WHO'S WHO
IN AMERICAN ART

WHO'S WHO IN AMERICAN ART

1973

A Biographical Directory
Edited by
THE JAQUES CATTELL PRESS

Foreword by
WILDER GREEN, Director
The American Federation of Arts

Jaques Cattell Press / R.R. Bowker Company
New York & London
Xerox Education Companies

Published by the R. R. Bowker Company
(A Xerox Education Company) 1180 Avenue of the Americas,
New York, New York 10036
Copyright © 1973 by Xerox Corporation.
International Standard Book Number: 0-8352-0611-4
International Standard Serial Number 0000-0191
Library of Congress Catalog Card Number: 36-27014
Printed and bound in the United States of America

CONTENTS

FOREWORD

The American Federation of Arts is pleased to join the R. R. Bowker Company in publishing the 1973 edition of *Who's Who in American Art.* AFA has a more than sixty-year history of bringing art to the American people through circulating exhibitions and, more recently, film and Visitor/Artist programs. This involvement with art institutions and individuals throughout the country makes participation in the publishing of *Who's Who in American Art* and its companion volume, *The American Art Directory,* particularly appropriate.

Both volumes originally appeared as part of the American Art Annual series which began in 1898. From 1913 to 1952 The American Federation of Arts published the series, and, in 1952, Bowker assumed this responsibility with AFA as its consultant. At that time *The American Art Directory* was first published as a separate volume, followed by *Who's Who in American Art* in 1953. New editions of each have been published triennially.

Publication of the 1973 edition marks the culmination of many months of cooperative effort by The American Federation of Arts and The Jaques Cattell Press (a division of the R. R. Bowker Company) to ensure the accurate and up-to-date information that makes *Who's Who in American Art* an invaluable reference source.

Wilder Green, *Director*
The American Federation of Arts

PREFACE

Biographical sketches of over 6,500 leading artists, key art administrators, collectors, scholars, and critics throughout North America are alphabetically listed in this newly revised edition of *Who's Who in American Art*. Under the editorship of The Jaques Cattell Press, a division of the R. R. Bowker Company, a new format has been developed which includes, in addition to the basic elements of biographees' data, the artists' preferred media, commissions, collections arranged, bibliography, publications, and dealers' names with addresses. New to this edition is a distinctive professional classification index which highlights the names of artists and their preferred media. The sections of necrology, open exhibitions, and the geographical index are continued features.

Information on the activities of entrants was edited from questionnaires, and biographees were submitted proofs for approval prior to publication. The editors have used their best efforts to include all material submitted within the scope of the established format, but no legal responsibility can be assumed for accidental omissions or errors. Candidates for inclusion, who did not return forms and for whom no confirmation of current activity or location could be found, have been omitted.

The editors and publishers wish to thank the officers of The American Federation of Arts, the leading art galleries, museums and other art or-ganizations of the United States, Canada, and Mexico for their valued assistance in continuance of this enterprise. To Goldthwaite H. Dorr III, Director of the Phoenix Art Museum, to Ben Goo and Hugh Broadley of the Art Department at Arizona State University, and to Rudy Turk, Director of the University Collections, the editors extend their grateful acknowledgment for encouragement and advice. Recognition is accorded David Biesel, Editor in Chief, and Olga Weber, Managing Editor of Directories, R. R. Bowker Company, for direction in planning and liaison guidance with national and international art organizations. Through them and the many others, this enhanced edition reflects the progressive interest of the Xerox Education Group in the field of art communication.

In planning future revisions, careful consideration will be given to the valuable suggestions and content evaluations received for this edition. Correspondence should be directed to The Editors, *Who's Who in American Art,* P.O. Box 25001, Tempe, Arizona 85282.

THE JAQUES CATTELL PRESS

Anne Rhodes, *Editor Art Directories*
Dorothy Hancock, *Managing Editor*
Fred Scott, *General Manager*
March 1973

ABBREVIATIONS

abstr—abstract(s)
acad—academia, academic, academica, academie, academique, academy
accad—accademia
acoust—acoustic(s), acoustical
actg—acting
addn—addition, additional
adj—adjunct
Adm—Admiral
admin—administration, administrative
adminr—administrator
admis(s)—admission
adv—adviser(s), advisory
advan—advance(d), advancement
advert—advertisement, advertising
aesthet—aesthetics
affil—affiliate, affiliation
agr—agricultural, agriculture
akad—akademi, akademia
Ala—Alabama
Alta—Alberta
Am—America, American
anal—analysis, analytic, analytical
analog—analogue
anat—anatomic, anatomical, anatomy
ann—annual
anthrop—anthropological, anthropology
antiq—antiquary, antiquities, antiquity
antiqn—antiquarian
app—appoint, appointed
appl—applied
approx—approximate, approximately
Apr—April
apt—apartment(s)
arch—archiv, archiva, archivies, archivio, archivo
archeol—archeological, archeologie, archeologique, archeology
archit—architectural, architecture
Arg—Argentina
Ariz—Arizona
Ark—Arkansas
asn—association
asoc—asociacion
assoc(s)—associate(s), associated
asst(s)—assistant(s)
atty—attorney
Aug—August
auth—author
AV—audiovisual
Ave—Avenue

b—born
B C—British Columbia
bd—board
Belg—Belgian, Belgium
bibliog—bibliografia, bibliographic, bibliographical, bibliography(ies)
bibliot—biblioteca, bibliotek, bibliotheca, bibliothek, bibliotheque
biog—biographical, biography
bk(s)—book(s)
Bldg—Building(s)
Blvd—Boulevard
br—branch(es)
Brit—Britain, British

bull—bulletin
bur—bureau
bus—business
B W I—British West Indies

Calif—California
Can—Canada, Canadian, Canadien, Canadienne
Capt—Captain
Cath—Catholic
CBS—Columbia Broadcasting System
cent—central
Cent Am—Central America
cert—certificate(s), certification, certified
chap—chapter
chmn—chairman
c/o—care of
co—companies, company
Co—County
co-auth—co-author
co-dir—co-director
co-ed—co-editor
co-educ—co-educational
C of C—Chamber of Commerce
Col—Colonel
col(s)—college(s), collegiate
collab—collaboration, collaborative
collabr—collaborator
com—commerce, commercial
comdr—commander
commun—communication(s)
comn(s)—commission(s), commissioned
comnr—commissioner
compos—composition
comt(s)—committee(s)
conf—conference
Cong—Congress, Congressional
Conn—Connecticut
conserv—conservacion, conservation, conservatiore, conservatory
construct—construction
consult—consult, consultant, consultantship, consultation, consulting
contemp—contemporary
contrib—contribute, contributing, contribution
contribr—contributor
conv—convention
coop—cooperating, cooperation, cooperative
coord—coordinate, coordinating, coordination
coordr—coordinator
corp—corporate, corporation
corresp—correspondent, corresponding
coun—councel, counceling, council
counr—councilor, counselor
Ct—Court
ctr—center
cult—cultural, culture
cur—curator
curric—curriculum
C Z—Canal Zone
Czech—Czechoslovakia

D C—District of Columbia
Dec—December
Del—Delaware
deleg—delegate, delegation
demonstr—demonstrator
dept—department, departmental
develop—development, developmental
dict—dictionaries, dictionary
dig—digest
dipl—diplom, diploma, diplomate, diplome
dir(s)—director(s), directory
dist—district
distribr—distributor
div—division, divisional, divorced
doc—document(s), documentary, documentation
Dom—Dominion
Dr—Doctor, Drive

E—East
econ—economic(s), economical, economist, economy
ed—edicion, edit, edited, editing, edition, editor(s), editorial, edizione
educ—educate, educated, educating, education, educational
elec—electric, electrical, electricity
elem—elementary
emer—emeritus, emeriti
encycl—encyclopedia
eng—engineering
Eng—England, English
environ—environment(s), environmental
equip—equipment
estab—established, establishment
estud—estudante, estudas, estudiante, estudio, estudo
Europ—European
exec(s)—executive(s)
exhib(s)—exhibit(s), exhibition
exped(s)—expedition(s)
explor—exploration(s), exploratory
expos—exposition
exten—extension

fac—faculty
Feb—February
fed—federal
fedn—federation
fel(s)—fellow(s), fellowship(s)
Fla—Florida
for—foreign
found—foundation
Fr—French
Ft—Fort

Ga—Georgia
gen—general, generale
Ger—German, Germany
Ges—Gesellschaft
gov—governing, governor
govt—government, governmental
grad—graduate, graduated
Gt Brit—Great Britain
gym—gymnasium

handbk(s)—handbook(s)
hist—historia, historic, historica, historical, historique, historisch(e), history
H M—Her Majesty
hochsch—hochschule
hon(s)—honor(s), honorable, honorary
hosp(s)—hospital(s), hospitalization
hq—headquarters
Hwy—Highway

Ill—Illinois
illum—illuminating, illumination
illus—illustrate, illustrated, illustration
illusr—illustrator
Inc—Incorporated
incl—include, included, includes, including
Ind—Indiana
indust(s)—industrial, industries, industry
info—information
inst—institut, instituto
inst(s)—institute(s), institution(s)
instnl—institutional, institutionalized
instr(s)—instruct, instruction, instructors
instrnl—instructional
int—internacional, international, internazionale
introd—introduction
ist—istituto
Ital—Italia, Italian, Italiana, Italiano, Italica, Italien, Italienisch, Italienne(s)

J—Journal (title)
Jan—January
jour—journal (descriptive)
jr—junior
juv—juvenile(s)

Kans—Kansas
Ky—Kentucky

La—Louisiana
lab(s)—laboratories, laboratory
lang—language(s)
lect—lecture(s)
lectr—lecturer(s)
lett—letter(s)
lib—liberal
libr—libraries, library, librerio
librn—librarian
lit—literary, literatur, literatura, literature, littera, litterature
Lt—Lieutenant
ltd—limited

mag—magazine
maj—major
Man—Manitoba
Mar—March
mat—material(s)
Md—Maryland
med—medical, medicine, medicinal
mem—member(s), membership(s), memoirs
Mem—Memorial
metrop—metropolitan
Mex—Mexican, Mexicano, Mexico
mgr—manager
mgt—management
Mich—Michigan
Minn—Minnesota
Miss—Mississippi
Mo—Missouri
mo—month
mod—modern, moderna, moderne, moderno
monogr—monograph
Mont—Montana
Mt—Mount
munic—municipal, municipalities
mus—musée, museo, museum(s)

N—North
nac—nacional
nat—nationaal, national, nationale, nationalis

naz—nazionale
N B—New Brunswick
N C—North Carolina
N Dak—North Dakota
Nebr—Nebraska
Neth—Netherland
Nev—Nevada
New Eng—New England
Nfld—Newfoundland
N H—New Hampshire
N J—New Jersey
N Mex—New Mexico
Norweg—Norwegian
Nov—November
N S—Nova Scotia
N S W—New South Wales
N Y—New York
N Z—New Zealand

Oct—October
off—office, official
Okla—Oklahoma
Ont—Ontario
oper(s)—operation(s), operational, operative
Ore—Oregon
orgn—organization, organizational

Pa—Pennsylvania
Pac—Pacific
Pan-Am—Pan-American
partic—participant, participating
P E I—Prince Edward Island
philos—philosophic, philosophical, philosophy
photog—photographic, photography
photogr—photographer(s)
Pkwy—Parkway
Pl—Place
P O Box—Post Office Box
polytech—polytechnic, polytechnical
Port—Portugal, Portuguese
P Q—Province of Quebec
P R—Puerto Rico
prehist—prehistoric, prehistory
pres—president
Presby—Presbyterian
preserv—preservation
prof—profession, professional, professor, professorial
prog(s)—program(s), programmed, programming
proj(s)—project(s), projection(s), projectional, projective
prov—province, provincial
pub—public
publ—publication(s), published, publisher(s), publishing
pvt—private

Quart—Quarterly

Rd—Road
R D—Rural Delivery
rec—record(s), recording
regist—register, registered, registration
registr—registrar
relig—religion, religious
rep—represent, representative
Repub—Republic
res—research
rev—review, revised, revision
R F D—Rural Free Delivery
R I—Rhode Island
Rm—Room
R R—Rural Route
Rte—Route
Russ—Russian

S—South
S Africa—South Africa
S Am—South America, South American
Sask—Saskatchewan
S C—South Carolina
Scand—Scandinavia, Scandinavian

sch(s)—school(s)
scholar—scholarship
sci—science(s), scientific
S Dak—South Dakota
sec—secondary
sect—section
secy—secretary
sem—seminar, seminary
Sen—Senator, Senatorial
Sept—September
ser—series
serv—service(s), serving
soc(s)—sociedad, sociesade, societa, societas, societate, société, societet, societies, society
Span—Spanish
spec—special
Sq—Square
St—Saint, Street
sta(s)—station(s)
Ste—Sainte
struct—structural, structure(s)
stud—studencheskii, studencheskikh, student, studentship, studentov, studien, studja, studi(a)
super—superieur, superior, superiore
suppl—supplement, supplemental, supplementary
supt—superintendent
supv—supervising, supervision
Swed—Swedish
Switz—Switzerland
symp—symposium(s)

tech—technical, technique
technol—technologic, technological, technology
tel—telegraph(y), telephone
Tenn—Tennessee
Terr—Terrace
Tex—Texas
transl—translation(s)
translr—translator
treas—treasurer, treasury

UN—United Nations
undergrad—undergraduate
UNESCO—United Nations Educational, Scientific & Cultural Organization
univ(s)—universidad, universite, universities, university
U S—United States
USA—United States Army
USAF—United States Air Force
USMC—United States Marine Corps
USN—United States Navy
U S S R—Union of Soviet Socialist Republics
Va—Virginia
var—various
v chmn—vice chairman
Vet—Veteran(s)
V I—Virgin Islands
vis—visiting
vol(s)—volume(s)
v pres—vice president
Vt—Vermont

W—West
Wash—Washington
Wis—Wisconsin
wk—week
W Va—West Virginia
Wyo—Wyoming

yearbk—yearbook
YMCA—Youth Men's Christian Association
YMHA—Youth Men's Hebrew Association
yr(s)—year(s)
YWCA—Youth Women's Chrisitan Association
YWHA—Youth Women's Hebrew Association

WHO'S WHO IN AMERICAN ART

A

AACH, HERB
Painter, Writer
b Cologne, Ger, Mar 24, 23; U S citizen.
Study & Training: Art Acad Cologne, 36-37; Pratt Inst, 41-42; Stanford Univ, 43-44; Escuela di Pintura Y Escultura, Mex, 48-50; Brooklyn Mus Art Sch, 47-48 & 50-51.
Work in Public Collections: Boston Mus, Mass; Everhart Mus, Scranton, Pa; Birla Acad, Calcutta, India; Chase Collection; William Penn Memorial Mus, Harrisburg, Pa.
Exhibitions: Whitney Ann, 52; Pa Acad Fine Arts, 55; Univ Ill Ann, 61; Childe Hassam Purchase Fund, Acad Arts & Lett, 71; Color Forum/Austin, Univ Texas, 72.
Teaching: Pratt Inst, 47-51 & 65-68; Brooklyn Mus; Skowhegan Sch Painting & Sculpture, 69 & 70; asst prof art & painting, Queens Col, 66-.
Bibliography: L Finkelstein (auth), Color as system, Craft Horizon, 70.
Memberships: Color Forum (founder, organizer & bd mem); Col Art Asn; Artists Workshop Club; Intersoc Color Coun; Experiments in Art & Technol.
Research: All phases of color, phenomenology, perception and fluorescence.
Publications: Ed & translr, Goethe's color theory, Van Nostrand Reinhold, 71; contrib ed, J Color & Appearance, 72; auth, articles in Arts, Craft Horizons, Color Eng & many other magazines & journals.
Dealer: Jacques Seligmann & Co, Inc, 5 E 57th St, New York, NY 10017.
Mailing Address: 523 E 14th St, New York, NY 10009.

AAKRE, RICHARD B
Painter, Photographer
Preferred Media: Ink.
b Duluth, Minn, Sept 9, 43.
Study & Training: Univ Minn, BA; Univ Iowa, MA & MFA; also asst to Robert Motherwell.
Exhibitions: New Eng Invitational, Boston, Mass, 71; Am Acad Arts & Lett & Nat Inst Arts & Lett, 72.
Teaching: Instr drawing, Univ Iowa, 68-69.
Awards: Award for painting, Am Acad Arts & Lett & Nat Inst Arts & Lett, 72.
Mailing Address: 909 North St, Greenwich, CT 06830.

AARONS, GEORGE
Sculptor
Preferred Media: Wood, Stone, Bronze & Welded Metals.
b Lithuania, Apr 6, 96; U S citizen.
Study & Training: Mus Fine Arts Sch, Boston, Mass; Beaux Inst Design, New York, N Y.
Work in Public Collections: Mus Art, Ein Harod, Israel; Fitchburg Art Mus, Mass; Musee de St. Denis, France; Hilles Libr, Radcliffe Col, Cambridge, Mass; Hillel House, Boston Univ, Mass.
Commissions: 5 Heroic figures & 10 ft relief, Old Harbor Village Housing Proj, S Boston, 38; reliefs, Siefer Hall, Brandeis Univ, Waltham, Mass, 50; reliefs, facade Baltimore Hebrew Congregation Bldg, 56; relief, Combined Jewish Philanthropies Bldg, Boston, Mass, 65; commemorative medal, 350th Anniversary, City of Gloucester, Mass, 72.
Exhibitions: Second & Third Int Exhib Sculpture, Philadelphia Mus, 40 & 49; Inst Contemp Art, Boston, 44; Ann Exhib Contemp Am Sculpture, Whitney Mus Am Art, 57, 59; Mass Inst Technol, Cambridge, 49; Sculpture Ctr, New York, 51.

Awards: Third prize, mem show, Inst Contemp Art, 44; Hayward Niedringhaus Memorial Prize, Rockport Art Asn, Mass, 53; hon mention, Gold Medal Exhib, Architectural League N Y, 58.
Bibliography: Abraham Kampf (auth), Contemporary synagogue art 1945-1965, Union Am Hebrew Congregations, N Y; Montreal Expo 67 Internation Exhibition of Contemporary Sculpture, 67; Israel Program for Scientific Translations, Encyclopaedia Judaica, 70.
Memberships: Nat Sculpture Soc; Rockport Art Asn.
Mailing Address: Eagle Rd, Gloucester, MA 01930.

ABANY, ALBERT CHARLES
Painter, Educator
Preferred Media: Oils, Graphics, Mixed Media.
b Boston, Mass, Mar 30, 21.
Study & Training: Sch Mus of Fine Arts, Boston, M O H Longstreth scholar, 42, dipl, 48; Tufts Univ, BS(educ), 49.
Exhibitions: One-man shows, Carl Siembab Gallery, Boston, Mass, 56; Clark Univ, 63; Northeastern Univ, 67; Wessell Libr, Tufts Univ, 71; Art Inst Boston, 72.
Teaching: Art teacher drawing & painting, Boston Ctr Adult Education, 49-51; art teacher materials & art hist, Art Inst Boston, 65-
Memberships: Col Art Asn Am; Am Fedn Arts.
Mailing Address: 42 MacArthur Rd, Natick, MA 01760.

ABBATE, PAUL S
Sculptor
Preferred Media: Marble, Bronze.
b Villarosa, Italy, Apr 9, 84; U S citizen.
Study & Training: Study in Italy & the U S.
Work in Public Collections: Dante Monument, Newburgh, N Y; Ruvolo Monument, Torrington Cemetery, Conn.
Exhibitions: Many exhibs in the U S & Europe.
Positions: Cur, Torrington Mus Art.
Memberships: Nat Sculpture Soc; Cenàcolo Dante Soc.
Mailing Address: 1169 Highland Ave, Torrington, CT 06790.

ABBE, ELFRIEDE MARTHA
Sculptor, Engraver
Preferred Media: Wood.
b Washington, D C.
Study & Training: Cornell Univ Col Archit, BFA, 40.
Work in Public Collections: Rosenwald Collection, Nat Gallery Art; Mus Fine Arts, Boston, Mass; Houghton Libr, Harvard Univ; Sloniker Collection, Cincinnati Art Mus; Mus Fine Arts, Venice, Italy.
Commissions: Large statue, The Hunter, New York World's Fair, 39; oak frieze, Mann Libr, Cornell Univ, 55 & bronze sculptures, Clive McCay Mem, 67; bronze head, Napoleon, McGill Univ Libr; walnut carving The Illuminator, Sterling Mem Hunt Library, Carnegie-Mellon Univ, 69.
Exhibitions: Nat Acad Design, New York; San Diego Fine Arts Gallery, 60; printing in the U S A and United Kingdom, London Chappel Exhib, Eng, 63; Int Botanical Artists, Hunt Libr, Carnegie-Mellon Univ, 68; Nat Arts Club, New York, 69 & 70.
Awards: Tiffany Fel, 48; Hunt Found Grant, 61; gold medal, Nat Arts Club, 70.
Bibliography: Norman Kent (auth), The Book Art of Elfriede Abbe, Am Artist Mag, 60.
Memberships: Nat Arts Club; fel Nat Sculpture Soc; Pen & Brush Club; Arts Club of Washington, D C.
Publications: Designed, illustrated & printed Garden spice and wild pot-herbs, Cornell Univ Press, 55; The American scholar, 56, Seven Irish tales, 57 & Significance of the frontier, 58.
Mailing Address: 24 Woodcrest Ave, Ithaca, NY 14850.

ABBOT, HAZEL NEWNHAM
Painter
Preferred Media: Watercolors.
b Montreal, P Q; U S citizen.
Study & Training: Sch Fine Arts, Boston, Mass; Charles H Woodbury Sch, Ogunquit, Maine.
Work in Public Collections: Wellesley Col Art Mus.
Exhibitions: Philadelphia Watercolor Club, 38; Royal Brit Artists, London, 58; Nat Asn Women Artists, New York, N Y, 66; Soc Artistes Français, Paris, 72; Fedn Brit Artists, London, 72.
Collections Arranged: Storms Over New Mexico, The Matterhorn, Canadian Forests & others, Colo Springs Fine Arts Ctr.
Memberships: Nat Asn Women Artists; Fedn Brit Artists.
Dealer: James Bourlet & Sons, Ltd, 17-18 Nassau St, London W1N 8BL, Eng.
Mailing Address: 1915 El Parque, Colorado Springs, CO 80907.

ABBOTT, DOROTHY
Sculptor, Lecturer
Preferred Media: Marble.
b Thibadoux, La, 35.
Study & Training: Tyler Col Fine Arts; Art Stud League; San Francisco State Col, BA; Columbia Univ, MA.
Work in Public Collections: Gallery Madison 90, New York, N Y; Parrish Mus, Southampton, N Y; Jersey City Mus, N J.
Exhibitions: Nat Arts Club, New York, 63-71; Audubon Artists, New York; Nat Acad Design, New York; 65-72; Painters & Sculptors Soc N J, 67; Parrish Mus, 69.
Awards: 1st prize, 26th & 27th Ann, Guild Hall, East Hampton, N Y, 64 & 65; Best in Show, 28th Ann, 66; medal of honor, Painter & Sculpture Soc N J, 67.
Memberships: Audubon Artists Am (bd selection, 72-74).
Mailing Address: c/o Gallery Madison 90, 1248 Madison Ave, New York, NY 10028.

ABDALLA, NICK
Painter, Educator
Preferred Media: Mixed Media.
b Albuquerque, N Mex, May 24, 39.
Study & Training: Eastern N Mex Univ, 57-59; Univ Ill, Champaign, 59-60; Univ N Mex, BFA, 61, MA, 63.
Work in Public Collections: El Paso Mus Art, Tex; Roswell Art Mus, N Mex; Fine Arts Mus, Santa Fe, N Mex.
Exhibitions: 16th Exhib Southwestern Prints & Drawings, Dallas Mus Fine Arts, Tex, 66; New Mexico Photographers '68 & N Mex Painting Invitational, 68, Fine Arts Mus, Santa Fe; 13th & 14th Ann Sun Carnival Nat Art Exhib, Art Mus El Paso, 68 & 69; First Nat Print & Drawing Exhib, McCray Gallery, Western N Mex Univ, Silver City, 69.
Teaching: Asst prof painting & drawing, Univ N Mex, 71-
Awards: C Troop Gallery Award, 16th Exhib Southwestern Prints & Drawings, Dallas Mus Fine Arts, 66; first purchase award, 13th Ann Sun Carnival Art Exhib, El Paso Mus Art, 68; first purchase award, Nat Print & Drawing Exhib, McCray Gallery, Silver City, N Mex, 69.
Dealers: Janus Gallery, 116 1/2 E Palace, Santa Fe, NM 87501; Tally Richards' Gallery of Contemporary Art, One Ledoux St, Taos, NM 87571.
Mailing Address: 515 11th St N W, Albuquerque, NM 87102.

ABELES, SIGMUND
Printmaker, Sculptor
b New York, N Y, Nov 6, 34.
Study & Training: Pratt Inst; Univ S C, BA, 55; Art Stud League; Skowhegan Sch Painting & Sculpture; Brooklyn Mus Sch; Columbia Univ, MFA, 57.
Work in Public Collections: Mus Mod Art, New York; Mus Arte, Ponce, P R; Pa Acad Fine Arts & Philadelphia Mus Art; Boston Mus Fine Arts, Mass; plus many others.
Exhibitions: Whitney Ann Sculpture & Prints, Whitney Mus Am Art, New York, 67; 28 American Printmakers, Rijksacademie, Amsterdam, Holland, 68; Human Concern & Personal Torment, Whitney Mus Am Art, 69; American Contemporary Prints—one, Inst Contemp Art, London, Eng, 70; Master Prints of the 20th Century, Boston Mus Fine Arts, 71; plus many other group and one-man shows.
Teaching: Swain Sch Design, New Bedford, Mass, 61-64; Wellesley Col, 64-69; Boston Univ, 69-70; Univ N H, 70-
Awards: Grant & award, Nat Inst Arts & Lett, 65; sabbatical grant, Nat Coun Arts & Humanities, 66; grant for graphics, Louis Comfort Tiffany Found, 67.
Dealer: Associated American Artists Gallery, 663 Fifth Ave, New York, NY 10022.
Mailing Address: R F D 1, Rte 107, Northwood, NH 03261.

ABLOW, JOSEPH
Painter, Educator
Preferred Media: Acrylic, Pastel, Watercolor.
b Salem, Mass, Aug 16, 28.
Study & Training: Sch Mus Fine Arts, Boston, Paige traveling fel, dipl with highest hons 51; Bennington Col, BA 54; Harvard Univ, MA, 55; Fulbright grant, Paris, 58; advanced study in painting with Oskar Kokoschka, Ben Shahn, Jack Levine & in design with Gyorgy Kepes.
Work in Public Collections: DeCordova Mus, Lincoln, Mass; Univ Mass, Boston; Middlebury Col, Vt; Skowhegan Sch Collection, Maine.
Exhibitions: Young Americans, Brandeis Univ, 54; 62nd Am Exhib, Art Inst Chicago, 57; New England Painting, DeCordova Mus, 64; Varieties of Figurative Art, Bard Col, 69; group show, Kunstsalon Wolfsberg, Zurich, Switz, 69.
Teaching: Asst prof art hist, Bard Col, 59-61; prof advan painting, Boston Univ, 63-, chmn div art, Sch Fine & Applied Arts, 64-67; vis assoc prof humanities, Mass Inst Technol, 70.
Dealer: Boris Mirski Gallery, 166 Newbury St, Boston, MA 02116.
Mailing Address: 16 Monmouth Ct, Brookline, MA 02146.

ABRAMOVITZ, MR & MRS MAX
Collectors
Mr Abramovitz b Chicago, Ill, May 23, 08.
Study & Training: Mr Abramovitz, Univ Ill, BS, 29; Columbia Univ, MS, 31; Ecole Beaux-Arts, 32-34; Univ Pittsburgh, hon DFA, 61, Univ Ill, 70.
Commissions: Mr Abramovitz, design of Univ Iowa Art Mus & Krannert Ctr Performing Arts, Univ Ill.
Teaching: Assoc prof Sch Fine Arts, Yale Univ, 39-42.
Mailing Address: 418 E 50th St, New York, NY 10022.

ABRAMS, HARRY N
Publisher, Collector
b London, Eng, Feb 23, 05.
Study & Training: Nat Acad Design; Art Stud League New York.
Positions: Pres, Harry N Abrams, Inc.
Collection: American and French twentieth century paintings, graphic arts and sculpture.
Mailing Address: 33 E 70th St, New York, NY 10021.

ABRAMS, HERBERT E
Painter, Lecturer
Preferred Media: Oils.
b Greenfield, Mass, Mar 20, 21.
Study & Training: Norwich Art Sch, Conn; Pratt Inst, hon grad in illus; Art Stud League with Frank Vincent Du Mond.
Work in Public Collections: Portraits, Gen William C Westmoreland, West Point Museum, N Y; Dr Philip Bard, Johns Hopkins Univ Collection, Baltimore, Md; Dr James T McCord, Princeton Theological Sem, N J; Gen Anna Mae Hays, Walter Reed Med Ctr Collection, Washington, D C.
Commissions: USAF Insignia, stars & tabs on aircraft, 42; portraits, Gen & Mrs Palmer Pierce, West Point Officer's Mess, 63.
Exhibitions: Dallas Mus Fine Arts, 48; One-Man shows, Grand Central Art Galleries, New York, N Y, 58, 64 & 68; S Vermont Art Asn, 65; Springfield Acad Artists, Mass, 68; Okla Mus Art, 69.
Teaching: Lectr & demonstr painting to art orgn & study groups; TV lect & demonstration, 71.
Awards: Best still life, Dr Byron Kenyon Award, Hudson Valley Art Asn, 68; best portrait, 70.
Memberships: Hudson Valley Art Asn; Art Stud League of New York.
Mailing Address: Heartwood, Warren, CT 06754.

ABRAMS, RUTH
Painter
b New York, N Y.
Study & Training: Columbia Univ; Art Stud League New York; New Sch Social Res; also workshops with Zorach, Archipenko & Harrison.
Work in Public Collections: Carnegie Inst Technol; Smith Col Mus Art; Rose A Mus, Brandeis Univ; New York Univ Art Col; Univ Caracas; also in pvt collections U S & S Am.
Exhibitions: Riverside Mus, N Y; Art: U S A, 58; Critics Choise, 60; Dallas Mus Fine Arts, 63; one-man show, Mus Fine Arts, Caracas, Venezuela, 63; plus others.
Positions: Art dir, New Sch Social Res Asn, 66.
Publications: Illusr, Ekistics, Athens, Greece & Arena-Interbuild, London, Eng, 67.
Mailing Address: 18 W Tenth St, New York, NY 10011.

ACCONCI, VITO
Sculptor
b New York, N Y, Jan 24, 40.
Study & Training: Holy Cross Col, AB; Univ Iowa, MFA.

Work in Public Collections: Mus Mod Art, New York; Los Angeles Co Mus, Los Angeles, Calif; Sonnabend Gallery, New York & Paris, France; Daniel Templon Gallery, Paris; L'Attico Gallery, Rome, Italy.
Exhibitions: Information, Mus Mod Art, 70; Software, Jewish Mus, New York, 70; Prospect, Kunsthalle, Dusseldorf, Ger, 71; Sonnabend Gallery, 72; Documenta 5, Kassel, 72.
Teaching: Lectr art theory, Sch Visual Arts, New York, 68-71.
Bibliography: J Perreault (auth), Cockroach Art, Village Voice, 3/71; P Schjeldahl (auth), Vito Acconci, Art in Am, 4/72; R Pincus-Witten (auth), Vito Acconci & the conceptual performance, Art Forum, 4/72.
Publications: Contribr, Information Catalogue, Mus Mod Art, 70; Conceptual art, Dutton, 72; Vito Acconci issue, Avalanche Mag, 72; Auth, Notes Toward the development of a show, Sonnabend Press, 72.
Dealer: Sonnabend Gallery, 420 W Broadway, New York, NY 10013.
Mailing Address: 102 Christopher St, New York, NY 10014.

ACHEPOHL, KEITH ANDEN
Printmaker, Painter
b Chicago, Ill, Apr 11, 34.
Study & Training: Knox Col, BA; Univ Iowa, MFA.
Work in Public Collections: Pennell Collection, Libr Cong, Washington, D C; New York Pub Libr; Philadelphia Mus Art, Art Inst Chicago; Achenbach Found for Graphic Arts, Calif Palace Legion of Honor, San Francisco; plus 32 others.
Exhibitions: Nat Print Exhib, Libr Congr, 60, 61, 63 & 69; Seattle Northwest Printmakers Int, 61, 67, 68 & 71; Philadelphia Print Club Int & Nat Exhibs, 62, 68, 71 & 72; Brooklyn Mus Invitational, 68; Graphics '71, West Coast, Am Fedn Arts Traveling Exhib, Univ Ky, 71-72.
Teaching: Instr printmaking, Univ Iowa, 64-67; vis artist printmaking, Univ Wash, summer 67; assoc prof, Pac Lutheran Univ, 69-72; vis artist printmaking, Univ Iowa, 72-
Awards: Purchase awards, Pennell Fund, Libr Cong, 60 & 61; Lynd Ward Prize, 67 & John B Turner Prize, 69, Soc Am Graphic Artists; Philadelphia Print Club, 70.
Memberships: Soc Am Graphic Artists; Philadelphia Print Club.
Dealer: Associated American Artists Gallery, 663 Fifth Ave at 52nd St, New York, NY 10022.
Mailing Address: 7473 Riverside Dr E, Sumner, WA 98390.

ACKERMAN, GERALD MARTIN
Art Historian, Educator
b Alameda, Calif, Aug 21, 28.
Study & Training: Univ Calif, BA, 52; Maximilliam Universität, 56-58, with Prof Sedlmayr; Princeton Univ, MFA, 60; PhD, 64, with Prof Lee & Panofsky.
Collections Arranged: Thiebaud Figures, Stanford Univ Mus, 65; Gerôme, Dayton Art Inst, Minneapolis Art Inst, Walters Art Gallery, Baltimore, 72-73.
Teaching: Instr art history, Bryn Mawr Col, 60-64; asst prof, Stanford Univ, 65-70; assoc prof, Pomona Col, 71-, chmn art dept, 72-
Memberships: Col Art Asn; Deutsche Verein für Kunstwissenschaft.
Research: 19th century realism in America and Europe, in particular academic realists such as Jean Leon Gerôme and Thomas Eakins; art theory.
Publications: Auth, Gerôme and Manet, Gazette des Beaux-Arts, 70: 163-176; Lomazzo's treatise on painting, Art Bulletin, 59: 317-326; Gerôme, the academic realist, Art News Ann, 33: 100-107; Thomas Eakins and His Parisian Masters, Gerôme and Bonnat, Gazette des Beaux Arts, 72: 235-256; Gerôme, exhibition catalogue, 72.
Mailing Address: Art Dept, Pomona College, Claremont, CA 91711.

ACOSTA, MANUEL GREGORIO
Painter, Sculptor
Preferred Media: Oils, Clay.
b Villa Aldama, Mex, May 9, 21; U S citizen.
Study & Training: Univ Tex, El Paso; Chouinard Art Inst, Los Angeles; also with Urbici Soler, sculptor.
Work in Public Collections: El Paso Mus, Tex; W Tex Mus, Lubbock; Baker Gallery, Lubbock; Time, Inc Collection, New York, N Y; also included in Harmsen's Western Collection, Colo.
Commissions: Pioneer murals (apprenticed with Peter Hurd), W Tex Mus, 52; Southwest History (aluminum mural), Casa Blanca Motel, Logan, N Mex, 56; fresco mural, First Nat Bank, Las Cruces, N Mex, 57; aluminum fresco mural & hist panels, Bank of Tex, Houston.
Exhibitions: Art U S A, Mo, 58; Tex Watercolor Soc, Austin, 60; one-man show, Chase Gallery, New York, 62; Am Watercolor Soc, New York, 65.
Positions: Adv, Tex Comn Arts & Humanities, 72-
Publications: Illusr, Cesar Chavez (cover), Time Mag, 69; Illusr, Canto y Grito mi Liberacion, Doubleday, 72.
Dealer: Baker Collector Gallery, 1301 13th St, Lubbock, TX 79408.
Mailing Address: 366 Buena Vista St, El Paso, TX 79905.

ACTON, ARLO C
Sculptor
b Knoxville, Iowa, May 11, 33.
Study & Training: Wash State Univ, BA, 58; Calif Inst Arts, MFA, 59.
Work in Public Collections: San Francisco Mus Art, Calif.
Exhibitions: Some Points of View for '62, Stanford Univ, 62; The Artist's Environment: The West Coast, Fort Worth, Tex, 62; Fifty California Artists, Whitney Mus Am Art, New York, N Y, 62-63; California Sculpture, Kaiser Ctr, Oakland, Calif, 63; Third Paris Biennial, 63; plus many other group & one-man shows.
Teaching: Univ Calif, Berkeley, 63.
Awards: Edgar Walter Mem Prize, San Francisco Mus Art, 61; second prize, Richmond Art Asn Ann, 61; award, San Francisco Art Asn, 64; plus others.
Bibliography: Peter Selz (auth), Funk, Univ Calif Press, Berkeley, 67; Maurice Tuchman (auth), American sculpture of the sixties, Los Angeles Co Mus Art, 67.
Mailing Address: c/o Hansen-Fuller Gallery, 228 Grant Ave, San Francisco, CA 94108.

ADAMS, ALICE
Sculptor
Preferred Media: Wood, Metal, Rubber.
b New York, N Y, Nov 16, 30.
Study & Training; Columbia Univ, BFA, 53; Fulbright travel grant, 53-54; French govt fel, 53-54; L'Ecole Nat d'Art Decoratif, Aubusson, France.
Work in Public Collections: L'Ecole Nat d'Art Decoratif; Univ Nebr, Lincoln; Hertz Corp, New York.
Exhibitions: Eccentric Abstraction, Fischbach Gallery, New York, 66; Am Abstract Artists Ann, Riverside Mus, New York, 67-68; Contemporary American Sculpture, Whitney Mus Am Art, 70-71; Penthouse Gallery Exhib, Mus Mod Art, New York, 71; American Women Artists, Kunsthaus, Hamburg, Ger, 72.
Teaching: Instr sculpture, Manhattanville Col, 61-; asst prof, Calif State Col, Los Angeles, 69.
Awards: MacDowall Colony, MacDowall Found, 67.
Bibliography: Barbara Kafka (auth), The woven structures of Alice Adams, Craft Horizons, 3/67; Ward Jackson (auth), monograph, color photo, Art Now, New York, 4/69.
Memberships: Am Abstract Artists (secy, 67).
Mailing Address: 246 Bowery, New York, N Y 10028.

ADAMS, CLINTON
Art Administrator, Lithographer
b Glendale, Calif, Dec 11, 18.
Study & Training: Univ Calif, Los Angeles, BEd, 40; MA, 42.
Work in Public Collections: Mus Mod Art, New York, N Y; Chicago Art Inst, Ill; Amon Carter Mus Western Art, Ft Worth, Tex; Achenbach Found Graphic Arts, San Francisco, Calif; Grunwald Graphics Art Found, Univ Calif, Los Angeles.
Exhibitions: 16th Nat Print Invitational, Brooklyn Mus, 68; Tamarind: Homage to Lithography, Mus Mod Art, New York, 69; 73rd Western Ann, Denver Art Mus, 71; 1972 Southwest Biennial, Mus New Mex, 72; Retrospective Exhibition: Paintings, 61-71, Roswell Mus & Art Ctr, N Mex, 72.
Teaching: Asst prof painting & lithography, Univ Calif, Los Angeles, 46-54; chmn, dept art, Univ Ky, 54-57; chmn dept art, Univ Fla, 57-60; dean, col fine arts, Univ New Mex, 61-
Positions: Assoc prof, Tamarind Lithography Workshop, Los Angeles, 60-61; dir, Tamarind Institute, Albuquerque, 70-
Awards: Purchase award, 17th Exhib Southwestern Prints & Drawings, Dallas Mus Fine Arts, 67; Nat Print & Drawing Exhib, Northern Ill Univ, 68; 1972 Southwest Biennial, Mus New Mex, 72.
Memberships: Col Art Asn Am; Mid-Am Col Art Asn (v pres, 71-72).
Publications: Co-auth, Tamarind book of lithography: art and techniques, Abrams, 71.
Mailing Address: 1917 Morningside Dr NE, Albuquerque, NM 87110.

ADAMS, GLENN NELSON
Painter
b Montreal, P Q, Jan 24, 28.
Study & Training: McGill Univ; Montreal Mus Fine Art; Mount Allison Univ, with Alex Colville & L P Harris.
Work in Public Collections: Montreal Mus Fine Arts; Can Indust, Ltd; Montreal Star.
Exhibitions: Banfer Gallery, 63 & 64; Galerie Agnes Lefort, 64; Montreal Mus Fine Art, 64.
Mailing Address: 1447 Painter Circle, Montreal, P Q, Can.

ADAMS, KATHERINE LANGHORNE
Painter, Sculptor
Preferred Media: Oils.
b Plainfield, N J.
Study & Training: Art Stud League New York; also studies at Lyme, Conn.
Work in Public Collections: Smithsonian Inst, Washington, D C.

Commissions: Murals in oil for Robert C Hill & Thomas Lamont, Palisades, N Y.
Exhibitions: One-man show, Babcock Gallery, N Y; invitational group shows, Art Inst Chicago, Ill, Detroit Mus Art, Mich, Buffalo Fine Arts Acad, N Y & St Louis Mus, Mo, plus many others.
Mailing Address: 225 S Lee St, Alexandria, VA 22314.

ADAMS, MARK
Designer, Painter
Preferred Media: Tapestry, Stained Glass.
b Fort Plain, N Y, Oct 27, 25.
Study & Training: Syracuse Univ; with Hans Hofmann & Jean Lurcat, France.
Work in Public Collections: Tapestries, Queen of Heaven, Dallas Mus Fine Arts, Tex; Phoenix and the Golden Gate, Marina Br, San Francisco Pub Libr; Rose, Santa Rosa-Sonoma Pub Libr, Santa Rosa, Calif; painting, Mounted Policeman, Hall of Justice, San Francisco, Calif.
Commissions: Stained glass, St Andrew's Episcopal Church, Saratoga, Calif, 63-70; baptistry, All Saints' Episcopal Church, Carmel, Calif, 68; tapestry, Man Flying, Bank Calif, San Francisco, 68; tapestry, Weyerhaeuser Co, Tacoma, Wash, 71; stained glass, Temple Emanu-el, 72.
Exhibitions: Int Biennial of Tapestry, Lausanne, Switz, 62 & 65; Collector: Object/Environment, Mus Contemp Crafts, New York, N Y, 65; San Francisco Art Inst Ann, San Francisco Mus Art, 65; Calif Design, Pasadena Art Mus, 66; 400 Years of Tapestry, Norfolk Mus Arts & Sci, 66.
Mailing Address: 3816 22nd St, San Francisco, CA 94114.

ADAMS, PAT
Painter, Educator
Preferred Media: Oil/Isobutyl Methacrylate, Gouache.
b Stockton, Calif, July 8, 28.
Study & Training: Univ Calif, Berkeley, BA, 49; Brooklyn Mus Art Sch with Max Beckmann & John Ferren; Fulbright fel, France, 56-57.
Work in Public Collections: Whitney Mus; Joseph Hirshhorn Collection; Univ Calif, Berkeley; Univ Mich; Univ N C, Greensboro.
Exhibitions: Whitney Mus Painting Ann, 56, 61; 41 Aquarellistes, Mus Mod Art traveling exhib in France, 57; Lyricism in Abstract Art, Am Fedn Arts traveling exhib, 62; Betty Parsons Collection, Finch Col, New York, N Y, 68; Color Forum, Univ Tex, Austin, 72.
Teaching: Art fac painting, Bennington Col, 64-
Positions: Vis critic painting, Yale Univ, 71-72; grad sem, Queens Col, fall 72.
Awards: Yaddo Found summer residences, 54, 64, 69 & 70; painting award, Nat Coun Arts, 68; MacDowell Colony fels, 68 & 72.
Bibliography: Bernard Chaet (auth), Interview with Pat Adams, Artists at Work, 61; Dore Ashton (auth), The symbolist legacy III, Art & Architecture, 12/64; Hilton Kramer (auth), Art: Pat Adams paintings, New York Times, 1/10/70.
Publications: Contribr, Private myth, Tanager Gallery, 61; Art now, 6/72.
Dealer: Virginia Zabriskie Gallery, 29 W 57th St, New York, NY 10019.
Mailing Address: Bennington College, Old Faculty Row, Bennington, VT 05201.

ADAMS, PHILIP RHYS
Art Administrator
b Fargo, N Dak, Nov 19, 08.
Study & Training: Ohio State Univ, BA, 29; New York Univ Inst Fine Arts, MA, 31, with Cook, C R Morey & Whittemore; Princeton Univ, Carnegie fel, with Mather, Baldwin Smith & Friend.
Collections Arranged: Near Eastern, Far Eastern, Egyptian, Classical, Medieval sculpture, painting and ceramics; Mary Hanna, Emilie Heine and Mary E Johnston painting collections; decorative arts—period rooms, furniture, ceramics, tapestries, glass and costumes, all at the Cincinnati Art Museum.
Teaching: Instr & lectr art hist, Newcomb College, Tulane Univ, 31-34.
Positions: Dir, Columbus Gallery Fine Arts, 34-35; dir, Cincinnati Art Museum, 45-
Mailing Address: Cincinnati Art Museum, Cincinnati, OH 45202.

ADAMS, ROBERT DAVID
Designer, Painter
Preferred Media: Acrylics
b Nelsonville, N Y, Feb 6, 25.
Study & Training: Pratt Inst, grad, 49.
Exhibitions: IBM Gallery Regional, Poughkeepsie, N Y, 66; Bennett Jr Col Regional, Millbrook, N Y, 66; Marist Col Regional, Poughkeepsie, 66; Vassar Col Regional, Poughkeepsie, 67; Regional Ann Open Show, Art Guild, Boca Raton, Fla, 72.
Teaching: Pvt classes in painting, 60-68.

Positions: Art dir, Periodical House, New York, N Y, 49-53; art dir, McFadden Publ, New York, 53-55; mem bd dirs, Dutchess Co Art Asn, Poughkeepsie, 59-61; pres, IBM Art Club, Poughkeepsie, 59-61.
Awards: First prize for Wharf (oil), IBM Watson Trophy Show, 67; first prize for Scene (oil), Dutchess Co Art Asn, 67; second prize for Lighthouse (acrylics), Art Guild Boca Raton, 72.
Bibliography: Lab artist, IBM News, 60; Artists, IBM Think, 71.
Memberships: Art Guild Boca Raton.
Mailing Address: 750 N E 40th St, Boca Raton, FL 33432.

ADAMS, WILLIAM HOWARD
Art Administrator, Collector
b Jackson Co, Mo.
Study & Training: Univ Mo; Washington & Lee Univ, LLB.
Positions: Trustee, Kansas City Art Inst, 56-62; chmn, Mo Coun Arts, 63-65; mem int coun, Mus Mod Art; asst adminr, Nat Gallery Art; mem, Truman Libr Bd; mem ed bd, Cult Affairs.
Collection: Contemporary and primitive art.
Publications: Ed, The community and the arts, 64; auth, Politics of art, 67.
Mailing Address: 2820 P St N W, Washington, DC 20007.

ADDAMS, CHARLES SAMUEL
Cartoonist
b Westfield, N J, Jan 7, 12.
Study & Training: Colgate Univ, 29-30; Univ Pa, 30-31; Grand Cent Sch Art, New York, 31-32.
Exhibitions: Fogg Art Mus; R I Sch Design; Original Drawings, Mus City New York, 56; Pa Univ Mus, 57; Metrop Mus Art Print Exhib.
Publications: Contribr, New Yorker Mag; auth, Night crawlers, 57, The groaning board, 64 & My crowd, 70, Simon & Schuster; auth, Black Maria, Pocket Books, Inc, 60; auth, The Charles Addams Mother Goose, Harper-Row, 67; plus others.
Mailing Address: c/o New Yorker Mag, 25 W 43rd St, New York, NY 10036.

ADELMAN, DOROTHY (LEE) McCLINTOCK
Printmaker, Painter
b Manhattan, N Y.
Study & Training: Art Stud League New York, with Roberto Delamonico & Michael Ponce de Leon; Westchester Art Workshop, White Plains, N Y, with John Ruddley & Stephen Rogers Peck; Silvermine Guild Artists, Inc, New Canaan, Conn, with Ray Riddaback; Hudson River Mus, Yonkers, N Y, with Harold Wollcott.
Work in Public Collections: Hudson River Mus; Westchester Art Workshop; in pvt collections throughout U S A & Israel.
Exhibitions: Carroll Condit Gallery, White Plains, 69-72; Yonkers Art Asn, Hudson River Mus, 71-72; Katonah Gallery, Katonah, N Y, 71-72; Miller Gallery, Cincinnati, Ohio, 72; Scarborough Galleries, Ossining, N Y, 71 & 72.
Teaching: Instr painting, Am Red Cross, White Plains, 71; instr painting, Westchester Art Workshop, 71.
Positions: Bd mem, White Plains Outdoor Art Exhib, Inc, 70-73.
Awards: Purchase award, Westchester Art Workshop, 69; Hudson River Mus Purchase Award, 71; first & third award, Mamaroneck Artist Guild, 72.
Memberships: Art Stud League New York; Mamaroneck Artists Guild; Westchester Art Soc; Yonkers Art Asn (publ/pub rels div, 72-73); Katonah Gallery (coun mem, 70-73).
Dealers: Scarborough Art Galleries, Arcadian Shopping Center, Rte 9, Ossining, NY 10562; Carroll Condit Gallery, 210 Mamaroneck Ave, White Plains, NY 10601.
Mailing Address: 1286 Hardscrabble Rd, Chappaqua, NY 10514.

ADKISON, KATHLEEN (GEMBERLING)
Painter
Preferred Media: Oils.
b Beatrice, Nebr.
Study & Training: With Mark Tobey.
Work in Public Collections: Paintings, Seattle Art Mus, Wash; Seattle First Nat Bank; Bank Wash, Tacoma & Spokane; Butler Inst Am Art, Youngstown, Ohio; Cheney Cowles Mus, Spokane.
Exhibitions: Northwest Ann, Seattle, 47-71; El Paso Nat, 60-70; five Butler Inst Am Art Ann, 61-69; World's Fair Northwest Artists, Seattle, 62; Pa Acad Fine Arts 159th Ann, 64.
Teaching: Instr painting, Wash State Univ Exten, 55-67.
Awards: Sun Carnival First Prize, El Paso Mus, 61; Dr Fuller Purchase Award, Northwest Ann, 61; prize for Winter Retreat, Friends Am Art, 69.
Dealer: Gordon Woodside Gallery, 803 E Union, Seattle, WA 98122.
Mailing Address: 1203 Overbluff, Spokane, WA 99203.

ADLER, A M
Art Dealer
b New York, N Y, Sept 2, 02.
Study & Training: Yale Col; Yale Sch Archit; Inst Fine Arts, New York Univ.
Positions: Past pres, Art & Antique Dealers Asn; past pres, Confedn Int Negociants Objets Art.
Mailing Address: Hirschl & Adler Galleries, 21 E 67th St, New York, NY 10021.

ADLER, BILLY (TELETHON)
Sculptor, Photographer
b New York, N Y, Sept 5, 40.
Study & Training: Univ Pa, BA; Annenberg Sch Commun, MA.
Work in Public Collections: Vancouver Art Gallery, B C; Pasadena Mus Art, Calif; Baltimore Mus Art, Md; Mus Mod Art, New York; Berkeley Mus Art, Calif.
Teaching: Vis prof archit, Calif Inst Arts, 71; vis prof archit, Univ Calif, Santa Barbara, 72.
Awards: Martin Lesuer achievement award, 72.
Bibliography: Pop art, Time Mag, 11/71.
Publications: Co-auth, Coffee shops, 71; Here's the scoop, 72 & Tube of Milhous, 72, West Mag; co-auth, Radical software, 72.
Mailing Address: 3666 Barry Ave, Los Angeles, CA 90066.

ADLER, LEE
Painter, Printmaker
Preferred Media: Oil, Silk Screen Printing.
b New York, N Y, May 22, 34.
Study & Training: Art Stud League, New York, 62-64; Brooklyn Mus Art Sch, N Y, 64-65; Pratt Graphics Ctr, New York, 69.
Work in Public Collections: Metrop Mus Art, New York; British Mus, London, Eng; Whitney Mus Am Art, New York, Art Inst Chicago, Ill; Corcoran Gallery Art, Washington, D C.
Exhibitions: Childe Hassam Fund Competition, Am Acad Arts & Lett, New York, 68-69; 20th New Eng Exhib, New Canaan, Conn, 69; Nat Acad Design, New York, 69; 17th Nat Print Biennial, Brooklyn Mus, 70; Print Acquisitions, Whitney Mus Am Art, 70.
Awards: Grumbacher Award, Jersey City Mus, 68; Burndy Corp Award, 69; purchase award, Childe Hassam Fund Competition, 69.
Bibliography: John Canaday (auth), Lee Adler, New York Times, 12/68; Lee Adler, Arts 1/69; J G Bowles (auth), Lee Adler, Art News, 3/72.
Memberships: Audubon Artists; Silvermine Guild Artists; Allied Artists Am.
Dealers: Bertha Schaefer Gallery, 41 E 57th St, New York, NY 10022; Associated American Artists, 663 Fifth Ave, New York, NY 10022.
Mailing Address: 168 Clinton St, Brooklyn, NY 11201.

ADLER, ROBERT
Painter
Preferred Media: Oil, Ink.
b New York, N Y, Jan 10, 30.
Study & Training: Syracuse Univ; Atelier 17, with Stanley Hayter, Paris, France.
Exhibitions: Silvermine Guild, Conn, 63; Drawings, U S A, 65; West Side Artists, Riverside Mus, New York, 66; Second Kent Invitational, Kent State Univ, Ohio, 68.
Dealer: Poindexter Gallery, 24 E 84th St, New York, NY 10028.
Mailing Address: 120 Riverside Dr, New York, NY 10024.

ADLER, SAMUEL (MARCUS)
Painter, Educator
Preferred Media: Oil, Collage.
b New York, N Y, July 30, 98.
Study & Training: Nat Acad Design, with Leon Kroll & Charles Louis Hinton.
Work in Public Collections: Whitney Mus Am Art, New York; Nat Collection Fine Arts, Smithsonian Inst, Washington, D C; Joseph H Hirshhorn Mus, New York; Brooklyn Mus, N Y; Munson-Williams-Proctor Inst, Utica, N Y, plus others.
Exhibitions: Pa Acad Fine Arts, Philadelphia, 48, 51, 52, 53 & 68; Univ Ill, 49-53, 55, 57, 59, 61, 63, 65, 67 & 71; American Painting Today, Metrop Mus Art, 50; Whitney Mus Art Painting Ann, 51, 52, 55, 56 & 57; Art U S A, New York, 62; and many others including 23 one-man exhib, 48-72.
Teaching: Prof art, New York Univ, 48-; prof art, Univ Ill, 59-60; vis prof art, Univ Ga, 67 & 68.
Positions: Pres, New York Chap, Artists Equity Asn, 54-55.
Awards: J Henry Schiedt Mem Prize, Pa Acad Fine Arts, 51; purchase award, Whitney Mus Am Art, 54; artist-in-residence award, Ford Found, 65.
Bibliography: Lee Nordness (auth), Art U S A now, Viking Press, 63; Allen Weller (auth), The joys & sorrows of recent American art, Univ Ill Press, 68; Graham Collier (auth), Form, space & vision, 3rd ed, Prentice Hall, 72.

Publications: Illusr, Candide, World Publ, 47; contribr, Education & the imagination, Univ Mich, 58; Education synopsis, New York Univ, 68; Samuel Adler, recent collages, Ga Mus Art, 68; Art Educ Mag, 72.
Dealer: Frank Rehn Gallery, 655 Madison Ave, New York, NY 10022.
Mailing Address: 27 E 22nd St, New York, NY 10010.

ADLER, SEBASTIAN J
Museum Director
b Chicago, Ill, Sept 11, 32.
Study & Training: Winona State Col, BS; Univ Minn, Duluth.
Positions: Founder-dir, Nobles Co Art Ctr, 58-60; dir, Sioux Falls Art Ctr, 60-62; asst dir, Wichita Art Mus, 63-64 & dir, 64-65; dir, Contemp Arts Mus, 66-
Memberships: Col Arts Asn; Am Asn Mus; Northwood Inst (adv comt); Tex Comn Arts & Humanities (adv comt).
Mailing Address: Contemporary Arts Museum, 5216 Montrose St, Houston, TX 77006.

ADRIAN, BARBARA (MRS FRANKLIN TRAMUTOLA)
Painter, Collector
Preferred Media: Oil.
b New York, N Y, July 25, 31.
Study & Training: Art Stud League New York with Reginald Marsh, 47-54; Hunter Col, 51; Columbia Univ, 52-54.
Work in Public Collections: Butler Inst Am Art, Youngstown, Ohio; Univ Southern Ill, Carbondale; City Hall, San Juan, Puerto Rico.
Exhibitions: Childe Hassam Fund Purchase Exhib, New York, 68; Nat Acad Design, New York, 68; Butler Inst Am Art, 70; Gallery Mod Art, New York, 70; Suffolk Mus, Stony Brook, New York, 71.
Teaching: Art instr painting & drawing, Art Stud League New York, 68-
Positions: Art consultant, R H Macy, New York, 60-61; Saks Fifth Ave, New York, 60; Doyle Dane & Bernbach, New York, 60.
Awards: Benjamin Altman Prize, Nat Acad Design, 68.
Bibliography: Edmund Burk Feldman (auth), Art as image & idea, Prentice-Hall.
Memberships: Life mem, Art Stud League New York.
Collection: Reginald Marsh, John Sloan, Will Barnet, Henry Pearson, Rouault, Versalius, Goya, Martin Lewis.
Dealers: Eileen Kuhlik, 23 E 67th St, New York, NY 10021; Capricorn Galleries, Washington, DC 20014.
Mailing Address: 420 E 64th St, New York, NY 10021.

AGOOS, HERBERT M
Collector
b Boston, Mass, Dec 12, 15.
Study & Training: Harvard Col, AB; also fine arts mus course with Paul Sachs.
Collection: Twentieth century modern art.
Mailing Address: 11 Kennedy Rd, Cambridge, MA 02138.

AGOPOFF, AGOP MINASS
Sculptor
Preferred Media: Clay, Granite, Marble, Bronze, Wood.
b Sliven, Bulgaria; U S citizen.
Study & Training: Basic art training with Kiril Shivarov & Prof George Nicholov, Varna, Bulgaria; Atelier Damian, Constantza, Roumania; Columbia Univ; Nat Acad Design with eminent sculptor Charles Keck.
Work in Public Collections: Off Commandant, USMC, Washington, D C; Nat Hist Mus, Erevan, Armenia; Diocese, Armenian Church of N & S Am, New York, N Y; Hall of Fame for Great Americans, New York Univ; J Edgar Hoover Bureau, U S Dept Justice, Washington, D C.
Commissions: Bronze mem, Rev Dr John Henry House, Thessaloniki, Greece, 34; heroic bronze statue, Gov H Bell, Belton, Tex, 37; Albert Dorne Award Medal for Famous Artists Sch, New York, N Y, 64; Heroic portrait plaque of John F Kennedy, J F Kennedy Memorial, Hyannis, Mass, 64; four large portrait tablets, Dow Chem Co, Midland, Mich, 70.
Exhibitions: Nat Acad Design, 43-; Nat Sculpture Soc, 60-; Hudson Valley Art Asn, 61-; Allied Artists Am, 62-; Am Artists Prof League, 69-
Awards: Gold medals of honor, Hudson Valley Art Asn, 63 & 71; Lindsey Morris Memorial Award, Nat Sculpture Soc, 64; Daniel Chester French Medal, Nat Acad Design, 71.
Memberships: Nat Acad Design (assoc); fel, Allied Artists Am; fel, Am Artists Prof League; fel, Hudson Valley Art Asn; fel, Nat Sculpture Soc.
Mailing Address: Summit Dr, Denville, NJ 07834.

AGOSTINELLI, MARIO
Painter, Sculptor
Preferred Media: Oils.
b Arequipa, Peru, Sept 18, 23; U S citizen.
Study & Training: Studied in Arg, Brazil, France & Italy.

Work in Public Collections: Acad Bellas Artes, Buenos Aires, Arg; Mus Mod Art, Rio de Janeiro; Springfield Mus Art, Mass.
Exhibitions: Allied Artists Am; Butler Inst Am Art; Conn Acad Fine Arts; Knickerbocker Artists; Nat Acad Design, New York, N Y; plus other group & one-man shows.
Awards: Samuel Morse Medal, Nat Acad Design; gold medal, Knickerbocker Artists; gold medal, Salon Watercolor, Lima, Peru; plus others.
Dealer: Beilin Gallery, 655 Madison Ave, New York, NY 10021.
Mailing Address: 420 E 79th St, New York, NY 10021.

AGOSTINI, PETER
Sculptor
b New York, N Y, Feb 13, 13.
Study & Training: Leonardo da Vinci Sch Art, N Y.
Work in Public Collections: Univ Tex; Univ Calif; Univ Southern Calif; Int Ladies Garment Workers Union; Whitney Mus Am Art.
Exhibitions: Whitney Mus Am Art, 64, 70 & 72; Sculpture of the 60's, Los Angeles, Calif, 67; Int Sculpture, Guggenheim Mus, 67 & Toronto, Ont, 68; Nat Inst Arts & Lett, 72; N Y State Pavilion, World's Fair; plus others.
Teaching: Lect & summer courses, Columbia Univ, 61; mem staff, Wagner Col, 68.
Awards: Longview Found Purchase Awards, 60-62; Brandeis Univ Creative Arts Award, 64; Guggenheim fel, 66.
Bibliography: Article, In: Time Mag, 11/13/64.
Dealer: Zabriskie Gallery, 613 E 12th St, New York, NY 10009.
Mailing Address: 151 Avenue B, New York, NY 10009.

AHLGREN, ROY B
Painter, Printmaker
Preferred Media: Acrylics.
b Erie, Pa, July 6, 27.
Study & Training: Erie Tech Sch with Joseph Plavcan; Villa Maria Col with Prof Zoltan Heya (portraiture); Famous Artists Sch, dipl.
Work in Public Collections: U S Info Agency, Washington, D C; Minn Mus Art, St Paul; Seattle Art Mus, Wash; Tex Tech Univ Mus, Lubbock; Miss Art Asn, Jackson.
Commissions: Edition of serigraphs, Assoc Am Artists, New York, N Y, 70; church bull cover designs, Lutheran Churches, Erie, Pa, 71-72.
Exhibitions: Nat Acad Design, Nat Galleries, New York, N Y, 68-69; 21st Nat Exhib Prints, Libr Cong, Washington, D C, 69; Northwest Printmakers Int Exhib, Seattle, 69-71; 164th Ann Exhib, Pa Acad Fine Arts, Philadelphia, 69; Expo-70, U S Pavilion, World's Fair, Osaka, Japan, 70.
Teaching: Instr art, Tech Mem High Sch, Erie, 70-
Positions: Assoc, Galerie 8, Erie, 67-; bd mem, Erie Art Ctr, 70-72.
Awards: First prize, graphics, 11th R I Arts Festival, Providence, 69; third award for painting, 13th Nat Jury Show, Chautauqua Art Asn, N Y, 70; purchase award, drawing, Drawings, USA, Minnesota Mus Art, St Paul, 70.
Bibliography: Jean Reeves (auth), One-man show, Buffalo Evening News, 69; Jane Abrams (auth), Educational slide collection, Univ New Mex, 71; Lynwood Kreneck (auth), Colorprint USA filmstrip, Tex Tech Univ, 71.
Memberships: Boston Printmakers; Philadelphia Water Color Club.
Publications: Contribr, Showcase sect, Famous Artists Mag, 69; Assoc Am Artists catalog, 71; Contemporary Artists, U S A, Livingston, 71; Contemporary American Printmakers, N Y Graphic Soc, 72; Ferdinand-Roten Catalog, 72.
Dealers: Associated American Artists, 663 Fifth Ave, New York, NY 10022; Bermond Art Ltd, Lake Success, NY 11040.
Mailing Address: 1012 Boyer Rd, Erie, PA 16511.

AHLSKOG, SIRKKA
Craftsman, Sculptor
b Finland, Apr 15, 17.
Study & Training: Suolahden Kansanopisto, Finland; Craft Stud League, New York.
Work in Public Collections: Atlanta Art Asn Mus; Norfolk Mus Arts & Sci; Arch Am Art, div Smithsonian Inst.
Exhibitions: Cooper Union Mus, 60, 61 & 63; Design Ctr, N Y, 60 & 62; one-man show, Columbia Mus Art, S C, 61; Princeton Art Asn, 64; Guild Hall, East Hampton, N Y, 67; plus others.
Teaching: Instr tapestry weaving, Penland Sch Handicrafts, 56-57; lectr tapestry weaving.
Awards: Pen & Brush Club Awards, 57-61 & 63.
Memberships: Pen & Brush Club; Artist-Craftsmen New York, Del (bd mem).
Mailing Address: 414 E 83rd St, New York, NY 10028.

AHLSTROM, RONALD GUSTIN
Painter
Preferred Media: Collage & Acrylic (mixed media).
b Chicago, Ill, Jan 17, 22.
Study & Training: Art Inst Chicago, BFA, with Paul Weighart; Univ Chicago; DePaul Univ.
Work in Public Collections: Art Inst Chicago; Tacoma Art Mus, Wash; Philbrook Art Ctr, Tulsa, Okla; Barat Col Collection Lake Forest, Ill; Container Corp Am, Chicago.
Exhibitions: 27th Corcoran Biennial, Washington, D C, 61; Chicago & Vicinity Exhib, Art Inst Chicago, 62; 12 Chicago Artists, McCormick Pl Gallery, Chicago, 62; 50th Northwest Ann, Seattle Art Mus, Wash, 64; 5 Abstractionists, Faulkner Main St Gallery, Chicago, 68.
Awards: Clyde Carr Prize for painting, Art Inst Chicago, 55 & Wm H Bartels Prize, 58; 50th Northwest Ann, Purchase prize, Ford Found, 64.
Bibliography: Meilach & Ten Hoor (auth), Collage & found art, Reinholt Pub, 64; H Haydon (auth), article in Chicago Mag, New Chicago Found, 68; Robert Glauber (auth), article in Art Scene Mag, 69.
Dealer: Joseph Faulkner Main Street Gallery, 100 East Walton St, Chicago, IL 60611.
Mailing Address: 902 E St Charles Rd, Lombard, IL 60148.

AHYSEN, HARRY JOSEPH
Painter, Educator
Preferred Media: Oils, Watercolors.
b Port Arthur, Tex.
Study & Training: Tulane Univ; Univ Houston, BFA; Univ Tex, Austin, MFA.
Work in Public Collections: Regent's Room, Univ Texas.
Commissions: Cover, The Texaco Star, Texaco, Inc, 57; mural, Buccaneer Hotel, Galveston, Tex, 66; murals, Flagship Hotel, Galveston, 67; related paintings, Huntsville Nat Bank, Tex, 70; landscape paintings, David Tinsley, Huntsville, 71.
Exhibitions: Miss Nat Exhib, Jackson, 62 & 65; Beaumont Tri-State Ann Art Mus Show, Tex, 63, 64 & 65; San Antonio Five-State Watercolor Show, Tex, 64; Houston Power & Light Co Exhib; one-man show, Port Arthur, Tex, 70; Southwestern Watercolor Soc Exhib, 72; plus others.
Teaching: Asst prof oil painting, Sam Houston State Univ, 63-
Awards: President's award, Beaumont Ann Mus Show, 63; first prize, Houston Art League Ann, 64; first prize, Miss Nat Exhib, 65.
Publications: Auth, Composition devices for landscapes, 70; Paul Schumann (monogr), 72.
Mailing Address: Art Dept, Sam Houston State University, Huntsville, TX 77340.

AIROLA, PAAVO
Painter, Writer
Preferred Media: Oil, Watercolor.
b Karelia, Finland; Can citizen.
Study & Training: Isaac Grünewald Art Sch, Stockholm Sweden, 48; Otte Sköid Art Sch, Sweden; Academie Libre, Stockholm.
Work in Public Collections: Nat Gallery, Stockholm; Örebro Mus Fine Art, Sweden; Hudikswal Art Mus, Sweden; London Art Mus, Ont; Zacks Collection, New York, N Y.
Exhibitions: Royal Can Acad Fine Art Ann, 54-61; Toronto Art Gallery, 59; Phoenix Art Mus, 60-64; Galleri Z, Stockholm, 67; Gallerie Raymond Duncan, Paris, France, 67.
Bibliography: Revue Moderne, Paris, 12/64.
Memberships: Royal Canadian Acad Fine Arts (assoc 58-); Ontario Soc Artists; fel Int Inst Arts & Lett; Can Soc Painters in Water Colour.
Mailing Address: P O Box 22001, Phoenix, AZ 85028.

AKSTON, JOSEPH JAMES
Collector, Patron
Study & Training: Sch For Serv, Georgetown Univ.
Positions: Pres & ed, Arts Mag, Art Voices Mag & Art Digest Newsletter, New York, N Y; mem bd overseers, art prog, Brandeis Univ, Waltham, Mass; bd dirs, Whitney Mus Am Art Coun, New York; mem nat coun & trustee, Mus African Art, Washington, D C.
Memberships: Four Arts Soc.
Mailing Address: Hotel Pierre, 2 E 61st St, New York, NY 10021.

ALAJALOV, CONSTANTIN
Painter, Illustrator
b Russia, Nov 18, 00; U S citizen.
Study & Training: Univ Petrograd.
Work in Public Collections: Brooklyn Museum, N Y; Philadelphia Mus Art, Pa; Mus Mod Art, New York, N Y; Mus City New York; Dallas Mus Fine Arts, Tex.

Commissions: Murals for S S America; The Hands of Leonard Bern Bernstein, 67; sets for Michael Mordkin's Ballet and posters for many theatrical productions.
Exhibitions: Many nat exhibs; one-man shows in Hollywood, Calif, New York & Dallas.
Teaching: Prof art, Phoenix Art Inst & Archipenko's Ecole Beaux-Arts.
Publications: Illusr, George Gershwin's Song Book, Alice Duer Miller's Cinderella, Our Hearts Were Young and Gay, Nuts in May, Bottoms Up & others; contribr to many nat mag.
Mailing Address: 140 W 57th St, New York, NY 10019.

ALAUPOVIĆ, ALEXANDRA V
Sculptor, Educator
Preferred Media: Bronze, Wood, Marble, Welded Steel.
b Slatina, Yugoslavia, Dec 21, 21; U S citizen.
Study & Training: Acad Visual Arts, Univ Zagreb, Academic sculptor and teaching certificate, 48; Acad Visual Arts, Prague, 49; Univ Ill, Urbana-Champaign, 59-60; Univ Okla, MFA, 66.
Work in Public Collections: Univ Okla Mus Art, Norman; Gradski muzej, Varazdin, Yugoslavia; Muzej otoka Hvara, Yugoslavia; Oklahoma City Pub Libr, Okla; Okla Art Ctr, Oklahoma City.
Commissions: Portrait-busts, Oklahoma City Libr, 62; Okla Med Res Found Off Bldg, 64; First Unitarian Church, Oklahoma City, 64.
Exhibitions: Exposition Asn Peintres, Graveurs et Sculpteurs de Croatie, Dubrovnik, Yugoslavia, 56; ULUH (association of visual artists in Croatia), Yugoslavia, Beograd, 56; 35th Ann Springfield Art Mus, Mo, 65; On Music, Univ Okla Mus Art, 68; Ann Eight State Exhib of Painting & Sculpture, Oklahoma City, 71.
Teaching: Instr drawing, basic form & sculpture, Univ Okla, 64-66; instr sculpture, Okla Sci & Arts Found, Oklahoma City, 69-
Awards: Jacobson Award, Univ Okla, 64; hon mention in sculpture, Philbrook Art Ctr, Tulsa, 67 & first sculpture award, 70.
Memberships: The MacDowell Club of Allied Arts.
Dealer: Sales & Rental Gallery, Oklahoma Art Center, 3113 Pershing Blvd, Oklahoma City, OK 73107.
Mailing Address: 11908 N Bryant, Rt 1, Box 167 A, Oklahoma City, OK 73111.

ALBEE, GRACE THURSTON ARNOLD
Engraver, Painter
Preferred Media: Wood.
b Scituate, R I, July 28, 90.
Study & Training: R I Sch Design, class of 1912; wood engraving with Paul Bornet, Institut D'Esthetique Contemporaine Cours D'Art, Paris, France, 28-29.
Work in Public Collections: Libr Cong, Washington, D C; Carnegie Inst, Washington, D C; Metrop Mus, New York, N Y; Brooklyn Mus, N Y; Cleveland Mus, Ohio; plus one other.
Commissions: Wood engravings, Forgotten Things, Cleveland Mus & Print Club, Ohio, 44; designer frontispiece, A little book of aphorisms, Scribner, 47; Co-op Farm, Benefit Scholar Fund Alumni Asn, R I Sch Design, 48; Bridge by the Golf Course, Buck Hiu Falls Print Club, Pa, 48; designer frontispiece, Unicorns & tadpoles, Exposition, 58.
Exhibitions: Venice Biennale, Italy, 40; Artists for Victory, Metrop Mus, 42; Nat Prints Exhib, Libr Cong, 43, 44; Nat Exhib, Brooklyn Mus, 47, 54; Nat Exhib Watercolors & Prints, Metrop Mus, 52.
Positions: Gov bd, Nat Alumni Asn, R I Sch Design, 44-47, class sect, 44-65.
Awards: Prizes for Artists for Victory, Metrop Mus, 42 & Nat Exhib Watercolors & Prints, 52; Samuel Finley Breese Morse Medal, Nat Acad Design, 62, 72; purchase award, Pennell Collection, Libr Cong, 43, 44.
Bibliography: Malcolm C Salaman (auth), A chat to the print lover, The Studio, London, Eng, 31; Ernest W Watson (auth), Wood engravings by Grace Albee, American Artist, 12/46; Albert Reese (auth), American prize prints of the 20th century.
Memberships: Boston Printmakers Soc; Soc Am Graphic Artists (selection jury, 54); Am Artists Prof League (chmn selection & awards jury, 66-, chmn mem comt, 69); life fel Metrop Mus Art; Nat Acad Design (chmn nominating comt, 52-).
Dealer: Kennedy Galleries, Inc, 20 E 56th St, New York, NY 10022.
Mailing Address: 84-43 123rd St, Kew Gardens, NY 11415.

ALBERS, ANNI
Designer, Graphic Artist
Preferred Media: Textiles.
b Berlin, Ger, June 12, 99; U S citizen.
Study & Training: Bauhaus, Weimar, Ger, dipl; Md Inst Col Art, DFA, 72.
Work in Public Collections: Metrop Mus Art, New York, N Y; Mus Mod Art, New York; Art Inst Chicago, Ill; Victoria & Albert Mus, London, Eng; Baltimore Mus Art, Md.
Commissions: Mem to Nazi victims, comn by List Family for Jewish Mus; Ark Curtain, Dallas.
Exhibitions: Mus Mod Art, New York; Mass Inst Technol, Cambridge; Carnegie Inst Technol, Pittsburgh, Pa; Yale Univ Art Gallery, New Haven, Conn; Honolulu Acad Art, Hawaii.
Teaching: Asst prof art, Black Mountain Col, 33-49; lects, leading univs & mus.
Awards: Gold medal, Am Inst Architects, 61; citation, Philadelphia Col Art, 62; Tamarind Lithography Workshop Fel, Los Angeles, 64.
Publications: Auth, Anni Albers: on designing, Wesleyan Univ Press, 62 & 71; Anni Albers: on weaving, Wesleyan Univ Press, 65 & 72; Anni Albers: pre-Columbian Mexican miniatures, Praeger, 70.

ALBERS, JOSEF
Painter, Printmaker
b Bottrop, Ger, Mar 19, 88; U S citizen.
Study & Training: Royal Art Sch, Berlin, Ger; Art Acad, Munich, Ger; Bauhaus, Weimar, Ger.
Work in Public Collections: Metrop Mus Art, New York, N Y; Solomon R Guggenheim Mus, New York; Mus Mod Art, New York; Whitney Mus Am Art, New York; Chicago Art Inst, Ill.
Commissions: America (brick mural), Harvard Univ, 50; Two Gates (glass mural), Time & Life Bldg, New York, 61; Manhattan (mural in plastic), Pan Am Bldg, New York, 63; Growth (two wall paintings), Rochester Inst Technol, 69; Repeat and Reverse (supraporta), Yale Univ Art Bldg.
Exhibitions: One-man traveling exhib, Homage to the Square, Mus Mod Art, S Am & U S, 64-66; Josef Albers White Line Squares, Los Angeles Co Mus, 66; Kunsthalle, Dusseldorf, W Ger, 70; Princeton Univ Art Mus, 71; Metrop Mus Art, 11/71-1/72.
Teaching: Design, Bauhaus, Weimar, Dessau & Berlin, 23-33; design & painting, Black Mountain Col, N C, 33-46; painting & design, Yale Univ, 50-60.
Awards: Commander's Cross, Order of Merit, Ger Fed Repub, 68; hon citizen, Bottrop, Ger, 70.
Bibliography: Monogr, Eugene Gomringer (auth), Josef Albers (Eng ed), Wittenborn, 68; Werner Spies (auth), Joseph Albers (Eng ed), Abrams, 70; Jurgen Wissmann (auth), Josef Albers (Ger ed), Bongers, Recklinghausen, W Ger, 71.
Memberships: Am Abstract Artists; Am Inst Graphic Arts; Print Coun Am; Nat Inst Arts & Lett.
Publications: Co-auth, Despite straight lines, Yale Univ Press, 61; auth, Poems and drawings, Wittenborn, 61; Interaction of color, Yale Univ Press, 63; Search versus re-search, Trinity Col, 69; Formulation: articulation, Abrams, 72.
Mailing Address: 808 Birchwood Dr, Orange, CT 06477.

ALBERT, CALVIN
Sculptor, Educator
Preferred Media: Plaster, Metal.
b Grand Rapids, Mich, Nov 19, 18.
Study & Training: Grand Rapids Art Gallery with Otto Karl Bach; Art Inst Chicago; Inst Design with Moholy-Nagy & György Kepes; Archipenko Sch Sculpture; Fulbright advan res grant, 61-62; Tiffany grant 63, 65; Guggenheim fel, 66.
Work in Public Collections: Metrop Mus, New York, N Y; Whitney Mus Am Art, New York; Art Inst Chicago; Jewish Mus, New York; Detroit Inst Arts.
Commissions: Ark Doors & Candelabra, Steinberg House, Park Ave Synagogue, New York, 54; Outdoor Candelabra, Temple Israel, Tulsa, Okla, 55; Eternal Light & Candelabra, Temple Israel, Bridgeport, Conn, 57; Crucifix, Tabernacle & Candlesticks, St Paul's Church, Peoria, Ill, 59.
Exhibitions: Unknown Political Prisoner Prizewinners, Mus Mod Art, New York, & Tate Gallery, London, Eng, 53; le Dessin Contemporains aux Etats Unis, Musée Nat d'Arte Moderne, Paris, France, 54; Whitney Ann Am Artists, 54-68; Univ Ill Contemp Painting & Sculpture, 57 & 65; 20th Century Masters of Drawing, Gallery Mod Art, New York, 64.
Teaching: Instr sculpture & design, Inst Design, Chicago, 42-46; instr color & drawing, Brooklyn College, 47-49; prof art & head grad sculpture program, Pratt Inst, 49-
Publications: Co-auth, Figure drawing comes to life, 57.
Mailing Address: 222 Willoughby Ave, Brooklyn, NY 11205.

ALBERTAZZI, MARIO
Painter, Art Critic
Preferred Media: Oil.
b Bologna, Italy, Dec 9, 20.
Study & Training: Istituto Tecnico, Bologna, Italy; Art Stud League, New York, N Y.
Work in Public Collections: Italian Consulate General & Casa Italiana, Columbia Univ, New York.
Exhibitions: Galerie Internationale, 68, Ligoa Duncan Gallery, 69, New York Pub Libr, 69, Caravan House Galleries, 70 & Pacem in Terris Gallery, New York, 71.

Positions: Art ed, Il Progresso Italo-Americano, New York, 64-;
corresp, Il Giornale d'Italia, Rome, Italy, 70-
Awards: First prize, collage, Composers, Authors & Artists of Am
Nat Contest, 69.
Memberships: Composers, Authors & Artists of Am; Burr Artists.
Mailing Address: 545 W End Ave, New York, NY 10024.

ALBIN, EDGAR A
Educator, Art Critic
b Columbus, Kans, Dec 17, 08.
Study & Training: Univ Tulsa, BA; State Univ Iowa, MA; Ariz State
Col; also with Grant Wood, Philip Guston & Donald Mattison; Ful-
bright res grant, India, 54-55.
Work in Public Collections: Little Rock Mus Fine Arts, Ark.
Exhibitions: 14th Int Exhib of Northwest Printmakers, Seattle, Wash,
42; Mid-Western Artists, Nelson Galleries, Kansas City, Mo, 42;
Southern Printmakers Circulating Exhib, 42; Tex State Art Asn
Int, Elizabeth Ney Galleries, Austin, 43; one-man exhib, Thayer
Mus, Univ Kans, 44.
Teaching: Instr art & humanities, Tulsa Pub Schs, Okla, 31-39; assoc
prof art hist & studio, Univ Tulsa, 39-47; prof art hist, Univ Ark,
47-62; vis prof, Stetson Univ, 50-52; prof & hd, Dept Art, South-
west Mo State Univ, 62-
Positions: Pres Mo Col Art Asn; mem seminar Am insts & cult, Tate
Inst, Bangalore, India, 55.
Memberships: Am Asn Univ Prof (pres, 67-68); Am Inst Architects;
Delta Phi Delta.
Research: Asian art and art of the twentieth century.
Publications: Co-auth, Syllabus for a basic course in the arts (2
vols) & Syllabus for humanities (2 vols), Univ Ark, 53; auth, Cul-
ture of the Orient, Col Art J, summer 55; auth, Howard J Whit-
lach, sculptor, Art Trends, Madras, India, 1/62; auth, The arts,
weekly column in Leader & Press, Springfield, Mo, 71-
Mailing Address: 1332 S Rogers St, Springfield, MO 65804.

ALBRECHT, MARY DICKSON
Sculptor, Painter
Preferred Media: Steel, Bronze, Metals, Plastics.
b Dothan, Ala, June 4, 30.
Study & Training: Univ Houston; Tex Woman's Univ, BS (sculpture
with honors), 70.
Work in Public Collections: Okla Art Ctr Mus, Oklahoma City; Univ
Tex Permanent Collection, Arlington; City Dallas Park & Rec-
reation Dept, Tex.
Exhibitions: 13th Nat Exhib Prints & Drawings, Okla Art Ctr, 71;
15th Tex Crafts Exhib, Dallas Mus Fine Arts, 71; Tex Fine Arts
Asn State Citation Show, 71 & 72 & 61st Ann Nat Exhib, 72, La-
guna Gloria Mus, Austin, Tex.
Awards: Juror's choice & circuit merit awards, Tex Fine Arts Asn
State Citation Show, 71 & 72; purchase award, art acquisition
comt, Univ Tex, Arlington, 72.
Mailing Address: 7646 La Bolsa Dr, Dallas, TX 75240.

ALBRIGHT, IVAN LE LORRAINE
Painter
b North Harvey, Ill, Feb 20, 97.
Study & Training: Northwestern Univ, 15-16; Ill Sch Archit, 16-17;
Ecole Regionale Beaux-Arts, Nantes, 19; Art Inst Chicago, 20-
23; Pa Acad Fine Arts, 23; Nat Acad Design, 24.
Work in Public Collections: Brooklyn Mus, N Y; Carnegie Inst,
Pittsburgh, Pa; Dallas Mus Fine Arts, Tex; Libr Cong, Washing-
ton, D C; Metrop Mus Art, New York, N Y; plus others.
Commissions: The Portrait of Dorian Gray (painting) for film, 43;
The Temptation of St Anthony (painting) for film, 43.
Exhibitions: Brussels World's Fair; Whitney Mus Am Art, New
York; Corcoran Gallery Art, Washington, D C; Nat Acad De-
sign, New York; retrospective, Art Inst Chicago, 64; plus other
group & one-man shows.
Awards: Nat Inst Arts & Lett Award, 57; Benjamin Altman Prize,
Nat Acad Design, 61; Dunn Int Award, Tate Gallery, 63; plus
many others.
Bibliography: George A Flanagan (auth), Understanding and enjoy-
ing modern art, Thomas Y Crowell, 62; Katharine Kuh (auth),
The artist's voice, talks with seventeen artists, Harper & Row,
62 & Break-up: the core of modern art, New York Graphic Soc,
65; plus others.
Memberships: Nat Acad Design; Chicago Soc Arts.
Mailing Address: c/o Kennedy Galleries, 20 E 56th St, New York,
NY 10022.

ALBRIGHT, MALVIN MARR
Painter, Sculptor
b Chicago, Ill, Feb 20, 97.
Study & Training: Univ Ill; Art Inst Chicago; Pa Acad Fine Arts.
Work in Public Collections: Corcoran Gallery Art; Toledo Mus
Art; Butler Inst Am Art; Univ Ga; Pa Acad Fine Arts; plus
others.

Exhibitions: Nat Acad Design; Whitney Mus Am Art; Mus Mod Art;
Pa Acad Fine Arts; Carnegie Inst; plus others.
Awards: Altman Prize, 42 & 62 & Palmer Mem Prize, Nat Acad
Design; Corcoran Silver Medal, Washington, D C; Dana Medal,
Pa Acad Fine Arts, 65; plus others.
Memberships: Academician Nat Acad Design; fel Royal Soc Arts;
Int Inst Arts & Lett; Nat Sculpture Soc; fel Pa Acad Fine Arts;
plus others.
Mailing Address: 1500 Lake Shore Dr, Chicago, IL 60610.

ALBRIGHT, THOMAS
Art Critic, Writer
b Oakland, Calif, June 10, 35.
Study & Training: Univ Calif, Berkeley, BA.
Positions: Art critic, San Francisco Chronicle, 66-; contrib ed, Vis-
uals, Rolling Stone, San Francisco, 68-; San Francisco ed, Art
Gallery, Ivoryton, Conn, 70-
Publications: Auth, catalogue of exhib, San Francisco Rolling Re-
naissance, 68; auth, articles, In: New York Times, 69.
Mailing Address: 4247 Terrace St, Oakland, CA 94611.

ALCALAY, ALBERT S
Painter
Preferred Media: Oils, Plexiglas.
b Paris, France, Aug 11, 17; U S citizen.
Study & Training: Studied in Paris & Rome, Italy.
Work in Public Collections: Fogg Mus, Harvard Univ; De Cordova &
Dana Mus; Mus Mod Art; Boston Mus Fine Arts; Rome Mus Mod
Art; plus others.
Exhibitions: Mus Mod Art, 55; Whitney Mus Am Art, 56, 58 & 60;
Inst Contemp Art, Boston, 60; Pa Acad Fine Arts, 60; 36 one-
man shows, De Cordova Mus, Lincoln, Mass; plus others.
Teaching: Lectr design, Carpenter Ctr, Harvard Univ, 59-
Awards: Guggenheim fel, 59-60; prize, Boston Art Festival, 60.
Dealer: Pucker-Safari Gallery, 171 Newbury St, Boston, MA 02116.
Mailing Address: 66 Powell, Brookline, MA 02146.

ALCOPLEY, L
Painter, Graphic Artist
Preferred Media: Oils, Acrylics, Watercolors, Inks.
b Ger, June 19, 10; U S citizen.
Study & Training: Studied in Dresden, Ger.
Work in Public Collections: Mus Mod Art, New York, N Y; Mus Mod
Art, Tokyo, Japan; Stedelijk Mus, Amsterdam, Holland; Israel
Mus, Jerusalem; Nat Gallery Iceland, Reykjavik; plus many
others.
Commissions: Mural, Univ Freiburg, Fed Repub Ger, 58.
Exhibitions: One-man shows, Galerie Bing, Paris, France, 56,
Suermondt Mus, Aachen, W Ger, 57 & Stedelijk Mus, 61; Byron
Gallery, New York, 64; Israel Mus, 69-70; also many others.
Positions: Co-ed, Leonardo, Int J of Contemp Artist, 68-
Bibliography: Willem De Kooning & Franz Kline (auth), On works of
Mr Alcopley, 52; Michael Seuphor (auth), Ecritures-dessins
d'Alcopley, 54; Will Grohmann (auth), Alcopley-voies et traces,
61.
Memberships: Am Abstract Artists; Groupe Espace, Paris.
Publications: Auth, Einsichten, drawings by Alcopley to poems by
S E Broese, 59, You don't say, 62 & Alcopley listening to
Heidegger and Hisamatsu, 69; contribr, Cimaise, Paris, Bokubi,
Kyoto, Japan, & numerous other publ.
Mailing Address: 50 Central Park W, New York, NY 10023.

ALDRICH, LARRY
Art Administrator, Collector
Positions: Pres & founder, Larry Aldrich Mus Contemp Art,
Ridgefield, Conn.
Collection: Contemporary painting and sculpture.
Mailing Address: Larry Aldrich Associates, 530 Seventh Ave,
New York, NY 10018.

ALDWINCKLE, ERIC
Designer, Painter
b Oxford, Eng, Jan 22, 09; Can citizen.
Work in Public Collections: Nat Gallery Can, Ottawa, Ont.
Commissions: Oil, Sunnybrook Hosp, Toronto, Ont, 47-48; Heraldy
(egg tempera), Oshawa Col, Ont, 53-; Hydro Electric Tempera,
York Twp, Toronto, 59.
Exhibitions: Ont Soc Artists, 37-49; New York World's Fair, 39;
Nat Gallery, London, Eng, 42-43.
Teaching: Vice prin design, Ont Col Art, 36-42; prin design &
colour, New Sch Design, 44-45.
Positions: Art dir, Stratford Festival, Ont, 55-58; art dir, Univ To-
ronto, 48-53.
Awards: Art direction award, Art Dir Club, 49; Can Dollar Award,
Govt Can, 71.
Bibliography: Paul Arthur (auth), Mural, Can Art Mag, 49; Design-
illustration, Graphis (Ger), 50.

Memberships: Ont Soc Artists; life mem Can Soc Graphic Arts; life mem Arts & Lett Club.
Publications: Illusr, Varsity story, 48 & Canada's tomorrow, 54.
Mailing Address: 135 Rose Ave, Toronto, Ont, Can.

ALEXANDER, ROBERT SEYMOUR
Educator, Designer
b Pittsburgh, Pa, Feb 1, 23.
Study & Training: Ad-Art Studio Sch, 41-42; Shrivenham Am Univ, Eng, 45; Carnegie Inst Technol, 47; Univ Ill, BFA, 51; Cranbrook Acad Art, MFA, 52.
Commissions: Indust designs for FMC Corp, Mich Dept Agr, Recordio Corp, Planet Corp & others.
Exhibitions: Exhib Mich Artists, Detroit Inst Arts, 59, 62 & 72; Mich Area Artists, Kalamazoo Inst Arts, 64; one-man show, The Little Gallery, Birmingham, Mich, 64.
Teaching: Prof in charge indust design, Mich State Univ, 54-
Positions: Artist-designer, James H Matthews Co, Pittsburgh, Pa, 46-47; training aids designer, USA, Ft Eustis, Va, 48; automotive designer, Ford Motor Co, Dearborn, Mich, 52-53; independent designer, 55-; univ res grants, 62-65, 67, 69-73; group leader, design for educ proj, Princeton Univ, 66.
Awards: First prize, Int furniture design competition, Nat Cotton Coun, 59.
Bibliography: J Fisher (auth), Education for design, Format Mag, 5/66.
Memberships. Indust Designers Soc Am; Soc Archit Historians; Mich Acad Sci, Arts & Lett.
Research: Study of environmental format; photographic study of visual evidence of human response to physical factors such as space, shape and light levels.
Mailing Address: Dept of Art, Michigan State University, East Lansing, MI 48823.

ALICEA, JOSE
Printmaker
b Ponce, P R, Jan 12, 28.
Study & Training: Acad Pov, Ponce; Inst Puerto Rican Cult, with Lorenzo Homar.
Work in Public Collections: Philadelphia Mus Art, Pa; Mus Mod Art, New York, N Y; Libr of Cong, Washington, D C; Boston Pub Libr, Mass; Mus Arte Ponce.
Commissions: Woodcut mural, Inst Puerto Rican Cult for Guayanilla H S, 70.
Exhibitions: 1st Muestra Int Grabado, Barcelona, Spain, 69; 9th & 10th Festival Arte de Cali, Colombia, 69-70; 3rd Int Graphic Biennial, Cracow, 1st & 2nd Biennial Latinamericana Grabado de San Juan, P R, 70-72; 3rd Biennial Int Della Grafica, Florence, Italy, 72.
Teaching: Instr printmaking, Escuela Artes Plasticas, San Juan, 67-
Positions: Asst to dir, Inst Puerto Rican Cult Workshop, 58-62; art dir, Revista del Cafe, Ponce, 62-
Awards: Prize for graphic, Ateneo Puertorriqueno, 65; Mildred Boerike Prize, Print Club Philadelphia, 67; travel grant, Casa Del Arte, San Juan, 68.
Bibliography: E Ruiz de la Mata (auth), The art of Jose R Alicea, San Juan Rev Mag, 7/66 & Graphics by Alicea, San Juan Star, 8/9/70; Gloria Borras (auth), El grabado en la vida de Jose R Alicea, El Mundo, 69.
Publications: Illusr, Trovas larenas, 68; auth, Rio grande de Loiza (portfolio of prints), 68; auth, Cancion de Baquine (portfolio of prints), 70; auth, En las manos del pueblo, 72; illusr, Calambrenas.
Dealer: Galeria Santiago, 207 Cristo St, San Juan, PR 00901.
Mailing Address: 911 Ave Campo Rico, Country Club, Rio Piedras, PR 00924.

ALJAMAN (ALTON JAMES CHAPMAN)
Painter, Educator
Preferred Media: Oils, Acrylics, Foil.
b River Junction, Fla, May 21, 26.
Study & Training: Art Inst Pittsburgh, dipl; Ad-Art Studio Sch, dipl; Merlin Enabnit Color Study Course; also with Roy Hilton, Raymond Simboli & Robert Brackman.
Work in Public Collections: Gov Palace, Vera Cruz, Mex; Sunland Training Ctr, Miami, Fla; Ligoa Duncan Gallery, New York, N Y; Mirell Gallery, Coconut Grove, Fla; Atterbury Acad Fine Arts, Miami, Fla.
Exhibitions: Mobile Gulf Coast Exhib, Ala, 67; Southeastern Art Exhib, Panama City, Fla, 68 & 69; Salon of the 50 States, New York, 69; Gold Coast Shrine Club Mahi Temple, Deerfield Beach, Fla, Sovereign Exhibs, Ltd, Winton-Salem, N C & Williamsburg, Va, 70; plus other group & one-man shows.
Teaching: Instr pvt classes, 62-; dir workshop, North Miami Beach Artists Guild, Fla, 68-69; instr art & asst dir, Atterbury Sch, 72-73.

Positions: Art dir, Whitman & Shoop, Pittsburgh, Pa, 51-53; art dir & owner, Creative Advert, Ashland, Ohio, 53-56; art dir, WMIE Radio Sta, Miami, 56-61; dir & owner, Creative Advert, Miami, 60-62.
Awards: Latham Found award, 46; Prix de Paris Award, Ligoa Duncan Galleries, New York, twice in 69; Antoni Gaudi I Cornet Medal award, Soc Gaudi, Barcelona, Spain, 70.
Memberships: Am Artists Prof League (secy, 69); Fla Artist Group, Inc; Allied Artists Am; Blue Dome Art Fel (pres, 71); Miami Art League, Inc (secy, 69).
Research: Developed & perfected Foillage, involving the use of color in relationship with colored foil & acrylic polymers.
Art Interests: Use of color in relation to creative non-figurative art to its fullest extent.
Collection: Oils & acrylics of both representational & non-figurative paintings.
Publications: Art ed, Independent Newspaper, Lawrenceville, Pa, 46-48.
Mailing Address: 921 N E 157th Terrace, North Miami Beach, FL 33162.

ALLAN, WILLIAM GEORGE
Painter
Preferred Media: Acrylics, Watercolors.
b Everett, Wash, Mar 28, 36.
Study & Training: San Francisco Art Inst, BFA.
Work in Public Collections: Santa Barbara Mus Art, Calif; San Francisco Mus Art, Calif; Univ Art Mus, Berkeley, Calif; R I Sch Design, Providence; Whitney Mus Am Art, New York, N Y.
Exhibitions: Carnegie Int Exhib, Pittsburgh, Pa, 57; Continuing Surrealism, La Jolla Mus Art, Calif, 71; Whitney Painting Ann, New York, 72; 70th Am Exhib, Art Inst Chicago, 72; Indianapolis Mus Art Exhib, 72.
Teaching: Instr painting, Univ Calif, Davis, 65-67; instr painting, Univ Calif, Berkeley, 69; asst prof art, Calif State Univ, Sacramento, 68-
Dealers: Hansen-Fuller Gallery, 228 Grant Ave, San Francisco, CA 94108; Galleria Odyssia, 41 E 57th St, New York, NY 10022.
Mailing Address: 327 Melrose, Mill Valley, CA 94941.

ALLEN, CLARENCE CANNING
Painter, Writer
Preferred Media: Oil.
b Cleveland, Ga, Nov 29, 97.
Study & Training: Southeastern State Col with Dr Allen Berger & Ola Forbes; Art Stud League New York, N Y, with George Bridgman & R P R Neilson; San Antonio Art Acad, Tex, with Jose Arpa', Xavier Gonzalez & Rolla Taylor; also with Molly Guion, Dimitri Romanovsky, Charles H Owens & Bettina Steinke.
Work in Public Collections: Libr of Pres Truman, Eisenhower & Johnson. Portraits: Sen Robert S Kerr, Mus of Poteau, Okla; Will Rogers, Will Rogers Mem Hosp, Saranac Lake, N Y; Indian Mus of Creek Tribe, Okmulgee, Okla; Osage Mus, Pawhuska, Okla. Also numerous private, hist & found collections.
Commissions: Early and Late Means of Disseminating News, Newspaper Printing Corp, 53; Press Media Symbology, Tulsa Press Club, Okla, 57; Creek Tribe Council Tree, Tulsa City Hall, 69.
Exhibitions: Freedoms Found, Valley Forge, Pa, 53-56, 58 & 61; Giornate Mediche Int, Verona, Italy, 63; La Caricature de Par le Monde, Troisieme Salon Int, Place Victoria, Montreal, P Q, 67.
Teaching: Instr graphic art, Cent High Sch, San Antonio, Tex, 24-27; instr fine art, private classes, Tulsa; instr oil painting, Tulsa Garden Ctr.
Positions: Artist, art dir, ed & cartoonist, Tulsa World & Tulsa Tribune, 29-68.
Awards: Five nat awards, Freedoms Found, 53, 55, 56, 58, 61 & top nat award, 54.
Bibliography: John Chase (auth), Today's Cartoon, Hauser Press, New Orleans, 62.
Memberships: Am Artists Prof League; Nat Soc Mural Painters; Soc Illus; Asn Am Editorial Cartoonists; Nat Cartoonists Soc.
Publications: Auth, Sketching, 32; Biographical sketches of prominent Tulsans, 49; Originality, 50; Are you fed up with modern art?, 52; also articles in numerous nat & regional mag.
Mailing Address: 1645 E 17th Pl, Tulsa, OK 74120.

ALLEN, COURTNEY
Illustrator, Sculptor
b Norfolk, Va, Jan 16, 96.
Study & Training: Corcoran Art Sch, Washington, D C, 15-16; Nat Acad Art Sch, New York, N Y, 20-21; also with Charles W Hawthorne, Provincetown, Mass, 19-21 & C W W Bicknell, 19.
Exhibitions: Allied Artists Am; Provincetown Art Asn; Chrysler Art Mus; Provincetown Hist Mus.
Positions: Trustee, Chrysler Art Mus, Provincetown, 60-68; pres, Truro Hist Soc, Mass, 69.

Memberships: Provincetown Art Asn (pres, 56-58); Soc Illusr; Allied Artists Am.
Mailing Address: Box 237, Hughes & 6A Rds, North Truro, MA 02652.

ALLEN, LORETTA B
Painter, Designer
b Caney, Kans.
Study & Training: Univ Okla, with Marshall Lackey; Fed Arts Schs, Minneapolis, Minn; Famous Artists Sch; also with Grace Chadwick, Oklahoma City, Molly Guion & Dimitri Romanofsky, New York, N Y.
Exhibitions: Oklahoma City Art Ctr; Tulsa Studio Group, 61 & 62; Osage Co Hist Mus, 69; plus others.
Positions: Illusr, children's bks; fashion designer; fashion illusr, local publ.
Memberships: Am Artists Prof League.
Mailing Address: 1645 E 17th Pl, Tulsa, OK 74120.

ALLEN, MARGARET PROSSER
Painter, Educator
b Vancouver, B C, Jan 26, 13; U S citizen.
Study & Training: Univ Wash, BA, MFA; also with Alexander Archipenko & Amadee Ozenfant.
Work in Public Collections: Pastel, Del Art Mus; mixed media print, Univ Del Permanent Collection.
Exhibitions: Six exhibs, Northwest Ann, 38-48; over ten exhibs, Del Ann, 42-64; Weyhe Gallery, New York, N Y, 47; The Carvings of Sanchi, photog exhib circulated by Smithsonian Inst, 68-72; Univ Del Faculty Group Show, Del Art Mus, 72.
Teaching: Instr design, Univ Del, 42-48, asst prof design, 49-72, assoc prof design, 72-
Awards: Hon mention, 47 & first prize, 49, Wilmington Soc Fine Arts; popular prize (one of five), Northwest Ann, 48; grant, Univ Del, 68.
Mailing Address: 119 Briar Lane, Newark, DE 19711.

ALLEN, MARGO
Sculptor, Painter
Preferred Media: Bronze, Terra-Cotta.
b Lincoln, Mass.
Study & Training: Boston Mus Sch Fine Arts; Naum Los Sch Anat, Rome, Italy; Venturini Sch Encaustic Painting, Rome; marble carving at Gelli Studio, Querceta, Italy.
Work in Public Collections: Dallas Mus Fine Arts, Tex; Mus Mod Art, Mexico City, Mex; Palace Legion of Honor, San Francisco, Calif; Butler Mus Am Art, Youngstown, Ohio; Art Mus N Mex, Santa Fe.
Commissions: 34 terra-cotta reliefs, First Nat Bank, Lafayette, La; bronze eagle, New Iberia Bank, Iberia, La; U S S Constitution (bronze Mem plaque), U S Navy; garden fountains, Tex, Mass, Bermuda & others; many portrait commissions in bronze.
Exhibitions: Nat Acad Design, New York, N Y; Pa Acad Fine Arts, Philadelphia; Boston Mus Fine Arts, Mass; New York Archit League, N Y; Addison Gallery Am Art, Andover, Mass.
Memberships: Nat Sculpture Soc; Nat League Am Pen Women; Ringling Mus; New England Asn Contemp Sculpture; Sarasota Art Asn, Fla.
Mailing Address: 501 Sloop Lane, Sarasota, FL 33577.

ALLEN, PATRICIA (PATRICIA ALLEN BOTT)
Painter, Art Critic
Preferred Media: Oils.
b Old Lyme, Conn.
Study & Training: With George Burr & Malcolm Fraser; Art Stud League New York, with Ivan Olinsky & Harry Sternberg.
Work in Public Collections: Greenville Mus Art, S C; Hickory Mus Art, N C; Bronx Zoo Galleries, New York, N Y; Riveredge Found, Calgary, Alta; E African Wildlife Soc, Nairobi, Africa.
Exhibitions: Soc Animal Artists Travel & Ann Shows, New York, 55-; Grand Cent Art Galleries, New York, 65-; E African Wildlife Galleries, Nairobi, 71-72; one-man shows, Mexico, Burr Galleries, New York, 55 & African Wildlife, Hilton Galleries, Nairobi, 70.
Positions: Dir, Burr Galleries, New York, 50-61; auth, Soc Animal Artists Newsletter, 59-; secy & sales, Salmagundi Club, 62-66, in charge sales, Grand Cent Art Galleries, New York, 66-
Awards: Medal, Fla Fedn Arts, 44; best in show medal, 69 & medal, 70, Gotham Painters.
Bibliography: Articles, In: The Standard, 71 & Christian Sci Monitor, 71.
Memberships: Nat Arts Club; Soc Animal Artists (founder & secy, 59-); Am Artists Prof League; Nat Asn Women Artists.
Publications: Contribr, reviews of art shows, In: The Host, 56-; contribr, reviews of art shows, In: The Villager, 56-70; contribr, reviews of art shows, In: The Pendulum, 59-

Dealer: Grand Central Art Galleries, 40 Vanderbilt Ave, New York, NY 10017.
Mailing Address: 151 Carroll St, Bronx, NY 10464.

ALLEN, RALPH
Painter, Educator
b Eng, 1926.
Study & Training: Sir John Cass Sch Art & Slade Sch Fine Arts, London, Eng.
Work in Public Collections: Nat Gallery Can; Art Gallery Toronto; Queen's Univ, Ont; Queen's Park, Toronto; also in pvt cols.
Exhibitions: Montreal, 60; Kingston, 60 & 67; Ottawa, 64; Toronto, 68.
Teaching: Lect on Daniel Fowler, Kingston, Ont & Nat Gallery Can, Ottawa, 65; assoc prof art hist & dir Agnes Etherington Art Ctr, Queen's Univ, Ont.
Awards: Jessie Dow Award, Montreal, 59; Can Coun scholar, 59 & sr fel, 68; Baxter Award, Toronto, 60.
Memberships: Ont Soc Artists.
Publications: Auth, Catalogue permanent collection of paintings, drawings and sculpture, Agnes Etherington Art Ctr, 68.
Mailing Address: Art Centre, Queen's University, Kingston, Ont, Can.

ALLIN, WARREN
Painter
Preferred Media: Oil.
b New Haven, Conn, June 30, 30.
Study & Training: Univ Md BA, with Herman Maril & Maurice Ziegler; Cranbrook Academy of Art, MFA, with Zoltan Sepeshy & John S DeMartelly.
Work in Public Collections: D C Municipal Ct, Washington, D C; Butler Inst Am Art, Youngstown, Ohio.
Commissions: Famous Composers, Bethesda-Chevy Chase High Sch, Bethesda, Md, 48.
Exhibitions: Michiana Show, South Bend, Ind, 58; Smithsonian Exhib, Washington, D C, 58 & 59; Corcoran Regional, Washington, D C, 59; Butler Inst Am Art, 70; Mainstreams 71 & 72, Marietta, Ohio, 71 & 72.
Teaching: Instr art, Arlington County Pub Schs, Va, 58-71.
Awards: Purchase award, Butler Inst Am Art, 70; audience choice award, Mainstreams 71 & award of excellence, Mainstreams 72, Marietta Col.
Mailing Address: c/o Capricorn Galleries, 8003 Woodmont Ave, Bethesda, MD 20014.

ALLING, CLARENCE (EDGAR)
Museum Director, Craftsman
b Dawson Co, Nebr, Jan 28, 33.
Study & Training: Washburn Univ, BFA; Ohio State Univ, with Edgar Littlefield; Univ Kans, MFA, with Sheldon Carey.
Work in Public Collections: Excelsior Ins Co, New York.
Exhibitions: One-man shows, Mulvane Art Ctr, Topeka, Kans, 63 & Sioux City Art Ctr, Iowa, 63; Area Artists, Sioux City, 63 & 65 & Des Moines, Iowa, 64; two-man show, L'Atelier, Cedar Falls, Iowa, 65; plus others.
Positions: Dir, Waterloo Munic Galleries, at present.
Awards: Prizes, Designer-Craftsman Show, Lawrence, Kans, 59-61; purchase award, Ceramic Nat, Everson Mus, Syracuse, N Y, 60; merit award, Sioux City, 65.
Mailing Address: Waterloo Municipal Galleries, 225 Cedar St, Waterloo, IA 50704.

ALLOWAY, LAWRENCE
Educator, Art Critic
b London, Eng, Sept 17, 26.
Collections Arranged: For Solomon R Guggenheim Mus—Morris Louis-Memorial Exhibition, 63; Francis Bacon, 63; Guggenheim International Award Exhibition, 63; William Baziotes-Memorial Exhibition, 65; Barnett Newman: the Stations of the Cross 66; Jean Dubuffet, 66.
Teaching: Instr, Bennington Col, Vt, 61-62; prof, State Univ N Y Stony Brook, 68-
Positions: Cur, Solomon R Guggenheim Mus, 62-66; art ed, The Nation, 68; assoc ed, Artforum, 72.
Awards: Foreign Leader Grant, U S State Dept, 68; award for distinction in art criticism, Frank Jewett Mather, 72.
Research: 20th century American art and the cinema.
Publications: Auth, The metallization of a dream, 64; The Venice Biennale 1895-1968, 68; Christo, 69; Violent America: the movies 1946-1964, 71; Mechanismus der Bedeutung (introduction), 71.
Mailing Address: 330 W 20th St, New York, NY 10011.

ALLWELL, STEPHEN S
Sculptor
Preferred Media: Bronze.
b Baltimore, Md, Oct 15, 06.
Study & Training: Md Inst, Baltimore.

Commissions: Folksinger, Mrs Robert Lindner, Baltimore, 69; copier, Alan Elkin, Baltimore, 70; Lacrosse, James F Welsh, Baltimore, 71.

Exhibitions: Four shows, Miniature Painters, Sculptors & Gravers Soc, Washington, D C, 67-71; Acad Arts, Easton, Md, 67 & 71; Mariner's Mus Marine Art Exhib, Newport News, Va, 69; Washington Co Mus, Hagerstown, Md, 69; Peale Mus, Baltimore, 70.

Awards: Grand prize outdoor exhib, Baltimore Outdoor Art Show, 67; purchase award, Metromedia-WCBM, 67; Reese E McLeod Prize Sculpture, Miniature Painters, Sculptors & Gravers Soc Washington, D C, 69.

Bibliography: L'art a l'etranger, La Rev Mod, 7/68.

Memberships: Artists' Equity Asn; fel Md Fedn Art; Alumni Asn Md Inst; Baltimore Art Guild; Rehoboth Art League.

Mailing Address: 803 Evesham Ave, Baltimore, MD 21212.

ALONZO, JACK J
Art Dealer, Collector
b Brooklyn, N Y, July 3, 27.
Study & Training: Brooklyn Col; N Y Univ.
Positions: Owner, Alonzo Gallery, 65-
Specialty of Gallery: Contemporary paintings, sculpture, graphics, drawings and others, predominately abstract.
Collection: Catholic.
Publications: Contribr, Arts Mag, 4/71.
Mailing Address: Alonzo Gallery, 26 E 63rd St, New York, NY 10021.

ALPS, GLEN EARL
Educator, Printmaker
b Loveland, Colo, June 20, 14.
Study & Training: Univ Northern Colo, BA; Univ Wash, MFA; Univ Iowa, advanced study with Mauricio Lasansky.
Work in Public Collections: Mus Mod Art, New York, N Y; Philadelphia Art Mus, Pa; Chicago Art Inst, Ill; Los Angeles Co Mus Art, Los Angeles, Calif; Libr Cong, Washington, D C.
Commissions: Sculptural panel, Seattle Pub Libr, 60; fountain, Munic Bldg, City of Seattle, 61; wall sculpture, Magnolia Br, Seattle Pub Libr, 64; edition of prints, Washington State Arts Comn, 71; bronze fountain, First Christian Church, Greeley, Colo, 72.
Exhibitions: 17th Nat Print Exhib, Brooklyn Art Mus, N Y, 70; Graphic's '71 West Coast U S A, Univ Ky, circulated by Smithsonian Inst, 71; 35th Nat Graphics Exhib, Wichita Art Mus, Kans, 71; 2nd Ann Nat Print Exhib, Ga State Univ, 71; 51st Ann Print Exhib, Soc Am Graphic Artists, Kennedy Galleries, New York, 71.
Teaching: Prof printmaking, Univ Wash, 45-
Positions: Treas, Northwest Printmakers, 49-51, pres, 51-53 & 62-64.
Awards: Tamarind fel, Ford Found, 60 & artist-in-residence, 65.
Bibliography: Russell O Woody, Jr (auth), Polymer painting and related techniques, Van Nostrand Reinhold, 71; Jules Heller (auth), Printmaking today, Holt Reinhart & Winston, 72.
Memberships: Col Art Asn; Soc Am Graphic Artists; Am Fedn Arts; Print Club; Print Coun Am.
Publications: Auth, The collagraph, 16mm color film.
Dealer: Francine Seders Gallery, 6701 Greenwood Ave N, Seattle, WA 98103.
Mailing Address: 6523 40th Ave NE, Seattle, WA 98115.

ALSDORF, JAMES W
Patron, Collector
b Chicago, Ill, Aug 16, 13.
Study & Training: Wharton Sch Finance & Commerce, Univ Pa.
Positions: V pres, mem exec comt & trustee, Art Inst Chicago, also chmn, comn Oriental art, comn primitive art, comn exhibs, v chmn, comn bldgs, comn Buckingham fund and acquisitions, mem, comn 20th century paintings & sculpture & comn prints & drawings; mem nat comn, univ art mus Univ Calif, Berkeley; adv coun, univ art gallery, Univ Notre Dame, Ind, Am Fedn Arts, Mus Contemp Art, Chicago & Field Mus, Chicago; benefactor, Art Asn Indianapolis, John Herron Art Gallery; pres, Alsdorf Found, Chicago, 49-
Memberships: Gov life mem Chicago Hist Soc; assoc Arch Am Art.
Collections: Modern drawings, paintings and sculpture; American nineteenth century Trompe l'oeil School; Early Americana and folk art, archaic and classical art.
Mailing Address: 301 Woodley Rd, Winnetka, IL 60093.

ALSTON, CHARLES HENRY
Painter, Educator
Preferred Media: Oil, Stone, Wood, Mosaic.
b Charlotte, N C, Nov 28, 07.
Study & Training: Art Stud League New York; Arthur Wesley Dow fel, Columbia Univ, BA, MA.
Work in Public Collections: Whitney Mus Am Art, New York, N Y; Metrop Mus Art; Detroit Mus; International Business Machines Corp; Atlanta Univ.

Commissions: Oil mural, History of California, Golden State Mutual Life Ins Co, 48; Mosaic, Emerging Man, Harlem Hospital, New York; Man on the Threshold of Space, Harriet Tubman Sch, New York, 67; bronze, Martin Luther King, Community Church, New York; two mosaic murals, Bronx Co Family & Criminal Court Bldg, in progress.
Exhibitions: Metrop Mus Art, 50; Whitney Mus Am Art, 54-56; Pa Acad Fine Arts, 55-65; retrospective, Gallery Mod Art, New York, 69; Mus Mod Art, 70.
Teaching: Instr drawing & painting, Art Studs League New York 50-; assoc prof, City Col New York, 60-
Positions: Mem, Nat Coun Arts, 67; painter mem, New York City Art Comn, 70-
Awards: Grant for achievement in arts, Inst Arts & Lett, 58; Thomas B Clarke Award, Nat Acad Design, 71.
Bibliography: Alain Locke (auth), The Negro in art, Assocs Negro Folklore, Washington, D C, 40; Bardolph (auth), The Negro vanguard, Rinehart, 59; Cedric Dover (auth), American Negro art, Studio Press, London, Eng, 60.
Memberships: Nat Soc Mural Painters (dir, 66).
Dealer: Kennedy Galleries, 20 E 56th St, New York, NY 10022.
Mailing Address: 1270 Fifth Ave, New York, NY 10029.

ALTABÉ, JOAN BERG
Painter, Educator
Preferred Media: Opaque Watercolor, Acrylics.
b New York, N Y, Apr 27, 35.
Study & Training: Hunter Col, BA 56; Advanced Study with Robert Motherwell (oils), William Baziotes (watercolor), Richard Lippold (design) & Gabor Peterdi (graphics).
Exhibitions: Artists Equity Asn of New York, 70; Slidell Nat Festival Exhib, City Auditorium, 70; Ogunquit 50th, 51st Ann Nat Exhib, Maine, 70; Greater New Orleans Nat Exhib, 71; Centro Studi Rassegna Int Arte Mod, Italy, 71-72.
Teaching: Teacher fine arts, New York City sec schs, 57-
Memberships: Artists Equity Asn of New York; Index Contemp Artists, Art Resources Inst San Francisco; Am Fedn Arts; Guild Hall, East Hampton, N Y.
Publications: Contribr, Fine arts discovery mag, 70; illustr, Translation of Becquer, Gustavo: la ajorca de oro, 72.
Mailing Address: 511 W Fulton St, Long Beach, NY 11561.

ALTMAN, HAROLD
Etcher, Educator
b New York, N Y, Apr 20, 24.
Study & Training: Art Stud League New York; Cooper Union Sch Art; Acad Grande Chaumiere, Paris, France.
Work in Public Collections: Mus Mod Art; Whitney Mus Am Art; Boston Mus Fine Arts; Philadelphia Mus Art; Metrop Mus Art.
Commissions: Print ed, Jewish Mus, New York Hilton Hotel, Soc Am Graphic Artists, Container Corp Am Great Ideas of Western Man Series.
Exhibitions: Four shows, Pa Acad Fine Arts Ann, 63-69; Five American Printmakers, Basel, Switz, 65; Second Inter-Am Biennial Printmaking, Santiago, Chile, 65; A Decade of American Drawings, Whitney Mus Am Art, 65; one-man show, Everson Mus Art, Syracuse, N Y, 69; more than 150 one-man shows plus other group shows throughout Europe, Japan, Israel & others.
Teaching: Prof drawing & painting, Pa State Univ, University Park.
Awards: Guggenheim fels, 60-62; Nat Acad Arts & Lett Award, N Y, 63; Fulbright res fel, 64-65; plus many others.
Memberships: Soc Am Graphic Artists.
Mailing Address: Box 57, Lemont, PA 16851.

ALTMAYER, JAY P
Collector
b Mobile, Ala, Mar 1, 15.
Study & Training: Tulane Univ La, BA & LLB.
Collection: American paintings mostly dealing with plantation life and workers; paintings by William Aiken Walker, Sully, Rembrandt Peale, Gilbert Stuart, Severn Rosen, Jarvis and others; large collection of precious metal and Jewelled historical American presentation swords.
Publications: Auth, American presentation swords.
Mailing Address: 55 S McGregor St, Mobile, AL 36608.

ALTORFER, GLORIA FINCH
Painter, Designer
Preferred Media: Acrylic, Oil, Watercolor, Collage.
b Peoria, Ill, Apr 19, 31.
Study & Training: Bradley Univ, BA; with Hermann Kosak & Reynold Weidenaar.
Exhibitions: 14th Nat Exhib, Greater Fall River Art Asn, Mass, 70; Juried Arts 7th Nat Exhib Painting & Sculpture, Tyler, Tex, 70; 37th Nat Ann, Miniature Painters, Sculptors & Gravers Soc, Wash-

ington, D C, 70; 73rd Ann Nat Exhib for Prof Women Artists, Catharine Lorillard Wolfe Art Club, Nat Acad Design, New York, N Y, 70; Miniature Art Soc N J, 71.
Teaching: Pvt instr painting, YMCA, Roeckers Decorative Galleries and others, 68-
Positions: Interior Designer, E G Lehmann Assos, 71-
Awards: Best of show, Lacon Old Settler's Art Show, 70; best of show, Brown Co Art Gallery Asn, 70; best of show, Pekin Palette Club, 71.
Memberships: Ill Art League (exec bd 68-); Peoria Art Guild (chmn all mem show, 72); Fine Arts Soc; Lakeview Ctr for Arts & Sci.
Dealer: Collectors Upstairs Gallery-Lakeview Ctr, 1125 W Lake St, Peoria, IL 61614.
Mailing Address: 4010 N War Memorial Dr, Peoria, IL 61614.

ALTSCHUL, ARTHUR G
Collector, Patron
b New York, N Y, Apr 6, 20.
Positions: Trustee, Whitney Mus Am Art; trustee, Am Fed Arts; mem, Int Coun, Mus Mod Art; fel in perpetuity, Metrop Mus Art.
Collection: American impressionists and The Eight; cubists and lesser known members of the neo-impressionist school; the Nabis and the Pont-Aven schools.
Mailing Address: 55 Broad St, New York, NY 10004.

ALTVATER, CATHERINE THARP
Painter
Preferred Media: Watercolor.
b Little Rock, Ark, July 26, 07.
Study & Training: Grand Cent Sch Contemp Arts & Crafts; Art League Long Island with F Spradling & E Whitney; Nat Acad Fine Arts with Mario Cooper, Ogden Pleissner, Louis Bouché & Robert Phillips.
Work in Public Collections: Museums in U S, Europe, Japan & Can; also many private collections.
Exhibitions: Nat Acad Design; Nat Arts Club; Hudson Valley Art Asn, Metrop Mus Fine Arts; Mus Fine Arts, Mexico City; plus others.
Teaching: Workshops & demonstrations throughout the U S.
Awards: Over 60 awards including 20 first prizes.
Memberships: Am Watercolor Soc; Hudson Valley Art Asn; Am. Artists Prof League; Catherine Lorillaird Wolfe Art Club; Allied Artists Am; and others.
Mailing Address: Rte 2, Box 44, Scott, AR 72142.

ALTWERGER, LIBBY
Painter, Graphic Artist
Preferred Media: Watercolors.
b Toronto, Ont, July 13, 21.
Study & Training: Ont Col Art.
Exhibitions: Royal Can Acad, 60; Ont Soc Artists, 61; one-man shows, Pascall Gallery, Toronto, 64 & Sonneck Gallery, Kitchener, Ont, 68.
Teaching: Instr drawing, Ryerson Polytech Inst.
Awards: Lt Gov Gen Medal, 59; Grand Prix Gold Medal, Int Feminine Culturelle, Vichy, France, 63; Sterling Trust Award for lithograph, 65; plus others.
Memberships: Can Soc Graphic Artists; Can Soc Painters in Water Colour; Can Soc Painter-Etchers & Engravers.
Mailing Address: 526 Dovercourt Rd, Toronto 173, Ont, Can.

AMAROTICO, JOSEPH ANTHONY
Painter, Conservator
Preferred Media: Acrylic on Rag Board or Canvas.
b Bronx, N Y, Sept 3, 31.
Study & Training: Am Art Sch, New York, N Y, with Raphael Soyer; Pa Acad Fine Arts, Philadelphia, with Franklin Watkins, Walter Stuempfig, Hobson Pittman & Theodor Siegl.
Work in Public Collections: Pa Acad Fine Arts; George Washington Univ, Washington, D C; Glassboro Col, N J; Washington, D C, District Court.
Exhibitions: Nat Exhib, Pa Acad Fine Arts, 59, 61, 64, 66, 67, 68 & 69; Nat Traveling Exhib, Am Fedn Arts, 64; Tenth Mary Washington Exhib Mod Art, Fredricksburg, Va, 65; Art for Embassies, U S Dept State, Jamaican Embassy, Kingston, 67; Ann Exhib, Butler Inst, Youngstown, Ohio, 69, 70 & 72.
Teaching: Instr painting, Pa Acad Fine Arts, 66-
Positions: Conservator paintings, Pa Acad Fine Arts, 68-
Awards: Mary Butler Award, Pa Acad Fine Arts Fel Exhib, 62; painting prize, Cheltenham Art Ctr, Philadelphia, 68; endowment fund prize, Woodmere Art Ctr, Chestnut Hill, Pa, 72.
Memberships: Fellowship of Pa Acad Fine Arts (mem bd, 72-); American Group, Int Inst for Conservation Hist & Artistic Works.
Dealers: Pearl Fox Galleries, 103 Windsor Ave, Philadelphia, PA 19126; Mickelson Galleries, 709 G St, NW, Washington, DC 20001.
Mailing Address: Box 239, Plumsteadville, PA 18949.

AMATEIS, EDMOND ROMULUS
Sculptor
Preferred Media: Stone, Bronze, Acrylic, Wood.
b Rome, Italy, Feb 7, 97; U S citizen.
Study & Training: Beaux-Arts Inst Design; Acad Julienne; fel Am Acad Rome, 21-24.
Work in Public Collections: Brookgreen Gardens, S C; Hall Am Artists, Columbia Univ.
Commissions: War Horses, Baltimore War Memorial, 27; pediment & metopes, Buffalo Hist Soc, 28; large relief, Kansas City Liberty War Memorial, 33; relief & spandrels, Labor & Interstate Com Comn Bldg, 35; Wall of Fame, Ga Warm Springs Found, 52; also numerous medals, garden figures & portraits.
Exhibitions: Biennale Romana Int d'Arte, 23; Nat Acad Design; Philadelphia Mus Art; Philadelphia Acad Fine Arts; Metrop Mus Art.
Teaching: Instr sculpture, Sch Am Sculpture, 27; instr sculpture, Columbia Univ, 28-32; instr sculpture, Bennett Sch, 38-40.
Awards: Henry O Avery Prize, Architectoral League N Y, 29; James E McClese Prize, Pa Acad Fine Arts, 33.
Bibliography: Breving (auth), A sculptor with plastic vision, Int Studio, 26; Ernest Watson (auth), Edmond Amateis, Am Artist, 40; D DeLue (auth), Edmond Amateis, Nat Sculpture Rev, 67.
Memberships: Nat Acad Design; Nat Sculpture Soc (pres, 42-44); Nat Inst Arts & Lett.
Publications: Auth, A sculptor speaks his mind, Liturgical Arts, 43.
Mailing Address: 1620 Fifth St, Clermont, FL 32711.

AMAYA, MARIO ANTHONY
Museum Director, Writer
b Brooklyn, N Y, Oct 6, 33.
Study & Training: Brooklyn Col, BA in art hist; London Univ exten courses at Nat Gallery Gt Brit.
Collections Arranged: Obsessive Image, Inst Contemp Arts, London, Eng, 68, British Painting Here and Now for Brit Trade Coun traveling exhib to U S, 69, Young and Fantastic for Macy's, New York, N Y; The Sacred and Profane in Symbolist Art & Six Centuries of Treasures for Art Gallery of Ont, 69; Realisms for Montreal Mus Fine Arts & Art Gallery Ont, 70; Eduoard Vuillard for Art Gallery Ont, Calif Palace of Legion of Honour & Chicago Art Inst; French 17th and 18th century Drawings in North American Collections with Pierre Rosenberg of the Louvre for Ottawa, Toronto, New York and San Francisco, 72.
Teaching: Vis prof Symbolism to Surrealism, State Univ N Y Buffalo, 71-72; seminar on The Exiles (artists who left Paris in 39).
Positions: Art critic, London Financial Times, Apollo, Punch, Sunday Times Colour Suppl & Vogue, London, Eng, 57-; founding assoc ed, About the House, London, 62; founding ed, Art & Artists, London, 65-68; contrib ed, Art in America; chief cur, Art Gallery Ont, 69-72; dir, New York Cultural Ctr, 72-
Memberships: Col Art Asn Am; Am Mus Asn.
Research: Tiffany glass, art nouveau and pop art as well as symbolist art, surrealism and contemporary avant garde art.
Collection: Old Masters, 17th century Italian and 19th century French drawings plus pop art.
Publications: Auth, Pop as art, Studio Vista & Viking Press, 65; Art nouveau, Dutton/Vista Picturebooks, 66; Tiffany glass, Walker & Co, 67; contribr, Holiday, Nova and many others.
Mailing Address: 15 W 75th St, PH B, New York, NY 10023.

AMBROSE, CHARLES EDWARD
Painter
Preferred Media: Watercolor, Oil.
b Memphis, Tenn, Jan 6, 22.
Study & Training, Univ Ala, BFA, 49, MA 50.
Work in Public Collections: Univ Southern Miss; Carey Col; Biloxi Art Asn; Miss Art Asn; First National Bank, Hattiesburg, Miss.
Commissions: Portrait reliefs, Univ Southern Miss, 58 & portraits, 60; Pat Harrison Waterways Bldg, 65; Carey Col; Miss Archives Bldg, 72.
Exhibitions: Miss Art Asn Ann, 50-; Birmingham Watercolor Soc, 50-; New Orleans Art Asn Ann Spring Exhib, 52-; Edgewater Ann, Biloxi, Miss, 68; Mid-Continent Exhib, Mo, 71.
Teaching: Assoc prof drawing & painting (resident artist), Univ Southern Miss, 50-70; hd art dept, Miss State Col Women, 70-72.
Awards: Best watercolor award, New Orleans Art Asn, 52; first place watercolor, Miss Art Asn, 68; first place drawing, Edgewater Ann, 70.
Memberships: Southeastern Col Arts Conference; Miss Art Educ Asn; Southern Asn Sculptors; Col Art Asn; Miss Art Asn.
Mailing Address: Box 70, Mississippi State College for Women, Columbus, MS 39701.

AMELIO, GILBERT NEIL
Sculptor, Painter
Preferred Media: Terra Cotta, Oil on Canvas.
b Bronx, N Y, Dec 14, 24.
Study & Training: Univ Southern Calif, BFA; painting with Francis de Erderly & sculpture with Merrell Gage.

Commissions: Bas-relief, pioneer founder, Farmers Market, Los
Angeles, Calif; statue, Lady of Loyola, Loyola Univ Los Angeles,
51; heroic bust of Michelangelo in terra cotta, William Lasky,
Jr, Hollywood, Calif, 54; mural, oil on board, St Thomas More
Cath Church, San Antonio, Tex, 67; plus another.
Exhibitions: Sculpting Face of Christ while lecturing throughout U S
with 757 performances since 61.
Positions: Dir art hist properties, U S Air Force Acad, 70-72,
chief admin serv, March Air Force Base, 72-
Awards: Silver cup, Am Educ & Theatrical Asn, 66-67; gold award
for excellence, New York Int Film & TV Festival; Christopher
Award, Columbus Film Festival, 72; plus others.
Bibliography: Face to Face, Audio Prod, Inc, New York, N Y, 71;
Joe Landis (producer), Repertoire Workshop, CBS TV, Holly-
wood, 3/30/72.
Publications: Auth, The Air Force Academy Chapel, its art and
architecture, 72; illusr, Talon cadet mag & newspapers; per-
formance of Face of Christ in terra cotta, CBS TV, 72.
Mailing Address: Administrative Services, March Air Force Base,
CA 92508.

AMEN, IRVING
Painter, Printmaker
Preferred Media: Oils.
b New York, N Y, July 25, 18.
Study & Training: Pratt Inst, scholar, 32-39; study in Paris, France,
50 & Italy, 53.
Work in Public Collections: Mus Mod Art, New York; Metrop Mus,
New York; Albertina Mus, Vienna, Austria; Victoria & Albert
Mus, London, Eng; Bibliot Nat, Paris.
Exhibitions: Master Prints, Mus Mod Art, New York; Int Ausstellung
Von Holzschnitten, Zurich, Switz; I Mednarodna Graficna Razs-
tava, Ljubljana, Yugoslavia; LV Biannale di Pittura Americana,
Bordighera, Italy; Dessins Americains Contemporains, U S Info
Serv.
Teaching: Instr art, Pratt Inst & Univ Notre Dame.
Memberships: Int Inst Arts & Lett; Int Soc Wood Engravers; Accad
Fiorentina delle Arti Disegno; Soc Am Graphic Artists; Am
Color Print Soc; plus others.
Publications: Print ed, Irving Amen woodcuts 1948-1960, Irving
Amen: 1964, Amen: 1964-1968 & Amen: 1968-1970.
Dealer: Amen Gallery, 1049 Madison Ave, New York, NY 10028.
Mailing Address: 153 Waverly Pl, New York, NY 10014.

AMES, ARTHUR FORBES
Painter, Educator
b Tamaroa, Ill, May 19, 06.
Study & Training: San Francisco Art Inst.
Work in Public Collections: Mus Contemp Crafts, New York, N Y;
Pasadena Mus, Calif; Calif State Fair, Sacramento; Harvey Mudd
Col, Claremont, Calif; Wichita Art Asn, Kans.
Commissions: Tapestries, Garrison Theater, Univ Ctr, Claremont;
enamel mural, Rose Hills, Whittier, Calif; enamel door panels,
Emanual Temple, Beverly Hills, Calif; mosaic, Ahmanson Bank,
Los Angeles, Calif; mosaic, Apostle Cath Church, Westwood,
Calif.
Exhibitions: Syracuse Ceramic Nat, N Y, 49, 51 & 54; Brussels
World's Fair, Belg; Mus Contemp Crafts; Contemp Arts Exhib,
Univ Ill, 52 & 53; Objects, U S A, Smithsonian Inst & traveling
exhib, 69.
Teaching: Prof design & head dept, Otis Art Inst, Los Angeles, 54-
71.
Awards: First prize for ferro enamel, 14th Ceramic Nat, Syracuse,
49; first prize for drakenfield, 16th Ceramic Nat, 57; purchase
award for painting, Pasadena Mus.
Mailing Address: 4094 Olive Hill Dr, Claremont, CA 91711.

AMES, JEAN GOODWIN
Designer, Painter
Preferred Media: Acrylics.
b Santa Ana, Calif, Nov 5, 03.
Study & Training: Pomona Col; Art Inst Chicago, grad, 26; Univ
Calif, Los Angeles, BE, 31; Univ Southern Calif, MFA, 37.
Work in Public Collections: Mus Contemp Crafts, New York, N Y;
Everson Mus, Syracuse, N Y.
Commissions: Ceramic mural (with Arthur Ames), 56 & enamel
mural, 58, Rose Hills Mem Park, Whittier, Calif; ceramic mural
(with Arthur Ames), Guarantee Savings & Loan, Fresno, Calif,
58; & tapestry designed for Garrison Theater, Claremont, Calif,
64; tapestry designed for Fed Plaza Bldg, Los Angeles, Calif, 68.
Exhibitions: French & American Tapestries, Otis Art Inst, Los Angeles & La Jolla Art Ctr, Calif, 61; Mus Contemp Crafts Traveling Exhib, 67; Enamels, Everson Mus Fine Art, Syracuse, N Y,
69; Scripps Col, 69-
Teaching: Prof drawing & design, Scripps Col & Claremont Grad
Sch, 40-69.
Awards: First award, Seventh Nat Decorative Arts & Ceramics,

Wichita Art Asn, 52; award for distinguished archit decoration,
Am Inst Architects, Southern Calif Br, 56 & 58; woman of the
year in art, Los Angeles Times, 58.
Memberships: Am Crafts Coun.
Mailing Address: 4094 Olive Hill Dr, Claremont, CA 91711.

AMES, LEE JUDAH
Illustrator, Writer
Preferred Media: Mixed Media.
b New York, N Y, Jan 8, 21.
Study & Training: Columbia Univ, with Carnahan.
Work in Public Collections: Many pieces, layouts & finished illustra-
tions in Univ Southern Miss permanent collection.
Exhibitions: Instr comic art, Sch Visual Arts, New York, 58-59;
lectr advert art, Dowling Col, 70-
Teaching: Instr comic art, Sch Visual Arts, New York, 58-59; lectr
advert art, Dowling Col, 70-
Positions: Art dir, Weber Assocs, New York, 47-52; pres, Ames Ad-
vert, New York, 53-54; artist-in-residence, Doubleday Publ Co,
New York, 55-60.
Publications: Illusr, Exploring chemistry, Doubleday, 58; auth &
illusr, Draw, draw, draw, Doubleday, 62; co-auth & illusr, City
street games, Holt, Rinehart & Winston, 63; illusr, If I were,
Western Publ, 70; illusr, Hide and seek A B C, Platt, 71; plus
illusr for over 100 addn bks.
Mailing Address: 44 Lauren Ave, Dix Hills, NY 11746.

AMES, (POLLY) SCRIBNER
Painter, Sculptor
b Chicago, Ill.
Study & Training: Univ Chicago, PhB; Art Inst Chicago; scholar Chi-
cago Sch Sculpture; also with Jose de Creeft and Hans Hofmann,
New York, N Y; Hans Schwegerle, Munich, Ger.
Work in Public Collections: Death mask drawing of Marsden Hart-
ley, Univ Minn Gallery, Minn; bronze, Ill State Mus; portrait
of singer Povla Frijsh, Town Hall, New York; five panel carving,
Univ Chicago High Sch; oil painting, Quadrangle Club, Univ Chi-
cago; plus others.
Commissions: Wood carving, Western Springs First Congregational
Church, Ill, 64; portraits of Geraldine Page, 61, Mrs E E Cum-
mings, 68, Maureen Ting-Klein, comn by Richard Klein, 68 &
Anne Rothnie, comn by Brit Consul Gen Allen Rothnie, 70.
Exhibitions: One-man shows, Culture Ctr, Neth, W Indies, 47,
Galerie Chardin, Paris, France, 49; Cercle Univ, Aix-en-
Provence, 50 & Esher-Surrey Gallery, The Hague, Holland, 50;
also Closson Gallery, Cincinnati & many others.
Teaching: Instr art, City & Country Sch, New York, 39-42; instr life
class, private studio, New York, 39-45; pvt classes in oils, New
York & Chicago, 39-68; talks on Greece on educ TV & to var
clubs.
Positions: Libr, Univ Chicago, 58-59; Recording for Blind, 58-;
slide dept, publicity, Art Inst Chicago, 64-65.
Awards: Bronze award for Young Satyr and Friend, Ill State Mus,
62.
Memberships: Arts Club Chicago (bd dir, 57-); Oriental Inst; Chi-
cago Quadrangle Club; Chicago Archeol Inst; Renaissance Soc,
Univ Chicago.
Publications: Auth, two articles, In: Progressive Educ Mag, 41; auth
& illusr, Marsden Hartley in Maine, Univ Maine, 72.
Mailing Address: 5834 S Stony Island Ave, Chicago, IL 60637.

AMINO, LEO
Sculptor
Preferred Media: Plastics.
b Tokyo, Japan, June 26, 11; U S citizen.
Study & Training: New York Univ; Am Artists Sch, New York, N Y.
Work in Public Collections: Whitney Mus Am Art, New York; Study
Collection, Mus Mod Art, New York; Des Moines Art Ctr, Iowa;
Provincetown Mus, Mass; Olsen Found, New Haven, Conn.
Exhibitions: Mus Mod Art, New York, 50; Metrop Mus Art, New York,
51; Whitney Mus Am Art, 56; Jewish Mus, New York, 70; San
Francisco Mus Art, Calif, 70.
Teaching: Instr sculpture, Black Mountain Col, 46 & 50; instr sculp-
ture, Cooper Union Sch Art, 52-
Dealer: Sculpture Center, 167 E 69th St, New York, NY 10021.
Mailing Address: 58 Watts St, New York, NY 10013.

AMOROSO, JACK LOUIS
Painter, Collector
Preferred Media: Acrylics, Lacquer, Graphics.
b Brighton, Mass, Apr 28, 30.
Study & Training: Practical Arts Sch, Boston; Lacedra Sch Fine
Arts, Boston.
Work in Public Collections: Univ Miami Lowe Art Mus, Fla.
Commissions: Surrealistic Roman Ruins, commissioned by Play-
house M, Miami, Fla, 54; Calypso-Island Motif, commissioned by
Famous Door Nightclub, Bimini, 60; Harlequin Theme, 56 & Old

Western Scenes, 62, commissioned by Coconut Grove Playhouse, Miami; London, Along the Thames (acrylic mural), cinema lounge, Queen Elizabeth II, Cunard Line, 72.
Exhibitions: Houston Int Exhib, Tex, 56; Inst Contemp Arts, Boston, Mass, 56; Corcoran Gallery Art, Washington, D C, 56; Carnegie Inst, Pittsburgh, Pa, 56; New York City Ctr Gallery, 57 & 58.
Positions: Art dir, Coconut Grove Playhouse, Miami, 55-59; v pres & dir, Playhouse Gallery, Miami, 58-59; dir, Artist Equity Miami, 58-59; dir, Soc Fla Printmakers, 58-62.
Awards: Outstanding New Talent in U S A, Art in Am, 57; best over all, rep Fla in New York World's Fair, 64.
Bibliography: A Bower (auth), Outstanding new talent, Art in Am, 57; L Campbell (auth), Miami artist, Art News, 58; Hal Corrington (auth), Amoroso, produced on Channel 4-TV in Miami, 58.
Collection: Eskimo sculptures; Pre-Columbia sculptures; African sculptures; Picasso ceramics.
Publications: Auth, Art festivals, 54 & auth, The arts of New England, 56, Miami Herald; auth, State of mind, Coconut Grove, 60.
Dealer: DeLigny Art Galleries, 709 E Las Olas, Fort Lauderdale, FL 33301.
Mailing Address: 3539 Poinciana Ave, Miami, FL 33133.

ANARGYROS, SPERO
Sculptor
Preferred Media: Bronze, Marble, Stone, Wood.
b New York, N Y, Jan 23, 15.
Study & Training: Study with William Zorack, New York, 34-35; asst to Mahonri Sharp Young, This is the Place monument, Salt Lake City, Utah, 44-47.
Commissions: Bronze bust, Sheik Khalid ben Mohammed Al-Qasimi, 70; bronze heroic figure, Pedro Martinez, Knight Comdr of Pope St Sylvester, Agana, Guam, 72; bronze bust, Ralph K Davies, Ralph K Davies Med Ctr, San Francisco, 72; plus many others.
Exhibitions: Nat Acad Design, 38-40, 53-56 & 59; M H De Young Mem Mus, 53 & 62-63; one-man shows, Houston & Corpus Christi, Tex, 68, San Francisco, Calif, 69 & Egyptian Mus, San Jose, Calif, 69; plus many others.
Awards: St Gaudens Medal fine draughtsmanship, 34; first hon mention, Nat Competition Sculpture, Pomona Co, Calif, 38; first award sculpture, Tenth Ann Nat Exhib, Acad Artists Asn, 59.
Bibliography: Terence Busch (auth), Spero Anargyros and his 23 ton rock, San Francisco Mag, 11/65; Frederick Whitaker (auth), Spero Anargyros, sculptor, Am Artist, 2/67; Valerie Shields (auth), Man with a masterful thumb, Spectator, 2/57.
Memberships: Life mem, Art Stud League New York; fel Nat Sculpture Soc; fel Int Inst Arts & Lett.
Mailing Address: 2503 Clay St, San Francisco, CA 94115.

ANAYA, STEPHEN RAUL
Printmaker
b Los Angeles, Calif, June 29, 46.
Study & Training: San Fernando Valley State Col with Tom Fricano; Univ Calif, Los Angeles, BA, currently studying with David Glines & Raymond Brown.
Work in Public Collections: Chicago Inst Art, Ill; San Diego State Col, Calif; Davidson Col, N C; William Hayes Mem Art Ctr, Univ N C, Chapel Hill; Ga State Univ, Atlanta.
Exhibitions: Fourth Ann Nat Print Exhib, San Diego State Col, 71; Davidson Nat Print & Drawing Exhib, Davidson Col, 72; Fifth Nat Stud Printmakers Exhib, Univ N C, 72; Third Nat Print Exhib, Ga State Univ, 72; Nat Print Exhib, Calif Soc Printmakers, Richmond Art Ctr, Calif, 72.
Teaching: Teaching asst printmaking, Univ Calif, Los Angeles, 70-71; assoc printmaking, 71-
Awards: Los Angeles Chap winner, Nat Soc Arts & Lett, 71; prize for graphics, fourth Nat Print Exhib, San Diego State Col, 71; prize for graphics, Davidson Nat Print & Drawing Exhib, 72.
Memberships: Los Angeles Printmaking Soc.
Mailing Address: 6309 Canby Ave, Reseda, CA 91335.

ANDERSEN, ANDREAS STORRS
Educator, Painter
Preferred Media: Oils, Acrylics.
b Chicago, Ill, Oct 6, 08.
Study & Training: Carnegie-Mellon Univ; Brit Acad Fine Arts, Rome, Italy, dipl; Acad Belli Arti, Rome; Art Inst Chicago.
Work in Public Collections: IBM Corp; Univ Ariz.
Exhibitions: Metrop Mus Art, New York, N Y; Whitney Mus Am Art, New York; Corcoran Gallery Art, Washington, D C; M H De Young Mem Mus, San Francisco, Calif; Tucson Art Ctr, Ariz.
Teaching: Prof art, Univ Ariz, 35-62; head art dept, 40-62; prof art, Otis Art Inst, Los Angeles, Calif, 62-
Positions: Pres emer, Tucson Art Ctr; dir, Univ Ariz Art Gallery, 49-56; pres, Otis Art Inst, 62-

Awards: Hon award, I B M Corp, 40.
Memberships: Nat Asn Schs Art; Nat Art Educ Asn; Am Asn Univ Prof.
Publications: Art ed, signs and symbols in Christian art, 54.
Mailing Address: Otis Art Institute, 2401 Wilshire Blvd, Los Angeles, CA 90057.

ANDERSEN, WAYNE VESTI
Art Historian, Educator
b July 7, 28; U S citizen.
Study & Training: Univ Calif, BA; Columbia Univ, William Bayard Cutting fel, 61-62, MA & Ph D.
Teaching: Prof art hist, Mass Inst Technol, 62-
Awards: Belg-Am Found CRB fel, 62; Ford Found grant humanities, 62-63.
Memberships: Col Art Asn Am.
Research: Late nineteenth century painting.
Publications: Auth, Cezanne's portrait drawings, 69; auth, Gauguin's paradise lost, 71; plus numerous articles in scholarly mags.
Mailing Address: Massachusetts Institute of Technology, 7-143, Cambridge, MA 02139.

ANDERSON, BRAD J
Cartoonist
b Jamestown, N Y, May 14, 24.
Study & Training: Syracuse Univ, BFA, 51.
Work in Public Collections: Albert T Reid Col; William Allen White Found, Univ Kans; Complete Collection Grandpa's Boy Original Comic Strips, Syracuse Univ Mss Libr.
Exhibitions: San Diego Fair Fine Arts & Cartoon Exhib; Punch, Brit-Am Exhib, 54; Cartoon Exhib, The Selected Cartoons of 14 Saturday Evening Post Cartoonists; Cartoon Americana, overseas exhib.
Positions: Art dir, graphic art dept, Syracuse Univ, 50-52; freelance cartoonist, 50-; int syndicated cartoonist, Marmaduke, 54- & Grandpa's Boy, 54-
Memberships: Mag Cartoonist Guild; Newspaper Comics/Coun.
Publications: Illusr, Marmaduke, 55, Marmaduke rides agin' & Marmaduke rides again, 68; contribr cartoons, In: Sat Eve Post, Look Mag & others.
Mailing Address: 514 W Ivy, San Diego, CA 92101.

ANDERSON, DAVID K
Art Dealer, Collector
b Buffalo, N Y, June 26, 35.
Positions: Pres & owner, Martha Jackson Gallery, Inc, New York, N Y.
Specialty of Gallery: Art of 20th century since 1945.
Mailing Address: 32 E 69th St, New York, NY 10503.

ANDERSON, DAVID PHILLIP
Painter, Lecturer
Preferred Media: Acrylics.
b Charleroi, Pa, Nov 26, 26.
Study & Training: Calif State Teachers Col; also portraiture with Christopher Clark.
Work in Public Collections: State Capitol Bldg, Tallahassee, Fla.
Commissions: Series of oils, operatic themes, Stanley Levine, Metrop Opera, 61; muralistic oil, Huegenot Soc, Fla, 62; portrait of Carlo Bergonzi in role of Canio, Metrop Opera, 68; representation of Justice, William R Fleece, State Rep, 70; portrait, Doc Severinsen, comn by Suncoast Hosp Guild, 72.
Exhibitions: Ninth Ann Nat Exhib, Ringling Mus, Sarasota, Fla, 59; Harmon Gallery, Naples, Fla, 65; Fla Pavilion, New York World's Fair, 65; Fla Showcase Offices, Rockefeller Plaza, New York, N Y, 66; State Dept Art, Embassy Int, 67.
Teaching: Instr art, Portsmouth Art Gallery, 61; instr art, Sun Tan Art Gallery, 68-72; guest lectr & demonstr, Art League Treasure Island, Portsmouth Art League, Ohio, Sun Tan Art Ctr & Beaux Art Gallery, 61-
Awards: First & grand awards, Beaux Arts Gallery, 63-72.
Publications: Illusr, cover of St Petersburg Times Church News & Leisure & Arts Sect, 60; contribr, Together, 62 & St Petersburg Mag, 64.
Dealer: Galerie Lucile, 6409 Renaldo Way S, St Petersburg, FL 33707.
Mailing Address: 1034 Farragut Dr, Saint Petersburg, FL 33710.

ANDERSON, DOUG
Illustrator
b N H, Oct 2, 19.
Study & Training: New Sch, N Y; Art Stud League New York.
Publications: Auth, How to draw with the light touch, New things to draw & how to draw them, Let's draw a story & Humorous drawing made easy; illusr, New Yorker Mag, Fortune, Good Housekeeping & many others.
Mailing Address: 35 E 63rd St, New York, NY 10021.

ANDERSON, GUNNAR DONALD
Painter, Illustrator
Preferred Media: Oil.
b Berkeley, California, Mar 3, 27.
Study & Training: Calif Sch Fine Arts with Clifford Still; Art Ctr Col Design, BFA, with Lorser Feitelson.
Work in Public Collections: Brown-Forman Distillers, Louisville, Ky; Dalzell Hatfield Galleries, Los Angeles, Calif; Guildhall Galleries, Chicago, Ill; Conacher Galleries, San Francisco, Calif; Meredith Long Galleries, Houston, Tex.
Commissions: Paintings of children, Mr & Mrs Stephen Bechtel, Piedmont, Calif, 65; Mr & Mrs Lowell Dillingham, Hawaii, 66; Mrs Robert E Norcross, Tyronza, Ark, 68; Mr & Mrs Meredith Long, Houston, Tex, 71; Mr & Mrs George Weyerhauser, Tacoma, Wash, 72.
Exhibitions: Fifth Winter Invitational, Palace of Legion of Honor, San Francisco, 64; M H de Young Memorial Museum, San Francisco, 25th Annual, Society of Western Artists, 68; Charles & Emma Frye Mus, Seattle, Wash, 71; Calif State Fair, Sacramento, 71; Mainstream 72, Grover M Hermann Fine Arts Ctr, Marietta College, Ohio, 72.
Awards: Best figure or portrait, 29th Ann, Soc Western Artists, 71; third prize, California State Fair, 71; best in fine art, Exhib One, Soc Art Center, Alumni, 72.
Bibliography: Mrs Linda Hardwick (auth), Collage, Educational TV, Memphis Community TV found, 71-72; TV interview, Memphis, Tenn, 71; Don J Anderson (auth), Paintings of children, Chicago Today, 72.
Memberships: Soc Western Artists; Soc Art Center Alumni.
Publications: Illusr, Oscar Lincoln Busby Stokes, Harcourt, Brace & World Inc, 70.
Dealer: Mrs Laddie Andrews, Lord & Taylor Art Gallery, 424 Fifth Ave, New York, NY 10018.
Mailing Address: 4583 Belmont Ct, Sonoma, CA 95476.

ANDERSON, GUY IRVING
Painter
Preferred Media: Oil, Watercolor.
b Edmonds, Wash, Nov 20, 06.
Study & Training: Private classes; Tiffany Found fel.
Work in Public Collections: Seattle Art Mus, Wash; Santa Barbara Mus, Calif; Munson Williams Proctor Inst, Utica, N Y; Art Mus Greater Victoria, B C; Univ Ore, Eugene.
Commissions: Mural (oil on wood), Seattle Opera House, 62; cement & metal panels, Hilton Inn, Seattle; panel, workers, Edmonds Pub Libr; stone inlay, terrace, Seattle First Nat Bank; pebble mosaics, John H Hauberg Garden, Seattle.
Exhibitions: Eight-man show toured in Europe & Asia, U S Info Agency, 56-57; Fine Arts Pavilion, Seattle World's Fair, 62; A University Collects: Oregon, circulated by Am Fedn Arts, 67-68; 73rd Western Ann, Denver Art Mus, 72; The Drawing Society Nat Exhib, circulated by Am Fedn Arts, 70-72.
Awards: Music & Art Found Award, Seattle, 52; first prize, Anacortes Art Festival, Wash, 64; award of merit, Am Inst Archit, Seattle, 65; plus others.
Bibliography: Holiday Mag, 59; Art in Am, 62; Guy Anderson, Gear Press, Seattle, 65.
Mailing Address: Box 217, La Conner, WA 98257

ANDERSON, GWENDOLYN ORSINGER, see ORSINI.

ANDERSON, HOWARD BENJAMIN
Graphic Artist, Painter
b Racine, Wis, June 26, 03.
Study & Training: Univ Wis-Madison, BA; Art Inst Chicago, Ill; Corcoran Gallery Art Sch, Washington, D C.
Exhibitions: 150th Anniversary Exhib Lithography, Print Club Rochester, N Y, 48; 69th Ann Exhib Chicago Artists & Vicinity, Chicago Art Inst, 66; Print Ann, Soc Am Graphic Artists, 50-59, 67 & 68; Am-Japanese Contemp Print Exhib, Tokyo, 67; 9th Union League Art Show, Union League Club, Chicago, 72.
Positions: Package designer, R Loewy & Assocs, Chicago, 45-49; package designer, Cermak Studio, Chicago, 49-55; com artist, Artists Inc, & Koopman Neumer, Chicago.
Memberships: Soc Am Graphic Artists; Chicago Soc Artists.
Mailing Address: 2725 Devon Ave, Chicago, IL 60659.

ANDERSON, JEREMY RADCLIFFE
Sculptor, Educator
Preferred Media: Wood
b Palo Alto, Calif, Oct 28, 21.
Study & Training: Calif Sch Fine Arts, cert, 50.
Work in Public Collections: Doxie, San Francisco Mus; untitled redwood, Pasadena Art Mus; Map # 12, Mus Mod Art, New York, N Y; Riverrun, Univ Calif, Berkeley.
Exhibitions: One-man show, Stable Gallery, New York, 54; one-man retrospective, San Francisco Mus, San Francisco & Pasadena,

66 & 67; Funk Show, Univ Calif, Berkeley, 67; American Sculpture of the 60's, Los Angeles Mus, 67; Expo 70, San Francisco Pavilion, Osako, Japan, 70.
Teaching: Instr sculpture, San Francisco Art Inst, 58-
Awards: I N Walter Sculpture Prize, Calif Sch Fine Arts, 48; Rosenberg traveling fel, San Francisco Art Asn, 50.
Bibliography: Assignment 4 (film), archives of KRON-TV, San Francisco, 2/19/62; Gerald Nordland (auth), Jeremy Anderson, introd to catalog, Retrospective, San Francisco Mus, 66; Jose Pierre (auth), Funk Art, L'Oeil, No. 190, Paris, 10/70.
Publications: Auth, The artist's view, 2, San Francisco, 9/52.
Dealer: Ruth Bronstein, Quay Gallery, 2 Jerome Alley, San Francisco, CA 94133.
Mailing Address: 534 Northern Ave, Mill Valley, CA 94941.

ANDERSON, JOHN S
Sculptor
Preferred Media: Wood.
b Seattle, Wash, Apr 29, 28.
Study & Training: Los Angeles Art Ctr, Pratt Inst.
Work in Public Collections: Mus Mod Art, New York, N Y; Whitney Mus Am Art, New York.
Exhibitions: Int Arts Festival, Providence, R I, 65; Albert A List Show, New Sch Social Res, 65; Cummer Gallery Art, Jacksonville, Fla, 66; six one-man shows, Allan Stone Gallery, New York, 65-71.
Teaching: Instr sculpture, Pratt Inst, 59-62; instr sculpture, Sch Visual Arts, 68-70; instr sculpture, Cooper Union, 70-
Awards: Guggenheim Found grant, 65-66; Mini grant, N J State Coun Art, 72.
Dealer: Allan Stone Gallery, 48 E 86th St, New York, NY 10028.
Mailing Address: Box 59, School St, Asbury, NJ 08802.

ANDERSON, LENNART
Printmaker, Instructor
b Detroit, Mich, Aug 22, 28.
Study & Training: Art Inst Chicago, BFA; Cranbrook Acad Art, MFA.
Work in Public Collections: Detroit Inst Art; Whitney Mus Am Art; Hudson Co, Detroit.
Exhibitions: Carnegie Inst Mus Art, 64 & 67; Contemp Art U S A, Norfolk, Va, 66; Whitney Mus Am Art Ann, 67; Vassar Col, 68; Ravinia Festival, High Park, Ill, 68; plus others.
Teaching: Instr, Chatham Col, 61-62; instr, Pratt Inst, 62-64; instr, Swain Sch, New Bedford, Mass, summers 63-64; instr, Art Stud League New York; instr, Yale Univ, 67; instr, Skowhegan Sch, 68.
Awards: Tiffany Found grants, 57 & 61; Prix de Rome, 58-61; Raymond A Speiser Mem Prize, Pa Acad Fine Arts, 66; plus others.
Dealer: Graham Gallery, 1014 Madison Ave, New York, NY 10021.
Mailing Address: 877 Union St, Brooklyn, NY 11215.

ANDERSON, RONALD TRENT
Painter, Printmaker
b Madison, Wis, Oct 10, 38.
Study & Training: Univ Wis, BS, MS & MFA.
Work in Public Collections: Dalhousie Univ, Halifax; Univ Wis; Madison Art Ctr; Park Forest Art Ctr, Ill; also in many pvt collections U S & Can.
Exhibitions: Wis Printmakers, Smithsonian Inst, Washington, D C, 62; Nat Drawing & Sculpture Exhib, Muncie, Ind, 62 & 63; Watercolors: U S A, Springfield, Mo, 62, 64 & 65; Nat Drawings & Print Athens, Ohio, 63; Union League Chicago, Nat Design Ctr, 67; plus others.
Teaching: Teaching fel, Univ Wis, 61-63; instr art, Bloom Twp High Sch, Chicago Heights, Ill, 63-67; asst prof art educ & head dept, N S Col Art, 67-
Awards: Awards, 62 & 66 & purchase award, 64, Madison Art Asn; purchase award, Ill Midwest Art Fair, 66; purchase award, Dalhousie Univ, 67; plus others.
Mailing Address: 3000 Olivet St, Apt 402, Halifax, N S, Can.

ANDRADE, EDNA WRIGHT
Educator, Painter
Preferred Media: Acrylic, Silkscreen.
b Portsmouth, Va, Jan 25, 17.
Study & Training: Pa Acad Fine Arts, 33-38; Cresson European traveling scholar, Pa Acad Fine Arts, 36-37; Univ Pa Sch Fine Arts, BFA, 37.
Work in Public Collections: Philadelphia Mus Art, Pa; Pa Acad Fine Arts, Philadelphia; Yale Art Gallery, New Haven, Conn; Albright-Knox Art Gallery, Buffalo, N Y; Montclair Art Mus, N J.
Commissions: Mosiac mural, Columbia Br, Free Libr Philadelphia, 62; marble intarsia mural, Welsh Rd Br, Free Libr Philadelphia, 67; geometric paintings, Smith Kline & French Co, Philadelphia, 68; mobile sculpture, Roxborough Br, Free Libr Philadelphia, 69; granite paving, Salvation Army Div Hdq, Philadelphia, 72.
Exhibitions: Art with Optical Reaction, Des Moines Art Ctr, Iowa,

66; East Coast-West Coast Painting, Univ Okla Philbrook Art Ctr, 68; Master Painters of Three Centuries, Montclair Art Mus, N J, 69; New Accessions USA, Colo Springs Art Ctr, 70; Silkscreen: History of a Medium, Philadelphia Mus Art, 72.
Teaching: Prof art, Philadelphia Col Art, 57-72; prof art, Temple Univ, Philadelphia, 72-
Awards: Childe Hassam Memorial Purchase Awards, Am Acad Arts & Lett, 67-68; Mary Smith Prize, Pa Acad Fine Arts, 68.
Memberships: Pa Acad Fellowship; Print Club (mem bd, 72); Artists Equity Asn; Am Color Print Soc; Peale Club.
Dealer: Marian Locks Gallery, 1524 Walnut St, Philadelphia, PA 19102.
Mailing Address: 415 S Carlisle St, Philadelphia, PA 19146.

ANDRE, CARL
Sculptor
b Quincy, Mass, Sept 16, 35.
Study & Training: With Patrick Morgan & Frank Stella.
Work in Public Collections: Brandeis Univ; Inst Contemp Art, Chicago, Ill; Walker Art Ctr, Minneapolis, Minn; Haus Lange, Krefeld, Ger.
Exhibitions: Primary Structure, New York, N Y, 66; Sculpture of the '60's, Los Angeles, Calif & Philadelphia, Pa, 67; Art of the Real, Mus Mod Art, New York, 68; Minimal Art, The Hague, Dusseldorf, Paris & Berlin, 68; Solomon R Guggenheim Mus, New York, 70; plus others.
Awards: Nat Endowment Arts Award, 68.
Memberships: Art Workers Coalition.
Dealer: John Weber Gallery, 420 W Broadway, New York, NY 10012.
Mailing Address: Box 540, Cooper Station, New York, NY 10003.

ANDRE, FRANÇOISE
Painter
Preferred Media: Oils, Acrylics.
b Les Sables d'Olonne, France, Aug 13, 26; Can citizen.
Study & Training: Acad Royale Beaux-Arts, Brussels; Inst Nat Superieur Beaux-Arts, Antwerp; Int Nat Superieur Arts Decora Tifs, Gromaire.
Work in Public Collections: Vancouver Art Gallery, B C; Univ Western Ont; Sir George Williams Univ; Princeton Univ; Queens Univ.
Commissions: Mural, Redemptorist Sem, Edmonton, 61.
Exhibitions: Quadriennal de Liege, Belg, 48; Western Art Circuit, 52 & 53; Vancouver Art Gallery Centennial Exhib, 59; Artists Ann, Art Inst Chicago, Ill, 63; Chicago Centennial Exhib, 63.
Awards: Prix Koenigsberg, Miss Koenigsberg, Brussels, 47; Prix Georgette Baes, Baes Found, Brussels, 48; first prize with highest distinction, Acad Royale, Brussels, 48.
Dealer: Harold Patton, 17500 Fenway Dr, Detroit, MI 48221.
Mailing Address: 1930 Lafayette Rd, Gladwyne, PA 19035.

ANDREJEVIC, MILET
Painter
Preferred Media: Egg Tempera.
b Yugoslavia, Sept 25, 25; U S citizen.
Study & Training: Belgrade Acad Appl Arts, 41-44; Belgrade Acad Fine Arts, BFA, 50, MFA, 52.
Work in Public Collections: Whitney Mus Am Art, New York, N Y; Allentown Mus; R I Sch Design, Providence; Nicholas Wilder Collection, Los Angeles.
Commissions: Portrait, Robert C Scull, New York, 72.
Exhibitions: Formalist Exhib, Washington Gallery Mod Art, 63; 28th Biennale, Corcoran Gallery Art, 63; Am Painting Ann, Whitney Mus Am Art, 64 & 66; R I Sch Design, 69 & 70; Green Gallery Revisited, Hofstra Univ, 72.
Teaching: Instr art hist & lib arts, exten, New York Univ, 65-66; instr design, Brooklyn Col, 72-
Bibliography: Paul Katz (auth), Art now New York, 12/69; Whee K Muller (auth), Iconography of past and present, Arts Mag, fall 72; Claes Oldenburg (auth), Store days.
Dealer: Noah Goldowsky Gallery, 1078 Madison Ave, New York, NY 10021.
Mailing Address: 35 W 82nd St, New York, NY 10024.

ANDREWS, BENNY
Painter, Lecturer
Preferred Media: Oil & Collage, Ink.
b Madison, Ga, Nov 13, 30.
Study & Training: Fort Valley State Col, 48-50; Univ Chicago, 56-58; Chicago Art Inst, BFA, 58; John Hay Whitney opportunity fel, 65-66.
Work in Public Collections: Mus Mod Art, New York, N Y; Detroit Inst Art, Mich; Mus African Art, Washington, D C; High Mus, Atlanta, Ga; Butler Inst Am Art, Youngstown, Ohio.
Exhibitions: 30 Contemporary Black Americans, Minneapolis Inst Arts, Minn, 68; Martin Luther King Memorial, Mus Mod Art, 69;

Afro-Americans: Boston and New York, Mus Fine Arts, Boston, Mass, 70; Symbols, Studio Mus Harlem, New York, 71; Artists as Adversary, Mus Mod Art, 71.
Teaching: Instr art, New Sch Social Research, 67-70; lectr art, Queens College, 68-72; Dorne vis prof, Univ Bridgeport, 70.
Positions: Co-chmn, Black Emergency Cultural Coalition, New York, 69-
Awards: N Y State Creative Arts Prog Awardee, 71.
Bibliography: Samella Lewis & Ruth Waddy (auth), Black artists on art, Vol II, Contemp Crafts, 71; Elton Fax (auth), 17 black artists, Dodd, 71; Rhoda L Goldstein (ed), Life and culture in the U S A black, Thomas Y Crowell, 71; plus others.
Publications: Illusr, I am the darker brother, Macmillan, 68; auth, On understanding black art, New York Times, 1/21/70; The B E C C (Black Emergency Cultural Coalition), Arts Mag, 4/70; To date, M O D E Mag, 4/71.
Dealer: ACA Gallery, 25 E 73rd St, New York, NY 10021.
Mailing Address: 31 Beekman St, New York, NY 10038.

ANDREWS, LADDIE E
Art Dealer
b Tenn.
Positions: Owner, private business, 52-63; dir, Lord & Taylor Gallery, 63-
Memberships: Nat Arts Club; Parrish Art Mus.
Specialty of Gallery, Select and arrange six one-man shows yearly plus group and rotating shows.
Mailing Address: c/o Lord & Taylor Gallery, 38th St & Fifth Ave, New York, NY 10018.

ANDREWS, OLIVER
Sculptor
Study & Training: Univ Southern Calif; Stanford Univ, BA; Univ Calif, Santa Barbara; also with Jean Helion, Paris, France.
Work in Public Collections: Work in many pvt collections.
Commissions: Stage design, Theatre Group's King Lear, Univ Calif, Los Angeles & Hollywood Pilgrimage Theatre, 64; sculptural lighting fixture, Yale Univ; bronze fountain, W Valley Prof Ctr, San Jose, Calif.
Exhibitions: One-man shows, 50, 56 & 63 & group shows, 57, 59 & 68, Santa Barbara Mus Art; Whitney Mus Am Art, 56 & 62; San Francisco Mus Art, 60-63 & 66; Southwestern Col, Chula Vista, Calif, 66 & 68; Southern Asn Sculptors Traveling Exhib, 67-68; plus others.
Teaching: Asst prof drawing & sculpture, Univ Calif, Los Angeles, 57-70; lectr sculpture, mus, schs, art, stud & faculty groups, radio & TV, 59-69; assoc prof sculpture, San Fernando Valley State Col, 62-70.
Awards: Prizes, Los Angeles Co Mus Art, 57 & 61; Univ Calif, Los Angeles res grant, 61-68; awards, Inst Creative Art, Univ Calif, 63 & 67.
Dealer: David Stuart Galleries, 807 N La Cienega Blvd, Los Angeles, CA 90069.
Mailing Address: 408 Sycamore Rd, Santa Monica Canyon, CA 90402.

ANDREWS, SYBIL (SYBIL ANDREWS MORGAN)
Graphic Artist
Preferred Media: Oils, Watercolors.
b Bury St Edmunds, Eng, Apr 19, 98.
Study & Training: Heatherley Sch Fine Art, London, Eng, with Henry G Massey; also with Boris Heroys, London.
Work in Public Collections: Victoria & Albert Mus, London; Nat Gallery South Australia; Dublin Mus, Ireland; Los Angeles Co Mus Art, Calif; Leeds Mus, Eng.
Exhibitions: 200 Years of British Graphic Art, Prague, Vienna & Bucharest, 35-36; Sybil Andrews Exhib Colour Linocut Prints, Vancouver Art Gallery, 48; Primera Expos Arte Sacro Moderno, Buenos Aires, Arg, 54; Print Makers Soc Calif.
Teaching: Pvt classes.
Awards: G A Reid Award, Soc Can Painter, Etchers & Engravers, 51.
Memberships: Soc Can Painter, Etchers & Engravers.
Art Interests: Color linocut prints.
Mailing Address: 2131 South Island Hwy, Campbell River, BC, Can.

ANDRUS, JAMES ROMAN
Printmaker, Painter
Preferred Media: Oils.
b St George, Utah, July 11, 07.
Study & Training: Otis Art Inst, Los Angeles, Calif; Colorado Springs Fine Arts Ctr; Art Stud League New York, N Y; Brigham Young Univ, BA & MA; Columbia Univ; Univ Colo, EdD.
Work in Public Collections: Utah State Capitol Collection (three), Salt Lake City; Brigham Young Univ, Provo, Utah; Dixie Col Collection, St George; Provo City Schs Collection; Granite Sch Dist Collection, Salt Lake City.

Commissions: Mural, St George Temple, Utah, 43; oil painting, Cent Utah Ment Health Ctr, 72; portraits of Charles E Maw & Joseph K Nicoles, Brigham Young Univ, portrait of J C Moffitt, Provo Sch Dist.

Exhibitions: Calif State Fair Exhib, 39; Utah State Inst Fine Arts Exhibs; Boston Mus Ann, Mass; Wichita Print Asn, Kans; Univ Utah Ann, Salt Lake City.

Teaching: Spec instr painting, Brigham Young Univ, 40-43, asst prof painting & printmaking, 50-53, prof art, 58-, chmn art dept.

Positions: Mem, Utah State Fair Art Comt, Salt Lake City; chmn visual arts div, Utah State Inst Fine Arts; mem, Utah State Bd Educ Elem Art Curric.

Awards: Faculty award of merit, Otis Art Inst, 38; Univ Colo art fel, 52; purchase prizes, Utah State Inst Fine Arts, 45, 50 & 54.

Memberships: Nat Art Educ Asn; Western Art Educ Asn; Utah Acad Sci, Arts & Lett; Cent Utah Art Bd.

Mailing Address: 1765 N 651 East, Provo, UT 84601.

ANDRUS, MOULTON LOYAL
Sculptor, Architect
Preferred Media: Epoxy, Aluminum.
b New York, N Y, May 28, 40.
Study & Training: Yale Col, BA, 62, Sch Archit, Yale Univ, March, 68.
Work in Public Collections: Work in pvt collections only.
Commissions: Relief, pvt collection, Conn, 70; integral relief, pvt collection, Fla, 71; constructions for pvt collections, New York, Pa & Minn, 72.
Exhibitions: Grennwich Art Soc, Conn, 66-68; 23rd New Eng Exhib Painting & Sculpture, 72; Sculptors Guild, New York, 72.
Positions: Proj architect, Hobart D Betts, Architect, 68-70; principal, Moulton Andrus, Architect, 70-72; designer, Bloodworth, Hawes & Peterson, Architects, 72-
Awards: First prize in sculpture, 65 & 66 & best work in show, Greenwich Art Soc, 67.
Memberships: Sculptors Guild; Archit League.
Mailing Address: 7532 S W Corbett Ave, Portland, OR 97219.

ANDRUS, VERA EUGENIA
Painter, Lithographer
b Plymouth, Wis, Dec 9, 95.
Study & Training: Univ Minn; St Paul Sch Art; Minneapolis Inst Art; Art Stud League, New York, N Y, with Boardman Robinson, Eugene Fitsch & George Grosz.
Work in Public Collections: Metrop Mus Art, New York; Libr Cong, Washington, D C; Boston Pub Libr, Mass; Minneapolis Inst Art, Minn; Smithsonian Inst, Washington, D C; plus others.
Exhibitions: New York World's Fair, 39-40; Venice Bienniale, 40; Int Print Exhib, Carnegie Inst, Pittsburgh, Pa, 49; invited one-man exhib, Am Mus Natural Hist, New York, 49; 22nd Am Drawing Biennial, Norfolk Mus Arts & Sci & Smithsonian Traveling Exhib, 67-68.
Teaching: Elem drawing, Adult Educ, City Col, 40's.
Positions: Asst information & sales desk, Metrop Mus Art, 29-49, supvr, photograph research & sales dept, 52-57.
Awards: First award in watercolor, Twin City Artists, Minneapolis Art Inst, 28; medal hon, Nat Asn Women Artists, 41; Stow Wengenroth Award, Rockport Art Asn, Mass, 61; plus others.
Bibliography: Dorothy Adlow (auth), several articles accompanying reproductions of lithographs, Christian Science Monitor.
Memberships: Rockport Art Asn, (juror, 71); Nat Asn Women Artists; Hudson Valley Art Asn (former pres).
Collection: Paintings in oil and watercolors; pastels and drawings in all media; lithographs.
Publications: Auth & illustr, Sea-bird island, Harcourt, Brace, 39; Sea dust, poems, drawings and lithographs, Wake-Brook House, 55; auth, Black river, a Wisconsin story, Little, 67; Fragile vase has a history-north shore: 71, Essex Co-newspapers, 71; also a number of poems in magazines and newspapers.
Mailing Address: 17 Parker St, Rockport, MA 01966.

ANGEL, RIFKA
Painter
Preferred Media: Encaustic.
b Kalvaria, Russia, Sept 16, 99; U S citizen.
Study & Training: Art Stud League with Boardman Robinson; also with John Sloan, Alfred Maurer & Emil Ganso; Moscow Art Acad.
Work in Public Collections: Honolulu Acad Fine Arts; Chicago Art Inst; Nelson Art Gallery & Mary Atkins Mus Fine Arts; Brandeis Univ.
Exhibitions: Chicago Art Inst, 31, 33, 35 & 39; 16 Cities Exhib, Mus Mod Art, New York, N Y, 34; Brooklyn Mus, 37; one-man show & ann, Honolulu Acad, 40-41; one-man show, Nelson Art Gallery & Mary Atkins Mus Fine Arts, 43; plus many other one-man shows in galleries.
Awards: For originality in painting, Art Inst Chicago, 33; City Mus St Louis, 45; Design for Democratic Living, Am Fedn Arts, 48.

Bibliography: C J Builiet (auth), Apples and madonnas, 30; Jacobson (auth), Art of today, Chicago, Stein Publ, 33; F Pratt & B Firzel (auth), Encaustic - materials and methods, Lear publ, 49.
Memberships: Artists Equity Asn New York; fel Int Inst Arts & Lett.
Mailing Address: 79-81 MacDougal St, New York, NY 10018.

ANGELINI, JOHN MICHAEL
Painter, Art Director
Preferred Media: Watercolors.
b New York, N Y, Nov 18, 21.
Study & Training: Newark Sch Fine & Indust Art; special studies in Europe, 61.
Work in Public Collections: Dominican Fathers, New York; David L Yunich Collection, Bambergers, N J; Bloomfield Col, N J; Paterson Main Libr, N J; St Vincent Col, Latrobe, Pa.
Exhibitions: Audubon Artists Nat Ann, Nat Acad Design, New York, 63; N J Watercolor Soc Ann, Newark, 63; N J Arts Club Watercolor Ann, New York, 64; N J Pavillion, New York World's Fair, 65; Watercolor U S A, Nat Ann & Traveling Exhib, Springfield Mus, Mo, 66.
Positions: Art dir, Berles Carton Co, Inc, Paterson, N J, 50-; adv bd, N J Music & Arts, Chatham, 72-
Awards: Medal of honor for watercolor, Audubon Artists, 63; silver medal for watercolor, N J Watercolor Soc, 63; medal of honor for watercolor, Nat Arts Club, 64.
Bibliography: L Pessolano (auth), John Angelini-a profile, 70 & R Williams (auth), John Angelini-A W S, 71, N J Music & Arts; John Angelini-interview (with R Williams), WDHA-FM New Jersey, 71.
Memberships: Am Watercolor Soc; Assoc Artists N J (bd dir, 69-); Audubon Artists; N J Watercolor Soc (treas); Allied Artists Am.
Publications: Contribr, Prize winning watercolors, Book II, 66; contribr, N J Music & Arts, 70, 71 & 72; auth, articles, In: Am Artist, 72.
Dealer: Heritage Arts Gallery, 24 First St, South Orange, NJ 07079.
Mailing Address: 5 Carey Ave, Butler, NJ 07405.

ANGELO, EMIDIO
Cartoonist, Painter
b Philadelphia, Pa, Dec 4, 03.
Study & Training: Philadelphia Mus Sch Indust Art.
Exhibitions: Pa Acad Fine Arts; Da Vinci Art Alliance.
Teaching: Instr advan art class, Samuel S Fleisher Art Mem, Philadelphia, Pa.
Positions: Ed cartoonist, Main Line Times, Ardmore, Pa.
Awards: Da Vinci Award, 45, silver medals, 58, 60 & 68, bronze medal, 61; Charles K Smith Prize, Woodmere Art Gallery, 60; gold medal, Philadelphia Sketch Club, 69; plus others.
Memberships: Da Vinci Art Alliance; fel Pa Acad Fine Arts; Nat Cartoonist Soc; Am Ed Cartoonists.
Publications: Producer, short color film of Alighieri's, The Inferno, 67; auth, Just be patient, The time of your life, Emily and Mabel & others.
Mailing Address: 7201 Wissachickon Ave, Philadelphia, PA 19119.

ANGELOCH, ROBERT (HENRY)
Painter
b Richmond Hill, N Y, Apr 8, 22.
Study & Training: Art Stud League New York; Acad Fine Arts, Florence, Italy; also with Fiske Boyd.
Work in Public Collections: Art Stud League New York; Munson-Williams-Proctor Inst.
Commissions: Murals, New York City Bd Educ, Kellogg Corp, Brunswick, N J & Queensboro Pub Libr.
Exhibitions: Many nat & regional exhibs.
Teaching: Supvr, Woodstock Summer Sch, Art Stud League New York, 60-68, instr, Art Stud League New York, 64-72; instr, Woodstock Sch Art, 68-72; instr, Russell Sage Col, 71-72.
Awards: Purchase award, Woodstock Art Asn, 64; Jane Peterson Prize, Allied Artists Am, 64; first prize, Springfield Mus Fine Arts, 68; plus others.
Bibliography: S R Day (auth), Creative Woodstock, Mead Mt Press, 66.
Memberships: Art Stud League New York; Woodstock Artists Asn.
Publications: Auth & illusr, Rillet, 65 & Monhegan (bks drawings), 65; auth, Basic oil painting techniques, Pitman, 70; auth, Outdoor sketching, Am Artist Mag, 70.
Dealer: Lewis Gallery, Mill Hill Rd, Woodstock, NY 12498.
Mailing Address: Box 95, Woodstock, NY 12498.

ANGULO, CHAPPIE
Painter, Illustrator
Preferred Media: Acrylics.
b Mar 3, 28; U S citizen.
Study & Training: Los Angeles City Col; Univ Calif, Los Angeles; Kahn Art School; Esmeralda, Inst Nac Bellas Artes, Mexico City; London Art Ctr.

Work in Public Collections: Mus Mod Art & Mus Cultures, Mexico City; Art Mus, Iguala Guerrero, Mex.
Commissions: Reproduction murals, Bonampak, 57, Chichen Itza & Tomb 7 Oaxaca, 58, Nat Mus Anthrop, Moneda; reproduction mural, Teotihuacan, Bauet Nac, Mex, 59.
Exhibitions: Pintores de Vanguardia, Mus Mod Art, Mexico City, 67; Confrontacion '68 - Mexico, Bellas Artes, Mexico City, 68; one-man show, Olympic Cultural Prog, 69; Contemporary Mexican Artists, Mus Mod Art, Mexico City, 70; one-man show, Mus Fronterizo, Juarez, Mex, 71.
Bibliography: M Vazquez (auth), Museo de las Culturas, Inst Nat Antropologia, 65; A Pastrana (auth), El concreto, Arquitectura Arte & Urbanism Mag, 68.
Publications: Illusr, Teotihuacan-un autoretrato cultural, 64; illusr, Tlalmanalli - encomtrade en tlatelolco, 66; illusr, Relieves de Chalcatzingo (in press); co-auth & illusr, El Amanecer (in press).
Mailing Address: A P Postal 1170, Cuernavaca, Morelos, Mex.

ANHALT, JACQUELINE RICHARDS
    Art Dealer
b Kansas City, Mo, Jan 6, 25.
Study & Training: Col William & Mary.
Memberships: Art Dealers Asn Southern Calif (bd mem-treas, 70-74).
Specialty of Gallery: Contemporary paintings and sculpture.
Mailing Address: Jacqueline Anhalt Gallery, 750 N La Cienega Blvd, Los Angeles, CA 90069.

ANLIKER, ROGER (WILLIAM)
    Painter, Educator
Preferred Media: Encaustic, Gouache, Silverpoint, Graphite.
b Akron, Ohio, Jan 27, 24.
Study & Training: Cleveland Inst Art, dipl, 47, BFA, 48.
Work in Public Collections: Cleveland Mus Art, Ohio; Mus Art, Carnegie Inst, Pittsburgh, Pa; Butler Inst Am Art, Youngstown, Ohio; Westmoreland Co Mus Art, Greensburg, Pa; Akron Art Inst, Ohio.
Exhibitions: Contemporary Drawings from 12 Countries—1945-1952, Art Inst Chicago & traveling to six mus, 52-53; Carnegie Int, 55 & 58; Dessins Americains Contemporains, Strasbourg & travel in France, 56; one-man exhib of 78 works, Westmoreland Co Mus Art, 63; retrospective exhib of 110 works, Temple Univ, Philadelphia, Pa, 65.
Teaching: Asst prof painting & drawing, Carnegie-Mellon Univ, 48-63; prof painting & drawing, Tyler Sch Art, Temple Univ, 63-
Awards: Carnegie Institute Prize, 52 & first watercolor prize, 56, Assoc Artists Pittsburgh; Guggenheim fel, 56.
Mailing Address: 1948 Lycoming Ave, Arlington, PA 19001.

ANSPACH, ERNST
    Collector
b Glogau, Ger, Feb 4, 13; U S citizen.
Study & Training: Univ Munich; Breslau Univ, PhD.
Positions: Gen partner, Loeb, Rhoades & Co, Investment Bankers, New York, N Y.
Memberships: Fel in perpetuity Metrop Mus Art, New York; fel Univ Mus, Philadelphia.
Collection: African tribal sculpture. Exhibited at Mus Primitive Art, New York, 67-68 & Univ Notre Dame, spring 68.
Mailing Address: 118 W 79th St, New York, NY 10024.

ANTHONY, LAWRENCE KENNETH
    Sculptor, Educator
Preferred Media: Metal, Wood.
b Hartsville, S C, May 27, 34.
Study & Training: Washington & Lee Univ, BA; Univ Ga, MFA; study with Lamar Dodd & Howard Thomas.
Work in Public Collections: Brooks Mem Art Gallery, Memphis, Tenn; Vanderbilt Univ Art Dept, Nashville, Tenn; Ark State Univ, Jonesboro; Univ S C, Columbia; Southwestern at Memphis; plus one other.
Commissions: Menorah form sculpture, Jewish Community Ctr, Memphis, 67; sculpture, Corinthian Broadcasting Co, New York, N Y, 71; wall sculpture, CBS-TV, Sacramento, Calif, 72.
Exhibitions: One-man shows, Ga Mus Art, 59, Univ S C, 61, Columbia Mus Art, 66, Brooks Mem Art Gallery, 68 & Vanderbilt Univ, 72.
Teaching: Prof sculpture & drawing, Southwestern at Memphis, 61-
Mailing Address: 1662 Forrest Ave, Memphis, TN 38712.

ANTHONY, WILLIAM GRAHAM
    Painter, Draftsman
Preferred Media: Pencil.
b Fort Monmouth, N J, Sept 25, 34.
Study & Training: Yale Univ, BA, 58, with Josef Albers; San Francisco Art Inst, 59-60; Art Stud League New York, 61; also with Theodoros Stamos.

Work in Public Collections: Whitney Mus Am Art, New York, N Y; Wallraf-Richartz Mus, Cologne, Ger; Art Inst Chicago, Ill; Yale Univ Art Mus, New Haven, Conn; Corcoran Gallery Art, Washington, D C; plus eight others.
Exhibitions: One-man show, Calif Palace of Legion of Honor, San Francisco, 62; Drawing: U S A-63, St Paul Art Ctr, Minn, 63; Maniacal Laughter, Westbeth Gallery, New York, 71; also group shows, Phoenix Gallery & Allan Stone Gallery, New York.
Teaching: Instr figure drawing, San Francisco Acad Art, 62-63.
Positions: Dir, Spectrum Art Gallery, New York, 65-66.
Bibliography: Laurie Anderson (auth), article, In: Art News, 9/71; Marjorie Welish (auth), article, In: Arts, 9-10/71; Gregory Battcock (auth), article, In: Art and Artists, 11/71.
Publications: Auth, A new approach to figure drawing, Crown Publ, 65, Odhams, Ltd, Eng, 67 & Bonanza Publ.
Dealer: Fischbach Gallery, 29 W 57th St, New York, NY 10019.
Mailing Address: H216 Westbeth, 463 West St, New York, NY 10014.

ANTONAKOS, STEPHEN
    Sculptor
Preferred Media: Neon.
b Greece, Nov 1, 26; U S citizen.
Work in Public Collections: Whitney Mus Am Art & Mus Mod Art, New York, N Y; Milwaukee Art Ctr, Wis; Weatherspoon Art Gallery, Univ N C, Greensboro; Newark Mus, N J.
Exhibitions: Neons, Fischbach Gallery, New York, 67-70 & 72; American Sculpture, Sheldon Mem Art Gallery, Univ Nebr, Lincoln, 70; Contemp Am Sculpture Ann, Whitney Mus Am Art, 70; Continuation of 1969 Sao Paulo Biennale, Smithsonian Inst, Washington, D C; American Sculpture of the Sixties, Los Angeles Co Mus Art & Philadelphia Mus Art.
Teaching: Vis artist, grad seminar, Yale Univ, fall 68; artist-in-residence, sculpture, Univ Wis-Madison, spring 71.
Awards: New York State Creative Artists Pub Serv Prog.
Mailing Address: 435 W Broadway, New York, NY 10012.

ANTONOVICI, CONSTANTIN
    Sculptor, Lecturer
Preferred Media: Marble, Bronze, Wood.
b Neamt, Romania, Feb 18, 11; U S citizen.
Study & Training: Fine Arts Acad, Romania; Fine Arts Acad, Vienna, Austria, with Prof Fritz Behn; Study with Constantin Brancusi, Paris, France.
Work in Public Collections: Le Salon des Artistes Independants, Paris; Vatican, Roma, Italy; St Joseph, Vienna; Museum Fine Arts Montreal, P Q; Cathedral of St John the Divine, New York, N Y.
Commissions: Monuments of St George, Fine Arts Comt, Vienna, 43, & of St Joseph, 47; General De Gaulle, French Army Commandment, Tyrol, Austria, 46; Gen Dwight D Eisenhower, Pres Nixon Collection; Bishop Manning, Cathedral St John the Divine, 54; St Luke, St Luke's Hospital, New York, 55.
Exhibitions: Asn Federative L'Art Libre, Paris, 51; Silver Anniversary, Canadian Artists Asn, 53; Art Alliance Gallery Am, Philadelphia, 62; N J Mus Art Ann, 64; Nat Sculpture Soc Ann Exhibition, New York, 71.
Awards: Awards for commissions through competitions.
Bibliography: Canon West, S T D (auth), The source of courage, The Living Church, 5/12/54; Frank Getlein (auth), Art and artists, Sunday Star, Washington, D C, 7/19/64; Ralph Fabri (auth), Sculpture, Today's Art, 3/70; plus others.
Memberships: Nat Sculpture Soc.
Mailing Address: 310 W 106th St, New York, NY 10025.

ANTREASIAN, GARO ZAREH
    Painter, Lithographer
b Indianapolis, Ind, Feb 16, 22.
Study & Training: Herron Sch Art, BFA; with Stanley William Hayter & Will Barnet.
Work in Public Collections: Metrop Mus Art, Mus Mod Art & Solomon R Guggenheim Mus, New York, N Y; Art Inst Chicago, Ill; Los Angeles Co Mus Art, Los Angeles, Calif.
Commissions: History of Indiana Univ, Bloomington, Ind, 54; Lincoln in Indiana, (with Ralph Peck), Ind State Off Bldg, Indianapolis, 63.
Exhibitions: Tamarind: Homage to Lithography, Mus Mod Art, New York, 69; Recent Suites, Jewish Mus, New York, 69; U S Pavilion, Venice Biennale, Italy, 70; Int Exhib Graphics, Montreal, P Q, 71; British Int Print Biennale, Bradford, Eng, 72.
Teaching: Instr art, Herron Sch Art, Indianapolis, 48-64; prof lithography & art, Univ N Mex, 64-
Positions: Tech dir lithography, Tamarind Lithography Workshop, Inc, Los Angeles, Calif, 60-61; tech dir lithography, Tamarind Inst, Univ N Mex, 70-72.
Awards: Purchase awards, Nat Print Exhib, Northern Ill Univ, 68; Nat Print Exhib, State Univ N Y Albany, 68; First Hawaii Int, Honolulu Acad Arts, 71.
Publications: Co-auth, The Tamarind book of lithography: art and techniques, 71.

Dealers: Martha Jackson Gallery, 32 E 69th St, New York, NY 10021; Malvina Miller Gallery, 3489 Sacramento St, San Francisco, CA 94118.
Mailing Address: 1300 Morningside Dr, NE, Albuquerque, NM 87110.

ANUSZKIEWICZ, RICHARD J
Painter
b Erie, Pa, May 23, 30.
Study & Training: Cleveland Inst Art, BFA, 53; Yale Univ, MFA, 55; Kent State Univ, BS in Educ, 56.
Work in Public Collections: Akron Art Inst, Ohio; Albright-Knox Art Gallery, Buffalo, N Y; Butler Inst Am Art, Youngstown, Ohio; Corcoran Gallery Art, Washington, D C; Whitney Mus Am Art, New York, N Y; plus others.
Exhibitions: Larry Aldrich Mus, Ridgefield, Conn, 68 & 71; Va Mus Fine Arts, Richmond, 70; Ind State Univ, Terre Haute, 70; Masur Mod Art, Monroe, La, 70; Birmingham Mus, Ala, 71; plus many other group & one-man shows.
Teaching: Artist-in-residence, Dartmouth Col, 67; Univ Wis, 68; Cornell Univ, 68; Kent State Univ, 68.
Awards: Philosophers Stone Prize, 63, first prize, 64, Silvermine Guild Artists; purchase prize, Flint Inst Art, Mich, 66.
Bibliography: Gregory Battcock (ed), Minimal art: a critical anthology, Dutton, 68; Douglas MacAgy (auth), Plus by minus: today's half-century, Albright-Knox Art Gallery, 68; Allen S Weller, The joys and sorrows of recent American art, Univ Ill Press, 68.
Dealer: Sidney Janis Gallery, 5 W 57th St, New York, NY 10019.
Mailing Address: 76 Chestnut St, Englewood, NJ 07631.

APARICIO, GERARDO
Painter
b Madrid, Spain, 43.
Study & Training: Escuela Bellas Artes; Escuela Artes Y Oficios; Escuela Nac Artes Graficas, 63-68.
Exhibitions: II Nac Artes Plasticas, 63; Munic Mus Mataro, Spain, 69; 25th Expos Painting, Casa Siglo SV, Segovia, 70; New Prints, Alonzo Gallery, New York, 70; one-man shows, Galeria Egam, Madrid & Galeria Seiquer, Madrid.
Awards: Medella, XII Salon Grabado; first prize for printmaking, Expos Bellas Artes, 64.
Mailing Address: c/o Alonzo Gallery, 26 E 63rd St, New York, NY 10021.

APGAR, NICOLAS ADAM
Painter, Educator
Preferred Media: Oils.
b Gaillon, France, Dec 8, 18; U S citizen.
Study & Training: Syracuse Univ, 39-41, 55-58, BFA, 58, MFA, 60; Univ Va, cert, 64; also with Louis Bouché, Fletcher Martin, Louis Bosa, Josef Albers & Jean Charlot.
Work in Public Collections: Syracuse Univ, N Y; Albany Inst Hist & Art, N Y; Hyde Collection, Glens Falls, N Y; Suksdorf Mem Collection, Hartwick Col, Oneonta, N Y; also included in private collections.
Exhibitions: One-man shows, Skidmore Col, Saratoga Springs, N Y, 45 & Albany Inst Hist & Art, 50; State Teachers Col, Albany, 58; Everson Mus Regional, Syracuse, 60; one-man show, Randolph-Macon Woman's Col, Lynchburg, Va, 69.
Teaching: Lectr anatomy, Syracuse Univ, 50-61; asst prof design & drawing, Richmond Prof Inst, 62-67; assoc prof design & drawing, Va Commonwealth Univ, 67-
Publications: Contribr, Interaction of color, 63; contribr, Search vs research, 71.
Mailing Address: 2207 Buford Rd, Richmond, VA 23235.

APOSTOLIDES, ZOE
Painter
Study & Training: Calif Sch Fine Arts, San Francisco; Univ Calif, Berkeley; Inst Fine Arts, New York Univ; Art Stud League New York; Hans Hofmann Sch Art, New York.
Work in Public Collections: In pvt collections, U S & abroad.
Exhibitions: Chelsea Art Festival, N Y, 65; Hilton Hotels Art Gallery, New York & Athens, Greece, 65; Pittsburgh Plan for Art, 65; Hartford Arts Found, 66; Palma de Mallorca & Corfu, 67; plus others.
Awards: Prizes, Va Artists Mart Gallery, 57, Va Intermont Col, 58 & Baltimore Mus Art, 58 & 59.
Mailing Address: c/o Capricorn Galleries, 8003 Woodmont Ave, Bethesda, MD 20014.

APPEL, KAREL
Painter, Sculptor
Preferred Media: Acrylic, Aluminum, Wood.
b Amsterdam, Holland, Apr 25, 21.
Study & Training: Royal Acad Fine Arts, Amsterdam, 40-43.
Work in Public Collections: Tate Gallery, London, Eng; Mus Mod Art, New York, N Y; Ctr Nat Art Contemp, Paris, France; Stedelijk Mus, Amsterdam; Mus Fine Arts, Boston, Mass.
Commissions: Mural, Questioning Children, Cafeteria, City Hall, Amsterdam, 49; Garden Hall, Stedelijk Mus, 65; mural, City People, Univ Econ, Rotterdam, Holland, 65; ceramic mural, Country People & City People, New Cong House, The Hague, Holland, 67.
Exhibitions: One-man exhib, Studio Fachetti, Paris, 54; Dutch Artists of the Twentieth Century, Stedelijk Mus, 62; Works from the Peggy Guggenheim Foundation, Guggenheim Mus, New York, 69; Karel Appel: Sculpture, Reliefs, Paintings, Kunsthalle, Basel, Switz, 69; Appel's Appels, presented by Rothmans of Pall Mall, Canada, LTD, museums throughout Canada, 72-73.
Awards: UNESCO Prize, 27th Int Biennale, Venice, 54; int painting prize, fifth São Paulo Biennale, 59; first prize for painting, Guggenheim Internation Exhib, New York, 60.
Bibliography: Sir Herbert Read, W Sandberg & Hugo Claus (auth), Karel Appel: painter, Abrams, 62; Michel Tapie (auth), Karel Appel, Le Grandi Monografie, Fratelli Fabbri Editori, Milano, 68; Simon Vinkenoog (auth), Appel's Oogappels & Het Verhaal van Karel Appel, Brunz & Zoon, Altrecht/Antwerpen, 70.
Publications: Illusr, Appel: a beast-drawn man, 62; Author, Karel Appel over Karel Appel, Triton Press, Amsterdam, 71.
Dealer: Martha Jackson Gallery, 32 E 69th St, New York, NY 10021.
Mailing Address: 333 E 69th St, New York, NY 10021.

APPEL, KEITH KENNETH
Painter, Printmaker
b Bricelyn, Minn, May 21, 34.
Study & Training: Mankato State Col, BA, BS & MS.
Exhibitions: Fur Rendezvous Exhib, Anchorage, 61-65; All Alaska Exhib, 61, 64-69; Festival of Music, 63-67; Alaska Centennial, 67; one-man shows, 64 & 65.
Teaching: Instr art, East High Sch, Anchorage; art consult, Anchorage Sch Dist, 68-69.
Awards: Landkammer Juried Show, Mankato, Minn, 60; Fur Rendezvous Exhibs, 61-65; Alaska Centennial, 67.
Memberships: Alaska Artists Guild (past pres); Nat Art Educ Asn.
Dealer: Artique Gallery, 314 G St, Anchorage, AK 99501.
Mailing Address: 4705 Malibu Dr, Anchorage, AK 99503.

APT, CHARLES
Painter
Preferred Media: Oil, Pastel, Watercolor.
b New York, N Y, Dec 10, 33.
Study & Training: Pratt Inst BFA, 56.
Work in Public Collections: Am Stock Exchange, Chem Bank, Bowery Bank, Celanese Corp & Paine, Webber, Jackson & Curtis, New York.
Commissions: Painting, Am Stock Exchange, 68; Painting of U S Navy Band, Premiere Concert, J F Kennedy Center for Performing Arts, U S Navy Dept, 71.
Exhibitions: Allied Artists Am, New York, 64, 65, 67 & 69; Am Watercolor Soc, New York, 65, 66, 68 & 69; Nat Acad Design, New York, 65 & 68; Exposition Intercontinentale, Monaco, France, 66 & 68; Nat Mus Racing Ann Saratoga, N Y, 67.
Awards: Best-in-show, Saratoga Mus Racing, 67; second Benjamin Altman Award, Nat Acad Design, 68; Le Prix Prince Souverain, Prince Rainier, Monaco, 68.
Bibliography: Reproduction of painting & artists statement, Prize Winning Paintings, Vol. VI, 66; Joan Hess Michael (auth), Charles Apt in Portugal, Am Artist Mag, 4/70.
Memberships: Nat Acad Design (assoc, 72-); Artists Fel (trustee, 69); Allied Artists of Am; Salmagundi Club; Nat Arts Club.
Dealer: FAR Gallery, 746 Madison Ave, New York, NY 10021.
Mailing Address: 280 Ninth Ave, New York, NY 10001.

AQUINO, EDMUNDO
Painter, Engraver
Preferred Media: Oils, Silkscreen, Lithograph
b Oaxaca, Mex, June 30, 39.
Study & Training: Nat Sch Plastics Art, Nat Univ Mex, Teacher of Fine Arts Degree, 62; Ecole Nat Superieure des Beaux-Arts, Paris, Fr Govt scholar, 67-69; Slade Sch Fine Arts, London, Brit Coun scholar, 69.
Work in Public Collections: Nat Libr Paris, France; Univ Mass Collection; London Co Coun, City Literary Inst London, Eng; Mus Mod Art, Mexico City, Mex.
Commissions: Mural and Plexiglas decorations for two theatres, Sterling Theatres, Los Angeles, Calif, 66-67.
Exhibitions: XVI Interministerial Exhibition, Gallery Contemp Art, City of Paris, 68; International Festival of Painting, Cagnes-Sur Mer, France, 69 & 72; Biennale of Paris, 69; Second British International Biennale of Prints, Bradford, Eng, 70; Biennale of Black and White, Lugano, Switz, 72.
Teaching: Instr drawing & painting & head plastic arts sect, Sch Fine Arts, Oaxaca, Mex, 63-67.

Positions: Dir, Galleries of Casa del Lago, Nat Univ Mex, Mexico
City, 71-
Awards: First prize for painting, Univ Mus Arts & Scis, Nat Univ
Mex, 61; first prize for painting & drawing, medal awarded by
Hotel Monnaie, Paris, at Exhib of Foreign Artists with Fr Govt
scholarships, 69.
Dealer: Ines Amor, Galeria de Arte Mexicano, Milan 18, Mexico 6
D F, Mex.
Mailing Address: Giotto 51-12, Mixcoac, Mexico 19 D F, Mex.

ARAKAWA, (SHUSAKU)
Painter
b Japan, July 6, 36.
Work in Public Collections: Mus Mod Art, New York, N Y; Basel
Mus, Switz; Japan Nat Mus, Tokyo; plus others.
Exhibitions: Documenta IV; Venice Biennial, 70; plus others.
Bibliography: L Alloway (auth), Introduction to the mechanism of
meaning, Bruckman Verlag, 71; N & E Calas (auth), Images &
icons, Dutton, 71.
Publications: Auth, The mechanism of meaning, 71.
Mailing Address: 124 W Houston St, New York, NY 10012.

ARBEIT, ARNOLD A
Painter, Educator
Preferred Media: Oil, Watercolor.
b New York, N Y, Oct 1, 16.
Study & Training: New York Univ, BArch, MArch, MA(educ); Beaux
Arts Inst Design, New York, cert; J C Smith Univ, ScD; with Hale
Woodruff, William Armstrong & Estelle Armstrong.
Work in Public Collections: Columbus Mus Arts & Crafts, Ga; Ham-
mond Mus, N Salem, N Y.
Commissions: Painting in lobby, 20 Vesey St Bldg, New York, N Y,
60.
Exhibitions: Scarsdale Gallery, N Y, 59-; Nat Traveling Exhib,
Addison Gallery Am Art, Andover, Mass, 60; Cooper Union, New
York, 66-67; Esperanto Gallery, New York, 67.
Teaching: Instr archit, Cooper Union, 47-64; prof archit, City Col-
lege, 64-68.
Positions: Univ Architect, City Univ New York, 67-
Awards: William Armstrong Award for watercolor; F B Morse
Medal; imaginative design award, New York Soc Architects, 70;
plus others.
Memberships: Nat Inst Archit Educ (chmn, 70-); New York Univ Sch
Art & Archit Alumni (pres, 70-); Military Govt Asn Monuments
Fine Arts & Archives (chmn, 67-); Am Inst Architects (var
comts, 47-).
Publications: Auth, The architect & the museum, Mus News, 10/64;
Space guides, City Univ New York, 67-; Arbeit in the land of black
& white, 71; plus various articles in Archit Forum, 60-.
Mailing Address: 116 Fox Meadow Rd, Scarsdale, NY 10583.

ARBUCKLE, FRANKLIN
Painter, Illustrator
Memberships: Royal Can Acad Arts.
Mailing Address: 278 Lawrence Ave E, Toronto, Ont, Can.

ARCHAMBAULT, LOUIS
Sculptor, Educator
Preferred Media: Metals.
b Montreal, Que, Apr 4, 15.
Study & Training: Univ Montreal, BA; Ecole des Beaux-Arts de
Montréal, dipl céramics.
Work in Public Collections: Nat Gallery Can, Ottawa; Art Gallery
Ont, Toronto; Mus Province Québec, Québec; Mus Int Della
Ceramica, Faenza, Italy; Can Imperial Bank Com, Montreal.
Commissions: Aluminum & terra cotta wall (with Norman Slater),
Can Pavilion, Brussels' Exp, 58; six aluminum screens & two
pool sculptures, Ottawa Airport, 60; mural sculpture, Place des
Arts, Montreal, 63; aluminum sculpture, Toronto Airport, 64; 12
steel sculptures, Can Pavilion, Montreal's Exp, 67.
Exhibitions: Int Sculpture Exhib, Festivals of Great Brit, London,
Eng, 51; Milan Triennials, 54 & 57; 28th Venice Biennale, 56;
Pittsburgh Int, 58; Int Exhib Contemp Sculpture, Expo 67, Mon-
treal, 67.
Teaching: Resident artist & prof sculpture, Univ Quebec, 69-
Awards: Can Gov & Can Coun fels, 53, 59, 62 & 69; Allied arts
medal, Royal Archit Inst Can, 58; service medal, Order Can, 68.
Bibliography: Flight from tradition, Time Mag, Can ed, 5/5/47; Bill
Stephenson (auth), Louis Archambault's wonderful wall, Mac-
Lean's, Can, 1/18/58; Guy Robert (auth), Archambault, Vie des
Arts, summer 72.
Memberships: Royal Can Acad Arts (academician, 68-).
Mailing Address: 278 Sanford Ave, St Lambert, Que, Can.

ARCHER, DOROTHY BRYANT
Painter, Educator
Preferred Media: Acrylic, Oil.
b Hampton, Va, Apr 18, 19.
Study & Training: Richmond Professional Inst; Kansas City Art
Inst with Wilbur Niewald; Honolulu Acad Art with John Young.
Exhibitions: Honolulu Acad Arts Ann, Hawaii, 62; Easter Art Festi-
val, Honolulu, 63; Texas Fine Arts Ann, Laguna Gloria Mus, 65 &
Texas Fine Arts Invitational, 66; one-man show, el Inst Relaciones
Culturales, Chihuahua, Mex, 69.
Teaching: Instr acrylics, El Paso Mus Art, Tex, 69-70; instr acryl-
ics, private nat workshops, 69-; instr acrylics, Carrizo Lodge,
Ruidoso, N Mex, 69-
Positions: Founder, Civic Art Guild, Killeen, 64; fine arts chmn, C
of C Festival, Killeen, Tex, 64-66.
Awards: Acrylic watercolor, El Paso Art Asn, 70.
Bibliography: Barbara Funkhouser (auth), Dorothy Archer-abstract
artist, El Paso Times, 70.
Memberships: Nat Soc Art Educators; Nat Soc Arts & Lett.
Dealer: Nancy Crook International Art Gallery, 1220 Wyoming Ave,
El Paso, TX 79902.
Mailing Address: 8717 Marble Dr, El Paso, TX 79904.

ARCILESI, VINCENT J
Painter, Educator
Preferred Media: Oil, Pastel.
b Saint Louis, Mo, May 5, 32.
Study & Training: Furman Univ, 49-50; Univ Okla, BFA(design), 53;
Art Inst Chicago, BFA(painting), 56, MFA, 61.
Work in Public Collections: Art Inst Chicago Mus; Ill State Mus,
Springfield.
Commissions: Mural (oil on canvas), Lake Shore Nat Bank, Chicago,
Ill, 66.
Exhibitions: 70th Ann, Art Inst Chicago, 67; one-man show, Joseph
Faulkner-Main St Galleries, Chicago, 68; one-man show, Ill Arts
Coun Gallery, Chicago, 70; Ten Downtown New York, N Y, 72;
The American Landscape/1972, Boston Univ, Mass, 72.
Teaching: Assoc prof painting & drawing, Southwest Col, 64-; adj
assoc prof painting & drawing, Finch Col, 72-73.
Positions: Artists comt, Art Rental & Sales Gallery, Art Inst Chi-
cago, 69-
Awards: Hon mention, lithography, 34th Ann Okla Artists, 52; hon
mention, painting, Festival of Arts, Univ Chicago, 64.
Bibliography: Marjorie Dell (auth), Vincent Arcilesi, Art Scene, 9/
68; Donald Key (auth), Mystic realism show opens Alverno series,
Milwaukee Jour, 9/14/69; Don J Anderson (auth), Arcilesi—
nature is sensuality, Chicago Today, 9/13/70.
Memberships: Alliance Figurative Artists (prog comt, 72-73); Participating Artists Chicago (exec comt, 67-70).
Publications: Illusr, The Loves of Franklin Ambrose, Playboy Mag,
72.
Dealers: Westbroadway Gallery, 431 W Broadway, New York, NY
10012; Capricorn Galleries, 8003 Woodmont Ave, Bethesda, MD
20014.
Mailing Address: 116 Duane St, New York, NY 10007.

ARENBERG, ALBERT L
Collector
b Des Moines, Iowa, Nov 16, 91.
Study & Training: Ill Inst Technol, BSEE.
Collection: Works by Miro, Giacometti, Soulages, Kline and others.
Mailing Address: 1214 Green Bay Rd, Highland Park, IL 60035.

ARGEROPOLOS, (BASIL) THEODORE
Painter, Printmaker
Preferred Media: Acrylics.
b Chicago, Ill, June 4, 46.
Study & Training: Univ Ill, Chicago Circle, BA; Sch Art Inst Chi-
cago, MFA; also with Vera Berdich, Roland Ginzel, Richard
Koppe, Martin Hurtig & Raymond Yosheda.
Work in Public Collections: Blue Cross-Blue Shield Bldg Collec-
tion, Chicago; Richard J Daley Collection; Earl Ludgin Collec-
tion; John Maxon Collection; T William Fejer Collection.
Commissions: Ed commemorative prints, Edgewater Beach Hotel,
Chicago, 70.
Exhibitions: Two & Three Dimensional Prints, Alonzo Gallery, New
York, N Y, 69; 19th & 20th Century Prints, Univ Conn Mus, 69;
Chicago Five, Wright Art Ctr, Beloit, Wis, 70 & Univ Chicago,
71; Five Exhib, Univ Chicago, 72.
Teaching: Instr painting, printmaking & two & three dimension de-
sign, Univ Ill, Chicago Circle, 70-
Bibliography: Franz Schulze (auth), Chicago five, Chicago Daily
News, 2/71 & Chicago art scene, Art News, 10/71; Amy Goldin
(auth), Five exhibition, Art Gallery Mag, 4/72.
Dealer: Alonzo Gallery, 26 E 63rd St, New York, NY 10021.
Mailing Address: 114 W Kinzie, Chicago, IL 60610.

ARGRAVES, HUGH OLIVER
Painter
Preferred Media: Oil.
b Decatur, Ill, July 7, 22.
Study & Training: Beloit Col; Beloit Vocational Sch with E M R Weirner, portrait artist.
Exhibitions: Burpee Art Gallery, Rockford, Ill, 57; Lynn Kottler Galleries, New York, N Y, 61-66; Ahda Artz Gallery, New York, 62 & 66; Ligoa Duncan Gallery, New York, 69; Belvidere Art Show, Ill, 70.
Awards: Third place, Belvidere Art Show, 70.
Bibliography: Clyde C Walton (auth), Illinois lives, Hist Rec Asn, 69-70.
Mailing Address: 519 N Main St, Rockford, IL 61103.

ARISS, HERBERT JOSHUA
Painter, Illustrator
b Guelph, Ont, Sept 19, 18.
Study & Training: Ontario Col Art; Can Coun sr fel, 60-61.
Work in Public Collections: Nat Gallery Can; Art Gallery Ont; Winnipeg Art Gallery; Vancouver Art Gallery; London Art Gallery, Ontario.
Commissions: Casein, Huron & Erie Co, Chatham, 58; ceramic, John Labatt Brewery, London, 59; multimedia, Sir Adam Beck Sec Sch, London, 67; multimedia, Ont Govt Bldg, Toronto, 68.
Exhibitions: Second & Third Can Biennial, Ottawa, 64-66; Can Soc Graphic Arts, 70; Can Printmakers, Nat Gallery, Can Int Show, 71; Can Soc Painters in Watercolour, London & New York, 72.
Teaching: Instr drawing & painting, Doon Sch Fine Arts, 55-58; hd dept art, H B Beal Art Sch, London, Ont, 65-
Positions: Pres, Western Art League, 57-60; mem, London Art Gallery Bd, 68-71; dir, London Art Gallery Asn, 69-72; chmn Acquisition Comte, London Pub Libr & Art Mus, 70-71.
Awards: Dirs purchase award, Vancouver Art Gallery, 63; honour award, Can Soc Painters in Watercolour, 65.
Bibliography: Brights lights of London, Time, 68; Barry Lord (auth), How Beal has made London an art centre, Toronto Star, 70; J Bryce (auth), Herb Ariss retrospective, Arts Can, 71.
Memberships: Ontario Soc Artists; Can Soc Painters in Watercolour (v pres, 58-60); Can Soc Graphics Art; Can Group Painters.
Publications: Illusr, Contes de nos jours, 56; Lectures variees, 58; La double mort de Frederic Belot, 58; Contes d'Aujour d'hui, 63; War, 71.
Dealer: Nancy Poole's Studio, London Ontario and Toronto Ont.
Mailing Address: 770 Leroy Crescent, London, Ont, Can.

ARKUS, LEON ANTHONY
Museum Director
b N J, May 6, 15.
Study & Training: City Col New York, with Townsend Harris.
Collections Arranged: Three Self-Taught Pennsylvania Artists: Hicks, Kane, Pippin, 66-67; Carl-Henning Pedersen: Paintings, Watercolors, Drawings, 68; The Art of Black Africa, 69-70; Pittsburgh International 1970, 71; The Fresh Air School, 72-73.
Positions: Asst dir, Mus Art, Carnegie Inst, Pittsburgh, Pa, 54-62, assoc dir, 62-68, dir, 68-
Memberships: Am Asn Mus; Assoc Artists Pittsburgh (bd mem, 54-); Asn Art Mus Dirs; Pittsburgh Plan for Art (gov, 58-); Three Rivers Arts Festival (bd mem).
Publications: Auth, Three self-taught Pennsylvania artists: Hicks, Kane, Pippin, 66; Carl-Henning Pedersen: paintings, watercolors, drawings, 68; The art of black Africa, 69; Pittsburgh international 1970, 71; John Kane, painter (catalogue raisonné), Univ Pittsburgh Press, 71; plus one other.
Mailing Address: Museum of Art, Carnegie Institute, 4400 Forbes Ave, Pittsburgh, PA 15213.

ARMAN
Sculptor
Preferred Media: Plastic
b Nice, France, 28.
Study & Training: École Nat Art Decoratif, B Ph; École Louvre.
Work in Public Collections: Mus Nat Art Mod, Paris, France; Mus Mod Art, New York, N Y; Stedelijk Mus, Amsterdam, Holland; Walker Art Ctr, Minneapolis, Minn; Albright-Knox Art Gallery, Buffalo, N Y.
Exhibitions: One-man show, Stedelijk Mus, 64; Walker Art Ctr, 64; Venice Biennale, Italy, 68; Dokumenta, Kassel, Ger, 68; Osaka Expo, Japan, 70.
Awards: Tokyo Biennel Second Prize, 64; Grand Marzotto Prize, 66.
Bibliography: Janis & Blish (auth), Collage; Peter Selz (auth), Assemblage; Lucy Lippard (auth), Pop art.
Mailing Address: c/o Lawrence Rubin Gallery, 49 W 57th St, New York, NY 10019.

ARMSTRONG, ROGER JOSEPH
Painter, Cartoonist
Preferred Media: Watercolors, Ink.
b Los Angeles, Calif, Oct 12, 17.
Study & Training: Pasadena City Col; Chouinard Art Inst; Sueo Serisawa Workshop.
Work in Public Collections: City of Santa Fe Springs, Calif; City of Pico Rivera.
Exhibitions: Calif Nat Watercolor Soc Ann & Traveling Exhibs, 64-69; All Calif Exhib, Laguna Beach Art Mus, Calif, 66-67; International Masters of Watercolor, Dalzell-Hatfield Galleries, Los Angeles, 67; one-man shows, Muckenthaler Cult Ctr, 69 & Newport Beach Munic Gallery, 70; plus many others.
Collections Arranged: Three Man Exhib - Keith Finch, Edgar Ewing, Robert Frame, 63; West Coast Figurative, 64; First Ann West Coast Sculpture Exhib, 64; plus others.
Teaching: Instr drawing & composition watercolor painting, Laguna Beach Sch Art, 65-; lect, history of cartooning.
Awards: Second award for watercolor, First Ann Orange Co Exhib, 63; first purchase award, First Ann Pio Pico Art Festival, 68; hon mention, East Meets West Exhib, Calif Nat Watercolor Soc, 72.
Bibliography: Raymond Fisher & John Barnard (auth), Roger Armstrong, triple threat artist, World of Comic Art, winter 66-67.
Memberships: Calif Nat Watercolor Soc (1st v pres, 69, 2nd v pres, 70); Laguna Beach Art Asn (dir, 63-66, pres, 66-67); Los Angeles Art Asn; San Luis Obispo Art Asn.
Publications: Auth & illusr, All Walt Disney & Warner Bros cartoon comic books, Western Publ, 40-50; illusr, Our country's national parks, Bobbs-Merrill, 41; co-auth & illusr, Ella Cinders comic strip, United Features Syndicate, 50-61 & Napoleon & Uncle Elby, Los Angeles Times Syndicate, 50-60; auth & illusr, Flintstones, Little Lulu & others, Western Publ, 60-72.
Mailing Address: 29612 Via Pan, Laguna Niguel, CA 92677.

ARNASON, H HARVARD
Art Historian, Writer
b Winnipeg, Man, Apr 24, 09; U S citizen.
Study & Training: Univ Man; Northwestern Univ, BS & MA; Princeton Univ, MFA.
Teaching: Instr art, Northwestern Univ, 36-38; lectr, Frick Col, 38-42; vis assoc prof, Univ Chicago, 47; prof art & chmn dept, Univ Minn, 47-60; Carnegie vis prof, Univ Hawaii, 59.
Positions: Sr field rep, Off War Info, Iceland, 42-44, asst dep dir for Europe, Off War Info, 44-45; chief prog planning & eval unit, Off Int Info & Cult Affairs, Dept State, 46-47; U S rep, Preparatory Comm, UNESCO, London & Paris, 46; tech adv to U S del, First Gen Conf UNESCO, 46; dir, Walker Art Ctr, Minneapolis, Minn, 51-60; v pres art admin, Solomon R Guggenheim Found, 60-69.
Awards: Chevalier, Ordre Arts et Lett, France; Knight, Order St Olav, Norway; Fulbright, Nat Endowment Humanities & Kress Found fels.
Memberships: Am Fedn Arts (trustee); T B Walker Found, Minneapolis (trustee); Solomon R Guggenheim Found (trustee); Joseph H Hirshhorn Mus, Washington, D C (trustee); Int Found Art Res (exec bd & chmn adv comt); plus others.
Art Interests: Modern painting, nineteenth and twentieth centuries; sculpture, eighteenth to twentieth centuries.
Publications: Auth, Sculpture by Houdon, 64; co-auth, Alexander Calder, Van Nostrand-Reinhold, 66; auth, History of modern art, Abrams, 68 & textbook ed, Prentice-Hall, 69; auth, Jacques Lipchitz: fifty years of sketches in bronze, Praeger, 69; co-auth, Alexander Calder, 69; also monogr, catalogues & articles on medieval, 18th century & mod art.
Mailing Address: River Rd, Roxbury, CT 06783.

ARNESON, ROBERT CARSTON
Sculptor, Educator
Preferred Media: Clay, Ceramics.
b Benicia, Calif, Sept 4, 30.
Study & Training: Calif Col Arts & Crafts, BA(educ), 54; Mills Col, MFA, 58; studied ceramics with Antonio Prieto.
Work in Public Collections: San Francisco Mus Art; Oakland Art Mus; Santa Barbara Mus Art; Univ Calif Art Mus, Berkeley; Nat Mus Mod Art, Kyoto, Japan.
Exhibitions: Funk Art, Univ Calif Art Mus, Berkeley, 67; Objects U S A, Johnson Wax Collection touring U S & Europe, 68-73; Human Concern/Personal Torment, Whitney Mus Am Art, New York, N Y, 69; Clay Works, 20 Americans, Mus Contemp Crafts, New York, 71; Contemporary Ceramic Art, Mus Mod Art, Kyoto & Tokyo, 71-72.
Teaching: Instr design, Mills Col, 60-62; prof art, Univ Calif, Davis, 62-

Bibliography: Ceramics, Time Mag, 4/26/68; David Zack (auth), The ceramics of Robert Arneson, Craft Horizons Mag, 1/70; Janet Malcolm (auth), On and off the avenue, New Yorker Mag, 9/4/71.
Dealer: Hansen-Fuller Gallery, 228 Grant Ave, San Francisco, CA 94108.
Mailing Address: Art Dept, University of California, Davis, CA 95616.

ARNEST, BERNARD
Painter
Preferred Media: Oil, Acrylic.
b Denver, Colo, Feb 17, 17.
Study & Training: Colo Springs Fine Arts Ctr.
Work in Public Collections: Walker Art Ctr, Minneapolis, Minn; Minneapolis Inst Arts; Colo Springs Fine Arts Ctr; Univ Nebr, Lincoln; Univ Georgia, Atlanta.
Exhibitions: Whitney Mus Ann Am Painting, New York, N Y; Carnegie Int, Pittsburgh, Pa; Corcoran Biennial Washington, D C; Pa Acad, Philadelphia; Univ Ill Ann, Urbana-Champaign.
Teaching: Assoc prof drawing & painting, Univ Minn, 49-57; prof drawing & painting, Colo Col, 57-
Positions: Chief war artist, European Theater Hq, U S Army, 44-45; chmn advan placement in art comt, Col Entrance Exam Bd, 69-72.
Awards: Guggenheim fel, 40; int exchange prog, U S Dept State, 60.
Dealer: Kraushaar Galleries, 1055 Madison Ave, New York, NY 10028.
Mailing Address: 1502 Wood Ave, Colorado Springs, CO 80907.

ARNHEIM, RUDOLF
Educator, Writer
b Berlin, Ger, July 15, 04; U S citizen.
Study & Training: Univ Berlin, PhD, 28; Guggenheim fel, 42-43.
Teaching: Mem fac psychol art, Sarah Lawrence Col, 43-68; prof, Harvard Univ, 68-
Memberships: Am Soc Aesthet (pres & trustee); Am Psychol Asn (pres, div arts, 70-72).
Publications: Auth, Art and visual perception, Univ Calif Press, 54, Film as art, 56, Toward a psychology of art, 66, Visual thinking, 69, Entropy and art, 71.
Mailing Address: Carpenter Center, Harvard University, Cambridge, MA 02138.

ARNHOLD, MR & MRS HANS
Collectors
Mailing Address: Ritz-Tower Hotel, Park Ave at 57th St, New York, NY 10022.

ARNHOLT, WALDON SYLVESTER
Painter, Instructor
Preferred Media: Oil, Pastel, Watercolor.
b Nankin, Ohio, Jan 1, 09.
Study & Training: Bloomfield Art Sch, N J, dipl; studied restoration fine art with C Fritz Hoelzer, Ger & portraiture with C Fritz Hoelzer, N Y.
Work in Public Collections: Mus Sci & Natural Hist, Tampa, Fla. (Restoration Works) Parthenon Gallery, Nashville, Tenn, Ringling Mus, Sarasota, Fla & State Capitol, Atlanta, Ga.
Commissions: Christ in Gethsamane (oil), United Brethren, Ashland Ohio, 26; portraits of City Fathers, Ashland, Ohio, 37-41; Christ at the Door (oil), United Presbyterian Church, Savannah, Ohio, 52; Timucan Indian & Ocean Room Fleurescent (oil), Mus Sci & Natural Hist, Tampa, Fla, 64; portrait of Joseph Brant, Brant Mus, Burlington, Ont, Can, 68.
Exhibitions: One-man shows, King Mus & Gallery, Mansfield, Ohio, 45; St Petersburg Art Gallery, Fla, 62; Indian Portraiture, Munic Art Mus, Tampa, 63; Mus Sci & Natural Hist Art Mus, 65; Indian Portraiture, Fla Fedn Art, DuBarry, 69.
Teaching: Instr art & adv, group classes, Ohio, 30-59; instr art, group classes, Florida Condominiums, 59-; instr art, private classes in studio, Fla, 59-
Positions: Interior decorator artist, Lakeland, Fla, 27-30; decorator, Tiffin Scenery Co, Ohio, 30-35; artist, lithographer, A L Garber Co, Ashland, Ohio, 36-59.
Awards: For Talk Sinks Ships, Am Artist Projs, 42 & Hist Events of City, New London Post Off, Ohio, 45.
Mailing Address: 1224 Sunset Point Rd, Clearwater, FL 33515.

ARNOLD, FLORENCE M
Painter
Preferred Media: Oil on canvas.
b Prescott, Ariz, Sept 16, 00.
Study & Training: Mills Col, degree in music; Univ Southern Calif, BA; Claremont Grad Sch.
Work in Public Collections: Long Beach Mus Art; Laguna Art Asn Gallery; Orlando Art Gallery, Encino, Calif; Calif State Univ, Fullerton; Media Art Gallery, Santa Ana, Calif.

Exhibitions: Gallerias Numero, Florence, Rome, Milan & Prato Venice, 63; Calif Hard-edge Painting Invitational, Newport Beach, 64; one-man shows, Long Beach Mus Art, 62-69; La Mirada Festival of Arts Purchase Award, 68; one-man show, Fresno Art Ctr, 69.
Awards: First prize, Muckenthater Cultural Ctr, 67 & 69; first prize, Orange Co Art Asn, 68; hon mention, Riverside Eighth Ann, 70.
Bibliography: Monogr, Calif State Univ, Fullerton, 69.
Memberships: Orange Co Art Asn (pres & bd mem, 50-65); Los Angeles Art Asn; Muckenthaler Cultural Ctr, (bd mem, 60-72); Laguna Art Asn (bd mem, 67-69); Long Beach Art Asn; Los Angeles Mus Art (charter mem).
Mailing Address: 1136 Valencia Mesa Dr, Fullerton, CA 92633.

ARNOLD, PAUL BEAVER
Educator, Printmaker
Preferred Media: Woodcut, Intaglio.
b Taiyuanfu, China, Nov 24, 18; U S citizen.
Study & Training: Oberlin Col, AB, 40, MA, 41; Cleveland Inst Art; Univ Minn, MFA, 55.
Work in Public Collections: Libr Cong, Washington, D C; Cleveland Mus Art, Ohio; Seattle Art Mus, Wash; Baltimore Mus, Md; Dayton Art Inst, Ohio.
Commissions: Color intaglio, Pheasant, Int Graphic Arts Soc, New York, N Y, 56 & color woodcut, White Peacock, 57; mural, Gilford Instrument Co, Oberlin, Ohio, 71.
Exhibitions: Audubon Artists, New York, 53, 54, 55, 56, 57, 59 & 67; two-man show, Howard Wise Gallery, Cleveland, 60; May Show, Cleveland Mus, 61, 63 & 66; one-man show, Jersey City State Col, N J, 66; one-man show, Miami Univ, Oxford, Ohio, 68.
Teaching: From instr to prof art & chmn dept, Oberlin Col, 41-, Ford Found fac fel prog, 51-52, Great Lakes Cols Asn res grant, 65-66.
Awards: Audubon Artists Medal, 57.
Memberships: Nat Asn Schs Art (bd dir); Col Art Asn; Mid-America Col Art Asn.
Publications: Illustr, General chemistry, & Laboratory experiments in general chemistry, Campbell and Steiner, 55; co-auth, The humanities at Oberlin, 57; auth, Printmaking today, Lalit Kala Contemp, New Delhi, India, 4/70.
Mailing Address: Dept of Art, Oberlin College, Oberlin, OH 44074.

ARNOLD, RALPH MOFFETT
Painter, Educator
b Chicago, Ill, Dec 5, 28.
Study & Training: Roosevelt Univ, BA; Art Inst Chicago with Vera Berdich.
Work in Public Collections: Whitney Mus Am Art, New York, N Y; Fisk Univ, Nashville Tenn; Rockford Col, Ill; Commonwealth Pa; Ill Bell Tel Co, Chicago; plus one other.
Commissions: Wall murals, James House, Arthur Rubloff Realty Co, 71.
Exhibitions: Violence in American Art, Mus Contemp Art, Chicago, 69; American Prints Today, Mus Art, Utica, N Y, 70; Afro-American Arts 1800-1969, Mus Philadelphia Civic Ctr, 70; Contemporary Black Artists in America, Whitney Mus Am Art, 71; All Collage Exhib, Ball State Univ, Muncie, Ind, 72.
Teaching: Instr painting, Rockford Col, 69-70; asst prof, Barat Col, Lake Forest, & Loyola Univ Chicago, 70-
Positions: Adv bd, Arts & Sales & Rental Gallery, Art Inst Chicago.
Awards: Artists-in-residence to help underprivileged children, Ill Art Coun, 69.
Memberships: Arts Club Chicago.
Dealer: William Van Straaten, 646 N Michigan Ave, Chicago, IL 60611.
Mailing Address: 1858 N Sedgwick St, Chicago, IL 60614.

ARNOLD, RICHARD R
Designer, Painter
b Detroit, Mich, July 14, 23.
Study & Training: Southwestern Univ; Wayne Univ, BFA; Cranbrook Acad Art, MFA, with Zoltan Sepeshy; Tulane Univ; Univ Mich.
Work in Public Collections: Cranbrook Mus Art; Northwestern Nat Life Ins Collection.
Commissions: Mural, Essex Bldg, Minneapolis, Minn; designs for Chrysler Corp, American Motors Corp, Gen Mills Co, Gen Elec Co, Am Standards, Gen Motors Corp, Ford Motor Co, Mich Bell Tel Co, Xerox Corp & others.
Exhibitions: Communication Through Art, Am Fedn Arts Traveling Exhib, Pakistan, Turkey, Iran; one-man show, White Mus, Cornell Univ, 56; Calif Palace of Legion of Honor, 60; maj exhibs in large cities in the U S.
Teaching: Instr, Univ Wis, 48-51; asst prof, Cornell Univ, 53-56; asst prof, San Jose State Col, 58-60; assoc prof, Rochester Inst

Technol, 60-64; prof & head design div, Minneapolis Sch Art, 64-; vis prof, Univ Victoria, summer 68; lect, Mass Production and Architecture, Univ Toronto; lect, Interior Architecture, Univ Mass.
Memberships: Col Art Asn Am.
Mailing Address: Design Division, Minneapolis School of Art, 200 E 25th St, Minneapolis, MN 55409.

ARON, KALMAN
Painter
b Riga, Latvia, Sept 14, 24.
Study & Training: Acad Art, Riga; Acad Fine Arts, Vienna, BA.
Work in Public Collections: Corcoran Gallery Art; La Jolla Mus Art; Henry Miller, Chancellow Speith, Univ Calif, Riverside.
Exhibitions: Los Angeles Co Mus, 56; Denver Art Mus, 60; Fine Arts Houston, 62; Calif Palace of Legion of Honor; O'Hana Gallery, London, Eng, 63; plus others.
Awards: Los Angeles Art Asn Awards; Ahmanson Award & bronze medal, Los Angeles Co Mus, 62.
Mailing Address: 921 N Westmount Dr, Los Angeles, CA 90069.

ARONSON, BORIS
Designer, Painter
b Kiev, Russia, Oct 15, 00.
Study & Training: State Art Sch, Kiev; Sch of the Theatre, Kiev, with Alexandra Exter; with Herman Struch, Berlin, Ger; Sch Mod Painting, Moscow, with Ilya Mashkov; also study in France.
Work in Public Collections: Paintings in pvt collections.
Commissions: Design, interior for Temple Sinai, Washington, D C; design of Coriolanus for Shakespeare Mem Theatre, Stratford, Eng; sets for more than 100 stage productions incl The Crucible, The Rose Tattoo, The Diary of Anne Frank, Fiddler on the Roof, Judith, Cabaret, Zorba & The Prince.
Exhibitions: Tel-Aviv Mus, Israel; Whitney Mus Am Art & Mus Mod Art, New York, N Y; Philadelphia Mus Art, Pa; retrospective exhib, Storm King Art Ctr, Mountainville, N Y; plus many others.
Teaching: Instr stage designing, Pratt Inst Art Sch, 57.
Awards: Guggenheim fel, 50; Am Theatre Wing Awards, 50 & 51; Ford Found grant.
Bibliography: Waldemar George (auth), Boris Aronson et l'art du theatre, Paris, 28.
Memberships: Ger Art Soc.
Publications: Auth, Marc Chagall, 23 & Modern graphic art, 24; illusr, The theatre in life & var children's bks; contribr, Theatre Arts, Show, Vogue & Interior.
Mailing Address: 1 W 89th St, New York, NY 10024.

ARONSON, DAVID
Painter, Sculptor
Preferred Media: Encaustic, Bronze.
b Shilova, Lithuania, Oct 28, 23; U S citizen.
Study & Training: Boston Mus Fine Arts Sch with Karl Zerbe, cert, 45; grant, Nat Soc Arts & Lett, 58; Guggenheim fel, 60.
Work in Public Collections: Smithsonian Inst, Washington, D C; Art Inst Chicago, Ill; Va Mus Fine Arts, Richmond; Boston Mus Fine Arts, Mass; Whitney Mus Am Art, New York, N Y.
Commissions: Great Ideas of Western Man, Container Corp Am, 63.
Exhibitions: Fourteen Americans, Mus Mod Art, 45; Va Mus Fine Arts Biennial, 45; Johnson Collection of American Art (travelled internationally), 62 & 63; New York World's Fair, 64-65; Nat Collection Fine Arts Opening Exhib, Smithsonian Inst, 65.
Teaching: Instr painting, Boston Mus Fine Arts Sch, 43-54; chmn div art, Boston Univ, 54-63, prof art, 62-
Awards: Grand prize, Boston Arts Festival, 52-54.
Bibliography: Time Mag, 11/63; Newman (auth), Wax as art form, Yosellof, 66; Grossman (auth), Art & tradition, Yosellof, 67.
Memberships: Nat Acad Design (academician, 72).
Publications: Auth, Encaustic, Artist Mag, 62; Real and unreal: the double nature of art, Boston Univ Press, 67.
Dealer: Bernard Danenberg Galleries, 1020 Madison Ave, New York, NY 10021.
Mailing Address: 137 Brimstone Lane, Sudbury, MA 01776.

ARONSON, IRENE HILDE
Designer, Painter
b Dresden, Ger, Mar 8, 18; U S citizen.
Study & Training: Eastbourne Sch Art, Eng; Slade Sch Fine Arts, Univ London; Ruskin Sch Drawing, Oxford Univ; Columbia Univ, BFA, 60, MA, 62; Art Stud League New York; Parsons Sch Design; also with Prof Schwabe, Polunin & William S Hayter.
Work in Public Collections: Bibliot Nat Print Dept, Paris, France; Victoria & Albert Mus, London; Brit Mus Print Dept; Mus Mod Art Print Dept, New York, N Y; Metrop Mus Art, New York.
Exhibitions: Pa Acad Fine Arts, Philadelphia, 54; Kunstmuseum, Bern, Switz, 57; Brooklyn Mus, N Y & Boston Mus, Mass, 58; Int Print Show, Ljubljana, Yugoslavia, 59; one-woman show, Mus

Arte Mod, Mexico City, 59; one-woman show, Towner Art Gallery, Eastbourne, Eng, 61.
Teaching: Instr art, continuing educ, Bryant Adult Ctr, 54-66; instr art (per diem), New York City Jr High Sch, at present.
Positions: Asst costume designer, Barnum & Bailey Circus, Broadway, 44.
Awards: Gold medal, Slade Sch Fine Arts, 39; medal of honor, Nat Asn Women Artists, 57; plus others.
Memberships: Nat Asn Women Artists; Asn Univ Women; Col Art Asn Am.
Publications: Auth, The printmaker, Design Mag, 55; contribr, articles, In: Artist Mag, 61-; auth, Setting up a printmaking workshop, Graphic Processes; auth, How to make a lithograph & An artist travels to Hong Kong, Am Artist; also illusr of var bks.
Mailing Address: 63-20 Haring St, Rego Park, NY 11374.

ARONSON, JOSEPH
Designer, Writer
b Buffalo, N Y, Dec 22, 98.
Study & Training: Univ Buffalo; Columbia Univ Sch Archit, BArch.
Positions: Critic design, Pratt Inst, Brooklyn, N Y.
Memberships: Victorian Soc; Archit League, New York; Soc Archit Historians; Int Castles Inst; plus others.
Publications: Auth, Furniture & decoration, 36, rev ed, 52; auth, Encyclopedia of furniture, 38, rev ed 65 & New encyclopedia of furniture, 67, Crown; contribr, Popular Sci Mag, Encycl Am & others.
Mailing Address: 118 E 37th St, New York, NY 10016.

ARP, HILDA DORA
Painter, Sculptor
Preferred Media: Oil, Watercolor, Pastel.
b Harburg, Ger, June 26, 09; U S citizen.
Study & Training: New Sch Social Res with Egas, 55; Brooklyn Mus with Reuben Tam, 56; Art Stud League with H Sternberg, 61; Pratt Graphic Ctr with C Romano, 66.
Work in Public Collections: Norfolk Mus, Va; Wagner Col, Staten Island; Union Church, Bay Ridge, Brooklyn, N Y. also private collections throughout U S, France, Ger & Norway.
Exhibitions: Int Watercolor Biennial, Brooklyn Mus, 63; Nat Acad Design Galleries, New York, 63-; Travel and Transportation & Administration Bldg, New York World's Fair, 64-65; Mus Cognac, France, Int Exhib Women Painters, Cannes, France, 65.
Positions: Dir, Colorama Galleries Inc, New York World's Fair, 64-65; comt mem, Bay Ridge Art Festival, Brooklyn, 65-
Awards: Am Heritage Award, JFK Mem Libr for Minorities, 72.
Memberships: Nat Asn Women Artists; Am Fedn Arts; Artists Equity Asn of N Y; Soc Arts & Lett; Int Platform Asn.
Dealer: Gallery International, 1098 Madison Ave, New York, NY 11220.
Mailing Address: 4516 Seventh Ave, Brooklyn, NY 11220.

ARTIS, WILLIAM ELLISWORTH
Educator, Ceramist
b Washington, N C, Feb 2, 14.
Study & Training: State Univ N Y Col Ceramics, Alfred Univ; Syracuse Univ; Chadron State Col; Pa State Univ.
Work in Public Collections: Walker Art Ctr, Minneapolis, Minn; IBM; Slater Mem Mus, Norwich, Conn; Howard Univ; Nat Portrait Gallery, Washington, D C; plus others.
Commissions: Ceramic tile rm divider, men's dormitory, Chadron State Col.
Exhibitions: Joslyn Art Mus, 62; Great Hall, City Col New York, 67; Creighton Univ, Omaha, Nebr, 69; Nat Sculpture Soc; Whitney Mus Am Art; plus others.
Teaching: Prof art, Mankato State Col, Minn.
Awards: Rosenwald fel, 47; nine purchase awards, Atlanta Univ, 44-65.
Memberships: Am Ceramic Soc; Nat Sculpture Soc; Col Art Asn Am; Nat Art Educ Asn.
Publications: Contribr, American Negro art, N Y Graphic Soc.
Dealer: Gallery 500, Mankato, MN 56001.
Mailing Address: 1904 Warren St, Mankato, MN 56001.

ARTSCHWAGER, RICHARD ERNST
Painter, Sculptor
b Washington, D C, Dec 26, 24.
Study & Training: Cornell Univ, AB; studio study with Amedee Ozenfant.
Work in Public Collections: Roswell Mus, New Mex; Univ Okla Mus Art, Norman; Kunstmus, Basle, Switz; Wallraf-Richartz Mus, Cologne, Ger; Detroit Mus, Mich.
Exhibitions: Primary Structures, Jewish Mus, New York, N Y, 66; Arp to Artschwager, Bellamy-Goldowsky, New York, 68; When Attitudes Become Form, Kunsthalle Berne, Switz, 69; Sonsbeek '71, Arnhem/Utrecht, Holland, 71; Documenta 5, Kassel, Ger, 72.

Bibliography: E Baker (auth), Artschwager's mental furniture, Art News, 1/68; Kotte et al (auth), Utrecht Project 1971, Mus Hedendagse Kunst, Utrecht, Holland, 72.
Dealer: Leo Castelli Gallery, 4 E 77 St, New York, NY 10021.
Mailing Address: Box 23, Charlotteville, NY 12036.

ARTZ, FREDERICK B
Art Historian, Writer
b Dayton, Ohio, Oct 19, 94.
Study & Training: Oberlin Col, AB, 16; Univ Toulouse, 19; Univ Paris, 22-23, Harvard Univ, PhD, 24; Oberlin Col, LittD, 66; Carthage Col, LittD, 70.
Teaching: Instr hist, Antioch Col, 16-17; instr hist, Harvard Univ, 23-24; from asst prof to prof hist, Oberlin Col, 24-66; vis prof, Harvard, 30-31, lectr, summer sch, 31 & 34.
Publications: Auth, France under the Bourbon restoration 1814-1830, Russell, 31 & 63; auth, Reaction & revolution: 1815-1832, 35 & 68, Harper-Row; auth, From the Renaissance to romanticism, trends in style in art, literature and music, Univ Chicago Press, 62; auth, Mind of the Middle Ages (rev ed), Knopf, 65; auth, Renaissance humanism 1300-1500 & The enlightenment in France, Kent State Univ Press; plus others.
Mailing Address: 157 N Professor St, Oberlin, OH 44074.

ARWIN, LESTER B
Art Dealer
b Rochester, N Y.
Study & Training: Columbia Univ; New York Univ, BS; painting with Carlos Lopez.
Teaching: Instr art appreciation, Wayne Co Comm Col, 70.
Memberhips: Am Fedn Arts; Founders Soc, Detroit Art Inst; Mus Mod Art; Mich Acad Sci & Arts.
Specialty of Gallery: 20th century paintings, graphics and sculpture.
Collection: Reginald Marsh, Burliuk, Geo Grosz, Rivera, Shahn, Antreasian, Domjan and others.
Mailing Address: 222 Grand River W, Detroit, MI 48226.

ASAWA, RUTH (RUTH ASAWA LANIER)
Sculptor, Graphic Artist
b Norwalk, Calif, Jan 27, 26.
Study & Training: Milwaukee State Teachers Col, with Robert von Neumann; Black Mt Col, with Josef Albers.
Work in Public Collections: Mus Mod Art; Whitney Mus Am Art; Chase Manhattan Bank; City of San Francisco; Gov & Mrs Nelson Rockefeller.
Commissions: Two bronze wire sculptures in fountains, Phoenix Civic Plaza; bronze fountain, Ghirradelli Sq; bronze fountain, Hyatt Hotel, San Francisco Union Sq.
Exhibitions: Whitney Mus Am Art, 55, 56 & 58; Mus Mod Art, 58; San Francisco Mus Art, 54, 63 & 73; one-man shows, de Young Mem Mus, San Francisco, 60 & Pasadena Mus Art, 65; U S Info Agency Junk Art Travel Show, 72-73; plus others.
Positions: Mem, San Francisco Art Comn, 68-70; co-founder, Alvarado sch art workshop, San Francisco Unified Sch Dist, 68-
Awards: Tamarind fel, 65; purchase award, San Francisco Art Festival, 66; Dymaxion Award, 66; plus others.
Mailing Address: 1116 Castro St, San Francisco, CA 94114.

ASCHENBACH, PAUL
Sculptor
Preferred Media: Steel, Marble.
b Poughkeepsie, N Y, May 25, 21.
Study & Training: R I Sch Design, 40-41; with Randolph W Johnson, Deerfield, Mass, 42-45; I Marshall, Philadelphia, Pa, 46-48.
Work in Public Collections: Sculpture on the Highway, Vermont Interstate Highway; Sculpture Park, St Margarethen, Austria; De Cordova & Dana Mus, Lincoln, Mass; Mem Art Gallery, Univ Rochester, N Y; Bundy Art Gallery, Waitsfield, Vt.
Commissions: Forged mild steel crucifix, Trinity Col, Burlington, Vt, 61; corten steel, Bundy Art Gallery, 66; fabricated bronze, Bailey Mem Libr, Univ Vt, Burlington, 63-64; forged steel, Mother Seton, St Josephs Col on the Ohio, Cincinnati, 65.
Teaching: Assoc prof art, Univ Vt, 56-
Positions: Trustee, Vt Coun on the Arts, 65-68; coordr Vermont Int Sculpture Symp, 68-; coordr Mill 21, sculpture prog in Vermont Marble Co, 69-70.
Mailing Address: Charlotte, VT 05445.

ASCHER, MARY G
Painter
Preferred Media: Oil, Watercolor.
b Leeds, Eng; U S citizen.
Study & Training: New York Sch Applied Design for Women; Hunter Col; Art Stud League; also with Will Barnet, Vaclav Vytlacil & Morris Kantor.
Work in Public Collections: Norfolk Mus, Va; Nat Mus Sports, New York, N Y, Bat Yam Mus & Ein Harod L'Osmanut, Israel; Nat

Collection Fine Art, Smithsonian Inst, Washington, D C; B'nai Brith Mus, Washington, D C.
Exhibitions: American Art in Our Time, Chrysler Exhib, Provincetown, 57; Art U S A, Coliseum, 58-59; Exchange Exhib with Japanese Women Artists (Centenary), 60; Exchange Exhib with Argentine Artists (men and women), USIA, 63; 18th New Eng Ann, Silvermine, 67.
Positions: 2nd v pres & chaplain, Nat Soc Arts & Lett (Empire State), 72-
Awards: Medal of honor, Printers & Sculptors Soc N J, 58; Huntington Hartford Found Fel, 61; career achievement award in the arts, Baruch Col Alumni Asn, 68.
Memberships: Fel Royal Soc Arts, London; Am Soc Contemp Artists; Nat Asn Women Artists (chmn publicity & pub rels, 57-71, ed newsletter, 61-69); Life mem Art Stud League; Am Fedn Arts.
Publications: Auth, Poetry-painting, 58; contribr, Anthology of readings for use in Christian education and worship, word alive, 69 & News extra, 71.
Mailing Address: 116 Central Park S, Apt 10-N, New York, NY 10019.

ASHER, BETTY M
Collector
b Chicago, Ill.
Collection: Contemporary art.
Mailing Address: 12921 Marlboro St, Los Angeles, CA 90049.

ASHER, FREDERICK M
Art Historian
b Chicago, Ill, May 25, 41.
Study & Training: Dartmouth Col, BA; Univ Chicago, MA & PhD.
Teaching: Instr art history, Lake Forest Col, 67-70; asst prof art history, Univ Minn, 70-
Positions: Actg dir, Univ Gallery, Univ Minn, 71-72; treas, Am Comt for S Asian Art, 72-
Research: South Asian art.
Publications: Various publications pertaining to the art of India.
Mailing Address: Dept of Art History, University of Minnesota, Minneapolis, MN 55455.

ASHER, LILA OLIVER
Printmaker, Educator
Preferred Media: Wood & Linoleum Block.
b Philadelphia, Pa.
Study & Training: With Gonippo Raggi, Joseph Grossman & Frank B A Linton; Philadelphia Col Art grad.
Work in Public Collections: Corcoran Gallery Art & Howard University, Washington, D C; Univ Va, Charlottesville; Univ Tex, El Paso; City of Wolfsburg, Ger collection.
Commissions: Oil paintings, two panels, Congregation Rodeph Shalom, Philadelphia, 40; three horizontal panels, Bolling Field Officers Club, Washington, D C; murals, two rooms, Indian Spring Country Club, Glenmont, Md; portraits, the late Justice Harold H Burton & Hon Cyrus Chyng.
Exhibitions: Pa Acad Fine Arts, Philadelphia; Pennell Print Exhib, Libr Cong, Washington, D C; Ann Print Exhib, Univ Va; Nat Collection Fine Arts, Washington, D C; Philadelphia Col Art; also one-woman shows, 51, 63, 65, 68, 70 & 72.
Teaching: Instr art, Howard Univ, 47-51; instr art, Wilson Teachers Col, 53-54; from lectr to prof art, Howard Univ, 61-
Awards: Corcoran Gallery Art, 55; Grumbacher Award, 60; Univ Va, 70.
Memberships: Am Asn Univ Prof; Soc Washington Artists (pres, 62-64); Soc Washington Printmakers (rec secy, 68-); Artist Equity Asn (treas, D C Chap, 71-).
Mailing Address: 4100 Thornapple St, Chevy Chase, MD 20015.

ASHLEY, FRANK NELSON
Painter
b Lincoln, Nebr, Mar 17, 20.
Study & Training: Univ Minn, 38-41; Am Acad Art, Chicago, Ill, 45-46; Minneapolis Art Inst, 47-48; Art Stud League New York, with Reginald Marsh, 48-50.
Exhibitions: Art U S A, Madison Square Garden, New York, N Y, 58 & 59; Legion of Hon Invitational, San Francisco, Calif, 62-64.
Awards: Grand prize, Art U S A, New York, 58; Spreckels Award, Legion of Hon Invitational, 64.
Dealers: Zantman Art Galleries, P O Box 5818, Carmel-by-the-Sea, CA 93921; Oehlschlaeger Galleries, 107 E Oak St, Chicago, IL 60611.
Mailing Address: Box 4951, Carmel, CA 93921.

ASHTON, DORE
Art Critic, Art Historian
b Newark, N J, May 21, 28.
Study & Training: Univ Wis, BA; Harvard Univ, MA.
Teaching: Hd dept art & archit hist, Cooper Union, 69-

Positions: Assoc ed, Art Digest, New York, N Y, 52-54; art critic, New York Times, 55-60; contrib ed, Studio Int, London, Eng, 68-; contrib ed, Opus Int, Paris, France, 65-.
Awards: Mather Award for art criticism, Col Art Asn, 63; Guggenheim Fels, 64 & 69; Ford Found Award, 65.
Memberships: Int Asn Art Critics (gov bd mem, 60-); Col Art Asn.
Research: Modern art.
Publications: Auth, The unknown shore, 62; A reading of modern art, 69; Richard Lindner, 69; The New York school: a cultural reckoning, 72; ed, Picasso on art, 72.
Mailing Address: 217 E 11th St, New York, NY 10003.

ASKIN, ARNOLD SAMUEL
Collector
b Utica, N Y, Aug 21, 01.
Study & Training: Yale Univ, BA.
Collection: Impressionist and post-impressionist paintings.
Mailing Address: Cross River Rd, Katonah, NY 10536.

ASMAR, ALICE
Painter, Designer
Preferred Media: Casein, Indelible India Inks, Acrylics, Oil.
b Flint, Mich.
Study & Training: Lewis & Clark Col, BA(magna cum laude); with Edward Melcarth & Archipenko, Univ Washington, MFA; Woolley fel, Ecole Nat Superieure des Beaux-Arts: Paris, France, with M Souverbie: Huntington Hartford Found residence fels, 61-64.
Work in Public Collections: Huntington Hartford Mus, New York, N Y; Roswell Mus & Art Ctr, New Mex; Security Pacific Int Bank, New York; Mutual Savings & Loan Asn, Pasadena, Calif; Joseph Magnin's El Paseo, Santa Barbara, Calif.
Commissions: Mural, Channel Island, Joseph Magnin's, 64; California Triptich, Security Pacific National Bank, Los Angeles, Calif, 70.
Exhibitions: Artists of Los Angeles & Vicinity Ann, Los Angeles Co Art Mus, 61; Drawings USA, St Paul Art Center Nat Traveling Exhib, 63-65; Mostra Rappresentativa Nazionale, Biennale Delle Regioni, Ancona, Italy, 68-69; Western Asn Art Mus Circulating Banner Exhib, 70-72; Drawings USA, Minn Mus Art Nat Travel Show, 71-73.
Teaching: Asst prof painting & drawing, Lewis & Clark College, 55-58; instr painting, Lennox Adult Educ, Calif, 63-65.
Positions: Eng draftsman, Boeing Aircraft, 52-54.
Awards: Menzione Onorevole, Biennale Delle Regione, 68-69; purchase award, Seattle Art Mus; first prize, Southern Calif Expos.
Bibliography: Elena Montez (auth), Art & artists of New Mexico & Alice Asmar's rice paper paintings, New Mex Mag, 3/68; Beverly Edna Johnson (auth), The roots of Asmar's imagery, brochure for two exhibs, 4/72; Janice Lovoos (auth), The linear design of Alice Asmar, Am Artist Mag, 4/72.
Memberships: Desert Art Ctr, Palm Springs; Am Fedn Arts; Southwest Mus; Los Angeles Co Art Mus.
Dealers: Adele Bednarz Galleries, 902 N La Cienega Blvd, Los Angeles, CA 90069; Mary Livingston's Gallery 2, 1211 N Broadway, Santa Ana, CA 92701.
Mailing Address: P.O. Box 1965, Hollywood, CA 90028.

ASOMA, TADASHI
Painter
Preferred Media: Oils.
b Iwatsuki, Japan, Apr 28, 23.
Study & Training: Saitama Teachers Col, Urawa, MS; Bijitsu Gakko, Tokyo, Japan, govt scholar; Grande Chaumiere, Paris, govt scholar; Art Stud League New York.
Work in Public Collections: Nelson Gallery, Kansas City; Andrew Dickson White Mus, Ithaca, N Y; Nat Bank, Des Moines, Iowa.
Exhibitions: One-man shows, Mi Chou Gallery, N Y, 60, Findlay Galleries, N Y, 65, 67, 69 & 71; Knott Gallery, San Francisco, Calif, 70, Alley Gallery, Tex, 72 & Elms Gallery, Midland, Tex, 72.
Teaching: Instr art educ, Iwatsuki Jr High Sch, 50-64.
Awards: Second prize, Saitama Bijitsu Ten, 55; second prize, Nat Exhib Prof Art, 68.
Bibliography: Articles, In: Art News, Sun New York Times & New York Post, 65, 67, & 69; plus others.
Dealer: Findlay Galleries, 11 E 57th St, New York, NY 10022.
Mailing Address: Philipse Brook Rd, Garrison, NY 10524.

ATKINS, DAVID
Painter
Preferred Media: Oils.
b Waterbury, Conn, Nov 28, 10.
Study & Training: Art Stud League New York, with George Bridgman; Nat Acad Design, with Leon Kroll, 27-30; Educ Alliance Art Sch, with Abbo Ostrowsky, 32-36.

Work in Public Collections: Butler Inst Am Art Mus, Youngstown, Ohio; Philathea Col Mus Mod Art, London, Ont, Can.
Exhibitions: Metrop Mus Art, New York, N Y, 36; Riverside Mus, New York, 43-62; Whitney Mus Am Art, New York, 54; Artists '72, Union Carbide, New York, 72; Lever House, New York, 72.
Positions: Pres, Group III, 71-72.
Awards: Prize for painting, League Present Day Artists, 47; painting prize, 8th St Gallery, Knickerbocker Artists, 48; Prix de Paris, Raymond Duncan, 57.
Bibliography: John Gruen (auth), Review of a one-man show, Herald Tribune, 11/9/63; Review of a one-man show, Pictures on Exhib, 11/9/63; Art Digest review, Art Digest, 12/65.
Memberships: Artists Equity New York (exec bd, 62-); League Present Day Artists (pres & secy, 43-50); Metrop Painters & Sculptors (chmn exhibs, 71-); Prof Art Studio Club; Artists Circle (founder, 68-).
Dealer: Werbin Gallery, 976 Lexington Ave, New York, NY 10021.
Mailing Address: 41 Union Square W, Rm 1426, New York, NY 10003.

ATKINSON, TRACY
Museum Director
b Middletown, Ohio, May 10, 28.
Study & Training: Ohio State Univ, BFA (summa cum laude), 50; Mex City Col, 50; Univ Pa, 50-55, MA, 51; Bryn Mawr Col, 53.
Collections Arranged: Antique Luster, Albright-Knox Art Gallery, Buffalo, N Y, 59; Contemporary American Painting & German Expressionism, Columbus Gallery Fine Arts, Ohio, 61-62. For Milwaukee Art Ctr: Wisconsin Collects, 64, Pop Art and the American Tradition, 65, The Inner Circle, 66, Botero, 67, Options & The Bradley Collection, 68, Seymour Lipton & A Plastic Presence, 69, Aspects of a New Realism, 70, Portraits Exhibition, 71 & Six Painters, 72.
Positions: Curatorial asst, Albright-Knox Art Gallery, 55-59; asst dir, Columbus Gallery Fine Arts, 59-61, actg dir, 61-62; dir, Milwaukee Art Ctr, 62-
Memberships: Milwaukee Landmarks Comn; Midwest Mus Conf (v pres, Wis, 68-71, exec v pres, 70-71, pres, 71-72); Am Asn Mus (state rep); Asn Art Mus Dirs (trustee & 2nd v pres, 72-73); Int Coun Mus.
Publications: Auth, German genre paintings from the Von Schleinitz collection, Antiques Mag, 11/69; David Black, recent work, introd to catalogue for the David Black in Berlin Exhib, 4-5/71; also articles in prof journals, nat art news magazines & newspapers.
Mailing Address: Milwaukee Art Center, 750 N Lincoln Memorial Dr, Milwaukee, WI 53202.

ATKYNS, (WILLIE) LEE, JR
Painter, Art Administrator
Preferred Media: Acrylics.
b Washington, D C, Sept 13, 13.
Work in Public Collections: Phillips Memorial Gallery, Washington, D C; Talladega Col, Ala; Rockville Civic Ctr, Md.
Exhibitions: Annuals, Soc Washington Artists & Landscape Club Washington; Carnegie Inst; Corcoran Gallery Art; Nat Collection Fine Arts; and many others.
Collections Arranged: Music Themes in Painting, 70-71; Dynamic Liberated Lines, 72-
Teaching: Instr painting, Lee Atkyns Studio Sch Art, Washington, D C, 45-68 & summer classes, Puzzletown, Pa, 45-50.
Positions: Dir, Lee Atkyns Studio & Gallery of Art, 50-
Awards: Landscape Club Washington, 54, 56, 60, 62, 68 & 71; Soc Washington Artists, 47-54; Am Artists Prof League, 61.
Memberships: Soc Washington Artists; Landscape Club of Washington; Artists Equity Asn.
Specialty of Gallery: Dynamic Liberated Lines series.
Mailing Address: 4712 Wisconsin Ave, Washington, DC 20016.

ATLEE, EMILIE DeS
Painter, Instructor
Preferred Media: Oils, Pastels.
b Bethlehem, Pa, July 6, 15.
Study & Training: Spring Garden Inst, Philadelphia; also with Roswell Weidner & Joseph & Gertrude Capolino.
Work in Public Collections: United Airlines, Philadelphia Airport; Palasaides High Sch, Bucks County, Pa; La Salle Col, Philadelphia; Univ Del, Wilmington; Del Co Mem Hosp, Drexel Hill, Pa.
Commissions: Portraits, Libr Univ Del & Berks Co Ct House, Pa.
Exhibitions: One-man shows, Little Gallery, Philadelphia, 63 & Newmans Gallery, Philadelphia, 70; Knickerbocker Artists Ann, New York, 64; Philadelphia Art Teachers Asn, 69-71; Pa 71, Harrisburg Mus, 71.
Teaching: Instr 53-69; instr, Main Line Ctr Arts, Bryn Mawr, Pa, 69-
Awards: Hon mention, Nat, Ogunquit Art Ctr, 59 & Nat Benedictine Art Awards, 69; gold medal, Newton Sq Arts Festival, 61.

Bibliography: Dorothy Grafly (ed), The changing moods of art, Art in Focus, 71.
Memberships: Artists Equity Asn; Pa Acad Fine Arts; Philadelphia Mus Art; Woodmere Art Gallery; Main Line Ctr Arts.
Dealer: Newman Galleries, 1625 Walnut St, Philadelphia, PA 19103.
Mailing Address: 2117 Chestnut Ave, Ardmore, PA 19003.

AUBIN, BARBARA
Painter, Educator
Preferred Media: Watercolor.
b Chicago, Ill, Jan 12, 28.
Study & Training: Carleton Col, BA 49; Art Inst Chicago, BAE, 54, MAE, 55; George D Brown for travel fel Art Inst Chicago, France & Italy, 55-56; Buenos Aires Conv Act grant, Haiti, 58-60.
Work in Public Collections: Art Inst Chicago; Ball State Univ, Muncie, Ind; Centre d-Art, Port-au-Prince, Haiti; Union League Club, Chicago,
Exhibitions: Artists of Chicago and Vicinity, Art Inst Chicago, 53, 55, 60, 61 & 68; Mid-Year Shows, Butler Inst Am Art Ohio, 61 & 62; American Drawing Ann, Norfolk Mus Arts & Sci, 63; Tenth Ann Nat Prints & Drawings Exhib, Okla Art Ctr, 68; Drawings U S A, St Paul Art Ctr, Minn & travelling, 68.
Teaching: Asst prof painting, drawing & watercolor, Art Inst Chicago, 60-68; asst prof painting, drawing & design, Loyola Univ (Chicago), 68-71; Chicago State Univ, 71-; St Joseph's Col, 71-
Awards: Hon mention for the Dana Medal, Pa Acad Fine Arts, 53; Huntington Hartford Found Grant, 63; Mich Watercolor Soc Award, 65 & 70.
Bibliography: Margaret Harold (compiler), Prizewinning watercolors & prizewinning art, Allied Publications, 66.
Memberships: Col Art Asn Am; Am Asn Mus; Mich Watercolor Soc; Chicago Soc Artists.
Dealer: Art Rental & Sales Gallery, Art Institute of Chicago, Michigan & Adams St, Chicago, IL 60603.
Mailing Address: 1925 N Hudson Ave, Chicago, IL 60614.

AULT, LEE ADDISON
Collector, Art Dealer
b Cincinnati, Ohio, Sept 30, 15.
Study & Training: Princeton Univ, 37.
Positions: Publisher, Art in America, 57-69; trustee, Skowhegan Sch Painting & Sculpture, 68-; adv coun, Princeton Univ Art Mus, 66-; trustee, Maine Coast Artists.
Collection: 20th century painting and sculpture; primitive art.
Mailing Address: Lee Ault & Company, 25 E 77th St, New York, NY 10021.

AUSTIN, DARREL
Painter
Preferred Media: Oil.
b Raymond, Wash, June 25, 07.
Study & Training: Univ Notre Dame; Univ Ore; also with Emil Jaques, European Sch Art.
Work in Public Collections: Metrop Mus Art & Mus Mod Art, New York, N Y; Mus Fine Arts, Boston, Mass; Nelson Gallery Art, Kansas City, Mo; Phillips Mem Gallery, Washington, D C.
Commissions: Four oil panels, med col, Univ Ore, 36.
Exhibitions: Whitney Mus, New York; Carnegie Inst, Pittsburgh, Pa; City Art Mus, St Louis, Mo; Contemporary Painting in the U S, toured in Latin Am countries; Inst Contemp Art, Boston, Mass.
Awards: Lippincot Award for figure oil, Pa Acad Art, 53.
Bibliography: Miller (auth), Americans 1942, Mus Mod Art, 42; Bird (auth), Darrel Austin, Art in Am, 43; Darrel Austin, Life Mag, 45.
Dealers: ACA Galleries, 25 E 73rd St, New York, NY 10021; Harmon Gallery, Naples, FL 33940.
Mailing Address: R D 4, Sawmill Hill Rd, New Fairfield, CT 06810.

AUSTIN, PHIL
Painter, Lecturer
Preferred Media: Watercolors.
b Waukegan, Ill, Jan 27, 10.
Study & Training: Univ Mich, AB, 33.
Work in Public Collections: Ill State Libr, Lincoln Collection, Springfield & Ill State Mus; Wheaton Col Art Collection, Ill.
Exhibitions: Five shows, Am Watercolor Soc Ann, New York, N Y, 61-69; Watercolor U S A, Springfield, Mo, 72; Mainstreams '72, Marietta, Ohio, 72; Am Artists Prof League Grand Nat, New York, 72; Acad Artists, Springfield, Mass, 72; plus others.
Teaching: Guest instr watercolor, Wheaton Col, 63-70; lectr.
Positions: Mem staff, Kling Studios, Chicago, Ill, 45-50; free lance artist, 50-66.
Awards: Best of show purchase award, Artists Guild Chicago, 66; William Schultz Art Sch Watercolor Award, Acad Artists, 70; hon mention, Mainstreams '72, Marietta Col, Ohio, 72.
Bibliography: Phil Austin, watercolorist, Am Artist, 10/71.
Memberships: Am Watercolor Soc; Acad Artists Asn; Am Artists Prof League.

Dealers: Anchor Lane Gallery, Wisconsin Bay Drive, Gills Rock, WI 54210; Deer Path Gallery, 253 Market Square, Lake Forest, IL 60045.
Mailing Address: Rte 1, Ellison Bay, WI 54210.

AUTH, ROBERT R
Painter, Sculptor
Preferred Media: Acrylics.
b Bloomington, Ill, Oct 27, 26.
Study & Training: Ill Wesleyan Univ, BFA; Wash State Univ, MFA.
Work in Public Collections: Salt Lake Art Ctr, Utah; Col Southern Idaho, Twin Falls; Ricks Col, Rexburg, Idaho; Boise Gallery Art, Idaho; Wash State Univ, Pullman.
Exhibitions: 4th Biennial Exhib, Intermountain Painting & Sculpture, Salt Lake Art Ctr, 69; Fedn Rocky Mountain States Invitational (traveling), 71-72; Invitational Inaugural Exhib, Denver Art Mus, Colo, 71; 48th Ann Invitational Nat April Art Exhib, Springville Mus Art, Utah, 72; Realist Painting: 12 Viewpoints, Minneapolis, Minn, 72.
Teaching: Instr art, Burley High Sch, Idaho, 60-61; instr art & humanities, Boise High Sch, 61-
Positions: From asst supt to supt, Fine Art Div, Western Idaho Fair, 64-; bd dir, Boise Gallery Art, 69-; chmn, art curric develop comt, Boise Independent Sch Dist, 71.
Awards: 4th Biennial Exhib Intermountain Painting & Sculpture, 69; 36th Ann Exhib for Idaho, 72; Allied Arts Coun Artist of the Year Award, 72.
Bibliography: Catalogs for Fedn Rocky Mountain States Ann, 71 & 72; Ann Nat, Springville, Utah, 70, 71 & 72; David Thomas (auth), Realist paintings: 12 viewpoints, Red River Art Ctr, Moorhead & Rochester Art Ctr, Minn, 72.
Memberships: Idaho Art Asn (conf chmn, 68, v pres, 70-72); Boise Art Asn (trustee, 69-).
Dealer: Elva Brooks, The Art Mart, 711 S Latah St, Boise, ID 83705.
Mailing Address: 530 Hillview Dr, Boise, ID 83702.

AUTORINO, ANTHONY MICHAEL
Painter
b Montclair, N J, Sept 29, 37.
Work in Public Collections: Univ Conn; Presidential Palace, the Ivory Coast.
Exhibitions: Greengate Invitational Art Show, Greensburg, Pa, 65; Am Vet Soc Artists, Union Carbide Bldg, 66; 101st Traveling Exhib, Am Watercolor Soc, 68; Nat Acad Design & Am Watercolor Soc, 68.
Awards: First prize, Greengate Invitational Art Show, 65; N J State Art Festival at Longbranch, 66.
Bibliography: Prize Winning Art: Book Six, Allied, 66; Dorothy Grafly (auth), art editorial in the Sunday Bulletin, Philadelphia, 68.
Mailing Address: 18 W Mechanic St, New Hope, PA 18938.

AUVIL, KENNETH WILLIAM
Educator, Printmaker
b Ryderwood, Wash, Dec 18, 25.
Study & Training: Univ Wash, BA, 50, MFA, 53.
Work in Public Collections: Achenbach Found, Palace of Legion of Honor, San Francisco, Calif; Seattle Art Mus, Wash; U S Embassy, Bonn, Ger; Wichita Art Asn, Kans; Victoria & Albert Mus, London, Eng.
Commissions: Ed of 170 screen prints, Hilton Collection, Hotel Hilton, New York, N Y, 62.
Exhibitions: Northwest Printmakers Int Exhibs, Seattle Art Mus, 53-67 & 70; Fourth Biennial di Pittura Americana, Bordighera, Italy, 57; Libr Cong Nat Exhibs, 59, 63 & 66; New Impressions for the Decade, Oakland Art Mus, Calif, 70; Int Print Exhib, Richmond Art Ctr, Calif, 72.
Teaching: Prof art (printmaking), Calif State Univ, San Jose, 56-
Memberships: Northwest Printmakers (pres, 55-56); Calif Soc Printmakers.
Publications: Auth, Serigraphy-silk screen techniques for the artist, Prentice-Hall, 65.
Mailing Address: 605 Olson Rd, Santa Cruz, CA 95060.

AVAKIAN, JOHN
Painter, Educator
b Worcester, Mass.
Study & Training: Yale Univ Sch Art & Archit, BFA & MFA; Boston Mus Sch, grad traveling scholar, diploma (hons) & cert.
Work in Public Collections: Kansas State Univ; Western Mich Univ; Bucknell Univ; Tulsa Civic Ctr, Okla; Cramer Electronic, Inc, Newton, Mass; plus one other.
Exhibitions: New Talent, New England, DeCordova Mus, Lincoln, Mass, 65; 20th Nat Exhib Prints, Libr Cong, Washington, D C, 66; 38th Int Printmakers Exhib, Seattle Art Mus, Wash, 67; one-man show, Higgins Wing, Worcester Art Mus, Mass, 71; 21st Ann Int Exhib, Beaumont Art Mus, Tex, 72.

Teaching: Instr color & design, Worcester Art Mus Sch, Mass, 65-; instr color & design, Mt Ida Jr Col, 65-, chmn art dept, 66-71, dir art, 72-
Awards: William E Brigham Prize, Providence Art Club, 68; Blanche E Colman Found Award, 70; Art Patrons League of Mobile Award, 72.
Memberships: Col Art Asn Am; Boston Visual Artist's Union; Worcester Art Mus.
Dealer: Lenore Gray Gallery, Inc, 15 Meeting St, Providence, RI 02903.
Mailing Address: 43 Morse St, Sharon, MA 02067.

AVEDISIAN, EDWARD
Painter
b Lowell, Mass, 36.
Study & Training: Boston Mus Sch Art.
Work in Public Collections: Guggenheim Mus, New York, N Y; Whitney Mus Am Art, New York; Metrop Mus Art; Los Angeles Mus Art; Pasadena Mus Art; plus others.
Exhibitions: John Powers Collection, Larry Aldrich Mus, 66; Robert Rowan Collection, San Francisco Mus Art, 67; Paintings from Expo '67, Montreal; Boston Inst Contemp Art, 67-68; Painters Under 40, Whitney Mus Am Art, 68; plus others.
Teaching: Artist-in-residence, Univ Kans, 69; instr, Sch Visual Arts, New York, 69-70.
Dealer: Robert Elkon Gallery, 1063 Madison Ave, New York, NY 10028.
Mailing Address: 650 Huntington Ave, Roxbury, MA 02115.

AVERY, RALPH HILLYER
Painter, Illustrator
Preferred Media: Watercolor.
b Savannah, Ga, Sept 3, 06.
Study & Training: Rochester Inst Technol; Louis Comfort Tiffany Found, Oyster Bay, N Y; also with Charles Woodbury, Harry Leith-Ross, Wayman Adams & Hilda Belcher.
Work in Public Collections: Mem Art Gallery, Rochester, N Y; Frye Free Art Mus, Seattle, Wash; Witte Mem Mus, San Antonio, Tex; Parrish Art Mus, South Hampton, N Y; State Univ N Y, Albany, N Y.
Exhibitions: One-man show, Telfair Acad Arts & Sci, Savannah, Ga, 52; Arnot Art Gallery, Elmira, N Y, 53; Finger Lakes Exhib, Rochester, N Y, 71; Am Watercolor Soc, New York, N Y, 71; Nat Acad Design, New York, N Y, 71; plus others.
Awards: Lillian Fairchild Award, Univ Rochester, 54; Rudolf Lesch Purchase Award, 66 & Marthe T McKinnon Award, Am Watercolor Soc, 70.
Bibliography: Ernest Watson (auth), Ralph Avery, American Artist Mag, 6/54; Anthony Cassen (auth), Ralph Avery, profile in paint, Blair Acad Bull, 11/66.
Memberships: Assoc Nat Acad Design; Am Watercolor Soc; fel Rochester Mus Arts & Sci.
Publications: Contribr, Watercolor methods, 55; Watercolor painting step-by-step, 56; 100 watercolor techniques, 68; Fundamentals of watercolor painting, 70; Complete guide to acrylic painting, 71.
Mailing Address: 60 N Fitzhugh St, Rochester, NY 14614.

AY-O
Painter, Printmaker
b Ibaragi-Ken, Japan, May 19, 31.
Study & Training: Tokyo Kyaiku Univ, BA.
Work in Public Collections: Many mus in Japan, U S A, W Ger, Holland, Poland & others.
Commissions: Murals, Kanazawa-Hakkey-Kaikan, 66; Environment, Expo '70, Japan.
Exhibitions: Galleries in Japan, 53-72; Happening, Japan, U S A & W Ger, 60-72; Environment, Japan, U S A, Italy & W Ger, 60-70; galleries in U S A, 63-70; Zwirner Gallery, Ger, 66; plus one one-man show.
Teaching: Assoc prof painting, Univ Ky, 68-70.
Awards: Sao Paulo Biennial, Brazil Bank, 71; Tokyo Int Print Biennial, Mus Mod Art, Tokyo, 71; Krakow Prints Biennial, Mus d'Art Lodz Prix, 72.
Bibliography: Article, In: Art & Artist, London, 67; article, In: Mizue Mag, Japan, 70; Joseph Love (auth), article, In: Kikan Hanga, Japan, 71.
Publications: Auth, Rainbow passes slowly, Nantenshi Gallery, 71; auth, Nashville skyline, 71; auth, Ouzel, Tikuma-shobo, 72.
Dealer: Mizuno Gallery, 669 N La Cienega Blvd, Los Angeles, CA 90069.
Mailing Address: 363 Canal St, New York, NY 10013.

AYASO, MANUEL
Painter, Sculptor
Preferred Media: Goldpoint, Mixed media.
b Riveira, Spain, Jan 1, 34; U S citizen.
Study & Training: Newark Sch Fine & Indus Arts, cert.

Work in Public Collections: Whitney Mus Am Art, New York, N Y; Worcester Mus, Mass; Pa Acad Fine Arts, Philadelphia; N J State Mus, Trenton; Newark Mus, N J.
Exhibitions: Drawings U S A Circulating Exhib, 62 & 64-65; 22nd Int Watercolor Biennial, Brooklyn Mus, N Y, 63; El Neo-Humanismo en el Dibujo de U S A, Italia y Mexico, Univ Mex, 63; American Painting & Sculpture, Pa Acad Fine Arts, 67; Contemporary American Artists, Nat Inst Arts & Lett, 71.
Awards: Tiffany Found scholar in painting, 62; Ford Found Purchase Award, 64; Childe Hassan Fund Purchase Award, 71.
Memberships: Am Fedn Arts.
Dealer: Forum Gallery, 1018 Madison Ave, New York, NY 10021.
Mailing Address: 127 New York Ave, Newark, NJ 07105.

AYLING, MILDRED SHOOB
Painter, Photographer
Preferred Media: Watercolors.
b Hesper, Iowa, Jan 24, 12.
Study & Training: San Francisco Acad Art; Inst San Miguel Allende, Mex; also with Eliot O'Hara, George Post & Vivian Goddard.
Work in Public Collections: Crocker Gallery, Sacramento, Calif; Haggin Gallery, Stockton, Calif; Triton Mus, Santa Clara, Calif; Royal Victoria Inst & Mus, Port of Spain, Trinidad, W I.
Exhibitions: Inst San Miguel de Allende, Mex, 66; Soc Western Artists Ann Exhib, De Young Mus, San Francisco, 68-70; Masters of Am Drawing, Crocker Gallery, Sacramento, 69; Salon d'Hiver U S A, R Duncan Galleries, Paris, France, 70; Montalvo Ctr Arts, Saratoga, Calif, 71.
Positions: Artist-photographer, 30-58.
Awards: Second prize & hon mention for watercolors, Mother Lode Nat, 56-57; first prize for watercolor, Mother Lode Women Artists, 62; purchase award for watercolor, Calif State Savings & Loan, 67.
Bibliography: H Svensgaard (auth), Mildred Shoob Ayling, pony express, 8/69; Lotta Pengel (auth), American artist in Surinam, Ochtenblad, 1/72; Yousef Ali (auth), The Ayling view of Trinidad & Surinam, produced on TTTV-TV, 2/72.
Memberships: Soc Western Artists; Am Artists Prof League; Am Watercolor Soc.
Dealers: Treehouse Gallery, Modesto, CA 90050; Art & Design Associates, Mono Hwy, Sonora, CA 95370.
Mailing Address: 7212 River Rd, Oakdale, CA 95361.

AYLON, HELÉNE
Painter
Preferred Media: Aluminum, Plexiglass & Acrylic.
b New York, N Y.
Study & Training: Brooklyn Col, BA(cum laude); with Ad Reinhardt.
Work in Public Collections: Whitney Mus Am Art, New York.
Commissions: Wall painting, chapel, John F Kennedy Airport, N Y, 66; mural, lobby, New York Univ Med Ctr, New York, 67.
Exhibitions: Lyrical Abstraction, Whitney Mus Am Art, Aldrich Mus Contemp Art, Phoenix Art Mus & Philadelphia Civic Ctr, 69; 2 Generations, Univ Mus, Univ Pa, 70; Season's Highlights, Aldrich Mus Am Art, 71; 4 Painters, Skidmore Col, Saratoga, N Y, 71; Painting & Sculpture Today, Indianapolis Mus Art, Ind, 72.
Teaching: Instr painting, Brooklyn Mus & Hunter Col, 72-
Awards: Macdowell fel, 72.
Bibliography: Grace Glueck (auth), Art: highlights of downtown scene, New York Times, 12/11/70; Gregoire Muller (auth), Materiality and painterliness, Arts Mag, 9-10/71; Carter Ratcliff (auth), New York letter, Art Int, 6/73.
Memberships: Archit League N Y (v pres painting).
Mailing Address: c/o Max Hutchinson Gallery, 127 Greene St, New York, NY 10012.

AYMAR, GORDON CHRISTIAN
Painter, Art Historian
Preferred Media: Watercolor.
b East Orange, N J, July 24, 93.
Study & Training: Yale Univ, AB, 14; Sch of Mus Fine Arts, Boston, 15-17.
Work in Public Collections: Yale Univ Art Gallery, New Haven, Conn; Addison Gallery Art, Phillips Acad, Mass; Nat Coun Churches, New York, N Y; New York Neurol Inst; Photographic Dept Permanent Study Collection, Mus Mod Art, New York.
Commissions: Portraits, Pres K Towe, American Cyanamid, New York, 55; Pres W Wheeler, Jr, Pitney Bowes, Stamford, Conn, 58; Dr H S Coffin, Madison Ave Presbyterian Church, New York, 61; Pres L W Wister, South Kent Sch, Conn, 69; Pres J Armstrong, Middlebury Col, Vt, 71.
Exhibitions: Mus Art, Montreal, P Q, 60; Royal Soc Painters in Water Colour, London, Eng, 62; Charles & Emma Frye Art Mus, Seattle, Wash, 64; Nat Acad Design, New York, 68; Am Watercolor Soc, New York, 71.

Awards: For Cat on Mikonos, Conn Classic Arts, 62; Deborah, thinking, Darien Art Festival, Darien, Conn, 64; portrait of Chris Aymar, Kent Art Asn, Conn, 71.
Bibliography: Salon des aquarellistes de New York, Rev Mod, Paris, 62; C R Cammel (auth), American masterpieces in water colour, New Daily, London, 62; Dorothy Brazier (auth), Crowd enjoys charming picture, Seattle Times, 64.
Memberships: Am Watercolor Soc (1st v pres, 63); Washington Art Asn, Conn (trustee, 66); Kent Art Asn, (exhib comt, 72).
Research: Portraits through the centuries.
Publications: Auth, The art of portrait painting, 67.
Mailing Address: Geer Mountain Rd, South Kent, CT 06785.

AYOROA, RODOLFO (RUDY) E
Painter
b La Paz, Bolivia, Sept 16, 27.
Study & Training: Acad Fine Arts, Cochabamba, Bolivia; Nat Univ Buenos Aires, Arg.
Work in Public Collections: Nat Collection Fine Arts, Washington, D C; plus collections in Colombia, Arg, P R, Can & U S A.
Commissions: Painting, Pres Palace, La Paz, 52.
Exhibitions: Latin Am Found Arts, San Juan, P R, 69; Coltejer Biennial Art, Medellin, Colombia, 70 & 72; Frostburg Col Mus Art, Md, 71; Biennial Art, Montevideo, Uruguay, 71; Univ P R Mus Art, San Juan, 72; plus many other group & one-man shows.
Teaching: Lectr art, George Washington Univ & Univ P R.
Bibliography: Rafael Squirru (auth), Ayoroa, Americas Mag, 68; E Ruiz de la Mata (auth), Ayoroa, San Juan Star Mag, 2/27/72.
Art Interests: Kinetic light sculpture; architectural design & painting.
Mailing Address: 6724 Wilson Lane, Bethesda, MD 20034.

AYRE, ROBERT HUGH
Writer, Critic
b Napinka, Man, Apr 3, 00.
Positions: Art critic, Montreal Star.
Awards: Can Drama Award, 42; Can Coun travel grant to Paris, London & Italy, 62.
Publications: Auth, Mr Sycamore (novella); auth, Sketco, The Raven (Indian legends), Macmillan, 61; contribr, var periodicals & yearbks & Art in Can.
Mailing Address: 5745 Cote St Luc Rd, Montreal, P Q, Can.

AZUMA, NORIO
Serigrapher, Painter
Preferred Media: Oils.
b Kii-Nagashima-cho, Japan, Nov 23, 28.
Study & Training: Kanazawa Art Col, Japan, BFA; Chouniard Art Inst, Los Angeles, Calif; Art Stud League, New York, N Y.
Work in Public Collections: Nat Collection Fine Arts, Smithsonian Inst, Washington, D C; Whitney Mus Am Art, New York; Philadelphia Mus Art, Pa; Brooklyn Mus Art, N Y; Art Inst Chicago, Ill.
Commissions: 1500 serigraph prints, IBM Corp, N Y, 66.
Exhibitions: Corcoran Biennial, Washington, D C, 63; Third Int Triennial Original Graphic, Grenchen, Switz, 64; Mus Mod Art, Tokyo Exhib, 65; Sculpture and Prints, Whitney Mus Am Art, 66; Silkscreen, History of a Medium, Philadelphia Mus Art, 72.
Awards: Int Print Show, Seattle Mus Art, 60; Print Exhib, Soc Am Graphic Artists, 68; Print Exhib, Boston Printmakers, 70.
Memberships: Soc Am Color Prints; Print Club; Soc Am Graphic Artists; Print Coun Am.
Dealers: AAA Gallery, 663 Fifth Ave, New York, NY 10022; Weinger Gallery 41 E 57th St, New York, NY 10022; Fendrick Gallery, 3059 M St NW, Washington, DC 20007.
Mailing Address: 276 Riverside Dr, New York, NY 10025.

B

BABER, ALICE
Painter
Preferred Media: Oils, Watercolors
b Charleston, Ill, Aug 22, 28.
Study & Training: Indiana Univ, BA, grad sch; also in Fontainebleau, France.
Work in Public Collections: Corcoran Gallery Art, Washington, D C; San Francisco Mus Art, Calif; Nat Collection Fine Arts, Washington, D C; Nat Mus of Israel; Peter Stuyvesant (Turmac) Collection, Holland.
Exhibitions: Deuxieme Biennale Paris, France, 61; Modern American Painting, U S Info Serv, Am Embassy, London, Eng & Edin-

burgh, Scotland, 61-62; Third Kent State Univ Invitational, Ohio, 68; group show, Eisenstadt Schloss, Austria, 69; Trends in 20th century art, Univ Calif, Santa Barbara, 70.
Teaching: Vis artist, Univ Minn, 70-71; vis artist, Univ Calif, Santa Barbara, fall 71; vis artist, State Univ N Y Col Purchase, 72-73.
Bibliography: James Jones (auth), Alice Baber and the tragedy of light, Studio Int, 9/65; Dorothy Beskind (producer), Alice Baber at work (film), 70; James Mellow (auth), Today's series lineup, New York Times, 4/11/71, reprint, Art Int, spring 71.
Dealer: A M Sachs Gallery, 29 W 57th St, New York, NY 10019.
Mailing Address: 73 Bedford St, New York, NY 10014.

BACH, DIRK
Painter, Educator
b Grand Rapids, Mich, Nov 27, 39.
Study & Training: Univ Denver, BFA(painting), 61, MA(painting), 62; Univ Mich, Ann Arbor, MA(orient art hist), 64.
Work in Public Collections: Denver Art Mus, Colo; Hopkins Ctr Art Galleries, Dartmouth Col, Hanover, N H; Lamont Gallery, Phillips Exeter Acad, N H; Loretto-Hilton Gallery, Webster Col, St Louis, Mo.
Commissions: Wall reliefs, Denver Art Mus, 62, N H Comn Arts for N H Voc Inst, Berlin, 68 & Grad & Music Schs, Univ N H, 68.
Exhibitions: Mid-America Ann, Nelson Gallery, Kansas City, Mo, 61; Western Ann, Denver Art Mus, 61; Young New England Painters, John & Mable Ringling Mus Art, Sarasota, Fla, 69; New England Drawing Exhib, Addison Gallery, Andover, Mass, 70; one-man touring show, Cloud Mandalas, Landscape Buddhism, Webster Col, Tucson Art Ctr, R I Sch Design & Nat Ctr Atmospheric Res, Boulder, Colo, 71-
Collections Arranged: One Hundred Years of American Art, Scudder Gallery, Durham, N H, 66; The Rose Art Museum Collection at New Hampshire, Scudder Gallery, 69.
Teaching: Asst prof painting, Univ. N H, 65-69; asst prof art hist, R I Sch Design, 69-; assoc & lectr, Asian Studies, Brown Univ, 70-
Positions: Dir, Scudder Gallery, Univ N H, 65-69; trustee, Arts R I, Providence, 71-
Awards: U S Nat Defense lang grant Mandarin Chinese, 64; Univ N H cent univ res grant commemorative stamp paintings, 68; Nat Endowment Humanities travel & res grant, Japan, 71
Bibliography: Young New England Painters, (catalogue), Ringling Mus, 69; J Canepa (auth), Cloud Mandalas/Landscape Buddhism, (catalogue), Webster Col, 71.
Memberships: Col Art Asn Am; Artists Equity Asn; N H Art Asn.
Research: Development of Ch'an painting in China; production of cosmic diagrams in the Far East.
Collection: Chinese and Japanese hanging scrolls.
Publications: Illusr, A new way to Paul Klee, Denver Art Mus, 46; contribr, The painting of Tao Chi, Univ Mich Mus Art, 67; auth, The stamp collection of Dirk Bach, Ramparts, 11/68; auth, The Rose Art Museum collection at New Hampshire, (catalogue), Univ N H, 69; auth, Selections from the oriental collections, R I Sch Design, 72.
Mailing Address: 216 Olney St, Providence, RI 02906.

BACH, OTTO KARL
Museum Director, Writer
b Chicago, Ill, May 26, 09.
Study & Training: Dartmouth Col; Univ Paris; Univ Chicago, MA; Univ Denver, hon DH, 55.
Positions: Dir, Grand Rapids Art Gallery, 43-44; dir, Denver Art Mus, Colo, 44-; originator, Living Arts Ctr Pilot Educ Progs, 59-
Awards: Extraordinary serv cert, City & Co Denver, 55; Am Creativity Award, 61; Chevalier Arts & Lett, 69.
Memberships: Am Asn Mus; Western Asn Art Mus Dirs; Col Art Asn Am; Int Soc Conserv Mus Objects.
Publications: Auth, A new way to Paul Klee, 45, American heritage, 49, Under every roof, 50, Pre Columbian gold, 51 & Life in America; plus others.
Mailing Address: 140 Krameria St, Denver, CO 80220.

BACHRACH, GLADYS WERTHEIM
Painter
Preferred Media: Oils.
b New York, N Y, June 10, 09.
Work in Public Collections: Fla Southern Col, Lakeland; Immobilaire, Vatican, Italy.
Exhibitions: Neville Pub Mus, Green Bay, Wis, 53; Ohio Wesleyan Univ, Delaware, Ohio, 53; Univ Ky, Lexington, 53; Condon Riley Gallery, New York, N Y, 58 & 59; plus other group and one-man exhibs.
Positions: Chmn art exhib, Berkshire Art Ctr, Canaan, N H, 53.
Awards: First prize for Nightfall (painting), Berkshire Art Ctr Exhib, 53; award, Fla Southern Col, 52.

Bibliography: Condon Riley (auth), Foreword in exhib catalog, 59.
Memberships: Artists Equity Asn; Metrop Mus Art.
Collection: Early abstract impressionism to current abstract realism.
Mailing Address: 305 E 72nd St, New York, NY 10021.

BACIGALUPA, ANDREA
Designer, Painter
b Baltimore, Md, May 26, 23.
Study & Training: Art Stud League, Woodstock, N Y, summer 49; Md Inst Fine Arts, BFA, 50; Acad Belli Arti, Florence, Italy, 50-51.
Commissions: Ceramic mural, Marquette Univ High Sch, Milwaukee, Wis, 61; oil mural, Holy Cross Sch, Las Cruces, N Mex, 66; ceramic mural, Church of Our Lady of Assumption, El Paso, Tex, 70; ceramic mural, Carmel of Santa Fe, N Mex, 71; sculptured font, Liturgy in Santa Fe, 72.
Exhibitions: Am Univ, Biarritz, France, 45; Ten Santa Fe Artists, Mus N Mex, Santa Fe, 58; Am House, New York, N Y, 60; one-man show, Mus N Mex, 60; Church Archit Guild, Pittsburgh, Pa, 61.
Positions: Owner-dir, Studio Gian Andres, Santa Fe, 54-; pres, Marelli-Lee Inc, Milan, Italy, 62-; rep, Gabriel Loire (stained glass), Chartres, France, 70-; dir media, Liturgy in Santa Fe, 70-
Awards: Bronze medallion, Md Inst Fine Arts, 50; purchase prize, Wichita Liturgical Arts Exhib, 67.
Bibliography: J Cudney (auth), Bacigalupa wall hangings, N Mexican, 10/13/68; full color article in N Mexico Mag, summer 69; Artists of Santa Fe, C R Wenzell Publ, 69.
Publications: Contribr, N Mexican, Santa Fe, 54-71; Liturgical Arts, 71; auth, Santos and Saints' Days, Sunstone Press, Santa Fe, 72.
Mailing Address: Studio of Gian Andrea, 626 Canyon Rd, Santa Fe, NM 87501.

BACKSTROM, FLORENCE (FLORENCE JENNIE ENGLERT)
Painter, Designer
Preferred Media: Watercolor.
b New York, N Y.
Study & Training: Cooper Union, cast drawing with Victor Perard; Art Stud League New York, anat with Robert Beverly Hale & sketching, painting & life with Frank Reilly.
Exhibitions: Diamond Jubilee, Art Stud League New York, Nat Acad Design Galleries, 50; Newark Mus, N J, 52; Pa Acad Fine Arts, 52; State Mus N J, Trenton, 53; Cherry Festival, Am Artists Prof League, Smithsonian Inst, Washington, D C, 63.
Teaching: Instr adult classes sketching, watercolor & oil, Bergenfield High Sch, N J, 59-61; also private instr.
Positions: Art dir, Takagi Greenwald, New York, 27-29; fashion designer, Alice Price Inc, Englewood, N J, 31-32; artist-illusr, Pattern Fashion, New York, 33-35.
Awards: Am Artists Prof League Gold Cup for Best Watercolor, Garden State Plaza, N J, 60; Am Artists Prof League Third Prize for Watercolor, Fairleigh Dickinson Univ, N J, 63; plus many others.
Bibliography: Philbrook Smith (auth), Florence Backstrom turns enthusiasm on American art week show, In: Music & Arts, Philbrook Smith Publ, N J, 60.
Memberships: Life mem Art Stud League New York; Am Artists Prof League; Painters & Sculptors Soc N J; Ringwood Manor Asn Arts; Bergen Co Artists Guild.
Mailing Address: 84 Carletondale Rd, Ringwood, NJ 07456.

BACKUS, STANDISH, JR
Painter, Illustrator
b Detroit, Mich, Apr 5, 10.
Study & Training: Princeton Univ, AB; Univ Munich.
Work in Public Collections: Santa Barbara Mus Art; Utah State Col; San Diego Fine Arts Soc; Calif Watercolor Soc; Los Angeles Mus Art.
Commissions: Mural, Beckman Instruments, Inc, 55; mosaic mural, Pac War Mem, Corregidor Island, Manila Bay, Panama, 67-68.
Exhibitions: Los Angeles Mus Art, 38-40; Art Inst Chicago, Ill, 40; IBM Corp; Denver Art Mus; one-man show, Santa Barbara Mus Art; plus others.
Teaching: Instr, Univ Calif Exten.
Positions: Naval combat artist, Pac area & Japan, 45; off Navy artist, Byrd Exped to S Pole, 55-56.
Awards: Prizes, Oakland Art Gallery, 39, Calif Watercolor Soc, 40 & Calif State Fair, 48 & 49.
Memberships: Calif Watercolor Soc; Am Fedn Arts; Artists Equity Asn; Am Watercolor Soc; Los Angeles Art Asn; plus others.
Mailing Address: 2626 Sycamore Canyon Rd, Montecito, CA 93103.

BACON, PEGGY
Painter, Writer
b Ridgefield, Conn, May 2, 95.
Study & Training: N Y Sch Fine & Appl Art; Art Stud League New York.

Work in Public Collections: Metrop Mus Art; Whitney Mus Am Art; Brooklyn Mus; Mus Mod Art; plus others.
Exhibitions: Work in many nat exhibs.
Awards: Guggenheim fel, 34; Nat Acad Arts & Lett Award, 44; Butler Inst Am Artists Prize, 55.
Memberships: Nat Acad Design; Soc Am Graphic Artists; Nat Inst Arts & Lett.
Publications: Auth, The inward eye, 52; auth & illusr, Good American witch, Hale, 57; auth, Ghost of Opalina, 57 & auth & illusr, Magic touch, 68, Little; auth, Oddity, Pantheon, 62; also illusr over 60 bks.
Dealer: Kraushaar Galleries, 1055 Madison Ave, New York, NY 10021.
Mailing Address: Box 156, Cape Porpoise, ME 04014.

BADER, FRANZ
Art Dealer, Collector
b Vienna, Austria, Sept 19, 03; U S citizen.
Study & Training: Univ Vienna.
Positions: Owner, Wallishussersche Bookshop, Vienna, 39; v pres & gen mgr, Whyte Gallery, Washington, D C, 39-52; pres, Franz Bader Gallery, Washington, D C, 52-
Specialty of Gallery: Contemporary American art, Washington artists, original graphics.
Collection: Original graphics, contemporary artists and sculpture.
Mailing Address: 2124 Pennsylvania Ave, N W, Washington, DC 20007.

BADERIAN, RUTH
Painter, Educator
Preferred Media: Watercolors.
b New York, N Y, July 2, 27.
Study & Training; Art Stud League New York, scholar; also with Jean Liberte, Harry Sternberg & Barbara Vassilieff.
Work in Public Collections: Long Island Lighting Co, N Y; Sen John D Caemmerer Collection, Albany, N Y.
Exhibitions: Am Artists Prof League, New York, 66-72; Hudson Valley Art Asn, White Plains, N Y, 66-72; Am Watercolor Soc, New York, 70-72; Allied Artists Am, New York, 70-72; Knickerbocker Artists, New York, 71-72.
Teaching: Instr watercolor, Manhasset High Sch, N Y, 67-; instr watercolor, Garden City High Sch, N Y, 71-; instr watercolor, Wheatley High Sch, Westbury, N Y, 71-
Awards: Awards, Am Artists Prof League, 70-71; Herbert Bonhert Award, Hudson Valley Art Asn, 70; traveling exhib award, Am Watercolor Soc, 72.
Memberships: Am Artists Prof League; Hudson Valley Art Asn; Catharine Lorillard Wolfe Art Club, New York; Nat Art League; Art League Nassau Co.
Dealer: Rita Capon, 56 Briarfield Lane, Huntington, NY 11743.
Mailing Address: 390 Congress Ave, East Williston, NY 11596.

BAER, ALAN
Art Administrator
b Philadelphia, Pa, Apr 15, 31.
Study & Training: Colby Col, 52.
Positions: Chmn & managing dir, Int Art Registry (U K) Ltd, London, Eng & New York, N Y, 70-
Memberships: Int Coun Mus; Int Inst Conserv Hist & Artistic Works; World Crafts Coun.
Mailing Address: 111 John St, New York, NY 10038.

BAER, JO
Painter, Writer
Preferred Media: Oils.
b Seattle, Wash, Aug 7, 29.
Study & Training: Univ Wash; Grad Faculty, New Sch Social Res.
Work in Public Collections: Mus Mod Art, New York, N Y; Solomon R Guggenheim Mus, New York; Kölnischer Kunstverein, Köln, W Ger; Suermondt Mus, Aachen, W Ger; James Michener Collection, Univ Tex, Austin.
Exhibitions: Systematic Paintings, Solomon R Guggenheim Mus, 66; Whitney Mus Am Art Painting Ann, New York, 67 & 69; Documenta IV, Mus Friedericianum, Kassel, Ger, 68; 31st Biennial, Corcoran Gallery Art, Washington, D C, 69; Other Ideas, Detroit Art Inst, Mich, 69.
Teaching: Instr painting, Sch Visual Arts, New York, 69-70.
Awards: Nat Coun Arts Award, 68-69.
Bibliography: P Schjeldahl (auth), Jo Baer: playing on the senses, N Y Times, 5/14/72; C Ratcliff (auth), Jo Baer: notes on 5 recent paintings, Artforum, 5/72; L R Lippard (auth), Color at the edge, Art News, 5/72.
Publications: Auth, Edward Kienholz: a sentimental journeyman, Art Int, 4/68; auth, Mach bands: art and vision & Xerography and edge-effects (collateral essay), Aspen Mag, fall-winter 70; con-

tribr, Symposium on art and politics, Artforum, 9/70; auth, Fluorescent light culture, Am Orchid Soc Bull, 9-10/71.
Dealer: Richard Bellamy, 1078 Madison Ave, New York, NY 10028.
Mailing Address: 53 E Tenth St, New York, NY 10003.

BAHM, HENRY
Painter
b Boston, Mass, Feb 26, 20.
Study & Training: Mass Sch Art, Boston; Boston Mus Fine Arts Sch.
Work in Public Collections: Walter P Chrysler Collection; Univ N C; John P Merriam Collection, Boston; Boston Mus Fine Arts; Dillard Collection, S C.
Commissions: Mural, Foxboro Clubhouse, Mass.
Exhibitions: Los Angeles Co Mus, Los Angeles, Calif, 50; Norfolk Mus, Va, 59; Univ N C, 60; Columbia Mus, S C, 62; Boston Arts Festival, 65.
Teaching: Pvt classes in painting.
Awards: Jordan Marsh Co Award; purchase prizes, Cooperstown Art Asn & Univ N C.
Memberships: Berwick Art Ctr, Pa; De Cordova Mus, Mass; Provincetown Art Asn; Boston Mus Fine Arts & Norfolk Mus; Copley Soc Boston.
Dealer: New England Picture Frame Co, 845 Allens Ave, Providence, RI 02905.
Mailing Address: 755 Beacon St, Newton, MA 02159.

BAILEY, CLARK T
Sculptor, Educator
Preferred Media: Welded Steel.
b Chickasha, Okla, Nov 10, 32.
Study & Training: Univ Houston, BFA; Inst Allende, San Miguel de Allende, Mex, MFA; also with Richard Hunt.
Commissions: Fountain, Mr & Mrs Charles Berry, Casady Sch, Oklahoma City, Okla, 70; and smaller works in many private collections.
Exhibitions: Ann Exhib, Nat Acad Design, New York, N Y, 67; 37th, 38th & 39th Ann Exhibs, Nat Sculpture Soc, New York, 70-72; Xerox Exhib, Rochester, N Y, 71.
Teaching: Prof art, Okla Col Lib Arts, 58-
Positions: Staff artist, Houston Pub Schs, Tex, 54-56; post illusr, U S Army, Ft Chaffee, Ark, 56-58.
Awards: Best in show, Tex-Okla Ann Exhib, 67 & 68; Mahonri Young Award, Nat Acad Design, 67; C Percival Dietsch Award, Nat Sculpture Soc, 70.
Memberships: Nat Sculpture Soc; Okla Mus Art.
Publications: Contribr, Prize winning sculpture, Allied, 66; contribr, La Rev Mod, 67 & Sculpture Rev, 70 & 71.
Mailing Address: 124 Farris Pl, Chickasha, OK 73018.

BAILEY, JAMES ARLINGTON, JR
Painter, Restorer
Preferred Media: Oils.
b Ft Lauderdale, Fla, May 26, 32.
Study & Training: Univ Fla; Univ Denver; Univ Md Overseas Exten, Saudi Arabia; Georgetown Univ, BSFS.
Work in Public Collections: Univ N C Mus, Greensboro; Norton Gallery, West Palm Beach, Fla; Princeton Univ, N J; Mus Contemp Art, Houston, Tex; Columbus Mus, Ohio.
Exhibitions: Gulf Coast Regional, Mobile, Ala, 66-68; Max 24 Exhibition, Purdue Univ, Lafayette, Ind, 68-69; Soc Four Arts, Palm Beach, Fla, 69-70; Art for Peace Exhibition, Dainenburg Gallery, New York, N Y, 70; Graphikbiennale, Vienna, Austria, 72.
Awards: Purchase award, Weatherspoon Mus, Univ N C, 67.
Publications: Contribr, Lo que es y ha sido la pintura, Vanidades, 12/70.
Dealer: Mirell Gallery, Florida & Rice Sts, Coconut Grove, FL 33133.
Mailing Address: 7719 S W 69th Ave, South Miami, FL 33143.

BAILEY, MALCOLM C W
Painter, Illustrator
Preferred Media: Acrylics, Enamels, Ink, Wash.
b New York, N Y, Aug 18, 47.
Study & Training: Pratt Inst, BFA, 69.
Work in Public Collections: Mus Mod Art, New York, Whitney Mus Am Art.
Exhibitions: Afro-American Artists since 1950, Brooklyn Col, 69; Whitney Ann Am Painting, 69 & 72 & one-man exhib, 71, Whitney Mus Am Art; Paperworks by 22 Young Artists, Mus Mod Art, New York, 70.
Teaching: Adj instr painting, Cooper Union, New York, spring 70.
Awards: Fel award, Yaddo, 69-70 & MacDowell Colony, 70.
Bibliography: Barbara Rose (auth), Black artists in America, Art in Am, 70; Grace Glueck (auth), Review of one-man show, Whitney Mus, N Y Times, 71.
Publications: Contribr, cover, Art Gallery Mag, 70.
Mailing Address: 462 Broome St, New York, NY 10013.

BAILEY, WALTER ALEXANDER
Painter, Art Administrator
Preferred Media: Oils, Acrylics.
b Wallula, Kans, Oct 17.
Study & Training: Kansas City Art Inst, Mo; Bus Col, Leavenworth, Kans; Fr Inst Lett, dipl; also with John Douglas Patrick, Anthony Angarola, Adolphe Blondheim, Charles A Wilimovsky, Randall Davey, Ross Braught, Thomas Hart Benton & Leon Gaspard.
Work in Public Collections: Springfield Pub Libr, Mass; Kansas City Pub Libr, Mo.
Commissions: Watercolor sketches, Univ Kans, Lawrence, 27; watercolor sketches, Univ Tex, Austin, 28; two murals, William Rockhill Nelson Gallery Art, Kansas City, Mo, 35; four murals, Orchestra Promenade, Music Hall, Munic Auditorium, Kansas City, 36; mural, E High Sch, Kansas City, 37.
Exhibitions: Louis Comfort Tiffany Guild Exhibs, Anderson Galleries, New York, N Y, 26, 27 & 29; Midwestern Art Exhib Ann, Kansas City Art Inst; one-man show, Mexico City, Mex, 30; 13th Ann W Coast Paintings Exhib, Charles & Emma Frye Mus, Seattle, Wash, 67; All-City Outdoor Art Festival, Los Angeles, Calif, 68.
Teaching: Instr landscape painting, Master Class, Taos, N Mex, 27-29; instr landscape painting, Master Class, Kansas City, Mo, 32-34; instr landscape painting, Kansas City Art Inst, 38-39.
Positions: Ed art dir, Kansas City Times, 17-27; motion picture story-bd artist, educ films, Douglas Aircraft Co, Santa Monica, Calif, 41-42; scenic artist, motion picture studios, Hollywood, Calif, 43-44; night art dir, Los Angeles Examr, Calif, 50-61; art ed, Los Angeles Herald-Examr, 62-67.
Awards: Louis Comfort Tiffany Found fel, 24; Am Inst Fine Arts fel, 65; Jose Drudis Found fel, 66; plus others.
Bibliography: Sally Sooner (auth), article, In: Daily Sun Okla, Oklahoma City, 11/23/30; Allen Charles (auth), article, In: Art Digest, 36; Howard Burke (auth), article, In: Los Angeles Examr, 12/11/59.
Memberships: Calif Nat Watercolor Soc; Am Inst Fine Arts (pres, 67-68); Calif Art Club (dir, 63 & 66-67); Valley Artists' Guild (v pres & dir, 62-64); Am Artists West (dir, 65-72); plus others.
Publications: Contribr, Kansas City Star & Art Digest, 27-28; contribr, South Pasadena Rev, Calif, 72.
Mailing Address: 1417 Twelfth Ave, Los Angeles, CA 90019.

BAILEY, WILLIAM H
Painter
Preferred Media: Oil.
b Council Bluffs, Iowa, Nov 17, 30.
Study & Training: Yale Univ, Alice Kimball English traveling fel & BFA, 55, MFA, 57; with Josef Albers.
Work in Public Collections: Mus Art, Aachen, Ger; Weatherspoon Mus, Greensboro, N C; Speed Art Mus, Louisville, Ky; Kresge Art Ctr, Mich State Univ, E Lansing; Ind Univ Mus Art, Bloomington.
Exhibitions: One-man show, Kans City Art Inst, Mo, 67; Realism Now, Vassar Col Art Mus, Poughkeepsie, N Y, 68; Twenty-two Realists, Whitney Mus Am Art, New York, N Y, 70; one-man shows, Robert Schoelkopf Gallery, New York, 71 & Univ Conn, Storrs, 72.
Teaching: Prof fine arts, Ind Univ, 62-69; prof art, Yale Univ, 69-
Awards: First prize painting, Boston Arts Festival, 57; Guggenheim Found fel painting, 65.
Bibliography: Hilton Kramer (auth), William Bailey and the artifice of realism, New York Times, 10/31/71; Jerrold Lanes (auth), Problems of representation—are we asking the right questions?, Art Forum Mag, 1/72; Robert Hughes (auth), The realist as corn god, Time Mag, 1/31/72.
Dealer: Robert Schoelkopf, 825 Madison Ave, New York, NY 10021.
Mailing Address: 344 Willow, New Haven, CT 06511.

BAILEY, WORTH
Museum Curator, Art Historian
b Portsmouth, Va, Aug 23, 08.
Study & Training: William & Mary Col; Univ Pa, BA.
Work in Public Collections: Univ Pa; Valentine Mus Art; Col William & Mary.
Commissions: Designed Christmas card series; Alexandria Commemorative Stamp, 49.
Exhibitions: Norfolk, Williamsburg & Richmond, Va.
Positions: Cur, Jamestown Archeol Proj, 33-38; cur, Mount Vernon, Va, 38-51; cur consult, Nat Trust Hist Preservation, Washington, D C, 51-56; consult, Our Town 1749-1865, spec exhib, Alexandria Asn, 56; cur, Alexander Hamilton Bicentennial Exhib, U S Treasury Dept, 57; archit consult, hist Am Bldgs Surv, Nat Park Serv, Washington, D C, 58-66; ed, Historic American buildings survey catalogue supplement, 59; historian, Am Bldgs Survey, Wis Archit, 65; fine arts comt, Sully Plantation, Fairfax Co, 63-69.
Awards: Norfolk Soc Artists Awards, 26-28; Brookings Inst Ctr Advan Study fel, 62.

Memberships: Am Asn Mus; Am Soc Archit Historians; Hist Alexandria Found.
Publications: Auth, Safeguarding a heritage, 63; illusr, Christmas with the Washingtons, Seaport in Virginia & George Washington's Alexandria; contribr, With heritage so rich, 66, Encycl Am & var art, antique & hist mags.
Mailing Address: 8029 Washington Rd, Alexandria, VA 22308.

BAILIN, HELLA
Painter
b Dusseldorf, Ger, Oct 17, 15; U S citizen.
Study & Training: Berlin Acad, 34, Reimann Sch, Berlin, 36, Newark Sch Fine & Indust Arts, 47 & 52-56.
Work in Public Collections: Washington Sch Psychiatry, Washington, D C; Temple Beth Ahm, Springfield, N J; plus others.
Commissions: Painting & mural, Marshall Sch, South Orange, N J, 63; murals, Mennen Prod, Morristown, N J, 63 & Consol Gas Co, Metuchen, N J, 63.
Exhibitions: Am Watercolor Soc; Nat Acad Design; Audubon Artists; Watercolor: U S A; Allied Artists Am.
Awards: Stanley Mem Award, Nat Asn Women Artists, 69; Ted Kautzky Award, Am Watercolor Soc, 70; David Wuject-Key Mem Prize, Allied Artists Am, 72.
Memberships: N J Watercolor Soc; Allied Artists Am; assoc Artists N J; Am Watercolor Soc; Portraits, Inc; plus others.
Mailing Address: 820 Bishop St, Union, NJ 07083.

BAIRD, JOSEPH ARMSTRONG, JR
Writer, Educator
b Pittsburgh, Pa, Nov 22, 22.
Study & Training: Oberlin Col, BA (magna cum laude), 44; Harvard Univ, MA, 47, PhD, 51.
Collections Arranged: Numerous exhib Calif Hist Soc, San Francisco, 62-63, 67-70, & Univ Calif, Davis, 53-
Teaching: Instr art hist, Univ Toronto, 49-53; from instr to prof, Univ Calif, Davis, 53-61, lectr, 61-
Positions: Cur, Calif Hist Soc, 62-63; art consultant, 67-70; cataloguer, Robert B. Honeyman, Jr Collection, Bancroft Libr, Univ Calif, Berkeley, 64-65.
Awards: Award merit, Calif Hist Soc, 62.
Memberships: Am Fedn Arts; Nat Trust Hist Preserv; Soc Archit Historians.
Research: Latin American architecture; California architecture, painting and graphic arts.
Collection: Art and life in the 19th and 20th century.
Publications: Auth, Time's wondrous changes: San Francisco architecture, 1776-1915, Calif Hist, 62; The churches of Mexico, Univ Calif Press, 62; Catalogue of the original paintings, drawings and water colors in the Robert B Honeyman, Jr Collection, Bancroft Libr, Univ Calif, Berkeley, 68; California's pictorial letter sheets, David Magee, S F, 67; Historic lithographs of San Francisco (in print), 72; also compiler & ed several exhib catalogues.
Mailing Address: 1830 Mt View Dr, Tiburon, CA 94920.

BAIRD, ROGER LEE
Sculptor, Instructor
Preferred Media: Wood, Metal, Plastics, Mixed Media.
b Washington, D C, May 20, 44.
Study & Training: Calif Col Arts & Crafts, BFA, 66, MFA, 68.
Work in Public Collections: City of Napa Collection, Calif; City of Walnut Creek Collection, Calif.
Commissions: Founders Medallion, Calif Col Arts & Crafts, Oakland, Calif, 68.
Exhibitions: One-man show, Richmond Art Ctr, Calif, 65; two-man show, Comara Gallery, Los Angeles, Calif, 65; Sculpture Los Angeles, 65, Munic Art Gallery, 65; Zellerbach Mem Competition Art Sculpture, Palace Legion of Honor, San Francisco, Calif, 65; Art Inst Centennial Exhib, San Francisco Mus Art, 71.
Teaching: Instr jewelry & metal arts, Merritt Col, 66-71; instr jewelry & metal arts, San Francisco City Col, 71-
Mailing Address: 1526 E 17th St, Oakland, CA 94606.

BAKANOWSKY, LOUIS J
Sculptor, Designer
Preferred Media: Mixed Media.
b Norwich, Conn, Oct 8, 30.
Work in Public Collections: Syracuse Univ, N Y.
Commissions: Mem structure, Brunswick, Maine, 73.
Exhibitions: View, 60 & Selection, 61, Inst Contemp Art, Boston, Mass; one-man show, Siembab Gallery, Boston, 60; Sculpture, DeCordova Mus, Lincoln, Mass, 64; New England Art Today, Boston, 65.
Teaching: Asst prof design, Cornell Univ, 61-62; prof design, Harvard Univ Grad Sch Design, 63-
Positions: Designer, Cambridge Seven Assocs, Inc, 62-

Awards: Sculpture prizes, Boston Arts Festival, 58 & Providence Art Festival, 59.
Bibliography: Sculpture of Louis J Bakanowsky, Connection Mag, 61; Louis J Bakanowsky, Kenchiku Bunka Mag, 71.
Mailing Address: 2 Barberry Rd, Lexington, MA 02173.

BAKER, ANNA P
Painter, Graphic Artist
b London, Ont, June 12, 28.
Study & Training: Univ Western Ont, BA; Art Inst Chicago, BFA & MFA.
Work in Public Collections: Libr Cong, Washington, D C; London Pub Libr & Art Mus; Cleveland Mus Art; Ball State Teachers Col, Muncie, Ind; Univ Western Ont.
Exhibitions: Saint Paul, Minn, 62; Philadelphia Art Alliance; Oklahoma Printmakers, 63; DeCordova Mus; Los Angeles, Calif, 66; G W Smith Mus, Springfield, Mass; plus others.
Awards: Mr & Mrs Frank Glogan Prize painting, Art Inst Chicago; purchase prize, Cleveland Mus Art; Can Coun grant, 68.
Memberships: Can Painters, Etchers & Engravers.
Mailing Address: Barton, VT 05822.

BAKER, CHARLES EDWIN
Art Historian, Writer
b Harlan, Iowa, Dec 16, 02.
Study & Training: State Univ Iowa, BA & MA; Columbia Univ.
Positions: Ed, Hist Records Surv, New York, 37-41; ed, New York Hist Soc, 44-71.
Memberships: Am Asn State & Local Historians; N Y State Hist Asn; Soc Am Historians.
Publications: Auth, The American art union, 53; auth, Dictionary of artists in America, 1564-1860, Yale Univ Press, 57; contribr to art mag & ed of bks on the hist Am art.
Mailing Address: 4652 Manhattan College Pkwy, New York, NY 10471.

BAKER, EUGENE AMES
Painter
Preferred Media: Oils, Acrylics, Watercolors, Serigraphy.
b Dyersberg, Tenn, Jan 6, 28.
Study & Training: Calif Col Arts & Crafts, BA (art educ, high distinction), 51.
Exhibitions: Monterey Co Fair, Calif, 54-62; Laguna Beach Invitational Festival Arts, Calif, 56-59; Young Collector's Show, Dallas Mus Fine Arts, Tex, 59; guest artist, Wash State Fair, Puyallup, 64-65; one-man shows, Zantman Art Galleries, Ltd, Carmel, Calif, 70-71.
Teaching: Instr arts & crafts, Pac Grove High Sch, Calif, 51-52; instr oil painting & drawing, Monterey Peninsula Col, Calif, 57-62.
Positions: Bd dirs, Am Fedn Arts, Carmel, Calif.
Awards: Watercolor award, Laguna Beach Festival Arts, 56; watercolor award, Monterey Co Fair, 54-57 & 59-62.
Bibliography: Carl Martin (auth), Reason and passion, Game & Gossip, 52.
Memberships: Carmel Art Asn (v pres-treas, 53-).
Dealers: Les Enfants Art Gallery, 416 Bourbon St, New Orleans, LA 70130; Zantman Art Galleries, Ltd, Sixth & San Carlos, Carmel, CA 93921.
Mailing Address: P O Box 335, Carmel Valley, CA 93924.

BAKER, GEORGE
Sculptor
Preferred Media: Bronze, Aluminum.
b Corsicana, Tex, Jan 23, 31.
Study & Training: Col Wooster; Occidental Col, BA; Univ Southern Calif, MFA.
Work in Public Collections: Mus Mod Art & Whitney Mus Am Art, New York, N Y; Mus 20th Century Art, Vienna, Austria; Forest of Sculptures, Hakone, Japan; San Diego State Col, Calif.
Commissions: Kinetic fountain, Int Sculptors Symposium, Expo '70, Osaka, Japan, 69; kinetic hanging sculpture, comn by State Calif for San Diego State Col, 72; kinetic sculpture, Linwood State Bank, Kansas City, Mo, 72.
Exhibitions: Erlangen, Ger, 68; Kaiser Ctr, Oakland, Calif, 68; Mus Mod Art, New York, 68; Whitney Mus Am Art, 68 & 70; Studio Marconi, Milan, Italy, 70.
Teaching: Instr sculpture, Univ Southern Calif, 60-64; asst prof sculpture, Occidental Col, 64-
Awards: Int Sculptors Symposium, Osaka, Japan, 69; artist-in-residence, Berlin, Ger, 71-72.
Bibliography: Articles, In: Quadrum, Brussels, 64, Art & Artists, London, 66 and Art in Am, 66 & 67.
Mailing Address: 2697 Tanoble Dr, Altadena, CA 91001.

BAKER, GRACE
Painter
Preferred Media: Oil.
b Riverdale, N Y.
Study & Training: Finch Col, BA; pvt study with William Oden-Waller.
Work in Public Collections: Am Int Underwriters Corp, New York, N Y; Art Loft, Williamsburg, Va; Loan-Own Art Gallery, Peninsula Art Asn, Newport News, Va; Art Graphic Gallery, Hampton, Va; Blue Ribbon Restaurant, Yulan, N Y.
Commissions: Portrait of Lawrence J Troiano, Riverdale, N Y, 66; oil still life, Blue Ribbon Restaurant, 67; portrait for Mrs James Henkel, Newport News, 70; The Old Mill, Mr & Mrs Henry F Henrici, Williamsburg, 72; Topaz, oil, Holly Paterson, Williamsburg, 72.
Exhibitions: Peninsula Art Asn Shows, 70-71; XXI Biennial, Tidewater Artists Asn, Chrysler Mus, Norfolk, Va, 70; Spec Maritime Exhib, Mariners Mus, Newport News, 71; World Health Day 1972, UN Postage Stamp Design Competition, 71-72; pvt exhib, Bank Hampton Roads, Hampton, Va, 72.
Positions: Mem int panel of artists, UN Postage Stamp Design, 70-
Awards: Second pl, Better Living Show, 71; second pl in oils, Todd Ctr Arts Festival, 72.
Memberships: Tidewater Artists Asn; Peninsula Arts Asn; Va Mus Fine Arts; Occasion for the Arts; Am Artists Prof League.
Dealers: The Art Loft, 439 Prince George St, Williamsburg, VA 23185; Famous French Galleries Ltd, Rte 3, Box 274B, Williamsburg, VA 23185.
Mailing Address: P O Box 2962, Williamsburg, VA 23185.

BAKER, MILDRED
Art Administrator
b Brooklyn, N Y, Aug 14, 05.
Study & Training: Univ Rochester, 23-25.
Collections Arranged: Owned in New Jersey, 46; Work by American Negro Artists, 46; Creative Photography in New Jersey; Modern Architecture in New Jersey; Newark Museum's First Exhibition of Work by New Jersey Artists, 52.
Positions: Asst to exec secy, Col Art Asn, 30-33; dir, Woodstock Art Gallery, 34-35; asst to dir & asst dir, Fed Art Proj, Works Progress Admin, Washington, D C, 35-43; asst to dir, Newark Mus, 44-49, asst dir, 49-53, assoc dir, 53-71; ed, Newark Mus News Notes, 45-68; ed, The Mus, 48-71.
Memberships: Am Asn Mus; Am Fedn Arts.
Mailing Address: 569 Mt Prospect Ave, Newark, NJ 07104.

BAKER, RICHARD BROWN
Collector
b Providence, R I, Nov 5, 12.
Study & Training: Yale Univ, BA, 35; Oxford Univ, Rhodes scholar, 35-38, BA & MA; Art Stud League New York; Hans Hofmann Sch Fine Arts.
Exhibitions: (Richard Brown Baker Collection) R I Sch Design Mus Art, 64 & 73; Staten Island Inst Arts & Sci, 60; Drew Univ, 60 & 62; Walker Art Ctr, 61; Jewett Art Ctr, Wellesley Col, 63; Yale Univ Art Gallery, 63; Univ R I, Kingston, 64; Larry Aldrich Mus Contemp Art, 66; Oakland Univ Art Gallery, Rochester, Mich & Univ Wis Art Gallery, Milwaukee, 67; Univ South Fla, 67 & 69; Mus Art Mod, Mexico City, 68; Univ Notre Dame, Ind, 69.
Positions: Mem, Comt on Art Gallery of Univ Coun, Yale Univ, 62-66, 71-; mem, Mus Comt, R I Sch Design Corp annually 66-
Bibliography: Kenneth B Sawyer (auth), Richard Brown Baker, U S collector of modern art, Studio Int, London, 1/65.
Memberships: Mus Mod Art; life fel Metrop Mus Art; assoc Solomon R Guggenheim Mus; Am Asn Mus; fel Pierpont Morgan Libr.
Collection: Recent art in all media (earliest 1945), international in origin, although preponderantly by U S artists.
Publications: Auth, Notes on the formation of my collection, Art Int, 9/20/61; co-auth, Two in the first row, Art in Am, 10/63.
Mailing Address: 1185 Park Ave, New York, NY 10028.

BAKER, MRS WALTER C
Collector
Collection: Graphic arts.
Mailing Address: 555 Park Ave, New York, NY 10022.

BAKKE, LARRY HUBERT
Educator, Painter
Preferred Media: Oils, Collage.
b Vancouver, B C, Jan 16, 32.
Study & Training: Univ Wash, BA & MFA; Syracuse Univ, PhD, art hist with Laurence Schmeckebier & art educ with Michael F Andrews.
Work in Public Collections: Everett Col; Syracuse Univ.
Exhibitions: Figure Painting Invitational, Univ B C Fine Arts Gallery, Vancouver, 63; Nat Exhib Small Paintings, Purdue Univ Art Gallery, Ind, 54; The Painter and the Photograph, Univ N Mex

Art Gallery, Albuquerque, 64-65; 97th Ann Exhib, Am Watercolor Soc, New York, N Y, 64; Cortland Invitational - Seven Syracuse Artists, Cortland Fine Arts Gallery, N Y, 70.
Teaching: Vis prof, Univ Victoria, summers 58-71; instr art hist, drawing & painting, Everett Col, 59-63; assoc prof aesthetics, painting & synaesthetics, Syracuse Univ, 63-; vis prof, Villa Giglucci, Florence, Italy, summer 68.
Awards: First prize, Northwest Watercolor, Seattle Art Mus, 62; Northwest Painters Award, Puget Sound Group Northwest Painters, 63; First prize for painting, Spokane-Northwest Painters, 63.
Bibliography: Margaret Harold (auth), Prize-winning watercolors, Allied Publ, 63; Van Deren Coke (auth), The painter and the photograph, Univ N Mex Press, 64; Laurence Schmeckebier (auth), Larry Bakke, drawings and paintings, 1957-1969, Syracuse Univ Press, 69.
Memberships: Nat Art Educ Asn.
Publications: Co-auth, Washington Education, 62; auth, Creative crafts, 63; auth, New York State Art Teachers Bull, 70; co-auth, Synaesthetic education, 71.
Mailing Address: 309 University Pl, Syracuse, NY 13210.

BALART, WALDO
Painter
Preferred Media: Constructions, Mixed Media.
b Banes, Cuba, Feb 10, 31; US citizen.
Study & Training: Univ Havana, 50-51, CPA, 54; Univ St Thomas Villaneuva, Havana, 55-56; Mus Mod Art New York, 59-62.
Work in Public Collections: Mus Mod Art, New York, N Y; Metrop Mus Art, New York; Museo Arte Contemporaneo, Madrid, Spain.
Exhibitions: Iris Olert Gallery, Paris, France, 67; Cisneros Gallery, New York, N Y, 69; Benson Gallery, Bridgehampton, N Y, 70; Graham Gallery, New York, 71; Museo Arte Contemporaneo, Madrid, 72.
Teaching: Instr art, Southampton Col, summer, 67.
Mailing Address: Covarrubias 9, Madrid 10, Spain.

BALES, GEORGE CARSON (BOB)
Painter, Illustrator
Preferred Media: Oils, Inks.
b Terre Haute, Ind, Apr 6, 20.
Study & Training: Univ Ill, BFA; Univ Calif, Los Angeles; Calif Inst Arts; Univ Southern Calif; Pepperdine Univ, MBA; also with Thomas Hart Benton, Robert Philipp, Will Foster, Robert Brackman, Don Graham & Ken Anderson.
Work in Public Collections: U S Air Force Art Collection, Washington, D C; Air Force Mus, Wright-Patterson Air Force Base, Ohio; Air Force Acad, Colorado Springs, Colo.
Commissions: Mural, dean, Col Fine Arts, Univ Ill, 41; mural, Rockford, Ill Ct House, 41; mural, The RB-70 in flight, U S Air Force, Dept Defense, Washington, D C, 62.
Exhibitions: Air Force Exhib, Soc Illus, New York, N Y, 54-60; World Premiere Exhibition of U S Air Force Art, Smithsonian Inst, Washington, D C, 60; USAF in the Pacific, Raymond Burr Galleries, Beverly Hills, Calif, 61; Air Force in Aerospace, Denver Art Mus, 62; one-man show, Pacific & Far East, Arts Club Washington, D C, 53.
Positions: Layout artist, Walt Disney Prods, 45-47; combat artist Korean conflict, U S Air Force, 50-51, off illusr, 52-62; dir, World-wide Air Force Documentary Prog, 54-62; res consult, Heritage of the Air, Leach Corp, Los Angeles, 62-69; art dir, The Last Moment (film), Yasin Prods, Hollywood, Calif, 65-67.
Awards: Art Dir Award Excellence, New York, 62; gold medal achievement, Soc Illus, New York, 63; arts & lett award, Air Force Asn, Washington, D C, 63.
Bibliography: Joe Dunford (auth), The Air Force on canvas, Pelican Films, 60.
Memberships: Soc Illus New York; Soc Desert Painters, Calif.
Publications: Auth, Artists & the USAF, Famous Artists Mag, 6/54; contribr, Art takes to the air, Am Artist Mag, 8/55; co-auth, Artists roam the world of the USAF, Nat Geog Mag, 5/60; illusr, Ernie Pyle's Southwest, 2/65; auth & illusr, The feasibility of an allied health program in the small independent college, 12/71.
Dealer: Hammer Galleries, 781 Fifth Ave, New York, NY 10022.
Mailing Address: 3500 Manchester Blvd, Townhouse 230, Inglewood, CA 90305.

BALES, (LEEOMA) JEWEL
Painter
Preferred Media: Watercolor.
b Purcell, Okla, Aug 28, 11.
Study & Training: With William B Schimmel, Douglas Greenbowe and others.
Work in Public Collections: Alhambra High Sch, Phoenix, Ariz; Mesa City Libr, Mesa, Ariz; Baptist Hosp, Phoenix.
Exhibitions: Am Watercolor Soc, Nat Acad Design Galleries, New York, N Y, 62; Tucson Regional, Art Ctr, Ariz, 63, 66 & 68; Ann,

Ariz State Fair, Phoenix; Ann Traveling Exhib, Ariz Watercolor Asn; Open Watercolor Show, Phoenix Art Mus.
Awards: First award for Tree Study, Mesa Art League, 61; People's Choice for Winter Fun, Ariz State Fair, 69; purchase award for Winter Fun, Ariz Bank, 69.
Memberships: Ariz Watercolor Asn (pres, 69-71, treas, 72-73); Ariz Artist Guild (v pres, 64-66); Nat. League Am Pen Women (treas, 71-72); Int Platform Asn.
Mailing Address: 8122 N Eighth Ave, Phoenix, AZ 85021.

BALKIND, ALVIN LOUIS
Art Administrator, Educator
b Baltimore, Md, Mar 28, 21; Can citizen.
Study & Training: Johns Hopkins Univ, BA; study at the Sorbonne.
Teaching: Assoc prof museology, Univ B C, 67-
Positions: Dir, Fine Arts Gallery, Univ B C, 67-
Research: Museology, contemporary art.
Mailing Address: Fine Arts Gallery, University of British Columbia, Vancouver 8, B C, Can.

BALLINGER, HARRY RUSSELL
Painter, Writer
Preferred Media: Watercolors, Oils.
b Port Townsend, Wash, Sept 4, 92.
Study & Training: Univ Calif, San Francisco, 10-11; Art Stud League New York, 12-13; with Harvey Dunn, Paris, 15-16; Acad Colorossi, Paris, France, 27.
Work in Public Collections: New Brit Mus Am Art; Wadsworth Atheneum, Hartford, Conn; Springfield Art Mus, Mass; Cent Conn State Col, Meriden; Arts & Crafts Soc; plus others.
Commissions: Murals, Plant High Sch, West Hartford, Conn.
Exhibitions: Salmagundi Club, New York, N Y; Nat Acad Design, New York; Audubon Artists; Allied Artists Am; Am Watercolor Soc, London, Eng & Traveling Exhibs; plus others.
Teaching: Instr art, Conn Cent Col, 45-59.
Awards: Nine prizes, Salmagundi Club, 44-64; five prizes, Rockport Art Asn, 53-63; N Shore Art Asn Prize, 64; plus others.
Memberships: Salmagundi Club; Allied Artists Am; Audubon Asn; Conn Acad Fine Arts; Am Watercolor Soc; plus others.
Publications: Auth, Painting surf and sea, 57 & Painting boats and harbors, 59; auth, Painting landscapes, 65 & Painting sea and shore, 66, Watson-Guptill; also auth many articles.
Mailing Address: R F D 2, New Hartford, CT 06057.

BALLINGER, LOUISE BOWEN
Educator, Writer
b Palmyra, N J, Feb 9, 09.
Study & Training: Philadelphia Col Art, BFA(art educ), 51; Univ Pa, MS(educ), 61; Pendle Hill; Barnes Found; also painting with Franklin Watkins.
Teaching: Cur schs, Pa Acad Fine Arts, 42-48; from assoc dir to dir dept art educ, Philadelphia Col Art, 48-62; instr, Grad Sch Educ, Univ Pa, 62-66, assoc, 66-
Memberships: Philadelphia Art Alliance; Nat Art Educ Asn (coordr & publicity chmn, 65 conf); Comt Art Educ; Eastern Art Asn (mem coun, 64-).
Publications: Co-auth, Design: sources and resources, 65 & auth, Perspective/space and design, 69, Van Nostrand Reinhold.
Mailing Address: 334 S Camac St, Philadelphia, PA 19107.

BALOG, MICHAEL
Painter, Sculptor
Preferred Media: Multimedia.
b San Francisco, Calif, Apr 30, 46.
Study & Training: Ventura Col, 66-67; Chouinard Art Sch, grad with hons, 69, studied with Stephan Von Huene.
Work in Public Collections: Herbert Distel Mus, Bern, Switz; Univ Iowa, Iowa City; Wichita Art Mus, Kans; Leo Castelli Gallery, New York, N Y.
Exhibitions: One-man shows, Irving Blum Gallery, Los Angeles, 70 & Leo Castelli Gallery, New York, 72; After-Quake, Denver, Colo, 71; The Last Plastic Show, Valencia, Calif, 72; Documenta Five, Kasel, Ger, 72 (via Herbert Distel Mus).
Bibliography: David Shirey (auth), Art, New York Times, 4/1/72; Barbara Rose (auth), Lively arts, New York Mag, 4/72; Brigid Polk (interviewer), Michael Balog, Interview, 5/72.
Dealer: Leo Castelli Gallery, 4 E 77th St, New York, NY 10021.
Mailing Address: 55 W 26th St, New York, NY 10010.

BALOSSI, JOHN
Sculptor, Educator
Preferred Media: Aluminum
b Staten Island, N Y, May 28, 31.
Study & Training: Columbia Univ, BFA & MA.
Work in Public Collections: Mus Mod Art, New York, N Y; Finch Col Mus, New York; Chase Manhattan Collection, San Juan, P R; Ponce Mus, P R.

Commissions: Mural, Stud Union Bldg, Univ P R, 69; aluminum wall relief, Inst Puerto Rican Cult, 71; mural, C R U V Pub Housing, Manati, P R, 72.
Exhibitions: Am Acad Arts & Lett, New York, 68; Primera Bienal Grabado, 70 & Segunda Bienal Grabado, 72, San Juan, P R.
Teaching: Asst prof fine arts, Univ P R Rio Piedras.
Bibliography: R Rivera Garcia (auth), John Balossi: escultor, Artes Visuales, 72; Maria Damoni (auth), Las nubes metalicas de John Balossi, Nuevo Dia, 3/4/72.
Dealer: Ruth White Gallery, 42 E 57th St, New York, NY 10022
Mailing Address: Dept of Fine Arts, University of Puerto Rico, Rio Piedras, PR

BAND, MAX
Painter, Sculptor
b Naumestis, Lithuania, Aug 21, 00; U S citizen.
Study & Training: Acad Art, Berlin, Ger, 20-22; also in Paris, France.
Work in Public Collections: Mus Luxembourg, Petit Palais, Paris & other Europ mus; Fr Art Inst, Philadelphia, Pa; Riverside Mus; Los Angeles Mus Art; Mus Mod Art; plus others.
Commissions: Sculpture F D Roosevelt, White House, Washington, D C, 34; bust President Roosevelt presented to President Kennedy, White House, 61.
Exhibitions: Art Inst Chicago, Ill, 54; Mus Petit Palais, Paris, 55; Calif Palace of Legion of Honor, 56; B'nai B'rith Mus, Washington, D C, 58; Jewish Community Ctr, Long Beach, Calif, 61; also exhibited extensively U S & Europe.
Teaching: Artist-in-residence, Univ Judaism, Los Angeles, 64.
Memberships: Hon mem Calif Art Club; fel Int Inst Arts & Lett.
Publications: Auth, History of contemporary art, 35 & Themes from the Bible.
Mailing Address: 6401 Ivarene Ave, Hollywood, CA 90028.

BANISTER, ROBERT BARR
Gallery Director, Painter
Preferred Media: Oils, Watercolors.
b Sheridan, Ore, May 10, 21.
Study & Training: Univ Ore, BS; Rochester Inst Technol, MA; Western Wash Col; Univ Utah; Univ Ill; Portland State Univ, EdD.
Work in Public Collections: Ford Collection, Detroit, Mich; Kipplinger Collection, Washington, D C; Int Biog, London, Eng; State Dept Collection, Calif; also in collection of Tomaso Campanella, Rome, Italy.
Exhibitions: Witte Mus Exhib, San Antonio, Tex, 60; Tours of Ford Collection, Rotunda, Detroit, 51-69; Kipplinger Publ, Washington, D C, 69; Rome Int, 69; London Int, 71; plus many others.
Collections Arranged: U S Army Touring Exhibitions, 54-55; Men of Art Guild National Touring Exhibition.
Positions: Art supvr, Ore Pub Schs, Klamath Falls, 48-51; art dir, Hq 5th USA, 51-55, 4th USA, 55-60 & 15th USAF SAC, 60-63; art supvr, Moreno Valley Schs, Calif, 63-71; art dir & owner, Lincoln Art Galleries, 71-
Awards: Purchase award, Witte Mus, 60; Tomaso Campanella Award, Rome, 69; Int Biog Award & Queen's Award, London, 71.
Memberships: Ore Arts Comn (bd dirs, 72); Arts in Ore Asn (bd, 72); Riverside Fine Arts Guild (pres bd, 68); Moreno Valley Allied Arts Asn (pres bd, 69-71); Men of Arts Guild (bd dirs, 60).
Specialty of Gallery: Paintings, crafts and sculpture of the Northwest.
Publications: Auth, Developing creativity in children: grades K through 12, 63-71.
Mailing Address: Lincoln Art Galleries, Lincoln County Art Center, 620 N E Hwy 101, Box 424, Lincoln City, OR 97367.

BANKS, ANNE JOHNSON
Painter, Lecturer
Preferred Media: Acrylics.
b New London, Conn, Aug 10, 24.
Study & Training: Wellesley Col, BA, 46; Honolulu Sch Art, with Willson Stamper, 48-50; George Washington Univ, with Thomas Downing, MFA, 68.
Work in Public Collections: Lyman Allyn Mus, New London; George Washington Univ, Washington, D C.
Exhibitions: Monthly Nat Juried Exhib, Madison Gallery, New York, N Y, 62; one-man show, Lyman Allyn Mus, 64; Virginia Artists 71, Va Mus, Richmond, 71; Fairfax Co Area Exhibs, 71 & 72; Northern Va Fine Arts Asn Area Exhib, 72.
Teaching: Lectr art, George Washington Univ, summer 68; instr art, George Mason Col, 68-69; lectr art, Northern Va Community Col, 71-72.
Awards: Hon mention, Fairfax Co Area Show, 71; four merit awards, Art League, Alexandria, Va, 71-72; merit award, Northern Va Fine Arts, 72.
Memberships: Northern Va Fine Arts Asn; Alexandria Art League.
Mailing Address: 1104 Croton Dr, Alexandria, VA 22308.

BANKS, RICHARD
Painter
Preferred Media: Oils.
b West Palm Beach, Fla, Mar 29, 29.
Study & Training: Norton Gallery Art, West Palm Beach, with Ann Norton; Art Stud League New York.
Work in Public Collections: City of New York Mus, N Y; Yale Univ, New Haven, Conn; Parrish Art Mus, Southampton, L I.
Dealer: Environment Gallery, 205 E 60th St, New York, NY 10022.
Mailing Address: 12 E 11th St, New York, NY 10003.

BANKS, VIRGINIA
Painter
Preferred Media: Watercolors.
b Boston, Mass, Jan 12, 20.
Study & Training: Smith Col, BA; State Univ Iowa, MA.
Work in Public Collections: Seattle Art Mus, Volunteer Park, Wash; IBM Collection, New York, N Y; San Francisco Mus Art, Calif; Univ Ill, Urbana-Champaign; Univ Ore Mus Art, Eugene.
Commissions: Portrait of Dr John Hogness (first pres of Inst Med, Acad Arts & Sci), Univ Wash Sch Med, Seattle, 72.
Exhibitions: Pa Acad Fine Arts, Philadelphia, 47-52; Brooklyn Mus, N Y, 49-61; Am Painting Today, Metrop Mus Art, New York, 50; Young American Painters, Imperial Mus, Tokyo & Osaka, Japan, 51; Jeanne Bucher Gallery, Paris, France, 53; plus many one-man shows.
Teaching: Instr studio & art hist, State Univ Iowa, 42-47; instr studio & art hist, Univ Buffalo, Albright Art Sch & N Y State Teachers Col, 47-48; instr studio & art hist, Cornish Art Sch, Seattle, 51-52.
Awards: Award, Pepsi-Cola Competition, 48; Hallmark Int Art Award, 49.
Bibliography: Lynch (auth), How to make collages, Viking, 61; Albe (auth), & Peck (auth), Artists of Puget Sound, Metrop Press, 62.
Mailing Address: 3879 51st Ave, Seattle, WA 98105.

BANNARD, WALTER DARBY
Painter, Art Critic
b New Haven, Conn.
Study & Training: Phillips Exeter Acad; Princeton Univ; Guggenheim Mem Found fel, 68-69.
Work in Public Collections: Whitney Mus Am Art, New York, N Y; Mus Mod Art, New York; N J State Mus, Trenton; Dayton Art Inst, Ohio; Albright-Knox Art Gallery, Buffalo, N Y; plus many others.
Exhibitions: Highlights of the 1969-1970 Art Season, Aldrich Art Mus, 70; Six Painters, Albright-Knox Art Gallery, Baltimore Mus Art & Milwaukee Art Ctr, 71; Whitney Mus Ann, New York, 72; Rubin Gallery, 72; Abstract Painting in the 70's, Mus Fine Arts, Boston, Mass, 72; plus many other group and one-man shows.
Teaching: Vis critic, Columbia Univ, 68; lect, Friends Mod Art, Detroit Mus Fine Art, 69; symposium & seminars, Princeton Univ, New York Univ, Mus Fine Arts, Boston & others, 66-.
Positions: Juror, 51st May Show, Cleveland Mus, 69.
Awards: Nat Found Arts Award, 68-69; purchase award, N J State Mus, 71.
Bibliography: M Tucker (auth), The structure of color, Whitney Mus Am Art, 71; Canvases brimming with color, Life Mag, 9/24/71; Abstract artmaking in the 70's, Christian Sci Monitor, 4/24/72; plus many others.
Publications: Auth, Notes on an auction, Artforum, 9/70; auth, The artist and politics, Artforum, 9/70; auth, Touch and scale: cubism, Pollock, Newman and Still, Artforum, summer 71; Nolands new paintings, Artforum, 11/71; Caro's new sculpture, Artforum, summer, 72; plus many others.
Dealer: Lawrence Rubin Gallery, 49 W 57th St, New York, NY 10019.
Mailing Address: 11 Madison St, Princeton, NJ 08540.

BANTA, E ZABRISKIE (MRS OLIVER SMITH)
Painter, Craftsman
Preferred Media: Oils, Watercolors.
b Philadelphia, Pa.
Study & Training: Cornell Univ; Art Stud League New York; also with Umberto Romano & William McNulty.
Work in Public Collections: Buena Vista Col, Storm Lake, Iowa.
Commissions: Mural of crucifixion, All Saint's Church, Tarpon Springs, Fla, 65.
Exhibitions: Art Club St Petersburg & Fla Fedn Arts, 52; Fla Gulf Coast Art Ctr, 66 & 71; Rockport Art Asn, Mass, 71; Philadelphia Watercolor Club, Pa, 72.
Teaching: Spec instr art, New York City Pub Schs, 35-46.
Positions: Dir & pres, Tarpon Springs Art Asn, 58-65.
Awards: First award, Fedn Fla Artists, 52; gold medal, Am Art Festival, Nags Head, N C, 65; first award, Gulf Coast Art Ctr, 67.

Memberships: Rockport Art Asn; Philadelphia Watercolor Club; Fla Gulf Coast Art Ctr, Fla Artists; Nat League Am Pen Women (v pres, 70).
Dealer: McNichols Art Gallery, Naples, FL 33940.
Mailing Address: 223 Shore Dr, Ozona, FL 33560.

BARANIK, RUDOLF
Painter
Preferred Media: Oil.
b Lithuania, Sept 10, 20; U S citizen.
Study & Training: Art Inst Chicago, 46; Art Students League New York, 47; Acad Julian, Paris, France, 48; with Fernand Leger, 49-50.
Work in Public Collections: Whitney Mus Am Art & Mus Mod Art, New York, N Y; Mod Mus, Stockholm, Sweden; New York Univ; Univ Mass.
Exhibitions: Recent Work by Young Americans, Mus Mod Art Traveling Exhib, 55; Ann Exhib, Whitney Mus Am Art, 58 & 61; Pa Acad Fine Arts, 64; Int Anti-War Exhib, Tokyo, Japan, 68; Nat Inst Arts & Lett, 72.
Teaching: Vis artist, Ball State Univ, 64; instr painting, Pratt Inst, 66-; instr painting, Art Stud League New York, 68-
Awards: First prize, N Eng Ann, 68; Raymond Speiser Mem Prize, Pa Acad Fine Arts, 64; Childe Hassam Purchase Prize, Nat Inst Arts & Lett, 68.
Memberships: Artists Equity Asn New York (bd mem, 60-61); Artists & Writers Protest Against the War in Vietnam; Artworkers Coalition, New York.
Publications: Co-auth, The Attica Book, 72.
Mailing Address: 97 Wooster St, New York, NY 10012.

BARBEE, ROBERT THOMAS
Painter, Graphic Artist
b Detroit, Mich, Sept 25, 21.
Study & Training: Cranbrook Acad Art, BA & MFA; Centenary Col; also in Mex.
Work in Public Collections: Butler Inst Am Art, Youngstown, Ohio; Cranbrook Acad Art, Bloomfield Hills, Mich.
Exhibitions: Five shows, Va Mus Fine Arts, Richmond, 53-65 & Traveling Exhibs, 58 & 62; Birmingham Mus Art, 59; Norfolk Mus Art & Sci, 60; Mus Art of Ogunquit, Maine, 62 & 63; Am Fedn Arts, New York, N Y, 65; plus others.
Teaching: Instr painting & drawing, Univ Va, assoc prof art, 70-
Awards: Prizes, Irene Leach Mem Exhib, Norfolk Mus Arts & Sci, 62 & prize, 64, Thalheimer's Invitational Exhib, Richmond, 63.
Mailing Address: Dept of Art, University of Virginia, Charlottesville, VA 22903.

BARBOUR, ARTHUR J
Painter, Illustrator
Preferred Media: Watercolors.
b Paterson, N J, Aug 23, 26.
Study & Training: Newark Sch Fine & Indust Art; also with Avery Johnson, Syd Brown & James Carlin.
Commissions: Watercolors, Women's Day Mag, Ford Motor Co & Essex Chem Corp; mural, Am Artists Christmas Card Group.
Exhibitions: Am Watercolor Soc; Watercolor: U S A; Nat Arts Club, New York, N Y; Am Artists Prof League; one-man show, Beaumont Mus Art, Tex, 65; plus others.
Teaching: Instr watercolor painting, Ringwood Sch Art, N J.
Awards: Awards, Urban Farms Exhib & Plainfield Art Asn, 64; Grumbacher Award, N J Watercolor Soc.
Memberships: Am Watercolor Soc; Knickerbocker Artists; Painters & Sculptors Soc N J; N J Watercolor Soc (traveling exhib chmn); Am Artists Prof League.
Mailing Address: 29 Voorhis Pl, Ringwood, NJ 07456.

BARDAZZI, PETER
Painter
b New York, N Y, Mar 5, 43.
Study & Training: Pratt Inst, BFA, 67; Yale Univ, MFA, 69.
Work in Public Collections: Mus Mod Art, New York.
Exhibitions: Art in Process, Finch Col Mus, 69; Human Concern, Whitney Mus Am Art, 69; one-man show, Cordier & Ekstrom Gallery, 71; Painting & Sculpture Today, Indianapolis Mus Art, 72; Whitney Mus Am Art Painting Ann, 72.
Awards: Fed work study prog award, 68; painting award, New Britain Mus, Conn, 69.
Bibliography: J Canaday (auth), articles, In: New York Times, 5/31/71 & 2/6/72; J Gruen (auth), From the top drawers, N Y Mag, 2/31/71.
Mailing Address: P O Box 502, Canal St Station, New York, NY 10013.

BARDIN, JESSE REDWIN
Painter, Instructor
Preferred Media: Oil on canvas.
b Elloree, S C, Mar 26, 23.
Study & Training: Univ S C, AB & cert in painting; Art Stud League New York with Will Barnet & Harry Sternberg, Bernay merit scholar for advanced study with Byron Browne & Vyclav Vytlacil; research in mus of U S, Europe & Cent Am.
Work in Public Collections: Mint Mus, Charlotte, N C; N C Mus, Raleigh; Williams Col Art Mus, Williamstown, Mass; La State Univ, Baton Rouge, La; S C State Art Collection, Columbia Mus Art.
Commissions: Paintings in business collections throughout the U S.
Exhibitions: 21 Americans, Berlin Acad Art, Ger; Pa Acad Fine Arts Ann, Philadelphia; Butler Inst Am Art, Youngstown, Ohio; 50 Artists-50 States (toured U S 2 years, Am Fed Arts), Burpee Mus, Ill; Contemp S C Artists Tri-centennial Exhib, Greenville Co Art Mus, S C, 71.
Teaching: Instr & supvr painting, Richland Art Sch of Columbia Mus Art, 56-
Awards: Ford Found Purchase Prize, N C State Mus, 60; first purchase prize, Hunter Ann, Hunter Gallery Art, 62; first prize, Springs Mill Art Exhib for N C & S C, three consecutive years.
Bibliography: Margaret Harold (auth), Prize winning paintings, Books II, III, IV & V, Allied Publ, 60-64; Jack Morris (auth), Contemporary artists of South Carolina, Greenville Co Mus Art, 70; Adger Brown (auth), South Carolina art, State Newspaper, 71.
Memberships: Life mem, Art Students League New York; Guild of S C Artists; S C Craftsmen; Columbia Art Asn; Am Craftsmen Coun.
Collection: Contemporary pottery.
Dealer: Betsy Havens Gallery, Inc, 1009 Gervais St, Columbia, SC 29201.
Mailing Address: 1723 Devine St, Columbia, SC 29201.

BAREISS, WALTER
Collector
b Tübingen, W Ger, May 24, 19.
Study & Training: Yale Univ, BS; Columbia Law Sch.
Positions: Trustee, Mus Mod Art, New York, N Y; trustee, Assocs in Fine Arts, Yale Univ; mem vis comt, dept Greek & Roman art, Metrop Mus, New York; mem purchasing comn 20th century art & chmn, Gallery Asn, Bavarian State Mus, Munich, Ger.
Collection: Twentieth century art; Greek vases, fifth and sixth centuries B C.
Mailing Address: 60 E 42nd St, New York, NY 10017.

BARETSKI, CHARLES ALLAN
Art Librarian, Art Historian
b Mount Carmel, Pa, Nov 21, 18.
Study & Training: New York Univ, with Demetrios Tselos, Unified Study Curric scholarships, 35-37; Newark Univ, BA(cum laude), 45; Columbia Univ, BSLS, 46, field res proj on Fine Arts Libr Collections in metrop New York & MSLS, 51; Am Univ, archival dipl, 51, advan archival admin dipl, 55; Univ Notre Dame, MA, 57, PhD, 58; Polish Arts Workshop, Univ Minn Exten, dipl, 60; New York Univ Grad Sch Arts & Sci, MA, 65, PhD, 69.
Collections Arranged: International Folk and Handicrafts Exhibitions (series), 54-56; individual exhibs arts & crafts of Spain, Cuba, Port, Ukraine, Poland, P R, Lithuania, Italy, Greece, Iraq, Hungary, W Cent Africa, Neth & others, 57-
Teaching: Dir-founder, Inst Polish Cult, Seton Hall Univ, 53-54.
Positions: Reporter, Newark Sun Ledger, 35; prof librn, Newark Pub Libr, 38-44, sr art libr asst, 44-47, sr art librn, 48-54, br libr dir, 54-56, 57-
Awards: New York Univ Founder's Day Award for distinguished achievement in doctoral studies, 70; Am Heritage Award for 40 yrs outstanding community serv, J F Kennedy Libr for Minorities, 72; Newark Pub Libr 30-yr serv award, 72.
Bibliography: Herbert S Allan (auth), The good librarian, Ameryka, Vol 38; Dorothy Rowe (auth), Man of letters—the whole alphabet, N J Music & Arts Mag, summer 53; Marina Antoniou (auth), The romance of the Ironbound: a community within a community, Newark, 1-2/70.
Memberships: Am Coun Polish Art Cult Clubs (mem Newark Coun, 54-, nat chmn info ctr, 71-); Polish Am Hist Asn (nat ed mo bull, 61-65); Middle States Coun Social Studies (chmn acad freedom dept, 65-66); Ethnic Res Archives (founder-dir, 72-); Am Soc Aesthet.
Research: Nineteenth century American painting; historical school of Polish painting in the nineteenth century; European folk art of nineteenth and twentieth centuries; history of Polish arts cultural clubs in the United States.
Publications: Auth, The Karolik collection: reappraisal and reaffirmation, Art in Am, winter 52; ed, The Polish pantheon: a roster of men and women of Polish birth or ancestry who have contributed to American culture and world civilization, 58; ed, High horizons education program in New York City, 61; ed, Commemorative history of the Polish University Club of New Jersey, 1928-1963, 63; ed & publ, Ironbound Counselor Community Newspaper, 65; also contribr to many nat arts mag.
Mailing Address: 229 Montclair Ave, Newark, NJ 07104.

BARILE, XAVIER J
Painter, Instructor
b Tufo, Italy, Mar 18, 91; U S citizen.
Study & Training: Cooper Union Art Sch; Art Stud League New York; also with Victor Perard, Louis Mora, Charles Chapman & John Sloan.
Work in Public Collections: Pvt collections in U S & Europe.
Exhibitions: Denver Art Mus, Colo; Newark Mus, N J; one-man show, Santa Fe Mus, New Mex; Whitney Mus Am Art, New York, N Y; Nat Soc Painters in Casein; plus others.
Teaching: Dir art dept, Pueblo Jr Col, 39-45; instr, various art schs, New York, N Y & St Augustine, Fla; lect oil, watercolor & casein painting & monotypes to cols, art ctrs, galleries & clubs.
Bibliography: James Britton (auth), The art of Xavier J Barile, Art Rev Int; article, In: Am Art News; plus others.
Memberships: Artists Equity Asn; Painters & Sculptors Soc N J; Nat Soc Painters in Casein; Am Monotype Soc; Audubon Artists; plus others.
Publications: Illusr, mag stories & covers.
Mailing Address: 180 West End Ave, Apt 25N, New York, NY 10023.

BARINGER, RICHARD E
Painter, Designer
b Elkhart, Ind, Dec 3, 21.
Study & Training: Inst Design, Chicago, with Lazlo Moholy-Nagy & Emerson Woelffer, BA, 48; Harvard Univ Grad Sch, with Walter Gropius, BArch, 50, MArch, 51.
Work in Public Collections: Busch-Reisinger Mus, Harvard Univ; Coop Ins Co, Manchester, Eng; Pac Indemnity Co, Los Angeles, Calif; Univ Mass; Mus Mod Art; plus others.
Exhibitions: Gallery Mod Art, Washington, D C, 63; Mus Mod Art, New York, N Y; Fort Worth Art Ctr, Tex; Finch Col, N Y, 67; Colgate Univ, 68; plus many others.
Teaching: Assoc prof archit, Inst Design, Ill Inst Technol, 55-60; asst prof archit, Columbia Univ, 62-63; vis critic, Univ Pa, 65-66; artist-in-residence, Inst Design, 66-67.
Positions: Pvt practice archit, Chicago, Ill, 55-61; pvt practice archit, New York, N Y, 61-
Awards: Progressive archit award, Progressive Archit Mag, 57; award for residential design, Am Inst Architects, 58; Archit Rec Award, 58; plus others.
Memberships: Fel Am Acad Rome; Am Inst Architects.
Publications: Auth, articles, In: Progressive Archit, Archit Rec, House & Home, Zodiac, Habitare, mags.
Mailing Address: 74 Grove St, New York, NY 10014.

BARKAN, BEBE (BEVERLY ADRIAN)
Painter, Illustrator
Preferred Media: Acrylics, Graphics.
b Brooklyn, N Y, Mar 8, 43.
Study & Training: Hunter Col, BA(art), 64; Inst Allende, Mex, 67; Hunter Col, MA(art), 69, with Ponce de Leon, Richard Lippold, Ray Parker, Tony Smith, George Sugarman & Richard C Zieman.
Commissions: Sculpted sterling silver jewelry, Brentano's, Manhassett, N Y, 68.
Exhibitions: Ninth Ann Nat Exhib Graphics, Mercyhurst Col, Erie, Pa, 69; 16th Ann Exhib, Community Arts Coun S Shore, Hempstead, N Y, 70; Ann Open Exhib, Long Beach Art Asn, N Y, 70; Invitational Show, Nat Coun Jewish Women, New Hyde Park, N Y, 70; 7 Artists on the Green, Merrick, N Y, 70.
Teaching: Instr art, New York City Bd Educ, 64-69.
Positions: Art ed, Bitterroot, Brooklyn, N Y, 72-; art ed, Cross-Cult Commun Press, Merrick, 72-
Awards: Second prize, graphics, Merrick Art League, 69; second prize, collage, Cerebral Palsy Third Ann Art Show, Merrick, 70.
Memberships: Merrick Art League; Long Beach Art Asn.
Publications: Contribr, Washington Sq J, 69; co-auth, The American Hototogisu, 69; illusr, Int poetry festival prog, L I Univ, 72; ed, Bitterroot, summer 72; contribr, Shantih, 72.
Mailing Address: Bebe Originals, 239 Wynsum Ave, Merrick, NY 11566.

BARKER, WALTER WILLIAM
Painter, Writer
b Coblenz, Ger, Aug 8, 21; U S citizen.
Study & Training: Wash Univ, BFA, 48, with Phillip Guston & Max Beckmann; Iowa Univ with Mauricio Lassansky; Univ Ind MFA, 50, with Alton Pickens & Henry Hope.
Work in Public Collections: Mus Mod Art, New York, N Y; Brooklyn

Mus, N Y; Boston Mus Fine Arts, Mass; City Art Mus St Louis, Mo; Los Angeles Co Mus, Los Angeles, Calif.
Exhibitions: Int Exhib Mod Graphic Art, Mus Mod Art, New York, 52; Carnegie Int, Pittsburgh, Pa, 56; American Painting, Va Mus Fine Art, Richmond, 62; Schrift und Bild, Stedelijk Mus, Amsterdam, Holland, 63; Painting and Sculpture Today, Herron Inst Art, Indianapolis, Ind, 67.
Teaching: Lectr art hist, Salem Col, 49-50; instr painting,Washington Univ, 50-62; instr basic found, Brooklyn Mus Sch, 63-66; assoc prof painting, Univ N C, 66-
Positions: Spec corresp, Saint Louis Post-Dispatch, 62-; consult visual arts, St Marks in the Bowery, New York, 63-66; mem vis comt arts, Washington Univ, 68-; chmn N C Chap, Save Venice Comt, 69-
Awards: New Talent U S A Award, 56; spec citation for art rev, Col Art Asn, 66; distinguished alumnus, Washington Univ, 72.
Bibliography: Ernest Smith (auth), Walter Barker, 1958-1968, Webster Col, 68; Mary King (auth), New work by Walter Barker, St Louis Post Dispatch, 68; Joseph Pulitzer, Jr (auth), Walter Barker, Fogg Mus Art, Harvard Univ, 71.
Memberships: Col Art Asn; Max Beckmann Gesellschaft, Munich, Ger (contrib mem, 72-).
Research: Max Beckmann's last years in the United States.
Publications: Auth, Introd to exhib, Max Beckmann in America, Viviano Gallery, 69; contribr, The May collection & Max Beckmann, review, Arts Mag, 12/1/69; Lucian Krokowski & Max Beckmann, The Joseph Pulitzer Collection, Vol 3, 71.
Dealer: Betty Parsons Gallery, 24 W 57th St, New York, NY 10019.
Mailing Address: Art Dept, University of North Carolina, Greensboro, NC 27412.

BARNES, ANNA MARYE
Painter
Preferred Media: Oils, Acrylics.
b Newport News, Va, Mar 31, 18.
Study & Training: Watkins Inst, Nashville, Tenn; Tex Woman's Univ, with Chapman Kelly.
Work in Public Collections: Riley Collection, Greenhow-Repton House, Williamsburg, Va.
Exhibitions: Natchez River Festival, Beaumont, Tex, 65; Tex Painting & Sculptor Show, Dallas Mus Fine Arts, Tex, 66; Tex Fine Art Asn Nat Laguna Gloria, Austin, Tex, 67; Richardson Civic Art Asn, Tex, 71; Tex Fine Art Asn Ann, Univ Tex, Arlington, 72.
Positions: Secy, Beaumont Art League, 60-61; v pres, Tyler Art League, 65-67; mem bd, Dallas Mus Fine Arts, 71-72.
Awards: Humble Oil Co Award, Tex Fine Art Asn Nat; first award, Tyler Art League; second award, Richardson Civic Art Asn.
Memberships: Tex Fine Art Asn (dir region, 72-); Richardson Civic Art Asn (secy, 72-).
Dealer: Edom Art Colony, Edom, TX 75756.
Mailing Address: 15655 Terrace Lawn Circle, Dallas, TX 75240.

BARNES, HALCYONE D
Painter
Preferred Media: Watercolors.
b Dallas, Tex, Mar 31, 13.
Study & Training: Allisons Art Colony, Way, Miss; Univ Tex; also with Karl Zerbe, Fred Conway, Lamar Dodd, Richard Zellner, Andrew Bucci & others.
Work in Public Collections: Brooks Mem Mus; Addison Gallery Am Art, Andover, Mass; Miss Art Asn; Miss State Col Women, Columbus; Miss State Univ, Starkville; also in many pvt cols.
Commissions: Murals, First Nat Bank, McComb, Miss, Delta Elec Co, Greenwood, Miss & Hankins Corp, Magnolia, Miss.
Exhibitions: Delgado Mus Art, New Orleans, 55-60; Birmingham Watercolor Soc, 56, 58 & 60; Mid-S Exhib, Memphis, Tenn, 56-61; Atlanta, Ga, 58-61; Provincetown Art Asn, 59 & 60; plus many others.
Awards: Prizes, Nat Watercolor Exhib, Birmingham, Ala, Miss Art Colony, Stafford Springs, Miss & La Font Exhib, Pascagoula, Miss; plus others.
Memberships: Miss Art Colony; Delgado Mus Art Asn; Nat Watercolor Soc; Provincetown Art Asn; Miss Art Asn.
Mailing Address: Summit, MS 39666.

BARNES, ROBERT M
Painter, Educator
b Washington, D C, Sept 24, 34.
Study & Training: Art Inst Chicago, BFA, 56; Univ Chicago, BFA, 56; Columbia Univ, 56; Hunter Col, 57-61; Univ London Slade Sch, Fulbright grants, 61-63.
Work in Public Collections: Mus Mod Art; Whitney Mus Am Art, New York, N Y; Art Inst Chicago, Ill; Pasadena Art Mus, Calif.
Commissions: Ed lithographs, New York Hilton Hotel, 62.
Exhibitions: Mus Civico, Bologna, 65; Galerie Dragon, Paris, France, 67; Univ Ill, 67; Kansas City Art Inst, 72; Galeria Fanta Spade, Rome, Italy, 72; plus others.

Teaching: Instr grad painting, Ind Univ, 60-61; vis artist, Kansas City Art Inst, 63-64; asst prof painting & drawing, Ind Univ, Bloomington, 65-70, prof, dept fine arts, 70-
Awards: Copley Found Award, 61.
Dealer: Allan Frumkin Gallery, 620 N Michigan Ave, Chicago, IL 60603.
Mailing Address: Palazzo di Mont Acuto 419, 06019 Umbertide (pg), Italy.

BARNET, MR & MRS HOWARD J
Collectors
Mr Barnet, b New York, N Y, Mar 8, 24.
Study & Training: Mr Barnet, New York Univ, BS.
Collection: Paintings.
Mailing Address: Barker's Point Rd, Sands Point, NY 11050.

BARNET, WILL
Painter, Printmaker
b Beverly, Mass, May 25, 11.
Study & Training: Boston Mus Fine Arts Sch, with Phillip Hale, 27-30; Art Stud League New York, with Charles Locke, 30-33.
Work in Public Collections: Boston Mus Fine Arts; Whitney Mus Am Art; Metrop Mus Art; Fogg Mus Art; Cincinnati Art Mus; plus others.
Exhibitions: Inst Contemp Art, Boston; Mus Mod Art; Univ Calif, 68; Univ Ill, 69; retrospective, Assoc Am Artists, 72; plus others.
Teaching: Instr, Art Stud League New York, 36-; instr, Cooper Union Art Sch, 45-65; summer instr, Mont State Col, 51; vis critic, Yale Univ, 52 & 53; guid faculty, Famous Artists Schs, 54-; summer instr, Univ Ohio & Univ Minn, Duluth, 58; instr, Univ Wash, Spokane, summer 63; instr, Des Moines Art Ctr, Iowa, 65; distinguished vis prof, Pa State Univ, 65-66; prof, Cooper Union Art Sch, 65-; instr, Pa Acad Fine Arts, 67-; vis prof, Cornell Univ, 68-69.
Awards: Third prize & purchase prize, 60, prize, 61, Corcoran Gallery Art; Walter Lippincott Prize, Pa Acad Fine Arts, 68.
Bibliography: James T Farrell (auth), The paintings of Will Barnet (monogr), Press Eight, New York, 50; Robert Beverly Hale (auth), introd, In: Will Barnet—27 paintings completed 1960-1968, New York, 68; Robert Doty (auth), foreword, In: Will Barnet—graphics 1932-1972, Catalogue Raisonne, N Y, 72.
Memberships: Am Abstr Artists; Fedn Mod Painters & Sculptors; Soc Am Graphic Artists; life mem Art Stud League New York.
Mailing Address: 43 W 90th St, New York, NY 10024.

BARNETT, EARL D
Designer, Painter
Preferred Media: Oil, Acrylic, Watercolor.
b Trenton, Tenn, Nov 9, 17.
Study & Training: Cleveland Sch Art, with Henry G Keller, Viktor Schreckengost, Willard Combes, Kenneth Bates & Frank Wilcox.
Work in Public Collections: Butler Inst Am Art, Youngstown, Ohio; Contracting Plasterers' & Lathers' Int Asn Union Hall, Washington, D C.
Commissions: Six past pres portraits, Bd Dir Room, Benefit Trust Life Ins Co, Chicago, Ill, 64-70; portrait, Hon Robert Downing, Glenville, Ill, 67; past pres portraits, Contracting Plasterers' & Lathers' Int Asn Union Hall, 67-71; portrait, Adm James Ross, Naval Armory, Chicago, Ill, 70.
Exhibitions: Cooperstown Art Asn Ann, N Y, 62, 63, 65 & 68; Allied Artists Ann, New York, N Y, 64, 67 & 69; Butler Inst Am Art, 65, 67 & 68; Union League Club Ann, Chicago, 67; Mainstreams '72, Marietta, Ohio, 72.
Positions: Art dir, W L Stensgaard & Assocs, Chicago, 46-47; asst art dir & designer, Kling Studios, Chicago, 48-51; v pres & creative dir, J M Callan Co, Chicago, 65-71; v pres & creative dir, Conway Displays, Inc, Niles, Ill, 71-
Awards: Second prize cover competition, Bantam Bks, 57; purchase prize, The Horn & Bell at S Haven, Butler Inst Am Art, 65; award, Out of Steam, Anderson Winter Show, Ind, 72.
Memberships: Cooperstown Art Asn; Munic Art League Chicago. Artists Guild Chicago.
Mailing Address: 2221 Prairie Ave, Glenview, IL 60025.

BARNWELL, JOHN L
Painter
Preferred Media: Oil, Graphics.
b Los Angeles, Calif, Mar 17, 22.
Study & Training: Univ Calif, Berkeley, BA; Newark Sch Fine & Indust Art, N J; Art Stud League New York, with Frank Reilly.
Exhibitions: Knickerbocker Artists, 68; Hunterdon Co Art Ctr State Show, 71; Am Artists Prof League Grand Nat Show, New York, 72; Painters & Sculptors Soc N J, 72; Benedictine Art Awards Finalist Show, New York, 72.
Awards: Spec award, Ringwood Manor Asn Arts State Show, 68; Permanent Pigments Materials Award, Painters & Sculptors Soc N J, 70; patrons award, Hudson Artists State Show, 70.

Memberships: Painters & Sculptors Soc N J; Salmagundi Club; fel Am Artists Prof League; Miniature Art Soc N J; Art Stud League New York.
Dealer: Robbins Art Galleries, Scotland Rd, East Orange, NJ 07018.
Mailing Address: 74 Addison Ave, Rutherford, NJ 07070.

BAROOSHIAN, MARTIN
Painter, Art Administrator
b Chelsea, Mass, Dec 18, 29.
Study & Training: Boston Mus Fine Arts Sch, full tuition scholars, dipls with highest hons, 52 & 55; Albert H Whitlin traveling fel, Europe, 52; Tufts Univ, BSEduc, 53; Boston Univ, MA(art hist), 58; also with Gaston Dorfinant & S W Hayter, Paris, France; master teacher grant, N Y State Dept Educ, 66; U S Dept Educ Asian studies grant, 70.
Work in Public Collections: Montreal Mus Fine Art, P Q; Mus Mod Art, New York, N Y; Metrop Mus Art, New York; Libr Cong, Washington, D C; Lincoln Ctr Mus Performing Arts, New York.
Exhibitions: Young American Printmakers, Mus Mod Art Traveling Show, Europe & Latin Am, 53-55; Boston Printmakers Traveling Exhibs; Soc Am Graphic Artists, New York; First Int Can Graphic Art Exhib, Montreal Mus Fine Art, 71; one-man shows, South Bend Art Ctr, Ind, Honolulu Acad Art, Hawaii & others.
Teaching: Chmn dept art, Burr's Lane Jr High Sch, Dix Hills, N Y, 65-
Positions: Trustee, Montclair Art Mus, N J, 59-60.
Awards: Albert H Whitlin traveling fel, 52; master teacher grant, dept educ, State N Y, 66; Asian studies grant, Dept Health, Educ & Welfare, 70.
Memberships: Boston Printmakers; Soc Am Graphic Artists (pres, 72-74).
Dealer: Dorsky Gallery, 111 Fourth Ave, New York, NY 10003.
Mailing Address: 95 Murray Ave, Port Washington, NY 11050.

BARR, ALFRED HAMILTON, JR
Art Historian, Art Administrator
b Detroit, Mich, Jan 28, 02.
Study & Training: Princeton Univ, AB, 22, univ fel, 22-23, AM, 23, Thayer fel, 24-25; Harvard Univ, PhD, 46; Princeton Univ, hon LittD, 49; Univ Bonn, hon PhD, 58; Univ Buffalo, hon DFA, 62; Yale Univ, hon PhD, 67; Columbia Univ, 69.
Teaching: Instr art, Vassar Col, 23-24; asst dept fine arts, Harvard Univ, 24-25; instr art & archaeol, Princeton Univ, 25-26; assoc prof art, Wellesley Col, 26-29; Mary Flexner Lectureship, Bryn Mawr Col, 46.
Positions: Dir, Mus Mod Art, New York, 29-43, trustee, 39-, v pres bd trustees, 39-43, dir res in painting & sculpture, 44-46, dir mus collections, 47-67, counr bd trustees, 67-; co-ed, Art in Am, 36; chmn New York Comt, Nat Art Wk, 40; mem adv comt art, Off Coordr Inter-Am Affairs, 40-43; mem adv comt, Inst Mod Art, Boston & Cincinnati Mod Art Soc; ed, Am Painters Series, Penguin Bks (London), 44-45; ed, 31 Mus Mod Art exhib catalogues; adv coun, dept art & archaeol, Princeton Univ, 46-; vis comt fine arts, Fogg Art Mus, Harvard Univ, 58-60, chmn, 65-70; bd overseers, Harvard Univ, 64-70.
Awards: Chevalier, Legion of Honor, 59; spec merit award for notable creative achievement, Brandeis Univ, 64; Nat Inst Arts & Lett Award for distinguished service to arts, 68; plus others.
Publications: Auth, Cubism and abstract art, 36, Fantastic art, dada, surrealism, 36, What is modern painting?, 43, Picasso: fifty years of his art, 46 & Matisse: his art and his public, 51.
Mailing Address: The Museum of Modern Art, 11 W 53rd St, New York, NY 10019.

BARR, DAVID JOHN
Sculptor, Painter
Preferred Media: Masonite.
b Detroit, Mich, Oct 10, 39.
Study & Training: Wayne State Univ, BFA & MA.
Work in Public Collections: Detroit Inst Arts; Wayne State Univ Alumni Bldg.
Commissions: Wall reliefs, Jewish Home for Aged, Detroit, 65; outdoor sculpture, comn by David Lebenbom, Beverly Hills, Mich, 71.
Exhibitions: Mich Artists Shows, Detroit, 62-66; Flint Nat Invitational, Mich, 66; Evanston Art Ctr, 69; Chicago Contemporary (Relief/Construction/Relief), Herron Mus, Atlanta High Mus & Cranbrook Art Mus, 69.
Teaching: Assoc prof sculpture, Macomb Co Col, 64-
Awards: Archit awards, Louis Redstone Assocs, 65 & Albert Kahn Assocs, 65.
Bibliography: Dennis Stone (auth), Young structurists, Midwest Art Scene, 67; Relief makers, Chicago Omnibus, 67; Chicago art, Art News, 68.

Publications: Auth, Notes on growth, 69, Notes, 70 & Notes III, 72, The Structurist.
Dealer: Kazimir Gallery, 620 N Michigan Ave, Chicago, IL 60611.
Mailing Address: 8469 Yale, Oak Park, MI 48237.

BARR, ROGER TERRY
Sculptor, Painter
b Milwaukee, Wis, Sept 17, 21.
Study & Training: Univ Wis; Nat Univ Mex; Pomona Col, BA; Claremont Col, MFA; Jepson Art Inst, Atelier 17.
Work in Public Collections: Va Mus Fine Arts; Pasadena Art Mus; Mus Arte Mod, Sao Paulo, Brazil; Boston Mus Fine Arts; Art Mus Göteborg, Sweden; plus others in pub & pvt collections.
Exhibitions: One-man shows, M H de Young Mem Mus, San Francisco, Galerie Philadelphie, Paris, Esther Robles Gallery, Los Angeles & Feingarten Gallery, New York, plus others; Int Sculpture Exhib, Mus Rodin, 66 & Mus Toulouse, 67, Paris; plus other group shows.
Teaching: Instr art, Univ Calif, Los Angeles, 50-52; instr art, Calif Sch Fine Arts, San Francisco, 54-56; founding dir, Col Art Study Abroad, Am Ctr Students & Artists, Paris, 58-71.
Awards: Oakland Art Mus, 55; Stanford Univ Purchase Prize, 56; Catherwood Found fel, 56; plus others.
Memberships: Col Art Asn Am; Am Fedn Arts.
Dealer: Galerie Smith-Andersen, 200 Homer St, Palo Alto, CA 94301.
Mailing Address: 920 McDonald Ave, Santa Rosa, CA 95404.

BARR-SHARRAR, BERYL
Painter, Writer
b Norfolk, Va.
Study & Training: Mt Holyoke Col, BA; Univ Calif, Berkeley, MA; Inst Fine Arts, New York Univ, MA.
Exhibitions: Seven Americans of Paris, Am Cult Ctr, U S Embassy, Paris, 62; Galerie Lutece, Paris, 66 & 67; Maisons Cult Amiens, Bourges, Mus Avignon, Besancon, Montpellier, Nancy & Ste-Etienne, 67; Galerie Lucian Durand, Paris, 67; Mus Bourdeux, Menton & le Havre, 68.
Teaching: Vis lectr painting, Mt Holyoke Col, 68-69.
Positions: Co-founder, Col Art Study Abroad, Paris, 61, assoc dir, 61-68.
Awards: Prix le France pour le jeune peinture, Paris, 64.
Publications: Ed, The artists' and writers' cookbook, 61; auth, Wonders, warriors and beasts abounding, Doubleday, 67; auth, Artistes en exil (exhib catalogue), Paris Am Ctr, 68; auth, Some aspects of early autobiographical imagery in Picasso's suite 347, Art Bull, 12/72.
Mailing Address: 54 E 11th St, New York, NY 10003.

BARRETT, BILL
Sculptor, Educator
b Los Angeles, Calif, Dec 21, 34.
Study & Training: Univ Mich, Ann Arbor, BS (design), 58, MS (design), 59, MFA, 60.
Work in Public Collections: Cleveland Mus Art, Ohio; Aldrich Mus Contemp Art, Ridgefield, Conn; Norfolk Mus Art, Va; Syracuse Univ, N Y; Univ of the South, Sewanee, Tenn.
Commissions: Cast bronze sculpture relief, Mr & Mrs Whitelaw Reid, New York, N Y, 59; plaster sculpture, Hanover Col, Ind, 65; welded aluminum sculpture, Class of '42 for Univ Mich Dent Sch, 71; welded aluminum sculpture, Mr & Mrs Gerber, Great Neck, N Y, 72.
Exhibitions: Nat Sculpture Exhib, Bundy Art Gallery, Vt, 63; Nat Art Inst Show, San Francisco Mus Art, Calif, 64; May Show, Cleveland Mus Art, 64; First Flint Nat Invitational Show, Flint Mus Art, Mich, 67; Whitney Mus Am Art Sculpture Ann, New York, 70.
Teaching: Assoc prof sculpture, Eastern Mich Univ, 60-68; instr sculpture, Cleveland Art Inst, 63-64; instr sculpture, City Col New York, 69-
Memberships: Sculptors Guild New York.
Mailing Address: 268 Bowery, New York, NY 10012.

BARRETT, THOMAS R
Painter, Instructor
Preferred Media: Acrylics, Casein.
b Woodhaven, N Y, Feb 17, 27.
Study & Training: Wesleyan Univ, BA; Brooklyn Mus Art Sch; Univ N H, MA.
Work in Public Collections: DeCordova & Dana Mus, Lincoln, Mass; New Eng Col, Henniker, N H; Portland Art Mus, Maine; Phillips Exeter Acad, Exeter, N H.
Exhibitions: Metrop Mus Art, 52; Boston Art Festivals, 52-61; Portland Art Festival, 56-60; DeCordova & Dana Mus, 65 & 68;

New England Art, Provincetown & Boston, 70; one-man show, Lamont Gallery, Exeter, N H, 71.
Teaching: Instr painting & art hist & head art dept, St Paul's Sch, Concord, N H.
Awards: Currier Gallery Art, 60 & 62; City of Manchester, N H, 65; DeKalb Award, 72.
Memberships: N H Art Asn (pres, 68-69).
Dealer: Klein-Vogel Gallery, 8104 E Jefferson, Detroit, MI 48214.
Mailing Address: St Paul's School, Concord, NH 03301.

BARRIE, ERWIN S
Painter
b Canton, Ohio, June 3, 86.
Study & Training: Art Inst Chicago.
Work in Public Collections: Famous Golf Holes I Have Played (collection of 30 golf paintings), U S Golf Asn, Far Hills, N J; Metrop Golf Asn; also in pvt collections.
Exhibitions: Permanent one-man exhib, The Carolina, Pinehurst, N C; Grand Cent Galleries, New York, N Y.
Positions: Dir & mgr, Grand Central Art Galleries, Inc.
Mailing Address: Grand Central Art Galleries, Inc, 40 Vanderbilt Ave, New York, NY 10017.

BARRON, HARRIS
Sculptor
Preferred Media: Bronze, Wood, Granite.
b Boston, Mass, Nov 15, 26.
Study & Training: Vesper George Sch Art; Kerr Sch Art; Mass Sch Art, BFA.
Work in Public Collections: Addison Gallery Am Art, Andover, Mass; Portland Mus Art; plus others.
Commissions: Relief wall, Sears Roebuck, Saugus, Mass; bronze sculpture, Temple Facade, Leominster, Mass; bronze sculpture, Temple Israel, Columbus, Ohio; wood relief, Alper-Wellesley Trust Bldg, Brookline, Mass; relief-frieze, West Hartford Community Ctr; plus others.
Exhibitions: Boston Art Festival, 55-57 & 60; Silvermine Guild Artists, 57; Smithsonian Inst, 57; Whicita Art Asn, 55; Inst Contemp Arts, Boston.
Awards: Art in Am Award, 60; first prize, Art in Architecture, Everson Mus Art, 62; first prize, Margaret Brown Award, Inst Contemp Art, Boston, 64.
Mailing Address: 30 Webster Pl, Brookline, MA 02146.

BARRON, ROS
Painter
b Boston, Mass, July 4, 33.
Study & Training: Mass Col Art, BFA; also with Carl Nelson; fel Radcliffe Inst, Harvard Univ, 66-68.
Work in Public Collections: Addison Gallery Am Art, Andover, Mass; Worcester Art Mus; Dartmouth Col Collection; Harvard Univ; Syracuse Mus Fine Arts; plus others.
Commissions: Seasons (wall painting), YMCA, Roxbury, Mass, 65; Rainbow, Rocket, Road (wall painting), Lawrence Sch, Brookline, Mass, 67; polarized light painting, comn by S D I, San Francisco, Calif, 69; ser wall paintings for Community Ctr, Wilmington, Del, 70; plus others.
Exhibitions: Whitney Ann Am Painting, Salon 71-72; Ward-Nasse Gallery, N Y; Surreal Image, de Cordova Mus; UNESCO Art in Architecture, Rotterdam, Holland; American Painting & Sculpture, U S Info Agency Exhib, Europe; plus many others.
Teaching: Asst prof, Univ Mass, Boston.
Positions: Dir, ZONE.
Awards: Design award, U S Dept HUD, 68; Rockefeller artist-in-television grant, WGBH-TV, 68-69; N Y Found Arts, Inc Award to ZONE, 72; plus others.
Mailing Address: 30 Webster Pl, Brookline, MA 02146.

BARRON, MRS S BROOKS
Collector
b Hartford, Conn, Sept 6, 02.
Study & Training: Conn Col Women, BA.
Memberships: Art Collectors Club.
Collection: Contemporary art.
Mailing Address: 19631 Argyle Crescent, Detroit, MI 48203.

BARSCHEL, H J
Designer, Photographer
Preferred Media: Graphics.
b Berlin-Charlottenburg, Ger, Feb 22, 12.
Study & Training: Munic Art Sch; Acad Free & Appl Art, Berlin, MA.

Work in Public Collections: Mus Mod Art; N Y Pub Libr; Libr Cong, Washington, D C.
Commissions: Created graphic arts prog brochure, Rochester Inst Technol.
Exhibitions: Am Inst Graphic Arts; Art Dir Club, 38, 39 & 50; A-D Gallery, 46; one-man shows, Bevier Gallery, Rochester Inst Technol, 54 & 65; Faculty Art Exhibs, 57, 59 & 61.
Teaching: Prof graphic commun & instr advan design for reproduction & creative drawings, Sch Art & Design, Rochester Inst Technol.
Positions: Assoc art dir, John P Smith Co, Rochester, N Y, 53-54, designer, graphic arts res dept, 54-; art dir exp jour, Matrix, Rochester Inst Technol; exec mem, Rochester Arts Coun.
Awards: Prize, Am Inst Graphic Arts, 38.
Publications: Contribr, Art & Indust Mag, London, 54, Publimondial Mag, Paris, 55 & Productionwise Mag, New York, 55; auth, A plea for substantialism & Personal reflections on my era, 64; plus others.
Mailing Address: School of Art & Design, Rochester Institute of Technology, 1 Lomb Memorial Dr, Rochester, NY 14623.

BARTLE, ANNETTE
Painter, Illustrator
b Warsaw, Poland.
Study & Training: Sorbonne, BA; Elmira Col, BA; Art Stud League, with Robert Hale, Louis Bouche, R Johnson, Menkes, Paul Fiene & John Carroll.
Work in Public Collections: Lincoln Life Inst Co Col, Nebr; Woodside Savings & Loan Asn, N Y; C V Starr Co; Union Carbide Co.
Commissions: Mural, Top of Fair Bldg, N Y World's Fair.
Exhibitions: U S Info Agency, 63-65; New York Univ, 64; Bass Mus Art, 64; Am Acad Arts & Lett, 64; Philbrook Art Ctr, 64 & 65; plus others.
Awards: Art Stud League New York scholar; Pan-Am traveling scholar; award, East Hampton Guild, N Y.
Bibliography: Article, In: Handbook of the American artists group, Am Artists Group Inc, 66-68; mentioned by: U S 90th Cong, 1/23/68.
Publications: Contribr, Esquire & Look Mags & Conn Mutual Life Ins Co Publ.
Mailing Address: 231 E 76th St, New York, NY 10021.

BARTLETT, FRED STEWART
Art Administrator
b Brush, Colo, May 15, 05.
Study & Training: Univ Colo, AB, 28; Univ Denver, grad study, 32-35; Harvard Univ, Carnegie fel, summer 37.
Collections Arranged: Average of 20-25 exhibs per yr including biennials Artists West of the Mississippi (odd yrs) & New Accessions U S A (even yrs).
Positions: Docent & actg dir, Denver Art Mus, 32-43; cur painting & asst dir, Colo Springs Fine Arts Ctr, 43-55, dir, 55-71, dir emer, 71-; int chmn art dept, Temple Buell Col, 71-72, consult, art dept, 72-
Memberships: Colo Coun on Arts & Humanities (bd mem, 71-); Friends Contemp Art, Denver (bd mem, 71-); Asn Art Mus Dirs (mem, 56-71, hon mem, 71-); Asn Am Mus; U S Air Force Acad Fine Arts Panel (chmn, 64-).
Mailing Address: 5440 Manitou Rd, Littleton, CO 80123.

BARTLETT, JENNIFER LOSCH
Painter, Writer
b Long Beach, Calif, Mar 14, 41.
Study & Training: Mills Col, BA, 63; Yale Univ, BFA, 64, MFA, 65, with Jack Tworkov, James Rosenquist, Al Held & Jim Dine.
Work in Public Collections: Walker Art Ctr, Minneapolis, Minn.
Exhibitions: 7 Walls, Mus Modern Art Lending Exhib, New York, N Y, 71; one-woman show, Reese Palley Gallery, New York, 72; Whitney Ann: 1972 Painting, Whitney Mus Am Art, New York, 72; New Options, Walker Art Ctr, 72; American Women Artists, Kunsthalle, Hamburg, Ger, 72.
Teaching: Instr painting, Univ Conn, 68-72; vis artist, Chicago Art Inst, Ill, Fall 72; instr painting, Sch Visual Arts, New York, 72-
Bibliography: Dean Swanson (auth), Painting: new options, (catalogue), Walker Art Ctr, 72; Ira Licht (auth), Art without limits, (catalogue), Rochester Mem Art Gallery, N Y, 72.
Publications: Auth, Cleopatra I-IV, Adventures in Poetry Press, 71.
Dealer: Reese Palley Gallery, 93 Prince St, New York, NY 10012.
Mailing Address: 78 Greene St, New York, NY 10012.

BARTLETT, ROBERT WEBSTER
Painter, Designer
Preferred Media: Oils.
b Hinsdale, Ill, Dec 14, 22.
Study & Training: Art Inst Chicago, 38-39; Art Stud League New York, 43-44.

Work in Public Collections: Grumbacher Col; Washington Co Mus
Fine Arts; William Penn High Sch, Harrisburg, Pa; Pangborn
Co Collection; Phoenix Galleries, Baltimore, Md.
Commissions: Murals, Sullivan High Sch, Chicago, State of Pa &
pvt comns.
Exhibitions: Carnegie Mus, Pittsburgh, Pa; Army Air Force,
Middletown, Pa; Phoenix Galleries, Baltimore, Md; many shows,
Harrisburg Art Asn & Washington Co Mus Fine Arts.
Teaching: Instr painting, Mechanicsburg Art Asn, Pa, 69-
Awards: Harrisburg Art Asn Ann, 71.
Bibliography: Baker (auth), Visual persuasion, 64; Margaret
Harold, Prize-winning paintings, Allied Publ, 64.
Memberships: Harrisburg Art Asn (Pres, 54); Mechanicsburg Art
Asn.
Mailing Address: 57 Center Dr, Camp Hill, PA 17011.

BARTOK, JOHN ANTHONY
Painter
Preferred Media: Oils, Watercolors.
b Bridgeport, Conn, Jan 22, 38.
Study & Training: Manhattan Col, BSME(mech eng), 60; also with
William C Ehrig.
Commissions: Portrait of the late Hon W J Landregan, Lynn, Bar
Asn, Dist Ct of Southern Essex, Lynn, Mass.
Exhibitions: Gran Nat, Am Artists Prof League, New York, N Y, 70-
72; Paintings by Contemporary Artists of New England, Jordan
Marsh Ann, 70-71; Hudson Valley Art Asn, Westchester Co Ctr,
N Y, 70-71; Mainstreams, 71, Marietta, Ohio, 71; Salmagundi
Club, New York, 71.
Awards: Richard Mitton Mem Award, Jordan Marsh, Boston, Mass,
70; Ralph Metzner Award, Ogunquint Art Ctr, 70; hon mention,
oils, Am Artists Prof League.
Memberships: Salmagundi Club; Am Artists Prof League (mem nat
bd dirs, 70-); Hudson Valley Art Asn; North Shore Art Asn;
Copley Soc Boston.
Mailing Address: 104 Shore Rd, Ogunquit, ME 03907.

BARTON, AUGUST CHARLES
Designer, Painter
Preferred Media: Watercolors, Tempera.
b Székesfehervár, Hungary, Nov 15, 97; U S citizen.
Study & Training: Ludovika Mil Acad, BS; Hungarian Tech Univ;
Hungarian Acad Com Arts; Art Stud League New York.
Work in Public Collections: Fabric designs for all maj printed fab-
ric mfrs in the U S A, Can, Eng, Australia, Mex, Holland &
Sweden.
Exhibitions: Am Watercolor Soc; Hudson Valley Art Asn; Silvermine
Guild Artists.
Teaching: Prof art, textile design, Moore Col Art, Philadelphia, Pa,
46-63; lectr, Silvermine Col Art, 62-65; lectr, Philadelphia Col
Textiles & Sci, 63-
Positions: Pres, Barton Studios, Inc, New York, 31-
Memberships: Am Watercolor Soc; Silvermine Guild Art; Hudson
Valley Art Asn; Textile Designers Guild Am.
Publications: Auth, articles, In: Women's Wear Daily & college publ.
Mailing Address: 110 W 40th St, New York, NY 10018.

BARTON, ELEANOR DODGE
Educator
b Willsborough, N Y, Jan 23, 18.
Study & Training: Vassar Col, AB, 38; Inst Fine Arts, New York
Univ, AM, 42; Radcliffe Col Grad Sch, PhD, 52.
Teaching: Lectr mod & Baroque sculpture; staff asst, Yale Univ,
40-42; teaching fel, Smith Col, 42-43, instr, 43-48, assoc prof,
48-53; prof art & chmn dept, Sweet Briar Col, 53-71; vis lectr,
Wellesley Col, 56-57; vis prof art, Vassar Col, 71; prof art hist
& chmn dept, Univ Hartford, 72-
Awards: Shirley Farr fel, Am Asn Univ Women, 60-61.
Memberships: Col Art Asn Am; Renaissance Soc Am; Archaeol Inst
Am; Am Asn Univ Women.
Publications: Contribr, Marsyas, Collier's Encycl, Encycl World
Art, New Cath Encycl & Renaissance Quart.
Mailing Address: Dept of Art History, University of Hartford, West
Hartford, CT 06117.

BARTON, GEORGIE READ
Painter, Educator
Preferred Media: Oils.
b Summerside, P E I; U S citizen.
Study & Training: Mt Allison Sch Fine Arts, cert fine arts, 24-27;
Art Stud League New York, N Y, 29-34, with Frank Vincent
Dumond, Edward McCartan & Arthur Lee.
Work in Public Collections: Art of the Western Hemisphere, IBM

Corp Collection; Bruckner Mus, Albion, Mich; Confederation Art
Gallery, Charlottetown, P E I.
Exhibitions: Expos Int, France, Monaco & U S, 67-68; Acad Artists
Springfield, Mass; Am Artists Prof League, New York; Hudson
Valley Art Asn, White Plains, N Y; Allied Artists Am, New York,
71-
Teaching: Art dir, Ottawa Ladies Col, Ont, 34-40; art dir, St Agnes
Sch, Albany, N Y, 40-44; private classes, 44-
Awards: Bronze medal, IBM Corp, 41; gold medal, Hudson Valley
Art Asn, 63 & gold medal & citation, 72.
Memberships: Hudson Valley Art Asn (secy, 58-65, pres, 65-69,
first v pres, 69-); Acad Art Asn; Coun Am Artists Socs (dir bd,
66-); Am Artists Prof League (dir nat bd, 64-); Catharine
Lorillard Wolfe Art Club.
Publications: Contribr, Am Artists Prof League Bull, 71.
Mailing Address: 66 Lockwood Rd, Scarsdale, NY 10583.

BARTON, JOHN MURRAY
Painter, Art Dealer
b New York, N Y, Feb 8, 21.
Study & Training: Art Stud League New York; Tschacbasov Sch Art,
New York.
Work in Public Collections: Metrop Mus Art, New York; Brooklyn
Mus, N Y; Mus Mod Art, Haifa, Israel; Butler Inst Am Art,
Youngstown, Ohio; Philadelphia Mus Art, Pa; plus others.
Commissions: Ceramic mural (with Lumin Martin Winter), New
York Bd Educ for P S 41; oil & sand mural (with Lumin Martin
Winter), New York Bd Educ for Riverdale Jr High Sch; History of
Money (oil, with Louise August), S C State Bank, Columbia; oil &
lacquer mural, Polyclinic Hosp, New York; acrylic on concrete
(with Louise August), Gilbert's Hotel, Fallsburgh, N Y.
Exhibitions: Numerous nat & regional exhibs.
Teaching: Pvt classes at studio on creative expression, 60-65;
lectr, creative expression, univ art depts, throughout the East
Coast, 60-65.
Positions: Pres, John Darton Assocs, Inc, 65-; pres, J M B Publ,
Ltd, 68-; pres, Multiple Reproductions, Inc, 70-; secy-treas, Int
Assoc Artists, Ltd, 72-
Memberships: Le Soc Int de Who's Who, Geneva, Switz.
Specialty of Gallery: Publisher of original fine art graphics; art
shows at colleges, universities, galleries and others.
Publications: Illusr, Space Aeronautics, Print Mag & Printers Ink.
Mailing Address: J M B Publishers, Ltd, 3 E 28th St, New York, NY
10016.

BARUCH, MR & MRS JOSEPH M
Collectors
Mailing Address: Doubling Rd (40), Greenwich, CT 06830.

BARUZZI, PETER B
Painter, Educator
b Fredericktown, Pa, Dec 3, 24.
Study & Training: Memphis Acad Art, BFA; Memphis State Teachers
Col; Syracuse Univ, MFA; State Univ Iowa; also with Mauricio
Lasansky.
Exhibitions: Brooks Mem Mus, 48-54; Union Col, Schenectady, N Y,
55; one-man show, Skidmore Col, 64; State Univ N Y Albany;
Munson-Williams Proctor Inst, Utica, N Y; plus others.
Teaching: Instr, Memphis Acad Art, 51-54; asst prof art, Skidmore
Col, 54-70; lectr art, Union Col, N Y, 63 & 64; assoc prof art,
Skidmore Col, 70-
Positions: Dir, Chautauqua Art Asn, 60.
Mailing Address: Dept of Art, Skidmore College, Saratoga Springs,
NY 12866.

BARZUN, JACQUES
Writer, Art Critic
b Creteil, France, Nov 30, 07; U S citizen.
Study & Training: Columbia Col, BA, 27; Columbia Univ, MA, 28,
PhD, 32.
Teaching: Instr hist, Columbia Col, 29-38; asst prof hist, Columbia
Univ, 38-42, assoc prof hist, 42-45, prof hist, 45-
Research: Forty years of study and teaching of intellectual history
and culture.
Publications: Auth, reviews & articles, In: Mag of Art, 43-53; auth,
articles, In: Am Scholar, Art Digest & Harper's, 56-; auth, Art—
by act of Congress, The Public Interest, fall 65; auth, Museum
piece, 1967, Mus News, 4/68; auth, The arts to-day; consolida-
tion or confrontation?, J of Royal Soc Arts, 3/72.
Mailing Address: 110 Low Library, Columbia University, New
York, NY 10027.

BASHOR, JOHN W
Educator, Painter
Preferred Media: Acrylics.
b Newton, Kans, Mar 11, 26.
Study & Training: Washburn Univ, BA, 49; Univ Iowa, MFA, 53.

Work in Public Collections: Rockhill-Nelson Mus, Kansas City, Mo; Washburn Univ, Topeka, Kans; Springfield Art Mus, Mo; Sandzen Mem Mus, Lindsborg, Kans; Kans State Univ, Manhattan.
Commissions: Murals, Kaw Valley State Bank, Topeka, 64, Bethany Col, Lindsborg, 65 & First Nat Bank, Grand Island, Nebr, 65.
Exhibitions: Mid-Am Ann, Rockhill-Nelson Mus, 56; Nebraska Invitational, Univ Nebr, Lincoln, 62; circulating one-man exhib, State of Pa, 62-63; Kansas' Artist, Nat Gov Circulating Exhib, 66; Fedn Rocky Mountain States Circulating Exhib, 68.
Teaching: Assoc prof painting & prints, Bethany Col, 54-66.
Positions: Dir, Sch Art, Mont State Univ, 66-
Memberships: Mid-Am Col Art Asn; Col Art Asn; Mont Art Educ Asn.
Mailing Address: School of Art, Montana State University, Bozeman, MT 59715.

BASKERVILLE, CHARLES
Painter
Preferred Media: Oils, Acrylics, Watercolors.
b Raleigh, N C, Apr 16, 96.
Study & Training: Cornell Univ; Art Stud League New York; Acad Julien, Paris, France.
Work in Public Collections: Nat Fine Arts Collection, Washington, D C; Nat Portrait Gallery, Washington, D C; 65 off portraits for USAAF, Pentagon, Washington, D C; Mus of City of New York, N Y; Nat Mus Racing, Saratoga Springs, N Y.
Commissions: Mural in relief lacquer, Main Lounge of S S America, 40; mural, Joint Comt Mil Affairs, U S Capitol, Washington, D C, 47; Two Tigers (mural), Princeton Univ, N J, 59; Mexican Pavilion (mural) comn by Cornelius Vanderbilt Whitney; Harlequin (mural) comn by Douglas Dillon, Hobe Sound, Fla, 70.
Exhibitions: Carnegie Int, Pittsburgh, Pa, 40; Army Air Force Portraits, Nat Gal Art, Washington, D C, 45 & Metrop Mus Art, New York, 47; Significant War Scenes, Chrysler Corp Collection, Corcoran Gallery Art, Washington, D C, 49; one-man show, Parrish Art Mus, Southampton, N Y, 65.
Bibliography: Many articles in magazines & newspapers.
Memberships: Nat Soc Mural Painters (pres, 3 yrs); Am Artists Prof League.
Dealer: FAR Gallery, 746 Madison Ave, New York, NY 10021.
Mailing Address: 130 W 57th St, New York, NY 10019.

BASKIN, LEONARD
Sculptor, Graphic Artist
b New Brunswick, N J, Aug 15, 22.
Study & Training: New York Univ, 39-41; Yale Sch Fine Arts, 41-43; Tiffany Found fel, 47; New Sch Social Res, AB, 49; Acad Grande Chaumiere, 50; Acad Fine Arts, Florence, Italy, 51; New Sch Social Res, DFA, 66; Clark Univ, LHD, 66; Univ Mass, DFA, 68.
Work in Public Collections: Mus Mod Art; Metrop Mus Art; Brooklyn Mus; Nat Gallery Art, Washington, D C; Fogg Mus Art; plus others.
Exhibitions: New Sch Social Res, 67; São Paulo, Brazil; Mus Art Mod, Paris; Yugoslavia; Zurich, Switz; plus others.
Teaching: Prof sculpture & graphic arts, Smith Col, 53-
Awards: Guggenheim Found fel, 53; medal, Am Inst Graphic Artists, 65; medal of merit graphic arts, Nat Inst Arts & Lett, 69; plus others.
Bibliography: Herbert Read (auth), article, In: A concise history of modern sculpture, 64; Raphael Soyer (auth), article, In: Homage to Thomas Eakins, etc, 65; Wayne Craven (auth), article, In: Sculpture in America, 68; plus others.
Memberships: Nat Inst Arts & Lett; William Morris Soc; Am Inst Graphic Artists.
Dealer: Kennedy Galleries, 20 E 56th St, New York, NY 10022.
Mailing Address: Fort Hill, Northampton, MA 01060.

BASS, JOHN
Collector, Patron
b Vienna, Austria, 91.
Positions: Dir, Bass Mus Art; adv coun, Dept Art, Hist & Archeol, Columbia Univ.
Memberships: Am Inst Graphic Arts.
Collection: John & Johanna Bass Collection donated to City of Miami Beach which provided a building to house collection; consists of paintings, sculpture, vestments, tapestries and other objects of art; loans and donations of art made to many museums and universities here and abroad.
Mailing Address: Bass Museum of Art, 2100 Collins Avenue, Miami Beach, FL 33139.

BASSFORD, WALLACE
Painter, Instructor
Preferred Media: Oils, Acrylics, Graphics.
b Saint Louis, Mo.
Study & Training: Wash Univ Sch Fine Arts; also with Pennell, Hoke, Wuerpel, Carpenter & G E Browne; foreign free-lance study.

Work in Public Collections: Mo State Capitol Bldg; Boca Raton Fla Club; Univ Syracuse; Univ Mo; De Beers Collection.
Exhibitions: Univ Ill Ann; Corcoran Biennials; Carnegie Inst; Boston Mus Fine Arts; Saint Louis Mus Fine Arts; plus others.
Teaching: Instr-dir figure, still-life & landscape, North Truro Sch Art, Mass, summers; instr, pvt classes, Palm Beach, Fla, winters.
Awards: Gold medal, Kans Art Inst; Boston Gardens Festival Pop Prize; all N E best of art, Silvermine Conn Guild Art.
Publications: Auth, Painting the female figure, Reinhold.
Dealers: Grand Central Art Gallery Inc, Vanderbilt Ave, New York, NY 10017; Palm Beach Galleries, Palm Beach, FL 33480.
Mailing Address: Box 63, North Truro, MA 02652.

BATCHELOR, JONATHAN DAVID
Painter, Sculptor
Preferred Media: Oil, Acrylic, Bronze, Stone, Wood.
b Vancouver, Wash, June 29, 13.
Study & Training: Calif Col Arts & Crafts; Lukits Art Sch; Otis Art Inst, MFA.
Work in Public Collections: Oakland Mus, Calif; St Mary's Art Gallery, Moraga, Calif.
Commissions: Requiem, Lakeside Park, Oakland, 46; St John, St John's Church, El Cerrito, Calif, 48.
Exhibitions: Oakland Art Gallery, 45; Calif State Fair, Sacramento, 46; Palace Legion of Honor, San Francisco, 49; De Young Mus, San Francisco, 52; Jack London Sq, Oakland, 58.
Teaching: Instr painting, Calif Col Arts & Crafts, 46-52; instr painting, Oakland High Sch, 46-
Awards: Silver medal, Calif State Fair, 48; gold medals, Oakland Art Gallery, 50 & 53.
Bibliography: N Rourkes & Jose Gutierrez (auth), Painting with acrylics, 66 & N Rourkes (auth), Sculpture in plastics, Watson-Guptill, 68.
Memberships: Calif Col Arts & Crafts Alumni Asn (mem coun, 67-71, v pres, 71-72).
Mailing Address: P O Box 81, Canyon, CA 94516.

BATE, NORMAN ARTHUR
Educator, Printmaker
b Buffalo, N Y, Jan 3, 16.
Study & Training: Pratt Inst, BFA, 54; Univ Ill, MFA, 57.
Work in Public Collections: Audubon Artists, New York, N Y; Univ Maine, Orono; Fogg Mus, Boston, Mass; Seattle Art Mus, Wash; also in collection of Dr Marland, Comnr Educ, Washington, D C.
Commissions: Etchings, 100 prints, Int Graphic Arts Soc, New York, 57, 200 prints, Assoc Am Artists, New York, 58 & 100 prints, Print Club Rochester, N Y, 61.
Exhibitions: Peabody Mus, Boston, Mass, 58; Audubon Artists Ann, 59; Libr Cong, Washington, D C, 59; one-man shows, Carnegie Gallery, Univ Maine, 59 & Nazareth Col, Rochester, 64.
Teaching: Asst prof drawing, Pratt Inst, 51-55; prof printmaking & illus, Rochester Inst Technol, 57-
Awards: Joseph Pennell Award for etching, Libr Cong, 59; John Taylor Arms Medal & Award for etching, Audubon Artists, 59; Greene Award for etching, Albright-Knox Art Gallery, Buffalo, N Y, 59.
Memberships: Can Soc Painter-Etchers & Engravers; Print Club Rochester (pres, 59-61).
Publications: Auth & illusr, Who built the highway?, 53, Who built the bridge?, 54, Who fishes for oil?, 55, What a wonderful machine is the submarine, 61 & When cave men painted, 63.
Mailing Address: Box 150, R D 2, Geneva, NY 14456.

BATE, STANLEY
Painter
Preferred Media: Oil.
b Nashville, Tenn, Mar 26, 03.
Study & Training: Watkins Inst, Nashville; Art Stud League New York, N Y; also studied in France & Switz.
Work in Public Collections: Berkshire Mus, Pittsfield, Mass; Albany Inst Hist & Art, N Y; Cooperstown Art Asn, N Y; Berkshire Community Col, Pittsfield.
Exhibitions: Metrop Mus Art, New York, 52; Whitney Mus Am Art, New York, 53; Corcoran Galleries, Washington, D C, 53; Nat Mus, Havana, Cuba, 56; Albany Coun Arts Exhib, Albany Inst Hist & Art, 70.
Positions: Art supvr, Encycl Britannica, New York, 27-29.
Awards: Purchase awards, Albany Inst Hist & Art, 70, Cooperstown Art Asn, 70 & Berkshire Community Col, 71.
Memberships: Berkshire Art Asn (dir, 72); Cooperstown Art Asn (dir, 72).
Mailing Address: Box 294, R R 1, Craryville, NY 12521.

BATES, CHARLES T, JR
Painter
b Rockford, Ill, Nov 24, 42.
Study & Training: Minneapolis Col Art & Design, scholar, 69-70, BFA, 70.
Work in Public Collections: McCannel Found; collections of Stuart Wells, Sharon Bredeson & Lillian Anthony.
Exhibitions: Martin Gallery, Minneapolis, 69; Minneapolis Col Art & Design, 70; Arts Festival, Gen Mills, 70; Rockford Col, Ill, 71.
Teaching: Lectr art symp, Wadena Pub Schs, Minn; instr, Minneapolis Col Art & Design Pre-Col Workshops, 70.
Positions: Dir, Thee Whole, Community Ctr, fall 68; art consult, Soul of City, Downtown Arts Festival, Minneapolis, summer 69; pres, Glenwood-Lyndale Residence Coun, 69-70; artist-in-residence, Holden Village, Chelan, Wash, summer 70.
Awards: Grants, Minn State Arts Coun for independent study, summer 69, McCannel Found for independent study, summer 69 & Louis Comfort Tiffany Found, 70.
Mailing Address: 3325 Columbus Ave S, Minneapolis, MN 55407.

BATES, GLADYS EDGERLY
Sculptor
Preferred Media: Wood, Stone, Cast Stone.
b Hopewell, N J, July 15, 96.
Study & Training: Corcoran Gallery Sch Art, Washington, D C, 10-16; Pa Acad Fine Arts, Cresson European scholar, 20, 16-21.
Work in Public Collections: Pa Acad Fine Arts, Philadelphia, Pa; Metrop Mus Art, New York, N Y; N J State Mus, Trenton.
Exhibitions: A Century of Progress, Art Inst Chicago, Ill, 34; Tex Centennial, Dallas, 36; Am Sculpture Exhib, Carnegie Inst, Pittsburgh, Pa, 38; Artists for Victory, Metrop Mus Art, New York, 42; Third Sculpture Int, Philadelphia Mus, Pa, 49.
Awards: George D Widener Gold Medal, Pa Acad Fine Arts, 31; Third purchase prize, Artists for Victory, Metrop Mus Art, 42; Nat Asn Women Artists prize, 48.
Memberships: Fel Nat Sculpture Soc; Nat Asn Women Artists; Pen & Brush Club; Conn Acad Fine Arts; Mystic Art Asn.
Dealer: Stone Ledge Studio Art Galleries, Noank, CT 06340.
Mailing Address: Stonecroft, P O Box 215, Mystic, CT 06355.

BATES, KENNETH
Painter
Preferred Media: Oils.
b Haverhill, Mass, Oct 28, 95.
Study & Training: Art Stud League New York, 14-15, with Bridgeman; Pa Acad Fine Arts, Sch, 16-17 & 19-21, studied with Garber, Cearson & Breckenridge, Cresson European scholar, 20.
Work in Public Collections: Pa Acad Fine Arts, Philadelphia; Woodmere Gallery, Philadelphia; Beach Mem Collection, Univ Conn, Storrs; Slater Mem Mus, Norwich, Conn.
Exhibitions: 24th Int Exhib, Carnegie Inst, Pittsburgh, Pa, 25; 39th Ann Exhib, Art Inst Chicago, Ill, 26; Carnegie Corp Traveling Exhib, Nat Gallery Can, Ottawa, Ont, 34-35; IBM Collection, New York World's Fair, 40; 18th Biennial Exhib, Corcoran Gallery Art, Washington, D C, 43.
Awards: Hon mem, 39th Ann, Art Inst Chicago, 26; Jennie Sesman Gold Medal, Pa Acad Fine Arts, 27; First Conn Acad Fine Arts Prize, 50.
Bibliography: Edward Alden Jewell (auth), Americans, Knopf, 30; Kenneth Bates, Am Artist Mag, 5/43; Ernest W Watson (auth), Composition in landscape & still life, Watson-Guptill, 59.
Memberships: Academician Nat Acad Design; Conn Acad Fine Arts; New Haven Paint & Clay Club; Mystic Art Asn.
Publications: Auth, Brackman, his art and teaching, Noank Publ Studio, 51.
Dealer: Stone Ledge Studio Art Galleries, Noank, CT 06340.
Mailing Address: Stonecroft, P O Box 215, Mystic, CT 06355.

BATES, KENNETH FRANCIS
Craftsman, Educator
b North Scituate, Mass, May 24, 04.
Study & Training: Mass Sch Art, BSEduc; also study abroad.
Work in Public Collections: Cleveland Mus Art, Ohio; Butler Inst Am Art, Youngstown, Ohio.
Commissions: Murals, Campus Sweater Co, Cleveland & Lakewood Pub Libr; ecclesiastical enamels, Washington D C, Bethesda Md, Youngstown, Ohio, Univ Notre Dame & others.
Exhibitions: Cleveland Mus Art, 28-61; European traveling exhibs; Smithsonian Inst Traveling Exhib; Nat Syracuse Traveling Exhib; one-man shows, Cleveland, New York, Brooklyn Mus & Art Inst Chicago, 61; plus others.
Teaching: Instr & lectr, Cleveland Inst Art, 27-71, emer instr, 71-
Awards: Prizes, 29-64 & silver medal, 49, 57 & 66, Cleveland Mus Art; Fine Arts Award of Cleveland, 63; first faculty grant for study abroad, 65; plus others.
Memberships: Fel Int Inst Arts & Lett.

Publications: Auth, Enameling, principles and practice, 51, Basic design, principles and practice, 60, The enamelist, 67 & Basic design, 70, World Publ; auth, articles on enameling, In: Design Mag, Ceramics Monthly, Encycl of the Arts & others.
Mailing Address: 7 E 194th St, Euclid, OH 44119.

BATES, MAXWELL BENNETT
Painter, Writer
Preferred Media: Oils, Watercolors, Lithography.
b Calgary, Alta, Dec 14, 06.
Study & Training: Prov Inst Technol & Art, with Lars Haukaness; Brooklyn Mus Art Sch, with Max Beckmann & Abraham Rattner; Univ Calgary, DUC, 71.
Work in Public Collections: Nat Gallery Can, Ottawa; Nat Gallery New Zealand, Auckland; Art Gallery Winnipeg, Man; Art Gallery Vancouver, B C; Art Gallery Greater Victoria, B C.
Exhibitions: Canadian Watercolors and Graphics Today, traveling exhib in U S, 59-60; Canadian Painting and Graphics, Mexico City, Mex, 60; Biennial Exhib, Nat Gallery Can, 69.
Awards: Ann honor award, Can Soc Painters in Watercolour, 57; Haspel-Seguin Award, Can Soc Graphic Art, 60.
Bibliography: John Graham (auth), Maxwell Bates, 12/68 & P K Page (auth), Maxwell Bates, 4/70, Arts Can; Robin Skelton (auth), Maxwell Bates: experience and reality, Malahat Rev, 71.
Memberships: Royal Can Acad Arts; Can Soc Painters in Watercolour (v pres, 58); Can Soc Graphic Art; The Limners (pres, 72).
Publications: Auth, Faraway Flags, 64.
Dealer: Canadian Art Galleries, 811 17th Ave S W, Calgary, Alta, Can.
Mailing Address: 931 Lakeview Ave, Victoria, B C, Can.

BATTCOCK, GREGORY
Art Critic, Lecturer
b New York, N Y, July 2, 1941.
Study & Training: Acad Delle Arti, Rome, Italy; Hunter Col, MA.
Teaching: Assoc prof art history, William Paterson Col, 69-
Positions: Spec corresp, Arts Mag, 67-; New York corresp, Art & Artists, London, 69-; columnist, Gay Newspaper, 70-
Bibliography: Pierre Restany (auth), Libres propos sur la nouvelle critique Americaine, Domus, 7/71.
Publications: Ed, The new art, 66 & Minimal art, 69, Dutton; auth, Why art & New ideas in art education, Dutton, 72; co-auth, Art of the sixties, Abrams, 72.
Mailing Address: William Paterson College, Wayne, NJ 07470.

BAUER, WILLIAM
Painter, Illustrator
Preferred Media: Oils.
b St Louis, Mo, June 13, 88.
Study & Training: Wash Univ Sch Art, with Oscar Berninghause; also with Fred Carpenter.
Work in Public Collections: Mo State Collection, Jefferson City; Ill State Mus; Old Capital Art Fair, Springfield, Ill.
Exhibitions: Carnegie Inst Int, 22; Kansas City Art Inst, 24; Mo State Fair, 26; St Louis Art League, 27; Ill State Mus, 63.
Awards: Purchase prize for The Brook in Winter, Kansas City Art Inst, 24; purchase prize for Cityscape, Ill State Mus, 63; Winter Landscape, Scada Old Capital Art Fair, 64.
Bibliography: Prize Winning paintings, Allied Publ, 62.
Memberships: Hon life mem, St Louis Artist Guild.
Mailing Address: 7741 Gen Sherman Lane, St Louis, MO 63123.

BAUERMEISTER, MARY HILDE RUTH
Sculptor
Preferred Media: Wood, Glass, Light.
b Frankfurt am Main, W Ger, Sept 7, 34.
Work in Public Collections: Mus Mod Art, Solomon R Guggenheim Mus & Whitney Mus Am Art, New York, N Y; Albright-Knox Art Gallery, Buffalo, N Y; Stedelijk Mus, Amsterdam, Holland.
Exhibitions: One-man show, Stedelijk Mus, Amsterdam, 62; Recent Acquisitions, Mus Mod Art, New York, 64; Whitney Mus Am Art Ann, 64-66; European Drawing Show, Solomon R Guggenheim Mus, 65; Carnegie Int, Pittsburgh, Pa, 67-68.
Bibliography: Solomon (auth), Mary Bauermeister, Bonino Kotelogue, 64; Fischer (auth), Das Werk M Bauermeister, Das Kunstwerk, 65; Pernezky (auth), Mary Bauermeister, Mittelrhein Mus, Koblenz, 72.
Dealer: Galeria Bonino, 7 W 57th St, New York, NY 10019.
Mailing Address: 546 Summer Hill Rd, Madison, CT 06443.

BAUM, WILLIAM
Painter
b New York, N Y, Oct 30, 21.
Study & Training: Design Labs; also with Theodore Roszak & I Rice Pereira.

Exhibitions: Brooklyn Mus, 60; four shows, Silvermind Guild Artists, 60-64; Hudson River Mus, 61; Pa Acad Fine Arts, Philadelphia, 62; Berkshire Mus, 63; plus others.
Awards: Award, Berkshire Art Asn, 63; Larry Aldrich Award, Silvermine Guild Artists, 64.
Mailing Address: 195 Lafayette St, Williston Park, NY 11596.

BAUMAN, LIONEL R
    Collector
Mailing Address: 2 W 45th St, New York, NY 10036.

BAUMBACH, HAROLD
    Painter, Printmaker
Preferred Media: Oils.
b New York, N Y, 05.
Study & Training: Pratt Inst; Educ Alliance.
Work in Public Collections: Whitney Mus Am Art, New York; Brooklyn Mus, N Y; Albright-Knox Art Gallery, Buffalo, N Y; Univ Iowa Art Mus, Iowa City; R I Sch Design Mus, Providence.
Commissions: Five lithograph editions in color, Bank St Atelier, New York, 72.
Exhibitions: Carnegie Int, 47; Arizona Museum Purchase Exhibition, Metrop Mus Art, New York, 47; Second Ann Summer Show, Park-Berne Galleries, New York, 64; one-man show, Univ Iowa Mus, 67; Free Form Exhibition, Whitney Mus Am Art, 72.
Teaching: Spec lectr art appreciation, Brooklyn Col, 60-66; adj asst prof art appreciation, Long Island Univ, 66-67; vis prof painting, Univ Iowa, summer 67, vis artist, 72-73.
Awards: Hon mention, Pepsi Cola Artists for Victory Competition, 46.
Memberships: Fedn Mod Painters & Sculptors.
Dealer: Krasner Gallery, 1061 Madison Ave, New York, NY 10021.
Mailing Address: 278 Henry St, Brooklyn, NY 11201.

BAUMHOFER, WALTER MARTIN
    Illustrator, Painter
Preferred Media: Oils, Casein.
b Brooklyn, N Y, Nov 1, 04.
Study & Training: Pratt Inst, scholar, 23, with Dean Cornwell.
Work in Public Collections: Custer Mus, Monroe, Mich; Northport Fed Savings Asn, N Y; 4H Clubs Nat Hqs, Dept Agr, Washington, D C; Union Free Sch Dist 4, Northport.
Commissions: West Indian Flora & Fauna, W Harry Baker, St Thomas, V I, 69; portrait, founder Northport Fed Savings & Loan Asn.
Exhibitions: Brooklyn Mus Art, 40; one-man show, Soc Illusr, New York, N Y, 43 & ann shows, 43-54; Stony Brook Mus, 51.
Awards: Most popular painting, Stony Brook Mus, 51.
Publications: Illusr, Argosy, Cosmopolitan, Redbook, American, Outdoor Life & other nat mags.
Dealer: American Artists Representatives, Inc, 60 W 45th St, New York, NY 10036.
Mailing Address: 56 School St, Northport, NY 11768.

BAUR, JOHN I H
    Museum Director, Writer
b Woodbridge, Conn, Aug 9, 09.
Study & Training: Yale Univ, BA, 32, MA, 34.
Teaching: Vis lectr Am art, Yale Univ, 51-52.
Positions: Supvr educ, Brooklyn Mus Art, N Y, cur, 36-52; cur, Whitney Mus Am Art, New York, N Y, 52-58, assoc dir, 58-68, dir, 68-
Publications: Auth, Philip Evergood, 60 & Bernard Reder, 61; co-auth, American art of our century, 61; auth, Revolution and tradition in modern American Art, 51 & 67 & Joseph Stella, 71, Praeger; plus others.
Mailing Address: Mt Holly Rd, Katonah, NY 10536.

BAVINGER, EUGENE ALLEN
    Painter, Educator
b Sapulpa, Okla, Dec 21, 19.
Study & Training: Univ Okla, BFA; Inst Allende, Mex, MFA.
Work in Public Collections: Addison Gallery Am Art, Andover, Mass; Nelson Gallery, Atkins Mus, Kansas City, Mo; Joslyn Art Mus, Omaha, Nebr; Masur Mus, Monroe, La; Mulvane Art Ctr, Topeka, Kans.
Exhibitions: American Painting Today, Metrop Mus Art, New York, N Y, 50; 12 Artists West of the Mississippi, Colo Springs Fine Art Ctr, Colo, 61; 70th Western Ann Invitational-19 artists, Denver Art Mus, Colo, 64; Fifty Artists from Fifty States, Am Fedn Arts Traveling Exhib, 66; one-man show, Sheldon Art Gallery, Lincoln, Nebr, 67.
Teaching: Prof art, Univ Okla, 47-
Awards: Grand award, 31st Okla Ann, Philbrook Art Ctr, Tulsa, 71; purchase award, 41st Ann Exhib, Springfield Art Mus, Mo, 71; first award, 22nd Ann Exhib, Fort Smith Art Ctr, Ark, 72.

Bibliography: Margaret Harold (auth), Prize-winning paintings, Book II & IV, Allied Publ, 62 & 64.
Mailing Address: 520 Parrington Oval, Rm 202, Norman, OK 73069.

BAYEFSKY, ABA
    Painter, Printmaker
Preferred Media: Graphics.
b Toronto, Ont, Apr 7, 23.
Study & Training: Cent Tech Sch, Toronto.
Work in Public Collections: Nat Gallery Can, Ottawa; Nat Gallery Victoria, Melbourne, Australia; Art Gallery Ont; Libr Cong, Washington, D C; Hebrew Univ, Jerusalem; plus others.
Commissions: Mural, Northview Colliate, Toronto; tapestry, Synagogue Ont; mural, Ont Govt Bldg.
Exhibitions: All major Can Art Soc Exhibs & 17 one-man shows.
Teaching: Instr, Ont Col Art, 56-
Positions: Off war artist, RCAF.
Awards: J W L Forster Award, Ont Soc Artists, 57; Can Coun grant to India, 58; Centennial Citation, Toronto, 67; plus others.
Memberships: Assoc Royal Can Acad Art (coun mem); Can Soc Graphic Art; Can Soc Painters in Water Colour; Can Group Painters.
Publications: Illusr, Rubaboo, 62, portfolio 18 lithographs, Tales from the Talmud, 63, The ballad of Thrym, (privately publ), 65 & portfolio colour blockprints, Indian legends, 68.
Mailing Address: 7 Paperbirch Dr, Don Mills, Ont, Can.

BAYER, HERBERT
    Painter, Designer
b Haag, Austria, Apr 5, 00; U S citizen.
Study & Training: Real-Gym, Linz, Austria; archit with Schmidthammer, Linz, 19; with Emanuel Margold, Darmstadt, Ger, 20; wall paintings with Vassily Kandinsky, 21; Bauhaus, Weimar, 21-23.
Work in Public Collections: San Francisco Mus Art; Mus Mod Art; Guggenheim Mus; Staatsgemäldesammlungen, Munich; Denver Art Mus; plus many others U S & Europe.
Commissions: Murals, Bauhaus Bldg, Weimar, Commons Bldg, Grad Ctr, Harvard Univ, Elem Sch, Bridgewater, Mass & Health Ctr, Aspen, Colo; designed articulated wall construction for 1968 Olympics, Mexico City, Mex; plus others.
Exhibitions: San Francisco Art Mus, 49; Germanisches Nationalmuseum, Nuremberg; Hochsch Bildende Künste, Berlin, 57; Städtische Kunsthalle, Dusseldorf, 60; Marlborough Gallery, New York, N Y, 71; plus others.
Positions: Art dir, Vogue, Ger; dir, Dorland Studio, Berlin, 28-38, art dir, Dorland Int, N Y; consult design, Aspen Inst; chmn dept design, Container Corp Am, 56-65; consult, Atlantic Richfield Co, 65-
Awards: Prizes, U S & Europe.
Bibliography: Included in: George Rickey (auth), Constructivism: origins and evolution, Braziller, 67, Hans M Wingler (auth), Graphic work from Bauhaus, N Y Graphic Soc, 68 & Eberhard Roters (auth), Painters of the Bauhaus, Praeger, 69; plus others.
Memberships: Alliance Graphique Int; Am Abstr Artists; Int Design Conf, Aspen, Colo.
Publications: Auth & designer, Herbert Bayer-visual communication, architecture, painting, 67; contribr, articles, In: Gebrauchsgraphik, Col Art J, Bauhaus Mag & Linea Grafica; plus others.
Dealer: Marlborough Gallery, 41 E 57th St, New York, NY 10022.
Mailing Address: P O Box B, Aspen, CO 81611.

BEACH, WARREN
    Painter
b Minneapolis, Minn, May 21, 14.
Study & Training: Phillips Acad, Andover, Mass; Yale Univ, BFA, 39; Univ Iowa, MA, 40; Harvard Univ, MA, 47.
Work in Public Collections: Addison Gallery Am Art, Andover; Columbus Gallery Fine Arts, Ohio.
Exhibitions: Minneapolis Art Inst; Art & Artists Along the Mississippi, 41; Minn State Fair, 41; one-man show, Grace Horne Gallery, Boston, Mass, 45; Columbus Art League, 48; plus others.
Teaching: Dean, Columbus Art Sch, 47-49.
Positions: Dir exten serv, Walker Art Ctr, Minneapolis, 40-41; asst art mus, Addison Gallery Am Art, 46-47; asst dir, Columbus Gallery Fine Arts, 47-55; dir, Fine Arts Gallery San Diego, 55-69.
Memberships: Addison Gallery Am Art; Am Asn Mus; Col Art Asn Am; Am Asn Mus Dirs; Western Asn Mus Dirs.
Mailing Address: 3740 Pio Pico St, San Diego, CA 92106.

BEAL, JACK
    Painter
Preferred Media: Oils.
b Richmond, Va, June 25, 31.
Study & Training: Norfolk Col, William & Mary & Va Polytechnic

Inst, 50-53; Art Inst Chicago, 53-56, with Briggs Dyer, Isobel Mackinnon & Kathleen Blackshear.
Work in Public Collections: Whitney Mus Am Art, New York, N Y; Walker Art Ctr, Minneapolis, Minn; Art Inst Chicago, Ill; San Francisco Mus Fine Arts, Calif; Delaware Mus, Wilmington.
Dealer: Allan Frumkin Gallery, 41 E 57th St, New York, NY 10022 & 620 N Michigan Ave, Chicago, IL 60611.
Mailing Address: 101 Prince St, New York, NY 10012.

BEALL, LESTER THOMAS
Painter, Designer
b Kansas City, Mo, Mar 14, 03.
Study & Training: Univ Chicago, PhB, 26.
Work in Public Collections: Mus Mod Art, New York, N Y.
Commissions: Two murals, comn by Pub Serv Co Northern Ill, 33 & Crane Co, 34, Chicago World's Fair; series of posters, U S Govt, 36-41; identification progs, var nat corps, 40-64; complete graphic prog for SS United States, U S Lines, 51-52; design of two postage stamps, U S Postmaster Gen, 58-67.
Exhibitions: Three Ann Int Watercolor Exhibs, 34-36 & two Ann Am Exhib Watercolors & Drawings, 48-49, Art Inst Chicago; one-man show, Posters, 36 & Word and Image, 68, Mus Mod Art, New York; Exhib of Advan Guard Advert Artists, Katharine Kuh Gallery, Chicago, 41; Modern Art Influences on Printing Design, Libr Cong, Washington, D C, 56; Alliance Graphique Int Mem Exhibs, London, 55, Milan, Italy, 61, Hamburg, Ger, 66, New York, 66, Vienna, Austria & Lucerne, Switz; plus others.
Teaching: Vis lectr, Yale Univ, R I Sch Design, Univ Mich & Pratt Inst.
Positions: Pres & dir, Lester Beall, Inc, 26-69.
Awards: Three U S Govt Citations, 43, 58 & 59; 15 awards for outstanding contrib to develop typographic art of 20th century, Int Ctr Typographic Arts, 64 & 69; Election First Hall of Fame, Art Dirs Club New York, 72.
Bibliography: Dr E Hölscher (auth), Lester Beall, New York, Gebrauchsgraphik, 4/39; Modern advertising: Lester Beall, Norte, 2/42; Franz Hermann Wills (auth), Lester Beall, Graphis, 40: 128-135.
Memberships: Alliance Graphique Int; Am Inst Graphic Arts; Fel Int Inst Arts & Lett; hon mem Soc Typographic Arts; Soc Illustrators.
Publications: Auth, Foundations of design, Fourth Prod Yearbk, 38; auth, Design as applied to advertising, Am Printer, 10/41; auth, What is new in American typography?, Type Dirs Club Prog Sem, 4/59; Auth, A plea for the individual and individuality, Art Dirs Club 9th Commun Conf, 64; auth, Graphic design in the human environment, Print, 3-4/68.
Mailing Address: Dumbarton Farm, Brookfield Center, CT 06805.

BEALMER, WILLIAM
Craftsman, Educator
b Atlanta, Mo, Sept 9, 19.
Study & Training: Northeast Mo State Teachers Col, BSc; Univ Colo, MFA; Chicago Inst Design; Des Moines Art Ctr; Univ Iowa.
Exhibitions: Univ Colo Art Ctr; Des Moines Art Ctr; Sioux City Art Ctr; Joslyn Art Mus, Omaha, Nebr; Art Dept, Grinnell Col & Iowa State Col.
Teaching: Assoc prof art, Northern Ill Univ, 70-
Positions: Spec consult, many univs, schs, filmmakers, TV, art confs & other orgns & insts; asst supt & state supvr art eudc, Springfield, Ill.
Memberships: Nat Art Educ Asn (pres-elect, 67-69, pres, 69-71); Int Soc Educ Through Art; Ill Educ Asn; Nat Educ Asn; Am Craftsmen's Coun; plus others.
Mailing Address: Dept of Art, Northern Illinois University, De Kalb, IL 60115.

BEAM, PHILIP CONWAY
Art Administrator, Educator
b Dallas, Tex, Oct 7, 10.
Study & Training: Harvard Col, AB, 33; Courtauld Inst, Univ London, cert, 36; Harvard Univ, MA, 43, PhD, 44.
Teaching: Asst prof art, Bowdoin Col, 39-46, assoc prof, 46-49, prof, 49-58, chmn dept art, 49-, Henry Johnson prof art & archaeol, 58-; vis prof, Wesleyan Univ, summer 60; lectr, Shelburne Mus, summer 67; vis prof, Wesleyan Univ, summer 69; lectr, Shelburne Mus, summer 70; vis prof art, Univ Vt.
Positions: Dir, Bowdoin Col Mus Art, 39-64; consult, The world of Winslow Homer, Time-Life Bks, 66; cur, Winslow Homer Collection, Bowdoin Col Mus Art, 67-
Memberships: Am Asn Univ Prof; Am Asn Mus; Maine Art Comn (chmn, 54-55).
Publications: Auth, The language of art, Ronald, 58, The art of John Sloan, 62 & Winslow Homer at Prouts Neck, Little, 66.
Mailing Address: 41 Spring St, Brunswick, ME 04011.

BEAMAN, RICHARD BANCROFT
Painter, Educator
Preferred Media: Acrylics.
b Waltham, Mass, June 28, 09.
Study & Training: Univ Exeter; Harvard Univ, SB, 32; Eliot O'Hara Sch Watercolor Painting; Univ Calif, Berkeley; Mass Inst Technol, with Gyorgy Kepes.
Work in Public Collections: Carnegie Inst Mus Art; Westmoreland Co Mus Art.
Commissions: Fused stained glass murals, Hilton Hotel, Rivers Suite, Pittsburgh, Pa, 59; fused stained glass windows, Wayne State Univ Col Educ, Detroit, Mich, 60; fused stained glass wall, Provident Inst for Savings, Prudential Ctr, Boston, Mass, 60's; fused stained glass window, Trinity Church, East Liverpool, Ohio, 61; fused stained glass wall, Commonwealth Bank, Trust Dept, Pittsburgh, 61.
Exhibitions: Regional Shows, New York, Philadelphia, Pa, Washington, D C, Los Angeles, Calif, Pittsburgh & Westmoreland, Pa, 33-72; Carnegie Int, Pittsburgh, 59; one-man show, Carnegie Inst & three one-man shows, Pittsburgh Plan for Art, 62-72.
Teaching: Asst prof art, Univ Redlands, 39-55; Stickney lectr painting, Calif Inst Technol, 48-50; prof painting & art hist, Carnegie-Mellon Univ, 55-
Positions: Pres, Assoc Artists Pittsburgh, 62.
Awards: Purchase prize, Westmoreland Co Mus Art, 62; purchase prize, Carnegie Inst, 63; Louis Comfort Tiffany Award, 65.
Memberships: Pittsburgh Plan for Art (pres, 64-68).
Publications: Auth, The cubist witch, S Atlantic Quart, 49; auth, Vitrail reconsidered, Stained Glass Mag, fall 67.
Dealer: Pittsburgh Plan for Art, 1251 N Negley Ave, Pittsburgh, PA 15206.
Mailing Address: 5718 Fifth Ave, Pittsburgh, PA 15232.

BEAMENT, HAROLD
Painter
Preferred Media: Oils.
b Ottawa, Ont, July 23, 98.
Study & Training: Osgoode Hall Law Sch, Toronto, Barrister-at-law; Ont Col Art.
Work in Public Collections: Nat Gallery Can, Ottawa; Archives Can, Ottawa; Montreal Mus Fine Arts, P Q; Quebec Provincial Mus, Quebec, P Q; Art Gallery Hamilton, Ont.
Exhibitions: British Empire Exhibition, Wembley, Eng, 24-25; Expos Art Can, Mus Jeu Paume, Paris, France, 27; Traveling Southern Dominions of British Empire, 36; A Century of Canadian Art: Tate Gallery, London, Eng; Canadian War Art, Nat Gallery Eng, 44; all arranged by Nat Gallery Can.
Teaching: Instr painting, Montreal Mus Fine Arts, 36-37; instr painting, N S Col Art, 62-63.
Awards: Jessie Dow Prize, Montreal Mus Fine Arts, 36; Can Govt Medal, 67.
Memberships: Academician Royal Can Acad Arts (secy-treas, 60-61, v pres, 62-63, pres, 64-67).
Publications: Auth, articles, In: The Studio (London), 11/15/24 & 2/46.
Mailing Address: 183 St Paul St E, Montreal 127, P Q, Can.

BEAMENT, TIB (THOMAS HAROLD)
Painter, Instructor
b Montreal, P Q, Feb 17, 41.
Study & Training: Fettes Col, Edinburgh, Scotland, O level cert; Ecole Beaux-Arts, Montreal, dipl; Acad Belle Arti, Rome, Italian Govt grant; Ecole Beaux-Arts, Montreal, postgrad studies & teaching cert; Sir George Williams Univ, MA(art educ); also in graphic studios of Shirly Wales, France; Richard Lacroix, Albert Dumouchel, & Atelier 838, Montreal.
Work in Public Collections: Montreal Mus Fine Art; Confederation Art Gallery, Charlottetown, P E I; London Pub Libr & Art Gallery, Ont; Mus Québec, P Q; Rothmans Art Gallery, Stratford, Ont.
Commissions: Decorative Trees (mural), Holiday Inn, Montreal, 65.
Exhibitions: Royal Can Acad Arts, various locations, 64-67 & 70; Fourth Biennale Paris, France, 65; Int Exhib Northwest Printmakers, Seattle, Wash, 65; First Biennial Graphics, Crakov, Poland, 66; Int Exhib Graphics, Montreal, 71.
Teaching: Dir art dept, Edgars & Cramps Sch, Montreal, 67-; also pvt classes in batik, Montreal; instr etching, Univ Que.
Awards: Can Coun grant, 66; spec mention, Price Fine Arts Awards, 70; Elizabeth T Greenshields Found grant, 71-72.
Memberships: Soc Can Painter-Etchers & Engravers.
Dealer: 1640 Gallery, 1445 Crescent St, Montreal, P Q, Can.
Mailing Address: 121 Lewis Ave, Montreal 215, P Q, Can.

BEAN, JACOB
Art Administrator
b Stillwater, Minn, Nov 22, 23.
Study & Training: Harvard Univ.
Teaching: Adj prof, Inst Fine Arts, New York Univ, 67-

Positions: Chargé Mission, Cabinet Dessins, Mus Louvre, Paris, France, 56-60; cur drawings, Metrop Mus Art, 62-; assoc ed, Master Drawings, 63-
Publications: Auth, Les Dessins Italiens de la Collection Bonnat, Bayonne, 60; auth, 100 European Drawings in the Metropolitan Museum of Art, 64; co-auth, Drawings in New York Collections I, The Italian Renaissance, 65, Drawings in New York Collections II, The Seventeenth Century in Italy, 67 & Drawings in New York Collections III, The Eighteenth Century in Italy, 71.
Mailing Address: Metropolitan Museum of Art, Fifth Ave at 82nd St, New York, NY 10028.

BEARD, MARION L PATTERSON
Educator, Painter.
Preferred Media: Watercolors.
b Vincennes, Ind.
Study & Training: Ind State Univ, BS Art; Syracuse Univ, MFA.
Exhibitions: Nat Asn Women Artists Ann, New York, N Y; Am Watercolor Soc, New York Watercolor Club, New York; Hoosier Art Salon, Indianapolis, Ind; Nat Prof Exhib Ann, Ogunquit, Maine; one-man show, H Lieber Art Gallery, Indianapolis.
Teaching: Art supvr, Vincennes City Schs, 36-; supvr art educ, Vincennes Community Schs Corp, 55-; art critic teacher, Indiana State Univ, 57-; art critic teacher, Ind Univ, 61-62; prof painting, Adult Educ Art Dept, Vincennes Univ & Ind Univ, 51-; prof painting, Vincennes Univ Educ Ctr, 51-
Awards: Margaret George Bridwell Mem Watercolor Award & William H Block Co Watercolor Award, Hoosier Art Salon; William E Tirey Mem Watercolor Award, Wabash Valley Artists.
Memberships: Nat Asn Women Artists; Ind Artists Club; Nat Art Educ Asn; Art Educ Asn Ind; Indianapolis Mus Art.
Mailing Address: Rte 1, Vincennes, IN 47591.

BEARDEN, ROMARE HOWARD
Painter
b Charlotte, N C, Sept 2, 14.
Study & Training: New York Univ, BS, 35; Art Stud League, 36-37; Columbia Univ, 43; Sorbonne, cert, 51.
Work in Public Collections: Mus Mod Art, New York, N Y; Whitney Mus, New York; Newark Mus, N J; Albright Mus, Buffalo, N Y.
Exhibitions: One-man shows, Corcoran Gallery, Washington, D C, 66, Mus State Univ N Y, Albany, N Y, 68, Univ Calif Mus Art, Berkeley, Calif, 10/71, retrospective, Mus Mod Art, 3/71-6/71.
Teaching: Vis lectr African & Afro-American art & culture, Williams Col, 69.
Positions: Dir, Cinque Gallery, New York, 69-
Bibliography: Dore Ashton (auth), Romare Bearden—projections, Quadrum—17, 65; Ralph Ellison (auth), foreword in catalogue, Albany Mus, State Univ N Y, 68; Carrol Greene (auth), foreword in catalogue, Mus Mod Art exhibition, 3/71.
Memberships: Black Acad Art & Lett; Am Inst Arts & Lett.
Publications: Auth, The painters mind (with Carl Holty), Crown, 69 & 5 black masters of American art (with Harry Henderson), Doubleday, 72.
Dealer: Cordier & Ekstrom Inc, 980 Madison Ave, New York, NY 10021.
Mailing Address: 357 Canal St, New York, NY 10013.

BEASLEY, BRUCE
Sculptor
Preferred Media: Acrylic Plastic, Metal.
b Los Angeles, Calif, May 20, 39.
Study & Training: Dartmouth Col; Univ Calif, Berkeley, BA.
Work in Public Collections: Mus Mod Art, New York, N Y; Solomon R Guggenheim Mus, New York; Los Angeles Co Mus Art, Los Angeles; Musee d'Art Moderne, Paris, France; Univ Art Mus, Berkeley.
Commissions: Apolymen, cast acrylic sculpture, State Calif, 70; cast acrylic sculptures, Oakland Art Mus & Southland Shopping Ctr, Hayward, Calif, 72.
Exhibitions: Art of Assemblage, Mus Mod Art, New York, 61; Biennale de Paris, Musee d'Art Moderne, 63; Selected Acquisitions, Solomon R Guggenheim Mus, 66; A Plastic Presence, Jewish Mus, New York & Milwaukee Art Ctr, San Francisco Mus Art, 69-70; American Sculpture in Perspective, Sheldon Art Gallery, Univ Nebr, 70.
Awards: Andre Malraux Purchase Award, Biennale de Paris, 63; Frank Lloyd Wright Memorial Purchase Award, Marin Mus Asn, 65; purchase prize, San Francisco Arts Festival, 67.
Bibliography: The crystal clear scene, Time Mag, 2/9/68; Shipley & Weller (auth), Contemporary American painting and sculpture, Univ Ill Press, 69; Hotaling (auth), The age of Lucite dawns in Sacramento, Art News, 5/70.
Dealers: Andre Emmerich Gallery, 41 E 57th St, New York, NY 10022; Hansen-Fuller Gallery, 228 Grant Ave, San Francisco, CA 94108.
Mailing Address: 322 Lewis St, Oakland, CA 94607.

BEATTIE, GEORGE
Educator, Painter
Preferred Media: Acrylics.
b Cleveland, Ohio, Aug 2, 19.
Study & Training: Cleveland Inst Art, 38-41.
Work in Public Collections: Whitney Mus Am Art, New York, N Y; Montclair Mus, N J; High Mus of Atlanta Mem Arts Ctr, Ga; Mead Painting of the Year; Larry Aldrich Collection, Conn.
Commissions: Paintings, History of Agriculture in State of Georgia, State Agr Bldg, Atlanta, 56 & History of Middle Georgia, Fed Post Off Bldg, Macon, Ga, 68.
Exhibitions: Mead Painting of the Year, 55 & 61; Int Drawing Ann, Uffizi Loggia, Florence, Italy, 57; Fulbright Exhib, Rome, Italy, 57; Smithsonian Traveling Exhib, 58-59; Art U S A, 59.
Teaching: Head creative drawing, Ga Inst Technol Sch Archit, 57-67.
Positions: Exec dir, Ga Comn on Arts, 67-
Awards: Nat Inst Arts & Lett grant, 55; Fulbright grant to Italy, 56-57; artist, Link Archaeol Expeds to Israel, 60 & Sicily, 62.
Bibliography: Margaret Harold (auth), Oil paintings and why they won the prize, Allied Publ, 60; Nina Kaiden & Bartlett Hayes (auth), Artist and advocate, Renaissance Ed, 67.
Memberships: Atlanta Mem Arts Ctr, High Mus (mem bd sponsors); Arts Festival Atlanta, Inc (hon life mem bd trustees).
Mailing Address: 857 Woodley Dr N W, Atlanta, GA 30318.

BEAUCHEMIN, MICHELINE
Painter, Weaver
Preferred Media: Wool, Acrylics, Metallic Threads.
b Longueuil, P Q, Oct 24, 31.
Study & Training, École Beaux Arts Montreal; École Beaux Arts Paris, France, with Zadkine; also with Tatsumura & Kawashima, Kyoto, Japan.
Work in Public Collections: Nat Art Gallery, Ottawa; Montreal Mus Fine Arts; Quebec Mus Fine Arts; Malton Int Airport, Toronto; Montreal Star.
Commissions: Tapestry, Place Arts, Salle Wilfrid Laurier, Montreal, 63; tapestry, Ont Prov Govt, Queens Park, 68; stage curtain tapestry, hand woven, Opera House, Nat Art Ctr, Ottawa, 69; tapestry, Sci & Humanities Bldg, York Univ, tapestry, 70; Can Pavilion, Expo 70, Osaka, Japan, 70.
Exhibitions: First Nat Can Craft Exhib, Ottawa, 57; Brussels World's Fair, 57; Solo Exhibs, Montreal Mus Fine Arts, 60 & Nihon Bashi Gallery, Tokyo, Japan, 68; Retrospective Solo, Ctr Cult Can, Paris, 71.
Awards: Silver medal, Gov Gen Can, 67; Can Coun Award, Can Govt, 72.
Bibliography: Claude Gauvreau (auth), L'itinéraire de l'ange, Cult Vivante No 3, 67; Michel Mercier (producer), Femme d'aujourd'hui (TV film), 71; Claude Lyse Gagnon, Au mur, Vie Arts, 72.
Memberships: Royal Can Soc Arts (mem coun, 71).
Publications: Illusr & auth, Minstra, Can Arts, 59; illusr, covers, Vie Arts, 59 & Can Arts, 59; Fin d'une enfance, Marie Claire Blais, Chatelaine, 63.
Mailing Address: 22 Chemin du Roy, Les Grondines, Cté Portneuf, P Q, Can.

BEAVER, FRED
Painter, Lecturer
Preferred Media: Watercolor.
b Eufaula, Okla, July 2, 11.
Work in Public Collections: Philbrook Art Ctr, Tulsa, Okla; Gilcrease Mus Art & Hist, Tulsa; Heard Mus, Phoenix, Ariz; Five-Tribes Mus, Muskogee, Okla.
Commissions: Indian Dancers, Thunderbird Motel, Oklahoma City, Okla, 57; Indian Dancers, 23rd & May Ave Bank, Oklahoma City, 59; Seminole Indian Life, Arts & Crafts Ctr, Bur Indian Affairs, Washington, D C, 61; Indian Outlook, Durwood Indian Church, Ardmore, Okla, 63.
Exhibitions: American Indian Paintings Exhibs, Tulsa, 47- & Heard Mus, 63-71; Indian Paintings, Scottsdale, Ariz, 65-71; Five-Tribes Mus exhibs, 67-71; regional art show, Tulsa, 70.
Awards: Trophy, Waite Phillips Found, Tulsa, 63; Heritage Award, Indian Heritage Found, Muskogee, 68; drawing award, Murray Col, Tishomingo, Okla, 70.
Bibliography: Dorothy Dunn (auth), American Indian Painting; article, Indian Art, S Dak Rev, 69; plus others.
Publications: Illusr, Creek-Seminole spirit tales, 71.
Mailing Address: 437 Locust St N W, Ardmore, OK 73401.

BECHTLE, C RONALD
Painter
Preferred Media: Watercolors, Gouache.
b Philadelphia, Pa, Nov 14, 24.
Study & Training: East Tenn Univ; Tyler Sch Fine Arts, Temple Univ; Fleisher Mem, Sch Indust Art; also with Benton Spruance, 52-53.

Work in Public Collections: Munson-Williams-Proctor Inst, Utica, N Y; Denver Art Mus, Colo; Santa Barbara Mus Art, Calif; Columbus Gallery Fine Art, Ohio; Phoenix Art Mus, Ariz.

Exhibitions: Pa Acad Fine Arts Regional, 65 & 69; one-man shows, Panoras Gallery, New York, N Y, 66, Santa Barbara Mus Art, 67, Miami Mus Mod Art, Fla, 68 & St Joseph's Col Gallery, Philadelphia, 70.

Positions: Pres, Group 55, 56-57; pres, Philadelphia Abstract Artists, 57-63.

Memberships: Artists Equity Asn; Philadelphia Art Alliance; Mus Mod Art, New York; Am Fedn Arts; Philadelphia Watercolor Club.

Publications: Auth, Information Theory of Art, Mensa J, 61.

Dealer: Storelli Gallery, 1130 Pine St, Philadelphia, PA 19107.

Mailing Address: Apt 5B, 26 Strawberry Hill Ave, Stamford, CT 06902.

BECHTLE, ROBERT ALAN
Painter
b San Francisco, Calif, May 14, 32.
Study & Training: Calif Col Arts & Crafts, BAA, MFA; Univ Calif, Berkeley.
Work in Public Collections: Whitney Mus Am Art, New York, N Y; Mus Mod Art, New York; Neue Gallerie, Aachen, Ger; Univ Calif Art Mus, Berkeley; City Art Mus, Saint Louis, Mo.
Exhibitions: Contemp Am Painting, 67 & 22 Realists, 69, Whitney Mus Am Art, New York; Aspects of a New Realism, Milwaukee Art Ctr, Wis, 68; Radical Realism, Mus Contemp Art, Chicago, Ill, 71; Documenta 5, Kassel, Ger, 72.
Teaching: Prof printmaking, Calif Col Arts & Crafts, 57-; guest artist, Univ Calif, Davis, 66-68; assoc prof painting, Calif State Univ, San Francisco, 68-
Awards: James D Phelan Award in painting, 65.
Bibliography: B Lord (auth), The eleven o'clock news in color, ArtsCan, 6/70; C Ratcliff (auth), article, In: Art Int, 2/72; U Kultermann (auth), Radical realism, New York Graphic Soc, 72.
Dealer: O K Harris Gallery, 465-69 W Broadway, New York, NY 10012.
Mailing Address: 850 Mendocino Ave, Berkeley, CA 94707.

BECK, MARGIT
Painter, Lecturer
Preferred Media: Oils.
b Tokay, Hungary.
Study & Training: Inst Fine Arts, Oradea Mare, Roumania; Art Stud League New York.
Work in Public Collections: Whitney Mus Am Art, New York, N Y; J B Speed Mus, Louisville, Ky; Washington Co Mus Fine Arts, Hagerstown, Md; Lyman Allyn Mus, New London, Conn; Norfolk Mus Arts & Sci, Norfolk, Va; plus others.
Commissions: Portrait of Bayonne (oil), N J Jewish Community Art Ctr, Bayonne, 72.
Exhibitions: Corcoran Gallery Art Biennial, 65; four shows, Pa Acad Fine Arts Ann, 57-68; Whitney Mus Am Art Ann, 58-60; four shows, Brooklyn Mus Int Watercolor Biennial, 59-67; Art Inst Chicago, 60-61; plus other group & one-woman exhibs.
Teaching: Lectr art, Hofstra Univ, 66-67; lectr art, New York Univ, 67-
Awards: Henry Ward Ranger Purchase Award, Nat Acad Design, 65; Childe Hassam Purchase Award, Am Acad Arts & Lett, 68, 70 & 71; medal of honor, Audubon Artists, 68 & 72; plus others.
Bibliography: Brian O'Doherty (auth), Unfashionable virtues of a personal cubism, New York Times, 5/12/62; Mel Shapiro (auth), Margit Beck (monogr), L I Mag, 12/62; John Gruen (auth), Wistful vista, New York Mag, 2/1/71.
Memberships: Artists Equity Asn (exec bd mem, 65-70); Audubon Artists (v pres, 66-70).
Dealer: Babcock Galleries, 805 Madison Ave, New York, NY 10021.
Mailing Address: 22 Florence St, Great Neck, NY 11021.

BECK, ROSEMARIE (ROSEMARIE BECK PHELPS)
Painter, Educator
Preferred Media: Oils.
U S citizen.
Study & Training: Oberlin Col; Columbia Univ; N Y Univ.
Work in Public Collections: Whitney Mus Am Art; Vassar Col Mus; State Univ N Y Col New Paltz; Hirshhorn Collection; Nebr Art Mus.
Commissions: Mural painting, Rotron Mfg Co, 58.
Exhibitions: Pa Acad Fine Arts; Nat Inst Arts & Lett; Whitney Mus Am Art; Art Inst Chicago; eleven one-man shows, Peridot Gallery.
Teaching: Lectr painting, Vassar Col, 57-58, 61-62 & 63-64; lectr painting, Middlebury Col, 58-60 & 63; lectr painting, Queens Col, 68-
Awards: Ingram-Merrill grant, 67.
Dealer: Peridot Gallery, 820 Madison Ave, New York, NY 10021.
Mailing Address: 6 E 12th St, New York, NY 10003.

BECK, STEPHEN R
Painter, Educator
Preferred Media: Acrylic Lacquer
b Salt Lake City, Utah, Dec 28, 37.
Study & Training: Univ. Utah, BFA; Cranbrook Acad Art, MFA.
Work in Public Collections: Cranbrook Acad Art Galleries, Bloomfield Hills, Mich; Kingswood Sch-Cranbrook, Bloomfield Hills; Salt Lake Art Ctr; Utah Mus Fine Arts, Salt Lake City; Univ. Utah, Salt Lake City.
Exhibitions: U S Senate Bldg, Washington, D C, 65; Mich Ann, Detroit, 65; Western Regional Biennial, Salt Lake City, 71; Westminster Col Invitational, Salt Lake City, 71; 73rd Ann Western Invitational, Denver, Colo, 71.
Teaching: Instr drawing & painting & admin asst, Univ Utah, 68-
Positions: Mem adv comt, Utah State Inst Fine Arts, Salt Lake City, 70-
Awards: Purchase awards, Salt Lake Art Ctr, 70 & 72.
Dealer, Max Hutchinson Gallery, 127 Greene St, New York, NY 10012.
Mailing Address: Dept of Art, University of Utah, Salt Lake City, UT 84112.

BECKER, BETTIE (BETTIE GERALDINE WATHALL)
Painter
Preferred Media: Collage, Acrylics.
b Peoria, Ill, Sept 22, 18.
Study & Training: Univ Ill, BFA; Art Stud League New York, with John Carroll; Art Inst Chicago, with Lewis Ritman; Inst Design, Ill Inst Technol, with Hans Weber.
Work in Public Collections: Witte Mem Mus, San Antonio, Tex; Union League Club, Chicago, Ill.
Commissions: Mural (with Frank Wiater), Talbot Materials Testing Lab, Univ Ill, Urbana, 40.
Exhibitions: Drawings U S A, St Paul, Minn, 66-68; Fifth Ann Tippecanoe Regional, Lafayette, Ind, 67; Festival De Arte De Las Dos Banderas, U S-Mexico, Douglas, Ariz, 72; Ninth Union League Art Show, Chicago, 72; Critic's Choice, Art Inst Chicago, 72.
Awards: Newcomb prize, Univ Ill Col Fine & Applied Arts, 40; George R Bailey purchase prize, Union League Club, Chicago, 72; hon mention, Artist's Guild, Chicago, 72.
Memberships: Chicago Soc Artists (rec secy, 68-); Renaissance Soc, Univ Chicago; Alumni Asn, Art Inst Chicago; Wis Arts Coun; Penninsula Arts Asn.
Publications: Auth, Life with liberty, 43; illusr, Sat Rev of Literature, 48, New York Times, 48, Chicago Tribune, 48 & 49 & Evanston Rev, 68.
Mailing Address: 1817 Asbury Ave, Evanston, IL 60201.

BECKER, CHARLOTTE (MRS WALTER COX)
Illustrator, Painter
Preferred Media: Oils.
b Dresden, Ger; U S citizen.
Study & Training: Cooper Union; Industrial Arts Night Sch; Art Stud League New York.
Memberships: New York Camera Club.
Art Interests: Painted over a thousand magazine covers, art calendars and art prints, all of children.
Publications: Auth & illusr, Helo Judy stories, 50, Stories for fun, 50, Unlike twin series, 52 & Three little steps series, 52, Scribner; auth & illusr, A chimp in the family, Messner (in prep); also many other children's bks.
Mailing Address: Pine Plains, NY 12567.

BECKMANN, HANNES
Painter, Educator
Preferred Media: Oils, Acrylics.
b Stuttgart, W Ger, Oct 8, 09; U S citizen.
Study & Training: Bauhaus, Dessau, Ger, dipl; also with Paul Klee, Wasily Kandinsky, & Josef Albers.
Work in Public Collections: Mus Fine Arts, Boston, Mass; Mus Fine Arts, Newark, N J; Busch-Reisinger Mus, Cambridge, Mass; Dartmouth Col, Hanover, N H.
Exhibitions: The Responsive Eye, Mus Mod Art, New York, 65.
Teaching: Prof psychol of perception & basic color & design, Cooper Union, 53-70; vis critic, Yale Univ, 59-60; lectr, Harvard Univ; fac mem, Dartmouth Col, 70-
Dealer: Kanegis Gallery, 244 Newbury St, Boston, MA 02116.
Mailing Address: 10 Woodrow Rd, Hanover, NH 03755.

BEDFORD, HELEN DE WILTON
Educator
b Columbia, Mo, Nov 12, 04.
Study & Training: Univ Mo, BS(educ), 25; Teachers Col, Columbia Univ, 31; Univ N Mex, 52.
Exhibitions: All Faculty Show, Southeast Mo State Univ, Cape Girardeau, 69.

Teaching: Prof ceramics, crafts & art educ, Southeast Mo State Univ, 25-, head art dept, 25-72; prof & head dept art, Kappa Pi, 62-70.
Memberships: Mo State Teachers Asn; Community Teachers Asn; Kappi Pi (sponsor, 62-70); Int Platform Asn; Southeastern Mo Art Educators (sponsor, 25-).
Collection: Indian arts and crafts; birds in paintings, prints & third dimensional.
Mailing Address: 1030 Merriwether, Cape Girardeau, MO 63701.

BEDNO, EDWARD
Designer, Educator
b Chicago, Ill, Mar 8, 25.
Study & Training: Art Inst Chicago, BFA; Inst Design, Ill Inst Technol, MS; Northwestern Univ; Univ Chicago.
Exhibitions: Art Dirs Club, Chicago; Soc Typographic Artists; Contemp Design Exhib, Los Angeles; Midwest Bk Clin; Am Inst Graphic Arts; plus others.
Teaching: Instr, Northwestern Univ, Evanston, 51-52; instr, Inst Design, Ill Inst Technol, 57, lectr, 60-64, asst prof, 64-
Positions: Pres, Bedno Assocs, Chicago, Ill.
Awards: Award, Midwest Film Festival.
Publications: Contribr, photog essay, Am Heritage Mag, 64.
Mailing Address: 5009 S Ellis Ave, Chicago, IL 60626.

BEELKE, RALPH G
Educator
Preferred Media: Oils, Acrylics.
b Buffalo, N Y, Dec 16, 17.
Study & Training: Buffalo Sch Fine Arts, dipl; Columbia Univ, MA, 47, EdD, 52.
Teaching: Instr art, pub schs & cols, 40-52; head, Dept Art, State Univ N Y, Col Fredonia, 51-56; head, Dept Creative Arts, Purdue Univ, 62-
Positions: Ed, Eastern Arts Asn Bull, 55-57; specialist educ in arts, Off Educ, Dept Health, Educ & Welfare, Washington, D C, 56-58; exec secy art educ, Nat Art Educ Asn, Washington, D C, 58-62; ed, Art Educ J & Western Arts Asn Bull, 58-62.
Awards: Art Educator of Yr, Nat Art Educ Asn, 63.
Memberships: Col Art Asn; Nat Art Educ Asn (pres, 65-67); Am Soc Aesthet & Art Criticism.
Publications: Contribr, Sch Arts Mag, 55-62; auth, Curriculum development art education, 62.
Mailing Address: 304 Hollowood Dr, West Lafayette, IN 47906.

BEERMAN, HERBERT
Painter, Educator
b Newark, N J, Nov 8, 26.
Study & Training: Rutgers Univ; Univ Miami, AB; Sch Design, Yale Univ, BFA, with Josef Albers.
Exhibitions: One-man shows, Artists Gallery, New York, N Y, Krasner Gallery, New York, Seton Hall Univ & Saratoga Springs, N Y; Newark Mus; Fairleigh Dickinson Univ; plus others.
Teaching: Lect contemp art, Rutgers Univ, Seton Hall Univ & Cornell Univ; instr painting, Arts Workshop, Newark Mus; from instr color theory & 2-D design to assoc prof art, Sch Art & Design, Pratt Inst, 60-
Awards: MacDowell fel, 58, 59 & 61; prize, Saratoga Centennial, 63; Yaddo fel, 63 & 64.
Memberships: Artists Equity Asn.
Mailing Address: School of Art & Design, Pratt Institute, Brooklyn, NY 11205.

BEERMAN, MIRIAM H
Painter
Preferred Media: Oils.
b Providence, R I.
Study & Training: R I Sch Design, BFA; Art Stud League New York, with Yasuo Kuniyoshi; New Sch Social Res, with Adja Yunkers; Atelier 17, Paris, France, with Stanley Hayter.
Work in Public Collections: Whitney Mus Am Art, New York, N Y; Brooklyn Mus, N Y; Andrew Dickson White Mus, Cornell Univ, Ithaca, N Y; New Sch Social Res, New York.
Exhibitions: The Humanist Tradition in Contemporary American Painting, New Sch Social Res, 68; American Drawings of the Sixties, New Sch Art Ctr, 69; Am Acad Arts & Lett, New York, 69; one-woman exhibs, Brooklyn Mus, 71-72 & Graham Gallery, New York, 72; plus many others.
Teaching: Instr art, Miami Univ, Ohio, 48-49; instr art, Roslyn Pub Schs, N Y, 54-61; instr art, MUSE (Brooklyn Children's Mus), 69-
Awards: Fulbright grant, 51-53; award, 11th R I Arts Festival, 69; Cult Coun Found grant, Creative Artist's Pub Serv Prog, 71.
Bibliography: Gene Thornton, The critical people (rev & anal), 10/27/68 & 1/26/69; The new grotesques, Time Mag, 6/13/69; Barry Schwartz (auth), Humanism in modern art, Praeger (in prep).

Publications: Ed & illusr, The enduring beast, Doubleday, 72.
Dealer: Graham Gallery, 1014 Madison Ave, New York, NY 10021.
Mailing Address: 25 Eastern Pkwy, Brooklyn, NY 11238.

BEERY, ARTHUR O
Painter
Preferred Media: Oil, Watercolor.
b Marion, Ohio, Mar 4, 30.
Work in Public Collections: Butler Inst Am Art, Youngstown, Ohio; Erie Art Ctr, Pa; Lessco Data, New York, N Y; J M Katz Collection, Pa.
Commissions: Murals of Athens, Greece, Monte Carlo, Stromboli, Rock of Gibralter & Charleston, S C for U S Navy Minecraft Base, Charleston, 54.
Exhibitions: Pa Acad Fine Arts, Philadelphia, 68; Butler Inst Am Art, 68-70 & 72; Watercolor U S A, Springfield, Mo, 71; 23rd Grand Prix Int, Deauville, France, 72; Contemp Am Art Invitational, Cernuschi Gallery, Paris, France, 72.
Awards: People's Choice, Ohio State Fair, 67; Inst Award, Butler Inst Am Art, 68; Richard P Stahl Award, Watercolor U S A, 71.
Memberships: Mansfield Fine Arts Guild, Ohio; Columbus Art League, Ohio.
Dealer: Watercolors of Columbus, Columbus, OH 44116.
Mailing Address: 378 Lynn Dr, Marion, OH 43302.

BEETZ, CARL HUGO
Painter, Instructor
Preferred Media: Oils, Acrylics, Watercolors, Lithography.
b San Francisco, Calif, Dec 25, 11.
Study & Training: Calif Sch Fine Arts, San Francisco, 29, with Spencer Macky; Grand Cent Sch Art, New York, 30-31, with Grant Reynard; Art Stud League New York, 31, with George Bridgman; Chouinard Art Inst, Los Angeles, with Pruett Carter, 31-35, cert, 35.
Work in Public Collections: San Francisco Mus Art, Calif.
Exhibitions: Western States Watercolor Exhib, Riverside Mus, New York, N Y, 40; 20th Int Exhib of Watercolors, Art Inst Chicago, Ill, 41; one-man shows, Los Angeles Co Mus, Calif, 42 & M H De Young Mem Mus, San Francisco, 44; J and E R Pennell Exhibition of Prints, Libr Cong, Washington, D C, 44-45.
Teaching: Instr life drawing, Chouinard Art Inst, 35-44; instr life drawing & illus, Acad Advert Art, San Francisco, 44-53; prof drawing & painting, Calif Col Arts & Crafts, Oakland, 44-58; instr drawing & painting, City Col of San Francisco, 45-71.
Awards: First prize, Calif Painters Exhib, Redlands Art Guild, 41; hon mention, Calif Watercolor Soc, 43.
Bibliography: Janice Lovoos (auth), The drawings and lithographs of Carl Beetz, Am artist Mag, 1/60.
Mailing Address: 266 27th Ave, San Francisco, CA 94121.

BEGG, JOHN ALFRED
Designer, Sculptor
Preferred Media: Bronze
b New Smyrna, Fla, June 23, 03.
Study & Training: Columbia Univ, BS; studied sculpture with Jose De Creeft & Ossip Zadkine.
Work in Public Collections: Addison Gallery Am Art, Andover, Mass; Hudson River Mus, Yonkers, N Y; New York Pub Libr, N Y.
Exhibitions: Am Sculpture of Our Time, 43 & Recent Work by Am Sculptors, 45, Buchholz Gallery; Contemporary American Sculpture, Watercolors and Drawings, Whitney Mus Am Art, 45 & 50; Sculpture at the Crossroads, Worcester Art Mus, 48; one-man shows, Hudson River Mus, 62 & 67.
Teaching: Lectr basic design, New York Univ, 50-58.
Positions: Art ed & bk designer, Am Bk Co, New York, 32-37; art dir, Oxford Univ Press, New York, 39-68, v pres, 60-68; art dir, Art in Am, 57-59.
Awards: First prize for sculpture, 58, 59 & 64 & purchase award, 70, Yonkers Art Asn, Hudson River Mus; first prize for sculpture, Greenburgh Arts & Cult Comt, 71.
Bibliography: Alfred Puhn (auth), Sculptor and model, Hellman, Williams & Co, 49; Bartlett Hayes, Jr (auth), The naked truth and personal vision, Addison Gallery Art, 55.
Memberships: Typophiles; Yonkers Art Asn (chmn, 72-73).
Collection: Primitive art.
Publications: Auth, Form and format (monogr), 49; auth, Book Design in U S A, Schweizer Graphische Mitt, 50; auth, Abstract art and typographic format, Mag of Art, 52.
Mailing Address: 137 S Broadway, Hastings-on-Hudson, NY 10706.

BEGGS, THOMAS MONTAGUE
Art Administrator, Painter
Preferred Media: Oil, Fresco, Tempera.
b Brooklyn, N Y, Apr 22, 99.
Study & Training: Pratt Inst; Art Stud League New York; Yale Univ, BFA; Ecole Am Beaux-Arts, Fontainebleu, France; Harvard Univ, Carnegie scholar, 28-29.

Work in Public Collections: Portrait of Jasper Newton Field, Redlands Univ.

Commissions: Club Room Overmantle, Miami Realty Bd, Fla, 26; Guild Hall Overmantle, Claremont Congregational Church, Calif, 28; Mem Court Bench, Pomona Col, 33.

Exhibitions: Los Angeles Co Fair, 27; Ebell Club, Los Angeles, 37; Washington Watercolor Club, 48.

Collections Arranged: Weather in Art, Pomona Col Art Gallery, 46; Pictorial Art of the American Indian, Nat Collection Fine Arts, 49; Art and Magic in Arnhem Land, 50 & Art and Archaeology of Viet Nam, 59, Smithsonian Inst.

Teaching: Prof art & head dept, Pomona Col, 26-47.

Positions: Dir, Nat Collection Fine Arts, Smithsonian Inst, 48-64, spec asst to secy fine arts, 65-

Awards: Fed Repub Ger Travel Grant, 54; gold medal for advan Am art, Am Artists Prof League, 63.

Publications: Auth, Artist in residence, Parnassus, 12/40; auth, The golden brush of Kristian Krekovic, Am Mag of Art; auth, Harriet Lane Johnston and the National Collection of Fine Arts, Smithsonian Report for 1954, 55.

Mailing Address: 6540 Hitt Ave, McLean, VA 22101.

BEHL, MARJORIE
Painter
Preferred Media: Watercolors, Oils.
b Pocahontas, Ark.
Study & Training: Layton Art Inst, William & Mary Col; Calif Col Arts & Crafts; Old Dominion Univ; also with George Post & Charles Sibley.

Work in Public Collections: Alfred Khouri Collection, Walter Chrysler Mus, Norfolk, Va; Valentine Mus, Richmond, Va; Univ Va Permanent Collection, Charlottesville, Va; Borden Chemical Co, Smith-Douglas Div, Virginia Beach, Va; Public School Purchase Collection, Norfolk, Va.

Exhibitions: One of Three Rotating Show, Va State Mus, Richmond; Soc Western Artists, M H De Young Mem Mus, San Francisco, 64; Tidewater Artists Asn Show & Am Drawing Biennial, Norfolk Mus, Va, 64; one-man show, Norfolk Mus, 66; State of Fla Watercolor Show, Sarasota Art Mus, 72; plus many others.

Teaching: Instr art, Carolton Oaks Sch, Norfolk High Schs & Jewish Community Ctr, Norfolk, 63-67; lectr, Tidewater Art Asn, Women's Club & others, 60-64.

Awards: First prize watercolor, Ark State Watercolor Exhib, 57; first prizes in watercolor, Va Beach Boardwalk Shows, 57-68; first prize for watercolor, Tidewater Artists Asn Biannual, 65.

Memberships: Sarasota Art Asn; Tidewater Artists Asn (bd mem, 60-64, chmn Azalea Festival, 57-60); Soc Western Artists.

Mailing Address: Villa 13, 6308 Midnight Pass Rd, Sarasota, FL 33581.

BEHL, WOLFGANG
Sculptor, Educator
Preferred Media: Wood, Bronze, Stone.
b Berlin, Ger, Apr 13, 18; U S citizen.
Study & Training: Acad Fine Art, Berlin, Ger; R I Sch Design.

Work in Public Collections: Pa Acad Fine Arts, Philadelphia; Addison Gallery Am Art; Conn Gen Ins Co; New Britain Mus Am Art; Cornell Univ.

Commissions: Welded cross & bronze stations of the cross, St Timothy Church, West Hartford, Conn, 61; bronze group of holy family, Rectory of St Joseph's Cathedral, Hartford, 63; welded menorah & eternal light, Temple Beth Sholom, Manchester, Conn, 64; bronze tabernacle & processional cross, Church of the Resurrection, Wallingford, Conn, 66; Reredos, Immanuel Lutheran Church, Attleboro, Mass, 69.

Exhibitions: Plastics U S A, Soviet Union, 60; Carnegie Int, Pittsburgh, Pa, 64; Fogg Art Mus, Harvard Univ, Cambridge, Mass, 66; Hemisfair 68, San Antonio, Tex, 68; Retrospective, New Britain Mus, 68.

Teaching: Asst prof sculpture & drawing, William & Mary Col, 45-53; prof sculpture, Univ Hartford, 55-

Awards: Sculpture awards, Conn Acad Fine Arts, 61, 63 & 64; Nat Inst Arts & Lett grant, 63; Ford Found Purchase Award, 64.

Bibliography: Retrospective catalogue, New Britain Mus, 69; Eye to Eye (film), WGBH Pub TV, Boston, 71.

Memberships: Nat Sculpture Ctr (adv bd, 68-); Sculptors Guild (dir, 72).

Dealer: New Bertha Schaefer Gallery, 41 E 57th St, New York, NY 10022.

Mailing Address: 179 Kenyon St, Hartford, CT 06105.

BEINEKE, DR & MRS J FREDERICK
Collectors
Dr Beineke, b Decatur, Ind, Apr 5, 27.
Collection: African and South Pacific art; Japanese woodblock prints; ancient art, ethnographica, old graphic art and modern Far East art.
Mailing Address: Romford Rd, Washington Depot, CT 06794.

BEITZ, LESTER U
Painter, Illustrator
b Buffalo, N Y, May 11, 16.
Study & Training: Art Inst Buffalo; also with Charles S Bigelow.
Work in Public Collections: In pvt collections only.
Commissions: Murals, Officer's Club, Royal Air Force Sta, Fairford, Eng & Enlisted Men's Club, Schilling Air Force Base, Salina, Kans, 62.
Art Interests: Specializes in the portrayal of the American West.
Publications: Auth, Illusr, A treasury of frontier relics; contribr, articles, illus & features on frontier Americana, In: Real West, Desert, Western Digest, Argosy, Ford Times & var other mag.
Mailing Address: 2407 Audubon Pl, Austin, TX 78741.

BEJAR, FELICIANO
Sculptor, Painter
Preferred Media: Crystal, Plastic
b Jiquilpan, Mex, July 14, 20.
Work in Public Collections: Mus Arte Mod, Mexico City, Mex; Birmingham City Mus, Eng; Herron Mus, Indianapolis, Ind; Lowe Mus, Univ Miami, Coral Gables, Fla; Mus Fine Art, Montreal, P Q.

Commissions: Series of 8 paintings, Roussel Labs, Mexico City, 67; series of 300 Magiscope sculptures in plastic, J Walter Thompson Co, New York, N Y, 71; series of 13 Magiscope sculptures in crystal, Carborundum Co, Niagara Falls, N Y, 72; series of 12 prints, Spode Porcelain Co, Stoke-on-Trent, Eng, 72; Magiscope sculpture, Banco Nacional de Mexico, Palacio De Iturbide, Mexico City, 72.

Exhibitions: One-man shows, Magiscopes, Bertha Schaefer Gallery, New York, 66, 68 & 71, The World of Feliciano Bejar, City Mus, Sheffield, Eng, 66, Magiscopes 1966-1970, Mus Arte Mod, Mexico City, 70, Magiscopes, 1964-1970, Grosvenor Gallery, London, Eng, 70 & Retrospective Exhib, Galerie Valentin, Zurich, Switz, 72.

Bibliography: Nelken, Fernandez, Xirau, De La Maza (authors), Feliciano Bejar 1947-1962, Nat Inst Fine Arts, Mexico City, 62; Ian Hugo (film dir), Through the Magiscope, 68; Edward Lucie-Smith (auth), Feliciano Bejar, Turret Bks, London, 72.

Memberships: Salon Plastica Mexicana; Mexico City; World Crafts Coun, New York.

Art Interests: Inventor of special form of optical sculpture using lenses and prisms and other reflective and refractive forms in plastic and crystal, given generic name of Magiscopes.

Dealer: Martin Foley, Arvil S A, Hamburgo 241, Mexico 6 D F, Mex.

Mailing Address: Apartado Postal 20-029, Mexico 20, D F, Mex.

BELINE, GEORGE
Painter, Sculptor
b Minsk, Russia, July 23, 87.
Study & Training: Nat Acad Design; Lycee Charlemagne, Ecole Beaux-Arts, Ecole Superieure Places Vosges, Paris, France.
Work in Public Collections: Many pub & pvt collections.
Exhibitions: Nat Acad Design, New York, N Y; Pa Acad Fine Arts, Philadelphia; Am Watercolor Soc, New York; Ogunquit Art Ctr, Maine; Am Artists Prof League, New York; plus others.
Memberships: Allied Artists Am; Hudson Valley Art Asn; Salmagundi Club; Am Artists Prof League; Hunterdon Co Art Ctr.
Mailing Address: Delaware River Dr, Frenchtown, NJ 08825.

BELING, HELEN
Sculptor, Instructor
Preferred Media: Reinforced Fiber Glass, Bronze.
b New York, N Y, Jan 1, 14.
Study & Training: Nat Acad Design, 30-37, with Paul Manship & Lee Lawrie; Art Stud League New York, 44-45, with William Zorach.
Work in Public Collections: Butler Inst Am Art, Youngstown, Ohio; Syracuse Univ Mus, N Y; Norfolk Mus Arts & Sci, Va; St Lawrence Univ, Canton, N Y; TV Mus Art & Sci, New York.
Commissions: Eternal Light (brass), Jewish Community Ctr, White Plains, N Y, 57; Menorah (bronze), Temple Israel, Waterbury, Conn, 59; Eternal Light (bronze), Temple B'nai Jacob, Woodbridge, Conn, 61; Candelabra Room (ceramic), Pleasant Valley Home, West Orange, N J, 62; Exodus (wall relief), Temple Emanu-el, Yonkers, N Y, 66.
Exhibitions: Nine one-man shows, Pa Acad Fine Arts, 50-66; Metrop Mus Art Sculpture Exhib, 51; Sculptors Guild Ann, 54-71; Whitney Mus Am Art, 55; Univ Ill, 57.
Teaching: Instr sculpture, Westchester Art Workshop, White Plains, 50-66; instr sculpture, Col New Rochelle, 70-71.
Awards: Sculpture award, Sabena Airline Int Co, 53; medals of honor, Nat Asn Women Artists, 58 & 68; medal of honor, Audubon Artists, 65.
Memberships: Nat Asn Women Artists (chmn sculpture jury, 68-70); Sculptors Guild (pres, 72); Fine Arts Fedn (bd dirs, 72).
Dealer: Krasner Gallery, 1061 Madison Ave, New York, NY 10021.
Mailing Address: 287 Weyman Ave, New Rochelle, NY 10805.

BELKIN, ARNOLD
Painter, Sculptor
Preferred Media: Acrylics.
b Calgary, Alta, Dec 9, 30.
Study & Training: Vancouver Art Sch, 45-47; Nat Polytech Inst, Mex, 47-50; asst to David Alfaro Siqueiros, 51.
Work in Public Collections: Mus Arte Mod, Mexico City; Phoenix Art Mus, Ariz; Betzalel Nat Mus, Jerusalem, Israel; Gen Motors Collection, Austin, Tex; Kresge Int Collection, Detroit, Mich.
Commissions: Mural, Fed Penitentiary, Mexico City, 61; Gov Sch Handicapped Children, Mex, 63; Jewish Community Cult Ctr, Mex, 67; portable mural, Mex Pavillion, Expo' 67, Montreal, 67; mural, Humanities Bldg, Lock Haven State Col, 71.
Exhibitions: Guggenheim Int Award Exhib, New York, N Y, 64; Biennale des Jeunes, Paris, France, 65; Mexico, The Emergent Generation, Univ Tex Art Mus, Austin, 67; Second Latin Am Graphics Biennale, San Juan, P R, 72; Third Biennale, Medellin, Colombia, 72.
Teaching: Asst prof mural techniques, Univ of the Americas, Mex, 54-60; vis instr painting, Pratt Inst, 67-71.
Awards: Theatre design award, Mex Theater Critics, 61; nat purchase prize for painting, Salon de la Plastica Mex, 63; purchase prize, Second Graphics Biennale, San Juan, 72.
Bibliography: Henry Seldis (auth), article in Los Angeles Times, 67; Raquel Tibol (auth), Secuencia y consecuencia de A Belkin, Excelsior, Diorama de la Cult, 71; Lawrence Alloway (auth), catalog text, The Marat Series, Lerner-Misrachi Gallery, New York, N Y, 72.
Memberships: Salon de la Plastica Mex, Salon de Los Independientes, Mex, Mus Latino Am, New York (co-organizer, 71).
Publications: Co-auth, Nueva Presencia- a humanist manifesto, 61.
Dealer: Richard Lerner, 789 Madison Ave, New York, NY 10021.
Mailing Address: 303 E Houston St, New York, NY 10002.

BELL, ALISTAIR MACREADY
Printmaker, Painter
Preferred Media: Woodcut, Intaglio, Watercolor.
b Darlington, Eng, Oct 21, 13; Can citizen.
Work in Public Collections: Nat Gallery Can, Ottawa, Ont; Mus Mod Art, New York, N Y; Victoria & Albert Mus, London, Eng; Mus Ugo Carpi, Italy; Vancouver Art Gallery, B C.
Exhibitions: First Int Biennial Graphics, Tokyo & Osaka, Japan, 57; Third Int Exhib Graphics, Lubljana, Yugoslavia, 59; Sixth Bianco e Nero, Lugano, Switz, 60; Recent Prints, Canada, Mus Mod Art, 67; First Int Triennial of Contemp Xylography, Carpi, 69.
Awards: Can Coun sr arts fel, 59, & sr arts award, 67.
Memberships: Assoc Royal Can Acad Art; Can Soc Graphic Art; Soc Can Painter-Etchers & Engravers.
Dealer: Bau-Xi Gallery, 3003 Granville St, Vancouver 9, B C, Can.
Mailing Address: 2566 Marine Dr, W Vancouver, B C, Can.

BELL, CLARA LOUISE (MRS BELA JANOWSKY)
Painter
b Newton Falls, Ohio.
Study & Training: Cleveland Sch Art; Art Stud League New York; also with Henry G Keller.
Work in Public Collections: Metrop Mus Art; Brooklyn Mus; Masonic Temple, Youngstown, Ohio; Butler Inst Am Art; Coast Guard Acad, Hamilton Hall, New London, Conn; plus others.
Exhibitions: Nat Asn Women Artists, New York, N Y, 28-64; Allied Artists Am, 54, 60 & 73; Royal Soc Miniature Painters, London, Eng, 58; Rehoboth Art League, Del, 60; Chester Art Guild, Vt, 60-64; plus others.
Awards: Four prizes, Cleveland Mus Art, 19-26; prizes, Nat Asn Women Artists, 49, 61 & 64 & medals, 30, 52, & 59.
Memberships: Am Soc Miniature Painters; Nat Asn Women Artists (jury mem, 62-63, exhib jury, 64-65).
Publications: Contribr, Art Digest, 51 & Am Artist, 58.
Mailing Address: 52 W 57th St, New York, NY 10019.

BELL, ENID
Sculptor, Educator
Preferred Media: Wood, Terra-cotta, Stone, Marble, Alabaster.
b London, Eng, Dec 5, 04; U S citizen.
Study & Training: Glasgow Sch Art, Scotland; study with Sir W Reid Dick, London; St John's Wood Sch Art, London; Art Stud League New York.
Work in Public Collections: Deaf Smith Hist Soc Mus, Hereford, Tex; Union City Pub Libr, N J.
Commissions: Carved wood relief panels, comn by Sect Fine Arts, U S Treas Dept, Mt Holly, N J, Post Office, 37; Boonton, N J, Post Office, 38 & Hereford, Tex, Post Office, 40.
Exhibitions: Distinguished American Sculptors, Brooklyn Mus, N Y, 30; Pa Acad Fine Arts Ann, 34, 40 & 46; Paris Int Expos, France, 37; American Art Today, New York World's Fair, 39; Artists for Victory, Metrop Mus Art, New York.

Teaching: Instr sculpture & head dept, Newark Sch Fine & Indust Art, 44-68.
Positions: Sculpture supvr, Fed Art Proj, N J, 40-41.
Awards: Sculpture medal, Montclair Mus Ann, N J, 33; gold medal dipl, Paris Int Expos, 37; first sculpture award, Montclair Mus Ann, 49.
Publications: Auth & illusr, Tincraft as a hobby, 34; auth, My wood sculpture, Am Artist Mag, 65; auth & illusr, Practical wood carving projects; auth, articles, In: Am Artists Mag, 66-68 & Nat Sculpture Rev, 66.
Mailing Address: 277 Walton St, Englewood, NJ 07631.

BELL, LELAND
Painter
b Cambridge, Md, 1922.
Exhibitions: Knoedler Gallery, 63; six shows, Schoelkoph Gallery, New York, N Y, 63-72; Hansa Gallery; Zabriskie Gallery; Poindexter Gallery; plus others.
Dealer: Robert Schoelkoph Gallery, 825 Madison Ave, New York, NY 10021.
Mailing Address: 241 W 16th St, New York, NY 10011.

BELL, PETER ALAN
Painter, Art Administrator
Preferred Media: Oil, Acrylics.
b Grantham, U K, Apr 21, 18.
Study & Training: Univ Cape Town; Rhodes Univ, S Africa, BA(fine art) & UED, 52.
Work in Public Collections: Confederation Art Ctr, Charlottetown, P E I; Dalhousie Univ Art Gallery, Halifax, N S; Erindale Col, Univ Toronto, Ont; Univ N B, Fredericton; Nat Gallery S Africa, Cape Town.
Commissions: Banner for entrance hall, Confederation Ctr, Charlottetown.
Exhibitions: Van Riebeck Festival, Cape Town, 53; various socs ann exhibs in Can, 65-; Quinquennial Exhib S African Art, 70; Atlantic Province Art Circuit Biennial, 70-71; Eastern Province Art Exhib, Port Elizabeth, S Africa.
Collections Arranged: Centennial Sculpture Proj, St John's, Nfld, 67; Graphics S Africa, Can tour, 67-68; Christopher Pratt, Retrospective, Can tour, 70-71; Greetings from the Artist (artists' Xmas card proj), 70-
Teaching: Head, Ndaleni Art Sch, Richmond, S Africa, 59-63; art specialist, Mem Univ Nfld, 63.
Positions: Cur, Mem Univ Art Gallery, 63-
Memberships: Can Soc Graphic Arts; Can Soc Painters in Water Colour; Soc Can Painter-Etchers & Engravers.
Mailing Address: 7 Appledore Pl, St John's, Nfld, Can.

BELL, R MURRAY
Collector
Study & Training: Univ Alta; Osgoode Hall Law Sch, Toronto.
Collection: Chinese ceramics, with special interest in blue and white Chinese porcelain.
Mailing Address: 134 Forest Hill Rd, Toronto 195, Ont, Can.

BELLAMY, RICHARD
Art Dealer
Positions: Co-dir, Noah Goldowsky Gallery.
Mailing Address: 1078 Madison Ave, New York, NY 10028.

BELLEFLEUR, LEON
Painter, Etcher
b Montreal, Que, Feb 8, 10.
Study & Training: Ecole Beaux-Arts, Montreal; Ecole Normale, Montreal.
Work in Public Collections: Nat Gallery Can; Art Gallery Toronto; Mus P Q; Mus Art Contemporain, Montreal.
Exhibitions: São Paulo, Brazil, 50 & 53; Spoleto, Italy, 60; retrospective, Nat Gallery Can, London Mus, Ont & Montreal Mus Contemp Art, 68; many others, Europe, U S, Japan, Mex & Can.
Awards: Jessie Dow Award, 50; Commonwealth Award, Vancouver, B C; Guggenheim award, 60.
Memberships: Asn Prof Artists Quebec.
Mailing Address: 417 St Joseph Blvd W, Montreal, P Q, Can.

BELSHE, MIRELLA MONTI
Sculptor, Art Historian
Preferred Media: Bronze, Plexiglas, Aluminum.
b Tuscany, Italy, July 28, 28; U S citizen.
Study & Training: Univ Hawaii, MA(eastern art), 67, MFA, 69.
Work in Public Collections: Bronze sculpture, Hawaii State Found Purchase, 69 & plexi-light sculpture, 72; bronze-plexi sculpture, AMFAC Collection, Honolulu, Hawaii, 71.
Commissions: Bronze sculpture, Waimea Kohala Airport, Hawaii Dept Transportation, 72.
Exhibitions: Hawaii Craftsmen Ann, 66-; Honolulu Artists Ann, 68-;

Hawaii Painters & Sculptors League Ann, 70-; Northwestern Regional, Oakland, Calif, 70; one-man show, Contemporary Arts, Honolulu, 71.
Teaching: Asst prof art, Univ Hawaii, 69-72.
Positions: Comnr, Mayor Comn Art & Cult, 71-
Awards: First prize sculpture, Univ Art Festival, 68; first prize over all categories, Easter Art Festival, 70 & second prize sculpture, 72.
Memberships: Hawaii Painters & Sculptors League (exhib chmn, 71); Hawaii Craftsmen (v pres & pres, 71-72); Art Educators Asn (v chmn, 70-71, secy, 72).
Research: Sculpture of the Nara Period; Japanese primitive art; early Hawaiian art.
Mailing Address: 3231 Beaumont Woods Place, Honolulu, HI 96822.

BEN-ZION
Painter, Sculptor
Preferred Media: Oils, Watercolors, Ironwork.
b Ukraine, July 7, 97; U S citizen.
Work in Public Collections: Mus Mod Art, New York, N Y; Metrop Mus Art, New York; Whitney Mus Am Art, New York; Art Inst Chicago, Ill; Jewish Mus, New York; plus others.
Exhibitions: Advancing American Art, State Dept Traveling Show, 47; Bezalel Mus, Jerusalem, Israel, 57; A Retrospect, Jewish Mus, New York, 59; Whitney Mus Am Art Rev, 60-61; Collector's Choice, Denver Art Mus, Colo, 61.
Teaching: Instr painting, Cooper Union, 43-50; instr painting, Ball State Univ, summer 56; instr painting, Univ Iowa, summer 59.
Bibliography: Ralph Pearson (auth), The modern renaissance in American art, Harper & Rowe, 54; Stephen S Kayser (auth), Ben-Zion 1933-59—a retrospect, Jewish Mus, New York, 59; Emery Grossman (auth), Art and tradition, Thomas Yoseloff, 67.
Mailing Address: 329 W 20th St, New York, NY 10011.

BENDA, RICHARD R
Painter
Preferred Media: Acrylic & Collage
b Chicago, Ill, Sept 22, 34.
Study & Training: Chicago Acad Fine Arts, Art Inst Chicago.
Work in Public Collections: Mus Mod Art, Mexico City, Mex; Columbia Col, Ill; Borg Warner Corp Collection, Chicago; Ill State Mus, Springfield; Ill Bell Tel Collection, Chicago.
Commissions: 14 Stations of the Cross, oil paintings, St Patricks Church, Elkhart, Ill, 68; Conference, acrylic & collage painting, Blue Cross Assn, Chicago, 70; St John's Church, Lostant, Ill.
Exhibitions: New Horizons in Painting & Sculpture, North Shore Art League, Winnetka, Ill, 68-72; 20th Ann Exhib Knickerbocker Artists, Nat Arts Club, New York, N Y, 70; Bertrand Russell Centenary Invitational Exhib, London, Eng; 29th Invitational Exhib Ill Artists, Ill State Mus, 71; Fr Inst Latin Am Gallery, Mexico City, 71.
Awards: Hon mention awards, Ill State Fair, Springfield, 69-71; A I Friedman Award, Painters in Casein Soc, New York, 69; first prize, Nat Juried Exhib, Slidell, La, 70.
Memberships: N Shore Art League; Audubon Artists Soc, New York; Arts Club Chicago.
Publications: Contribr, The journal, 12/67, 11/68 & 12/68; contribr, La Rev Mod, Paris, 7/68; contribr, Art Scene Mag, 1/69; contribr, Signature Mag; contribr, Vision Mag, Mexico City, 11/71.
Dealers: Welna Gallery, 105 E Ontario St, Chicago, IL 60610; Verzyl Gallery, 377 Ft Salonga Rd, Rte 25A, Northport, NY 11768.
Mailing Address: 3559 N Ashland Ave, Chicago, IL 60657.

BENDELL, MARILYN
Painter, Instructor
Preferred Media: Oil.
b Grand Ledge, Mich, Sept 19, 21.
Study & Training: Am Acad Art; also with Arnold E Turtle & Pierre Nuyttens.
Work in Public Collections: Principia Col, St. Louis, Mo; Saginaw Mus, Mich; Hadley Sch for Blind, Winnetka, Ill; Huntington Mus Fine Arts, W Va; Lester Kierstead Henderson Galleries, Monterey, Calif.
Commissions: The Juggler of Notre Dame, comn by Sen Schuch, Saginaw Mus, 50; portrait of founder Principia Col, comn by William E Morgan, St. Louis, Mo, 58; portrait of Helen Keller, Hadley Sch for Blind, 58; portrait of Mrs Paul Schulze, comn by Paul Schulze, Chicago, Ill, 60; David and Kim, Huntington Mus Fine Arts, 65.
Exhibitions: Chicago Galleries, Ill, 55; Ill State Fair, Springfield, Ill, 58; 16th Ann Mem Exhib, Acad Artists Asn, Springfield, Mass, 64; Famous Florida Artists, Frank Oehlschlaeger Galleries, Sarasota, Fla, 64 & 65; Acad Artists Asn Nat Show, Springfield, 72.
Teaching: Instr portrait, figure & still life, Longboat Key Art Ctr,

Fla, 52-68; instr still life, Oak Park-River Forest Art League, Oak Park, Ill, 57-59; instr portrait, figure & still life, Cortez Art Sch, Fla, 68-
Positions: Dir, Cortez Art Galleries, 68-
Awards: Popular award for Bus Stop, Ill State Fair, 61; first in portrait for Jeri, Springfield Mus Fine Arts, 64 & first in portrait & figure, Portrait of a Young Woman, 70.
Bibliography: Edith Weigle (auth), The wonderful world of art, Chicago Tribune, 8/17/58; W C Burnett (auth), Two art shows reviewed, Sarasota Herald Tribune, 64; Charles Benbow (auth), She reflects her colorful oil paintings, St Petersburg Times, 11/13/71.
Memberships: Brown Co Art Gallery Asn; fel Royal Soc Arts; Am Artists Prof League; Acad Artists Asn, Springfield; Sarasota Art Asn.
Dealer: Lester Kierstead Henderson Galleries, 712 Hawthorne, Monterey, CA 93940.
Mailing Address: P O Box 5, Longboat Key, FL 33548.

BENDER, BEVERLY STERL
Sculptor, Designer
Preferred Media: Marble, Alabaster, Wood.
b Washington, D C, Jan 14, 18.
Study & Training: Knox Col, BA; Art Stud League, New York, N Y, with Hovannes; Sculpture Ctr, New York, with Miss Denslow; Mus Natural Hist, New York.
Work in Public Collections: James Ford Bell Mus Natural Hist, Minneapolis, Minn.
Commissions: Memorial, Mrs Disco, Mystic Seaport, Conn, 69.
Exhibitions: Nat Sculpture Soc, New York, 65, 70 & 72; Southern Vt Art Ctr, Manchester, 68-71; Nat Arts Club, New York, 69; Smithsonian Inst, Washington, 70 & 71; James Ford Bell Mus Natural Hist, 71.
Positions: Artist & designer, Johns-Manville, New York, N Y, 43-72.
Awards: First prize, Beaux Arts, 64; bronze medal, Pen & Brush Club, 65; gold medal, Catharine Lorrillard Wolfe, 69.
Memberships: Soc Animal Artists; Southern Vt Art Ctr; Catharine Lorillard Wolfe Art Club; Knickerbocker Artists; Pen & Brush Club (bd dirs, 65-67, 69 & 70).
Mailing Address: R D 3, Pound Ridge, NY 10576.

BENDER, BILL
Painter
Preferred Media: Oils.
b El Segundo, Calif, Jan 5, 20.
Work in Public Collections: U S Air Force Acad, Colorado Springs, Colo; U S Navy, Pensacola, Fla; Palm Springs Mus, Calif; Pentagon, Washington, D C; White House, Washington, D C.
Exhibitions: Calif Home Show, Los Angeles, 70; Chriswood Gallery, Rancho Calif, Calif, 70; Round-up of Western Art, Palm Desert, Calif, 71; Am Artists Prof League, New York, N Y, 72; Catalina Festival Art, Catalina Island, Calif, 72.
Awards: Artists' Artist Award & First Place Award, Chriswood Gallery, 70; Artists' Artist Award, 20th Ann Death Valley Show, 70.
Bibliography: Ainsworth (auth), Painters of the desert, Desert Mag, 60; Frey (auth), Art and artists, Milton W Jones Co, 65; Ainsworth (auth), The cowboy in art, World Publ, 69.
Memberships: Life mem & fel Am Inst Fine Arts; fel Am Artist Prof League; Death Valley Artists (dir, 59-); hon mem Catalina Art Asn.
Publications: Illusr, Beckoning desert, Prentice-Hall, 62; illusr, Christmas cards, stationary & calendars, Leanin' Tree Publ Co, Boulder, Colo, 60-
Mailing Address: Star Rte, Box 154, Oro Grande, CA 92368.

BENDIG, WILLIAM CHARLES
Painter, Instructor
b Corry, Pa, Dec 1, 27.
Study & Training: Trinity Col; Chelsea Sch Art, Univ London, with Ceri Richards; pvt study in Greece & Italy.
Work in Public Collections: Trinity Col, Hartford, Conn.
Exhibitions: Essex Art Asn, 56-61; New York City Ctr, N Y, 57; Springfield Art League, 57; Mystic Art Asn, 57-58 & 61; Riverside Mus, New York, 60.
Teaching: Instr painting, drawing & art history, Brunswick Sch, Greenwich, Conn & Cheshire Acad, Conn; lect art hist, mediaeval art & archit, Trinity Col, 65.
Positions: Juror of exhibs, Silvermine Guild, Chautauqua Art Ctr & Va Beach Regional; publ, Art Gallery, 57-
Memberships: Essex Art Asn (v pres, 59-61); Mediaeval Acad Am.
Mailing Address: Hollycroft, Ivoryton, CT 06442.

BENEDICT, NAN M
Painter, Educator
b Lynchburg, Va, July 27, 37.
Study & Training: Pratt Inst, BFA, 59, MFA, 61.
Commissions: Mural, New York City Pub Libr Syst, 69.

Exhibitions: Pratt Inst Faculty Exhibs, 61, 62, 68 & 71; Detroit Art Inst, 63; Brooklyn Mus, 63 & 72; Gettysburg Col, Pa, 64; Manhattan Ctr, 71.
Teaching: From instr to prof art, Pratt Inst, 61-, acting dir grad progs, 70-71, chmn grad art, 71-
Memberships: Am Asn Univ Prof.
Mailing Address: 183 Steuben St, Brooklyn, NY 11205.

BENGERT, ELWOOD GEORGE
Painter
Preferred Media: Watercolors.
b Clifton, N J, Dec 16, 21.
Study & Training: Newark Sch Fine & Indust Art; Parsons Sch Design, grad, with Stephen Greene & Ralph Fabri, also grad work France & Italy, six months.
Commissions: Stained glass windows, Holy Family Church, Vernon, Tex, 51, St Paul's Church, Manchester, Vt, 52, St Mary's Cathedral, Ogdensburg, N Y, 52, Boston Col Chapel, Mass, 53 & St Nicholas of Tolentine Church, Bronx, N Y, 55.
Exhibitions: Parsons Best European Paintings, Mus Southampton, N Y, 50; Montclair Mus, N J, 52; Knickerbocker Artists 13th Ann, New York, N Y, 53; Audubon Artists 17th Ann, Nat Acad Galleries, New York, 55.
Teaching: Instr watercolors, Ridgewood Sch Art, 60-62.
Positions: Owner, Bengert Gallery, Inc, Franklin Lakes, N J, 60-
Memberships: N J Watercolor Soc.
Dealer: Munson Galleries, 275 Orange St, New Haven, CT 06510.
Mailing Address: 814 High Mountain Rd, Franklin Lakes, NJ 07417.

BENGLIS, LYNDA
Sculptor, Painter
b Lake Charles, La, Oct 25, 41.
Study & Training: Yale Norfolk summer fel, 63; Newcomb Col, Tulane Univ, with Ida Kohlmeyer, Pat Trivigno & Zolton Buki, BFA, 64; Brooklyn Mus Art Sch, Max Beckman scholar, 65, with Rubin Tam.
Work in Public Collections: Detroit Inst Arts, Mich; Fort Worth Art Ctr, Tex; Lannan Found, Palm Springs, Fla; Walker Art Ctr, Minneapolis, Minn; Milwaukee Art Ctr, Wis.
Commissions: Latex rubber corner piece, Univ Rhode Island, Kingston, 69; Rouge, polyurethane foam corner piece, Vera List, Byram, Conn, 70; Adhesive Products, pigmented polyurethane foam, Walker Mus, Minneapolis, Minn, 71; Totem, pigmented polyurethane foam, Hayden Gallery, Mass Inst Technol, Boston, 71.
Exhibitions: One-woman shows, Paula Cooper Gallery, New York, N Y, 71 & Hansen-Fuller Gallery, San Francisco, Calif; American Women Artists Show, GEDOK, Kunsthaus, Hamburg, 72; Painting: New Options, Walker Art Ctr, Minneapolis, 72; Video-Tape Festival, 12th Ann St Jude Invitational, De Saisset Art Gallery, Santa Clara, Calif & Everson Mus Art, Syracuse, N Y.
Teaching: Asst prof painting & sculpture, Univ Rochester, 70-72; asst prof sculpture, Hunter Col, 72-
Bibliography: Phantom (video tape), Kans State Univ, 71; Ann McIntoche (auth), Lynda Benglis paints with foam (video tape), Mass Inst Technol, 71-72; Klaus Kertess (auth), On Lynda Benglis, Studio Arts, 5-6/72.
Dealer: Paula Cooper Gallery, 96-100 Prince St, New York, NY 10012.
Mailing Address: 328 E Ninth St, Apt 21, New York, NY 10003.

BENGSTON, BILLY AL
Painter
Preferred Media: Mixed Media.
b Dodge City, Kans, June 7, 34.
Work in Public Collections: Mus Mod Art, New York, N Y; Art Inst Chicago, Ill; Los Angeles Co Mus Art, Calif; Whitney Mus Am Art, New York; Ft Worth Art Ctr Mus, Tex.
Exhibitions: Chicago Biennial Painting Exhib, Art Inst Chicago, 63 & 72; Eighth Biennial, Sao Paulo, Brazil, also shown Smithsonian Inst, 65; Whitney Ann Painting Exhib, Whitney Mus Am Art, New York, 67 & 69; Retrospective Exhib, Los Angeles Co Mus Art, Calif, 68; Kompas IV, Stekelijk van Abbemuseum, Eindhoven, Holland, 69.
Positions: Founder, Artist Studio, Venice, Calif, 60.
Awards: Nat Found Arts grant, 67; Tamarind fel, Tamarind Lithography Workshop through Ford Found, 68.
Bibliography: Walter Hopps (auth), VIII Sao Paulo Biennial Exhibition Catalog, Pasadena Art Mus, 65; Fidel Danieli (auth), Billy Al Bengston's Dentos, Artforum, 5/67; James Monte (auth), Retrospective Exhibition Catalog, 68.
Publications: Co-auth, Business cards, Heavy Indust Publ, 68; auth, Late fifteis at the Ferus, Artforum, 1/69; auth, Los Angeles artists' studios, Art in Am, 11-12/70.
Mailing Address: Artist Studio, 110 Mildred Ave, Venice, CA 90291.

BENGTZ, TURE
Museum Director, Painter
Preferred Media: Oils, Watercolors, Graphics.
Study & Training: In Finnish Schs & Sch Mus Fine Arts, Boston, Mass, dipl; Slade Sch, London, Eng; Fontainebleau, Paris, France; Paige traveling scholar to Europe, summers 33-37; Tiffany Found fels, 40-41.
Work in Public Collections: Mus Fine Arts, Boston; Addison Gallery, Andover, Mass; Libr Cong, Washington, D C; Seattle Art Mus, Wash; Cincinnati Art Mus, Ohio; plus many other public & pvt collections.
Commissions: Design of stained glass window, 12th century church, Finland, 68.
Exhibitions: Nat Acad Design, New York, N Y; Brooklyn Mus, N Y; Chicago Art Inst, Ill; Palace of Legion of Honor, San Francisco, Calif; Am Fedn Arts Watercolor Traveling Show, Australia, India & Japan; plus many other one-man shows, group exhibs & traveling exhibs.
Teaching: Instr drawing & painting, Sch Mus Fine Arts, Boston, 34-38, instr artistic anat, 38-39, instr graphic arts, 39-41, head drawing & graphic arts dept, 41-69; demonstr & lectr drawing & anat, WGBH TV, 57-60; lects & demonstrations drawing, composition, anat, painting & printmaking, U S & abroad.
Positions: Tech illusr radar equip, Raytheon Corp, Waltham, Mass, 41-45; mus dir, Art Complex, Inc, Duxbury, Mass, 69-
Awards: Palmer Mem Prize, Nat Acad Design, 44; Boston Mus Prize, Boston Printmakers, 65; Boston Printmakers Prize & Gendrot Prize, Boston Printmakers, 69; plus many others.
Publications: Illusr, White squaw, Heath.
Mailing Address: The Art Complex, Inc, P O Box 1411, Duxbury, MA 02332.

BENJAMIN, KARL STANLEY
Painter, Instructor
b Chicago, Ill, Dec 29, 25.
Study & Training: Northwestern Univ; Univ Redlands, BA, 49; Claremont Grad Sch, MA, 60.
Work in Public Collections: Whitney Mus Am Art, New York, N Y; Los Angeles Co Mus Art, Calif; San Francisco Mus Art, Calif; Wadsworth Atheneum, Hartford, Conn; Pasadena Art Mus, Calif.
Exhibitions: 4 Abstract Classicists (West Coast Hard Edge), Los Angeles Co Mus & San Francisco Mus Art, also shown Inst Contemp Art, London, Eng, 59; Purist Painting, Am Fedn Arts Traveling Exhib, shown at Andrew Dickson White Mus, N Y, Walker Art Ctr, Minneapolis, Minn, Speed Mus, Louisville, Ky & others, 60; Geometric Abstraction in America, Whitney Mus Am Art, 62; The Responsive Eye, Mus Mod Art, New York, 65; 30th Ann Exhib Am Painting, Corcoran Gallery, Washington, D C, 67.
Teaching: Instr, Calif Pub Schs, Chino & others, 49-
Dealers: Henri Gallery, 1500 21st St N W, Washington, DC 20036. William Sawyer Gallery, 3045 Clay St, San Francisco, CA 94115.
Mailing Address: 675 W Eighth St, Claremont, CA 91711.

BENN, BEN
Painter
b Russia, Dec 27, 84.
Study & Training: Nat Acad Design, 04-08.
Work in Public Collections: Albany Inst Art, N Y; Baltimore Mus Art, Md; Butler Art Inst, Youngstown, Ohio; Kroller-Mueller Found, The Hague, Holland; Metrop Mus Art, New York, N Y; Watkins Mem Gallery, Am Univ, Washington, D C; plus many others.
Exhibitions: Art: U S A, Madison Sq Garden, New York, N Y, 58; Art: U S A, Coliseum, New York, 59; The Decade of the Armory Show: New Directions in American Art 1910-1920, Friends of Whitney Mus Am Art Traveling Exhib, 63-64; Critics' Choice: Art Since World War II, Kane Mem Exhib, Providence Art Club, R I, 65; four one-man shows, Babcock Gallery, 63-70; plus many other group & one-man shows.
Awards: J Henry Schiedt Award, Pa Acad Fine Arts 147th Ann Exhib, 52; Carol H Beck Gold Medal, Pa Acad Fine Arts, 66; Peabody Waite Award, Am Acad Arts & Lett, 71.
Bibliography: Dorothy Adlow, Ben Benn Exhibition: Part I, Christian Sci Monitor, 2/18/63; Sidney Geist (auth), Letters to the editor, Arts Mag, 5-6/63; Sidney Tillim (auth), Month in review, Arts Mag, 3/63.
Dealer: Babcock Galleries, 805 Madison Ave, New York, NY 10021.
Mailing Address: Apt 4A, 110 W 96th St, New York, NY 10025.

BENNETT, HARRIET
Painter
Preferred Media: Oils.
b New York, N Y.
Study & Training: Art Stud League New York, with Robert Brackman & Byron Browne; Brooklyn Mus, with Minna Citron; New Sch Social Res; Pratt Graphic Art Ctr; YWCA Craft Ctr.

Work in Public Collections: Five paintings, Inst High Fidelity, New York; also included in many private collections.
Exhibitions: One-man shows, Marino Gallery, New York, 58; Condon Riley Gallery, New York, 59; Cichi Gallery, Rome, Italy, 62; Galerie de l'Univ A G, Paris, France, 62 & Woodstock Gallery, London, Eng, 65.
Awards: Falmouth Artists Guild Award, 62.
Bibliography: Mario Federici (auth), Harriet Bennett's paintings, Brochure, Rome, 1/62; Enrico Centardi (auth), Harriet Bennett, Voce Del Sud, Rome, 2/3/62; Raymond Charmet (auth), Fusion in light, Arts, Lettres, Spectacles du, Paris, 9/6/62.
Memberships: Mus Mod Art, New York; Whitney Mus Am Art; Long Beach Art Asn, N Y.
Dealer: Alexander Gallery, 117 E 39th St, New York, NY 10016.
Mailing Address: P O Box 225, Island Park, NY 11558.

BENNEY, ROBERT
Painter
b New York, N Y.
Study & Training: Cooper Union Art Sch; Art Stud League New York; Nat Acad Design; Grand Cent Art Sch.
Work in Public Collections: Corcoran Gallery Art; De Young Mus; IBM; Chrysler Corp; Mariners Mus; plus many others.
Commissions: Many portraits of prominent persons.
Exhibitions: Nat Gallery Art, Washington, D C; Metrop Mus Art, New York; Brooklyn Mus, N Y; Dc Young Mus, San Francisco, Calif; Corcoran Gallery Art, Washington, D C; plus many others.
Teaching: Assoc prof art, Duchess Community Col, Poughkeepsie, N Y.
Positions: Lectr various art groups.
Awards: First award, Philadelphia Mus Art.
Memberships: Soc Illustrators; Artists Equity Asn; Art Stud League New York; Artist & Writers Asn; Appraisers Asn Am.
Publications: Contribr, Our flying Navy; contribr, Pictures, painters & you, 49; contribr, Life's picture history of World War II, 50; contribr, Am Artist Mag, 56; contribr, Life of Joshua, 59; plus many others.
Dealer: Capricorn Galleries, 8003 Woodmont Ave, Bethesda, MD 20014.
Mailing Address: 50 W 96th St, New York, NY 10025.

BENNO, BENJAMIN G
Painter, Sculptor
b London, Eng, June 2, 01; U S citizen.
Study & Training: Mod Sch, New York, N Y, 12-16, with Robert Henri & George Bellows; Sch Archit & Beaux Arts New York, 14-17, with Solon Borglum, John Gutzon de la Mothe Borglum & others; Guggenheim Mem fel, Europe, 32-33.
Work in Public Collections: Fogg Mus Art, Cambridge, Mass; Brooklyn Mus Art, N Y; Baltimore Mus Art, Md; San Francisco Mus Art, Calif; also in many private collections in the U S and Europe.
Exhibitions: Pastels from the Years 1930-1959, Collector's Gallery, New York, 59; Poetic Image I, Paintings with Group, Amel Gallery, New York, 61; Drawings from the Years 1926-1961, Greer Gallery, New York, 62; Poetic Image II, Paintings & Drawings with Group, Amel Gallery, 62; Retrospective, Paintings and Drawings from the Years 1933-1961, Mont State Univ, Missoula, 64; plus many others.
Teaching: Instr drawing & painting, Brooklyn Children's Mus, 41-42; private classes in drawing & painting, 48-55; instr advan painting, Mont State Univ, summer 64.
Bibliography: Gertrude Stein (auth), Everybody's autobiography, William Heineman, Ltd, London & Toronto, 37; Henry Miller (auth), Chez Benno, London Bull, 6/38; Waldemar George (auth), Le salon de surindependents, Arts & Metiers Graphique, 1/1/39.
Mailing Address: Rear Bldg, Apt F3, 434 Lafayette St, New York, NY 10003.

BENSING, FRANK C
Painter, Illustrator
Preferred Media: Oils.
b Chicago, Ill, Oct 29, 93.
Study & Training: Art Inst Chicago; also with Wellington Reynolds & Walter Biggs.
Work in Public Collections: Portraits in pub bldgs, Bryn Mawr College, Pa, State Off Bldg, Albany, N Y, Notre Dame Univ, Ind, Columbia Univ, New York, N Y, Univ Miami, Fla & many others.
Exhibitions: Am Watercolor Soc, 70; Allied Artists Am, 71; Nat Acad Design, 71; plus many others.
Awards: Gold medal of honor, Nat Arts Club, 69; purchase prize, Louis Seeley, Salmagundi Club, 71; Artists' Fellowship Silver Medal, Michael M Engel Mem Award, 71.
Memberships: Allied Artists Am; Soc Illustrators; Artists' Fellowship, Artists Guild; Dutch Treat Club; Salmagundi Club.
Publications: Illusr for nat mag, 30-45.
Mailing Address: 1 W 67th St, New York, NY 10023.

BENSINGER, B EDWARD, III
Collector
b Chicago, Ill, Nov 27, 29.
Study & Training: Yale Univ, BA; Grad Sch Bus, Univ Southern Calif, MBA.
Positions: With Bensinger Enterprises, Beverly Hills, Calif; with Brunswick Corp, Chicago, Ill.
Collection: Beckmann and Corot.
Mailing Address: 613 N Canon Dr, Beverly Hills, CA 90210.

BENSON, ELAINE K G
Art Dealer, Writer.
b Philadelphia, Pa, Apr 30, 24.
Study & Training: Univ Pa, BA, 44.
Teaching: Coordr fashion fields, Phila Col Art, 63-64.
Positions: Dir pub rels, Phila Col Art, 57-64; dir, Benson Gallery, 65-; co-dir summer art prog, Southampton Col, 67-69.
Memberships: Am Fedn Art.
Specialty of Gallery: Contemporary European and American paintings, sculpture and fine crafts.
Publications: Criticism and articles on art and artists in Craft Horizons, On the Sound, and others.
Mailing Address: Benson Gallery, P O Box AJ, Bridgehampton, NY 11932.

BENSON, GERTRUDE ACHERMAN
Writer, Art Critic
b Romania, Aug 6, 04.
Study & Training: Hunter Col, BA; New Sch Social Res with Dr Alvin Johnson; New York Univ Inst Fine Arts, MA; also with Charles Morey, Princeton, Carnegie fels art & archaeol, 28-29 & for year abroad, 30-31.
Teaching: Asst prof, dept humanities, Philadelphia Col Art, 60-63; also lectures on special approach to art history as it affects contemporary art.
Positions: Art Ed, Philadelphia Inquirer, 50-57; feature writer, Philadelphia Bulletin, New York Times, Drexel Univ & Thomas Jefferson Univ, 60-71.
Publications: Auth, Greco-Roman influence on Utrecht Psalter, Art Bull, 31; Exploding the Van Gogh myth, Mag Art, 35; La tour & le Nain, Mag Art, 35; Lewis Carroll, New York Times Mag, 57; interviews with Marin, Jacob Epstein, DeKooning, Stuart Davis, Lipchitz, Knaths, Rouault, Nolde, Calder, Watkins Shalm & many others; also many articles & book reviews in Nat magazines & newspapers.
Mailing Address: Rittenhouse Claridge, Philadelphia, PA 19102.

BENTHAM, DOUGLAS WAYNE
Sculptor
Preferred Media: Steel
b Rosetown, Sask, Apr 16, 47.
Study & Training: Univ Sask, BA & advan degree in fine arts.
Work in Public Collections: Sask Arts Bd, Regina, Sask; Edmonton Art Gallery, Alta; Art Gallery Windsor, Ont; Univ Sask, Saskatoon; Univ Calgary, Alta.
Exhibitions: One-man show, Regina Pub Libr Art Gallery, 70; Saskatchewan-Art & Artists, Norman Mackenzie Art Gallery, Regina, 71; West '71, 71 & two-man show, spring, 73, Edmonton Art Gallery; Kingston Spring Exhib, Ont, 72.
Awards: For work in sculpture, Sask Arts Bd, 69; Can Coun arts bursaries, 70-71, 72-73; purchase award for sculpture, West '71, Edmonton Art Gallery, 71.
Bibliography: B Christie (auth), Douglas Bentham-sculptures, The Sheaf, 71; T Fenton (auth), Some Saskatchewan artists, 71 & T Heath (auth), Douglas Bentham-recent work, 72, Arts Can.
Mailing Address: 612 Seventh St E, Saskatoon, Sask S7H 0X9, Can.

BENTLEY, CLAUDE
Painter, Graphic Artist
Preferred Media: Acrylics.
b New York, N Y, June 9, 15.
Study & Training: Northwestern Univ; Art Inst Chicago.
Work in Public Collections: Univ Ill, Metrop Mus Art; Denver Art Mus; Art Inst Chicago; Ill State Mus; plus others.
Commissions: Murals, 3600 Lake Shore Dr Bldg, Chicago, Ill; comn as design consult, Plaza del Lago Shopping Ctr, Winnetka, Ill.
Exhibitions: Corcoran Gallery Art; San Francisco Mus Art; Whitney Mus Am Art; Art Inst Chicago; Sarasota Art Asn; plus others.
Awards: John G Curtis Jr Award, 63; Old Orchard Art Fair Award, 63; purchase award, Ill State Mus, 63; plus others.
Bibliography: Prize winning oil paintings, Allied, 60; Literary Times, 4/65; Creating art from anything, Meilach, 68.
Collection: African, oceanic and pre-Columbian art.

Dealer: Jacques Baruch Gallery, 900 N Michigan Ave, Chicago, IL 60611.
Mailing Address: 1911 N Cleveland Ave, Chicago, IL 60614.

BENTON, FLETCHER
Sculptor
b Jackson, Ohio, Feb 25, 31.
Study & Training: Miami Univ, BFA.
Work in Public Collections: Univ Calif; IBM Corp; Interchem Corp; New York Bank for Savings; Ridgefield/Aldrich; plus others.
Commissions: Sculpture, Atlantic Richfield Co.
Exhibitions: Univ Ill, 67 & 69; HemisFair '68, San Antonio, Tex; Whitney Mus Am Art Sculpture Ann, 68; Lytton Art Ctr, Los Angeles, 68; Electric Art, Univ Calif, Los Angeles, 69; plus others.
Teaching: Instr, Calif Col Arts & Crafts, 59; instr, San Francisco Art Inst, 64-68; instr, San Jose State Col, 68-69.
Bibliography: Peter Selz (auth), article, In: Directions in kinetic sculpture, Univ Calif, Berkeley, 66; George Rickey (auth), article, In: Constructivism: origins and evolution, Braziller, 67; Tracy Atkinson (auth), article, In: Directions I: options 1968, Milwaukee Art Ctr, 68.
Dealers: Bonino Gallery, 7 W 57th St, New York, NY 10019; Esther Robles Gallery, 665 N La Cienega, Los Angeles, CA 90069.
Mailing Address: 2100 Pine St, San Francisco, CA 94115.

BENTON, MARGARET PEAKE
Painter
b South Orange, N J.
Study & Training: Ont Col Art; Victoria Col, Univ Toronto; Toronto Conservatory Music; special study, portraiture with Archibald Barnes, Toronto, Ont.
Work in Public Collections: Queen's Pvt Collection, Eng; Pa Acad Fine Arts, Philadelphia; Nurmanzil Psychiatric Clin, Punjab, India; King's Col, Halifax, N S; Victoria Col Libr, Toronto.
Commissions: Christ Blessing the Children & Christ Healing the Sick (murals), Chapel of St John's Garrison Church, Toronto, Ont.
Exhibitions: Pa Soc Miniature Painters, Philadelphia, 45-51; Miniature Painters, Sculptors & Gravers Soc of Washington, D C, 45-71; Royal Can Acad Art, Toronto, Ont & Montreal, P Q, 48-49; Royal Acad Art, London, Eng, 50; Nat Miniature Art Show, Miniature Art Soc N J, Paramus, 71-72.
Awards: Elizabeth Muhlhofer Award, Miniature Painters, Sculptors & Gravers Soc of Washington, D C, 62; Levantia White Boardman Mem Second Prize, 70; R V Shope Second Place Award, Miniature Art Soc N J Nat Exhib, 71 & 72.
Memberships: Miniature Painters, Sculptors & Gravers Soc of Washington, D C; Int Platform Asn.
Mailing Address: Lansdowne Villa, Wesley Ave, Niagara-on-the-Lake, Ont, Can.

BENTON, THOMAS HART
Painter, Writer
b Beosho, Mo, Apr 15, 89.
Study & Training: Art Inst Chicago, 06-07; Acad Julian, Paris, France, 08-11; Univ Mo, hon DFA, 48; Lincoln Univ, hon LittD, 57; New Sch Social Res, hon DFA, 68.
Work in Public Collections: Metrop Mus Art; Wanamaker Gallery Col; Mus Mod Art; Brooklyn Mus; Pa Acad Fine Arts; plus others.
Commissions: Murals, Mo State Capitol, 35-36, Achelous & Hercules, Harzfeld Dept Store, Kansas City, Mo, 47, Lincoln Univ, 52-53, N Y State Power Auth, Massens, 57-61, Truman Libr, Independence, Mo, 58-61 & others.
Exhibitions: Whitney Mus Am Art; group exhibs, 39, 40 & 42, one-man exhibs, 39 & 41 & retrospective, 69, Assoc Am Artists, New York, N Y; Univ Kans, 58; traveling one-man show, Univ Ariz, 62; retrospective, Cranbrook Acad Fine Arts, 66; plus others.
Teaching: Instr, Art Stud League New York, 26-36; dir dept painting, Kansas City Art Inst & Sch Design, 35-40; lectr, many cols & univs.
Awards: Gold medals, Architects League, 33 & Am Inst Architects.
Bibliography: Calvin Tomkins (auth), article, In: The world of Marcel Duchamp, Time Inc, 66; Barbara Rose (auth), articles, In: American art since 1900, a critical history, 67 & Readings in American art since 1900, 68, Praeger; plus others.
Memberships: Hon mem Acad Bellas Artes; Am Acad Arts & Sci; Nat Acad Design.
Publications: Auth, An artist in America, McBride, 37 & Univ Mo Press, 68; auth, Drawings, 68, Univ Mo Press; auth, Thirty years' view, or, a history of the working of the American government for thirty years, from 1820-1850, Greenwood, Vols I & II, 68; auth, Thirty years' view, Garrett Press, Vols I & II, 69; auth, An American in art: a professional and technical autobiography, Univ Kans Press, 69; plus others.
Mailing Address: 3616 Belleview Ave, Kansas City, MO 64111.

BENTON, WILLIAM
Collector
b Minneapolis, Minn, Apr 1, 00.
Positions: Owner, Encyclopaedia Britannica & subsids, Praeger Publ, Inc & Phaidon Press, Ltd; hon trustee, Wadsworth Atheneum.
Memberships: Life fel Metrop Mus Art; Mus Mod Art, New York (mem int coun & bus comt for arts).
Collection: Twentieth century American art including Reginald Marsh, Ivan Albright, Bellows, Levine, Benton and many others; widely exhibited, and donated to universities, colleges and museums.
Mailing Address: 342 Madison Ave, New York, NY 10017.

BENTOV, MIRTALA
Sculptor
Preferred Media: Bronze.
b Kharkov, U S S R, Apr 29, 29; U S citizen.
Study & Training: Boston Mus Sch, cert; Grande Chaumière, Paris, France, with Zadkine; Ecole Arts Décoratifs, Paris, with Couturier; Tufts Univ, BFA.
Work in Public Collections: Park Synagogue Mus, Cleveland, Ohio, Universalist Unitarian Church, Brighton, Mass; Temple of Aaron Gallery, Saint Paul, Minn; Tufts Univ, Medford, Mass; Temple of Understanding, Washington, D C.
Commissions: Medal for Sixth Cong, Int Soc Hemat, 56; portraits of two founders, Missionary Order of Maryknoll, N Y, 62; portrait of Roman Jakobson, Slavic Depts of Harvard Univ & Mass Inst Technol, 69; portrait of pres Milton Grahm, Grahm Jr Col, Boston, Mass, 70.
Exhibitions: Traveling Scholars, Boston Mus Fine Arts, 61; Art Now, New City Hall, Boston, 71; one-woman shows, Pucker-Safrai Gallery, Boston, 69 & 72, Salem State Col, Mass, 72 & Tufts Univ, 72.
Awards: Second prize sculpture, Boston Art Festival, 56; Boston Mus Sch Albert Whitin traveling scholar, 57; prize, Providence Art Club, 72.
Publications: Auth (Mirtala Kardinalovska), Peoms (in Russian), 72.
Dealer: Pucker-Safrai Gallery, 171 Newbury St, Boston, MA 02116.
Mailing Address: 241 Glezen Lane, Wayland, MA 01778.

BENY, (WILFRED) ROLOFF
Photographer, Writer
b Medicine Hat, Alta, Jan 7, 24.
Study & Training: Banff Sch Fine Arts, scholar, 39; Trinity Col, Univ Toronto, BA & BFA, 45; State Univ Iowa fel, 46-47, with Mauricio Lasaksny, MA & MFA, 47; Columbia Univ; Inst Fine Art, New York Univ, scholar 47-48; study & travel in Europe, 48-49 & 51-52; Guggenheim fel for printmaking & painting, 53; Univ Lethbridge, LLD, 72.
Work in Public Collections: Nat Gallery Can, Ottawa, Ont; Art Gallery Toronto, Ont; Mus Mod Art, New York, NY; Milione Gallery, Milan, Italy, Redfern Gallery, London, Eng; plus many other pub & pvt collections.
Commissions: Photographic murals, Nesbitt-Thomson, Toronto-Dominion Bank Ctr, 67; Image Canada (38 photo-murals), comn for Fed Pavilion of Expo, Montreal, 67; The Renaissance (photo-exhib), Ontario Music Educ Asn & Govt Ont Coun Arts, 68; India (book with Aubrey Menen), Govt of India, 69; Island-Ceylon (book with John Lindsay), Govt of Ceylon, 71.
Exhibitions: Ont Soc Artists Show, Art Gallery Toronto, 45; 32nd Nat Exhib, Soc Am Etchers, Gravers, Lithographers, New York, 47; Second Nat Print Ann Exhib, Brooklyn Mus, N Y, 48; Exhib Current Am Prints, Dept Fine Arts, Carnegie Inst, 48; Nat Gallery Can, Ottawa; plus many other group & one-man shows.
Awards: Int Prize for Design for The thrones of earth and heaven, Leipzig Book Fair, 58; award for Comite des arts graphiques Français, 65; gold medal for world's finest book for Japan in colour, Int Bk Fair, 68, Can Gold Medal, 67 & Can Coun Award, 68.
Bibliography: Merle Shain (auth), Roloff Beny in Rome, Chatelaine, 5/7/70; Kay Kritzwiser (auth), Roloff Beny: breathtaking odyssey, Toronto Globe & Mail, 5/1/71; Arnold Edinborough (auth), Superb camera art of Roloff Beny, Financial Post, 5/22/71.
Publications: Co-auth, The thrones of earth and heaven, 58, A time of Gods, 62, Pleasure of ruins, 64, To every thing there is a season, 67 & Japan in colour, 67.
Mailing Address: 432 13th St S, Lethbridge, Alta, Can.

BENZ, LEE R
Printmaker, Sculptor
Preferred Media: Woodcut, Cast Stone (Metal), Wood, Alabaster, Marble.
b Neponset, Ill.
Study & Training: Bradley Univ, BA & MA.
Exhibitions: One-man shows, Metamora Court House, Ill, 68 & Caterpillar Tractor Co Gallery, Peoria, 70; Albany Print Show, N Y,

69; Mercyhurst Col Print Show, Erie, Pa, 70; Quincy Art Show, Ill, 71; Colorprint U S A, Univ Tex, 72.
Teaching: Instr design & sculpture, Ill Cent Col, 69-
Awards: Sears Award for Sculpture, Lakeview Area Show, 69; sculpture award, Quincy Art Show, 70; first prize for sculpture, Heart of Ill Shows, 70 & 71.
Memberships: Peoria Art Guild; Lakeview Ctr; Ill Art Educ Asn; Ill Art League.
Dealers: Peoria Art Guild, 1831 N Knoxville, Peoria, IL 61604; Lakeview Center, 1125 Lake St, Peoria, IL 61604.
Mailing Address: 1125 FonDuLac Dr, East Peoria, IL 61611.

BERAHA, ENRIQUE MISRACHI
Art Dealer
b Skopjle, Yugoslavia, Sept 11, 25.
Study & Training: Nat Univ Mex, Law degree; Escuela Artes del Libro, Mexico City; Nat Univ Mex Sch Philos.
Positions: Dir, Galeria Arte Misrachi; publ art bks.
Specialty of Gallery: Modern art, especially Mexican.
Publications: Ed, Siqueiros, 64; ed, Tamayo, 65; ed, Siqueiros escultopintura, 68; ed, Francisco Zuñiga, 69; ed, Jose Luis Cuevas, his world, 69.
Mailing Address: Génova 20, Mexico D F 6, Mex.

BERD, MORRIS
Painter, Educator
Preferred Media: Oils, Acrylics.
b Philadelphia, Pa, Mar 12, 14.
Study & Training: Philadelphia Col Art; Univ per Strangeri, Perugia, Italy, cert.
Work in Public Collections: Barnes Found, Merion, Pa; Philadelphia Mus Art; Pa Acad Fine Arts, Philadelphia; Philadelphia Col Art; Franklin Inst, Philadelphia.
Commissions: History of Oil (mural), comn by Sun Oil Co, Franklin Inst; History of Architecture (mural), Gimbel Bros, Philadelphia.
Exhibitions: Many Pa Acad Fine Arts Ann & Philadelphia Mus Art Regionals; also over fifteen one-man shows.
Teaching: Prof painting, Philadelphia Col Art, 36-, co-chmn dept, 50-71.
Awards: Gimbels Mural Award, 52; silver medal, YMHA Jubilee Show; Katzman prize, Philadelphia Print Club, 62.
Mailing Address: 350 Howarth Rd, Media, PA 19063.

BERDICH, VERA
Printmaker
Preferred Media: Intaglio.
b Chicago, Ill.
Study & Training: Sch Art Inst Chicago, BA, 46.
Work in Public Collections: Chicago Art Inst Print & Drawing Collection; Rosenwald Collection; Libr Cong Prints, Washington, D C; Mus Mod Art; Univ Chicago Print Libr.
Commissions: Symphonic Metamorphosis (100 prints), Ravinia Festival, 69.
Exhibitions: Prints, Yamada Gallery, Kyoto, Japan, 59; Int Exchange Prints (France), Boston Pub Libr, 61; Prints & Paintings, San Francisco Mus Art, 63; one-man show, Graphic Works, Art Inst Chicago, 66; Prints, Carnegie Mellon Univ, 67.
Teaching: Assoc prof etching, Sch Art Inst Chicago, 46-; instr printmaking, Univ Chicago, 57-58.
Awards: Frank G Logan second prize, 62 & first prize, 64 & John G Curtis prize, 66, Art Inst Chicago.
Memberships: Chicago Arts Club; Philadelphia Print Club; Sch Art Inst Chicago Alumni Asn; Am Asn Univ Prof.
Publications: Auth, The unquiet eye, 73.
Mailing Address: School of the Art Institute of Chicago, Michigan Ave at Adams, Chicago, IL 60603.

BERENSTAIN, STANLEY
Cartoonist, Writer
b Philadelphia, Pa, Sept 29, 23.
Study & Training: Philadelphia Mus Sch Indust Art; Pa Acad Fine Arts.
Work in Public Collections: Albert T Reid Col; Univ Kans; Farrell Lib Arts Col, Kans State Univ; Stanley & Janice Berenstain Collection, Syracuse Univ.
Commissions: Calendars & greetings cards, Hallmark, 02-
Awards: Nat Educ Asn Sch Bell Award, 60.
Memberships: Nat Cartoonists Soc; Auth League.
Publications: Auth & illusr (with Janice Berenstain), Are parents for real, Bantam, 71, What Dr Freud didn't tell you, 71, How to teach your children about sex, 72, Lover boy, 72 & Bedside lover boy, 72, Dell; plus others.
Mailing Address: 644 Stetson Rd, Elkins Park, PA 19117.

BERG, PHIL
Collector, Patron
b New York, N Y, Feb 15, 02.
Study & Training: Col Textiles & Sci,Pennsylvania, BS.
Work in Public Collections: Los Angeles Mus Art, Calif.
Positions: Trustee, Southwest Mus, Los Angeles & Los Angeles Co Mus, Los Angeles.
Memberships: Soc Am Archaeol; Am Anthrop Asn; Am Fedn Arts; Adventurers-Explorers Club.
Art Interests: Archaeological activities include excavations in Meso-America, Mestopotamian Valley and others. Donated over four hundred pieces and designed exhibition, Man Came This Way, 71-72; also supplied endowment. Several hundred pieces presently being donated to Los Angeles County Museum.
Collection: Material covered from Sumerian worshipper figures through history of art of man until Miro.
Publications: Auth, Man came this way, 71; Museums and people, 72.
Mailing Address: 10939 Chalon Rd, Los Angeles, CA 90024.

BERG, SIRI
Painter
Preferred Media: Oil, Acrylics.
b Stockholm, Sweden; U S citizen.
Study & Training: Inst Art & Archit, Univ Brussels; Pratt Graphics Ctr, New York, N Y.
Exhibitions: Ann, Hudson River Mus, Yonkers, N Y, 67 & 71; Philadelphia Mus Art, Pa, 70 & 72; Three New Women Painters, East Hampton Gallery, New York, N Y, 70; solo exhib, Phoenix Gallery, New York, 72; Salon 72-73, Ward Nasse Gallery, New York, 72-73.
Teaching: Lectr art, La Guardia Community Col, 71-
Positions; Dir art prog, Riverdale Ment Health Clin, Bronx, N Y, 66-
Publications: Auth, Therapeutic art programs around the world. Uses of art in educational day treatment center, Am J Art Ther, 70.
Dealer: Phoenix Gallery, 939 Madison Ave, New York, NY 10021.
Mailing Address: 530 W 236th St, Bronx, NY 10463.

BERGAMO, DOROTHY JOHNSON
Painter, Instructor
b Chicago, Ill, Feb 1, 12.
Study & Training: Univ Chicago, 34; Art Inst Chicago, BFA, 37; resident fel, 38; Northwestern Univ, MA, 41.
Work in Public Collections: Pub Health Serv Hosp, Lexington, Ky; Witte Mus Art, San Antonio, Tex; Olson Found, Guilford, Conn; Grand Canyon Col; Valley Nat Bank, Phoenix, Ariz.
Exhibitions: Chicago Art Inst; Texas Gen; Contemp Art Gallery, New York, N Y; Ariz Watercolor Asn.
Teaching: Instr, Munic Jr Col, Chicago, 38-43; instr, Art Inst, San Antonio, 43-46; assoc prof, Ariz State Col, 48-51; spec art instr, Madison Schs, Phoenix, 56-57; spec art instr, Carl Hayden Sch, Phoenix, 57-; chmn dept performing arts, Trevor G Browne High Sch, Phoenix.
Positions: Dir, Art Ctr, Phoenix, 51-56.
Memberships: Am Asn Univ Women; Nat League Am Pen Women (state pres); Ariz Watercolor Asn.
Mailing Address: 8828 N 17th Ave, Phoenix, AZ 85021.

BERGE, (EDWARD) HENRY
Sculptor
b Baltimore, Md, May 29, 08.
Study & Training: Md Inst Fine Arts; Rhinehart Sch Sculpture with J Maxwell Miller.
Work in Public Collections: Portrait head & 2 portrait reliefs, Hagerstown Mus Fine Arts; approx 300 portrait heads for figures in 12 waxworks mus in U S & Can.
Commissions: Portrait relief, Joseph D Baker, Mem Tower, City Park, Frederick, Md, 41; large tympanum relief, Angel of Truth, First Unitarian Church, Baltimore, Md, 55; portrait bust, Gov Millard Tawes, State Office Bldg, Baltimore, 61; portrait reliefs, Henrietta & Jacob Blaustein, Oheb Shalom Temple, Baltimore, 63; hundreds more.
Exhibitions: Baltimore Mus Art, 40; Nat Acad Design, New York, N Y; Pa Acad Fine Arts; Nat Sculpture Soc Ann, Lever House, New York, 68; Rhinehart Sch Sculpture 75th Anniversary, Baltimore, 71.
Memberships: Fel Nat Sculpture Soc; Charcoal Club, Baltimore; Md Inst Fine Arts Alumni Asn.
Mailing Address: 5 Merrymount Rd, Baltimore, MD 21210.

BERGEN, SIDNEY L
Art Dealer
b New York, N Y, Sept 27, 22.
Study & Training: Alfred Univ.
Positions: Owner & dir, ACA Galleries, New York, N Y.
Memberships: Art Dealers Asn Am.
Specialty of Gallery: Early twentieth century and contemporary American art.
Mailing Address: ACA Galleries, 25 E 73rd St, New York, NY 10021.

BERGER, JASON
Painter
b Malden, Mass, Jan 22, 24.
Study & Training: Boston Mus Fine Arts Sch, 42-43; Univ Ala, 43-44; Boston Mus Fine Arts Sch, 46-49; Ossip Zadkine Sch Sculpture, Paris, France, 50-52.
Work in Public Collections: Mus Mod Art; Chase Manhattan Bank, New York, N Y; Smith Col Mus Art; Guggenheim Mus Art; Brandeis Univ; plus others.
Exhibitions: Carnegie Inst Mus, 54 & 55; Recent Drawings U S A, Mus Mod Art, 56; Pa Acad Fine Arts, 62; Silvermine Guild; Providence Art Festival, R I, 69; plus others.
Teaching: Instr painting, Boston Mus Fine Arts Sch, 55-69; vis. prof, State Univ N Y Buffalo, 69-70.
Awards: Grand prize, 55 & first prize, 61, Boston Art Festival; Boston Mus Fine Arts Sch traveling fel; purchase prize, Sheraton-Boston Hotel, 65; plus others.
Publications: Illusr, Foundation course in French, 56.
Mailing Address: 12A Calzada de los Estrada, Cuernavaca, Morelos, Mex.

BERGER, KLAUS
Educator, Writer
b Berlin, Ger, Mar 24, 01.
Study & Training: Univ Munich; Univ Berlin; Univ Heidelberg; Univ Goettingen, PhD; Ecole du Louvre, Paris, France.
Teaching: Prof, Northwestern Univ; prof, Biarritz U S Army Univ; prof, Univ Mo, Kansas City; prof emer art hist, Univ Kans, Lawrence.
Awards: Fulbright fel as guest prof Univ Cologne, 54; Am Coun Learned Socs grant, 58; Guggenheim fel, 66.
Publications: Auth, Géricault, drawing and watercolors, 46; auth, French master drawings of the nineteenth century, 50 & Ger ed; auth, Géricault and his work, 52, & Ger & Fr ed; auth, Odilon Redon, fantasy and color, 65 & Ger ed; auth, Amen-Worte Jesu, De Gruyter, 70; also contribr to nat art mag.
Mailing Address: Dept of Art History, University of Kansas, Lawrence, KS 66044.

BERGER, SAMUEL A
Collector
b New York, N Y, Sept 29, 84.
Study & Training: City Col New York, AB, 02; New York Law Sch, LLB, 04.
Positions: Sr mem, Powers, Kaplan & Berger, 31-63; lawyer & sr mem, Reine, Mound & Cotton, New York, 63- ; founder, Albert Einstein Col Med.
Memberships: Asn Bar New York (v pres, 60-62).
Collection: Impressionist, post-impressionist and avante-garde American.
Publications: Auth, Revolutionary radicalism, 20, Dachis Case, 30 & Rosso Case, 31.
Mailing Address: 1095 Park Ave, New York, NY 10028.

BERGERE, RICHARD
Illustrator, Painter
Study & Training: New York Univ, BS; Columbia Univ, MA; Art Stud League New York; Parsons Sch.
Publications: Designer & illusr, From stones to skyscrapers, 60, Automobiles of yesteryear, 62 & Homes of the presidents, 62, Dodd; designer & illusr, When will my birthday be?, McGraw, 62 & The story of St Peter's, 66; plus others.
Mailing Address: 143-28 41st Ave, Flushing, NY 11355.

BERGGRUEN, JOHN HENRY
Art Dealer
b San Francisco, Calif, June 18, 43.
Study & Training: San Francisco State Col, AB, 67.
Positions: Pres & owner, John Berggruen Gallery, San Francisco, 68-
Memberships: Soc Encouragement Contemp Art (bd dirs).
Specialty of Gallery: Paintings, drawings and original prints of the twentieth century.
Mailing Address: 257 Grant Ave, San Francisco, CA 94108.

BERGLING, VIRGINIA CATHERINE (MRS STEPHEN J KOZAZCKI)
Art Book Dealer
b Chicago, Ill, Nov 6, 08.
Work in Public Collections: Books in large libraries throughout the world; also used as texts for designers' schools.
Memberships: Miami Art League; Brit Heraldry Soc, London, Eng.
Research: All phases of technical art and design.
Art Interests: Genealogy and heraldic art; coats of arms.

Publications: Ed, Art monograms & lettering, 20th ed, 64; ed, Ornamental designs and illustrations, 4th ed, 64; ed, Art alphabets and lettering, 9th ed, 67; ed, Heraldic designs & engravings, Illus Manual Rev, 66; ed, style charts for gen jewelry & silverware engraving; plus others.
Mailing Address: P O Box 523, Coral Gables, FL 33134.

BERKMAN, AARON
Painter, Instructor
Preferred Media: Oils, Watercolors, Casein.
b Hartford, Conn, May 23, 00.
Study & Training: Hartford Art Sch; Mus Art Sch, Boston; Yaddo Found fel; Huntington Hartford Found fel.
Exhibitions: Kaufman Art Gallery, New York, N Y, 60 & 63; Bercone Galleries, New York, 70; one-man show, Audubon Artists, 71.
Teaching: Instr & lectr art, 92nd St YMHA Art Ctr, New York, 43-65.
Positions: Art dir, 92nd St YMHA Art Ctr, 55-65; art dir, Bercone Studios, New York, 67-
Memberships: Artists Equity Asn; Audubon Artists.
Publications: Auth, Art and space, 49; auth, Amateur standing, monthly column in Art News, 55-61; auth, The functional line in painting, 57.
Dealer: Bercone Galleries, 1305 Madison Ave, New York, NY 10028.
Mailing Address: 230 E 88th St, New York, NY 10028.

BERKON, MARTIN
Painter
Preferred Media: Oils, Gouache, Ink.
b Brooklyn, N Y, Jan 30, 32.
Study & Training: Brooklyn Col, BA; New York Univ, MA; Pratt Inst.
Exhibitions: Brooklyn & Long Island Artists, Brooklyn Mus, 58; one-man shows, Smolin Gallery, New York, 62 & 20th Century W Gallery, 67; 5th Nat Exhib, Ohio Univ Gallery, 64; Butler Inst Am Art Ann Midyear Show, 65, 67 & 69.
Teaching: Instr elements of design, Fairleigh Dickinson Univ, 66-67; instr drawing & painting, City Col New York, 68-69.
Awards: Patron's Prize, Nat Soc Painters in Casein, 65.
Memberships: Col Art Asn Am.
Mailing Address: 51-25 Van Kleek St, Elmhurst, NY 11373.

BERKOWITZ, HENRY
Painter, Designer
Preferred Media: Oil, Watercolor, Mixed Media.
b Brooklyn, N Y, Feb 5, 33.
Study & Training: Brooklyn Mus Art Sch, with Sidney Simon; Workshop Sch Advert & Ed Art; Sch Visual Arts, New York, N Y.
Exhibitions: Alumni Exhib, Brooklyn Mus Art Sch, 58 & Alumni Graphic & Drawing Exhib, 59-60; Am Vet Soc Artists Show, New York, 63 & 68; Berkshire Mus Invitational, Pittsfield, Mass, 71.
Positions: Asst art dir, Pyramid Publ, New York, 63-
Awards: First prize for abstract watercolor, Amity Art League, 64; first prize for portrait (drawing), Lindenhurst Left Bank Show, 64; first prize for drawing, Babylon Art League, 66.
Memberships: Am Vet Soc Artists; Huntington Art League; Berkshire Art Asn; Awixa Pond Art Asn; Shore Arts Asn.
Dealer: Lynn Kottler Galleries, 3 E 65th St, New York, NY 10021.
Mailing Address: 1081 Hyman Ave, Bayshore, NY 11706.

BERKOWITZ, LEON
Painter
Preferred Media: Oils.
b Philadelphia, Pa.
Study & Training: Univ Pa, BFA; George Washington Univ, MA; Art Stud League New York; Corcoran Gallery Art Sch; Mexico City Univ; Acad Grande Chaumiere, Paris, France; Acad Bella Arti, Florence, Italy.
Work in Public Collections: Corcoran Gallery Art & Nat Collection Fine Arts, Washington, D C; James A Michener Collection, Houston, Tex; Wadsworth Atheneum, Hartford, Conn; Aldrich Mus Contemp Art, Ridgefield, Conn; High Mus, Atlanta, Ga.
Exhibitions: One-man show, Corcoran Gallery Art, Washington, D C, 69; Highlights of the 1968-1969 Art Season, Aldrich Mus Contemp Art, 69; one-man show, A M Sachs Gallery, New York, 69; Second Flint Invitational, Mich, 70; one-man show, Guelph Univ, Ont, 70.
Teaching: Prof art, Corcoran Sch Art, 68-
Positions: Co-founder & dir, Workshop Ctr of Arts, Washington, D C, 47-55.
Awards: Purchase prize, Second Flint Invitational, 70; Nat Found Arts & Humanities grant, 71.
Dealer: A M Sachs Gallery, 29 W 57th St, New York, NY 10019.
Mailing Address: 2003 Kalorama Rd, N W, Washington, DC 20009.

BERLIND, ROBERT
Painter
Preferred Media: Oil on Canvas.
b New York, N Y, Aug 20, 38.
Study & Training: Columbia Col, BA, 60; Sch Art & Arch, Yale Univ, BFA, 62, MFA, 63.
Exhibitions: Invitational at the Kultureel Centrum, Venlo, Neth, 67; one-man show, Maison de la Culture, L'Isle of Sorgire, Vaucluse, France, 69; Minneapolis Inst Art Biennial, Minn, 70; one-man show, Green Mountain Gallery, New York, 72; Yale Invitational (Yale at Norfolk summer prog), Norfolk, Conn, 72.
Teaching: Asst prof, Minneapolis Sch Art, 64-66, 69-70; asst prof art hist & humanistics, Haarlem, Neth, 66-68.
Dealer: Green Mountain Gallery, 135 Greene St, New York, NY 10011.
Mailing Address: R D 1, Orrtanna, PA 17353.

BERMAN, ARIANE R
Painter, Printmaker
Preferred Media: Acrylics, Wood.
b Freeport, Danzig, Mar 27, 37; U S citizen.
Study & Training; Hunter Col, BFA, 59; Yale Univ, scholar, 59-62 & MFA, 62; Am Asn Univ Women & Fondation Etats-Unis grants, École Beaux Artes, 62-63; also with Stanley William Hayter & lithography with Jacques Desjobert.
Work in Public Collections: Metrop Mus Art; Philadelphia Mus Art, Pa; Gallery Fine Arts, Purdue Univ, Ind; U S Info Agency via Am Color Print Soc Exhib; Am Petrol Inst, Washington, D C
Commissions: Paintings & sculpture, Fontana Gallery, Narberth, Pa, 63-71; painting, Philmont Country Club, Pa, 65; painting, Seventeen Mag, 71; painting, Shipley Sch, Bryn Mawr, Pa, 71; painting, Charles E Ellis Col, Newtown Square, Pa, 71.
Exhibitions: One-man shows, Fontana Gallery, 63 & 71, Harry Salpeter Gallery, New York, N Y, 66 & Eileen Kuhlik Gallery, New York, 71; Soc Four Arts, Palm Beach, Fla, 64; Philadelphia Art Alliance, 64 & 68; Nat Acad Design, New York, 65; Butler Inst Am Art 36th Ann, 72.
Awards: Painting prize, Yale Univ Sch Fine Arts, 62; Harriet Hale Wodley Award, Fondation Etats-Unis, 63; Edward H Stern Award, Philadelphia Art Alliance, 65.
Bibliography: Articles, In: La Rev Mod, Paris, France, 64, 66 & 71; cover story, In: Host Mag, 71; Joseph Yusif (auth), Assoc Press Sunday Mag, 71.
Memberships: Am Color Print Soc; Nat Asn Women Artists; Silvermine Guild Artists; Philadelphia Art Alliance; Yonkers Art Asn.
Dealers: Eileen Kuhlik Gallery, 23 E 67th St, New York, NY 10021; (graphics) Associated American Artists, 663 Fifth Ave, New York, NY 10022.
Mailing Address: 161 W 54th St, New York, NY 10019.

BERMAN, LEONID, see LEONID

BERMAN, MURIEL MALLIN
Collector, Patron
b Pittsburgh, Pa, June 21, 24.
Study & Training: Univ Pittsburgh; Carnegie-Mellon Univ; Pa Col Optom; Cedar Crest Col; Muhlenberg Col.
Teaching: Lects on African art and its origins, American, French, Picasso, Wyeth, Fakes, Forgeries and Reproductions.
Positions: Mem, Pa Coun Arts; hon chmn, Bucks Co Collectors Art Show, New Hope, Pa, 66; co-chmn, Episcopal Diocese Bicentennial Art Comt, 71; numerous other govt, civic & educ positions.
Memberships: Art Collectors Club Am; Am Fedn Arts; Friends Whitney Mus Am Art; Archives Am Art, Detroit; Mus Mod Art, New York: plus many others.
Art Interests: Collection on loan, Art in the U S Embassies Program; founder and donor, Carnegie-Berman College Art Slide Library Exchange; Berman Circulating Traveling Art Exhibitions, colleges and museums in the East.
Collection: Early twentieth century American modern, pop and op art; Eskimo, Japanese, Aboriginal Australian, French and African.
Mailing Address: 20 Hundred Nottingham Rd, Allentown, PA 18103.

BERMAN, NANCY MALLIN
Art Administrator, Art Historian
b Philadelphia, Pa, Oct 20, 45.
Study & Training: Wellesley Col, BA, 67; Hunter Col; Jewish Theol Sem, New York, N Y.
Positions: Cur, Lester Francis Avnet Collection, New York, 67-68; cur, Judaica Dept, Jewish Mus, New York, 68-72; cur, Skirball Mus, Hebrew Union Col, Los Angeles, Calif, 72-
Research: Jewish art, especially the development of the Hanukah Lamp in relation to prevailing architectural styles.
Mailing Address: 3077 University Mall, Los Angeles, CA 90007.

BERMAN, PHILIP I
Collector, Patron
b Pennsburg, Pa, June 28, 15.
Study & Training: Ursinus Col, hon LLD, 68; Lehigh Univ, LHD, 69.
Positions: Pres: Philip & Muriel Berman Found; chmn vis comt, Fine & Creative Arts, Lehigh Univ, 66-; many other positions in bus, govt, educ civic & art activities.
Awards: First Ann Am Jewish Comt Pa, Del, Md Region Award; Distinguished Serv Award, Allentown C of C; Outstanding Civic Leaders Am Award, 68; plus others.
Memberships: Life fel Metrop Mus Art, New York: Aspen Ctr Contemp Art; Am Fedn Arts; Art Collectors Club Am; Archives Am Art; many other art museums & associations.
Art Interests: Collections on traveling exhibitions and temporary loan in the United States; many paintings on permanent loan to civic and educational institutions in Lehigh Valley area; participant in Art in the Embassies Program.
Collection: American, French and Japanese art.
Mailing Address: 20 Hundred Nottingham Rd, Allentown, PA 18103.

BERMUDEZ, EUGENIA M, see DIGNAC, GENY

BERMUDEZ, JOSE YGNACIO
Sculptor, Painter
Preferred Media: Metals.
b Havana, Cuba, Aug 6, 22; U S citizen.
Study & Training: With Roberto Diago, Havana, Cuba, 52-53; Bell Voc Sch, Washington, D C, 61.
Work in Public Collections: Mus Mod Art, New York, N Y; Corcoran Gallery Art, Washington; Mus Bellas Artes, Caracas, Venezuela; Philadelphia Mus Art, Pa; Mus Mod Art, Cali, Columbia.
Commissions: Metal Relief 1961, First Americana Ann Mural Competition, 61.
Exhibitions: New Media-New Form I & II, Martha Jackson Gallery, New York, 60; Corcoran Gallery Art, Washington, 61; Mus Bellas Artes, Caracas, 67; Sculptures & Drawings, Pyramid Galleries, Washington, 70; Third Biennial Art Coltejer, Medellin, Colombia, 72.
Positions: Asst visual arts, cult dept, Org Am States, Washington, 53-58, chief graphic serv div, 58-71.
Awards: Fourth prize for painting, Sixth Ann Art Exhib, Havana, 53; second prize, Ninth Festival Art, Cali, 69; Cintas Fel Found fel, New York, 69-70.
Bibliography: L J Ahlander (auth), article, In: Washington Post, 7/29/62; T Alvarengo (auth), Imagen, Arte y Technologia, 71.
Dealer: Pyramid Galleries Ltd, 2121 P St N W, Washington, DC 20037.
Mailing Address: 4049 E Alan Lane, Phoenix, AZ 85028.

BERNARD, DAVID EDWIN
Printmaker, Educator
Preferred Media: Intaglio.
b Sandwich, Ill, Aug 8, 13.
Study & Training: Univ Ill, BFA; Univ Iowa, MFA; also studied with Mauricio Lasansky & Humbert Albrizio.
Work in Public Collections: Pennell Collection, Libr Cong, Washington, D C; Mid-Am Collection, Nelson Gallery, Atkins Mus, Kansas City, Mo; Otis Art Inst, Los Angeles, Calif; Free Pub Libr, Philadelphia, Pa; Joslyn Mus, Omaha, Nebr.
Commissions: Mural (steel & wood), Duerksen Fine Art Ctr, Wichita State Univ, 57; free standing tree symbol (steel), Camp Fire Girls Orgn, Wichita Art Mus, Kans, 60; sculpture (steel, wood & brass), Irene Vickers Baker Children's Theatre, Wichita; pair of standing tree shapes, Art Asn Wichita, 71-72.
Exhibitions: God and Man in Art, Am Fedn Arts Traveling Exhib, 57; First Ann Invitational Exhib, Otis Art Inst, 61; two-man traveling print exhib, Inst Cult Mexicano-Norte Americano, Guadalajara & five cities in Mex, 63; Univ Nebr Invitational Print Exhib, Sheldon Art Gallery, Lincoln, 67; one-man exhib prints, Philbrook Art Ctr, Tulsa, 67.
Teaching: Instr art prog, Maryville Col, 46-48; prof printmaking, Wichita State Univ, 49-
Awards: Purchase award for Hombre y Toro (intaglio), Pennell Collection, Libr Cong, 53; purchase award for Calvary (colored intaglio), Mid-Am Ann, Nelson Gallery, 55; purchase award for La Mer (colored intaglio), 10th Kans Artists Ann, Wichita Art Mus, 64.
Memberships: Soc Am Graphic Artists; Calif Soc Printmakers; Artists Guild Wichita (pres, 56); Mid-Am Col Art Asn; Wichita Art Mus Mem.
Publications: Auth, The collagraph print, Artists Proof, 62; Illusr, A west wind rises, 62 & Sun city, 64, Univ Nebr Press.
Mailing Address: 2243 N Yale Ave, Wichita, KS 67220.

BERNAY, BETTI
Painter
Preferred Media: Oil.
b New York, N Y, Sept 21, 26.
Study & Training: Pratt Inst; Nat Acad Design, New York, with
Louis Bouché; Art Stud League New York, with Frank Mason;
also with Robert Brackman.
Work in Public Collections: IOS Found, Geneva, Switz; Circulo
Amistad, Cordoba, Spain; Columbus Mus Arts & Crafts, Ga;
Columbia Mus Art, S C; André Weil Collection, Paris, France.
Commissions: Painting, pres of Renault, Madrid, Spain, 64; painting,
Children Have No Barriers, IOS Found, Geneva, 69; paintings,
Macaws, Seacost E Bldg, Miami Beach, Fla, 69 & mural, Sandy
Cove, S Bldg, 70.
Exhibitions: One-man shows, Columbus Mus Arts & Crafts, 60,
Columbia Mus Art, 60, André Weil Gallery, 60 & 63 & Mus
Malaga, Spain, 65; Salon des Artistes Indépendants, Grand Palais,
Paris, 63; Salon Populiste, Mus Mod Art, Paris, 63; plus many
others.
Awards: Artistic merit medal, City of New York, 42; Prix de Paris,
58; medal of honor, Mus Bellas Artes (Malaga), 65.
Memberships: Artists Equity Asn; Am Artists Prof League; Nat Asn
Painters & Sculptors Spain; Soc Artistes Français; Soc Artistes
Indépendants.
Mailing Address: 5001 Collins Ave, Miami Beach, FL 33140.

BERNE, GUSTAVE MORTON
Collector
b New York, N Y, Mar 4, 03.
Study & Training: Columbia Col, AB, Columbia Law Sch, LLB.
Positions: Pres, Long Island Jewish Med Ctr, N Y.
Collection: French impressionists.
Mailing Address: 9 Beech Lane, Great Neck, NY 11024.

BERNSTEIN, BENJAMIN D
Collector
b New York, N Y, June 24, 07.
Positions: Mem jury, Art Comn for Tercentenary, Fine Arts
Comn & Philadelphia Art Alliance; bd dirs, Philadelphia Art
Alliance.
Memberships: Buten Mus Wedgwood; fel Philadelphia Mus Art; life
mem Am Fedn Arts; Univ Pa Mus; Pa Acad Fine Arts; plus
others.
Collection: Contemporary art, mainly expressionist; large collec-
tion of oils, gouache, drawings, sculpture and lithographs.
Mailing Address: 901 Poplar St, Philadelphia, PA 19123.

BERNSTEIN, GERALD
Painter, Restorer
Preferred Media: Oils, Watercolors.
b Indianapolis, Ind, Aug 25, 17.
Study & Training: John Herron Art Inst; Art Stud League New York,
with George Bridgman & Yasuo Kuniyoshi; New York Univ, BA,
Inst Fine Arts, MA.
Work in Public Collections: Staten Island Inst Arts & Sci.
Exhibitions: Staten Island Inst Arts & Sci Ann, 50-72; Group Shows,
Pietrantonio Gallery, New York, N Y, 59-62; Downtown Gallery,
New York, 60; Edison Art Ctr, N J, 68.
Collections Arranged: Artist Look at Nature, Surveys of American
Painting & one-man & group exhibs, Staten Island Mus, 50-56.
Teaching: Artist-in-residence, States Island Community Col, 70-71.
Positions: Cur art, Staten Island Mus, 50-56; owner & dir, Island
Art Ctr, Staten Island, 58-
Awards: First landscape awards, Staten Island Mus Sect Art
Awards, 57, 59 & 61; first prize for watercolor, Edison Art
Ctr, 68; first prize, Staten Island Mus Spring Exhib Weissglass
Awards, 69.
Mailing Address: 1639 Richmond Rd, Staten Island, NY 10304.

BERNSTEIN, SYLVIA
Painter, Sculptor
Preferred Media: Watercolors.
b Brooklyn, N Y, Apr 11, 18.
Study & Training: Nat Acad Design; also with Arthur Covey, Gifford
Beal, Sidney Dickinson, Charles Hinton, Carl Anderson & Leon
Kroll.
Work in Public Collections: Whitney Mus Am Art, New York, N Y;
Wadsworth Atheneum, Hartford, Conn; Brooklyn Mus Art, N Y;
Munson-Williams-Proctor Inst, Buffalo, N Y; Pa Acad Fine Arts,
Philadelphia.
Exhibitions: 21st Nat Watercolor Biennial, Brooklyn Mus, 61; Childe
Hassam Fund Paintings Exhib, Am Acad Arts & Lett, 61; Con-
temporary American Drawings, Smithsonian Inst Traveling Exhib,
66-67; 200 Years of Watercolor Painting in America, Metrop Mus
Art, New York, 67; Philadelphia Art Alliance Invitational Water-
color Painting in America, Metrop Mus Art, New York, 67; Phila-
delphia Art Alliance Invitational Watercolor Show, 71-72.

Awards: Zimmerman Mem Award for most distinguished entry,
Philadelphia Watercolor Club, 62; medal of honor for watercolor,
Nat Asn Women Artists, 63; medal of honor for watercolor, Nat
Arts Club.
Bibliography: Margaret Harold (auth), Prize-winning watercolors,
Allied, 64.
Memberships: Nat Asn Women Painters (chmn watercolor jury, bd
dirs); Philadelphia Watercolor Soc; Am Watercolor Soc; Audubon
Artists; N Y Soc Women Artists.
Dealers: Bonfoey Gallery, 1710 Euclid Ave, Cleveland, OH 44115;
Four Winds Gallery, Kalamazoo, MI 49003.
Mailing Address: 8 Circle Rd, Scarsdale, NY 10583.

BERNSTEIN, THERESA
Painter, Art Historian
Preferred Media: Oils, Aquarelle, Graphics.
b Philadelphia, Pa.
Study & Training: Pa Acad Fine Arts; Art Stud League New York.
Work in Public Collections: Metrop Mus Art; Brooklyn Mus; Har-
vard Univ; Phillips Art Gallery, Washington, D C; Nat Mus,
Smithsonian Inst.
Commissions: First Orchestra in America, Treas Dept for Mann-
hein, Pa, 40; portrait of Prof David Lyons, Harvard Univ Biblical
Mus Faculty, 54; portrait of Prof Robert Pheiffer, Harvard Univ,
56; portrait of Henrietta Szold, Founder of Hadassah, comn by
mem of family, 59.
Exhibitions: Exhib Am Painters, Metrop Mus Art, New York, N Y,
50; Carnegie Inst, Pittsburgh, Pa, over six yrs; Biennial Am Art,
Corcoran Gallery Art, Washington, D C; Nat Mus, Smithsonian
Inst, Washington, D C, 56; New York Ann, Nat Acad Design.
Teaching: Dir summer art course, Gloucester, Mass, 32-69.
Awards: Shilliard Gold Medal, Plastic Club, 25; Jeanne d'Arc Medal,
Fr Inst Arts & Lett, 29; John A Johnson award, North Shore Arts
Asn, 71.
Bibliography: J B Nelson (auth), Theresa Bernstein, Int Studio, 25;
Dorothy Adlow (auth), article, In, Christian Sci Monitor, 29; E A
Jenell (auth), articles, In: New York Times, 45 & Menorah J, 48.
Memberships: Nat Asn Women Artists (jury awards, 38-59); Audu-
bon Artists Am (mem jury, 50-); Soc Am Graphic Artists; Allied
Artists Am; New York Soc Women Artists (dir, 28-).
Research: Graphic art; American art.
Publications: Auth, William Meyerowitz, 58 & auth, History of Jew-
ish artists, 58, Zukenft; auth, History-Cape Ann artists, Glouces-
ter Times, 70; auth, History North Shore Arts Association, 72;
auth, History New York Society of Women Artists, 72.
Dealers: Grand Central Galleries, 40 Vanderbilt Ave, New York, NY
10017; Bar Harbor Gallery, 23 Main St, Bar Harbor, ME 04653.
Mailing Address: 54 W 74th St, New York, NY 10023.

BERRESFORD, VIRGINIA
Painter, Art Dealer
Preferred Media: Oils, Watercolors.
b New Rochelle, N Y.
Study & Training: Teacher's Col, Columbia Univ, with Charles
Martin; Acad Mod, Paris, France, with Ozenfant.
Work in Public Collections: Whitney Mus Am Art, New York, N Y;
Detroit Mus, Mich; Columbus Gallery Fine Arts, Ohio.
Commissions: Juliet by Moonlight (mural), comn by Katharine
Cornell, Assoc Hall, Vineyard Haven, Mass.
Exhibitions: World's Fair, 39; Pa Acad Fine Arts; Mus Mod Art,
New York; Brooklyn Mus, N Y; Art Inst Chicago, Ill; plus many
other group and one-woman shows.
Positions: Owner & dir, Berresford Gallery, Menemsha, Mass, open
summers only.
Specialty of Gallery: Modern painting, sculpture and prints.
Dealer: Jacques Seligmann & Co, 5 E 57th St, New York, NY 10022.
Mailing Address: R F D, Vineyard Haven, MA 02568.

BERRY, GLENN
Painter, Educator
Preferred Media: Acrylics, Oils.
b Glendale, Calif, Feb 27, 29.
Study & Training: Pomona Col, BA; Sch Art Inst Chicago, BFA &
MFA.
Work in Public Collections: Storm King Art Ctr, Mountainville, N Y;
Joseph H Hirshhorn Collection, Washington, D C; Kaiser Alumi-
num & Chem Corp, Oakland, Calif; Palm Springs Desert Mus,
Palm Springs, Calif; Calif State Univ, Humboldt, Arcata, Calif.
Exhibitions: Phelan Awards Exhib & Artists Behind Artists, Calif
Palace of Legion of Honor, San Francisco, 67; one-man shows,
Ingomar Gallery, Eureka, Calif, 68, Ankrum Gallery, Los Ange-
les, Calif, 70 & Esther Bear Gallery, Santa Barbara, Calif, 71.
Teaching: Prof painting, Calif State Univ, Humboldt, 56-
Dealer: Ankrum Gallery, 657 N La Cienega Blvd, Los Angeles, CA
90069.
Mailing Address: P O Box 709, Arcata, CA 95521.

BERTOIA, HARRY
Sculptor, Craftsman
Preferred Media: Copper, Bronze.
b San Lorenzo, Italy, Mar 10, 15; U S citizen.
Study & Training: Arts & Crafts Sch, Detroit, Mich; Cranbrook Acad Art, Bloomfield Hills, Mich, 37-42.
Work in Public Collections: Va Mus Fine Art; San Francisco Mus Art; Mus Mod Art; Dallas Pub Libr, Tex; Denver Art Mus; plus others.
Commissions: Sculptural screens, Gen Motors Tech Ctr, Detroit, Mfrs Trust Bank, N Y & Mass Inst Technol Chapel; bronze sculpture,View of Earth from Space, Dulles Airport, Washington, D C, 62; copper & bronze fountain piece, Civic Ctr, Philadelphia, Pa, 67; plus others.
Exhibitions: Mus Non-Objective Art, New York, N Y; circulating exhib, Smithsonian Inst; Whitney Mus Am Art; Mus Mod Art; Int Sculpture Exhib, Battersea Park, London, Eng.
Awards: Gold medal, Archit League N Y, 55; gold medal, Am Inst Architects, 56; Graham fel, 57.
Bibliography: Tracy Atkinson (auth), included in: Directions I: options 68 (catalogue), Milwaukee Art Ctr, 68; Wayne Craven (auth), included in: Sculpture in America, Crowell, 68; Eduard Trier (auth), included in: Form and space: sculpture in the 20th century, Praeger, 68; plus others.
Dealers: Fairweather-Hardin Gallery, 101 E Ontario St, Chicago, IL 60611; Staempfli Gallery, 47 E 77th St, New York, NY 10021.
Mailing Address: R D 1, Barto, PA 19504.

BESON, ROBERTA (ROBERTA BESON HILL)
Painter, Art Administrator
Preferred Media: Oils.
b Minneapolis, Minn.
Study & Training: Univ Minn; Orange Co Jr Col, Newport Beach, Calif, with Stan Parkhouse; also with Pruett Carter & D Logan Hill.
Work in Public Collections: Monterey Civic Club, Calif.
Positions: Cur & mgr, D Logan Hill Fine Art Gallery, Carmel, Calif, 67-
Dealer: D Logan Hill Fine Art Gallery, Lincoln St between Fifth & Sixth, Carmel, CA 93921.
Mailing Address: P O Box 4381, Carmel, CA 93921.

BESS, FORREST CLEMENGER
Painter, Lecturer
b Bay City, Tex, Oct 5, 11.
Study & Training: Tex A&M Col, 29-32; Univ Tex, 32-33.
Work in Public Collections: Mus Fine Arts Houston; Brandeis Univ; Boston Mus Fine Arts; Univ St Thomas, Houston, Tex.
Exhibitions: One-man shows, DeYoung Mem Mus, San Francisco, 58; Wit & Whimsey in 20th Century Art, Am Fedn Arts, New York, N Y, 62; New Arts, Houston, 63; Contemp Arts Asn, Houston, 63 & 64; one-man show, Witte Mem Mus, San Antonio, Tex, 67; plus others.
Teaching: Lectr design, photog, Cartier-Bresson, Eve Arnold, Oliver Baker & Sumio Kuwabara.
Awards: Prize, Witte Mem Mus, 46.
Mailing Address: 1701 Avenue E, Bay City, TX 77414.

BESSEMER, AURIEL
Painter, Illustrator
Preferred Media: Oils.
b Grand Rapids, Mich, Feb 27, 09.
Study & Training: Western Reserve Acad, scholar, 24-27; Columbia Univ, Columbia Univ Club scholar, 27-30; Master Inst United Arts, Roerich Mus scholar, 31-33, with Howard Giles; Nat Acad Design, 27-30, with Arthur Covey & Leon Kroll; Art Stud League New York; State Univ N Y, 49; George Washington Univ; Wilson Teacher's Col.
Commissions: Southern Tapestry (mural), Post Off, Winnsboro, S C, 37-38; Life in the Southern Cotton Belt (mural), Post Off, Hazlehurst, Miss, 38-39; six murals, Post Off, Arlington, Va, 39-40; six murals, Wabash Railroad parlor cars, 49; twelve murals, Pa Railroad parlor cars, Congressionals N Y to Washington run, 51-52; plus many other murals & portraits.
Exhibitions: One-man shows at sixteen art ctrs in the U S including Pub Libr, Washington, D C, City Hall, Asheville, N C, Art Ctr, Raleigh, N C, Currier Gallery, Manchester, N H & Bowdoin Col Mus Fine Arts, Brunswick, Maine, 35-43.
Teaching: Instr art, Nat Art Sch, Washington, D C, 45-46; instr art, Jean Morgan Art Sch, New York, 47-49, Roerich Acad Arts, 48-52 & Pan Am Art Sch, 49-51; instr art, Catan-Rose Art Inst, Forest Hills, N Y & Montclair Sch Art, N J, 50; also lectr on aesthetics, mysticism in art & lit, philos & relig; pvt art classes, 63-70; artist-illusr, The Summit Lighthouse, Colorado Springs, 72-
Positions: Art gallery dir, Gallery Mod Masters, 36-42; creative designer, L & A Studios, Philadelphia & Pentone Co, New York,

61; spec asst to dir, Univ Sci & Philosophy, Waynesboro, Va, 62; staff artist, Summit Lighthouse, Colorado Springs, Colo, 72-
Awards: Maximillian Toch Prize, Nat Acad Design, 30; first hon mem, Chaloner Prize, 32; dipl & silver medal, Tommaso Campanella Int Acad Rome, 70; plus others.
Bibliography: Marian Slater (auth), Auriel Bessemer—artist, philosopher, poet, Voice Universal, 11/62; article, In: Georgetown Times, S C, 10/8/64; Margaret Odom (auth), Internationally known artist with teach at YWCA, Columbia Record, 10/6/66.
Publications: Illusr, Climb the highest mountain, The Summit Lighthouse, 72.
Mailing Address: First & Broadmoor, Colorado Springs, CO 80906.

BETSBERG, ERNESTINE (MRS ARTHUR OSVER)
Painter
b Bloomington, Ill, Sept 6, 09.
Study & Training: Art Inst Chicago, Raymond traveling fel, with Boris Anisfeld.
Exhibitions: One-man shows, Munson-Williams-Proctor Inst & Whitney Mus Am Art, 55; N Y, 56, 58 & 59; Saint Louis, Mo, 60; Pa Acad Fine Arts, 62 & 68; plus others.
Mailing Address: 465 Foote St, Saint Louis, MO 63119.

BETTMANN, OTTO LUDWIG
Art Historian
b Leipzig, Ger, Oct 15, 03; U S citizen.
Study & Training: Univ Leipzig, MS in LS, 27; PhD, 32.
Exhibitions: The Bettmann Panopticon Exhib, New York, N Y, 63.
Positions: Assoc ed, C F Peters Co, Leipzig, 27-28; ed, Axel Juncker Publ, Berlin, 28-30; cur rare bks, State Art Libr, Berlin, 30-33; founder & pres, Bettman Archive, Inc, 36-
Awards: Award of merit, Inst Graphic Arts, 67, 68 & 71.
Bibliography: John Tebell (auth), Picture man of 57th St, Sat Rev, 2/11/61; Friedof Johns (auth), One million pictures, Am Artist, 67.
Memberships: Am Inst Graphic Arts; Fr Inst; Am Fedn Arts.
Research: Pictorial documentation of all aspects of cultural history.
Publications: Co-auth, A pictorial history of American sports, 52; auth, A pictorial history of medicine, 56; co-auth, Our literary heritage, 56; co-auth, Pictorial history of music, 60; auth, Bettmann portable archive, 66; also auth graphic hist bks.
Mailing Address: 136 E 57th St, New York, NY 10022.

BETTS, EDWARD HOWARD
Painter, Educator
Preferred Media: Acrylics, Watercolors.
b Yonkers, N Y, Aug 4, 20.
Study & Training: Art Stud League New York; Yale Univ, BA, 42; Univ Ill, MFA, 52.
Work in Public Collections: Fogg Mus Art, Cambridge, Mass; Butler Inst Am Art, Youngstown, Ohio; Va Mus Fine Arts, Richmond, Va; Univ Rochester Mem Art Gallery, N Y; Indianapolis Art Mus, Ind.
Exhibitions: Five Corcoran Biennials, Washington, D C, 47-59; American Painting Today - 1950, Metrop Mus Art, New York, N Y, 50; Int Watercolor Exhibs, Brooklyn Mus, N Y, 53, 55 & 61, four shows, Watercolor U S A, Springfield Art Mus, Mo, 63-71.
Teaching: Prof painting, Univ Ill, Champaign, 49-
Awards: Silver medal of honor, Am Watercolor Soc, 53 & 59; First Altman Landscape Prize, Nat Acad Design, 57, 59 & 66; purchase award, Childe Hassam Purchase Fund Exhib, 66.
Bibliography: A S Weller (auth), Edward Betts Art in Am, New Talent Issue, 2/55.
Memberships: Nat Acad Design; Am Watercolor Soc; Audubon Artists; life mem Art Stud League New York.
Publications: Auth, Edward Betts discusses his lacquer paintings, 3/55, & Painting in polymer and mixed-media, 10/64, Am Artist Mag.
Dealer: Midtown Galleries, 11 E 57th St, New York, NY 10022.
Mailing Address: 804 Dodds Dr, Champaign, IL 61820.

BEVILACQUA, FRANCIS
Sculptor, Painter
Preferred Media: Chisel on marble & granite.
b Nicastro, Italy, Mar 31, 11; U S citizen.
Study & Training: Fine Art Acad, Rome, Italy, Ital Ministry Educ scholar, 28; sculpture with Domenico Trentacoste, painting with Felice Carena.
Work in Public Collections: Boca Mus Fine Art, Buenos Aires, Arg; Capitol Bldg, Washington, D C; Nat. Football League Bldg, New York, N Y; Shrine of Memories, Hartsdale, N Y; Jose Roger Balet Collection, Buenos Aires.
Commissions: Figures on granite panels, St Raphael's Sch, East Meadow, N Y, 60; emerald granite mural, R E A Express Bldg,

New York, 63; allegoric groups of figures, Stanley Warner-Bergen Mall, Paramus, N J, 65; black granite mural, City of New York Bd Educ, Pub Sch, 54, 70; black marble portraits, Shrine of Memories, Hartsdale, N Y, 71.
Exhibitions: Ital Pavilion, Belgrade Int Fair, Yugoslavia, 39; Muller Gallery, Buenos Aires, 52-55; Van Riel Gallery, Buenos Aires, 53; Religious Art of Western Hemisphere, Buenos Aires, 54; Grand Nat Exhib, Am Artists Prof League, New York, 71-72.
Awards: Gold Medal, Coun Corps, Rome, 39.
Bibliography: A Merlino (auth), Artistas plasticos de Argentina, Jorge J Batmalle, 54; Fred Shapiro (auth), New technique in art, Philadelphia Inquirer, 4/6/56; D Grafly (auth), The art world, Sunday Bull, 9/23/56.
Memberships: Fel Am Artists Prof League.
Art Interests: Pointsculpture, a self-developed technique of chiseled marble or granite.
Mailing Address: 333 E 79th St, New York, NY 10021.

BHALLA, HANS
Painter, Art Historian
Preferred Media: Collages, Prints.
Study & Training: Talladega Col, AB; Cranbrook Acad Art, MFA; Columbia Univ.
Work in Public Collections: Pub & pvt collections in U S A, Europe, Can, India, Jamaica & Japan.
Exhibitions: 37th Int Exhib, Northwest Printmakers; Seattle Art Mus, Wash; 15th Nat Print Exhib, Brooklyn Mus, New York; Boston Mus Fine Arts, Mass; Butler Inst Am Art, Youngstown, Ohio; plus many others.
Teaching: Lectr mod art, Middleburg Col, Cedar Crest Col, Ursinus Col & Fordham Univ; lectr Afro-Am art, Columbia Univ; from asst to assoc prof painting & printmaking, Talladega Col, 63-67; assoc prof art & chmn dept, Spelman Col, 67-
Positions: Actg coord, Centerwide Art Prog, Atlanta Univ Ctr Cols, at present.
Awards: Grant, Atlanta Univ Corp, 70; IBM faculty fel, 71; grant, Bd Home Missions, United Church Christ, New York, 71.
Memberships: Col Art Asn Am; Am Asn Mus; Mus Mod Art; Am Asn Univ Prof.
Mailing Address: Dept of Art, Spelman College, Atlanta, GA 30314.

BHAVSAR, NATVAR PRAHLADJI
Painter
Preferred Media: Dry Pigment, Acrylic.
b Gothava, India, Apr 7, 34.
Study & Training: Bombay State Higher Art Exam, India, AM, 58, Govt Dipl Art, 59; Gujarat Univ, India, BA, 60; Univ Pa, MFA, 65, John D Rockefeller III Fund fel, 65-66.
Work in Public Collections: Whitney Mus Am Art, New York, N Y; Mass Inst Technol, Cambridge, Mass; Power Inst, Univ Sydney, Australia; Boston Mus Fine Arts, Mass; Lannan Found, Palm Springs, Fla.
Exhibitions: Seventh Int Print Exhib, Mod Gallery Ljubljana, Yugoslavia, 67; Painting and Sculpture Today, Indianapolis Mus Art, Ind, 70; Whitney Mus Am Art Painting Ann, 70-71; Two Generations of Color Painting, Inst Contemp Art, Univ Pa, Philadelphia, 70; Beautiful Paintings and Sculpture, Jewish Mus, New York, 70.
Teaching: Art instr, Univ R I, spring semesters 67-69.
Bibliography: Christopher Andreae (auth), Painters philosophy, goal beyond objects, Christian Sci Monitor, 1/24/70; Carter Ratcliff (auth), Reviews--New York, Art Int, 3/70; Elwyn Lynn (auth), Power Bequest Exhib 1970, (catalogue), 9/70.
Dealer: Max Hutchinson Gallery, 127 Greene St, New York, NY 10012.
Mailing Address: 131 Greene St, New York, NY 10012.

BIANCO, PAMELA RUBY
Painter
Preferred Media: Oils.
b London, Eng, Dec 31, 06; U S citizen.
Study & Training: John Simon Guggenheim fel for creative painting abroad, 30.
Work in Public Collections: Mus Mod Art, New York, N Y; Chase Manhattan Bank, New York; Queens Col, New York; New York Pub Libr; Kerlan Collection, Univ Minn, Minneapolis.
Exhibitions: One-woman exhibs, Leicester Galleries, London, 19-20, Anderson Galleries, New York, 21, Knoedler Galleries, New York, 24, Graham Gallery, New York, 69 & Santa Barbara Mus Art, 70.
Bibliography: J B Manson (auth), The drawings of Pamela Bianco, The Studio, 11/25/20; Louis Untermeyer (auth), The drawings of Pamela Bianco, Century Mag, 7/22; Joseph Stella (auth), Pamela Bianco, an appreciation, Playboy, 25.
Publications: Illusr, Flora, William Heinemann, London, 20; illusr, Natives of rock, Francesco Bianco, 25; illusr, The skin horse,

George H Doran, 27; auth & illusr, Beginning with a, Oxford Univ Press, 47; auth & illusr, The valentine party, Lippincott, 54.
Dealer: Graham Gallery, 1014 Madison Ave, New York, NY 10021.
Mailing Address: 428 Lafayette St, New York, NY 10003.

BIBERMAN, EDWARD
Painter, Lecturer
Preferred Media: Oils.
b Philadelphia, Pa, Oct 23, 04.
Study & Training: Univ Pa, BS(econ); Pa Acad Fine Arts, Philadelphia.
Work in Public Collections: Butler Inst Am Art, Youngstown, Ohio; Mus Pa Acad Fine Arts; Mus Fine Art, Houston, Tex; Brandeis Univ, Waltham, Mass; Los Angeles Co Mus, Los Angeles, Calif.
Commissions: Wall murals, Fed Bldg, Los Angeles, 37 & 40 & Venice, Calif, 39.
Exhibitions: 46 Under 35, Mus Mod Art, New York, N Y, 30 & Mural Projs Exhib, 32; various ann exhibs, Whitney Mus Am Art, New York, 30-40; Los Angeles Co Mus Art, 36-65 & Los Angeles Munic Art Gallery, 71.
Teaching: Instr drawing, Art Ctr Sch Design, 38-50; lectr art hist, Univ Calif, Los Angeles, Irvine & San Diego Campuses, 67-
Awards: Lambert Fund Purchase Prize, Pa Acad Fine Arts, 30; Tupperware fel, Orlando, Fla, 57; Los Angeles City Ann Award, 68.
Memberships: Nat Soc Mural Painters.
Publications: Auth, The best untold, Blue Heron Press, 54; Time and circumstance, Ritchie, 68.
Dealer: Heritage Gallery, 718 N La Cienega Blvd, Los Angeles, CA 90069.
Mailing Address: 3332 Deronda Dr, Los Angeles, CA 90028.

BICE, CLARE
Art Administrator, Painter
Preferred Media: Oils.
b Durham, Ont, Jan 24, 09.
Study & Training: Univ Western Ont; Art Stud League New York; Can Gov fel for study in France, 52-53; Univ Western Ont, LLD, 62.
Work in Public Collections: Imperial Oil Collection; Seagram Collection; Nat Gallery Can, Ottawa, Ont.
Exhibitions: Royal Can Acad Arts, maj Can cities, 40-70; Ont Soc Artists, Toronto, 40-70.
Collections Arranged: Canadian Painting 1850-1950; Young Contemporaries (Canada), 50-65; Annual Western Ontario Exhibitions, 40-72.
Positions: Cur, London Art Mus, Ont, 40-
Awards: Can Coun Sr Arts fel, 62-63; Can Coun fel for writing, 72-73.
Memberships: Can Art Mus Dirs Orgn (pres, 66-68); Royal Can Acad Arts (pres, 67-70); Ont Soc Artists.
Publications: Auth-illusr, Jory's cove, 41, Across Canada, 48, The great island, 54, A dog for Davie's hill, 57 & Hurricane treasure, 65.
Mailing Address: 1010 Wellington St, London, Ont, Can.

BICHLER, LUCILLE MARIE PARIS, see PARIS, LUCILLE M.

BICKFORD, GEORGE PERCIVAL
Collector
b Berlin, N H, Nov 28, 01.
Study & Training: Harvard Col, AB, 22, Harvard Law Sch, LLB, 26.
Teaching: Lectr Indian hist & cult, Cleveland Col, 48-50.
Positions: Trustee & v pres, Cleveland Inst Art, Ohio, 55-; v pres & trustee, Cleveland Mus Art, 57-; trustee, Am Comt S Asian art.
Memberships: Am Asn Mus; Am Oriental Soc; Am Coun Asian Studies; Harvard Univ (vis comt, dept fine arts).
Collection: East Indian antiquities.
Mailing Address: 2247 Chestnut Hills Dr, Cleveland, OH 44106.

BIDDLE, GEORGE
Painter, Sculptor
b Philadelphia, Pa, Jan 24, 85.
Study & Training: Harvard Univ, AB, 08, LLB, 11.
Work in Public Collections: Mod Mus Art, Tokyo, Japan; Butler Inst Am Art, Youngstown, Ohio; Fogg Art Mus, Cambridge, Mass; Corcoran Gallery Fine Arts, Washington, D C; Walter E Chrysler Collection; plus mus in U S, Berlin, Ger & Mexico City, Mex.
Commissions: Fresco & sculpture (with Helene Sardeau), Supreme Ct Bldg, Mexico City; fresco, Nat Libr, Rio de Janeiro, Brazil; murals, Justice Bldg, Washington, D C.
Exhibitions: Retrospective of prints circulated by U S Info Agency in Japan, India, Italy & other European countries; over 100 one-man shows in U S, Europe, Asia & Mexico City.
Positions: Chmn art adv comt, War Dept, N Africa, 43; art adv comt, State Dept; mem, Fine Arts Comn, 50; mem, Nat Comn for Effective Cong.

Awards: Huntington Hartford Found fel, 54; Edward MacDowell
    Colony art award, 56; purchase prize, Brandeis Univ.
Memberships: Soc Painters, Gravers & Sculptors (v pres, 34); Nat
    Soc Mural Painters (pres, 35); Mural Artists Guild (pres, 37-
    38); Nat Soc Arts & Lett (v pres, 62).
Publications: Auth & illusr, George Biddle's war drawings, 44;
    auth & illusr, The yes and no of contemporary art, 57; auth &
    illusr, Indian impressions, 60; auth & illusr, Tahitian journal,
    68; contribr, nat mag.
Mailing Address: Mt Airy Rd, Croton-on-Hudson, NY 10520.

BIDDLE, JAMES
    Art Administrator, Collector
b Philadelphia, Pa, July 8, 29.
Study & Training: Princeton Univ, BA, 51.
Positions: Cur, Am Wing, Metrop Mus Art, 63-67; pres, Nat Trust
    Hist Preservation, Washington, D C, 67-; bd gov, Corcoran Gal-
    lery Art.
Memberships: Drawing Soc (pres); Am Fedn Arts (trustee); White
    House Hist Asn (bd dirs).
Publications: Ed, Jackson Pollock: works on paper, 69.
Mailing Address: 2425 Wyoming Ave, Washington, DC 20008.

BIDNER, ROBERT D H
    Painter, Designer
b Youngstown, Ohio, Mar 14, 30.
Study & Training: Cleveland Inst Art, BFA, 53.
Work in Public Collections: Nat Collection Fine Arts, Washington,
    D C; Andrew Dickson White Mus Art, Cornell Univ, Ithaca, N Y;
    Butler Inst Am Art, Youngstown; Nat Acad Design, New York,
    N Y; Canton Mus Art, Ohio.
Commissions: Murals, Bd Educ, Cleveland, Ohio, 53, William A
    Stenson, Greenwich, Conn, 69 & Fordham Univ, New York, 70.
Exhibitions: Mid-Year Shows, Butler Inst Am Art, 51-55 & 72; 25th
    Biennial Exhib, Corcoran Gallery Art, Washington, D C, 57; Dark
    Mirror, Am Fedn Arts, New York, 64-65; Contemporary Ameri-
    can Artists, Westmoreland Co Mus Art, Pa, 69; Art in Embassies
    Prog, U S State Dept, Washington, D C, 69-72.
Positions: Asst art dir, G M Basford, Inc, New York, 57-58; art dir,
    Fuller Smith & Ross, Inc, New York, 58-66; art dir, Ted Bates &
    Co, Inc, New York, 66-72.
Awards: Best in show, Butler Inst Am Art, 53; purchase award, Nat
    Acad Design, 56; Medal for a Creative Painting, Allied Artists
    Am, 66.
Bibliography: John Gruen (auth), article, In: New York Herald
    Tribune, 4/7/67; John Canady (auth), article, In: New York Times,
    4/8/67; Vito Acconci (auth), New York one man shows, Art News
    Mag, 4/69.
Dealer: A M Sachs Gallery, 29 W 57th St, New York, NY 10019.
Mailing Address: 559 First St, Brooklyn, NY 11215.

BIEDERMAN, CHARLES (KAREL JOSEPH)
    Sculptor
Preferred Media: Painted Aluminum.
b Cleveland, Ohio, Aug 23, 06.
Study & Training: Art Inst Chicago, 26-29.
Work in Public Collections: Tate Gallery, London, Eng; Kröller-
    Müller Mus, Otterlo, Holland; Walker Art Ctr, Minneapolis,
    Minn; Des Moines Art Ctr, Iowa; Univ E Anglia, Norwich, Eng.
Commissions: Three constructionist pieces, Interstate Med Clin,
    Red Wing, Minn, 40; work in pub plaza, Nat Endowment Arts,
    Red Wing, 71.
Exhibitions: One-man shows, Pierre Matisse Gallery, New York,
    N Y, 36, Arts Club, Chicago, Ill, 41 & Gallery 12, Minneapolis,
    71; retrospectives, Walker Art Ctr, Minneapolis, 65 & Hayward
    Gallery, London, 69.
Awards: Sikkens Paintworks Award, 62; Ford Found purchase
    award, 64; Nat Coun Arts Grant, 66.
Bibliography: Jan van der Marck (auth), Charles Biederman and the
    structurist direction in art, Feistbundel F vanderMeer, 66;
    Robyn Denny (auth), Retrospective (catalogue), Hayward Gallery,
    69; Leif Sjoberg (auth), London ahead of New York?, Studies in
    the 20th Century, 71.
Art Interests: Three dimensional art (neither sculpture nor paint-
    ing); writing books and articles on art.
Publications: Auth, Art as the evolution of visual knowledge, 48;
    auth, Letters on the new art, 51; auth, The new Cezanne, 58;
    auth, Dialogue II, creative or conditioned vision, Faber, 68; auth,
    A note on new arts, Studio Int, 70.
Mailing Address: Rte 2, Red Wing, MN 55066.

BIEDERMANN, MAX
    Painter
Preferred Media: Acrylic.
b New York, N Y, Dec 11, 14.
Study & Training: Cooper Union, with John Rogers.

Exhibitions: New Eng Exhib, Silvermine Guild Artists, 71; Grand
    Nat Show, Am Artists Prof League, New York, 72; Hudson Valley
    Art Asn, White Plains, N Y, 72; Art League Nassau Co, Garden
    City Art Gallery, N Y, 72; Nat Art League, Douglaston, N Y, 72.
Memberships: Am Artists Prof League; Hudson Valley Art Asn; Nat
    Art League; Art League Nassau Co.
Mailing Address: 245 Brompton Rd S, Garden City, NY 11530.

BIEHL, ARTHUR OLIVER
    Painter, Educator
Preferred Media: Acrylics.
b Norfolk, Va, Nov 18, 26.
Study & Training: Va Commonwealth Univ, BFA, 50.
Work in Public Collections: Va Mus Fine Arts, Richmond.
Exhibitions: 17th-22nd Va Artists Biennial, Va Mus, 63 & 66-71;
    33rd Ann Mid-Year Show, Butler Inst Am Art, 68; Realist Invita-
    tional Shows, Winston-Salem, N C, 69-70; 32nd Semi-Ann South-
    eastern Exhib, Gallery Contemp Art, Winston-Salem, 70; Main-
    streams '70, Marietta Col, Ohio, 71.
Teaching: Prof design & illus, Va Commonwealth Univ, 54-
Positions: Self employed free lance designer; illusr, 50-
Awards: Va Artist Biennial award of distinction, 63 & purchase
    award, 65, Va Mus Fine Arts; award of excellence, Mainstreams
    '70, Marietta Col, 70.
Bibliography: Barclay Sheaks (auth), Painting with acrylics, Davis,
    72.
Memberships: Am Asn Univ Prof.
Publications: Contribr, Graphis Packaging, 60.
Dealer: Gallery of Contemporary Art, Main St, Winston-Salem, NC
    27101.
Mailing Address: 1906 Floyd Ave, Richmond, VA 23220.

BIELER, ANDRE CHARLES
    Painter, Printmaker
Preferred Media: Acrylics, Oils; Can citizen.
b Lausanne, Switz, Oct 8, 96; Can citizen.
Study & Training: Art Stud League New York, Woodstock, with
    Charles Rosen & Eugene Speicher; Acad Ranson, Paris, France,
    with Paul Serusier & Maurice Denis; also execution of frescoes
    with Ernest Biéler, Switz.
Work in Public Collections: Nat Gallery Can, Ottawa; Mus Québec,
    P Q; Montreal Mus Fine Art, P Q; Agnes Etherington Art Centre,
    Queen's Univ, Kingston, Ont; Art Gallery Ont, Toronto.
Commissions: Saguenay: People and Hydro-Electric Development,
    Shipshaw (on aluminum panels), Aluminum Co Can, 48; Rehabili-
    tation (oil on canvas glued to wall), Vet Welfare Serv, Ottawa, 55;
    Scènes de Québec (oil on canvas attached to wall), Proctor &
    Gamble, Pointe Claire, P Q, 57; aluminum foil, plaster & alumi-
    num plates, comn by Aluminum Labs, Tokyo Aluminum Co,
    Japan.
Exhibitions: A Century of Canadian Art, Tate Gallery, London, Eng,
    38; Int Water Colour Exhib, Chicago, Ill, 39; Golden Gate Int
    Exhib Contemp Art, San Francisco, Calif, 39; one-man retro-
    spective, André Biéler—50 Years 1920-1970, 11 cities, 70-71;
    Int Exhib Graphics, Montreal Mus Fine Arts & Traveling Exhib,
    71-
Teaching: Resident artist & prof art hist, appreciation & painting,
    Queen's Univ, 36-63.
Positions: Dir, Agnes Etherington Art Centre, 57-63.
Awards: J W L Forster Award, Ont Soc Artists, 57; C W Jefferi
    Award, Can Soc Graphic Art, 64; Centennial Medal, Can Govt,
    67.
Bibliography: M Barbeau (auth), Painters of Quebec, Toronto Press,
    46; R Allen (auth), Introduction to André Biéler: 50 Years (cata-
    logue), Queen's Univ, 70; Frances K Smith (auth), A Canadian
    artist in the market place, Can Collector, 2/71.
Memberships: Academician Royal Can Acad Arts; Ont Soc Artists;
    Can Soc Graphic Art; Can Group Painters; Can Soc Painters in
    Watercolour.
Collection: French Canadian furniture and artifacts; Canadian and
    European paintings.
Publications: Ed, Kingston Conf Proc, 41; contribr, Can Art, IX:
    70-71; auth, Twelve Pines Press (monogr), Agnes Etherington
    Art Ctr, 72.
Dealer: Walter Klinkhoof, 1200 Sherbrooke W, Montreal, P Q,
    Can.
Mailing Address: R R 1, Glenburnie, Ont, Can.

BIER, JUSTUS
    Museum Director, Writer
b Nürnberg, Ger, May 31, 99; U S citizen.
Study & Training: Univs Munich, Erlangen, Jena & Bonn, 18-24;
    Univ Zurich, PhD, 24; Duke Univ, DFA, 70.
Teaching: Lectr, Tilmann Riemenschneider, Franconian & twentieth
    century sculpture; docent & instr art hist, Munic Univ, Nürnberg,
    25-30; asst prof art hist & actg head dept fine arts, Univ Louis-

ville, 37-41, assoc prof, 41-46, prof, 46-60; vis prof, Free Univ Berlin, 56; vis prof, Univ Southern Calif, 59; Fulbright lectr & vis prof, Univ Wurzburg, 60-61.
Positions: Dir & cur, Kestner-Gesellschaft Art Inst, Hanover, Ger, 30-36; founder & dir, Mus Vorbildliche Serienprodukt, Hannover, 30-36; critic & art ed, Courier-J, Louisville, Ky, 44-53; dir, Allen R Hite Art Inst, 46-60; critic & art ed, Courier-J, 54-56; dir, N C Mus Art, Raleigh, 61-70, emer dir & cur res, 70-
Awards: Res grant, Inst Advan Study, 53-54; Guggenheim fel, 53-54 & 56-57; Fulbright award, 60-61; plus others.
Memberships: Col Art Asn Am (chmn comt regional socs, 51 & 52, mem nominations comt, 52); Am Soc Aesthet (ed coun, 52-54, chmn session, 54); assoc Int Asn Art Critics; Am Fedn Arts; Am Asn Univ Prof; plus others.
Publications: Auth, Tilmann Riemenschneider, 48; contribr, Art Bull, Art in Am, Art Quart, Gazette Beaux-Arts; plus others.
Mailing Address: 201 Peartree Rd, Raleigh, NC 27610.

BILCHER, A EARLE
Painter
Preferred Media: Watercolor, Pastel, Charcoal.
b Philadelphia, Pa, Sept 18, 16.
Study & Training: Newark Sch Fine & Indust Arts; also with John R Grabach, Clara Stroud & Gustave Cimmiotti.
Work in Public Collections: York Jr Col, Pa; Permanent Palette Collection (traveling), Maurice J Stein, New York, N Y.
Exhibitions: Baltimore Mus Art Regional, 43; Academic Artists Asn, Inc, Springfield, Mass, 65, 66, 70 & 71; 31st Mid-Year Show, Butler Inst Am Art, Youngstown, Ohio, 66; Watercolors-Prints-Drawings, Pa Acad Fine Arts, Philadelphia, 69; Am Watercolors, Wichita Centennial 1970, Kans, 70.
Awards: Grumbacher Artists Award, 68 & Mem Award, Baltimore Watercolor Club, Inc, 70; Center Club Award, 70.
Bibliography: Gaston Janet (auth), A Earle Bilcher, painter, Rev Mod, Paris, 70.
Memberships: Baltimore Watercolor Club, Inc (treas, 65-); Acad Artists Asn, Inc, Md Inst Alumni Asn, Charter Chap.
Dealer: Artists Attic, 8511 Loch Raven Blvd, Baltimore, MD 21234.
Mailing Address: 5403 Remmell Ave, Baltimore, MD 21206.

BILECK, MARVIN
Printmaker, Illustrator
Preferred Media: Graphics.
b Passaic, N J, Mar 2, 20.
Study & Training: Cooper Union Sch Art.
Work in Public Collections: Shapiro Collection, Portland Mus, Ore.
Teaching: Asst prof drawing, graphics, calligraphy & art of the bk, Philadelphia Col Art, 60-67; asst prof drawing & graphics, Queens Col, N Y, 67-
Awards: Fulbright grant to France, 58; runner-up, Caldecott Medal, Am Inst Graphic Artists, Fifty Bks of Yr, Chicago Bk Clin.
Publications: Illusr, Sugarplum, 55 & Nobody's birthday, 61, Knopf, Rain makes applesauce, Holliday, 64, Penny, Viking Pr, 66 & Walker in the City, Harcourt Brace; plus others.
Mailing Address: 302 E Third St, New York, NY 10009.

BILLINGS, HENRY
Painter, Illustrator
Preferred Media: Oils.
b Bronxville, N Y, July 13, 01.
Study & Training: Art Stud League New York.
Work in Public Collections: Whitney Mus Am Art; William Allen White Libr, Kans State Teachers Col.
Commissions: Painting, Ford Motor Co, New York World's Fair, 38; paintings comn by U S Treas Dept Fine Arts Div for Saranac Post Off, N Y, 37, Medford Post Off, Mass, 38, Wappinger Falls Post Off, N Y & Columbia Ct House, Tenn, 40.
Exhibitions: Carnegie Int, Pittsburgh, Pa, 47; Whitney Mus Ann, 32, 37 & 40.
Teaching: Vis lectr painting, Bard Col, 35-53; instr painting, Art Stud League New York, 40; instr painting, Art Stud League Summer Sch, Woodstock, N Y, 60-61.
Positions: Designer, United Neighborhoods, Inc, 75th Anniversary Exhib, 59-61; consult, UNICEF Photo Exhib, New York World's Fair.
Publications: Auth & illusr, Construction ahead, 50, All down the valley, 52 & Bridges, 55, Viking Press.
Mailing Address: P O Box 1014, Main St, Sag Harbor, NY 11963.

BILLMYER, JOHN EDWARD
Craftsman, Educator
b Denver, Colo, Aug 17, 12.
Study & Training: Univ Denver; Kirkland Sch Art; Case Western Reserve Univ, BA & MA; also study abroad.
Work in Public Collections: Cleveland Mus Art; Denver Art Mus.
Exhibitions: Cleveland Mus Art; Denver Art Mus, 47-68 & Metrop

Show, 52-67; five shows, Syracuse Mus Fine Art, 48-56; Wichita Mus Art, 51, 55 & 57; Metrop Show, Denver Art Mus, 52-67; Colorado Springs Fine Arts Ctr, 60; plus others.
Teaching: Prof graphics & hist Romanesque & Baroque archit, Univ Denver.
Memberships: Am Asn Univ Prof; Denver Art Mus (trustee, 62-71); Col Art Asn Am.
Mailing Address: 1519 E Mexico Ave, Denver, CO 80210.

BINAI, PAUL FREYE
Painter, Art Curator
Preferred Media: Oils.
b Lancaster, Pa, July 3, 32.
Study & Training: Indiana Univ, AB, MFA, with Alton Pickens & Leo Steppat; Yale Univ; John Herron Art Inst; Ecole Fontainebleau, Paris, France, Walter Damrosch fel for study in painting, 62.
Work in Public Collections: Purdue Univ Art Ctr; Miami Mus Mod Art.
Exhibitions: Palais Fontainebleau, France, 62; Am. Fedn Arts, 64-65; Akron Art Inst, 64; one-man shows, Miami Mus Mod Art, Ligoa Duncan Gallery, New York, N Y, & Raymond Duncan Gallery, Paris, 64; plus many others.
Teaching: Instr art & design, Purdue Univ, 60-64; instr art, Akron Art Inst, 64-68.
Positions: Asst dir, Project Outreach, Detroit Inst Arts, 68-70, asst cur graphic arts, 71-
Awards: Purdue Univ Res Found grant, 61.
Memberships: Col Art Asn Am; Am. Asn Mus.
Mailing Address: Detroit Institute of Arts, 5200 Woodward Ave, Detroit, MI 48202.

BINFORD, JULIEN
Painter, Sculptor
Preferred Media: Oils, Egg Tempera, Acrylics, Marbles, Limestones, Beeswax.
b Richmond, Va, Dec 25, 08.
Study & Training: Emory Univ; Art Inst Chicago, with Boris Anisfeld; Ryerson traveling fel for France & Spain.
Work in Public Collections: Boston Mus Fine Arts, Mass; Springfield Art Mus, Mass; New Britain Mus, Conn; Phillips Gallery, Washington, D C; Va Mus Fine Arts, Richmond.
Commissions: Seven mural panels in banking room, Greenwich Savings Bank, 3 W 57th St, New York, N Y; one mural panel, Greenwich Savings Bank, 14th St at 6th Ave, New York; mural panel in lobby, Va State Libr, Richmond; church panel (mural) behind rostrum, Shiloh Baptist Church, Fine Creek, Va; mural panel for libr, Thomas Jefferson High Sch, Richmond.
Exhibitions: Salon Tuileries, Paris, France; Carnegie Int, Pittsburgh, Pa; Int Watercolor Show, Chicago Art Inst; Pa Acad Fine Arts, Philadelphia; Corcoran Gallery Art Biennial, Washington, D C.
Teaching: Prof art, Mary Washington Col, Univ Va, 46-62, 64-
Positions: Artist corresp, Life Mag, 44-46; chmn Int Exhib Contemp Art, Mary Washington Col, Univ Va, 55-66.
Awards: Springfield Mus Art Purchase Award, 42; Rosenwald Found fel, 43; purchase award, Buck Hill Falls Art Asn, 46.
Bibliography: River Jordan Mural, Life Mag, 42; Harry Salpeter (auth), Julien Binford, Esquire, 44; Elizabeth Binford (auth), Julien Binford, Am Artist Mag, 53.
Publications: Paintings for hist record of New York Harbor at War, Life Mag, 44.
Dealer: Midtown Galleries, 11 E 57th St, New York, NY 10022.
Mailing Address: P O Box 187, Powhatan, VA 23139.

BINGHAM, MRS HARRY PAYNE
Collector
Collection: Paintings.
Mailing Address: 834 Fifth Ave, New York, NY 10021.

BINGHAM, LOIS A
Art Administrator, Lecturer
b Iowa Falls, Iowa, July 8, 13.
Study & Training: Oberlin Col, scholar, BA & MA; Sch Fine Arts, Yale Univ, scholar; Inst d'Art & Archeol, Univ Paris, Carnegie grant for grad study.
Collections Arranged: More than 200 exhibs arranged & supervised incl Nation of Nations, to inaugurate Berlin Cong Hall, 54, Modern Painting and Sculpture, Moscow, 59 & biennial exhibs at Sao Paulo, Venice, Santiago, New Delhi & Paris, 61-
Teaching: Lects, The Medici: Patrons of Art, The Index of American Design, Dutch Painting, Manuscripts of the Middle Ages & Duccio's Maestra, Nat Gallery Art.
Positions: Staff, Nat Gallery Art, 43-48, assoc cur educ, 48-54; chief fine arts div, exhib br, U S Info Agency, 54-65; chief, Int Art Prog, Smithsonian Inst, Nat Collection Fine Arts, Washington, D C, 65-

Publications: Auth, How to look at works of art, Nat Gallery Art; auth, Highlights of American painting, CARE, N Y; contribr, Favorite paintings from The National Gallery of Art.
Mailing Address: National Collection of Fine Arts, Smithsonian Institution, Washington, DC 20560.

BINNING, BERTRAM CHARLES
Painter
b Medicine Hat, Alta, 09.
Study & Training: Vancouver Sch Art; Art Stud League New York; Univ Ore; London, Eng, with Henry Moore, Ozenfant & Meninsky.
Work in Public Collections: Nat Gallery Can, Ottawa; Art Gallery Toronto; Hart House, Univ Toronto; Vancouver Art Gallery.
Exhibitions: Can Biennial, 54; Venice Biennale, 54; Three Can, 55; Valencia, Venezuela, 55; Milan Triennial, 57; plus others.
Awards: Carnegie scholar, 36 & 51; medal, Vancouver, 51.
Memberships: Fedn Can Artists; B C Soc Fine Arts; Can Soc Graphic Art; Can Group Painters; assoc Royal Can Acad.
Mailing Address: 2968 Mathers Crescent, West Vancouver, B C, Can.

BIRMELIN, AUGUST ROBERT
Painter, Printmaker
b Newark, N J, Nov 7, 33.
Study & Training: Cooper Union Art Sch; Yale Univ, BFA & MFA; Slade Sch, Univ London.
Work in Public Collections: Mus Mod Art; San Francisco Mus Art; Sheldon Mem Gallery, Lincoln, Nebr; Mus Contemp Art, Nagaoka, Japan; Michener Found, Univ Tex, Austin; plus others.
Exhibitions: Nat Inst Arts & Lett, 68; Finch Col Art Mus, New York, N Y, 69; San Francisco Mus, 70; Boston Univ, 71-72; Indianapolis Mus Art, 72; plus others.
Teaching: Instr, Yale Summer Sch, 60; assoc prof art, Queens Col, N Y, 64-73; instr, Columbia Univ, summers 65-66; instr, Skowhegan Sch Painting, 67.
Awards: Fel award, Am Acad in Rome, 61-64; purchase award drawing, San Francisco Mus Art, 70; Childe Hassam Purchase Award, Nat Inst Arts & Lett, New York, 71.
Dealer: Terry Dintenfass Inc, 18 E 67th St, New York, NY 10021.
Mailing Address: 547 Riverside Dr, New York, NY 10027.

BISACCIO, PHILIP
Painter
b New York, N Y, Mar 15, 07.
Study & Training: Art Stud League New York, with Reginald Marsh.
Exhibitions: Knickerbocker Artists, 71.
Positions: Former ed, Art Times; exhibitor, Grafton Potter Art Gallery, 71-
Memberships: Life mem, Art Stud League New York.
Mailing Address: 101 W 78th St, New York, NY 10024.

BISCHOFF, ELMER NELSON
Painter, Educator
Preferred Media: Oils.
b Berkeley, Calif, July 9, 16.
Study & Training: Univ Calif, Berkeley, BA, 38, MA, 39.
Work in Public Collections: Mus Mod Art, New York, N Y; Whitney Mus Am Art, New York; Art Inst Chicago, Ill; New Sch Art Ctr, New York; San Francisco Mus Art, Calif.
Exhibitions: Whitney Mus Am Art Ann Exhib Contemp Am Painting, 59; Recent Painting U S A: The Figure, Mus Mod Art, New York, 62; '54 to '64, Painting & Sculpture of a Decade, Tate Gallery, London, Eng, 64; Pittsburgh Int Exhib Contemp Painting & Sculpture, 67; Expo '70, Osaka, Japan, 70.
Teaching: Instr painting & drawing, San Francisco Art Inst, Calif, 46-52, 56-63; prof painting & drawing, Univ Calif, Berkeley, 63-
Awards: Ford Found grant, 59; Nat Inst Arts & Lett grant, 63.
Dealer: Staempfli Gallery, 47 E 77th St, New York, NY 10021.
Mailing Address: 2571 Shattuck Ave, Berkeley, CA 94705.

BISGARD, JAMES DEWEY
Collector, Patron
b Harlan, Iowa, Apr 17, 98.
Study & Training: Univ Nebr, BA; Harvard Univ Med Sch, MD.
Positions: Trustee, Josiyn Art Mus, 45-
Art Interests: Impressionist and contemporary art.
Collection: Contemporary European, American and Mexican; also ash can group.
Mailing Address: 26349 Ocean View, Carmel, CA 93921.

BISGYER, BARBARA G (BARBARA G COHN)
Sculptor
b New York, N Y, June 7, 33.
Study & Training: Sarah Lawrence Col; Sculptors & Ceramic Workshop, New York; also indust design with R R Kostellow.
Work in Public Collections: U S Info Agency Permanent Collection, U S embassy.

Commissions: Pvt comns.
Exhibitions: Princeton Univ, 69; First Nat City Bank, New York, 68-70; Young Sculptors For Channel 13, 70; Lever House, 70-72; Union Carbide, 71; plus other group & one-man shows.
Teaching: Pvt instr sculpture.
Awards: Medal for Creative Sculpture, 68 & Today's Art Medal, 71, Audubon Artists; Merrit Award for outstanding design & craftsmanship in sculpture, Artist Craftsmen New York, 71.
Bibliography: Candidates for fame, Cue Mag, 64; articles, In: Art News, 66 & 68; article, In: Today's Art, 71.
Memberships: Artists Craftsmen New York (mem bd gov, 64-69 & 72-, exhib chmn, 67-69); Mamaroneck Artists Guild (v pres, 72-73); New York Soc Women Artists (exhib chmn, 72-73); Am Soc Contemp Artists.
Dealer: Environment Gallery, 205 E 60th St, New York, NY 10022.
Mailing Address: 50 Lake Rd, Rye, NY 10580.

BISHOP, BENJAMIN
Painter, Educator
Preferred Media: Oils.
b New York, N Y, Feb 10, 23.
Study & Training: Art Stud League New York, 45-47; Univ Nebr, BFA; N Y Univ Inst Fine Arts, 50-51; Columbia Univ; Univ Calif, Berkeley, MA, 65.
Work in Public Collections: Norfolk Mus Art & Sci, Va; State Univ N Y Col Potsdam; Univ Mass, Amherst; Syracuse Univ Mus, N Y; State Univ N Y Binghamton.
Exhibitions: Drawing Soc Nat Exhib, 65, circulated to 11 mus by Am Fedn Arts, 65-66.
Teaching: Instr art, Memphis Acad Art, Tenn, 47-48; instr art, Vassar Col, 51; instr art, Univ Mo-Columbia, 52-54; instr art, Santa Catalina Sch Girls, Monterey, Calif, 64-65; prof art, State Univ N Y Col New Paltz, 65-
Awards: Delta Pi Delta Award, Joselyn Art Mus, 48; first prize for drawing, Monterey Co Fair, Calif, 65; Childe Hassam Fund purchase award, Am Acad Arts & Lett, 68.
Dealer: Alonzo Gallery, 26 E 63rd St, New York, NY 10021.
Mailing Address: Box 958, Tillson, NY 12486.

BISHOP, BUDD HARRIS
Art Administrator
b Canton, Ga, Nov 1, 36.
Study & Training: Shorter Col(Ga), AB, 58; Univ. Ga, MFA, 60, with Lamar Dodd & Howard Thomas; Arts Admin Inst, Harvard Univ, 70.
Collections Arranged: Tennessee Sculpture 1971, Chattanooga Art Asn, Inc.
Teaching: Lectr art hist, Vanderbilt Univ, 61-62; art dir children's prog, Ensworth Sch, Nashville, Tenn, 61-64; lectr art surv, Univ. Chattanooga, 67-68.
Positions: Dir creative serv, Transit Advert Asn, New York, N Y, 64-66; exec dir, Chattanooga Art Asn, Inc, 66-
Memberships: Am Asn Mus; Southeastern Mus Conf (coun mem, 72); Tenn Asn Mus (coun mem, 68-70, pres, 71-).
Research: Early Tennessee artists; early southern American painting.
Mailing Address: 415 Park Rd, Lookout Mountain, TN 37350.

BISHOP, ISABEL (MRS HAROLD G WOLFF)
Painter, Etcher
b Cincinnati, Ohio, Mar 3, 02.
Study & Training: Wicker Art Sch, Detroit, Mich; New York Sch Appl Design for Women; Art Stud League New York; Moore Inst, hon DFA.
Work in Public Collections: Metrop Mus Art, New York, N Y; Whitney Mus Am Art, New York; Boston Mus Fine Art, Mass; Des Moines Art Ctr, Iowa; Philips Mem Gallery, Washington, D C.
Commissions: Mural for post off in New Lexington, Ohio, U S Govt Sect Fine Arts.
Exhibitions: Venice Biennials; Pittsburgh Int; Nat Exhib Prints, Brooklyn Mus; One-man shows, Berkshire Mus, Pittsfield, Mass & Midtown Galleries, New York.
Teaching: Instr figure painting & drawing, Art Stud League New York, 35-37; instr art, Skowhegan Sch Painting & Sculpture, 56 & 58.
Awards: Many awards.
Memberships: Am Soc Graphic Artists (v pres, 69-72); Nat Arts Club; Audubon Artists; Royal Soc Arts, London.
Dealer: Midtown Galleries, 11 E 57th St, New York, NY 10022.
Mailing Address: 355 W 246th St, New York, NY 10471.

BISHOP, MARJORIE CUTLER
Painter
Preferred Media: Oil.
b Melrose, Mass.
Study & Training: Art Stud League, New York, N Y; New Sch Social

Res; also with Guy Pene du Bois, Moses Soyer, Sol Wilson & Valero, Paris, France.
Work in Public Collections: Walker Art Ctr, Minneapolis, Minn.
Exhibitions: Carnegie Inst, Pittsburgh, Pa, 45; Pa Acad Fine Arts, Philadelphia, 45; Audubon Artists, New York, 47, 52 & 54; Hecksher Mus, Huntington, N Y & Guild Hall, Easthampton, N Y, 65; plus 20 one-man shows.
Teaching: Instr creative painting & art hist, Bishop Art Studio, Oldfield, N Y, 56-
Positions: Art Coun, Suffolk Mus, Stony Brook, N Y, 61-65.
Awards: Purchase prize, Walker Art Ctr, 45; exhib award, St Paul-de-Vence, France, 53.
Dealer: Gallery North, North Country Rd, Setauket, NY 11733.
Mailing Address: Flax Bond Woods, Setauket, NY 11733.

BISONE, EDWARD GEORGE
Painter, Illustrator
Preferred Media: Acrylic, Watercolor, Charcoal, Mixed Media.
b Buffalo, N Y, Nov 19, 28.
Study & Training: Univ Buffalo, with Seymour Drumlevitch.
Exhibitions: 27th Ann, Butler Inst Am Art, Youngstown, Ohio, 62; 99th Ann Exhib, Am Watercolor Soc, New York, NY, 66; 13th Nat Show, Chautauqua Exhib Am Art, New York, 70; Ann Drawing & Small Sculpture Show, Ball State Univ, Muncie, Ind, 70; 145th Ann Exhib, Nat Acad Design, New York, 70.
Awards: First prize painting, Burnhams Gallery Sight & Sound, 63; Tony Sisti Award, Leisureland Show, 68; first prize graphics, McAlpine United Presby Church, 72.
Bibliography: Discussed in La Rev Mod, Paris, France, 67; Art Rev Mag, 68.
Memberships: Artists Equity Asn.
Publications: Auth, Art notebook, Vol 1, No 2; illusr, Tour the world of cooking in 15 minutes, 72.
Dealer: Galerie des Beaux Arts, 352 Adams Ave, Scranton, PA 18503.
Mailing Address: 17 Pleasant St, Cheektowaga, NY 14225.

BISSELL, (CHARLES) PHIL
Cartoonist, Illustrator
Preferred Media: Ink, Tempera
b Worcester, Mass, Feb 1, 26.
Study & Training: Sch Practical Art, Boston, Mass; Art Instr Inc, Minneapolis, Minn, grad.
Work in Public Collections: Baseball Hall of Fame, Cooperstown, N Y; Basketball Hall of Fame, Springfield, Mass; Football Hall of Fame, Canton, Ohio; Eisenhower Libr, Abilene, Kans.
Commissions: New Eng Patriots (Nat Football League) insignia.
Exhibitions: Southern Calif Expo, 64; Nat Cartoonists Soc, New York, N Y, 71 & Washington, D C, 72; Man and his world, Ninth Int Salon Cartoons, Montreal, P Q, 72.
Memberships: Nat Cartoonists Soc.
Mailing Address: 162 W Main St, Westborough, MA 01581.

BITTLEMAN, ARNOLD (IRWIN)
Painter
b New York, N Y, July 4, 33.
Study & Training: R I Sch Design; Yale Univ, BFA & MFA.
Work in Public Collections: Mus Mod Art; Whitney Mus Am Art; Brooklyn Mus; Fogg Mus Art; Addison Gallery Am Art; plus others.
Exhibitions: Whitney Mus Am Art, 58-59 & 62-63; Pa Acad Fine Arts, 59; Mus Mod Art, 59 & 65; Yale Sch Art, 63; Univ Mich, Ann Arbor, 65; plus others.
Teaching: Instr drawing & color, Parsons Sch Design, New York, N Y; instr, Yale Univ Sch Art & Archit; instr painting & printmaking, Skidmore Col; assoc prof, dept arts & artist-in-residence, Union Col, N Y.
Awards: Alice K English traveling fel, Yale Univ, 56-57; prize, Metrop Young Artists Show, New York, 59.
Bibliography: Articles with reproductions of work, In: Art in Am & Artists at Work.
Dealer: Kanegis Gallery, 244 Newbury St, Boston, MA 02116.
Mailing Address: 4 Douglas Rd, Schenectady, NY 10304.

BITTNER, HANS OSKAR
Painter, Illustrator
b Breslau, Ger, Jan 25, 05; U S citizen.
Study & Training: Breslau Kunstschule; Munich Acad.
Work in Public Collections: Collection of Crown Prince William of Ger; Breslau Kunst Mus; Breslau Art Galleries; Chicago Art Galleries; also in private collections.
Exhibitions: Ill Festival Art, Chicago, 64; three Main Libr, Chicago; Chicago Chap Artists Equity Asn; Rockford Col, Kenosha Col & Univ Wis-Stevens Point; work also exhibited on ABC & NBC.
Positions: Glass & display designer, Goldblatt Stores, Chicago, 30-35; commercial artist, Vogue Wright, 35-45; artist & designer, Wilding Picture Studio, 52-68.

Awards: Several second pl & hon mentions, Palette & Chisel Acad & Munic Art League, Chicago; gold medal, Col Frank Chesrow, Chicago, 72.
Memberships: Palette & Chisel Acad (dir, 68-); Munic Art League (dir, 69-); Artist Guild Chicago.
Mailing Address: 3843 N Sawyer Ave, Chicago, IL 60618.

BLACK, DAVID EVANS
Sculptor
Preferred Media: Plastics, Metals.
b Gloucester, Mass, May 29, 28.
Study & Training: Skowhegan Sch, Maine, summer, 49; Wesleyan Univ, AB, 50; Ind Univ, Bloomington, 53, with Karl Martz & George Rickey.
Work in Public Collections: Neue Nat Galerie, W Berlin, Ger; Addison Gallery Am Art, Mass; Dayton Art Inst; Butler Inst Am Art, Youngstown, Ohio; Ind Univ.
Commissions: Ceramic reliefs for apt bldgs, Lane & Neil Aves, Columbus, Ohio; bronze fountain, Independence Square, Columbus, 63; ceramic sculpture, Hardesty Village, Columbus, 65; cast stone wall reliefs, Forum Theatre, Columbus, 69; outdoor sculpture in clear plastics & steel, Neue Nat Galerie Sculpture Ct, 72.
Exhibitions: One-man shows, Contemporaries Gallery, New York, N Y, 67 & Amerika-Haus, W Berlin, 71; Am Painting & Sculpture, Krannert Mus, Univ Ill, 69 & Indianapolis Mus, 72; Plastics, Jewish Mus, New York, Milwaukee Art Ctr, Wis & San Francisco Mus Art, Calif, 69-70.
Teaching: Prof sculpture, Ohio State Univ, 54-
Positions: Mem visual arts panel, Ohio Arts Coun, Columbus, 67-
Awards: Fulbright grant to Italy, 62-63; Nat Arts Coun Award, 66; artists-in-residence prog, Berlin & W Ger Govt, 70-71.
Bibliography: David Black, sculptor (half hr prog), Ohio State Univ TV Ctr, 67; Tracy Atkinson (auth), David Black, recent work & George Rickey (auth), David Black, Art Int, 12/72.
Publications: Auth, Transparent sculpture, Ohio State Univ Arts, 2/72.
Mailing Address: 145 E Tulane Rd, Columbus, OH 43202.

BLACK, FREDERICK (EDWARD)
Painter, Art Administrator
Preferred Media: Oils, Acrylics.
b Providence, R I, May 24, 24.
Study & Training: Univ N Mex, BS, BA, MA.
Work in Public Collections: Univ N Mex; Roswell Art Mus; Long Beach Mus Art.
Exhibitions: Phoenix Art Mus, 63; Univ Ill Biennial Invitational; one-man exhib, Calif Palace of Legion of Honor; Whitney Mus Am Art Invitational; one-man show, Paul Rivas Gallery, Los Angeles, 65; plus many others.
Collections Arranged: Arts of Southern California series, contemp art, organized by Long Beach Mus Art, circulated by Western Asn Art Mus, 62-65; period & contemp exhibs, N Mex State Art Mus; Tucson Art Ctr.
Teaching: Vis prof art, Univ Colo, summers 60 & 61; prof art, Univ Ariz Exten, 60-61; vis prof art, Otis Art Inst, summers 65 & 66; vis prof art hist, Univ Calif, Los Angeles, 65; vis prof art hist, Calif State Col, Long Beach, summer 66; assoc prof art, Univ Albuquerque, 66-69.
Positions: Dir, State Art Mus, Santa Fe, N Mex; dir, Tucson Art Ctr, Ariz; adv prof painting, Art Ctr Sch, Los Angeles; art juror, state & regional, 61-64; dir, Long Beach Mus Art, 61-66; mem fine arts adv bd, Albuquerque City Comn, 70-
Awards: First prize, Providence Art Club, 53; nominee for New Talent, Art in Am, 58; Ford Found grant nominee, 59.
Memberships: Western Mus League (past pres); Long Beach Arts Coun (pres); Artists Equity Asn; Am Asn Mus; Western Asn Art Mus.
Publications: Contribr, bk revs, N Mex Quart, 53 & 64; contribr, Director's choice, Art in Am, 62; auth, Long & Evangel, Craft Horizons, 3-4/70.
Mailing Address: 7300 Arroyo Del Oso Ave N E, Albuquerque, NM 87109.

BLACK, LISA
Painter
Preferred Media: Ink, Acrylics.
b Lansing, Mich, June 19, 34.
Study & Training: Univ Paris, Sorbonne, dipl, 55; Univ Mich, BA, 56.
Exhibitions: New Haven Paint & Clay Club 70th Ann Art Exhib, Conn, 71; Art Asn Newport 60th & 61st Am Ann Exhib, Newport, R I, 71; Springfield Art League 53rd Nat Exhib, Mass, 72; 32nd Ann Invitational Art Exhib, Cedar City, Utah, 72; 15th Nat Exhib Am Art, Chautauqua, N Y, 72.
Awards: Merit award, New Rochelle Art Asn Juried Ann, 71; William Holland Drury Prize, Art Asn Newport 60th Am Ann, 71; second award, graphics, Springfield Art League Nat, 72.

Memberships: Artists Equity Asn New York & Nat; Westchester Art Soc; Stamford Art Asn; Rowayton Arts Ctr; Greenwich Art Soc.
Mailing Address: 17 Brushy Hill Rd, Darien, CT 06820.

BLACK, MARY McCUNE
Art Administrator, Painter
Preferred Media: Watercolors.
b Broadwell, Ohio, Feb 14, 15.
Study & Training: Ohio Univ, BS(educ), 37, MFA, 58; Amagansett Sch Art, Sarasota, Fla; workshop study with Charles Burchfield, William Thon, Aaron Bohrod, Paul Sample, Elliot O'Hara & Hilton Leech.
Work in Public Collections: FMC Corp; McJunkin Corp; Kanawha Co Pub Libr; Art in Embassies Prog, 67-68; Lutheran Church, Parkersburg, W Va.
Commissions: Three murals for Pediatric Ward, Charleston Gen Hospital Auxiliary, W Va, 53.
Exhibitions: Ohio Valley Regional, Ohio Univ, 45; Huntington Galleries Regional, 54; Intermont Col Regional, Bristol, Va, 57; Nat League Am Pen Women, Tulsa, Okla, 68 & Smithsonian Inst, Washington, D C, 63.
Collections Arranged: Permanent collection exhibition; Fiber and Fabrics; Collectors Exhibition of Kanawha Valley.
Teaching: Instr art, Sandusky Jr High Sch, 37-39; instr painting, adult prog, Kanawha Co Bd Educ, 58-04; instr art, Valley Day Sch, 60-63; instr painting, YMCA & Charleston Art Gallery, 63-68.
Positions: Dir, Charleston Art Gallery of Sunrise, W Va, 63-
Awards: Seven first prizes in watercolor, Allied Artists W Va, 42-56; fourth prize in oil, Nat League Am Pen Women, 61; first prize for watercolor, Centennial Art Show, Clarksburg, W Va, 63.
Memberships: Am Asn Mus; Allied Artists W Va (pres, 58-59); Nat League of Am Pen Women (pres, 59-60); W Va Art Educ Asn.
Mailing Address: Charleston Art Gallery, 755 Myrtle Rd, Charleston, WV 25314.

BLACK, SHIRLEY
Painter
Preferred Media: Watercolors.
b New York, N Y, June 20, 21.
Study & Training: Art Stud League New York, with E Yaghijian, G Grosz, M Glasier & Morris Kantor; Phillips Mem Gallery, Washington, D C, 42; Columbia Univ Teachers Col, with Arthur Young, 56-57; Mus Mod Art, with Zoltan Hecht, 57-58; Nat Acad Design, with Federico Castellon & Mario Cooper.
Work in Public Collections: Alfred Univ, N Y; Bridgeport Univ, Conn; Marine Midland Trust Co Rochester, N Y; Mount Holyoke Col, South Hadley, Mass.
Exhibitions: Butler Inst Am Art, Youngstown, Ohio, 57; The Importance of the Small Painting, Nordness Gallery, New York, 60; The Fifth Season, Alonzo Gallery, New York, 69; Am Watercolor Soc, Nat Acad Sch Fine Arts, New York, 70-71; Philbrook Mus, Tulsa, Okla, 71.
Bibliography: Martha B Scott (auth), Watercolors of Shirley Black bring some response as poetry, Bridgeport Sunday Post, 10/17/71.
Memberships: Silvermine Guild Artists.
Dealer: Alonzo Gallery, 26 E 63rd St, New York, NY 10021.
Mailing Address: 360 E 72nd St, New York, NY 10021.

BLACKBURN, LENORA WHITMIRE
Collector
b Midland, Tex, Aug 21, 04.
Study & Training: Univ Tex, Austin, BA, 27; also grad study.
Memberships: Mobile Art Asn; Art Patrons League of Mobile.
Art Interests: Exhibiting collection for groups and giving lectures on artists.
Collection: Old Masters including Titian, Ghirlandaio, Rubens, Hals, Van der Helst, Bol, Franz van Mieris, Van Dyck, Constable, Turner, Watteau, Ingres, Vigée-Lebrun, Gainsborough, Richard Wilson, Bonington, Alma-Tadema, T Rousseau, Daubigny, Jules Breton, John F Herring, Sr, Claude Monet, Rouault, Sir Alfred East and many others. Americans including Charles Wilson Peale, Inness, Sully, Eakins, William Marshall (Lincoln's portrait of which Marshall made an engraving), Bierstadt, Blakelock, Robert Henri, John Sloan, Childe Hassam, Alexander Wyant, George Phippen, Peter Hurd, Joe Rader Roberts and many others.
Mailing Address: 4505 N Sunset Dr, Mobile, AL 36608.

BLACKBURN, MORRIS (ATKINSON)
Painter, Printmaker
Preferred Media: Oil, Watercolor, Gouache, Sumi.
b Philadelphia, Pa, Oct 13, 02.
Study & Training: Pa Acad Fine Arts; also with Arthur B Carles, Jr.

Work in Public Collections: Pa Acad Fine Arts; Philadelphia Mus Art; N J State Mus, Trenton; Mus New Mex, Santa Fe; Libr Cong, Washington, D C.
Exhibitions: Pa Acad Fine Arts Ann, 30-72; 37 one-man shows, 30-72; plus many exhibs, Nat Acad Design, Am Watercolor Soc & Audubon Artists.
Teaching: Instr painting, Philadelphia Mus Art, 45-72; instr painting, drawing & graphics, Pa Acad Fine Arts, 52-
Awards: Guggenheim fel, 52; watercolor medal, Philadelphia Watercolor Club, 69; Percy M Owens Prize, Fellowship Pa Acad Fine Arts, 72.
Bibliography: Henry Pitz (auth), Morris Blackburn, Am Artist Mag, 11/70; film, Portrait of a painter, Philadelphia Mus Art.
Memberships: Philadelphia Watercolor Club (mem bd & chmn exhib comt, 69-71); Am Watercolor Soc; Audubon Artists; Allied Artists Am; Fellowship Pa Acad Fine Arts.
Mailing Address: 2104 Spring St, Philadelphia, PA 19103.

BLACKETER, JAMES RICHARD
Painter, Art Dealer
Preferred Media: Oils.
b Laguna Beach, Calif, Sept 23, 31.
Study & Training: Santa Ana Col; also with Bennett Bradbury.
Exhibitions: Laguna Beach Invitational Marine Show, Calif, 59; Los Angeles Co Fair Invitational Exhib, Pomona, Calif, 60; Hunt-Wesson Foods Show, Fullerton, Calif, 72.
Teaching: Pvt classes oil painting, 60-
Positions: Art dir, Fed Sign & Signal Corp, Los Angeles, Calif, 58-60; Santa Ana, Calif, 60-72; owner, The Studio (art gallery), Laguna Beach.
Awards: Laguna Beach Art Asn Awards, 51, 58, 59 & 60; Festival of Arts Award, 58; Ebell Club Los Angeles Award, 60.
Memberships: Laguna Beach Art Asn(secy, 60); Am Inst Fine Arts; Laguna Beach Festival of Arts; Showcase 21.
Specialty of Gallery: Marine oil paintings.
Mailing Address: 2260 Glenneyre St, Laguna Beach, CA 92651.

BLACKWELL, JOHN VICTOR
Art Historian, Educator
b Yale, Okla, Oct 25, 19.
Study & Training: James Millikin Univ, BA; State Univ Iowa, MA, MFA & PhD.
Teaching: Prof & dean col arts & sci, Univ Nebr, Omaha.
Research: Medieval art history.
Mailing Address: College of Arts & Sciences, University of Nebraska at Omaha, 60th & Dodge Sts, Omaha, NE 68101.

BLACKWELL, THOMAS LEO
Painter
Preferred Media: Oils.
b Chicago, Ill, Mar 9, 38.
Work in Public Collections: Many in private collections.
Commissions: Many private commissions.
Exhibitions: Human Concern-Personal Torment, Whitney Mus Am Art, New York, N Y, 69; Whitney Mus Am Art Painting Ann, 72; New Realism, Lowe Mus, Univ Miami, Fla, 72; New Painting, Indianapolis Mus Art, Ind, 72; Sharp Focus Realism, Sidney Janis Gallery, 72; Hyperrealistes Americains, Galerie 4 Movements, Paris, France, 72.
Bibliography: Masters & Houston (auth), Psychedelic art, Grove, 68; Chase & McBurnett (auth), interview, In: Art in Am, 11/72; Linda Chase (auth), Hyperrealism Americains, Publ Fillipacchi, 73.
Dealer: Allan Stone Gallery, 48 E 86th St, New York, NY 10028.
Mailing Address: 131 Prince St, New York, NY 10012.

BLACKWOOD, DAVID (LLOYD)
Painter, Printmaker
Preferred Media: Watercolors.
b Wesleyville, Nfld, Nov 7, 41.
Study & Training: Ont Col Art, Toronto, 59-64.
Work in Public Collections: Nat Gallery Can; Nat Gallery Australia; London Mus & Art Gallery; N B Mus; Art Gallery Hamilton.
Exhibitions: Northwest Printmakers, Seattle, Wash, 68; International Graphics '71, Montreal Mus Fine Arts; Can Printmakers, Can Embassy, Washington, D C, 71; First Norweg Biennial, Frederickstad, Norway, 72; Calgary Stampede Exhib Can Art, 72.
Teaching: Art master drawing & painting, Trinity Col Sch Port Hope, Ont, 63-72; artist-in-residence, Erindale Col, Univ Toronto, 69-
Awards: Ingres Medal, Ministry Cult, Govt France, 63; purchase award, Can Biennial, Nat Gallery Can, 64; Hornyansky Award, Int Graphics 71, Montreal Mus, 71.
Bibliography: Farley Mowat (auth), The survivor, Gallery Pascal, 71; Peter Bell (auth), David Blackwood paintings, drawings, prints, Mem Univ, 65; Farley Mowat (auth), The survivor, Gallery Pascal, 71; Rex Bromfield (auth), David Blackwood (film), Can Broadcasting Corp, 72.

Memberships: Assoc Ont Col Art; Ont Soc Artists; Can Soc Graphic
Art; Can Soc Painters, Etchers & Engravers; Can Soc Painters in
Watercolor.
Publications: Illusr, A whale for the killing, 72; co-auth, The lost
party, McClelland, 73.
Dealer: Gallery Pascal, 104 Yorkville Ave, Toronto, Ont, Can.
Mailing Address: Erindale College, University of Toronto, Clark-
son, Ont, Can.

BLADEN, RONALD
Sculptor
b Vancouver, B C, July 13, 18.
Study & Training: Vancouver Art Sch; Calif Sch Fine Arts.
Work in Public Collections: Mus Mod Art; Los Angeles Co Mus Art.
Exhibitions: Whitney Mus Am Art, 66 & 68; Guggenheim Mus Art,
67; Corcoran Gallery Art, 67; Minimal Art, The Hague, 68;
Documenta, Kassel, 68; plus others.
Awards: Rosenberg fel, Nat Arts Coun, San Francisco.
Dealer: Fischbach Gallery, 29 W 57th St, New York, NY 10019.
Mailing Address: 182 Fifth Ave, New York, NY 10010.

BLAGDEN, (FREDERIC) ALLEN
Painter
Preferred Media: Watercolors.
b New York, N Y, Feb 21, 38.
Study & Training: Hotchkiss Sch; Yale Univ Summer Art Sch; Cor-
nell Univ, BFA.
Work in Public Collections: Berkshire Mus, Pittsfield, Mass;
Garvan Collection, Peabody Mus, New Haven, Conn.
Commissions: portrait, Hotchkiss Sch, Lakeville, Conn, 70; plus
many private portrait commissions.
Exhibitions: Silvermine Guild Artists, Conn, 67; St Gaudens Mus,
N H, 67; Wadsworth Atheneum, Hartford, Conn, 68; Albright-
Knox Art Gallery, Buffalo, N Y, 69; Lenox Hill Hosp Benefit Ex-
hib, Gimbel's East, New York, 72; plus six one-man shows.
Teaching: Instr painting, Hotchkiss Sch, 68-69.
Positions: Illusr, dept ornith, Smithsonian Inst, Washington, D C,
62-63.
Awards: Allied Artist Award, 63; Century Club Art Prize, 71.
Memberships: Century Club, New York.
Dealer: Frank Rehn Gallery, 655 Madison Ave, New York, NY
10021.
Mailing Address: Falls Village, CT 06031.

BLAGDEN, THOMAS P
Painter
Preferred Media: Oils, Watercolors.
b Chester, Pa, Mar 29, 11.
Study & Training: Yale Univ, BA, 33; Pa Acad Fine Arts, 33-35; spec
study with Henry Hensche & George Demetrios.
Work in Public Collections: Addison Gallery Am Art, Andover,
Mass; Wadsworth Atheneum, Hartford, Conn; Albany Inst Hist &
Art, N Y; Berkshire Mus, Pittsfield, Mass; Chrysler Mus,
Provincetown, Mass.
Exhibitions: Pa Acad Fine Arts, Philadelphia, 38; Corcoran Gallery
Art, Washington, D C, 41; Metrop Mus Art, New York, N Y, 50;
Am Acad Arts & Lett, N Y, 61; Loeb Drama Ctr, Harvard Univ,
Cambridge, Mass, 71.
Teaching: Instr art, Hotchkiss Sch, Lakeville, Conn, 35-56.
Awards: Purchase prize, Wadsworth Atheneum & Berkshire Mus.
Memberships: Conn Watercolor Soc.
Mailing Address: Lime Rock Rd, Lakeville, CT 06039.

BLAI, BORIS
Educator, Sculptor
Preferred Media: Bronze, Wood, Stone.
b Russia, July 24, 98; U S citizen.
Study & Training: Imperial Acad Russia; Ecole Beaux-Arts, Paris,
France; student of Rodin, France.
Work in Public Collections: Rhythm of the Sea (bronze), Philadelphia
Mus Art, Pa; busts of all five presidents & other portraits, Tem-
ple Univ, Philadelphia; busts of Frank Lloyd Wright & Pres
Spivey, Fla Southern Col, Lakeland; also in many pvt collections.
Exhibitions: First Open Air Show, Rittenhouse Square, Philadelphia,
27; Chicago Art Inst, 32; Philadelphia Art Alliance, 37; Phila-
delphia Acad Ann, 40; retrospective shows, Long Beach Island
Found Arts & Sci, N J, 68 & Harcum Jr Col, Bryn Mawr, Pa, 69.
Teaching: Dir & instr art, Oak Lane Country Day Sch, 27-30;
founder, prof art & dean, Tyler Sch Fine Arts, Temple Univ, 30-
60, emer dean, 60-; dean, DuCret Sch Art, Plainfield, N J, 69-72;
founder, Blai Master Workshop, Melrose Park, Pa, 72-
Positions: Founder & hon pres, Long Beach Island Found Arts & Sci,
49-
Awards: Page One Award, Newspaper Guild Greater Philadelphia,
60; Philadelphia Art Alliance Medal, 60; Samuel S Fels Medal,
Fels Jr High Sch, 62.
Bibliography: Dr Millard E Gladfelter & Dr Herman S Gunderheimer

(auth), The Stella Elkins Tyler School of Fine Arts of Temple
University, 53; Louis A deFuria (auth), Boria Blai . . . sculptor,
educator, N J Music & Arts Mag, 10/70
Publications: Auth, The arts in education, Educ & the Exceptional
Child, 35; auth, The future of art in America, Dept of Art Educ
Bull, 41; auth, Your happiness is in your hands, Am Mag, 40 &
Reader's Digest, 40 & 62.
Mailing Address: Fourth & High Ave, Melrose Park, Philadelphia,
PA 19126.

BLAINE, NELL
Painter
Preferred Media: Oils, Watercolors, Ink.
b Richmond, Va, July 10, 22.
Study & Training: Richmond Prof Inst (Col William & Mary Exten,
Richmond Sch Art, now Va Commonwealth Univ), 39-42; Hans
Hofmann Sch Fine Arts, 42-43; Atelier 17, etching & engraving
with William S Hayter, 45; New Sch Social Res, 52-53.
Work in Public Collections: Whitney Mus Am Art, New York, N Y;
Brooklyn Mus, N Y; Mus Mod Art, New York; Va Mus Fine Arts,
Richmond; Univ Art Mus, Univ Calif, Berkeley; plus many others.
Commissions: Two murals, landscapes & cityscapes of Paris,
Revlon, Inc, New York, 58.
Exhibitions: The Women, Art of this Century, Peggy Guggenheim
Gallery, New York, 45; American Abstract Artists Ann, 44-57;
Stable Gallery Ann, 50-59; 50's Revisited, Tibor de Nagy Gallery,
70; Six Figurative Painters, Kansas City Art Inst, Mo, 72; plus
23 one-woman shows & many other group shows.
Teaching: Instr landscape & studio, Great Neck Pub Sch Adult Prog,
56; instr, Great Lakes Col Asn, New York, 70, 72-
Positions: Ceramic artist, Warner Prins Co, New York, 48-49;
costume & set designer for dancers, Midi Garth & E Goff, New
York, 49-54; art dir, United Jewish Appeal, New York, 50; set
designer, Artists Theatre, New York, 55.
Awards: Va Mus Fine Arts fels for painting, 43 & 46; Hallmark Int
Award, 60; Longview Found grants, 64 & 70.
Bibliography: Lawrence Campbell (auth), Blaine paints a picture,
Art News Mag, 5/59; Homage to Nell Blaine, Art News Mag,
12/59; James R Mellow (auth), The flowering summer of Nell
Blaine, New York Times, 10/11/70.
Memberships: Artists Equity Asn.
Publications: Co-auth, Prints/Nell Blaine - Poems/Kenneth Koch,
53; illusr, In memory of my feelings, Mus Mod Art, 68; contribr,
Art Now, 1/70; auth, Getting with Lester and Mondrian in the
forties, Jazz and Painting, 72; contribr, A sense of place—the
artist & the American landscape, 72.
Dealer: Poindexter Gallery, 24 E 84th St, New York, NY 10028.
Mailing Address: Apt 8A, 210 Riverside Dr, New York, NY 10025.

BLAIR, CARL RAYMOND
Painter, Educator
Preferred Media: Oil.
b Atchison, Kansas, Nov 28, 32.
Study & Training: Univ Kans, BFA, 56; Kans City Art Inst; Sch De-
sign,MFA, 57.
Work in Public Collections: Mint Mus Art, Charlotte, N C; Greenville
Co Mus Art, S C; Greenville Col, Ill; S C Arts Comn, Columbia;
Clemson Univ, S C.
Exhibitions: 33rd Butler Ann Painting Exhib, Youngstown, Ohio; Soc
Four Arts, Palm Beach, Fla; Piedmont Painting & Sculpture Ex-
hib, Charlotte, 65; Appalachian Corridors I, Charleston, W Va,
68; Int Platform Asn, Washington, D C, 71.
Teaching: Prof drawing & painting, Bob Jones Univ, 57-; summer
school, Kans City Art Inst & Greenville Co Mus Art.
Awards: Piedmont Painting & Sculpture Exhib, Mint Mus Art, 65;
Appalachian Corridors I, S C Arts Comn, 68; Int Platform Asn,
68.
Bibliography: La Revue Moderne, Paris, France, 65-68; Margaret
Harold (auth), Prizewinning art book VI, 66; Jack A Morris Jr
(auth), Contemporary artists of South Carolina, 70.
Memberships: S C Artists Guild, (adv bd, 57-); Int Platform Asn;
Greenville Artists Guild (pres, 71-); South Carolina Arts Comn
(acquisitions comt, 69-).
Dealer: Hampton III Gallery Ltd, Hampton Corners, Taylors, SC
29687.
Mailing Address: 41 Blythewood Dr, Greenville, SC 29607.

BLAIR, HELEN (HELEN BLAIR CROSBIE)
Sculptor, Illustrator
Preferred Media: Bronze.
b Hibbing, Minn, Dec 29, 10.
Study & Training: Mass Sch Art, with Cyrus Dallin; Boston Mus
Sch; Archipenko Sch Art, with Archipenko.
Commissions: Plaques, of Dr Waring, Colo Med Sch, 69 & Dr
Porter, Porter Mem Hosp, Denver, 70.
Exhibitions: One-man shows, Ardan Studios, New York, N Y, 34,

Portraits, Inc, New York, 41-42, Vose Galleries, Boston, 44 &
Saint Paul Art Ctr, Minn, 62.
Teaching: Instr art educ, Boston Univ, 37-40.
Bibliography: K S Thompson (auth), Figurines step into a new role,
Boston Transcript, 34; Peter Martin (auth), Moulder of youth,
Am Mag, 46; Marjorie Barrett (auth), Helen Blair's little people,
Denver Post, 70.
Memberships: Artists Equity Asn; Nat Arts & Lett Soc; Ariz Art-
ists Guild.
Publications: Illusr, Jeanne-Marie, 34, Great day in the morning,
46, Assorted sisters, 47, The house under the hill, 49 & Hetly and
the grand deluxe, 51, Houghton Mifflin.
Dealer: Downtown Galleries, 1635 Broadway, Denver, CO 80202.
Mailing Address: 1919 E Claremont St, Phoenix, AZ 85016.

BLAIR, ROBERT NOEL
Painter, Sculptor
Preferred Media: Watercolors, Oils, Acrylics.
b Buffalo, N Y, Aug 12, 12.
Study & Training: Sch of Mus Fine Arts, Boston, Mass.
Work in Public Collections: Metrop Mus Art, New York, N Y; Butler
Inst Am Art, Youngstown, Ohio; Munson-Williams-Proctor Inst,
Utica, N Y; State Univ N Y Col Buffalo; Ford Motor Co Collection,
Dearborn, Mich.
Commissions: Sermon on the Mount (oil, tempera) USA Chapel, Fort
McClellan, Ala, 43; Open Hearth (oil), Bethlehem Steel Plant,
Lackawanna, N Y, 47; Olean in 1890's (two tempera panels), Olean
House, Olean, N Y, 61; Venetian Feast (oil panel), Lakeview
Hotel, N Y; fountain with three figures (fiberglass-epoxy sculp-
ture), Dr & Mrs Hal Meisburger, Patchen, N Y, 62-65.
Exhibitions: Corcoran Biennial, Corcoran Gallery Art, Washington,
D C, 47; Watercolor International, Art Inst Chicago, Ill, 48; Pa
Acad Fine Arts Nat, Philadelphia, 48; Butler Art Inst Nat &
Metrop Mus Art Watercolor Nat, 53; one-man retrospective,
Community Tribute Exhibition, State Univ N Y Col Buffalo, 66;
also thirty one-man shows.
Teaching: Instr painting, Art Inst Buffalo, 38-55, Albright Art Sch,
55 & State Univ N Y Col Buffalo, 71.
Positions: Dir, Art Inst Buffalo, 46-49.
Awards: Guggenheim fels, 46 & 51; Watowsky prize, Art Inst Chi-
cago, 48; first watercolor prize, Butler Inst Am Art, 53;
Bibliography: Dr Kenneth Winebrenner (auth), Robert N Blair retro-
spective, community tribute exhibit, State Univ N Y Col Buffalo,
66.
Memberships: Patteran Soc, Buffalo; Buffalo Soc Artists.
Research: Expansion of technical possibilities in painting.
Publications: Illusr, St Lawrence Seaway, 57; illusr, Ford Times
Mag, 58-61; illusr, Am Artist Mag, 66; illusr, Jeannie's world,
66.
Mailing Address: R D 1, Olean Rd, Holland, NY 14080.

BLAIR, WILLIAM McCORMICK
Patron
b Chicago, Ill, May 2, 84.
Study & Training: Yale Univ, BA, 07; Lake Forest Col, LittD, 63;
Northwestern Univ, LLD, 64.
Positions: Pres bd trustees, Art Inst Chicago, 58-; trustee, Chi-
cago Natural Hist Mus, Univ Chicago.
Awards: Chevalier, Fr Legion Hon.
Memberships: Am Fedn Arts (trustee).
Mailing Address: 1416 Astor St, Chicago, IL 60610.

BLAKE, LEO B
Illustrator, Instructor
b Galesburg, Ill, July 7, 87.
Study & Training: Art Inst Chicago; also with Alfred East, W J Rey-
nolds & Birge Harrison.
Work in Public Collections: Rochester Inst Technol; Ill Acad Fine
Arts; Foxhollow Sch; Lee, Adams & Meriden Savings Banks.
Exhibitions: Berkshire Mus Art; Springfield Art League; Philadel-
phia Art Alliance; Jordan Marsh Co, Boston, 57; Meriden Arts &
Crafts Asn, Conn, 57, 58 & 63; plus others.
Teaching: Instr, pvt classes, Cheshire, Mass.
Awards: Award, Vixseboxes Gallery, Cleveland, Ohio; hon mention,
52 & 58, best portfolio award, 60 & prize, 63, Meriden Arts &
Crafts Asn; awards, Jordan Marsh Co, 57, 59 & 60.
Memberships: Salmagundi Club; N Shore Art Asn; Conn Acad Fine
Arts; Grand Cent Art Gallery; New Haven Paint & Clay Club.
Mailing Address: Blake Studios, Cheshire, MA 01225.

BLAKE, PETER JOST
Art Critic, Architect
b Berlin, Ger, Sept 20, 20; U S citizen.
Study & Training: Univ London, 39; Regent St Polytech Sch Archit;
Univ Pa, 40; Pratt Inst, BArch, 48.
Positions: Writer, Archit Forum, New York, N Y, 42-43, assoc ed,
50-54 & 58-61, managing ed, 61-64, ed, 64-72; cur archit & design,

Mus Mod Art, New York, 48-50; archit ed, House & Home, 55-57;
partner, Peter Blake & Julian Neski, 58-61; partner, James Ba-
ker & Peter Blake, Architects, New York, 64-; ed-in-chief,
Archit Plus, New York, 72-
Awards: Howard Myers Award Archit Jour, 60; citation for design
Am archit exhib sent to Iron Curtain countries, 58; fel, Am Inst
Architects, 70.
Memberships: Am Inst Architects (mem comt aesthet, 65-66, juror,
medal hon & award merit, 68-69, mem urban design comt, 69);
Archit League New York (v pres archit, 66-68, mem scholar &
awards comt, 68-69, pres, 71-72); Int Design Conf, Aspen, Colo
(bd dirs, 65-70); Regional Plan Asn (mem comt second regional
plan).
Publications: Auth, Master builders, Knopf, 60; auth, God's own junk-
yard: the planned deterioration of America's landscape, Holt,
Rinehart & Winston, 64; auth, Frank Lloyd Wright, 64, LeCorbu-
sier, 64 & Mies van der Rohe, 64, Penguin; also contribr articles
popular mags & newspapers.
Mailing Address: 55 W 55th St, New York, NY 10019.

BLAKELY, JOYCE (CAROL)
Painter, Instructor
Preferred Media: Oils.
b New Orleans, La, July 1, 29.
Study & Training: Delgado Art Mus; S Ga Col; also with Bill Hend-
rix, St Simon's Island.
Commissions: Old Timer, Portrait of a Girl & Relic of the Past,
comn by Sam Fisher, Tel Aviv, 71; Boatscape, First Presby
Church, Hendersonville, N C, 72; River Jordan Mural, Green
River Baptist Church, 72.
Exhibitions: Sovereign Exhibs, Hendrix Gallery, St Simon's Island,
69-70; Winston-Salem, N C & London, Eng, 70; Williamsburg,
Va, 71 & Myrtle Beach, S C, 71; USS Hope Exhib, Butler Inst Am
Art, 72; B Russell Contemp Art Exhib, Rotunda Gallery, London,
72.
Teaching: Instr oil painting, Opportunity House, Hendersonville,
N C, 71-; pvt instr.
Memberships: Nat League Am Pen Women; League Pen Women
Asheville, N C (secy, 72-); Henderson Art League, N C.
Mailing Address: 800 Fleming St, Hendersonville, NC 28739.

BLAKESLEE, SARAH (SARAH BLAKESLEE SPEIGHT)
Painter
Preferred Media: Oils.
b Evanston, Ill, Jan 13, 12.
Study & Training: Corcoran Sch Art; Pa Acad Fine Arts; Cresson
Europ traveling scholars; also with Catherin Critcher.
Work in Public Collections: Pa Acad Fine Arts; Nat Acad Design;
Greenville Art Ctr, N C.
Commissions: Portraits, E Carolina Univ, Greenville, N C & St
Mary's Col, Raleigh, N C; portraits, still life & landscapes in
many pvt collections.
Exhibitions: Art Inst Chicago Ann, 39 & 40; Corcoran Gallery Art
Biennial, 40; Pa Acad Fine Arts Ann, Philadelphia; Nat Acad
Deisgn Ann; N C Mus Art Collectors Exhib, 68.
Teaching: Instr art, Lankenau Sch, Philadelphia, 52-61; instr art,
var art ctrs, N C, 61-
Awards: Mary Smith Prize, Pa Acad Fine Arts, 41; first prize,
Woodmere Art Gallery, Chestnut Hills, Philadelphia, 56; first
prize & gold medal, Penn-Nat-Ligonier Pa, 61.
Mailing Address: 508 E Ninth St, Greenville, NC 27834.

BLAMEUSER, MARY FLEURETTE, B V M
Painter, Instructor
Preferred Media: Watercolors, Oils, Lithography.
b Skokie, Ill.
Study & Training: Art Inst Chicago; Univ Colo; Columbia Univ;
Clarke Col, BA; State Univ Iowa, MA; Georgio Cini Found fel,
Venice, Italy, 65; watercolor with Noël Quinn & Edgar Whitney.
Work in Public Collections: Wichita Art Asn, Kans.
Commissions: Mosaic mural, 61 & bronze tabernacle, 63, Sisters of
Charity, B V M, Wichita.
Exhibitions: Cath Art Asn Traveling Show, 40; Contemporary, State
Univ Iowa, Iowa City, 48; Wichita Women Artists, 57; Kans Water-
color Soc Exhib, Wichita, 70 & 71; Kans Cult Arts Comn Travel-
ing Show, 72.
Teaching: Instr sec art, Holy Angels Acad Milwaukee, Wis, 33-45;
instr sec art, Bishop Conaty Mem High Sch, Los Angeles, Calif,
45-56; instr art educ & painting, Clarke Col, Dubuque, Iowa, 51 &
58; instr sec art, Mt Carmel Acad, Wichita, 56-
Positions: Chmn art educ, Archdiocese Los Angeles, 46-56; mem,
Diocese Liturgical Art Comn, Wichita, 64-; active comt, Scholastic Art Awards, Kans Regional, 69-
Awards: Watercolor award, Wichita Women Artists, 57.
Bibliography: S M Cathlin (auth), The story of a mosaic, Vista, Sisters of Charity, B V M, 63; John Simoni (auth), Nun exhibits sen-

sitivity, Wichita Eagle & Beacon, 5/9/65; Connie Close (auth), Nun finishing mosaic mural, Wichita Eagle, 65.
Memberships: Wichita Art Asn; Wichita Art Mus Mem; Kans Watercolor Soc (bd mem-publicity, 70-72).
Dealer: Wichita Art Mus, 619 Stackman Dr, Wichita, KS 67203.
Mailing Address: 8506 E Central Ave, Wichita, KS 67206.

BLANC, PETER (WILLIAM PETERS BLANC)
Sculptor, Painter
Preferred Media: Wood.
b New York, N Y, June 29, 12.
Study & Training: Harvard Univ, BA; St John's Univ, LLB; Corcoran Sch Art; Am Univ, MA.
Work in Public Collections: Va Mus Fine Arts, Richmond; Fort Worth Art Ctr, Tex; New York Univ; Tweed Mus, Duluth, Minn.
Exhibitions: Contemporary American Painting, City Art Mus, St Louis, Mo, 51; Contemporary American Sculpture, Watercolors & Drawings, Whitney Mus Am Art, New York, 52; Watercolors, 1953, Baltimore Mus Art, Md, 53; 18th Biennial, Brooklyn Mus, N Y, 55; Artists of the Hamptons, Benson Gallery, Bridgehampton, N Y, 67; also 13 one-man shows in New York, 50-71.
Teaching: Pvt classes in painting & drawing, 47-54; instr painting & drawing, Am Univ, 50-53.
Awards: First prize for drawing, Corcoran Gallery Art, 59; special award, Washington Water Color Club, 52; hon mention, Soc Washington Artists, 53.
Memberships: Artists Equity Asn New York (bd dir, 63-71).
Publications: Auth, The artist and the atom, Mag of Art, 51.
Dealer: Thomson Gallery, 19 E 75th St, New York, NY 10021.
Mailing Address: 161 W 75th St, New York, NY 10023.

BLANCHARD, CAROL
Painter, Graphic Artist
b Springfield, Mass, Aug 29, 18.
Study & Training: Colby Jr Col; Art Stud League New York; Painter's Workshop, Boston, Mass.
Work in Public Collections: Pasangrahn, Saint Martin, B W I; Bay Roe, Jamaica, B W I; San Miguel Allende, Mex; also in pvt collections.
Commissions: Illusr, Christmas cards, UN.
Exhibitions: Art Inst, Zanesville, Ohio, 50; Carnegie Inst, Pittsburgh, Pa, 51-59; Univ Ill, 53; Walker Art Ctr, Minneapolis, Minn, 60; Kalamazoo Inst Art, Mich; plus others.
Awards: Awards, Carnegie Inst Art, 51-53 & 59 & Art Dirs Club, 55 & 56; Benedictine Art Award creative arts, 67 & 68; plus others.
Publications: Illusr, Always ask a man; illusr, seven bks by Mary Stolz; illusr, Village Voice, Women's Wear Daily & other newspapers.
Mailing Address: 375 Bleecker St, New York, NY 10014.

BLANKENSHIP, ROY
Painter, Conservator
Preferred Media: Oils.
b Philadelphia, Pa, Nov 26, 43.
Study & Training: Twistback Conserv Ctr, Oxford, Pa, 72; Univ Del, BA, 72; Westlawn Sch Design, Westport, Conn, current study.
Work in Public Collections: Univ Del, Newark, Atlas Chem Industs, Wilmington, Del; Brandywine High-Marbrook Sch, Wilmington; The Gallery, Centerville, Del; Schoonover Galleries, Wilmington.
Commissions: Oil paintings, Mr & Mrs Dimeler, Wilmington, 70; Mrs Alberta Hartmann, Wilmington, 71, Class of 62, Brandywine High, 72 & Wigwam Cottage, Gloucester, Mass, 72.
Exhibitions: Univ Del Regional Ceramic Show, 68; Nat Graphic & Print Exhib, San Diego, Calif, 69; N Shore Art Asn Am, Gloucester, Mass, 72; Univ Del Ann Sculpture Show, 72; Del Valley Regional Invitational, Roy Rogers Family Restaurants, Wilmington, 72.
Teaching: Instr art hist & restoration & conserv oil paintings, Univ Del, spring 72; instr art, Ursuline Acad, Wilmington.
Positions: Conservator & restorer, Del Art Mus, Wilmington, 72-; adv arts, New Castle Parks & Recreation, Wilmington, 72-
Awards: Vietnam Combat Artists Award & Citation, Dept Navy, 65-66.
Bibliography: Harry Conner (auth), University of Delaware artist in national publication, Wilmington Eve Jour, 11/71 & University of Delaware artist on top list, Weekly Post, Newark, Del, 12/71; Laura H Southerland (auth), Roy Blankenship—a man for all arts, Del Today Mag, 1/72.
Memberships: Int Inst Conserv Hist & Artistic Works; N Shore Arts Asn; Del Art Mus; Winterthur Mus, Wilmington.
Publications: Auth, Albert Insley—81 years of American art, Deme Publ, 72.
Dealer: Roger Curtis, Riverview Rd, Riverview, Gloucester, MA 01930.
Mailing Address: 2B Rector Ct, Lancashire, Wilmington, DE 19810.

BLANKFORT, DOROTHY
Collector
Study & Training: Bates Col; Cornell Univ.
Memberships: Los Angeles Co Mus (exec bd, contemp art coun).
Collection: Chiefly contemporary American.
Mailing Address: 1636 Comstock Ave, Los Angeles, CA 90024.

BLANKFORT, MICHAEL
Collector
b New York, N Y, Dec 10, 07.
Positions: Mem bd trustees, Los Angeles Co Mus Art.
Collection: Contemporary American art.
Mailing Address: 1636 Comstock Ave, Los Angeles, CA 90024.

BLATTNER, ROBERT HENRY
Painter, Illustrator
Preferred Media: Watercolors.
b Lynn, Mass, Dec 8, 06.
Study & Training: Mass Col Art, BS(educ).
Teaching: Instr design, Boston Univ, 37-38; instr design, Col New Rochelle, 39-41.
Positions: Illusr, Christian Sci Monitor, 34-42; art dir, Marschalk & Pratt Advert Agency, 43-45; art dir, Reader's Digest, 45-71; retired.
Awards: Award of merit, Soc Illustrators, 71.
Memberships: Soc Illustrators; Art Dirs Club (pres, 60-61); Am Inst Graphic Arts (dir, 58-59); hon mem Am Watercolor Soc.
Mailing Address: Loch Lane, Port Chester, NY 10573.

BLAUSTEIN, ALFRED H
Painter, Printmaker
b Bronx, N Y, Jan 23, 24.
Study & Training: Cooper Union Art Sch, grad fine arts; Prix de Rome fel, 54-57; Am Acad Arts & Lett grant in painting, 58; Guggenheim fel painting, 58, printmaking, 61.
Work in Public Collections: Whitney Mus Am Art, New York, N Y; Metrop Mus Art, New York; Chicago Art Inst, Ill; Libr Cong, Washington, D C; Pa Acad Fine Arts, Philadelphia.
Commissions: Drawing assignment, Life & Brit Overseas Food Corp, Tanzania, E Africa, 48-49; fresco mural, S Solon Meeting House, Maine, 53; printing assignment, Fortune Mag, 70.
Exhibitions: Four shows, Pa Acad Fine Arts, 51-67; Metrop Mus Art, 50 & 66; Carnegie Int, Pittsburgh, Pa, 52 & 64; Whitney Mus Am Art Ann, 53 & 57; six shows, Brooklyn Mus Print Ann, 57-70, plus many one-man shows.
Teaching: Lectr fine arts, Yale Univ, 59-62; instr printmaking, Pratt Graphic Ctr, 64-69; assoc prof fine arts, Pratt Inst, 59-
Dealer: Terry Dintenfass Gallery, 18 E 67th St, New York, NY 10021.
Mailing Address: 141 E 17th St, New York, NY 10003.

BLAZEJE, ZBIGNIEW
Sculptor, Painter
b Barnaul, U S S R, Jan 2, 42; Can citizen.
Study & Training: Royal Conserv Music, Toronto.
Work in Public Collections: Art Gallery Ont, Toronto; Norman McKenzie Art Gallery, Regina, Sask; Confedn Art Gallery, Charlettetown, P E I; Hart House Univ Toronto; Sir George William Univ, Montreal, Que.
Commissions: Structural sculpture, Libr-Ross Bldg, York Univ, 72.
Exhibitions: Tenth Winnipeg Show, Winnipeg Art Gallery, Man, 65; Canadian Art, Art Gallery Can Pavillion Expo 67, Montreal, 67; Sculpture 67, City Hall Toronto, 67; Electric Art, Univ Calif, Los Angeles Art Gallery & Phoenix, Ariz, 69; Sensory Perceptions Art Gallery Ont, touring eight Ont art ctrs, 70-71.
Teaching: Instr environ, Ont Col Art, 70-72; instr environ, New Sch Art, Toronto, 71-72.
Awards: Can Coun jr grants, 66, 67 & 69.
Bibliography: H Malcomson (auth), Sculpture in Canada, Artforum, 10/67; G M Dault (auth), In the galleries Toronto, Arts Can, 6/71; Electric gallery + 3, McCurdy-Bursell Films, Toronto, 4/72.
Dealer: Electric Gallery, 272 Avenue Rd, Toronto, Ont, Can.
Mailing Address: 1254 Dundas St W, Toronto 145, Ont, Can.

BLEIFELD, STANLEY
Sculptor, Instructor
Preferred Media: Bronze.
b Brooklyn, N Y, Aug 28, 24.
Study & Training: Albert C Barnes Found, Meryon, Pa, 42-43; Tyler Sch Art, Temple Univ, BFA, 49, BS(educ), 49, MFA, 50.
Work in Public Collections: Temple Univ, Philadelphia, Pa; Tampa Bay Art Ctr, Fla; Congregation B'nai Israel, Elmont, N Y.
Commissions: The Prophets (relief), Vatican Pavilion, New York World's Fair, 64; The Magic Carpet (relief), Pub Libr, Kokomo, Ind, 69; Mediterranean Landscape (relief), Washington, D C, 72.
Exhibitions: One-man shows, Peridot Gallery, New York, 63, 65 &

68; Am Fedn Arts, 66-67; one-man show, Kenmore Galleries, Philadelphia, 67; I F A Galleries, Washington, D C, 68 & 71; FAR Gallery, New York, 71.
Teaching: Asst prof art, Southern Conn State Col & Western Conn State Col, 53-63; instr sculpture, Silvermine Guild, New Canaan, Conn, 63-66; dir sculpture, Bleifeld Studio, Westport, Conn, 66-
Positions: Fel, Tyler Sch Fine Arts, 64-; ed bd, Nat Sculpture Rev, 70.
Awards: John Gregory Award, 64 & bronze medal, 70, Nat Sculpture Soc; Tiffany Found fel, 65 & 67.
Bibliography: A sculptor hails the Bible, Life Mag, 6/28/63; article, In: Am Artist Mag, 72.
Memberships: Nat Sculpture Soc.
Publications: Illusr, A day at the county fair, 60 & Elly the elephant, 62.
Dealer: FAR Gallery, 746 Madison Ave, New York, NY 10021.
Mailing Address: 27 Spring Valley Rd, Weston, CT 06880.

BLEY, ELSA W
Painter
b New York, N Y, Mar 10, 03.
Study & Training: Art Stud League New York; Grand Cent Sch Art; also with George Luks, George Pearse Ennis, Wayman Adams & Henry B Snell.
Exhibitions: Nat Arts Club, New York, N Y, 36-39 & 61-65; Southern Vt Art Ctr, 38-65; Nat Asn Women Artists, 48-63; Pen & Brush Club, 59-65; Am Artists Prof League, 63; plus others.
Teaching: Instr, Southern Vt Art Ctr, 51-58; instr, Garden City Community Club, 57-58; instr, Southern Vt Art Ctr, 63-65.
Positions: Founder & dir, Scarsdale Art Guild, 34-45.
Awards: Medal, Sch Art League; four awards, Scarsdale Art Asn, 36-45.
Memberships: Nat Arts Club; Pen & Brush Club; Southern Vt Art Ctr; Scarsdale Art Asn; Nat Asn Women Artists (chmn watercolor jury, 59-61).
Mailing Address: P O Box 357, Main St, Dorset, VT 05251.

BLISH, CAROLYN BULLIS
Painter
Preferred Media: Watercolor, Oil.
b Washington, D C, Jan 14, 28.
Study & Training: Watercolor with Edgar Whitney.
Exhibitions: Am Watercolor Soc, 65-; Catharine Lorillard Wolfe Art Club, 68; Hudson Valley Art Asn, 69; Allied Artists Am, 69-; one-woman show, Grand Cent Art Galleries, New York, N Y 70.
Awards: Gold medal of honor, Hudson Valley Art Asn, 69; Washington Sch Art Award, Am Watercolor Soc, 71 & C F S Award, 72.
Memberships: Am Watercolor Soc; Allied Artists Am; Hudson Valley Art Asn; Am Artists Prof League; Philadelphia Watercolor Club.
Publications: Illusr calendars, Collecting, Conn Mutual, 68, May apples, N Y Life Ins, 71 & Sweep of dunes, Provident Mutual, 73.
Dealer: Grand Central Art Galleries, 40 Vanderbilt Ave, New York, NY 10017.
Mailing Address: 107 Rockwood Rd, Wilmington, DE 19809.

BLIZZARD, ALAN
Painter, Educator
b Boston, Mass, Mar 25, 29.
Study & Training: Mass Sch Art, Boston, with Lawrence Kupferman; Univ Ariz, with Andreas Andersen; Univ Iowa, with Stuart Edie, James Lechay & Byron Burford.
Work in Public Collections: Brooklyn Mus, N Y; Metrop Mus Art, New York, N Y; Art Inst Chicago, Ill; Denver Art Mus, Colo, La Jolla Mus Art, Calif.
Exhibitions: Many exhibs in leading mus, cols, univs & art centers.
Teaching: Vis asst prof, Univ Okla; asst prof, Univ Calif, Los Angeles; prof art, Scripps Col & Claremont Grad Sch.
Mailing Address: Dept of Art, Scripps College, Claremont, CA 91711.

BLOCH, E MAURICE
Art Historian, Educator
b New York, N Y.
Study & Training: New York Univ Sch Archit, BFA; Harvard Univ; New York Univ Inst Fine Arts, MA & Ph D; Nat Acad Design; Art Stud League New York, with Brackman; Belg-Am Educ Found fel, 51.
Teaching: Lectr, Univ Mo, 43-44; lectr, New York Univ, 44-45; lectr, Univ Minn, Minneapolis, 46-47; asst prof & cur, Cooper Union, 49-55; prof Am art, hist prints & hist drawings & dir, Grunwald Graphic Arts Found, Univ Calif, Los Angeles, 56-
Awards: Founders Day Award of Achievement, New York Univ, 57; Western Heritage Ctr Award, 68.
Memberships: Print Coun Am (bd dirs); Univ Calif, Los Angeles, Art Coun (bd dirs); Tamarind Lithography Workshop (bd dirs); life mem, Art Stud League New York; Art Historians Southern Calif.

Research: American art of the eighteenth and nineteenth centuries; history of European and American drawings and graphic arts.
Publications: Auth, George Caleb Bingham: evolution of an artist and a catalogue raisonné, Vols I & II, 67; auth, articles, In: Gazette Beaux Arts, New York Hist Soc Quart, The Connoisseur, Art in Am & others.
Mailing Address: 2253 Veteran Ave, Los Angeles, CA 90064.

BLOCK, ADOLPH
Sculptor, Instructor
Preferred Media: Bronze.
b New York, N Y, Jan 29, 06.
Study & Training: Beaux Arts Inst Design; Fontainebleau Sch Fine Arts; also with Hermon MacNeil & Sterlin Calder.
Work in Public Collections: Bryant High Sch, New York, N Y; Bayonne Pub Libr, N J; Queens Vocational High Sch, N Y; Beth-El Hosp, Brooklyn, N Y; Garfield Restaurant, N Y, plus others.
Commissions: Panels, Nat Shrine Immaculate Conception, Washington, D C; bronze mem portrait panel, Dr Franz J Kallmann, Columbia-Presby Med Ctr, N Y, 67; Washington Irving Medal, 68 & Simon Newcomb Medal, 70, New York Univ Hall Fame Series; Nathan Hale Coin Medal, Nat Commemorative Soc, 69; plus others.
Exhibitions: Nat Acad Design; Pa Acad Fine Arts; Archit League N Y; Nat Sculpture Soc; Whitney Mus Am Art; plus others.
Positions: Del to Fine Arts Fedn, 54-60; dir, Fine Arts Fedn New York, 54-62; Nat Sculpture Soc del, Int Coun Plastic Arts, 58-62; ed, Nat Sculpture Rev, 58-; instr sculpture, Nat Acad Design, 59-; v pres, Int Coun Plastic Arts, 60-63,
Awards: Lindsay Morris Prize medals, 58, Herbert Adams Mem Medal & Citation, 61, silver medal, 67 & award for most notable serv, 70, Nat Sculpture Soc; plus others.
Memberships: Academician Nat Acad Design; fel Nat Sculpture Soc (rec secy, 53-55, secy, 56-58, chmn mem comt, 56-62, first v pres, 59-62, pres, 63-65); Allied Artists Am; Fontainebleau Alumni Asn.
Mailing Address: 319 W 18th St, New York, NY 10011.

BLOCK, AMANDA ROTH
Painter, Printmaker
Preferred Media: Acrylics, Oils.
b Louisville, Ky, Feb 20, 12.
Study & Training: Smith Col; Univ Cincinnati; Art Acad Cincinnati; Art Stud League New York; Herron Sch Art, Ind Univ-Purdue Univ, Indianapolis, BFA; also with Garo Antreasian.
Work in Public Collections: J B Speed Mus, Louisville, Ky; Cincinnati Art Mus, Ohio; Brooklyn Mus, N Y; New York Pub Libr, N Y; Philadelphia Mus Art, Pa.
Exhibitions: American Sculpture Show, Chicago Art Inst, Ill, 41; Soc Am Graphic Artists Show, 67-; Philadelphia Print Club; Watercolor, Drawing & Print Biennial, Pa Acad Fine Arts, Philadelphia, 69; Butler Inst Am Art, Youngstown, Ohio.
Teaching: Lectr lithography & drawing, Herron Sch Art, 69-
Awards: Katherine Mattison Watercolor Award, Indianapolis Mus Art, 63; Watercolor Award, Indiana Artists Exhib, Sheldon Swope Art Gallery, 64; Ben & Beatrice Goldstein Award, Soc Am Graphic Artists Exhib, Kennedy Gallery, New York, 71.
Memberships: Philadelphia Print Club; Soc Am Graphic Artists.
Dealers: E Wehye Gallery, 794 Lexington Ave, New York, NY 10021; Editions Limited Gallery, 919 Westfield Blvd, Indianapolis, IN 46220.
Mailing Address: 6000 Spring Mill Rd, Indianapolis, IN 46208.

BLOCK, IRVING ALEXANDER
Painter, Educator
b New York, N Y, Dec 2, 10.
Study & Training: New York Univ, BS; Nat Acad Design; Acad Grande Chaumiere, Paris, France.
Work in Public Collections: Joseph H Hirshhorn Collect, Washington, D C; Palm Springs Mus, Calif; Storm King Mountain Art Ctr, N Y; Univ Mass Art Collect, Amherst; Victoria & Albert Mus, London, Eng.
Commissions: Mural, Am Med Asn, Med Bldg, New York World's Fair, 39; murals, comn by U S Treas Dept, Post Off Bldg, Batesburg, S C, 40 & Post Off Bldg, Wakefield Sta.
Exhibitions: Group shows, Los Angeles Co Art Mus, Metrop Mus Art, New York, Colorado Springs Art Ctr, La Jolla Mus & others, 40-; one-man shows, Ankrum Gallery, Los Angeles, 68-71.
Teaching: Prof art, Calif State Univ, 63-
Awards: Third Int Art Film Festival Award, 57; Hirshhorn Found grant in painting, 69; Calif State Cols Outstanding Prof Award, 70.
Bibliography: C Perkins (auth), Irving Block, Artforum, 5/63; taped biog interviews, Arch Am Art, 66; V Shears (auth), California painters in oil, Am Artist, 5/68.

Memberships: Hon mem Accad Int Tommaso Campanella, Rome.
Publications: Co-auth, dir & producer (films), Rembrandt, poet of light, 53, Goya, 55 & World of Rubens, 57.
Dealer: Ankrum Gallery, 657 N La Cienega Blvd, Los Angeles, CA 90069.
Mailing Address: 3880 Carpenter Ave, Studio City, CA 91604.

BLOCK, JOYCE
Calligrapher, Instructor
Preferred Media: Sumi Ink.
b Chicago, Ill.
Study & Training: Univ Calif, Los Angeles, BA; Teachers Col, Columbia Univ, MA; also pvt study with Kakei Fujita.
Exhibitions: Nihon Shodo Bijutsuin (Japan Calligraphy Art Acad), Tokyo, 63-73; Yokohama Shodo Renmei (Yokohama Calligraphy League), 68-72; Gen Nichi Sho Ten (Gen Nichi Calligraphy Exhib), 70-73; Japanese Calligraphy of Joyce Block, Lynn Kottler Galleries, New York, N Y, 71.
Teaching: Instr art, Kinnick Middle Sch, Yokohama, 71-
Memberships: Photog Soc Am; Nat Educ Asn; Overseas Educ Asn; N E Asia Teachers Asn.
Mailing Address: Box 412, Fleacts Detachment, FPO Seattle 98761.

BLOCK, MR & MRS LEIGH B
Collectors
Mr Block, b Chicago, Ill, Apr 7, 05.
Study & Training: Mr Block, Univ Chicago.
Positions: Mr Block, dir, Nat Scholar Serv & Fund for Negro Stud, Med Res Inst, Michael Reese Hosp; trustee, Northwestern Univ, Chicago; trustee, Art Inst Chicago.
Memberships: Mr Block, Art Collectors Club.
Mailing Address: 1260 N Astor St, Chicago, IL 60610.

BLOEDEL, LAWRENCE HOTCHKISS
Collector
b Bellingham, Wash, Mar 21, 02.
Study & Training: Williams Col, BA, 23; Columbia Univ, BS, 37; Williams Col, LHD, 67.
Collection: Twentieth century American art.
Mailing Address: Sloan Rd, Williamstown, MA 01267.

BLOOM, DONALD STANLEY
Painter
Preferred Media: Oils, Watercolors, Inks, Pastels.
b Roxbury, Mass, Sept 3, 32.
Study & Training: Mass Col Art, BFA, 53; Art Stud League New York, 53-55, with Barnet, Levi & Trafton; Inst Allende, San Miguel Allende, Mex, MFA, 57.
Work in Public Collections: New Brunswick Pub Libr, N J; Upsala Col, East Orange, N J; Fairleigh Dickinson Univ, Madison, N J; Bloomfield Col, N J; Montclair State Col, N J.
Commissions: Mural (ceramic in concrete), Judge Raymond del Tufo, Newark, N J, 64.
Exhibitions: Whitney Ann Am Painting, Whitney Mus Am Art, New York, N Y, 60; Silvermine Ann, New Canaan, Conn, 63; Audubon Artists Ann, Nat Acad Galleries, New York, 63; N J Pavilion, New York World's Fair, 65; Springfield Watercolor Ann & Traveling Show, Mo, 65.
Teaching: Instr painting & collage, Morris Co Art Asn, N J, 60-68; instr painting, Bloomfield Col, 65-66; dist chmn art dept, Piscataway Schs, N J, 66-
Awards: Guggenheim fel creative painting, 61; Huntington Hartford Found fel, 64; Silvermine Guild Award, 65.
Bibliography: E Genauer (auth), rev, In: New York Herald Tribune, 9/61; J Beck (auth), rev, In: Art News, 10/61; V Raynor (auth), rev, In: Arts, 10/61.
Memberships: Assoc Artists N J; Art Educators N J.
Publications: Auth, We learned about color & design, Sch Arts Mag, 58; illusr, Seventeen Mag, 61; illusr, Country & Western Issue, Billboard Mag, 63; auth, Batik in the classroom & Woodcuts by children, Instr Mag, 72.
Dealers: Lawrence Gallery, 901 Westport Rd, Kansas City, MO 64111; Ryder Gallery, 667 N La Cienega Blvd, Los Angeles, CA 90069.
Mailing Address: 31 Dexter Rd, East Brunswick, NJ 08816.

BLOORE, RONALD LANGLEY
Painter, Educator
Preferred Media: Oil on Panel.
b Brampton, Ont, May 29, 25.
Study & Training: Univ Toronto; New York Univ; Washington Univ, MA; Courtauld Inst, Univ London.
Work in Public Collections: In major Can pub & pvt cols.
Commissions: Murals, Montreal Int Airport, Confedn Ctr, Charlottetown, P E I & York Univ.

Teaching: Prof humanities, faculty arts, York Univ.
Awards: Can Coun grants.
Bibliography: Withrow (auth), Contemporary Canadian printing.
Art Interests: Canadian art.
Dealer: Morris Gallery, 15 Prince Arthur St, Toronto, Ont, Can.
Mailing Address: 206 Vanier College, York University, Downsview, Ont, Can.

BLOS, MAY (ELIZABETH)
Illustrator, Painter
b Sebastopol, Calif, May 1, 06.
Study & Training: Univ Calif, Berkeley, AB(cum laude), 26; also with Perham Nahl, Eugen Neuhaus, M Heymann & Hans Hoffman, Munich.
Commissions: Murals, Tree of Life, 62, Echinodermata, 64, Paleobotany, 65, Migration of Molluscs, 68 & display, Carboniferous, 71, Paleontology Dept, Univ Calif, Berkeley (with help of staff).
Exhibitions: Hunt Botanical Libr, Carnegie Inst Technol, Pittsburgh, Pa, 63; Canessa Gallery, San Francisco, Calif, 70; Univ Calif, Berkeley, 71.
Positions: Adv, Am Indian Artists, San Francisco, 68-70.
Memberships: Oakland Mus Asn.
Publications: Illusr, Nicotiana, Chronica Botanica Press, 54; illusr, Cactus & Succulent J, 58-; illusr, Field Mus Natural Hist Bull, 62; illusr, Cuyama Valley Badlands, Calif, Geol Sci, 63.
Mailing Address: 29 Live Oak Rd, Berkeley, CA 94705.

BLOS, PETER W
Painter, Instructor
Preferred Media: Oils, Acrylics.
b Munich, Ger, Oct 29, 03; U S citizen.
Study & Training: State Acad Art, Munich, with Groeber & von Stuck; also French Schs in Paris.
Work in Public Collections: Oakland Art Mus, Calif; Wilshire Methodist Church, Los Angeles, Calif.
Commissions: Thirteen portraits of faculty members, Univ Calif, Berkeley, 62-71.
Exhibitions: Nat Acad Design, 41; Soc Western Artists Ann, M H De Young Mem Mus, San Francisco, Calif, 55-71; Rosicrucian Art Gallery, San Jose, Calif, 63; St Mary's Col, Moraga, Calif, 64 & 72; Haggin Gallery, Pioneer Mus, Stockton, Calif, 67.
Teaching: Instr portraits & figures, Walnut Creek Civic Arts Ctr, 62-
Positions: Adv, Am Indian Artists, San Francisco, 68-70.
Awards: Klumpke Figure Painting Award, Soc Western Artists, 41 & 70; gold medal, Oakland Mus, 51; second prize for oils, Springville Invitational, Utah, 69.
Memberships: Oakland Mus Asn; Oakland Art Asn; East Bay Artists Asn; Soc Western Artists.
Collection: Navaho rugs, Indian baskets and paintings.
Mailing Address: 29 Live Oak Rd, Berkeley, CA 94705.

BLOWER, DAVID HARRISON
Painter
Preferred Media: Oils, Watercolors.
b Fontanet, Ind, Sept 18, 01.
Study & Training: Wicker Sch Fine Art, Detroit, Mich; Colorossi Acad, Paris, France; Acad Grande Chaumiére, Paris; also painting with Paul Honore, Detroit.
Work in Public Collections: Home Savings & Loan Asn, Los Angeles, Calif; Swope Art Gallery, Terre Haute, Ind; DePauw Univ, Greencastle, Ind.
Exhibitions: Mich Artists Ann, Detroit Inst Arts, 31, 50 & 51; Los Angeles Co Art Mus, 41, 45 & 50; one-man shows, Swope Art Gallery, 57 & Brand Art Ctr, Glendale, Calif, 57 & 68; seven shows, Los Angeles Art Festival, 63-72.
Bibliography: N Kent (auth), 101 watercolor techniques, Watson-Guptill, 68.
Publications: Auth, David Blower—watercolorist, Am Artist Mag, 65.
Mailing Address: 3504 Glenhurst Ave, Los Angeles, CA 90039.

BLUHM, NORMAN
Painter
Preferred Media: Oil.
b Chicago, Ill, Mar 28, 20.
Study & Training: Ill Inst Tech; also with Mies Van der Rohe.
Work in Public Collections: Whitney Mus Am Art, New York, N Y; Corcoran Gallery Art, Washington, D C; High Mus Art, Atlanta, Ga; Albright-Knox Art Gallery, Buffalo, N Y; New York Univ Collection.
Exhibitions: Carnegie Int, 58; Am Abstract Image, Solomon R Guggenheim Mus, 61; Two Decades Am Painting, Mus Mod Art, 66; Large Scale Am Painting, Jewish Mus, 67; one-man show, Corcoran Gallery Art, 69.
Dealer: Martha Jackson Gallery, 32 E 69th St, New York, NY 10021.
Mailing Address: P O Box 729, Millbrook, NY 12545.

BLUM, SHIRLEY NEILSEN
Art Historian, Educator
b Petaluma, Calif, Oct 14, 32.
Study & Training: Stockton Col, AA; Univ Chicago, MA; Univ Calif, Los Angeles, PhD.
Teaching: Assoc prof art hist, Univ Calif, Riverside.
Awards: Distinguished teaching award, Univ Calif, Riverside, 69.
Publications: Auth, Jawlensky and the serial image & Early Netherlandish Triptychs: a study in patronage, Univ Calif Press, 69.
Mailing Address: Dept of Art, University of California, Riverside, CA 92502.

BLUMBERG, RON
Painter, Instructor
Preferred Media: Oils, Watercolors.
b Reading, Pa.
Study & Training: Nat Acad Design; Art Stud League New York; Acad Grande Chaumière, Paris, France.
Work in Public Collections: Los Angeles Co Mus, Calif; Calif Executive Mansion, Sacramento; Bart Lytton Collection, Los Angeles.
Exhibitions: One-man shows, Esther Robles Gallery, Los Angeles, 58, Raymond Burr Galleries, Los Angeles, 62-63, Dallas North Galleries, Tex, 66, Cowie Galleries, Los Angeles, 70 & Rosequist Galleries, Tucson, Ariz, 71.
Teaching: Pvt classes painting & drawing, 50-
Positions: Cult chmn, Westwood C of C, West Los Angeles, 69-
Awards: Jr Coun Prize & Purchase Award, Los Angeles Co Mus, 50; Calif Watercolor Soc Award, 63; award, Inland VI, San Bernardino, 71.
Memberships: Calif Watercolor Soc; Los Angeles Art Asn.
Mailing Address: 10930 Le Conte Ave, Los Angeles, CA 90024.

BLUME, PETER
Painter
b Russia, Oct 27, 06; U S citizen.
Study & Training: Educ Alliance Sch Art, N Y, 19-24; Art Stud League New York; Beaux Arts Acad Art.
Work in Public Collections: Boston Mus Fine Arts; Columbus Gallery Fine Arts; Mus Mod Art; Metrop Mus Art; Whitney Mus Am Art; plus others.
Commissions: Murals, U S Post Off, Cannonsburg, Pa, Rome, Ga & Geneva, N Y.
Exhibitions: Boston Mus Fine Arts; Whitney Mus Am Art; Metrop Mus Art; Mus Mod Art; plus many others.
Awards: Guggenheim fel, 32 & 36; prizes, Carnegie Inst, 34; Nat Inst Arts & Lett grant, 47.
Bibliography: Lloyd Goodrich & I H Baur (auth), included in: American art of our century, Whitney Mus Am Art, 61; George A Flanagan (auth), included in: Understanding and enjoying modern art, Crowell, 62; Frank Getlein (auth), Peter Blume. New York: Kennedy Galleries (exhib catalogue), 68; plus others.
Memberships: Assoc Nat Acad Design; Nat Inst Arts & Lett; Am Acad Arts & Lett.
Mailing Address: Rte 1, Box 140, Sherman, CT 06784.

BLUMENTHAL, MARGARET M
Designer
Preferred Media: Textiles.
b Latvia, Sept 7, 05.
Study & Training: Berlin, Ger, with B Scherz & Bruno Paul.
Exhibitions: Monza, Italy; Metrop Mus Art; Pratt Inst Gallery.
Positions: Indust & textile designer, 43-; freelance designer & stylist, Libbey-Owens Co, Fallani & Cohn Co, Drulane Co, Toscony Fabrica, Franco Mfg Co, Colortex Co & Astorloid Co.
Mailing Address: 689 Columbus Ave, New York, NY 10025.

BOAL, SARA METZNER
Painter, Instructor
Preferred Media: Oils.
b Wheeling, W Va, Jan 10, 96.
Study & Training: Wellesley Col, BA; Cornell Univ; Columbia Univ; also with M A Rasko, Richard Marwede, Dmitri Romanovsky & Carle Blenner.
Work in Public Collections: Libr, Barnesville, Ohio & Libr, Wheeling, W Va; Starr Mus, Albion, Mich; Barbizon Plaza Hotel, New York, N Y; Wellesley Col, Mass.
Commissions: Many pvt commissions.
Exhibitions: Academic Artists of Springfield, Mass, Springfield Mus Art, 55; Fifty American Artists, Schoneman Gallery Art, New York; Belgian Pavilion, New York World's Fair, 64-66; Catharine Lorillard Wolfe Art Club, Nat Acad Design, 69-71.
Teaching: Pvt classes in art.
Awards: Norbury Mem Prize, Catharine Lorillard Wolfe Art Club, 53; Kramer Montgomery Medal of Honor, Ogunquit Art Studio, 59; First prize in landscape, Ahde Arzt Gallery, Soc Composers, Authors & Artists, 69.

Memberships: Catharine Lorillard Wolfe Art Club (pres, 65-68); Composers, Authors & Artists Am (pres, N Y Chap, 70-72); life fel Royal Soc Arts; Hudson Valley Art Asn (mem bd, 55-65); Nat Arts Club New York.
Publications: Auth, Sketches of the Alps, 60, Sketches of Greece, 63, Sketches of New York, 65, Sketches of Japan, 67 & Sketches of Segovia, 71.
Mailing Address: 246 Corona Ave, Pelham, NY 10803.

BOARDMAN, SEYMOUR
Painter
b Brooklyn, N Y, Dec 29, 21.
Study & Training: City Col New York, BS, 42; Art Stud League New York; Ecole Beaux Arts, Paris, France; Acad Grande Chaumiere, Paris; Atelier Fernand Leger, Paris, 46-52.
Work in Public Collections: Whitney Mus Am Art; Guggenheim Mus; Walker Art Ctr, Minneapolis, Minn; Santa Barbara Mus Art; New York Univ; plus others.
Exhibitions: Whitney Mus Am Art, 55, 61 & 67; Nebr Art Asn, 56; Kunsthalle, Basel, Switz, 64; Santa Barbara Art Mus, 64; Albright-Knox Gallery, Buffalo, N Y, 67; plus others.
Awards: Longview Found Award, 63; Guggenheim fel, 72.
Mailing Address: 334 E 30th St, New York, NY 10016.

BOAZ, WILLIAM G
Sculptor, Educator
b Hickory, Ky, July 6, 26.
Study & Training: Murray State Col, with Clara Eagle; Univ Louisville, with Wilkje & Brause; Univ Ga, with Lamar Dodd, Ferdinand Warren & Sibyl Browne, MA; Hans Hofmann Sch Art, Provincetown, Mass; New York Univ, with Margaret Naumburg; Teachers Col, Columbia Univ, with Edwin Ziegfeld.
Exhibitions: Louisville Art Ctr, 52, 56 & 57; H C E Gallery, Provincetown, 56; Oxford, Miss, 56 & 57; Purcell Gallery, Orange, Calif, 63; New York Univ, 63.
Teaching: Instr art educ, Univ Ga; asst prof sculpture & art educ, Murray State Col; asst prof art educ & sculpture & head dept art, Chapman Col.
Positions: Supvr art, Gainesville, Ga; Cambodian govt consult art educ, U S Opers Mission, Unitarian Serv Comt.
Awards: Royal Cambodian Govt Chevalier Medal, 62.
Research: Haniwa sculpture, in Japan.
Mailing Address: Dept of Art, Chapman Col, Orange, CA 92666.

BOBBITT, VERNON L
Painter, Educator
b Pella, Iowa, July 27, 11.
Study & Training: State Univ Iowa, BFA & MA; Denison Univ; Columbia Univ.
Exhibitions: One-man shows, Weyhe Gallery, New York, N Y, 56; Lowe Art Gallery, Univ Miami, Fla, 64; Ft Lauderdale Fine Art Gallery, Fla, 65; Civic Art Ctr, Battle Creek, Mich, 65; Ankrum Gallery, Los Angeles, Calif, 69.
Teaching: Chmn art dept, Albion Col, 46-
Memberships: Mich Comn on the Arts; Am Asn Univ Prof; Midwestern Col Art Asn; Col Art Asn.
Mailing Address: Dept of Art, Albion College, Albion, MI 49224.

BOBICK, BRUCE
Painter, Educator
Preferred Media: Watercolor.
b Clymer, Pa, Oct 25, 41.
Study & Training: Indiana Univ Pa, BS, 63, MS, 67; Univ Notre Dame, MFA, 68.
Work in Public Collections: Ill State Mus, Springfield; Mt Mercy Col, Cedar Rapids, Iowa; Little House on Linden Art Ctr, Birmingham, Ala; Denison Art Asn, Iowa; Tyler Jr Col, Tex.
Exhibitions: Watercolor U S A, 7th 8th & 10th Ann Exhibs, Springfield Art Mus, Mo, 68, 69 & 71; 49th & 51st Ann Calif Nat Watercolor Soc Exhib, Laguna Beach & Oakland, 69 & 71; 164th Ann Am Watercolors, Prints & Drawings, Pa Acad Fine Arts, Philadelphia, 69; 145th & 146th Ann, Nat Acad Design, New York, N Y, 70 & 71; 12th Midwest Biennial Exhib, Joslyn Art Mus, Omaha, Nebr, 72.
Teaching: Assoc prof art, Western Ill Univ, 68-
Awards: Wm Holland Drury Prize in Aquamedia, Newport Art Asn, R I, 70; hon mention, Springfield Art Mus, 71; purchase award, Ill State Mus, 71.
Memberships: Calif Nat Watercolor Soc; Pittsburgh Watercolor Soc; Watercolor Soc Ala; La Watercolor Soc; Col Art Asn Am.
Research: Study of communication between artist and viewer.
Mailing Address: 635 Memorial Dr, Macomb, IL 61455.

BOBLETER, LOWELL STANLEY
Educator, Painter
b New Ulm, Minn, Dec 24, 02.
Study & Training: Bishop Brissman Inst, 20-23; St Paul Sch Art, 23-25; pvt study with George Resler & Cameron Booth; Sch Assoc Arts, hon DFA, 65.

Work in Public Collections: Libr Cong, Washington, D C; Metrop Mus Art, New York, N Y; Nat Gallery Art, Washington, D C; Smithsonian Inst, Washington, D C; Minneapolis Inst Art, Minn; plus many others.
Exhibitions: Corcoran Gallery Art, Washington, D C, 38-47; Carnegie Inst, Pittsburgh, Pa, 40-42; Art Inst Chicago, Ill, 40-45; Metrop Mus Art, 44-47; plus many exhibs in mus in Rome, Paris, Philadelphia, Boston, San Francisco, Los Angeles & others.
Teaching: Chmn art dept, Hamline Univ Sch Fine Arts, 42-48.
Positions: Dir, St Paul Gallery & Sch Art, 40-42; supt, Minn State Fair, 42-48; pres, Sch Assoc Arts, 48-
Awards: Numerous first awards & medals in int & nat exhibs.
Memberships: Nat Asn Interior Designers; Minn Artists Asn; Col Art Asn Am; Artists Equity Asn; Nat Asn Mus Dirs.
Mailing Address: c/o Associated Arts Galleries, 344 Summit Ave, St Paul, MN 55102.

BOCCIA, EDWARD EUGENE
Painter, Craftsman
b Newark, N J, June 22, 21.
Study & Training: Pratt Inst Art Sch, N Y; Art Stud League New York; Columbia Univ, BS & MA.
Work in Public Collections: City Art Mus Saint Louis; Denver Art Mus; Univ Mass; Drury Col, Springfield, Mo; Saint Louis Univ; plus others.
Commissions: Stained glass, Clayton Inn, Mo; four wall paintings, First Nat Bank, Saint Louis; Stations of the Cross, Old Cathedral, Saint Louis; mural, Stations of the Cross & stained glass windows, Newman Chapel, Washington Univ, Saint Louis; religious drawings & 14 mural paintings, Temple Brith Sholom Kneseth Israel, Saint Louis; plus others.
Exhibitions: One-man shows, Jewish Community Ctr, Saint Louis & Webster Col, Webster Groves, 63; Nat Liturgical Art Show, Saint Louis, 64; one-man show, Drury Col, 65; traveling exhib, sponsored by Mo State Coun Arts, 68; one-man show, drawings, Gallery Tournabuoni, Florence, Italy, 71; plus others.
Teaching: Dean, Columbus Art Sch, Ohio, 48-51; guest instr, Univ Sask, summer 60; guest instr, Webster Groves Col, summer 65; prof fine arts, Wash Univ.
Awards: Ital Govt fel award res & painting in Italy, 58-59; bronze medal, Temple Israel, Saint Louis, 62.
Publications: Contribr, Saint Louis Post-Dispatch & Wash Univ Mags.
Mailing Address: 600 Harper Ave, Webster Groves, MO 63119.

BOCK, VERA
Illustrator, Designer
b Saint Petersburg, Russia.
Study & Training: Pvt study in Europe.
Work in Public Collections: Kerlan Collection, Univ Minn Libr.
Exhibitions: New York Pub Libr; Woodmere Art Gallery, Philadelphia, Pa; Art Dirs Club, N Y; one-man show, William Farnsworth Mus, Rockland, Maine, 52 & group, 57.
Positions: Illusr & designer bks, leading publ.
Publications: Illusr, Life & Coronet Mags.
Mailing Address: 318 W 105th St, New York, NY 10025.

BODIN, PAUL
Painter
Preferred Media: Oils, Watercolors.
b New York, N Y, Oct 30, 10.
Study & Training: Nat Acad Design; Art Stud League New York.
Work in Public Collections: Albright-Knox Art Gallery, Buffalo, N Y; Univ W Va, Morgantown.
Exhibitions: Brooklyn Mus Int Watercolor Exhib, 49 & 59; Metrop Mus Art Watercolor Exhib, 52; one-man shows, Laurel Gallery, 48 & 50, New Gallery, 52 & Betty Parsons Gallery, 59 & 61.
Awards: Special distinction award, Art: U S A, 58; Longview Found Award, Art: U S A, 59.
Mailing Address: 207 W 86th St, New York, NY 10024.

BODO, SANDOR
Painter, Sculptor
b Szamosszeg, Hungary, Feb 13, 20; U S citizen.
Study & Training: Col Fine & Appl Art, Budapest, Hungary.
Work in Public Collections: (Restoration works) President Andrew Jackson Home in the Hermitage, Nashville, Tenn; President James K Polk Mus, Columbia, Tenn; Tenn State Mus, Nashville; Tenn Fine Arts Ctr, Nashville.
Commissions: Bronze reliefs, Hungarian Reformed Fedn Am, 65; portrait of Andrew Jackson, Royal Palace, Copenhagen, Denmark, 71.
Exhibitions: Nat Housing Ctr, Washington, D C; Butler Inst Am Art, Youngstown, Ohio; Nat Acad Galleries, New York, N Y; Smithsonian Inst, Washington, D C; Brooks Mem Art Gallery, Memphis, Tenn.

Positions: Self employed artist & art restorer.
Awards: Gold medal of honor for watercolor, Am Art Week Exhib, 61; gold medal of honor for sculpture, Nat Arts Club, New York, N Y, 63 & gold medal of honor for oil painting, 66.
Memberships: Fel Am Artists Prof League; Nat Arts Club; Allied Artists Am.
Mailing Address: Bodo's Art Studio, 6513 Hwy 100, Nashville, TN 37205.

BODOLAI, JOSEPH STEPHEN
Film Maker, Sculptor
Preferred Media: Film, Tape, Contemporary Materials.
b Youngstown, Ohio, May 11, 48.
Study & Training: Allegheny Col, BA, 70; Univ Manchester, with Alistair Smith; King's Col, Univ Cambridge, 68, with Sir Francis Warner.
Commissions: Tableaux, Cliche Guild of Can, Toronto, 72.
Exhibitions: Thrill Factory, D W Griffith Film Festival, Louisville, Ky, 70; Univ Film Asn Film Festival, 71; Art Gallery Ont, Toronto, 72; Entertainment from the Thrill Factory, A Space, Toronto, 72; Electric Poetry, York Univ, Toronto, 72.
Positions: Cur contemp art, The Electric Gallery, Toronto, 71-
Awards: Foster P Doane Prize, Allegheny Col, 70.
Memberships: Alliance Technol & Art.
Publications: Contribr, Essays on kinetic art, The Electric Gallery, 72; contribr, Leonardo, Paris & London, 72.
Dealer: A Space, 85 St Nicholas St, Toronto, Ont, Can.
Mailing Address: 390 Huron St, Toronto, Ont, Can.

BOE, ROY ASBJÖRN
Art Historian, Educator
b Fredrikstad, Norway, Sept 27, 19; U S citizen.
Study & Training: Univ Minn, BS, 41, MA, 47; Univ Oslo, Fulbright fel, 50-51; N Y Univ, grad fel, 49-50, PhD, 70; Moorhead State Col, faculty res grant, 72-73.
Teaching: Instr art hist, Univ Minn, 46-47, 55-56; asst prof art hist, La State Univ, 56-57; asst prof art hist, Pa State Univ, 57-60; assoc prof art hist, Univ Miss, 60-66, chmn dept art, 61-64; assoc prof art hist, Moorhead State Col, 67-
Memberships: Col Art Asn Am; Norweg-Am Hist Asn; Am Asn Univ Prof.
Research: Nineteenth and twentieth century European and American art; north European art; Edvard Munch; artists of American western frontier; panoramas.
Publications: Auth, Edvard Munch's murals for the University of Oslo, Art Quart, 60; auth, Edvard Munch og J P Jacobsen's Niels Lyhne, Oslo, 60; auth, The panoramas of the Mississippi, Miss Quart, 63.
Mailing Address: 1106 Fifth Ave S, Moorhead, MN 56560.

BOEDEKER, ARNOLD E (BOEDIE)
Illustrator, Painter
Preferred Media: Watercolors, Oils, Acrylics.
b Sheboygan, Wis, June 5, 93.
Study & Training: Art Inst Chicago; also with John Pike, Edgar Whitney, Jerry Farnsworth, Don Stone, Tom Nichols, Dong Kingman, Millard Sheets, Rex Brandt & George Post.
Work in Public Collections: Canton Art Inst; Massillon Art Mus; Akron Art Inst; Cuyahoga Valley Art Ctr; Drawing Room Gallery.
Exhibitions: Mainstreams '72, Am Watercolor Soc; Butler Inst Am Art; Wichita Centennial Exhib; Canton Art Inst; Massillon Art Mus; plus many others.
Positions: Art dir, Goodyear Tire & Rubber Co, Akron, Ohio, 15-61.
Awards: Awards for paintings, The Quarry, Canton Jewish Ctr, 67, Lowtide, Massillon Art Inst, 68 & Market at San Miguel, 70, Wichita Centennial Nat Art Exhib.
Memberships: Am Artists Prof League; Akron Soc Artists (pres, 66-68); Cuyahoga Valley Art Ctr (trustee, 61-, pres, 62-63).
Mailing Address: 2965 Silver Lake Blvd, Cuyahoga Falls, OH 44224.

BOESE, ALVIN WILLIAM
Researcher, Collector
b Saint Paul, Minn, Mar 24, 10.
Positions: Mgr dept devoted to res & develop improved surfaces for artists, 3M Co, Saint Paul.
Collection: Mainly contemporary American art, all media except sculpture.
Mailing Address: 803 Lincoln Ave, Saint Paul, MN 55102.

BOGART, GEORGE A
Painter
b Duluth, Minn, Oct 30, 33.
Study & Training: Univ Minn, Duluth, BA; Univ Wash, MFA; also with Fletcher Martin, Philip Evergood & Dong Kingman.
Work in Public Collections: Witte Mem Mus; Delgado Mus Art, New Orleans, La; Ill State Univ; Washburn Univ, Topeka, Kans.

Exhibitions: Delgado Mus Art, 61 & 64; New York World's Fair, 64; Dallas Mus Fine Arts, 64 & 65; Univ Tex, 67; Ill State Univ, 69; plus others.
Teaching: Instr, Univ Wash; prof art, Univ Tex, Austin; prof art, Pa State Univ, State College; prof art, Univ Okla.
Awards: Purchase prize, Delgado Mus Art, 64; purchase prize, Ill State Univ, Normal, 69; purchase prize, Washburn Univ, 71.
Publications: Contribr, Southwestern art; illusr, George Bogart drawings and paintings, 67.
Mailing Address: 1210 Beverly Hills, Norman, OK 73069.

BOGART, RICHARD JEROME
Painter
Preferred Media: Oils.
b Highland Park, Mich, Oct 30, 29.
Study & Training: Art Inst Chicago, grad, 52.
Exhibitions: Riverside Mus, New York, 64; The American Landscape, A Living Tradition, circulated by Am Fedn Arts, Peridot Gallery, New York, 68; one-man shows, Poindexter Gallery, New York, 68-70.
Bibliography: Alan Gussow (auth), A sense of place—the artist and the American land, Sat Rev Press.
Dealer: Poindexter Gallery, 24 E 84th St, New York, NY 10028.
Mailing Address: Monroe, CT 06468.

BOGEN, BEVERLY
Painter
Preferred Media: Acrylic.
b Jersey City, N J.
Study & Training: Syracuse Univ, BA; Art Stud League; Pratt Graphic Art Ctr; with Victor Perard, Benton Spruance, Harry Sternberg & Leo Manso.
Work in Public Collections: Charles Z Mann Gallery, New York, N Y; Vera Lazuk Gallery, Cold Spring Harbor, N Y; Sally Robbins Gallery, South Orange, N J; Robert Aaron Young Assoc, New York; Award Studios, New York; also over 300 private collections in U S & abroad.
Exhibitions: Silvermine Guild Artists, Conn, 66; Mus Sec, Guild Hall, East Hampton, N Y, 69; Allied Artists, Nat Acad Galleries, New York, 70; one-man shows, Charles Z Mann Gallery & Vera Lazuk Gallery, 71.
Bibliography: Gorden Brown (auth), review, Arts Mag, 5/71; Malcolm Preston (auth), Progress in a palette, News Day, 1/71; Virginia Seward (auth), review, Long Island Press, 1/71.
Memberships: Artists Equity Asn New York; Am Fedn Arts.
Dealers: Charles Z Mann Gallery, 1226 Third Ave at 71st St, New York, NY 10021; Vera Lazuk Gallery, Main St, Cold Spring Harbor, NY 11724.
Mailing Address: 19 Kay St, Jericho, NY 11753.

BOGERT, GRACE WARREN
Painter, Educator
Preferred Media: Oils.
b New York, N Y.
Study & Training: Art Stud League New York, with Charles Chapman, John Costigan & Robert Brackman.
Work in Public Collections: Bergen Community Mus, Paramus, N J; Leonia Pub Libr, N J.
Exhibitions: Am Artists Prof League, Smithsonian Inst, Washington, D C, 63; Expos Int, Monaco & Dieppe, France, 67-68; Nat Arts Club, New York, 68; Allied Artists Am, Nat Acad Design, New York, 70; Catharine Lorillard Wolfe Art Club, Nat Acad Design, 71.
Teaching: Private instr oil painting, 56-
Awards: Award, Catharine Lorillard Wolfe Art Club, 58; Ann Waldron Mem Award, Am Artists Prof League, 63; first prize portrait, Bergen Co Artists Guild, 65.
Memberships: Allied Artists Am; Am Artists Prof League (dir nat bd, 65-); Catharine Lorillard Wolfe Art Club (bd dir, 65-); Burr Artists; Bergen Co Artists Guild.
Mailing Address: 134 Reldyes Ave, Leonia, NJ 07605.

BOGGS, FRANKLIN
Painter, Educator
b Warsaw, Ind, July 25, 14.
Study & Training: Fort Wayne Art Sch, Ind; Pa Acad Fine Arts.
Work in Public Collections: Abbott Labs; U S War Dept; U S Post Off, Newton, Miss; Mayo Clin, Rochester, Minn; Merchants & Savings Bank, Janesville, Wis; plus others.
Commissions: Mural, Vocational Sch, Janesville, 01; concrete murals, Yates Am Mach Co, Madison, Wis, 61; Univ Wis Math Bldg, 62 & Cancer Res Bldg, Madison, 63; Univ Wis-Milwaukee 64 & Cutler-Hammer Off Bldg, Milwaukee, 65; plus others.
Exhibitions: Pa Acad Fine Arts.
Collections Arranged: Supvr Assembling, American Indian Exhib.
Teaching: Prof & artist-in-residence, Beloit Col, 45-, chmn art dept, 55-71; lectr Am Indian Exhib, Finland & Sweden, 58-59.

Positions: Illusr, Tenn Valley Auth, 40-44; war artist, 44.
Awards: Gimbels Wis Exhib Prize, 52; Milwaukee J Prize, Freedom of the Press Exhib; Fulbright res grant to Finland, 58; plus others.
Publications: Illusr, Men without guns; army med paintings reproduced in art mags.
Mailing Address: Dept of Art, Beloit College, Beloit, WI 53511.

BOGGS, JEAN SUTHERLAND
Museum Director, Art Historian
b Negritos, Peru, June 11, 22; Can citizen.
Teaching: Asst prof art, Skidmore Col, 48-49; asst prof art Mt Holyoke Col, 49-52; assoc prof art, Univ Calif, 54-62; Steinberg prof hist art, Washington Univ, 64-66.
Positions: Dir, Nat Gallery Can, 66-
Memberships: Am Asn Mus (mem coun, 69-); Can Art Mus Dirs Asn; Asn Art Mus Dirs (v pres, 72-); fel Royal Soc Can.
Publications: Auth, Portraits by Degas, 62, Drawings by Degas, 66 & The National Gallery of Canada, 71.
Mailing Address: Elgin at Slater, Ottawa, Ont. K1A 0M8, Can.

BOGHOSIAN, VARUJAN
Sculptor, Educator
Preferred Media: Constructions.
b New Britain, Conn, June 26, 26.
Study & Training: Vesper George Sch Art, Boston; Yale Univ Sch Art & Archit, BFA & MFA.
Work in Public Collections: Mus Mod Art, New York, N Y; Whitney Mus Am Art, New York, N Y; Addison Gallery Am Art, Andover, Mass; Worcester Mus, Mass; Currier Gallery Art, Manchester, N H.
Exhibitions: One-man shows, Stable Gallery, New York, 63-66 & Cordier & Ekstrom, New York, 70 & 72.
Teaching: Prof sculpture, Dartmouth Col, 68-
Awards: Fulbright grant, 53; sculptor-in-residence, Am Acad Rome, 67; Nat Inst Arts & Lett Award, 72.
Bibliography: Dore Ashton (auth), article, In: Studio Int, 4/65; article, In: Time Mag, 2/9/70.
Dealer: Cordier & Ekstrom, Inc, 980 Madison Ave, New York, NY 10021.
Mailing Address: Dept of Art, Dartmouth College, Hanover, NH 03755.

BOHAN, PETER JOHN
Art Historian, Painter
Preferred Media: Acrylic Resins.
b New York, N Y.
Study & Training: Bristol Univ, 47-48; Rensselaer Polytech Inst, BEng, 50; Columbia Univ, 54-55; Yale Univ, MA, 57; Courtauld Inst Art, Univ London, Fulbright scholar, 58-59; Yale Univ, PhD, 61; SUNY res fel archit & urban planning, Europe, 69-70.
Exhibitions: 32nd Regional Exhib, Albany Inst Hist & Art, 67; First SUNY Artists Exhib, Albright-Knox Art Gallery, Buffalo & traveling exhib, 67-68; 19th Ann N Eng Exhib, Albany Inst Hist & Art, 69; Convocation of the Arts, State Univ N Y, Albany & traveling exhib, 69.
Collections Arranged: American Gold 1700-1860, Yale Univ Art Gallery, 63; From Victor Hugo to Jean Cocteau (French portrait drawings), 65 & First Intercollegiate Student Exhibition, 66, State Univ N Y Col New Paltz Art Gallery; plus others.
Teaching: Asst prof art hist, Southern Conn State Col, 62-63; prof art hist, State Univ N Y Col New Paltz, 63-
Positions: Asst cur, Garvan Collection, Yale Univ Art Gallery, 59-63; dir, College Art Gallery, State Univ N Y Col New Paltz, 63-
Awards: Perkin-Elmer Prize in Painting, Silvermine Guild Artists Ann, 68.
Memberships: Soc Archit Historians.
Research: Architecture and design, 1870-1930.
Publications: Auth, American gold, 1700-1860, Yale Univ Art Gallery, 63; auth, From Victor Hugo to Jean Cocteau, New Paltz Col Art Gallery, 65; auth, Early American gold, Antiques, 12/65; auth, First New Paltz intercollegiate student exhibition, New Paltz Col Art Gallery, 66; auth, Early Connecticut silver, 1700-1840, Wesleyan Univ Press, 70.
Mailing Address: History of Art Dept, State University of New York College at New Paltz, New Paltz, NY 12561.

BOHNEN, BLYTHE
Painter
Preferred Media: Acrylics.
b Evanston, Ill, July 26, 40.
Study & Training: Smith Col, BA; Boston Univ, BFA; Hunter Col, MA.
Exhibitions: Annual Survey of American Painting, Whitney Mus Am Art, 71-72; group show, Penthouse, Mus Mod Art, New York, N Y, 72; Painting and Sculpture Today, Indianapolis Mus Art, Ind, 72; New American Abstract Painting, Vassar Col Mus, 72; American Women Artists, Kunsthaus, Hamburg, Ger, 72.

Teaching: Lectr, Metrop Mus Art, 67-
Bibliography: Lucille Naimer (auth), The Whitney annual, Arts Mag, 3/72; Carter Ratcliff (auth), The Whitney annual, Art Forum, 4/72; Kenneth Baker (auth), New York commentary, Studio Internation, 5/72.
Dealer: A I R Gallery, 97 Wooster St, New York, NY 10012.
Mailing Address: 504 E 84th St, Apt 5E, New York, NY 10028.

BOHNERT, ROSETTA
Painter, Lecturer
b Brockton, Mass.
Study & Training: Univ R I; Sch Appl Design, N Y; also with Olaf Olesen, Maud Mason & Walter Farndon.
Work in Public Collections: Brueckner Mus.
Exhibitions: Am Artists Prof League; Nat Arts Club, New York, N Y; Allied Artists Am; Hudson Valley Art Asn; Catharine Lorillard Wolfe Art Club; plus others.
Teaching: Lectr.
Positions: Dir nat bd, Am Artists Prof League; v pres, Hudson Valley Art Asn; nat dir, Coun Am Artists Soc.
Awards: Gold medal & citation, Hudson Valley Art Asn, 61; prizes, Nat Arts Club, Catharine Lorillard Wolfe Art Club & others.
Memberships: Contemp Club, Greenwich, Conn; Am Artists Prof League; Hudson Valley Art Asn (past pres); Allied Artists Am; Catharine Lorillard Wolfe Art Club; plus others.
Mailing Address: 243 S Broadway, Hastings-on-Hudson, NY 10706.

BOHROD, AARON
Painter, Educator
b Chicago, Ill, Nov 21, 07.
Study & Training: Art Inst Chicago; Art Stud League New York, N Y, with John Sloan.
Work in Public Collections: Art Inst Chicago; Corcoran Gallery of Art, Washington, D C; Metrop Mus Art, New York; Philippines Mus Art, Manila; Whitney Mus Am Art, New York.
Exhibitions: Art Inst Chicago Int Watercolor Exhibs, 32-40; Carnegie Int Exhib, 36-38, 40; Artists for Victory Exhib, Metrop Mus Art, 42; Pa Acad Fine Arts, 42; Nat Acad Fine Arts Exhibs, 53-72; plus many others.
Teaching: Artist-in-residence, Southern Ill Univ, Carbondale, 41-42; artist-in-residence, Univ Wis-Madison, 48-
Positions: Artist war corresp, U S Corps Engrs & Life Mag, 42-45.
Awards: Clark Prize & Silver Medal, Corcoran Gallery Art; prize, Artist for Victory Exhib, Metrop Mus Art; First Logan Prizes, Art Inst Chicago, 37 & 45.
Bibliography: Harry Salpeter (auth), Bohrod: Chicago's gift to art, Esquire Mag, 40; article, In: Life Mag, 41; Frank Getlein (auth), review, In: Washington Star; John Lloyd Taylor (auth), Bohrod Retrospective Catalogue, Milwaukee Art Ctr, 66.
Publications: A pottery sketch book, 59 & A decade of still life, 66, Univ Wis Press.
Mailing Address: 4811 Tonyawatha Trail, Madison, WI 53716.

BOLINSKY, JOSEPH ABRAHAM
Sculptor, Educator
Preferred Media: Bronze, Stone, Wood.
b New York, N Y, Jan 17, 17.
Study & Training: Columbia Univ, MA; Stourbridge Col Art, Eng; Skowhegan Sch Painting & Sculpture, with José de Creeft; Iowa Univ, MFA.
Work in Public Collections: Newark Mus Art, N J; Tel Aviv Mus Art, Israel; State Univ N Y Col Buffalo.
Commissions: Carved ark doors & welded menorah, Sons Jacob Synagogue, Waterloo, Iowa, 52; three welded forms & facade, Dr Diamond Med Ctr, Waterloo, 60; cast bronze group of six figures, Jewish Community Fedn Bldg, Cleveland, Ohio, 66; bronze screen, St Mary's Hosp, Rochester, N Y, 70; carved ark doors, Temple Shaarey Zedek, Amhurst, N Y, 71.
Exhibitions: Des Moines Art Ctr, Iowa, 52; Western N Y Regional, Albright-Knox Gallery, Buffalo, N Y, 59; Art on Paper, Skowhegan Sch Painting & Sculpture, 69; Rochester Festival of Religious Art, N Y, 70; Our Legacy of Art in Western New York, Charles Birchfield Ctr, 72.
Teaching: Instr sculpture, Univ Northern Iowa, 49-54; prof sculpture, State Univ N Y Col Buffalo, 54-; vis sculptor, Stanislaus State Univ, summer 71.
Awards: First prize, stone carving, Des Moines Art Ctr, 52; first prize for Moon Mountain, stone carving, Albright-Knox Gallery, 59; award, bronze casting, Rochester Festival of Religious Art, 70.
Memberships, Patteran Art Asn, Buffalo.
Publications: Contribr, Jewish form symbolism, Ethos Mag, 58, Demonstrator, Carved sculpture, (film), U S Info Serv, 68.
Dealer: Gallery West, 311 Bryant St, Buffalo, NY 14222.
Mailing Address: 10 Ames Ave, Tonawanda, NY 14150.

BOLLES, JOHN S
Art Dealer, Collector
b Berkeley, Calif, June 25, 05.
Study & Training: Univ Okla, BS; Harvard Univ, MArch.
Positions: Owner & dir, Bolles Gallery, 58-
Awards: Artists Equity Award, Artists Equity Asn & Calif Coun Architects, 50.
Memberships: Am Inst Architects; Calif Coun Architects (pres, 46); San Francisco Art Inst (chmn bd, 61-64).
Specialty of Gallery: Contemporary, mostly California and the West Coast art.
Collection: Contemporary, includes Dove, Soulage, Hoffman, Olivera and many others; gifts to University of Oklahoma Museum and Oakland Museum, California.
Publications: Auth, La Iglesia, Chichen Itza Yucatan, 65; auth, var archaeol reports for Carnegie Inst & Oriental Inst, Univ Chicago.
Mailing Address: 14 Gold St, San Francisco, CA 94133.

BOLLEY, IRMA S
Painter, Designer
Preferred Media: Watercolors.
b Turku, Finland; U S citizen.
Study & Training: Mass Col Art, dipl; Art Stud League New York; special study with Jerry Farnsworth, F D Greenbowe & Joe Jones.
Exhibitions: 32nd Ann N J State Exhib, Montclair Mus, 63; Exhibition of Finnish-American Art, Riverside Mus, New York, N Y, 64; 9th Westfield Art Asn Ann, Union Col, Cranford, N J, 70; Crafts for Fun and Function, Union Carbide Corp, New York (courtesy McCalls Needlework & Crafts), 70; Art from New Jersey, New Jersey State Mus, Trenton, 71.
Positions: Art dir, Gray Advert Agency, New York, 41-44; designer-consult, Needlework & crafts, McCall Pattern Co, 49-
Awards: First prize for oil, Waiting, Finlandia Found, 63; first prize for mixed media, Growth, Summit Art Ctr, 68 & Beneath the Earth, Westfield Art Asn, 70.
Bibliography: Irma Bolley, designer-artist, McCall Publ, 65; Peggy Ann Darbie (auth), Leisure crafts appeal to young, Courier News, Plainfield, N J, 9/24/69; Randy Stiles (auth), The joys of creation, Scene Publ, 3/70.
Memberships: Nat Asn Women Artists; N J Watercolor Soc; Summit Art Ctr; World Crafts Coun.
Publications: Contribr, articles, In: McCall Needlework & Crafts, 68-
Mailing Address: 79 Redmont Rd, Watchung, NJ 07060.

BOLOMEY, ROGER HENRY
Sculptor, Art Historian
Preferred Media: Steel, Aluminum
b Torrington, Conn, Oct 19, 18; U S & Swiss citizen.
Study & Training: Acad Bella Arte, Florence, Italy, 47; Univ Lausanne, 47-48; Calif Col Arts & Crafts, Oakland, 48-50.
Work in Public Collections: Mus Mod Art, New York, N Y; Whitney Mus Am Art, New York; Oakland Mus, Calif; Los Angeles Co Mus, Calif; Univ Calif Mus Art, Berkeley.
Commissions: Aluminum sculpture, Southridge Mall, Milwaukee, Wis, 70; two reliefs, Mutual of N Y, Syracuse, 71; aluminum sculpture, Eastridge Mall, San Jose, Calif, 71; two bronze sculptures, S Mall Proj, Albany, N Y, 71; cor-ten steel sculpture, Lehman High Sch, Bronx, N Y, 71-72.
Exhibitions: Carnegie Inst Int, Pittsburgh, Pa, 64; Whitney Mus Am Art Sculpture Ann, 64; Quatriène Exposition Suine Sculpture, Bienne, Switz, 66; Contemporary American Paintings & Sculpture, Univ Ill, Urbana, 67; American Sculpture, Univ Nebr, Lincoln, 70.
Teaching: Assoc prof art, Herbert H Lehman Col, 68-
Awards: First prize & purchase award, Bundy Art Mus Sculpture Int, Waitsfield, Vt, 63; sculpture prize, San Francisco Art Inst 84th Ann, 65; Res Found Award, City Univ N Y, 70.
Memberships: San Francisco Art Inst; Am Fedn Arts.
Mailing Address: Wingdale, NY 12594.

BOLOTOWSKY, ILYA
Painter, Educator
Preferred Media: Oils, Acrylics, Wood, Metal, Plastics.
b St Petersburg, Russia, July 1, 07; U S citizen.
Study & Training: Col St Joseph, Constantinople, Turkey, cert, 23; Nat Acad Design, dipl, 30.
Work in Public Collections: Mus Mod Art, New York, N Y; Solomon R Guggenheim Mus, New York; Whitney Mus Am Art, New York; Chase Manhattan Bank Collection, New York; Hirshhorn Collection, Washington, D C; plus many others.
Commissions: Abstract mural, comn by Works Progress Admins, Williamsburg Housing Proj, N Y, 36-37; mural, comn by Works Progress Admins, Hall of Med Sci, New York World's Fair, 38-39; mural, comn by Works Progress Admins, Men's Day Room, Hospital for Chronic Diseases, Welfare Island, N Y, 41; Mosaic,

comn by Works Progress Admins, Theodore Roosevelt High Sch, Bronx, N Y, 41; abstract mural, Cinema I Lobby, New York, 63.
Exhibitions: The Classic Spirit in XX Century Art, Janis Gallery, New York, 64; Plus by Minus, Albright-Knox Gallery, Buffalo, N Y, 67; The 1930's Painting & Sculpture in America, Whitney Mus Am Art, 68; The Nonobjective World, 1924-1939, Gallerie Jean Chauvelin, Paris, France, Annalee Jude Fine Art, London, Eng, Galleria Milano, Italy & others, 71; also many other gallery and one-man shows.
Teaching: Prof painting & drawing, Black Mountain Col, 46-48; assoc prof painting, drawing & design, Univ Wyo, 48-57; prof painting, drawing & design, State Univ N Y Col New Paltz, 57-65; prof painting, drawing & design, Southampton Col, 65-
Awards: First Hallgarten prize for painting, Nat Acad Design, 29 & 30; first prize for film, Metanoia, Midwest Film Festival, Univ Chicago, 63; abstract painting award, Nat Inst Arts & Lett, 71.
Bibliography: Lawrence Campbell (auth), Squaring the circle and vice-versa, Art News, 2/70; Knute Stiles (auth), Ilya Bolotowsky, Artforum, 3/70; Robert M Ellis (auth), Ilya Bolotowsky-paintings & columns art museum, Univ N Mex, 70.
Memberships: Am Abstract Artists (co-founder, charter mem, former pres); Fedn Mod Painters & Sculptors (co-founder, charter mem, former v pres); Fine Arts Fedn N Y (bd dirs); Nat Soc Mural Painters; Audubon Soc.
Publications: Co-auth, An interview of Naum Gabo, Harvard Univ Press & Wittenborn, 55; auth, Metanoia (film), Grove Press, 63; auth, A Russian-English dictionary of painting, Telberg Book Co, 65; auth, On neoplasticism and my own work, Leonardo, 6-7/69.
Dealer: Grace Borgenicht Gallery, 1018 Madison Ave, New York, NY 10021.
Mailing Address: Box 288-A, John St, Sag Harbor, NY 11963.

BOLSTER, ELLA S
Designer-Weaver, Lecturer
b Helena, Mont, Dec 8, 06.
Study & Training: Mont State Univ; art metalwork with Alexander Bick, Colo State Univ; handweaving with Mary Meigs Atwater, Univ Mont; handweaving gold brocades, Nat Col Arts & Crafts, Tehran, Iran; pottery with Pieter Grueneveld, The Hague, Netherlands; handweaving with Anni Albers, Haystack Mountain Sch Crafts, Maine.
Work in Public Collections: Handwoven formal tablecloth, Wichita Art Mus, Kans.
Commissions: Handwoven altar hanging, pulpit antipendijm, burse & veil, St. Mary's Episcopal Church, Arlington, Va, 62; plus several individual handweaving & stitchery commissions.
Exhibitions: Int Textile Exhib, Greensboro, N C, 54; Fiber, Clay, Metal, St. Paul Gallery & Sch Art, Minn, 55; Decorative Arts & Ceramics Exhib, Wichita, 55-57; Contemp Handweaving, Univ Nebr Art Gallery, Lincoln, 61; Textiles by Outstanding Am Designer-Weavers, Univ Gallery Fine Art, Lafayette, La, 61; plus many others including one-man shows.
Teaching: Instr art metalwork, Mont State Univ, summer 44; instr canvaswork & Macramé, Univ Ariz, Tucson, summer 71, 72; also traveling lectr, Weavers' Guilds, east & midwestern states, & other organizations throughout the U S.
Awards: Purchase prize, Ann Nat Exhib, Wichita Art Asn, 55; First in Fiber, St Paul Gallery & Sch Art, 55; First in Textiles, Nat League Am Pen Women Diennial Exhib, Smithsonian Inst, Washington, D C, 64; plus 11 nat & int awards, 54-64.
Bibliography: Mickey Gates Maker (auth), Her weaving is a creative art, Alpha Gamma Delta Quart, 58; Mary Alice Smith (auth), Ella Bolster, experiments in many techniques, Handweaver & Craftsman Mag, 61; Opal Johnston (auth), Weaver magna cum laude, Southwest Art Scene Mag, 68; many others.
Memberships: Designer Weavers of Washington (1st pres, 57); Am Craftsmen's Coun (state rep, D C, 62-63); Nat League Am Pen Women (br art chmn, 64-68, Ariz state pres, 68-70 & art chmn, 72-74); Craft Guild, Tucson Art Ctr.
Publications: Auth, magazine articles.
Dealers: Tucson Art Center, 325 W Franklin St, Tucson, AZ 85705; Davis Sorokin Gallery, 2559 E Ft Lowell Rd, Tucson, AZ 85716.
Mailing Address: 6391 E Printer Udell, Tucson, AZ 85710.

BOLTON, MIMI DU BOIS
Painter, Lecturer
Preferred Media: Oils.
b Gravlotte, France, Dec 12, 02; U S citizen.
Study & Training: Corcoran Sch Art; Phillips Sch; also with Karl Knath.
Work in Public Collections: Corcoran Gallery Art, Washington, D C; Mus Mod Art, Tyler, Tex; Kauffman Collection, Washington Evening Star.
Exhibitions: Corcoran Gallery Art Biennial; Baltimore Mus Art; Butler Inst Am Art; Boston Mus Fine Arts; Nat Acad Design.
Collections Arranged: For Soc Washington Artists, 55-59.

Teaching: Instr painting, Corcoran Sch Art, 50-52; pvt classes painting & drawing, 52-70.
Awards: Purchase award, Corcoran Area Show, 54; first award, Chautauqua Nat, 61; first award, Juried Arts Show, Tyler, Tex, 62.
Bibliography: Margaret Harold, Prizewinning paintings, Allied Publ, 62 & 63; articles, In: Art News, 64 & 65.
Memberships: Artists Equity Asn; Soc Washington Artists (secy, 46-55).
Dealer: Franz Bader Gallery, 2124 Pennsylvania Ave N W, Washington, DC 20037.
Mailing Address: 18900 Montgomery Village Ave, Gaithersburg, MD 20760.

BOMAR, BILL
Painter
b Fort Worth, Tex.
Work in Public Collections: Brooklyn Mus; Mus Fine Arts Houston; Fort Worth Art Ctr; Dallas Mus Fine Arts; Des Moines Art Ctr.
Exhibitions: Six one-man shows, Weyhe Gallery, New York, N Y.
Mailing Address: Hotel Chelsea, 222 W 23rd St, New York, NY 10010.

BONAMARTE, LOU
Painter, Designer
Preferred Media: Watercolor.
b New London, Conn, Jan 18, 33.
Study & Training: Mitchell Col; and with John Pike & Frank Reilly.
Work in Public Collections: Slater Mem Mus, Norwich, Conn.
Commissions: Yuletide watercolors, Gen Dynamics Corp, 66 & 68; watercolor illus, Combustion Eng, 72.
Exhibitions: Ebell Art Soc, Los Angeles, Calif, 70; Providence Watercolor Club, R I, 71; Acad Artist Asn, Springfield, Mass, 71-72; Am. Watercolor Soc, New York, N Y, 72; Knickerbocker Artist, Nat Arts Club, New York, 72.
Positions: Graphic designer, Gen Dynamics Corp, 60-69; freelance designer, 69-
Awards: W Alden Brown Mem Award, Providence Watercolor Club, 71; prize for watercolor, Salmagundi Club, New York, 71 & 72; Canelli Gold Medal Award, Acad Artists Asn, Springfield, Mass, 72.
Memberships: Salmagundi Club; Acad Artist Asn; Providence Watercolor Club; Am Artists Prof League; assoc mem Grand Cent Art Gallery, New York.
Publications: Illusr, Mike's world your world, Educ Ventures Inc, 71; Let's give a party, Am Educ Publ, 72.
Mailing Address: 62 Norwood Ave, New London, CT 06320.

BOND, ORIEL EDMUND
Illustrator, Painter
Preferred Media: Polymer.
b Altus, Okla, July 18, 11.
Study & Training: Rockford Col, exten courses with Marquis E Reitzel, Einar Lundquist & Alice McCurry.
Work in Public Collections: Works in private collections only.
Exhibitions: 6 shows, Rockford Art Asn, Ill, 56-63; Ill State Fair, Springfield, 59-61; Sovereign Exhibs Ltd, Winston-Salem, N C & Williamsburg, Va, 70; Am Artists Prof League, New York, N Y, 71 & 72.
Positions: Chief artist, J L Clark Mfg Co, Rockford, 38-
Awards: Popular award, Ill State Fair, 59; first pl display award, Trading Post Days, Rockton, 72; first pl & popular award, Colonial Village Mall, 72.
Memberships: Fel Am Artists Prof League.
Mailing Address: 7816 Bond Dr, The Ledges, Roscoe, IL 61073.

BOND, ROLAND S
Collector
b Van Alstyne, Tex, Dec 25, 98.
Positions: Trustee, Dallas Mus Fine Arts.
Collection: Fifty paintings by various contemporary French artists.
Mailing Address: 2600 Republic National Bank Bldg, Dallas, TX 75201.

BONET, JORDI
Sculptor, Muralist
Preferred Media: Cast Aluminum, Fired Clay, Cement, Plastic.
b Barcelona, Spain, May 7, 32; Can citizen.
Work in Public Collections: Exterior sculpted mural, Orthogenic Sch, Univ Chicago; sculpted ceramic mural, Queen's Park Bldg, Toronto; cast aluminum doors, Nat Art Ctr, Ottawa; five cast aluminum sculptures, Expo '67, Place des Nations, Montreal; sculpted cement walls, Grand Theatre Quebec.
Commissions: Ceramic mural, Trade Bank & Trust Co, New York, N Y, 63; cast aluminum mural, Charleston Nat Bank, W Va, 66;

sculpted aluminum mural, Pac Gas & Elec Co, San Francisco, Calif, 71; ceramic mural, Zale Corp, Dallas, Tex, 71; ceramic mural, Continental Bank, Chicago, Ill, 72.
Exhibitions: Can Govt Exhib, Triennial Milan, Italy, 68; Nat Art Gallery, Ottawa, 69; Am Inst Architects IRAIC Convention, Chicago, 69; Mus Rodin, Paris, France, 70; Exhib Quebec Pavilion, Expo 70, Osaka, Japan, 70.
Awards: Drawing award, Spring Salon, Montreal Mus Fine Arts, 59; sculpture award, Abramowitz Chap of Hadassah, 63 & 65; allied arts medal, Royal Archit Inst Can, 65.
Bibliography: J Folch-Ribas (auth), The sign and the earth, 64; Guy Robert (auth), L'infinie a remplir, 71; Paul Vezina (auth), Jordi Bonet, Film Off, Quebec, 72.
Memberships: Royal Can Acad Arts; Asn Prof Artists Quebec; Art Guild Quebec.
Mailing Address: Manoir Campbell, Mont St Hilaire, P Q, Can.

BONGART, SERGEI R
Painter, Educator
Preferred Media: Oils, Acrylics.
b Kiev, Russia.
Study & Training: Kiev Art Acad.
Work in Public Collections: Theater Mus, Kiev, Russia; Nat Acad Design, New York, NY; Laguna Beach Art Mus, Calif; Long Beach Art Mus, Calif; Charles & Emma Frye Art Mus, Seattle, Wash.
Exhibitions: Charles & Emma Frye Art Mus; Los Angeles Co Mus Art, Los Angeles, Calif; Nat Acad Design, New York; M H De Young Mem Mus, San Francisco, Calif; Metrop Mus Art, New York.
Teaching: Instr drawing & painting, Sergei Bongart Sch Art, Santa Monica, Calif, 49-
Awards: Grand Nat Gold Medal, Am Artists Prof League, New York, 59; first prize in West Coast Oil Painting Exhib, Frye Mus, 62; silver medal of honor, Am Watercolor Soc, 69.
Bibliography: Janice Lovoos (auth), The paintings of Sergei Bongart, Am Artist, 9/62; Nancy Kalis (auth), Sergei Bongart: romantic realist with a Russian soul, Art Rev, 69; Wendon Blake (auth), Complete guide to acrylic painting, Watson-Guptill, 71.
Memberships: Nat Acad Design; Am Watercolor Soc; Royal Soc Arts; Soc Western Artists.
Dealer: Zachary Waller Gallery, 904 N La Cienega Blvd, Los Angeles, CA 90069.
Mailing Address: 533 W Rustic Rd, Santa Monica, CA 90402.

BONGIORNO, LAURINE MACK
Art Historian
b Lima, Ohio, Apr 17, 03.
Study & Training: Oberlin Col, AB, 25; Radcliffe Col, PhD, 30.
Teaching: Asst prof art hist, Wellesley Col, 30-42, assoc prof art hist, 42-44; lectr art hist, Oberlin Col, 55-66.
Positions: Ed, Allen Art Mus Bull, 50-67.
Research: Italian Renaissance sculpture; Giotto.
Publications: Auth, Notes on art of Silvestro dell'Aquila, 42 & Date of altar of madonna in S M del Soccorso, 44, Art Bull; A fifteenth century stucco & art of Verrocchio, Allen Art Mus Bull, 62; Theme of old and new law in Arena Chapel, Art Bull, 68; Umbrian statue of Saint Sebastian, Allen Art Mus Bull, 71.
Mailing Address: 19 N Park St, Oberlin, OH 44074.

BONINO, ALFREDO
Art Dealer
b Naples, Italy, July 29, 25.
Positions: Pres, Galeria Bonino, Buenos Aires, Arg, 45-, Rio de Janeiro, Brazil, 52 & New York, N Y, 61-
Memberships: Mus Mod Art, New York; Solomon R Guggenheim Mus; Mus Mod Art, Rio de Janeiro; Mus Mod Art, Buenos Aires.
Specialty of Gallery: Contemporary art.
Mailing Address: 7 W 57th St, New York, NY 10019.

BONSIB, LOUIS WILLIAM
Painter
Preferred Media: Oils, Watercolors.
b Vincennes, Ind, Mar 10, 92.
Study & Training: Indiana Univ, AB, 16; Univ Cincinnati; Univ Ill; Vincennes Univ, hon DH, 71.
Work in Public Collections: Union Bldg, Ind Univ, Bloomington; 15 paintings, Fort Wayne Pub Schs, Ind; Fort Wayne Art Mus; Brown Co Art Gallery, Nashville, Ind; Vet Hosp, Marion, Ind; plus many others.
Exhibitions: Hoosier Salon Ann, Indianapolis, Ind, 35-71; Ft Wayne Woman's Club Ann, 14 yrs; also many exhibs, Indiana Artists Ann, Indianapolis, Fort Wayne Art Inst Mus & Northern Indiana Art Salon, Hammond.
Positions: Pres, Fort Wayne Art Sch, 48-49, bd mem, 48-52; bd mem, Brown Co Art Gallery.

Awards: First prize for landscape in oil, Northern Ind Art Salon, 48; third prize for landscape in oil, Ogunquit, Maine, 50; J O Holcomb Prize for landscape, Ind Artists Asn, 61; plus many others.
Memberships: Life mem Brown Co Art Gallery Asn (bd dirs); Ind Artists Asn; Hoosier Salon.
Mailing Address: 2015 St Joe Center Rd, Fort Wayne, IN 46825.

BOOKATZ, SAMUEL
Painter, Sculptor
b Philadelphia, Pa, Oct 3, 10.
Study & Training: Cleveland Inst Art; Boston Mus Sch Art; Harvard Univ; Acad Grande Chaumière & Colarossi, Paris, France; Am Acad Rome, Italy; also with Oskar Kokoschka & Ivan Mestrovic.
Work in Public Collections: Corcoran Gallery Art, Washington, D C; The Phillips Gallery, Washington, D C; Smithsonian Inst, Washington, D C; Cleveland Mus Art, Ohio; Norfolk Mus Art & Sci, Va.
Commissions: Portraits of Pres & Mrs F D Roosevelt, 41; murals, comn by U S Govt, U S Naval Hosp, Norfolk, Va & San Diego, Calif, 42-45; murals, pvt comn, Americana, Des Moines, Iowa, 66; murals, Govt Turn Key Housing for Aged, Prince George's Co, Md & Della Ratta Off Bldg, Bethesda, Md, 71; portrait, Gov David L Lawrence, Pa, 65.
Exhibitions: One-man shows, Cleveland Mus Art, 40 & Corcoran Gallery Art, 46; Pa Acad Fine Arts, Philadelphia, 52; Va Mus Art, Richmond, 55; Baltimore Mus Art, Md, 60.
Teaching: Dir art, Samuel Bookatz Sch Art, Washington, D C, 45-
Positions: Govt artist & White House artist, 41-43.
Awards: William Page Award & Prix de Rome Award in the Arts, Boston Mus, 37; Inst Allende fel, 54; Ford Found grant, 62.
Mailing Address: 2700 Que St N W, Washington, DC 20007.

BOOKBINDER, JACK
Painter, Writer
Preferred Media: Oils.
b Odessa, Ukraine, Jan 15, 11; U S citizen.
Study & Training: Univ Pa, BS in Educ; Pa Acad Fine Arts; Tyler Sch Art, Temple Univ, MFA.
Work in Public Collections: Pa Acad Fine Arts, Philadelphia; Philadelphia Mus Art; Libr Cong, Washington, D C; Nat Gallery Art, Washington, D C; Yale Univ Art Gallery, New Haven, Conn.
Commissions: Mosaic mural (with Frederick Geasland), Church of the Redeemer, Bryn Mawr, Pa, 64; painting of Hahnemann Med Col, Squibb Pharmaceut Co, 66.
Exhibitions: One-man show, Nessler Gallery, New York, N Y; 100 American Water Colorists Exhibition, Royal Acad Arts, London, Eng, 62; American Printmakers Abroad, U S State Dept Exhib, 62; Two Hundred Years of American Watercolors, Metrop Mus Art, 66; Fifty American Watercolorists, Mexico City, Mex, 68.
Teaching: Lectr art, Barnes Found, Merion, Pa, 36-44; lectr art, Univ Pa, 47-59; lectr art, Pa Acad Fine Arts, 49-61.
Positions: Consult, Dept Educ, Philadelphia Mus Art, 45-46; spec asst to dir of art educ, Sch Dist of Philadelphia, 46-59, dir of art educ, 59-
Awards: Mong Q Lee Mem Award, 61 & William Church Osborn Mem Award, 68, Am Watercolor Soc; New Eng Heritage Award, Acad Artists Asn, 71.
Bibliography: Henry Pitz (auth), Jack Bookbinder, painter & educator, Am Artists Mag, 3/61.
Memberships: Artists Equity Asn; Philadelphia Watercolor Club; Audubon Artists; Print Coun Am; Am Watercolor Soc.
Publications: Auth, Invitation to the arts & The gifted child, his education in the Philadelphia Public Schools; auth, History of sculpture & Art in the life of children, Compton's Encycl; contrib ed, Sch Arts Mag.
Dealers: Newman Galleries, 1625 Walnut St, Philadelphia, PA 19103; Little Gallery, 211 S 17th St, Philadelphia, PA 19103.
Mailing Address: 323 S Smedley St, Philadelphia, PA 19103.

BOOTH, CAMERON
Painter
Preferred Media: Oils.
b Erie, Pa, Mar 11, 92.
Study & Training: Sch Art Inst Chicago, 12-17; also with Andre L'Hote, Paris, 27 & Hans Hofmann, Munich, Ger, 28.
Work in Public Collections: Minneapolis Art Inst, Minn; Guggenheim Mus, New York, N Y; Walker Art Ctr, Minneapolis; Butler Mus Am Art, Youngstown, Ohio; Univ Minn, Minneapolis.
Exhibitions: Five shows, Carnegie Int, 23-64; 16 American Cities, Mus Mod Art, New York, 33; Booth Retrospective Exhib, circulated by Am Fedn Arts, 61; American Abstract Expressionists, Imagists, 62; Art Across America, Mead Corp, 65.
Teaching: Instr drawing & painting, Minneapolis Sch Art, 22-28; instr drawing & painting, Art Stud League New York, 44-48; instr drawing & painting, Queens Col, 46-47; instr drawing & painting, Univ Minn, 48-60; vis artist, Univ Calif, Berkeley, 57-59.
Awards: John Simon Guggenheim Mem Found fel, 40.
Bibliography: Booth (monogr), Am Fedn Arts, 61.

Memberships: Fedn Mod Sculptors & Painters.
Dealer: Paul Kramer Gallery, 507 Wabasha, Saint Paul, MN 55102.
Mailing Address: 3408 Park Terr, Minneapolis, MN 55406.

BOOTH, LAURENCE OGDEN
Sculptor, Architect
Preferred Media: Plexiglas, Felt, Steel.
b Chicago, Ill, July 5, 36.
Study & Training: Stanford Univ, BA, 58; Mass Inst Technol, BArch, 60.
Work in Public Collections: Sch Soc Sci, Univ Chicago.
Exhibitions: Young Structurists, Oregon & Chicago, 68; one-man show, Kansas City Libr, 68; Black & White, Kouler Gallery, Chicago, 70; Beloit Col, 71; Group 5, Chicago, 71-72.
Teaching: Instr archit, Univ Ill, Chicago Circle, 69-71.
Bibliography: Amy Goldin (auth), Vitality vs greasy kid stuff, Art Gallery Mag, 72.
Publications: Auth, Spiritual content of order, Arc Mag, 68; auth, Review of Stanley Tigerman sculpture, Art Scene Mag, 69.
Mailing Address: 553 W Fullerton, Chicago, IL 60614.

BOPP, EMERY
Painter, Educator
b Corry, Pa, May 13, 24.
Study & Training: Pratt Inst Art Sch, N Y; Yale Sch Painting & Design, with Josef Albers & William de Kooning, BFA; New York Univ; Rochester Inst Technol, MFA.
Work in Public Collections: Addison Gallery Am Art, Andover, Mass; Greenville Co Mus Art, S C.
Exhibitions: Bob Jones Univ, 62-64; Butler Inst Am Art Exhib, 66; Birmingham Mus Art, 66; Southeastern Exhib, Atlanta, Ga, 67; Greenville Co Mus Art, 68; plus others.
Teaching: Chmn div art, Bob Jones Univ, 55-
Awards: Purchase award, Hunter Gallery Art, Chattanooga, Tenn, 65; merit award, Southeastern Exhib, Atlanta, 67; purchase award, Greenville Co Mus Art, 68.
Memberships: Southeastern Col Art Conf; Guild S C Artists (treas, 61-62, v pres, 63-64, pres, 64-65); Col Art Asn Am; Int Platform Asn.
Mailing Address: Division of Art, Bob Jones University, Greenville, SC 29614.

BORGATTA, ISABEL CASE
Sculptor, Lecturer
Preferred Media: Stone, Wood.
b Madison, Wis, Nov 21, 21.
Study & Training: Smith Col, 39-40; Yale Univ Sch Fine Arts, BFA, 44; New Sch Social Res, 44-45; Studio of Jose de Creeft, 44-45; Art Stud League New York, 46.
Work in Public Collections: Wadsworth Atheneum, Hartford, Conn; Yeshiva Univ, New York, N Y; Krannert Mus, Univ Ill, Champaign; Norfolk Mus, Va.
Commissions: Mem sculpture, City of New Rochelle Pub Schs, 72.
Exhibitions: Pa Acad Fine Arts Ann, Philadelphia, 49-55; Nat Acad Fine Arts Ann & Nat Asn Women Artists Ann, 50-52; Whitney Mus Am Art, 51-52; Hudson River Mus, 60-61; retrospective, Briarcliff Col Mus, 71; plus ten solo exhibs.
Teaching: Instr art, Halsted Sch, Yonkers, N Y, 45-49; lectr sculpture, City Col New York, 60-71.
Awards: First prize for sculpture, Hudson River Mus, 60; Jacques Lipchitz Award, 61; Edward MacDowell fel, 68 & Yaddo fel, 71.
Bibliography: Roxanne Guerrero (auth), A maternal art, Life Mag, 54; Mark van Doren (auth), The sculptures of Isabel Case Borgatta, Galerie St Etienne Brochure, 54; William D Allen (auth), Borgatta's marbles, Arts Mag, 68.
Memberships: Sculptors League; Women in the Arts.
Dealer: Frank Rehn Gallery, 655 Madison Ave, New York, NY 10022.
Mailing Address: 320 Clinton Ave, Dobbs Ferry, NY 10522.

BORGATTA, ROBERT EDWARD
Painter, Educator
Preferred Media: Oils, Marble.
b Havana, Cuba, Jan 11, 21; U S citizen.
Study & Training: Nat Acad Design, 34-37; New York Univ Sch Archit & Allied Arts, BFA, 40; Yale Univ Sch Fine Arts, MFA, 42; New York Univ Inst Fine Arts, 46-53.
Work in Public Collections: Norfolk Mus, Va; Ford Found.
Commissions: Mural & sculpture, Gutman Assocs, New York, N Y; design, stained glass, Temple Emanu-el, Yonkers, N Y, 60.
Exhibitions: Audubon Artists Ann, 53-72; Whitney Mus Am Art Prizewinners Show, 54; Schettini Gallery, Milan, Italy, 57; one-man shows, Babcock Galleries, 64 & 68; group show, Corcoran Gallery Art, 68.
Teaching: Prof painting & drawing, City Col New York. 47-
Awards: Tiffany fel, 42; Emily Lowe Found Award, 57; Newman Medal, Nat Soc Painters in Casein, 69.

Bibliography: American artists in Italian exhibit, Valligia Diplomatica, 10/57; An artist in his studio, House Beautiful, 3/60; John Canaday (auth), review, In: New York Times, 3/15/69.
Memberships: Audubon Artists; Am Watercolor Soc; Nat Soc Painters in Casein.
Dealer: Babcock Galleries, 805 Madison Ave, New York, NY 10051.
Mailing Address: 320 Clinton Ave, Dobbs Ferry, NY 10522.

BORGENICHT, GRACE (GRACE BORGENICHT BRANDT)
Art Dealer, Collector
b New York, N Y, Jan 25, 15.
Study & Training: Columbia Univ, MA, 37; also with Andre Lhote, Paris, France, 34.
Positions: Dir & owner, Grace Borgenicht Gallery, 51-
Specialty of Gallery: Contemporary American painting and sculpture.
Collection: Cezanne, Matisse, Picasso, de Kooning, Bonnard, Mondrian, Degas, Vuillard, Avery, Leger, de Rivera, Watteau, Kupka and Hartley.
Mailing Address: 1018 Madison Ave, New York, NY 10021.

BORGZINNER, JON
Writer, Art Critic
b New York, N Y, Jan 14, 38.
Study & Training: Yale Univ, BA; Inst Art & Archeol, Univ Paris, Fulbright grant.
Positions: Art ed, Time Mag, New York, 63-67; consult, Anonymous Arts Recovery Soc, 64-; assoc ed, Life Mag, 67-69; for bus ed, Business Wk Mag, 70; asst news ed, CBS, 70; managing ed, Oui Mag; free-lance writer & critic.
Awards: Bausch & Lomb Medal outstanding criticism optical art, 64; Chaddford Soc Prize essays on contemp Brit graphics, 65; Daumier Soc Award res contemp posters, 68.
Memberships: Munic Art Soc.
Mailing Address: Jericho Lane, East Hampton, Long Island, NY 11937.

BORIS, BESSIE
Painter
Preferred Media: Acrylics, Ink, Pastels.
b Johnstown, Pa, June 6, 19.
Study & Training: Art Stud League New York, 40-42; study with George Grosz & Vaclav Vytlacel.
Work in Public Collections: Mills Col, New York, N Y; Norfolk Mus Arts & Sci, Va; Univ Mass, Amherst; Slater Mem Mus, Norwich, Conn; New York Univ Collection; plus others.
Exhibitions: 21st Biennial, Corcoran Gallery Art, Washington, D C, 49; Inst Contemp Art, Boston, Mass, 51; Pa Acad Fine Arts Ann Drawing Show, 63 & 69; Fairleigh-Dickinson Univ, Madison, N J, 64; Acad Arts & Lett (paintings invited for Childe Hassam Award selections), 70; plus many other one-man and group shows.
Awards: First painting award, Butler Inst Am Art, 46; first prize purchase award, Mo Valley Artists, Mulvane Mus, 48; Dana Watercolor Medal, Pa Acad Fine Arts, 61; plus others.
Dealer: Babcock Galleries, 805 Madison Ave, New York, NY 10021.
Mailing Address: 444 W 20th St, New York, NY 10011.

BORNE, MORTIMER
Sculptor, Painter
b Poland; U S citizen.
Study & Training: Art Stud League New York; Nat Acad Design; Ecole Beaux Arts.
Work in Public Collections: Etchings & drypoints, Metrop Mus Art, New York, N Y; chromatic wood sculpture, Munic Mus Ramat-Gan, Israel, 70; oil paintings, Univ Judaism Mus, Los Angeles, Calif; color drypoints, Nat Gallery Art & drypoints, Libr Cong, Washington, D C.
Exhibitions: One-man shows, Spec Exhib of Drypoints, Corcoran Gallery Art, Washington, D C, 41, Drypoints, Mus Fine Arts, Montreal, Can, 42, Color Drypoints-A New Medium, U S Nat Mus, Smithsonian Inst, Washington, 44 & Color Drypoints, Currier Gallery, Manchester, N H.
Teaching: Lectr art, New Sch, New York, 45-67.
Awards: Talcott Prize, 39 & Noyes Prize, 43, Soc Am Etchers.
Bibliography: Leila Mechlin (auth), The art world, Washington Sun Star, 12/10/44; H M (auth), Mortimer Borne and a note on color prints, New York Pub Libr Bull, 5/44; The chromatic wood sculpture of Mortimer Borne, Nat Hist, 11/70.
Publications: Auth, Idiomatic specialization, 52; auth, Modern art goes below the surface, Rotarian, 10/60; auth, New art techniques, 69 & auth, Chromatic versus polychrome sculpture, 71, Leonardo.
Dealer: Kennedy Galleries, 20 E 56th St, New York, NY 10022.
Mailing Address: 107 S Broadway, Nyack, NY 10960.

BORNSTEIN, ELI
Educator, Sculptor
b Milwaukee, Wis, Dec 28, 22.
Study & Training: Univ Wis, BS, 45, MS, 54; Art Inst Chicago; Univ
Chicago, 43; Acad Montmartre of Fernand Leger, Paris, France,
51; Acad Julien, Paris, 52.
Work in Public Collections: Walker Art Ctr, Minneapolis, Minn;
Nat Gallery Can, Ottawa, Ont.
Commissions: Aluminum construction, Sask Teacher's Fed, Saska-
toon, 56; structurist relief, Univ Sask, Saskatoon, 58; structurist
relief, Int Air Terminal, Winnipeg, Man.
Exhibitions: Retrospective 1941-1964, Mendel Art Gallery, Saska-
toon, 64; one-man shows, Kazimir Gallery, Chicago, Ill, 65 & 67;
Nat Gallery Can Biennial, Ottawa, 67; Second Int Biennial,
Medellin, Colombia, 70.
Teaching: Instr drawing, painting & sculpture, Milwaukee Art Inst,
43-47; instr design, Univ Wis, 49; prof art, Univ Sask, 50-,
head dept art, 63-71.
Positions: Ed, The Structurist, 60-72.
Awards: Allied Arts Medal, Royal Archit Inst Can, 68; hon men,
Second Int Biennial Exhib, Medellin, Colombia, 70.
Publications: Auth, articles, In: The Structurist No 1-11; auth,
Structurist art and creative integration, Art Int, 67; auth, Notes
on structurist process, data directions in art, theory and
aesthetics, Faber & Faber, Ltd, 1968; auth, Notes on structurist
vision, Canadian art today, Studio Int, 69; auth, Toward an organic art, The Structurist, 71.
Mailing Address: Dept of Art, University of Saskatchewan, Saskatoon, Sask S7N 0W0, Can.

BOROCHOFF, (IDA) SLOAN
Painter, Art Dealer
Preferred Media: Oils.
b U S citizen.
Study & Training: High Mus Art, 39; Univ Ga, 39-40; Ga State Univ,
40; Chicago Sch Interior Decorating, dipl, 66; Atlanta Art Inst,
68.
Work in Public Collections: Ga Inst Technol, Atlanta; Nat Acad Eng,
Washington, D C; Vet Admin Hospital, Atlanta; Lovett Sch, At-
lanta; The Temple, Atlanta.
Commissions: Noah's Ark (print), Atlanta Jewish Welfare Fedn, 71;
painting, Am Art Campaign, Atlanta, 72.
Exhibitions: One-woman show, Dzikalas Gallery, 61; Third Nat Art
Competition, B'nai B'rith Woman, Washington, D C, 65; Int Plat-
form Asn Art Exhib, Washington, D C, 71; invited one-woman
shows, Ga Inst Technol Stud Ctr & Lovett Sch Show, 71.
Teaching: Lectr, schools & pvt parties, 70-
Positions: V pres, Designs Unlimited, Inc, Atlanta, 64-; pres, Sloan
Borochoff Gallery, 70-; co-ed, Musical musings, 71-72.
Awards: Award for Three Boats, Sandy Springs Jr Woman's Club,
71; award for Designs in Art, Scottdale Enterprises, Inc, 72.
Memberships: Atlanta Artists Club; Atlanta Writers Club; High Mus
Art; Atlanta Music Club (co-ed newsletter, 70-72); Atlanta Press
Club.
Specialty of Gallery: Varied group in graphics, oils, commissioned
art works and original art.
Publications: Auth, Story prints, 69-71; auth, Story graphics, 71.
Mailing Address: 3450 Old Plantation Rd, N W, Atlanta, GA 30327.

BOROS, BILLI (MRS PHILIP BISACCIO)
Painter, Writer
b New York, N Y.
Study & Training: Art Stud League New York, with Edwin Dickinson,
Reginald Marsh & Iver Rose; Aviano Acad Art.
Work in Public Collections: Private collections only.
Exhibitions: Studio 41, the Cortile; Nat Arts Club, 65; Am Artists
Prof League, 65-67; Nat Art League, 69; Catharine Lorillard
Wolfe Art Club, 66 & 69; plus others.
Positions: Publ, Art Times, 58-60, 63-64; dir, Grafton Potter Art
Gallery, 70-
Awards: Catharine Lorillard Wolfe Art Club Award, 69.
Memberships: Am Art Prof League; life mem Art Stud League New
York.
Publications: Auth, Boros' Hall (monthly column), Grafton Potter
Art Gallery, 71-
Mailing Address: 101 W 78th St, New York, NY 10024.

BORZEMSKY, BOHDAN
Painter, Graphic Artist
b Kolomya, Ukraine, July 7, 23.
Study & Training: Art Sch & Art Acad, Lviv, Western Ukraine;
Cooper Union Art Sch, N Y; also with Edwin Dickinson & Robert
Gwathmey.
Work in Public Collections: Ukrainian Inst Am; St Peters Col Libr,
Jersey City, N J.

Exhibitions: New Britain Mus Am Art, Conn; Libr Cong, Washing-
ton, D C; Nat Acad Design; Nat Arts Club; Boston Printmakers;
plus others.
Awards: Two prizes, Cooper Union.
Memberships: Ukrainian Art & Lit Club; Ridgewood Art Asn.
Mailing Address: 211 Oakdene Ave, Teaneck, NJ 07666.

BOSCH, GULNAR KHEIRALLAH
Art Historian, Educator
b Lake Preston, S Dak, Oct 31, 09.
Study & Training: Art Inst Chicago & Univ Chicago, BAE, 29; Fine
Arts Inst Art & Archaeol, New York Univ, MA, 40; Oriental Inst,
Univ Chicago, PhD, 52.
Teaching: Catherine Comer Chair & head dept art hist, Wesleyan
Col, 45-57; prof art hist, La State Univ, 57-60; prof art hist &
head dept, Fla State Univ, 60-; dir art hist, Fla State Univ Study
Ctr, Florence, Italy, 67-68.
Memberships: Am Oriental Soc; Col Art Asn Am; Southeastern Col
Art Conf (v pres, 56-57, 65-66, pres, 57-58); Archaeol Inst Am
(pres, Tallahassee Chap, 65-66, 69-70).
Publication: Auth, Ibn Khaldun on evolution, Islamic Rev, Vol 38,
No 5; auth, Staff of the scribes and implements of the discern-
ing: an excerpt, 61; auth, Review of Arab painting by Richard
Ettinghausen, Col Art J, 63; auth, Review of der Islamische
bucheinband des mittelalters by M Weisweiler, 64; auth, Medi-
eval Islamic leather book-bindings: doublures as a dating factor,
Summaries of papers 26th international congress of Orientalists,
64.
Mailing Address: Dept of Art, Florida State University, Tallahassee, FL 32304.

BOSIN, BLACKBEAR
Painter, Designer
Preferred Media: Watercolors, Gouache, Acrylics, Charcoal, Pencil.
b Anadarko, Okla, June 5, 21.
Work in Public Collections: Wichita Art Mus, Kans; Wichita Art Asn;
Philbrook Art Ctr, Tulsa, Okla; Heard Mus, Phoenix, Ariz; Whit-
ney Gallery of Western Art, Cody, Wyo.
Commissions: Sculpture design for city, Kans Gas & Elec, Wichita,
69; mural, comn by Schafer, Schirmer & Eflin for Farmers
Credit Land Bank, Wichita, 72; painting, Southern Plains Mus,
Anadarko, 72.
Exhibitions: Festival of Arts, White House, Washington, D C, 65;
Whitney Gallery of Western Art, 66; Nat Indian Ann, Philbrook
Art Ctr, 67; Heard Mus, 67; Wichita Art Asn, 71.
Awards: Grand award, Philbrook Art Ctr, 59-63; Waite Phillips Spe-
cial Indian Artists Award, 67.
Bibliography: Articles, In: Life Int, 60 & Newsweek; Lilian West-
phal (auth), article, In: Woche, 72.
Memberships: Wichita Artists Guild (v pres, 63-66); Wichita Advert
Asn.
Research: American Indian in the Great Plains Region.
Collection: American Indian artifacts.
Mailing Address: 710 W Douglas, Wichita, KS 67203.

BOSTELLE, THOMAS (THEODORE)
Painter, Sculptor
Preferred Media: Oils, Wood.
b West Chester, Pa, Nov 16, 21.
Work in Public Collections: Wilmington Soc Fine Arts, Del; West
Chester State Col; Southeast Nat Bank, West Chester; Hist Soc
West Chester; plus other work in private collections.
Commissions: For private collections.
Exhibitions: Calif Palace Legion Honor, 48; Pa Acad Fine Arts,
Philadelphia, 48-52; Walker Art Gallery, 52.
Teaching: Instr drawing & painting, Fleisher Art Mem, 52-55;
instr, Wilson Soc Fine Arts, 56-60; private classes, 60-
Positions: Aesthetic adv, One world or none & Stuff for stuff
(documentaries), Phillip Ragan Assocs, 47-49.
Awards: Four Christian Brinton First Prize Awards & three N C
Wyeth First Prize Awards, 46-72.
Bibliography: Clint Collins (auth), People are talking about, Vogue,
3/57; Nancy Mohr (auth), article In: Del Today, 4/72.
Dealer: Franz Bader Inc, 2124 Pennsylvania Ave N W, Washington,
DC 20037.
Mailing Address: 408½ E Lancaster Ave, Downingtown, PA 19335.

BOSTICK, WILLIAM ALLISON
Painter, Art Administrator
Preferred Media: Watercolors, Acrylics, Oils.
b Marengo, Ill, Feb 21, 13.
Study & Training: Carnegie Inst Technol, BS; Cranbrook Acad Art,
with Zoltan Sepeshy; Detroit Soc Arts & Crafts, with John Foster;
Wayne State Univ, MA(art hist); Berlitz Sch Lang.
Work in Public Collections: Detroit Inst Arts, Mich; Evansville Mus
Arts & Sci, Ind; Cranbrook Acad Art Mus, Detroit; Detroit Pub
Libr; Wayne State Univ, Detroit.

Commissions: 32 calligraphic panels on wood, 11 calligraphic lecterns & 1 large calligraphic quotation (with Christopher Bostick), Cath Cemeteries of Chicago for Resurrection Mausoleum, Justice, Ill, 71

Exhibitions: Exhibition for Michigan Artists, Detroit Inst Arts, 36-63; Pepsi-Cola Exhib, 45; Scarab Club Gold Medal Exhib, 47-71; Mich Water Color Soc, 48-71; Mich Acad Sci, Arts & Lett Arts Exhib, 55-65.

Collections Arranged: Mich Artists Ann, Detroit Inst Arts, 47-57.

Teaching: Instr drawing, Wayne State Univ, 46-47; instr calligraphy, Detroit Soc Arts & Crafts Art Sch, 61-63; instr hist of the book, Wayne State Univ Grad Sch, 62-67.

Positions: Typographer & graphic designer, Evans-Winter-Hebb, Detroit, 36-37; exec secy, Founders Soc, Detroit Inst Arts, 46-60; Adminr & secy, Detroit Inst Arts, 46-; ed, Midwest Mus Quart, 59-60.

Awards: Maximilian Jaeger Mem Award, Mich Water Color Soc, 61; Scarab Gold Medal, 62 & 68; Garelick's Gallery purchase prize, Mich Artists Exhib, 63.

Memberships: Mich Water Color Soc (chmn, 46-47); Scarab Club Detroit (pres, 62-63); Midwest Mus Conf (pres, 55-56); Am. Inst Graphic Arts (regional v pres, 60-65); Am Asn Mus.

Publications: Illusr, Many a watchful night, 45; co-auth, The amphibious sketch, 45; auth & illusr, England under G I's reign, 46; illusr, The mysteries of Blair House, 48.

Dealer: Arwin Galleries, 222 W Grand River, Detroit, MI 48226.

Mailing Address: 9340 W Outer Dr, Detroit, MI 48219.

BOSTWICK, MR & MRS DUNBAR W
Collectors
Mailing Address: 778 Park Ave, New York, NY 10021.

BOTERF, CHESTER ARTHUR (CHECK)
Painter, Lecturer
Preferred Media: Acrylics.
b Fort Scott, Kans, Apr 27, 34.
Study & Training: Univ Kans, BA, 59; Art Stud League New York; Hunter Col, 63-64; Columbia Univ, MFA, 65.
Work in Public Collections: Mus Mod Art, New York, N Y; Larry Aldrich Mus, Ridgefield, Conn; Des Moines Art Ctr, Iowa; Chase Manhattan Bank, New York; Columbia Univ, New York; plus others.
Commissions: 3-D wall piece (acrylic on canvas), First City Nat Bank Houston, Tex, 72.
Exhibitions: Larry Aldrich Mus, Ridgefield, 68; Des Moines Art Ctr, 68; Indianapolis Mus Art, Inc, 68-69; Finch Col, New York, 71; Recent Acquisitions, Mus Mod Art, New York, 71; plus others.
Teaching: Lectr design & drawing, Hunter Col, 65-71.
Dealer: John Bernard Myers, 50 W 57th St, New York, NY 10012.
Mailing Address: 46 MacDougal St, New York, NY 10012.

BOTHMER, BERNARD V
Museum Curator, Art Historian
b Ger, Oct 13, 12; U S citizen.
Collections Arranged: Egyptian Sculpture of the Late Period, 60; Art from the Age of Akhenaten, 73.
Teaching: Adj prof fine arts, Grad Sch Arts & Sci, New York Univ, 60-
Positions: From asst to asst cur, Dept Egyptian Art, Mus Fine Arts, Boston, 46-56; assoc cur ancient art, Brooklyn Mus, 56-64, cur ancient art, 64-
Memberships: Am Res Ctr in Egypt (field dir, 54-56); Egypt Explor Soc; Archaeol Inst Am; Col Art Asn Am.
Research: Ancient Egyptian portraiture, Egyptian sculpture of the late period.
Publications: Co-auth, Egyptian sculpture of the late period, 700 BC to 100 AD, 60; co-auth, The Pomerance collection of ancient art, 66; ed, Wilbour monographs, Vols I-V, 68-72; co-auth, Brief guide, Dept Ancient Art, Brooklyn Mus, 70.
Mailing Address: The Brooklyn Museum, 188 Eastern Parkway, Brooklyn, NY 11238.

BOTHMER, DIETRICH FELIX VON
Art Historian, Art Administrator
b Eisenach, Ger, Oct 26, 18; U S citizen.
Study & Training: Friedrich Wilhelm Univ, Berlin, Ger; Oxford Univ, dipl classical archaeol; Univ Chicago; Univ Calif, PhD.
Teaching: Adj prof Greek art, Inst Fine Arts, New York Univ, 65-
Positions: Asst cur, Dept Greek & Roman Art, Metrop Mus Art, 46-51, assoc cur, 51-59, cur, 59-
Awards: Guggenheim fel, 67.
Memberships: Archaeol Inst Am; Soc Promotion Hellenic Studies; Vereinigung der Freunde antiker Kunst; Deutsches Archaol Inst; Mus Asn.
Research: Greek and Roman art and archaeology.

Publications: Auth, Amazons in Greek art, 57; auth, Ancient art from New York private collections, 60; co-auth, An inquiry into the forgery of the Etruscan terra-cotta warriors, 61; auth, Corpus Vasorum Antiquorum U S A, Fascicule 12, 63 & co-auth, Fascicule 14, 73.
Mailing Address: 1040 Fifth Ave, New York, NY 10028.

BOTHWELL, DORR
Painter, Printmaker
Preferred Media: Oils, Acrylics.
b San Francisco, Calif, May 3, 02.
Study & Training: Calif Sch Fine Arts, San Francisco; Rudolph Schaeffer Sch Design, San Francisco; Univ Oregon; Abraham Rosenberg fel for art study abroad, 49-51.
Work in Public Collections: Metrop Mus Art, New York, N Y; Whitney Mus Am Art, New York; Fogg Mus, Cambridge, Mass; Victoria & Albert Mus, London, Eng; Bibliotheque Nat, Paris, France.
Exhibitions: Pittsburgh Int, 52 & 58; Third Bienale, Sao Paulo, Brazil; Meltzer Gallery, New York, 58; one-man shows, De Young Mem Mus, San Francisco, 58 & 63; Bolles Gallery, San Francisco, 72.
Teaching: Instr design, Calif Sch Fine Arts, 44-48; instr design, Parsons Sch Design, New York, 52; instr design, Calif Sch Fine Arts, 53-58; instr design, San Francisco Art Inst, 59-61; instr, Mendocino Art Ctr, 61-; instr, Ansel Adams Photog Workshop, Yosemite Nat Park, Calif, 64-
Memberships: Mendocino Art Ctr, Calif.
Publications: Co-auth, Notan dark-light design, Van Nostrand Reinhold, 68.
Mailing Address: P O Box 27, Mendocino, CA 95460.

BOTKIN, HENRY
Painter, Writer
Preferred Media: Oils, Collage.
b Boston, Mass.
Study & Training: Mass Sch Art; Art Stud League New York.
Work in Public Collections: Metrop Mus Art, Mus Mod Art & Whitnew Mus Am Art, New York, N Y; Phillips Mem Gallery, Washington, D C; plus many others.
Exhibitions: One-man shows, Phillips Mem Gallery, 37, Art Club Chicago, 38, Riverside Mus, 61, Syracuse Univ, 71 & Frank Rehn Gallery, 72; 65 one-man shows plus many other group shows.
Positions: Art adv to leading collectors.
Awards: Four awards incl Nat Inst Arts & Lett grant, 65.
Memberships: Artists Equity Asn New York (pres, 51); Group 256, Provincetown, Mass (pres, 55-58); Am Abstr Artists (pres, 54-55); Fedn Mod Painters & Sculptors (pres, 57-61, 68-69); fel Int Asn Plastic Arts & Lett.
Dealer: Frank Rehn Gallery, 655 Madison Ave, New York, NY 10021.
Mailing Address: 56 W 11th St, New York, NY 10011.

BOTTO, RICHARD ALFRED
Painter, Educator
Preferred Media: Oil.
b Union City, N J, May 5, 31.
Study & Training: Pratt Inst, cert, 56, AS (appl sci), 58, with Walter Klett, Charles Mazoujian, Walter Murch, Stephen Peck & Edgar Whitney; Art Stud League New York, N Y & Woodstock, N Y, with Frank Reilly.
Exhibitions: Nat Acad Design, New York, 71; Allied Artists Am, New York, 72; Am Artists Prof League, New York, 72; Hudson Valley Art Asn, White Plains, N Y, 72; State Exhib, N J State Mus, Trenton, 72.
Teaching: Instr fine art, Frank Reilly Sch Art, New York, 64-68, pres, 67-68.
Positions: Chmn dept fine arts, Jersey City Mus, N J, 68-69.
Awards: Best-in-show medal, Jersey City Mus, 67; Gerald Lubeck Prize, Allied Artists Am, 71; gold medal, Grand Nat, Am Artists Prof League, 72.
Memberships: Allied Artists Am; Am Artists Prof League; Hudson Valley Art Asn; Painters & Sculptors Soc N J; Hudson Artists (pres, 66-68).
Mailing Address: 138 Union Pl, Ridgefield Park, NJ 07660.

BOUCHARD, LORNE HOLLAND
Painter, Illustrator
Preferred Media: Oils.
b Montreal, P Q, Mar 19, 13.
Study & Training: Drawing with W M Barnes; also with Prof Felix, Ecole Beaux-Arts, Montreal.
Work in Public Collections: Mus Fine Arts, Montreal; Quebec Prov Mus, P Q; Tom Thomson Mem Mus & Art Gallery, Owen Sound, Ont; also in pvt collections in Can, U S, England & Brazil.

Commissions: Numerous pvt commissions from advertising agencies for large paintings for bd rms of Can Iron, Nordair, Seagrams, Hewitt Equipment Co & others.
Exhibitions: First group show, 31, two-man show, 62, Montreal Mus; Royal Can Acad Arts Ann Exhib & Traveling Shows, 40-70; one-man shows, Continental Galleries, Montreal, 40-49, 52-55; eight one-man shows, Walter Klinkhoff Gallery, Montreal, 60-71; four-man show, Ont Mus Art, London, 62.
Awards: Award of merit, Advertising & Editorial Art Exhib, Art Directors Club, Montreal, 56; first prize, Montreal Hadassah Exhib, 59; hon mention, Price Fine Arts Award, Montreal, 70.
Bibliography: Magic of the mountains, 60 & The Mackenzie river-Mississippi of the north, 63, Week End Mag; Alex Mogelon (auth), Art profile: Lorne Bouchard, Montrealer Mag, 4/68; John Basset (producer), An artist's impression of the Arctic-Lorne Bouchard (film), Nat Can TV, 69.
Memberships: Academician Royal Can Acad Arts.
Publications: Illusr, Trapping is my life, 70.
Dealer: Walter Klinkhoff Gallery, 1200 Sherbrooke St W, Montreal, P Q, Can.
Mailing Address: 4070 Jauron St, Montreal 390, P Q, Can.

BOUGHTON, WILLIAM HARRISON
Painter, Educator
Preferred Media: Oil.
b Dubuque, Iowa, Feb 19, 15.
Study & Training: Univ Iowa, BA, 43; Univ Calif, Berkeley, MA, 45; James Phelan Fel (foreign travel & independent study), 45-47; with Earl Loran, Fletcher Martin, Grant Wood, Emil Ganso, Lester Longman, Worth Ryder, Stephen Peper, H W Janson & Shaefer-Simmern.
Work in Public Collections: New York City Schs; Luxury Liners, S S Constitution & S S Independence; Am Embassy, Paris, France; Libr Congress, Washington, D C; Fla State Univ Gallery.
Commissions: Mural, Student Union, Lamar Univ, 55 & sculpture, Quadrangle, 57.
Exhibitions: Serigraphies Americaines, Paris, 53; Dix Peintres Americaines, Paris, 54; L'aquarelles Contemporarines Aux Etats Unis, France, 55; Kunst Uit Amerika, Breda, Netherlands, 57; L'arte Grafica, Villa Giula, Rome, Italy, 57.
Teaching: Asst prof art, Fla State Univ, 47-54; head, art dept Lamar Univ, 54-70, prof art, 54-
Awards: Elected mem & silver medal, Int Acad Arts, Tommaso Campanella, Rome, 70.
Bibliography: F Dugas (auth), Texas professor has shown his work world wide, Facets, Tex Fine Arts Soc, 71.
Memberships: Nat Serigraph Soc; Col Art Asn; Am Color Print Soc; Beaumont Art Asn.
Publications: Auth, Maskoid and the silk screen, Art Mat Trade News, 50; Maskoid stencil technique, Fla Newspaper News & Radio Digest, 50.
Dealer: Meredith J Long Galleries, 2323 San Felipe Rd, Houston, TX 77019.
Mailing Address: 4625 Corkwood Lane, Beaumont, TX 77706.

BOULTON, JACK
Art Administrator
U S citizen.
Study & Training: Col Design, Archit & Art, Univ Cincinnati, BS, 67, MA, 70.
Collections Arranged: Kent State, traveling loan exhib, Kent State Univ & other univs in the U S, 71-
Teaching: Instr art & chmn dept, Hughes High Sch, Cincinnati, 68-70.
Positions: Display designer, H & S Pogue Co, 63-64; advert prod artist, Northlich Stolley, 65-66; assoc dir, Carl Solway Gallery, 70-72; dir, Contemp Arts Ctr, 72-
Mailing Address: Contemporary Arts Center, 115 E 5th St, Cincinnati, OH 45202.

BOULTON, JOSEPH L
Sculptor, Designer
b Fort Worth, Tex, May 26, 96.
Study & Training: Nat Acad Design; Art Stud League New York; Beaux-Arts Inst Design; apprentice to Herman A MacNeil.
Work in Public Collections: Fort Worth Mus Art; Southern Plains Indian Mus, Anadarko, Okla; New J State Mus, Trenton; Mus Fine Arts, Springfield, Mass; Detroit Art Inst Mus, Mich; plus many other public & pvt collections.
Commissions: Coins & medals for Med Soc, State of Pa, Am Acad Gen Practice, Pa, Franklin Mint, Polish-Am Asn & others; also many plaques & busts.
Exhibitions: Many shows, Hudson Valley Art Asn, 51-68; Nat Acad Design, New York, N Y, 53; Allied Artists Am; Arts & Crafts Asn, Meriden, Conn, 68 & 70; Silvermine Guild, New Canaan, Conn, 71; plus many others.

Awards: Anna Hyatt Huntington Award, Hudson Valley Art Asn, 54, 56 & 68; Arts & Crafts Asn Awards, 68 & 70; Olivetti Award, Silvermine Guild, 71; plus many others.
Memberships: Nat Sculpture Soc; Allied Artists Am; Painters & Sculpturers Soc N J; Acad Artists Asn; Royal Soc Arts; plus others.
Mailing Address: 43 Old Hill Rd, Westport, CT 06880.

BOUQUET, GUS
Painter, Sculptor
Preferred Media: Oils, Watercolors, Clay, Graphics.
b San Francisco, Calif, Feb 14, 15.
Study & Training: BSArch & MFA; art educ through apprenticeships.
Work in Public Collections: Kaiser Found, State Capitol Bldg, Sacramento, Calif; Am Automobile Asn, San Francisco.
Commissions: Sculptures, The Firefighter, Dept Forestry, Eaglerock, Calif, 63-64 & JFK, Boy Scouts Am, Vacaville, Calif, 64; decorative sculpture & design, Kern Co Fair, Bakersfield, 68.
Exhibitions: Brandeis Univ Alumni Show, San Francisco, 63-64; three one-man shows, Calif, 67; Kernville Art Festival, 67-68; CBS Art Festival, Bakersfield, 68; Wasco Art Festival, 71; plus others.
Teaching: Pvt instr, Bakersfield, Vallejo & San Francisco.
Positions: Parade dir, City of Bakersfield, 67-68; art dir, Fifth Agr Dist, State of Calif, 67-69; lectr-demonstr, TV Channels 17, 23 & 29.
Awards: Brandeis Univ Alumni Award, 63-64; CBS Festival Silver Medal, 68; Wasco Festival Award, 71.
Memberships: Soc Western Artists; Art Village (v pres, 67-68); Bakersfield Art Asn; Kernville Art Asn; Taft Art Asn; plus others.
Publications: Auth, The ceramic project book, 67.
Dealer: Beverly Shea, Box 112, Canyon, CA 94516.
Mailing Address: 510 Alameda, Vallejo, CA 94590.

BOURAS, HARRY D
Sculptor
Preferred Media: Steel, Concrete, Bronze.
b Rochester, N Y, Feb 13, 31.
Study & Training: Univ Rochester, BA, 51; Univ Chicago, 55-56.
Work in Public Collections: Mus Mod Art, New York, N Y; Art Inst Chicago, Ill; Mus Fine Arts, Rochester, N Y; Ishibashi Mus, Tokyo, Japan; Palais Beaux Artes, Brussels, Belg.
Exhibitions: Five shows, American Exhib, Art Inst Chicago, 58-72; Art of Assemblage, Mus Mod Art, New York, 66; Corcoran Ann, Washington, D C, 66 & 68; Beyond Illustration, Rotunda Bella Besana, Milan, Italy, Gemeentemuseum, Arnhem, Holland, Kunstverein, Munich, Ger, Mus Mod Art, Tokyo & others, 71-73
Teaching: Artist-in-residence, Univ Chicago, 62-64; artist-in-residence, Columbia Col, Chicago, 64-
Awards: Pauline Palmer Award, 62 & Logan Gold Medal for Sculpture, 65, Art Inst Chicago; Guggenheim Found fel, 71-72.
Bibliography: William Seitz (auth), Art of assemblage, Simon & Schuster, 66; M Kirby (auth), Happenings, Dutton, 69; Meilach & Selden (auth), Direct metal sculpture, Crown, 69; plus reviews in nat art mag.
Memberships: Cliff Dwellers; Arts Club Chicago.
Publications: Contribr, Prize-winning sculpture, Bk I, Allied Publ, 64; contribr, The arts and the public, Univ Chicago Press, 67; auth, Burlington diner (film), Film Group, 68.
Dealers: Noah Goldowsky, 1080 Madison Ave, New York, NY 10021; B C Holland, 260 Ontario St, Chicago, IL 60611.
Mailing Address: 850 Castlewood Terr, Chicago, IL 60640.

BOURGEOIS, LOUISE
Sculptor
Preferred Media: Wood, Latex, Plastic & Marble.
b Paris, France; U S citizen.
Study & Training: Lycee Fenelon, Paris, France, baccalaureate, 32; Sorbonne, 32-35; Ecole du Louvre, 36-37; Acadèmie des Beaux-Arts, 36-38; Acadèmie de la Grande Chaumiere, 37-38; Atelier Fernand Léger, 38.
Work in Public Collections: Mus Mod Art, New York, N Y; Whitney Mus Am Art, New York; New York Univ; Mus Rhode Island Sch Design, Providence; Harvard Univ, Cambridge, Mass.
Exhibitions: Les Etats-Unis, Sculpture du XX siecle, Musée Rodin, Paris, 65; The New American Painting and Sculpture, The First Generation, Mus Mod Art, 69; La Biennale de Carrara, Italy, 69; L'Art Vivant aux Etats Unis, Fondation Maeght, Vence, France, 69; American Sculpture, Univ Nebr, Lincoln, 70.
Teaching: Instr sculpture, Pratt Inst, 64-65; instr sculpture, Brooklyn Col, 63 & 68; field fac sculpture, Goddard Col, 71-
Bibliography: Daniel Robbins (auth), Sculpture by Louise Bourgeois, Art Int 10/64, William Rubin (auth), Some reflections on the work of Louise Bourgeois, 4/69, J P Marandel (auth), Louise Bourgeois, 12/71.
Mailing Address: 347 W 20 St, New York, NY 10011.

BOUSSARD, DANA
Sculptor
Preferred Media: Fabric.
b Salem, Ore, Feb 7, 44.
Study & Training: St Mary's Col; Art Inst Chicago; Univ Chicago; Univ Mont, BFA, MFA, 68.
Work in Public Collections: Am Mus Contemp Crafts, New York, N Y; Minneapolis Art Inst, Minn.
Commissions: Altar hanging banner, 70 & vestment, 71, Newman Ctr Church, Missoula, Mont; vestment, St Francis Church, Missoula, 71; portrait of Art Longpre family, Seattle, Wash, 71; portrait of Mr Evans, comn by family, Seattle, 72.
Exhibitions: Face Coverings, Mus Contemp Crafts, New York, 71; 10 New Talents, Friends of the Crafts, Seattle, 72; Deliberate Entanglements of UCLA, Portland, Ore, 72; Am Crafts Coun Northwest Exhib, New York, 72; Women in Art, Henry Gallery, Seattle, 72.
Teaching: Instr design, Univ Mont, 70-71; instr fabric, Factory Visual Arts Workshop, 71 & 72; instr fabric, Arts & Crafts Soc, Portland, 72.
Positions: Secy, Missoula Area Art Coun, 71-72.
Awards: C M Russell drawing award, 70.
Bibliography: Lee Snow (auth), Soft jewelry & body ornaments, Simon & Schuster, 73.
Memberships: Am Crafts Coun (mem at large); Friends of the Crafts, Seattle.
Research: Fabric sculpture.
Dealers: Fountain Gallery, 115 S W Fourth Ave, Portland, OR 97204; William Sawyer Gallery, 3043 Clay St, San Francisco, CA 94115.
Mailing Address: 141 S Third St W, Missoula, MT 59801.

BOWEN, HELEN EAKINS
Painter
Preferred Media: Oil, Polymer.
b Bluefield, W Va.
Study & Training: Univ Alaska; Art Stud League New York, N Y; Nat Acad Sch Fine Arts; with Raymond Huit, Paris; also with José de Creeft, Hugh Gumpel, Marshall Glasier & Vincent Malta.
Work in Public Collections: Finch Col Mus Art, New York; Crysler Mus, Norfolk, Va; Gibbes Art Gallery, Charleston, S C; Miami Mus Mod Art, Fla; George Thomas Hunter Gallery Art, Nashville, Tenn.
Exhibitions: Catherine Lorillard Wolfe Art Club, Inc, New York, 64; Am Artists Prof League, New York, 67; Nat Arts Club Gallery, New York, 68; one-artist show, Gibbes Art Gallery, 69; Allied Artists Am, Nat Acad Design Galleries, New York, 70.
Positions: Mem adv coun, sch visual & performing arts, Syracuse Univ, 71-
Awards: Mark Trafton Fowler fel, 63; Louis Jambor Mem Award, 64; James A Suydam Bronze Medal, 66.
Memberships: Life mem Art Stud League New York; Mus Mod Art, New York; Gibbes Art Gallery; Metrop Mus Art.
Dealer: Van der Straeten Gallery of Contemporary Artists, 981 Madison Ave, New York, NY 10021.
Mailing Address: 531 W 122nd St, New York, NY 10027.

BOWEN, WAYNE
Painter
Preferred Media: Oils, Graphics.
b Akron, Ohio.
Study & Training: With Sandra Chessman Turk & Harold Clay.
Exhibitions: Ogunquit Art Ctr 52nd Ann Nat Exhib, Maine, 72; New Rochelle Art Asn 58th Juried Exhib, N Y, 72; 4th W&J Col Nat Painting Show, Washington, Pa, 72; one-man show, Butler Libr, State Univ N Y Col Buffalo, 72; Assoc Art Orgn 1st Ann Juried Exhib, Buffalo, 72.
Awards: Cathalbe Prize, Ogunquit Art Ctr Nat Exhib, 72; Shiva Prize, New Rochelle Juried Exhib, 72.
Bibliography: D K Winebrenner (auth), Bowen paints incredible, Record-Courier Express, 10/5/69; Jessie Nazaret (auth), Interview with Wayne Bowen, Voice of the Alchemist, 6/71; Jean Reeves (auth), Evolution of a painter, Buffalo Evening News, 1/19/72.
Memberships: Towne Art Guild, Tonawanda, N Y (pres, 69-71); Guild Allied Artists (v pres, 71); Fine Arts League, Buffalo, N Y (juror of selection, 72); Chautauqua Art Asn; Springfield Art League, Mass.
Mailing Address: 194 Cleveland Ave, Buffalo, NY 14222.

BOWIE, WILLIAM
Sculptor
Preferred Media: Metal.
b Youngstown, Ohio, Feb 15, 26.
Study & Training: Youngstown Univ; Bethany Col.
Work in Public Collections: Skyline of New York, New York Bank Savings, N Y; Globe-Wernicke Showroom, New York; Hertz Skyctr Airport, Huntsville, Ala; Brown & Williamson Tobacco Corp, Louisville, Ky; Glass Container Div, Owens-Ill, Scarsdale, N Y.
Commissions: Exec off, Am Brands, Inc, New York; Brooklyn Col Stud Ctr; Honeywell, Inc, Framingham, Mass; Irving Trust Co, Caracas, Venezuela, Frankel Rare Book Room, Univ Houston Libr.
Exhibitions: Meltzer Gallery; George Jensen's; Am House; Sculpture Exhib, Butler Inst Am Art, 65; For Your Home, Krannert Art Mus, Univ Ill; Symposium 66, Purdue Univ, 66; plus many others.
Positions: Judge Sculpture Exhib, Butler Inst Am Art, 66.
Awards: Purchase award, Sculpture Exhib, Butler Inst Am Art, 65; good design award, Purdue Univ, 66; spec award outstanding merit in craftsmanship, Artist-Craftsmen New York.
Mailing Address: Sculpture Studio, 202 E 77th St, New York, NY 10021.

BOWMAN, DOROTHY (LOUISE)
Painter, Printmaker
b Hollywood, Calif, Jan 20, 27.
Study & Training: Chouinard Art Inst, with Rico Lebrun & Jean Charlot; Jepson Art Inst, Los Angeles, Calif; Otis Co Art Inst, Los Angeles.
Work in Public Collections: Brooklyn Mus; Mus Mod Art; Libr Cong; Los Angeles Co Mus Art; De Cordova & Dana Mus.
Commissions: Ed serigraphs, Int Graphics Art Soc, New York, 58-69; Hilton Hotel, New York, 62; panels of stained glass, Methodist Church, San Luis Obispo, 67; paintings, St Andrew's Priory, Volyermo, Calif, 72.
Exhibitions: Brooklyn Mus Nat Print Show, N Y, 54-62; Boston Mus Print Ann, 60; Mus Arte Mod, São Paulo, Brasil, 61; 50 Am Printmakers, Am Fedn Arts Traveling Show, Japan & Moscow, 64; Manila Hilton Art Ctr, Phillipines, 71.
Awards: Many awards, Brooklyn Mus Print Shows, Libr Cong Nat Print Shows & Boston Mus Shows, 54-71.
Bibliography: Enciclopedia internazionale degli artisti, 70; Bruce Cody (auth), American printmaking since 1940.
Memberships: Western Serigraphic Soc.
Dealer: Oscar Salzer, P O Box 36523, Los Angeles, CA 90036.
Mailing Address: Big Sur, CA 93920.

BOWMAN, JEAN (JEAN BOWMAN MAGRUDER)
Painter, Illustrator
Preferred Media: Oils.
b Mount Vernon, N Y, Sept 27, 17.
Study & Training: Grand Cent Art Sch, with Jerry Farnsworth; Nat Acad Design, with Leon Kroll; also with Scott Carbee, Boston, Mass.
Work in Public Collections: Mus of Racing, Saratoga Springs, N Y; plus over 350 paintings in pvt collections.
Commissions: Horse & equestrian portraits, including landscape & archit for Paul Mellon, Richard K Mellon, HM Queen Elizabeth II, Robert Kleberg, Walter Chrysler & Walter Jeffords.
Exhibitions: Knoedler Gallery, New York, N Y; Horse Painters of the World, Tryon Gallery, London, Eng, 69; one-man shows, Vose Galleries, Boston, Mass, 40, Scott & Fowles, New York, 52, Grand Cent Galleries, New York, 53 & Ackermann's, London, 68.
Memberships: Grand Cent Galleries; Soc Animal Artists; Portraits Inc.
Publications: Illusr, Maryland Horse, 40-45; illusr, British Race Horse, 54; illusr, Know about horses, 60; illusr, Spur of Virginia, 70-72; illusr, Chronicle of the Horse.
Dealer: Ackermann Gallery, 3 Old Bond St, London, Eng.
Mailing Address: Bonnycastle Studio, Middleburg, VA 22117.

BOWMAN, KEN
Painter
Preferred Media: Acrylic Polymer, Collage.
b Denver, Colo, Mar 28, 37.
Study & Training: Univ Colo; Art Inst Chicago, BFA, 63.
Work in Public Collections: Utah Mus Fine Arts, Salt Lake City; Univ Art Mus, Berkeley, Calif.
Exhibitions: One-man exhibs, Tibor de Nagy Gallery, Inc, New York, N Y, 70 & 72; Art on Paper, Weatherspoon Gallery, Univ N C, 71; Third Biennial Art, Medellin, Colombia, S Am, 72; Painting and Sculpture Today 1972, Indianapolis Mus Art, Ind, 72.
Mailing Address: c/o Tibor de Nagy Gallery, Inc, 29 W 57th St, New York, NY 10019.

BOWMAN, RICHARD
Painter.
b Rockford, Ill, Mar 15, 18.
Study & Training: Art Inst Chicago, 38-42; Univ Iowa, MFA, 49.
Work in Public Collections: San Francisco Mus Art; Oakland Mus; Stanford Univ; Univ Tex Mus; Santa Barbara Art Mus; plus others.

Exhibitions: Retrospectives, Stanford Univ, 56 & San Francisco Mus Art, 61; Whitney Mus Am Art, 62; Carnegie Int, 61 & 63; Rockford Art Asn 50 California Artists, 65, selected for Am Fedn Arts circulating exhib, 66-68; one-man show, San Francisco Mus Art, 70 & retrospective (1943-1972), Roswell Mus & Art Ctr, N Mex, 72; plus others.
Teaching: Instr, N Park Col, 44-46; instr, Chicago Art Inst Sch, 44-47; instr, State Univ Iowa, 47-49; instr, Stanford Univ, 49-50 & 57, 58 & 63; instr, Univ Man, 50-54.
Awards: Prizes, Montreal, 52 & Winnipeg Art Gallery, 53; hon mention, Oakland Art Mus, 55; artist-in-residence grant painting, Roswell Mus & Art Ctr, 72; plus others.
Mailing Address: 178 Springdale Way, Redwood City, CA 94062.

BOWMAN, RUTH
Educator, Art Administrator
b Denver, Colo, June 14, 23.
Study & Training: Bryn Mawr Col, BA; New York Univ Inst Fine Arts, MA; Columbia Univ Sch Archit.
Collections Arranged: Exhibs at New York Univ to tour with Am Fedn Arts incl One Hundred Years of Impressionism, Wildenstein Gallery, 70, The New York Painter, A Century of Teaching: From Morse to Hofmann, Marlborough-Gerson Gallery, 67, A University Collects, 65-68 & Twentieth Century Painting and Sculpture from the New York University Art Collection, Hudson River Mus, 71.
Teaching: Adj asst prof art hist, Sch Continuing Educ, New York Univ, 65-, adj asst prof art hist, Sch Educ, 70-, lectr art, Washington Sq Col, 72- (Sunrise Semester-CBS); also many free lance courses & lects on mod art; radio & TV weekly-WNYC.
Positions: Coordr, Forms from Israel exhib, circulated by Am Fedn Arts, 58-60; res dir, World House Galleries, 61-62; asst cur, Jewish Mus, 62-63; cur, New York Univ Art Collect, 63-; mem nat exhibs comt, Am Fedn Arts, 63-; consult educ prog, Guggenheim Mus, 69-.
Memberships: New York City Cult Coun (chmn, visual arts comt, 71-); D A L T Proj, Bank St Col Educ (adv comt, 71-).
Publications: Auth, catalog introd, The thirtieth anniversary exhibition, American Abstract Artists, 66; auth, Double exposure (catalog), Am Fedn Arts, 69; co-auth, Development and handling of school and university art collections, Col Art Asn, 72; auth & ed, exhib catalogs, mag articles & teaching aids for New York Univ Art Collection & various educ & cult orgn.
Mailing Address: 200 E 66th St, New York, NY 10021.

BOWRON, EDGAR PETERS
Art Administrator, Art Historian
b Birmingham, Ala, May 27, 43.
Study & Training: Colgate Univ, AB, 65; Univ Pa, 65-66; Inst Fine Arts, N Y Univ, AM; Ford Found mus training fel, 66-69; Metrop Mus Art, Ford Found fel, 68-69, cert mus training, 69.
Collections Arranged: Cur-in-charge, J Paul Getty Collection Exhib, Minneapolis Inst Arts, Minn, 72.
Teaching: Educ lectr, Metrop Mus Art, 69-70.
Positions: Registr, Minneapolis Inst Arts, 70-
Memberships: Col Art Asn Am; Am Eighteenth Century Soc.
Research: Italian painting, sixteenth to eighteenth centuries; French painting, seventeenth and eighteenth centuries.
Publications: Auth, Scarsellino's nymphs at the bath, 70 & Vasari's Portrait of six Italian poets, 71-73, Minneapolis Inst Arts Bull; co-auth, The J Paul Getty collection, Minneapolis, 72.
Mailing Address: 201 E 24th St, Minneapolis, MN 55404.

BOXER, STANLEY (ROBERT)
Sculptor, Painter
b New York, N Y, June 26, 26.
Study & Training: Brooklyn Col; Art Stud League New York.
Work in Public Collections: Whitney Mus Am Art, New York; Chase Manhattan Bank, New York; Santa Barbara Mus, Calif; Mus Mod Art, New York; Newark Mus, N J.
Commissions: Sculptures, white marble, Mr & Mrs Stuart Caplin, Redding, Conn, 70; white marble, Mr & Mrs Sam Dorsky, Great Neck, N Y, 71; marble & wood, Sy Wittlin, Briarcliff Manor, N Y, 71; marble & wood, Milton Goldman, Fort Lauderdale, Fla, 71; black marble, Mr & Mrs Gene Gorman, New York, 72.
Exhibitions: One-man exhibs, painting, Tibor de Nagy Gallery, New York, 72, sculpture, 72 & drawing, Santa Barbara Mus, Calif, 72; paintings, Houston Mus Art, Tex, 72; sculptures, Minneapolis Mus Art, Minn, 72.
Bibliography: John Cauman (auth), article, In: Art Int, 72; Hilton Kramer (auth) & Grace Glueck (auth), articles, In: New York Times, 72.
Dealer: Tibor de Nagy Gallery, 29 W 57th St, New York, NY 10019.
Mailing Address: 167 Crosby St, New York, NY 10012.

BOYCE, GERALD G
Educator, Painter
Preferred Media: Mixed Media.
b Embarrass, Wis, Dec 29, 25.
Study & Training: Wis State Col, BS; Milwaukee Art Inst; American Guatemalan Inst, Guatemala City; Univ Iowa, MFA.
Work in Public Collections: Ball State Univ; DePauw Univ; Earlham Col; Evansville Col; St John's Univ.
Exhibitions: Los Angeles Co Mus; San Francisco Mus Art; Art Inst Chicago, 54; Mus Mod Art, New York, N Y, 56; Corcoran Gallery Art, Washington, D C, 71.
Teaching: Prof art hist & studio, Indiana Cent Col, 50-; lectr art hist, DePauw Univ, 68-
Positions: Consult, Ind Bell Tel Co, 67-70; consult, U S Post Off Dept, 72.
Awards: First prizes, Indiana Artist Club, St John's Univ Nat & Minot Col Show, 71.
Memberships: Nat Col Art Conf; Am Crafts Coun (secy, N Cent Regional, 62-66).
Mailing Address: R R 1, Box 239A, Morgantown, IN 46160.

BOYCE, RICHARD
Sculptor, Lecturer
Preferred Media: Stone, Bronze.
b New York, N Y, June 11, 20.
Study & Training: Mus Fine Arts Sch, Boston, Mass, William Paige grant, 49, Bartlett grant, 56.
Work in Public Collections: Whitney Mus Am Art, New York; Joseph H Hirshhorn Found; Mus Art, R I; Addison Gallery Am Art, Andover, Mass; Harvard Univ, Cambridge, Mass.
Commissions: Andromeda Fountain, Dr & Mrs Morton Grossman, Los Angeles, Calif, 64.
Exhibitions: Univ Ill, 55 & 67; Art Inst Chicago, 60; Pa Acad Fine Arts, Philadelphia, 64; The New Vein, European traveling exhib of Smithsonian Inst, 68-69; The Partial Figure in Art, Baltimore Mus Art, 70
Teaching: Asst prof painting, Wellesley Col, 53-62; lectr design, Boston Univ, 59-61; lectr sculpture, Univ Calif, Los Angeles, 62-
Dealer: Silvan Simone Gallery, 11579 Olympic Blvd, Los Angeles, CA 90064.
Mailing Address: 1419 W Washington Blvd, Venice, CA 90291.

BOYCE, WILLIAM G
Art Administrator, Educator
b Fairmont, Minn, July 25, 21.
Study & Training: Univ Minn, Minneapolis, BS, 49, MEd, 52; Mills Col, 54-55.
Collections Arranged: Cataloged the George P Tweed Memorial Art Collection; Dedicatory Exhibition Honoring Mrs Alice Tweed Tuohy; Tweed at Twenty Exhibition; A University Collects-Tweed Gallery, Traveling Exhibition; David Ericson Exhibition plus many others.
Teaching: Prof art & head dept, Univ Minn, Duluth, 70-
Positions: Ed cur, Tweed Gallery, Univ Minn, Duluth, 57-65, assoc dir, 65-69, dir, Tweed Mus Art, Univ Minn, Duluth, 69-
Memberships: Life mem Nat Educ Asn; Minn Art Educ Asn (pres, 63-65); Midwest Mus Conf (v pres for Minn, 67-70); Am Asn Mus; Am Asn Univ Prof.
Publications: Auth, David Erickson (monogr), Edgewater Press, 63; also many catalogs.
Mailing Address: 2700 Minnesota Ave, Duluth, MN 55802.

BOYD, DONALD EDGAR
Sculptor, Educator
Preferred Media: Fiberglass, Fabrics, Bronze, Wood.
b Sparta, Ohio, Feb 20, 34.
Study & Training: Ohio State Univ, BFA(cum laude), 56; Harvard Univ, with Mirko Basadella, MAT, 61; Univ Iowa, MFA, 66; with Elliot Offner & Robert Laurent; Hobart Welding Sch, with Richard Stankiewicz, 68.
Work in Public Collections: Dayton Art Inst, Ohio.
Exhibitions: Boston Arts Festival, Mass, 62 & 64; Ninth Midwest Biennial, Joslyn Art Mus, Omaha, Nebr, 66; First Ann Nat Slide Competition, Univ Buffalo, N Y, 69; Blossom Music Ctr Sculpture Invitational, Kent, Ohio, 71.
Teaching: Asst prof sculpture & drawing, Kenyon Col, 66-72.
Awards: Boit prize for graphics, Boston Mus Sch Eve Div, 61; first prize, First Ann Nat Slide Competition, Univ Buffalo, 69; purchase prize for sculpture, Dayton Art Inst, 69.
Bibliography: R Stevens (auth), Donald Boyd, La Rev Mod, 1/63.
Memberships: Col Art Asn; Am Asn Univ Prof.
Dealer: Ross Widen Galleries, 11308 S Euclid Ave, Cleveland, OH 44121.
Mailing Address: 18209 Glen Rd, Gambier, OH 43022.

BOYD, E
Art Administrator, Writer
b Philadelphia, Pa, Sept 23, 03.
Study & Training: Pa Acad Fine Arts.
Commissions: Renderings of regional folk art, Index Am Design; restoration & preservation interior paintings, regional colonial churches; conserv altar-pieces, missions, Laguna Pueblo, N Mex, Ranchos de Taos & San Miguel, Santa Fe; plus others.
Collections Arranged: Religious Art of the Western World, Dallas Mus Fine Arts, 58; Popular Arts of Colonial New Mexico, 59 & Santeros of New Mexico, 69, Mus Int Folk Art, Santa Fe, N Mex.
Teaching: Lectr N Mex arts & crafts.
Positions: Registr, Los Angeles Mus Art, 49-51; cur, Span Colonial Dept, Mus N Mex, Santa Fe, 51-69, cur emer, 70-
Memberships: Int Inst Conserv Mus Objects; Span Colonial Art Soc; N Mex Archaeol Soc.
Publications: Auth, Saints and saintmakers, 46, sect on N Mex Span colonial art, In: The concise encyclopedia of American antiques, 58 & Popular arts of colonial New Mexico, 69; auth, Popular arts of Spanish New Mexico (in press); contribr, Arts & Archit, Antiques & other publ.
Mailing Address: International Folk Art Museum, Museum of New Mexico, P O Box 2087, Santa Fe, NM 87501.

BOYD, JAMES HENDERSON
Printmaker, Sculptor
b Ottawa, Ont, Dec 16, 28.
Study & Training: Art Stud League New York, with Wil Barnet; Nat Acad Design; Contemporaries Graphic Workshop, with M Ponce de Léon.
Work in Public Collections: Nat Gallery Can, Ottawa; Mus Mod Art, New York, N Y; Victoria & Albert Mus, London, Ont; Lugano Art Mus; Sorsbie Art Gallery, Nairobi, S Africa.
Commissions: Carved doors, Centennial Libr, Campbellton, N B, 67 & 72; carved doors, Pub Serv Alliance Bldg, Ottawa, 69; entrance sculpture, Can Pavilion, Osaka World's Fair, 70.
Exhibitions: Cincinnati Biennial of Prints, 62; First Biennial of Prints, Santiago, Chile, 63; Eighth Int Black & White Exhib, 64; Tokyo Invitational Biennial of Prints, 64; Centennial Art Exhib, Toronto, 67.
Teaching: Resident artist, Univ Western Ont, 67-69; prof printmaking, Ont Col Art, 71-, head dept, 70-71; prof painting, Munic Art Ctr, Ottawa, 70-72.
Positions: Hon cur, Univ Western Ont, 67-69.
Awards: Purchase award, Eighth Int Black & White Exhib, 64; first prize, First Nat Print Exhib, Burnaby, B C; Venezuela Prize, best foreign artist, Second Biennial of Prints, Santiago, Chile, 65.
Memberships: Fel & life mem Int Inst Arts & Lett; Can Graphic Art Soc.
Dealer: Isaacs Gallery, Yonge St, Toronto, Ont, Can.
Mailing Address: P O Box 2400, Station D, Ottawa, Ont K1P 5W5, Can.

BOYER, JACK K
Museum Director, Curator
b Van Houten, N Mex, Sept 2, 11.
Positions: Dir & cur, Kit Carson Home & Mus, Taos, N Mex, 54-
Memberships: Am Asn Mus; Archaeol Soc N Mex; N Mex State Hist Soc; Clearing House Western Mus.
Publications: Contribr, newspapers & other publ.
Mailing Address: Kit Carson Home & Museum, Kit Carson St, Taos, NM 87571.

BOYER, MRS RICHARD C
Collector, Patron
b New York, N Y, Mar 5, 17.
Study & Training: Barnard Col, BA.
Collection: Louisiana artists.
Mailing Address: 6237 Jefferson Hwy, Baton Rouge, LA 70806.

BOYLE, KEITH
Painter, Educator
b Defiance, Ohio, Feb 15, 30.
Study & Training: Ringling Sch Art, Sarasota, Fla; Univ Iowa, BFA.
Work in Public Collections: State of Iowa, Des Moines; San Francisco Mus Art, Calif; Stanford Univ Mus, Calif; Mead Paper Corp, Atlanta, Ga; Pa State Univ, Altoona.
Exhibitions: Current Bay Area Art, Stanford Univ Mus, 64; The Colorists, San Francisco Mus Art, 65; Drawings by 100 American Artists, Ann Arbor, Mich, 65; A Century of California Painting, 1870-1970, 70; Looking Westward, Joslyn Art Mus, Omaha, Nebr, 70.
Teaching: Assoc prof painting & drawing, Stanford Univ, 62-
Dealer: Smith-Andersen Gallery, Homer St, Palo Alto, CA 94303.
Mailing Address: 515 Newell Rd, Palo Alto, CA 94303.

BOYLE, RICHARD J
Art Administrator, Art Historian
b New York, N Y, June 3, 32.
Study & Training: Adelphi Univ, BA; Oxford Univ, with Edgar Wind & John Pope-Hennessy; Art Stud League New York, with Will Barnet.
Collections Arranged: John Trachtman Retrospective, 66, Laser Light: A New Visual Art, 69, The Early Work of Paul Gauguin, 71 & Robert S Duncanson: A Centennial Exhibition, 72, Cincinnati Art Mus; American Paintings from Newport, Wichita Art Mus, 69.
Positions: Cur, Int Art Found, Newport, R I, summer 62; dir, Middletown Fine Arts Ctr, Ohio, 63-65; cur painting, Cincinnati Art Mus, 65-
Memberships: Nat Trust Hist Preservation.
Research: Late nineteenth and twentieth century painting, especially late nineteenth century American painting.
Publications: Co-auth, Rediscovery: Thomas Cole's voyage of life, Art in Am, 67; auth, From Hiram Powers to laser light, Apollo, 71; contribr, French impressionists influence American impressionists, Lowe Art Mus, Fla, 71; contribr, Genius of American painting, Weidenfeld & Nicolson, 73; auth, American impressionism (in prep).
Mailing Address: Cincinnati Art Museum, Eden Park, Cincinnati, OH 45202.

BOYNTON, JAMES W
Painter, Printmaker
Preferred Media: Graphics
b Fort Worth, Tex, Jan 12, 28.
Study & Training: Tex Christian Univ, BFA & MFA.
Work in Public Collections: Dallas Mus Fine Arts; Mus Fine Arts, Houston; Witte Mem Mus; Tex Fine Arts Asn; Fort Worth Art Ctr; plus others.
Exhibitions: San Francisco Mus Art, 52, 62 & 69; Mus Mod Art, 56, 62 & 69; Whitney Mus Am Art, 57, 58 & 67-68; Tex Pavillion, HemisFair, San Antonio, 68; Los Angeles Mus Art, 69; plus others.
Teaching: Instr, Univ Houston, 55 & 57; instr, San Francisco Art Inst, 60 & 62; instr, Univ N Mex, summer 63; instr, Houston Mus Sch, 68-69; instr, Northwood Inst, Dallas, 68-69; instr, Univ St Thomas, Tex, 69-70.
Awards: Awards, Beaumont Art Mus & Oklahoma City Art Ctr, 68; Tamarind Workshop fel, 67; plus others.
Bibliography: Douglas MacAgy (auth), James Boynton (monogr), Barone Gallery Inc, 59.
Dealer: Atelier Chapman Gallery, 2526 Fairmont St, Dallas, TX 75201.
Mailing Address: 3723 Albans St, Houston, TX 77005.

BOZ, ALEX (ALEX BOZICKOVIC)
Painter, Lecturer
Preferred Media: Casein, Oils.
b Sarajevo, Yugoslavia, July 8, 19; U S citizen.
Study & Training: Univ Belgrade, BFA, 43; Belgrade Acad Fine Arts, 43-50; Belgrade, 48-50.
Work in Public Collections: Contemp Mus Art, Rijeka, Yugoslavia; Contemp Mus Art, Novisad, Yugoslavia; City of Bremen, W Ger; Bell Tel Co, Chicago, Ill; City Hosp, Bremen.
Commissions: Murals, Zopas Corp, Rome, Italy, 53 & City Planning Comn, Bremen, W Ger, 55.
Exhibitions: One-man shows, Los Angeles, Milwaukee, Chicago, New York, Toronto & Europe, 52-72; Kunsthall Exhib, Bremen, 55; Gallery Boheme, Copenhagen, Denmark, 55; Old Orchard Festival, Chicago, Ill, 59-67; Art Inst Chicago, 60.
Teaching: Prof art, Rijeka, Yugoslavia, 50-52; instr painting & printmaking, Americana Art Ctr, Northfield, Ill, 65-68.
Awards: Awards from Gallery Boheme, Copenhagen 55 & Old Orchard Festival, Chicago, 66.
Mailing Address: Americana Galleries, 271 Waukegan Rd, Northfield, IL 60093.

BRACH, PAUL H
Painter, Educator
Preferred Media: Oils.
b New York, N Y, Mar 13, 24.
Study & Training: State Univ Iowa, BFA, 48, MFA, 49.
Work in Public Collections: Mus Mod Art, New York; Whitney Mus Am Art, New York; Los Angeles Co Mus, Calif; St Louis Mus, Mo; New York Publ Libr.
Exhibitions: One-man shows, Leo Castelli Gallery, New York, 57 & 59; Cordier-Ekstrom Gallery, 62 & 64 & Kornblee Gallery, 68; plus many other group and one-man shows.
Teaching: Instr art, Univ Mo, 49-51; prof art, Univ Calif, San Diego, 66-68; dean art, Calif Inst Arts, 68-
Dealer: Kornblee Gallery, 58 E 79th St, New York, NY 10021.
Mailing Address: 642 Moreno Ave, Los Angeles, CA 90049.

BRACKETT, TRUMAN H, JR
Art Administrator, Educator
b Boston, Mass, Oct 18, 33.
Study & Training: Dartmouth Col, AB; Univ Pa, MA.
Teaching: Lectr art hist, Philadelphia Col Art, 61-62; lectr art hist, 64-72, adj assoc prof art hist, 72-
Positions: Asst dir, Hopkins Ctr Art Galleries, Dartmouth Col, 62-65, dir, 65-
Mailing Address: R F D, Orford, NH 03777.

BRACKMAN, ROBERT
Painter, Educator
b Odessa, Russia, Sept 25, 98.
Study & Training: Francisco Ferrer Sch; Nat Acad Design; also with George Bellows & Robert Henri.
Work in Public Collections: Metrop Mus Art, New York, N Y; Whitney Mus Am Art, New York; Colonial Williamsburg; West Point Acad Collection; plus 35 other art mus in the U S.
Commissions: Portraits of Gen Charles Lindbergh, Mr & Mrs John D Rockefeller, Jr, Hon Herbert H Lehman, John Foster Dulles, Gen Nathan F Twining & many others.
Exhibitions: Nat Acad Design, New York; Audubon Artists, New York; Allied Artists Am, New York; Pa Acad Fine Arts, Philadelphia; Art Inst Chicago, Ill; plus many others
Teaching: Instr art, Art Stud League New York, 34-
Awards: N Grumbacher Purchase Prize, Audubon Artists Exhib, 60; Adolph & Clara Obrig Prize, 135th Ann Exhib, Nat Acad Design, 60; Andrew Carnegie Prize, 65 & gold medal of honor, 66, Nat Acad Design; also many other awards.
Bibliography: Peyton Boswell (auth), Modern American Painter; Homer St Gaudens (auth), Art and Artist.
Memberships: Royal Soc Arts, London, Eng; Nat Acad Design; Am Watercolor Soc; Audubon Artists; Int Soc Arts & Lett; plus many others.
Mailing Address: Noank, CT 06340.

BRADFORD, HOWARD
Serigrapher, Painter
b Toronto, Ont, July 14, 19; U S citizen.
Study & Training: Chouinard Art Inst, Los Angeles, Calif; Jepson Art Institute, Los Angeles; Calif Sch Fine Arts, San Francisco.
Work in Public Collections: Philadelphia Mus Fine Arts, Pa; Boston Mus Fine Arts, Mass; Bibliotheque Nat France; Los Angeles Co Mus; New York Pub Libr, N Y.
Commissions: Print editions(100), Dallas Mus Fine Arts, Tex, 53, Hilton Hotel, New York, 64 & Assoc Am Artists, New York, 67-69.
Exhibitions: Libr Cong Nat Print & Drawing Exhib, 51; Brooklyn Mus Print Ann, 52; Dallas Mus Fine Arts Nat Print Exhib, 53; 60 American Printmakers via U S Info Serv in Europe, 56; Carmel Art Asn, Calif, 72.
Positions: Dir, Serigraphs Ltd Gallery, Monterey, Calif, 69-
Awards: Birds by Beach (serigraph), Libr Cong, 51 & Dallas Mus Fine Arts, 53; award for serigraph, Philadelphia Mus Art, 59.
Memberships: Am Color Print Soc; Western Serigraph Inst, Los Angeles; Carmel Art Asn (bd dirs, 72-, treas, 72-73).
Dealer: Oscar Salzer, 448 N Detroit St, Los Angeles, CA 90036.
Mailing Address: 417 Cannery Row, Monterey, CA 93940.

BRADLEY, MRS HARRY LYNDE
Collector
Collection: Contemporary art.
Mailing Address: 136 W Greenfield Ave, Milwaukee, WI 53204.

BRADLEY, IDA FLORENCE
Painter, Instructor
Preferred Media: Watercolor.
b Johnstown, Pa, Oct 24, 08.
Study & Training: Puzzletown Art Sch, with Lee Atkyns; Art League Ligonier Valley, with Lucile Banks & Ralph Reynolds, Ind.
Work in Public Collections: Watercolor, Govt Bldg; painting, Penelec Elec Co; First Methodist Church; painting, Pitt Col.
Commissions: Three oils, Bethlehem Steel Corp, Johnstown, 58.
Exhibitions: Allied Artists Johnstown, 40-; Am Artists Prof League, New York, N Y, 72; Johnstown Area Arts Coun, 72; Arts Assocs, Johnstown, 72.
Teaching: Instr painting, private sch, 45-
Awards: Best of show, Allied Artists Johnstown, 53, best watercolor prize, 59; best of show, St Vincent Col, 71.
Memberships: Allied Artists Johnstown (mem bd dir, 60-70); Am Artists Prof League; Johnstown Area Arts Coun; Arts Assocs.
Mailing Address: 2139 Pitt Ave, Johnstown, PA 15905.

BRADLEY, PETER ALEXANDER
Painter, Art Dealer
Preferred Media: Acrylics.
b Connellsville, Pa, Sept 15, 40.
Study & Training: Cranbrook Acad Art, Bloomfield, Mich, 63; Soc Arts & Crafts, Detroit, Mich; Yale Univ.

Work in Public Collections: Drawing, Mus Mod Art, New York, N Y; engraving, Metrop Mus Art, New York.
Commissions: Sculpture, de Menil Found, Houston, Tex, 71.
Exhibitions: American Print Makers, U S Info Agency, circulated in U S S R, 66; Some American History, Rice Univ, Houston, 71; The Deluxe Show, Houston, 71; Toward Color and Field, Mus Fine Arts, Houston, 71; one-man show, Andre Emmerich, New York, 72.
Positions: Art dealer, Perls Gallery, New York, 64-; guest cur, The Deluxe Show, 71.
Bibliography: Simone Swan (auth), The deluxe show (catalogue), De Menil Publ, 71; E A Carean (auth), Toward color and field, Mus Fine Arts, 71; John Canady (auth), Peter Bradley, New York Times, 6/3/72.
Specialty of Gallery: Twentieth century modern masters; French paintings.
Dealer: Andre Emmerich, 41 E 57th St, New York, NY 10022.
Mailing Address: 654 Broadway, New York, NY 10012.

BRADSHAW, GLENN RAYMOND
Painter, Educator
Preferred Media: Watercolors, Collage.
b Peoria, Ill, Mar 3, 22.
Study & Training: Ill State Univ, BS, 47; Univ Ill, MFA, 50.
Work in Public Collections: Butler Inst Am Art, Youngstown, Ohio; Springfield Art Mus, Mo; Pasadena Mus, Calif; El Paso Mus, Tex; Ill State Mus, Springfield.
Exhibitions: Am Watercolor Soc Exhib, Royal Watercolor Soc, London, Eng, 62; 200 Years of Watercolor Painting in America, Metrop Mus Art, New York, N Y, 66-67; A View of Contemporary Watercolor, Cleveland Inst Art, Ohio, 68; Watermedia '70, Univ Colo, Boulder, 70; Illinois Painters II, Ill Arts Coun Invitational Touring Exhib, 71-72.
Teaching: Prof art, Univ Ill, 52-
Awards: Grand purchase prize, Watercolor U S A 2nd Ann, Springfield Art Mus, 63; Am Artist Medal, Am Watercolor Soc Ann, 64; Best of Show, Calif Water Color Soc Mem Show, 65.
Bibliography: L Mouat (auth), On the importance of being midwestern, Christian Sci Monitor, 10/21/67; N Kent (auth), 100 watercolor techniques, Watson-Guptill, 68; E Reep (auth), The content of watercolor, Rheinhold Van Nostrand, 69.
Memberships: Am Watercolor Soc; Calif Nat Water Color Soc; Nat Soc Painters in Casein.
Publications: Contribr, Illustrators 10, 68; auth, Are juried exhibitions worth saving, 2/69 & Jackson's prairie, 5/69, Am Artist; contribr, Illustrators 13, 71 & Illustrators 14, 72.
Dealer: The Bonfoey Co, 1710 Euclid Ave, Cleveland, OH 44115.
Mailing Address: 906 Sunnycrest St, Urbana, IL 61801.

BRADSHAW, ROBERT GEORGE
Painter, Educator
b Trenton, N J, Mar 13, 15.
Study & Training: Princeton Univ, AB; Columbia Univ, MA.
Exhibitions: N J State Mus; Am Watercolor Soc; Boston Mus Fine Art; Cape Ann Soc Mod Art; New York World's Fair, 65; plus others.
Teaching: Lectr art appreciation & hist; prof art, Douglass Col, Rutgers Univ, New Brunswick, 46-, actg chmn dept art, 64-65.
Awards: Hons art & archaeol, Princeton Univ, 37; prize, N J Watercolor Soc, 59 & Montclair Art Mus, N J, 63.
Memberships: Col Art Asn Am; N J Watercolor Soc; Hunterdon Co Art Ctr.
Mailing Address: 48 Hilltop Blvd, East Brunswick, NJ 08816.

BRADY, CHARLES MICHAEL
Painter
Preferred Media: Oil.
b New York, N Y, July 27, 26.
Study & Training: Art Stud League New York, 48-51, with John Groth & Morris Kantor.
Work in Public Collections: Three works in Irish Arts Coun Col, Dublin.
Exhibitions: Am Painting, 1950, Metrop Mus Art, New York, 50; Living Art, Dublin, 59-71; Royal Hibernian Acad, Dublin, 65; Pa Acad Fine Arts, Philadelphia, 67; Harrison S Morrison Exhib, Newport, R I, 68.
Teaching: Artist-Instr graphics, dept archit, Col Technol, Dublin, 70-71.
Awards: Player-Wills Third Prize, 66.
Memberships: Life mem Art Stud League New York; United Arts Club (hon chmn artist group, 71), Dublin.
Dealer: Babcock Galleries, 805 Madison Ave, New York, NY 10021.
Mailing Address: 1 Royal Terr W, Dún Laoghaire, Ireland.

BRAINARD, OWEN
Painter, Educator
Preferred Media: Acrylics.
b Kingston, N Y, June 9, 24.
Study & Training: Columbia Univ, 46, with Dong Kingman; Syracuse Univ, BFA, 48, with Stephen Peck; State Univ N Y Albany, 51; Syracuse Univ, MFA, 52, with Fred Haucke.
Work in Public Collections: Iowa Art Educ Asn; Fort Collection Am Art; Chicago Pub Libr; Univ Ryukyus, Okinawa; Mich State Univ. and in pvt collections.
Commissions: Mosaic wall mural, Everett High Sch, Lansing, Mich, 59.
Exhibitions: Walker Art Ctr Biennial, Minneapolis, Minn, 53; Regional Art Today, Joslyn Mus, Omaha, Nebr, 57; Art: U S A, Madison Sq Garden, N Y, 58; 16th Nat Print Exhib, Libr Cong, 58; 3rd Nat Print Exhib, New Canaan, Conn, 60; plus many others.
Teaching: Asst prof design & painting, Drake Univ, 52-57; prof painting & serigraphy, Mich State Univ, 57-
Positions: Free-lance designer & illusr, Lincoln-Mercury Times Mag, Iowa Children's Home Soc, Mich State Univ Publ & others, 49-
Awards: Iowa Artists Ann Award, 55; Western Mich Ann Award, Friends of Art, 60; Midland Art Asn Ann Award, 62.
Memberships: Col Art Asn.
Dealer: 420 Gallery, Union St, Traverse City, MI 49684.
Mailing Address: 850 Tarleton Ave, East Lansing, MI 48823.

BRAITSTEIN, MARCEL
Sculptor, Educator
Preferred Media: Welded Steel, Bronze, Stainless Steel.
b Charleroi, Belg, July 11, 35; Can citizen.
Study & Training: Ecole Beaux-Arts Montréal, dipl; Inst Allende, San Miguel Allende, Mex.
Work in Public Collections: Montreal Mus Fine Arts, P Q; Art Gallery Ont, Toronto; Winnipeg Art Gallery, Man; Confederation Ctr, P E I.
Commissions: Sunscreen, comn by Architect L Lapierre, Firemen's Bank, Montreal, 65; monument to Rt Hon A Meighen, comn by Dept Pub Works, Can Govt, 69.
Exhibitions: Quebec Prov Competition, Quebec, P Q, 59; Spring Show, Montreal Mus Fine Arts, 61; Vermont U S A, Bundy Art Gallery, 66; Panorama of Quebec Sculpture, Mus Rodin, Paris, France, 70; First Int Biennial of Small Sculpture, Budapest, Hungary, 71.
Teaching: Instr advan sculpture, Montreal Mus Fine Arts, 63-65; prof sculpture, Ecole Beaux-Arts Montreal, 65-69; prof sculpture, Univ Quebec, Montreal, 69-
Awards: Sculpture prizes, Quebec Govt, 59 & Montreal Mus Fine Arts, 61.
Bibliography: Guy Robert (auth), Marcel Braitstein (rev), Vie des Arts, Montreal, 62; E H Turner (auth), Sculpture in Canada, Can Art, 62; Jean Simard (auth), Marcel Braitstein, sculpteur (monogr), Quebec Sculptors Asn, 69.
Memberships: Quebec Sculptors Asn (v pres, 69-71); assoc Royal Can Acad Arts.
Mailing Address: 1061 Richelieu Blvd N, St Hilaire, P Q, Can.

BRAMS, JOAN
Painter, Sculptor
Preferred Media: Acrylics.
b Montreal, P Q, Mar 30, 28; U S citizen.
Study & Training: Ont Col Art.
Exhibitions: Fort Lauderdale Mus Arts, Fla; Columbia Mus Art, S C; Birmingham Mus Art, Ala; John Herron Mus Art, Indianapolis, Ind; plus others.
Dealers: Contemporary Gallery, 2800 Routh St, Dallas, TX 75201; Gallery 99, 1135 Kane Concourse, Miami, FL 33154.
Mailing Address: 324 Eden Rd, Palm Beach, FL 33480.

BRANDON, WARREN EUGENE
Painter, Writer
Preferred Media: Oils, Acrylics.
b San Francisco, Calif, Nov 2, 16.
Study & Training: Milligan Col; also with Raymond Brose, Jack Feldman, Jack Davis & Eliot O'Hara.
Work in Public Collections: Am Collection, Didrichsen Art Found, Helsinki, Finland; eight paintings, Kaiser Ctr, Oakland, Calif; Milligan Col, Tenn.
Commissions: Mural, Cochran Bldg, Seattle, Wash.
Exhibitions: Nat Art Roundup, Las Vegas, Nev, 60-64; Calif State Fair, 62-69 incl one-man show, 63; Knickerbocker Nat Ann, New York, 64; M H De Young Mem Mus, San Francisco; San Francisco Mus Art Nat Ann; plus many other group & one-man shows.
Teaching: Pvt classes, San Francisco, Calif & Hawaii, twice a yr; summer teaching tours in Can, Seattle, Wash, Reno, Nev, Carmel, Calif & abroad.

Positions: Judge & juror, Calif State Fair, three yrs.
Awards: First prize in oils, West Coast Painters Ann, Seattle, Southwestern Painters Ann, Tucson, Ariz & San Francisco Mus Art Ann; plus many others.
Bibliography: Margaret Harold (auth), Prize-winning Oil Paintings, Bk II.
Memberships: Art Guild Am; Southwest Artists; fel Royal Soc Art, London; Artists' Coop San Francisco; Marin Soc Artists (chmn art counc, bd dirs); plus others.
Publications: Auth, Six paintings in search of an artist, 61.
Dealers: Artists' Cooperative Gallery, 2224 Union St, San Francisco, CA 94123; Friedlander Gallery, 95 Yesler Way, Seattle, Wash 98104.
Mailing Address: 2441 Balboa St, San Francisco, CA 94121.

BRANDT, FREDERICK ROBERT
Painter, Museum Exhibition Director
Preferred Media: Acrylics.
b Paterson, N J, June 7, 36.
Study & Training: Pa State Univ, BA, 60, MA, 63.
Work in Public Collections: Chrysler Mus Norfolk, Va; Va Polytech Inst & State Univ, Blacksburg, Va; Richmond Humanities Ctr, Va; St Mary's Hosp, Richmond; Retreat for the Sick, Richmond.
Commissions: Slide-tape pub permanent presentations for Agecroft Hall, Richmond, 69 & Stratford Hall, Va, 72.
Exhibitions: 27th Juried Exhib, Gallery Contemp Art, Winston-Salem, 68; 9th Dixie Ann, Montgomery Mus Fine Arts, Ala, 68; Piedmont Ann, Mint Mus, Charlotte, N C, 68; 20th Irene Leache Biennial Exhib, Chrysler Mus Norfolk, 70; Virginia Artists 1971, Va Mus Fine Arts, Richmond, 71.
Collections Arranged: Homer and the Sea, 64; The World of Shakespeare, 65; Greek Gold, 66; William Hogarth, 67; Architectural Drawing in Virginia, 69; Church Silver of Colonial Virginia, 70; American Painting 1970, Art Nouveau, 71; Francisco Goya: Portraits in Paintings, Prints and Drawings, 72.
Positions: Interpretation asst, gallery div, Va Mus Fine Arts, 60-61; teaching asst, Pa State Univ, 61-63; asst progs dir, Va Mus Fine Arts, 63-
Awards: Juror's spec mention for prints, 9th Dixie Ann, Montgomery Mus Fine Arts, 68; purchase award, 20th Irene Leache Biennial Exhib, 68; cert of distinction, Va Artists 1971, Va Mus Fine Arts, 71.
Memberships: Am Asn Mus; James River Mus Conf.
Publications: Contribr, Art nouveau (catalog), 71; contribr, Francisco Goya: portraits in paintings, prints and drawings (catalog), 72; auth, var articles in antique periodicals, 71-72.
Dealer: Eric Schindler Gallery, 2305 E Broad St, Richmond, VA 23223.
Mailing Address: 3207 Monument Ave, Richmond, VA 23221.

BRANDT, GRACE BORGENICHT, see BORGENICHT, GRACE.

BRANDT, REXFORD ELSON
Painter, Writer
Preferred Media: Watercolors.
b San Diego, Calif, Sept 12, 14.
Study & Training: Univ Calif, Berkeley, AB(art), 36; Stanford Univ, 38.
Work in Public Collections: San Diego Fine Arts Gallery, Calif; San Francisco Mus Art, Calif; Currier Gallery Am Art, Andover, N H; Nat Acad Design Galleries, New York, N Y; Crocker Gallery Art, Sacramento, Calif; Los Angeles Co Mus Art, Calif.
Commissions: Metropolitan Aqueduct, portfolio for Fortune Mag, 37; scraffiti tile murals (with William O. Payne), Corona del Mar State Beach Park, 65; San Diego County, Calif, portfolio for Copley Found, La Jolla, Calif, 68; carved wall relief (with John Svenson), Irvine Coast Country Club, 68; murals, Southern Calif First Nat Bank, Newport, 69.
Exhibitions: Int Watercolor Exhib, Chicago Art Inst, 36 & 37; Nat Gallery Art, Washington, D C, 41; Royal Soc Painters in Watercolour, London, Eng, 62; Am Watercolor Soc Ann, 71; Nat Acad Design Ann, 72; plus many others.
Teaching: Dir of Brandt Painting Workshops, Corona del Mar, Calif, also in Europe & Mexico, 46-
Awards: First prize, Calif Watercolor Soc, 38 & 70; Samuel F B Morse Medal, Nat Acad Design Ann, 68 & 70; bronze medal, Am Watercolor Soc, 70.
Bibliography: Norman Kent (auth), Seascapes & landscapes, Am Artist, 56; Ernest Watson (auth), Composition in landscape & still life, Watson-Guptill, 59; Cynthia Lindsay (auth), The natives are restless, New Am Libr, 60.
Memberships: Calif Watercolor Soc (pres, 48-49); Am Watercolor Soc (v pres, 66-70); assoc Nat Acad Design; plus many regional soc.
Publications: Auth, Watercolor landscape, 63, The artists' sketchbook and its uses, 66, San Diego, land of the sundown sea, 69 & The winning ways of watercolor, 72; co-auth, Rex Brandt, 72.

Dealer: Challis Gallery, 1370 S Coast Blvd, Laguna Beach, CA 92652.
Mailing Address: 405 Goldenrod, Corona del Mar, CA 92625.

BRANDT, WARREN
Painter
Preferred Media: Oils.
b Greensboro, N C, 18.
Study & Training: Pratt Inst, 35-38; Washington Univ, BFA(hons); with Philip Guston & Max Beckmann; John J Milliken traveling fel; Univ N C, Greensboro, MFA.
Work in Public Collections: Chase Manhattan Bank; Chrysler Mus; Nat Collection Fine Arts, Smithsonian Inst; James Michener Collection; plus many other public & pvt collections.
Exhibitions: Metrop Mus Watercolor Exhib; Am Fedn Arts; Whitney Mus Am Art; Artists by Artists, 67 & Drawings of the Sixties, 69, New Sch Social Res; one-man retrospective, Allentown Art Mus, 69; plus many other group and one-man shows.
Teaching: Head art dept, Salem Col, 49-50; instr art, Pratt Inst, 50-51; instr art, Guilford Col, Greensboro, 52-54; chmn dept art, Univ Miss, 57-59; Southern Ill Univ, 59-61; dir, New York Studio Sch, 67.
Bibliography: Kenneth Sawyer (auth), Notes on the painter, Warren Brandt, Art Int, 66; Herman Cherry (auth), Brandt, the mystery of the commonplace, Art News, 68; Jay Jacobs (auth), The French touch, Art Gallery, 72.
Publications: Auth, Painting with oils, Van Nostrand Reinhold, 71.
Dealer: A M Sachs Gallery, 29 W 57th St, New York, NY 10022.

BRANNER, ROBERT
Art Historian
b New York, N Y, Jan 13, 27.
Study & Training: Yale Univ, BA, 48, PhD, 53.
Teaching: Prof art hist & archaeol, Columbia Univ, 57-
Awards: Alice Davis Hitchcock Book Award, Soc Archit Historians, 63.
Memberships: Soc Nat Antiq France; Soc Française Archeol; Mediaeval Acad Am; Col Art Asn; Soc Archit Historians.
Research: Mediaeval art and architecture.
Publications: Auth, Burgundian Gothic architecture, 60; auth, Gothic architecture, 61; auth, La Cathedrale de Bourges, 62; auth, Saint Louis and the court style in Gothic architecture, 65; auth, Chartres Cathedral, 69.
Mailing Address: Dept of Art History, Columbia University, New York, NY 10027.

BRANSOM, (JOHN) PAUL
Painter, Illustrator
b Washington, D C, July 26, 85.
Exhibitions: Retrospective exhib, Woodmere Art Gallery, Chestnut Hill, Philadelphia, Pa, 63.
Memberships: Am Watercolor Soc New York; Salmagundi Club; Soc Animal Artists; Am Artists Prof League.
Publications: Illusr, Call of the wild, spec ed, 12, Wind in the willows, 13 & An argosy of fables, 21; illus, Wilderness champion: the story of a great hound, 44, Wolf king, 49 & Phantom deer, 54, Lippincott; illusr, Wilderness champion, G&D, 70; also illusr over 40 bks.
Mailing Address: 15 W 67th St, New York, NY 10023.

BRAUNER, ERLING BERNHARDT
Painter, Educator
Preferred Media: Oils.
b Ithaca, N Y, Apr 16, 06.
Study & Training: Cornell Univ, BFA & MFA.
Work in Public Collections: Denison Univ Libr, Granville, Ohio.
Exhibitions: Flint Art Inst, 50 & 52; Detroit Art Inst, 53 & 56; South Bend Art Asn, 54 & 60; Ohio State Univ, 56; Grand Rapids Art Inst, 56.
Teaching: Instr art, Mich State Univ, 35-40, asst prof, 40-42, assoc prof, 42-58; prof, 58-71, chmn art dept, 62-71, prof & chmn emer, 71-
Memberships: Mich State Coun for Arts (exec comt, 66-69, chmn visual arts comt, 66-69).
Mailing Address: 2527 Arrowhead Rd, P O Box 119, Okemos, MI 48864.

BRAZEAU, WENDELL (PHILLIPS)
Painter
b Spokane, Wash, May 19, 10.
Study & Training: Univ Wash, BFA, 33, MFA, 47; Calif Sch Fine Arts, 32; Archipenko Art Sch, 48.
Work in Public Collections: Seattle Art Mus, Wash; Henry Gallery, Seattle; Marylhurst Col, Ore.
Exhibitions: Northwest Ann, Northwest Printmakers & Northwest Watercolor Shows, Seattle, 45-; Denver Ann, Colo, 51; Gov Invitational, Olympia, Wash & Japan, 67.

Teaching: Prof design Univ Wash Sch Art, 45-
Awards: Several purchase awards, Northwest Ann, Seattle Art Mus.
Mailing Address: 2631 29th St W, Seattle, WA 98199.

BRCIN, JOHN DAVID
Sculptor
b Gracac, Yugoslavia, Aug 15, 99.
Study & Training: Valparaiso Univ, BFA, 17; Art Inst Chicago, Bryan Lathrop European traveling fel, 20, cert merit, 22; Ohio State Univ, MA, 30; Art Inst Chicago, 46.
Work in Public Collections: Univ Ill, Champaign; Roosevelt Univ, Chicago; Pioneer Mus Art, Stockton, Calif; Evansville Mus Arts, Ind; various pub sch collections.
Commissions: Portrait bust of Judge Elbert H Gary, Gary Com Club; Mem Tablet to Newton, Mann, First Unitarian Church, Omaha, Nebr; Rudolph Hering Medal, Am Soc Chem Engrs; Cyrus Hall McCormick Monument, Washington & Lee Univ; Gov Henry Horner Monument, Grant Park, Chicago; plus many others.
Exhibitions: Nat Acad Design, New York, N Y; Pa Acad Fine Arts, Philadelphia; Art Inst Chicago; Detroit Inst Arts, Mich; Mus Fine Arts, Houston, Tex; plus others.
Teaching: Instr modeling & drawing, Minneapolis Sch Art, 22-23; head sculpture dept, Layton Sch Art, Milwaukee, 23-24; instr modeling, Rockford Col, Ill, 34-36.
Awards: Hickox prize, 36; Catherine Barker Spaulding Prize, Hoosier Salon; Munic Art League Portrait Prize, 45; plus others.
Memberships: Nat Sculpture Soc.
Publications: Auth, The sculpture of John David Brcin, 67.
Mailing Address: 4 E Ohio St, Chicago, IL 60611.

BREASTED, JAMES HENRY, JR
Art Historian, Lecturer
b Chicago, Ill, Sept 29, 08.
Study & Training: Princeton Univ, AB; Heidelberg Univ; Queen's Col, Oxford Univ; Univ Chicago, MA; Inst Advanced Study, Princeton.
Teaching: Instr art & archaeol, Colo Col, 37-39; asst prof art hist, Univ Calif, Los Angeles, 41-46; lectr & master art hist, Kent Sch, 52-70; chmn dept art & art hist, 52-70.
Positions: Dir, Los Angeles Co Mus, 46-51; chmn bd dirs, The Barnstormers, Inc, Tamworth Summer Theatre, N H, 67-
Awards: Officier de l'Académie, Fr Govt, 49.
Memberships: Archaeol Inst Am; Col Art Asn Am; Egypt Explor Soc; Soc Archit Historians; Soc Italic Handwriting.
Research: Art historical and archaeological scholarship in the chief periods, cultures and areas; synthesizing new information and new insights into illustrated lectures.
Publications: Auth, Arab nationalism in the Near East, in Africa, the Near East and the war, Univ Calif Press, 43; auth, Egyptian servant statues, Vol XIII, In: Bollingen Series, Bollingen Found, 48.
Mailing Address: Mt Mexico Farm, Tamworth, N H 03886.

BRECHER, SAMUEL
Painter, Educator
Preferred Media: Oils.
b Boryslaw, Austria, July 4, 97.
Study & Training: Cooper Union; Nat Acad Design; spec study with Charles W Hawthorne Provincetown, Mass & New York, N Y.
Work in Public Collections: Metrop Mus Art, New York; Walker Art Ctr, Minneapolis, Minn; Newark Mus Art, N J; Fla Southern Col, Lakeland; Tel Aviv Mus & Ein Harod Mus, Israel.
Exhibitions: American Art Today, New York World's Fair, 39; Directions in American Painting, Carnegie Inst, Pittsburgh, Pa, 41; Sawdust and Spangles, San Francisco Mus Art, Calif, 42; 4th Biennial Exhib Contemp Am Paintings, Va Mus Fine Arts, Richmond, 44; 23rd Biennial Exhib, Corcoran Gallery Art, Washington, D C, 53.
Teaching: Instr painting, Newark Sch Fine & Indust Art, 46-
Awards: First prize in oil painting, Salmagundi Club, 50; prize in oil painting, 14th Ann Audubon Exhib, 56; first prize, 8th Ann Exhib Nat Soc Casein Painters, 62.
Bibliography: Charles Z Offin (auth), Cape Cod on canvas, Pictures on Exhib, 1/42; Zelda Ormont (auth), Samuel Brecher, artist, Caravan, 11/46; Howard Devree (auth), Portrait of Staten Island, New York Times Mag, 1/13/57.
Memberships: Audubon Artists; Allied Artists; Nat Soc Casein Painters; N J Painters & Sculptors Soc.
Dealer: Winston Gallery, 1350 16th St, Fort Lee, NJ 07024.
Mailing Address: 124 W 23rd St, New York, NY 10011.

BRECKENRIDGE, JAMES D
Art Historian
b New York, N Y, Aug 8, 26.
Study & Training: Cornell Univ, BA; Princeton Univ, MFA & PhD.

Teaching: Lectr art hist, Johns Hopkins Univ, 57-59; vis prof art hist, Univ Pittsburgh, 60-61; prof art hist, Northwestern Univ, 61-, chmn dept, 64-

Positions: Cur, Corcoran Gallery Art, 52-55; cur, Baltimore Mus Art, 55-60.

Awards: Res fel, Am Coun Learned Socs, 59-60; sr fel, Nat Endowment for Humanities, 70-71.

Memberships: Int Ctr Medieval Art (dir, 72-); Col Art Asn Am (dir, 67-71); fel Royal Soc Arts; fel Am Numis Soc.

Research: History of portraiture.

Publications: Auth, Likeness: a conceptual history of ancient portraiture, 69.

Mailing Address: Dept of Art History, Northwestern University, Evanston, IL 60201.

BREED, CHARLES AYARS
Sculptor, Educator

Preferred Media: Plastics.

b Paw Paw, Mich, Jan 31, 27.

Study & Training: Western Mich Univ, BS; Univ Wis, MA.

Work in Public Collections: Midland Ctr Arts, Mich.

Commissions: 12 Stations of the Cross, Indian River Cath Church, 55; Cross (glass & brass), Mem Presby Church, Midland, Mich, 57; window panels (plastic), William Dixon Home, Midland, 60; Eternal Flame (plexiglass), Temple Beth El, Spring Valley, N Y, 66; Icon Screen (polyester), Hellenic Orthodox Church, Bloomfield Hills, Mich, 68.

Exhibitions: Craftsman U S A 66, 66 & Plastic as Plastic Nat Invitational, 68, Mus Contemp Crafts, New York, N Y; Made of Plastic Nat Invitational, Flint Inst Art, Mich, 68; Exhib 70, Columbus Art Gallery, Ohio, 70; First Biennial Int Small Sculpture Exhib, Budapest, Hungary, 71.

Teaching: Dir art, Nat Music Acad, 58-62; assoc prof art & chmn dept, Delta Col, 62-

Positions: Bd dirs, Awareness Inc, Lansing, Mich, 62-64; bd dirs, Midland Art Coun, Mich, 65-68; bd dirs, Midland Ctr Arts, 67-72; mem, Coun Arts, Lansing, 71-72.

Awards: Res fel, Dow Found, 61; nat merit award, Mus Contemp Crafts, New York, 66; Outstanding Teacher Yr, Bergstein Found, 67.

Bibliography: Jack Brickhouse (auth), Everything is double in Paw Paw, produced by Paramount Films, 48; Curtis Bessinger (auth), Where does the design of a house begin?, House Beautiful, 1/62; John Krafft (auth), Plastic as plastic, Detroit News Sunday Mag, 66.

Memberships: Life mem Nat Educ Asn; Mich Art Educ (treas, 55, pres, 56); Am Craftsmen Coun; Mich Coun Arts.

Publications: Auth, Plastic a new art form, House Beautiful, 2/62; co-auth, Plastic-the visual arts in crafts, Crafts & Craftsmen, 67.

Dealer: Lee Nordness Galleries, 236 E 75th St, New York, NY 10021.

Mailing Address: 4202 Sherwood Ct, Midland, MI 48640.

BREER, ROBERT C
Sculptor, Film Maker

b Detroit, Mich, Sept 30, 26.

Study & Training: Stanford Univ, BA.

Work in Public Collections: Mus Mod Art, New York, N Y; Mod Mus, Stockholm, Sweden; Anthology Film Archives, New York; Mod Art Mus, Krefeld, Ger; Cinematheque Française, Paris, France.

Commissions: Design for Pavilion, Expo '70, Japan, Pepsi-Cola Co, 70.

Exhibitions: New York & London Film Festivals, 64-71; Salon des Galeries Pilotes, Lausanne, Switz, 66; The Machine as Seen at the End of the Mechanical Age, Mus Mod Art, New York, 68; Plans and Projects as Art, Kuntshalle, Berne, Switz, 70; Kinetics-Arts Coun of Great Britain, Hayward Gallery, London, Eng, 70.

Teaching: Vis instr kinetics, Cooper Union, 71-

Positions: Mem bd dirs, Filmmakers Coop, New York, 67-72.

Awards: Creative Film Found Award, 59; Oberhausen Film Festival Award, Femme, 69.

Bibliography: Noel Burch (auth), The films of Robert Breer, Film Quart, 59; Adrienne Mancia & William Van Dyke (auth), 4 artists as film makers, Art in Am, 1/67; Calvin Tompkins (auth), Onwards and upwards with the arts, New Yorker, 10/70.

Art Interests: Film and kinetic sculpture.

Mailing Address: Ludlow Lane, Palisades, NY 10964.

BREESKIN, ADELYN DOHME
Art Administrator

b Baltimore, Md, July 19, 96.

Study & Training: Bryn Mawr Col; Radcliffe Col; Sch Fine Arts, Boston; Goucher Col, hon LittD, 53; Washington Col, hon DFA, 61, Wheaton Col, 63, Hood Col, 66, Morgan State Col, 66.

Teaching: Instr art, McCoy Col, Johns Hopkins Univ, 37-50; lect, U S & abroad; also radio & TV appearances; Am specialist lect tour of Orient, State Dept, 64-65.

Positions: Cur prints & drawings, Baltimore Mus Art, 30-, gen cur, 38, actg dir, 42, dir, 47-62; art consult & cur contemporary art, Nat Col Fine Arts, Smithsonian Inst, 66-

Awards: Star of Solidarity for promoting intercultural betterment, Italian Govt, 54.

Memberships: Am Asn Mus Dirs (secy-treas, 53-56, pres, 56-57); Print Coun Am (secy); Int Graphic Arts Soc (selection jury, 55-64); Am Fedn Arts (trustee, 60-).

Mailing Address: Rm 256, National Collection of Fine Arts, Smithsonian Institution, Washington, DC 20560.

BREIGER, ELAINE
Painter, Printmaker

Preferred Media: Acrylics, Oil.

b Springfield, Mass.

Study & Training: Art Stud League New York; Cooper Union, cert fine arts; spec master printing with Krishna Reddy.

Work in Public Collections: Lessing Rosenwald Collection, Jenkintown, Pa; New York Pub Libr, N Y; State Univ N Y Col Potsdam; Univ Nev, Reno; New York Univ.

Commissions: Print of etching & acrylic painting for Great Ideas of Western Men series, Container Corp Am, 70.

Exhibitions: Boston Printmakers, Boston Mus Fine Arts, Mass, 69; 17th Nat Print Exhib, Brooklyn Mus, N Y, 70; 4th Am Biennial of Engraving, Santiago, Chile, 70; State Univ N Y Col Potsdam, 72; Nat Print & Drawing Exhib, Okla Art Ctr, Okla City, 72.

Teaching: Instr techniques etching & intaglio printing, 92nd St YMHA-YWHA, New York, 71-, chmn dept art, 72-

Positions: Mgr Printmaking Workshop, 68-70.

Dealers: Associated American Artists, 663 Fifth Ave, New York, NY 10022; Alonzo Gallery, 26 E 63rd St, New York, NY 10021; Pace Gallery, 32 E 57th St, New York, NY 10022.

Mailing Address: 155 E 91st St, New York, NY 10028.

BREININ, RAYMOND
Painter, Sculptor

b Vitebsk, Russia, Nov 30, 10.

Study & Training: Chicago Acad Fine Arts, with Uri Penn.

Work in Public Collections: Metrop Mus Art; Mus Mod Art; Brooklyn Mus; Art Inst Chicago; Phillips Collection, Washington, D C; plus others.

Commissions: Costumes & settings, Ballet Theatre's Undertow; murals, Winnetka High Sch, Ill, State Hosp, Elgin, Ill, U S Post Off, Wilmette, Ill & Pump Rm, Ambassador E Hotel, Chicago, Ill; plus others.

Teaching: Artist-in-residence, Univ Southern Ill; instr art, Univ Minn; instr, Breinin Sch Art, Chicago, Ill; instr painting & drawing, Art Stud League New York, N Y; instr, Nat Acad Design, New York.

Awards: Prizes, Art, U S A, 58, Art Inst Chicago (seven) & Pa Acad Fine Arts (two); plus others.

Bibliography: Rosamond Frost (auth), included in: Contemporary art: the march of art from Cezanne until now, Crown, 42; Dorothy C Miller (ed), included in: Americans 1942. 18 artists from 9 states (catalogue), Mus Mod Art, 42; Emily Genauer (auth), included in: Best of art, Doubleday, 48; plus others.

Memberships: Nat Acad Design.

Mailing Address: 121 Inwood Rd, Scarsdale, NY 10583.

BREITENBACH, EDGAR
Art Historian

b Hamburg, Ger, June 26, 03.

Study & Training: Univ Munich, 21-22; Univ Hamburg, 22-27, PhD, 27; Univ Berlin, libr dipl, 29.

Teaching: Vis lectr, Mills Col, 42-43.

Positions: Res assoc, Fine Arts Ctr, Colorado Springs, 45-55; monuments officer; adv to high comnr for Ger on fine arts; Libr Cong rep to Berlin; chief, Prints & Photographs Div, Libr Cong.

Memberships: Col Art Asn Am; Spec Libr Asn.

Publications: Auth, Speculum Humanae Salvationis, Strassburg, 30; auth, Santos, the religious folk art of New Mexico, 43.

Mailing Address: Reference Dept, Prints & Photographs Div, Library of Congress, Washington, DC 20540.

BREITENBACH, WILLIAM JOHN
Sculptor, Draughtsman

Preferred Media: Cast Aluminum, Polyester Resin; India Ink

b Milwaukee, Wis, Jan 21, 36.

Study & Training: Univ Wis-Milwaukee, BS, 62, MS, 65; Stephen F Austin State Univ, MFA, 71.

Work in Public Collections: Brentwood Col, N Y; Del Mar Col, Corpus Christi, Tex; Stephen F Austin State Univ, Nacogdoches, Tex.

Commissions: Sculptural fountain, William Robert Murfin, Houston, Tex, 72.

Exhibitions: 49th Regional Exhib, R S Barnell Art Ctr, Shreveport, La, 72; 5th Ann Del Mar Col Drawing & Small Sculpture Show, 71; Creative Collab, Rice Univ, Houston, Tex, 72; 9th Monroe Ann, Masur Mus Art, Monroe, La, 72; Southwest Graphics Invitational, Mexican-Am Cultural Exchange Inst, San Antonio, Tex, 72.
Teaching: Supvr elementary art, South Door Co Sch Dist 1, Brussels, Wis, 62-65; asst prof art educ & drawing, Sam Houston State Univ, 65-
Awards: 1st prize in sculpture, 5th Ann Exhib, Del Mar Col, 71; merit award for creative collab, Rice Univ, 71.
Memberships: Tex Art Educ Asn; Tex Asn Schs Art.
Publications: Auth, Art education and the modern age, Tex trends in art education, 68.
Dealer: Henkle Galleries, 6405 Richmond Ave, Houston, TX 77029.
Mailing Address: Box 2023, Sam Houston State University, Huntsville, TX 77340.

BREITHAUPT, ERWIN M
Educator, Art Historian
b Columbus, Ohio, Nov 12, 20.
Study & Training: Miami Univ, BFA; Ohio State Univ, MA & PhD; Oak Ridge Inst Nuclear Studies.
Exhibitions: Design of the Future, Mus Mod Art, New York, N Y, 54 & Merchandise Mart, Chicago, Ill, 55.
Collections Arranged: F L Wright Centennial Exhib, 66.
Teaching: Assoc prof art hist & design, Univ Ga, 47-62; prof art & chmn dept art hist & design, Ripon Col, 62-
Awards: Gen Educ Bd fel, Rockefeller Found, 51; Severy Award, 65 & Uhrig Award, 69, Ripon Col.
Memberships: Col Art Asn.
Research: Area of the art institution and creativity.
Publications: Auth, A new approach to art education, 56; auth, The basic art course at Georgia, 57; co-auth, An institutional approach to aesthetics, 59; contrib, The creative life of man, 70.
Mailing Address: Dept. of Art, Ripon College, Ripon, WI 54971.

BRENDEL, BETTINA
Painter, Lecturer
b Luneburg, Ger; U S citizen.
Study & Training: Kunstschule Schmilimsky, Hamburg 41-42; Landes Hochschule Bildende Künste, Hamburg, 45-47 with Erich Hartmann; Univ Southern Calif, 55-58.
Work in Public Collections: San Francisco Mus Art, Pasadena Art Mus, Long Beach Mus Art & La Jolla Art Mus, Calif.
Exhibitions: Los Angeles Co Mus Art Ann, 55, 57, 59 & 61; Pasadena Art Mus, 55, 57, 58 & 62; Strutture e Stile, Stadtische Gallerie, Bochum, Ger & Galleria Moderna, Torino, Italy, 62; 58th Ann, San Francisco Mus Art, 66; On Mass and Energy, Santa Barbara Mus Art, 66; also 11 one-man shows.
Teaching: Instr, The Emergence of Mod Painting, Univ Calif, Los Angeles, 58-61.
Awards: Award, La Jolla Art Mus, 58 & 59; Long Beach Mus Art, 60; first purchase award, San Francisco Mus Art, 66.
Bibliography: Michel Tapié (auth), Musee manifeste, Fratelli Pozzo Editori, Torino, 62; Constance Perkins (auth), article in Art Forum, 4/62; H Von Breton (auth), article in Santa Barbara News Press, 2/66.
Memberships: Col Art Asn Am; Am Fedn Arts; Mus Mod Art, New York; Solomon R Guggenheim Mus.
Research: Theoretical physics and its relation to the arts.
Publications: Auth, The painter and the new physics, Art J, fall 71.
Mailing Address: 1061 N Kenter Ave, Los Angeles, CA 90049.

BRENDEL, OTTO J
Art Historian
b Nuremberg, Ger, Oct 10, 01; U S citizen.
Study & Training: Univ Heidelberg, PhD, 28.
Teaching: Prof art hist & archaeol, Columbia Univ, 56-69.
Memberships: Fel Am Acad in Rome; life mem Ger Archaeol Inst.
Research: Art, especially painting and sculpture: Greek, Etruscan, Roman, classical survivals in later art including contemporary.
Publications: Contribr, bks & periodicals, U S & abroad, 24-
Mailing Address: 315 Riverside Dr, New York, NY 10025.

BRENNAN, FRANCIS EDWIN
Collector, Writer
b Maywood, Ill, July 14, 10.
Study & Training: Univ Wis; Art Inst Chicago.
Positions: Secy, Am Fedn Arts; design consult, Washington Post Co & Newsweek Mag; picture ed, Life picture hist World War II; art adv to ed-in-chief, Time Inc.
Awards: Order Mérite Commercial, France, 50; Legion Hon, France, 60.
Mailing Address: 40 E 62nd St, New York, NY 10021.

BRENNAN, HAROLD JAMES
Designer, Craftsman
b Indianapolis, Ind, Oct 25, 03.
Study & Training: Carnegie Inst, BA & MA; Harvard Univ; Univ Paris.
Exhibitions: Assoc Artists Pittsburgh.
Teaching: Prof art, Westminster Col, 33-46, chmn div arts, 46-48; lectr, Asn Am Cols Arts Prog, 34-53; dir, Sch Am Craftsmen, Alfred Univ, 48-50; dir, Sch Am Craftsmen, Rochester Inst Technol, 50-54, chmn div arts, 53-56, dean, Col Fine & Appl Arts, 59-70, emer dean, 70-
Awards: Scholar, Inst Int Educ, Univ Paris, 38; Grogan Prize, Assoc Artists Pittsburgh, 38.
Memberships: Am Indust Art Asn (comt art educ); Midwest Designer-Craftsmen.
Publications: Contribr, Craft Horizons, Handweaver & Craftsman, Am Indust Art Asn J & others.
Mailing Address: 920 Lake Rd, Webster, NY 14580.

BRENNER, MABEL
Painter
Preferred Media: Oil, Casein, Tempera, Acrylic.
b New York, N Y, Mar 27, 06.
Study & Training: With Fred Patrone, Fla; Boston Univ with Vincent Ferrini & Sydney Hurwitz; also with Victor Candell, New York & Provincetown.
Work in Public Collections: Goddard Mem Hosp; Chaim Gross Collection; North Easton Savings Bank.
Exhibitions: One-man shows, Cape Cod Art Asn, Cape Cod, Mass, 63 & Robert Brooks Studio, Hyannis, 69; 15 New England Artists, Brockton Art Asn, Brockton Pub Libr, 65; one-man show, Attleboro Art Mus, Mass, 66; New England Artists, Brockton Art Ctr, 70; South Shore Art Festival, Scituate, Mass, 70; plus one other.
Awards: Award, Brockton Art Asn, 60; award, South Shore Art Festival, 70; award, Lutheran Church Exhib, 71.
Memberships: Brockton Art Asn (v pres, 60-); Attleboro Art Mus; Fuller Mem, Brockton Art Ctr; Copley Art Soc; Cape Cod Art Asn.
Dealer: Robert Brooks Studio, 762 Falmouth Rd, Hyannis, MA 02601.
Mailing Address: Bancroft 6, 15 Foundry St, South Easton, MA 02375.

BRESCHI, KAREN LEE
Sculptor
Preferred Media: Clay, Mixed Media.
b Oakland, Calif, Oct 29, 41.
Study & Training: Calif Col Arts & Crafts, BFA, 63; Sacramento State Univ, 60-61; San Francisco State Univ, MA, 65.
Work in Public Collections: Oakland Mus, Calif; Crocker Art Gallery, Sacramento, Calif.
Exhibitions: Calif State Fair, 62-63; Mus Contemp Crafts Group Show, 63; San Francisco Art Inst Ann, 65, Small Sculpture Show, 71 & Faculty Show, 72.
Teaching: Instr design & drawing, San Francisco Community Col, 71-72; instr sculpture, San Francisco Art Inst, 71-72.
Awards: First pl for The Painted Flower, Oakland Art Mus, 62; Women's Archit League Award, Crocker Art Mus, 63; award, Calif State Fair, 63.
Memberships: West/East Bag.
Dealer: Berkeley Gallery, 370 Brannan St, San Francisco, CA 94107.
Mailing Address: 3342 Grand Ave 2, Oakland, CA 94610.

BREVERMAN, HARVEY
Painter, Printmaker
b Pittsburgh, Pa, Jan 7, 34.
Study & Training: Univ Pittsburgh; Carnegie Inst Technol, with Samuel Rosenberg & Balcomb Greene & BFA; Ohio Univ, MFA.
Work in Public Collections: Whitney Mus Am Art, New York, N Y; Albright-Knox Art Gallery, Buffalo, N Y; Butler Inst Art, Youngstown, Ohio; Baltimore Mus, Md; Philadelphia Mus, Pa.
Exhibitions: American Painting Biennial, Corcoran Gallery Art, Washington, D C 63; Brooklyn Mus Biennial, New York, 64; Pa Acad Fine Arts Ann, Philadelphia, 65; New Talent-65, Assoc Am Artists Galleries, New York, 65; Third Brit Int Print Biennial, Bradford, Eng, 72.
Teaching: Prof art, State Univ N Y Buffalo, 61-; artist-in-residence, State Acad Fine Arts, Amsterdam, Netherlands, 65-66; vis artist, Falmouth Sch Art, Cornwall, Eng, fall 69.
Awards: Tiffany Found grant painting, 62; Netherlands Govt grant, 65; N Y State Coun Arts, 72.
Dealers: FAR Galleries, Inc, 746 Madison Ave, New York, NY 10021; Associated American Artists, 663 Fifth Ave, New York, NY 10022.
Mailing Address: 76 Smallwood Dr, Buffalo, NY 14226.

BREWER, DONALD J
Museum Director, Art Historian
b Los Angeles, Calif, July 22, 25.
Study & Training: Univ Calif, Santa Barbara, BA, 50; special study with Donald J Bear, Santa Barbara, 48-50.
Collections Arranged: Henry Moore Sculpture and Drawing, 63; The Work of Louis I Kahn, 65; The Reminiscent Object—Harnett, Peto & Haberle, 65; Beyond the Actual—Contemporary California Realism, 70; Other Landscapes and Shadow Land, San Francisco Visionary Painting, 71.
Teaching: Instr 20th century art, Univ Calif Exten, 55-64; instr mus & gallery world, Fresno State Col, 68-70; instr art of collecting art, Pioneer Mus, Stockton, Calif, 71-
Positions: Registr, cur & dir, La Jolla Mus Art, Calif, 51-68; dir art galleries, Fresno State Col, 68-70; dir, Pioneer Mus & Haggin Galleries, 70-71; dir univ art galleries, Univ Southern Calif, 71-
Memberships: Western Asn Art Mus (v pres, 62).
Publications: Co-auth, John Marin & Marsden (exhib catalogue), La Jolla Mus Art, 66; auth, Georges Rouault, 66 & The Louis and Charlotte Bergman collection, 67 (exhib catalogues), La Jolla Mus Art; auth, Contemporary California realism (exhib catalogue), Pioneer Mus, 70; auth, Other landscapes & shadow land (exhib catalogue), Univ Southern Calif, 71.
Mailing Address: Art Galleries, University of Southern California, University Park, Los Angeles, CA 90007.

BREWINGTON, MARION VERNON
Art Historian, Writer
b Salisbury, Md, June 23, 02.
Study & Training: Univ Pa, BS, 25.
Positions: Asst dir, Peabody Mus, Salem, Mass, 56-66; dir Kendall Whaling Mus, 66-
Memberships: Mass Hist Soc; Am Antiqn Soc; Md Hist Soc; Salem Marine Soc; Soc Nautical Res.
Research: Marine painters.
Publications: Co-auth, Kendall Whaling Museum paintings & Kendall Whaling Museum prints; auth, Marine paintings in the Peabody Museum of Salem; auth, Chesapeake Bay, a pictoral maritime history; auth, Shipcarvers of North America.
Mailing Address: 27 Everett St, Sharon, MA 02067.

BREZIK, HILARION, C S C
Painter, Educator
Preferred Media: Watercolors.
b Houston, Tex, Aug 5, 10.
Study & Training: Univ Notre Dame, BFA, MA & MFA.
Commissions: Stage sets for Beautiful Dreamer, New Moon & The Golden Trail, Stud Theater, Cathedral High Sch, Indianapolis, Ind, 37-40; three walls, God Bless America, Recreation Rm, St Charles Boys Home, Milwaukee, Wis, 41; Winter Wonderland (painting), Dining Hall, Boysville of Mich, Clinton, 54; Signs of Zodiac (mural), Mary Moody Northern Theater, St Edward's Univ, Austin, Tex, 72.
Exhibitions: Wis Art Asn, Milwaukee Mus Art, 43; Tex Fine Arts Asn, Laguna Gloria Mus, Austin, 61; Brothers of Holy Cross Biennial, St Edward's Univ, Austin, 63-69; Art Dept, Univ Notre Dame, Ind, 71; Watercolor Exhib, Elizabeth Ney Mus, Austin, 72.
Collections Arranged: Brothers of Holy Cross Nat Exhib Biennial, Austin, 61-69.
Teaching: Asst prof watercolor, printmaking & art hist, St Edward's Univ, 67-
Positions: Ed, The South West Rev, Austin, 58-68; dir, St Edward's Univ Exhib Prog, 67-
Awards: Hon mention, Wis Art Asn, 43.
Memberships: Am Fedn Arts; Tex Asn Schs Art.
Publications: Auth, A man from Texas sees a parade, Christian Art Quart, Vol II, No 3; auth, Art and the Catholic artist, Assoc St Joseph, Vol XXVI, No 4 & Vol XXVII, No 1; illusr, The happy heart, Dujarie Press.
Mailing Address: Dept of Art, St Edward's University, Austin, TX 78704.

BRIANSKY, RITA PREZAMENT
Painter, Printmaker
b Grajewa, Poland, July 25, 25; Can citizen.
Study & Training: Montreal Mus Fine Arts, with Jacques de Tonnancour; also with Alexandre Bercovitch, Montreal; Ecole Beaux-Arts Montreal; Art Stud League New York.
Work in Public Collections: Vancouver Art Gallery, B C; Art Gallery Hamilton, Ont; London Art Mus, Ont; Willistead Art Gallery, Windsor, Ont; Lambton Col, Sarnia, Ont.
Exhibitions: Second Int Biennial Exhib of Prints, Tokyo & Osaka, Japan, 60-61; Salon Int Femme Vichy, France, 60-61; UNICEF Int, United Nations, New York, 65; Seventh Calgary Graphics Exhib Centennial Show, Alta, 67; Fourth Biennial Exhib Prints, Invitational Sect, Burnaby, B C, 67.
Awards: Third prize, First & Second Nat Exhib of Prints, Burnaby,

B C, 60 & 63; dipl honneur, Salon Int Femme Vichy, 61; Can Coun grant 62 & arts award, 67.
Bibliography: E Kilbourn (auth), 18 print-makers, Can Art, 61.
Memberships: Can Painter-Etchers & Engravers; Can Soc Graphic Arts.
Publications: Illusr, Rubaboo 4, 65; illusr, The pollution reader, 68; illusr, Ten etchings from Wm Shakespeare's Sonnets, 72.
Dealer: Waddington Galleries, 1456 Sherbrooke St W, Montreal, P Q, Can.
Mailing Address: 4832 Wilson Ave, Montreal 253, P Q, Can.

BRICE, BRUCE RAYMOND
Painter
Preferred Media: Oils, Acrylics, Watercolors.
b New Orleans, La, May 4, 42.
Work in Public Collections: New Orleans Mus Art, La.
Commissions: Wall Murals, Tribute to Tremé Community, Allan Jaffe, New Orleans, 71; Dedication to the Desire Project, Metrolink, New Orleans, 71; I Have a Dream, New Orleans Pub Sch, 72.
Exhibitions: 26th Ann State Art Exhib, Baton Rouge, La, 70; Artists of the Southeast & Texas Biennial, Issac Delgado Mus, New Orleans, 71; Am Civil Liberties Union Art Show, New Orleans, 71; New Orleans Jazz and Heritage Festival, 71 & 72; New York Jazz Festival, N Y, 72.
Teaching: Instr painting, New Orleans Pub Sch, spring 71.
Awards: Award, Isaac Delgado Mus Art, 71.
Bibliography: Maurice Guillerman (auth), Desire Project wall mural, discussion WWL-TV, 1/16/72; Bella Jarrett (auth), Community centers are no longer child's play, Response, 4/72; Jennifer Quale (auth), Keep time rolling...reach the people, Times-Picayune Newspaper, 10/8/72; plus others.
Mailing Address: 2611 Chartres St, New Orleans, LA 70117.

BRICE, WILLIAM
Painter, Educator
b New York, N Y, Apr 23, 21.
Study & Training: Chouinard Art Inst; Art Stud League New York.
Work in Public Collections: Metrop Mus Art; Whitney Mus Am Art; Mus Mod Art; Los Angeles Mus Art; Santa Barbara Mus Art.
Exhibitions: Va Mus Fine Arts, 66; Des Moines, 67; one-man shows, Univ Calif, San Diego, Dallas Mus Fine Arts & San Francisco Mus Art, 67; plus others.
Teaching: Prof art, Univ Calif, Los Angeles, 53-
Awards: Awards, Los Angeles, 47 & Los Angeles City Exhib, 51.
Bibliography: Nathaniel Pousette-Dart (auth), included in: Paintings, watercolors, lithographs, Clayton Spicer Press, 46.
Memberships: Artists Equity Asn.
Mailing Address: 427 Beloit St, Los Angeles, CA 90049.

BRIEGER, PETER H
Art Historian, Educator
Teaching: Prof art & archaeol & head dept, Univ Toronto, emer prof art & archaeol, 70-
Mailing Address: 51 Woodlawn Ave W, Toronto 5, Ont, Can.

BRIGADIER, ANNE
Painter, Lecturer
Preferred Media: Oils, Acrylics, Collage, Encaustics.
b New York, N Y.
Study & Training: Art Stud League New York with Kimon Nicolaides & Morris Kantor; also with Rudolph Ray; study in France, Italy & Spain.
Work in Public Collections: Syracuse Univ Mus, N Y; N C Mus Art, Raleigh; Univ Md, Baltimore; Finch Col Mus, New York; Newark Mus Art, N J & Norfolk Mus, Va; plus others.
Exhibitions: Eastern States Exhib of Contemporary Painting, Springfield Mus Fine Arts, Mass, 60; solo shows, ROKO Gallery, 61-66; one-woman show, 30 Collages - 1954-1964, Mansfield State Col, Pa, 64; Mus Mod Art Lending Serv, Libr, New York, 66-68; Philadelphia Mus Art Lending Serv, Pa, 70-72; plus others.
Teaching: Pvt classes & lect demonstrations in collage.
Awards: Oil painting award, November Woods, Cape Cod Art Asn, 57.
Bibliography: F Crotty (auth), Why try to imitate the past says noted Provincetown Artist, Worcester Sun Telegram, 11/9/58, Provincetown Advocate, 11/13/58 & Interior Design Mag, 10/58.
Memberships: Am Fedn Arts; Provincetown Art Asn (hon v pres, 65-70, trustee 58-64 & 71-).
Publications: Auth & illusr, Collage, a complete guide for artists, Watson-Guptill, New York & London, 11/70.
Dealer: Roko Gallery, 90 E Tenth St, New York, NY 10003.
Mailing Address: 69 Fifth Ave, New York, NY 10003.

BRIGGS, AUSTIN
Illustrator, Collector
b Humboldt, Minn, Sept 8, 08.
Study & Training: Wicker Art Sch, Detroit, Mich; Art Stud League New York.

Awards: Gold medal, 63 & hall of fame award, 69, Soc Illustrators; gold medal, Pa Art Dirs Club, 63.
Memberships: Life mem Soc Illustrators.
Collection: Sculpture—Calder, Stabile, Henry Moore, Nadelman and others.
Mailing Address: 4, Rue Lhomond, 75005 Paris, France.

BRIGGS, ERNEST
Painter
b San Diego, Calif, Dec 24, 23.
Study & Training: Calif Sch Fine Arts, San Francisco, with Clyfford Still, David Park & Mark Rothko, 47-50.
Work in Public Collections: Carnegie Inst, Pittsburgh, Pa; Mich State Univ, East Lansing; Rockefeller Inst, New York, N Y; Whitney Mus Am Art; San Francisco Mus Art; also in pvt cols.
Exhibitions: Carnegie Inst, 61; Dallas Mus Fine Arts, 61 & 62; San Francisco Mus Art, 62 & 63; Jewish Mus, New York, 67; Yale Art Gallery, 68; plus others.
Teaching: Instr drawing & painting, Univ Fla, 58; instr, Pratt Inst, New York, 61-
Dealer: Alonzo Gallery, 26 E 63rd St, New York, NY 10021.
Mailing Address: 128 W 23rd St, New York, NY 10011.

BRIGGS, JUDSON REYNOLDS
Painter
b Philadelphia, Pa, May 17, 06.
Study & Training: Art Inst Chicago; Art Stud League New York, N Y.
Work in Public Collections: Mus Mod Art, New York; Maison Cult, France; Mus Bellas Artes, Caracas, Venezuela; Mex Am Cult Inst, Mexico City; UN Bldg, New York; plus many others.
Exhibitions: Metrop Mus Art, New York; Mus Mod Art Traveling Exhib; one-man shows, Nat Gallery Sect & Sala Int Friendship, 57, Palacio Bellas Artes, Mex; Paris Exhib, sponsored by Picasso, Malraux & Leger, Maison Club, 38; Span Children's Milk Fund World Tour, 38; plus many others.
Teaching: Instr graphic arts, New York Sch Fine & Indust Arts, 36; dir painting, Artes Contemporaneos, Cuernavaca, Mex; instr drawing, Sch Archit, Univ Morelos; instr, St Mary's Univ, Tex; instr, San Antonio Jewish Community Ctr; instr, Our Lady of the Lakes Col; pvt instr.
Bibliography: Enrique Gaul (auth), bk, Ed Arte Universal.
Dealers: Fairmont Gallery, 6040 Sherry Lane, Dallas, TX 75225; Village Group, 303 S Almo, San Antonio, TX 78205.
Mailing Address: c/o Artists Showroom, 167 E 33rd St, New York, NY 10016.

BRIGHT, BARNEY
Sculptor
Preferred Media: Bronze, Other Metals.
b Shelbyville, Ky, July 8, 27.
Study & Training: Davidson Col; Univ Louisville; Art Ctr, Louisville, Ky.
Work in Public Collections: J B Speed Art Mus, Louisville; Milwaukee Art Ctr, Wis; Childrens Art Gallery, Louisville; Univ Ky, Lexington; Libr Bldg, Jeffersonville, Ind.
Commissions: Sculpture for Old Stag Distillery, Frankfort, Ky, 65; sculpture at Louisville Zool Garden, Louisville Zoo, Ky; sculpture at WAVE Garden, WAVE Inc, Louisville; sculpture of Dean A C Russell, Univ Louisville Law Sch; plus many others.
Exhibitions: Friendship Exhib, France, 58; Sculpture Today, John Herron Art Inst, Indianapolis, Ind, 61; Tri-State Exhib, Evansville Mus Arts & Sci, Ind, 62; Parrish Art Mus, South Hampton, N Y, 70; Suffolk Co Mus, Stony Brook, N Y, 71.
Mailing Address: 2031 Frankfort Ave, Louisville, KY 40206.

BRIGHTWELL, WALTER
Painter
Preferred Media: Oil, Watercolor.
b Del Rio, Tex, July 14, 19.
Study & Training: Art Stud League New York, N Y, with Frank Dumond.
Work in Public Collections: U S Navy Combat Art Collection, Washington, D C.
Commissions: Mural, West Side Savings Bank, New York, 57.
Exhibitions: Mus Marine, Paris, France, 63; Allied Artists Am, Nat Acad Design, New York, 66 & Am Watercolor Soc, New York, 69; Coun Am Artist Socs, New York, 66; Ft Lauderdale Mus Arts, Fla, 69.
Awards: George Burr Gold Medal, Nat Arts Club, New York, 59; Gwynne Lennon Award, Salmagundi Club, New York, 63; purchase award, Am Watercolor Soc, 66.
Memberships: Allied Artists Am; Am Watercolor Soc (dir, 69-71); Artists Fel (corresp secy, 63-69); Salmagundi Club (art chmn, 63-67); Grand Cent Art Galleries.

Dealer: Grand Central Art Galleries, 40 Vanderbilt Ave, New York, NY 10017.
Mailing Address: 946 Reef Lane, Vero Beach, FL 32960.

BRINK, GUIDO PETER
Painter, Sculptor
b Dusseldorf, W Ger, Jan 8, 13; U S citizen.
Study & Training: State Acad Fine Arts, Dusseldorf; Acad Beaux Arts-Mètiers Art, Paris, France.
Work in Public Collections: Busch-Reisinger Mus, Harvard Univ, Cambridge, Mass; Ministry Cult, N Rhine Prov, W Ger; Inland Steel Corp, Chicago, Ill; State Acad Fine Arts; Art Ctr & Performing Art Ctr, Milwaukee, Wis.
Commissions: Sculpture fountain, Milwaukee Co Zoo, 68; hanging sculpture, Tippecanoe Libr, Milwaukee, 68; perforated metal screen, E Side Libr, Milwaukee, 69; wall relief, Supersteel Prod Inc, Milwaukee; sculpture, aluminum with baked enamel, Frank W Ladky Assoc, Inc, Milwaukee.
Exhibitions: Art in Architecture, Archit League New York Int, 53; Sculptures of Painters, Fairweather-Hardin Gallery Int, Chicago, 59; Nat Painting & Sculpture Show, Butler Inst Am Art, Youngstown, Ohio, 60; 22nd Watercolor Biennial Int, Brooklyn Mus, N Y, 63; Int Outdoor Sculpture Exhib, Mus Arte Mod, Milan, Italy, 70.
Teaching: Instr painting, Layton Sch Art & Design, Milwaukee, 55-, chmn, Sophomore Comprehensive Study Prog, 72-
Awards: Layton Sch Art & Design fel, 61; award of merit, Am Inst Architects, 70; nat merit award, Indust Perforators Asn, Chicago, 70.
Bibliography: M Graham (auth), Sculpture and engineering, Milwaukee Eng Mag, 1/67; M Fish (auth), Guido Brink, Wis Architects Mag, 68; M Kirkhorn, Modern artist abandons his studio for a factory, Milwaukee J, 69.
Memberships: Wis Painters & Sculptors; Art Ctr, Milwaukee; Friends of Art, Milwaukee Art Ctr.
Dealers: Irving Galleries, 400 E Wisconsin Ave, Milwaukee, WI 53202; Benjamin Galleries, 900 N Michigan Ave, Chicago, IL 60611.
Mailing Address: 2827 N Farwell Ave, Milwaukee, WI 53211.

BRITSKY, NICHOLAS
Painter, Educator
Preferred Media: Oils, Casein, Watercolors.
b Weldirz, Ukraine, Dec 11, 13; U S citizen.
Study & Training: Yale Univ, BFA; Syracuse Univ; Cranbrook Acad Art; Fulbright fel to Italy, 56-57; Portugal, 65-66.
Work in Public Collections: Evansville Mus, Ind; Ill State Mus, Springfield; Ford Motor Co Collection, Dearborn, Mich; Univ Ill, Chicago; Prudential Life Ins Co, New York, N Y; also 65 in pvt collections.
Commissions: Bronze grille, Bell Tel Co, Waterloo, Iowa, 40; mosaic tile mural, Allen Park High Sch, Galesburg, Ill, 54; com mural, E B Evans Co, Philadelphia, Pa, 64; painting for print reproduction, Donald Art Co, Mamaroneck, N Y, 65.
Exhibitions: Denver Mus, Colo, 51, 53 & 55; Butler Inst Am Art, Youngstown, Ohio, 52-54; Nat Acad Design, New York, 60; Evansville Mus, 61, 67 & 68; Mainstreams U S A, Mariette Col, Ohio, 69-72.
Teaching: Prof art, Univ Ill, 39-
Awards: First painting prize, Evansville Mus, 64; critics award in painting, Marietta Col, 71; first prize, watercolor, Ohio Univ; plus one other.
Memberships: Am Fedn Arts.
Publications: Contribr, Encycl Slavonica, Philos Press, 49; illusr, Ford Times Mag, 64.
Dealer: Grand Central Galleries, 40 Vanderbilt Ave, New York, NY 10017.
Mailing Address: Dept of Art, University of Illinois, Champaign, IL 61820.

BRITTON, EDGAR
Sculptor
Preferred Media: Bronze.
b Kearney, Nebr, Apr 15, 01.
Study & Training: Univ Iowa, 18-20; also with Grant Wood, 20-24.
Work in Public Collections: Doors & tower, United Bank Denver, Colo; column, Fed Ctr Bldg, Denver; Orpheus, Colorado Springs Libr, Colo; Genesis, Antlers Plaza, Colorado Springs; The Family, Denver Gen Hosp.
Commissions: Frescoes for Chicago Heights H S & Deerfield Shields H S, Works Proj Admin, 35; frescoes, Lane Tech H S, Chicago, Ill, 37; frescoes, 39 & frescoes for Waterloo Post Off, Iowa, 40, U S Dept Interior Fine Arts Comn.
Exhibitions: Opening show, 72 & one-man show, 72, Denver Art Mus; one-man & group shows, Fine Arts Ctr, Colorado Springs.
Teaching: Instr painting, Fountain Valley Sch Boys, Colo; instr painting, Colorado Springs Fine Arts Ctr.

Positions: Pres, Artists Equity, Colorado Springs; mem, Fine Arts Comn City & Co Denver, 67-71; mem, Arts & Humanities, 67-68.
Awards: Anne Evans Mem prize for painting, Denver Art Mus, 48; first prize for painting, Pasadena Art Inst, 49; award, Denver Chap, Am Inst Architects, 71.
Memberships: Allied Sculptors Colo.
Dealer: Littledale Gallery, 2309 W Main St, Littleton, CO 80120.
Mailing Address: 6427 S Hill St, Littleton, CO 80120.

BROADD, HARRY ANDREW
Painter, Art Historian
Preferred Media: Oils, Acrylics.
b Chicago, Ill, Feb 17, 10.
Study & Training: Univ Chicago, PhB, 30; Columbia Univ, AM, 31; Art Inst Chicago; Univ Mich, PhD, 46.
Exhibitions: Int Exhib Watercolors, Art Inst Chicago, 32; Artists of Chicago & Vicinity Show, Art Inst Chicago, 33, 36 & 37; Mich Artists Exhib, Detroit Inst Arts, 46; One-man retrospective 1931-1961, Philbrook Art Ctr, Tulsa, Okla, 61.
Teaching: Asst prof art & art educ, Eastern Mich Univ, 37-47; prof art hist, Univ Tulsa, 47-67; prof art hist, Northeastern Ill Univ, 67-
Memberships: Col Art Asn Am; Nat Art Educ Asn; Ill Art Educ Asn.
Publications: Auth, Music as a stimulus to design & Literature as a stimulus to expression, Design, 35; auth, articles on graphic arts, block printing & others, In: World Bk Encycl, 62; auth, Sandpaper lithographs, 69 & Art appreciation & history/who needs it?, 70, Arts & Activities.
Mailing Address: Dept of Art, Northeastern Illinois University, Bryn Mawr at St Louis Ave, Chicago, IL 60625.

BROADLEY, HUGH T
Art Historian, Art Administrator
b Sacramento, Calif, June 5, 22.
Study & Training: Park Col, AB; Yale Univ, AM; New York Univ, PhD.
Teaching: Prof art hist, Bowling Green State Univ, 61-65; prof art hist, Ariz State Univ, 69-
Positions: Mus cur, Nat Gallery Art, 54-61; cur art collections, Ariz State Univ, 65-67; dir, Phoenix Art Mus, 67-69; pres, Western Asn Art Mus, 68.
Memberships: Col Art Asn Am; Am Asn Mus; Friends of Mexican Art (1st v pres, 71-).
Research: Flemish painting of the fifteenth and sixteenth centuries.
Mailing Address: 4102 N 50th Pl, Phoenix, AZ 85018.

BROCHSTEIN, I S
Collector
Mailing Address: 2322 Braeswood Blvd, Houston, TX 77025.

BRODERSON, MORRIS
Painter
b Los Angeles, Calif, Nov 4, 28.
Study & Training: Pasadena Mus, life drawing classes with De Erdeley; Univ Southern Calif, spec studies in art, four yrs.
Work in Public Collections: Whitney Mus Am Art, New York, N Y; Mus Fine Arts, Houston, Tex; Joseph H Hirshhorn Collection, Washington, D C; Nat Collection Fine Arts, Washington, D C; San Francisco Mus Art, Calif.
Exhibitions: Young America, Whitney Mus Am Art, 60; one-man show, M H De Young Mem Mus, San Francisco, 61; Twelve Artists Invitational, Corcoran Gallery Art, Washington, D C, 64; Pittsburgh Invitational, Carnegie Int, 66; one-man show, Fine Arts Gallery, San Diego, Calif, 69.
Awards: New Talent, U S A, Art in Am, 60; excellence in art, Art Dirs Club Philadelphia, 63; Great Ideas of Western Man, Container Corp Am, 63.
Bibliography: Bruce Barton, Jr (auth), That heavy secret, Time Mag, 3/1/63; Dorothy Adlow (auth), Broderson's fantastic reach, Christian Sci Monitor, 63; John Canaday (auth), The special world of Broderson, New York Times, 11/13/71.
Dealers: Ankrum Gallery, 657 N La Cienega Blvd, Los Angeles, CA 90069; Staempfli Gallery, 47 E 77th St, New York, N Y 10021.
Mailing Address: 657 N La Cienega Blvd, Los Angeles, CA 90069.

BRODERSON, ROBERT
Painter
b West Haven, Conn, July 6, 20.
Study & Training: Duke Univ, AB, 50; State Univ Iowa, with Mauricio Lasansky, James Lechay & Stuart Edie, MFA, 52.
Work in Public Collections: Nat Inst Arts & Lett, N Y; Whitney Mus Am Art; Wadsworth Atheneum, Hartford, Conn; Colorado Springs Fine Arts Ctr; Princeton Univ Art Mus.
Exhibitions: Four shows, Pa Acad Fine Arts, 51-67; Denver Art Mus, 63; Univ Ill, 63 & 65; Nebr Art Asn, 64; Carnegie Inst, 64; plus others.

Teaching: Instr, Duke Univ, 57-64.
Awards: Duke Univ summer res fel, 63; Guggenheim fel, 64; Childe Hassam Purchase Award, 68; plus others.
Dealer: Terry Dintenfass Inc, 18 E 67th St, New York, NY 10021.
Mailing Address: P O Box 190, Raleigh, NC 27602.

BRODEY, STANLEY CARL
Painter
Preferred Media: Watercolors.
b New York, N Y, Sept 17, 20.
Study & Training: Pratt Inst; Art League Long Island & Nat Art League, with Edgar Whitney; John Pike Watercolor Sch; also with Tom Nicholas & Don Stone, Rockport, Mass.
Work in Public Collections: Sayville Pub Libr, N Y; Awixa Pond Art Ctr, Bayshore, N Y; State Col Va, Petersburg.
Exhibitions: Themes & Variations, Heckscher Mus, Huntington, N Y, 62; Am Watercolor Soc 101st Ann, New York, 68; Nat Art League Ann, Adelphi Univ, Garden City, N Y, 71; Fine Arts Festival, Parrish Art Mus, Southampton, N Y, 71; Am Artists Prof League Grand Nat, Lever House, New York, 72.
Positions: Publicity chmn, Malverne Artists of Long Island, 62-; publicity chmn, Long Beach Art Asn, N Y, 68-
Awards: Forbes Indust Award, 65; Kiwanis Award, 68; Grumbacher Award, 72.
Bibliography: Freda Stern (auth), Artist finds beauty, Sun Mag, New York Daily News, 59; R Savage (auth), First night, Saskatoon Star-Phoenix, 65; M Engels (auth), He's bachelor & in love... with Island Sunday News, 72.
Memberships: Am Artist Prof League; Hudson Valley Art Asn; Nat Art League; Prof Art Guild; Art League Nassau Co.
Dealer: M M Michaels, 13 W 30th St, New York, NY 10001.
Mailing Address: 424 Woodmere Blvd, Woodmere, NY 11598.

BRODIE, GANDY
Painter, Designer
b New York, N Y, May 20, 24.
Study & Training: Columbia Univ; Hans Hofmann Sch Fine Arts; art hist with Meyer Schapiro.
Work in Public Collections: Mus Mod Art; Whitney Mus Am Art; Phillips Collection, Washington, D C; Baltimore Mus Art; Chrysler Mus, Provincetown, Mass; plus others.
Exhibitions: Recent Acquisitions, Whitney Mus Am Art, 57; Mus Mod Art, 57 & 61; one-man shows, Obelisk Gallery, Boston, 65, Zabriskie Gallery, New York, N Y, 67 & Richard Gray Gallery, Chicago, Ill, 67; plus others.
Teaching: Artist-in-residence, Hollins Col, 68.
Awards: Nat Arts Coun Award, 68; Guggenheim fel, 68-69; State of Wash cult enrichment grant, 69; plus others.
Mailing Address: West Townshend, VT 05359.

BRODSKY, JUDITH KAPSTEIN
Printmaker, Painter
Preferred Media: Intaglio.
b Providence, R I, July 14, 33.
Study & Training: Radcliffe Col, BA(art hist); Tyler Sch Art, Temple Univ, MFA.
Work in Public Collections: Libr Cong, Washington, D C; Fogg Art Mus, Cambridge, Mass; N J State Mus, Trenton; First Nat Bank Boston, Mass; Princeton Univ, N J.
Commissions: The Magic Muse, traveling art environ (with Ilse Johnson, M K Johnson & Jane Teller), Asn Arts N J State Mus, 72.
Exhibitions: Art from New Jersey, N J State Mus, 67, 70 & 71; Boston Printmakers, De Cordova Mus, 71 & Rose Art Mus, Brandeis Univ, 72; Soc Am Graphic Artists, Kennedy Gallery, New York, N Y, 71; Philadelphia Print Club, Pa, 72; California Printmakers, Richmond, 72.
Teaching: Lectr art hist, Tyler Sch Art, 66-71; asst prof printmaking, Beaver Col, 72-
Positions: Assoc dir, Princeton Graphic Workshop, Inc, 66-68.
Awards: Purchase prizes, Washington Printmakers, Libr Cong, 69, N J State Mus, 70 & 71 & Boston Printmakers, 71.
Memberships: Col Art Asn Am; Philadelphia Print Club; Calif Soc Printmakers; Boston Printmakers.
Dealers: Princeton Gallery of Fine Art, 9 Spring St, Princeton, NJ 08540; Associated American Artists, 663 Fifth Ave, New York, NY 10022.
Mailing Address: 59 Castle Howard Ct, Princeton, NJ 08540.

BRODSKY, STAN
Painter
Preferred Media: Oils, Casein, Watercolor.
b Brooklyn, N Y, Mar 23, 25.
Study & Training: Univ Mo, B Jour; Univ Iowa, MFA, with Jim Lechay, Byron Burford; Columbia Univ, EdD.
Work in Public Collections: N Y Univ; Univ Del; C W Post Col, Long Island Univ.

Commissions: Lobby mural, Electronic Abstract Symbols, PRD Electronics, Syosset, N Y, 70.
Exhibitions: Festival of Art, Phila Mus Art, Pa, 59; Young Artists of Promise, Mortimer Brandt Gallery, New York, N Y, 62; Art Today, N Y State Fair, Syracuse, 67; 33rd midyear ann, Butler Inst Am Art, Youngstown, Ohio, 68; The New Landscape, Artists of Suffolk Co Exhib, Heckscher Mus, Huntington, N Y, 70.
Teaching: Assoc prof art, C W Post Col, L I Univ, 60-
Awards: First prize, Wilmington Mus Art, Del, 58; second prize, Huntington Twp Art League, 68; second prize, N Shore Community Art Ctr, Great Neck, N Y, 71.
Memberships: Prof Artists Guild.
Dealer, Roko Gallery, 90 E Tenth St, New York, NY 10003.
Mailing Address: 16 Bittersweet Pl, Huntington, NY 11743.

BRODY, JACOB JEROME
Art Administrator, Educator
b Brooklyn, N Y, Apr 24, 29.
Study & Training: Brooklyn Mus Art Sch, with Gross & Ferren, 46-50; Art Stud League New York, with Groth, 47; Cooper Union, cert, 50; Brooklyn Col, 50-52; Univ N Mex, BA, 56, MA, 64, PhD, 71.
Collections Arranged: The Collection of George May, Everhart Mus, Scranton, Pa, 57; Oriental Spring, 58-59 & Early Masters of Modern Art, 59, Isaac Delgado Mus Art, New Orleans, La; Indigo, Mus Int Folk Art, Santa Fe, N Mex, 61; The Corn Series of Joseph Imhof, 64, Hopi Kachina Dolls, 65 & Navajo Weaving, the Maxwell Collection, 63, Maxwell Mus Anthrop, Univ N Mex, Albuquerque, 63; American Indian Art, Univ N Mex Fine Arts Mus, 71.
Teaching: Assoc prof museology, Univ N Mex, 63-, assoc prof Am Indian Art, 65-
Positions: Curator art, Everhart Mus, 57-58; curator collection, Isaac Delgado Mus Art, 58-60; curator collection, Mus Int Folk Art, 61-62; dir & curator, Maxwell Mus Anthrop, N Mex, 62-
Awards: Nat Found Humanities mus internship, 68; best southwestern non-fiction award, Border-Regional Libr Asn, 71; Tom L Popejoy Dissertation Award, Univ N Mex, 72.
Bibliography: John Ewers (auth), rev, In: Am West, 71.
Publications: Auth, The Kiva murals of pottery mound, 70; auth, Indian painters and white patrons, 71; auth, In advance of the ready-made (in press).
Mailing Address: Maxwell Museum of Anthropology, University of New Mexico, Albuquerque, NM 87106.

BRODY, MR & MRS SIDNEY F
Collectors
Positions: Mr Brody, trustee, Los Angeles Co Mus Art, 59-, pres, 66-70, chmn trustees, 70-
Collection: Contemporary paintings and sculpture.
Mailing Address: 360 S Mapleton Dr, Los Angeles, CA 90024.

BROEMEL, CARL WILLIAM
Painter, Illustrator
Preferred Media: Watercolors, Oils.
b Cleveland, Ohio, Sept 5, 91.
Study & Training: Cleveland Sch Art, 06-10; Royal Sch Appl Arts, Munich, Ger, 13-15; Art Stud League New York & Nat Acad, 17-18.
Work in Public Collections: Cleveland Mus Art; New Brit Mus Am Art; Brooklyn Mus Art, N Y; USAF Art Mus, Washington, D C.
Exhibitions: American Paintings & Sculpture, Art Inst Chicago, 32-33; Exhib Am Paintings, Cleveland Mus Art, 37; Am Watercolor Soc, New York, 41; Nat Watercolor Competition, Springfield Art Mus, Mo, 68; Berkshire Art Mus, Pittsfield, Mass, 69.
Teaching: Instr watercolor, pvt classes, 25-28.
Positions: Art studio painting & illus, Cleveland, Ohio, 19-40; archit designing & decorating, Cleveland, 22-26; art studio painting & illus, New York, 41-57; mem USAF art staff to Gaffin Island, 55; art studio painting, Sharon Co, Conn, 57-
Awards: First watercolor prizes, May Show Cleveland Mus, 28 & 29; third prize abstr, Berkshire Art Asn, Mass, 67.
Memberships: Life mem Am Watercolor Soc; Kent Art Soc (juror, 59-); USAF Art Prog (partic artist).
Publications: Auth, Specialty shops, Archit Forum, 24; auth, American watercolor (series), Am Artist, 59; auth, article, In: North Light-Fletcher, 71.
Dealer: The Bonfoey Co, 1710 Euclid Ave, Cleveland, OH 44115.
Mailing Address: R D 2, Sharon, CT 06069.

BROH, MINERVA LEEDY
Painter, Sculptor
b Highspire, Pa.
Study & Training: York Col (Pa); Art Stud League New York; Art Asn Harrisburg, Pa; sculpture with Jose de Creeft, New York, N Y; color with Ben Cunningham; color & compsition with Morris Kantor, New York.

Work in Public Collections: Middletown Area High Sch, Pa; Fonteyne Gallery, New Hope, Pa; and many others, both private & public.
Exhibitions: Semi-ann Southeast Pa Pictorial Arts Juried Art Exhib, 61; Washington Co Mus Ann Exhib, Hagerstown, Md, 64; Prof Invitational Art Show, Solanco High Sch, Quarryville, Pa, 71-72; plus five one-man shows.
Teaching: Instr art & art hist, Broh Gallery, 64-
Awards: Second prize, Boardwalk Show, City of Ocean City, 68.
Bibliography: Local artist is honored, Home Star, Harrisburg, Pa, 1/5/66; Interview, Harrisburg Evening News, 6/5/68; Broh at Lynn Kottler, Park E News, 12/4/69.
Collection: Lithographs, etchings, paintings, serigraphs & woodblocks.
Mailing Address: R D 1, New Cumberland, PA 17070.

BROKAW, LUCILE
Painter
Preferred Media: Collage.
b New York, N Y, Mar 12, 15.
Study & Training: Grand Cent Sch Art, 27-29; sculpture, Paris, France, 30-32; George Grosz Art Sch, New York, 33-34.
Work in Public Collections: Many pvt collections.
Exhibitions: San Francisco Mus Art Ann, 59; Theatre Collects American Art, Whitney Mus Am Art, New York, 61; Craftsmen U S A, Los Angeles Co Mus, 66; California Stitchery, Calif Arts Comn Traveling Exhib, 69-70; People Figures, Smithsonian Traveling Exhib, 69-70; plus others.
Awards: Nat Orange Show Award, San Bernardino, 55; Eighth All City Outdoor Art Festival Award, 60; first prize, Artist-Craftsman-Westside Jewish Community Ctr, 64.
Bibliography: Bentley Schaad (auth), The realm of contemporary still life painting, Reinhold, 62; Dona Meilach (auth), Contemporary rugs and wall hangings, Abelard, 70; Meilacht Snow (auth), Creative stitchery, Reilly & Lee, 70.
Memberships: Los Angeles Art Asn (trustee).
Dealer: Adele Bednarz Galleries, 902 La Cienega, Los Angeles, CA 90069.
Mailing Address: 831 Paseo Miramar, Pacific Palisades, CA 90272.

BROMBERG, MR & MRS ALFRED L
Collectors
Mailing Address: 3201 Wendover Rd, Dallas, TX 75214.

BRONER, ROBERT
Printmaker, Painter
b Detroit, Mich, Mar 10, 22.
Study & Training: Wayne State Univ, BFA, 44, MFA, 46; Soc Arts & Crafts, Detroit, 42-45; painting with Stuart Davis, 49-50; Atelier 17, Paris, France, with S W Hayter, 49-52.
Work in Public Collections: Mus Mod Art, New York, N Y; Boston Pub Libr Collection; Los Angeles Co Mus; Nat Gallery Art, Washington, D C; Cincinnati Art Mus.
Commissions: Ed etchings, Detroit Inst Arts, 67 & London Arts Gallery, 67-69.
Exhibitions: Six shows, Brooklyn Mus Prints Nat, 51-69; Print Coun Am Show, 18 mus, U S A & Europe, 59-60; Brit Int Print Biennale, 68 & 70; Salon de Mai, Mus Art Mod, Paris, 69; Soc Am Graphic Artists, 69 & 71.
Teaching: Assoc prof art & humanities, Wayne State Univ, 64-
Awards: Print purchase prize, Brooklyn Mus, 64; purchase prize, Soc Am Graphic Artists, Assoc Am Artists Gallery, 69.
Memberships: Brit Printmakers Coun; Soc Am Graphic Artists; Philadelphia Print Club; Mich Asn Printmakers (pres); Drawing & Print Club, Detroit Inst Arts (bd dirs).
Mailing Address: 18244 Parkside, Detroit, MI 48221.

BROOK, ALEXANDER
Painter
Preferred Media: Oils
b Brooklyn, N Y, July 14, 98.
Study & Training: Art Stud League New York; also with Kenneth Hayes Miller.
Work in Public Collections: Metropolitan Mus Art, New York, N Y; Carnegie Inst, Pittsburgh, Pa; Art Inst Chicago, Ill; Boston Mus, Mass; Corcoran Gallery Art, Washington, D C.
Exhibitions: Art Inst Chicago, 29; Corcoran Gallery Art, 34; City Art Mus, St Louis, Mo, 38; American Painting, Worcester Mus, Mass, 38; Carnegie Inst Int, 39.
Awards: Temple Gold Medal, Philadelphia Acad Art, 29; first prize, Los Angeles Mus, Calif, 54; first prize, Georgia Jungle, Carnegie Inst, 39.
Dealer: Larcada Gallery, 23 E 63rd St, New York, NY 10021.
Mailing Address: Point House, Sag Harbor, NY 11963.

BROOKE, DAVID STOPFORD
Museum Director
b Walton-on-Thames, Eng, Sept 18, 31.
Study & Training: Harvard Univ, AB, 58 & AM, 63.

Positions: Asst cur, Fogg Art Mus, Cambridge, Mass, 60-61; asst to dir, Smith Col Mus, Northampton, 63-65; chief cur, Art Gallery Ont, Toronto, 65-68; dir, Currier Gallery Art, Manchester, N H, 68-
Memberships: Asn Am Art Mus Dirs.
Research: British painting of the eighteenth and nineteenth centuries.
Publications: Co-auth, James Tissot (catalogue), Art Gallery Ont, 68; auth, Mortimer at Eastbourne and Kenwood, Burlington Mag, 68; auth, James Tissot's amateur circle, Boston Mus Bull, 69; co-auth, The Dunlaps of New Hampshire, Antiques, 70; auth, Raeburn's portrait of John Clerk of Eldin, Currier Gallery Bull, 71.
Mailing Address: 365 Ray St, Manchester, NH 03104.

BROOKS, (JOHN) ALAN
Painter, Educator
Preferred Media: Oil, Watercolor.
b Burbank, Calif, Oct 11, 31.
Study & Training: City Col San Francisco; San Jose State Col, MA with Eric Oback; San Francisco Art Inst with William Morehouse.
Work in Public Collections: State of Calif, Sacramento; City of San Francisco, Calif.
Exhibitions: Pioneer Mus & Haggan Galleries, Stockton, Calif, 62; Phelan Awards Biennial, San Francisco, 65, 67 & 69; one-man shows, St Marys Col Calif, 67; John Bolles Gallery, San Francisco, 68-71; Newman Ctr, Univ Calif, Berkeley, 69.
Teaching: Instr painting, City Col San Francisco, 71-
Awards: Second award, Santa Clara Co Fair, 59; purchase award, Calif State Fair, 60; hon mention, San Francisco Ann Art Festival, 70.
Publications: Contribr, Sch Arts Mag, 71.
Dealer: John Bolles Gallery, 10 Gold St, San Francisco, CA 94133.
Mailing Address: 633 Alvarado St, San Francisco, CA 94114.

BROOKS, CHARLES M, JR
Art Historian, Educator
b East Orange, N J, 1908.
Study & Training: Yale Univ, MFA.
Teaching: Head art dept, Lawrence Univ, Myra Goodwin Plantz Prof art & archit, 69-
Positions: Dir, John Nelson Bergstrom Art Ctr, Neenah, Wis.
Awards: Six-time medalist, Nat Inst Archit Educ; prize, Fontainebleau.
Memberships: Am Soc Archit Historians.
Publications: Auth, Texas missions, their romance and architecture; co-auth, Vincent Van Gogh. A Monograph, Arno, 42.
Mailing Address: Art Dept, Lawrence University, Appleton, WI 54511.

BROOKS, FRANK LEONARD
Painter, Writer
b London, Eng, Nov 7, 11; Can citizen.
Study & Training: Ont Col Art, Toronto.
Work in Public Collections: Nat Gallery Can; Art Gallery Ont; Worcester Art Mus, Mass; Mus Mod Art, Mex; Ayala & Samuel J Zacks Collection, Can.
Exhibitions: Can Artists Abroad, Nat Gallery Can, 56; Bienal Interam, Mex, 58; New York World's Fair, 59; Fourth Biennial Exhib Can Art I, 61; plus major exhibs across Can.
Teaching: Instr art, Northern Voc Sch, Toronto; also guest art prof, various univs & art schs.
Positions: Official war artist, Royal Can Navy, 42-45.
Memberships: Royal Can Acad Arts.
Publications: Auth, Watercolor ... a challenge, 57, Painting and understanding abstract art, 64, Painter's workshop, 69 & Oil painting—basic and new techniques, 71, Van Nostrand Reinhold.
Dealer: Roberts Gallery, 641 Yonge St, Toronto 5, Ont, Can.
Mailing Address: P O Box 84, San Miguel de Allende, Guanajuato, Mexico.

BROOKS, JAMES
Painter
b St Louis, Mo, Oct 18, 06.
Study & Training: Southern Methodist Univ, 23-25; Dallas Art Inst, 25-26, with Martha Simkins; Art Stud League New York, with Kimon Nicolaides & Boardman Robinson; pvt study with Wallace Harrison, 45.
Work in Public Collections: Brooklyn Mus, N Y; Solomon R Guggenheim Mus, Mus Mod Art & Metrop Mus Art, New York, N Y; Tate Gallery, London, Eng; plus many others.
Commissions: Murals, Woodside Libr, N Y, La Guardia Airport, New York & U S Post Off, Little Falls, N Y.

Exhibitions: San Francisco Mus Art, Calif, 63; retrospective, Whitney Mus Am Art, 63-64; Dunn Int, Tate Gallery, London, 64; one-man show, Philadelphia Art Alliance, Pa, 66; The New American Painting and Sculpture, Mus Mod Art, New York, 69; plus many other group & one-man exhibs.
Teaching: Instr drawing, Columbia Univ, 46-48; instr lettering, Pratt Inst Art Sch, 48-59; vis critic, Yale Univ, 55-60; artist-in-residence, Am Acad Rome, 63; vis artist, New Col, Sarasota, Fla, 65-67; Miami Beach Art Ctr, Fla, 66; prof art, Queens Col, 66-67, 68-69.
Awards: Norman Wait Harris Silver Medal & Prize, 61; Ford Found Purchase Award, 62; Guggenheim Found fel, 67-68; plus others.
Bibliography: George A Flanagan (auth), Understanding and enjoying modern art, Thomas Y Crowell, 62; Sam Hunter (auth), James Brooks, Whitney Mus Am Art, 63; Sam Hunter (ed), New art around the world, Abrams, 66; plus many others.
Dealer: Martha Jackson Gallery, 32 E 69th St, New York, NY 10021.
Mailing Address: 128 Neck Path, The Springs, East Hampton, NY 11937.

BROOKS, LOUISE CHERRY
Collector, Ceramist
b Phoenix City, Ala, Aug 28, 06.
Study & Training: With Kelly Fitzpatrick & Charles Shannon.
Positions: Mem bd trustees, Montgomery Mus Fine Arts & Montgomery Art Guild.
Awards: Ala Art League & Nat Soc Arts & Lett.
Collection: Early English Staffordshire figures, especially ceramic bird groups.
Mailing Address: 3604 Narrow Lane Rd, Montgomery, AL 36106.

BROOKS, PHYLLIS FEATHERSTONE
Painter, Instructor
Preferred Media: Oils, Mixed Media, Tempera, Graphics.
b Minneapolis, Minn.
Study & Training: Col William & Mary; Am Univ, BA; self study prog in Europe, 69-71; also with Robert Gates, Ben Summerford, Helene Hertzbrun, Arthur Smith & Sara Baker.
Exhibitions: One-woman show, Fed Reserve Bd, Washington, D C, 64; Landon Sch, Azalea Festival, Bethesda, Md, 65; Watkins Gallery, Washington, D C, 65; Third Ann Juried Show, Northern Va Fine Arts Asn, 72.
Teaching: Instr art, Alexandria Pub Schs, Va, 65-66; instr painting, pvt classes, Heidelberg, W Ger, 69-71.
Awards: Northern Va Fine Arts Asn Cert Merit, 72.
Bibliography: Alice Digilio (auth), In the galleries, Alexandria J, 4/27/72; article, In: Alexandria Gazette, 5/22/72.
Memberships: Northern Va Fine Arts Asn; Art League, Inc.
Dealer: Art League, Inc, 315 Cameron St, Alexandria, VA 22314.
Mailing Address: 319 S Pitt St, Alexandria, VA 22314.

BROOKS, WENDELL T
Printmaker, Educator
b Aliceville, Ala, Sept 10, 39.
Study & Training: Ind Univ, BS (art educ), 62, Martin Luther King, Jr fel, 68-70, scholar, 69-71, Southern fel, 70-71, MFA (printmaking), 71; Woodstock Artist's Asn, scholar, summer 61; Pratt Graphic Art Asn, scholar, 62; Univ Md, 65-66; Howard Payne Col, 66-67.
Work in Public Collections: Libr of Cong, Washington, D C; Nasson Col; Mount Union Col; Carleton Col; Bethel Col; plus others including pvt collections.
Exhibitions: A Return to Humanism, Burpee Art Mus, Rockford, Ill, 71; Social Comment in Recent Art, Concordia Teachers Col, Seward, Nebr, 71; The Black Experience in Prints, Pratt Graphic Ctr, New York, N Y, 72; Black Artists of America, N J State Mus, Trenton, 72; New Jersey, 1972, Seventh Ann Exhib, Trenton, 72; plus many other group & one-man shows.
Teaching: Instr printmaking, Ala A & M Univ, 67-68; asst prof printmaking & artist-in-residence, Nassan Col, 70; asst prof printmaking, Trenton State Col, 71-; lectr art at various art groups, cols & univs, 69-72.
Awards: Am Spirit Hon Medal, Citizens Comt for Army, Navy & Air Force, Inc, 63.
Bibliography: Article, In: Negro Heritage, 10/68; article, In: Chalkboard, 11/68; article, In: Christian Sci Monitor, 6/22/70; plus many other newspapers.
Memberships: Philadelphia Print Club.
Mailing Address: Dept of Art, Trenton State College, Trenton, NJ 08625.

BROOMFIELD, ADOLPHUS GEORGE
Painter, Designer
Preferred Media: Oils, Watercolors, Crayon.
b Toronto, Ont, Aug 26, 06.
Study & Training: Ont Col Art, Toronto & Port Hope, Ont; addn

studies with group of seven Can painters; also with Lismer, MacDonald & Carmichael.

Work in Public Collections: War Collection, Nat Gallery Can, Ottawa Ont; Imperial War Col, Ottawa; Can Wire & Cable Co Collection, Toronto.

Exhibitions: RCAF World Wide Exhib, Can & Eng, 45; Can Traveling Show, Montreal, P Q & Vancouver, B C, 62; Royal Can Acad Arts, Nat Gallery Can, 65.

Bibliography: L de Corriveau (auth), Broomfield, Can Rev, 46; G Broomfield ARCA, Roundel, RCAF, 64; L Schrag (auth), Broomfield, Globe & Mail, 64.

Memberships: Assoc Royal Can Acad Arts.

Mailing Address: 232 Isabella Ave, Cooksville, Mississauga, Ont, Can.

BROSE, MORRIS
Sculptor
b Wyszkow, Poland, May 16, 14.
Study & Training: Detroit Inst Arts & Crafts; Wayne State Univ; Cranbrook Acad Art, Bloomfield Hills, Mich.
Work in Public Collections: Detroit Inst Art; Grosse Pointe Libr, Mich; Chase Manhattan Bank Collection, New York; Zieger Osteop Hosp, Detroit; J L Hudson Eastland Ctr, Mich; plus others.
Exhibitions: Mich Artists Ann, 54-; Mus Mod Art, 61; Spoleto Festival, Italy, 61; Westminster Sculpture Exhib, 69; Cranbrook Acad Art Alumni Exhib, 68; plus others.
Teaching: Lectr contemp sculpture, Detroit Inst Art, Wayne State Univ, Montieth Col & others; instr sculpture, Cranbrook Acad Art & Soc Arts & Crafts; instr, Oakland Univ.
Awards: Prize, Detroit Soc Women Painters & Sculptors, 59; Leon & Joseph Winkleman Found Prize, 59; Mich Artists Founders Prize, 62; plus others.
Mailing Address: 65 McLean St, Highland Park, MI 48203.

BROSS, ALBERT L JR
Painter
Preferred Media: Oil.
b Newark, N J, June 29, 21.
Study & Training: Art Stud League New York, N Y, with Messrs Dumond, Bridgeman & McNulty.
Work in Public Collections: N J State Mus, Trenton; Roebling Collection; Springville Mus Art, Utah; Hanover Park High Sch.
Exhibitions: Nat Arts Club Print Show, New York, 72; Hudson Valley Art Asn Regional Show, White Plains, N Y, 72; Acad Artists Asn, Springfield, Mass, 72; Springville Mus Art, 72.
Awards: West Orange Civic Award, Art Ctr Orange, 66; oil award, Nat Show, Springville, 70; award, Am Asn Univ Women, 72.
Memberships: Life mem, Art Stud League; Hudson Valley Art Asn; Acad Artists Asn; Hunterdon Co Art Ctr, N J; Summit Art Ctr, N J.
Mailing Address: Village Rd, New Vernon, NJ 07976.

BROUDO, JOSEPH DAVID
Educator, Ceramist
b Baltimore, Md, Sept 11, 20.
Study & Training: Alfred Univ, BFA, 46; Boston Univ, MEd, 50.
Work in Public Collections: Int Mus Ceramics, Faenza, Italy; Prieto Collection, Mills Col, Calif.
Exhibitions: Int Exhib, Ostend, Belg, 60; Ten Boston Area Craftsmen, New York World's Fair, 64-65.
Teaching: Prof hist art, ceramics, drawing & painting, Endicott Jr Col, 46-, chmn art dept.
Awards: Grand prize, Int Exhib, Ostend, Belg, 60; top honors, Eastern States Expos & De Cordova Craftsmen Exhib; plus others.
Memberships: Mass Asn Craftsmen (chmn, 55-56, dir, 72); Am Crafts Coun (chmn Bennington Craft Fair, 71-72, exec coun, 71-72); Boston Soc Arts & Crafts (dir, 62-).
Mailing Address: 5 Gary Ave, Beverly, MA 01915.

BROUDY, MIRIAM LEVINE
Painter
Preferred Media: Oil.
b Altoona, Pa, Sept 30, 05.
Study & Training: Pa Mus Sch Art, Philadelphia; Academie Colorassi, Paris, France; Arts Stud League; New Sch Social Res; and with Kuniyoshi.
Work in Public Collections: Burndy Corp, Norwalk, Conn; Cosmopolitan Mutual Casualty; Gen Time, Stamford, Conn; Leo & Murial Rogers Collection, New York, N Y; Everhart Mus, Scranton, Pa.
Exhibitions: Nat Asn Women Artists; Riverside Mus; Nat Acad Design; Art USA; Sivermine Guild Artists, New Britian Mus.
Awards: Howard Penrose Award, Conn Acad Fine Arts, 60; Henry Ward Ranger Award, Nat Acad Design, 61; Nat Asn Women Artists, 63.

Memberships: Sivermine Guild of Artists (exec v pres, 72); Conn Acad Fine Arts; New Haven Paint & Clay Club; Nat Asn Women Artists (mem chmn, New Eng); Artists Equity Asn.
Mailing Address: Cloverly Circle, East Norwalk, CT 06855.

BROUGH, RICHARD BURRELL
Educator, Designer
Preferred Media: Watercolors.
b Salmon, Idaho, May 31, 20.
Study & Training: Chouinard Art Inst, Los Angeles, Calif, dipl; Witte Mem Mus, San Antonio, Tex.
Work in Public Collections: Montgomery Mus Fine Arts, Ala; Birmingham Art Mus, Ala; Gulf States Paper Corp, Tuscaloosa, Ala; Ford Motor Co, Dearborn, Mich; Witte Mem Mus.
Commissions: Mural for Service Club, USAF, Sheppard Field, Tex, 41; 6 hist paintings, Univ of the South, Sewanee, Tenn, 58; 12 hist paintings, Gulf States Paper Corp, 60.
Exhibitions: American Painting Today, Metrop Mus Art, New York, N Y, 50; Witte Mem Mus, 58; U S Variety Show, U S Info Agency, traveling exhib to Middle East, 60; Ford Exhib, New York World's Fair, 64; 21 paint in Hyplar, Grumbacher U S Traveling Collection, 69.
Teaching: Prof graphics, Univ Ala, 48-
Awards: First award, Loveman, Joseph & Loeb, 60; purchase award, Maron Pittman Allen, 66; first purchase award, Bluff Park Asn, 70.
Bibliography; Margaret Harold (auth), Award winning art, Allied Publ, 65; Meet the Artist, TV Spec, Birmingham, Ala, 69.
Memberships: Am Asn Univ Prof; Birmingham Art Asn (bd mem, 69-); Miss Art Asn; Ala Watercolor Soc; Tex Watercolor Soc.
Publications: Illusr, 99 Fables, 65; illusr, Ford Times (200 illus), 50-70.
Mailing Address: Dept of Art, University of Alabama, University, AL 35486.

BROUSSARD, JAY REMY
Museum Director, Painter
b New Iberia, La, Dec 20, 20.
Study & Training: La State Univ; Univ Southwestern La.
Exhibitions: Butler Inst Am Art; Fla Int, Lakeland; Southeastern Ann, Atlanta; Denver Mus Art; New Orleans Art Asn; plus others.
Teaching: Mem fine arts faculty, La State Univ, 49-56.
Positions: Juror selections & awards, many major regional & nat art exhibs, Tex Gen, Univ Miami, Lowe Gallery Ann, Jacksonville Mus Ann, Miss Art Asn Ann, Beaumont Art Mus & others; dir, State La Art Comn, Baton Rouge, 47-
Awards: Silver medal, First Nat Amateur Painters Exhib, Art News Mag, 50; prize, Delgado Mus Art, 50; spec mention, Southeastern Ann, Atlanta, 52.
Memberships: Southeastern Mus Conf (past pres); Southern Art Mus Dirs Asn; Am Asn Mus; Nat Trust Hist Preservation.
Mailing Address: 3640 Marigold Ave, Baton Rouge, LA 70808.

BROWN, BO
Cartoonist
Preferred Media: Inks.
b Philadelphia, Pa, July 2, 06.
Study & Training: Univ Pa, AB & Law Sch.
Work in Public Collections: Various cartoon collections, 50-
Positions: Free lance cartoonist, 30-
Memberships: Nat Cartoonists Soc; Guild Mag Cartoonists.
Publications: Contribr, Best cartoons of year, 42-; contribr, Jokes Wagen, 69; contribr, Sons & hair, 70; contribr, Tee Party, 70.
Mailing Address: 218 Wyncote Rd, Jenkintown, PA 19046.

BROWN, BRUCE ROBERT
Painter, Sculptor
Preferred Media: Oil.
b Philadelphia, Pa, July 25, 38.
Study & Training: Tyler Sch Art, Temple Univ, BFA(painting), 61, MFA(sculpture), 64.
Work in Public Collections: Telfair Acad Arts & Sci, Savannah, Ga; Arts & Humanities Coun W Va; Festival Arts Collection, Erie, Pa.
Exhibitions: Carnegie Inst, 55-57; Nat Show, Pa Acad Fine Arts, Philadelphia, 62; Nat Show, Butler Inst Am Art, Youngstown, Ohio, 62 & 63; Am Acad Arts & Lett, New York, N Y, 68; 21st Ann Int Exhib, Beaumont, Tex, 72; plus many others.
Teaching: Instr, Adult Ceramics Prog, Dept Recreation, City of Philadelphia, 61-64; instr ceramics & art, Philadelphia Pub Sch, 65-66; instr art, West Liberty State Col, 67-68; asst prof art, Monroe Community Col, State Univ N Y, 69-
Awards: Award painting, Appalachian Corridors: Exhibition I, Charleston, W Va, 68; purchase award, Arts & Humanities Coun W Va, 67; purchase award, Am Acad Arts & Letters, 68.

Memberships: Col Art Asn Am; Tyler Alumni Asn (mem adv bd);
Southern Sculptors Asn; Rochester Print Club; Philadelphia
Watercolor Club.
Mailing Address: 781 Harvard St, Rochester, NY 14610.

BROWN, CHARLES MOSES (CHARLIE)
Potter
Preferred Media: Clays.
b Mayport, Fla, Sept 8, 04.
Work in Public Collections: Jacksonville Art Mus, Fla; Mus Arts &
Sci, Daytona Beach, Fla; Mint Mus Art, Charlotte, N C; Wichita
Art Asn, Kans; Objects U S A, Johnson Wax Co.
Commissions: Ten planters, Univ Marion Bldg, Jacksonville, 63;
altar cross, vases & candelabra, 67 & chalice & platton, 71,
Lutheran Church, Jacksonville; baptismal font, Presby Church,
Jacksonville, 68; wall hanging, Childrens Mus, Jacksonville, 70.
Exhibitions: 3000 Years of Pottery, Univ Fla, Gainesville, 66;
Craftsmen '66, Mint Mus Art, Charlotte, 66; 25th Anniversary,
Scripps Col, Clermont, Calif, 69; Mus Arts & Sci Invitational,
Daytona Beach, 72; Fla Craftsmen, St Augustine, 72.
Awards: Award for hanging raku pot, Miami Nat Ceramic Show, 70;
best in show for large raku pot, Winter Park Arts Festival, 70;
burnished black pot, Fla Craftsmen Ann Show, 72.
Bibliography: Hal Riegger (auth), Charles Brown-potter, Ceramics,
64; The new craftsmen, Newsweek, 2/70; Ann Connor (auth), He
decks the necks with beads of clay, Fla Times Union, 71.
Memberships: World Crafts Coun; Am Crafts Coun (state rep, 69-
70); Fla Craftsmen (treas, 56).
Mailing Address: P O Box 23216, Mandarin, FL 32217.

BROWN, DANIEL QUILTER
Illustrator, Cartoonist
Preferred Media: Ink, Wash, Watercolors, Pencil.
b Fremont, Ohio.
Exhibitions: Butler Art Inst, Youngstown, Ohio, 40; Mansfield Art
Club, Ohio, 41; Am Soc Mag Cartoonists War Show, 43; San-
dusky, Ohio, 44.
Positions: Art dir, Ferrando Publicidad, Buenos Aires, Arg, 49-
50.
Publications: Contribr, cartoons, In: Am Weekly, Sat Eve Post, Am
Weekly, Wall St Jour, King Features Syndicate & many other
publ in U S & abroad; works publ in many books & anthologies.
Mailing Address: 930 W Adams St, Sandusky, OH 44870.

BROWN, HARRY JOE, JR
Collector, Writer
Study & Training: Phillips Exeter; Stanford Univ; Yale Univ, BA
(magna cum laude); Oxford Univ, Marshall fel & MA.
Positions: Producer, 20th century Fox; pres, Little Antigone
Theaters.
Awards: Rice Awards, best prod & best new play, The Zoo Story,
60; New York Critics' Award for best orig screenplay, Duffy.
Collection: Major abstract expressionists; pop; Los Angeles school.
Publications: Auth, Duffy, 68.
Mailing Address: 952 Fifth Ave, New York, NY 10021.

BROWN, JAMES MONROE, III
Art Administrator
b Brooklyn, N Y, Oct 7, 17.
Study & Training: Amherst Col, AB, 39, hon MA, 54; Harvard Univ,
MA, 46, Advan Mgt Prog, 58.
Positions: Asst to dir, Inst Contemp Art, Boston, Mass, 41; asst to
dir, Dumbarton Oaks Res Libr & Collection, Washington, D C, 46;
asst dir, Inst Contemp Art, Boston, 46-48; dir, William A Farns-
worth Art Mus, Rockland, Maine, 48-51; dir, Corning Glass Cen-
ter, 51-63, dir pub affairs, 56-59, dir mgt develop, 59-61; pres,
Corning Found, 61-63; pres, Corning Mus of Glass, 61-63; dir,
Oakland Mus, Calif, 64-67; dir, Norton Simon, Inc Mus Art, 68-
69; dir, Va Mus Fine Arts, Richmond, 69-
Memberships: Coun Am Asn Mus (past v pres & treas, pres, 70-72);
Am Asn Art Mus Dirs; Am Fedn Arts; Int Coun Mus (past U S A
chmn); Int Exhibs Found.
Mailing Address: Virginia Museum of Fine Arts, Blvd & Grove Ave,
Richmond, VA 23221.

BROWN, JOHN CARTER
Museum Director
b Providence, R I, Oct 8, 34.
Study & Training: Harvard Univ, AB, 56, MBA, 58; Munich Univ, 58;
with Bernard Berenson, Florence, Italy, 58-59; Neth Inst Art
Hist, 60; New York Univ Inst Fine Arts, MA, 62; Brown Univ,
hon LLD, 70.
Positions: Asst to dir, Nat Gallery Art, 61-63, asst dir, 64-68, dep
dir, 68-69, dir, 69-
Awards: Gold medal of honor, Nat Arts Club, 72.
Memberships: Asn Art Mus Dirs; Col Art Asn Am; Am Asn Mus;
Soc Archit Historians; Int Coun Mus.

Research: Seventeenth century Dutch art.
Publications: Auth & dir, American vision (film), 65.
Mailing Address: National Gallery of Art, Washington, DC 20565.

BROWN, JOHN HALL
Painter, Designer
Preferred Media: Watercolors.
b Houston, Tex, June 6, 10.
Study & Training: Tex A&M Col, BA, 33, post-grad study, 35-36.
Work in Public Collections: City of Richardson Pub Libr, Tex; Art
Soc Permanent Collection, Sherman, Tex.
Exhibitions: Southwest Watercolor Soc Regional; Tex Fine Arts Soc
Regional; Artists & Craftsmen Regional; Richardson Civic Art
Soc Regional; Jefferson Arts Festivel, New Orleans, La.
Positions: Architect.
Awards: Harold Michler Purchase Prize, 70; first & second award
watercolor, Artists & Craftsmen, 70; best of show, Richardson
Civic Art Soc, 71.
Memberships: Southwest Watercolor Soc (v pres, 70); Richardson
Civic Art Soc (v pres, 72); Artists & Craftsmen; Tex Fine Arts
Soc.
Dealer: Curl Gallery, 4843 Massachusetts Ave NW, Washington, DC
20016.
Mailing Address: 120 Westshore Dr, Richardson, TX 75080.

BROWN, JOSEPH
Sculptor, Educator
Preferred Media: Bronze.
b Philadelphia, Pa, Mar 20, 09.
Study & Training: Temple Univ, BS(educ); apprentice & studio asst
to R Tait McKenzie, 31-38.
Work in Public Collections: Pa Acad Fine Arts, Philadelphia; R I
Sch Design Mus Art, Providence; N C Art Mus, Raleigh; Univ
Tex, Austin; Yale Univ, New Haven, Conn.
Commissions: Portraits from life, Robert Frost, 63 & John Stein-
beck, 64, Univ Tex, Austin; Discus Thrower & Runner (bronzes),
Johns Hopkins Univ, Baltimore, Md, 65; Gymnasts (bronze),
Temple Univ, Philadelphia, Pa, 69; four heroic athletic statues
(bronze), City of Philadelphia, Vet Stadium, 70.
Exhibitions: Pa Acad Fine Arts Ann, Philadelphia, 32-; Nat Acad
Design, New York, N Y, 33-; Art Exhib, Olympic Games, Berlin,
36; Int Sculpture Exhib, Philadelphia Mus Art, 49; Expo 67,
Montreal, P Q, 67.
Teaching: Sculptor-in-residence, Princeton Univ, 39-
Positions: Mem Philadelphia Art Comn.
Awards: First prize for sculpture, Montclair Mus Art, N J, 40;
Barnett Prize, Nat Acad Design, 44; distinguished serv citation,
Am Asn Health, Phys Educ & Recreation, Nat Educ Asn, 67.
Bibliography: Red Smith & Norman Thomas (auth), Introd to Joe
Brown, retrospective catalogue, 32-66; Harry Olesker (auth),
Shaping things & vice-versa (TV film), NBC TV, 55.
Memberships: Fel Nat Sculpture Soc; Pa Acad Fine Arts; Artists
Equity Asn.
Publications: Auth, Unpredictability—margin for inspiration,
Archit Rec, 9/55; auth, Dynamics of group interaction, viewpoint
of an artist, Am J Psychiat, 3/66; auth, And you hear your name,
Univ Mag, summer-fall 66.
Mailing Address: 185 Nassau St, Princeton, NJ 08540.

BROWN, JUDITH
Sculptor
b New York, N Y, Dec 17, 32.
Study & Training, Sarah Lawrence Col, BA.
Work in Public Collections: Mem Art Gallery, Rochester, N Y;
Evansville Mus Art; Riverside Mus, New York; Larry Aldrich
Mus; Cathedral Cuernavaca, Mex; plus others.
Commissions: Mural sculpture, Lobby, Radio Sta WAVE, Louisville,
Ky; sculpture, Electra Film Prod, New York; wall sculpture,
Youngstown Res Ctr, Ohio; plus others.
Exhibitions: Boston Art Festival, 60 & 64; Silvermine Guild Artists,
63 & 64; Dallas Mus Fine Arts, 64; Riverside Mus, 64; Hopkins
Art Ctr, Dartmouth Col, 64; plus others.
Awards: Frank J Lewis Award, Univ Ill, 59; award, Silvermine
Guild Artists, 64.
Dealer: Kendall Art Gallery, Box 742, Wellfleet, MA 02667.
Mailing Address: c/o Coe Kerr Gallery, 49 E 82nd St, New York,
NY 10028.

BROWN, MARION B
Painter
Preferred Media: Watercolor.
b Brooklyn, N Y, Oct 15, 13.
Study & Training: Pratt Inst, Sch Fine & Appl Arts, cert teaching;
also with Edgar A Whitney.
Work in Public Collections: Dimes Savings Bank New York, Brook-
lyn; First Nat City Bank, Syosset, N Y.

Exhibitions: Hudson Valley Art Asn, White Plains, N Y, 61-72; Am Watercolor Soc, Nat Acad Design Galleries, New York, N Y, 62, 69, 71 & 72; Audubon Artists, Nat Acad Design Galleries, 65 & 66; Am Artists Prof League, New York, 66-72; Catharine Lorillard Wolfe Art Club, Nat Acad Design Galleries, 67-71.
Teaching: Instr watercolor, Malverne High Sch, N Y, 53-65; instr watercolor, Garden City Community Club, N Y, 67-
Awards: Herb Olsen Award, Am Watercolor Soc, 71; gold medal, Hudson Valley Art Asn, 71; Coun Am Artists Socs Award, Catharine Lorillard Wolfe Art Club, 71.
Memberships: Am Watercolor Soc; Hudson Valley Art Asn; Am Artists Prof League; Catharine Lorillard Wolfe Art Club; Nat Art League.
Dealer: Garden City Galleries Ltd, 923 Franklin Ave, Garden City, NY 11530.
Mailing Address: 18 Nassau Ave, Freeport, NY 11520.

BROWN, MARVIN PRENTISS
Painter, Sculptor
Preferred Media: Industrial Materials.
b New York, N Y, July 2, 43.
Study & Training: Brooklyn Mus Art Sch, 61-62, with Donald Fabricant & Peter Forakis; Yale Univ Summer Sch, Yale-Norfolk fel, 64, with Leland Bell & Richard Ziemann; Philadelphia Col Art, BFA, 65, with Robert Keyser, Natalie Charkow & Jean Cohen; Ind Univ, 65-66, with Ronald Slowinski; Brooklyn Col, 67, with Carl Holty.
Work in Public Collections: Philadelphia Pub Sch Syst, Pa; Eastern Mich Univ, Ypsilanti; Corp Design Ctr, Westinghouse Corp, Gateway Ctr, Pittsburgh, Pa.
Commissions: Wall sculpture, Howard Beach Br, Queensborough Pub Libr, Dept Pub Works, New York City, 71.
Exhibitions: Ann Exhib Contemp Am Painting, 69 & 72, Ann Exhib Contemp Am Sculpture, 70, Whitney Mus Am Art; Afro-American Artists: New York and Boston, Mus Fine Arts, Boston, 70; Untitled I, Art Lending Serv, Mus Mod Art, New York, 71; American Drawings: The Last Decade, Katonah Gallery, N Y, 71; Painting or Sculpture?, Newark Mus, N J, 72.
Teaching: Lectr painting, Philadelphia Col Art, Pa, 70-71; vis artist, Univ R I, summer 72; adj lectr art, Hunter Col, 71-; lect, Calif State Univ, Hayward, 72-73.
Awards: Corp Yaddo residence award, 68; Edward MacDowell Asn fel, 70.
Bibliography: Hilton Kramer (auth), Black artists' show on view in Boston, N Y Times, 5/22/70; Barbara Rose (auth), Black art in America, Art in Am, 9-10/70; Carter Ratcliff (auth), The Whitney annual: part I, Artforum, 4/72.
Mailing Address: 171 Spring St, New York, NY 10012.

BROWN, MARY RACHEL, see MARAIS

BROWN, PAUL LOUIS
Painter
Preferred Media: Acrylics.
b Boston, Mass, June 25, 39.
Study & Training: Brandeis Univ, 57-61, BA; Yale Univ, 61-65, MFA.
Exhibitions: Indianapolis Mus Show, Ind, 70; Project '70, Boston City Hall, Mass, 70; one-man show, Poindexter Gallery, New York, N Y, 70.
Teaching: Asst prof fine arts, Brandeis Univ, 69-
Mailing Address: 15 Cooney St, Somerville, MA 02143.

BROWN, RICHARD F
Museum Director
b New York, N Y, Sept 20, 16.
Study & Training: Bucknell Univ, AB, 40; Inst Fine Arts, New York Univ, 40-42; Harvard Univ, MA, 48, Bacon-Rich traveling fel, 49, PhD, 52.
Teaching: Teaching fel art hist, Harvard Univ, 47-49; res scholar & lectr, Frick Collection, New York, 49-54; vis prof 19th century Fr painting, Harvard Univ, 54.
Positions: Chief cur, Los Angeles Co Art Mus, Calif, 55-62, dir, 62-65; dir, Kimbell Art Found, Fort Worth, Tex, 66-
Awards: Phi Beta Kappa Award; decoration arts & lett, Repub France, 62.
Memberships: Col Art Asn Am (pres); Asn Art Mus Dirs (pres); Am Asn Mus (mem coun).
Mailing Address: Kimbell Art Museum, Fort Worth, TX 76107.

BROWN, ROGER
Painter
Preferred Media: Oil.
b Hamilton, Ala, Dec 10, 41.
Study & Training: Am Acad Art, Chicago, Ill; Art Inst Chicago Sch, BFA & MFA.
Work in Public Collections: Art Inst Chicago; Elmhurst Col, Ill; Kresge Found, Detroit, Mich; Ill Bell Tel Collection, Chicago; Playboy Collection, Chicago.

Commissions: Painting, Main Bank Chicago, 72.
Exhibitions: Spirit of the Comics, Inst Contemp Art, Philadelphia, 69 & Am Fedn Arts, 70-71; Works by Chicago Artists, San Francisco Art Inst, 70; one-man show, Phyllis Kind Gallery, Chicago, 71; one-man show, Sacramento State Art Gallery, 71; Chicago School: Imagist Art 1947-72, Mus Contemp Art, Chicago, 72.
Awards: Renaissance Prize, Art Inst Chicago, 69 & Walter Campana Prize, 71; Art Inst Chicago Sch Joseph Ryerson foreign travel fel, 70.
Bibliography: Halstead (auth), Chicago, 69 & Linville (auth), New York, 70, Artforum; Franz Schulze (auth), Fantastic images: Chicago art since 1945, Follet, 72.
Publications: Illusr, Song of Susan, 10/70, Four poems by Yevtushenko, 10/71 & Encounter in Munich, 3/72, Playboy Mag.
Dealer: Phyllis Kind Gallery, 226 E Ontario St, Chicago, IL 60611.
Mailing Address: 3647 N Wilton Ave, Chicago, IL 60613.

BROWN, WILLIAM FERDINAND II
Illustrator, Writer
b Jersey City, N J, Apr 16, 28.
Study & Training: Princeton Univ, AB, 50.
Memberships: Nat Cartoonists Soc; Artists & Writers.
Publications: Auth & illusr, Tiger tiger, 50, Beat beat beat, 49, The girl in the Freudian slip, 60, The abominable showmen, 60 & The world is my yo-yo, 63.
Mailing Address: 44 Grahampton Lane, Greenwich, CT 06830.

BROWN, WILLIAM HENRY
Painter
Preferred Media: Oil on Canvas.
b Oakland, Calif, Mar 19, 31.
Study & Training: Univ San Francisco; San Francisco Art Inst, BFA & MFA.
Work in Public Collections: Oakland Art Mus, Calif; De Young Mus, San Francisco, Calif; San Francisco Art Comn.
Exhibitions: Drawing Show & Summer Painting Show, San Francisco Mus Art, 64; Foreign Artists in Rome I, Artists & Stud Ctr Gallery, Italy, 66; one-man show, John S Bolles Gallery, San Francisco, 68; 4B, Pinturas, Cascais, Port, 70.
Teaching: Instr painting & drawing, San Francisco Art Inst, 61-64.
Awards: Purchase prize, Oakland Art Mus, 59; award, Calif Palace Legion of Honor, San Francisco, 61.
Dealer: John S Bolles Gallery, 10 Gold St, San Francisco, CA 94133.
Mailing Address: 31 West Mall, Bristol BS8 4BG, Eng.

BROWN GREENE, LUCILLE
Painter, Lecturer
Preferred Media: Acrylics, Oils, Watercolors, Collages.
b Los Angeles, Calif.
Study & Training: Univ Calif, Los Angeles, with Richard Haines, Rice Hebrun & Stanton MacDonald-Wright.
Work in Public Collections: Long Beach Mus Art, Calif; Dixie Col, St George, Utah; Utah State Agr Col, Logan; Long Beach State Col Art Dept, Calif.
Exhibitions: Butler Inst Am Art; Calif Nat Watercolor Soc; Los Angeles Co Mus Art, Calif; Pasadena Mus, Calif; Mus Belle Arts, Mexico City, Mex.
Teaching: Chmn dept art, Santa Monica H S, Calif, 50-58; instr art, Santa Monica Col, 58-69.
Positions: Lectr Modern Art, Playa del Rey Women's Club, Calif, 72; lectr Modern Art, Women Painters of West, Ebell Club, Los Angeles, 72.
Awards: Stairway of the Stars Award, Santa Monica City & Bd Educ, 68; Am Watercolor Soc Award, Calif Nat Watercolor Soc, 71; two awards, Women Painters of the West, 71 & 72.
Memberships: Calif Nat Watercolor Soc (secy, 1 yr, historian, 4 yrs); Women Painters of the West (juror, 72-73).
Publications: Illusr, Passover to freedom, Ritchie, 68; auth, Art, Calif J Secondary Educ.
Mailing Address: c/o Galerie Internationale, 1095 Madison Ave, New York, NY 10028.

BROWNE, ROBERT M
Collector, Patron
b Brooklyn, N Y, Apr 12, 26.
Exhibitions: (Of Collection) Oceanic Arts, Honolulu Acad Arts, Hawaii, 67; Sculpture of Polynesia, Art Inst Chicago, Ill, 67 & Mus Primitive Art, New York, N Y, 68; Arts of Oceania, Dallas Mus Fine Arts, Tex, 70; Art of the Sepik River, Art Inst Chicago, 71.
Bibliography: Allen Wardwell (auth), The sculpture of Polynesia, 67 & The art of the Sepik River, 71, Art Inst Chicago; John Lunsford (auth), The arts of Oceania, Dallas Mus Fine Arts, 70.
Memberships: Catholic Art Asn Hawaii (pres, 65-); Honolulu Acad Arts; Bishop Mus Asn; Anthrop Soc Hawaii.
Art Interests: Primitive art; Japanese Mingei ceramic collection.
Mailing Address: 3625 Anela Pl, Honolulu, HI 96822.

BROWNE, SYD J
Painter
Preferred Media: Oils, Watercolors.
b Brooklyn, N Y, Aug 21, 07.
Study & Training: Pratt Inst; Art Stud League New York.
Work in Public Collections: Libr Cong, Washington, D C; New
Britain Inst, Conn; New York Pub Libr, N Y; Staten Island Inst,
N Y; Fairleigh Dickinson Univ, N J.
Awards: Mischa Lempert Mem Purchase Prize, Salmagundi Club,
50; William Church Osborn Purchase Prize, Am Watercolor Soc,
50; Soc Am Artists Award, Salmagundi Club, 70.
Memberships: Nat Acad Design; Salmagundi Club.
Dealer: Grand Central Galleries, Hotel Biltmore, New York, NY
10017.
Mailing Address: Winter Harbor, ME 04693.

BROWNETT, THELMA DENYER
Painter
Preferred Media: Oil.
b Jacksonville, Fla, Oct 26, 24.
Study & Training: Wesleyan Conserv, BFA(magna cum laude), 46,
with Emile Holzhauer; Columbia Univ, 48, with Dr Edwin Zieg-
field; Univ Ga, MFA, 52, with Lamar Dodd, James Johnson
Sweeny & William Zorack.
Work in Public Collections: Ga Mus Art, Athens; Gertrude Herbert
Art Mus, Augusta, Ga; Atlanta Art Mus, Ga; Ringling Mus Art,
Sarasota, Fla; also private collections in the U S and abroad.
Commissions: Mural, Puppet Playhouse, Augusta, Ga, 51; hundreds
of portraits, 56-; Reredos, St Peter's Church, Jacksonville, Fla,
58; Triptych, St Mark's Episcopal Church, Jacksonville, 63;
mural, Off Bldg, San José Plaza, Jacksonville, 65.
Exhibitions: Am Artists Prof League Nat Exhib, New York, N Y, 52;
Nat Asn Women Artists, Argent Gallery, New York, 54; A C A
Gallery Nat, New York, 55; Arts Festival Twelve, Regional Inter-
national, Jacksonville, 71; Fla Artist Group State Exhib, St
Augustine, Fla, 72.
Teaching: Chmn dept art, Augusta Col, 52-55; chmn dept art, Jack-
sonville Univ, 56-58; chmn dept art, Fla Jr Col, 65-70.
Positions: Dir Gertrude Herbert Art Inst, 51-55; art comnr, State
of Ga, 54-57; chmn visual arts, Arts Festival Eleven, Jackson-
ville, 68-69.
Bibliography: Articles in Mademoiselle, 6/53 & La Rev Mod, Paris,
France, 55.
Memberships; Asn Ga Artists (pres, 55); Fla Artist Group (secy-
treas, 59-61); Fedn Fla Artists (mem bd dirs, 62-63); Jackson
Coun Arts (mem bd dirs, 69-).
Publications: Auth, Painting, Student Handbook, 71.
Mailing Address: 4774 Apache Ave, Jacksonville, FL 32210.

BROWNHILL, HAROLD
Painter, Illustrator
Preferred Media: Watercolours.
b Sheffield, U K; Can citizen.
Study & Training: Abbeydale & Cent Schs; Lancasterian schol,
Ecclesall Bierlow Schol; Sheffield Col Art, scholar, 7 yrs.
Exhibitions: N S Traveling Exhib, 18 months; A Quiet Prospect (oil
painting), N S Soc Artists 50th Anniversary Golden Jubilee Exhib,
Halifax, 72, plus numerous other ann exhibs.
Memberships: N S Soc Artists (pres, 2 yrs, treas, 6 yrs).
Publications: Auth, Acadia - a response to some questions, 71.
Mailing Address: 6322 Norwood St, Halifax, N S, Can.

BROWNING, COLLEEN
Painter
Preferred Media: Oils.
b Eire; U S citizen.
Study & Training: Slade Sch Art, London, Eng.
Work in Public Collections: Calif Palace Legion of Honor, San Fran-
cisco; Detroit Art Inst, Mich; Columbia Mus, S C; Rochester Mem
Art Gallery, N Y; Milwaukee Art Ctr, Wis.
Exhibitions: Five shows, Whitney Mus Am Art Contemp Ann, New
York, N Y, 51-63; Carnegie Int, Pittsburgh, Pa, 52 & 55; Art Inst
Chicago, 54; five shows, Nat Acad Design, New York, 57-72; Bi-
ennial Inter-Americana, Mexico, 61.
Teaching: Instr painting & drawing, City Col New York, 60-
Awards: Figure composition award, Stanford Univ, 56; second prize
for oils, Butler Inst Am Art, 60; Adolph & Clara Obrig Prize,
Nat Acad Design, 70.
Bibliography: Articles, In: Newsweek, 52 & 54; Norman Kent (auth),
Colleen Browning, Am Artist, 57; John Canaday (auth), Art -
against the current, New York Times, 65.
Memberships: Academician, Nat Acad Design (coun mem, 69-72,
jury of selection, 72, corresp secy, 72-73); Audubon Artists (jury
of awards, 72).

Publications: Illusr, Portrait of a lady, Ltd Ed Club, 67; illusr, The
poet's eye, Prentice-Hall, 69; illusr, Every man heart look down,
Crowell-Collier, 70; illusr, Downtown is, McGraw-Hill, 72.
Dealer: Kennedy Galleries, 20 E 56th St, New York, NY 10022.

BRUCKER, EDMUND
Painter, Educator
Preferred Media: Oils.
b Cleveland, Ohio, Nov 20, 12.
Study & Training: Cleveland Inst Art, Dipl in painting, 34, postgrad
study, 34-36; Wayman Adams Summer Sch, 44.
Work in Public Collections: Cleveland Mus Art; Indianapolis Mus
Art, Ind; Butler Inst Am Art, Youngstown, Ohio; Evansville Mus
Arts & Sci, Ind; Dartmouth Col, Hanover, N H.
Commissions: Portrait of founder, School Mfg Co, Inc, Chicago, Ill, 61;
portrait of L G Balfour, L G Balfour Co, Attleboro, Mass, 63;
portrait of Gov, Off of Gov, Ind State Capitol, Indianapolis, 64;
portrait of Col H Weir Cook, Munic Airport, Indianapolis, 67;
portrait of pres, Vincennes Univ, Ind, 70.
Exhibitions: Directions in American Painting, Carnegie Inst, Pitts-
burgh, Pa, 41; Paintings of the Year, Pepsi-Cola 3rd Ann, New
York, 46; 145th Ann of Painting & Sculpture, Pa Acad Fine Arts,
Philadelphia, Pa, 50; Contemporary Arts of United States, Los
Angeles, Calif, 56; La State Univ Int Drawing Invitational, Baton
Rouge, 65.
Teaching: Instr drawing, Cleveland Inst Art, 36-38; instr drawing &
painting, John Herron Art Sch, Indianapolis, 38-67; prof drawing
& painting, Herron Art Sch, Ind Univ, Indianapolis, 67-
Positions: Portrait cover artist, Ind Bus & Indust Mag, Culver, 60-
71.
Awards: First prize in oils, Ill State Fair 12th Prof Art Exhib, 58;
William H Block Co first prize, Hoosier Salon Patrons Asn, 62;
Millikin Award for artistic achievement, Art Asn Indianapolis,
63.
Bibliography: Jacob Getlar Smith (auth), The drawings of Edmund
Brucker, Am Artist Mag, 56; Medium of the ancients, Indianap-
olis Star Mag, 59; Margaret Harold (auth), Prize-winning paint-
ings, Bk III, Allied Publ, 63.
Memberships: Ind Artists Club (first v pres, 70); Hoosier Salon
Patrons Asn; Ind Soc Printmakers (dir, 50).
Mailing Address: 545 King Dr, Indianapolis, IN 46260.

BRUDER, HAROLD JACOB
Painter, Educator
Preferred Media: Oils.
b Bronx, N Y, Aug 31, 30.
Study & Training: Cooper Union, cert, 51; New Sch Soc Res; Pratt
Graphic Art Ctr.
Work in Public Collections: N J State Mus, Trenton; Palm Springs
Desert Mus; Joseph H Hirshhorn Mus.
Exhibitions: Corcoran Gallery Biennale, Washington, D C, 63;
Modern Realism & Surrealism, Am Fedn Arts traveling show, 64;
22 Realists, Whitney Mus Am Art, New York, N Y, 70; Painting
from the Photo, Riverside Mus, New York, 70; The Realist Re-
vival, Am Fedn Arts traveling show, 72-73; plus many one-man
shows.
Teaching: Assoc prof art, Kansas City Art Inst, 63-65; vis lectr,
Pratt Inst, 65-66; assoc prof art, Queen's Col (N Y), 65-; artist-
in-residence, Aspen Sch Contemp Art, summer 67.
Bibliography: The paintings of Harold Bruder, Ohio Rev, 6/61;
Ralph Pomeroy (auth), Harold Bruder and immediate family, Art
& Artists, 10/68; Alan Gussow (interviewer), A sense of place,
Saturday Rev Press, 72.
Dealer: Forum Gallery, 1018 Madison Ave, New York, NY 10021.
Mailing Address: 45-10 Kissena Blvd, Flushing, NY 11355.

BRULC, DENNIS
Printmaker, Painter
b Milwaukee, Wis, Aug 30, 46.
Study & Training: Univ Wis, BFA, 69.
Work in Public Collections: Winston Collection, Detroit, Mich. Mil-
waukee Art Ctr; S Johnson Collection, Racine, Wis; Akron Art
Inst, Ohio; Univ Wis-Milwaukee & Univ Wis-Madison.
Commissions: Pneumatic Matrice (with Richard Tupper & Orrel
Thompson), Akron Art Inst, 69; Pneumatic Matrice II (with John
Loyd Taylor), Milwaukee Art Ctr, 70; Homage to Sharon Tate,
print/sculpture, Lawrence Esser, Milwaukee, 71.
Exhibitions: One-man exhibs vapour dye prints, Univ Wis-Milwaukee
Fine Art Galleries, 68, Univ Wis-Green Bay Galleries, 69, Mil-
waukee Art Ctr, 69 & J Henry Galleries, St Thomas, V I, 70; Into
the Seventies, Akron Art Inst, 70; Reflection Thru A Collectors
Eye, Milwaukee, 71; 20 American Printmakers, Oneonta, N Y, 72;
Albrecht Durer Print & Drawing Show, Milwaukee, 72.
Awards: Award, Wis Painters & Sculptors, Milwaukee Art Ctr; first
prize, 37th Madison Salon Art, Univ Wis-Madison, 71; first prize,
Albrecht Durer Print & Drawing Show, Goethe House, 72.

Bibliography: M Kirkhorn (auth), Review of Brulc, Milwaukee Jour, 68; R Manglesdorff (auth), Multiple reality flow arte, Kaleido-scope, 71.
Memberships: Arts Technol Found (pres, 68-); Wis Painters & Sculptors; Negative Movement (dir, 66-69).
Publications: Contribr, Cheshire Mag & Fashions of Moving Times, 67; contribr, La Guardia, 68-71; co-auth, Pneumatic matrice (color movie), Milwaukee Art Ctr, 70; contribr, Los Angeles Staff, 71; contribr, Kaleidoscope, 71.
Mailing Address: c/o Bressler Galleries, 727 N Milwaukee St, Mil-waukee, WI 53202.

BRUMBAUGH, THOMAS BRENDLE
Art Historian, Writer
b Chambersburg, Pa, May 23, 21.
Study & Training: Indiana Univ Pa, BS; State Univ Iowa, MA; Ohio State Univ, PhD; fel East Asian Studies, Harvard Univ, 59; Ful-bright fel, India, 60.
Teaching: Instr, Ohio State Univ, 53-54; from asst prof to assoc prof, Emory Univ, 55-63; from assoc prof to prof, Vanderbilt Univ, 64-
Memberships: Col Art Asn; Archaeol Inst Am.
Research: Nineteenth century American painting, sculpture and architecture; J A D Ingres.
Publications: Ed, Middle Tenn Archit, 73; auth, articles on art and artists, In: Art News, Art Quart, Art J, Gazette Beaux-Arts & others.
Mailing Address: Box 1648, Station B, Nashville, TN 37235.

BRUMER, SHULAMITH
Sculptor
Preferred Media: Stone.
b Russia, July 5, 24; U S citizen.
Study & Training: Art Stud League New York, with William Zorach; Columbia Univ, with Oronzio Malderelli.
Exhibitions: One-man shows, Sculpture Ctr, New York, N Y, 65, 68 & 73; Philbrook Mus, Tulsa, Okla; Nat Acad Design, New York; Riverside Mus, New York; Brockton Art Ctr, Mass.
Teaching: Instr stone & wood carving, Sculpture Ctr Art Sch, 71-
Awards: Hon mention, Audubon Artists, 58-63; Allied Artists, 60 & Architectural League, 66.
Memberships: Sculpture Ctr (trustee, 71-); Allied Artists; Knicker-bocker Artists.
Dealer: Sculpture Center, 167 E 69th St, New York, NY 10021.
Mailing Address: 473 Franklin D Roosevelt Dr, New York, NY 10002.

BRUN, THOMAS
Sculptor, Instructor
b London, Eng, Nov 1, 11; U S citizen.
Study & Training: Soc Arts & Crafts, Detroit, Mich, with John Foster, Sarkis Sarkisian, Guy Palozolla, Jay Bursma & Lilly Saarimen.
Work in Public Collections: Detroit Inst Arts; Edison Elec Co; and several pub schs in Detroit.
Commissions: Lansing Birdman, Forbes Cohen, Lansing, Mich, 70; 4 wood figures, bronze hippo & bird mobile, Kalamazoo, Mich, 71; bronze hippo & bird in flight, Jackson, Mich, 72.
Exhibitions: Detroit Inst Arts, 50-70; regional exhibs, Ill, Mich, Minn & Wis, 53-57; Pa Acad Fine Arts, 64.
Teaching: Instr clay modeling, Detroit Inst Arts, 60-65; instr clay modeling, Birmingham Art Asn, 65-67; instr wax modeling, De-troit Jewish Community Ctr, 67-
Awards: Purchase prize, Detroit Inst Arts, 49, Lawrence Fleisch-man Award. 53.
Bibliography: Work reviewed by Broner, Detroit Times, M Driver, Detroit Free Press & H Shiff, Detroit News, 49-72.
Dealer: Arwin Galleries Inc, 222 Grand River, Detroit, MI 48226.
Mailing Address: 4811 Orion Rd, Rochester, MI 48063.

BRUNDAGE, AVERY
Collector
Collection: Asiatic art (Chinese, Japanese, Korea, Khmer, Thai-land, Burma, Nepal, India, Tibet & Persia) consisting of eight or ten thousand objects, given to City of San Francisco, which has built Museum Center of Asian Art and Culture to house it.
Mailing Address: 229 Lake Shore Dr, Chicago, IL 60611.

BRUNEAU, KITTIE
Painter
Preferred Media: Acrylics, Graphics.
b Montreal, P Q, Oct 12, 29.
Study & Training: Ecole Beaux Arts Montreal, EBA.
Work in Public Collections: Mus d'Art Contemporain, Montreal; Mus Que; Univ Montreal Libr; Univ Que Libr, Montreal; Sir Georges William Univ.
Exhibitions: Peintures Dessins, Mus d'Art Contemporain, Montreal, 66; Vancouver Print Int, 67; l'Expo Centenaire l'Ont, Toronto, 67;

2nd Biennale Gravure Cracovie, Pologne, 68; Foire Int Bale, Suisse, 72; plus many other group & one-man shows.
Bibliography: Guy Viau (auth), Kittie Bruneau-peintre et sculpteur, Cite Libre, Montreal, 62; J de Roussan (auth), Kittie Bruneau, Lidec, Montreal, 67.
Memberships: Asn Artistes Prof Que; Guild Graphique.
Mailing Address: c/o Galerie Libre, 2100 rue Crescent, Montreal, P Q, Can.

BRUNER, LOUISE KATHERINE
Art Critic, Writer
b Cleveland, Ohio, June 13, 10.
Study & Training: Denison Univ, BA; Bowling Green State Univ.
Teaching: Instr reviews & criticism, Univ Toledo, 72-
Positions: Art critic, Cleveland News, 40-56; art critic, Toledo Blade, 58-
Awards: First prize for critical writing, Ohio Newspaperwomen's Asn, 71; Roy Neuberger Found Award, Am Fedn Arts Nat Coun Arts Criticism Workshop, 68; alumni citation, Denison Univ, 71.
Memberships: Toledo Artists Club (trustee, 60-); Toledo Mod Art Group (trustee, 68-71); Art Interests, Inc (trustee, 69-); Archaeol Inst Am (trustee, Toledo Chap, 55-).
Publications: Ed, Blade art directory-public and private collections, 59; contribr, Arts Mag, 64-67; contribr, Craft Horizons, 71; contribr, Am Artist, Art Gallery Mag & Saint Louis Post-Dispatch, 72.
Mailing Address: 2200 Scottwood, Toledo, OH 43620.

BRUNO, PHILLIP A
Art Dealer, Collector
b Paris, France.
Study & Training: Columbia Col, hist fine arts & archit, BA; Inst Fine Arts, New York Univ.
Commissions: Restored 17th century house on Martha's Vineyard, Mass, 64.
Collections Arranged: First one-man exhib in Europe of Jose Luis Cuevas, Paris, 55; first one-man show in the South of El-mer Livingston Macrae, Nashville, Tenn, 63; first retrospective exhib, Ralph Rosenborg, Washington, D C, 52.
Positions: With Weyhe Gallery, New York, 50-51; co-founder, Grace Borgenicht Gallery & assoc dir, 51-55; dir, World House Gal-lery, New York, 56-60; dir, Am Exhibs for La Napoule Found, New York & France; co-dir, Staempfli Gallery, New York, 60-
Memberships: Hon life mem Saint Paul Art Ctr; first hon mem Tenn Fine Arts Ctr Cheekwood, Nashville; Dukes Co Hist Soc, Edgartown, Mass; Nat Trust Hist Preservation.
Collection: Mainly mid-twentieth century American watercolors and drawings, ranging from Marin to Gatch, including Lachaise, Demuth, Arthur B Davies, Robey, Kline & Corbett. Part of collection has been exhibited at the Krannert Art Museum, Ten-nessee Fine Arts Center, Finch College Museum of Art & Saint Paul Art Center.
Mailing Address: 419 E 57th St, New York, NY 10022.

BRUNO, SANTO MICHAEL
Painter, Instructor
Preferred Media: Acrylics, Plastics, Wood.
b Reading, Pa, June 29, 47.
Study & Training: Tyler Sch Art, Temple Univ, Philadelphia, Pa, BFA, 69; Tyler Sch Art, Rome, Italy, grant, 69-71, MFA, 71; also with Stephen Green, Romas Viesulas & David Pease.
Work in Public Collections: High Mus Art, Atlanta, Ga.
Exhibitions: Woodmere Gallery Invitational Painting & Sculpture Exhib, Philadelphia, 69; three-man invitational, Am Studies Ctr, Naples, Italy, 71; Painting & Sculpture Invitational, Loyola Univ, Rome, Italy, 71; Image, South Gallery, Atlanta, Ga, 72; First Im-pressions of Atlanta (one-man show), Atlanta, 72.
Teaching: Instr painting & drawing, Atlanta Sch Art, 71-
Awards: Italian-Am Origination grant, 68; Nathon Margolis Mem Award, Temple Univ, 69.
Bibliography: Neville Compton (auth), 3 young American painters, Rome Daily Am, Apr/71.
Dealer: Galerie Illien, 123 14th St N E, Atlanta, GA 30309.
Mailing Address: 275 Collier Rd N W, Atlanta, GA 30306.

BRUSCA, JACK
Painter
Preferred Media: Acrylic.
b New York, N Y, Nov 18, 39.
Study & Training: Univ N H; Sch Visual Arts, New York, with Alex Gottlieb, Alex Katz, Joe Tilson & Helen Frankenthaller.
Work in Public Collections: Aldrich Mus Contemp Art, Ridgefield, Conn; Powers Gallery, Univ Sydney, Australia; R I Sch Design; Albright-Knox Art Gallery, Buffalo, N Y; Cleveland Mus Art, Ohio.
Exhibitions: Plastic Presence, Jewish Mus, New York, 69; Flint In-vitational, Mich, 70; Toledo Mus Art, Ohio, 70; Paintings & Sculp-

tures of Today, Indianapolis Mus Art, Ind, 70; Highlights of the Season, Aldrich Mus Contemp Art, 70.
Dealer: Bonino Gallery, 7W 57th St, New York, NY 10002.
Mailing Address: 171 Bowery, New York, NY 10002.

BRYAN, WILHELMUS B
Art Administrator, Educator
b Washington, D C, Oct 9, 98.
Study & Training: Princeton Univ, BA & MA; Univ Minn; Macalester Col, LHD.
Teaching: Lectr, schs, cols, church & art educ groups; dean, Macalester Col, Saint Paul; dir, Blake Sch, Minneapolis, Minn; emer dir, Minneapolis Sch Art.
Positions: Dir Westminster Found, Princeton Univ; dir, Atlanta Art Asn; chmn, Ga State Art Comn.
Memberships: Nat Asn Schs Art (pres); Soc Artists & Art Dirs.
Mailing Address: 3171 Ringewood Rd N W, Atlanta, GA 30327.

BRYANT, OLEN L
Sculptor, Educator
Preferred Media: Wood, Clay.
b Cookeville, Tenn, May 4, 27.
Study & Training: Murray State Col, BS; Cranbrook Acad Art, MFA; Inst Allende, San Miguel, Mex; Cleveland Inst Art; Art Stud League New York.
Work in Public Collections: Tenn Fine Arts Ctr Collection, Nashville, Hunter Gallery, Chattanooga, Tenn; Carroll Reece Mus, Johnson City, Tenn.
Exhibitions: One-man shows, Tenn Fine Arts Ctr, 68, Hunter Gallery, Chattanooga, Tenn, 69, Evansville Mus, Ind, 70, Haas Gallery, Bloomsburg, Pa, 71 & Morehead Univ, Ky, 71.
Teaching: Instr art, Shaker Heights Schs, Ohio, 58-61; instr art, Union Univ, 62-65; assoc prof art, Austin Peay Univ, 66-
Memberships: Nashville Artists Guild; Am Crafts Coun; World Crafts Coun.
Mailing Address: Dept of Art, Austin Peay University, Clarksville, TN 37040.

BRZOZOWSKI, RICHARD JOSEPH
Painter
Preferred Media: Watercolors, Acrylics.
b New Britain, Conn, Sept 9, 32.
Study & Training: Paier Art Sch, New Haven, Conn.
Work in Public Collections: Grumbacher Collection, New York, N Y; Phoenix Mutual Inst, Hartford, Conn; Springfield Mus Art, Mass.
Exhibitions: Nat Acad, New York, 68; Watercolor U S A, Springfield, Mo, 68; Am Watercolor Soc, New York, 71; Decordova Mus, Springfield, Mass, 72; Audubon Artists, New York, 72.
Awards: Grumbacher Purchase Award, Am Watercolor Soc, 63; best watercolor award, Conn Watercolor & Conn Acad, 66; famous artist sch award, Conn Watercolor Soc, 67.
Memberships: Am Watercolor Soc; Conn Watercolor Soc (bd dirs, 69-70); Conn Acad; Silvermine Guild Artists; Acad Artists Am.
Mailing Address: 13 Fox Rd, Plainville, CT 06062.

BUBA, JOY FLINSCH
Sculptor, Illustrator
b Lloyd's Neck, N Y, July 25, 04.
Study & Training: Eberle Studio, New York, N Y; Staedel Kunst Inst, Frankfurt, Ger; Art Acad, Munich, Ger; and with Theodor Kaerner & Angelo Yank.
Work in Public Collections: David Mannes, Metrop Mus Art, New York; Florence Sabin, Statuary Hall, Capitol Bldg, Washington, D C; Norman Thomas & Margaret Sanger, Nat Portrait Gallery, Washington, D C; John D Rockefeller, Jr, Rockefeller Plaza, New York; Konrad Adenauer, Palais Schaumberg, Bonn, Ger.
Publications: Illusr, Elephants, Proboscidea memoir; Elephants, rabbits; Frogs & toads, goldfish; Written in sand; Lyrico, the only horse of his kind.
Mailing Address: 521 Park Ave, New York, NY 10021.

BUCCI, ANDREW A
Painter
Preferred Media: Oils, Watercolors.
b Vicksburg, Miss, Jan 12, 22.
Study & Training: Sch Art Inst Chicago, BFA, 51, MFA, 54.
Work in Public Collections: Brooks Mem Gallery, Memphis, Tenn; Ark Arts Ctr, Little Rock; Miss Art Asn, Jackson; Florence Mus, S C; Delta State Col, Cleveland, Miss.
Commissions: Designer, Miss Statehood Commemorative U S Postage Stamp, U S Post Off Dept, 67.
Exhibitions: Butler Inst Midyear Ann, Youngstown, Ohio, 56; Fifth Delta Ann, Ark Art Ctr, 62; Washington Watercolor Asn Ann, 64; Eastern Region Drawing Exhib, Philadelphia Mus, 65; Ala Watercolor Soc Ann, 67; plus four one-man shows.
Awards: First, Miss Art Asn Nat Oil Show, 61; purchase prize watercolor, Fifth Delta Ann, Ark Arts Ctr, 62; Bellaman Found

Award, 64.
Memberships: Miss Art Asn; Washington Watercolor Asn (past pres & v pres, treas, 72-); Artists Equity Asn; Soc Washington Artists; Watercolor Soc Ala.
Mailing Address: 13711 Piscataway Dr, Oxon Hill, MD 20021.

BUCHER, GEORGE ROBERT
Educator, Sculptor
Preferred Media: Fibers, Polyester.
b Sunbury, Pa, Oct 14, 31.
Study & Training: Univ Pa & Pa Acad Fine Arts, BFA, 57; Barnes Found, Merion, Pa, 56-58; Univ Pa & Pa Acad Fine Arts, MFA, 59.
Work in Public Collections: Civic Fine Arts Ctr, Philadelphia, Pa; Sioux Falls Col, S Dak; Kleinberg, Ont.
Exhibitions: Nat Coun Jewish Women, Philadelphia, Pa, South Orange, Teaneck & Essex Co, N J, 67-70; Binder Twine Festival, Toronto, Ont, 69-72; one-man show, New Holland Sperry Rand, Pa, 71; Art 71, William Penn Mus, Harrisburg, Pa, 71; Fellowship Show, Pa Acad Fine Arts, Philadelphia, 72; plus many others.
Collections Arranged: Med Exhibs, Wistar Inst Anat Mus, Philadelphia, 55; Mayan Art, 58, Phrygian Art, 59, Philadelphia Artists, 59, Copic Art, 60 & Ruins of Rome, 61, Univ Pa Mus; designed permanent N Am Art Sect, Univ Pa Mus, 61.
Teaching: Artist, Wistar Inst Anat, 55-56; artist & asst to mgr exhibs, Univ Pa Mus, 58-61; instr art & mech drawing, Salem High Sch, N J, 59-60; instr & artist, Univ Pa Fine Arts Sch & Mus, 60-61; assoc prof & chmn art dept, Sioux Falls Col, 61-65; assoc prof art, Susquehanna Univ, 65-
Memberships: Col Art Asn Am.
Collection: Fiber sculpture.
Publications: Auth, No island is a man (cartoon book), 65.
Mailing Address: Freeburg, PA 17827.

BUCK, RICHARD D
Conservator
b Feb 3, 03; U S citizen.
Study & Training: Harvard Univ, AB, AM.
Teaching: Tutor fine arts, Harvard Univ, 28-32; instr fine arts, Wheaton Col, 32-34; lectr conserv, Harvard Univ, 48-51.
Positions: Res asst & chief conservator, Dept Conserv, Fogg Mus, Harvard Univ, 37-51; spec wood panels, Nat Gallery London, 49-50; dir, Intermuseum Conserv Asn, Oberlin, Ohio, 52-
Memberships: Int Inst Conserv Hist & Artistic Works (v pres, 60-70, mem coun, 60-, chmn, Am group, 59-61).
Research: Wood technology and application to works of art.
Publications: Ed, On picture varnishes and their solvents, 71.
Mailing Address: Intermuseum Laboratory, Allen Art Bldg, Oberlin, OH 44074.

BUCK, ROBERT TREAT, JR
Art Historian, Art Administrator
b Fall River, Mass, Feb 16, 39.
Study & Training: Williams Col, BA; N Y Univ, MA with Dr Walter Friedlaender.
Collections Arranged: Sam Francis: Paintings 1947-1972; Paintings by Auguste Herbin; Here and Now: 13 Young Americans; Modernist Painting; Pollock to the Present; Master Drawings from the Art Inst Chicago and the Mus Modern Art; Homage to Albers.
Teaching: Adj assoc prof mus training, Univ Toledo, 65-66; adj assoc prof mus training & 19th & 20th century art, Wash Univ, 66-70; adj assoc prof mus training, State Univ N Y Buffalo, 72-
Positions: Lectr-researcher, Toledo Mus Art, 64-65; asst cur & instr, Wash Univ, 65-67 & dir, gallery of art, 65-70; asst dir, Albright-Knox Art Gallery, Buffalo, N Y, 70-73, dir, 73-
Awards: N Y State Coun Arts traveling fel, summer 71.
Research: Nineteenth century French painting; art of the twentieth century.
Publications: Auth, Sam Francis, Paintings 1947-1972, 72.
Mailing Address: 1285 Elmwood Ave, Buffalo, NY 14222.

BUCKLEY, CHARLES EDWARD
Art Administrator, Art Historian
b South Hadley, N H, April 29, 19.
Study & Training: Art Inst Chicago, BFA; Harvard Univ, MA.
Teaching: Teaching fel, Dept Fine Arts, Harvard Univ; also Loomis Sch, Windsor, Conn & Hartford Col, Hartford, Conn.
Positions: Keeper, W A Clark Collection, Corcoran Gallery Art, Washington, D C, 49-51; gen cur, Wadsworth Atheneum, 51-55; dir, Currier Gallery, Manchester, N H, 55-64; dir, St Louis Art Mus, Mo, 64-
Memberships: Am Asn Mus (pres, 72-74); Asn Art Mus Dirs (secy-treas, 68-71, trustee & v pres, 71-72; Col Art Asn Am; Soc Archit Historians.

Research: Seventeenth to twentieth century American art; eighteenth
century American art; eighteenth century English painting;
twentieth century European painting and sculpture.
Publications: Contribr, articles, In: Connoisseur, Art Quart, Art
Bull & Antiques.
Mailing Address: 665 S Skinker, St Louis, MO 63110.

BUDD, DAVID
Sculptor, Painter
Exhibitions: Whitney Mus Am Art Ann, New York, N Y, 69 & 70.
Mailing Address: 333 Park Ave S, New York, NY 10010.

BUDD, MRS HUDSON WARREN, see LIVINGSTON, VIRGINIA

BUECHNER, THOMAS SCHARMAN
Art Administrator, Painter
b New York, N Y, Sept 25, 26.
Study & Training: Princeton Univ, 44-45; Art Stud League New
York, 46-47; Ecole Beaux-Arts, Fontainebleau & Paris, France,
47-48.
Commissions: Portraits, Lewis Francis, Packer Col Inst, 64, Paul
Sheaffer, Brooklyn Hosp, 65, David Atwater, Grace Episcopal
Church, 70 & Joseph Hill, Downstate Med Ctr, 72.
Collections Arranged: Vincent Van Gogh (arranged), Metrop Mus
Art, 49; Glass 1959 (assembled), Corning Mus Glass, 59;
Levine-Shikler (cataloged), Brooklyn Mus, 71.
Teaching: Head art dept, Corning Community Col, 58-60; head
painting & drawing, Heights Casino, Brooklyn, 65-68; prof draw-
ing arts & social change, Salzburg Sem Am Studies, 71.
Positions: Dir, Corning Mus Glass, 50-60; dir, Brooklyn Mus, 60-
71; pres, Corning Mus Glass, 71-
Awards: Brooklyn Man of Year, Brooklyn Col, 63; Forsythia
Award, Brooklyn Botanic Garden, 71; Gari Melcher's Gold
Medal, Artist's Fellowship, 71.
Memberships: Am Asn Mus (councilman, 60); Nat Collection Fine
Arts Adv Bd, 72; Louis Comfort Tiffany Found (trustee, 71);
Chemung Valley Arts Coun (pres, 72); fel Royal Soc for En-
couragement of Arts.
Research: American illustration, emphasis on cover artists; glass
history with emphasis on art glass.
Publications: Auth, Glass vessels in Dutch painting in the 17th
century, 52; auth, Life and work of Frederick Carder, 52; auth,
A guide to The Corning Museum of Glass, 55; contribr, A guide
to The Brooklyn Museum, 67; auth, Norman Rockwell: artist and
illustrator.
Mailing Address: Corning Glass Works, Corning, NY 14830.

BUENO, JOSE
Sculptor, Painter
Preferred Media: Woods, Oils.
b Oklahoma City, Okla, Mar 23, 37.
Work in Public Collections: Mus Mod Art, New York, N Y; Pasadena
Art Mus, Calif; Los Angeles Co Mus Art, Calif; Victoria & Al-
bert Mus, London, Eng; Fort Worth Art Mus, Tex.
Awards: Cassandra Found award; Am Fedn Arts award.
Mailing Address: 725 N Western Ave, Los Angeles, CA 90029.

BUGGEL, WILLIAM LEE
Art Administrator, Painter
Preferred Media: Clay, Polymer.
b Columbia, S C, May 8, 39.
Study & Training: Univ S C, BA(fine arts), 67; study with Hiram
Williams, summer 67.
Work in Public Collections: Greenville Co Mus Art, S C; Gibbes Art
Gallery, Charleston, S C.
Commissions: Mural, C of C, Columbia, 71.
Exhibitions: Guild of S C Artists, 67; Seventh & Ninth Piedmont Ann
Painting & Sculpture, Charlotte, N C; Gallery Contemp Art,
Winston-Salem, N C, 68; 23rd Ann S C Artists Exhib, 69; Tri-
centennial Show, Contemp Artists S C, 70; plus five one-man
shows.
Positions: Asst dir, Gibbes Art Gallery, 68-
Awards: Ben Winestein Award, Greenville Mus, 67; Lewis & Dowis
Archit Award, 71; Thomas J Tobias Award, 72.
Bibliography: Jack A Morris (auth), Contemporary Artists of South
Carolina Tricentennial Publication, Keys Printing, 70.
Memberships: Guild S C Artists (pres, 71).
Mailing Address: 15 Broad St, Charleston, SC 29401.

BUHRMAN, RUTH EWING
Painter
Preferred Media: Acrylic.
b Easthampton, Mass, Mar 3, 23.
Study & Training: Corcoran Sch Art; Art League Northern Va,
Alexandria, with Joy Luke, James Twitty & Frank Getlein.

Exhibitions: Ann Exhibs, Washington Soc Artists, Smithsonian Mus
Nat Hist, Washington, D C, 62, 63 & 65; Ann Exhibs, Va Mus Fine
Arts, Alexandria, 71 & 72; Art League Northern Va, 72.
Awards: Blue ribbon, Va Mus Fine Arts, 70; Aschille Gorky Award,
Waterford Found, 71; cert merit, Va Mus Fine Arts, 72.
Memberships: Art League Northern Va (mem judging comt, 70-);
Studio 213; Va Mus Fine Arts; Va Fedn Women's Clubs (chmn
fine arts, 68-70).
Mailing Address: 8516 Culver Pl, Alexandria, VA 22308.

BULLARD, EDGAR JOHN III
Museum Curator, Art Historian
b Los Angeles, Calif, Sept 15, 42.
Study & Training: Univ Calif, Los Angeles, BA, 65, MA, 68; Harvard
Univ Inst Arts Admin, 71.
Collections Arranged: German Expressionist Watercolors in Amer-
ican Collections, 69, Mary Cassatt 1844-1926, 70 & John Sloan
1871-1951, 71, Nat Gallery Art, Washington, D C.
Positions: Asst cur, J Paul Getty Mus, Malibu, Calif, 67; mus cur,
Nat Gallery Art, 68-70, asst to dir, 70-71, cur spec projs, 71-
Awards: Samuel H Kress Found fel, Nat Gallery Art, 67-68.
Memberships: Am Asn Mus; U S-Int Coun Mus; Col Art Asn Am;
Archives Am Art; Nat Trust for Hist Preserv.
Research: Late nineteenth and twentieth century American and
European art.
Publications: Auth, John Sloan as an illustrator, Am Artist, 10/71;
auth, The Centennial year of artist John Sloan, Smithsonian Mag,
10/71; auth, Edgar Degas, McGraw-Hill, 71; co-auth, John Sloan
1871-1951 (exhib catalog), Nat Gallery Art, 71; auth, Mary
Cassatt: oils and pastels, Watson-Guptill, 72.
Mailing Address: National Gallery of Art, Washington, DC 20565.

BULTMAN, FRITZ
Sculptor, Painter
b New Orleans, La, Apr 4, 19.
Study & Training: With Morris Graves, 31; New Bauhaus, Chicago,
37-38; Hans Hofmann Sch Fine Arts, 38-41.
Work in Public Collections: Whitney Mus Am Art; Rockefeller Art
Gallery, Seal Harbor, Maine; Mus Art, R I Sch Design; Riverside
Mus; Univ Nebr; plus others.
Exhibitions: One-man show, Delgado Mus, New Orleans, 59; also
exhibs in U S, Paris, Cologne, Turino, Milan & Japan.
Teaching: Lectr, univs, cols, art clubs & mus; instr painting, sch
educ, Pratt Inst, New York, 58-63; instr painting, grad art sch,
Hunter Col, 59-63; instr & artist-in-residence, Fine Arts Work
Ctr, Provincetown, Mass, 68-70.
Awards: Ital Govt grant, 50-51; prize, Art Inst Chicago, 64; Ful-
bright res grant, Paris, 64-65.
Bibliography: Nathaniel Pousette-Dart (ed), included in: American
painting today, Hastings, 56.
Publications: Contribr, article on Hans Hofmann, In: Art News, 63.
Mailing Address: 176 E 95th St, New York, NY 10028.

BUMBECK, DAVID A
Printmaker, Educator
Preferred Media: Intaglio.
b Framingham, Mass, May 1, 40.
Study & Training: R I Sch Design, BFA, 62; Syracuse Univ, MFA, 66,
with Robert Marx.
Work in Public Collections: Everson Mus, Syracuse, N.Y; New York
Pub Libr, N.Y; Rochester Mem Galleries, N Y; Ithaca Mus, N Y;
Wiggin Collection, Boston Pub Libr, Mass.
Exhibitions: Boston Printmakers Nat Exhib, 67-72; Graphics 69, Nat
Print Exhib, N Y State Fair, 69; Nat Print Exhib, Northern Ill
Univ, 70; Nat Exhib, Soc Am Graphic Artists, 71; Silvermine Nat
Print Exhib, 72.
Teaching: Instr painting & printmaking, Mass Col Art, Boston, 66-68;
asst prof printmaking, Middlebury Col, 68-
Awards: Purchase award, Everson Mus, 66; David Berger Mem
Award, Boston Printmakers Nat Exhib, 68; purchase awards, Ga
State Univ Nat Print Exhibs, 70 & 71.
Memberships: Boston Printmakers (mem exec bd, 68-); Silvermine
Guild Artists.
Dealer: Far Gallery, 746 Madison Ave, New York, NY 10021.
Mailing Address: 18 College St, Middlebury, VT 05753.

BUNCE, LOUIS DeMOTT
Painter
Preferred Media: Oils, Acrylics.
b Lander, Wyo, Aug 13, 07.
Study & Training: Mus Art Sch, Portland, Ore; Art Stud League
New York, N Y.
Work in Public Collections: San Francisco Mus Art, Calif; Whitney
Mus Am Art, New York; Portland Mus; Seattle Art Mus, Wash;
Butler Inst Am Art, Youngstown, Ohio.
Commissions: Mural, Port of Portland, Portland Int Airport, 58;
600 serigraphs, Hilton Hotel, Portland, 63.

Exhibitions: Third Biennial, São Paulo, Brazil, 55-56; Print Coun Am, 62-63; Univ Ill Art Mus, 67; Nat Drawing Soc, 70; Denver Mus Art, 71.
Teaching: Instr painting, Mus Art Sch, Portland, 46-; vis prof painting, Univ Calif, Berkeley, 60; vis prof painting, Univ Ill, Urbana, 66-67.
Awards: Ford Found fel, Tamarind Lithographic Workshop, 61; Ford Found Purchase Award, Seattle Art Mus Ann, 65; painting award, Portland Art Mus Ann, 71.
Bibliography: New painters, Art in Am, 55; West coast painters, Life Mag, 11/57.
Dealer: Fountain Gallery, 115 S W Fourth Ave, Portland, OR 97204.
Mailing Address: 1800 S E Harold St, Portland, OR 97202.

BUNKER, EUGENE FRANCIS, JR (GENE)
Potter, Educator
Preferred Media: Stoneware, Porcelain.
b Bozeman, Mont, Aug 11, 28.
Study & Training: Mont State Univ, BS, 53; Mills Col, MA, 55.
Work in Public Collections: Portland Mus, Ore; Henry Gallery, Univ Washington, Seattle; Stetson Univ Permanent Collection, Deland, Fla; Prieto Mem Collection, Mills Col, Oakland, Calif; Art Inst Chicago, Ill.
Commissions: Two large stoneware covered jars, Rot Harris, Am composer, 56; two red porcelain bottles, A A D'Amico Collection of Contemp Crafts, Bangor, Maine, 62; baptismal font, Good Shepherd Lutheran Church, Sanford, Fla, 62; baptismal font, Christ the King Episcopal Church, Orlando, Fla, 63; complete altar appointments, Episcopal Church, Port Saint Lucie, Fla, 63.
Exhibitions: Ninth Nat Decorative Arts Ceramic Exhib, Wichita, Kans, 54; Finer-Clay-Metal Nat Exhib, Saint Paul, Minn, 54; Calif State Fair, 55; Midwest Designer Craftsmen's Exhib, Art Inst Chicago, 57; Winter Park Festival, Fla, 63 & 64.
Teaching: Asst prof art, Stetson Univ, 59-64; assoc prof art & head dept, Asheville Biltmore Col, 64-68; prof art & chmn dept, Univ N C, Asheville, 68-72.
Awards: First prize for stoneware, Calif State Fair, 55; hon award, Midwest Designer Craftsmen's Exhib, Art Inst Chicago, 57; first prize for sculpture, Winter Park Festival, 63 & 64; plus others.
Bibliography: F Messersmith (auth), The pottery of Gene Bunker, Am Artist Mag, 3/62; Eugene F Bunker, La Rev Mod, 8/67.
Memberships: Am Craftsmen's Coun; Southern Col Art Conf; Fla Craftsmen; Southern Highland Handicraft Guild; Asheville Art Mus (chmn recruiting comt & bd dirs, 64-68).
Publications: Auth, Art in the community, Ill Art Educ Asn Yearbook, 56; auth, twenty five articles on ceramics related fields, World Bk Encycl, 64; illusr, The year of the swan, 66; auth, Pottery lab outline, 66.
Dealer: America House, 57th St, New York, NY 10019.
Mailing Address: Bunker Hill Kiln Site, 948 Fairview Rd, Asheville, NC 28803.

BUNKER, GEORGE (RAYMOND)
Painter, Educator
Preferred Media: Oils, Lithography.
b Denver, Colo, May 27, 23.
Study & Training: Yale Univ BA, 46; Art Stud League New York, with Reginald Marsh, Yasuo Kuniyoshi & Vaclav Vytlacil, 46-48; Brooklyn Mus Art Sch, with Victor Candell, 48-49; Acad Julien, Paris, France, 49-50.
Work in Public Collections: Philadelphia Mus Art, Pa; Libr Cong, Washington, D C; Lessing Rosenwald Collection, Nat Gallery, Jenkintown, Pa; Samuel S Fleischer Found, Philadelphia; Rosenbach Found, Philadelphia.
Exhibitions: Am Fedn Arts Traveling Exhibs, 48, 55 & 57; Philadelphia Mus Art Second & Third Festivals; Pa Acad Fine Arts Biennials, 57, 63 & 65; Brooklyn Mus Art Print Nat, 58; Cincinnati Mus Art Int Exhib Lithography, 58.
Teaching: Instr drawing & painting, Swarthmore Col, 55-57; prof fine arts, Philadelphia Col Art, 58-, chmn dept, 58-65, dean faculty, 65-72.
Positions: Pres, Artists Equity Asn, Philadelphia, 59-60; bd dirs, Philadelphia Old Town Hist Soc, 71-72.
Awards: Award, Philadelphia Art Alliance Regional Prints & Drawings, 56; Print Club Philadelphia Purchase Prizes, 56, 57 & 61; third prize, Cheltenham Art Ctr First Nat Drawing Exhib, 64.
Memberships: Print Club Philadelphia (bd gov, 56-62 & 71-); Philadelphia Mus Art; Mus Mod Art, New York; Am Asn Univ Prof; Union Independent Cols Art (acad dean's bd, 66-72).
Publications: Ed, Leon Karp portfolio, Artists Equity Asn, 60; ed, Alexey Brodovitch and his influence, 72 & Mitzi Melnicoff, 73, Philadelphia Col Art.
Dealer: Socrates Perakis Gallery, 18 Bank St, Philadelphia, PA 19106.
Mailing Address: 324 S 12th St, Philadelphia, PA 19107.

BUNN, KENNETH RODNEY
Painter
b Denver, Colo, June 1, 38.
Study & Training: George Washington Univ; Univ Md; Am Univ; also taxidermy with Jonas Bros, Denver.
Work in Public Collections: In pvt collections.
Exhibitions: 145th-147th Ann, Nat Acad Design; 36th-38th Ann, Nat Sculpture Soc; World Wildlife Exhib, Palm Beach, Fla.
Awards: Bronze medal, Nat Sculpture Soc 36th Ann; Helen Foster Barnett Prize, Nat Acad Design 146th Ann.
Memberships: Fel Nat Sculpture Soc; Soc Animal Artists; Salmagundi Club.
Mailing Address: 2496 W Second Ave, Denver, CO 80223.

BUNSHAFT, MR & MRS GORDON
Collectors
Mr Bunshaft, b Buffalo, N Y, May 9, 09.
Study & Training: Mr Bunshaft, Mass Inst Technol, BArch, 33, fel & MArch, 35; Univ Buffalo, hon DFA, 62.
Commissions: Mr Bunshaft, design of Lever House, New York, N Y, Beinecke Rare Bk & Mss Libr, Yale Univ, New Haven, Conn, Albright-Knox Art Gallery, Buffalo & Joseph H Hirshhorn Mus & Sculpture Garden, Washington, D C.
Positions: Mr Bunshaft, mem Pres Comt on Fine Arts, 63-; mem, Int Coun Mus Mod Art.
Awards: Mr Bunshaft, Brunner Award, Nat Inst Arts & Lett, 55; medal honor, N Y Chap Am Inst Architects, 61; Chancellor's Medal, Univ Buffalo, 69.
Memberships: Mr Bunshaft, Academician Nat Acad Design; Nat Inst Arts & Lett; Munic Art Soc New York; hon mem Buffalo Fine Arts Acad; fel Am Inst Architects.
Collection: Contemporary art.
Mailing Address: 200 E 66th St, New York, NY 10021.

BURANABUNPOT, PORNPILAI
Designer
Preferred Media: Textiles.
b Nakorn-Pathom, Thailand, Jan 5, 45.
Study & Training: Univ Calif, Berkeley, BA, 68; Cranbrook Acad Art, Bloomfield Hills, Mich, MFA, 70; weaving with Ed Rossbach & Lilian Elliot, Berkeley.
Work in Public Collections: Mint Mus Art, Charlotte, N C; Art Comn Collection, State Ky.
Exhibitions: Third Biennial Craft Exhib, Birmingham, Mich, 69; one-woman show, Fabric Design, Paducah Col, Ky, 72; Mid-States Craft Exhib, Evansville Mus Arts, 72; Ninth Ann Piedmont Craft Exhib, Mint Mus Art, 72; Second Biennial Lake Superior Craft Exhib, Univ Minn, Duluth.
Teaching: Instr art, Murray State Univ, 70-71, asst prof art, 71-72; asst prof art, Gustavus Adolphus Col, 72-
Awards: Stud design competition textile design, P Kaufman Co, 69 & 70; purchase award, Mint Mus Art, 72.
Memberships: Am Craftsmen Coun; Ky Guild Artists & Craftsmen.
Mailing Address: 621 W St Paul St, Saint Peter, MN 56082.

BURCH, CLAIRE R
Painter, Writer
Preferred Media: Watercolors, Collage.
b New York, N Y, Feb 19, 25.
Study & Training: Wash Sq Col, New York Univ, BA, 43-47.
Work in Public Collections: Butler Institute Am Art, Youngstown, Ohio; Guild Hall, East Hampton, New York; Birmingham Mus, Ala; Brooklyn Mus, N Y; Beth Israel Hospital, New York.
Exhibitions: One-man shows, Ruth White Gallery, New York, 63, Galerie L'Antipoete, Paris, France, 63, Southampton Col, 64-65 & Roko Gallery, 64; Maniacal Laughter, Westbeth Gallery, New York, 71.
Awards: First prize for representational painting, Guild Hall, 65; first prize for watercolor, North Shore Community Art Ctr, 65; third prize for watercolor, Brooklyn Mus, 65.
Memberships: New York Playwrights Coop; Schizophrenics Anonymous Int.
Publications: Auth, Ten cents a dance (three-act play), 68; auth, Careers in psychiatry, Macmillan, 68; auth, Stranger in the family, Bobbs-Merrill, 72; auth & illusr, Notes of a survivor, Westbeth Poets Press, 72; auth, The secret songs of Claire Burch & auth (music, lyrics & bk), Blues to be called crazy when crazy's all there is (play), 72.
Mailing Address: 463 West St, New York, NY 10014.

BURCHESS, ARNOLD
Painter, Sculptor
Preferred Media: Watercolor, Bronze.
b Chicago, Ill, June 7, 12.
Study & Training: City Col New York, BSS; and with George W Eggers & Robert Garrison.

Commissions: Three bas reliefs (with Robert Garrison), Radio City Music Hall New York, N Y, 35.
Exhibitions: Butler Art Inst, 55; Am Watercolor Soc, New York, 55-; Birmingham Mus Art, Ala, 55; one-man show, Van Dimant Gallery, Southampton, N Y, 57; Mus Mod Art, New York, 59.
Teaching: Lects, Shapes in Clay, Metrop Mus Art, New York, 39; Prof & chmn dept fine art, Fashion Inst Technol, New York, 59-
Awards: Watercolor prize, Birmingham Mus Art, 55.
Bibliography: Article in La Rev Mod, 56; Arnold Burchess—watercolorist, Am Artist Mag, 59; Norman Kent (auth), 100 watercolor techniques, Watson-Guptill, 70.
Memberships: Am Watercolor Soc; Audubon Artists.
Dealer: Aries East Art Gallery, Rte 6A, East Brewster, MA 02640.
Mailing Address: South Harpswell, ME 04079.

BURDEN, CARTER
Collector
b Los Angeles, Calif, Aug 25, 41.
Study & Training: Harvard Univ; Columbia Univ Law Sch.
Positions: Founder & pres, The Studio Mus in Harlem.
Memberships: Exec Comt, Jr Coun of Mus Mod Art, New York; Int Coun Mus Mod Art (acquisitions comt).
Collection: Works of the contemporary period, mainly American abstract paintings since 1950.
Mailing Address: 1457 Lexington Ave, New York, NY 10028.

BURFORD, BYRON LESLIE
Painter, Educator
Preferred Media: Oil, Acrylics.
b Jackson, Miss, July 12, 20.
Study & Training: Univ Iowa, BFA & MFA.
Work in Public Collections: Worcester Art Mus, Mass; Walker Art Ctr, Minneapolis, Minn; Nelson/Atkins Gallery, Kansas City, Mo; Sheldon Art Mus, Lincoln, Nebr; George Eastman House, Rochester, N Y.
Exhibitions: Pa Acad Fine Arts, Philadelphia, 65; Am Acad Arts Ann, New York, N Y, 67; New York Gallery Mod Art, 68; Venice Biennale, Italy, 68; Bienal Arte Coltejer, Colombia, 70.
Teaching: Prof painting, Univ Iowa, 47-; prof painting, Univ Minn & Univ Mass, summer 67.
Awards: Guggenheim Found fel, Ford Found award & Nat Inst Arts & Lett grant, 60.
Dealer: Babcock Galleries, 805 Madison Ave, New York, NY 10021.
Mailing Address: 113 S Johnson, Iowa City, IA 52240.

BURGARD, RALPH
Art Administrator
b Buffalo, N Y, June 22, 27.
Study & Training: Dartmouth Col, AB.
Positions: Dir, Arts Coun Winston-Salem, N C & Saint Paul Coun Arts & Sci; dir bldg, Arts & Sci Ctr, Saint Paul; organizer, ann united cult fund campaign; bd mem, Nat Coun Arts & Govt, Dartmouth Arts Coun, Urban Arts Corps & Cunningham Dance Found; founding mem, Community Arts Couns, Inc; mem adv comt, Inst Int Educ & New York City Cult Coun; first exec dir, Assoc Couns Arts, 65-70; arts consult, many states, cities & U S Govt.
Publications: Auth, Arts in the city; also numerous articles.
Mailing Address: 10 Rectory Lane, Scarsdale, NY 10583.

BURGART, HERBERT JOSEPH
Educator
b St Marys, Pa, Apr 27, 32.
Study & Training: Calif State Univ Long Beach, BA, 54; Pa State Univ, MEd, 56, DEd, 61.
Collections Arranged: For Cohen Mus, George Peabody Col, Nashville, Tenn, Univ South Fla Gallery, Tampa, Holbrook Mus, Univ Ga, Athens, La State Univ Mus, Baton Rouge & Anderson Gallery, Va Commonwealth Univ, Richmond.
Teaching: Chmn art educ, Univ Ga, 62-65; chmn the arts, George Peabody Col, 65-66; dean, Sch Arts, Va Commonwealth Univ, 66-
Memberships: Southeastern Arts Asn (pres, 70); Southeastern Col Art Conf (pres, 71); La Art Asn (pres, 57); Pa State Univ Grad Arts (pres, 61).
Publications: Auth, articles, In: Sch Arts, 59, 60 & 62, Ceramics Monthly, 60 & Studies in Art Educ, 61 & 62; auth, Creative art: the child & the school, Univ Ga Press, rev ed, 64.
Mailing Address: 3903 Brook Rd, Richmond, VA 23227.

BURGESS, DAVID LOWRY
Painter.
b Philadelphia, Pa, Apr 27, 40.
Study & Training: Pa Acad Fine Arts, Philadelphia; Univ Pa; Inst Allende, San Miguel, Mex; Ohio State Univ.
Work in Public Collections: Houghton Libr; Harvard Univ, Cambridge, Mass; Mus Fine Arts, Boston, Mass.

Exhibitions: Earth Air, Fire, Water, The Elements, Mus Fine Arts, Boston, 71 & Drawings of the 19th & 20th Centuries, 72; Am Acad Arts & Lett & Nat Inst Arts & Lett, New York, N Y, 72; CAYAC traveling exhib, Spain, Peru, Arg & Chile, 72; Multiple Interaction Team, Chicago, San Francisco, Cincinnati & Philadelphia, 72.
Teaching: Asst prof visual fundamentals, Mass Col Art, Boston, 70-
Positions: Mem, Nat Humanities Faculty, 69-; fel, Ctr Advan Visual Studies, Mass Inst Technol, 71-
Awards: Prize, Am Acad Arts & Lett & Nat Inst Arts & Lett, 72.
Bibliography: Baker (auth), articles in Archit Forum, 6/69 & Art Forum, 3/71; Kepes (auth), Art of the environment, 72.
Publications: Auth, Fragments, 69; Looking and listening, 72.
Mailing Address: 4 Malcolm Rd, Cambridge, MA 02138.

BURGGRAF, RAY LOWELL
Painter, Educator
Preferred Media: Acrylic.
b Mt Gilead, Ohio, July 26, 38.
Study & Training: Ashland Col, BS, 61; Cleveland Inst Art, BFA, 68; Univ Calif, Berkeley, MA, 69, MFA, 70.
Work in Public Collections: Drawing, Mint Mus Art, Charlotte, N C, 71; drawing, De Kalb Col, Clarkston, Ga, 71.
Exhibitions: Artists of the Southeast and Texas, Isaac Delgado Mus Art, New Orleans, La, 71; 16th Nat Sun Carnival Art Exhib, El Paso Mus Art, Tex, 71; 12th Ann Calgary Graphics Exhib, Alta Col Art, 72; 13th Dixie Ann, Montgomery Mus Fine Arts, Ala, 72; 61st Ann Exhib, Laguna Gloria Art Mus, Austin, Tex, 72.
Teaching: Asst prof painting & drawing, Fla State Univ, 70-
Awards: Purchase award, Mint Mus Art, 71; First Nat Bank Award, Mobile Art Patrons League, Ala, 71; award, Ball State Univ, Muncie, Ind, 72.
Memberships: Col Art Asn Am.
Mailing Address: 1507 Marion Ave, Tallahassee, FL 32303.

BURGY, (DONALD) (THOMAS)
Conceptual Artist
b New York, N Y, Aug 3, 37.
Study & Training: Mass Col Art, BFA, 59; Rutgers Univ, MFA, 63.
Work in Public Collections: Rutgers Univ Collection, New Brunswick, N J; Addison Gallery Am Art, Andover, Mass; Salem State Col, Mass.
Commissions: Hello Day (city-wide art work), Salem State Col, 71; Mirror (mural), Subway Sta, City of Boston, 72.
Exhibitions: Concept Art, Stadtisches Mus, Lever Kusen, Ger, 69; Software, Jewish Mus, New York, 70; Information, Mus Mod Art, New York, 70; Elements, Mus Fine Arts, Boston, 71; Colombia Bienal, S Am, 72.
Teaching: Instr, Bradford Col, 66-; Mass Col Art, 72; Nat Humanities Fac, 72.
Bibliography: Schley (auth), Software (film), Jewish Mus, 69-70; Burnham (auth), Introduction to Art ideas for the year 4000, 70; Ursula Meyer (auth), article, In: Conceptual art.
Publications: Auth, Check-up, Art in Am, 70; auth, Art ideas for the year 4000, 70; auth, Context completion ideas, Centro Communication y Arte, Buenos Aires, 71 & Schuring Galerie, Krefeld, Ger, 71.
Mailing Address: 294 S Main St, Bradford, MA 01830.

BURICKSON, ZOEL
Sculptor, Lecturer
Preferred Media: Stone, Bronze, Steel, Wood.
b Europe; U S citizen.
Study & Training: Study in Europe; Md Inst Col Art.
Work in Public Collections: Wash Co Mus Fine Arts, Md; bas relief, Temple Beth Israel, York, Pa; Cumberland Valley High Sch libr.
Commissions: Steel sculpture, Borger Steel Co, York, 71.
Exhibitions: William Penn Mus, Harrisburg, Pa, 60 & 72; Hist Soc Mus, York, 64; Lever House, New York, N Y, 69; Salmagundi Club, New York, 70.
Teaching: Instr sculpture, York Col (Pa), 66-
Awards: Best of show for Melody, Wash Co Mus Fine Arts, 62 & first prize for In the Park, 68.
Memberships: Burr Artists (chmn field exhibs, 69-); Artists Equity Asn; York Art Asn.
Mailing Address: 204 Elmwood Blvd, York, PA 17403.

BURKE, DANIEL V
Painter, Educator
Preferred Media: Acrylics.
b Erie, Pa, Apr 21, 42.
Study & Training: Columbus Col Art & Design; Mercyhurst Col, BA (art); Edinboro State Col; MacDowell Colony, Peterborough, N H, summer fel.
Work in Public Collections: Del Mar Col Art Gallery, Corpus Christi, Tex; Erie Art Ctr; also in numerous private collections.

Exhibitions: 16th Ann Drawing & Small Sculpture Show, Ball State Univ, Muncie, Ind, 70; Mainstreams '70, 3rd Ann Int, Marietta Col, Ohio, 70; Greater New Orleans Nat, Metairie, La, 71; 6th Ann Nat Drawing & Small Sculpture Show, Del Mar Col, 72; 32nd Ann Invitational Art Exhib, Cedar City, Utah, 72.
Teaching: Asst prof two-dimensional arts, Mercyhurst Col, 69-
Awards: Award, 16th Ann Ball State Univ Show, 70; award of excellence, Mainstreams '70; best of show, Greater New Orleans Nat, 71.
Mailing Address: 738 E Ninth St, Erie, PA 16503.

BURKE, E AINSLIE
Painter, Educator
b Omaha, Nebr, Jan 26, 22.
Study & Training: Md Inst Fine Arts; McCoy Col, John Hopkins Univ; Inst Allende, San Miguel, Mex; Art Stud League New York; Fulbright fel, 57-58.
Work in Public Collections: Springfield Mus, Mass; Lamont Art Mus, Exeter, N H; Lehigh Univ, Pa; Munson-Williams-Proctor Mus, Utica, N Y; Lowe Art Gallery, Syracuse Univ, N Y.
Exhibitions: 17th Biennial Int Exhib, Brooklyn Mus, N Y, 53; four one-man shows, Kraushaar Galleries, New York, N Y, 60-71; Pa Acad Fine Arts Ann, Philadelphia, 69; Finger Lake Exhib, Rochester Mem Gallery, N Y, 69; Munson-Williams-Proctor Mus Ann, 70-71.
Teaching: Vis artist, Exeter Acad, 64-; vis artist, Syracuse Univ Sch Art, 62-64, prof drawing & painting, 64-69; chmn studio arts dept Syracuse Univ Col Visual & Performing Arts, 70-
Awards: Woodstock Found Award, 57; Hermine Klienert Award, 59.
Memberships: Am Asn Univ Prof; life mem Art Stud League New York; Woodstock Artists Asn (pres, 60-62).
Dealer: Kraushaar Galleries, 1055 Madison Ave, New York, NY 10028.
Mailing Address: 3435 Ransom Rd, Jamesville, NY 13078.

BURKERT, ROBERT RANDALL
Painter, Graphic Artist
b Racine, Wis, Aug 20, 30.
Study & Training: Wustum Art Ctr, Racine; Univ Wis-Madison, with John Wilde & Alfred Sessier, 48-55; Jacques Desjobert Atelier, Paris, France, summer 70.
Work in Public Collections: Metrop Mus Art, New York, N Y; Boston Mus Fine Arts, Mass; Butler Art Inst, Youngstown, Ohio; Philadelphia Mus Art, Pa; Nat Collection Fine Arts, Washington, D C.
Commissions: Outdoor wall (with Derse Outdoor Advert), Mortgage Guarantee Ins Co, 72.
Exhibitions: Recent Drawings, U S A Exhib, Mus Mod Art, New York, 56; Presentation Artist, Boston Printmakers, 62; Butler Art Inst Ann, 65; New Talent Graphics Show, Assoc Am Artists, New York, 66; Univ Ill Graphics Invitational, Champaign-Urbana, 70.
Teaching: Prof graphics & drawing, Univ Wis-Milwaukee, 56-
Bibliography: James Schineller (auth), Art: search and self discovery, Int Textbook Co, 69; Fritz Eichenberg (auth), Graphics, Abrams, 72; Wall painting: summer of '72 (film), Ted Acheson, 72.
Dealers: Associated American Artists, 605 Fifth Ave, New York, NY 10022; Bradley Galleries, 2565 N Downer Ave, Milwaukee, WI 53211.
Mailing Address: 3228 N Marietta Ave, Milwaukee, WI 53211.

BURKHARDT, HANS GUSTAV
Painter, Collector
Preferred Media: Oils, Pastels.
b Basel, Switz, Dec 20, 04; U S citizen.
Study & Training: Cooper Union, 25-28; Grand Cent Sch Art, 28-29; Arshile Gorky Studio, 29-36.
Work in Public Collections: Los Angeles Co Mus Art, Los Angeles, Calif; Joslyn Art Mus, Omaha, Nebr; Joseph Hirshhorn Collection, New York, N Y; Mod Mus, Stockholm, Sweden; Kunstmuseum Basel, Switz.
Exhibitions: American Painting Today, Metrop Mus Art, New York, 50; 46th Ann, Pa Acad Fine Arts, 51; Chicago Art Inst Ann, 52; Art in the Twentieth Century, San Francisco Mus, 55; Weihnachts Ausstellung, Kunsthalle, Basel, 64.
Teaching: Prof painting & drawing, Univ Southern Calif, 59-60; asst prof painting & drawing, Univ Calif, Los Angeles, 61-63; assoc prof painting & drawing, San Fernando Valley State Col, 63-
Awards: Award for oil, Jr Art Coun, Los Angeles Co Mus Art, 57; Ala Story Purchase Award for oil, Santa Barbara Mus Art, 58; first purchase award for oil, Howard Ahmanson, 61.
Bibliography: Henry Seldis (auth), Abstractionist defends his sensitive craft, Los Angeles Times, 4/23/61; Artist in his studio, KHJ TV, Los Angeles, 9/10/61; Thirty-year retrospective, KHJ TV, Los Angeles, 4/21/62.

Collection: Arnoldo Pomadoro sculptures; deKooning watercolors and lithographs; numerous works of Mark Tobeys; also prints by Picasso, Kollwitz, Tamayo, Rapael Sawyer, Roualt and many others; large collection of Gorky oils and drawings.
Dealer: Michael Smith, 936 N La Cienega, Los Angeles, CA 90069.
Mailing Address: 1914 Jewett Dr, Los Angeles, CA 90046.

BURNETT, CALVIN
Painter, Educator
Preferred Media: Oils.
b Cambridge, Mass, July 18, 21.
Study & Training: Mass Col Art, BFA; Sch Boston Mus Fine Arts (printmaking); Mass Col Art, BS Educ; Boston Univ, MFA.
Work in Public Collections: Boston Mus Fine Arts, Mass; Oakland Mus, Calif; Fogg Art Mus, Harvard Univ, Cambridge, Mass; Wiggins Collection, Boston Pub Libr; Wellesley Col; plus others.
Teaching: Prof art, Mass Col Art, 56-
Awards: Second award, Assoc Am Artists, 59; first award for printmaking, Boston Printmakers, 64; first award for painting, Atlanta Univ Ann, 66.
Bibliography: Della Taylor (auth), Skill adds to communication, Charleston Gazette, 66; M Holsen (auth), Introducing some Boston printmakers, The Connoiseur, London, 67; V E Atkinson (auth), Black dimensions in contemporary American art, New Am Libr, 71.
Publications: Auth-designer, Objective drawing techniques, Van Nostrand Reinhold, 66.
Mailing Address: 13 Hillside Terr, West Newton, MA 02165.

BURNETT, LOUIS ANTHONY
Painter
Preferred Media: Oils, Acrylics.
b New York, N Y, Dec 25, 07.
Study & Training: Art Stud League New York; Educ Alliance, New York; New Sch Social Res.
Work in Public Collections: Norfolk Mus Fine Arts, Va; Smithsonian Inst, Washington, D C; City of Atlantic City, N J.
Exhibitions: Whitney Mus Am Art, New York, 51; Allied Artists Am, New York; Norfolk Mus Fine Arts, 59; Nat Acad Design, New York, 68; Rockport Art Asn, Mass, 72; plus others.
Teaching: Demonstr oil painting, Rockport Art Asn, 61-67.
Awards: Grand art prize (trip to Europe), Atlantic Art Festival, 67; Henry Ward Ranger Fund Award, Nat Acad Design, 68; most creative & imaginative prize, Rockport Art Asn, 69.
Memberships: Allied Artists Am (pub relations, 63); Art Stud League New York (bd of control, 55); Rockport Art Asn; Hunterdon Art Ctr.
Dealer: Doll & Richards Art Gallery, 172 Newbury St, Boston, MA 02116; Burnett & Moore Gallery, 17 Dock Sq, Rockport, MA 01966.
Mailing Address: 4 Hoffman Rd, High Bridge, NJ 08829.

BURNHAM, LEE
Sculptor, Painter
Preferred Media: Bronze, Stone, Ceramics, Wood, Synthetics, Glass.
b New York, N Y, Feb 16, 26.
Study & Training: Cranbrook Acad Art, 43-45, sculpture with Carl Milles; Art Stud League New York, 46-47, sculpture with W Zorach; Syracuse Univ, 47-51, sculpture with Ivan Mestrovic; Porta Romano Scuola, Firenze, Italy, 51-52; Reinhold Sch Art, Baltimore, Md, with Sidney Waugh & Cecil Howard.
Work in Public Collections: Bronze head of Christ, Inst Cath, Paris, France; bronze crucifix, Visitation Convent, St Paul, Minn; bronze head, Daytona Hist Soc, Fla; bronze statue, Dixie Plantation, Quitman, Ga.
Commissions: Bronze bust of Pierre Henry, comn by family & Cath Univ Louvaine; head of Marjorie Kinnen Rawlings, comn by Norton Baskin; stations; appointments & sculpture, St Joseph's Cath Church, Zephyrhills, Fla, 60; stone figure, Sch Ment Retarded, Downington, Pa, 65; ceramic tile, St Patrick-St Joseph Chapels, 66.
Exhibitions: One-man shows, Firenze, Italy 51 & St Augustine, Fla, 58; Gallerie St Placide, Paris, France, 59; Bicentennial Medal Design Competition, Franklin Mint, 72.
Awards: Award, Mus Mod Art, 40; watercolor award, Fla Fedn Art, 57.
Memberships: Nat Sculpture Soc.
Mailing Address: P O Box 385, Hawthorne, FL 32640.

BURNSIDE, KATHERINE TALBOTT
Painter
Preferred Media: Paint, Plastics, Metal.
b Fort Worth, Tex.
Study & Training: Colo Springs Fine Art Ctr; Claremont Col; Ohio Univ; also with Henry Lee McFee, Maurice Sterne, Josef Albers, Victor Candell & Leo Manso.

Work in Public Collections: Arts & Humanities W Va Collection; Zanesville Art Inst, Ohio; IBM Corp Collection; Charleston Art Gallery, W Va; Huntington Gallery, W Va.
Exhibitions: Interior Valley, Fleishman Show, Cincinnati, Ohio, 55; Dayton Art Inst, Ohio, 62; Nine Artists of W Va, traveling show, 63; Four Arts, Palm Beach, Fla, 65; Provincetown Art Asn Invitational, Mass, 71.
Awards: Prize, Cape Cod Art Asn, 65; graphics & drawings award, Charleston Art Gallery, 70; purchase award, Allied Artists W Va, 72.
Memberships; Allied Artists W Va; Provincetown Art Asn; East Coast Gallery, Provincetown (bd mem); Studio 7, Parkersburg, W Va.
Mailing Address: 922 Juliana St, Parkersburg, WV 26101.

BUROS, LUELLA
Painter, Designer
Preferred Media: Watercolors.
b Canby, Minn.
Study & Training: Teachers Col, Columbia Univ, 29-30; Rutgers Univ, 31-32; Teachers Col, Columbia Univ, 33-34; Ohio State Univ, 34-35.
Work in Public Collections: Newark Mus, N J; Montclair Art Mus, N J; City of Cape May, N J.
Exhibitions: Five Watercolor & Print Exhibs, Pa Acad Fine Arts, Philadelphia, 37-47; Contemp Exhib Painting & Sculpture, Golden Gate Int Expos, San Francisco, Calif, 39; Corcoran Biennial Art, Corcoran Gallery Art, Washington, D C, 39, 43 & 45; Four Int Exhibs of Watercolors, Art Inst Chicago, 40-43; Contemp Am Art Exhib, Artists for Victory, Metrop Mus Art, New York, N Y, 43.
Awards: Hon mention in watercolor, Springfield Art League, 41; first prize in watercolor, Contemp Va Oil & Watercolor Exhib, Norfolk Mus Arts & Sci, 44-45; medal of honor in oils, Nat Asn Women Artists, Nat Acad, 53.
Memberships: N J Watercolor Soc; Assoc Artists N J (dir, 58-60); Nat Asn Women Artists; Philadelphia Watercolor Soc.
Mailing Address: 220 Montgomery St, Highland Park, NJ 08904.

BURROWS, SELIG S
Collector, Patron
b New York, N Y, 13.
Study & Training: Fordham Univ, grad, 33; New York Univ Law Sch, grad, 36.
Positions: Mem, Bd Dirs, Friends of Whitney Mus Am Art; mem, Adv Bd, Skowhegan Sch Painting & Sculpture; trustee, Long Island Theater Soc.
Collection: Late nineteenth and twentieth century American art.
Mailing Address: Serena, Mill Neck, NY 11765.

BURROWS, TOM
Sculptor, Educator
Preferred Media: Fiberglass.
b Can, May 9, 40.
Study & Training: Univ B C, BA (fine arts), 67; Saint Martin's Sch Art, London, Eng, 67-69; Can Coun bursary, 67-71.
Work in Public Collections: Can Coun Collection, Ottawa; Galleria Ariete, Milan; Brock Hall Collection, Univ B C; City of Auckland, N Z; Vancouver Art Gallery.
Commissions: Childrens sculpture, Vancouver Art Gallery, 65; wood sculpture, Habitat, Expo '67, 67; two way mirror & linkchain, Dept Pub Works, Chilliwack, B C, 70; City Auckland, 71.
Exhibitions: Sculpture '67, Toronto City Hall, 67; Edinburgh Festival, 68; Galleria Ariete, Milan, 69; Univ B C Fine Arts Gallery, 70; Pacific Rim, N Z Sculpture Symp, 71.
Teaching: Chmn studio art, Univ B C, 72-
Bibliography: Lee Nova (auth), West Coast art, 71 & Burrows (auth), Take only for granted the things that you can touch, 72, Arts Can.
Mailing Address: Dept Fine Arts, University of British Columbia, Vancouver, BC, Can.

BURT, DAVID SILL
Sculptor, Writer
Preferred Media: Sheet Metal, Electrified Plastics.
b Evanston, Ill, Feb 20, 17.
Study & Training: Harvard Univ, BA, 40.
Work in Public Collections: Fine art ctr, Univ Wis-Milwaukee; U S Embassy, New Delhi, India; Chapellier Gallery, New York, N Y.
Commissions: Suspended metal screen, Anaconda Copper Co, 66; fountain, Ital Steamship Lines, 66; two mobiles, Pavillion Apt, 67; wall sculpture, Am Can Co, 69; fountain, Dr Leo Wade, 72.
Exhibitions: Pa Acad Fine Arts Exhib, 64; New Eng Exhib, 65-67 & 69.
Positions: Promotion writer, Archit Forum, Indust Design & Interiors, 52-

Awards: First sculpture award, Time-Life Employee Exhib, 64; first sculpture award, Stamford Art Asn Exhib, 72.
Memberships: Sculptors League; Silvermine Guild Artists; Stamford Mus Art Comt.
Publications: Auth, Detour to sculpture, Am Artist Mag.
Dealer: The Sculpture Center, 167 E 69th St, New York, NY 10021.
Mailing Address: 111 West Hill Rd, Stamford, CT 06902.

BUSA, PETER
Painter, Sculptor
Preferred Media: Oils, Woods, Plaster.
b Pittsburgh, Pa, June 23, 14.
Study & Training: Carnegie Inst Technol, with Raymond Simboli, Sam Rosenberg, Alex Kostellow & Tom Benton; Art Stud League New York; Hans Hofmann Sch Fine Art.
Work in Public Collections: Smithsonian Inst; Peggy Guggenheim; Smith Col Mus; Walker Art Ctr; Whitney Mus Am Art; plus others.
Exhibitions: Art of this Century, Peggy Guggenheim, 46; Bertha Schaefer Gallery, 49-51; Albright-Knox Art Gallery, 54; Retrospective, Chrysler Art Mus, 59; Selections from Permanent Collections, Whitney Mus Am Art, 72; plus many others.
Teaching: New York Univ, 45-53; Cooper Union, 45-54; prof art, State Univ N Y Col Buffalo, 54-57; prof art, Univ Minn, Minneapolis, 60-, chmn dept studio arts.
Positions: Dir summer art prog, Southampton Col, 71.
Awards: William Heugerer Award, Albright-Knox Art Gallery, 54; purchase award, Ford Found, 62; spec donor award, Walker Art Ctr, 66.
Bibliography: Peter Busa, Tweed Gallery, Univ Minn, 66; Sidney Simon (auth), Concerning the beginnings of the N Y School, Art Int, 67.
Memberships: Col Art Asn Am; Artists Equity Asn (past pres Minn chap, 62-65); life mem Art Stud League New York.
Publications: Auth, Creative imagination in science & art, 57; auth, Art to eat & diet, 67.
Mailing Address: 2124 Riverside Ave, Minneapolis, MN 55404.

BUSCAGLIA, JOSE
Sculptor
Preferred Media: Bronze.
b San Juan, P R, Sept 15, 38.
Study & Training: Harvard Univ, BA(cum laude), 60; also with Enrique Monjo, sculptor, 58-59 & 60-62.
Work in Public Collections: Robert Frost, Nat Portrait Gallery, Washington, D C; Dean Delmar Leighton, Harvard Univ; Autobiography of an Inspiration, Ponce Mus Art; Ramos Antonini, Capitol P R; Justice, U S Fed Dist Ct.
Commissions: Monuments, Gov Jesús T Piñero, Gov, Carolina, P R, 65; Pres John F Kennedy, Lions Club, Arecibo, P R, 67; Tree of Life, Univ Puerto Rico, Mayagüez Campus, 67; Santiago Iglesias Government-San Juan, 68; Luis Muñoz Rivera, Gov, Muñoz Rivera Park, San Juan, 69.
Exhibitions: One-man shows, Harvard Univ, Banco Popular at Rockefeller Ctr, Lisner Auditorium at George Washington Univ, 67; also several exhibs Univ P R Mus & Inst Puerto Rican Cult.
Teaching: Prof art, University of P R, Rio Piedras, 63-
Awards: Gran Premio Puertorrigueño, Acad Arts & Sci of P R, 67.
Bibliography: Film, Not by bread alone, Esso Co, 65.
Memberships: Acad Arts & Sci P R (bd mem 64 & 69); Nat Sculpture Soc.
Publications: Auth, Anatomia del proceso creativo, 66 & Creatiology as a new approach to the teaching of the arts, Acad Arts & Sci Bull, 67; La intuicion y la uclosidad del reflejo, 71.
Mailing Address: Fine Arts Dept, University of Puerto Rico, Rio Piedras, PR 00931.

BUSH, BEVERLY
Painter, Sculptor
b Kelso, Wash.
Study & Training: Univ Wash, BA; Nat Acad Design Sch Fine Arts; Art Stud League New York.
Exhibitions: Nat Asn Women Artists, 58; City Ctr, New York, N Y, 58; Art: U S A, 59; Audubon Artists, 59; Seattle Art Mus, 64; plus others.
Positions: Ed Nat News Lett & exec secy, Artists Equity Asn, 58-
Awards: Youth Friends Asn scholar, Nat Acad Design, 54-55; Joseph Isador merit scholar, 55-57.
Memberships: Artists Equity Asn.
Mailing Address: 3521 E Spruce St, Seattle, WA 98102.

BUSH, JACK
Painter
b Toronto, Ont, Mar 20, 09.
Study & Training: Ont Col Art, Toronto; Royal Can Acad.

Exhibitions: Represented Can at São Paulo, Brazil, 67; Carnegie Int, 67; Expo '67; Nat Gallery Can, 67 & traveling to Europe, 68; Can Coun Exhib, Edinburgh Festival, Scotland, 68; plus others.
Teaching: Vis artist, Mich State Univ, spring 65; vis artist, Cranbrook Acad Art, Bloomfield Hills, Mich, 68.
Awards: Can Arts Coun sr fel study in Europe & N Y, 62; grand award, Montreal Mus Fine Arts, 65; Guggenheim fel, 68; plus others.
Memberships: Can Soc Painters in Water Colour (pres); Ont Soc Artists; Painters Eleven.
Publications: Contribr, article, In: Art Int, 2/65.
Dealer: David Mirvish Gallery, 596 Markham St, Toronto 174, Ont, Can.
Mailing Address: 1 Eastview Crescent, Toronto, Ont, Can.

BUSH, LUCILE ELIZABETH
    Painter, Educator
b Mount Sterling, Ky, July 26, 04.
Study & Training: Univ Ky, AB; Teachers Col, Columbia Univ, MA, Columbia Univ, PhD; Art Stud League New York; also with Leger, L'Hote & Marcoussis, Paris, France.
Work in Public Collections: Skidmore Col, Saratoga Springs, N Y.
Commissions: Portraits, pvt cols; scenery & costume design, Harwich Jr Theatre, Mass.
Exhibitions: One-man shows, Saratoga Springs, Schenectady & Glens Falls, N Y.
Teaching: Lectr var aspects mediaeval iconography; instr art, Skidmore Col, 28-43; instr art & chmn dept, Wheaton Col, Mass, 47-65, prof art, 66-
Positions: Dir, Watson Gallery, 02-00.
Awards: Carnegie scholar, 30; Elizabeth Avery Colton fel, Am Asn Univ Women, 45-46.
Memberships: Col Art Asn Am; Am Asn Univ Prof; Mediaeval Acad; Renaissance Soc; Soc Archit Historians.
Publications: Auth, Bartolo di Fredi, Sienese painter of the late 14th century (microfilm), 50.
Mailing Address: Art Dept, Wheaton College, Norton, MA 02766.

BUSH-BROWN, ALBERT
    Writer, Educator
b West Hartford, Conn, Jan 2, 26.
Study & Training: Princeton Univ, AB, 47, MFA, 49, PhD, 58; Emerson Col, hon LLD, 65; Providence Col, hon HHD, 66.
Teaching: Instr art & archaeol, Princeton Univ, 49-50; asst prof art & archit, Western Reserve Univ, 53-54; asst prof archit, Mass Inst Technol, 54-58; assoc prof & exec off archit, 58-62; pres, R I Sch Design, 62-68; Bemis vis prof, Mass Inst Technol, 68-69; chancellor, Long Island Univ.
Positions: Nat adv comt, Archives Am Art, 62-; Nat Coun on The Arts, White House, 64-70; dir-at-large, Nat Coun Arts in Educ, 65-71.
Awards: Woodrow Wilson fel in art & archaeol, Princeton Univ, 47-48; Howard Found fel, Brown Univ, 59-60; Ford Found fel, 68-69.
Memberships: Century Asn; hon mem Am Inst Architects.
Publications: Co-auth, Louis Sullivan, 60; auth, The architecture of America: a social interpretation, 61; auth, Books, Bass, Barnstable, 67; auth, numerous articles in encycl, art & archit journals, 52-65.
Mailing Address: Piping Rock Rd, Locust Valley, NY 11560.

BUSHMILLER, ERNIE PAUL
    Cartoonist
b New York, N Y, Aug 23, 05.
Study & Training: Nat Acad Design.
Positions: Cartoonist, syndicated comic strip, Nancy & Sun comic strip, Fritzi Ritz, United Features, 31-
Memberships: Soc Illusr; Nat Cartoonists Soc; Dutch Treat Club; Artists & Writers Asn.
Publications: Auth & illusr, sev bks on comic strip, Nancy.
Mailing Address: 552 Haviland Rd, Stamford, CT 06903.

BUTCHKES, SYDNEY
    Painter, Sculptor
Preferred Media: Acrylic Paint, Acrylic Sheet.
b Covington, Ky, Oct 13, 22.
Study & Training: Cincinnati Art Acad, Ohio; Art Stud League New York, N Y; New Sch Soc Res, New York.
Work in Public Collections: Brooklyn Mus, N Y; Cincinnati Art Mus; Wadsworth Atheneum, Hartford, Conn; Nat Collection Fine Arts, Smithsonian Inst, Washington, D C; Sheldon Mem Art Gallery, Lincoln, Nebr.
Commissions: Sculpture, lobby of Financial Progs Bldg, Denver, Colo, 69; hanging sculpture, bar of Ritz Carlton Hotel, Boston, Mass, 69; painting, lobby of Skidmore, Owings, Merrill, Chicago, Ill, 70; paintings, World Trade Ctr, N Y & Continental Tel Co, Washington, D C.

Exhibitions: Art for the Collector, San Francisco Mus Art, 65; Painting without a Brush, Inst Contemp Art, Boston, 65; Painting out from the Wall, Des Moines Art Ctr, Iowa, 67; Plastic as Plastic, Mus Contemp Crafts, New York, 69; Mus Acquisitions, Colo Springs Art Ctr, Colo, 69.
Memberships: Abstr Am Artists.
Dealer: Bertha Schaefer Gallery, 32 E 57th St, New York, NY 10022.
Mailing Address: Sagg Main St, Sagaponack, NY 11962.

BUTLER, JOSEPH (GREEN)
    Art Administrator, Painter
Preferred Media: Oils, Watercolors.
b Youngstown, Ohio, Sept 5, 01.
Study & Training: Dartmouth Col.
Work in Public Collections: Columbus Gallery Fine Arts, Ohio; Dartmouth Col Collection, Hanover, N H; Kalamazoo Inst Art, Mich; Phillips Exeter Col, N H; Butler Inst Am Art, Ohio.
Exhibitions: Mid-Year Shows, Butler Inst Am Art, 38-60; Oil & Watercolor Shows, Pa Acad Fine Arts, Philadelphia, 46-48; Am Watercolor Soc, New York, N Y, 47-50; Miss Art Asn, 48-49; Audubon Artists, New York, 50-52.
Collections Arranged: National Annual Mid-Year Shows, 38-; Ohio Painters of the Past; David G Blythe; William T Richards & Anna Richards Brewster; Art of the Carrousel; Area Artists Annuals, 40-; Ohio Ceramic & Sculpture Shows, 49-
Positions: Dir, Butler Inst Am Art, 34-
Awards: Patron of Am Art Award, Chautauqua Art Asn, 62; Ohio Arts Coun Award for 35 yrs serv, 71.
Memberships: Archives Am Art; Artists Equity Asn.
Mailing Address: The Butler Institute of American Art, 524 Wick Ave, Youngstown, OH 44502.

BUTLER, JOSEPH THOMAS
    Art Historian, Writer
b Winchester, Va, Jan 25, 32.
Study & Training: Univ Md, BS, 54; Univ Ohio, MA, 55; Univ Delaware, Winterthur fel & MA, 57.
Teaching: Adj assoc prof archit, Columbia Univ, 71-
Positions: Cur, Sleepy Hollow Restorations, Tarrytown, N Y, 57-; Am ed, The Connoisseur, 68-
Memberships: Nat Arts Club; Furniture Hist Soc; Irish Georgian Soc.
Research: American decorative arts.
Publications: Co-auth, World furniture, 65; auth, American antiques, 1800-1900, 65; Candleholders in America, 1650-1900, 67 & The family collections at Van Cortlandt Manor, 67; co-auth, The arts in America, the 19th century, 70.
Mailing Address: 269 Broadway, Dobbs Ferry, NY 10522.

BUTTERBAUGH, ROBERT CLYDE
    Sculptor, Educator
Preferred Media: Plastics, Metals, Woods.
b Freeport, Ill, May 28, 31.
Study & Training: Univ of the Pac, BA, 54; Claremont Grad Sch, MFA, 62, with Paul Darrow & David Scott.
Work in Public Collections: Sunderland Col Art, Eng.
Commissions: Sculpture relief, copper sheet, Temple Beth El, Salinas, Calif, 64; sculpture, welded corten steel, T Merrill Hall, Hartnell Col, Salinas, 65; fountain, redwood & cast bronze, Cent Plaza Bldg, Salinas, 66; sculpture, redwood & plastic, Salinas City Hall Foyer, 68; sculpture group & low relief, cast concrete, aquatic complex, Hartnell Col, currently.
Exhibitions: Midland Group Gallery, Nottingham, Eng, 69; Sunderland Col Art, 69; Cerritos 70, Norwalk, Calif, 70; Form and the Inner Eye, Los Angeles, Calif, 71; Southern Ore Col Gallery, Ashland, 71.
Teaching: Prof art, Hartnell Col, 62-; lectr sculpture, Sunderland Col Art, 68-69.
Awards: Fulbright-Hays travel grant, 68-69.
Dealer: Bolles Gallery, 10 Gold St, San Francisco, CA 94133.
Mailing Address: 908 Riker St, Salinas, CA 93901.

BUTTON, JOHN
    Painter
b San Francisco, Calif, 1929.
Study & Training: Univ Calif, Berkeley; Calif Sch Fine Arts.
Work in Public Collections: Columbia Univ; Art Inst Chicago, Ill; also in pvt collections.
Exhibitions: David Herbert Gallery, New York, Hirschl & Adler Galleries, Tibor de Nagy Gallery, Tanager Gallery, Kornblee Gallery.
Mailing Address: c/o Kornblee Gallery, 58 E 79th St, New York, NY 10021.

BUTTS, PORTER
    Art Historian, Art Administrator
b Pana, Ill, Feb 23, 03.

Study & Training: Univ Wis-Madison, BA, MA(art hist), with Prof O F L Hagen.
Collections Arranged: Wis Salon of Art Ann, 34-; Wis State Centennial Art Exhib, 36; Wis Union Collection of Art (some 700 paintings, watercolors, graphics & sculptures principally by Wis artists).
Positions: Dir, Wis Union Galleries, Univ Wis-Madison, 28-68; planning consult, Milwaukee Arts Ctr & 110 col & univ cult-social centers, 46-
Awards: Creative Arts Award, given annually by Univ Wis, Madison, in recognition of Porter Butts' contribution to the arts.
Memberships: Madison Art Asn (secy-treas, 29-32).
Research: Regional art history, especially development of art in Wisconsin in the nineteenth and twentieth centuries.
Publications: Auth, Art in Wisconsin: the art experience of the middle west frontier, 36; auth, Regional studies, Art in Am, 10/45.
Mailing Address: 2900 Hunter Hill, Madison, WI 53705.

BUZZELLI, JOSEPH ANTHONY
Painter, Sculptor
Preferred Media: Enamels, Oils, Metals, Woods, Plastics.
b Old Forge, Pa, May 6, 07.
Study & Training: Art Stud League New York; Univ Southern Calif; Beaux-Arts & Grande Chaumiere, Paris, France.
Work in Public Collections: Philadelphia Pub Libr, Pa.
Commissions: Murals in churches; One Religion, Early New York City to Present & Man Striving for Peace (murals), Fed Detention House, New York, N Y, 44; The Pool, Wiltwyck Sch for Boys, 45.
Exhibitions: Whitney Mus Am Art; Smithsonian Inst; Art U S A, Madison Sq Garden, New York; Metrop Mus Art; Carnegie Art Inst; plus many other group and one-man shows.
Teaching: Instr, Henry St Settlement House, Educ Alliance, Long Beach Art Ctr & Brooklyn Mus Wiltwyck Sch for Boys & Youth House.
Awards: First prize in watercolor, Nat Emily Lowe Seventh Ann Award Show, first prize in oils, New York City Ctr; spec award for enamels fired on steel, Guild Hall Galleries, East Hampton; plus others.
Bibliography: Reviews, In: Art News Int, Arts Digest, New York Herald Tribune & many others.
Art Interests: Fired enamels on steel.
Publications: Auth, The dirty book (on anti-pollution).
Mailing Address: 608 N Casey Key, Osprey, FL 33559.

BYE, RANULPH (DeBAYEUX)
Painter, Educator
Preferred Media: Watercolors, Oils.
b Princeton, N J, June 17, 16.
Study & Training: Philadelphia Col Art; Art Stud League New York.
Work in Public Collections: Mus Fine Arts, Boston, Mass; Munson-Williams-Proctor Inst, Utica, N Y; Reading Pub Mus, Pa; Smithsonian Inst, Washington, D C; Pa Hist & Mus Comn, Harrisburg, Pa.
Commissions: Mine Force (paintings of naval base), U S Navy Dept, Charleston, S C, 66.
Exhibitions: Ann Exhibs, Allied Artists Am, Am Watercolor Soc, Philadelphia Water Color Club, Salmagundi Club & Nat Arts Club New York.
Teaching: Assoc prof art, Moore Col Art, Philadelphia, Pa, 48-
Awards: John L Ernst Award, 66 & William Church Osborne Mem Prize, 71, Am Watercolor Soc; Eastman Prize for Watercolor, Salmagundi Club, 72.
Bibliography: Wendy Buehr (auth), Station closed, Am Heritage Press, 66.
Memberships: Salmagundi Club; Am Watercolor Soc; Allied Artists Am; Philadelphia Water Color Club; Garden State Watercolor Soc; plus others.
Art Interests: Pictorial record in watercolor of railroad stations in eight eastern states, circa 1900.
Publications: Auth, Seascapes and landscapes, 56 & Watercolor technique American artist, 66, Watson-Guptill.
Mailing Address: Church School Rd, Doylestown, PA 18901.

BYRD, D GIBSON
Educator, Painter
Preferred Media: Oils.
b Tulsa, Okla, Feb 1, 23.
Study & Training: Univ Tulsa, BA, with Alexandre Hogue; Univ Iowa, MA.
Work in Public Collections: Butler Inst Am Art, Youngstown, Ohio; Philbrook Art Ctr, Tulsa, Okla; Kalamazoo Art Ctr, Mich; Wright Art Ctr, Beloit Col, Wis; Univ Wis-Green Bay.
Exhibitions: The Midwest, Joslyn Art Mus, Omaha, Nebr, 52; Walker Art Ctr Biennial Exhib, Minneapolis, Minn, 58; Wisconsin Renaissance, Marine Bank Invitational, Milwaukee, Wis, 65; Second Nat Invitational Drawing Exhib, Univ Wis-Green Bay, 70; Arts: U S A II, Northern Ill Univ, DeKalb, 71.

Teaching: Prof art, Univ Wis-Madison, 55-; vis lectr, Sch Art Educ, Birmingham, Eng, 65-66.
Positions: Dir, Kalamazoo Art Ctr, 52-55.
Memberships: Madison Art Ctr (v pres); Inst for Study Art in Educ, New York (bd mem); Col Art Asn Am; Nat Art Educ Asn; Wis Art Educ Asn.
Publications: Auth, The artist-teacher in America, Col Art J, winter 63-64; auth, Theodore Robinson (exhib Monogr), Univ Wis Press, 64; auth, Artist-teacher in America: John Sloan, Sch Arts Mag, 66; auth, Visiting artists: thoughts & second thoughts, Visual Arts Educ, 70; auth, Thomas Hart Benton (exhib catalog), Madison Art Ctr, 70.
Dealer: Bradley Galleries, 2565 N Downer Ave, Milwaukee, WI 53211.
Mailing Address: Dept of Art, University of Wisconsin, Madison, WI 53711.

BYRNES, JAMES BERNARD
Museum Director, Art Historian
b New York, N Y, Feb 19, 17.
Study & Training: Nat Acad Design, New York, 36-38; Am Artists Sch, New York, 38-40; Art Stud League New York, 41-42; Ist Meschini, Univ Perugia, Rome, 51-52.
Collections Arranged: Edgar Degas, His Family and Friends in New Orleans (exhib & catalog), 65; Odyssey of an Art Collector—the Collection of Mr & Mrs Frederick S Stafford, Paris (exhib & catalog), 66; Arts of Ancient and Modern Latin America (exhib & catalog), 68.
Teaching: Vis prof hist 20th century art, Univ Fla, 60-61.
Positions: Cur mod & contemp art, Los Angeles Co Mus, 46-54; dir, Colo Springs Fine Arts Ctr, 54-56; assoc dir, N C Mus Art, 56-58, dir, 58-60; dir New Orleans Mus Art, 62-
Awards: Knight in the Order of Leopold II, Belg Govt, 72.
Memberships: Asn Art Mus Dirs; Am Asn Mus; Int Coun Mus; hon life mem Am Inst Designers.
Research: Nineteenth and twentieth century art; seventeenth century Dutch art; pre-Columbian and African art.
Mailing Address: New Orleans Museum of Art, Lelong Ave, City Park, New Orleans, LA 70119.

BYRON, CHARLES ANTHONY
Art Dealer
b Istanbul, Turkey, Dec 15, 20.
Study & Training: Ecole Libre Sci Polit, Paris, France; Univ Paris; Harvard Univ, BA, LLB & MA.
Positions: Dir, Byron Gallery, New York, N Y.
Specialty of Gallery: Contemporary and surrealist art.
Mailing Address: 25 E 83rd St, New York, NY 10028.

BYRUM, MARY
Painter
Preferred Media: Oils.
b Louisville, Ky, Sept 15, 32.
Study & Training: Art Ctr of Louisville; Univ Louisville; also portrait painting with John Dempsey & life drawing with Eugene Leake.
Work in Public Collections: Bellarmine Col Gallery, Louisville.
Exhibitions: Hunter Gallery, Chattanooga, Tenn, 63; Evansville Mus, Ind, 64; one-man shows, Brescia Col, Owensboro, Ky, 66, Seaton House Gallery, Jeffersontown, 68 & Port O'Call Gallery, Louisville, 70; plus others.
Awards: Best representational award, Ky State Fair, 62; second place, Ky State Fair, 64; first in representational, Louisville Women's Club, 66.
Memberships: Crit Club of Louisville (pres, 65-66); Louisville Sch Art.
Mailing Address: 8127 Blake Lane, Louisville, KY 40258.

BYWATERS, JERRY
Painter, Art Historian
b Paris, Tex, May 21, 06.
Study & Training: Southern Methodist Univ, AB; Art Stud League New York; spec study in Europe & Mex.
Work in Public Collections: Mus Fine Arts, Dallas, Tex; Southern Methodist Univ, Dallas; murals in Post Off Bldgs, Houston, Quanah, Farmersville & Trinity, Tex.
Exhibitions: Golden Gate Int Expos, San Francisco, Calif, 39; New York World's Fair, 39 & 40; City Art Mus, St Louis, Mo, 40; 53rd Ann Am Painting & Sculpture, Art Inst Chicago, 42; Am Painting & Sculpture, Metrop Mus Art, New York, 50.
Collections Arranged: 200 Years of American Painting, 46; Six Southwestern States, 47; Pre-Columbian Art, 50; Lasker Collection, 53; Otis Dozier, 56; Survey of Texas Painting, 57; Andrew Dasburg, 58; Religious Art of the Western World, 58; South American Art Today, 59; Century of Art & Life in Texas, 61; The Arts of Man, 62; Indian Art, 63; Texas Painting & Sculpture. 71.

Teaching: Asst prof painting, Southern Methodist Univ, 36-63, prof arts of N Am, 64-71, emer prof, 71-

Positions: Art critic, Dallas Morning News, 33-39; dir, Dallas Mus Fine Arts, 43-64; dir Pollock Galleries, Southern Methodist Univ, 65-70.

Awards: First prize, Tex Ann, Houston Mus, 40; Dealey Purchase Prize, Dallas Mus Fine Arts, 42; Caller-Times Purchase Prize, Corpus Christi Mus, 47.

Publications: Auth, Diego Rivera and Mexican popular art, Southwest Rev, 28; auth, Twelve from Texas, Southern Methodist Univ Press, 52; co-auth, Everett Spruce, Univ Texas Press, 58; auth, Andrew Dasburg, Am Fedn Arts, 59; co-auth, Texas painting & sculpture: the 20th century, 71.

Mailing Address: 3625 Amherst, Dallas, TX 75225.

C

CABALLERO, EMILIO
Educator, Painter
Preferred Media: Watercolors, Enamel.
b Newark, N J, July 4, 19.
Study & Training: Amarillo Col, AA, 40; W Tex State Univ, BA, 42; Columbia Univ, MA, 49, DEd, 55.
Work in Public Collections: Col Southwest, Hobbs, N Mex; Lovett Mem Libr, Pampa, Tex; St Anne's Cath Church, Canyon, Tex, YWCA, Amarillo, Tex; Pampa Youth Ctr.
Commissions: Mosaic facade, Tex Midland Pub Libr, 58; copper enamels, Amarillo Savings & Loan, 68, Hosea Foster Ins Co, 69, Amarillo Munic Bldg, 69 & Bank Southwest, Midland, 70.
Exhibitions: Tex Oil 58, Dallas Pub Libr, Tex, 58; Tex Fine Arts Circuit Show, 68; 104th Ann Am Watercolor Soc Exhib, New York, 71; 9th Ann Southwestern Exhib Prints & Drawings, Dallas; Mid-Am Ann, William Parkhill Nelson Gallery, Kansas City.
Teaching: Spec art instr, Amarillo Pub Schs, 46-49; prof art & chmn dept, W Tex State Univ, 49-, faculty excellence award, 72.
Positions: Art consult, Agnes Russell Ctr, Columbia Univ, 51-52; consult art, Ed Comt Amarillo Art Alliance, 70-; lectr, Friends of Fine Arts, 70-
Awards: Accolade Award for 20 Yrs Art, Amarillo Globe Times, 62; Kappa Pi Gold Plaque Hall of Fame, 70.
Bibliography: Elsie Wilbanks (auth), Art on the Texas plains, Lubbock Art Asn, 59; L Sumner (auth), Plains party line, Amarillo Globe News, 60; G Denko (auth), Caballero heads festival, Amarillo Globe, 70.
Memberships: Fel Royal Soc Gt Brit; Llano Estacado Heritage N Mex (art ed, 70); Soc Archit Historians; Soc Art Ther.
Publications: Contribr, Expression through puppetry, Tex Outlook, 47; contribr, Evocative painting, Design, 49; contribr, Watercolor painting in elementary grades, Am Crayon Co, 49.
Dealer: Canyon Art Gallery, 2710 Fourth Ave, Canyon, TX 79015.
Mailing Address: 6317 Calumet, Amarillo, TX 79016.

CABOT, HUGH
Painter, Sculptor
Preferred Media: Oils, Charcoal, Ink.
b Boston, Mass, Mar 22, 30.
Study & Training: Vesper George Sch Fine Arts, Boston; Boston Mus Fine Arts Sch; Col of the Americas, Mexico City; Oxford Univ.
Work in Public Collections: USN Dept Hist & Records; Combat Art Collection, USN Mus Combat Art.
Exhibitions: Tokyo Press Club; USN Korean Combat Art Coverage; Mitsubichi Gallery, Tokyo; Operation Palette, USN Show, exhibited in every major city in the free world.
Bibliography: The twister (feature film), Seiler-Van Belle, 72; Sisk (auth), International, Mex-Ariz Publ, 72.
Publications: Illusr, Korea, 56; illusr, The mountain of gold, 62.
Mailing Address: Box 2078, Nogales, AZ 85621.

CADDELL, FOSTER
Painter, Instructor
Preferred Media: Oils, Pastels.
b Pawtucket, R I, Aug 2, 21.
Study & Training: R I Sch Design; pvt study with Peter Helck, Robert Brackman & Guy Wiggins of Nat Acad.
Commissions: Off portrait, Sen Thomas J Dodd of Conn, Washington, D C & Judge L P Moore, U S Circuit Ct Appeals, Second Dist, New York; Dr George S Avery, dir, Brooklyn Bot Gardens, N Y; Carl Cuttler, founder, Marine Hist Asn Mystic Seaport, Mystic, Conn; relig paintings for many denominations incl Church of England; portraits of many bus & civic leaders.
Exhibitions: Providence Art Club Ann, 64-; Academic Artists of America, Springfield Mus Fine Arts, 71; Am Watercolor Soc Ann, Nat Acad Galleries, 71; Am Artists Prof League Grand Nat, 72.
Teaching: Pvt classes, Southern New Eng, 60-
Positions: Lithograph artist, Providence Lithograph Co, 39-52; artist with Far East Air Force, 43-46.
Awards: Ward Mem Award for painting, Acad Artists Am, 68; first hon mention, Am Artists Prof League Grand Nat, 71; Windsor-Newton Award, Am Artists Prof League Grand Nat, 72.
Bibliography: Norman Kent (auth), Foster Caddell-artist & teacher, Am Artist Mag, 12/68.
Memberships: Providence Art Club; Am Artists Prof League; Acad Artists Am; Salmagundi Club.
Publications: Illusr, educ bks, Ginn & Co, 53-68; illusr, series sports bks, Little, Brown & Co; also relig illus for most Protestant denominations educ & instrnl bks & mat.
Mailing Address: Northlight, Rte 49, Voluntown, CT 06384.

CADE, WALTER III
Painter
Preferred Media: Acrylics, Collage.
b New York, N Y, Jan 17, 36.
Study & Training: Inst Mod Art, New York.
Exhibitions: Brooklyn Mus Fench Show, New York, 67 & 68; group show, C W Post Col, Long Island Univ, Brookville, N Y, 68; Whitney Mus Am Art Ann, New York, 69-70; Huntington Township Art League Show, Hechsher Mus, Huntington, N Y, 69 & 71; Contemporary Black Artists in America, Whitney Mus Am Art, 71; plus others.
Awards: Best in show, Allendale Community Arts Asn, 67; first prize, Jamaica Chamber Com, N Y, 72; best in show, Corcoran Gallery Art, Riggs Nat Bank, Washington, D C, 72.
Bibliography: Jeanne Paris (auth), The ghetto sparkles, Long Island Sun Press, 5/7/72; article, In: Playboy Mag, 72; article, In: New York Amsterdam News, 5/6/72.
Mailing Address: c/o Studio Gallery, 172-03 119th Ave, Jamaica, NY 11434.

CADLE, RAY KENNETH
Painter, Craftsman
b Ravenswood, W Va, Sept 26, 06.
Study & Training: Dayton Art Inst; woodblock printing with Kiyoshi Saito & suiboku painting with Ryukyu Saito, Tokyo.
Exhibitions: Hanga Group Exhib, Metrop Gallery, Ueno Park, Tokyo, 52; one-man show, Int House Gallery, Tokyo, 54; Morris Harvey Col, Charleston, W Va, 59; one-man show, Centenary Col Gallery, Shreveport, La, 65; La State Mus, Shreveport, 72.
Positions: Staff arts & crafts dir, Hq Fifth Air Force, Nagoya, Japan, 49-50; staff arts & crafts dir, Hq Far E Air Force, Tokyo, 50-57; staff arts & crafts dir, Hq Pac Air Forces, Honolulu, Hawaii, 57-58; command arts & crafts dir, Hq Second Air Force, Barksdale AFB, La, 61-
Awards: Nat Recreation & Park Asn fel award arts & crafts, 64.
Memberships: Allied Artists, W Va; Honolulu Printmakers; Men's Art Guild, Shreveport (bd mem, 66-); Int Suiboku Soc, Japan.
Dealer: C C Hardman, 712 Texas St, Shreveport, LA 71101.
Mailing Address: Apt 523, Towne House, 726 Cotton St, Shreveport, LA 71101.

CADMUS, PAUL
Painter, Printmaker
Preferred Media: Tempera.
b New York, N Y, Dec 17, 04.
Study & Training: Nat Acad Design, 16-26; Art Stud League New York, with Joseph Pennell, 28.
Work in Public Collections: Whitney Mus Am Art, New York; Metrop Mus Art, New York; Mus Mod Art, New York; Fogg Art Mus, Cambridge, Mass; Smithsonian Inst, Washington, D C.
Commissions: Costumes & scenery, Filling Station Ballet, Ballet Caravan, 38; mural, Parcel Post Bldg, Richmond, Va, 38.
Positions: V pres, Bd Control, Art Stud League New York, 35-
Awards: Flora Mayer Witkowsky Prize, Art Inst Chicago, 45; Nat Inst Arts & Lett grant, 61; purchase prize, Norfolk Mus Arts & Sci, 67.
Bibliography: Paul Cadmus of Navy fame has his first art show, Life Mag, 3/29/37; Harry Salpeter (auth), Paul Cadmus: enfant terrible, Esquire Mag, 7/37; Una E Johnson (auth), Paul Cadmus/prints and drawings, Brooklyn Mus, 68.
Memberships: Soc Am Graphic Artists.
Dealer: Midtown Galleries, 11 E 57th St, New York, NY 10022.
Mailing Address: 128 Remsen St, Brooklyn, NY 11201.

CAGE, ROBERT FIELDING
Painter, Sculptor
Preferred Media: Oil, Brass, Copper, Wood.
b Charlotte Co, Va, Oct 7, 23.
Study & Training: De Bourgos Sch Art, Washington, D C; Salisbury Sch Art, Rhodesia, BFA; Am Stud & Arts League, Paris, France.

Work in Public Collections: Sculptures, Lynchburg Art Club, Va &
Great Atlantic Real Estate Co, Newport News, Va; paintings,
Averett Col, Danville, Va, Tobacco Auctions Ltd, Salisbury &
Banks Haley Mus Fine Arts, Albany, Ga.
Exhibitions: Nat Gallery Rhodesia, Salisbury, 64-65; Norfolk Mus
Art, Va, 70; Va Mus Fine Art, Richmond, Va, 71; N C Mus Art,
Raleigh, N C, 71; Crafts, Mint Mus, Charlotte, 71; plus 12 one-
man shows.
Awards: Mariners Mus Top Sculpture Award, Great Atlantic Real-
tor, 71.
Bibliography: Revs, In: Eve Capitol, Annapolis, Md & Lynchburg
News, Va.
Memberships: Va Mus Art; Contemp Gallery Art, Winston-Salem,
N C; Md Fedn Artists.
Dealers: Schindler Gallery, 2305 E Broad St, Richmond, VA 23223;
Haynesworth, Inc, Danville, VA 24541.
Mailing Address: P O Box 63, South Boston, VA 24592.

CAGLIOTI, VICTOR
Painter, Sculptor
Preferred Media: Acrylics, Oils, Constructions.
b Inwood, N Y, July 20, 35.
Study & Training: Pasadena City Col; State Univ N Y Buffalo, with
Peter Busa; New York Univ, BS, with Howard Conant, John Opper,
Hale Woodruff & Martin Craig; Columbia Univ, with Stephen
Greene.
Work in Public Collections: New York Univ, N Y; Drury Univ, Mo;
Housatonic Col, Conn; St Louis Park Ctr, Minn.
Commissions: Wall relief (an assemblage), comn by Dept Health,
Educ & Welfare, Nassau Co, N Y, 69; comn to experiment with
indust process works of art, Colwell Press, 72.
Exhibitions: Albright-Knox Regional, Buffalo, 55; six one-man
shows, Buffalo, New York & Minneapolis, Minn, 56-71; Nat Inst
Arts & Lett Ann Invitational, New York, 70; Collectors Invita-
tional, Parrish Art Mus, New York, 71.
Teaching: Asst prof drawing & painting & asst chmn dept, Univ Minn,
70-
Awards: Albright Art Sch fel, 54; artists-writers revolving fund
award, Nat Inst Arts & Lett, 68; nat competition for govt comn,
69.
Bibliography: Jack Azarch (auth), interview, In: Avanti, 70; Gordon
Brown (auth), Editorial focus, Arts Mag, 70; Don Morrison (auth),
news rev, In: Minneapolis Star, 71.
Memberships: New Art Asn (exec comt, 71-); Artists Equity Asn.
Publications: Illusr, Opera News, 53; ed & auth, Pictures on exhibit,
69 & 70.
Dealers: Avanti Galleries, 145 E 72nd St, New York, NY 10028; Mar-
tin Gallery, 2116 Second Ave S, Minneapolis, MN 55404.
Mailing Address: 167 Bedford St S E, Minneapolis, MN 55414.

CAHILL, JAMES FRANCIS
Art Historian, Educator
b Fort Bragg, Calif, Aug 13, 26.
Study & Training: Univ Calif, Berkeley, BA, 50; Univ Mich, MA, 53,
PhD, 58, with Prof Max Loehr.
Collections Arranged: Guest-dir, The Art of Southern Sung China,
62, Fantastics and Eccentrics in Chinese Painting, 67 & Scholar-
Painters of Japan: the Nanga School, 72 (with catalogs), Asia
House Gallery, New York.
Teaching: Prof hist of art, Univ Calif, Berkeley, 65-
Positions: Cur Chinese art, Freer Gallery Art, Washington, D C, 58-
65.
Awards: Louise Wallace Hackney scholar, 50-52; Fulbright scholar,
54-55; Guggenheim fel, 72-73.
Memberships: Col Art Asn Am.
Research: Chinese painting; Japanese painting; Chinese bronzes.
Publications: Auth, Chinese painting (Geneva, Skira), 60; auth,
Chinese paintings, XI-XIV centuries, 60; co-auth, The Freer
Chinese bronzes, 67; ed, The restless landscape: Chinese paint-
ing of the late Ming period, 71.
Mailing Address: 2422 Hillside Ave, Berkeley, CA 94704.

CAIN, JAMES FREDERICK, JR
Printmaker, Museum Curator
b Philadelphia, Pa, June 24, 38.
Study & Training: Assumption Col, Mass, AB; Tyler Sch Art,
Temple Univ, MA; Laval Univ; Harvard Univ; Univ Pa.
Work in Public Collections: Prints, Mus Mod Art, Los Angeles Co
Mus; Art Inst Chicago; Pasadena Art Mus & Mus Fine Arts San
Diego; plus others.
Positions: Mus cur, dept graphic arts, Nat Gallery Art, Washing-
ton, D C.
Awards: Ford Found cur training grant, Tamarind Lithography
Workshop, Los Angeles, 67; Eng Speaking Union grant study at
Brit Mus, 68.

Memberships: Eng Speaking Union; Philobiblon Club; Philadelphia
Print Club.
Publications: Designed illus sect, Fifteenth century engravings of
northern Europe (catalogue), Nat Gallery Art, 67.
Mailing Address: 3334 Prospect St N W, Washington, DC 20007.

CAIN, JOSEPH (LAMBERT)
Painter, Educator
b New Orleans, La, Apr 16, 04.
Study & Training: Chicago Acad Fine Arts; Art Inst Chicago; Art
Stud League New York; Hans Hofmann Sch Fine Arts, New York;
Sorbonne Inst Art & Archeol, Paris, France.
Commissions: Murals, N Y State Training Sch, Warwick.
Exhibitions: Pa Acad Fine Arts; Nat Acad Design; Addison Gallery
Am Art, Andover, Mass; Fleming Mus; R I Sch Design; plus
others.
Teaching: Prof art, Univ R I, 44-, head art dept, 44-58.
Positions: Co-dir with Matene Rachotes Cain, Summer Art Work-
shop.
Awards: Carnegie Inst fel; Tiffany Found fel & Medal.
Memberships: Am Asn Univ Prof; Contemp Art Group.
Publications: Auth, Art is the artist.
Mailing Address: Dept of Art, University of Rhode Island, Kingston,
RI 02881.

CAIN, JOSEPH ALEXANDER
Painter, Educator
Preferred Media: Acrylics.
b Henderson, Tenn, May 27, 20.
Study & Training: Univ Calif, Berkeley, BA, 47, MA, 48.
Work in Public Collections: Butler Inst Am Art, Youngstown, Ohio;
Seton Hall Univ, South Orange, N J; Calif Nat Watercolor Soc
Collection; Witte Mus, San Antonio, Tex; Univ Utah Permanent
Collection.
Commissions: Oil mural, C of C, Corpus Christi, Tex, 59; mosaic
mural, comn by Freeman Martin, Spohn Hosp, 62; mosaic
murals, comn by Joe Williams, Buccanneer Bowl, 65.
Exhibitions: Philadelphia Watercolor Club Exhib, Pa Acad Fine
Arts, 65; Butler Inst Am Art Mid-Year Ann, 65; Nat Soc
Painters in Casein Exhib, New York, N Y, 67; Southeastern
Watercolor Soc Regional Show, Dallas, Tex, 69; Calif Nat Wa-
tercolor Soc Ann, Los Angeles, 69.
Teaching: Prof art, Del Mar Col, 50-
Positions: Art critic, Corpus Christi Caller-Times, 56-; chmn,
Munic Arts Coun, Corpus Christi, 72-73.
Bibliography: Margaret Harold (auth), Prize-winning art, Bk 6, Al-
lied Publ, 66.
Memberships: Fel Royal Soc Arts; Calif Nat Watercolor Soc (spec
rep, 71-72); Tex Watercolor Soc (third v pres, 71-72); Nat Soc
Painters in Acrylics & Casein; Tex Fine Arts Asn (regional dir,
70).
Publications: Auth, Art news and reviews, weekly column of art
criticism in Corpus Christi Caller-Times, 56-
Mailing Address: 402 Troy Dr, Corpus Christi, TX 78412.

CAIN, MICHAEL PETER
Painter, Sculptor
Preferred Media: Acrylics.
b Boston, Mass, July 3, 41.
Study & Training: Harvard, AB(cum laude), 64; Yale Univ, BFA &
MFA, 67.
Commissions: Underwater environ strobe piece, Boston Pub Garden,
68; computerized outdoor feedback environ, Mus Mod Art sculp-
ture garden, 70; pub environ, Park near Walker Art Ctr, 71; in-
terior video feedback piece, Automation House, New York, N Y,
71; mirrorized wind rotor environ near Kline Biology Tower,
Yale Univ, 72.
Teaching: Res assoc, Sch Art & Archit, Yale Univ, 67-
Positions: Mem, Pulsa Group.
Bibliography: Lucy Lippard (auth), Pulsa, Arts Can, 12/68; John
Chandler (auth), Art in the electric age, Arts Int, 2/69; Gregory
Battcock (auth), The politics of space, Arts Mag, 2/70.
Publications: Contribr, Time: a panel discussion, Art Int, 11/69;
contribr, A report on the art and technology program of the Los
Angeles County Museum, 71.
Mailing Address: R R 2, Wigwam Rd, Litchfield, CT 06759.

CAISERMAN-ROTH, GHITTA
Painter, Printmaker
Preferred Media: Acrylics, Oils, Mixed Media, Graphics.
b Montreal, P Q, Mar 2, 23.
Study & Training: Parsons Sch Design, BA; Am Artists Sch;
Ecole Beaux-Arts, with Albert Dumouchel.
Work in Public Collections: Montreal Mus Fine Arts; Vancouver
Art Gallery, B C; Confederation Art Gallery, Charlottetown,
P E I; London Pub Libr & Art Mus, Ont; Beaverbrook Art Gal-
lery, Fredericton, N B.

Commissions: Hommage à Dumouchel, Univ Quebec Press, 72.
Exhibitions: Expo '67, 67; Joint Int Exhib, Soc Can Etcher-Painters & Engravers & Can Soc Graphic Arts, 70; group show, Can Embassy, Washington, D C, 70; solo show, Waddington Galleries, Montreal, 70.
Teaching: Instr art, Sir George Williams Univ, 60-; instr art, Queen's Univ, 63; instr art, Saidye Bronfman Ctr, Montreal, 70-
Awards: Can Coun Sr fel, 62; Can Centennial Medal, Can Govt, 67; plus various purchase awards.
Memberships: Can Soc Painter Etchers; Can Soc Graphic Art; Royal Can Acad Art.
Dealer: Waddington Gallery, 1452 Sherbrooke W, Montreal, P Q, Can.
Mailing Address: 5 Bellevue Ave, Westmount, P Q, Can.

CAJORI, CHARLES F
Painter
Preferred Media: Oils, Pencil.
b Palo Alto, Calif, Mar 9, 21.
Study & Training: Colo Springs Fine Arts Ctr; Cleveland Art Sch; Columbia Univ; Skowhegan Sch Painting & Sculpture.
Work in Public Collections: New York Univ, N Y; Geigy Chem Corp, Ardsley, N Y; Mitchner Collection, Univ Tex, Austin; Walker Art Ctr, Minneapolis, Minn; Whitney Mus Am Art, New York.
Exhibitions: Festival of Two Worlds, Spoletto, Italy, 58; one-man show, Howard Wise Gallery, New York, 63; Decade of American Drawings, Whitney Mus Am Art, 65; Drawings of the Sixties, New Sch Social Res, New York, 69; three-man show, Loeb Ctr, New York Univ, 70.
Teaching: Instr drawing & painting, Cooper Union Art Sch, 56-65; instr drawing & painting, New York Studio Sch, 64-69; prof drawing & painting, Queens Col, Flushing, 65-
Awards: Longview Found Purchase Award, 62; Ford Found Purchase Award, 63; award in painting, Inst Arts & Lett, 70.
Bibliography: L Finkelstein (auth), Cajori: figure in the scene, Art News, 63.
Memberships: Col Art Asn Am.
Mailing Address: Litchfield Rd, Watertown, CT 06795.

CALAMAR, GLORIA
Painter, Lecturer
Preferred Media: Watercolors, Inks, Acrylics, Oils, Graphics.
b New York, N Y, Sept 7, 21.
Study & Training: Otis Art Inst, scholar, 39-43; Art Stud League New York, scholar, 45-46; Orange Co Community Col, AA (humanities), 69; State Univ N Y Col New Paltz, BA (art hist), 70.
Work in Public Collections: Cent Theatre, Oslo, Norway; Santa Barbara Mus, Calif; Mount Saint Mary Col, Newburgh, N Y.
Exhibitions: Albany Inst Art, N Y, 47; Delgado Mus, New Orleans, La, 50; San Francisco Art Asn, Calif, 53; Los Angeles Co Mus Art, Calif, 54; Univ Calif, Berkeley, 69; plus other group & one-man shows.
Teaching: Instr studio courses & art hist, Orange Co Community Col (N Y), 63-68; instr art hist, Mount Saint Mary Col (N Y), 68-69.
Bibliography: A gift is indicated, Trumpeteer Mag, 49; Gloria Calamar has affinity for her subject, Am Artist Mag, 4/69; plus other articles in Fr, Belg, Norwegian & Am mags.
Memberships: Woodstock Art Asn; Artists Equity Asn; alumni assoc Otis Art Inst; Art Stud League New York.
Dealer: George Furnémont, 47 Rue des Esperonniers, Brussels, Belgium.
Mailing Address: Box 468, Woodstock, NY 12498.

CALAPAI, LETTERIO
Printmaker, Instructor
b Boston, Mass.
Study & Training: Mass Sch Art; Sch Fine Arts & Crafts; Art Stud League New York; Am Artists Sch; also with Robert Laurent, Ben Shahn & Stanley Hayter.
Work in Public Collections: Metrop Mus Art, New York, N Y; Fogg Art Mus, Cambridge, Mass; Art Inst Chicago, Ill; Libr Cong, Washington, D C; Bibliot Nat, Paris, France; Kyobashi Mus Mod Art, Tokyo, Japan; plus many other pub & pvt collections.
Exhibitions: Intag One, Calif, 71; 20-yr retrospective of graphic work, touring univ & cols throughout the U S, 72-73; plus many other one-man & group nat & int exhibs.
Teaching: Chmn graphic arts dept, Albright Art Sch, Univ Buffalo, 49-55; instr graphics, New Sch Social Res, 55-62; instr graphics, New York Univ, 62-65; vis assoc prof fine arts, Brandeis Univ, 64-65; instr, Univ Ill, Chicago Circle, 65.
Positions: Founder-dir, Intaglio Workshop for Advance Printmaking, 60-65.
Awards: Tiffany Found grant, 59; Rosenwald Found, 60; New York World's Fair, 64-65; plus others.
Memberships: Soc Am Graphic Artists (past v pres); Audubon Artists (former dir); Adv Panel, Ill Arts Coun.
Mailing Address: 344 Tudor, Glencoe, IL 60022.

CALAS, NICOLAS
Writer
b Lausanne, Switz, 07; U S citizen.
Study & Training: Univ Athens, Greece, Law Degree.
Teaching: Prof art hist, Fairleigh Dickinson Univ, 63-
Publications: Auth, Foyers d'incendie, Paris Denoel, 38; auth, Confound the wise, Arrow Ed, New York, 42; co-auth, The Peggy Guggenheim collection of modern art, 66; auth, Art in the age of risk, Dutton, 68; co-auth, Icons and images of the sixties, Dutton, 71.
Mailing Address: 210 E 68th St, New York, NY 10021.

CALCAGNO, LAWRENCE
Painter
b San Francisco, Calif, Mar 23, 13.
Study & Training: Calif Sch Fine Arts, San Francisco, 47-50; Acad Grande Chaumiere, Paris, France, 50-51; Acad Delgi Belli Arte, Florence, Italy, 51-52.
Work in Public Collections: San Francisco Mus Art, Calif; Whitney Mus Am Art, New York, NY; Brooklyn Mus, N Y; New York Univ Collection, N Y.
Exhibitions: Am Pavilion, Brussels World's Fair, 58; Carneige Inst Mus Int, 61; Nat Collect Fine Arts, Smithsonian Inst, Washington, D C, 68; Whitney Mus Am Art, 70.
Teaching: Vis Andrew Mellon prof painting, Carnegie-Mellon Univ, 55-58.
Awards: Ford Found grant, 65.
Mailing Address: 215 Bowery, New York, NY 10002.

CALCIA, LILLIAN ACTON
Educator
b Paterson, N J, Mar 28, 07.
Study & Training: Montclair State Normal Sch, dipl, 25; Teachers Col, Columbia Univ, BS, 31, MA, 35, EdD, 42.
Teaching: Instr elem art, Passaic, N J, 25-28; instr art, Elem & Jr High Sch, Passaic, 28-29; instr art, elem grades, Patterson, N J, 29-35; assoc prof, Newark State Teachers Col, 35-54, chmn art dept, 49-54; prof fine arts & chmn dept, Montclair State Col, 54-69, emer prof fine arts, 69-
Awards: Lillian A Calcia Visual Arts Ctr dedicated Montclair State Col, 69.
Memberships: Life mem Nat Educ Asn; N J Educ Asn; Asn Supv & Curric Dirs; N J Art Educ Asn (founder & past pres); Eastern Art Asn; plus others.
Mailing Address: 301 Rea Ave Exten, Hawthorne, NJ 03104.

CALDER, ALEXANDER
Sculptor
b Philadelphia, Pa, July 22, 98.
Study & Training: Stevens Inst Technol, ME, 19; Art Stud League New York, 23-26, with George Luks, Guy Du Bois, Boardman Robinson & John Sloan.
Work in Public Collections: Mus Mod Art & Metrop Mus Art, New York, N Y; Wadsworth Atheneum; Mus Western Art, Moscow, Russia; Philadelphia Mus Art; plus others.
Commissions: Gen Motors Corp, 54; New York Int Airport, 58; UNESCO, Paris, France, 58; plus many others.
Exhibitions: Many one-man, two-man & group exhibs nat & abroad.
Awards: First prize for non-Italian sculptor, Biennale Venice, 52; first prize sculpture, Int Exhib Contemp Painting & Sculpture, Pittsburgh, Pa, 58; gold medal award, Nat Inst Arts & Lett, 71; plus others.
Memberships: Nat Inst Arts & Lett.
Publications: Co-auth, Animal sketching, Bridgemen Publ, 41; auth & illusr, Three young rats, Mus Mod Art, 46; auth, Calder: an autobiography with pictures, Pantheon Bks, 66.
Mailing Address: R F D, Painter Hill Rd, Roxbury, CT 06783.

CALDWELL, HENRY BRYAN
Museum Director
b Larchmont, N Y, June 22, 18.
Study & Training: Harvard Univ, AB; School Fine Arts, grad, New York Univ, MA.
Positions: Asst dir, Corcoran Gallery Art, Washington, D C, 50-54; dir, Fort Worth Art Ctr, Tex, 55-60; Norfolk Mus Arts & Sci, Va, 60-70; dir, Allentown Art Mus, 70-72.
Mailing Address: R D 2, Allentown, PA 18103.

CALE, ROBERT ALLAN
Printmaker
Preferred Media: Graphics.
b Stonington, Conn, Jan 9, 40.
Study & Training: R I Sch Design, BFA, 64; S W Hayter's Atelier 17, Paris, France, 69-70.
Work in Public Collections: Bibliot Nat, Paris; Lessing J Rosenwald Collection, Alverthorpe Gallery, Jenkintown, Pa; Libr Cong,

Washington, D C; New York Pub Libr, N Y; Yale Univ Art Collection, New Haven, Conn.
Commissions: Ed of 100 black & white prints, New York Graphics Soc, Greenwich, 71; ed of 225 three color prints from several plates (with Will Barnet, artist & Elisabeth Egbert, asst), Ferdinand Roten Galleries, Baltimore, Md, 71-72; Karl Shrag, New York, 72.
Exhibitions: 4 Young American Printmakers in Paris, Europ Tour, 69-72; Atelier 17 Exhib, Mus Mod Art, Haifa, Israel, 70; 3rd Ann Print Exhib, Atlanta, Ga, 72; Silvermine 9th Nat Print Exhib, Conn, 72; Potsdam Prints 1972, N Y, 72.
Teaching: Instr printmaking, Printmaking Workshop, New York, 71-73; instr printmaking, Pratt Graphics Ctr, New York, 72-73; artist in residence graphics, Trinity Col, 72-73.
Positions: Asst curator, Pratt Graphics Ctr, 71-72; master printer, Printmaking Workshop, 71-
Awards: Margarete Walters Fund for Young Printmakers, Retina Gallery, Cambridge, Mass, 71; award print, mem exhib, Pratt Graphics Ctr, 71.
Bibliography: 8 young Americans in Paris, U S Embassy, Paris, 70; Ellen Zeifer (auth), The marine prints of Bob Cale, Am Artist, 7/72.
Publications: Auth, Description of methods involved in the prints of Robert A Cale in the Rosenwald Collection, 71.
Dealer: Eleanor Kanegis, Retina Gallery, Gloucester, MA 01930.
Mailing Address: c/o Printmaking Workshop, 248 W 23rd St, New York, NY 10011.

CALFEE, WILLIAM HOWARD
Sculptor
b Washington, D C, 09.
Study & Training: École Beaux-Arts, Paris, France; Cranbrook Acad Arts.
Work in Public Collections: Philadelphia Mus Art, Pa; Metrop Mus Art, New York, N Y; Cranbrook Acad Arts, Bloomfield Hills, Mich; Philbrook Art Ctr, Tulsa, Okla; Baltimore Mus Art, Md.
Commissions: Eight murals & two sculptures, comn by Sect Fine Arts, U S Treas Dept, 36-41; font, altar & candlesticks, St Augustine Chapel, Washington, D C, 69.
Exhibitions: One-man shows, Southern Vt Art Ctr, Manchester, Baltimore Mus Art, Corcoran Gallery Art, Washington, D C & Franz Bader Gallery, Washington, D C; also many group shows in mus.
Teaching: Instr drawing & painting, Phillips Gallery, Washington, D C; chmn dept painting & sculpture, Am Univ, 46-54; instr mural tech, Centre Art, Port au Prince, Haiti, 49; guest assoc prof painting, Univ Calif, Berkeley, 51.
Publications: Collabr design & auth, introd, In: Tradition and experiment in modern sculpture.
Mailing Address: 4817 Potomac Ave N W, Washington, DC 20007.

CALIFF, MARILYN ISKIWITZ
Painter, Designer
Preferred Media: Oils, Collage.
b Memphis, Tenn, Apr 27, 32.
Study & Training: Memphis Acad Arts, BFA.
Work in Public Collections: Brooks Mem Art Gallery, Overton Park, Memphis.
Commissions: Glass mosaic murals (with Barbara Shankman), Memphis Hebrew Acad, 62, Baron Hirsch Synagogue, 66 & Memphis Jewish Community Ctr, 68.
Exhibitions: 8th & 13th Delta Exhib, Little Rock, Ark, 65 & 70; Juried Arts, 4th Nat Exhib, Tyler, Tex, 67; 13th Ann Mid-South Exhib, Memphis, Tenn, 68; 10th All-State Artists Exhib, Nashville, 70; Ball State Drawing Exhib, Muncie, Ind, 71.
Awards: First in oils, 13th Mid-South Exhib, Brooks League, 68; three purchase prizes, First Tenn Artists & Craftsman Show, 72.
Publications: Auth, Your first quilt, 72.
Mailing Address: 5305 Denwood Ave, Memphis, TN 38117.

CALKIN, CARLETON IVERS
Painter, Lecturer
b Grand Rapids, Mich, July 27, 14.
Study & Training: Univ S Dak, BFA; Minneapolis Inst Art Sch; Chouinard Art Inst; Ohio Univ, MA; Univ Calif, PhD; Univ Michoacan, Mex; Inter-Am Univ, Panama.
Work in Public Collections: Portraits of Indian chiefs, S Dak Hist Mus, Vermillion; portraits, Tex Christian Univ, Fort Worth; hist mural, Ohio Univ; war murals, Rio Hato AFB, Panama.
Exhibitions: Regional exhibs, Fort Worth, Tex; local, regional & state fair shows, Ind.
Teaching: Lectr pre-Colombian, Latin Am archaeol & colonial & contemp Latin Am art; instr art, Ohio Univ, Univ Calif & Tex Christian Univ; head dept art, Purdue Univ, Lafayette, 55-62, prof art hist, 62-66.
Positions: Cur, Hist Saint Augustine Pres Bd, 66-

Memberships: Col Art Asn Am; Am Archaeol Soc; Am Asn Mus.
Publications: Contribr, Latin Am art sect, In: Encycl Britannica, 57.
Mailing Address: 265 Matanzas Blvd, Saint Augustine, FL 32084.

CALLAHAN, JACK
Painter, Instructor
b Somerville, Mass, Apr 13, 11.
Study & Training: Vesper George Sch Art; Mass Sch Art; Art Stud League New York.
Work in Public Collections: Portraits, Univ Mass & many pvt cols.
Exhibitions: Addison Gallery Am Art, Andover, Mass, 63; Endicott Jr Col; Nat Acad Design, 63; Smith Mus Fine Arts, Springfield; Am Watercolor Soc; plus others.
Teaching: Instr fine arts, Vesper George Sch Art.
Positions: Demonstr, N Shore Art Asn, Rockport Art Asn, Eastern States Exhib, Springfield & Lexington Arts & Crafts, Mass; jury mem, N Shore Art Asn, 59 & 62 & Rockport Art Asn, 61; maintains studio & gallery, Rockport, Mass.
Awards: Six hon mentions, 53-64 & Carl R Matson Mem Award, 58, 62 & 64, Rockport Art Asn; Archer M Huntington Award, Hudson Valley Art Asn, 63; Hatfield Award of Merit, Boston Soc Watercolor Painters, 65; plus others.
Memberships: Boston Watercolor Soc; Portraits, Inc, N Y; Portrait Asn New Eng; Copley Soc, Boston; Springfield Art Asn; plus others.
Mailing Address: 37 South St, Rockport, MA 01966.

CALLAHAN, KENNETH
Painter
b Spokane, Wash, Oct 30, 05.
Work in Public Collections: Whitney Mus Am Art, Mus Mod Art & Metrop Mus Art, New York, N Y; Pa Acad Fine Arts, Philadelphia; Brooklyn Mus, N Y; plus many other pub & pvt collections.
Commissions: Murals, U S Post Off Bldgs, Centralia & Anacortes, Wash & Rugby, N Dak; murals, Wash State Libr, Olympia, 60, Seattle Civic Theater, 62, Syracuse Univ, 64 & Wash Mutual Savings Bank, 70; plus others.
Exhibitions: Many nat & int group & one-man shows.
Teaching: Vis artist, Syracuse Univ, Pa State Univ, Boston Univ, Univ Southern Calif, Skowhegan Sch Painting & Sculpture & others.
Positions: Panel selection, Tamarind Lithography Workshop, 59-69.
Awards: Guggenheim fel, 54-55; Nat Inst Arts & Lett grant, 68; Am Acad Arts & Lett Purchase Award, New Orleans Art Mus, 72; plus others.
Bibliography: Sheldon Cheney (auth), Expressionism & Story of modern art; S H Richardson (auth), Painting in America; Henry Geldzahler (auth), 20th century art; plus many others.
Memberships: Wash State Arts Comn.
Publications: Auth, articles, In: Seattle Times, Art News, Art Digest, Creative Art & Am Mag Art.
Dealer: Kraushaar Galleries, 1055 Madison Ave, New York, NY 10021.
Mailing Address: Box 493, Long Beach, WA 98631.

CALLAN, ELIZABETH PURVIS
Painter
Preferred Media: Watercolors.
b Hamilton, Ont; U S citizen.
Study & Training: Vesper George Sch Art, Boston, Mass; Pratt Inst, Brooklyn, N Y; Nat Acad Design, New York, N Y; Art Stud League New York.
Exhibitions: Catharine Lorillard Wolfe Art Club, 72; Hudson Valley Art Asn, 72; Allied Artist Am, 72; Am Watercolor Soc Ann, 73.
Teaching: Lectr for private group teaching.
Memberships: Am Watercolor Soc (chmn of demonstrations, 67-, chmn of int exhibs, 72-, first v pres, 72-).
Mailing Address: 626 James St, Pelham Manor, NY 10803.

CALLCOTT, FRANK
Painter
Preferred Media: Oils.
b San Marcos, Tex, May 28, 91.
Study & Training: Southwestern Univ, AB; Columbia Univ, MA, PhD; Art Stud League New York; also with Nicolaides & Bridgeman.
Work in Public Collections: Metrop Mus Art, New York, N Y; Dallas Mus, Tex; Columbia Univ, New York; Southwestern Univ, Tex; Wesleyan Retirement Home, Georgetown, Tex.
Commissions: Portrait of pres of Tex Club, 38; portrait of wife, comn by pres of Scudder Sch, New York, 40; homestead of Atkins Family, Georgetown, 58; altar piece of chapel, 60 & portrait of patroness, 68, Wesleyan Retirement Home.
Exhibitions: Nat Acad Design Ann, New York, N Y, 33; Allied Artists Am, New York, several from 40-70; Audubon Artists, New York; Am Artist Prof League; Tex Art Asn Ann, Austin.

Teaching: Instr Spanish lang, lit & hist, Columbia Univ, 19-23, asst prof Spanish lang, lit & hist, 23-45, assoc prof Spanish lang, lit & hist, 45-50, prof Spanish lang, lit & hist, 50-56; instr, Riverside Church Arts & Crafts Prog, 49-53.
Positions: Bd control & treas, Art Stud League New York, 30-34; trustee, Am Fine Arts Soc, 32-34.
Awards: Hon mention, Southern States Art League, 36; award of merit in art & educ, Alumni Asn Southwestern Univ, 70.
Bibliography: Articles in New York Times, New York Tribune, Southwestern Univ Megaphone, Art News New York, Fort Worth Star Tel & many others from 35-72.
Memberships: Audubon Artists; Allied Artists Am; Am Artists Prof League; Tex Fine Arts Asn.
Publications: Auth, The supernatural in early Spanish literature, 23; auth, When Spain was young, 32; auth, articles in: Rev Hispanica, Mod Lang Asn Mag & others.
Dealers: Buchanan Dam Art Gallery, Buchanan Dam, TX 78609; House of Arts & Gifts, Georgetown, TX 78626.
Mailing Address: Box 62, Georgetown, TX 78626.

CALLERY, MARY
Sculptor
b New York, N Y, June 19, 03.
Study & Training: Art Stud League New York, 24-28.
Work in Public Collections: Mus Mod Art, New York; Mus Fine Arts Toledo, Ohio; San Francisco Mus Fine Arts; Addison Gallery, Andover, Mass; Va Mus Fine Arts, Richmond; plus others.
Commissions: Laughlin Children's Ctr, Sewickley, Pa; Int Expos, Brussels, 58; three hanging birds & portrait heads, Pittsburgh Pub Comn, Pa; relief, Brooklyn Court House; Sculpture arch, Lincoln Ctr Opera, New York; plus others.
Exhibitions: One-man shows, Art Club Chicago & galleries in Boston, New York & Paris, France.
Dealer: Coe Kerr Gallery, 49 E 82nd St, New York, NY 10028.
Mailing Address: 168 E 68th St, New York, NY 10021.

CALLICOTT, BURTON HARRY
Painter, Calligrapher
Preferred Media: Oils.
b Terre Haute, Ind, Dec 28, 07.
Study & Training: Cleveland Sch Art, cert, 31.
Work in Public Collections: Brooks Art Gallery, Memphis, Tenn; Tenn Art Comn, Nashville; Miss Art Asn, Jackson; Ark Art Ctr, Little Rock.
Commissions: Three mural panels, Pub Works Admin Proj, 34-35.
Exhibitions: New York World's Fair Exhib Am Painting, 39; Iron Horse in Art, Fort Worth Mus Art, Tex, 58; one-man shows, Brooks Art Gallery, 65, Miss Art Asn, 69 & Memphis Acad Arts, 71.
Teaching: Prof drawing, painting & calligraphy, Memphis Acad Arts, 37-
Awards: Purchase award, 69 & Hors Concour Award, 70, Ark Art Ctr, Little Rock; Worthen Bank Award, Little Rock, 71.
Bibliography: Edward Faiers (auth), catalog foreword, Memphis Acad Arts, 61.
Mailing Address: 3395 Douglass Ave, Memphis TN 38111.

CALLISEN, STERLING
Educator
b New York, N Y, Mar 30, 99.
Study & Training: Princeton Univ, AB, 20; Harvard Univ, MA, 34, PhD, 36.
Teaching: Asst fine arts, Harvard Univ, 34-36; asst prof, Rochester Univ, 36-41; assoc dean, Wesleyan Univ, 45-49; dean educ, Metrop Mus Art, 49-59; prof art hist, Pace Col, 64-
Positions: Pres, Parsons Sch Design, 59-64, emer pres, 64-
Memberships: Sch Art League (pres); Col Art Asn Am; Scarsdale Art Asn; Am Asn Archit Historians; Mus Asn Clubs; plus others.
Mailing Address: 10 Ridgecrest W, Scarsdale, NY 10583.

CAMACHO, PAUL
Painter
Preferred Media: Acrylics.
b Morovis, P R, Sept 7, 29.
Exhibitions: New England Annual, Silvermine Guild Artists, New Canaan, Conn, 64-71; Eastern States Exhibition, Springfield Art Inst, Mass, 67; Painting and Sculpture Today, Indianapolis, Ind, 70; Puerto Rican Art, Newark Mus, N J, 71; Inverse Illusionism, Am Fedn Arts Circulating Exhib, 71-72; plus others.
Awards: Ray Ridabock Mem Award for Painting, Silvermine Guild, 70.
Bibliography: Carter Ratcliff (auth), article, In: Art Int, 3/70; Atirnomis (auth), article, 2/71 & William D Case (auth), article, 2/72, In: Arts Mag.
Dealer: William Zierler Gallery, 956 Madison Ave, New York, NY 10021.
Mailing Address: West Rd, R F D 1, Weston, CT 06880.

CAMERON, DUNCAN F
Art Administrator, Writer
b Toronto, Ont, Feb 1, 30.
Positions: Sr adminr, Royal Ont Mus, Toronto, 56-62; pres & chmn bd, Janus Mus Consultants, Ltd, Toronto, 64-71; dir, Brooklyn Mus, 71-
Memberships: Int Coun Mus; Asn Art Mus Dirs; Am Asn Mus; Int Comt Pub & Mod Art (coordr, 71); Int Ctr Mus Archit (mem bd, 72).
Research: Museological.
Publications: Auth, Museums for moderns, UNESCO Courrier, 10/70; auth, Surveys can improve programs, reduce costs by predicting size and character of audience, Arts Mgt Handbk, 70; auth, The museum's dilemma of social responsibility, 8/70, The museum: a temple or forum, 71, ICOM Newsletter; auth, Problems in the language of museum interpretation, 71.
Mailing Address: Brooklyn Museum, 188 Eastern Pkwy, Brooklyn, NY 11238.

CAMINS, JACQUES JOSEPH
Painter, Printmaker
Preferred Media: Oils.
b Odessa, Russia, Jan 1, 04; U S citizen.
Study & Training: Paris, France; Art Stud League New York; special study with Jean Liberty & Byron Browne; Pratt Graphics Ctr, with Naoko.
Work in Public Collections: Israel Mus, Jerusalem; Negev Mus, Bersheba, Israel; Fr Embassy Cult Inst in Israel; Mem Art Mus & Gallery of Lidice, Czech; Tel-Aviv Univ.
Exhibitions: Veverly Gallery, New York, N Y, 64; Cript Gallery, Columbia Univ, 65; 50th Anniversary Audubon Artists at the Nat Acad Galleries, New York, 67; Artists Equity Asn Gallery, 71; Provincetown Art Asn, Mass, many years.
Teaching: Instr painting, Lakewood, N J, Bd Educ, 67.
Bibliography: Frank Crotty (auth), profiles, In: Worchester Sunday Telegram & Provincetown Advocate, 65; Barbara Sloan (auth), profile, The Observer, 67.
Memberships: Artists Equity Asn; Provincetown Art Asn; Art Stud League New York; Westbeth Graphics Workshop; Am Fedn Arts.
Dealer: East Coast Gallery, Commercial St, Provincetown, MA 02657.
Mailing Address: Westbeth Studio A923, 463 West St, New York, NY 10014.

CAMPANELLI, DANIEL
Painter, Illustrator
Preferred Media: Pencil, Ink.
b Bronx, N Y, Mar 18, 49.
Study & Training: Sch Visual Arts, N Y, grad.
Commissions: Cover illus, Prentice Hall, Englewood Cliffs, N J, 70; five hist sites prints, Friends of Hermitage, Inc, Bergen Co, N J, 72.
Exhibitions: One-man show, Edward Williams Col, Hackensack, N J, 69; Hudson Valley Juried Show, White Plains, N Y, 71; one-man show, Bloomfield Civic Ctr, N J, 71; invitational show, Garden State Arts Ctr, Holmdel, N J, 72; three-man show, Ringwood Manor State Park, N J, 72.
Teaching: Instr drawing, YWCA, Ridgewood, N J, 69-72; instr drawing, Edward Williams Col, 71.

CAMPANELLI, PAULINE EBLÉ
Painter, Instructor
Preferred Media: Oils.
b New York, N Y, Jan 25, 43.
Study & Training: Ridgewood Sch Art, N J, grad; Art Stud League New York.
Commissions: Illustrations of New York area geol hist, Paterson Mus, N J, 69; still life oils, Scafa-Tornabene Art Publ Co, White Plains, N Y, 71.
Exhibitions: One-man show, Am Art Gallery, Greenwich, Conn, 67; Exhibition of Contemporary American Realism, Hammond Mus, North Salem, N Y, 68; Am Artists Prof League Grand Nat Show at Lever House, New York, 68 & 70-72; one-man show, Edward Williams Col, Hackensack, N J, 69; Hudson Valley Juried Show, White Plains, N Y, 71.
Awards: Three best in show awards, Community Arts Asn State Show, N J, 67-69; spec award, Urban Farms State Show, N J, 71; distinguished serv award, Am Artists Prof League Grand Nat, 72.
Memberships: Federated Art Asns N J (rep, 71-72, bd judges & juries, 72); Am Artists Prof League (exhib chmn, N J chap, 70-71, trustee, 71-72).
Mailing Address: 39 Riverside Dr, Oakland, NJ 07436.
Teaching: Hd instr oil painting, Art Workshop & Gallery, Hawthorne, N J, 67-69; instr oil painting, Edward Williams Col, 71.
Awards: Gold medal award for oils, Catharine Lorillard Wolfe Art Club, 71; best in show award, Garden State Plaza Art Exhib, 71; distinguished serv award, Am Artists Prof League, 72.

Memberships: Catharine Lorillard Wolfe Art Club; Federated Art Asn of N J (rep, 71, bd judges & juries, 71-72); Am Artists Prof League (trustee, N J Chap, 72).
Mailing Address: 39 Riverside Dr, Oakland, NJ 07436.

CAMPBELL, DAVID PAUL
Painter
Preferred Media: Watercolor, Oils, Tempera.
b Washington, D C, Mar 31, 36.
Study & Training: Art Stud League New York.
Exhibitions: Smithsonian Inst, Washington, D C, 59; Concorso Donatello, Florence, 66; The Representational Spirit, State Univ N Y Albany, 70.
Teaching: Instr landscape painting, Garland Col, Florence, summers 68 & 69.
Awards: Fourth prize extemporaneous landscape, Community Casale, Italy, 66.
Dealer: Bowery Gallery, 135 Greene St, New York, NY 10012.
Mailing Address: 102 Forsyth St, New York, NY 10002.

CAMPBELL, DOROTHY BOSTWICK
Painter, Sculptor
b New York, N Y, Mar 26, 99.
Study & Training: Study with Eliot O'Hara, Washington, D C & Marilyn Bendell, Cortez, Fla.
Work in Public Collections: Cooperstown Art Asn, N Y; Mystic Mus, Conn; Pioneer Gallery, Cooperstown.
Exhibitions: Cooperstown Art Asn, various group shows & one-man show, 65; various shows, Sarasota Art Asn, Fla, Pioneer Gallery, Cooperstown, N Y & Am Art League, Washington, D C; Cortez Art Sch, Fla, 72.
Awards: First prize for watercolor, Collectors Corner, Washington, D C; purchase prize for watercolor, Cooperstown Art Asn, 65; merit award for oils, Cortez Sch Art Exhib, 72.
Memberships: Am Art League; Am Fedn Arts; Cooperstown Art Asn (dir); Sarasota Art Asn; Longboat Art Asn, Fla.
Publications: Auth & illusr, Passing thoughts, Bks I-VI, 67-72.
Mailing Address: 3111 Woodland Dr, N W, Washington, DC 20008.

CAMPBELL, GRETNA
Painter
Preferred Media: Oil.
b New York, N Y, Mar 23, 23.
Study & Training: Cooper Union; Art Stud League New York with Morris Kantor.
Work in Public Collections: Long View Found.
Exhibitions: Whitney Mus Am Art; Corcoran Gallery Art; Pa Acad Fine Arts; Mus Mod Art.
Teaching: Lectr painting, Phila Col Art, 63-71; instr painting, New York Studio Sch, 71-72.
Awards: Pearl Fund grant, 47-50; Tiffany Found grant, 52-53; Fulbright fel, 53-54.
Memberships: Artists Alliance.
Dealer: Green Mountain Gallery, 17 Perry St, New York, NY 10011.
Mailing Address: 145 W 88th St, New York, NY 10024.

CAMPBELL, KENNETH
Sculptor, Painter
b West Medford, Mass, Apr 14, 13.
Study & Training: Mass Sch Art, with Ernest Major, Cyrus Darlin, Richard Andrews & William Porter; Nat Acad Design, with Leon Kroll & Gifford Beal; Art Stud League New York, with Arthur Lee.
Work in Public Collections: Kalamazoo Art Inst; Walker Art Ctr, Minneapolis, Minn; Whitney Mus Am Art.
Exhibitions: Audubon Artists, 64 & 65; Sculptors Guild, N Y, 64, 65 & 67; Univ Ill, 65; Univ N C, 66; retrospective exhib, Univ Ky, 67; plus others.
Teaching: Instr drawing, painting & sculpture, Studio Five, Boston & Provincetown, Mass, 47-51; instr, Erskine Sch, Boston, 47-48; instr, Silvermine Col Art, 62 & 63; instr, Queens Col, N Y, 63-66; artist-in-residence, Univ Ky, 66; Univ R I, 67; lectr, Columbia Univ & Univ Md, 68-69.
Awards: Ford Found Purchase Award, 63 & 64; Richard Davis Mem Award, Audubon Artists, 65; Guggenheim fel, 65; plus others.
Memberships: Artists Club (treas & bd mem, 53-61); Art Stud League New York; Sculptors Guild (bd mem); Audubon Artists; Boston Soc Independent Artists (bd dirs).
Mailing Address: 79 Mercer St, New York, NY 10012.

CAMPBELL, (JAMES) LAWRENCE
Painter, Writer
Preferred Media: Oils, Watercolors.
b Paris, France, May 21, 14; U S citizen.
Study & Training: London Cent Schs Arts & Crafts; Acad Grande Chaumiere, Paris; Art Stud League New York.

Work in Public Collections: Joseph H Hirshhorn Mus & Sculpture Garden, Washington, D C.
Exhibitions: One-man show, Contemp Arts, New York, N Y, 51; Am Fedn Arts Traveling Exhib, 55-56; Pa Acad Fine Arts Ann, Philadelphia; Weatherspoon Gallery, Univ N C; Realist Shows, circulating through State Univ N Y, 70-72; plus other group & one-man shows.
Teaching: Assoc prof studio art, Brooklyn Col, prof, 72-; vis lectr art hist, Pratt Inst, 68-
Positions: Ed assoc, Art News Mag, 49-; dir publ, Art Stud League
Memberships: Am Sect, Int Asn Art Critics; Art Stud League New York.
Research: Nineteenth century European and American painting; also Ruskin; history of Art Students League of New York.
Publications: Auth, feature articles & reviews, In: Art News, 49-; contribr, The mosaics of Jeanne Reynal; auth, Thomas Sills, 65; ed, The elements of drawing, Dover, 71; auth, articles, In: Vogue, Craft Horizons, Washington Post, J Aesthetic Criticism & others.
Dealer: Kornblee Gallery, 58 E 79th St, New York, NY 10021; Green Mountain Gallery, 17 Perry St, New York, NY 10011.
Mailing Address: 215 W 98th St, New York, NY 10025.

CAMPBELL, MALCOLM
Art Historian, Educator
b Hackensack, N J, May 12, 34.
Study & Training: Princeton Univ, AB, MFA & PhD.
Teaching: Assoc prof hist art & chmn dept, Univ Pa.
Research: Sixteenth and seventeenth century Italian art.
Publications: Contribr, Art Bull, Burlington Mag & Rivista Arte.
Mailing Address: Dept of History of Art, G-29 Fine Arts Bldg, University of Pennsylvania, Philadelphia, PA 19104.

CAMPBELL, MARJORIE DUNN
Painter, Educator
b Columbus, Ohio, Sept 14, 10.
Study & Training: Ohio State Univ, BS & MA; Claremont Col Grad Inst Art; Teachers Col, Columbia Univ; also with Hans Hofmann, Emil Bisttram & Millard Sheets.
Teaching: Instr appl art, Univ Mo, 42-45; asst prof fine arts, Ohio State Univ, 45-49; asst prof art, Univ Northern Iowa, 49-71, assoc prof, 71-
Memberships: Art Educ Asn Iowa; Int Soc Educ through Art; Western Art Asn; Nat Art Educ Asn.
Publications: Contribr, Sch Arts, Art Educ J & Everyday Art Mags.
Mailing Address: Dept of Art, University of Northern Iowa, Cedar Falls, IA 50613.

CAMPBELL, RICHARD HORTON
Painter, Printmaker
Preferred Media: Oils.
b Marinette, Wis, Jan 11, 21.
Study & Training: Cleveland Sch Art; Art Ctr Sch, Los Angeles, Calif; Univ Calif, Los Angeles.
Work in Public Collections: Theater Guild Am, New York, N Y; Hilton Hotel, Denver, Colo.
Exhibitions: Butler Inst Am Art, Youngstown, Ohio; Denver Mus, Colo; Frye Mus, Seattle, Wash; Oakland Art Mus, Calif; Sarasota Nat, Fla.
Positions: Bd dirs, Santa Monica Art Gallery.
Awards: Second prize, Los Angeles All-City Exhib, 51; first prize, Cleveland May Show, 54; first prize, Seventh Festival of Arts, Los Angeles, 58.
Memberships: Calif Nat Watercolor Soc; Los Angeles Art Asn; fel Int Inst Arts & Lett.
Mailing Address: 643 Baylor St, Pacific Palisades, CA 90272.

CAMPBELL, ROSAMOND SHEILA
Painter, Designer
b Bareilly, India, Mar 25, 19.
Study & Training: Adelaide Sch Fine Arts, Australia; Melbourne Gallery Painting Sch; Cent Sch, London, Eng, with John Farleigh; Regent St Polytech, London, with Auerbach.
Work in Public Collections: Collections in N S, P E I & N B.
Exhibitions: N B Mus, 57 & 58; Maritime Art Asn, 57-61; Saint John Pub Libr, 59; Dalhousie Univ, 61; one-man show, Acadia Univ, Wolfville, N S; plus others.
Teaching: Lectr art.
Positions: Free lance artist; display dir, N B Mus.
Awards: Purchase prizes, Maritime Art Asn, 57, 58 & 61; prizes, Saint John Exhib, 58-61.
Memberships: Maritime Asn; Saint John Art Club.
Publications: Illusr children's bks for leading publ, London & Australia.
Mailing Address: New Brunswick Museum, 277 Douglas Ave, Saint John, N B, Can.

CAMPBELL, VIVIAN (VIVIAN CAMPBELL STOLL)
Collector, Writer
b Belmont, Mass, May 20, 19.
Positions: Asst cur, Fogg Art Mus, Harvard Univ, 37-42; dir, Harry Stone Gallery, New York, 42-44; prod mgr & art ed, Woman's Press Mag, 44-47; ed art publ, UNESCO, Paris, 48-50; art reporter & ed, Life mag, Paris & New York, 48-66; free lance writer, 60-
Memberships: ARC Directions (ed bd, 66-); New York Printmakers Workshop (bd dirs, 69-).
Research: Flemish painting.
Publications: Auth, A Christmas anthology of poetry and painting, 47; contribr, Life Mag, L'Oeil, Am Scholar & other publ.
Mailing Address: 408 W 20th St, New York, NY 10011.

CAMPBELL, WILLIAM PATRICK
Art Historian
b Essex Fells, N J, Sept 4, 14.
Study & Training: Yale Univ, BA, 36; Harvard Univ, MA, 46.
Positions: Cur, Worcester Art Mus, Mass; actg chief cur, Nat Gallery Art, Washington, D C.
Memberships: Am Asn Mus.
Research: American painting.
Mailing Address: National Gallery of Art, Sixth St at Constitution Ave, Washington, DC 20565.

CAMPOLI, COSMO
Sculptor, Educator
b South Bend, Ind, Mar 21, 22.
Study & Training: Art Inst Chicago, grad, 50, Anna Louise Raymond traveling fel to Italy, France & Spain, 50-52.
Work in Public Collections: Mus Mod Art, New York, N Y; Richmond Art Mus, Va; Unitarian Church, Chicago, Ill; City of Chicago Park Dist; Exchange Nat Bank, Chicago; plus many pvt collections.
Exhibitions: The New Images of Man, Mus Mod Art, New York, 59; U S Info Agency Show, Moscow & Petrograd; The Chicago School Exhibition, Galerie due Dragone, Paris, France; Festival of Two Worlds (sculpture exhib), Spoleto, Italy; 30-yr retrospective, Mus Contemp Art, Chicago, 71; plus many others.
Teaching: Instr adult art group, Hull House, 47-49; instr sculpture, Contemp Art Workshop, Chicago, 52-; Assoc prof sculpture, Inst Design, Ill Inst Technol, 53-, chmn dept sculpture, 55-; vis prof, Univ Chicago, summers 63-65; lectr original artist-mkt-concept, Conf World Affairs, Univ Colo, 72.
Positions: Juror, var shows in Chicago area, Nelson Gallery - Atkins Mus, Columbus Art League & Walker Art Ctr.
Awards: Bronze medal, Deleg Nat Educ-Fisica, Madrid, 69; Automotive Asn Spain Award, An Expression of the Automobile Obsession, 69; appointed Knight of Mark Twain, 71; plus others.
Bibliography: Harold Haydon (auth), rev, In: Chicago Sun-Times, 5/9/71; Franz Schulze (auth), rev, In: Chicago Daily News, 5/29/71; Rev of 30 yr Retrospective, Fr TV, 6/71; plus many others.
Publications: Auth, Artists Market, Alumni Asn Newspaper, Sch Art Inst Chicago, 71.
Mailing Address: 5326 S Cornell St, Chicago, IL 60615.

CAMURATI, ALBERT
Painter
Preferred Media: Oils.
b New York, N Y, Apr 13, 17.
Study & Training: Cooper Union; Queens Col.
Exhibitions: L I Art League, 65-67; Nat Art League, 67-70; Hudson Valley Art Asn, 68, 70 & 71; Long Island Art 72.
Teaching: Instr camouflage, USA, 42-45; instr oil painting, Bishop Loughlin High Sch, Brooklyn, N Y, 67-70.
Memberships: Am Artists Prof League; Hudson Valley Art Asn; Nat Art League (pres, 72-).
Mailing Address: 148-45 60th Ave, Flushing, NY 11355.

CANADAY, JOHN EDWIN
Art Critic
b Fort Scott, Kans, Feb 1, 07.
Study & Training: Univ Tex, BA; Yale Univ, MA; Ecole Louvre, Paris, France.
Teaching: Assoc prof art hist, Univ Va, 38-50; prof art hist & head, Sch Art, Newcomb Col, Tulane Univ, 50-52.
Positions: Chief, Div Educ, Philadelphia Mus Art, 51-59; art critic, New York Times, 59-
Publications: Auth, Mainstreams of modern art, Metropolitan seminars in art, Lives of the painters, Embattled critic & Culture gulch.
Mailing Address: New York Times, 229 W 43rd St, New York, NY 10036.

CANDELL, VICTOR
Painter, Educator
b Budapest, Hungary, May 11, 03; U S citizen.
Study & Training: Pvt study in Budapest & Paris, France.
Work in Public Collections: Metrop Mus Art, New York, N Y; Clark Fund, Whitney Mus Am Art, New York; Corcoran Gallery Art, Washington, D C; Krannert Mus, Urbana, Ill; Carnegie Inst, Pittsburgh, Pa; plus over one hundred other pub & pvt collections.
Commissions: Outdoor mural, Govt Iraq, New York World's Fair, 39.
Exhibitions: Many Carnegie Int & Whitney Mus Am Art ann; Chicago Graphic Int; Am-French Art Exchange Exhib, Galerie Jean Bucher, Paris, 54; UNESCO sponsored European tour of Am painting, 56-57.
Teaching: Instr painting, Brooklyn Mus Sch Art, 46-54; instr painting, Cooper Union, 54-68; co-dir & instr, Provincetown Workshop, Mass, 58-; asst prof painting, New York Univ, 69-
Positions: Adv, Marquis Biog Libr Soc, 68-; trustee, Provincetown Art Asn, 71-
Awards: Second prize, Artist as Reporter Exhib, Mus Mod Art, 40; purchase award, Whitney Mus Am Art, 52; painting prize, Silvermine New Eng Show, 68.
Memberships: Artists Equity Asn New York (dir); fel Edward MacDowell Art Colony; life fel Int Acad Arts & Lett; Am Asn Univ Prof; Audubon Artists (dir).
Dealer: Grand Central Art Galleries, 40 Vanderbilt Ave, New York, NY 10017.
Mailing Address: 22 E Tenth St, New York, NY 10003.

CANFIELD, JANE (WHITE)
Sculptor
Preferred Media: Marble, Stone, Bronze, Terra-cotta.
b Syracuse, N Y, Apr 29, 97.
Study & Training: Art Stud League New York; James Earle & Laura Gardin Fraser Studio; Borglum Sch; also with A Bourdelle, Paris, France.
Work in Public Collections: Whitney Mus Am Art; Cornell Univ Mus Art.
Commissions: Six animals in lead for gate posts, Paul Mellon, Upperville, Va, 40; animals in lead for gym entrance, Miss Porters Sch, Farmington, Conn, 60; St John Apostle in stone, Church of St John of Lattington, Locust Valley, N Y, 63; herons in stone, Mem Sanctuary, Fishers Island, 69; Can geese in bronze for pool, Long Lake, Minn, 71.
Exhibitions: Sculpture pavilion, World's Fair, New York, N Y, 39; one-man show, Brit-Am Art Gallery, New York, 55; one-man shows, Far Gallery, New York, 61 & 65; Country Art Gallery, Locust Valley, 71.
Publications: Auth, The Frog Prince, Harper & Row, 70.
Dealer: Far Gallery, 746 Madison Ave, New York, NY 10021.
Mailing Address: Guard Hill Rd, Bedford Village, NY 10506.

CANIFF, MILTON ARTHUR
Cartoonist, Writer
Preferred Media: Ink, Watercolors, Oils.
b Hillsboro, Ohio, Feb 28, 07.
Study & Training: Ohio State Univ, BA, with James Hopkins, Ralph Fanning & Guy Brown Wiser; Rollins Col, hon FAD.
Work in Public Collections: Metropolitan Mus Art, New York, N Y; Louvre (graphics), Paris, France; Air Force Mus, Dayton, Ohio; Nat Aviation Club, Washington, D C.
Commissions: Murals, Nat Aviation Club, 60, Flag Plaza, Pittsburgh, Pa, 68, Alumni House, Ohio State Univ, 71 & Conv Ctr, Dayton, Ohio, 72.
Exhibitions: One-man shows, Levy Gallery, 36 & Soc Illustrators Gallery, 47, New York; one-man show, Jean Renoir Gallery, Paris, 65; Art of the Cartoon, Graphics Hall, Louvre, Paris, 66; Art of the Cartoon, Lever Gallery, New York, 71.
Awards: Reuben Award, Nat Cartoonists Soc, 47 & 72; Arts & Lett Award, U S Air Force Asn, 49; Seegar Award, Nat Cartoonists Soc, 71.
Bibliography: Stephen Becker (auth), Comic art in America, Simon & Schuster.
Memberships: Nat Cartoonists Soc (pres, 48-50, hon chmn, 70-); Soc Illustrators.
Publications: Auth & illusr, Dickie Dare, 32-34; auth & illusr, Terry and the pirates syndicated newspaper feature, 34-46; auth & illusr, Male call, U S Serv newspapers, 42-45; auth & illusr, Steve Canyon, syndicated newspaper feature, 47-
Dealer: Toni Mendez, 140 E 56th St, New York, NY 10022.
Mailing Address: 443 Chuckwalla Rd, Palm Springs, CA 92262.

CANIN, MARTIN
Painter
Preferred Media: Oil on Canvas.
b Brooklyn, N Y, Oct 1, 27.
Study & Training: Syracuse Univ, BFA.

Work in Public Collections: Philadelphia Mus Art; San Francisco Mus Art; Saint Petersburg Mus Art; Yale Univ Art Gallery; Boston Mus Fine Arts.
Exhibitions: Pa Acad Fine Arts Ann, 54; Hard Edge Painting, Mus Mod Art, New York Penthouse, 63; group show, Mus Mod Art Penthouse, 68; Int Drawing Show, Darmstaat, Ger, 70; Prints from Kelpra Studio, Hayward Gallery, London, 71.
Teaching: Instr painting, drawing & design, Parsons Sch Design, 61-69.
Dealer: Graham Gallery, 1014 Madison Ave, New York, NY 10021.
Mailing Address: 2231 Broadway, New York, NY 10024.

CANNON, MARGARET ERICKSON
Painter, Instructor
Preferred Media: Oils, Acrylics.
b Marquette, Mich, May 26, 23.
Study & Training: Univ of the Americas, BA(art educ); Univ Calif, Los Angeles; Long Beach City Col; Calif State Univ, Fullerton, MA(drawing & painting); Univ Barcelona; also special study in Spanish & Mex art.
Work in Public Collections: Univ of the Americas, Mex; Hunt Gallery, Fullerton, Calif; Cerritos Col Gallery, Calif; Paideia Gallery, Hollywood, Calif; Calif State Univ, Fullerton.
Exhibitions: Artes Graficas, Univ of the Americas, Mex, 53; Nat Metaphys Inst, Hollywood, 64; Cerritos Col Invitational, Norwalk, Calif, 64-65; Whittier Invitational, Calif, 65-66; Warsaw Fine Arts Invitational, Poland, 66-67.
Teaching: Prof art hist, Univ of the Americas, 53-54; instr art hist & lectr community servs, Cerritos Col, 62-66; lectr art appreciation, Calif State Univ, Fullerton, 67.
Positions: Art critic, Am News & Radio, Mex, 53-54; co-founder, Fullerton Art League, 65-66.
Awards: Award for painting, Univ of the Americas, 52; Orange Co Art Asn, Calif; La Mirada Art Festival, Calif.
Memberships: Los Angeles Art Asn; Calif Art Educ Asn; Nat Art Educ Asn; Southern Calif Art Ther Asn; Am Asn Univ Women.
Research: Symbology-psychology in art; Greek art.
Art Interests: Art therapy.
Publications: Auth, History of the Waves, U S Naval Reserve; illusr, Patriots-female version.
Dealer: Paideia Gallery, 765 N La Cienega Blvd, Los Angeles, CA 90069.
Mailing Address: 1711 E Grove Pl, Fullerton, CA 92631.

CANNON, T C (TOM WAYNE)
Painter, Printmaker
Preferred Media: Oils, Acrylics.
b Lawton, Okla, Sept 27, 46.
Study & Training: Inst Am Indian Arts, Santa Fe, N Mex; San Francisco Art Inst; Cent State Univ (Okla).
Work in Public Collections: Southern Plains Mus, Anadarko, Okla; Hon Collection, Inst Am Indian Affairs; Washington Arts & Crafts Bd, Bur Indian Affairs, Washington, D C
Exhibitions: Young Indian Painters, Fine Arts Mus N Mex, Santa Fe, 66; Scottsdale Nat, Ariz, 66; one-man shows, American Before Columbus, Dennis Larkins Gallery, 70 & Paintings & Graphics, Southern Plains Mus, 71; Two American Painters, Smithsonian Inst, Washington, D C, 72.
Awards: First prize, Southwestern Interscholastic Meet, 62, 63 & 64; Gov Trophy, Scottsdale Nat, 66.
Publications: Illusr, Tales of the Kiowa Indians, 72.
Dealer: Joachim Jean Aberbach, 241 W 72nd St, New York, NY 10023.
Mailing Address: 400 E Danforth, Apt 134, Edmond, OK 73034.

CANRIGHT, SARAH ANNE
Painter
Preferred Media: Oils, Acrylics.
b Chicago, Ill, Aug 20, 41.
Study & Training: Art Inst Chicago, BFA.
Work in Public Collections: Kresge Found, New York, N Y; Sam Koffler Found & Ill Bell Tel Co, Chicago, Gould Corp, Ill.
Exhibitions: Nonplussed Some, Hyde Park Art Ctr, Chicago, 68-69; Famous Artists, Mus Contemp Art, Chicago, 69; Famous Artists, Another Load, San Francisco Art Inst, 70; 73rd Vicinity Show, Art Inst Chicago & Phyllisteens, Phyllis Kind Gallery, Chicago, 71.
Awards: Armstrong Award, Art Inst Chicago, 71.
Bibliography: W Halsted (auth), Chicago, Artforum, 68; F Schulze (auth), Chicago, Art News, 71, various articles, Chicago Daily News.
Mailing Address: c/o Phyllis Kind Gallery, 226 E Ontario St, Chicago, IL 60611.

CANTEY, SAM BENTON, III
Collector
Study & Training: Culver Mil Acad; Washington & Lee Univ, BA.
Collections Arranged: School of Fontainebleau, Fort Worth Art Ctr & Univ Texas Art Mus, Austin, 65.
Collection: Modern prints, drawings and watercolors; School of Fontainebleau prints and drawings; work of Fort Worth and Texas artists.
Publications: Auth, articles in various newspapers, catalog introductions on Tex artists and catalog for School of Fontainebleau Exhib.
Mailing Address: 1220 Washington Terrace, Fort Worth, TX 76107.

CANTINI, VIRGIL D
Painter, Sculptor
Preferred Media: Enamels.
b Italy, Feb 28, 20.
Study & Training: Carnegie Inst Technol, BFA, 46; Univ Pittsburgh, MA, 48.
Work in Public Collections: Wichita Mus Art, Kans; Carnegie Mus Art, Pittsburgh, Pa; Westmoreland Co Mus Art, Greensburg, Pa; Hillman Libr, Univ Pittsburgh, Pa; Point Park Col, Pittsburgh, Pa.
Commissions: New Horizons & Skyscape (sculpture), Joseph Horne Co, Pittsburgh, 64-65; Man (sculpture), Grad Sch Pub Health, Univ Pittsburgh, 66; three sculptures & two tapestries, Hillman Libr, Univ Pittsburgh, 69; Joy of Life (fountain sculpture), Urban Redevelop Authority Pittsburgh, 69; Skyscape (enamel mural), Oliver Tyrone Co, Pittsburgh, 71.
Exhibitions: Assoc Artists Pittsburgh, 45-70; World's Fair, Brussels, Belg, 58; Pittsburgh Int, Carnegie Mus Art, 61, 64 & 67; one-man shows, Westmoreland Co Mus Art, 62 & Pittsburgh Plan for Arts, 62, 67 & 71.
Teaching: Chmn dept studio arts & prof sculpture, drawing, painting & design, Univ Pittsburgh, 52-
Positions: V pres, Pittsburgh Coun for Arts, 68-70.
Awards: Guggenheim fel, 58; Pope Paul VI Bishop's Medal, 64; Davinci Medal - Ital Sons & Daughters Am, Cultural Heritage Found, 68.
Bibliography: Dorothy Sterling (auth), article, In: Am Artist, 52; Helen Knox (auth), article, In: Pitt Mag, 64; Lloyd Davis (auth), article, In: Appalachian, 67.
Memberships: Assoc Artists Pittsburgh (pres, 62-64); Arts & Crafts Ctr (v pres, 55-57); Pittsburgh Plan for Arts; Col Art Asn Am; Am.Crafts Coun.
Dealer: Pittsburgh Plan for Arts, 1251 N Negley Ave, Pittsburgh, PA 15206.
Mailing Address: Dept of Studio Arts, University of Pittsburgh, Pittsburgh, PA 15213.

CANTOR, ROBERT LLOYD
Educator, Designer
b New York, N Y, Aug 14, 19.
Study & Training: N Y Univ, PhD.
Exhibitions: One-man show, Charleston Art Gallery.
Teaching: Prof fine & indust arts, W Va Inst Technol; instr art, N Y Univ; instr art, City Col New York; instr art, Fashion Inst Technol; instr art, Columbia Univ.
Positions: Exec dir, Artists Equity Asn, New York; educ dir, Am Craftsmen Sch, New York.
Memberships: Eastern Artists Asn; Nat Educ Asn; Indust Art Asn; Comn Art Educ, Mus Mod Art; Soc Plastic Eng.
Publications: Auth, History of art workbook & auth, Plastics for the layman; also training film scenarios, manuals, textbooks & contributor to art, educational & political journals.
Mailing Address: 15 Gulf Rd, Lawrence Brook, East Brunswick, NJ 08816.

CAPARN, RHYS (RHYS CAPARN STEEL)
Sculptor
Preferred Media: Bronze, Stone.
b Onteora Park, N Y, July 28, 09.
Study & Training: Bryn Mawr Col, 27-29; Ecole Artistique Animaux, with Edouard Navellier, 30; Archipenko Art Sch, New York, 31-33.
Work in Public Collections: Morton May Collection, City Art Mus, Saint Louis; Riverside Mus Collection, Brandeis Univ; drawings, Fogg Mus; Whitney Mus Am Art, New York.
Commissions: Figures on armillary sphere (with Harold A Caparn), Brooklyn Bot Garden, 32; wall reliefs in concrete, bronze screen, drawings in ceramic tile & fountain head (with O'Conner & Kilham), Wollman Libr, Barnard Col, 58-59.
Exhibitions: 15 Sculptors, Mus Mod Art Traveling Exhib, 41; 5 Ann, Whitney Mus Am Art, 41-60; New York Six, Petit Palais, Paris, 50; Unknown Political Prisoner, Tate Gallery, London, 53; Drawings, 56-57 & 8 Americans, 57-58, U S Info Agency Exhibs, Europe & Far East.

Teaching: Instr sculpture, Dalton High Sch, New York, 46-55 & 60-
Positions: Mem Mayors Comt Beautification City of New York, 63-64; founding mem Harlem Cult Coun, 64.
Awards: Am Sculpture Second Prize, Metrop Mus Art, 51; medals of honor for sculpture, Nat Asn Women Artists, 60 & 61.
Bibliography: Robert Beverly Hale (auth), Rhys Caparn, Retrospective Press, 72.
Memberships: Sculptors Guild; Am Abstr Artists; fel Int Inst Arts & Lett.
Publications: Illusr, Down the mountain, 62.
Mailing Address: R D 1, Taunton Hill Rd, Newtown, CT 06470.

CAPLAN, JERRY L
Sculptor, Educator
Preferred Media: Terra-cotta.
b Pittsburgh, Pa, Aug 9, 22.
Study & Training: Carnegie-Mellon Univ, BFA & MFA; Art Stud League New York; Univ N C.
Work in Public Collections: N C State Art Gallery, Raleigh; Pittsburgh Bd Educ.
Commissions: Terra-cotta sculptures, Friendship Fed Plaza, Pittsburgh, 68; ceramic panels, Temple Emmanuel foyer, Pittsburgh, 71; porcelain symbols, Westinghouse Ceramic Div, Derry, Pa, 72; terra-cotta, Kossman Group, Kossman Assocs, Pittsburgh, 72; symbol, Rockwell Corp, Pittsburgh, 72.
Exhibitions: Five shows, Butler Inst of Am Art, 55-72; Norfolk Drawing Biennial, Norfolk Mus, 67-69; Drawing U S A, St Paul, Minn, 68; Kent State Univ Sculpture Invitational, 69; Carnegie Inst, 71.
Teaching: Instr sculpture & ceramics, Chatham Col, 59-; instr painting, Arts & Crafts Ctr, Pittsburgh, 62-; lectr, Frick Educ Comn, Pittsburgh, 64-
Awards: Purchase award, Raleigh State Art Gallery, 52; purchase award, Assoc Artists Pittsburgh, 65; Soc Sculptors Award, 70.
Memberships: Assoc Artists Pittsburgh (v pres, pres, 66); Soc Sculptors (treas); Am Crafts Coun; Craftsmen's Guild Western Pa; Pittsburgh Plan for Art (bd dirs, 71-).
Mailing Address: 5812 Fifth Ave, Pittsburgh, PA 15232.

CAPLES, BARBARA BARRETT
Printmaker, Painter
b Providence, R I, Oct 28, 14.
Study & Training: Smith Col AB(magna cum laude), 36; Yale Univ Sch Fine Arts, 36-38; also with George Laurence Nelson & Ruth Starr Rose.
Work in Public Collections: Smith Col Mus, Northampton, Mass; Univ Va, Charlottesville.
Exhibitions: Am Watercolor Soc, 38; Soc Washington Printmakers, 68-; one-man shows, Smith Col & Art League, Alexandria, Va, 70; Boston Printmakers, 71.
Teaching: Instr art & art hist, Rye Country Day Sch, N Y, 38-40; instr art, Walter Reed Hosp, Washington, D C, 43-45; instr serigraphy, YWCA, Alexandria, 65-
Awards: First prize for watercolor, C Z Art Asn, 47; numerous awards, Art League, Alexandria, 65-71; hon mention, Fairfax Co Cult Asn, 71; plus one other.
Memberships: Soc Washington Printmakers; Art League, Alexandria (mem bd, 69); N Va Fine Arts Asn.
Mailing Address: 1111 Roan Lane, Alexandria, VA 22302.

CAPONI, ANTHONY
Sculptor, Educator
Preferred Media: Stone.
b Pretare, Italy, May 7, 21.
Study & Training: Univ Flore, Italy; Cleveland Sch Art; Walker Art Ctr, Minn; Univ Minn, BS & MEd.
Work in Public Collections: Minneapolis Inst Art; Saint Cloud State Col; Minn Mus Art.
Commissions: Sculpture, columns & figures, St Joseph Sch, Red Lake Falls, Minn, St Mary's Church, Warroad, Minn; St Johns Church, Rochester, Minn; wax models for all bronze motifs in Eisenhower Libr, Abilene, Tex; two bronze relief sculptures, Ascoli, Italy; plus others.
Exhibitions: Walker Art Ctr, Minneapolis, Minn, 47-58; Saint Paul Gallery Art, 47-58; Iowa State Teachers Col, 58; Minneapolis Art Inst Ann; Augustana Col, Sioux Falls, S Dak, 71; plus other group & one-man shows.
Teaching: Prof art & chmn dept, Macalester Col, 58-
Positions: Co-dir, Sculpture in Minnesota (film), 50; pres, Minn Sculpture Group, 52; v pres, Minn Soc Sculptors, 58; producer, Forms that live and forms (film), Univ Minn, 59.
Awards: Ford Found grant & four prizes, Minneapolis Inst Art, 47-59; six awards, Minn State Fair, 48-65; awards, Saint Paul Gallery Art, 49 & 55.
Memberships: Artists Equity Asn; Soc Minn Sculptors.

Publications: Auth, Boulders and pebbles of poetry and prose, Independence Press, 72.
Mailing Address: Art Dept, Macalester College, Saint Paul, MN 55105.

CAPP, AL
Cartoonist
b New Haven, Conn, Sept 28, 09.
Study & Training: Pa Acad Fine Arts; Mus Fine Arts, Boston.
Positions: Auth, syndicated comic strip, Li'l Abner; columnist, New York Daily News; commentator, daily syndicated radio-TV prog.
Mailing Address: Capp Enterprises, 122 Beacon St, Boston, MA 02116.

CARDOSO, ANTHONY
Painter, Instructor
Preferred Media: Oils.
b Tampa, Fla, Sept 13, 30.
Study & Training: Univ Tampa, BS(art); Art Inst Minn, BFA; Univ S Fla.
Work in Public Collections: Minn Mus Art, St Paul; Newsboy, Tampa Tribune; sculpture, Del Webb Corp, Sun City, Fla.
Commissions: Mural painting, Spain, Dr Louis Passetti, Tampa, 70; Sports Authority, Tampa Stadium Office, 71; sports theme paintings, Leto High Sch & Pierce High Sch, Tampa, 71; plus many others.
Exhibitions: 22nd Smithsonian Biennial Traveling Show, 69-70; Prix de Paris, Raymond Duncan Galleries, Paris, France, 70; Salon of 50 States, Ligoa Duncan Gallery, New York, N Y, 70; New York Int Art Show, 70; Drawings U S A, Minn Mus Art, St Paul, 71.
Teaching: Head art dept, Jefferson High Sch, 57-65; instr & head fine arts dept, Leto High Sch, 65-
Positions: Rep of high schs, Tampa Arts Coun, 70-
Awards: Smithsonian 22nd Biennial Award, Norfolk Mus & Smithsonian Inst, 69-70; Prix de Paris Award, Raymond Duncan Galleries, 70; Drawings U S A Purchase Award, Minn Mus Art, 71.
Bibliography: Bob Martin (auth), article, In: Tampa-Times & Tribune, 71; Bertrand Sorlot (auth), article, In: La Rev Mod, 71.
Memberships: Fla Arts Coun (rep, 70-72); Ringling Art Mus; Tampa Realists Artists; Latin Quarter.
Publications: Contribr, La Rev Mod, 71 & 72.
Dealer: S Arnold Gallery, 1705 Broadway, Tampa, FL 33605.
Mailing Address: 3208 Nassau St, Tampa, FL 33607.

CAREWE, SYLVIA
Painter, Designer
b New York, N Y.
Study & Training: New Sch Social Res, with Kunoyshi; also with Hans Hofmann, New York & Provincetown.
Work in Public Collections: Whitney Mus Am Art, New York; Mus Art Mod, Paris, France; Tel-Aviv Mus, Israel; Howard Univ, Washington, D C; Joseph H Hirshhorn Collection; plus many other pub & pvt collections.
Exhibitions: Tapestries, Butler Inst Am Art, Youngstown, Ohio, 60; Pastel Paintings for Tapestry, Donnell Art Libr, New York, 68; Poster Exhib, Am Embassies throughout the world, 69; Paintings, Fordham Univ, 70; 300 Years of Women's Paintings & Sculpture, N C Show of Women, 72; plus many others.
Teaching: Lect tapestry, Columbia Univ.
Awards: ACA Gallery prize, one-man show, 47.
Memberships: Artists Equity Asn; Am Soc Contemp Artists; Am Watercolor Soc; Philadelphia Print Club; New York Soc Women Artists; plus many others.
Publications: Illusr, many covers for nat art mag.
Mailing Address: 500 E 83rd St, New York, NY 10028.

CAREY, JAMES SHELDON
Educator, Potter
Preferred Media: Ceramics, Glass.
b Bath, N Y, July 28, 11.
Study & Training: State Univ N Y Col Ceramics, Alfred Univ, BS; Teachers Col, Columbia Univ, AM; also with Fritz Dreisbach, Toledo Mus Art & Andre Billeci, Alfred Univ.
Work in Public Collections: Metrop Mus Art, New York, N Y; Everson Mus Art, Syracuse, N Y; Scripps Col, Calif; Univ South Fla, Tampa; Joslyn Art Mus, Omaha, Nebr.
Exhibitions: 20th Ceramic Int, Everson Mus, 50; 2nd Int Ceramic Exhib, Ostend, Belg; Int Cult Exchange, Geneva, Switz; Wichita Nat Ceramic Exhib, Wichita Art Asn, Kans.
Teaching: Lectr ceramics & sculpture, Teachers Col, Columbia Univ, 40-42; instr ceramics & sculpture, R I Sch Design, 42-43; prof ceramics & glass, Univ Kans, 44-; vis prof, San Jose State Col, summers 45 & 47.
Positions: Adv ed, Ceramics Mo. 53-55.

Awards: Prize for textured urn (stoneware), Syracuse Mus Fine
Arts, 58; award for Out of Orbit (glass), First Nat Space Art
Exhib, 69.
Bibliography: Fruit of the wheel, Time Mag, 2/16/69; Glenn Nelson
(auth), Ceramics: a potter's book, Holt, Rinehart & Winston, 71.
Memberships: Fel Am Ceramic Soc; Am Crafts Coun (trustee, 67-
69); Nat Coun Educ for Ceramic Arts (bd dirs, 66-71).
Research: Originator of throwing on an upside-down wheel, pulling
clay down to make tall pots; developer of new liquid for throwing.
Mailing Address: Design Dept, University of Kansas, Lawrence, KS
66044.

CAREY, JOHN THOMAS
Educator, Art Historian
b Wilmont, Minn, Aug 23, 17.
Study & Training: Milwaukee State Teachers Col, BA; Univ Wis, MS;
Ohio State Univ, PhD; Harvard Univ.
Teaching: Art instr, Univ Wis-Madison, 47-48; asst prof art, Ill
State Univ, 49-51; instr art, Ohio State Univ, 53-54; asst prof art,
Bowling Green State Univ, 54-56; prof art & chmn dept, Northern
Ill State Univ, 56-66; vis prof, Rollins Col, 66-67; prof art &
chmn dept, Univ West Fla, 67-; vis prof, World Campus Afloat,
Chapman Col, spring 69 & spring 73.
Memberships: Col Art Asn Am; Southeastern Col Art Asn (ed, news-
letter & rev, 71-).
Research: Introduction and development of lithography in America.
Publications: Ed, Ill Art Educ Yearbk, 57; contribr, William
Fendrick, early American lithographer (monogr), Libr Cong, 57.
Mailing Address: 412 Sunnydale Lane, Cantonment, FL 32533.

CAREY, TED
Collector, Designer
b Chester, Pa, June 3, 32.
Study & Training: Philadelphia Mus Sch Art, BFA.
Teaching: Former instr, Pratt Inst, Brooklyn, N Y.
Positions: Textile designer & free lance illusr.
Collection: Contemporary paintings, sculpture and drawings.
Mailing Address: 20 Oyster Pond Lane, East Hampton, NY 11937.

CARIOLA, ROBERT J
Painter, Sculptor
b Brooklyn, N Y, Mar 24, 27.
Study & Training: Pratt Inst Art Sch; Pratt Graphic Ctr.
Work in Public Collections: Fordham Univ, New York, N Y; De
Pauw Univ, Greencastle, Ind; La Salle Col, Philadelphia, Pa;
Hofstra Col, Hempstead, N Y; Topeka Pub Libr, Kans.
Commissions: Metal sculpture, Col Art Coordr, La Salle Col, 67;
metal sculptures, comn by Jonynas & Shepherd Studio, St Bren-
dan's Church, Bronx, N Y, 68; stained glass windows, comn by
Contemp Christian Art Gallery, Trinity Lutheran Church, N J.
69, metal mural, altar & artifacts, comn by Contemp Christian
Art Gallery, St Gabriel's Church, Oakridge, N J, 70-71.
Exhibitions: Boston Mus Printmakers Exhib, 62; Corcoran Gallery
Art, Washington, D C & Pa Acad Fine Arts, Philadelphia, 63;
Vatican Pavilion, New York World's Fair, 64; Nat Acad Design,
New York, 70.
Teaching: Instr art, La Salle Acad, Oakdale, N Y, 63-65; instr art,
Catholic Youth Orgn Summer Workshop; instr art, Huntington
Twp Art League, 71.
Positions: Art consult, Catholic Youth Orgn, Rockville Ctr, N Y,
67-; art coordr, St John's Cloister, Queens, N Y, 72-
Awards: First prize & purchase award, Hofstra Col, 57; Emily
Lowe Award, 62; Tiffany grants, 64-65, 66-67.
Bibliography: A V LesMez (auth), Cariola, Long Island Rev Mag,
64; Walt Carlson (auth), Vatican Pavilion gets Long Island ex-
hibit, New York Times, 8/27/64; Jeanne Paris (auth), Cariola's
works on exhibit at Merrick Gallery, Long Island Press,
5/28/67.
Memberships: Prof Artists Guild (pres, 69-70); hon mem Cath
Fine Arts Soc.
Publications: Illusr, Writer's Ann, 58; illusr, Sign Mag, 71; con-
tribr, Liturgical Arts Mag, 71-72.
Dealers: Merrick Art Gallery, 8 Merrick Ave, Merrick, NY 11566;
Contemporary Christian Art Gallery, 1060-A Lexington Ave,
New York, NY 10021.
Mailing Address: 1844 Gormley Ave, Merrick, NY 11566.

CARLIN, ELECTRA MARSHALL
Art Dealer
b Fort Worth, Tex.
Study & Training: George Washington Univ, BA.
Positions: Dir, Carlin Galleries; mem, Art Comn Bd, Fort Worth,
Tex, 63-
Memberships: Fort Worth Art Asn; Dallas Mus Art Asn; Northwood
Inst; Am. Fedn Arts.

Specialty of Gallery: American artists and craftsmen; Eskimo prints
and carvings. Mailing Address: 710 Montgomery St, Fort Worth,
TX 76107.

CARLIN, JAMES
Painter
Preferred Media: Oils, Watercolors.
b Belfast, Ireland, June 25, 10; U S citizen.
Study & Training: Belfast Munic Col, grad; apprenticeship stained
glass painting studios with Ger, Eng & Irish instrs; London Art
Schs; Newark Sch Fine & Indust Art.
Work in Public Collections: Montclair Art Mus, N J; also in pvt
collections of Dore Schary, Hollywood & many others.
Commissions: Design of stained glass windows (in collaboration),
Londonderry Guild Hall & several prominent churches in Ire-
land, 26-28.
Exhibitions: 12th Brooklyn Mus Int, N Y, 41; Victory Exhib, Met-
rop Mus Art, New York, N Y, 42; Allied Artists Am Exhib, New
York, 45; Portrait of America, Pepsi-Cola Co, New York, 45;
Allied Artists Am Oils Exhib, Nat Acad Galleries, New York, 46.
Teaching: Mem faculty, Queen's Col, N Y; instr fine arts & head
dept, Newark Sch Fine & Indust Art, 46-
Awards: Silver medal of honor, N J Watercolor Soc, 58; George A
Zabriskie Award in Watercolor, Nat Acad Design; first prize in
oils, Audubon Artists.
Bibliography: Norman Kent (auth), The artist speaks his mind, Wat-
son-Guptill, 69; Michael Jenson (auth), Carlin and nature, New-
ark News, 71; Wendon Blake (auth), Acrylic watercolor painting,
Watson-Guptill, 71.
Memberships: Am Watercolor Soc; Philadelphia Watercolor Soc;
N J Watercolor Soc; Audubon Artists; Assoc Artists N J; plus
others.
Dealer: Grand Central Art Galleries, 40 Vanderbilt Ave, New York,
NY 10017.
Mailing Address: 73 Cathedral Ave, Nutley, NJ 07110.

CARLOS, (JAMES) EDWARD
Painter, Art Administrator
Preferred Media: Oils.
b Kingsville, Pa, Nov 8, 37.
Study & Training: Ind Univ Pa, BS(art educ), 59; Colo Col, with En-
rique Montenegro, summer 60; Cath Univ Am, with Ken Noland,
Alexander Giampietro & Bernard Leach, MFA, 63; Univ Hawaii,
with Gustav Ecke; Ohio Univ, fel & PhD.
Exhibitions: Mainstreams '72, Marietta, Ohio, 72.
Teaching: Vis prof art, Portland State Col, summer 65; asst prof
art, Western Ill Univ, 65-66; instr art, Ohio Univ, 67-69; instr
art & chmn dept fine arts, Univ of the South, 69-72; chmn dept
fine arts, Fordham Univ, Lincoln Ctr Campus, 72-
Positions: Lectr various art groups & schs.
Awards: Int Snapshop, East-Kodak, 71.
Mailing Address: Dept of Art, Fordham University at Lincoln Center Campus, New York, NY 10023.

CARLSON, CYNTHIA J
Painter
Preferred Media: Oils
b Chicago, Ill, Apr 15, 42.
Study & Training: Chicago Art Inst, BFA; Pratt Inst, New York,
MFA.
Exhibitions: Towards a New Metaphysics, Allan Frumkin, N Y;
Paris Biennale for Young Artists, 71; 26 Women, Larry Aldrich
Mus, Conn, 71; first one-man exhib, Gallery Marc, Washington,
spring 72.
Teaching: Instr. drawing, design & painting, Philadelphia Col Art,
67-
Mailing Address: 101 W 27th St, New York, NY 10001.

CARMACK, PAUL R
Cartoonist
b Madisonville, Ky, Dec 18, 95.
Study & Training: Art Inst Chicago.
Positions: Staff cartoonist, Christian Sci Monitor, 25-61.
Awards: Eight Freedoms Found Hon Medals, 51-62.
Memberships: Am Asn Ed Cartoonists.
Publications: Auth & illusr, The diary of Snubs, our dog, Vols I, II.
II & IV; illusr, Huttee boy, the elephant.
Mailing Address: 780 Boylston St, Boston, MA 02199.

CARMEL, HILDA ANNE
Painter
b New York, N Y.
Study & Training: City Col New York; New York Univ; Art Stud
League New York, with Reginald Marsh.
Work in Public Collections: Jewish Mus, New York; Evansville Mus
Arts & Sci, Ind; Bat Yam Mus & Sholom Ash Mus, Israel; Long
Island Univ Mus, Brooklyn, N Y.

Exhibitions: Soc Ecole Francaise Expos, Paris, France, 70; Yonkers Art Asn, Hudson River Mus, Yonkers, N Y, 71; Painters & Sculptors N J, Jersey City, 72; Lehigh Univ, Bethlehem, Pa, 72; Opening Exhib, Bronx Mus Art, 72.
Positions: Gallery dir, Hilda Carmel Gallery, 59-63.
Awards: First prize, Soc Ecole Francaise Expos, Mus Mod Art, Paris, 70; hon mention, Bronx Coun on Arts, 70; medal of honor, Cent Studi e Scambi Int. Italv. 71.
Memberships: Artist Equity Asn New York (exhib chmn & corresp secy, 70-); League Present Day Artists (exhib chmn & pres, 71-); hon mem Gallery 84; Bronx Coun on Arts (visual art comt, 70).
Mailing Address: 3210 Fairfield Ave, Riverdale, NY 10463.

CARMICHAEL, DONALD RAY
Painter, Educator
Preferred Media: Watercolors, Oils.
b Elnora, Ind, Dec 26, 22.
Study & Training: Herron Art Inst, Indianapolis, Ind, BFA, 51; also with John Taylor & David Freidenthal, New York, N Y, Edwin Fulwler, Ford Times & Garo Antreasian, N Mex.
Work in Public Collections: Cheekwood Fine Arts Ctr, Nashville, Tenn; Jackson-Madison Co Pub Libr, Jackson, Tenn; Dyersburg Pub Libr, Tenn; Jackson Ment Health Ctr.
Commissions: Life-size minuteman statue, stoneware mounted on face of bldg (with Warren Kessler), Carl Smith Agency, Jackson, Tenn, 67; official seal (engraving), Jackson State Community Col, 67; five panel mural, History of Jackson, McDonalds, Inc, Jackson. 68.
Exhibitions: Enjay Chem Nat, Trenton, N J, 66; Tennessee Painting Today, Cheekwood Fine Arts Ctr, 67; one-man invitational, Int Banana Festival, Fulton, Ky, 70; three man invitational, Lynn Kottler Galleries Spring Festival, New York, 71; 23rd Grand Prix Int, Deauville, France, 72.
Teaching: Instr painting, Shelbyville Art League, Ind, 51-55; instr art appreciation, Union Univ, Tenn, 64-66, instr drawing, painting & composition, 66-
Positions: Pres, Jackson Art Asn, 65-67; pres, Jackson Arts Coun, 68-70; chmn visual arts adv panel, Tenn Arts Comn, 72.
Awards: Purchase award, Enjay Chem Nat, 66; purchase award, Tennessee Painting Today, Tenn Arts Comn, 67.
Bibliography: Neuman Jones (auth), Art leagues in small communities, Delta Rev, 68; William T Alderson (auth), Tennessee lives, Historical Record Asn, 71; article, In: La Rev Mod, 72.
Memberships: Artists Equity Asn; Tenn Col Arts Coun (chmn nominating comt, 70-); Hoosier Salon; Tenn Watercolorist (dir & mem chmn, 71-); Memphis Watercolor Soc.
Publications: Illusr, (cover), The Old Hickory Review, Jackson Writers Guild, 69; contribr, The Torch, Union Univ, 70-72.
Dealer: Golden Fleece Gallery, Overton Square-Madison Ave, Memphis, TN 38104.
Mailing Address: 110 Carlisle Dr, Jackson, TN 38301.

CARMICHAEL, JAE
Painter, Art Administrator
b Hollywood, Calif, Aug 22, 25.
Study & Training: Mills Col, 42-44; Univ Southern Calif, BFA, 51, PhD(art & cinematography), 72; Claremont Grad Sch, MFA, 55.
Work in Public Collections: Long Beach Mus Art; Mills Col; Scripps Col; Charles & Emma Frye Mus; Computer Measurements Corp; plus many others including pvt collections.
Exhibitions: Over 100 Int, Nat & Regional Shows since 45; plus 21 one-man shows.
Teaching: Instr drawing & painting, Palos Verdes Arts Asn; lectr art hist & film, Otis Art Inst.
Positions: Dir, Pacificult Asian Mus; dir, Pasadena Sch Fine Arts.
Awards: Over thirty major awards including Jury of Selection Hors Concours Award, Pasadena Soc Artists Ann, 70.
Bibliography: Kim Blair (auth), Pacificulture Center becomes a reality, Los Angeles Times, 10/25/71; Ray McConnell (auth), More or less personal, 11/19/71 & Margaret Stovall (auth), Jae Carmichael fulfills dreams at Pacificulture Foundation, 12/11/71, Star News.
Memberships: Calif Watercolors Soc (mem bd, 59-60 & 70-72); Pasadena Soc Artists (mem bd, 58-60, 62 & 63, pres, 70-72); Women Painters West; Laguna Beach Art Asn (mem exhibs comt, 60-72); Los Angeles Art Asn (mem bd, 65-69).
Mailing Address: 985 San Pasqual St, Pasadena, CA 91106.

CARO, FRANK
Art Dealer
b Gouezec, France, July 17, 04.
Specialty of Gallery: Chinese antique arts and contemporary Chinese painters; arts of India and southeast Asia; pre-Colombian arts.
Mailing Address: 41 E 57th St, New York, NY 10022.

CARONE, MATTHEW DAVID
Painter, Art Dealer
Preferred Media: Oils, Acrylics.
b Hoboken, N J, Apr 10, 30.
Study & Training: Univ Miami, BEd; also with Nicolas Carone, New York, N Y.
Work in Public Collections: Lowe Mus, Coral Gables, Fla; Fort Lauderdale Mus Arts, Fla; Peabody Col Mus, Nashville, Tenn; Ill State Mus, Springfield; Lowe Mus, Syracuse Univ, N Y; plus many others.
Commissions: Many private commissions.
Exhibitions: Fort Lauderdale Mus Arts, 64; Fla Pavillion, New York World's Fair, 65; Soc Four Arts, Palm Beach, Fla, 65; Mercer Univ, Macon, Ga, 67; Hortt Mem Competition, Fort Lauderdale Mus Arts, 71; plus many other group & one-man shows.
Teaching: Leader mod art, Univ Miami, 65.
Positions: Owner-dir, Carone Gallery, Fort Lauderdale, 64-
Awards: First prize, Hortt Mem Competition, 63; first prize of merit, Brandeis Chapter, Palm Beach, Fla, 64; third prize, Broward Co Artists Show, Fort Lauderdale Mus Arts, 67.
Bibliography: Maurice La Reau (auth), articles, In: Fort Lauderdale News, 5/20/62 & 2/7/65; Griffin Smith (auth), article, In: Miami Herald, 4/2/72.
Specialty of Gallery: Master graphics.
Publications: Contribr, Prize winning paintings, 64; contribr, Miami Herald Sunday Mag, 3/19/67.
Dealer: Galerie 99, 1135 Kane Concourse Blvd, Bay Harbor Island, FL 33154.
Mailing Address: 904 N Rio Vista Blvd, Fort Lauderdale, FL 33301.

CARPENTER, E
Painter
Preferred Media: Watercolors.
b Mianus, Conn, July 11, 17.
Study & Training: Nat Acad Design, with Mario Cooper; also with Edgar Whitney.
Commissions: Calendar & cards, New Eng Biol Lab, Point Judith, R I, 69; cover for calendar & watercolor pad, Aquabee, Bee Paper Co, Passaic, N J, 69-70.
Exhibitions: Nat Miniature Painters-Sculptors & Gravers Soc Show, Washington, D C, 69; Knickerbocker Artists, Nat Arts Club, 69-70; Nat Am Artists Prof League, Lever House, New York, N Y, 69-71; Catharine Lorillard Wolfe, Nat Gallery, N Y.
Awards: Salmagundi scholar, 68 & N Y Phoenix Sch Design Award, 69, Washington Square Art Exhib, New York; Minor S Jamison Award, Nat Miniature Painters, Sculptors & Gravers Soc, 69.
Memberships: Am Artists Prof League; Catharine Lorillard Wolfe Art Club; Bergen Co Artists Guild.
Mailing Address: 248 Wyckoff Ave, Wyckoff, NJ 07481.

CARPENTER, GILBERT FREDERICK (BERT)
Painter, Educator
b Billings, Mont, July 14, 20.
Study & Training: Stanford Univ, AB; Chouinard Art Inst; Ecole Beaux Arts, Paris, France; Columbia Univ.
Work in Public Collections: Honolulu Acad Art, Hawaii; Sheldon Mem Mus, Lincoln, Nebr; Weatherspoon Gallery, Univ N C, Greensboro; Kresge Found, Mich State Univ.
Exhibitions: Honolulu Acad Art, 51, 59, 60 & 61; American Painting, Va Mus Fine Arts, 66; Zabriskie Gallery, New York, N Y, 70; one-man shows, Calif Palace Legion of Hon, 52 & Joslyn Mus, Omaha, Nebr, 52 & 54.
Teaching: Instr art, Columbia Univ, 54-60; head dept art, Univ Hawaii, 60-64; prof art & permanent head dept, Univ N C, Greensboro, 64-
Memberships: N C State Art Soc.
Publications: Art critic, Honolulu Star Bull, 61-62.
Dealer: Zabriskie Gallery, 29 W 57th St, New York, NY 10019.
Mailing Address: 2505 W Market St, Greensboro, NC 27403.

CARPENTER, HARLOW
Museum Director
b Calif, Oct 20, 26.
Study & Training: Harvard Univ Sch Design, BArch.
Positions: Dir, Bundy Art Gallery, Waitsfield, Vt.
Mailing Address: Bundy Art Gallery, Waitsfield, VT 05673.

CARPENTER, JAMES MORTON
Educator, Art Historian
b Glens Falls, N Y, Dec 7, 14.
Study & Training: Harvard Univ, AB & PhD.
Teaching: From instr to asst prof fine arts, Harvard Univ, 43-50; from assoc prof to prof art, Colby Col, 50-, chmn dept, 55-
Positions: Dir, Colby Col Art Mus, 59-66; bd gov, Skowhegan Sch Painting & Sculpture, 65-; bd trustees, Haystack Mountain Sch Crafts, 68-; mem, Maine State Comn Arts & Humanities, 68-

Memberships: Col Art Asn; Archives Am Art (New Eng Bd).
Research: Aspects of art theory; history of Maine art.
Publications: Co-auth, Maine and its role in American art, 63.
Mailing Address: 1 Edgewood St, Waterville, ME 04901.

CARR, J GORDON
Architect, Painter
Preferred Media: Watercolor.
b Batavia, N Y, Feb 20, 07.
Study & Training: Mass Inst Technol, BS(archit), 29, MS(archit), 30; Harvard Univ, MBA, 34; study with Gordon Grant, Herb Olsen & John Pike.
Work in Public Collections: Grand Cent Art Galleries, New York N Y; Etchings Int, New York; Silvermine Guild Artists, New Canaan, Conn; Quadrangle Galleries, Dallas, Tex; Navy Dept, Washington, D C.
Exhibitions: Two one-man shows, Grand Cent Art Galleries, New York; Parker Playhouse, Fort Lauderdale, Fla; several shows, Am Watercolor Soc & Knickerbocker Artists, New York; Nat Acad Design, New York, 68.
Awards: Prize, Salmagundi Club, 63; Muriel Alvord Mem Award, Hudson Valley Art Asn, 64; New Eng Artists Exhib, John Kellam Award, Silvermine Guild Artists, 70.
Memberships: Am Watercolor Soc; Silvermine Guild Artists; Hudson Valley Art Asn; Salmagundi Club; Conn Watercolor Soc.
Dealer: Grand Central Art Galleries, Hotel Biltmore, New York, NY 10017.
Mailing Address: 46 Beechcroft Rd, Greenwich, CT 06830.

CARR, SALLY SWAN
Sculptor
Preferred Media: Stone.
b Minong, Wis.
Study & Training: N Y Univ; advan sculpture, Phoenix Sch Design; life sketch, Clay Club; also with John Hovannes, Frederick Allen Williams & wax tech with Paul Manship; Art Stud League New York, N Y.
Work in Public Collections: Am Numismatic Soc, New York; Basketball Hall of Fame, Springfield, Mass; Cayuga Mus Art & Hist, Auburn, N Y; Florentine Craftsmen, New York.
Commissions: Indian Queen, woodcarving & Eagle, reliefs, Sheraton Hotel, Philadelphia, Pa, 57; Great Seal of U S, woodcarving, M Ketchum, Jr, U S Embassy, Rabat, Morocco, 59; Lion of St Marks, bronze relief, Marco Polo Club, Waldorf Astoria Hotel, New York, 60; Cardinal Virtues, cararra marble reliefs. Riverside Mem Park, St Joseph, Mich, 65; Dr A Schweitzer, bust, Town Hall, Kaysersburg & Gunsbach, France, 70.
Exhibitions: Archit League New York, 55-71; Catharine Lorillard Wolfe Art Club, New York, 60-; Nat Arts Club, New York, 67-70; Nat Acad Design, Allied Artists, 69-70; Acad Artists, Springfield Mus Art, Mass, 70.
Awards: A H Huntington First Prize Trophy, Catharine Lorillard Wolfe Art Club, 70; Founders Prize & Plaque, Pen & Brush Club, New York, 70; bronze & silver medals, City of Kaysersburg, 70.
Memberships: Archit League New York (mem exhibs comt, 60); Burr Artists (second v pres, 69-); Catharine Lorillard Wolfe Art Club (first v pres, 66-71, pres, 71-); Composers, Auth & Artists Am (dir & historian, 69-); hon mem Smithsonian Inst.
Mailing Address: 530 E 23rd St, New York, NY 10010.

CARREL, CLAUDIA
Painter, Sculptor
b Paris, France, Jan 11, 21.
Study & Training: Boston Mus Fine Arts Sch Fine Arts; Art Stud League New York; Pratt Graphic Art Ctr; Hans Hofmann Sch Art.
Work in Public Collections: Rose Art Mus, Brandeis Univ; Andrew Dickson White Mus, Cornell Univ; Boston Mus Fine Arts; Norfolk Mus Arts & Sci; Columbia Univ Art Collection; plus others.
Exhibitions: Am Fedn Arts Traveling Exhib, 68; Fine Arts Found, Hartford, Conn; Parrish Art Mus, Southampton, N Y & others; seven one-man shows, New York, N Y.
Awards: Prizes, Nat Acad Design, 62; Grumbacher Award, Aububon Artists, 63.
Mailing Address: 25 Eastern Pkwy, Brooklyn, NY 11238.

CARRILLO, LILIA
Painter
Preferred Media: Oils, Acrylics.
b Mexico City, Mex, Nov 2, 29.
Study & Training: Escuela Pintura y Escultura, Mexico City; La Grande Chaumiere, Paris.
Work in Public Collections: Mus Arte Mod, Mex; Inst Arte Contemporáneo, Lima, Perú; Unión Panamericana, Washington, D C; Banco Cedulas Hipotecarias, S A, Mex; IBM, Mex.
Commissions: Mural, Mex Govt for World Fair in Osaka, Japan, 70.

Exhibitions: Artistes Etrangeres en France, Petit Palais, Paris, 55; I Bienal Jòvenes, Paris, 59; VI Bienal Tokio, Japan, 61; VI Bienal São Paulo, Brazil, 61; Salón ESSO, Mus Art Mod, Mex, 65.
Awards: ESSO Second Prize, 65.
Bibliography: Octavio Paz (auth), Puertas al campo, UNAM, Mexico City, 66; Pintura actual: México 1966, Artes Mex y Mundo, 66; J Garcia Ponce (auth), Nueve pintores Mexicanos, Era, Mex, 68.
Dealer: Galeria Juan Martin, Amberes 17, Mexico City 6, Mex.
Mailing Address: Galeana 37 bis, Mexico City 20, Mex.

CARRINGTON, JOY HARRELL
Painter, Illuminator
Preferred Media: Oils.
b Jacksonville, Tex.
Study & Training: Kansas City Art Inst, three years; Am Acad Art, Chicago; Nat Acad Chicago; Chicago Art Inst, with Pougialis; Art Stud League New York, four years; also with Frank Peyraud, Highland Park, Ill & Robert Brackman, Noank, Conn.
Work in Public Collections: Oil portrait of Clara Driscoll, Long Barrack Mus, Alamo; illuminated mem bk, First Methodist Church, Jacksonville; illuminated page of miniature watercolor portraits, Alamo Libr; illuminated page, Coppini Acad Fine Arts, San Antonio; Tex State Reverse Seal, State Capitol Bldg, Austin.
Exhibitions: One-man show, Witte Mem Mus, San Antonio, 63 & St Marys Univ, 64; Ann Invitational Western Art Show, Coliseum in in San Antonio, 64-72; Am Artists Prof League Grand Nat Exhib, 67-72; Meinhard Galleries, Houston, 67-72.
Positions: Commercial artist for Frank Bros, San Antonio, Hartman Furniture Co & Handelan & Staff Shoe Agency, Chicago & Loesers, Brooklyn.
Awards: Coppini Acad Award for oil painting, Witte Mus, 57; Grumbacher Award for Oil Painting, Am. Artists Prof League, 69; sculpture award, Kansas City Art Inst.
Bibliography: Glenn Tucker (auth), Arts Rev, San Antonio Light, 8/63; Herweck (auth), article, In: The Record, spring 72.
Memberships: Am Artists Prof League; Nat Soc Arts & Letters; Coppini Acad Fine Arts; Kerrville Art Club; Hill Country Arts Found.
Dealer: Meinhard Galleries, 1714 S Post Oak Rd, Houston, TX 77027.
Mailing Address: T Anchor Ranch, Route 16, Box 30, Medina, TX 78055.

CARROLL, ROBERT JOSEPH
Painter, Illustrator
b Syracuse, N Y, Oct 11, 04.
Study & Training: Crouse Col Fine Arts, Syracuse Univ, 23-27; Parsons Sch Design, N Y.
Work in Public Collections: In many pvt collections.
Exhibitions: Brooklyn Mus; Syracuse Mus Fine Arts; Albright Art Gallery, Buffalo, N Y; Rochester Mus Art; N Y Galleries, 68; plus others.
Positions: Free lance illusr; illusr, rec covers for var co.
Publications: Illusr, Vogue, Harpers Bazaar & McCall's Mags; illusr bk jackets, Doubleday.
Mailing Address: 327 W 11th St, New York, NY 10014.

CARSON, SOL KENT
Painter, Printmaker
Preferred Media: Oils, Acrylics.
b Philadelphia, Pa, June 7, 17.
Study & Training: Tyler Sch Fine Arts, Temple Univ, Barnes Found scholar, 37-39, univ scholar & fel, 39-44, BFA(hons), 44; Teachers Col, Temple Univ, BS Educ(hons), 45, MEd(hons), 46; Temple Univ, 57; New York Univ, 58; Minerva Univ Grad Sch, Bari, Italy, PhD, 60; also with Raphael Sabatini, Boris Blai, Russell & Howard Conant.
Work in Public Collections: Temple Univ, Philadelphia; Millersville State Col Collection, Pa; Philadelphia Libr Collection; also in many pvt collections.
Commissions: Bronze bust of Dean Ladd Thomas, Temple Univ Sch Theology; Stone head of Mother Katherine Drexel, Convent, Cornwells Heights, Pa; Paul Bunyan stone plaque & mural, Forests for Israel Awards, Pa; portrait of wife of Pres D'Aragond, Italy; also many pvt comns for paintings.
Exhibitions: New York World's Fair, 39; Pa Acad Fine Arts Invitational, 64-66; Temple Univ, Tyler Galleries, 66-72; William Penn Mem Mus, Harrisburg, Pa, 67; Artist Equity Int, Civic Ctr Mus, Philadelphia, 68-72.
Teaching: Assistantship graphic arts dept, Temple Univ, 40-45, dir dept visual educ, 44-47, dir dept art, Eckels Col, 46-55; instr art, Philadelphia Bd Educ, 47-58; art consult, Bristol Twp Sch Dist, 56-66; fac art, Wis State Univ, Superior, summers 65-67, assoc prof art, Millersville State Col, 66-
Positions: Mus consult, Univ Pa, 45-46.
Awards: First prize for painting, Int League for Peace & Freedom.

Memberships: Artists Equity Asn; Am Asn Univ Prof; Asn Higher Educ; Pa State Educ Asn; Nat Educ Asn.
Mailing Address: Adams House, Millersville, PA 17551.

CARSTENSON, CECIL C
Sculptor, Lecturer
Preferred Media: Wood.
b Marquette, Kans, July 23, 06.
Study & Training: Kansas City Art Inst; Univ Nebr; Art Inst Chicago; also with several sculptors in Italy.
Work in Public Collections: Joslyn Mus, Omaha, Nebr; Phoenix Art Mus, Ariz; Univ Mo-Kansas City; Nelson Gallery Art, Kansas City; Jewish Community Ctr, Kansas City; and others.
Exhibitions: Mid America, Nelson Gallery Art; Joslyn Art Gallery Show; Mo Pavilion, World's Fair Exhib, New York, N Y; St Louis Mus Show; Denver Art Gallery Show.
Teaching: Instr sculpture, Univ Mo-Kansas City, 51-53.
Positions: Comt mem, Mo Coun on Visual Arts, 68-72.
Awards: Hon mention & purchase award, Mid America, Nelson Gallery Art.
Publications: Auth, Film, sculpture, Nelson Gallery Art, 62; Craft and creation of wood sculpture, Scribner, 71.
Dealer: Pucker Safrai Gallery, 171 Newbury St, Boston, MA 02116.
Mailing Address: 1018 W 38th St, Kansas City, MO 64111.

CARTER, ALBERT JOSEPH
Museum Curator
b Washington, D C, Apr 20, 15.
Study & Training: Howard Univ, BS; Teachers Col, Columbia Univ, MA; Teamer Schs Educ, Charlotte, N C, DHL in Educ.
Collections Arranged: Ceramics, Textiles, Metals & Wood, 47-48; Japanese Wood Block Color Prints, 47-48; Contemporary Indian Paintings, 47-48; Expressionism in Graphic Arts, 48-49; Miniatures for Illuminated Books of the Middle Ages, 49-50; Contemporary American Paintings, 49-50; New Vistas in American Art, 61.
Teaching: Instr commercial art, G I Sch, Letchers Art Ctr, Washington, D C, 46-59.
Positions: Cur, Howard Univ Art Gallery, Washington, D C.
Awards: Fel, Corning Mus Glass, N Y, 57.
Memberships: Am Asn Mus; D C Art Asn.
Mailing Address: 6337 16th St N W, Washington, DC 20011.

CARTER, BERNARD SHIRLEY
Painter, Instructor
Preferred Media: Watercolors.
b Boston, Mass, Oct 22, 17.
Study & Training: Art Stud League New York, with Raphael Soyer & Arnold Blanch; Ogunquit Sch Art, Maine, with Bernard Karfiol.
Work in Public Collections: Metrop Mus Art, New York, N Y; Boston Mus Fine Arts, Mass.
Exhibitions: Int Watercolor Exhib, Brooklyn Mus, N Y, 51; Am Watercolor Soc Ann, New York, 60 & 61; 100th Ann Exhib, Am Watercolor Soc, Metrop Mus Art, 67; Audubon Ann Exhib, Nat Acad Galleries, New York, 70.
Teaching: Instr painting, Parsons Sch Design, New York, 46-65; instr painting & dir, Bedford Art Ctr, N Y, 65-
Awards: Non-mem award, Am Watercolor Soc, 60; Katonah Gallery award, 65; first prize for watercolor, Artists Northern Westchester, N Y, 65.
Memberships: Am Watercolor Soc; Century Asn.
Mailing Address: 350 Cherry St, Bedford Hills, NY 10507.

CARTER, CLARENCE HOLBROOK
Painter, Designer
b Portsmouth, Ohio, Mar 26, 04.
Study & Training: Cleveland Sch Art, 23-27; Capri, Italy, with Hans Hofmann, summer 27.
Work in Public Collections: Metrop Mus Art; Mus Mod Art; Cleveland Mus Art; Corcoran Gallery Art; Joseph H Hirshhorn Collection; plus others.
Commissions: Murals, sect painting & sculpture, Treasury Dept, Portsmouth, Ohio, & Ravenna, Ohio Post Off & Cleveland Pub Auditorium.
Exhibitions: Carnegie Inst; one-man shows, Butler Inst Am Art, Suffolk Mus, Stony Brook, Long Island, High Mus Art, 57 & Allentown Art Mus, 59; plus many Europ, S Am, Can mus & others.
Teaching: Lectr art, mus, cols & art schs; asst prof painting & design, Carnegie Inst, 38-44; dir art, Chautauqua Inst, New York Univ, 43; guest instr painting, Cleveland Inst Art, summer 48; guest instr, Minneapolis Sch Art, fall 49; guest instr, Lehigh Univ, 54; guest instr, Ohio Univ, 55; guest instr, Atlanta Art Inst, 57; vis lectr, Lafayette Col, 61, artist-in-residence, 61-69; guest artist, Univ Iowa, spring 70; consult, Lafayette Col, 70-71.
Positions: Dir, FAP for Northeastern Ohio, 37-38.
Awards: Prizes, Cleveland Arts & Crafts, 27-39, Butler Inst Am Art, 37, 40, 43 & 46 & Carnegie Inst, 41, 43 & 44; plus others.

Memberships: Assoc Nat Acad Design; Del Valley Art Asn (pres, 62-63); Am Watercolor Soc (bd dirs, 61-62, v pres, 62).
Publications: Auth, chap, In: Work for artists; contribr, articles, In: Col Art J & Am Artist.
Dealer: Gimpel & Weitzenhoffer Galleries, 1040 Madison at 79th St, New York, NY 10021.
Mailing Address: Spring Mills, R D 1, Milford, NJ 08848.

CARTER, DAVID GILES
Art Administrator, Art Historian
b Nashua, N H, Nov 2, 21.
Study & Training: Princeton Univ, AB, 44, with C R Morey & A M Friend; Harvard Univ Grad Sch Arts & Sci, MA, 49, with P Sachs, C R Post, C Kuhn & others; Inst Fine Arts, New York Univ, 51, with W Cook, E Panofsky & G Schoenberger.
Collections Arranged: Turner in America (with Wilbur D Peat), 56; The Young Rembrandt and His Times, 58; The G H A Clowes Collection, 59; Dynamic Symmetry, 61; El Greco to Goya (with Curtis Coley), 63; The Weldon Collection, 64; Masterpieces from Montreal, 66; The Painter and the New World, 67; Rembrandt and His Pupils, 69; plus many others.
Teaching: Vis lectr, Art of the Northern Renaissance, Indiana Univ, Bloomington, 58-59.
Positions: Curatorial asst, Metrop Mus Art, New York, 50-54; cur paintings & prints, John Herron Art Mus, 55-59; dir Mus Art, R I Sch Design, 59-64; dir, Montreal Mus Fine Arts, 64-
Awards: Gold Medal of Ital Cult, Ital Ministry Foreign Affairs, 63.
Memberships: Asn Art Mus Dirs; Can Art Mus Dirs Orgn (past pres); Mediaeval Acad; Armor & Arms Club Am; Royal Soc Arts; plus others.
Research: Primary focus on fifteenth century Netherlands; secondary interest in Mannerist and Northern Baroque painting.
Collection: Minor masters of seventeenth century Netherlands and Italianized Dutch artists.
Publications: Auth, Two Romanesque frescoes from San Baudelio de Berlanga, Herron Art Inst Bull, 3/54; auth, A portrait by Rembrandt, Herron Art Inst Bull, 8/56; Auth, Christ's triumphal entry into Jerusalem, Herron Art Inst Bull, 6/58; Auth, The Providence crucifixion its place and meaning for Dutch XVth century painting, Mus Notes, 5/62; auth, Rencontre avec Valentin, l'Genil, 70.
Mailing Address: 1379 Sherbrooke St W, Montreal 109, P Q, Can.

CARTER, DEAN
Sculptor, Educator
Preferred Media: Bronze, Wood.
b Henderson, N C, Apr 24, 22.
Study & Training: Corcoran Sch Art; Am Univ, BA; Ogunquit Sch Painting & Sculpture; Indiana Univ, MFA; Ossip Zadkine Sch Art, Paris, France.
Work in Public Collections: Cranbrook Acad Art, Mich; Hollins Col, Va; Washington & Lee Univ, Lexington, Va; Wichita Art Asn Galleries, Kans; First Colony Life Ins Co of Jamestown, Lynchburg, Va.
Commissions: Limestone relief, Foreign Students, Indiana Univ, 48; welded bronze relief, Wesley Found Bldg, Blacksburg, Va, 62; bronze screen, Providence Bldg, Seven Corners, Va, 64; bronze portrait, Walter Gropius, Col Archit, Va Polytech Inst, 65; welded bronze screen, Roanoke Mem Hosp, Va, 70.
Exhibitions: Pa Acad Fine Arts, Philadelphia, 54; Cini Found, Venice, Italy, 64; Smithsonian Circulating Exhib, 69-71; one-man show, Artists' Mart, Washington, D C, 70; Contemp Gallery Art Ann Sculpture Show, Winston-Salem, N C, 71.
Teaching: Chmn art prog, Va Polytech Inst & State Univ, 63-
Positions: Mem art adv bd, Va Highlands Community Col, Abigdon, 69-71 & Mountain Empire Community Col, Wise, 71-72; consult, U S Fine Arts Surv, 72.
Awards: Best in sculpture, Roanoke Fine Arts Show, 63; Cini Found fel, 64; hon mention for sculpture, Contemp Gallery Art, Winston-Salem, 65.
Bibliography: Ted Kliman (auth), A world of sculpture (film), Va Polytech Inst & State Univ, 62; W M White, Jr (auth), Sculpturing by Dean Carter, Maelstrom, 66; W C Burleson (auth), On campus—Dean Carter, Context, summer 69.
Memberships: Soc Washington Artists; Southern Sculptors Asn (v pres, 66-68); Southern Highlands Handicraft Guild (stand & ed comts); Am Crafts Coun (state rep, 65); Blacksburg Regional Art Asn (pres).
Dealer: Artists' Mart, 1361 Wisconsin Ave N W, Washington, DC 20007.
Mailing Address: 1011 Highland Circle, Blacksburg, VA 24060.

CARTER, GRANVILLE W
Sculptor
Preferred Media: Wood, Stone, Metals.
b Augusta, Maine, Nov 18, 20.
Study & Training: Coburn Class Inst; Portland Sch Fine & Applied

Art; New York City Sch Indust Art; Nat Acad Sch Fine Arts; Grande Chaumiere, Paris, France; Scuolo Circolare Int, Rome, Italy; in residence Am Acad Rome.

Work in Public Collections: Smithsonian Inst, Washington, D C; Thomas Alva Edison Mus, West Orange, N J; Hall of Fame for Great Americans, New York Univ; Morristown Hist Mus, N J; Maine State Mus, Augusta.

Commissions: Michael & Gabriel (heroic archangels in limestone), S Transept, 62 & 31 clerestory bosses & over 60 figures from Passion, Nave, 64-67, Washington Nat Cathedral; bronze bust of Jane Addams, Hall of Fame, 68; monumental bust of Alexander Stewart, Garden City, N Y, 69; West Texas Pioneer Family Monument (heroic bronze), Lubbock, Tex, 71.

Exhibitions: Am Acad Rome Ann, 55; Archit League, New York, 56-58; Nat Sculpture Soc, Lever House, New York, several yrs; Int Expos Medals, Paris & Prague, 67 & 70; Am Artists Prof League Ann, New York, 70.

Teaching: Instr sculpture, Nat Acad Design, 66-; lectr sculpture, Washington Cathedral & Hofstra Univ, 66-

Positions: Deleg, Fine Arts Fedn New York, 72.

Awards: Louis Comfort Tiffany Found fels, 54 & 55; Henry Hering Mem Medal, Nat Sculpture Soc, 68; gold medal, Am Artists Prof League, 70.

Bibliography: Fishwack & Feller (auth), For thy great glory, Community Press, 65; Charles Guy (auth), editorial, In: Lubbock Avalanche J, 6/10/71; Ford Mitchell (auth), West Texas pioneer family monument (film), KCBD TV, 71.

Memberships: Fel Nat Sculpture Soc (coun mem, 60-72, rec secy, 63-65); Fel Am Artists Prof League (bd dirs, 72-); Academician Nat Acad Design; Coun Am Artist Socs (bd dirs, 69-).

Publications: Contribr, Nat Sculpture Rev, spring 67; contribr, Hall of Fame for Great Americans Brochures, 63-72.

Mailing Address: 625 Portland Ave, Baldwin, NY 11510.

CARTMELL, HELEN
Painter
Preferred Media: Oils.
b Bridgeport, Conn, Jan 6, 23.
Study & Training: Detroit Soc Arts & Crafts, Mich, scholar; Wayne State Univ.
Work in Public Collections: Ossabaw Island Proj Found, Savannah, Ga; Wayne State Univ Collection, Detroit; Chrysler Corp, Detroit; Sen Philip Hart, Washington, D C; Int Nickel Co, New York, N Y; also in pvt collections.
Exhibitions: Nine Univ Mich Regional Invitationals, 63-72; Willistead Gallery, Ont, 65; six shows, Mich Acad Sci, Arts & Lett, 65-72; Grand Rapids Art Mus, Mich, 69 & 71; one-man show, Arwin Galleries, Detroit, 70.
Positions: Dir prod dept, Ctr Instrnl Technol, Wayne State Univ, 68-
Awards: Silver medal award, Scarab Club Detroit; Oil award, Mich Acad Sci, Arts & Lett; Oil & Esther Longyear Mem Awards, Mich Soc Women Painters & Sculptors; plus others.
Memberships: Mich Acad Sci, Arts & Lett; Scarab Club Detroit; Detroit Soc Women Painters & Sculptors.
Dealer: Arwin Galleries, 222 W Grand River, Detroit, MI 48226.
Mailing Address: 21700 Winshall Rd, St Clair Shores, MI 48081.

CARULLA, RAMON A
Painter
Preferred Media: Oils.
b Havana, Cuba, Dec 7, 36.
Study & Training: San Alejandro Sch Art.
Work in Public Collections: Havana Mus Fine Arts; Montreal Mus Fine Art, P Q; Princeton Gallery Collection; Mirell Gallery, Coconut Grove, Miami, Fla; Beaux Art Lowe Art Mus, Miami; plus private collections.
Commissions: Young Artist's Mural, Lyceum Lawn Tennis Asn, 65; also private comns.
Exhibitions: Ann Lawn Tennis Art Exhib, Havana, 65; Fall & Spring Salons, Lowe Art Mus, 67-69; Foremost Art Competition, 70-71; Beaux Art Lowe Art Mus Ann Exhib, 71; Third & Fourth Ann Pan Am Art Exhibs, 71-72; and others.
Awards: Best Young Artist, Ann Lawn Tennis Art Exhib, 65; best painting award, Sobot Gallery, Can, 69; hon mention, Fourth Ann Pan Am Exhib, 71-72.
Bibliography: K Flanders (auth), article, In: Times Guide, 70-71; Nat Coun Culture (auth), Young Artists at Work, Ministry Pub Works, Havana.
Memberships: Miami Art Ctr; North Miami Guild.
Dealer: Robert Draper, 3421 Main Highway, Coral Gables, FL 33133.
Mailing Address: 4735 N W 184th Terr, Miami, FL 33054.

CASARELLA, EDMOND
Graphic Artist, Painter
b Newark, N J, Sept 3, 20.
Study & Training: Cooper Union Art Sch, 38-42; Brooklyn Mus Art Sch, with Gabor Peterdi, 49-51.

Work in Public Collections: Brooklyn Mus; Victoria & Albert Mus, London, Eng; Libr Cong; Bibliot Nat; Univ Ill; plus others.
Exhibitions: Brooklyn Mus, 53-60, 62 & 64; J L Hudson Art Gallery, Detroit, Mich, 64; New York World's Fair, 64 & 65; Poland, 65; retrospective print show, Skopje & Bitola, Yugoslavia, 67; retrospective sculpture, Young Men's Hebrew Asn, Hackensack, N J, 69; plus others.
Teaching: Instr graphics & sculpture, Brooklyn Mus Graphic Workshop, 56-60; instr, Yale-Norfolk Summer Art Sch, 58; instr, New York Univ, 64-65; instr, Pratt Inst, 64-65; instr, Hunter Col, 64-65; instr, Yale Univ, 64-65; instr, Rutgers Univ, 64-65; instr graphics, Teachers Col, Columbia Univ, 64-65 & 66-67; instr, Pratt Graphic Art Ctr, 65; instr, Manhattanville Col Sacred Heart, 65-66; instr graphics & sculpture, Cooper Union, 65-68, instr sculpture, 65-70; instr graphics & sculpture, Finch Col, 69-; former instr graphics, Art Stud League New York.
Positions: Mem adv bd, Cooper Union, 59-60.
Awards: Guggenheim fel, 60; prizes, Soc Am Graphic Artists, N Y, 62 & 63; Tiffany Award graphics, 66; plus others.
Bibliography: Gabor Peterdi (auth), included in: Printmaking: methods old and new, Macmillan, 59; Bernard Chaet (auth), included in: Artists at work, Webb, 60; The complete printmaker, 72.
Memberships: Sculptors Guild; Soc Am Graphic Artists; Print Coun.
Mailing Address: 83 E Linden Ave, Englewood, NJ 07631.

CASCIERI, ARCANGELO
Sculptor, Educator
b Civitaquana, Italy, Feb 22, 02; U S citizen.
Study & Training: Sch Archit, Boston Archit Ctr, 22-26; Boston Univ 32-36.
Work in Public Collections: Boston Col; Holy Cross Col; Buffalo Courier Express Bldg; Parlin Jr High Sch, Everett, Mass; Lexington Jr High Sch, Mass.
Commissions: Am War Mem World War I, Belleau Woods, France & World War II, Margraten, Holland; exterior Mem Auditorium, Lynn, Mass; exterior Boys' Stadium, Franklin Field, Dorchester, Mass; sculpture on fountain, Parkman Plaza, Boston; plus sculpture statues in many cathedrals & churches in the U S.
Exhibitions: Sculpture Exhib, Boston Mus Fine Arts; sev Sculpture Exhibs, New Eng Sculpture Asn; one-man exhib, Sch Design, Harvard Univ; Lit Arts Soc Exhib, New York, N Y.
Teaching: Pvt classes, Boston, 32-37; instr, Craft Ctr Sch, Boston, 39-40; instr design, New London Jr Col, Conn, 41-43; instr design, Boston Archit Ctr, 36-, head Sch Archit, 38-, mem bd dirs.
Positions: Asst dir sculpture & wood carving, W F Ross Studio, Cambridge, 23-41; sculptor & asst dir, Schwamb Assocs Studio, Arlington, 41-46, sculptor & dir, 46-52; partner studio for sculpture & decorations, Boston & Arlington, 52-
Awards: Gold medal & citation, Nat Sculpture Soc, 61; Anniversary Citation, Boston Archit Ctr, 64.
Memberships: Fel Am Inst Architects (chmn cmt collaborative arts); hon mem Dante Alighieri Soc; New Eng Sculptors Asn; Boston Soc Architects; Mass Asn Architects.
Mailing Address: 500 Concord Ave, Lexington, MA 02173.

CASE, ANDREW W
Painter, Educator
Preferred Media: Watercolors.
b Peru, Ind, July 19, 98.
Study & Training: Pratt Inst; Pa State Univ, BS & MA.
Work in Public Collections: William Penn Mem Mus, Harrisburg, Pa; State Col High Sch, Pa; also in pvt collections in the U S & Europe.
Exhibitions: One-man show, Warwick Gallery, Philadelphia, Pa; Retrospective Exhib, Hist Soc York Co, 65; Here and There, Hist Soc York Co, 68; New York Watercolor Club; Am Watercolor Soc.
Teaching: Instr art, Calif State Col, Pa, 25-26; prof art, Pa State Univ, 26-62, emer prof, 62-; dean art, York Acad Arts, 62-72.
Mailing Address: 450 Roosevelt Ave, York, PA 17404.

CASEY, ELIZABETH TEMPLE
Museum Curator
b Providence, R I, Sept 24, 01.
Study & Training: Pembroke Col, Brown Univ.
Collections Arranged: Exhibs from permanent collection of Mus Art, R I Sch Design, Providence.
Positions: Mus asst, Mus Art, R I Sch Design, 26-35, cur textiles, 35-43; cur Aldrich Collection, 50-, cur Oriental art, 56-
Research: English, Chinese and Japanese ceramics; Oriental costumes and textiles; Japanese color prints.
Publications: Auth, The Lucy Truman Aldrich Collection of European porcelain figures of the eighteenth century, 65.
Mailing Address: 89 Ingleside Ave, Edgewood, RI 02905.

CASSARA, FRANK
Painter, Printmaker
Preferred Media: Intaglio.
b Partinice, Sicily; U S citizen.
Study & Training: Colorado Springs Sch Fine Arts, Colo; Univ Mich, MS(design); also spec study, Atelier 17, Paris, France.
Work in Public Collections: Libr Cong, Washington, D C; Bibliot Nat, Paris, France; Stedelijk Mus, Amsterdam, Neth; Detroit Inst Arts, Mich; Free Libr Philadelphia, Pa.
Commissions: Murals, U S Post Off, East Detroit, Mich, 39, Donald Thompson Sch (fresco), Highland Park, Mich, 39, U S Post Off, Sandusky, Mich, 40 & Water Conditioning Plant, Lansing, Mich, 41.
Exhibitions: 7th Int Exhib Lithography & Wood Engr, Art Inst Chicago, Ill, 39; Int Asn Plastic Arts, U S Info Agency Tour, S Am, 59; 1st Int Calif Soc Etchers, San Francisco, 64; 1st Exhib Am Printmakers, Gallerie Nees Morphes, Athens, Greece, 65; 22nd Nat Exhib Prints, Libr Cong, 71.
Teaching: Instr drawing, Detroit Soc Arts & Crafts, 46-47; prof printmaking, Univ Mich, 47-
Positions: Pres, Ann Arbor Art Asn, 56-57.
Publications: Contribr, Prize winning graphics, 63, 64 & 66 & Artists' proof, a collectors edition, 71.
Dealer: Forsythe Gallery, 201 Nickels Arcade, Ann Arbor, MI 48104.
Mailing Address: Art Dept, University of Michigan, Ann Arbor, MI 48104.

CASSILL, HERBERT CARROLL
Printmaker, Educator
Preferred Media: Intaglio, Wood.
b Percival, Iowa, Dec 24, 28.
Study & Training: State Univ Iowa, BFA, 48, MFA, 50, with Maricio Lasansky.
Work in Public Collections: Mus Mod Art, New York, N Y; Cleveland Mus Art; Brooklyn Mus; Libr Cong, Washington, D C; Oakland Art Mus, Calif.
Exhibitions: Libr Cong, 52, 54 & 60; six shows, Philadelphia Print Club, 53-60; Int Exhib Graphic Arts, Mus Mod Art shown in Europe, 54; Modern Art in the U S A, Mus Mod Art (shown in Europe), 55; Society of American Graphic Artists Overseas Exhib, U S State Dept, 60.
Teaching: Instr printmaking, State Univ Iowa, 53-57; head dept printmaking, Cleveland Inst Art, 57-
Awards: Louis Comfort Tiffany Found fel printmaking, 53; purchase prize, Philadelphia Print Club, 56; first prize, Print Show, State Univ N Y Col Potsdam, 61.
Mailing Address: 3084 Coleridge Rd, Cleveland, OH 44118.

CASTELLI, LEO
Art Dealer
b Trieste, Italy, Sept 4, 07.
Study & Training: Univ Milan; Columbia Univ, grad work hist.
Positions: Dir, Leo Castelli Gallery.
Specialty of Gallery: American vanguard painting and sculpture.
Mailing Address: Leo Castelli Gallery, 4 E 77th St, New York, NY 10021.

CASTER, BERNARD HARRY
Painter, Enamelist
b Wolcott, N Y, May 27, 21.
Study & Training: Syracuse Univ, AA(fine arts), 56, BA, 60.
Exhibitions: 21st Ann Western N Y Regional, Buffalo, 55; 19th Ceramic Nat, Syracuse Mus, 56; N Y State Artists Invitational Exhib, N Y State Fair, 58; The Kentucky Guild Train, 66; 14th Ann Rochester Festival of Religious Arts, 72.
Awards: Marie Wilner Award, Cayuga Mus Hist & Art, Auburn, N Y, 62 & ceramic award, 64; hon mention, Eighth Ann Westchester Outdoor Art Exhib, New Rochelle, N Y, 67.
Dealer: Galerie Paula Insel, 987 Third Ave, New York, NY 10022.
Mailing Address: Box 154, South Butler, NY 13154.

CASTLE, WENDELL KEITH
Designer, Sculptor
Preferred Media: Wood.
b Emporia, Kans, Nov 6, 32.
Study & Training: Univ Kans, BFA & MFA.
Work in Public Collections: Addison Gallery Am Art, Andover, Mass; Rochester Mem Art Gallery, N Y; Nordenfieldske Kunstindustrimus, Norway; Mus Contemp Crafts, New York, N Y; Ithaca Col Art Mus, N Y.
Commissions: Interior, comn by Douglass Baker, Rochester, 67; interior, comn by Lee Nordness, New York, 69; sculpture, Marine Midland Bank, Rochester, 71; furniture, Stendig, Inc, New York, 71-72; furniture, comn by Sam Johnson, Racine, Wis.

Exhibitions: Int Kunsthandwerk, 66; Attitudes, Brooklyn Mus, N Y, 69; Objects U S A, traveling show, U S & Europe, 70-; Wooden Work, Smithsonian Inst, 72; 13th Triennale, Milan, Italy.
Teaching: Instr drawing, Univ Kans, 60-61; assoc prof furniture design, Rochester Inst Technol, 62-70; prof sculpture, State Univ N Y Col Brockport, 70-
Awards: Jurors prize for one-man show, Rochester Mem Art Gallery, 66; Louis Comfort Tiffany Found & N Y State grants, 72.
Bibliography: Wilson (auth), The music rack, produced by ACC, 66; Limber Timber, Newsweek, 5/13/68; Pierce (auth), Transitions, film produced by Nat Educ TV, 69.
Memberships: Am Craftsman Coun (N Y rep).
Publications: Auth, George Sugarman, 68, Mike Nevelson, 69 & Wharton Esherick, 71, Craft Horizons.
Dealer: Shop 1, 127 Alexander St, Rochester, NY 14607.
Mailing Address: 18 Maple St, Scottsville, NY 14546.

CASTORO, ROSEMARIE
Painter, Sculptor
b Brooklyn, N Y, Mar 1, 39.
Study & Training: Mus Mod Art, N Y, scholar, 54-55; Pratt Inst, BFA(cum laude), 56-63.
Work in Public Collections: Berkeley Mus, San Francisco, Calif; Woodward Found, Washington, D C.
Commissions: Procession of Strokes, N Y State Coun Arts, 72.
Exhibitions: Distillation, Tibor de Nagy Art Gallery, New York, N Y, 66 & solo exhibs, 71 & 72; The Drawn Line, 470 Parker St Gallery, Boston, Mass, 71; Highlights of the 70-71 Art Season, Aldridge Mus Contemp Art, Conn, 71; Painting & Sculpture, Storm King Mountain, N Y, 72.
Awards: Woodward Found, 70; Guggenheim fel, 71-72; N Y State Coun Arts, 72.
Bibliography: E C Goosen (auth), Distillation, Artforum, 11/66; April Kingsley (auth), Rev of the second solo show, Art News, 2/72; Denise Wolher (auth) Rev of the second solo show, Arts Mag, 4/72.
Publications: Auth, Open hearing, Art Workers Coalition, 69; auth, The artist & politics, Artforum, 9/70; auth, Artists transgress all boundaries, Art News, 1/72; ed, Art in the mind, 70; ed, Conceptual art, 72.
Dealer: Tibor de Nagy Art Gallery, 29 W 57th St, New York, NY 10019.
Mailing Address: 151 Spring St, New York, NY 10012.

CASTRO (PACHECO FERNANDO)
Painter
b Merida, Mex, Jan 26, 18.
Study & Training: Escuela Artes Plasticas, 34.
Work in Public Collections: Museo Arte Mod, Bosque Chapultepec, Mex; Palacio Bellas Artes, Mex; Libr of Cong, Washington, D C; Dallas Mus Fine Arts, Tex.
Commissions: Cosmogonia Maya (mural), Palacio Gobierno, Palacio Estado, Merida, 70-71; Jacinto (mural), Sala de Recepciones, Gobierno Estado; Canek (mural) & Yucatan en la Historia (mural), Palacio Gobierno, Merida, 72.
Exhibitions: 3rd & 4th Exposicion Internacional de Arte, Tokyo, Japan, 55 & 57; 5th Muestra Internacional de Blanco y Negro, Lugano, Suiza, 58; 10th Int Biennial Watercolor Exhib, Brooklyn, N Y, 59; Exposicion de Pintura Mexicana, Rome, Italy, 67; plus many others.
Teaching: Instr art, Escuela Pintura y Escultura, La Esmeralda, Mex, 46-61, dir, 61-; instr art, Escuela Nacional Artes Plasticas, Nat Univ Mex, 49-
Positions: Juror, Oposiciones y Examines Profesionales, Escuela Nacional Artes Plasticas, 55-; juror, Salon Plastica Mexicana, Eventos Pintura, Dibujo y Grabado.
Awards: First prize in painting, Salon Plastica Mexicana, 54, 55 & 61.
Bibliography: Antonio Mediz Bolio (auth), article, In: Diario del Sureste, 51; Justino Fernandez (auth), article, In: El Universal, 72; Raquel Tibol (auth), article, In: Diorama Cultura, Excelsior, 72.
Memberships: Soc Mex Grabadores (pres); Plastica Mex (consejero, 58, asesor, 60); Escuela Nacional Artes Plasticas U N A M (consejero technico, 57); Escuela Pintura y Escultura S E P (consejero technico, 56).
Publications: Illusr, Acabo su camino con la muerte, 52, La nube esteril, 52, Los pozos sagrados, 54, Voz y sangra del hijo de Yucatan, 55 & La flauta de la caña, 60.
Dealer: Galeria de Arte Mexicano, Milan 18, Mexico D F, Mex.
Mailing Address: Beta 59, Mexico D F 21, Mex.

CASWELL, HELEN RAYBURN
Painter, Writer
Preferred Media: Oils
b Long Beach, Calif, Mar 16, 23.
Study & Training: Univ Ore Sch Fine Arts.

Commissions: Murals, Federated Church, Saratoga, Calif, 65; Mem Paintings, San Jose Hosp, Calif, 67 & Emanuel Lutheran Church, Saratoga, 69.
Exhibitions: DeYoung Mus Show, Soc Western Artists, 61; one-man shows, Northwest Mo State Col, 66 & Rosicrucian Mus, San Jose, 70; Montalvo Cult Ctr, Saratoga, Calif, 68.
Awards: James D Phelan Award for Narrative Poetry, 58; San Francisco Browning Soc Award, 66.
Memberships: Soc Western Artists.
Publications: Auth & illusr, Jesus, my son, John Knox, 62; auth & illusr, A wind on the road, 64 & A new song for Christmas, 66, Van Nostrand Reinhold; Shadows from the singing house, Charles Tuttle, 67; auth & illusr, You are more wonderful, Gibson, 70.
Dealer: Park's Art Gallery, 322 Town & Country Village, San Jose, CA 95128.
Mailing Address: 15095 Fruitvale Ave, Saratoga, CA 95070.

CATALDO, JOHN WILLIAM
Educator, Film Maker
b Boston, Mass, Nov 28, 24.
Study & Training: Mass Col Art, BSEd; Columbia Univ, MA & EdD; spec study completed at Sch Am Craftsmen, Rochester, N Y, with L Copeland, Univ Calif, Los Angeles, with J P Jones, Teachers Col, Univ Buffalo & Pa State Univ.
Work in Public Collections: Wichita Art Asn, Univ Mo; Albright-Knox Art Gallery, Buffalo, N Y; N Y State Crafts Fair, Ithaca; Teachers Col, Columbia Univ; Munic Art Ctr, Long Beach, Calif.
Commissions: Films on art, Nat Educ Asn, 61; screen-divider, Sheraton-Palace Hotel, San Francisco, Calif, 62; sculpture, Lithuanian Social Ctr, DuBois, Pa, 65; 30 films, Nat Inst TV, Bloomington, Ind, 70-72.
Exhibitions: Young Americans, U S A, Contemp Crafts Show, 56; Wichita Art Asn Sculpture & Jewelry Show, 56 & 61; Albright-Knox Art Gallery Show, 60; Graphic Design Invitational, Syracuse Univ, 61; Ball State Drawing & Sculpture Ann, 63-64.
Teaching: Assoc prof art, Teachers Col, Columbia Univ, 60-61; assoc prof art, Penn State Univ, 61-65; dir art educ & prof art, Philadelphia Col Art, 65-70; acad dean & instr calligraphy, Mass Col Art, 70-
Positions: Assoc ed, Art Educ, 60-63; ed, Sch Arts, 62-67.
Awards: Lacey Print Prize, 56 & ceramic sculpture prize, 58, Western N Y Ann, Albright-Knox Art Gallery; Words & calligraphy selected for AIGA 50 Best Books Award, Van Nostrand Reinhold, 70.
Memberships: Nat Art Educ Asn (bd dirs, 66-70, pres, Eastern Regional, 68-70); Educ Press Asn; Am Asn Univ Prof; Col Art Asn Am.
Publications: Auth, Lettering—a guide for teachers, David Publ, 58; auth, Graphic design & visual communication, Intext, 66; auth, Words & calligraphy for children, Van Nostrand Reinhold, 69.
Mailing Address: 29 Forty Acres Dr, Wayland, MA.

CATAN-ROSE, RICHARD
Painter, Educator
b Rochester, N Y, Oct 1, 05.
Study & Training: Royal Acad Fine Arts, Italy, MFA; St Andrews Univ, London, Eng, LLD; Cooper Union Art Sch; also with Pippo Rizzo, Antonio Quarino, J Joseph & A Shulkin.
Work in Public Collections: Our Lady Queen of Martyrs Church, Forest Hills, Long Island, N Y; Royal Acad Fine Arts, Italy.
Exhibitions: Allied Artists Am, 39 & 40; Vendome Gallery, 39-41; one-man shows, Forest Hills, Long Island, 44-46 & Argent Gallery, 46; also in Europe.
Positions: Pres, Catan-Rose Inst Art, Jamaica, Long Island.
Memberships: Am Fedn Arts.
Mailing Address: 72-72 112th St, Forest Hills, Long Island, NY 11375.

CATCHI (CATHERINE O CHILDS)
Painter, Sculptor
Preferred Media: Oils, Watercolors, Bronzes.
b Philadelphia, Pa, Aug 27, 20.
Study & Training: Briarcliff Jr Col, 37; Com Illus Studios, 38-39; Paul Wood Studio, 49-55; with Leon Kroll, Harry Sternberg & Hans Hofmann; also with Angelo Savelli, Positano, Italy.
Work in Public Collections: Hofstra Univ, Hempstead, N Y.
Exhibitions: Rayburn Hall (by Congressional invitation), Washington, D C, 68; Alfredo Valente Gallery, New York, N Y, 68; Lever House, New York, four times; Royal Acad Galleries, Edinburgh, Scotland; Royal Birmingham Soc Artists Galleries, Eng.
Awards: Grumbacher Award, 63; Lillian Cotton Mem Award & medal of hon, Nat Asn Women Artists, 66; Irene Sickle Feist Mem Prize, 71.

Bibliography: Nan Ickeringill (auth), Art & at home with Catchi, New York Times, 68; Doris Herzig (auth), She has painted since she was 12, Newsday, 68; Molly Sinclair (auth), Oil, brush & canvas, Atlanta Constitution, 69.
Memberships: Nat Register Prominent Americans (exec adv coun, 69); Exec & Prof Hall Fame; Nat Asn Women Artists (second v pres, 72-73); Audubon Artists; Int Platform Asn.
Publications, Contribr, Prize winning oil paintings, 66 & 67.
Dealer: Harbor Gallery, Cold Spring Harbor, NY 10516.
Mailing Address: 2 Gristmill Lane, Manhasset, NY 11030.

CATLIN, STANTON L
Museum Director, Art Historian
b Portland, Ore, Feb 19, 15.
Study & Training: Oberlin Col, AB; Acad Fine Arts, Prague, Czech; Am Sch Class Studies, Athens, Greece; Fogg Mus, fel mod art; Inst Fine Arts, New York Univ, MA.
Teaching: Prof N Am art, faculty fine arts, Univ Chile, 42-43; lectr hist of art, Yale Univ, 62-64; dir, art of Latin Am since independence, Yale Univ-Univ Tex, 65-67; vis assoc prof art, Hunter Col, 72-
Positions: Asst to dir circulating exhibs, Mus Mod Art, 39; secy, comt art, Coordr Inter-Am Affairs, 41-42; supvr, exhib contemp Am painting sent to S & Cent Am, by Mus Mod Art, 41; exec dir, Am Inst Graphic Arts, 46-50; from ed to cur Am Art, Minneapolis Inst Arts, 52-58; asst dir, Yale Univ Art Gallery, New Haven, Conn, 58-67; dir, art gallery, Ctr Inter-Am Rels, N Y, 67-71.
Memberships: Grolier Club; Latin Am Studies Asn; Am Asn Mus; Col Art Asn Am.
Research: History of modern Latin American art, foundation sponsored textbook project.
Publications: Auth, La peinture Mexicaine, 52; co-auth, Art of Latin America since independence (exhib catalog); contribr, articles, In: Minneapolis Inst Art Bull, Art News, New York Times, New Yorker, Columbia Rec Legacy Album (Mexico), Art in Am, Am Indigena & exhib catalogs of Ctr Inter-Am Rels.
Mailing Address: 44 Meyer Pl, Riverside, CT 06878.

CATOK, LOTTIE MEYER
Painter
Preferred Media: Oils, Watercolors.
b Hoboken, N J.
Study & Training: New York Sch Appl & Fine Arts; also with Guy Wiggins, W Lester Stevens & Robert Brackman.
Work in Public Collections: Fla Southern Col, Lakeland; dorm living rms, Smith Col, Northampton, Mass; Rental Gallery, Mus Fine Arts, Springfield, Mass; plus many portraits in pub bldgs.
Commissions: Portraits of judges of law, Law League, Superior & Probate Cts, Mass, 61, 66 & 69; portrait of pres of Am Int Col, commissioned by col, Springfield, 63; portraits of clergymen, churches & temples, Springfield, 63-67; portrait of Ted Shawn (ballet), Jacob's Pillow, Lenox, Mass, 64; portrait of med men, Wesson Women's Hosp, Springfield, 66-71.
Exhibitions: Grand Cent Art Galleries, New York, N Y, 55-57; North Shore Art Asn, Gloucester, Mass, 63-72; Hudson Valley Art Asn, White Plains, N Y, 69-72; Allied Artists Am, New York, 70; Am Artists Prof League, New York, 70-71.
Awards: First for landscape, Springfield Artist Guild; patron's prize, Springfield Art League; figure award, Acad Artists, 71.
Bibliography: Jack Steiner (auth), I know what I like, New York World Tel, 66.
Memberships: Fifty Am Artists; Royal Soc Art, London, Eng; Baltimore Watercolor Club; Acad Artists (pres, 69-70); Copley Soc Boston.
Publications: Contribr, Art News, 58; contribr, The fifty American artists' book, 69; contribr, Robbins reproductions, 69.
Mailing Address: 45 May Fair Dr, Longmeadow, MA 01106.

CATTELL, RAY
Painter, Art Director
Preferred Media: Acrylic, Watercolor, Oil.
b Birmingham, Eng, May 5, 21; Can citizen.
Study & Training: Birmingham Col Art, Eng; Univ Toronto.
Work in Public Collections: London Art Gallery, Ont; Sarnia Art Gallery, Ont; Saskatoon Art Gallery, Sask, Alta.
Exhibitions: Royal Can Acad Art, 60-71; Ont Soc Artists, 60-71; Flint Inst Fine Arts, Mich, 65; Can Soc Painters in Watercolour, 66-72; Am Watercolor Soc, 72.
Positions: Exec coun mem, Royal Can Acad Art, 70-72.
Awards: Watercolour award, City of Toronto, 63; hon award, Can Soc Painters in Watercolour, 65, 68 & 72; Baxter Purchase Award, 66.
Memberships: Royal Can Acad Art; Ont Soc Artists (v pres, 67-68); Can Soc Painters in Watercolour; Arts & Letters Club; Art Dir Club Toronto (pres, 64-65).
Publications: Auth, Article on creativity, Marketing Mag, 60.
Dealer: Gallery Moos, 138 Yorkville Ave, Toronto 5, Ont, Can.
Mailing Address: 58 Russell Hill Rd, Toronto, Ont, Can.

CATTI (CATHERINE JAMES)
Painter
Preferred Media: Acrylics, Plexiglas, Enamel, Copper.
b Mount Vernon, N Y, Oct 8, 40.
Study & Training: Boston Univ, BFA; Columbia Univ, MA.
Commissions: Acrylic for The Last Jesus (film), Sepia Theater, Toledo, Ohio, 72.
Exhibitions: Contemporary Black Artists in America, 71 & Whitney Ann, Whitney Mus Am Art, 72; one-woman show, Cinque Gallery, New York, N Y, 71; Projected Art: Artists At Work, & Women in the Arts, Finch Mus, 71 & 72; Black Artists Nat, Smith Mason Gallery, Wash, D C, 72.
Teaching: Art specialist, Wittwyck Sch for Boys, 68-70; instr anat, Col New Rochelle, 72-; lectr African art, educ & PSI Systs.
Awards: Creative Artists Coun Grant in painting, N Y State Coun on Arts, 71.
Bibliography: Black artists in America (slide collection), Univ S Ala & H Kress Found.
Memberships: Am Crafts Coun.
Publications: Auth, three articles, In: Arts & Activities Mag, 67-70.
Dealer: Summerfield Gallery, 303 Broadway, Dobbs Ferry, NY 10522.
Mailing Address: 6 Fulton St, Hastings-on-Hudson, NY 10706.

CAVALLI, DICK
Cartoonist
b New York, N Y, Sept 28, 23.
Exhibitions: Punch Exhib Humor, London, Eng, 53.
Positions: Cartoonist, syndicated comic strip Winthrop, Newspaper Enterprise Asn; mem founding fac, Famous Cartoonists Course, Famous Artists Schs.
Memberships: Nat Cartoonists Soc; Newspaper Comics Coun.
Publications: Contribr cartoons, numerous bks, anthologies & cartoon collections; contribr, cartoons, In: Sat Eve Post, Collier's, Look, This Wk, True & many other U S & for mags.
Mailing Address: P O Box 966, New Canaan, CT 06840.

CAVALLON, GIORGIO
Painter
Preferred Media: Oils.
b Sorio, Italy, Mar 3, 04; U S citizen.
Study & Training: Nat Acad Design; also with Charles Hawthorne.
Work in Public Collections: Solomon R Guggenheim Mus, New York, N Y; Mus Mod Art, New York, N Y; Whitney Mus Am Art, New York; Michener Collection, Univ Tex, Austin; Chase Manhattan Bank Collection, New York.
Exhibitions: Yale Univ Art Gallery, New Haven, Conn, 67; Large Scale American Paintings, Jewish Mus, New York, 67; Painting as Painting, Art Mus, Univ Tex, Austin, 68; The 1930's, Painting & Sculpture in America, Whitney Mus Am Art, 68; The New American Painting & Sculpture, Mus Mod Art, New York, 69; plus many others.
Teaching: Artist-in-residence, Univ N C, Greensboro, 64; vis critic in art, Yale Univ, 66-67; instr art, Columbia Univ, 69.
Awards: Guggenheim fel, 66; award in painting, Nat Inst Arts & Lett, 70; award in painting, New Eng Art/Painting & Sculpture Invitational Show, 71.
Bibliography: Frank O'Hara (auth), Cavallon paints a picture, Art News, 12/58; John Sedgwick (auth), Discovering modern art, Random House, 66; Barbara Rose (auth), American art since 1900, Praeger, 67.
Dealer: A M Sachs Gallery, 29 W 57th St, New York, NY 10028.
Mailing Address: 178 E 95th St, New York, NY 10028.

CAVANAUGH, TOM RICHARD
Painter, Educator
Preferred Media: Oils.
b Danville, Ill, July 19, 23.
Study & Training: Univ Ill, BFA, 47, McLellan fel & MFA, 50; Fulbright grant to Italy, 56-57.
Work in Public Collections: William Rockhill Nelson Gallery Art, Kansas City, Mo; Mulvane Art Mus, Topeka, Kans; Joslyn Art Mus, Omaha, Nebr; Ark Art Ctr, Little Rock; Isaac Delgado Mus Art, New Orleans, La.
Exhibitions: American Painting Today, Metrop Mus Art, New York, 50; Whitney Mus Am Art Ann Exhib, 51; Corcoran Biennial Exhibs, Washington, D C, 59 & 61; Maine: 100 Artists of the 20th Century, Colby Col, Waterville, 64; American Painting, 62, Va Mus Quadriennial, Richmond, 62.
Teaching: Instr painting & drawing, Kansas City Art Inst, 52-55; instr painting & drawing, Wash Univ Sch Fine Arts, 55-56; prof painting & drawing, La State Univ, 57-
Positions: Art & educ dir, Springfield Art Asn, Ill, 47-49; dir, Bay St Studio, Boothbay Harbor, Maine, summers 50-
Awards: Painting prize, Athletics, La State Univ Union, 69.

Bibliography: Margaret Harold (auth), Prize-winning oil paintings, Bk 1 & 7, 60 & 67, Allied Publ; Bartlett H Hayes (auth), Artist and advocate, Renaissance Ed, 68.
Publications: Auth, A city is not built in a day: the architecture of Springfield, Illinois, 1819-1949, 49; contribr, Maine Artists Calendar, 67.
Mailing Address: 3365 Tyrone Dr, Baton Rouge, LA 70808.

CAVAT, IRMA
Painter, Educator
Preferred Media: Acrylics, Oils, Mixed Media.
b New York, N Y.
Study & Training: New Sch Social Res; Archipenko Art Sch; Acad Grande Chaumiere, Paris; also with Ozenfant, Paris & Hans Hofmann.
Commissions: Murals, Vodun, Port-au-Prince, Haiti, 48 & pvt hotel, Athens, Greece, 70; wall of portraits, Faculty Club, Univ Calif, Santa Barbara, 68; wall piece, Los Angeles, Calif, 70.
Exhibitions: Recent Drawings, Mus Mod Art, New York, 50; Ill Nat, Urbana, 59; Festival of Two Worlds, Spoleto, Italy, 58-59; Ten Americans, Palazzo Venezia, Rome, Italy, 60; one-man shows, Santa Barbara Mus & Phoenix Mus, Ariz, 66-67; plus one-man shows, Detroit, Chicago, Los Angeles, New York, Paris, Rome & Trieste.
Teaching: Assoc prof painting & drawing, Univ Calif, Santa Barbara, 64-
Awards: Yaddo fel, Trask Found, 50; Fulbright fels, 56-58; Creative Arts Inst award, Univ Calif, 70.
Dealer: Arwin Galleries, 222 Grand River W, Detroit, MI 48226.
Mailing Address: Dept of Art, University of California, Santa Barbara, CA 93106.

CAVER, WILLIAM RALPH
Sculptor, Painter
Preferred Media: Metal.
b Longview, Tex, Oct 11, 32.
Study & Training: N Tex State Univ, BS; Univ Guanajuanto, MFA; Univ Barcelona.
Work in Public Collections: Houston Mus Fine Arts, Tex; N Tex State Gallery, Denton; Patio Gallery, Fort Worth, Tex; Inst Allende Gallery, San Miguel de Allende, Mex.
Commissions: Sculpture, Louisville Libr, 71; sculpture, Texarkana Col Libr, Tex, 72.
Exhibitions: Dallas Ann Libr Exhib, 63 & 64; Inst Allende Ann Show, 66; Texarkana Regional Art Show, 67-69; Denton Regional Art Show, 70.
Teaching: Instr art, Dallas Pub Sch Syst, 58-67; asst prof art, Texarkana Col, 67-
Awards: First prize each yr, Texarkana Regional Art Show, 67-69 & Denton Regional Art Show, 70.
Memberships: Tex Asn Art Sch.
Dealer: Pandora's, 3201 New Boston, Texarkana, TX 75501.
Mailing Address: Rt Six, Box 453, Texarkana, TX 75501.

CECERE, ADA RASARIO
Painter
Preferred Media: Oils, Watercolors.
b New York, N Y.
Study & Training: Art Stud League New York; Beaux-Arts Inst New York; Nat Acad Design.
Work in Public Collections: Norfolk Mus Arts & Sci, Va; Ohio Univ Founder's Collection, Athens; Oklahoma City Mus, Okla; Children's Hosp Founder's Libr, Baltimore, Md.
Commissions: Sand-carved mural, U S Treas Dept Nat Competition, 47; Triptych, altar for Ft Gordon, USA; mural, Hyde Park Restaurant, New York, N Y; mural, Lobby of Hotel Newton, New York.
Exhibitions: Brooklyn Mus, N Y, 60; Am Watercolor Soc Traveling Exhibs, 60 & 69; seven one-man shows, New York, N J & Pa, 60-72; Richmond Mus Traveling Exhibs, 60-72; Asn Women Artists, U S, Can, France & Italy, 72.
Teaching: Pvt painting classes in studio, 47-72.
Awards: Medal of honor for pastel, Nat Asn Women Artists, 55; solo exhib award, Fairleigh Dickinson Univ, 63; Maria Cantarella Mem Prize, Allied Artists Am, 68.
Memberships: Audubon Artists (dir, 60-72); Nat Asn Women Artists (adv bd, 50-72); Allied Artists Am (award jury, 61-); Knickerbocker Artists (v pres, 57-59); Pen & Brush Club (off, Brush Sect, 60-72).
Mailing Address: 240 Waverly Pl, New York, NY 10014.

CECERE, GAETANO
Sculptor, Lecturer
b New York, N Y, Nov 26, 94.
Study & Training: Nat Acad Design; Beaux-Arts Inst Design; Am Acad in Rome, fel, 20-23.

Work in Public Collections: Metrop Mus Art; Numismatic Mus, N Y; Norfolk Mus Art.
Commissions: Plaques, U S Capitol, Washington, D C; reliefs, Fed Reserve Bank, Jacksonville, Fla; war mem, Clifton, Plainfield & Princeton, N J; plus others.
Exhibitions: Nat Sculpture Soc, 24-58; Nat Acad Design, 24-69; Allied Artists Am, 62-64; Knickerbocker Artists, 62-64; Audubon Artists, 62, 64 & 65; plus others.
Teaching: Lectr contemp & ecclesiastical sculpture; former dir sculpture dept, Beaux-Arts Inst Design; former mem faculty, Mary Washington Col & Sch Fine Arts, Nat Acad Design.
Awards: Award in sculpture, Nat Arts Club, 68; sculpture award, Audubon Artists, 69; Therese Richard Mem Award, Allied Artists Am, 70; plus others.
Memberships: Academician Nat Acad Design; Nat Sculpture Soc; New York Archit League.
Mailing Address: 240 Waverly Pl, New York, NY 10014.

CELENDER, DONALD DENNIS
Art Historian, Painter
b Pittsburgh, Pa, Nov 11, 31.
Study & Training: Carnegie-Mellon Univ, BFA, 56; Univ Pittsburgh, MEd, 59, A W Mellon scholar, 60-63, PhD, 63.
Work in Public Collections: Centro Arte y Communicacion, Buenos Aires, Arg; Mus Arte Mod, Buenos Aires; Allen Mem Art Mus, Oberlin Col, Ohio; Latrobe Mus, Pa; Gen Mills Collection, Minneapolis, Minn.
Commissions: Stained glass panels, Children's Hosp, Pittsburgh, 61; moving water sculpture, Nokomis Br, Minneapolis Pub Libr, stained glass mural, Main Br, & Eva Rhodes Freeman Mem (stained glass mural), Lake St Br, 67; Mem (stained glass panels), St James Lutheran Church, Minneapolis, 68.
Exhibitions: Walker Art Ctr Biennial, 64; Art in the Mind, Allen Mem Art Mus, 70; 2,972,453, Centro Arte y Comunicacion, Buenos Aires, 70; one-man shows, O K Harris Gallery, New York, 70-72; Art Systems I and II, Mus Arte Mod, Buenos Aires, 71-72.
Teaching: Edith M Kelso prof art hist, Macalester Col, 64-
Positions: Cur, Nat Gallery Art, 61-63; dir educ & pub activities, Minneapolis Inst Arts, 63-64.
Awards: Man of Year in Art, Pittsburgh Jaycees, 61; faculty, foreign & res fels, 67-72; Ford fel in Humanities, 70-71.
Bibliography: Sue Chastain (auth), Fill all manholes with cherry jello, Minneapolis Star, 2/23/72; Grace Glueck (auth), Art Notes, New York Times, 2/27/72; Gareth Hiebert (auth), Grand Canyon sweet and other delicacies, St Paul Pioneer Press & Dispatch, 5/28/72.
Memberships: Col Art Asn Am; Am Mus Asn; Delta Phi Delta; Minn Arts Forum; Minneapolis Soc Fine Arts.
Research: Development of conceptual art movements.
Publications: Auth, articles on Bellows, Caneletto, Duccio, De-Hooch, Grunewald, Manet & Turner for Nat Gallery Art, 61-63; auth, Musical instruments in art, 65; auth, The dance, 72; auth, Eight conceptual art movements, 72.
Dealer: O K Harris Gallery, 465 W Broadway, New York, NY 10012.
Mailing Address: 15 Duck Pass Rd, St Paul, MN 55110.

CELENTANO, FRANCIS MICHAEL
Painter
Preferred Media: Acrylics.
b New York, N Y, May 25, 28.
Study & Training: N Y Univ Inst Fine Arts, MA, 57; Fulbright fel, 57; Acad Fine Arts, Rome, Italy, 58.
Work in Public Collections: Mus Mod Art, New York; Albright-Knox Art Gallery, Buffalo, N Y; Columbia Broadcasting Co, New York; Seattle Art Mus, Wash; Rose Art Gallery, Brandeis Univ, Waltham, Mass.
Commissions: Painting, hwy bldg, Wash State Hwy Dept, 70; mural, Port of Seattle, Seattle-Tacoma Airport, 71.
Exhibitions: The Responsive Eye, Mus Mod Art, New York, 65; Kinetic & Optical Art Today, 65 & Plus by Minus: Today's Half Century, 68, Albright-Knox Art Gallery; Whitney Ann, Whitney Mus Am Art, 67; Pacific Cities, Auckland City Art Gallery, New Zealand, 71.
Teaching: Assoc prof drawing, painting & design, Univ Wash, 66-
Awards: Int Artist's Sem, Fairleigh Dickinson Univ, 65.
Bibliography: Faulkner (auth), Art today, Holt, Rinehart & Winston, 69; Moore (auth), Letters from 31 artists, Albright-Knox Art Gallery, 70; Kingsbury (auth), Art, Seattle Mag, 1/70.
Dealer: Richard White Art Gallery, 311 Occidental S, Seattle, WA 98104.
Mailing Address: 1919½ Second Ave, Seattle, WA 98101.

CERNUSCHI, ALBERTO C
Art Dealer, Art Critic
b U S citizen.
Study & Training: Univ Milan, PhD; Univ Lausanne, PhD.

Teaching: Lectr mod art, Ecole du Louvre, Mus Cernuschi.
Positions: Founder, Cernuschi & Caravan de France Galleries, Paris, France & New York, N Y; trustee, Cernuschi Mus, Paris.
Specialty of Gallery: Modern art.
Publications: Auth, Theory of Autodeism, Philos Libr.
Mailing Address: 121 E 57th St, New York, NY 10022; also 49 Faubourg Saint Honore, Paris 8, France.

CERVANTES, PEDRO
Sculptor
Preferred Media: Welded Steel.
b Mexico City, Mex, Oct 10, 33.
Study & Training: Escuela Nac Artes Plasticas, San Carlos, Mex, 51-52.
Work in Public Collections: Banco Fomento Cooperativo, Mex; Banco Attantico, Mex; Financiera Nuevo Leon, Mex; Leona Textil Bldg, Monterrey, Mex; Entrance to Port of Alvarado, Mex.
Commissions: Welded iron sculpture, Jorge Gonzalez Reyna, 62; iron sculpture, Inst Nac Vivienda, 65; Incongruente, chromed steel, Hojalata & Lamina Hylsa, 71; Euridice, steel, Club Industriales, A C, 72; Septentrion, chromed steel, Nylon Mex, 72.
Exhibitions: New Values Show, Salón Plastica Mex, 62; Exhibition Young Artists Show, 65 & one-man show, 72, Mus Mod Art, Mexico City, Mex; Contemporary Mexican Painting, La Habana, Cuba, 65; Expo 67, Montreal, Que, 67.
Awards: First prize, Solar Exhib, Mex Ministry Educ, 68; first prize, Ann Salon Sculpture & Engraving, Salón Plástica Mex, 72.
Bibliography: Alfonso de Neuvillate & Luis Cardoza y Aragón (auth), Mexico pintura actual, Artes Mex; Raquel Tibol (auth), Pedro Cervantes o/a ahbivalencia, Excelsior, 2/72; Jorge Crespo de la Serna (auth), La escultura de Pedro Cervantes, Novedades, 3/72.
Mailing Address: c/o Galeria de Arte Misrachi, S A, 20 Genova, Mexico City 6, Mex.

CESAR, GASTON GONZALEZ
Sculptor
b San Felipe del Progreso, Mex, Feb 6, 40.
Study & Training: Escuela Nac Artes Plasticas, Prof (artes plasticas).
Work in Public Collections: Stone sculpture, Fine Arts Gallery San Diego, Calif.
Commissions: Figure of Fray Bernardino de Sahagin en Cuidad Sahagin, Hidalgo, Mex, 62; figure of Guadalupe Victoria en Gomez Palacio, Durango, Mex, 64; stone sculpture, Inst Mexicano del Seguro Social, Oaxtepec; stone sculpture, Medicos de la Colonia (Epoca).
Exhibitions: 2nd & 3rd Vienal Escultura Mexico, 64 & 66; Seccion Arte Pabellon Mexicano, World's Fair, New York, N Y, 65 & Expo '67, Montreal, Can, 67; Tendencias del Arte Abstracto en Mexico, Mus Univ Mex, 67.
Teaching: Prof art, Escuela Diseno Indust, Nat Univ Mex, 71-
Mailing Address: Hidalgo 30-B, Coyocan 21, D F, Mex.

CHADEAYNE, ROBERT OSBORNE
Painter, Educator
Preferred Media: Oils, Pastels.
b Cornwall, N Y, Dec 13, 97.
Study & Training: Colgate Univ; Art Stud League New York; also with C K Chatterton, Henry Martin Hoyt, George Luks & John Sloan.
Work in Public Collections: John Lambert Collection, Pa Acad Fine Arts; permanent collections, Columbus Gallery Fine Arts & Butler Inst Am Art; I B M Collection Am Art; Schumacker Collection, Capital Univ.
Commissions: Paintings, Broad and High St 1920, Trautman Off Bldg, Columbus, Ohio, 64 & Central Ohio, 65; cityscape, Huntington Nat Bank, Columbus, 70.
Exhibitions: Art Inst Chicago Ann; Pa Acad Fine Arts Ann; Nat Acad Design Ann, New York, N Y; Corcoran Biennial, Washington, D C; Butler Inst Am Art Midyear Nat Exhib, Youngstown, Ohio, 65-70.
Teaching: Dir drawing & painting, Columbus Art Sch, 27-42; prof fine arts, Ohio State Univ, 42-63.
Awards: Norman Waite Harris Medal, Art Inst Chicago, 20; purchase prize, Pa Acad Fine Arts, 20; I B M Medal for contribution to world of art.
Memberships: Columbus Art League (v pres, pres, 29-32, bd dirs); Columbus Gallery Fine Arts (bd mgrs).
Dealer: Capricorn Galleries, 8003 Woodmont Ave, Bethesda, MD 20014.
Mailing Address: Riverside Dr, Dublin, OH 43017.

CHAET, BERNARD
Painter, Educator
b Boston, Mass, Mar 7, 24.
Study & Training: Boston Mus Sch, with Karl Zerbe, 42-45; Tufts Univ, BS, 49.

Work in Public Collections: Fogg Art Mus, Harvard Univ, Cambridge, Mass; Univ Calif Art Gallery, Los Angeles; Brooklyn Mus, N Y; Addison Gallery Am Art, Andover, Mass; R I Sch Design Mus, Providence.
Exhibitions: Univ Ill Biennial Am Painting, 51, 53 & 60; Golden Years of American Drawing 1900-56; Brooklyn Mus, 56; Recent Drawings U S A, Mus Mod Art, New York, N Y, 56; Corcoran Biennial Am Painting, Washington, D C, 62; Pa Acad Fine Arts Ann, Philadelphia, 62.
Teaching: Prof drawing & painting, Yale Art Sch Yale Univ, 51-
Awards: Grant, Nat Found Humanities Arts, 66-67.
Publications: Auth preface, 20th Century Drawing (catalogue), Yale Art Gallery, 55; auth, Studio talk, monthly articles in Art Mag, 56-59; auth, Artists at work, Webb, 61; auth, The art of drawing, Holt, Rinehart & Winston, 71.
Dealer: Alpha Gallery, 121 Newbury St, Boston, MA 02116.
Mailing Address: 141 Cold Spring St, New Haven, CT 06511.

CHAFETZ, SIDNEY
Printmaker, Educator
b Providence, R I, Mar 27, 22.
Study & Training: R I Sch Design, BFA, 47; Acad Julian, Paris, France, 47-48; L'Ecole Am Beaux Arts, Fontaine Bleau, 47; with Fernand Leger, Paris, 48; Atelier 17, with S W Hayter, Paris, 50-51.
Work in Public Collections: Libr of Cong, Washington, D C; Cincinnati Art Mus; Nat Woodblock Inst, Tokyo, Japan; Philadelphia Mus Art; New York Pub Libr.
Commissions: Dedication etching, Ohio State Univ Col Law, 64; Hawthorne keepsake, Ohio State Univ, 64; Robert Lowell Poster, Int Poetry Forum, Pittsburgh, Pa, 67; F Scott Fitzgerald Keepsake, Fitzgerald Newsletter, Ohio State Univ, 68; Poor Richards Almanacks Original Woodblock Portrait, Imprint Soc, Barre, Mass, 70.
Exhibitions: Ten Years of American Prints, 1947-57, Brooklyn Mus, N Y, 57; Young American Printmakers, Mus Mod Art, New York, N Y, 58-59; Ninth Int Expos Gravure, Switz, Norway & Sweden, 66; First Biennial Int Gravure Sur Bois, Banska Bystrica, Czech, 70; Second Triennial Int Graphica Contemp, Capri, Italy, 72.
Teaching: Prof art, Ohio State Univ, 48-; vis prof art, Univ Ariz, spring 65, Univ Wis-Madison, summer 67 & Univ Denver, summer 71.
Awards: Tiffany Found Award, 49; Fulbright fel, 50-51; purchase prize & awards, First Biennial Int Gravure, Banska Bystrica, Czech, 70.
Memberships: Soc Am Graphic Artists; Am Color Print Soc; Am Asn Univ Prof.
Dealer: Associated American Artists, 663 Fifth Ave, New York, NY 10022.
Mailing Address: Division of Art, Ohio State University, Columbus, OH 43210.

CHALK, MR & MRS O ROY
Collectors
Collection: Contemporary Art.
Mailing Address: 1010 Fifth Ave, New York, NY 10028.

CHAMBERLAIN, BETTY
Art Administrator, Writer
b Feb 10, 08.
Study & Training: Smith Col, AB; Sorbonne, Paris, France, grad studies with Henri Focillon.
Positions: Metrop Mus Art, 29-32; Philadelphia Mus Art, 38-40; compiler & auth, weekly art sect, Time Mag, 40-42; Off War Info Domestic Graphic Program, 42-43; publicity dir, Mus Mod Art, New York, 48-54, asst to dir; managing ed, Art News, 54-56; publicity & community develop dir, Brooklyn Mus, 56-59; founder & dir, Art Info Cntr, Inc, 59-; mem adv comn, Mus Am Folk Art & Malcolm X Art Ctr, New York.
Memberships: Am Asn Mus.
Publications: Auth, Artist's guide to his market, 70; auth, mo art column, Lincoln Ctr & Carnegie Hall Programs, Sat Rev, 69-; auth, mo column & features, Am Artist Mag, 71-; ed, mo bull, Mus Mod Art, New York.
Mailing Address: Art Information Center, 189 Lexington Ave, New York, NY 10016.

CHAMBERLAIN, ELWYN
Painter
b Minneapolis, Minn, May 19, 28.
Study & Training: Minneapolis Sch Art; Univ Idaho, BA, 49; Univ Wis, MS, BA, MA, 51.
Work in Public Collections: Sarah Roby Found; Whitney Mus Am Art; Johnson Wax Collection, Art: U S A: Now.

Exhibitions: R I Sch Design; Deerfield Acad; Provincetown Art Festival; Spoleto Festival Two Worlds, Italy, 58; Art: U S A, 63; plus others.
Teaching: Asst instr art, Univ Wis, 50; guest instr painting, Univ Idaho, spring 55; guest lectr mod art, Bard Col, 66-67.
Bibliography: Lee Nordness (ed), included in: Art: U S A: Now, C J Bucher, 62.
Publications: Auth, Art voices (bibliog), 66.
Mailing Address: 222 The Bowery, New York, NY 10012.

CHAMBERLAIN, JOHN ANGUS
Sculptor
b Rochester, Ind, Apr 16, 27.
Study & Training: Art Inst Chicago, 50-52; Univ Ill; Black Mt Col, 55-56.
Work in Public Collections: Albright-Knox Gallery, Buffalo, N Y; Los Angeles Co Mus Art, Calif; Mus Mod Art, New York, N Y; Univ N C; Rome Naz; plus others.
Exhibitions: Contemporary American Sculpture, Selection I, Whitney Mus Am Art, 66; one-man show, Cleveland Mus Art, 67; HemisFair '68, San Antonio, Tex, 68; York Univ, Toronto, Ont, 69; Guggenheim Mus, 71; plus others.
Awards: Guggenheim fel, 66.
Bibliography: Sam Hunter (ed), included in: New art around the world: painting and sculpture, Abrams, 66; Wayne Craven (auth), included in: Sculpture in America, Crowell, 68; Gregory Battcock (ed), included in: Minimal art: a critical anthology, Dutton, 68; plus others.
Dealer: Leo Castelli Inc, 4 E 77th St, New York, NY 10021.
Mailing Address: 333 Park Ave S, New York, NY 10010.

CHAMBERLAIN, SAMUEL
Printmaker, Writer
Preferred Media: Graphics.
b Cresco, Iowa, Oct 28, 05.
Study & Training: Univ Wash, 13-15; Mass Inst Technol, 15-16 & 19-20; Paris, France, with M Edouard Leon, 25; Royal Col Art, London, Eng, 26-27; Marlboro Col, hon MA, 68.
Work in Public Collections: Libr Cong; New York Pub Libr; Metrop Mus Art; Boston Mus Fine Arts; Art Inst Chicago; plus others.
Exhibitions: Nat Acad Design Ann; var etching exhibs.
Teaching: Asst prof archit, Univ Mich, 25-26.
Awards: Kate W Arms Prize, Soc Am Etchers Exhib, 33; John Taylor Arms Prize, 36; ann award, New Eng Soc, 55; plus others.
Memberships: Academician Nat Acad Design; Soc Am Graphic Artists; fel Am Acad Arts & Sci; hon mem Am Inst Architects; assoc Photog Soc Am; plus others.
Publications: Auth, New England scene: a camera profile, Archit, 65; auth, Cape Ann, 67, Stroll through historic Salem, 69, A tour of old Starbridge Village, 69 & 72 & Rockefeller Center: a photographic narrative, 72, Hastings; plus many others.
Mailing Address: 5 Tucker St, Marblehead, MA 01946.

CHAMBERS, JOHN
Painter, Film Maker
Preferred Media: Oils, Ink, Pencil.
b London, Ont, Mar 25, 31.
Study & Training: Univ Western Ont, 52-53; Royal Acad Fine Arts, Madrid, Spain, DFA, 59; Univ Western Ont, hon LLD.
Work in Public Collections: Nat Gallery Can, Ottawa, Ont; Vancouver Art Gallery, B C; Art Gallery Ont, Toronto; Mus Mod Art, New York, N Y; Philadelphia Mus Fine Arts, Pa.
Exhibitions: Forum Art Gallery, New York, 65; New York World's Fair, 65; Int Exhib, Paris, France, Brussels, Belg & Switz, 67; Art Gallery of Ontario Retrospective, Vancouver Art Gallery, 70; Gallery Contemp Art, Chicago, Ill, 70.
Awards: Can Coun grants, 67-68, 69-70; Univ Alta Nat Award, Banff Sch Fine Arts, 72.
Bibliography: Chambers (film), Fraser Boa Prod, 70; Pierre Berton (interviewer), Jack Chambers, CBC TV, 71; Man alive, CBC TV, 71.
Memberships: Assoc Royal Can Acad Arts; Nat Asn Artists, Can Artists Representation (pres, 68); London Film Co-op, Ont (founder, pres & dir, 68-).
Publications: Contribr, Chambers, Coach House Press, 67; auth, Perceptual Realism, Arts Can, 69; auth, articles, In: Art in Am & Arts Int, 70; contribr, Modern Canadian Painting, McClelland & Stewart Ltd, 72; auth, article on perceptualism, Arts & Artists, London, 12/72.
Mailing Address: c/o Nancy Poole's Studio Ltd, 554 Waterloo St, London 14, Ont, Can.

CHAMNESS, RUBY HILL
Painter
b St John, Ill, June 11, 00.
Study & Training: Mason Col Music & Fine Arts; Morris Harvey

Col; also with Leo Manso, New York & watercolor with Fred Messersmith, Stetson Univ.
Work in Public Collections: Charleston Art Gallery; U S Embassy Montevideo, Uruguay; painting, Nat Mus, Brazil.
Exhibitions: Butler Inst Am Art, Youngstown, Ohio, 57; one-man show, W Va State Col, 59; W Va Centennial Exhib & Exhibition 180, Huntington Galleries, 63; Art in the Embassies Prog, Sofia, Bulgaria & Columbo, Ceylon, 67; Exhibit 280, Huntington, W Va, 72.
Awards: Award for Pale Moon, Yellow Moon, Exhibition 180, Huntington Galleries, 63; purchase award for Silhouette, Allied Artists W Va, 67.
Memberships: Allied Artists W Va; Tri-State Art Asn, Huntington.
Mailing Address: 4212 Staunton Ave S E, Charleston, WV 25304.

CHANDLER, ELISABETH GORDON
Sculptor
Preferred Media: Bronze, Marble.
b St Louis, Mo, June 10, 13.
Study & Training: Pvt study with Edmondo Quattrocchi; anatomy at Art Stud League New York.
Work in Public Collections: Columbia Univ Sch Law, New York, N Y; Sch Pub & Int Affairs, Princeton Univ; Aircraft Carrier U S S Forrestal; Gov Dummer Acad Libr; Storm King Art Ctr, Mountainville, N Y.
Commissions: Forrestal Mem Award Medal, Nat Security Indust Asn, 54; portrait bust of James L Collins, comn by estate for James L Collins Parochial sch, Corsicana, Tex, 55; Timoshenko Medal for Applied Mechanics, Am Soc Mech Engrs, 56; Benjamin Franklin Medal, New York Univ Hall of Fame, 62; bust of Owen R Cheatham, Founder, Entrance Hall, Georgia Pacific Corp, Portland, Ore, 70.
Exhibitions: Mattituck Mus, Waterbury, Conn, 49; Nat Acad Design Ann, New York, 50-72; Nat Sculpture Soc Ann, 53-72; Acad Artists, Springfield, Mass, 61; Smithsonian Inst, Washington, D C, 63.
Positions: Dir, Coun Am Artist Socs, 71-
Awards: First prize, Brooklyn War Mem Competition, 45; Thomas R Proctor Prize, 56 & Dessie Greer Prize, 60, Nat Acad Design.
Memberships: Fel Nat Sculpture Soc; fel Int Inst Arts & Lett; fel Am Artists Prof League (dir, 71-); Nat Arts Club; Pen & Brush Club.
Mailing Address: Mill Pond Lane, Old Lyme, CT 06371.

CHANDLER, JOHN WILLIAM
Painter, Educator
b Concord, N H, Sept 28, 10.
Study & Training: Exeter Sch Art, Boston; Manchester Inst Arts & Sci; St Anselms Col, AB; Boston Univ, scholar, 59-60, EdM; Harvard Univ; Columbia Univ; study in Europe & with Aldro T Hibbard.
Work in Public Collections: Pvt collections only.
Exhibitions: Represented N H in Pasadena Nat, 46; Currier Gallery Art Regional, 47; one-man show, Keene State Col, 51; De Cordova & Dana Mus, 52; Nebraska Wesleyan Univ, 58.
Collections Arranged: Cataloged Richard J Healey Collection, Currier Gallery Art.
Teaching: Exec dir & instr design & painting, Manchester Inst Arts & Sci, 33-46; assoc prof art & head dept, Lycoming Col, 52-70; instr painting, Concord Artists, Inc, 71-
Positions: From asst to dir to actg dir, Currier Gallery Art, 42-52.
Awards: First watercolor award, Currier Gallery Art, 47; Danforth Found Award, 52.
Memberships: Concord Artists (founding mem); N H Art Asn (charter mem & former pres).
Publications: Auth, various articles on glass & silver.
Mailing Address: 2 Coolidge Ave, Concord, NH 03301.

CHAPELLIER, GEORGE
Art Dealer, Collector
b Liege, Belg, 1890.
Collections Arranged: Exhibs since 1930: G E Browne, I R Wiles, C K Chatterton, E Glicenstein, Robert Henri, Edward Potthast, Charles Schreyvogel & W M Chase.
Positions: Dir, Chapellier Galleries, New York, N Y.
Specialty of Gallery: American art, 1850-1930.
Mailing Address: Chapellier Galleries, 22 E 80th St, New York, NY 10021.

CHAPELLIER, ROBERT
Art Dealer
b Brussels, Belg.
Study & Training: N Y Univ; Brooklyn Polytech Inst; State Univ N Y, PE.
Positions: Partner, Chapellier Galleries; mem adv coun, Caramoor; mem N Y Coun Hofstra Univ.

Memberships: Assoc Inst Conserv Hist & Artistic Works.
Specialty of Gallery: American art, 1850-1930.
Mailing Address: 22 E 80th St, New York, NY 10021.

CHAPIAN, GRIEG HOVSEP
Painter, Lecturer
Preferred Media: Oils.
b Varna, Bulgaria, May 27, 13; U S citizen.
Study & Training: Cooper Union, 30-31; Nat Acad Design, 31-36, with Leon Kroll, Karl Anderson, Charles C Curran, Arthur S Covey, Francis Scott Bradford, Jr, Gifford Beal, Charles S Chapman & Ivan Olinsky.
Commissions: Two murals for Auto Racing Syndicate, Johannesburg, S Africa, 39.
Exhibitions: Allied Artists Am, New York, N Y, 36; Pa Acad Fine Arts, Philadelphia, 37; First Nat Wartime Art Show, Camden, N J, 44; N Mex State Fair Art Exhib, Albuquerque, 71; Grand Nat Exhib, Am Artists Prof League, New York, 72.
Teaching: Dir hist art & landscape, Murray Art Schs, Scranton & Wilkes-Barre, Pa, 48-50; dean & dir figure drawing & painting, Cooper Sch Art, Cleveland, 50-55; dean fashion illus & philos of art, Pan-Am Art Sch, New York, 60-66.
Positions: Mem bd dir, N Mex Art League, 69-71.
Awards: Grand prize & first for oils, Local 1, CIO, 44; first for oils & best of show for graphics, N Mex Art League, 69.
Bibliography: Flo Wilks (auth), Magic realism in noted artist's work reflects his wide range of interests, Albuquerque J, 6/14/70.
Memberships: Am Artists Prof League; Southwest Watercolor Soc; Artists Equity Asn; Nat Art League.
Dealer: Mesilla Gallery, P O Drawer 486, Mesilla Park, NM 88047.
Mailing Address: 1850 Gretta St N E, Albuquerque, NM 87112.

CHAPIN, LOUIS (LE BOURGEOIS)
Writer, Art Critic
b Brooklyn, N Y, Feb 6, 18.
Study & Training: Principia Col, BA; Boston Univ, AM.
Teaching: Asst prof fine arts, Principia Col, 46-60.
Positions: Staff critic, Christian Sci Monitor, 60-66; dir, The Earl Rowland Found, New York, 67-; theater critic, Christianity & Crisis, New York, 70-
Art Interests: Audio filmstrips documenting major art exhibitions.
Publications: Contribr, Music at the Cross-roads, Macmillan; auth, numerous reviews & articles in nat publ.
Mailing Address: 444 E 20th St, New York, NY 10009.

CHAPLIN, GEORGE EDWIN
Painter, Educator
Preferred Media: Oil.
b Kew Gardens, N Y, Aug 30, 31.
Study & Training: Yale Univ Sch Art, BFA & MFA, with Josef Albers.
Work in Public Collections: Yale Univ Gallery, New Haven, Conn; State Univ N Y Cortland.
Exhibitions: Feingarten Galleries, Los Angeles, Calif, 64-65; Bednarz Galleries, Los Angeles & La Jolla Mus, Calif, 67; State Univ N Y Cortland, 69; Silvermine Guild Artists, New Canaan, Conn, 71.
Teaching: Head dept painting, Silvermine Col Art, 65-71; dir studio prog, Trinity Col, Hartford, Conn, 72-
Mailing Address: Box 488, ORS, Oxford, CT 06483.

CHAPMAN, ALTON JAMES, see ALJAMAN

CHAPMAN, DAVE
Designer
b Gilman, Ill, Jan 30, 09.
Study & Training: Armour Inst Technol, BS, 32.
Teaching: Lectr phases of indust design.
Positions: Head prod design div, Montgomery Ward & Co, 34-36; sr partner, Dave Chapman, Indust Design, 36-58; pres, Design Res, Inc, 55-; pres, Dave Chapman Design, Inc, 58-
Awards: Design award medal, Indust Designers Inst, 54 & 60; numerous awards & citations, Am Inst Graphic Arts, Soc Typographic Arts & Art Dirs Club.
Memberships: Fel Am Soc Indust Designer (bd dirs & past pres); life mem Art Inst Chicago; Soc Typographic Arts; Benjamin Franklin fel Royal Soc Arts; fel Int Inst Arts & Lett.
Mailing Address: 3240 N Lake Shore Dr, Chicago, IL 60657.

CHAPMAN, MRS GILBERT W
Collector, Patron
b Evanston, Ill.
Study & Training: Atelier Julien, Paris, France; Art Inst Chicago; also with Fernand Leger.
Positions: Pres, Art Club Chicago, 31-40.
Memberships: Int Coun Mus Mod Art, New York; fel Metrop Mus Art, New York; fel Pierpont Morgan Libr; Whitney Mus Am Art; Mus Primitive Art.

Collection: Modern art; Polynesian art; pre-Columbian art.
Mailing Address: 1 Sutton Pl S, New York, NY 10022.

CHAPMAN, HOWARD EUGENE
Designer, Cartoonist
b Martinsburg, W Va, Dec 20, 13.
Study & Training: Corcoran Sch Art, with Richard Lahey; George Washington Univ, BS; Tiffany Found, with Hobart Nichols.
Work in Public Collections: Corcoran Gallery Art.
Positions: Art dir, Cong Quart Serv, Inc, Washington, D C; creator & dir, Asn Art Aids, Alexandria, Va; creator self-syndicated daily comic panel, Federal Fidgets; designer, publ, ed graphics, bk covers, direct mail promotion, ed cartoons & caricatures.
Awards: Prize, Washington Co Mus Fine Arts, Hagerstown, Md, 39; Tiffany Found scholar; bronze medal, Washington Art Club, 48.
Mailing Address: 3213 Wessynton Way, Alexandria, VA 22309.

CHAPPELL, WARREN
Illustrator, Designer
b Richmond, Va, July 9, 04.
Study & Training: Univ Richmond, BA; Art Stud League New York; Offenbacher Werkstatt, Ger; Colo Springs Fine Arts Ctr; also with George Bridgman, Allen Lewis, Boardman Robinson & Rudolf Koch; Univ Richmond, hon DFA, 68.
Work in Public Collections: Newberry Libr, Chicago, Ill; Alderman Libr, Charlottesville, Va; New York Pub Libr, N Y.
Teaching: Instr drawing & graphic arts, Art Stud League New York, 32-35; instr drawing & graphic arts, Colo Springs Fine Arts Ctr, 35-36.
Awards: Goudy Award, Rochester Inst Technol, 70.
Bibliography: Isabel Bishop (auth), foreword to Sixty-three drawings by Warren Chappell, The Typophiles (New York), 55.
Publications: Auth, The anatomy of lettering, Loring & Mussey, 35; illusr, The temptation of Saint Anthony, Ltd Ed Club, 43; illusr, The history of Tom Jones, Illus Mod Libr, 43; illusr, The complete novels of Jane Austen, Random House, 50; auth, A short history of the printed word, New York Times, 70.
Mailing Address: James St, R R 3, Norwalk, CT 06850.

CHAPPS, JOHN
Sculptor
b Hartford, Conn, Dec 23, 41.
Study & Training: R I Sch Design, 59-61; Univ Hartford, with Wolfgang Behl, 61-65, BFA, 65; Rinehart Sch Sculpture, Md Inst, MFA, 67.
Exhibitions: Work has been widely exhibited in regional galleries.
Teaching: Instr design & drawing, Minneapolis Col Art & Design, 67-70; asst prof sculpture, Md Inst, 70-
Mailing Address: 68 Sequin St, Newington, CT 06111.

CHARLES, CLAYTON (HENRY)
Sculptor, Educator
b Goodman, Wis, Sept 11, 13.
Study & Training: Univ Wis, BA & MA, with Wolfgang Stechow, Oskar Hagen, John Kienitz & James Watrous.
Work in Public Collections: IBM Collection; City of Milwaukee; Univ Wis; Beloit Col; Gimbel's Wis Collection; plus others.
Exhibitions: Grand Central Art Galleries; Art Inst Chicago; Wis Salon; Milwaukee Art Inst; Gimbel's.
Teaching: Educ dir, Milwaukee Art Inst, 46-47; assoc prof, Beloit Col, 47-49, chmn dept art, 49-51; prof art, Univ Miami, 51-
Awards: Wis Salon, 47; Milwaukee Art Inst, 50; Assoc Fla Sculptors, 61; plus others.
Mailing Address: Dept of Art, Univ Miami, Coral Gables, FL 33124.

CHARLOT, JEAN
Painter, Art Historian
b Paris, France, Feb 7, 98; U S citizen.
Work in Public Collections: Metrop Mus Art & Mus Mod Art, New York, N Y; Philadelphia Mus Art, Pa; Mus Arte Mod, Mex; Acad Arts, Honolulu, Hawaii.
Commissions: Fresco, comn by Mex Govt, Escuela Preparatoria, Mexico City, 22; fresco, Univ Ga, Athens, 44; fresco, Tempe, Ariz, 51; fresco, First Nat Bank, Hawaii, 66; ceramic sculpture, Ala Moana Hotel, Honolulu, 71; plus others.
Exhibitions: One-man show, Palace of Legion of Honor, San Francisco, Calif, 42; Smith Col Mus, 48; Fifty Years Retrospective, 1916-1966, Honolulu Acad Arts, 66; one-man show, U S Cult Ctr, Maracaibo, Venezuela, 67; retrospective at Mus Arte Mod, Mexico City (cult event for Olympics), 68.
Teaching: Instr painting, Art Stud League New York, 33-42; artist-in-residence, Univ Ga, 42-44; vis prof painting, Smith Col, 44-45; Ryerson lectr, Yale Univ, 47; dir art sch, Colo Springs Fine Arts Ctr, 47-49; sr prof painting & art hist, Univ Hawaii, 49-67, emer sr prof, 67-

Awards: Guggenheim fel, 45-47; fel in perpetuity, Metrop Mus Art, 60; sr specialist, E-W Ctr, U S Govt, 67; Nat Coun Arts grant, 68.
Bibliography: Charlot murals in Georgia, Univ Ga Press, 45; George Tahara (producer), three films, For: Cine-Pic & Syracuse Univ, 55, 60 & 72.
Memberships: Benjamin Franklin fel Royal Soc Arts; Col Art Asn Am; Hawaiian Hist Soc; Hawaiian Painters & Sculptors.
Research: Hawaiian historical research; archaeology of Yucatan; Mexican art both colonial and modern.
Collection: Mexican pre-Hispanic; Pacific Island artifacts; modern art.
Publications: Co-auth, The temple of the warriors at Chichen Itza, Carnegie Inst of Washington, 29; auth, Mexican art and the Academy of San Carlos, Univ Tex Press, 62; auth, Mexican mural renaissance: 1920-1925, Yale Univ Press, 63; auth, Three plays of ancient Hawaii, Univ Hawaii Press, 63; An artist on art, Univ Hawaii Press, 72.
Mailing Address: 4956 Kahala Ave, Honolulu, HI 96816.

CHASE, ALICE ELIZABETH
Educator, Writer
b Ware, Mass, Apr 13, 06.
Study & Training: Radcliffe Col, with G H Edgell & P J Sachs, AB; Yale Univ, with Henri Focillon, Sumner Crosby & G H Hamilton, MA.
Teaching: Lectr iconography hist art; docent, art gallery, Yale Univ, 31-, asst prof hist art, 46-70, emer prof, 70-
Positions: Cur educ, Brooklyn Mus, 46-47.
Awards: Citations, Wilson Col & Radcliffe Col, 69.
Memberships: Soc Archit Historians; Archaeol Inst Am; Col Art Asn Am.
Publications: Auth, Famous paintings, an introduction to art for young people, 51, rev ed, 61 & 62 & Famous artists of the past, 64, Platt; auth, Looking at art, Crowell, 66.
Mailing Address: 18 Pleasant St, Ware, MA 01082.

CHASE, ALLAN (SEAMANS)
Sculptor, Designer
Preferred Media: Steel, other metals.
Study & Training: Univ Ga, BFA.
Commissions: Brass on steel, Sherwood Theatre, Gainesville, Ga, 66; brass on steel, Oxford Chem Co, Atlanta, Ga, 67; welded steel, Woodward Acad, College Park, Atlanta, 68; five steel murals, Gi-Gi's Restaurant, Rochester, N Y & six steel & polyester murals, St Petersburg, Fla, 71.
Exhibitions: Fifth Biennial Nat Relig Art Exhib, Bloomfield, Mich, 66; Southeastern Ann Exhib, Atlanta, 66 & 68; Piedmont Park Arts Festival, Atlanta, 66-72; Mus Arts & Sci, Macon, Ga, 67.
Positions: Designer, Gi-Gi's Restaurants, Tampa, Fla, Atlanta & Athens, Ga & Rochester, N Y, 65-
Memberships: High Mus Art, Atlanta.
Art Interests: Reflective quality of metal as an art media.
Dealer: Joseph Coggins, North Lake Mall, Collectors Cove, Atlanta, GA 30340.
Mailing Address: 5435 Peachtree Rd, Atlanta, GA 30341.

CHASE, DORIS (TOTTEN)
Sculptor, Film Maker
b Seattle, Wash, Apr 29, 23.
Study & Training: Univ Wash; also with Mark Tobey.
Work in Public Collections: Mus Mod Art, Kobe, Japan; Art Inst Chicago; Pa Acad Fine Arts, Philadelphia; Nat Collection Fine Arts, Washington, D C; Mus Fine Arts, Boston, Mass; plus many others.
Commissions: Monumental Kinetic Sculpture, Expo '70, Osaka, Japan, Atlanta Sculpture Park, Ga, Kerry Park, Seattle, Wash & four ballets, Seattle Opera Asn, Wash; Play-Ground of Tomorrow, Los Angeles, Calif.
Exhibitions: One-man shows, Ruth White Gallery, New York, N Y, 67, 69 & 70, Formes Gallery, Tokyo, Japan, 63 & 70, Henry Gallery, Univ Wash, Seattle, 71 & Western Mus Asn Circulating Exhib, 70-72; Wadsworth Atheneum, Hartford, Conn, 73; plus many other one-man and group shows.
Bibliography: Article, In: Geijutsh-Schincho, Tokyo, 4/70; Robert Heyer & Richard Payne (auth), Discovery Patterns, S I Paulist-Newman, 71; Louis Chapin (auth), article, In: Christian Sci Monitor, 2/10/71; plus many others.
Publications: (Films) The expanding universe of sculpture, Hartley Prod; Mantra, ABC TV, Seattle; Doris Chase - sculpture on the move, William Jenson Prod; Tondo, King Screen; Circles II (computer animated), Creative Film Soc.
Mailing Address: 6801 17th N E, Seattle, WA 98115.

CHASE, JEANNE NORMAN
Painter
b Spokane, Wash.
Study & Training: San Fernando State Col, BA(fine arts), 59.

Work in Public Collections: Bendix Avionics Corp; J Morris Stone Assocs; incl in over 400 pub & pvt collections throughout U S.
Exhibitions: Fort Lauderdale Mus Arts, Fla, 68; Music in Art Exhib, Collection of Dr Artine Artinian, Henry Flagler Mus, Palm Beach, Fla, 72; Art for Heart, United Fund, Broward Co Invitational, 72; one-woman exhib, Upstairs Gallery, Erie, Pa, 72; Four Women Artists, Parker Playhouse, Fort Lauderdale, Fla, 73; plus others.
Awards: Drawing award, Fort Lauderdale Mus, 68; second place in painting, Coconut Grove Art Festival, 72; first prize in drawing, Gold Coast Art Exhib, 72.
Bibliography: Mary Lavarett (auth), A fund of art, Fort Lauderdale Mag, 11/71.
Memberships: Lauderdale-by-the-Sea Art Guild; Boca Raton Art Guild.
Mailing Address: 440 N E Third Ave, Fort Lauderdale, FL 33301.

CHASE, SAUL ALAN
Painter
Preferred Media: Acrylics.
b New York, N Y, Apr 7, 45.
Study & Training: City Col New York, BFA, 65, MFA, 68.
Work in Public Collections: Detroit Inst Art, Mich; Ga Mus Art, Univ Ga, Athens; Brooklyn Mus Art, N Y; Sara Roby Found, New York; Univ Wyo Mus Art, Laramie.
Exhibitions: Nat Acad Design Ann, 69 & 72; Childe Hassam Purchase Award Exhib, 71; Trends in Realism, St Mary's Col Md, 72; Audubon Artists Soc Ann, 72; Butler Art Inst Midyear Exhib, 72.
Awards: S J Wallace Truman Prize, Nat Acad Design, 69 & 72; Salmagundi Club Award, Audubon Artists, 72.
Dealer: ACA Galleries, 25 E 73rd St, New York, NY 10021.
Mailing Address: 152 Wooster St, New York, NY 10012.

CHASE-RIBOUD, BARBARA DEWAYNE
Sculptor
Preferred Media: Cast Bronze, Cast Aluminum.
b U S, June 26, 39.
Study & Training: Temple Univ, BFA; Yale Univ, MFA.
Work in Public Collections: Mus Mod Art, New York, N Y; Berkeley Mus, Univ Calif; Newark Mus, N J; Inst Contemp Arts, Mus Mod Art, Paris, France; Geigy Found, New York.
Commissions: Aluminum wall relief, Pierre Simon, New York; bronze & silk wall relief, Keystone Bldg, Boston, Mass; aluminum screen fountain, Wheaton Plaza Ctr, Washington, D C; forged steel sculptures, Pierre Cardin, Paris; cast bronze sculpture, Boussois-Souchon-Neuvecelle, Paris.
Exhibitions: Festival of Two Worlds, Speleto Int, 58; Carnegie Inst Int, Pittsburgh, Pa, 59; Drawing & Painting Nat, Pa Acad, 59; Salon de Mai, Mus Mod Art, Paris, 71-72; Whitney Sculpture Ann, New York, 72.
Awards: Philadelphia Art Alliance Purchase Prize, 57; John Hay Whitney Found fel, 58; Nat Endowment Arts individual grant, 73.
Bibliography: Alvin Yudkoff (auth), Five, Silvermine Films, 72; Françoise Nora (auth), Another country, Art News, 72; Sam Hunter (auth), American sculpture, Abrams, 73.
Dealer: Betty Parsons Gallery, 24 W 57th St, New York, NY 10019.
Mailing Address: 199, Rue de Vaugirard, 75015 Paris, France.

CHATTERTON, CLARENCE KERR
Painter
Preferred Media: Oils, Watercolors, Gouache.
b Newburgh, N Y, Sept 19, 80.
Study & Training: New York Sch Art, 1900-1904, with William M Chase, Robert Henri, Luis Mora & Kenneth Hayes Miller.
Work in Public Collections: Brooklyn Mus; Nat Collection Fine Arts, Smithsonian Inst; Sheldon Mus, Omaha, Nebr; Canajoharie Mus; Vassar Col.
Exhibitions: First Nat Exhib Am Art at Rockefeller Ctr, New York, N Y, 36; Carnegie Inst Int Exhib, Pittsburgh, Pa, 36, 41 & 43; Golden Gate Expos, San Francisco, Calif, 40; Corcoran Gallery Art, Washington, D C, 41-43; one-man exhibs, Chapellier Gallery, New York, 65 & 70; plus many others.
Teaching: Prof art & artist-in-residence, Vassar Col, 15-48.
Awards: Isidor prize for best work in watercolor, Salmagundi Club, 13; honored by Hudson Valley Art Asn, 69.
Bibliography: Articles, In: New York Times, 4/12/36, New York Herald Tribune, 11/6/65, & Vassar Alumnae Mag, 2/66; plus many others.
Mailing Address: c/o Chapellier Gallery, 22 E 80th St, New York, NY 10021.

CHAUDHURI, PATRICIA M
Sculptor, Painter
b New York, N Y, July 6, 26.
Study & Training: Simmons Col, BS; Boston Mus Fine Arts, five year cert, painting with Karl Zerbe & David Aronson; summer schol-

ars, Skowhegan Sch Painting & Sculpture, 51 & Yale Summer Art Sch, 52; also sculpture with George Demetios.
Exhibitions: Painting, Boston Arts Festival, 55 & sculpture, 63; sculpture, Nat Acad Design Am Ann Exhib, 61 & 63; New Eng Sculpture Asn, 69-71.
Teaching: Instr stone carving & nature drawing, De Cordova & Dana Mus, Lincoln, Mass, 71-; instr wood carving, Millbrook Art Ctr, Arlington, 71-
Awards: Louis T Comfort Tiffany Award for Sculpture, 61.
Bibliography: Nat Sculpture Rev, summer, fall & winter, 70.
Memberships: Nat Sculpture Soc; New Eng Sculptor's Asn (recording secy, 69-70, v pres, 71-72).
Mailing Address: Deer Foot Trail, Harvard, MA 01451.

CHAVEZ, EDWARD ARCENIO
Painter, Sculptor
b Wagonmound, N Mex, Mar 14, 17.
Study & Training: Colo Springs Fine Arts Ctr, Colo with Boardman Robinson, Frank Mechau, Arnold Blanch & Peppino Mangravite; painting grants, Tiffany Found, 48, Fulbright, Inst Int Educ, Italy, 51.
Work in Public Collections: Libr Congress Print Collection, Washington, D C; Watkins Gallery, Washington, D C; Mus Mod Art, New York, N Y; Detroit Mus Art, Mich; Butler Inst Am Art, Youngstown, Ohio.
Commissions: Murals, Govt Art Com, Post Office, Center, Tex, 38, Post Office, Geneva, Nebr; Post Office, Glenwood Springs, Colo, West High Sch, Denver, Colo; mural, U S A 200th Sta Hosp, Recife, Brazil.
Exhibitions: Nat Inst Arts & Lett, New York; Whitney Mus Am Art, New York; Nat Acad Design, New York; Pa Acad Art Ann, Philadelphia; Am Art Exhib, Metrop Mus Art, New York.
Teaching: Instr painting, Art Stud League New York, 54-58; vis. prof art, Colo Col Art Dept, Colorado Springs, 59-60; prof art, Syracuse Univ Sch Art, 60-62.
Awards: Childe Hassam Award, for painting, Nat Inst Arts & Let, 53.
Memberships: Woodstock Art Asn (chmn, 49-); academician Nat Acad Design.
Mailing Address: 32 Plochman Lane, Woodstock, NY 12498.

CHEE, MAY
Potter
b Honolulu, Hawaii, May 31, 21.
Study & Training: Univ Hawaii, with Claude Horan & Harue McVay.
Work in Public Collections: Hawaii State Found Cult & Arts; Hawaii State Dept Educ.
Exhibitions: Hawaii Craftsman Ann, 68-70; one-man show, Contemp Arts Ctr Hawaii, 71; Windward Artists Guild Easter Ann, 72; Honolulu Acad Arts, 72.
Awards: Purchase award, Hawaii Found Cult & Arts, 68; Gima Award, Windward Artists Guild, 72.
Memberships: Hawaii Potters Guild; Hawaii Craftsmen.
Dealer: Daisy, Contemporary Arts Gallery, 463 Kapahulu, Honolulu, HI 96815.
Mailing Address: 2633 Anuenue, Honolulu, HI 96822.

CHENEY, SHELDON
Writer, Art Historian
b Berkeley, Calif, June 29, 86.
Study & Training: Univ Calif, Berkeley, AB; Calf Sch Arts & Crafts; Harvard Univ.
Teaching: Hon fel in art, Union Col, 37-40.
Memberships: Benjamin Franklin fel, Royal Soc Arts; Am Fedn Arts; Authors League Am; Soc Am Historians; Univ Art Mus Coun, Univ Calif, Berkeley.
Research: Theatre arts; sculpture; modern painting.
Publications: Auth, a new world history of art, 56; auth, The story of modern art, 58; auth, Sculpture of the world: a history, 68; auth, The theatre, 72; contribr to many magazines, symposia, encyclopedias & others.
Mailing Address: 12 Stony Hill Rd, New Hope, PA 18938.

CHEREPOV, GEORGE
Painter, Instructor
Preferred Media: Oils.
b Lithuania, Mar 28, 09; U S citizen.
Study & Training: With profs Konstantin Wisotzky, Riga, Latvia & Aalexis Hansen, Dubrovnic, Yugoslavia.
Work in Public Collections: Mus, Kempten, W Ger; Town Hall, Memmingen, W Ger; State Bank, Munich W Ger; Stamford Mus, Conn; Mus of Art, Tucson, Ariz.
Exhibitions: Allied Artists Am, New York, N Y; Acad Artists Asn, Springfield, Mass; Southern Vt Art Ctr, Manchester; Grand Cent Art Galleries New York; Hudson Valley Art Asn.
Teaching: Art instr, Greenwich Art Ctr, Conn, 55-57; art instr Westchester Co Ctr, White Plains, N Y, 61-67; art instr, Scarsdale Adult Educ, 62-70.

Awards: Best in Show, First Award, Allied Artists Am, 68; gold
medal, Hudson Valley Art Asn, 69; medal of honor, Kent Art Asn,
Conn, 71.
Memberships: Fel Allied Artists Am; Hudson Valley Art Asn(mem
bd dirs); Acad Artists Asn; Grand Cent Art Galleries; Southern
Vt Art Ctr.
Publications: Auth, Discovering oil painting, 71.
Dealer: Grand Central Art Galleries, Biltmore Hotel, 40 Vanderbilt
Ave, New York, NY 10017.
Mailing Address: 1050 King St, Greenwich, CT 06830.

CHERMAYEFF, IVAN
Designer, Painter
b London, Eng, June 6, 32; U S citizen.
Study & Training: Harvard Univ, 50-52; Inst Design, Ill Inst Technol, four Moholy-Nagy scholarships, 52-54; Yale Univ Sch Design, Mohawk Paper Co fel, BFA, 55.
Commissions: Moveable Paintings (mounted on tracks), Gen Fire-
proofing Co Showroom, New York, N Y, 66; Exploding Triangles
(shaped canvases), IBM Data Processing Hq, Harrison, N Y, 70;
Dimensional Abstractions (plastic laminate wall constructions),
Bartholomew Consolidated Sch Corp, Columbus, Ind, 71; Abstrac-
tion (Aubusson tapestry), Westinghouse Elec Corp, Pittsburgh, Pa,
72; Metal Construction (wall with painted steel components), Am
Repub Ins Co, Des Moines, Iowa.
Exhibitions: One-man show, Gimpel-Weitzenhoffer, New York, 71;
First Am Biennial Graphic Arts, Columbia, S Am, 71; Art from
Industry Sculpture Show, Butler Inst Am Art, Youngstown, Ohio,
71; Venice Biennale, 72.
Teaching: Instr design, Brooklyn Col, 56-57; instr design, Sch
Visual Arts, 59-65.
Positions: Partner, Brownjohn, Chermayeff & Geismar, 57-60;
partner, Chermayeff & Geismar Assocs, 60-; partner, Cambridge
Seven Assocs, 63-; trustee & comt mem painting & sculpture,
film, design, Mus Mod Art, New York, 65-; v pres, Yale Arts
Asn, 68-; mem comt arts & archit, Yale Univ Coun, 71-; mem
comt arts & archit, Harvard Univ Bd Overseers, 72-
Awards: Indust arts medal, Am Inst Architects, 67; gold medal,
Philadelphia Col Art, 71.
Bibliography: Douglas Davis (auth), article, In: Newsweek Mag, 71.
Memberships: Am Inst Graphic Arts (v pres, pres, bd dirs, 60-);
Int Design Conf Aspen (v pres, co-chmn, bd dirs, 67-); Indust
Designers Soc Am; Alliance Graphique Int; Benjamin Franklin fel
Royal Soc Arts; plus one other.
Publications: Illusr, The Thinking book, Keep it like a secret, The
new nutcracker suite & Blind mice and other numbers; auth, Ob-
servations on American architecture, Viking Press, 72.
Dealers: Gimpel-Weitzenhoffer Galleries, 1040 Madison Ave, New
York, NY 10021; Pace Editions, 115 E 23rd St, New York, NY
10010.
Mailing Address: 830 Third Ave, New York, NY 10022.

CHERNER, NORMAN
Designer
b New York, N Y, June 7, 20.
Study & Training: New York Sch Fine & Appl Arts; Columbia Univ,
BS, MA.
Exhibitions: Inst Contemp Arts, Boston, Mass; Akron Art Inst, Ohio;
Mus Fine Arts, Houston, Tex; Brooklyn Mus Art, N Y; traveling
exhib archit interiors, Am Fedn Arts-Archit League, 61; plus
many other group & one-man shows.
Teaching: Instr design, Mus Mod Art, New York & Fieldston Sch
Indust Design, 46-49; instr design, Teachers Col, Columbia Univ,
49-53; lectr design City Col New York & New York Pub Libr, N Y.
Positions: Design consult, Helikon Furniture Corp; dir, Norman
Cherner Assoc, New York & Norwalk, Conn, 46-; designer house
for Int Trade Fair, U S Dept Commerce in Vienna, Austria, 58;
design consult, Remington Rand Libr Bur; design consult, Gift &
Art Ctr, New York; design consult, Pilgrim Glass Corp, W Va
Pavilion, New York Worlds Fair, 64-65; continual prog furniture
design, Robert Benjamin Co, Inc; design consult for all hotels,
Marriott Corp, Washington, D C, 68-; design consult, Rudin Mgt
Co, Inc, 72; pres, Westport Designs, Inc.
Awards: Work selected as one of best interiors of yr, Interiors Mag.
Publications: Auth, Make your own modern furniture, How to build
children's toys & furniture, How to build under $5,000 &
Fabricating houses from component parts, 57.
Mailing Address: 293 Saugatuck Ave, Westport, CT 06880.

CHERNOW, ANN
Painter, Educator
Preferred Media: Acrylics, Oil, Silkscreen.
b New York, N Y, Feb 1, 36.
Study & Training: Syracuse Univ, 53-55; New York Univ, BS, 57, MA,
69; with Irving Sandler, Jules Olitski, Hale Woodruff & Robert
Kaupelis.
Work in Public Collections: Butler Inst Am Art, Youngstown, Ohio;

Lyman Allyn Mus, New London, Conn; Housatonic Mus Art,
Bridgeport, Conn; Musee de L'Art/Contemporain, Skopje, Yugo-
slavia; Bridgeport Mus Art, Sci & Indust.
Exhibitions: Butler Inst Am Art, 68; one-woman exhibs, Greenwich
Art Soc, Conn & Silvermine Guild Art, New Canaan, Conn, 69;
New Eng Ann, Silvermine Guild Art, 69 & 70; 13 Women Artists,
Westport Weston Arts Coun, Conn, 71.
Teaching: Instr studio work, Mus Mod Art, New York, N Y, 66-70;
art history, Univ Conn, summer 69; painting & drawing, Silver-
mine Col & Silvermine Guild, 68-
Awards: Founders Day Award, New York Univ, 56; Virginia Murphy
Mem Scholar, Sch art league, New York, 57; First prize, painting,
Bridgeport Mus, 67.
Memberships: Silvermine Guild Art; Westport Weston Arts Coun (bd
dir to 70).
Publications: Auth, Prescription for playtime, Co Mag, Conn, 68;
Let's remember, Palette, Mag of Conn Art Asn, 69 & Reuben
Nakian, sculptor, 69.
Dealer: Silvermine Guild of Artists, Silvermine Road, New Canaan,
CT 06840.
Mailing Address: 38 Gorham Ave, Westport, CT 06880.

CHERNOW, BURT
Educator, Museum Director
b New York, N Y, July 28, 33.
Study & Training: New York Univ, BA, 58; MA, 60; with Lawrence
Alloway, Jules Olitski, Irving Sandler & Hale Woodruff.
Work in Public Collections: Jacksonville Mus, Fla; Bridgeport Mus
Art, Sci & Indust, Conn; Col Art Mus, Hampton, Va; Le Musee de
L'Art Contemporain, Skopje, Yugoslavia; Housatonic Mus Con-
temp Art, Bridgeport, Conn.
Exhibitions: New York Univ, Loeb Stud Ctr, N Y; Bridgeport Mus;
U N Pavilion, New York World's Fair, 64-65; U S Info Agency
traveling exhib; Silvermine Guild, New Canaan, Conn.
Collections Arranged: 20th Century American and European Con-
temporary Art, Housatonic Mus Art.
Teaching: Staff, Mus Mod Art, New York, 67-70; chmn art dept,
Housatonic Community Col, Bridgeport, 68-; staff, Silvermine
Guild Artists, 70-
Positions: Mem, Nat Comt Art Educ, 61-64; mem, Inst for Study Art
Educ, 68-70; consult, Col Art Asn, 69-70; consult, writer, Educ
Directions, 68-; dir, Housatonic Mus Contemp Art, 68-
Awards: 1st prize, sculpture, Barnum Art Festival, Bridgeport Mus,
Conn, 60.
Bibliography: M Bishop (auth), For arts sake, Conn Mag, 3/72.
Memberships: Westport-Weston Arts Coun, Conn (bd dir, 69-);
Conn Art Asn (bd dir, 64-65); Silvermine Guild Artists.
Publications: Auth, An interview with Alexander Calder, Sch Arts
Mag, Dec, 63; The college art collection, Jr Col J, Sept, 68; The
new ambiguity, Art Educ J, Jan, 69; Paper, paint & stuff, Vol I
& II, Educ Directions, 69.
Mailing Address: 38 Gorham Ave, Westport, CT 06880.

CHERRY, HERMAN
Painter, Educator
Preferred Media: Oils.
b Atlantic City, N J, Apr 10, 09.
Study & Training: Otis Art Inst; Stud Art League, Los Angeles, with
S McDonald Wright; Art Stud League New York, with Thomas
Hart Benton.
Exhibitions: Metrop Mus Art, New York, N Y; Mod Mus Art, New
York; Pa Acad Fine Arts, Philadelphia; Walker Art Ctr, Minn;
one-man show, Benson Gallery, Bridgehampton, N Y, 72; plus
many other group shows in U S A, Paris, France & Athens,
Greece also many other one-man shows.
Teaching: Univ Miss, 57; Southern Ill Univ, 58; vis prof art, Univ
Calif, Berkeley, 59-65; Univ Sask, summer 63; Colo Col, 64;
artist-in-residence, Univ Ky, 66-67; Univ Ore, 68; Southampton
Col, summer 68, 69 & 70; Univ Minn, 69; New Paltz Col, 70;
Kingsborough Community Col; New York Studio Sch; plus many
lectures on Italian & Fr painters & sculptors & contemp art at
various cols, univs & mus.
Positions: Instr pvt classes; chmn First & Second Nat Art Conf,
Woodstock, N Y, 47-48; mem, Art Proj, Los Angeles.
Bibliography: Article, In: Life Mag; article, In: Arts Mag; Mrs Syd-
ney Janis (auth), Mobiles, Art Int; plus others.
Publications: Assoc ed, Contemporary slides; auth, G I artists in
Italy & France, Numero; auth, The art of the artist, Craft Hori-
zon; auth, Warren Brandt, Art News; auth, article, In: Leonardo;
plus others.
Mailing Address: 121 Mercer St, New York, NY 10012.

CHESNEY, LEE R, JR
Printmaker, Painter
Preferred Media: Intaglio.
b Washington, D C, June 1, 20.
Study & Training: Univ Colo, BFA, 46; Univ Iowa, MFA, 48; Univ

Michoacan, Morelia, Mex; also with James Boyle, James Lechay & Mauricio Lasansky.
Work in Public Collections: Rosenwald Collection, Nat Gallery Art, Washington, D C; Mus Mod Art, New York, N Y; Tate Gallery Art, London, Eng; Bibliot Nat, Paris, France; Nat Gallery Art, Stockholm, Sweden.
Exhibitions: 4th Int Biennale, Bordighera, Italy, 56; Nihon Sosaku Hanga Kyokai Exhib, Japan Print Asn Int Ann, Tokyo & Osaka, 57-71; Two Decades of American Prints—'47-'68, Brooklyn Mus 16th Print Nat, N Y, 68; Epinal Print Invitational Biennial, France, 70-71; Int Print Biennial, Seoul, Korea, 70 & 72.
Teaching: Instr drawing, Univ Iowa, 48-50; prof painting & printmaking, Univ Ill, 50-67; assoc dean fine arts, Univ Southern Calif, 67-72; prof painting & printmaking, Univ Hawaii, 72-
Awards: Fulbright sr res award, 56-57; Francis G Logan Medal for Painting, Art Inst Chicago, 62; Vera List Purchase Award, Soc Am Graphic Artists, 65.
Memberships: Japan Print Asn; Soc Am Graphic Artists; Col Art Asn Am; Los Angeles Printmaking Soc (exec bd, 67-).
Publications: Contribr, Printmaking today, Col Art J, Vol XIX, No 2; contribr, A brief glance at Ukiyo-e and Hanga, Japan Print Quart, winter 67.
Dealer: Comsky Gallery, 8432 Melrose Pl, Los Angeles, CA 90069.
Mailing Address: 2110 Brown Way, Honolulu, HI 96822.

CHESTER, CHARLOTTE WANETTA
Painter, Sculptor
Preferred Media: Oils, Mixed Media, Pastels, Watercolors, Silkscreen.
b Columbus, Ohio.
Study & Training: Capitol Univ; Okla City Univ; Pa Acad Fine Arts, with Blackburn & Sloan; Philadelphia Col Art, with Niebert; also with Eric Irmer, Frankfurt, Ger, two years, Hlena De Hellebrandth, Ned Hergelroth, Cape May, N J, Laimons Eglitis & Emanuel Finkel.
Work in Public Collections: Artist and Space, Nat Air & Space Mus, Smithsonian Inst, Washington, D C; The Barn, Millville, N J; Atlantic City Hall.
Commissions: Many paintings.
Exhibitions: Frankfurt Ger Juried Exhib, 65; juried exhibs, Atlantic City Art Ctr, N J, 65-70 & Cult Art Ctr of Ocean City, 68; Kerr Mus, Okla, 70.
Teaching: Instr advan oil painting, Atlantic Community Col, 68-69; instr art, private studio, 65-70.
Awards: Hon mention for untitled watercolor & cert merit for Abstract #12, Atlantic City Art Ctr, 69; cert merit for oil, Atlantic City Chamber Commerce, 70.
Memberships: Am Fedn Art; League South Jersey Artist (pres, 68-70); Federated Art Asn N J (chmn South Jersey, 71); Green Co Art Asn; Watercolor Soc London.
Publications: Contribr, Yearbook Ocean City, 68.
Mailing Address: 7 S Wyoming Ave, Ventnor, NJ 08406.

CHESTER, DONOVAN T
Painter
Preferred Media: Acrylics.
b Sask, Can.
Study & Training: Univ Sask, Regina; Emma Lake Artists Workshop, 69, with Michael Stiener.
Work in Public Collections: Sask Arts Bd, Regina; Mendel Art Gallery, Saskatoon, Sask; Kitchener-Waterloo Gallery, Ont.
Exhibitions: Saskatchewan: Regina & Saskatoon, Kitchener, Ont, 70; Saskatchewan: Art & Artists, Regina, 71; West '71, Edmonton, Alta, 71.
Awards: Can Coun Arts bursary, 70-71.
Bibliography: T Fenton (auth), Some artists from Regina to Saskatoon, Arts Can, 2/71; K Wilkin (auth), A report from the west, Art in Am, 5/72.
Mailing Address: 3132 Victoria Ave, Regina, Sask S4T 1L2, Can.

CHETHAM, CHARLES
Museum Director
U S citizen.
Teaching: Prof art, Smith Col.
Positions: Dir, Smith Col Mus Art.
Mailing Address: Smith College Museum of Art, Northampton, MA 10160.

CHETHLAHE (DAVID CHETHLAHE PALADIN)
Painter, Designer
Preferred Meida: Acrylics, Sand.
b Chinle, Ariz, Nov 4, 26.
Study & Training: Santa Fe Indian Sch; Art Inst Chicago.
Work in Public Collections: William Penn Mem Mus, Harrisburg, Pa; U S Dept Interior, Washington, D C; U S State Dept, Washington, D C; UNICEF, United Nations, New York, N Y.

Commissions: Sand painted mural, Howard Johnson's, Detroit, Mich, 69; four tapestries, comn by City of Phoenix for Phoenix Civic Plaza, Ariz, 72.
Exhibitions: One-man show, Heard Mus, Phoenix, 68; one-man invitational, William Penn Mem Mus, Harrisburg, 69; Scottsdale Indian Nat, Ariz, 69-72; American Indians Today, Mem Mus, Santa Ana, Calif, 70; one-man show, Martin Gallery, Scottsdale, 71-72.
Teaching: Dir fine arts workshop, Prescott Col, 71-
Awards: Spec purchase award, 69, first prize, 70 & grand prize, 71, Scottsdale Nat.
Bibliography: Peterson (auth), Indian art '70, KAET TV, Phoenix, 70; Jules Power (auth), Chethlahe, Indian artist, Discovery '71, ABC TV, 71; Peterson (auth), 3 Indians, KAET TV, Phoenix, 72.
Memberships: Am Craftsmen Coun; Artists Equity Asn; Am Indian Designer Craftsmen (pres, 68-69); Coun Am Indian Artists.
Dealer: Martin Gallery, 7257 First Ave, Scottsdale, AZ 85251.
Mailing Address: 2206 Sandia, Prescott, AZ 86301.

CHEW, PAUL ALBERT
Art Administrator, Lecturer
b Norristown, Pa, Apr 22, 25.
Study & Training: Univ Pittsburgh, BA, 50, Henry Clay Frick Fine Arts Dept grad assistantship, 50-51, MA, 52; Univ Manchester, Eng, fel, 55-57, PhD, 57.
Collections Arranged: 250 Years of Art in Pennsylvania, 59; One-Man Show: Lawrence Calcagno, 67; Recent Trends in American Art, 69; One-Man Show: Henry Koerner, 71.
Teaching: Instr art hist, Univ Pittsburgh, Greensburg, 63-
Positions: Asst to dir, Carnegie Mus, 52-53; exec to dir, Circulating Exhibs, Mus Mod Art, New York, 53-54; dir, Westmoreland Co Mus Art, 57-
Memberships: Westmoreland Community Concerts, Greensburg (pres); Col Art Asn Am; Am Asn Mus.
Publications: Ed, 250 years of art in Pennsylvania, 59.
Mailing Address: 208 N Maple Ave, Greensburg, PA 15601.

CHI, CHEN
Painter
Preferred Media: Watercolors, Oils.
b Wu-sih, China, May 2, 12.
Study & Training: In China.
Work in Public Collections: Metrop Mus Art, New York, N Y; Pa Acad Fine Arts, Philadelphia; Butler Inst Am Art, Youngstown, Ohio; Fort Worth Art Mus, Tex; Charles & Emma Frye Art Mus, Seattle, Wash.
Exhibitions: American Watercolors, Drawings & Prints, Metrop Mus Art, 52; Four Whitney Mus Am Art Ann, New York, 54-63; 24th Biennial, Corcoran Gallery Art, Washington, D C, 55; Contemporary American Painting & Sculpture, Univ Ill, Urbana, 57; Brooklyn Mus 22nd Int Watercolor Biennial, 63; also one-man exhibs in mus & galleries in the U S, 47-72.
Teaching: Instr watercolor, St Johns Univ, Shanghai, 42-46; vis prof watercolor, Pa State Univ, 59-60; artist-in-residence, city schs, Ogden, Utah, 67; artist-in-residence, Utah State Univ, 71.
Awards: Watercolor of the Year Award, Am Watercolor Soc, 55; Nat Inst Arts & Lett grant for creative work in art, 60; Saltus Gold Medal of Merit, Nat Acad Design, 69.
Memberships: Nat Acad Design (counr, 69-71); Am Watercolor Soc (dir, 56-59); Audubon Artists (dir, 64-69 & 72-); Allied Artists Am (dir, 58-60); Nat Arts Club (gov, 72-).
Publications: Illusr, American cities: Chicago, Collier's Mag, 51; illusr, The magic of Mardi Gras—New Orleans, Collier's Mag, 52; illusr, American cities: San Francisco, Collier's Mag, 52; illusr, A single pebble, In: Readers Digest Condensed Bks, 56; illusr, Pagentry of VIII Winter Olympics, Squaw Valley, Sports Illus, 60; plus others.
Dealer: Grand Central Art Galleries, 40 Vanderbilt Ave, New York, NY 10017.
Mailing Address: 23 Washington Square N, New York, NY 10011.

CHIARA, ALAN ROBERT
Painter
Preferred Media: Watercolors.
b Cleveland, Ohio, May 5, 36.
Study & Training: Cooper Sch Art, Cleveland; Cleveland Inst Art.
Work in Public Collections: Butler Inst Art, Youngstown, Ohio; Springfield Art Mus, Mo; Cent Nat Bank Cleveland; Bethany Col, Lindsborg, Kans; Nat Acad Design, New York, N Y.
Exhibitions: Butler Inst Art, 68; Watercolor U S A, Springfield, Mo, 68; Nat Art Exhib, Wichita, Kans, 70; Nat Acad Design, New York, 71; Am Watercolor Soc, New York, 72.
Positions: Master designer, Am Greetings, Cleveland, 58-70; pres, Chiara Galleries, Cleveland, 69-
Awards: Silver medal award, Am Watercolor Soc, 66; Adolph & Clara Obrig Prize, 67 & William A Paton Prize, 70, Nat Acad Design.

Memberships: Am Watercolor Soc; assoc Nat Acad Design.
Specialty of Gallery: Living American artists.
Publications: Auth, watercolor page, In: Am Artist Mag, 11/67.
Mailing Address: 8316 Glen Oak, Cleveland, OH 44147.

CHIARANDINI, ALBERT
Painter, Instructor
Preferred Media: Oils.
b Udine, Italy, Sept 30, 15; Can citizen.
Study & Training: Ont Col Art; portrait painting with F Challener &
J Alfsen.
Work in Public Collections: Univ Toronto, Holy Blossom Synagogue,
Galleon Collection & Scarborough Gen Hospital, Toronto.
Commissions: Portraits in many pvt collections.
Exhibitions: Royal Can Acad Arts; Ont Soc Artists; Hamilton Art
Gallery Ann.
Teaching: Instr portrait painting, Holy Blossom Synagogue, 62-,
Northern Secondary Sch, Toronto, 63-, Ont Col Art, 66-70.
Bibliography: Pearl McCarthy (auth), Portrait of Mr DeJourno,
Globe & Mail, 62; Sidney Katz (auth), Derelicts, Toronto Daily
Star, 66; The masses, 67 & Forgotten man, 70, The Telegram.
Mailing Address: 72 Bowerbank Dr, Willowdale, Ont, Can.

CHICAGO, JUDY
Painter
b Chicago, Ill, July 20, 39.
Study & Training: Univ Calif, Los Angeles, BA, 62, MA, 64.
Work in Public Collections: Mus Mod Art, New York, N Y; Legion
of Hon.
Exhibitions: Primary Structures, Jewish Mus, New York, 66; Sculp-
ture of the Sixties, Los Angeles Co Mus Art, Calif & Philadel-
phia Mus Art, Pa, 67; West Coast Now, Seattle Art Mus, Port-
land Mus Art & San Francisco Mus Art, 68; one-woman show,
Pasadena Art Mus, 69; Color as Structure, Whitney Mus Am
Art, 70.
Positions: Dir feminist art prog, Calif Inst Arts, Valencia.
Bibliography: Judith Dancoff (producer), Miss Chicago & California
girls (film), 72; Susan Stocking (auth), Thru the feminist looking
glass with Judy Chicago, Los Angeles Times Calendar, 7/72;
Priscilla English (auth), Womanhouse article, New Woman,
3/72.
Art Interests: Sprayed painting on acrylic sheet.
Dealer: Jack Glenn Gallery, 2831 East Coast Hwy, Corona Del
Mar, CA 92625.
Mailing Address: 14120 Van Nuys Blvd, Pacoima, CA 91331.

CHICOINE, RENE
Painter, Instructor
b Montreal, P Q, 1910.
Study & Training: Beaux-Arts, Montreal.
Work in Public Collections: Mus Quebec; Court House, Montreal.
Exhibitions: Regional & nat exhibs, 28-
Teaching: Instr, Ecole Beaux-Arts, Montreal.
Mailing Address: Ecole des Beaux-Arts, Pavillon des Arts, Voir
Université du Québec, Montreal, P Q, Can.

CHIEFFO, CLIFFORD TOBY
Painter, Printmaker
Preferred Media: Graphics.
b New Haven, Conn, July 23, 37.
Study & Training: Southern Conn State Col, BS; Teachers Col, Co-
lumbia Univ, MA.
Work in Public Collections: Baltimore Mus Art; Berkshire Mus Art;
Georgetown Univ; U S State Dept Art in Embassies Prog; Nat
Collection Fine Art, Washington, D C; plus others.
Exhibitions: Corcoran Gallery Art, 63, 65 & 67; Baltimore Mus Art,
65 & 66; Washington Gallery Mod Art, 68; Munson-Williams-
Proctor Inst, Ithaca, N Y, 68; Four American Printmakers, Am
Embassy, Ireland, 68; plus others.
Teaching: Instr painting, drawing & silk-screen, Univ Md; Corcoran
Sch Art; assoc prof fine arts & chmn dept, Georgetown Univ,
presently.
Awards: Teaching fel, Italy, 63; artist-in-residence grant, Am Fedn
Arts, Colo, 65; artist-in-residence grant, Mo Coun Arts, 67;
plus others.
Memberships: Am Soc Aesthet & Art Criticism; Col Art Asn Am.
Publications: Auth, Silk-screen as a fine art, Van Nostrand-Rein-
hold, 67.
Mailing Address: 5412 Nevada Ave N W, Washington, DC 20015.

CHILDS, CATHERINE O, see CATCHI

CHINNI, PETER ANTHONY
Sculptor, Painter
Preferred Media: Bronze, Stainless Steel.
b Mount Kisco, N Y, Mar 21, 28.
Study & Training: Art Stud League New York; Acad Belle Arti,

Rome, Italy; also with Roberto Melli, Rome and Felice Casorati,
Turin.
Work in Public Collections: Whitney Mus Am Art, New York, N Y.
Denver Art Mus, Colo; New Sch Social Res, New York; St Louis
Art Mus, Mo; The Readers Digest Collection, New York.
Exhibitions: Carnegie Int, Pittsburgh, Pa, 64-65; Whitney Mus Am
Art Ann, 64-65; New Sch Social Res, 69; Biennale Roma, 69; Gal-
lery Mod Art, Rome, 70.
Mailing Address: Lungotevere Portuense 158, Rome, Italy 00153.

CHIPP, HERSCHEL BROWNING
Educator, Museum Curator
b New Hampton, Mo, Nov 9, 13.
Study & Training: Univ Calif, Berkeley, BA & MA; Columbia Univ,
PhD; Univ Paris; Fulbright fel to France, 51-52; Belg-Am Educ
Found fel, 52.
Teaching: Chmn art dept, Univ Calif, Berkeley, 61-
Positions: Dir, Univ Art Gallery, Univ Calif, Berkeley, 61-; dir, Am
Exhib, Paris Biennale, 63.
Memberships: Col Art Asn Am (dir, 61-65); Soc Hist Art Fr.
Research: Twentieth century painting and sculpture.
Publications: Auth, Viennese Expressionism, 63, Jugendstil and ex-
pressionism in German posters, 65, Theories of modern art, 68
& Friedrich Hundertwasser, 69; contribr, articles in nat maga-
zines, newspapers & journals.
Mailing Address: Dept of History of Art, University of California,
Berkeley, CA 94720.

CHO, DAVID
Sculptor
b Los Angeles, Calif, Aug 13, 50.
Study & Training: Calif State Univ, Los Angeles, BA, 72.
Work in Public Collections: Long Beach Mus Art, Calif.
Exhibitions: Funk: Cho, Phillips, Tunberg, Downey Art Mus, Calif,
71; Sound Show, Civic Art Gallery, Walnut Creek, Calif, 71; Long
Beach Mus Art 10th Ann, Calif, 72; Small Environments, South-
ern Ill Univ & Wis Art Ctr, Madison, 72.
Awards: Dr & Mrs Maurice Rosenbaum purchase award, 72.
Dealer: Joyce/Jeannette, 11831 S Park Ave, Los Angeles, CA 90066.
Mailing Address: 1787 Sunny Heights Dr, Los Angeles, CA 90065.

CHRIST-JANER, ALBERT WILLIAM
Painter, Printmaker
Preferred Media: Watercolors, Lithography.
b Appleton, Minn, June 13, 10.
Study & Training: St Olaf Col, BA; Art Inst Chicago, with Francis
Chapin; Yale Univ Art Sch; Fogg Art Mus, with Arthur Pope &
Paul Sachs; also spec study with Boardman Robinson & Adolf
Dehn.
Work in Public Collections: Metrop Mus Art & Whitney Mus Am
Art, New York; Phillips Gallery & Libr Cong, Washington, D C;
Brooklyn Mus, N Y; plus others.
Commissions: Lithographs for Int Graphic Art Soc, 70, Asn Am
Artists, 70, Lublin, 71 & New York Graphic Soc, 72.
Exhibitions: Brit Int Print Biennale, 70; Print Club Ann, Philadel-
phia, Pa, 71-; Northwest Printmakers Int, Seattle, Wash, 71;
Boston Printmakers, Mass, 71; Addison Gallery Am Art, An-
dover, Mass, 72; plus one other.
Teaching: Head art dept, Stephens Col, 35-42; head art dept, Mich
State Univ, 42-45; dir, Cranbrook Acad Mus & Libr, 45-47; dir
humanities div, Univ Chicago, 47-52; dir arts ctr, New York
Univ, 52-56; dir sch art, Pa State Univ, 56-58; dean, Pratt Inst
Art Sch, 58-68; dir, Pratt Inst Manhattan Ctr, 68-70; Fuller E
Callaway prof art, Univ Ga, 70-
Awards: Am Philos Soc Award, 68 & 69; Lessing J Rosenwald Pur-
chase Prize, Philadelphia Print Club, 69; Tamarind artist-in-
residence grant, 72; plus others.
Publications: Auth, George Caleb Bingham of Missouri, Dodd, 40;
auth, Boardman Robinson, Univ Chicago Press, 46; auth Eliel
Saarinen: Finnish American architect and educator, Univ Chicago
Press, 48; auth, Art in Child Life, 59; auth, Forms, 68; plus
others.
Dealers: (paintings) Frank Rehn Gallery, 655 Madison Ave, New
York, NY 10021; (prints) Associated American Artists Gallery,
663 Fifth Ave at 52nd St, New York, NY 10022.
Mailing Address: Art Dept, University of Georgia, Athens, GA
30601.

CHRIST-JANER, ARLAND F
Painter, Printmaker
Preferred Media: Graphics.
b Garland, Nebr, Jan 27, 22.
Work in Public Collections: Am Repub Ins Co, Des Moines, Iowa;
Bankers Trust Co, New York, N Y; Hershey Foods Corp, Pa;
Montclair Art Mus, N J; Motion Picture Asn Am, New York.

Exhibitions: Boston Univ, 67; Yale Divinity Sch Visual Arts Festival, New Haven, Conn, 68; Krasner Gallery, New York, 68; Davis Art Gallery, Stephens Col, Columbia, Mo, 69.
Dealers: (prints) Associated American Artists, 663 Fifth Ave, New York, NY 10022 & Nielson Gallery, 179 Newbury St, Boston, MA 02116; (paintings) Krasner Gallery, 1061 Madison Ave, New York, NY 10028.
Mailing Address: College Entrance Examination Board, 888 Seventh Ave, New York, NY 10019.

CHRISTENSEN, ERWIN OTTOMAR
Art Historian, Writer
b St Louis, Mo, June 23, 90.
Study & Training: Armour Inst; Art Inst Chicago, 10-12; Univ Ill, BS(arch), 14; Harvard Univ, MArch, MA.
Teaching: Instr art, Syracuse Univ, 34-36; instr art, Univ Pa, 37-39; instr art, Carl Schurz Found, 39-40; instr art, Coe & Monmouth Cols in art seminar, Nat Gallery Art, 63-69; lectr Am Folk Art, hist of European Art & hist of archit.
Positions: Cur, Index Am Designing & Decorating Artists, Nat Gallery Art, Washington, D C, 46-60; dir publs, Am Asn Mus, 60-, consult, 64-
Publications: Auth, A history of western art, 59; ed, Museums directory, U S & Can, 61; auth, A pictorial history of western art, 64; auth, American crafts & folk arts, 64; auth, A guide to art museums in the U S, 68.
Mailing Address: 9030 Stevens Lane, Lanham, MD 20801.

CHRISTENSEN, HANS-JORGEN THORVALD
Designer, Craftsman
Preferred Media: Sterling Silver, Metals.
b Copenhagen, Denmark, Jan 21, 24.
Study & Training: Sch for Arts & Crafts, Copenhagen, 39-44; apprentice at Georg Jensen Silver; Sch for Arts & Crafts, Copenhagen, dipl, 50; Col Tech Soc, Copenhagen, 51-53; Sch for Arts & Crafts, Oslo, Norway, 52.
Work in Public Collections: Johnson Wax Collection, Objects U S A; silver pieces in pvt collections & churches.
Exhibitions: Expo, Universal & Int Exhib, Brussels, Belg, 58; one-man show, Albright-Knox Art Gallery, Buffalo, N Y, 60; one-man show, Security Trust Co, Rochester, N Y, 69; Johnson Wax Collection, Object U S A, traveled in U S & Europe, 69; Radial 80, Xerox Art Show, Rochester, N Y, 72.
Teaching: Instr design, Sch Arts & Crafts, Copenhagen, 52-54; instr silversmithing & design, Sch Am Craftsmen, Rochester Inst Technol, 54-59; assoc prof, 59-63, prof, 63-
Positions: Head model dept, Georg Jensen Silver, Copenhagen, 52-54.
Awards: Hertz Legazy, King Christian X of Denmark, 44; Damascene Plate of Leo Brom, Utrecht, Huntington Gallery, 55; Rochester Silversmith Guild Award, Mem Art Gallery, Rochester, 60.
Bibliography: Herald Brennan (auth), Why handmade?, Craft Horizon, 5-6/55; Talis Bergmanis (auth), Hans Christensen and the silver pots, Democrat & Chronicle, 68; Lee Nordness (auth), Objects U S A, Viking Press, 70.
Mailing Address: 119 Faircrest Rd, Rochester, NY 14623.

CHRISTIANA, EDWARD
Painter, Instructor
b White Plains, N Y, May 8, 12.
Study & Training: Pratt Inst, dipl; Munson-Williams-Proctor Inst Sch Art, with William C Palmer.
Work in Public Collections: Currier Gallery Art, Manchester, N H; Syracuse Mus Fine Arts, N Y; Columbus Mus Art, Ohio; Albany Inst Hist & Art, N Y; Cooperstown Art Asn, N Y.
Exhibitions: 53rd & 55th Watercolor & Drawing Ann, Art Inst Chicago, 42 & 44; Four Am Watercolor Soc Ann, New York, N Y, 45-50; Audubon Artists, New York, 50; 37th Allied Artists Am Ann, New York, 50; 146th Painting & Sculpture Ann, Pa Acad Fine Arts, Philadelphia, 51.
Teaching: Instr painting, drawing & design, Munson-Williams-Proctor Inst Sch Art, 42-
Awards: William Church Osborn Purchase Prize, Am Watercolor Soc, 49 & 51; award, 27th Ann Exhib, Assoc Artists Syracuse, 54; award, 21st Ann Upper Hudson Exhib, Albany Inst Hist & Art, 56.
Memberships: Cooperstown Art Asn (bd dirs, 50-).
Dealer: Sales & Rental Gallery, Munson-Williams-Proctor Institute, 310 Genesee St, Utica, NY 13502.
Mailing Address: 6 Steuben St, Holland Patent, NY 13354.

CHRISTISON, MURIEL B
Art Administrator, Instructor
b Minneapolis, Minn.
Study & Training: Univ Minn, BA & MA; Univ Paris Inst Art & Archaeol, dipl art hist; Univ Brussels, dipl art hist.

Collections Arranged: The Impressionists & Post-Impressionists, Va, 51; Goya, Va, 53; Masterpieces of Chinese Art, Va, 55; Les Fetes Galantes, Va, 55; Masterpieces of American Silver, Va, 60; Sport & the Horse, Va, 60; Art of India & Southeast Asia, Univ Ill, 63; For Your Home, Univ Ill, 66 & 70; plus many others.
Teaching: Instr art in civilization & Am art, Univ Minn, Minneapolis, 45-47; instr visual awareness, Univ Ill, Champaign, 71-72, instr art museology, 72-
Positions: Head educ dept, Minneapolis Inst Arts, 44-47; assoc dir, Va Mus Fine Arts, Richmond, 48-61; consult, Ark Art Ctr, Ill Art Coun & Ill Off Pub Instr, 61-; assoc dir & oper dir, Krannert Art Mus, Champaign, 62-71, actg dir, 71-
Awards: Carnegie scholar, Inst Int Educ, 36; C R B fel, Belg-Am Educ Found, 38.
Memberships: Am Asn Mus (constnl comn & state rep, 71-72; Midwest Mus Conf (v pres, 69-); Int Inst Conserv Hist & Artistic Works; Int Coun Mus; Soc Preservation Va Antiq; plus others.
Publications: Auth, Circular on museum education: 7 titles, 51-55; auth, The artmobile, an experiment in education, Art J, 55; auth, Le Museobus du Virginia Museum of Fine Arts, Mus, 55; auth, 25th anniversary in Virginia, 60 & The design game, 71, Mus News; plus others.
Mailing Address: Krannert Art Museum, 500 Peabody Dr, Champaign, IL 61820.

CHRISTMAN, REID AUGUST
Painter
Preferred Media: Oils.
b Brooklyn, N Y, Oct 28, 48.
Study & Training: Nat Acad Fine Art, scholar, 71, with Daniel Greene; Art Stud League New York, scholar, 72, with Robert Brackman & Everett R Kintsler.
Work in Public Collections: Harbor Gallery, Cold Spring Harbor, N Y.
Exhibitions: Hudson Valley Art Asn, 71; Grand Nat, Am Artists Prof League, Lever House, New York, 72.
Awards: Grand Nat Award, Am Artists Prof League, 72; Salmagundi Club Award, 72; spec award, Malverne Artists Prof League, 72.
Memberships: Am Artists Prof League; Salmagundi Club; Malverne Artists Prof League; Guild Hall, East Hampton.
Mailing Address: 8615 Broadway, Elmhurst, Queens, NY 11373.

CHRISTO (JAVACHEFF)
Sculptor
b Gabrovo, Bulgaria, June 13, 35.
Study & Training: Fine Arts Acad, Sofia, 52-56; work-study, Burian Theatre, Prague, Czech, 56; Vienna Fine Arts Acad, Austria, 57.
Exhibitions: First Air-Package and Wrapped Tree, Stedelijk van Abbemuseum, Eindhoven, Holland, 66; Packed Fountain and Packed Medieval Tower, Spoleto, 68; Wrapped Coast, Little Bay, Sydney, Austrailia, 69; Wrapped Monuments, Vittorio Emanuele, Piazza Duomo & Leonardo, Piazza Scala, Milan, Italy, 70; Valley Curtain, Rifle, Colo, 71-72; plus others.
Mailing Address: 48 Howard St, New York, NY 10013.

CHRISTOPHER, WILLIAM R
Painter
Preferred Media: Acrylics, Oils, Pencil.
b Columbus, Ga, Mar 4, 24.
Study & Training: Sorbonne, Paris, France, 46-47; Acad Julien, Paris, 46-48; Ossip Zadkine, Paris, 47; Ecole Americaines, Fontainebleau, France, 47; also with Amedee Ozenfant, 48-50 & Hans Hofmann, 50, New York, N Y.
Work in Public Collections: Mus Fine Arts, Boston, Mass; Whitney Mus Am Art, New York; Addison Gallery Am Art, Andover, Mass; Seattle Art Mus, Wash; Inst Contemp Arts Libr, London; plus many other pub & pvt collections.
Exhibitions: Inst Contemp Arts, Boston; Inst Contemp Arts, London; Nat Acad Design, New York; one-man shows, Mus Mod Arte, Paris, 71 & U S Embassy, Madrid, Spain, 72; plus many other group & one-man shows.
Teaching: Vis artist, Dartmouth Col, 66, instr summers 68-73.
Awards: Gold medal for Fallen Rock Zone, Boston Univ, 64; Carroll Reece Mus Purchase Award, East Tenn State Univ, 68; grant, Inst Arts & Lett, New York; plus others.
Dealer: Joan Peterson Gallery, 561 Boylston St, Copley Sq, Boston, MA 02116; Galeria Juana Mordo, Villanueva, 7, Madrid I, Espana.
Mailing Address: Hartland VT 05048.

CHRYSSA, VARDA
Sculptor
b Athens, Greece, 33; U S citizen.
Study & Training: Acad Grande Chaumiere, Paris, 53-54; Calif Sch Fine Art, 54-55.
Work in Public Collections: Mus Mod Art, Whitney Mus Am Art & Solomon R Guggenheim Mus, New York, N Y; Albright-Knox Art

Gallery, Buffalo, N Y; Walker Art Ctr, Minneapolis, Minn; plus others.
Exhibitions: One-man shows, Pace Gallery, 66 & 67, Harvard Univ, 68 & Galerie Rive Droite, Paris, 69; Documenta IV, Kassel, Ger, 68; Whitney Mus Am Art, New York, 72.
Bibliography: Lucy R Lippard (auth), included in Pop art, Praeger, 66; Gregory Battcock (ed), Minimal art: a critical anthology, Dutton, 68; Diane Waldman (auth), Chryssa: selected works 1955-1957, Pace Gallery, 68.
Mailing Address: 712 Madison Ave, New York, NY 10021.

CHUBB, FRANCES FULLERTON
Painter, Educator
b Saint Mary's, Idaho, Oct 6, 13.
Study & Training: Univ Puget Sound, BFA; Univ Wash, MFA; also with George Z Heuston.
Exhibitions: Seattle & Tacoma Galleries, Wash, 39-
Teaching: Instr art, art appreciation, painting & art hist, Univ Puget Sound, 42-53, asst prof, 53-58, assoc prof, 58-68, prof, 68-
Awards: Prize, Tacoma Art Asn, 40 & Olympia Ann, 53 & 57.
Memberships: Tacoma Art Mus; Women Painters of Washington; Washington Art Asn.
Publications: Illusr, Lumber industry in Washington, 39.
Mailing Address: Dept of Art, University of Puget Sound, Tacoma, WA 98416.

CHUEY, ROBERT ARNOLD
Painter, Lecturer
Preferred Media: Oils, Ink.
b Barberton, Ohio, Nov 15, 21.
Study & Training: Los Angeles Art Ctr Sch, 45-46; Los Angeles Co Art Inst, 47-49; Jepson Art Inst, 49-52, with Rico LeBrun.
Work in Public Collections: Los Angeles Co Mus, Calif; City Mus St Louis, Mo.
Exhibitions: Seven Los Angeles Co Mus Ann, 49-60; Carnegie Inst, Pittsburgh, Pa, 53; São Paulo Biennial, Brazil, 55; Pa Acad Fine Arts, Philadelphia, 58; Santa Barbara Mus Art, 57.
Teaching: Lecturer art, Los Angeles Co Art Inst, 54-56, Chouinard Art Inst, 58-63, Univ Calif, Los Angeles, 63-65, Univ Calif, Santa Barbara, 65-67, Chouinard Art Inst & Univ Southern Calif, 67-68, Univ Calif, Los Angeles, 68-69.
Publications: Contribr, Realm of contemporary still-life, 63; contribr, Drawing—a search for form, 66; contribr, Painting techniques, 68.
Dealer: Jacqueline Anhalt Gallery, 750 N La Cienega Blvd, Los Angeles, CA 90069.
Mailing Address: 2460 Sunset Plaza Dr, Los Angeles, CA 90069.

CHURCH, C HOWARD
Painter, Educator
b South Sioux City, Nebr, May 1, 04.
Study & Training: Art Inst Chicago, with Boris Anisfeld, John Norton & William P Welsh, 28-32, BFA, 35; Univ Chicago, BA, 38; Ohio State Univ, MA, 39.
Commissions: Murals, Morgan Park Mil Acad, Chicago, Ill, 32-36.
Exhibitions: One-man shows, Mulvane Art Mus, Thayer Mus Art, Univ Nebr, Joslyn Art Mus & Kresge Art Ctr, East Lansing, Mich; plus others.
Teaching: Head art dept, Washburn Univ, 40-45; head art dept, Mich State Univ, 45-60, prof, 60-72; retired.
Positions: Dir, Morgan Park Sch Art, Chicago, 33-36; dir, Mulvane Art Mus, Washburn Univ, 40-45.
Awards: Fine arts medal, 63 & purchase award, mem exhib, 66, Mich Acad Sci, Arts & Lett; print purchase award, Mich Artists Exhib, Mich Educ Asn, 69 & 70; plus others.
Memberships: Mich Acad Sci, Arts & Lett (art prog chmn, 53-54 & 54-55, chmn fine arts sect, 56-59, pres, 59-60); Midwest Col Art Asn (v pres, 59-60, pres, 60-61).
Mailing Address: 271 Lexington Ave, East Lansing, MI 48823.

CIARROCHI, RAY
Painter
Preferred Media: Oils.
b Chicago, Ill.
Study & Training: Chicago Acad Fine Arts; Wash Univ, BFA, with Fred Conway & Stephen Pace; Boston Univ, MFA.
Work in Public Collections: Ciba-Geigy Collection, Ardsley, N Y; Univ Mass Collection, Amherst.
Exhibitions: Art on Paper, Weatherspoon Gallery, Univ N C, 71; Artists in Residence, Westby Gallery, Glassboro State College N J, 71; one-man shows, Tibor De Nagy Gallery, 71 & 72; Nat Inst Arts & Lett, New York, N Y, 72.
Teaching: Instr painting & drawing, Parsons Sch Design, New York, 66-71; lectr drawing, Columbia Univ Sch Arts, 69-71; instr painting, Md Inst Col Art, 71-72.

Awards: Fulbright grant to Italy, 63-64; Tiffany grant, 67.
Dealer: Tibor de Nagy Gallery, 29 W 57th St, New York, NY 10019.
Mailing Address: 463 West St, New York, NY 10014.

CICERO, CARMEN LOUIS
Painter, Instructor
Preferred Media: Acrylics.
b Newark, N J, Aug 14, 26.
Study & Training: Newark State Col, BS, 51; Hans Hofmann Sch Art, 52; Hunter Col, 53, with R Motherwell.
Work in Public Collections: Solomon R Guggenheim Mus, Mus Mod Art & Whitney Mus Am Art, New York, N Y; Mus Mod Arte, Paris, France; Stedelijk Mus, Holland; Aldrich Mus, Ridgefield, Conn.
Exhibitions: Corcoran Gallery Art, Washington, D C, 51 & 59; Guggenheim Mus Inaugural Show, 59; New York-Rome Found, Italy, 59; Mus 20 Jahrhunderts, Austria, 63; Am-Japan Int Young Artists, Tokyo, Japan, 67.
Teaching: Instr art, Sarah Lawrence Col, 59-68; instr painting, New Sch Social Res, 67-70.
Awards: Guggenheim Mem Found fel, 57-58 & 63-64; Ford Found Purchase Prizes, 61 & 65.
Bibliography: William Gerdts (auth), Painting and sculpture in N J, 64; Barbara Rose (auth), New talents, Art in Am, 64; N Knobler (auth), The visual dialogue, 66.
Memberships: Artists Equity Asn; Provincetown Art Asn.
Dealer: Peridot-Washburn Gallery, 820 Madison Ave, New York, N Y 10021.
Mailing Address: 268 Bowery, New York, NY 10012.

CIKOVSKY, NICOLAI
Painter, Printmaker
b Pinsk, Russia, Dec 10, 94.
Study & Training: Vilna Art Sch, Russia, 10-14; Penza Royal Art Sch, Russia, 14-18; Moscow High Tech Art Inst, 21-23.
Work in Public Collections: Mus Mod Art; Brooklyn Mus; Art Inst Chicago; Pa Acad Fine Arts; City Art Mus Saint Louis; plus others.
Commissions: Murals, Dept Interior, Washington, D C & U S Post Off, Towson & Silver Spring, Md.
Exhibitions: Toledo Mus Art; Mus Mod Art; Art Inst Chicago, 60 & 61; Newark Mus Art; Glasgow Mus; plus others.
Teaching: Instr, Ekaterinenburg Higher Tech Art Inst, Russia, 19-21; instr, St Paul Sch Art, summers 34 & 35; instr, Cincinnati Art Acad, 35-36; instr, Art Inst Chicago, 37.
Awards: Purchase prize, 59, purchase prize, Ranger Fund, 60 & Isaac N Maynard Prize, 64, Nat Acad Design; plus others.
Bibliography: Jerome Mellquist (auth), included in: The emergence of American art, Scribner, 42; Grace Pagano (auth), Contemporary American painting, In: The Encyclopedia Britannica collection, Meredith, 45; William H Gerdts, Jr (auth), included in: Painting and sculpture in New Jersey, Van Nostrand, 64; plus others.
Memberships: Assoc Nat Acad Design; Nat Inst Arts & Lett.
Mailing Address: 500 W 58th St, New York, NY 10019.

CIKOVSKY, NICOLAI JR
Art Historian, Educator
b New York, N Y, Feb 11, 33.
Study & Training: Harvard Col, AB; Harvard Univ, AM & PhD.
Collections Arranged: Sanford Robinson Gifford, Univ Tex Art Mus, 70-71; The White Marmorean Flock; 19th Century American Women Neoclassical Sculptors, Vassar Col Art Gallery, 72.
Teaching: Assoc prof art, Vassar Col, 71-
Positions: Dir, Vassar Col Art Gallery, 71-
Research: Nineteenth century American painting & sculpture.
Publications: Auth, George Inness, 71.
Mailing Address: Vassar College Art Gallery, Poughkeepsie, NY 12601.

CIMBALO, ROBERT W
Sculptor
Preferred Media: Graphics, Wood.
b Tiriolo, Italy; U S citizen.
Study & Training: Pratt Inst, Brooklyn, N Y; Syracuse Univ; Sorita Dante Alighari, Rome, Italy; Belle Arte, Rome; Univ Studi Roma.
Work in Public Collections: Kirkland Art Ctr, Clinton, N Y; Munson-Williams-Proctor Inst, Utica, N Y; Syracuse Univ, N Y; State Univ N Y Col Cortland; Pratt Inst, Brooklyn, N Y.
Commissions: Ltd ed fine arts bk, East Utica, Munson-Williams-Proctor Inst, 70.
Dealer: FAR Gallery, 746 Madison Ave, New York, NY 10021.
Mailing Address: 748 South St, Utica, NY 13501.

CIPRIANO, ANTHONY GALEN
Sculptor
b Buffalo, N Y, Sept 30, 37.
Study & Training: Syracuse Univ, 54; Univ Notre Dame, 55-58, with

Ivan Mestrovic; Art Stud League New York, 58-59, with George Grosz; fel Fontainebleau Sch Painting & Sculpture, France, 60; Kokoschka Sch, Salzburg, Austria, 61.
Work in Public Collections: Bass Mus, Miami, Fla; Gallery Mod Art, New York, N Y; Huntington Hartford Collection; also pvt collections.
Exhibitions: Nat Inst Arts & Lett, 63; Bass Mus, 65 & 69; Salmagundi Club, 66; Greenwich Gallery, 68; Portraits, Inc, New York, 69; plus others.
Teaching: Pvt classes in sculpture.
Awards: Leopold Schrepp Found grant, 56; Artist of the Year, Am Artists Prof League, 63; first prize, Salmagundi Club, 66.
Memberships: Salmagundi Club.
Mailing Address: 24 W 56th St, New York, NY 10019.

CISNEROS, FLORENCIO GARCIA (FRANK GARCIA)
Art Dealer
b Victoria las Tunas, Cuba, Feb 1, 24; U S citizen.
Positions: Dir, Galeria Cubana, Havana, 52-59; dir, Sardio Gallery, Caracas, Venezuela, 55-57; dir, Cisneros Gallery, New York, N Y, 65-
Awards: Cintas fel, 54-55.
Bibliography: G Chase (auth), Art in Latin America, Free Press, 70.
Memberships: Circulo Pan Americano de Cultura.
Specialty of Gallery: Latin American art.
Publications: Auth, Latin American painters in New York, 64; auth, Maternity in Precolumbian art, 70.
Mailing Address: Cisneros Gallery, 1316 Madison Ave, New York, NY 10028.

CITRON, MINNA WRIGHT
Painter, Printmaker
b Newark, N J, Oct 15, 96.
Study & Training: Brooklyn Inst Arts & Sci; New York Sch Applied Design; Art Stud League New York; City Col New York; also with K Nicolaides & Kenneth Hayes Miller; Atelier 17.
Work in Public Collections: Nat Collection Fine Arts, Smithsonian Inst; Rosenwald Collection, Nat Gallery Art; The White House & U S Info Agency, Washington, D C; Mus Mod Art, Whitney Mus Am Art, Metrop Mus Art & Joseph H Hirschhorn Collection, New York, N Y; plus many others.
Exhibitions: Dulin Gallery, Knoxville, Tenn, 66; Am Color Print Soc, Philadelphia Mus Art, 67; Calif State Col, Long Beach, 69; N J State Mus, Trenton, 68 & 70; plus one-man shows throughout U S, Europe & S Am.
Teaching: Inst art, Brooklyn Mus, 40-44; lectr U S & abroad; instr art, Pratt Inst Manhattan Ctr, 71-72.
Positions: Rep, U S Govt, Congrès Int Educ Artistique, Paris, France, 47; mem, Washington Conf Women in Arts, Corcoran Gallery, 72.
Awards: Soc Am Graphic Artists Award, Los Angeles Co Mus, 69; awards, N J State Mus, 68 & 70; Yaddo fel, artist-in-residence, Lakeside Studio, Mich, 70; plus others.
Bibliography: Herta Wecher (auth), Cimaise, Paris, 56; Adela Jaume (auth), El Diario de la Marina, Havana, Cuba, 57; Dario Suro (auth), Cuadernos Hispano-Americanos, 60; plus others.
Dealer: Spectrum Gallery, 464 W Broadway, New York, NY 10012.
Mailing Address: 145 Fourth Ave, New York, NY 10003.

CIVITELLO, JOHN PATRICK
Painter
Preferred Media: Acrylics.
b Paterson, N J, Aug 17, 39.
Study & Training: William Paterson Col, BA, 61; New York Univ, MA, 62.
Work in Public Collections: N J State Mus, Trenton; Broadway Bank & Trust Co, Paterson.
Exhibitions: Awards Artists Exhib, Montclair Mus, N J, 66; Fourteen Contemporary New Jersey Artists, N J State Mus, 67; 30th Biennial of American Art, Corcoran Gallery Art, Washington, D C, 67; John Civitello: Paintings, Am Acad Art Gallery, Rome, Italy, 70; What's Happening in Soho, Univ Md Art Gallery, 71.
Awards: Prix-de-Rome in painting, Am Acad Rome, 68-70; Gov N J Purchase Award, N J State Mus, 71; creative artists pub serv grant, Cult Coun Found, 72.
Bibliography: E Bilardello (auth), Pittori Americani a Roma, Margutta-Periodico d'Arte Contemporanea, Rome, 70.
Dealer: A M Sachs Gallery, 29 W 57th St, New York, NY 10019.
Mailing Address: 83 Murray St, New York, NY 10007.

CLAGUE, JOHN ROGERS
Sculptor
Preferred Media: Steel, Bronze, Fiberglass.
b Cleveland, Ohio, Mar 14, 28.
Study & Training: Cleveland Inst Art, BFA.

Work in Public Collections: Cleveland Mus Art; Larry Aldrich Mus, Ridgefield, Conn; Mass Univ Mus.
Commissions: Limestone sculpture, Cleveland Recreation Ctr, 56; Israel (bronze sculpture), Jewish Community Ctr, Cleveland, 61; limestone motif, Child Guid Ctr, Cleveland, 64; kinetic sound-making sculpture (stainless steel), Ashland Col, Ohio, 72.
Exhibitions: Cleveland Mus Art May Show, 55-72; Whitney Mus Am Art Ann, New York, N Y, 64-65; Waddell Gallery, New York, 66; Highlights of 1966-1967 Art Season, Larry Aldrich Mus, 67; Int Monumental Sculpture Exhib, Blossom Music Ctr, 68.
Teaching: Instr sculpture, Oberlin Col, 57-61; instr sculpture, Cleveland Inst Art, 56-72.
Awards: Yale Norfolk fel, 54; Catherwood Found traveling fel, 56; Nat Scholastic Mag Hall of Fame, 70.
Mailing Address: 11625 County Line Rd, Gates Mills, OH 44040.

CLANCY, JOHN
Art Dealer
Positions: Dir, Frank Rehn Gallery.
Mailing Address: 655 Madison Ave, New York, NY 10021.

CLARE, STEWART
Research Artist, Lecturer
b Montgomery City, Mo, Jan 31, 13.
Study & Training: Univ Kans, scholar, BA, 35; Iowa State Univ, fel, MS, 37; Univ Chicago, fel, PhD, 49; Kansas City Art Inst & Univ Mo, Kansas City, 47-49.
Work in Public Collections: Chromatological studies in pvt collections in the U S & Can; scientific illustrations in form of monographs in libr in the U S, Eng, Can, Australia & nat libr of other countries.
Exhibitions: 18 major one-man shows & fifteen major group exhibs incl Univ Alberta, 50-54, pvt invitational showings in Australia & Africa, 54-57, The Science of Color & Design, 62-66, Chromatology: The Science of Color, 65-66, Scientific Illustrations & Diagrams, Designs & Writings, 68, at univs, cols & mus, U S; Brit Asn for Advan Sci (group exhib), Durham Mus & Art Ctr, 70.
Teaching: Lectr, dept fine art, Univ Alberta, 50-53, Union Col, 58-61 & State Univ N Y Col Twin Valleys, 62-66.
Positions: Res artist, proj in sci of color, Kansas City Art Inst, Univ Mo, Kansas City, Univ Alberta, Univ Adelaide, Union Col & others, 58-66; res in chromatology, Col Emporia, 67-72; color consult & info resource, Vol for Int Tech Assistance, 62-, Nat Referral Ctr for Sci & Technol, Libr Cong, 70-
Awards: Awards for Scientific Illustrations, Univ Mo, Columbia, 29-31; var res grants from above-mentioned univs, 46-72.
Memberships: Am Fedn Arts; Nat Art Educ Asn; Soc N Am Artists (adv bd, 71-); Int Soc Educ through Art; Inter-Soc Color Coun & others.
Publications: Contribr, scientific illustrations, var periodicals & textbooks, nat & int, 37-72; contribr, Fine arts registry, 72-73; auth, The theory of color & design, Abstracts Int (in press); plus others.
Mailing Address: 4000 Charlotte St, Kansas City, MO 64110.

CLARK, ANTHONY MORRIS
Museum Director, Collector
b Chestnut Hill, Pa, Oct 12, 23.
Study & Training: Harvard Univ, BS, 45.
Exhibitions: Philadelphia Art Alliance, Pa, 48.
Teaching: Fac asst, Salzburg Sem of Harvard Univ, 50.
Positions: Conserv asst, Mus Art, R I Sch Design, 53; field worker, Byzantine Inst, Istanbul, 54; secy mus & ed mus notes, Mus Art, R I Sch Design, 55-59; David E Finley fel, Nat Gallery Art, 59-61; cur paintings & sculpture, Minneapolis Inst Arts, 61-63, actg dir, 63, dir, 63-
Awards: Order of the North Star, Sweden, 71; Comdr, Order of Merit, Italy.
Memberships: The Athenaeum, London, Eng; Soc Benemerito, Amici Musei Roma; life mem Friends of The Courtauld.
Research: Eighteenth century Roman art, Roman baroque and neo-classical art.
Collection: Eighteenth century Roman art.
Publications: Auth, The age of Canova, 57; also auth, scholarly studies pub in U S, Gr Brit, Ger, Italy & elsewhere.
Mailing Address: Minneapolis Institute of Arts, 201 E 24th St, Minneapolis, MN 55404.

CLARK, CHEVIS DELWIN
Painter, Instructor
Preferred Media: Watercolors.
b Charleston, S C, Sept 5, 22.
Study & Training: High Mus Sch Art, grad, 50; also with Dong Kingman, Atlanta, Ga.

Work in Public Collections: Gibbes Art Gallery, Charleston, S C; Beaufort Art Gallery, S C; S C Arts Comn, Columbia; C & S Bank Collections: Columbia; U S Navy Combat Art Gallery, Washington, D C.

Commissions: Murals, U S Navy, Charleston, 67-69.

Exhibitions: New South Show, Norfolk Mus, Va, 53-54; Carolina Art Asn Shows, Charleston, 53-71; Southeastern Ann Exhibs, Atlanta, 54-57; Ala Watercolor Soc, 54-57; Spring Mills Traveling Exhib, Lancaster, S C, 70-71.

Teaching: Private classes, 50-; instr acrylics & watercolors, Hastie Sch Art, 70-72; instr acrylics & watercolors, Gibbes Art Gallery, Charleston, S C, 72-

Positions: Artist-illusr, Charleston, 50-

Awards: First award, purchase award & third award, Carolina Art Asn State Show, 60-70; first award, Fripp Island First Ann State Show, 69; purchase award, Guild S C Artists State Show.

Bibliography: Jack Morris (auth), Contemporary artist of South Carolina.

Memberships: Carolina Art Asn; S C Artist Guild (treas); Charleston Artist Guild (pres).

Mailing Address: 1540 Heron, Mt Pleasant, SC 29464.

CLARK, ELIOT CANDEE
Painter

Preferred Media: Oils, Watercolors, Pastels.

b New York, N Y, Mar 27, 83.

Study & Training: Art Students League New York, with Clark & John Twachtman; also study in Europe.

Work in Public Collections: Metropolitan Mus Art, New York; Baltimore Mus Art, Md; Dayton Mus Art, Ohio; San Antonio Art Mus, Tex; Nat Acad Design, New York; plus others.

Exhibitions: Nat Acad Design, Soc Am Artists & Am Watercolor Soc, New York; Art Inst Chicago, Ill; St Louis Art Mus, Mo; plus many others.

Teaching: Instr painting, Art Stud League New York, Univ Va & Savanah Art Club; staff lectr arts of India, Asia Inst & hist art, Roerich Mus.

Positions: Art critic, The Studio, London, Eng.

Awards: Third Hallgarlen Prize & Ranger Fund Purchase Prize, Nat Acad Design; Allied Artist of Am Burton Prize.

Memberships: Nat Acad Design (pres, 56-59); Am Watercolor Soc (pres, 20-23); Allied Artists of Am (pres, 45-53); hon mem Nat Sculpture Soc; life mem Nat Arts Club; plus one other.

Publications: Auth, Alexander Wyant, 16; auth, John Twachtman, 24; auth, J Francis Murphy, 26; auth, History of the National Academy of Design (1825-1951), 54; auth, Theodore Robinson (mss).

Mailing Address: Rio Rd, Charlottesville, VA 22901.

CLARK, G FLETCHER
Sculptor

Preferred Media: Wood.

b Waterville, Kans, Nov 7, 99.

Study & Training: Univ Calif, BA; Beaux-Arts Inst Design in Europe.

Work in Public Collections: Wood Mem Gallery, Montpelier, Vt; also in pvt collections in U S & abroad.

Exhibitions: One-man shows, Calif Palace of Legion of Honor, San Francisco, 33 & Avant-Garde Gallery, New York, N Y, 59; Gilbert Gallery, San Francisco, 68; Paris Art Gallery, San Francisco, 72.

Mailing Address: 1360 Lombard St, San Francisco, CA 94109.

CLARK, JOHN DEWITT
Sculptor

Preferred Media: Black Granite, Bronze, Wood.

b Kansas City, Mo.

Study & Training: Kansas City Art Inst; San Diego State Col, MA; also with Lowell Houser & Everett Jackson.

Work in Public Collections: Palomar Col; Southwestern Col.

Exhibitions: Invitational W Coast Sculpture Exhib, 59; Eleven California Sculptors, Western Mus Asn, 62-64; Jefferson Gallery, La Jolla & Los Angeles, Calif, 63, 65 & 69; Mex N Am Cult Inst, Mexico City, Mex, 66; Fein Garten Gallery, Los Angeles, 70; plus others.

Teaching: Prof sculpture & design, Southwestern Col (Calif), 66-

Awards: Southern Calif First Nat Bank, San Diego, 71; Med Growth Industs, San Diego, 71; M H Golden Construct Co, San Diego, 72.

Bibliography: Rev, In: Artforum, 58.

Dealer: Esther Robles Art Gallery, 665 N La Cienega Blvd, Los Angeles, CA 90069.

Mailing Address: 6981 San Miguel Ave, Lemon Grove, CA 92045.

CLARK, MARK A
Museum Curator

b Dayton, Ohio, Jan 20, 31.

Collections Arranged: The Lipton Collection of Antique Tea Silver, 58; Glass from Area Collections, 66; The Folger Collection of Antique Silver Coffee Pots, 67; Paul Storr Silver in American Collections, 72; Vermeil Collection (cataloger), White House, 72.

Positions: Mus Registr, Dayton Art Inst, 57-61, assoc cur decorative arts, 61-68, cur of decorative arts & mus registr, 68-

Memberships: Am Asn Mus; Montgomery Co Hist Soc (nat trust & adv bd).

Publications: Auth, Paul Storr silver in American collections, 72.

Mailing Address: P O Box 941, Dayton, OH 45401.

CLARK, PARASKEVA
Painter

b Saint Petersburg, Russia, Oct 28, 98.

Study & Training: Leningrad Acad Arts, 18-21; also with S Zaidenberg, V Schoukhaeff & C Petrov-Vodkin.

Work in Public Collections: Nat Gallery Can; Art Gallery Ont; Napier Art Gallery, N Z; Dalhousie Univ.

Commissions: Winnipeg Art Gallery, Man; Assumption Univ, Windsor; Art Gallery Hamilton; Hart House, Univ Toronto; Victoria Col, Univ Toronto.

Exhibitions: Two-man shows, Art Gallery Toronto, 53 & Art Asn Montreal, 55-56; one-man show, Hart House, Univ Toronto, 56; Walker Art Ctr, Minneapolis, Minn, 58; N Z, 58; plus others.

Awards: Award, Hamilton, Ont, 48; purchase prize, Winnipeg Art Gallery, 54; purchase award, Art Gallery Hamilton, 64.

Memberships: Can Soc Painters in Water Colour; Royal Can Acad.

Mailing Address: 56 Roxborough Dr, Toronto 5, Ont, Can.

CLARK, ROBERT CHARLES
Painter, Lecturer

Preferred Media: Tempera, Watercolor, Oil.

b Minneapolis, Minn, Aug 31, 20.

Study & Training: Minneapolis Sch Art; Walker Gallery Art Sch, Minneapolis.

Work in Public Collections: Palos Verdes Estates Art Gallery, Calif; Los Angeles Co Mus Hist, Sci & Art, Los Angeles, Calif; Norton B Simon, Inc & Hunt's Foods & Industs Found, Los Angeles.

Commissions: Mural, The Resurrection, Forest Lawn Mem Park, Glendale, Calif, 65.

Exhibitions: Artists of Los Angeles & Vicinity Ann, Los Angeles Co Mus Art, 55-58; Illusion & Reality, Santa Barbara Mus Art, Calif, 56; one-man show, Calif Palace Legion of Honor, San Francisco, 56; Charles & Emma Frye Mus, Seattle, Wash, 57-58; John & Mabel Ringling Mus, Sarasota, Fla, 59.

Positions: Background Artist, Natural Hist Dept, Los Angeles Co Mus, 54-62.

Awards: Artists of Los Angeles & Vicinity, Los Angeles Co Mus Art, 55; purchase award, Palos Verdes Estates Art Gallery, 56.

Bibliography: Janice Lovoos (auth), The Tempera Paintings of Robert Clark, Am Artist, 12/69.

Memberships: Am Artists Prof League; fel Am Inst Fine Arts.

Dealer: Zantman Art Galleries, Ltd, Sixth & Dolores Sts, Carmel, CA 93921.

Mailing Address: P O Box 597, Cambria, CA 93428.

CLARKE, JOHN CLEM
Painter

Preferred Media: Oils.

b Bend, Ore, June 6, 37.

Study & Training: Ore State Univ; Univ Ore, BFA, 60; Mex City Col.

Work in Public Collections: Whitney Mus Am Art, New York, N Y; Milwaukee Art Ctr, Wis; Akron Art Inst, Ohio; Palm Springs, Calif; Oakland Mus, Calif.

Exhibitions: Whitney Mus Am Art Ann, New York, 67-70 & 72; Mus Mod Art, New York, 68; Younger Artists from O K Harris, Dayton Art Inst, Ohio, 70; Spray, Santa Barbara Mus Art, Calif, 71; New Landscapes, Moore Col Art, Philadelphia, Pa, 71; plus many other group & one-man shows.

Dealer: O K Harris Gallery, 469 W Broadway, New York, NY 10012.

Mailing Address: 465 W Broadway, New York, NY 10012.

CLARKE, RUTH ABBOTT
Painter

b Greensboro, N C, Dec 10, 09.

Study & Training: Univ N C, AB, 31, MFA, 55; Hans Hofmann Sch Art, 55; Art Stud League New York, 56; Teachers Col, Columbia Univ, 62.

Work in Public Collections: Univ N C at Greensboro; Wake Forest Col; Elliott Hall Collection; Wachovia Bank Collection.

Exhibitions: Winston-Salem Gallery Contemp Art, 64; Mint Mus Art, Charlotte, N C, 65; Wilmington Col, N C, 67; Asheville Mus Art, N C, 67; Greensboro Col, 67; plus others.

Teaching: Instr art, Univ N C Greensboro, 54-56; asst prof art & head art dept, Meredith Col, 57-61; art specialist, Frederick Co Pub Schs, Md, 61-62; vis lectr art, Greensboro Col, 65-

Awards: Prizes, Assoc Artists N C, 61; Winston-Salem Gallery Fine Arts, 61, 63 & 64; Greensboro Art League, 64; plus others.
Memberships: Assoc Artists N C (treas, 64-68); N C Art Soc; Southeastern Col Art Asn.
Mailing Address: 2605 Springwood Dr, Greensboro, NC 27403.

CLAWSON, REX MARTIN
Painter
b Dallas, Tex, Nov 2, 30.
Study & Training: Colorado Springs Fine Arts Ctr, with William Johnstone.
Exhibitions: Dallas Mus Fine Arts, 47-51; Tex Ann, 51-53; Knoedler Gallery, 52; one-man shows, Edwin Hewitt Gallery, 55 & Royal Athena II Gallery, N Y, 63 & 64.
Awards: Tex fel, 48; prize, Dallas Mus Fine Arts, 51.
Mailing Address: 78 Third Ave, New York, NY 10003.

CLEARY, FRITZ
Sculptor, Art Critic
Preferred Media: Bronze.
b New York, N Y, Sept 26, 14.
Study & Training: St John's Univ; Nat Acad Design; Beaux-Arts Inst, with Alexander Finta.
Commissions: Presidential heads, Long Br Jr High Sch, N J; Robert Mount Mem, Monmouth Col, N J; World War II Mem, Point Pleasant, N J; John F Kennedy Mem, Asbury Park, N J.
Exhibitions: Nat Acad Design, New York; Pa Acad Fine Arts, Philadelphia; Oakland Art Mus, Calif; Nat Sculpture Soc Ann, 72; also in col art mus & city mus in Eastern U S.
Positions: Art critic, Asbury Park Press, weekly 45-62, Sun, 62-
Awards: Warren Prize, Am Artists Prof League; Oakland Art Mus Award; gold medal, Allied Artists, 67.
Memberships: Allied Am Artists; Nat Sculpture Soc (deleg, New York Fedn Arts, 71-73); Asbury Park Soc Fine Arts (pres, cur mus, 66-).
Publications: Auth & illusr, Sixty days around the world, 56; auth, editorial, In: Nat Sculpture Rev, spring 72.
Mailing Address: 205 Grassmere Ave, Interlaken, Asbury Park, NJ 07712.

CLEM (CLEM ALBERT GOUVEIA)
Painter
Preferred Media: Watercolors, Oils, Graphics.
b Nov 29, 17; U S citizen.
Study & Training: Watercolor with Edgar Whitney; oils with Peter Hayward.
Exhibitions: Hudson Valley Art Asn Nat, Westchester Co Ctr, N Y, 66-72; Am Artists Prof League Grand Nat, Lever House, New York, N Y, 68-72; Berkshire Mus Nat, Pittsfield, Mass, 71; Am Watercolor Soc Nat, Nat Acad Design, New York, 71; Springfield Mus Nat, Mass, 71-72.
Awards: Acad Artists Asn Award, Springfield Mus, 71; first prize for watercolor, Am Artists Prof League, 71-72; gold medal of hon, Hudson Valley Art Asn, 72.
Memberships: Salmagundi Club; Hudson Valley Art Asn (dir, 72-); Acad Artists Asn; Am Artists Prof League; Woodmere Art Gallery, Philadelphia, Pa.
Dealer: Jamison Galleries West, 1741 N Campbell Ave, Tucson, AZ 85719.
Mailing Address: 27-50 Gillmore St, East Elmhurst, NY 11369.

CLEMENSON, VAN CLARK
Painter
Preferred Media: Oils.
b Johnstown, Pa, Oct 23, 10.
Commissions: Coal & Railroads, Slovenian Savings & Loan Asn, 59; Coal & Steel Industry, Johnstown Chamber Commerce, 60; Johnstown-Pitt Campus, Johnstown Savings Bank, Richland Br, 68; Casino, Monte Carlo, Monte Carlo Hotel, 68; Johnstown Flood 1889, Johnstown Savings Bank, Johnstown Br, 70.
Exhibitions: Allied Artists Johnstown, Pa, 60; Penn Nat, Rector, Pa, 65; Three Rivers, Pittsburgh, Pa, 68-69; Am Artists Prof League, New York, NY, 71-72; Hudson Valley Art Asn, White Plains, N Y, 71-72.
Awards: Allied Artists Johnstown, Best of Show, Johnstown Bank & Trust Co, 62; Best of Show, Cambria Co Fair Asn, 64; Grand Nat Gold Medal, Am Artists Prof League, 71.
Memberships: Allied Artists Johnstown, Pa (dir, 54-58 & 72, pres, 58-63); Am Artists Prof League (pres, Pa chap, 71-72).
Mailing Address: 1715 Jaffa Dr, Johnstown, PA 15905.

CLENDENIN, EVE
Painter, Printmaker
Preferred Media: Acrylics, Ink.
b Baltimore, Md.
Study & Training: Banff Sch Fine Arts, 44, with H G Glyde of Royal

Acad, London, Eng; study with Eliot O'Hara, 45; also with Hans Hofmann, New York, N Y & Provincetown, Mass, 46-56.
Work in Public Collections: Chrysler Mus, Norfolk, Va; also in pvt collections in New York, Las Vegas, Nev & elsewhere.
Exhibitions: Réalities Nouvelles, Paris, France, 55; Nat Mus Mod Art, Tokyo, Japan, 55; Baltimore Mus, Md, 58; Karlis Gallery, Provincetown, Mass, 60-61; N C Mus Art, Raleigh, 69.
Awards: Award, Baltimore Mus, 58; Nat Asn Women Artists Award, 57; two awards, Cape Cod Art Asn, 62 & 65.
Bibliography: L'art a l'etranger, La Rev Mod, 12/1/61.
Memberships: Am Abstract Artists; Nat Asn Women Artists; Artists Equity Asn; Cape Cod Art Asn; Provincetown Art Asn.
Collection: Picasso drawings, Matisse drawing, Hans Hofmann painting, Bonnard watercolor, Dufy watercolors, Paul Klee watercolor, Jan Mueller painting, and others.
Mailing Address: 150 Central Park S, New York, NY 10019.

CLERK, PIERRE
Painter
b Atlanta, Ga, Apr 26, 28.
Study & Training: Loyola Col; McGill Univ; Montreal Sch Art & Design; Acad Julien, Paris, France; Acad Grande Chaumiere, Paris.
Work in Public Collections: Mus Mod Art, Guggenheim Mus & Whitney Mus Am Art, New York, N Y; Nat Gallery Can, Ottawa, Ont; Mus Contemp Art, Montreal, P Q.
Exhibitions: Venice Biennale, Italy, 56 & 58; Carnegie Int, Pittsburgh, Pa, 59; Expo 67, Montreal, 67; Rosc Int, Dublin, Ireland, 71; Third Brit Int Print Biennial, 71.
Awards: Can Coun travel grant & P Q Govt travel grant, 71.
Dealer: Gimpel Gallery, 1040 Madison Ave, New York, NY 10021.
Mailing Address: 70 Grand St, New York, NY 10012.

CLEVELAND, HELEN BARTH
Art Administrator, Instructor
Preferred Media: Oils, Pastels.
b Alliance, Ohio.
Study & Training: Mt Union Col, with George A Gibbs & Eric Johanson; Kent State Univ, with Novotny; Syracuse Univ, with George SanderSluis, & James A Smith; New York Univ; London Acad Art, Eng; Univ San Juan; Acad Arts Honolulu, Hawaii.
Work in Public Collections: Art Gallery Ont, Toronto; Light House Gallery, Tequesta, Fla; Artists Unlimited, Key West, Fla; Chautauqua Gallery Art, N Y.
Commissions: Murals, Wildwood Gallery, Lake Orion, Mich, 67, Prendergast Libr, Jamestown, N Y, 68 & Galerie 8, Erie, Pa, 69; correlate & design art ctr, Patterson Libr, Westfield, N Y, 70-71; nat hist murals, Hist Ctr, Governor Gilligan's Art Exhibit, Alliance, 71.
Exhibitions: Chautauqua Gallery Art Nat & Regional, 52, 56 & 63; Albright-Knox Regional, Buffalo, N Y, 65; Cleveland Art Mus, Ohio, 67; Hemingway Gallery, New York & Jamestown, N Y, 68-70; Canton Cult Ctr, Ohio, 70.
Collections Arranged: Directed & assembled Nat Jury Shows, Am Exhib Art, Chautauqua, 57-72; New York Univ Shows, 50-51; Syracuse Univ Shows arranged & assembled, 53-55 & 65-68.
Teaching: Instr art, Alliance Pub Schs, 27-; instr crafts, Syracuse Univ, Chautauqua & New York Univ, 50-52 & 61-64; instr art, Sierra Leone, Africa, 63.
Positions: Chmn, Masonic Cult Arts, Alliance, 45-; collabr creativity in art, Syracuse Univ, 63-65; pres & dir, Chautauqua Gallery Art, 63-; chmn, Patterson Libr Art Grant, Westfield, N Y, 70-71.
Awards: Chautauqua Art Asn Ribbons, Bestor Plaza Art Festival, 50, 54 & 57; community meritorious award as art judge, Am Legion, Alliance, 66-67; citation for winning poster, State of Ohio, 69.
Bibliography: Lee Nelson (auth), Outstanding woman of today, Erie Times, Pa, 65-66; Jean Reeves (auth), The director, Chautauqua Gallery of Art, Buffalo Eve News, N Y, 71.
Memberships: Am Fedn Art; Nat Educ Asn; life mem Ohio Educ Asn; Asn Am Univ Women; Canton Cult Art Ctr; plus others.
Publications: Co-auth, Arts and crafts, Grade Teacher, 55; co-auth, Art in poetry, Solvay Publ Co, 59; co-auth, Creativity in elementary schools, 63-64; co-auth, Arts illustrated (children's series), Rowe-Peterson, 65; co-auth, Chautauqua Gallery of Art, Art Gallery Mag, 66.
Mailing Address: 1192 Parkside Dr, Alliance, OH 44601.

CLIVE, RICHARD R
Painter
Preferred Media: Oils, Pastels.
b New York, N Y, Jan 8, 12.
Study & Training: Nat Acad Design, 30; N Y Univ, BFA, 35; also with Dan Greene & Harold Wolcott.

Work in Public Collections: U S Navy Combat Art Collection, Washington, D C; Munic Collection, Ossining, N Y; Arts & Sci Ctr, Nashua, N H.
Commissions: WAVES at U S Naval Training Ctr, Bainbridge, Md; Marines and Civilians, S Vietnam, Dept of Navy, Washington, D C.
Exhibitions: Westchester Year of History Celebration, 59; Salmagundi Club Ann Exhibs, 61-72; Am Friends of the Hebrew Univ Art Festivals, 63-65; four presentations, Naval Art Coop & Liaison Comt, 63-72; Stevens Ctr Invitational Art Exhib, Stevens Inst Technol, 68.
Awards: Varied awards, Women's Clubs of Westchester, 60-67; prize for portrait, New Rochelle Art Asn, 67 & first for graphic, 68; Lt Harry E Breng Award, Am Legion, 68.
Memberships: Salmagundi Club (mem NACAL Comt); Am. Artists Prof League; Acad Artists Asn; Artists Fellowship; Rockport Art Asn (v pres, 70).
Dealer: Imperator Galleries Ltd, 747 W Boston Rd, Mamaroneck, NY 10543.
Mailing Address: 29 Holly St, Yonkers, NY 10704.

CLOAR, CARROLL
Painter
Preferred Media: Acrylics.
b Earle, Ark, Jan 18, 18.
Study & Training: Southwestern of Memphis, BA; Memphis Acad Arts; Art Stud League New York, McDowell fel, 40.
Work in Public Collections: Metrop Mus Art, New York, N Y; Mus Mod Art, New York; Brooks Mem Art Gallery, Memphis, Tenn; Whitney Mus Am Art, New York; Joseph H Hirshhorn Mus, Washington, D C.
Exhibitions: Retrospective, New York Univ at Albany; Pittsburgh Int; Whitney Ann, New York; Pa Acad Fine Arts Ann, Philadelphia; Brooks Mem Art Gallery, Memphis.
Positions: Bd trustees, Brooks Mem Art Gallery, 69-71.
Awards: Guggenheim fel, 46; prize, Am Acad Arts & Lett, 67.
Bibliography: An Arkansas boyhood, Horizon, 11/58; Summer dies as slowly, Time Mag, 8/19/66; Growing up in the Arkansas Delta, Esquire, 6/69.
Dealer: Kennedy Galleries, 20 E 56th St, New York, NY 10022.
Mailing Address: 235 S Greer, Memphis, TN 38111.

CLOSE, CHUCK
Painter
Preferred Media: Acrylics.
b Monroe, Wash, July 5, 40.
Study & Training: Everett Community Col, Wash, 58-60; Yale Univ Summer Sch Music & Art, Norfolk, Conn, 61; Univ Wash Sch Art, Seattle, BA, 62; Yale Univ Sch Art & Archit, New Haven, BFA & MFA, 64; Fulbright scholar to Vienna, Austria, 64-65.
Work in Public Collections: Minneapolis Art Inst, Minn; Walker Art Ctr, Minneapolis; Whitney Mus Am Art, New York, N Y; Ludwig Collection, Aachen, W Ger; Art Gallery Ont, Toronto.
Exhibitions: 22 Realists, 70 & Whitney Ann Exhib, 71, Whitney Mus Am Art; Contemp Art Show, Mus Contemp Art, Chicago, Ill, 71; Contemp Art Show, Los Angeles Co Mus, Calif, 71; Documenta V, Kassel, W Ger, 72.
Teaching: Instr art, Univ Mass Sch Art, Amherst, 65-67.
Bibliography: Barbara Rose (auth), Real, realer, realist, New York Mag, 1/31/72; Robert Hughes (auth), Art—the realist as corn god, Time Mag, 1/31/72; Lucille Naimer (auth), rev, In: Arts Mag, 3/72.
Dealer: Bykert Gallery, 24 E 81st St, New York, NY 10028.
Mailing Address: 101 Prince St, New York, NY 10012.

CLOSE, MARJORIE (PERRY)
Painter, Lecturer
Preferred Media: Oils.
b Chloride, Ariz, Nov 11, 99.
Study & Training: Calif Sch Fine Arts, 4 yr scholar; Univ Calif, 18-20; Chicago Art Inst, 20-22; Wana Derge Studio, Berkeley, Calif; San Francisco Art Inst; George Post, 36; San Francisco City Col, 51-57; Rudolf Schaeffer Sch, 56; also with Matteo Sandona, 52-56 & Thomas Leighton, 56-68.
Commissions: Portraits, Marjorie Markel & Molly Parker, 53 & Admiral John Redman, 54, San Francisco, Calif; still life, Cinerarias, Col & Mrs R F Elliott, Arlington, Va, 60; Elizabeth Stoddard Huntington, Southern Pac Railroad Co, San Francisco, 69.
Exhibitions: 13 Shows, Soc Western Artists Ann, De Young Mus, San Francisco, 56-71; Calif State Fair, Sacramento, 67, 70 & 71; 4 Shows, Nat Asn Women Artists, Nat Acad Design, New York, 61-72; Soc Western Artists, Charles & Emma Frye Mus, Seattle, Wash, 71; Acad Art Asn 23rd Ann, Springfield, Mass, 72.
Teaching: Lectr & demonstr, San Francisco Pub Schs & art orgns.
Positions: Deleg, Art Adv Bd, Calif State Fair.
Awards: Trompe l'Oeil Still Life Award, Dan Le Gear Mem Award, San Francisco, 66, 67 & 71; Pres Award & best still life award,

Am Artists Prof League, New York, 69-71; Premier Grand Prix Award, still-life painting, 23rd Int Grand Prix, Deauville, France, 72.
Bibliography: Virginia Lee (auth), Hidden Realities, San Francisco Trumpeteer, spring 59; Marjorie Close, U S Artist, La Rev Mod, 61; Frederic Whitaker (auth), Marjorie Close, Am Artist Mag, 1/70.
Memberships: Soc Western Artists (treas, 66-67, pres, 68-69, dir exhibs, 71-72); Nat Asn Women Artists; Am Artists Prof League; Catharine Lorillard Wolfe Art Club.
Publications: Co-auth, Color, form & composition, 66.
Mailing Address: 50 Beachmont Dr, San Francisco, CA 94132.

CLOVER, JAMES B
Sculptor, Educator
b Oskaloosa, Iowa, Apr 13, 38.
Study & Training: Kans City Art Inst, BFA; Tulane Univ, MFA.
Work in Public Collections: High Mus Art, Atlanta, Ga; Emory Univ, Atlanta, Brandeis Univ; Univ Southern Ill; Ga Comn Arts.
Commissions: Playground, Atlanta League Jewish Women, 70; sculpture, Civic League, Conyers, Ga, 72.
Exhibitions: Emory Univ, 66; Heath Gallery, Atlanta, 70; Arts Festival Atlanta, 72.
Teaching: Head sculpture, Atlanta Sch Art, 64-
Awards: Southeastern Award of Merit, High Mus Art, 65; purchase awards, Western Mich Univ & Univ Southern Ill, 69.
Dealer: Heath Gallery, 34 Lombardy Way N E, Atlanta, GA 30309.
Mailing Address: 1280 Peachtree St N E, Atlanta, GA 30309.

CLOWES, ALLEN WHITEHILL
Collector, Patron
b Buffalo, N Y, Feb 18, 17.
Study & Training: Harvard Univ, BS(fine arts), 39; Fogg Mus, with Chanler Post, Benjamin Rowland, Leonard Opdyke, Kuhn & Paul Sachs; Harvard Univ Grad Sch Bus Admin, MBA, 42; Franklin Col, hon DFA, 64.
Positions: Dir, Clowes Fund Collection Old Masters, 58-71; cur, Clowes Fund Collection Old Masters, Indianapolis Mus Art, 71-
Awards: Resolution of thanks, Indianapolis Mus Art, for Clowes Pavilion housing Clowes Fund Collection.
Art Interests: Clowes Fund Collection originally formed by the late Dr G H A Clowes and now belongs to Clowes Fund, Inc, located in Clowes Pavilion, Indianapolis Museum of Art.
Collection: Paintings by the Old Masters from the fourteenth to nineteenth century, including Bellini, Bosch, Bruegel, Caravaggio, Clouet, Constable, Cranach, Duccio, Durer, El Greco, Goya, Hals, Holbein, Rembrandt, Rubens and Titian.
Mailing Address: 250 E 38th St, Indianapolis, IN 46205.

CLUTZ, WILLIAM
Painter
b Gettysburg, Pa, Mar 19, 33.
Work in Public Collections: Mus Mod Art, New York, N Y; Joseph H Hirshhorn Collection, Washington, D C; Fogg Mus, Cambridge, Mass; Newark Mus, N J; Chase Manhattan Bank, New York, plus others.
Exhibitions: Recent Painting U S A: The Figure, Mus Mod Art, New York, 62; The Figure International, Am Fedn Arts, 63; Pa Acad Fine Arts Ann, Philadelphia, 64-66; one-man shows, Bertha Schaefer Gallery, New York, 63, 64, 66 & 69 & Graham Gallery, New York, 72; plus many other group and one-man shows.
Mailing Address: 485 Central Park W, New York, NY 10025.

CLYMER, JOHN F
Painter, Illustrator
b Ellensburg, Wash, Jan 29, 07.
Study & Training: Vancouver Sch Art; Ont Col Art; Wilmington Acad Art; Grand Cent Art Sch, with Harvey Dunn.
Work in Public Collections: Glen Bow Found, Calgary; Mont Hist Soc, Helena; Cowboy Hall of Fame, Oklahoma City, Okla; Whitney Gallery Western Art, Cody, Wyo.
Exhibitions: Hudson Valley Art Asn, 62-65; Soc Animal Artists, 62-72; Whitney Gallery Western Art, 69; Cowboy Artists Am, 69-72; Mont Hist Soc, Helena, 72.
Awards: Silver medal, 69, gold medals, 70 & 72, Cowboy Artists Am.
Memberships: Soc Animal Artists; Salmagundi Club; Ont Soc Artists; Hudson Valley Art Asn; Cowboy Artists Am.
Publications: Contribr, illus, In: Sat Eve Post & Field & Stream; prior to 65.
Mailing Address: Box 194, Teton Village, WY 83025.

COATES, ROBERT M
Writer, Art Critic
b New Haven, Conn, Apr 6, 97.
Study & Training: Yale Col, BA, 19.
Work in Public Collections: Books in most pub libr & art schs.

Positions: Former art critic, New Yorker Mag.
Memberships: Int Art Critics Asn; Nat Inst Arts & Lett.
Publications: Auth, The hour after westerly, 57, The view from here,
60, Beyond the Alps, 61, The man just ahead of you, 63 & South of
Rome, 65; plus other books & articles in journals.
Mailing Address: Old Chatham, NY 12136.

COBB, RUTH
Painter
Preferred Media: Watercolors.
b Boston, Mass, Feb 20, 14.
Study & Training: Mass Col Art, cert.
Work in Public Collections: Boston Mus Fine Arts; Va Mus Fine
Arts, Richmond; Butler Inst Am Art, Youngstown, Ohio; Munson-
Williams-Proctor Inst, Utica, N Y; Brandeis Univ, Waltham,
Mass.
Exhibitions: Am Watercolor Exhib, Metrop Mus Art, New York, 52;
22nd Biennial Int Watercolor Exhib, Brooklyn Mus, N Y, 63; Am
Watercolor Soc Ann, 68-72; Watercolor U S A, Springfield Art
Mus, Miss, 69; 35 Years in Retrospect, Butler Inst Am Art, 71.
Awards: Purchase award, Nat Acad Design, 68; Mr & Mrs William
H C Lehmann Award, 68 & Lena Newcastle Mem Award, 70, Am
Watercolor Soc.
Bibliography: Norman Kent (auth), Ruth Cobb, Am Artist Mag,
9/61; reprod & article, In: Prize-winning watercolors, Allied
publ, 67; Norman Kent (auth), reprod & article, In: 100 water-
color techniques, Watson-Guptill, 69.
Memberships: Am Watercolor Soc; Allied Artists Am; Philadelphia
Watercolor Soc; Boston Watercolor Soc.
Dealer: Shore Galleries, 8 Newbury St, Boston, MA 02116.
Mailing Address: 38 Devon Rd, Newton Centre, MA 02159.

COBURN, BETTE LEE DOBRY
Painter, Designer
Preferred Media: Oils, Acrylics, Graphics.
b Chicago, Ill.
Study & Training: Grinnell Col; Art Inst Chicago; Univ N C; studied
watercolor with Eliot O'Hara, Flat Rock, N C; Art Stud League
New York, with E de Kooning.
Work in Public Collections: Univ S C, Columbia; Univ N C, Greens-
boro; Greenville Co Mus Art, Greenville, S C; S C State Arts
Collection; U S Army Air Corps, Washington, D C.
Commissions: Abstract mural, First Fed Bank Hendersonville, N C,
65; space murals, Astro Theatre, 70 & Astro II Theatre, Green-
ville, S C, 71.
Exhibitions: Hunter Art Ann, Chattanooga, Tenn, 68; 23rd South-
eastern Ann Exhib, High Mus Art, Atlanta, Ga, 69; Nat U S A
Traveling Exhib of Oils, Nat Asn Women Artists, 70-72; Int
Grand Prix Art, Deauville, France, 72; Mostra Italia 1972, Nat
Asn Women Artists' For Exhib, 72.
Teaching: Instr oils, Greenville Co Mus Art, 68-70; instr mixed
media, adult classes, Furman Univ, 68-70.
Awards: Purchase award, Univ S C, 66; top merit award, Guild
S C Artists, Gibbes Gallery, 67; Greenville Co Mus Merit
Award, Greenville Artists Guild, 68.
Bibliography: Charles E Thomas (auth), B L Coburn abstract artist,
Sandlapper, 69; J A Morris, Jr (auth), 39 contemp artists of
South Carolina, Greenville Co Mus Art, 70.
Memberships: Nat Asn Women Artists (mem chmn, 70); Soc Am
Pen Women; Guild S C Artists (treas & awards chmn, 58-);
Greenville Artists Guild (pres & awards chmn, 72); Artists
Equity Asn.
Mailing Address: 436 Henderson Rd, Greenville, SC 29607.

COCHRAN, GIFFORD ALEXANDER
Painter
Preferred Media: Watercolors.
Study & Training: Study with Hans Stangl, Munich, Ger, 29-32.
Work in Public Collections: Hudson River Mus, Yonkers, N Y;
Farmsworth Mus, Rockland, Maine; Colby Col, Waterville, Maine;
Pub Art Gallery, Amarillo, Tex.
Exhibitions: New York World's Fair, 39; Farnsworth Mus, Rockland,
Maine; Van Diemen-Lilienfeld Galleries, New York; Ahda Arzt
Galleries, New York: Burr Galleries, New York; Oklahoma Art
Ctr, Oklahoma City; plus many others.
Memberships: Am Artists Prof League.
Publications: Auth, Grandeur in Tennessee, J J Augustin, 47.
Mailing Address: 227 Eden Rd, Palm Beach, FL 33480.

COCKER, BARBARA J
Painter, Designer
Preferred Media: Acrylics.
b Uxbridge, Mass, Oct 16, 23.
Study & Training: Becker Jr Col, AA; Mt St Mary Col; New York Sch
Interior Design; also pvt study with artist mother.
Work in Public Collections: Riverview Hosp, Red Bank, N J; Mon-

mouth Med Ctr, Long Branch, N J; Cent Jersey Bank & Trust Co,
Freehold & Rumson, N J; also in many pvt collections.
Commissions: Two seascapes, Judge William Kirkpatrick, Rumson,
65 & 72; two seascapes, Mr & Mrs John Holton, Rumson, 66 & 70;
seascape, Dr J Putnam Brodsky, Rumson, 68; seascape, V Pres
Jack A Baird, Bell Tel Labs, Holmdel, N J, 70; sailboat scene,
Virgin Islands, Mr & Mrs William Crawford, Washington, D C,
72.
Exhibitions: Catharine Lorillard Wolfe Exhib, Nat Acad Design, New
York, 70; Burr Artists Ann, Lever House & Burr Artists Show
Salmagundi Club, New York, 70; one-man shows, Little Gallery
at the Barbizon, New York, 71, The Old Mill Asn, N J, 71, Pacem
in Terris Gallery, New York, 72 & Cent Jersey Bank & Trust Co,
71 & 72.
Awards: First prize, Oceanport Hist Soc Art Show, 66 & Monmouth
Med Ctr Art Show, 69; highest award, Art for Arthritis Benefit,
72.
Bibliography: Feature article, In: Becker Jr Col Alumni Mag, 5/71.
Memberships: Old Mill Asn; Burr Artists; Guild Creative Art; Mon-
mouth Arts Gallery.
Mailing Address: 3 Rumson Rd, Rumson, NJ 07760.

COE, MATCHETT HERRING
Sculptor
Preferred Media: Bronze, Stone, Wood, Marble.
b Loeb, Tex, July 22, 07.
Study & Training: Cranbrook Acad Art, with Carl Milles.
Work in Public Collections: USN C B Mus, Port Hueneme, Calif;
Am Numismatic Soc, New York, N Y; Metrop Mus Art, New
York; Carnegie Mus, Pittsburgh, Pa; Corcoran Gallery Art,
Washington, D C.
Commissions: Bronze statues, Dick Dowling, State of Tex, Sabine
Pass, 36 & The Texan, Vicksburg Nat Mil Park, 60; New London
Sch Mem (granite relief), New London Mem Asn, Tex, 38; en-
trance to zoo (stone relief), City of Houston, 52; 75th Issue, Soc
Medalists, New York, 67.
Exhibitions: Patron Church, Mus Contemp Crafts, 57; Church Archit
Guild Am, Los Angeles, Calif, 59; Nat Sculpture Soc 75th Anni-
versary Exhib, 68 & Medals By Mem Show, Smithsonian Inst, 68;
Am Numismatic Asn Convention, San Diego, Calif, 68.
Awards: First place for Dick Dowling Monument, Nat Competition;
first place for frieze on New London Sch Mem, State Competi-
tion; selected by noted panel of sculptors to design 75th Issue,
Soc Medalists.
Memberships: Nat Sculpture Soc.
Mailing Address: 2554 Gladys St, Beaumont, TX 77702.

COES, KENT DAY
Painter, Designer
Preferred Media: Watercolor.
b Chicago, Ill, Feb 14, 10.
Study & Training: Grand Central Sch Art, New York, N Y; Art Stud
League New York; N Y Univ.
Work in Public Collections: Frye Mus Art, Seattle, Wash; Montclair
Art Mus, N J; Holyoke Mus Fine Arts, Mass; Norfolk Mus Arts &
Sci, Va; Univ Pa, Philadelphia; plus one other.
Exhibitions: Annual exhibs for Nat Acad Design, New York, Allied
Artists Am, New York, Acad Artists Asn, Springfield, Mass, Am
Watercolor Soc, New York; also exchange exhibs in London, Eng,
Mexico City, Mex & Ontario, Canada.
Positions: Art editor, elec construct & maintenance mag, McGraw-
Hill, 47-
Awards: Gold medal of honor, Allied Artists Am, 59; Gerhard
Miller Award, Am Watercolor Soc, 71; bronze medal, Nat Arts
Club, N Y, 72.
Bibliography: Kent Day Coes insists—, Am Artist mag, 10/57;
Norman Kent (auth), 100 watercolor techniques, 68 & Norman
Kent & Susan Meyer (auth), Watercolorists at work, 72, Watson-
Guptill.
Memberships: Nat Acad Design, assoc (aquarelle), 63-; Am Water-
color Soc (dir, var terms, 52-); Allied Artists Am (dir, sec, v
pres, 50); N J Watercolor Soc (founder-mem, pres, 47-48); Acad
Artists Asn.
Dealer: Grand Central Art Galleries, 40 Vanderbilt Ave, New York,
NY 10017.
Mailing Address: 463 Valley Rd, Upper Montclair, NJ 07043.

COFFEY, DOUGLAS ROBERT
Painter, Educator
Preferred Media: Polymers, Oils.
b Cleveland Heights, Ohio, Dec 27, 37.
Study & Training: Cleveland Inst Art, dipl, 59; Univ Denver, BFA,
61; Western Reserve Univ, MA, 65.
Work in Public Collections: Xerox Corp, New York, N Y; Kodak
Corp, Rochester, N Y; Cleveland Mus Art.

Exhibitions: Cleveland May Show, 62; Butler Inst Am Art Exhib, Youngstown, Ohio, 63; Rochester Fingerlakes Exhib, 71; 13th Ann Rochester Festival of Religious Art, 71; 16th Nat Print Exhib, Hunterdon Art Ctr, 72.
Teaching: Asst prof fine arts, Rochester Inst Technol, 67-
Awards: Sullivan Award for Painting, Fingerlakes Exhib, 70; first award, 13th Ann Festival of Religious Art, 71.
Dealer: Memorial Art Gallery, 490 University Ave, Rochester, NY 14607.
Mailing Address: 81 Langpap Rd, R D 1, Honeoye Falls, NY 14472.

COFFEY, KARITA JOYCE
Ceramist
Preferred Media: Clay.
b Lawton, Okla, Aug 10, 47.
Study & Training: Inst Am Indian Art, with Ralph Pardington; Univ Okla, with Roger D Corsaw & BFA.
Commissions: Clay war shields, Bur Indian Affairs, 71.
Exhibitions: First Am Indian Art Exhib, Europe, 65; one-woman show, Southern Plains Indian Mus, Anadarko, Okla, 71.
Bibliography: Institute of American Indian arts, 7/65 & Exhibits, 12/71, Craft Horizons.
Mailing Address: No 2 Rivercrest, Hanover, NH 03755.

COGGESHALL, CALVERT
Painter
Preferred Media: Oils.
b Utica, New York, 07.
Study & Training: Univ Pa, 29; study with Bradley Walker Tomlin, 49.
Work in Public Collections: Yale Univ Art Gallery, New Haven, Conn; Boston Mus Fine Arts, Mass; N Y State Collection; Albright-Knox Art Gallery, Buffalo, N Y; Chase Manhattan Collection; plus others.
Exhibitions: Abstract painting and Sculpture in America, 54 & Young American Painters, 67, Mus Mod Art, New York, N Y; Toledo Art Mus, Ohio, 54; Whitney Mus Am Art Painters Ann, New York, 67; Pittsburgh Plan for Art, Pa, 68; Univ Colo, Boulder, 68; plus one-man shows.
Bibliography: Reviews, In: Art News, summer 67, 2/69 & 5/70, New York Times, 5/6/67 & 12/14/68 & Arts Mag, 2/69.
Mailing Address: Newcastle, ME 04553.

COGSWELL, DOROTHY McINTOSH
Educator, Painter
Preferred Media: Watercolors, Acrylics.
b Plymouth, Mass, Nov 13, 09.
Study & Training: Yale Univ, BFA & MFA.
Work in Public Collections: Springfield Mus Fine Arts, Mass; Wisteriahurst, Holyoke Mus, Mass; Newport Art Asn; Mt Holyoke Col.
Commissions: Egg tempera mural, Libr, 44, acrylic mural, Buckland Hall, 61 & acrylic mural & relief, Torrey Hall, 63, Mt Holyoke Col.
Exhibitions: New Haven Paint & Clay Club, 29-; New York Watercolor Soc, 32-; Am Watercolor Soc, 33-; Conn Acad, 37; New York World's Fair, 39; plus others.
Collections Arranged: Caroline R Hill Collection of Medieval and Renaissance Art.
Teaching: Prof art hist, Mt Holyoke Col, 39-
Positions: Dir collections, Mt Holyoke Col, 70-
Awards: First prize in watercolor, Eastern States Exhib, 41; Fulbright lectr, Nat Art Sch, Sydney, Australia, 57-58.
Memberships: Springfield Art League (pres, 42-43); New Haven Paint & Clay Club; Am Asn Mus; Mt Holyoke Friends of Art (chmn 47-60); Col Art Asn Am.
Art Interests: Renaissance and modern art.
Publications: Auth, A visitor's impressions of Australian art, Soc Artists, Sydney, 58; auth, Mt Holyoke College art collection, Col Art J, 72.
Mailing Address: 23 Jewett Lane, South Hadley, MA 01075.

COGSWELL, MARGARET PRICE
Art Administrator
b Evanston, Ill, Sept 15, 25.
Study & Training: Wellesley Col, BA, 47; Pratt Inst; Art Inst Chicago; Columbia Univ; Art Stud League New York.
Collections Arranged: Communication through Art, 64; The American Poster, 68; American Exhib, 34th & 35th Venice Biennales, 68 & 70; Explorations, 70; The Audio-Visual Magazine, 72.
Teaching: The Poster & The Collector (seminar), Smithsonian Inst, 70.
Positions: Head dept publ & assoc foreign exhib, Am Fedn Arts, 55-66; ed, The Am Artists Series, 59-63; chmn, 50 Books of the Year, Am Inst Graphic Arts, 64; dep chief, Int Art Prog, Nat Collection Fine Arts, Smithsonian Inst, 66-

Awards: Gold medal for printmaking, Am Artist Mag, 53.
Memberships: Am Asn Mus; Ben and Abby Grey Found, St Paul (trustee, 63-).
Publications: Ed, The ideal theater: eight concepts, 63; co-ed, The cultural resources of Boston, 64; ed, Sao Paulo 9, 67; ed, The American poster, 68.
Mailing Address: 2929 Connecticut Ave N W, Washington, DC 20008.

COHELEACH, GUY JOSEPH
Painter, Illustrator
Preferred Media: Oils, Tempera.
b New York, N Y.
Study of Training: Cooper Union, grad, with Don Eckelberry.
Work in Public Collections: Nat Wildlife Gallery, Washington, D C; Nat Audubon Soc; Am. Mus Nat Hist; Dean Amadon Collection; Beware, presented to President Nixon.
Commissions: Snowy Egrets, Nat Audubon Soc, 68; American Eagle, U S Govt, presented to Vice President Agnew, 71; Elephant, African Safari Club Washington, D C, for President Nixon, 72; Leopard and Elephant, World Wildlife Fund, 72; Elephant and Leopard, Mzuri Safari Found, 72.
Exhibitions: Wildlife Art of America, Frame House Gallery, Louisville, Ky, 68 & 72; Linnean Soc Exhib, Am Mus Natural Hist, New York, 69; Bird Artists of the United States, Graham Gallery, New York, 72; Bird Artists of the World, Tryon Gallery, London, Eng, 72.
Awards: Blue ribbon awards for Peregrine, 69, Great Horned Owl, 70 & Leopard Stare, 71, Printing Indust Am.
Bibliography: Les Line (auth), Guy Coheleach, Audubon Mag, 67; R B Kirkpatrick, National Wildlife visits Guy Coheleach, Nat Wildlife Mag, 70; Herman Kitchen (auth), Guy Coheleach and the bald eagle, Unit One Films, 70.
Memberships: Soc Animal Artists; Explorer's Club; African Safari Club; Adventurer's Club.
Publications: Illusr, Audubon, 65-; illusr, Saturday Evening Post, 67; illusr, Nat Wildlife Mag, 67-; illusr, Readers Digest, 67-; illusr, Int Wildlife Mag, 71-
Dealer: Graham Gallery, 1014 Madison Ave, New York, NY 10021.
Mailing Address: 12 Fenimore Lane, Huntington, NY 11743.

COHEN, MR & MRS ARTHUR A
Collectors
Mr Cohen, b New York, N Y, June 25, 28.
Study & Training: Univ Chicago, BA & MA
Positions: Managing ed, The Documents of 20th Century Art, Viking Press, 68-72.
Art Interests: Organizer of opening exhibition, The Hebrew Bible in Christian, Jewish & Muslim Art, Jewish Mus, 63.
Collection: Primitive & ancient arts; modern painting & sculpture.
Publications: Auth, Rhythm and color: the writings of Robert and Sonia Delaunay, Viking Press, 73; auth, Sonia Delaunay, Abrams, 73.
Mailing Address: 160 E 70th St, New York, NY 10021.

COHEN, DAVID H
Painter
Preferred Media: Oils, Graphics.
b New York, N Y, Jan 9, 27.
Study & Training: Pratt Inst; Nat Acad Design, with Morton Roberts & Daniel Greene; Pratt Graphic Ctr, with David Finkbeiner & Jeff Stone.
Work in Public Collections: Naval Mus, Washington, D C; Gallery Madison 90, New York; also collections in London, Eng, Berlin, Ger, Amsterdam, Holland & Lima, Peru.
Commissions: Viet Nam Wounded (military) for Dept Navy, St Alban's Hosp, New York & numerous portraits of celebrities & race horses for private comns, 61-
Exhibitions: Salmagundi Club, New York; Nat Arts Club Ann, New York; Nat Acad Design Ann, New York; Hudson Valley Artists Asn Ann, 69 & 70; Am Artists Prof League Grand Nat Exhib, 71 & 72.
Awards: Grand Nat Award, Am Artists Prof League, 68; Anonymous Award, Hudson Valley Artists Asn, 69; Grand St Boys Found Award, 72.
Memberships: Fel Am Artist Prof League; Salmagundi Club; Am. Vet Soc Artists.
Dealer: Gallery Madison 90, 1248 Madison Ave, New York, NY 10028.
Mailing Address: 142-01 41st Ave, Flushing, NY 11355.

COHEN, ELAINE LUSTIG
Painter, Designer
b N J, Mar 6, 27.
Study & Training: Tulane Univ, 45-46; Univ Southern Calif, BFA, 48.
Work in Public Collections: Mus Mod Art, New York.

Commissions: Graphic designs for Am Fedn Arts, Philip Johnson, Architect, Lincoln Ctr, Fed Aviation Agency & Meridian Bks.
Exhibitions: Greetings Exhib, Mus Mod Art, New York, 66; Fifty Years Graphic Arts in America, Am Inst Graphic Arts, 66; group show, Tibor de Nagy Gallery, New York, 69; John Bernard Myers Gallery, New York, 70 & 72; Women, N C Mus, 72; plus others.
Positions: Designer, with Alvin Lustig, to 55; freelance designer, 55-67; mem adv comt art & archit, Yale Univ Sch Design, 57-62.
Dealer: John Bernard Myers Gallery, 50 W 57th St, New York, NY 10019.
Mailing Address: 160 E 70th St, New York, NY 10021.

COHEN, H GEORGE
Painter, Educator
b Worcester, Mass, Sept 14, 13.
Study & Training: Worcester Mus Art Sch, 33-36; Inst Design, Chicago, 49; also with Herbert Barnett & Kenneth Shopen.
Work in Public Collections: Mt Holyoke Col Mus; Univ Mass; De-Cordova & Dana Mus Art; Slater Mem Mus, Norwich, Conn; Loeb Ctr, New York Univ; plus others.
Exhibitions: Va Mus Fine Arts, Richmond, 61; Brooklyn Mus, 64; DeCordova & Dana Mus, 64 & 68; Brockton Art Mus, 68; Amherst Col, 68; plus many others.
Teaching: Lectr mod painting, mod art, art of film & kinetic art; instr Smith Col, 42-46, prof art, 46-62, prof, 62-
Awards: Prizes, Springfield Art League, 45-49, 51-58 & 60; Macdowell fel, 58; prize, Berkshire Art Asn, 59; plus others.
Memberships: Springfield Art League; Soc Cinematologists; Col Art Asn Am; Am Asn Univ Prof; Am Film Inst; plus others.
Publications: Contribr, Lincoln Times & Ford Times.
Mailing Address: Hillyer Bldg, Smith College, Northampton, MA 01060.

COHEN, HAROLD LARRY
Designer, Lecturer
b Brooklyn, N Y, May 24, 25.
Study & Training: Pratt Inst Art Sch, Brooklyn; Northwestern Univ; Inst Design, BA.
Teaching: Lectr; formerly prof design, chmn dept & dir, design res & develop, Southern Ill Univ, Carbondale.
Positions: Dir, Inst Behav Res, Silver Spring, Md.
Awards: Five good design awards, with Davis Pratt; awards, Mus Mod Art, 49-53; design of chair selected by U S Govt for traveling exhib of one hundred leading U S prod.
Memberships: Fel Int Inst Arts & Lett; AAAS.
Mailing Address: Institute for Behavioral Research, 2429 Linden Lane, Silver Spring, MD 20910.

COHEN, HY
Painter
b London, Eng, June 13, 01.
Study & Training: Nat Acad Design; City Col New York, BS.
Exhibitions: Corcoran Gallery Art; Brooklyn Mus; Am Watercolor Soc; Wash Univ; Art Inst Chicago; plus others.
Positions: Organized & moderated, Let's talk about art, weekly radio prog, 45-46.
Memberships: Artists Equity Asn New York (pres, 63-70, hon pres, 70-); life mem Am Watercolor Soc.
Mailing Address: 166 W 72nd St, New York, NY 10023.

COHEN, WILFRED P
Collector, Patron
b New York, N Y, Aug 24, 99.
Study & Training: New York Univ; City Col New York.
Awards: Award, Nat Conf Christians & Jews, 64.
Collection: Giacometti, Arps & California painters, exhibited collections at Country Art Gallery, Westbury, Long Island & Galerie Chassaing, Paris, France.
Mailing Address: 1290 Avenue of the Americas, New York, NY 10019.

COHOE, GREY
Printmaker, Writer
Preferred Media: Intaglio, Oil.
b Tocito, N Mex, Sept 9, 44.
Study & Training: Inst Am Indian Arts, Santa Fe, N Mex, printmaking with Seymour Tubis & writing with Terry P Allen; Haystack Mountain Sch of Crafts, Deer Isle, Maine; Univ Ariz, BFA, printmaking with Andrew Rush & Lynn Schroder.
Work in Public Collections: Private collections only: Robert Putsch, Parker, Colo; John Humphrey, Cleveland, Ohio; Chris Isentberg, Pasadena, Calif; John Espy, New Orleans, La; Carl F Diener, Tucson, Ariz.
Commissions: N Mex State Parks & Recreation Emblem, State of N Mex, 66; Mountain Bell Calendar, Mountain Bell Tel Co, Denver, Col, 70.

Exhibitions: The Am Indian Heritage Art Exhib, Nat Cowboy Hall of Fame, Oklahoma City, Okla, 66; Am Discovers Indian Art Show, Smithsonian Inst, Washington, D C, 67; Scottsdale Nat Indian Arts Exhib, Ariz, 67; 1967 Biennial Exhib of Am Indian Arts & Crafts, Washington, D C, 67; Ariz State Mus, Tucson, 68.
Awards: Vincent Price Writing Award, 66; Nat Indian Short Story Contest, 70.
Bibliography: Articles, In: Interior Design, 67, Native American Arts I, 68 & Pembroke Mag, 72.
Publications: Contribr prose, In: Design for good reading, Harcourt, 69; contribr poem & prose, In: S Dak Rev, 69-71; contribr poem & prose, American Indian literature, Houghton Mifflin, 72; contribr poem & prose, Red Eagle, & illusr, The king of thousand islands, Doubleday, 72.
Mailing Address: P O Box 852, Shiprock, NM 87420.

COINER, CHARLES TOUCEY
Painter
Preferred Media: Oils.
b Santa Barbara, Calif, Aug 20, 97.
Study & Training: Chicago Acad Fine Arts; Art Inst Chicago.
Work in Public Collections: Philadelphia Mus Art, Pa; Pa Acad Fine Arts, Philadelphia; Whitney Mus Am Art, New York, N Y; Univ Wichita, Kans; Syracuse Univ, N Y.
Exhibitions: Nat open shows & regional exhibs in Pa.
Memberships: Philadelphia Art Alliance; New York Art Dirs Club; Nat Acad Design; Pa Acad Fine Arts.
Publications: Auth, articles on painting & conserv of wildlife, Esquire, Can, 9/63, Ireland, 2/65 & Scotland, 2/68.
Dealer: Midtown Galleries, 11 E 57th St, New York, NY 10022.
Mailing Address: Mechanicsville, Bucks Co, PA 18934.

COKE, F VAN DEREN
Educator, Photographer
b Lexington, Ky, July 4, 21.
Study & Training: Univ Ky, BA; Ind Univ, MFA; Harvard Univ.
Work in Public Collections: Mus Mod Art, New York, N Y; Int Mus Photog, Rochester, N Y; Nat Gallery Can, Ottawa, Ont; San Francisco Mus Art, Calif; Bibliot Nat, Paris, France.
Exhibitions: Photographers of the New Generation, Int Biennale, Milan, Italy, 60; Creative Photography—The Sixties, Sheldon Mem Art Gallery, Univ Nebr, Lincoln, 66; Photography—U S A, De Cordova Mus, Lincoln, Mass, 67; 13 Photographers, Pratt Inst, Brooklyn, N Y, 69; Focus Gallery, San Francisco, 72.
Collections Arranged: Taos and Santa Fe: the Artist's Environment, 63; Impressionism in America, 65; The Drawings of Andrew Dasburg, 66; John Marin in New Mexico, 68; Photo/Graphics, 71; Wider-View, 72; Nordfeldt the Painter, 72.
Teaching: Asst prof photog & art hist, Univ Fla, 58-61; assoc prof photog & art hist, Ariz State Univ, 61-62; prof & chmn dept of art, Univ N Mex, 63-70; lectr, St Martin's Sch Art, London, Eng, 71; prof art hist, Univ Rochester, 71-72; prof photog & art hist, Univ N Mex, 72-
Positions: Dir, Univ N Mex Art Mus, 72-
Awards: Int competition award, Mod Photog Mag, 56; int competition awards, U S Camera Mag, 57, 58 & 60; New Talent U S A Award, Art in Am, 60.
Bibliography: Henry Smith (auth), Van Deren Coke, Photog, Eng, 59; Joan Murry (auth), Two views of the west, Artweek, 1/22/72; A Frankenstein (auth), A creative photographer, San Francisco Chronicle, 1/13/72.
Memberships: Col Art Asn Am; Soc Photog Educ (bd dirs, 67-70); Friends of Photog (bd adv, 68-72).
Research: The use of photographs by artists; twentieth century American painters; contemporary photographers.
Publications: Auth, Taos and Santa Fe: the artist's environment, Univ N Mex Press, 63; auth, The drawing of Andrew Dasburg, Univ N Mex Art Mus, 66; auth, Marin in New Mexico/1929 & 1930, Univ N Mex Art Mus, 68; auth, Nordfeldt the painter, Univ N Mex Press, 72; auth, The painter and the photographer: from Delacroix to Warhol, Univ N Mex Press, 72.
Dealer: The Witkin Gallery, 243 E 60th St, New York, NY 10022.
Mailing Address: Art Museum, University of New Mexico, Albuquerque, NM 87106.

COLBURN, CAROL (HARRIET)
Painter, Photographer
Preferred Media: Acrylics, Watercolors.
b Milwaukee, Wis, Jan 23, 32.
Study & Training: Phoenix Col; Univ Ariz, Exten; also private studio workshops of Emily Hargarves & Dorothy Fratt of Phoenix.
Work in Public Collections: Mem Union Art Collection, Ariz State Univ, Tempe; Art Collection, Alhambra High Sch, Phoenix.
Exhibitions: 10th Ann Sun Carnival, El Paso, Tex, 65; Father Garce's Celebration of the Arts, Southwest Invitational, Yuma Art Ctr, Ariz, 71 & 72; 21st & 22nd Ann Tucson Festival, Tucson

Art Ctr, 71 & 72; 1st Four Cornerstates Biennial of Painting & Sculpture, Phoenix Art Mus, 71 & Painting & Sculpture Invitational, 72.
Awards: First four Cornerstates Biennial, Ariz Artists Guild, 71.
Memberships: Phoenix Fine Art Asn.
Mailing Address: 1614 E Rancho Dr, Phoenix, AZ 85016.

COLBY, VICTOR E
Sculptor, Educator
Preferred Media: Wood
b Frankfort, Ind, Jan 5, 17.
Study & Training: Corcoran Sch Art; Ind Univ, AB, 48; Cornell Univ, MFA, 50.
Work in Public Collections: Cornell Univ Mus, Ithaca, N Y; Ithaca Col Mus, N Y; Munson-Williams-Proctor Inst, Utica, N Y; St Lawrence Univ, Canton, N Y; State Univ N Y Col Cortland.
Commissions: Wall sculpture, Wilson Nuclear Physics Lab, Cornell Univ, 68.
Exhibitions: One-man shows, Hewitt Gallery, 58 & The Contemporaries, 66.
Teaching: Prof sculpture, Cornell Univ, 50-
Mailing Address: R D 1, Groton, NY 13073.

COLE, ALPHAEUS PHILEMON
Painter
Preferred Media: Oils, Watercolors.
b Jersey City, N J, July 12, 76.
Study & Training: Julien Acad, Paris, France; Ecole Beaux-Arts, Paris; with Jean Paul Laurens & Benjamin Constant; also study in Italy for many years.
Work in Public Collections: Portraits of Rev William Orchard & Sir Edwin Arnold, Nat Portrait Gallery, London, Eng; portrait of Dr Gerald Simpson, Newcastle-on-Tyne, Eng; portrait of Timothy Cole, Brooklyn Mus, N Y; portrait of Ernest Roth, Metatuke Mus, Waterford, Conn; also numerous portraits in Univ Ala, Univ Va, Fordham Univ, Univ London & others.
Exhibitions: Pan-Am Exhib, World's Fair at Buffalo, 1900; plus many others.
Teaching: Portrait & still life class, Cooper Union, 24-31.
Awards: Archer Huntington Prize, Hudson Valley Art Asn, 56; George Beline Prize, Salmagundi Club, 70; Allied Artists Am Prize, 72.
Memberships: Nat Acad Design (rec secy, 50); Allied Artists Am (pres, 52-53); hon life mem Nat Arts Club; mem emer Salmagundi Club; Lyme Art Asn.
Publications: Co-auth, Timothy Cole, wood engraver, 35.
Mailing Address: 222 W 23rd St, New York, NY 10011.

COLE, DONALD
Painter
Preferred Media: Acrylics.
b New York, N Y, Oct 31, 30.
Study & Training: Bucknell Univ, BS(civil eng); Univ Iowa, MFA; also apprenticeship with Bruce Mitchell, Lewisburg, Pa.
Exhibitions: Younger Painters, Sch Visual Arts Gallery, New York, 70; Mus Mod Art (lending serv), New York, 70-71; New Work: New York, Am Fedn Arts Circulating Exhib, 70-72; Painting & Sculpture Today, Indianapolis Mus Art, 72.
Bibliography: Grace Glueck (auth), article, In: New York Times, 70; Willis Domingo, (auth), article, In: Arts Mag, 71; Robert Pincus-Witten (auth), article, In: Artforum, 72.
Dealer: Nancy Hoffman Gallery, 429 W Broadway, New York, NY 10012.
Mailing Address: 53 Mercer St, New York, NY 10013.

COLE, FRANCES
Painter
Preferred Media: Watercolors.
b St Louis, Mo, Sept 2, 10.
Study & Training: Antioch Col; Univ Mich; Univ Dayton; Schimmel Sch Art, Scottsdale, Ariz.
Work in Public Collections: Ariz Bank, Yuma & Phoenix; Valley Nat Bank, Phoenix; First Nat Bank, Yuma; Thunderbird Bank, Glendale, Ariz.
Exhibitions: Am Watercolor Soc Ann Exhib, Nat Acad Design Galleries, New York, N Y, 64 & 65; Ariz Artists Guild Traveling Exhib, St Louis, Mo, Louisville, Ky & Kansas City, Mo, 65; Southwestern Invitational, Yuma Fine Arts Asn, 67-70; Fine Arts Festival Watercolor Exhib, S Dak State Univ, Brookings, 69; Nat Diamond Biennial Art Exhib, Nat League Am Pen Women, Washington, D C, 72.
Awards: Spring Nat Exhib Gold Medal, Low Ruins Gallery, Tubac, Ariz, 65; Regional Art Exhib First Award in Watercolor, Nat League Am Pen Women, 67; First Nat Bank Award, Yuma, 70.
Bibliography: C Bower (ed), Artists of the southwest, Western Rev, winter 67; Gabriel Wills (auth), Scottsdale artists busy in co-op gallery, Southwestern Art Scene, 2/68; H L Cowle (auth), The Arizona bit, West Art, 1/71.

Memberships: Nat League Am Pen Women (Ariz state pres, 72-); Ariz Watercolor Asn (v pres, 69-70, pres, 71-); Ariz Artists Guild (pres, 63-65); Arts Coun Greater Phoenix (pres, 68-70); assoc Am Watercolor Soc.
Publications: Auth, Art over four decades, Ariz, Ariz Repub, 68.
Dealer: Thompson Gallery, 2020 N Central Ave, Phoenix, AZ 85004.
Mailing Address: 1701 E Cinnabar, Phoenix, AZ 85020.

COLE, SYLVAN, JR
Art Dealer, Writer
b New York, N Y, Jan 10, 18.
Study & Training: Cornell Univ, BA, 39.
Positions: Pres & dir, Assoc Am Artists, 58-; adv bd, Pratt Graphics Ctr, 64-
Memberships: Art Dealers Asn Am (v pres, 68-); Print Coun Am (dealers adv comt, 66-); Alumni Friends of Herbert F Johnson Mus (v pres, 72-).
Specialty of Gallery: Original prints.
Publications: Auth, Raphael Soyer: fifty years of printmaking, 67; auth, The graphic work of Joseph Hirsch, 70; auth, Will Barnet—prints 1932-1972, 72.
Mailing Address: 1112 Park Ave, New York, NY 10028.

COLE, THOMAS CASILEAR
Painter
Preferred Media: Oils.
b Staatsburgh, N Y.
Study & Training: Riverview Mil Acad, Poughkeepsie, N Y; Harvard Univ; Mus Fine Arts Sch, Boston, Mass, with Philip Hale, Edmond C Tarbell & Frank W Benson; Acad Julien, Paris, France, with Jean Paul Laurens.
Work in Public Collections: Portrait of Dorothy, Butler Inst Am Art, Youngstown, Ohio; portrait of lady, San Francisco Art Mus, Calif; portrait of William S Halsted, Duke Univ, N C; portrait of Col Walter Taylor, Battle Abbey, Richmond, Va; portrait of Judge Samuel C Williams, Tenn Hist Soc, Nashville.
Commissions: Portrait of Judge Alfred C Coxe, Fed Ct House, New York, N Y, 20; portrait of Gov Stickney, Vt State Capitol, Montpelier, 21; portrait of Judge Edward P Pierce, Mass Supreme Ct, Boston, 30; portrait of Father Mathew, Father Mathew Soc, Salem, Mass, 40; hist portrait of Pres James K Polk, comn by State of Tenn, presented to U S Naval Acad, Annapolis, Md, 45.
Exhibitions: Several shows at Nat Acad Design, New York, Pa Acad Fine Arts, Philadelphia & Allied Artists Am, New York; Art Inst Chicago, Ill, 16; Soc Francais, The Salon, Paris, 24.
Teaching: Instr portrait painting, Phoenix Art Inst, New York, 30-32; instr portrait & figure painting, New York Sch Fine & Indust Arts, 32-35.
Publications: Illusr, Gunston Hall (bk for children), 56.
Dealer: Portraits, Inc, 41 E 57th St, New York, NY 10022.
Mailing Address: Van Dyck Studio Bldg, 939 Eighth Ave, New York, NY 10019.

COLEMAN, MICHAEL
Painter, Etcher
Preferred Media: Oils.
b Provo, Utah, June 25, 46.
Study & Training: Brigham Young Univ.
Work in Public Collections: White House, Washington, D C.
Exhibitions: Springville Mus Nat Invitational.
Awards: 1st Place, Springville Mus, 71.
Bibliography: George Dibble (auth), Artists still excel within tradition, Salt Lake Tribune, 68; Ian Mandan (producer), Rocky Mountain Artists Series, Nat Educ TV, 69.
Dealer: Zantman Art Galleries, Ltd, P O Box 5818, Carmel, CA 93921.
Mailing Address: 2843 Marrcrest East, Provo, UT 84601.

COLESCOTT, WARRINGTON W
Printmaker, Educator
b Oakland Calif, Mar 7, 21.
Study & Training: Univ Calif, Berkeley, BA & MA; Acad Grande Chaumiere, Paris, France; Slade Sch Art, Univ Col, London, Eng.
Work in Public Collections: Metrop Mus Art, New York, N Y; Mus Mod Art, New York; Milwaukee Art Ctr, Wis; Art Inst Chicago, Ill; Minneapolis Inst Art, Minn.
Commissions: Death in Venice (suite of ten color etchings), Ferdinand Roten, Inc, Baltimore, Md, 71.
Exhibitions: Soc Am Graphic Artists, New York, annually; The Artist as Adversary, Mus Mod Art, New York, 71; The Indignant Eye, Boston Univ Fine Arts Gallery, 71; Primera Bienal Americana Artes Graficas, Colombia, S Am, 71; Colorprint U S A, Texas Tech Univ, 71 & 72.
Teaching: Prof art, Univ Wis-Madison, 49-, chmn dept art, 63-65.
Positions: Aquisitions comt, Elvehem Art Ctr, Univ Wis, 69-71; accessions comt, Madison Art Ctr, 71-

Awards: Fulbright fel, 57; Guggenheim fel, 66; Durer Award, Goethe Soc, Milwaukee, 72.
Bibliography: John Lloyd Taylor (auth), Warrington Colescott: graphics, 68 & Toby Olson et al (auth), Warrington Colescott, 72, Madison Art Ctr; Warrington Colescott, environmental artist, Arts & Soc Mag, spring-summer 72.
Memberships: Soc Am Graphic Artists; Philadelphia Print Club; Wis Arts Coun (bd mem, 64); Midwestern Col Art Conf.
Publications: Illusr, Songs from the decline of the West, Perishable Press, 70; illusr, Death in Venice, Aquarius Press, 71; illusr, Mariposa poems, Tetrad Press (London), 71; illusr, After the funeral of Assam Hamady, Perishable Press, 71.
Dealer: Associated American Artists Gallery, 663 Fifth Ave, New York, NY 10022.
Mailing Address: Rte 1, Hollandale, WI 53544.

COLETTI, JOSEPH ARTHUR
Sculptor, Writer
Preferred Media: Bronze, Marble, Granite, Limestone, Wood.
b San Donato, Italy, Nov 5, 98; U S citizen.
Study & Training: Quincy Art Sch; Mass Col Art; Harvard Col, AA, 23; Fogg Art Mus traveling fel, 23; Am Acad Rome, Harvard Univ Sachs fel, 24-26.
Work in Public Collections: Lyman Allyn Mus, New London, Conn; Fogg Art Mus, Cambridge, Mass; Crapo Art Gallery, New Bedford, Mass; Bibliot Nat, Paris, France; Pitti Palace, Florence, Italy.
Commissions: St George's Chapel, John Nicholas Brown, Newport, R I, 24; narthex, Harvard Univ World War I Mem Chapel, 30; facade & fifteen heroic panels for interior, Cathedral of Mary Our Queen, Baltimore, Md, 54-59; Gen Logan Statue, Logan Int Airport, Boston, Mass, 55; Father McGivney Statue, Knights of Columbus, Waterbury, Conn, 60.
Exhibitions: One-man invited show, Fogg Art Mus, 28; Nat Sculpture Soc Show, Palace of Legion of Honor, San Francisco, Calif, 29; Paintings & Sculpture from 16 American Cities, Mus Mod Art, New York, N Y, 33; Artists for Victory, Metrop Mus Art, New York, 42; Sculpture International, Philadelphia Mus Art, 49.
Positions: Mem, Mass State Art Comn, 48-53, chmn, 60-65; mem adv comt, Univ Va Art Ctr, 62-63; trustee, Va Ctr Creative Arts, 70-
Awards: First prize medal, Boston Tercentenary Fine Arts Exhib, 30; decorated Cavaliere Ufficiale nell Ordine al Merito, Repub Italy, 61; decorated Commendatore dell'Ordine, Stella della Solidarietá Italiana, 70.
Bibliography: Harry E Hurd (auth), Joseph Artur Coletti, sculptor, Art & Archaeol, Vol 27, No 2; The sculpture of Joseph Coletti, Am Artist, 2/44; Alan Priest (auth), The sculpture of Joseph Coletti, Macmillan, 68.
Memberships: Fel Nat Sculpture Soc; Guild Boston Artists; Mediaeval Acad Am; Am Fedn Arts.
Research: Stone carving and stone carving tools.
Publications: Auth, Foreword to Maillol (catalog), Inst Mod Art, Boston, 36; auth, The preservation of Commonwealth Ave, Boston City Coun, 63; auth, Beacon Hill, journey through New England, a guide, 65; auth, Government and the arts: a program, Boston Forum, 66; auth, Sculpture techniques: stone carving & stone carving tools, Encycl Britannica, 67.
Mailing Address: 30 Ipswich St, Boston, MA 02215.

COLGROVE, RONALD B
Illustrator, Painter
Preferred Media: Inks, Acrylics.
b Buffalo, N Y, July 17, 30.
Study & Training: Albright Art Sch.
Work in Public Collections: Many in pvt collections.
Exhibitions: Washington Square Show, New York, N Y, 68; Western New York Art Show, 69; Butler Inst Am Art, Ohio, 69; Chautauqua Nat Jury Show, N Y, 70; one-man show, Chautauqua.
Positions: Prin artist, Cornell Aeronautical Lab, 65-67, chief artist, 67-
Awards: Mrs Carmine G DeSapio Award for black & white, 64; Chautauqua traditional oil award, 67; traditional oil award, Buffalo Soc Artists, 68.
Memberships: Buffalo Soc Artists; Chautauqua Art Asn.
Dealer: Walter Meibohm Gallery, 478 Main St, East Aurora, NY 14052.
Mailing Address: S 6679 Maple Hill Rd, South Wales, NY 14139.

COLIN, GEORGIA T
Collector, Designer
b Boston, Mass.
Study & Training: Smith Col; Univ Grenoble, Sorbonne, Paris, France; Ecole de Louvre.
Memberships: Am Inst Interior Designers; Nat Soc Interior Designers.

Collection: With husband, Ralph F Colin, have for forty years collected painting, sculpture, drawings and graphics mainly School of Paris 1890-1970.
Mailing Address: 941 Park Ave, New York, NY 10028.

COLIN, RALPH FREDERICK
Collector
b New York, N Y, Nov 18, 00.
Study & Training: City Col New York, BA, 19; Columbia Univ Law Sch, LLB, 21.
Positions: Founder, admin v pres & gen coun, Art Dealers Asn Am, 62-
Memberships: Mus Mod Art, New York (trustee, 54-69, v pres, 60-69; Fogg Art Mus (vis comt, 51-); Am Fedn Arts (trustee, 45-56); Adv Comt on Arts Ctr Prog, Columbia Univ.
Collection: Paintings, sculpture, drawings and graphics concentrated on School of Paris 1890-1970.
Mailing Address: 941 Park Ave, New York, NY 10028.

COLKER, EDWARD
Painter, Designer
b Philadelphia, Pa, Jan 5, 27.
Study & Training: Philadelphia Col Art, grad; New York Univ, grad; spec study with E & J Desjobert, Paris, France.
Work in Public Collections: Mus Art, Philadelphia; N J State Mus, Trenton; New York Pub Libr Print Collection; Mus Mod Art, New York, N Y; Nat Mus, Stockholm, Sweden; plus others.
Commissions: Lithography ed, Print Club, Philadelphia, 66 & Int Graphic Art Soc, New York, 66 & 69.
Exhibitions: One-man shows, Amel Gallery, New York, 65, East Hampton Gallery, New York, 69 & Hunterdon Art Ctr, N J, 72; Stampe di due Mondi, Rome, Italy & Philadelphia Mus Art, 67; American Art Today, Pa Acad Fine Arts, Philadelphia, 68.
Collections Arranged: Spec Exhibs, Symbol and Vision, Calif Painters & Sculptors, 70 & Depth and Presence, Environmental Sculpture, Corcoran Gallery Art, Washington, D C, 71.
Teaching: Assoc prof fine arts, Univ Pa Grad Sch Fine Arts, 68-70; prof & chmn dept art, Univ Ill, Chicago Circle, 72-
Awards: Rosenwald Prizes, Print Club Philadelphia, 56 & 63; Guggenheim fel, 61-62; Noyes, Coleman Prizes, N J State Mus, 67 & 69.
Bibliography: Zigrosser (auth), The appeal of prints (appreciation), Leary Publ, 70.
Memberships: Col Art Asn Am; Am Inst Graphic Arts; Print Coun Am.
Mailing Address: College of Art and Architecture, University of Illinois, Chicago Circle, Box 4348, Chicago, IL 60680.

COLLIER, ALAN CASWELL
Painter
Preferred Media: Oils.
b Toronto, Ont, Mar 19, 11.
Study & Training: Ontario Col Art; Art Stud League New York, with Howard Trafton.
Work in Public Collections: Nat Gallery Can, Ottawa, Ont; Art Gallery Ont, Toronto; Art Mus London, Ont; Hamilton Art Gallery, Ont; Frye Mus, Seattle, Wash.
Commissions: Murals, Ryerson Polytech Inst, Toronto, 58 & 62; mural, Bank Can, Toronto Agency, 59; mural, Ont Govt Bldg, Queen's Park, Toronto, 68; many portraits, educ & bus orgn.
Exhibitions: First Biennial Can Art, Nat Gallery Can, 55; Dept Can External Affairs, Nat Gallery Can, 57; Fourth Biennial Can Art, Nat Gallery Can, 61; Faces of Canada, Stratford, Ont, 64; Canadian Artists '68, Art Gallery Ont, 68.
Teaching: Instr drawing & painting, Ont Col Art, 55-67.
Memberships: Ont Soc Artists (pres, 58-61); Royal Can Acad Art (hon treas, 65-72).
Dealers: Roberts Gallery, 641 Yonge St, Toronto, Ont, Can; Kensington Gallery, 328 Tenth St, N W, Calgary, Alta, Can.
Mailing Address: 115 Brooke Ave, Toronto 380, Ont, Can.

COLLINS, GEORGE R
Art Historian
b Springfield, Mass, Sept 2, 17.
Study & Training: Princeton Univ, BA, 35, MFA, 42.
Positions: From instr to prof art hist, Columbia Univ, 46-
Awards: Guggenheim fel, 62-63.
Research: Modern architecture and city planning; Spanish art and architecture.
Publications: Auth, Antonio Gaudi, Broziller, 60; co-auth, Architecture of fantasy (transl & rev, Phantastische Architektur), 60; co-auth, Camillo Sitte..., Vols I & II, Random House & Phaidon, Eng, 65; auth, numerous articles in journals; ed, a number of bks on hist Am art & planning.
Mailing Address: 448 Riverside Dr, New York, NY 10027.

COLLINS, JIM (LEE)
Educator, Sculptor
Preferred Media: Wood, Metals.
b Huntington, W Va, Sept 12, 34.
Study & Training: Marshall Univ, AB, 57; Univ Mich, Ann Arbor, MPH, 61; Ohio Univ, MFA, 66.
Work in Public Collections: Wichita Art Asn, Kans; Univ S C, Columbia; Huntington Galleries, W Va; Am Repub Ins Co, Des Moines, Iowa; Berea Col, Ky.
Commissions: Outdoor sculpture, St Augustine Church, Signal Mountain, Tenn, 70; outdoor sculpture, Arlen Realty, Chattanooga, Tenn, 71.
Exhibitions: Benedictine Art Awards, New York, N Y, 64 & 65; Miami Mus Mod Art Invitational, Fla, 65; Contemp Southern Sculpture Invitational, S C, 68; Ann Delta Art Exhib, Ark Arts Ctr, 68; Atlanta Festival Sculpture Invitational, 68 & 69.
Teaching: Assoc prof art, Univ Tenn, Chattanooga, 66-
Awards: Sculpture award, Ball State Univ, 67; purchase award, Atlanta Art Festival, Ga, 67; purchase & achievement awards, Appalachian Corridors, W Va, 72.
Bibliography: Prize winning sculpture, Allied Publ, 64; articles, In: Travel West Virginia, 66 & Appalachian Rev, 68.
Memberships: Tenn Watercolorists; Southern Asn Sculptors (pres, 70-71).
Publications: Auth, Introduction to A Handbook to British landscape painters, 70.
Dealer: Heath Gallery, 34 Lombardy Way N E, Atlanta, GA 30309.
Mailing Address: 109 Louisiana Ave, Signal Mountain, TN 37377.

COLLINS, JOHN IRELAND
Painter
Preferred Media: Oil, Watercolor.
b Atlantic City, N J, Dec 31, 26.
Study & Training: Corcoran Sch Art, Washington, D C, grad; also with Karl Knaths, Provincetown, Mass.
Exhibitions: Int Watercolor Show, Brooklyn Mus, N Y, 66; one-man show, Farnsworth Mus, Rockland, Maine, 67; 20th Exhibition of New England Artists, Silvermine Guild Artists, New Canaan, Conn, 69; Landscape I, 135 Watercolors by 45 New England Artists, DeCordova Mus, Lincoln, Mass, 70 & Landscape II, 90 Oils by 45 New England Artists, 71.
Awards: Emily Lowe Award, 53; Thomas E Saxe Jr Award, Silvermine Guild Artists, 69; Guggenheim Mem Grant, 72.
Bibliography: Lawrence Kent (auth), John Ireland Collins, artist in residence, Maine Digest, 66; Leo Chabot (auth), Nature artist at work, Bangor Daily News, 67; Jim Moore (auth), Cushing, mecca for art, awards, Portland Press Herald, 72.
Dealer: Joan Peterson Gallery, 561 Boylston St, Boston, MA 02130.
Mailing Address: Pleasant Point, ME 04563.

COLLINS, KREIGH
Illustrator
b Davenport, Iowa, Jan 1, 08.
Study & Training: Cincinnati Art Acad; Cleveland Art Sch.
Commissions: Murals, East Grand Rapids High Sch, Ottawa Hills High Sch & E Congregational Church, Grand Rapids, Mich (now at Grand Valley State Col); portraits & landscapes in pvt collections; murals, city auditorium, Newberry, Mich.
Exhibitions: Grand Rapids Art Gallery, 30 & 33.
Positions: Creator, Up anchor!, Sun feature; creator, Kevin the bold.
Publications: Illusr, World history, 46, Make way for the brave, McKay, 50 & Marconi: pioneer of radio, Messner, 53; auth & illusr, Christopher Columbus, 58 & David Livingstone, Rev & Herald, 61; plus others.
Mailing Address: 6174 Grand River Dr, Ada, MI 49301.

COLLINS, LOWELL DAUNT
Painter, Art Dealer
Preferred Media: Oils.
b San Antonio, Tex, Aug 12, 24.
Study & Training: Colo Springs Fine Art Ctr, with B Robinson; Mus Fine Arts, Houston; Art Stud League New York; Acad Grande Chauniere, Paris, France; Univ Houston, BFA & ML.
Work in Public Collections: Mus Fine Arts, Houston, Tex; Mus Fine Arts, Dallas, Tex; U S Info Agency.
Commissions: Painting for Nelson Found.
Exhibitions: Provincetown Arts Festival; New York World's Fair; Hemisfair, San Antonio; Columbia Biennial, S C; New Zealand Exchange Exhib; plus many others.
Teaching: Instr art & archit, Univ Houston, 51-58; dean art dept, Mus Fine Arts, Houston, 58-66; dir art sch, Lowell Collins Gallery, 66-
Positions: Art ed, Tex Cancer Bull, 47-49; cur pre-Columbian art, Mus Nat Sci, Houston, 70-; dir Lowell Collins Gallery, 70-

Awards: First prize, Tex Fine Arts Asn, 49; second prize, D D Feldman Art Exhib, 56; first prize & purchase award, Motorola Corp, 60.
Memberships: Sr mem Houston Philos Soc; sr mem Am Soc Appraisers; hon mem Hanzen Col, Rice Univ; Archaeol Soc Am.
Speciality of Gallery: Pre-Columbian art; African art; Oriental art; contemporary paintings and sculpture.
Publications: Illusr, Houston, Land of big rich, 51; illusr, Houston, the feast years, 61; illusr, The Galveston era, 65; illusr, Unhappy medium, 68.
Mailing Address: 2903 Saint St, Houston, TX 77027.

COLLINS, WILLIAM CHARLES
Painter, Educator
Preferred Media: Acrylics.
b Cambridge, Mass, Jan 18, 25.
Study & Training: R I Sch Design, BFA; Univ Ill, Urbana, MFA; Akad Bildenoe Kunste, Munich.
Work in Public Collections: Wash Univ, St Louis, Mo; Cincinnati Art Mus, Ohio; Univ Ill, Urbana.
Commissions: Mural, St Johns Unitarian Church, 62 & paintings, Hunter Savings & Loan, 66, Bethesda Hosp, 71, O K Transfer Corp, 72 & Stone Corp, Cincinnati, Ohio.
Exhibitions: Western New York Shows, Albright-Knox Art Gallery, Buffalo, N Y, 53-54; Dayton Art Inst, 63, 65 & 71; American Art, Whitney Mus Am Art, New York, N Y, 64; American Landscape, Fort Worth Art Ctr, Tex, 65; Mid-America Exhibs, Butler Inst Am Art, Youngstown, Ohio.
Teaching: Instr drawing, Albright Art Sch, Buffalo, 51-54; instr drawing & painting, Art Acad Cincinnati, 64-67; vis prof drawing & painting, Wash Univ, 67-72; dir, Portland Sch Fine & Appl Art, Maine, 72-
Awards: Morton D May purchase prize, City Art Mus, Saint Louis, 57; Fulbright fel, Ger, 57-58; painting prize, Interior Valley Exhib, Contemp Art Ctr, Cincinnati, 61.
Dealer: Carl Solway Gallery, 204 W Fourth St, Cincinnati, OH 45202.
Mailing Address: Portland School of Fine & Applied Art, 93 High St, Portland, ME 04101.

COLSON, CHESTER E
Painter, Educator
b Boston, Mass, June 17, 17.
Study & Training: Mass Sch Art, BS, 46; Teachers Col, Columbia Univ, MA, 49; with Edwin Ziegfeld; also pvt study.
Work in Public Collections: Everhart Mus, Scranton, Pa; Wilkes Col, Wilkes-Barre, Pa; Norwich Univ, Northfield, Vt.
Exhibitions: One-man show, Little Gallery, Wilkes-Barre, 68; Philadelphia Drawing & Print Show, Pa, 68; one-man show, Everhart Mus, 69; Fleming Mus, Burlington, Vt, 69; Norwich Armory Show, Northfield, Vt, 72.
Teaching: Chmn dept fine arts, Wilkes Col, 59-
Awards: Sordoni Prize, 62; purchase prize, Everhart Mus, Scranton, Pa, 68; purchase prize, Norwich Univ, Vt Artists, Northfield, Vt, 69; plus others.
Memberships: Col Art Asn Am; Nat Art Educ Asn; Philadelphia Watercolor Soc.
Dealer: Jeanne Fairbanks, Bethany Colony, PA 18701.
Mailing Address: Dept of Fine Arts, Wilkes College, Wilkes-Barre, PA 18703.

COLT, JOHN NICHOLSON
Painter, Educator
Preferred Media: Oils, Acrylics, Pastels.
b Madison, Wis, May 15, 25.
Study & Training: Univ Wis, BS & MS.
Work in Public Collections: Whitney Mus Am Art; Milwaukee Art Ctr; Munson-Williams-Proctor Mus, Utica, N Y; Le Centre d'Art, Port au Prince, Haiti; Beloit Col, Wright Art Ctr, Wis.
Commissions: Mural, Marquette Univ, 59.
Exhibitions: Butler Inst Am Art Exhib Am Painting, Youngstown, Ohio, 55; Whitney Ann Exhib Am Painting, Whitney Mus Am Art, New York, N Y, 60; Chicago Vicinity, Chicago Art Inst, Ill, 62 & 64; Walker Biennial, Walker Art Ctr, Minneapolis, Minn, 62, 64 & 66; Art Across America, Knodler Gallery, New York, 68.
Teaching: Prof painting, Univ Wis-Milwaukee, 58-
Awards: Medal of Hon, Milwaukee Art Ctr; Ford Found award & the Top Award, Walker Art Ctr.
Mailing Address: 2840 N Stowell Ave, Milwaukee, WI 53211.

COLT, PRISCILLA C
Art Administrator, Lecturer
b Kalamazoo, Mich, Oct 15, 17.
Study & Training: Kalamazoo Col, AB; Western Reserve Univ, MA; Harvard Univ; Inst Fine Arts, New York Univ.
Collections Arranged: Portland Art Mus.

Teaching: Instr hist art & art theory, Sch Dayton Art Inst, Ohio, 58-69.
Positions: Asst, Jr Mus, Metrop Mus Art, 43-44; asst & cur educ, Va Mus Fine Arts, 44-47; ed & cur, Minneapolis Inst Art, 48-49; res asst, Portland Art Mus, Ore, 49-56; consult contemp art, Dayton Art Inst, 67-
Publications: Contribr, articles, In: Art J & Art Int, 64-65.
Mailing Address: 330 W Schantz Ave, Dayton, OH 45419.

COLT, THOMAS C, JR
Museum Director
b Orange, N J, Feb 20, 05.
Study & Training: Dartmouth Col, BS, 26; Columbia Univ; Cambridge Univ.
Positions: Writer & critic, New York, 26-27; assoc, Rehn Galleries, New York, 27-29; trustee, Richmond Acad Arts, 33-35; secy, Va Art Alliance, 34-35; dir, Va Mus Fine Arts, Richmond, 35-42, 45-48; dir, Portland Art Mus, Ore, 48-56; adv ed, J Aesthet & Art Criticism, 51-53; dir, Dayton Art Inst, 57-
Awards: Star of Solidarity, Ital Govt, 53.
Memberships: Asn Art Mus Dirs; Int Inst Conserv Mus Objects; Intermus Conserv Asn (pres, 68-70); hon mem Ore Archaeol Soc; Ohio Arts Coun (exec comt, 65-70); plus others.
Publications: Ed, C S Price, 1874-1950, Prehistoric stone sculpture of the Pacific Northwest, Samuel H Kress collection of paintings of the Renaissance & Fifty treasures of the Dayton Art Institute; plus others.
Mailing Address: Dayton Art Inst, Forest & Riverview Acres, Dayton, OH 45401.

COLVILLE, ALEXANDER
Painter, Graphic Artist
b Toronto, Ont, Aug 24, 20.
Study & Training: Mt Allison Univ, with Stanley Royle, BFA.
Work in Public Collections: Nat Gallery Can; Mus Mod Art, New York, N Y; Wallraf-Richarts Mus, Cologne, Ger; Kestner Gesellschaft, Hannover, Ger; Centre Nat Art Contemporain, Paris, France.
Exhibitions: Tate Gallery, London, Eng, 64; Venice Biennale, 66; Bologna Biennale, 67; Kestner Gesellschaft, Hannover, 69; Marlborough, London, Eng, 70; plus others.
Mailing Address: P O Box 253, Sackville, N B, Can.

COLWAY, JAMES R
Painter
Preferred Media: Watercolor, Acrylics.
b Oneida, N Y, Nov 12, 20.
Study & Training: Syracuse Univ Sch Art, 45-48, Univ Col, 46-48.
Work in Public Collections: U S Embassy Prog, Washington, D C; Butler Inst Am Art, Youngstown, Ohio; Lyman Allyn Mus, Univ Conn, New London; St Lawrence Univ, Canton, N Y; Eisenhower Col, Geneva, N Y.
Exhibitions: Munson-Williams-Proctor Inst, Utica, N Y, 52-53; Grumbacher Invitational Show, Grand Cent Art Gallery, New York, 64; one-man show, Chase Gallery, New York, 69; one-man shows, St Lawrence Univ & Grand Haven Art Ctr, Mich, 70.
Positions: Art dir, Oneida Silversmiths, N Y, 48-53, dir advert, 64-
Bibliography: Fred A Mohr (auth), Upstate art goes around the world, Empire Mag, Syracuse Herald-American, 1/72.
Dealer: Chase Gallery, 31 E 64th St, New York, NY 10021.
Mailing Address: 101 The Vineyard, Oneida, NY 13421.

CONANT, HOWARD SOMERS
Educator, Painter
Preferred Media: Acrylics, Inks.
b Beloit, Wis, May 5, 21.
Study & Training: Art Stud League New York, with Kunyiyoshi; Univ Wis, BS & MS; Univ Buffalo, EdD.
Work in Public Collections: Andrew Dickson White Gallery, Cornell Univ, Ithaca, N Y; Trenton State Col, N J; Drury Col, Springfield, Mo; Tex Technol Col, Lubbock; Milton Col, Wis.
Commissions: Mural painting, Molloy Col, Rockville Ctr, N Y, 70; environmental mural, N Y State Art Teachers Asn, Sperry High Sch, Henrietta, N Y, 71; Art for schools: a study of children's responses to original works of art, comn by Ctr for Appl Res in Educ.
Exhibitions: One-man shows, Molloy Col, 70, Cape May Art League, N J, 71 & Philadelphia Art Alliance, Pa, 72.
Teaching: Prof art, State Univ N Y Buffalo, 47-55; prof & chmn dept, New York Univ, 55-
Awards: Distinguished Serv to Art Educ, Nat Gallery Art, 66; distinguished alumnus, Univ Wis-Milwaukee, 68.
Memberships: Int Soc Educ through Art; Inst for Study Art in Educ; Nat Art Educ Asn; N Y State Art Teachers Asn.
Publications: Auth, Art workshop leaders planning guide, 58; co-auth, Art in education, 63; auth & ed, Masterpieces of the arts,

63; auth, Art education, 64; auth, Seminar on elementary and secondary school education in the visual arts, 65.
Dealer: Galleria Propersi, 225 Magnolia Ave, Mount Vernon, NY 10552.
Mailing Address: 80 Washington Sq E, New York, NY 10003.

CONDIT, (ELEANOR) LOUISE
Art Administrator
b Baltimore, Md, May 7, 14.
Study & Training: Vassar Col, AB, 35; Teachers Col, Columbia Univ, MA, 41.
Positions: Supvr educ, Brooklyn Children's Mus, 35-42; supvr jr mus, Metrop Mus Art, 43-61, asst dean jr mus, 61-68, assoc dean jr mus, 68-, mus educator, in charge jr mus, 72-; pres, Am Asn Youth Mus, 72-
Awards: Carnegie Corp grant for mus educ, 39; Metrop Mus Art travel grants, 61 & 70.
Memberships: Am Asn Mus (counr, 57-63, v pres, 60-63); Int Coun Mus; Mus Coun New York (secy-treas, 60-64); Metrop Mus Employees Asn (pres, 68-70); New York Film Coun (secy-treas, 47-50).
Publications: Auth, Paul Revere, a Metropolitan Museum picture book, 44; contribr, Museums and education, In: UNESCO museums and monuments series, 72; contribr, prof journals.
Mailing Address: The Metropolitan Museum of Art, Fifth Ave at 82nd St, New York, NY 10028.

CONGDON, WILLIAM (GROSVENOR)
Painter
Preferred Media: Oils.
b Providence, R I, Apr 15, 12.
Study & Training: Provincetown Sch Art, with Henry Hensche; Demetrious Sch Sculpture, Boston & Folly Cove, Mass.
Work In Public Collections: Metrop Mus Art, New York, N Y; Whitney Mus Am Art, New York; Mus Mod Art, New York; Cleveland Mus, Ohio; Duncan Phillips Gallery, Washington, D C.
Commissions: Bronze head, Stephen O Metcalf, R I Sch Design, Providence Mus, 39.
Exhibitions: Landmarks, American Painting—50 years, Wildenstein Gallery, New York, 50; Painters under 35, Metrop Mus Art, 50; Biennale Venezia, 52 & 58; Carnegie Int, Pittsburgh, Pa, 52 & 58; New Decade, Whitney Mus Am Art, 55.
Awards: Temple Gold Medal, Pa Acad Fine Arts, 51; purchase prize, Univ Ill, 52; Clark Award, Corcoran Gallery Art, 53.
Bibliography: Dorothy Seiberling & George Hunt (auth), William Congdon, Life Mag, 4/30/51; Peggy Guggenheim (auth), Pittore di Venezia, Biennale Venezia, 2/53; Emily Genauer (auth), Congdon converted, New York Herald Tribune, 8/21/68.
Publications: Auth, In my disc of gold, Reynal, 62; auth, An artist, his art, and the Christian community, Jaca Bk, Italy, 72.
Dealer: Betty Parsons Gallery, 24 W 57th St, New York, NY 10019.
Mailing Address: Vicolo Bovi 1, Assisi, Italy 06081.

CONLON, GEORGE
Sculptor
Preferred Media: Marble, Bronze.
b Lonaconing, Md, June 25, 88.
Study & Training: Md Inst Art; Rinehart Sch Sculpture, Baltimore; Acad Julian, Paris; Acad Colarossi, Paris.
Work in Public Collections: Kremlin; Washington, D C; Nat Hq Am Legion, State Dept, Washington, D C; plus others.
Commissions: Jemmet Mem, Biarritz, France, 33; Gen Pershing, Nat Hq Am Legion; plus others.
Exhibitions: Soc Salon Artistes Français, 12-14 & 20-39.
Awards: Rinehart scholar study of sculpture abroad, 11-15.
Memberships: Nat Sculpture Soc.
Mailing Address: 2032 Belmont Rd N W, Washington, DC 20009.

CONLON, WILLIAM
Painter, Educator
b Albany, N Y, 41.
Study & Training: Sch Visual Arts, New York, N Y, 60-63; Sch Art & Archit, Yale Univ, BFA, MFA, 67.
Exhibitions: One-man exhibs, Reese Palley Gallery, New York, 70 & 72; Four Painters, Dallas Mus Fine Arts, 71; Kunstmarket Koln, 71; Duchamp Festival, Univ Calif, Irvine, 71; Whitney Mus Am Art Ann, New York, 72; plus others.
Teaching: Instr painting, Sch Art & Archit, Yale Univ, 68-70; instr art, Hunter Col, 70-71; prof art, Univ Calif, Irvine, 71-
Bibliography: Jane Gollin (auth), Reviews and previews: Conlon at Reese Palley, Art News, Vol 69, No 8; Robert Pincus-Witten (auth), New York, Artforum, Vol 9, No 4; Carter Ratcliff (auth) New York letter: exhibition at Reese Palley, Art Int, Vol 14, No 10; plus others.
Mailing Address: c/o Reese Palley, 93 Prince St, New York, NY 10012.

CONNAWAY, INA LEE WALLACE
Painter, Sculptor
Preferred Media: Oils, Stone, Wood, Bronze.
b Cleburn, Tex, Dec 27, 29.
Study & Training: Baylor Univ; also with Rhinhold Ewald, Hanau, Ger & Junicero Sekino, Alaska; Famous Artist Course, Univ Alaska; Corcoran Sch Art; George Washington Univ, BA.
Work in Public Collections: Alaskan State Mus, Juneau; John F Kennedy Elem Sch, Fort Richardson, Alaska; P E Wallace Jr High Sch, Mt Pleasant, Tex; Cora Kelly Elem Sch, Alexandria, Va; Kate Duncan Smith DAR Sch, Ala.
Exhibitions: Lasting Americana, A Series on the United States, Ft Richardson, Juneau & Anchorage, Alaska, 62-65; Am Artists Prof League Grand Nat, 66; Soverign Exhibs Ltd, Va, N C & S C, 70-71; U S Mil Acad Libr Exhib, 70; DAR Army & Navy Chap Exhib, 71.
Teaching: Instr sculpture, Int Sch, Washington, D C, fall 69; instr painting, Welcome to Washington, 70-71.
Awards: Prizes, Beaux Arts Ball, Artist of the Mo & Am Art Wk, Anchorage, 63; Alaska State Fair, Palmer, 64.
Bibliography: Pub Info Off Revs, Army Times, 64-68; Mario Pescara (auth), Ina Connaway, Am Rev, spring 70; E Lewis (auth), TV film, U S Mil Acad, 12/70.
Memberships: Am Fedn Arts; Nat Soc Arts & Lett; Int Platform Asn; Am Asn Mus; Am Artist Prof League.
Mailing Address: c/o Lynn Kottler Gallery, 3 E 65th St, New York, NY 10021.

CONNER, BRUCE
Painter, Film Maker
b McPherson, Kans, Nov 18, 33.
Study & Training: Wichita Univ, with David Bernard; Univ Nebr, BFA, with Rudy Pozzatti; Brooklyn Mus Art Sch, with Reuben Tam; Univ Colo.
Work in Public Collections: Mus Mod Art, New York, N Y; Art Inst Chicago, Ill; Los Angeles Co Art Mus, Calif; San Francisco Mus Art, Calif; Whitney Mus Am Art, New York.
Commissions: Poster, New York Film Festival, Am Fedn Arts, 65; film portrait, Audrey Sabol, Pa, 68.
Exhibitions: The Art of Assemblage, Mus Mod Art, New York, 60; Whitney Biannual, Whitney Mus Am Art, American Sculpture of the Sixties, Los Angeles Co Art Mus, 67; Edible Art Show, San Francisco Mus Art, 68; Belly-Button Art of the Seventies, Newport Harbor Art Gallery, 72.
Teaching: Instr filmmaking, Calif Col Arts & Crafts, 65-66; undergrad seminar, Wasted Time, San Francisco Art Inst, 66-67.
Positions: Pres & founder, Rat Bastard Protective Asn, San Francisco, 58-61; dir, bd dirs, Canyon Cinema Corp, San Francisco, 69-70, 71-72.
Awards: Ford Found grant, 65; Copley Found Award, 65; gold medal award, Milan Biennale Nuovo Techniques in Arts, 67.
Bibliography: Thomas Garver (auth), Bruce Conner (catalog), Rose Art Mus, Brandeis Univ, 64; Carl Belz (auth), 3 films by Bruce Conner, Film Cult Mag, spring 67; Joan Siegfried (auth), Bruce Conner (catalog), Inst Contemp Arts, Philadelphia, 67.
Memberships: Nat Art Workers Community.
Publications: Co-auth, Book: Bruce Conner/Mike McClure, Averhahn Press, 67; auth, The Dennis Hopper one-man show, Crown Point Press, Vols I-III, 71-73.
Dealer: Quay Gallery, 2 Jerome Alley, San Francisco, CA 94124.
Mailing Address: 4696 18th St, San Francisco, CA 94114.

CONNERY, RUTH M
Painter, Instructor
Preferred Media: Oils, Acrylics.
b New York, N Y.
Study & Training: Mills Col, AA; Art Stud League New York, with William von Schlegell & Hans Hoffmann.
Work in Public Collections: First Nat Bank Rye, N Y; Henry Bruckner Jr High Sch, Bronx, N Y.
Commissions: Portraits, comn by Mr & Mrs Peter Sulon, Rye, Mr & Mrs Victor Wook, New York, Mr & Mrs Anthony Rizzo, Jupiter Island, Fla & Mr & Mrs H Canale, Larchmont, N Y.
Exhibitions: Nat Asn Women Artists, New York, 49-69; Jersey City Mus, 55; Mus of Southern France, 67; Leger Bldg, Park Ave, New York, 67-68; Norton Gallery, West Palm Beach, Fla, 70-71.
Teaching: Instr creative painting, Westchester Arts Workshop & Mamaroneck Artists Guild, 60-69; instr creative painting, Palm Beach Adult Educ Inst, 70-72.
Awards: Pres prize, New Rochelle Art Asn, 65; group show award, Westchester Arts Workshop, 67; One-man show award, Contemporaries, Inc, New York.
Memberships: Nat Asn Women Artists (secy, 65); Artists Guild Norton Gallery, Palm Beach.
Mailing Address: 1612 Treemont Ave, Jupiter, FL 33458.

CONNETT, (DELORES) DEE M
Educator, Painter
Preferred Media: Acrylics.
b Mulvane, Kans, May 25, 35.
Study & Training: Kans State Teachers Col, BS(art educ), 53; Wichita State Univ, MA, 64; Am Univ, Mex, 64; art sem, Florence, Italy, 70; also with Mary Kretsinger & Dorothy MacCray.
Work in Public Collections: Wichita Art Mus, Kans; Halstead Art Asn, Kans; Nebr Wesleyan Univ, Lincoln; Centre House, Swannanoa, N C; MacCray Gallery, Western N Mex State Univ, Silver City.
Commissions: Cement sculpture, Sch Dist 191, Wichita, 68; paintings commissioned by Harry Litwin, Litwin Enterprises, Wichita, 70.
Exhibitions: 18th Ann Mo Valley Exhib, Mulvane Gallery, Topeka, Kans, 65; Nebr Wesleyan Univ Show, 66; Centre House, 68; Drawing: Mid-U S A, Spiva Art Ctr, Joplin, Mo, 70; Graphics '71, Nat Print & Drawing Show, MacCray Gallery, 71.
Teaching: Instr art, Wichita Pub Schs, 57-64; instr painting, Wichita Art Mus, 69-70; chmn dept art, Friends Univ, Wichita, 64-
Positions: Mem, Fine Arts Coun Comt, Wichita, 66-70; bd mem, Wichita Art Mus, 66-; state & local pres, Nat League Am Pen Women, Wichita, 70-72; mem, Century II Sculpture Planning Comt, Wichita, 70-72.
Awards: Outstanding Teacher of Year Award, Friends Univ, 70; Outstanding Young Women of Am, Wichita, 70; plus many purchase awards in paintings from various museums, 53-
Bibliography: Elma Byrne (auth), Wichita Spotlight, Wichita Eagle-Beacon, 8/67; article, In: Apartment Living Mag, 11/71.
Memberships: Artist Guild Wichita; Kappa Pi (sponsor, 69); Kans Artist-Craftsmen Asn.
Dealers: Sales & Rental Gallery, Wichita Art Museum, Wichita, KS 67203; Art Barn, W 13th St, Wichita, KS 67203; Blue Huron Gallery, Glenwood, NM 88039.
Mailing Address: 1635 N Sheridan, Wichita, KS 67203.

CONNOLLY, JEROME PATRICK
Painter, Illustrator
Preferred Media: Oils.
b Minneapolis, Minn, Jan 14, 31.
Study & Training: Univ Minn, BS(art educ); also with Francis Lee Jaques.
Work in Public Collections: Diorama backgrounds, William Penn Mem Mus, Harrisburg, Pa, Ill State Mus, Springfield, The Sci Ctr, St Paul, Minn, Mid-Fairfield Co Youth Mus, Westport, Conn & Mus Hist & Technol, Smithsonian Inst, Washington, D C.
Exhibitions: Soc Animal Artists Ann, New York, N Y, 65-; Hudson Valley Art Asn Ann, White Plains, 69-; one-man show, Abercrombie & Fitch, New York, 72.
Positions: Staff artist, Ill State Mus, Springfield, 58-60; staff artist, Natural Sci Youth Found, Westport, Conn, 60-65; free lance artist, 65-
Memberships: Soc Animal Artists; Soc Illustrators; Hudson Valley Art Asn.
Publications: Illusr, The story of monarch x, 66; illusr, The cat family, 68; illusr, Adelbert the penguin, 69; illusr, The deer family, 69; illusr, Aise-ce-bon: a raccoon, 71.
Mailing Address: 55 Cambridge Rd, Stamford, CT 06902.

CONOVER, ROBERT FREMONT
Printmaker, Painter
Preferred Media: Graphics, Oils.
b Trenton, N J, July 3, 20.
Study & Training: Philadelphia Mus Sch Art; Art Stud League New York; Brooklyn Mus Sch.
Work in Public Collections: Smithsonian Inst, Washington, D C; Brooklyn Mus, N Y; Whitney Mus Am Art, New York; New York Pub Libr; Philadelphia Mus, Pa.
Commissions: Print ed, 200 woodcuts, 57 & 75 woodcuts, 61, Int Graphic Art Soc; print ed, 75 woodcuts, Hilton Hotels, 62; print ed, 30 woodcuts, Assoc Am Artists Galleries, 69; print ed, 60 relief prints, Ferdinand Roten Galleries, 71.
Exhibitions: Painter of the 20th Century, Mus Mod Art, New York, 50; Whitney Mus Am Art Ann, 50-54; Carnegie Int, Pittsburgh, Pa, 54; Pa Acad Fine Arts Painting Ann, 54; Brooklyn Mus Print Biennial, 70.
Teaching: Instr painting & graphics, New Sch Social Res, 51-; instr painting, Brooklyn Mus Sch, 60-; instr graphics, Newark Sch Fine & Indust Arts, 67-
Awards: Purchase prize, Brooklyn Mus, 54; purchase prize, Soc Am Graphic Artists, Assoc Am Artist Gallery, 67; purchase prize, Philadelphia Print Club.
Bibliography: Article, In: Art in Am, 57; Seuphor (auth), Dictionary of abstract painting, 58; Jules Heller (auth), Printmaking today, Holt, Rinehart & Winston, 72.

Memberships: Soc Am Graphic Artists (mem coun); Am Abstract Artists.
Dealer: Associated American Artists Gallery, 663 Fifth Ave, New York, NY 10022.
Mailing Address: 162 E 33rd St, New York, NY 10016.

CONRAD, GEORGE
Educator, Painter
Preferred Media: Oil.
b Newark, N J, Feb 10, 16.
Study & Training: Newark Sch Fine & Indust Arts; New York Univ, BS; Columbia Univ, MA & EdD.
Work in Public Collections: Butler Inst Am Art, Ohio; La Jolla Mus Art, Calif; Univ. Ga; Columbus Pub Libr, Ohio; Univ Ore.
Exhibitions: Artists from N J, Newark Mus; Independent, New York, N Y; N J Art in Cols, State Mus, N J.
Teaching: Prof art educ, Ill State Univ, 49-58; prof art hist, Glassboro State Col, 58-
Positions: Ed, The Arts, 62-72; mem, N J Arts Coun, 66-71.
Memberships: N J Art Educ Asn (pres, 69); Eastern Arts Asn (coun, 69); Nat Art Educ Asn (state assembly, 69).
Publications: Auth, Process of art educ, Prentice-Hall, 64.
Mailing Address: 163 N Mansfield Blvd, Cherry Hill, NJ 08034.

CONSTABLE, ROSALIND
Collector, Writer
b England.
Positions: Researcher, Fortune Mag, 38-47; cult corres, Time, Inc, 48-67; free lance writer.
Collection: Contemporary paintings, lithographs, drawings and sculpture.
Publications: Contribr, articles, In: Life Mag, New Yorker, Bk Wk, New York & others.
Mailing Address: 609 Old Taos Hwy, Santa Fe, NM 87501.

CONSTABLE, WILLIAM GEORGE
Art Historian, Writer
b Derby, Eng, Oct 27, 87.
Study & Training: Cambridge Univ, MA; Slade Sch, London, Eng, with Wilson Steer & Harvard Thomas:
Positions: Formerly, asst dir, Nat Gallery, London, dir, Courtauld Inst Art, Univ London, Slade prof, Univ Cambridge, cur paintings, Boston Mus Fine Arts, Mass & lectr, Yale Univ.
Awards: Chevalier, Legion Hon; Commendatore, Crown of Italy; off, Ordre Arts & Lett, France.
Memberships: Fel Soc Antiquaries; Art Workers Guild, London; Goldsmiths Co, London; Am Acad Arts & Sci; fel Int Inst Conserv (past pres); plus others.
Publications: Auth, Flaxman: English painting 17th & 18th centuries, Richard Wilson, The painters workshop, Beacon Press, 63, Canaletto & Art collecting in the U S; contribr, articles, In: art mags & bull.
Mailing Address: 23 Craigie St, Cambridge, MA 02138.

CONSTANT, GEORGE
Painter
b Greece, Apr 17, 92; U S citizen.
Study & Training: Wash Univ, 12-14; Art Inst Chicago, 14-18; also with Charles Hawthorne & George Bellows.
Work in Public Collections: Metrop Mus Art; Brooklyn Mus; Detroit Inst Art; Dayton Art Inst; San Francisco Mus Art; plus others.
Exhibitions: New York World's Fairs, 39 & 64-65; 10 Years of American Prints, 47-56, Brooklyn Mus, 56; U S Info Agency, 56-57 & 60-61; Art: U S A, New York, 59; Humanists of the 60's, New Sch Social Res, 63 & 65; plus others.
Awards: Award, Parrish Mus, Southampton, Long Island, 50, 51 & 66; awards, 62 & 63 & Carolyn Tyson Award, 66, Guild Hall; Emily Lowe Award, Audubon Artists, 68; plus others.
Memberships: Fedn Mod Painters & Sculptors; Audubon Artists.
Publications: Contribr, reproductions, In: The art museum in America, The naked truth and personal vision & Twentieth century highlights of American painting; auth, George Constant, Arts, Inc, 61 & George Constant, Argonaut, Athens, Greece, 68.
Mailing Address: 187 E Broadway, New York, NY 10002.

CONSUEGRA, HUGO
Painter, Architect
Preferred Media: Oils.
b Havana, Cuba, Oct 26, 29.
Study & Training: San Alejandro Acad Arts, Havana, 43-46; Univ Havana, 49-55, grad archit; Univ Madrid, 69-70.
Work in Public Collections: Nat Mus, Havana; Isaac Delgado Mus, New Orleans; New York Univ; Nat Gallery, Sofia, Bulgaria; New York Pub Libr.
Commissions: Mural painting, Sch Nursery, Havana, 61; ceramic mural, Ministry Transp, 62.

Exhibitions: Third, Sixth & Seventh Bienal Sao Paulo, Brazil, 55, 61 & 63; Pittsburgh Int, Carnegie Inst, 58; Comparisons, Mus Mod Art, Paris, France, 59; Second Bienal Mex, 60; Third Bienal Paris, France, 63.
Teaching: Prof hist art, Sch Archit, Univ Havana, 60-65.
Positions: Dir, Dept Plastic Arts, Ministry Pub Works, Havana, 59-63.
Awards: Hon mention, Second Bienal Mex, 60; second prize, Second Ann, Barranquilla, Colombia, 60; Cintas Found fel, 70-71.
Bibliography: Gaston Diehl (auth), La galerie des hommes celebres, L Mazenod, Paris, 63; Rene Huyghe (auth), L'art et l'homme, Larousse, Paris & Planeta, Barcelona, 66; Chase (auth), Contemporary Latin American art, Free Press, 70.
Mailing Address: 142-02 84th Dr, Jamaica, NY 11435.

CONWAY, FRED
Painter, Educator
b Saint Louis, Mo, 1900.
Study & Training: Saint Louis Sch Fine Arts; Julian Acad, Acad Mod, Paris, France.
Work in Public Collections: City Art Mus Saint Louis; Springfield Mus Art; Univ Mo; Denver Art Mus; Joslyn Mem Art Mus; plus others.
Commissions: City Art Mus Saint Louis; Saint Louis Art Guild; Denver Art Mus; Nat Acad Design; Va Mus Fine Arts, Richmond; plus many others including numerous one-man shows.
Teaching: Prof painting, Wash Univ, 23-
Awards: Silver medal, Corcoran Gallery Art, 49; Art Dirs Club Awards, Chicago & New York, 53; gold medal, Architects League, 56; plus others.
Memberships: Saint Louis Art Guild; Art Dirs Club; Architects League.
Mailing Address: 265 Union Blvd, Senate Apt, Saint Louis, MO 63108.

COOK, AUGUST CHARLES
Painter, Engraver
Preferred Media: Oils.
b Philadelphia, Pa, Mar 15, 97.
Study & Training: Pa Acad Fine Arts; Harvard Univ.
Work in Public Collections: Paintings, La Salle Col, Philadelphia; Pennell Collection Print, Libr of Cong, Washington, D C; print, Butler Mus Am Art, Youngstown, Ohio; prints, Gibbs Art Gallery, Charleston, S C; print, S C Art Comn Collection.
Exhibitions: Pa Acad Fine Arts; Soc Am Graphic Artists; Libr of Cong Print Exhib; Nat Acad Design, New York, N Y; Carolina 25th Ann, Gibbs Art Gallery.
Teaching: Prof fine arts & head dept, Converse Col, Spartanburg, S C, 24-66.
Awards: Purchase prize, Furman Univ, Greenville, S C.
Bibliography: Jack Morris (auth), Contemporary artists of South Carolina, 70.
Memberships: Guild S C Artists.
Mailing Address: 438 S Fairview Ave Ext, Spartanburg, SC 29302.

COOK, GLADYS EMERSON
Illustrator, Painter
Preferred Media: Pastels, Oils.
b Haverhill, Mass.
Study & Training: Skidmore Col, BS; Univ Wis, MS.
Work in Public Collections: Metrop Mus Art, New York, N Y; Cincinnati Mus, Ohio; Boston Mus, Mass; Libr Cong, Washington, D C; Smithsonian Inst; also in many pvt collections.
Commissions: Dog portfolio (8 plates in full color) & cat portfolio (8 plates in full color), 60; U S Equestrian Team Portraits, 68; folio of four Lipizzaner Horses, 70; also many animal portraits, pvt comns, 50-72.
Exhibitions: Metrop Mus Art, New York, 50; Soc Illustrators; also others.
Teaching: Substitute instr art, New York City Jr High Schs, 63-70.
Awards: Artist of the year, Albany Print Club, 68; artist of accomplishment, Skidmore Col, 72.
Memberships: Fel Royal Soc Arts, 65.
Publications: Auth & illusr, Hiram and other cats, How to draw cats, How to draw dogs, How to draw horses & Circus Clowns on parade; plus many others.
Mailing Address: Hotel Wolcott, 4 W 31st St, New York, NY 10001.

COOK, HOWARD NORTON
Painter, Lecturer
Preferred Media: Oils, Watercolors, Pastels, Graphics.
b Springfield, Mass, July 16, 01.
Study & Training: Art Stud League New York; also with Bridgeman, Dumond, Morgan & Pennell & abroad.
Work in Public Collections: Metrop Mus Art, New York, N Y; Mus Mod Art, New York; Whitney Mus Am Art, New York; Philadelphia Mus Art, Pa; Minneapolis Art Inst, Minn.

Commissions: Two fresco murals, comn by Works Progress Admin, Law Libr, Springfield, Mass, 34; fresco mural, comn by Sect Fine Arts, Pittsburgh Court House, Pa, 36; sixteen mural panels, Fed Bldg, San Antonio, Tex, 37-39; two tempera murals, Post Off Bldg, Corpus Christi, Tex, 41; mural, Mayo Clin Diag Bldg, Rochester, Minn, 52-54.
Exhibitions: Archit League New York Ann, 37; Artists for Victory, Metrop Mus Art, 51; Corcoran Gallery Art Ann, Washington, D C, 53; Detroit Pub Libr Mural Exhib, 56; also all important graphic arts exhibs, U S & abroad, 31-50.
Teaching: Prof painting, Minneapolis Inst Art, 45 & 58; guest prof painting, Univ New Mex, 47, 50 & 60; prof painting, Univ Calif, Berkeley, summer 48; prof painting, Scripps Col, summer 51; guest prof painting, Wash Univ, 54; prof painting, Highlands Univ, summer 57.
Positions: Mem jury, U S Govt Sect Fine Arts, Washington, D C, 37; mem jury Am art, Metrop Mus Art, 51.
Awards: Logan Medal, Art Inst Chicago, 33; gold medal for mural painting, Archit League New York, 37; Samuel F B Morse Gold Medal, Nat Acad Design, 63.
Bibliography: Carl Zigrosser (auth), The artist in America, 42; Carl Zigrosser (auth), Howard Cook, New Mex Quart, 50.
Memberships: Life mem, Art Stud League New York; life mem Nat Acad Design; life mem Taos Art Asn.
Publications: Auth, From prints to frescoes, Am Mag Art, 1/42; auth, Sammi's army, Doubleday, 43; Auth, Making a watercolor, Am Artist Mag, 45.
Dealers: Kennedy Galleries, 20 E 56th St, New York, NY 10022; Mission Gallery, Taos, NM 87571.
Mailing Address: Box 73, Ranchos de Taos, NM 87557.

COOK, RICHARD LEE
Sculptor, Educator.
Preferred Media: Light, Sound, Movement, Neon, Plastic, Electronics.
b Big Spring, Tex, Oct 30, 34.
Study & Training: Univ N Mex, BA & MA; computer drawing & sculpture with Charles Mattox; also sculpture with Ron Grow.
Work in Public Collections: Permanent collection, Masur Mus Art, Monroe, La; Contemp Am Collection, Mobile Art Gallery, Ala; permanent collection, Univ N Mex Fine Arts Ctr, Albuquerque; permanent collection, Nicholls State Univ Fine Arts Gallery, Thibodaux, La.
Exhibitions: One-man shows, Glade Gallery, New Orleans, La, 69-71; Sculpture: 70, traveling exhib, Southern Asn Sculptors, 70; 13th Ann 8-State Exhib, Okla Art Ctr, Oklahoma City, 71; 6th Nat Drawing & Small Sculpture Show, Del Mar Col, Corpus Christi, Tex, 72; four-man show, Tulane Univ La, New Orleans, 73.
Teaching: Assoc prof art & chmn dept, Nicholls State Univ, 68-
Awards: Purchase award, Masur Mus, 69; first award, La Art Comn, Baton Rouge, 70; second award, Southern Asn Sculptors, 70.
Memberships: Southern Asn Sculptors (pres, 71-); Col Art Asn Am; Nat Art Educ Asn; Artists Equity Asn.
Dealer: Michael Ledet Fine Arts, Ltd, 1126 S Carrolton Ave, New Orleans, LA 70118.
Mailing Address: 617 Pine, Thibodaux, LA 70301.

COOKE, DONALD EWIN
Writer, Designer
Preferred Media: Watercolors.
b Philadelphia, Pa, Aug 5, 16.
Study & Training: Philadelphia Mus Sch Art.
Exhibitions: Pa Acad Fine Arts Watercolor Show, 37 & 38.
Teaching: Instr illustration, Philadelphia Mus Sch Art, 38-40.
Position: Art dir, David McKay Co, 40-41; art dir & managing ed, John C Winston Co, 45-60; pres, Edraydo, Inc, 60-
Awards: Hon mention, Int Bookplate Exhib, 33.
Memberships: Philadelphia Sketch Club.
Publications: Auth, Color by overprinting, 55; auth & illusr, The silver horn of Robin Hood, 56; auth, Men of Sherwood, 61; auth, Fathers of America's freedom, 69; auth, America's great document-The Constitution, 70.
Mailing Address: 106 Oakford Circle, Wayne, PA 19087.

COOKE, EDWY FRANCIS
Painter, Educator
b Toronto, Ont, Mar 10, 26.
Study & Training: Univ Toronto, BA; Univ Iowa, MFA.
Work in Public Collections: Art Gallery Toronto; London Mus Art, Ont; Beaverbrook Art Gallery, Fredericton, N B; Sir George Williams Univ, Montreal; Loyola Col, Montreal; plus others.
Exhibitions: Royal Can Acad, 44-58; Nat Gallery Can; one-man shows, Hart House, Univ Toronto, 47 & 52, London Art Mus, Ont, 55 & Art Ctr, Univ N B, 62; plus others.
Teaching: Instr drawing & painting, Art Workshop, 51-59; instr, Art Gallery Toronto, 51-59; instr, Univ Toronto, 54-59; lectr

hist art, Univ Toronto, 52-59; head dept fine arts, Univ N B, 59-64; assoc prof fine arts, Sir George Williams Univ, 64-
Positions: Cur Lee collection, Hart House, Univ Toronto, 53-59; dir, Beaverbrook Art Gallery, Frederickton, N B, 59-64; dir, Sir George Williams collection art & art galleries, 66-
Awards: Can Coun grant overseas res, 58.
Memberships: Can Soc Painters in Water Colour; Can Mus Asn; Univs Art Asn Can; Col Art Asn Am.
Mailing Address: Dept of Fine Arts, Sir George Williams University, Montreal, P Q, Can.

COOKE, HEREWARD LESTER
Art Historian, Painter
Preferred Media: Watercolors.
b Princeton, N J, Feb 16, 16.
Study & Training: Oxford Univ, BA, 37; Yale Univ Sch Fine Arts, 39-41; Princeton Univ, MFA, 51; Sorbonne, Fulbright fel, Paris, France, 51-52; Princeton Univ, PhD, 56; Art Stud League New York, with George Bridgeman.
Work in Public Collections: Phillips Collection, Washington, D C; Nat Gallery Sweden, Stockholm; Corcoran Gallery Art, Washington, D C; Princeton Univ Gallery; U S Govt Art Collections of Marines, Air Force, Army, NASA.
Exhibitions: One-man shows, New York, Philadelphia, Princeton Univ Mus, Bowdoin Col Mus, Augusta Richmond Co Mus, & others.
Collections Arranged: Chinese Imperial Collection, 59, Art of Iran, 62 & Turkish Govt Collection, 64, Nat Gallery Art.
Teaching: Artist-in-residence, Princeton Univ, 48-51; instr drawing, Corcoran Gallery Art, 57-58.
Positions: Cur, Nat Gallery Art, 55-62, cur painting, 62-
Awards: Prix de Rome in art hist, Am Acad Rome, 52-54; Order of Merit, Italian Govt, 64.
Bibliography: Donald Holden (auth), H Lester Cooke, painter and scholar, Am Artist Mag, 2/67.
Memberships: Am Asn Mus.
Research: Old Master drawings and Am watercolors.
Publications: Co-auth, Roman drawings at Windsor Castle, Phaidon Press, 60; auth, Galleria Nacional de Washington, Aquilar Press, 65; auth, Painting lessons from the Great Masters, Watson-Guptill, 67; auth, The National Gallery (in four lang), Knorr & Hirth, 68.
Dealer: Franz Bader Gallery, 2124 Pennsylvania Ave N W, Washington, DC 20037.
Mailing Address: 808 Swinks Mill Rd, McLean, VA 22101.

COOKE, KATHLEEN McKEITH
Painter, Sculptor
Preferred Media: Oils, Dry Point, Clay.
b Belfast, Ireland, Sept 30, 08; U S citizen.
Study & Training: With Arthur Sweden, Samuel Adler, Madeleine Gekiere, Collette Roberts & Theodoros Stamos.
Work in Public Collections: Univ Utah, Cornell Univ & Arts Coun Ireland, plus many others.
Exhibitions: American Drawings of the Sixties, New Sch Art Ctr, New York, 69-70; David Hendriks Gallery, Dublin, Ireland, 70; Sculpture-The Artists Plus Discoveries, Betty Parsons Gallery, 70-71; Hillsborough Art Ctr, N Ireland, 71; ROSC Int Exhib, 71; plus many others.
Bibliography: Brian Fallon (auth), Animals by Kathleen Cooke, Irish Times, 8/9/71; Bruce Arnold (auth), Kathleen Cooke, Irish Independent, 8/16/71; Hilary Pyle (auth), article, In: Sunday Independent, 8/15/71.
Mailing Address: 95 Lexington Ave, New York, NY 10016.

COOLIDGE, DAVID
Painter
Preferred Media: Watercolor, Oil.
b Lincoln, Nebr.
Study & Training: Drake Univ, BFA; studies with John Falter; Pa Acad Fine Arts; Tyler Sch Art, Rome, Italy.
Work in Public Collections: U S Nat Bank, Omaha, Nebr; Continental Western Ins Co, Des Moines, Iowa; Meredith Corp, Des Moines; I M T Ins Co, Des Moines; Arthur Anderson & Co, Philadelphia, Pa.
Commissions: The Heritage Plate, J M Smucker Co, Orrville, Ohio, 72.
Exhibitions: Pennsylvania '71, William Penn Mem Mus, Harrisburg, Pa, 71; Hazelton Art League, Pa, 71; Philadelphia Watercolor Club Ann, Philadelphia Art Alliance, 71; Philadelphia Watercolor Club Traveling Exhib, 71-72.
Positions: Art dir, Ivey Advert, Inc, Philadelphia, Pa, 66-70.
Awards: Best of Show, Chestnut Hill Develop Group, 69; second prize, Stone Harbor Art Fair, N J, 71; purchase prize, Pennsylvania '71, William Penn Mem Mus, 71.

Memberships: Philadelphia Watercolor Club; assoc mem Am Water-
color Soc; Woodmore Art Gallery.
Mailing Address: c/o Sulgrave Studios, P O Box 359, Bryn Mawr,
PA 19010.

COOLIDGE, JOHN
Art Historian, Educator
b Cambridge, Mass, Dec 16, 13.
Study & Training: Harvard Univ, BA, 35; New York Univ, PhD, 48.
Teaching: Prof fine arts, Harvard Univ, 47-
Positions: Dir, Fogg Art Mus, Harvard Univ, 48-68.
Memberships: Col Art Asn Am (v pres); Soc Archit Historians
(v pres).
Research: History of American architecture, Italian renaissance
architecture.
Publications: Auth, Mill and Mansion, 42; auth, The Villa Guilea,
Art Bull, 42.
Mailing Address: Fogg Art Museum, Harvard University, Cam-
bridge, MA 02138.

COONEY, BARBARA (MRS CHARLES TALBOT PORTER)
Illustrator, Writer
b Brooklyn, N Y, Aug 6, 17.
Study & Training: Smith Col, BA, 38; Art Stud League New York, 40.
Positions: Illusr, bks, also var mags & anthologies.
Awards: Caldecott Medal for Chanticleer and the fox, 58.
Publications: Auth & illusr, Captain Pottle's house; illusr, Christ-
mas folk, 69 & auth & illusr, Garland of games and other diver-
sions, 69, HR & W; illusr, Dionysus and the pirates, 70 &
Hermes, lord of robbers, 71, Doubleday; illusr, Wynken, Blynken
& Nod, Hastings, 70; plus many others.
Mailing Address: Pepperell, MA 01463.

COONEY, JOHN DUCEY
Art Administrator, Writer
b Boston, Mass, Aug 23, 05.
Study & Training: Harvard Col, BA; Harvard Univ Grad Sch; Univ
Pa.
Collections Arranged: Five Years of Collecting Egyptian Art,
Brooklyn Mus, N Y, 56-57.
Teaching: Adj prof Egyptian art, Case Western Reserve Univ.
Positions: Asst cur ancient art, Brooklyn Mus, N Y, 37-39, cur
ancient art, 40-63; cur ancient art, Cleveland Mus Art, Ohio, 64-
Memberships: Am Res Ctr Cairo (dir, 52-53); Archaeol Inst Am;
Cleveland Soc (pres, 65-67); Hon mem Deutsches Archaeol Inst.
Research: Egyptian glass; minor arts; Amarna reliefs.
Publications: Auth, Egyptian art in the collection of Albert Gallatin,
J Near Eastern Studies, 53; auth, Glass sculpture in Ancient
Egypt, J Glass Studies, 60; auth, Fragment of a great saite
monument, Am Res Ctr Egypt J, 64; auth, Amarna reliefs
Hermopolis in American collections, 65; auth, Catalogue of the
Egyptian Glass in the British Mus, 72.
Mailing Address: Cleveland Museum, 11150 East Blvd, Cleveland,
OH 44106.

COOPER, JOANNE BECKMAN
Painter
Preferred Media: Polymer.
b Columbus, Ohio, Apr 14, 30.
Study & Training: Art Stud League New York, with Edwin Dickinson
& Harry Sternberg; Carnegie Hall & Mus Mod Art, with Zoltan
Hecht; Northwestern Univ, three yrs; Ohio State Univ.
Work in Public Collections: Iona Inst Arts, Iona Col, New Rochelle,
N Y.
Exhibitions: Nat Acad Design, New York, N Y, 66; Max 24-66, Pur-
due Univ, Ind, 66; Benedictine Art Awards, 71; Nat Soc Painters
in Casein & Acrylic, 71 & 72.
Teaching: Instr art, Ethical Cult Schs Children's Assembly, 68-69.
Awards: First prize, Riverdale Art Show, 68; first prize, Haddon-
field Arts & Crafts League, 69; hon mention, Benedictine Art
Awards, 71.
Memberships: Nat Soc Painters in Casein & Acrylic (publicity dir,
72); Artists Equity Asn New York; Silvermine Guild Artists; Al-
lied Artists; Yonkers Art Asn.
Publications: Illusr (cover), Sounds of language, Rinehart, Holt &
Winston, 71.
Dealer: Art Adventures Unlimited, 816 Madison Ave, New York, NY
10021.
Mailing Address: 4483 Douglas Ave, Riverdale, NY 10471.

COOPER, LUCILLE B
Painter, Sculptor
Preferred Media: Oils, Watercolors, Clays, Acrylics.
b Shanghai, China, Nov 5, 24; U S citizen.
Study & Training: Univ Calif, Los Angeles; Univ Hawaii; Honolulu
Acad Art.
Work in Public Collections: Painting, Hawaii Loa Col.

Commissions: 48 collages, Polynesian Hotel, Honolulu, Hawaii, 60;
oil painting, Fiji Hotel, 71.
Exhibitions: 3 + 1 Show, Ala Moana, Honolulu; Honolulu Acad Art
Ann; Easter Art Festival; Hawaii Painters & Sculptors League
Ann; Honorary Retrospective, Hawaii Loa Col, 70.
Teaching: Lectr ceramic jewelry design, Univ Hawaii Curriculum
Ctr, lectr painting, at present.
Positions: Chmn, Comn Cult & Art, Honolulu.
Awards: Best in show for watercolor, Watercolor & Serigraph Soc;
hon mention for watercolor.
Memberships: Hawaii Painters & Sculptors League (secy); Hawaii
Potters Guild; Hawaii Craftsmen (v pres); hon mem Windward
Art Guild (pres).
Dealer: Downtown Gallery, Merchant St, Honolulu, HI 96813.
Mailing Address: 1005 Kailua Rd, Kailua, HI 96734.

COOPER, MARIO
Painter, Sculptor
Preferred Media: Watercolors.
b Mexico City, Mex, Nov 26, 05.
Study & Training: Otis Art Inst, Los Angeles, 24; Chouinard Art
Sch, Los Angeles, 25; Grand Cent Art Sch, New York, N Y, 27-37;
also with F Tolles Chamberlin, Louis Trevisco, Purett Carter &
Harvey Dunn.
Work in Public Collections: Metrop Mus Art; Col USAF; Butler Inst
Am Art; St Lukes Hosp, Denver, Colo.
Commissions: Processional cross, Chapel of Intercession & St
Martin's, New York; painting of Atlas ICBM & planes, USAF,
Marianas Hall, Armed Serv Staff Col, Norfolk, Va; comn by
USAF to paint the capitals of Europe, 60; invited by Nat Gallery
to doc flight Apollo Ten & Eleven for NASA, 69.
Exhibitions: Audubon Artists; Allied Artists Am; Sarasota Art Asn;
Conn Acad Fine Arts; first nat exhib, USAF art, Smithsonian Inst,
60; plus many others.
Teaching: Instr, Art Stud League New York, 57-; instr, Nat Acad De-
sign Sch Fine Arts, City Col New York, 61-68.
Positions: Pres, Audubon Artists, 54-58; Del to U S Comn, Inter-Am
Press Asn, 54-; in charge team artists to Japan, Korea & Oki-
nawa, USAF, 56 & in charge team artists to Japan, 57; pres, Am
Watercolor Soc, 59-; art consult, USAF, 60.
Awards: Prize, Audubon Artists, 61; prizes, 67-69, citation, 67 &
medal, 69, Am Watercolor Soc; medal of achievement, Inst Art
Mex, 70; plus many others.
Bibliography: Included in: The U S Air Force, a pictorial history,
66, One hundred watercolor techniques, 68 & History of the
American Watercolor Society, 69; plus others.
Memberships: Academician Nat Acad Design; Am Watercolor Soc;
Audubon Artists; Allied Artists Am; Knickerbocker Asn; Brook-
lyn Soc Artists; plus others.
Publications: Auth, Flower painting in watercolor, 66; auth, Drawing
and painting the city, 67 & co-auth, Painting with watercolor, 71,
Van Nostrand-Reinhold; illusr, short stories of: P G Wodehouse,
Quentin Reynolds & many others; also contribr, nat mags.
Mailing Address: 1 W 67th St, New York, NY 10023.

COOPER, PHILLIS
Sculptor
Preferred Media: Ceramics.
b Oakland, Calif, July 22, 45.
Study & Training: Univ Calif, Davis, BA.
Exhibitions: Kingsley Sculpture Ann, Crocker Art Gallery, Sacra-
mento, Calif, 69; All Girls Show, Candy Store Gallery, Folsom,
Calif, 71; Deep Source of Trouble, San Francisco State Col,
Calif, 72; Reno's Clay Diggings, Wenger Gallery, San Francisco,
72; The Cup Show, David Stuart Gallery, Los Angeles, Calif, 72.
Awards: Kingsley Art Club Educ Found Award, 69.
Bibliography: Thomas Albright (auth), Another side of Reno, San
Francisco Chronicle, 7/27/72.
Dealer: Wenger Gallery, 855 Montgomery St, San Francisco, CA
94133.
Mailing Address: 948 Washington, Reno, NV 89503.

COPE, DOROTHY
Painter
b Vancouver, B C, Sept 5, 15.
Study & Training: Vancouver Art Sch.
Work in Public Collections: Vancouver Art Gallery.
Exhibitions: B C Soc Artists, 49-58; Can Soc Painters in Water
Colour, 54-58; Ont Soc Artists, 58; 100 Years of British Colum-
bia Art, 58; four-man show, Toronto Art Gallery, 59; plus others.
Awards: Award, Winnipeg Show, 57; dipl of hon, Int Salon, Vichy,
France, 61.
Memberships: B C Soc Artists; Can Soc Painters in Water Colour.
Mailing Address: 840 Evelyn Dr, West Vancouver, B C, Can.

COPELAND, LAWRENCE GILL
Educator, Designer
Preferred Media: Metal.
b Pittsburgh, Pa, Apr 12, 22.
Study & Training: Ohio State Univ, BFA, 46; Univ Stockholm, Sweden, cert, 47; study with Baron Eric Fleming, 47-48, Emeric Gomery, 48-49; Cranbrook Acad Art, MFA, 51.
Work in Public Collections: Nat Gallery Art, Washington, D C.
Commissions: Mrs Vanderbilt Webb Award, Rochester Inst Technol, N Y, 55; Sterling Awards, Gannett Newspapers, Rochester, N Y, 59-61; off identifications, Phillips Petroleum, Hackensack, N J, 65.
Exhibitions: Davidson Art Ctr, Middletown, Conn, 55; Craftsmanship in a Changing World, Mus Contemp Crafts, 56; Brussels World's Fair, 58; New York Crafts, Munson-Williams-Proctor Inst, Utica, N Y, 61; Mus Contemp Crafts, New York, 66.
Teaching: Asst prof metal design, Sch for Am Crafts, Rochester Inst Technol, 51-59; Assoc prof design, City Col New York, 63-, chmn art dept, 67-69.
Memberships: Am Crafts Coun; Artist-Craftsmen New York (bd mem, 67-68); N Y State Craftsmen (v pres & bd mem, 56-71); Col Art Asn Am; Metrop Mus Art.
Mailing Address: 442 Hamilton Pl, Hackensack, NJ 07601.

COPELAND, LILA
Painter, Printmaker
Preferred Media: Oils, Crayon, Lithography.
b New York, N Y.
Study & Training: Art Stud League New York, with George Grosz; Pratt Graphic Art Ctr.
Work in Public Collections: Brit Mus, London, Eng; Bibliot Nat, Paris, France; Nat Collection Fine Arts, Washington, D C; Philadelphia Mus Art, Pa; Boston Mus Fine Arts, Mass.
Exhibitions: Art Inst Chicago; De Pauw Univ; Oklahoma Mus Art; Staten Island Mus; Wis State Univ.
Awards: Norman Waite Harris Bronze Medal & Prize, Art Inst Chicago.
Bibliography: Joan Hess Michel (auth), Children—the drawings of Lila Copeland, Am Artist, 12/70; Joyce Hill (auth), Sketch of Lila Copeland, Lower Cape Newspaper, 12/12/72.
Memberships: Provincetown Artists Asn.
Dealer: Associated American Artists, 663 Fifth Ave, New York, NY 10022.
Mailing Address: 31 W Ninth St, New York, NY 10011.

COPLAN, KATE M
Designer, Writer
b Baltimore, Md, Dec 25, 01.
Study & Training: Johns Hopkins Univ.
Positions: Chief exhibs & publ, Enoch Pratt Free Pub Libr, Baltimore, 35-63.
Awards: Prize, gold, silver & bronze medals, Int Window Display Competition, 50; Ten Women of Achievement, Baltimore, 50; Baltimore's Hadassah's Award, 67.
Memberships: Md Libr Asn; Am Libr Asn; Baltimore Pub Rels Coun.
Publications: Auth, Effective library exhibits: how to prepare and promote good displays, 58, Poster ideas and bulletin board techniques: for libraries and schools, 62 & co-auth, Guide to better bulletin boards, 70, Oceana; co-auth, The library reaches out, 65; contribr, Libr J & Publ Weekly.
Mailing Address: 130 Slade Ave, Apt 112, Baltimore, MD 21208.

COPLANS, JOHN (RIVERS)
Art Editor, Art Critic
b London, Eng, June 24, 20.
Positions: Ed-at-large, Artforum Mag, 62-66, assoc ed, 66-70, ed, 71-; dir, art gallery, Univ Calif, Irvine, 65-68; cur, Pasadena Art Mus, 67-70; organizer, numerous exhibs & catalogue essays.
Awards: Guggenheim fel, 69.
Publications: Auth, Cezanne watercolors, Ward Ritchie Press, 67; auth, Serial imagery, 68 & Andy Warhol, 71, New York Graphic; auth, Roy Lichtenstein, Praeger, 72; auth, Ellsworth Kelly, Abrams, 72; contribr, Artforum, Art News, Art in Am, Art Int & others.
Mailing Address: c/o Artforum, 667 Madison Ave, New York, NY 10021.

CORCOS, LUCILLE
Painter, Illustrator
Preferred Media: Tempera, Acrylics, Gouache, Watercolors, Ink, Crayon.
b New York, N Y, Sept 21, 08.
Study & Training: Art Stud League New York, with Richard Lahey & Jan Matulka.
Work in Public Collections: Whitney Mus Am Art, New York, N Y; Mus Tel-Aviv, Israel.
Commissions: Kaleidoscope, Waldorf-Astoria (mural), Waldorf-Astoria Hotel, New York, 45; Boston Pops Concert (painting), Am Brewers Asn, 45; Children's Games (painting in egg tempera), Life Mag, New York, 51; This is Macy's (painting), Fortune Mag, New York, 54; White Christmas (painting), Am Weekly, 57; plus others.
Exhibitions: Five Shows, Art Inst Chicago Int Exhib Watercolors, 38-42; Ann Exhib Sculpture, Watercolors & Drawings, Whitney Mus Am Art, 38-54; La Peintura Contemporanea Norte Americana, travelled to mus in S Am cities, 41; Five Shows, American Painting Today, Metrop Mus Art, New York, 41-50; Nine Shows, Portrait of America, Carnegie Inst, 45-72.
Awards: Hon mention, Portrait of Am Exhib, Pepsi-Cola Co, 44; hon mention, Audubon Artists, 46; purchase award, Audubon Artists, Grumbacher Co, 56.
Bibliography: Jean Lipman (auth), The composite scene in primitive painting, Gazette Beaux Arts, 42; A double view of artists' life, Life Mag, 7/54; Gailanne Repetti (auth), The big river on canvas, The Record Mag, 12/10/66.
Memberships: Artists Equity Asn New York.
Publications: Illusr, A treasury of Gilbert & Sullivan, Simon & Schuster, 41; illusr, Grimm's Fairy Tales, four Vols, Ltd Ed Club, 62; auth & illusr, From Ungskah to Oyaylee, Pantheon, 65; illusr & ed, Seeking & finding (multi-media educ prog), Fordham Publ, 69; auth & illusr, The city book, Golden Press, 72; plus many others.
Mailing Address: 167 S Mountain Rd, New City, NY 10956.

CORD, ORLANDO
Painter
b New Orleans, La, Nov 22, 22.
Study & Training: Self-taught; spec study, Univ Color, 46, under Hans Hofmann, 49, Art Stud League New York, 51 & periodic study with Fairfield Porter, 60-63.
Work in Public Collections: Guild Hall Mus; Heckscher Mus; Mus Mod Art, Paris; N J State Mus; Parrish Art Mus; plus other pub & pvt collections.
Exhibitions: Long Island Univ, Parrish Art Mus & Heckscher Mus, 71; Tower Gallery, Southampton, N Y & Guild Hall, London, Eng, 72; plus many others.
Mailing Address: c/o Harmon Gallery, 1258 Third St S, Naples, FL 33940.

CORDINGLEY, MARY BOWLES
Painter
Preferred Media: Oils, Pencils, Inks, Acrylics, Pastels.
b Des Moines, Iowa, Jan 1, 18.
Study & Training: Minneapolis Sch Art & Design; Minneapolis Art Inst; Univ Minn; Colorado Springs Fine Arts Ctr; also with Steve Rettegi, New York, Hilton Leech, Fla & Paul Olsen, Minneapolis.
Work in Public Collections: In over 140 pvt collections.
Commissions: Numerous portraits.
Exhibitions: Traveling Exhibs, 66 & 67 & Print Show, 70, Mont Inst Arts; Nat League Am Pen Women Nat Biennial, Washington, D C, 67 & 70; Jr League Print Show, Great Falls, Mont, 71; plus seven one-man shows including, C M Russell Mus, Great Falls, 67 & 71, Univ Mont, 70 & Univ Minn.
Positions: Creator & owner, Orig Pioneer Prints Notepaper Co.
Memberships: Mont State Arts Coun; Mont Inst Arts; Prof Women Artists Mont.
Mailing Address: 42 Prospect Dr, Great Falls, MT 59405.

CORISH, JOSEPH RYAN
Painter
Preferred Media: Oils.
b Somerville, Mass, Apr 9, 09.
Study & Training: Boston Univ, JD, 32; Harvard Univ, Adj in Arts, 38.
Work in Public Collections: U S Naval Acad Mus; U S Naval War Col; Boston Univ; also in various state capitols, foreign embassies & Brit, Ger, Span, Japanese, Port & U S Navies.
Commissions: Golden memories in sport history for Case Mem, Boston Univ, 68; U S Naval Acad Mus, 71; Spruance Mem Bldg, U S Naval War Col, 71; Ger Embassy, Washington, D C, 71; Ark State Capitol Rotunda.
Exhibitions: Boston Mus Fine Arts: Soc Independent Artists, Mass, 57; Jordon Exhib Contemp New Eng Artists, Boston, 58; one-man shows, Golden Age of Sail, U S Naval Acad, Md & Birmingham Mus Art Centennial Exhib, Ala, 71; Bertrand Russell Centennial Exhib, London, Eng, 72; Man and the Sea, Olympic Int Exhib, Kiel, Ger, 72.
Teaching: Guest lectr painting, Harvard Univ, Regis Col, Univ Conn, Copley Soc, & other colleges, museums & art associations.
Positions: Art dir, Castle Hill Found, Ipswich, Mass, 58-63; artist-in-residence, U S Navy First Naval Dist, 71-
Awards: First prize, Hamilton Wenham Open, 54, Diamond Jubilee Nat Exhib, Am Bar Asn, 56 & Portsmouth Art Asn Open, 60.

Memberships: North Shore Arts Asn (dir & trustee, 56-); Copley
Soc (dir & trustee, 62-64); Winchester Art Asn.
Publications: Paintings reproduced in full color as mag covers, U S
Naval War Col Rev, Down East Mag, Wilmington Report & many
others.
Mailing Address: 421 Highland Ave, Somerville, MA 02143.

CORMIER, ROBERT JOHN
Painter, Instructor
b Boston, Mass.
Study & Training: R H Ives Gammell Studios, cert.
Work in Public Collections: Maryhill Mus, Goldborough, Wash;
Boston Col Libr, Chestnut Hill, Mass; Superior Courthouse,
Cambridge, Mass.
Commissions: Portraits for St Michael's Church, Charleston, S C,
60 & Cent Savings Bank, Lowell, Mass, 72; also pvt comns for
portraits of prominent individuals.
Exhibitions: New Eng Artists Contemp Ann, 54-69; Am Artists Prof
League Grand Nat, 59-69; Guild of Boston Artists, 60-72; Boston
Arts Festival, 62; Coun Am Artists Socs, New York, 66.
Teaching: Instr drawing & painting, Vesper George Sch Art, 69-
Awards: Grand prize, Boston Arts Festival, 62; gold medal of
honor, Coun Am Artists Socs, 65.
Memberships: Guild of Boston Artists (secy, bd gov, 70-72); Copley
Soc Boston (v pres, 70-72); Am Artists Prof League (dir, Mass
Chap, 65-71).
Mailing Address: 30 Ipswich St, Boston, MA 02115.

CORNELIUS, FRANCIS DuPONT
Conservator, Painter
b Pittsburgh, Pa, Oct 19, 07.
Study & Training: Univ Pa, BArch; Univ Pittsburgh, MA.
Exhibitions: Assoc Artists Pittsburgh, annually.
Teaching: Lectr conserv art, Colo Col, 61-68; lectr conserv methods
at various univs & cols.
Positions: Res fel conserv, 44-45; fel conserv, Metrop Mus Art, New
York, N Y, 45-52; tech adv, Colorado Springs Fine Arts Ctr,
Colo, 52-55, restorer, 55-68; conservator, Mus N Mex Art Gal-
lery, 55-61; conservator, Univ Nebr Art Gallery, 58-; El Paso
Mus Art, 60-; private studio for preservation of works of art,
Colorado Springs, Colo, 52-68; independent lab for preservation
works of art, Cincinnati, Ohio, 68-; conservator, Cincinnati Art
Mus, 68-
Memberships: Am Asn Mus; Spanish Colonial Art Soc, Santa Fe,
N Mex (bd trustees, 64-); fel Int Inst Conserv Mus Objects.
Research: Surface films & disintegration of canvas supports.
Art Interests: Partic, Brit Coun course conserv, London, Eng, 56.
Publications: Auth, Frick pieta panels; auth, Further developments
in the treatment of fire-blistered oil paintings, 66; auth, Move-
ment of wood & canvas for paintings in response to high & low RH
cycles, 68.
Mailing Address: Cincinnati Art Museum, Cincinnati, OH 45202.

CORNELIUS, MARTY
Painter, Illustrator
Preferred Media: Oils.
b Pittsburgh, Pa, Sept 18, 13.
Study & Training: Carnegie-Mellon Univ, BA, 35; Pittsburgh Play-
house, 38-39; art therapy, VA Hosp & Menninger's, Topeka, Kans;
also with Reginald Marsh, New York, N Y & Alexander Kostel-
low, Pittsburgh.
Work in Public Collections: 100 Friends of Pittsburgh Art; 100
Friends Labrobe Art; New Bethlehem High Sch; Mus Mod Art,
New York, N Y; others in pub schs & hosps.
Exhibitions: Whitney Mus Am Art, New York; Corcoran Gallery Art
Biennial, Washington, D C; Palace of Legion of Honor, San Fran-
cisco, Calif; Assoc Artists Pittsburgh Ann, Carnegie Inst, 37-;
Regional Painting & Sculpture Exhib, Westmoreland Co Mus Art,
Greensburg, Pa; plus many others.
Teaching: Instr art, VA Hosp, Pittsburgh; art therapist drawing,
Carnegie-Mellon Univ, 59-61, prof drawing, 65-69.
Positions: Designer, Aluminum Co Am, New Kensington, Pa, 50-
51; Joseph Horne Co, Pittsburgh, 55-56.
Awards: Awards, Martin Leisser Sch Design, 46 & 48, Butler Inst
Am Art, 48, Assoc Artists Pittsburgh, 39, 45 & 53 & others.
Memberships: Fel Int Inst Arts & Lett; Int Platform Asn; Assoc
Artists Pittsburgh (mem bd dirs, 39-40); plus others.
Publications: Illusr, Pittsburgh, the story of an American city, 58.
Mailing Address: Phoenix Nest, Ligonier, PA 15658.

CORNFELD, MELISSA MAREIN
Weaver
b New York, N Y, Oct 11, 45.
Study & Training: Foreningen Handarbetets Vanner, Stockholm,
Sweden, 66; Carnegie Inst Technol, BFA, 67.
Work in Public Collections: W Va Arts & Humanities Coun Collec-
tion.

Exhibitions: Young Americans, Mus Contemp Crafts, New York, 62
& 69; Piedmont Show—Crafts, Mint Mus, Charlotte, N C, 67;
Louisville Art Ctr Regional Craft Biennial, Ky, 68; Appalachian
Corridors, Charleston, W Va, 68, 70 & 72; Ann Invitational Craft
Show, Northern Ill Univ, De Kalb, 70.
Teaching: Instr drawing, Huntington Galleries, W Va, 67-68.
Awards: Tag Galayan Award for Weaving, Appalachian Corridors,
68; W Va Arts & Humanities Award for three pieces, Exhibition
180, 69.
Memberships: Am Crafts Coun.
Mailing Address: 132 N Blvd W, Huntington, WV 25201.

CORNFELD, MICHAEL I
Craftsman, Educator
Preferred Media: Graphics.
b Brooklyn, N Y, Oct 13, 42.
Study & Training: Ind Univ, BA; Univ Ky; Carnegie Inst Technol,
MFA.
Work in Public Collections: W Va Arts & Humanities Coun Collec-
tion, Charleston.
Commissions: Room of Macrame, Huntington Galleries, W Va, 72.
Exhibitions: Appalachian Corridors, Charleston, W Va, 68, 70 & 72;
Nat Polymer Exhib, Eastern Mich Univ, Ypsilanti, 68; Exhibition
180, Huntington Galleries, 68; Allied Artists Charleston, W Va,
68 & 72; Piedmont Graphics Exhib, Mint Mus, Charlotte, N C, 70.
Teaching: Asst prof art, Marshall Univ, 67.
Awards: Award for graphics, Exhibition 180, Huntington Galleries,
68; award for weaving & Tag Galayan Purchase Award, Appala-
chian Corridors, 72; first in crafts Allied Artists, W Va Arts &
Humanities Coun, 72.
Memberships: Am Crafts Coun; Col Art Asn Am.
Mailing Address: 132 N Blvd W, Huntington, WV 25201.

CORSAW, ROGER D
Educator, Craftsman
Preferred Media: Ceramics.
b Ithaca, N Y, Nov 27, 13.
Study & Training: New York State Col Ceramics, Alfred Univ, BS;
Inst Design, Ill Inst Technol, with Gyorgy Kepes & Moholy Nagy.
Work in Public Collections: Everson Mus Fine Arts, Syracuse, N Y;
Smithsonian Inst, Washington, D C; Mus Contemp Crafts, New
York, N Y; Denver Art Mus, Colo; Philbrook Art Ctr, Tulsa,
Okla.
Exhibitions: 11 Nat Ceramic Exhibs, Everson Mus, Syracuse Fine
Arts, 37-68; 2nd Int Exhib Ceramics, Ostend, Belg, 59; Designer-
Craftsmen U S A, Mus Contemp Crafts, 60; Int Cult Exchange Ex-
hib, Geneva, Switz, 60; Forms from the Earth—1000 Years of
Pottery in America, Mus Contemp Crafts, 61.
Teaching: Prof ceramic art, Univ Okla, 36-
Awards: First prize for pottery, 6th Nat Ceramic Exhib, 37; pur-
chase award, Nat Acad Arts, Smithsonian Inst, 55; first prize,
Oklahoma Artists Ann, Tulsa, 56, 60, 61 & 62.
Memberships: Nat Coun Educ for Ceramic Arts (chmn mem comt,
68-72); Am Crafts Coun; Okla Designer Craftsmen.
Mailing Address: 725 Juniper Lane, Norman, OK 73069.

CORSE, MARY ANN
Painter, Sculptor
b Berkeley, Calif, Dec 5, 45.
Study & Training: Univ Calif, 63; Calif Inst Arts, Chovinard scholar
& BFA, 68.
Work in Public Collections: Los Angeles Co Mus Art, Los Angeles,
Calif; Solomon R Guggenheim Mus, New York, N Y; Robert
Mitchner Collection, Univ Tex.
Exhibitions: Whitney Sculpture Ann, Whitney Mus Am Art, New York,
70; Permutations, Light & Color, Mus Contemp Art, Chicago, 70;
24 Young Artists, Los Angeles Co Mus, 71; Theodoron Awards,
Solomon R Guggenheim Mus, 71; 15 Los Angeles Artists, Pasa-
dena Art Mus, 72.
Awards: New Talent Award, Los Angeles Co Mus, 68; Theodoron
Award, Solomon R Guggenheim Mus 70.
Bibliography: Andy Eason (producer), White Light (film), Eason De-
sign, 69.
Mailing Address: c/o Dick Bellamy, 1078 Madison Ave, New York,
NY 10028.

CORSO, PATRICK
Painter
Preferred Media: Oils.
b New York, N Y, June 1, 26.
Study & Training: Art Stud League New York, with F Dumond; Nat
Acad Design, with Leon Krolle, Robert Phillips & Belskie.
Work in Public Collections: U S Marine Corps Hq, Washington, D C;
Great Lakes U S Naval Sta, Chicago, Ill; Butler Inst Am Art,
Youngstown, Ohio.
Commissions: Trinity, Cath Church, Great Lakes U S Naval Sta, 53;
Our Lady of Fatima, Barstow U S Marine Corps Supply Depot, 54.

Exhibitions: Allied Artists Am, 69; Salmagundi Club, New York, 69; Nat Arts Club, 72; Am Artists Prof League, 72; Butler Inst Am Art, 72.
Awards: Second prize oil, Salmagundi Club, 71; first prize oil, Am Artists Prof League, 72.
Memberships: Salmagundi Club; Allied Artists Am; Am. Artists Prof League.
Dealer: Harbor Gallery, 43 Main St, Cold Spring Harbor, NY 11724.
Mailing Address: 8615 Broadway, Elmhurst, NY 11373.

CORSON, GORDON MELVIN
Painter
Preferred Media: Oils.
b Oakland, Calif, May 29, 36.
Study & Training: Univ San Francisco; Calif Col Arts & Crafts; Univ Calif; apprenticed to James E Constant, Oakland; San Francisco City Col, with Carl Beetz.
Work in Public Collections: Oakland Art Mus; Richmond Art Ctr, Calif; Park's Art Gallery, San Jose, Calif; Kaiser Ctr, Oakland; Brandeis Univ, New York, N Y.
Exhibitions: Brandeis Univ Art Show, San Francisco, 64-65; four San Francisco Art Festivals, 66-71; four Jack London Art Shows, Oakland, 66-70; Soc Western Artists, de Saisset Art Gallery, Santa Clara, Calif, 67; Soc Western Artists Nat Cystic Fibrosis Show, San Francisco, 68.
Awards: Best of show, Brandeis Univ, 64, first place for mixed media, 64 & third place purchase award, 65.
Memberships: Oakland Art Asn; Soc Western Artists; East Bay Artists Asn.
Mailing Address: P O Box 112, Canyon, CA 94516.

CORTLANDT, LYN
Painter
Preferred Media: Oils.
b New York, N Y.
Study & Training: Chouinard Art Inst & Jepson Art Inst, Los Angeles, Calif; Art Stud League New York; Pratt Inst Art Sch; Columbia Univ Sch Painting & Sculpture; Hans Hofmann Sch Fine Arts; China Inst Am; Also pvt study.
Work in Public Collections: Metrop Mus Art, New York; Mus Nat Art Mod, Paris, France; Stedelijk Mus, Amsterdam, Neth; Mus Fine Arts, Boston, Mass; Fogg Mus Art, Cambridge, Mass; plus many others.
Exhibitions: Pa Acad Fine Arts, Philadelphia; Nat Acad Design, New York; Art U S A, many mus, galleries & cols; Munic Mus Art, Tokyo, Japan; Kunstmus, Bern, Switz; plus many others.
Awards: Nat Asn Women Artists; Painters & Sculptors Soc N J; Centro Studi e Scambi Int Medal of Honor; plus others.
Memberships: Fel Royal Soc Arts; fel Int Inst Arts & Lett; Marquis Biog Libr Soc (adv mem); Allied Artists Am; plus many others.
Mailing Address: 1070 Park Ave, New York, NY 10028.

CORWIN, SOPHIA M
Sculptor, Painter
Preferred Media: Steel, Marble, Oils, Acrylics.
b New York.
Study & Training: Nat Acad Sch Fine Arts; Art Stud League New York; Hoffman Sch; Archipenko Sch; Phillips Gallery Art Sch, Washington, D C, with Karl Knaths, scholar, 45; N Y Univ, BA & MA(creative arts).
Exhibitions: Art: U S A: 58, City Ctr, Lever House & Contemp Arts Gallery, New York, N Y; four one-man shows, Capricorn Gallery & Creative Arts Gallery, New York, Colony Galleries, Washington, D C & others, 68-70; Group Shows, Baltimore Mus; Nat Collection Fine Arts, Corcoran Gallery Art & Phillips Mem Galleries, Washington, D C; Silvermine Guild, Conn.
Teaching: Asst instr painting, N Y Univ, 61-62; instr painting & drawing & dir, Studio Workshop, Bronx House, N Y, 62-; lectr art hist, Coop Col Ctr Westchester, State Univ N Y Col Purchase, 71-
Positions: Juror for art show, N Y State Coun Arts, 70.
Awards: Nat competition award for one-man show, Creative Arts Gallery, 54.
Memberships: Nat Soc Women Artists; Am. Soc Contemp Artists; League Present Day Artists; Sculptors League, Artists Equity Asn.
Mailing Address: 79 Franklin Ave, Yonkers, NY 10705.

CORZAS, FRANCISCO
Painter
Preferred Media: Oils.
b Mexico City, Mex, Oct 4, 36.
Study & Training: La Esmeralda, Inst Nac Bellas Artes, Mexico City, 51-55; Acad San Giacoma, Rome, Italy, 56-58; French Govt scholarship, 67.

Work in Public Collections: Mus Mod Art, Mexico City; Los Angeles Co Mus Art, Calif; Phoenix Art Mus, Ariz; Mus Mod Art, Tel-Aviv, Israel; Banco de Comercio, Mexico City.
Commissions: Painting, Hotel Princess. Acapulco, Mex, 72.
Exhibitions: Confrontacion 66, Palacio Nac Bellas Artes, 66; Ninth São Paulo Biennial, Brazil, 67; Mex pavilion, Expo '67, Montreal, Can, 67 & Expo '70, Osaka, Japan, 70; Young Mexican Painters, Ctr Inter-Am Relations, New York, N Y, 71.
Awards: Second prize for Via Margutta, Rome, Italy, 58; hon mention, 62 & acquisition prize, 64, Salon de la Plastica Mexicana.
Bibliography: Toby Joysmith (auth), Moods of modern romantic, The News, 67; John Canaday (auth), Young Mexicans, N Y Times, 70; Roberto Sanesi (auth), Rigattiere D'ombre, Corriere della Sera, 71.
Dealer: Galeria Juan Martin, Amberes 17, Mexico City 6, Mex.
Mailing Address: Ferrocarril del Valle 68, Col Tizapan, Mexico 20, D F.

COSGROVE, STANLEY
Painter
b Montreal, P Q, Dec 23, 11.
Study & Training: Beaux-Arts, Montreal; Art Asn Montreal; also with Orozco, Mex.
Work in Public Collections: Nat Gallery Can; Vancouver Art Gallery; Mus Mod Art, New York; Winnipeg Art Gallery.
Exhibitions: Yale Univ; UNESCO; Montreal Mus Fine Arts; Quebec Provincial Mus; Nat Gallery Can, Ottawa, Ont; plus others.
Awards: Medal, Beaux-Arts, Montreal; travel scholar in Quebec, Fr Govt, 53.
Memberships: Royal Can Acad Arts.
Mailing Address: P O Box 11, R R 1, Hudson, P Q, Can.

COSLA, DR & MRS O K
Collectors
Dr Cosla b Rumania, May 21, 99.
Study & Training: Dr Cosla, studied Berlin, Ger, with Wilhelm von Bode.
Collection: French, German, Dutch, Flemish, English paintings, twelfth to twentieth century. Paintings from the Cosla Collection are in the Museums of Brigham Young University, Furman University, Baldwin Wallace College, Montclair State College and Mills College.
Mailing Address: 575 West End Ave, New York, NY 10024.

COSTA, OLGA
Painter, Collector
Preferred Media: Oils.
b Lepzig, Ger, Sept 28, 13; Mex citizen.
Study & Training: San Carlos Art Sch, Nat Univ Mex, with Carlos Merida, painter & Jose Chavez Morado, painter, muralist.
Work in Public Collections: Mus Arte Mod, Mexico City; Mus Art, Warsaw, Poland; Mus Mod Art, New York, N Y; Banco Nac de Mex, Mexico City.
Commissions: Mural mosaic, Banco Hipotecario for Spain Cuantla City, 53; ballet costumes & sets, Coreographer Waldeen, Mexico City.
Exhibitions: Mus Nat d'Art Mod, Paris, France, 52; Nat Mus Tokyo, Japan 55; Fifth Int Art Exhib, Japan, 59; Mus Nac Arte Mod, Mexico City, 61; XIX Olympic Games Cultural Exhib, Galeria Arte Mod, Mexico City, 68.
Bibliography: Luis Cardosa Aragon (auth), Pintura Mexicana, Fondo de Cultura Economica, Mexico City, 64; Toby Joysmith (auth), Perpetuating the Mexican Barbizon, The News (Novedades), Mexico City, 69; Maria Sten (auth), Olga Costa, Tyija Mag, Varsovia, 70.
Collection: Preh-hispanic, colonial and folk art.
Dealers: Ines Amor, Galeria Arte Mexicano, Milan 18, Mexico City, Mex.
Mailing Address: Pastita 158, Guanajuato, Guanajuato, Mex.

COTE, ALAN
Painter
b Conn, May 9, 37.
Study & Training: Mus Fine Arts Sch, Boston, 55-60, European fel, 61-64.
Work in Public Collections: Whitney Mus Am Art, New York, N Y; Dallas Mus Fine Art, Tex; James A Michener Collection, Univ Tex; Ludwig Collection, Swermont Mus, Aachen, Ger; Phoenix Art Mus, Ariz.
Exhibitions: Paintings for Museum Collections, Am Fedn Arts, 68; A Tendency in Contemporary Painting, Köln, W Ger, 69; Whitney Ann, 69-72 & The Structure of Color, 71, Whitney Mus Am Art, New York; New York Painting, Univ Calif, Berkeley, 72; plus many other group & one-man exhibitions.
Bibliography: Willoughby Sharp (auth), Points of view, Arts Mag, 12/70-1/71; Canvases brimming with color, Life Mag, 9/24/71; Robert Pincus-Witten (auth), New York, Artforum, 3/71.

Publications: Contribr, Nine notes on color (catalogue of The Structure of Color), Whitney Mus Am Art, 71; contribr, Kunst, Praxis Heute, K Thomas-Dumont-Köln, W Ger, 72.
Dealers: Dunkleman Gallery, 15 Bedford Rd, Toronto, Ont, Can; Ricke Gallery, Linderstrasse 22, Koln, Ger.
Mailing Address: c/o Cuningham Ward, 94 Prince St, New York, NY 10012.

COTSWORTH, STAATS
    Painter, Illustrator
b Oak Park, Ill, Feb 17, 08.
Study & Training: Philadelphia Mus Sch Indust Art; Art Stud League New York, with Reginald Marsh; also with Thornton Oakley & Herbert Pullinger.
Work in Public Collections: Norfolk Mus Fine Art.
Commissions: Murals, pvt homes & pub bldgs.
Exhibitions: Corcoran Gallery Art; Philadelphia Watercolor Club; Nat Arts Club; one-man show, Am-Brit Art Ctr, 48; Whitney Mus Am Art, 54; plus others.
Positions: Chmn & custodian, Art Collection of the Players, New York, N Y.
Awards: Prizes, Conn Acad Fine Arts, 54 & Knickerbocker Artists, 55.
Memberships: Philadelphia Watercolor Club; Salmagundi Club; Am Soc Painters in Casein; Am Watercolor Soc; Audubon Artists.
Publications: Illusr, A Bacchic pilgrimage & Deep water days.
Mailing Address: 360 E 55th St, New York, NY 10022.

COUCH, URBAN
    Painter, Designer
b Minneapolis, Minn, Apr 27, 27.
Study & Training: Minneapolis Sch Art, BFA, 51; Skowhegan Sch Painting & Sculpture, 51; Cranbrook Acad Art, MFA, 59; Kyoto, Japan, 64-65.
Work in Public Collections: Minneapolis Inst Arts; Walker Art Ctr, Minneapolis; Sioux City Art Ctr, Iowa; Cranbrook Mus, Bloomfield Hills, Mich; Gray Found Collection; plus others.
Exhibitions: Neville Mus Invitational, Green Bay, Wis, 67; Art in the Embassies, U S State Dept, Sophia, Bulgaria & Canberra, Australia, 68, extended prog, 69-71; Minneapolis Inst Arts Faculty Exhib, 68; Difference of a Decade, Lee Nordness Galleries, New York, N Y, 69; Suzanne Kohn Gallery, Minneapolis, Minn, 69; plus many other group & one-man shows.
Teaching: Instr art, Minneapolis Col Art & Design, 55-70, chmn found prog, 59-62, actg dir, 62-63, asst to dir, 63-64, actg chmn fine arts div, 65-66, chmn painting dept, 68-71; instr advan painting, Walker Art Ctr, 57-61; instr art, Kingswood Sch, Bloomfield Hills, Mich & Bloomfield Hills Art Ctr, 58-59; grad workshop, Univ Minn, 59-61; instr advan painting, Minnetonka Art Ctr, Minneapolis, 59-61; artist-in-residence, Minnesota Jr Cols, summers, 67-69; instr grad painting, Calif Col Arts & Crafts, summer 70; chmn div art, W Va Univ, 71-
Positions: Graphic designer, USN, Calif, 45; alumni dir, Minneapolis Col Art & Design, 57; design consult, Control Data Corp, 60-62; consult-examiner prog, Comn on Cols & Univs, Chicago, 62-63; consult & examiner, N Cent Asn, 63-
Mailing Address: 508 Grand St, Morgantown, WV 26505.

COUGHLIN, JACK
    Graphic Artist, Printmaker
b Greenwich, Conn, Feb 19, 32.
Study & Training: Art Stud League New York; R I Sch Design, BFA, 54, MS, 61.
Work in Public Collections: Metrop Mus Art, New York, N Y; Mus Mod Art, New York; Norfolk Mus Arts & Sci, Va; Staedelsches Kunst Inst, Frankfort, Ger; Nat Collection Fine Arts, Washington, D C.
Commissions: Ed original prints, Assoc Am Artists, 62, 67 & 68, Int Graphic Arts Soc, 66 & 68, Silvermine Guild Artists, New Canaan, Conn, 67 & Graphic Studio, Dublin, Ireland, 71.
Exhibitions: Am Drawing Biennials, Norfolk Mus Arts & Sci, 62, 64 & 66; Contemp Artists Eligible for Awards, Nat Inst Arts & Lett, New York, 70; 17th Biennial Am Printmaking, Brooklyn Mus Art, N Y, 70; 2nd San Diego Nat Print Exhib, Fine Arts Gallery San Francisco, Calif, 71; 51st Print Exhib, Soc Am Graphic Arts, New York, 71.
Teaching: Assoc prof drawing & printmaking, Univ Mass, Amherst, 60-
Awards: E K Sloane Purchase Award, 21st Am Drawing Biennial, Norfolk Mus, 65; first prize printmaking, 60th Ann Exhib, Conn Acad Fine Arts, Wadsworth Atheneum, Conn, 70; H P Shope Purchase Award, Soc Am Graphic Artists, 51st Print Exhib, 71.
Bibliography: Robin Skelton (auth), The imagination of Jack Coughlin, 70 & Jack Coughlin: Irish portraits, 72, Malahat Rev, Univ Victoria, B C.

Memberships: Assoc Nat Acad Design; Soc Am Graphic Artists; Boston Printmakers; Silvermine Guild Artists.
Publications: Illusr, Twelve birds, Univ Mass Press, 64; illusr, Mnemosyne lay in dust, 66 & Synge-Petrarch, 71, Dolmen Press, Dublin, Ireland; illusr, Grotesques, 20 etchings by Jack Coughlin, Aquarius Press, 70.
Dealer: Associated American Artists, 663 Fifth Ave, New York, NY 10022.
Mailing Address: N Leverett Rd, Montague, MA 01351.

COUGHTRY, JOHN GRAHAM
    Painter, Sculptor
b Saint Lambert, P Q, June 8, 31.
Study & Training: Montreal Sch Art & Design; Ont Col Art.
Work in Public Collections: Toronto Art Gallery; Winnipeg Art Gallery; Nat Gallery Can; Mus Mod Art; Albright-Knox Art Gallery; plus others.
Commissions: Relief, Beth David Synagogue, Toronto.
Exhibitions: Commonwealth Exhib, London, Eng, 62; Vancouver Art Gallery, 62; Art Gallery Toronto, 63; Dunn Int Exhib, Tate Gallery, London, 63; Guggenheim Int, N Y, 64.
Awards: Prizes, Winnipeg Nat Exhib, 57 & 62, Vancouver Art Gallery, 62 & Art Gallery Toronto, 63; plus others.
Mailing Address: 832 Yonge St, Toronto, Ont, Can.

COULING, GORDON ROBERT
    Painter, Educator
Preferred Media: Oils, Tempera, Stained Glass.
b Guelph, Ont, Nov 21, 13.
Study & Training: Ont Col Art, hon dipl; New York Univ.
Work in Public Collections: Univ Guelph; Guelph Creative Arts Collection.
Teaching: Asst prof studio & art hist, Macdonald Inst, 49-65; assoc prof art & chmn dept fine art, Univ Guelph Col Arts, 65-69, prof art, 72, actg chmn, 72-
Research: North American architecture, especially stone building in Ontario.
Mailing Address: 5 Simpson Way, Guelph, Ont, Can.

COUPER, JAMES M
    Painter, Instructor
b Atlanta, Ga, Nov 21, 37.
Study & Training: Atlanta Art Inst; Ga State Univ; Fla State Univ.
Work in Public Collections: Fla State Univ; Miami Art Ctr; John & Mable Ringling Mus Art.
Commissions: Mural, 20th Century Fox, 68.
Exhibitions: Young Americans Nat, New York, N Y, 62; Soc Four Arts Nat, Palm Beach, Fla, 65; Isaac Delgado Mus Art Nat, New Orleans, La, 66; Drawings '72, Fort Lauderdale, Fla, 72; Fla State Dept Invitational, 72.
Collections Arranged: Art of the Asian Mountains, 69; The Artist & The Sea, 69; Art of Italy, 69; Up & Out, 69-70.
Teaching: Instr painting, Miami-Dade Jr Col, 64-68; instr painting, Miami Art Ctr, 65-72; instr painting, Fla Int Univ, 72-
Positions: Asst to dir, Miami Art Ctr, 67-70.
Mailing Address: 8950 S W Red Rd, Miami, FL 33156.

COURT, LEE WINSLOW
    Painter
Preferred Media: Oils.
b Somerville, Mass, Dec 10, 03.
Study & Training: Mass Col Art; also with Aldro T Hibbard, Rockport, Mass & Harry Leith-Ross, Philadelphia, Pa.
Work in Public Collections: Polar Archives, Nat Archives, Washington, D C; Farnsworth Mus, Rockland, Maine; Evansville Mus, Ind; Proctor Acad, N H; Sanford Sch, Del.
Commissions: Cat-Bow Farm, comn by Sinclair Weeks, Lancaster, N H, 66; Beach Aircraft Co, Wichita, Kans, 67; M S Lindblad, Explorer, comn by Lars-Eric Lindblad, Norway, 70.
Exhibitions: Salmagundi Club, New York, N Y, 53-; Acad Artists Asn, Springfield, Mass, 55-; Am Artists Prof League, New York, 58-; Guild Boston Artists, Mass, 65-; Southern Vt Artists, Manchester, 69-
Positions: Dir, Coun Am Artist Socs, New York, 56-59; producer, Int Trade Fairs, 57-62; pres, Copley Soc, Boston, 57-64; chmn, Comt Fair Representation in Art Exhibs, Boston, 61-
Awards: Citation, Govt Mex, 44; Legion of Honor Govt France, 49; Woodman Award, Ogunquit, Maine, 67.
Memberships: Am Artists Prof League (dir, 58-62); Guild Boston Artists; Salmagundi Club; Acad Artists Asn; N Shore Art Asn, Gloucester, Mass.
Publications: Ed, An appreciation, Joseph Rodover De Camp, 25.
Mailing Address: Rte 30, West Townshend, VT 05359.

COURTICE, RODY KENNY
 Painter
Preferred Media: Tempera, Oils, Watercolours.
b Renfrew, Ont.
Study & Training: Ont Col Art; Art Inst Chicago; Hans Hoffman Summer Sch, Provincetown.
Work in Public Collections: Numerous pub & pvt collections.
Exhibitions: Nat & int exhibs.
Memberships: Assoc Royal Can Acad Arts; Can Group Painters; Can Soc Painters in Watercolour; Ont Soc Artists; Can Soc Graphic Art.
Mailing Address: Rosedale Court 204, 30 Elm Ave, Toronto 5, Ont, Can.

COVI, DARIO A
 Art Historian
b Livingston, Ill, Dec 26, 20.
Study & Training: Eastern Ill State Col, BEd, 43; State Univ Iowa, MA, 48, with Prof William S Heckscher; New York Univ, PhD, 58, with Prof Richard Offner.
Teaching: From instr to prof art hist, Univ Louisville, 56-70; prof art hist, Duke Univ, 70-
Positions: Mem exec comt, Ky Arts Comn, 65-70.
Awards: Am Coun Learned Socs fel, 64; Fulbright-Hays fcl, 68-69.
Memberships: Col Art Asn Am; Southeastern Col Art Conf.
Research: Italian renaissance art.
Publications: Auth, Prints . . . from the Allen R Hite Art Institute Collection (exhib catalog), 63; contribr, McGraw-Hill Dict Art, Art Bull, Burlington Mag, Renaissance News & other nat art publ.
Mailing Address: Dept of Art, Duke University, 6605 College Station, Durham, NC 27708.

COVINGTON, HARRISON WALL
 Painter, Educator
b Plant City, Fla, Apr 12, 24.
Study & Training: Univ Fla, 42-43; Hiram Col, 43; Univ Fla, BFA (hons), 49, MFA, 53.
Work in Public Collections: Herron Mus Art, Indianapolis, Ind; Mead Corp, Atlanta, Ga; Everson Mus Art, Syracuse, N Y; John & Mable Ringling Mus Art, Sarasota, Fla; Jacksonville Mus Art, Fla.
Exhibitions: Museum Director's Choice, circulated throughout Southeast U S, 56 & 59; Nat Home Furnishings Show, New York, N Y, 59; Painting U S A: The Figure, Mus Mod Art, New York, 62; New York World's Fair, 64; Florida 17, Pan-Am Union, Washington, D C, 68.
Teaching: Instr art, Univ Fla, 49-61; prof art, Univ S Fla, 61-, chmn visual arts prog, 61-67, dean, Div Fine Arts, 67-72.
Awards: Sloan Found grant, 47; Guggenheim fel, 64.
Mailing Address: Dept of Art, University of South Florida, Tampa, FL 33618.

COWAN, WOODSON MESSICK
 Cartoonist, Painter
Preferred Media: Watercolors.
b Algona, Iowa, Nov 1, 86.
Study & Training: Art Inst Chicago.
Exhibitions: Paintings exhib Westport, Conn, 64, Darien, Conn, 68, Norwalk, Conn, 70 & Jekyll Island, Ga, 72.
Positions: Sports writer & cartoonist, George Mathew Adams Syndicate, New York, 20-27; comic strip artist, Nat Ed Asn Serv, Cleveland, 28-42; ed cartoonist, Bridgeport Eve Post, 49-59; ed cartoonist, New Haven Eve Regis, 60-69.
Awards: Best of yr for ed cartoon Christmas Tragedy, Nat Found Hwy Safety, 66.
Memberships: Westport Artists (pres, 49); Artists & Writers; Jekyll Island Art Asn.
Publications: Auth & illusr, Them were the days, 26; illusr, Teen topics, 48; illusr, Popularity plus, 50; auth & illusr, Flying Andy, 55; auth & illusr, Famous figures of the old west, 62; auth & illusr, Iowa cracker barrel, 72.
Mailing Address: 18 Godfrey Rd, Weston, CT 06880.

COWDREY, MARY BARTLETT
 Art Historian, Art Critic
b Passaic, N J, June 16, 10.
Study & Training: Douglass Col, Rutgers Univ, AB, 33, LittD, 64.
Work in Public Collections: Publ in all art libr in U S.
Collections Arranged: American 18th-19th Century Paintings, Harry Saw Newman Gallery; American 18th-20th Century, English 18th-19th Century Paintings, Smith Col Mus Art.
Positions: Cur paintings, Harry Shaw Newman Gallery, 43-49; cur & actg dir, Smith Col Mus Art, 49-55; archivist, Archives Am Art, New York Off, 55-61; cur prints & drawings, N J Hist Soc, 61-62.
Memberships: Victorian Soc Am (adv comt, 69-).
Research: History of American art.

Publications: Auth, National Academy of Design exhibition record (compilation), 43; co-auth, William Sidney Mount, 44; auth, American Academy of Fine Arts & American Art Union, exhibition record, 53; auth, Winslow Homes: illustrator, 51; auth, Fanny Palmer, an American lithographer in prints, 62; plus many other books, articles & monographs.
Mailing Address: 33 Randolph St, Passaic, NJ 07055.

COWING, WILLIAM R
 Painter, Instructor
b Hartford, Conn, Nov 8, 20.
Study & Training: Univ Hartford, BFA; Univ Mex, grad study.
Work in Public Collections: New Brit Mus; Springfield Mus Art; Dayton Art Inst.
Exhibitions: Conn Acad Fine Arts, 41-72; Springfield Art League, 49-72; Eastern States Exhib, 51, 61 & 62; Boston Art Festival, 55 & 56; Conn Watercolor Soc, 48-72; plus others.
Teaching: Instr, Westminster Sch, Simsbury, Conn; instr, Conn Acad Coun, 62-
Positions: Bd dirs, Conn Watercolor Soc, 52-53 & 62-64, pres, 64-66; pres, Housatonic Art Asn, 60-64; coun mem, Conn Acad Fine Arts, 62-70.
Awards: Int Hallmark Art Award, 52; prize, Conn Acad Fine Arts, 60; prize, Silvermine Guild Artists, 54; plus others.
Memberships: Conn Watercolor Soc; Conn Acad Fine Arts; Springfield Art League, Mass.
Mailing Address: 30 Great Pond Rd, Simsbury, CT 06070.

COWLES, CHARLES
 Publisher, Collector
b Santa Monica, Calif, Feb 7, 41.
Study & Training: Stanford Univ.
Positions: Pres & publisher, Artforum Mag.
Memberships: Studio Mus Harlem (trustee); Mus Mod Art (mem int coun); Fine Arts Coun Fla.
Collection: Contemporary art.
Mailing Address: 59 Wooster St (5), New York, NY 10012.

COWLES, MR & MRS GARDNER
 Collectors
Mr Cowles, b Algona, Iowa, Jan 31, 03.
Positions: Mr Cowles, trustee, Mus Mod Art, New York.
Collection: Contemporary paintings.
Mailing Address: Cowles Communications, Inc, 488 Madison Ave, New York, NY 10022.

COWLES, RUSSELL
 Painter
b Algona, Iowa, Oct 7, 87.
Study & Training: Dartmouth Col, AB, 09; Nat Acad Design; Art Stud League New York; Am Acad in Rome; Century Asn; Grinnell Col, hon DFA, 45; Dartmouth Col, DHL, 51; Cornell Univ, hon DFA, 58; mural painting with Douglas Volk & Barry Faulker.
Work in Public Collections: Denver Art Mus; Terre Haute Mus; Encycl Britannica Collection; Murdock Col, Univ Wichita; Dartmouth Col; plus others.
Exhibitions: Carnegie; Pa Acad Fine Arts; Whitney Mus Am Art; Los Angeles Co Mus Art; Calif Palace of Legion of Honor; plus many other group & one-man shows.
Awards: Medal, Art Inst Chicago; prizes, Denver Art Mus & Santa Barbara Mus Art.
Bibliography: Monroe Wheeler (auth), included in: Painters and sculptors of modern art, Crowell, 42; Ernest W Watson (auth), included in: Twenty painters and how they work, Watson-Guptill, 50; Ralph M Pearson (auth), included in: The modern renaissance in American art, Harper & Row, 54; plus others.
Dealer: Kraushaar Galleries, 1055 Madison Ave, New York, NY 10028.
Mailing Address: 179 E 70th St, New York, NY 10021.

COWLEY, EDWARD P
 Educator, Painter
Preferred Media: Oils.
b Buffalo, N Y, May 29, 25.
Study & Training: Albright Art Sch; Buffalo State Col, BS, 48; Columbia Univ, MA, 49; Nat Col Art, Dublin, Ireland, Ford Found fel, 55.
Work in Public Collections: Albany Inst Hist & Art, N Y; Schenectady Mus, N Y; Smith Col, Northhampton, Mass; Colgate Univ, Hamilton, N Y; Berkshire Mus, Pittsfield, Mass.
Teaching: Prof art & chmn art dept, State Univ N Y Albany, 56-
Awards: State Univ N Y res grant, 66.
Mailing Address: Box 198, Altamont, NY 12009.

COX, ALLYN
Painter
b New York, N Y, June 5, 96.
Study & Training: Nat Acad Design; Art Stud League New York; Am
Acad Rom fel, 16-21.
Work in Public Collections: Butler Inst Am Art, Youngstown, Ohio;
Princeton Univ Mus, N J; Nat Collection, Washington, D C.
Commissions: Ceilings & others, W A Clark Mem Libr, Univ Calif,
Los Angeles, 24-28; six mural panels & others, Law Bldg, Univ
Va, 31-33; murals & stained glass, George Washington Masonic
Nat Mem, 47-58; frescos & others, U S Capitol, Washington, D C,
52-; mosaics, U S Grant Mem, New York, N Y, 64-66.
Exhibitions: Drawings & Paintings, Southampton Mus, N Y, 53.
Positions: Art comnr, New York City, 52-58.
Awards: Rome Prize, Am Acad Rome, 16; gold medal of honor,
Archit League New York, 53; gold medal for serv to arts, Royal
Arch Masons, 62.
Memberships: Academician Nat Acad Design; Nat Soc Mural Paint-
ers (pres, 7 yrs); Am Artists Prof League (pres, 50-52); Archit
League New York (past v pres).
Mailing Address: 165 E 60th St, New York, NY 10022.

COX, E MORRIS
Collector
b Santa Rosa, Calif, Feb 5, 03.
Study & Training: Univ Calif, AB; Harvard Univ Grad Sch Bus, MBA.
Positions: Pres, San Francisco Mus Art, 55-60, now trustee; treas,
Calif Acad Sci, 63-67, now chmn bd trustees; dir, Bay Area Educ
TV Asn.
Collection: Contemporary sculpture and painting.
Mailing Address: 2361 Broadway, San Francisco, CA 94115.

COX, GARDNER
Painter
Preferred Media: Oils, Watercolors, Tempera, Acrylics.
b Holyoke, Mass, Jan 22, 06.
Study & Training: Art Stud League New York, 24; Harvard Univ, 24-
27; Boston Mus Sch, 28-30; Mass Inst Technol, 29-31.
Work in Public Collections: Nat Gallery Art, Washington, D C; Nat
Portrait Gallery, Washington, D C; Boston Mus Fine Arts, Mass;
Fogg Art Mus, Harvard Univ, Cambridge, Mass; Addison Gallery
Am Art, Andover, Mass.
Commissions: Portraits, Lessing Rosenwald, Nat Gallery Art, Hon
Dean Acheson, State Dept, Washington, D C, 50, Robert Frost,
Frost Libr, Amherst Col, Mass, 57, Justice Felix Frankfurter,
Harvard Univ Law Sch, 60 & Robert F Kennedy, Nat Portrait
Gallery, 68.
Exhibitions: Carnegie Int, Pittsburgh, Pa, 41; Va Mus Fine Arts,
Richmond, 46; Art Inst Chicago, Ill, 48, 49 & 51; Metrop Mus
Art, New York, N Y, 50; Corcoran Gallery Art, Washington, D C.
Teaching: Head dept painting, Boston Mus Sch, 54-56.
Positions: Exec Comt, Boston Arts Festival, 55-65; exec comt,
Mass Art Comn, 65-
Awards: M V Kohnstamm Prize, Am Exhib Watercolors, Art Inst
Chicago, 49; Norman Wait Harris Bronze Medal, 60th Am Exhib,
Art Inst Chicago, 51; popular prize, Boston Arts Festival, 60.
Bibliography: Portrait painters, Life Mag, 2/3/41; Experiments in
New England, Time Mag, 7/21/52; Portraits by Cox, Newsweek
Mag, 6/15/53.
Memberships: Nat Inst Arts & Lett; Nat Acad Design; Am Acad Arts
& Sci; Am Acad Rome (trustee, 63); Cambridge Art Asn.
Dealer: Portraits, Inc, 41 E 57th St, New York, N Y 10022.
Mailing Address: 30 Ipswich St, Boston, MA 02215.

COX, J HALLEY
Painter, Educator
Preferred Media: Watercolors.
b Des Moines, Iowa, May 20, 10.
Study & Training: San Jose State Univ, BA, BFA, 34; Univ Calif,
Berkeley, MA, 37.
Work in Public Collections: Honolulu Acad Arts, Hawaii; State Found
Cult & Arts, Honolulu; Contemp Arts Ctr, Honolulu; Boston Mus
Fine Arts, Mass; Dept Educ, State of Hawaii.
Commissions: Mural & paintings, Waiaka Lodge, Kailua, Hawaii, 54;
exhib & area design, B P Bishop Mus, Honolulu, 63-66.
Exhibitions: Artists of Hawaii Ann, Honolulu Acad Arts, 46-71; Ha-
waii Painters & Sculptors League Ann, Contemp Arts Ctr, Hono-
lulu, 67-71.
Teaching: Instr art, Calif Pub Schs, 37-45; asst prof art, Calif Col
Arts & Crafts, 46-48; prof art, Univ Hawaii, 48-
Awards: Purchase award for drawing, Wattumul Found, 52; first
awards for watercolors, Honolulu Acad Arts, 52 & 55; purchase
awards, State Found Cult & Arts, 69 & 71.
Memberships: Hawaii Painters & Sculptors League (pres, v pres &
treas, 48-72).
Publications: Auth, articles, In: Paradise of the Pac Mag, 60; auth,
Lei Niho Palaoa, Polynesian Cult Hist, 67; auth, Hawaiian petro-
glyphs, Bishop Mus Press, 70; co-auth, Hawaiian sculpture, Univ
Hawaii Press, 72.
Dealer: Gima's Gallery, Ala Moana Center, Honolulu, HI 96814.
Mailing Address: 3279-F Beaumont Woods Pl, Honolulu, HI 96822.

COX, J W S
Painter, Instructor
b Yonkers, N Y, May 18, 11.
Study & Training: Pratt Inst Art Sch; Acad Colorossi, Paris, France,
with Othon Friesz; Boston Univ; Eliot O'Hara Sch Art.
Work in Public Collections: Boston Mus Fine Arts, Mass; Ford Publ.
Exhibitions: Audubon Artists; Am Watercolor Soc; Ala Watercolor
Soc; Miss Watercolor Soc; Springfield Art League; plus others.
Positions: Pres, New Eng Sch Art, 61-
Awards: Prizes, Rockport, Mass, 51 & 60 & Washington Watercolor
Club, 57.
Publications: Contribr, articles & illus to Christian Sci Monitor.
Mailing Address: 368 Longwood Ave, Roxbury, MA 02215.

COX, JAN
Painter
b The Hague, Holland, Aug 27, 19.
Study & Training: Higher Inst Fine Arts, Antwerp, Belg, 36; Univ
Ghent, 37-41.
Work in Public Collections: Mus Royale Beaux-Arts, Brussels,
Belg; Koninklijk Mus Schone Kunsten, Antwerp; Boston Mus Fine
Arts; Cincinnati Mus Asn; Brooklyn Mus; plus others.
Exhibitions: Salon de Mai, Paris, France, 59, 60 & 64; Prix Mar-
zotto Traveling Exhib, 64; Acad Antwerp, 64; Utrecht, 64; Art
Inst Chicago, 65; plus many other group & one-man shows.
Teaching: Head dept painting, Sch Mus Fine Arts, Boston, Mass,
56-; guest prof, Acad Ghent, Belg.
Memberships: Founding mem La Jeune Pienture Belge, Antwerp.
Mailing Address: 177 Babcock, Brookline, MA 02146.

COX, JOSEPH H
Painter, Educator
b Indianapolis, Ind, May 4, 15.
Study & Training: John Herron Art Inst, with Donald Mattison &
Eliot O'Hara, BFA; Univ Iowa, with Jean Charlot & Philip
Guston, MFA.
Work in Public Collections: Atlanta Paper Co Collection; N C State
Mus; Ford Motor Co Collection; Norfolk Mus Art; Atlanta Art
Asn; plus others.
Commissions: Exterior murals: (mosaic), N Greenville Jr Col,
Tigerville, S C & (aluminum & stained glass), Br Banking Co,
Raleigh, N C; interior murals: (anodized aluminum & colored
light), Southern Nat Bank, Lumberton, N C, Cent Carolina Bank,
Durham, N C & Libr Tower, N C State Univ, Raleigh.
Exhibitions: N C State Mus Art Ann; Mint Mus, Charlotte, N C; High
Mus Art, 69; Ten Southern Artist Traveling Show.
Teaching: Instr art, Univ Iowa, asst prof, 45-48; asst prof, Univ
Tenn, 48-54; assoc prof design, sch design, N C State Univ, 54-
63, prof, 63-72.
Awards: Atlanta Paper Co Painting of the Year Exhib, 55 & 56;
Southeastern Exhib Award, Atlanta, Ga, 56 & 58; purchase award,
66, hon mention, 68, N C State Mus; plus others.
Mailing Address: School of Design, North Carolina State University,
P O Box 5398, Raleigh, NC 27607.

COX, WARREN EARLE
Collector, Art Dealer
b Oak Park, Ill, Aug 27 95.
Positions: Art ed & art dir, Encycl Britannica, 14th ed, 29-39; pres,
Warren E Cox & Assocs, Inc.
Specialty of Gallery: Near and Far Eastern art.
Collection: Large collection of pre-Ming ceramics; Islamic pieces.
Publications: Auth, Pottery & porcelain; auth, Chinese ivory
sculpture; auth, articles, In: The Connoisseur, Oriental Art,
Far Eastern Ceramic Bull & others.
Mailing Address: Warren E Cox & Associates, Inc, 6 E 39th St,
New York, NY 10016.

COZE-DABIJA, PAUL
Painter, Writer
Preferred Media: Oils, Acrylics, Watercolors, Pastels, Plastics.
b Beyrouth, July 29, 03; Fr & U S citizen.
Study & Training: Lycee Janson Sailly; Ecole Nat Arts Decoratifs,
Paris, France; also with J F Gonin.
Work in Public Collections: Victoria Mus, Ottawa, Ont; Southwest
Mus, Los Angeles, Calif; Heard Mus, Phoenix, Ariz; Mesa Verde
Mus, Colo; plus many others in nat parks & mus.
Commissions: Mural, Skyharbor Airport, Phoenix, 61; stations of
the cross & altars, St Thomas Apostle, Phoenix; mural, Golden
Door, Escondido, Calif; fountain & sculptured shrine, U S Indian
Med Ctr, Phoenix, 70; mural, Blue Cross/Blue Shield outdoor
facade, Ariz Vet Mem Coliseum, Phoenix, 71; plus many others.

Exhibitions: Paris Nat Salon; Pasadena Art Inst, Calif; Los Angeles Co Mus Art; Mus N Mex, Santa Fe; also Tucson & Phoenix, Ariz, Canada & France.

Teaching: Co-founder, Scouts of France, 16, later nat comnr; pvt classes in quick sketching, 35-; instr art, Pasadena Art Inst, 42-46; dir studio workshop, Pasadena, 44-51; dir, Phoenix Art Studio, 53-

Positions: Tech dir, Twentieth Century Fox, Universal & Warner Bros Studios, Hollywood, Calif; dir & co-founder, Fr Res Found, Hollywood; head ethno exped for Paris Mus Man to Northwest Can; Fr Consul for Ariz.

Awards: Chevalier, Legion of Honor, France; silver medal, Paris Salon, Paris; prizes, Ariz State Fair; plus others.

Bibliography: Galitzine (auth), selection, In: Fr Readers Digest; many appearances on TV.

Memberships: Soc Nat Beaux-Arts; & many other Paris, Ariz & Calif asns.

Publications: Auth, Moeurs et histoire des Peaux Rouges, Quatre Feux & other bks; auth & illusr, articles, In: Nat Geographic Mag, Ariz Hwys Mag & other publ; auth, Quick sketching with Paul Coze, Foster Publ, 70.

Mailing Address: 4040 E Elm St, Phoenix, AZ 85018.

CRAFT, DOUGLAS D
Painter, Educator
b Greene, N Y, Oct 20, 24.
Study & Training: Univ Iowa: Univ Chicago; Art Inst Chicago, BFA; Syracuse Univ; Univ N Mex, MA.
Work in Public Collections: Mus Mod Art, New York, N Y; Whitney Mus Am Art, New York; Art Inst Chicago, Ill; Univ Ky, Lexington; Univ N Mex, Albuquerque.
Exhibitions: One-man shows: Royal Col Art Galleries, London, Eng, 64; Univ Ky Art Galleries, 64; Traverse Festival Gallery, Edinburgh, Scotland, 65; Mus Art, Carnegie Inst, Pittsburgh, Pa, 68; XXth Century West Galleries, Ltd, New York, 68.
Teaching: Assoc prof painting, Art Inst Chicago, 55-66; assoc prof painting, Carnegie Inst Technol, 66-69; vis artist, Cooper Union, 69-71.
Positions: Vis artist in residence, Univ Ky, 64; Am artist in residence, Royal Col Art, 64-65; vis artist-critic, Sunderland Col Art, Eng, 65; vis critic-artist, Gloucestershire Col Art, Cheltenham, 65.
Awards: Harry Allison Logan Mem Award, Chautauqua Inst, N Y, 63; Logan Bronze Medal & Prize, Art Inst Chicago, 66.
Bibliography: R B Freeman (auth), D Craft, Univ Ky, 64; Max Wykes-Joyce (auth), Douglas Craft, Arts Rev, London, 64; Cordelia Oliver (auth), Exhibitions at Edinburgh, The Guardian, 65.
Dealer: Fischboch Gallery, 29 W 57th St, New York, NY 10019.
Mailing Address: 240 Ogden Ave, Jersey City, NJ 07307.

CRAFT, JOHN RICHARD
Art Administrator
b Uniontown, Pa, June 15, 09.
Study & Training: Phillips Acad, Andover, Mass; Yale Univ; Art Stud League New York; Univ Paris, 36-38; Acad Julien; with Andre l'Hôte; Am Sch Classical Studies, Athens, Greece, 37-39; Johns Hopkins Univ, MA & PhD.
Positions: Dir, Wash Co Mus Fine Arts, Hagerstown, Md, 40-49; dir, Columbia Mus Art, S C, 50-
Memberships: Am Asn Mus; Southeastern Mus Conf (pres, 52-55); S C Fedn Mus (pres, 70-71); Am Inst Designers.
Mailing Address: Columbia Museum of Art, Senate & Bull Sts, Columbia, SC 29201.

CRAIG, EUGENE
Cartoonist, Lecturer
b Fort Wayne, Ind, Sept 5, 16.
Commissions: Designer U S Postage Stamp Battle of Brooklyn, 51.
Teaching: Lectr, Jour Clins, Serv Clubs & others.
Positions: Cartoonist, Fort Wayne News-Sentinel, 34-51; cartoonist, Brooklyn Eagle, 51-55; cartoonist, Columbus Dispatch, 55-
Awards: Six Freedoms Found Awards, 50-62.
Memberships: Am Asn Ed Cartoonists; Nat Cartoonists Soc.
Mailing Address: 73 E Kramer St, Canal Winchester, OH 43110.

CRAIG, MARTIN
Sculptor
Preferred Media: Metal.
b Paterson, N J, Nov 2, 06.
Study & Training: City Col New York, BS.
Work in Public Collections: Gov Nelson A Rockefeller Collection; Kalamazoo Art Inst, Mich; Montreal Star, P Q.
Commissions: Eternal light & three candelabra, Temple Mishkan Tefila, Newton, Mass; ark & two candelabra, Fifth Ave Synagogue,

New York, N Y; ten commandments sculpture, Temple Beth El, Providence, R I; candelabrum, ten commandments sculpture & eternal light, Temple Israel, New Rochelle, N Y.
Exhibitions: Galerie Siècle, Paris, France, 49; Salon Jeune Sculpture Ann, Paris, 50-54; Salon Mai, Paris, 52-54; Galerie Colette Allendy, Paris, 54; New Talent Exhib, Mus Mod Art, New York, 55.
Teaching: Lectr sculpture, Cooper Union Art Sch, 55-57; lectr sculpture, New York Univ, 56-68; asst prof sculpture & drawing, Sarah Lawrence Col, 57-58.
Positions: Welder & chaser, Sculptors Workshop & Foundry, Yonkers, 67-68.
Awards: First prize, Organic Design Competition, Mus Mod Art, 40; purchase award, Longview Found, 62; Mark Rothko Award, 71.
Mailing Address: 795 Accabonac Hwy, East Hampton, NY 11937.

CRAIG, NANCY ELLEN
Painter
Preferred Media: Oils.
b Bronxville, N Y.
Study & Training: Acad Julien, Paris, France; Art Stud League New York, N Y; Hans Hoffman Sch, Provincetown, Mass.
Work in Public Collections: Metrop Mus Art, New York; Baltimore Mus; New Britain Art Inst.
Commissions: Portrait, comn by Assoc Justice Stanley Reed, Supreme Ct Bldg, Washington, D C, 55; portraits, comn by Gov & Mrs Herbert Lehman, New York, 59; mural, five walls of dining room, comn by T S Hyland, Greenwich, Conn, 61; portrait, Mrs Franklin D Roosevelt, Jr, New York, 64; portrait, Lady Symonette, Nassau, Bahamas, 70.
Exhibitions: Nat Acad Design, New York; Audubon Artists, New York; Allied Artists Am, New York; Nat Asn Women Artists, New York; Nat Watercolor Soc, New York.
Awards: First Benjamin Altman Figure Prize, Nat Acad Design, 57; gold medal of honor, Allied Artists Am; Patron's Prize, Audubon Artists.
Bibliography: Nardi Campion (auth), Nancy Ellen Craig & her portraits, Am Artist, 12/54.
Publications: Auth, Portrait painting in oil, 60.
Dealer: Grand Central Galleries, Hotel Biltmore, Madison Ave & 43rd St, New York, NY 10017; Graham Gallery, 1014 Madison Ave, New York, NY 10021.
Mailing Address: Box 57, Truro, MA 02666.

CRAMER, ABRAHAM
Painter, Cartoonist
Preferred Media: Oils, Watercolors, Pastels.
b Kiev, Russia; U S citizen.
Study & Training: Kiev Sch Fine Arts, Russia; Acad Fine Arts, Mexico City, Mex.
Commissions: Portraits & landscapes.
Exhibitions: Paintings, Mexico City, 30.
Publications: Contribr, cartoons, In: Sat Eve Post, New Yorker, Ladies Home J, Red Book, King Features Syndicate, Esquire, True & various other mag.
Mailing Address: 1909 Quentin Rd, Brooklyn, NY 11229.

CRAMER, RICHARD CHARLES
Painter, Educator
b Appleton, Wis, Aug 14, 32.
Study & Training: Layton Sch Art, BFA; Univ Wis-Milwaukee, BS, Univ Wis-Madison, MS, 61, MFA, 62.
Work in Public Collections: Pa Acad Fine Arts; Everhart Mus, Scranton, Pa; Everson Mus, Syracuse, N Y; Univ Wis; Southern Univ, New Orleans; plus others.
Exhibitions: Syracuse Regional, 63-65; Drawing Biennial, Norfolk Mus Art, 65; Drawings, Smithsonian Inst Traveling Exhib, 65; Printmakers, N Y, 66; Philadelphia Art Festival, 67; plus others.
Teaching: Instr drawing & design, Univ Wis, 60-62; instr painting & drawing, Elmira Col, 62-66; instr painting & drawing, Tyler Sch Art, Temple Univ, 66-70, assoc prof, 70-
Awards: Prizes, Milwaukee Art Inst, 54, Syracuse Allied Artists, 64 & Munson-Williams-Proctor Inst, Utica, N Y, 65; plus others.
Memberships: Col Art Asn Am.
Mailing Address: 39 N Tenth St, Philadelphia, PA 19107.

CRANE, JAMES
Painter, Cartoonist
b Hartshorne, Okla, May 21, 27.
Study & Training: Albio Col, BA; State Univ Iowa, MA; Mich State Univ, MFA.
Teaching: Prof art & head collegium creative arts, Eckerd Col, presently.
Awards: Awards, Fla State Fair, 65, Fla Art Group, 65 & Soc Four Arts, Palm Beach, Fla, 67; plus others.
Publications: Auth, On edge, 65, The great teaching machine, 66 &

Parables, 71, John Knox; auth, Inside out, 67; illusr, A funny
thing happened on the way to heaven, 69; plus others.
Mailing Address: Dept of Art, Eckerd College, Saint Petersburg,
FL 33733.

CRANE, ROY (CAMPBELL)
Cartoonist, Writer
Preferred Media: Ink.
b Abilene, Tex, Nov 22, 01.
Study & Training: Hardin-Simmons Univ, 18-19; Univ Tex, 19-22;
Chicago Acad Fine Arts, 20; asst to H T Webster, 23-24; Rol-
lins Col, hon LHD, 57.
Work in Public Collections: Carnegie Libr, Syracuse Univ, N Y;
Univ Tex Libr, Austin.
Exhibitions: Mus Arts Decoratifs, Palais Louvre, Paris, France,
68; Smithsonian Inst, 69; various exhibs with Nat Cartoonists
Soc & Newspaper Comics Coun Collections.
Positions: Staff mem, art dept, New York World, 22-24.
Awards: Billy De Beck Mem Award, Nat Cartoonists Soc, 50; U S
Navy Distinguished Pub Serv Award, 57; Best Story Strip Car-
toonist, Nat Cartoonists Soc, 65.
Memberships: Nat Cartoonists Soc; Newspaper Comics Coun.
Publications: Auth-cartoonist, Wash Tubbs & Captain Easy (comic
strips), Newspaper Enterprise Asn Serv, Cleveland, Ohio, 24-
43; auth-cartoonist, Buz Sawyer (comic strip), King Features
Serv, New York, 43-
Mailing Address: 5585 Jessamine Lane, Orlando, FL 32809.

CRAVEN, ROY CURTIS, JR
Painter, Educator
b Cherokee Bluffs, Ala, July 29, 24.
Study & Training: Univ Chattanooga, BA, 49; Art Stud League New
York, 49-50, with George Grosz, Yasuo Kuniyoshi & Byron
Browne; Univ Fla, MFA, 56.
Work in Public Collections: Va Mus Art, Richmond; Mus Arqueolgia
y Etnologia Guatemala, Guatemala City; Esso Stand Oil Collec-
tion, New York, N Y; New Col, Sarasota, Fla; Chattanooga Art
Asn, Tenn.
Commissions: Sculptural relief, Civic Auditorium, Jacksonville, Fla,
62; sculptural relief, Duval Fed Savings & Loan Asn, Jackson-
ville, 62; archit relief, facade of Med Bldg, Wesley Manor Re-
tirement Village, St Johns Co, Fla, 63; archit relief, facade of
Music & Fine Arts Bldg, Jacksonville Univ, Fla, 64.
Exhibitions: American Prints & Watercolors, Metrop Mus Art, New
York, N Y, 50; Forecast, 57-58 & Painting of the Year, 61-62, Am
Fedn Arts touring exhibs, U S; also exhibs at Delgado Mus, New
Orleans, La & Four Arts Club, Palm Beach, Fla, several yrs.
Collections Arranged: Miniatures & Small Sculptures from India,
66; Spec loan retrospective exhib of works by Yasuo Kuniyoshi,
69; The Maya, a spec exhib of photog & artifacts, 70.
Teaching: Prof art, Univ Fla, 54-, head advert design, 55-65.
Positions: Dir Univ Gallery, Univ Fla, 66-, dir Ctr Latin Am &
Tropical Arts, 72-
Awards: Fulbright sr res scholar to India, 62-63; three Ctr Latin
Am Studies travel grants to Cent Am, 68-69; various awards in
painting & graphic design.
Memberships: Am Asn Mus; Southeastern Mus Conf (bd mem, ed
jour, 67-); Asia Soc; Asn Asian Studies; Fla Art Mus Dirs Asn.
Research: Publications in ancient and contemporary art of India;
pre-Columbian art.
Publications: Auth, Indian sculptures in the John & Mable Ringling
Mus Art (monogr), 61; auth, Ten contemporary painters from
India (catalog), 63; auth, Miniatures & small sculptures from
India (catalog), 66; contribr, A short report on contemporary
painting in India, Art J, spring 65; contribr, A Pallava-Type
Vishnu Icon, Oriental art, autumn 70.
Mailing Address: Rte 3, Box 191 V-1, Gainesville, FL 32601.

CRAWFORD, CATHERINE BETTY
Painter
Preferred Media: Watercolors, Prints.
b Ingersoll, Ont, Feb 5, 10.
Study & Training: Univ Toronto, BA; summer study with Eliot
O'Hara, & at Doon Sch & Queen's Univ; also study with Gordon
Payne, E H Varley & Carl Schaeffer.
Work in Public Collections: London Art Gallery, Ont; Archives Can
Painter-Etchers, Toronto; Loan Collections: Woodstock, Ont.
Exhibitions: Western Art League Shows, London, Ont & Soc of Can
Painter-Etchers, various yrs; one-man shows, London, Burling-
ton & Woodstock, 48-67 & London, 73.
Awards: Purchase award, London Women's Comt at Gallery, 53;
first prize for watercolor, Western Fair, London, 64.
Memberships: Soc Can Painter-Etchers.
Mailing Address: 1 Duke Lane, Ingersoll, Ont, Can.

CRAWFORD, JOHN McALLISTER, JR
Collector, Patron
b Parkersburg, W Va, Aug 6, 13.
Study & Training: Brown Univ, AB, 37, hon LittD, 64; Harvard Univ
Sch Educ; Syracuse Univ, hon LHD, 67.
Exhibitions: William Morris Collection shown at Brown Univ, 59;
Grolier Club, New York, N Y, 64; Nat Mus, Stockholm, Sweden,
65; Mus Cernuschi, Paris, France, 66; Chinese Calligraphy &
Painting Collection shown at Morgan Libr, New York, 62, Fogg
Art Mus, Harvard Univ, 63, William Rockhill Nelson Gallery
Art, Kansas City, Mo & Victoria & Albert Mus, London, Eng, 65.
Positions: Trustee, Asheville Sch, N C, 50; libr comt, Brown Univ,
58-; vis comt, Fogg Art Mus, Harvard Univ, 61-66; mem coun
friends, Columbia Univ Libraries, 67-
Bibliography: William Morris & the Kelmscott Press (catalogue),
Brown Univ Libr, 60; Chinese calligraphy & painting in the col-
lection of John M Crawford, Jr (catalogue), Morgan Libr, 62;
Chinese calligraphy, Philadelphia Mus, 71.
Memberships: China Inst Am (chmn art comt, 67-, trustee, 71-);
Friends of the Asia House Gallery (treas, 64-); fel Morgan Libr
(music comt, 63-); Century Asn; Grolier Club (coun, 58-, chmn
exhib comt, 65).
Art Interests: Chinese art in calligraphy, painting, also early
bronzes, gilt bronzes, sculpture, jade & ceramics.
Collection: Chinese calligraphy & painting; William Morris & the
Kelmscott Press; Medieval manuscripts; early printed books;
other printed masterpieces & modern painting.
Mailing Address: 46 E 82nd St, New York, NY 10028.

CRAWFORD, RALSTON
Painter, Illustrator
b Saint Catherines, Ont, Sept 25, 06; U S citizen.
Study & Training: Otis Art Inst, Los Angeles, 27; Pa Acad Fine
Arts, with Henry Breckenridge & Henry McCarter, 27-30; Barnes
Found, 28-30; Acad Colarossi & Acad Scandinave, Paris, 32-33;
Columbia Univ, 33.
Work in Public Collections: Metrop Mus Art; Munson-Williams-
Proctor Inst; Whitney Mus Am Art; Albright-Knox Art Gallery;
Libr Cong; Mus Fine Arts Houston; plus others.
Exhibitions: Corcoran Gallery Art; Metrop Mus Art; Whitney Mus
Am Art; Retrospective Exhibs, Univ Ill, 66 & Creighton Univ,
Omaha, Nebr, 68; plus others.
Teaching: Lectr mod art, instr, Cincinnati Art Acad, 40; instr, Buf-
falo Sch Fine Arts, 41-42; guest dir, Honolulu Sch Art; instr, Art
Sch Brooklyn Mus, 48; instr, Cincinnati Art Acad, 49, Univ Minn, 49,
La State Univ, 50, Univ Colo, 52, New Sch Social Res, 52-57, Univ
Colo, 58, Univ Southern Calif, 60, Univ Ky High Sch Wk, 60, Hofstra
Col, 60-62 & Univ Minn, 61; Ford Found & Am Fedn Arts vis art-
ist, Sheldon Art Gallery, Univ Nebr, 65; vis artist, Univ Ill, 66.
Positions: Res consult, New Orleans Jazz Arch, Tulane Univ, 45;
art observer, Bikini Atom Bomb Test, 46.
Awards: Tiffany Found Award, 31; purchase prize, Metrop Mus Art,
42; Tamarind fel, 66; plus others.
Bibliography: Selden Rodman (auth), included in: The eye of man,
Devin, 55; Lee Nordness (ed), included in: Art: U S A: now, C J
Bucher, 62; Barbara Rose (auth), included in: American art since
1900, a critical essay, Praeger, 67; plus others.
Publications: Illusr, Stars: their facts and legends, 40; illusr, covers
& articles, In: Fortune Mag, 44-46; contribr, Le Figaro, Brit
Jazz J, Le Jazz Hot & others.
Dealer: Zabriskie Gallery, 29 W 57th St, New York, NY 10019.
Mailing Address: 60 Gramercy Park, New York, NY 10010.

CRAWFORD, WILLIAM H
Cartoonist, Sculptor
b Hammond, Ind, Mar 18, 13.
Study & Training: Chicago Acad Fine Arts; Ohio State Univ, BA, 35;
Grande Chaumiere, Paris.
Work in Public Collections: Syracuse Univ; Libr Cong; cartoons,
Can Pavilion, Montreal.
Exhibitions: Italy, Paris, Israel.
Teaching: Instr, Newark Sch Fine & Applied Arts & Rutgers Univ.
Positions: Ed cartoonist, Newark Eve News, N J, 38-61; chief ed
cartoonist, Newspaper Enterprise Asn, New York, 62-
Awards: Prize, Cleveland Mus Art, 34; best ed page cartoonist, Nat
Cartoonists Soc, 56-58 & 66.
Memberships: Nat Cartoonists Soc (pres, 60-61); Asn Am Ed Car-
toonists.
Publications: Contribr, nat mags; illusr, Barefoot boy with cheek,
43, Zebra derby, 46 & others.
Mailing Address: 128 E 28th St, New York, NY 10016.

CRAWLEY, WESLEY V
Sculptor, Educator
b Akron, Ohio, Mar 1, 22.
Study & Training: Chicago Art Inst, 37; Univ Ariz, 47-48; Univ Ore,
AB, 58, MS, 59.

Work in Public Collections: Dream & Mass, Space & Motion, Univ South Carolina, Columbia; Requiem, Greenville Art Ctr, N C; Study for Tomorrow, E Carolina Univ, Greenville; Superstition, Pembroke State Univ, N C.

Commissions: Cascades (stone carving), Bethel Sch Dist, Ore, 58; Tomorrow (life size bronze), People's Bank & Trust Co, 65; Garden Figure (cast lead), Wright Chem Corp, Acme, N C, 66; Portrait of W E Debnam, comn by family, Greenville, 67; portrait of Mary True, comn by Mr & Mrs E P David, Jr, Dunn, D C, 72; plus many other portraits & garden sculpture.

Exhibitions: Pac Northwest Inst of Sculpture, Portland Art Mus, Ore, 56 & Vancouver Art Mus, B C, 58; North Carolina Artists Traveling Show, Raleigh Art Mus & through state, 64; Southern Asn Sculptors Traveling Show, galleries of the South & Southwest, 67; Contemporary Southern Sculpture, Univ S C, 68.

Teaching: Prof drawing & sculpture, E Carolina Univ, 59-, coordr grad studies, 69-

Awards: First award, Pac Northwest Inst Sculpture, Ore State Sculpture Exhib, 56; Contemp Southern Sculpture Purchase Award, Univ S C, 68; Small Southern Sculpture Purchase Award, Southern Asn Sculptors, 67.

Bibliography: J Hall (auth), Hall Marks (interview), Raleigh News & Observer, 8/4/63; L Holmes (auth), article, In: Rocky Mount News & Observer, N C, 56; L Siegel (auth), rev, In: Art Rev, summer 66.

Memberships: Southern Asn Sculptors (former bd mem).

Mailing Address: 104 Dogwood Dr, Greenville, NC 27834.

CREAMER, PAUL LYLE
Art Dealer

b Chicago, Ill, Sept 3, 28.

Study & Training: Albion Col, BA; New York Univ, grad study.

Positions: Dir, New Bertha Schaefer Gallery, Inc.

Specialty of Gallery: Contemporary American and European paintings, sculpture, and graphics.

Mailing Address: 41 E 57th St, New York, NY 10022.

CREECH, FRANKLIN UNDERWOOD
Painter, Instructor

Preferred Media: Conte, Charcoal, Aluminum, Bronze, Clay, Acrylics.

b Smithfield, N C, Oct 14, 41.

Study & Training: Univ N C, Chapel Hill, summers 63 & 64; Duke Univ, BA, 64; Fla State Univ, MS, 66; Det Danske Selskab, Holbaëk, Denmark, printing with Hugo Arne Bock.

Work in Public Collections: Mint Mus, Charlotte, N C.

Exhibitions: 33rd & 34th N C Artist Exhib, 71 & 72; 1971 Invitational Crafts Exhib, Gallery Contemp Art, Winston-Salem, N C, 71; 8th Int Gran Prix du Cote d'Azur, Cannes, France, 72; 1972 Regional Painting Exhib, Lauren Roger Mus, Laurel, Miss, 72.

Teaching: Instr art, Hugh Morson Jr High Sch, Raleigh, N C, 64-65; instr design & graphics, Gaston Col, Dallas, N C, 66-, chmn dept, 69-

Awards: Purchase award, Piedmont Drawing & Graphic Show & hon mention, Piedmont Crafts Show, Mint Mus.

Bibliography: Artist in the 33rd North Carolina Artists exhibition, La Rev Mod, 10/71.

Memberships: Am Crafts Coun; World Crafts Coun; Nat Art Educ Asn.

Mailing Address: P O Box 461, Dallas, NC 28034.

CREECY, HERBERT LEE
Painter, Sculptor

b Norfolk, Va, Aug 14, 39.

Study & Training: Atlanta Sch Art, 60-64; Atelier 17, Paris, France; also with Stanley Hayter.

Work in Public Collections: High Mus Art, Atlanta, Ga; Ga Comn Arts, State of Ga.

Exhibitions: Atlanta Art Asn, 64; Art in the Embassies Prog, U S Dept State, 66; Clark Col, Atlanta, 67; High Mus Art, 70; OK Harris Gallery, New York, N Y, 72.

Dealer: OK Harris Gallery, 469 W Broadway, New York, NY 10013.

Mailing Address: P.O. Box 186, Suwanee, GA 30174.

CREESE, WALTER LITTLEFIELD
Educator

b Danvers, Mass, Dec 19, 19.

Study & Training: Brown Univ, AB; Harvard Univ, MA & PhD; Columbia Univ.

Teaching: Instr & teaching fel, Harvard Univ, 44-45; instr, Wellesley Col, 45; instr, Univ Louisville, 46-47, asst prof, 47-52, assoc prof, 52-55, prof, 56-58; prof, Univ Ill, Urbana, 58-63; vis prof, summer sch, Harvard Univ, 61-63; dean sch archit & allied arts, Univ Ore, 63-68; prof archit, Univ Ill, Urbana, 68-

Positions: Ed, jour, Soc Archit Historians, 50-53; chmn, Louisville & Jefferson Co Planning & Zoning Comt, 54-55; ed adv, Col Art J.

Awards: Rehmann fel, Am Inst Architects, 60; Smithsonian fel, 69; Guggenheim fel, 72-73; plus others.

Memberships: Soc Archit Historians (pres, 58-59); hon mem Am Inst Architects; Col Art Asn Am.

Mailing Address: Dept of Architecture, University of Illinois, Urbana, IL 61801.

CREMEAN, ROBERT
Sculptor

b Toledo, Ohio, Sept 28, 32.

Study & Training: Alfred Univ, 50-52; Cranbrook Acad Art, BA, 54, MFA, 56.

Work in Public Collections: City Art Mus Saint Louis; Detroit Inst Art; Santa Barbara Mus Art; Univ Nebr; Univ Miami; plus others.

Exhibitions: Univ Iowa, 64; Newport Harbor, 64; Denver Mus Art, 64; Venice Biennale, 68; Smithsonian Traveling Exhib, Europe & S Am, 68-69; plus many others.

Teaching: Instr, Detroit Inst Arts; instr, Univ Calif, Los Angeles, 56-57; instr, Art Ctr La Jolla, Calif, 57-58.

Awards: Fulbright scholar to Italy, 54-55; Tamarind Lithography Workshop grant, 66-67.

Mailing Address: c/o Esther Robles Gallery, 655 N La Cienega Blvd, Los Angeles, CA 90069.

CREO, LEONARD E
Painter, Sculptor

Preferred Media: Oils, Graphics.

b New York, N Y, Jan 10, 23.

Study & Training: Mexico City Col; Art Stud League New York; also with Pietro Annigoni.

Work in Public Collections: New Britain Mus, Conn; Lyman Allyn Mus, Conn; Amherst Col Mus Fine Arts, Mass; Washington Co Mus Fine Arts, Hagerstown, Md; Long Beach Mus Fine Arts, Calif.

Commissions: Passage of Life (mural), St Paul's Within the Walls, Rome, 50; Last Supper (mural), Chapel of Parioli Sch, Rome, 62.

Exhibitions: One-man shows, Chase Gallery, New York, 58-63, A C A Gallery, Rome, Italy, 64 & 65, A C A Gallery, New York, 65-69 & 71, Carter Gallery, Los Angeles, 67, 69 & 71 & Portal Gallery, London, 68, 69 & 71; plus others.

Dealers: A C A Gallery, 25 E 73rd St, New York, NY 10021; Carter Gallery, 900 N La Cienega Blvd, Los Angeles, CA 90069.

Mailing Address: Leys Hill, Walford, Ross on Wye, Herefordshire, Eng.

CRESS, GEORGE AYERS
Painter, Educator

b Anniston, Ala, Apr 7, 21.

Study & Training: Emory Univ; Univ Ga, BFA, MFA.

Work in Public Collections: Tenn Fine Arts Ctr; Mead Corp; Ford Motor Co; murals, Tenn Valley Auth; High Mus Art; plus many others.

Exhibitions: Pa Acad Fine Arts; Springfield Watercolor Ann; Univ Ga; Grand Cent Moderns, N Y; one-man shows, Addison Gallery Am Art 20 Yr Retrospective, Hunter Gallery & various southeastern mus; plus many other group & one-man shows.

Teaching: Instr art, Judson Col, Marion, Ala, 45-46; instr art, Mary Baldwin Col, Staunton, Va, 46-47; instr art, Univ Md, 47-48; instr art, Univ Ga, 49, 65 & 69; instr art, Univ Tenn, 49-51; instr art, Ont Dept Educ, 63; instr art, Univ S C, 67; prof art & head dept, Univ Tenn, Chattanooga, 51-

Positions: Chmn, Tenn Col Arts Coun, 66-68.

Awards: Southeastern Ann, Birmingham Mus Ann & Atlanta Arts Festival; plus many others.

Memberships: Southeastern Col Conf (pres, 65-66); Col Art Asn Am.

Mailing Address: Dept of Art, University of Tennessee, Chattanooga, TN 37404.

CRESSON, MARGARET FRENCH
Sculptor, Writer

Preferred Media: Bronze.

b Concord, Mass, Aug 3, 89.

Work in Public Collections: Berkshire Mus, Pittsfield, Mass; Corcoran Gallery Art; New York Univ; Monroe Shrine, Fredericksburg, Va; Rockefeller Inst; plus others.

Exhibitions: Ten shows, Nat Acad Design, 21-44; nine shows, Pa Acad Fine Arts, 22-42; Art Inst Chicago, 28-29, 37 & 40; Whitney Mus Am Art, 40; Carnegie Inst, 41; plus others.

Positions: Secy, Nat Sculpture Soc, 41-42; v pres, Archit League, 44-46; founder, Chesterwood Studio Mus.

Awards: Medal, Soc Washington Artists, 37; award, Dublin Hill Art Exhib, 39 & 44; gold medal, Am Artists Prof League, 59; plus others.

Memberships: Academician Nat Acad Design; Nat Sculpture Soc; Archit League; Nat Trust Hist Preservation.
Publications: Auth, Journey into fame & Laurel Hill; contribr, New York Times, Am Artist, Am Heritage & others.
Mailing Address: Chesterwood, Stockbridge, MA 01262.

CRIMI, ALFRED D
Painter, Instructor
Preferred Media: Oils, Watercolors.
b San Fratello, Italy, Nov 21, 24; U S citizen.
Study & Training: Nat Acad Design; life drawing with Ivan Olinsky, Beaux Arts Inst; Preparatory Sch Ornamental Arts; fresco painting & Pompeian encaustic with Prof Venturini Paperi, Rome, Italy.
Work in Public Collections: Norfolk Mus Arts & Sci, Va; Butler Inst Am Art, Youngstown, Ohio; Columbia Mus, S C; Libr Cong, Washington, D C.
Commissions: Fresco, Rutgers Presby Church, New York, N Y, 35-37; fresco, sect painting & sculpture, Post Off Dept, Washington, D C, 37-38; oil mural, sect painting & sculpture, Northampton, Mass, 38-39; mosaic, comn by New York Bd Educ, Einstein Jr High Sch, 66-67 & Adlai Stevenson High Sch, 68-69.
Exhibitions: Mus Mod Art, New York, 36; Art Inst Chicago, Ill, 36; Whitney Mus Am Art, New York, 46; Metrop Mus Art, New York, 52-53; First Int Exhib Liturgical Art, Trieste, Italy, 61.
Teaching: Instr drawing & painting, City Col New York, 47-53; instr advan drawing, Pratt Inst, 48-51; instr painting, Pa State Univ, 63; also instr, lectr & critic, cols & univs, 44-
Positions: Mural decorator, Barnett Philip, New York, 28-32; consult, Meyer & Frank Dept Store, Portland, Pa, 31-32; field artist, Sperry Gyroscope Co, Lake Success, N Y, 42-45.
Awards: Mainstream Int, Marietta Col, Ohio, 69 & 70; top purchase award, Butler Inst Am Art, 69; gold medal of honor, Audubon Artists, 71.
Bibliography: Ernest Watson (auth), Making of fresco, Am Artist, 10/41; Mechanical brains (artist's drawings of war machinery), Life Mag, 1/21/44; Carrie Timpane (photographer & collabr), The making & fascination of fresco painting (color film), 57-59.
Memberships: Audubon Artists (pres, 51-52, chmn admis comt, 69-72); Allied Artists Am (bd dir, 47-72); Art Comn City New York; Am Watercolor Soc; Col Art Asn Am.
Publications: Auth, articles, In: Am Artist Mag, 1/47 & 2/62.
Mailing Address: 186 W Fourth St, New York, NY 10014.

CRIQUETTE (RUTH DuBARRY MONTAGUE)
Painter, Writer
Preferred Media: Oils.
b Paris, France; U S citizen.
Study & Training: Ecole Beaux Arts, Paris; Univ Nev, MFA; seminars at Metrop Mus Art; Lumis Art Acad; also with Roland Pierson Prickett.
Work in Public Collections: Many in pvt collections.
Exhibitions: Da Vinci Exhib Artes, Rome, Italy, 69; Repertorium Artis Exhib, Monaco, 70; Int Exhib Artes, Rome, 71; 14th-15th Int Exhib, Gallerie Int, New York, N Y, 72; Int Inst Arts & Lett Perpetual Exhib, Switz.
Teaching: Dir & instr oil painting, Prickett Sch Color, 48-60; dir & instr oil painting, Montague Sch Painting, Washington, D C, 61-68; instr oil painting, Ecole Marsan, Vernon, Normandy, France, 69-70.
Positions: Dir, Montague Studio-Gallery, Orlando, Fla, 71-
Awards: Community Leader of America, Community Leaders of Am, 68.
Memberships: Int Arts Guild, Monte Carlo, Monaco; Centro Studi E Scambi Int, Rome (hon rep); Acad Int Leonardo Da Vinci, Rome (hon rep); life fel Int Inst Artes et Lett, Switz; Metrop Mus Art, New York.
Publications: Contribr, New Yorker, 53; co-auth, 5 Home study courses in oil painting, 60; contribr, Let's live, 60-61; auth & illusr, Bahamian ah-h-h, 69; auth & illusr over 100 monogrs in oil painting field, 71-72.
Dealer: Gallerie Internationale, 1095 Madison Ave, New York, NY 10028.
Mailing Address: 1400 Clouser Ave, Orlando, FL 32804.

CRISPO, ANDREW JOHN
Art Dealer, Collector
b Philadelphia, Pa, Apr 21, 45.
Study & Training: St Joseph's Col (Pa).
Positions: Assoc dir ACA Galleries & dir, mus sect, 69-72.
Specialty of Gallery: American and European art of the twentieth century.
Collection: Morris Louis, John Marin, Georgia O'Keefe, Sam Francis, Horace Pippin, and other Americans.
Mailing Address: 126 E 79th St, New York, NY 10021.

CRIST, RICHARD
Painter, Writer
b Cleveland, Ohio, Nov 1, 09.
Study & Training: Carnegie Inst Technol; Art Inst Chicago.
Work in Public Collections: Mineral Industs Col; Pa State Univ; Pub Schs Collections, Pittsburgh, Somerset & Latrobe, Pa; Mary Washington Col, Univ Va.
Commissions: Mural, Prospect Sch, Pittsburgh, Pa.
Exhibitions: Whitney Mus Am Art, 56 & 57; Albany Inst Hist & Art, 57; N Y State Col Teachers, Albany, 57; Audubon Artists, 67; Rennselaer Polytech Inst, Troy, N Y, 69; plus many other group & one-man shows.
Awards: Am Traveling scholar, Art Inst Chicago; prizes, Carnegie Inst, 40 & Berkshire Mus Art, 57 & 68; plus others.
Memberships: Assoc Artists Pittsburgh; Woodstock Art Asn (exec bd).
Publications: Auth & illusr, The cloud catcher, 56, Secret of turkeyfoot mountain, 57, Broken horse chimneys, 60, The Queekup Spring, 61 & Cub Scout Donny, Abingdon; plus others.
Mailing Address: 24 Boltwood Ave, Castleton, NY 12033.

CRITE, ALLAN ROHAN
Painter, Illustrator
b Plainfield, N J, Mar 20, 10.
Study & Training: Boston Mus Fine Arts Sch; Mass Sch Art; Boston Univ, CBA; Harvard Univ, BA.
Work in Public Collections: Boston Mus Fine Arts; Spellman Col, Atlanta, Ga; Addison Gallery Am Art, Andover, Mass; Marine Hosp, Carville, La; Villanova Col, Pa; plus others.
Commissions: Insignia, USS Wilson; mural, Grace Church, Martha's Vineyard, Mass; stations of the cross, Holy Cross Church, Morrisville, Vt, 57; plus many others.
Exhibitions: One-man shows, Boston Mus Fine Arts, Fogg Mus Art & Farnsworth Mus Art; Religious Art Festival, Brandon, Vt, 61; Festival Arts, Ecumenical Youth Assembly N Am, Ann Arbor, Mich, 61; plus many other group and one-man shows.
Teaching: Lectr Christian art, Oberlin Col, 58; past lectr, Regis Col.
Awards: Awards, Boston Mus Fine Arts Sch & Seabury Western Theol Sem, 52; fourth prize, Franklin Mint Bicentennial Medal Design.
Memberships: Boston Soc Independent Artists; Boston Inst Mod Art; Boston Mus Fine Arts Sch (alumni bd); Children's Art Ctr, Boston (bd mem); Archaeol Inst Am.
Publications: Auth & illusr, Cultural heritage of the United States, 68 & Were you there when they crucified my Lord, McGrath, 69; contribr, mags & bulls; auth & illusr, many relig bks & articles.
Mailing Address: 410 Columbus Ave, Boston, MA 02116.

CROFT, LEWIS SCOTT
Painter
Preferred Media: Oils, Watercolors.
b Chester Basin, N S, Mar 25, 11.
Study & Training: Study with M Denton-Burgess, Vancouver, B C & William S Schwartz, Chicago, Ill.
Work in Public Collections: Swope Art Gallery, Terre Haute, Ind; Parish Art Mus, Southampton, N Y; N C Mus Art, Raleigh; Elliott Mus, Stuart, Fla; Philbrook Art Ctr, Tulsa, Okla; plus 40 others.
Exhibitions: Am Artists Prof League, New York, N Y, 57-58; Fla State Fair, Tampa, 58-59; Southeastern Ann, Delgrado Mus, New Orleans, La, 60; Allied Artists Am, New York, 61, 63 & 65; Audubon Artists Ann, New York, 62.
Awards: Best of show, Sunshine Art Festival, Fla, 58; best oil, Mystic, Conn, 62-64; grand prize gold medal, Washington Sq Outdoor Art Show, 65.
Memberships: Allied Artists Am; Int Platform Asn; Int Inst Arts & Lett.
Publications: Auth, article, In: Am Artist Mag, 3/68.
Dealer: Christopher Gallery, 766 Madison Ave, New York, NY 10021.
Mailing Address: 56 Lincoln Ave, South Hamilton, MA 01982.

CRONBACH, ROBERT M
Sculptor
Preferred Media: Direct Metal, Bronze, Concrete, Terra Cotta.
b Saint Louis, Mo, Feb 10, 08.
Study & Training: Saint Louis Sch Fine Arts, with Victor Holm, 25-26; Pa Acad Fine Arts, with Charles Grafly & Albert Laessle, 27-30; Cresson scholar to Europe, 29-30.
Work in Public Collections: Nat Collection of Smithsonian Inst, Washington, D C; Saint Louis Art Mus; Springfield Art Mus, Mo; Walker Art Ctr, Minneapolis, Minn; Mus Fine Arts, Skopje, Yugoslavia; plus others.
Commissions: Bronze screen, Dorr Oliver Bldg, Stamford, Conn, 60; bronze & steel wall sculpture, UN Gen Assembly Bldg, New York, N Y, 60; fountain, Fed Off Bldg, Saint Louis, 63; fountain, Kanawha Co Pub Libr, Charleston, W Va, 66; Tribute to Leroy

Grumman (stainless steel sculpture), Long Island Asn Hall of Fame, 72; plus many others.
Exhibitions: Whitney Mus; HemisFair, San Antonio, Tex; Pa Acad Fine Arts; Houston Mus Fine Arts; Brooklyn Mus; plus many other group & one-man shows.
Teaching: Instr, Adelphi Univ, 48-62; instr, N Shore Community Arts Ctr, 50-55; instr, Skowhegan Sch Painting & Sculpture, 59, 60, 64, 65 & 72.
Positions: Chmn bd gov, Skowhegan Sch Painting & Sculpture; mem, Nassau Co Fine Arts Comn; mem, Mayor's Comt Beautification of New York.
Awards: Nat competition for sculpture for Social Security Bldg, Washington, D C, 39; competition for sculpture for UN Bldg, New York, 60; Reynolds Metals Sculpture Trophy, 61; plus others.
Bibliography: John I H Baur (auth), Revolution and tradition in modern American art, Harvard Univ Press, 59; Minor L Bishop (auth), Fountains in contemporary architecture, Am Fedn Arts, 65; Louis G Redstone (auth), Art in architecture, McGraw-Hill, 68.
Memberships: Sculptors Guild; Munic Art Soc; Archit League New York; Fedn Mod Painters & Sculptors; Artist-Craftsmen New York.
Publications: Auth, New new deal art projects, an anthology of memoirs, Smithsonian Inst Press, 72.
Dealer: New Bertha Schaefer Gallery, 41 E 57th St, New York, NY 10022.
Mailing Address: 170 Henry St, Westbury, Long Island, NY 11590.

CRONIN, ROBERT (LAWRENCE)
Sculptor
Preferred Media: Welded Steel.
b Lexington, Mass, Aug 10, 36.
Study & Training: R I Sch Design, BFA, 59; Cornell Univ, MFA, 62.
Work in Public Collections: Worcester Art Mus, Mass; Boston Mus Fine Arts, Mass.
Exhibitions: Boston Fine Arts Festival, 63; Minneapolis Art Inst Ann, 64; Detroit Art Inst Ann, 65.
Teaching: Instr painting, Bennington Col, 66-68; instr art, Sch Worcester Art Mus, 68-
Awards: First prize in painting, Boston Fine Arts Festival, 63.
Mailing Address: 55 Salisbury St, Worcester, MA 01608.

CROSBY, RANICE
Medical Illustrator, Educator
b Regina, Sask, Apr 26, 15.
Study & Training: Conn Col, AB; Johns Hopkins Med Sch, with Max Broedel; also with Robert Brackman.
Teaching: Asst to N J Eastman, Johns Hopkins Hosp; asst prof art as appl to med & dir dept, Johns Hopkins Med Sch, 44-
Memberships: Asn Med Illusr; Am Asn Univ Prof.
Publications: Illusr, med textbks & contribr illus, med jours.
Mailing Address: 3926 Cloverhill Rd, Baltimore, MD 21218.

CROSBY, SUMNER McKNIGHT
Art Historian
b Minneapolis, Minn, July 29, 09.
Study & Training: Yale Univ, BA, 32, PhD, 37; Minneapolis Col Art, hon DFA.
Teaching: Prof medieval art, Yale Univ, 36-
Awards: Chevalier, Legion of Honor, 50.
Memberships: Col Art Asn Am (pres, 44-45); Am Fedn Art (trustee, 41-44, 47-); Int Ctr Medieval Art (chmn, 70-); Archeol Inst Am (trustee, 65-69).
Research: Excavations in the Abbey Church of Saint-Denis.
Publications: Auth, The Abby of St-Denis, 42; auth, L'Abbaye Royale de Saint-Denis, 53; ed, Art through the ages, fourth ed, 59; auth, The apostle bas-relief at Saint-Denis, 72.
Mailing Address: 29 Fairgrounds Rd, Woodbridge, CT 06525.

CROSS, MARIA CONCETTA
Painter, Art Dealer
Preferred Media: Oils, Watercolors.
b Fort Worth, Tex, Jan 25, 11.
Study & Training: Tex Christian Univ; Tex Woman's Univ; also study in Europe, Italy, Mex & Taos, N Mex.
Work in Public Collections: Dr M E Houtzager, Dir, Cent Mus Art, Utrecht, Netherlands; Dr Orsla Sarzana, Pres, Inst Learning, Palermo, Italy; Tex Wesleyan Col; Jon Starnes, Houston, Tex.
Exhibitions: Fort Worth Art Ctr; Beaumont Art Mus; Dallas Mus Fine Arts; Witte Mem Mus, San Antonio; Springfield Mo Art Gallery; plus many others.
Positions: Owner & instr painting, Cross Gallery, Fort Worth.
Awards: Awards for Old House, Tex Wesleyan Col, Old Ruins, Tex Art Guild & Melons, Beaumont Art Mus, Tex.

Specialty of Gallery: Western Americana art and bronzes; contemporary American art.
Collection: Western paintings and bronzes.
Mailing Address: 3629 W Seventh St, Fort Worth, TX 76107.

CROSS, WATSON, JR
Painter, Instructor
Preferred Media: Watercolors, Oils, Mixed Media.
b Long Beach, Calif, Oct 10, 18.
Study & Training: Chouinard Art Inst, scholarship, 38-42.
Commissions: Illustrations of Air Bases, USAF, Alaska, 63.
Exhibitions: San Francisco Mus Art Ann, 47-48; Calif Watercolor Soc Traveling Exhib, Riverside Mus, New York, N Y, 48; John Herron Art Inst Invitational, 48; Los Angeles Co Mus Art Ann, 53-54.
Teaching: Prof drawing & painting, Chouinard Art Inst, 44-71; guest prof drawing, Calif State Univ, Los Angeles, summer 71; instr drawing & painting, Laguna Beach Sch Art, 69-
Positions: Secy, Calif Watercolor Soc, 51-53, pres, 53-54; judge, Princeton Univ's Creativity Testing, 65.
Publications: Contribr, Content of watercolor, Van Nostrand Reinhold, 69.
Mailing Address: 1238 E Workman Ave, West Covina, CA 91790.

CROSSGROVE, ROGER LYNN
Painter, Educator
Preferred Media: Pastels, Watercolors.
b Farnam, Nebr, Nov 17, 21.
Study & Training: Kearney State Col; Univ Nebr, BFA; Univ Ill, MFA; Univ Michoacan.
Work in Public Collections: Butler Inst Am Art, Youngstown, Ohio; Montclair Art Mus, N J; Des Moines Art Ctr, Iowa; Inst Mex-Norteamericano Relac Cult, Mexico City.
Exhibitions: Whitney Mus Am Art, New York, N Y, 56; Pa Acad Fine Arts, Philadelphia, 64; Audubon Artists, New York, 68; Conn Watercolor Soc, Wadsworth Atheneum, Hartford, Conn, 70; Monotypes, Pratt Graphics Ctr, New York, 72.
Teaching: Prof art & assoc chmn dept graphic arts, Pratt Inst, 52-68; prof art & head dept, Univ Conn, 68-
Awards: Emily Lowe Award, 51; gold medal, Nat Arts Club, 67; Am Watercolor Soc Award, 67.
Bibliography: Henry N Rasmusen (auth), Printmaking with monotype, Chilton, 60.
Memberships: Col Art Asn Am; Am Watercolor Soc; Mystic Art Asn; Delta Phi Delta; Kappa Pi.
Publications: Contribr, Paperbound books in print, 63; contribr & ed, Artists proof, 67-
Mailing Address: Storrs Heights, Storrs, CT 06268.

CROTTO, PAUL
Painter, Sculptor
Preferred Media: Oils.
b New York, N Y, Oct 24, 22.
Study & Training: Art Stud League New York; Beaux-Arts, Florence, Italy; also with Fernand Léger, Paris, France.
Work in Public Collections: Villeneuve-sur-Lot Mus, France; Mus Art Int, San Francisco, Calif; Galerie Grave, Munich, Ger.
Commissions: Portraits, L E Kaplan, New York & Robert Aries, Paris.
Exhibitions: Mostra Artisti Am, Florence, 51; Mostra Int, Bordighera, Italy, 53; Am Painters in France, Galerie Craven, Paris, 53; Salon Automne, Paris, 56; Salon Comparaisons, Mus Mod Art, Paris, 68.
Awards: Prix Int de peinture, Villeneuve-sur-Lot, 63.
Bibliography: T Ehrenmark (auth), American artist in Sweden, Dagens Nyheter, 63; A Blasco Ibanez (auth), American artist in Paris, Los Angeles Herald Examr, 68; Betty Werther (auth), Art, Time-Life, Paris, 69.
Memberships: Soc Coop Entre Aide Artistes.
Dealer: Van der Straeten Gallery of Contemporary Artists, 981 Madison Ave, New York, NY 10021.
Mailing Address: 19 Rue Cauchois, Paris, France.

CROVELLO, WILLIAM GEORGE
Painter, Sculptor
Preferred Media: Marble, Steel, Acrylics.
b New York, N Y, Sept 1, 29.
Study & Training: R I Sch Design, BFA, 51; also Japanese calligraphy with Taiun Yanagida, Tokyo, 57-61.
Work in Public Collections: Sculpture, Cubed Curve, New York City Dept Parks, Recreation & Cult Affairs.
Exhibitions: Carnegie Int, Pittsburgh, Pa, 61; one-man shows, Tokyo Gallery, 61, Galeria Juana Mordo, Madrid, 68; Grosvenor Gallery, London, Eng, 70, A M Sachs Gallery, New York & Agra Gallery, Washington, D C, 71; plus many others.
Bibliography: Jose De Castro Arines (auth), La Dinamica de Crovello, Informaciones, 4/68; James Burr (auth), Review of

Grosvenor Exhibitions, Apollo Mag, 10/70; Frank Getlein (auth), Two Art Exhibitions Expressing a Single Image, Washington Star, 3/70; plus others.
Dealer, A M Sachs Gallery, 29 W 57th St, New York, NY 10019.
Mailing Address: 84 Ave Legrand, 1050 Brussels, Belgium.

CROWN, KEITH ALLEN
Painter, Educator
Preferred Media: Watercolors, Oils.
b Keokuk, Iowa, May 27, 18.
Study & Training: Art Inst Chicago, 36-40, 45-46, BFA, 46.
Work in Public Collections: Ackland Mus, Chapel Hill, N C; Long Beach Mus Art, Calif; Univ Mass, Amherst; Rio Hondo Col, Whittier, Calif; Univ Calgary.
Exhibitions: Important California Artists, Witte Mus Art, San Antonio, Tex, 65; Crown, Long Beach Mus, Calif, 66; Painting as Painting, Univ Texas, Austin, 68; one-man retrospective, The Idea Painter, Occidental Col, 69; one-man show, Univ Ill Stud Union, Champaign-Urbana, 71.
Teaching: Prof painting & drawing, Univ Southern Calif, 46-; prof painting, Univ N C, summer 68; prof painting, Univ Ill, 70-71.
Awards: Los Angeles All-City Art Festival Purchase Award, 61; student purchase award, Media '70, Rio Hondo Col, 70; award, Calif Nat Watercolor Soc 51st Ann, 71.
Bibliography: Crown, Long Beach Mus Art Catalog, 66.
Memberships: Calif Nat Watercolor Soc (v pres, 58, pres, 59); Col Art Asn Am.
Publications: Contribr, Introduction to Arts of Southern California XVII: watercolor (catalog), Long Beach Mus Art, 66; contribr, rev of Faber Birren's ed of Chevraul's The Principles and Harmony of Color, Art Bull, 69; contribr, The content of watercolor, Van Nostrand Reinhold, 69; auth (films), Painting in New Mexico-1969, 69 & Painting in the Middle West-1971, 71.
Dealer: Jacqueline Anhalt Gallery, 750 N La Cienega Blvd, Los Angeles, CA 90069.
Mailing Address: Fine Arts Dept, University of Southern California, Los Angeles, CA 90007.

CRUTCHFIELD, WILLIAM RICHARD
Painter, Printmaker
Preferred Media: Watercolors.
b Indianapolis, Ind, Jan 21, 32.
Study & Training: Herron Sch Art, Ind Univ, Indianapolis, BFA, 56; Tulane Univ, La, MFA, 60.
Work in Public Collections: Mus Mod Art, New York, N Y; Art Inst Chicago, Ill; Cleveland Mus Art, Ohio; Philadelphia Mus Art, Pa; Libr of Cong, Washington, D C.
Exhibitions: Minneapolis Inst Art, Minn, 67; Fort Lauderdale Mus Arts, Fla, 71; N J State Mus, Trenton, 71 & 72; California Prints 1972, Mus Mod Art, New York, 72; Dorsky Gallery, New York, 72.
Awards: Mary Milliken award for travel in Europe, Herron Sch Art, Ind Univ, Indianapolis, 56; Fulbright scholar, State Art Acad, Hamburg, Ger, 61.
Bibliography: Jane Livingston (auth), Crutchfield phenomena, Art in Am, 1-2/71; article, In: Horizon, winter 72.
Publications: Illusr, Americana 67, Owl feathers, 70, Air, land, sea, 70, Six rainbow trains, 71 & A report on the art & technology program of the Los Angeles County Museum of Art 1967-1971, 71.
Mailing Address: 8285 Sunset Blvd, Los Angeles, CA 90046.

CRUZ, EMILIO
Painter, Educator
b New York, N Y, Mar 38.
Study & Training: John Hay Whitney fel, 64-65; Cintas Found fel, 65-66.
Work in Public Collections: Mus Mod Art; World Trade Ctr; Ciba-Geigy Collection; plus many others in pvt collections.
Exhibitions: Nat Collection Fine Arts, Smithsonian Inst, Washington, D C, 68; San Francisco Mus Art, Calif, 69; Univ Tex Mus, Austin, 69; Spanish Pavillion, Saint Louis, Mo, 70; one-man show, Loretto-Hilton Gallery, Webster Col, Mo, 69; plus many other group & one-man shows.
Teaching: Ramblerny Sch Performing Arts, Bucks Co, Pa, 67; mem bd educ, South Bronx Multi-Purpose Educ Serv, New York, 67-68; artist-in-residence team, Rockefeller-Danforth grant, Metrop Educ Coun Arts, Saint Louis, Mo, 69; asst prof painting, Art Inst Chicago Sch, 70-
Positions: Chmn events & exhibs comt & dir, Wabash Transit Gallery, 72-
Awards: Walter Gutman Found, 62; Nat Endowment Arts, 70-71.
Mailing Address: 541 W North Ave, Chicago, IL 60610.

CRUZ, HECTOR
Painter
Preferred Media: Oils.
b Chimalhuacan, Mex, July 2, 33.
Study & Training: La Esmeralda Sch Painting & Sculpture, grad 51; Taller de Integracion Plastica; Inst Bellas Artes, 55.

Work in Public Collections: Mus Arte Mod, Mexico City, Mex; Mus Bellas Artes, Mexico City; Salon Plastica Mex Belles Artes, Mexico City; Misrachi Gallery Mod Art, Mexico City; Gallery Plastica de Mex, Mexico City.
Exhibitions: Collective Exhib Contemp Mex Art, Moscow, Russia, 57; Salon de Plastica Mexicana, Mexico City, 57 & 69; Art Mexicain Contemporain, France, 58; New Masters of San Carlos, Mexican Art Gallery, San Antonio, Tex, 62; New Vision of Landscape, Misrachi Gallery Mod Art, Mexico City, 71.
Awards: Gold medal, Collective Exhib Contemp Mex Art, Moscow, 57; New Year's prize & first place, Salon Plastica Mex, 57 & 69.
Mailing Address: Camelia 14, Tizapan, Mexico 20, D F.

CRYDERMAN, MACKIE
Painter, Graphic Artist
b Dutton, Ont.
Study & Training: Winnipeg Sch Art, with Franz Johnston; Ont Col Art; Artisans Guild, Detroit, with Arthur Neville Kirk; Guild Allied Arts & Crafts; Soc Arts & Crafts, with Sarkis Sarkisian; also with Francis de Erdly.
Work in Public Collections: Medway High Sch; H B Beal Tech Sch; also in pvt cols.
Commissions: Scenery & sets, London Little Theatre Dom Drama Festival, 49; murals & decor, Park Towers Club, London, Ont, 61.
Exhibitions: Western Art League, 36-69; Can Soc Painter-Etchers & Engravers, 56-65; London Art Gallery, Ont, 57; Expo '67; Montreal Mus Fine Arts; plus others.
Teaching: Dir art, H B Beal Tech & Commercial High Sch, London, Ont, 27-; instr art, summer sch, Univ Western Ont, 46.
Positions: Mem dept educ, Ont, 47 & 48; bd gov, Fanshawe Cole Appl Art & Technol, London, Ont.
Awards: Prize, Western Fair, 55.
Memberships: Can Soc Painter-Etchers & Engravers.
Mailing Address: 12 Chalmers Ave, London 24, Ont, Can.

CSOKA, STEPHEN
Painter, Etcher
b Gardony, Hungary, Jan 2, 97; U S citizen.
Study & Training: Budapest Royal Acad Art, 22-27.
Work in Public Collections: Budapest Mus Art; Libr Cong; Brit Mus Art; Metrop Mus Art; Norfolk Mus Art; plus others.
Exhibitions: Nat Acad Design, 40-45; one-man shows, Philadelphia Art Alliance, 43 & Minn State Fair, 43; Carnegie Inst, 43-45; Corcoran Gallery Art, 45; retrospective, Pacem in Terris Gallery, New York, N Y, 68; plus others.
Teaching: Instr, Fashion Inst Technol; instr, Nat Acad Design Sch Fine Arts.
Awards: Awards, Soc Am Graphic Artists, 42, 45 & 52 & Assoc Am Artists, 47, 53 & 58; Acad Arts & Lett grant; plus others.
Memberships: Academician Nat Acad Design; Soc Am Graphic Artists; Audubon Artists.
Publications: Auth, Pastel painting, 62.
Mailing Address: 85-80 87th St, Woodhaven, NY 11421.

CUEVAS, JOSÉ LUIS
Painter, Illustrator
b Mexico City, Mex, Feb 26, 34.
Study & Training: Sch Painting & Sculpture (La Esmeralda, Inst Nac Bellas Artes), Mexico City.
Work in Public Collections: Mus Mod Art, New York, N Y; Solomon R Guggenheim Mus, New York; Brooklyn Mus, N Y; Mus of Albi & Lyons, France; plus others.
Exhibitions: Spec rm at V Biennial of Sao Paulo, Brazil, 59; VII Mostra Int Bianco a Nero, Lugano, Switz, 62; Rosc 67, Nat Mus Dublin, Ireland, 67; I Biennial New Delhi, India, 68; Biennial Venize, Italy, 72.
Teaching: Resident artist, Philadelphia Mus Sch Art, 57; lect art, San Jose State Col, 70.
Awards: First int prize for drawing, V Biennial of Sao Paulo, Brazil, 59; first int award, Mostra Bianco e Nero, 62; first prize for engraving, I Biennial of New Delhi, India, 68.
Bibliography: Carlos Fuentes (auth), Los mundos de José Luis Cuevas, Misrachi Gallery, Mexico City, 70.
Publications: Illusr, Recollections of childhood, Kanthos Press, 62; illusr, Cuevas charenton, Tamarind Workshop, 65; auth, Cuevas by Cuevas, Era, Mexico City, 65; illusr, Crime by Ceuvas, Lublin Ed, 68; illusr, Homage to Quevedo, 69 & Cuevas comedies, 71, Collectors Press; plus others.
Dealer: Grace Borgenicht Gallery, 1018 Madison Ave, New York, NY 10021; Misrachi Gallery, Genova 20, Mexico City, Mex.
Mailing Address: Galeana 109, San Angel, Mexico City, 20, Mex.

CULBERTSON, JANET LYNN (MRS DOUGLAS KAFTEN)
Painter, Instructor
Preferred Media: Acrylics, Silver Point.
b Greensburg, Pa, Mar 15, 32.
Study & Training: Carnegie Inst Technol, BFA, 53; Art Stud League New York, N Y, 54; graphics, Atelier 17, New York, 55; N Y Univ, MA, 63; Pratt Graphic Arts Inst, 64-65; Calif State Col, Long Beach, 70.
Work in Public Collections: Univ Mass, Amherst Mus Collection.
Exhibitions: Bucknell Univ Ann, Pa, 67-69; Los Angeles Ann, Calif, 69; Nat Ann Drawing Exhib, San Francisco Mus, Calif, 70; All Calif 16th Ann, Laguna Beach, 70.
Teaching: Instr art, Pace Col, 64-68.
Awards: Third prize, Palos Verdes Art Asn Calif, 70.
Memberships: Women's Ad Hoc Comt of Art, New York.
Dealer: Lerner-Heller Gallery, 789 Madison Ave, New York, NY 10021.
Mailing Address: 315 E 86th St, New York, NY 10028.

CULLER, GEORGE D
Art Administrator, Educator
b McPherson, Kans, Feb 27, 15.
Study & Training: Cleveland Inst Art, grad, 36; Western Reserve Univ, BS & MA.
Exhibitions: Painting & Prints, Midwestern Exhib, Kansas City, Mo; May Shows, Cleveland, Ohio; New Years Exhibs, Butler Inst Am Art, Youngstown, Ohio; plus others.
Teaching: From instr to asst prof art, Kansas State Teachers Col, 39-42; instr painting, Cleveland Inst Art, 46.
Positions: Head illusr, Dept Prod Illus, Boeing Airplane Co, Wichita, Kans, 42-45; from suprvr to asst cur educ, Cleveland Mus Art, 46-49; dir, Akron Art Inst, 49-55; dir mus educ, Art Inst Chicago, 55-58; dir, San Francisco Mus Art, 58-65; pres, Philadelphia Col Art, 65-; dir, Nat Asn Schs Art, 65-69, v pres, 69-; mem bd, Union Independent Cols Art, 69-
Mailing Address: Philadelphia College of Art, Broad & Pine Sts, Philadelphia, PA 19102.

CUMING, BEATRICE
Painter
b Brooklyn, N Y, Mar 25, 03.
Study & Training: Pratt Inst, grad; also study in France.
Work in Public Collections: Lyman Allyn Mus, New London, Conn; Syracuse Mus Fine Arts, N Y; Conn Col, New London; Libr Cong, Washington, D C.
Exhibitions: Solo exhibs, Guy Mayer Gallery, 42, Contemp Arts Gallery, 46, New Gallery, 46, New York, N Y & Mystic Art Asn, Conn, 56; Retrospective, Lyman Allyn Mus, 68; plus many others.
Teaching: Instr art, Parsons Sch Design & Sch Visual Arts, New York; dir, young peoples' art prog & adult classes, Lyman Allyn Mus.
Awards: Recipient of var comns and resident grants to continue creative work.
Memberships: Mystic Art Asn (mem dir, 15 yrs); Essex Art Asn; Am Artists; Conn Watercolor Soc; Am Watercolor Soc.
Mailing Address: 241 A Massapeag Rd, Uncasville, CT 06389.

CUMMINGS, FREDERICK JAMES
Art Administrator, Art Historian
b Floydayda, Tex, Aug 19, 33.
Study & Training: Willamette Univ, BA, 54; Harvard Univ, MA, 56; Univ Chicago, PhD(hons), 66; Courtauld Inst Art, Univ London, 60-61.
Collections Arranged: American Decorative Arts from the Pilgrims to the Revolution, 67; Art in Italy, 1600-1700, 65; Romantic Art in Britain: Paintings and Drawings, 1760-1860; Painting in France, 1774-1830 (in prep).
Teaching: Instr art hist, Univ Mo, 61-64; adj prof art hist, Wayne State Univ, 65-
Positions: Actg dir, Mus Art & Archaeol, Univ Mo, 63-64; asst dir & cur European art, Detroit Inst Arts, 64-; ed, Art Quart, 66-69.
Awards: Hon fine arts silver medal award, Mich Acad Sci, Arts & Lett, 72.
Memberships: Col Art Asn Am (bd dirs, 71-); Am Asn Mus; Am Soc Eighteenth Century Studies.
Research: Romantic painting in Western Europe.
Publications: Co-auth, Romantic art in Britain: painting and drawings, 1760-1860; auth, Charles Bell and anatomy of expression, Art Bull, 64; auth, Wright's Boothby, Rousseau, and the romantic malady, Burlington Mag, 68; auth, Folly and mutability in Joseph Wright's alchemist and democritus, Art Quart, 70; contribr, Proceedings of the American Society for Eighteenth Century Studies, 72.
Mailing Address: Detroit Institute of Arts, 5200 Woodward Ave, Detroit, MI 48202.

CUMMINGS, NATHAN
Collector
b St John, N B.
Collection: Impressionists; post-impressionists; Fauves; cubits.
Mailing Address: Waldorf Towers 28A, 100 E 50th St, New York, NY 10022.

CUNNINGHAM, BENJAMIN FRAZIER
Painter, Educator
Preferred Media: Oil, Acrylic.
b Cripple Creek, Colo, Feb 10, 04.
Study & Training: Univ Nev; Calif Sch Fine Arts.
Work in Public Collections: Mus Mod Art, New York, N Y; Solomon R Guggenheim Mus, New York; Whitney Mus Am Art, New York; Michener Collection, Univ Texas, Austin; Tweed Gallery, Univ Minn, Duluth.
Commissions: Mural, Ukiah Post Office, Calif, Pub Works Admin Proj, U S Treas Dept, 37; Nevada (painting), States Series, Container Corp, 48; mini-multiple, Art Gallery Mag, 1/70.
Exhibitions: Directions in American Painting, Carnegie Inst, 41; The Responsive Eye, Mus Mod Art, 65; Highlights of the Season, Aldrich Mus, Conn, 66; Pa Acad ann, 68; II Bienal de Arte Coltejer, Medellin, Colombia, 70.
Teaching: Instr design, Cooper Union, New York, 60-68; instr painting, Univ Minn, Duluth, summers, 67 & 68; instr painting & color, Art Stud League New York, 67-
Positions: Suprvr mural painting for Northern Calif, Fed Art Proj, 36-39.
Awards: Art on Paper purchase award, Dillard Paper Co & Weatherspoon Guild, 70.
Bibliography: Lawrence Campbell (auth), The well-tempered colorwheel, Art News, 4/69.
Dealer: A M Sachs Gallery, 29 W 57th St, New York, NY 10019.
Mailing Address: 44 Carmine St, New York, NY 10014.

CUNNINGHAM, CHARLES CREHORE
Art Curator, Collector
b Mamaroneck, N Y, Mar 7, 10.
Study & Training: Harvard Univ, AB, 32; Courtauld Inst, Univ London, BA, 34; Harvard Univ Grad Sch, 35; Univ Hartford, hon DFA, 59; DePaul Univ, hon LittD, 70.
Collections Arranged: Fifty Painters of Architecture, 47 & Life in 17th Century Holland, 50-51, Wadsworth Atheneum, Hartford, Conn; Rembrandt after Three Hundred Years, Art Inst Chicago, 69.
Positions: Asst cur paintings, Mus Fine Arts, Boxton, 35-42; dir, Wadsworth Atheneum, 46-66; dir, Art Inst Chicago, 66-72; chief cur, Sterling & Francine Clark Art Inst, Williamstown, Mass, 72-
Awards: Order of Merit, Italy, 69.
Memberships: Asn Art Mus Dirs (pres, 58); Am Asn Mus (coun, 70-72); U S Comt, Int Coun Mus (chmn, 70-72); Benjamin Franklin fel Royal Soc Arts; Chicago Comn Hist & Archit Landmarks (comnr, 68-72).
Research: Dutch painting; Rembrandt and Rembrandt school; French nineteenth century painting.
Collection: French, Dutch and American paintings.
Publications: Auth, The medicine man, 54 & The Pierpont Morgan treasures, 64.
Mailing Address: 89 South St, Williamstown, MA 02167.

CUNNINGHAM, FRANCIS
Painter
Preferred Media: Oils.
b New York, N Y, Jan 18, 31.
Study & Training: Art Stud League New York, with Edwin Dickinson & Robert Beverly Hale.
Work in Public Collections: Berkshire Mus, Pittsfield, Mass.
Exhibitions: One-man shows, Hirschl & Adler Galleries, New York, 67 & 70; Butler Inst Am Art, Youngstown, Ohio, 67 & 72; Nat Acad Design, New York, 67, 69 & 72; one-man show, Welles Gallery, Lenox Libr, Mass, 71; The Contemporary Figure, Suffolk Mus, Stony Brook, N Y, 71.
Teaching: Lectr art hist, painting & drawing, City Col New York, 62-65; instr painting & drawing, Brooklyn Mus Art Sch, 62-
Awards: Peebles Award, Berkshire Mus, 65; Berkshire Art Asn Purchase Award, Berkshire Mus, 68.
Publications: Co-auth, Polykleitos' Diadoumenos: measurement and animation, Art Quart, summer 62; illusr, Fundatmentals of roentgenology, 64.
Dealer: Hirschl & Adler Galleries, 21 E 67th St, New York, NY 10021.
Mailing Address: 789 West End Ave, New York, NY 10025.

CURRIE, BRUCE
Painter
Preferred Media: Oil.
b Sac City, Iowa, Nov 27, 11.
Work in Public Collections: Nat Acad Design, New York, N Y; State

Univ N Y Albany; Butler Inst Am Art, Youngstown, Ohio; Dwight Art Mem, Mt Holyoke Col, South Hadley, Mass; Kalamazoo Inst Arts, Mich.
Exhibitions: Butler Inst Am Art, 66; Nat Acad Design, 69-72; Conn Acad Fine Arts, Hartford, 70; Schenectady Mus, N Y, 71; Colorado Springs Fine Arts Ctr, Colo, 71; plus many others including one-man shows.
Awards: Thomas B Clarke Prize, Nat Acad Design, 66; Charles Noel Flagg Mem Prize, Conn Acad Fine Arts, 68; Emily Lowe Mem Award, Audubon Artists, New York, 71.
Memberships: Nat Acad Design; Conn Acad Fine Arts; Am. Watercolor Soc; Audubon Artists; Woodstock Artists Asn.
Mailing Address: RFD Box 284, Woodstock, NY 12498.

CURTIS, PHILIP CAMPBELL
　　Painter
Preferred Media: Oils.
b Jackson, Mich, May 26, 07.
Study & Training: Albion Col, BA, 30; Univ Mich Law Sch; Yale Univ Sch Fine Arts, cert, 35; Harvard Univ, 41; Albion Col, hon DFA, 71.
Exhibitions: Twenty-yr Retrospective Exhib, Northern Ariz Univ, 67; one-man shows, Palm Springs Desert Mus, Calif, 71, Dickson Art Ctr, Univ Calif, Los Angeles, 72, Univ Nev, Las Vegas, 72 & Utah Mus Fine Arts, Salt Lake City, 72; plus 15 other one-man shows.
Positions: Supvr mural painting, Works Progress Admin Proj, New York, N Y, 35; Founder & first dir, Phoenix Art Ctr & Phoenix Art Mus, 36-39; designer, WPA Art Proj Exhib, De Young Mus, San Francisco, Calif, 38; mem staff, Des Moines Art Ctr, 39-41.
Memberships: Benjamin Franklin fel Royal Soc Arts.
Dealer: Coe Kerr Gallery, 49 E 82nd St, New York, NY 10028.
Mailing Address: 109 Cattle Track, Scottsdale, AZ 85253.

CUSHING, GEORGE
　　Industrial Designer
b Plainfield, N J, Oct 14, 06.
Study & Training: Rutgers Univ, 26-27; New York Univ, 28-32; Watson-Guptill Sch, 34; New Sch Social Res, 35-36.
Teaching: Dir indust design, Newark Sch Fine & Indust Arts, 40-54; lectr design, New York Univ, Pratt Inst, N J Art Teachers Asn & New York Hist Mus.
Positions: Partner & pres, Cushing & Nevell, New York, 33-; chmn bd, Cushing & Nevell Tech Design Corp, New York; pres, Cushing & Nevell, Inc, Calif; owner, Penbuck Farms, Pa.
Awards: Modern plastic award, 39; elec mfg award, 40; Indust Designers Inst Award, 51.
Memberships: Nat Tech Serv Asn (pres, 62-63, v chmn bd, 64-65); Indust Designers Inst; Am Soc Indust Design.
Mailing Address: 101 Park Ave, New York, NY 10017.

CUSICK, NANCY TAYLOR
　　Painter, Educator
Preferred Media: Constructions, Mixed Media, Acrylics, Oils.
b Washington, D C.
Study & Training: Am Univ, BA, 59, MA, 61, Elizabeth Van Swinderin scholar & with Gates, Calfee, D'Arista & Summerford; Corcoran Art Sch, 68; Univ Calif, 71, with Lindgren.
Exhibitions: Washington Watercolor Soc Nat Exhib, Smithsonian Inst, Washington, D C, 63; three man show, Art Asn Newport, R I, 65; Corcoran Gallery Art Area Exhib, Washington, 67; area show, Washington Co Mus, Hagerstown, Md, 67; Washington Artists Today, Massillon Mus, Ohio, 69; plus one other.
Teaching: Instr art hist, Dunbarton Col Holy Cross, 67-72, instr advan painting, 69-72; instr art hist & drawing, Prince George's Col, 72-73.
Awards: First prize for painting, Blue Boots, Soc Washington Artists, 66; best in show, Hagerstown Mus, Pangborn Corp, 67.
Bibliography: Article, In: Washington Artists Today, Acropolis, 67.
Memberships: Artists Equity Asn (mem chmn, 71-); Nat Art Educ Asn; Soc Washington Artists (ann exhib chmn, 64 & 68).
Dealer: The Studio Gallery, 1735 Connecticut Ave N W, Washington, DC 20009.
Mailing Address: 2015 Hillyer Pl N W, Washington, DC 20009.

CUSUMANO, STEFANO
　　Painter, Educator
Preferred Media: Oils.
b Tampa, Fla, Feb 5, 12.
Study & Training: Cooper Union Sch Art & Archit, 27; Metrop Art Sch, 28-30; also with Arthur Schwieder, 31.
Work in Public Collections: Nat Gallery Art, Washington, D C; Metrop Mus Art, New York, N Y; Whitney Mus Am Art, New York; Brooklyn Mus, N Y; Krannert Art Mus, Champaign, Ill.
Exhibitions: Carnegie Int, Pittsburgh, Pa, 48; Recent Drawings U S A, Mus Mod Art, New York, 56; Whitney Mus Am Art Ann,

62; Art on Paper, Weatherspoon Art Gallery, Greensboro, N C, 69; Am Acad Arts & Lett Paintings Exhib, New York, 71.
Teaching: Adj prof art, New York Univ, 54-; adj asst prof art, Cooper Union Sch Art & Archit, 55-
Awards: Purchase award, Ford Found, 62; Dillard Purchase Award, Weatherspoon Gallery, 69; Childe Hassam Award, Am Acad Arts & Lett, 71.
Mailing Address: 170 W 73rd St, New York, NY 10023.

CUTHBERT, VIRGINIA
　　Painter, Instructor
Preferred Media: Oils.
b West Newton, Pa, Aug 27, 08.
Study & Training: Syracuse Univ, BFA, 30; Acad Grande Chaumiere, Acad Colarossi, Paris, France & Chelsea Polytech Inst, Eng, Augusta-Hazard fel, 30-31; study with George Luks, 32; Univ Pittsburgh, 33-34; Carnegie Inst Technol, 34-35.
Work in Public Collections, Albright-Knox Art Gallery, Buffalo, N Y; Princeton Univ Art Mus, N J; Rutgers Univ Libr Collection, N J; also in collections of Seymour H Knox, Buffalo & Vincent Price, Los Angeles, Calif.
Commissions: Mural, comn by Works Progress Admin, Munic Bldg, Mt Lebanon, Pa, 34; Fortune Mag covers, 51 & 56; Southwestern Rev cover, 52; painting comn by Nat Gypsum Co, Buffalo.
Exhibitions: 8 Pa Acad Fine Arts Ann, Philadelphia, 35-53; 10 Carnegie Int & Am Ann, Carnegie Inst, Pittsburgh, Pa, 37-52; Metrop Mus Art, New York, N Y, 43, 44 & 50; 7 Whitney Mus Am Art Ann, New York, 44-53; Good Will Exhib to Brazil, 60.
Teaching: Instr painting, Albright Art Sch, 42-54; instr painting, Univ Buffalo, 42-54; instr painting, State Univ N Y Buffalo, 54-66.
Positions: Art columnist, Buffalo Courier Express, 54-55.
Awards: First prize, Western N Y Exhib, Albright-Knox Art Gallery, 46-52; Nat Inst Arts & Lett grant for painting, 54; prize, Chautauqua Nat Exhib, N Y, 55.
Bibliography: Virginia Cuthbert (catalog), Carnegie Inst, 38; Virginia Cuthbert & Philip Elliott (catalog), Albright-Knox Art Gallery, 44; Retrospective: Virginia Cuthbert & Philip Elliott (catalog), Charles Burchfield Ctr, State Univ N Y Buffalo, 71.
Memberships: Patteran Artists, Buffalo.
Publications: Auth, spec art reviews, In: Buffalo Eve News, 54-56.
Dealer: Frank Rehn Gallery, 655 Madison Ave, New York, NY 10021.
Mailing Address: 147 Bryant St, Buffalo, NY 14222.

CUTLER, ETHEL ROSE
　　Painter, Designer
Preferred Media: Watercolors, Oils.
b New York, N Y, Mar 13, 15.
Study & Training: Hunter Col, with Joseph Cummings Chase, BA; Columbia Univ, MA; Sch Prof Arts, cert advert & interior design; New York Univ; ceramics & sculpture with Michael Lekakis & Rudolph Staffel; Univ Mo; Inst Design, Ill Inst Technol; Am Artist Sch, grant & with Nahum Tschachbasov; New Sch Social Res, with Yasua Kunyioshi & Alexei Brodovitch.
Exhibitions: New York City Ctr Gallery; Design Derby, Hialeah, Fla; Young American Artist Group, New York; Lynn Kottler Galleries, New York; Sch Home Econ, Univ Mo-Columbia; plus others.
Teaching: Instr fine arts, Women's Col, Univ N C, Greensboro, 43-47; instr, Adelphi Col, 47-50; asst prof interior design, Univ Mo-Columbia, 50-55; asst prof surface design, R I Sch Design, 55-59.
Positions: Design consult, artist & designer, Cutler Designs, 50-
Awards: Award for Boats, New York City Ctr Gallery, 59; award for Brothers, Macy's Gallery; grant, Metrop Mus Art, New York, 68.
Memberships: Col Art Asn Am; Artists Equity Asn; Allied Bd Trade; Nat Soc Interior Designers; Am Craftsmen's Coun.
Research: Techniques of William Morris and the arts and crafts movement of the Beaux Arts, the Bauhaus and other influences of the nineteenth century.
Publications: Illusr, New York City & its parks, Institutional & historic buildings, Miami Beach, Florida & Floral studies.
Mailing Address: 230 E 88th St, New York, NY 10028.

CUTLER, GRAYCE E
　　Painter, Writer
Preferred Media: Watercolors, Acrylics, Oils.
b Salt Lake City, Utah.
Study & Training: Univ Utah; Art Stud League New York, with Kuniyoshi & Morris Kantor; New York Sch Design, cert; Hans Hofmann Sch Art, Provincetown, Mass; also with Eliot O'Hara.
Work in Public Collections: Granite Schs Admin Art Collection, Salt Lake City; Pollard Collection, Greater Victoria Art Gallery, B C; Alice Merrill Horne Collection, Utah; also Royal Family of Saudi Arabia & numerous other private collections.
Exhibitions: Springville Art Mus Ann Invitational, 64-; Burr Artists, New York, New York World's Fair, 65; Soc Western Artists Ann, De Young Mus, San Francisco, Calif, 66, 68 & 69; San Francisco

Women Artists Invitational, Kaiser Ctr, Oakland, 68; one-woman invitational, Rosicrucian Egyptian Mus & Gallery, San Jose, 68 & 71; plus others.
Teaching: Instr art.
Positions: Western regional dir Am Art Month promoting Am art & artists, Am Artists Prof League, 55-65; pres & organizer traveling exhibs in Western States for Utah artists, Utah Creative Artists, 56-58; mem judiciary comt, Utah High Schs Ann, 62.
Awards: First prize for watercolor, Utah State Fair, 69; watercolor award of honor, representing Utah in Intermountain States Traveling Exhib, Utah Inst Fine Arts, 70; watercolor first award representing Northern Calif, hon mention, Nat League Am Pen Women Biennial, Washington, D C, 72; plus one other.
Bibliography: Articles, In: Rosicrucian Digest, 68 & 71 & Relief Soc Mag, 69.
Memberships: Soc Western Artists; Nat Soc Interior Designers (bd mem, San Francisco Chapter, 68-70); Assoc Utah Artists; Burr Artists, N Y; San Francisco Women Artists.
Research: Early writings and drawings as an art form.
Mailing Address: 470 S 13th East St, Salt Lake City, UT 84102.

CUTTLER, CHARLES DAVID
 Art Historian
b Cleveland, Ohio, Apr 8, 13.
Study & Training: Ohio State Univ, BA & BFA; Inst Art & Archeol, Paris, France; Univ Bruxelles; Inst Fine Arts, New York Univ, PhD.
Exhibitions: Cleveland May Show, Ohio, 35 & 36; Philadelphia Watercolor Ann, Pa, 37.
Teaching: Asst instr art hist, Ohio State Univ, 35-37; from instr to asst prof art hist, Mich State Univ, 47-57; from assoc prof to prof art hist, Univ Iowa, 57, res prof, 65; guest lectr, Sem Europ Art & Civilisation Belg, Ghent, summer 69.
Awards: Award, Ann Watercolor Competition, Ohio State Univ, 35; C R B fel, Brussels, 53-54; Fulbright-Hays sr fel, 65-66.
Memberships: Col Art Asn Am; Mid-Am Col Art Asn; Renaissance Soc Am; Medieval Acad Am; Int Ctr Medieval Art.
Research: Netherlandish and German art of the fourteenth to sixteenth centuries; the art of Hieronymus Bosch.
Publications: Auth, Some Grünewald sources, Art Quart, 56; auth, The Lisbon Temptation of St Anthony by Jerome Bosch, Art Bull, 57; auth, Northern painting, from Pucelle to Bruegel, XIVth, XVth and XVIth centuries, 68; auth, Bosch and the Narrenschiff: a problem in relationships, Art Bull, 69; auth, Two aspects of Bosch's Hell imagery, Miscellanea F Lyna (Scriptorium, 23), 69.
Mailing Address: 1691 Ridge Rd, Iowa City, IA 52240.

CYRIL, (RUTH)
 Painter, Printmaker
Preferred Media: Graphics.
b New York, N Y.
Study & Training: Art Stud League New York; New Sch Soc Res; N Y Univ; The Sorbonne, Paris, France, Fulbright fel.
Work in Public Collections: Metrop Mus Art, New York; Victoria & Albert Mus, London, Eng; Bibliotheque Nationale, Paris; Nat Gallery Art, Washington, D C; State Dept, Washington, D C; plus many others.
Exhibitions: Invited to exhibit by the State Dept in foreign countries, Redfern Gallery, London, Schneider Gallery, Rome, Italy & La Guilde de la Gravure, Switz, 60-72; plus many group & one-man shows in mus & univs in U S A.
Teaching: Invited instr painting, graphic art, design & crafts, Adelphi Univ, 63-66.
Awards: First prize, Dallas Mus Fine Art, Tex; first prize, Print Club, Philadelphia, Pa.
Mailing Address: 800 West End Ave, New York, NY 10025.

CZUMA, STANISLAW J
 Art Historian
b Warsaw, Poland, Oct 26, 35; U S citizen.
Study & Training: Jagiellonian Univ, BA & MA; Paderewski Found scholar studies in India, 58-60; Nat Defense Foreign Lang fel studies in India, 65-67; Banares Hindu Univ, with Vasudeva S Agrawala; Univ Calcutta, with S K Saraswati; Sorbonne, with Louis Renou; Univ Mich, PhD, 68, with Walter Spink.
Collections Arranged: Cambodian Art, Asian House Gallery, New York, 69; Permanent Indian Gallery, Brooklyn Mus.
Teaching: Res asst Oriental art, Univ Mich, Ann Arbor, 62-64.
Positions: Ford Found curatorial trainee, Cleveland Mus, 68-70; cur Oriental art, Brooklyn Mus, 70-72; cur Indian art, Cleveland Mus, 72-
Memberships: Asn Asian Studies; Asia Soc; China Inst; Japan Soc; Int Coun Mus, Paris.
Research: Art of India and Southeast Asia, especially Gupta and Medieval India.

Publications: Co-auth, Cambodian art (catalogue), Asia Soc, 69; auth, Gupta style bronze Buddha, Bull Cleveland Mus, 2/70.
Mailing Address: Oriental Dept, Cleveland Museum, East Blvd, Cleveland, OH 44106.

CZURLES, STANLEY A
 Painter, Educator
b Elizabeth, N J, Sept 14, 08.
Study & Training: Syracuse Univ, BFA, 29, MFA, 38; Univ Iowa, PhD, 42.
Exhibitions: Albright Art Gallery; Syracuse Mus Fine Arts; one-man show, Buffalo Town Club.
Teaching: Asst prof art, State Univ N Y Buffalo, 41-46, dir visual educ, 43-46, prof art & dir art educ, 46-
Positions: Adv, N Y State Coun Arts, 64-65; consult, N Y State Art Teachers Asn.
Memberships: Nat Educ Asn; Nat Art Educ Asn (coun mem); Eastern Art Asn (pres, 62-64).
Publications: Auth, The art process and learning: in the child and the articulated curriculum, 68; contribr, art educ mags & bulls.
Mailing Address: 244 Wardman Rd, Kenmore, NY 14217.

D

D'AGOSTINO, VINCENT
 Painter
Preferred Media: Oils, Watercolors.
b Chicago, Ill, Apr 7, 98.
Study & Training: Art Inst Chicago, grad(cum laude); also with George Bellows & Charles Hawthorne.
Work in Public Collections: Whitney Mus Am Art, New York, N Y; Logan Collection, Art Inst Chicago, Ill.
Commissions: Mural, Mexican Village, Chicago World's Fair, 33; mural for Gloucester Post Off, N J, U S Treas Dept, 35; mural for college, Mt Loretto, N Y, commissioned by Patrick Cardinal O'Boyle, 41; mural, Riccardo's Studio Restaurant, Chicago, 48.
Exhibitions: Metrop Mus Art, New York, 39; New York World's Fair Fine Art Exhib, 40; 100 Years of American Art, Los Angeles Co Fair, Calif, 53; Los Angeles Co Mus Art, 54; Graham Gallery Nat Invitational Show, New York, 66; plus many others.
Teaching: Artist-in-residence, Mt Loretto, N Y, 41-42; prof art, Woodbury Col, Calif, 49-54.
Awards: Tiffany Found Award, 31 & 32; Ford Found grant nominee, 54.
Bibliography: Whitney Museum of Art, Macmillan, 31; Ben Hecht (auth), Wistfully yours, Theatre Arts Mag, 7/51; Arthur Millier (auth), Painting in the U S A: 1721 to 1953, Los Angeles Co Fair Asn, 53.
Memberships: Nat Soc Mural Painters; Artists Equity; United Scenic Artists.
Mailing Address: 11133 Hesby St No 3, North Hollywood, CA 91601.

DAGYS, JACOB
 Sculptor
Preferred Media: Wood, Bronze, Marble & Artificial Materials.
b Lithuania, Dec 16, 05; Can citizen.
Study & Training: Kaunas Art Sch, Lithuania.
Work in Public Collections: Balzekas Mus, Chicago, Ill; Ciurlionis Gallery, Chicago.
Commissions: Crucifix, sacre coeur, & others, St Monicas Church, Toronto, Ont, 58; St Anthony, & others, Church Resurrection, Toronto, 67.
Teaching: Instr art, Raseiniai High Sch, Lithuania, 32-44.
Bibliography: Album, Dagy's sculptures and paintings, Am Lithuanian Art Asn, 67.
Memberships: Sculptor Soc Can.
Publications: Articles about art for Lithuanian Press.
Mailing Address: 78 Chelsea Ave, Toronto, Ont, Can.

DAHILL, THOMAS HENRY, JR
 Painter, Educator
b Cambridge, Mass, June 22, 25.
Study & Training: Tufts Col, BS, 49; Harvard Univ, summer 53; Sch Mus Fine Arts, Boston, dipl, 53, cert, 54; Skowhegan Sch Painting & Sculpture; Am Acad in Rome, fel, 55-57; Max Beckmann Gesellschaft, Murnau, Ger, resident, 56; Emerson Col, AM, 67.
Commissions: Mural, Unitarian Church, Brockton, Mass, 58; film strips, series of paintings on Old & New Testaments, 61-62; film strip, life of George Washington Carver, 61.
Exhibitions: Boston Art Festival, 55, 56 & 63; Archit League, N Y, 58; Int Bienale Relig Art, Salzburg, Austria, 58-59; Emerson Col,

64 & 67; Drawings of N Africa exhibited through Mus Fine Arts
Boston to galleries of New Eng Prep Schs, 67-69; plus others.
Teaching: Lectr gen art hist & contemp use of art in churches; instr
hist art, Tufts Univ, 54-55 & 60-65; instr, dept drawing, Sch Mus
Fine Arts, Boston, 58-65; prof fine arts & chmn dept, Emerson
Col, 67-
Awards: Abbey Mem fel to Am Acad in Rome, 55-57.
Memberships: Inst Contemp Art, Boston; MacDowell Colonists;
Alumni Asn, Sch Mus Fine Arts, Boston.
Mailing Address: 223 Broadway, Arlington, MA 02174.

DAHL, FRANCIS W
Cartoonist
b Wollaston, Mass, Oct 21, 07.
Positions: Cartoonist, Boston Herald-Traveler, 28-72; cartoonist,
Boston Globe, 72-
Publications: Auth & illusr, Left handed compliments, 41 & Dahl's
cartoons, 43; illusr, Dahl's Boston, 46 & Dahl's brave new world,
47; auth & illusr, Birds, beasts and Bostonians, 54.
Mailing Address: 47 Central Ave, Newtonville, MA 02160.

DAHLBERG, EDWIN LENNART
Painter
Preferred Media: Watercolors.
b Beloit, Wis, Sept 20, 01.
Study & Training: Art Inst Chicago, grad.
Work in Public Collections: Charles & Emma Frye Mus, Seattle,
Wash; Wesleyan Univ.
Exhibitions: Am Watercolor Soc Ann, 54-; Nat Acad Design; Pa Acad
Fine Arts, 54-61; Art Inst Chicago, 54-61; Royal Soc Watercolor
Painters, London, Eng, 66.
Awards: Henry Ward Ranger Fund purchase prize, Nat Acad Design,
58; medal of merit for best in show for all media, Knickerbocker
Artists, 70; gold medal of Hon, Am Watercolor Soc, 72.
Bibliography: Edwin L Dahlberg Seeks mood in a motif, Am Artist,
2/65; Norman Kent (auth), 100 watercolor techniques, Watson-
Guptill, 68; Edwin L Dahlberg paints a watercolor on location
(film), produced by Electrographic Corp Am, 71.
Memberships: Am Watercolor Soc (bd dirs, 65-68); Allied Artists
Am (bd dirs, 67-71); Hudson Valley Art Asn; Knickerbocker
Artists.
Mailing Address: 6 South Boulevard, Nyack, NY 10960.

DAILEY, CHARLES ANDREW (CHUCK)
Museum Director, Painter
b Golden, Colo, May 25, 35.
Study & Training: Univ Colo, BA(art), 61; study in Western Europe,
62-63.
Work in Public Collections: Mus N Mex Permanent Collection, Santa
Fe; Vincent Price Collection, Hollywood, Calif.
Exhibitions: Fiesta Biennial, 64 & 65 & 1968 Southwest Biennial, 68,
Mus N Mex; 1968 N Mex State Fair, Albuquerque, N Mex, 68; one-
man show, Gallery 5, Santa Fe, 64.
Collections Arranged: Afro-Arabic World, 66-67, The New Mexican
Santero, 70-71 & World of Folk Costume, 71-72, Museum Inter-
national Folk Art, Three Culture-sculpture exhibition & The Rain
Cloud Callers (Indian art), Fine Arts Mus & The Spanish Endohe
(Spanish history in Southwest), Palace of Governors, Museum of
New Mexico.
Teaching: Mus training dir, Inst Am Indian Arts, Santa Fe, 71-
Positions: Mus preparator, Univ Colo Mus, Boulder, 59-61; exhibs
tech, Mus Northern Ariz, Flagstaff, 62-63; cur-in-charge exhib
div, Mus N Mex, 64-71.
Bibliography: Catherine Wenzell (auth), Artists of Santa Fe, pri-
vately pub, 68; Artists U S A 1971, Livingstone, 71; Rauschen-
busch (auth), International directory of arts, Deutsches Zen-
traldruckerei A G, 71-72.
Memberships: N Mex Asn Mus (mem chmn, at present); Am Asn
Mus; Midwest Mus Asn; Far West Mus Asn.
Publications: Auth, Creating a crowd (maniken development & how
to), N Mex Asn Mus, 72.
Dealer: Jamison Gallery, 111 E San Francisco, Santa Fe, NM 87501.
Mailing Address: 412 Sosaya Lane, Santa Fe, NM 87501.

DAILEY, JOSEPH CHARLES, see JOCDA

DAILEY, MICHAEL DENNIS
Painter, Educator
Preferred Media: Oils, Watercolors.
b Des Moines, Iowa, Aug 2, 38.
Study & Training: Univ Iowa, BA & MFA.
Work in Public Collections: Univ Iowa, Iowa City; Western Ill Univ,
Macomb; Mercyhurst Col, Erie, Pa; Art Gallery Greater Victoria,
B C; Anacortes City Mus, Wash.
Exhibitions: Art Across America, regional exhib San Francisco Mus
Art, 65; Ultimate Concerns Drawing Exhib, Ohio Univ, Athens, 65;
Drawings U S A, St Paul Art Ctr, Minn, 66 & 68; 73rd Western
Ann Invitational, Denver Art Mus, Colo, 71.

Teaching: Assoc prof drawing & painting, Univ Wash, 63-
Awards: Purchase award, Mercyhurst Nat Graphics Exhib, Erie, Pa,
65; first pl award in painting, Wash State Ann Art Exhib,
Wenatchee, 67; Northwest Watercolor Soc Award, 30th Ann
Northwest Watercolor Exhib, Seattle Art Mus, 70.
Mailing Address: c/o Francine Seders Gallery, 6701 Greenwood
Ave N, Seattle, WA 98105.

DAILY, EVELYNNE B
Painter, Printmaker
b Indianapolis, Ind, Jan 8, 03.
Study & Training: Herron Sch Art, Ind Univ; Art Inst Chicago; But-
ler Univ; Ecole Beaux Arts, Fontainebleau, France, dipl; Way-
man Adams Sch Portrait Painting, New York; also Bauhaus with
Moholy-Nagy, Chicago.
Work in Public Collections: Indianapolis Mus Art; Fort Wayne Mus;
Richmond Art Asn; Libr Cong, Washington, D C.
Exhibitions: Nat Acad Design, New York; Pa Acad Fine Arts; Brook-
lyn Mus, N Y; Seattle Art Mus Int Print Show; Libr Cong Exhib
Prints.
Teaching: Instr drawing & painting, pub & pvt schs, Indianapolis, 40-
60; instr painting & printmaking, Oxbow Acres Summer Art Sch,
Brown Co, Ind, 64-
Positions: Dir, Brown Co Art Gallery Asn, 62-64 & 69-71; pres, Ind
Fedn Art Clubs, 67-69; secy, Ind Artists Club.
Awards: Hugh J Baker Mem Prize for best group of etchings,
Hossier Salon Exhibs, 50; J T Holcomb Prize for Painting, Her-
ron Mus, 58; Festival of Arts Award, Nat Soc Arts & Lett, 66.
Memberships: Nat Soc Arts & Lett (dir); Ind Artists Club; Ind Art-
ist-Craftsmen; Hoosier Salon.
Dealer: Daily Studio, Box 515, Nashville, IN 47448.
Mailing Address: 6237 Central Ave, Indianapolis, IN 46220.

DAINGERFIELD, MARJORIE JAY
Sculptor
Preferred Media: Bronze, Marble.
b New York, N Y.
Study & Training: Sch Am Sculpture; Grand Cent Sch Art; also with
Solon Borglum, Edmond Amateis, Brenda Putnam, Mahonri
Young, Isadore Konti & Ann Hyatt.
Work in Public Collections: Sch Trop Med, San Juan, P R; Mus of
City New York; Georgetown Univ, Washington, D C; N C Mus Art,
Raleigh; Mint Mus, Charlotte, N C.
Commissions: Indian head (bronze), Hobart Col, New York; Dr Bai-
ley Ashford (portrait head in bronze), Sch Trop Med, San Juan,
34; Dr C C Carpenter (portrait head), Bowman Gray Sch Med,
Winston-Salem, N C, 69; The Offering (bronze statue), St Mary's
of the Hills, Blowing Rock, N C, 72.
Exhibitions: One-man shows, Duke Univ, N C & Mint Mus, Charlotte;
group shows, Nat Sculpture Soc, Pen & Brush Club, New York,
Catharine Lorillard Wolfe Art Club & Nat Acad Design, New York.
Teaching: Instr sculpture, Grand Cent Sch Art, 25-27; instr sculp-
ture, Rollins Col, 35-37; instr sculpture, Norton Gallery & Sch
Art, 40.
Positions: Lectr & demonstr on sculpture at various univ clubs,
Richmond, Va, Winter Park & Palm Beach, Fla & art groups in
New York.
Awards: Ann Hyatt Huntington award for bronze; Catharine Lorillard
Wolfe Art Club award for Life with Father.
Memberships: Fel Nat Sculpture Soc; Pen & Brush Club(chmn sculp-
ture sect); Catharine Lorillard Wolfe Art Club; Blowing Rock Art
Asn.
Publications: Auth, The fun & fundamentals of sculpture, Scribners,
63.
Mailing Address: 1 W 67th St, New York, NY 10023.

DALE, WILLIAM SCOTT ABELL
Art Historian, Art Administrator
b Toronto, Ont, Sept 18, 21.
Study & Training: Univ Toronto, BA & MA; Harvard Univ, PhD.
Teaching: Prof art hist, Univ Western Ont, 67-
Positions: Res cur, Nat Gallery Can, Ottawa, Ont, 51-57; cur,
Art Gallery Toronto, 57-59; dir, Vancouver Art Gallery, B C,
59-61; asst dir, Nat Gallery Can, 61-66, dep dir, 66-67.
Memberships: Col Art Asn Am; Mediaeval Acad Am.
Research: Romanesque ivories; the Bulwer Collection; Canadian
art.
Publications: Contribr, The arts in Canada, 58; contribr, Oxford
companion to art, 70.
Mailing Address: University of Western Ontario, London, Ont, Can.

DAL FABBRO, MARIO
Sculptor, Writer
Preferred Media: Wood.
b Cappella Maggiore, Italy, Oct 6, 13; U S citizen.
Study & Training: Inst Indust Art, Venice, Italy; Magistero Art,
Venice.

Work in Public Collections: Collection Sant' Andrea, Vittorio Veneto, Italy; Allentown Art Mus, Pa; Dieruff High Sch Collection, Allentown.
Exhibitions: Nat Art Exhib, Vittorio Veneto, 69; Allentown Art Mus Exhibs, 69-72 & one-man show, 72; Cheltenham Art Ctr, Philadelphia, Pa, 71; Phillips Mill Art Gallery, New Hope, Pa, 71; Ctr Artistico Ital Belle Arti, Trieste, Italy, 72.
Awards: Awards, Three Sq, Lehigh Art Alliance, 69; wood construction, Woodmere Art Gallery, Philadelphia, 70; archaic construction, Phillips Mill Art Gallery, 71.
Memberships: Int Acad Tommaso Campanella, Rome, Italy; Allentown Art Mus; Woodmere Art Gallery; Lehigh Art Alliance.
Publications: Auth, Costruzione e funzionalita' del mobile moderno, Hoepli, Italy, 50; auth, Furniture for modern interiors, Van Nostrand Reinhold, 52; auth, How to make built-in furniture, McGraw-Hill & Ceac, Spain, 55; auth, How to build modern furniture, McGraw-Hill & Hoepli, 57; auth, Upholstered furniture, its design and construction, McGraw-Hill & Hoepli, 69.
Mailing Address: 1251 Tacoma St, Allentown, PA 18103.

D'ALMEIDA, GEORGE
Painter
Preferred Media: Acrylics, Watercolors
b Paris, France, June 30, 34; U S citizen.
Exhibitions: American Artists, Palazzo Venezia, Rome, Italy, 60; Carnegie Inst, Pittsburgh, 64; 5th Rassegna Arte Figurativa, Rome, 65; U S Info Serv Exhib, Rome, 68.
Dealers: M Knoedler & Co, 21 E 70th St, New York, NY 10021; Fairweather Hardin Gallery, 101 E Ontario St, Chicago, IL 60611.
Mailing Address: Casina di Selvole, Radda in Chianti (Siena), Italy.

DALTON, FRANCES LOUISA
Painter, Instructor
Preferred Media: Oils, Mixed Media, Ink, Watercolors, Pencil.
b Amesbury, Mass, Dec 28, 06.
Study & Training: Sch Mus Fine Arts, cert; Ecole Beaux Arts, Paris; Paige Traveling scholar, 30-33; also sculpture with Robert Laurent.
Work in Public Collections: Royal Hawaiian Hotel; Andover High Sch; also pvt comns.
Exhibitions: Jordan Marsh Exhibs, Boston; Whistler Gallery, Lowell; Springfield Mus; Boston Art Festival; Silvermine Guild, Conn.
Collections Arranged: Exhibs at Whistler House Gallery, Addison Gallery & John Ester Gallery & Boston Mus Guild Artists.
Teaching: Supvry instr art, Andover Jr & Sr High Schs.
Positions: Chmn, Andover High Art Festivals; chmn, Andover Art Asn; chmn Am Art Wk, 58-64.
Awards: Lawrence Centennial Exhib, 53; Richard Mitton Gold Medal & Award, 54; Painting & Graphic Awards, 70-71.
Memberships: Guild Scholars & Mus Sch, Boston.
Mailing Address: 70 Chestnut St, Andover, MA 01810.

DALTON, HARRY L
Collector, Patron
b Winston-Salem, N C, June 13, 98.
Study & Training: Duke Univ, AB & hon LHD; Brit Univ; N Y Univ.
Memberships: N C Art Soc; Mint Mus; N C Mus; N C Arts Coun; Weatherspoon Gallery.
Collection: Various schools of European and American art; collection has been loaned to various galleries.
Mailing Address: 1212 Wachovia Bank Bldg, Charlotte, NC 28202.

DALY, KATHLEEN (KATHLEEN DALY PEPPER)
Painter
Preferred Media: Oils, Crayon.
b Napanee, Ont, May 28, 98.
Study & Training: Ont Col Art, assoc, with Arthur Lismer, J eh MacDonald & J W Beatty; Acad Grande Chaumiere, Paris; Ont Col Art; also woodcuts with Rene Poitier, Paris.
Work in Public Collections: Nat Gallery Can, Ottawa, Ont; Art Gallery Ont, Toronto; London Libr & Art Gallery, Ont; McMichael Mus, Kleinburg, Ont; Dept Nat Affairs, Ottawa.
Commissions: Portraits, Dr Thomas Cullen, Baltimore, 41, Premier Herbert Greenfield, 46 & Señor Hach, Tangiers, Morocco.
Exhibitions: Group of Seven, 31; Brit Empire Exhib, 37-38; Great Lakes Exhib, 38-39; New York World's Fair, 39; Ann, Ont Soc Arts, Royal Can Acad & Can Group Painters.
Bibliography: Life in Eskimoland, London Press, 62.
Memberships: Royal Can Acad; Ont Soc Artists.
Publications: Co-illusr, Kingdom of Saguenay, 36; illusr, North, Dept Northern Affairs, 62; auth, Morrice, Clarke, Irwin, Toronto, 66.
Mailing Address: 441 Walmer Rd, Toronto, Ont, Can.

DALY, NORMAN DAVID
Sculptor, Painter
b Pittsburgh, Pa, Aug 9, 11.
Study & Training: Univ Colo, BFA; Ohio State Univ, MA; N Y Univ Grad Inst.
Work in Public Collections: White Art Mus, Cornell Univ, Ithaca, N Y; Munson-Williams-Proctor Inst, Utica, N Y; Univ Wash, Seattle; Walker Art Ctr, Minneapolis, Minn; State Univ N Y Col Cortland.
Commissions: Carved plaque of zodiac symbols, meditation rm, State Univ N Y Col Cortland; Time (stained glass windows), crypt, Mt Saviour Monastery, Pine City, N Y.
Exhibitions: Metrop Mus Art; Whitney Mus Am Art; Pa Acad Fine Arts; Art Inst Chicago; Carnegie Inst; plus others.
Teaching: Prof art, Cornell Univ, 42-, dir Llhuroscian studies, 68-
Bibliography: Kenneth Evett (auth), The civilization of Llhuros, New Republic, 2/12/72; Charles Michener (auth), The fabulous Llhoroscians, Newsweek, 2/28/72; Thomas Leavih (auth), Norman Daly at Cornell, Art in Am, 3-4/72.
Publications: Auth, The civilization of Llhuros (catalogue), 72.
Mailing Address: 110 N Quarry St, Ithaca, NY 14850.

DAMAZ, PAUL F
Writer, Collector
b Portugal, Nov 8, 17; U S citizen.
Study & Training: Ecole Speciale Archit, Paris, France, BA(Arch); Inst Urbanisme, Sorbonne, Paris, MA(Town Planning).
Teaching: Design critic archit, Columbia Univ, 52-53.
Positions: Coun mem, Arts Acquisition Comt, Stony Brook Univ, 70; deleg, Fine Arts Fedn New York, 72-75.
Awards: Arnold Brunner fel, Archit League New York, 58.
Bibliography: Anne Le Crenier (auth), Names, Archit & Eng News, 67.
Memberships: Am Inst Architects (collab arts comt, 67-70); Am Inst Planners; Ordre Architectes, France; Archit League New York (v pres, 63); Munic Arts Soc.
Research: Integration of art in modern architecture; art in public spaces.
Collection: Contemporary art, mostly North and Latin American.
Publications: Auth, Art in European architecture, 56 & Art in Latin American Architecture, 62, Van Nostrand Reinhold.
Mailing Address: 302 E 88th St, New York, NY 10028.

DAME, LAWRENCE
Art Critic, Writer
b Portland, Maine, July 2, 98.
Study & Training: Harvard Univ; Univ Paris; Univ Grenoble, France; Inst de Burgos, Spain.
Teaching: Lect on art & ruins & relics of Yucatan; rev of art bks & other publ.
Positions: Art ed, Boston Herald, 50-60; art ed, Sarasota Herald-Tribune, Fla, 60-65; art ed, Post, Palm Beach, Fla, 69-73.
Research: World's leading museums.
Publications: Auth, Yucatan, Random House, 40; auth, Maya mission, Doubleday, 69; auth, Der Dschungel missionar, Reinhardt, Basel, Switz, 70; plus others; contribr, Sat Eve Post, Reader's Dig, Am Mercury, Mag Dig, Arts Mag, New York Times & others.
Mailing Address: P O Box 2392, Palm Beach, FL 33480.

D'AMICO, AUGUSTINE A
Collector, Patron
b Lawrence, Mass, May 15, 05.
Study & Training: Colby Col, BS, MA.
Exhibitions: Paintings & graphics, 61 & contemp ceramics, 63, Univ Maine, Orono; paintings & graphics, Colby Col Art Mus, Waterville, Maine, 63; contemp ceramics, Lincoln Co Mus, Wiscasset, Maine, 65; selected graphics from collection, tour sponsored by Maine Comn Arts & Humanities, 71.
Positions: Trustee & pres, Haystack Mountain Sch Crafts, Deer Isle, Maine; mem art adv coun, fellow & former trustee, Colby Col, Waterville, Maine; chmn, patron fine arts, Univ Maine; mem, Maine State Comn Arts & Humanities.
Memberships: Am Fedn Arts; Mus Mod Art; Am Craftsmens Coun;
Art Interests: Advancement of art & craft programs in teaching institutions.
Collection: Twentieth century paintings, graphics & ceramics.
Mailing Address: 201 Broadway, Bangor, ME 04401.

D'AMICO, VICTOR EDMOND
Educator, Writer
b New York, N Y, May 19, 04.
Study & Training: Cooper Union; Pratt Inst; Teachers Col, Columbia Univ, BS & MA; studied & worked with Norman Bel Geddes in Theatre Design; Philadelphia Mus Col Art, hon DFA, 64.
Work in Public Collections: Madonna (mezzotint), New York Pub Libr.

Collections Arranged: Creator of Children's Art Carnival, exhibited at Mus Mod Art, New York, 42-56, Milan, Italy, 57, Barcelona, Spain, 57, New Delhi, 63, Brussels World's Fair, 68, Harlem Sch Arts, 69 & Mus Mod Art, 72.

Teaching: Head art dept, Fieldston Sch, New York, 26-48; dir, dept educ, Mus Mod Art, 37-70, dir art ctr, 49-70; prof art & art educ, New York Univ, 62-

Awards: Citation of merit, State Univ N Y Col Buffalo, 64; medal of honor, Nat Gallery Art, Washington, D C, 66.

Publications: Auth, Theatre arts, Manual Press, 31; auth, Creative teaching in art, Intext, 42; auth, Experiments in creative art teaching, Mus Mod Art, New York, 60; co-auth, Assemblage, Mus Mod Art, 72.

Mailing Address: 30 Palmer Ave, White Plains, NY 10603.

DAMRON, JOHN CLARENCE
Painter, Illustrator
Preferred Media: Oils, Watercolors.
b Brooklyn, N Y.
Study & Training: Pratt Inst, N Y; Grand Cent Sch Art, with Harvey Dunn; also with Edmund Oppenheim & Henry Gasser.
Commissions: Portraits, U S Banknote Corp, 66, pres Bloomfield Col, N J, 69 & Barrington Col, R I, 71.
Exhibitions: Am Artists Prof League Grand Nat, Lever House, New York, N Y, 68, 71 & 72; Am Watercolor Soc 104th Ann, Nat Acad Design Galleries, New York, 71; Hudson Valley Art Asn 43rd Ann, White Plains, N Y, 71.
Teaching: Instr portraiture, Art Ctr Sch, East Orange, N J, 65-70.
Awards: First award, McCandlish Lithograph Co, Philadelphia, 51; Grand Nat First Award for Oil & N J State Show First Award for Watercolor, Am Artists Prof League, 71.
Memberships: Am Artists Prof League (dir nat bd, 70-); Grand Cent Art Galleries; Art Ctr Oranges (pres, 66, hon dir, 71-72); Millburn-Short Hills Arts Ctr.
Publications: Illusr, covers for Colliers & Liberty Mag, 43 & Capper's Farmer Mag, 46; illusr, Toronto Star Weekly, 46.
Dealer: Grand Central Art Galleries, 40 Vanderbilt Ave, New York, NY 10017.
Mailing Address: 742 Sterling Dr, Orange, NJ 07050.

DANBY, KEN
Painter, Printmaker
Preferred Media: Egg Tempera.
b Sault Ste Marie, Ont, 40.
Study & Training: Ont Col Art, Toronto, 58-60.
Work in Public Collections: Nat Gallery Can, Ottawa, Ont; Mus Mod Art, New York, N Y; Montreal Mus Art, P Q; Art Gallery Vancouver, B C; Univ Calif Art Gallery, Berkeley.
Exhibitions: Magic Realism in Canadian Art, London Art Gallery, Ont, 66; Third Int Drawings & Watercolours Exhib, Darmstadt, Ger, 70; First Int Graphics Mart, Zurich, Switz, 71; Biennale Jeunes, Paris, France, 71; Third Brit Int Print Biennale, Bradford, Yorkshire, Eng.
Awards: Jessie Dow Best Painting Award, Montreal Mus Fine Arts, 64.
Bibliography: Rex Bromfield (producer), See: Ken Danby, Can Broadcasting Corp, 71.
Mailing Address: c/o Gallery Moos Ltd, 138 Yorkville Ave, Toronto 5, Ont, Can.

d'ANDREA, ALBERT PHILIP
Educator, Sculptor
Preferred Media: Bronze, Terra Cotta.
b Benevento, Italy, Oct 27, 97; U S citizen.
Study & Training: Nat Acad Design; Pratt Inst; Univ Rome; City Col New York, BA, 18.
Work in Public Collections: Nat Portrait Gallery, Smithsonian Inst, Washington, D C; Lib of Cong, Washington; City Col New York; Biblioteca Apostolica Vatican, Vatican City, Italy; Jewish Mus, N Y.
Commissions: Bernard M Baruch Medal, Baruch Col, City Univ New York, 54; Thomas A Edison Medal, Edison Elec Inst, New York, 59; Grover Cleveland Medal, N Y Univ Hall Fame, New York, 66; Townsend Harris bas-relief, Hudson Falls Cent Sch, 68; Lincoln Medal, Lincoln Mem Univ, Cumberland Gap, Tenn, 71.
Exhibitions: Nat Acad Design Graphics Ann, 44; Portrait Sculpture Exhib, 71 & Nat Sculpture Soc 39th Ann Exhib, 72, Nat Sculpture Soc Gallery, New York; Audubon Artists 30th Ann Exhib, New York, 72; Am Artists Prof League Grand Nat Exhib, New York, 72.
Teaching: Mem faculty art, City Col New York, 18-48, prof art & chmn dept, 48-68, emer prof, 68-
Positions: Dir planning & design, City Col New York, 48-67; pres, Gamma Chapter, Phi Beta Kappa, New York, 65-66.

Awards: Pennel Award, Libr of Cong, Nat Acad Design, 44; Townsend Harris Medal, City Col New York Alumni Asn, 55; Lindsey Morris Mem Prize for bas-relief sculpture, Nat Sculpture Soc, 63.
Bibliography: I E Levine (auth), Portrait of an artist, City Col New York Alumnus, 56.
Memberships: Nat Sculpture Soc; Audubon Artists; Am Artists Prof League; Fedn Int Medaille; Royal Soc Arts.
Publications: Contribr, Nat Sculpture Rev, 63, 67 & 72.
Mailing Address: 2121 Bay Ave, Brooklyn, NY 11210.

DANE, WILLIAM JERALD
Art Librarian
b Concord, N H, May 8, 25.
Study & Training: Drexel Inst Technol, MLS; New York Univ Inst Fine Arts; Sorbonne, Paris, France; Attingham Park Summer Sch, Eng.
Collections Arranged: Fine Print Collection, Newark Pub Libr; 150 Years of Graphic Art in New Jersey, N J State Coun on the Arts.
Positions: Supv art & music libr, Newark Pub Libr, 67-
Memberships: Grolier Club; Victorian Soc Am (chmn, N Y Chap, 72-).
Publications: Auth, The picture collection subject headings, 69; auth, rev of art publ, In: Libr J, Ref Bks Am.
Mailing Address: 5 Washington St, Newark, NJ 07101.

DANENBERG, BERNARD
Art Dealer
Positions: Owner & dir, Danenberg Gallery.
Specialty of Gallery: Nineteenth and twentieth century American art.
Mailing Address: 1020 Madison Ave, New York, NY 10021.

DANES, GIBSON ANDREW
Educator
b Starbuck, Wash, Dec 13, 10.
Study & Training: Univ Ore; Art Inst Chicago, BFA; Northwestern Univ, BS & MA; Yale Univ, univ fel, 46, PhD; Lake Erie Col, hon DFA.
Teaching: Prof art, Univ Tex, Austin, 40-43; prof art, Ohio State Univ, 48-52; chmn dept art, Univ Calif, Los Angeles, 52-58; dean, Sch Art & Archit, Yale Univ, 58-68; dean & prof visual arts, State Univ N Y Col Purchase, 68-
Awards: Rockefeller post-war fel, 46; Ford Found fel, 51.
Memberships: Col Art Asn Am; hon mem, Conn Chap, Am Inst Architects.
Publications: Auth, Looking at modern painting, 67; contribr, nat art mag & col journals.
Mailing Address: School of Visual Arts, State University of New York, College at Purchase, Purchase, NY 10577.

DANHAUSEN, ELDON
Sculptor
b U S citizen.
Study & Training: Sch Art Inst Chicago, BFA, James Nelson Raymond foreign traveling fel, 47.
Work in Public Collections: Hackley Art Gallery, Muskegon, Mich; Civic Ctr, New Orleans, La; Standard Club Chicago, Ill; Roosevelt Univ, Chicago.
Commissions: Sculpture, Int Minerals & Chem Corp, Skokie, Ill, 60; sculpture, Home Mutual Appleton, Wis, 63; sculpture, WOC-TV, Davenport, Iowa, 64; sculpture, Civic Ctr, New Orleans, 67; sculpture, 150 N Wacker Dr Bldg, Chicago, 71.
Exhibitions: Downtown Gallery, New York, N Y; Chicago Ann Show, Art Inst Chicago, 45-60; Rivinia Festival Art Exhib, 57, 59 & 60; American Business & the arts, San Francisco Mus Art, 61; Sculpture 70, Art Inst Chicago, 70.
Teaching: Assoc prof sculpture, Sch Art Inst Chicago, 48-
Awards: Linde Co prize, Chicago Ann Show, Art Inst Chicago, 60; citation for art in archit, Am Inst Archit Iowa Chap, 63.
Bibliography: Something to talk about in Chicago, Mademoiselle Mag, 1/54; Art in Chicago, produced on CBS-TV, 67; Meilach (auth) & Seiden (auth), Direct metal sculpture, Crown.
Publications: Auth, Art in the market place, sculptor's viewpoint, Chicago Mkt Scene, 3/70; contribr, Contemporary stone sculpture, Crown.
Mailing Address: 1418 N LaSalle St, Chicago, IL 60610.

DANIEL, ROXANNE
Painter, Photographer
Preferred Media: Oils.
b Nashville, Tenn, Aug 3, 27.
Study & Training: Prix de Rome, with Loren Fisher & Eau Gallie, Fla; Peabody Demonstration Sch, Nashville; Univ Miss.
Work in Public Collections: Univ of the South, Sewanee, Tenn.
Commissions: Diamond Mine, poured polyester hanging mural, Aardvark Advert Agency, Atlanta, Ga, 70.

Exhibitions: Nassau Festival Arts, Bahamas, 62; Univ of the South, 63; three-man show, Lynn Kottler Galleries, New York, N Y, 71.
Awards: Hon award, first & third, Tenn C of C, Nashville, 62; Tenn Art League Award; Bertrand Russell Centenary Art Exhib, London, Eng, 72.
Memberships: Artists Asn; High Mus Art.
Dealer: Copeland-Hill, Inc, 3834 Peachtree Rd N E, Atlanta, GA 30319.
Mailing Address: 18-B Lombardy Way N E, Atlanta, GA 30309.

DANIELS, DAVID M
Collector, Patron
b Evanston, Ill, Apr 10, 27.
Study & Training: Yale Univ; Curtis Inst Music.
Positions: Trustee & accessions comt, Minneapolis Inst Fine Arts, 65-; trustee, Skowhegan Art Sch, 69-; pres, Drawing Soc, 71-
Collection: Drawings and sculpture of all periods; medals and paintings.
Publications: Contribr, The drawings of Morris Graves, New York Graphics, 73.
Mailing Address: 4 Sutton Place, New York, NY 10022.

DANIKIAN, CARON LE BRUN
Writer, Art Critic
b Rochester, N Y, May 2, 42.
Study & Training: Marymount Manhattan Col, BA, 64.
Positions: Art ed & critic, Boston Herald Traveler, Mass, 66-72; exhib coordr, State St Bank, Boston, 67-71; art ed & critic, Boston Herald Am, 72-
Research: Turn-of-the-century Boston artists.
Publications: Contribr, Sunday Herald Traveler Mag, Boston Arts Mag & Nat Antiques Rev.
Mailing Address: 790 Boylston St, 19B, Boston, MA 02199.

DANSON, EDWARD B
Museum Director, Writer
b Glendale, Ohio, Mar 22, 15.
Study & Training: Univ Ariz, BA, 40; Harvard Univ, MA, 48, PhD (anthrop), 52.
Teaching: Asst prof anthrop, Univ Colo, 48-50; Univ Ariz, 50-56.
Positions: Asst dir, Archaeol Field Sch, Univ Ariz, 52-53, actg dir, 54; asst dir, Mus Northern Ariz, 56-58, dir, 59-; pres, Ariz Acad Sci, 58-59; Nat Park Serv Adv Bd, 58-64, adv coun, 64-; adv comt multiple-use mgt, Coconino Nat Forest, 64-
Memberships: Southwest Parks & Monuments Asn (adv bd); Ariz Archaeol & Hist Soc (pres, 55-56); Am Asn Mus; fel Am Anthrop Asn; AAAS; plus others.
Publications: Auth, New dimensions in Hopi ceramic crafts & Last of the frontier merchants, Nat Parks Mag; auth, An important archaeological gift, Plateau; co-auth, A petrographic study of Gila polychrome, Am Antiq; also numerous small papers & rev.
Mailing Address: P O Box 674, Flagstaff, AZ 86001.

DAOUST, SYLVIA
Sculptor
b Montreal, P Q, May 24, 02.
Study & Training: Ecole Deaux-Arts, Montreal.
Work in Public Collections: Mus P Q; Col St Laurent; Monastère St Benoît-du-lac, Montreal; Univ Montreal; plus others.
Commissions: IBM Corp; portraits, Can Bar Asn; Govt P Q.
Exhibitions: Nat Gallery Can; Mus P Q; Art Gallery Toronto; Royal Can Acad Art, 30-; Expos Relig Art, Rome, 50; plus others.
Teaching: Instr, Ecoles Beaux-Arts, Montreal.
Awards: Award, Royal Can Acad, 51; Can Govt scholar, France, 55-56; medal, Royal Archit Inst Can, 61; plus others.
Memberships: Royal Can Acad Art; Sculptors' Soc Can.
Mailing Address: 2105 Bord du Lac, Dorval, P Q, Can.

DAPHNE, ANNETTE
Painter
Preferred Media: Oils.
b Paris, France.
Study & Training: Acad Grande Chaumiere, Paris; Art & Publicite, Paris; Acad Art Bezalel, Jerusalem, with Ardon; Acad Art Avni, Tel Aviv, with Marcel Janco.
Work in Public Collections: Acad Art Bezalel.
Exhibitions: Exhibs Israel Painters, Tel Aviv, 56-58; Exhib Govt Israel, Jerusalem, 56; one-man show, Theodor Herzl Gallery, New York, 61 & Panoras Gallery, New York, 73; Rose Sheskin Gallery, New York, 65.
Positions: Bks illusr, Tel Aviv, Israel, 50-60; textile designer, New York, 64-
Awards: First prize, Israel Govt, 56.
Mailing Address: 127 E 39th St, New York, NY 10016.

DAPHNIS, NASSOS
Painter, Sculptor
Preferred Media: Epoxy, Plexiglas.
b Krokeai, Greece, July 23, 14; U S citizen.
Work in Public Collections: Mus Mod Art, New York, N Y; Whitney Mus Am Art, New York; Albright-Knox Gallery Art, Buffalo, N Y; Carnegie Inst, Pittsburgh, Pa; Larry Aldrich Mus, Ridgefield, Conn.
Commissions: Wall paintings, City Walls, Inc, 70 & Nat Endowment on Arts, 71; art environment, Arlen Realty Develop Corp, 71.
Exhibitions: Contemp Am Painting Ann, Whitney Mus Am Art, 69; Contemporary American Painting & Sculpture, Krannert Art Mus, Univ Ill, 69; 31st Biennial Exhib, Corcoran Gallery Art, Washington, D C, 69; Painting and Sculpture Today—1969, Indianapolis Mus Art, Ind, 69; Highlights of the 68-69 Season, Larry Aldrich Mus, 69.
Positions: Mem bd dirs, City Walls, Inc, 69-
Awards: Ford Found Award, 62; Nat Found Arts & Humanities Award, 66; Nat Endowment on Arts grant, 71.
Bibliography: Robert M Murdock (auth), Nassos Daphnis: work since 1951, Albright-Knox Art Gallery, 69; Hilton Kramer (auth), The Corcoran Biennial, 2/23/69 & 12 artists join in an uncommon show, 3/18/71, New York Times.
Memberships: Am Abstract Artists.
Dealer: Leo Castelli Gallery, 4 E 77th St, New York, NY 10021.
Mailing Address: 400 W 23rd St, New York, NY 10011.

DAPHNIS-AVLON, HELEN
Painter, Sculptor
Preferred Media: Acrylics, Ceramics, Metal, Graphics, Photo-silk Screen.
b Manhattan, N Y, June 18, 32.
Study & Training: Brooklyn Mus, 50-53; Colorado Springs Fine Arts Mus, 53; Hunter Col, BFA, 53, MA, 57.
Work in Public Collections: Chrysler Mus; Sonnabend Art Collection, N Y.
Commissions: Painting, 59.
Exhibitions: Bertha Schaeffer Gallery, New York, N Y, 59-62; Provincetown Art Asn, Mass, 60-72; Wadell Gallery, New York, 69; Peace Exhib, Mus Mod Art, New York, 70; Westbeth Gallery, New York, 70; plus others.
Teaching: Art instr graphics, Brooklyn Mus, 53-62; instr art, pub & pvt schs, N Y & Mass, 60-; adult instr art, Brooklyn Col, 68-69.
Positions: Dir, Avlon's Art Co-op Gallery, Provincetown, Mass, 69-72; chmn window display & multi-media films, Westbeth Graphic Arts Workshop, 70-72.
Awards: Ten yr outstanding achievement award, Hunter Col, 63.
Memberships: Westbeth Tenants (grants & health, 70); Provincetown Art Asn; Mus Mod Art, New York; Village Community Sch (class rep, 72).
Mailing Address: 463 West St, New York, NY 10014.

D'ARCANGELO, ALLAN M
Painter
b Buffalo, N Y, June 16, 30.
Study & Training: Univ Buffalo, AB(hist); City Col New York; Mexico City Col.
Work in Public Collections: Whitney Mus Am Art, New York, N Y; Mus Mod Art, New York; Albright-Knox Mus, Buffalo; Gemeenee Mus, The Hague, Netherlands; Mus Mod Art, Nagaoka, Japan.
Exhibitions: American Landscape Painting, Mus Mod Art Traveling Exhib, U S A & Spoleto, Italy, 64; Two Decades of American Painting, Japan, India & Australia, 66; New Forms, Stedelijk Mus, Amsterdam, Holland, 66; Environment U S A, Biennial of São Paulo, Brazil, 67; L'art Vivant Americain, Found Maeght, St Paul de Vence, France, 69.
Teaching: Instr painting, Sch Visual Arts, New York, 63-68; instr painting, Cornell Univ, 68.
Awards: Artist-in-residence, Aspen Inst Humanistic Studies, 65 & 67; Nat Inst Arts & Letters ann award, 70.
Bibliography: Dienst (auth), Pop art, R Bechtold, 65; N Calas (auth), Art in the age of risk, 68 & N Calas (auth), Icons & images of the sixties, 71, Dutton.
Memberships: Soc Am Graphic Artists; City Walls Inc.
Dealer: Marlborough-Gerson Gallery, 41 E 57th St, New York, NY 10022.
Mailing Address: P O Box 33, Kenoza Lake, NY 12750.

D'ARISTA, ROBERT
Painter, Educator
Preferred Media: Oils.
b New York, N Y, 29.
Study & Training: Washington Sq Col, New York Univ; Columbia Univ; Acad Grande Chaumiere, Paris, France; Fulbright scholar, Florence, 55.

Work in Public Collections: Yale Univ Art Gallery, New Haven, Conn; Toledo Mus Art, Ohio; Hirshhorn Collection, Washington, D C; Neuburger Collection; Nat Collection Fine Arts, Washington, D C.
Exhibitions: Carnegie Inst, Pittsburgh, Pa; Solomon R Guggenheim Mus, New York; Whitney Mus Am Art, New York; four one-man shows, Nordness Gallery, New York, 64-72.
Teaching: Prof Art, Am Univ, 61-
Awards: Rosenthal Found Award, Inst Arts & Lett, 67; distinguished vis artist, Boston Univ, spring 73.
Publications: Auth, Reflections on painting, In: Painters on painting, Grosset & Dunlap.
Mailing Address: 3125 Quebec Pl N W, Washington, DC 20008.

DARIUS, DENYLL
Painter
Preferred Media: Acrylics.
b Chicago, Ill, Mar 12, 42.
Study & Training: Phoenix Col, AA; Ariz State Univ, BFA.
Work in Public Collections: Ariz State Univ, Tempe; Northern Ariz Univ, Flagstaff; Loomis Savings & Loan, Chicago; Yares Gallery, Scottsdale, Ariz.
Exhibitions: Scottsdale Artists League Exhib, 65; Tucson Art Ctr Ann, Ariz, 68; Yuma Art Ctr Invitational, Ariz, 70; Firebird Festival Fine Arts, Phoenix Civic Plaza, 70; Four Corners Biennale, Phoenix Art Mus, 71.
Awards: First prize in painting, Tucson Art Ctr, 68; Firebird Purchase Award, Goldwater's, Inc, 70; hon mention, Phoenix Art Mus, 71.
Dealer: Yares Gallery, 3625 Bishop Lane, Scottsdale, AZ 85252.
Mailing Address: 4902 W Cheery Lynn Rd, Phoenix, AZ 85031.

DARRICARRERE, ROGER DOMINIQUE
Sculptor, Craftsman
Preferred Media: Steel, Glass.
b Bayonne, France, Dec 15, 12; U S citizen.
Study & Training: Beaux-Arts, Bayonne, 30-35; Ecole Nat Superieure Decoratifs Paris, dipl, 38; Inst Metiers, Paris, 45.
Commissions: Spatial kaleidoscope, Lytton Ctr, Los Angeles, Calif, 59; revolving steel & glass sculpture depicting moving picture indust; leaded glass window wall, World's Fair Contest, St Stephen's Lutheran Church, Granada Hills, Calif; Columbia Savings & Loan Asn, Los Angeles, 66; massive bronze sculpture, Atlantis, Lytton Savings & Loan Asn Northern Calif, Oakland, Calif, 67; plus others.
Exhibitions: Pasadena Art Mus, 59-63; Otis Art Inst, Los Angeles, 61-65; New York World's Fair, 64-65; Mus Contemp Crafts, New York, N Y, 66; Craftsman U S A, Los Angeles Co Mus, 66; plus others.
Teaching: Instr int design & painting, Coe Col, 48-51; workshop prof glass in archit, Calif State Col Long Beach, 68 & 69; lectr stained glass & sculpture, Mt St Mary's Col, spring 69.
Awards: Awards fine arts & craftsmanship, Am Inst Architects, 58, 59, 61 & 63; first prize, Nat Competition stained glass panel, New York World's Fair, 64-65; nat merit award, Craftsman U S A, 66; plus others.
Memberships: Southern Calif Designer-Craftsmen; Guild Relig Archit.
Mailing Address: 1937 San Fernando Rd, Los Angeles, CA 90065.

DARROW, PAUL GARDNER
Painter, Educator
Preferred Media: Graphics.
b Pasadena, Calif.
Study & Training: Colorado Springs Fine Art Ctr, Colo; Claremont Grad Sch & Univ Ctr.
Work in Public Collections: Pasadena Art Mus, Calif; Times-Mirror Collection, Los Angeles, Calif; U S Navy, Washington, D C; Lytton Savings & Loan Collection, Los Angeles; Long Beach Mus Art, Calif.
Commissions: Murals, Air France, Los Angeles, 61, Balboa Yacht Club, 63 & Newport Bank, Calif, 71.
Exhibitions: Mus Mod Art, São Paulo, Brazil, 55; Pasadena Art Mus, Calif, 55; Downtown Gallery, New York, N Y, 57; San Francisco Mus Art, Calif, 59; Calif Inst Technol, Pasadena, 70.
Teaching: Prof art & chmn dept, Scripps Col, 60-; prof art, Claremont Grad Sch, 70-
Positions: V pres, Calif Watercolor Soc, 60-62; founder, Los Angeles Printmaking Soc, 62; artist-corresp, U S Navy 7th fleet, Viet Nam & Japan, 63.
Awards: Purchase awards, Los Angeles Mus Art, 55 & Pasadena Art Mus, 58; res grant, Ford Found, 69.
Bibliography: Bently Schaad (auth), The realm of contemporary still life painting, 62 & Edmondson (auth), Printmaking, 72, Van Nostrand Reinhold; David Smith (auth), Darrow C Sentery (monograph & catalogue), Calif Inst Technol, 70.

Publications: Illusr, Aldous Huxley, Paris Rev, 62; illusr, The concrete wilderness, Meredith, 67; illusr, The guide for the married man, Price Stern, 68; illusr, Psychological perspectives, C G Jung Inst, 70.
Dealer: Comara Gallery, La Cienega, Los Angeles, CA 90034.
Mailing Address: 690 Cuprien Way, Laguna, CA 92651.

DARROW, WHITNEY, JR
Cartoonist
b Princeton, N J, Aug 22, 09.
Study & Training: Princeton Univ; Art Stud League New York, N Y.
Publications: Auth & illusr, Happiness is a dry martini, 65 & Misery is a blind date, 67; illusr, Whtiney Darrow, Jr's unidentified flying elephant, 68; illusr, Whitney Darrow Jr's animal etiquette, 69 & Sex and the single child, 69.
Mailing Address: Box 212, Saugatuck, Westport, CT 06880.

DASBURG, ANDREW MICHAEL
Painter
b Paris, France, May 4, 87.
Study & Training: Art Stud League, with Kenyon Cox & Frank V DuMond; also with Birge Harrison & Robert Henri.
Work in Public Collections: Whitney Mus Am Art; Denver Art Mus; Los Angeles Mus Art; Calif Palace of Legion of Honor; Dallas Mus Fine Arts; plus others.
Exhibitions: Whitney Mus Am Art; San Francisco Mus Art; Mus Mod Art; one-man show, Dallas Mus Fine Arts, 57; retrospective, Am Fedn Arts-Ford Found, 59; plus others.
Awards: Guggenheim fel, 32; Ford Found grant; Nat Found Arts Award, 67; plus others.
Bibliography: Lloyd Goodrich & John I H Baur (auth), included in: American art of our century, Whitney Mus Am Art, 61; Van Deren Coke (auth), included in: Taos and Santa Fe. The artistic environment. 1882-1942, Univ N Mex Press, 63; Barbara Rose (auth), included in: American art since 1900, a critical essay, Praeger, 67; plus others.
Mailing Address: P O Box 643, Taos, NM 87571.

DASH, HARVEY DWIGHT
Educator, Painter
Preferred Media: Oils.
b Brooklyn, N Y, June 28, 24.
Study & Training: Pratt Inst; Tyler Sch Fine Arts, Temple Univ, BFA, BSEd & MFA; Rutgers Univ; Columbia Univ; Montclair State Col.
Exhibitions: Pa Acad Fine Arts, Philadelphia; Temple Univ, Philadelphia; one-man shows, Fairleigh Dickinson Univ, Teaneck, N J & Brighton Gallery, New York, N Y.
Teaching: Instr fine art, Temple Univ, 46-47; chmn dept art, Tenafly High Sch, 51-57 & Paramus High Sch, N J, 57-63.
Positions: Supvr art, Boundbrook Bd Educ, 48-51; dir creative arts, Paramus Sch Syst, 63-67; dir Lighthouse Art Gallery, Nyack, N Y, 67-69; dir Lighthouse Sch Art, Upper Grandview, N Y, 67-
Awards: Paramus Bd Educ grants, 65 & 66.
Memberships: N Y State Art Teachers Asn; Nat Art Educ Asn.
Mailing Address: 654 Rte 9W, Upper Grandview, NY 10960.

DASH, ROBERT (WARREN)
Painter
Preferred Media: Acrylics; Pastels.
b New York, N Y, June 8, 34.
Work in Public Collections: Univ Art Mus, Univ Calif, Berkeley; Brooklyn Mus, N Y; Mod Art Mus of Munich, Ger; New York Univ; Chase Manhattan Bank Collection.
Commissions: Stage set for Port, 64; Garden (lithographs with lines by James Schuyler, 72; var covers for vols of poetry.
Exhibitions: The New York Season, 60-61; Yale Univ Exhib, 61; Landscapes by Five Americans, Festival of Two Worlds, Mus Mod Art Traveling Exhib, 66; Inform & Interpret, Am Fedn Arts Traveling Exhib, 68; A Sense of Place, Guild Hall, East Hampton, N Y, 72.
Teaching: Adj prof advan painting, Southampton Col, spring 70.
Bibliography: James Schuyler (auth), Notes on the paintings (catalog), Graham Gallery, 70; John Ashbery (auth), Recent paintings by Robert Dash (catalog), Allentown Mus, 71; article, In: Art Now, Vol 9, No 2.
Dealer: FAR Gallery, 746 Madison Ave, New York, NY 10021.
Mailing Address: Sagg Main, Saggaponnack, NY 11962.

DATUS, JAY
Painter, Art Administrator
b Jackson, Mich, Mar 24, 14.
Study & Training: Worcester Mus Sch; Yale Univ Sch Fine Arts.
Work in Public Collections: Univ Wis; Beloit Col.
Commissions: Murals, Ariz State Capitol Bldg, First Nat Bank, Phoenix Ariz, Southern Ariz Bank & Trust Co, Tucson, Ariz.

Exhibitions: Art Inst Chicago; one-man shows, O'Brien Gallery, Chicago, Ill & Phoenix Fine Arts Ctr.
Positions: Founder & dir, Kachina Sch Art, Phoenix, 48- ; mem bd trustees, Heart Mus Art, Phoenix.
Memberships: Phoenix Fine Arts Asn (bd trustees & first v pres); fel Royal Soc Arts, London.
Publications: Auth, The paint box, Ariz Repub Newspaper.
Mailing Address: 3801 N 30th St, Phoenix, AZ 85016.

DAUGHERTY, JAMES HENRY
Painter, Writer
b Asheville, N C, June 1, 89.
Study & Training: Corcoran Sch Art; Pa Acad Fine Arts; London, Eng, with Frank Brangwyn.
Work in Public Collections: Yale Mus Fine Arts; N Y Pub Libr; Wilmington Pub Libr; Achenbach Found; Calif Palace of Legion of Honor; plus others.
Commissions: Murals, Stanford High Sch & Loew's Theatre, Cleveland, Ohio.
Exhibitions: Silvermine Guild Artists; Archit League; Bridgeport Art League; Fairfield Univ, Conn; Univ Minn; plus others.
Awards: Newbery Medal, 39.
Memberships: Silvermine Guild Artists; Auth Guild; PEN.
Publications: Illusr, Robert Goddard: trail blazer to the stars, Macmillan, 64; auth & illusr, Rainbow book of American history, World Publ, 68; Their weight in wildcats, Avon, 69; auth & illusr, Andy and the lion, 70 & auth, Sound of trumpets: Ralph Waldo Emerson, 71, Viking Press; also contribr, mags & periodicals.
Dealer: Robert Schoelkopf Gallery, 825 Madison Ave, New York, NY 10021.
Mailing Address: Broad St, Weston, CT 06880.

D'AULAIRE, EDGAR PARIN
Illustrator, Lithographer
Preferred Media: Mixed Media.
b Munich, Ger, Sept 30, 98; U S citizen.
Study & Training: Gym Technische Hochschule; Kunstgewerbeschule (Sch Appl Arts); Hans Hofmann Sch; Ecole Andre L'hote; Ecole Pola Gaugin, Paris, France.
Commissions: Fresco in church, Drammen, Norway; Hopkin Ctr, Hanover, N H; pub libraries & cols in U S A & Europe.
Exhibitions: Salon d'Automne, Paris; Galerie Wang, Oslo, Norway.
Awards: Caldecott Medal, Am Libr Asn, 40; Regina Award, Catholic Libr Asn, 70.
Bibliography: Esther Flverill (auth), Caldecott medal books, Vol II, Horn Book, 57; B Hürlimann (auth), Die welt im Bilderbuch, Atlantis Verlag Zurich, 65; L B Hopkins (auth), Books are by people, Citation, 69.
Memberships: Artists Guild.
Publications: Co-auth & illusr, Ola, 32, Greek myths, 62; Norse gods & giants, 67 & Trolls, 72, Doubleday, 72; Children of the northlights, Viking, 36.
Mailing Address: 74 Mather Rd, Wilton, CT 06897.

D'AULAIRE, INGRI (MORTENSON) PARIN
Writer, Illustrator
Preferred Media: Oils, Pastels, Lithographs.
b Kongsberg, Norway, Dec 27, 04; U S citizen.
Study & Training: Kunstindustriskolen, Oslo, 23-24; Hans Hofmann Sch Art, Munich, Ger, 24-25; Acad l'Hote; also with Pola Gaugin & Scandinaie, Paris, France, 25-29.
Work in Public Collections: Hopkin Ctr, Hanover, N H; pub libr & col collections both in U S A & Europe.
Exhibitions: Salon d'Automne, Paris, 27-29.
Awards: Caldecott Medal, Am Libr Asn, 40; Regina Medal, Catholic Literary Asn, 70.
Bibliography: B Hürliman (auth), Die welt in bilderbuck, Atlantic Verlag Zurich, 65; L B Hopkins (auth), Books are by people, Citation Press, 69.
Memberships: Authors Guild Am.
Publications: Co-auth & co-illusr, Ola, 32, Children of the northlights, 35, Abraham Lincoln, 39, D'aulaires book of Greek myths, 62 & D'aulaires trolls, 72.
Mailing Address: Lia Farm, 74 Mather, Wilton, CT 06897.

DAUTERMAN, CARL CHRISTIAN
Art Historian, Lecturer
b Newark, N J.
Study & Training: Newark Sch Fine & Indust Art; Newark Mus Apprentice Training Course; New York Univ, BA; Columbia Univ MA Art Hist.
Collections Arranged: Numerous exhibs in decorative arts, especially ceramics.
Teaching: Adj prof Europ & Am decorative arts, Columbia Univ, 51-

Positions: Mgr spec exhibs, Cooper Union Mus Arts of Decoration, 38-42; catalogue writer, Parke-Bernet Galleries, 46-53; spec admin consult, Metrop Mus Art, 53-55, from assoc cur to cur Western Europ arts, 55-
Memberships: Am Friends Attingham (dir, 70-72); Am Ceramic Circle (pres, 70-); Wedgwood Int Sem (dir & hon dir, 64-); Col Art Asn Am; Am Asn Mus.
Research: Analyzing eighteenth century archives of Manufacture Nationale de Sèvres.
Publications: Co-auth, Decorative art in the Kress Collection at the Metropolitan Museum of Art, 64; auth, Checklist of American silversmiths' work in the Metropolitan Museum of Art, 68; auth, Sèvres, 69; co-auth, Catalogue of the Wrightsman Collection III: furniture, snuffboxes, silver, 70; auth, Catalogue of the Wrightsman Collection IV: porcelains, 70.
Mailing Address: Metropolitan Museum of Art, Fifth Ave at 82nd St, New York, NY 10028.

DAVES, DELMER
Collector
b San Francisco, Calif.
Study & Training: Los Angeles Polytech, grad, 22; Stanford Univ, 27.
Memberships: Am Fedn Arts; Mus Mod Art, New York.
Mailing Address: 107 N Bentley Ave, Los Angeles, CA 90049.

DAVEY, RONALD A
Art Administrator, Art Historian
b United Kingdom.
Study & Training: Wallasey Sch Art; Courtauld Inst, Univ London; Ecole Hautes Etudes, Univ Paris.
Teaching: Asst lectr art, Slade Sch Fine Art, Univ London, 54-58; lectr art, Univ Newcastle upon Tyne, 58-64; prin, West Sussex Col Art, 64-67; prof art & design & chmn dept, Univ Alta, 67-
Memberships: Fel Royal Soc Arts.
Mailing Address: Dept of Art & Design, University of Alberta, Edmonton, Alta, Can.

DAVID, DIANNE
Art Dealer, Collector
b Corpus Christie, Tex, Nov 9, 38.
Study & Training: Mount Vernon Jr Col; Univ Ariz; Parsons Sch Design.
Positions: Owner-dir, David Gallery, Houston, 64-
Specialty of Gallery: Contemporary drawings, paintings & sculpture.
Collection: Contemporary American artists-magic realism.
Mailing Address: 2243 San Felipe Rd, Houston, TX 77019.

DAVID, DON RAYMOND
Painter, Instructor
Preferred Media: Acrylics, Watercolors.
b Springbrook, Ore, May 2, 10.
Study & Training: Art Ctr Sch Los Angeles, Calif; Chouinard's, Los Angeles; Hans Hoffman Sch, New York, N Y.
Exhibitions: One-man shows, Webb Gallery, Los Angeles, 47, three shows, Camino Gallery, New York, 56, 58 & 60, one show, New Sch Soc Res, New York, 65, Baruch Col, New York, 72 & three one-man shows, Alonzo Gallery, New York, 69, 70 & 72.
Teaching: Instr drawing, Art Ctr Sch, 46-48; instr hist pictorial art & illus, Newark Sch Fine & Indust Art, N J, 68-
Dealer: Alonzo Gallery, 26 E 63rd St, New York, NY 10012.
Mailing Address: 32 E 22nd St, New York, NY 10010.

DAVIDEK, WILLIAM STEFAN
Painter
Preferred Media: Oils, Watercolors.
b Flint, Mich, May 15, 24.
Study & Training: Flint Inst Arts, with Jaroslav Brozik; Art Stud League New York, with Morris Kantor; Cranbrook Acad, with Fred Mitchell.
Work in Public Collections: Flint Inst Arts, Mich; Detroit Inst Arts, Mich; N Muskegon Community Col, Mich; Albion Col, Mich.
Commissions: Dioramas, Carol Churchill Pierson for Sloan Mus, Flint, 65-72; mosaic, St Luke Cath Church, Flint, 69; sanctuary wall, Luke M Powers Sch, Flint, 70.
Exhibitions: Mich Artists Show, 46-61; Flint Ann, 46-72; Butler Midyear Show, 59; Pa Acad Fine Art, 59; Flint Invitational, 70.
Awards: Founder's Prize, 61 & Lou R Maxon Prize, Detroit Inst Art.
Dealer: Tadlow Gallery, N Scenic Dr, Whitehall, MI 49461.
Mailing Address: 5391 W Coldwater Rd, Flint, MI 48504.

DAVIDOVICH, JAIME
Painter
b Buenos Aires, Arg, Sept 27, 36; U S citizen.
Study & Training: Univ of the Republic, Uruguay, scholar, 59; Sch Visual Arts, New York, N Y, 63.

Work in Public Collections: Mus Arte Mod, Buenos Aires, Mus
  Belas Artes, Rio de Janiero, Brazil.
Commissions: Carroll Wall Proj, John Carroll Univ, Cleveland,
  Ohio, 71.
Exhibitions: One-man show, Retrospective 1962-1972, Drake Univ,
  Des Moines, Iowa, 71; Exp in Art & Technol Show, Lake Erie
  Col, Ohio, 71; Five Artists, New Gallery, Cleveland, Ohio, 72;
  Arte de Sistemas, Mus Mod Art, Buenos Aires & Mus Fine Arts,
  Santiago, Chile, 72; Akron Art Inst, 72.
Teaching: Prof painting, Sch Visual Arts, Bahia Blanca, Arg, 61-62.
Positions: Off rep to U S, Di Tella Found, 63-64; coun mem, Int Soc
  Educ Through Art, 63-
Awards: Di Tella Found grant to rep Arg at Int Cong Educ Through
  Art, Montreal, 63.
Bibliography: R Squirru (auth), International art exhibit, Mus Art
  Mod, Buenos Aires, 60; R Welchans (auth), Carroll project 1971,
  Fine Arts Mag, 71.
Mailing Address: 16410 Fernway, Cleveland, OH 44120.

DAVIDSON, ABRAHAM A
  Educator, Writer
b Dorchester, Mass, June 27, 35.
Study & Training: Harvard Univ, AB, 57; Hebrew Teachers Col, Bos-
  ton, BJEd, 60; Boston Univ, AM(art hist), 60; Columbia Univ,
  PhD(art hist), 65.
Teaching: Instr art hist, Wayne State Univ, 64-65; asst prof art hist,
  Oakland Univ, 65-68; from asst. prof art hist to assoc prof,
  Tyler Sch Art, Temple Univ, 68-
Research: History of nineteenth and twentieth century American
  painting and sculpture.
Publications: Auth, Cubism and the early American modernist, Art
  Jour, winter 66-67; auth, Charles DeMuth: stylistic development,
  Bull R I Sch Design Mus Notes, 68; auth, Catastrophism and
  Peale's Mammoth, Am Quart, 69; auth, John Marin; dynamism
  codified, Art Forum, 71; auth, Beginnings of modernism in Amer-
  ican art, Abrams, 73.
Mailing Address: Tyler School of Art, Temple University, Beech &
  Penrose Ave, Elkins Park, PA 19126.

DAVIDSON, ALLAN ALBERT
  Painter, Sculptor
Preferred Media: Watercolors, Marble, Bronze, Oils, Graphics.
b Springfield, Mass, Feb 24, 13.
Study & Training: Sch Mus Fine Art, Boston; Ecole Beaux Arts,
  Paris; Fogg Mus, BA; Maitre Arts.
Exhibitions: Am Watercolor Soc; Am Artists Prof League; Boston
  Watercolor Soc; N Shore Art Asn; Provincetown Art Asn; plus
  others.
Positions: Pres, Cape Ann Soc Mod Art; set designer, S Shore Play-
  house, Cohasset, Mass, 41; corresp, Stars & Stripes, World War
  II; mem Commonwealth Mass Art Comn, 61-
Awards: Hendy Gold Medal; Chase Mem Prize; Benson-Hayes-
  Stuart Award; plus many others.
Memberships: Am Watercolor Soc; Boston Watercolor Soc; Am
  Artists Prof League; Rockport Art Asn; N Shore Art Asn.
Mailing Address: 8 Dean Rd, Rockport, MA 01966.

DAVIDSON, HERBERT LAURENCE
  Painter
Preferred Media: Oils.
b Green Bay, Wis, Sept 6, 30.
Study & Training: Art Inst Chicago, Ill, Anna Raymond Foreign
  Traveling fel, 56.
Exhibitions: Butler Mus, Youngstown, Ohio, 65; Rotond Della
  Besana, Milan, Italy, 71; Royal Col Art, London, Eng, 71; Kon-
  inlijk Mus Schone Kunsten, Belg, 72; Kunstverein, Hanover, Ger,
  72.
Dealer: Oehlschlaeger Galleries, 107 E Oak St, Chicago, IL 60611.
Mailing Address: 406 W Webster Ave, Chicago, IL 60614.

DAVIDSON, J LeROY
  Art Historian
b Cambridge, Mass, Mar 16, 08.
Study & Training: Harvard Univ, AB; Inst Fine Arts, New York Univ,
  MA; Yale Univ, PhD.
Teaching: Asst prof Asian art, Yale Univ, 47-55; prof Asian art,
  Claremont Grad Sch, 56-61; prof Asian art, Univ Calif, Los An-
  geles, 61-
Research: Oriental art.
Publications: Numerous articles and books on Asian art.
Mailing Address: Art Dept, University of California at Los Angeles,
  Los Angeles, CA 90024.

DAVIDSON, MARSHALL BOWMAN
  Art Critic, Writer
b New York, N Y, Apr 26, 07.
Study & Training: Princeton Univ, BS, 28.

Teaching: Lectr Am decorative graphic & fine arts.
Positions: Asst cur, Am Wing, Metrop Mus Art, New York, N Y,
  35-41, assoc cur, 41-47, ed publ, 47-60; ed, Horizon Bks, 61-64;
  ed, Horizon Mag, Am Heritage Publ, New York, 64-66, sr ed, 66-
Awards: Carey-Thomas Award creative publ, 51.
Publications: Auth, Life in America, 2 vols, 51; auth, Antiques:
  from the Civil War to World War One, 69 & The American heritage history of notable American houses, 71, Am Heritage Press;
  auth, Colonial antiques, 70, American antiques, 70 & Horizon concise history of France, 72, Am Heritage; plus others; also contribr, art, hist & other mags & Metrop Mus Bull.
Mailing Address: 140 E 83rd St, New York, NY 10028.

DAVIDSON, MORRIS
  Painter, Art Administrator
Preferred Media: Oils, Watercolors, Acrylics.
b Rochester, N Y, Dec 16, 98.
Study & Training: Md Inst Design, dipl, 16; Art Inst Chicago, with
  Harry Walcott, 17-18; with George Elmer Browne, 20; Acad
  Grande Chaumière, Paris, France, 25.
Work in Public Collections: Baltimore Mus Art, Md; Univ N C; Gal-
  lery Living Art, N Y Univ; Sarah Lawrence Col; Jerusalem Mus,
  Israel.
Exhibitions: Whitney Mus Am Art, New York, N Y, 34; American
  Modern Artists, Riverside Mus, New York, 50; New Sch Soc
  Res, New York, 53; Detroit Inst Arts, Mich, 60; Pa Acad Fine
  Arts, Philadelphia, 60; plus over 40 one-man shows.
Teaching: Instr drawing, Art Inst Chicago, 17-18; instr painting,
  Minneapolis Sch Art, 22-23; instr painting, Master Inst New
  York, 31.
Positions: Dir, Morris Davidson Sch Mod Painting, New York, 35-
  65; dir, Provincetown, Mass Summer Sch, 45-
Memberships: Provincetown Art Asn (v pres, 50-60); Am Artists
  Cong (N Y exec bd, 39); Fedn Mod Painters & Sculptors (pres,
  50-); Rockland Found (chmn bd, 50-).
Publications: Auth, Understanding modern art, 31 & auth, An ap-
  proach to modern painting, 48, Coward; auth, Painting for
  pleasure, Hale, Cushman & Flint, 38; auth, Painting with
  purpose, Prentice, 64.
Mailing Address: 7 Orchard Terrace, Piermont, NY 10968.

DAVIDSON, SUZETTE MORTON
  Designer, Collector
b Chicago, Ill, Aug 24, 11.
Study & Training: Vassar Col, AB, 34; Art Inst Chicago, 36-40.
Exhibitions: Printing Design by Suzette Morton Zurcher (former
  name), Chicago Pub Libr, Albion Col, Mich & Univ Calif, Santa
  Barbara.
Positions: Trustee, Art Inst Chicago; trustee, Newberry Libr;
  trustee (chmn), Morton Arboretum, Lisle, Ill; owner, The Poca-
  hontas Press, 37-
Awards: Five selections, 50 Books of the Year Award, Am Inst
  Graphic Arts, 42-67.
Memberships: Am Fedn Arts (trustee); Am Inst Graphic Arts; Soc
  Typographic Arts; Metrop Mus; Mus Mod Art.
Collection: From classical antiquity to Picasso, with emphasis on
  seventeenth century Italian painting, pre-Raphaelite paintings and
  drawings; pre-Columbian gold; old and rare books pertaining to
  gardens and botany.
Publications: Designer, numerous exhib catalogs, Art Inst Chicago.

DAVIES, JORDAN ALAN
  Painter
Preferred Media: Acrylics
b Chicago, Ill, Oct 8, 41.
Study & Training: Art Inst Chicago, BFA, 63, MFA, 66.
Work in Public Collections: Art Inst Chicago; Larry Aldrich Mus,
  Ridgefield, Conn.
Exhibitions: Contemporary Reflections, 1971-1972, Larry Aldrich
  Mus, 72.
Teaching: Instr painting & drawing, Chicago Teachers Col, 67-68.
Positions: Pres, Partic Artists Chicago, 67-68.
Awards: Logan Prize & Medal, Art Inst Chicago, 66; Nat Endow-
  ment Arts fel, 70-71.
Dealer: Phyllis Kind Gallery, 226 E Ontario St, Chicago, IL 60611.
Mailing Address: 87 Bowery, New York, NY 10002.

DAVIES, KENNETH SOUTHWORTH
  Painter, Educator
Preferred Media: Oils.
b New Bedford, Mass, Dec 20, 25.
Study & Training: Mass Sch Art, Boston; Yale Sch Fine Arts, BFA,
  50.
Work in Public Collections: Wadsworth Atheneum, Hartford, Conn;
  New Britain Mus Am Art, Conn; Detroit Inst Arts, Mich; Spring-
  field Mus Fine Arts, Mass; Univ Nebr, Lincoln.

Commissions: U S Postage Stamp commemorative for pharmacy,
U S Postal Serv, 72.
Exhibitions: American Symbolic Realism, London, Eng, 50; Carne-
gie Int, 52; Whitney Mus Am Art Ann, 52; Univ Ill Ann, 52; 25
yr retrospective exhib, New Britain Mus Am Art, 71.
Teaching: Dean drawing, painting & perspective, Paier Sch Art,
Hamden, Conn, 53-
Awards: Louis Comfort Tiffany scholar, 50; purchase award, Berk-
shire Mus, Pittsfield, Mass; purchase award, Springfield Mus,
Mass, 50.
Memberships: Silvermine Guild Artists; New Haven Paint & Clay
Club (v pres, 69); Conn Acad Fine Arts (coun mem, 70).
Mailing Address: 40 Walnut Hill Rd, Madison, CT 06443.

DAVIES, THEODORE PETER
Printmaker, Painter
Preferred Media: Wood.
b Brooklyn, N Y, Oct 9, 28.
Study & Training: Sch Mod Photog, New York, N Y, 52; Art Stud
League New York, John Sloan merit scholar, 58, with George
Grosz & Harry Sternberg, 57-60.
Work in Public Collections: Photograms, Mus Mod Art, New York;
woodcuts, Nat Gallery Art, Washington, D C; woodcuts, Phila-
delphia Mus Art, Pa; Art Stud League New York; Brigham Young
Univ, Utah.
Commissions: Six woodcuts on process of papermaking, Scott
Paper, 60; three ed, woodcuts of New York financial dist, Pic-
ture Decorator, 68.
Exhibitions: Print Club Philadelphia Ann; Silvermine Guild Ann;
Boston Printmakers Ann, 59; The Sense of Abstraction, Mus Mod
Art, New York, 59; Big Prints, State Univ N Y Albany, 68; plus
others.
Awards: First prize graphics, Washington Sq Outdoor Art Exhib, 58;
first prize graphics, Atlantic City Ann Art Exhib, 59; hon men-
tion, Boston Printmakers, 59.
Bibliography: Laurence Campbell (auth), article, In: Art Stud League
News, 12/61; Gene Paris (auth), article, In: Long Island Press,
4/23/67; plus others.
Memberships: Life mem Art Stud League New York (mem bd con-
trol, 61-63, recording secy, 63-64); Print Coun Am; Print Club
Philadelphia; Queens Coun Arts (show coordr, 72).
Publications: Contribr, Woodcuts, 60; contribr, Realistic abstract
drawing, 60; illusr, Picture framing, 60.
Dealer: Harbor Gallery, 43 Main St, Cold Spring Harbor, NY 11724.
Mailing Address: 87-38 Santiago St, Hollis, NY 11423.

DAVILA, CARLOS
Painter, Printmaker
b Lima, Peru, Feb 1, 35.
Study & Training: Nat Sch Fine Art, Lima.
Work in Public Collections: Pan Am Union, Washington, D C; Mus
Mod Art, Miami, Fla; Univ San Marcos, Lima; Ctr Inter-Am
Rels, New York, N Y; Mus Arte, Lima.
Commissions: Restoration pre-Colombian archaeol monuments
(collabr), Chan-Chan, Peru, 63-65.
Exhibitions: Fifth Biennale, Mus Art Mod, Paris, 65; Miami Mus
Mod Art, Fla, 66; Mus Arte, Lima, 68; Painting in the Richard
Brown Baker Collection, Univ Tampa, Fla, 69; Young Artists
from Around the World, Int Play Group, New York, N Y, 71.
Awards: First award, Soc Hebraica Nat Competition, 64; first
award, Jovenes Artistas, Univ San Marcos, 67; first award, Adela
Investment, Mus Arte, 68.
Publications: Auth, articles, In: Artes Visuales Mag, Washington,
D C, 66-67.
Dealer: Nabis Fine Art Inc, 276 Park Ave S, New York, NY 10010.
Mailing Address: 88 Bleecker St, New York, NY 10012.

DAVIS, ALICE
Painter
b Iowa City, Iowa, Apr 1, 05.
Study & Training: Univ Iowa, BA & MA; Nat Acad Design.
Exhibitions: Kansas City Art Inst; Joslyn Art Mus; Des Moines Art
Ctr.
Teaching: Prof art & head dept, Lindenwood Col, 45-47; asst prof
art, Grinnell Col, 47-51; assoc prof appl art, Iowa State Univ,
51-70.
Memberships: Col Art Asn Am; Nat Art Educ Asn; Art Educators
of Iowa.
Mailing Address: 810 Gaskill Dr, Ames, IA 50010.

DAVIS, BRADLEY DARIUS
Painter
Preferred Media: Acrylics.
b Duluth, Minn, Apr 24, 42.
Study & Training: Univ Minn, BA; Hunter Col, MA.
Work in Public Collections: Univ Minn, Minneapolis; Walker Art
Ctr, Minneapolis; Whitney Mus Am Art, New York, N Y.

Exhibitions: Minneapolis Inst Art Biennial, Minn, 65; Walker Art
Ctr Biennial, 66; Some Young Minnesota Artists, Univ Minn,
Minneapolis, 67; Whitney Mus Am Art Painting Ann, New York,
72; one-man show, Holly Solomon's 98 Greene St Loft, New York,
72.
Awards: First prize & spec jury award, Minneapolis Inst Art Bi-
ennial, 65; second prize & purchase prize, Walker Art Ctr, 66.
Dealer: Dave Hickey, 306 E 50th St, New York, NY 10022.
Mailing Address: 392 Broadway, New York, NY 10013.

DAVIS, DAVID ENSOS
Sculptor
Preferred Media: Steel, Aluminum, Bronze, Wood.
b Rona de Jos, Romania, Aug 27, 20; U S citizen.
Study & Training: Beaux Art, Paris, France, 45; Cleveland Inst Art,
scholar & BFA, 48; Case Western Reserve Univ, MA, 61.
Exhibitions: 53rd May Show, Cleveland Mus Art, 72; 24th Ann Ohio
Ceramic & Sculpture, Butler Inst Am Art, Youngstown, 72; Ohio
Sculptors Invitational, Blossom Music Ctr, Cleveland, 72; group
show, Sloane-O'Sickey Gallery, Cleveland, 72; one-man show,
Akron Art Inst, 72.
Positions: Staff artist, Am Greetings Corp, Cleveland, 48-49, dir
creative dept, 49-54, asst to v pres creative dept, 54-58, v pres
creative dept, 58-61.
Memberships: Art Community (steering comt); Cleveland Inst Art
(bd trustees & alumni asn).
Mailing Address: 26611 Fairmount Blvd, Beachwood, OH 44122.

DAVIS, DONALD ROBERT
Painter, Art Dealer
Preferred Media: Mixed Media, Oils, Acrylics.
b Toronto, Ont, July 30, 09; U S citizen.
Study & Training: Syracuse Univ; Art Stud League New York, N Y.
Work in Public Collections: Berkshire Mus, Pittsfield, Mass; also in
many private collections.
Commissions: Prehistoric Lascaux cave fresco, Bandag, Inc,
Jamaica, W I.
Exhibitions: Berkshire Art Asn Ann Exhib, 67 & 68; one-man shows,
Berkshire Mus, 67 & Tyringham Gallery, Mass, 69; Albany Inst
Art Regional Exhib, N Y, 68.
Positions: Owner & dir, Tyringham Gallery.
Memberships: Am Asn Mus; Berkshire Art Asn.
Specialty of Gallery: Paintings, sculpture, prints, objets d'art.
Collection: Prints by American and European contemporaries; pre-
Columbian; ivories.
Publications: Auth, article, In: Am Artist Mag.
Mailing Address: Tyringham Art Gallery, Tyringham, MA 01264.

DAVIS, DOUGLAS MATTHEW
Art Critic, Artist
Preferred Media: Videotape.
b Washington, D C, Apr 11, 33.
Study & Training: Abbott Art Sch, Washington, D C; Am Univ, BA,
56; Rutgers Univ, New Brunswick, MA, 58.
Exhibitions: Videotape, Whitney Mus Am Art, New York, N Y, 71;
Ten Videotape Performances, 71 & Projected Art, Finch Col Mus
Art; retrospective, Everson Mus, Syracuse, N Y, 72; Videotape,
Galerie Aubry, Paris, 73.
Collections Arranged: Walking, Smithsonian Inst, Washington, D C,
69; Look-Out!, 70 & Electronic Hokkadim, 71, Corcoran Gallery
Art, Washington, D C.
Teaching: Vis artist videotape, Corcoran Gallery Art, 70-71; vis
artist, Northwood Exp Art Inst, Dallas, Tex, 72.
Positions: Art critic, Nat Observer, 65-69; contrib ed, Art Am, 68-
70; art critic, Newsweek Mag, 70-; artist-in-residence, TV Lab,
WNET-TV, New York.
Awards: Nat Endowment for Arts grant to create a TV event, 70;
N Y State Coun Arts grant for creative work in mixed media, 70.
Publications: Auth, For a new esthetic, Am Scholar, 3-4/66; auth,
Art as act, Art Am, 70; auth, Media/art/media, Arts Mag, 9/71;
auth, Video obscura, Artforum, 4/72; auth, Art and the future,
Praeger, 73.
Mailing Address: 27 Washington Sq N, New York, NY 10011.

DAVIS, ESTHER M
Sculptor, Painter
b Brunswick, Ga, Aug 10, 93.
Study & Training: Teacher's Diploma Parson's Art School; Columbia
Univ; New Sch Social Res; studied with Chaim Gross, Norman
Raeben, Bruno Lucchesi & Sol Swarz.
Work in Public Collections: Mayfield Librr, Syracuse Univ Mus, N Y;
Colby Col, Maine; Drew Univ, Madison, N J; Community Church
Woman's Asn Hq, New York, N Y.
Commissions: Paintings of characters & scenes, Dark of the Moon,
Carnegie Theater Lobby, New York, 60; sculpture, Samarai, New
Sch Assocs Gallery, New York, 72.

Exhibitions: New Gallery, New York, 53; Bodley Gallery, New York, 59; New York World's Fair, 65; Roko Gallery, New York, 70; Allied Artists Am, 70.
Positions: Art dir, Lane Bryant, New York, 17-19; art dir, Bambergers, N J, 19-20; art consultant & ed, art books, Davis, Delaney & Arrow, 66-; dir, Community Church Art Gallery, 68-71.
Awards: Three first prizes in group shows, New Sch Social Res, 65-70; four first prizes in Elberon, N J, art shows, 66-71.
Bibliography: Reviews of work in New Yorker Mag, 53, Art News, 60 & Arts Mag, 70.
Memberships: Artists Equity Asn; Am Fed Arts; Allied Artists Am.
Dealer: Roko Gallery, 90 E 10th St, New York, NY 10003.
Mailing Address: 10 Park Ave, New York, NY 10016.

DAVIS, GENE
Painter
b Washington, D C, Aug 22, 20.
Study & Training; Maryland Univ; Wilson Teachers Col.
Work in Public Collections: Mus Mod Art, New York, N Y; Whitney Mus Am Art, New York; Tate Gallery, London, Eng; San Francisco Mus Art, Calif; Corcoran Gallery Art, Washington, D C; plus many others.
Commissions: Mural, South Mall Proj, N Y State Capitol Bldg, Albany, 69; mural, Neiman-Marcus, Bal Harbour, Fla, 70; official poster, comn by List Found, Lincoln Ctr Concert Series, N Y.
Exhibitions: One-man show, Corcoran Gallery Art, Washington, D C, 64 & 68; Whitney Ann Exhib Am Painting, Whitney Mus Am Art, 67 & 68; one-man shows, San Francisco Mus, 68 (with Robert Irwin & Richard Smith), Jewish Mus, N Y, 68 & Univ Utah Art Mus, Salt Lake City, 72; plus many other one-man & group shows.
Teaching: Instr painting, Corcoran Gallery Sch Art, 67-68, instr painting, Am Univ, 68-70; artist-in-residence, Skidmore Col, summer 69; instr painting, Corcoran Gallery Sch Art, 70-; artist-in-residence, Univ Va, spring 72
Awards: Bronze medal for painting & award, Am Painting Biennial, Corcoran Gallery Art, 65; Nat Coun Arts grant, 67.
Bibliography: Gene Baro (auth), Preoccupation with colour, Studio Int, 11/67; Donald Wall (auth), The micro-paintings of Gene Davis, Artforum, 12/68; Barbara Rose (auth), Conversation with Gene Davis, Artforum, 3/71.
Publications: Auth, Statement by the artist, Art Now, 2/70; auth, Random thoughts on art, Studio Int, 11/70.
Mailing Address: 4120 Harrison St N W, Washington, DC 20015.

DAVIS, GEORGE
Cartoonist, Illustrator
Preferred Media: Ink.
b Newark, N J, Feb 6, 14.
Study & Training: Cartoonist's & Illustrator's Sch; Art Stud League New York.
Work in Public Collections: New York Pub Libr, N Y.
Positions: Med Illusr, Vet Admin, 50-54.
Publications: Contribr, Saturday Evening Post, Look Mag, True Mag, King Features Syndicate & other national publications, 50-
Mailing Address: 108 Charles St, New York, NY 10014.

DAVIS, GERALD VIVIAN
Painter, Educator
Preferred Media: Oils, Gouache, Charcoal, Pastels, Inks.
b Brooklyn, N Y, Sept 8, 99.
Study & Training: Ecole des Beaux Arts, Paris, France; Julian Acad, cert; Acad Grande Chaumiére, Paris; also with Déchenard & Royer.
Work in Public Collections: Many works in private collections around the world.
Commissions: Portrait of Pres of Danish Eng, Soc Danish Eng, Copenhagen, 38; portrait of Rev Dr Clayton Williams, Am Church in Paris, France, 40; portrait of Dr Knutson, Dir Watkins Hosp, Univ Kans, Lawrence, 51; painting, Univ Kans Dept Archit, 51; Summit & Copenhagen Hosps, Overlook Hosp Summit, City Hosp Copenhagen, 65 & 69.
Exhibitions: Art Inst Chicago, 28; Soc Nat Beaux Arts & Salon d'Automne, Paris, 39; Nat Acad Design, New York, N Y, 40; Kansas City Nelson Art Mus, 51; Trenton Art Mus & Newark Mus, 68; plus many other group & one-man shows.
Teaching: Instr art, Univ Ill, Champaign, 25-28; asst prof art, Univ Kans, 47-51.
Awards: Contemp N J Artists, 60; N J State Show, East Orange Art Ctr, 68 & Summit Art Ctr, 69.
Memberships: Assoc, Soc Nat Beaux Arts.
Mailing Address: 86 Elm St, Summit, NJ 07901.

DAVIS, HARRY ALLEN
Painter, Educator
Preferred Media: Acrylics, Ink, Watercolors.
b Hillsboro, Ind, May 21, 14.
Study & Training: Herron Sch Art, Ind Univ-Purdue Univ, Indianapolis, BFA, 38; Am Acad Rome, FAAR, 41.
Work in Public Collections: Butler Inst Am Art, Youngstown, Ohio; Indianapolis Mus Art, Ind; Springfield Art Mus, Mo; Evansville Mus Arts & Sci, Ind; Grover M Hermann Fine Arts Ctr, Marietta Col, Ohio.
Commissions: Panorama of Indianapolis (acrylics), Am Fletcher Nat Bank (now owned by Indianapolis Mus Art), 66.
Exhibitions: Five Butler Midyear Exhibs, Youngstown, 61-71; Watercolor U S A, Nat Watercolor Exhib, Springfield, Mo, 65-72; Governors' National Art Tour, representing Ind throughout the U S A, 66; Mainstreams Int Exhib, Marietta, Ohio, 68-72; 24th Am Drawing Biennial, Norfolk, Va, 71.
Teaching: Artist-in-residence, Beloit Col, 41-42; prof painting & drawing, Herron Sch Art, Ind Univ-Purdue Univ, Indianapolis, 46-
Awards: Prix de Rome, Am Acad Rome, 38; award of distinction & purchase award, Mainstreams '71, Marietta Col, 71; Mo Sesquicentennial Award, State of Mo, 71.
Bibliography: Clifford (auth), Hoosier artists: Harry A Davis, Indianapolis Star Mag, 6/13/65; Mendelowitz (auth), Drawing: guide to drawing, Holt, 66.
Memberships: Fel Am Acad Rome; Ind Artists Clu (pres, 55-56, dir, 72); Assoc Prof Artists (v pres, 69-70).
Mailing Address: Herron School of Art, Indiana University-Purdue University at Indianapolis, Indianapolis, IN 46202.

DAVIS, J RAY
Painter, Printmaker
Study & Training: Cent State Univ (Okla), BA; Univ Okla, MFA (painting & printmaking).
Work in Public Collections: State of Okla Collection & Traveling Exhib.
Exhibitions: Kans State Univ Invitational To Grad Midwestern Univs, 69; one-man shows, Painting Prints & Vacum Forms, Contemp Arts Found, Oklahoma City, Okla, 70 & Graphic Retrospective, Emporia, Kans, 70; 31st Ann Exhib Okla Artists, Philbrook Art Ctr, Tulsa, 71; Okla Featured Artist of Month, Okla Art Ctr, Apr, 72.
Teaching: Instr art, Okla Sci & Arts Found, 67-70; asst prof art, Okla City Univ, 69-; instr art, state supported art classes for all fifth graders in Okla City Pub Sch Syst, 71-72.
Awards: Graphics awards, 30th & 31st Ann Exhib Okla Artists, Tulsa 70 & 71 & 57th Ann Tulsa Regional Exhib, 71.
Mailing Address: 1421 N W 19th St, Oklahoma City, OK 73106.

DAVIS, JERROLD
Painter
b Chico, Calif, Nov 2, 26.
Study & Training: Univ Calif, Berkeley, BA, 53, MA.
Work in Public Collections: Carnegie Inst, Pittsburgh, Pa; Santa Barbara Mus Art, Calif; Los Angeles Mus Art, Calif; Flint Inst Art, Mich; Oakland Mus Art, Calif; plus others.
Exhibitions: Calif Palace of Legion of Honor, 60-64; Especially for Children, Los Angeles Co Mus, 65; Art in the Embassies Prog; Univ Ariz, 67; Lytton Ctr, Los Angeles, 67 & 68; plus others.
Teaching: Instr, Univ Calif, summer 67.
Awards: Guggenheim fel, 58-59; Am Fedn Arts-Ford Found artist-in-residence grant, Flint, Mich, 64; prizes, Calif Palace of Legion of Honor, 60 & 62; plus others.
Dealer: Jacqueline Anholt Gallery, 750 N La Cienega Blvd, Los Angeles, CA 90069.
Mailing Address: 66 Twain Ave, Berkeley, CA 94708.

DAVIS, JOHN HAROLD
Art Administrator, Illustrator
b Milwaukee, Wis, Feb 8, 23.
Study & Training: Layton Art Inst, Milwaukee; Art Inst Chicago.
Commissions: Stations of the Cross, Mount St Frances, Iowa, 49; new altar & reconstruct of church, Monsefú, Perú, 64-66; Veracruz (tapestry applique), Chimbote, Perú, 68; mural of cast concrete, San Antonio de Padua, Lima, Perú, 69; decoration of interior, Church of San Juan de Miraflores, 70.
Exhibitions: Am Printmakers, Philadelphia, Pa, 45-55; Art Ctr, Lima, 56, 58 & 70; Charles Allis Art Libr, Milwaukee, 71; Inst Cult Peruano Norteamericano, Lima; Munson-Williams-Procter Inst, Utica, N Y, plus many others.
Collections Arranged: 15 Impressionists, 50; Spanish painting included in prog exhibs, Iowa Art Ctr & Syracuse Univ, 52; Folk Art of Perú, Los Angeles Co Fair, 68; Peruvian Crafts Exhibition, Fardoms & Masions, London, Eng; First Biennial Crafts of Peru (Artesania del Peru), Museo Arte Lima, 68; plus 120 smaller exhibs.

Teaching: Instr painting & drawing, Syracuse Univ, 48-55; dir painting & drawing, Art Ctr Gallery & Shop, Miraflores, 55-
Bibliography: Petterson (auth), Folk art of Perú, Scripps Col Press; Serven Rodman (auth), South American of the poets & The Perú traveler, Meredith.
Memberships: World Crafts Coun (dir for Latin Am, 68-); Asociacion Nacional de Artesanos del Perú (founder, 68-); Inst Art Ctr; Fundacion Peruana Pro-Arte y Educacion (pres, 65-).
Collection: Peruvian folk art; twentieth century drawings.
Publications: Illusr, Mis antepasados, 54, Manuel Pardo Rivadeneyra, 55, Conquest of Perú, New Am Libr Ed, 58 & The New Testament In Quechua, 72-73; auth & illusr, Slice of life (limited ed).
Mailing Address: Art Center Gallery & Shop, Calle Berlin 917, Miraflores, Lima, Perú.

DAVIS, LEROY
Art Dealer
Positions: Owner & dir, Davis Galleries.
Specialty of Gallery: Contemporary art.
Mailing Address: 231 E 60th St, New York, NY 10022.

DAVIS, LEW E
Painter
Preferred Media: Oils.
b Jerome, Ariz, Nov 2, 10.
Study & Training: Nat Acad Design, New York, N Y.
Work in Public Collections: Newark Mus, N J; Coe Col, Cedar Rapids, Iowa; Ariz State Collection Am Art, Tempe; Univ Ariz Art Gallery, Tucson; Phoenix Art Mus, Ariz.
Commissions: U S Post Off, Los Banos, Calif, 38 & Marlow, Okla, 41.
Exhibitions: 107th Ann, Nat Acad Design, 32; Corcoran Gallery, Washington, D C, 37; Whitney Mus Am Art Ann, New York, 37-41; Los Angeles Mus, Calif, 38; San Francisco Mus, Calif, 38-40.
Bibliography: Harry Wood (auth), 25 year retrospective, Ariz State Univ, 40; Jon Hopkins (auth), The art of Lew Davis, Northland, 70.
Mailing Address: Pinnacle Peak, Scottsdale, AZ 85255.

DAVIS, MARIAN B
Art Historian, Curator
b St Louis Co, Mo, Sept 24, 11.
Study & Training: Wash Univ, BA, 32, MA, 35; Radcliffe Col, MA, 39; PhD, 48.
Collections Arranged: Sch of Fontainebleau, 65; plus many others.
Teaching: Instr art hist, Worcester Art Mus, 41-44; from instr to assoc prof art hist, Univ Tex, Austin, 44-50; prof art hist, 50-
Positions: Chief cur & acting dir, Art Teaching Gallery, Univ Tex, Austin, 63-
Memberships: Col Art Asn (dir, 51-55); Soc Archit Historians; Archaeol Inst Am; Renaissance Soc; Nat Trust Hist Preserv.
Research: Italian Renaissance; U S architecture.
Publications: Auth, Two eighteenth century paintings, Worcester Art Mus Ann V, 46; auth, Summer travel for students, Col Art J, 54; auth, Some first impressions of Sicily, Tex Trends in Art Educ, autumn 59; auth, Art history—contribution to understanding, Western Arts Asn Bull, 61.
Mailing Address: 2701 Wooldridge Dr, Austin, TX 78703.

DAVIS, PHILIP CHARLES
Photographer, Educator
b Spokane, Wash, Oct 15, 21.
Study & Training: Albright Art Sch, Buffalo, N Y, cert.
Work in Public Collections: Mus Art Inst Chicago; Int Mus Photog, Rochester, N Y; Detroit Art Inst, Mich.
Commissions: Outdoor exhib photos, Univ Mich Sesquicentennial Comt, 66.
Exhibitions: One-man show photographs, Kalamazoo Art Ctr, Mich, 62; The University, Univ Mich, Ann Arbor, 64; three-man show photographs, 831 Gallery, Birmingham, Mich, 71; Group Invitational, Kresge Art Ctr, Mich State Univ, 72.
Teaching: From instr to prof art, Univ Mich, Ann Arbor, 48-
Positions: Photogr, var photo-illus studios, Detroit, Mich, 52-
Awards: Gold medal, 59, silver medal, 60 & Bravo Gold Medal, 61, Art Dirs Club Detroit.
Bibliography: Irving Destor (auth), Camera angles, Assoc Press Newsfeatures, 72.
Memberships: Soc Photog Educ.
Publications: Auth & illusr, The university, 67; auth & illusr, Take photography step by step, 70; auth & illusr, Photography, 72; auth & illusr, The Dexter port-folio (50 set ed), 72.
Dealer: 831 Gallery, 831 E Maple Rd, Birmingham, MI 48011.
Mailing Address: 7385 Webster Church Rd, Whitmore Lake, MI 48189.

DAVIS, ROBERT TYLER
Art Administrator, Art Historian
b Los Angeles, Calif, Aug 11, 04.
Study & Training: Harvard Univ, BA & MA; Fogg Mus, with Paul J Sachs & also painting & design with Arthur Pope & Martin Mower.
Teaching: Prof art, McGill Univ, 47-52; coord humanities, Univ Miami, 57-59.
Positions: Dir, Portland Art Mus, Ore, 39-47; dir, Mus Fine Arts, Montreal, Can, 47-52; dir, Vizcaya-Dade Co Art Mus, Miami, Fla, 52-57; asst dir, Nat Collection Fine Arts, Smithsonian Inst, 69-72; spec asst for collections, 72-
Research: The American Renaissance, paintings & patrons, late nineteenth to early twentieth centuries.
Mailing Address: Eighth & G Sts N W, Washington, DC 20560.

DAVIS, RONALD WENDEL
Painter, Collector
Preferred Media: Polyester Resin, Fiberglass.
b Santa Monica, Calif, June 29, 37.
Study & Training: San Francisco Art Inst, 60-64.
Work in Public Collections: Los Angeles Co Mus, Calif; Mus Mod Art, New York, N Y; Tate Gallery, London, Eng; Albright-Knox Art Gallery, Buffalo, N Y; San Francisco Mus Art, Calif.
Exhibitions: A News Aesthetic, Washington Gallery Mod Art, D C, 67; Documenta 4, Kassel, Ger, 67; Whitney Mus Am Art Ann, New York, 67; Color, Univ Calif, Los Angeles Art Galleries, 69; Venice Biennial, Italy, 72.
Awards: Nat Ednowment Arts, 68.
Bibliography: M Fried (auth), Ronald Davis: surface & illusion, Artforum, 4/67; R Hughes (auth), Ron Davis at Kasmin, Studio Int, 176, 12/68; B Rose (auth), American painting, Vol 2, 70.
Collection: Contemporary art.
Dealer: Nicholas Wilder Gallery, 8225½ Santa Monica, Los Angeles, CA 90046.
Mailing Address: 6950 Grasswood Ave, Malibu, CA 90265.

DAVIS, STEPHEN A
Painter
b Fort Worth, Tex, Apr 24, 45.
Study & Training: Univ Madrid, 66; Claremont Men's Col, BA(polit sci), 67; Univ Tex, 67-68; Claremont Grad Sch, MFA, 71.
Exhibitions: Fullerton Col Painting Show, 71; two-man show, Pomona Col, 71; Off The Stretcher, Oakland Mus, 72; Bay Area Underground, Univ Calif Art Mus, Berkeley, 72; Hansen Fuller Gallery Artists Show, 72.
Collections Arranged: Conceptual Show 11 Young Bay Area Artists & Collectors & 4 Young Berkeley Artists, Hansen Fuller Gallery.
Positions: Mus asst, Univ Tex, 67-68; gallery asst, Pomona Col, 68-69; asst Hansen Fuller Gallery, 70.
Mailing Address: c/o Hansen Fuller Gallery, 228 Grant Ave, San Francisco, CA 94108.

DAVIS, MR & MRS WALTER
Collectors, Patrons
Mr Davis, b New Orleans, La; Mrs Davis, b Natchez, Miss.
Study & Training: Mr Davis, Tulane Univ Law Sch; Mrs Davis, Newcomb Art Sch.
Positions: Mr Davis, Bd New Orleans Opera. Mrs Davis, trustee & women's bd, New Orleans Mus Art; women's bd, New Orleans Symphony; women's bd, New Orleans Opera; trustee comt, Am Asn Mus.
Collection: Drawings by Mary Cassat, Louis Valtat, Chagall & Krebs; gouaches by Tamayo, Raoul Dufy, Cuevas; sculpture by Henry Moore, L Nierman & L Wercollier; watercolors by John Marin, Raoul Dufy, David Smith, Jean Dufy, Merida & Montenegro; oils by Modigliani, R Dufy, de Chirico, Rouault, Utrillo, Harold Carney, Merida & Montenegro.
Mailing Address: 1819 Octavia St, New Orleans, LA 70115.

DAVIS, WAYNE LAMBERT
Painter, Illustrator
Preferred Media: Tempera, Watercolors, Oils.
b Oak Park, Ill, Jan 3, 04.
Study & Training: Art Stud League New York, with Joseph Pennell; Columbia Univ; N Y Univ, State N Y cert art teacher.
Work in Public Collections: Smithsonian Inst, Washington, D C; First Nat City Bank New York; Kennedy Galleries, New York; Newman Galleries, Philadelphia, Pa; Country Art Gallery, Locust Valley, N Y; plus others.
Commissions: Mural of skiing, Vail, Colo, comn by Vernon Taylor, Denver, 68; Stairway murals of Brooklyn Bridge area, First Nat City Bank New York, 53rd St Br, 69.
Exhibitions: One-man shows, Kennedy Galleries, 67, Country Art Galleries, 69 & Hunter Gallery, Aspen, Colo, 69; Grand Cent Gallery, New York, 69; Harbor Gallery, Cold Spring Harbor, N Y, 69.

Teaching: Instr art, Hit Sch Art, Locust Valley, 53-63; instr water-color, Great Neck High Sch, N Y, 54-
Positions: Art dir & staff artist, Grumman Aircraft Eng Corp, Beth-page, N Y, 41-53.
Awards: First in watercolor for the Lobster Weir, Stony Brook Mus, N Y, 68; first in oil for The Salmon Run, Oper Democracy, Locust Valley, 71.
Memberships: Nassau Art League.
Publications: Illusr, Fortune & Liberty, 43, Vanity Fair, 44 & Sport-man Pilot, 45; auth, Pathway to expression (color film), privately publ, 66.
Dealer: Country Art Gallery, The Plaza, Locust Valley, NY 11560.
Mailing Address: R F D 1, Five Mile River Rd, Putnam, CT 06260.

DAVISON, ROBERT
Painter, Designer
b Long Beach, Calif, July 17, 22.
Study & Training: Los Angeles City Col.
Work in Public Collections: James Philip Gray Collection, Spring-field Mus Fine Arts, Mass.
Commissions: Designer scenery & costumes, Galileo, Hollywood, 47, Cirque de Deaux, Ballet Russe Monte Carlo, 48, Constanzia, Ballet Theatre, 51, La Barca di Venetia per Padova, Festival Due Mondi, Spoleto, Italy, 63 & Natalia Petrovna, Opera Soc Washington, 65; plus others.
Exhibitions: Am Watercolor Soc, 59; Boston Art Festival, 59; East-ern States Exhib, Springfield, Mass, 59; Allied Artists Am, 59; The Life of Christ Exhib, Birmingham, Mich, 60; plus others.
Mailing Address: 21-18 45th Ave, Long Island City, NY 11101.

DAWLEY, JOSEPH WILLIAM
Painter, Writer
Preferred Media: Oils.
b Nashville, Ark, June 19, 36.
Study & Training: With Raymond Froman, 58-61; Southern Methodist Univ, BFA, 59; Dallas Mus Fine Arts, 60; Art Stud League New York, 61.
Work in Public Collections: Mus Arts & Crafts, Columbus, Ga; Davenport Mus Art, Iowa; Henderson Arts Coun, Tex; Southern Methodist Univ, Dallas, Tex; Grand Cent Gallery, New York, N Y.
Exhibitions: Allied Artists Show, New York, 69 & 70; Acad Artists Show, Springfield, Mass, 69 & 70; Hudson Valley Art Show, White Plains, N Y, 69 & 70; Am Artists Prof League, New York, 69-71; Salmagundi Club Show, New York, 70 & 72.
Awards: Figure or Portrait Anonymous Award, Acad Artists, 69; William Collins Award, Hudson Valley Art Asn, 69; Jane Peter-son Portrait Award, Allied Artists, New York, 70.
Bibliography: Kolbe (auth), Dawley reasserts realism, Am Artist Mag, 70; Singer (auth), Meet the artist—Joseph Dawley, Suburban Life Mag, 70; Calaway (auth), Bringing sanity back to art, South-west Scene Mag, 70.
Memberships: Allied Artists Asn; Hudson Valley Art Asn; Am Artist Prof League; Acad Artists; Salmagundi Club.
Publications: Auth, Character studies in oil, Watson-Guptill, 72.
Dealer: Grand Central Gallery, 40 Vanderbilt Ave, New York, NY 10017.
Mailing Address: 13 W Holly St, Cranford, NJ 07016.

DAWSON, BESS PHIPPS
Painter, Art Dealer
b Tchula, Miss.
Study & Training: Belhaven Col; Southwest Miss Jr Col; workshops, Allisons Art Colony, Way, Miss & Miss Art Colony, Laurel.
Work in Public Collections: Art in Embassy Prog, Taiwan; Old Capitol Hist Mus, Jackson, Miss; Miss Art Asn Gallery, Jackson; Miss State Col Women, Columbus; First Nat Bank Miss Collec-tion, Jackson.
Commissions: Murals, (with Ruth A Holmes), Church of God, Mc-Comb, Miss, 58, (with Halcyone Barnes & Ruth A Holmes), Delta Elec Co, Greenwood, Miss, 58, First Nat Bank, McComb, 59 & Hankins Container Corp, Magnolia, Miss, 59; painting, Order Eastern Star, Jackson, 69.
Exhibitions: High Mus Art, Atlanta, Ga, 65; Delgado Mus Art, New Orleans, La, 67; Brooks Mem Gallery, Memphis, Tenn, 69; Ark Arts Ctr, Little Rock, 70; Art Asn Gallery, Jackson, 70.
Teaching: Supvr art, McComb Pub Schs, 68-
Positions: Co-owner & dir, Gulf S Galleries, 71-
Awards: First purchase prize, S Cent Bell, 69; purchase prize, Eastman Mem-Lauren Rogers Mus, 69; award of merit, Miss Art Colony, 71.
Memberships: Southwest Miss Art Asn (secy, 66-); Miss Art Colony (bd dirs, 62-); Allisons Art Colony (bd dirs); Miss Art Asn (coordr state bd, 68-69).
Specialty of Gallery: Continuous showing of invited Mississippi artists in all media
Publications: Co-auth, Manual for classroom teachers, 69 & illusr, Elementary art (TV doc), 69, McComb Pub Schs.

Dealers: Gulf South Galleries, 211 Llewellyn Ave, McComb, MS 39648; Mainstream Mall, Greenville, MS 38701.
Mailing Address: P O Box 32, Summit, MS 39666.

DAWSON, EVE
Painter
Preferred Media: Oils.
b Somersetshire, Eng; U S citizen.
Study & Training: Art Stud League New York, N Y.
Work in Public Collections: In private collections in U S, Eng, Malta & Australia.
Exhibitions: 15 one-man shows in New York & Vt; Nat Acad Design; Nat Arts Club; plus two- and three-man shows.
Awards: First award, Nat Pen Women Am; two first awards, Pen & Brush Club; two hon mentions, Nat Arts Club.
Memberships: Nat Arts Club; Knickerbocker Art Club; Pen & Brush Club; Catharine Lorillard Wolfe Art Asn; Burr Artists.
Dealer: Lord & Taylor Gallery, Fifth & 39th, New York, NY 10016.
Mailing Address: 15 Grammercy Park, New York, NY 10003.

DAY, CHON (CHAUNCEY ADDISON)
Cartoonist
b Chatham, N J, Apr 6, 07.
Study & Training: Art Stud League New York, with Boardman Robin-son & John Sloan.
Exhibitions: Metrop Mus Art, 42; Pa Acad Fine Arts.
Awards: Best gag cartoonist, Nat Cartoonists Soc, 56 & 61.
Memberships: Mag Cartoonists Guild; Nat Cartoonists Soc.
Publications: Auth & illusr, I could be dreaming, 45, What price dory, 55, Brother Sebastian, 57, Brother Sebastian carries on, 59 & Brother Sebastian at large, 61; contribr cartoons, New Yorker, Good Housekeeping, Ladies Home J & others.
Mailing Address: 22 Cross St, Westerly, RI 02891.

DAY, HORACE TALMAGE
Painter, Educator
Preferred Media: Oils, Watercolors.
b Amoy, China, July 3, 09; U S citizen.
Study & Training: Art Stud League New York, 28-32; with Kimon Nicolaides & Kenneth H Miller; Tiffany Found, Oyster Bay, 30-35.
Work in Public Collections: Va Mus Fine Arts, Richmond; Norfolk Mus, Va; Addison Gallery, Andover, Mass; Nelson Gallery, Kan-sas City, Mo; Fleming Mus, Burlington, Vt.
Commissions: Mural, Tenn Treas Dept, 38; three paintings, Dept Reclamation, Dept Interior, Washington, D C, 69.
Exhibitions: Whitney Mus Am Art Ann, New York, N Y, 39-41 & 44; one-man shows, Va Mus Fine Arts, 48 & Bodley Gallery, New York, 58; Biennial Am Painting, Va Mus Fine Arts, 58; Biennial Am Drawing, Norfolk Mus, 70.
Teaching: Prof art, Mary Baldwin Col, Staunton, Va, 42-63; instr painting, Kansas City Art Inst, 47-48.
Positions: Dir painting, Herbert Inst Art, Augusta, Ga, 36-41; dir, Northern Va Fine Arts Ctr, Alexandria, 72-
Memberships: Southern Vermont Art Asn.
Publications: Contribr, Art in the armed forces, Hyperion, 45; illusr, Staunton in the valley of Virginia (folio), McClure, 47.
Mailing Address: c/o Hensley Gallery, 113 N Fairfax St, Alexandria, VA 22314.

DAY, MARTHA B WILLSON
Painter, Collector
b Providence, R I, Aug 16, 85.
Study & Training: R I Sch Design; Julian Acad, Paris, France; also with Lucia F Fuller.
Work in Public Collections: Philadelphia Mus Art; Smithsonian Inst.
Exhibitions: Am Soc Miniature Painters Ann & Pa Miniature Paint-ers Soc Ann.
Teaching: Lectr miniatures.
Awards: Prize, Pa Acad Fine Arts, 32; McCarty Medal, Pa Minia-ture Painters Soc.
Memberships: Providence Art Club; Am Soc Miniature Painters; Pa Miniature Painters Soc.
Mailing Address: 88 Congdon St, Providence, RI 02906.

DAY, ROBERT JAMES
Cartoonist
b San Bernardino, Calif, Sept 25, 00.
Study & Training: Otis Art Inst, 18-27.
Exhibitions: Many cartoon exhibs throughout U S & Europe.
Art Interests: Line & wash drawings.
Publications: Illusr, Seen any good movies lately?; illusr, The mad world of bridge, 60; illusr, Over the fence is out, 61; illusr, What every bachelor knows, 61; illusr, Rome wasn't burned in a day, 72; plus many others & contribr to New Yorker & other nat mags.
Mailing Address: c/o The New Yorker Magazine, 25 W 43rd St, New York, NY 10036.

DAY, WÖRDEN
    Sculptor, Printmaker
b Columbus, Ohio, June 11, 16.
Study & Training: Randolph-Macon Womans Col, BA; New York
    Univ, MA; also with Jean Charlot, Emilio Amero, Maurice
    Sterne, Vaclav Vylacil, Hans Hofmann & Stanley William Hayter.
Work in Public Collections: Nat Gallery Art & Libr Cong, Washing-
    ton, D C; Philadelphia Mus Art, Pa; Metrop Mus Art & Whitney
    Mus Art, New York; State Mus, N J; plus others.
Exhibitions: Nat Print Exhibs, Libr Cong, Brooklyn Mus, Philadel-
    phia Mus Art, 48-62; Int Print Exhibs, Europe, Asia & Mex, 50-
    62; Abstract Painting and Sculpture in America, Mus Mod Art,
    New York, 51; Carnegie Third Int, Pittsburgh, Pa, 53; Int Water-
    color Exhib, Brooklyn Mus, N Y, 62.
Teaching: Instr design, Pratt Inst, 55-56; vis artist, Iowa State Univ,
    61; instr woodcut & watercolor, New Sch Social Res, 61-66; instr
    multi-media, Art Stud League New York, 66-69.
Awards: Va Mus Fine Arts grant, 40-42; J Rosenwald Awards, 42-
    44; Guggenheim fel, 51-52 & 61-62.
Bibliography: Una Johnson (auth), Solo prints - paintings (catalog),
    Montclair Art Mus, 59; Printmakers, U S A (film), U S Info
    Serv, 61; 3 Mid-Atlantic artists, Kalamazoo Art Ctr, 63.
Memberships: Artists equity Asn; Fedn Mod Painters & Sculptors;
    Montclair Art Mus; MacDowell Colony; Art Stud League New
    York.
Dealers: Sculpture Center of New York, 167 E 69th St, New York,
    NY 10021; Discovery Gallery, Clifton, NJ 07015.
Mailing Address: 285 Claremont Ave, Montclair, NJ 07042.

DAYTON, BRUCE B
    Collector
b Minneapolis, Minn, Aug 16, 18.
Study & Training: Yale Univ, BA, 40.
Positions: Trustee, Minneapolis Soc Fine Arts.
Mailing Address: 777 Nicollet Ave, Minneapolis, MN 55402.

DEADERICK, JOSEPH
    Painter, Educator
Preferred Media: Oils, Acrylics, Watercolors.
b Memphis, Tenn, Jan 17, 30.
Study & Training: Univ Ga, BFA, 52; Cranbrook Acad Art, MFA, 54;
    Ind Univ, 58-59.
Work in Public Collections: Kalamazoo Col, Mich.
Commissions: Ceramic tile mural, Univ Wyo, Laramie, 68; faceted
    glass window, Lutheran Campus Ctr, Laramie, 68.
Exhibitions: Sixth Midwest Biennial, Joslyn Art Mus, Omaha, Nebr,
    60; Brooklyn Mus Biennial Print Show, N Y, 64; Drawing U S A
    traveling show, St Paul, Minn, 66-68; one-man show, Colorado
    Springs Fine Arts Ctr, Colo, 67; Fedn Rocky Mountain States
    Traveling Show (exhibited in eight states), 72.
Teaching: Instr design, Ind Univ, Bloomington, 56-59; prof art, Univ
    Wyo, Laramie, 59-
Awards: Two grants, Univ Wyo Grad Res Coord Comt, 64 & 69; hon
    mention, Survey '69, Univ Mont, 69; first place award for design
    of medal commemorating Bicentennial Celebration of the U S,
    Franklin Mint, 72; nat award for excellence in design, Printing
    Indust Am Graphic Arts Competition, 72; plus others.
Dealer: Gilbert Galleries, 590 Sutter St, San Francisco, CA 94102.
Mailing Address: Art Dept, University of Wyoming, Laramie, WY
    82070.

DEAN, ABNER
    Illustrator, Writer
b New York, N Y.
Study & Training: Nat Acad Design; Dartmouth Col, BA.
Memberships: Soc Illustrators.
Publications: Auth (books of drawings), It's a long way to heaven, 45,
    What am I doing here?, 47, And on the eighth day, 49, Cave draw-
    ings for the future, 54 & Abner Dean's naked people, 63; also two
    bks verse & drawings plus illusr other bks & mags & for indust.

DEAN, PETER
    Painter, Sculptor
Preferred Media: Oils.
b Berlin, Mont, July 9, 39.
Study & Training: Cornell Univ; Univ Wis, BA; Pratt Graphic Art
    Ctr; also with Andre Girard.
Work in Public Collections: Delgado Mus Art, New Orleans, La;
    Mus Mod Art, New York, N Y; Brooklyn Mus, New York; Los An-
    geles Co Mus, Los Angeles, Calif.
Exhibitions: 2nd Bienal Int, Madrid, Spain, 69; one-man shows, Bien-
    ville Gallery, New Orleans, 70 & 73, Allan Stone Gallery, New
    York, 70 & 73 & New Orleans Mus Art, 72; 32nd Corcoran Bien-
    nial Am Painting, Washington, D C, 71.
Positions: Geologist, Anaconda Co, Butte, Mont, 57-61; geologist,
    Hanna Coal & Ore Corp, Belo Horizonte, Brazil, 58-59.

Bibliography: A Molass (auth), Under earth works, Geol World, 57;
    E Bisson (auth), Art & earth works, Mining Engrs, 59.
Dealer: Allan Stone Gallery, 48 E 86th St, New York, NY 10028.
Mailing Address: 686 Academy St, New York, NY 10034.

DeANDREA, JOHN LOUIS
    Sculptor
Preferred Media: Fiberglass.
b Denver, Colo, Nov 24, 41.
Study & Training: Univ Colo, BFA; Univ N Mex.
Work in Public Collections: Sammuel Ludwig Collection, Neue
    Mus, Aachen, Ger; Everson Mus, Syracuse, N Y; Rudolf Zwir-
    ner Gallery, Cologne, Ger; Fey & Northelfer Gallery, Berlin,
    Ger.
Commissions: Nude female figure, William Kaufman Bldg, New
    York, N Y, 71; seated negro youth, Countess Susanna Ratazzi,
    New York.
Exhibitions: Whitney Mus Am Art Ann, New York, 70; Sharp Focus
    Realism, Sidney Janis Gallery, New York, 71; New Realism, Old
    Realism-Oanenburg & Roman Contemporaries, New York, 71;
    Paris Biennale, France, 71; Documenta 5, Kassel, Ger, 72; plus
    other group & one-man shows.
Teaching: Asst art, Univ N Mex.
Bibliography: Bodies for sale, Village Voice, 71; The new corn god,
    Time Mag, 72; Udo Kulterman (auth), Radical Realism, 72.
Dealer: O K Harris Gallery, 465 W Broadway, New York, NY 10013.
Mailing Address: 4646 Grove St, Denver, CO 80211.

DE ANGELI, MARGUERITE
    Writer, Illustrator
Preferred Media: Watercolors, Pencil.
b Lapeer, Mich, Mar 14, 89.
Awards: Newberry Medal, 50 & Distinguished Daughter Pa, 58, Am
    Libr Asn; Award, Drexel Univ, 50.
Memberships: Philadelphia Art Alliance.
Publications: Auth & illusr, Black fox of Lorne, 56; ed & illusr, Old
    Testament, 60; auth, Book of nursery & Mother Goose rhymes;
    plus many others.
Mailing Address: 2601 Parkway, Apt 445, Philadelphia, PA 19130.

DEATON, CHARLES
    Sculptor, Architect
Preferred Media: Concrete, Mixed Media.
b Clayton, N Mex, Jan 1, 21.
Commissions: Designs for sculptured bank, Key Savings & Loan,
    Littleton, Colo, 67 & sculptured stadia (with Kivett & Meyers,
    Architects), Jackson Co Sports Complex Auth, 72.
Teaching: Instr design, Franklin Sch Prof Art, 45-48; also lectr
    various art & archit depts, 60-
Bibliography: Len Leddington (auth), Architecture as sculpture, To-
    day Show, NBC TV, 66; Hermine Mariaux (auth), Freedom in
    space, Town & Country, 67; Mary Roblee Henry (auth), Live-in
    sculpture, Vogue, 70.
Publications: Auth, The sculptured house, Art Am, 66.
Mailing Address: Genesee Mountain, Golden, CO 80401.

DE BELLIS, HANNIBAL
    Sculptor, Medalist
Preferred Media: Bronze.
b Accadia, Italy, Sept 22, 94; U S citizen.
Study & Training: Univ Ala, MD, 20; also with Gaetano Cecere, Jean
    De Marco & George Lober.
Work in Public Collections: Navy Art Mus, Navy Combat Mus,
    Pentagon & Smithsonian Inst, Washington, D C; Numismatic Soc;
    Bronze medallions, Rudolph Matas, Tulane Univ Libr, La & R
    Tagore, Consulate India, New York, N Y.
Commissions: Portrait medallions of Adm King, Burke & Richets &
    Navaquila, Navy eagle, U S Navy; Groedal Medal, Am Col Cardiol,
    49; bronze plaques for St Vincent's Hosp & Med Ctr, New York;
    Adm Arleigh Burke Fleet Trophy, Navy Mus, Washington, D C;
    Salmagundi Club Honor Award Medal, 72.
Awards: Salmagundi Sculpture Prizes, 60 & 71; Adm A Burke
    Sculpture Award, 62; Am Artists Prof League Award, 64.
Medalist Memberships: Nat Sculpture Soc; Am Artists Prof League; Salma-
    gundi Club (art cur, 60-).
Mailing Address: 10 Holder Pl, Forest Hills, NY 11375.

DE BLASI, ANTHONY ARMANDO
    Painter
Preferred Media: Acrylics.
b Alcamo, Italy, Jan 1, 33; U S citizen.
Study & Training: Pan Am Sch Art, New York, N Y; Art Stud League
    New York, with Sidney Dickenson & Will Barnet; Univ R I, BA;
    Ind Univ, Bloomington, MFA, with William Bailey, James Mc-
    Garrell, Henry Hope & Albert Elsen.

Work in Public Collections: Riverside Mus Collection, Rose Art
Mus, Brandeis Univ; Wichita State Univ Mus Fine Arts, Kans;
Detroit Art Inst, Mich; Ind Univ, Bloomington; Bethany Col, W Va.
Exhibitions: Midyear show Contemp Am Art, Butler Inst, Youngs-
town, Ohio, 67; Penthouse Exhib, Mus Mod Art, New York, 68;
Exhib Permanent Collection, Riverside Mus, New York, 70; one-
man shows, Spectrum Gallery, New York, 68, 69 & 71 & Detroit
Art Inst, 72.
Teaching: Chmn & artist-in-residence, Washington & Jefferson Col,
63-66; assoc. prof. painting & drawing, Mich State Univ, 66-
Awards: Louis Comfort Tiffany Found grant, 66-67; first prize,
Exhib Am Art, Chatauqua Art Asn, 67; Founders Purchase Prize,
Detroit Art Inst, 70.
Bibliography: Emily Wasserman (auth), review, In: Artforum, 4/68;
Rita Simon (auth), review 4/68 & Atirnomis (auth), review,
12-1/70, In: Arts Mag.
Memberships: Col Art Asn Am; Midwest Col Art Asn; Art Stud
League New York.
Dealer: Spectrum Gallery, 464 W Broadway, New York, NY 10012.
Mailing Address: Dept Art, Michigan State University, East Lansing,
MI 48223.

DE BORHEGYI, STEPHAN
Museum Director, Writer
b Budapest, Hungary, Oct 17, 21.
Study & Training: Péter Pazmány Univ, Budapest, PhD; Yale Univ,
fel.
Collections Arranged: Primitive Art, Milwaukee, 60; Pre-Columbian
Arts of Peru, Milwaukee, 61; Art in Ivory, Milwaukee; Underwa-
ter Archaeology traveling exhib, 63; Polish Folk Art, 63; Arts
of the Ancient Mayas, 64; plus many others.
Teaching: Lectr pre-Columbian art, folk art & Maya art & archit;
prof anthrop, San Carlos Univ Guatemala, 49-51; asst prof an-
throp, Univ Okla, 54-59; former lectr & prof anthrop, Univ Wis-
Milwaukee; former instr, Marquette Univ.
Positions: Asst cur, Hungarian Nat Mus Sci & Hist, 47-48; dir,
Stovall Mus, Univ Okla, 54-59; dir, Milwaukee Pub Mus, 59-71.
Awards: Dipl of merit for reorganization of Guatemalan Nat Mus,
Guatemalan Govt, 51.
Memberships: Am Anthrop Asn; Soc Am Archaeol; Am Asn Mus;
Span Colonial Arts Soc; fel Royal Anthrop Soc Gt Brit & Ireland;
plus others.
Publications: Contribr, American university museums, Mus J, 56,
The Spanish colonial art museum of Guatemala, Mus, 56, The
public relations function in American colleges and university
museums, Museologist, 56, Aqualung archaeology, Natural Hist
Mag, 58 & A primitive art exhibit, Curator, Vol 4, No 1; plus
others.
Mailing Address: 2370 N Terrace Ave, Milwaukee, WI 53211.

DE BOTTON, JEAN PHILIPPE
Painter, Sculptor
Preferred Media: Oils.
French & U S citizen.
Study & Training: Ecole Beaux-Arts, Paris, France; Sorbonne,
Paris; Rollins Col, PhB; also with Antoine Bourdelle, Georges
Braque & Jules Romains.
Work in Public Collections: Metrop Mus Art, New York, N Y; Mus
Art Mod, Paris; Albertina Mus, Vienna, Austria; Dallas Mus Art,
Tex; Wallraff-Richards, Cologne, Ger; plus others.
Commissions: Paris Int Expos (painting), Fr Govt, 25; Seine River
Bridge (painting), Int Paris Colonial Exhib, 37; HM King George
VI, Coronation at Westminster Abbey (painting), HM King George
VI, Eng, 38; San Francisco War Mem Poster, City San Fran-
cisco, 42; America at War with H J Kaiser, San Francisco City
for Marine Mus, 45.
Exhibitions: Carnegie Int, Pittsburgh, Pa, 32 & 38; Brit Empire
Bldg, New York, 37; Knoedler & Wildenstein Galleries, New York
& Paris, 39 & 56; Calif Palace of Legion of Honor, San Fran-
cisco, 45.
Teaching: Prof fresco, Ecole Beaux-Arts, Paris, 32-37; prof paint-
ing, Acad Montmartre, Paris, 32-38; prof fine arts, Acad Mont-
martre, New York, 57-59.
Awards: Grand Prix, Salon Honneur Beaux-Arts, Fr Govt, 25 &
Grand Prix, Expos Int, Paris, Fr Govt, 37; City Honor, Scran-
ton, Pa, 70.
Bibliography: A Frankenstein (auth), Jean de Botton, Calif Palace
Legion of Honor Publ, 45; Frank Elgar (auth), Jean de Botton,
Georges Fall, Paris, 68; Eric Newton (auth), Jean de Botton,
Parrish Art Mus, 70.
Memberships: Salon Autonme Paris (jury mem, 28-); Salon Mod
Paris (v pres, 37-); Salon France Nouvelle (pres, 38); Nat Soc
Mural Painters (bd dirs, 68-69); Am Fedn Arts.
Research: Chiaroscuro killed painting, Cezanne revived it; modern
conception and the approach to contemporary art; French art
through the ages; the art of the fresco through the ages.

Collection: El Greco, The Last Supper, Venitian period, signed
Theodocopoulis.
Publications: Auth, Fou-Fou discovers America, San Francisco, 45;
auth, Triumph of Hope (ballet), San Francisco Opera, 45.
Dealers: M Knoedler & Co, E 70th St, New York, N Y 10021; Dal-
zell-Hatfield Galleries, Ambassador Box K, Los Angeles, CA
90070.
Mailing Address: 930 Fifth Ave, New York, NY 10021.

DE BRUN, ELSA, see NUALA

DE CESARE, SAM
Sculptor, Painter
b New York, N Y, May 31, 20.
Study & Training: N Y Univ, BSEd & MA; also with Ruth Canfield &
Oliver Connor Barrett.
Work in Public Collections: Springfield Mus Art, Mo.
Commissions: War Mem Murals, John Jay High Sch, New York, 67-
69.
Exhibitions: YMHA, New York, 47 & 48; ACA Gallery, New York, 49-
51; Audubon Artists, 52; Springfield Mus Art, 54; Med Benefit
Fund Exhib, Flower Fifth Ave Hosp, 63; plus others.
Teaching: Lectr sculpture & art appreciation.
Positions: Chmn indust arts, New York Secondary Schs; tech adv,
Yorkville Housing Comn, N Y, 56-57; mem comt indust arts, Bd
Educ, New York, 57-58; chmn, standing Adv Comt Indust Arts,
New York, 60-62.
Awards: Soc Four Arts Award, Palm Beach, 44; purchase award,
Springfield Mus Art, 45; Grumbacher Award, Long Island Univ,
63.
Memberships: Indust Arts N Y (chmn); Asn Supvr & Adminr.
Publications: Co-auth, tech manuals for USNR, 42-45 & General
crafts course of study, New York Bd Educ, 48.
Mailing Address: 9-05 150th St, Whitestone, NY 11357.

de CHAMPLAIN, VERA CHOPAK
Painter
Preferred Media: Oils, Watercolors.
b Ger; U S citizen.
Study & Training: Art Stud League New York; spec studies with
Edwin Dickinson.
Work in Public Collections: Permanent Collection of Fusco Galler-
ies, New York, N Y & in collections abroad.
Exhibitions: Interlaken, Switz, 66; Rudolph Gallery, Wood-
stock, N Y, 67; Seamen's Bank for Savings, New York, New
York, 69; Artists Equity Gallery, New York, 70 & 72; Fontaine-
bleau Gallery, New York, 72.
Teaching: Art dir & instr oil painting, Emanu-El Ctr, 10 E 66th St,
New York, 68-
Positions: Art chmn, Nat Soc Arts & Lett, Empire State, 69-
Awards: Second prize, Twilight & Onteora Club, Haines Falls,
N Y, 65.
Bibliography: Samuel M La Corte (auth), Creative Images, Clifton
Leader, 70.
Memberships: Fel Royal Soc Arts; Artists Equity Asn New York;
Kappa Pi; Int Platform Asn; Art Stud League New York.
Mailing Address: 230 Riverside Dr, New York, NY 10025.

DECHAR, PETER
Painter
Preferred Media: Oils.
b New York, N Y, Apr 19, 42.
Work in Public Collections: Mus Mod Art, New York; Whitney Mus
Am Art, New York; Larry Aldrich Mus, Conn; Walker Art Ctr,
Chicago, Ill; Fiberglass Tower Art Collection.
Exhibitions: Highlights from the 1967 Season, Larry Aldrich Mus,
Conn, 67; Contemp Painting & Sculpture, Krannert Art Mus, 67;
Whitney Mus Am Art Ann, New York, 67 & 69; one-man show,
Cordier & Ekstrom Gallery, New York, 67 & 69; Twentieth Cen-
tury Art from the Rockefeller Collection, Mus Mod Art, New
York, 69
Dealer: Cordier & Ekstrom Gallery, 980 Madison Ave, New York,
NY 10021.
Mailing Address: 169 Garfield Pl, Brooklyn, NY 11215.

DE CHRISTOPHER, EUGENE LOUIS
Sculptor, Designer
Preferred Media: Wood, Metal, Plexiglas.
b Philadelphia, Pa, Jan 1, 18.
Study & Training: Philadelphia Col Art, sculpture with Renzetti;
Pratt Inst, New York, N Y; Art Stud League New York; also sculp-
ture with family, Avalino, Italy.
Work in Public Collections: Gilbert Galleries, San Francisco, Calif;
multiples, Knoll Int & Mus Mod Art; Pace Gallery, New York.
Exhibitions: Gilbert Galleries; Bank Am Gallery, San Francisco;
Pace Gallery, 72.

Teaching: Instr art appreciation, Northeast Cath High Sch, Philadephia, 36-39; instr design, Calif Inst Art, 61.
Positions: Independent graphic designer, 47-; creative dir, Creative Playthings, 61-63.
Awards: Graphics awards, for prod design, Archit Forum, 67 & Gold Medal, Paperboard Packaging Coun, 71; plus others.
Dealer: Pace Gallery, 115 E 23rd St, New York, NY 10010.
Mailing Address: Box 658, Belvedere, CA 94920.

DE COSTA, ARTHUR (ARCHANGELO)
Painter, Lecturer
Preferred Media: Oils.
b New York, N Y, Aug 19, 21.
Study & Training: Univ Pa; Pa Acad Fine Arts.
Work in Public Collections: Pa Acad Fine Arts; Woodmere Art Gallery, Chestnut Hill, Pa; Philadelphia Col Textiles & Sci.
Exhibitions: Philadelphia Mus Art, 62; Pa Acad Fine Arts Ann, 64; Nat Acad Design Ann Exhib, New York, 65; Wilmington Arts Ann, 65; one-man show, Peale House Gallery, 69.
Teaching: Instr painting & drawing, Pa Acad Fine Arts, 65-, lectr painting procedures, 70-; lectr, Norristown Art League, 68-70; lectr painting procedures, Chestnut Hill Col & Studio Group, Wilmington, Del, 70-
Research: Materials and procedures for classic painting techniques.
Dealer: Pearl Fox Gallery, 103 Windsor Ave, Philadelphia, PA 19126.
Mailing Address: 336 S Juniper St, Philadelphia, PA 19107.

DE COUX, JANET
Sculptor
Preferred Media: Stone, Wood.
b Niles, Mich.
Study & Training: Carnegie Inst Technol, two yrs; N Y Sch Indust Design; R I Sch Design; Art Inst Chicago; asst to C Paul Jennewein, A B Cianfarani, Gozo Kawamura, Alvin Meyer & James Earl Fraser.
Work in Public Collections: Many in private collections.
Commissions: William Penn, William Penn Mem Mus, Harrisburg, Pa; Madonna (black granite), Manhasset, Long Island, N Y; St Benedict, St Vincent's Archabbey, Latrobe, Pa; St Benedict sculpture proj, Liturigcal Art Soc; five pieces sculpture, St Scholastica's Church, Aspinwall, Pa; plus many others.
Exhibitions: One-man show, Carnegie Inst; Artist of Year Show, Arts & Crafts Ctr, Univ Pittsburgh; plus many other group shows.
Teaching: Resident instr art, Cranbrook Acad Art, 42-45.
Awards: Guggenheim fel; Widener Gold Medal, Pa Acad Fine Arts; Lindsay Mem prize, Nat Sculpture Soc; plus many others.
Memberships: Nat Acad Design; Nat Sculpture Soc; Pittsburgh Assoc Artists.
Mailing Address: Gibsonia, PA 15044.

DE CREEFT, JOSE
Sculptor, Educator
Preferred Media: Stone, Marble.
b Guadalajara, Spain, Nov 27, 84; U S citizen.
Study & Training: Acad Julien, Paris, France, 06; Maison Greber, Paris, 11-14.
Work in Public Collections: Mus Mod Art, New York, N Y; Whitney Mus Am Art, New York; Philadelphia Mus Art, Pa; Smithsonian Inst, Washington, D C; Metrop Mus Art, New York; plus others.
Commissions: Soldier War Mem (granite), Saugues, Puy de Dome, France, 18; 200 sculptures in stone, Forteleza de Ramonje, Mallorca, Spain, 27-29; Alice in Wonderland (bronze group), Delacorte Found, Cent Park, New York, 59; Nurses (mosaic mural), Bronx Munic Hosp, N Y, 62; The Gift of Health to Mankind (bronze relief), Pub Health Lab, Bellevue Hosp, New York, 67.
Exhibitions: El Circulo Bellas Artes, Madrid, Spain, 03; Artists for Victory, Metrop Mus Art, New York, 42; Critics Choice, Armory Show, New York, 45; U S Contemporary Art, Moscow, U S S R, 59; Festival of the Arts, Rose Garden, White House, Washington, D C, 65.
Teaching: Instr sculpture, New Sch Social Res, 32-39 & 57-65; instr sculpture, Art Stud League New York, 44-
Awards: First prize for Maternity, Artist for Victory, Metrop Mus Art, 42; G D Widener Mem Gold Medal for portrait of Rachmaninoff, Pa Acad Fine Arts, 45; Ford Found Retrospective Traveling Show (13 U S mus), 59-60.
Bibliography: Robert Hanson (auth), Jose de Creeft (film), CBS Camera 3, 67; Alfredo Gomez-Gil (auth), Cerebros Espanoles en U S A, 71; Jules Campos (auth), Jose de Creeft, 72.
Memberships: Am Acad Arts & Lett; Audubon Artists (v pres, 58); fel Nat Inst Arts & Lett; academician Nat Acad Design (v pres, 72); founding mem Sculptors Guild (exec bd, 40, v pres, 58); plus others.
Mailing Address: c/o Kennedy Galleries, Inc, 20 E 56th St, New York, NY 10022.

DE DIEGO, JULIO
Painter, Illustrator
Preferred Media: Oils, Watercolors, Tempera, Metals, Jewelry.
b Madrid, Spain, May 9, 00; U S citizen.
Study & Training: Study in Madrid, Paris & Rome.
Work in Public Collections: Metropolitan Mus Art, New York, N Y; Washington Univ, St Louis, Mo; Montclair Art Mus, N J; Encycl Britannica, New York; Santa Barbara Mus Art, Calif; plus others.
Commissions: Murals & chapel doors, St Gregory Church, Chicago, Ill, 29; Bullfight (mural), Hotel Sherman, Chicago, 33; Fort Sheridan (mural), Fort Sheridan, Chicago, 36; Story of Wine (mural), Hotels Ambassador & Sherman, Chicago, 37; metal sculptures & murals, Ling Nang Restaurant, New York, 59; also many others.
Exhibitions: One-man show, Art Inst Chicago, 35; Surrealist Exhib, Paris, France & London, Eng, 47; Int Cult Affairs Exhib, Dept of State, Paris, London & Rome, 48; Pa Acad Fine Arts; Philadelphia & Carnegie Inst, Pittsburgh, Pa, several yrs; plus others.
Teaching: Prof painting, Art Inst Chicago, 39-40; prof painting, Univ Denver, 48-52; prof painting, Artist Equity Workshop, 55-57; plus others.
Awards: First prize, Men & Steel Show, 54 & first prize, Cotton Exhib, 56, Birmingham Mus, Ala; first prize for The Figure, Arvida Corp, Sarasota, Fla, 71; plus others.
Bibliography: Bruce Henderson (auth), He paints weird war & peace, Life Mag, 46; Ralph M Pearson (auth), Julio de Diego work shop, Desingne, 50; Bruce Barton (auth), 38 views of the Armada, Time Mag, 62; plus others.
Memberships: Artist Equity Asn New York (pres); Sarasota Artist Asn.
Collection: African, Mexican, Indian toys and artifacts; imaginative junk.
Publications: Auth, Comentaries: Europe 1952, Col Art J, 52; illusr, Have you seen birds . . . ?, 68; illusr, A stranger in the Spanish village, 64; auth, The book of ah!, 70; auth, Cuckoo heads, 71.
Dealer: Frank J Oehlscchlaeger, 107 E Oak St, Chicago, IL 60611 & 28 Blvd of the Presidents, St Armands Key, Sarasota, FL 33578.
Mailing Address: 2235 Alameda Ave, Sarasota, FL 33580.

DEDINI, ELDON LAWRENCE
Cartoonist
b King City, Calif, June 29, 21.
Study & Training: Hartnell Col, AA; Chouinard Art Inst, Los Angeles, Calif.
Work in Public Collections: Achenbach Collection, Legion of Hon, San Francisco, Calif; Libr of Cong, Washington, D C; N Y Univ, New York.
Exhibitions: Nat Cartoonists Soc Group Exhib, New York; Int Cartoonale, Heist-Duinbergen, Belgium, 64-66; 3 Cartoonists Show, Richmond Art Mus, Calif, 68.
Positions: Cartoonist, Salinas-Index-Jour, Calif, 40-42; story cartoonist, Walt Disney Studios, Burbank, Calif, 44-46; cartoonist-gagman, Esquire, Inc, Chicago, Ill, 46-50; cartoonist, New Yorker Mag, N Y, 50-; cartoonist, Playboy Inc, Chicago, 60-
Awards: Best mag cartoonist, Nat Cartoonist Soc, 58, 61 & 64.
Memberships: Nat Cartoonists Soc; Mag Cartoonists Guild (second v pres, 71).
Publications: Contribr, Esquire, 43-50; contribr, The New Yorker, 50-72; contribr, Playboy Mag, 60-72; auth, The Dedini Gallery, 61 & illusr, La clef, 70, Holt.
Mailing Address: P O Box 1630, Monterey, CA 93940.

DE DONATO, LOUIS JOHN
Painter
Preferred Media: Oils.
b Bronx, N Y, Aug 29, 34.
Study & Training: Art Stud League New York, with Frank J Reilly.
Work in Public Collections: Uplands Gallery of Grafton, Vt.
Exhibitions: Acad Artists Asn, Springfield, Mass, 67; 72nd Ann Oil Show, Nat Arts Club, New York, N Y, 70; Salmagundi Club, New York, 71; Allied Artists Am, New York, 71; Am Artists Prof League, New York, 71.
Awards: Acad Artists Asn Award, 67; Grumbacher Award, 72nd Ann Oil Show, Nat Arts Club, 70; first prize, Salmagundi Club Auction, 72.
Memberships: Salmagundi Club (co-chmn scholar comt, 71-72); Allied Artists Am; Am Artists Prof League; Acad Artists Asn; life mem Art Stud League New York; plus others.
Mailing Address: 247 W 72nd St, New York, NY 10023.

DEE, LEO JOSEPH
Painter
Preferred Media: Oils.
b Newark, N J, July 8, 31.
Study & Training: Newark Sch Fine & Indust Art, dipl, with Hans Weingartner, Benjamin Cunningham, James Rosati & Ruben Nakian.

Work in Public Collections: Newark Mus Art; Springfield Mus Art, Mass; Cooper-Hewitt Mus, New York, N Y; Fannie E Rippel Found, Newark.

Exhibitions: 6 exhibs, N J Artists, 58-71 & Arts Festival, 59, Newark Mus; Drawing Soc Regional, Philadelphia Mus & Nat (circulated by Am Fedn Arts), 65-66; Meticulous Realism, Tawes Art Ctr, Univ Md, 66; Art from New Jersey & other exhibs, N J State Mus, Trenton, 66-70; Fourth Invitational Painting & Sculpture, Van Deusen Gallery, Kent State Univ, 70.

Teaching: Instr drawing & painting, Newark Sch Fine & Indust Art, 58-

Bibliography: William H Gerdts (auth), Painting and sculpture in New Jersey, Vol 24, In: New Jersey Historical Series, Van Nostrand Reinhold, 64 & 150 years of American still life painting, Coe Kerr Gallery, 70.

Dealer: Coe Kerr Gallery, 49 E 82nd St, New York, NY 10028.

Mailing Address: 38 Ridgewood Terr, Maplewood, NJ 07040.

DEERING, ROGER
Painter, Lecturer
b East Waterboro, Maine, Feb 2, 04.
Study & Training: Grad Sch Fine Arts, Portland Soc Art; also with Wayman Adams, Penrhyn Stanlaws, Aldro Hibbard, Anson Cross, George Elmer Browne & Jay Connaway.
Work in Public Collections: Irving Trust Co, N Y; Gorham State Teachers Col, Maine; Woodsfords Congregational Church, Portland; Ennis Libr, Farmington, Maine; Newcomen Soc Eng in N Am; plus others.
Commissions: Murals, Portland & Scarboro Beach.
Exhibitions: Salmagundi Club, 52-69; Rockport Art Asn, 59-69; Am Artists Prof League, 53-58, 65 & 68; Univ Maine Art Dept Traveling Exhibs, 64-69 & Univ Maine Gallery, 67-69; Old Bergen Art Guild Traveling Exhib, N J, 69-70; plus many other group & one-man shows.
Teaching: Lectr marine painting; instr & dir, Roger Deering Studio-Gallery & Sch Outdoor Painting; former instr landscape & painting, Kennebunkport, Maine & Pinehurst, N C.
Positions: Maine state chap chmn, Am Artists Prof League, 38-, mem adv bd.
Awards: Prizes, Rockport Art Asn, 60-63; paintings selected for reproduction on calendar of prize winning paintings, N Y Life Ins Co, 61, 62 & 68; prize, Copley Soc Boston, 63; plus others.
Memberships: Rockport Art Asn; Grand Cent Art Gallery; Copley Soc Boston; Salmagundi Club; Am Artists Prof League; plus others.
Mailing Address: Ocean Ave, Kennebunkport, ME 04046.

DEFENBACHER, DANIEL S
Designer, Lecturer
b Dover, Ohio, May 22, 06.
Study & Training: Carnegie Inst; Ind Univ; Lawrence Col, hon DFA, 50.
Teaching: Lectr mod art & mus admin.
Positions: Asst to nat dir, Fed Art Proj, Works Proj Admin, 36-39; dir, Walker Art Ctr, Minneapolis, Minn, 39-51; dir, Fort Worth Art Ctr, Tex, 51-54; mem exec comt, Int Design Conf, 51-; pres, Calif Col Arts & Crafts, Oakland, 54-57; mgt consult design & assoc, Victor Gruen Assoc, Architects, Beverly Hills, Calif, 57-59; dir design & commun, Raychem Corp, Menlo Park, Calif, 59-
Awards: Carnegie fel, 29-30.
Publications: Ed, Jades, 44 & American Watercolor and Winslow Homer, 45; auth, Watercolor—U S A; contribr, Sch Arts, Better Design & others.
Mailing Address: Raychem Corp, 300 Constitution Dr, Menlo Park, CA 94025.

DE FOIX-CRENASCOL, LOUIS
Art Historian, Art Administrator
b Italy, June 2, 21; U S citizen.
Study & Training: Maffeo Vegio State Col, Italy, MA; Pontif Univ St Anselm, Rome, LL D; Inst Archaeol & Art Hist, Univ Rome, dipl, with Cesare Brandi.
Collections Arranged: Joseph Stella Retrospective, 64, Haitian Artists, 65 & Religion in the Art of Haiti, 68, Seton Hall Univ.
Teaching: Prof art hist, Seton Hall Univ, 61-, chmn dept art, 68-
Positions: Inspector antiquities & fine art, Ital Govt, 53-57. Dir art Gallery, Seton Hall Univ, 63-
Awards: Fulbright scholar, 65.
Memberships: Asn Int Archeol Classique; Col Art Asn Am; Soc Archit Historians.
Research: Italian Renaissance painting and architecture; Indian and Tantric art.
Publications: Co-auth, Franchino Gaffurio (1451-1522), 51; auth, The Pallavicino chorals and the Lombard miniature of the 15th century, 55; auth, The incoronata of Lodi, 56; also contribr to many Europ & Am art jour & mag.
Mailing Address: Dept of Art, Seton Hall University, South Orange, NJ 07079.

DeFOREST, JULIE MORROW
Painter, Writer
Preferred Media: Oils.
b New York, N Y.
Study & Training: Wellesley Col, AB; Columbia Univ, AM.
Work in Public Collections: Wellesley Col Collection, Mass; Cincinnati Mus Art Permanent Collection, Ohio; Univ Cincinnati Permanent Collection; Aurora Mus, Ind; Nat Women's Fedn Clubs.
Exhibitions: Newhouse Galleries, New York; Milch Galleries, New York; Loring Andrews Gallery, Cincinnati; Classons' Gallery, Cincinnati; one-man shows, Cincinnati & New York.
Awards: Award for Landscape (painting), Cincinnati Mus Art, Women's Art Club; citation, Dict Int Biography, London, Eng; two regional poetry awards, Col Club Cincinnati.
Memberships: Allied Artists Am; Nat Arts Club; Prof Artists Cincinnati; MacDowell Soc, Cincinnati; Cincinnati Mus Art Asn.
Mailing Address: Vernon Manor Hotel, Suite 303, Oak St & Burnet Ave, Cincinnati, OH 45219.

DE FOREST, ROY DEAN
Painter, Sculptor
b North Platte, Nebr, Feb 11, 30.
Study & Training: Yakima Jr Col, 48-50; Calif Sch Fine Arts, 50-52; San Francisco State Col, BA, MA.
Work in Public Collections: San Francisco Mus Art, Calif; Art Inst Chicago, Ill; Oakland Art Mus, Calif; Joslyn Art Mus, Omaha, Neb; Crocker Art Mus, Sacramento, Calif.
Exhibitions: Third Biennial São Paulo, Brazil, 55; Int Exhib Pioneer Galleries, Lausanne Mus Cantonal Beaux Arts, Switz, 66; West Coast Now, group exhibs at Portland, Ore, San Francisco & Los Angeles, Calif, 68; 1969 Biennial Painting & Sculpture, Univ Ill, 69; The Spirit of the Comics, Am Fedn Arts, Philadelphia, 70-71; plus many other group & one-man shows.
Teaching: Instr painting & drawing, Calif Col Arts & Crafts, 63-65; assoc prof painting & drawing, Univ Calif, Davis, 65-
Positions: Dir, Larsen Gallery, Yakima Jr Col, 58-60.
Awards: Purchase prize, Oakland Art Mus, Bay Printmakers Soc, 56; Neallie Sullivan award, San Francisco Art Asn, 64; purchase prize, La Jolla Art Mus, 65.
Bibliography: Article, In: Art Int, Vol 12; Thomas Allbright (auth), Wildest of funk art, San Francisco Chronicle, 2/6/69; Charles Johnson (auth), The new symbolism, Sacramento Bee, 4/13/69.
Memberships: San Francisco Art Asn (chmn artists coun, 64).
Dealers: Hansen-Fuller Gallery, 228 Grant Ave, San Francisco, CA 94108; Allan Frumkin Gallery, 41 E 57th St, New York, NY 10022.
Mailing Address: P O Box 47, Port Costa, CA 94569.

de GARTHE, WILLIAM EDWARD
Painter, Sculptor
Preferred Media: Oils.
b Finland, Apr 14, 07; Can citizen.
Study & Training: Studied art in Montreal.
Work in Public Collections: Oil painting, Mt Allison Univ, Sackville, N B; painting & sculpture, Art Stud League New York; life class painting, Acad Belle Art, Rome, Italy; oil painting, Acad Grande Chaueière, Paris, France; Acad Julian, Paris; plus others in pvt collections.
Exhibitions: One-man shows at Montreal, Toronto, Rothesay, Fla, West Indies & others; group shows, Royal Soc Marine Painters, London, Eng, also in Europe, West Indies, Can & U S A.
Awards: Various awards.
Memberships: Int Platform Asn; fel Int Inst Art & Lett; Nova Scotia Mus Fine Arts (past pres); Am Artist Prof League; Royal Soc Marine Painters.
Publications: Auth, Painting the sea & auth, This is Peggy's Cove.
Mailing Address: Ocean Gallery, Peggy's Cove, Nova Scotia, Can.

DE GERENDAY, LACI ANTHONY
Sculptor
Preferred Media: Wood, Bronze.
b Budapest, Hungary, Aug 17, 11.
Study & Training: S Dak Sch Mines & Technol; Ursinus Col; Nat Acad Design; Beaux Arts Inst, New York, N Y.
Work in Public Collections: Salle D'Honneur, Mus Africa, Algiers; Adm Farragut Medal, N Y Univ Hall of Fame Mus.
Commissions: Wood reliefs, Fed Govt, Tell City, Ind, 39 & Aberdeen, S Dak, 41; gold medal, Soc Electrical Engrs, 60; bronze relief, St Francis of Assisi Sch, Torrington, Conn, 65; bronze medal, N Y Univ Hall of Fame, 70.

Exhibitions: Pa Mus, Philadelphia; Acad Arts & Lett, New York,
N Y; Nat Acad Design, New York; Smithsonian Inst, Washington,
D C; Gold Medal Exhib, Archit League, New York.
Awards: Ellen Speyer Awards, Nat Acad Design, 47 & 63; Lindsey
Morris Mem Awards, Nat Sculpture Soc, 55 & Allied Artists
Am, 69.
Memberships: Fel Nat Sculpture Soc; Allied Artists Am.
Mailing Address: 22-27 76th St, Jackson Heights, NY 11370.

DE GRAAFF, MR & MRS JAN
Collectors, Patrons
Collection: Structurist, Barbizon paintings and sculpture.
Mailing Address: 14 Sutton Pl S, New York, NY 10022.

DE GRAZIA, ETTORE TED
Painter
b Morenci, Ariz, June 14, 09.
Study & Training: Univ Ariz, BA, 44, BS & MA, 45.
Work in Public Collections: Way of the Cross (paintings depicting
fifteen stations of the cross); Kino Collection (scenes from life of
Jesuit priest Father Eusebio Kino).
Commissions: Los Ninos (painting), reproduced as UNICEF greet-
ing card, 60.
Exhibitions: Numerous one-man shows, 32-
Awards: Achievement award, Univ Ariz, 68.
Publications: Auth, Yaqui Easter, 68, The Seri Indians, 70, M-Col-
lection, 71 & De Grazia and his mountain the Superstition, 72;
works have appeared in Ariz Hwys & other maj publs.
Mailing Address: 6300 N Swan, Tucson, AZ 85718.

DEHNER, DOROTHY
Sculptor, Printmaker
Preferred Media: Bronze.
b Cleveland, Ohio.
Study & Training: Univ Calif, Los Angeles; Skidmore Col, BS; Art
Stud League New York, with Nicolaides, K H Miller & Jan
Matulka; Atelier 17, New York, N Y.
Work in Public Collections: Metrop Mus Art & Mus Mod Art, New
York; Seattle Art Mus, Wash; Minn Art Mus, Minneapolis; Mun-
son-Williams-Proctor Inst, Utica, N Y.
Commissions: Aluminum grill, 59 & bronze room divider, 61, James
Marston Fitch, Stony Point, N Y; plexiglas relief, Great South-
west Indust Park, Atlanta, Ga, 68; plexiglas relief, New York
Med Col, Valhalla, N Y, 72; bronze sculpture, Union Camp Corp,
Wayne, N J, 72.
Exhibitions: Whitney Mus Am Art, New York, 49-63; Recent Sculp-
ture, Mus Mod Art, New York, 60; Hirshhorn Collection, Guggen-
heim Mus, New York, 61; Carnegie Inst Ann, 63; one-man retro-
spective, Jewish Mus, N Y, 65; plus others.
Awards: First prize for sculpture, Kane Mem Exhib, Providence,
65; Tamarind Lithography Inst Artist-in-Residence, 70-71; Yaddo
Found fel, 71.
Memberships: Sculptor's Guild (bd mem, 60-62); Fedn Mod Paint-
ers & Sculptors; Artists Equity Asn.
Publications: Auth, Buying art, 47 & Review of exhibition of
oceanic art, Mus Mod Art, 48, Archit Forum; auth, Making &
fabricating plexiglas sculpture, 68 & John Graham, 69,
Leonardo; auth, Foreword for John Graham's system & dialec-
tics of art, John Hopkins Press, 71.
Dealer: Marian Willard, 29 E 72nd St, New York, NY 10021.
Mailing Address: 33 Fifth Ave, New York, NY 10003.

DE HOYOS, LUIS
Collector
b New York, N Y, Mar 6, 21.
Study & Training: Colage Univ, BA, 43.
Collection: Contemporary Latin American paintings; lithographs of
Orozco, Rivera, Siqueiros; paintings and drawings of Covarrubias
of primitive art objects, exhibited at the Museum of Primitive
Art, New York; Guerrero stone sculpture, circulated by the
American Federation of Arts.
Mailing Address: 30 Lake St, Monticello, NY 12701.

DE ICAZA, FRANCISCO, see ICAZA

DE JONG, GERRIT, JR
Educator, Writer
b Amsterdam, Netherlands, Mar 20, 92.
Study & Training: Univ Utah, AB, 20, MA, 25; Nat Univ Mex, 21;
Stanford Univ, PhD, 33; Univ Munich.
Positions: Pub lectr art appreciation, Brigham Young Univ, 25-,
dean Col Fine Arts, 25-59, lectr aesthetics, 40-; dir, Centro
Cult Brasil-Estados Unidos, Santos, 47-48.
Awards: Distinguished Serv Arts & Lett, Utah Acad Sci, Arts & Lett,
53; David O McKay Humanities Award, Brigham Young Univ, 72.
Memberships: Fel Utah Acad Sci, Arts & Lett (pres, 48); Coun
Latin Am Studies.

Research: Art appreciation.
Publications: Auth, An approach to modernity in art, 50; auth, Art
in Brazil, Brazil, portrait of half a continent, 50; auth, The quest
for beauty, Instr, 5/63; auth, Evolution of art in Brazil, 72 &
auth, Brazilian architecture, 72, Modern Brazil.
Mailing Address: 640 N University Ave, Provo, UT 84601.

DE KANELBA, SITA GOMEZ
Painter
Preferred Media: Acrylics.
b Paris, France, Apr 5, 32; U S citizen.
Study & Training: Parsons Sch Design, New York, N Y.
Work in Public Collections: Art Ctr, South Bend, Ind; Life & Time,
New York.
Commissions: Mural, Wayne Country Club, N J, 65; 20 paintings,
Dorado Beach Hotel, P R, 65; poster for musical Ben Franklin
in Paris, George W George, 66; collage, Ernest Lowenstein, Inc,
New York, 66; mural, Eagle, Fabrics, New York, 69.
Exhibitions: Mus Contemp Crafts, New York; two one-man shows,
Bakerkamp Gallery & Cisneros; Studio Gallery, Alexandria, Va;
J Walter Thompson; Albert White Gallery, Toronto.
Awards: First prize, Nat Competition, Koscuisko Found, New York,
66.
Dealer: Cisneros Gallery, Madison Ave at 92nd St, New York, NY
10021.
Mailing Address: 427 E Ninth St, New York, NY 10009.

DeKAY, JOHN
Painter
b Ithaca, N Y, Apr 8, 32.
Study & Training: Ithaca Col, BS, 55.
Commissions: Portraits, John F Kennedy, Nat Arch, Washington,
D C; painting, President Johnson's Inauguration, Johnson pvt
collection; portrait, Gen Eisenhower, President's Mus, Abilene,
Kans; portrait, Pope Paul VI, Vatican City; portrait, Martin
Luther King, Mrs King; murals, Sterling Forest Conf Ctr.
Exhibitions: Athens, Greece; Paris, France; Madrid, Spain; Spoleto,
Italy & Palm Beach, Fla; paintings of animals & birds publ world-
wide.
Awards: Maurice Fromkes scholar to Segovia, Spain, 61.
Mailing Address: 251 E 51st St, New York, NY 10022.

DEKNATEL, FREDERICK BROCKWAY
Art Historian, Educator
b Chicago, Ill, Mar 9, 05.
Study & Training: Princeton Univ, AB, 28; Harvard Univ, PhD, 35;
Alfred Univ, LHD, 66.
Teaching: Instr & tutor, Harvard Univ, 32-40, assoc prof fine arts,
40-46, chmn dept, 44-49, prof, 46-55, William Dorr Boardman
prof fine arts, 55-
Awards: Knight, First Class, Order of St Olaf, Norway.
Memberships: Col Art Asn Am (pres, 47-48).
Research: Nineteenth and twentieth century painting.
Publications: Auth, Edward Munch, 50.
Mailing Address: 146 Brattle St, Cambridge, MA 02138.

DE KNIGHT, AVEL
Painter
Preferred Media: Gouache, Oils.
b New York, N Y, 33.
Study & Training: Ecole Beaux-Arts, Paris, France; Acad Grande
Chaumiere, Paris; Acad Julien, Paris.
Work in Public Collections: Metrop Mus Art, New York; Walker
Art Inst, Minneapolis, Minn; Norfolk Mus Arts & Sci, Va; Spring-
field Art Mus, Mo; Massillon Art Mus, Ohio.
Exhibitions: Afro-American Artists, Boston Mus Fine Arts, 70;
Black American Artists, Ill Arts Coun, 71; Projected Art/Art-
ists at Work, Finch Col Mus, New York, 71; Nat Acad Design,
New York, 72; Mus Mod Art, New York, 72.
Teaching: Instr painting, Brooklyn Mus Art Sch, 69.
Positions: Art critic, France-Amerique, 58-68.
Awards: Childe Hassam Purchase Awards, Am Acad Arts & Lett,
60 & 70; gold medal grand award, Am Watercolor Soc Centenniel,
67; William A Paton Prize, Nat Acad Design, 67-71.
Memberships: Academician Nat Acad Design; Am Watercolor Soc.
Dealer: Babcock Galleries, 805 Madison Ave, New York, NY 10021.
Mailing Address: 81 Perry St, New York, NY 10014.

de KOLB, ERIC
Collector, Writer
b Vienna, Austria, Mar 10, 16; U S citizen.
Study & Training: Acad Art, Vienna, Austria; Graphic Inst, Vienna;
Archit Acad, Vienna.
Work in Public Collection: Art Mus, Toronto, Can.
Exhibitions: Sculpture, Kleeman Galleries, 63.
Awards: Welsh Award for best graphic package, 53 & 55, prizes, 54
& 55, Package Designer Coun.

Memberships: Art Dir Club; Package Design Coun.
Art Interests: Sculpture in gold.
Collection: Romanesque, Greek, Etruscan & African Art;
  Romanesque Madonnas.
Publications: Auth, Primitive Negro art, 43, African collection, Eric
  de Kolb, 44, Romanesque madonnas, 62, Ashanti goldweights, 70
  & Senufo soothsayer bronzes, 71.
Mailing Address: 1175 Park Ave, New York, NY 10028.

de KOONING, ELAINE MARIE CATHERINE
  Painter, Writer
Preferred Media: Oils.
b New York, N Y, Mar 12, 20.
Study & Training: With Willem de Kooning & Arshile Gorky; Moore
  Col Art, Philadelphia, Pa, DFA; Western Col Women, DFA.
Work in Public Collections: Mus Mod Art, New York, N Y; N Y Univ;
  Elmira Col, N Y; Greenville Mus, S C; Drew Univ, Madison, N J.
Commissions: Portrait of Casey Stengel, Eddie Robinson, Baltimore,
  Md, 58; portrait of Joseph Hirshhorn, commissioned by Mr
  Hirshhorn, 62; portrait of John F Kennedy, Truman Libr, Inde-
  pendence, Mo, 62-63; two portraits of John F Kennedy, John F
  Kennedy Libr, 62-63; portrait of Allen Ginsberg, Channel 13, NET
  TV, 71.
Exhibitions: Fourth Int Exhib, Tokyo, Japan, 54; Sixty American
  Painters, Walker Art Ctr, 60; Carnegie Int, 60; Whitney Mus Am
  Art Ann, New York, 62; Figure Painting, Mus Mod Art, New York,
  63.
Teaching: Prof painting, Yale Univ Grad Sch, 67-68; Mellon chair
  painting, Carnegie-Mellon Univ, 69-70; prof painting, Univ Pa
  Grad Sch, 71-
Awards: Hallmark Award.
Bibliography: In quest of a famous likeness, Life Mag, 64; Lawrence
  Campbell (auth), Elaine de Kooning paints a picture & Rene Arp,
  They're painting their way, Art News.
Memberships: Artists Equity.
Publications: Auth, articles, In: Art News, 49-; auth, three articles,
  In: It Is.
Dealer: Graham Gallery, 1014 Madison Ave, New York, NY 10021.
Mailing Address: 51 Raynor St, Freeport, NY 11520.

DE KOONING, WILLEM
  Painter
b Rotterdam, Holland, Apr 24, 04.
Study & Training: Acad Beeldende Kunsten ed Technische Weten-
  schappen, Amsterdam, 16-24.
Work in Public Collections: Art Inst Chicago; Metrop Mus Art;
  Mus Mod Art; Whitney Mus Am Art; Walker Art Ctr, Minneapo-
  lis, Minn; plus others.
Commissions: Murals, New York World's Fair, 39 & French Line
  Pier (with Fernand Leger), New York, N Y.
Exhibitions: Two Decades of American Painting, Melbourne Nat, 67;
  Frankfurter Kunstverein, Kimpass New York, 68; retrospective,
  Stedelijk Mus, Amsterdam, 68; retrospective, 68 & The New
  American Painting and Sculpture, 69, Mus Mod Art; Whitney
  Mus Am Art Ann, 69 & 70; plus many other group & one-man
  shows.
Teaching: Instr, Black Mt Col, 48; instr, Yale Univ, 50-51.
Awards: Silver medal, Acad Plastic Arts, Rotterdam; Mr & Mrs
  Frank G Logan Medal, Art Inst Chicago, 51; President's Medal,
  63; plus others.
Bibliography: Dore Ashton (auth), included in: The unknown shore,
  Little, 62; Oto Bihalji-Merin (auth), included in: Adventures of
  modern art, Abrams, 66; Gregory Battcock (ed), included in:
  Minimal art: a critical anthology, Dutton, 68; plus others.
Memberships: Nat Inst Arts & Lett.
Publications: Auth, articles, In: popular & prof publ.
Dealer: M Knoedler Co, 21 E 70th St, New York, NY 10021.
Mailing Address: Woodbine Dr, The Springs, East Hampton, Long
  Island, NY 11973.

DE LAMA, ALBERTO
  Painter, Instructor
Preferred Media: Oils.
b Havana, Cuba.
Study & Training: De La Salle Sch, Havana, Cuba; Univ Havana; Am
  Acad Art, Chicago, with William Mosby & Joseph Van den
  Broucke.
Work in Public Collections: Pullman Bank Art Collection, Chicago;
  Home Fed Savings Art Collection, Chicago.
Exhibitions: Third Ann Sports in Art Competition & Exhib, Aber-
  crombie & Fitch & Nat Art Mus Sport, 67; Ill State Fair Prof Art
  Exhib, 67 & 70; Palette & Chisel Acad Fine Arts, 67-72; Munic
  Art League Chicago, 68 & 70.
Teaching: Instr painting & drawing, Am Acad Art, 69-
Awards: Diamond award, 70 & 71 & gold medal, 70, Palette & Chisel
  Acad Fine Arts.

Memberships: Munic Art League Chicago; Palette & Chisel Acad
  Fine Arts (bd dir, 70-).
Dealer: Talisman Gallery, 115 E 12th, Bartlesville, OK 74003.
Mailing Address: P O Box 17, Chicago, IL 60690.

DELANEY, JOSEPH
  Painter, Writer
Preferred Media: Oils.
b Knoxville, Tenn, Sept 13, 04.
Study & Training: Art Stud League New York, N Y, 29-35 & con-
  tinuing educ; N Y Univ, writing with Horce Coohn; also with
  George Bridgeman, Thomas Hart Benton & Alexander Brook.
Work in Public Collections: Nat Gallery, Smithsonian Inst, Washing-
  ton, D C; Univ Ariz, Tucson; Truman Libr, Independence, Mo;
  Huntington Hartford Collection, New York; Univ Tenn, Knoxville.
Commissions: Environment, mural of 126th St & 7th Ave, Harlem
  Mus, New York, 71.
Exhibitions: Ariz Collection, Metrop Mus Art, New York, 42; Con-
  temporary American Painters, Whitney Mus Am Art, New York,
  50; Univ Tenn, Knoxville, 70; Berkshire Mus, Pittsfield, Mass,
  70; Studio Mus, Harlem, 71.
Teaching: Art instr anat, Vt Acad, summer 68.
Positions: Art instr & researcher, Works Progress Admin Fed Art
  Proj, 34-40; researcher, Am Wing, Metrop Mus Art, 36-38 &
  38-39.
Awards: Rosenwald fel, 42.
Bibliography: Evelyn Brown (auth), Artist at work, Horman Found,
  42; Hilton Kramer (auth), article, In: New York Times, 70.
Memberships: Life mem Art Stud League New York; Old Independent
  Art Soc; Bumshell Art Group; Artists Equity Asn.
Research: European museum art work in Paris and London.
Publications: Auth, Dralen Locke, Negro in art, 44; auth, Robert
  Dincus-Witten, Artforum, 70; also articles in Ebony, 68 & New
  York Post, 71.
Mailing Address: 704 Sixth Ave, New York, NY 10010.

DeLAP, TONY
  Sculptor
b Oakland, Calif, Nov 4, 27.
Study & Training: Menlo Jr Col, Calif; Calif Col Arts & Crafts, Oak-
  land; Claremont Grad Sch, Calif.
Work in Public Collections: Whitney Mus Am Art, New York, N Y;
  Walker Art Inst, Minneapolis; San Francisco Mus Art, Calif;
  Mus Mod Art, New York; Tate Gallery, London, Eng.
Commissions: 13 sculptures, Carborundum Abrasive Mkt Awards,
  Niagara Falls, N Y, 69; sculpture-fountain complex, C C H Bldg,
  San Rafael, Calif, 70.
Exhibitions: Whitney Mus Am Art Sculpture Ann, 64 & 66; The Re-
  sponsive Eye, Mus Mod Art, New York, 65; Primary Structures,
  Jewish Mus, New York, 66; Sculpture of the 60s, Los Angeles Co
  Mus Art, 67; West Coast 1945-69, Pasadena Art Mus, 69.
Teaching: Lectr fine arts, Univ Calif, Davis, 63-64; assoc prof fine
  arts, Univ Calif, Irvine, 65-
Positions: Mem, San Francisco Art Comn, 64-65.
Awards: Am Fedn Arts & Ford Found grants, Mus-in-Residence
  Prog, Haverford, Pa; Nealie Sullivan Award, San Francisco Art
  Inst, 64.
Bibliography: John Coplans (auth), DeLap, space and illusion, Art-
  forum, 64; Alan Solomon (auth), Tony DeLap: the last five years,
  Univ Calif, Irvine, 68; Lawrence Alloway (auth), Trio (catalogue),
  Owens-Corning Fiberglass, 70.
Dealer: Nicholas Wilder Gallery, 8225 Santa Monica Blvd, Los Ange-
  les, CA; Robert Elkon Gallery, 1063 Madison Ave, New York, NY
  10028.
Mailing Address: 225 Jasmine St, Corona del Mar, CA 92625.

DeLAURO, JOSEPH NICOLA
  Sculptor, Educator
Preferred Media: Bronze, Marble, Wood, Plastics.
b New Haven, Conn, Mar 10, 16.
Study & Training: Yale Univ, BFA, 41; Univ Iowa, MFA, 47; also in
  Italy, 53, 62, 66 & 71.
Work in Public Collections: Private collections only.
Commissions: Mankato stone sculpture, St Columba Cathedral,
  Youngstown, Ohio, 59; glass & plastic mural, Windsor Bd Educ,
  Ont, 64; bronze sculpture, Hiram Walker & Sons, Ltd, Ont, 67;
  bronze sculpture, Detroit Pub Libr, Mich, 67; bronze sculpture,
  Jewish Community Centre, Windsor, Ont, 70.
Exhibitions: Walker Gallery, Minneapolis, Minn, 47; Mich Regional
  Exhib, Detroit, 48; Ecclestical Art Guild, Detroit, 50; Fine Arts
  Dept Faculty Exhib, Art Gallery Windsor, Ont, 70-72; Biannale
  del Fiorino, Florence, Italy, 71.
Teaching: Prof sculpture & drawing, Marygrove Col, Detroit, 47-59;
  Prof Sculpture & Drawings & head dept, fine arts, Univ Windsor,
  60-
Awards: Alice Kimball fel, 40 & Tiffany Fel, 41 & Elizabeth Pardee
  Scholar, 41, Yale Univ.

Memberships: Fel Royal Soc Arts; Nat Sculpture Soc; Col Art Asn; Mid Am Col Art Asn; Univ Art Asn Can.
Mailing Address: 7560 Bircklan Dr, Plymouth, MI 48170.

DE LAWTER, DR & MRS HILBERT H
Collectors
Study & Training: Dr De Lawter, Indiana Univ, BS, MD.
Positions: Dr De Lawter, primitive acquisitions comt, Detroit Inst Arts, Mich, 66-, exec bd, African art gallery comt, 67-; bd mem, Wayne State Univ Press, Detroit, 67. Mrs De Lawter, exec bd & nominating comt, Friends Mod Art; founders soc & acquisitions comt exec bd, Detroit Inst Art; mem bd, Acquisitions comt, galleries comt, Cranbrook Acad Art; founding mem & past bd mem, Bloomfield Art Asn. Both on exec comt & sponsors of first arts symposium, Oakland Univ, Detroit.
Art Interests: Arranging and exhibiting items from collection in institutions and galleries in Detroit.
Collection: Modern paintings and sculpture; African art; the colorists Louis, Noland, Olitski and others.
Mailing Address: 2081 W Valley Rd, Bloomfield Hills, MI 48013.

DE LEEUW, CATEAU WILHELMINA
Painter, Writer
Preferred Media: Oils, Wood.
b Hamilton, Ohio, Sept 22, 03.
Study & Training: Metrop Art Sch; Art Stud League New York; Acad Grande Chaumiere, Paris.
Exhibitions: One-man shows, New Brit Inst, 30 & N J Col Women, 38 & 42; Am Watercolor Soc, 31; Nat Asn Women Artists, 33; Montclair Art Mus, 33, 34 & 44; N J State Mus, 53 & 54.
Awards: Laura E Hayford Prize, Pen & Brush Club, 34; Citation, for distinguished serv to Ohio through writing for children, Ohioana Libr, 58.
Memberships: Hon mem Plainfield Art Asn (first pres, 27-29); Pen & Brush (second v pres); Am Artists Prof League.
Publications: Illusr, Future for sale, 46; auth, Where valor lies, 59; auth, Give me your hand, 60; auth, Fear in the forest, 60; auth, The turn in the road, 61.
Mailing Address: 1763 Sleepy Hollow Lane, Plainfield, NJ 07060.

DE LEEUW, LEON
Painter, Sculptor
b Paris, France, May 5, 31; U S citizen.
Study & Training: Art Stud League New York, N Y; N Y Univ, with Philip Guston; also with Hans Hofmann.
Exhibitions: N J Artists, N J State Mus, 69; Montclair Artists, Montclair Mus, 70; one-man shows, Montclair Libr, 71, Highgate Gallery, 71 & Fairlong Libr, 71; plus others.
Teaching: Instr painting & sculpture, Wilson Col, 59-60; asst prof painting, sculpture & drawing, Montclair State Col, 63-
Bibliography: Russel Woody (auth), Painting in polymer media (two reproductions of paintings), Van Nostrand Reinhold, 71.
Dealer: Midday Gallery, Six Dean St, Englewood, NJ 07631.
Mailing Address: 317 N Fullerton Ave, Montclair, NJ 07042.

de LESSEPS, TAUNI
Sculptor, Painter
Preferred Media: Bronze, Lacquer.
b Paris, France, Mar 10, 20; U S citizen.
Work in Public Collections: 3 Bronzes in The White House; also works in private collections of Sen Claiborne Pell, Baronne La Caze, Paris, France, Princesa Jose de Baviera y Borbon, Madrid, Spain, Mr & Mrs Nicholas du Pont; plus others.
Commissions: Cranes & Cattails, wrought iron sculpture, Lipton Tea Co, New York, N Y; Headless Horseman, metal, Sleepy Hollow Country Club, Scarborough, N Y; large mural, Scenic View of London, Cumberland Ct, London, Eng; entire collection in solid 18 kt gold & silver for F J Cooper, Philadelphia, Pa.
Exhibitions: Cooper's Int Gallery, San Juan, P R, 68 & Amsterdam, Holland, 69; Lyford Cay Gallery, Nassau, Bahamas, 70 & 71; Palm Beach Galleries, Fla, 71; AGRA Gallery, Washington, D C, 71.
Memberships: Soc Illusr; Nat Art Mus of Sports.
Mailing Address: 535 E 86th St, New York, NY 10028.

DELGADO-GUITART, JOSE
Painter
b Tanger, Spain, Sept 24, 47.
Study & Training: Univ Madrid.
Work in Public Collections: Nommo Gallery, Kampala, Uganda; Galeria Circulo 2, Madrid, Spain; Galeria Catafau, Barcelona, Spain; also many works in private collections.
Exhibitions: One-man shows, Galeria Circulo 2, 70, Galeria Panorama, Lisbon, Portugal, 70, Nommo Gallery, 71 & Franklin & Marshall Col, Lancaster, Pa, 72; Cincinnati Art Mus Group Show, Ohio, 72; plus many other group & one-man shows.

Bibliography: Manuel Morero (auth), Talking about painting, Sol de Espana, 7/70; E Molero Pujos (auth), La inquieta juventud de Jose Delgado-Guitart, Arte.
Memberships: Whitney Mus Am Art; Am Fedn Arts.
Mailing Address: 237 E Market St, York, PA 17403.

DELIHAS, NEVA C
Sculptor
Preferred Media: Plastics.
b New Haven, Conn, Dec 29, 40.
Study & Training: Univ Conn; Southern Conn State Col.
Work in Public Collections: Assoc Univs, Brookhaven Nat Lab, Upton, N Y.
Exhibitions: Huntington Art League Ann, Long Island, N Y, 70-72; Cooperstown Art Asn Ann, N Y, 71; 20th Anniversary Competition in Painting & Sculpture, Berkshire Mus, Pittsfield, Mass, 71; Long Island Artists Alliance 14th Ann, Great Neck, N Y, 72; 23rd Ann New Eng Exhib, Silvermine Guild Artists, New Canaan, Conn, 72; plus many one-woman shows.
Awards: First in sculpture, Huntington Art League, 71; award for sculpture, Long Island Artists Alliance, 72; Silvermine Guild Artists 50th Ann Award, 72.
Memberships: Artists Equity Asn; Long Island Artists Alliance; Guild Hall, East Hampton.
Dealer: Hundred Acres Gallery, 456 W Broadway, New York, NY 10013.
Mailing Address: 25 Locust Rd, Brookhaven, NY 11719.

DE LISIO, MICHAEL
Sculptor
Preferred Media: Terra Cotta, Bronze.
b New York, N Y.
Work in Public Collections: Joseph H Hirshhorn Collection; Minneapolis Inst Arts; Wichita Art Mus, Kans; Christ Church Col, Oxford Univ.
Exhibitions: One-man shows, N S Col Art, Halifax, 69, Hanover Gallery, London, Eng, 70 & Minneapolis Inst Arts, 71; Acquisitions Show, Wichita Art Mus, 71.
Bibliography: Ralph Pomeroy (auth), Literary figures, Art & Artists, 7/70; Anthony Clark (auth), Michael de Lisio, Minneapolis Inst Arts Catalogue, 1/71; Robert Phelps (auth), Portraits by a knowing naif, Life Mag, 1/29/71.
Mailing Address: 32 E 64th St, New York, NY 10021.

DEL JUNCO, EMILIO
Collector, Patron
b Havana, Cuba, July 29, 15.
Study & Training: Sch Archit, Univ Havana; Kungliga Konstakademi, Stockholm, Sweden; pvt study with Dean J L Sert of Harvard Univ.
Teaching: Lectr & critic, Sch Archit, Univ Toronto, 61-64.
Art Interests: Promotion and organization of exhibitions in Cuba, Sweden, U S and Canada; donor of paintings to Mus Modern Art and Solomon R Guggenheim Museum, New York and Art Gallery of Toronto, Ontario.
Collection: Contemporary art.
Mailing Address: 196 Roxborough Dr, Toronto, Ont, Can.

DELLA-VOLPE, RALPH EUGENE
Painter, Educator
Preferred Media: Oils.
b N J, May 10, 23.
Study & Training: Nat Acad Design; Art Stud League New York.
Work in Public Collections: Chase Manhattan Bank Collection, New York, N Y; Gallery Mod Art, New York; Slater Mus, Norwich, Conn; Pennell Collection, Libr of Cong, Washington, D C; Wichita Art Asn, Kans.
Exhibitions: Pa Acad Fine Arts, Philadelphia, 52; Butler Inst Am Art, Ohio, 63; Final, Nat Inst Arts & Lett, New York, 63 & 64; Seattle Art Mus, Wash; Berkshire Mus, Pittsfield, Mass; plus many one-man shows.
Teaching: Prof drawing & painting & artist-in-residence, Bennett Col, 49-
Awards: Wichita Art Asn purchase award, 50; Libr of Cong purchase award, 52; Berkshire Mus drawing prize, 54.
Bibliography: Reviews of shows in N Y Times, Art News & Arts Mag, 60-63; Arts 7: New York art world, Art Digest, 64.
Mailing Address: Bennett College, Millbrook, NY 12545.

DELLIS, ARLENE B
Art Administrator
b Brooklyn, N Y, Apr 12, 27.
Study & Training: Antioch Col; Univ N C, Greensboro, BA.
Positions: Head lending serv, Brooklyn Mus, N Y, 49-55; head traveling exhibs & registr, Solomon R Guggenheim Mus, New York, N Y, 55-63; registr, Gallery Mod Art, New York, 64; registr,

Marlborough-Gerson Gallery, New York, 64-67; registr, ed-designer & dir circulating exhibs, Bernard Danenberg Galleries, New York, 69-72.
Publications: Ed (exhib catalogues), Archipenko: the American years, 1923-63, 70, The rediscovered years: Leon Kroll, 70, auth & ed, Sculpture by William Zorach, 70, ed, Max Weber: early works on paper, 71 & Max Weber drawings, 72.
Mailing Address: 351 W 57th St, New York, NY 10019.

DELONEY, JACK CLOUSE
Painter, Illustrator
Preferred Media: Watercolors, Acrylics.
b Enterprise, Ala, Nov 2, 40.
Study & Training: Auburn Univ, BFA, 64; Watercolor Workshop, with Marc Moon, 72.
Work in Public Collections: First Nat Bank, Montgomery, Ala; People's Bank & Trust Co, Tupeo, Miss; Pope & Quit Co, Mobile, Ala; Fla Gas Corp, Winter Park, Fla.
Exhibitions: Va Beach Boardwalk Festival, 70-72; 49th Regional Exhib, Shreveport, La, 71; La Watercolor Soc Exhib, New Orleans, 71-72; Ala Watercolor Soc Exhib, Birmingham, 71-72; 7th Juried Art Exhib, Mobile Art Gallery, 72; plus one-man shows.
Positions: Book Designer, Methodist Publ House, Nashville, Tenn, 64-65; illusr, Fort Rucker, Ala, 65-
Awards: Pope & Quint Purchase Prize, 72; purchase award, People's Bank & Trust, Tupeo, 72; hon mention, Greenbriar Watercolor Show, Atlanta, Ga, 72.
Memberships: Ala Watercolor Soc; La Watercolor Soc; Atlanta Artist Club; Ala Art League; Ozark Art Club (pres).
Publications: Illusr, Aviation Digest, 66-
Mailing Address: Rte 4, Box 425, Ozark, AL 36360.

DeLONGA, LEONARD ANTHONY
Sculptor, Educator
Preferred Media: Steel, Stone, Wood, Bronze.
b Cannonsburgh, Pa, Dec 18, 25.
Study & Training: Univ Miami, BA, 50; Univ Ga, MFA, 52.
Work in Public Collections: Delaware Art Mus, Wilmington; Lowe Art Gallery, Univ Miami, Coral Gables, Fla; Montclair Mus, N J; Ga Mus Art, Athens; Nat Collection Fine Arts, Smithsonian Inst, Washington, D C.
Commissions: Marshalltown Iowa Community Ctr.
Exhibitions: One-man exhibs, Allentown Art Mus, Pa, 65, Univ Mass, Amherst, 65 & Univ N H, Durham, 67; Nat Inst Arts & Letters, New York, N Y, 61; Humanism in Sculpture, DeCordova & Dana Mus, Lincoln, Mass, 70.
Teaching: Head dept art, Tex Wesleyan Col, Fort Worth, 54-56; instr art, Univ Ga, 56-62, asst prof art, 62-64; prof art, Mt Holyoke Col, 65-
Bibliography: Leonard DeLonga (catalogues of one-man exhibs), Kraushaar Galleries, 61, 64, 67 & 70.
Dealer: Kraushaar Galleries, 1055 Madison Ave, New York, NY 10028.
Mailing Address: 23 Woodbridge St, South Hadley, MA 01075.

DE LUE, DONALD
Sculptor
Preferred Media: Bronze.
b Boston, Mass, Oct 5, 97.
Study & Training: Boston Mus Fine Arts Sch.
Commissions: Spirit of American Youth (22' bronze figure), Omaha Beach Figure, U S Mil Cemetery Mem, Saint Laurent, Normandy; The Rocket Thrower (45' bronze), World's Fair, 1964-1965, New York, N Y; Quest Eternal (27' bronze figure), Prudential Ctr, Boston, Mass; two heroic figures (22' golden bronze), State La Mem, Gettysburg, Pa, 71; two figure group (16' bronze), State Miss Mem, Gettysburg, Pa; plus many others.
Positions: Chmn art comt, Hall Fame for Great Am, New York Univ; adv ed, Am Artist Mag.
Awards: Guggenheim fel, 43-44; Hering Mem Gold Medals, 60; Am Artists Prof League Gold Medal; plus others.
Memberships: Assoc Nat Acad Design; Nat Sculpture Soc; Nat Inst Arts & Lett; Archit League; Am Artists Prof League; plus others.
Mailing Address: 82 Highland Ave, Leonardo, NJ 07737.

DE MARCO, JEAN ANTOINE
Sculptor
b Paris, France, May 2, 98; U S citizen.
Study & Training: Ecole Nat Arts Decoratif, Paris.
Work in Public Collections: Sculpture, Brooklyn Mus, N Y, engraving print, Metrop Mus Art, New York, N Y; sculpture, Norfolk Mus Art & Sci, Va; sculpture, Nat Art Collection, Smithsonian Inst, Washington, D C; prints, Joslyn Art Mus, Omaha, Nebr.
Commissions: Twelve stone high reliefs, Cathedral of the BVM, Baltimore, Md; sculpture for two chapels & three heroic size statues (with Magginis Walsh & Kennedy), Nat Shrine Immaculate

Conception, Washington, D C; two heroic size marble portrait medallions (with J George Stewart, Architect), House of Cong, Washington, D C; sculpture for West Coast War Mem Second World War (with Clark & Beutler Architects), commissioned by Am Comn Battles Monuments, Presidio, San Francisco, Calif; two marble statues for House of Theology (with Brother Cajetan, Architect), Centerville, Ohio; plus others.
Exhibitions: Nat & regional exhibs & in mus in U S.
Teaching: Instr sculpture, Colombia Univ, Boston Mus Fine Arts Sch, Nat Acad Design & Bennett Jr Col; instr bronze casting & drawing, Iowa State Univ.
Positions: Mem joint comt artists & writers revolving funds, Nat Inst Arts & Letters-Am Acad Arts & Letters, 60.
Awards: Nat Inst Arts & Letters grant, 50; medal of merit, Am Acad Arts & Letters, 59; Saltus Gold Medal & Elizabeth Watrous Gold Medal, Nat Acad Design; plus others.
Memberships: Nat Inst Arts & Letters (mem dept comt, mem gen comt, mem comt on progress, 61-64); Nat Acad Design; Nat Sculpture Soc (chmn comt hons & awards, 63, mem coun, 63-69).
Mailing Address: c/o National Academy of Design, 1083 Fifth Ave, New York, NY 10028.

DeMAREE, ELIZABETH ANN (BETTY)
Painter, Collector
Preferred Media: Watercolors.
b Denver, Colo, Oct 19, 18.
Study & Training: Cooper Union Sch Art; with Robert E Wood, Calif; also with Edgar A Whitney, Herb Olsen & Mario Cooper, New York.
Work in Public Collections: Kissinger Oil Bldg, Denver; Van Schack, Littleton, Colo; Marathon Oil Bldg, Littleton; Cheyenne Pub Libr, Wyo.
Commissions: Ceramic plaque of oil scene, Indust of Lowell Williamson, Calgary, Can, 62; ceramic, Off Gov Colo, 62; watercolor scenics of Denver bldgs, Cassidy Paint, Hilb & Co & J Signs, Denver, 70; Old Main (painting), Colo State Univ, Fort Collins, 70; watercolor portraits of children, James F Kuhns, Dallas, Tex, 71-72.
Exhibitions: Denver OYO, Denver Art Mus, 68; Gilpin Co Arts Asn, Central City, Colo, 68-72; Southwestern Watercolor Soc, Dallas, 69-72 & Albuquerque, N Mex, 72; Cheyenne Artist Guild Ann Exhib, 70-72.
Teaching: Instr pvt classes, 68-; demonstr & lectr, art asns of Colo & Wyo, 68-
Awards: Best of show, Southwestern Watercolor Soc, Dallas, 69; second place award, Cheyenne Artists Guild, 70 & 71.
Memberships: Denver Artists Guild; Cheyenne Artists Guild; Southwestern Watercolor Soc; Assoc Am Watercolor Soc; Artists Equity Asn.
Collection: Watercolors by Robert E Wood, Chen Chi, Dale Meyers, Edgar A Whitney, Gerry Pierce, Buffalo Kaplinski, Robert L Pratt & others.
Dealers: Applewood Art Gallery, 12975 W 24th Pl, Applewood, CO; Gallery A, E Kit Carson Rd, P O Box 1221, Taos, NM 87571.
Mailing Address: 4989 E Iliff Ave, Denver, CO 80222.

DE MARIA, WALTER
Sculptor
Preferred Media: Earth.
b Oct 1, 35; U S citizen.
Study & Training: Univ Calif, Berkeley, MA, 59.
Work in Public Collections: Mus Mod Art, New York, N Y; Whitney Mus Am Art, New York, N Y; Basel Knustmuseum, Basel, Switz.
Exhibitions: Primary Structures, Jewish Mus, New York, 66; Sculpture of the 60's, Los Angeles Co Mus, Calif, 67; Whitney Mus Am Art Sculpture Ann, 68; When Activities Become Form, Bern, Switz, 69; Information, Mus Mod Art, New York, 70.
Awards: Guggenheim fel, 69-70.
Bibliography: O Bourdon (auth), Walter De Maria, the singular experience, Art Int, 12/68.
Publications: Contribr, Hard core (land film ed 100), 69.
Dealer: Noah Goldowsky Gallery, 1078 Madison Ave, New York, NY 10021.
Mailing Address: P O Box 258, New York, NY 10013.

DE MARTINI, JOSEPH
Painter
b Mobile, Ala, July 20, 96.
Study & Training: Nat Acad Design, with Leon Krill & Ivan Olinsky.
Work in Public Collections: Addison Gallery Am Art, Andover, Mass; City Art Mus Saint Louis; Boston Mus Fine Arts; Mus Mod Art; Metrop Mus Art; plus many others.
Exhibitions: City Art Mus Saint Louis, 38, 41, 42 & 46; Corcoran Gallery Art, 41, 43 & 45; Va Mus Fine Arts, Richmond, 42, 44 & 46; John Herron Art Inst, 45; Nebr Art Asn, 45 & 46; plus many others.

Teaching: Artist-in-residence, Univ Ga, 52-53.
Awards: Prize, Nat Acad Design, 50; Guggenheim fel, 51; gold medal, Pa Acad Fine Arts, 52; plus others.
Bibliography: Rosamond Frost (auth), included in: Contemporary art: the march of art from Cezanne until now, Crown, 42; Emily Genauer (auth), included in: Best of art, Doubleday, 48; John I H Baur (auth), included in: Revolution and tradition in modern American art, Harvard Univ Press, 59; plus others.
Memberships: Assoc Nat Acad Design; Audubon Artists.
Mailing Address: 103 W 27th St, New York, NY 10001.

DE MATTIES, NICK FRANK
Printmaker
b Honolulu, Hawaii, Oct 19, 39.
Study & Training: Long Beach State Col, BA, 64; Inst Design, Chicago, MS, 67, with Misch Kohn.
Work in Public Collections: Cabinet Estampes, Bibliot Nat Paris; Libr Cong; Sheldon Mem Art Gallery; San Francisco Mus Mod Art; Columbia Univ.
Exhibitions: 22nd Am Drawing Biennial, Norfolk, Va, 67; 9th & 11th Nat Exhib Prints and Drawings, Okla, 67 & 69; 2nd Dulin Nat Print and Drawing Competition, Knoxville, Tenn, 68; 40th Int Exhib, Northwest Printmakers, 70; Printmakers in Oregon, Eugene, 71.
Teaching: Instr printmaking & drawing, San Diego State Col, 67-69; asst prof printmaking & drawing, Mt St Mary's Col (Calif), 69-70; vis prof printmaking, Univ Ore, 72.
Positions: Founder & dir, Pac Northwest Graphics Workshop, 70-
Awards: Purchase award, Miniature Painters, Sculptors & Gravers Soc Washington, D C, 68; Continental Art Award, Los Angeles Printmaking Soc, 68.
Bibliography: Article, In: Vol 11, Artists Proof, Pratt Graphics Ctr & N Y Graphic Soc Ltd.
Memberships: Los Angeles Printmaking Soc.
Mailing Address: Box 78, Star Rte, Cheshire, OR 97419.

DE MENIL, JOHN
Collector
b Paris, France, Jan 4, 04; U S citizen.
Study & Training: Univ Paris, BA, 22, Sch Polit Sci, grad, 25, BLaw, 35.
Positions: Trustee, Mus Primitive Art, Mus Mod Art & R I Sch Design; v pres, Int Coun Mus Mod Art.
Collection: Contemporary painting.
Mailing Address: 3363 San Felipe Rd, Houston, TX 77019.

DEMETRION, JAMES THOMAS
Art Administrator
b Middletown, Ohio, July 10, 30.
Positions: Dir, Des Moines Art Ctr, Iowa.
Mailing Address: Des Moines Art Center, Greenwood Park, Des Moines, IA 50312.

DE MILLE, LESLIE BENJAMIN
Painter
Preferred Media: Oils, Pastels.
b Hamilton, Ont, Apr 24, 27; U S citizen.
Study & Training: Hamilton Tech Inst; Art Stud League New York, N Y; also with Leon Franks, Laguna Beach, Calif.
Work in Public Collections: Portraits, President Nixon & others, Whittier Col Collection; Death Valley 49ers Collection.
Commissions: Portrait, Gov Ronald Reagan, Gov Mansion, Calif, 67; oil painting, Princess Lorayne Kamienski, Rynn-Berry, London, Eng, 71; three portraits, Daylin, Inc, Beverly Hills, Calif, 72; oil paintings & sketches, U S Sixth Fleet, Mediterranean (naval combat artist), Off Naval Art Collection, 72.
Exhibitions: Laguna Beach Festival Arts, 65-; Death Valley 49ers Ann Invitational Exhib, Calif, 69-; Lahaina Art Soc, Maui, Hawaii, 70; Grand Nat Exhib, Am Artists Prof League, New York, 71-72; San Gabriel Fine Arts Asn Open Show, Calif, 72.
Teaching: Organizer, dir & instr, one week sem for art orgn in western U S, 66-
Positions: Judge, San Gabriel Fine Arts Asn, 70 & 71 & Catalina Festival Arts, Avalon, Calif, 71.
Awards: Best of Show, Catalina Festival Arts Invitational, 71; Best of Show for All Media, Am Artists Prof League, 71; Best of Show, Gold medal & one second prize for portrait & still-life, San Gabriel Fine Arts Asn, 72.
Memberships: Am Inst Fine Arts (dir, 72), fel Am Artists Prof League; Laguna Beach Festival Arts; Lahaina Art Soc; San Gabriel Fine Arts Asn.
Dealer: Desert-Southwest Art Gallery, 74-119 Hwy 111, Palm Desert, CA 92260.
Mailing Address: 1432 S Coast Hwy, Laguna Beach, CA 92651.

DE MONTEBELLO, GUY-PHILIPPE LANNES
Museum Director
b Paris, France, May 16, 39.
Study & Training: Harvard Col, BA, 61; New York Univ Inst Fine Arts, 61-63.
Collections Arranged: The Spingold Collection Exhibition, Brandeis Univ, 65, 67 & 68; Summer Loan Exhibition, Metrop Mus Art.
Teaching: Lectr Fr art, romanticism & 18th century women painters.
Positions: Assoc cur Europ paintings, Metrop Mus Art, 63-69; dir, Mus Fine Arts Houston, Tex, 69-
Awards: Woodrow Wilson fel, 61-62.
Memberships: Col Art Asn Am; Am Asn Mus; Am Asn Mus Dirs.
Publications: Auth, Peter Paul Rubens, McGraw, 69; contribr, articles, In: Metrop Mus Art Bull & others.
Mailing Address: The Museum of Fine Arts of Houston, P O Box 6826, Houston, TX 77005.

DE NAGY, EVA
Painter
b Hungary.
Study & Training: Acad Royal Beaux-Arts, Brussels, Belg.
Work in Public Collections: Color slides, Guild Libr, Church Archit Guild Am, Washington, D C.
Exhibitions: Provincetown Art Asn, 60 & 61; Ecclesiastical Crafts Exhib, Pittsburgh, Pa, 61 & 62; Painters & Sculptors Soc N J, 61 & 62; Am-Hungarian Art Asn, New York, N Y, 62 & 63; Catharine Lorillard Wolfe Art Club, 62 & 64; plus many other group & one-man shows.
Positions: Owner-dir, Eva de Nagy Gallery, Provincetown, Mass; state art chmn, N J Fed Women's Clubs, 60 & 62; mem art comn, Trenton State Mus, 60 & 62; chmn, Roebling-Boehm art scholar, 62 & 64.
Awards: Prizes, N J State Fed Women's Club, 54 & 59; bronze medal, Seton Hall Univ, 56; prize, N J State Med Asn Convention Art Exhib, 58 & 60; plus others.
Memberships: Provincetown Art Asn; Cape Cod Art Asn; Am Artists Prof League (publicity chmn, N J chap); Painters & Sculptors Soc N J (treas).
Mailing Address: 462 Commercial St, Provincetown, MA 02657.

DENES, AGNES C
Conceptual Artist, Theoretician
Preferred Media: Graphics, Mixed Media.
b Budapest, Hungary; U S citizen.
Study & Training: City Col New York; New Sch Social Res; Columbia Univ, M L Robinson scholar, 64-65.
Work in Public Collections: Mus Mod Art, New York, N Y; Whitney Mus Am Art, New York; Smithsonian Inst, Washington, D C; Roy R Neuberger Mus, Purchase, N Y; Israel Mus, Jerusalem; plus others.
Exhibitions: One-woman shows, Columbia Univ, 65, Granite Gallery, New York, 66, Ruth White Gallery, 68, 69 & Blue Parrot Gallery, New York, 72; Nat Acad Gallery, 70; Oversized Prints, Whitney Mus Am Art, 71; Software, Jewish Mus, New York, 71; Mus Mod Art, Buenos Aires, 71-72; plus many others.
Teaching: Guest lect, N Y Univ, 71, City Univ New York, 72 & Guilford Col, 72.
Awards: John J Myers Art Sch Awards, 59-63; Alfred P Cohen Art Sch Awards, 61 & 62; Cult Coun Found Creative Artists Serv Prog grant, 72.
Bibliography: Lucy Lippard (auth), Six years, Praeger.
Mailing Address: 93 Crosby St, New York, NY 10012.

DE NIKE, MICHAEL NICHOLAS
Sculptor
Preferred Media: Wood.
b Regina, Sask, Sept 14, 23; U S citizen.
Study & Training: Nat Acad Fine Arts; also with Jean de Marco & Carl Schmitz.
Commissions: Bas relief, Hudson Trust Bank, Union, N J, 66; Sperm Whale, Camden Manor Inn, Maine, 70; Albert Payson Terhune Memorial, Nat Collie Fanciers, Paramus, N J, 71.
Exhibitions: Ann, Nat Sculpture Soc, New York, N Y, 64, Audubon Artists, New York, 64, Nat Acad Fine Arts, New York, 65, Knickerbocker Artists, 66 & Hudson Valley Artists, White Plains, N Y, 69.
Teaching: Instr woodcarving, Fair Lawn Adult Educ, 68-
Positions: V pres, Paterson Art League, N J, 67-68; co-chmn, Mayor's Coun Cult Develop, 68-69.
Awards: Dr Ralph Weiler Award, Nat Acad Design, 64; Herald News Award, Paterson, 69.
Mailing Address: 2343 Hamburg Turnpike, Wayne, NJ 07470.

DE NIRO, ROBERT
Sculptor, Painter
b Syracuse, N Y, May 3, 22.
Study & Training: Black Mountain Col; also with Hans Hofmann.

Work in Public Collections: Brandeis Univ; Houston Mus Fine Arts; Longview Found; Univ N C.
Exhibitions: Whitney Mus Am Art Ann, New York, N Y; Jewish Mus, New York; Inst Contemp Art, Boston, Mass; Ball State Univ, Muncie, Ind; Colo Springs Fine Arts Ctr; plus others.
Teaching: Instr, Sch Visual Arts, New Sch Social Res & State Univ N Y Buffalo.
Awards: V Hallmark Int Competition; Longview Found grant; Guggenheim Found fel, 68.
Dealer: Zabriskie Gallery, 29 W 57th St, New York, NY 10019.
Mailing Address: 463 West St, New York, NY 10014.

DENNIS, CHARLES HOUSTON
Cartoonist
b Springfield, Mo, Nov 11, 21.
Study & Training: Art League Calif, San Francisco; Acad Art, San Francisco.
Positions: Staff artist, Springfield Leader & Press, 39-42; free lance mag cartoonist, 50-
Publications: Contribr, numerous mags, 50-; auth, Cartoon gag writing principles and techniques, 55.
Mailing Address: 1831 Magnolia Way, Walnut Creek, CA 94597.

DENNIS, CHERRE NIXON
Painter, Etcher
Preferred Media: Watercolors.
b Raton, N Mex.
Study & Training: Univ Tulsa, with Adah M Robinson; Univ N Mex, with Emil Bisttram; Okla State Univ, with Doel Reed; also with Rexford E Brandt & Phillip L Dike.
Exhibitions: Midwestern Exhib, Kansas City, Mo, 39; Watercolor & Print Ann, Oakland Art Gallery, Calif, 42; Philbrook Art Ctr, Tulsa, Okla, 56; Nat Representational Art Ann, Thomas Gilcrease Inst, Tulsa, 58; Southwestern Biennial, Mus N Mex, Santa Fe, 62.
Teaching: Art instr etching & drawing, Philbrook Art Ctr, 40-41.
Positions: Pres & chmn bd, Adah M Robinson Mem Fund, Tulsa, 67-69.
Awards: First award for graphics, Tulsa Art Ann, 35 & 36 & second award for watercolor, Philbrook Art Ctr, 50.
Memberships: N Mex Art League; Lake Region Arts & Crafts Colony.
Dealer: 3000 Monterey Dr S E, Albuquerque, NM 87106.
Mailing Address: Lakeview on Gibson, Rte 1, Box 304B, Wagoner, OK 74467.

DENNIS, ROGER WILSON
Painter
Preferred Media: Oils, Watercolors.
b Norwich, Conn, Mar 11, 02.
Study & Training: Art Stud League New York.
Exhibitions: Lyme Art Asn; Conn Acad; Copley Soc, Boston.
Positions: Conservator painting, Lyman Allyn Mus, New London, Conn, 45-
Memberships: Lyme Art Asn; Copley Soc.
Dealer: Peter's Gallery, Jay St, New London, CT 06320.
Mailing Address: Columbus Ave, Niantic, CT 06357.

DENNISON, DOROTHY (DOROTHY DENNISON BUTLER)
Painter, Lithographer
Preferred Media: Oils.
b Beaver, Pa, Feb 13, 08.
Study & Training: Pa Acad Fine Arts, Cresson traveling scholar, 29.
Work in Public Collections: Columbus Gallery, Ohio; Canton Art Inst, Ohio; Pa Acad Fine Arts, Philadelphia; Butler Inst Am Art, Ohio; Olsen Found, Conn.
Exhibitions: Pa Acad Fine Arts, Philadelphia; Butler Inst Am Art, Ohio; Newport Art Asn, R I; Portland Mus, Maine; Northwest Territory Exhib, Ill.
Teaching: Head art dept, Knox Sch, Cooperstown, N Y, 40-41; instr drawing, Syracuse Univ, 41-43; head art dept, Russell Sage Col, 43-44.
Awards: Purchase prize, Butler Inst Am Art, 50; first prize, Ohio State Fair, 69.
Memberships: Fel Pa Acad Fine Arts.
Dealer: Kennedy Galleries, 20 E 56th St, New York, NY 10022.
Mailing Address: 1915 Walker Mill Rd, Poland, OH 44514.

DENNISON, KEITH ELKINS
Art Administrator, Art Historian
b Oakland, Calif, Sept 20, 39.
Study & Training: San Francisco State Univ, BA, with Dr Ernest Mundt; spec training, M H de Young Mem Mus, San Francisco, Calif.
Collections Arranged: Horizons, A Century of California Landscape Painting.

Positions: Asst cur educ, M H de Young Mem Mus, 68-70; visual arts adv, Calif Arts Comn, Sacramento, Calif, 70-71; dir, Pioneer Mus & Haggin Galleries, Stockton, Calif, 71-
Publications: Auth, Horizons, a century of California landscape painting, 70.
Mailing Address: Pioneer Museum & Haggin Galleries, 1201 N Pershing, Stockton, CA 95203.

DE NORONHA, MARIA M (MRS HAROLD SHAFRON)
Painter, Lecturer
b Cascais, Port; U S citizen.
Study & Training: Jr Col Sagrado Coração, Port; Hunter Col, BA; Montclair Col; Art Stud League New York; Am Ctr Stud & Artists, Paris, France; also with Doug Kingman, New York & Roger Barr, Paris.
Work in Public Collections: Grumbacher Co, New York; Oglethorpe Univ, Atlanta, Ga; George Washington Carver Mus; Col Charleston; Am Ctr Stud & Artists, Paris.
Exhibitions: U S Embassy, Saigon, Vietnam, 70; Nat Acad Design, New York, 71; State Dept, Washington, D C, 71; Washington Mus, Md, 71; Southeastern Art Exhib, 72; plus others.
Teaching: Instr art & chmn dept, Lyndhurst High Sch, N Y, 58-60; instr art, Oglethorpe Univ, 64-67; asst prof art, Atlanta Univ, 68-70; also lectr, Atlanta Univ Grad Sch & Alice Lloyd Col, Ky.
Positions: Owner, Art Studio, Charleston, 60-62; mem art comt, off & lectr, Int Platform Asn, 68-72; dir, Noronha Art Studio, Atlanta, 69-
Awards: M Grumbacher Award as Painter of the Yr, 62; Southeastern Art Exhib Award for Seas, 65; Oglethorpe Univ Res Grant, 66.
Bibliography: Armando Troni (auth), Int Contemp Art Mag, 71.
Memberships: Life fel, Royal Soc Arts; Am Asn Univ Prof; Southeastern Art Conf.
Mailing Address: P O Box 9606, Atlanta, GA 30319.

DENTZEL, CARL SCHAEFER
Museum Director, Writer
b Philadelphia, Pa, Mar 20, 13.
Study & Training: Univ Calif, Los Angeles; Univ Berlin; Univ Mex.
Teaching: Former lectr, Pomona Col.
Positions: Pres, Los Angeles Co Mus Asn; mem bd, Univ Calif Art Coun, Los Angeles; pres, Western Mus Conf, 57-58; dir, Southwest Mus, Los Angeles; pres, Cult Heritage Bd, City Los Angeles, 63-64.
Memberships: Univ Calif Art Coun, Los Angeles; Los Angeles Mus Art (exec comt).
Publications: Auth, introduction & bibliog, In: Diary of Titian Ramsay Peale: Oregon to California, overland journey September and October, 1841, 57; auth, Cinco de Mayo—an appraisal, 60 & The universality of local history, 60; auth, The art of Leon Gaspard (introduction), A memorial exhibition of paintings and sketches by Leon Gaspard (catalog), 64; auth, introduction, In: Edward H Davis and the Indians of the southwest United States and northwest Mexico, 65; plus many others.
Mailing Address: Southwest Museum, 10 Highland Park, Los Angeles, CA 90065.

DENYS, GEORGE FREDERICK
Painter
Preferred Media: Oils.
b Beaumont, Tex, Jan 22, 46.
Study & Training: Utah Tech Col; Col Southern Utah; Brigham Young Univ, with Michael Coleman & Archie Higgenbottham.
Exhibitions: Utah Inst Fine Arts, 71; Nat & All Utah Shows, Springville Mus, 71 & 72; Capricorn Gallery, Bethesda, Md, 71-72; Four Seasons, Jackson, Wyo, 71-72; Morman Festival Arts, 72.
Dealer: Capricorn Galleries, 8003 Woodmont Ave, Bethesda, MD 20014.
Mailing Address: 446 E 1910 S, Orem, UT 84057.

DE PAUW, VICTOR
Painter
b Belg, Jan 21, 02.
Study & Training: Calif Sch Fine Arts; Art Stud League New York.
Work in Public Collections: Mus Mod Art; N Y Pub Libr; Philadelphia Mus Art; Brooklyn Mus; Cleveland Mus Art; also in pvt collections, U S & abroad.
Exhibitions: Nessler Gallery, 54; 30 yr retrospective, Eastside Gallery, New York, N Y, 65; Parrish Art Mus, Southampton, Long Island, N Y, 65; Pace Col, New York; Inst Estudios Norteamericanos, Barcelona, Spain; plus others.
Teaching: Former instr, Art Stud League New York, Peoples Art Ctr, Mus Mod Art & Country Art Sch, Westbury, N Y; lectr mod art & art of Am Indian, Southampton Col, Long Island Univ, 64.
Awards: Purchase prize, Southampton Col, Long Island Univ, 69.
Publications: Auth, art rev, In: East Hampton Star; illusr, The spirit of Christmas (spec ed) & other bks.
Mailing Address: 30 Osborn Lane, East Hampton, NY 11937.

DE PEDERY-HUNT, DORA
Sculptor, Designer
b Budapest, Hungary, Nov 16, 13.
Study & Training: Royal Sch Appl Art, Budapest, MA.
Work in Public Collections: Nat Gallery Can; Art Gallery, Toronto, Ont; Art Gallery Ont; Dept External Affairs, Ottawa; Mus Contemp Crafts, Charlottetown, P E I; plus others.
Exhibitions: Canadian Religious Art Today, Regis Col, Toronto, 63 & 66; Int Exhib Contemp Medals, The Hague & Rome, 63, Athens, 66, Paris, 67 & Prague, 69; Biennial Christian Art, Salzburg, 64; Can Pavillion, Expo' 67; all major group shows in Can plus others.
Positions: Can rep, Fedn Int Medaille, Paris.
Awards: Purchase prizes, Uno-a-Erre, Arezzo, Italy, 64-66; Nat Coun Jewish Women Award, 66; Can Govt Centennial Medal, 67; plus others.
Memberships: Assoc Royal Can Acad; Sculptors' Soc Can (past pres); Ont Soc Artists.
Mailing Address: 88 Walker Ave, Toronto 7, Ont, Can.

DE POL, JOHN
Engraver, Designer
Preferred Media: Wood.
b New York, N Y, Sept 16, 13.
Study & Training: Art Stud League New York, N Y; Sch Technol, Belfast, Northern Ireland.
Work in Public Collections: Libr Cong; New York Pub Libr; Metrop Mus Art; Syracuse Univ Libr; Bucknell Univ Libr.
Commissions: Presentation prints, Woodcut Soc, 52, Miniature Print Soc, 53 & Albany Print Club, N Y, 58-59.
Exhibitions: One-man exhibs, Albany Print Club, Bucknell Univ, Syracuse Univ & Lycoming Col; Nat Acad Design Ann, 72.
Positions: Free lance art dir & design consult for various corp; illusr, Franklin Keepsake Ann Ser.
Awards: Albany Print Club Purchase Prize, 68; John Taylor Arms Mem Prize, Nat Acad Design, 68; Nat Arts Club Purchase Prize, 68.
Bibliography: P K Thomajan (auth), John De Pol, wood engraver, Print Mag, 8/54; Norman Kent (auth), The wood engravings of John De Pol, 3/56 & William Caxton, Jr (auth), A new chiaroscuro wood engraving by John De Pol, 2/68, Am Artist.
Memberships: Soc Am Graphic Artists; Albany Print Club; life mem Art Stud League New York; assoc Nat Acad Design.
Mailing Address: 280 Spring Valley Rd, Park Ridge, NJ 07656.

DERGALIS, GEORGE
Painter
b Athens, Greece, Aug 31, 28; U S citizen.
Study & Training: Sculpture with Ambrose, 48-50; Accad Belle Arti, Rome, MA, 51; Boston Mus Fine Arts, dipl, 58.
Work in Public Collections: De Cordova Mus, Lincoln, Mass; Brockton Mus, Mass; Inst Sarro, Barcelona, Spain; Mus Sch Fine Arts, Boston; St Matthew Church, Fichburg, Mass.
Exhibitions: Prima Mostra Int, Rome, 50; Quadrienale, Mus Mod Art, Rome, 51; Kurhaus Wiesbaden, Ger, 53; De Cordova Mus, 62; Brockton Mus, 72.
Teaching: Prof painting, De Cordova Mus, 61-; art instr, Mus Sch Fine Arts, Boston, 61-70; instr art, YMHA, Boston, 62-64; prof color design & drawing, Dergalis Studio, Wayland, Mass, 67-
Positions: V pres, Alumni Mus Sch Fine Arts, 64-65; pres, Mus Sch Fine Arts, 66-68.
Awards: Prix Rome, Accad Belli Arti, 51; Paige scholar, 59; gold medal, Concord Art Asn, 69.
Bibliography: Art and antiques, Melrose Press, London, 72.
Memberships: Copley Soc (gov off, 67); Int Soc; Int Soc Arts & Lett; Boston Mus Sch Alumni (pres, 68); Cambridge Art Asn.
Dealer: Frederick R Schaeffer, 549 Technology Sq, Cambridge, MA 01432.
Mailing Address: 72 Oxbow Rd, Wayland, MA 01778.

DE RIVERA, JOSE
Sculptor
Preferred Media: Stainless Steel, Bronze.
b West Baton Rouge, La, Sept 18, 04.
Study & Training: With John W Norton, Chicago; also study in Spain, Italy, France, Greece & Egypt.
Work in Public Collections: Mus Mod Art, New York, N Y; Art Inst Chicago, Ill; San Francisco Mus Art, Calif; Smithsonian Inst, Washington, D C; Tate Gallery, London, Eng; plus many others.
Commissions: Steel Century Two (sculpture), Am Iron & Steel Inst, 65.
Exhibitions: Whitney Mus Am Art Ann, New York, 34-68; Grace Borgenicht Gallery, New York, 52-72; White House, Washington, D C, 66; Sculpture of the '60's, Los Angeles Co Mus Art, Calif & Philadelphia Mus Art, Pa, 67; Retrospective 72, La Jolla Mus Contemp Art, Calif & Whitney Mus Am Art, New York, 72; plus many other group & one-man shows.

Teaching: Instr sculpture, Brooklyn Col, 53; critic in sculpture, Yale Univ, 53-55; instr sculpture, Sch Design N C State Col, 57-60.
Awards: Watson F Blair Prize, Art Inst Chicago, 57; Nat Inst Arts & Lett grant, 59; creative awards medal, Brandeis Univ, 69; plus others.
Mailing Address: c/o Grace Borgenicht Gallery, 1018 Madison Ave, New York, NY 10003.

DERUJINSKY, GLEB W
Sculptor, Craftsman
Preferred Media: Wood, Bronze.
b Smolensk, Russia, Aug 13, 88; U S citizen.
Study & Training: Univ & Fine Arts Acad, Petrograd.
Work in Public Collections: Metrop Mus Art; Memphis Mus; Cranbrook Acad Art; plus others.
Commissions: Stations of the Cross, House of Theol, Cincinnati, Ohio; four statues, Church of St Vincent Ferrer, New York, N Y; statue of St Joseph, St Mary's Church, Flushing, N Y; statues in marble, Cathedral of Immaculate Conception, Washington, D C; Franz Liszt statue, Haifa Mus Mus, Israel; plus many others.
Exhibitions: Pa Acad Fine Arts; Metrop Mus Art; Royal Acad, Eng & Belg; one-man show, Knoedler Gallery, London; Grand Cent Art Gallery, New York, N Y, 71.
Awards: Awards, Nat Acad Design, 38 & 68; Lindsey Mem Prize, 54 & 65; Daniel French Prize, 58 & gold medal, 66, Allied Artists Am; plus others.
Memberships: Academician Nat Acad Design; Nat Sculpture Soc; Am Artists Prof League; Allied Artists Am.
Mailing Address: 29 W 65th St, Apt 2D, New York, NY 10023.

DE RUTH, JAN
Painter, Writer
Preferred Media: Oils.
b Karlovy Vary, Czech, July 31, 22; U S citizen.
Study & Training: Rotter Art Sch, Prague, Czech; Ruskin Sch Drawing, Oxford Univ, Eng; Art Stud League New York; New Sch Soc Res, New York, N Y; also with Frederic Taubes.
Exhibitions: 38 nat juried exhibs, 14 mus one-man shows & 51 gallery one-man exhibs.
Awards: Gold medal, Nat Arts Club; purchase award, Butler Inst Am Art; purchase award, Audubon Artists.
Memberships: Allied Artists Am (v pres); Audubon Artists; Am Artists Prof League; Royal Soc Art, London; Artists Fel.
Publications: Auth, portrait painting, 64; auth, Painting the nude, 68.
Dealer: Kuhlik Gallery, 23 E 67th St, New York, NY 10021.
Mailing Address: 1 W 67th St, New York, NY 10023.

DESHAIES, ARTHUR
Printmaker
Preferred Media: Graphics.
b Providence, R I, July 6, 20.
Study & Training: Cooper Union Art Sch, 39-42; R I Sch Design, BFA, 48; Ind Univ, MFA, 50.
Work in Public Collections: Bradley Univ; Brooklyn Mus; in many mus U S & Europe & in univ & pvt collections.
Exhibitions: American Prints Today, Print Coun Am Traveling Exhib, 59-62; Brooklyn Mus; Third Int Biennial Exhib Prints, Tokyo, 62; Otis Art Inst, Los Angeles, Calif; Whitney Mus Am Art.
Awards: Fulbright fel to France, 52; Tiffany Found grant, 60; Guggenheim fel creative printmaking, 61; plus others.
Bibliography: Gabor Peterdi (auth), included in: Printmaking: methods old and new, Macmillan, 59; S W Hayter (auth), included in: About prints, Oxford Univ Press, 62.
Publications: Contribr, Am Prints Today (catalogue), 62.
Mailing Address: 1314 Dillard St, Tallahassee, FL 32303.

DESIND, PHILIP
Art Dealer, Collector
b New York, N Y, Feb 28, 10.
Study & Training: City Col New York, BS, 34, MS, 38.
Positions: Dir, Capricorn Galleries, Bethesda, Md, 64-
Specialty of Gallery: Current U S artists, with emphasis on realism.
Collection: Contemporary American realism.
Mailing Address: 8003 Woodmont Ave, Bethesda, MD 20014.

DESKEY, DONALD
Designer
b Blue Earth, Minn, Nov 23, 94.
Study & Training: Univ Calif; Mark Hopkins Art Sch; Art Inst Chicago; Art Stud League New York; Grande Chaumiere, Paris, France.
Exhibitions: Seattle World's Fair, 62; New York World's Fair, 64; U S Pavillions, Int Trade Fairs, Salonika, Greece, 60 & Zagreb,

Yugoslavia, 61; Dept Agr Fairs, Verona, Milan, Madrid, Manchester & Cologne; Union Carbide Exhib, Moscow; plus many others.
Teaching: Lectr indust design.
Positions: Pres, Donald Deskey Assocs, Indust Design Consults, 27-; design consult to var exhibitors, New York World's Fair, 64-65; mem adv bd, Soc Plastic Engrs, Inc U S A; dir, Donald Deskey Assocs, Ltd, Eng; dir, Sculley, Deskey & Scott, Inc.
Awards: Prizes, Pittsburgh Plate Glass Co, Art Dirs Club, 61 & Am Inst Graphic Arts, 61; plus others.
Memberships: Nat Inst Archit Educ; fel Am Soc Indust Designers; Am Inst Graphic Arts; Package Design Coun (dir); Benjamin Franklin fel Royal Soc Art, London; plus others.
Mailing Address: 575 Madison Ave, New York, NY 10021.

DESPORTES, ULYSSE GANDVIER
Painter, Art Historian
Preferred Media: Oils.
b Winnsboro, S C, Apr 12, 20.
Study & Training: Richmond Prof Inst, Col William & Mary, BFA, with Julien Binford, Marion Junkin & Theresa Pollack; Ecole Normale Super Beaux-Arts, Paris, France, with Maurice Brianchon; Inst Art & Archeol, Univ Paris, with Pierre Lavedan & André Chastel.
Work in Public Collections: Va Mus Fine Arts, Richmond; Washington & Lee Univ, Lexington, Va; Va Commonwealth Univ, Richmond.
Exhibitions: Va Artists, 1961 & Va Artists 1963, Va Mus Fine Arts; S C Artists, Gibbs Art Mus, Charleston, 62.
Teaching: Asst prof art hist & painting, Hollins Col, 57-62; prof art & chmn dept, Mary Baldwin Col, 62-
Positions: Dir catalogues, Kende Galleries, New York, N Y, 46-48; dir Florence Mus, S C, 57.
Awards: Second prize, S C Artists Asn, 62, cert of merit, Va Mus Fine Arts, 63.
Research: Neoclassic art; sculptor Giuseppe Ceracchi; painter Louis David.
Publications: Contribr, Bull Mus Bernadotte, 62; contribr, Princeton Libr Chronicle, 62; contribr, Art Quart, 63 & 64; contribr, Antiques Mag, 69.
Mailing Address: 322 N New St, Staunton, VA 24401.

DESSNER, MURRAY
Painter
b Philadelphia, Pa, Nov 11, 34.
Study & Training: Pa Acad Fine Arts, William Emlen Cresson traveling scholar, 65 & J Henry Schiedt traveling scholar, 66; also with Franklin C Watkins & Hobson Pittman.
Work in Public Collections: Painting & Print Collection, Philadelphia Mus Art; Pittman Collection, Bryn Mawr Col, Pa; Penn Fed Collection.
Exhibitions: Int Arts Festival P R, 69; two-man show, East Hampton Gallery, New York, N Y, 69; Cheltenham Ann, 69-72; one-man shows, Peale Galleries, Pa Acad Fine Arts, 70 & Marion Locks Gallery, Philadelphia, 72.
Teaching: Instr painting, Pa Acad Fine Arts, 70-
Awards: Philadelphia Mus Art Purchase Prize, Cheltenham Art Ctr, 69.
Bibliography: Two Philadelphians, Time Mag, 69; work reviewed in Art News, 69.
Dealer: Marion Locks Gallery, 1530 Walnut St, Philadelphia, PA
Mailing Address: 802 Sansom St, Philadelphia, PA 19107.

DE TOLNAY, CHARLES
Art Historian, Writer
b Budapest, Hungary, May 27, 99; U S citizen.
Study & Training: Univ Berlin, 20-21; Univ Frankfurt, 22; Univ Vienna, PhD, 25; Inst Advan Study, 39-48; Univ Rome, hon DLitt, 64; hon DPl, Univ Budapest, 70.
Teaching: Vis prof, Columbia Univ, 53-64.
Positions: Dir, Casa Buonarroti, Florence, Italy.
Awards: Laureat Acad Inscriptions & Belles-Lett, Inst France, 37; Guggenheim & Bollingen fels.
Memberships: Col Art Asn Am; hon mem Accad Disegno, Florence; Accad Naz dei Lincei, Rome.
Publications: Auth, The youth of Michelangelo, Vol 1, 43 & 69, The Sistine Chapel, Vol 2, 45 & 69, The Medici Chapel, Vol 3, 48 & 70, The tomb of Julius Two, Vol 4, 54 & 70, The final period, Vol 5, 60 & 70 & Michelangelo, architect, Vol 6, In: Michelangelo, Princeton Univ Press; plus others.
Mailing Address: Casa Buonarroti, Via Ghibellina 70, Florence, Italy.

DE TONNANCOUR, JACQUES G
Painter, Instructor
b Montreal, P Q, Jan 3, 17.
Study & Training: Col Brébeuf; Ecole Beaux-Arts, Montreal; Art Asn Montreal, with G Roberts.

Work in Public Collections: Nat Gallery Can; Art Gallery Toronto.
Commissions: Murals, Dow Planetarium, Montreal, 67 & Univ Montreal, 68.
Exhibitions: Yale Univ, 44; Rio de Janeiro, 44 & 46; UNESCO; retrospective exhib, Vancouver Art Gallery, 66; Mus Art Contemporain, 67; plus others.
Teaching: Lectr Can art; instr, Ecole Beaux-Arts, Montreal.
Awards: Brazilian Govt scholar to Rio de Janeiro, 45-46; Can Coun fel, 58 & medal, 68; second prize, Quebec Ann Art Competition, 64.
Memberships: Royal Can Acad Art.
Publications: Auth, Roberts.
Mailing Address: 211 Walnut Ave, Saint Lambert, P Q, Can.

DE TORE, JOHN E.
Painter, Educator
Preferred Media: Watercolor.
b Syracuse, N Y, Sept 14, 02.
Work in Public Collections: Ranger Fund; Princeton Univ; Butler Inst Am Art, Youngstown, Ohio; Munson-Williams-Proctor Inst, Utica, N Y; Springfield Mus Fine Arts, Mass.
Exhibitions: Butler Inst Am Art; Am Watercolor Soc, New York, N Y; Audubon Artists; Watercolor U S A, Springfield Art Mus, Mo; Cooperstown Art Asn, N Y.
Teaching: Private classes in watercolor.
Awards: Best-in-show award, Cooperstown Art Asn, 61; Rudolph Lesch Award, Am Watercolor Soc, 62; first prize, watercolor, Butler Inst Am Art, 64.
Memberships: Grand Cent Galleries; Am Watercolor Soc; fel Royal Soc Arts; Allied Artists Am; Audubon Artists.
Publications: Contrib, Am Artist, 60.
Dealer: Grand Central Galleries, Biltmore Hotel, New York, NY 10017.
Mailing Address: 811 Grant Blvd, Syracuse, NY 13203.

DEUTSCH, PETER ANDREW
Painter
Preferred Media: Acrylics.
b Truava, Czech, July 31, 26; Can citizen.
Study & Training: Univ St Andrews, BSc(hon).
Work in Public Collections: Nat Gallery Can, Ottawa, Ont; Art Gallery Ont, Toronto; Agnes Etherington Art Gallery, Queen's Univ (Ont); Rothmans Art Gallery, Stratford, Ont.
Exhibitions: Sixth Can Biennial Exhib, Nat Gallery Can, Ottawa, 65; Ont Centennial Exhib Can Art, Art Gallery Ont, 67; Royal Can Acad Ann, 67, 68, 70 & 71; Ont Soc Artists Exhibs, 67 & 69; Art Gallery Hamilton Ann, 69 & 70.
Dealer: Gallery Moos, 138 Yorkville Ave, Toronto, Ont, Can.
Mailing Address: 20 Skipton Ct, Downsview, Toronto, Ont, Can.

DEVERELL, TIMOTHY
Painter
b Regina, Sask, 1939.
Study & Training: Regina Sch Art, Univ Sask; Art Stud League New York.
Exhibitions: Mus Fine Arts Houston, 61; one-man show, Kornblee Gallery, 61 & 62; Yale Univ Art Gallery, 62; one-man show, Art Stud League New York, 65; Seventh Biennial Can Painting, Nat Gallery Can, Ottawa, 68.
Awards: Allen Tucker merit scholar; Edward MacDowell traveling scholar, 63.
Mailing Address: 53 W 29th St, New York, NY 10001.

DE VINNA, MAURICE (AMBROSE, JR)
Critic, Educator
b Tulsa, Okla, Apr 12, 07.
Study & Training: Harvard Univ, AB; Inst d'Art Contemp, Paris, France; with Jacques Loutschansky, Paris; Inst Art & Archaeol of Univ Paris; Brevet d'Art Sorbonne; Harvard Grad Sch.
Teaching: Lectr art hist, Tulsa Exten Ctr, Univ Okla, 32-33; spec lectr, Benedictine Heights Col, Tulsa, 56-58; lectr art hist & aesthetics.
Positions: Asst state dir, Works Proj Admin Art Prog, 36-42; monuments, fine arts & archives sect, OMGUS, 46-47.
Memberships: Press Assoc Am Inst Designers; Hon Consul France.
Publications: Ed fine arts, Tulsa World, 34-
Mailing Address: Tulsa World, Tulsa, OK 74102.

DeVIS-NORTON, MARY M
Museum Educator
b Vancouver, Wash, Aug 22, 14.
Study & Training: Univ Calif, Los Angeles, BE; Univ Hawaii, MFA.
Teaching: Mus instr, Honolulu Acad Arts, Hawaii, 41-53, 71-
Positions: Dir educ, Honolulu Acad Arts, 53-63, cur jr educ, 63-71.
Memberships: Nat Art Educ Asn.
Mailing Address: 2552 Sonoma Pl, Honolulu, HI 96822.

DE VITIS, THEMIS
Painter, Designer
b Lecce, Italy, Nov 3, 05.
Study & Training: Acad Beaux-Arts, Rome, Venice & Milan, Italy; Fashion Inst Technol, N Y, cert.
Work in Public Collections: Mus Art, Prov Bldg & Munic Bldg, Lecce, Italy; Univ Ciudad Trujillo, Dom Repub; Norfolk Mus Arts & Sci; Butler Inst Am Art, Youngstown, Ohio; also in pvt collections.
Commissions: Murals, portraits & designs, Thibaut, Renverne Originals, Louis Bowen & others; murals, Italy.
Exhibitions: Salon Independents, Paris; Salon Art Murals, Artists Equity Asn, 51, 52 & 54; Am Fedn Arts, 55; Adirondack Ann, 62 & 63; Norfolk Mus Arts & Sci, 66 & 68; plus others.
Positions: Mem welfare comt, New York chap, Artists Equity Asn, 52-, dir exec bd, 60-62.
Awards: Scholar, Lecce, Italy, 22; nat award, Beaux-Arts, Venice, 27.
Memberships: Artists Equity Asn; hon mem Kappa Pi.
Publications: Contribr, art criticisms, In: Fr & Ital publ.
Mailing Address: 111 Bank, New York, NY 10014.

DE VITO, FERDINAND A
Painter, Educator
b Trenton, N J, Jan 4, 26.
Study & Training: Cleveland Inst Art, BFA; Yale Univ, MFA; Univ Denver; Philadelphia Mus Sch Art; studied painting with Josef Albers & Conrad Marca-Relli, graphics with Gabor Peterdi.
Exhibitions: One-man show, East Hampton Gallery, N Y, 65; Mickelson Gallery, Washington, D C, 66; retrospective, Univ Art Gallery, Binghamton, N Y, 68; Am Fedn Arts, 68 & 69.
Teaching: Assoc prof art, State Univ N Y Binghamton, 71-
Awards: Mary C Page Award, Cleveland, Ohio.
Mailing Address: Dept of Art, State University of New York at Binghamton, Binghamton, NY 13901.

DEW, JAMES EDWARD
Educator, Painter
Preferred Media: Acrylics, Watercolors, Oils.
b Barnesville, Ohio, Sept 15, 22.
Study & Training: Univ Ala, 43-44; Oberlin Col, AB, 46, AM, 47.
Teaching: Prof painting, Univ Mont, 47-
Memberships: Col Art Asn Am.
Mailing Address: 531 E Sussex Ave, Missoula, MT 59801.

DE WAAL, RONALD BURT
Collector
b Salt Lake City, Utah, Oct 23, 32.
Study & Training: Univ Utah, BS, 55; Mexico City Col, summer 55 & 58; Univ Denver, MA, 58.
Positions: Humanities librn & exhibs chmn, Colo State Univ, Fort Collins, 66-
Memberships: Col Art Asn Am; Nat Sculpture Soc.
Collection: Beethoven statuary and paintings; pewter, porcelain, and wood figure sculptures. Beethoven in the Arts, exhibited Univ Utah, 65 & Colo State Univ, 66, 67 & 70.
Publications: Auth, The world bibliography of Sherlock Holmes and Dr Watson, New York Graphic Soc, 73; auth, Beethoven in the fine arts (in prep).
Mailing Address: 719 S Washington, Fort Collins, CO 80521.

DE WELDON, FELIX GEORGE WEIHS
Sculptor, Architect
b Vienna, Austria; U S citizen.
Study & Training: Univ Vienna Sch Archit, BA, MA, MS & PhD; Oxford Univ; also study in Italy, Spain & France.
Work in Public Collections: Bronze statue of John Glenn, Air & Space Mus, Washington, D C; Truman Libr, Independence, Mo; Kennedy Libr, Boston, Mass.
Commissions: Flag raising on Iow Jima, Marine Corps War Mem Found, Washington, D C, 54; Simon Bolivar (equestrian statue), Washington, D C, 58; Red Cross Monument, Washington, D C, 59; Truman Monument, Athens, Greece, 63; Nat Monument, Govt Malaysia, Kuala Lampur, 66.
Exhibitions: Royal Acad, London, Eng, 36; Salon, Paris, France, 38; Archit League New York, 39; Mus Montreal, Can, 40; Art Asn, Newport, R I, 46.
Teaching: Dir, Newport Acad Fine Arts, 52-60.
Positions: Comnr, Comn Fine Arts, 50-63; chmn, Comn Arts & Sci for President Eisenhower, 52-60; chmn, Arts & Sci Comt Taft Inst Govt, 71.
Awards: Medal of Honor for Arts & Sci, Austria, 62; Award for Outstanding Serv, Daughters Am Revolution, 72; knight, Order of Malaysia Brit Commonwealth.
Bibliography: Uncommon valour (film), USN, 52; U S Marines, Nat Geog Mag, 52; Tribute in transit, Life Mag, 54.
Memberships: Art Asn Newport, R I.
Mailing Address: 9320 Falls Bridge Lane, Potomac, MD 20854.

DEWEY, MR & MRS CHARLES S, JR
Collectors
Mailing Address: 50 E 77th St, New York, NY 10021.

DEWEY, KENNETH FRANCIS
Painter, Illustrator
Preferred Media: Pen & Ink, Watercolors, Oils.
b New York, N Y, Oct 5, 40.
Study & Training: Sch Visual Arts, New York; also with B Hogarth & Philip Hayes.
Work in Public Collections: Yares Gallery, Scottsdale, Ariz.
Exhibitions: One-man shows, Dal Bohrer's Design Gallery, 69 & Yares Gallery, 72; Firebird Festival Fine Arts, 70; Strathmore Paper Int, 70; Southwest Graphics Int, 72.
Awards: Strathmore Paper Award, 70; Mod Publicity Int Award, 70; bronze medal, two awards, Communigraphics, 71.
Publications: Illusr, Rip Van Winkle, Simon & Schuster, 70; auth & illusr, Don's trek, Ariz Repub & Gazette, 70; illusr, Spirit of Cochise, Scribner, 72; auth & illusr, Onyamarks, The Studio, 72.
Dealer: Yares Gallery, P O Box 1662, Scottsdale, AZ 85252.
Mailing Address: c/o 1901 E Oak St, Phoenix, AZ 85006.

DeWITT, FLOYD TENNISON
Sculptor, Painter
Preferred Media: Bronze, Iron, Oils.
b Wolf Point, Mont, Aug 25, 34.
Study & Training: Minneapolis Sch Art, Minn, scholar, 57, with Paul Granlund; Rijksakademie Van Beeldende Kunsten, Amsterdam, Netherland, scholar, 61-66, sculpture with V P S Esser.
Work in Public Collections: Rijksakademie Collection, Amsterdam; City Collection, Utrecht; Royal Collection, Princess Benedicte, Denmark; Nat Medallion Soc, Hague, Netherlands; Rijks Collection, Amsterdam.
Commissions: Seven welded reliefs, Michaels Supper Club; Rochester, Minn, 60; Eleanor Roosevelt Medallion, Royal Begeer, Vorschaten, Netherlands, 64; Inheritor (bronze equestrian monument), City of Amsterdam, 67; bronze donkeys, Utrecht, Netherlands, 67; Pegasus (cast bronze), Utrecht, 72.
Exhibitions: 20th Century Sculpture, Walker Art Ctr, Minneapolis, 58; Interacademial Exhib Sculpture, Hague, 63; Het Paard, Paardenburg on Amstel, Netherland, 64; Mod Dutch Sculpture, Singer Mus, Harlem, Netherlands, 69; Ann Salons Arti Et Amicitiae, Amsterdam, 70-72.
Awards: Purchase awards, Rijksacademie, 61-66 & Denmark, 63.
Memberships: Arti & Amicitiae Amsterdam (mem jury, 68-); Int Asn Art, Paris; Amsterdam Soc Medallion Art.
Dealer: Chapellier Galleries, 22 E 80th St, New York, NY 10021.
Mailing Address: Gijsbrecht van Aemstelstraat 29, Amsterdam, Netherlands.

DIAO, DAVID
Painter
b Szechuan, China, Aug 7, 43; U S citizen.
Study & Training: Kenyon Col.
Work in Public Collections: Whitney Mus Am Art, New York, N Y; San Francisco Mus, Calif; Art Gallery Ont, Toronto; Mus Mod Art, New York; Va Mus, Richmond.
Exhibitions: Beaux Arts 25th Anniversary Exhib, Columbus Gallery Fine Arts, Ohio, 71; Paintings & Sculpture Today, Indianapolis Mus Art, Ind, 72; 8 Painters, New York, Mus Art, Univ Calif, Berkeley, 72; plus others.
Teaching: Instr painting, Cooper Union, 70-; vis critic painting, Yale Univ Grad Sch Art, 71-72.
Bibliography: James Harithas (auth), David Diao, Arts Mag, 4/70; Carter Ratcliff (auth), Painted vs painterly, Art News Ann, 71; Peter Schjeldahl (auth), Two on the move, New York Times, 3/19/72.
Dealer: Dunkelman Gallery, 15 Bedford Rd, Toronto, Ont, Can.
Mailing Address: 231 Bowery, New York, NY 10002.

DICE, ELIZABETH JANE
Craftsman, Educator
b Urbana, Ill, Apr 3, 19.
Study & Training: Univ Mich, BDesign, 41, MDesign, 42; Ind Univ, MA, 66; Int Sch Art, Mex; Inst Allende, Mex; Columbia Univ Teachers Col; Norfolk Art Sch; painting with Jerry Farnsworth.
Exhibitions: Miss Art, 48-51, 67 & 68; Nat Crafts Exhib, Wichita, 50; Nat Watercolor Show, Jackson, 51; Starkville Craft Exhib, Miss, 54; New Orleans Art Asn, 55; plus many others.
Teaching: Assoc prof art, Miss State Col Women, 45-
Awards: Prizes, Jackson, 46 & 51; Miss River Craft Exhib Award, 63.
Memberships: Col Art Asn Am; Handweavers Guild Am (state rep, 72); Miss Art Asn; Miss Educ Asn; Southeastern Col Art Conf.
Mailing Address: 134 King St, Columbus, MS 39701.

DICKERSON, DANIEL JAY
Painter, Educator
Preferred Media: Acrylics, Oils.
b Jersey City, N J, Dec 22, 22.
Study & Training: Cooper Union Art Sch, 41-43 & 45-46; Cranbrook Acad Art, BFA, 47, MFA, 49.
Work in Public Collections: Joseph H Hirshhorn Collection; Adelphi Univ Mus; Ill Wesleyan Mus; Cranbrook Mus.
Exhibitions: Whitney Mus Am Art Ann, 47; Pa Acad Fine Arts, 53; Audubon Artist Exhib, 64; Nat Inst Arts & Lett, 68; Mus Mod Art group show works in art lending service, 68.
Teaching: Lectr art, Manhattanville Col, 65-69; chmn art dept, Finch Col, 69-
Awards: First prize, Springfield Art Mus, 54; Emily Lowe Award for painting, Audubon Artists, 64; first prize, Hartford Temple Art Show, 70.
Dealer: Terry Dintenfass Inc, 18 E 67th St, New York, NY 10021.
Mailing Address: 104 High St, Leonia, NJ 07605.

DICKERSON, WILLIAM JUDSON
Painter
Preferred Media: Oils, Watercolors.
b El Dorado, Kans, Oct 29, 04.
Study & Training: Art Inst Chicago, dipl, 30; lithography with Bolton Brown & painting with B J O Nordfeldt, Santa Fe, N Mex.
Work in Public Collections: Libr of Cong, Washington, D C; Nelson Art Gallery, Kansas City, MO; Wichita Art Mus, Kans; Wichita Art Asn; portraits of judges, Kans Supreme Ct, Topeka.
Exhibitions: Metrop Mus Art, New York, N Y, 52; Kans State Univ, Manhattan, 70; Kans Watercolor Soc, Wichita, 70-72; Philadelphia Watercolor Club, Pa, 71; Watercolor U S A, Springfield, Mo, 72.
Collections Arranged: Nat Decorative Arts Exhib, Wichita, 64, 68 & 70; Nat Graphic Arts Invitational, Wichita, 67 & 69.
Teaching: Instr drawing, painting & lithography, Wichita Art Asn Sch, 30-71.
Positions: Dir, Wichita Art Asn Sch, 30-64, dir sch & gallery, 65-71, emer dir, 72-
Memberships: Soc Can Painters, Etchers & Engravers; Kans Watercolor Soc; Philadelphia Watercolor Club.
Mailing Address: 509 N Martinson, Wichita, KS 67203.

DICKEY, HELEN PAULINE
Painter, Instructor
Preferred Media: Polymers, Oils.
b Cleveland, Ohio.
Study & Training: Mus Sch, Toledo Univ; West Reserve Univ; Tampa Univ, with Harold Nosti; Cleveland Art Sch, with Carl Gaertner.
Work in Public Collections: Contemp Gallery, St Petersburg, Fla; Jassada of Clearwater, Loew's Hotels, New York, N Y; Fla Presby Col, St Petersburg; Merritt-Phinney-Southard, Cleveland.
Exhibitions: Hunter Ann, Chattanooga, Tenn, 67; 22nd Southeastern Ann Exhib, High Mus, Atlanta, Ga, 67; Juried Arts 6th Nat Exhib, Tyler, Tex, 69; Chautauqua Nat Exhib Am Art, 69-70; Gulf Coast Art Exhib, Mobile, Ala.
Teaching: Instr, Studio Four, 64-69; instr Arts Ctr, 71-72; instr Art Club St Petersburg, 72.
Positions: Dir Art Gallery, Main Pub Libr, St Petersburg, 68-; dir, Arts Ctr Gallery, St Petersburg, 71-
Awards: Many state awards, 62-
Bibliography: Mariane Kelsey (auth), Artist says, I paint for myself, 67; Charles Benbow (auth), reviews, In: St Petersburg Times, 67-; Henry Fink (auth), reviews, In: Times Independent, 67-
Memberships: Fla Artist Group; Fla League Arts; Arts Ctr Asn St Petersburg (v pres, 71-72); Fine Arts Mus; Ringling Mus.
Specialty of Gallery: Original paintings, sculpture and craft.
Publications: Contribr & illusr, A brighter dawn awaits the human day, Churchman Mag, 12/68.
Dealer: Contemporary Gallery, 110 First Ave N E, St Petersburg, FL 33701.
Mailing Address: 1723 Lakewood Dr S, St Petersburg, FL 33712.

DICKINSON, EDWIN
Painter
b Seneca Falls, N Y, Oct 11, 91.
Study & Training: Pratt Inst Art Sch, 10-11; Art Stud League New York, 11-12; Paris, France, 19-20; also with William M Chase & C W Hawthorne.
Work in Public Collections: Metrop Mus Art; Albright-Knox Art Gallery; Mus Mod Art; Whitney Mus Am Art; Art Inst Chicago; plus others.
Exhibitions: Fifteen Americans, 52, Mus Mod Art, 59 & Traveling Exhib, 61; retrospectives, Boston Univ, 58 & Whitney Mus Am Art, 65; Brooklyn Mus; Boston Mus Fine Arts; Venice Biennale, 68; plus others.

Teaching: Lectr, Hartford, Boston & Columbia Univs; instr art, Art Stud League New York, 22-23 & 45-65; instr art, Cooper Union Art Sch, 45-50; instr art, Brooklyn Mus, 49-53.
Awards: Creative arts medal, Brandeis Univ, 59; Ford Found grant, 59; Brevoort-Eickenmeyer Prize, Columbia Univ, 65; plus others.
Bibliography: Werner Haftman (auth), included in: Painting in the twentieth century, Praeger, 60; Lloyd Goodrich (auth), The drawings of Edwin Dickinson, Yale Univ Press, 63 & Edwin Dickinson (catalog), Whitney Mus Am Art, 65; plus others.
Memberships: Fedn Mod Painters & Sculptors; Nat Acad Design; Patteran Soc, Buffalo; Am Acad Arts & Lett; Nat Inst Arts & Lett; plus others.
Mailing Address: Box 793, Wellfleet, MA 02667.

DICKINSON, ELEANOR CREEKMORE
Painter, Sculptor
Preferred Media: Mixed Media.
b Knoxville, Tenn, Feb 7, 31.
Study & Training: Univ Tenn, BA, 52, with C Kermit Ewing; San Francisco Art Inst, 61-63, with James Weeks.
Work in Public Collections: Corcoran Gallery Art, Washington, D C; San Francisco Mus Art, Calif; Butler Inst Am Art, Youngstown, Ohio; Libr Cong Collection, Washington, D C; Oakland Mus, Calif.
Exhibitions: One-artist shows, McClung Mus, Knoxville, Tenn, 64, San Francisco Mus Art, 65, Santa Barbara Mus Art, Calif, 66, Corcoran Gallery Art, 70 & Poindexter Gallery, New York, N Y, 72.
Teaching: Lectr drawing & painting, Univ Calif, 69-71; vis prof life drawing, Calif Col Arts & Crafts, Oakland, 71-
Positions: Trustee, San Francisco Art Inst, 63-66.
Awards: San Francisco Women Artists Pres Prize, San Francisco Mus, 59; purchase award, Butler Inst Am Art, 60; purchase award, City of San Francisco, 71.
Bibliography: Aline Saarinen (auth), Revival!, NBC Today Show, 70; Nina Osnos (auth), Revival by Eleanor Dickinson, Corcoran Gallery Art, 70; James R Mellow (auth), Eleanor Dickinson, New York Times, 72.
Memberships: Artists Equity Asn Northern Calif (mem bd dirs).
Publications: Contribr, Sculpture from junk, Van Nostrand Reinhold, 67; auth, Tennessee revival services, Libr Cong Arch Folk Song, 71.
Dealers: Poindexter Gallery, 24 E 84th St, New York, NY 10028; William Sawyer Gallery, 3045 Clay St, San Francisco, CA 94115.
Mailing Address: 2125 Broderick St, San Francisco, CA 94115.

DICKINSON, WILLIAM STIRLING
Educator, Art Administrator
b Chicago, Ill, Dec 22, 09.
Study & Training: Princeton Univ, BA(cum laude); Art Inst Chicago; Fontainebleau Ecole des Beaux Artes, France.
Teaching: Lectr survey of Mex, Inst Allende, San Miguel de Allende, Mex, 45-, lectr Mex: writers viewpoints, 71-
Positions: Dir, Escuela Univ Bellas Artes, San Miguel de Allende, 38-51; dir & pres, Inst Allende, 51-
Publications: Co-auth & illusr, Mexican odyssey, 35; co-auth & illusr, Westward from Rio, 36; co-auth & illusr, Death is incidental, 37; co-auth, San Miguel de Allende, 71; transl, Imperial Cuzco, 71.
Mailing Address: Sto Domingo 38, San Miguel de Allende, Guanajuato, Mexico.

DICKSON, HAROLD EDWARD
Educator, Writer
b Sharon, Pa, July 18, 00.
Study & Training: Pa State Univ, BS; Harvard Univ, MA & PhD.
Teaching: Prof art hist, Pa State Univ, University Park, 23-64, emer prof art hist, 64-; vis prof art hist, Univ N C, 65-67.
Memberships: Col Art Asn Am; Am Asn Univ Prof; Soc Archit Historians; Scarab Club.
Publications: Auth, John Wesley Jarvis, American painter, 49, A hundred Pennsylvania buildings, 54, Pennsylvania painters, 55, George Grey Barnard, 64 & Arts of the young republic: the age of William Dunlap, Univ N C Press, 68; plus others.
Mailing Address: Dept of Art History, Pennsylvania State University, University Park, PA 16802.

DIEBENKORN, RICHARD
Painter
b Portland, Ore, Apr 22, 22.
Study & Training: Stanford Univ, 40-43; Univ Calif, 43-44; Calif Sch Fine Arts, 46; Univ N Mex, MA, 52
Work in Public Collections: Toronto Mus; Phoenix Mus; Albright-Knox Gallery, Buffalo; Oberlin Col Gallery; San Francisco Mus Art; plus others.
Exhibitions: Five shows, Whitney Mus Am Art Ann, 55-70; one-man shows, DeYoung Mem Mus, San Francisco, 63 & Jewish Mus, 65;

Venice Biennale, 68; one-man show, Los Angeles Co Mus, 69 & 72; plus many other group and one-man shows.
Teaching: Prof art, Univ Calif, Los Angeles, 68-
Awards: Albert M Bender fel, 46; purchase prize, Olivet Col; gold medal, Pa Acad Fine Arts, 68.
Bibliography: David M Mendelowitz (auth), included in: A history of American art, Holt, Rinehart & Winston, 61; Lee Nordness (ed), included in: Art: U S A: now, C J Bucher, 62; Alfred Neumeyer (auth), included in: The search for meaning in modern art, Prentice-Hall, 64; plus others.
Memberships: Am Acad Arts & Lett.
Publications: Auth, Drawing, 65.
Dealer: Marlborough Gallery, 41 E 57th St, New York, NY 10022.
Mailing Address: 334 Amalfi Dr, Santa Monica, CA 90402.

DIENES, SARI
Painter, Sculptor
b Debrecen, Hungary, Oct 8, 99; U S citizen.
Study & Training: With Fernand Leger & Andre Lhote in Paris, France; Ozenfant Sch Art, London, Eng, & with Henry Moore.
Work in Public Collections: Brooklyn Mus, N Y; Mus Mod Art Print Collection, New York; also in many pvt collections.
Commissions: Stage set & costume designs for Fire, Univ Ill Art Festival, 52; 400 rubbings of prehistoric Indian carvings on stones bordering Columbia River, comn by Archaeol Dept, Univ Wash, 55-58; figures & masks for Questions from the Floor, Buffalo Art Festival, 68; Electric Circus, 68; two screens, Hearing Rooms, Legislative Bldg, Albany, N Y, 72.
Exhibitions: Plastic Show, John Daniels Gallery, New York, 65; Stout State Univ, Faculty Show, Menomonie, Wis, 66; Petroglyphs, Wesleyan Univ, Middletown, Conn, 68; Prints and Projections, Rockland Community Col, Suffern, N Y, 71; Christmas Show, 71 & Retrospective, 72, Rockland Found, West Nyack, N Y; plus many other group & one-man shows.
Teaching: Asst dir, Ozenfant Sch Art, London; Instr art, Parsons Sch Design & Brooklyn Mus Art Sch, New York; artist-in-residence, Stout State Univ, 66.
Awards: MacDowell Colony fels, 52, 53 & 55; Am Fedn Art grant, 71; Mark Rothko Found grant, 71; plus others.
Bibliography: Articles, In: Life Mag, 11/15/55, Craft Horizons, 10/57 & 10/62 & Domus, 7/63; plus others.
Mailing Address: Gate Hill, Stony Point, NY 10980.

DIERINGER, ERNEST A
Painter
Preferred Media: Acrylics.
b Chicago, Ill, July 6, 32.
Study & Training: Art Inst Chicago.
Work in Public Collections: Dayton Art Inst, Ohio; Cleveland Mus, Ohio; Pet Milk Collection; Ill Bell Tel Collection.
Exhibitions: Six one-man shows, Poindexter Gallery, 62-72; Post Painterly Abstraction Traveling Show, 64; Park Bernet Summer Show, 64; Am Painting, Champaign-Urbana, Ill, 65; Chicago Expatriates, 72.
Awards: New Eng Ann Awards, Edwin C Andrews, 71 & Am Tobacco Co, 72.
Mailing Address: R D 1, Lonetown Rd, West Redding, CT 06896.

DIGNAC, GENY (EUGENIA M BERMUDEZ)
Sculptor, Painter
Preferred Media: Plastics.
b Buenos Aires, Arg, June 8, 32.
Work in Public Collections: Mus Mod Art, Cali, Colombia; Galeria Banco Cent, Quito, Ecuador; Latin Am Art Found, San Juan, P R.
Exhibitions: Some More Beginnings, Exp in Art & Technol, Brooklyn Mus, N Y, 68; IX Festival of Art, Cali, Colombia, 69; Earth, Air, Fire, Water Elements of Art, Boston Mus Fine Arts, Mass, 71; Arte de Sistema, Centro de Arte y Comunicacion, Mus Art Mod, Buenos Aires, 71; III Biennial of Art Coltejer, Medellin, Colombia, 72; also many one-woman shows, 67-71.
Awards: Uranus II light & plastic sculpture, IX Festival of Art, Mus Mod Art, Cali, 69.
Bibliography: J Bermudez (producer), Dignac, 67-68 & Three fire gestures (films), 70-71; R Osuna (producer), D Dig Dignac (film), 68.
Publications: Auth, 3 Fire Gestures, limited ed, produced & designed by J Bermudez.
Dealer: Pyramid Gallery, 2121 P St N W, Washington, DC 20037.
Mailing Address: 4049 E Alan Lane, Phoenix, AZ 85040.

DIKE, PHILIP LATIMER
Painter, Designer
Preferred Media: Watercolors, Oils.
b Redlands, Calif, Apr 6, 06.
Study & Training: Chouinard Art Inst; Art Stud League New York; Am Acad, Fontainebleau, France; also with Clarence Hinkle, F Tolles Chamberlin, George Luks & M St Hubert.

Work in Public Collections: Hearne Collection, Metrop Mus Art, New York, N Y; Butler Inst Am Art, Youngstown, Ohio; Pennell Collection, Libr Cong, Washington, D C; Springfield Mus; Pasadena Art Inst, Calif.
Commissions: Painted altar piece, First M E Church, Redlands, Calif, 46; ceramic tile, Gladding McBean, Los Angeles, Calif, 51; ceramic tile entrance, St San Antonio Col Fine Arts Ctr, 52; ceramic tile pool area, Scripps Col, 52; mosaic, chapel, Claremont Community Congregational Church, 62.
Exhibitions: Calif Nat Watercolor Soc, 26-71; Am Watercolor Soc, New York, 29-72; one-man & juried exhibs, Los Angeles Co Mus, 31-55; Carnegie Int, Pittsburgh, Pa, 36-58; Nat Acad Design Exhib, 51.
Teaching: Instr painting, Chouinard Art Inst, 30-49; prof painting, Scripps Col & Claremont Grad Sch, 49-69, prof emer, 70-
Positions: Color coordr, Walt Disney Prod, 34-44.
Awards: First prize for oil, Los Angeles County Mus, 31; first prize for watercolor, Butler Inst Am Art, 59; purchase prizes, Springfield Nat Watercolor Exhibs, 67-72.
Memberships: Nat Acad Design; Am Watercolor Soc (hon v pres, 57); Calif Nat Watercolor Soc (pres, 38-39); West Coast Watercolor Soc (hon v pres, 64).
Publications: Auth, Watercolors, Am Artist Mag, 11/40.
Dealer: Richard Challis Gallery, 9390 S Coast Hwy, Laguna Beach, CA 92652.
Mailing Address: 3110 Forbes Ave, Claremont, CA 91711.

DILL, GUY GIRARD
Sculptor
Preferred Media: Mixed Media.
b Duval Co, Fla, May 30, 46.
Study & Training: Chouinard Sch Art, Los Angeles, BFA.
Work in Public Collections: Guggenheim Mus, New York, N Y; Staedelijk Mus, Amsterdam; Pasadena Mus, Los Angeles, Calif.
Commissions: 20 timbers, Thomas E Inch, Brentwood, Calif, 71.
Exhibitions: Los Angeles Artists, Los Angeles Co Mus Art, 70; Guggenheim Mus, 71; Earth, Air, Fire, Water, La Jolla Mus Art, Calif, 71; Ace Gallery, Los Angeles, 72; Felicity Samuel Gallery, London, Eng, 72.
Awards: Theodoron Award, Guggenheim Mus, 71.
Bibliography: D Waldman, Theodoron (catalogue), Guggenheim Mus, 71; Bill Packer (auth), Interview with Guy Dill, Art & Artists, London, 72.
Dealer: Irving Blum, 811 N La Cienega Blvd, Los Angeles, CA 90069.
Mailing Address: 201 San Juan, Venice, CA 90291.

DILLER, MARY BLACK
Painter, Writer
b Lancaster, Pa.
Study & Training: Carnegie Inst, with Petrovits; Pa Acad Fine Arts, with MacCarter, Garber & Carles; Art Stud League New York, with Fogarty & Du Mond; Metrop Art Sch, with Jacobs.
Work in Public Collections: Columbia Mus Art, S C; Albany Inst Hist & Art, N Y; Fla Southern Col, Lakeland; Tiffany Found; Seton Hall Univ, Newark, N J.
Exhibitions: Isochromatic, Aquachromatic, Casein & Palettes Traveling Exhibs, 36-55; Audubon Artists Ann, New York, N Y, 42-60; Art Stud League New York Vet Show, 44; Pa Acad Fine Arts, Philadelphia; one-man exhibs, New York Pub Libr, Lancaster & Reading, Pa.
Teaching: Dir dept art, Shippen Sch, Lancaster, 27-39.
Positions: Pa State Dir Am Art Wk, Am Artists Prof League, 38.
Awards: Awards for Ellen, Iris Club, 26 & The Witness Tree, Ogunquit Art Ctr, 40; St Vincent's Col Purchase Prize, Audubon Artists, 64.
Bibliography: Michael M Engel (auth), Basic shapes, Design Mag, 53; For the young in art, Today's Art, 54.
Memberships: Lancaster Co Art Asn (pres, 37-39); Audubon Artists; Nat Soc Arts & Lett; Tiffany Found; Kappa Pi.
Publications: Auth & illusr, Holiday Drawing Book, 54; contribr, How to draw, Child's book of knowledge, 55; auth & illusr, Drawing for young artists, 55; auth & illusr for Design Mag, Every Child's Mag & Jack & Jill; auth, articles, In: Poetry, Town & Country & Sun News.
Mailing Address: 220 Cabrini Blvd, New York, NY 10033.

DILLON, C DOUGLAS
Art Administrator, Collector
b Geneva, Switz, Aug 21, 09.
Study & Training: Harvard Univ, AB.
Positions: Trustee, Metrop Mus Art, 51-, pres, 70-
Collection: French impressionist painting; eighteenth century continental and British porcelain; eighteenth century French furniture and decorative objects.
Mailing Address: 767 Fifth Ave, New York, NY 10022.

DILLON, MILDRED (MURPHY)
  Painter, Printmaker
  Preferred Media: Wood.
  b Philadelphia, Pa, Oct 12, 07.
  Study & Training: Philadelphia Col Art, 25-28; Pa Acad Fine Arts, 28-29; Barnes Found, 29-31, with Henry McCarter & Earle Horter.
  Work in Public Collections: Philadelphia Mus Art; Barnes Found, Merion, Pa; Free Libr Philadelphia; Arch Can Painters & Etchers; Am Coloprint Soc Collection, Philadelphia.
  Exhibitions: Four-man show, Nat Serigraph Soc, 49 & Print Club Philadelphia, 59; Libr Cong Nat, 57; Mus Bellas Artes, Contemp Graphics Overseas, Caracas, Venezuela, 60; Color Prints of the Americas, N J State Mus, 70.
  Positions: V pres, Am Color Print Soc, Philadelphia, 55-; chmn, Rittenhouse Sq Outdoor Exhib, 58-70; demonstr, Print Club Philadelphia, 61-70.
  Awards: Harrison Morris Prize, Pa Acad Fine Arts, 53; George Lear Mem Prize, Woodmere Art Gallery, 58; Klein Prize, Print Club Philadelphia, 67.
  Memberships: Artists Equity Asn; Philadelphia Art Alliance (mem bd dirs, 60-); fel Pa Acad Fine Arts; Woodmere Art Gallery; Alumnae Philadelphia Col Art.
  Mailing Address: 627 E Wadsworth Ave, Philadelphia, PA 19119.

DIMAN, HOMER
  Painter
  Preferred Media: Oils, Watercolors.
  b New York, N Y, July 31, 14.
  Study & Training: Ecole Beaux Artes; Parsons Sch Fine Art, New York; Art Stud League New York; Franklin Acad Art, New York; Newark Sch Fine Art; also with John Sloan, miniature illum with Arthur Szyk & anat with George Bridgeman.
  Work in Public Collections: Am Univ Mus, Beirut, Lebanon; Arch Fla Art, Ringling Mus, Sarasota, Fla.
  Exhibitions: Masters Invitational, Boston, Mass, 35; World's Fair, New York, 39 & 40; Big Bend Nat, Tallahassee, Fla, 68; De Bary Hall, Hq Fla Fedn Art, 70-71; Latin Quarter Gallery, Tampa, Fla, 70-71.
  Positions: V pres & mem exec bd, Fla Fedn Art, De Bary, 70-71.
  Awards: Int Art Dirs Award, Advert Arts, New York, 39; W Shore Exhib Awards, Tampa Realistic Artists, 69 & 70.
  Memberships: Art Club St Petersburg; Latin Quarter Gallery; Sarasota Art Asn; Soc N Am Artists.
  Dealer: Arts International, 2957 West Bay Dr, Belleair Bluffs, FL 33540.
  Mailing Address: 7200 34th St S, Apt 3-B, St Petersburg, FL 33711.

DI MEO, DOMINICK GENEROSO
  Painter, Sculptor
  Preferred Media: Mixed Media.
  b Niagara Falls, N Y, Feb 1, 27.
  Study & Training: Art Inst Chicago, four year dipl, 50, BFA, 52; Univ Iowa, MFA, 53.
  Work in Public Collections: Art Inst Chicago, Ill; Whitney Mus Am Art, New York, N Y; Ill Bell Tel Co, Chicago.
  Exhibitions: 12th Exhib Contemp Am Painting & Sculpture, Krannert Art Mus, Champaign-Urbana, Ill, 65; Ann Exhib Contemp Am Painting, Whitney Mus Am Art, 67-68; Fantasy & Figure, Am Fedn Arts, New York & traveling show, 68-69; Violence in Recent American Art, Mus Contemp Art, Chicago, 68-69; The Crowd: Exhibit of Sculpture, Painting and Graphics, Arts Club Chicago, 69.
  Awards: John Simon Guggenheim Mem Found fel graphics, 72-73.
  Bibliography: Whitney Halstead (auth), Introduction, In: Di Meo, work: 1959-1966, Galaxie, 67.
  Dealer: Fairweather-Hardin Gallery, 101 E Ontario St, Chicago, IL 60611
  Mailing Address: 868 Broadway, New York, NY 10003.

DIMONDSTEIN, MORTON
  Sculptor, Painter
  Preferred Media: Wood, Bronze.
  b New York, N Y, Nov 5, 20.
  Study & Training: Am Artists Sch, New York, N Y, 37-39; Art Stud League New York, 39-41; Otis Art Inst, Los Angeles, Calif, 45-48; Inst Politecnico Nac, Mexico City, Mex, 50-51.
  Work in Public Collections: World Bank, Washington, D C; Libr of Cong, Washington; Pushkin Art Mus, Moscow, U S S R; Seattle Art Mus, Wash; Portland Art Mus, Ore.
  Exhibitions: One-man shows, ACA Gallery, New York, 53, Galleria Penelope, Rome, Italy, 61 & Jacqueline Anhalt Gallery, Los Angeles, 67-72; Third Int Biennial of Sculpture, Carrara, Italy, 62; Int Biennial Art, Palermo, Italy, 64.
  Teaching: Instr all media, Sch Fine Art, Los Angeles, 63-72; instr drawing & sculpture, Univ Southern Calif, 64-68.
  Positions: Staff artist, UNESCO, Patzcuaro, Mex, 52-53.

Memberships: Soc Am Graphic Artists.
  Publications: Mexico (portfolio of woodcuts), Posada Graphics, 54.
  Dealer: Jacqueline Anhalt Gallery, 530 N La Cienega Blvd, Los Angeles, CA 90069.
  Mailing Address: 749 Longwood Ave, Los Angeles, CA 90005.

DIMSON, THEO AENEAS
  Designer
  Preferred Media: Graphics.
  b London, Ont, Apr 8, 30.
  Study & Training: Ont Col Art, Toronto.
  Work in Public Collections: Typomundus 20, France.
  Exhibitions: Art Dirs Club New York; Am Inst Graphic Arts, New York; Graphica Club Toronto; Graphica Club Montreal; Int Poster Art, Bulgaria.
  Positions: V pres creative design, Art Assocs Ltd, Toronto, 59-65; pres & creative dir, Reeson Dimson & Smith Ltd, Toronto, 65-
  Awards: Medal awards, Graphica Club Toronto, 66 & Graphica Club Montreal, 71; award of excellence, Am Inst Graphic Arts, 71.
  Bibliography: Hara (auth), Designers, Graphic Design Mag, 62; Republic of childhood, Oxford Univ, 67.
  Memberships: Graphica Club Toronto; Am Inst Graphic Arts; assoc Royal Can Acad Arts.
  Publications: Illusr, The sunken City, 60 & The double knights, 63, Oxford Univ; illusr, Rubaboo five, Sage, 65.
  Mailing Address: 232 Seaton St, Toronto, Ont, Can.

DINE, JAMES
  Painter, Sculptor
  b Cincinnati, Ohio, June 16, 35.
  Study & Training: Univ Cincinnati; Boston Mus Sch.
  Work in Public Collections: Mus Mod Art, New York, N Y; Tate Gallery, London, Eng; Stedelijk Mus, Amsterdam, Holland; Whitney Mus Am Art, New York; Albright-Knox Art Gallery, Buffalo, N Y.
  Exhibitions: Six Painters & the Object, Guggenheim Mus, New York, 63; 23rd Int Venice Biennial, Italy, 64; Art of U S A, 1670-1966, Whitney Mus Am Art, 66; Dokumenta IV, Kassel, Ger, 67.
  Teaching: Vis prof, Oberlin Col, 65 & Cornell Univ, 67.
  Awards: Norman Harris Silver Medal & prize, Art Inst Chicago, 64.
  Bibliography: John Gordon (auth), Jim Dine, Whitney Mus Am Art, 70; Christopher Finch (auth), Jim Dine, Abrams (in press).
  Publications: Illusr, The poet assassinated, 68; auth & illusr, Welcome home lovebirds, 69; co-auth, Work from the same house, 69; co-auth & illusr, The adventures of Mr & Mrs Jim & Ron, 70.
  Mailing Address: c/o Sonnabend Gallery, 924 Madison Ave, New York, NY 10021.

DINGLE, ADRIAN
  Painter
  Preferred Media: Acrylics.
  b Barmouth, Wales, Feb 4, 11; Can citizen.
  Work in Public Collections: Nat Gallery Can; London Gallery & Art Mus, Ont, Can; Royal Bank Can Collection; Ont Club Collection, Toronto; Arts & Lett Club Collection, Toronto.
  Exhibitions: Royal Can Acad Arts, Ottawa, Montreal; Ont Soc Artists, Toronto; 22nd & 23rd Ann Exhibs Contemp Can Art, Hamilton.
  Memberships: Ont Soc Artists (pres, 67-70); Royal Can Acad Arts (exec coun, 71-72); life fel Int Inst Arts & Lett; Arts & Lett Club, Toronto.
  Publications: Illusr, Redcoat sailor, 56; illusr, Logging with Paul Bunyon, 57; illusr, Tecumtha, 58; Life in Ontario, a social history, 68; contribr, The great Canadian comic books, Peter Martin Assocs, 71.
  Dealers: Roberts Gallery, 641 Yonge St, Toronto, Ont, Can; Gallery 1667, 1246 Hollis St, Halifax, N S, Can.
  Mailing Address: 830 Queensway West, Mississauga, Ont, Can.

DINTENFASS, TERRY
  Art Dealer
  U S citizen.
  Positions: Dir, Terry Dintenfass, Inc.
  Specialty of Gallery: Contemporary American art and American folk art.
  Mailing Address: 18 E 67th St, New York, NY 10021.

DIODA, ADOLPH T
  Sculptor, Educator
  Preferred Media: Wood.
  b Aliquippa, Pa, Sept 10, 15.
  Study & Training: Carnegie Inst Technol; Cleveland Sch Art; Art Stud League New York, N Y; also with John B Flannagan, New York.

Work in Public Collections: Carnegie Mellon Mus, Pittsburgh, Pa;
Pa Acad Fine Arts, Philadelphia; Philadelphia Mus Art; Ogonquit
Mus Art, Maine; Westmoreland Mus Art, Greensburg, Pa.
Commissions: Crucifix, St Michael Sch, Pittsburgh, 49; figure, comn
by Dahlen K Ritchey, Pittsburgh, 51; steel panel, Dept Recreation,
City of Philadelphia, 71.
Exhibitions: Whitney Mus Am Art Ann, New York, 40; Sculpture Int,
Philadelphia Mus Art, 40-49; Carved in Stone, Bucholtz Gallery,
New York, 45; Pa Acad Fine Arts Ann, 46, 47 & 69; 60th Ann
Exhib Am Paintings & Sculpture, Art Inst Chicago, 51.
Teaching: Instr sculpture, Tyler Sch, Temple Univ, 59-69; instr
sculpture, Haverford Col, 62-69; instr wood & stone carving, Pa
Acad Fine Arts, 62-
Awards: Guggenheim Found grant, 45; George D Widener Medal, Pa
Acad Fine Arts, 47; Eben Demarest Scholar Fund grant, Carnegie
Inst Technol, 48.
Memberships: Artists Equity Asn, Philadelphia chap; Peale Club.
Mailing Address: c/o 411 Healy St, Jenkintown, PA 19046.

DIRUBE, ROLANDO LOPEZ
Painter, Sculptor
b Havana, Cuba, Aug 14, 28; U S citizen.
Study & Training: Univ Havana Col Archit & Eng, 48; Art Stud
League New York, with George Grosz & Kuniyoshi, 49; Brooklyn
Mus Art Sch, with Gabor F Peterdi & Max Beckman, 50; Escuela
Nac Artes Graficas, Madrid, Spain, 51-52.
Work in Public Collections: Metrop Mus Art, New York, N Y; Phila-
delphia Univ, Pa; Nat Mus, Havana, Cuba; Mus Mod Art, Madrid,
Spain; Ponce Mus, P R.
Commissions: Nat Asn Architects, 56; Nat Theatre & Nat Sport Col-
iseum, Cuban Govt, Havana, 58; Int Theatres, G H G Enterprises,
San Juan, P R, 70; One Biscayne Tower, G H G Enterprises, Mi-
ami, Fla, 72.
Exhibitions: I Bienal Hispanoamericana Arte, Madrid, 51; Latein-
amerikanische Kunst Gegenwart, Ger, 51; II Bienal São Paulo,
Brazil, 53; Int Colour Woodcut Exhib, Victoria & Albert Mus,
London, 54-55; IX Biennale Int Art Menton, France, 72.
Teaching: Prof design anal, Inter-Am Univ P R Sch Archit, 64-65;
lectr design, Sch Archit, Univ P R, San Juan, 67; prof painting,
Art Stud League, San Juan, 68-
Awards: First prize woodcut, I Bienal Hispanoamericana Arte, 51;
gold medal in painting & gold medal in woodcut, Univ Tampa, 51.
Bibliography: E S Santovenia (auth), Historia de la nación Cubana,
Ed Hist Nación Cubana, S A, 52; R Guastela (auth), Dirube painter
& sculpture (film), Viguie Guastela, 68; J Gómez Sicre (auth), San
Juan muralists, Pan Am Unión Revista Am, 71.
Publications: Illusr, En la Habana ha muerto un turista, 63; illusr
Los combatientes, 68.
Mailing Address: 124 W Ocean Dr, Bay View Cataño, PR 00632.

DI SUVERO, MARK
Painter
b Shanghai, China.
Study & Training: Univ Calif, BA.
Work in Public Collections: Wadsworth Antheneum, Hartford, Conn;
New York Univ, N Y.
Exhibitions: Art Inst Chicago, Ill, 63; Peace Tower, Los Angeles,
Calif, 66; American Sculpture of the Sixties, Los Angeles Co
Mus Art, Calif, 67; Whitney Mus Am Art, New York, 67; San
Francisco Mus Art, Calif, 69; plus others.
Awards: Longview Found grant; Walter K Gutman Found grant; Art
Inst Chicago, 63.
Mailing Address: c/o Noah Goldowsky Gallery, 1078 Madison Ave,
New York, NY 10028.

DIX, GEORGE EVERTSON
Art Dealer
b Evanston, Ill, Apr 6, 12.
Study & Training: Yale Col, BA, Yale Univ, MA.
Positions: Asst dir, Am-Brit Art Ctr, New York, 46-47; owner,
George Dix Gallery, 47-48; co-owner, Durlacher Bros, New
York, 48-67; pvt dealer, 67-
Specialty of Gallery: Paintings and drawings before 1900.
Mailing Address: 19 E 55th St, New York, NY 10022.

DIXON, SALLY FOY
Art Administrator, Lecturer
Preferred Media: Film.
b Seattle, Wash.
Study & Training: Carnegie-Mellon Univ; Chatham Col.
Positions: Cur film sect, Carnegie Inst Mus Art, 70-
Memberships: Pittsburgh Film-Makers Asn (bd dirs, 71); Pitts-
burgh Plan for Art (bd gov, 72-).
Research: First two decades of film in Pittsburgh.
Publications: Contribr, Carnegie Mag, 70-72; contribr, QED Renais-
sance, 12/71.
Mailing Address: Film Section, Carnegie Institute Museum of Art,
4400 Forbes Ave, Pittsburgh, PA 15213.

DMYTRUK, IHOR
Painter, Lecturer
Preferred Media: Acrylics.
b Ukraine, Feb 11, 38; Can citizen.
Study & Training: Univ Alta; Vancouver Sch Art.
Work in Public Collections: Edmonton Art Gallery, Alta; Univ
Calgary, Alta; Stud Union Art Gallery, Univ Alta; Art Gallery
Hamilton, Ont; Art Gallery Windsor, Ont.
Exhibitions: Winnipeg Show, 64, 66 & 68; All Alberta Show, 64-67, 69
& one-man show, 71; Edmonton Art Gallery; Canadian Drawings
and Prints, Cardiff Arts Festival, Gt Brit, 65; West 71, Edmonton
Art Gallery & traveling show, 71.
Teaching: Instr drawing & painting, exten dept, Univ Alta, 63-;
instr drawing & painting, Northern AHA Inst Technol, 63; instr
drawing & painting, art dept, Univ Alta, 70-72.
Awards: All Alberta 1966 Award, Reeves & Sons Ltd; Can Coun
travel grant, 66 & arts bursary, 72.
Bibliography: E N Yates (auth), Four Edmonton artists, 10/69 &
Myra Davies (auth), Recent work by Ihor Dmytruk, 10-11/71,
Arts Can; Karen Wilkin (auth), A report on the West, Art Am,
5/72.
Memberships: Can Artists Representation.
Mailing Address: 11139-110 A Ave, Edmonton, Alta T5H 1K2, Can.

DOBBS, JOHN BARNES
Painter
Preferred Media: Oils.
b Passaic, N J, Aug 2, 31.
Study & Training: R I Sch Design; Brooklyn Mus Art Sch, with
Gregorio Prestopino; Skowhegan Sch Painting & Sculpture, with
Jack Levine.
Work in Public Collections: Syracuse Mus Art, N Y; Fairleigh Dick-
inson Univ; Butler Inst Am Art, Youngstown, Ohio; Univ Mass;
Springfield Mus Art, Mass.
Exhibitions: Five one-man shows, ACA Gallery, New York, N Y,
64-72, Long Island Univ, 71 & Wesleyan Univ, 71; Nat Acad De-
sign, New York, 67, 68 & 71; Nat Inst Arts & Lett, New York, 68-
71.
Teaching: Instr, Brooklyn Mus Art Sch, 56-59; instr New Sch Soc
Res, 65-; instr, City Col New York, 70-71; lectr, John Jay Col
Criminal Justice, 72-
Awards: Emily Lowe Award, Audubon Artists, 65; Louis Comfort
Tiffany Found grant, 67; Childe Hassam Purchase Prize, Nat
Inst Arts & Lett, 71.
Publications: Auth & illusr, Drawings of a draftee, 59; illusr, Death
and justice frescoes, 70; illusr, Fortune Mag, 70; illusr, Libera-
tion Mag, 4/72.
Dealer: ACA Gallery, 25 E 73rd St, New York, NY 10014.
Mailing Address: 463 West St, New York, NY 10014.

DOBKIN, ALEXANDER
Painter
b Genoa, Italy, May 1, 08; U S citizen.
Study & Training: City Col New York, BS; Columbia Univ, MA; Art
Stud League New York.
Work in Public Collections: Mus Mod Art, New York, N Y; Butler
Inst Am Art, Youngstown, Ohio; Newark Mus, N J; Joseph H
Hirshhorn Collection, Washington, D C; Philadelphia Mus Art,
Pa; plus other pub & pvt collections.
Exhibitions: Art Inst Chicago, Ill; Corcoran Gallery Art, Washing-
ton, D C; Pa Acad Fine Arts, Philadelphia; Carnegie Inst, Pitts-
burgh, Pa; Brooklyn Mus, N Y; plus most major mus in U S & in
Europe, Australia & S Am.
Positions: Dir, Art Sch Educ Alliance, 55-
Awards: Two Pennell Purchase Awards for Prints, Libr Cong; two
Childe Hassam Purchase Awards, Am Acad Arts & Lett.
Bibliography: Gerald Zwag (auth), Le sexe de la femme; Bruce
Hooten (auth), Drawing; Herman Baron (auth), American con-
temporary artists.
Memberships: Assoc Nat Acad Design.
Publications: Auth, Principles of figure drawing & Alexander Dob-
kin's travel sketchbook; illusr, Songs of Patricia, A child's
garden of verses, Two years before the mast & others.
Dealer: Forum Gallery, 1018 Madison Ave, New York, NY 10021.
Associated American Artists, 663 Fifth Ave, New York, NY
10022.
Mailing Address: 737 Greenwich St, New York, NY 10014.

DOCKSTADER, FREDERICK J
Museum Director, Collector
b Los Angeles, Calif, Feb 3, 19.
Study & Training: Arizona State Univ, AB & MA; Western Reserve
Univ, PhD.
Work in Public Collections: Cleveland Mus Art, Ohio.
Exhibitions: Cranbrook Acad Art, Bloomfield Hills, Mich, 48; Cleve-
land Mus Art, 49-51.

Collections Arranged: Specialized in exhib installation & reorganization at Cranbrook Inst Sci, Dartmouth Col Mus & Mus Am Indian.

Teaching: Instr silversmithing, Cranbrook Acad Art; instr silversmithing, N H League Arts & Crafts, 52-55; prof, dept art & archaeol, Columbia Univ, 61-64, mem adv coun, 61-; lects, silversmithing, American Indian art & arts & crafts.

Positions: Staff ethnologist, Cranbrook Inst Sci, 46-53; cur anthrop, Dartmouth Col Mus, 53-56; asst dir, Mus Am Indian, 56-59, dir, 59-; comnr, U S Indian Arts & Crafts Bd, 56-68, chmn, 61-68.

Awards: Second prize in silversmithing, 50 & first prize in silversmithing, 51, Cleveland Mus Art; Lotos Award, Lotos Club, New York, 72.

Memberships: Cosmos Club, Washington, D C; Century Club, New York.

Publications: Auth & illusr, The Kachina and the white man, 54; auth & illusr, Indian art in America, 61, Indian art in Middle America, 64 & Indian art in South America, 67; contribr, articles on arts & crafts to various nat publ.

Mailing Address: Museum of the American Indian, Broadway at 155th St, New York, NY 10032.

DODD, ERIC M
Art Administrator, Educator
Can citizen.
Study & Training: Univ Durham, BA, 49, dipl(educ), 50; Ohio State Univ, MA, 51.
Teaching: Assoc prof art, Univ Calgary, 67-, head dept, 68-
Positions: Dir, Univ Calgary Art Gallery, 67-
Mailing Address: Dept of Art, University of Calgary, 2920 24th Ave N W, Calgary, Alta T2N 1N4, Can.

DODD, LAMAR
Painter, Educator
b Fairburn, Ga, Sept 22, 09.
Study & Training: Ga Inst Technol, 26-27; Art Stud League New York, with George Luks, Boardman Robinson, John Steuart Curry, Jean Charlot & George Bridgeman, 29-33; LaGrange Col, LHD, 49; Univ Chattanooga, DFA, 59; Univ Fla, DFA.
Work in Public Collections: Atlanta Art Inst; Art Inst Chicago; Metrop Mus Art; Montclair Art Mus; Pa Acad Fine Arts; plus others.
Exhibitions: Am Acad Arts & Lett; Am Fedn Arts; Art Inst Chicago; Am Watercolor Soc; Brooklyn Mus; plus others.
Teaching: Lectr, U S A, Denmark, Ger, Turkey, Italy, Austria & Greece; assoc prof art, Univ Ga, 37-40, regent's prof art, Lamar Dodd prof art, head dept art & chmn div fine arts, 40-; lectr, United Chap Phi Beta Kappa, 67-68.
Positions: Pres, Col Art Asn Am, 54-56; mem, U S Dept State Comt Arts Tour, India Thailand, Belg, Japan, Korea, Manila & others; NASA artist, Apollo 7 & 10, 68-69.
Awards: Award, Nat Arts Club, 54; purchase prizes, Pa Acad Fine Arts & Whitney Mus Am Art, 58; plus others.
Bibliography: Monroe Wheeler (auth), included in: Painters and sculptors of modern America, Crowell, 42; Ray Bethers (auth), included in: How paintings happen, Norton, 51; John I H Baur (auth), included in: Revolution and tradition in American art, Harvard Univ Press, 59; plus others.
Memberships: Assoc Nat Acad Design; Col Art Asn Am; Southeastern Art Asn; Asn Ga Artists; Athens Art Asn; plus others.
Publications: Illusr, The Savannah and the Santee, Rivers of Am Series; contribr, Col Art J, Bk Knowledge & others.
Mailing Address: Dept of Art, University of Georgia, Athens, GA 30601.

DODD, LOIS
Painter, Educator
b Montclair, N J, Apr 22, 27.
Study & Training: Cooper Union, with Byron Thomas & Peter Busa.
Work in Public Collections: Cooper Union Mus, New York, N Y; Wadsworth Atheneum, Hartford, Conn; Kalamazoo Art Ctr, Mich; Ciba-Geigy Chem Corp, Ardsley, N Y; Hilton Hotel Print Collection, New York.
Exhibitions: Five one-man shows, Tanager Gallery, New York, 54-62; Americans in Rome, U S Info Agency, Rome, 60; Drawings, Univ Ky, 61; Drawings & Watercolors, Yale Univ, 64; three one-man shows, Green Mt Gallery, New York, 69-71.
Teaching: Instr, Philadelphia Col Art, 63; instr, Wagner Col, 63-64; instr, Philadelphia Col Art, 65; instr, Brooklyn Col, 65-72, asst prof, 72-
Positions: Co-founder, Tanager Gallery.
Awards: Ital Govt study grant, 59-60; Longview Found Purchase Award, 62; Ingraham, Merrill Found grant, 71.
Dealer: Green Mountain Gallery, 135 Greene St, New York, NY 10012.
Mailing Address: 30 E Second St, New York, NY 10003.

DODGE, ERNEST STANLEY
Museum Director
b Trenton, Maine, Mar 18, 13.
Study & Training: Harvard Univ, 37-38; Marlboro Col, hon MA, 61; hon DLitt, Boston Univ, 70.
Teaching: Lowell lectr, Boston Pub Libr, 62.
Positions: Mus asst, Peabody Mus, Salem, 31-37, asst cur, 37-43, cur, 43-46, asst dir, 46-50, dir, 50-; dir, Salem Chamber Commerce, 53-55 & 66-68; mem Mass Coun Arts & Humanities, 65-67; sr specialist, Univ Hawaii East-West Ctr, 68; chmn, Int Historians Arctic Voyagers Sem, Moscow, 70; trustee, Penobscot Marine Mus, Searsport, Merrimack Valley Textile Mus, North Andover, Maine, Fruitlands Mus, Harvard & Fund Educ Liberia, Boston.
Awards: Guggenheim fel, 60-61.
Memberships: Fel Am Acad Arts & Sci; Am Anthrop Asn; Royal Anthrop Inst; Royal Geog Soc; Mass Hist Soc; plus many others.
Publications: Auth, Gourd growers of the South Seas, 43; auth, Northwest by sea, Oxford Univ Press, 61; auth, New England and the South Seas, Harvard Univ Press, 65; auth, Beyond the capes: Pacific exploration from Cook to the Challenger 1776-1877, Little, Brown & Co, Boston, 71 & Victor Gollancz, London, 71; auth, The polar Rosses, Faber & Faber, London (in press); plus others.
Mailing Address: Peabody Museum, 161 Essex St, Salem, MA 01970.

DODGE, JOSEPH JEFFERS
Painter, Art Administrator
Preferred Media: Oils.
b Detroit, Mich, Aug 9, 17.
Study & Training: Sch Fine Arts, Harvard Univ, BS(hons), 40; also study with Yasuo Kuniyoshi, Woodstock, N Y, 44.
Work in Public Collections: Cummer Gallery Art, Jacksonville, Fla; The Hyde Collection, Glen Falls, N Y; Ft Edward Art Ctr, N Y; Munson-Williams-Proctor Inst, Utica, N Y; Gulf Life Ins Co, Jacksonville.
Exhibitions: Artists of the Upper Hudson, Albany Inst Hist & Art, N Y, 42-61; Pa Acad Fine Arts, Philadelphia, 45; 64th Am Art Exhib, Art Inst Chicago, Ill, 61; Realist Invitational, Galley Contemp Art, Winston-Salem, N C, 69; Florida Creates, var mus, 71-72.
Collections Arranged: French Art of the Sixteenth Century, 64 & Artists of Victoria's England, 65, Cummer Gallery Art; The Age of Louis XIII, Cummer Gallery Art & Mus Fine Arts, Saint Petersburg, Fla, 69-70; plus others.
Teaching: Instr drawing & painting, The Hyde Collection, 41-62; substitute prof art hist, Hamilton Col, 47; instr art hist, Adirondack Community Col, 61-62.
Positions: Cur, The Hyde Collection, 41-62; dir, Cummer Gallery Art, 61-72.
Collection: Nineteenth century realists and academic; drawings.
Dealer: Art Sources, Inc, Universal Marion Bldg, Jacksonville, FL 32201.
Mailing Address: 1836½ Elizabeth Pl, Jacksonville, FL 32205.

DODWORTH, ALLEN STEVENS
Art Administrator, Printmaker
b Long Beach, Calif, Nov 19, 38.
Study & Training: Stanford Univ, BA(fine arts & design); Portland State Univ, art hist.
Collections Arranged: 34th-36th Ann Exhibs for Artists of Idaho, 69-72 & Painters of the Idaho Scene, 72, Boise Gallery Art.
Positions: Chmn, White Gallery, Portland State Univ, 67-69; dir Boise Gallery Art, Boise Art Asn, 69-
Memberships: Western Asn Art Mus (regional rep, 71-); Western Regional Conf, Am Asn Mus; Idaho Art Asn; Boise Allied Arts Coun (dir, 71-); Am. Fedn Arts.
Specialty of Gallery: International graphics; Oriental art; Idaho art; all media.
Mailing Address: c/o Boise Gallery of Art, P O Box 1505, Boise, ID 83701.

DOGANCAY, BURHAN CAHIT
Painter
b Istanbul, Turkey, Apr 24, 25.
Study & Training: Ankara Halk Evi; Acad Grande Chaumiere, Paris, France.
Work in Public Collections: Guggenheim Mus, New York, N Y; Georgia Mus Art; Brooklyn Mus, New York; Mus Mod Art, New York; Los Angeles Co Mus Art.
Exhibitions: Devlet Resim Heykel Sergisi, Ankara, 60; About New York 1915-1965, Huntington Hartford Mus, New York, 65; Contemporary Turkish Paintings, U S A, 71; Artist's at Work, Finch Col Mus, New York, 71; Printmakers at Pace, New York, 72.
Awards: City New York Cert Appreciation, 64; Tamarind Lithography Workshop fel, 69.

Bibliography: Jay Jacobs (auth), Back to the walls, Gallery Mag, 70; Louise Schultz (auth), Dogancay and his work, 71; E G Bowles & Tonny Russell (auth), This book is a movie, 71.
Dealer: Gimpel & Weitzenhoffer, 1040 Madison Ave, New York, NY 10021.
Mailing Address: 220 E 54th St, New York, NY 10022.

DOHANOS, STEVAN
Illustrator, Painter
b Lorain, Ohio, May 18, 07.
Study & Training: Cleveland Sch Art.
Work in Public Collections: Whitney Mus Am Art, New York, N Y; Cleveland Print Club; Avery Mem, Hartford, Conn; New Britain Inst; Dartmouth Col.
Commissions: Murals, Charlotte Amalie, St Thomas, V I, Forest Serv Bldg, Elkins, W Va & U S Post Off, West Palm Beach, Fla.
Exhibitions: New Britain Mus Am Art, Conn, 72.
Teaching: Founding fac mem, Famous Artists Sch, Westport, Conn.
Awards: Medal, Philadelphia Watercolor Club; Art Dirs Club; prize, Cleveland Printmakers.
Memberships: Soc Illustrators (pres, 61-63); Am Watercolor Soc.
Publications: Illusr, nat mag.
Mailing Address: 279 Sturges Hwy, Westport, CT 06880.

DOHERTY, ROBERT J, JR
Art Administrator, Educator
b Everett, Mass, Jan 16, 24.
Study & Training: R I Sch Design, BFA, 51; Yale Univ, MFA, 54; Fulbright travel grant to Ger, 65-66.
Commissions: Design & supvr construction, Rice River House, Louisville, Ky, 62.
Exhibitions: Taft Sch, Watertown, Conn, 51; Photographs & Graphic Design, Louisville Art Ctr Asn Sch, 55 & 58; Photographs, Arts-Club Louisville, 56; Photographs, Allen R Hite Art Inst, Univ Louisville, 64.
Collections Arranged: Visual Arts in Louisville, U S Info Serv, circulated throughout France, 57; Graphic Design, Allen R Hite Art Inst, 61; USA-FSA Photo Exhib, Univ Louisville, 61; 19th Century Photographs, Univ Louisville, 64; The Art of Typeface, traveling exhib, Ky Arts Comn, 67; 19th Century Coal Hole Covers, Ky Arts Comn, 69.
Teaching: Assoc prof fine arts, Univ Louisville, 59-65, prof, 65-, chmn fine arts dept, 67-, comt on Photog Archives, 68-72; instr, Free Univ, 70-71 & 71-72.
Positions: Consult, Atomic Energy Comn, Visual Commun Ctr, Washington, D C, 52; dir graphic design, Reynolds Metals Co, 53-57; dir develop, R I Sch Design, 57-59; art ed, R I Sch Design, 57-59; art ed, Landscape Archit, 60-62; cur photog collection, Allen R Hite Art Inst, 62-68, acting dir, 64-65, dir, 67-72; graphic designer, Firma Dorland GmbH, Munich, Ger, 65-66; dir, Int Mus Photog, George Eastman House, Rochester, N Y, 73-
Awards: Am Inst Architects Design Award, 56; Am Inst Graphic Arts design award, 57; Lithographers & Printers Nat Asn Award for Aluminum Foil Design, 60.
Memberships: Designer-Craftsmen R I (pres, 59); Louisville Jr Art Gallery (dir, 60-65, v pres, 63-65); Louisville Art Ctr Asn (trustee, 67-70).
Research: Photographic collections as sources of historic information.
Publications: Auth, Aluminum foil design, 59; auth, USA-FSA, Camera, 10/62 & Foto, 64; picture ed, Documenting a decade, 72.
Mailing Address: International Museum of Photography at George Eastman House, 900 East Ave, Rochester, NY 14907.

DOLE, GEORGE
Cartoonist, Painter
Preferred Media: Oils, Ink, Wash.
b New York, N Y, July 24, 20.
Study & Training: Nat Acad Design; Pratt Inst; Art Stud League New York.
Work in Public Collections: George Dole permanent manuscript collection, Syracuse Univ; Farrell Libr permanent collection, Kans State Univ; plus others in private collections.
Exhibitions: Sixth Int Salon Cartoons, Montreal, Can, 69.
Memberships: Mag Cartoonists Guild.
Publications: Contribr, Playboy Mag, Sat Rev, Pageant, Parade, Cosmopolitan & many others.
Mailing Address: 6 David Rd, Portland, ME 04102.

DOLE, WILLIAM
Painter, Educator
b Angola, Ind, Sept 2, 17.
Study & Training: Olivet Col, with George Rickey & Harris King Prior, AB, 37; Mills Col, 40; Univ Calif, Berkeley, MA, 47; Mills Col, 49.

Work in Public Collections: Amherst Col; Phoenix Mus Art; Santa Barbara Mus Art; Mills Col; Rockefeller Inst; plus others.
Exhibitions: Calif Watercolor Soc, 50-52; one-man show, DeYoung Mem Mus, 51; group, 55 & 57 & one-man shows, 51, 58 & 68, Santa Barbara Mus Art; one-man show, La Jolla Mus, 64; retrospective, Univ Calif, Santa Barbara, 65; plus many other group & one-man shows.
Teaching: Lectr, Univ Calif, 47-49; instr art, Univ Calif, Santa Barbara, 49-51, asst prof art, 51-58, assoc prof art & chmn dept, 58-62, prof art, 62-
Mailing Address: Dept of Art, University of California, Santa Barbara, CA 93106.

DOLPH, CLIFFORD R
Museum Director
b Chicago, Ill, July 29, 01.
Study & Training: Univ Chicago; Univ Colo.
Positions: Ed, gen & spec exhib catalogs, Maryhill Mus Fine Arts, dir, 38-
Memberships: Western Asn Art Mus.
Mailing Address: Maryhill Museum of Fine Arts, Maryhill, WA 98620.

DOMAREKI, JOSEPH THEODORE
Painter, Sculptor
Preferred Media: Oils, Multi-Media, Steel, Bronze.
b Newark, N J, May 17, 14.
Study & Training: Newark State Col, BS, 37; Univ Iowa, MA, 47; New York Univ, 48-50.
Work in Public Collections: Norfolk Mus Arts & Sci, Va; Navy Dept, Pentagon Bldg, Washington, D C; Columbia Mus Art, S C; Broad Nat Bank, Newark; Monmouth Col, West Long Branch, N J.
Commissions: Bronze & stone wall mural, Sinclair Res Ctr, Tulsa, Okla, 63; hammered lead relief sculpture (exterior side), St Luke's Episcopal Church, Haworth, N J, 65; oil painting, Newark Brush Co, Kenilworth, N J; Corten free-standing mural (exterior), Clean-Way Laundry, South Orange, N J; multi-media painting, Secord Mem, Columbia High Sch, Maplewood, N J.
Exhibitions: Newark Mus Triennial State Exhib, 62-71; Art Gallery 64, Hall of Educ, New York World's Fair, 64-65; American Art Today, Pavilion Fine Arts, New York World's Fair, 64; Silvermine Ann Exhib, Conn, 65; N J Artists Ann, Trenton State Mus, 66, 68 & 70.
Teaching: Head dept art, Sch Dist South Orange & Maplewood, N J, 64-
Awards: Medal of honor for painting, Knickerbocker Artists Ann, 55 & 64; John J Newman Mem Medal, Nat Soc Painters in Casein, 62; medal of honor for painting, Audubon Artists Ann, 64.
Memberships: Audubon Artists (pres, 64-68); Assoc Artists N J (v pres, 58-60); Nat Soc Painters & Sculptors (v pres, 56-58); N J Watercolor Soc; Knickerbocker Artists.
Dealer: Gallery Madison/90, 1248 Madison Ave, New York, NY.
Mailing Address: 1482 Fox Trail, Mountainside, NJ 07092.

DOMBEK, BLANCHE M
Sculptor
Preferred Media: Bronze, Wood, Metal, Clay.
b New York, N Y.
Study & Training: With Alexandre Zeitlin & Leo Amino.
Work in Public Collections: Brooklyn Mus, N Y; Currier Gallery Art, Manchester, N H; Randolph-Macon Woman's Col, Lynchburg, Va; Broëse Collection, Ger.
Commissions: Portrait of Melissa, comn by Mrs R Tompkins, Rolling Hills, Calif, 65; The Accuser (welded iron & steel), comn by Mrs T Ortner, Palos Verdes Peninsula, Calif, 66; Capricornus (bronze), comn by Isabella Gardner, New York, 69; Gemini (sculptured fountain), comn by Mrs Bess Harris, Worcester, Eng, 72; Portrait of Felicity, comn by Patricia Joudry, Glos, Eng, 72.
Exhibitions: Colette Allendy Gallery, Paris, France, 54; Peridot Gallery, 54; Pasadena Mus, Calif, 60; Thorne Gallery, Keene, N H, 69; Currier Gallery Art, Manchester, 71-72.
Bibliography: Evelyn Eaton (auth), Progression (film), Draco Found, 65; American visitor's sculpture helps launch new play, Stroud Daily, Glos, Eng, 12/8/71; Kate Kendall (auth), Sculptor's range to mark Dombek show, Peterborough Transcript, 1/23/69.
Mailing Address: R F D, Hancock, NH 03449.

DOMINIQUE, JOHN AUGUST
Painter
Preferred Media: Oils, Watercolors.
b Virserum, Sweden, Oct 1, 93; U S citizen.
Study & Training: Portland Art Asn Sch, 13; San Francisco Inst Art, 15-16; Van Sloan Sch Painting, 17; Santa Barbara Sch Arts, 21 & 27-29; also with Colin Campbell Cooper, Armin Hanson & Carl Oscar Borg.
Work in Public Collections: Univ Va Art Gallery, Richmond.

Exhibitions: Portland Art Mus, Ore, 36; Oakland Art Mus, Calif, 41; Los Angeles Art Mus, Calif, 44; Calif Watercolor Soc, Pasadena Art Mus, 61; Charles & Emma Frye Art Mus, Seattle, Wash, 62.
Awards: Covered Bridge (painting), 40 & Oregon Landscape (painting), 41, Ore State Fair; Peach Tree in Bloom (painting), Glendale Art Asn, 50.
Bibliography: Arthur Millier (auth), article, In: Los Angeles Times, 10/8/33; Maxine Buren (auth), article, In: Ore Statesman, 10/9/38; Melba Meredith (auth), article, In: Ojai Valley News, 7/5/62.
Memberships: Calif Nat Watercolor Soc.
Mailing Address: 216 N Pueblo Ave, Ojai, CA 93023.

DOMIT, MOUSSA M
Art Administrator, Art Historian
b Lebanon, May 24, 32; nat U S.
Study & Training: Ohio State Univ, BA(art hist); Southern Conn State Col, MS(art educ); Yale Univ, spec courses art hist.
Collections Arranged: Sculpture of Thomas Eakins, Corcoran Gallery Art, 69; The Art of Wilhelm Lehmbruck, Nat Gallery Art, Washington, D C, 72.
Teaching: Instr hist art, Columbus Col Art & Design, Ohio, 62-64; lectr art appreciation, Corcoran Sch Art, Washington, D C, 68-70; lectr art hist, Hood Col, 71-72.
Positions: Cur intra-univ loan collection & registrar collections, Yale Univ Art Gallery, New Haven, Conn, 66-68; assoc dir, Corcoran Gallery Art, Washington, 68-70; mus cur, Nat Gallery Art, Washington, 70-72; assoc dir, N C Mus Art, Raleigh, 72-
Memberships: Am Asn Mus.
Research: American impressionist painting.
Publications: Auth, The sculpture of Thomas Eakins, 69 & auth, George Lee: recent color photography, 69, Corcoran Gallery Art; auth, American impressionist painting, Nat Gallery Art, 73.
Mailing Address: North Carolina Museum of Art, Raleigh, NC 27611.

DONAHUE, KENNETH
Art Administrator, Art Historian
b Louisville, Ky, Jan 31, 15.
Study & Training: Univ Louisville; Inst Fine Arts, N Y Univ.
Positions: Asst art dept & art librarian, Univ Louisville, 36-38; staff lectr, Mus Mod Art, New York, N Y, 38-43; res fel, Am Coun Learned Soc, Rome, Italy, 47-49; lectr & cur asst, Frick Collection, New York, 49-53; cur, Ringling Mus Art, Sarasota, Fla, 53-57; dir, 57-64; dep dir, Los Angeles Co Mus Art, 64-66; dir, 66-; mem, Internal Revenue Commissioner's Art Adv Panel, Washington, D C, 70-
Memberships: Col Art Asn (bd dirs, 67-71); Asn Art Mus Dirs (v pres, 71-72); Am Asn Mus (coun, 68-, v pres, 70-72).
Publications: Auth, articles in professional journals & exhibition catalogues; contribr, Enciclopedia degli Italiani.
Mailing Address: Los Angeles County Museum of Art, 5905 Wilshire Blvd, Los Angeles, CA 90036.

DONATI, ENRICO
Painter, Sculptor
b Milan, Italy, Feb 19, 09; U S citizen.
Study & Training: Univ Pavia, Italy, Dr(soc & econ sci), 29; Art Stud League New York, 40; New Sch Soc Res, New York, 41.
Work in Public Collections: Albright-Knox Art Gallery, Buffalo, N Y; Univ Art Mus, Univ Calif, Berkeley; Mus Mod Art, New York; Whitney Mus Am Art, New York; Baltimore Mus Art, Md.
Exhibitions: Eight Carnegie Int Exhibs, 45-61; Embellished Surfaces, Mus Mod Art, New York, 53-54; Younger American Painters, Solomon R Guggenheim Mus, 54-55; Palais des Beaux-Arts, Brussels, Belgium, 61; Friends Collection, Whitney Mus Am Art, 64.
Teaching: Vis lectr & critic, Yale Univ, 60-62.
Positions: Mem adv bd, Brandeis Univ, Waltham, Mass, 56-72; mem adv bd, Parsons Sch Design, New York, 59; mem pres coun arts & archit, Yale Univ, 62-72; chmn nat comn, Univ Art Mus, Univ Calif, Los Angeles, 70-72; mem exec bd, Art Ctr Col Design, Calif, 70-72.
Bibliography: Peter Selz (auth), Enrico Donati, Mus de Poche, 65.
Dealer: Staempfli Gallery, 47 E 77th St, New York, NY 10021.
Mailing Address: 222 Central Park South, New York, NY 10019.

DONNESON, SEENA
Graphic Artist, Painter
b New York, N Y.
Study & Training: Pratt Inst; Art Stud League New York, with Morris Kantor; Pratt Graphic Arts Ctr, with Michael Ponce de Leon; New Sch Social Res.
Work in Public Collections: Mus Mod Art, New York; Brooklyn Mus; Los Angeles Co Mus Art, Calif; Smithsonian Mus, Washington, D C; N J State Mus, Trenton.

Commissions: Ed of prints, Touchstone Press.
Exhibitions: 4th Int Triennale of Original Colored Graphics, Grentchen, Switz, 65; 15th Biennale, Brooklyn Mus, 65; 15th Nat Print Exhib, Am Fedn Arts, 66-68; 2nd, 3rd, 4th Int Miniature Prints, Pratt Inst & N Y State Coun Fine Arts, 66-72; Projected Art: Artists at Work, Finch Col, New York, 71.
Teaching: Lect hist mod art, New York Univ, 61-63.
Positions: App mem, Nassau Co Fine Arts Comn, 70-; exhib coordr, Dept Parks, Recreation & Cult Affairs, New York, 72-
Awards: Res fel, MacDowell Colony, 63, 64; guest artist, Tamarind Lithography Workshop, 68; purchase award, W Wash State Col, 70.
Bibliography: Gordon Brown (auth), Young artists rebel against rectangular format, Art Voices, Winter, 63.
Memberships: Artists Equity Asn N Y; Philadelphia Water Color Club; Print Club Philadelphia; Nat Asn Women Artists; Prof Artists Guild (pres, 66-67).
Dealer: Associated American Artists, 663 Fifth Ave, New York, NY 10022.
Mailing Address: 319 Greenwich St, New York, NY 10013.

DONOHOE, VICTORIA
Art Critic, Writer
b Philadelphia, Pa.
Study & Training: Rosemont Col, BA; Univ Pa Grad Sch Fine Arts, MFA; Pius XII Inst Fine Arts Advan Study, Florence, Italy, scholar, 52-53, cert; Am Fedn Arts Workshop Art Criticism, scholar, 68.
Collections Arranged: Relig & Liturgical Art From the Eastern U S, Philadelphia Civic Ctr, 63.
Teaching: Lab asst studio art & art hist, Rosemont Col, 50-52, lectr, 54-55.
Positions: Art critic, Standard & Times, Philadelphia, 59-62; art critic, Philadelphia Inquirer, 62-; appointed to Philadelphia Archdiocesan Lit Comn, 72-
Memberships: Philadelphia Mus Art; Mus Mod Art; Soc Archit Historian; Univ Mus, Univ Pa; Pa Acad Fine Arts.
Research: Late nineteenth century American sculpture.
Publications: Contribr, Outdoor sculpture in Philadelphia, colonial times to the present, 73; also contribr to anthologies, mags & Sun supplements.
Mailing Address: 34 Narbrook Park, Narberth, PA 19072.

DONSON, JEROME ALLAN
Educator, Sculptor
Preferred Media: Wood.
b New York, N Y, Mar 20, 24.
Study & Training: Univ Southern Calif, BA, 49, MSEd, 50, with Prof DeErdely & Prof Don Goodall; Am Grad School, Denmark, Jean Hershholt Fund scholar, 50; Univ Copenhagen, 51, with Johannes Brøndsted & Dr Vagn Poulsen; New Sch Social Res, with Seymour-Lipton & Camillo Egas; Univ Calif, Berkeley, MA(art), 57, with Prof Herschel Chipp & Clark Winter.
Exhibitions: Guild S C Artists, Florence, 55.
Collections Arranged: Arts of Southern California, 56-61; The Exodus Group, 60; Landscape Past and Present, 61.
Teaching: Lectr art hist, Long Beach City Col Exten, 57; lectr mod art hist, Univ Calif, Los Angeles, 58-60; dir art & assoc prof art hist, Fairleigh-Dickinson Univ & appreciation chmn art depts, Rutherford, Madison & Teaneck, 62-63; prof & art consult, Long Island Univ, 65; vis prof visual hist, Inst Design, Ill Inst Technol & Chicago Bd Educ, 70-72; prof, Louisville Sch Art, 72-
Positions: Dir, Florence Mus, S C, 54-56; munic art dir, Long Beach, Calif, 56-61; Am art spec, U S State Dept, U S Info Agency, Washington, D C & Europe, 61-62; exec dir, Off Cult Affairs, New York, 63-64; ed, Art J, Col Art News, quart, 64-70; exec dir, Fine Arts Ctr, Anderson, Ind, 66-68; dir, Louisville Sch Art & Art Ctr Asn, Louisville, 72-
Awards: First prize in sculpture, Guild S C Artists, 55; cult award of yr, Long Beach C of C, 61; award of merit, Prof Photog Calif, 62.
Memberships: Col Art Asn Am (ed, Col Art News, 64-70); Am Coun Educ (pres, 72); Am Asn Higher Educ; Western Mus League (regional v pres, 61); Western Asn Art Mus Dirs (stand chmn, 60); plus others.
Research: Scandinavian arts, modern and contemporary, primitive.
Collection: Living artists of Southern California, the Midwest, New York, and internationally known artists.
Publications: Auth, A survey of early Scandinavia and its arts, Denmark Nat Mus, 51; auth, Clearinghouse for western museums, Arts of Southern California, Ceramics Mo; auth, University & college courses for potential art museum professionals, 60; auth, Light and shadow, ceramic exploration, Design, fall 60; auth, American vanguard exhibitions in Europe, Art J, summer 63.
Mailing Address: 2315 Raleigh Lane, Louisville, KY 40206.

DOOLEY, HELEN BERTHA
Painter, Art Dealer
Preferred Media: Oils, Watercolors.
b San Jose, Calif, July 27, 07.
Study & Training: San Jose State Col, AB; Claremont Grad Sch, MA; Douglas Donaldson Sch Design; Calif Sch Fine Arts, San Francisco; Chouinard Art Inst, Los Angeles; Univ Calif, Berkeley; Teachers Col, Columbia Univ.
Work in Public Collections: Univ Pac, Stockton, Calif; Shimizu Mus, Japan.
Commissions: Portrait of Dr D Elton Trueblood (oil), 55-56; portrait of Mrs Lloyd Bertholf (oil), Stockton, 56; portrait of Dr Irving Goleman (oil), comn by Mrs Irving Goleman, Stockton, 62; Summer Floral (oil), G Douglas Burck, pres, Am Inst For Studies, 69.
Exhibitions: Pa Acad Fine Arts, Philadelphia, 41; De Young Mus, San Francisco, 51; Am Watercolor Soc, Nat Acad Galleries, New York, N Y, 63; Lord & Taylor Galleries, New York, 69; Los Angeles Co Mus Art Exhib & West Coast Watercolor Soc, Sacramento, Calif, 71.
Teaching: Instr art, Oakland City Schs, 28-30; com artist, Hale Bros, San Jose, 31-32; instr art, adult educ, San Jose City Schs, 33-37; instr art, Scripps Col, 37-39; supvr art, Kern Co Schs, Bakersfield, Calif, 39-47; prof art, Univ Pac, 48-68.
Positions: Owner, Dooley Gallery, Carmel, Calif, 64-
Awards: Mist on the Bay (watercolor), Soc Western Artists, 51; How Green the Valley (oil), Calif State Fair, 65; Festival (oil), Monterey Peninsula Mus Art, 67.
Memberships: Soc Western Artists; Carmel Art Asn (bd dirs, 70-71); West Coast Watercolor Soc.
Research: Art education.
Publications: Auth, Figure drawing teaching charts, 48-49; auth, Elementary crafts in a nutshell, 63.
Dealer: Arts & Design Associates, Sonora, CA 95370.
Mailing Address: Dooley Gallery, Box 5577, Carmel, CA 93921.

DOOLITTLE, WARREN FORD, JR
Art Administrator, Painter
b New Haven, Conn, April 3, 11.
Study & Training: Yale Univ, BFA; Syracuse Univ, MFA.
Work in Public Collections: Evansville Mus Art, Ind; Eastern Ill Univ, Charleston, Ill; Univ Fla, Gainesville; Seattle Art Mus, Wash; mural, New Haven Pub Sch Syst, New Haven.
Commissions: Asst to Eugene Savage, N Y Worlds Fair, 38; plus many private & public portraits.
Exhibitions: Pepsi Cola's Paintings of the Year, New York, 46; Second Exhib Contemp Art, Univ Iowa Summer Show, 58; Art Inst Chicago Ann Drawing Exhib, 63; First Spring Ann, Calif Palace Legion of Hon, San Francisco; Corcoran Gallery Art 20th Biennial, Washington, D C.
Teaching: Asst drawing, Yale Univ, 34-35; instr painting, Univ Fla, 35-38; prof painting, Univ Ill, Urbana, 38-41, prof-in-charge undergrad & grad painting, 48-68, chmn grad progs art, 56-71, emer prof art, 71-
Awards: Scholarships, Yale Univ, 33-35; faculty fel, Ford Found, 54; first prize, Washington Ann Nat Exhib, Nat Watercolor Soc, 60.
Mailing Address: P O Box 1225, Crystal River, FL 32629.

DORFMAN, BRUCE
Painter, Educator
b New York, N Y, Aug 15, 36.
Study & Training: Art Stud League New York, with Yasuo Kuniyoshi & Arnold Blanch; Univ Iowa, BA.
Work in Public Collections: Butler Inst Am Art, Youngtown, Ohio; Syracuse Univ, N Y; Collection Mourlot, Paris, France; Commerce Trust Co Found; plus others.
Exhibitions: Fla Art, New York World's Fair Invitational, 64; Modern American Paintings, Mus Art, Univ Kans, 67; Professionals who Teach, New York Cult Ctr, 69; Litografias Coleccion Mourlot, Mus of Univ P R, 71; Butler Inst Am Art Ann, 72.
Teaching: Guest artist, Norton Mus, W Palm Beach, Fla, 62-64; instr painting & drawing, Art Stud League New York, Woodstock, N Y, 64-, coordr & moderator, Friday Noon Forum, 68-71; resident artist, Syracuse Univ, 71; instr painting & drawing, Everson Mus Art, Syracuse, 71-
Positions: Dir, Young People's Studio & Workshop Studio, Woodstock, N Y, 68-72; dir, Hudson River Sch, Hyde Park, N Y, 72-
Awards: Julius Hallgarten Award, Nat Acad Design, 62; New York World's Fair Invitational Exhib Award, State Fla, 64; purchase award, Butler Inst Am Art Ann, 72; plus others.
Bibliography: John Canaday (auth), article, In: New York Times, 10/67; Joseph Morgenstern (auth), Bruce Dorfman, Kennedy Galleries, 1/72; Henry A La Farge (auth), article, In: Art News, 3/72.
Memberships: Life mem Art Stud League New York; Woodstock Artists Asn.

Publications: Auth, Color mixing, Pitman, 68.
Dealer: Kennedy Galleries, 20 E 56th St, New York, NY 10022.
Mailing Address: Art Students League of New York, 215 W 57th St, New York, NY 10019.

DORN, CHARLES MEEKER
Educator, Art Administrator
b Minneapolis, Minn, Jan 17, 27.
Study & Training: George Peabody Col, BA & MA, 50; Univ Tex, EdD, 59.
Teaching: Prof art educ & head dept art, San Fernando Valley State Col, 70-72; prof art educ & head creative arts, Purdue Univ, Lafayette, 72-
Positions: Exec secy, Nat Art Educ Asn, 62-70.
Awards: 25th Anniversary Award for Distinguished Serv in Art in Educ, Nat Gallery Art, 66.
Memberships: Nat Art Educ Asn (exec secy); Int Soc Educ Art (prog chmn, 69); Nat Coun Arts Educ (prog chmn, 67); Tenn Art Educ Asn (pres); Calif Art Educ Asn (higher educ bd).
Publications: Auth, Childrens art, 12/62 & Student art, 3/64, NEA J; auth, Art education in the U S, Biiku Bunka, 6/67; auth, Directions in art education, The National Elementary School Principal, 11/67; auth, Art education in the silent 70's, Art Education, 1/72.
Mailing Address: Dept Creative Arts, Purdue University, Lafayette, IN 47907.

DORR, GOLDTHWAITE HIGGINSON, III
Art Administrator
b New York, N Y, Jan 11, 32.
Study & Training: Harvard Univ, BA, 56; Univ Minn, 61-62.
Collections Arranged: David Park: A Retrospective Exhibition, 69; Robert McCall: Space Artist, 72; numerous others in the past eleven years.
Positions: Cur & chief preparator, Minneapolis Inst Arts, 61-68; dir, Santa Barbara Mus Art, 68-70; dir, Phoenix Art Mus, 70-
Memberships: Asn Art Mus Dirs; Am Asn Mus; Col Art Asn Am.
Publications: Auth, Minneapolis Inst Arts Bull, 12/61; contribr, Minneapolis Inst Arts Bull, 3/62, 65, 67 & 68.
Mailing Address: Phoenix Art Museum, 1625 N Central Ave, Phoenix, AZ 85004.

DORR, WILLIAM SHEPHERD
Collector
b Augusta, Ga.
Study & Training: Univ Ga, with Lloyd Miller; Emory Univ.
Positions: Purchasing Comt, Whitney Mus Am Art, 65-66.
Awards: Awards, Asn Ga Artists, 48 & Southern Artists Exhib, 49.
Collection: Contemporary artists and sculptors, including Arakawa, Calder, Chamberlain, Conner, Dine, Johns, Lindner Oldenburg, Rivers, Rauschenberg, Woodburn and others.
Mailing Address: 15 Charles St, New York, NY 10014.

DORRA, HENRI
Art Historian, Educator
b Alexandria, Egypt, Jan 17, 24; U S citizen.
Study & Training: Univ London, BSc, 44; Harvard Univ, MS & MA, 50, PhD, 53.
Collections Arranged: Years of Ferment, Univ Calif, Los Angeles; Visionaries and Dreamers & Ryder, Corcoran Gallery Art, San Francisco Mus Art & Cleveland Mus Art, 55-60.
Teaching: Lectr art hist; stud fel, Metrop Mus Art, 51-52; mem faculty, Univ Calif, Los Angeles, 63-65; prof art, Univ Calif, Santa Barbara, 65-
Positions: Asst dir, Corcoran Gallery Art, 54-61; asst dir, Philadelphia Mus Art, 61-62; exec v pres, Indianapolis Art Asn, 62-63; trustee, Santa Barbara Mus Art.
Awards: Bowdoin Prize, Harvard Univ, 49.
Memberships: Am Asn Mus; Col Art Asn Am.
Publications: Auth, Gauguin, Metrop Mus Art, 53, Seurat, Beaux-Arts, Paris, 60 & The American muse, 61; contribr, Gazette Beaux-Arts; Metrop Mus Art Bull & others.
Mailing Address: Dept of Art, University of California, Santa Barbara, CA 93106.

DORRANCE, NESTA
Art Dealer
b Swansea, Wales.
Study & Training: London Sch Econ.
Positions: Dir, Jefferson Place Gallery.
Specialty of Gallery: Contemporary art.
Mailing Address: Jefferson Place Gallery, 2144 P St N W, Washington, DC 20037.

DORST, CLAIRE V
Painter, Educator
b Plymouth, Wis, June 4, 22.
Study & Training: Beloit Col, BA, 49; Univ Iowa, MA, 53; Univ Wis-Madison, United Lutheran Church Am synodical faculty scholar, 62-63, MFA, 63.
Work in Public Collections: Univ Iowa Collection; Univ Wis Collection; also in private collections.
Exhibitions: Wisconsin at Work, Mem Mus, Milwaukee, 50 & Wisconsin Painters and Sculptors Ann, 64; Fla State Fair Show, Tampa, 65; Nat Exhib Contemp Painting, Soc 4 Arts, Palm Beach, Fla, 66 & 70; Hortt Mem Exhib, Mus Arts, Fort Lauderdale, Fla, 68 & 70.
Teaching: Asst prof studio art, Wayne State Col, 53-59; prof art & art hist & chmn dept art, Carthage Col, 59-64; prof studio art, Fla Atlantic Univ, 64-, chmn dept art, 68-
Awards: Tellus Madden Award, Wis Spring Show, 63; first prize in painting, Winter Park Art Fair, 65; Atwater Kent Award, Soc 4 Arts Nat Exhib, 66.
Memberships: Fla League Arts (mem bd dirs, 71-); Fla Craftsmen; Am Crafts Coun; Col Art Asn Am.
Dealer: Tahir Gallery, 823 Chartres St, New Orleans, LA 70116.
Mailing Address: Dept of Art, Florida Atlantic University, Boca Raton, FL 33432.

DOSTER, ROSE WILHELM
Painter, Sculptor
Preferred Media: Watercolors, Ceramics.
b Baltimore, Md, May 11, 38.
Study & Training: Art Instr Schs, Minn, cert illus & design; Md Inst Col Art, cert design, also eve classes with Leonard Bahr & Mr Meiser.
Work in Public Collections: Goodman Gallery, Taylor Manor Hosp, Ellicott City, Md; Cafritz Hosp Gallery, Washington, D C.
Exhibitions: Latham Found Int Poster Contest, Stanford, Calif, 54-59 & 61; Nat League Am Penwomen State Art Show, Annapolis, Md, 69; Md Inst Alumni Asn Ann, Baltimore, 70-72; Baltimore Watercolor Club Ann, 71 & 72; York Art Asn, Pa, 72.
Teaching: Instr, pvt studio.
Awards: Latham Found Inst Poster Contest Cert Award of Merit, 54-59 & Sch Arts Mag Bk Award & Cert Merit, 56, Latham Found; George Peabody Award, Peabody Inst, Baltimore, 60.
Bibliography: Val LeVander (auth), Rose Doster, Carroll Rec, 6/22/72.
Memberships: Nat League Am Penwomen (art chmn & second v pres, 70-72, mem chmn & first v pres, 72-74); Rehoboth Art League; Md Craft Coun; Md Inst Alumni Asns; Hanover Art Guild.
Mailing Address: Shiloh Ave, Hampstead, MD 21074.

DOTY, ROBERT McINTYRE
Art Administrator, Curator
b Rochester, N Y, Dec 23, 33.
Study & Training: Harvard Univ, AB; Univ Rochester, MA.
Collections Arranged: Photo-Secession, 1960; Photog Am, 65; Whitney Ann, 66-71; Adolph Gottlieb, 68; Light: Object & Image, 68; Human Concern, Personal Torment, 69; Contemp Black Artists Am, 71.
Positions: Cur, Whitney Mus Am Art.
Mailing Address: Whitney Museum of American Art, 945 Madison Ave, New York, NY 10021.

DOUBRAVA, JAN
Painter
b Brno, Czech, July 21, 12; U S citizen.
Study & Training: Art Stud League New York, N Y; New Sch Soc Res; also with Julian Levi, Stuart Davis, Kuniyoshi & Lewis Daniel.
Work in Public Collections: New Brit Mus; Univ Iowa.
Exhibitions: Butler Art Inst, 53, 60 & 61; Audubon Artists, 54, 57, 58 & 60; Springfield Mus Fine Arts, 57 & 59; Nat Inst Arts & Letters, 61 & 63; Pa Acad Fine Arts, 64.
Teaching: Asst head dept art, New Sch Soc Res, 52-
Awards: Nat Inst Arts & Letters grant, 63 & Childe Hassam Fund Purchase Award, 71; Ford Found Purchase Award, 64.
Mailing Address: 463 West St, New York, NY 10014.

DOUGLAS, EDWIN PERRY
Painter, Educator
b Lynn, Mass, June 18, 35.
Study & Training: R I Sch Design, BFA; San Francisco Art Inst, MFA.
Work in Public Collections: Montreal Mus Fine Arts, Can; San Francisco Art Inst Art Bank, Calif; Dayton Art Mus, Ohio; Cincinnati Art Mus, Ohio; Lincoln Land Community Col Art Mus, Springfield, Ill.
Exhibitions: San Francisco Art Inst Nat Painting & Sculpture Tour, Calif, 63; 11th Ann Can Young Contemporaries Exhib, Montreal, 64; 81st Ann Spring Exhib, Montreal Mus Fine Arts, 64; 31st

Ann Can Soc Graphic Art, Kingston, Ont, 64; Cincinnati Invitational Biennial, Cincinnati Art Mus, Ohio, 69.
Teaching: Instr painting, Univ Man Sch Art, 63-64; instr painting & drawing, Cincinnati Art Acad, Ohio, 64-68; asst prof drawing, Cincinnati Art Acad, Ohio, 64-68; asst prof drawing, Wash Univ Sch Fine Arts, 69-72; vis lectr painting, Univ Cincinnati, 72-73.
Bibliography: Dialogue on painting, produced by Miami Univ TV, 67.
Mailing Address: 4854 Gray Rd, Cincinnati, OH 45232.

DOWDEN, ANNE OPHELIA TODD
Painter, Illustrator
Preferred Media: Watercolors.
b Denver, Colo, Sept 17, 07.
Study & Training: Univ Colo; Carnegie Inst Technol; Art Stud League New York.
Work in Public Collections: Hunt Bot Libr, Pittsburgh, Pa; New York Bot Garden, N Y.
Commissions: 22 paintings for reproduction as facsimile prints, Frame House Gallery, Louisville, Ky, 69-72; painting of three azaleas, Callaway Gardens, Pine Mt, Ga, 71; painting of tulip tree flowers, New York Bot Garden, 72.
Exhibitions: American Textiles, Metrop Mus Art, New York, 48; Decorative Arts Today, Newark Mus, 48; Int Group Shows, 64, 68 & 72, one-man show, 65, Hunt Bot Libr.
Teaching: Instr drawing, Pratt Inst, 30-32; head dept art, Manhattanville Col, 32-53.
Awards: Tiffany Found fel, 29-31.
Publications: Auth & illusr, Look at a flower, 63, illusr, Shakespeare's flowers, 69 & auth & illusr, Wild green things in the city, 72, Crowell; auth & illusr, The secret life of the flowers, 64 & auth & illusr, Roses, 65, Western Pub.
Mailing Address: 205 W 15th St, New York, NY 10011.

DOWLING, DANIEL BLAIR
Editorial Cartoonist
Preferred Media: Ink, Crayon.
b O'Neil, Nebr, Nov 16, 06.
Study & Training: Univ Calif, Berkeley; Chicago Acad Fine Arts.
Positions: Ed cartoonist, Omaha World Herald, 40-48; ed cartoonist, New York Herald Tribune, 48-65; ed cartoonist, Kansas City Star, 67-
Awards: Awards, Sigma Delta Chi & Freedoms Found; Christopher Award.
Memberships: Assoc Am Ed Cartoonist (pres, 58-60).
Mailing Address: Kansas City Star, Kansas City, MO 64108.

DOWLING, ROBERT W
Patron
b New York, N Y, Sept 9, 95.
Study & Training: Adelphi Col, DFA, 61; Fairleigh Dickinson Univ, 63; Dowling Col, hon LHD, 69; Ithaca Col, hon LLD, 70.
Positions: Real estate & bldg bus, New York, N Y, 18-; mem nat shrines adv bd, Dept Interior; chmn adv comt arts, John F Kennedy Ctr for Performing Arts, 59-67, trustee, 68-; chmn, trustee Dowling Col, 68-
Awards: Cert merit, C of C; spec award, Nat Conf Christians & Jews; Antoinette Perry award; plus others.
Memberships: Inst Int Educ (co-chmn, trustee); Carnegie Hall Soc; Nat Inst Social Sci (v pres); plus many others.
Mailing Address: Pierre Hotel, 2 E 61st St, New York, NY 10021.

DOWNEY, JUAN
Sculptor, Instructor
Preferred Media: Electronics.
b Santiago, Chile, May 11, 40.
Study & Training: Sch Archit, Cath Univ Chile, BArch, 61; Atelier 17, Paris, France, 63-65, printmaking with S W Hayter; Pratt Inst, 67-69.
Work in Public Collections: Mus Mod Art, New York, N Y; Casa Americas, Havana, Cuba; Tel Aviv Mus, Israel; Bibliot Nat, Paris; Nat Collection Fine Arts, Washington, D C; plus others.
Exhibitions: Cibernetic Serendipity, Washington, D C & San Francisco, Calif, 69; Galeries Pilotes, Mus Cantonale Beaux Arts, Lausanne, Switz, 70; Nature et Technologie, Bordeaux, France, 71; Lucht-Kunst, Stedelijk Mus, Amsterdam, 71; Art and Science, Tel Aviv Mus, 71; plus many others.
Teaching: Instr art, Smithsonian Inst, Washington, D C, 69-70; instr archit, Pratt Inst, New York, 70-; instr art, Hunter Col, New York, 70-
Awards: First prize, Casa Americas, Havana, 64; Orgn Am States fel, 70; Guggenheim Found fel, 71.
Bibliography: Howard Wise (auth), Pollution robot (film), 70.
Publications: Auth, Electronic sculpture, Leonardo, Paris, France, 69.
Dealer: Howard Wise, 2 W 13th St, New York, NY 10019.
Mailing Address: 12 E 20th St, New York, NY 10003.

DOWNING, GEORGE ELLIOTT
Painter, Educator
b Marquette, Mich, June 19, 04.
Study & Training: Univ Chicago, PhB; Harvard Univ, MA & PhD.
Teaching: Instr art, Univ Chicago, 26-30; asst prof art, Brown Univ, 32-46, assoc prof art, 46-53, prof art, 53-70, emer prof art, 70-
Mailing Address: 144 Power St, Providence, RI 02906.

DOYLE, EDWARD A
Illustrator, Painter
b Cranston, R I, May 22, 14.
Study & Training: R I Sch Design.
Exhibitions: R I Artists; Providence Art Club, 58; Fall River Art Asn, 63-65; Jordan Marsh Ann, 65; one-man shows, Attleboro Mus, 68 & Fall River Art Asn, 72.
Teaching: Instr figure drawing, Fall River Art Asn, 66-69.
Positions: Archit illusr, 46-
Awards: Awards, Warren Art Festival, 66 & 72, Fall River Art Asn, 67 & 69 & Fall River Arts Festival, 69 & 72.
Mailing Address: 150 Hornbine Rd, Swansea, MA 02777.

DOYLE, THOMAS J
Sculptor, Instructor
b Jerry City, Ohio, May 23, 28.
Study & Training: Ohio State Univ, BFA, 52, MA, 53, with Roy Lichtenstien & Stanley Twardewicz.
Work in Public Collections: Brooklyn Mus, N Y; Carnegie Inst, Pittsburgh, Pa; Kley Collection, Ger.
Commissions: Fiberglass sculpture, Pub Arts Coun, City of New York, 72.
Exhibitions: Kunsthalle, Bern, Switz, 64; Kunsthalle, Dusseldorf, Ger, 65; Dwan Gallery, New York, 66 & 67; Sculpture of the Sixties, Los Angeles Co Art Mus, Calif, 67; Primary Structures, Jewish Mus, New York, 67.
Teaching: Instr sculpture, Brooklyn Mus Art Sch, 60-68; instr sculpture, New Sch Social Res, 61-68; lectr sculpture, Queens Col, 70-
Bibliography: Lucy R Lippard (auth), Tom Doyle, Kunsthalle, Dusseldorf, 65 & Space embraced: Tom Doyle's recent sculpture, Arts, 4/66; Irving Sandler (auth), Gesture & non-gesture in recent sculpture, Los Angeles Co Mus Art, 67.
Dealer: 55 Mercer Gallery, 55 Mercer St, New York, NY 10013.
Mailing Address: 189 Bowery, New York, NY 10002.

DOYON, GERARD MAURICE
Art Administrator, Art Historian
b Manchester, N H, Apr 6, 23.
Study & Training: Manchester Inst Arts, dipl fine arts, 49; St Anselm's Col, AB, 51; Fulbright scholar to Paris, 51-52; Ecole Beaux-Arts, Paris, 52; Ecole Mus du Louvre, AE, 52; Boston Univ, MA, 54, PhD, 64.
Teaching: Chmn art dept, St Anselm's Col, 52-61; chmn art dept, Miami-Dade Jr Col, 61-64; assoc prof art hist, Fla Atlantic Univ, 64-68; prof art hist & chmn art dept, Washington & Lee Univ, 68-
Positions: Dir, duPont Gallery, Washington & Lee Univ, 68-
Awards: Danforth scholar, 60-61 & 62-63.
Memberships: Col Art Asn Am.
Research: French art of the eighteenth and nineteenth centuries, especially painting.
Publications: Auth, The mural paintings of Theodore Chasseriau, Gazette Beaux-Arts, Paris, 69.
Mailing Address: 911 Shenandoah Rd, Lexington, VA 24450.

DOZIER, OTIS
Painter, Printmaker
Preferred Media: Graphics.
b Forney, Tex, Mar 27, 04.
Work in Public Collections: Univ Nebr; Dallas Mus Fine Arts; Denver Art Mus; Metrop Mus Art; Wadsworth Atheneum; plus others.
Commissions: Murals, U S Post Off, Arlington, Giddings & Fredericksburg, Tex.
Exhibitions: Whitney Mus Am Art, 45; Carnegie Inst, 46; Dallas Allied Artists, 46; one-man shows, Witte Mem Mus, 48 & Dallas Mus Fine Arts, 56.
Teaching: Instr, Dallas Mus Fine Arts, 45-69.
Awards: Awards, Dallas Allied Artist, 32 & 46, Southwestern Art Asn, 48 & New Orleans Arts & Crafts, 48; plus others.
Mailing Address: 7019 Dellrose Dr, Dallas, TX 75214.

DRABKIN, STELLA
Painter, Designer
Preferred Media: Mosaics.
b New York, N Y, Jan 27, 06.
Study & Training: Nat Acad Design; Philadelphia Graphic Sketch Club; also with Earl Horter.

Work in Public Collections: Pa Acad Fine Arts; Philadelphia Mus Art; Rosenwald Collection, Nat Gallery Art, Washington, D C; Metrop Mus Art; Libr Cong; also in many pvt collections.
Exhibitions: Am Color Print Soc; Soc Am Graphic Artists; Audubon Artists; Pa Acad Fine Arts; Philadelphia Mus Art; plus many other group and one-man shows.
Positions: Chmn, Philadelphia Art Alliance; mem coun, Am Color Print Soc, v pres, 65-
Awards: Prizes, Am Color Print Soc, 44; purchase award, N J State Mus; prizes, Philadelphia Print Club, 55 & 67.
Memberships: Soc Am Graphic Artists; Artists Equity Asn; Philadelphia Art Alliance; Am Color Print Soc; Audubon Artists; plus others.
Publications: Auth, Pennsylvania: painting in Pennsylvania, Printing with Monotype.
Mailing Address: 2404 Pine St, Philadelphia, PA 19103.

DRAGO, GABRIELLE D
Painter
Preferred Media: Oils.
b Union, Ore.
Study & Training: Calif Sch Fine Arts, San Francisco; Art Stud League New York; also with Rico Lebrun, Alexander Brook & Sidney Gross.
Work in Public Collections: Dallas Mus Fine Arts, Tex.
Exhibitions: Nat Arts Club, New York, N Y, 65; Knickerbocker Artists Asn, New York, 65 & 70; Artists Equity Asn New York, 70-71; N J State Mus, Newark, 70-72; Nat Asn Women Artists, New York; plus others.
Memberships: Artists Equity Asn New York; Nat Asn Women Artists; Art Stud League New York.
Mailing Address: 27 E 22nd St, New York, NY 10010.

DRAPER, LINE BLOOM
Painter
b Verviers, Belg; U S citizen.
Work in Public Collections: Univ Toledo; First Unitarian Church; Int Inst, Toledo.
Exhibitions: Nine Midwest Tri-State Art Shows, Montpelier, Ohio, 54-70; Nat Jefferson Ann, New Orleans, 69; Am Artists Nat Show, 55; Nat Painters Casein Touring Exhibs, 70, 71 & 72-73; Five Women in Art Invitational Exhib, Defiance Col, 73; plus many other group & one-man shows.
Teaching: Instr art, Defiance Col, summers 57-58.
Awards: Hon mentions for watercolor, 56 & oil, 57, Ohio State Fair; many awards for oil, watercolor, graphics & drawing, Port Clinton Ann Regional Art Show, 57-71; honor award for outstanding contrib to art, Toledo Fedn Art Socs, 64 & 66; plus many others.
Memberships: Fedn Art Socs (past v pres & rec secy); life Toledo Artists Club (past pres); Toledo Womens Art League; Athena Art Soc (past pres); Am Watercolor Soc; plus many others.
Publications: Auth, articles, In: Art Rev, Toledo Blade, Ohio Poetry Rev, Sylvania Sentinel & D'Art.
Mailing Address: 4210 Corey Rd, Toledo, OH 43623.

DRAPER, ROBERT SARGENT
Painter, Art Dealer
b Rutland, Vt, Feb 18, 20.
Study & Training: Univ Fla, BA; Norton Gallery & Sch Art; Hans Hofmann Sch Art.
Work in Public Collections: Norton Gallery Art; Lowe Mus, Coral Gables, Fla; Columbus Mus Arts & Crafts, Ga; Emory Univ, Atlanta, Ga; Am Sch Madrid Mus, Spain; also in pvt collections.
Exhibitions: Lowe Art Mus, 53-55; Ringling Mus, Sarasota, Fla, 55; Springfield Mus Fine Arts, 56; Riverside Mus, N Y, 58; Fla Artists Group, 61-63, 65, 67 & 69; plus others.
Teaching: Lectr pre-Columbian art, contemp art & class art of Fr 17th century; Blue Dome fel, 57-58, 60-61 & 67-69.
Positions: Pres, Miami Art League, 54-55; pres, Miami Artists Asn, 54-55 & 56-59; owner, Mirell Gallery, Miami, Fla.
Awards: Prizes, Miami Art League, 48, 50, 51 & 55, Soc Four Arts, Palm Beach, Fla, 54 & Am Artists Prof League, 55; plus others.
Memberships: Artists Equity Asn; Fla Artists Group.
Mailing Address: Mirell Gallery, 3333 Rice St, Coconut Grove, FL 33133.

DRAPER, WILLIAM FRANKLIN
Painter
Preferred Media: Oils.
b Hopedale, Mass, Dec 24, 12.
Study & Training: Harvard Univ, 31-32; Nat Acad Design, 31-34; Grande Chaumiere, Paris, France, 35; Art Stud League New York, 37; also with Jon Corbino, Leon Kroll & Henry Hensche.
Work in Public Collections: Nat Portrait Gallery; Pavilion, Music Ctr, Los Angeles, Calif; Off Housing & Urban Develop; C I A; NASA.

Commissions: Portraits, President John F Kennedy, 62, Shah of Iran, 67, Terrence Cardinal Cooke, 71, Gen Lauris Norsted, 72 & Ambassador Walter Annenberg.
Exhibitions: Nat Gallery, London, Eng, 44; Metrop Mus Art, 45; Cent Asn Ann; Graham Gallery, New York, N Y, 69 & 71; Palm Beach Gallery, Fla, 72.
Teaching: Instr, Art Stud League New York, 65-
Memberships: Boston Allied Artists; Century Asn.
Dealers: Portraits, Inc, 41 E 57th St, New York, NY 10022; Graham Gallery, 1014 Madison Ave, New York, NY 10021.
Mailing Address: 535 Park Ave, New York, NY 10021.

DREIBAND, LAURENCE
Painter
Preferred Media: Oils, Acrylics.
b New York, N Y, Nov 8, 44.
Study & Training: Chouinard Art Inst, Los Angeles, Calif, 61; Art Ctr Col Design, Los Angeles, BFA(with distinction), 67, fel & MFA, 68.
Work in Public Collections: Home Savings & Loan Collection; Container Corp Am Collection.
Commissions: Great Ideas of Western Man, Container Corp Am, 70.
Exhibitions: West Coast 70, E B Crocker Art Gallery, Sacramento, Calif, 70; Beyond the Actual, Pioneer Mus, Stockton, Calif, 70; one-man shows, David Stuart Galleries, 70-72; California Artists, Long Beach Mus Art, 71; L A-14 Painters, Art Galleries, Univ Calif, Santa Barbara, 72.
Teaching: Instr painting & photog, Art Ctr Col Design, 70-; chmn fine arts dept, 72-; instr painting, Calif State Col, Los Angeles, 71.
Awards: First prize, Fine Arts Gallery San Diego, 70; Great Ideas of Western Man Purchase Award, Container Corp Am, 70; 19th All City Festival Purchase Award, Municipal Art Gallery, Los Angeles, 71.
Bibliography: Joseph Young (auth), Los Angeles artist—Laurence Dreiband, Art Int, 70; Barbara Witus (auth), Paintings of Laurence Dreiband, Los Angeles Free Press, 3/31/72; Dr Udo Kulterman (auth), New realism, New York Graphic Soc, 72.
Publications: Auth, Laurence Dreiband, paintings and drawings, David Stuart Galleries, 72.
Dealer: David Stuart Galleries, 807 N La Cienega Blvd, Los Angeles, CA 90069.
Mailing Address: 4317½ W Second St, Los Angeles, CA 90004.

DREISBACH, CLARENCE IRA
Painter, Lecturer
Preferred Media: Oils, Watercolors.
b Union Hill, Pa, Jan 28, 03.
Study & Training: With Orlando G Wales; Baum Art Sch, Allentown, Pa.
Work in Public Collections: Allentown Art Mus, Pa; Reading Pub Mus & Art Gallery, Pa; Call-Chronicle Publ Co, Allentown; Swain Country Day Sch, Allentown; Liberty High Sch, Bethlehem, Pa; plus many others.
Exhibitions: Fla Southern Col Int Exhib, 52; St Augustine Art Asn, 56; Am Artists Prof League Grand Nat, 57; one-man show, Burr Galleries, New York, N Y, 60; Norton Galleries, West Palm Beach, Fla, 71; plus many others.
Teaching: Lectr landscape painting, Allentown Community Col; lectr landscape painting, Wyomissing Inst Fine Arts, 63-64; lectr landscape painting, Baum Art Sch.
Awards: First award, St Augustine Art Asn, 56; Grand Nat finalist, Am Artists Prof League, 57.
Memberships: Norton Gallery & Artists Guild, West Palm Beach; Lake Worth Art League, Fla; Allentown Art Mus; Art Guild Boca Raton, Fla; Buck Hill Art Asn.
Publications: 25 paintings reproduced in Ideals.
Dealer: Darrah Cooper, Inc, 310 Royal Poinciana Plaza, Palm Beach, FL 33480.
Mailing Address: 916 N St Lucas St, Allentown, PA 18104.

DREITZER, ALBERT J
Collector, Patron
b Sept 6, 02; U S citizen.
Collection: French Impressionists & Post Impressionists.
Mailing Address: 45 Sutton Pl South, New York, NY 10022.

DRESKIN, JEANET STECKLER
Painter, Educator
Preferred Media: Polymers.
b New Orleans, La, Sept 29, 21.
Study & Training: Newcomb Col, Tulane Univ La, BFA, 42, with Xanvier Gonzales; Johns Hopkins Univ, med art cert, 43; John McCrady Sch, New Orleans.

Work in Public Collections: S C State Art Collection, Columbia Mus Art; Ga Mus Art, Athens; Greenville Co Mus Art, Greenville S C; Furman Univ, Greenville; Wachovia Nat Bank N C, Winston-Salem; plus many others.
Commissions: Seals, painting & plaque, S C State Bd Health, Columbia, 57 & S C Heart Asn, Greenville, 58; painting, Fiber Industs, Imp Chem, Dorchester, Eng, 66; mural, mixed media, Piedmont Industs, New York, N Y, 67; print, wood block, S C Tricentennial Comn, Greenville, 70.
Exhibitions: Nat Watercolor Exhib, Dulin Gallery Art, Knoxville, Tenn, 64; Hunter Ann, George Thomas Hunter Gallery Art, Chattanooga, Tenn, 67; Piedmont Ann, Mint Mus Art, Charlotte, N C, 69-71; Chautauqua Exhib Am Art, Chautauqua Art Gallery, N Y, 70; U S A Traveling Exhib, Nat Asn Women Artists, 70-73; plus many others.
Teaching: Faculty head painting & graphics, Greenville Co Mus Sch Art, 50-52 & 62-, head sch, 68-; instr art, exten div, Univ S C, 71-73.
Positions: Staff artist, Am Mus Nat Hist, New York, 43-45; staff artist, Univ Chicago Med Sch, 45-50; juror, S C Scholastic Art Awards, 66 & 71.
Awards: Owen H Kenan Mem Award of Merit, Am Contemp Exhib, Soc Four Arts, Fla, 68; W J Kaplan Award of Merit, Nat Soc Painters Casein, 69; M May Purchase Award, Appalachian Corridors III, Charleston, W Va, 72; plus many others.
Bibliography: Lucien Felli (auth), Jeanet Steckler Dreskin, 67 & National association of women artists, 72, La Rev Mod, Paris, France; Jack A Morris, Jr, (auth), Contemporary artists of South Carolina, Tricentennial Comn, 70; Lucille Green (auth), Jeanet S Dreskin, artist-educator, Sandlapper, 3/70; plus many others.
Memberships: Guild S C Artists (mem bd, 55-, treas, 68, v pres, 71, pres, 72); Nat Asn Women Artists (mem comt, 71-); Nat League Am Pen Women (S C pres, 59-60, 65-66); Nat Asn Med Illusr; Watercolor Soc Ala.
Publications: Illusr, Anatomy of the gorilla, for Am Mus Nat Hist, Columbia Univ, 43-46; illusr, What's new, Abbot Labs (& Latin Am ed), 46, 47 & 49; illusr, Surgery of repair, Lippincott, 50; illusr, Williams obstetrics, Stander-Appleton, 50; paintings reproduced as covers for Pen Women, 64 & 66; plus many others.
Dealers: Hampton III Gallery, Ltd, 11 Hampton Village Shopping Center, Greenville, SC 29609; Aronson Midtown Gallery, 798 Peachtree N E, Atlanta, GA 30308.
Mailing Address: 60 Lake Forest Dr, Greenville, SC 29609.

DRESSER, LOUISA
Art Administrator, Art Historian
b Worcester, Mass, Oct 25, 07.
Study & Training: Vassar Col, BA; Fogg Art Mus, Harvard Univ; Courtauld Inst, Univ London.
Collections Arranged: New England Painting, 1700-1775, 43, Christian Gullager, 49, Edward Savage, 51, The Dial and The Dial Collection, 59, Worcester Art Mus.
Positions: Assoc in decorative arts & cur decorative arts, Worcester Art Mus, 32-49, actg dir, 43-46, cur of collection, 49-72, trustee, 72-
Awards: Guggenheim fel, 56-57.
Memberships: Am Antiqn Soc; Soc Arts & Crafts, Boston (secy, 67-); Salisbury Mansion Assocs (pres, 71-); Worcester Craft Ctr (corporator, 64-); Am Asn Mus.
Research: American painting of the seventeenth and eighteenth centuries, primarily New England.
Publications: Co-auth, Seventeenth century painting in New England, 35; auth, Early New England printmakers, 39; co-auth, Maine and its role in American art, 63; auth, Portraits in Boston, 1630-1720, J Archives Am Art, 66; auth, The background of colonial American portraiture, 66.
Mailing Address: Worcester Art Mus, 55 Salisbury St, Worcester, MA 01608.

DREW, JOAN
Printmaker, Sculptor
Preferred Media: Graphics.
b Indianapolis, Ind, Dec 21, 16.
Study & Training: Mass Col Art; Art Stud League New York; graphics with Sternberg.
Work in Public Collections: Rochester Mem Art Gallery; Philadelphia Mus Art; Lyman Allyn Mus Art; N Y Pub Libr; Princeton Univ; plus others.
Exhibitions: Mus Mod Art, 57, 58 & 60; Boston Printmakers, Boston Mus Fine Arts, 57-68; one-man show, Lyman-Allyn Mus, 59; Albright-Knox Art Gallery, 64; Art in Embassies, 64-65; plus many other group & one-man shows.
Teaching: Lectr, serigraph-collage.
Bibliography: Included in: Prize-winning graphics II, 64.
Memberships: Boston Printmakers.

Publications: Contribr, children's bk sect cover, New York Times, 60.
Mailing Address: 19 Elmwood Ave, Rye, NY 10580.

DREWELOWE, EVE
Painter, Sculptor
Preferred Media: Mixed Media.
b New Hampton, Iowa.
Study & Training: Univ Iowa, BA, 23, MA, 24; Univ Colo, 54.
Work in Public Collections: Univ Iowa Mus, Iowa City; Univ Colo, Boulder; Harkness House, London, Eng; Utah State Univ, Cedar City; Wartburg Col, Waverly, Iowa.
Commissions: Two oil paintings, First Nat Bank Fort Collins, 61.
Exhibitions: 18th Int Watercolor Exhib, Art Inst Chicago, 39; New York World's Fair, 39-40; UNESCO Travel Exhib, Eng, 48-49; Midwestern Show, Nelson Gallery & Atkins Mus, Kansas City, Mo, 60; The West—80 Contemporaries, Univ Ariz, Tucson, 67.
Positions: Pres, Boulder Chap Artists Equity, 63-68, acting pres, 69; mem art adv comt, Boulder Pub Libr, 63-69; pres, Boulder Artists Guild.
Awards: Flower Subject Contest Award, Denver Art Mus, 32; Award, Tri-State Exhib, Cheyenne, Wyo, 56; first prize in oil, Boulder Art Asn Regional, 63.
Memberships: Hon life mem, Artists Equity Asn; Colo Chap Artists Equity; Boulder Artists Guild.
Publications: Illusr, In denim and broadcloth, 53.
Mailing Address: 2025 Balsam Dr, Boulder, CO 80302.

DREWES, WERNER
Painter, Printmaker
Preferred Media: Oils, Watercolors, Woodcut.
b Canig, Ger, July 27, 99; U S citizen.
Study & Training: Charlottenburg Technische-Hochschule, Berlin, Ger; Stuttgart Sch Archit, Ger; Stuttgart Sch Arts & Crafts; Weimar Staatliches Bauhaus, with Itten & Klee; Dessau Staatliches Bauhaus, with Kandinsky & Feininger.
Work in Public Collections: Nat Collection Fine Arts, Washington, D C; Busch-Reisinger Mus, Cambridge, Mass; City Art Mus, St Louis, Mo; Libr of Cong, Washington; Yale Univ, New Haven, Conn.
Exhibitions: Carnegie Int, Pittsburgh, Pa, 45-47; one-man shows, Prints, Drawings & Painting, Cleveland Mus Art, Ohio, 61, Prints, Achenbach Found, Legion of Hon, San Francisco, Calif, 62, Paintings, Prints, Retrospective, Wash Univ, St Louis, Mo, 65 & Prints, Retrospective, Nat Collection Fine Arts, Washington, 69.
Teaching: Instr painting, drawing & printmaking, Columbia Univ, 37-40; instr design, Inst Design, Chicago, 45; dir design & first yr prog, Wash Univ Sch Fine Arts, 46-65.
Positions: Founding mem, Am Abstract Artists, New York, N Y, 37-46.
Awards: Plexiglas sculpture competition, Mus Mod Art, 39; award for Autumn Harvest (painting), City Art Mus, 59.
Bibliography: R Frost (auth), Werner Drewes, nature & abstract, Art News, 2/15/49; Germain Bazin (auth), History of modern painting, Hyperion, 51; Caril Dreyfuss (auth), Werner Drewes, woodcuts, Smithsonian Inst, 69.
Memberships: Philadelphia Print Club; Color Print Soc.
Dealers: Hom Gallery, Inc, 7315 Wisconsin Ave, Washington, DC 20014; Associated American Artists, 653 Fifth Ave, New York, NY 10022.
Mailing Address: 2006 Colts Neck Rd, Reston, VA 22070.

DREXLER, LYNNE
Painter
Preferred Media: Oils
b Newport News, Va.
Study & Training: Richmond Prof Inst, BFA; Hunter Col; Col William & Mary; Hans Hoffman Sch Fine Arts, scholar.
Work in Public Collections: Prentice Hall Collection, Englewood Cliffs, N J; Ciba-Geigy Collection, Hudson River Mus; Tammarind Print Collection, Mus Mod Art, New York, N Y; Univ Mass, Amherst.
Exhibitions: One-man show, Tanager Gallery, 59; Norfolk Mus Regional Show, 60; Galleria, San Miguel de Allende, Mex, 62; Tetra-centennial, Va Mus Fine Arts, Richmond, 66; Traveling Show, mus in West & South, 66; plus others.
Dealer: Alonzo Gallery, 26 E 63rd St, New York, NY 10021.
Mailing Address: 222 W 23rd St, New York, NY 10011.

DREYER, MARGARET WEBB
Painter, Art Dealer
Preferred Media: Acrylics, Watercolors, Mixed Media.
U S citizen.
Study & Training: Westmoreland Col, San Antonio, Tex; Univ Tex Sch Archit & Fine Arts; Mus Fine Arts, Houston, Tex; Inst Allende, San Miguel de Allende, Mex.

Work in Public Collections: Witte Mus, San Antonio; Elizabeth Ney Mus; Thomas P Creaven Estate; Inst Int Educ; Abe Issa Interests, Kingston, Jamaica.
Commissions: Mosaic murals, plexiglas, comn by Buffington, McAllister for Mading Pub Sch, Houston, 66, face of Cavallini Mosaic Co Bldg, San Antonio, 66 & face of Crawford Bldg, Joseph Holland, 67; mosaic mural & fountain for home, comn by Rudy Dean, 67.
Exhibitions: 11th Midwest Biennial, Joslyn Art Mus, Omaha, Nebr, 70; 15th Ann Sun Carnival Exhib, El Paso Mus, Tex, 71; Tex Watercolor Soc 21st Ann, San Antonio, 71; 60th Ann Exhib Tex Fine Arts Asn, Austin, Tex, 71; also circuit selections & invitationals for all major Tex mus.
Teaching: Dir fine arts, Tex Recreation Dept, City of Houston, 50-60.
Positions: Owner & dir Mural Originals, Houston, 60-; owner & dir Dreyer Galleries, Houston, 61-
Awards: First purchase award for Blueprint for Survival II, Tex Watercolor Soc, 70; Sibley Mem Purchase Award for Pendulum, 22nd Tex Watercolor Soc Nat, 71; King Award for Blueprint for Survival V, 60th Ann Tex Fine Arts Asn, 71.
Bibliography: David Dolin (auth), Fine arts feature Margaret Webb Dreyer, artist, 70 & Ann Holmes (ed), Feature Margaret Webb Dreyer, 72, Houston Chronicle; plus other articles in Houston Chronicle & Houston Post.
Memberships: Tex Watercolor Soc; Tex Fine Arts Asn; Art League Houston; Mus Fine Arts, Houston; Mus Fine Arts, Beaumont.
Research: Pre-Columbian works; African works; contemporary paintings and sculpture; murals; antique art objects.
Mailing Address: 4713 San Jacinto, Houston, TX 77004.

DRIESBACH, DAVID FRAISER
Printmaker, Educator
Preferred Media: Intaglio.
b Wausau, Wis, Oct 7, 22.
Study & Training: Univ Ill, Beloit Col; Univ Wis; Pa Acad Fine Arts; Iowa State Univ; Atelier 17, with S W Hayter, 69.
Work in Public Collections: Seattle Mus, Wash; Dayton Art Inst, Ohio; Columbus Gallery Fine Arts, Ohio; Bibliot Nat, Paris, France; Univ Windsor, Can.
Commissions: Fiscal Flight (ed 150 color etching), Sears Roebuck Co, 67; series of bronze reliefs, Assoc Am Artists, N Y, 68.
Exhibitions: Contemporary Art in U S A, Worcester Mus, Mass, 51; Young Printmakers of America, Mus Mod Art, New York, N Y, 53; Ten Printmakers of U S A, Purdue Univ, 66; 162nd Ann Am Watercolors, Prints & Drawings, Pa Acad Fine Arts, 67; American Graphics 1969, Col of the Pac, San Francisco, 69.
Teaching: Prof printmaking, Northern Ill Univ, 64-
Awards: Ford Found purchase prize for intaglio, 60; Carlton Col prize for intaglio, 66; Uris Bros prize for intaglio, 66.
Bibliography: Bob White (auth), David Driesbach, Chicago Art Scene, 1/68; The complex world of David Driesbach, Northern Alumnus, 3/68.
Memberships: Midwest Col Art Asn.
Dealer: Van Straaten Gallery, 646 N Michigan Ave, Chicago, IL 60611.
Mailing Address: 520 Kendall Lane, Dekalb, IL 60115.

DRIESBACH, WALTER CLARK, JR
Sculptor, Instructor
Preferred Media: Stone, Wood.
b Cincinnati, Ohio, July 3, 29.
Study & Training: Sch Dayton Art Inst, 47-52, with Robert Koepnick; studio asst to Joseph Kiselewski, New York, 54-55; Art Acad Cincinnati, 55-56, with Charles Cutler.
Commissions: St Anthony of Padua (relief in limestone), St Anthony of Padua Church, Cincinnati, 59; limestone entablature of 165 figures, St Teresa Church, Cincinnati, 62; The Lord's Supper (walnut relief), Mt St Mary Seminary, Norwood, Ohio, 64; limestone relief & incised designs of Apostles, Immaculate Conception Church, Dayton, Ohio, 65; granite figure, Fireman Monument, Cincinnati, Ohio, 68.
Exhibitions: Ohio Sculptors, Akron and Canton Art Institutes, 60; Northwest Territory Sculpture Show, Cincinnati Art Mus & John Herron Inst Art, Indianapolis, Ind, 61; one-man shows, Wilmington Col, Ohio, 63 & Univ Dayton, 69; two-man show, Col Mt St Joseph, Ohio, 64.
Teaching: Instr sculpture & drawing, Memphis Acad Arts, 56-58; instr sculpture, Dayton Art Inst Eve Sch, 58-60; instr sculpture & drawing, Wilmington Col, 63-66; instr sculpture, drawing & 3-D design, Univ Dayton, 66-72; instr drawing, Thomas More Col Eve Sch, 70-71; instr sculpture, Art Acad Cincinnati, 70-; instr sculpture, Col Mt St Joseph, 72-
Awards: Fleischmann Purchase Prize, Zoo Arts Festival, Cincinnati, 64; first prize, 66 & second prize, 68, Prof Sculpture Div, Ohio State Fair Fine Arts Exhib.
Publications: Contribr, Contemporary stone sculpture, Crown Publ, 70.

Dealer: Herbert E Feist, 1125 Madison Ave, New York, NY 10028.
Mailing Address: 2541 Erie Ave, Cincinnati, OH 45208.

DRIGGS, ELSIE
Painter
Preferred Media: Oils.
b Hartford, Conn, Aug 5, 98.
Study & Training: Art Stud League New York; also with Maurice
Sterne, Rome.
Work in Public Collections: Whitney Mus Am Art; Baltimore Mus
Art; Yale Univ Mus; Phillips Gallery, Washington, D C; Sheldon
Mem Gallery, Lincoln, Nebr.
Commissions: Animal cartoons & W African gold weights, Works
Prog Admin, Harlem House, New York, N Y, 34; La Salle, Post
Off, Huntsville, La, 35; Indian Village, pvt comn, New York, 38.
Exhibitions: 35 Under 35, Mus Mod Art Opening Show, 30; A Mile
of Art, Munic Art Exhib R C A Bldg, 34; Edward J Gallagher,
III Collect, Baltimore Mus Art, 53; Root Collect, Metrop Mus
Art, 54; The Precisionists, Whitney Mus Am Art, 63.
Teaching: Instr, 45-48.
Positions: Asst, Metrop Mus Art, 23.
Bibliography: Samuel M Kootz (auth), Modern American painters,
Brewer & Warren, 30; Sheldon Cheney (auth), The story of
modern art, Viking Press, 41.
Mailing Address: 31 Grove St, New York, NY 10014.

DRISCOLL, EDGAR JOSEPH, JR
Art Critic
b Boston, Mass, Sept 1, 20.
Study & Training: Cambridge Sch Weston; Univ Iowa, with Grant
Wood; Yale Univ Sch Fine Arts.
Teaching: Lectr art, var groups.
Positions: Juror, many art shows & panels; art critic, Boston
Globe.
Memberships: St Botolph Club; Yale Club; Harvard Club.
Mailing Address: 75 Hancock St, Boston, MA 02114.

DRISKELL, DAVID CLYDE
Painter, Educator
Preferred Media: Oils, Tempera, Watercolors.
b Eatonton, Ga, June 7, 31.
Study & Training: Skowhegan Sch Painting & Sculpture, scholarship,
53, with Jack Levine & Henry V Poor; Howard Univ, BA, 55, with
James A Porter & Morris Louis; Cath Univ Am, MFA, 62, with
Nell Sonnemann & Ken Noland; Riksbureau voor Kunsthistorisches
Documentatie, The Hague, Neth, cert, 64.
Work in Public Collections: Smithsonian Inst, Washington, D C;
Birmingham Mus Art, Ala; Corcoran Gallery Art, Washington,
D C, Carl Van Vechten Gallery Fine Arts, Fisk Univ, Nashville,
Tenn; Howard Univ Collection Fine Arts, Washington, D C.
Commissions: Mountain and Tile Suite (10 woodcuts-color), Tenn
Arts Comn, 72.
Exhibitions: Atlanta Univ Ann, 59; Baltimore Mus Area Exhib, 65;
Corcoran Area Exhib, 66; Birmingham Festival Exhib, 72; Cent
South Ann, Nashville, 72.
Collections Arranged: Modern Masters from the Solomon R Guggen-
heim Museum (catalogue-Modern Masters, Klee, Kandinsky and
Picasso), Talladega Col, Ala, 56; The Afro-American Series, 12
exhibs each with 16 page catalogue of the work of 12 black
artists, Fisk Univ, Univ Miami & others.
Teaching: Prof painting & art hist, Talledega Col, 55-62; prof paint-
ing & art hist, Howard Univ, 62-66; prof art & chmn dept, Fisk
Univ, 66-
Positions: Mem bd adv, Mus African Art, 67-; mem visual arts adv
panel, Tenn Arts Comn, 69-, mus adv bd, 71-
Awards: John Hope Award in Art, Atlanta Univ, 59; Museum Donor
Award, Am Fedn Art, 62; Graphics Art Award, Corcoran Gallery
Art, 65.
Bibliography: Afro-American Series: 12 monographs, Fisk Univ;
Moss (auth), Missing pages (film), Fisk Univ, 71.
Memberships: Col Art Asn Am; Nat Conf Artists; Am Mus Asn; Am
Fedn Art (trustee, 69-); Tenn Col Art Coun (co-chmn, 68-71).
Research: Role of the black artist in American society and tradi-
tional African art, its impact on Afro-American art.
Dealers: Franz Bader Gallery, 2124 Pennsylvania Ave, Washington,
DC 20037; Frost Gully Gallery, Freeport, Maine 04032.
Mailing Address: 1601 Phillips St N, Nashville, TN 37208.

DRIVER, MORLEY-BROOKE LISTER
Art Critic, Collector
b London, Eng, Jan 13, 13.
Study & Training: Slade Sch, London; Univ Calif, BA & MA; also
with Roger Fry & Bernard Berenson.
Positions: Writer & art critic, Detroit Free Press & Ward's Quart.
Collection: All media—impressionists, Braque to Giacometti,
Shahn, Baskin, Piper, Moore, Robert Parker, Picasso, Matisse
and others.

Publications: Auth, series articles art for beginners; contribr,
articles, mags, TV, bk rev & others.
Mailing Address: 8120 Jefferson E, Detroit, MI 48214.

DRUMM, DON
Sculptor, Craftsman
b Warren, Ohio, Apr 11, 35.
Study & Training: Hiram Col; Kent State Univ, BFA & MA.
Work in Public Collections: Akron Art Inst; Cleveland Mus Art;
Bowling Green State Univ; Columbus Gallery Fine Arts; Massil-
lon Mus; plus others.
Commissions: Reliefs, walls, aluminum & steel sculpture & foun-
tains, Alcoa Co, Pittsburgh, Pa, Episcopal Diocese, São Paulo,
Brazil, Richard Gossar Mem Sculpture, Toledo, Ohio, Curtain
Bluff Hotel, Antigua, BWI & City of Akron, Ohio; plus others.
Exhibitions: Group shows, 64 & 65, traveling exhib circulated by
Am Fedn Arts, 65-67 & 72, Mus Contemp Crafts, N Y; Cleve-
land Mus Art, 64-68; Columbus Gallery Fine Arts, 66 & 67;
plus others.
Teaching: Instr sculpture, Akron Art Inst; artist-in-residence,
Bowling Green State Univ, 66-71; instr, Penland Sch Crafts,
66-72.
Awards: Purchase Prize, Cleveland Mus Art, 64; prizes, Nat Soc
Interior Design, 65 & Columbus Gallery Fine Arts.
Bibliography: Oppi Untracht (auth), Metal techniques for the crafts-
man; Louis G Redstone (auth), Art and architecture; Meilach &
Seiden (auth), Direct metal sculpture.
Memberships: Ohio Designer Craftsmen; Am Craftsmen's Coun.
Research: Investigation into the use of contemporary materials and
construction techniques to create urban sculpture specializing in
the use of cast aluminum and concrete.
Mailing Address: Don Drumm Studio, 110 Corson Ave, Akron, OH
44302.

DRUMMOND, (I G)
Painter, Sculptor
Preferred Media: Concrete.
b Edmonton, Alta, Apr 11, 23; U S citizen.
Study & Training: Pa Acad Fine Arts & Univ Pa, BFA, 51, MFA, 52;
also, murals with George Harding.
Commissions: World's Fair Trade Ctr, New York, N Y, 63-64;
murals, Aeromatic Travel Corp, 69, A C Camera, Grand Cent
Sta, New York, 70, Ahi Ezer Synagogue, Brooklyn, N Y, 71 &
Blake Equip Corp, Englewood, N J, 72.
Exhibitions: Pa Acad Fine Arts, Philadelphia, 50; Silvermine Guild,
Conn, 64; East Hampton Gallery, N Y, 68-69; Art Image, Man-
hattan, 69-70.
Mailing Address: 18-44 21 Rd, Astoria, NY 11105.

DRUMMOND, ARTHUR A
Painter, Illustrator
Preferred Media: Oils, Watercolors.
b Toronto, Ont, May 28, 91.
Study & Training: Ont Col Art; pvt study with W M Cutts, J W
Beatty, C M Manley & others.
Work in Public Collections: In pub & pvt collections in Can, U S,
Eng, Norway, Japan, Australia, Turkey, S Africa, Port, W Africa,
Bermuda & elsewhere.
Exhibitions: Royal Can Acad Arts; Ont Soc Artists; Can Nat Exhib;
Am Watercolor Soc; Montreal Art Asn; plus others.
Positions: Former illusr, Can Home Jour.
Awards: Jessie Dow Prize best water colour, Montreal Art Gallery,
30.
Memberships: Am Watercolor Soc; formerly founder-mem Can Soc
Graphic Art.
Mailing Address: R R 1, Orono, Ont, Can.

DRUMMOND, SALLY HAZELET
Painter
Preferred Media: Oils.
b Evanston, Ill, June 4, 24.
Study & Training: Rollins Col, 42-44; Columbia Univ, BS, 48; Inst
Design, Chicago, 49-50; Univ Louisville, MA, 52.
Work in Public Collections: Mus Mod Art, New York, N Y; Whitney
Mus Am Art; Speed Mus Art, Louisville; Univ Iowa Mus, Iowa
City; Joseph Hirshhorn Collection, Greenwich, Conn.
Exhibitions: Am Artists Ann, Whitney Mus Am Art, New York, 60;
Lyric Abstraction in America, Am Fedn Arts Traveling Exhib,
62-63; Americans 63, Mus Mod Art, New York, 63; Focus on
Light, N J State Mus, Trenton, 67; 21st New Eng Painting &
Sculpture Ann, Silvermine, Conn, 70.
Awards: Fulbright grant, Venice, 52; Guggenheim grant, France, 67.
Bibliography: Lawrence Campbell (auth), Dotted light, Art News
Mag, 4/72.
Dealer: Fishbach Gallery, 29 W 57th St, New York, NY 10019.
Mailing Address: 371 Wilton Rd E, Ridgefield, CT 06877.

DRUTZ, JUNE
Painter, Educator
Preferred Media: Tempera, Watercolors.
b Toronto, Ont, Feb 14, 20.
Study & Training: Cent Tech Sch; Ont Col Art, hon grad, 65.
Work in Public Collections: McMaster Univ, Hamilton, Ont; Ont Dept Educ, Toronto; North Bay Dept Educ, Ont.
Commissions: Seeds of Spring Returning (serigraph ann print), Glenhyrst Art Asn, Brantford, Ont, 68-69.
Exhibitions: Ont Soc Artists, 67; Soc Graphic Artists, Ottawa, 67; Can Soc Painters & Etchers, Toronto, 69; Can Soc Graphic Artists, Ottawa, 69; Int Juried Print Show, Montreal, P Q, 71; plus one-man shows.
Teaching: Instr hist res, watercolour & life drawing, Ont Col Art, Toronto, 67-71; instr costume drawing, life drawing & watercolour, Ont Dept Educ, summers, 68-72; instr life drawing, printmaking & hist res, Ryerson Polytech Inst, Toronto, 72-
Positions: Exec off, Can Soc Graphic Artists, Toronto, 72-
Awards: Ont Soc Artists, 67; metrop award, Soc Graphic Artists, 69; A G Reid Award, Soc Painters & Etchers, 69.
Memberships: Royal Can Acad (designer assoc, 72-); Ont Soc Artists; Soc Graphic Artists (exec mem, 71-); Can Painters & Etchers.
Dealer: Nancy Poole Studios Ltd, 16 Hazelton Ave, Toronto 5, Ont, Can & 554 Waterloo St, London 14, Ont, Can.
Mailing Address: 352 Spadina Rd, Toronto 349, Ont, Can.

DRYFOOS, NANCY
Sculptor
Preferred Media: Marble.
b New Rochelle, N Y.
Study & Training: Sarah Lawrence Col, dipl, sculpture with Oronzio Maldarelli & painting with Curt Roesch; Columbia Univ Sch Archit, with Oronzio Maldarelli, also sculpture with Jose de Creeft.
Work in Public Collections: Brandeis Univ; Columbia Univ; Sarah Lawrence Col; Evanston Mus Fine Arts; N Y Univ.
Commissions: Am Jewish Tercentenary, 54; reliefs for Kingsbridge House Synagogue, Home For Aged Hebrews, 57; Edel Award for Fine Arts, Wedgwood-Dickenson Col, 59; Naomi Lehman Mem Award, 62; Jos M Proskauer Bar Asn Award, N Y, 62.
Exhibitions: Allied Artists Am Ann, Nat Acad Design Gallery, 48-72; Pa Acad Fine Arts Biennale; Syracuse Mus Ann, N Y, 54; Brooklyn Mus Ann, N Y, 56; Nat Sculpture Soc Ann, New York, N Y, 65-72.
Awards: Gold Medal of Honor, Allied Artists Am, 58; second prize, Knickerbocker Artists, 60; Constance K Livingston Award, Am Soc Contemp Artists, 70.
Memberships: Fel Nat Sculpture Soc (secy, 72-); N Y Soc Women Artists (v pres, 71-73); Nat Asn Women Artists (mem jury, 71-73); Allied Artists Am (juror, 72); Am Soc Contemp Artists (dir, 70-72).
Publications: Contribr, Nat Sculpture Rev, 70-71.
Mailing Address: 301 E 47th St, New York, NY 10017.

DUBANIEWICZ, PETER PAUL
Painter
b Cleveland, Ohio, Nov 17, 13.
Study & Training: Cleveland Inst Art, scholar, 31, grad, 35; Agnes Gund Traveling scholar, 35; Mus Sch Fine Arts, Boston, Mass; Albert Whitin Traveling fel, France, Ger & Italy, 38.
Work in Public Collections: Ohio Bell Tel Co; Sunny Acres Hosp, Cleveland; Ford Motor Co; St Paul's Episcopal Church; Lake Co Sch; plus many other pub & pvt collections.
Exhibitions: Human Equations, Women's City Club, Cleveland Intown Club; Cleveland Print Mkt; Ten-Thirty Art Gallery, Cleveland; Ohio State Fair; Springfield Mus, Mass; plus many others.
Teaching: Instr, Boston Mus Sch Fine Art, 38-41; instr, Cleveland Inst Art, 45-; lectr, Skowhegan Sch Painting & Sculpture; instr, Oberlin Col, winter 72.
Positions: Pres, Cleveland Soc Artists, 49-51; pres, Poloniase Arts Cleveland, 49-50.
Awards: Buffalo Art Club Prize, 63; second prize, Int Platform Asn Show, 66; H M Newman Relig Art Show, Cleveland, Ohio, 70.
Publications: Illusr, color cover, Cleveland Palin Dealer.
Mailing Address: 3289 Fairmount Blvd, Cleveland Heights, OH 44118.

DUBIN, RALPH
Painter, Sculptor
Preferred Media: Oils.
b New York, N Y, Sept 2, 18.
Study & Training: Am Artist Sch, with Moses Soyer & James Lechay; New Sch Soc Res, with Robert Gwathmey & Stuart Davis; Brooklyn Mus Art Sch, with Gabor Ptererdi & Ben Shahn; Brooklyn Col, BA; also with Hans Hofmann.

Work in Public Collections: Pa Acad Fine Art, Philadelphia; Smithsonian Inst, Washington, D C.
Exhibitions: Nat Inst Arts & Lett, New York, 68; Pa Acad Fine Arts; Cornell Univ; Whitney Mus Am Art; eight one-man shows, Kraushaar Gallery, New York; plus others.
Teaching: Lectr art, Queen's Col(N Y), 61-68; instr art, New York Community Col, 65-68.
Dealer: Antoinette Kraushaar, 1055 Madison Ave, New York, NY 10028.
Mailing Address: 463 West St, New York, NY 10014.

DUCA, ALFRED MILTON
Sculptor, Painter
Preferred Media: Polymers, Metals.
b Milton, Mass, July 9, 20.
Study & Training: Pratt Inst, 38-41; Boston Mus Fine Arts, 43-44.
Work in Public Collections: Addison Gallery Am Art, Andover, Mass; Fogg Mus & Divinity Sch, Cambridge; Worcester Art Mus, Mass; Munson Procter Inst, Utica, N Y; Boston Univ Sch Basic Studies.
Commissions: Sculptures, Prudential Ins Co, Boston, 68-69, Castle Sq, Boston, 70-71, Standard Oil Co Ind Res Ctr, 71-72 & Computer Sphere, J F Kennedy Post Off, Boston, 71-72; steel screen, Proj 57, Boston, 71-72.
Exhibitions: Local, regional & nat exhibs, 58-72.
Teaching: Proj dir youth aid, Gloucester Community Develop Corp.
Positions: Beaux art dir, Brandeis Univ, 52-53; vis lectr, Boston Univ, 57-58; res assoc, Mass Inst Technol, 58-65; consult, White House Conf Children & Youth, 70-71.
Awards: Grants, Rockefeller Found, 58 & Ford Found, 60; New Eng Res Ctr Educ Award, 72.
Memberships: Mass Coun Arts & Humanities.
Research: Development of polymer processes for painters and sculptors; development of the foam vaporization process for casting metal for sculpture.
Publications: Auth, Polymer tempera, a handbook for artists, 52; auth, Polymer tempera, significant teaching aid, 54; auth, Art casting, Mass Inst Technol Jour, 62; co-auth, Plastics as art form, Newman, 64; co-auth, Synthetic pating media, Jensen, 64.
Mailing Address: Annisquam, Gloucester, MA 01930.

du CRET, DUDLEY VAUGHAN
Art Administrator, Art Historian.
b Brooklyn, N Y, Oct 8, 19.
Study & Training: Colgate Univ; Columbia Univ, 40; N Y Univ, 49; Pratt Inst, 51-52; Munich Art Acad, Ger, 59-60.
Teaching: Prof art hist, du Cret Sch Arts, North Plainfield, N J, 64-
Positions: Art consult, Heumann Werbegesellschaft, 53-58; radio & TV consult, Radio Hamburg & WERA, Plainfield, 63-64; dir & pres bd trustees, du Cret Sch Arts, 64-
Memberships: Salmagundi Club; Artists Fel; Am Artists Prof League.
Research: Major museum works of Europe and America.
Collection: Antique pipes from all over the world; antique firearms; African masks; paintings; sculptures.
Publications: Auth, Brief history of Western civilization for the art student; co-ed, Sketching as a hobby.
Mailing Address: 1234-B Hamilton Ct, Leisure Village East, Lakewood, NJ 08701.

DUFOUR, PAUL ARTHUR
Painter, Designer
Preferred Media: Sumi, Stained Glass.
b Manchester, N H, Aug 31, 22.
Study & Training: Univ N H, BA, 50; Yale Univ, BFA, 52; with Takahiko Fujita & Ikuo Hirayama, Japan, 64.
Work in Public Collections: Masur Mus Art, Munroe, La.
Commissions: Stained glass, sculpture & mosaic (with Desmond-Miremont-Burks, Architects), St Joseph Prep Sch, Baton Rouge, La, 68; stained glass (with Desmond-Miremont-Burks, Architects), Chapel of Unity, Greenwell Springs, La, 68; stained glass for chapel, Slidell Mem Hosp, La, 70; stained glass (rose window), Christ the King Episcopalian Church, Covington, La, 71; stained glass, mosaic mural & bronze sculpture (with Smith & Barr Architects), St Thomas Church, Ruston, La, 72.
Exhibitions: St Paul Drawing Biennial, Minn, 62; Tokyo Invitational & Kyoto Invitational, 64; Artists of Louisiana, Delgado Mus, New Orleans, 65; Dufour Retrospect, Sumi Painting, La State Univ, Baton Rouge, 66; Witherspoon Invitational, Univ N C, 68.
Teaching: Asst prof painting, St John's Univ, Collegeville, Minn, 55-58; vis prof design, Siena Heights Col, Adrian, Mich, 57; prof design & stained glass, La State Univ, Baton Rouge, 58-
Positions: Supvr educ, Currier Gallery Art, Manchester, N H, 52-55; artist-in-residence, Viterbo Col, La Crosse, Wis, 60-
Awards: Top award, La State Exhib Prof Artists, 66; top award & purchase prize, Mazur Mus Art, 67; top award, La Nat Watercolor Exhib, 69.

Bibliography: Marold (auth), Prize winning art, Allied, 66; This is their South, Southern Living, 69.
Memberships: Am Asn Univ Prof; Col Art Asn; Am Craft Coun; La Watercolor Soc.
Dealer: River Oaks Galleries, 2501 River Oaks Blvd, Houston, TX 77019.
Mailing Address: Dept of Art, Louisiana State University, Baton Rouge, LA 70803.

DUGMORE, EDWARD
Painter
Preferred Media: Oils.
b Hartford, Conn, Feb 20, 15.
Study & Training: Hartford Art Sch, scholarship, 4 yrs; Calif Sch Fine Arts; Univ Guadalajara, Mex, MA.
Work in Public Collections: Albright-Knox Art Gallery, Buffalo, N Y; Geigy Chem Corp, Ardsley, N Y; Walker Art Inst, Minneapolis, Minn; Des Moines Art Ctr, Iowa; Mus Purchase Fund, New York, N Y.
Exhibitions: Solomon R Guggenheim Mus, New York, 61; San Francisco Mus Art, Calif, 63; Painting as Painting, Univ Tex, Austin, 68; New England Art/Painting and Sculpture, Boston Ctr for Arts, Mass, 71; Albright-Knox Permanent Collection Show, 72; plus others.
Teaching: Vis artist, Montana Inst, Great Falls, 65; vis artist, Univ Minn, Minneapolis, spring 70; vis artist, Des Moines Art Ctr & Drake Univ, 72.
Awards: Kohnstamm Award, Art Inst Chicago, 62; Guggenheim fel, 66-67.
Bibliography: Mary Fuller (auth), Was there a San Francisco school?, Artforum, 1/71; Eric Protter (auth), Painters on painting, Grosset & Dunlap, 71; Harold Rosenberg (auth), The art world, New Yorker, 3/6/71.
Mailing Address: 100 W 14th St, New York, NY 10011.

DUHME, H RICHARD, JR
Sculptor, Educator
Preferred Media: Bronze, Stone, Terra Cotta.
b St Louis, Mo, May 31, 14.
Study & Training: Pa Acad Fine Arts, 32-38; Univ Pa, 34; Barnes Found, Marion, Pa, 40-41; Am Sch Classical Studies, Athens, Greece, summer 51; Wash Univ, BFA, 53.
Commissions: Fish & Frog Fountain (hammered copper & brass), Myron Loomstein, Architect, Clayton, Mo, 60; Girl with Dog (bronze), Nat Humane Educ Ctr, Waterford, Va, 68; Lion Club Fountain (bronze), Mycenaean Found, Mycenae, Greece, 69; Mo Sesquicentennial Medallions (silver & bronze), Sesquicentennial Comt, 71; St Martin & the Beggar (monumental bronze group), Bishop of Erie, Pa, 71.
Exhibitions: Pa Acad Fine Arts Ann, Philadelphia, 38-41 & 50; Metrop Mus Art Summer Sculpture Show, New York, N Y, 42; St Louis City Art Mus Group Show, 49-50 & 52; Cincinnati Art Mus, Ohio, 61; Expos Int Medaile Contemporaine, Nat Mus, Athens, Greece, 66.
Teaching: Prof sculpture, Wash Univ, 47-; head dept sculpture, Chautauqua Inst Summer Schs, 53-; head dept sculpture, Syracuse Univ Chautauqua Ctr, 53-69.
Awards: Cresson Foreign Travel award, 35 & May Audubon Post Prize fel, 41, Pa Acad Fine Arts; first hon mention, Prix de Rome, Am Acad Rome, 39.
Memberships: Fel Nat Sculpture Soc; Allied Artists Am.
Mailing Address: 8 Edgewood Rd, St Louis, MO 63124.

DU JARDIN, GUSSIE
Painter, Printmaker
Preferred Media: Oils.
b San Francisco, Calif, Feb 19, 18.
Study & Training: Univ Colo, BA; Univ Iowa, MA; also painting with Phillip Guston.
Work in Public Collections: N Mex Mus Art, Santa Fe; N Mex Highlands Univ, Las Vegas; Univ Iowa, Iowa City.
Commissions: Fresco (with Elmer Schooley), Las Vegas Hosp, N Mex.
Exhibitions: Mus N Mex, 61, Southwest Biennial Exhib, 72; Butler Inst Am Art 26th Ann, 61; Tucson Festival Art Exhib, 64.
Awards: First purchase award, Mus N Mex, 61.
Mailing Address: P O Box 5, Montezuma, NM 87731.

DULAC, MARGARITA WALKER
Painter, Educator
Preferred Media: Oils.
b Asheville, N C.
Study & Training: Art Inst Chicago, summer 38, 40, 54 & 55; Acad André Lhote, Paris, France, Woolley fel with André Lhote, 38-39, cert, 39; Northwestern Univ, scholar & BS(cum laude), 42; Univ Chicago, fel & MA, 44; Univ Iowa, fel; also with F Leger, Paris, 52.

Work in Public Collections: New Trier Twp High Sch, Winnetka, Ill; Northwestern Univ, Deering Libr & mural in Patten Gym, Evanston, Ill; Wilmette Pub Libr, Ill; Poetry Soc Am, New York, N Y; Ministère Affaires Etrangères, Paris.
Commissions: Portraits, Hans Lange, dir Chicago Symphony Orch, Chicago, Ill, 37, Julius Huehn, New York, N Y, 37, André Gérard, (Pertinax), 44, Gen de Gaulle, Paris, 44 & Andrès Segovia, New York, 47.
Exhibitions: Chicago Artists Exhib, Art Inst Chicago, 35, 36 & 38; Salon Tuileries, Paris, 39 & 50; Int Exhib Drawings, Bodley Gallery, New York, 58; Jersey Painters & Sculptors Nat Exhib, Jersey City Mus, 69 & 70; plus many others.
Teaching: Head dept art, De Kalb High Sch, Ill, 37-38; art instr painting, Heidelberg Univ, 44-46; art instr painting, Acad Leger, Paris, 47-51.
Positions: Art critic, Arts Mag, summer 66; art critic, Jersey Jour, 67-70; art critic, The Herald, New York, 70-; plus others.
Awards: First prize painting & first prize poetry, Univ Chicago, 42; first prize pastel, Univ Guild, Evanston, 42; first prize, N H Poetry Soc, 72; plus many other awards in poetry.
Bibliography: C J Bulliet (auth), Chicago painter Margarita McKee Walker, Chicago Daily News, 37; Winning honors easy for artist, Chicago Am, 7/13/38; André Lhote (auth), Un peintre Américain, Nouvelle Rev Française, 6/1/60.
Memberships: Poetry Soc Am; Hudson Valley Artists Asn; Composers, Authors & Artists Am (chmn publicity).
Publications: Auth, Cyclorama, Univ Chicago Press, 42; auth, Moonrise, Household Mag, Heritage, Chicago Mag & other poems; auth, Ivan Albright—mystic-realist, 1/66, Raymond Katz, master of mixed media, 1/69 & Werner Goshans, realism and fantasy, 6/70, Am Artist; plus many other articles in various newspapers.
Mailing Address: Box 334, Murray Hill Station P O, New York, NY 10016.

DULCAN, CARIL E
Art Dealer, Writer
b New Haven, Conn, Apr 6, 33.
Study & Training: Smith Col, BA; Am Univ; Smithsonian Inst, art hist with Jacob Kainen.
Collections Arranged: Washington Color Sch, Washington Gallery Mod Art; W P A Prints, 68 & Werner Drewes, Woodcuts, 69, Nat Collection Fine Arts.
Positions: Researcher, Washington Gallery Mod Art, 62-66; res asst print dept, Nat Collection Fine Arts, Washington, D C, 67-69; dir, Studio Gallery, Washington, D C, 70-
Research: Washington Color School artists.
Specialty of Gallery: Contemporary art.
Publications: Contribr (Caril Dreyfuss), Highlights of the National Collection of Fine Arts, 68; auth (Caril Dreyfuss), Drewes, woodcuts, Smithsonian, 69.
Mailing Address: 3116 Cathedral Ave N W, Washington, DC 20008.

DUNBAR, GEORGE BAUER
Painter
Preferred Media: Collage.
b New Orleans, La, Sept 20, 27.
Study & Training: Tyler Sch Fine Arts, Temple Univ; Acad Grande Chaumeire, Paris, France.
Commissions: Lykes Bros Steamship; Arthur Davis Collection, New Orleans; Latter Bldg, New Orleans; First Nat Bank, Slidell, La; New Orleans Clin.
Exhibitions: Rose Mus, Brandeis Univ, Waltham, Mass; Temple Univ, Philadelphia, Pa; Riverside Mus, New York, N Y; Delgado Mus, New Orleans, La; Bressler Gallery, Milwaukee, Wis.
Teaching: Lectr art, Tulane Univ La.
Awards: Awards, Rose Mus, Brandeis Univ, Tyler Sch Fine Arts, Philadelphia & Delgado Mus.
Publications: Contribr, Art News & La Rev Mod.
Dealer: Simone Stern Gallery, 516 Royal St, New Orleans, LA 70130.
Mailing Address: P O Box 524, Rt 2, Slidell, LA 70458.

DUNCALFE, WALTER JOHN DOUGLAS
Painter, Designer
Preferred Media: Oils, Watercolors.
b Victoria, B C, Sept 11, 09.
Study & Training: Art Stud League New York, N Y, with Robert B Hale, 47; New Sch Soc Res, with Huang Wen-Shan; Pratt Inst, BFA(hon), 61.
Exhibitions: San Francisco Mus Art Ann Watercolor Exhib, 43; Am Watercolor Soc Ann, 47; Audubon Artists Seventh Ann, 48; Whitney Mus Am Art Contemp Sculpture, Watercolor & Drawing Exhib, 48; Brooklyn & Long Island Biennial, Brooklyn Mus, 60.
Teaching: Instr, City Col New York, 51-55; head advert design, Jamesine Franklin Sch Prof Art, 52-55; instr, Fairleigh Dickinson Col, 53-54; from assoc art to prof, Pratt Inst, 55-; lectr hist art, N Y Univ, summer 56.

Memberships: Life mem, Art Stud League New York.
Mailing Address: 224 Willoughby Ave, Brooklyn, NY 11205.

DUNCAN, RUTH
 Painter
Preferred Media: Oils, Watercolors.
b Greeley, Colo, Feb 19, 08.
Study & Training: Stephens Col, AA; Univ Okla, BFA; also with Harold A Roney, Simon G Michael & Warren Hunter.
Work in Public Collections: Stephens Col, Columbia, Mo; Admin Bldg, San Antonio Jr Col, Tex; Royal Bldg, Dallas, Tex.
Commissions: Many.
Exhibitions: 10 Exhibs, Am Artists Prof League; U S Nat Galleries, Smithsonian Inst, Washington, D C, 62; Stephens Col, 68; Witte Mem Mus, San Antonio; Univ Tex, Austin; plus others.
Awards: Wonderland Gallery Award, River Art Group, 71; Coppini Acad Fine Arts Award for best conserv painting, River Art Group, 72.
Memberships: Fel Am Artists Prof League; Coppini Acad Fine Arts (recording secy, 60-67); River Art Group.
Mailing Address: 1511 Fulton Ave, San Antonio, TX 78201.

DUNN, ALAN (CANTWELL)
 Cartoonist, Writer
Preferred Media: Lithographic Crayon, Ink.
b Belmar, N J, Aug 11, 00.
Study & Training: Columbia Univ; Nat Acad Design Art Sch; Louis Comfort Tiffany Found; Fontainebleau École Des Arts, France; hon vis fel Am Acad Rome.
Work in Public Collections: Libr Cong; Alan Dunn Manuscript Collection, Syracuse Univ; Metrop Mus Art, New York, N Y; plus many others.
Exhibitions: One-man exhib, Social Comment Art, Hamilton Col, 68; Syracuse Univ; Princeton Mus Art; also other nat & int exhibs.
Positions: Contrib staff, New Yorker Mag, 26-; editorial cartoonist, Architectural Record, 36-
Memberships: Author's Guild.
Publications: The last lath, 47; East of fifth, 48; Should it gurgle, 57; Is there intelligent life on earth, 60; Portfolio of social cartoons, 1957 to 1968, 68; plus three others.
Mailing Address: c/o New Yorker Magazine, 25 W 43rd St, New York, NY 10036.

DUNN, CAL
 Painter
Preferred Media: Oils, Watercolors.
b Georgetown, Ohio, Aug 31, 15.
Study & Training: Cincinnati Art Acad, 27; Cent Acad Commercial Art, 32-34.
Work in Public Collections: Ford Motor Co, Detroit, Mich; Allstate Ins Co, Chicago, Ill; Am Artists Group, New York, N Y; Tavern Club Chicago.
Commissions: Numerous watercolor story assignments for Ford Motor Co, throughout U S, 50-62.
Exhibitions: Am Watercolor Soc Exhibs, New York, N Y, 55 & 56 & Traveling Exhib, 63; Chicago & Vicinity Exhib, Art Inst Chicago, 57; 100 American Watercolorists, Royal Gallery, London, 63.
Positions: Animation art dir, U S A A F, Wright Field, Dayton, Ohio, 43-44; art dir, Sarra, Inc, 44-47; pres, Cal Dunn Studios, Chicago, 47-
Awards: for Edge of Town, Am Artist Mag, 56, The City, Nat Offset & Lithographic Asn, 57 & Manscape, Artist Guild Chicago, 65.
Memberships: Am Watercolor Soc; Artist Guild Chicago (pres, 55-57).
Publications: Illusr, Ford Times—Lincoln Mercury Times, 50-62; auth, article, In: Am Artist Mag, 56.
Mailing Address: 141 W Ohio St, Chicago, IL 60610.

DUNN, NATE
 Painter, Instructor
Preferred Media: Oils, Acrylics.
b Pittsburgh, Pa, July 4, 96.
Study & Training: Carnegie Inst Technol, with Arthur Sparks, Alfred Taylor & Geo Sotter.
Work in Public Collections: Butler Inst Am Art; Thiel Col; Pa State Univ.
Exhibitions: Butler Inst Am Art, Youngstown, Ohio; Mansfield Col; Playhouse, Pittsburgh, Pa; Canton Art Gallery, Ohio; Thiel Col, Greenville, Pa.
Teaching: Instr painting & drawing, Girls Buhl Club, 58-
Awards: Purchase Prizes, Butler Inst Am Art Area Shows, 64 & Steubenville Art Asn, 72; St John's Episcopal Church Award, 66.
Memberships: Friends Am Art, Youngstown; Steubenville Art Asn; Canton Gallery; fel Royal Soc Arts.
Dealer: Shoestring, 1505 Elm, Youngstown, OH 44505; Queen's Gallery, Cleveland, OH 44101.
Mailing Address: 490 Carley Ave, Sharon, PA 16146.

DUNN, O COLEMAN
 Collector
b Raymond, Alta, Can, Mar 27, 02; U S citizen.
Collection: British and American paintings and drawings; European old masters.
Mailing Address: 917 Kearns Bldg, 136 S Main St, Salt Lake City, UT 84101.

DUNNINGTON, MRS WALTER GREY
 Collector, Patron
b Long Branch, N J, Aug 17, 10.
Study & Training: Smith Col, BA; Bryn Mawr Col.
Positions: Treas, women's comt, Philadelphia Mus Art, 38-41; pres, bd trustees, Parrish Art Mus, Southampton, N Y; dir, N Y Hort Soc.
Collection: Furniture, porcelain, paintings, drawings.
Mailing Address: 960 Fifth Ave, New York, NY 10021.

DUNWIDDIE, CHARLOTTE
 Sculptor
b Strasbourg, France.
Study & Training: Acad Arts, Berlin, Ger, with Wilhelm Otto; also with Mariano Benlliure y Gil, Madrid, Spain & Alberto Lagos, Buenos Aires, Arg.
Work in Public Collections: Cardinal's Palace, Buenos Aires; Church of Good Shepherd, Lima, Peru; Marine Corps Mus, Washington, D C; Aquaduct Racecourse, New York, N Y; Mt St Alfonsus, Suffield, Conn.
Exhibitions: Salon Bellas Artes, Buenos Aires, 40-45; Allied Artists Am, 56-72; Nat Sculpture Soc, 58-72; Nat Acad Design, 59-72; Am Artists Prof League, 59-70.
Positions: Pres, Pen & Brush Club, 66-70; mem ed bd, Nat Sculpture Rev, 70-
Awards: Speyer Award, 69 & Artists Fund Prize for best in show, 72, Nat Acad Design; Lindsey Mem Prize, Nat Sculpture Soc, 70; plus others.
Memberships: Nat Acad Design (secy, 66-69); Nat Sculpture Soc; Allied Artists Am; Royal Soc Arts, London, Eng; Am Artists Prof League (dir, 60-).

DU PEN, EVERETT GEORGE
 Sculptor, Educator
Preferred Media: Bronze, Wood, Terra Cotta, Marble.
b San Francisco, Calif, Dec 12, 12.
Study & Training: Univ Southern Calif, with Merril Gage; Yale Sch Fine Arts, Clara Kimball English Traveling fel, 37, BFA, with George Eberhard, George Snowden & Alexander Archipenko.
Work in Public Collections: Seattle Art Mus; Washington Mutual Savings Bank, Seattle; Univ Wash Faculty Club, Seattle; Aberdeen City Hall, Wash.
Commissions: Three limestone carvings, Elec Eng Bldg, Univ Wash, 48; bronze sculptures for fountains, State of Wash, Olympia Libr, 60 & World's Fair, Seattle, 62; crucifix & wall carving, St John Episcopal Church, Seattle, 63; carved walnut screens, Munic Bldg, City of Seattle, 63.
Exhibitions: Nat Acad Design, New York, 50, 59 & 72; Seattle Art Mus Northwest Ann, 47-63; Pa Acad Fine Art, 50, 54 & 58; Nat Sculpture Soc, 50, 59 & 72; Mainstreams 72, Marietta Col, 72.
Teaching: Asst sculpture, Carnegie Inst Technol Art Sch, 39-40; asst sculpture, Wash Univ Art Sch, 40-42; from instr to prof sculpture, Univ Wash Sch Art, 45-
Positions: Sculpture mem, Munic Art Comn, Seattle; sculpture adv, Art Adv Bd Seattle World's Fair, 60-62.
Awards: Saltus Gold Medal, Nat Acad Design.
Bibliography: Minor L Bishop (auth), Fountains in contemporary architecture, Am Fedn Arts, 65; Louis G Redstone (auth), articles, In: Art Archit, 68 & Nat Sculpture Rev.
Memberships: Fel Nat Sculpture Soc.
Mailing Address: 1231 20th Ave E, Seattle, WA 98102.

DU PRE, GRACE ANNETTE
 Painter
Preferred Media: Oils.
b Spartanburg, S C.
Study & Training: Converse Col & Converse Col Sch Music; Grand Cent Sch Art, with Greacen, Wolfe, Karl Anderson, Hildebrandt, Wayman Adams & Frank V Dumond.
Work in Public Collections: Charleston City Hall Collection of Portraits, S C; U S Supreme Court, Washington, D C; New York City Main Post Off Collection; State House, Columbia, S C; Church of the Ascension Collection of Rectors' Portraits, New York, N Y.
Commissions: 14 paintings of judges from life, U S Court Appeals, 7th Circuit, Chicago, Ill, 54-61; double portrait of Pres Truman & his mother, now in Truman Collection; Dr Hu Shih (portrait from life), Columbia Univ Lowe Libr; plus many others incl four portraits of James F Byrnes, now in pub collections.

Exhibitions: Allied Artists Am Ann, New York, N Y, 42-63; Nat Arts Club Ann, 42-63; Am Artists Prof League Ann, 43-62; Audubon Artists Ann, 46; Nat Exhib Am Paintings, Ogunquit, Maine, 51 & 58.
Teaching: Pvt classes, Spartanburg, S C, 32-42.
Awards: Second prize for portrait, Mint Mus Regional Exhib, 43; award, 31st Nat Exhib Am Painting, 51; prize for portrait, Catharine Lorrillard Wolfe Art Club Ann, 55.
Bibliography: Articles, In: The State Mag, S C Mag & many newspapers.
Memberships: Allied Artists Am; Grand Cent Art Galleries; Nat Arts Club; Catharine Lorrillard Wolfe Art Club; Am Artists Prof League (nat exec bd, 50-55).
Dealer: Grand Central Art Galleries, Vanderbilt Ave, New York, NY 10017.
Mailing Address: 361 Mills Ave, Spartanburg, SC 29302.

DURAND, LUCILLE MURPHY
Illustrator
Preferred Media: Watercolors, Graphics.
b Fort Lee, N Y.
Study & Training: Art Stud League New York, N Y; Nat Acad Design, New York.
Exhibitions: Mus Mod Art, New York; almost all local shows, N J & Pa, 70-72; First Ann Regional Art Exhib, Cult Arts Ctr, Ocean City, N J, 72; Philadelphia Art Mus, Pa, 72.
Teaching: Pvt instr, 62-
Positions: Illusr, The J, New York, Curtis Publ, Relig Publ & var greeting card co, to 62.
Memberships: Cult Arts, Ocean City; Cape May Co Art League, N J.
Mailing Address: R R 1, Box 123, Woodbine, NJ 08270.

DUREN, TERENCE ROMAINE
Painter, Illustrator
b Shelby, Nebr, July 9, 06.
Study & Training: Art Inst Chicago, 29; Fontainebleau, France, 32; Kunstgewerbliche Hochsch, Vienna, 36.
Work in Public Collections: Art Inst Chicago; Cleveland Mus Art; Corcoran Gallery Art; Carnegie Inst; Joslyn Mem Mus; plus others.
Commissions: Murals, pub bldgs, Cleveland & Columbus, Ohio.
Exhibitions: Los Angeles Mus Art, 45; Carnegie Inst, 45 & 46; San Francisco Mus Art; Dallas Mus Fine Arts; Art: U S A, 58; plus others.
Awards: Prizes, Fla Southern Col, 52, Franklin Co, Nebr, 52 & Lincoln Art Guild, 52; plus others.
Memberships: Nat Soc Mural Painters; fel Int Inst Arts & Lett; Int Platform Asn.
Publications: Illusr, cover drawings, World Herald, Omaha, Nebr, The American West, 55, World Bks, 60-61, Funk & Wagnall's Encycl, 60-61, Fortune Mag & other publ.
Mailing Address: Shelby, NE 68662.

DURIEUX, CAROLINE WOGAN
Printmaker
b New Orleans, La, Jan 22, 96.
Study & Training: Newcomb Col, BA(art educ), 17; fel, Pa Acad Fine Arts, 18-20; La State Univ, MA, 49.
Work in Public Collections: Rosenwald Collection, Nat Gallery Art, Washington, D C; Mus Mod Art, New York, N Y; Philadelphia Mus Fine Arts, Pa; Libr of Cong, Washington, D C; Bibliot Nat, Paris, France.
Exhibitions: Libr of Cong Print Ann, Washington, D C, 46; Cincinnati Mus Fine Arts Int Biennial, Ohio, 56; San Francisco 24th Ann, Calif, 61; Print Coun Am, Europe & Far East, 62; Second Nat Lithography Exhib, Fla State Univ, 66.
Teaching: Instr life class painting, Newcomb Col, 20-21 & 38-43; from asst prof to prof graphics, La State Univ, Baton Rouge, 43-65, emer prof, 65-
Positions: Consult, Fed Art Proj, Works Proj Admin, 38-43.
Awards: Res grants for develop of electron prints & Clichés Verres, La State Univ Coun Res, 51-60 & 72-73.
Bibliography: Salpeter (auth), About Caroline Durieux, Coronet, 37; Caroline Durieux, La State Univ Press, 49; Zigrosser (auth), The appeal of prints, N Y Graphics, 70.
Memberships: Audubon Artists; Baton Rouge Gallery.
Publications: Illusr, Gumbo Yaya, Houghton, 38; illusr, New Orleans City guide, Works Proj Admin, 38; co-auth, Mardigras day, Holt, 48.
Dealer: Taylor Clark Prints, 2623 Government St, Baton Rouge, LA 70806.
Mailing Address: 772 W Chimes, Baton Rouge, LA 70802.

DUTTON, BERTHA P
Museum Director, Writer
b Algona, Iowa, Mar 29, 03.
Study & Training: Univ Nebr, 29-31; Univ N Mex, BA, 35, MA, 37; Columbia Univ, PhD, 52.

Teaching: Instr anthrop, TV & adult classes, Mus N Mex, 47-57; instr anthrop, St Michael's Col, 65.
Positions: Secy, dept anthrop, Univ N Mex, 33-36; cur ethnol, Mus N Mex, Santa Fe, 39-59, cur interpretation, 60-62, cur, div res, 62-65; dir, Mus Navaho Ceremonial Art, Inc, 66-
Awards: Nat Sci Found grant-in-aid, 62-63; Columbus Explor Fund grant, 64, 65 & 68; cert appreciation, Indian Arts & Crafts Bd, U S Dept Interior, 67; plus others.
Memberships: Northern Ariz Soc Sci & Art; Ariz Archaeol & Hist Soc; Southwestern Asn Indian Affairs (bd mem); Archaeol Soc N Mex; Southwest Anthrop Asn; plus others.
Publications: Auth & illusr, History of Plumbate Ware, Gannon, 43; co-auth & illusr, Excavations at Tajumulco, Guatemala, 43 & auth & illusr, Sun father's way: the Kiva murals of Kuaua, 63, Univ N Mex Press; contribr, Am Antiq & N Mex Quart; plus many others.
Mailing Address: Museum of Navaho Ceremonial Art, Inc, Box 5153, Santa Fe, NM 87501.

DUVOISIN, ROGER
Writer, Illustrator
Preferred Media: Gouache, Collage, Ink.
b Geneva, Switz, Aug 28, 04; U S citizen.
Study & Training: Col Mod, Geneva; Ecole Arts Decoratifs, Geneva.
Work in Public Collections: Univ Libr Collection, Minneapolis; Rutgers Univ Libr Collection; Univ Southern Miss Libr Collection.
Exhibitions: Am Fedn Arts Traveling Exhib U S Mus, 44-45; Mus Mod Art Touring Exhib, 46-49; Philadelphia Mus Sch Art, 52; U S Graphic Art Touring Exhib, Russia & E Europe, 63-66; Univ Minn, 67.
Teaching: Vis prof illus, Parsons Sch Design, New York, N Y, 43-51.
Awards: Caldecott Medal, Am Libr Asn; Rutgers Univ Bicentennial Award; Ger Govt Award, Bonn, 56.
Bibliography: Henry Pitz (auth), article, In: Am Artist, 12/49; John Hutchins (auth), article, In: Herald Tribune Bk Rev Mag, 11/16/52; Hashel Frankel (auth), article, In: Sat Rev, 8/22/64.
Memberships: Am Inst Graphic Art.
Publications: Auth & illusr, Petunia books, 50-66; illusr, Happy lion books, 54-70; illusr, The three cornered hat, 60; auth & illusr, Veronica books, 60-71; auth & illusr, The crocodile in the tree, 72.
Mailing Address: Box 116, Gladstone, NJ 07934.

DWIGHT, EDWARD HAROLD
Museum Director
b Cincinnati, Ohio, Aug 2, 19.
Study & Training: St Louis Sch Fine Arts; Yale Univ; Art Acad Cincinnati.
Collections Arranged: Juan Gris, 48; Paintings by the Peale Family, 54; Rediscoveries in American Painting, 55; Still Life Painting since 1470, 56; El Greco, Rembrandt, Goya, Cézanne, Van Gogh, Picasso, 57; Ralston Crawford, 58; American Painting, 1760, 60; Masters of Landscape: East and West, 63; Audubon Watercolors and Drawings, 65; John Quidor, 65-66; Worthington Whittredge Retrospective, 69.
Positions: Cur Am art, Cincinnati Art Mus, 54-55; dir, Milwaukee Art Ctr & cur, Layton Col, 55-62; dir, Mus Art, Munson-Williams-Proctor Inst, 62-
Awards: Ford Found fel, Humanities & the Arts Prog, for res on J J Audubon, 61.
Memberships: Asn Art Mus Dirs.
Publications: Auth, Audubon watercolors and drawings, 65; auth, John Quidor, 65-66; auth, Worthington Whittredge retrospective, 69.
Mailing Address: Munson-Williams-Proctor Institute, 310 Genessee St, Utica, NY 13502.

DWORZAN, GEORGE R
Painter, Sculptor
Preferred Media: Oils on Canvas, Wood.
b New York, N Y, Mar 28, 24.
Study & Training: Cooper Union, with Morris Cantor; Art Stud League New York, with Harry Sternberg; Acad Grande Chaumiere, Paris, France; Acad Leger, Paris, with Fernand Leger.
Work in Public Collections: N Y Univ, New York; Chase Manhattan Bank, New York; Univ Mass, Amherst; Ohio State Univ; Herron Mus Art, Indianapolis, Ind.
Exhibitions: Salon Realities Nouvelles, Mus Art Mod, Paris, 48-49; Art U S A, Coliseum, New York, 59; Nat Print Competition, AAA Gallery, New York, 60; Contemp Arts Soc Ann, Herron Mus, 64 & 68; Univ N C Ann Invitation, Chapel Hill, 68.
Teaching: Instr painting & drawing, New York Univ.
Dealer: East Hampton Gallery, 450 W 27th St, New York, NY 10025.
Mailing Address: 463 West St, New York, NY 10014.

DYCK, PAUL
Painter, Lecturer
Preferred Media: Oils.
b Chicago, Ill, Aug 17, 17.
Study & Training: With Johann Von Skramlik, Florence, Italy, Prague, Czech, Rome, Italy & Paris, France, 26-33.
Work in Public Collections: Phoenix Art Mus, Ariz; Mus Northern Ariz, Flagstaff; Franklin Inst, Philadelphia, Pa; plus private collections in U S A, Can & Europe.
Commissions: Indians of the Overland Trail (painting), sponsored by pub mus, 56; Flame of Man (painting), F O Hess, Franklin Inst, Philadelphia, 70.
Exhibitions: One-man exhibs, Southwest Mus, Los Angeles, Calif, Mont Hist Soc, Helena, Chicago Mus Nat Hist, Phoenix Art Mus & Ariz State Univ Mus, plus 43 others, 54-72.
Teaching: Lectr, Am Indian Cult.
Awards: Artist commendation, U S Navy, 45; lifetime mem, Buffalo Bill Hist Ctr, Cody, Wyo, 71.
Publications: Auth, Brule, Sioux people of the Rosebud, 69; contribr, articles, In: Montana, Mag of Western Hist, 72; contribr, articles, In: Buffalo Bill Hist Ctr, 72.
Mailing Address: P O Box 217, Rimrock, AZ 86335.

DZUBAS, FRIEDEL
Painter
b Berlin, Ger, Apr 20, 15; U S citizen.
Work in Public Collections: Solomon R Guggenheim Mus & Whitney Mus Am Art, New York, N Y; Boston Mus Fine Arts, Mass; San Francisco Mus Art, Calif; Everson Mus, Syracuse, N Y.
Exhibitions: Post Painterly Abstraction, Los Angeles Co Mus Art, Calif, 64; Form, Color, Image, Detroit Inst Arts, Mich, 67; American Painting Now, Am Pavilion, Expo 67, Montreal, P Q, 67; Color and Field, Albright-Knox Art Gallery, Buffalo, N Y, Cleveland Mus, Ohio & Dayton Art Inst, Ohio, 70-71; Abstract Painting in the 70's, Boston Mus Fine Arts, 72.
Teaching: Artist-in-residence, Dartmouth Col, 62; vis artist critic, Inst Humanistic Studies, 65-66; vis artist critic, Univ Pa, 68-69; vis artist critic, Cornell Univ, 69-
Awards: Guggenheim fel, 66 & 68; Nat Coun on the Arts Award, 68.
Bibliography: Barbara Rose (auth), In absence of anguish, Arts Int, 10/63; Max Kosloff (auth), Friedel Dzubas, an interview, Artforum, summer 65; John Elderfield (auth), Abstraction in the 70's, Arts Int, summer 72.
Publications: Auth, statement & color plate, In: Art in Am, 67 & Art now: New York, 72.
Dealers: Lawrence Rubin Gallery, 49 W 57th St, New York, NY 10019; David Mirvish, 596 Markham St, Toronto, Ont, Can.
Mailing Address: 119 The Knoll, Ithaca, NY 14850.

E

EADES, LUIS ERIC
Painter, Educator
Preferred Media; Oils, Acrylics.
b Madrid, Spain, June 25, 23; U S citizen.
Study & Training: Bath Sch Art, Eng; Slade Sch, Univ London; Inst Polytech Nac, Mexico City, Mex; Univ Ky, Lexington, BA.
Work in Public Collections: Whitney Mus Am Art, New York, N Y; Mus Fine Arts, Houston, Tex; Dallas Mus Fine Arts, Tex; Fort Worth Art Ctr, Tex; Mus Fine Arts, Holyoke, Mass.
Commissions: Airport mural, Govt Honduras, Toncontin, Tegucigalpa, 48.
Exhibitions: Recent Painting U S A: The Figure, Mus Mod Art, New York, 62; Forty Artists Under Forty, Whitney Mus Am Art, 62; State of Man, New Sch Soc Res, New York, 64; Second Intermountain Biennial Exhib, Salt Lake Art Ctr, Utah, 65; Colo Springs Fine Arts Ctr, Colo, 69.
Teaching: Prof painting & drawing, Univ Tex, 54-60; prof painting & drawing, Univ Colo, 61-
Publications: Illusr, The precipice, Univ Tex Pr, 69.
Dealer: Carlin Galleries, 710 Montgomery, Fort Worth, TX 76107.
Mailing Address: 1627 Fifth St, Boulder, CO 80302.

EAGERTON, ROBERT PIERCE
Printmaker, Painter
b Florence, S C, Mar 17, 40.
Study & Training: Atlanta Sch Art, BFA; Acad Fine Arts, Vienna, Austria; Cranbrook Acad Art, Bloomfield Hills, Mich.
Work in Public Collections: Nat Collection Fine Art, Smithsonian Inst, Washington, D C; Art Inst Chicago Mus; Lessing J Rosenwald Collection, Jenkins Town, Pa; Sheldon Swope Gallery Art; Mus Graphic Art, New York, N Y.
Commissions: Portfolio of six lithographs, NABIS Fine Arts, New York, 72.
Exhibitions: Drawings U S A, Saint Paul Art Ctr, 66; New Talent in Printmaking, Assoc Am Artist Gallery, New York, 69; Biennale Int l'Estampe, Paris, France, 70; Contemporary American Prints, Krannert Mus, Univ Ill, 71; Lithographs de la Collection Mourlot, P R, 71.
Teaching: Assoc prof lithography, Herron Sch Art, Ind Univ-Purdue Univ, Indianapolis, 66-, head dept printmaking, 69-, chmn dept fine arts, 70-; guest artist printmaking, Univ Ill, Champaign, 70; vis prof printmaking, Tyler Sch Art, summer 72.
Positions: Co-founder, Transfigurations Press, Sarasota, Fla, 64-66.
Awards: Southeastern Arts grant, Atlanta Arts Comn, 65; first prize, 59th Ann Ind Print Exhib, Indianapolis Mus, 68; res grant, Ind Univ, 70.
Dealer: Associated American Artists Gallery, 663 Fifth Ave, New York, NY 10022.
Mailing Address: 4004 Arthington Blvd, Indianapolis, IN 46226.

EAGLE, CLARA M
Craftsman, Educator
b Columbus, Ohio, June 16, 08.
Study & Training: Ohio State Univ, BS & MA; Sch Am Craftsmen; also with John Huntington.
Exhibitions: Louisville-Ind Ann, 59 & 60; Evansville Tri-State Exhib, 59 & 65; Am Craftsmen's Coun Show, Gatlinburg, 60; Miss River Craft Show, 65; Louisville Kentuckiana Exhib, 65.
Teaching: Prof art & chmn dept, Murray State Univ, 46-
Positions: Art supvr, Mayfield Heights, Ohio, 30-36, Mount Vernon, Ohio, 36-44, Findlay, 43-46, Ashtabula, 44-45 & Rio Grande Col, summer 46; Ky state art chmn, Am Asn Univ Women 58-62; pres, Ky Art Educ Asn, 54-55 & 61-62; mem ed bd educ curric guide, Ky Dept Educ; sponsor, Kappa Pi.
Awards: Hon mention, silversmithing, Evansville Tri-State Exhib, 59; prize, Louisville-Ind Ann, 61.
Memberships: Am Asn Univ Prof; Am Asn Univ Women; Col Art Asn Am; Western Art Asn (Ky rep); Southeastern Col Art Asn; plus others.
Mailing Address: Division of Art, Murray State University, Murray, KY 42072.

EAMES, JOHN HEAGAN
Etcher, Painter
b Lowell, Mass, July 19, 00.
Study & Training: Harvard Univ, AB, 22; Royal Col Art, with Malcolm Osborne & Robert Austin, 33, 35 & 37.
Work in Public Collections: Metrop Mus Art, New York, N Y; Libr of Cong, Washington, D C; Albany Inst Hist & Art, N Y.
Exhibitions: Royal Acad, London, Eng, 35, 37 & 40; New York World's Fair, N Y, 39; Int Print Exhib, Art Inst Chicago, 39; Biennial Exhib, Venice, Italy, 40; Contemp Am Drawings, Metrop Mus Art, New York, 42 & 52.
Awards: Kate W Arms Mem Prize, 52, 54 & 57, John Taylor Arms Prize, 53 & Henry B Shope Prize, 57, Soc Am Graphic Artists.
Memberships: Soc Am Graphic Artists; Nat Acad Design; Royal Soc Painters-Etchers, London, Eng.
Mailing Address: Boothbay Harbor, ME 04538.

EARL, JACK EUGENE
Sculptor
Preferred Media: Ceramics.
b Uniapolis, Ohio, Aug 2, 34.
Study & Training: Bluffton Col, BA; Ohio State Univ, MA.
Work in Public Collections: Butler Mus Art, Youngstown, Ohio; Columbus Gallery Fine Arts, Ohio; Emerson Art Ctr, Syracuse, N Y.
Exhibitions: Toledo Mus Art, Ohio, 68; Objects U S A, Smithsonian Inst, Washington, D C, 69; Mus Contemp Crafts, New York, N Y, 71; Fort Wayne Mus Art, Ind, 71; Int Exhib Ceramics, Victoria & Albert Mus Art, London, Eng, 72.
Teaching: Instr ceramics, Toledo Mus Art, 64-72; asst prof ceramics, Va Commonwealth Univ, 72-
Awards: Nat Coun Educ Ceramic Arts prize, Emerson Art Ctr, 68; merit award, Louisville Art Ctr, 68-70; purchase award, Columbus Gallery Fine Arts, 72.
Memberships: Nat Coun Educ Ceramic Arts.
Mailing Address: 4717 W Hundred Rd, Chester, VA 23831.

EASBY, DUDLEY T, JR
Art Administrator, Art Historian
b Lock Haven, Pa, Dec 3, 05.
Study & Training: Princeton Univ, BS(magna cum laude), 28; Univ Pa Law Sch, LLB(cum laude), 31.

Positions: Secy, Metrop Mus Art, New York, 45-69, chmn dept primitive art, 70-71, secy emer, 71-; consult fel, Univ Pa Mus, Philadelphia, 56-
Awards: Comdr, Orden al Merito, Peru, 61; Off, Orden del Sol, Peru; Orden del Aguila Azteca, Mex, 70.
Memberships: Inst Andean Res (past pres); Archaeol Inst Am (former gen coun).
Mailing Address: 2221 Rittenhouse Sq, Philadelphia, PA 19103.

EASLEY, LOYCE ROGERS
Painter, Potter
Preferred Media: Oils.
b Weatherford, Okla, June 28, 18.
Study & Training: Univ Okla, BFA; grad work at Univ Okla & Eastern N Mex Univ; also with Frederic Taubes.
Work in Public Collections: U S Air Force Acad, Colorado Springs, Colo; Mus N Mex, Santa Fe; West Tex Mus, Tex Tech Univ, Lubbock; Rosewell Mus Art, N Mex; Southwest Tex State Col, San Marcus.
Commissions: Many portrait & easel painting commissions.
Exhibitions: Bon Marche Gallery Invitational, Seattle, Wash, 64; Nat Invitational Exhib, The Gallery, Fort Lauderdale, Fla, 64; 6th Ann Exhib Southwest Am Art, Oklahoma City Art Ctr, Okla, 65; 51st Allied Artists Am Ann Exhib, 65; N Mex Mus Painting Invitational, N Mex, 68.
Awards: First award, 48th Fiesta Exhib, 61 & second award, 50th Fiesta Exhib, Mus N Mex; distinguished former student, Univ Okla, 63.
Bibliography: Margaret Harold (auth), Prize winning paintings, 60; Montez (auth), New Mexico artists, N Mex Mag, 63; Wendes (auth), article, In: New Mexican, 65.
Memberships: Hon mem New Mexico Art League.
Dealers: Ojo del Sol, 612 N Oregon, El Paso, TX 79901; Jamison Gallery, 111 E San Francisco, Santa Fe, NM 87501.
Mailing Address: 812 N Dal Paso, Hubbs, NM 88240.

EAST, N S, JR
Designer, Sculptor
Preferred Media: Metals.
b Delaware County, Pa, Mar 21, 36.
Study & Training: Philadelphia Col Art, 62-65; also with Herman Cohen.
Work in Public Collections: Glassboro Col, N J; Univ City Arts League, Philadelphia, Pa; Philadelphia Bd Educ, Tilden Jr High Sch; Bell Tel Co Pa, Philadelphia.
Exhibitions: Color 65, one-man show, Allentown, Pa, 65; Sculpture 68, Grabar Gallery, Philadelphia, 68; Nat Forum Prof Artists, Philadelphia, 68-72; one-man show, Antonio Souza Gallery, Mexico City, Mex, 69; two-man show, Wood-Type Workshop, 72.
Teaching: Instr AV art, Philadelphia Sch Syst, 65-67; instr lang of art, Bell Tel Co & Univ City Arts League, 67-70; instr welding, Univ City Arts League, 70-
Positions: Pres, NE: Design Consults, 70-; owner, ornamental iron studio, The Iron Men.
Memberships: Univ City Arts League (v pres, 65-66); Nat Forum Prof Artists (bd mem); Philadelphia Mus Art; Upper Merion Cult Ctr; Alumni Asn, Philadelphia Col Art.
Publications: Auth, The language of art/toward another Bauhaus, 67; auth, Beachead of the stars, Apollo Mission, 69; auth, Design and the social dimension, 69; auth, The combined graphics department, 70; auth, The city of '76, Philadelphia Bicentennial, 71.
Mailing Address: 4820 Chester Ave, Philadelphia, PA 19143.

EATON, MYRWYN LAKE
Educator, Painter
Preferred Media: Oils, Watercolors, Casein, Ink.
b Strawberry Point, Iowa, July 30, 04.
Study & Training: State Univ Iowa, BA,26; Chicago Acad Fine Arts; Art Inst Chicago; Harvard Univ, Bacon scholar, 31, MA, 32, Harvard traveling scholarships, 33-34 & 38.
Exhibitions: George Binet Gallery, New York, N Y, 48-50; Gallery Andre Maurice, Paris, France, 49; N Y Univ, New York, 62; Rossmoor, Walnut Creek, Calif, 67; Univ Calif, Santa Cruz, 68.
Teaching: Instr studio courses & art hist, N Dak State Col, 26-29; asst & tutor studio courses & art hist, Harvard Univ, 32-38; from instr to assoc prof studio courses & art hist, N Y Univ, 38-66.
Mailing Address: 2125 Skycrest Dr, Walnut Creek CA 94595.

EBERMAN, EDWIN
Art Administrator, Educator
Preferred Media: Watercolors.
b Black Mountain, N C, Feb 20, 05.
Study & Training: Carnegie-Mellon Col Fine Arts, BA.
Teaching: Dir educ, painting, illustrating & cartooning, Famous Artists Schs, 48-65.

Positions: Art dir, Arts & Decorative Mag, 33-35; art dir, McCalls Mag, 36-38; art dir, Look Mag, 41-46; dir & co-founder, Famous Artists Schs, 47-65.
Publications: Co-auth, Techniques of the picture story, 45; auth, Nantucket sketchbook, 46; co-auth, numerous textbooks for Famous Artists Sch, 48-65.
Mailing Address: 370 Wahackme Rd, New Canaan, CT 06840.

EBIE, WILLIAM DENNIS
Art Administrator, Painter
Preferred Media: Acrylics.
b Akron, Ohio, Feb 7, 42.
Study & Training: Akron Art Inst Sch Design, scholar, 60, Univ Akron & Akron Art Inst Sch Design, BFA, 64; Calif Col Arts & Crafts, scholarships, 67-68, MFA, 68.
Work in Public Collections: Calif Col Arts & Crafts Gallery.
Exhibitions: Two-man show, Fla A&M Univ Art Gallery, Tallahassee, 70; Five States Art Exhib, Port Arthur, Tex, 71; Four Corner States Biennial, Phoenix, Ariz, 71.
Teaching: Instr painting, Fla A&M Univ, 69-70; instr painting, Roswell Mus Adult Educ, N Mex, 71-
Positions: Ceramic specialist, Peace Corps, Cuzco, Peru, 64-66; graphic artist, Alameda Co Health Dept, Oakland, Calif, 67-68; asst dir, Roswell Mus & Art Ctr & managing dir, Roswell Mus Artist-in-Residence Prog, 71-
Mailing Address: Route 1, Box 244 A, Roswell, NM 88201.

ECKE, BETTY TSENG YU-HO
Painter, Art Historian
Preferred Media: Watercolors, Collage, Plexiglass.
b Peking, China, Nov 29, 23; U S citizen.
Study & Training: Fu-jen Univ, Peking, BA, 42; Univ Hawaii, MA, 66; Inst Fine Arts, New York Univ, PhD, 72.
Work in Public Collections: Honolulu Acad Arts, Hawaii; Walker Art Ctr, Minneapolis, Minn; Nat Mus Mod Art, Stockholm, Sweden; Mus Cernuschi, Paris, France; Stanford Art Gallery, Calif.
Commissions: Mura, St Katherine's Church, Kaui, Hawaii, 57; mural, Manoa Chinese Pavilion, Honolulu, Hawaii, 58; mural, Golden West Savings & Loan, San Francisco, Calif, 64; wall painting, Castle & Cook Co, Ltd, Honolulu, 68; wall painting, Honolulu Int Airport, 72.
Exhibitions: Contemporary American Painting & Sculpture, Univ Ill, Urbana, 58, 61 & 65; Carnegie Inst Painting & Sculpture Int, Pittsburgh, Pa, 61 & 65; Kunstverein, Munich & Frankfurt, Ger; Walker Art Ctr; San Francisco Mus Art, Calif; plus others.
Teaching: Instr studio art, Honolulu Acad Art, 50-63, consultant Chinese art, 53-; assoc prof Chinese art hist, Univ Hawaii, 63-; Fulbright visitor Chinese art hist, Acad Bildenden Künste & Univ, 66-67; prog chmn art hist, Univ Hawaii, 71-
Awards: Award, Am Artists of the Western States, Stanford Art Gallery; New York Univ Founders Day Award for outstanding scholarship, 72.
Bibliography: Contemporary American painting & sculpture (catalog), 58, 61 & 65; rev of exhib at Downtown Gallery, New York, In: Time Mag, 1/19/62; Seldis (auth), Pacific heritage, Art in Am, 65; plus one other.
Memberships: Honolulu Acad Art; Am Col Art Asn; Asian Soc; Asian & Pacific Art Asn Hawaii (organizer, 72).
Research: Chinese art; some contemporary elements in Chinese classic pictorial art; Chinese calligraphy.
Publications: Contribr, four articles, Studies of 16th century Chinese artists, 54-63; contribr, Encyclopedia world art, Rome, 64; auth, Some contemporary elements on Chinese claassic pictorial art, 65 & 71; illusr, The analects of Confucius, 70; auth, Chinese calligraphy.
Mailing Address: 3460 Kaohinani Dr, Honolulu, HI 96817.

ECKERT, WILLIAM DEAN
Painter, Art Historian
Preferred Media: Acrylics.
b Coshocton, Ohio, Oct 10, 27.
Study & Training: Ohio State Univ, BA(with distinction), BFA(cum laude) & MA; Univ Iowa, PhD.
Work in Public Collections: Butler Inst Am Art, Youngstown, Ohio.
Exhibitions: Columbus Art League, Columbus Gallery Fine Arts, Ohio, 50; Mid-Am Regional, Nelson Gallery, Kansas City, 52; Midwest Regional, Joslyn Mus, Omaha, Nebr, 52; Upper Hudson Valley Regional, Albany Art Inst, N Y, 66; Quincy Art Ctr Regional, Ill, 71.
Teaching: Assoc prof art hist, Western Ill Univ, Macomb, 59-65; assoc prof art hist, Union Col, Schenectady, N Y, 65-68; assoc prof art hist, Lindenwood Cols, 68-
Awards: Award in painting & graphics, Akron May Show, 54; first prize in graphics, Ohio State Fair Exhib, 56; third award in painting, Quincy Art Ctr Regional, Ill, 71.
Memberships: Col Art Asn; Soc Archit Historians; Midwest Col Art Conf; Mo Col Art Asn.

Research: Renaissance stage in Italy; evolution of the perspective scene.
Publications: Contribr, The college gallery and the liberal arts, Symposium, summer 67.
Mailing Address: 620 Yale Blvd, St Charles, MO 63301.

ECKHARDT, FERDINAND
Art Historian, Art Administrator
b Vienna, Austria; Can citizen.
Study & Training: Univ Vienna; hon LLD, Univ Man, 71.
Positions: Dir educ, State Mus, Vienna; dir Winnipeg Art Gallery, 53-
Awards: Austrian Cross of Honor for Sci & Art, 72.
Memberships: Can Mus Asn; Can Art Mus Dirs Asn (past pres); Int Coun Mus—Can; Am. Asn Art Mus Dirs.
Research: Author of several books and articles.
Mailing Address: 300 Memorial Blvd, Winnipeg, Man R3C 1V1, Can.

ECKMAIR, FRANK C
Printmaker
b Norwich, N Y, June 21, 30.
Study & Training: Whitney Sch Art, New Haven, Conn, 48; State Univ N Y Col Oneonta, 50; State Univ Iowa, with M Lasansky & Warshaw, 50-53, BA, 53; Ohio Univ, MFA, 62; State Univ N Y Col Buffalo, faculty fels, 68, 71 & 72.
Work in Public Collections: Metrop Mus Art, New York, N Y; Libr of Cong, Washington, D C; Smithsonian Inst, Washington; Philadelphia Mus Art, Pa; New York Pub Libr, N Y.
Commissions: Editions of woodcuts, Roten Galleries, Baltimore, Md, 63-73 & Assoc Am Artists, New York, 64-72.
Exhibitions: Northwest Printmakers Int, Seattle, Wash, 61; Philadelphia Print Club Invitational Int, Philadelphia, 62; Five American Printmakers, Ball State Univ Invitational, Ind, 66; Libr of Cong Nat Print Exhib, Washington, 67; Big Prints, State Univ N Y Albany, 68.
Teaching: Prof printmaking, State Univ N Y Col Buffalo, 63-
Positions: Dir gallery, art ctr, Millikan Univ, 62-63; dir gallery, State Univ N Y Col Buffalo, 63-65; pres, TAROT Designing & Printing, Buffalo, 69-
Awards: First prize for graphics, 180 Exhib, Huntington, W Va, 61; hon mention, Silvermine Print Exhib, Conn, 63; first prize for graphics, Cooperstown Art Asn, N Y, 66.
Bibliography: B Cody (auth), American printmaking since 1940, N Y Graphic Arts Soc.
Memberships: Patteran, Buffalo, N Y; Cooperstown Art Asn (exhib chmn, 72); Col Art Asn.
Art Interests: Relief printmaking.
Publications: Auth, Relief printmaking-an outline, 69; contribr, A pride of rabbis (portfolio), 71; ed, Centennial 1971 (portfolio), State Univ N Y Col Buffalo, 71; contribr, Witches of Salem (portfolio), 72.
Dealer: Associated American Artists, 663 Fifth Ave, New York, NY 10022.
Mailing Address: 17 Berkeley Pl, Buffalo, NY 14209.

ECKSTEIN, JOANNA
Collector, Patron
b Seattle, Wash, July 28, 03.
Study & Training: Goucher Col, BA.
Positions: Cur, USIA exhib of Am paintings & sculpture, Eng & France, 57-58; trustee & docent, Seattle Art Mus.
Collection: Contemporary paintings.
Mailing Address: 802 33rd St East, Seattle, WA 98112.

ECKSTEIN, RUTH
Printmaker, Painter
Preferred Media: Acrylics, Collage, Intaglio Print.
b Nuremberg, W Ger, May 11, 16; U S citizen.
Study & Training: New Sch Soc Res, New York, N Y, with Stuart Davis; Art Stud League New York, with Harry Sternberg, Julian Levy & V Vitlacyl; Pratt Graphic Ctr, New York, with Seong Moy & Roberto Delamonica.
Work in Public Collections: Philadelphia Mus Art; Brooklyn Mus; Israel Mus, Jerusalem; Univ Mass, Amherst; U S Info Agency, Graphic Arts Proj.
Exhibitions: Prints & Watercolors, Pa Acad Fine Arts, Philadelphia, 59, 64 & 65; Nat Print Exhib, Libr Cong, Washington, D C, 60; Triennial of Original Colored Graphics, Grenchen, Switz, 64; Carroll Reece Mus, Johnson City, Tenn, 68; one-woman shows, Alonzo Gallery, New York, 68, 70 & 72.
Awards: Purchase option, Art Stud League New York, 55; purchase award, Hofstra Univ, Hempstead, N Y, 56; Village Art Ctr Award, New York, 63.
Bibliography: Prize winning Graphics II, 64.
Memberships: Am Abstr Artists (secy, 70-); Soc Am Graphic Artists; Audubon Artists.
Dealer: Alonzo Gallery, 26 E 63rd St, New York, NY 10021.
Mailing Address: 5 Cricket Lane, Great Neck, NY 11024.

EDER, EARL
Painter
b Poplar, Mont, Nov 17, 44.
Study & Training: Inst Am Indian Arts, Santa Fe, N Mex, 62-65; San Francisco Art Inst, Calif, 65-70; Univ Mont, MA, 71.
Exhibitions: Edenbourgh Art Festival, 65; Alaska Centennial, 66; Riverside Mus Biennial Exhib, 68; 7 + 3, Am Indian Hist Soc Show, 68; Univ San Francisco, 69.
Awards: First pl in Biennial Exhib, Am Indian Arts & Crafts, 67; second pl, Scottsdale Nat Indian Arts Exhib, 70; first pl, Heard Mus, 70.
Bibliography: The dance in contemporary American Indian art, Harkness House, 67; Alfred Frankenstein (auth), 7 + 3, San Francisco Chronicle, 68; Return of red man, Life Mag, 68.
Mailing Address: 1627½ South 11th St West, Missoula, MT 59801.

EDGERLY, BEATRICE (BEATRICE EDGERLY MACPHERSON)
Painter, Writer
Preferred Media: Oils.
b Washington, D C, Jan 30, 98.
Study & Training: Gunston Hall, Washington, D C; Corcoran Gallery Sch Arts; Pa Acad Fine Arts, fel.
Work in Public Collections: Pa Acad Fine Arts, Philadelphia.
Commissions: Pen & ink decorative spots, Mc Call's Mag, 27; Gateway (pen & ink), Horace Lorimer, Sat Eve Post, 29; portrait in oil, Pres Danish Puddings, 46; two portraits in oil, comn by Margaret Sanger Slee, 50.
Exhibitions: Pa Acad Fine Arts, Philadelphia, 20-30; Nat Acad Design, New York, 30; Philadelphia Art Alliance, 33; Ariz State Univ, Tempe, 53; Franklin & Marshall Col, Lancaster, Pa, 66.
Positions: Founder & co-dir, Southern Ariz Sch Art, Tucson, 47-64.
Awards: Thouron prize, Pa Acad Fine Arts; Cooper prize, Nat Asn Women Artists.
Publications: Illusr, Peter & Peggy primer, Macmillan, 30; illusr, Ararat cocktail, 40; auth, From the hunter's bow, 42; art ed, Ariz Daily Star, 52-59.
Mailing Address: 6161 E Pima St, Tucson, AZ 85712.

EDIE, STUART
Painter, Educator
Preferred Media: Oils, Acrylics.
b Wichita Falls, Tex, Nov 10, 08.
Study & Training: Kansas City Art Inst; Art Stud League New York.
Work in Public Collections: Whitney Mus Am Art, New York, N Y; Toledo Art Mus, Ohio; Newark Mus, N J; Brooklyn Mus, N Y; Metrop Mus Art, New York.
Commissions: Mural, comn by Treas Dept, Honeoye Falls, N Y, 42.
Exhibitions: Carnegie Int, Pittsburgh, Pa, 48; many exhibs, Whitney Mus Am Art Ann, Art Inst Chicago Ann, Ill, Pa Acad Fine Arts Ann, Philadelphia & Corcoran Biennial, Washington, D C.
Teaching: Instr painting, Am Artists Sch, 40-51; instr painting, Univ Iowa, 44-70.
Awards: Artists of the Midwest Award, Kansas City Art Inst, 55; Artists of the Miss Valley Award, Davenport Mus, 58; Walker Biennial Award, 60.
Mailing Address: Apartado 129, Guanajuato, Guanajuato, Mex.

EDMONDS, NICHOLAS BIDDLE (NICK)
Sculptor
Preferred Media: Wood.
b Boston, Mass, Feb 21, 37.
Study & Training: Ogunquit Sch Painting & Sculpture, with Robert Laurent, 53-55; Boston Mus Sch, with Harold Tovish, 55-58 & Ernest Morenon, 60-61.
Work in Public Collections: Chappel Hill Art Ctr, Manchester, N H.
Exhibitions: New Eng Sculptor's Exhibs, Boston, 67, 69 & 71; Inst Contemp Art, Boston, 70; one-man shows, Chappel Hill Art Ctr, Manchester, 69, Addison Gallery, Andover, Mass, 71 & Art Ctr Hargate, Concord, N H, 72.
Teaching: Asst prof sculpture, Boston Univ, 65-
Awards: Travelling scholar, 62 & grad scholar study of wooden structures in Europe, 69, Boston Mus Sch.
Mailing Address: 136 S Main St, Sharon, MA 02067.

EDMONDSON, LEONARD
Etcher
b Sacramento, Calif, June 12, 16.
Study & Training: Univ Calif, Berkeley, AB, 40, MA, 42.
Work in Public Collections: Metrop Mus Art, New York, N Y; Bibliotheque Nat, Paris, France; New York Pub Libr, N Y; San Francisco Mus Art; Pasadena Art Mus.
Commissions: Edition of etchings, Int Graphic Arts Soc, N Y, 60, Hilton Hotel, N Y, 62, Ferdinand Roten Galleries, Inc, N Y, 66 & U S Info Agency, Washington, D C, 67.
Exhibitions: American Watercolors, Drawings & Prints, Metrop Mus Art, 52; Younger American Painters, Guggenheim Mus, 54;

American Prints Today, Print Coun Am, 62; Int Triennial of Original Colored Graphics, Switz, 64; Graphics '71 West Coast U S A, Univ Ky, 71.
Teaching: Prof art, Calif State Univ, Los Angeles, 64-
Awards: Purchase prize for oil, Univ Ill, 55; purchase prize for etching, Brooklyn Mus, 56; purchase prize for etching, Pasadena Art Mus, 58.
Bibliography: Mugnaini (auth), Oil painting, techniques & materials, 69 & Reep (auth), The content of watercolor, 69, Van Nostrand; Heller (auth), Printmaking today, Holt, 71.
Publications: Auth, Etching, Van Nostrand, (in prep).
Mailing Address: 714 Prospect Blvd, Pasadena, CA 91103.

EDWARDS, ELLENDER MORGAN
Printmaker, Photographer
b Hagerstown, Md.
Study & Training: Tyler Sch Art; pvt study art hist in Europe; Md Inst Col Art, BFA, 58; Art Stud League New York, with Jean Liberté; Hunter Col, grad study; Corcoran Art Sch, George Washington Univ; Md Inst Col Art; also with Reuben Kramer.
Exhibitions: 28th Ann Cumberland Valley Photo Salon, Washington Co Mus Art, 59, 29th & 30th Cumberland Valley Artists, 61 & 62, Hagerstown, Md; Md Regional, Baltimore Mus Art, 61; 21st Ann Life in Baltimore, Peale Mus, Md, 61.
Positions: Secy, Montgomery Co Art Educators Asn, Rockville, Md, 70-
Awards: Third prize color print, 28th Ann Cumberland Valley Photo Salon, Md, 59; second prize serigraph, Waterford Found, Inc, Va, 60; first prize graphics, Shepherd Col, Shepherdstown, W Va, 71.
Memberships: Nat League Am Penwomen; Nat Art Educ Asn.
Mailing Address: Box 106, Rockville, MD 20850.

EDWARDS, ETHEL (MRS XAVIER GONZALEZ)
Painter
b New Orleans, La.
Study & Training: Newcomb Col Art Sch; also with Xavier Gonzalez.
Work in Public Collections: IBM Collection; Chase Manhattan Bank, N Y; Commerce Trust Bank, Kansas City, Mo; Boston Mus Fine Arts; Springfield Mus Fine Art; plus others.
Exhibitions: Butler Inst Am Art, Youngstown, Ohio, 64-69; Whitney Mus Am Art, 64 & 65; Hartford Atheneum, 67 & 68; Watercolor: U S A, Springfield, Ill, 67-69; Cape Cod Art Asn, 69.
Awards: Larry Aldrich Prize, Silvermine Guild Artists; prizes, Watercolor: U S A, Springfield, Ill, 67 & Ball State Univ, Muncie, Ind, 67.
Memberships: McDowell Colony Alumni.
Mailing Address: 222 Central Park S, New York, NY 10019.

EDWARDS, KATE FLOURNOY
Painter
Preferred Media: Oils.
b Marshallville, Ga, July 29, 77.
Study & Training: Art Inst Chicago; Acad Grande Chaumière, with Charles Hawthorne; Nashville Col Young Ladies.
Commissions: Eight portraits in Ga Inst Technol, Atlanta; portrait of Dr W L Funkhouser, Aidmore Children's Hosp, Atlanta; two portraits for First Presby Church, Atlanta; three portraits for Wesleyan Col, Macon, Ga; portrait of Gen Blanton Winship, Gov Palace, P R; plus many others.
Exhibitions: One-man shows, Anderson Galleries, Chicago, Ill, Thurber Galleries, Chicago, Med Bldg, Augusta, Ga & Washington Libr, Macon, Ga.
Bibliography: Newspaper & mag articles, also TV.
Memberships: Atlanta Art Asn; Poetry Soc Ga.
Publications: Auth, Rhymes for good times, 71; plus articles & verses for N Y Times, Christian Sci Monitor & Ga Rev.
Mailing Address: Darlington Apartments, Apt No 1105, 2025 Peachtree Rd N E, Atlanta, GA 30309.

EDWARDS, STANLEY DEAN
Painter, Illustrator
Preferred Media: Oils, Acrylics.
b Joliet, Ill, Dec 5, 41.
Study & Training: Art Inst Chicago; Univ Chicago, BFA; Saugatuck Summer Sch.
Work in Public Collections: Corcoran Gallery Art, Washington, D C; Ball State Univ Art Gallery.
Exhibitions: 12 Chicago Painters, Walker Art Ctr, 65; Corcoran Biannual, Washington, D C, 65; Protest & Hope Group Show, New Sch Social Res, 67; Butler Ann, Youngstown, Ohio, 68; Violence in Art, Mus Contemp Art, Chicago, Ill, 69; plus others.
Teaching: Instr art, Trinity Sch, New York, 69-70; instr, Chicago Acad Fine Arts, 72.
Awards: Hon mention & purchase prize, Corcoran Gallery, 65; Vanderbilt Purchase Fund, 69.

Bibliography: Whitney Halsted (auth), article, In: Artforum, 66; Franz Schultz (auth), article, In: Panorama Mag, Chicago Daily News, 65-68 & 69.
Dealer: Fairweather-Hardin Gallery, 101 E Ontario, Chicago, IL 60611.
Mailing Address: 825 W Diversey Ave, Chicago, IL 60614.

EGAN, CHARLES
Art Dealer
b Philadelphia, Pa, June 29, 11.
Positions: Owner, Egan Gallery, New York, N Y, 45-
Specialty of Gallery: Modern American art.
Mailing Address: Egan Gallery, 1005 Second Ave, New York, NY 10022.

EGRI, TED
Sculptor
Preferred Media: Metals, Wood, Mixed Media.
b New York, N Y, May 22, 13.
Study & Training: Master Inst Roerich Mus, dipl, 31-34; Duncan Phillips Mem Gallery Art Sch, 42; Hans Hofmann Sch Art, New York & Provincetown, Mass, 48.
Work in Public Collections: William Rockhill Nelson Mus, Kansas City, Mo; Mus N Mex, Santa Fe; Millicent A Rogers Mem Mus, Taos, N Mex; Northern Iowa Univ, Cedar Falls.
Commissions: Sculpture (welded Cor-ten steel), Northern Iowa Univ, 65; ark doors & eternal light, Mt Sinai Temple, El Paso, Tex, 65; fountain (welded brass) Exec Life Bldg, Beverly Hills, Calif, 66; monument on pedestal (welded of Kaiseloy steel), City Albuquerque, N Mex, 69; menorah & eternal light (welded & stained glass), Temple Shalom, Dallas, Tex, 72.
Exhibitions: Four Shows, Contemporary American Painting & Sculpture, Univ Ill, Champaign, 52-61; Pa Acad Fine Arts Ann, Philadelphia, 53; Denver Art Mus Regional Ann, Colo, 54; Art: U S A 58, Madison Sq Garden, New York, 58; Southwestern Art Invitational, Dallas Mus Fine Arts, Tex, 60.
Teaching: Instr oil painting & life drawing, Kansas City Art Inst, 48-50; lectr art sculpture, life drawing & painting, Univ Wyo, 59-60; vis lectr art, Univ Ill, 60-61; Nat Endowment Arts & U S Off Educ artist-in-residence, Taos Co Schs, 72-73.
Positions: Mem art adv comt, Mus N Mex, 58, 62-63; mem art adv comt, N Mex Arts Comn, 69-70.
Awards: A I Friedman Award, Audubon Artists Ann, 47; top award for sculpture & hon mention for drawing, Mus N Mex Fiesta Biennial, 65; top award for sculpture, Mus N Mex Five-State Regional, 69.
Bibliography: Willard Spence (auth), Ted Egri, Taos artist, Christian Art, 12/66.
Memberships: Artists Equity Asn (nat v pres, 67-68, 71-72); Taos Art Asn (art comt, 71-72).
Dealers: Stables Gallery, Taos, NM 87571; Gallery of Contemporary Art, Taos, NM 87571.
Mailing Address: Taos, NM 87571.

EHRENREICH, EMMA
Painter
Preferred Media: Oils, Acrylics.
b New York, N Y, Sept 19, 06.
Study & Training: City Col New York; Long Island Univ; Hunter Col; Nat Acad Design; Brooklyn Mus; New Sch Social Res; Art Stud League New York; also with Abraham Rattner, Morris Davidson & Robert Motherwell.
Work in Public Collections: Rose Art Mus, Brandeis Univ, Boston, Mass; Denver Mus Art, Colo; Portland Mus, Ore; Norfolk Mus Arts & Sci, Va; Glickenstein Mus, Safed, Israel.
Exhibitions: Artists League Am, 46; Five Brooklyn Mus Invitational Int Exhibs, 53-61; eight one-man exhibs, Contemp Arts Gallery, New York, 53-63; Silvermine Guild for Artists, Conn, 58; Gallerie Vendome, Pittsburgh, Pa, 65.
Teaching: Lectr mod art, Bd Educ, New York City High Schs, 64-68.
Awards: Medal of honor in casein, Brooklyn Soc Artists, 51; purchase award for oil painting, Riverside Mus, 60; medal of honor for oil painting, Audubon Artists, 62.
Bibliography: Margaret Harold (auth), Prize-winning watercolors, Allied Publ, 62.
Memberships: Col Art Asn Am; Audubon Artists; Nat Asn Women Artists (chmn, oil jury, 70-72); New York Soc Women Artists (pub relations, 60-72); Am Soc Contemp Artists (mem chmn, 70-72).
Dealer: Beryl Mills, 10 W 33rd St, New York, NY 10001.
Mailing Address: 132 E 35th St, New York, NY 10016.

EHRMAN, FREDERICK L
Collector
b San Francisco, Calif, Jan 3, 06.
Study & Training: Univ Calif, AB, 27.

Collection: Paintings and sculptures.
Mailing Address: Lehman Brothers Inc, 1 William St, New York, NY 10004.

EICHENBERG, FRITZ
Illustrator, Printmaker
Preferred Media: Graphics.
b Cologne, Ger, Oct 24, 01; U S citizen.
Study & Training: State Acad Graphic Arts, Leipzig, MFA, 23; Southeastern Mass Univ, hon degree, 72.
Work in Public Collections: Metrop Mus Art, New York, N Y; Philadelphia Mus Art, Pa; Libr Cong, Washington, D C; Rosenwald Collection, Nat Gallery Art, Washington, D C; Bibliot Nat, Paris, France; Hermitage Mus, Leningrad, U S S R.
Commissions: Illustrations of more than one hundred classics, children's bks, comn by publ in the U S & abroad.
Exhibitions: Soc Am Graphic Artists Ann; Xylon Int Exhibs in Geneva, Switz, Yugoslavia & elsewhere; U S Info Agency Traveling Exhibs; Assoc Am Artists, New York, 67; one-man show, Pratt Manhattan Ctr, New York, 72.
Teaching: Prof & chmn art dept, Pratt Inst, 56-63; chmn art dept, Univ R I, 66-69; mem art faculty, Univ R I, 69-72; mem art faculty, Albertus Magnus Col, 72-
Positions: Dir emer, Pratt Graphic Arts Ctr, 56-; mem Pennell Comt, Libr Cong, 59-65; ed, Artist's Proof Ann (Pratt Inst), 60-; sr adv, U S graphics exhib, U S Info Agency, U S S R, 63; graphic survey Southeast Asia, J D Rockefeller III Fund, 68.
Awards: Joseph Pennell Medal, Pa Acad Fine Arts, 44; distinguished serv medal, Ltd Ed Club.
Bibliography: G Amberg (auth), Fritz Eichenberg, graphic artist, Graphis Mag; E Ettenberg (auth), Fritz Eichenberg, Am Artist; Eichenberg, artist and the book, Libr Cong Quart, 65.
Memberships: Soc Am Graphic Artists; Nat Acad Design; Royal Soc Arts; Xylon Int.
Research: Graphic arts, printmaking, art education, art history.
Publications: Illusr, Wuthering heights & Jane Eyre, Random, 43; illusr, The brothers Karamazov & many Russian classics, 49; illusr, Erasmus In Praise of Folly, Aquarius, 72; auth, The print: art, history & technique, Abrams (in prep).
Dealer: Associated American Artists, 663 Fifth Ave, New York, NY 10022.
Mailing Address: 142 Oakwood Dr, Peace Dale, RI 02879.

EIDE, PALMER
Sculptor, Designer
Preferred Media: Oils, Acrylics, Wood, Stone, Mixed Media.
b Sioux Falls, S D, July 5, 06.
Study & Training: Augustana Col, BA; Art Inst Chicago; Harvard Univ; Yale Univ; Cranbrook Acad Art; Saint Olaf Col, DFA, 68.
Work in Public Collections: Civic Fine Arts Ctr, Sioux Falls.
Commissions: Sculpture, City Hall, Sioux Falls, 36; mosaic, First Presby Church, Sioux Falls, 54; sculpture, First Lutheran Church, Sioux Falls, 62; sculpture, Jehovah Lutheran Church, St Paul, Minn, 64; sculpture, St Philips Lutheran Church, Minneapolis, Minn, 66.
Exhibitions: Sioux City Art Ctr, 61, 62 & 66; Fine Arts in Serv of Church, Seattle, Wash, 63; Sixth Ann Ecclesiastical Arts Exhib of the Church Archit Conf, Dallas, Tex, 64; Lutheran Art U S A Traveling Exhib, 67; Cult Opportunities Resource Ctr Traveling Exhib, Minn, 69.
Teaching: Prof painting, Augustana Col, 31-71; Fulbright prof art, Nat Col Art, Lahore, W Pakistan, 64-65.
Awards: Award in sculpture, Fine Arts in Serv Church, Seattle, 63; award in painting, 29th Ann Fall Show, Sioux City Art Ctr, 66.
Bibliography: Mary Roche (auth), New ideas & inventions, N Y Times, 3/14/48; Louis G Redstone (auth), Art in architecture, McGraw, 68.
Memberships: Col Art Asn; Midwest Col Art Asn.
Mailing Address: 2025 Austin Dr, Sioux Falls, SD 57105.

EIDLITZ, DOROTHY MEIGS
Patron, Photographer
b New Haven, Conn.
Study & Training: Vassar Col, AB, 14; Univ Pa, grad study; Columbia Univ; New Sch Social Res; photog with Ansel Adams, Berenice Abbott & Konrad Cramer.
Exhibitions: Exhibs in many art galleries in U S.
Positions: Founder & hon pres, Sunbury Shores Arts & Nature Centre, Inc, Saint Andrews, N B; Artist-in-residence, Res Studio Art Ctr, Maitland, Fla, 61; bd mem, Orlando Art Asn & Loch Haven Art Ctr, Orlando, Fla, 65; pres, Dorothy Meigs Eidlitz Found, Inc.
Awards: Numerous medals & purchase awards.
Memberships: Fel Royal Photog Soc Gt Brit; fel Photog Soc Am; Metrop Mus Art; Mus Mod Art; Am Fedn Arts; plus others.

Collection: Chiefly twentieth century American painting, sculpture, ceramics, Japanese, both antique and contemporary.
Publication: Contribr, Poet's Camera & other publ & bks.
Mailing Address: 4 E 62nd St, New York, NY 10021.

EILERS, FRED (ANTON FREDERICK)
Painter, Designer
Preferred Media: Oils.
b Wilmington, N C.
Study & Training: William & Mary Col, BS; Richmond Prof Inst, with Theresa Pollack.
Work in Public Collections: Evansville Mus, Ind; Old Nat Bank, Evansville; St Marys Hosp, Evansville; First Lutheran Church, Richmond, Va; Univ Evansville, Ind.
Commissions: Mural, Colonial Nat Bank, 69.
Exhibitions: Hoosier Salon, Indianapolis, Ind; Ohio Valley Watercolor, Athens; Mid States Exhib, Evansville; one-man shows, Gallery R, Evansville Mus Gallery, Univ Evansville, Old Gallery, Evansville, Hoosier Gallery, Ind & Thor Gallery, Louisville.
Teaching: Instr portrait painting, Univ Evansville, 46-, instr figure drawing, 50-
Positions: Bd dirs, Evansville, 58-60; consult art purchases, Old Nat Bank, 69-
Awards: Bronstein purchase award, 60 & graphics purchase award, 68, Evansville Mus; Hoosier Salon Merit Award, 65.
Dealers: Risley, Evansville, IN 47708; Thor Gallery, 734 S First St, Louisville, KY 40202.
Mailing Address: 2140 E Chandler Ave, Evansville, IN 47714.

EISENBERG, MARVIN
Art Historian, Educator
b Philadelphia, Pa.
Study & Training: Univ Pa, BA, 43; Princeton Univ, MFA, 49, PhD, 54.
Teaching: Instr art hist, Univ Mich, 49-53, asst prof art hist, 54-58, assoc prof art hist, 58-61, prof art hist, 61-, chmn dept, 61-69.
Positions: Mem Inst for Advan Study, winter 70.
Awards: Guggenheim fel, 59; Star of Solidarity, Ital Govt, 61.
Memberships: Col Art Asn Am (pres, 68-69); Benjamin Franklin fel Royal Soc Arts.
Research: Italian late mediaeval painting.
Publications: Auth, articles on early Italian painting in journals & museum bulletins.
Mailing Address: Dept of History of Art, University of Michigan, Ann Arbor, MI 48104.

EISENSTAT, BENJAMIN
Painter, Illustrator
b Philadelphia, Pa, June 4, 15.
Study & Training: Fleisher Art Mem; Pa Acad Fine Arts; Albert Barnes Found.
Work in Public Collections: Philadelphia Mus Art; Fleisher Art Mem, Philadelphia; Springfield Art Mus, Mo; Woodmere Gallery, Philadelphia; Jefferson Hosp, Philadelphia.
Commissions: Official painting of nuclear ship Savannah, U S Maritime & N Y Ship Comn, Washington, D C, 59; three panel historical mural, First Bank N J, Philadelphia, 60; three panel historical mural, Provident Mutual Life Ins Co, Philadelphia, 62; two panel historical mural, Burlington Co Trust Co, Moorestown, N J, 63; two panel historical mural, Oreland Episcopal Church, Pa, 70.
Exhibitions: Artists for Victory, 45 & Nat Drawing Show, 55, Metrop Mus Art, New York, N Y; Norfolk Mus Art Nat Drawing Show, 71; Watercolor U S A, Springfield, Mo, number of times including 72; Nat Acad Design Ann, New York; Am Watercolor Soc Ann, New York.
Teaching: Assoc prof painting & drawing, Philadelphia Col Art, 46-69, prof painting & drawing & chmn illustrating dept, 69-; instr watercolor, Philadelphia Mus Art, 62-66.
Awards: Ann medal achievement, Philadelphia Watercolor Club, 62; Harrison Morris prize, Fellowship, Pa Acad Fine Arts, three times; Watercolor U S A prize, Springfield Mus, 72.
Bibliography: Hugh Scott, Mural on Market Street, Today Mag, 6/12/60; Henry Pitz (auth), Documentary drawings of Benjamin Eisenstat, Am Artist, 12/65.
Memberships: Am Watercolor Soc; Philadelphia Watercolor Club (bd dirs); Philadelphia Art Alliance (bd dirs, 62-68); Artists Equity (bd dirs, 67-71); Fellowship, Pa Acad Fine Arts (bd dirs, 55-60).
Collection: Original illustrations.
Publications: Auth & illusr, articles, In: Today Mag, 54-71; auth & illusr, articles, In: Ford Times, 54-72; auth & illusr, articles in travel sect, N Y Sunday Times, 55-61; auth & illusr, Coming Events in Britain, 61.
Dealer: Newman Gallery, 1625 Walnut St, Philadelphia, PA.
Mailing Address: 438 Camden Ave, Moorestown, NJ 08057.

EISENSTEIN, MR & MRS JULIAN
Collectors
Mr Eisenstein, b Warrenton, Mo, Apr 3, 21.
Study & Training: Mr Eisenstein, Harvard Univ, BS, 41, MA, 42, PhD, 48.
Positions: Mr Eisenstein, pres & trustee, Washington Gallery Mod Art, 61-65.
Collection: Contemporary art.
Mailing Address: 82 Kalorama Circle N W, Washington, DC 20008.

EISLER, COLIN T
Educator
Study & Training: Yale Univ, AB, 52; Harvard Univ, AM, 54, PhD, 57.
Teaching: Prof fine arts, Inst Fine Arts, New York Univ.
Mailing Address: Institute of Fine Arts, New York University, 1 E 78th St, New York, NY 10021.

EISNER, ELLIOT WAYNE
Educator
b Chicago, Ill, Mar 10, 33.
Study & Training: Roosevelt Univ, BA; Ill Inst Technol, MS; Univ Chicago, MA & PhD.
Teaching: Instr art educ, Ohio State Univ, 60-61; asst prof educ, Univ Chicago, 61-65; prof educ & art, Stanford Univ, 65-
Awards: Palmer Johnson Award, Am Educ Res Asn, 67; Guggenheim fel, 70.
Memberships: Nat Art Educ Asn (chmn res, 64); Am Educ Res Asn.
Publications: Co-auth, Readings in art education, Ginn, 66; auth, Confronting curriculum reform, Little, 71; auth, Educating vision, Macmillan, 72.
Mailing Address: 820 Tolman Dr, Stanford, CA 94305.

EITEL, CLIFFE DEAN
Painter, Designer
b Salt Lake City, Utah, June 18, 09.
Study & Training: With Roy C Eitel; Nat Acad Art; Art Inst Chicago; Inst Design; also with Joseph Binder, Gyorgy Kepes, Hubert Ropp & Charles Wilimovsky.
Work in Public Collections: Seattle Art Mus, Wash.
Commissions: Four ceramic tile murals, Mercy Hosp, Canton, Ohio, 56; two ceramic tile murals, Tampa Munic Hosp, Fla, 57; mural (oil), Flavorama Prods, Northfield, Ill, 59; ceramic tile mural, Augustinian Seminary, Olympia Fields, Ill, 59; two mosaic tile murals, St Marys Hosp, Kankakee, Ill, 60.
Exhibitions: Libr of Cong, Washington, D C, 46; Art Inst Chicago, Ill, 50; Brooklyn Mus, N Y, 50; in Ger with State Dept Exhib, 51; Benjamin Galleries, Chicago, 56.
Teaching: Instr abstract & mod art, Chicago Prof Sch Art, 41-43; demonstr printmaking, Northbrook Pub & Jr H S, 71-72.
Positions: Art dir, Swan Studios, Chicago, 37-39; art dir, Hanks & Assoc, Chicago, 39-41; free lance designer & artist, Chicago, 41-
Awards: Landscape in Motion, Artists Guild Chicago, 45.
Bibliography: Alex Weaver (auth), Evolution of a Cliffe Eitel design, Am Artist Mag, 50; Kunst des gestaltens, Der Polygraph, Frankfurt, Ger, 50; Clyde Walton (auth), Historical records, Illinois Lives, 69.
Memberships: Northbrook Art League (design dir, 70-72); Northshore Art League; Renaissance Soc, Univ Chicago.
Mailing Address: 1819 Oakwood Rd, Northbrook, IL 60062.

EITELJORG, HARRISON
Collector, Patron
b Indianapolis, Ind, Oct 1, 04.
Study & Training: Ind Univ Law Sch.
Memberships: Indianapolis Mus Art (trustee, gov & mem fine arts adv comt); Contemp Art Soc.
Art Interests: Sponsor of museum of western artifacts.
Collection: Abstract & modern American art; Sch of Paris; Western painting and sculptor; African art.
Mailing Address: 4567 Cold Spring Rd, Indianapolis, IN 46208.

EITNER, LORENZ E A
Art Historian, Educator
b Brünn, Czech, Aug 27, 19; U S citizen.
Study & Training: Duke Univ, AB, 40; Princeton Univ, 40-43, 46-49, MFA, 48, PhD, 52.
Collections Arranged: Masterdrawings, Guggenheim Mus, New York & Univ Gallery, Univ Minn, 60; Gericault, Los Angeles Co Mus, Detroit Inst Art & Philadelphia Mus Art, 71-72; numerous art exhibs at Stanford Mus.
Teaching: Prof art, Univ Minn, 49-63; prof art & chmn art dept, Stanford Univ, 63-
Positions: Dir, Stanford Mus, 63-
Memberships: Col Art Asn Am (v pres, dir, 56-71).
Research: European painting of the latter half of the eighteenth century and the beginning of the nineteenth century.

Publications: Auth, The Flabellum of Tournus, Col Art Asn, 44; auth, Introduction to art, Burgess, 60; auth, Gericault, Univ Chicago Press, 60; auth, Neoclassicism and romanticism, Prentice-Hall, 69; auth, Gericault's raft of the Medusa, Phaidon (London), 72.
Mailing Address: Dept. of Art, Stanford University, Stanford, CA 94305.

EKSTROM, ARNE H
Art Dealer
Positions: Dir, Cordier & Ekstrom Inc.
Specialty of Gallery: Contemporary American art.
Mailing Address: 980 Madison Ave, New York, NY 10021.

ELAM, CHARLES HENRY
Art Administrator
b Ashland, Ky, Feb 13, 15.
Study & Training: Univ Cincinnati, AB, 38; Inst Fine Arts, New York Univ, AM, 52; Courtauld Inst, Univ London, 53.
Collections Arranged: Catalogued & asst assembler, Rendezvous for Taste, Peale Mus, 56, French Paintings 1789-1929 from the Collection of Walter P Chrysler, Jr, Dayton Art Inst, 60 & The Peale Family, Detroit Inst Arts, 67.
Positions: Archivist, Peale Mus, 54-59; chief cur, Dayton Art Inst, 59-64; cur Am art, Detroit Inst Arts, 64-67; ed, Wayne State Univ Press, 67-70; mus registr, Detroit Inst Arts, 70-
Publications: Auth, The Peale family, Detroit, 67; co-ed, The Detroit Institute of Arts illustrated handbook, 71.
Mailing Address: 25 E Palmer Ave, Detroit, MI 48202.

ELDER, MULDOON
Painter, Sculptor
Preferred Media: Oils.
b Los Angeles, Calif, June 24, 35.
Work in Public Collections: Long Beach Mus Art; Downey Mus Art; Pentagon Collection; Syntex Collection; Vorpal Gallery Permanent Collection.
Exhibitions: Long Beach Mus Art, 57; Houston Mus, 58; Dallas Mus Art, 58; Downey Mus Art, 60; San Francisco Mus Art, 69.
Awards: Purchase awards, Long Beach Mus Art, Pentagon Collection & Downey Mus Art.
Bibliography: R Ellsworth (auth), Muldoon Elder (catalogue), Vorpal Gallery.
Mailing Address: c/o Vorpal Gallery, 1168 Battery St, San Francisco, CA 94111.

ELDREDGE, MARY AGNES
Sculptor
Preferred Media: Copper, Stone, Wood.
b Hartford, Conn, Jan 21, 42.
Study & Training: Vassar Col, BA, with Concetta Scaravaglione; Pius XII Inst, Florence, Italy, MFA, with Josef Gudics.
Work in Public Collections: Dartmouth Col Collection, Hanover, N H.
Commissions: Risen Christ Corpus, St Mary's Church, Horseheads, N Y, 68; Virgin Mary, Newman Chapel, Univ Wis-Stevens Point, 69; copper wall relief, Green Mountain Col Libr, Poultney, Vt, 70; cemetery monument, Children's Cath Cemetery, Portland, Ore, 71; exterior copper relief, Our Lady of Mt Carmel Church, Staten Island, 72.
Exhibitions: Mostra dell' Arte Religiosa per Pasqua, Florence, 65; Nat Arts Club Religious Art Exhib, New York, N Y, 66; Acad Artists Asn Nat Exhib, Springfield, Mass, 67; Modern Art and the Religious Experience, Fifth Ave Presby Church, New York, 68; 6th Biennial Nat Religious Art Exhib, Cranbrook Acad Art, 69.
Awards: Therese Richard Mem Prize, Nat Arts Club, 66; Acad Artists Asn Award, 67.
Dealer: Contemporary Christian Art, Inc, 1060 A Lexington Ave, New York, NY 10021.
Mailing Address: R F D 1, Box 472, Springfield, VT 05156.

ELDREDGE, STUART EDSON
Painter, Instructor
Preferred Media: Gouache, Watercolors, Tempera, Oils.
b South Bend, Ind, July 1, 02.
Study & Training: Dartmouth Col, AB; Art Stud League New York, with Kimon Nicolaides; Beaux Arts Inst, New York.
Work in Public Collections: Butler Inst Am Art, Youngstown, Ohio; Springfield Art Mus, Mass; Southern Vt Artists, Inc, Manchester; Dartmouth Col, Hanover, N H; Robert Hull Fleming Mus, Burlington, Vt.
Commissions: Murals, First Nat Bank, Springfield; mural, Springfield Hosp; stations of cross, St Joseph's Church, Chester, Vt; murals in textile bldg, World's Fair, New York, N Y, 39.
Exhibitions: 9th Ann Print Exhib, Libr of Cong, Washington, D C, 51; Philadelphia Watercolor Club, 52 & 53; Ind Artists 50th Ann Invitational, 57; Am Watercolor Soc, 61 & 63; plus 18 one-man shows, 50-72.

Teaching: Instr drawing & painting, Cooper Union, 32-40; instr drawing & painting, Art Stud League New York Summer Sch, 34 & 35; prof drawing, Pius XII Inst, Florence, Italy, summer 64.
Awards: Tiffany fel, 32.
Memberships: Southern Vt Artists (trustee, 50-72); Springfield Art & Hist Soc (trustee, 59-).
Dealer, Gallery 2, Woodstock, VT 05091.
Mailing Address: RFD No 1, Box 472, Springfield, VT 05156.

ELIAS, HAROLD JOHN
Painter, Lecturer
Preferred Media: Oils, Watercolors, Wire.
b Cleveland, Ohio, Mar 12, 20.
Study & Training: Art Inst Chicago; De Paul Univ; Mich State Univ, BFA, MFA; also with John Rogers Cox & Katherine Blackshear.
Work in Public Collections: Art Inst Chicago, Ill; Upjohn Collection, Kalamazoo, Mich; Ill State Mus, Springfield; Massillon Mus, Ohio; Univ Idaho, Moscow.
Commissions: Mich scenes, Fraternal Order Eagles, Muskegon Heights, Mich, 56; Mich scenes, Round Lake Lodge, Watervliet, Mich, 64; mobile, Mercy Hosp, Benton Harbor, Mich, 66; Triligy (mobile), Cath Church, Muskegon Heights, 67; aluminum & plastic mural, Letourneau Col, Longview, Tex, 72.
Exhibitions: American Art Today 1950, Metrop Mus Art, New York, N Y, 50; Pa Acad Fine Art, 51; Detroit Inst Art, 52, 53 & 55; Int Sculpture Competition, Brussels, Belg, 53; Baltimore Mus Art, 53; plus many others.
Teaching: Instr art hist & oil painting, Muskegon Community Col Eve Div, 52-57; instr drawing & oil painting, Lake Mich Col Eve Div, 60-66; instr drawing & oil painting, Kilgore Col Eve Div, 69-
Positions: Asst dir, Hackley Art Gallery, Muskegon, 52-56, acting dir, 56-57.
Awards: Awarded one-man show, Chicago Esquire Theatre Exhib, 50; Hollis S Baker best of show, Western Mich Artists Exhib, 52; Schiller award for watercolor, Mich Exhib, 65.
Bibliography: Review of show, Art News, 50; New talent, Art in Am, 57.
Memberships: Mich Acad Sci, Arts & Letters; Centro Studi E Scambi Internazionali; Mich State Coun Arts; Tex Comn Arts & Humanities.
Publications: Auth, Why not beauty, Longview Daily News; many exhib reviews as gallery dir; many articles for local papers.
Mailing Address: 1800 McCann Rd, Longview, TX 75601.

ELIASOPH, PAULA
Painter, Writer
b New York, N Y, Oct 26, 95.
Study & Training: Pratt Inst; Columbia Univ; Art Stud League New York; murals with Augustus Vincent Tack; paint, materials, technique with Dr Maximillian Toch.
Work in Public Collections: Metrop Mus Art, New York; Brooklyn Mus, N Y; New York Pub Libr, N Y; Libr Cong, Washington, D C; Franklin D Roosevelt Libr; plus many others.
Commissions: Tree of Life, YMHA, 57; Tree of Life, Hillcrest Hollis Jewish Ctr, Jamaica, 60.
Exhibitions: Am Watercolor Soc, 30-72; Philadelphia Soc Etchers, 40; Fedn Mod Painters & Sculptors, 40-71; Am Fedn Art Traveling Exhib, 55-57; Inst Mod Art, Boston, Mass, 64; plus many others.
Teaching: Instr pvt classes, 41-; instr art, Forest Hills Jewish Ctr, 49-66; instr & supvr art & art hist, Yeshiva of Central Queens, 49-66.
Positions: Secy, League of Am Pen Women, 50; res, stud counseling bur, psychol ctr, Univ Minn, 67-68; res, dept hist, Univ Mo-Columbia, 69; mem comt study art in educ, N Y Univ, 69.
Awards: Award for Interior, Long Island Art League; Etchings of Trees in Central Park, YWHA & YMHA, 43; award, Alexander Kriesel Art Gallery, 55.
Bibliography: Carlyle Burrows (auth), On Paula Eliasoph, New York Herald Tribune, 31; E C Sherburne (auth), Form rhythms in space, Christian Sci Monitor, 32; Edward Alden Jewell (auth), On exhibition by Paula Eliasoph, New York Times, 32-57; plus others.
Memberships: Fedn Mod Painters & Sculptors (incorporating trustee, 41-; treas, 41); life mem Am Watercolor Soc; life mem Art Stud League New York; life mem Long Island Art League; Inst Study Art Educ, N Y Univ.
Publications: Auth, Etchings & drypoints of Childe Hassam, Smithsonian Inst, 33; auth, art educ articles, In: Yeshiva of Central Queens Bull, 41-69; auth, article, In: Group Psycho Ther Mag, 59; auth, Art in our classrooms, 63; contribr, Monk's Pond Mag, 68.
Dealer: Chapellier Galleries, 22 E 80th St, New York, NY 10021.
Mailing Address: 148-25 89th Ave, Jamaica, NY 11435.

ELISCU, FRANK
Sculptor
b New York, N Y, July 13, 12.
Study & Training: Beaux-Arts Inst Design; Pratt Inst, 30-33.
Commissions: Busts, Aeronaut Hall Fame; fountain, Brookgreen Gardens, S C; Atoms for Peace figure, Ventura, Calif; war mem, Cornell Med Col; heroic horses in slate, Bankers Trust Bldg, N Y; plus others.
Exhibitions: Pa Acad Fine Arts; Conn Acad Fine Arts; Cleveland Mus Art; Springfield Mus Art; Detroit Inst Art; plus others.
Awards: Bennet Prize sculpture, Nat Sculpture Soc, 53; prize, 55 & silver medal, 58, Archit League New York; Henry Hering Award, 60; plus others.
Memberships: Fel Nat Sculpture Soc (pres, 67-70); Academician Nat Acad Design; Archit League New York.
Publications: Auth, Sculpture: three techniques-Wax, slate, clay & Direct wax sculpture.
Mailing Address: 440 Rock House Rd, Easton, CT 06612.

ELISOFON, ELIOT
Painter, Photographer
b New York, N Y, Apr 17, 11.
Study & Training: Fordham Univ, BS.
Work in Public Collections: Mus Mod Art, New York; Philadelphia Mus Art, Pa; Fogg Art Mus, Cambridge, Mass; Metrop Mus Art, New York; Tokyo Mus Western Art, Japan.
Commissions: Four one-hr doc films, Black African Heritage, on African art & its environ.
Positions: Color consult (films), Moulin Rouge, Bell, Book & Candle & The Greatest Story Ever Told; hon res assoc primitive art, Peabody Mus Archaeol & Ethnog, Harvard Univ; curatorial assoc, Mus African Art, Washington, D C.
Awards: Watercolor purchase prize, Philadelphia Mus Art.
Publications: Ed & auth, The sculpture of Africa, 58; auth & illusr, The Nile, 64; auth & illusr, Color photography; illusr, The art of Indian Asia; co-auth & illusr, Erotic spirituality.
Mailing Address: 145 E 27th St, New York, NY 10016.

ELKON, ROBERT
Art Dealer, Collector
b Belg, 28.
Study & Training: Univ Wis-Madison, BA; Harvard Univ Law Sch; Columbia Univ; New York Univ Inst Fine Arts.
Positions: Owner-dir, Robert Elkon Gallery.
Memberships: Art Dealers Asn; Harvard Club.
Specialty of Gallery: Twentieth century masters; contemporary painters and sculptors.
Publications: Auth, literary revs, In: New York Times & Art News.
Mailing Address: 1063 Madison Ave, New York, NY 10028.

ELLINGER, ILONA E
Painter, Educator
b Budapest, Hungary, June 12, 13.
Study & Training: Royal Hungarian Univ Sch Art, MFA; Royal Swedish Art Acad; Johns Hopkins Univ, with David M Robinson & W F Albright, PhD; Univ Freiburg; Univ Wis.
Exhibitions: Soc Washington Artists; one-man show, Am-Brit Art Ctr, George Washington Univ, 50; Silver Spring Art Gallery, 51; Corcoran Gallery Art, 58; plus others.
Teaching: Prof art & head dept, Trinity Col, Washington, D C, 43-; Fulbright prof hist art & archit, Nat Col Arts, Lahore, W Pakistan, 63-64; lectr Am art, U S Info Serv, Lahore, Rawalpindi, Dacca; vis prof, State Univ N Y Stony Brook, 69-71.
Memberships: Soc Washington Artists; Archaeol Inst Am.
Mailing Address: 2800 Woodley Rd N W, Washington, DC 20008.

ELLIOTT, B CHARLES, JR
Art Administrator, Art Historian
b Grove City, Pa, Apr 9, 24.
Study & Training: Allegheny Col, BA, 47; Syracuse Univ, grad study scholar, 52, 53 & 55, MA, 55; Univ Pittsburgh, study travel grants, 53 & 56.
Collections Arranged: Moses Soyer Retrospective, 68, Valfred Thelin, 69, Joseph Domjan, 70, George Papashvily, 70 & Gloria Vanderbilt, 71.
Positions: Dir Cult Exchange Prog, Univ Pittsburgh, 56-58; dir, Cheekwood Fine Arts Ctr, 59; dir, Reading Pub Mus & Art Gallery, 67-
Awards: Eben Demarst Award, 63.
Memberships: Archeol Soc Lorraine, France; Am Asn Mus; Nat Sci Youth Found.
Research: History of the fêtes of Lorraine.
Publications: Auth, catalogues, Moses Soyer, 68, Valfred Thëlin, 69, Joseph Domjan, 70, George Papashvily, 70 & Gloria Vanderbilt, 71.
Mailing Address: 500 Museum Rd, Reading, PA 19602.

ELLIOTT, BRUCE ROGER
Printmaker, Educator
b New York, N Y, Aug 3, 38.
Study & Training: Silvermine Artists Guild; State Univ N Y Buffalo,
BS; State Univ N Y Col Oswego; Univ Md, MA.
Exhibitions: Graphics 68, Ultimate Concerns, Ohio Univ, Athens, 68;
Graphics U S A 1970, Clarke Col, Dubuque, Iowa, 70; 13th Nat
N Dak Print & Drawing Exhib, Univ N Dak, 70; 9th Ann Nat Print
& Drawing Exhib, Olivet, Mich, 70; Nat Print & Drawing Exhib,
Minot State Col, N Dak, 70.
Teaching: Asst prof drawing, R I Col, 69-71; printmaker, Holy
Cross Col, 71-, spec studies adv, 72.
Positions: Chmn dept art, Kings Park High Sch, N Y, 65-67; co-
chmn Grad Art Asn, Univ Md, College Park, 68-69.
Awards: Lewisboro Fine Arts Comn Fine Arts scholar, N Y, 56; fine
arts award, State Univ N Y Buffalo, 59; graphics award, 41st Nat
Print & Drawing Exhib, Springfield, Mass, 70.
Memberships: Springfield Art League; Holden Exp; Worcester Art
Mus; Am. Asn Univ Prof; Col Art Asn Am.
Dealer: Franz Bader Galleries, 2124 Pennsylvania Ave, Washington,
DC 20037. The Galleries, 464 Washington St, Wellesley, MA 02181.
Mailing Address: R F D, 152 Pleasant St, Spencer, MA 01562.

ELLIOTT, JAMES HEYER
Art Administrator
b Medford, Ore, Feb 19, 24.
Study & Training: Willamette Univ, AB, 47; Harvard Univ, AM, 49,
teaching fel fine arts, 50-51; Fulbright scholar to Europe, 52-53.
Teaching: Assoc prof hist of the art mus, Hunter Col, 67-68.
Positions: Cur & actg dir, Walker Art Ctr, 53-56; cur mod art &
asst chief cur, Los Angeles Co Mus, 56-63, chief cur, 63-66; dir,
Wadsworth Atheneum, 66-
Memberships: Am Asn Mus (mem coun, pres, New Eng Conf, 71, Int
Comn Art Mus); Asn Art Mus Dirs; Conn Comn on the Arts
(comnr & v pres).
Publications: Auth, title essay for catalogue, Pierre Bonnard Exhi-
bition, 65.
Mailing Address: Wadsworth Atheneum, Hartford, CT 06103.

ELLIOTT, LILLIAN
Weaver, Designer
Preferred Media: Textiles.
b Detroit, Mich.
Study & Training: Wayne Univ, BA; Cranbrook Acad Art, Bloom-
field Hills, Mich, MFA.
Work in Public Collections: Mus Contemp Crafts, New York, N Y;
Detroit Inst Arts; San Francisco City Art Collection, Calif; Ob-
jects, U S A—Johnson's Wax Collection of Contemporary Crafts,
Smithsonian Inst Traveling Exhib; Univ Art Collections, Ariz
State Univ, Tempe.
Exhibitions: Calif Design Exhibs, Pasadena Art Mus, Calif, 62-71;
Fabric Collage Invitational, Mus Contemp Crafts, New York, 65;
Collagen—Collage Invitational Exhib, Kunstgewerbe Mus, Zur-
ich, Switz, 68; Objects, U S A—Johnson's Wax Collection,
Smithsonian Inst Traveling Exhib, 70-72; Tapestry, Tradition &
Technique Invitational, Los Angeles Co Mus Art, Calif, 71.
Teaching: Instr art, Univ Mich Col Archit & Design, Ann Arbor, 59-
60; lectr textiles, dept design, Univ Calif, Berkeley, 66-
Positions: Fabric designer, Ford Motor Co Styling Div, Dearborn,
Mich, 56-59.
Awards: Tiffany Found grant in weaving, 64; San Francisco Art
Festival Purchase Award, 65 & 69; Founder's Soc Purchase
Award, Mich Craftsmen's Show, Detroit Inst Arts, 69.
Publications: Contribr, Chap, In: The new American tapestry, Van
Nostrand Reinhold, 68.
Dealer: Anneberg Gallery, 2721 Hyde St, San Francisco, CA 94109.
Mailing Address: 1775 San Lorenzo, Berkeley, CA 94707.

ELLIOTT, PHILIP CLARKSON
Painter, Educator
b Minneapolis, Minn, Dec 5, 03.
Study & Training: Univ Minn, 21-23; Yale Univ, BFA, 26.
Work in Public Collections: Univ Pittsburgh; Albright-Knox Art Gal-
lery; also in pvt collections.
Exhibitions: Carnegie Inst, 43 & 45; Mus Mod Art, 52; N Y State
Fair, 62; Albright-Knox Art Gallery, 62-68; Western New York
Exhib, 62-68; plus others.
Teaching: Lectr techniques of painting; asst prof fine arts, Univ
Pittsburgh, 34-40; prof painting & drawing, State Univ N Y Buf-
falo, 54-, chmn art dept, 54-71.
Positions: Dir, Albright Art Sch, Buffalo, N Y, 41-54.
Awards: Prizes, Albright Art Gallery, 49 & 52, Springville, N Y, 62
& Western New York Exhib, 65; plus others.
Memberships: Patteran; Col Art Asn Am; Nat Asn Schs Art.
Mailing Address: 147 Bryant St, Buffalo, NY 14222.

ELLIOTT, RONNIE ROSE
Painter
Preferred Media: Oils, Collage, Charcoal, Assemblage, Gouache.
b New York, N Y, Dec 16, 16.
Study & Training: Hunter Col; New York Univ; Art Stud League New
York.
Work in Public Collections: Mus Mod Art, New York; Whitney Mus
Am Art, New York; Carnegie Inst, Pittsburgh, Pa; Andrew Dick-
son White Mus, Cornell Univ, Ithaca, N Y; Jewett Arts Ctr &
Farnsworth Mus, Wellesley Col, Mass.
Exhibitions: Col Int Exhib, Mus Mod Art, New York, 48; one-man
exhib, Paintings, Galerie Colette Allendy, Paris, France, 52;
one-man exhib, Collage Retrospective, 1943-1963, 63; one-man
shows, Rose Fried Gallery, New York, 58 & 67.
Awards: Wellesley Col Purchase Award, through sr art majors,
Jewett Arts Ctr, 70.
Bibliography: Gabrielle Buffet Picabia (auth), Ronnie Elliott, L'Art
d'Aujourd'hui, Paris, 1/53; Michel Seuphor (auth), Dictionaire de
la peinture abstraite, Paris, 57; Harriet Janis & Rudi Blesh
(auth), Collage, 1961, Chilton, 61.
Mailing Address: 68 E Seventh St, New York, NY 10003.

ELLIS, CARL EUGENE
Art Administrator, Instructor
b Oklahoma City, Okla, Oct 12, 32.
Study & Training: Univ Ark, BA; Univ Ark Grad Sch; Harvard Univ
Grad Sch.
Collections Arranged: John Willard Raught 1857-1931, A Retro-
spective Exhibition, 61; Dorflinger Glass Gallery (permanent),
69; Art of the Far East Gallery (permanent), 72.
Teaching: Instr art hist, Akron Art Inst, 58-59; instr art hist, Ever-
hart Mus, 59-
Positions: Asst cur exhibs, Akron Art Inst, 58-59; cur art, Ever-
hart Mus, 59-, assoc dir, 66-
Memberships: Am Asn Mus; Am Fedn Arts; Northeastern Mus Asn;
Nat Early Am Glass Club; Lackawanna Hist Soc (trustee).
Publications: Auth, Dorflinger glass, Everhart Mus, 60; auth, John
Willard Raught 1857-1931, Everhart Mus, 61; auth, Drawings and
prints by Peter Takal, Everhart Mus, 67; auth, American jewelry
today, Everhart Mus, 69; auth, Dorflinger glass, Nat Early Am
Glass Club Bull, 69.
Mailing Address: Nay Aug Park, Scranton, PA 18510.

ELLIS, EDWIN CHARLES
Educator
b Iowa City, Iowa, May 29, 17.
Study & Training: State Univ Iowa, BFA, MA & MFA; also with
Grand Wood, Fletcher Martin, Philip Guston & Maurico Lasanky.
Teaching: Head dept & prof art hist & drawing, Cent Mo State Univ, 49-
Art Interests: Drawing with felt tip pens.
Mailing Address: 207 Broad St, Warrensburg, MO 64093.

ELLIS, FREMONT F
Painter
b Virginia City, Mont, Oct 2, 97.
Study & Training: Art Stud League New York.
Work in Public Collections: El Paso Mus, Tex; Mus N Mex, Santa
Fe; Thomas Gilcrease Inst Am Hist, Tulsa, Okla; Art Inst, Lub-
bock, Tex; Univ Calif, Los Angeles.
Commissions: S S America (mural).
Awards: When Evening Comes Navajo Girls purchase prize, Spring-
ville Utah Mus; Henry E Huntington Award, Los Angeles Co Mus
Art, 24; Adele Hyde Morrison Prize & bronze medal, Oakland
Mus, Calif, 50.
Mailing Address: 553 Canyon Rd, Santa Fe, NM 87501.

ELLIS, GEORGE RICHARD
Museum Director
b Birmingham, Ala, Dec 9, 37.
Study & Training: Univ Chicago, BA & MFA.
Positions: Art supvr, Jefferson Co Schs, 62-64; former cur, Bir-
mingham Mus Art; asst dir, Mus Cult Hist, Univ Calif, Los An-
geles, presently.
Memberships: Nat Art Educ Asn; Ala Art Educ Asn (v pres); Bir-
mingham Art Asn; Ala Watercolor Soc (v pres, 64-65, pres, 65-).
Mailing Address: Museum of Cultural History, Rm 55A, Haines
Hall, University of California, Los Angeles, CA 90024.

ELLIS, RAY G
Painter
b Apr 24, 21.
Study & Training: Philadelphia Mus Sch.
Work in Public Collections: Columbus Mus Arts & Crafts; McGraw-
Hill, Inc; Nat Newark & Essex Bank; M Grumbacher Collection;
Du Cret Sch Arts; plus other pub & pvt collections.

Exhibitions: Am Watercolor Soc, 66 & 68-72 & Traveling Exhibs, 69-72; Audubon Artists; Nat Arts Club; Salmagundi Club; Jersey City Mus; one-man shows, Pa Acad Fine Arts & Columbia Mus Art, S C; plus others.
Positions: Trustee, De Cret Sch Arts, 71-72.
Awards: Grumbacher Award, Am Watercolor Soc, 69; Hudson Valley Art Asn Awards, 70-72; Winsor & Newton Medal, Audubon Artists, 71.
Bibliography: The watercolors of Ray G Ellis, Twin City Printery, 71; Norman Kent (auth), Watercolorists at work, Watson-Guptill, 72.
Memberships: Artists Fel (pres, 71-72); N J Watercolor Soc (pres, 67-68); Salmagundi Club (bd dirs & first v pres, 72); Nat Arts Club; Am Watercolor Soc; plus others.
Mailing Address: 76 Main St, Chatham, NJ 07928.

ELLISON, J MILFORD
Painter, Graphic Artist
b Sioux City, Iowa, Sept 16, 09.
Study & Training: Chicago Acad Fine Arts; Am Acad Art, Chicago; Chouinard Art Inst, Los Angeles; San Diego State Col, AB; Univ Colo; Univ Southern Calif; Banff Sch Fine Arts; Mexico City Col, MA.
Work in Public Collections: San Diego Fine Arts Soc; First Presby Art Collection; San Diego City Hall; San Diego Art Inst; Prince Kuhio Hotel, Kawai.
Commissions: Prince Kuhio Hotel, Kawai; Int Expo in San Diego, 35.
Exhibitions: 12 shows, San Diego Fine Arts Soc, 30-63; Laguna Beach Art Asn, 46, 48-56 & 61; 3 shows, La Jolla Mus Art; 15 shows, San Diego Art Inst, 52-71; 20 shows, La Jolla Art Asn, 54-72; plus others.
Collections Arranged: Fine Arts & Crafts, S Pac Art Festival, Suva, Fiji, 72.
Teaching: Chmn art dept, Point Loma High Sch, San Diego, 46-69; instr, exten, Univ Calif, 49-54 & 58; instr watercolor, U S Int Univ, Calif Western Campus, 54-61.
Positions: Dir art exhibs, Southern Calif Expo, Del Mar, 70-73.
Awards: Six awards, San Diego Art Inst, 54-70; awards, La Jolla Art Asn, 59-71 & La Jolla Art Festival, 63 & 64; plus others.
Memberships: La Jolla Art Asn (pres, 71-72); San Diego Art Inst (pres, 52-55); San Diego Watercolor Soc (pres, 64-65); plus others.
Mailing Address: 7421 Via Capri, La Jolla, CA 92037.

ELOUL, KOSSO
Sculptor
Preferred Media: Stainless Steel, Concrete.
b Jan 22, 20; U S citizen.
Study & Training: Art Inst Chicago, 39-43; sculptor symposiums, Austria, 60, Jugoslavia, 61, Italy & Israel, 62, Berlin, Ger, 63, Montreal, 64 & Long Beach, Calif, 65.
Work in Public Collections: Shalom 7 (painted steel), Rose Mus, Brandeis Univ; Art Gallery Ont, Toronto; Mus d'Art Contemp, Montreal; Mus Tel-Aviv, Israel; Bezalel Mus, Jerusalem, Israel.
Commissions: Hardfact (concrete & stainless steel), Calif State Univ, Long Beach, 65; Silent Thunder (painted steel), J Patrick Lannan Found, Palm Beach, Fla, 67; Morning Night (gunite fountain), Beverly Woods, Los Angeles, Calif, 68; Double You (stainless steel), Greenwin Housing Proj, Davisville, Toronto, 69; Now (environ sculpture), Fanshawe Col, London, Ont, 71.
Exhibitions: 29th Venice Biennial, 59; Middleheim Park Int, Antwerpen, 59; Fifth Festival Spoleto, Italy, 62; Carnegie Int, 64 & 67; Calif Artists in U S Mus, Lytton Art Ctr, Los Angeles, 67.
Teaching: Artist-at-residence sculpture, Calif State Univ, Long Beach, 65-66; artist-at-residence form & space, Univ Toronto Sch Archit, 69-70.
Bibliography: T H Heinrich (auth), The razor's edge, Vol 156/157 & Gilles Hemault (auth), Kosso Eloul, Arts Can; Fernande St Martin (auth), Lettre de Montreal, Art Int, 11/64; Curt Oplinger (auth), article, In: Artforum, 1/66.
Memberships: L'Accademia Tiberina, Rome, Italy.
Dealers: OK Harris Gallery, 345 W Broadway, New York, NY 10013; Dunkelman Gallery, 15 Bedford Rd, Toronto, Ont, Can.
Mailing Address: 61 W 74th St, New York, NY 10023.

ELSEN, ALBERT EDWARD
Art Historian
b New York, N Y, Oct 11, 27.
Study & Training: Columbia Col, AB; Columbia Univ, MA & PhD.
Teaching: Asst prof art hist, Carleton Col, 52-58; prof art hist, Indiana Univ, Bloomington, 58-68; prof art hist, Stanford Univ, 68-
Awards: Fulbright fel, 49-50; Am Coun Learned Socs grant, 60; Guggenheim fel, 66-67.
Memberships: Col Art Asn Am (bd dirs, 66-70, secy, 70-72, v pres, 72-).

Research: Modern art, principally modern sculpture.
Publications: Auth, Rodin's Gates of Hell, 60; auth, Rodin, 63; auth, Purposes of art, 63, 67 & 72; auth, The partial figure in modern sculpture: from Rodin to 1969, 69; auth, The sculpture of Henri Matisse, 72.
Mailing Address: 723 Alvarado Row, Stanford, CA 94305.

ELSKY, HERB
Sculptor
Preferred Media: Cast Polyester Resin.
b 1944.
Study & Training: Univ Calif, Los Angeles, MA.
Work in Public Collections: Nat Collection Fine Arts, Washington, D C.
Exhibitions: San Fernando Valley State Col; Univ Art Mus, Univ N Mex, Albuquerque; one-man show, Esther-Robles Gallery, 71.
Teaching: Vista instr, Philadelphia, Pa.
Mailing Address: c/o Esther-Robles Gallery, 665 N La Cienega Blvd, Los Angeles, CA 90069.

ELSNER, LARRY EDWARD
Sculptor, Educator
Preferred Media: Wood.
b Gooding, Idaho, 30.
Study & Training: Utah State Univ, BS; Columbia Univ, MFA.
Work in Public Collections: Ariz State Univ, Tempe; Salt Lake City Art Ctr, Utah; Archie Bray Found, Helena, Mont; Utah State Univ, Logan.
Commissions: Wood relief, Edith Bowen Sch, Logan, 68; metal relief, Col Family Life, Utah State Univ, 69.
Exhibitions: Intermountain Painting & Sculpture, Salt Lake Art Ctr, 63; 23rd Ceramic Nat, Everson Mus, Syracuse, N Y, 64; Southern Sculpture, 67, Columbia, S C, 67; Smithsonian Inst Invitational Show Sculpture, Washington, D C, 69; one-man show, 100 Pieces of Pottery, Tokyo, Japan, 71.
Teaching: Assoc prof sculpture, Utah State Univ, 60-
Awards: Ford Found Sculpture Purchase Award, 63; hon mention, Southern Sculpture 67, 67.
Memberships: Am Craftsmen Coun.
Mailing Address: 1229 Thrushwood Dr, Logan, UT 84321.

ELZEA, ROWLAND PROCTER
Museum Curator, Painter
Preferred Media: Acrylics.
b Columbia, Mo, Sept 19, 31.
Study & Training: Univ Mo, BA & MA; Hunter Col, MSEd; also privately with Esteban Vicente, New York.
Work In Public Collections: Del Art Mus, Wilmington.
Collections Arranged: Regional Sculpture Exhib, 67; Contemporary British Painting, 69; American Painting Since World War II, 71; American Painting 1840-1940, 72; Golden Age of American Illustration: 1880-1914, 72.
Teaching: Instr art hist & painting, Sch Art & Design, Philadelphia, Pa, 69-71, pres, 69-70.
Positions: Cur collections, Del Art Mus, 58-
Memberships: Col Art Asn Am.
Publications: Auth, Samuel and Mary R Bancroft English Pre-Raphaelite collection, 62; auth, Howard Pyle Collection, 71; auth, Golden age of American illustration: 1880-1914, 72.
Mailing Address: Sharpless Rd, Landenberg, PA 19350.

EMBRY, NORRIS
Painter
Preferred Media: Mixed Media.
b Louisville, Ky, Jan 14, 21.
Study & Training: Acad Fine Arts, Florence, Italy.
Work in Public Collections: Solomon R Guggenheim Mus, New York, N Y; also in pvt collections.
Exhibitions: Inst Contemp Art, Boston, Mass, 57; Rochester Mem Art Gallery, N Y; one-man shows, Robert Elkon Gallery, New York, 63 & 65; 100 American Drawings, Mus Mod Art, New York, 65; Baltimore Mus; plus others.
Dealers: Robert Elkon Gallery, 1063 Madison Ave, New York, NY 10028; André Emmerich Gallery, 41 E 57th St, New York, NY 10022.
Mailing Address: 1 W Biddle St, Baltimore, MD 21201.

EMERSON, EDITH
Painter, Curator
Preferred Media: Oils, Watercolors.
b Oxford, Ohio.
Study & Training: Art Inst Chicago; travel in Japan & Mex; Pa Acad Fine Arts; two Cresson scholarships to Europe; travel to Europe & India.
Work in Public Collections: Mural decorations, Plays & Players Theatre, Philadelphia, Pa; Philadelphia Mus Art; mural decorations, Church of the Nativity of the Blessed Virgin Mary & Con-

vent, Philadelphia; Woodmere Art Gallery, Philadelphia; Pa Acad Fine Arts, Philadelphia; plus others.
Commissions: Stained glass window in memory of Theodore Roosevelt, Temple Keneseth Israel, 19; two panels, The Sacred Heart & St Joseph with the Christ Child, lower Church of the Nativity of the Blessed Virgin Mary; five triptych altarpieces for Army & Navy, 42-43; four panels, The Life of St Joseph & chancel decorations, Nativity Convent, Sisters of St Joseph, 46; plus others.
Exhibitions: Nat Acad Design, New York, N Y; Archit League, New York; Pa Acad Fine Arts, Philadelphia; Corcoran Gallery Art, Washington, D C; Woodmere Art Gallery, Philadelphia; plus many others.
Collections Arranged: Exhib chmn, Woodmere Art Gallery, 42-
Teaching: Instr hist art, Agnes Irwin Sch, 16-27; lectr art appreciation, Philadelphia Mus Sch Indust Art, 29-36; instr hist art, Chestnut Hill Col, 48-56; plus lectr at var cols & clubs.
Positions: Libr asst, Art Inst Chicago, 08-11; pres, Woodmere Art Gallery, 45, cur, 46-; chmn, Regional Coun Community Art Ctrs, Philadelphia, 50-; pres & cur, Violet Oakley Mem Found, 61-
Awards: Granger prize, Fellowship Pa Acad Fine Arts; medal of honor, Philadelphia Watercolor Club, 69.
Bibliography: S Mechlin (ed), Mural decorations for Little Theatre, Philadelphia, Am Mag Art, 5/18; H Eberbein (auth), Moorestown Trust Co, Archit Forum, 4/27; M A Barney (auth), E Emerson's bookplate designs, Am Soc Bookplates Designers & Collectors, 33.
Memberships: Nat Soc Mural Painters; fellowship Pa Acad Fine Arts (jury, 45); Philadelphia Watercolor Club (dir jury, 44); Art Inst Chicago Alumni Asn; Philadelphia Mus Art; plus one other.
Publications: Auth, Splendid Spain, 3/24, Age of innocence, 6/25 & Opening book of the law, 1/27, Am Mag Art; auth, The Madonna in East Christian art, Asia Mag, 12/30; illusr, Song of Roland, 38 & Pageant of India's history, 48, Longmans.
Mailing Address: 627 Saint George's Rd, Philadelphia, PA 19119.

EMERSON, ROBERTA SHINN
Art Administrator
b Indianapolis, Ind, Feb 14, 22.
Study & Training: Northwestern Univ; Univ Chicago; Marshall Univ.
Collections Arranged: W Va Artists on the Move (traveling exhib), 67; A Room Full of Ropes (participatory exhib), 72.
Teaching: Asst prof art appreciation, Marshall Univ, 68-69.
Positions: Interim dir, Huntington Galleries, 67-68, dir, 71-
Mailing Address: Huntington Galleries, Huntington, WV 25701.

EMERSON, STERLING DEAL
Museum Director
b Saint Albans, Vt, May 21, 17.
Study & Training: Champlain Col, 37.
Teaching: Lectr mus collections & hist meetings throughout New Eng.
Positions: Dir, Shelburne Mus, Vt, 53-; pres, Vt Attractions Asn; mem adv comt, Mus Am Folk Arts, New York, N Y; v pres, Shelburne Enterprises, Inc, 65-; secy & treas, New Eng Heritage, Inc.
Memberships: Nat Trust Hist Preservation in U S; Early Am Industs Asn (dir, 53-); Vt Hist Soc; Green Mt Folklore Soc; Newcomen Soc N Am; plus others.
Mailing Address: Shelburne Museum, Inc, Shelburne, VT 05482.

EMERY, CHARLES ANTHONY
Art Administrator, Educator
b Farnborough, Eng, Apr 30, 19; Can citizen.
Study & Training: Oxford Univ, BA, 48, MA, 53.
Teaching: Assoc prof art hist, Univ Victoria, B C, 56-67.
Positions: Dir, Vancouver Art Gallery, 67-
Mailing Address: 1145 W Georgia St, Vancouver, BC, Can.

EMERY, LIN (LIN EMERY BRASELMAN)
Sculptor
Preferred Media: Kinetics, Metals.
b New York, N Y.
Study & Training: Ossip Zadkine Studio, Paris, France; Sculpture Ctr, New York.
Work in Public Collections: DeWaters Art Ctr, Flint, Mich; Delgado Mus, New Orleans, La; Norton Art Galleries, West Palm Beach, Fla; Huntington Mus Art, W Va; Walter P Chrysler Mus, Provincetown, Mass.
Commissions: Aquamobile, Germantown Nat Bank, Philadelphia, Pa, 65; monument & aquamobile, State of La, Civic Ctr, New Orleans, 68-71; aquamobile, Univ S C, Columbia, 70-72; aquamobile, Fidelity Nat Bank, Oklahoma City, Okla, 71; magnetmobile, S Cent Bell, Birmingham, Ala, 72.
Exhibitions: One-man show, Southern Art Mus Dirs Asn, six-mus tour, 55-56; Pa Acad Fine Arts Ann, Philadelphia, 60 & 64; Far East Tour, Int House & U S Info Serv, three countries, 62; New

Directions, Am Fedn Arts Tour, 62-63; Sculpture: 1900-1965, DeWaters Art Mus, 65.
Positions: Vis critic, Tulane Univ Sch Archit, 67-68.
Bibliography: Lansford (auth), New talent, Art in Am, 55; Moore & Allen (auth), Metal that moves, La Mag, 67; Pierce (auth), Lin Emery's aquamobiles, Art Int, 69.
Dealer: Sculpture Center, 167 E 69th St, New York, NY 10021.
Mailing Address: 7520 Dominican St, New Orleans, LA 70118.

EMIL, ALLAN D
Collector, Patron
b New York, N Y, Mar 25, 98.
Study & Training: Columbia Univ, 15-16; N Y Law Sch, 16-18; Brooklyn Law Sch, LLB, 19.
Positions: Patron, Mus Mod Art; trustee, Am Fedn Arts; Friends of Whitney Mus Am Art.
Memberships: Mus Mod Art; Solomon R Guggenheim Mus.
Collection: Ancient and modern sculpture; impressionist, abstract and modern art.
Mailing Address: 575 Madison Ave, New York, NY 10022.

EMIL, ARTHUR D
Collector
b New York, N Y, Dec 29, 24.
Study & Training: Yale Univ; Columbia Law Sch.
Positions: Exec comt, jr coun, Mus Mod Art.
Collections: Modern painting; ancient sculpture.
Mailing Address: 540 Madison Ave, New York, NY 10022.

EMMERICH, ANDRE
Art Dealer, Writer
b Frankfort, Ger, Oct 11, 24.
Study & Training: Amsterdam Lyceum, Neth; Kew Forest Sch, New York; Oberlin Col, BA, 44.
Memberships: Art Dealers Asn Am (pres, 72-74).
Specialty of Gallery: Contemporary art; pre-Columbian art.
Publications: Auth, Art before Columbus, Simon & Schuster, 63; auth, Sweat of the sun & tears of the moon—gold and silver in pre-Columbian art, Univ Wash Press, 65.
Mailing Address: 41 E 57th St, New York, NY 10022.

ENGEL, MICHAEL MARTIN, II
Painter
Preferred Media: Watercolors.
b New York, N Y, Mar 20, 19.
Study & Training: With A Katchemakoff; Art Stud League New York, with Kimon Nicolaides & George Picken; Am Sch Design, with Cherkasoff.
Work in Public Collections: Parrish Art Mus, Southampton, N Y; St Lawrence Univ, Canton, N Y; U S Navy Combat Art Collection; Antioch Col, Yellow Springs, Ohio; Clayton-Liberatore Gallery, Bridgehampton, N Y.
Exhibitions: Hofstra Col Invitational, 59; Audubon Artists Ann; Salmagundi Club; Suburban Art League, N Y; Wall St Art Asn, N Y.
Awards: First prize for watercolor, Suburban Art League, 64; prof award, Wall St Art Asn.
Memberships: Audubon Artists (historian, 45-, pres, 62-63); Int Asn Arts (v pres, 70-); Salmagundi Club; Artists Fellowship (trustee, 63-, chmn finance comn); life fel Royal Soc Arts.
Mailing Address: 22 Lee St, Huntington, NY 11743.

ENGELHARD, MR & MRS CHARLES
Collectors
Collection: Paintings.
Mailing Address: Waldorf Towers, 50th St & Park Ave, New York, NY 10022.

ENGGASS, ROBERT
Art Historian
b Detroit, Mich, Dec 20, 21.
Study & Training: Harvard Univ, AB, 46; Univ Mich, MA, 50, PhD, 55.
Teaching: Assoc prof art hist, Pa State Univ, 58-65, prof art hist, 66-71; prof art hist, Univ Kans, 71-
Awards: Grants-in-aid, Am Coun Learned Socs, 58 & 70; Fulbright res scholar, Univ Rome, 63-64; four res grants, Kress Found, 66-70.
Publications: Auth, The painting of Baciccio, Giovanni Battista Gaulli: 1609-1709, 64; contribr, Life of Bernini, 67; auth, Bernardino Ludovisi, Burlington Mag, 68; co-auth, Italy & Spain 1600-1750: sources & documents in the history of art, 70; co-auth, Atti del congresso internazzionale di studi sul Tiepolo, 72.
Mailing Address: Spooner Hall, University of Kansas, Lawrence, KS 66044.

ENGLAND, PAUL GRADY
Painter, Educator
Preferred Media: Oils.
b Hugo, Okla, Jan 12, 18.
Study & Training: Carnegie Inst Technol, BA, 40; Univ Tulsa, MA, 59; Art Stud League New York, 43-46; Zadkine Studio, Paris, France, 48 & 49.
Work in Public Collections: Philbrook Art Ctr, Tulsa, Okla; permanent print collection, N Y Pub Libr, New York; Joslyn Mus Art, Amaha, Nebr; Williams Col Mus, Mass; Staten Island Mus, New York.
Exhibitions: One-man shows, Le Centre d'Art, Port-au-Prince, Haiti, 47, Creuze Gallery, Paris, France, 49, Iolas Gallery, New York, 51, Grand Central Moderns, New York, 55 & Philbrook Art Ctr, Tulsa, 71.
Teaching: Asst prof painting, Hofstra Univ, 59-
Awards: Graphics award, Joslyn Mus Art, 57; grand awards, Philbrook Art Ctr, 57 & 63.
Bibliography: Margaret Harold (auth), Prize winning paintings, Allied, 64.
Memberships: Art Stud League New York.
Publications: Auth, Dust to dust, New Yorker Mag, 9/14/41; auth, Art critiques, France-Amerique, 55-57.
Dealer: Herbert Benevy, 1317 First Ave, New York, NY 10021.
Mailing Address: 01 Christopher St, New York, NY 10014.

ENGLANDER, GERTRUD
Ceramist
b Ger, Jan 29, 04; U S citizen.
Study & Training: Kunstgewerbeschule Cologne; Craft Students League, YWCA, New York, N Y; N Y Univ.
Exhibitions: Designer-Craftsmen U S A 1960, Mus Contemp Crafts, 60, Am Craftsmen's Coun Touring Exhib, 61; Craftsmen of Northeastern States, Worcester Art Mus, 63; Artist Craftsmen New York Ann, Lever House, 71.
Teaching: Instr ceramics, Craft Students League YWCA, New York, 52-; instr ceramics, Little Art Workshop, New York, 53-55.
Awards: Award of Merit for outstanding craftsmanship, Artist Craftsmen New York, 71.
Memberships: Artist Craftsmen New York; Am Craftsmens Coun; Craft Stud League YWCA.
Mailing Address: 345 E 52nd St, New York, NY 10022.

ENGLE, BARBARA JEAN
Painter, Printmaker
Preferred Media: Oils.
b Grandin, N Dak.
Study & Training: Honolulu Acad Arts, Hawaii; Chouinard Art Inst, Los Angeles, Calif; Otis Art Inst, Los Angeles.
Exhibitions: Three plus one, (paintings), Ala Moana Galleries, Honolulu, 69; Nat Print Exhib, Honolulu Acad Arts, 71; one-woman shows, Silk Screen Prints, Honolulu Acad Arts, 71, Barbara Engle, Serigraphs, Santa Fe, N Mex, 72 & Barbara Engle, Jewelry, Santa Barbara, Calif, 72.
Teaching: Instr drawing & painting, Honolulu Acad Arts, 64, 69, 70 & 72; instr abstr painting, printmaking & silk screen, Bishop Mus Honolulu, 70-
Bibliography: Helen Hutton (auth), Technique of collage, Batsford, Eng & Watson-Guptill, New York, N Y, 68; Lee Nordness (auth), Objects U S A, Viking Press, 70.
Dealer, Downtown Gallery, 125 Merchant St, Honolulu, HI 96813.
Mailing Address: 2257 Noah St, Honolulu, HI 96816.

ENMAN, TOM KENNETH
Painter, Art Administrator
Preferred Media: Oils, Watercolors.
b Salt Lake City, Utah, Feb 22, 28.
Study & Training: Univ Wash, Exten, 48-49; Chicago Acad Fine Arts, Ill, cert, 52; Cape Sch Art, Provincetown, Mass, scholar, 52; Calif Col Arts & Crafts, Oakland, 53-54; Univ Calif, Los Angeles, Exten, 58-61; Laguna Beach Sch Art, Calif, 69; also with Alex Villumsion & Plya Del Ray, Calif, 62.
Exhibitions: 19th Newport Ann, Newport Beach, Calif, 64; Laguna Beach Art Gallery Ann Fall Mem, 64; All Calif Exhib, Laguna Beach, 65; 7th Nat Ann Art Round Up, Las Vegas, 66; Laguna Beach Art Asn Graphic & Drawing Exhib, 67.
Positions: Dir, Artist Guild Laguna Beach, 64-65; dir, Laguna Beach Art Gallery, 65-
Awards: First in graphic (pen & ink), 64 & hon mention in oil, 65, Laguna Beach Art Asn.
Memberships: Laguna Beach Art Asn (dir); Antiquarian Soc Calif (chmn mem comt).
Mailing Address: 31781 National Park Dr, Laguna Niguel, CA 92677.

ENRIQUEZ, GASPAR
Designer, Instructor
b El Paso, Tex, July 18, 42.
Study & Training: Univ Tex, El Paso, BA; printmaking with Loren Janzen & jewelry with Walt Harrison.
Work in Public Collections: State Nat Bank; Univ Tex, El Paso.
Exhibitions: Designer Craftsman Exhib, El Paso Mus Art, 70.
Teaching: Instr art, El Paso Pub Schs, 70-
Memberships: El Paso Art Asn; Int Designers Craftsman.
Dealer: Jinx Gallery, 6513 N Mesa, El Paso, TX 79912.
Mailing Address: Box 17112, El Paso, TX 79917.

EPPINK, HELEN BRENAN
Educator, Painter
Preferred Media: Acrylics, Oils.
b Springfield, Ohio, Aug 19, 10.
Study & Training: Cleveland Art Inst; John Huntington Polytech Inst, Cleveland, Ohio; Colorado Springs Fine Art Ctr.
Work in Public Collections: Wichita Art Mus, Kans; Kans State Univ, Manhattan; Kans Fedn Womens Clubs Collection.
Exhibitions: Cleveland May Show, Ohio, 34; Third Air Capitol Show, Wichita Art Mus, 56; Midwest Biennial, Joslyn Art Mus, Omaha, Nebr, 56; Eighth Biennial Regional Exhib, Kans State Univ, 65; 22nd Ann Exhib Oils by Kans Artists, Manhattan, 70.
Teaching: Instr art, Col Emporia, 44-53; instr art, Ottawa Univ, Kans, 48-51; instr art, Kans State Teachers Col, 51-52, 60-61; head dept art, Col Emporia, 61-
Awards: Second prize for watercolor, Midwestern Show, Kansas City Art Inst, 39; purchase prize for watercolor, Wichita Art Mus, 56; purchase prize for oil, Eighth Biennial Exhib, Kans State Univ, 65.
Memberships: Am Asn Univ Prof (local secy-treas, 70-71); Kans Fedn Art; Kans State Art Teachers Asn.
Mailing Address: 2101 Canterbury Rd, Emporia, KS 66801.

EPPINK, NORMAN R
Printmaker, Painter
Preferred Media: Oils, Watercolors.
b Cleveland, Ohio, July 29, 06.
Study & Training: Cleveland Art Inst, BEA; Western Reserve Univ, MA.
Work in Public Collections: Brit Mus, London, Eng; Metrop Mus Art, New York, N Y; Art Inst Chicago, Ill; Nat Gallery Art, Washington, D C; Cleveland Mus Art.
Commissions: Court of Romance (mural), comn by Lakewood Bd Educ for Harding Jr High Sch, Ohio, 30; industrial mural, Mansfield Pub Libr, Ohio, 35.
Exhibitions: Third Int Color Lithography, Cincinnati Art Mus, Ohio, 54; Pratt Inst Int Print Show, 64 & 68; one-man show, 101 Prints, Linda Hall Libr, Kansas City, Mo & circulating exhib, Nat Gallery Art, Washington, D C, 68.
Teaching: Instr art, Lakewood Pub Schs, 28-30; instr art, Cleveland Pub Schs, 35-37; instr art, Kansas State Teachers Col, 37-, head dept art hist, 47-68, lectr (prof) art hist, 68-
Positions: Med illusr, Cleveland Clinic Found, 30-33; mem, Kans Cult Arts Comn, 66-67.
Awards: Second prize lithography, 53, first prize, 54 & first prize color lithography, 55, Cleveland Mus Art.
Bibliography: Norman Eppink, printmaker, The Rotarian, 12/68.
Memberships: Am Inst Graphic Arts; Am Asn Univ Prof; Kans Fedn Art (trustee, 72); Kans State Art Teachers Asn.
Research: Printmaking processes.
Publications: Auth & illusr, 101 prints, ltd ed, pvt press, 67, trade ed, Univ Okla Press, 71.
Mailing Address: 2101 Canterbury Rd, Emporia, KS 66801.

ERBE, JOAN (MRS JOAN ERBE UDEL)
Painter
b Baltimore, Md, Nov 1, 26.
Work in Public Collections: Munic Court, Washington, D C; Peale Mus, Baltimore; Baltimore Mus Art; Morgan Col.
Exhibitions: Peale Mus, 51-61; seven shows, Baltimore Mus Art, 54-65; Smithsonian Inst, 56; Corcoran Gallery Art, 57-60; Butler Inst Am Art, 60 & 61; plus others.
Awards: Prizes, Artists Equity Asn, 60 & 61, Corcoran Gallery Art, 60 & 62 & Baltimore Mus Art, 63, 64 & 66; plus others.
Memberships: Artists Equity Asn.
Mailing Address: 5603 Wexford Rd, Baltimore, MD 21209.

ERDMAN, R H DONNELLEY
Art Critic, Art Dealer
b Pasadena, Calif, Jan 19, 38.
Study & Training: Princeton Univ BA (Arch), MFA (Arch) & PhD (Arch); Univ Calif, BArch.
Teaching: Asst prof archit, Rice Univ Sch Archit.
Positions: Dir, Tex Gallery.
Memberships: Contemp Art Mus, Houston (trustee).

Publications: Auth, Christmas in Houston, Architex, 71; auth, The museums of fine arts, Rice Univ Sch Archit, 72.
Mailing Address: Rice University School of Architecture, Houston, TX 77001.

ERICSON, BEATRICE
Painter
Preferred Media: Acrylics.
b Paris, France, U S citizen.
Study & Training: With Morris Davidson & Boris Margo, Provincetown, Mass; also with Max Schnitzler, New York, N Y.
Work in Public Collections: N Y Univ Fine Arts; Marist Col, Poughkeepsie, N Y; Miami Mus Mod Art; also Gov Nelson A Rockefeller collection.
Exhibitions: Silvermine Guild Artists, New Canaan, Conn; Norfolk Mus Arts & Sci; one-man shows, Angeleski Gallery, New York, 60, Letters to the Unknown, Brata Gallery, New York, 67 & Archaic Past, Caravan House, New York, 72.
Bibliography: Reviews, In: Art News & Arts Mag, 57-72; Leo Soretsky (auth), article, In: FM Guide, 4/72.
Art Interests: Structure, balance & inventive calligraphy; interplay of color.
Dealer: Caravan House Gallery, 132 E 65th St, New York, NY 10021.
Mailing Address: 14 Watkins Ave, Middletown, NY 10940.

ERICSON, DICK
Cartoonist, Illustrator
b New York, N Y, Apr 12, 16.
Work in Public Collections: Nat Cartoonists Soc Collection; Libr Cong.
Teaching: Lectr cartooning & advert, schs, serv clubs, bus conventions & others.
Positions: Advert & pub rels consult, writer & illusr; v pres, bd gov, Nat Cartoonists Soc, chmn ACE awards comt, pub rels comt, slide shows & overseas tours; creator, syndicated newspaper features, Citizen Sibley & Trixie the Trader, Al Smith Features, Imagene, publ by Banking & Stewart the Steward.
Awards: Spec award outstanding pub rels achievements, Nat Automobile Dealers Pub Rels Comt, 54; ENIT trophy, cartoon category, 13th Int Humor Festival, Bordighera, Italy, 60.
Memberships: Nat Cartoonists Soc.
Publications: Contribr, cartoons, In: Best cartoons of the year; contribr, Sat Eve Post, True, Playboy, Ladies Home J & many others.
Mailing Address: Roxbury, CT 06783.

ERICSON, ERNEST
Illustrator, Instructor
b Boston, Mass.
Study & Training: Boston Mus Fine Arts Sch; Art Inst Chicago; Art Stud League New York; Grande Chaumiere, Paris, France.
Exhibitions: Detroit Inst Art, Mich; New York Watercolor Soc, N Y; Pa Acad Fine Arts, Philadelphia; Soc Illustrators, New York.
Teaching: Instr advan design, Sch Visual Arts, 56-
Positions: Illusr, Kenyon & Eckhardt, New York, 55-70.
Memberships: Soc Illustrators.
Mailing Address: 305 E 86th St, New York, NY 10028.

ERICSON, SUSAN KUNCE
Designer, Painter
Preferred Media: Acrylics, Oils.
b St Louis, Mo, May 3, 27.
Study & Training: Sch Fine Arts, Wash Univ, Scholastic Arts Mag scholar, 44, BFA, 48, with Max Beckman & Phillip Guston; Univ Ill; Brooklyn Mus Sch; Boston Univ; Inst Allende, Mex.
Work in Public Collections: Mural of Christ, Rock Hill Presby Church, Mo; Gibby Med Bldg, Miami, Fla.
Commissions: Many privately commissioned portraits & paintings.
Exhibitions: Ann Mo Exhib, St Louis Art Mus, 48; Metrop State Art Contest, Smithsonian Inst, 51; Conn Acad Fine Arts Ann Exhib, 58; Northeastern Univ Show, Copley Soc, Boston, 67; one-man show, Lahey Clin, Boston, 71.
Positions: Free lance commercial illusr, Nat Educ Asn, Washington, D C, Ketchum, McCleod & Groves, Creative Arts Studio, & many others, 48-60; free lance fine & commercial artist, Studio V, Ipswich, Mass, 60-
Specialty of Gallery: Portraits in landscape settings; landscapes emphasizing construction of natural objects.
Dealer: Sally Maren Gallery, Orchard Rd, Swampscott, MA 09107.
Mailing Address: 18 Lakeman's Lane, Ipswich, MA 01938.

ERLANGER, ELIZABETH N
Painter, Lecturer
Preferred Media: Casein, Oils.
b Baltimore, Md, Oct 23, 01.
Study & Training: Art Stud League New York; also with Ralph M Pearson, Umberto Romano, Jean Liberte & Hans Hofmann.

Work in Public Collections: Metrop Mus Art, New York, N Y; Brandeis Mus Art, Waltham, Mass; New York Univ; Evansville Mus, Ind; Peabody Mus, Nashville, Tenn.
Exhibitions: Twelve one-man shows; Nat Asn Women Artists juried foreign exhibs, Greece, 57, Japan, 60, Arg, 63, Scotland, 63 & France, 66.
Teaching: Lectr painting, Sch Art League, 58-65.
Positions: Liaison Off from U S Comn of Int Art Asn to U S Nat Comn for UNESCO, 64-68.
Awards: Var awards, Am Soc Contemp Artists, 53-63; prize in casein, Nat Soc Painters in Casein, 63; first spec citation awarded woman for outstanding civic achievement in the arts, Gov Rockefeller, 66.
Memberships: Audubon Artists; Am Soc Contemp Artists (pres, 63-65); Soc Am Graphic Arts; Nat Soc Painters in Casein (exec bd, 60-69); Nat Asn Women Artists (exec bd, 56-63).
Mailing Address: 156 W 86th St, New York, NY 10024.

ERNST, JAMES ARNOLD
Painter, Instructor
Preferred Media: Watercolors.
b New York, N Y, Aug 5, 16.
Study & Training: Pratt Inst Sch Art, 37-39; Grand Cent Art Sch, 40.
Work in Public Collections: Acad Arts, Easton, Md.
Exhibitions: Drawings-U S A, first-third biennials, St Paul Gallery Art, Minn, 61-66; Acad Arts Juried Show, Easton, Md, 67; Regional Invitational Exhib, WCBM Art Gallery, Baltimore, Md, 69; Land of Pleasant Living Exhib, Baltimore, 69.
Teaching: Instr drawing, beginning & advanced watercolor, City Col New York, 51-62.
Positions: Specialist in design & line drawing, Batten, Barton, Durstine & Osborne, Inc, New York, 51-62.
Awards: Best watercolor, Md State Fedn Arts, Annapolis, 67; best watercolor, Acad Arts, Easton, 67; first prize & purchase award, Land of Pleasant Living Exhib, 69.
Memberships: Joint Ethics Comt; Artists Guild, New York (v pres; mem bd, 56-); Baltimore Watercolor Club; Acad Arts, Easton.
Publications: Auth, Drawing the line, Reinhold, 62.
Dealer: Phoenix-Chase Galleries, 5 W Chase St, Baltimore, MD 21201.
Mailing Address: Crescent Coves, Bozman, MD 21612.

ERNST, JIMMY
Painter, Educator
b Cologne, Ger, June 24, 20; U S citizen.
Study & Training: Altona Arts & Crafts Sch, 38.
Work in Public Collections: Metrop Mus Art; Whitney Mus Am Art; Brooklyn Mus; Wadsworth Atheneum; Art Inst Chicago; plus many others.
Commissions: Sculpture, NBC Producer's Showcase, 54; paintings, Abbott Labs, 55 & Fortune Mag, 55 & 61; murals, USS Adams, 56 & Continental Bank, Lincoln, Nebr, 58-59.
Exhibitions: Pa Acad Fine Arts, 53, 55, 57 & 65; Bielefeld Mus, Ger, 64; Berlin, 65; one-man show, Grand Rapids Mus Art, 68; Whitney Mus Am Art Ann, 69 & 70; plus many others.
Teaching: Lectr contemp art, art asns & mus, U S; prof art, Brooklyn Col, 51-; vis artist, Univ Colo, 54 & 56; vis artist, Mus Fine Arts, Houston, Tex, 56; lectr, U S Info Serv, U S S R & Ger, 61 & 63.
Awards: Norman Wait Harris Award, Art Inst Chicago, 54; creative arts award, Brandeis Univ, 57; Guggenheim grant, 61.
Dealer: Borgenicht Gallery, 1018 Madison Ave, New York, NY 10021.
Mailing Address: 39 Arrowhead Trail, New Canaan, CT 06840.

ESCOBEDO, AUGUSTO ORTEGA
Sculptor, Painter
Preferred Media: Bronze, Marble.
b Mexico City, Mex, Nov 22, 14.
Work in Public Collections: Mus of Virginia, Minn; Eisenhower Mus, Abilene, Kans; Mus Mod Art, Mexico City; Gallery of Int Airport, Mexico City.
Commissions: Fountain & 11 bronze figures, Ministry of Educ, Mexico City, 57; bronze equestrian group, Govt Tabasco, Villahermosa City, 61; 9 bronze figures, Nat Inst Children's Welfare, Mexico City, 61; 3 figures, polyester, Pl Versailles Shopping Ctr, Montreal, Can, 66; fountain & 16 bronze figures, Universal Studios, Universal City, Calif, 69.
Exhibitions: Mex Art Show, Tokyo, Japan, 55; Int Telecommun Union Sculpture Contest, Geneva, Switz, 65; Mex Art Show, Denver Mus Fine Arts, Colo, 67; Mex Art, Waddington Galleries, Montreal, 68; Contemp Mex Artists, HemisFair Plaza, San Antonio, Tex, 72.
Teaching: Prof sculpture, Univ Morelia, Michoacan, Mex, 56.
Awards: Man of Vision Award, Vision Mag, 56; Contemp Sculpture Show Award, Univ Chihuahua, 64 & 65.

Bibliography: A Luna Arroyo (auth), Panorama de la escultura Mexicana, Ed Inst Nac Bellas Artes, 64; Raquel Tibol (auth), Historia del arte Mexicano, Ed Hermes, 64; M Monteforte Toledo (auth), Las piedras vivas, Univ State of Mex, 71.
Mailing Address: Callejon de las Flores 4, San Francisco, Coyoacan, Mexico D F 21, Mexico.

ESCOBEDO, HELEN
Sculptor, Art Administrator
b Mexico City, Mex, July 28, 36.
Study & Training: Royal Col Art, scholar, three yrs, with Frank Dobson, Leon Underwood & John Skeaping, ARCA.
Work in Public Collections: Narodni Galerie, Prague, Czech; Stanley Marcus Collection, U S A; Banco Comercio, Mexico City; Mus Arte Moderno, Mexico City.
Commissions: 3 Striding Figures (bronze), Mario Gaidano, San Francisco, Calif, 64; Terrace Environment (concrete), Hotel Aristos, Mexico City, 68; Dinamic Wall (wood), Mex Pavilion, Hemisfair, San Antonio, Tex, 68; Gateway to the Wind (concrete), Olympic Hwy, Mex Olympics, 68; Signals (aluminum), Int Sculpture Symp, Auckland, N Z, 71.
Exhibitions: Uluv Galerie, Prague, 69; Park Lazienkowski, Warsaw, Poland, 70; Kunstindustrimuseet, Oslo, Norway, 70; Graphic Environment, Eleventh Biennial Middelheim, Antwerp, Belg, 71; First Biennial Am Graphic Arts, Mus Tertulia, Cali, Colombia, 71.
Positions: Dir fine arts, Mus Univ Ciencias y Arte, Nat Univ Mex, 61-; mem adv bd, Nat Sculpture Ctr, Univ Kans, Lawrence, 70-
Awards: Tlatilco prize for sculpture, Mus Arte Moderna, 64.
Memberships: Founding mem Salon Independiente.
Art Interests: Environmentalist.
Dealer: Galeria de Arte Mexicano, Milan 18, Mexico D F 6, Mex.
Mailing Address: Avenida San Jeronimo 162, Mexico D F 20, Mex.

ESHOO, ROBERT
Painter
Preferred Media: Oil, Watercolor.
b New Britain, Conn, Apr 27, 26.
Study & Training: Boston Mus Fine Arts Sch Mass, cert & dipl; Syracuse Univ, BFA, MFA.
Work in Public Collections: Boston Mus Fine Arts; Wadsworth Atheneum, Hartford, Conn; Currier Gallery Art, Manchester, N H; Munson-Williams-Proctor Inst, Utica, N Y; Addison Gallery Am Art, Andover, Mass.
Exhibitions: Chicago Art Inst Ann, Ill, 57; Young America, Whitney Mus Am Art, New York, N Y, 57; Quadrennial, Am Painting 1962, Va Mus Fine Arts, Richmond, 62; 28th Biennial Exhib, Corcoran Gallery, Washington, D C, 63; Retrospective, Currier Gallery Art, 67.
Teaching: Supvr painting & graphics, Currier Art Ctr, 58-; instr studio art, Derryfield Sch, Manchester, 65-
Dealer: Pucker/Safrai Gallery, 171 Newbury St, Boston, MA 02146.
Mailing Address: 1015 Chestnut St, Manchester, NH 03104.

ESLER, JOHN KENNETH
Printmaker
b Pilot Mound, Man, Jan 11, 33.
Study & Training: Univ Mann, BEd, Univ Man Sch Art, BFA.
Work in Public Collections: Mus Mod Art, New York, N Y; Victoria & Albert Mus, London, Eng; Albright-Knox Gallery, Buffalo, N Y; Nat Gallery Can, Ottawa, Ont; Montreal Mus Fine Arts, P Q.
Exhibitions: Third Biennal Am Grababo, Santiago, Chile, 68; Third Int Gravure, Krakow, Poland, 70; Second Int Print Biennale, Bradford, Eng, 70; Premio Int Biella, Italy, 71; Int Buchkunst-Ausstellung, Leipzig, 71.
Teaching: Instr printmaking, Alta Col Art, Calgary, 64-68; asst prof printmaking, Univ Calgary, 68-
Awards: C W Jefferies Award, Can Soc Graphic Arts, 68; first purchase award, Burnaby Biennial Print Exhib, 69; first purchase award, Graphic Exhib, Art Alliance Cent Pa, 70.
Memberships: Can Soc Graphic Art (Western rep, 68-); Soc Can Etchers & Engravers.
Mailing Address: Box 2, Site 14, R R 4, Calgary, Alta T2M 4L4, Can.

ESMAN, BETTY (BETTY ESMAN SAMUELS)
Painter
b New York, N Y.
Study & Training: Syracuse Univ Col Fine Arts; Nat Acad Design; Ecole Beaux-Arts, Paris, France; also in Europe & S Am.
Work in Public Collections: Fla Southern Col; Brandeis Univ; Ball State Teachers Col; Univ S C; Peabody Mus; also in pvt collections.
Exhibitions: Art Inst Chicago; San Francisco Mus Art; Mus Beaux Arts, Dijon, France, 54; N Y World's Fair, 64 & 65; U S Info Serv Traveling Exhibs, Holland, Yugoslavia & Mex, 65-66; plus many other group & one-man shows.

Awards: Prizes, Nat Asn Women Artists, 55 & 59 & Brooklyn Soc Artists, 55 & 59.
Memberships: Nat Asn Women Artists; Brooklyn Soc Artists; Nat Soc Painters in Casein; Painters & Sculptors Soc N J; Artists Equity Asn.
Mailing Address: 1230 Park Ave, New York, NY 10028.

ESMAN, ROSA M
Art Dealer, Collector
b New York, N Y, Nov 29, 27.
Study & Training: Smith Col, BA.
Work in Public Collections: (Limited Editions) New York 10 & 7 Objects in a Box, Mus Mod Art, New York, N Y; New York International, Whitney Mus Am Art, New York; Metropolitan Scene, Metrop Mus Art, New York; 7 Objects 69, Brit Arts Coun, London, Eng; Armam Paintbox, Princeton Mus.
Positions: Pres & dir, Tanglewood Press, New York, 64-69; dir, Abrams Original Editions, 69-72; pres & dir, Tanglewood Press & Rosa Esman Gallery, 72-
Specialty of Gallery: Graphics and multiple objects in signed limited editions; drawings.
Collection: (With Aaron H Esman, MD) Contemporary drawings, prints and paintings, with emphasis on New York artists of the 60's and 70's; also African and pre-Columbian art.
Publications: Ed, Seven objects in a box, 66; ed, New York 10/69, 69; ed, Six drawing tables by Saul Steinberg, 71; ed, Four Pochoirs by Helen Frankenthaler, 71; ed, No gas by Red Grooms, 72; plus others.
Mailing Address: 24 E 80th St, New York, NY 10021.

ESSERMAN, RUTH
Painter
b Chicago, Ill, May 21, 27.
Study & Training: Univ Ill, BA & MA; Univ Mex; Art Inst Chicago.
Exhibitions: Roosevelt Univ-Pan-Am Exhib, 57; New Horizons, 58; Denver Art Mus, 59 & 60; Chicago Sun-Times Competition, 60-62; Minneapolis Inst Art, 64; plus others.
Teaching: Instr art, Highland Park High Sch, Ill, 57-, chmn art dept, 60-
Positions: Adv, U S Off Educ, 67-68.
Awards: Recipient of numerous prizes & awards.
Memberships: Ill Art Educ Asn (pres, 65-66); Ill Educ Asn.
Mailing Address: 4333 Vine St, Highland Park, IL 60035.

ETNIER, STEPHEN MORGAN
Painter
Preferred Media: Oils.
b York, Pa, Sept 11, 03.
Study & Training: Yale Art Sch; Pa Acad Fine Arts; also with Rockwell Kent & John Carroll; hon degrees from Bowdoin Col & Bates Col.
Work in Public Collections: Metrop Mus Art; Boston Mus; Yale Univ; Toledo Mus; Duncan Phillips, Washington, D C.
Commissions: Many private commissions.
Exhibitions: Carnegie Inst; Corcoran Gallery Art; Pa Acad Fine Arts; Nat Acad Fine Arts; Milch Gallery, 31-64; Midtown Gallery; plus others.
Awards: Samuel F B Morse Gold Medal, Altman Prize & Saltus Gold Medal, Nat Acad Design.
Bibliography: Harry Saltpeter (auth), Stephen Etnier, bad boy artist, Esquire, 39; Howard Deoree (auth) & Ernest Watson (auth), Stephen Etnier, 56 & Betty Chamberlain (auth), Stephen Etnier, a long voyage home, 72, Am Artist.
Dealer: Midtown Gallery, 11 E 57th St, New York, NY 10022.
Mailing Address: Old Cove, South Harpswell, ME 04079.

ETROG, SOREL
Sculptor, Painter
b Jassy, Roumania, Aug 29, 33.
Study & Training: Inst Painting & Sculpture, Tel-Aviv, Israel; Brooklyn Mus Sch Art.
Work in Public Collections: Art Gallery Toronto; Montreal Mus Fine Arts; Mus Art Contemporain, Montreal; Nat Gallery Can; Boymans Mus, Rotterdam, Holland; plus many others, U S & Can.
Exhibitions: Venice Biennial, 66; Legnano, Italy, 66; Expo '67; Retrospective, 1958-1968, Palazzo Strozzi, Florence, Italy, 68; Ont Cols Traveling Exhib, Art Gallery Toronto, 68-69; plus many other group & one-man shows.
Mailing Address: 229 Yonge St, Toronto, Ont, Can.

ETS, MARIE HALL
Illustrator, Writer
b North Greenfield, Wis, Dec 16, 95.
Study & Training: N Y Sch Fine & Appl Art, 16-17; Univ Chicago, PhB, 24; Art Inst Chicago; also with Frederick V Poole.

Work in Public Collections: Kerlan Collection, Univ Minn Libr; Iowa City Pub Libr; Milwaukee Pub Libr.
Commissions: Set of illus, Childcraft & How & Why Libr.
Exhibitions: First Ann Exhib Selected Bks for Children, Am Fedn Arts, 45; one-man show, original drawings, Libr Exhib Gallery, Teachers Col, Columbia Univ, 63; Albright-Knox Gallery Art, 64.
Awards: Hans Christian Andersen Award for, Play with me, Stockholm, Sweden, 56; award for, Play with me, Am Inst Graphic Arts, 58-60; Caldecott Award, 60.
Publications: Auth & illusr, Gilberto and the wind, 69, Talking without words, 70, Just me, 70, In the forest, 70 & Elephant in a well, 72, Viking Press; plus many others.
Mailing Address: Morningside Gardens, 501 W 123rd St, Apt 11H, New York, NY 10027.

ETTENBERG, EUGENE M
Designer, Educator
b Westmount, P Q, Oct 21, 03; U S citizen.
Study & Training: Pratt Inst, BFA; Columbia Univ, MA, EdD(fine arts).
Exhibitions: Metrop Mus Art; Archit League; Am Inst Graphic Arts; Columbia Univ Teachers Col Libr; Pratt Inst.
Teaching: Instr typography, Pratt Inst, 47-59; lectr graphic arts, Columbia Univ, 53-64.
Positions: Ed, Advert & Publ Prod Yr Bk, 36-41; contrib ed, Am Artists Mag, 51-; graphics consult, U S Dept Interior & Nat Endowment Arts, 72.
Awards: Carey-Thomas Award, 58; Golden Keys Award, 69.
Memberships: Am Inst Graphic Arts (v pres & dir, 50-55); Type Dirs Club (pres, 65-67); Typophilies (pres, 68-69); Nat Art Educ Asn.
Research: History of typography, 1450 to present; type faces; type foundries; designers & backgrounds.
Art Interests; Graphic arts.
Publications: Auth, Type for books & advertising, Van Nostrand, 47 & Macmillan, 49.
Mailing Address: 284A Heritage Village, Southbury, CT 06488.

ETTENBERG, FRANKLIN JOSEPH
Painter, Draughtsman
Preferred Media: Pen & Ink, Oils.
b Brooklyn, N Y, May 7, 45.
Study & Training: Univ Mich, BS(design), 66, with Milton Cohen, Fred Bauer & John Stephenson; Univ N Mex, MA, 71, with John Kacere.
Work in Public Collections: Detroit Inst Art, Mich; Univ N Mex Fine Arts Mus, Albuquerque; Roswell Mus & Art Ctr, N Mex.
Exhibitions: Mich Artists Ann, Detroit Inst Arts, 65; Mus N Mex Biennial, Santa Fe, 72; 19th Exhib Southwestern Prints & Drawings, Dallas Mus Fine Arts, 72.
Awards: Nat Found Arts & Humanities travel grant, 66; artist-in-residence grant, Roswell Mus & Art Ctr, 72.
Dealer: Artium Orbis Gallery, 558 Canyon Rd, Santa Fe, NM 87501.
Mailing Address: 204 Jefferson, Santa Fe, NM 87501.

ETTING, EMLEN
Painter, Illustrator
Preferred Media: Oils, Acrylics.
b Philadelphia, Pa, Aug 24, 05.
Study & Training: Harvard Univ, BS, 28; Grande Chaumière & André Lhote, Paris.
Work in Public Collections: Whitney Mus Am Art, New York, N Y; Pa Acad Fine Arts, Philadelphia; Addison Gallery Am Art, Andover, Mass; Philadelphia Mus Art; Atwater Kent Mus, Philadelphia.
Commissions: Philadelphia Industries (oil on canvas), Market St Nat Bank, 47; oil on canvas, Italian Consulate, Philadelphia, 55.
Exhibitions: Whitney Mus; Carnegie Inst, Pittsburgh, Pa; Corcoran Gallery Art, Washington, D C; Pa Acad Fine Arts; San Francisco World's Fair.
Teaching: Instr painting & drawing, Sch Indust Art, Philadelphia Mus Art, Philadelphia Col Art & Tyler Sch Art, Temple Univ.
Positions: U S artist-deleg, Second Int Cong Plastic Arts, Dubrovnik, 57.
Awards: Chevalier, Legion d'Honneur, Fr Govt; Star Solidarity, Italian Govt.
Bibliography: Mary Rupert (auth), Emlen Etting, paintings of an American romantic, London Studio, 39.
Memberships: Artists Equity Asn (pres, 55-58, hon pres, pres, Philadelphia Chap, 50-53, hon pres); Nat Soc Mural Painters; Century Asn; Philadelphia Art Alliance; Alliance Française (hon pres); plus others.
Publications: Illusr & translr, Valery, Le cimetiere Marin, Centaur Press, 32; illusr, Amerika & Ecclesiastes, New Directions, 40; illusr, Born in a crowd, Crowell-Collier; auth & illusr, Drawing the ballet, Studio Bks, 44.
Dealer: Midtown Galleries, 11 E 57th St, New York, NY 10022.
Mailing Address: 1921 Manning St, Philadelphia, PA 19103.

ETTINGHAUSEN, RICHARD
Art Historian, Educator
b Frankfort-on-Main, Ger, Feb 5, 06; U S citizen.
Study & Training: Univ Frankfort, PhD, 31; also in Eng.
Teaching: Lectr Persian miniatures, art of the Islamic Bk, Near Eastern pottery, arts of the Muslim E; res assoc, Iranian Inst, N Y, 34-37; lectr, New York Univ, 37-38; assoc prof hist of Islamic art, Univ Mich, 38-44; assoc Near Eastern art, Freer Gallery Art, Washington, D C, 44-58; res prof Islamic art, Univ Mich, 48; adj prof, Inst Fine Arts, New York Univ, 61-67, Hagop Kevorkian prof Islamic art, 67-
Positions: Ed, Ars Islamica, 38-51; co-ed, Ars Orientalis, 51-58; cur Near Eastern art, Freer Gallery, 58-61, head cur Near Eastern Art, 61-67; consult chmn, Islamic dept, Metrop Mus Art, New York, N Y, 69-
Memberships: Col Art Asn Am; Am Oriental Soc; Asia House, N Y; Am Res Ctr in Egypt.
Publications: Auth, Studies in Muslim Iconography & Paintings of the sultans & emperors of India, in American collections, Verry, 61; auth, introduction, In: Turkish miniatures from the thirteenth to eighteenth century, NAL, 65; contribr, Bull Iranian Inst & Gazette Beaux-Arts; plus others.
Mailing Address: Institute of Fine Arts, New York University, Washington Square, New York, NY 10003.

ETTLING, RUTH (DROITCOUR)
Printmaker, Painter
b Pittsburgh, Pa, Mar 30, 10.
Study & Training: R I Sch Design; Marshall Univ, BA; spec study with Charles Burchfield, Arnold Blanch, William Thon, Fletcher Martin, Victor Candell & Walter Murch.
Work in Public Collections: Charleston Gallery Sunrise, W Va; Dayton Art Inst, Ohio; Hunterdon Co Art Ctr, Clinton, N J; Huntington Galleries, W Va; W Va Arts & Humanities Collection, Charleston.
Exhibitions: Hunterdon Co Nat Print Show, Clinton, 62; Ohio Printmakers, Dayton, 62; Exhib 180, Huntington, 70; Ruth Ettling's Recent Prints, Huntington Galleries, 71; Allied Artists W Va, Charleston, 72.
Teaching: Instr drawing & painting, Huntington Galleries, 52-66, summer dir, print workshop, 72; instr art, Putnam Jr High Sch, Ashland, Ky, 66-72.
Awards: Huntington Galleries Juror's Award, 59; Charleston Gallery Sunrise First Graphics Award, 71; W Va Coun Arts & Humanities Award, 72.
Memberships: Tri-State Arts Asn (pres, 72); Nat Art Educ Asn.
Publications: Illusr, Dear Bob, love mother, 67.
Mailing Address: 1475 Spring Valley Circle, Huntington, WV 25704.

EUGENIE (EUGENIE MUELHAUSER MURPHY)
Painter
Preferred Media: Watercolors, Oils.
b Brooklyn, N Y, Jan 10, 13.
Study & Training: With Edgar Whitney, John Rogers, Don Stone, Paul Puzinas, Emile Gruppe & Wayne Morrell.
Exhibitions: La Bldg, World's Fair, New York, N Y, 64; Am Artists Prof League Grand Nat, Lever House, New York, 66-68; Huntington Hartford's Gallery, Cent Park, New York, 67; Nat Art League, Douglaston, N Y, 69; Nat Arts Club, Catharine Lorillard Wolfe Art Club, New York, 69; plus others.
Teaching: Instr watercolors & china painting, pvt studio, Bellerose, N Y, 63-70; instr oil painting, Great Neck Women's Club, N Y, 67-70; instr oil painting, Nat Art League, Douglaston, 68-70; instr watercolors & china painting, pvt studio, Sayville, N Y, 72-
Positions: Corresp secy, Douglaston Art League, 60-66.
Awards: Travel exhib award, Washington Square Outdoor Exhib, West Side Savings Bank, 66; Winsor Newton Award, Am Artists Prof League Grand Nat, 68; second prize for watercolor, Sayville C of C, 72; plus over 25 others.
Memberships: Am Artists Prof League; Catharine Lorillard Wolfe Art Club; Nat Art League (corresp secy & recording secy, 60-70); Art League, Nassau Co; Wet Paints Art League.
Art Interests: China painter.
Mailing Address: 39 Sejon Dr, Sayville, NY 11782.

EVANS, BRUCE HASELTON
Art Administrator, Art Historian
b Rome, N Y, Nov 13, 39.
Study & Training: Amherst Col, BA; N Y Univ Inst Fine Arts, MA.
Collections Arranged: The Paintings of Edward Edmondson, 72; Jean-Léon Gérôme—The Paintings, 72.
Positions: Cur asst to dir, Dayton Art Inst, 65-67, chief cur, 68-72, asst dir, 72-
Memberships: Am Asn Mus; Col Art Asn.

Publications: Auth, Fifty treasures of the Dayton Art Institute, 69; auth, Edward Edmondson—a biography & critical study of his paintings, 72; co-auth, The paintings of Jean-Léon Gérôme, 72; plus numerous articles in mus bulletins & exhib catalogues.
Mailing Address: P O Box 941, Dayton, OH 45401.

EVANS, EDWARD ARTHUR
Painter
Preferred Media: Watercolors, Pastels.
b Muskogee, Okla, Sept 17, 95.
Study & Training: Watercolor with John Vawter, Elliot O'Hara & Irving Shapiro; pvt study in Oriental, fine & commercial arts; pastel with Ernest Savage.
Exhibitions: Am Artists Prof League Ann, Miami, Fla, 56-72 & New York, N Y, 60-72.
Memberships: Am Artist Prof League (pres, 56, bd dir, 57-60, 66-69 & 70-72).
Mailing Address: 13291 Old Cutler Rd, Miami, FL 33156.

EVANS, GROSE
Art Administrator, Art Historian
b Columbus, Ohio, Dec 14, 16.
Study & Training: Ohio State Univ, BFA, 39, MA, 40; Inst Fine Arts, New York Univ, 41-43 & 45-46; Johns Hopkins Univ, PhD, 53.
Teaching: Prof lectr Baroque-mod art, George Washington Univ, 53-61; prof lectr Am painting, Johns Hopkins Univ, 65; curric dir art teachers' training, George Washington Univ & Nat Gallery Art, 66 & 67.
Positions: From lectr to assoc cur, dept educ, Nat Gallery Art, 46-60, cur exten serv, decorative arts & index Am design, 60-70, cur exhibs & loans, 70-73, cur decorative arts, 73-
Memberships: Col Art Asn Am.
Research: Anglo-American Art of the eighteenth century.
Publications: Auth, Benjamin West & the taste of his time, Southern Ill Univ Press, 59; auth, Vincent Van Gogh, McGraw, 68.
Mailing Address: 2308 Glasgow Rd, Alexandria, VA 22307.

EVANS, HENRY
Printmaker
b Superior, Wis, May 16, 18.
Work in Public Collections: Albertina, Vienna; Libr Cong, Washington, D C; Hunt Bot Inst, Pittsburgh; Clark Libr, Calif, Los Angeles; Oakland Mus, Calif.
Exhibitions: One-man shows, Royal Hort Soc, London, 65, Hunt Bot Inst, 66, Biomed Libr, Univ Calif, Los Angeles, 68, Calif Acad Sci, San Francisco, 70 & Oakland Mus, 71; plus many others.
Bibliography: A Frankenstein (auth), Evans' botanical portfolios, San Francisco chronicle, 8/25/68; staff (auth), Henry Evans, printmaker (doc film), KQED, 69; Johan Kooy (auth), Henry Evans, printmaker, Pac Discovery, 12/70.
Publications: Illusr, Champagne and shoes, Peregrine Pr, 62; illusr, Hortulus, 66; illusr, Flower pot gardens, Crowell Collier, 67; auth, illusr & printer, State flowers, Vol 1-5, hand printed at Peregrine Pr, 68-72.
Mailing Address: 555 Sutter, Apt 406, San Francisco, CA 94102.

EVANS, MINNIE
Painter
Preferred Media: Watercolors.
b Wilmington, N C, Dec 12, 92.
Work in Public Collections: Newark Mus, N J; Indianapolis Mus, Ind; Mus Am Folk Art, New York, N Y; Ill Bell Tel, Chicago; Am Fedn Arts, New York.
Exhibitions: One-man shows, The Art Image, New York, 69, Davison Art Ctr, Wesleyan Univ, Middletown, Conn, 69 & 70, Dorothy Yepez Gallery, Saranac Lake, N Y, 70, Portal Gallery, London, Eng, 70 & St John's Art Gallery, Wilmington, 70.
Bibliography: Nina Howell Starr (auth), The lost world of Minnie Evans, Bennington Rev, summer 69; Suzanne Ulamis (auth), Artist Minnie Evans, gifted primitive, Am Illus, May 71; Geoffrey Ashe (auth), Camelot and vision of Albion, Heinmann, 71.
Dealer: Mr Nina Howell Starr, 333 E 68th St, New York, NY 10021.
Mailing Address: Rte 3, Box 377, Wilmington, NC 28401.

EVANS, RICHARD
Painter, Educator
Preferred Media: Oils, Acrylics, Intaglio.
b Chicago, Ill, Oct 1, 23.
Study & Training: Otis Art Inst, dipl; Calif Col Arts & Crafts; Studio of George Miller, New York, N Y; Univ Wyo, MA; fels, Stacey Found, 47 & Tiffany Found, 48 & 50.
Work in Public Collections: San Francisco Fine Arts Comn; Univ Wyo; Col Southern Utah.
Commissions: Tile mural, Univ Wyo, 68; portrait of Sam S Knight, Univ Wyo Geol Mus; twenty sculptures of prominent personages for private commissions.

Exhibitions: Northwest Printmakers Int, 65; Gov Nat Touring Art Exhib, 66-67; Otis Art Inst 50th Anniversary Exhib, 68; Denver Mus Inaugural Exhib, 72; Joslyn Mem Mus Midwest Biennial, 72.
Teaching: Instr drawing, Calif Col Arts & Crafts, Oakland, 50-52; instr drawing & painting, Miami Univ, Oxford, Ohio, 56-57; prof printmaking, drawing & painting, Univ Wyo, 57-
Awards: San Francisco Art Festival purchase award for drawing, 50; 26th Cedar City Invitational purchase award, 66; anonymous donor award, Otis Art Inst 50th Anniversary Exhib, 68.
Bibliography: Victor Flach (auth), The making of Ikon # 13 (film & TV tape), produced by Univ Wyo, 70; Bruce Cady (auth), American printmaking today, N Y Graphics Soc (in prep).
Publications: Auth, On large scale prints, Am Artist, 11/62.
Mailing Address: Dept. of Art, University of Wyoming, Laramie, WY 82070.

EVANS, ROBERT JAMES
Painter, Museum Curator
b Chicago, Ill, May 2, 44.
Study & Training: Parsons Col; Univ Iowa; Northeast Mo State Col, BSEduc; Drake Univ; Southern Ill Univ, Carbondale, MFA.
Work in Public Collections: Univ Galleries, Southern Ill Univ, Carbondale.
Exhibitions: Mid-States Ann, Evansville Mus Art & Sci, Ind, 69-70; Ark Nat Exhib, Ark State Univ Gallery, Jonesboro, 70; one-man shows, Strawn Art Ctr, Jacksonville, Ill, 71 & Ill Bell Tel Gallery, Chicago, 72; Illinois Painters II, Ill Arts Coun Circulating Exhib, 71-73.
Teaching: Instr drawing & painting, Springfield Art Asn, Ill, 71-
Positions: Res asst, Univ Galleries, Southern Ill Univ, Carbondale, 69-70; cur art, Ill State Mus, Springfield, 70-
Awards: 22nd Ann Exhib First Prize Painting, Quincy Art Club, Ill, 71; resident award, Va Ctr Creative Arts, Charlotteville, summer 72.
Memberships: Am Crafts Coun; Am. Asn Mus.
Publications: Auth, articles, In: Living Mus, 70- & rev, In: Craft Horizons.
Mailing Address: 2129 S State, Springfield, IL 62704.

EVERETT, LEN G
Painter
Preferred Media: Oils, Pastels.
b Burlington, Iowa.
Study & Training: State Univ Iowa, BFA & MFA; Art Stud League New York, N Y, with Robert Brackman, Joseph Hirsch & Robert Hale; Nat Acad Design, New York, with Robert Philipp; also with Henry Hensche, Provincetown, Mass.
Work in Public Collections: Washington & Jefferson Col, Washington, Pa.
Exhibitions: One-man show, Mus Conservative Art, Oklahoma City, Okla, 63; Audubon Artists, Nat Acad Design Galleries, New York, 69 & 72; Butler Inst Am Art Midyear Ann, Youngstown, Ohio, 69 & 72; Mainstreams 71, Marietta, Ohio, 71; 32nd Ann Cedar City Nat Invitational Art Exhib, Utah, 72.
Awards: Silvermine Tavern Award for oil painting, 17th Ann New Eng Exhib, 66; Audubon Artists Medal & Cash Award for creative oil painting, 69; second prize in oil painting, 15th Ann Nat Art Round Up, 71.
Bibliography: Ralph Fabri (auth), Medal of merit in Allied Artists Annual, Today's Art, 70.
Memberships: Allied Artists Am; Am Artists Prof League; Hudson Valley Art Asn; Am Vet Soc Artists (v pres, 68-70); Berkshire Art Asn.
Dealers: Talisman Gallery, 115 E 12th St, Bartlesville, OK 74003. Owen Gallery, Inc, 1430 Larimer St, Denver, CO 80202.
Mailing Address: 150 E 27th St, New York, NY 10016.

EVERGOOD, PHILIP
Painter, Graphic Artist
b New York, N Y, Oct 26, 01.
Study & Training: Trinity Hall, Cambridge Univ, 18-20; Slade Sch, Univ London, with Henry Tonks, 20-23; Art Stud League, with George Luks & William Von Schlegell, 23-25; Acad Julian, Paris, France, with Jean Paul Laurens & Andre Lhote, 25.
Work in Public Collections: Encycl Britannica Collection; Pepsi-Cola Collection; Metrop Mus Art; Mus Mod Art; Whitney Mus Am Art; plus others.
Commissions: Murals, Richmond Hill Pub Libr, Long Island, N Y, U S Post Off, Jackson, Ga & Kalamazoo Col.
Exhibitions: Am Exhib, Moscow, 59; Retrospective Exhib, 27-60 & Whitney Mus Am Art Ann, 67; Gallery Mod Art, Huntington Hartford Mus, 67; Art Stud League New York, 67-68; Smithsonian Inst, 68; plus many others.
Teaching: Lectr art & aesthet.
Awards: Gold medal, Pa Acad Fine Arts, 50 & 58; Nat Inst Arts & Lett grant, 56; Ford Found purchase award, 62; plus others.

Bibliography: John I H Baur (auth), Philip Evergood, Praeger, 60; Lloyd Goodrich & John I H Baur (auth), included in: American art of our century, Whitney Mus Am Art, 61; Lucy R Lippard (auth), The graphic work of Philip Evergood. Selected drawings and complete prints, Crown, 66; plus others.
Memberships: An Am Group; Artists Equity Asn; Nat Inst Arts & Lett; hon mem Kappa Pi.
Publications: Auth, Evergood-twenty years of his work, 46; illusr, Short stories of Gogol, 51 & Evergood graphics, 66; illusr, Fortune & Time Mags; contribr, art mags.
Mailing Address: c/o Kennedy Galleries, 20 E 56th St, New York, NY 10022.

EVERSLEY, FREDERICK JOHN
Sculptor
Preferred Media: Multicolored Cast Transparent Plastic.
b Brooklyn, N Y, Aug 28, 41.
Study & Training: Carnegie Inst Technol, BSEE, 63; Inst Allende, San Miguel de Allende, Mex.
Work in Public Collections: Smithsonian Inst, Washington, D C; Whitney Mus Am Art, New York, N Y; Milwaukee Art Ctr, Wis; Oakland Art Mus, Calif; Boyman's Mus Art, Rotterdam, Netherlands.
Commissions: Plastic sculpture, Bayshore Properties, San Francisco, Calif, 70.
Exhibitions: One-man show, 70 & Sculpture Ann, 71, Whitney Mus Am Art; Permutations-Light and Color, Mus Contemp Art, Chicago, Ill, 70; Art & Technology, Los Angeles Co Mus Art, Calif, 71; American Kunst 1950-1970, La Mus Contemp Art, Denmark, 71.
Positions: Tech consult, Art & Technology Exhib, Los Angeles Co Mus Art, 71.
Awards: First purchase prize, Fourth Ann Calif Small Images Exhib, Calif State Col, Los Angeles, 70; Nat Endowment Arts fel, 72; purchase prize, Tenth Ann Southern Calif Exhib, Long Beach Mus, 72.
Bibliography: Henry Seldis (auth), Eversley show in New York, Los Angeles, Times, 6/8/70; Barbara Rose (auth), Black art in America, Art in Am, 9/70; John Canaday (auth), Review of Whitney Sculpture Annual, New York Times, 4/7/71.
Mailing Address: c/o Engineered Aesthetics, 1110 W Washington Blvd, Venice, CA 90291.

EVETT, KENNETH WARNOCK
Painter, Writer
Preferred Media: Watercolors, Oils.
b Loveland, Colo, Dec 1, 13.
Study & Training: Colo State Col, AB; Colo Col, MA; also with Boardman Robinson, George Biddle & Henry V Poor.
Work in Public Collections: Montclair Mus, N Y; Colorado Springs Fine Arts Ctr, Colo; Munson-Williams-Proctor Inst, Utica, N Y; Andrew Dickson White Mus, Cornell Univ, N Y; Univ Ariz.
Commissions: Three murals for rotunda of Nebr State Capitol, 54.
Exhibitions: Pa Acad Fine Arts, 52; Whitney Mus Am Art Ann, 52-54; Metrop Mus Art, 53; Corcoran Gallery Art Biennial, 54; Art Inst Chicago Biennial, 54.
Teaching: Prof art, Cornell Univ, 48-
Positions: Art critic, New Republic.
Awards: Drawing prize, Norfolk Mus, 66; drawing prize, Rochester Mus, 68; purchase prize, Munson-Williams-Proctor Inst, 68.
Publications: Auth, The civilization of Liboros, 72 & auth, The new realism, 72, New Republic.
Dealer: Antoinette Kraushaar Galleries, 1055 Madison Ave, New York, NY 10028.
Mailing Address: 402 Oak Ave, Ithaca, NY 14850.

EWALD, LOUIS
Painter, Designer
Preferred Media: Oils, Mosaic, Gold Leaf.
b Minneapolis, Minn, Dec 19, 91.
Study & Training: Pa Mus & Sch Indust Art.
Commissions: Altar paintings, murals, gilding & color on walls, ceilings & entrance doors in 85 churches, 16-72.
Memberships: Church Archit Guild Am; Nat Soc Mural Painters; Alumni Asn Philadelphia Col Art.
Mailing Address: P O Box 242, Bryn Athyn, PA 19009.

EWING, CHARLES KERMIT
Painter, Educator
b Bentleyville, Pa, May 27, 10.
Study & Training: Carnegie-Mellon Univ, AB & AM; Univ Iowa, with Jean Charlot; Harvard Univ.
Work in Public Collections: Pittsburgh Pub Schs; State College, Pa; Univ Pittsburgh; High Mus Art, Atlanta, Ga; Univ Ga Mus, Athens.
Commissions: Murals, New Johnsonville Steam Plant, Tenn.

Exhibitions: Nat Acad Design; Butler Art Inst; Carnegie Inst; All Artists Philadelphia; Assoc Artists, Pittsburgh, 38-72; plus others.
Teaching: Prof art & head dept, Univ Tenn, Knoxville.
Positions: Former art consult, Tenn Valley Auth.
Awards: Prizes, Assoc Artists, Pittsburgh, 40, 43, 45 & 56 & Mid-Ann, Memphis, Tenn, 63; Mead Co Painting of the Year, Atlanta; plus others.
Memberships: Assoc Artists, Pittsburgh (pres); Artists Asn, Atlanta.
Dealer: Dulin Gallery of Art, 3100 Kingston Pike, Knoxville, TN 37919.
Mailing Address: Topside Rd, Knoxville, TN 37920.

EWING, EDGAR LOUIS
Painter
Preferred Media: Oils.
b Hartington, Nebr, Jan 17, 13.
Study & Training: Art Inst Chicago, grad, 35, Edward L Ryerson fel, 35-36 & also with Boris Anisfeld.
Work in Public Collections: Richmond Mus Fine Arts, Va; Los Angeles Co Mus Art, Calif; Santa Barbara Mus, Calif; De Young Mem Mus, San Francisco, Calif; San Diego Mus, Calif.
Exhibitions: Sao Paulo Mus Art Int, Brazil; Carnegie Mus Int, Pittsburgh, Pa; Art Inst Chicago; Metrop Mus Art, New York, N Y; Pa Acad Fine Arts, Philadelphia; plus many others.
Teaching: Instr painting, Art Inst Chicago, 37-43; prof fine arts, Univ Southern Calif, 46-72; Mellon prof painting, Carnegie Mellon Univ, 68-69.
Awards: Louis Comfort Tiffany grant, 49; Samuel Goldwyn award, Los Angeles Co Mus Art, 57; Floresheim Award, Art Inst Chicago.
Bibliography: Schaad (auth), The realm of contemporary still life painting, 62 & Mugraini (auth), Oil painting-techniques & materials, 69, Van Nostrand.
Memberships: Am Asn Univ Prof; Calif Nat Watercolor Soc (pres); Col Art Asn; Los Angeles Mus Asn.
Publications: Auth, Syllabus for drawing & painting, Univ Southern Calif Press, 66.
Dealer: Esther Bear Gallery, 1125 High Rd, Santa Barbara, CA 93108.
Mailing Address: 4222 Sea View Lane, Los Angeles, CA 90065.

EWING, THOMAS R
Painter, Instructor
Preferred Media: Acrylics, Oils, Plastics.
b Pittsburgh, Pa, Nov 5, 35.
Study & Training: Corcoran Sch Art, 58; Pa Acad Fine Arts, 60-63.
Work in Public Collections: Pa Acad Fine Arts, Philadelphia; Phoenix Art Mus, Ariz.
Exhibitions: 159th, 161st & 163rd Ann Exhib Am Painting & Sculpture, Pa Acad Fine Arts, 64-68; Atlier Chapman Kelly Galleries, Dallas, Tex, 66; one-man show, Makler Gallery, Philadelphia, 69.
Teaching: Instr painting, Pa Acad Fine Arts, 70-; instr painting & life drawing, Philadelphia Mus Art, 72-
Awards: Emily Lowe Competition Award, 66; Lois Comfort Tiffany grant, 72.
Dealers: Marion Locks Gallery, Philadelphia, PA 19104; Atlier Chapman Kelly Galleries, 2526 Fairmount, Dallas, TX 75201.
Mailing Address: 114 Linwood Ave, Ardmore, PA 19003.

EYEN, RICHARD J
Art Dealer, Designer
b Lincoln, Nebr, Mar 24, 30.
Study & Training: Univ Calif, Los Angeles, Univ Cincinnati, BS(design).
Positions: Owner & dir, Environ Gallery, New York, N Y, 63-
Memberships: Artist-Craftsmen Soc New York.
Specialty of Gallery: Contemporary American artists, especially sculptors.
Mailing Address: 205 E 60th St, New York, NY 10022.

F

FABE, ROBERT
Painter, Educator
Preferred Media: Tempera, Watercolors.
b Chicago, Ill, May 24, 17.
Study & Training: Art Acad Cincinnati, cert fine art, 38; Art Stud League New York, Out of Town scholar & with George Grosz, Arnold Blanch & Raphael Soyer, 38-39.

Work in Public Collections: Cincinnati Art Mus, Ohio; Dayton Art Inst, Ohio; Univ Cincinnati; Miami Univ, Oxford, Ohio; Proctor & Gamble, Cincinnati; plus other pub & private collections.
Commissions: Murals, Shrimp Boat Restaurant, Dayton, Otter Bein Press, Dayton & Highland Towers, Marvin Warner Corp, Cincinnati.
Exhibitions: Butler Inst Am Art, Youngstown, Ohio, 40-68; Cincinnati Ann, 40-70 & Laser Art Exhib, 71, Cincinnati Art Mus; one-man shows, Mt St Joseph Col, Cincinnati, 70 & Ohio State Capitol, 71; plus many other group & one-man shows.
Teaching: Assoc prof art, Univ Cincinnati, 58-
Awards: Dayton Art Inst purchase award; Butler Inst Am Art purchase award; Ohio Univ Show award.
Memberships: MacDowell Soc (pres, 70-72); Cincinnati Prof Artists (pres, 70-72).
Mailing Address: 4235 Rose Hill Ave, Cincinnati, OH 45229.

FABRI, RALPH
Painter, Writer
Preferred Media: Acrylic, Oil, Graphics.
b Budapest, Hungary, Apr 23, 94; U S citizen.
Study & Training: Royal State Gymnasium, Budapest, BA; Royal Univ Technol, Budapest; Royal Acad Fine Arts, Budapest, MA; Nat Acad Sch Fine Arts, New York, N Y, sculpture with Robert Aitkin.
Work in Public Collections: Metrop Mus Art, New York; Libr Cong, Washington, D C; Norfolk Mus Art & Sci; Smithsonian Inst, Washington, D C; Mus Fine Arts, Budapest.
Exhibitions: Nat Acad Design, Ann, New York, 42-; Audubon Artists Ann, New York, 44-; Am Watercolor Soc Ann, New York, 63-; Butler Inst Am Art, Youngstown, Ohio, 68-70; 20th Century Hungarian-Born Artists Abroad, Budapest, 70.
Teaching: Instr life, still life, Parsons Sch Design, New York, 47-49; assoc prof painting & art hist, City Univ New York, 51-67; instr painting & drawing, Nat Acad Sch Fine Arts, 64-
Positions: Staff critic, Pictures on Exhibit, New York, 49-61; assoc ed, Today's Art, New York, 61-70, ed, 70-
Awards: Etching prize, Nat Acad Design, 50; medal of hon (watercolor), Painters & Sculptors Soc N J, 64; purchase prize, Butler Inst Am Art, 68.
Memberships: Nat Acad Design (recording secy, 52-55; treas, 61-68); Audubon Artists, Inc (hon life pres, 54-); Nat Soc Painters Casein & Acrylic (hon life pres, 61-); Am Watercolor Soc (historian); Allied Artists Am (v pres).
Publications: Auth, Color, a complete guide for artists, 67; Complete guide to flower painting, 68; History of the American Watercolor Society, 69; Painting cityscapes, 69; Artist's guide to composition, 70.
Mailing Address: 54 W 74 St, New York, NY 10023.

FACCI, DOMENICO (AURELIO)
Sculptor, Instructor
b Hooversville, Pa, Feb 2, 16.
Study & Training: Roerich Acad Arts, 36.
Work in Public Collections: Norfolk Mus Arts & Sci, Va; Fla Southern Col, Lakeland.
Commissions: St Rita (bronze sculpture), comn by Rambusch, St Rita's Church, Long Island City, N Y, 66; St Paul (aluminum sculpture), comn by Rambusch, Fredericksburg, Va, 67; St Vincent de Paul (aluminum sculpture), comn by Rambusch, Guam, 68; St Ann & St Mary (stone sculptures), comn by Rambusch, St Ann's Church, Hagerstown, Md, 69; figures of Martin Luther King, Abraham Lincoln, Mary McLeod Bethune & W Wilberforce, comn by Episcopalian Diocese, St Thomas' Church, New York, 71; also 16 Corbels carved in situ on facade.
Exhibitions: 20th Century Sculpture, Silvermine Guild, New Canaan, Conn; Art: U S A, Coliseum, New York, N Y, 59; First Int Art Exhib, Fla Southern Col; Artists Equity Exhib, Whitney Mus Am Art; Butler Inst Am Art.
Teaching: Vis prof sculpture & stone carving, Fla Southern Col, 52-; instr sculpture & stone carving, Ridgewood Art Sch, N J, 61-65; instr sculpture & stone carving, Craft Stud League, New York, 66-
Positions: Treas, League Present Day Artists, 65-; treas, Sculptors' League, 71-
Awards: Louisa Robins Award, Silvermine Guild, 54; medal of honor, Sculptors & Painters Soc N J, 56; Albert Dorne Prize, Audubon Artists, 56-61.
Bibliography: Domenico Facci, sculptor (film), WEDO-TV, Tampa, Fla, 70.
Memberships: Audubon Artists (exec v pres); Am Soc Contemp Artists (dir); Sculptors League (treas); League of Present Day Artists (treas); fel Nat Sculpture Soc.
Mailing Address: 248 W 14th St, New York, NY 10011.

FAGG, KENNETH (STANLEY)
Art Administrator, Illustrator
Preferred Media: Tempera.
b Chicago, Ill, May 29, 01.
Study & Training: Univ Wis, BA; Art Inst Chicago; Art Stud League New York; Pa Acad Fine Arts; Otis Art Inst, Los Angeles, Calif; also with Harvey Dunn & Joseph Pennell.
Work in Public Collections: Art Inst Chicago, Ill; U S Mil Acad, West Point, N Y; U S Naval Acad, Annapolis, Md; Smithsonian Inst, Washington, D C; Nat Mus Can, Ottawa.
Exhibitions: Am Watercolor Soc, New York, N Y, 52-60.
Teaching: Instr illus, Workshop Sch, New York, 48-49; instr drawing & painting, Chappaqua Adult Sch, 51-54.
Positions: Art dir, advert dept, Fox Films, New York, 30-35; art dir, Kayton Spiero Advert, New York, 35-36; free lance illusr, 36-60; creative dir geophys dept, Rand McNally & Co, 61-
Memberships: Art Stud League New York; Soc Illustrators.
Research: Creator of geo-physical relief globes of the earth, ocean floors & moon.
Publications: Illusr, Holiday, 46, Sat Eve Post, 53, Look, 54-58, Life, 54-70 & Mechanix Illustrated, 55-58.
Mailing Address: Box 76, Chappaqua, NY 10514.

FAHLSTROM, OYVIND
Painter
b São Paulo, Brazil, 28.
Commissions: Organizer & dir intermedia events incl Ur Mellanöl, Fahlström's Hörna, Mod Mus, Stockholm, 64, Kisses Sweeter than Wine, Armory, New York, 66 & Du Gamla Du Fria (feature film), Stockholm, 69-70 (Venice Film Festival, 72).
Exhibitions: D Cordier, Paris, France, 58 & 62; Venice Biennale, 66; Chicago Mus Contemp Art, 67; S Janis, 67, 69 & 71; Mus Arts Décoratifs, Paris, 68; plus many other group & one-man shows.
Bibliography: Fahlstrom, Bonniers Ed, Stockholm, Sweden, 67.
Publications: Auth, Bord (poetry in Swed), 64, Den Helige T Nilsson (novel in Swed), 68 & Om Livskonst (essays in Swed), 70, Bonniers Ed, Stockholm.
Dealer: Janis Gallery, 15 E 57th St, New York, NY 10022.
Mailing Address: 121 Second Ave, New York, NY 10003.

FAILING, FRANCES ELIZABETH
Painter, Educator
Preferred Media: Watercolors, Oils.
b Canisteo, N Y.
Study & Training: Pratt Inst, dipl; Western Reserve Univ, BS; Columbia Univ, MA.
Work in Public Collections: Phoenix Pub Libr Gallery Awards Collection, Ariz; John Herron Art Inst, Indianapolis, Ind; Plymouth Art Club Collection, City Mus, Eng; Washington High Sch Libr, Indianapolis.
Exhibitions: Indiana Artists, John Herron Art Mus, Indianapolis, 33-51; Hoosier Salon, Chicago & Indianapolis, 34-47; Le Salon-148 Expos Beaux Arts, Grand Palais, Paris, France, 35; Int Watercolor Exhib, Art Inst Chicago, 37; Ninth Biennial Int Exhib Watercolors, Brooklyn Mus, 37; plus many one-man shows in mus, galleries & univs.
Teaching: Chmn art dept, Washington High Sch, Indianapolis, Ind, 27-55; exchange instr art, Girls Grammar Sch, Farnham Surrey, Eng, 34-35; exchange instr art, Farmington High Sch, Honolulu, Hawaii, 49-50; asst prof art, Ariz State Univ, 56-63.
Awards: Leidy prize, Nat Asn Women Artists, 37; purchase prize, Ariz State Fair, O'Brien Gallery Art, Scottsdale, Ariz, 56; first premium for watercolor, Maricopa Fair, Ariz, 58.
Bibliography: Society of Women Artists (exhibition), Royal Inst Galleries London, 1/36; Anson B Cutts (auth), Watercolors by Frances Failing, Ariz Rep, 12/30/56; Flora Lauter (auth), Active Indiana artists.
Memberships: Nat Asn Women Artists; Mus Fine Arts, St Petersburg; Plymouth Art Club, Eng.
Mailing Address: 516 12th Ave N E, Apt 7, St Petersburg, FL 33701.

FAIRBANKS, JONATHAN LEO
Art Administrator
b Ann Arbor, Mich, Feb 19, 33.
Study & Training: Brigham Young Univ & Univ Utah, BFA, 53; Univ Pa & Acad Fine Arts, MFA, 57; Univ Del, MA, 61.
Teaching: Teaching fel, Pa Acad Fine Arts, 55-57; adj prof, Boston Univ; lectr, many univs.
Positions: Cur asst, Winterthur Mus, 61-62, asst cur, 62-67, assoc cur, 67-; cur Am decorative arts, Mus Fine Arts, Boston, Mass, 71-
Awards: Winterthur fel, 59-61; mural, Acad Natural Sci.
Memberships: Int Inst Conserv of Hist & Artistic Works; Am Asn Mus; Soc Archit Historians; Washington Region Conserv Guild (adv coun); Victorian Soc in Am (v pres, 69-71); plus others.

Publications: Auth, Benjamin Ferris: a friend of many talents (catalogue), Del Antiques Show, 66; auth, American antiques in the collection of Mr and Mrs Charles L Bybee, Antiques, 12/67 & 1/69; auth, Address to the friends of Wilmington for the 150th anniversary celebration of the building of the meetinghouse at 4th and West Streets, Wilmington, privately publ, 68; auth, Friends of Wilmington, Quaker Hist, spring, 69; auth, The craftsman in early America, Role of Crafts in Educ, Dept Health Educ & Welfare, 6/69; plus others.
Mailing Address: Museum of Fine Arts, Boston, MA 02115.

FAIRCHILD, ISABEL SHELTON
Designer, Painter
Preferred Media: Watercolors.
b Pittsburgh, Pa, Nov 3, 15.
Study & Training: Carnegie-Mellon Univ, BA; Trinity Col, MA.
Work in Public Collections: Cent Conn State Col, New Britain; Carnegie Inst, Pittsburgh.
Commissions: Design of exhibition areas, Children's Mus, Hartford, Conn, 57; diorama design, Roaring Brook Nature Ctr, Canton, Conn, 65.
Exhibitions: Assoc Artists Pittsburgh, Carnegie Mus, 38; New England Invitational, Trinity Col, 67; Conn Acad Fine Arts, Wadsworth Atheneum, 69; Conn Watercolor Soc, New Britain Mus Am Art, 70.
Teaching: Instr design, Pratt Inst, 38-39; instr design, Hartford Art Sch, 44-47; prof art & mus dir, Cent Conn State Col, 64-
Positions: Delineator, Hartford architect firms, 45-60; dir, New Britain Mus, 60-63.
Awards: Oil painting prize, Conn Soc Women Painters, 55; prize for drawing, Conn Acad Fine Arts, 59; Sage-Allen Award, Conn Watercolor Soc, 70.
Memberships: Conn Acad Fine Arts (pres, 71-72); Conn Watercolor Soc (secy, 55-59); Conn Soc Women Painters (secy, 68-70).
Publications: Auth & illusr, weekly art column in New Britain Herald, 61-63; auth, A review of Islamic painting, Muslim World, 70; illusr, Shade swamp, 71.
Dealer: Wiley Gallery, 23 High St, Hartford, CT 06101.
Mailing Address: 2793 Albany Ave, West Hartford, CT 06117.

FAIRWEATHER, SALLY H
Art Dealer
b Chicago, Ill, Sept 29, 17.
Study & Training: Art Stud League New York, 36; Art Inst Chicago, BA 39.
Teaching: Instr life drawing, Katherine Lord Sch, Evanston, Ill, 39-43.
Positions: Dir, Fairweather-Hardin Gallery, Chicago, 47-; dir, Art Dealers Asn Am, 62-63; dir, Found for Arts Scholarships, Chicago, 64-; co-founder, Chicago Art Dealers Asn, 66.
Specialty of Gallery: Modern paintings, graphics and sculpture.
Mailing Address: 101 E Ontario St, Chicago, IL 60611.

FAISON, SAMSON LANE, JR
Museum Director, Educator
b Washington, D C, Nov 16, 07.
Study & Training: Williams Col, BA, 29; Harvard Univ, MA, 30; Princeton Univ, MFA, 32; Williams Col, hon LittD, 71.
Collections Arranged: Traveling & locally generated exhibs, Williams Col Mus Art.
Teaching: From instr to asst prof art, Yale Univ, 32-36; from asst prof to prof art, Williams Col, 36-, chmn dept, 40-69; vis prof, Univ Pa, New York Univ, Columbia Univ, Univ Calif, Berkeley & Harvard Univ, summers; vis res prof, Univ Ga, spring 68.
Positions: Exec secy, Comt on Visual Arts, Harvard Univ, 54-55; dir, Williams Col Mus Art, 48-
Awards: Chevalier, Legion of Honor, Fr Govt, 47; Guggenheim fel, 60-61.
Memberships: Col Art Asn Am (pres, 51-53); Asn Art Mus Dirs; Int Asn Art Critics; Mass Coun Arts & Humanities.
Research: German eighteenth century architecture; nineteenth and twentieth century French and American painting.
Publications: Auth, Barna and Bartolo di Fredi, Art Bull, 36; auth, Dominkus Zimmermann, Mag Art, 52; auth, Manet, Abrams, 53; auth, Guide to art museums of New England, Harcourt Brace Jovanovich, 58; auth, Art tours & detours in New York State, Random, 64.
Mailing Address: Scott Hill Rd, Williamstown, MA 01267.

FALCONIERI, VIRGINIA
Painter, Instructor
Preferred Media: Oils.
b Paterson, N J, Mar 18, 43.
Study & Training: Entwistle Sch Art, Ridgewood, N J, one year; Ridgewood Art Sch, three years.
Commissions: Mural of the universe, Paterson Mus, 64.

Exhibitions: Acad Artists Asn, Mus Fine Arts, Springfield, Mass, 64; Miniature Painters, Sculptors and Gravers Soc, Washington, D C, 71; Catharine Lorillard Wolfe Art Club, Nat Art Club, New York, 71; Allied Artists Am, Nat Acad Galleries, New York, 71; Composers, Authors & Artists Am, New York Chapter, 72.
Teaching: Pvt classes in oil painting, 66-
Positions: Assoc curator art, Paterson Mus, 64-
Awards: Best in Show Gold Medal, Gotham Painters New York, 68; first prize in traditional oils, Bergen Co Park Comn, N J, 70; third prize, Composers, Authors & Artists Am, 72.
Memberships: Assoc mem Allied Artists Am; Catharine Lorillard Wolfe Art Club; Composers, Authors & Artists Am; Miniature Painters, Sculptors & Gravers Soc; Burr Artists.
Mailing Address: 228 Lafayette Ave, Hawthorne, NJ 07506.

FALK, GATHIE
Sculptor, Painter
Preferred Media: Clay.
b Alexander, Man, Jan 31, 28.
Study & Training: Univ B C, art educ.
Work in Public Collections: Vancouver Art Gallery, B C; Faculty Club & Brock Collection, Univ B C; Dept External Affairs Collection, Can; Toronto Dominion Bank Collection.
Commissions: Two ceramic & paint wall murals, Dept External Affairs Bldg, 72.
Exhibitions: Younger Vancouver Sculptors, Univ B C, 68; one-man show, Douglas Gallery, Vancouver, 68; New Vancouver Art, Newport Harbor Art Mus, Univ Calif, Santa Barbara, 69; Works Mostly on Paper, Inst Contemp Art, Boston, 70; two-man show, 29 Pieces, Vancouver Art Gallery, 70.
Awards: Arts bursary, Can Coun, 68, 69 & 71.
Bibliography: Elfleda Wilkinson (auth), Artists of Pacific, Can, Nat Film Bd, 71; Karen Wilkin (auth), Canadian art in the west, Art in America, 5/72; Doris Shodball (auth), Gathie Falk, Arts Can, 6-7/72.
Mailing Address: 2861 W Third Ave, Vancouver, B C, Can.

FALKENSTEIN, CLAIRE
Sculptor
b Coos Bay, Ore.
Study & Training: Univ Calif, Berkeley.
Work in Public Collections: Addison Gallery Am Art, Andover, Mass; Baltimore Mus Art, Md; Boston Mus Fine Arts, Mass; Solomon R Guggenheim Mus, New York, N Y; Los Angeles Mus Art, Calif; plus many others.
Commissions: Floor to ceiling stair railing for Gallery Sapzio, Milan, Italy & for Gallery Stadler, Paris, France; fire-screen for Baron de Rothschild's chateau; fountain, Wilshire Blvd, Los Angeles; plus other fountains, gates & murals for pvt homes, U S & abroad.
Exhibitions: Il Segno Gallery, Rome, Italy, 58; Inst Contemp Art, Boston, 59; Art for Use, Louvre, Paris, 62; Carnegie Inst, Pittsburgh, Pa, 64; Whitney Mus Am Art, New York, 64; plus many other group & one-man shows.
Dealer: Martha Jackson Gallery, 32 E 69th St, New York, NY 10021.
Mailing Address: 719 Ocean Front Walk, Venice, CA 90291.

FALTER, JOHN
Illustrator
b Plattsmouth, Nebr, Feb 28, 10.
Study & Training: Kansas City Art Inst; Art Stud League New York; Grand Cent Sch Art.
Memberships: Soc Illustrators; Artists & Writers Club.
Publications: Illusr, A ribbon and a star, 46; illusr, The horse of another color, 46; contrib, covers to Sat Eve Post.
Mailing Address: 21 Summit St, Philadelphia, PA 19118.

FALZONE, MICHAEL JOSEPH
Painter, Sculptor
Preferred Media: Acrylics, Mixed Media.
b Garwood, N J, Sept. 29, 42.
Study & Training: Santa Barbara Art Inst, BFA, 70; Claremont Grad Sch, MFA, 72; San Francisco Art Inst; Newark Sch Fine & Indust Art.
Work in Public Collections: Long Beach Mus Art, Calif.
Exhibitions: Calif-Hawaii Regional Painting & Sculpture Show, Fine Arts Gallery, San Diego, Calif, 71; Eighth Ann Nat Small Sculpture & Drawing Exhib, Western Wash State Col, Bellingham, 71; San Francisco Art Inst Centennial Exhib, San Francisco Mus Art, Calif, 71; Tenth Ann Southern Calif Exhib, Long Beach Mus Art, 72.
Teaching: Instr drawing, Pasadena City Col, 72-
Awards: Purchase award, Long Beach Mus Art, 72.
Mailing Address: 1729 N San Antonio Ave, Pomona, CA 91767.

FANGOR, VOY
Painter
Preferred Media: Oils.
b Warsaw, Poland, Nov 15, 22; U S citizen.
Study & Training: Warsaw Acad Fine Arts, MFA.
Work in Public Collections: Guggenheim Mus, New York, N Y; Mus
Mod Art, New York; Univ Calif Art Mus, Berkeley; Muzeum
Sztuki, Lodz, Poland; Stedelijk Mus, Amsterdam, Holland.
Exhibitions: The Responsive Eye, Mus Mod Art, 65; 34th Biennale
Venezia, Padiglione Centrale, 68; Guggenheim Mus, 70.
Teaching: Asst prof painting, Warsaw Acad Fine Arts, 53-61; assoc
prof painting, Fairleigh Dickinson Univ, 65.
Bibliography: R C Kennedy (auth), Notes on Fangor, Art Int, 66; Jay
Jacobs (auth), Pertinent and impertinent: illusionist, Art Gallery
Mag, 69; John Canaday (auth), Fangors romantic op, New York
Times, 2/15/70.
Dealer: Galerie Chalette, 9 E 88th St, New York, NY 10028.
Mailing Address: 2 Green Village Rd, Madison, NJ 07940.

FARAGASSO, JACK
Illustrator, Painter
Preferred Media: Oils.
b Brooklyn, N Y, Jan 23, 29.
Study & Training: Art Stud League New York, 48-52, with Frank J
Reilly.
Work in Public Collections: George Washington Carver Mus, Tuske-
gee Inst, Ala.
Exhibitions: Gallery Mod Art, New York, 69; Am Artists Prof
League, 69-71.
Teaching: Instr drawing, painting & illustration & dir, treas &
trustee, Frank Reilly Sch Art, New York, 67-68; instr drawing,
painting & illustration, Art Stud League New York, 68-
Memberships: Art Stud League New York; fel Am Artists Prof
League.
Art Interests: Realistic school of painting, ranging from illustrative
to Surrealistic to Malerische.
Publications: Paperback illustrations for Ballantine, Paperback Lib
& Curtis Pub, 57-; also many covers & book illustrations for
Pocket Bks, Macfadden, Berkeley Bks, Belmont Bks, Lancer,
Pinnacle Bks, Harcourt, Brace Jovanovich & Signet Bks.
Mailing Address: 340 E 55th St, New York, NY 10022.

FARBER, GEORGE W
Collector
b Southbridge, Mass, July 11, 01.
Study & Training: Clark Univ.
Collection: Graphics.
Mailing Address: 138 Newton Ave N, Worcester, MA 01609.

FARBER, MAYA M
Painter
Preferred Media: Oils, Acrylics, Collage.
b Timisoara, Rumania, Jan 24, 36; U S citizen.
Study & Training: Pratt Inst, with Edwin Oppler; Hunter Col; Hans
Hoffman Sch; Art Stud League New York, with Reginald Marsh.
Work in Public Collections: Butler Inst Am Art, Youngstown, Ohio;
Int Tel & Tel, New York; Columbia Mus Art, S C; Ga Mus Art,
Athens; Jacksonville Art Mus, Fla.
Exhibitions: Silvermine Guild Artists Festival, 66; Jamaica Festival
Art, 67; Twilight Park Ann, 69; N Y State Fair, 70; Rochester
Festival Relig Art, 72.
Awards: Second prize, Jamaica Festival Art, 67.
Dealer: Chase Gallery Inc, 31 E 64th St, New York, NY 10021.
Mailing Address: 435 E 52nd St, New York, NY 10022.

FARIAN, BABETTE S
Painter, Designer
Preferred Media: Acrylics, Ink, Graphics.
b New York, N Y, June 6, 16.
Study & Training: New York Sch Fine & Applied Art, two years;
Cooper Union, three years; Art Stud League New York, three
months, with Bridgman; Mus Mod Art, three years, with Donald
Stacy; also with Addison Lamar, Joseph Margulies & Morris
Kantor.
Work in Public Collections: First Unitarian Church, Flushing, N Y;
Tamassee D A R Sch Gallery; also in several pvt collections.
Exhibitions: Am Artists Prof League; Long Island Art League; Burr
Artists; U S Fine Arts Registry; Gotham Painters.
Teaching: Instr color & design, Cooper Union Art Sch, 40-41.
Positions: Textile designer-artist, Krasom Co, New York, 55-57;
free lance designer, 58-59; asst head studio, Manhattan Shirt Co,
New York, 60-64; designer, Hanscom Fabrics.
Awards: Blue ribbon for oils, watercolors & graphics, Martha's
Vineyard Fair, 67 & Blue ribbon for graphics, 68; medal for best
oil, Gotham Painters, 68.

Bibliography: Article, In: Jackson Heights News, 7/18/66; photos of
work, In: Artist Mag, 66.
Memberships: Artist's Equity Asn New York; Burr Artists (cata-
logue chmn); Composers, Authors & Artists Am (jury & hanging
comt); Gotham Painters; Jackson Heights Art Club (asst ed news-
letter, currently former ed & chmn hospitality & mem comts).
Publications: Auth, The pendulum of time and the arts, 68.
Dealer: Celia Gross, South Bay Art Gallery Ltd, 44 S Ocean Ave,
Patchogue, NY 11772.
Mailing Address: 34-48 81st St, Jackson Heights, NY 11372.

FARIS, BRUNEL DE BOST
Painter, Educator
Preferred Media: Collage.
b Oklahoma City, Okla, Aug 9, 37.
Study & Training: Univ Okla, BFA & MFA.
Work in Public Collections: Univ Okla Art Mus, Norman; State of
Okla Collection.
Exhibitions: Mid-Am Ann, Nelson Gallery Art, Kansas City, Mo, 65;
35th Ann Exhib, Springfield Art Mus, 65; 8 State Exhib South-
western Art, Okla Art Ctr, Oklahoma City, 68 & 71; Okla Ann,
Philbrook Art Ctr, Tulsa, 69.
Teaching: Instr art, Tulsa Pub Schs, 61-64; instr art, Okla City Pub
Schs, 65-66; asst prof art & chmn dept, Okla City Univ, 69-
Positions: Art dir, Okla Sci & Arts Found, 66-69.
Memberships: Col Art Asn.
Art Interests: Magnetic elements on steel.
Mailing Address: 1012 N W 39th St, Oklahoma City, OK 73118.

FARNHAM, ALEXANDER
Painter, Writer
Preferred Media: Oils.
b Orange, N J, May 5, 26.
Study & Training: Art Stud League New York, with George Bridge-
man, W C McNulty & Frank Vincent DuMond; also with Van Dear-
ing Perrine & Anne Steel Marsh.
Work in Public Collections: Newark Mus, N J; Nat Arts Club, New
York; Monmouth Col; James A Michener Collection; Harkness
Collection.
Commissions: Naval subjects murals, Naval Repair Base, New Or-
leans, La, 45; portrait of dir, Am Found for the Blind, 50; paint-
ing of off bldg, N J Mfrs Ins Co, Trenton, 69.
Exhibitions: Methods & Materials of the Painter, Montclair Art Mus,
circulated in Can, 54; Nat Acad Design 135th Ann Exhib, New
York, 60; Eastern States Art Exhib, Springfield, Mass, 65-67;
N J Award Artists Exhib, Montclair Art Mus, 66; N J Artists,
Newark Mus Invitational, 68.
Positions: Artist, U S Navy, 45-46.
Awards: Agnes B Noyes Award, Montclair Art Mus, 50; second
award, N J Tercentenary, State of N J, 63; purchase award,
Newark Mus, 68.
Bibliography: Diana Bainbridge (auth), art review & commentaries,
N J Mus & Arts, 6/69.
Memberships: Assoc Artists N J (pres, 72-); Hunterdon Art Ctr.
Publications: Auth & illusr, Tool collectors handbook, 70; auth,
Architectural forms, subjects for the artist's brush, 72.
Dealer: Heritage Arts, 24 First St, South Orange, NJ 07079.
Mailing Address: R D 2, Box 365, Stockton, NJ 08559.

FARNSWORTH, JERRY
Painter, Author
Preferred Media: Oils.
b Dalton, Ga, Dec 31, 95.
Study & Training: Corcoran Art Sch, Washington, D C; also with
C W Hawthorne.
Work in Public Collections: Metrop Mus Art & Whitney Mus Am
Art, New York, N Y; Pa Acad Fine Arts, Philadelphia; Houston
Mus Art, Tex; Toledo Mus Art, Ohio.
Exhibitions: Carnegie Inst Nat & Int Exhibs; American Painting
Today, Metrop Mus Art; San Francisco World's Fair; Century of
Progress, Chicago, Ill; retrospective, Univ Ill, Champaign; plus
others.
Teaching: Instr figure & portrait painting, Farnsworth Sch Art.
Awards: Altman Prize, Thomas Proctor Prize & Maynard Portrait
Prize, Nat Acad Design.
Bibliography: Articles, In: Am Artist Mag.
Memberships: Nat Acad Design (coun mem); Nat Arts Club.
Art Interests: Preparation of archives of American art at Syra-
cuse University and archives of American art, Smithsonian.
Publications: Auth, Painting with Jerry Farnsworth, Learning to
paint in oil & Portrait and figure painting.
Dealer: Frank Oehlschlaeger Galleries, 107 E Oak St, Chicago, IL
60611; 28 S Blvd of Presidents, Sarasota, FL 33578.
Mailing Address: 3482 Flamingo, Sarasota, FL 33581.

FARR, FRED WHITE
Sculptor
Preferred Media: Bronze.
b St Petersburg, Fla, Aug 9, 14.
Study & Training: Portland Art Mus Sch, Ore; Univ Oregon; Art
Stud League New York.
Work in Public Collections: Portland Art Mus; Ball State Univ,
Muncie, Ind; Detroit Inst Art, Mich; Philadelphia Mus Art, Pa;
Krannert Art Mus, Champaign, Ill.
Commissions: Mural, Social Security Bldg, Washington, D C; mural,
S S Argentina.
Exhibitions: One-man shows, Stable Gallery, 54 & 55, Bertha
Schaefer Gallery, 55 & Paul Rosenberg Gallery, New York, 57,
61, 64 & 69; Art: U S A, 59 & 60; also exhibited extensively in
mus throughout U S.
Awards: Prize, Portland Art Mus, 49; silver medal, Port-au-Prince,
50; purchase award, Krannert Art Mus, 59.
Memberships: Am Educ Asn; McDowell Colonists.
Publications: Auth, Jewelry, Collier's New Encycl.
Mailing Address: 463 West St, New York, NY 10014.

FARRELL, PATRIC
Art Administrator, Writer
b New York, N Y, July 22, 07.
Study & Training: Private & independent study.
Collections Arranged: Jack B Yeats Show, Wild Earth, 31; Robert
Flaherty, Man of Aran, 34; Sir William Orpen Mem, 34; Power
O'Malley, 35; Irish Painting, New York World's Fair, 39; Nuala
(Elsa de Brun), Carstairs Gallery, 47; James Joyce/Finnegans
Wake, Lyman Allyn Mus; also arranged exhibitions at other lead-
ing galleries.
Positions: Dir, Irish Theatre, New York, 27-30; dir, Mus Irish Art,
New York, 30-
Research: Visual arts & theatre; Irish art from pre Christian to
present; illuminated manuscripts.
Publications: Auth, Jack B Yeats, 30; auth, Power O'Malley, 34; ed,
James Joyce/Finnegans wake exhibition, 54; ed, Images & illumi-
nations, 60; ed, Kierkegaard's either/or exhibition, 71.
Mailing Address: 161 E 81st St, New York, NY 10028.

FARRELL, STEPHANIE KRAUSS
Art Adminstrator
b Jackson Heights, N Y, Sept 28, 40.
Study & Training: Univ Chicago, BA
Collections Arranged: The Art of George R M Heppenstall, 72.
Positions: Registrar, Carnegie Inst Mus Art, 66-70, asst curator
painting & sculpture, 70-
Awards: Special honors in art, Univ Chicago, 62.
Memberships: Life mem, Art Stud League New York.
Publications: Contrib numerous articles on the collection, Carnegie
Mag, 66-72; auth, The art of George R M Heppenstall (brochure),
72.
Mailing Address: 720 Ivy St, Pittsburgh, PA 15232.

FARRIS, JOSEPH G
Cartoonist, Painter
b Newark, N J, May 30, 24.
Study & Training: Art Stud League New York; Biarritz Univ; Whitney
Sch Art.
Work in Public Collections: Paintings in private collections.
Exhibitions: One-man show, Ward Eggleston Gallery, New York,
N Y.
Awards: Emily Lowe award.
Memberships: Mag Cartoonists Guild.
Art Interests: Advertising cartoons & decorative murals.
Publications: Contribr cartoons to Sat Eve Post, True, Am Legion,
Am Weekly, Ladies Home J, Playboy, This Week, Redbook, Look,
New Yorker, Punch & other nat mag; illusr, Slave boy in Judea;
illusr bk jackets for others; auth & illusr, UFO ho ho.
Mailing Address: Long Meadow Lane, Bethel, CT 06801.

FARRUGGIO, REMO MICHAEL
Painter
b Palermo, Italy, Mar 29, 06.
Study & Training: Nat Acad Design; Educ Allied Indust Art Sch,
with Bogdonov.
Work in Public Collections: Metrop Mus Art; Portland Art Mus,
Ore; Butler Art Inst; Saint Paul Mus Art; Dallas Mus Fine Arts;
also in pvt cols.
Exhibitions: Metrop Mus Art; Whitney Mus Am Art; Va Mus Fine
Arts, Richmond; Detroit Inst Art; Pa Acad Fine Arts; plus
others.
Awards: Prizes, Detroit Inst Art, 46 & Butler Inst Am Art, 56.
Memberships: Artists Equity Asn.
Mailing Address: 47 W 28th St, New York, NY 10001.

FASANO, CLARA
Sculptor
Preferred Media: Terra-cotta, Bronze.
b Castellaneta, Italy; U S citizen.
Study & Training: Cooper Union Art Sch; Art Stud League New
York; also with Prof Arturo Dazzi, Rome, Italy; Acad Julien &
Colarossi Acad, Paris, France.
Work in Public Collections: Metrop Mus Art, New York, N Y; Nat
Collection Fine Arts, Smithsonian Inst, Washington, D C; Norfolk
Mus Arts & Sci, Va.
Commissions: Sculpture for Middleport Post Off, Ohio, Richmond
High Sch, Staten Island, N Y & Tech High Sch, Brooklyn, N Y;
many portraits for pvt comns.
Exhibitions: Whitney Mus Am Art, New York; Metrop Mus Art; Nat
Acad Design, New York; Pa Acad Fine Arts, Philadelphia; Salon
Automne in Paris, London, Rome & others.
Teaching: Instr sculpture, Indus & Fine Arts Sch of New York &
adult educ, Bd Educ, New York, 46-56; instr sculpture, Man-
hattanville Col, 56-66.
Awards: Nat Inst Arts & Lett grant, 52; medal of honor for sculp-
ture, Nat Asn Women Artists, 55; Daniel Chester French Medal,
Nat Acad Design, 65.
Bibliography: Fred Whitaker (auth), Clara Fasano and her terra
cotta, Am Artist Mag, 2/57.
Memberships: Academician, Nat Acad Design; fel Nat Sculpture Soc
(coun, 52, 60-63); Sculptors Guild; Audubon Artists (bd dirs); Nat
Asn Women Artists (adv bd).
Mailing Address: c/o National Academy of Design, 1083 Fifth Ave,
New York, NY 10028.

FASBENDER, WALTER
Museum Director
Positions: Exec dir, Vanderbilt Mus Comn Suffolk Co, Centerport,
N Y.
Mailing Address: Vanderbilt Mus, Little Neck Rd, Centerport, NY
11721.

FASTOVE, AARON (AARON FASTOVSKY)
Painter
Preferred Media: Oils.
b Kiev, Russia, Aug 20, 98; U S citizen.
Work in Public Collections: Nat Gallery Art, Washington, D C.
Exhibitions: Nat Acad Design, 63; Univ Notre Dame, 64; Expos
Intercontinental, Monaco, 66 & 68; Prix de Paris, Raymond Dun-
can Gallery, Paris, France, 67; two one-man shows, New York,
N Y; plus many other group exhibs.
Awards: Munic Art Gallery, 39, spec mention for contribution to
first index of American Design, Metrop Mus Art, 42.
Memberships: Am Fedn Arts.
Publications: Contribr, Art Digest, 50.
Mailing Address: 2720 Bronx Park E, Bronx, NY 10467.

FAUL, ROBERTA HELLER
Writer
b York, Pa, Dec 11, 46.
Study & Training: Wilson Col, 65-67; George Washington Univ, BA
(hons), 69.
Positions: Ed, Mus News, 71-
Mailing Address: 2233 Wisconsin Ave N W, Washington, DC 20007.

FAULCONER, MARY (FULLERTON)
Painter, Designer
Preferred Media: Gouache.
b Pittsburgh, Pa.
Study & Training: Pa Mus Sch Art; also with Alexey Brodovitch.
Work in Public Collections: Mr & Mrs Paul Mellon; Mrs Gilbert
Miller; Mr & Mrs Richard Rheem; Mr & Mrs John Hay Whitney;
Duchess of Windsor; plus many others.
Commissions: Designed stamp, U S Postal Serv, Philatelic Affairs
Div, Washington, D C, 72; two paintings for UNICEF, 72; paintings
for Steubin Glass.
Exhibitions: Alex Iolas Gallery, New York, N Y, 55, 58 & 61; Phila-
delphia Art Alliance, Pa, 62; Bodley Gallery, New York, 64, 66,
69 & 72; Tenn Fine Arts Ctr, Nashville, 67; De Mers Gallery,
Hilton Head, S C, 71-72.
Teaching: Instr advert, Philadelphia Mus Sch Art, 36-40.
Positions: Art dir, Harper's Bazaar Mag, 40; art dir, Mademoiselle
Mag, 45.
Awards: Distinctive merit award, 54, 57 & 61 & silver medal, 58 &
59, Art Dir Club.
Dealer: Bodley Gallery, 787 Madison Ave, New York, NY 10021.
Mailing Address: 303 E 57th St, New York, NY 10022.

FAULKNER, KADY B
Painter, Educator
Preferred Media: Oils, Watercolors.
b Syracuse, N Y, June 23, 01.
Study & Training: Syracuse Univ, BFA, 25, MFA, 36; Art Stud League

New York, with Boardman Robinson; Colo Springs Art Ctr; also with Hans Hofmann & Henry Varnum Poor.
Work in Public Collections: Univ Nebr, Lincoln; Kenosha Pub Mus, Wis; Univ Colo, Boulder; Brigham Young Univ, Provo, Utah; Pa Fine Arts Gallery, Philadelphia.
Commissions: Mural, U S Post Off, Valentine, Nebr; outdoor mosaic mural, Kemper Hall, Kenosha, Wis; altar piece, De Koven Found, Racine, Wis; altar piece, St Mary's Church, Mitchell, Nebr; mural, Union Col, Lincoln, Nebr.
Exhibitions: Nat Asn Women Artists, New York, N Y; Springfield Mo Ann; Norfolk Art Gallery, Va; one-man shows, Kenosha Pub Mus, Wis, 71, Florissant Gallery, St Louis, Mo, 72 & Kemper Hall, Kenosha, 72.
Teaching: Prof art, Univ Nebr, Lincoln, 30-50; vis prof watercolors, Univ Colo, Boulder, summers 34-37; chmn dept fine arts, Kemper Hall, Kenosha, 50-72.
Awards: Award for landscape in oil, Springfield Art Gallery, Mo; In Joy & In Sorrow (oil), Nat Asn Women Artists; The Wall (painting), Univ Wis Gallery.
Memberships: Delta Phi Delta (pres); Kenosha Art Asn (pres, 50-55, mem bd); Racine Art Asn; Kenosha Arts Coun (mem bd).
Dealer: Little Gallery, Wustum Museum, Racine, WI 53404.
Mailing Address: 6018 Third Ave, Kenosha, WI 53140.

FAULKNER, RAY N
Educator, Writer
b Charlevoix, Mich, June 3, 06.
Study & Training: Univ Mich, AB (with distinction), 27; Harvard Univ, MLA, 29; Univ Minn, PhD, 37.
Teaching: Instr to asst prof art & art educ, Univ Minn, Minneapolis, 32-36; prof art & head dept fine arts, Teachers Col, Columbia Univ, 39-46; prof art & archit & head dept, Stanford Univ, 46-71.
Publications: Co-auth, Art today, 1st-5th ed, 41, 49, 56, 63, 69; co-auth, Inside today's home, 1st-3rd ed, 54, 60, 68.
Mailing Address: 765 Frenchman's Rd, Stanford, CA 94305.

FAUNCE, SARAH CUSHING
Museum Curator
b Tulsa, Okla, Aug 19, 29.
Study & Training: Wellesley Col, BA; Washington Univ, MA; Columbia Univ.
Collections Arranged: New Black Artists, 69; Peruvian Colonial Painting, 71.
Teaching: Lectr art theory & criticism, Barnard Col, 64.
Positions: Cur art collections, Columbia Univ, 65-69; exhib consult, Jewish Mus, 68-70; cur painting & sculpture, Brooklyn Mus, 69-
Memberships: Col Art Asn Am; Victorian Soc; Nat Trust for Hist Preserv.
Publications: Auth, criticisms & articles, In: Art News, 62-71.
Mailing Address: The Brooklyn Museum, Eastern Parkway, Brooklyn, NY 11238.

FAUSETT, (WILLIAM) DEAN
Painter, Etcher
b Price, Utah, July 4, 13.
Study & Training: Brigham Young Univ; Art Stud League New York; Nat Inst Archit Educ; Colorado Springs Fine Arts Ctr.
Work in Public Collections: Metrop Mus Art; Mus Mod Art; Whitney Mus Am Art; Toledo Mus Art; New Brit Mus; plus many others.
Commissions: Murals, U S Post Off, Augusta, Ga, Grant's Tomb, N Y, Bldg for Brotherhood, New York, N Y, U S Air Acad, Colorado Springs, Colo & Global Power, USAF, Armed Forces Comn Rm, U S Capitol, Washington, D C; plus many others.
Exhibitions: Seven shows, Whitney Mus Am Art Ann, 32-46; one-man shows, Southern Vt Art Asn, 40-43 & 54-55; Carnegie Inst, 41-46; Univ Utah, 60 & 68; one-man show, Springville Art Mus, Utah, 68; plus many other group & one-man shows.
Awards: Guggenheim fel, 43-45; prize, Nat Soc Mural Painters, 45 & Salmagundi Club, 46; plus others.
Memberships: Nat Soc Mural Painters; Southern Vt Art Asn.
Mailing Address: 1 W 67th St, New York, NY 10023.

FAUSETT, LYNN
Painter
Preferred Media: Oils, Tempera
b Price, Utah, Feb 27, 94.
Study & Training: Brigham Young Univ, 10-12; Univ Utah, 14-16; Art Stud League New York, with Kenneth Hayes Miller, 22-27; Am Sch Fontainebleau, summer 28.
Commissions: Making of A City (mural), city Hall, Price, Utah, 38-40; Organization of 1st Primary, chapel, Church Latter Day Saints, Farmington, Utah, 40; Kennecott Copper Opers, Chrysler Bldg, New York, N Y, 52; Mormon Pioneer Trek, Utah Pioneer Park, Salt Lake City, 60; scenic & hist murals, Harman Cafes, Salt Lake City, 67-68.

Exhibitions: One-man shows, Villita Gallery, San Antonio, Tex, 48, Univ Utah, Salt Lake City, 57, Retrospective, Utah Hist Soc, Salt Lake City, 61, Canyonlands, Old Supreme Ct Chambers, Washington, D C, 62 & West Ala Art Asn, Tuscaloosa, 62.
Positions: Pres, Assoc Utah Artists, 48.
Awards: Meritorious serv award for art dir, Ninth Serv Comd, U S Army, 45; purchase prize, Utah Inst Fine Arts, 47 & 75th Anniversary Exhib, Art Stud League New York, 50; merit hon award, Emer Club, Univ Utah, 72.
Memberships: Art Stud League New York; Nat Soc Mural Painters.
Mailing Address: 1105 Parkway Ave, Salt Lake City, UT 84106.

FAX, ELTON CLAY
Painter, Writer
Preferred Media: Oils.
b Baltimore, Md, Oct 9, 09.
Study & Training: Syracuse Univ Col Fine Arts.
Work in Public Collections: U S Navy & Marine Corps Exhib Ctr, Washington, D C.
Awards: Louis E Seley Naval Art Coop & Liaison Comt award, 72; Coretta Scott King Award, 72; Areana Players Award, 72.
Bibliography: Brawley (auth), The Negro genius, 36; Locke (auth), The Negro in art, 37; Dover (auth), American Negro art, 61.
Memberships: Salmagundi Club (Naval Art Coop & Liaison Comt); Author's Guild Am.
Publications: Auth, West Africa vignettes, 61; auth, Seventeen black artists, 71; auth, Garvey, 72.
Mailing Address: 51-28 30th Ave, Woodside, NY 11377.

FEARING, KELLY
Painter, Educator
Preferred Media: Oils, Acrylics.
b Fordyce, Ark, Oct 18, 18.
Study & Training: La Tech Univ, BA; Columbia Univ, MA.
Work in Public Collections: Dallas Mus Fine Arts, Tex; Fort Worth Art Ctr, Tex; Mus Fine Arts Houston, Tex; Inst Contemp Arts, Boston, Mass; Tex Fine Arts Asn.
Exhibitions: Contemporary Painting & Sculpture, Univ Ill, Urbana, 55, 57 & 63; Carnegie Int, Pittsburgh, Pa, 56; Museum Director's Choice, Colorado Springs Fine Arts Ctr, Colo, 61; one-man show, Witte Mem Mus, San Antonio, Tex, 69; Texas Painting & Sculpture: 20th Century, 71-72.
Teaching: Prof art & educ, Univ Tex, Austin, 47-
Bibliography: Frank H Lyell (auth), Leaves from an artist's notebook (Kelly Fearing), Tex Quart, summer 58; Allen S Weller (auth), The new romanticism, Art in Am, 60; New talent U S A, Art in Am, 62.
Research: Art activities for elementary and secondary school children; art education for elementary teachers.
Publications: Co-auth, Our expanding vision, Benson, 60; illusr, Confabulario & other inventions, Univ Tex Press, 64; co-auth, The creative eye, Benson, Vols I & II, 69; co-auth, Art and the creative teacher, Benson, 71.
Dealer: Valley House Gallery, 6616 Spring Valley Rd, Dallas, TX 75240.
Mailing Address: 1315 W Ninth St, Austin, TX 78703.

FeBLAND, HARRIET
Painter, Sculptor
Preferred Media: Acrylics, Plexiglass.
b New York, N Y.
Study & Training: Art Stud League New York; Am Artists Sch; Pratt Inst; Brooklyn Mus; New York Univ.
Work in Public Collections: Emily Lowe Gallery, Univ Miami, Coral Gables, Fla; Cincinnati Art Mus, Ohio; Tweed Gallery, Univ Minn, Duluth, Minn; Hempstead Bank of Long Island Collection Am Art, N Y; Sealy Co Collection Contemp Art, Chicago, Ill, plus one other.
Exhibitions: Retrospective, Hudson River Mus, 63; Plastics as an Art Form, Newark State Col, 64; L'Ecole Francaise, Mus Mod Art, Paris, France, 70; Int Expos, Alwin Gallery, London, Eng, 70; Women in Art, Brainerd Hall Art Gallery, State Univ N Y Col Potsdam, 72.
Teaching: Mod art lectr, Looking at Modern Painting, New York Univ, 60-62; instr & dir, Advan Painters Workshop, Iona Col Inst Arts, 62-; instr, Westchester Art Workshop, White Plains, 65-72.
Awards: Westchester Art Asn Painting Award, 63; Yonkers Art Asn First Prize, 69; Dea Camhi Mem Award for sculpture, 71.
Bibliography: Benjamin D Allen (auth), Plastics in Art, Rohm & Haas Reporter Mag, 66; Harriet FeBland, Encycl Polymer Sci & Technol, 67; Thelma Newman (auth), Plastics as an art form, Chilton, 67.
Memberships: Artists Equity Asn New York (v pres, 70-, prog dir, 69-72); League Present Day Artists (adv bd, 71-72); Nat Asn Women Artists; Col Art Asn Am; Silvermine Guild Artists.
Mailing Address: Premium Point, New Rochelle, NY 10801.

FEDER, BEN
Designer, Painter
b New York, N Y, Feb 1, 23.
Study & Training: Parsons Sch Design; Vet Ctr, Mus Mod Art, with Prestopino.
Exhibitions: Stamford Mus Art, Conn, 60; Bodley Gallery, N Y, 64; Inst Allende, San Miguel Allende, Mexico City, Mex.
Teaching: Lectr design & typography.
Positions: Designer, major bk publ, U S & abroad; designer, bks & bk jackets; designer & graphic arts consult, New Bk Knowledge, Grolier, Inc; pres, Ben Feder, Inc, New York, N Y.
Memberships: Int Ctr Typographic Arts.
Mailing Address: 50 Rockefeller Plaza, New York, NY 10021.

FEDERE, MARION
Painter, Graphic Artist
Preferred Media: Oils, Woodcuts.
b Vienna, Austria; U S citizen.
Study & Training: Early art educ in Vienna with Frances Haendel; Brooklyn Col, Brooklyn Mus, Beckman scholar, two yrs & Charles Seiden's Workshop, two yrs; Pratt Graphics Ctr.
Work in Public Collections: New York Hilton Gallery, N Y; Skylight Gallery, New York; Butler Inst Am Arts, Ohio; Union Steel Chest Co, Rochester; also in collection of Dr & Mrs Herbert Drobes, Suffern, N Y; plus many others.
Exhibitions: Allied Artists Am, Nat Acad Galleries, New York, 58; Colo-rama, New York Worlds Fair, 64-65; Prospect Park Centennial Invitational, Brooklyn, N Y, 66; Artists Equity of New York Invitation Show & Westchester Art Soc, N Y, 67; Brooklyn Mus Gallery, N Y, 69 & 72; plus many others.
Awards: 19th ann drawing award, Village Art Ctr, 64; Floyd Bennett Field First Prize, First Place Prof Award, 69.
Bibliography: Gordon Brown (auth), article, In: Arts Mag, 3/72; H G L (auth), Federe at Skylight, Park East, 3/16/72; Marion Federe, France-Amerique: Le Courier des Etats Unis, 3/23/72; plus others.
Memberships: Artists Equity Asn New York (treas, Group Three, 68-); Contemp Artists Brooklyn (treas, 69-72).
Dealer: Skylight Gallery, One Union Square W, New York, NY 10003.
Mailing Address: 2277 E 17th St, Brooklyn, NY 11229.

FEHER, JOSEPH
Designer, Painter
Preferred Media: Oils.
b Hungary, Apr 23, 08; U S citizen.
Study & Training: Royal Hungarian Acad Fine Arts, Budapest, Acad Bella Arti, Firenze, Italy; Art Inst Chicago, Ill.
Work in Public Collections: Abbott Labs, Chicago; Nemes Collection, Budapest; Honolulu Acad Arts, Hawaii; United Air Lines Collection, Chicago; Ely Lilly Collection, Indianapolis, Ind.
Commissions: Mural, Across the U S, United Air Lines, 46; watercolor drawings, The Navy in Micronesia-Documentation, U S Navy, 50-51, Hawaii Statehood commemorative postage stamp, U S Govt, 59.
Exhibitions: Int Watercolor Exhib, Chicago Art Inst, 28; invitational one-man show, Univ Ill, Urbana, 45; Hawaii Painters & Sculptors, 48; The Navy in Micronesia, 51 & invitational three-man show, 68, Honolulu Acad Arts.
Teaching: Instr graphic design, Inst Design, Chicago, 45-46; instr painting, drawing & design, Honolulu Acad Arts.
Positions: Artist-historian, Bishop Mus, Honolulu, 55-69; designer publ, Honolulu Acad Arts, 47-, dir art school, 62-, cur prints & drawings, 66.
Awards: Distinctive merit award, 20th Ann New York Art Dirs Show, 41; six medal awards, Chicago Art Dirs Ann, 42-48; award cert, Soc Typographic Arts, Chicago, 46.
Publications: Auth, Tale bearing winds (portfolio), Bishop Mus, 58; illusr, The voyage of the flying bird, Dodd, 65; illusr, Claus Spreckels, Univ Hawaii Press, 67; auth, Hawaii; a pictorial history, Bishop Mus, 69.
Dealer: Downtown Gallery Ltd, 125 Merchant St, Honolulu, HI 96813.
Mailing Address: Honolulu Academy of Arts, Honolulu, HI 96814.

FEHL, PHILIPP P
Painter, Art Historian
Preferred Media: Inks, Watercolors.
b Vienna, Austria, May 9, 20; U S citizen.
Study & Training: Sch Art Inst Chicago; Stanford Univ, BA, MA; Univ Chicago, PhD.
Work in Public Collections: Neue Galerie Joanneum, Graz, Austria.
Exhibitions: One-man shows, Chapel Hill Art Gallery, N C, 69 & 70, Neue Galerie Joanneum, Graz, 71 & Krannert Art Mus, Univ Ill, 71.
Teaching: Prof hist art, Univ N C, Chapel Hill, 63-69; prof hist art, Univ Ill, Urbana-Champaign, 69-
Positions: Art historian-in-residence, Am Acad Rome, Italy, 66-67; assoc, Ctr Advan Study, Univ Ill, 70-71.

Awards: Res fel, Warburg Inst, Univ London, 57-58.
Bibliography: Wilfried Skreiner (auth), Capricci by Philipp Fehl, Neue Galerie, Graz, 71.
Memberships: Col Art Asn Am (bd dirs, 68-71); Renaissance Soc Am; Am Soc Aesthetics & Art Criticism; Southeastern Renaissance Conf; Midwestern Renaissance Conf.
Research: Renaissance art; history of the classical tradition in art; history of art criticism.
Collection: Prints, Renaissance to modern.
Publications: Ed, A course in drawing, Univ Chicago Press, 54; illusr, The bird: a series of capricci, Final Press, 70; auth, The classical monument, New York Univ Press, 72; auth, articles in Art Bull, Burlington Mag, J Warburg & Courtauld Inst, Gazette Beaux Arts & others; illusr, Voyager, Lillabulero & other mags.
Mailing Address: Dept of Art, University of Illinois at Urbana-Champaign, Champaign, IL 61820.

FEIGEN, RICHARD L
Art Dealer, Collector
b Chicago, Ill, Aug 8, 30.
Study & Training: Yale Univ, BA, 52; Harvard Univ, MBA, 54.
Positions: Pres, Richard L Feigen & Co, Inc, 57-
Memberships: Arts Club Chicago; Art Inst Chicago (sponsor); life fel Metrop Mus Art; life fel Minneapolis Soc Fine Arts.
Specialty of Gallery: Paintings, drawings and sculpture, fourteen hundred to the present.
Collection: Old Master paintings; Beckmann, Grosz, Kandinsky, Cornell, Dubuffet; the younger generation.
Publications: Contribr, Arts Mag, 67; auth, Dubuffet & the anti-culture, 69; contribr, Office design, 70; auth, George Grosz: dada drawings, 72.
Mailing Address: 27 E 79th St, New York, NY 10021.

FEIGENBAUM, HARRIET (MRS NEIL CHAMBERLAIN)
Sculptor
Preferred Media: Hay.
b New York, N Y, May 25, 39.
Study & Training: Art Stud League New York; Nat Acad Sch Fine Arts; Columbia Univ.
Work in Public Collections: Andrew Dickson White Mus, Cornell Univ; Colgate Univ Mus.
Exhibitions: Nat Acad Design, New York, 63; one-person show, Ruth White Gallery, New York, 69; two-person show, Fontana Gallery, Philadelphia, Pa, 71; Hundred Acres First Sculpture Ann, New York, 71; one-person show, Warren Benedek Gallery, 72.
Awards: Hallgarten traveling fel, 61.
Memberships: Archit League New York.
Dealer: Warren Benedek Gallery, 380 W Broadway, New York, NY 10012.
Mailing Address: 801 Greenwich St, New York, NY 10014.

FEIGL, DORIS LOUISE
Painter
Preferred Media: Oils.
b Bayonne, N J, Aug 19, 16.
Study & Training: Portrait study with Emily Nichols Hatch, 35-37; Grand Cent Sch Art, 38-40, with Edmund Graecon & Jerry Farnsworth; Art Stud League New York, five years, with Joseph Hirsch, Bruce Dorfman & Sidney Dickenson.
Exhibitions: Bergen Mall Ann, Paramus, N J, 65-72; Bergen Co Artist Guild Ann, Paramus, 66-72; Catharine Lorillard Wolfe Club Ann, Nat Arts Club, New York, N Y, 66-72; Allied Artists Show, Nat Acad Design, New York, 67; Am Artists Prof League Grand Nat, Lever House, New York, 68-71; plus others.
Teaching: Instr painting, Englewood Women's Club, N J, 68-72.
Awards: Best in Show, Bergen Co Artists Guild, 66 & first prize for oil, 69; award for oil, Catharine Lorillard Wolfe Art Club, 70.
Memberships: Bergen Co Artists Guild (secy, 66-68); Am Artists Prof League; Catharine Lorillard Wolfe Art Asn.
Mailing Address: 728 Catalpa Ave, Teaneck, NJ 07666.

FEIN, STANLEY
Painter, Illustrator
Preferred Media: Oils, Inks.
b Brooklyn, N Y, Dec 21, 19.
Study & Training: Parsons Sch Design; N Y Univ.
Work in Public Collections: N Y Univ Collection.
Commissions: Paintings of New York State history, 71 & paintings of the cities of New York State, 72, Bank of New York.
Teaching: Instr design & color, Pratt Inst, 56-58.
Awards: Art Dirs Club N Y, 56-65; Wall St Art Asn, 60; Soc Illustrators, 70 & 71.
Dealer: Phoenix Gallery, 939 Madison Ave, New York, NY 10022.
Mailing Address: 250 Warren St, Brooklyn, NY 11201.

FEININGER, T LUX
Painter, Writer
Preferred Media: Oils, Watercolors.
b Berlin, Ger, June 11, 10; U S citizen.
Study & Training: Bauhaus, Dessau, Ger, 26-32; stage design with Oskar Schlemmer; also with Paul Klee, W Kandinsky & Josef Albers, dipl, 29; Inst Fine Arts, New York Univ, 46-47, with Salmony, Lopez-Rey, Cook & Friedlaender.
Work in Public Collections: Mus Mod Art, New York, N Y; Busch-Reisinger Mus, Harvard Univ, Cambridge, Mass; Fogg Art Mus, Harvard Univ; Altonaer Mus, Hamburg, Ger.
Exhibitions: American Realists & Magic Realists, Mus Mod Art, New York, 43; Revolution & Tradition in Modern American Art, Brooklyn Mus, N Y, 51; Whitney Mus Am Art Ann, New York, 51; Four American Painters, Mass Inst Technol, Cambridge, 54; Retrospective, Busch-Reisinger Mus, 62.
Teaching: Instr design, Sarah Lawrence Col, 50-52; lectr drawing & painting, Harvard Univ, 53-62; instr drawing & painting, Boston Fine Arts Mus Sch, 62-
Awards: Hon mention, Arts & Crafts Club, New Orleans, La, 48; hon mention, Cambridge Art Asn, 63.
Bibliography: Thomas B Hess (auth), Profile, Art News, 2/47; Feininger family, Life Mag, 11/51; E Bitterman (auth), Art in modern architecture, Van Nostrand Reinhold, 52.
Memberships: Cambridge Art Asn; Westport Art Group.
Publications: Auth, The Bauhaus: evolution of an idea, Criticism, summer 60; auth, Lyonel Feininger: city at the edge of the world, Praeger, 65; auth, Address on modern art, Harvard Art Rev, 66; auth, The heritage of Lyonel Feininger, Am-Ger Rev, 66.
Mailing Address: 22 Arlington St, Cambridge, MA 02140.

FEITELSON, LORSER
Painter
b Savannah, Ga, Feb 11, 98.
Work in Public Collections: Mus Mod Art, New York, N Y; Brooklyn Mus, New York; San Francisco Mus, Calif; Los Angeles Co Mus Art; Joseph F Hirshhorn Collection.
Exhibitions: Dada, Surrealism & Fantastic Art, Mus Mod Art, 36-37; Abstract Classicism, Los Angeles Co Mus Art & Inst Contemp Art, London, 59; Geometric Abstraction in America, Whitney Mus Am Art, New York, 62; Whitney Mus Am Art Ann, 65; Retrospective Exhib, Munic Art Gallery, Los Angeles, 72.
Bibliography: Jules Langsner (auth), Permanence & change in the art of Lorser Feitelson, 9/25/63 & Henry Seldis (auth), Lorser Feitelson, 5/20/70, Art Int.
Memberships: Los Angeles Art Asn (chmn bd trustees).
Mailing Address: 8307 W Third St, Los Angeles, CA 90048

FELD, AUGUSTA
Painter, Instructor
Preferred Media: Mixed Media.
b Philadelphia, Pa, Apr 18, 19.
Study & Training: Fleisher Art Mem & Music Settlement Sch, Philadelphia; Philadelphia Col Art, BA; Tyler Sch Fine Arts, Temple Univ; Pa Acad Fine Arts, MA.
Work in Public Collections: Woodmere Art Gallery, Philadelphia; Marple-New Town Libr, Broomall, Pa; Pa Mil Col, Chester; Pa Acad Fine Arts, Philadelphia; permanent collection of Philadelphia Sch Dist.
Commissions: Tree of Life (mural of wood inlays, gold paint & vinyl, with Joseph Brahim), Del Co Community Ctr, Springfield, Pa, 64; dance mural (oil painting), Melita Dance Studio, Philadelphia, 68.
Exhibitions: Woodmere Art Gallery, 61-; Pa Acad Fine Arts, 64-69; Philadelphia Art Alliance Golden Anniversary, 70; Wilmington Soc Fine Arts, Del, 71; Pennsylvania '71, Harrisburg Art Mus, 71.
Teaching: Instr art, Philadelphia, 54-65; instr art, Wallingford Art Ctr, Pa, 63-64; instr art, Haverford, Pa, 63-65.
Positions: Dir art, Hillview-Trout Nursery Sch, Broomall, Pa, 61-
Awards: Van Sciver Award, Woodmere Art Gallery, 62; first prize for oils, Atlantic City Chamber Com, 68; first prize, print exhib, Cheltenham Art Ctr, 71.
Bibliography: Margaret Harold (auth), Prize-winning watercolors, Allied Fla, 63; article, In: La Rev Mod, 64.
Memberships: Artists Equity Asn; Pa Acad Fine Arts; Philadelphia Art Alliance; Community Art Ctr Wallingford; Woodmere Art Gallery.
Mailing Address: 2207 Gilham Rd, Broomall, PA 19008.

FELDMAN, EDMUND BURKE
Art Historian, Art Critic
b Bayonne, N J, May 6, 24.
Study & Training: Newark Sch Fine & Industrial Arts, with John R Grabach & Emile Alexay, 38-41, dipl, 41; Syracuse Univ, BFA, 49; Univ Calif, Los Angeles, with Karl With, Stanton MacDonald Wright & Abraham Kaplan, 50-51, MA(art hist), 51; Columbia Univ, with Lyman Bryson & George Counts, 51-53, EdD, 53.

Teaching: Assoc prof art, Livingston State Col, 53-56; assoc prof painting, sculpture & design, Carnegie-Mellon Univ, 56-60; chmn art div, State Univ N Y Col New Paltz, 60-66; prof art, Ohio State Univ, summer 66; prof art, Univ Ga, 66-
Positions: Cur paintings & sculpture, Newark Mus, 53.
Memberships: Kappa Pi; Col Art Asn Am; Nat Art Educ Asn.
Research: Theory of art criticism.
Publications: Auth, Engaging art in dialogue, Sat Rev, 7/15/67; auth, The critical act, J Aesthetic Educ, 2/67 & Rivista di Estetica, 67; auth, Art as image & idea, 67 & Becoming human through art, 70, Prentice-Hall; auth, Varieties of visual experience, Prentice-Hall & Abrams, 72.
Mailing Address: 140 Chinquapin Pl, Athens, GA 30601.

FELDMAN, HILDA (MRS NEVILLE S DICKINSON)
Painter, Educator
Preferred Media: Watercolors.
b Newark, N J, Nov 22, 99.
Study & Training: Newark Sch Fine & Indust Art, grad; Pratt Inst, alumni class, 5 yrs.
Work in Public Collections: Reading Mus & Art Gallery; Marine Hist Asn, Mystic Seaport, Conn; Ford Motor Co, Detroit, Mich; Seton Hall Univ, South Orange, N J; many in pvt collections.
Exhibitions: Am Watercolor Soc, New York, N Y; Nat Asn Women Artists, New York; Audubon Soc, New York & N J Galleries; plus traveling shows in Can, Holland, Belgium, Japan & Switz.
Teaching: Instr design & watercolor, Newark Sch Fine & Indust Art, 23-72; instr painting, Millburn Adult Sch, N J, 46-63.
Awards: Winsor Newton prize, 55 & B W Hamm prize, 68; Nat Asn Women Artists; plus others from several N J exhibs.
Memberships: Nat Asn Women Artists (chmn watercolor jury & traveling watercolor jury); Am Watercolor Soc; N J Watercolor Soc; Maplewood & South Orange Gallery.
Mailing Address: 507 Richmond Ave, Maplewood, NJ 07040.

FELDMAN, LILIAN
Painter
Preferred Media: Acrylics.
b Brooklyn, N Y, July 8, 16.
Study & Training: Cooper Union; Pratt Inst; also with Harry Shulberg & Harry Sternberg.
Work in Public Collections: Nassau Community Col, Garden City, N Y; Panoras Gallery, New York, N Y.
Commissions: Many murals for private commissions.
Exhibitions: Lever House, 70, New York; Nassau Community Col, 70; Fordham Univ, 71; N Y Sch Technol, Old Westbury, N Y, 72; Land Hall Show, U S Merchant Marine Acad, 72.
Awards: First prize, Art Unlimited Juried Show, 60.
Memberships: Prof Artists Guild Long Island (pres, 71-); Long Island Artists Alliance.
Mailing Address: 214-12 16th Ave, Bayside, NY 11360.

FELDMAN, RONALD
Art Dealer
Positions: Owner & dir, Ronald Feldman Gallery, New York, N Y.
Specialty of Gallery: Contemporary artists; contemporary and modern European and American prints.
Mailing Address: Ronald Feldman Gallery, 33 E 74th St, New York, NY 10021.

FELDMAN, WALTER (SIDNEY)
Painter, Educator
b Lynn, Mass, Mar 23, 25.
Study & Training: Yale Univ Sch Fine Arts, BFA, 50, Sch Design, MFA, 51; also with W de Kooning, Stuart Davis & Josef Albers.
Work in Public Collections: Addison Gallery Am Art, Andover, Mass; Metrop Mus Art, New York, N Y; Fogg Art Mus, Cambridge, Mass; Israel Mus, Jerusalem; Mus Mod Art, New York.
Commissions: Mosaic pavements, Temple Beth-El, Providence, R I, 57; stained glass windows, Sugarman Mem Chapel, Providence, R I, 61; World's Fair poster, IBM Corp, 63; Quezalcoatl (mural), Pembroke Col, Brown Univ, 66; 32 panel mural, Temple Emanu-El, Providence, R I, 68.
Exhibitions: American Watercolors, Drawings and Prints, Metrop Mus Art, 52; Recent Drawings U S A, Mus Mod Art, New York, 55; Mostra Int, Milan, Italy, 57; 26th Biennial, Corcoran Gallery, Washington, D C, 59; Nat Inst Arts & Lett, New York, 61.
Teaching: Instr painting & design, Yale Univ Sch Design, 50-53; prof painting & printmaking, Brown Univ, 53-; vis prof drawing, Harvard Univ, 68.
Awards: Metrop Mus Art Award, 52; gold medal, Mostra Int, Milan, Italy, 57; first painting award, Boston Arts Festival, Mass, 64.
Bibliography: G Y Loveridge (auth), Providence practitioner of ancient art, The Rhode Islander, 4/25/54; Michael Forster (auth), The color of Mexico is black, Nivel 41, German P Garcia (Mexico City), 5/25/62; Jane Shelton (auth), Walter Feldman, Harvard Art Rev, spring 66.

Memberships: Am Color Print Soc.
Dealer: Obelisk Gallery, 470 Parker St, Boston, MA 02116.
Mailing Address: 224 Bowen St, Providence, RI 02906.

FELGUEREZ, MANUEL
Painter, Sculptor
Preferred Media: Oils, Acrylics, Plastics, Metals.
b Zacatecas, Mex, Dec, 1928.
Study & Training: With Ossip Zadkine, Paris.
Work in Public Collections: Mus Arte Mod, Mex, Israel, Tokyo, New Delhi & Bogotá.
Commissions: Spec murals, World Fair Seattle, Mex Govt, 62; mural, Concamin, Mexico City, 64; mural, World Fair Montreal, Mex Govt, 67; mural, Hemisfair San Antonio, Mex Govt, 68; sculpture, Olympic Games, Mex Govt, 68.
Exhibitions: I Bienal Jóvenes, Paris, 59; II Salón Anual de Pintura, Barranquilla, Colombia, 60; VI Bienal Tokyo, 61; VI Bienal São Paulo, 61; I Trienal India, New Delhi, 68.
Teaching: Prof sculpture, Iberoamerican Univ, Mex, 56-62; vis prof sculpture, Cornell Univ, 66; prof format design, Nat Univ Mex, 69-70, dean cols visual invest, 71.
Awards: Segundo premio, II Salón Anual, Barranquilla, 60; segundo premio int, I Trienal India, 68.
Bibliography: L Cardoza (auth), Mexico: pintura activa, Era, Mex, 61; Pintura actual: Mexico 1966, Artes Mex y Mundo, 66; J García Ponce (auth), Nueve pintores Mexicanos, Era, Mex, 68.
Dealer: Galeria Juan Martin, Amberes 17, Mexico City 6, Mex.
Mailing Address: Galeana 37 bis, Mexico City 20, Mex.

FELT, MR & MRS IRVING MITCHELL
Collectors
Collection: Contemporary painting and sculpture.
Mailing Address: 911 Park Ave, New York, NY 10021.

FENCI, RENZO
Sculptor
Preferred Media: Bronze.
b Florence, Italy, Nov 18, 14; U S citizen.
Study & Training: Royal Inst Art, Florence; also with Libero Andriotti & Bruno Innocenti.
Work in Public Collections: Permanent Gallery Mod Art, Florence; Santa Barbara Mus Art, Calif.
Commissions: Entrance at Milan Fair, Italy, 36; nine banks in Los Angeles area, Home Savings & Loan Asn, Calif; Dr Charles Leroy Loman Mem, Orthopedic Hosp, Los Angeles, 68; Stanford Athletic Bd Distinguished Serv Medal, Stanford Univ, 69.
Exhibitions: Art Inst Chicago, Ill, 41; Calif State Fair, 50; Los Angeles Co Mus Art, 55; Nat Exhib Contemp Arts U S, Pomona, Calif, 56; one-man show, Santa Barbara Mus Art, 68.
Teaching: Instr sculpture, Univ Wash, Pullman, 42; asst prof sculpture, Univ Calif, Santa Barbara, 46-54; prof sculpture & head dept, Otis Art Inst, 54-
Awards: Calif State Fair, 47, 49 & 50; Los Angeles Co Mus Art, 55; Santa Barbara Mus Biennial Show.
Bibliography: Bette Howell (auth), Twelve California sculptors, Am Artist Mag, 68; Dialogues in art, produced by KNBC-TV in Los Angeles, in cooperation with Univ Calif, Los Angeles Exten Serv & Los Angeles Co Mus Art, 69.
Mailing Address: 3206 Deronda Dr, Los Angeles, CA 90028.

FENDELL, JONAS J
Educator, Painter
Preferred Media: Plastic Resins.
b Brooklyn, N Y.
Study & Training: New Sch Soc Res; Brooklyn Mus Art Sch; Syracuse Univ, BFA, MFA.
Work in Public Collections: Print collection, Mus Mod Art, New York, N Y; painting, Baltimore Mus Art, Md; print, Syracuse Univ, N Y; print, Univ Maine; IBM Collection.
Exhibitions: Butler Inst Am Art; Provincetown First Nat; Brooklyn Mus Print Show; Baltimore Mus Art; Whitney Mus Am Art; Mus Mod Art.
Teaching: Instr design & materials, Md Inst Col Art, 58-; assoc prof design, printing & painting, Essex Col, 68-
Positions: Designer, Hurdell/Designs, 56-57; asst dir, Syracuse Mus, 57-58.
Awards: Purchase award, Mus Mod Art, New York; purchase prize, Baltimore Mus Art.
Memberships: Col Art Asn Am.
Research: Investigation of commercial and/or industrial adhesives, fastening agents processes and supports useful to the general artist.
Dealer: Ifa Gallery, 2623 Connecticut Ave N W, Washington, DC 20008.
Mailing Address: Maryland Institute College of Art, 1300 Mount Royal Ave, Baltimore, MD 21217.

FENDRICK, BARBARA COOPER
Art Dealer
U S citizen.
Positions: Dir, Fendrick Gallery.
Specialty of Gallery: Graphics, works on paper.
Mailing Address: 3059 M St N W, Washington, DC 20007.

FENICAL, MARLIN E
Painter, Art Administrator
Preferred Media: Watercolors, Oils, Ink.
b Harrisburg, Pa, July 22, 07.
Study & Training: Wellfleet Sch Art; also with Xavier Gonzales & Ben Wolff.
Work in Public Collections: Univ Detroit, Mich; Rehoboth Art League, Del; Munic Ct, Washington, D C.
Exhibitions: Washington Watercolor Asn, 53-71; Rehoboth Art League (invitational & juried), 58-71; Southeastern Exhib, Atlanta, Ga, 60; Va Biennial, Va Mus Fine Arts, 65; Va Beach, Va, 68.
Positions: Chief art dir, U S Army Publs, 47-
Awards: Washington Watercolor Asn award, 53; Rehoboth Art League award, 59, 61 & 70; Am Art League award, 59 & 63.
Bibliography: Beryl Dill Kneen (auth), Artist prepares booklet, Northern Va Sun, 63; Sara Wright (auth), The army's art dir, Fed Times, 67.
Memberships: Washington Arts Club (treas, 63); Arts Club Washington (chmn pictorial photo comn, 72); Soc Washington Artists; Rehoboth Art League & Artists Equity; Washington Watercolor Asn.
Publications: Auth & illusr, A picture tour of historic Harpers Ferry, privately pub, 61.
Mailing Address: 3192 Key Blvd, Arlington, VA 22201.

FENTON, ALAN
Painter, Instructor
Preferred Media: Oils, Liquitex.
b Cleveland, Ohio, July 29, 27.
Study & Training: Pratt Inst, BFA; Art Stud League New York; New Sch Social Res; also pvt study with Adolph Gottlieb & Jack Tworkov; Cleveland Sch Art.
Work in Public Collections: Corcoran Gallery Art, Washington, D C; Pace Gallery, New York, N Y; Baltimore Gallery Art, Md; Ivan Karp Collection & Vincent Melzac Collection.
Exhibitions: Cleveland Mus Art, 59-61; SECA Exhib, San Francisco Mus Art, Calif, 63; Pace Gallery, New York, 65-66; Larry Aldrich Mus, Ridgefield, Conn, 68; Corcoran Gallery Art, 71-72.
Teaching: Instr drawing, Pratt Inst, 69-; instr drawing, Housatonic State Col, 71-
Awards: Jury mention, Cleveland Mus Art, 59; jury mention, City Ctr, New York, 59; first prize, Cleveland Mus Art, 60-61.
Mailing Address: 333 Park Ave S, New York, NY 10010.

FENTON, BEATRICE
Sculptor
Preferred Media: Bronze.
b Philadelphia, Pa, July 12, 87.
Study & Training: Philadelphia Mus Sch Indust Art, Pa, 03-04; Pa Acad Fine Arts, 04-11; Cresson scholars to Europe, 09-10; Moore Inst Art, Sci & Indust, hon DFA, 54.
Commissions: Fountain figure, Brookgreen Gardens, S C; mem tablet, Pratt Libr, Baltimore; mem drinking fountain, Hahnemann Med Col, Philadelphia; mem sun-dial, Rittenhouse Square, Philadelphia; two fish fountains, Fairmount Park, Philadelphia; plus many others.
Exhibitions: Pa Acad Fine Arts, 20-68; Philadelphia Art Alliance, 24-65; Nat Sculpture Soc; DaVinci Alliance, 57; Woodmere Art Gallery, 58-68.
Teaching: Instr sculpture, Moore Inst Art, Sci & Indust, Philadelphia, 42-53.
Awards: DaVinci Alliance Bronze Medal, 54; Violet Oakley Mem Prize, Woodmere Art Gallery, 62; Percy M Owens Mem Award, 67; plus others.
Memberships: Philadelphia Art Alliance; fel Nat Sculpture Soc.
Mailing Address: 621 Westview St, Philadelphia, PA 19119.

FENTON, HOWARD CARTER
Painter
Preferred Media: Acrylics, Oils.
b Toledo, Ohio, July 2, 10.
Study & Training: Chouinard Art Inst; Univ Calif, Los Angeles, BA, MA; also with S McDonald Wright.
Work in Public Collections: Santa Barbara Mus Art Calif; Univ Calif, Santa Barbara Libr; Esther Bear Gallery Santa Barbara; Alwin Gallery, London, Eng; Galleria Piazza di Spagna, Rome, Italy.
Exhibitions: One-man shows, Santa Barbara Mus Art, 64, Esther Bear Gallery, 66, Univ Calif Art Galleries, 67, Galleria Piazza di Spagna, 67 & Alwin Gallery, 68.

Teaching: Prof art, Univ Calif, Santa Barbara, 48-
Bibliography: David Gebhard (auth), Howard Fenton, Haagen Press, 68.
Memberships: Santa Barbara Mus Art; Col Art Asn.
Collection: Contemporary American artists.
Dealer: Esther Bear Gallery, 1125 High Rd, Santa Barbara, CA 93103.
Mailing Address: 1000 Ladera Lane, Santa Barbara, CA 93108.

FENTON, JOHN NATHANIEL
Painter, Etcher
b Mountaindale, N Y, June 29, 12.
Study & Training: Art Stud League New York, with Kenneth Hayes Miller, Allen Lewis & Samuel Adler.
Work in Public Collections: Brooklyn Mus; N Y Pub Libr; Pratt Contemp Print Ctr; Miami Mus Mod Art; Mus Panama; plus others.
Commissions: Ed of prints, Assoc Am Artists.
Exhibitions: Columbus Mus Fine Arts, 58; Butler Inst Am Art, 58; Ill Wesleyan Univ, 58; Art Inst Chicago, 61; Audubon Artists, 61; plus others.
Teaching: Instr art, adult educ, New York Univ; instr, Goddard Col; instr, adult educ prog, Scarsdale High Sch, N Y.
Positions: Creator, film short on Poe's, The black cat, shown theatres throughout U S & invited for showing, Cannes Film Festival, 61.
Awards: Joseph Isador Gold Medal, Nat Acad Design, 58; Hassam Purchase Prize, Am Acad Arts & Lett, 58; award, Pratt Inst, Brooklyn, N Y, 68.
Dealer: Babcock Galleries, 805 Madison Ave, New York, NY 10021.
Mailing Address: 63 Broadview Rd, Woodstock, NY 12498.

FENTON, MICHAEL IRWIN
Painter, Instructor
Preferred Media: Oils.
b New York, N Y, May 22, 42.
Study & Training: Ohio State Univ, BS, with Hoyt Sherman; Cranbrook Acad Art, MFA, with Donald Willett.
Work in Public Collections: Cleveland Mus Art & Canton Art Inst, Ohio.
Exhibitions: Juried exhibs, Butler Inst Am Art, Youngstown, 67 & Cleveland Mus Art, Ohio, 67-69; one-man exhibs, Kent State Univ, 70, Massillon Mus & Cincinnati Mus Art, Ohio, 71.
Teaching: Instr painting, Cooper Sch Art, 67-70; instr drawing, Kent State Univ, 70-71; sr instr painting, Art Acad Cincinnati, 71-
Awards: Spec prize, Akron Art Inst, 69; purchase prize, Canton Art Inst, 69 & third prize, 70.
Bibliography: Elizabeth McClelland (auth), cover article, In: WCLV Radio Publ, Cleveland, 71.
Mailing Address: 3566 Michigan Ave, Cincinnati, OH 45208.

FERBER, HERBERT
Sculptor, Painter
b New York, N Y, Apr 30, 06.
Study & Training: Beaux-Arts Inst Design; City Col New York; Columbia Univ.
Work in Public Collections: Metrop Mus Art, Whitney Mus Am Art & Mus Mod Art, New York; Allbright-Knox Art Gallery, Buffalo, N Y; Detroit Inst Art, Mich; plus others.
Commissions: Copper sculpture, John F Kennedy Off Bldg, Boston, Mass; copper sculpture, Rutgers Univ, N J; environment sculpture, Rutgers Univ; plus others.
Exhibitions: Whitney Mus Am Art; Mus Mod Art, New York; Pa Acad Fine Arts; Boston Mus Fine Arts; Documenta 5, Kassel, Ger; plus others.
Teaching: Vis prof sculpture, Univ Pa, Rutgers Univ & Bennington Col.
Bibliography: Many articles in nat art periodicals.
Mailing Address: 44 MacDougal St, New York, NY 10012.

FERGUSON, CHARLES
Painter, Art Historian
b Fishers Island, N Y, June 30, 18.
Study & Training: Williams Col, AB; Art Stud League New York, painting with Frank Dumond & graphics with Harry Sternberg; Trinity Col, MA.
Work in Public Collections: New Britain Mus Am Art, Conn; Mattatuck Mus, Waterbury, Conn.
Commissions: Stained glass window, Fishers Island, 71; murals, Williston Acad, Easthampton, Mass, Renbrook Sch, West Hartford, Conn & private home, Fishers Island.
Exhibitions: Conn Acad Fine Arts; Conn Watercolor Soc; Greater Hartford Civic Arts Festival.
Collections Arranged: Aaron Draper Shattuck, 70; Robert B Brandegee, 71 & Ken Davies, 71.

Teaching: Instr hist art & studio painting, Trinity Col; instr hist art & studio painting, Loomis Sch.
Positions: Dir, New Britain Mus Am Art, 65-; chmn, New Britain Design Rev Comt.
Awards: Sage Allan Prize, 69; New Britain Herald Prize, 70; Sanford Low Prize, Conn Acad Fine Arts, 71.
Memberships: Conn Acad Fine Arts; Henry L Ferguson Mus, Fishers Island (off).
Mailing Address: 56 Lexington St, New Britain, CT 06052.

FERGUSON, EDWARD ROBERT
Painter, Printmaker
Preferred Media: Oils, Acrylics.
b Pueblo, Colo, Mar 21, 14.
Study & Training: Flint Inst Arts, 33-37.
Work in Public Collections: Flint Inst Arts, Mich; Detroit Inst Arts, Mich; Carter Mus Western Art, Fort Worth, Tex; Hunterdon Co Art Ctr, Clinton, N J; Panama Art Asn, Panama City Auditorium, Fla.
Commissions: Portrait murals, Genessee Co Court House, Flint, Mich, 39-68.
Exhibitions: 18th Nat Exhib Prints, Libr of Cong, Washington, D C, 60; Contemp Graphic Arts Overseas Exhib, Soc Am Graphic Artists, 61; Print Fair, Burr Galleries, New York, N Y & Free Libr Philadelphia, Pa, 62; Northwest Printmakers 35th Int Exhib, Seattle Art Mus & Portland Art Mus, 64; First Ann Exhib Lithography, Fla State Univ, 64.
Awards: Dr Herbert Schiller purchase award, South Bend Art Asn, Ind, 62; Seventh Nat Print Exhib purchase award, Hunterdon Co Art Ctr, 63; 11th Bay Ann Art Show purchase award, Panama Art Asn, 72.
Mailing Address: 1618 Carolina Ave, Lynn Haven, FL 32444.

FERGUSON, THOMAS REED
Painter, Educator
b Lancaster County, Pa, May 11, 15.
Study & Training: Pa State Univ, BS; Univ Pa; Harvard Univ; also with Charles W Dawson & Hobson Pittman.
Exhibitions: Lehigh Univ, 45; Lehigh Co Art Asn, 45; Pa State Univ Summer Exhib.
Teaching: Asst prof art, Pa State Univ, 46-
Positions: Dir univ rels, Pa State Univ, 58-69, v pres pub affairs, 69-
Mailing Address: 304 Old Main, Pennsylvania State University, University Park, PA 16802.

FERIOLA, JAMES PHILIP
Painter, Art Administrator
Preferred Media: Watercolors.
b Great Notch, N J, July 4, 25.
Study & Training: Phoenix Sch Design, New York, grad.
Work in Public Collections: Nassau Co Mus, Syosset, N Y; R Peerman Corp & H Butt Corp, Corpus Christi, Tex; Country Art Gallery, Locust Valley, N Y.
Exhibitions: Smithsonian Inst, Washington, D C; Nat Acad Design, New York; World's Fair Fine Arts Pavilion, New York; Hammond Mus; Prince Rainier III Palace, Monaco.
Teaching: Instr watercolor, Baldwin Art Ctr, N Y.
Positions: Supvr art & exhib dept, Nassau Co Mus, presently.
Awards: Gold Medal of Honor, Smithsonian Inst; travel grant to Europe, Greenwich Village Art Show; Silver Medal Hon, Am Vet Soc Artists.
Bibliography: Famous People of Hempstead, N Y (film).
Memberships: Am Watercolor Soc; Hudson Valley Artists; Am Artists Prof League; Am Vet Soc Artists; Art League of Nassau Co.
Publications: Illusr, Of plates and purlins; illusr, A rural heritage for today.
Mailing Address: 226 Perry St, Hempstead, NY 11550.

FERN, ALAN MAXWELL
Art Historian, Art Administrator
b Detroit, Mich, Oct 19, 30.
Study & Training: Univ Chicago, AB, 50, MA, 54, PhD, 60; Courtauld Inst, Univ London, res scholar.
Collections Arranged: Diverse print, poster & photo shows, Libr Cong, 62-; Leonard Baskin, Nat Collection Fine Arts, Smithsonian Inst, 70.
Teaching: From asst to instr to asst prof, The Col, Univ Chicago, 52-61.
Positions: From asst cur to cur to asst chief, Prints & Photographs Div, Libr Cong, 61-
Awards: Fulbright fel, 54-55.
Memberships: Print Coun Am (dir, 63-, pres, 69-71); Col Art Asn Am; Am Inst Graphic Arts (dir, 68-71); Spec Libr Asn; Grolier Club.

Research: History of prints, posters, book design, nineteenth and twentieth century art.
Publications: Auth, A note on the Eragny Press, Cambridge Univ Press, 57; co-auth, Art nouveau, Mus Mod Art, New York, 60; co-auth, Word and image, Mus Mod Art, New York, 69; auth, Leonard Baskin, Smithsonian Press, 70; contribr, Edward Johnston, In: Heritage of the graphic arts, Bowker, 72.
Mailing Address: Prints & Photographs Division, Library of Congress, Washington, D C, 20540.

FERNANDEZ-YANEZ, ALVARO
Painter
b Arg.
Study & Training: Univ Buenos Aires, archit degree.
Work in Public Collections: Many pvt collections in Arg, Brazil, Uruguay, U S A, Spain, Sweden, Syria, Switz, Austria, France & Italy.
Exhibitions: Bacardi Gallery, Miami, Fla; Galeria Fortuny, Madrid, Spain; Jockey Club, Miami, 70; Art Show Extraordinaire, Palm Bay Club, Miami, 70; Fourth Ann Pan-Am Art Exhib, Miami, 72; Mus Mod Art, Miami, 72; plus many other group & one-man shows.
Dealer: Bay Harbor Galleries Art Gallery, 1007 Kane Concourse, Bay Harbor Island, Miami, FL 33154.
Mailing Address: 800 West Ave, Penthouse 46, Miami Beach, FL 33139.

FERNIE, JOHN CHIPMAN
Sculptor, Instructor
Preferred Media: Wood, Paper, Cardboard.
b Hutchinson, Kans, Oct 22, 45.
Study & Training: Colo Col, 63-65; Kans City Art Inst, BFA, 68; Univ Calif, Davis, grant, 69, teaching fel & MFA, 70.
Exhibitions: One-man shows, Worth Ryder Gallery, Univ Calif, Berkeley, 70, Reese Palley Gallery, 70 & 72, & Sacramento State Col, 72; group shows, Young Bay Area Sculptors, San Francisco Art Inst, 70 & Documenta 5, Kasel, Ger, 72.
Teaching: Asst, Univ Calif, Davis, 69; instr sculpture, Calif Col Arts & Crafts, 70-72; instr sculpture, Stephens Col, 72-
Bibliography: Richardson (auth), article, In: Arts Mag, 2/71; Albright (auth), Exciting, compelling show, San Francisco Chronicle, 7/1/71.
Publications: Auth, Petit trianon, twikkel, I worship you, God bless your symmetry, 70; auth, Masters survey, 70.
Dealer: Reese Palley Gallery, 550 Sutter St, San Francisco, CA 94102 & 19 Prince St, New York, NY 10012.
Mailing Address: Stephens College, Columbia, MO 65203.

FERRARA, FRANK VINCENT
Sculptor, Painter
Preferred Media: Marble, Bronze, Terra-cotta, Oils.
b New York, N Y, Oct 8, 19.
Study & Training: Greenwich House Workshop; Leonardo da Vinci Art Sch; Cooper Union; Scuola Belle Arte, Florence, Italy; also with Victor Salvatore, Attillio Piccirilli, James E Frazer & Frederick Mac Monies.
Commissions: Bronze horse, 38 & Fenimore Cooper Statue, Fine Arts Proj, City New York; Robert E Lee (bronze bust), Mr Marwall, New York, 63.
Exhibitions: Nat Acad Design, New York, 37; Grand Cent Art Gallery, 39; Viaegi Gallery, Rome, Italy, 48; Loeb Ctr, New York Univ, 58.
Teaching: Art specialist sculpture & tech adv painting & drawing, Dept Cult Affairs, City of New York, 72.
Awards: Bronze medal (first prize), Fiorella La Guardia, 34.
Memberships: Nat Sculpture Soc.
Collection: Contemporary sculpture.
Mailing Address: 1903 Edenwald Ave, Bronx, NY 10466.

FERRIS, EDYTHE
Painter, Graphic Artist
Preferred Media: Oil.
b Riverton, N J, June 21, 97.
Study & Training: Philadelphia Sch Design for Women, dipl.
Work in Public Collections: Free Libr Philadelphia, Pa; Philadelphia Mus Art; Archive Collection, Can Painters & Etchers, Toronto Mus; Randolph-Macon Woman's Col, Lynchburg, Va; Philadelphia Art Alliance.
Exhibitions: Drawings USA, Minneapolis, Minn, 63; Norfolk Drawing Biennial, Va, 64; Artists Equity Asn Mem, Civic Ctr, Philadelphia, 68 & 71; Fibonocci Exhib, Art Alliance, Philadelphia, 72; Am Color Print Soc Ann, Philadelphia Art Alliance, 72.
Collections Arranged, 78 exhibs of living artists of German origin or ancestry in Old Customs House for Carl Schurz Asn, 53-64; 20 traveling exhibs of original prints, German Expressionists, with notes & catalogue, 57-67.

Teaching: Dir crafts, adult educ, Cent YWCA, Philadelphia, 34-38; dir crafts, Fletcher Farm, Proctorsville, Vt, summers 34, 35 & 36; instr crafts, Montgomery Co Day Sch, Wynnewood, Pa, 42-49; lectr art appreciation, Junto, Philadelphia, Pa, 50-54.
Positions: Art adv, Nat Carl Schurz Asn, 53-67.
Awards: J Lessing Rosenwald Prize for woodcut, Print Club, 55; hon mention, Am Automobile Asn, 70.
Bibliography: Bet Jones (auth), Two bird pictures, Randolph Macon Woman's Col, 68, Janet Mowery (auth), The birds of Edythe Ferris and Morris Graves, 69.
Memberships: Am Color Print Soc (pres, 50-51); Artists Equity Asn; Moore Col Art Alumnae; Univ City Arts League (founder, 65).
Publications: Contrib, American German Review, various years during 50's.
Dealer: Sidney Rothman—The Gallery, Barnegat Light, NJ 08006.
Mailing Address: 240 S 45th St, Philadelphia, PA 19104.

FERRIS, (CARLISLE) KEITH
Illustrator, Painter
b Honolulu, Hawaii, May 14, 29.
Study & Training: Tex A&M Col; George Washington Univ; Corcoran Sch Art.
Commissions: Ser of paintings, Pratt & Whitney Aircraft, Chandler Evans Div, Colt Industs, Repub Aviation Div, Fairchild Industs, Gen Dynamics & Sperry Rand Corp; plus many others.
Exhibitions: USAF Exhib, N Y Soc Illusr, 61-69; N Y World's Fair, 64; USAF Hq, The Pentagon, Washington, D C; one-man shows, Aerospace Hall, Nat Air & Space Mus, Smithsonian Inst, Washington, D C, 69-70 & Soc Illusr N Y, 70.
Positions: Ed & advert art, Aviation Wk & Space Technol, Flying, Popular Aviation & Air Progress; chmn, Air Force Art Comt, Soc Illusr, 68-70.
Awards: Citation of merit, Soc Illusr, 66.
Memberships: N Y Soc Illusr.
Art Interests: Aviation/aerospace art.
Mailing Address: 50 Moraine Rd, Morris Plains, NJ 07950.

FERRITER, CLARE
Painter, Instructor
Preferred Media: Oils.
b Dickinson, N Dak, June 18, 13.
Study & Training: Mass Col Art, Boston; Yale Univ, BFA; Stanford Univ, MA.
Work in Public Collections: Butler Inst Am Art, Youngstown, Ohio; Univ Del, Newark; George Washington Univ, Washington, D C; Massillon Mus, Ohio; Addison Gallery Am Art, Andover, Mass.
Commissions: Portrait of Miss H D Lamont, commissioned by Class of 1909 for Westover Sch, Middlebury, Conn, 59.
Exhibitions: One-man shows, Univ P R Mus, 62 & Corcoran Gallery Art, Washington, D C, 63; regional invitationals, Delaware Art Ctr, Wilmington, 66, Baltimore Mus, Md, 68 & Univ Del, Newark, 71.
Teaching: Instr art, MacMurray Col, 36-38; instr art, Westover Sch, 40-42; lectr painting, Catholic Univ Am, 66-
Awards: Nat Asn Women Artists, 63 & 66; Baltimore Mus, 66; Soc Washington Artists, 64, 66 & 72.
Memberships: Nat Asn Women Artists; Washington Watercolor Asn; Soc Washington Artists (v pres, 62-63) Artists Equity Asn (chap pres, 67-69).
Publications: Illusr, Manila lights & shadows (weekly page), Manila Sunday Tribune Mag, 10/4/31-8/32; illusr, covers, In: Philippine Mag, 9/32-2/33.
Dealer: Franz Bader Gallery, 2124 Pennsylvania Ave, Washington, DC 20037.
Mailing Address: 4722 Rodman St N W, Washington, DC 20016.

FERRO, WALTER
Graphic Artist
Preferred Media: Wood.
b Brooklyn, N Y.
Study & Training: Art Stud League New York, 46-48; Brooklyn Mus Art Sch, color theory with John Ferren, 48-52.
Work in Public Collections: Permanent print collection, Metrop Mus Art, New York, N Y.
Exhibitions: Audubon Artists, 53; Am Inst Graphic Artists, 56 & Soc Am Graphic Artists, New York, 59; United Nations Traveling Exhib, 66; one-man show, Kings Col, Briarcliff, N Y, 67.
Awards: Kenneth Hays Miller Mem Prize, Audubon Artists, 53; Kate W Arms Mem Award, Soc Am Graphic Artists, 59; Guggenheim fel, 72.
Bibliography: Norman Kent (auth), The woodcuts of Walter Ferro, Am Artist Mag, 1/62.
Publications: Illusr, The best of two worlds, Morrow, 53; illusr, Beowulf, Random, 62; illusr, Hold April, McGraw, 62; illusr, U N calendar, U N, 66; illusr, The invisible pyramid, Scribner, 70.
Mailing Address: R D 2, Salem Rd, Pound Ridge, NY 10576.

FESSLER, MARY THOMASITA, see SISTER THOMASITA.

FFRENCH (PHYLLIS MARJORIE LINNELL-FFRENCH)
Painter
Preferred Media: Oils, Watercolors, Pencils, Inks, Crayons.
b Melbourne, Australia, June 16, 21; U S citizen.
Study & Training: With Caroline Weir, Melbourne; Melbourne Nat
   Gallery; with Sir John Langstaff, Melbourne; with Dr George
   Wang Wu, Shanghai, China; with Max Meldrum, Melbourne; Cor-
   coran Gallery Art, Washington, D C.
Work in Public Collections: Yellow Roses (painting), Hornsby Col,
   N S W, Australia; Easter Lily (painting), Rosenberg Found & Mus,
   Philadelphia, Pa.
Commissions: Mrs Helen Caskin (portrait in oils), Philadelphia, 47;
   Col George Donnelly (portrait in oils), New York, N Y, 48; two
   portraits in oil of Dr Mary Roos Podea & Charles Roos, Jr, New
   York, 49; Prince Siradje Ali ed Din (portrait in oils), Algiers,
   Algeria, 53; Kenneth Huebner (portrait in oils), New York, 64.
Exhibitions: One-man shows, Proud's, Sydney, Australia, 44, Mc-
   Clees, Philadelphia, 45, Galerie de Bennecaze, Algiers, 53, Grife
   y Escoda, Barcelona, Spain, 54 & Solo Retrospective, Church of
   St Vincent Ferrer, New York, 69.
Teaching: Instr art, pvt classes, 43-53.
Awards: First prize for Fuschia (pastels), Canterbury Hort Soc, 29;
   first prize for Gladioli (watercolor), Caroline Weir, 32.
Bibliography: Carol Wharten (auth), Perceptual painting, Baltimore
   Sun, 47; R Rostagny (auth), Mme Phyllis Linnell-Ffrench,
   Derniere Heure, Algiers, France, 54; M Irurozqui (auth), Phyllis
   M Linnell-Ffrench, La Prensa, Spain, 54.
Memberships: Burr Artists.
Mailing Address: 118 W 57th St, New York, NY 10019.

FIERO, EMILIE L
Sculptor
Preferred Media: Bronze, Marble.
b Joliet, Ill, Jan 16, 89.
Study & Training: Art Inst Chicago; also in Florence, Italy &
   Paris, France.
Work in Public Collections: Blue Heron Fountains (bronze), Fine
   Arts Garden, Cleveland Mus Art, Ohio.
Commissions: St Francis Fountain (bronze), Stevenson, Md; Trip-
   tych, Calvary Episcopal Church, Gramercy Park, New York,
   N Y.
Exhibitions: Metrop Mus Art, Nat Acad Design & Nat Sculpture Soc,
   New York; Pa Acad Fine Arts, Philadelphia; Art Inst Chicago,
   Ill.
Awards: Wheeler Williams Award for The Cock (bronze), Am
   Artists Prof League Exhib, Smithsonian Inst, Washington, D C.
Memberships: Nat Sculpture Soc; Allied Artists Am; Am Artists
   Prof League.
Mailing Address: 4701 Sheboygan Ave, Madison, WI 53705.

FIFE, MARY
Painter
Preferred Media: Oils.
b Canton, Ohio.
Study & Training: Carnegie Inst Technol, BA; Cooper Union; Acad
   Russe, Paris, France; Art Stud League New York.
Exhibitions: One-man shows, Pen & Brush Inc, New York & Brook-
   lyn Art Gallery, N Y; group shows, Metrop Mus Art, New York,
   Whitney Mus Am Art, New York & Art Inst Chicago, Ill; plus
   others.
Teaching: Instr drawing, Kansas City Art Inst, Mo, 45-50; head
   dept art, Birch-Wathem Sch, New York, 61-70.
Awards: Figure prize, Nat Acad Design, 67; Pen & Brush Prize, 69;
   Elizabeth McGenius Award, 70.
Memberships: Pen & Brush Inc (mem bd); Nat Asn Women Artists
   (mem bd).
Dealer: Brooklyn Art Gallery, 1358 Flatbush Ave, Brooklyn, NY
   11210.
Mailing Address: 82 State St, Brooklyn, NY 11201.

FILIPOVIC, AUGUSTIN
Sculptor, Painter
Preferred Media: Bronze.
b Davor, Yugoslavia, Jan 8, 31; Can citizen.
Work in Public Collections: Art Gallery Ont, Toronto; Fort William
   Libr, Ont; Palazzo Braschi, Rome, Italy; The Inn on the Park,
   Toronto, Ont.
Commissions: Cardinal Stepinac (bronze bust), 60 & fiberglass cru-
   cifiction, 66, Our Lady of Croatia Church, Toronto; Spirit of the
   Dance (cement), Colonial Tavern, Toronto, 60; reclining figure
   (bronze), Parkin & Assocs for Don Mills Post Off, 69.
Exhibitions: Mostra Arte Lazio, Rome, Italy, 55; Nat Gallery Art,
   Ottawa, Ont, 62; Gallery Moos, Toronto, 67; Gallery Agnes Le-
   fort, Montreal, P Q, 68; Bertha Schaefer Gallery, New York,
   N Y, 71.

Teaching: Resident sculptor, Univ Toronto Sch Archit, 62.
Awards: Second prize, Mostra Arte Lazio, Rome, 52; prize of the
   mayor of Rome, via Margutta, Rome, 58; prize in centennial
   competition, Niagara Falls, 66.
Memberships: Sculpture Soc Can.
Dealer: Gallery Moos, Toronto 5, Ont, Can.
Mailing Address: 585 Markham St, Toronto 4, Ont, Can.

FILIPOWSKI, RICHARD E
Sculptor, Educator
Preferred Media: Bronze, Brass, Silver, Steel, Aluminum.
b Poland, May 29, 23; U S citizen.
Study & Training: Inst Design, Ill Inst Technol, BA, with L
   Moholy-Nagy.
Work in Public Collections: Addison Gallery Am Art, Andover, Mass
   State St Bank & Trust Co, Boston, Mass; Boston Safe Deposit &
   Trust Co; Chase Manhattan Bank, New York, N Y; First Nat Bank,
   Boston.
Commissions: Sculptural ark, Temple B'rith Kodesh, Rochester,
   N Y, 62; sculptural cross, Trinity Lutheran, Chelmsford, Mass,
   63; sculpture, Atlantic, Sheraton Corp, Prudential Ctr, Boston,
   64; sculptural cross, Trinity Evangelical Lutheran, Philadelphia,
   65; sculpture, Echo, Revere Copper & Brass Corp, New York, 65.
Exhibitions: Art for U S Embassies, Inst Contemp Art, Boston, 66;
   Nat Exhib Art, Ogunquit, Maine, 67; one-man shows, Fitchburg
   Art Mus, Mass, 68 & State Univ N Y Col Oneonta, N Y, 69; Out-
   door Sculpture Exhib, De Cordova Mus, Lincoln, Mass, 72.
Teaching: Assoc prof, Mass Inst Technol, 53-
Awards: First prize for sculpture, Boston Arts Festival, 58; Aleck
   & Ruth McLean Award, Nat Exhib Art, Ogunquit, 67.
Bibliography: Katherine Kuh (auth), Abstract & surrealist American
   art, Art Inst Chicago, 48; Patricia Boyd Wilson (auth), The home
   forum, Christian Sci Monitor, 65; Phoebe Cutler (auth), Richard
   Filipowski's sculpture, Harvard Art Rev, 67.
Dealer: Joan Peterson Gallery, 561 Boylston St, Boston, MA 02130.
Mailing Address: 10 Round Hill Rd, Lexington, MA 02173.

FILKOSKY, JOSEFA
Sculptor, Educator
Preferred Media: Aluminum, Plexiglas.
b Westmoreland City, Pa, June 15, 33.
Study & Training: Seton Hill Col, BA, 55; Carnegie-Mellon Univ,
   BFA, 63; Cranbrook Acad Art, MFA, 68; Art Inst Chicago, sum-
   mer sculpture sem, 68.
Work in Public Collections: Pipe Dream IV, Gateway Ctr, City of
   Pittsburgh, Pa; Pipe Dream V, Hudson River Mus, Yonkers, N Y;
   Red-Winged, Alcoa Collection, Merwin Tech Ctr, Pittsburgh;
   Pipe Dream VIII, Harlan Corp, Southfield, Mich.
Commissions: Pipe Dream IX, Taubman Corp, Southfield.
Exhibitions: Young Americans 1962, Mus Contemp Art, N Y, 62,
   plus two years travel exhib; one-man shows, The Art Image In
   All Media, N Y, 70, Ind Univ, 72 & Bertha Schaefer Gallery,
   New York, N Y, 73; two-man show, Pittsburgh Plan For Art, 71;
   Contemp Sculpture Invitational, Vassar Col, 71.
Teaching: Assoc prof art & chmn dept, Seton Hill Col, 56-
Positions: Design consult, Guild Hall Studios, Paramus, N J, 70-
Awards: Three Rivers Purchase Award, 72.
Bibliography: Donald Miller (auth), Sister Josefa's Pipe Dreams,
   Art Int, 12/71; Suzanne Vlamis (auth), Pipe Dream Nun, M D Mag,
   5/72.
Memberships: Assoc Artists Pittsburgh; Pittsburgh Plan for Art.
Dealers: Bertha Schaefer Gallery, 41 E 57th St, New York, NY
   10022; Dorothea Silverman, 500 E 83rd St, New York, NY 10028.
Mailing Address: Seton Hill College, Greensburg, PA 15601.

FILLMAN, JESSE R
Collector
b Pittsburgh, Pa, May 5, 05.
Study & Training: Amherst Col, BA; Columbia Univ, LLB.
Collection: Mostly American paintings and sculpture.
Mailing Address: 28 State St, Boston, MA 02109.

FILMUS, TULLY
Painter, Lecturer
Preferred Media: Oil.
b Otaki, Russia, Aug 29, 08; U S citizen.
Study & Training: Pa Acad Fine Arts, Philadelphia; New York Univ,
   N Y; Barnes Found, Philadelphia; Arts Stud League, New York;
   Crisson traveling scholar for study in Paris & Rome.
Work in Public Collections: Metrop Mus Art, New York; Whitney
   Mus Am Art, New York; Joslyn Art Mus, Omaha, Nebr; Syracuse
   Univ Mus, N Y; Canton Art Inst, Ohio.
Exhibitions: Whitney Mus Am, Art, 40-46; Art Inst Chicago, Ill, 41;
   Carnegie Inst, Pittsburgh, Pa, 41-46; Pa Acad Fine Arts, Phila-
   delphia, Pa, 41-46; Corcoran Gallery Art, Washington, D C, 42.
Teaching: Instr painting & drawing, Am Artist Sch, New York, 36-
   38 & Cooper Union Art Sch, New York, 38-50.

Awards: Fellowship prize, Pa Acad Fine Arts, 48; Salmagundi prize, Audubon Artists, 69.
Bibliography: Dr Alfred Werner (auth), The painter Tully Filmus, World Publs, 63; Tully Filmus—selected drawings, Jewish Publ, 71.
Memberships: Artist Equity Asn N Y; Audubon Artists; Art Comn Nassau Co, N Y.
Dealer: A C A Gallery, 25 E 73rd St, New York, NY 10021.
Mailing Address: 17 Stuart St, Great Neck, NY 11023.

FINCH, KEITH BRUCE
Painter
Work in Public Collections: Calif Dept Agr; Los Angeles Co Mus Art; Whitney Mus Am Art; Home Savings & Loan Asn; Denver Art Mus; plus others.
Exhibitions: Santa Barbara Mus Art; Corcoran Gallery Art; Pa Acad Fine Art; Am Watercolor Soc; Art Inst Chicago; plus others.
Teaching: Kann art instr; instr, Finch-Warshaw Studio; instr, Univ Calif, Los Angeles; instr, Long Beach Mus Art; instr painting, Serisawa Studio.
Awards: Awards, Nat Orange Show, Nat Acad Design & Soc Illusr; plus others.
Mailing Address: c/o Serisawa Gallery, 8320 Melrose Ave, Suite 103, Los Angeles, CA 90069.

FINCHER, JOHN H
Painter, Educator
Preferred Media: Oils, Ink.
b Hamilton, Tex, Aug 4, 41.
Study & Training: Hardin-Simmons Univ, 60-61; Tex Tech Col, BA, 64; Univ Okla, teaching fel, 64-66, MFA, 66.
Work in Public Collections: Dallas Mus Fine Arts; Univ Okla Mus Fine Arts; Bethel Col Art Collection, Kans; Wichita Mus Art.
Exhibitions: Southwestern Biennial, Mus N Mex, Santa Fe, 63; 15th Exhibition of Southwestern Prints & Drawings, Dallas Mus Fine Arts, 65; Watercolor U S A, Springfield Art Mus, Mo, 68; Ball State Univ Ann Exhib Drawings & Small Sculptures, Ind, 68-70; The Drawing Society, Mus Fine Arts, Houston, 70.
Teaching: Asst prof art, Wichita State Univ, 66-
Awards: Wurlitzer Found Grant, Taos, N Mex, 72.
Mailing Address: Division of Art, Wichita State University, Wichita, KS 67218.

FINCK, FURMAN J
Painter, Educator
Preferred Media: Oils.
b Chester, Pa, Oct 10, 00.
Study & Training: Pa Acad Fine Arts, dipl; Ecole des Beaux Arts, Paris, France; Acad Julian, Paris; Am Acad, Rome, Italy; Muhlenberg Col, DFA.
Work in Public Collections: Mass Gen Hosp; Temple Univ Health Sci Ctr; Nat Portrait Gallery; Toledo Mus; Dartmouth House, London, Eng.
Commissions: Med faculty (series of portraits), Temple Univ, 44-; med clinics (series), Med Schs U S, 45-; portrait of President Truman, Nat Dem Club, New York, N Y, 50; portrait of President Eisenhower, Union League, Philadelphia, Pa, 54; deans schs pharm U S (series), Wyeth Labs, 60-64.
Exhibitions: Pa Acad Fine Arts Ann; Carnegie Int; Nat Acad Design Ann; Corcoran Gallery Art Biennial; Portraits Inc Ann.
Teaching: Instr drawing & painting, Cheltenham Art Ctr, Pa, 67-; mem staff painting, Philadelphia Mus Art, 69-; dean, du Cret Sch Art, Plainfield, N J, 70-
Awards: Cresson European traveling scholar, Pa Acad Fine Arts, 24; first Altman prize, Nat Acad Design, 55; Krindler prize, Salmagundi Club Ann, 64.
Bibliography: Henry Pitz (auth), Furman Finck, Am Artist Mag, 3/56; Martin Zipin (auth), Finck paints a portrait (film), produced by WFIL-TV.
Memberships: Salmagundi Club (chmn pub rels, 50-); Twenty Five Year Club of Temple Univ (art comt, 51-); Players (v chmn art comt, 70-); Saint George's Soc New York; Dutch Treat.
Publications: Auth, The meaning of art in education, Columbia Univ Publ, 38; co-auth, The artist as teacher, Appleton, 50; auth, The artist and the architect, Am Inst Architects J, 59; auth, Complete guide to portrait painting, Watson-Guptill, 70.
Mailing Address: 285 Central Park W, New York, NY 10024.

FINDLAY, DAVID B
Art Dealer
Positions: Co-dir, Findlay Galleries.
Mailing Address: 11 E 57th St, New York, NY 10022.

FINDLAY, HELEN T
Art Dealer
b Kansas City, Mo, July 21, 09.
Study & Training: Vassar Col, AB, 30.

Positions: Pres, Jr League Kansas City, 35-36; art secy, Asn Jr Leagues Am, 36-39; fund raising, Nat Recreation Asn, 39-43; secy & mgr, Wally F Findlay Galleries, Chicago, Ill, 62-; bd mem, Chicago Vassar Club.
Awards: Named one of Nine Women of the Year, Chicago Munic Art League, 59.
Mailing Address: Wally F Findlay Galleries, 320 S Michigan Ave, Chicago, IL 60604.

FINE, JUD
Sculptor
Preferred Media: Mixed Media.
b Los Angeles, Calif, Nov 20, 44.
Study & Training: Univ Calif, Santa Barbara, BA; Cornell Univ, MFA.
Work in Public Collections: Minneapolis Inst Arts; Los Angeles Co Art Mus; Lannon Found.
Exhibitions: Documenta 5, Kassel, Ger, 72; Akron Art Inst, 72; Pasadena Art Mus, 72; one-man exhibs, Mazuno Gallery, Ron Feldman Gallery & Brand Art Ctr, Los Angeles, 72 & Daytons Gallery 12, Minneapolis, Minn, 73.
Awards: New Talent 1972, Los Angeles Co Art Mus, 72.
Mailing Address: Ronald Feldman Fine Arts Inc, 33 E 74th St, New York, NY 10021.

FINE, PERLE
Painter, Educator
Preferred Media: Oils, Acrylics, Collage.
b Boston, Mass, May 1, 08.
Study & Training: Atelier 17, with William Hayter; also with Hans Hofmann.
Work in Public Collections: Whitney Mus Am Art, New York, N Y; Brandeis Univ, Waltham, Mass; Munson-Williams-Proctor Inst, Utica, N Y; Solomon R Guggenheim Mus, New York; Brooklyn Mus, N Y; plus others.
Exhibitions: Carnegie Int, Pittsburgh, Pa; Art of This Century, Peggy Guggenheim Gallery, New York; Geometric Abstraction in America & Nature in Abstraction, Whitney Mus Am Art; Mex Biennial, Palacio Bellas Artes, Mexico City, 60; Art of Assemblage, Mus Mod Art, New York, 61; plus others.
Teaching: Vis prof fine arts, Cornell Univ; assoc prof fine arts, Hofstra Univ.
Awards: First prize for oil painting, 61 & first prize for collage, Silvermine Guild, Conn; purchase award for wood-collage, Brooklyn Mus.
Bibliography: Article, In: It Is & monogr, In: Arts & Archit; John Baur (auth), Nature in abstraction (catalog).
Memberships: Am Abstract Artists; Fedn Mod Painters & Sculptors; Guild Hall, East Hampton.
Mailing Address: 58 Third Ave, New York, NY 10003.

FINE, STANLEY M
Cartoonist
Preferred Media: Inks.
b Pittsburgh, Pa, May 24, 22.
Study & Training: Hussian Sch Art; Philadelphia Mus Col Art.
Commissions: 30 action posters, Clemprint Inc, Concordville, Pa, 71.
Positions: Asst, Ted Key's panel cartoon-Hazel, 70.
Publications: Contribr, This fabulous century, Time-Life, 70; cartoonist, Homedingers (cartoon panel), Philadelphia Eve Bull, 70-; contribr, Best cartoons of the year, Dodd, 70-72; contribr, The involved generation, Holt, 71; contribr, Teensville U S A, Noble & Noble, 71.
Mailing Address: 3901 Conshohocken Ave, Philadelphia, PA 19131.

FINGESTEN, PETER
Sculptor, Educator
Preferred Media: Concrete, Watercolors.
b Berlin, Ger, Mar 20, 16; U S citizen.
Study & Training: Hochschule fuer Bildende Kuenste, Berlin, prof dipl; Pa Acad Fine Arts; Asia Inst, New York, cert.
Commissions: Archit relief, Villa Mantero, Como, Italy, 38; sculpture of Christ (bust), First Presby Church, Washington, D C, 48; portrait, Glycerine Corp Am, New York, N Y, 54; Mem plaque, Pace Col, New York, 68.
Exhibitions: Int Exhib Black & White, Milan, Italy, 38; Art of Democratic Living, Am Fedn Arts Nat Traveling Show, 46.
Teaching: Instr art hist, Manhattan Col, New York, 46-50; lectr Asian art, Asia Inst, 50-51; prof art hist, Pace Col, 50-, chmn dept art, 68-
Awards: First sculpture award, Int Exhib Black & White, 38; Louis Comfort Tiffany grant, 48.
Bibliography: Fortunate Fingesten, Time Mag, 3/4/40; J K Reed (auth), Fingesten's 30th, Art Digest, 3/1/47.
Memberships: Am Soc Aesthetics (secy Eastern region, 71-); Col Art Asn Am.

Research: Symbolism of art.
Publications: Auth, East is east, Muehlenberg Press, 56; auth, The eclipse of symbolism, Univ S C Press, 70; auth, Symbolism & reality, J Psycholinguistic Res, 71; auth, Surrealism & the symbolic paradox, Humanitas, spring 72.
Mailing Address: Pace College, 41 Park Row, New York, NY 10038.

FINK, ALAN
Art Dealer
b Chicago, Ill, July 17, 25.
Study & Training: Univ Ill, BA.
Positions: Dir, Alpha Gallery.
Memberships: Asn Boston Art Dealers (pres).
Specialty of Gallery: Contemporary American painting, sculpture and graphics; modern master prints.
Mailing Address: c/o Alpha Gallery, 121 Newbury St, Boston, MA 02116.

FINK, HERBERT LEWIS
Painter, Educator
b Providence, R I, Sept 8, 21.
Study & Training: Carnegie Inst Technol, 41; R I Sch Design, BFA, 49; Yale Univ, MFA, 56; Art Stud League; also with John Frazier, Gabor Peterdi, Arshile Gorky & Rico Lebrun.
Work in Public Collections: Univ Mich; Univ Iowa; Baltimore Mus Art; Md Inst; Brown Univ; plus others.
Commissions: Mural, R I Post Off Lobby, Providence, 59; metal sculpture, Sen Green Airport, 60; archit screen, Hartford Bank & Trust Bldg.
Exhibitions: Am Color Print Soc, 59; Soc Am Graphic Artists, 59; Art Dirs Ann, 59; Libr Cong, 59; Philadelphia Mus Art, 59; plus others.
Teaching: Instr painting & drawing, R I Sch Design, 51-61; instr, Yale Univ, 56-61; prof art & chmn dept, Southern Ill Univ, Carbondale, 61-
Positions: Print ed, Int Graphic Arts Soc; trustee, Tiffany Found.
Awards: Purchase prizes, Soc Am Graphic Artists, 59 & Libr Cong, 59; Guggenheim fel, 65-66; plus others.
Mailing Address: 1003 W Hillcrest Dr, Carbondale, IL 62901.

FINK, SAM
Painter, Illustrator
b New York, N Y, May 27, 16.
Exhibitions: One-man show, Kretschmer Gallery, New York, 70.
Teaching: Instr advert concepts, Pratt Inst, 70-71.
Positions: V pres & head print prod, Young & Rubicam, 48-68; art supvr, creative dir & dir print & graphic prod, William Esty Agency, 68-70; art consul, 70-
Publications: Auth & illusr, The 56 who signed, Sat Rev Press, 71.
Mailing Address: 7 Crampton Ave, Great Neck, NY 11023.

FINKE, LEONDA FROELICH
Sculptor, Draughtsman
Preferred Media: Bronze, Wood, Ink, Silverpoint.
b Brooklyn, N Y, Jan 23, 22.
Study & Training: Art Stud League New York; Educ Alliance; Brooklyn Mus Art Sch; drawing with Arthur Lee; sculpture with Chaim Gross.
Work in Public Collections: Norfolk Mus Arts & Sci, Va.
Exhibitions: Long Island & Brooklyn Artists Exhib, Brooklyn Mus, 60; Norfolk Mus Drawing Biennial, 65 & 67; Pa Acad Fine Arts Painting & Sculpture Ann, 66; invitational one-man show, Nassau Community Col, 69; Nat Sculpture Soc, Lever House, 69-72.
Teaching: Instr sculpture & drawing, Nassau Community Col, 70-; instr sculpture, Baldwin Adult Sch, 67-
Awards: Malvina Hoffman Prize, Nat Asn Women Artists, 67; Lindsay Morris Award for bas-relief, Nat Sculpture Soc, 70; medal for creative sculpture, Audubon Artists, 72.
Memberships: Nat Asn Women Artists (sculpture jury, 70-71, recording secy, 71-72); Audubon Artists (sculpture selection jury, 72); New York Soc Women Artists (exhib comt, 70); Manhasset Art Asn.
Dealer: Harbor Gallery, 43 Main St, Cold Spring Harbor, NY 11724.
Mailing Address: 623 Garden Lane, East Meadow, NY 11554.

FINKELSTEIN, MAX
Sculptor, Instructor
Preferred Media: Metals.
b New York, N Y, June 15, 15.
Study & Training: Los Angeles City Col; Sculpture Ctr, New York, N Y; Calif Sch Art, Los Angeles; Univ Calif, Los Angeles.
Work in Public Collections: Krannert Art Mus, Univ Ill, Champaign; Hirshhorn Mus, Washington, D C; Univ Calif Mus, Berkeley; Santa Barbara Mus Art, Calif; Los Angeles Co Mus Mod Art; Michener Found Collection, Univ Tex, Austin.
Exhibitions: Krannert Art Mus Biennial, Univ Ill, Champaign, 67; Highlights of the 1967-1968 Art Season, Larry Aldrich Mus,

Ridgefield, Conn, 68; Microcosm, Long Beach Mus Art, Calif, 69; Painting & Sculpture Today, Indianapolis Mus Art, Ind, 70; one-man shows, La Jolla Mus Art, Calif, 68 & Esther Robles Gallery, 70; plus many other group & one-man shows.
Teaching: Instr sculpture, Univ Judaism, 63-
Awards: Los Angeles Munic Gallery, 65; Long Beach Mus, 65 & 67; Krannert Mus, Univ Ill, Champaign, 67.
Bibliography: Ray Faulkner (auth) & Edwin Ziegfield (auth), Art today, Holt, 69.
Mailing Address: 621 N Curson Ave, Los Angeles, CA 90036.

FINLEY, DAVID EDWARD
Art Administrator
b York, S C, Sept 13, 90.
Study & Training: Univ S C, BA, 10; George Washington Univ Law Sch, LLB, 13.
Positions: Dir, Nat Gallery Art, 38-56; trustee, Corcoran Gallery Art; mem Nat Protrait Gallery Comn, Smithsonian Inst; mem Nat Collection Fine Arts Comn, Smithsonian Inst; chmn, U S Comn Fine Arts, 50-63.
Awards: Theodore Roosevelt Distinguished Serv Medal, 57; Henry Medal, Smithsonian Inst, 67.
Memberships: Am Asn Mus (pres, 45-49); Am Fedn Arts.
Mailing Address: 1616 H St N W, Washington, DC 20006.

FIORE, JOSEPH A
Painter, Educator
Preferred Media: Oils, Watercolors.
b Cleveland, Ohio, Feb 3, 25.
Study & Training: Black Mountain Col, 46-48; Calif Sch Fine Arts, 48-49; also with Josef Albers, Ilya Bolotowsky & William De Kooning.
Work in Public Collections: Whitney Mus Am Art, Columbia Univ Law Sch Collection & Chase Manhattan Collection, New York, N Y.
Exhibitions: Whitney Ann, 59; one-man show, Staempfli Gallery, 60; Maine: Fifty Artists of the Twentieth Century, Colby Col, Waterville, Maine & Am Fedn Arts, 64; one-man shows, Robert Schoelkopf Gallery, New York, 65 & 69; Painterly Realism, Smith Col, Northampton, Mass & Am Fedn Arts, 70.
Teaching: Instr painting & drawing, Black Mountain Col, 49-56, chmn dept art, 51-56; instr painting, Philadelphia Col Art, 62-70; instr painting, Maryland Inst Col Art, 70-
Awards: Prize for painting, San Francisco Mus Art Ann Show, 49; first prize, Metrop Young Artists First Ann, Nat Arts Club, 58.
Publications: Illusr, The Dutiful Son, Jargon Bks, 56.
Mailing Address: c/o Green Mountain Gallery, 35 Greene St, New York, NY 10013.

FISCH, ARLINE MARIE
Goldsmith, Educator
Preferred Media: Precious Metals.
b Brooklyn, N Y.
Study & Training: Skidmore Col, BS(art); Univ Ill, Urbana, MA(art); Fulbright student grant to Denmark, Inst Int Educ, 56-57; Fulbright res grant to Denmark, Bd for Scholars, 66-67; Sch Arts & Crafts, Copenhagen, Denmark; also with Bernhard Hertz Guldvaerefabrik, Copenhagen.
Work in Public Collections: Objects: U S A, Johnson Wax Collection; Worshipful Company of Goldsmiths, London, Eng; Minn Mus Art, St Paul; Western Ill Univ, Macomb; Crocker Art Gallery, Sacramento, Calif.
Exhibitions: California Design, Pasadena Art Mus Triennial, 65, 68 & 71; Form & Quality, Int Handicraft Fair, Munich, Ger, 68-72; Goldsmith 70, Minn Mus Art, St Paul, 70; Jewellery 71, Art Gallery Toronto Int Exhib, 71; Schmuck-Objekte, Mus Bellerive, Zurich, Switz, 71; plus many solo exhibs.
Teaching: Instr design & weaving, Skidmore Col, 58-61; prof jewelry & weaving, San Diego State Univ, 61-; guest lectr design, Guldsmedshøjskole, Copenhagen, Denmark, 67 & 71.
Awards: Gold medal, Int Handicraft Fair, Munich, 71.
Bibliography: R Radakovich (auth), The expanding wonderland of Arline Fisch, Craft Horizons, 9/68; Arline Fisch, creadora de joyas extraordinarias, Temas, 2/69; Lee Nordness (auth), Objects: U S A, Viking, 70.
Memberships: World Crafts Coun (mem bd, U S sect, 69-); Soc N Am Goldsmiths (founder, 70); Am Crafts Coun (Calif rep, southwest regional assembly, 69-72, craftsman-trustee, 72-75); Allied Craftsmen San Diego (pres, 65).
Dealer: Lee Nordness Galleries, 236 E 75th St, New York, NY 10021.
Mailing Address: 4316 Arcadia Dr, San Diego, CA 92103.

FISCHBACH, MARILYN COLE
Art Dealer, Collector
b New York, N Y.
Study & Training: New York Univ; New York Sch Interior Design; painting with Nicolas Takis & Victor D'Amico.

Positions: Owner, Fischbach Gallery, New York, N Y.
Specialty of Gallery: Avante garde.
Collection: Contemporary.
Mailing Address: Fischbach Gallery, 29 W 57th St, New York, NY 10019.

FISCHER, JOHN J
Painter, Sculptor
b Antwerp, Belgium, Aug 11, 30; U S citizen.
Study & Training: Educ Alliance Art Sch.
Work in Public Collections: Carnegie Inst, Pittsburgh, Pa; Univ Ky, Lexington; Keebler Co, Elmhurst, Ill.
Commissions: Wall piece, Keebler Co, Elmhurst, 68.
Exhibitions: Modern Masters, Univ St Thomas, Tex, 64-66; All Fur Show, Alan Stone Gallery, New York, N Y, 65; Cookies & Breads-The Bakers Art, Mus Contemp Crafts, New York, 65; Jewelry by Contemp Painters & Sculptors, Mus Mod Art, New York, 67; Critics, Curators, Collectors Choice, A M Sachs, New York, 68.
Teaching: Lectr & instr sculpture, N Y Univ Continuing Educ.
Positions: Dir, Loafers-Homebakers Asn, 70-
Bibliography: Grace Glueck (auth), Vie de Bohemia in a project, N Y Times, 64; Howard Smith (auth), article, In: Village Voice, 68.
Publications: Contribr, Cookies & breads-the bakers art, Am Craftsman Coun, 66.
Dealer: Lerner-Heller Gallery, 789 Madison Ave, New York, NY 10021.
Mailing Address: 83 Leonard St, New York, NY 10013.

FISCHER, MILDRED (GERTRUDE)
Designer, Weaver
Preferred Media: Fibers.
b Berkeley, Calif, Sept 15, 07.
Study & Training: Mount Holyoke Col, AB; Wiener Kunstgewerbe Schule; Art Inst Chicago; Cranbrook Acad Art; Wetterhoff Inst, Finland, cert in tapestry; tapestry with Martta Taipale, Finland & Else Halling, Oslo, Norway; papermaking with Eishiro Abe, Japan.
Work in Public Collections: Mus Contemp Crafts, New York, N Y; Grand Rapids Art Mus, Mich; Witherspoon Gallery, Univ N C Woman's Col, Greensboro; Davis Gallery, Stephens Col, Columbia, Mo; Univ Cincinnati Art Collection, Ohio.
Exhibitions: Midwest Designer-Craftsmen, circulated by Smithsonian Exhib Servs, 59-60; Designer-Craftsmen U S A, circulated by Am Fedn Arts, 60-61; Woven Wall Hangings by Eleven Americans, circulated by Victoria & Albert Mus, London, Eng, 62-63; Magic of Fibers, Grand Rapids Art Mus, 70; Exhibition '72, circulated by Columbus Art Gallery, 72.
Teaching: Asst prof art & head dept, Knox Col, 46-49; assoc prof art, Lindenwood Col, 52-55; assoc prof design, Univ Cincinnati Col Design, Archit & Art, 55-
Awards: Third purchase award, Int Textile Exhib, 47; first prize for tapestry, Nat Decorative Arts Exhib, 53; award for wall hanging, Ohio Designer/Craftsmen, Columbus Art Mus, 62.
Memberships: Ohio Designer/Craftsmen (standards comt, 63-68); Am Crafts Coun.
Dealer: Miller Gallery, 3453 Edwards Rd, Cincinnati, OH 45208.
Mailing Address: 1306 Michigan Ave, Cincinnati, OH 45208.

FISH, GEORGE A
Painter
Preferred Media: Watercolors.
b Cornwall, Eng; U S citizen.
Study & Training: Nat Acad Design; Art Stud League New York; Grand Cent Sch Art.
Exhibitions: Audubon Artists, Allied Artists Am & Am Watercolor Soc Shows, Nat Acad Galleries, New York, N Y; Nat Arts Club, New York; Salmagundi Club, New York; plus many others.
Awards: Nell Broadman scholarship, Washington Sq Outdoor Art Exhib, 66; purchase award, Salmagundi Club, 67; best in show, Hudson Artists, 68; plus many others.
Memberships: Salmagundi Club; Am Watercolor Soc; Allied Artists Am; N J Watercolor Soc; Am Artists Prof League; plus others.
Mailing Address: 281 Oak Ave, River Edge, NJ 07661.

FISH, ROBERT (ROBERT JAMES FIELD)
Sculptor, Educator
Preferred Media: Rubber.
b Kelowna, B C, July 24, 48.
Study & Training: Univ B C, BEd, with G Smith & J Macdonald; Vancouver Sch Art; also apprenticeship with Michael Morris & Gary Lee Nova.
Work in Public Collections: Nat Gallery Can, Ottawa.
Teaching: Instr painting, Banff Sch Fine Arts, 72.
Awards: Coutts-Hallmark scholar, 66; Eagle Pencil scholar, 66; B C Art Teachers Asn scholar, 66.

Memberships: Intermedia Soc; Image Bank (mgr off br, 71-72); Citizens of Sea.
Mailing Address: 1956 Graveley St, Vancouver 6, B C, Can.

FISHER, LEONARD EVERETT
Painter, Illustrator
b New York, N Y, June 24, 24.
Study & Training: With Moses Soyer, New York, 39; Art Stud League New York, with Reginald Marsh, 41; Brooklyn Col, with Serge Chermayeff, 41-42; Yale Univ Sch Fine Arts, BFA, 49, MFA, 50.
Work in Public Collections: Butler Inst Am Art, Youngstown, Ohio; Libr of Cong, Washington, D C; Univ Ore, Eugene; Fairfield Univ, Conn; Kerlan Collection, Univ Minn, Minneapolis.
Commissions: Illustrations for 200 children bks for major Am publ, 54-; three panels (silk screen) for wall montage in main elevator lobby, Washington Monument, Washington, D C, commissioned by U S Dept Interior, 64; 14 stations of cross (painted wall decoration), St Patricks Church, Armonk, N Y, 70; Am Bicentennial (four block eight cent commemorative postage stamps), U S Postal Serv, Washington, D C, 72.
Exhibitions: Twelfth Ann Spring Invitational, Springfield Mus, Mass, 53; Painters Panorama Invitational, Am Fedn Arts Sponsored Tour, 54-56; New England Painting Ann, Silvermine Guild Artists, 68, 69 & 71; Mainstreams '71, Marietta Ohio, 71; Butler Inst Am Art Invitational, Youngstown, Ohio, 72.
Teaching: Asst design theory, Yale Univ Sch Fine Arts, 49-50; dean studies, Whitney Sch Art, 51-53; instr painting & bk illus, Paier Sch Art, 66-
Awards: William Wirt Winchester traveling fel, Yale Univ, 49; Pulitzer fel art, 50; premio grafico, Fifth Int Book Fair, Bologna, Italy, 68.
Bibliography: G Alan Turner (auth), Leonard Everett Fisher, Pulitzer prize winner, Design, 6-9/52; Joan Hess Michel (auth), Leonard Everett Fisher, illustrator & painter, Am Artist, 9/66.
Memberships: Am Inst Graphic Arts; New Haven Paint & Clay Club (pres, 68-70); Authors Guild/Authors League Am; Silvermine Guild Artists (bd dirs, 70-); Conn Arts Coun (v pres, 72-73).
Publications: Auth & illusr, The colonial Americans, Watts, Vols 1-17, 64-71; auth & illusr, Two if by sea, Random, 70; auth & illusr, Revolutionary war heroes, Stackpole, 70; illusr, The wicked city, Farrar, Straus & Giroux, 72; auth & illusr, The death of evening star, Doubleday, 72.
Dealer: Capricorn Galleries, 8003 Woodmont Ave, Bethesda, MD 20014.
Mailing Address: 7 Twin Bridge Acres Rd, Westport, CT 06880.

FISHKO, BELLA
Art Dealer
b Russia; U S citizen.
Study & Training: Hunter Col.
Positions: Dir, Forum Gallery.
Memberships: Art Dealers Asn Am; Friends of Whitney Mus Am Art.
Specialty of Gallery: American art of the twentieth century, painting and sculpture.
Publications: Contribr to various nat art magazines.
Mailing Address: 1018 Madison Ave, New York, NY 10021.

FITCH, GEORGE HOPPER
Collector, Patron
b New York, N Y, Nov 29, 09.
Study & Training: Yale Univ, BA, 32.
Positions: Trustee, Yale Univ Art Gallery.
Memberships: Patrons Soc, De Young Mus & Calif Palace of Legion of Honor (chmn, 71-72); Am Fedn Arts (trustee, 51-72, 1st v pres, 55-64); Munic Art Soc New York (pres, 58-60); Art Comn City New York (v pres, 67-68); Art Collectors Club Am (founder, chmn, 57-64).
Art Interests: Increasing art appreciation and availability.
Collection: Twentieth century American watercolors; East Indian miniatures; African Bobbins.
Publications: Auth, So you're going to heaven, 71.
Mailing Address: 1960 Broadway, San Francisco, CA 94109.

FITE, HARVEY
Sculptor
Preferred Media: Stone, Wood.
b Pittsburgh, Pa, Dec 25, 03.
Study & Training: St Stephen's Col; with Corrado Vigni, Florence, Italy.
Work in Public Collections: Whitney Mus Am Art, New York, N Y; Albany Inst Hist & Art, N Y.
Commissions: Restoration of Ancient Maya sculpture in Copan, Honduras, Carnegie Inst Washington, D C, 38.
Exhibitions: One-man shows, Rome, Italy, Paris, France & New York, N Y, 49-51; U S Dept State traveling group shows in Europe & Africa, 53 & 54; Opus 40 (monumental landscape sculp-

ture, terraced rock & fountains covering six & one half acres of bluestone quarry), Woodstock, N Y.
Teaching: Prof sculpture, Bard Col, 32-69.
Awards: Asia Found grant for Cambodia, 56.
Memberships: Woodstock Artists Asn.
Mailing Address: High Woods, Saugerties, NY 12477.

FITZGERALD, HARRIET
Painter, Lecturer
Preferred Media: Oils.
b Sept 14, 04; U S citizen.
Study & Training: Randolph-Macon Woman's Col, BA; Art Stud League New York, two years with John Sloan; also with Maurice Stern, New York, N Y, two years & Ambrose Webster, Provincetown, Mass, three summers.
Work in Public Collections: Swope Gallery, Terre Haute, Ind; Staten Island Mus, New York; Hine's Gallery, Rocky Mountain Art Ctr, N C; Westminster Col, Fulton, Mo; Lawrence Col, Appleton, Wis.
Commissions: Portrait, Dean Mabel H Kennedy, 48 & pres John Childs Simpson, 62, Stratford Col, Danville, Va; v pres Samuel Hatcher, Randolph-Macon Col, Ashland, Va, 55; pres William A Webb, 70 & alumnae secy Anne J Ribble, Randolph-Macon Woman's Col, Lynchburg, Va.
Exhibitions: One-man show, Va Mus Fine Arts, 42; six one-man shows, Charles Barzansky Gallery, New York, 44-46; Irene Lynch Exhib, Norfolk Mus, Va, 62; Mary Washington Col Int, 65; Abingdon Square Painters Traveling Exhib, 69-72.
Teaching: Lectr, Va Area Univ Ctr, 49-51, 60-62; lectr arts prog, Asn Am Cols, 55-64, 67-69; vis lectr, Stratford Col, 57-
Awards: Am Artists Cong Award, 39; citation for distinguished work in the arts as painter & lectr, Randolph-Macon Woman's Col, 62.
Memberships: Artists Equity, New York; Abingdon Square Painters (bd dirs, 48-); Womans Press Club New York.
Publications: Auth, American art between the wars, Randolph-Macon Col Mag, Vol 36, No 1; auth, Art, philosophy and religion, (spec publ), Randolph-Macon Woman's Col, 64; auth, Georgia O'Keeffe, 44, Exploring new dimensions in creativity & What kind of culture, 69, Randolph-Macon Woman's Col Alumnae Bull.
Dealer: Abingdon Square Painters, 242 W 14th St, New York, NY 10011.
Mailing Address: 62 Bank St, New York, NY 10014.

FITZSIMMONS, JAMES JOSEPH
Painter, Architect
Preferred Media: Watercolors.
b Springfield, Mass, July 12, 08.
Study & Training: Pratt Inst Sch Archit, cert, 33.
Work in Public Collections: Springfield Mus Fine Arts, Mass; Travelers Ins Co, Hartford, Conn.
Exhibitions: Southern Vt Art Ctr, Manchester, 57; Audubon Artists, New York, N Y, 62; Knickerbocker Artists, New York, 62; Nat Acad Design, New York, 63; Eastern States Art Exhibs, Springfield, 64.
Awards: Am Artist Mag hon award, 54; purchase prize, Springfield Mus Fine Arts, 55; first prize for watercolor, Acad Artist, 63.
Memberships: Springfield Art League; Acad Artist; Essex Art Asn.
Mailing Address: 308 Enfield St, Enfield, CT 06082.

FLACK, AUDREY L
Painter, Instructor
Preferred Media: Oils.
b New York, N Y, May 30, 31.
Study & Training: Cooper Union, grad, 51; Cranbrook Acad Art; Yale Univ, scholar & study with Josef Albers.
Work in Public Collections: Whitney Mus Am Art, New York; Rose Art Mus, Brandeis Univ; N Y Univ Art Collection; Riverside Mus, New York; French & Co, New York.
Commissions: Family portrait commissioned by Oriole Farb, Dir, Riverside Mus.
Exhibitions: 22 Realists, Whitney Mus Am Art, 70; The Painter and the Photograph, Riverside Mus, 70; Indianapolis Mus Art Ann, Ind, 72; Whitney Mus Am Art Ann, 72; Women in Art, State Univ N Y Col Potsdam, 72.
Teaching: Instr drawing, Pratt Inst, Brooklyn, N Y, 65-71; instr anat, N Y Univ, 68-71; instr drawing, Sch Visual Arts, N Y, 71-
Bibliography: Oriole Farb (auth), Paintings from the photo, Riverside Mus, 70; Van Deren Coke (auth), The painter & the photograph, Univ N Mex Press, 72; Udo Kulterman (auth), Radical realism, Praeger, 72.
Publications: Illusr, New realism, St Cloud St Col, 70; illusr & contribr, 22 Realists (catalogue), Whitney Mus, 70; illusr, The close up vision, Arts Mag, 5/72; illusr, Painting & sculpture today 1972, Indianapolis Mus Art, 72; illusr, Whitney Ann 1972 (catalogue), 72.
Dealer: French & Co, 980 Madison Ave, New York, NY 10021.
Mailing Address: 110 Riverside Dr, New York, NY 10024.

FLAGG, MR & MRS RICHARD B
Collectors
Mr Flagg, b Frankfurt Am Main, Ger, Feb 8, 06.
Study & Training: Mr Flagg, Acad Arts, Vienna, Austria; sculpture with Joseph Heu, Vienna.
Collection: European wood sculpture of the fifteenth, sixteenth and seventeenth century; European furniture—Gothic, Renaissance and Baroque; silver and metalcraft of the same periods; important private collection of European clocks with emphasis on the early sixteenth and seventeenth centuries.
Mailing Address: 7170 N River Rd, Milwaukee, WI 53217.

FLAVIN, DAN
Artist, Writer
Preferred Media: Electric Light.
b New York, N Y, Apr 1, 33.
Study & Training: Self-educated as artist.
Work in Public Collections: Stedelijk Mus, Amsterdam, Neth; Ludwig Collection, Wallraf-Richartz Mus, Cologne, Ger; Mus Mod Art, New York; Tate Gallery, London, Eng; Solomon R Guggenheim Mus, New York.
Exhibitions: alternating pink & gold (an expos of Dan Flavin), Mus Contemp Art, Chicago, Ill, 67-68; fluorescent light, etc from Dan Flavin, Nat Gallery Can, Ottawa, Ont, Vancouver Art Gallery, B C & Jewish Mus, New York, 69-70; Spaces, Mus Mod Art, New York, 69; New York Painting & Sculpture: 1940-1970, Metrop Mus Art, New York, 70; Sixth Int Exhib, Solomon R Guggenheim Mus, New York, 71.
Teaching: Lectr grad faculty, Univ N C, Greensboro, spring 67.
Awards: William & Noma Copley Found Award, 64; award, Nat Found Arts & Humanities, 66.
Publications: Auth, ...in daylight or cool white (brief autobiog), 12/65, auth, some remarks..., 12/66 & auth, ...on an American artist's education, 3/68, Art Forum; auth, several more remarks..., Studio Int, 4/69; co-ed & contribr, fluorescent light, etc from Dan Flavin (catalogue of expos), Nat Gallery of Can, 69.
Dealers: Leo Castelli Gallery, 4 E 77th St, New York, NY 10021; John Weber Gallery, 420 W Broadway, New York, NY 10012.
Mailing Address: Indian Brook Rd, Garrison, NY 10524.

FLAX, SERENE
Painter
Preferred Media: Watercolors.
b Chicago, Ill, May 25, 25.
Study & Training: Northwestern Univ; Chicago Acad Fine Arts, degree; Art Inst Chicago; Inst Design; also with Kwok Wailau & Paul Wieghardt.
Work in Public Collections: Caravan Gallery, Tulsa, Okla; Deerfield High Sch, Ill.
Exhibitions: Drawings U S A, St Paul Art Ctr, Minn, 63; Calif Watercolor Soc, Los Angeles, 64-67; Am Watercolor Soc, Nat Acad Design, New York, N Y, 64-69; Watercolor U S A, Springfield Art Mus, Ill, 66-68; Ill State Mus, Springfield, 68 & 72.
Teaching: Instr painting & techniques, Highland Park High Sch, Ill, spring 68 & 70; lectr, local cols.
Positions: Chmn, Old Orchard Art Festival, 65.
Awards: Award for transparent watercolor, Brugger's Fine Arts Serv, 04; purchase award, Caravan Gallery, 66; munic art award, Art Inst Chicago, 69; plus var local awards.
Bibliography: Franz Schulze (auth), Chicago art scene, Panorama, 66.
Memberships: Arts Club Chicago; North Shore Art League (chmn various comts, 64-67); Deerpath Art League; Calif Watercolor Soc; Am Watercolor Soc.
Publications: Auth, article, In: Am Artist Mag, 1/67; contribr, Art League News.
Mailing Address: 268 Moraine Rd, Highland Park, IL 60035.

FLEISCHMAN, LAWRENCE
Art Dealer, Collector
b Detroit, Mich, Feb 14, 25.
Study & Training: Western Mil Acad, Alton, Ill; Purdue Univ; Univ Detroit, BS.
Positions: Comn mem, Fine Arts Comt, U S Info Agency, 57-59; pres, Arch Am Art, 59-66; pres, Detroit Inst Arts, 62-66; White House Comt Fine Arts, 62-66; pres, Detroit Arts Comn; dir, Kennedy Galleries; trustee, Skowhegan Sch Art, 68-; fel, Morgan Libr, New York, 68-; ed, Am Art J, 69-
Awards: Spec award, City Detroit, 66; Lotus Club Art Award, 67.
Memberships: Arch Am Art (trustee); life mem Pa Acad Fine Arts; life mem Pa Hist Soc; Art Dealers Asn New York; Soc Arts & Crafts (treas art sch, 55-66, hon trustee).
Specialty of Gallery: Eighteenth, nineteenth and twentieth century American art.
Collection: American art and Roman and Greek antiquities.

Publications: Auth, Ben Shahn (catalogue), 68-69 & American Masters Exhibition (catalogue), 71, Kennedy Galleries.
Mailing Address: 20 E 56th St, New York, NY 10022.

FLEMING, ALLAN ROBB
Designer, Calligrapher
b Toronto, Ont, May 7, 29.
Study & Training: Western Tech Sch.
Work in Public Collections: Mus Mod Art, New York.
Commissions: 19th Century Signage, Upper Can Village, comn by Anthony Adamson, Toronto, 58; Can Nat Railways symbol, comn by James Valkus, New York, 59; interior calligraphy, Massey Col, 62; Ont Hydro symbol, Ont Hydro-Elec Power Comn, 65; Hall of Memory, Toronto City Hall, 65.
Exhibitions: Several exhibs at Art Dir Club New York & Type Dir Club New York; Twenty Five Books of the Year, Am Asn Univ Press, 68-72; Am Inst Graphic Arts Covers, 71; Fifty Books of the Year, Am Inst Graphic Arts.
Teaching: Instr typographic design, Ont Col Art, 58-61.
Positions: V pres & dir creative serv, Cooper & Beatty Ltd Typographers, Toronto, 57-62; v pres & dir creative serv, Maclaren Advert Co Ltd, 63-68; chief designer, Univ Toronto Press, 68-
Awards: Gold Medal for distinguished contrib to the art of typographic design, Royal Can Acad Arts, 65; Centennial Medal, Can Govt, 67; gold medal for design of The Econ Atlas of Ontario, Int Bk Fair, Leipzig, 70.
Bibliography: Robert Fulford (auth), Allan Fleming, Can Art, 60; Arnold Rockman (auth), Visual communication in Canada, Idea, Japan, 61.
Memberships: Fel Graphic Designers Can; academician Royal Can Acad Arts; Nat Design Coun.
Mailing Address: 6 South Dr, Toronto 5, Ont, Can.

FLEXNER, JAMES THOMAS
Writer, Art Historian
b New York, N Y, Jan 13, 08.
Study & Training: Lincoln Sch, Teacher's Col; Harvard Col, grad (magna cum laude), 25.
Awards: Life in America Prize, Houghton Mifflin, 46; Guggenheim fel, 53; Parkman Prize, Soc Am Historians, 62.
Memberships: Century Asn; Soc Am Historians; PEN Am Ctr (pres, 54-55).
Research: American painting as an expression of American life.
Publications: Auth, America's old masters, 39, rev ed, 67; auth, American painting, first flowers of our wilderness, 47 & 69; auth, The pocket history of American painting, 50; American painting, the light of distant skies, 54 & 69; auth, American painting, that wilder image, 62 & 70; plus others.
Mailing Address: 530 E 86th St, New York, NY 10028.

FLINSCH, HAROLD, JR
Collector, Patron
b Minneapolis, Minn, Mar 4, 38.
Study & Training: Miss State Univ; Univ Minn; Univ S C.
Positions: Past v pres & trustee, Columbia Art Asn, S C; dir, Newberry Arts Asn, at present.
Collection: J Bardin, E Yaghjian, Chagall, Baskin, Parker, Whistler, Buffet, Abeles, Van Hook Chitty and others.
Mailing Address: Rte 1, Box 117, Lexington, SC 29072.

FLINT, JANET ALTIC
Curator, Art Historian
b Louisville, Ky, Aug 24, 35.
Study & Training: Louisville Art Ctr; Univ Louisville, BS(painting & art hist); Univ Minn, MA(art hist).
Collections Arranged: Prints: 1800-1945, 66; The Watercolors of William Henry Holmes, 70; Boris Anisfeldt: 20 Years of Designs for the Theatre, 71; Drawings by William Glackens, 72; J Alden Weir, An American Printmaker, 72.
Positions: Assoc curator, Minneapolis Inst Arts, 59-66; asst curator & curator prints & drawings, Nat Collection Fine Arts, Smithsonian Inst, 69-
Memberships: Print Coun Am.
Research: American prints and drawings.
Publications: Co-auth, Prints: 1800-1945 (catalogue), 66; auth, Boris Anisfeldt: 20 years of designs for the theatre (catalogue), 71; auth, Drawings by William Glackens (catalogue), 72; auth, J Alden Weir: an American printmaker (catalogue), 72; auth, Art nouveau: American posters & prints, Discovering Antiques, 4/72.
Mailing Address: c/o National Collection of Fine Arts, Eighth & G Sts N W, Washington, DC 20560.

FLINT, LEROY W
Painter, Educator
Preferred Media: Tempora, Acrylic, Aluminum.
b Ashtabula, Ohio, Jan 29, 09.
Study & Training: Univ Minn; Cleveland Inst Art; West Reserve Univ; Cleveland Col.

Work in Public Collections: Cleveland Mus Art; Akron Art Inst; Libr Cong; Butler Mus Am Art.
Commissions: Relief & painted mural, Cleveland Metrop Housing Authority, 38; mobile, Akron Pub Libr, Northfield Br, 70; mobile & mobile sculpture in private collections.
Exhibitions: Cleveland Mus Art May Shows, 37-50; Akron Art Inst Spring Shows, 50-55; Few Are Chosen, Columbus Gallery Fine Arts & Houston, Tex, 53; Butler Inst Am Art, Youngstown, Ohio, 71; one-man shows, 50-54, 56, 65 & 66.
Collections Arranged: A Bourdelle, Akron Art Inst, Ann Collection Show, 60-65, Ann Spring Show, 56-65; Ann Invitational, Kent State Univ, 67-72.
Teaching: Assoc prof painting & gallery docent, Cleveland Mus Art, 49-50; assoc prof painting, drawing, & art hist, Akron Art Inst, 56-65; assoc prof painting & drawing, Kent State Univ, 65-
Positions: Cur educ, Akron Art Inst, 53-56, dir, 56-65; gallery dir, Kent State Univ, 65-
Awards: Awards & mentions, Cleveland May Show, 38-41 & 46-50.
Memberships: Am Asn Mus; Int Inst Conserv; Col Art Asn; Am Soc Aesthet.
Publications: Auth, The volunteer and museum education, Curator, winter 59.
Mailing Address: 2910 14th St, Cuyahoga Falls, OH 44223.

FLOCH, JOSEPH
Painter
Preferred Media: Oils.
b Vienna, Austria, Nov 5, 95; U S citizen.
Study & Training: State Acad Fine Arts, Vienna, Masters degree.
Work in Public Collections: Mus Mod Art, Paris, France; Metrop Mus Art & Whitney Mus Am Art, New York, N Y; Belvedere Mus, Vienna; Albertina Mus, Vienna; plus many others.
Commissions: Murals for Col of Brive, France, comn by Fr Govt, 40.
Exhibitions: Int Shows in Bordeaux, 27, Paris, 37, New York World's Fair, 39 & 66; many one-man shows in New York galleries; retrospectives, M H De Young Mus, San Francisco, Calif, 64 & Belvedere Mus, Vienna, 72.
Teaching: Instr painting, New Sch Social Res, 64-67.
Awards: Lippincott prize, Philadelphia Acad Fine Arts, 44; Brevoort-Eickmeyer Prize, Columbia Univ, 55; Chevalier, Fr Order of Arts & Lett, 62.
Bibliography: M Gautier (auth), Joseph Floch, Ed Gemaux, Paris, 52; Held et al (auth), Joseph Floch, A S Barnes & Co, 67; H Aurenhammer (auth), Joseph Floch (catalog), Ed Austrian Galery, 72.
Memberships: Nat Acad Design (coun mem, 61-); Salon Automne, Paris; Fedn Mod Painters & Sculptors.
Dealer: Forum Gallery, 1018 Madison Ave, New York, NY 10021.
Mailing Address: 61 W 74th St, New York, NY 10023.

FLOETHE, RICHARD
Illustrator, Designer
b Essen, Ger, Sept 2, 01; U S citizen.
Study & Training: Acad Appl Arts, Dortmund, Ger; Acad Appl Arts, Munich, Ger, with Willy Geiger & Edward Ege; Bauhaus Weimar, Ger, with Maholy Nagy & Paul Klee.
Work in Public Collections: Metrop Mus Art, New York, N Y; Libr of Cong, Washington, D C; Philadelphia Mus Art, Pa; Kerlan Collection, Univ Minn; Spencer Collection, Fifth Ave Libr, New York.
Commissions: Hist mural, Pressa, Cologne, Ger, 28.
Teaching: Instr com design, Cooper Union, 41-42; instr illus, Ringling Sch Art, 55-67.
Positions: Art dir, Fed Art Proj, 36-39; art dir, New York City War Serv, 42-43.
Awards: Int Contest for Best Illus Bks award for Tyl Ulenspiegl, 35 & award for Pinocchio, 38, Limited Ed Club; Am Inst Graphic Arts award for English is our Language, 50.
Bibliography: Ronald K Floethe (auth), Kids stuff, Gordon Kerckhoff Prod, 70.
Publications: Illusr, If I were captain, 56, Blueberry pie, 62, Jungle people, 71 & Fishing around the world, 72, Scribner's; illusr, A thousand & one Buddhas, Ariel, 67; plus eighty one other titles, 32-72.
Mailing Address: 1391 Harbor Dr, Sarasota, FL 33579.

FLORIO, SAL ERSENY
Sculptor
Preferred Media: Bronze, Marble.
b San Piezo Patti, Messina, Italy, Dec 17, 90; U S citizen.
Study & Training: Nat Acad Design; also with Herman MacNeil & A Sterling Calder.
Commissions: Created models as chief sculptor assoc of Rene Chiambellan firm, New York, N Y, 28-33 & during this period created: group of 20 figures, symbols of Am Democracy for facade of News Bldg, New York, 29-30; models for Yale Sterling Mem Libr & Sterling Quadrangle, Law Sch & Divinity Col (with

Gamble-Rogers, archit) for Yale Univ, New Haven, Conn, 32; clay models for figure sculpture work, Charity Crucifix Tower, Royal Oak, Mich (Henry J McGill, archit), 33; co-designed American Culture Moving West (sculpture figure panels, high relief, north facade (with Herman A MacNeil), Mo State Capitol, Jefferson City, 34.
Exhibitions: Queen of Atlantis, Nat Sculpture Soc, New York, 25; American Venus, New York Main Pub Libr, 25; Hudson Valley Virgin, Nat Sculpture Soc, 70.
Awards: First prize for sculpture figure, silver medal & hon mention, group composition, Nat Acad Design; bronze medal for sculpture, Int Expos, San Francisco, 15; hon mention for medallion of Rear Adm Christian Joy Peoples, Philadelphia Exhib, 21.
Memberships: Nat Sculpture Soc (mem emer, 70); mem Ital Hist Soc Am.
Mailing Address: 52 Clifford Pl, Bronx, NY 10453.

FLORSHEIM, RICHARD A
Painter, Printmaker
Preferred Media: Oil, Lithography.
b Chicago, Ill, Oct 25, 16.
Study & Training: Univ Chicago.
Work in Public Collections: Mus Mod Art, New York, N Y; Metrop Mus Art, New York; Art Inst Chicago; Libr Cong, Washington, D C; Musée Nationale d'Art Moderne, Paris, France; plus many others.
Exhibitions: Rijksakademie, Amsterdam, 68; Art Inst Chicago, 70; Am Acad Arts & Lett, New York, 71; Ill State Mus, Springfield, 71; Nat Acad Design, New York, 72; plus many other group & one-man exhibs.
Teaching: Instr painting, Layton Sch Art, Milwaukee, 49-50; Contemp Art Workshop, Chicago, 52-63; artist-in-residence, Atlanta Mus, Ga, 64.
Publications: Illusr, Furman Univ Mag covers, winter 67, summer 68 & 5/69; illusr, Springs Cotton Mills Ann Report cover, 69; illusr, Images, Univ N C, Asheville, summer 69.
Dealer: Hampton III Gallery Ltd, 14 Hampton Corners, Greenville, SC 29601.
Mailing Address: Box 28606, Furman University, Greenville, SC 29613.
Positions: Asst dir, Arts Ctr Asn, Chicago, 51-52; bd mem, Ill Arts Coun, Chicago, 65-
Awards: Chicago Newspaper Guild Award, Art Inst Chicago, 54; Pennell Fund Award, Libr Cong, 56; Silvermine Guild Artists, 59.
Bibliography: A Eliot (auth), Richard Florsheim, Time, 59; N Kent (auth), Color lithographs of Richard Florsheim, Am Artist, 66; E Barry (auth), The artist is busy, Chicago Tribune Mag, 70; also many others.
Memberships: Nat Acad Design; Soc Am Graphic Artists; Audubon Soc Artists; Provincetown Art Asn (trustee & v pres, 62-71); Artists Equity Asn (pres, 53-54; now hon pres).
Publications: Articles in Col Art J, Art League News, Motive, Chicago Sun-Times, Cape Cod Standard Times plus others.
Dealers: ACA Galleries, 25 E 73rd St, New York, NY 10021 (painting); Associated American Artists, 663 Fifth Ave, New York, NY 10022 (prints).
Mailing Address: 5 E Ontario St, Chicago, IL 60611.

FLOWERS, THOMAS EARL
Painter, Educator
Preferred Media: Acrylics, Oils, Mixed Media.
b Washington, D C, Feb 17, 28.
Study & Training: Furman Univ, BA; Univ Iowa, MFA.
Work in Public Collections: Greenville Co Mus Art, S C; Columbia Mus Art, S C; Chase Manhattan Bank, New York, N Y; S C Arts Comn, Columbia; Vincent Price Enterprises, Chicago, Ill.
Commissions: Mural, Vince Perome, Greenville, S C, 62; mural, Saad Rug Co, Greenville, 63; mace & medallion, Furman Univ, Greenville, 65.
Exhibitions: 18th Ann Guild S C Artists Exhib, 68; 11th Ann Southern Contemp Art Exhib, Mobile, Ala, 69; 12th Ann Springs Art Exhib, Lancaster, S C, 70; Atlanta Artists Club, Nat 1, Ga, 70; Southeastern Painter's Choice Exhib, Ga Col, Milledgeville, Ga, 71.
Teaching: Asst prof art & chmn dept, Ottawa Univ, 56-58; instr sculpture, E Carolina Col, 58-59; assoc prof art & chmn dept, Furman Univ, 59-
Positions: State rep, Am Craftsman's Coun, 62-64.
Awards: First purchase award, Southeastern Painter's Choice Exhib, 71; purchase award, S C Arts Comn, 71; second award, Franklin Mint, 72.
Bibliography: Jack A Morris (auth), Contemporary artists of South Carolina, Greenville Co Mus Art, 70; R Smeltzer (auth), article, In: Southern Living Mag, 12/70; M Hays (auth), article, In: Furman Univ Mag, spring 72.
Memberships: Guild S C Artists (pres, 61-62; bd dirs, 71-72); Greenville Artists Guild (pres, 72-73); Southeastern Col Art Asn.

FLUEK, TOBY
Painter
Preferred Media: Oils.
b Czernica, Poland, Feb 20, 26; U S citizen.
Study & Training: Art Stud League N Y, with Robert Beverly Hale; also with Joe Hing Lowe & Irving Koenig.
Exhibitions: Greater New York Outdoor Art Exhib, Rego Park, 66, 71 & 72; Brush and Palette Society Exhibs, Bronx & Manhattan, 70-72; Bronx Mus Ann, Bronx Mus Arts, N Y, 72; Am Artists Prof League Grand Nat Exhib at Lever House, N Y, 72; one-woman show, Fellowship Gallery, Queens, 72.
Teaching: Instr oil painting, Woodside Jewish Ctr, N Y, 72.
Awards: First prize, Brush & Palette Soc, 71; third prize, Greater New York Outdoor Exhib, 72; best in show, Fellowship Art Gallery, 72.
Bibliography: Jack Besterman (auth), Two talentful women artists of Woodside Queens, Big Six Chapel & Pensioners News, 5/2/71; Jeanne Paris (auth), Art, Long Island Press, 10/8/72.
Memberships: Am Artists Prof League; Bronx Coun Arts; Brush & Palette Soc.
Mailing Address: 60-10 47th Ave, Woodside, NY 11377.

FOGEL, SEYMOUR
Painter, Sculptor
b New York, N Y, Aug 25, 11.
Study & Training: Art Stud League New York, 29, with George Bridgeman; Nat Acad Design, 29-32.
Work in Public Collections: Whitney Mus Am Art, New York; Joseph II Hirshhorn Collection, Washington, D C; Dallas Mus Art, Tex; Houston Mus Art, Tex; City of St Louis Art Mus, Mo.
Commissions: Sand sculpture wall, Hoffmann-La Roche Res Tower, Nutley, N J, 64; mosaic mural, U S Customs Courts Bldg, New York, 68; mosaic mural, Gouverneur Hosp, New York, 71; mosaic mural, Sch 29, New York, 71; stained glass screen, Bellevue Hosp, New York, 72.
Exhibitions: Metrop Mus Art, New York, 51; Carnegie Int, Pittsburgh, Pa, 58-59; many shows, Archit League New York, Whitney Mus Am Art & Nat Gallery Art, Washington, D C.
Teaching: Asst prof life drawing, design & mural, Univ Tex, Austin, 46-54; guest prof life drawing & grad painting, Mich State Univ, 61.
Positions: V pres, Archit League & Int Fine Arts Coun.
Awards: First prize, Gulf Carribean Int, Houston, 56; first prize, Tex Gen, Dallas, 56; first prize in design, Archit League New York, 58.
Bibliography: Zeigfield et all (auth), Art Today, Henry Holt; Ralph Pearson (auth), Modern renaissance in American art, Harper & Rowe, 54; Redstone (auth), Art and architecture, McGraw, 70.
Memberships: Archit League New York; Int Platform Asn.
Publications: Auth, Ethyl silicate & architecture, Archit & Engr News, 60; auth, The painter & architect, Am Inst Architects J, 60; auth, Art and the church, Liturgical Arts, 60; auth, Architect discovers painting & sculpture, Mich Am Inst Architects J, 61; auth, Painting & sculpture as architecture, Art in Am, 62.
Mailing Address: Torandor, 68 Georgetown Rd, Weston, CT 06880.

FOLDS, THOMAS McKEY
Art Consultant, Educator
b Connellsville, Pa, Aug 8, 08.
Study & Training: Yale Col, BA, 30; Yale Univ Sch Fine Arts, BFA, 34.
Commissions: Mural, U S Govt, Pub Works Admin, 34.
Exhibitions: Painting a Mural & Art in Advertising, traveling exhibs for Am Fedn Arts.
Teaching: Art dir, Phillips Exeter Acad, 35-46; prof art hist & chmn dept art, Northwestern Univ, 46-60; dean educ, Metrop Mus Art, 60-73.
Memberships: Col Art Asn Am; Am Asn Mus; Sch Art League New York (pres, 68-).
Publications: Auth & illusr, Where is the fire?, 47; auth, A critique of color reproductions, Col Art J, 48-49; co-auth, Masterpieces of painting in the Metropolitan Museum of Art, 70; auth, Abstract painting (exhib), Macmillan, 70.
Mailing Address: 535 E 86th St, New York, NY 10028.

FONDREN, HAROLD M
Art Dealer
b Canton, Ohio, Feb 5, 22.
Study & Training: Harvard Col, AB
Positions: Asst dir, Stable Gallery, 54-55; asst dir, Poindexter Gallery, 55-
Specialty of Gallery: Contemporary painting and sculpture.
Mailing Address: Poindexter Gallery, 24 E 84th St, New York, NY 10028.

FONELLI, J VINCENT
Painter, Sculptor
b Salerno, Italy, Sept 28, 06; U S citizen.
Study & Training: Cooper Union, BS(eng), 24; Univ Calif, Los Angeles, 48-50; Columbia Univ, 51-55; Hunter Col, 54-57; Corcoran Sch Art, 58-61.
Commissions: Many private commissions in U S & Mex, 60-71.
Exhibitions: The American Liberty, Palazzo dell'Arti Gallery, Washington, D C, 60-71; The Italian Boy, Interstate Bank Bldg, & Air India Dist Off, Washington, D C, 65; three life size busts (Ficondita, Diana & Beauty in Stone), Galleria delle Belli Arti, Florence, Italy, 71-
Positions: Archit designer, Baltimore, Md, 46-48; archit design, J Vincent Fonelli & Assocs, Beverly Hills, Calif, 48-50; founder & pres, Fonelli Studios of Fine Arts, Washington, D C, 60-71; founder & pres, Fonelli Studii delle Belli Arti, Florence, 71-
Memberships: Am Fedn Arts; Int Arts Guild, Monte Carlo.
Art Interests: Portrait painting & figure sculpture.
Publications: Auth, Beauty in sculpture & painting, 64; auth, art brochure, 65-68.
Mailing Address: Fonelli Studios of Fine Arts, Casella Postale Nr 612, 50100 Florence, Italy.

FONTANEZ, CARMELO
Painter, Instructor
Preferred Media: Watercolors.
b Rio Piedras, P R, July 16, 45.
Study & Training: Univ P R, BA (art educ); N Y Univ, MA (art educ).
Exhibitions: Univ P R Mus; Ateneo Puertorriqueño, 68; Ponce Art Mus, 68; Galeria Santiago, San Juan, 68, 69, 70 & 72; Inst Cult Puertorriqueño, 69.
Teaching: Instr art, Univ P R, 67-
Awards: First prize for watercolors, 67-69 & first prize for drawing, 69, IBEC Contest; first prize for watercolor, Ateneo Puertorriqueño, 69.
Dealer: Galeria Santiago, Calle Cristo 207, San Juan, PR 00901.
Mailing Address: Calle Pedro Diaz Correa 412, Urb del Carmen, Rio Piedras, PR 00923.

FONTANINI, CLARE
Educator, Sculptor
Preferred Media: Stone, Wood, Metals.
b Rutland, Vt.
Study & Training: Col St Catherine, AB; Columbia Univ, with Josef Albers & Oronzio Maldarelli, MA.
Work in Public Collections: Lammentations of Jerimiah (marble), Barnett-Aden Gallery, Washington, D C; Seat of Wisdom (walnut), Col St Catherine, St Paul, Minn; Copper Crucifix, Trinity Col Libr, Washington, D C.
Commissions: Assumption (stone), St Mary's Church, Winnsboro, La, 52; Stations of the Cross, private chapel, Cardinal Patrick O'Boyle, Washington, D C, 57; St John Evangelist (aluminum), church in McLean, Va, 59; St Michael Archangel (aluminum), church in Annandale, Va, 60; Rood Figures (walnut), All Saints Episcopal Church, Chevy Chase, Md, 66.
Exhibitions: Mint Mus Art, Charlotte, N C; Walker Art Gallery, Minneapolis, Minn; Va Mus Fine Arts, Richmond; Corcoran Gallery Art, Washington, D C; Nat Collection Fine Arts, Smithsonian Inst, Washington, D C; plus many others.
Teaching: Instr design, Phillips Mem Gallery, Am Univ, Washington, D C, 46-47; asst prof sculpture, Cath Univ Am, 47-58, prof sculpture, 58-, head dept art, 47-68.
Positions: Pres, Washington Sculptor's Group, 50; pres, Washington Artists Guild, 55.
Awards: First prize medal for sculpture, Nat Christian Arts Festival, Univ Wis, 55; Frank E Jellef award for sculpture, Washington, D C, 57; first prize for sculpture, Corcoran Gallery Art Ann Area Show, 59.
Memberships: Artists Equity Asn; Soc Washington Artists (secy, 43-45, v pres, 47).
Mailing Address: 1029 Perry St N E, Washington, DC 20017.

FOOSANER, JUDITH ANN
Painter
Preferred Media: Acrylics, Oils.
b Sacramento, Calif, Aug 10, 40.
Study & Training: Univ Calif, Berkeley, BA(Eng), 64, dean's award, 61; univ grant, 68, MA(art), 68.
Exhibitions: Group show, San Diego Fine Arts Gallery, Calif, 70; one-woman show, Wenger Gallery, 71.
Teaching: Instr painting & drawing, Calif Col Arts & Crafts, 70-
Publications: Auth, articles, In: Art Week, 11/71 & Art Gallery Mag, 1/72.
Dealer: Wenger Gallery, 855 Montgomery St, San Francisco, CA 94133.
Mailing Address: 5326 James Ave, Oakland, CA 94618.

FORAKIS, PETER
Painter, Sculptor
b Hanna, Wyoming, Oct 2, 27.
Study & Training: Calif Sch Fine Arts, BFA, 57.
Commissions: Tower of the Lakotas (steel tubing sculpture), Mass Inst Technol, Cambridge, 66; Gateway (cast iron tubing sculpture), Great Southwest Corp, Atlanta, Ga, 66-67; Earth Handle (wood sculpture), Denver City Park, Colo, 68; Tower of the Cheyenne (corten steel tubing sculpture), Univ Houston, Tex, 72.
Exhibitions: New Forms New Media, Martha Jackson Gallery, New York, N Y, 61; one-man show, Tibor de Nagy, New York, 63-64; American Artists Drawings, Guggenheim Mus New York, 64; Primary Structures, Jewish Mus, New York, 65; Sculpture of the 60's, Los Angeles Co Mus, Los Angeles, 66.
Publications: Auth & illusr, Grope Comics, Vol I & II, 63 & 66.
Dealer: Paula Cooper Gallery, 100 Prince St, New York, NY 10012.
Mailing Address: R F D 1, Putney, VT 05346.

FORD, CHARLES HENRI
Painter, Photographer
b Mississippi.
Work in Public Collections: Univ Southern Ill, Carbondale (complete run of poem posters); Univ Tex Archives, Austin.
Exhibitions: Photographs, Inst Contemp Art, London, Eng, 54; Drawings & Paintings, Galerie Marforen, 56, Galerie du Dragon, 57 & 58, Paris, France; Photographs & Lithographs, Cordier & Eckstrom, New York, N Y, 65.
Bibliography: Parker Tyler (auth), article, In: Screening the sexes, Holt, Rinehart & Winston, 72.
Publications: Auth, The overturned lake, 41, Sleep in a nest of flames, 49, Spare parts, 66, Silver flower coo, 68 & Flag of ecstasy, 72.
Mailing Address: c/o Minotaur Films, Inc, Zambeliou 73, Xania (Crete), Greece.

FORD, JOHN CHARLES
Painter
b Choudrant, La, Sept 29, 29.
Study & Training: La Polytech Inst, BFA, 50; Univ Tex; Austin Presby Theol Sem, BD, 53; Art Stud League New York, 57; Univ Ore, MFA, 60; also with Mark Tobey.
Work in Public Collections: Seattle Art Mus, Wash; Victoria Art Mus, B C; N Y Univ, New York; Notre Dame Univ; Nuffield Found, London.
Commissions: Altarpiece, Chapel La Grande, Ore, 65; outdoor painted screen construction, Lady Peter Norton, London, 69.
Exhibitions: San Francisco Art Mus, 59 & 60; Seattle Art Mus, 63; Contemp Am Drawings, Smithsonian Inst, Washington, 63; Cambridge Sch Archit, Eng, 69; plus many others.
Awards: Second prize, Art Stud League Universal Int Drawings & Painting Competition, New York, 57; prize winning drawing, Little Rock Art Mus, Ark, 57; award, Boise Art Mus, 60.
Dealers: Leicester Galleries, 22A Cork St, London W1, England; The Avanti Galleries, 145 E 72nd St, New York, NY 10021.
Mailing Address: 41 Bond St, New York, NY 10012.

FORD, JOHN GILMORE
Collector
b Baltimore, Md, Dec 23, 28.
Study & Training: Baltimore City Col, degree; Johns Hopkins Univ; Loyola Col; Md Inst Col Art, BFA.
Exhibitions: Indo-Asian Art(personal collection), Walters Art Gallery, Baltimore, 71.
Positions: Nat v pres, Am Inst Interior Designers, 70-
Awards: Citation of merit, Md Inst Col Art, 60.
Bibliography: P Pal (auth), Indo-Asian art, 71, Walters Art Gallery, Apollo Mag & Connoisseur Mag.
Memberships: Am Fedn Arts; Asia Soc.
Collections: Indian, Nepalese, Tibetan, Javanese, Chinese & Japanese bronzes, stone sculptures & paintings.
Mailing Address: 2601 N Charles St, Baltimore, MD 21218.

FORD, RUTH VANSICKLE
Painter, Educator
Preferred Media: Watercolors, Oils.
b Aurora, Ill, Aug 8, 98.
Study & Training: Chicago Acad Fine Arts, cert; Art Stud League New York; summers with John Carlson and spec classes with George Bellows, Guy Wiggins, Jonas Lie & Bruce Crane.
Work in Public Collections: Aurora Col, Ill; Lafayette Col, Ind; Aurora Pub Libr; Northern Ill Gas Co; Aurora YMCA.
Commissions: Portrait of Freeman for Freeman Room, Aurora YMCA, 68; portrait of head of drama dept, Aurora Col, commissioned by sr class for gift to col, 69.
Exhibitions: One-man show, Chicago Art Inst, 34; Grand Cent Galleries, New York, N Y, 47; Watercolor U S A, Springfield, Mo,

62-63; Nat Acad Design; Am Artists, Chicago Art Inst; plus many others.

Teaching: Prof life class, Chicago Acad Fine Arts, 30-60; prof painting, Aurora Col, 64-

Positions: Pres-dir, Chicago Acad Fine Arts, 37-60.

Awards: Fine Arts Bldg Prize, 30 & Chicago Woman's Aid Prize, 31, Chicago Art Inst; gold medal award for oil painting, Palette & Chisel Acad, 63; plus many others.

Memberships: Am Watercolor Soc; hon mem Artist Guild Chicago; Am Artists Prof League; Palette & Chisel Acad; Rockport Art Asn, Mass.

Art Interests; Portraits, landscapes & still lifes.

Dealer: Schramm Galleries, 215 S W Second St, Fort Lauderdale, FL 28315.

Mailing Address: 69 Central Ave, Aurora, IL 60506.

FORMAN, ALICE
Painter, Designer
b New York, N Y, June 1, 31.
Study & Training: Cornell Univ, with Kenneth Evett & Norman Daly, BA; Art Stud League New York, with Morris Kantor.
Exhibitions: Whitney Mus Am Art, 60; White Mus Art, Cornell Univ, 61; Phoenix Gallery, N Y, 66, 68 & 71; Marist Col, 68 & 71; Butler Inst Exhib, 72; plus others.
Awards: Nat Stud Asn Regional Awards; Daniel Schnackenberg merit scholar, Art Stud League New York.
Dealer: Phoenix Gallery, 939 Madison Ave at 74th St, New York, NY 10021.
Mailing Address: 8 Croft Rd, Poughkeepsie, NY 12603.

FORMAN, KENNETH WARNER
Painter, Educator
Preferred Media: Oils, Watercolors.
b Landour, India, June 5, 25; U S citizen.
Study & Training: Wittenberg Col, AB, BFA; Ohio State Univ, MA.
Work in Public Collections: Wittenberg Col, Springfield, Ohio; Univ R I, Kingston; Hartford C of C Festival Collection, Conn; Univ Conn Hon Col, Storrs.
Exhibitions: Nat Drawing Exhib, Ball State Teachers Col, Muncie, Ind, 65; 12th Biennial Exhib Contemp Am Prints, Brooklyn Mus, 65; 23rd Int Exhib Soc Printmakers, U S Nat Mus, 66; Contemp Am Painting, Mem Art Mus, Rochester, N Y, 67; Nat Watercolor Exhib, Peoria Art Ctr, Ill, 67.
Teaching: Instr media & techniques, painting, Am archit & art hist, Univ Conn, 57-, prof art, 68-
Awards: First painting award, Silvermine Guild Artists, 57; first painting award, Mystic Art Asn, Conn, 63; Hartford Art Festival purchase award, Hartford C of C, 72.
Memberships: Conn Watercolor Soc; Mystic Art Asn; Victorian Soc Am; Victorian Soc Eng; Am Fedn Arts.
Research: Victorian architecture in England & New England; traditional media with synthetic media in painting.
Publications: Auth, Understanding in the arts, 59 & illusr, 61, Fine Arts Mag; illusr, spec ed, The Penny Paper, 64; auth, Salvador Dali's moustache, The Floating Opera, 67.
Mailing Address: R F D 1, Mansfield Center, CT 06250.

FORRESTALL, THOMAS DE VANY
Sculptor, Painter
Preferred Media: Tempera, Steel, Iron, Bronze.
b Middleton, N S, Mar 11, 36.
Study & Training: Mt Allison Univ, 54-58; Can Coun grant to travel & study in Europe, 58-59, sculpture grant, 67.
Work in Public Collections: Can Coun; Winnipeg Art Gallery; Art Gallery Windsor; Confederation Mem Gallery; New Brunswick Mus.
Commissions: Kennedy & Churchill Mem, Prov N B, 64; steel sculpture, Atlantic Pavilion, Expo 67; welded relief mural, Centennial Bldg Fredericton, 68; two large welded steel sculptures, Can Govt, Fed Bldg, Antigonish, N S, 70; mural abstract for playhouse, Beaverbrook Can Found, Fredericton, 72.
Exhibitions: Exhib of Can Sculpture, Nat Gallery Can, Ottawa, 64 & Artists of Atlantic Can, 66; 26 paintings exhibited at Dartmouth Col, 66; 54 paintings organized by Beaverbrook Art Gallery for travel across Can, 71-72; Canada Visits Boston, 31 paintings exhibited at City Hall Art Gallery, Boston, Mass, 72; Centre Culturel, Paris, France, 72; plus others.
Positions: Asst curator, Beaverbrook Art Gallery, 59-60.
Awards: Citation of art merit, Secy State, Commonwealth Mass, 72.
Bibliography: Alex Mogelon (auth), Art Profile, Montrealer, 68; D S Richardson (auth), Tom Forrestall Exhibition, Beaverbrook Art Gallery, 71; Berry Lord (auth), Shaped by this land.
Memberships: Assoc Royal Can Acad Arts.
Publications: Co-auth, Shapes, 72.
Dealer: Roberts Gallery Ltd, 641 Yonge St, Toronto 5, Ont, Can.
Mailing Address: 329 University Ave, Fredericton, N B, Can.

FORSBERG, JAMES ALFRED
Painter, Printmaker
Preferred Media: Oils.
b Sauk Ctr, Minn, Nov 21, 19.
Study & Training: Minneapolis Art Sch; St Paul Sch Art; Art Stud League New York; Hans Hofmann Sch Fine Art.
Work in Public Collections: Mus Mod Art, New York, N Y; Smith Col, Mass; Cincinnati Art Mus, Ohio; Philadelphia Mus, Pa; Chrysler Mus, Norfolk, Va.
Exhibitions: Print Show & Drawing Show, Mus Mod Art, New York; nat & int print shows, 50-63.
Teaching: Chmn visual arts dept, Fine Arts Work Ctr, Provincetown, Mass, 69-70 & 72-
Mailing Address: 441 Commercial St, Provincetown, MA 02657.

FORSLUND, CARL VICTOR, JR
Painter
Preferred Media: Acrylics.
b Grand Rapids, Mich, Nov 12, 27.
Study & Training: Univ Mich, BS, advan study with Guy Palazolla & Rich Wilt.
Exhibitions: Mich Biennial, Grand Rapids, 54-68; four Mich Acad Ann, state cols, 63-68; Hackley Regional, Muskegon, Mich, 64-68 & 70; Butler Inst Am Art Ann, Youngstown, Ohio, 67.
Positions: Bd dirs, Grand Valley Artists Asn, 57-63; bd dirs, Friends Art, 62-69, pres, 65-68; bd trustees, Grand Rapids Art Mus, 62-71.
Awards: Lois Hall Mem, Grand Rapids Art Mus, 60; first prize oil, Mich Acad, Grand Valley State Col, 64; first prize oil, Hackley Art Gallery, Muskegon, 65.
Memberships: Mich Acad Fine Arts; Nat Soc Interior Designers.
Dealer: Hefner Galleries, 52 Market N W, Grand Rapids, MI 49507.
Mailing Address: 2141 Elmwood S E, Grand Rapids, MI 49506.

FORST, MILES
Painter, Educator
b Brooklyn, N Y, Aug 18, 23.
Study & Training: Mus Mod Art Veterans Ctr; Art Stud League New York, with Morris Kantor; Esquela Obrera, Mexico City, Mex; Hans Hofmann Sch Fine Arts.
Work in Public Collections: Mus Mod Art, New York, N Y; Newark Mus, N J; Mass Inst Technol, Cambridge; Chrysler Mus, Provincetown, Mass; Bowdin Col Mus.
Exhibitions: Green Gallery, New York, 64 & 66; Goldowsky-Bellamy Gallery, New York, 69; Notre Dame Univ, Ind, 69; Univ N C, 70; Sch Visual Arts, New York, 70.
Teaching: Instr painting & drawing, Sch Visual Arts, 63-71; assoc prof painting, San Francisco State Univ, 71-72; prof design, Otis Art Inst, 71-
Positions: Charter mem, Hansa Gallery, New York, 53-58; organizer, Radiance Prod, 72-
Awards: Working artist award, Walter K Gutman Found, 60, 62 & 65; working artist award, Longview Found, 61 & 62; artist-in-residence, Ford Found, 65.
Bibliography: Article, In: Art Collectors Ann, 67; Kaprow (auth), Happenings, 68; Drs P & E Kronhausen (auth), Erotic art, Grove, 69.
Memberships: Col Art Asn Am; Am Asn Univ Prof.
Dealer: Richard Bellamy, 1078 Madison Ave, New York, NY 10021.
Mailing Address: 122 S Ave 64, Los Angeles, CA 90042.

FORSTER, PEGGY LUCILLE
Art Administrator
b Drummond, Idaho, Apr 3, 25.
Study & Training: Brigham Young Univ.
Collections Arranged: National Invitational, All Utah Show & several one-man shows, Springville Museum Art, 70-72; Universities & Colleges of Utah Faculty Show, 70 & 71; High School Students of Utah, 71.
Positions: Dir, Springville Mus Art.
Mailing Address: 126 E 400 S, Springville, UT 84663.

FORSYTH, CONSTANCE
Painter, Printmaker
Preferred Media: Watercolor, Aquatint.
b Indianapolis, Ind, Aug 18, 03.
Study & Training: Butler Univ, BA; John Herron Art Sch, dipl, & study with W Forsyth & Clifton Wheeler; Pa Acad Fine Arts, with Henry McCarter & George Harding; Broadmoor Art Acad, Colorado Springs, Colo, with Ward Lockwood & Boardman Robinson.
Work in Public Collections: Indianapolis Art Mus, Ind; Tex Fine Arts Asn; Ball State Teachers Col, Muncie, Ind; Joslyn Mem Mus, Omaha, Nebr; Dallas Mus Fine Arts, Tex; plus others.
Exhibitions: Watercolor, Bern, Switz, 57, Tokyo, Japan, 60, traveling print show to India, 65 & foreign exhib, Florence, Italy, 72, Nat Asn Women Artists; Sixteenth Libr of Cong Print Exhib, Esslingen on the Necker, Ger, 59.

Teaching: Instr art, John Herron Art Sch, Indianapolis, 31-33; interim instr art, Western Col, Oxford, Ohio, spring 39; prof art, Univ Tex, Austin, 40-
Awards: Naomi Goldman prize for Surf (aquatint), Nat Asn Women Artists, 61; Maco Press prize for The Deluge (aquatint), John Herron Art Mus, 61; purchase prize for Up Close (watercolor), Tex Fine Arts Asn, 72.
Memberships: Nat Asn Women Artists; Tex Fine Arts Asn; Tex Printmakers Soc.
Publications: Illusr, The friends, Steck Co, 51.
Mailing Address: 4112 Ave B, Austin, TX 78751.

FORSYTH, ROBERT JOSEPH
Art Historian, Collector
b Neligh, Nebr, Sept 4, 21.
Study & Training: Univ Ore, BA, 43, MA, 47; Univ Minn, PhD, 65.
Teaching: Tex Christian Univ, 47-49; Univ Minn, 49-51; Hamline Univ, 57; Univ Minn, St Paul, 58-68; prof art hist, Colo State Univ, 68-; Univ Notre Dame, summer, 71.
Positions: Educ curator, Minneapolis Inst Arts, Minn, 51-55.
Memberships: Col Art Asn; Am Fedn Arts; Nat Trust for Hist Preservation.
Research: American art with emphasis on sculpture.
Collection: Twentieth century American drawings, sculpture and prints.
Publications: Auth, Sculpture and drawings: John B Flannagan, Univ Notre Dame, 63; auth, The early Flannagan and carved furniture, Col Art J, fall 67; auth, New jewel beveled and set, Art Week, 12/25/71; auth, Colorado collects (catalogue) & Thomas Moran in Yellowstone (catalogue), Colo State Univ, 72.
Mailing Address: Dept. of Art, Colorado State University, Fort Collins, CO 80521.

FORSYTH, WILLIAM H
Museum Curator, Writer
b Chicago, Ill, May 21, 06.
Study & Training: Hotchkiss Sch; Princeton Univ, BA & MFA; also with C R Morey, A M Friend & F Stohlman.
Positions: Asst, medieval dept, Metrop Mus Art, New York, N Y, asst cur, 36-41, assoc cur, 41-60, cur medieval art, 60-70, cur emer, 70-
Memberships: Assoc corres mem Soc Antiq France; Soc Archeol Limousin; Soc Acad de Dijon; Century Asn.
Publications: Auth, Entombment of Christ; French sculptures of the 15th and 16th centuries, Harvard Univ Press, 70; contribr, articles, In: Metrop Mus Studies & J, Art Bull & Metrop Mus Art Bull & Jour.
Mailing Address: 172 Mercer St, Princeton, NJ 08540.

FORTESS, KARL EUGENE
Painter, Printmaker
Preferred Media: Oils.
b Antwerp, Belgium, Oct 13, 07; U S citizen.
Study & Training: Art Inst Chicago; Art Stud League New York; Woodstock Sch Painting, with Yasuo Kuniyoshi.
Work in Public Collections: De Cordova Mus; Mus Mod Art, New York, N Y; Brooklyn Mus; Nat Collection Fine Arts, Smithsonian Inst; Butler Inst Am Art; plus many others including private collections.
Exhibitions: Art Inst Chicago; Mus Mod Art, New York; Whitney Mus Am Art; Nat Inst Arts & Letters; Nat Acad Design; plus many other group & one-man shows.
Teaching: Instr art, Art Stud League New York, Brooklyn Mus Art Sch, La State Univ, Am Art Sch; vis artist, Fort Wright Col; prof art, Boston Univ Sch Fine & Appl Arts, at present.
Positions: Artist fed art projects, Works Proj Admin; contract with U S Dept Health, Educ & Welfare for tape-recorded interviews with contemp Am artists.
Awards: First hon mention, Carnegie Inst, 41; Guggenheim fel, 46; Childe Hassam Fund purchase award, 52; Nat Endowment Arts grant.
Bibliography: Holger Cahill (auth), New horizons in American art; Ralph Pearson (auth), The modern renaissance in American art; Arthur Zaidenberg (auth), Prints, and how to make them; plus many others.
Memberships: Artists Equity Asn; Soc Am Graphic Artists; Art Stud League New York; Am Asn Univ Prof; Brit Film Inst.
Research: Participated in making a pictorial record of the Territory of Alaska for the U S Dept of Interior.
Publications: Auth, On the nature of things or the things of nature, In: The art of the artist, Crown, 51; auth, The comics as non-art, In: The funnies: an American idiom, Free Press, 63.
Mailing Address: 96 Bay State Rd, Boston, MA 02115.

FOSBURGH, JAMES WHITNEY
Painter, Writer
Preferred Media: Oils, Watercolors.
b New York, N Y, Aug 1, 10.
Study & Training: Yale Univ, BA, 33; Univ Rome, lauria degree, 33-34; Yale Univ, MA, 35.
Work in Public Collections: Metrop Mus Art; Boston Mus Fine Arts; Pa Acad Fine Arts; Toledo Mus Fine Arts; Hirshhorn Collection, Smithsonian Inst, Washington, D C; also in pvt collections.
Exhibitions: Corcoran Gallery Art; Pa Acad Fine Arts; one-man shows, Durlacher Bros, 50-63, Calif Palace of Legion of Honor, 55 & Los Angeles Mus Art, 55.
Teaching: Lectr painting & art hist, Frick Collection, Nat Gallery Art, Yale Univ & Metrop Mus Art, 34-60.
Positions: Chmn, Comt Paintings for the White House, 61-63; mem, Landmarks Preservation Comn, New York, 62-; mem, Comt Preservation of the White House, 64-; trustee, assoc in fine arts & mem comt, Garvin Collection, Yale Univ, presently.
Awards: Hallmark Award, 60.
Publications: Auth, Winslow Homer in the Adirondacks (catalogue), Adirondacks Mus, 59; contribr, Art News, Harper's Bazaar & Art in Am, 55-65.
Dealer: Coe-Kerr Gallery, 49 E 82nd St, New York, NY 10028.
Mailing Address: 32 E 64th St, New York, NY 10021.

FOSSUM, SYDNEY (GLENN)
Painter, Illustrator
Preferred Media: Oils, Watercolors, Pastels.
b Aberdeen, S Dak, Nov 13, 09.
Study & Training: Northern State Col; Minneapolis Sch Art, BFA; Univ Michoacana, Mex.
Work in Public Collections: Mus Mod Art, New York, N Y; Minneapolis Inst Arts, Minn; Walker Art Ctr, Minneapolis; Des Moines Art Ctr, Iowa; Joslyn Art Mus, Omaha, Nebr.
Commissions: Mural panels, Nat Co-op Cong, Minneapolis, 42; oil painting, Minn Centennial, Minneapolis, 49; mem gift print, Denver Art Mus, Colo, 54; pastel portrait, San Francisco Examiner, Calif, 60.
Exhibitions: Ann Watercolors, Prints, Drawings, Pa Acad Fine Arts, Philadelphia, 33-59; Int Watercolors, Chicago Art Inst, 34-46; Northwestern Printmakers Int, Seattle Art Mus, Wash, 42-60; Am Painting, Metrop Mus Art, New York, NY, 50; Ann Exhib Western Art, Denver Art Mus, 51-58.
Teaching: Instr drawing & painting, Minneapolis Sch Art, 45-50; instr drawing & painting, Wash Univ, 50-51; artist-in-residence, Des Moines Art Ctr, Iowa, 53-57.
Positions: Dir, Duluth Art Ctr, Minn, 60-62.
Awards: First in oils, Twin City Ann, Minneapolis Inst Arts, 39; first in oils & purchase award, Midwest Biennial, Walker Art Ctr, 47; purchase award for watercolor, St Paul Art Ctr, 62.
Memberships: Artists Equity Asn (dir, St Louis Chapter, 50-51, pres, Cent Area, 55-57, pres, North Calif Chapter, 58-60, pres, Minn Chapter, 65-67).
Publications: Illusr, We're the people, 42; illusr, The farmer builds his co-ops, 47; illusr, Ford Times, 53-58; illusr, Plain Song Mag, 67.
Mailing Address: 2700 12th Ave S, Minneapolis, MN 55407.

FOSTER, HAL
Cartoonist, Painter
b Halifax, N S, Aug 16, 92.
Positions: Creator & artist, Prince Valiant.
Awards: Banshees' Silver Lady; Nat Soc Cartoonists Reuben.
Publications: Auth & illusr, Prince Valiant and the three challenges, 60, Prince Valiant on the Inland Sea, 68, Prince Valiant in the new world, 68, Prince Valiant and the golden princess, 68 & Prince Valiant in the days of King Arthur, 69, Hastings.
Mailing Address: c/o Hastings House Publishers, Inc, 10 E 40th St, New York, NY 10016.

FOSTER, JAMES W, JR
Art Administrator
b Baltimore, Md, Jan 4, 20.
Study & Training: Johns Hopkins Univ, 38-41; George Washington Univ; Corcoran Sch Art, 45-46; Am Univ, BA, 47.
Positions: Exec asst, Baltimore Mus Art, 47-52, asst dir, 52-57; dir, Santa Barbara Mus Art, 57-63; dir, Honolulu Acad Arts, 63-
Memberships: Asn Art Mus Dirs; Am Asn Mus; Western Asn Art Mus; Hawaii Mus Asn.
Mailing Address: 900 S Beretania St, Honolulu, HI 96814.

FOULKES, LLYN
Painter
Preferred Media: Oils, Acrylics.
b Yakima, Wash, Nov 17, 34.
Study & Training: Cent Wash Col Educ; Univ Wash; Chouinard Art Inst.

Work in Public Collections: Whitney Mus Am Art, New York, N Y; Art Inst Chicago, Ill; Los Angeles Co Mus Art, Calif; Mus Mod Art, New York; Mus des 20 Jahrhunderts, Vienna, Austria.
Exhibitions: Seventh & Ninth São Paulo Biennial, Mus Mod Art, São Paulo, 63 & 67; New York World's Fair, 65; Fifth Paris Biennial, Mus Mod Art, Paris, France, 67; Whitney Mus Ann Am Painting, 67 & 69 & Am Art of Our Century, 71, Whitney Mus Am Art, New York; one-man shows, Pasadena Art Mus, Calif, 62, Oakland Mus Art, Calif, 64 & Galerie Darthea Speyer, Paris, France, 70.
Teaching: Prof painting & drawing & artist-in-residence, Univ Calif, Los Angeles, 65-71; resident painter, painting workshop, Art Ctr Sch, Los Angeles, 71-72.
Awards: First award for painting, San Francisco 82nd Ann, San Francisco Mus Art, 63; new talent purchase grant, Los Angeles Co Mus Art, 64; Medal of France (first award for painting), Fifth Paris Bienniale, Mus Mod Art, Paris, 67.
Bibliography: Demetrion (auth), U S A, fifth Paris biennale, Pasadena Art Mus, 67; Michael Compton (auth), Pop art, Movements Mod Art, 68; Henry Seldis (auth), Hollywood collects, Otis Art Inst, 70.
Memberships: Hon mem Pasadena Mus Art; hon mem Whitney Mus Am Art.
Mailing Address: c/o David Stuart Gallery, 807 N La Cienega Blvd, Los Angeles, CA 90042.

FOURCADE, XAVIER
Art Dealer
b Paris, France, Sept 20, 26.
Study & Training: Politic Sci Sch, Paris; Univ Paris Law Sch; Sch Oriental Languages, Paris; Univ Paris Sch Advan Studies; Oxford Univ.
Positions: V pres & dir, M Knoedler & Co, Inc, New York, N Y, 66-72; pres, Fourcade, Droll, Inc, New York, 72-
Specialty of Gallery: Twentieth century art & contemporary artists such as De Kooning, Gorky, Newman, Tony Smith, Moore, Eva Hesse, Heizer & others.
Mailing Address: Fourcade, Droll, Inc, 36 E 75th St, New York, NY 10021.

FOURNIER, ALEXANDER PAUL
Painter, Printmaker
Preferred Media: Acrylics.
b Simcoe, Ont, Oct 11, 39.
Study & Training: McMaster Univ, with Prof George Wallace.
Work in Public Collections: Art Gallery Ont, Toronto, Nat Gallery Can, Ottawa, Can Coun Collection, Ottawa & Art Gallery of Hamilton, Ont; Winnipeg Art Gallery, Man.
Commissions: Acrylic painting for lobby of apt bldg, Greenwin Construction Co, Toronto, 72.
Exhibitions: Ont Centennial Art Exhib, Art Gallery Ont, 67; 3rd Int Miniature Print Exhib, IBM Gallery, New York, N Y, 68; Five Lyrical Painters, Art Gallery Ont, 71; 3rd Int Exhib of Original Drawings, Mus Mod Art, Yugoslavia, 72; Graphic Art Today, 36th Int Venice Biennale, Italy, 72; plus many others.
Positions: Artist-in-residence, Waterloo-Lutheran Univ, 69-70.
Awards: First prize, Hadassah Art Auction, 64 & second prize, 66; C W Jeffery's Award, Can Soc Graphic Art, 67.
Bibliography: George Wallace (auth), Paul Fournier at the Westdale Gallery, Hamilton, Can Art, 7-8/62 & Alan Jarvis (auth), Canadian art to-day, Can Art, 7/66.
Mailing Address: c/o Pollock Gallery, 356 Dundas St W, Toronto, Ont, Can.

FOUSHEE, OLA MAIE (MRS JOHN M, SR)
Painter, Writer
b Avalon, N C.
Study & Training: Univ N C, Greensboro; Univ N C, Chapel Hill; also with Gregory D Ivy, Earl Mueller, John Opper, Francis Speight & Eliot O'Hara.
Exhibitions: Exhib in many group & one-man shows, N C, S C & Va.
Collections Arranged: Organized, Mile of Art, filmed by TV, Greensboro, N C, 62; plus other exhibs.
Teaching: Lectr art educ to various orgn.
Awards: Butler Inst Am Art; citation, N C State Art Soc, 62; plus others.
Memberships: N C State Art Soc; Assoc Artists N C; Durham Artists Guild; Allied Artists Durham (charter mem); Am Fedn Arts.
Publications: Contribr, Town & gown, Chapel Hill Weekly, annually; auth, Art in North Carolina: episodes and developments—1585-1970, Bks; columnist & feature writer.
Mailing Address: Box 866, Chapel Hill, NC 27514.

FOWLER, MARY BLACKFORD
Sculptor, Painter
b Findlay, Ohio, Feb 20, 92.
Study & Training: Oberlin Col, AB, 13; Columbia Univ, 18; Cor-

coran Sch Art, 33-36; Famous Artists Sch, 63-67; also with George Demetrios & Hans Hofmann.
Commissions: Commemorative sculpture, Findlay, Ohio, 37; five sculptured murals, Fed Bldg, Newport News, Va, 41-43; portrait bas-reliefs, Western Reserve Univ, Springfield Pub Libr, Mass & Am Sch Class Studies, Athens, Greece; plus others.
Awards: Prize, Findlay Art League, 61.
Memberships: Findlay Art League.
Publications: Co-auth, The picture book of sculpture, 29.
Mailing Address: 613 S Main St, Findlay, OH 45840.

FOX, CHARLES HAROLD
Craftsman
b Clarks Harbour, N S, Jan 15, 05.
Commissions: Jewelry, as gift to Princess Elizabeth & Duke of Edinburgh, by Govt N S, 51.
Exhibitions: Crafts Exhib, Nat Gallery, Can, 57; Brussels World's Fair, 58; Int Exhib, Dept External Affairs, Ottawa, Ont, 66 & 68; Expo '67.
Awards: Prizes, Can Nat Exhib, Toronto, 51, 53 & 55, Nat Exhib, Saint John, N B, 57 & Montreal, 61.
Mailing Address: 18 Caldwell Ave, Kentville, N S, Can.

FOX, JOHN
Painter
Preferred Media: Acrylics.
b Montreal, P Q, July 26, 27.
Study & Training: Montreal Mus Fine Arts; Slade Sch, London, Eng.
Work in Public Collections: Nat Gallery Can, Ottawa; Montreal Mus Fine Arts; Mus Que, P Q; Beaverbrook Art Gallery, Frederickton, N B; Art Gallery Greater Victoria, B C.
Mailing Address: c/o Marlborough Godard, 1490 Sherbrooke W, Montreal 109, P Q, Can.

FOX, ROY CHARLES W
Painter, Etcher
Preferred Media: Watercolors.
b Oneonta, N Y, Apr 14, 08.
Study & Training: Elmira Col, with Ernfred Anderson; also with Arthur R Abrams, Lars Hoftrup, Armand Wargny & James Swann.
Work in Public Collections: Arnot Art Mus, Elmira, N Y; Fla Southern Col, Lake Land; Elmira Col, N Y; Chemung Co Hist Soc, Elmira.
Exhibitions: Arnot Art Mus Regional, Elmira, 36-70; Finger Lakes Exhib, Rochester, N Y, 38-48; Am Soc Etchers, New York, N Y, 46; Cooperstown Art Asn, N Y, 57-70; The Etchers, Philadelphia Sketch Club, Pa, 60.
Awards: 100 Selected Prints of the Yr, Am Soc Etchers, 46.
Memberships: Elmira Art Club; Cooperstown Art Asn.
Publications: Contribr, Print Collectors Quart, 60; contribr, La Rev Mod, 66.
Mailing Address: Arnot Art Museum, 235 Lake St, Elmira, NY 14901.

FOX, TERRY ALAN
Sculptor
Preferred Media: Mixed Media.
b Seattle, Wash, May 10, 43.
Study & Training: Acad Belli Arti, Rome, Italy, 62-63.
Work in Public Collections: Sternum, Univ Calif Med Ctr, San Francisco.
Exhibitions: Arte de Sistemas, Mus Mod Art, Buenos Aires, Arg, 71; Prospect 71, Kuntshalle, Dusseldorf, Ger, 71; Projektion, Louisiana Mus, Denmark, 72; Dokumenta 5, Kassel, Ger, 72; Venice Biennale, Italy, 72; plus many others.
Teaching: Instr, art I levitation & art II singing, Mus Conceptual Art, San Francisco, 69-
Positions: Curator, Mus Conceptual Art, 69-71; west coast ed, Art Info, Dusseldorf, 69-
Bibliography: Sharp (auth), I want my mood to affect their looks, Avalanche, 71; Plagens (auth), Terry Fox: the impartial nightmare, Artforum, 72; Lippard (auth), excerpts, Praeger, 72.
Memberships: Fluxus West.
Publications: Contribr, Bevys and fox, Interfunktionen 6, 71; contribr, Pisces, Interfunktionen 7, 71; contribr, Environmental surfaces, Interfunktionen 8, 72; plus films & video tapes.
Dealer: Sonnabend Gallery, 420 W Broadway, New York, NY 10013 & 12 Rue Mazarine, Paris 6, France.
Mailing Address: 16 Rose St, San Francisco, CA 94102.

FOX, WINIFRED GRACE
Craftsman, Painter
b Avondale, N S, Nov 26, 09.
Study & Training: Sch Fine Arts, Mt Allison Univ; Art Stud League New York, with George Bridgman.
Work in Public Collections: Saint John Mus, N B; Centennial Permanent Collection, N S.

Commissions: Jewelry, as gift to Princess Elizabeth & Duke of
Edinburgh, by Govt N S.
Exhibitions: N S Soc Artists Ann; Nat Gallery Can, 57; Brussels
World's Fair, 58; Int Exhib, Dept External Affairs, Ottawa, Ont,
66 & 68; Expo '67; plus others.
Positions: Designer, dept handcrafts, N S Prov Govt, 45-60.
Awards: Prizes, Can Nat Exhib, Toronto, 51, 53 & 55, Nat Exhib,
Saint John, N B, 57 & Montreal, 61; plus others.
Memberships: N S Soc Artists.
Publications: Illusr, We keep a light & The flowing summer.
Mailing Address: 18 Caldwell Ave, Kentville, N S, Can.

FRACASSINI, SILVIO CARL
Painter, Educator
b Louisville, Colo, Nov 4, 07.
Study & Training: Univ Denver, BFA, 36; pvt study with John
Thompson & Walt Kuhn; Univ Iowa, MFA, 51.
Work in Public Collections: Denver Art Mus, Colo; Sioux City Art
Ctr, Iowa; Davenport Munic Gallery, Iowa; Elder Gallery, Lin-
coln, Nebr; Univ Iowa Mus, Iowa City.
Commissions: Mural (oil), Southern Hotel, Durango, Colo; mural
(oil), Philip Serafini residence, Denver; supvr decoration, Teller
House, Central City, Colo.
Exhibitions: Int Watercolor Exhib, Denver Art Mus, Colo, 39; Nat
Invitational Ceramics Exhib, Scripps Col, Claremont, Calif, 47;
Am Watercolor Soc 83rd Ann, Nat Acad Design, New York, N Y,
49; Am Color Print Soc 13th Ann, Philadelphia Print Club, Pa,
52; Wichita Nat Ceramics Exhib, Kans, 59.
Teaching: Instr art, Univ Denver, 34-42; prof art & head dept, Iowa
Wesleyan Col, 46-56; prof art, Univ Iowa, 56-
Positions: Docent, Denver Art Mus, 31-39; secy-registrar, Chappell
Sch, Univ Denver, 33-37.
Awards: Friends of Art purchase prize, Denver Art Mus, 43; first
Younkers award for watercolor, 55 & first prof award for ce-
ramics, 12th Ann, 60, Des Moines Art Ctr.
Memberships: Kappa Pi; Midwest Art Conf.
Mailing Address: Dept of Art, University of Iowa, 911 Iowa Ave,
Iowa City, IA 52240.

FRAME, ROBERT (AARON)
Painter
Preferred Media: Oils.
b San Fernando, Calif, July 31, 24.
Study & Training: With Henry Lee McFee, 47-50; Pomona Col, BA,
48; Claremont Col, MFA, 51.
Work in Public Collections: Pasadena Art Mus, Calif, 52; State
Calif, Sacramento, 58; Nat Acad Design, New York, N Y; Scripps
Col, Claremont, Calif; Munic Art Dept, City Los Angeles.
Exhibitions: Ill Biennial, Urbana, 61-65; American Painting, Rich-
mond, Va, 65; De Young Mus, San Francisco; Los Angeles Co
Mus; plus twenty one one-man exhibs.
Awards: Purchase prize, Pasadena Art Mus, 52; Guggenheim fel,
57-58; first prize, James D Phelan Awards, 65.
Bibliography: Schaad (auth), Realm of contemporary still life, Rein-
hold, 61; Harold (auth), Prize-winning paintings, Allied, 64;
Mugniani (auth), Oil painting, Van Nostrand, 69.
Dealer: Adele Bednarz Galleries, 902 La Cienega, Los Angeles, CA
90069.
Mailing Address: 112 Chapala St, Santa Barbara, CA 93101.

FRANCES, HARRIETTE ANTON
Painter, Printmaker
Preferred Media: Acrylics.
b San Francisco, Calif.
Study & Training: Jean Turner Sch Fashion Design, San Francisco,
scholar, 41; San Francisco Sch Fine Arts, 42-45; Univ Pac, 55-
57; San Francisco Art Inst, 63, 65-66; also with painters, James
Weeks & William H Brown, & with printmaker, Richard Graf.
Work in Public Collections: Fresno Art Ctr, Calif; Charles D Clark
Collection, McAllen, Tex.
Exhibitions: James D Phelan Award Exhib, De Young Mus, San Fran-
cisco, 63 & Palace Legion of Honor, 65; Fifth Winter Invitational,
Palace Legion of Honor, 64 & California Printmakers, 71; West-
ern Asn Art Mus invitational traveling one-man shows at mus &
univ galleries throughout U S, 68-70; San Francisco Women
Artists, Sonoma State Col & Oakland Art Mus, 69.
Awards: Northern Calif Art Ann Award, 63-65; Calif State Fair
Award, 64; James D Phelan Award in Art, 65.
Bibliography: George Christy (auth), Are you with it, Town &
Country Mag, 67; Martin Fox (ed), A graphic artist depicts her
LSD trip, Print Mag, 67.
Memberships: San Francisco Women Artists; Marin Soc Artists
(juror, calendar chmn & receiving chmn, 68-72);

Publications: Contribr, Macleans Mag, 64; contribr, Ramparts Mag,
66; contribr, U S A & Espanol issue, M D Mag, 66; contribr, Print
Mag & Psychedelic Art, 67.
Dealer: Contemporary Gallery, 2800 Routh St, Dallas, TX 75201.
Mailing Address: 60 Steven Ct, Fairfax, CA 94930.

FRANCIS, AL (ALFRED KADE)
Painter, Lecturer
Preferred Media: Watercolors, Oils.
b Amity, Ark, Feb 10, 27.
Study & Training: Norton Art Inst, Kansas City, Mo, 46; Centenary
Col La, BA, 52, with Don Brown, Edgar Whitney, Milford Zornes,
John Pike & L G Sicard.
Work in Public Collections: Watercolor, North Little Rock Times
Collection, Ark; Helen Anderson Collection, Little Rock, Ark;
Sovolos Advertising Agency & B & B Outdoor Advertising,
Shreveport, La; staff of permanent artists, Barnwell Art Ctr,
Shreveport, and many other public & private collections.
Exhibitions: Holiday in Dixie Art Show, 64; Regional & Nat Shreve-
port Art Club Ann Fall Exhib, 67; Hoover Watercolor Soc Ann
Fall Exhib, 67; Ark State Festival Arts 11th Ann Show, Little
Rock, 68; La Tourist Develop Comn, 68; plus others.
Teaching: Private art instr, 71-, plus many lectr demonstrations.
Positions: Art dir, B & B Outdoor Advertising, 67-72.
Awards: First prize for watercolor, Hoover Watercolor Soc, 67;
two purchase awards, Shreveport Art Club Fall Show, 67; two
awards & one first purchase award, Ark State Festival Arts, 68.
Bibliography: Margaret McDonald, The rooftop Rembrandt, Shreve-
port J, 5/12/67; Shreveport artist in local lecture, Marshall
Forecast, 11/16/71.
Memberships: Shreveport Art Club (bd dirs, 67); Hoover Water-
color Soc (rec secy, 67); Mens Art Guild (rec secy, 66); Mens
Prof League; Southwestern Watercolor Soc.
Mailing Address: 9138 Simmons Blvd, Shreveport, LA 71108.

FRANCIS, HAROLD CARLETON
Painter, Illustrator
b Culloden, Ont, Feb 19, 19.
Study & Training: Art Stud League New York, with Robert Brackman.
Exhibitions: Western Ont Exhib, 42-65; Can Soc Graphic Artists, 43,
44 & 53; Can Soc Painter-Etchers & Engravers, 49-61; Hamilton
Art Gallery, 54 & 60; Can Nat Exhib, 57.
Memberships: Can Soc Painter-Etchers & Engravers; fel Int Inst
Arts & Lett.
Publications: Contribr, articles & illus, In: Can Forum.
Mailing Address: 548 Kininvie Dr, London, Ont, Can.

FRANCIS, SAM
Painter
b San Mateo, Calif, June 25, 23.
Study & Training: Univ Calif, Berkeley; BA, 49, MA, 50; Atelier
Fernand Leger, Paris, France; Univ Calif, Berkeley, hon DFA,
69.
Work in Public Collections: Guggenheim Mus, N Y; Mus Mod Art;
Albright Art Gallery; Kunsthaus, Zurich, Switz; Dayton Art Inst;
plus others.
Commissions: Murals, Kunsthalle, Berne, Switz, 57, Sofu Sch Flower
Arrangement, Tokyo, Japan, 57 & Chase Manhattan Bank, New
York, N Y, 59.
Exhibitions: One-man shows, Seattle Art Mus, 59, Pasadena Mus
Art, 59, San Francisco Mus Art, 59 & 67 & Mus Fine Arts Hous-
ton, 67; retrospective, Stedelijk Mus, Amsterdam, 68; plus many
other group & one-man shows, U S & abroad.
Awards: First prize, Third Int Biennial Exhib Prints, Tokyo, 62;
Dunn Int Prize, Tate Gallery, London, 63; Tamarind fel, 63;
plus others.
Bibliogrphy: Werner Haftman (auth), included in: Paintings in the
twentieth century, Praeger, 60; Sam Hunter (ed), included in: New
art around the world: painting and sculpture, Abrams, 66; James
Johnson Sweeney (auth), Sam Francis (catalogue), Mus Fine Arts
Houston, 67; plus many others.
Dealer: Galerie Smith-Anderson, 200 Homer St, Palo Alto, CA
94301.
Mailing Address: 345 W Channel Dr, Santa Monica Canyon, Los An-
geles, CA 90402.

FRANCK, ALBERT JACQUES
Painter
b Middleburg, Holland, Apr 2, 99.
Exhibitions: Royal Can Acad Ann; Ont Soc Artists Ann; Can Soc
Painters in Water Colour Ann; Can Soc Graphic Arts Ann.
Awards: Purchase awards, Can Coun & Univ Western Ont.
Memberships: Ont Soc Artists; Can Soc Painters in Water Colour.
Art Interests: Restoration.
Mailing Address: 90 Hazelton Ave, Toronto 5, Ont, Can.

FRANCK, FREDERICK S
Painter, Writer
b Maastricht, Holland, Apr 12, 09; U S citizen.
Study & Training: Belg, Eng & U S; Univ Pittsburgh, hon DFA, 63.
Work in Public Collections: Whitney Mus Am Art, New York, N Y; San Francisco Mus Art, Calif; Stedelijk Mus, Holland; Mus Nat France, Paris; Tokyo Nat Mus, Japan; plus many others.
Commissions: Murals, Temple Beth-El, Elizabeth, N J, Albert Schweitzer Publ Sch, Levittown, N J, & Nat Mus Tokyo; stage designs for off-Broadway shows; drawings for New Yorker; built a chapel with own sculpture, stained glass & mosaics, Warwick, N Y, 65-68.
Exhibitions: Group shows in Whitney Mus Am Art & Metrop Mus Art, New York, Corcoran Gallery Art, Washington, D C, Butler Inst Am Art, Youngstown, Ohio, Calif Palace Legion of Honor, San Francisco & shows in Paris, Amsterdam, Geneva, London, Brussels, Rome & Japan; plus many other group & one-man shows.
Awards: Purchase prizes, Carnegie Inst, Am Acad Arts & Lett & others; Living Arts Found Award, Maastricht Mus, Holland, 58; Medal of the Pontificate, Pope John, 63; plus others.
Memberships: Fel Int Inst Arts & Lett; Found for Arts, Relig & Cult; Artists Equity Asn (hon dir, New York).
Publications: Auth, Open book, 67, Croquis Parisien, 69, Tutte le Strade portano a Roma, 69; Le Paris de Simenon, 69 & Simenon's Paris, 70; plus many other bks & articles in leading nat mag.
Mailing Address: Rte 1, Covered Bridge Rd, Warwick, NY 10990.

FRANCO, BARBARA
Curator
b New York, N Y, Mar 16, 45.
Study & Training: Bryn Mawr Col, BA; Cooperstown Grad Progs, MA.
Collections Arranged: White's Utica Pottery, 69-70 & Shaker Arts and Crafts, 70-71, Munson-Williams-Proctor Inst, Utica, N Y.
Positions: Cur decorative arts, Munson-Williams-Proctor Inst, 66-
Publications: Auth, White's Utica pottery (catalogue), 69; auth, Shaker arts and crafts (catalogue), 70; auth, Stoneware made by the White Family in Utica, N Y, Antiques, 71.
Mailing Address: 310 Genesee St, Utica, NY 13502.

FRANK, DAVID
Potter, Educator
Preferred Media: Clay.
b St Paul, Minn, Sept 13, 40.
Study & Training: Univ Minn, Duluth, with Glenn C Nelson & BS(art); Tulane Univ La, MFA.
Work in Public Collections: Tweed Gallery, Duluth; Newcomb Art Sch Collection; Mid Tenn State Univ Collection, Murfreesboro; Miss State Col Women, Columbus.
Exhibitions: Wichita Craft Exhib, Kans; 7th Miami Ceramic Nat, Fla; Southeast Craftsmen 66, N C; Mid South Ceramics & Crafts Exhib, Tenn; 14th Ann Delta Art Exhib, Ark.
Teaching: Asst prof ceramics, Miss State Col Women, 65-
Memberships: Am Craftsman's Coun.
Mailing Address: Box 243, Rte 1, Steens, MS 39766.

FRANK, HELEN SOPHIA
Painter, Designer
Preferred Media: Oils.
b Berkeley, Calif.
Study & Training: Calif Col Arts & Crafts, grad; Art Stud League New York, scholarship; Polakov Studio, New York, N Y.
Work in Public Collections: Norfolk Mus Arts & Sci, Va; Crocker Art Gallery, Sacramento, Calif; many pvt collections in the U S & abroad.
Exhibitions: One-man shows, Pinacotheca, New York, 43, Vancouver Art Gallery, B C, 47, Curacao Mus, Neth W Indies, 49, Parsons Gallery, London, Eng, 54, Chase Gallery, New York, 58 & Am Bible Soc, New York, 72.
Positions: Costumer, Roundabout Theatre & Joffrey Ballet Co, New York, 70.
Memberships: United Scenic Artists; Int Platform Asn.
Mailing Address: 241 Lexington Ave, New York, NY 10016.

FRANK, MARY
Sculptor
b London, Eng, Feb 4, 33.
Study & Training: With Max Beckmann, 50 & Hans Hofmann, 51.
Work in Public Collections: Art Inst Chicago; Kalamazoo Inst Art; Mus Mod Art; Southern Ill Univ; Worcester Mus Art, Mass; plus others.
Exhibitions: Mass Inst Technol; Yale Univ; Brandeis Univ; Mus Mod Art; Hans Hofmann & His Stud Traveling Exhib, 63-64; plus others.
Awards: Ingram Merril Found grant, 61; Longview Found grant, 62-64; Nat Coun Arts Award, 68.
Dealer: Zabriskie Gallery, 29 W 57th St, New York, NY 10019.
Mailing Address: 463 West St, New York, NY 10014.

FRANKEL, DEXTRA
Sculptor, Craftsman
b Los Angeles, Calif, Nov 28, 24.
Study & Training: Long Beach State Col.
Work in Public Collections: Philadelphia Free Libr; La Jolla Art Mus, Calif; Saint Paul Art Ctr, Minn; Pac View Mem Park, Corona Del Mar, Calif; Kennecott Copper Co, Salt Lake City, Utah; also in pvt collections.
Exhibitions: Los Angeles Co Mus Art, 59, 62 & 66; five shows, Pasadena Art Mus, Calif, 59-68; Tucson Art Ctr, Ariz, 64 & 66; Mus Contemp Crafts, N Y, 66 & 68; Los Angeles State Col, 69; plus many other group & one-man shows.
Collections Arranged: Recorded Images/Dimensional Media, 67, Intersection of Line, 67, Frazer/Lipofsky/Richardson, 68, Transparency/Reflection, 68 & others, Art Gallery, Calif State Univ, Fullerton.
Teaching: Asst prof art, Calif State Univ, Fullerton, 64-
Positions: Dir art gallery, Calif State Univ, Fullerton, 67-
Awards: Purchase awards, Am Color Print Soc, 61 & Philadelphia Free Libr, 61; award, Calif Craftsmen, Oakland Art Mus, 63; plus others.
Memberships: Calif Soc Printmakers; Am Color Print Soc; Am Craftsmen's Coun.
Mailing Address: Dept of Art, California State University, 800 N State College Blvd, Fullerton, CA 92631.

FRANKENSTEIN, ALFRED VICTOR
Art Critic, Art Historian
b Chicago, Ill, Oct 5, 06.
Study & Training: Univ Chicago, PhB, 32; Yale Univ.
Teaching: Prof art hist, Mills Col, 50-72; lectr art hist, Univ Calif, Berkeley, 55-; vis prof art hist, N Y Univ, 70-71; lectr art hist, Stanford Univ, presently.
Positions: Art Critic, San Francisco Chronicle, Calif, 34-
Awards: Guggenheim fel, 48; Frank Jewett Mather Award, Col Art Asn, 70.
Memberships: Col Art Asn.
Publications: Auth, After the hunt, William Harnett & other American still life painters, 53-61; auth, Angels over the alter (folk art in South Seas), 61; ed, William Sidney Mount, documentary biography, 73.
Mailing Address: c/o San Francisco Chronicle, San Francisco, CA 94119.

FRANKENTHALER, HELEN
Painter
b New York, N Y, Dec 12, 28.
Study & Training: Horace Mann, Brearley & Dalton Schs; Bennington Col, BA, 49; also with Rufino Tamayo, Wallace Harrison, Paul Feeley & Hans Hofmann.
Work in Public Collections: Metrop Mus Art, New York; Mus Mod Art, New York; Art Inst Chicago, Ill; Cleveland Mus Art; Pasadena Art Mus, Calif.
Exhibitions: Nature in Abstraction, Whitney Mus Am Art, New York, 58; American Abstract Expressionists & Imagists, Solomon R Guggenheim Mus, New York, 61; Post Painterly Abstraction, Los Angeles Co Mus Art, Calif, Walker Art Ctr, Minn & Art Gallery Ont, Toronto, 64; New York Painting & Sculpture: 1940-1970, Metrop Mus Art, New York, 69-70; Abstract Painting in the 70's, Mus Fine Arts, Boston, Mass, 72.
Teaching: Instr contemp painting sem, Yale Univ, spring 70; instr contemp painting sem, Princeton Univ & Hunter Col, 70.
Positions: Trustee, Bennington Col, 67-; fellow, Calhoun Col, Yale Univ, 68-
Awards: First prize, First Paris Biennial, 59; Commune of Catania gold medal, Third Biennial Int Grafica d'Arte, 72; Garrett Award, 70th Am Exhib, Art Inst Chicago, 72.
Bibliography: Eugene C Goossen (auth), Helen Frankenthaler, Praeger, 69; Barbara Rose (auth), Frankenthaler, Abrams, 72.
Dealer: Andre Emmerich Gallery, 41 E 57th St, New York, NY 10022.
Mailing Address: 173 E 94th St, New York, NY 10028.

FRANKLIN, ERNEST WASHINGTON, JR
Collector
b Apex, N C, Apr 13, 05.
Study & Training: Univ N C, BS; Univ Pa, MD.
Collection: Contemporary art.
Mailing Address: 1141 Linganore Pl, Charlotte, NC 28203.

FRANSIOLI, THOMAS ADRIAN
Painter
Preferred Media: Oils, Acrylics, Gouache, Pencil; Silk Screen.
b Seattle, Wash, Sept 15, 06.
Study & Training: Univ Pa, BArch; Art Stud League New York.

Work in Public Collections: Mus Fine Arts, Boston, Mass; Whitney Mus Am Art, New York, N Y; Seattle Art Mus, Wash; Dallas Mus Fine Arts, Tex; Farnsworth Mus, Rockland, Maine.
Commissions: Murals in dining rm, Aetna Life Bldg, Hartford, Conn, 62; four paintings of old New York, Univ Club, New York, 64; mural in stair hall, Princeton Club, New York, 66; mural in lobby, Brevoort East Hotel, New York, 67.
Exhibitions: Boston Art Festival, 48-49; Whitney Mus Ann, New York, 48-52 & 58; Carnegie Inst, Pittsburgh, Pa, 49 & 52; Am Art Today, Metrop Mus Art, New York, 50; Maine & Its Role in American Art, Colby Col, Waterville, Maine & Whitney Mus Am Art, New York, 63.
Awards: Purchase prize, Boston Arts Festival, 52; hon citizen of state of Maine, 54.
Dealer: Gallery 3, Greenwich Plaza, Greenwich, CT 06830.
Mailing Address: Cornwall Hollow, Falls Village, CT 06031.

FRASCONI, ANTONIO
Illustrator, Painter
Preferred Media: Graphics.
b Buenos Aires, Arg, Apr 28, 19.
Study & Training: Art Stud League New York; New Sch Social Res.
Work in Public Collections: Metrop Mus Art, New York, N Y; Mus Mod Art, New York; Mus Nac Bellas Artes, Montevideo, Uruguay; Bibliot Nat, Paris, France; Arts Coun Gr Brit, London, Eng.
Exhibitions: Casa Americas, Habana, Cuba, 65-68; Venice Biennale, Italy, 68; Art of the Americas, Yale Univ; Smithsonian Inst, Washington, D C; var ann, Pa Acad Fine Arts, Philadelphia.
Awards: Joseph Pennell Mem Medal, Pa Acad Fine Arts, 53; Grand Prix, Venice Film Festival, 60; Premio La Habana, Casa Americas, 68.
Bibliography: Leona E Prasse (auth), The work of A Frasconi, Baltimore Mus Art, 63; Manuel Gasser (auth), A Frasconi, Graphis Press (Switz), 67.
Publications: Illusr, Twelve fables of Aesop, 54; illusr, Bestiary, 65; illusr, Overhead the sun, 69; illusr, Unstill life, 69; illusr, On the slain collegians, 71.
Dealers: Weyhe Gallery, 794 Lexington Ave, New York, NY 10021; Terry Dintenfass, Inc, 18 E 67th St, New York, NY 10021.
Mailing Address: 26 Dock Rd, Norwalk, CT 06854.

FRASER, DOUGLAS (FERRAR)
Art Historian, Educator
b Hornell, N Y, Sept 3, 29.
Study & Training: Columbia Col, AB, Columbia Univ, AM & PhD.
Teaching: Prof art hist & archaeol, Columbia Univ.
Research: Primitive and pre-Columbian art.
Mailing Address: 445 Riverside Dr, New York, NY 10027.

FRATER, HAL
Painter
b New York, N Y, Mar 3, 09.
Exhibitions: Nat Acad Design; Chrysler Mus, Provincetown, Mass; Brooklyn Mus; Seton Hall Univ; Allied Artists Am; plus others.
Memberships: Painters & Sculptors Soc N J; Allied Artists Am; Soc Illusr; Artists Equity Asn.
Mailing Address: 215 Park Row, New York, NY 10038.

FRAUWIRTH, SIDNEY
Collector
b Smerekowjec, Poland, Nov 2, 08; U S citizen.
Collection: American paintings, drawings, and sculpture.
Mailing Address: 21 Cove St, New Bedford, MA 02744.

FRAZER, JOHN THATCHER
Film Maker, Painter
b Akron, Ohio, Apr 2, 32.
Study & Training: Univ Tex, BFA; Yale Univ, MFA, also with Joseph Albers.
Work in Public Collections: Davison Art Ctr, Wesleyan Univ, Middletown, Conn; Libr of Cong, Washington, D C; Cullinan Collection, Houston Mus Fine Arts, Tex; Nicholson Mem Libr, Longview, Tex.
Exhibitions: Tex Ann, Dallas Mus Fine Arts, Tex, 58; New Haven Arts Festival, Conn, 60; Boston Arts Festival, Mass, 61; Flaherty Film Festival, Lakeville, Conn, 66; Am Film Festival, New York, N Y, 68.
Teaching: Prof art, motion pictures & drawing, Wesleyan Univ, 59-
Bibliography: New talent, U S A, Art in Am, 62; Bernard Chaet (auth), The art of drawing, Holt, 70.
Memberships: Am Asn Univ Prof; Col Art Asn; Univ Film Study Ctr (v pres, 70-72).
Art Interests: Motion pictures.

Publications: Auth, Documentary films & books on documentary films, Choice Mag, 69.
Mailing Address: Art Center, Wesleyan University, Middletown, CT 06457.

FRAZIER, LE ROY DYYON
Painter, Sculptor
b Fort Meyers, Fla, May 2, 46.
Work in Public Collections: Mus Mod Art, New York, N Y; Whitney Mus Am Art, New York.
Exhibitions: Cleveland Top Artists, In Town Club, Cleveland, Ohio, 69; Int Exhib Art, Cleveland, 70; Whitney Mus Am Art Ann, New York, 72.
Mailing Address: George Washington Hotel, 23rd St & Lexington Ave, New York, NY 10010.

FRAZIER, PAUL D
Sculptor
Preferred Media: Metals, Plastics.
b Pickaway Co, Ohio, May 6, 22.
Study & Training: Ohio State Univ, BFA; Cranbrook Acad Art, MFA; Skowhegan Sch Painting & Sculpture, with Jose de Creeft; Acad Grande Chaumière, with Ossip Zadkine.
Work in Public Collections: Cranbrook Mus; Skowhegan Sch Painting & Sculpture Collection; Munson-Williams-Proctor Inst; Rochester Mus Arts & Sci.
Exhibitions: Primary Structures, Solomon R Guggenheim Mus, New York, N Y, 67; plus many other group & one-man shows.
Teaching: Instr sculpture, ceramics & design, Univ Minn, 50-53; instr sculpture, Munson-Williams-Proctor Inst, 53-58; assoc prof 3-D area & drawing, Queens Col, 64-
Awards: Gov award, State of Ohio, 47; Cranbrook Found medal for sculpture, 49; first prize for sculpture, Cooperstown Mus, 57.
Bibliography: Americans with a future, Art in Am, winter 54; Robert Coates (auth), Young & old, New Yorker, 3/9/57; Ralph Pomeroy (auth), Confirmed out-of-towner, Art Int, 10/28/68.
Mailing Address: Box 33, Washington Depot, CT 06794.

FREDERICKS, MARSHALL MAYNARD
Sculptor
Preferred Media: Granite, Bronze, Marble, Stone, Aluminum, Wood, Polyesters.
b Rock Island, Ill, Jan 31, 08.
Study & Training: John Huntington Polytech Inst, Cleveland, Ohio; Cleveland Sch Art, grad, 30; Heimann Schule, Munich, Ger; Schwegerie Schule, Munich; Acad Scandinav, Paris, France; private studies in Copenhagen, Rome & London; Carl Milles Studio; Cranbrook Acad Art; Gund fel; Matzen Traveling fel & Cranbrook fel.
Work in Public Collections: Detroit Inst Arts, Mich; Cleveland Sch Art, Ohio; Cranbrook Mus Art, Bloomfield Hills, Mich; Saginaw Mus, Mich; Milwaukee Pub Mus, Wis.
Commissions: Spirit of Detroit, City of Detroit, 59; Christ on the Cross, Catholic Church, Indian River, Mich, 59; Cleveland War Mem Fountain, City of Cleveland, 64; State Dept Fountain, Washington, D C, 64; Freedom of the Human Spirit, N Y World's Fair Comt, Flushing Meadow, 64.
Exhibitions: Carnegie Inst Nat, Pittsburgh, Pa; Philadelphia Int Invitational, Pa; Art Inst Chicago Nat, Ill; Detroit Art Inst, Mich; Whitney Mus Am Art Nat Invitational.
Teaching: Instr sculpture, Cranbrook Sch, Bloomfield Hills, 32-38; instr sculpture, Kingswood Sch, 32-42; instr sculpture, Cranbrook Acad Art, 32-42.
Positions: Mem, Gov Comt New State Capitol, Lansing, Mich; mem, Mich Asn Professions; trustee, Am-Scand Found; bd trustees, People-to-People Prog, Inc.
Awards: Fine arts gold medal, Am Inst Architects, 52; gold medal of hon, Mich Acad Sci, Arts & Letters, 53; gold medal of hon, Archit League New York, 56.
Memberships: Academician Nat Acad Design; fel Nat Sculpture Soc; hon mem Mich Soc Architects; fel Royal Soc Arts, London, Eng; fel Int Inst Arts & Letters.
Mailing Address: 440 Lake Park Dr, Birmingham, MI 48009.

FREDMAN, FAIYA R
Sculptor, Painter
Preferred Media: Poly-foam, Pencil.
b Columbus, Ohio, Sept 8, 25.
Study & Training: Calif State Univ, San Diego; Univ Calif, Los Angeles; also with S MacDonald Wright, Clinton Adams & Dr Harold Gregor.
Work in Public Collections: Univ Calif, San Diego; Ariz State Univ, Tempe.

Exhibitions: Invisible-Visible, Long Beach Mus Invitational, Calif, 72; Six San Diegans, La Jolla Mus Invitational, Calif, 72; Small Images, Calif State Univ, Los Angeles, 72; one-man shows, Skin '68, La Jolla Mus Contemp Art, 68 & Ariz State Univ, Tempe, 71.
Mailing Address: 121-27th St, Del Mar, CA 92014.

FREED, DAVID
Printmaker, Photographer
Preferred Media: Graphics.
b Toledo, Ohio, May 23, 36.
Study & Training: Miami Univ; Univ Iowa; Royal Col Art, London.
Work in Public Collections: Art Inst Chicago, Ill; Nat Collection Fine Arts, Washington, D C; Va Mus Fine Arts, Richmond; Libr Cong, Washington, D C; Mus Boymans van Beuningen, Rotterdam, Holland.
Exhibitions: Photography in Printmaking, AAA Gallery, New York, N Y, 68-70; one-man show, Franz Bader Gallery, Washington, D C, 68, 70 & 73; Human Concern/Personal Torment, Whitney Mus Am Art, 69; Second Int Print Biennial, Bradford, Eng, 70; one-man show, Gorner & Millard Gallery, London, Eng, 70 & 73.
Teaching: Asst prof printmaking, Va Commonwealth Univ, 66-; guest lectr etching, Cent Sch Art, London, 69.
Awards: Fulbright grant, 63-64.
Memberships: Soc Am Graphic Artists.
Mailing Address: 1825 W Grace, Richmond, VA 23220.

FREED, ERNEST BRADFIELD
Printmaker, Painter
b Rockville, Ind, July 20, 08.
Study & Training: Ind State Univ; Univ Ill, BS, DFA; Pa Acad Fine Arts, with George Harding; Univ Iowa, with Grant Wood & Mauricio Kasansky, MA.
Work in Public Collections: Libr of Cong; Metrop Mus Art; Baltimore Mus; Mod Mus, São Paulo, Brazil; Victoria & Albert Mus, London, Eng.
Exhibitions: Libr of Cong, 41, 49 & 50; Brooklyn Mus, 44; State Dept Tour Europe, 59; Korean Mus, Seoul, 70; State Univ Iowa, Ames, 72.
Teaching: Instr art, Northwest State Univ, 37-39; supvr art, Flagstaff Pub Schs, 39-41; instr art, Fairmont State Col, 41-49; head art dept, Bradley Univ, 49-54; head printmaking, Otis Art Inst, 54-
Awards: Eyre Medal, 53; Am Artists; Soc Graphic Artists; plus others.
Memberships: Soc Am Graphic Artists; Am Color Soc; Los Angeles Printmakers.
Mailing Address: Otis Art Institute, 2401 Wilshire Blvd, Los Angeles, CA 90057.

FREEDBERG, SYDNEY JOSEPH
Art Historian, Educator
b Boston, Mass, Nov 11, 14.
Study & Training: Harvard Col, AB(summa cum laude), 36, Sachs res fel fine arts, 36-37; Harvard Univ, AM, 39, PhD, 40.
Teaching: Asst & tutor fine arts, Harvard Univ, 38-40; asst prof art, Wellesley Col, 46-49, assoc prof art, 50-54; vis lectr fine arts, Inst Mod Art, Boston, 47; assoc prof fine arts, Harvard Univ, 54-60, chmn dept fine arts, 59-63, prof, 60-
Positions: Bd dirs, Col Art Asn Am, 62-66; nat v chmn, Comt to Rescue Italian Art, 66-71; dir, Save Venice, Inc, 71-
Awards: Hon Mem, Order of the British Empire; Grand Off, Order of Solidarity, Italian Repub.
Publications: Auth, Parmigianino: his works in painting, Harvard Univ Press, 50; auth, Painting of the high renaissance in Rome and Florence, Harvard Univ Press, Vols I & II, 61; auth, Andrea del Sarto, Harvard Univ Press, Vols I & II, 63; auth, Painting in Italy, 1500-1600, Penguin Bks (London & Baltimore), 71.
Mailing Address: Fine Arts Dept, Fogg Art Museum, Harvard University, Cambridge, MA 02138.

FREEDMAN, DORIS C
Art Administrator
b New York, N Y, Apr 25, 28.
Study & Training: Albright Col, BS; Columbia Univ Sch Social Work, MSW.
Positions: Dir, New York City Dept Cult Affairs, 67-70; producer-moderator, weekly radio show, Artists in the City, WNYC-FM, 69-; chmn, Pub Arts Coun, New York City, 71-; chmn Citizens for Artists Housing, 70-; pres, City Walls, Inc, 70-; co-chmn, Parks, Environ, Recreation & Cult Affairs Comt, 71-
Awards: Jeane Dale Katz Award, Queens Coun on Arts, 69; Louise Waterman Wise Laureate Award, Women's Div of Am Jewish Cong, 72.
Memberships: Fine Arts Fedn (exec bd); Metrop Mus Art (vis comt community relations, 71-); Parks Coun New York City (pub art chmn, 72); Munic Arts Soc (bd dirs, 71-).

Publications: Auth, Sculpture in environment (catalogue), New York City Dept Cult Affairs, 10/67; auth, Can government get with it in the arts?, A Further Mag of Arts, 68; auth, foreword to A guide for film teachers, 68, introduction to Neighborhood Street Festivals, 68 & A celebration for people, 70, New York City Dept Cult Affairs.
Mailing Address: Public Arts Council, 25 Central Park W, Apt 25-R, New York, NY 10023.

FREEDMAN, MAURICE
Painter
Preferred Media: Oils, Gouache.
b Boston, Mass, Nov 14, 04.
Study & Training: Boston Mus Fine Arts, scholarship class, 19-21; Mass Normal Art Sch, with Andrew, Sharman & Porter, 21-25; Boston Mus Sch, 30; Acad Lhôte, Paris, France, 30.
Work in Public Collections: Nat Collection Fine Arts, Smithsonian Inst, Washington, D C; Carnegie Inst, Pittsburgh, Pa; City Art Mus, St Louis, Mo; Brooklyn Mus, N Y; Los Angeles Co Mus, Calif.
Exhibitions: Carnegie Int, 50; American Painting Today & American Watercolors, Metrop Mus Art, New York, 50-52; Am Acad Arts & Lett, New York, 70; Maurice Freedman Retrospective, Wash Univ Gallery Art, St Louis, 72; Contemporary American Oil Painting 23rd Biennial, Corcoran Gallery Art, Washington.
Awards: Jane Peterson Medal, Audubon Artists, 72.
Bibliography: Sheldon Cheney (auth), A primer of modern art, 45; A O Gruskin (auth), Painting in U S A, 46; Walter Barker (auth), catalogue, Wash Univ, 72.
Dealer: Midtown Galleries, 11 E 57th St, New York, NY 11203.
Mailing Address: 121 Edgars Lane, Hastings-on-Hudson, NY 10706.

FREEDMAN, ROBERT J
Collector
Mailing Address: 120 E 71st St, New York, NY 10021.

FREELAND, WILLIAM LEE
Painter, Sculptor
Preferred Media: Oils, Pastels: Charcoal, Wood, Steel, Plastics.
b Pittsburgh, Pa, June 16, 29.
Study & Training: Philadelphia Mus Sch Art, Pa; Hans Hofmann Sch, Provincetown, Mass.
Work in Public Collections: Wilmington Mus & Soc Fine Arts, Del; Univ. Del, Newark; Chester Co Fed Savings & Loan, West Chester, Pa.
Exhibitions: One-man show, Philadelphia Art Alliance, 56; 25th Corcoran Biennial Exhib, Washington, D C, 57; color show, Birmingham Mus, Ala, 63; Artists Tribute to J F K, Swarthmore Col, 64; Nat Watercolor Show, Pa Acad Fine Arts, Philadelphia, 69.
Teaching: Asst prof fine arts, Moore Col Art, 69-
Awards: Copeland purchase award, Wilmington Mus; purchase award, Univ Del, 71.
Mailing Address: 516 N Scott's Lane, West Chester, PA 19380.

FREEMAN, DAVID L
Painter, Educator
Preferred Media: Acrylics.
b Columbia, Mo, Nov 10, 37.
Study & Training: Univ Mo, BA & MA; State Univ Iowa, MFA; Penland Sch Crafts & Penland Weavers.
Work in Public Collections: Mint Mus Art, Charlotte, N C; Minn Mus Art, St Paul; S C Nat Bank, Columbia; S C State Art Collection; Oshkosh Mus, Wis.
Exhibitions: One-man shows, Columbia Mus Art, S C, 71 & 501 Gallery, Mint Mus Art, 72; four-man show, Gallery Contemp Art, Winston-Salem, 71; 11th Piedmont Painting & Sculpture Show, Mint Mus Art, 71; 18th Drawing & Small Sculpture Show, Ball State Univ, 72.
Teaching: Asst prof studio art, Univ Wis, Madison, 63-70; assoc prof studio art, Winthrop Col, 70-
Awards: Purchase awards, Drawings U S A, Minn Mus Art, St Paul & 8th Ann Piedmont Graphics Exhib, Mint Mus Art, 71; 24th Exhib S C Artists Award, Gibbs Gallery, Charleston, NC, 71.
Memberships: Nat Col Art Asn.
Dealer: McDonald Art Gallery, 753 Providence Rd, Charlotte, NC 28207.
Mailing Address: 630 University Dr, Rock Hill, SC 29730.

FREEMAN, MARGARET B
Museum Curator, Writer
b West Orange, N J.
Study & Training: Wellesley Col, BA; Columbia Univ, MA; Sorbonne, Summer Sch.
Teaching: Instr, Dana Hall Sch, 25-27; instr, Metrop Mus Art, New York, N Y.

Positions: Res asst, Newark Mus, 24-25; secy, art mus, Wellesley
Col, 27-28; asst cur, Metrop Mus Art, 40-43, assoc cur, 43-55,
cur Cloisters, 55-70.
Awards: Phi Beta Kappa Award.
Memberships: Medieval Acad Am; Am Asn Mus; Medieval Club,
New York; Mus Coun New York; Int Ctr Romanesque Art.
Publications: Auth, Herbs for the medieval household & The story
of the three kings; co-auth, The belles heures of Jean, Duke of
Berry; contribr, articles, In: Bull Metrop Mus Art.
Mailing Address: 16 E 84th St, New York, NY 10028.

FREEMAN, MARK
Painter, Printmaker
Preferred Media: Oils, Acrylics.
b Austria, Sept 27, 09.
Study & Training: Columbia Col, BA; Columbia Univ, BArch; Int
Inst Educ fel, Sorbonne, Paris, France, 30.
Work in Public Collections: Libr of Cong, Washington, D C; Phila-
delphia Mus Art, Pa; Norfolk Art Mus, Va; Hengelose Kunstzaal,
Holland; Butler Art Inst, Ohio.
Exhibitions: Int Biennial Color Lithography, Cincinnati Mus, 52-53;
80 Prints U S A, State Dept Traveling Exhib, Europe & Africa, 54;
Artists of the Region, Easthampton Guild Hall Mus, 56 & 66;
Major Am Artists, Southampton Col, 68; Nat Inst Arts & Scis, 68
& 69.
Awards: Gold medal, Nat Soc Artists in Casein, 64; medal, Audubon
Artists, 69; medal, Painters & Sculptors N J, 72.
Memberships: Audubon Artists (exhib chmn, 72); Nat Soc Artists in
Casein & Polymer (pres, 72); League Present Day Artists (v
pres, 72); Am Soc Contemp Artists (exhib Comt, 72); Allied Art-
ists Am.
Mailing Address: 307 E 37th St, New York, NY 10016.

FREEMAN, RICHARD BORDEN
Art Historian, Educator
b Philadelphia, Pa, Oct 7, 08.
Study & Training: Yale Univ, AB, 32; Harvard Univ, AM, 34; Univ
Paris, summer 35.
Collections Arranged: Picasso-Gris-Miro, San Francisco Mus Art,
Calif, 48; Graphics Annuals, 58-72, The Lithographs Ralston
Crawford, 61, Niles Spencer (retrospective), 65 & Lithographs
by William Walmsley, 71, Univ Ky.
Teaching: Prof art & head dept, Univ Ala, Tuscaloosa, 50-56; vis
prof art, Hamilton Col, 57; prof art, Univ Ky, 58-, head dept, 58-
66.
Positions: Asst, Nelson Gallery, Kansas City, Mo, 34-36; registrar,
Fogg Mus Art, Cambridge, Mass, 36-38; asst cur, Cincinnati Art
Mus, 38-41; dir, Flint Inst Art, Mich, 41-47; art dir-in-charge,
San Francisco Mus Art, 47-50; dir, Hartford Art Sch, 56-57.
Memberships: Southeastern Col Art Conf (v pres, 51-52, pres, 52-
53); Mid Western Col Art Conf (v pres, 65-66, pres, 66-67); Col
Art Asn.
Research: Work of Ralston Crawford & the paintings of Niles Spen-
cer.
Publications: Auth, Ralston Crawford, Univ Ala Press, 52; auth, The
lithographs of Ralston Crawford, Univ Ky Press, 63; auth, Niles
Spencer (monograph), 65; plus many articles in Am J Archaeol,
Col Art J & Art J.
Mailing Address: Dept of Art, University of Kentucky, Lexington, KY
40506.

FREIFELD, ERIC
Painter, Educator
Preferred Media: Watercolors, Graphics.
b Saratov, Russia, Mar 13, 19; Can citizen.
Study & Training: St Martin's Sch Art, London, Eng; Art Stud League
New York.
Work in Public Collections: Montreal Mus Art, Can; Vancouver Gal-
lery Art; Univ Alta, Edmonton; St Michaels Col & Hart House,
Univ Toronto; Brook St Galleries, London.
Exhibitions: Can Soc Painters in Watercolor, 48-62; Royal Can Acad
Exhibs, 51-71; Can Soc Graphic Art, 55-62; Brooklyn Mus Int
Biennial, 59; Allied Artists Am, 60; plus many one-man, group
& nat shows in Can, Eng & U S A.
Teaching: Prof watercolor painting, figure drawing & artistic anat,
Ont Col Art, 46-
Positions: Chmn welfare comt, Ont Col Art Faculty Asn, 65-70, mem
exec comt, 65-70, mem governing coun, Ont Col Art, 72-
Awards: Carnegie Trust Fund scholar, 37; C W Jeffries Award, 57;
Can Coun Sr Arts fel, 61 & 71; plus many others.
Bibliography: Doris Shadbolt (auth), Eric Freifeld (exhib catalogue),
68 & Essay on Eric Freifeld, Arts Can Mag, 69; Nancy Beckett
(auth), articles, In: Can Press, Nat Release & Can Newspapers,
70.
Memberships: Can Soc Graphic Art (past pres); Can Soc Painters in
Watercolour; assoc Royal Can Acad Arts (assoc rep on coun);
Arts & Letters Club.

Dealer: Jerrold Morris Gallery, Prince Arthur St, Toronto, Ont,
Can.
Mailing Address: 48 Eccleston Dr, Toronto 16, Ont, Can.

FREILICH, ANN
Painter
Preferred Media: Oils, Watercolors.
b Czestochowa, Poland; U S citizen.
Study & Training: Educ Alliance Art Sch.
Work in Public Collections: Brooklyn Mus, New York, N Y; Peabody
Mus, Nashville, Tenn; Art Lending Collections, Philadelphia
Mus Art & Mus Mod Art; Syracuse Univ, N Y.
Exhibitions: Five one-man shows, Roko Gallery, 65-72; Riverside
Mus, 64; Bucknell Univ Drawing Exhib, 65; Gallery Mod Art,
Huntington Hartford Mus, 67; Am Acad Arts & Lett, 70-72.
Teaching: Santa Agata Art Workshop, Italy, 67; pvt classes in
studio.
Dealer: Roko Gallery, 90 E Tenth St, New York, NY 10003.
Mailing Address: 250 W 94th St, New York, NY 10025.

FREILICH, MICHAEL LEON
Art Dealer, Collector
b Czestochowa, Poland, May 1, 12; U S citizen.
Study & Training: City Col New York, BA, 35; Columbia Univ, 35-
36; City Col New York, 40-41.
Teaching: Group worker arts & crafts, Madison House, 38-39; lectr
art, Mus Mod Art, New York, 39-40; lectr mod art, adult educ
exten, New York Univ, 58-59; lectr to mus touring groups.
Positions: Owner & dir, Roko Gallery, 46-; v pres, Positano Art
Workshop, Italy, 70-; mem bd dirs, Arthur Williams Gallery
(photography), dir, 71-72; juror for art exhibs, New York area
mus & art asns.
Specialty of Gallery: Contemporary American painting, sculpture
and graphics; Ukiy-o Japanese prints and scrolls.
Collection: American painting, sculpture and graphics; Japanese
prints and scrolls; Netsukes; sculpture of India and the Orient;
arts of antiquity.
Publications: Auth, introductions to art catalogues.
Mailing Address: 90 E Tenth St, New York, NY 10003.

FREILICHER, JANE
Painter
Preferred Media: Oils.
b New York, N Y, Nov 29, 24.
Study & Training: Brooklyn Col, AB; Columbia Univ, AM; Hans Hof-
man Sch; art hist with, Meyer Schapiro.
Work in Public Collections: Brooklyn Mus, N Y; Mus Mod Art, New
York; Brandeis Art Mus, Mass; R I Mus Fine Arts; N Y Univ.
Exhibitions: Fourteen one-man shows, Tibor de Nagy Gallery, New
York, 52-; Whitney Mus Am Art Ann, 55-; Figurative Painting,
Vassar Col, 68; Painterly Realism, Am Fedn Arts, 70; one-man
show, John Bernard Myers Gallery, New York, 71.
Teaching: Vis critic & lectr, Univ Pa Grad Sch Fine Arts, Skow-
hegan Sch Art & Carnegie-Mellon Inst.
Awards: Hallmark Int Art Award, 60.
Bibliography: Fairfield Porter (auth), Jane Freilicher paints a pic-
ture, 9/55 & Peter Schjeldahl (auth), Urban pastorals, 2/71, Art
News; James Schuyler (auth), The painting of Jane Freilicher,
Art & Litt, autumn 66.
Publications: Illusr, Turandot and other poems, 53; illusr, Paris
review (portfolio of drawings), 65.
Mailing Address: 51 Fifth Ave, New York, NY 10003.

FREIMARK, ROBERT (MATTHEW)
Printmaker, Painter
b Doster, Mich, Jan 27, 22.
Study & Training: Univ Toledo, BEd; Cranbrook Acad Art, MFA; in-
dependent study, Mex.
Work in Public Collections: Nat Gallery, Prague, Czech; Libr of
Cong, Washington, D C; U S Info Agency; Seattle Mus, Wash; Los
Angeles Co Mus, Calif.
Commissions: Mem print, Des Moines Art Ctr, Iowa, 61.
Exhibitions: Drawings of 12 Countries, Art Inst Chicago, Ill, 52; Pa
Acad Fine Art Painting Ann, 52-53; Brooklyn Mus Biennial Water-
color Exhib, 64; one-man shows, Northamerican Cult Inst, Mex-
ico City, Mex, 63 & Moravske Mus, Brno, Czech, 70.
Teaching: Instr drawing, Toledo Mus Art, 52-55; instr painting, Ohio
Univ, 56-59; artist-in-residence, Des Moines Art Ctr, 59-63;
prof graphics, San Jose State Col, 64-
Positions: Guest artist, Joslyn Mem Mus, Omaha, Nebr, 61; guest
artist, Huntington Galleries, W Va, 63; guest artist-lectr, Co-
lumbia Univ, New York, 63; guest artist, Riverside Art Ctr,
Calif, 64.
Awards: New Talent in the U S A, Art in Am, 57; Ford Found grant,
W Va, 65; spec creative leave, Calif State Col Syst, 67.

Bibliography: Eva Gatling (auth), Robert Freimark, Motive, 4/63; Yar Chomicky (auth), Watercolor painting, Univ Pa Press, 68; Igor Zhor (auth), Robert Freimark (catalogue), Galeria Jaroslava Kral, 70.
Research: Mexican popular culture; rehabilitation through art; environmental planning for contemporary living.
Art Interests: Graphics, film & environmental art.
Mailing Address: Route 2, Box 539A, Morgan Hill, CA 95037.

FRELINGHUYSEN, MR & MRS PETER H B, JR
Collectors
Collection: Paintings.
Mailing Address: Morristown, NJ 07960.

FRENCH, JAMES C
Museum Curator, Lecturer
b Hayward, Wis, Sept 16, 07.
Study & Training: Minneapolis Col Music & Art, BA & MA; MacPhail Col Music & Art.
Teaching: Lectr.
Positions: Cur, Rosicrucian Egyptian, Oriental Mus & Art Gallery, San Jose, Calif, 51-
Memberships: Am Asn Mus; Am Fedn Arts; Int Inst Conserv Mus Objects.
Publications: Contribr, Rosicrucian Digest.
Mailing Address: 1471 McDaniel Ave, San Jose, CA 95126.

FRENCH, JARED
Painter, Sculptor
Preferred Media: Tempera.
b Ossining, N Y.
Study & Training: Amherst Col, BA; Art Stud League New York.
Work in Public Collections: Whitney Mus Am Art, New York, N Y; Baltimore Mus Art, Md; Baseball Mus, Cooperstown, N Y; Art Collection of Dartmouth Col, Hanover, N H.
Commissions: Cavalry Fording Stream (mural), Parcel Post Off, Richmond, Va; food murals, Coxsachie, New York; mural, Plymouth Post Off, Pa.
Exhibitions: Carnegie Int, Pittsburgh, Pa & Realism Show, Rochester Mus, N Y, 64; one-man shows, Banfer Gallery, New York, 68-69; Magic Realism Show & 20th Century Portraits Show, Mus Mod Art, New York; Whitney Mus Am Art Ann, New York; Four Anonymous Collectors, New York Cult Ctr, 72.
Awards: Nat Inst Arts & Lett Award, 67.
Mailing Address: Piazza Cucchi 3, Rome, Italy 00152.

FRERICHS, RUTH COLCORD
Painter
Preferred Media: Watercolors.
b White Plains, N Y.
Study & Training: Conn Col, BA(fine arts); Art Stud League New York, lithography with Armin Landeck; study in watercolor with William B Schimmel & F Douglas Greenbowe.
Work in Public Collections: Thunderbird Bank, Phoenix, Ariz; Valley Nat Bank, Prescott.
Exhibitions: Southwest Watercolor Soc Regional Exhib, Dallas, Tex, 69; Wichita Nat Centennial Watercolor Exhib, Kans, 70; Am Watercolor Soc Ann, New York, 70; Watercolor U S A, Springfield, Mo, 72; Watercolor West, Nat Exhib, Riverside, Calif, 72.

FREUDENHEIM, TOM LIPPMANN
Art Administrator
b Stuttgart, Ger, July 3, 37; U S citizen.
Study & Training: Harvard Col, AB; N Y Univ, MA
Collections Arranged: Pascin, 66 & Arnaldo Pomodoro, 70, Univ Art Mus, Berkeley, Calif.
Positions: Cur, Jewish Mus, New York, N Y, 62-65; asst dir, Univ Art Mus, Berkeley, 66-71; dir, Baltimore Mus Art, 71-
Memberships: Col Art Asn Am; Asn Art Mus Dirs; Am Asn Mus; hon mem Artists Equity Asn; hon mem Am Inst Interior Designers.
Publications: Auth, Myer Myers, American silversmith, 65; auth, Illuminated Hebrew manuscripts, 65; auth, Pascin, 66; auth, A Persian faience mosaic wall, Kunst Orients, 68; auth, Arnaldo Pomodoro, 70.
Mailing Address: Baltimore Museum of Art, Art Museum Dr, Baltimore, MD 21218.
Awards: Gold Medal, Low Ruins Nat Exhib, Tubac, 65; award, Southwest Watercolor Soc Regional, 69; purchase award, Phoenix Jewish Community Ctr Invitational, 70.
Memberships: Ariz Artists Guild (pres, 69-71); Ariz Watercolor Asn (corresp secy, 68-69).
Dealer: Thompson Gallery, 2020 N Central Ave, Phoenix, AZ 85004.
Mailing Address: 321 E Pomona Rd, Phoenix, AZ 85020.

FREUND, HARRY LOUIS
Painter, Illustrator
Preferred Media: Oils.
b Clinton, Mo, Sept 16, 05.
Study & Training: Univ Mo, 23-25; St Louis Sch Fine Arts, Wash Univ, 25-29; D H Wuerpel travel scholar, 29; Colarossi Acad, Paris, 29-30; Carnegie fel, 40; Princeton Univ, 40-41; Colorado Springs Fine Arts Ctr, 46-47; Carnegie-Stetson grant, Mex, 53; Stetson Univ grant, Cent Am, 59.
Work in Public Collections: IBM Corp; Libr of Cong, Washington, D C; Seattle Art Mus, Wash; St Louis Sch Fine Arts, libr murals, Bishop Col & Shaw Univ; plus many others in pub & pvt collections.
Exhibitions: Contemp Am Art Exhib, New York World's Fair; Nat Acad Design; Pa Acad Design; Carnegie Inst; Corcoran Gallery Art; plus many others in mus, schs & libraries in U S A & abroad.
Teaching: Resident artist, Hendrix Col, 39-41, head dept art, 41-46; founder dept art, Little Rock Jr Col, 40; founder & dir, Art Sch Ozarks, seven yrs; lectr & faculty artist vis, Asn Am Cols, five seasons; head dept art, Stetson Univ, 49-59, resident artist, 59-69.
Positions: Free lance illusr, Crowell Publ & Ford Motor Co Publs; mural designer, State of Mo at Chicago World's Fair, 33; mural artist, sect fine arts, U S Treas Dept, 34-40; visual aids dir, Eighth Serv Comd, U S Army, 45-46.
Memberships: Fla Artist Group (past pres); Nat Soc Mural Painters; Fla Craftsmen (past pres).
Mailing Address: 31 Steel St, Eureka Springs, AR 72632.

FREUND, TIBOR
Painter, Architect
Preferred Media: Acrylics.
b Budapest, Hungary, Dec 29, 10; U S citizen.
Study & Training: Fed Tech Univ, Zurich, dipl archit, 32; Vilmos Aba-Novak Art Sch, Budapest, 34; studies Oriental techniques of mosaics, Meshed, Iran, 40.
Work in Public Collections: Mus Fine Arts, Budapest; James A Michener Collection, Univ Tex, Austin; Goucher Col, Md; Ravinia Art Festival Asn, Chicago, Ill; Ball State Univ, Muncie, Ind.
Commissions: First moving mural on ridged surface, Bd Educ, Pub Sch 111, New York, N Y, 63; first moving mural on flat surface, Bd Educ Sch 162, New York, 70.
Exhibitions: Five one-man shows, New York, 60-72; Am Fedn Arts Traveling Exhibs, 63-65, 66-67 & 71-72; Abstract Art, Riverside Mus, New York, 65; An American Report on the Sixties, Denver Art Mus, Colo, 69; Painting & Sculpture Today, Indianapolis Mus Art, Ind, 70.
Awards: Silvermine Guild Award, first prize at 19th Ann New Eng Exhib, 68.
Bibliography: Jeanne Paris (auth), Tibor Freund, Long Island Press, 9/28/69; John Canaday (auth), Tibor Freund, New York Times, 10/4/69; Peter Schfeldahl (auth), Fourth show in New York 1969, Art Int, 11/69; plus others.
Memberships: Fel Royal Soc Arts; Am Fedn Arts; Nat Soc Mural Painters.
Research: Developed motion painting from a crude nineteenth century invention called three-sided picture.
Publications: Auth, Motion in painting—a new art form, Am Artist Mag, 11/64.
Dealer: Bertha Schaefer Gallery, 41 E 57th St, New York, NY 10022.
Mailing Address: 34-57 82nd St, Jackson Heights, NY 11372.

FREUND, WILL FREDERICK
Painter, Educator
Preferred Media: Oils, Watercolors, Mixed Media.
b Madison, Wis, Jan 20, 16.
Study & Training: Univ Wis, BS, MS; Univ Mo; Tiffany Found fel, 49.
Work in Public Collections: William Rockhill Nelson Gallery Art, Kansas City, Mo; Joslyn Mus Art, Omaha, Nebr; Okla Art Ctr, Oklahoma City; Mulvane Mus Art, Topeka, Kans; Univ Nebr Art Galleries, Lincoln.
Exhibitions: Mo Pavilion, New York Worlds Fair, N Y, 64; New Talent U S A, Art in Am Mag, 65; Watercolor U S A, Springfield Art Mus, Mo, 70 & 72.
Teaching: Instr art, Stephens Col, 46-64; assoc prof fine art, Southern Ill Univ, Edwardsville, 64-
Awards: First award for oil painting, Wis Painters & Sculptors, 46; first prize for oil painting, Mulvane Mus Art, 56; Ruth Renfro Award (first prize for watercolor), St Louis City Art Mus, 63.
Bibliography: Prize winners, Life Mag, 9/12/55; A B Louchheim (auth), Prize $, Art News, 10/56; Will Freund, painter potter woodworker boombass player, Wis Alumnus, 1/61.
Memberships: Ala Watercolor Soc, Birmingham.
Research: Aesthetic potential of the aqueous emulsion technique.
Mailing Address: 301 Prospect St, Alton, IL 62002.

FREUNDLICH, AUGUST L
Educator
b Frankfurt, Ger, May 9, 24; U S citizen.
Study & Training: Antioch Col, BA, Antioch Col & Teachers Col, Columbia Univ, MA; New York Univ, PhD.
Exhibitions: Competitive exhibs in Ohio, Ark, Tenn, N C, Ga, Ky, N J, Mich & N Mex; also exhibs in com galleries.
Teaching: Art educ spec, Antioch Lab Sch, 49-50; instr art educ, Univ Ark, 40-53; vis prof, State Univ N Y Col New Paltz, 53-54; head art dept, Eastern Mich Univ, 54-58; chmn arts div, George Peabody Col, 58-64; chmn art dept & dir, Lowe Art Mus, Univ Miami, 64-70; dean sch art, Syracuse Univ, 70; dean, Col Visual & Performing Arts, Syracuse Univ, 70-
Memberships: Nat Asn Schs Art; Col Art Asn Am; Nat Art Educ Asn; Nat Asn Schs Music; Am Asn Mus.
Research: Contemporary painting in East and West Germany.
Publications: Auth, William Cropper, retrospective, 68; auth, Frank Kleinholz—the outsider, 69; auth, numerous brochures, monographs & catalogs.
Mailing Address: Syracuse University, Syracuse, NY 13201.

FREYBERGER, RUTH MATILDA
Educator, Painter
b Reading, Pa, Nov 15, 12.
Study & Training: Kutztown State Col, BS; Pa State Univ, University Park, MEd & EdD; Univ Pa, with David Robb; also with Hobson Pitman & Andrew Case.
Work in Public Collections: Reading Pub Mus & Art Gallery, West Reading.
Commissions: Watercolor for Alumni Room, Reading High Sch, 55.
Exhibitions: Butler Art Mus, Youngstown, Ohio, 46; Reading Pub Mus & Art Gallery, 48; Berks Co Art Alliance, Reading, 48; one-man shows, Byndenwood, Pa, 52 & Lebanon Valley Col, Annville, Pa, 53.
Teaching: Instr art & supvr, New Holland Borough Schs, Pa, 35-41; instr art & supvr, Huntingdon Borough Schs, Pa, 41-45; instr art, Derry Twp High Sch & Jr Col, Hershey, Pa, 45-50; assoc prof art educ, Ill State Univ, 51-62; instr creative stitchery & early Am design, Bloomington-Normal Adult Educ, 56-; prof art, Ill State Univ, 62-
Awards: Carnegie fel art hist, Univ Pa, 46; purchase prize watercolor, Reading Pub Mus & Art Gallery, 48; first prize watercolors, 48 & second prize watercolors, 51, Pa State Univ.
Memberships: Ill Art Asn; Eastern Arts Asn; Nat Art Educ Asn.
Research: Differences in creative drawings of children of varying ethnic and socio-economic backgrounds, grades 1-6 in state of Pennsylvania.
Publications: Contribr, A school mural, a senior high school unit of teaching, 49; auth, The language arts approach to art, 60; auth, Problems in perspective, 61; auth, Understanding children's art expression (three films), 62; auth, An approach to design for the intermediate grades, 62.
Mailing Address: 211 A N University, Normal, IL 61761.

FRIBERG, ARNOLD
Illustrator, Painter
b Winnetka, Ill, Dec 21, 13.
Study & Training: Art Instr Schs; Chicago Acad Fine Arts; Am Acad Art, Chicago.
Work in Public Collections: Work in pvt collections.
Commissions: Series 15 monumental paintings, The Ten Commandments, Cecil B De Mille, 56; series 12 paintings, The Book of Mormon, Church of Jesus Christ of Latter Day Saints, 60; series of paintings, 100 Years of Football, Chevrolet Sports Asn Collection, 68; series over 100 paintings, The Northwest Mounted Police, Northwest Paper Co, 69; series hist paintings, American West, Sharp Rifle Co, 69.
Exhibitions: Ten Commandments Series, toured every continent, 57-58; Motion Picture Indust Exhib, N Y World's Fair, 64-65.
Teaching: Lectr vitality in relig painting, art as serv & Russell & Remington.
Positions: Chief artist-designer, Cecil B De Mille, 54-57.
Memberships: Life mem Royal Soc Arts, London; Art Instr Schs, Minneapolis, Minn (mem nat adv bd).
Publications: Auth & illusr, The ten commandments, 57 & Arnold Friberg's little Christmas books, 58.
Mailing Address: 5867 Tolcate Lane, Salt Lake City, UT 84121.

FRICK, HELEN CLAY
Art Library Director
Positions: Dir, Frick Art Ref Libr.
Mailing Address: 10 E 71st St, New York, NY 10021.

FRIED, ALEXANDER
Art Critic
b New York, N Y, May 21, 02.
Study & Training: Columbia Col, AB, 23, Columbia Univ, MA, 24.
Positions: Art ed, San Francisco Chronicle, 30-34; art ed, San Francisco Examr, 34-
Mailing Address: 22 Crown Terr, San Francisco, CA 94114.

FRIED, HOWARD LEE
Sculptor
b Cleveland, Ohio, June 14, 46.
Study & Training: Syracuse Univ, 64-67; San Francisco Art Inst, BFA, 68; Univ Calif, Davis, MFA, 70.
Work in Public Collections: Cleveland Mus Art, Ohio; Syracuse Univ, N Y; Univ Calif, Davis.
Commissions: Mural, Syracuse Univ, 66.
Exhibitions: Looking West, Joslyn Art Mus, Omaha, Nebr, 70; The 80's, Univ Art Mus, Univ Calif, Berkeley, 70; Prospect 71; Projection, Kunsthalle, Dusseldorf, Ger, 71 & Louisiana Mus, Denmark, 72; Documenta 5, Kassel, Ger, 72; plus many others.
Teaching: Instr sculpture, San Francisco Art Inst, 68-
Awards: Augusta Hazard Award, Syracuse Univ, 66; Adeline Kent Award, San Francisco Artist's Comt, 71-72.
Bibliography: Grace Glueck (auth), New York: big thump on the bass drum, Art in Am, 5-6/71; Brenda Richardson (auth), Howard Fried; paradox of approach-avoidance, Arts Mag, 6/71; Steve Davis (auth), Howard Fried installation piece, Art Week, 3/25/72.
Memberships: San Francisco Artist Comt (v chmn, 71-72).
Publications: Auth, Inside the harlequin, Flash Art, 71; auth, Studio relocation, Breakthroughs in Fiction, 72; auth, Cheshire cat 4, Avalanche, (in press); plus films & video tapes.
Dealer: Reese Palley Gallery, 550 Sutter St, San Francisco, CA 94012 & 93 Prince St, New York, NY 10021.
Mailing Address: 16 Rose St, San Francisco, CA 94102.

FRIED, MICHAEL
Art Critic
Positions: Art critic, Artforum Mag.
Publications: Auth, Morris Louis, In: Contemporary Art & Artists, Abrams.
Mailing Address: c/o Artforum Magazine, 667 Madison Ave, New York, NY 10021.

FRIED, RAYMOND JOHN
Art Administrator, Painter
b Cleveland, Ohio, Oct 29, 42.
Study & Training: Cleveland Inst Art, BFA, 64; Univ Pa, MFA, 66; also with Piero Dorazio & Helen Frankenthaler.
Exhibitions: Cleveland Mus Art May Show, 61-68; Philadelphia Inst Contemp Art Grad Show, 66; Nat Polymer Show, Eastern Mich State Univ, 68; area artists show & one-man show, Toledo Mus Art, 70.
Collections Arranged: Works Progress Admin Exhib, 70, Ceramics Invitational, 70, Old Master Prints, 71 & Sculpture of David Black, 71, Fort Wayne Mus Art.
Teaching: Instr painting, Toledo Mus Sch Design, 66-70.
Positions: Dir, Fort Wayne Mus Art, 70-
Memberships: Am Asn Mus; Am Fedn Arts.
Mailing Address: Fort Wayne Museum of Art, 1202 W Wayne St, Fort Wayne, IN 46804.

FRIED, ROBERT SAMUEL
Printmaker, Painter
b Brooklyn, N Y, Apr 7, 37.
Study & Training: New York City Community Col, AA; Cooper Union, cert fine art; San Francisco Art Inst, MFA.
Work in Public Collections: Metrop Mus Art, New York, N Y; Mus Mod Art, New York; San Francisco Mus Art, Calif; Brooklyn Mus, N Y; Los Angeles Co Mus Art, Calif.
Commissions: Exp theater, Deleyi Found, San Francisco, 69.
Exhibitions: Oversize Prints, Whitney Mus Am Art, New York, 71; Bay Area Printmakers, Achenback Found, 71; Potsdam Invitational Print Exhib, 72; 18th Nat Print Exhib, Brooklyn Mus, 72; California Prints, Mus Mod Art, New York, 72.
Teaching: Instr printmaking, San Francisco Art Inst, 69-72; instr painting, Univ Santa Clara, 72.
Positions: Art dir, Escapade Mag, 62-63; artist posters, Family Dog Concerts, 67-69.
Awards: Fulbright scholar, 63-65.
Bibliography: Beck (auth), Arts review, Art News, 66; J Albright (auth), Visionaries, Rolling Stone, 71.
Memberships: San Francisco Art Inst (artist comt & bd trustees, 69-).
Art Interests: Screen painting.
Dealer: Hansen-Fuller Gallery, 228 Grant Ave, San Francisco, CA 94108.
Mailing Address: 7 Ridgeway, Fairfax, CA 94930.

FRIED, THEODORE
Painter, Etcher
b Budapest, Hungary, May 19, 02; U S citizen.
Study & Training: Acad Fine Arts, Budapest, 20-23; also with Julius Rudnay.
Work in Public Collections: Mus Nat Art Mod, Paris, France; Albertina & Osterreichische Galerie, Vienna, Austria; Butler Inst Am Art, Youngstown, Ohio; Walker Art Ctr, Minneapolis, Minn; Mem Art Gallery, Rochester, N Y.
Exhibitions: November-Gruppe, Berlin, Ger, 29; Carnegie Shows, Pittsburgh, 43 & 49; Roy & Mary Neuberger Collection, Whitney Mus Am Art, New York, N Y, 54; Contemporary Trends, Am Fed Arts traveling show, 55-57; Westbeth Printmakers, Palacio de Belles Artes, Mexico City, Mex, 72; plus many others.
Teaching: Instr painting, Hudson Guild, New York, 49-69.
Bibliography: F Grossmann(auth), Theodore Fried, Forum, 33; L Campbell (auth), Theodore Fried, Art News, 61; C O Ennen (auth), Malerei Lexicon, Kindler, 65.
Memberships: Fedn Mod Painters & Sculptors (v pres, 55-60, treas, 69-72); Westbeth Graphic Artists.
Publications: Illusr, Jimmy the jeep, Lothrop, 45; illusr, The tune of the calliope, 58.
Dealer: Tyringham Gallery, Tyringham, MA 01264.
Mailing Address: 463 West St, New York, NY 10014.

FRIEDEBERG, PEDRO
Painter, Sculptor
Preferred Media: Wood.
b Florence, Italy, Jan 11, 37; U S citizen.
Study & Training: Iberoamerican Univ, Mex; sculpture with Mathias Goeritz.
Work in Public Collections: Worcester Mus Art, Mass; Isaac Delgado Mus, New Orleans, La; Panamerican Union, Washington, D C; Rose Art Mus, Brandeis Univ, Mass; Mus Arte Mod, Mexico City, Mex; The Israel Mus, Jerusalem.
Commissions: Sculptures, garden of Andre Bloc, Paris, France, 63; mural, Hotel Camino Real, Mexico City, 68; several murals, pvt homes, Mexico City, 70-72.
Exhibitions: Biennale Cordoba, Art, 66; Fantastic Furniture, Mus Contemp Crafts, N Y, 66; Labyrinths, Kunstakademie, Berlin, 66; Expo 67, Toronto, Ont, 67; 20th Biennale São Paulo, Brazil, 69 & Bienal Coltejer, Medellin, Colombia, 72.
Positions: Art ed, Mexico this month, 60-64.
Awards: Premio antrax, Biennale Cordoba, 66; second prize, Expos Solar, 68.
Bibliography: Ida Rodriguez (auth), Pedro Friedeberg, Programa Cult 19th Olimpiada, Mex, 68; Alfonso Neuvillate (auth), P Friedeberg (catalog), Biennale São Paulo, 69; Ida Rodriguez (auth), Pedro Friedeberg, Univ Mex, 72.
Memberships: Salon Plastica Mex; founding mem Los Hartos.
Publications: Auth, Autobiography, Archit Jour, Archit Fantastique, Paris, 62; auth, Autobiography, 2, Motive, 62; auth, Dialogos Mag, 71
Dealers: Galeria Misrachi, Genova 20, Mexico City 6, Mex; Kiko Galleries, 419 Lovett, Houston, TX 77006.
Mailing Address: Paseo De La Reforma 334-4, Mexico City 6, Mex.

FRIEDENSOHN, ELIAS
Painter, Educator
Preferred Media: Oils.
b New York, N Y, Dec 12, 24.
Study & Training: Tyler Sch Fine Arts, Temple Univ, 42; with Gabriel Zendel, Paris, France, 46; Queens Col, BA, 48; N Y Univ Inst Fine Arts, 49-51.
Work in Public Collections: Whitney Mus Am Art; Art Inst Chicago; Minneapolis Mus Art; Walker Art Ctr; Sarah Roby Found Collection; Krannert Mus Art, Univ Ill.
Exhibitions: Young American Painters, 59 & Whitney Mus Ann, 61-64, Whitney Mus Am Art; Art Inst Chicago Ann, 59 & 61; Corcoran Gallery Art Ann, Washington, D C, 62; Minneapolis Mus Art Drawing Ann, 71.
Teaching: Prof art, Queens Col, 59-; prof art & chmn arts div, Kirkland Col, 70-71.
Positions: Chmn, Nat Screening Comt for Painting, Fulbright Prog, Inst Int Educ New York, 66-69.
Awards: Fulbright grant, Italy, 57; Guggenheim fel, 60; purchase award, Minneapolis Mus Art, 71.
Memberships: Col Art Asn.
Dealer: Terry Dintenfass, 18 E 67th St, New York, NY 11210.
Mailing Address: Harding Rd, Clinton, NY 13323.

FRIEDMAN, B H
Writer
b New York, N Y, July 27, 26.
Study & Training: Cornell Univ, BA, 48.
Teaching: Lectr Eng, Cornell Univ, 66-67.
Positions: Adv council mem, Cornell Univ Arts Col; trustee, Am Fedn Arts; presently trustee, Whitney Mus Am Art & dir, Fine Arts Work Ctr, Provincetown, Mass.
Publications: Ed, School of New York: some younger artists, 59; auth, Circles, 62; Yarborough, 64; Jackson Pollock: energy made visible (biog), 72; Alfonso Ossorio (monogr), 72; and other titles as well as magazine publications.
Mailing Address: 237 E 48th St, New York, NY 10017.

FRIEDMAN, KENNETH SCOTT
Sculptor, Instructor
Preferred Media: Intermedia.
b New London, Conn.
Study & Training: Calif Western Univ; Shimer Col; San Francisco State Col, BA & MA; also spec study with Dr G David Cahoon & Dr Robert Smith.
Work in Public Collections: Oakland Mus, Calif; Vancouver Art Gallery, B C; La Jolla Mus Contemp Art, Calif; Archiv Sohm, Markgröningen, W Ger; Centro Arte y Communicacion, Buenos Aires, Arg.
Commissions: Eingepacktes (wrapped sculpture), Galerie Vice Versand, Remscheid, Ger, 69; Friedmanswerk, Edition Hundertmark, Berlin, Ger, 70; G T M (with Barbara Smith & Greg Sweigert), San Francisco, Calif, 70; Friedmansmuseum, Dr Alexander Thomas, Münster, Ger, 71; Collected Works, Mrs Leonard Brown, Springfield, Mass, 72.
Exhibitions: One-man shows, Time, Space, Light & Forgetfullness, Galerie Vice Versand, fall 71, Early Works, Starr King Sch, Berkeley, Calif, 71, The One Year One-Man Show, Oakland Mus, 72, Ken Friedman & Friends in Process, Vancouver Art Gallery, 72 & Work in Progress, Henry Gallery, Univ Wash, Seattle, 72; plus many other group & one-man shows.
Teaching: Instr expanded art & educ, Exp Col, San Francisco State Col, 66-69; instr intermedia & expanded art, Free Univ Berkeley, 70-71; spec lectr art, Univ Sask, Regina, 72.
Positions: Dir, Fluxus, exec dir, Fluxus West & ed, Fluxus West Publ, 66-; prog dir & dir gallery, de Benneville Pines, Angelus Oaks, Calif, 72-; cur contemp art, Intersection, San Francisco, Calif, 72-
Bibliography: Dietrick Albrecht (auth), Ken Friedman, Reflection Press, 71; Thomas Albright (auth), Informed sources, Art Gallery Mag, 4/72; Dallas Selman (auth), Ken Friedman in Vancouver (video tape documentary), Metromedia, 72.
Memberships: Col Art Asn; Aktual Czech Group (dir, Aktual/U S A, 67, dir, Ann KTM, 71-); Religious Arts Guild (editorial consult, 71-); Western Asn Art Mus; Soc Aesthet Res (gen ed publs).
Research: Psychological & social implications & meanings of art & art acitivty; educational potential.
Publications: Auth, The stone forest: an existential approach to education, privately publ, 71; illusr, Thomas Onetwo, Something Else Press, 71; auth, The aesthetics, Beau Geste Press, 72; auth, Friedmanstijl, 73; plus many other papers & small booklets.
Dealer: Armin Hundertmark/Edition Hundertmark, 1 Berlin 42, Kolonie Kleeblatt, Blumenweg 12, Ger.
Mailing Address: 6361 Elmhurst Dr, San Diego, CA 92120.

FRIEDMAN, MARTIN
Museum Director
b Pittsburgh, Pa, Sept 23, 25.
Study & Training: Univ Pa, BA, 45; Univ Wash, MA, 47; Univ Calif, Los Angeles, 49; Columbia Univ, 56-57; Belg-Am Educ Found grant, Brussels, 57-58; Univ Minn, Am art fel, 59-60.
Collections Arranged: School of Paris 1959: The Internationals, 59; The Precisionist View in American Art, 60; New Art of Brazil, 62; Adolph Gottlieb - Paintings, 63; Ten American Sculptors, 63; Am Sect São Paulo Bienal for U S Info Agency, 63; London: The New Scene, 64; Eight Sculptors: The Ambiguous Image, 66; Light/Motion/Space, 67; Art of the Congo, 67; 6 Artists, 6 Exhibitions, 68; 14 Sculptors: The Industrial Edge, 69; Figures/Environments, 70; Works for New Spaces, 71; American Indian Art: Form and Tradition, 72.
Positions: Fel, Brooklyn Mus, 56-57; sr cur, Walker Art Ctr, 58-60, dir, Walker Art Ctr, 61-
Awards: Ford Found fel, 61-62.
Memberships: Am Fedn Arts (trustee); Nat Collection Fine Arts Comn; Guthrie Theater Found (bd dirs); Asn Art Mus Dirs; Col Art Asn Am (dir).
Publications: Auth, Charles Sheeler, Abrams, 72; contribr, Arts, Art News, Art Int, Quadrum & Art & Artists.
Mailing Address: Vineland Pl, Minneapolis, MN 55403.

FRIEDMAN, STANLEY
Painter, Instructor
Preferred Media: Oils.
b Newark, N J, May 3, 41.
Teaching: Instr fine arts, Md Inst Col Art.
Mailing Address: 2001 South Rd, Baltimore, MD 21209.

FRINTA, MOJMIR SVATOPLUK
Art Historian, Writer
b Prague, Czech, July 28, 22; U S citizen.
Study & Training: Col Fine & Applied Arts, Prague; Karlova Univ,
Prague, BA; Ecole des Beaux Arts, Paris, France; Ecole du
Louvre, Paris; Univ Mich, MA, 53, PhD (hist art), 60.
Teaching: Prof art hist, State Univ N Y Albany, 63=
Positions: Sr restorer, Metrop Mus Art, New York, N Y, 55-63.
Memberships: Col Art Asn; Int Inst Conserv Art; Int Ctr Medieval
Art; Archaeol Soc Am.
Research: Late medieval painting & sculpture; art technology.
Publications: Auth, A portrait bust by the master of beautiful ma-
donnas, 60 & auth, The authorship of the Merode altarpiece, 68;
Art Quart; auth, The master of the Gerona martyrology & Bo-
hemian illumination, 64 & auth, The investigation of the punched
decoration of medieval Italian & non-Italian panel paintings, 65,
Art Bull; auth, The genius of Robert Campin, Mouton, 66.
Mailing Address: Dept of Art, State University of New York at
Albany, Albany, NY 12203.

FRISHMUTH, HARRIET WHITNEY
Sculptor
b Philadelphia, Pa, Sept 17, 80.
Study & Training: With Rodin & Injalbert, Paris, France; also with
Cuno Von Enchtritz, Berlin, Ger; Art Stud League New York,
with Borglum & McNeil.
Work in Public Collections: Slavonic Dance, also Vine, Metrop Mus
Art, New York; Play Days, Dallas Mus Fine Arts.
Commissions: Fountain, Joy of the Waters, Mus Fine Arts, Dayton,
Ohio; Mem sundial, Englewood, N J; Morton Mem, Windsorville,
Conn; marble portrait bust of Woodrow Wilson, Capitol, Rich-
mond, Va; fountain, Crest of the Wave, Bot Gardens, St Paul; plus
others.
Exhibitions: Nat Acad Design; Archit League; Nat Asn Women Paint-
ers & Sculptors; Acad Fine Arts, Philadelphia, Pa; San Francisco
Expos.
Awards: Joan of Arc Silver Medal, Nat Asn Women Painters &
Sculptors, 24; gold medal, Catharine Lorillard Wolfe Art Club;
first recipient award, Coun Am Artists Soc; plus others.
Memberships: Fel Nat Acad Design; Nat Sculpture Soc; Nat Asn
Women Painters & Sculptors; Allied Artists Am; League of Am
Artists; plus others.
Mailing Address: Heritage Village, Southbury, CT 06488.

FROMAN, RAMON MITCHELL
Painter
Preferred Media: Oils.
b Louise, Tex, Oct 13, 08.
Study & Training: Am Acad Art, Chicago; also with E F Van Am-
burg, Charles Schroeder, Gerry Peirce, Rex Brandt & John
Pike.
Work in Public Collections: Univ Tex, Austin; Southern Methodist
Univ, Dallas, Tex; Koshare Indian Mus, La Juanta, Colo; Repub
Nat Ins Co, Dallas; Taos Art Gallery, N Mex.
Commissions: Oil portraits, Disabled Am Vet, Dallas, 50, Kerrville
Lions Club, Tex, 55 & Dallas Crippled Children's Hosp, 58; oil
portrait of Hilory G Bedford, Mrs Archie Farr, Midland, Tex, 64;
oil portrait of Nancy Amiel, Virginia King, Southwestern Med
Ctr, Grand Prairie, Tex, 69.
Exhibitions: All Ill Soc Fine Arts, Chicago, 50; Joseph Sartor Gal-
lery, Dallas, 55; Am Artists Prof League, New York, N Y, 66;
Artists & Craftsmen Assoc, Dallas, 67; Koshare Indian Mus, La
Juanta, 71.
Teaching: Instr portraiture, Ramon Froman Sch Art Summer Sch,
58-
Awards: Miriam Y Burrill Award, Am Artists Prof League, 63; Am
Artists Prof League Gold Medal, Grand Nat Exhib, New York, 66;
best of show award, Am Coun Art, Artists & Craftsmen Exhib,
Dallas, 67.
Memberships: Am Artists Prof League; Artists & Craftsmen Assoc
(pres, 69); Coppini Acad Fine Art.
Dealer: Taos Art Gallery, Kit Carson Rd, Taos, NM 87571.
Mailing Address: 8483 Stults Rd, Dallas, TX 75231.

FROMER, MRS LEON
Collector
Collection: French impressionist paintings.
Mailing Address: 1035 Fifth Ave, New York, NY 10028.

FRUDAKIS, EVANGELOS WILLIAM
Sculptor
b Rains, Utah, May 13, 21.
Study & Training: Greenwich Workshop, New York, N Y, with Merli
& Albino Cavalitto, 35-39; Beaux Arts Inst Design, New York,
40-41; Pa Acad Fine Arts, with W Hancock, P Manship, E J Fer-
ris, J F Harbeson, D M Robb & W M Campbell; asst to sculptors
P Manship & J Davidson; Cresson traveling scholar, 47; Henry
Scheidt Mem scholar, 49; Louis Comfort Tiffany scholar, 49; Am
Acad Rome, Italy, Prix de Rome fel, 50-52.
Work in Public Collections: Pa Acad Fine Arts, Philadelphia; Le-
high Valley Art Alliance; Woodmere Art Gallery; Nat Acad Fine
Arts, New York; Dupont Co Collection: plus many others.
Commissions: Many commissions.
Exhibitions: Pa Acad Fine Arts Ann, 41-62; Nat Acad Design Ann,
48-63; Woodmere Art Gallery, Chestnut Hill, Pa, 55-59; Phila-
delphia Mus Art, 59 & 62; one-man show, Philadelphia Art Al-
liance, 58; plus many other group & one-man shows.
Teaching: Many lectures in art & sculpture demonstrations;
instr, Nat Acad Fine Art, New York; instr, Pa Acad Fine Arts,
Philadelphia, 71.
Awards: Winner, Nat Fountain Competition, Little Rock, Ark, 65;
Elizabeth N Watrous Gold Medal, 68 & Dessie Greer Prize, 70,
Nat Acad Design; gold medal & Therese-Edwin H Rochards
Prize, 72, Nat Sculpture Soc; plus many others.
Memberships: Fel Pa Acad Fine Arts (bd mgrs); fel Am Acad Rome;
fel Nat Sculpture Soc (mem coun); academician Nat Acad Design;
Allied Artists Am.
Research: Collaborated research on reconstruction of statues of
Roman Forum; viewings of Michelangelo's Rondanini Pieta;
problems with archit dept, Univ Pa.
Mailing Address: 1621 Sansom St, Philadelphia, PA 19103.

FRUHAUF, ALINE
Painter, Printmaker
Preferred Media: Graphics.
b New York, N Y, Jan 31, 07.
Study & Training: Parsons; Art Stud League New York; also with
Boardman Robinson, Kenneth Hayes Miller & Charles Locke.
Work in Public Collections: Phillips Gallery, Washington, D C; Libr
Cong, Washington, D C; Nat Collection Fine Arts, Washington,
D C; Smithsonian Inst, Washington, D C; Baltimore Mus Fine Art,
Baltimore, Md.
Exhibitions: Corcoran Gallery, Washington, D C; one-woman shows,
Univ Nebr, 41, Caricatures of American Artists, 44, Caricatures
of Washington Artists, 50 & The Face of Music in Washington,
Baltimore Mus & Making Faces, Smithsonian Inst, 65-66.
Memberships: Soc Washington Printmakers; Washington Watercolor
Club; Artists Equity Asn.
Publications: Contribr, America today, Equinox Press, 36; contribr,
Libr Cong Catalog, 70; contribr, The new deal art projects,
Smithsonian Press, 72; contribr, Art for the millions, New York
Graphic Soc, (in prep).
Dealer: Jem Hom, Wisconsin Ave, Bethesda, MD 20015.
Mailing Address: 7202 44th St, Chevy Chase, MD 20015.

FRUMKIN, ALLAN
Art Dealer
b Chicago, Ill, July 5, 26.
Study & Training: Univ Chicago.
Positions: Dir, Allan Frumkin Gallery, New York, N Y.
Specialty of Gallery: Contemporary American artists; nineteenth
and twentieth century drawings.
Mailing Address: 41 E 57th St, New York, NY 10022.

FUCHS, MARY THARSILLA, CDP
Educator
Preferred Media: Clay, Watercolors.
b Westphalia, Tex, Apr 19, 12.
Study & Training: Our Lady of the Lake Col, BA, 38; Columbia Univ,
MA, 42; Univ Sch Handicrafts, 42; Art Inst Chicago, 45; Univ Tex,
49-51; with Buckley McGurrin, 50-54; N Y Univ, 52; Pratt
Graphics Ctr, 69.
Commissions: Twelve faceted glass windows, St Timothy Church,
San Antonio, Tex, 71.
Exhibitions: Seventh & eighth Tex Gen, Witte Mus, San Antonio, 45
& 46; First Ann Tex Watercolor Soc, San Antonio, 50; San An-
tonio Press Club, 65.
Teaching: Elem sch instr, St Joseph Acad, 32-37, high sch instr
eng, hist, Ger & sci, 38-41; instr art, Our Lady of the Lake Col,
42-54, asst prof art, 54-58, assoc prof art, 58-68, prof art, 68-,
chmn dept, 42-72.
Memberships: Col Art Asn; Nat Art Educ Asn & Western Arts Asn;
Tex Art Educ Asn; Tex Watercolor Soc; San Antonio Art League.

Publications: Designer, Toddler's rosary, 54; auth, Rocky personalities, Sch Arts Mag, 3/57; auth, Religion worksheets for beginners, Confraternity of Christian Doctrine, 62.
Mailing Address: 411 S W 24th St, San Antonio, TX 78285.

FUGAGLI, ALFONSO
Painter
b Meadville, Pa, Jan 23, 12.
Study & Training: Teachers Col, Columbia Univ; Acad Fine Arts & Art Stud League New York; Cleveland Sch Art.
Work in Public Collections: Thiel Col, Greenville, Pa; Holiday Inn, Erie, Pa; also in many pvt collections U S & S Am.
Exhibitions: Cleveland May Show, 39; Butler Inst Am Art, 50; Santa Fe Gallery Art, 52; New Mex State Fair, 52; Chautauqua Art Exhib, 67; plus others.
Awards: Erickson Mem Award, Erie, Pa; prize, Chautauqua Art Exhib, N Y, 61; plus others.
Memberships: Erie Art Club.
Mailing Address: 564 Chestnut St, Meadville, PA 16335.

FUGE, PAUL H
Sculptor
Preferred Media: Electronic Environments, Video Communication.
b Plainfield, N J, June 9, 46.
Study & Training: Yale Univ, BA, 68.
Exhibitions: Boston Pub Gardens, outdoor environments sponsored by Housing & Urban Develop, 68; Spaces, Mus Mod Art, New York, 70; Work for New Spaces, Walker Art Mus, Minneapolis, Minn, 71; Pulsa & Television Sensoriums, Automation House, 71; Pulsa, Philadelphia Mus Fine Arts, 71.
Teaching: Instr art, Yale Univ Sch Art & Archit, 68-72; vis artist, Calif Inst Arts, 71-73.
Positions: Mem pulsa group environ art.
Art Interests: Environmental art.
Mailing Address: 161 Bowers Hill Rd, Oxford, CT 06483.

FUHRMAN, ESTHER
Sculptor
Preferred Media: Bronze, Acrylics.
b Pittsburgh, Pa, Feb 25, 39.
Study & Training: Pa State Univ, 56-57; Frick Dept Fine Arts, Univ Pittsburgh, BA, 60; also with Sabastiano Mineo & Hana Geber, New York, N Y.
Work in Public Collections: Port of New York Authority, N Y; Deere & Co, Moline, Ill.
Commissions: Marble lobby piece, Int Educ & Training, Inc, N Y, 70; bronze & acrylic wall sculptures, Hon & Mrs I D Davidson, New York, 71 & 72.
Exhibitions: Nat Asn Women Artists, Nat Acad Art, New York, 70-72; Six Contemp Artists, Montclair Mus Art N J, 72; Sculptors League, Columbia Univ Club, New York, 72; Three Contemp Sculptors, Queens Coun Arts, Queens Co Supreme Ct Bldg, 72; Am Soc Contemp Arts, Lever House, New York, 72; plus one other.
Teaching: Lect, Sculpture today, Sands Point Acad, L I, 71 & Kimberley Sch, N J, 72, Studio secrets, Montclair Mus Art, 71-72 & Building a ½ ton wall sculpture, Nat Acad Art, 72.
Awards: Ann exhib award, Nat Asn Women Artists, 72.
Bibliography: Marilyn Goldstein (auth), Massive sculpture shapes her life, Newsday, 3/69; Esther Fuhrman, La Rev Mod, 3/72.
Memberships: Nat Asn Women Artists; New York Soc Women Artists; Am. Soc Contemp Artists; Sculptors League; Silvermine Guild Artists.
Dealer: Mari Gallery, 133 E Prospect Ave, Mamaronek, NY 10543.
Mailing Address: 4 Essington Lane, Dix Hills, NY 11746.

FUKUI, NOBU
Painter
Preferred Media: Acrylics.
b Tokyo, Japan, June 2, 42.
Work in Public Collections: Mus Mod Art N Y; Indianapolis Mus Art, Ind; Larry Aldrich Mus, Conn; State Univ N Y Col Potsdam; Dartmouth Col, N H.
Exhibitions: One-man shows, Daniels Gallery, New York, 65, Max Hutchinson Gallery, 70 & 72 & Gallery Contemp Art, Pittsburgh, Pa, 71; Japanese Artists In Europe and America, Nat Mus Mod Art, Tokyo, 65; Painting and Sculpture Today, Indianapolis Mus Art, 70 & 72.
Dealer: Max Hutchinson Gallery, 127 Greene St, New York, NY 10012
Mailing Address: 53 Greene St, New York, NY 10013.

FULLER, ADELAIDE P & WILLIAM MARSHALL
Collectors.
Collection: American impressionists.
Mailing Address: 27 Valley Ridge Rd, Fort Worth, TX 76107.

FULLER, DIANA
Art Dealer
b New York, N Y, Jan 14, 31.
Study & Training: Sorbonne, two years study in art history.
Positions: Co-dir, Hansen-Fuller Gallery.
Specialty of Gallery: Contemporary art.
Mailing Address: c/o Hansen-Fuller Gallery, 228 Grant Ave, San Francisco, CA 94108.

FULLER, HARVEY KENNETH
Painter, Illustrator
Preferred Media: Oils.
b New York, N Y, Sept 9, 18.
Study & Training: Grand Cent Sch Art; Art Stud League New York; also with Jerry Farnsworth, Cape Cod.
Exhibitions: Am Artists Prof League; Nat Arts Club; Acad Arts Asn, Springfield, Mass; Meriden Arts Club; one-man show, Mystic Art Asn, 70.
Awards: Best painting, Meriden Arts Club, 60; Grumbacher print prize, Nat Arts Club, 68; hon mention for oil painting, Am Artists Prof League, 68.
Memberships: Nat Arts Club; Am Artists Prof League; Mystic Art Asn; Acad Artists, Springfield; Meriden Arts Club.
Publications: Auth & illusr, Manuel goes to sea, McGraw, 47.
Dealer: Stan Ledge Gallery, Noank, CT 06340.
Mailing Address: 4 Bindloss Rd, Mystic, CT 03655.

FULLER, RICHARD EUGENE
Museum Director
b New York, N Y, June 1, 97.
Study & Training: Yale Univ; Univ Washington, BS, MS & PhD, Summa Laude Dignitus, 61; hon LLD, Washington State Univ & Seattle Univ.
Teaching: Lect, History of Oriental Art.
Positions: Co-donor (with mother), Seattle Art Mus, 33 & Eugene Fuller Mem Collection, pres & dir, 33-; pres, Western Asn Art Mus Dirs, 35-37; U S Nat Comt, Int Coun Mus, 58-64.
Awards: Assoc Comdr, Order St John of Jerusalem, 69.
Memberships: Western Asn Art Mus; Chinese Art Soc Am; Am Asn Mus (coun, 54-64); Asn Art Mus Dirs (v pres, 56-57, 60-61, pres, 63-64).
Publications: Auth, Japanese art in the Seattle Art Museum.
Mailing Address: Seattle Art Museum, Volunteer Park, Seattle, WA 98102.

FULLER, SUE
Sculptor, Instructor
Preferred Media: Plastics.
b Pittsburgh, Pa.
Study & Training: Carnegie Inst Technol, BA, 36; Columbia Univ Teachers Col, MA, 39; also with Hans Hofmann, S W Hayter & Josef Albers.
Work in Public Collections: Metrop Mus Art, New York, N Y; Mus Mod Art, New York; Whitney Mus Am Art, New York; Art Inst Chicago, Ill; Nat Collection Fine Arts, Smithsonian Inst, Washington, D C.
Commissions: String Composition No 52, comn by M Greef for bd rm, Commercial Investment Trust, New York, 53; String Composition No 200, Mr & Mrs Ed Forst, San Diego, Calif, 60; String Composition No 900, Ruth Walker, Brookline, Mass, 69; String Composition No 901, Martha Lou Schove, Pittsburgh, Pa, 70; String Composition No T-250, Emerson Crocker Mem for Gail Borden Pub Libr, Elgin, Ill, 72.
Exhibitions: First Biennial São Paulo, Brazil, 50; Abstract Art in America, Mus Mod Art, New York, 51; Edward Root Collection, Metrop Mus Art, New York, 53; Plastics U S A, U S Info Agency traveling exhib, U S S R, 61; The Responsive Eye, Mus Mod Art, New York, 65.
Teaching: Instr mobile design, Mus Mod Art, New York, 45-47; guest artist, Univ Ga, 51-52; instr art, Columbia Univ Teachers Col, 52 & 58; instr two-dimensional design, Pratt Inst, 65-66.
Positions: Artist for indust design firm, 55-57.
Awards: Guggenheim fel, 48; Tiffany fel, 49; Nat Inst Arts & Lett grant, 50.
Bibliography: Ruth Lester (auth), String patterns, artist works with colorful twine, Life Mag, 8/31/49; Stacy Jones (auth), Artist devises a three dimensional effect, New York Times, 6/21/69; Rosalind Browne (auth), Sue Fuller: threading transparency, Art Int, 1/20/72.
Memberships: Soc Am Graphic Artists (v pres, Soc Am Etchers, 46-51); Comt Art Educ, Mus Mod Art (coun mem, 49-52); Artists Equity Asn New York (v pres, 52-53).
Publications: Auth, Mary Cassatt's use of soft-ground etching, Mag Art, 2/50; auth, Twentieth century cat's cradle, Craft Horizons,

4/54; auth, A Japanese artist and his tradition (calligraphy), Arts Digest, 8/55; auth, String composition (movie), N Y State Coun Arts, 70.
Dealer: Gallerie Chalette, 9 E 88th St, New York, NY 10028.
Mailing Address: 44 E 63rd St, New York, NY 10021.

FULTON, RUTH (McCONNELL)
Painter
Preferred Media: Oils, Watercolors, Pastels.
b Rome, Ga.
Study & Training: Shorter Col; Famous Artists Sch; Univ Tenn, with Prof Kermet Ewing, Joe Cox & Robert Taugner; also with Marian Greenwood, New York & Mex, 49-64.
Work in Public Collections: Pi Kappa Alpha Nat Hq, Memphis, Tenn; portraits of presidents, Univ Tenn Pi Kappa Alpha Chap; plus many in pvt collections.
Commissions: First Pi Kappa Alpha to be killed in Spanish Am War; Two Mears Daughters, Knoxville, 70; plus many pvt commissions.
Exhibitions: Dulin Gallery Art Rental Gallery, McClung Mus, Univ Tenn, 49-65; Crossroads Gallery, 70-; one-man show, Parthenon, Nashville, 65; one-man & group shows, Carousel, 65-66, 70-
Teaching: Pvt classes.
Awards: Schlitz Art Competition; Motorola Art Competition; art competition, Knoxville Pen Women, 70 & 71.
Bibliography: Articles, In: Famous Artists Mag, News Sentinel & Nashville newspapers.
Memberships: Knoxville Watercolor Soc (secy-treas, 66-68, pres, 68-70); charter mem Tenn Watercolorists; Nat League Am Pen Women (art chmn, 72-73); Knoxville Art Soc.
Art Interests: Portraits from life or photograph; scenes in Smokies; childrens portraits.
Mailing Address: 3639 Taliluna Ave, Knoxville, TN 37919.

FULTON, W JOSEPH
Museum Director, Educator
b Longmont, Colo, Apr 8, 23.
Study & Training: Univ Colo, joint-hon scholar, 40-44, BFA, 44; Harvard Univ, James Rogers Rich & Townsend scholarships, 45-46, AM, 46, grad fel, 46-47; Belg-Am Educ Found fel, 51; Fulbright fel to France, 53-54.
Collections Arranged: Pioneer American Moderns, Norfolk Mus, Va, 53; The Blue Four, 55 & California Design, 57, Pasadena Art Mus, Calif; Marsden Hartley, Univ Southern Calif & Univ Tex, 68-69.
Teaching: Lect, The Museum and the Community; 19th & 20th Century Art; American Decorative Arts, clubs & civic groups; other lect to cols & univs; asst prof art hist, Mass Col Art, 60-63; vis prof, Univ Tex, 68-69; lectr, 69-
Positions: Asst dir, Norfolk Mus, 51-53; dir, Pasadena Art Mus, 53-57; assoc, Maury A Bromsen Assocs, 58-63; v pres, 63-; asst dir, Okla Art Ctr, summer 63; cur collections, La State Mus, 66-68; actg chief cur, Univ Art Mus, Univ Tex, 68-69; mus consult, 69-
Memberships: Col Art Asn Am; Am Asn Mus; Soc Archit Historians; Am Asn Univ Prof.
Mailing Address: 547 Pratt St, Longmont, CO 80501.

FULWIDER, EDWIN L
Painter, Educator
b Bloomington, Ind, Aug 15, 13.
Study & Training: John Herron Art Sch, BFA.
Work in Public Collections: Herron Art Inst; Dayton Art Inst; Libr Cong; Seattle Art Mus.
Exhibitions: John Herron Art Inst, 36-46 & 57; Cincinnati Mus Asn, 39, 41 & 56-60; Dayton Art Inst, 56 & 58; Libr Cong, 57; Butler Inst Am Art, 58; plus others.
Teaching: Instr, John Herron Art Sch, Indianapolis, Ind, 45-47; instr, Cornish Sch, Seattle, Wash, 47-49; prof art, Miami Univ, 63, chmn dept art, 63-68.
Awards: Prizes, Herron Art Inst, 40 & 43 & 45, Dayton Art Inst, 53 & Massillon Art Mus, 56; plus others.
Publications: Contribr, articles, In: Ford Times & Am Artist Mag, 61.
Dealer: Capricorn Galleries, 8003 Woodmont Ave, Bethesda, MD 20014.
Mailing Address: 101 E Central Ave, Oxford, OH 45056.

FURMAN, GLORIA VIOLET
Painter, Art Dealer
Preferred Media: Collage, Oils, Acrylics.
b New York, N Y, Mar 21, 27.
Study & Training: Hunter Col, BA; Art Stud League New York; Brooklyn Mus Sch, with Reuben Tam.
Exhibitions: Provincetown Artists Asn; Art Stud League, Woodstock, N Y; Brooklyn Mus Summer Show; Christ Church Ann, Cobble Hill, N Y; one-man show, Gallery 91, 72.

Positions: Dir & organizer, Gallery 91, Brooklyn, N Y, 71-
Memberships: Provincetown Artists Asn.
Dealer: Gallery 91, 91 Atlantic Ave, Brooklyn, NY 11201.
Mailing Address: 263 Hicus St, Brooklyn, NY 11201.

FUSSINER, HOWARD
Painter
Preferred Media: Oils.
b New York, N Y, May 25, 23.
Study & Training: Am Peoples Sch, 38-42, with C G Nelson & John Heliker; Art Stud League, 46-47; Cooper Union, 47-49, with Robert Gwathmey & John Ferren; Hans Hofmann Sch, 48; New York Univ, 49-52, with Hale Woodruff.
Work in Public Collections: Everhart Mus, Scranton, Pa; Staten Island Inst Mus, New York; Slater Mus, Norwich, Conn; Mattatuck Mus, Waterbury, Conn; Colby Jr Col, New London, N H.
Commissions: Mural, comn by New York Univ, 51-52.
Exhibitions: Pa Acad Fine Arts Biennial, Philadelphia, 62; Silvermine Guild Artists Ann, 62; Boston Arts Festival, 63; Hartford Plaza 7, 64; New Haven Arts Festival, 64.
Teaching: Humanities, Morehouse col, 51-55; art, Colby Jr Col, 57-60; asst prof art, Southern Conn State Col, 60-
Awards: Best in show, New Haven Arts Festival & Hartford Plaza 7, 64 & Waterbury Arts Festival, 68.
Memberships: Col Art Asn Am; Conn Acad Fine Arts.
Publications: Auth, Organic integration in Cezanne's painting, summer 56, Van Gogh (poem), spring 58 & The use of subject matter in recent art, spring 61, Art J; auth, Uccello's Battle of San Romano (poem), summer 60 & Giotto (poem), winter 61-62, Art J.
Dealer: Athena Gallery, 278 Orange St, New Haven, CT 06510.
Mailing Address: 1 Everitt St, New Haven, CT 06511.

G

GABIN, GEORGE JOSEPH
Painter, Educator
Preferred Media: Oils.
b Brooklyn, N Y, Apr 16, 31.
Study & Training: Brooklyn Mus Art Sch; Art Stud League New York, with Reginald Marsh, Ivan Olinsky & Will Barnett.
Work in Public Collections: Repub Savings & Loan, Washington, D C.
Exhibitions: One-man shows, Carl Siembab Gallery, 63 & 67; Gallery 7, 65 & Guild Boston Artists, 72; group shows, Nat Acad Design, Allied Artists Am & Audubon Artists, 60-72 & Am Fedn Arts Nat Traveling Show, 64-65.
Teaching: Instr illus & drawing, New Eng Sch Art, Boston, Mass, 64-70; instr illus, drawing & painting, Montserrat Sch Visual Arts, 70-
Awards: Matson Mem prize for portraiture, Rockport Art Asn, 64; Jane Peterson Prize for portraiture, 65 & for landscape, 71, Allied Artists Am.
Memberships: Allied Artists Am; Guild Boston Artists; Rockport Art Asn (chmn arts comt, 65-69.
Mailing Address: 121 Main St, Rockport, MA 01966.

GABLIK, SUZI
Writer, Painter
b New York, N Y, Sept 26, 34.
Study & Training: Black Mountain Col, N C, summer 51; Hunter Col, BA, 55, with Robert Motherwell.
Work in Public Collections: Hirshhorn Collection; Sarah Robbie Found.
Exhibitions: Terry Dintenfass, Inc, New York, 72.
Bibliography: L Alloway (auth), rev, In: The Nation, 5/8/72; H Rose (auth), New York letter, Studio Int, 5/72.
Memberships: Int Asn Art Critics.
Publications: Co-auth, Pop art redefined, 68 & auth, Magritte, New York Graphic Soc, 71.
Dealer: Terry Dintenfass, Inc, 18 E 67th St, New York, NY 10021.
Mailing Address: 5 Westmoreland St, London W1, England.

GABRIEL, ROBERT A
Sculptor
b Cleveland, Ohio, July 21, 31.
Study & Training: Cleveland Inst Art; Skowhegan Sch Painting & Sculpture.
Commissions: Design, Pittsburgh Hilton Hotel; sculpture, Allegheny Ludlum Steel Co; design for Peter Muller-Munk, Gov Proj in Ankara, Turkey, 57-58.

Exhibitions: Cleveland Mus Art, Pittsburgh, Pa, 53-55; Western Pa Sculpture Exhib, 55 & 56; one-man shows, Carnegie Inst, Pittsburgh, 62 & Carnegie-Mellon Univ, Pittsburgh, 68; Mainstreams 69, Marietta, Ohio; plus many others.
Teaching: Assoc prof design, Carnegie Inst Technol; instr art, Allegheny Col, 54.
Positions: Dir educ, Arts & Crafts Ctr Pittsburgh, Pa, 71-
Awards: Prize, Wichita, Kans, 53; Mary Page traveling scholar, Cleveland Inst Art, 54.
Memberships: Assoc Artists of Pittsburgh (pres, 66-67); Pittsburgh Soc Sculptors (pres, 59-61).
Mailing Address: 6307 Hampton St, Pittsburgh, PA 15206.

GACH, GEORGE
Painter, Sculptor
Preferred Media: Wax, Wood, Oils, Plastic, Bronze.
b Budapest, Hungary, Jan 27, 09; U S citizen.
Study & Training: Hungarian Acad Fine Art, BA.
Commissions: Bas reliefs, Methodist Church, Dallas, Tex, 69-70; bronze bas reliefs of Okla hist, Liberty Bank Okla, 72.
Exhibitions: Audubon Artists, Allied Artists, Nat Sculpture Soc; plus many others.
Teaching: Instr sculpture, Acad Beirut Lebanon, 48-52.
Awards: Gold medal, Hudson Valley Art Asn, 59; Audubon Artists Medal of Honor, 66; gold medal, Nat Sculpture Soc, 71.
Memberships: Allied Artists Am; Nat Sculpture Soc; Nat Art League; Hudson Valley Art Asn; Nassau Art League.
Dealers: Country Art Gallery, Birth Hill Rd, The Plaza, Locust Valley, NY 11560; Crest Gallery, 125 Turtle Creek Village, Dallas, TX 75219.
Mailing Address: 212 Willow, Roslyn Heights, NY 11577.

GAGE, FRANCES M
Sculptor
b Windsor, Ont, Aug 22, 24.
Study & Training: Ont Col Art; Art Stud League New York; Ecole Beaux-Arts, Paris, France, Royal Soc Can scholar.
Work in Public Collections: Rothmans of Can; Univ Western Ont Med Sch; Med Sci Bldg, Toronto; Univ Guelph; bronze on Prince Arthur, Toronto.
Commissions: Crest, Ont Hydro Seaway, Cornwall; Metro Rd Bridges; fountain head, Cancer Hostel, Toronto; fountain, Albright Gardens, London, Ont; figure & reliefs, Prov Inst Trades Bldg, London, Ont; plus many portraits & other sculpture.
Exhibitions: Royal Can Acad Art; Sculptors Soc Can; Ont Soc Art.
Mailing Address: 60 Birch Ave, Toronto, Ont, Can.

GAGE, HARRY (LAWRENCE)
Painter, Educator
Preferred Media: Watercolors.
b Battle Creek, Mich, Nov 20, 87.
Study & Training: Art Inst Chicago, foreign travel scholar; Tucson Watercolor Guild, Ariz.
Exhibitions: Am Artists Prof League; Rockport Art Asn; North Shore Arts Asn, Gloucester; Concord Art Asn; Ogunquit Art Asn.
Teaching: Prof graphic arts, Carnegie Inst Technol, 12-19; lectr graphic arts, Pratt Inst, 25-30; ed graphic arts, Encycl Americana.
Positions: Treas, Am Fedn Arts, 26-30; co-founder & chmn, Annisquam Art Gallery, 54-
Awards: Gold medal for achievement in graphic arts, Am Inst Graphic Arts, 42; first New England Benjamin Franklin Award, Indust Asns New England, 59.
Memberships: Am Inst Graphic Artists (founding chmn bk clin, 30-36, pres N Y chap, 32-35); Am Artists Prof League; North Shore Arts Asn; Rockport Art Asn.
Publications: Auth, Applied design for printers, United Typothetae Am, 20; co-auth, A composition manual, Printing Indust Am, 53.
Mailing Address: 16 River Rd, Annisquam, Gloucester, MA 01930.

GAHMAN, FLOYD
Painter
Preferred Media: Oils, Watercolors.
b Elida, Ohio.
Study & Training: Valparaiso Univ; Columbia Univ; also with Hobart Nichols & Henry Varnum Poor.
Work in Public Collections: Pa State Univ; Ind Univ.
Exhibitions: Allied Artists Am Ann, New York, N Y, 30; Nat Acad Design Ann, New York, 32-; New York World's Fair, N Y, 39; Hudson Valley Art Asn Ann, New York, 50-; Acad Artists, Springfield, Mass, 59.
Teaching: Lectr painting, Pa State Univ, Ogontz Ctr, 46-59.
Awards: Tiffany Found fel, 33-36; landscape prize, Allied Artists Am, 42 & Acad Artists, 59.
Memberships: Nat Acad Design; Salmagundi Club; Acad Artists; Allied Artists Am; Hudson Valley Art Asn.
Mailing Address: 90 La Salle St, New York, NY 10027.

GAILIS, JANIS
Painter
Preferred Media: Oils.
b Courland, Latvia, Oct 19, 03; U S citizen.
Study & Training: Acad Fine Arts, Riga, Latvia, landscape painting with Vilhelms Purvitis, 25-32, dipl, 32.
Work in Public Collections: State Mus Latvia, Riga; City Mus Liepaja, Latvia.
Exhibitions: One-man shows, Kuntshaus, Duesseldorf, Ger, 49, Galerie Int, New York, N Y, 58, Ligoa Duncan Gallery, New York, 63, Raymond Duncan Gallery, Paris, France, 66 & 72.
Teaching: Instr art, State High Sch, Rezekne, Latvia, 32-44.
Bibliography: Janis Silins (auth), Janis Gailis, W Kohlhammer, Stuttgart, Ger, 48; Hugo Vitols & George W Weber, Jr (auth), Janis Gailis, Amber Printers & Publ, Toronto, 71.
Dealers: Ligoa Duncan Gallery, 825 Madison Ave, New York, NY 10021, & 31 Rue Seine, Paris VI, France.
Mailing Address: 101-54 106th St, Ozone Park, NY 11416.

GAINES, NATALIE EVELYN
Sculptor, Lecturer
Preferred Media: Metal, Plastics.
b Detroit, Mich, Dec 11, 29.
Study & Training: Detroit Soc Arts & Crafts; Greason Sch, Detroit, with Pearl Greason.
Work in Public Collections: Glassboro State Col.
Exhibitions: Ann Mich Artists, Detroit Inst Art, 49 & 50; Contemp Am Art, Creative Gallery, New York, N Y, 51; Allied Artists Am, New York, 58; one-man shows, Crespi Gallery, New York, 58 & Glassboro State Col, 61.
Awards: Third prize, Crespi Gallery Second Ann Competition Award Show, 58.
Memberships: Archit League New York.
Mailing Address: 410 E 79th St, New York, NY 10021.

GAINES, WILLIAM ROBERT
Art Historian, Painter
Preferred Media: Oils, Acrylics.
b Madison, Va, Aug 12, 27.
Study & Training: Pa Mil Col; Va Commonwealth Univ, BFA; Columbia Univ, MFA; also with Renato Guttuso.
Work in Public Collections: Univ Va, Charlottesville; Va Polytech Inst & State Univ, Blacksburg; St Mary's Hosp, Richmond, Va; Retreat for the Sick, Richmond.
Exhibitions: Five Va Artists Biennials, 49-63; Abingdon Sq Painters, New York, N Y, 53; Va Beach Boardwalk Exhib, 58; Va Commonwealth Univ, 64; one-man exhib, Tappahannock, Va, 72.
Collections Arranged: Art Nouveau, 71; Francisco Goya: Portraits in Paintings, Prints & Drawings, 72; Sculpture by Willi Gutmann, 72
Teaching: Instr painting, drawing & art hist, Va Mus, Richmond, 54-56, 57 & 62.
Positions: Registr, Va Mus, 51-53, artmobile cur, 53-54, supvr educ, 54-56, 57-62, head progs div, 62-
Awards: Best in Show Awards, Va Beach Boardwalk Exhib, 58 & Thalimers Invitational, 63.
Memberships: Am Asn Mus (chmn accreditation comt).
Publications: Auth, The art kits, Arts Va, Vol VI, No I; co-auth, Art Nouveau (catalogue), 71; auth, Virginia Museum: two pioneer programs, Mus News, Vol 50, No 2; ed, Francisco Goya: portraits in paintings, prints, and drawings (catalogue), 72.
Mailing Address: 206 N Meadow St, Richmond, VA 23220.

GAINS, JACOB
Painter
Preferred Media: Oils.
b Vilna, Poland; U S citizen.
Study & Training: Nat Acad Design; New York Sch Fine & Appl Art; Educ Alliance; also with Adja Yunkers & William Baziotes.
Work in Public Collections: Montclair Art Mus, N J; Bay Harbor Galleries, Miami Beach, Fla.
Exhibitions: Knickerbocker Artists, Riverside Mus, New York, N Y, 57; Newark Mus, N J, 59; Nat Acad Design Ann, New York, 61; Painters & Sculptors Soc Exhib, Jersey City Mus, N J, 63; Montclair Art Mus, 66.
Awards: Jersey City Mus Tercentenary Award, 60; first prize & medal of honor, Painters & Sculptors Soc, 63; Permanent Collection Purchase Award, Montclair Art Mus, 66.
Memberships: Painters & Sculptors Soc.
Dealer: Mrs Freda Kruse, 1007 Kane Concourse, Bay Harbor Island, Miami Beach, FL 33154.
Mailing Address: 400 Kings Point Dr, Miami Beach, FL 33160.

GAITHER, EDMUND B
Art Administrator, Art Historian
b Great Falls, S C, Oct 6, 44.
Study & Training: Morehouse Col; Ga State Col; Brown Univ.

Collections Arranged: Afro-American Artists: New York and Boston, Mus Fine Arts, Boston, Mass, 70.
Teaching: Asst prof art hist, Boston Univ, 70-72; lectr art hist, Wellesley Col & Harvard Col, 71-72.
Positions: Cur, Mus of Nat Ctr Afro-Am Artists, Boston, 69-; dir visual arts prog, Elma Lewis Sch Fine Arts, Boston, 69-; spec consult, Mus Fine Arts, Boston, 69-
Memberships: Nat Conf Artists; Col Art Asn.
Research: Historical & critical discussion of Afro-American Art.
Publications: Contribr, A new criticism needed, N Y Times, 5/70; auth introd, Afro-Am artists: New York & Boston, 70; ed & contribr, Affairs of black artists, 71; contribr, Negro reference book, 72 & Artists proofs, 72.
Mailing Address: 598 Walk Hill St, Mattapan, MA 02126.

GALLAGHER, EDWARD J, JR
Collector
Mailing Address: 3501 Ednor Rd, Baltimore, MD 21218.

GALLENKAMP, CHARLES & PATRICIA
Art Dealers
Positions: Co-owners & co-dirs, Janus Gallery.
Specialty of Gallery: Contemporary art of the Southwest; painting, sculpture, graphics and designer crafts.
Mailing Address: Janus Gallery, 116½ E Palace Ave, Santa Fe, NM 87501.

GALLO, FRANK
Sculptor, Educator
b Toledo, Ohio, Jan 13, 33.
Study & Training: Toledo Mus Sch Art, BFA, 54; Cranbrook Acad Art, 55; Univ Iowa, MFA, 59.
Work in Public Collections: Mus Mod Art & Whitney Mus Am Art, New York, N Y; Art Inst Chicago, Ill; Los Angeles Mus Art, Calif; Cleveland Mus Art, Ohio; plus others.
Commissions: Commemorative Medal for Civil Eng, Univ Ill.
Exhibitions: Whitney Mus Am Art Ann, 64-67, Young America, 65; Butler Inst Am Art, Youngstown, Ohio, 65; Toronto Int Sculpture Symposium, 67; Kennedy Mem Exhib; Venice Biennale, 68; plus others.
Teaching: Prof sculpture, Univ Ill, 60-
Awards: First Prize, Des Moines, 58; Prize, Interior Valley Competition, Cincinnati, 61; Guggenheim Found fel, 66.
Mailing Address: 804 W Nevada St, Urbana, IL 61801.

GAMBLE, KATHRYN ELIZABETH
Museum Director
b Van Wert, Ohio, Aug 19, 15.
Study & Training: Oberlin Col, AB, 37; Atelier year of study, Dayton Art Inst, 38; Newark Mus, cert, 41; New York Univ Grad Sch Fine Arts, MA, 48.
Collections Arranged: Montclair in Manhattan, exhib of permanent collection, 61; American Painting Collection (catalog), Montclair Art Mus; Asher B Durand Retrospective, 71; A B Durand (catalog).
Teaching: Supvr art, Covington Pub Schs, Ohio, 38-40.
Positions: Dir, Montclair Art Mus, 52-
Memberships: Am Asn Mus; N J Mus Coun.
Mailing Address: Montclair Art Museum, 3 S Mountain Ave at Bloomfield Ave, Montclair, NJ 07042.

GAMMON, JUANITA-LA VERNE
Painter, Educator
Preferred Media: Acrylics, Oils, Watercolors.
b McLeansboro, Ill.
Study & Training: Univ Ill, BFA & MFA.
Work in Public Collections: Work in many private collections.
Commissions: Many private comns.
Exhibitions: Dream Mus, Champaign, Ill, 70; McKinley Found, Urbana, Ill, 70; Nat Acad Design, New York, N Y, 70-71; Illini Union Gallery, Univ Ill, 71.
Teaching: Head dept art, Parkland Col, Champaign, 67-
Positions: Judge, local & regional art exhibs, 67-; art lectr & critic, Classroom Serv Clubs, 67-; supvr, Champaign Co Art Show, 69-
Memberships: Ad Club Champaign-Urbana (treas, mem bd, 71-); Col Art Asn Am; Am Asn Jr Cols; Nat Art Educ Asn; Ill Art Educ Asn.
Mailing Address: 711 W Healey, Champaign, IL 61820.

GARBISCH, EDGAR WILLIAM & BERNICE CHRYSLER
Collectors
Mr Garbisch, b LaPorte, Ind, Apr 7, 99; Mrs Garbisch, b Oelwein, Iowa.
Study & Training: Mr Garbisch, Washington & Jefferson Col, BA, 21; U S Military Acad, BS, 25.

Art Interests: Parts of collection donated to Nat Gallery of Art, Metropolitan Museum of Art, Philadelphia Museum of Art, Baltimore Museum of Art and other museums; selections from collection exhibited in museums in the United States, Canada, Europe and Japan.
Collection: American furniture and paintings; American and European brass and wrought iron fixtures; European and Chinese porcelains of the seventeenth, eighteenth and early nineteenth centuries; French furniture and French paintings of the nineteenth and early twentieth centuries.
Mailing Address: Pokety, Castle Haven Rd, Cambridge, MD 21613.

GARDINER, HENRY GILBERT
Art Administrator, Art Historian
b Boston, Mass, Aug 27, 27.
Study & Training: Harvard Col, BA(arch), 50; Harvard Univ, MA (fine arts), 59.
Collections Arranged: Color and Form 1909-1914, Fine Arts Gallery San Diego, 71-72, Oakland Mus, 72, Seattle Art Mus (pavilion), 72.
Positions: Asst cur painting, Philadelphia Mus Art, 60-69; dir, Fine Arts Gallery San Diego, 69-
Memberships: Asn Art Mus Dirs; Am Asn Mus; Col Art Asn Am.
Publications: Auth, Checklist of paintings in the Philadelphia Museum of Art, 65; auth, The collection of Mrs John Wintersteen, Calif Palace of Legion of Honor, 66; auth, The Samuel S White III and Vera White Collection, Philadelphia Mus Art, 68; auth, Arthur Carles: a critical & biographical study, Philadelphia Mus Art, 70; auth, Color and Form 1909-1914, Fine Arts Gallery San Diego, 71; plus others.
Mailing Address: Fine Arts Gallery, Balboa Park, San Diego, CA 92101.

GARDINER, ROBERT DAVID LION
Collector
b New York, N Y.
Study & Training: Columbia Col; Cornell Univ; Princeton Univ; Long Island Univ, hon LHD.
Collection: Paintings, silver, furniture, sculpture, porcelain, textiles.
Mailing Address: 990 Fifth Ave, New York, NY 10021.

GARDNER, ANDREW BRADFORD
Printmaker, Painter
b Chicago, Ill, Nov 17, 37.
Study & Training: Antioch Col, BA, 61; Ohio State Univ, MA, 66; Escuela Cent Bellas Artes San Fernando, Madrid, Spain, 64.
Work in Public Collections: Metrop Mus Art, New York, N Y; Mansfield State Col, Pa; Colgate Univ, Hamilton, N. Y.
Exhibitions: The Door, Mus Contemp Crafts, New York, 68; 16th & 18th Nat Print Exhibs, Brooklyn Mus, N Y, 68 & 72; New Talent in Printmaking-1969, Asn Am Artists Gallery, New York, 69; 2nd Biennale Int Estampe, Paris, France, 70; 4th Am Print Biennial, Santiago, Chile, 70.
Teaching: Instr art & design, Rochester Inst Technol, 66-67; asst prof fine arts, Rutgers Univ, Newark, 67-
Mailing Address: 108 Wyckoff St, Brooklyn, NY 11201.

GARDNER, JOAN A
Painter, Film Maker
b Joliet, Ill, May 3, 33.
Study & Training: Univ Ill, Kate Neal Kinley Mem fel, 55, BFA & MFA; Norfolk Summer Art Sch, Yale Univ, fel, 56, with Rico Lebrun & Gabor Peterdi.
Work in Public Collections: Univ Ill; Am Fedn Art.
Exhibitions: Art Inst Chicago, 56; Conn Acad Fine Arts Invitational, 69; John Slade Flyhouse, New Haven, Conn, 70; Conn Arts Festival, Hartford, 71; New Britain Mus Art, Conn, 71.
Teaching: Instr art, Southern Conn State Col, 65-71; instr art, Univ New Haven, 71-72.
Awards: Conn Acad Fine Arts Award, New Britain Mus, 69.
Memberships: Conn Acad Fine Arts.
Publications: Co-auth, The robot (film), Crowell Collier, 70.
Dealer: Mercer Gallery, 55 Mercer St, New York, NY 10013.
Mailing Address: 548 Orange St, New Haven, CT 06511.

GARDNER, ROBERT EARL
Printmaker, Educator
Preferred Media: Intaglio, Lithography.
b Indianapolis, Ind, June 29, 19.
Study & Training: John Herron Art Sch, BFA, 48; Atelier 17, New York, N Y, 48-49; Cranbrook Acad Art, MFA, 52.
Work in Public Collections: Carnegie Mus, Pittsburgh; Univ Okla Mus, Norman; Wichita Mus Art, Kans; Ohio Univ, Athens; Ga Comn Arts.
Exhibitions: Pa Acad Fine Arts Exhibs; Brooklyn Mus Print Biennials; Libr Cong Print Exhibs; Northwest Printmakers Exhibs; Philadelphia Print Club Exhibs.

Teaching: Assoc prof printmaking, Carnegie-Mellon Univ, 53-
Positions: Artisan-printer, Tamarind Lithography Workshop, Los Angeles, Calif, summer 62 & 63-64.
Mailing Address: Dept of Painting & Sculpture, Carnegie-Mellon University, Pittsburgh, PA 15213.

GARRETT, STUART GRAYSON, JR
Painter, Educator
b Oklahoma City, Okla.
Study & Training: Cooper Union; Art Stud League New York.
Work in Public Collections: USN Hist Collection; Norfolk Mus Art, Va; New York Univ; Johns Hopkins Univ; Univ Md.
Exhibitions: Nat Acad Design, New York, N Y; Am Watercolor Soc, New York; Am Artists Prof League, New York; Audubon Artists, New York; Mus Marine, Paris; plus others.
Teaching: Assoc prof art, City Col New York.
Awards: Gold medal, Am Artists Prof League, 59; Am Watercolor Soc prizes, 61, 65, 67 & 72; Salmagundi Club, 62, 63, 65 & 67; plus others.
Memberships: Am Watercolor Soc (dir); Allied Artists Am (past pres); Southern Vermont Artists; Salmagundi Club; Artists Fel.
Mailing Address: 517 E 84th St, New York, NY 10028.

GARRISON, EVE
Painter
Preferred Media: Oils, Casein.
b Boston, Mass, Apr 22, 08.
Study & Training: Art Inst Chicago, grad, 31; Wayne Univ; Lawrence Inst Technol; Lewis Inst Chicago.
Work in Public Collections: Miami Mus Mod Art, Fla; Union League Club Chicago; Drian Gallery, London, Eng; Mt Sinai Hosp, Chicago.
Exhibitions: One-man shows, Drian Gallery, London, 70, Galerie Vallombreuse, Biarritz, France, 72, Maharaj Gallery, Boston, 72 & retrospectives, Ill Inst Technol, Chicago, 72 & Miami Mus Mod Art, 72.
Awards: Awards for Old Colored Maid, Corcoran Mus, 34 & Bride & Groom, Union League Club Chicago, 61.
Bibliography: Dona Meilach (auth), Collage & found art, 65.
Dealer: Drian Gallery, London, Eng; Galerie Vallombreuse, Biarritz, France.
Mailing Address: 542 S Dearborn, Chicago, IL 60605.

GARSTON, GERALD DREXLER
Painter
Preferred Media: Oils.
b Waterbury, Conn, May 3, 25.
Study & Training: Johns Hopkins Univ, BA, 51; Art Stud League New York, N Y, 52, painting with Louis Bouche & printmaking with Harry Sternberg.
Work in Public Collections: Rose Mus, Brandeis Mus, Waltham, Mass, Los Angeles Co Mus, Los Angeles, Calif; William Rockhill Nelson Gallery Art, Kansas City, Mo; Philadelphia Mus Art, Pa; Wadsworth Atheneum, Hartford, Conn.
Exhibitions: Poindexter Gallery, New York, 62; A M Sachs Gallery, New York, 65; Susan Morse Hilles Collection, Mus Fine Arts, Boston, Mass, 66; Graham Gallery, New York, 67; Pucker-Safrai Gallery, Boston, 71.
Dealer: Pucker-Safrai Gallery, 171 Newbury St, Boston, MA 02116.
Mailing Address: 131 Oliver Rd, New Haven, CT 06515.

GARVER, THOMAS H
Art Administrator, Writer
b Duluth, Minn, Jan 23, 34.
Study & Training: Barnes Found, Merion, Pa; Haverford Col, BA; Univ Minn, MA.
Collections Arranged: Rose Art Mus, Brandeis Univ; Bruce Conner; Assemblages, Drawings & Films; 12 Photographers of the American Social Landscape, Newport Harbor Art Mus; Just Before the War: Urban America From 1935-1941 as seen by Photographers of the Farm Security Administration; Robert Rauschenberg in Black and White; Tom Wesselman: Early Still Lifes, 1962-64; Wood, The Sculpture of Gabriel Kohn; Edward Hopper: 15 Paintings; Don Potts: My First Car; New Art of Vancouver; Reginald Marsh Retrospective.
Positions: Asst dir, Krannert Art Mus, Univ Ill, 60-62; asst dir, Seattle World's Fair, 62; asst dir, Rose Art Mus, 62-68; dir, Newport Harbor Art Mus, Newport Beach, Calif, 68; consult art gallery design, Univ Chicago & Calif Inst Arts, 69; cur exhibs, Calif Palace of Legion of Honor/M H de Young Mem Mus, San Francisco, Calif, 72.
Memberships: Western Asn Art Mus (bd mem, 70-71, pres, 71-72); assoc Int Inst Conserv Hist & Artistic Works.
Research: Contemporary American art.
Publications: Contribr, Artforum & Los Angeles Reviewer, 68-70; contribr, Handbook of college and university administration, 69;

contribr, An interview with George Sawchuck, Artscan, 69; contribr, Balboa and the fun zone, Art Am, 71.
Mailing Address: M H de Young Memorial Museum, Golden Gate Park, San Francisco, CA 94118.

GARVEY, ELEANOR
Art Administrator
Positions: Assoc Cur, Printing & Graphic Arts, Harvard Col Libr.
Mailing Address: 60 Brattle St, Cambridge, MA 02138.

GARWOOD, AUDREY
Painter, Printmaker
Preferred Media: Oils, Wood.
b Toronto, Ont, July 7, 27.
Study & Training: Ont Col Art; Rijksacad, Amsterdam, scholar; Le Chaumiere, Paris.
Work in Public Collections: London Gallery & Art Mus, Ont; McLaughlin Art Gallery, Oshawa, Ont; Burnaby Art Gallery, B C; Hamilton Art Gallery, Ont.
Exhibitions: Royal Can Acad; Ont Soc Artists; Can Graphic Art Soc; Can Painters & Etchers; Nat Gallery Showcase.
Awards: Can Graphic Art Soc Award; Sterling Trust Award, Can Painters & Etchers; J Forester Award, Ont Soc Artists.
Memberships: Royal Can Acad Art; Ont Soc Art; Can Graphic Art Soc; Can Painters & Etchers.
Mailing Address: c/o Mazelow Gallery, 3463 Yonge St, Toronto 319, Ont, Can.

GARY, DOROTHY HALES
Collector, Writer
b San Francisco, Calif, Nov 21, 17.
Study & Training: Stanford Col.
Positions: Owner, pvt gallery.
Specialty of Gallery: Abstract, contemporary art.
Collection: Abstract art.
Publications: Auth, Sun, stones & silence, Simon & Shuster, 63; co-auth, Splendors of Asia, Viking Press, 65; co-auth, Splendors of Byzantium, Viking Press, 67.
Mailing Address: 730 Park Ave, New York, NY 10021.

GARY, JAN (MRS WILLIAM D GORMAN)
Painter, Printmaker
Preferred Media: Acrylics, Casein.
b Fort Worth, Tex, Feb 13, 25.
Study & Training: Art Ctr Sch, Los Angeles; San Antonio Art Inst, Tex; Art Stud League New York.
Work in Public Collections: Butler Inst Am Art, Youngstown, Ohio; Pensacola Art Ctr, Fla; Wis State Univ-Eau Claire; Brandeis Univ, Waltham, Mass; Rosenberg Libr, Galveston, Tex.
Exhibitions: N J Pavilion, New York World's Fair, 65; one-man shows, Centenary Col Women, Hackettstown, N J, 67 & Ringwood Manor State Mus, N J, 68; Am Acad Arts & Lett, 67-68; Four N J Artists, Canton Art Inst, Ohio, 71.
Awards: M Grumbacher Purchase Award, Audubon Artists Ann, 66; Janet Berne Mem Award, Nat Asn Women Artists Ann, 67; Childe Hassam Fund Purchase Award, Am Acad Arts & Lett, 68.
Bibliography: Margaret Harold (auth), Prize-winning watercolors, Bk 5, 67 & Prize-winning art, Bk 7, 67; Henry Gasser (auth), article, In: Am Artist, 10/70.
Memberships: Nat Soc Painters Casein & Acrylic; Nat Asn Women Artists; Audubon Artists; Painters & Sculptors Soc N J; Assoc Artists N J.
Mailing Address: 43 W 33rd St, Bayonne, NJ 07002.

GASPARRO, FRANK
Sculptor, Instructor
b Philadelphia, Pa, Aug 26, 09.
Study & Training: Pa Acad Fine Arts; also with Charles Grafly.
Commissions: Designed, Kennedy half-dollar (reverse), Am Numismatic Asn Medal, 69, Pres Richard M Nixon Medal (obverse & reverse), 69; Eisenhower dollar (obverse & reverse) & Lincoln Mem U S one cent (reverse); also many medals for U S mint.
Exhibitions: Phila Mus Art Sculpture Exhib, Pa, 40; Pa Acad Fine Arts, Philadelphia, 46; Medals at French Mint, Paris, France, 50; Spanish Int Medallic Art Exhibition, Madrid, 52 & 68; Woman on the Medal, Int Medallic Exhib.
Teaching: Instr, Fleisher Art Sch, Philadelphia, 46-
Positions: Engraver, U S Mint, Philadelphia, 42-65, chief engraver, 65-
Awards: Braverman Sculpture Prize, 59, 62-65; Am Numismatic Soc Gold Medal as outstanding numismatic sculptor of year, 68; gold medal, Numismatic Expos at Pistoia Montecatini, 72; plus others.
Memberships: Soc Medalists; Pa Acad Fine Arts Fel (bd dirs, 58-); Fr Soc of the Medal; Artists Equity Asn.
Mailing Address: 216 Westwood Park Dr, Manor, PA 19083.

GASSER, HENRY MARTIN
Painter, Writer
Preferred Media: Watercolors.
b Newark, N J, Oct 31, 09.
Study & Training: Newark Sch Fine & Indust Art, cert; Grand Cent Sch Art; Art Stud League New York, with Robert Brackman & John R Grabach.
Work in Public Collections: Metrop Mus Art, New York; Philadelphia Mus Art, Pa; Newark Mus, N J; Hist Properties Sect, Dept War, Washington, D C; Boston Mus Art.
Exhibitions: American Traditional Artists of the 20th Century, Columbus Mus, Ga, 63; Twentieth Century Realists, Fine Arts Gallery San Diego, 66; Nat Acad Design, 71; Am Watercolor Soc, 71.
Teaching: Instr painting & compos, Art Stud League New York, 64-70; instr painting workshop, Heritage Arts, South Orange, N J, 70-
Positions: Dir, Newark Sch Fine & Indust Art, 46-54.
Awards: Julius Hallgarten Prize, Nat Acad Design, 43; Philadelphia Watercolor Club Prize, 45; Am Watercolor Soc Award, 69.
Bibliography: Exploring casein (film), M Grumbacher, 60; Albert Teh Eyeck Gardner (auth), History of watercolor in America, Van Nostrand Reinhold, 66; Norman Kent (auth), Paintings of Newark, Am Artist Mag, 66.
Memberships: Nat Acad Design (rec secy, 60-67); Am Watercolor Soc (v pres, 53); Philadelphia Watercolor Club; Audubon Artists; Allied Artists Am.
Publications: Auth, Oil painting methods and demonstrations, 53, How to draw and paint, 55, Techniques of painting, 58, Picture making, 62 & Guide to painting, 64.
Dealer: Grand Central Art Galleries, 40 Vanderbilt Ave, New York, NY 10017.
Mailing Address: 654 Varsity Rd, South Orange, NJ 07079.

GAST, MICHAEL CARL
Painter
Preferred Media: Polymers, Oils.
b Chicago, Ill, June 11, 30.
Study & Training: Sch Art Inst Chicago, BFA, 52; Univ of the Americas, Mex, MFA(cum laude), 60.
Exhibitions: Washington Watercolor Asn 66th Ann Nat Exhib, Smithsonian Inst, 63 & Metrop Area Exhib, Howard Univ, Washington, D C, 70; Soc Washington Artists 70th & 71st Ann Exhib, Smithsonian Inst, 63 & 64; four-man show, Mickelson Gallery, Washington, D C, 66.
Teaching: Asst prof painting, George Washington Univ, 71.
Positions: Mus technician, div ceramics & glass, Nat Mus Hist & Technol, 61-64 & mus specialist, Nat Collection Fine Arts, 69-71, Smithsonian Inst.
Bibliography: Andrea O Cohen (auth), Mike Gast, D C Gazette, 4/19/72.
Memberships: Artists Equity Asn; Col Art Asn Am; Washington Watercolor Asn; Nat Art Workers Community.
Mailing Address: P O Box 848, Benjamin Franklin Station, Washington, DC 20044.

GASTON, MARIANNE BRODY
Painter, Illustrator
b New York, N Y.
Study & Training: Washington Irving Art Sch; Metrop Mus Art & Mus Natural Hist, scholar, 34-36; Parsons Inst for Fashion Illus, scholar, 36; Art Stud League New York, with Brackman, Vytlacil & R Soyer; Parsons Sch Design; Great Neck Art Asn, with M Soyer & Irving Maranz; pvt study with Jack Levine.
Work in Public Collections: New York Pub Libr; Art Dir Club New York.
Commissions: Cover art & color ads, Vogue, Harpers Bazaar, Cue, Glamour & others.
Exhibitions: Nat Asn Women Artists, 50-60; Best & Co, New York, 58; Gilgolde Gallery, Great Neck, N Y, 59 & 60; The Art Gallery, Dallas, Tex, 61; Hotel Fontainebleau, Miami Beach, Fla, 61; plus others.
Teaching: Instr art, New York, Great Neck & Miami Beach.
Awards: Alexander Medal, Sch Art League, 34; Art Dirs Club Award for Fashion Illus, 41; Atkins Award, Nat Asn Women Artists, 55.
Memberships: Art Stud League New York; Nat Asn Women Artists; Knickerbocker Artists; Artists Equity Asn; Art Dirs Club; plus others.
Mailing Address: 226 W San Marino Dr, Miami Beach, FL 33139.

GATES, HARRY IRVING
Sculptor, Painter
b Elgin, Ill, Dec 8, 34.
Study & Training: Univ Ill, BFA, 58, MFA, 60.
Work in Public Collections: Baltimore Mus Art, Md; Chase Manhattan Bank, New York, N Y; Corcoran Gallery Art, Washington,

D C; Int Art Prog Div, Nat Collection Fine Art, Washington, D C; Washington Co Mus Fine Arts, Hagerstown, Md.
Exhibitions: 53 Painters of Chicago, circulated in France & Ger, 58-59; 24th Ann Butler Inst Show, Youngstown, Ohio, 59; 25th Drawing, Print & Sculpture Exhib, San Francisco Mus Art, 61; one-man show, Baltimore Mus Fine Art, Md, 64; Small Sculpture Purchases for Int Art Prog, Nat Collection Fine Art, 69.
Teaching: Asst prof art, George Washington Univ, 64-
Awards: First Prize, 21st Ann Contemp Art, Palm Beach, Fla, 59; Artists Coun Award, 25th Ann Exhib for Sculpture, 61; Gov Prize, Md Ann, 70.
Dealer: Babcock Gallery, 805 Madison Ave, New York, NY 10021.
Mailing Address: P O Box 166, Frederick, MD 21701.

GATES, JOHN MONTEITH
Designer, Painter
b Elyria, Ohio, June 25, 05.
Study & Training: Harvard Col, 23-26; Sch Archit, Columbia Univ, BArch, 29.
Work in Public Collections: Steuben glass designs in many mus.
Exhibitions: Nat & int exhibs.
Positions: V pres & dir design, Steuben Glass, 33-70; dir design, Corning Glass Works, 59-70; retired.
Awards: First prize, Int Competition Design, Stockholm, Sweden, 33.
Memberships: Benjamin Franklin fel Royal Soc Art; Indust Design Soc Am; Am Inst Architects.
Mailing Address: 131 E 66th St, New York, NY 10021.

GATEWOOD, MAUD FLORANCE
Painter, Educator
Preferred Media: Polymers.
b Yanceyville, N C, Jan 8, 34.
Study & Training: Univ N C, Greensboro, AB; Ohio State Univ, MA; Univ Vienna; Fulbright grant, 62-63; Acad Appl Arts, Vienna; Harvard Summer Sch.
Work in Public Collections: Mint Mus Art, Charlotte, N C; Witherspoon Gallery, Univ N C, Greensboro; Emory Univ Libr, Atlanta, Ga.
Exhibitions: N C Artists Ann, N C Mus Art, Raleigh, 61-71; Peidmont Painting & Sculpture Ann, Charlotte, 65-71; Art on Paper, Greensboro, 65 & 67; Am Acad Arts & Lett & Nat Inst Arts & Lett, 72.
Teaching: Assoc prof painting, Univ N C, Charlotte, 64-
Positions: N C Nat Bank Art Comt, Charlotte, 66-
Awards: Am Acad Arts & Lett Award, 72.
Dealer: Heath Gallery, 34 Lombardy Way N E, Atlanta, GA 30309.
Mailing Address: 2309 Pender Pl, Charlotte, NC 28209.

GATLING, EVA INGERSOLL
Museum Director, Art Historian
b Mobile, Ala, Dec 28, 12.
Study & Training: Richmond Prof Inst, Col William & Mary, cert art, 35; Univ Ala, BA, 41; Yale Univ, MA, 44.
Collections Arranged: Eliel Saarinsen Memorial Exhib, Cranbrook Acad Art, 51; Whence Pop, 65, The Moran Family, 65 & Salute to Small Museums, 70, Heckscher Mus.
Positions: Dir exhib & supvr art equip, Duke Univ, 45-49; cur, Mus Cranbrook Acad Art, 49-54; asst dir, Des Moines Art Ctr, 59-61; dir, Heckscher Mus, 62-
Memberships: Am Asn Mus; Soc Archit Historians; Col Art Asn Am.
Research: American art, particularly after 1900; American architecture of the nineteenth and twentieth centuries; Buddhist art.
Collection: Twentieth century American painting, drawing and sculpture.
Publications: Auth, exhib catalogues, Mus Cranbrook Acad Art, 50-54 & Heckscher Mus, 63-; contribr, Soc Art Historians J, 51; contribr, Art J, 55; contribr, Artibus Asiae, 57.
Mailing Address: 32 Soundview Rd, Huntington, NY 11743.

GATRELL, MARION THOMPSON
Educator, Painter
Preferred Media: Graphics, Watercolors.
b Columbus, Ohio, Nov 13, 09.
Study & Training: Ohio State Univ, BSEd, 31, MA, 32.
Work in Public Collections: Butler Inst Am Art, Youngstown, Ohio; Columbus Gallery Fine Arts; Massillon Mus Art, Ohio; Otterbein Col, Westerville, Ohio; Steubenville Col, Ohio.
Exhibitions: Audubon Artists Nat, 45; Butler Art Inst Regional Ann, 50 & 57; Nat Asn Women Artists, Scotland, Eng & India, 64-65; Int Womens Competition, Cannes, France, 69; Nat Asn Women Artists, Florence & Naples, Italy, 72.
Teaching: Instr drawing & painting, Ohio State Univ, 43-47, asst prof, 47-56, assoc prof, 56-

Awards: Purchase Award for Cat in the Grass, Butler Art Inst, 57;
Baldwin Purchase Award for Prissy Ludden, Massillon Mus, 64;
Pace Gallery Award for Multiple Minimal Cat, Shoemacher Gallery, Capitol Univ, 68.
Bibliography: Top 10 Women of the year, Columbus Citizen,
12/31/54; Frances Piper (auth), Hurd and Gatrell featured,
Colubmus Dispatch, 1/8/67; Mrs Jerry Baughman (auth), Keystones at Ohio State, Ohio State Univ Monthly, 3/72.
Memberships: Nat Asn Women Artists; Columbus Art League (v pres, 41, mem bd, 43-).
Mailing Address: 1492 Perry St, Columbus, OH 43201.

GATRELL, ROBERT MORRIS
Educator, Painter
b Marietta, Ohio, May 18, 06.
Study & Training: Ohio State Univ BSEd, 29, MA, 33.
Work in Public Collections: Libr Cong, Washington, D C; Stanley
Grumbacher Collection Contemp Am Art, New York, N Y; E B
Crocker Art Gallery, Sacramento, Calif; Columbus Gallery Fine
Arts, Ohio; Canton Mus, Ohio; plus many others.
Commissions: Portraits, of Paul L Dunbar, Ohio State Archeol Mus,
38, Dean C Dye, 38 & George Rightmire, 42, Ohio State Univ, A A
Shaw, Denison Univ, 38 & Dean F J Smull, Ohio Northern Univ,
43.
Exhibitions: Am Watercolor Soc Ann, New York, 58 & 60; Water
color U S A, Springfield, Mo, 62 & 65; Am Drawing Ann, Norfolk,
Va, 63; Hunterdon Art Ctr Nat Print Exhib, 64-71.
Teaching: Instr drawing & painting, Ohio State Univ, 29-36, asst
prof, 36-55, prof, 55
Awards: Gov Award for Ceres, Ohio State Fair, 52; Purchase Prize
for Magic Dreamer, Butler Art Inst, 56; M Grumbacher Purchase
Award, Am Watercolor Soc, 60; plus one other.
Bibliography: Bram Dijkstra (auth), Award winning artist, Ohio
State Lantern, 60; F Piper (auth), Winter showcase of the arts,
66 & Hurd and Gatrell featured, 67, Columbus Dispatch.
Memberships: Am Watercolor Soc; Hunterdon Co Art Asn; Columbus Art League (pres, 42-43, bd gov, 48-52, 57-59).
Mailing Address: 1492 Perry St, Columbus, OH 43201.

GAUL, ARRAH LEE
Painter
b Philadelphia, Pa.
Study & Training: BFA; also study in Europe, Middle East, China,
Japan, India & Can.
Work in Public Collections: Reading Mus; Pa Acad Fine Arts; Rochester Mem Art Gallery.
Exhibitions: Philadelphia Sesqui-Centennial; one-man shows, Philadelphia Art Club, Beaux Arts Gallery, London & U S Embassy,
Tokyo; Grand Palais Champs Elysees, Paris; Neno Gallery Ann,
& Women Artists Asn Exhib, Neno Gallery, Tokyo; exhib, Acad
Music, Philadelphia; plus others.
Mailing Address: 1530 Locust St, Philadelphia, PA 19102.

GAUTHIER, JOACHIM GEORGE
Painter
b North Bay, Ont, Aug 20, 97.
Study & Training: Study under Frank Carmichael, Toronto.
Work in Public Collections: Work in pvt collections only.
Memberships: Can Soc Painters Watercolour; Ont Soc Arts; sr assoc Royal Can Acad Arts.
Mailing Address: 184 Ranleigh Ave, Toronto, Ont, Can.

GAWBOY, CARL
Painter
Preferred Media: Acrylics.
b Cloquet, Minn, May 21, 42.
Study & Training: Univ Minn, Duluth, BS, with Henry Pearson; Wis
State Univ-Superior, with Len Petersen; Univ Mont, with Don
Bunse & Rudy Autio.
Work in Public Collections: Navajo Community Col; also in many
private collections in Minn.
Commissions: Murals, Ely Chamber Commerce, Minn, 60 & Minn
Hist Soc, St Paul, 72.
Exhibitions: Arrowhead Art Exhib, Duluth, 66; Scottsdale Nat Indian
Art Exhib, Ariz, 72; Rainy River Jr Col, 72; Theatre-in-the-
Round, Minneapolis, Minn, 72.
Awards: Best in Show, Arrowhead Art Exhib, 66; first in painting,
Navajo Community Col, 72.
Bibliography: Gerald Vizenor (auth), Everlasting sky, Doubleday, 72.
Publications: Co-auth & illusr, Everything you ever wanted to ask
about Indians but were afraid to find out, 71.
Mailing Address: State Rte 1, Box 379, Ely, MN 55731.

GAY, ERIC LYNN
Painter, Photographer
Preferred Media: Oils.
b Flint, Mich, Feb 27, 43.
Study & Training: De Waters Art Ctr, Flint Inst Art, painting with
Stefan Davidek; photography with James McLendon.
Work in Public Collections: De Waters Art Ctr; Univ Chicago; Detroit Inst Arts.
Commissions: Bronze casting, Southwestern High Sch, Flint, 63;
landscape, Mr & Mrs John Mair, Flint, 67; seascape, comn by
Dr James Hill, Great Falls, Mont, 70; landscape, George DeSaint-
Rat, Great Falls, Mont, 72.
Exhibitions: Saginaw Valley Regional, Flint, 66; Mich Invitational,
Ann Arbor, 67; Bicentennial Medal Design, Mich, 72; Regional
juried show, C M Russell Gallery, Great Falls, 72.
Teaching: Instr painting, Sculpture Assocs, Flint, 66-67; instr
photog, U S Air Force, Great Falls, Mont, 69-72.
Positions: Graphics designer, Genesee Co Metrop Planning Comn,
Flint, 67-68; photogr, U S Air Force, 69-72.
Awards: Graphics Award, City of Flint, 67; two first prizes for
photog, in world wide contest, U S Air Force, 70.
Memberships: Mont Inst Art; C M Russell Gallery.
Art Interests: Visual expression and interpretation of landscape.
Publications: Illusr photog, Malmstrom AFB Guide, 71.
Mailing Address: 915 Sixth Ave N, Great Falls, MT 59401.

GAYLORD, FRANK CHALFANT
Sculptor, Designer
Preferred Media: Granite.
b Clarksburg, W Va, Mar 9, 25.
Study & Training: Carnegie Inst Technol Col Fine Arts; Tyler Sch
Fine Arts, Temple Univ, BFA.
Commissions: Firemens Mem, Mamaroneck Fire Dept, N Y, 62;
series of religious monuments, Archdiocese of Chicago, Ill,
62, Archdiocese of Detroit, Mich, 63 & in New Haven, Conn, 64;
Faith, Hope, Love (relief), New Britain, Conn, 67.
Exhibitions: Nat Sculpture Soc Ann Exhib, 65.
Teaching: Lectr advan of progressive philos on art, Am Inst Commemorative Arts, 65.
Memberships: Assoc Nat Sculpture Soc; assoc Vt Coun Arts.
Publications: Auth, Why Christ? & auth, A portrait of Hector, 68,
Monumental News Rev.
Mailing Address: 25 Delmont Ave, Barre, VT 05641.

GEBER, HANA
Sculptor, Instructor
Preferred Media: Silver, Bronze.
b Praha, Czech, Feb 14, 10; U S citizen.
Study & Training: Teachers Col, Prague; Art Stud League New York;
Sculpture Ctr, New York.
Work in Public Collections: Jewish Mus, New York; Rose Art Mus,
Brandeis Univ, Mass; Montclair Art Mus, N J; Int Synagogue,
Kennedy Airport, N Y; Univ Amherst Mus, Mass; plus many
other mus.
Commissions: Wedding Altar (silver & bronze), Temple Emanu El,
Yonkers, N Y; Mem in Bronze (wall piece), Verona High Sch, N J;
statue, Riverdale Temple, Bronx; Silver Wallpiece, Free West-
chester Synagogue, Mount Vernon, N Y; Judaica, Jewish Com-
munity Ctr, Harrison, N Y.
Exhibitions: Montclair Art Mus; Union Am Hebrew Congregations,
New York; Sculpture Ctr, New York: Am Jewish Hist Soc,
Waltham & Boston, Mass; Pa Acad Fine Arts, Philadelphia.
Teaching: Instr, Sculpture Ctr; instr, Riverdale Neighborhood House;
also private instr.
Awards: Mem Found Jewish Cult fel, 69; gold medal, Nat Asn Women
Artists; first prize in sculpture, Am Soc Contemp Artists.
Memberships: Audubon Artists; Nat Asn Women Artists; Sculpture
League; Artists Equity Asn; Sculpture Ctr.
Dealer: Sculpture Center, 167 E 69th St, New York, NY 10021.
Mailing Address: 168 W 225th St, New York, NY 10463.

GEBHARD, DAVID
Art Administrator, Art Historian
b Cannon Falls, Minn, July 21, 27.
Study & Training: Univ Minn, BA, MA & Ph D.
Collections Arranged: Purcell & Elmslie, Architects, 69, Walker Art
Ctr, 53; The Enigma of Ralph A Blakelock 1847-1919, 69, &
Charles Demuth, 71, Art Galleries, Univ Calif, Santa Barbara.
Teaching: Prof art hist, Univ Calif, Santa Barbara, 61-
Positions: Instr art hist, Univ N Mex, 53-55; dir, Roswell Mus &
Art Ctr, 55-60; dir, Art Galleries, Univ Calif, Santa Barbara, 61-
Research: Nineteenth and twentieth century architecture; architec-
ture of California; rock art of North America.

Publications: Auth, George Washington Smith, 64, Purcell and Elmslie, Architects, 65, 1868-1958 Architecture in California, 68, Charles F A Voysey, Architect, 70, Lloyd Wright, 71 & Schindler, 72.
Mailing Address: Art Galleries, University of California, Santa Barbara, CA 93106.

GEBHARDT, ANN STELLHORN
 Painter, Educator
b Leavenworth, Kans, Mar 13, 16.
Study & Training: Lake Erie Col; Ohio State Univ, BFA & MA, with Carolyn G Bradley, James R Hopkins & Alice Schille.
Exhibitions: Two-man show, Mint Mus Art.
Teaching: Asst prof art, Queens Col, N C, at present.
Memberships: Charlotte Art Guild.
Mailing Address: 2500 Sherwood Ave, Charlotte, NC 28207.

GEBHARDT, HAROLD
 Sculptor, Educator
b Milwaukee, Wis, Aug 21, 07.
Study & Training: Layton Sch Art.
Work in Public Collections: Milwaukee Pub Libr; Univ Wis-Milwaukee; Los Angeles Mus Art; also in pvt collections.
Exhibitions: Fleischer Anhalt Gallery, Los Angeles; Doane Col, Crete, Nebr; two-man shows, Occidental Col, Los Angeles & Trinity Univ Gallery, San Antonio, Tex; one-man shows, Santa Barbara Mus & San Bernardino Col; plus others.
Teaching: Prof sculpture, Univ Southern Calif, now emer prof.
Awards: Milwaukee Art Inst Award, 37; Los Angeles Mus Art, 46 & 50; City of Los Angeles, 48.
Memberships: Los Angeles Mus Art.
Mailing Address: 13186 Glenoaks Blvd, Sylmar, CA 91342.

GEBHARDT, PETER MARTIN
 Sculptor
Preferred Media: Metals.
b Los Angeles, Calif, Dec 10, 43.
Study & Training: Univ Southern Calif, 61-65; San Fernando State Col, 62-66.
Exhibitions: Scripps Col Gallery Group Show, Claremont, Calif, 55; two-man shows, Quinn Gallery, Univ Southern Calif, 58, The Egg & the Eye, Los Angeles, 67 & Univ Southern Calif, 68; one-man show, Seattle Pac Col, Wash, 69.
Mailing Address: 13186 Glenoaks Blvd, Sylmar, CA 91342.

GEBHARDT, ROLAND
 Sculptor, Painter
Preferred Media: Marble, Fiberglass, Concrete.
b Paramaribo, Surinam, Sept 24, 39; U S citizen.
Study & Training: Art Acad Hamburg, Ger, under Theo Ortner; Kuntsgewerbeschule, Zurich, Switz; also apprenticeship in stained glass, Marburg, Ger.
Work in Public Collections: Art Acad, Hamburg; Brandeis Univ, Waltham, Mass.
Exhibitions: Group shows, Ger & Eng, 63-64; group show, Gallery 84, New York, N Y, 71; one-man sculpture & painting exhib, Hudson River Mus, 71; 20th Century Sculpture in Westchester Collection, Yonkers, N Y, 72.
Awards: Ann prize, Art Acad Hamburg, 62.
Bibliography: Roland Gebhardt—sculptor (film), Fred Salaff, 72.
Dealer: Gallery 84, Inc, 1046 Madison Ave, New York, NY 10021.
Mailing Address: 102 N Highland Ave, Ossining, NY 10562.
Awards: First prize for painting, Santa Barbara Mus Art, 56; purchase award, San Francisco Mus Art, 57; Ford Found fel, Tamarind Lithography Workshop, 63.
Bibliography: Hilton Kramer (auth), rev, In: Arts Mag, 60; U S Info Serv color film for overseas distrib, 70-71; Howard Spivak (auth), Fine artists at work (film), Audiovisual instrnl devices, 71.
Mailing Address: 463 West St, New York, NY 10014.

GECHTOFF, SONIA
 Painter
b Philadelphia, Pa, Sept 25, 26.
Study & Training: Philadelphia Mus Col Art, BFA, 50.
Work in Public Collections: San Francisco Mus Art, Calif; Woodward Found for U S Embassies, Washington, D C; Singer Co, New York, N Y; Univ Mass, Amherst; Oakland Art Mus, Calif.
Exhibitions: Younger American Painters, Guggenheim Mus, New York, 54; American Painters, U S Pavilion, Brussels Fair, Belg, 58; Carnegie Int, Pittsburgh, Pa, 58; First Paris Bienale, France, 59; Sao Paulo Bienale, Brazil, 61.
Teaching: Instr painting & drawing, Calif Sch Fine Arts, 57-58; adj asst prof art, New York Univ, 61-71; lectr art, Queens Col, 70-

GECK, FRANCIS JOSEPH
 Painter, Educator
b Detroit, Mich, Dec 20, 00.
Study & Training: New York Sch Fine & Appl Art, N Y & Paris Atelier, France, dipl; Syracuse Univ, MFA, 46.
Exhibitions: Washington Watercolor Club 54th Ann, Smithsonian Inst, Washington, D C, 50; Pavilion of American Interiors, New York World's Fair, 65; Boulder Nat Bank, Colo, 66; Village Theatre Lobby, Boulder, 67-71; Manufacturers Hanover Trust Gallery, New York, 71; plus many others.
Teaching: Instr interior design, New York Sch Fine & Appl Art, Paris Atelier, France, 24-27; prof interior design, Univ Colo, Boulder, 30-69.
Positions: Interior architect & designer, William Wright Co, Detroit, Mich, 27-30.
Awards: Gold medal winner, Grand Nat Show, Am Artists Prof League, 53; Tommaso Campanella silver medal, Acad Int Lettre-Arti-Scienze, 70; Benedictine Art Award for hon mention, 71; plus many others.
Memberships: Boulder Artists Guild (secy-treas, 30-37, 51-52, pres, 44-46 & 71); Boulder Hist Soc (chmn, 37-44, trustee, 44-71, first v pres, 44-46, 56 & 69, pres, 48-50, 52-53 & 70); hon fel Am Inst Interior Designers (educ assoc, 54-71, chmn Rocky Mountain chap comt educ, 57-58); Interior Design Educ Coun (exec comt, 63-66).
Publications: Auth, Art: the period styles, 45; auth, Exercises in perspective, 48; auth, Introduction to interior decoration, 55; auth, Dial-a-style: English period furniture, 66; auth, Interior design & decoration, 67; plus others.
Mailing Address: 407 16th St, Boulder, CO 80302.

GECSE, HELENE
 Painter, Etcher
Preferred Media: Graphics.
b Astoria, N Y.
Study & Training: Glendale Col, Calif, with Jean Abel; Otis Art Inst, Los Angeles, Calif, with Joseph Mugnaini, Shiro Ikegawa & Guy Maccoy.
Work in Public Collections: Brand Libr Art Ctr, Glendale.
Exhibitions: One-man show, Huntington Galleries, W Va, 65; 11th Ann Drawing & Sculpture Show, Ball State Univ, Muncie, Ind, 65; 6th Nat Prints & Drawings, Ultimate Concerns, Ohio Univ, 65; 32nd Nat Graphics Arts Exhib, Wichita Art Asn, Kans, 65; Arts Southern Calif, Long Beach Mus, 66-67.
Dealer: Collector's Choice Gallery, 959 El Camino Real, Menlo Park, CA 94025.
Mailing Address: 3366 Pierce St, San Francisco, CA 94123.

GEE, HELEN
 Art Dealer
U S citizen.
Positions: Dir, Helen Gee Gallery.
Specialty of Gallery: Contemporary painting, sculpture and drawing.
Mailing Address: 263 W 11th St, New York, NY 10014.

GEESLIN, LEE GADDIS
 Painter, Educator
b Goldthwaite, Tex, June 28, 20.
Study & Training: Univ Tex; New Orleans Art & Crafts; Art Inst Chicago, BFA, MFA.
Exhibitions: Annually with local & regional shows of the Southwest; one-man shows, Brownsville, San Angelo, Houston, Corpus Christi, Brady, Lufkin, Dallas & Texarkana, Tex, also Shreveport, La, 63-
Teaching: Prof art & dean, Col Fine Arts, Sch Art, Sam Houston State Univ, at present.
Memberships: Tex Watercolor Soc; Tex Fine Arts Soc; Tex Art Educ Asn; Am Asn Univ Prof; Col Art Asn Am.
Mailing Address: School of Art, Sam Houston State University, Huntsville, TX 77340.

GEHNER, MARJORIE NIELSEN
 Painter
Preferred Media: Oils, Watercolors.
b Florence, Wis, May 26, 09.
Study & Training: Ripon Col, 26-28; Univ Wis-Milwaukee, with Gustav Miller, BE, 31; New Sch Social Res, with Emilio Egas, 35-36; Columbia Univ, with Arthur Young, prof dipl, 61.
Work in Public Collections: Oil, Ripon Col, Wis; oil, Leonia Pub Libr, N J.
Exhibitions: Traveling exhibs, Am Watercolor Soc, 68, Nat Asn Women Artists, France, 69 & U S A, 72.
Teaching: Instr art, Milwaukee Pub Schs, Wis, 30-31; instr art, Children's Mus, Long Island, N Y, 34-38; instr art, Leonia Pub Schs, N J, 54-55.

Awards: Goldie Paley award, Nat Asn Am Women, 61; ann show award, Fed Womens Club, Leonia, 64; ann show award, Am Asn Univ Women, 70.
Memberships: Am Watercolor Soc; Nat Asn Women Artists.
Mailing Address: 189 Park Ave, Leonia, NJ 07605.

GEHR, MARY (MARY RAY)
Printmaker, Painter
Preferred Media: Intaglio, Oils, Acrylics.
b Chicago, Ill.
Study & Training: Smith Col; Art Inst Chicago, with Paul Wieghardt; Inst Design of Ill Inst Technol, with Misch Kohn.
Work in Public Collections: Art Inst Chicago; Philadelphia Mus, Pa; Libr of Cong, Washington, D C; Nelson Rockefeller Collection.
Commissions: Golden Santorini (intaglio-edition of 210 etchings printed by Leterio Calapai), commissioned by Int Graphic Arts Soc, 67.
Exhibitions: Chicago & Vicinity Exhibs & Soc Contemp Am Art, Art Inst Chicago; Brooklyn Mus Nat Print Exhib; Boston Printmakers, Mass; Print Club, Philadelphia, Pa.
Awards: Print Fair, Philadelphia; first purchase award, Artist Guild Chicago; award for graphics, Old Orchard Festival, Chicago.
Bibliography: John Fink (auth), The Greece of Mary Gehr, Chicago Tribune Mag, 67; T J Carbol (ed), The printmaker in Illinois, Ill Art Educ Asn, 71-72; plus many articles in local papers.
Memberships: Arts Club Chicago; Print Club Philadelphia; Alumnae of Art Inst Chicago; Soc Typographic Arts; Archaeological Inst Am (Chicago br).
Publications: Illusr, designer & art ed, Exploring the world of archaeology, 66 & Exploring the world of pottery, 67.
Dealer: Jacques Baruch Gallery, 900 N Michigan Ave, Chicago, IL 60611.
Mailing Address: 1829 N Orleans, Chicago, IL 60614.

GEIGER, EDITH ROGERS
Painter
Preferred Media: Mixed Media.
b New Haven, Conn, July 13, 12.
Study & Training: Smith Col, BA, 34; Art Stud League New York, 34-35; Yale Univ, with Joseph Albers.
Work in Public Collections: Wadsworth Atheneum, Hartford; Tryon Art Mus, Smith Col; Springfield Art Mus, Mass; Art Mus, Ann Arbor, Mich; Bridgeport Univ Art Collection.
Exhibitions: Brooklyn Mus 21st Int Watercolor Biennial; Detroit Nat Watercolor Exhib; Boston Art Festival; Providence Festival, R I; solo exhibs, Bodley Gallery, New York, 56, Ruth White Gallery, New York, 59 & 62, Naples Art Gallery, Fla, 69 & 70.
Awards: Best-in-Show Awards, New Haven Festival Arts, 57 & 62; Woman's Award, Am Watercolor Soc, 62; Nat Asn Women Artists Award, 63.
Memberships: Nat Asn Women Artists; Am Watercolor Soc; Conn Watercolor Soc.
Dealer: Naples Art Gallery, Third St, Naples, FL 33940.
Mailing Address: 2082 Gulf Shore Blvd, Naples, FL 33940.

GEISEL, THEODOR SEUSS (DR SEUSS)
Illustrator, Writer
b Springfield, Mass, Mar 2, 04.
Study & Training: Dartmouth Col, AB, 25; Lincoln Col, Oxford Univ, 25-26; Dartmouth Col, hon LHD, 56, Am Int Col, 68.
Work in Public Collections: All Dr Seuss book illustrations & manuscripts in Libr of Univ Calif, Los Angeles.
Exhibitions: One-man show, Fine Arts Gallery, San Diego, 58.
Teaching: Lect on illustrating & writing children's books.
Positions: Advert illusr for industrial firms; ed cartoonist, PM (newspaper), New York; former pres & publ, Beginner Books, Inc; publ, Bright & Early Bks; pres, Beginner Bk Div, Random House, Inc; designer, Dr Seuss-Mattel Toy Line; designer children's furniture, Sears & Roebuck; producer animated cartoons for TV.
Awards: Legion of Merit, World War II, for educ & info films; Acad Awards, for best doc short, 46, for best doc feature, 51 & for best animated cartoon, 51.
Publications: Auth & illusr, The Foot Book, 68, I can lick 30 tigers today and other stories, 69, My book about me, 69, I can draw it myself, 70, Mr Brown can moo! can you?, 70, The Lorax, 71 & Marvin K Mooney, will you please go now!, 72; plus many others.
Mailing Address: Random House, 201 E 50th St, New York, NY 10022.

GEISSBUHLER, ARNOLD
Sculptor
b Delémont, Switz, Aug 9, 97; U S citizen.
Study & Training: Apprentice with Otto Münch, Zurich, Switz, 14-19; Acad Julian, Paris France, 19-20; Acad Grande Chaumière, with Bourdelle, 20-25.
Work in Public Collections: Art Mus, Bern, Switz; Mus Jurassien, Delémont, Switz; Fogg Art Mus, Harvard Univ, Cambridge, Mass; Fansworth Mus, Wellesley Col, Mass; Chester Dale Collection, Nat Gallery Art, Washington, D C.
Commissions: Somloire (stone war Mem), Town of Somloire, Maine-Loire, France, 24; plaques & reliefs in wood, Foxboro Post Off, Mass, 40; plus many private commissions.
Exhibitions: One-man show, Delémont, Switz, 24; Philadelphia Sculpture Int Invitational, Pa, 40; Sculpture in U S, Metrop Mus, New York, N Y, 51; Art in U S A, Madison Garden, N Y, 58; New Eng Painting & Sculpture Invitational, Boston, Mass, 71; plus many other group & one-man shows.
Teaching: Instr drawing & sculpture techniques, N Y Sch Design, 29-30; instr drawing & sculpture techniques, Stuart Sch Design, Boston, Mass, 36-42; instr drawing & sculpture techniques, Wellesley Col, 37-58.
Awards: Bronze medal for figure, Acad Julian, Paris, 19; outstanding award, Art U S A, 1958, 58; Cambridge Centennial Award, Cambridge Art Asn.
Memberships: Sculptor's Guild, New York; New Eng Sculptors; Cape Cod Art Asn.
Mailing Address: Scargo Pines, Box 202, Dennis, MA 02638.

GEIST, SIDNEY
Sculptor, Art Critic
Preferred Media: Wood, Stone.
b Paterson, N J, Apr 11, 14.
Study & Training: St Stephen's Col, N Y; Art Stud League New York; Acad Grande Chaumiere, Paris.
Work in Public Collections: Bard Col, Annandale-on-Hudson, N Y.
Exhibitions: Salon Jeune Sculpture, Paris, 50; one-man shows, Paris, 50, New York, 51, 57, 60 & Bard Col, 69; Pittsburgh Int, 58; Am Artists Ann, Chicago, 62.
Teaching: Instr sculpture, Pratt Inst, 61-65; instr sculpture, New York Studio Sch, N Y, 64-; instr sculpture, Vassar Col, 67-
Positions: Dir, New York Studio Sch, N Y, 64-66; guest cur, Brancusi Retrospective, Guggenheim Mus, 69.
Awards: Olivetti Award, Silvermine Guild, Conn, 60.
Bibliography: Thomas B Hess (auth), U S sculpture: some recent directions, Portfolio, 59.
Memberships: Col Art Asn Am.
Publications: Auth, Brancusi: a study of the sculpture, Grossman, 68; auth, Constantin Brancusi: a retrospective exhibition, Guggenheim Mus, 69.
Mailing Address: 11 Bleecker St, New York, NY 10012.

GEKIERE, MADELEINE
Painter, Educator
Preferred Media: Inks, Oils.
b Zurich, Switz, May 15, 19; U S citizen.
Study & Training: Art Stud League New York, with Kantor; Brooklyn Mus Art Sch, with Tamayo; New York Univ, with Sam Adler.
Work in Public Collections: Worcester Art Mus, Mass; Fogg Mus Art, Cambridge, Mass; New York Univ Collection, New York, N Y; Brooklyn Mus, N Y; Norfolk Mus Arts & Sci, Va.
Exhibitions: Norfolk Mus Arts & Sci, 67 & 68; Univ Ga, Athens, 67; many group shows, Audubon Artists & New York Univ Loeb Ctr, New York; also eight N Y one-man shows.
Teaching: Asst prof painting, New York Univ, 58-67; asst prof painting, City Col New York, 67-; vis prof painting, Univ Ga, 67.
Awards: Best illus bk of yr, New York Times, 57, 59 & 63; Audubon Medal of Honor, 69.
Memberships: Artists Equity Asn.
Publications: Auth & illusr, Who gave us?, 53; illusr, Switch on the night, 57; auth & illusr, The princess & the frilly lilly, 60; illusr, The reason for the pelican, 60; illusr, John J Plenty and Fiddler Dan, 63.
Dealer: Babcock Galleries, 805 Madison Ave, New York, NY 10021.
Mailing Address: 427 W 21st St, New York, NY 10011.

GELB, JAN
Painter, Printmaker
b New York, N Y, July 18, 06.
Study & Training: Yale Univ Sch Fine Arts, 26-27; Brittany, with Sigurd Skou, 28-29; Art Stud League New York, 29-32.
Work in Public Collections: Whitney Mus Am Art, New York; Metrop Mus Art, New York; Mus Mod Art, New York; Rosenwald Collection, Nat Gallery, Washington, D C; Libr Cong, Washington, D C.
Exhibitions: Am Watercolors, Metrop Mus Art, 51; 14 Painter-Printmakers, Brooklyn Mus & other mus, 56; Nature in Abstraction, Whitney Mus Am Art & other mus, 58; Contemp Am Painting, Birmingham Mus, Ala, 62; Candidates for Purchase Awards, Am Acad Arts & Lett, 67.

Awards: Philadelphia Print Club Purchase Award, Philadelphia Mus, 58; purchase award, Dulin Gallery, Knoxville, 68; Vera List Purchase Award, Soc Am Graphic Artists, 68.
Bibliography: August I Freundlich (auth), Catalogue of graphic works 1929-1972.
Memberships: Soc Am Graphic Artists (v pres, 66-67); Provincetown Art Asn; fel MacDowell Colony.
Dealer: Associated American Artists, 663 Fifth Ave, New York, NY 10017.
Mailing Address: 749 West End Ave, New York, NY 10025.

GELBER, SAMUEL
Painter, Educator
Preferred Media: Oils, Watercolors.
b Brooklyn, N Y, Mar 14, 29.
Study & Training: Brooklyn Col, BA; N Y Univ, MA.
Exhibitions: Brooklyn Mus Biennial, 56; Newark Mus, 58; one-man shows, Harry Salpeter Gallery, New York, N Y, 67 & Green Mountain Gallery, New York, 72; New Realism 70, St Cloud State Col, Minn, 70.
Teaching: Instr drawing, Pratt Inst, Brooklyn, 62-65; asst prof painting & drawing, Brooklyn Col, 62-
Awards: Crane & Co Award for Painting, Berkshire Mus, 66.
Bibliography: Gabriel Laderman (auth), Unconventional realists, Artforum, 11/67; Lee Wallin (auth), New realism 70, St Cloud State Col, 70; Alan Gussow (auth), A sense of place—the artist and the American land, Friends of Earth, 72.
Memberships: Artists Equity Asn.
Dealer: Green Mountain Gallery, 135 Greene St, New York, NY 10012.
Mailing Address: 215 W 98th St, New York, NY 10025.

GELDZAHLER, HENRY
Curator
b Antwerp, Belg, July 9, 35; U S citizen.
Study & Training: Yale Univ, BA; Harvard Univ.
Positions: Curatorial asst, Dept Am Paintings & Sculpture, Metrop Mus Art, 60-62, asst cur, 62-63, assoc cur, 63-67, cur twentieth-century art dept, 67-
Publications: Auth, American painting in the Twentieth Century, Metrop Mus Art; New York painting and sculpture 1940-1970, Dutton, 69.
Mailing Address: Metropolitan Museum of Art, Fifth Ave at 82nd St, New York, NY 10028.

GELINAS, ROBERT WILLIAM
Painter, Educator
Preferred Media: Acrylics.
b Springfield, Mass, Mar 1, 31.
Study & Training: Univ Conn; Univ Ala, BFA & MFA; also with Lawrence Calgagno & Tatsuiko Heima.
Work in Public Collections: Kelley Fitzpatrick Mus, Montgomery, Ala; Mead Corp Collection, Atlanta, Ga; Brooks Mem Gallery, Memphis, Tenn; Carroll Reese Mus, Johnson City, Tenn; Mus Fine Arts, Little Rock, Ark.
Commissions: Chapel sculpture, Wesley Found Stud Ctr, Memphis, 60.
Exhibitions: Art U S A, 58, New York, 58; 26th & 27th Corcoran Biennials, Washington, D C, 59 & 61; Painting of the Yr Ann, Mead Corp, Atlanta, 61; Bon Marche Nat Gallery Invitational, Seattle, Wash, 63; Fla Showcase, Rockefeller Ctr, New York, 64.
Teaching: Guest artist instr, Allisons Wells Art Colony Workshops, Canton, Miss, 58-62; asst prof art, Memphis State Univ, 58-63; assoc prof art, Univ S Fla, 63-
Positions: Art dir, Tuscaloosa News, Ala, 55-57; artist-in-residence, Maitland Res Ctr, 65; artist-in-residence Upham Studio, Naples, 66-69.
Awards: Painting of the Yr Award, Mead Corp, Atlanta, 61; first purchase prize, Mid South Ann, 61; 18th Ann Purchase Exhib Prize, Carrol Reese Mus, 67.
Bibliography: Margaret Harald (auth), Prize-winning paintings, Bk 2, Allied Publ, 61; Benbow (auth), All out war, St Pete Times, 8/65; Gelinas the modern master, Tampa Tribune, 66.
Dealer: Trend House Gallery, 3629 Henderson Blvd, Tampa, FL 33609.
Mailing Address: Rte 1, Box 202, Odessa, FL 33556.

GELLER, ESTHER (ESTHER GELLER SHAPERO)
Painter, Printmaker
Preferred Media: Encaustic, Watercolors.
b Boston, Mass, Oct 26, 21.
Study & Training: Mus Fine Arts Sch, Boston, dipl; also with Karl Zerbe.
Work in Public Collections: Mus Fine Arts, Boston; Addison Gallery Am Art, Andover, Mass; Brandeis Univ, Waltham, Mass; Walters Gallery, Regis Col, Weston, Mass; St Mark's Sch Gallery, Southboro, Mass.

Exhibitions: Art Inst Chicago Ann, Ill; Univ Ill Ann, Urbana; Boston Art Festivals; U S Info Serv Circulating Exhibs in the U S & Far East; one-man show, Am Acad Art Gallery, Rome, 71.
Teaching: Instr painting & drawing, Sch Mus Fine Arts, Boston, 43; instr painting & drawing, Boris Mirski Art Sch, 46-48; instr painting & drawing, Natick Art Asn Sch, 55-61.
Awards: Pepsi-Cola Prize; Cabot fel, 49; studios at MacDowell Colony, Yaddo & Am Acad, 50-71.
Bibliography: Pratt & Fizell (auth), Encaustic, Lear Publ, 49; Bern Chaet (auth), Artists at work, Webb, 60; B Hayes (auth), The layman's guide to modern art.
Dealer: Boris Mirski Art Gallery, 166 Newbury St, Boston, MA 02116.
Mailing Address: 9 Russell Circle, Natick, MA 01760.

GELLMAN, BEAH (MRS WILLIAM C McNULTY)
Painter, Sculptor
b Philadelphia, Pa, Nov 20, 04.
Study & Training: Univ Pa, BS(educ), 25; Art Stud League New York, with Kenneth Hayes Miller, Morris Kantor, Robert Beverly Hale & William C McNulty, 43-46.
Work in Public Collections: Sneed Gallery, Rockford, Ill; Berthold Gallery, Rockport, Mass & many in pvt collections.
Exhibitions: One-man & group shows, Rockport Art Asn, to 61; One-man shows, Granite Shore Hotel Gallery, Rockport, 65, Gallery Seven, Boston, Mass, 66 & three-man show, Lobby Gallery, Rockport, 69.
Teaching: Lectr, styling & design principles in the works of masters of painting.
Memberships: Rockport Art Asn; life mem Art Stud League New York.
Mailing Address: 20 Main St, Rockport, MA 01966.

GENAUER, EMILY
Art Critic, Writer
b New York, N Y.
Study & Training: Hunter Col, grad; Sch Jour, Columbia Univ, BLit.
Teaching: Lect, American Art Today, Functions of Art Criticism & others.
Positions: Staff writer & art feature writer, New York World, 29-31; art critic & ed, New York World-Tel, 32-49; art critic, New York Herald Tribune, 49-66; art critic & ed, New York World Jour Tribune, 66-67; art commentator, educ TV, New York, 67-; art critic-columnist, Newsday Syndicate, 67-; adv bd, Sch Jour, Columbia Univ.
Awards: New York Newspaper Women's Club Award for outstanding writing in spec field, 37, for outstanding column in any field, 49, 56, 58, 60 & 69; Columbia Univ Jour Alumni Award, 60.
Memberships: Nat Coun Humanities; Int Asn Art Critics; New York Newspaper Women's Club.
Publications: Auth, Toulouse-Lautrec (monogr), Met Mus Art, 53, Biography of Chagall, 57, Hommage a l'Ecole de Paris, 62, Biography of Tamayo & Chagall at the Met 71; plus others.
Mailing Address: 243 E 49th St, New York, NY 10017.

GENDERS, RICHARD ATHERSTONE
Painter
Preferred Media: Watercolors, Gouache.
b London, Eng, Aug 3, 19; U S citizen.
Study & Training: Herron Sch Art, Ind Univ-Purdue Univ, Indianapolis, with Edwin Fulwider, John Williams Taylor & Donald M Mattison, grad, 50.
Work in Public Collections: U S Navy Combat Art Collection, Washington, D C.
Commissions: Mural, Naval Sta, Dam Neck, Va, 55; many landscapes in private collections, 50-72.
Exhibitions: Operation Palette Worldwide Traveling Exhib, 50-72; John Herron Art Inst, Indianapolis, 55; Norfolk Mus Arts, Va, 58; Royal Scottish Mus, Edinburgh, 60; Mus Marine, Paris, France, 63.
Teaching: Instr fine arts, Indianapolis Art Inst, 48-51; instr com art, Atherstone's Studio, Indianapolis, 50-53; instr fine arts, Naval Training Ctr, Gt Lakes, Ill, 62-65.
Positions: Art dir, U S Navy, Norfolk, Va & Washington, D C, 52-65; art dir, NASA, 65-66; art dir, Blair, Inc, Baileys Crossroads, Va, 66-67; dir prod div, Naval Facilities Eng Comd, Washington, D C, 69-
Awards: First for watercolor, Ind Artist Club, 50; postage stamp design, U S Post Off, Washington, D C, 58; first for watercolor, Waukegan Art League, 65.
Bibliography: Artist with a mission, Indianapolis Star Mag, 55; Operation palette, Chicago Tribune Mag, 64; Lois De Nauw (auth), Variety is the key, Alexandria Gazette, 68.
Memberships: New Castle Art Asn; Indianapolis Art Asn; Tidewater Art Asn (pres, 55); Waukegan Art Asn (pres, 65); Northern Va Art League (v pres, 69).

Art Interests: Motion picture producing & directing.
Publications: Contribr, Aviation Safety Rev, 52-58; contribr, U S Naval Acad Inst Proceedings, 59; contribr, Civil Engr, 71.
Mailing Address: 4220 Peachtree Pl, Alexandria, VA 22304.

GENIUS, JEANNETTE (JEANNETTE M McKEAN)
Painter, Designer
Preferred Media: Oils, Pastels.
b Chicago, Ill.
Work in Public Collections: Ga Mus Art, Univ Ga, Athens; Columbus Mus Art, Ga; Winter Park City Hall, Fla; Univ Club, Winter Park; San Joaquin Mus, Stockton, Calif.
Exhibitions: Currier Art Gallery, Manchester, N H; Nat Arts Club, New York, N Y; Nat Asn Women Artists, New York Soc Four Arts, Palm Beach, Fla; Stetson Univ, Deland, Fla.
Positions: Dir exhibs, Morse Gallery Art, Rollins Col.
Awards: First prize, Fla Fedn Art, 48; second prize, Soc Four Arts, 50; first prize, Pen & Brush Club, 58.
Memberships: Nat Asn Women Artists; Nat Arts Club; Artists Equity Asn; Soc Four Arts; N H Art Asn.
Mailing Address: P O Box 40, Winter Park, FL 32789.

GENTRY, WARREN MILLER
Educator, Painter
Preferred Media: Oils.
b Manville, Wyo, Oct 3, 21.
Study & Training: Ariz State Univ, BA, 50, MA, 55; Univ Calif, Berkeley, 64, with Frank Lobdell.
Work in Public Collections: Munic Collection, Orange, France.
Exhibitions: Ariz State Fair Fine Arts Exhib, 49-63; First Ariz Ann, Phoenix, 59; Fresh Paint Show, M H de Young Mus, 59; Old Phoenix Art Mus.
Teaching: Prof art hist & painting, Glendale Community Col, 63-, founding dir art exhibs & Col Collection, 67-
Awards: Valley Bank Purchase Award, First Ariz Ann, 59.
Mailing Address: 1819 N 69th St, Scottsdale, AZ 85257.

GEORGE, THOMAS
Painter
Preferred Media: Oils, Gouache, Ink.
b New York, N Y, July 1, 18.
Study & Training: Dartmouth Col, BA, 40; Art Stud League New York; Acad Grande Chaumiere, Paris, France; Ist Statale Arte, Florence, Italy.
Work in Public Collections: Mus Mod Art, New York; Whitney Mus Am Art, New York; Nat Collection Fine Arts, Washington, D C; Tate Gallery, London, Eng; Rose Art Mus, Brandeis Univ; plus many others.
Commissions: Tapestry, Slatkin Art Gallery, New York, 68.
Exhibitions: Carnegie Int, 58 & 61; Whitney Mus Am Art Ann, 60-62 & 65; Japan Int Biennial Art, Tokyo, Japan, 63; Ill Univ Ann, 65; Nat Collection Fine Arts Inaugural Exhib, 68; plus many other group & one-man shows.
Awards: Purchase awards, Whitney Mus Ann, for painting, 61 & drawing, 62; Salon Int Galeries Pilote, Lausanne, Switz, 66 & N J State Mus, 72.
Bibliography: Gordon Washburn (auth), Forward, Ten year retrospective (catalogue), Dartmouth, 65; Martica Sawin (auth), The nature of symbols of Thomas George, Art Int, 65; J Jacobs (auth), Norway series drawings, Art Gallery Mag, 72.
Memberships: Fel Edward MacDowell Colony.
Publications: Illusr, A line of poetry, a row of trees, Jargon, 65.
Dealer: Betty Parsons Gallery, 24 W 57th St, New York, NY 10019.
Mailing Address: 20 Greenhouse Dr, Princeton, NJ 08540.

GEORGE, WALTER EUGENE, JR
Designer, Educator
b Wichita Falls, Tex, Oct 28, 22.
Study & Training: Univ Tex, BArch, 49; Harvard Univ, MArch, 50, with Walter Gropius.
Commissions: Many archit comn, 52-65.
Teaching: From asst to assoc prof archit, Univ Tex, 56-62; prof archit & chmn dept, Univ Kans, 62-67; dean, Col Archit, Univ Houston, 67-69.
Positions: With archit firms, 48-57, 69-; resident architect, Colonial Williamsburg, Va, 71-
Awards: First ann southwestern furniture competition award, Dallas Mus Fine Arts; Mont San Michele & Chartres Award, Am Inst Architects, 49.
Memberships: Soc Archit Historians; Am Inst Architects; Archaeol Inst Am.
Research: History of architecture of southwest United States.
Mailing Address: Colonial Williamsburg, Drawer C, Williamsburg, VA 23185.

GEORGES, PAUL
Painter
b Portland, Ore, 23.
Study & Training: Univ Ore; Hans Hofmann Sch Art; Atelier Fernand Leger, Paris, France, 49-52.
Work in Public Collections: Longview Found; Newark Mus Art, N J; Mass Inst Technol Collection; Reed Col, Portland; Mus Mod Art & Whitney Mus Am Art, New York, N Y; plus others.
Exhibitions: Pa Acad Fine Arts, Philadelphia, 64; Mus Mod Art, New York, 64; Boston Univ, 64; Sch Visual Arts, 65; New Sch Social Res, 65; plus many other group & one-man shows.
Teaching: Instr painting, Univ Colo, 60; artist-in-residence, Dartmouth Univ, 64; head, sem in art, Yale Univ, 64; mem staff, Sch Art, Yale Univ, 64-
Awards: Longview fel; Hallmark Purchase Award, 61; Carol Beck Gold Medal, Pa Acad Fine Arts, 64; plus others.
Publications: Contribr, Art News.
Mailing Address: Sagaponack, NY 11962.

GERARD, ALLEE WHITTENBERGER
Painter
Preferred Media: Oils.
b Fulton Co, Ind, Feb 9, 95.
Study & Training: Second Ft Wayne Art Sch; Miami Art Sch, Fla; also with Emil Gruppe, Elliot O'Hara, Marlyn Bendell, Curie Bohm & Homer Davisson.
Work in Public Collections: Warsaw Pub Schs, Ind; Rochester Pub Schs, Ind.
Exhibitions: Fort Wayne Art Mus, Ind, 44; Miami Beach Art Ctr, 48; Hoosier Salon Gallery, Indianapolis, 48, 50, 57 & 62; Sheldon Swope Gallery, Terre Haute, Ind, 56; Tri-State Col, Angola, Ind, 69.
Memberships: Life mem Miami Art League; Blue Dome Fel; Am Artists Prof League; Nat League Am Pen Women; Hoosier Salon Patrons Asn.
Dealer: Hoosier Salon, 115 E Washington St, Indianapolis, IN 46204.
Mailing Address: 1322 Country Club Dr, Warsaw, IN 46580.

GERARD, PAULA (MRS HERBERT RENISON)
Graphic Artist, Painter
Preferred Media: Silverpoint, India Ink, Sumi Ink, Watercolors, Tempera.
b Brighton, Eng; U S citizen.
Study & Training: Pvt study in Florence & Venice, Italy; Univ Florence, with Prof Toesca; Inst Francais, Florence, with Prof Soulier; lithography & etching in Paris & Brussels; Art Inst Chicago; painting with Boris Anisfeld.
Work in Public Collections: Libr of Cong, Washington, D C; Evansville Mus, Ind; Epstein Archives, Univ Chicago, Ill; George F Harding Mus, Chicago; Ringling Mus, Sarasota, Fla.
Exhibitions: One-man show, dept prints & drawings, 47 & First Biennial Prints, Drawings & Watercolors, 61, Art Inst Chicago; Images on Paper 70, Miss Art Asn, Jackson, 70; one-man show, Montgomery Mus Fine Arts, Ala, 71; 14th Ann Nat Exhib Prints & Drawings, Okla Art Ctr, Oklahoma City, 72.
Teaching: Instr figure drawing & anat, Layton Sch Art, Milwaukee, Wis, 45-62; vis instr graphics & printmaking, Midway Studios, Univ Chicago, 58-65; prof figure drawing & anat, Art Inst Chicago Sch, 62-
Positions: Juror, 11th Dixie Ann Exhib, Montgomery, Ala, 70.
Memberships: Alumni Asn of Art Inst Chicago Schs; Renaissance Soc, Univ Chicago (mem bd, 64-); Artists Equity (dir Chicago Chap, 72); Am Asn Univ Prof; Chicago Soc Artists.
Publications: Illusr, Is your contemporary painting more temporary than you think?, 62; illusr, The great speckled bird, Regnery, 64.
Mailing Address: 2043 N Mohawk St, Chicago, IL 60614.

GERARDIA, HELEN
Painter
b Russia; U S citizen.
Study & Training: New York Training Sch; Art Stud League New York; Brooklyn Mus Art Sch; Hans Hofmann Sch.
Work in Public Collections: Metrop Mus Art, New York; Brooklyn Mus, N Y; Philadelphia Mus, Pa; Libr Cong, Washington, D C; Tokyo Artists Ctr, Japan.
Exhibitions: Whitney Mus Am Art, New York; Corcoran Gallery Art Bienniel; Brooklyn Mus Print Ann; Norfolk Mus Drawing Ann; San Francisco Mus Painting Ann.
Awards: Maganini Award, New Eng Regional, Silvermine Guild, 57; two Medals of Honor in Graphics, Nat Asn Women Artists, 61 & 64; Medal of Merit, Nat Soc Painters Casein & Acrylic, 70.
Bibliography: Margaret Harold (auth), Award-winning art, Bk 3, 65 & Prize-winning art, Bk 7, 67; Gordon Brown (auth), The new look in art, Art Voices Quart, spring 65.

Memberships: Nat Asn Women Artists (pres, 72-74); Audubon Artists (treas, 70-72); Soc Am Graphic Artists (secy, 68-74); Int Asn Artists (deleg U S Comn, 66-74, deleg Int Cong, 68).
Research: The monoprint.
Dealer: Bodley Gallery, 787 Madison Ave, New York, NY 10021.
Mailing Address: 490 West End Ave, 4C, New York, NY 10024.

GERDTS, WILLIAM H
Art Historian, Educator
b Jersey City, N J, Jan 18, 29.
Study & Training: Amherst Col, BA; Harvard Univ, MA.
Collections Arranged: Exhibitions, New Jersey Artists, 57, Nature's Bounty and Man's Delight, 59, Old Master Drawings, 60, Nineteenth Century Master Drawings, 61, A Survey of American Sculpture, 62, Classical America 1815-1845, 63, The Golden Age of Spanish Still Life, 64 & Women Artists of America (1707-1964), 65.
Teaching: Assoc prof, Univ Md, 66-69; assoc prof art, Brooklyn Col, 71-; lect, American Art, Collecting Art & Conservation and Restoration, in cols, univs & adult schs.
Positions: Dir, Myers House, Norfolk, Va, 53-54; cur painting & sculpture, The Newark Mus, N J, 54-66; dir gallery, Univ Md, 66-69; assoc with Coe Kerr Gallery, New York, 69-71.
Publications: Ed, Drawings of Joseph Stella, 62; auth, Painting and sculpture in New Jersey, Rutgers Univ Press, 65; contribr to Antiques, Art Quart & N J Hist Soc Proc.
Mailing Address: 150 E 27th St, New York, NY 10016.

GERHOLD, WILLIAM HENRY
Painter, Educator
Preferred Media: Oils, Watercolors.
b Ashtabula, Ohio, Mar 30, 29.
Study & Training: Oberlin Col, BA, with Jeanne Miles; Ohio State Univ, MA.
Work in Public Collections: Army-Navy Club, Charleston, W Va; Marietta Col, Ohio; Capricorn Gallery, Bethesda, Md; Chiara Gallery, Cleveland, Ohio.
Commissions: Oil paintings, comn by Mr & Mrs William Gann, Chicago, Ill, 58 & by Ms Ruth Eells, Yellow Springs, Ohio, 58; watercolors, comn by Mrs Lessie Phipps, Beckley, W Va, 69, Mr & Mrs Gilbert Whitney, Huntington, W Va, 70 & Dr & Mrs Albert Kishler, McConnelsville, Ohio, 72.
Exhibitions: Butler Midyear, Youngstown, Ohio, 70; Appalachian Corridors II, Charleston, 70; Perspectives 1970, Cincinnati, Ohio, 70; Forest Festival, Elkins, W Va, 71 & 72; Ohio State Fairs, 70-72.
Teaching: Assoc prof educ, Antioch Col, 57-58; assoc prof art hist & painting, Marietta Col, 62-, dir Mainstreams Exhib, 68-
Awards: First prize for watercolor, Appalachian Arts & Crafts Fair, 70; Best Prof & Best W Va Landscape, Forest Festival, 71 & 72.
Memberships: Cent Ohio Watercolor Soc; Am Artists Prof League; W Va Artists & Craftsmen Guild.
Publications: Auth & illusr, Trinity Rev, 58.
Dealer: Capricorn Gallery, 8003 Woodmont Ave, Bethesda, MD 20014.
Mailing Address: 510 Caroline Ave, Williamstown, WV 26187.

GEROWITZ, JUDY see CHICAGO, JUDY

GERSOVITZ, SARAH VALERIE
Printmaker, Painter
Preferred Media: Silkscreen.
b Montreal, P Q.
Study & Training: MacDonald Col; Montreal Mus Fine Arts, drawing with de Tonnancour & design with Gordon Webber; l'Ecole Arts Appliques, seminars with Gabor Peterdi, Toshi Yoshida & Michael Rothenstein.
Work in Public Collections: Libr Cong, Washington, D C; Art Gallery Australia, Adelaide; Nat Gallery Can, Ottawa, Ont; Montreal Mus Fine Arts; Art Gallery Greater Victoria, B C.
Exhibitions: Royal Soc Painter-Etchers & Engravers, London, Eng, 59, 60, 62 & 63; Int Triennial Coloured Graphics, Grenchen, Switz, 61; Centennial Traveling Exhib Can Prints, Australia, 67; Int Print Show, Manchester Inst Arts & Sci, N H, 69; Int Exhib Prints, Montreal Mus Fine Arts, 71 & Art Gallery Ont, 72.
Teaching: Instr silkscreen & printmaking, Sadye Bronfman Ctr, Montreal, 72-
Awards: Graphic Art Prize, Winnipeg Art Gallery, 62; Anaconda Award, Can Soc Painter-Etchers & Engravers, 63 & 67; Graphic Art Prize & Gold Medal, Seagram Co, 68.
Bibliography: L Sabbath (auth), Sarah Gersovitz, Cong Bull, 67; Robert Ayre (auth), Silkscreen finesse, Montreal Star, 70; John Graham (auth), Gersovitz serigraphs, Winnipeg Free Press, 72.
Memberships: Royal Can Acad Arts; Can Soc Graphic Art (mem jury); Can Soc Painter-Etchers & Engravers (mem jury); Soc Artistes Prof Que (mem exec).

Publications: Illusr, cover, Figures in a landscape, Oberon, 67; auth, Discrimination—how it works, Montreal Star, 70.
Dealer: Galerie Marlborough-Godard Limitee, 1490 Sherbrooke St W, Montreal 109, P Q, Can.
Mailing Address: 5173 Mayfair Ave, Montreal 265, P Q, Can.

GERST, HILDE W
Art Dealer

U S citizen.
Study & Training: Ploner Acad, Italy.
Positions: Owner, Hilde Gerst Gallery, New York, N Y.
Memberships: Am Asn Mus.
Specialty of Gallery: French painting from Impressionist to contemporary; sculpture.
Mailing Address: Hilde Gerst Gallery, 681 Madison Ave, New York, NY 10021.

GESKE, NORMAN ALBERT
Art Administrator
b Sioux City, Iowa, Oct 31, 15.
Study & Training: Univ Minn, BA; New York Univ Inst Fine Arts, MA; Doane Col, hon DFA, 69.
Collections Arranged: Ernst Barlach (first Am mus exhib), 55; American Participation, 34th Venice Biennale, 68; American Sculpture, 70.
Positions: Asst dir, Univ Nebr Art Galleries, 50-53, actg dir, 53-56; dir, 56-
Memberships: Col Art Asn Am; Am Asn Mus; Asn Art Mus Dirs; Nebr Arts Coun (dir, 72).
Research: Nebraska Blakelock Inventory.
Publications: Auth, The figurative tradition in recent American art, 68; contribr, Int Art Exhibs, Arts Mag Yearbk No 10, 69; auth, Rudy Pozzatti, American Printmaker, 71.
Mailing Address: 2628 High St, Lincoln, NE 68502.

GETTY, J PAUL
Collector, Writer
b Minneapolis, Minn, Dec 15, 92.
Study & Training: Univ Calif, Los Angeles; Univ Calif, Berkeley; Oxford Univ, London, grad; Ohio Northern Univ, hon LLD, 66.
Publications: Auth, Europe in the 18th century, 47; Co-auth, Collector's choice, 56; auth, The joys of collecting, 65.
Mailing Address: 17985 Pacific Coast Hwy, Malibu, CA 90265.

GETZ, DOROTHY
Sculptor, Educator
b Grand Junction, Iowa, Sept 7, 01.
Study & Training: Ohio State Univ, BA, 23, MA, 32; Acad Belle Arti, Perugia, Italy, summers 62, 63 & 65.
Work in Public Collections: Columbus Gallery Fine Arts, Ohio; Akron Inst Am Art, Ohio; Sassaferato, Italy.
Exhibitions: Ceramic Nat, Syracuse, N Y, 52 & 54; Five Ohio Ceramic & Sculpture Shows, Akron, 55-64; Drawing & Small Sculpture Ann, Ball State Art Gallery, 56, 58 & 59.
Teaching: Prof art hist, drawing & interior design, Ohio Wesleyan Univ, 45-72.
Positions: Fashion illusr, Fashion Co, Columbus, Ohio, 32-38; fashion illusr, The Union Co, Columbus, 38-45.
Awards: Salvi Prize, 4th Piccolo Europa, Sassaferato, Italy, 63; purchase prize, Ohio Ceramic & Sculpture Show, Akron Inst Am Art, 64; purchase prize, Columbus Gallery Fine Arts, 66.
Mailing Address: 40 W Winter St, Delaware, OH 43015.

GETZ, ILSE
Painter
b Nuremberg, Ger, Oct 24, 17; U S citizen.
Study & Training: Art Stud League New York, with Morris Kantor & George Grosz.
Work in Public Collections: Carnegie Inst, Pittsburgh, Pa; Hinkhouse Collection, Coe Col, Cedar Rapids, Iowa; Phoenix Art Mus, Ariz; Tel-Aviv Mus, Israel; Nelson Gallery, Kansas City, Mo; plus others.
Commissions: Designed set for Ionesco's The Killer, New York, N Y, 60.
Exhibitions: Gump's Gallery, San Francisco, 58; Tibor de Nagy Gallery, New York, 63; Phoenix Art Mus, 64; Davis Art Ctr, Wesleyan Univ, Middletown, Conn, 67; Hopkins Ctr, Dartmouth Col, Hanover, N H, 67.
Teaching: Instr art, Positano, Italy, summers 56 & 58.
Awards: Yaddo fel, 59.
Dealer: Gimpel & Weitzenhoffer, 1040 Madison Ave, New York, NY 10021.
Mailing Address: Saw Mill Rd, Newtown, CT 06470.

GHENT, HENRI
Art Administrator, Art Consultant
b Birmingham, Ala, June 23, 26.
Study & Training: U S Armed Forces Inst, Honolulu, Hawaii, 45-46; New England Conservatory, Boston, Mass, 47-51; Georges Longy Sch, Cambridge, Mass, 51-53; Univ Paris, 58-60; also pvt study in Ger & Eng.
Collections Arranged: The Invisible Americans: Black Artists of the 1930s, 69; 10 Afro-American Artists, Mount Holyoke Col, Hadley, Mass, 69; 15 International Artists, 69, Allusions, 2nd Anniversary Exhibit, 70 & Native North American Art: Mixed Media Works by Contemporary American Indian Artists, 72, Community Gallery, Brooklyn Museum; Afro-American Artists: Since 1950, Brooklyn Col, N Y, 69; 8 Afro-American Artists, Rath Museum, Geneva, Switz, 71; 1972 All-Ohio Painting & Sculpture Biennial, Art Inst, Dayton, 72.
Teaching: Vis lectr, Col of Finger Lakes Series, 70-71; vis lectr, Moorhead State Col, 71-72; vis lectr, Dayton Art Inst, Ohio.
Positions: Consult, Minn Mus Art, Saint Paul, Dayton Art Inst, Mt Holyoke Col, Rath Mus, Geneva & Musd'Art Haitien, Port-au-Prince, Haiti; dir, Community Gallery, Brooklyn Mus, 68-72.
Awards: Martha Baird Rockefeller grant, 57; Bourse Speciale, Fr Govt, 58-60; Samuel H Kress Found res fel, 72-73.
Bibliography: Protesting the instant experts & their Black Art, New York Times, 8/15/71; Brooklyn Museum director serving as art consultant, New York Amsterdam News, 12/11/71; Saint Paul Art Museum gets Ghent's aid, Afro-American, 12/18/71; plus many others.
Memberships: Metrop Mus Art (vis comt, 71-); Sch Art League, New York (bd trustees, 69-); Smithsonian Assocs; Int Soc Educ Through Art.
Art Interests: Eclectic art with emphasis on contemporary painting, sculpture & graphics.
Collection: Contemporary painting, sculpture & graphics.
Publications: Auth, White is not superior, New York Times, 12/8/68; auth, Contemporary Puerto Rican artists, Sch Arts Mag, 10/69; auth, Black creativity in quest of an audience, Art in Am, 5-6/70; auth, articles, In, Art Gallery, 4/70 & 11/71; contribr, Eight Afro-American artists (catalogue), Rath Mus, 6/71; plus others.
Mailing Address: 310 E 75th St, Apt 1f, New York, NY 10021.

GHEZ, OSCAR
Collector
b Sousse, Tunisia, 05.
Study & Training: Univ Rome.
Collections Arranged: From Renoir to Picasso and Chagall, Petit Palais, Mod Art Mus.
Positions: Founder, Petit Palais, Geneva, Switz & Mod Art Found.
Mailing Address: 2 Terrasse Saint-Victor, Geneva, Switz.

GHIKAS, PANOS GEORGE
Painter, Educator
Preferred Media: Egg Tempera.
b Malden, Mass.
Study & Training: Yale Univ Sch Fine Arts, BFA, 46, MFA, 47; Akademie der Bildenden Kunste, Stuttgart, Ger, with Willi Baumeister, 53-54.
Work in Public Collections: Wadsworth Atheneum, Hartford, Conn; Walker Art Mus, Bowdoin Col, Brunswick, Maine; Fred Olsen Found, New Haven, Conn; State St Bank & Trust Co, Boston, Mass; Mass Col Art, Boston.
Exhibitions: Abstract & Surrealist Show, Chicago Art Inst, 47; Second Int Salon des Realites Nouvelles, Paris, France, 48; Annual of American Painting, Whitney Mus Am Art, 49; American Painting Annual, Univ Ill, 50; Worcester Mus Biennial Contemp Am Painting, 52.
Teaching: Vis artist design, Carpenter Ctr, Harvard Univ, 64-66; vis prof drawing, Bowdoin Col, 70-71; prof painting, R I Sch Design, Providence, 71-
Positions: Asst conservator, Yale Univ Art Gallery, New Haven, Conn, 57-59.
Awards: Fulbright fel, 53; MacDowell Colony fel, 67; Blanche E Colman Found grant, 69.
Bibliography: Chaet (auth), Artists at work, Webb, 61.
Publications: Illusr, Tales of Christophilos, 54, Again Christophilos, 56, The golden bird, 57 & The golden sword, 60.
Dealer: Joan Peterson Gallery, 561 Boylston St, Boston, MA 02116.
Mailing Address: 30 Ipswich St, Boston, MA 02215.

GIACOMANTONIO, ARCHIMEDES ARISTIDES, see MANTON, JOCK

GIAMBERTONE, PAUL
Sculptor
Preferred Media: Welded & Cast Bronze.
b Italy; U S citizen.
Study & Training: Beaux Arts Inst Design, New York, with Caetano Cercere; Educ Alliance, New York, with Chaim Gross.

Work in Public Collections: Safad Mus, Israel; Philothea Mus, London, Ont.
Exhibitions: Nat Arts Club, New York, N Y, 57; Silvermine Guild Artists, New Canaan, Conn, 58; N J Soc Painters & Sculptors, Jersey City Mus, 59 & 60; Knickerbocker Artists, Nat Arts Club, New York, 70.
Awards: Ivan R Laskins Award for sculpture, 70.
Bibliography: M Eder (auth), In the art galleries, East, 6/6/57; E Pollet (auth), In the galleries, 6/57 & Margaret Breuning (auth), Margaret Breuning writes, 7/59, Arts Mag.
Memberships: Artists Equity Asn New York; League Present Day Artists (dir, 60); Am Soc Contemp Artists (dir, 63); Sculptors League.
Dealer: Artemis East Gallery, 166 Lexington Ave, New York, NY 10016.
Mailing Address: 121 E 23rd St, New York, NY 10010.

GIAMBRUNI, TIO
Sculptor
b San Francisco, Calif, Aug 30, 25.
Study & Training: Univ Calif, Berkeley, BA & MA, with Glenn Wessels, John Haley, Jacques Schnier, Richard O'Hanlon.
Commissions: Golden Gateway Redevelop Proj, San Francisco.
Exhibitions: San Francisco Mus Art Ann, 51-; Bay Area Artists, New Orleans Mus Art, La, 63; one-man shows, Mills Col, 63 & Berkeley Gallery, 63, 64 & 66; The Artist's Reality, New Sch Social Res, 64; plus others.
Teaching: Modesto High Sch, Calif, 51-52; Liberty High Sch, 53-56; Miramonte High Sch, Calif, 56-59; Calif Col Arts & Crafts, 59-60; Univ Calif, Davis, 60-
Awards: Patrons of Music & Art Award, San Francisco Mus Art, 59.
Mailing Address: c/o Berkeley Gallery, 370 Brannan St, San Francisco, CA 94107.

GIBBONS, HUGH (JAMES)
Painter, Educator
Preferred Media: Oils, Inks.
b Scranton, Pa, Oct 26, 37.
Study & Training: Pa State Univ, with Elaine de Kooning & Robert Mallary, BA(painting), 59, MA(painting), 61.
Work in Public Collections: West Tex Mus, Lubbock; Bucknell Univ Collection, Lewisburg, Pa.
Exhibitions: Second Otis Art Inst Biennial Invitational, Los Angeles, Calif, 66; Hemis Fair '68, Tex Pavilion, San Antonio, Tex, 68; Fourth Biennial Drawings U S A, Saint Paul Art Ctr, Minn, 68; 35th Ann, Wichita, Kans, 71; one-man show, St Peter's Gallery, New York, N Y, 72.
Teaching: Assoc prof painting & drawing, Tex Tech Univ, 63-
Awards: Award for drawing, Mus N Mex, 64 & 66; first prize in graphics, Midland, Tex, 71.
Bibliography: Article, In: Prize Winning Graphics No 7, 67.
Mailing Address: 3432 53rd St, Lubbock, TX 79413.

GIBBONS, MARGARITA
Painter
Preferred Media: Oils.
b New York, N Y, Aug 18, 06.
Study & Training: Art Stud League New York; Pratt Inst; Paris, France & Amsterdam, Holland.
Work in Public Collections: New York Univ Permanent Collection; Slater Mus, Norwich, Conn; New York Bd Trade; Vatican.
Awards: First prize oils, Village Art Ctr, 60; N J Soc Painters & Sculptors Medal, 66; Seligson Mem Prize, Nat Asn Women Artists, 70.
Memberships: Nat Asn Women Artists (adv comt & dir, 67-72); Provincetown Art Asn; League Present Day Artists; Audubon Artists; Am Soc Contemp Artists (publicity chmn, 70).
Dealer: Carlsson Gallery, 791 Madison Ave, New York, NY 10021.
Mailing Address: Hotel Chelsea, 222 W 23rd St, New York, NY 10011.

GIBRAN, KAHLIL GEORGE
Sculptor
Preferred Media: Steel.
b Boston, Mass, Sept 29, 22.
Study & Training: Boston Mus Sch, 40-43, painting with Karl Zerbe.
Work in Public Collections: Chrysler Collection, Va Mus, Norfolk; Pa Acad Fine Art, Philadelphia; Cheekwood Art Ctr, Nashville, Tenn; Elmira Col, N Y.
Commissions: Bronze wall mural, Forsythe Dental, Boston, 71.
Exhibitions: Whitney Mus Am Art Ann, 56; Art U S A, 58; Art Festival, Boston, 64; Int, Trieste, Italy, 66; New Eng Artists, Provincetown Art Asn & Cyclorama, Boston, 71.
Awards: George Wiedner Medal, Pa Acad Fine Arts, 58; John S Guggenheim fel, 59-60 & 60-61; Nat Inst Arts & Lett Award & fel, 61.

Bibliography: Gregory MacDonald (auth), Kahlil Gibran a Boston sculptor, Boston Globe Mag, 67; Nathan Hale (auth), Welded sculpture, Watson-Guptil, 68; Donald Irving (auth), Sculpture material and process, Van Nostrand Reinhold, 70.
Memberships: Nat Sculpture Soc; New Eng Sculpture Soc; Cambridge Art Asn (v pres, 68-); Provincetown Art Asn.
Publications: Auth, Sculpture in process, Nat Sculpture Rev, 70; auth, Sculpture Kahlil Gibran, 72.
Mailing Address: 160 W Canton St, Boston, MA 02118.

GIBSON, GEORGE
Painter, Art Administrator
Preferred Media: Watercolors.
b Edinburgh, Scotland, Oct 16, 04; U S citizen.
Study & Training: Edinburgh Col Art; Glasgow Sch Art Scotland; W E Glover Scenic Studios, Glasgow; Chovinard Sch Art, Los Angeles, Calif; also with F Tolles Chamberlain, Pasadena, Calif.
Work in Public Collections: Calif Nat Watercolor Soc Collection, Los Angeles Co Mus Art; Home Savings & Loan, Los Angeles; Laguna Beach Mus Art, Calif; Santa Barbara Mus Art, Calif; Santa Paula C of C, Calif.
Exhibitions: Calif Nat Watercolor Soc Ann, 47-71; Am Watercolor Soc Ann, 49-72; Nat Acad Design, New York, N Y, 54-58; Phoenix Art Mus, Ariz, 72.
Positions: Supvr scenic art prod, MGM Studios, Culver City, Calif, 34-69.
Awards: Calif Nat Watercolor Soc 32nd Ann award, 51; Nat Acad Design 134th Ann watercolor award, 59; Verda Karen McCracken Young Award, Am Watercolor Soc 105th Ann, 72.
Bibliography: V Hewtschy (auth), From any angle, 10/54 & Ron Ross (auth), Cameramans comments, 12/54, Int Photographer; G Gibson (auth), Scenic art in motion picture industry, Soc Motion Picture & TV Eng J, 10/62.
Memberships: Assoc Nat Acad Design; Am Watercolor Soc; Calif Nat Watercolor Soc (secy, 47, first v pres, 49, pres, 51); West Coast Watercolor Soc; Acad Motion Picture Arts & Sci.
Publications: Contribr, Am Artist, 5/68 & 9/69.
Dealer: Emerson Galleries, 17230 Ventura Blvd, Encino, CA 91316.
Mailing Address: 12157 Leven Lane, Los Angeles, CA 90049.

GIBSON, ROLAND
Collector, Educator
b Potsdam, N Y, Feb 4, 02.
Study & Training: Dartmouth Col, AB, 35; Columbia Univ, MA, 40, PhD(econ), 47.
Exhibitions: Exhibs circulated by Roland Gibson Art Found during past six yrs at col & univ art galleries throughout U S.
Positions: Pres & treas, Roland Gibson Art Found, Inc, Potsdam, 65-; dir, Roland Gibson Mus Art, Dunbarton, N H, 67-70; cur art, State Univ N Y Col Potsdam, 70-
Collection: 300 works of contemporary abstract painting, prints & sculpture; Japanese & Italian abstract art.
Publications: Auth, Japanese abstract art collected in Japan in 1963 (catalogue), 64, Italian abstract art collected on a visit to Italy in 1966 (catalogue), 67 & A retrospective of the paintings of Mary Sloane (catalogue), 69.
Mailing Address: 9 Garden St, Potsdam, NY 13676.

GIFFORD, J NEBRASKA
Painter
Preferred Media: Acrylics.
b Omaha, Nebr, Nov 25, 39.
Study & Training: Bennington Col, BA; Atelier 17, Paris, France, with S W Hayter.
Work in Public Collections: Owens-Corning Fiberglas Collection, Toledo, Ohio.
Commissions: Acrylic painting, indoor wall, Omaha Community Playhouse, 61; oil & enamel painting, outdoor wall, Old Market, Omaha, 69.
Exhibitions: Cite Univ, Paris, France, 60; Chelsea Ann Art Show, 63; Windham Col, Putney, Vt, 65; Contemporary Reflections (1971-72), Aldrich Mus, Ridgefield, Conn, 72; Whitney Mus Am Art Ann, New York, N Y, 72.
Mailing Address: 4 Great Jones St, New York, NY 10012.

GIFFUNI, FLORA BALDINI
Painter, Designer
Preferred Media: Pastels.
b Naples, Italy, Oct 26, 19; U S citizen.
Study & Training: N Y Univ, BFA; Columbia Univ Teacher's Col, MFA; also with Frank Reilly, S Dickenson & R Brackman.
Exhibitions: Am Artist Prof League, Lever House, 66 & 72; Catharine Lorillard Wolfe Art Club, Nat Acad Design Galleries, 70; Nat Art League, Douglaston, N Y, 71; Nat Arts Club, New York, 72; Knickerbocker Artists, Nat Arts Club.
Teaching: Instr art, Immaculate Conception Sch, Jamaica, N Y, 50-62; pvt instr, 42-72.

Awards: Hon mention, Am Artist Prof League, 66; Talens Award, Catharine Lorillard Wolfe Art Club, 70; Bocour Award, Nat Art League, 71.
Memberships: Am Artist Prof League; Catharine Lorillard Wolfe Art Club (ed, 72); Nat Arts Club; Nat Art League.
Mailing Address: 180-16 Dalny Rd, Jamaica Estates, NY 11432.

GIKAS, CHRISTOPHER
Educator, Painter
Preferred Media: Stained Glass.
b Lincoln, Nebr, Jan 26, 26.
Study & Training: Okla State Univ, BFA; Univ N Mex, MA, stained glass with Hans Tatschl.
Work in Public Collections: Okla State Univ Collection; Univ N Mex Collection; W Tex State Univ, Canyon.
Commissions: Window wall, Univ N Mex, 62.
Teaching: Instr art, W Tex State Univ, 55-62; assoc prof art & art educ, Eastern N Mex Univ, 62-, Univ Pres faculty award, 69.
Publications: Co-auth, Tole' painting for the decorative artists, Vols I & II, 70 & 72; illusr, Journey through the history of New Mexico (pub sch text), 72.
Mailing Address: 700 Canadian St, P O Box 600, Portales, NM 88130.

GIKOW, RUTH (RUTH GIKOW LEVINE)
Painter
Preferred Media: Oils.
b Ukraine; U S citizen.
Study & Training: Cooper Union; also with John Stuart Curry & Raphael Soyer.
Work in Public Collections: Springfield Mus, Mo; Whitney Mus Am Art, New York, N Y; Smithsonian Inst, Washington, D C; prints, Metrop Mus Art, New York; prints, Mus Mod Art, New York.
Commissions: Mural for Bronx Hosp, N Y, comn by Works Proj Admin, 39.
Exhibitions: Carnegie Inst Mus Art, Pittsburgh, Pa; Corcoran Gallery Art, Washington, D C; Whitney Mus Am Art, New York; traveling shows to Japan, Ger & Eng.
Teaching: Instr painting, New Sch Social Res, 65-69.
Awards: Grant, Nat Inst Arts & Lett.
Bibliography: Mathew Josephson (auth), Ruth Gikow, Random, 70.
Art Interests: Drawing & printmaking.
Dealer: Forum Gallery, 1018 Madison Ave, New York, NY 10021.
Mailing Address: 231 W 11th St, New York, NY 10014.

GILBERT, CLYDE LINGLE
Painter, Commercial Artist
Preferred Media: Oils, Watercolors.
b Medora, Ind, Oct 15, 98.
Study & Training: Sch Applied Art, Battle Creek, Mich; Nat Acad Com Art, Chicago, Ill; Studio Fine Arts, Brazil, Ind.
Exhibitions: Wawasee Art Gallery, Syracuse, Ind, 49; Howe Mil Sch, Ind, 49; one-man show, Weddleville Sch, Ind, 66; Battle Creek Sanatorium, Mich, 66; State-wide Show, French Lick Hotel, Ind, 66.
Awards: Gold medal for highest packaging hons, 38.
Memberships: Ind Fedn Art Clubs; Elkhart Art League.
Mailing Address: 139 Riverview Ave, Elkhart, IN 46514.

GILBERT, CREIGHTON EDDY
Art Historian
b Durham, N C, June 6, 24.
Study & Training: N Y Univ, with Walter Friedlaender, Richard Offner, Lionello Venturi, Erwin Panofsky, Meyer Schapiro & Richard Krautheimer, BA, 42, PhD, 55.
Collections Arranged: Baroque Painters of Naples, Ringling Mus, 61; Major Masters of the Renaissance, 63 & 17th Century Paintings from the Low Countries, 66, Rose Art Mus, Brandeis Univ.
Teaching: Instr hist art, Emory Univ, 46-47; from instr to asst prof hist art, Univ Louisville, 47-56; asst prof hist art, Ind Univ, Bloomington, 56-58; from assoc prof to Sidney & Ellen Wien prof hist art, Brandeis Univ, 61-69; prof hist art, Queens Col (N Y), 69-, chmn dept, 69-72.
Positions: Cur, Ringling Mus, Sarasota, Fla, 59-61.
Awards: Fulbright sr lectr, Univ Rome, 51-52; Mather Award for best art criticism of yr, Col Art Asn Am, 64; fel, Netherlands Inst Advan Study, 72-73.
Memberships: Fel Am Acad Arts & Sci; Col Art Asn Am; Alumni Asn Inst Fine Arts, New York Univ (chmn bd dirs, 70-).
Research: Italian Renaissance.
Publications: Transl, Complete poems & selected letters of Michelangelo, 63, Mod Libr Ed, 65, Vintage, 70; auth, Michelangelo, McGraw, 67; auth, Change in Piero della Francesca, Augustin, 68; ed, Renaissance art, Harper, 70; auth, History of Renaissance art, Abrams, 72.
Mailing Address: Dept of Art, Queens College, Flushing, NY 11367.

GILBERT, LIONEL
Painter, Instructor
Preferred Media: Oils.
b Newark, N J, May 29, 12.
Study & Training: Newark Sch Fine & Indust Art, grad, 29; Acad Grande Chaumiere, Paris, 33; with Suzanne Valadon, Paris, 34; Chicago Sch Design, with Maholy-Nagy, 41; New York Univ, with Sam Adler, 55.
Work in Public Collections: Chase Manhattan Bank, New York, N Y; Joslyn Mus Art, Omaha, Nebr; Slater Mus, Conn; Eureka Col Collection, Ill; Silver Springs Acad, Colo; also in many pvt & corp collections.
Exhibitions: One-man shows, Gallery Contemp Art, Toronto, 58, New Sch Social Res, New York, 66 & Alonzo Gallery, New York, 68, 70 & 71; Childe Hassom Fund Exhib, Acad Arts & Lett, 69; Nat Acad Design, 70-71; plus others.
Teaching: Instr drawing & painting, YMHA, New York, 67-73; instr drawing & painting, New York Univ, 68-69.
Mailing Address: c/o Alonzo Gallery, 26 E 63rd St, New York, NY 10021.

GILBERTSON, (BERNICE) CHARLOTTE
Painter
Preferred Media: Oils, Acrylics, Mixed Media.
b Boston, Mass.
Study & Training: Boston Univ, BA; Art Stud League New York; Pratt Inst; also with Fernand Leger, Paris, France.
Exhibitions: Light Show, Inst Contemp Arts, Philadelphia, Pa, 65; Games Without Rules, Fishbach, N Y, 66; Invitational Show, Flint Col, N Y, 67; Destructivist Show, Finch Col, N Y, 68; E A T Show, Brooklyn Mus, New York, 68-69; plus many other group & one-man shows.
Memberships: Mus Mod Art; Am Fedn Arts.
Dealer: Bodley Gallery, 787 Madison Ave, New York, NY 10021.
Mailing Address: Old School House Rd, Harwich Port, MA 02646.

GILCHRIST, AGNES ADDISON
Art & Architectural Historian
b Philadelphia, Pa, Dec 25, 07.
Study & Training: Wellesley Col, AB, 30; Univ Pa, MA 33; Brenet Art Sorbonne, Paris, Carnegie scholar & cert art, 34; Courtauld Inst Art, Univ London, cert, 36, Carnegie scholarships, Fogg Mus, Harvard Univ, summers 35 & 40.
Teaching: Instr hist art, Univ Pa, 34-41; adj prof hist art, Randolph-Macon Woman's Col, 41-42; lectr hist art, Washington Sq Col, New York Univ, 48-49.
Positions: Archit historian, Nat Park Serv, Philadelphia, 57-58; researcher in Holland, Sleepy Hollow Restorations, Tarrytown, N Y, 59-60; researcher, New York Landmarks Preservation Comn, 62-64.
Awards: Brunner fel, New York Archit League, 55; Am Coun Learned Socs grant-in-aid, 66.
Memberships: Soc Archit Historians (pres, 54); Munic Art Soc New York (dir & researcher, 51-57); Landmark & Hist Soc Mt Vernon, N Y (pres, 64-66); Col Art Asn Am; New York Hist Soc.
Publications: Auth, Romanticism & the Gothic revival, 38 & 68; ed, Portraits in the University of Pennsylvania, 40; auth, Early American Gothic, Romanticism, 40; auth, articles, In: J of Soc Archit Historians, 42-72; auth, William Strickland, architect & engineer, 50 & 69.
Mailing Address: 286 E Sidney Ave, Mount Vernon, NY 10553.

GILES, NEWELL WALTON, JR
Painter
Preferred Media: Watercolors, Oils.
b Flushing, N Y, June 20, 28.
Study & Training: Wesleyan Univ, BA(art hist); New York-Phoenix Sch Design; also studied watercolor with Herb Olsen, Westport, Conn.
Commissions: Watercolor renderings, Stanwich Presby Church, Greenwich, Conn, 69, main lobby, Innis Arden Golf & Country Club, Old Greenwich, Conn, 71; Pan Ocean Oil Corp, New York, N Y, 72, plus various private comns.
Exhibitions: Greenwich Art Soc Ann Juried Show, Greenwich Libr, 66-70; Hudson Valley Art Asn Ann Show, White Plains, N Y, 66-72; Am Watercolor Soc Ann Show, New York, 68; Hammond Mus Exhib Contemp Am Art, North Salem, N Y, 68; Am Artists Prof League Regional Show, New York, 72.
Teaching: Private instr watercolor, 70-71.
Positions: Art dir, J M Mathes Inc, New York, 55-63; art & prod dir, J J Lane Inc, Advert, New York, 63-
Awards: Puck Award for newspaper advert, N Y J-Am, 60; first prize for watercolors, Greenwich Art Soc, 68 & Old Greenwich Art Soc, 70.
Bibliography: Article, In: La Rev Mod, 69.

Memberships: Assoc Am Watercolor Soc; Am Artists Prof League; Hudson Valley Art Asn; Greenwich Art Soc; Old Greenwich Art Soc (mem bd dirs).
Mailing Address: 3 Old Wagon Rd, Old Greenwich, CT 06870.

GILHOOLY, DAVID JAMES, III
Sculptor
Preferred Media: Clay.
b Auburn, Calif, Apr 15, 43; Can citizen.
Study & Training: Univ Calif, Davis, BA, 65, MA, 67.
Work in Public Collections: Mother & Child Hippo Fountain, Oakland Mus, Calif; Johnson's Wax Collection; Bronfman Collection Can Art, Nat Gallery, Ottawa, Ont; Mus Contemp Craft, New York, N Y; Joseph Monsen Collection, San Francisco Mus Art, Calif; plus many other pub & pvt collections.
Exhibitions: Funk Show, Univ Calif, Berkeley & Inst Contemp Art, Boston, Mass, 67; Realisms '70, Montreal Mus Art & Art Gallery Ont, 70; Whitney Mus Am Art Sculpture Ann, New York, 70; Clayworks, Mus Contemp Craft, New York, 71; Contemp Ceramic Art, Kyoto & Tokyo Mus Art, 72; plus many other group & one-man shows.
Teaching: Instr ceramic sculpture, Univ Calif, Davis, 66-70; instr drawings & watercolor, San Jose State Col, 67-69; instr ceramics & sculpture, Univ Sask, Regina, 69-71; instr ceramics & sculpture, York Univ, 71-
Bibliography: David Zack (auth), Basic art, Univ Sask Press, 71; Jeannette Arneson (auth), David Gilhooly, Crafts Horizon, 8/71; Gary Dault (auth), with David Gilhooly in the frogworld, Arts Can, spring 72.
Dealers: Hansen-Fuller Gallery, 228 Grant Ave, San Francisco, CA 94108; Candy Store Gallery, 608 Sutter, Folsom, CA 95630.
Mailing Address: 133 Gurnett, Aurora, Ont, Can.

GILKEY, GORDON WAVERLY
Printmaker, Educator
b Linn Co, Ore, Mar 10, 12.
Study & Training: Albany Col, BA, 33; Univ Ore, MFA, 36; Lewis & Clark Col, hon Arts D, 57.
Work in Public Collections: Metrop Mus Art, New York, N Y; Libr Cong, Washington, D C; Brit Mus, London; Bibliot Nat, Paris; San Francisco Art Mus.
Commissions: Etchings, Univ Ore Libr Construction, Univ Ore, 36 & New York World's Fair, 1939, New York World's Fair & Chas Scribner's Sons, 38-39.
Exhibitions: Many Northwest Printmakers Int, 50-72; Soc Am Graphic Artists, New York, 52-72; Expos Int Gravure, Ljubljana, Yugoslavia, 65-72; Biennale Int Gravure, Cracow, Poland, 68-70; Expos in Dessins Originaux, Rijeka, Yugoslavia, 68, 70 & 72.
Collections Arranged: Dir, Int Exchange Print Exhibs, U S Prints in Europe & Africa, 56 & 65; imported & circulated Contemp Prints France, 56, 61 & 66; Contemp Prints Italy, 57; Contemp Prints Gt Brit, 58 & 65; Contemp Prints Norway, 58, 63 & 71; Contemp Prints Yugoslavia, 59, 64, 69 & 72; Contemp Prints Holland, 59; Contemp Prints Ger, 60, 63 & 70; Contemp Prints Japan, 61, 65 & 69 & Contemp Japanese Sumi Paintings, 63; Contemp Prints Denmark, 62; Contemp Prints Greece, 62; Contemp Prints Czech, 68 & Contemp Prints Sweden—Woodcuts, 69.
Teaching: Instr art & studio, Stephens Col, 39-42; prof art hist & studio & head dept, Ore State Univ, 47-64, dean, Sch Humanities & Social Sci, 63-
Positions: Chief, U S War Dept Spec Staff Art Proj Europe, 45-47; trustee & chmn Art Comt, Portland Art Mus, 61-67; chmn, Gov Planning Coun Arts & Humanities Ore, 65-67.
Awards: Comdr, Order of Merit, Italy, 67 & Fed Ger Repub, 68; Off Order of Palms Acad, Repub France, 69.
Memberships: Am Soc Aesthetics (exec bd, N W Div); Am Asn Mus; Soc Am Graphic Artists; Print Coun Am; Col Art Asn Am.
Research: History of printmaking.
Art Interests: Donor of prints to national collections, state and university museums.
Collection: Historical and contemporary prints.
Publications: Auth, Etching showing construction progress of the University of Oregon library, 36 & Etchings: New York world's fair, 1939, 39; auth, numerous articles on printmaking.
Mailing Address: 350 N W 35th St, Corvallis, OR 97330.

GILL, FREDERICK JAMES
Painter, Educator
Preferred Media: Acrylics, Watercolors.
b Philadelphia, Pa, May 30, 06.
Study & Training: Pa Mus Sch Art; Univ Pa, BFA, 29; with Charles Woodbury, summer 31 & 32; Tyler Sch Art, MFA, 53.
Work in Public Collections: Philadelphia Mus Art; Lehigh Univ, Bethlehem, Pa; Temple Univ, Philadelphia; Temple Sch Pharm; Beaver Col, Philadelphia.
Exhibitions: Philadelphia Watercolor Club Ann & traveling exhibs, 42-; Am Watercolor Soc Ann & traveling exhibs, 47-; 200 Years

of Watercolor in America, Metrop Mus Art, New York, 67; one-
man retrospective, Wallingford Art Ctr, Pa; one-man show, Phil-
adelphia Art Alliance.
Teaching: Instr oil painting, Philadelphia Col Art, 55-71; instr wa-
tercolor & acrylics, Philadelphia Mus Art, 65-; instr watercolor
& acrylics, Philadelphia Mus Art, 65-; instr watercolor &
acrylics, Cult Art Ctr Ocean City, 67-
Awards: Medal of award for achievements in watercolor, 66 & Dana
Medal, 70, Philadelphia Watercolor Club; Paul Remmey Mem
Award, Am Watercolor Soc, 69.
Memberships: Philadelphia Art Alliance (oil color comt, 72); Am
Watercolor Soc; Philadelphia Watercolor Club (bd dirs, 60); Art-
ists Equity Asn (bd dirs Philadelphia Chap, 62).
Dealers: Benjamin Mangel Gallery, 159 Bala Ave, Baba-Cynwyd,
PA 19004; (summer) Bell Gallery, Harvey Cedars, NJ 08008.
Mailing Address: 7461 Sunset Dr, Avalon, NJ 08202.

GILL, GENE
Painter, Printmaker
b Memphis, Tenn, June 18, 33.
Study & Training: Memphis State Univ; Chicago Art Inst, Ill;
Chouinard Art Inst, Los Angeles, Calif, BFA.
Work in Public Collections: Los Angeles Co Mus, Los Angeles; Palm
Springs Desert Mus, Calif; Atlantic Richfield Corp, Los Angeles;
Home Savings, Los Angeles; Northrop Corp, Los Angeles.
Exhibitions: Second Los Angeles Ann, Munic Art Mus, 69; All Calif
Print Exhibs, Los Angeles, 69-71; Scrips Col Int Print Exhib, Los
Angeles, 70; Ninth Ann Southern Calif Exhib, Long Beach Mus
Art, 71; Laguna Beach Art Mus Exhib Ten, Calif, 71.
Awards: Purchase awards, Home Savings, 69 & Westside Jewish
Community Ctr, 70; Jurors Award, Laguna Beach Art Mus, 70.
Bibliography: Joseph E Young (auth), articles, In: Art Int, 70 & 71.
Dealer: Comara Gallery, 617 N La Cienega Blvd, Los Angeles, CA
90069.
Mailing Address: 2430 Cascadia Dr, Glendale, CA 91206.

GILL, JAMES (FRANCIS)
Painter, Sculptor
b Tahoka, Tex, Dec 10, 34.
Study & Training: San Angelo Jr Col; Univ Tex, fel, 60.
Work in Public Collections: Mus Mod Art, New York, N Y; Art
Inst Chicago, Ill; Whitney Mus Am Art, New York; Univ Calif
Mus Art, Berkeley; Mead Corp, Dayton, Ohio; Container Corp
Am; plus one other.
Commissions: Cover painting, Time, Inc.
Exhibitions: Art Inst Chicago, 64; Mus Mod Art, 65; San Francisco
Art Inst, Calif, 65; Whitney Mus Am Art, 66-68; Sao Paulo,
Brazil, 67; Nat Collection Fine Art traveling exhib, Europe,
68-69.
Teaching: Instr painting & lectr, Univ Idaho, Univ Ore & Univ Calif,
Irvine.
Awards: Purchase prize, Art Inst Chicago, 64.
Publications: Auth, Metamage, 69.
Mailing Address: Whale Gulch, Whitethorn, CA 95489.

GILL, ROBERT WAYNE
Painter
Preferred Media: Oils.
b Oconomowoc, Wis, Jan 17, 25.
Study & Training: Art Stud League New York, with Edwin Dickinson
& George Grosz.
Work in Public Collections: Butler Inst Am Art, Youngstown, Ohio;
Joslyn Art Mus, Omaha, Nebr; Syracuse Univ Mus Art, N Y; Ga
Mus Art, Athens; Tyler Mus Art, Tex.
Exhibitions: Realists, Gallery Mod Art, New York, N Y, 68; Butler
Inst Am Art, 70; Am Acad Arts & Lett, New York, 72; Primates
in Art, Portland Mus Art, Ore, 72; 147th Ann, Nat Acad Design,
New York, 72.
Publications: Co-auth, Painting the human figure, 64.
Dealer: ACA Galleries, 25 E 73rd St, New York, N Y 10021.
Mailing Address: 122 W 29th St, New York, NY 10001.

GILL, SUE MAY
Painter, Sculptor
b Sabinal, Tex.
Study & Training: Pa Acad Fine Arts, 20-26; Acad Colorosi, Paris,
France, 23-24; Art Inst Chicago.
Commissions: Sculpture, West Point Military Acad; numerous foun-
tain sculptures in pvt gardens; portraits of many prominent per-
sons in pvt collections in U S.
Exhibitions: Philadelphia Country Club, 66 & 68; Philadelphia Sketch
Club, 66; Auburn Mus, N Y, 67; Plastics Club, 69; Pa Acad Fine
Arts, Nat Acad Design & many others.
Teaching: Instr painting, Syracuse Univ, summer sessions; lect
painting, Pa Acad Fine Arts & pvt clubs.

Awards: Medal 42 & prize, 43, Philadelphia Sketch Club, Philadel-
phia Plastic Club Prizes, 42-44; Wayne Art Ctr, Pa, 66; plus
others.
Memberships: Philadelphia Artists Alliance; Philadelphia Plastic
Club; Nat Asn Women Artists; Fellowship Pa Acad Fine Arts;
Philadelphia Mus Art.
Mailing Address: 639 Love's Lane, English Village, Wynnewood, PA
19096.

GILLESPIE, GREGORY JOSEPH
Painter
Preferred Media: Oils, Acrylics.
b Elizabeth, N J, Nov 29, 36.
Study & Training: Cooper Union Art Sch; San Francisco Art Inst,
MFA.
Work in Public Collections: Whitney Mus Am Art; N J State Mus,
Trenton; Hirshhorn Collection.
Exhibitions: Whitney Ann, 66, 68 & 72; Personal Concern—Human
Torment, New Sch Soc Res, 69; Smith Col Mus Art, 71; Univ Ga,
71; Nat Acad Design, 72.
Awards: Am Acad Rome Award, 65-68; Fulbright fel, 67; Nat Inst
Arts & Lett Award, 69.
Bibliography: Gregory Gillespie (paintings Italy, 1962-70), Forum
Gallery, 71.
Memberships: Nat Acad Design.
Dealer: Forum Gallery, 1018 Madison Ave, New York, NY 10021.
Mailing Address: Depot Rd, Haydenville, MA 01039.

GILLIAM, SAM
Painter
b Tupelo, Miss, 33.
Study & Training: Univ Louisville, MA.
Work in Public Collections: Mus African Art, Phillips Collection,
Nat Collection Fine Arts, Corcoran Gallery Art & Howard Univ,
Washington, D C; plus many others.
Exhibitions: Works for New Spaces, Walker Art Ctr, Minneapolis,
Minn, 71; Washington Art, Madison Art Ctr, Wis, 71 & State Univ
N Y Albany, 71; Am Exhib, Indian Triennale, New Delhi, 71; Mus
Mod Art, New York, N Y, 71; Venice Biennale, Italy, 72; plus
many other group & one-man shows.
Awards: Norman Walt Harris Prize, Art Inst Chicago, 70; Longview
Found Purchase Award, 70; Guggenheim Mem Found fel, 71;
plus others.
Bibliography: LeGrace Benson (auth), Sam Gilliam: certain attitudes,
Artforum, 9/70; Elsie Carper (auth), Gilliam's giants in a Paris
show, Washington Post, 11/6/70; Douglas Davis (auth), Washing-
ton letter, Arts, 12-1/70; plus many others.
Mailing Address: 1752 Lamont St N W, Washington, DC 20010.

GILLING, LUCILLE
Printmaker
b Hamilton, Mo.
Study & Training: Kansas City Art Inst; New York Sch Fine & Appl
Arts, dipl; study in Paris, France, Eng & Italy; Queens Univ
Summer Sch.
Work in Public Collections: Nat Libr Can, Ottawa; Montreal Mus
Fine Art; Victoria & Albert Mus, London, Eng; Ohio State Univ;
Wayne State Univ.
Exhibitions: Soc Can Painters, Etchers & Engravers, Toronto, Ont,
56-; Can Soc Graphic Arts, Toronto, 57, 58 & 64; one-man shows,
Pascall Gallery, Toronto, 66, Sobot Gallery, Toronto, 69 &
Marjorie Kauffmann Graphics, 72.
Awards: Sterling Trust award, 59; Anaconda Award of Merit, 68.
Memberships: Soc Can Painters, Etchers & Engravers (exec coun,
57-); Prof Artists Can (secy/treas, 68-); Toronto Heliconian
Club (exec coun, 71-72).
Publications: Portfolios of etchings, The Canterbury Tales, 66 &
Don Quixote, 69, original signed etchings Ed 100.
Dealer: Marjorie Kauffmann Graphics, 5015 Westheimer, Houston,
TX 77027.
Mailing Address: 178 Alfred Ave, Willowdale, Ont, Can.

GILLINGWATER, DENIS CLAUDE
Painter
Preferred Media: Acrylics.
b Glendale, Calif, Feb 15, 46.
Study & Training: Univ Cincinnati, BFA, 68, MFA, 70.
Exhibitions: All Ohio Painting & Sculpture Exhib, Dayton Art Inst,
69; Cincinnati Art Mus Biennial, 70; Four Corner States Biennial,
Phoenix Art Mus, 71; Seventh Southwest Invitational, Yuma, Ariz,
72; Phoenix Art Mus Invitational, Ariz, 72.
Teaching: Vis art instr, Mesa Community Col, Ariz, 70-; artist-in-
residence, Nat Endowment for the Arts, Mesa, Ariz, 72-73.
Awards: Artist-in-residence, Mesa Pub Sch System, Nat Endow-
ment for the Arts, 72-73.
Mailing Address: $32\frac{1}{2}$ E Second Ave, Mesa, AZ 85202.

GILMORE, ETHEL (MRS CHARLES J ROMANS)
Painter, Instructor.
Preferred Media: Oils.
b New York, N Y.
Study & Training: Hunter Col, with A Dasburg & G E Brown & BA; Columbia Univ, with C J Martin & Hibbard & MA; Art Stud League New York, with P Kapple & H Snell.
Work in Public Collections: Jersey City Mus, N J; Junior Mus, Albany, Ga; La Salle Col, Philadelphia, Pa.
Exhibitions: Atlantic City Art Asn Ann, 69; Prof Artist South Jersey, 71; Allied Artist Am Ann, 71; Nat Asn Women Artists Ann, 72; Painters & Sculptors Soc N J Ann, 72.
Teaching: Instr fine arts, De Witt Clinton High Sch, New York, 23-50, chmn dept, 50-52.
Positions: Chmn art dept, Women's Community Club, 57-73.
Awards: Award for Bleak December, Allied Artists Am, 51; award for landscape, Jersey City Mus Asn, 53; best in show, Atlantic City Art Asn, 67.
Bibliography: A P Smith (auth), Careers, John C Romans & Ethel M Gilmore, N J Music & Arts, 3/69.
Memberships: Allied Artists Am (rec secy, 50-54, corresp secy, 54-55); Nat Asn Women Artists (jury art selection, 59-60); Painters & Sculptors N J; life mem Atlantic City Art Asn; Prof Artists South Jersey.
Mailing Address: Romans Studio, 1033 New York Ave, Cape May, NJ 08204.

GILMORE, ROGER
Art Administrator, Educator
b Philadelphia, Pa, Oct 11, 32.
Study & Training: Dartmouth Col, AB; Univ Chicago Divinity Sch, grad study.
Teaching: Dean, Sch Art Inst Chicago, Ill, 65-
Memberships: Soc Archit Historians, Cliff Dwellers.
Mailing Address: 4371 Central Ave, Western Springs, IL 60558.

GILVARRY, JAMES
Collector
Collection: Contemporary art.
Mailing Address: 210 E 47th St, New York, NY 10017.

GIMBEL, MRS BERNARD F
Collector, Patron
Collection: Paintings.
Mailing Address: Upper King St, Greenwich, CT 06830.

GINNEVER, CHARLES
Sculptor
Preferred Media: Steel.
b San Mateo, Calif, Aug 28, 31.
Study & Training: With Zadkine & Hayter, Europe, 53-55; Calif Sch Fine Arts, San Francisco, BFA, 57; Cornell Univ, MFA, 59.
Work in Public Collections: Wadsworth Atheneum, Hartford, Conn; Chrysler Mus, Provincetown, Mass.
Commissions: Aluminum sculpture, Vt Coun Arts, Southern Vt Art Ctr, 71-72.
Exhibitions: Art in Environment Show, New York, 67.
Teaching: Chmn dept art, Windham Col, Putney, Vt, 67-
Dealer: Paula Cooper Gallery, 100 Prince St, New York, NY 10012.
Mailing Address: P O Box 411, Putney, VT 05346.

GINSBURG, MAX
Painter, Illustrator
b Paris, France, Aug 7, 31.
Study & Training: Syracuse Univ, BFA; Nat Acad Design; City Col New York, MA.
Work in Public Collections: N Y Cult Ctr.
Exhibitions: Allied Artists Am, 56-72; Am Vet Soc Artists, 61-72; Audubon Artists, 62-72; Harbor Gallery, Cold Spring Harbor, 66, 68, 69, 71 & 72.
Teaching: Instr art, High Sch Art & Design, New York.
Awards: Prize, 61 & gold medal, 62 & 65, Am Vet Soc Artists; Allied Artists Am, 61 & 62; Nat Art Club, 63.
Memberships: Allied Artists Am; Audubon Artists; Am Vet Soc Artists; Artists Equity Asn.
Dealer: Harbor Gallery, 43 Main St, Cold Spring Harbor, NY 11724.
Mailing Address: 939 Eighth Ave, New York, NY 10019.

GINZEL, ROLAND
Painter, Printmaker
b Lincoln, Ill, 21.
Study & Training: Art Inst Chicago, BFA; State Univ Iowa, MFA; Slade Sch, London.
Work in Public Collections: Univ Southern Calif; Univ Mich; Ill Bell Tel Co; Art Inst Chicago; U S Embassy, Warsaw, Poland; plus others.

Exhibitions: Chicago Artists, Des Moines, Iowa, 68; Art Inst Chicago, 69; Madison, Wis, 69; Notre Dame Univ, 69; one-man show, Phyllis Kind Gallery, 69.
Teaching: Prof printmaking, Univ Chicago, 57-58; prof prints & painting, Univ Ill, Chicago Circle, 58-69; instr painting, Univ Wis, 60; instr art, Saugatuck Summer Sch, 61-62.
Awards: Oppenheim prize, 55, purchase prize, 56, print & drawing prize, 67 & Campana prize, 69, Art Inst Chicago; Fulbright fel to Rome, 62.
Dealer: Phyllis Kind Gallery, 226 E Ontario St, Chicago, IL 60611.
Mailing Address: 412 N Clark St, Chicago, IL 60610.

GIOBBI, EDWARD GIOACHINO
Painter
Preferred Media: Oils, Mixed Media.
b Waterbury, Conn, July 18, 26.
Work in Public Collections: Tate Gallery Art, London, Eng; Boston Mus Fine Arts, Mass; Whitney Mus Am Art, New York, N Y; Art Inst Chicago, Ill; Brooklyn Mus, N Y; plus others.
Exhibitions: Young America, Whitney Mus Am Art, 60; Recent Figure U S A, Mus Mod Art, New York, 60; 40 Painters under 40, Whitney Mus Am Art, 62; plus others.
Teaching: Artist-in-residence, Memphis Acad, Tenn, 59-60; artist-in-residence, Dartmouth Col, 72.
Awards: Emily Lowe Award, 49; Ford Found artist-in-residence program, 66; Guggenheim fel, 72.
Mailing Address: 161 Croton Lake Rd, Katonah, NY 10536.

GIORGI, VITA
Printmaker, Painter
b Mazara, Italy; U S citizen.
Study & Training: Wash Univ; La Ciudadela, Mexico City, Mex.
Work in Public Collections: New York Pub Libr, N Y; Manchester Inst Arts & Sci, N H; Potsdam Col, N Y; Mus Arte Contemp, Bogotá, Colombia; Mus Mod Art, Santiago, Chile.
Exhibitions: New Eng Art & Prints, De Cordova Mus, Lincoln, Mass, 65; Int Print Show, Manchester Inst Arts & Sci, 68; Salon Independente, Mexico City, 69; First Panam Graphics Biennal, Mus Latertulia, Cali, Colombia, 71; Third Brit Int Print Biennale, Bradford Mus, Eng, 72.
Bibliography: Toby Joy Smith (auth), Two painter poets, The News, Mexico City, 68; Thomas M Cranfill (auth), Image of Mexico, I, Tex Quart, 69; R Brown (auth), Ten downtown, New York, Arts Mag, 71.
Publications: Contribr, 66 & 68 & illusr, 66 & 68, Rev Mañana, Mexico City; illusr, El Mendrugo, New York, 72.
Dealer: Lerner-Misrachi Gallery, 789 Madison Ave, New York, NY 10021.
Mailing Address: P O Box 442, Canal St Station, New York, NY 10013.

GIRAUDIER, ANTONIO
Painter, Writer
Preferred Media: Acrylics, Mixed Media.
b Havana, Cuba, 26, U S citizen.
Work in Public Collections: Fordham Univ, Lincoln Ctr & Bronx Campuses; Univ Palm Beach, W Palm Beach, Fla; Am Poets Fel Soc, Charleston, Ill; also in private Am & foreign collections.
Exhibitions: 50 exhibs incl 6 group shows & 1 one-man show, New Masters Gallery, New York, N Y, 65-68; 2 two-man shows & 3 group shows, Wellfleet Gallery, Cape Cod & Palm Beach, 67 & 68; Long Beach Ann, New York, 68; 13 group shows, 1 two-man show & 3 one-man shows, Avanti Gallery, New York, 68-72; one-man show, Univ Palm Beach; plus others in U S & abroad.
Awards: Premier Prix de Printemps, Paris, 59; Laureat Marguerite d'Or, Paris, 60; Prix de Paris, 66; plus others.
Bibliography: Reviews, In: Arts Mag, 12/71-1/72 & The Inner Loom, 72; art work reproduced in 19 publ, US & abroad; plus many others.
Publications: Auth, 15 definitive works in Eng, 9 in Span; writings publ in 24 books & 17 magazines & newspapers (several incl art work), U S & abroad; poetry incl in anthologies U S & abroad.
Dealer: Avanti Galleries, 145 E 72nd St, New York, NY 10021.
Mailing Address: 215 E 68th St, New York, NY 10021.

GIRONELLA, ALBERTO
Painter, Illustrator
b Mexico City, Mex, Sept 26, 29.
Work in Public Collections: Mod Art Mus, Kamakua, Japan; Tel Aviv Mus; Mus Arte Mod, Mex; Pan-Am Union, Washington, D C.
Commissions: Mural, The Burial of Zapata, Fine Arts Inst, Mex.
Exhibitions: Inst Torcuato Tella, Buenos Aires, 64; 19th & 20th Salon Mai, Paris, 64-65; 50 Years of Collage, Mus Decorative Arts, Paris, 65; Alternative Attuli 12 L'Aquila, Cartello Spagoli, Italy, 65; Int Surrealistic Expos L'Oeil Gallery, Paris, 65.
Awards: Jouth Bienal, Paris, Govt France.

Bibliography: E Jaguer (auth), Gironella, Ed Era, 64; A Breton (auth), Le surrealisme et la pinture, Ed Gallimard, Paris, 65; J Pierre (auth), Le surrealisme, Ed Rencontre, Lausanne, 66.
Dealer: Galeria Juan Martin, Amberes 19, Mexico City 76, Mex.
Mailing Address: San Jose 201, Valle de Bravo, Mex.

GIUSTI, GEORGE
Designer, Sculptor
Preferred Media: Metals.
b Milan, Italy; U S citizen.
Study & Training: Acad Brera, Milan, Italy.
Work in Public Collections: Graphic Sect, Mus Mod Art, New York, N Y; also in several art cols, U S & abroad.
Exhibitions: New York, Philadelphia, Boston, Chicago, Los Angeles, Louvre in Paris, London, Milan, Vienna, Latin Am, Japan & the Orient.
Teaching: Instr, Cooper Union, New York.
Awards: More than 80 major awards & 15 gold & silver medals; art dir of year, 58.
Bibliography: Articles, In: Graphis, Switz, Communication Art, U S & Daily Tel Mag, London.
Memberships: Alliance Graphique Int; Am Inst Graphic Arts; Int Ctr Typographic Arts.
Publications: Auth & illusr, The human heart, 61; portfolios, Graphis, Switz, Idea & FAS, Japan, Pagina, Milano, Gebrauchsgrafik, Ger, Communication Art, U S & Daily Tel Mag, London; auth, articles, In: Fortune, Sat Eve Post, Time, Holiday, U S Info Agency Publ & others.
Mailing Address: Chalburn Rd, West Redding, CT 06896.

GIVLER, WILLIAM HUBERT
Painter, Instructor
b Omaha, Nebr, Mar 17, 08.
Study & Training: Portland Mus Art Sch, Ore; Art Stud League New York.
Work in Public Collections: Portland Art Mus; Philadelphia Mus Art, Pa; Seattle Art Mus, Wash.
Exhibitions: Pa Acad Fine Arts, Philadelphia; Nat Acad Design, New York, N Y; San Francisco Mus Art, Calif; Worcester Mus Art, Mass.
Teaching: Instr art, Portland Mus Art Sch, 31-44, dean, 44-
Awards: Prizes, Seattle Art Mus, Northwest Printmakers, Portland Art Mus & others.
Memberships: Ore Guild Painters & Sculptors.
Mailing Address: 2637 N W Northrup St, Portland, OR 97210.

GLASER, DAVID
Designer, Painter
Preferred Media: Oils, Mixed Media.
b Brooklyn, N Y, Sept 29, 19.
Study & Training: Art Stud League New York; New York Sch Indust Art; New York Sch Contemp Art, with Philip Evergood; Brooklyn Mus Art Sch, with Moses Soyer, Xavier Gonzales & Edwin Dickinson.
Commissions: Poster series for U S Army, 43-44.
Exhibitions: Hofstra Univ, 52-58; Nat Arts Club, 59; Art Directions, 59; City Ctr, New York, N Y, 60; Allied Artists Am, 60-71.
Positions: Art dir & designer, 46-48; art dir, 54-60; dir & designer, Studio Concepts, 60-
Awards: One-man shows, Almus Gallery, Great Neck, 60 & Heckscher Mus, Huntington, 63; best house redesign, Levitt & Sons, Am Home, 68.
Memberships: Allied Artists Am; Vet Soc Am Artists.
Research: Experimental silk screen production for industry; developed process for reproducing mosaics; new approaches in advertising & media including all communication skills.
Publications: Illusr, Planets, 61; illusr for Popular Sci, Popular Mechanix & Electronics Illustrated, 61-65.
Mailing Address: 33 Downhill Lane, Wantagh, NY 11793.

GLASER, SAMUEL
Collector
b Riga, Latvia, Jan 21, 02.
Study & Training: Mass Inst Technol, BS & MA.
Collection: Late nineteenth and twentieth century drawings, paintings, sculpture and rare illustrated books.
Mailing Address: 381 Dudley Rd, Newton Center, MA 02159.

GLASGALL, MRS HENRY W
Collector
Mailing Address: 930 Fifth Ave, New York, NY 10021.

GLASIER, ALICE GENEVA, see KLOSS, GENE

GLASS, HENRY P
Designer, Educator
b Vienna, Austria, Sept 24, 11.
Study & Training: Tech Univ, Vienna; Master Sch Archit, with Theiss.
Commissions: Design of furniture, products, com interiors display & archit.
Teaching: Prof indust design, Art Inst Chicago, 46-67, retired.
Positions: Design ed, Hitchcock's Woodworking Digest; chief designer, Morris B Sanders, New York, 40-41; head archit design dept, W L Stensgaard, Chicago, 42-45; owner, Henry P Glass Assocs, 46-; chmn Chicago chap, Indust Designers Inst, 57-59.
Awards: Gold medal, Indust Designers Inst, 52; Fine Hardwoods Asn Award, 55.
Memberships: Fel Indust Designers Soc Am.
Publications: Contribr, articles, In: Interiors, Plastics & other trade mag.
Mailing Address: 245 Dickens Rd, Northfield, IL 60093.

GLEZER, NECHEMIA
Art Dealer, Art Historian
b Vilno, Lithuania, 10; U S citizen.
Study & Training: Acad Fine Arts, Vilno; Stefana Batorego Univ, Vilno; Brera Acad Fine Arts, Milan, with Aldo Carpi.
Collections Arranged: Fourteen Italian Artists, sponsored by Italian Ambassador to U S A, Veerhoff Gallery, Washington, D C, 60; French Artists, C W Post Col, Long Island Univ, N Y, 61; I Pailes, Maison Française, New York Univ, sponsored by French Cultural Atache to U S A, 63; Ferruccio Steffanutti, Vatican Pavilion, New York World's Fair, 64-65; Trento Longaretti, Casa Italiana, Columbia Univ, New York, 67; I Pailes, Maison Française, Columbia Univ, 72.
Positions: Pres, Nechemia Glezer Gallery, New York, 53-
Awards: Award for cultural enrichment, Fr Cult Attache, 63; award for introducing Italian artists to USA, Italian Consul Gen, 69; academician, Accademia Tiberina di Roma, 72; plus one other.
Bibliography: Elspeth Flynn (auth), Southeby at Glezer Gallery, Brit Info Serv, 2/5/63; Mr Glezer from N Y visits Museum at Castelleone, La Notte, Milan, 5/24/64; Mario Pescara (auth), Collection of Nechemia Glezer, Am Rev Art & Sci, 4/69.
Research: Macchiaioli; Italian nineteenth century artists.
Specialty of Gallery: School of Paris artists; contemporary Italian artists.
Art Interests: Bringing contemporary French & Italian art to the attention of the American public.
Collection: Daumier, Chagall, Pailes, Kikoine, Kremegne, Bai, Brindisi, Carpi, Carena, Quidi, Gino Moro & Longaretti.
Publications: Introductions to catalogues.
Mailing Address: 870 Madison Ave, New York, NY 10021.

GLICK, PAULA FLORENCE
Art Dealer, Collector
b Baltimore, Md, Jan 8, 36.
Study & Training: Am Univ; George Washington Univ.
Positions: Assoc dir, Capricorn Galleries, 64-
Specialty of Gallery: American contemporary realists.
Collection: Contemporary realists.
Mailing Address: 9536 Lawnsberry Terr, Silver Spring, MD 20901.

GLICKMAN, MAURICE
Sculptor, Writer
Preferred Media: Bronze, Wood, Stone
b Jassy, Romania, Jan 6, 06; nat U S.
Study & Training: Educ Alliance Art Sch, New York, N Y, 21-26; Art Stud League New York, 27 & 29-30.
Work in Public Collections: Yvonne (bronze head), Roberson Mem Art Ctr, Binghamton, N Y; Girl with Braids (bronze head), Albany Inst History & Art, N Y; Siesta (alabaster), Joseph Hirshhorn Collection, Washington, D C; Football Players (marble), Queens Col Collection, N Y.
Commissions: Negro Mother & Child (bronze), Dept Interior, Washington, D C, 34; Construction (Philippine mahogany bas-relief), U S Treas Dept, South River, N J, 38; Mailmen (stone composition bas-relief), U S Post Off, Northampton, Pa, 40.
Exhibitions: Government in Art, Mus Mod Art, New York, 35; Carnegie Sculpture Invitational, Philadelphia Mus, Pa, 38; Whitney Mus Am Art Ann, New York, 38-61; Artists for Victory, Metrop Mus Art, New York, 41; Heritage of American Art, Nat Archives Bldg Rotunda, Washington, D C, 71; plus others.
Positions: Founder/dir, Sch Art Studies, New York, 45-55.
Awards: Guggenheim fel, 34.
Bibliography: Karl Schwartz (auth), Jewish sculptors, Newman Publ; Merwyn Eaton (auth), The sculpture of Maurice Glickman, Design, 10/48; Oliver Larkin (auth), Art & life in America, Rinehart, 49.
Memberships: Nat Sculpture Soc; Sculptors Guild (founding mem, 38-, exec secy, 54-55).

Research: Inter-relation of the arts with emphasis on the relation of sculpture & architecture, stressing the master sculptors contributions.

Publications: Auth, The sculptor and his market, Mag Art, 41; auth, On wood carving, Am Artist, 43; auth, The tools of the sculptor, Design Mag, 49; auth, Techniques in sculpture, Am Artist, 60; auth, Six lectures on six master sculptors (in prep); plus others.

Dealer: Florence Lewison Gallery, 30 E 60th St, New York, NY 10022.

Mailing Address: 165 E 66th St, New York, NY 10021.

GLIMCHER, ARNOLD B
Art Dealer, Writer
b Mar 12, 38; U S citizen.
Positions: Pres, Pace Gallery, New York, N Y, 63-
Specialty of Gallery: Twentieth century art.
Publications: Auth, Jean Duffet—simulacres (catalogue), 70 & auth, Ernest Trova—recent sculpture (catalogue), 71, Pace Ed; auth, Louise Nevelson, Praeger, 72.
Mailing Address: Pace Gallery, 32 E 57th St, New York, NY 10021.

GLINSKY, VINCENT
Sculptor, Educator
b Russia, Dec 18, 95; U S citizen.
Study & Training: Columbia Univ; City Col New York; Beaux Arts Inst Design.
Work in Public Collections: Brookgreen Gardens, Georgetown, S C; Norfolk Mus, Va; Bethesda Health Ctr, Md; Hall of Fame for Great Americans, N Y Univ; U S Air Force Acad, Colorado Springs, Colo.
Commissions: Expeditionary medal, U S Navy, 36; interior fountain, All Faith's Mem Tower, Paramus, N J, 64; Theodore Roosevelt coin-medal, Nat Commemorative Soc, 68; Eleanor Roosevelt portrait, U S Dept Labor, Washington, D C; Our Lady of Lourdes Shrine, St Paul's Col, Washington, D C.
Exhibitions: New York World's Fair, N Y, 39-40; Fairmount Park Int Sculpture Inst, Philadelphia Mus Art, 40 & 49; Am Sculpture, Carnegie Inst, Pittsburgh, Pa, 41; Contemp Am Art, London, Eng, 41; 150 Yrs of Am Sculpture, Westbury Gardens, N Y, 60.
Teaching: Instr sculpture, Brooklyn Col, 49-55; adj asst prof sculpture, N Y Univ Sch Continuing Educ, 50-; instr sculpture, Columbia Univ, 57-61.
Awards: Guggenheim fel, 30-31; grant in sculpture, Am Acad Arts & Lett & Nat Inst Arts & Lett, 45; gold medal, Nat Sculpture Soc, 67.
Bibliography: Enid Bell (auth), The compatibles, Am Artist Mag, summer 68.
Memberships: Audubon Artists; Archit League N Y (v pres, 56-58); Sculptors Guild (exec secy, 56-60); Nat Sculpture Soc (chmn exhib comt, 50-51); Nat Acad Design.
Art Interests: Carving & modeling.
Publications: Co-auth, Direct carving in stone, Nat Sculpture Rev, summer 65.
Mailing Address: 5 W 16th St, New York, NY 10011.

GLORIG, OSTOR
Painter
b New York, N Y, Feb 14, 19.
Study & Training: Am Art Sch, New York, four yr cert, with Robert Brackman, Raphael Soyer & Gordon Samstag.
Work in Public Collections: Mark Twain Portrait, Mark Twain Libr & Mem, Hartford, Conn.
Exhibitions: One-man shows, Lynn Kottler Galleries, 56, 59, 61, 64 & 72, Clarksville Gallery, 65 & Col Mt St Vincent, 67; Nat Soc Arts & Lett Empire State Chap Showing, 69.
Awards: Interior Design Cover, 51; Grumbacher Merit Award, 61.
Bibliography: Elaine Israel (auth), From diamond to canvas, Long Island Star-J, 5/9/67.
Memberships: Life fel Royal Soc Arts Eng; life mem Nat Soc Arts & Lett; hon mem Kappa Pi.
Dealer: Lynn Kottler Galleries, 3 E 65th St, New York, NY 10021.
Mailing Address: 21-56 47th St, Long Island City, NY 11105.

GLOVER, DONALD MITCHELL
Curator
b Cleveland, Ohio, May 23, 30.
Study & Training: Allegheny Col; Cleveland Inst Art; Brooklyn Mus; Case Western Reserve Univ, MA.
Positions: Cur educ, Dayton Art Inst.
Mailing Address: Dayton Art Institute, Forest & Riverview Aves, Dayton, OH 45405.

GLOVER, EUPHEMIA W
Sculptor
Preferred Media: Bronze, Stone.
b Windygates, Scotland; U S citizen.
Study & Training: Cent Tech Sch, Toronto; Ont Col Art, Toronto;

Cleveland Inst Art; also with William McVey, Cleveland, Ohio & Harold Castor, New York, N Y.
Commissions: Bronze dancer, Stafford Giles, London, Eng, 66; bronze balloon girls, Unitarian Church All Souls, New York, 69.
Exhibitions: Can Nat Exhib; Ceramic Nat, Syracuse; New Eng Regional, Silvermine, Conn; Nat Relig Art Exhib, 69.
Awards: Cert merit, Artist Craftsmen New York, 65 & 67; first prize, Pen & Brush Club, 67.
Memberships: Artist Craftsmen New York; New York Soc Women Artists; Pen & Brush Club.
Dealer: Environment Gallery, 205 E 60th St, New York, NY 10022.
Mailing Address: 45 E 85th St, New York, NY 10028.

GLUCKMAN, MORRIS
Painter
b Kiev, Russia, Aug 7, 94.
Study & Training: Odessa Art Sch; Nat Acad Design; Brooklyn Mus Sch Art; Davidson Sch Mod Art.
Work in Public Collections: Norfolk Mus, Va; Cambridge Gallery, Roslyn, N Y.
Exhibitions: Nat Acad Design; Nordness Gallery; City Ctr; Art: U S A; Contemp Arts; plus many other group & one-man shows.
Awards: Windsor Award, Brooklyn Mus; Albert Dorn Award, Am Watercolor Soc; Shannon Award, Brooklyn Soc Artists; plus many others.
Memberships: Artists Equity Asn; Am Watercolor Soc; Brooklyn Soc Artists; League Present Day Artists.
Mailing Address: 463 West St, Apt 1019 H, New York, NY 10014.

GLUECK, GRACE (HELEN)
Writer
b New York, N Y.
Study & Training: Washington Sq Col, New York Univ, BA; Columbia Univ.
Positions: Reporter, reviewer & art columnist, New York Times, 63-
Publications: Contribr, Museums in crisis, Braziller, 72.
Mailing Address: c/o New York Times, 229 W 43rd St, New York, NY 10036.

GLYDE, HENRY GEORGE
Painter, Educator
b Luton, Eng, June 18, 06.
Study & Training: Hastings Sch Art & Sci; Royal Col Art, London, hons; sr fel, Can Arts Coun, 58-59.
Work in Public Collections: Art Gallery Toronto; Edmonton Art Gallery; Nat Gallery Can.
Exhibitions: Royal Brit Artists; Royal Acad, London; Ont Soc Artists; Can Soc Graphic Art; Royal Can Acad; plus others.
Teaching: Instr, Borough Polytech, London, Croydon Sch Art, High Wycombe Sch Art; head art dept, Prov Inst Technol & Art, Alberta; prof fine arts emer, Univ Alta & Banff Sch Fine Arts.
Awards: Univ Alta Nat Award, 66.
Memberships: Royal Can Acad Arts.
Mailing Address: R R 1, Port Washington, B C, Can.

GOBIN, HENRY (DELANO)
Painter
Preferred Media: Watercolors.
b Tulalip Indian Reservation, May 29, 41.
Study & Training: San Francisco Art Inst, BFA, 70; Sacramento State Col, MA, 71.
Work in Public Collections: Am Embassy, Kenya, Africa; Am Embassy, Madrid, Spain.
Exhibitions: Am Indian Hist Soc Mus, San Francisco, Calif, 68; Mus Nac Bellas Artes, Buenos Aires, Arg, 68; San Francisco Art Inst, 70; Civic Art Gallery, San Jose, Calif, 71; Jamison Gallery, Santa Fe, N Mex, 71.
Teaching: Asst prof native Am art, Sacramento State Col, 70-71; training instr humanities, Inst Am Indian Arts, 71-
Awards: First prize, N Mex Wildlife Mag, 62; first prize, 17th Ann Navajo Fair, Gallup, N Mex, 63; first prize, Scottsdale Nat Indian Art Exhib, Ariz, 64.
Bibliography: Articles, In: Crafts Horizon, 65, Am Indian Hist Soc Mus, 68 & Artforum, 70.
Mailing Address: 1612 Young St, Santa Fe, NM 87501.

GODDARD, VIVIAN
Painter
Preferred Media: Oils.
b San Francisco, Calif.
Study & Training: Calif Sch Fine Art; Art Stud League New York; Stanford Univ, with Ed Farmer & Dan Mendelowitz; Art League San Francisco; Robert Brackman Summer Sch, Noank & Madison, Conn; Otis Art Sch, Los Angeles; Grande Chaumiere, Paris, France; Simi Studio, Florence, Italy.

Work in Public Collections: Pioneer Mus & Hagan Gallerie, Stockton, Calif, Hall Justice, San Francisco, Calif; City Sacramento, Calif; Stanislaus State Col, Turloc, Calif.
Commissions: Portraits, Richard Cragin, Alexander Capurso, Otto Kruger, Mrs Bernard McFadyen, Hubert Latimer, plus many others.
Exhibitions: One-man show, Windblad Gallerie, San Francisco, 68; Soc Western Artists, De Young Mus, 68-70; one-man shows, Pioneer Mus & Hagan Gallerie, 69, Stanislaus State Col, Turloc, 69 & Rosecrucian Mus, San Jose, Calif, 69 & 72.
Teaching: Head art dept, Miss Harker's Sch, Palo Alto, Calif, 38-48; instr painting, own studio, 69-71.
Positions: Demonstrations, Soc Western Artists, Calif, Burlingame Art Asn, Calif, Fresno Art Asn, Calif & Am Fine Arts Asn, Los Angeles, Calif; juror.
Awards: First award for graphics & award for oil portrait, Soc Western Artists, 67; award for portrait, Mother Lode Nat, 70.
Memberships: Soc Western Artists; Nat League Am Pen Women; life mem Art Stud League New York; Am Artists Prof League; life mem Am Inst Fine Arts.
Dealers: Portraits Inc, 41 E 57th St, New York, NY 10022; Hunter Gallery, 384 Post St, San Francisco, CA 94108.
Mailing Address: 712 Bay St, San Francisco, CA 94109.

GODWIN, ROBERT KIMBALL
  Painter
Preferred Media: Oils.
b Binghamton, N Y, Aug 4, 24.
Exhibitions: Soc Washington Artists 70th Ann, Smithsonian Inst, Washington, D C, 63; Yutenji Gallery, Tokyo, Japan, 67; one-man show, Potter's House Gallery, Washington, D C, 70; Fairfax Co Cult Asn & N Va Community Col Area Exhib, Annandale, Va, 72; N Va Fine Arts Asn 3rd Ann, Alexandria, Va, 72.
Mailing Address: 7423 Saville Ct, Alexandria, VA 22306.

GODWIN, ROBERT LAWRENCE
  Painter, Sculptor
Preferred Media: Metals.
b Enterprise, Ala, Oct 20, 34.
Study & Training: Auburn Univ, BAA, 57.
Work in Public Collections: Montgomery Mus Fine Art; Fisk Univ; Ala Coun Arts.
Commissions: Murals, Holiday Inn, Troy, Ala, 64, Kindergarten, Eufaula, Ala, 65 & W A Gayle Planetarium, Montgomery, Ala, 66; monuments, Welded Eagle, Goshen High Sch, Ala, 71 & Brick & Bronze, Troy City Schs, 72.
Exhibitions: Relig in Art Exhib, Birmingham, 66; Callaway Gardens Ann, Ga, 66, 69 & 70; Birmingham Festival Arts, 72.
Teaching: Instr drawing, painting & sculpture, U S Army Aviation Ctr, Fort Rucker, Ala, 65-71.
Positions: Artist-in-residence, Proj Impact, Troy, Goshen & Union Springs Schs, 70-71, Proj Impact, 71-72.
Awards: Best of show for painting, Contemp Southern Arts Festival, 64; Ala Art League Mus Purchase Award, 68; best of show & purchase prize for sculpture, Ocala Art Asn, Fla, 70.
Bibliography: Larry Godwin, artist-in-residence, State Printer, 71.
Mailing Address: R F D 1, Brundidge, AL 36010.

GOEDIKE, SHIRL
  Painter
Preferred Media: Oils.
b Los Angeles, Calif, 23.
Study & Training: Univ Calif, Los Angeles; Art Ctr Sch, Los Angeles.
Work in Public Collections: Los Angeles Co Mus Art; Pasadena Mus Art; Palm Springs Mus; Home Savings & Loan, Los Angeles; Seattle Nat Bank, Wash.
Exhibitions: Los Angeles Co Mus, 55-56; Stanford Univ, 56; one-man show, Palace Legion of Honor, San Francisco, Calif, 59; Santa Barbara Biennial, Santa Barbara Mus & nat tour, 59; 26th Biennial, Corcoran Gallery Art, Washington, D C.
Awards: Los Angeles Co Art Mus Purchase Prize, 55; All-City Art Festival Hon Mention, Home Savings & Loan Los Angeles, 56 & 57; first hon mention, James D Phelan Award, 57.
Bibliography: Alfred Frankenstein (auth), article, In: San Francisco Chronicle, 60; Arthur Millier (auth), article, In: Los Angeles Herald Exam, 66; Henry Seldis (auth), Los Angeles Times, 72.
Mailing Address: c/o Ankrum Gallery, 657 N La Cienega Blvd, Los Angeles, CA 90069.

GOERITZ, MATHIAS
  Sculptor, Designer
Preferred Media: Concrete, Steel.
b Danzig, Ger, Apr 4, 15.
Study & Training: Friedrich-Wilhelms Univ, PhD; Kunstgewerbeschule, Berlin-Charlottenburg.
Work in Public Collections: Steel structure, Mus Arte Mod, Mexico City, Mex; wood sculptures, Kunsthalle Hamburg, Ger, Riverside

Mus, New York, N Y & Mus Nat Bezalel, Jerusalem, Israel; bronze sculpture, Univ Ariz Art Gallery, Tucson.
Commissions: El Eco (total environ), comn by Daniel Mont, Exp Mus, Mexico City, 52-53; environ sculptures, Towers of Satellite City, comn by L Barragán & M Pani, 57, Towers of Automex, comn by R Legorreta, Toluca, Mex, 63-64, & Pyramid of Mixcoac, PIAC, Mexico City, 70-72; Route of Friendship (hwy environ), Mex Olympic Comt, Mexico City, 68.
Exhibitions: Art of Assemblage, Mus Mod Art, New York, 61; Pittsburgh Int Exhib, Carnegie Inst, 61; Concrete Poetry?, Stedelijk Mus, Amsterdam, Holland, 70-71; Art and Science, Tel Aviv Mus, Israel, 71; 11th Biennial, Open-air Mus Sculpture, Middelheim, Belg, 71.
Teaching: Prof basic design, Nat Univ Mex, 54-
Positions: Dir Sch Fine Arts & Indust Design, Iberoamericano Univ, Mex, 57-60; ed & auth, art sect Arquitectura-Mex, 59-
Awards: Artist-in-residence, Aspen Inst Humanistic Studies, Aspen, Colo, 70-72.
Bibliography: Olivia Zuñiga (auth), Mathias Goeritz, Ed Intercontinental, Mexico City, 63; Clive B Smith (auth), Builders in the sun, Architectural, New York, 67; H Harvard Arnason (auth), History of modern art, Abrams, New York, 68.
Publications: Illusr, Los amantes y la noche, ed Eco, Mex, 53; auth & illusr of books & articles in several mags.
Mailing Address: Calle Dr Manuel Mazari, 112, Cuernavaca, Morelos, Mexico.

GOETZ, PETER HENRY
  Painter, Lecturer
Preferred Media: Watercolors.
b Slavgorod, Russia, Sept 8, 17; Can citizen.
Study & Training: Waterloo Col, 45; Doon Sch Fine Art, with F H Varley; study watercolor in Japan.
Work in Public Collections: London Pub Libr & Art Mus, Ont; Sarnia Pub Libr & Art Mus, Ont; Kitchener Waterloo Art Gallery; Univ Waterloo, Ont; Univ Guelph, Ont.
Commissions: Series of twelve paintings from around the world, Waterloo Co Health Bldg, 65; painting of Parliament bldgs, Nat Club, Toronto, 67; The Peace Tower, Sen John B Aird, Toronto, 69; painting of Budapest, CFTO-TV, Toronto, 69; View of Prague, Toronto Stock Exchange, 69.
Exhibitions: Royal Can Acad; Ont Soc Artists; Can Soc Painters Watercolour; Nat Gallery Ottawa; Am Watercolor Soc, New York, N Y, 72.
Teaching: Lectured & demonstrated adult educ classes throughout Ont for Dept Educ.
Awards: Grand prize, Que Nat Exhib; watercolour prize, Western Ont Exhib; first prize, Brmpton Ann Exhib.
Memberships: Ont Soc Artists; Can Soc Painters Watercolour; Centro Studi & Scambi Int, Rome; fel Int Inst Arts & Letters; Am Fedn Art.
Dealer: Shaw-Rimmington Gallery, 20 Birch Ave, Toronto, Ont, Can.
Mailing Address: 784 Avondale Ave, Kitchener, Ont, Can.

GOETZ, RICHARD VERNON
  Painter, Educator
Preferred Media: Oils.
b Lawrenceburg, Tenn, Apr 6, 15.
Study & Training: Okla City Univ; Univ Okla; Cape Sch Art; Nat Acad Design; Art Stud League New York; with Robert Brackman, Henry Henche, George Bridgman, Sidney Dickenson & Jonas Lee.
Work in Public Collections: Butler Inst Am Art, Youngstown, Ohio; Okla Art Ctr, Oklahoma City; Okla Hist Soc, Oklahoma City; Fort Smith Art Ctr, Ark.
Exhibitions: Butler Inst Am Art, 68; Allied Artists Am, 68; Okla Mus Art, 68; Am Artists Prof League, 71; Okla-Tex Spring Ann, 72.
Teaching: Dir, Goetz Art Sch—Oklahoma City, 46- & Goetz Art Sch Santa Fe, 71-; co-dir, Malden Bridge Art Sch, New York, 64-71.
Awards: Best in Show, Tex-Okla Spring Show, 68 & Am Artists Prof League, 69; McDonnough Award, Butler Inst Am Art, 68.
Memberships: Am Artists Prof League.
Publications: Auth, Painting a still life, Am Artist, 68.
Dealer: Grand Central Art Galleries, Vanderbilt & 44th St, New York, NY 10017.
Mailing Address: 800 N E 21st St, Oklahoma City, OK 73105.

GOFF, LLOYD LOZES
  Painter, Illustrator
Preferred Media: Mixed Media.
b Dallas, Tex, Mar 29, 19.
Study & Training: Louis Comfort Tiffany Found Fel, Daniel Schnakenberg Scholar, Art Stud League with Nicolaides; Univ New Mex.
Work in Public Collections: Whitney Mus Am Art, New York, N Y; Wadsworth Atheneum, Hartford, Conn; West Point Mus, N Y; Dallas Mus Fine Arts, Dallas, Tex; Museo Nacionale de Bellas Artes, Mexico City, Mex.

Commissions: Mural (with Paul Cadmus), U S Embassy, Ottawa, Can, 38; South American Beauty (oil panel), Helena Rubinstein, New York, 39; Delta C Before Fencing (oil on canvas), U S Treas, Post Office, Cooper, Tex, 40; Planning The Route (oil on canvas), US Treas, Post Office, Hollis, Okla, 42; home mural (Duco on wall), Sailtops Farm, Rudgwick, Sussex, Eng, 70.

Exhibitions: Whitney Mus Ann, New York, 38-43; San Francisco Art Asn Exhibs, 41, 42 & 43; Carnegie Inst, Pittsburgh, Pa, 43; Acad Art Gallery, New York, 54 & 55; Am Artists & Water Conserv, Nat Gallery, Washington, D C, 72.

Teaching: Assoc prof art, painting & drawing, Univ New Mex, 44-47.

Bibliography: Ten Eyk Gardner (auth), History of watercolor painting in America, Reinhold, 66.

Memberships: Life mem, Art Stud League, New York; Artists Equity Asn N Y; N Mex chap, Artists Equity Asn, Inc.

Publications: Auth-illusr, Run Sandpiper Run, Lothrop, 57 & Fly Redwing Fly, 59.

Dealer: ROKO Gallery, 90 E Tenth St, New York, NY 10003.

Mailing Address: 136 W 75th St, New York, NY 10023.

GOINGS, RALPH LADELL
Painter

Preferred Media: Oils, Watercolors.

b Corning, Calif, May 9, 28.

Study & Training: Calif Col Arts & Crafts, Oakland, BFA; Sacramento State Col, MA.

Work in Public Collections: Neue Galerie, Aachen, Ger.

Commissions: Flower Painting, Florist Transworld Delivery, Inc, 71.

Exhibitions: Directions 2: Aspects of a New Realism, Milwaukee Art Ctr, 69; Radical Realism, Mus Contemp Art, Chicago, 71; Sharp-Focus Realism, Sidney Janis Gallery, New York, N Y, 72; New American Realism, Gallery Gestlo, Bremen, Ger, 72; Documenta 5, Kassel, Ger, 72.

Bibliography: John Lloyd Taylor (auth), Directions 3: eight artists, Milwaukee Art Ctr, 70-; Ivan Karp (auth), Rent is the only reality, Arts Mag, Vol 46, No 3; Dave Hickey (auth), Sharp focus realism at Janis, Art in Am, Vol 60, No 2.

Mailing Address: c/o Ivan C Karp, 469 West Broadway, New York, NY 10012.

GOLD, ALBERT
Painter, Educator

Preferred Media: Oils, Watercolors.

b Philadelphia, Pa, Oct 31, 16.

Study & Training: Philadelphia Mus Sch Art, 35-39, dipl.

Work in Public Collections: New York Pub Libr, N Y; Libr of Cong, Washington, D C; Pentagon, Washington, D C; Philadelphia Mus Art, Pa; Univ Pa Collection.

Commissions: Twelve paintings of Pa, Gimbel Brothers, 47-48; murals, Bur Agr; plus many others in pub & private collections.

Exhibitions: Nat Acad Design, New York, N Y, 40-68; Pa Acad Fine Arts Ann, 40-68; Artists for Victory, Metrop Mus Art, New York, 42; Mus Galliera, Paris, France, 44.

Teaching: Prof illus & materials of artist, Philadelphia Col Art, 46-, dir illus dept, 59-

Awards: Prix de Rome, Am Acad Rome, 42; Tiffany Found grant, 47-48; Sesnan Gold Medal for landscape, Pa Acad Fine Arts, 50.

Bibliography: Henry C Pitz (auth), Albert Gold, painter, draughtsman, Am Artist, 11/56.

Memberships: Philadelphia Watercolor Club; Philadelphia Art Alliance (past chmn, 46-72, chmn watercolor, 49-65); Artists Equity; Am Watercolor Soc.

Research: History of American illustration.

Art Interests: Representational, people & urban aspects in art.

Publications: Illusr, Our Philadelphia, 50; illusr, The commodore, 54; illusr, This was our war, 63; illusr, The captive rabbi, 65.

Dealer: 252 Gallery, 252 S 16th St, Philadelphia, PA 19103.

Mailing Address: 6814 McCallum St, Philadelphia, PA 19119.

GOLD, FAY
Painter

Preferred Media: Oils, Watercolors, Ink, Collage.

b Brooklyn, N Y.

Study & Training: Elmer Hayley-Lever Studio; Parsons Int; Master Inst United Arts Riverside Mus; Art Stud League New York, N Y.

Work in Public Collections: Eight drawings, Libr Performing Arts, Lincoln Ctr; watercolor, Evansville Mus, Ind.

Exhibitions: One-man shows, Norlyst Gallery, 46, Roke Gallery, 49 & 51, Village Art Ctr, 64 & John J Myers Gallery, New York, 64.

Awards: Munic Art Ctr, 39; Yaddo grant, Saratoga Springs, N Y, 49; John J Karpnick Prize, Audubon Artists, 64.

Memberships: Life mem Art Stud League New York; Am Watercolor Soc.

Mailing Address: Box 256, Times Square Station, New York, NY 10036.

GOLD, LEAH
Painter, Printmaker

Preferred Media: Casein, Graphics, Stained Glass.

b New York, N Y.

Study & Training: With Ruth Reeves & Hans Hofmann.

Work in Public Collections: Birmingham Mus Art, Ala.

Exhibitions: Int Watercolor Exhib, Brooklyn Mus, N Y, 52; Int Airpost Exhib, Nat Philatelic Mus, 54; Am Jewish Tercentenary Exhib, Riverside Mus, Corcoran Gallery Art, Albright-Knox Art Gallery, Cleveland Mus Art & Dallas Mus Fine Arts, 54-55; Second Biennial Exhib, Birmingham Mus Art, 56; Nat Print Exhib, Brooklyn Mus, 56.

Awards: Mrs John T Pratt Prize for woodcut, Nat Asn Women Artists, 57; prize for casein painting, Painters & Sculptors Soc N J 18th Ann, 59; award for stained glass sculpture, Brooklyn Soc Artists, 59.

Memberships: Artists Equity Asn New York (bd dirs, 65-); Am Soc Contemp Artists (asst treas & graphics jury, 71-); Nat Asn Women Artists; Painters & Sculptors Soc N J; League Present Day Artists (chmn mem comt, 70-).

Mailing Address: 330 W 28th St, New York, NY 10001.

GOLDBERG, CHAIM LEIB
Painter, Engraver

Preferred Media: Oils, Watercolors.

b Kazimierz, Poland, Mar 20, 17.

Study & Training: Art High Sch-Krakow, with Zbigniew Pronashko; Acad Fine Arts-Warsaw, with Tadeusz Pruszkowski; Govt Poland fel study in Paris, 47.

Work in Public Collections: Metrop Mus Art, New York, N Y; Nat Collection Fine Art, Washington, D C; Mus Mod Art, New York; Mus Fine Art, Boston, Mass; Mus Petit Palais, Geneva, Switz.

Commissions: Monument, Polanica Zdroj, Govt Poland, 54; mosaic fountain, 56 & embossed copper door, 57, Hotel Ramat Aviv, Tel Aviv, Israel; engravings, Govt Israel, 59-64.

Exhibitions: Mus Fine Art, Moscow, U S S R, 43; Nat Mus Fine Art, Warsaw, 50-52; one-man shows, Mus Yad Labanim, Israel, 66; Lys Gallery, New York, 67 & St John's Univ, New York, 71; Am Cong, Washington, D C, 72.

Awards: Silver Medal, Artists Guild-Novosibirsk, 44.

Bibliography: I Luden (auth), articles, In: Art Mag, Israel, 66; D Shirey (auth), rev, In: New York Times, 71; Isaac Bashevis Singer (auth), Mem Catalog, 72.

Mailing Address: 141-18 72nd Dr, Flushing, NY 11367.

GOLDBERG, JOSEPH WALLACE
Painter

Preferred Media: Oils.

b Seattle, Wash, Apr 27, 47.

Work in Public Collections: Art Gallery Greater Victoria, B C; Carpenter Art Galleries, Dartmouth Col, Hanover, N H; Henry Art Gallery, Univ Wash, Seattle; Whatcom Mus Hist & Art, Bellingham, Wash; Seattle Pub Libr.

Exhibitions: Gov Invitational, State Capitol Mus, Olympia, Wash, 70; Northwest Ann, Seattle Art Mus, 70; San Francisco Centennial Exhib, 71; Northwest Drawings, Henry Art Gallery, 72.

Mailing Address: c/o Francine Seders Gallery, 6701 Greenwood N, Seattle, WA 98103.

GOLDBERG, MICHAEL
Painter

b New York, N Y, Dec 24, 24.

Study & Training: Art Stud League New York, 38-42; City Col New York, 40-42; Hans Hofmann Sch Art, 41-42; Art Stud League New York, 46, with Jose de Creeft; City Col New York, 46-47; Hans Hofmann Sch Art, 48-50.

Work in Public Collections: Mus Mod Art, Israel; Art Inst Chicago, Ill; Dayton Art Inst, Ohio; Nat Gallery Art, Washington, D C; Mus Western Art, Tokyo, Japan; plus many others.

Exhibitions: Am Fedn Arts, 65; Am Art Gallery, Copenhagen, Denmark, 65; Smithsonian Inst, 66; Mus Mod Art, New York, 68; Corcoran Bienale, 69; plus many other group & one-man shows.

Teaching: Instr art, Univ Calif, Berkeley, 61-62; Yale Univ, 67; Univ Minn, 68.

Dealer: Paley & Lowe, Inc, 59 Wooster St, New York, NY 10012.

Mailing Address: 222 Bowery, New York, NY 10012.

GOLDBERG, NORMAN LEWIS
Writer, Art Historian

b Nashville, Tenn, Feb 10, 06.

Study & Training: Univ Toledo, BS; Vanderbilt Univ, MD.

Collections Arranged: Landscapes of the Norwich School, Cummer Gallery Art, Jacksonville, Fla, 67.

Teaching: Lectr, Victoria & Albert Mus, London, Eng, Castle Mus, Norwich, Eng, Fine Arts Ctr, Nashville, Tenn, Vanderbilt Univ, Isaac Delgado Mus Art, Cummer Gallery Art & Metrop Mus Art, 61-69.

Memberships: Col Art Asn Am.
Research: Norwich School of Painting, specializing in John Crome, the Elder and John Sell Cotman.
Publications: Auth, On John Crome & connoisseurship: the present day problem, 63 & auth, America honors the Norwich School, 67, Connoisseur; auth, Landscapes of the Norwich School, Cummer Gallery Art, 67; auth, Crome and some Cromesque mimicries, Times Literary Suppl, 69; auth, John Crome, the Elder, N Y Univ Press, 72; plus others.
Mailing Address: 721 Brightwaters Blvd N E, St Petersburg, FL 33704.

GOLDBERG, RAYMOND ROBERT
Painter, Instructor
Preferred Media: Watercolors.
b Rockville Centre, N Y, Jan 9, 11.
Study & Training: Pratt Inst Sch Fine & Appl Arts, cert spec studies, with Anna Fisher & John Pike.
Work in Public Collections: Watercolors, Abe Sharpe Found, Nashua, N H, Treadway Gallery, Lebanon, Pa, Gallery North, Setauket, N Y & Gregory Mus, Hicksville, N Y; graphic, Trencher Gallery, Garden City, N Y.
Commissions: Watercolors, San Georgio Bldg, Hershey Corp, Pa, 66, Old Courthouse Bldg, Dr Luther Long, Lebanon, 66, Race Horses, Quentin Riding Club, Pa, 70, Landscape, pres Fed Builders, Inc, Westbury, N Y, 71 & portrait, comn by Larry G Brown, Fuchinobe, Japan, 71.
Exhibitions: Am Artists Prof League Representational Traveling Show, 69 & Grand Nat, 72; Nat Art League Show, N Y World's Fair Bldg, 68; Nat Arts Club Watercolor Exhib, New York, N Y, 69; Salmagundi Club Ann Watercolor Exhib, New York, 71.
Teaching: Instr adult educ, Rockville Ctr High Sch, 67-; demonstr & lectr for art socs N Y & Pa, 68-; scholar-in-residence, Bd Coop Educ Serv, Nassau Co, N Y, 70-
Positions: Artist & adminr, Raymond R Goldberg Advert, Rockville Ctr, 45-; chmn art socs comt, Nassau Co Off Cult Develop, 72-
Awards: First prize for St George's Church, Malverne Artists Long Island, 69; first prize for Home, Salmagundi Club, 71; second prize for The House, Am Artists Prof League, 72.
Memberships: Salmagundi Club (mem entertainment comt, 68-); fel Am Artists Prof League; Nat Art League (chmn exhibs, 71-); Malverne Artists Long Island; Art League Nassau Co (past pres & adv, 65-).
Mailing Address: 126 Princeton Rd, Rockville Centre, NY 11570.

GOLDBERG, VIRGINIA EAGAN
Painter, Illustrator
Preferred Media: Oils.
b Lebanon, Pa, Feb 27, 14.
Study & Training: Univ Buffalo; also privately with Florence Hauer, Lebanon, Raymond R Goldberg, George Tschamber & John Pike.
Work in Public Collections: Treadway Gallery, Lebanon; Trencher Gallery, N Y; also in many private collections.
Commissions: Portraits, comn by H W Arnold, Wheaton, Md, 68; watercolor still life, comn by Dr George Jaspin, Manhasset, N Y, 69; watercolor landscape, comn by E F Nasierowski, Lynbrook, N Y, 70; oil, flowers, comn by Mrs N Koopman, Cornwall, Pa, 71.
Exhibitions: Nassau Co Cult Develop—Bankers Trust Open, Long Beach Art Asn Nat Open, 71; Malverne Artists Long Island Open, 72; Nat Art League Ann, 72; Am Artists Prof League Grand Nat, 72.
Teaching: Instr oils & watercolor, art weekends by Raymond R Goldberg, Mass & N Y, 69-; instr watercolor, Adult Educ, Rockville Ctr High Sch, N Y, 71-
Positions: Fashion illusr & copy writer, Raymond R Goldberg Advert, Rockville Ctr, 48-; art dir, Trencher's, Garden City, N Y, 50-; asst chmn Art Socs Comt, Nassau Co Off Cult Develop, 72-
Awards: First prize for oil Retired, 69 & second prize for From the Bride's Table, 72, Long Beach Art Asn; third prize for oil Day of Rest, Malverne Artists Long Island, 71.
Memberships: Fel Am Artists Prof League; Nat Art League (exhib co-chmn, 71-); Art League Nassau Co (ed newslett, 65-71); Malverne Artists Long Island (exhib reception hostess, 65-); Long Beach Art Asn (historian & bd mem, 68-).
Publications: Illusr, Long Island Cath Newspaper, Bridal Issue, 72.
Mailing Address: 126 Princeton Rd, Rockville Centre, NY 11570.

GOLDBERGER, MR & MRS EDWARD
Collectors, Patrons.
Collection: Modern sculpture; abstract and modern art.
Mailing Address: 1367 Flagler Dr, Mamaroneck, NY 10543.

GOLDEN, LIBBY
Printmaker, Painter
b New York, N Y, Nov 18, 13.
Study & Training: Cooper Union Art Sch, dipl, 34; Hunter Col, N Y

Univ & Art Stud League New York, 34-42; Pratt Graphic Arts Inst, 58-60.
Work in Public Collections: Philadelphia Mus Art, Pa; Detroit Inst Arts, Mich; Grand Rapids Mus Art, Mich; Colby Col Mus Art, Mass; U S State Dept.
Exhibitions: Silvermine Guild, Conn, 66-68; Boston Printmakers, Boston Mus Fine Arts, Mass, 66-69; Northwest Printmakers, Seattle Mus Art & Portland Mus Art, 68 & 69; Audubon Artists, New York, 70 & 71; Colorprint, U S A, Lubbock, Tex, 71; plus five one-man shows.
Awards: Print prizes, Mich State Fair, 65-69 & Nat Acad Design, New York, 69; purchase prize, Mich Painters & Printmakers.
Dealer: Arwin Galleries, 222 W Grand River, Detroit, MI 48226.
Mailing Address: 26764 York Rd, Huntington Woods, MI 48070.

GOLDHAMER, CHARLES
Painter, Instructor
b Philadelphia, Pa, Aug 21, 03.
Study & Training: Ont Col Art.
Work in Public Collections: Art Gallery Toronto; Hart House, Univ Toronto; War Records, Nat Gallery Art.
Exhibitions: Coronation, 37; Tate Gallery Art, London, 38; Gloucester, 39; Can Soc Painters in Watercolour, 39; War Art, Nat Gallery Can, 46; plus others.
Teaching: Dir art, Cent Tech Sch, Toronto, 23-69.
Positions: Official war artist, RCAF, 43-46.
Awards: Adamson prize for life drawing, Ont Col Art.
Memberships: Ont Soc Artists; Can Soc Graphic Art; Can Soc Painters in Watercolour (past pres); Arts & Lett Club Toronto.
Mailing Address: 1 Brule Gardens, Toronto, Ont, Can.

GOLDIN, LEON
Painter, Educator
Preferred Media: Oils, Gouache.
b Chicago, Ill, Jan 16, 23.
Study & Training: Art Inst Chicago, BFA, 48; Univ Iowa, MFA, 50.
Work in Public Collections: Brooklyn Mus, N Y; Addison Gallery Am Art, Andover, Mass; City Mus St Louis, Mo; Pa Acad Fine Arts, Philadelphia; Munson-Williams-Proctor Inst, Utica, N Y.
Exhibitions: American Painting at Mid-Century, Metropolitan Mus Art, New York, N Y, 51; American Drawings, Mus Mod Art, New York, 56; Corcoran Gallery Art Biennial, Washington, D C, 62; Carnegie Inst Int, Pittsburgh, Pa, 64; Pa Acad Fine Arts Ann, 66.
Teaching: Instr painting & drawing, Calif Col Arts & Crafts, 50-55; instr painting & drawing, Cooper Union, 61-64; assoc prof painting & drawing, Columbia Univ, 64-
Awards: Prix de Rome, Am Acad Rome, 55; Guggenheim fel, 59; award in painting, Nat Inst Arts & Lett, 68.
Dealer: Kraushaar Gallery, 1055 Madison Ave, New York, NY 10021.
Mailing Address: 438 W 116th St, New York, NY 10027.

GOLDOWSKY, NOAH
Art Dealer
b Minsk, Russia, Jan 16, 09; U S citizen.
Positions: Dir, Noah Goldowsky Gallery.
Specialty of Gallery: Twentieth century American art.
Mailing Address: 1078 Madison Ave, New York, NY 10028.

GOLDSCHMIDT, LUCIEN
Art Dealer
b Brussels, Belg, Mar 3, 12.
Positions: Dir, Lucien Goldschmidt, Inc; v pres, Art Dealers Asn Am, Inc.
Specialty of Gallery: Continental European art, circa 1500-1950, mainly prints and drawings.
Publications: Co-auth, Unpublished correspondence of Henri de Toulouse-Lautrec, 69.
Mailing Address: 1117 Madison Ave, New York, NY 10028.

GOLDSMITH, BARBARA
Writer, Art Critic
b New York, N Y, May 18, 31.
Study & Training: Wellesley Col, BA, 53; Columbia Univ, MA, 56.
Positions: Ed, Town & Country Mag & New York Mag; sr ed, Harper's Bazaar, 68-
Awards: New York Times Reporting Award, 68.
Memberships: Whitney Mus Am Art; Mus Mod Art (jr coun, 60-); Mus City New York (pres coun, 70-); Park Asn City New York (trustee, 63-).
Publications: Auth, articles, In: New York Mag, Esquire, Harpers Bazaar, McCalls & New York Times Mag Sect; plus others.
Mailing Address: 655 Park Ave, New York, NY 10021.

GOLDSMITH, C GERALD
Collector, Patron
b Orlando, Fla, Aug 2, 28.
Study & Training: Univ Mich; Harvard Univ Bus Sch.

Memberships: Friends of Whitney Mus Am Art; Am Fedn Arts.
Collection: Contemporary American art.
Mailing Address: 540 Madison Ave, New York, NY 10022.

GOLDSMITH, MORTON RALPH
Collector, Patron
b Cleveland, Ohio, Apr 26, 82.
Study & Training: Harvard Univ, BA.
Collection: Includes Matisse, Rousseau, Utrillo, Gris, Delacroix, Courbet, Rouault, Klee, Moro, Monticello, Derain, Maillol, Daumier, Cezanne, Orozco, Braque, Beckmann, Pascin, Redon, Vuillard, Renoir, Masson, Feininger, Marin, Weber, Kuniyoshi, Knaths, Hartley, Gatch, Bombois, Baziotes, Eilshemius, Kane, Dickinson, Spencer, Fiene, Avery, Bluemner, Grigoviev, Brook, Rivera, Hokusai, Mouillot, Blakelock, Hidalgo, Hogarth, Legrand, Maurer, Merida, Manigault, Hans Moller, Paalen, Turner, Bonhomme, and many others including American contemporaries.
Mailing Address: 2 Stonehouse Rd, Scarsdale, NY 10583.

GOLDSTEIN, MILTON
Printmaker, Educator
b Holyoke, Mass, Nov 14, 14.
Study & Training: Art Stud League New York, 46-49; also with Harry Sternberg, Morris Kantor & Will Barnet.
Work in Public Collections: Philadelphia Mus Art, Pa; Metrop Mus Art, New York, N Y; Mus Mod Art, New York; Smithsonian Nat Mus, Washington, D C; Brooklyn Mus, N Y.
Commissions: Collection of etchings for Europe & U S A (200 ed), Int Graphic Arts Soc, New York, 52; collection of etchings (150 ed), Book Find Club, New York, 54.
Exhibitions: Libr of Cong, Washington, D C, 48; Smithsonian Inst, Washington, 55; Outstanding Prints Produced in America, Brooks Mem Mus, Memphis, Tenn, 59; Am Printmakers in Italy, sponsored by Boston Pub Libr, Mass, 60; Masters Engraving Show, Queens Col, New York, 64.
Teaching: Prof printmaking, Adelphi Univ, 53-
Awards: Guggenheim fel, 50; first prize & purchase award, Philadelphia Mus, Pa, 52; first prize & purchase award, Nat Print Show, Western N Mex Univ, 71.
Bibliography: Milton Goldstein (auth), How to make an etching (film), Almanac Films, 51; Carl Zigrosser (auth), Fine prints, Crown, 60; Jules Heller (auth), Printmaking today, Holt, 60.
Memberships: Soc Am Graphic Artists (coun, 72); fel Royal Soc Arts, London; Am Color Print Soc; Kappa Pi (sponsor, Adelphi Univ, 60); Print Club.
Publications: Auth, A new color etching process, Everyday Art; auth, Reprint, Design Mag, 55.
Dealer: Weyhe Gallery, 794 Lexington Ave, New York, NY 10021.
Mailing Address: 56-16 219th St, Bayside, NY 11364.

GOLDSTONE, MR & MRS HERBERT
Collectors
Collection: Contemporary art.
Mailing Address: 25 Sutton Pl S, New York, NY 10022.

GOLDWATER, ROBERT
Art Historian
b New York, N Y, Nov 23, 07.
Study & Training: Columbia Col, BA, 29; Harvard Univ, MA, 31; New York Univ, PhD, 37.
Collections Arranged: Bambara Sculpture, 60; Senufo Sculpture, 63.
Teaching: Instr fine arts & art hist, New York Univ, 34-39; from asst prof to prof fine arts & art hist, Queens Col, 39-57; prof fine arts, New York Univ Inst Fine Arts, 57-
Positions: Bk rev ed, Col Art Asn Art Bull, 44-47; ed, Am Fedn Arts Mag of Art, 47-53; dir, Mus Primitive Art, 57-62, chmn admin comt, 62-
Research: West African sculpture; modern painting and sculpture, 1875 to the present; criticism.
Publications: Auth, Primitivism in modern painting, 38; auth, Gauguin, 57; auth, Bambara sculpture from the Western Sudan, 60; auth, Senufo sculpture from West Africa, 64; auth, What is modern sculpture?, 69.
Mailing Address: 347 W 20th St, New York, NY 10011.

GOLLIN, MR & MRS JOSHUA A
Collectors, Patrons
Mr Gollin b New York, N Y, Aug 16, 05.
Study & Training: Mr Gollin, Washington Univ.
Memberships: Sustaining mem, Metrop Mus Art, Mus Mod Art, Solomon R Guggenheim Mus & Am Fedn Arts.
Art Interests: Gave two prizes at 1964 Biennale in Venice for a painter and a sculptor under 40 years of age.
Collection: Sculpture of the past fifty years and African primitive carvings.
Mailing Address: 1025 Fifth Ave, New York, NY 10028.

GOLUB, LEON ALBERT
Painter
Preferred Media: Acrylics.
b Chicago, Ill, Jan 23, 22.
Study & Training: Univ Chicago, BA(hist art), 42; Art Inst Chicago Sch, BFA, 49, MFA, 50.
Work in Public Collections: Mus Mod Art, New York, N Y; Art Inst Chicago, Ill; Nat Collection Fine Arts, Smithsonian Inst, Washington, D C; Univ Calif, Berkeley; Nat Gallery Victoria, Melbourne.
Exhibitions: Carnegie Int, Pittsburgh, Pa, 54, 64 & 67; New Images of Man, Mus Mod Art, New York, 59; Sao Paulo Biennial, 62; Second Biennial Int Deporte Ballas Artes, Madrid, Spain, 69; Chicago Imagist Art, Mus Contemp Art, Chicago, 72; plus many oneman shows.
Teaching: Prof art, Livingston Col, Rutgers Univ, 70-
Awards: Ford Found grant, 60; Cassandra Found grant, 67; Guggenheim Found grant, 68.
Bibliography: Henry McBride (auth), Americans looking East, looking West, 5/54 & Max Kozloff (auth), The late Roman Empire in the light of Napalm, 11/70, Art News; Irving Sandler (auth), An interview with Leon Golub, Arts Mag, 2/70.
Publications: Auth, Bombs & helicopters, the art of Nancy Spero, Caterpillar I, 67; auth, Regarding the Lehman & Rockefeller gifts to the Metropolitan Museum, 11/70 & auth, Utopia/antiutopia, 5/72, Artforum.
Dealers: Galerie Darathea Speyer, 6 rue Jacques Callot, Paris 6e, France; Bienville Gallery, 539 Bienville, New Orleans, LA 70130.
Mailing Address: 171 W 71st St, New York, NY 10023.

GOLUBIC, THEODORE ROY
Sculptor
Preferred Media: Stone, Plastics, Metals.
b Lorain, Ohio, Dec 9, 28.
Study & Training: Miami Univ, BFA; Art Stud League New York, with John Corbino; Univ Notre Dame, MFA, asst to Ivan Mestrovic.
Commissions: Corpus, bronze for main altar, Little Flower Church, South Bend, Ind, 58; Angels in Mourning (with Ivan Mestrovic), St Joseph the Worker Church, Gary, Ind, 60; Circe, bronze bas relief panel, comn by Mrs H Fredrick Willkie, Elwood, Ind, 62; Crypt Relief Series, Rock of Ages Corp, Barre, Vt, 65-67; Nativity, limestone heroic relief, Church of Nativity, Dubuque, Iowa, 68.
Exhibitions: Art U S A, Madison Sq Garden, New York, N Y, 58; 134th Ann Exhib, Nat Acad Design, New York, 59; 2nd Biennial Am Painting & Sculpture, Detroit Inst Arts, 60; 34th Ann Exhib, Nat Sculpture Soc, New York, 67; Art for 1970, Southern Calif Expo, Del Mar, 70.
Teaching: Guest instr sculpture, Univ Notre Dame, summer 59; guest instr, Art Sch Air of Educ TV & ABC-TV, Elkhart, Ind, 62-63.
Positions: Sculpture consult, Rock of Ages Corp, 65-67; artist-in-residence, Roswell Mus & Art Ctr, N Mex, 71-72.
Memberships: Am Soc Aesthetics; Col Art Asn Am; Liturgical Art Soc; Croatian Acad Am.
Publications: Contribr, guest ed, 3/67 & cover & In art there is victory, 4/07, Am Art Stonc.
Mailing Address: 8626 N 37th Ave, Phoenix, AZ 85021.

GOMEZ-QUIROZ, JUAN MANUEL
Painter, Printmaker
Preferred Media: Oils, Acrylics, Intaglio.
b Santiago, Chile, Feb 20, 39.
Study & Training: R I Sch Design, Fulbright fel, 62-63; Yale Univ, Fulbright fel, 63-64; invited by Gabor Peterdi; Pratt Graphic Art Ctr, Pan Am Union fel, 64-66.
Work in Public Collections: Metrop Mus Art, New York, N Y; Boston Mus Fine Art, Mass; Mus Mod Art, New York; Libr Cong, Washington, D C; Brooklyn Mus Art, N Y.
Exhibitions: Magnct New York, Bonino Gallery, New York, 64; Modern Painter as Printmaker, Mus Mod Art, 64; 14th-17th Nat Print Shows, Brooklyn Mus, 64-70; 200 years of Latin American Art, Yale Univ Art Gallery, 66; Int Print Exhib, Montreal Mus Fine Art, 71; plus one-man shows & other exhibs.
Teaching: Lectr studio art, Univ Calif, Santa Barbara, 67-68; lectr studio art, N Y Community Col, 69-70; adj prof studio art, N Y Univ, 69-
Awards: Salon Alumnos First Prize, Univ Chile, 60; Guggenheim Found fel painting, 66.
Bibliography: Cleve Gray (auth), Experiment grows in Brooklyn, Arts in Am, No 5, 66; Gabor Peterdi (auth), Printmaking, Macmillan, rev ed, 71; Gordon Brown (auth), article, In: Arts Mag, 4/71.
Dealer: Alonzo Gallery, 26 E 63rd St, New York, NY 10021.
Mailing Address: 44 Grand St, New York, NY 10013.

GOMEZ-SICRE, JOSE
Art Administrator, Art Critic
b Matanzas, Cuba, 16.
Study & Training: Univ Havana, dipl law, 39; Columbia Univ & New York Univ, 44.
Commissions: (Direction of films) Easter Island; Chancay, the forgotten culture; World of a primitive painter: Jose Antonio Velasquez of Honduras; Manabu Mabe of Brazil paints a picture; Vicus; Art of Central America and Panama; Nine Artists of Puerto Rico; plus others.
Collections Arranged: Permanent Collection of Latin American Contemporary Art & exhib prog, Orgn Am States, 46-; assisted or directed assembling of collections for numerous mus & corp, incl Esso Stand Oil Collection, now property of Lowe Mus Art, Miami Univ.
Teaching: Lect art hist & Latin Am art, cols, univs & mus throughout U S, Latin Am & Europe, 50-
Positions: Art corresp, El Mundo, Norte, Havana & New York, 42-50; organized exhibs Cuban art for mus abroad & assisted in direction foreign & nat exhibs, Havana, 42-45; chief, Visual Arts Unit, Orgn Am States, Washington, D C, 46-
Research: Contemporary Latin American art.
Publications: Auth, Cuban painting today, 44, Spanish master drawings, 51, Museum guide in the U S, Vols I & II, 56 & Four artists of the Americas, 57; auth, Cuevas, Art Int, 11/71.
Mailing Address: Organization of American States, 17th St & Constitution Ave N W, Washington, DC 20006.

GONGORA, LEONEL
Painter, Educator
b Cartago, Colombia.
Study & Training: Wash Univ.
Work in Public Collections: Mus Mod Art, New York, N Y; New York Pub Libr; Wash Univ Permanent Collection, St Louis, Mo; Staatsgalerie Mus, Stuttgart, Ger; Mus Mod Art, Bogotá, Colombia.
Commissions: Paintings, comn by Fernando Gamboa for Mex Pavilion, Expo 67, Montreal, P Q & Expo 70, Osaka, Japan; lithographs, Lublin, Inc, New York, 69, Bank St Atelier, New York, 70 & Aquarius Press, New York, 71.
Exhibitions: Confrontacion 66, Mus Bellas Artes, Mexico City, 66; Am Acad Arts & Lett, New York, 69; First Panam Graphics Biennial, Mus Latertulia, Cali, Colombia, 71; Fourth Int Miniature Print Exhib, AAA Gallery, New York, 71; Third Brit Int Print Biennale, Bradform Mus, Eng, 72.
Teaching: Instr painting & drawing, People's Art Ctr, St Louis, Mo, 56-59; prof painting & drawing, Iberoamericano Univ, Mex, 60-61; prof painting & drawing, Univ Mass, Amherst, 63-
Awards: First prize in drawing, Nat Mus, Bogota, 64; Nat Acad Arts & Lett Award in Painting, New York, 68; Tenth Nat Arte Prize in Lithography, Mus Latertulia, 70.
Bibliography: Toby Joysmith (auth), Two painter poets, The News, Mexico City, 8/69; Roberto Paramo (auth), Góngora, el erotismo en persona, El, Mexico City, 10/71; Anna Mayo (auth), Never on Good Friday, Village Voice, New York, 11/71.
Publications: Illusr, Mass Rev, 67; illusr, Minn Rev, 69; illusr, The intricate land, New Rivers Press, 70; illusr, Poemas podridos, Villa Miseria Press, 72; contribr, Requirements of yesterday and today, Spectrum, 72.
Dealer: Lerner-Misrachi Gallery, 789 Madison Ave, New York, NY 10021.
Mailing Address: P.O. Box 442, Canal St Station, New York, NY 10013.

GONZALES, BOYER
Painter, Educator
Preferred Media: Oils.
b Galveston, Tex, Feb 11, 09.
Study & Training: Univ Va, BS(archit); also with Henry Lee McFee & Yasuo Kuniyoshi.
Work in Public Collections: Rochester Mem Gallery, N Y; Elisabet Ney Mus, Austin, Tex; Witte Mem Mus, San Antonio, Tex; Dallas Mus Fine Arts; Seattle Art Mus.
Exhibitions: New York Worlds Fair, N Y, 39; Pa Acad Fine Arts Ann, 52; Corcoran Gallery Art Biennial, 52; Pac Coast Invitational, 62-63; Artists West of the Mississippi, Colorado Springs Fine Arts Ctr, Colo, 65.
Teaching: Instr painting, Univ Tex, Austin, 39-42, from asst to assoc prof painting, 46-54, chmn dept art, 46-48; prof painting, Univ Wash, 54-, dir sch art, 54-66.
Positions: Dir, Nat Asn Schs Art, 60-62, v pres, 62-63.
Awards: Tex Fine Arts Asn Ann, 51; Tex Exhib Painting & Sculpture, 53; Northwest Ann Exhib Painting, Seattle Art Mus, 56.
Mailing Address: School of Art, University of Washington, Seattle, WA 98195.

GONZALES, CARLOTTA (MRS RICHARD LAHEY)
Painter, Sculptor
Preferred Media: Oils, Stone.
b Wilmington, N C, Apr 3, 10.
Study & Training: Pa Acad Fine Arts; Nat Acad Design; Art Stud League New York; Corcoran Sch Art; Ogunquit Sch Art.
Work in Public Collections: Am Battle Monuments Mem, Honolulu, Hawaii; Francis Bangs Collection, Ogunquit Mus Art, Maine; print collection, Corcoran Gallery Art, Washington, D C; star charts, Nat Geog Soc, Washington; plus many in private collections.
Commissions: The Heavens Above (star charts), 41, state seals, 45 & flags of America, 47, Nat Geog Soc, Washington, D C; mural (battle maps), Am Battle Monuments Commissions, 60; plus many portraits in private collections.
Exhibitions: Nat Acad Design, New York, N Y, 30; Corcoran Gallery Art Biennial, Washington, D C, 36-38; Goucher Col, Towson, Md, 43; Montclair Art Mus, N J, 46; Baltimore Mus, Md, 56.
Teaching: Instr sculpture, Goucher Col, 35-37; instr sculpture, Corcoran Sch Art, 35-45; instr pvt classes, 55-71.
Positions: Staff artist, Nat Geog Soc, 41-47.
Awards: Sculpture, Nat Acad Design, 30.
Memberships: Ogunquit Mus Art.
Publications: Co-auth, Life of Rembrandt & co-auth, Life of Picasso, Stravon.
Mailing Address: 9530 Clark Crossing Rd, Vienna, VA 22180.

GONZALEZ, XAVIER
Painter, Sculptor
b Almeria, Spain, Feb 15, 98; U S citizen.
Study & Training: Art Inst Chicago, 21-23.
Work in Public Collections: Whitney Mus Am Art, New York, N Y; Metrop Mus Art, New York; New Orleans Mus Art, La; Witte Mus, San Antonio, Tex; Mus Fine Arts, Seattle, Wash; plus others.
Exhibitions: Grand Central Moderns, New York, 51-53; Pa Acad Fine Arts, Philadelphia; Carngeie Inst, Pittsburgh, Pa; Brooklyn Mus, N Y; retrospective, Witte Mus, San Antonio, 68; plus many others.
Teaching: Instr art, San Antonio, 24; prof art, Newcomb Col, Tulane Univ, 30; instr art, Brooklyn Mus, 45; lectr, Nat Col Asn, 46; Western Reserve Univ, 53-54; Summer Sch Art, Wellfleet, Mass; lectr, Metrop Mus Art, New York.
Awards: Am Acad Arts & Lett grant; Guggenheim fel, 47; Ford Found grant, 65 plus others.
Memberships: Am Watercolor Soc; Am Nat Acad; Nat Asn Mural Painters (pres, 68).
Publications: Auth, Notes about painting, 55.
Mailing Address: 222 Central Park S, New York, NY 10019.

GOO, BENJAMIN
Sculptor, Painter
Preferred Media: Metals, Stone, Wood.
b Honolulu, Hawaii, July 12, 22.
Study & Training: State Univ Iowa, BFA, 53; Cranbrook Acad Art, MFA, 54; Brera Acad Fine Art, Sch of Marino Marini, Milan, Italy, 54-55.
Work in Public Collections: Roswell Mus & Art Ctr, N Mex; Phoenix Art Mus, Ariz; Tucson Art Ctr, Ariz; Yuma Art Ctr, Ariz; Ariz State Univ Art Collection, Tempe.
Commissions: Two non-objective white marble sculptures, Phoenix Civic Plaza, 71.
Exhibitions: Tenth Anniversary Exhib of Living Am Painters & Sculptors, Silvermine Guild Artists, New Canaan, Conn, 59; 155th Ann Exhib Am Painting & Sculpture, Pa Acad Fine Arts & Detroit Inst Art, 60; 24th Ann Drawing, Print & Sculpture Exhib, San Francisco Mus Art, Calif, 61; Creative Casting: Exhib of Art in Bronze, Mus Contemp Crafts, New York, 63; 73rd Western Ann, Denver Art Mus, Colo, 71.
Teaching: Prof art, Ariz State Univ, 55-; artist-in-residence, Nat Endowment for the Arts, Mesa, Ariz, 72-73.
Awards: First Ann Southwestern States purchase award, Roswell Mus & Art Ctr, 62; Fourth Southwestern Invitational purchase award, Yuma Art Ctr, 69; 21st Ann Tucson Festival Art Exhib, Tucson Art Ctr, 71.
Publications: Auth, Education and the craftsman, 1-2/62 & auth, Dick Seeger: artist craftsman in plastics, 7-8/62, Creative Crafts Mag.
Dealer: Art Wagon Galleries, 7120 Main St, Scottsdale, AZ 85251.
Mailing Address: 5312 Wilkinson Rd, Scottsdale, AZ 85253.

GOOCH, DONALD BURNETTE
Educator, Painter
Preferred Media: Watercolors, Tempera, Oils.
b Bloomingdale, Mich, Oct 17, 07.
Study & Training: Univ Mich Col Archit & Design, BS(educ), with

J P Slusser, 32-39, MA(design), 39; Detroit Art Acad, with C F
Lopez, 33-36; Fontainebleau Sch Fine Arts, France, 37.
Work in Public Collections: Detroit Inst Arts, Mich; Ford Motor
Co, Dearborn, Mich.
Commissions: Seven educ film strips, McGraw Hill, New York, N Y,
49-55; seven illus, Ford Times, Dearborn, 50-60; mural (oil),
Mich Consolidated Gas Co, Detroit, 51; oil painting, Mich Union,
Ann Arbor, 56; literary map of Mich, Mich Coun Teachers Eng,
64.
Exhibitions: San Francisco Watercolor Show, 40; Am Fedn Arts
Traveling Show Selected Watercolors, 41; Pepsi Cola's Painting
of the Year, 46; Pa Acad Fine Art, 47; Terry Nat Exhib, Miami,
Fla, 52.
Teaching: Instr design, Detroit Art Acad, 33-36; prof design, Univ
Mich Col Archit & Design, Ann Arbor, 36-73.
Awards: Alumni prize, collaborative competition, Am Acad Rome,
35; Detroit Inst Arts Founders Prize, 47; faculty res grants,
Horace H Rackham Sch Grad Studies, Univ Mich, 60-65.
Memberships: Ann Arbor Art Asn (pres, 47-48); Mich Watercolor
Soc (dir, 46-50); Mich Acad Sci, Arts & Lett (v chmn fine arts,
51-52); Mich Art Educ Asn (treas, 51-52); fel Int Acad Arts &
Lett.
Research: Pictographic techniques for communication with non-
literates, Nepal, 1961 and 1965.
Publications: Ed, Advertising to the American taste, 56, ed, Search
for certainty in advertising, 59 & ed & illusr, Theatre & Main
Street, 64, Univ Mich Press; illusr, The third crusade (film
strip), McGraw, 58; contribr, Picture talk in Kathmandu, Mich
Acad Sci, Arts & Lett, 63.
Mailing Address: 1633 Leaird St, Ann Arbor, MI 48105.

GOOCH, GERALD
Artist, Painter
b Mainington, W Va, 33.
Study & Training: Calif Col Arts & Crafts, BFA, 65; San Jose State
Col, MA, 67.
Work in Public Collections: Time, Inc, New York, N Y; Achenbach
Found, Palace Legion of Honor, San Francisco, Calif; Stanford
Univ, Palo Alto, Calif; Johnson Wax Co; Mus Mod Art, New York;
plus others including many in pvt collections.
Exhibitions: Calif Palace of Legion of Honor, Achenbach Found, San
Francisco, 67; Ill Biennial Exhib Contemp Painting, 67; Int Exhib
Tokyo, Japan, 67; A Decade in the West, Collection of Harry W
Anderson, Santa Barbara Mus Art, Calif, 71; West Coast '72,
Painters & Sculptors, Crocker Gallery, Sacramento, Calif, 72.
Teaching: Instr art, San Francisco Art Inst, 66-71; instr art, Laney
Col, Oakland, 69-
Awards: Calif State Fair, 65; Western Mich Univ Print Show, 66;
Okla Art Ctr Print Show, Oklahoma City, 66; plus others.
Mailing Address: c/o Hansen Fuller Gallery, 228 Grant Ave, San
Francisco, CA 94108.

GOOD, LEONARD
Painter, Educator
Preferred Media: Oils, Acrylics, Watercolors.
b Chickasha, Okla, June 25, 07.
Study & Training: Univ Okla, BFA & Letzeisen Medal, 27; Art
Stud League New York, with Nicolaides, 30; Univ Iowa, with Jean
Charlot, 40.
Work in Public Collections: Des Moines Art Ctr, Iowa; Milwaukee
Art Ctr, Wis; Oklahoma City Art Ctr, Okla; Philbrook Art Ctr,
Tulsa, Okla; Kans State Fedn Art, Manhattan.
Commissions: Portrait, Okla Hist Mus, Oklahoma City, 49; two
portraits, Univ Okla, Norman, 49-50; three portraits, Drake
Univ, Des Moines, Iowa, 54-60; portrait, Iowa Hist Mus, Des
Moines, 62; series of Iowa scenes for Sun features, Des Moines
Register, 65.
Exhibitions: First & Second Nat Exhibs Am Art, Metrop Mus Art,
New York, N Y, 36 & 37; Gallery of States Touring Exhib, Am
Fedn Arts, Washington, D C, 45; Mid America Annual, Joslyn
Mus Art, Omaha, Nebr, 55; Judged Juried Arts Ann, Tyler, Tex,
69.
Collections Arranged: Assembled permanent collection of paintings
for Preferred Risk Life Ins Co Home Off Bldg, Des Moines, 69.
Teaching: Prof painting & drawing, Univ Okla, 30-50; prof drawing
& painting, Univ Wis, 50-52; prof art hist, Drake Univ, 52-, head
dept art, 52-68.
Positions: Vis artist-in-residence, Iowa State Univ, 60-61; artist-in-
residence, Nat Endowment Arts & Iowa Arts Coun, Shenandoah,
Iowa, 70-71.
Awards: Zadok purchase prize for Hard Winter (painting), Milwau-
kee Art Ctr, 51; first prize for Survivor (drawing), Iowa Ann, Des
Moines Art Ctr, 58; first prize for Panorama (Iowa scene), Iowa
State Fair, 71.
Memberships: Delta Phi Delta (nat v pres, 54-58, nat pres, 58-60);
Art Dir Asn Iowa; Des Moines Art Ctr (var comts, 50-).

Publications: Illusr, A certain young widow, Univ Okla Press, 30;
illusr, instructional manuals for U S Air Force, Tinker Field,
Okla, 43-44; auth, Art today, U S Armed Forces Inst, 51; con-
tribr, Widening horizons: Oklahoma edition, Oklahoma City Art
Ctr, 60.
Dealer: Maka Gallery, 323½ 18th St, Rock Island, IL 61201.
Mailing Address: 750 34th St, Des Moines, IA 50312.

GOODALL, DONALD BANNARD
Art Administrator
b Los Angeles, Calif, Oct 8, 12.
Study & Training: Univ Ore, BA; Art Inst Chicago; Univ Chicago,
MA; Harvard Univ, PhD.
Teaching: Chmn dept art, Univ Southern Calif, 49-59; chmn dept art,
Univ Tex, Austin, 59-, dir Univ Art Mus, 63-, actg dean fine arts,
71-72.
Memberships: Col Art Asn Am; Nat Schs Art.
Mailing Address: Dept of Art, University of Texas at Austin, 23rd St
& San Jacinto, Austin, TX 78712.

GOODBRED, RAY EDW
Painter, Instructor
Preferred Media: Oils, Pastels.
b Brooklyn, N Y, Dec 7, 29.
Study & Training: Art Students League New York, N Y, with Robert
Brackman, 48-51; Nat Acad Sch Fine Art, with Ogden Pleissner,
51; N Y Univ Sch Educ, 53-56.
Work in Public Collections: Gibbes Art Gallery, Charleston, S C;
portrait, The Citadel; Med Univ S C; Roper Hosp, Charleston;
Hibernian Soc S C.
Commissions: Portraits of ten mem bd, Home Fed Savings & Loan
Asn, 71; plus other portrait comns throughout the Southeast.
Exhibitions: Knickerbocker Artists, Riverside Mus, New York, 56;
S C Artists Ann, 58-; Tricentennial S C Contemp Artists Invita-
tional, 70; Allied Artists Am, Nat Acad Design, 70-71; Salma-
gundi Club, New York.
Teaching: Private instr, 54-; demonstr oil portraits, Atlanta Art
Asn, Ga, 68, Colleton Co Art Asn, 69 & Beaufort, S C, 69; instr,
Hastie Sch Art, Gibbes Art Gallery, 69-
Positions: Juror exhibs, S C & N Y, 68-
Awards: First prize, Saul Alexander Award & purchase award, 67 &
Saul Alexander Award, 72, S C Artists Ann, Gibbes Art Gallery,
first prize & hon mention, Beaufort Art Asn Ann, 69; plus
others.
Bibliography: Jack A Morris, Jr & Robert Smeltzer (auth), Con-
temporary artists of South Carolina, Greenville Co Mus Art, 70. ;
Memberships: Salmagundi Club; life mem Art Students League New
York; Guild S C Artists; Charleston Artist Guild; Grand Cent
Art Galleries.
Dealers: Grand Central Art Galleries, Hotel Biltmore, 40 Vander-
bilt Ave, New York, NY 10017; Portraits, Inc, 41 E 57th St,
New York, NY 10022.
Mailing Address: 147 Beaufain St, Charleston, SC 29401.

GOODE, JOE, see BUENO, JOSE

GOODMAN, BENJAMIN
Patron
b Memphis, Tenn, Jan 18, 04.
Study & Training: Princeton Univ, AB, 24; Harvard Univ, LLB, 27.
Positions: Patron of regional art (mid-south); trustee & former
pres, Memphis Acad Arts; chmn, Memphis Munic Art Comn, 60-
Mailing Address: 115 S Rose Rd, Memphis, TN 38117.

GOODMAN, CALVIN JEROME
Art Consultant, Lecturer
b Chicago, Ill, Mar 1, 22.
Study & Training: Harvard Univ, AB(hon), 49.
Teaching: Instr bus methods for artists, Tamarind Lithography
Workshop, 61-71; instr prof practices, Calif Inst Arts, 67-71;
instr prof practices, Otis Art Inst, 68-71.
Positions: Mgt consult in the Arts, 60-; v pres, Tamarind Lithogra-
phy Workshop, 59-; v pres, Orgn Arts Sponsors, Los Angeles, 70-
Bibliography: Antreasian & Adams (auth), The Tamarind book of
lithography, Abrams, 71.
Research: The art market and specialized schools of art and music.
Collection: Contemporary original prints and oils, Wayne, Francis,
Burkhardt and others.
Publications: Auth, A management study of an art gallery, 66, Gal-
lery facility planning, 67 & Business methods for a lithography
workshop, 68, Tamarind; auth, The Artist's own business, 71 &
Marketing art, a handbook for artists and art dealers, 72.
Mailing Address: 11901 Sunset Blvd, Suite 102, Los Angeles, CA
90049.

GOODMAN, ESTELLE
Sculptor
b New York, N Y.
Study & Training: Barnard Col, BA.
Work in Public Collections: Norfolk Mus Art, Va; also pvt collections in U S.
Exhibitions: Knickerbocker Artists, 61-64; Allied Artists Am, 63-65; Audubon Artists, 65; Nat Design Ctr, New York, 66; W & J Sloane Co Galleries, 67; plus others.
Awards: Prizes, Painters & Sculptors of N J, 63 & 67; Yonkers Art Asn; Vt Art Ctr; plus others.
Memberships: Artist-Craftsmen of New York; Painters & Sculptors N J; Yonkers Art Asn; Knickerbocker Artists; League Present Day Artists; plus others.
Mailing Address: 115 Central Park W, New York, NY 10023.

GOODMAN, JAMES NEIL
Art Dealer, Collector
b Rochester, N Y, Apr 11, 29.
Positions: Dir, James Goodman Gallery.
Specialty of Gallery: Modern American and European masters, including Calder, Cornell, de Kooning, Klee, Leger, Matisse, Moore, Picasso & Tanguy.
Mailing Address: 55 E 86th St, New York, NY 10028.

GOODMAN, SIDNEY
Painter
b Philadelphia, Pa, Jan 19, 36.
Study & Training: Philadelphia Mus Sch Art, with Jacob Landau, Larry Day & Morris Berd.
Work in Public Collections: Art Inst Chicago, Ill; Libr Cong, Washington, D C; Mus Mod Art & Whitney Mus Am Art, New York, N Y; Philadelphia Mus Art.
Exhibitions: Two-man show, Peale House, Philadelphia, 69; Herron Inst Art, Indianapolis, Ind, 69; Univ Ill, 69; Southern Methodist Univ, 69; Philbrook Art Ctr, Tulsa, Okla, 69; plus many other group & one-man shows.
Teaching: Instr drawing & composition, Philadelphia Col Art.
Awards: Guggenheim fel, 63; Ford Found Purchase Award, 63; Philadelphia Print Club Purchase Award, 65; plus others.
Dealer: Terry Dintenfass, Inc, 18 E 67th St, New York, NY 10021.
Mailing Address: 323 Harrison Ave, Elkins Park, PA 19117.

GOODNOUGH, ROBERT
Painter
b Cortland, N Y, Oct 23, 17.
Study & Training: Syracuse Univ, Hiram Gell fel, 40, BFA; New York Univ, MA; New Sch Social Res; Ozenfant Sch Art; Hans Hofman Sch Fine Arts.
Work in Public Collections: Albright-Knox Art Gallery, Buffalo, N Y; Solomon R Guggenheim Mus, Mus Mod Art & Metrop Mus Art, New York, N Y; Wadsworth Atheneum, Hartford, Conn; plus others.
Exhibitions: One-man shows, Univ Minn, Univ Notre Dame & Arts Club Chicago, 64; Nat Inst Arts & Lett, 64; The New American Painting and Sculpture, Mus Mod Art, 69; plus many other group & one-man shows.
Teaching: Instr painting, Cornell Univ, New York Univ & Fieldston Sch, New York.
Positions: Art critic, Art News, 50-57; secy, Documents of Mod Art, 51.
Awards: Ada Garrett Award, Art Inst Chicago, 61; Ford Found Purchase Prize, 63.
Mailing Address: 122 Christopher St, New York, NY 10014.

GOODNOW, FRANK A
Painter, Educator
Preferred Media: Oil, Acrylic.
b Evanston, Ill, Dec 14, 23.
Study & Training: Northwestern Univ, Evanston; Art Inst Chicago, BFA; Anna L Raymond traveling fel, 48; also with Boris Anisfeld.
Work in Public Collections: Philadelphia Mus Art, Pa; New York State Univ; Univ Rochester, N Y; Everson Mus Art, Syracuse, N Y; Syracuse Univ.
Exhibitions: Salon des Jeunes Peintres, Paris, France, 49; Pa Acad Fine Arts, 53, 57 & 65; Whitney Mus Am Art, 55; one-man shows, Schuman Gallery, Rochester, 65, 69, 71 & 72; Am Acad Arts & Lett, 69.
Teaching: Prof painting, Syracuse Univ, 50-
Awards: Helen Everson Mem Purchase Prize, Everson Mus Art, 67; B Forman Award, Rochester Mem Gallery, 69.
Dealer: Schuman Gallery, 267 Oxford St, Rochester, NY 14607.
Mailing Address: 214 Dawley Rd, Fayetteville, NY 13066.

GOODRICH, LLOYD
Art Administrator, Writer
b Nutley, N J, July 10, 97.
Study & Training: Art Stud League New York, with Kenneth Hayes Miller; Nat Acad Design; Cornell Col, hon DFA, 63, Colby Col, 64.
Positions: Res cur, Whitney Mus Am Art, 35-47, assoc cur, 47-48, assoc dir, 48-58, dir, 58-68, adv dir, 68-71, consult, 71-: founder & dir, Am Art Res Coun, 42-; chmn ed bd, Mag of Art, 42-50; mem ed bd, Art in Am, 46-70; N Y Regional bd Archives of Am Art, chmn, Comt on Govt & Art, 48-; mem, Nat Coun Arts & Govt, 54-, v chmn, 62-; secy, Sara Roby Found, 56-; dir, trustee & hon v pres, Am Fedn Arts; mem Smithsonian Art Comn; co-chmn Joint Artists-Mus Comt; mem coun, Sci Int Enciclopedia Arte; assoc sem, Am Civilization, Columbia Univ; mem bd trustees, Whitney Mus Am Art; mem adv comt Art for the White House, 60-63; bd dirs, Edward MacDowell Asn; plus many other prior art positions.
Awards: Art in Am Award, 59; Nat Art Materials Trade Asn award, 64; award of merit, Philadelphia Mus Col Art, 64.
Memberships: Asn Art Mus Dirs; Int Art Critics Asn; Drawing Soc; hon mem Am Inst Interior Designers; fel Am Acad Arts & Sci.
Research: American art and artists.
Publications: Auth, Thomas Eakins, 33 & 70, Praeger; auth, Winslow Homer, 44 & 59 & Albert P Ryder, 59: co-auth, Georgia O'Keeffe, Praeger; auth, Edward Hopper, 71, Raphael Soyer, 72 & Reginald Marsh, 72, Abrams; plus many other bks & articles in nat art mag.
Mailing Address: Whitney Museum of American Art, 945 Madison Ave, New York, NY 10021.

GOODRIDGE, LAWRENCE WAYNE
Painter, Sculptor
Preferred Media: Acrylics, Electronics.
b Cincinnati, Ohio, Mar 18, 41.
Study & Training: Univ Cincinnati, BFA(hon), 63; Univ Cincinnati & Art Acad Cincinnati, MFA, 67.
Exhibitions: All-Ohio Painting & Sculpture Exhib, Dayton Art Inst, 67; Mid-States Art Exhib, Evansville Mus Arts & Sci, Ind, 70; one-man show & Louisville Biennial, J B Speed Art Mus, Ky, 71; 17th Ann Drawing & Sculpture Show, Ball State Univ, Muncie, Ind, 71.
Teaching: Instr found design & color theory, Art Acad Cincinnati, 69-, co-dean, 72-
Positions: Toy designer, Kenner Prod Co, 63-65.
Awards: Second prize, Eastern Fine Paper Graphic Design, 65.
Publications: Auth & illusr, European diary, 70 & Truck stop, 71, Cincinnati Mag.
Dealer: Richard Feigen Gallery, 226 E Ontario St, Chicago, IL 60611.
Mailing Address: 29 Kathryn St, Florence, KY 41042.

GOODSTEIN-SHAPIRO, see WALTON, FLORENCE GOODSTEIN.

GOODWIN, ALFRED
Collector
b Ger, Aug 4, 14.
Positions: Chmn exhibs, Salt Lake Art Barn, 55-61; hon lifetime trustee, Salt Lake Art Ctr, 63-
Mailing Address: 4325 S W 34th Ave, Portland, OR 97201.

GOOSSEN, EUGENE COONS
Art Critic, Educator
b Gloversville, N Y, Aug 6, 20.
Study & Training: Hamilton Col; Corcoran Sch Fine Arts; Sorbonne, Paris, France, cert; New Sch Social Res, BA.
Collections Arranged: Kenneth Noland, Morris Louis & First Barnett Newman Retrospective, Bennington Col, Vt, 58-61; 8 Young Artists, Hudson River Mus, N Y, 64; The Art of the Real, Mus Mod Art, New York, N Y, Grand Palais, Paris, Kunsthalle, Zurich Switz & Tate Gallery, London, Eng, 68-69; Helen Frankenthaler, Whitney Mus Am Art, New York, Whitechapel Gallery, London, Herrenhausen, Hannover & Kongresshalle, Berlin, Ger, 69; Ellsworth Kelly, Mus Mod Art, New York, 73.
Teaching: Prof art, Bennington Col, 58-61, mem visual arts comt, 61-; prof art & chmn dept, Hunter Col, 61-
Positions: Art critic, Monterey Peninsula Herald, 48-58; dir exhibs, Bennington Col, 58-61; adv comt, Archives Am Art, 67-; mem, New York City Cult Coun, 70-
Awards: Frank Jewett Mather Citation for excellence in art criticism, 58; Guggenheim fel, 70; City Univ New York res grant, 72.
Bibliography: Article, In: Time Mag, 4/7/67; Michael Murphy (auth), The art of the real (film), U S Info Agency, 68.
Memberships: Int Art Critics Asn; Am Asn Univ Prof; Col Art Asn.

Publications: Auth, Ellsworth Kelly, 58; auth, Stuart Davis, 59; auth, The art of the real, Eng, Fr & Ger ed, 68-69; auth, Helen Frankenthaler, 69; co-auth, Encyclopaedia of American art, Chanticleer Press, 72.
Mailing Address: R F D 1, Buskirk, NY 12028.

GORCHOV, RON
Painter
Preferred Media: Oil on Canvas.
b Chicago, Ill, Apr 5, 30.
Study & Training: Art Inst Chicago, 47-50; Univ Ill, 50-51.
Work in Public Collections: Whitney Mus Am Art, New York, N Y; Hartford Atheneum, Conn; Everson Mus Art, Syracuse, N.Y.
Teaching: Asst prof art, Hunter Col, presently.
Mailing Address: 74 Grand St, New York, NY 10013.

GORDER, CLAYTON J
Painter, Educator
Preferred Media: Acrylics.
b Fargo, N Dak, Mar 20, 36.
Study & Training: Concordia Col, Moorhead, Minn, BA; Univ Iowa, MA.
Work in Public Collections: San Francisco Mus Art; Container Corp Am, Rock Island, Ill; Des Moines Art Ctr, Iowa.
Exhibitions: Container Corp Am, 63; one-man shows, Davenport Munic Art Gallery, 68 & William Sawyer Gallery, 70 & 72; two-man show, Richard Feigen Gallery, 71; one-man show, Des Moines Art Ctr, 72.
Teaching: Asst prof painting & drawing, Augustana Col(Ill), 63-
Awards: First prize purchase award, Container Corp Am, 63; Edmundson Award for best work in show, any medium, Ann Iowa Artists Exhib, 69; Esther & Edith Younker Award in painting, 24th Ann Iowa Artist Exhib, 72.
Dealer: Richard Feigen Gallery, 226 Ontario St, Chicago, IL 60611. William Sawyer Gallery, 3045 Clay St, San Francisco, CA 94115.
Mailing Address: 910 Dodge St, Iowa City, IA 52240.

GORDLEY, METZ TRANBARGER
Painter
Preferred Media: Oils.
b Cedar Rapids, Iowa, May 24, 32.
Study & Training: Wash Univ, BFA; Univ Okla, MFA; Ohio State Univ; Univ N C, Chapel Hill.
Work in Public Collections: Greenville Art Ctr, N C; N C State Soc Print & Drawings, Raleigh.
Commissions: Aycock portrait for E Carolina Univ.
Exhibitions: Juried Arts Third Nat Exhib, Tyler, Tex, 66; 18th Irene Leache Mem Exhib, Norfolk, Va, 66; Watercolor U S A, Springfield, Mo, 66, traveling show, 66-67; Frontal Images, Miss Art Asn, Jackson, 69, traveling show, 69-70; Central South Exhib Tenn, Art League Parthenon, Nashville, 69.
Teaching: Prof painting, E Carolina Univ, 59-
Awards: First prize N C Print & Drawing Soc, 66; second prize for watercolor & second prize for oil, Kinston Art Show, 68.
Bibliography: Book review, In: Southeastern Art Rev, 72; Emily Farnham (auth), Behind a laughing mask, Charles Demuth.
Memberships: Assoc Artists N C(bd mem, 66-67); Col Art Asn.
Mailing Address: 105 Dalebrook, Greenville, NC 27834.

GORDON, JOHN
Art Administrator, Art Historian
b Brooklyn, N Y, Jan 20, 12.
Study & Training: Dartmouth Col, AB, 34.
Positions: Admin asst circulating exhibs, Mus Mod Art, New York, 44-46; secy, Brooklyn Mus, 46-52, cur paintings & sculpture, 52-59; cur, Whitney Mus Am Art, 59-69; dir, Soc Four Arts, Palm Beach, Fla, 69-
Memberships: MacDowell Colony (corp mem); Drawing Soc (adv bd); Am Fedn Arts; Arch Am Art; Nat Trust Hist Preserv.
Research: Nineteenth and twentieth century American paintings and sculpture.
Publications: Auth, Geometric abstraction in America, 62; auth, Louise Nevelson, 67; auth, Isamu Noguchi, 68; auth, Franz Kline, 69; auth, Jim Dine, 70.
Mailing Address: 596 N County Rd, Palm Beach, FL 33480.

GORDON, MAXWELL
Painter
b Chicago, Ill, Sept 4, 10.
Study & Training: Cleveland Sch Art, Ohio; John Huntington Polytech Inst, Cleveland.
Work in Public Collections: Brandeis Univ; Ein Harod Mus, Israel; Palacio Bellas Artes, Mexico City, Mex.
Exhibitions: Mus Mod Art, New York, N Y, 43 & 61; nine Pa Acad Fine Arts Nat Ann, 45-59; Whitney Mus Am Art, New York, 48; one-man shows, ACA Gallery, New York, 48-62 & Sala Int, Palacio Bellas Artes, 65 & 70.

Awards: First prize for oils, Butler Inst Am Art, Youngstown, Ohio, 47; second hon mention Corcoran Bienal, 47; Yaddo fels, 57 & 60.
Mailing Address: Apartado Postal 5-503, Mexico City 5, D F, Mex.

GORDY, ROBERT P
Painter
Preferred Media: Acrylics, Ink.
b Jefferson Island, La, Oct 14, 33.
Study & Training: La State Univ, Baton Rouge, BA & MA; State Univ Iowa; Yale Univ, Yale-Norfolk fel, 53, with Hans Hofmann.
Work in Public Collections: Whitney Mus Am Art, New York, N Y; Corcoran Gallery, Washington, D C; Dallas Mus Fine Arts, Tex; Fort Worth Art Ctr, Tex; New Orleans Mus Art.
Exhibitions: Whitney Mus Am Art Exhib, 67; Winners of Exhib Artists of Southeast & Tex, New Orleans Mus Art, 68 & 72; 14 Artist Award Winners in Southeast & Southwest, Selected by Nat Coun Arts, Witte Mem Mus, San Antonio, 68; New Acquisitions, Whitney Mus Am Art, 68; Spirit of the Comics, Inst Contemp Art Philadelphia.
Awards: Purchase prizes, New Orleans Mus Art, 58, 67 & 71 & Dallas Mus Fine Arts, 69; Nat Coun Arts grant, 67.
Bibliography: Joseph Mashek (auth), Interview with R Gordy, Studio Int, 12/69; The character of collecting-modern, Peoria Art Mus, 70; Ted Calas (auth), The art gallery guide, 5/72.
Dealer: Galerie Simonne Stern, 516 Royal St, New Orleans, LA 70130.
Mailing Address: 813 Barracks St, New Orleans, LA 70160.

GORMAN, CARL NELSON (KIN-YA-ONNY BEYEH)
Painter, Lecturer
Preferred Media: Oils, Watercolors.
b Chinle, Ariz, Oct 5, 07.
Study & Training: Los Angeles Co Art Inst, cert, fine arts night courses, 47-51, with Ejnar Hansen & Joseph Mugnaini; also illus with Norman Rockwell; blue print reading, Santa Monica Tech Sch, 54.
Work in Public Collections: Southwest Mus, Los Angeles, Calif; Navajo Tribal Mus, Window Rock, Ariz; Indian Arts & Crafts Bd, Dept Interior, Washington, D C; Col Ganado, Ariz.
Commissions: Watercolor for cover illus, 56 & mosaic for cover illus, 62, Westways Mag; cover illus for Vital Issues, 72.
Exhibitions: Am Indian Painting Competition, M H De Young Mem Mus, San Francisco, Calif, 54; Seven Douglas Aircraft Art Ann, Santa Monica & El Segundo, Calif, 54-60; Inter-Tribal Indian Ceremonial, Gallup, N Mex, 62 & 65; Scottsdale Indian Arts Nat, Ariz, 62, 63 & 65; First Ann Invitational Am Indian Paintings, U S Dept Interior, Washington, D C, 64.
Teaching: Instr sketching, Tuller Col, Window Rock, Ariz, 68-70; lectr art, Native Am Art Workshop, Univ Calif, Davis, 70-
Positions: Tech illusr, Douglas Aircraft Co, Los Angeles, Santa Monica, Lawndale, El Segundo & Torrance, 55-63; partner, Desert Designs (silk screening), Window Rock, 63-64; mgr, Navajo Arts & Crafts Guild, Window Rock, 64-66.
Awards: First prize for sculpture (mosaic), Ninth Art Ann, Douglas El Segundo Mgt Club, 61; first award for paintings with new vistas, Scottsdale Indian Arts Nat, 63; first award for oils, Inter-Tribal Indian Ceremonial, 65.
Bibliography: Fred E Huff (prog dir), Vet Day Spec, KPHO TV, Phoenix, 69; Carl Gorman, Navajo artist, Smoke Signals, Reno, fall 70.
Dealer: Navajo Gallery, Ledoux St, Taos, NM 87571.
Mailing Address: Apt 267, 619 Pole Line Rd, Davis, CA 95616.

GORMAN, R C
Painter, Art Dealer
Preferred Media: Acrylics, Oils, Pastels.
b Chinle, Ariz, July 26, 33.
Study & Training: Northern Ariz Univ, with Jack Salter & Ellery Gibson; Mexico City Col.
Work in Public Collections: Heard Mus, Phoenix, Ariz; Philbrook Art Ctr, Tulsa, Okla; Northern Ariz Univ, Flagstaff; Gonzaga Univ, Spokane, Wash; Santa Fe Fine Arts Mus, N Mex.
Commissions: Dance of the Hohokam Masked Figures, St Luke's Hosp, Phoenix, 71.
Exhibitions: Am Indian Art Exhib, Kaiser Ctr, Oakland, Calif, 66; Scottsdale Nat Indian Exhib, Ariz, 69; Santa Fe Ann Biennial Exhib, N Mex, 69; Philbrook Art Ctr, Tulsa, 69; Heard Mus Guild Exhib, Phoenix, 70.
Collections Arranged: U S Indian Arts & Crafts Board, Washington, D C, 68.
Positions: Owner, Navajo Gallery, Taos.
Awards: Grand award, Am Indian Art Exhib, Oakland, 66; first award, Scottsdale Nat Indian Exhib, 67; first award, Heard Mus Guild Exhib, 69.
Bibliography: Ronald Leal (auth), R C Gorman-the two worlds of a Navajo artist, Mankind Mag, 70; John Milton (auth), R C Gorman-

interview-the American Indian speaks, S Dak Rev, 70; Robert A Ewing (auth), An Indian artist and his art-this is Gorman, N Mex Mag, 71.
Memberships: Taos Art Asn.
Specialty of Gallery: Southwest art; Indian painters.
Art Interests: Modern Indian painters.
Collection: F Scholder, Tavlos, Pletka, C Counter, C Bissell, C Lovato, C Cannon, Kin-ya-onny Beyeh & Bob Hoasous.
Publications: Contribr, 23 contemporary Indian artists, Art in Am, 72; contribr, American deserts, Nat Geog Mag, 72.
Dealers: Jamison Galleries, 111 E San Francisco, Santa Fe, NM 87501; Mary Livingston, Gallery II, 1211 N Broadway, Santa Ana, CA 92701.
Mailing Address: c/o Navajo Gallery, P O Box 1756, Taos, NM 87571.

GORMAN, WILLIAM D
  Painter, Graphic Artist
Preferred Media: Casein Tempera, Graphics.
b Jersey City, N J, June 27, 25.
Study & Training: Newark Sch Fine & Indust Arts, N J.
Work in Public Collections: Newark Mus; Butler Inst Am Art, Youngstown, Ohio; Springfield Art Mus, Mo; Colo Springs Fine Art Ctr, Colo; U S Dept State, Washington, D C.
Exhibitions: One-man show, Philadelphia Art Alliance, 65; U S Dept State Art in Embassies Prog, Europe, Africa & Orient, 67-72; N J Artists, Newark Mus, 68; U S Watercolor Invitational, Chico State Col, Calif, 72.
Positions: Dir, Old Bergen Art Guild, Bayonne, N J, 62-
Awards: Henry Ward Ranger Fund Purchase Prizes, Nat Acad Design, 65 & 71; Watercolor U S A Purchase Prize, Springfield Art Mus, Mo, 66; Famous Artists Sch Award, Am Watercolor Soc, 71.
Bibliography: Margaret Harald (auth), Prize-winning watercolors, Bks 2, 4 & 5, 64, 65 & 67 & Prize-winning art, Bks 6 & 7, 66 & 67, Allied Publ; Henry Gasser (auth), article, In: Am Artist, 10/70.
Memberships: Audubon Artists; Am Watercolor Soc; Allied Artists Am; Nat Soc Painters Casein & Acrylic; Assoc Artists N J.
Publications: Auth, article, In: Today's Art Mag, 69.
Mailing Address: 43 W 33rd St, Bayonne, NJ 07002.

GORSKI, DANIEL ALEXANDER
  Sculptor, Painter
Preferred Media: Mixed Media.
b Cleveland, Ohio, Oct 26, 39.
Study & Training: Cleveland Inst Art, dipl, 61; Yale Univ Sch Art & Archit, with Jack Tworkov & Al Held, BFA, 62 & MFA, 64.
Work in Public Collections: Yale Univ, New Haven, Conn.
Exhibitions: Primary Structures, Jewish Mus, New York, N Y, 66; Cool Art, Larry Aldrich Mus, Ridgefield, Conn, 68; Yale Norfolk Summer Sch, Conn, 69; Hanging and Leaning, Emily Lowe Gallery, Hofstra Univ, Hampstead, L I, 70; 26 x 26, Vassar Col Art Gallery, Poughkeepsie, N Y, 71.
Teaching: Instr design, painting, color & drawing, Md Inst Col Art, 71-; vis lectr art hist & fashion design, Drexel Univ, 72.
Bibliography: W Berkson (auth), In the galleries, Arts Mag, 1/66; L Lippard (auth), Recent sculpture as escape, 2/66 & Escalation in Washington, 1/68, Art Int.
Mailing Address: R D 2, Box 297, Seven Valleys, PA 17360.

GORSLINE, DOUGLAS WARNER
  Painter, Illustrator
Preferred Media: Oils, Watercolors.
b Rochester, N Y, May 24, 13.
Study & Training: Yale Univ Sch Fine Arts; Art Stud League New York.
Work in Public Collections: Butler Inst Am Art, Pa; Harvard Univ Houghton Libr, Cambridge, Mass; Libr of Cong, Washington, D C; Lehigh Univ; St Paul Gallery Art, Minn.
Commissions: Oil painting on basketball, Sports Illustrated, New York, N Y; oil painting on sports, Westvaco, New York.
Exhibitions: Pa Acad Fine Arts, 63; Am Acad Arts & Lett, 64; 20th Century Am Art, San Diego Invitational, 65-66; Mainstreams, 68 & 70; Butler Inst Am Art, 72; plus many one-man shows.
Teaching: Instr art, Nat Acad Sch Fine Arts.
Awards: Childe Hassam Fund purchase award, Am Acad Arts & Lett, 62; Henry Ward Ranger Fund purchase award, Nat Acad Design, 63; Tiffany Found grant, 63.
Memberships: Nat Acad Design.
Mailing Address: c/o Robert Schoelkopf Gallery, 825 Madison Ave, New York, NY 10021.

GOTH, MARIE
  Painter, Designer
Preferred Media: Oils.
b Indianapolis, Ind.
Study & Training: Cincinnati Art Sch; Art Stud League New York,

with Frank Vincent Dumond & others; scholar to study with John Johansen, Martha's Vineyard Island.
Work in Public Collections: Portrait & still life, Frank Daily Collection & several portraits including Paul V McNutt, Ind Univ; portraits of T C Steel & Charles W Dahlgreen, Herron Art Inst; portrait of Gov Henry Schreiker, Ind State Capitol, Indianapolis; portrait of Will Hays, Wabash Col, Crawfordsville, Ind.
Commissions: Portrait of Mrs Honeywell commissioned by Mr Honeywell, Honeywell Mem Ctr, Wabash, Ind, 55; portrait of Izlar Solomon, conductor Indianapolis Symphony, 63; portrait of Dr A R Allen, commissioned by Mrs Allen for Mem at Terre Haute, Ind, 71; portrait of J Abraham Eyed, writer, Nashville, Ind, 72; portraits of John T McCutcheon, Purdue Univ & Wabash Col.
Exhibitions: Hoosier Salon, Chicago, Ill & Indianapolis, 24-72; Nat Acad Design, New York, N Y, 31; Speed Mem Mus, Louisville, Ky; Cincinnati Art Club, Ohio; Brooklyn Mus, N Y; plus others.
Teaching: Pvt classes.
Awards: Award for portrait of Florence, Nat Acad Design, 41; Ind Soc prize for portrait of Will Hays, 42 & outstanding award for portrait of Joe Hadley, 61, Hoosier Salon.
Mailing Address: R R 3, Box 2, Nashville, IN 47448.

GOTO, JOSEPH
  Sculptor
b Hilo, Hawaii, Jan 7, 20.
Study & Training: Art Inst Chicago; Roosevelt Univ.
Work in Public Collections: Art Inst Chicago, Ill; Indiana Univ; Mus Mod Art, New York, N Y; Univ Mich; Union Carbide Corp.
Exhibitions: Art Inst Chicago; Carnegie Inst; Univ Ill; J B Speed Art Mus, Louisville, Ky; Whitney Mus Am Art, New York; plus others.
Awards: Graham Found fel, 57; John Hay Whitney fel; Guggenheim fel, 69; plus others.
Bibliography: William S Rubin (auth), Dada, surrealism, and their heritage (catalog), Mus Mod Art, 68.
Mailing Address: 17 Sixth St, Providence, RI 02906.

GOTTLIEB, ABE
  Collector, Patron
b Poland, Apr 17, 08.
Study & Training: New Sch Social Res.
Positions: Chmn bd, Fedn Jewish Philanthropies & United Jewish Appeal.
Collection: From Renoir to Vlaminck; School of Paris; German expressionism; paintings, sculpture from Daumier to Moore.
Mailing Address: 387 Grand Ave, New York, NY 10002.

GOTTLIEB, ADOLPH
  Painter
b New York, N Y, Mar 14, 03.
Study & Training: Art Stud League New York; also in Paris, France & Berlin, Ger.
Work in Public Collections: Metrop Mus Art, Whitney Mus Am Art & Mus Mod Art, New York; Tel Aviv Mus, Israel; New Orleans Mus Art, La; plus others.
Commissions: Mural, Yerington Post Off Bldg, Nev, 39; Ark curtains, Congregation B-nai Israel, Millburn, N J, 52 & Congregation Beth El, Springfield, Mass, 53; stained glass facade, Park Ave Synagogue, New York, 54.
Exhibitions: One-man shows var pvt galleries, 30-; exhibs, Paris, London & Tokyo, 47-59; ten-year retrospective, Bennington Col & Williams Col, 54; retrospective, Jewish Mus, 57; one-man shows, Solomon R Guggenheim Mus & Whitney Mus Am Art.
Awards: Purchase award, Univ Ill, 51; third prize, Carnegie Int, 61; Grand Prix, Sao Paulo Bienal, 63; plus others.
Publications: Auth, articles, In: Col Art J & Art in Am.
Dealer: Marborough Gallery, 41 E 57th St, New York, NY 10022.
Mailing Address: 380 W Broadway, New York, NY 10013.

GOUGH, ROBERT ALAN
  Painter
Preferred Media: Oils, Pencil.
b Quebec, P Q, Aug 13, 31; U S citizen.
Study & Training: Am Acad Art, Chicago, Ill, with William H Mosby & J Allen St John.
Work in Public Collections: Am Fedn Arts; Butler Inst Am Art; Univ Nebr; Ill Arts Coun; Cent Col, Pella, Iowa.
Exhibitions: Univ Ill Biennial, 63; Pa Acad Fine Arts Ann, 64; Painting & Sculpture Today, Herron Mus Art, 66; one-man show, Gilman Galleries, Chicago, 67 & 69; 35 Years in Retrospect, Butler Inst Am Art, 71.
Awards: Henry Ward Ranger Purchase Prize, Nat Acad Design, 62; Friends of Am Art Purchase Prize, Butler Inst Am Art, 62; first prize, Ill Seven States Exhib, 63.
Dealers: Gilman Galleries, 103 E Oak St, Chicago, IL 60611; Harmon Gallery, 1258 Third St S, Naples, FL 33940.
Mailing Address: 220 Brookside Dr, Chillicothe, OH 45601.

GOULD, JOHN HOWARD
Painter, Film Maker
b Toronto, Ont, Aug 14, 29.
Study & Training: Ont Col Art, AOCA, 52; Acad Julian, Paris, France, 52.
Work in Public Collections: Nat Gallery Can; Montreal Mus Fine Arts; Beaverbrook Mus, Fredericton, N B; plus others in pvt collections.
Commissions: Portrait of Alan Jarvis, head of Nat Gallery Can, Ottawa, 62; Pikangikum (drawn film of Indians), Nat Film Bd Can, 67; performance drawings of Marcel Marceau, City Ctr, New York, N Y, 71; drawn film of Marceau, Paris, France, 71.
Exhibitions: Canadian Surrealism Today, touring exhib, 64; Focus on Drawing, Int Drawing Survey, Art Gallery Toronto, 65; Retrospective, Univ Toronto, 65; Can rep, Films on Art Category, Venice Biennale, 66; Flint Inst Arts Survey Exhib, 66.
Awards: Greenshield Found Award for figurative painting, Spain, 60; Can Coun grants, drawn film of Peru, 67 & drawn film of Japan, 70.
Bibliography: Alan Jarvis (auth), John Gould, Can Art Mag, 61; Ontario artist, Ont Homes & Living, 8/64; John Griffin (dir), John Gould on drawing (film), produced by Gesture Prod, 72.
Dealer: Arwin Galleries, 222 Grand River W, Detroit, MI 48226.
Mailing Address: Cedar St, Waubaushene, Ont, Can.

GOULD, STEPHEN
Sculptor, Art Administrator
Preferred Media: Bronze.
b New York, N Y, Dec 25, 09.
Study & Training: New Sch Social Res, with Prof Manola Pascal.
Work in Public Collections: Newark Mus, N J; Morris Mus Fine Art, Morristown, N J; Miami Mus Mod Art, Fla; Washington Co Mus Fine Arts, Hagerstown, Md; Allen R Hite Art Inst, Univ Louisville, Ky.
Exhibitions: Nat Soc Arts & Lett, Washington, D C, 69; Salmagundi Club, New York, 70; Famous Art (chosen as art of month on permanent exhib), Washington Co Mus Art, 70; American Art of Mid-Century, Nat Coun Jewish Women, South Orange, N J, 71; Salle Expos Int, Soc Ecole Francaise, Paris, France, 71-72.
Teaching: Art dir, World Univ Tucson, Ariz, 69-, lectr, affiliated cols.
Awards: Art-of-the-month Award for Heart of Humanity (sculpture), Washington Co Mus Art, 70; awards for I Protest (sculpture), Dr Bellis of Salmagundi Club, 70 & Soc Ecole Francaise, 71-72.
Bibliography: M Pescara (auth), Sculptor Stephen Gould, Am Rev Art & Sci, 10/69; Dr John Zitko (auth), Contemporary sculpture in the arts, World Univ, 3/72.
Memberships: Fel Royal Soc Arts; Nat Soc Arts & Lett; Salmagundi Club.
Dealer: Kottler Galleries, 3 E 65th St, New York, NY 10021.
Mailing Address: c/o Clearbrook, 29 A Larch Plaza, Cranbury, NJ 08512.

GOULET, LORRIE (LORRIE H DE CREEFT)
Sculptor, Instructor
Preferred Media: Stone, Wood, Ceramics.
b Riverdale, N Y, Aug 17, 25.
Study & Training: Inwood Potteries Studios, New York, N Y, 32-36, with Mrs Amiee Voorhees; Black Mountain Col, with Josef Albers; also sculpture with Jose de Creeft, 43-44.
Work in Public Collections: Sarah Roby Found; Joseph H Hirshhorn Collection; N J State Mus; Sen William Benton; Ball State Univ Art Gallery.
Commissions: Ceramic relief, New York Pub Libr, Grand Concourse, Bronx, 58; ceramic relief, Nurses' Residence & Sch, Bronx Munic Hosp, 61; stainless steel relief, 48th Precinct Police & Fire Sta, Bronx, 71.
Exhibitions: Mother and Child in Modern Art, Am Fedn Arts, 63; World Trade Fairs, Algiers, Barcelona & Zagreb, 64; Collectors Choice, Philbrook Art Ctr, 64; Dimensions 69, Temple Emein, N J, 69; Outdoor Sculpture Show, Van Saun Park, N J, 71; plus many other group & one-man shows.
Teaching: Instr sculpture & var media & staff mem, Mus Mod Art, New York, 57-64; sculpture staff mem, Scarsdale Studio Workshop, 59-61; sculpture staff mem, New Sch Social Res, 61-
Positions: Guest demonstr, Around the Corner, New York Dept Educ, CBS TV, 64-65.
Awards: First sculpture prize, Norton Gallery, 49 & 50; first sculpture prize, Westchester Art Soc, 64; Soltan Engel Mem Award, Audubon Artists, 67.
Memberships: Sculptors Guild; Audubon Artists; Nat Comt Art Educ; Rye Art Ctr (bd dirs); Westchester Art Soc.
Publications: Contribr, 20th century sculptors look at their work, The Palette; contribr, article on greenstone, In: Slate and soft stones, 71.
Dealer: Kennedy Galleries, 20 E 56th St, New York, NY 10022.
Mailing Address: 241 W 20th St, New York, NY 10011.

GOUREVITCH, JACQUELINE
Painter
Preferred Media: Oils.
b Paris, France, Oct 28, 33; U S citizen.
Study & Training: Black Mountain Col, N C, 50; Art Stud League New York, N Y, 52; Univ Chicago, BA, 54; Art Inst Chicago, 54-55.
Work in Public Collections: Chase Manhattan Bank, New York; Amstar Corp, New York; First Nat Bank, Worcester, Mass; Skidmore, Owings & Merrill, New York; Ball State Univ Mus, Muncie, Ind.
Exhibitions: One-woman shows, Roko Gallery, New York, 65, Rigelhaupt Gallery, Boston, Mass, 67 & 69 & Tibor de Nagy Gallery, New York, 71 & 72; (group shows), Skying, Rutgers Univ Art Gallery, New Brunswick, N J, 72 & Painting & Sculpture Today, Indianapolis Mus Art, 72; plus others.
Teaching: Docent & lectr, Philadelphia Mus Art, Pa, 59-62; vis artist drawing & painting, Wesleyan Univ, 67-71; artist-in-residence, Tamarind Inst, Albuquerque, N Mex.
Awards: Silvermine Guild Award, 66; Silver Bowl Award, Berkshire Mus, Pittsfield, Mass, 67.
Bibliography: Skying (catalogue), Rutgers Univ, New Brunswick, N J, 72.
Publications: Contribr, article & reproduction, In: Art Now: New York, fall 71.
Dealer: Tibor de Nagy Gallery, 29 W 57th St, New York, NY 10019.
Mailing Address: 13 Red Orange Rd, Middletown, CT 06457.

GOUVEIA, CLEM ALBERT, see CLEM

GOVAN, FRANCIS HAWKS
Educator, Painter
Preferred Media: Oils, Watercolors.
b Marianna, Ark, Dec 19, 16.
Study & Training: Hendrix Col, BA; Art Inst South, Memphis; Univ Wis; Layton Sch Art; Columbia Univ, MA; San Miguel, Mex.
Exhibitions: Am Watercolor Exhib, France, 53-55; one-man shows, Feigl Gallery, N Y, 54, 55 & 56; Retrospective, Brooks Mem Art Gallery, Memphis, 57 & 66; Kunst Am, 57-58; Art in the Embassies & Smithsonian Inst, 67-68.
Teaching: Instr art & creative dramatics, Milwaukee Univ Sch, 43-45; assoc prof art, Hendrix Col, 45-52; prof art, Memphis State Univ, 56-
Positions: Instr & occup therapist, Rockland State Hosp, Orangeburg, N Y, 52-54; freelance artist, New York, 54-55; educ dir, Brooks Mem Art Gallery, 55-56; cur exhibs, Memphis State Univ, 57-67.
Awards: First prize in watercolor, Memphis Biennial, 46; Carnegie Found grants res Ark pottery clays, 49 & mus fine art, 50.
Publications: Illusr, Arkansas pioneer days, Ark Gazette Sun Suppl, 48-49; auth, Art—what is it?, 59 & My last duchess, 65, Educ Quest.
Mailing Address: 3602 Spottswood Ave, Memphis, TN 38111.

GOWANS, ALAN
Educator, Writer
b Toronto, Ont, Nov 30, 23; U S citizen.
Study & Training: Univ Toronto, BA, MA, 46; Princeton Univ, MFA, 48, PhD, 50.
Teaching: Instr art hist, Rutgers Univ, 48-53; asst prof art hist, Middlebury Col, 53-54; chmn dept art & art hist, Univ Del, 56-, prof art hist, 60-; vis prof Univ Edinburgh, fall 64; vis prof Univ Stockholm, spring 65; chmn hist in art, Univ Victoria, 66-; vis prof, Harvard Univ.
Positions: Dir, Fleming Mus, Univ Vt, 54-56.
Awards: Am Coun Learned Socs grant, 49; Alice Davis Hitchcock Award, 65; Can Coun sr fel, 72.
Memberships: Soc Archit Historians (bd dirs, 59-66, secy, 61-64, first v pres, 70-71, pres, 71-); Inst for Study Universal Hist (pres, 70-).
Publications: Auth, Looking at architecture in Canada, 58 & 66, Images of American living, four centuries of architecture and furniture, 64, The restless art, a study of painting and painters, 1750-1950, 66, King Carter's Church, 69 & The unchanging arts, a study of illustration, comics, cartoons, advertising, TV, etc, 70; plus others.
Mailing Address: 3980 Locarno Lane, Victoria, B C, Can.

GRABACH, JOHN R
Painter, Educator
b Greenfield, Mass.
Study & Training: Art Stud League New York, with George B Bridgeman, Frank V DuMond, Kenyen Cox & H August Schwabe.
Work in Public Collections: Philadelphia Art Alliance, Pa; Art Inst Chicago, Ill; Vanderpoel Art Asn, Chicago; John Herron Art Inst, Indianapolis, Ind; Corcoran Gallery Art, Washington, D C; plus many private collections.

Exhibitions: Springfield Art Mus, Mass; Audubon Artists, Nat Acad
Galleries; Pa Acad Fine Arts, Philadelphia; Nat Acad Design,
New York; Detroit Inst Arts; plus many other group & one-man
shows.
Teaching: Heritage, South Orange, N J.
Awards: Peabody prize, Art Inst Chicago; Sesnan gold medal, Pa
Acad Fine Arts; Preston Harrison prize, Los Angeles Co Mus
Art; plus many others.
Memberships: Philadelphia Watercolor Club; Audubon Artists;
Salmagundi Club; Nat Acad Design; Irvington Art Mus Asn (dir);
plus others.
Mailing Address: 915 Sanford Ave, Irvington, NJ 07111.

GRACE, CHARLES M
    Collector
b Manhasset, N Y, Sept 13, 26.
Study & Training: Mount St Mary's Col, AB; Columbia Univ Sch Bus,
MBA.
Memberships: Liturgical Arts Soc; Antique Collectors Club Am;
Art Collectors Club; Am Fedn Arts; life fel Metrop Mus Art.
Mailing Address: Suite 607, 50 E 42nd St, New York, NY 10017.

GRADO, ANGELO JOHN
    Painter, Illustrator
Preferred Media: Oils, Pastels.
b New York, N Y, Feb 17, 22.
Study & Training: Art Stud League New York, with Robert Brack-
man; Nat Acad Design, with Robert Philipp.
Exhibitions: Am Watercolor Soc Exhibs, 58, 60, 63 & 65-71; Allied
Artists Am Exhibs, 61-69; Nat Acad Design, New York, 63; Am
Artists Prof League, New York, 63-72; Hudson Valley Art Asn,
69, 70, 71 & 72.
Positions: Art dir, Freelance, New York, 55-70.
Awards: Salmagundi Club Prize, 69; Am Artists Prof League Award,
70; George F Haight Award, Hudson Valley Art Asn, 72.
Bibliography: Billi Boros (auth), New talent, Art Times Mag, 64.
Memberships: Am Watercolor Soc; Am Artists Prof League; Hudson
Valley Art Asn.
Dealer: Portraits, Inc, 41 E 57th St, New York, NY 10022.
Mailing Address: 641-46th St, Brooklyn, NY 11220.

GRAFLY, DOROTHY (MRS CHARLES H DRUMMOND)
    Art Critic, Writer
b Paris, France, July 29, 96; U S citizen.
Study & Training: Wellesley Col, BA, 18; Radcliffe Col, Harvard
Univ, with Prof George P Baker.
Teaching: Instr art, Drexel Inst, 34-45.
Positions: Art critic & feature writer, Philadelphia North Am, 20-25;
corresp, Christian Sci Monitor, 20-63; art ed, Philadelphia Public
Ledger, 25-34; Philadelphia Record, 34-42; dir res & art & dir
Artists Gallery, Philip Ragan Assoc, Philadelphia, 42-48; ed-
publr, Art in Focus, 49-; art ed, Evening & Sunday Bull, 54-70.
Awards: Distinguished daughter Pa, State Pa, 60; citation of merit,
Da Vinci Art Alliance, 61; citation for civic & cult contrib, City
of Philadelphia, 72.
Memberships: Fel perpetuity, Pa Acad Fine Arts; Altrusa Club
Philadelphia (pres, 30-32); hon mem, Philadelphia Water Color
Club, Am Asn Mus, Am Fedn Arts, plus others.
Publications: Auth, articles in various mags incl Am Mag Art &
Am Artist; contribr, Dict Am Biog & Encycl Britannica.
Mailing Address: 131 N 20th St, Philadelphia, PA 19103.

GRAHAM, BILL (WILLIAM KARR)
    Cartoonist
b Coshocton, Ohio, Dec 14, 20.
Study & Training: Centenary Col, BS(social sci), 42.
Work in Public Collections: Syracuse Univ; Univ Mo; Univ Kans;
Univ Cincinnati; Va Mil Inst.
Exhibitions: Pavilion D'Humor, Montreal, Can, 71; Nat Cartoonists
Soc Traveling Exhib; Asn Am Ed Cartoonists Traveling Exhib.
Memberships: Nat Cartoonists Soc; Asn Am Ed Cartoonists.
Publications: Ed cartoonist, Ark Gazette, 48-
Mailing Address: Arkansas Gazette, Little Rock, AR 72203.

GRAHAM, F LANIER
    Art Historian, Art Administrator
b Shawnee, Okla, Mar 6, 40.
Study & Training: Kenyon Col, 58-60; Am Univ, 61-63, BA, 63; Co-
lumbia Univ, 63-66, MA, 66; N Y Univ Inst Fine Arts, 66-67.
Work in Public Collections: Chess set, Mus Mod Art, New York,
N Y; chess set, Muse Arts Décoratifs, Paris, France.
Positions: Mus asst, Phillips Collection, Washington, D C, 62-63;
assoc cur, Mus Mod Art, New York, 65-70; V dir & chief cur,
M H de Young Mem Mus & Calif Palace Legion of Hon, San Fran-
cisco, 70-
Memberships: Col Art Asn (local chmn nat convention, 72); Soc
Archit Historians.

Publications: Auth, A history of chess sets, Walker, 68; auth, Hector
Guimard, Mus Mod Art, 70; auth, T Edward & Tullah Hanley
Memorial collection, 70; auth, Three centuries of American
painting, 71 & auth, Masterpieces of French art from the Norton
Simon Collections, 73, San Francisco Mus.
Mailing Address: M H De Young Memorial Museum, Golden Gate
Park, San Francisco, CA 94118.

GRAHAM, FRANK P
    Art Administrator
b Grove City, Pa, Oct 21, 23.
Study & Training: Pa State Univ, BS in Arch; Ecole Am Beaux-Arts,
Paris, France; Sch Planning & Res for Regional Develop, London,
Eng.
Positions: Chief, Div Educ, Philadelphia Mus Art, presently.
Art Interests: Architecture, architectural history, art history and
city planning.
Mailing Address: Philadelphia Museum of Art, Division of Education,
Parkway at 26th St, Philadelphia, PA 19101.

GRAHAM, JAMES
    Art Dealer
Positions: Owner, Graham Gallery.
Mailing Address: 1014 Madison Ave, New York, NY 10021.

GRAHAM, JOHN MEREDITH, II
    Museum Director
b Floyd Co, Ga, Dec 23, 05.
Study & Training: Lehigh Univ, 27-28; study in Paris, France, 29-
31; New York Sch Fine & Applied Arts, grad, 31; study in Rome,
Italy, 35-36.
Teaching: Lectr fine arts; frequent radio & TV speaker.
Positions: Cur decorative arts, Brooklyn Mus, 39-60; dir & cur col-
lections, Colonial Williamsburg, 50-70, v pres, 61-70; circulated
Wedgwood Exhib throughout mus in U S & Can, 48; completed
restoration & furnishings interior, Van Cortlandt Manor House
for Sleepy Hollow Restoration, 58; adv, White House Fine Arts
Comt; mem hon bd gov, Wedgwood Int Sem; trustee & consult,
Campbell Mus.
Memberships: Soc Archit Historians; Eng Ceramic Circle; Pewter
Collectors Club New York (past v pres).
Publications: Auth, Popular art in America, 39; ed, Old pottery and
porcelain marks, 47; co-auth, Wedgwood, a living tradition, 48;
auth, American pewter, 49; contribr, Antiques & Am Collector.
Mailing Address: Libby House, Mentone, AL 35984.

GRAHAM, ROBERT CLABERHOUSE
    Art Dealer, Collector
b New York, N Y, Apr 28, 13.
Study & Training: Yale Univ, BFA, 36; New York Univ, 38-39.
Positions: Dir, Graham Gallery.
Specialty of Gallery: Nineteenth and twentieth century American art.
Collection: American and Oriental art.
Mailing Address: 1014 Madison Ave, New York, NY 10021.

GRAMATKY, HARDIE
    Painter, Writer
Preferred Media: Watercolors, Acrylics.
b Dallas, Tex, Apr 12, 07.
Study & Training: Stanford Univ, 26-28; Chouinard Art Sch, Los
Angeles, 28-30.
Work in Public Collections: Art Inst Chicago, Ill; Brooklyn Mus,
N Y; Mus Fine Arts, Springfield, Mass; Toledo Mus Art, Ohio;
Marietta Col, Ohio; Univ Ore, Eugene.
Exhibitions: Am Watercolor Soc, Nat Acad Design Galleries, New
York, N Y, 38-72; Nat Acad Design, 40-72; Chicago Int Exhib,
Art Inst Chicago, 42; America Observed, Soc Illusr, New York,
70; Mainstreams 72, Marietta Col, 72.
Awards: Awards, for Calhoun Street, Art Inst Chicago, 42, Memphis
Levee, Soc Illusr, 70 & Tiptonville Ferry, Marietta Col, 72.
Bibliography: Montgomery (auth), Story behind modern books, Dodd,
49; Helen Painter (auth), Little toot-hero, Elementary English
Mag, 10/60.
Memberships: Nat Acad Design (juror, 41-); Am Watercolor Soc
(dir, 39-); Soc Illusr; Author's Guild.
Publications: Auth, Little toot, 39, Hercules, 40, Nikos & the sea
god, 63, Little toot on the Thames, 66, Happy's Christmas, 70 &
Little toot on the Mississippi, 73, Putnam.
Mailing Address: 60 Roseville Rd, Westport, CT 06880.

GRAMBERG, LILIANA
    Painter, Printmaker
Preferred Media: Graphics.
b Treviso, Italy; U S citizen.
Study & Training: Univ Rome, with Laurea; Escuela Nac Bellas
Artes, Madrid; Atelier Gravure, with Bersier; Ecole Nat Super

Beaux Arts, Paris; Atelier 17, Paris with Hayter; Calif Col Arts & Crafts, MFA.
Work in Public Collections: Mus Art Mod Ville Paris; Brit Mus, London; Nat Collection Fine Arts, Washington, D C; Albertina Graphische Sammlung, Vienna; Rosenwald Collection, Jenkintown, Pa; plus others.
Exhibitions: Northwestern Printmakers; Silvermine Guild; Pa Acad Fine Arts; Alvarez Penteado Found, Sao Paulo, Brazil; plus 14 one-man shows, Smithsonian Inst, Univ Chile, Kunstnerforbundet, Oslo & other insts.
Teaching: Prof fine arts, Trinity Col (D C), 67.
Awards: Treadwell Award, Nat Asn Women Artists, 63; silver medal, Asn Incisori Italia, 64.
Bibliography: Margarita Nelken (auth), El patetico grabado de Liliana Gramberg, Arte (Mex), 3/59; Cajide (auth), Tecnica y poesia de los grabados de Liliana Gramberg, Artes (Spain), 2/61.
Dealer: Franz Bader Gallery, 2124 Pennsylvania Ave, Washington, DC 20037.
Mailing Address: 6322 32nd St N W, Washington, DC 20015.

GRANDEE, JOE RUIZ
Painter, Art Gallery Director
Preferred Media: Oils, Inks.
b Dallas, Tex, Nov 19, 29.
Study & Training: Aunspaugh Art Sch, Dallas.
Work in Public Collections: White House, Washington, D C; Xavier Univ Mus, Cincinnati, Ohio; Mont State Hist Soc Mus, Great Falls; Marine Corps Mus, Quantico, Va; Univ Tex, Arlington.
Commissions: Twenty Mules of Death Valley, U S Borax Co, Hollywood, Calif, 65; Linda Bird & Chuck Robb Off Portrait, Pres Family & Friends, 67; portrait of Johnny Carson, Rudy Tellez, assoc producer NBC, New York, N Y, 67; portrait of Robert Taylor, U S Borax Co for Robert Taylor, Hollywood, Calif, 68; Leander II McNelly, Texas Ranger, Tex Rangers, East Wing of White House, Washington, D C, 72.
Exhibitions: Custer Exhib, Amon Carter Mus Western Art, Fort Worth, Tex, 66; one-man shows, Mont Hist Soc Mus, Great Falls, 64, Los Angeles Music Ctr, Calif, 66, Norton Art Gallery Mus, Shreveport, La, 71 & El Paso Mus Fine Art, Tex, 72; Tex Ranger Mus Show, Waco, Tex, 72.
Positions: Owner, Joe Grandee Gallery & Mus of Old West.
Awards: U S Marine-spec award plaque, U S Marine 4th Div, 69; Grandee Day in Arlington, City of Arlington & Mayor, 69; first off artist of Tex, Tex Legis & Gov, 71; plus others.
Bibliography: Wayne Gard (auth), Joe Grandee—painter of the old west, Am Artist Mag, 67; Grandee paintings, TV film produced by U S Borax Co, 68; Joy Schultz (auth), The west still lives: Grandee, Heritage, 70.
Research: Ruizeem water medium.
Specialty of Gallery: Paintings, drawings & sculpture works of Joe Ruiz Grandee & displays of historical artifacts.
Publications: Illusr, Indian wars of Texas, 65; illusr, Pictorial history of the Texas Rangers, 69; illusr, The Grand Duke Alexis in the U S A, 72; illusr, The life of Jim Baker (mountain man) 1818-1898, 72; contribr, Cowboy series, In: Time-Life Bks, 72.
Dealers: Gene McDaniel, P O Box 433, Midland, TX 79701; Bob Hoff, P O Box 231, Houston, TX 77001.
Mailing Address: 1419 E Abram, Arlington, TX 76010.

GRANLUND, PAUL THEODORE
Sculptor, Instructor
b Minneapolis, Minn, Oct 6, 25.
Study & Training: Gustavus Adolphus Col, BA, 52; Univ Minn; Cranbrook Acad Art, George A Booth scholar, 53, MFA, 54.
Work in Public Collections: Am Swedish Inst; Cranbrook Acad Art; Walker Art Ctr; Va Mus Fine Arts; Sheldon Mem Mus Art Gallery, Lincoln, Nebr; plus others.
Commissions: Sculpture, Gustavus Adolphus Col & Lutheran Church of the Good Shepherd, Minneapolis.
Exhibitions: One-man shows, Calif Palace of Legion of Honor, 62, Univ Nebr, 64 & Washington Univ, 65; group show, La State Univ, 64; Art of Two Cities, Minneapolis Sch Art, 65; plus others.
Teaching: Cranbrook Acad Art, 54; Minneapolis Inst Sch, 55-
Awards: Fulbright fel, 54; Guggenheim fels, 57 & 58.
Memberships: Am Asn Univ Prof.
Dealer: Allan Frumkin Gallery, 41 E 57th St, New York, NY 10022 & 620 N Michigan Ave, Chicago, IL 60611.
Mailing Address: 5320 Russell Ave S, Minneapolis, MN 55410.

GRANSTAFF, WILLIAM BOYD
Painter, Illustrator
Preferred Media: Oils.
b Paducah, Ky, May 17, 25.
Study & Training: Kansas City Art Inst, with Ross Braught & Ed Lanning, grad; Am Acad Art, with William Mosby & Bill Fleming.

Commissions: Mural, Cadet Club, Garden City, Kans, 45; Old Homeplace, B J Farless, Princeton, Ky, 70; Old Log Cabin, Li Henderson, Golden Pond, Ky, 72.
Exhibitions: Mid South, Nashville, Tenn, 53; one-man show, Planters Bank, Hopkinsville, Ky, 72.
Teaching: Instr illus, Famous Artist Sch, 59-61.
Positions: Mem, Art Dir Club, Nashville, 55-58.
Awards: Brackman blue ribbon, Nashville, 53.
Bibliography: Meet your instructors, Famous Artist Mag, 61.
Publications: Illusr, Whats in a word, Abingdon 65, The way out, Moody, 70, Golden treasury of bible stories, Southern, 71 & Man-U S & Americas, 72 & Americans all, 72, Benefic.
Dealer: Bettye-Jos Gallery, Skyline Shopping Ctr, Hopkinsville, KY 42240.
Mailing Address: Old Eddyville Rd, Princeton, KY 42445.

GRASSO, DORIS (TEN-EYCK)
Painter, Sculptor
Preferred Media: Oils, Watercolors, Inks, Pastels, Terra-cotta.
b Fremont, N Y, May 3, 14.
Study & Training: Educ Alliance, New York, N Y, with Moses Soyer, Alex Dobkin & John Hovannes; N Hudson Arts Sch, with Fabian Zaccone; Rutherford Art Sch, with Lucille Hobbie.
Work in Public Collections: Paul Whitener Mem Collection, N C Mus Art; George B Burr Collection, New York; Jersey City Mus Art permanent collection; Staten Island Pub Schs Collection, N Y; Women's Club Collection, Lynhurst, N J.
Exhibitions: Knickerbocker Artists Int, New York, 63-65; Painters & Sculptors Soc N J Nat, 65-72; Nat Casein Soc, New York, 68; Acad Artists Regional, N J, 68-71; Am Artists Prof League Nat, New York, 69-70.
Teaching: Instr art, YWCA, Bayonne, N J, 50-55; instr art, Doris Grasso Sch Fine Arts, 52-62; instr art, Bayonne's Womans Club Eve Dept, 65-68.
Awards: Patrons award for oils, Nat Painters & Sculpture Soc, 67; Pauline Wick award for oils, Am Artists Prof League, 68; first award for sculpture, State Fedn Women's Clubs, 70.
Memberships: Fel Am Artists Prof League (pres, N J Chap; nat dir, 60-62); Painters & Sculptors Soc N J (bd dirs & secy, 62-65); Burr Artists (pub rels, 66-68); Gotham Painters Soc; Hunterdon Art Asn.
Mailing Address: 15 Langsford St, Lanesville, Cape Ann, Gloucester, MA 01930.

GRAUSMAN, PHILIP
Sculptor
Preferred Media: Metals, Stone.
b New York, N Y, Aug 16, 35.
Study & Training: Syracuse Univ, BA(cum luade), 57; Skowhegan Sch Painting & Sculpture, summers 56 & 57; Cranbrook Acad Art, MFA, 59; Art Stud League New York, with Jose de Creeft, 59.
Work in Public Collections: Baltimore Mus Art, Md; Munson-Williams-Proctor Inst, Utica, N Y; Cornell Univ, Ithaca, N Y; Jewish Mus, New York; Univ Mass, Amherst.
Exhibitions: Pa Acad Fine Arts Ann, 60 & 62; Whitney Mus Am Art, 62, 64 & 66; Alpha Gallery, Boston, Mass, 68; one-man shows, Grace Borgenicht Gallery, New York, 66 & Dartmouth Col, 72.
Teaching: Instr design, Cooper Union, 65-67; instr design & drawing, Pratt Inst, 65-69.
Positions: Artist-in-residence, Dartmouth Col, 72.
Awards: Nat Inst Arts & Letters grant, 61; Ford Found purchase grant, 61; Prix de Rome fel, 62-65.
Dealer: Alpha Gallery, 121 Newbury St, Boston, MA 02116.
Mailing Address: c/o Grace Borgenicht Gallery, 1018 Madison Ave, New York, NY 10021.

GRAVES, ARTHUR EARLE
Painter
Preferred Media: Oils.
b Duxbury, Vt, May 1, 07.
Study & Training: Wright Sch Art, Stowe, Vt, with Stan Marc Wright.
Exhibitions: Northern Vt Artists Asn Exhibs, Fleming Mus, Burlington, Vt; Cracker Barrel Exhibs, Newbury, Vt; Champlain Valley Exhibs, Essex Jct, Vt; Chittendon Trust Co, Burlington, 72.
Memberships: Northern Vt Artists Asn (treas, 57-60); Southern Vt Artists.
Mailing Address: 914 North Ave, Burlington, VT 05401.

GRAVES, MAITLAND
Writer, Painter
b New York, N Y, June 27, 02.
Study & Training: Art Stud League New York.
Commissions: Many portrait comns.
Exhibitions: Nat Acad Design, New York; Nat Arts Club, New York; Newark Mus, N J; Allied Artists Am, New York; Archit League, New York.
Teaching: Prof art, Pratt Inst, 29-59; prof art, Univ R I, 61.

Awards: First prizes for mural, portraits & still life & Europ
Traveling scholar, Nat Arts Club.
Memberships: Nat Arts Club; life mem Art Stud League New York.
Publications: Auth, The art of color and design & Color fundamen-
tals, McGraw-Hill; auth, The Graves design judgment test,
Psychol Corp; auth, articles, In: Reader's Digest publ in all int
ed.
Mailing Address: Vineyard Haven, MA 02568.

GRAVES, MORRIS
Painter
Preferred Media: Tempera, Oils.
b Fox Valley, Ore, Aug 28, 10.
Work in Public Collections: Seattle Art Mus; Mus Mod Art, New
York, N Y; Phillips Mem Gallery; Whitney Mus Am Art, New
York; Metrop Mus Art, New York.
Exhibitions: One-man shows, Seattle Art Mus, 36, Willard Art
Gallery, 42-71, Detroit Art Inst, 43, Los Angeles Co Mus,
48 & Art Inst Chicago, 48.
Awards: Guggenheim Found fel, 46; Blair Prize, Art Inst Chicago,
48; Windsor Award, Duke & Duchess of Windsor, 57.
Bibliography: Duncan Phillips (auth), article, In: Mag Art, 12/47;
Frederick Wight (auth), Morris Graves, Univ Calif Press, 56;
Katherine Kuh (auth), The artist's voice, Harper & Rowe, 60.
Memberships: Hon mem Am Watercolor Soc.
Mailing Address: c/o Willard Gallery, 29 E 72nd St, New York, NY
10021.

GRAVES, NANCY STEVENSON
Painter, Sculptor
b Pittsfield, Mass, 40.
Study & Training: Vassar Col, fel, 71, BA; Yale Univ Sch Art &
Archit, BFA & MFA.
Work in Public Collections: Mus Mod Art, New York, N Y; Whitney
Mus Am Art; Berkeley Mus Art; Nat Gallery Ottawa; Wallraf-
Richartz Mus, Cologne, Ger.
Exhibitions: Individual exhibs, Whitney Mus Am Art, 69, Neue
Galerie Alten Kurhaus, Aachen, 71 & Projects, Mus Mod Art,
New York, 71; Paris Biennale, Paris, France, 71; Documenta,
Kassel, Ger, 72.
Awards: Fulbright-Hays grant painting, Paris, 64-68.
Bibliography: E Wasserman (auth), Interview, Artforum, 3/70; P
Tuchman (auth), Nancy Graves, sculpture, drawings, films 1969-
1971, Neue Galerie, 9/71; B Richardson (auth) article, In: Arts,
4/72.
Mailing Address: 164 Mulberry St, New York, NY 10013.

GRAY, CLEVE
Painter, Sculptor
b New York, N Y, Sept 22, 18.
Study & Training: Princeton Univ, BA, 40.
Work in Public Collections: Guggenheim Mus, New York; Whitney
Mus Am Art, New York; Phillips Collection, Washington, D C;
Addison Gallery Am Art, Andover, Mass; Univ Art Gallery,
Berkeley, Calif.
Exhibitions: Most nat exhibs contemp art, 47-
Awards: Univ Ill Purchase Award, 51; Ford Found Award, 61.
Bibliography: Daniel Robbins (auth), Cleve Gray, Art Int, 3/64; Kim
Levin (auth), Gray's ceres series, Art News, 11/67.
Publications: Ed, David Smith, 68; ed, John Marin, 70; ed, Hans
Richter, 71.
Dealer: Betty Parsons Gallery, 24 W 57th St, New York, NY 10019.
Mailing Address: P O Cornwall Bridge, CT 06754.

GRAY, FRANCINE DU PLESSIX
Writer
b Warsaw, Poland, Sept 25, 30.
Study & Training: Bryn Mawr Col; Barnard Col, BA.
Positions: Writer, United Press, 53-54; ed asst, Realities, 54-55;
mem ed bd, Art in Am, 65-
Awards: Putnam Award for creative writing, Barnard Col, 52.
Publications: Contribr essays, fiction, profiles, In: New Yorker,
Vogue, Mademoiselle & House & Garden.
Mailing Address: Editorial Board, Art in America, 150 E 58th St,
New York, NY 10022.

GRAY, JIM
Painter, Instructor
Preferred Media: Watercolors.
b Middleton, Tenn, June 4, 32.
Work in Public Collections: Carnegie Libr, Regar Mus, Anniston,
Ala; Int Trade Ctr, Mobile, Ala; City of Malaga, Spain; First Fed
Collection, Mobile; Sevier Co Libr, Sevierville, Tenn.
Exhibitions: One-man shows, Frame House Gallery, Louisville, Ky,
69 & Percy Whiting Mus, Fairhope, Ala, 70; three-man show,

Long Boat Key Art Ctr, Sarasota, Fla, 70; Watercolor U S A,
Springfield, Mo, 70; Realist Invitational, Gallery Contemp Art,
Winston-Salem, N C, 71.
Teaching: Instr painting, Buckhorn Art Workshop, Gatlinburg, Tenn,
68-; instr watercolor, Atlanta Artist Club, Ga, 69-; lectr art &
humanities, Univ Tenn, Knoxville, 70-71.
Positions: Gov appointee, Ala State Comn Arts, 63-68.
Awards: Three times Best in Show & Permanent Trophy, Azalea
Trail Arts Festival, 57-59; twice Best of Show, Hammel-Adams
Glass, Mobile, 62-63.
Bibliography: P Winfrey (auth), Living & painting in the Smokies,
Great Smoky Mountains, spring-summer 67; Gordon Young (auth),
article, In: Nat Geog Mag, 10/68; K Lingo (auth), Southern per-
sonalities, Southern Living Mag, 11/72.
Memberships: Tenn Watercolorists; Atlanta Artist Club; Knoxville
Watercolor Soc.
Publications: Illusr, covers, Port Mobile, 62-66.
Dealer: Jim Gray Gallery, Parkway, Gatlinburg, TN 37738.
Mailing Address: Rte 1, Buckhorn Rd, Gatlinburg, TN 37738.

GRAY, RICHARD
Art Dealer
b Chicago, Ill, Dec 30, 28.
Positions: Owner & dir, Richard Gray Gallery.
Memberships: Art Dealers Asn Am (dir); Chicago Art Dealers Asn
(pres); Col Art Asn.
Specialty of Gallery: Paintings, sculpture, drawings & prints by
established European & American artists & the avante garde.
Mailing Address: Richard Gray Gallery, 620 N Michigan Ave, Chi-
cago, IL 60611.

GRAY, ROBERT WARD
Art Administrator
b Tallahassee, Fla, June 26, 16.
Study & Training: Univ Fla; Tri-State Col; Grad Sch Am Craftsmen,
with Herbert H Sanders.
Collections Arranged: Co-dir, New England Craft Exhib, 55.
Positions: In charge pottery shop & coordr craft prog, Old Stur-
bridge Village, 49-51; dir, Worchester Craft Ctr, 51-61; dir,
Southern Highland Handicraft Guild, 61-
Mailing Address: Southern Highlands Handicraft Guild, 15 Reddick
Rd, Asheville, NC 28805.

GRAY, WELLINGTON BURBANK
Educator, Designer
Preferred Media: Tempera, Watercolors.
b Albany, N Y, Apr 25, 19.
Study & Training: Univ Philippines, 46; Kutztown State Col, BS, 47;
N Y Univ, MA, 48, EdD, 54.
Work in Public Collections: Edinboro State Col, Pa; Erie Pub Mus,
Pa; Carnegie Libr, Connellsville, Pa; E Carolina Univ, Green-
ville, N C; Gov Gen Off Novmea, New Caledonia.
Exhibitions: One-man show, E Carolina Univ, Greenville, 67; two-
man shows, Greenville Art Ctr, 68, Mt Olive Col, N C, 68, Wayne
Community Col, Goldsboro, N C, 69 & Lenoir Community Col,
Kinston, N C, 69.
Teaching: Dir art, Highland Park Ill High Sch, 49-54; dir art educ,
Edinboro State Col, 54-56; prof art educ & interior design &
dean, E Carolina Univ Sch Art, 56-
Awards: Alumni citation, Kutztown State Col, 63.
Memberships: Nat Soc Interior Design (chap v pres); N C Art Educ
Asn (chmn higher educ); Southeastern Arts Asn (co-chmn col
teachers, 64-66); Inst Asn Fine Arts Deans; Southern Col Art
Conf.
Publications: Auth, Historical status of graduate degrees in art
education, J Educ Res, 57; auth, Student teaching in art, Int Text-
book, 60; auth, A minority report, 9/60, auth, Four crises in the
arts, 12/64 & auth, Teacher surplus: not in art, 3/71, N C Educ.
Mailing Address: 2001 Brook Rd, Greenville, NC 27834.

GRAZIANI, SANTE
Painter, Designer
b Cleveland, Ohio, Mar 11, 20.
Study & Training: Cleveland Sch Art, 38-41; Sch Fine Arts, Yale
Univ, BFA, 43, MFA, 48.
Commissions: Murals, Bluffton Post Off, Ohio, 41, Columbus Junc-
tion Post Off, Iowa, 42 & Holyoke Pub Libr, Mass, 49-51; murals,
Am Battle Monument, Henri-Chapelle, Belgium, 55-58 & Mayo
Clinic, Rochester, Minn, 69; plus others.
Exhibitions: Six one-man shows, Babcock Galleries, New York, 62-
71, Kanegis Gallery, Boston, 64-70, Univ Conn, Storrs, 70, Fair-
weather-Hardin Gallery, Chicago, 70 & Allentown Art Mus, 70;
plus others.
Teaching: Instr drawing & painting, Sch Fine Arts, Yale Univ, 46-
51; dean, Whitney Sch Art, 50-51; head Worcester Art Mus Sch,
51-

Positions: Officer-in-charge arts & crafts, USA, Pacific Theatre, 45-46.
Awards: Pulitzer Prize, 42; Boston Art Dirs Club Award, 54; spec drawing award, Norfolk Mus, 61; plus others.
Memberships: Nat Soc Mural Painters.
Dealers: Fairweather-Hardin Gallery, 101 E Ontario St, Chicago, IL 60611; Kanegis Gallery, 244 Newbury St, Boston, MA 02116.
Mailing Address: Worcester Art Museum, 55 Salisbury St, Worcester, MA 01545.

GRAZIANO, FLORENCE V MERCOLINO
Painter, Sculptor
Preferred Media: Oils, Pastels, Charcoals, Watercolors, Clays, Graphics.
b Plainfield, N J.
Study & Training: Columbus Col Art & Design; Art Stud League New York, with Robert Brackman, R B Hale, R de Lamonica & John Hovannes; Cape Sch Art; John Pike Watercolor Sch.
Work in Public Collections: Washington Co Mus Fine Arts, Hagerstown, Md; Sheldon Swope Mus Art, Terre Haute, Ind; Univ Maine, Orono; Rutgers Univ, N J; Eisenhower Col, Seneca Falls, N Y.
Commissions: Portrait of Henri Nosco, conductor of NBC Symphony Orchestra, 58; portrait & brochure, comn by Hildegarde, New York, N Y, 65 & 70; portrait comn by Mrs Jimmy Durante, Beverly Hills, Calif, 71; portrait comn by Claude Philippe, New York, 72; program & brochure, Plainfield Symphony, N J, 72-73.
Exhibitions: Int Art Show, New York, 70; Hudson Valley Art Asn Ann Exhib, New York, 70-71; Salon Soc l'Ecole Francaise, Paris, France, 71; Biennale Int Officielle d'Art Contemporain de Vichy, France, 72; Allied Artists Am, N Y, 72.
Teaching: Dir & instr art, Graziano Sch Arts, Marion, Ohio, 59-68; dir & instr art, Graziano Studio Fine Arts, Plainfield, N J, 69-; lectr & demonstr various art orgn, 59-
Positions: Dir first art show & sales, Marion Co Fair, 67; asst chmn & publ dir, Plainfield Festival Arts, 70.
Awards: First prize for sculpture & second prize for painting, Convention Hall Art Exhib, Las Vegas, Nev, 68; first prize for oils, Plainfield Art Asn, 68, 69 & 70; first for drawing & oil, Washington Hilton Art Show, D C, 69.
Bibliography: R Clermont (auth), La Rev Mod, Paris, 4/72; Lee Leary (auth), article, In: Spotlight Mag, 7/72; Leo Soretsky (auth), Opus artis, FM Guide, 8/72.
Memberships: Nat Arts Club; Am Artist Prof League (bd mem N J chap, 71-); Miniature Art Soc N J (mem comt, 72-); Plainfield Art Asn (bd mem, 69-); Hunterdon Art Ctr.
Mailing Address: 1413 Highland Ave, Plainfield, NJ 07060.

GREACEN, NAN (NAN GREACEN FAURE)
Painter, Instructor
Preferred Media: Oils.
b Giverny, France; U S citizen.
Study & Training: Brearley Sch, New York, N Y; Grand Cent Sch Art, New York.
Teaching: Instr art, Grand Cent Sch Art, New York, 31-42; instr pvt classes, 42-
Awards: Hallgarten Prize, Nat Acad Design, 36; gold medal, Montclair Art Mus, 38; Nat Arts Club Medal, 40.
Memberships: Nat Acad Design; Allied Artists Am; Audubon Artists; Hudson Valley Art Asn.
Publications: Auth, Still life is exciting, 69; auth, The magic of flower painting, 72.
Dealers: Grand Central Art Galleries, 40 Vanderbilt Ave, New York, NY 10017; McNichol Gallery, Naples, FL 33940.
Mailing Address: 184 San Juan Dr, Ponte Vedra Beach, FL 32082.

GREAVER, HANNE
Printmaker
b Copenhagen, Denmark, Aug 1, 33.
Study & Training: Kunsthaandvaerkerskolen, Copenhagen.
Work in Public Collections: Beloit Col, Wis; Univ Calif, Davis; Columbus Mus Arts & Crafts, Ga; Univ Ga; Univ Maine, Orono.
Exhibitions: Two-man show, Univ Ga, 64; Left Bank Gallery, Flint, Mich, 68, Univ Maine, Orono, 70 & Brick Store Mus, Kennebunk, Maine, 71; Five Women Printmakers, Kalamazoo Inst Arts, Mich, 69.
Mailing Address: 314 S Park St, Kalamazoo, MI 49006.

GREAVER, HARRY
Art Administrator, Painter
Preferred Media: Watercolors.
b Los Angeles, Calif, Oct 30, 29.
Study & Training: Univ Kans, BFA & MFA.
Work in Public Collections: Amherst Col, Mass; Colby Col, Maine; Univ Maine, Orono; New York Pub Libr; Norfolk Mus Arts & Sci, Va.

Exhibitions: Drawings U S A, St Paul, Minn, 63; Am Drawing Biennial, Norfolk Mus, 65; Drawing & Small Sculpture Show, Ball State Univ, Ind, 68; Second Nat Print Show, San Diego, Calif, 71; Watercolor Invitational, Chico State Col, Calif, 72.
Collections Arranged: Paintings by American Masters, 66, Western Art, 67 & The Surrealist, 71, Kalamazoo Inst Arts, Mich.
Teaching: Assoc prof art, Univ Maine, Orono, 55-66.
Positions: Dir, Kalamazoo Inst Arts, 66-
Awards: Purchase Awards, Norfolk Mus, 63 & 64.
Mailing Address: 314 S Park St, Kalamazoo, MI 49006.

GREBE (E P GREBE RIMMEL)
Painter, Lecturer
Preferred Media: Oils.
b Royersford, Pa, Mar 5, 09.
Study & Training: Moore Col Art; Univ Pa, Am Foundrymen's Asn cert; also with Sam Feinstein & Hans Hofmann.
Work in Public Collections: Royersford Jr H S, Pa; Embreville State Hosp, Pa.
Exhibitions: 16 Philadelphia Women Painters, Carl Schurz Found Invitational, 57; Norfolk Mus Drawing Show, Va, 65; Childe Hassam Purchase Exhib, Am Acad Arts & Lett, 68; 125th Anniversary Invitational, Moore Col Art, 69; two-man invitational show, Ursinus Col, 69.
Teaching: Instr pvt studio, 50-
Memberships: Alumnae Asn Moore Col Art; West Chester Art Asn; Art Resources Inst, Los Angeles, Calif.
Mailing Address: 406 N Lewis Rd, Royersford, PA 19468.

GREBENAK, DOROTHY
Craftsman
b Oxford, Nebr.
Work in Public Collections: Work in pvt collections only.
Exhibitions: Kansas City Art Inst, 64; Milwaukee Art Ctr, 65; Larry Aldrich Mus, Ridgefield, Conn, 67; Am Fedn Arts Traveling Exhib, 69; Money in Art, Chelsea Nat Bank, New York, 69; plus others.
Mailing Address: 16 Montgomery Pl, Brooklyn, NY 11215.

GRECO, ANTHONY JOSEPH
Painter, Sculptor
b Cleveland, Ohio, Apr 24, 37.
Study & Training: Cleveland Inst Art, with Louis Bosa, BFA, 60; Kent State Univ, with Joseph O'Sickey, MFA, 66.
Work in Public Collections: Butler Inst Am Art, Youngstown, Ohio; Kent State Univ; Ga State Art Comn.
Exhibitions: Butler Inst Am Art Ann, Youngstown; Akron Art Inst Spring Exhibs, Ohio; Cleveland Mus Art May Shows, Ohio; Hunter Gallery Art Ann Exhibs, Chatanooga, Tenn, 68-69; Alumni from Twenty Years, 1949-1969, Cleveland Inst Art, 70.
Teaching: Chmn drawing dept, Atlanta Sch Art, 66-; vis instr drawing & painting, Univ Wis-Madison, summer 69.
Awards: Hon mention & purchase award, Butler Inst Am Art Midyear, 61; B F Goodrich Mem Award, Akron Art Inst Ann, 70.
Dealer: Image South Gallery, 1931 Peachtree Rd N E, Atlanta, GA 30309.
Mailing Address: 839 Crestridge Dr N E, Atlanta, GA 30306.

GREEN, DAVID OLIVER
Sculptor, Educator
Preferred Media: Stone, Wood, Metals.
b Enid, Okla, June 29, 08.
Study & Training: Am Acad Art; Nat Acad Art.
Work in Public Collections: Los Angeles Co Mus Natural Hist, Calif.
Commissions: Dragonfly Fountain, Welton Beckett Asn, Hillsdale Shopping Ctr, San Mateo, Calif, 55; five figure group, Lytton Savings & Loan Asn, Hollywood, Calif, 60; children's sculpture, Women's Club for Bruggemeyer Mem Libr, Monterey Park, Calif, 68; Owl Tree (wall relief), dedicated to daughters of Maurice Fletcher & Tree of Life (fountain), Guyer Mem, Altadena Libr, Calif, 69.
Exhibitions: Los Angeles Co Mus Art Ann, 61; Tucson Art Ctr, Ariz, 63; Southern Calif Expos, San Diego Fair, Del Mar, 66; Citrus Col Invitational, Glendora, Calif, 68; 17th Ann All Calif Exhib, Laguna Beach Art Gallery, Calif, 71.
Teaching: Asst prof sculpture, Otis Art Inst, 47-; instr sculpture, Pasadena Art Mus, Calif, 56-59; asst prof sculpture, Scripps Col, Claremont, Calif, 66.
Awards: First prize for sculpture, Laguna Beach Art Asn, 62 & 67; first prize for sculpture, Pasadena Soc Artists, 71.
Bibliography: Jarvis Barlow (auth), David Green, Pasadena Independent, 7/13/47; Bev Johnson (auth), Owls, cats & bats, Los Angeles Times Sun Sect, 3/13/60; Peg Powell (auth), A way with animals, Independent Star-News, 12/15/63.
Memberships: Int Inst Arts & Lett; Pasadena Soc Artists.
Mailing Address: 176 W Jaxine Dr, Altadena, CA 91001.

GREEN, EDWARD ANTHONY
Art Administrator, Designer
Preferred Media: Watercolors.
b Milwaukee, Wis, Apr 20, 22.
Study & Training: Univ Wis-Madison, BS & MS, with Misch Kohn, Al
Sessler, Dean Meeker & Warrington Colescott; Layton Sch Art,
Milwaukee, 52; Univ Wis-Milwaukee, MFA, 66.
Work in Public Collections: Alverno Col, Milwaukee; Marine Bank,
Milwaukee; Manpower, Milwaukee; Cherokee Art Mus, Iowa;
Univ Wis-Madison.
Commissions: Church for Baptist Mission, Bamenda, British
Cameroons, 62; outdoor fountains, Conrad Mem, 66.
Exhibitions: Wis State Fair, 49-72; Wis Painters & Sculptors, 50-
72; Wis Printmakers, 54-72; Beloit & Vicinity, Wis, 58-72; Wis
Watercolors, 67-72.
Collections Arranged: Streets of Old Milwaukee; Hanseatic League;
Hopi Pueblo; Kwakiutl Plank House; Guatemala Market; Japanese
House & Garden; Mexican Courtyard; plus many others.
Teaching: Instr watercolor & life drawing, Univ Wis-Milwaukee, 55-;
instr outdoor sketching, Whitnall Park, Milwaukee, 68-.
Positions: Archit designer, Off Martin White, 40-42; archit model
maker, Off Allen Wadsworth, 47-48; art dir, Milwaukee Pub Mus,
51-; art & landmarks comnr, City of Milwaukee, 67-
Awards: First awards, for watercolor, Grumbacher, 62, serigraph,
Wis Printmakers, 64 & watercolor, Wis State Fair, 67.
Bibliography: Frank Getlein (auth), 55 & Jane Moynihan (auth), 63,
articles, In: Milwaukee J; Margaret Rahill (auth), article, In;
Milwaukee Sentinel, 56.
Memberships: Milwaukee Art Comn (chmn, 67-); Mus Artisans Guild
(pres, 68-); Midwest Mus Asn; Am Asn Mus; Milwaukee Art Ctr.
Publications: Illusr, West African art, 53, East Indians in the West
Indies, 60, Cameroons village, 62, Masks of the Northwest coast,
66 & Iroquois false-face masks, 69.
Dealer: Bradley Gallery, 2565 N Downer Ave, Milwaukee, WI 53211.
Mailing Address: 3173 S 31st St, Milwaukee, WI 53215.

GREEN, SAMUEL MAGEE
Art Historian, Painter
Preferred Media: Oils.
b Oconomowac, Wis, May 22, 09.
Study & Training: Harvard Univ, BA & PhD(cum laude); Pennsyl-
vania Acad Fine Arts.
Work in Public Collections: Fogg Mus Art; Smith Col Mus; Dart-
mouth Col; Libr Cong.
Exhibitions: Lyman Allyn Mus, New London, Conn; Speed Mem Mus,
Louisville, Ky, 50; one-man shows, Doll & Richards Gallery,
New York, N Y, 52 & 56; Acad Arts & Lett, New York, 53.
Teaching: Prof art hist & chmn dept, Wesleyan Univ, 48-; spec
lectr art hist, Salzburg Sem Am Studies, Austria, 53, 54 & 58;
vis prof art hist, Yale Univ, 60-61.
Awards: First prize, Conn Watercolor Soc, 55.
Memberships: Col Art Asn Am (chmn Am panel, 53); Soc Am His-
torians.
Publications: Auth, American art: an historical survey, Ronald
Press, 66.
Mailing Address: Davison Art Center, Wesleyan University, Middle-
town, CT 06457.

GREEN, WILDER
Art Administrator, Architect
b Paris, France, Apr 17, 27; U S citizen.
Study & Training: Yale Col, 45-47; Ill Inst Technol, & Design Inst,
Chicago, Ill, 47-48; Yale Univ Sch Archit, BArch, 52.
Teaching: Asst prof, Yale Sch Archit, 56-57; Hunter Col, 67-68.
Positions: Asst dir (cur), dept archit & design, Mus Mod Art, New
York, 57-61, coordr planning for bldg prog, 61-63, coordr prog,
63-67, dir exhib prog, 67-69, dep to actg dir, 69-70, dir exhib
prog, 70-71; pres, Cunnigham Dance Found, 69-; dir, Am Fedn
Arts, 71-
Memberships: Munic Art Soc New York; Archit League New York;
Archives Am Art; Am Asn Mus; Drawing Soc (mem exec comt,
62-).
Mailing Address: American Federation of Arts, 41 E 65th St, New
York, NY 10021.

GREENAMYER, GEORGE MOSSMAN
Sculptor, Educator
Preferred Media: Steel, Aluminum.
b Cleveland, Ohio, July 13, 39.
Study & Training: Philadelphia Col Art, BFA; Univ Kans, MFA.
Commissions: Bronze relief, Exhib Serv Int, New York, N Y, 65;
ceramic fountain, Collaborative Workshop, New York, 66; steel
column, comn by Malcolm Wells, Cherry Hill, N J, 68; bell tower,
Haystack Mountain Sch Arts & Crafts, Deer Isle, Maine, 70; steel
mountain, Basteille-Neilly Architects, Boston, Mass, 72.

Exhibitions: Five New Eng Sculptors, Phillips Exeter Acad, N H, 72;
one-man show, Univ Mass, Boston, 72; New Work, Inst Contemp
Art, Boston, 72; Outdoor Sculpture Show, De Cordova Mus, Lincoln, Mass, 72; Puritans Exhib Galleries, Boston City Hall, 72.
Teaching: Asst prof sculpture, at present, Mass Col Art, chmn dept,
71-
Awards: First award, Greater Fall River Nat Exhib, Mass, 65; third
award & hon mention, Greater Fall River Art Asn Nat, 66; hon
mention, Things Show, Brockton Art Ctr, Mass, 72.
Bibliography: Hilton Kramer (auth), Art in Boston kindles hope for
cities, New York Times, 5/70; Ellen Dyer (auth), Life and shape
of glass, clay and steel, Patriot Ledger, 4/71; Robert Taylor
(auth), Work of 3 sculptors nicely tied in at City Hall, Boston
Globe, 10/72.
Memberships: Boston Visual Artists Union; New Eng Sculptors Asn.
Mailing Address: 994 Careswell St, Marshfield, MA 02050.

GREENBAUM, DOROTHEA SCHWARCZ
Sculptor
Preferred Media: Lead, Stone, Bronze.
b New York, N Y, June 17, 93.
Study & Training: New York Sch Fine & Appl Art; Art Stud League
New York.
Work in Public Collections: Whitney Mus Am Art; Philadelphia Mus;
N J State Mus; Pa Acad Design; Mus Art, Ogunquit.
Commissions: Princeton Pub Libr, N J; Mus Art, Ogunquit.
Exhibitions: 15 one-man shows, Whitney Mus Am Art, Art Inst Chi-
cago, Pa Acad Design & other mus.
Awards: George Widener Mem Medal, 41; gold medal for sculpture,
Pa Acad Design, 47; Ford Found grant, Asn Women Artists, 56.
Memberships: Nat Inst Arts & Lett; assoc Nat Acad Design.
Dealers: Sculpture Center, 167 E 69th St, New York, NY 10021;
Princeton Gallery of Fine Arts, 9 Spring St, Princeton, NJ
08540.
Mailing Address: 104 Mercer St, Princeton, NJ 08540.

GREENBERG, CLEMENT
Writer, Art Critic
b Bronx, N Y, Jan 16, 09.
Study & Training: Art Stud League New York, 24-25; Syracuse Univ,
AB, 30.
Publications: Auth, Joan Miro, 48, Matisse, 53, Art and Culture, 61
& Hofmann, 61.
Mailing Address: 275 Central Park W, New York, NY 10024.

GREENBERG, GLORIA
Painter, Designer
Preferred Media: Acrylics.
b New York, N Y, Mar 4, 32.
Study & Training: Cooper Union Art Sch, cert, 52; Yale-Norfolk Art
Sch, scholar, 52, painting with Nicholas Marsicano; Brooklyn Mus
Art Sch, scholar, 53, printmaking with Gabor Peterdi.
Work in Public Collections: 4 Squares, acrylic panels, Kennedy Air-
port, 72.
Exhibitions: Brooklyn Mus Print Ann, 53; Soc Beaux Arts Dordogne,
France, 59; 14th Ann New Eng Exhib, Silvermine Guild Artists,
63.
Positions: Art consult & book designer, jr books div, Harper & Row
Publ, 65-72.
Awards: Medal of honor, Soc Beaux Arts Dordogne, 59.
Memberships: Mus Mod Art.
Publications: Co-auth & illusr, Away we go, 63 & Strange plants and
animals, 64, Harvey.
Dealer: Fifty-Five Mercer Gallery, 55 Mercer St, New York, NY
10013.
Mailing Address: 118 E 17th St, New York, NY 11003.

GREENBERG, SHIRLEE BERNICE
Painter
Preferred Media: Acrylics.
b Brooklyn, N Y, Apr 5, 25.
Study & Training: Pratt Inst, cert in illus; Brooklyn Mus, with Isaac
Soyer; Art Stud League New York, with Sidney Dickenson; also
with Alexander Dobkin & Paul Margin.
Work in Public Collections: Reflections No 11, Mont State Univ,
Bozeman; drawing, Univ Mass, Amherst.
Exhibitions: North Shore Community Ann, 67; Berkshire Art Asn
Fall Show, Mass, 68; 19th Ann New England Exhib, Conn, 68;
Second Ann N Y Exhib for Painters & Sculptors, 69; Am Acad
Arts & Lett Ann, New York, 69.
Awards: Eloise Egan Mem award, Silvermine Guild Artists, 68;
Charles Pincu Mem award, Berkshire Art Mus, 68; Childe Has-
sam purchase award, Am Acad Arts & Lett, 69.
Memberships: Prof Artists Guild; Silvermine Guild Artists.
Dealer: Alonzo Gallery, 26 E 63rd St, New York, NY 10021.
Mailing Address: 620 Mohawk Rd, West Hempstead, NY 11552.

GREENBOWE, F DOUGLAS
Painter
Preferred Media: Watercolors.
b Bayonne, N J, Sept 19, 21.
Study & Training: Art League New York, with Frank DuMond.
Work in Public Collections: Butler Inst Am Art, Youngstown, Ohio; Dayton Art Inst, Ohio; Phoenix Mus Art, Ariz; Art Inst Chicago, Ill; Seattle Art Mus, Wash; plus others.
Commissions: Paintings, Bank of Douglas, Tucson & Ariz Bank of Tucson.
Exhibitions: Am Watercolor Soc Ann; Brooklyn Mus, N Y; Pa Acad Fine Arts, Philadelphia; New J Watercolor Soc; Am Acad Arts & Lett; plus others.
Awards: Medal, Nat Arts Club, 53; two medals, Arizona State Fair, 63.
Memberships: Am Watercolor Soc; Ariz Watercolor Asn.
Mailing Address: 41 W First Ave, Scottsdale, AZ 85251.

GREENE, BALCOMB
Painter
b Niagara Falls, N Y, May 22, 04.
Study & Training: Syracuse Univ, AB, 26; New York Univ, AM, 40; Univ Vienna, 26-28.
Work in Public Collections: Mus Mod Art, Whitney Mus Am Art, Metrop Mus Art & Solomon R Guggenheim Mus, New York, N Y; Carnegie Inst, Pittsburgh, Pa; plus many others.
Exhibitions: Art Ctr Los Angeles, Calif, 64; Tampa Art Inst, Fla, 66; Santa Barbara Mus Art, Calif, 66; Phoenix Art Mus, Ariz, 66; Fairweather-Hardin Gallery, Chicago, 69; plus many others.
Teaching: Instr art, Dartmouth Col, 28-31; assoc prof, Carnegie Inst Technol, 42-59.
Positions: Ed, Art Front, 35-36.
Awards: Carol H Beck Medal; Critic's Choice, Art News, four times.
Memberships: Am Fedn Arts; fel Int Inst Arts & Lett; Am Abstract Artists (first chmn, 36-37, 38-41); Century Club.
Dealers: Forum Gallery, 1018 Madison Ave, New York, NY 10021; Bednarz Gallery, 902 N La Cienega Blvd, Los Angeles, CA 90069.
Mailing Address: 345 E 52nd St, New York, NY 10022.

GREENE, DANIEL E
Painter
b Cincinnati, Ohio, Feb 26, 34.
Study & Training: Art Acad Cincinnati; Art Stud League New York, N Y, Thelka M Bernays scholar, 54-55, with Robert Brackman; Nat Acad Design, with Robert Philipp.
Work in Public Collections: Norfolk Mus; Greenshields Mus, Montreal; Shelburne Mus; Yale Univ; U S Senate; plus many others.
Commissions: Portraits, of Keith Funston, New York Stock Exchange, George Romney, State of Mich, Elmer Bobst, Warner Lambert Pharmaceut Co, George D Aiken, State of Vt & Archibald Davis & John Watlington, Wachovia Nat Bank; plus many others.
Awards: Hilldebrand Portrait Prize, Hudson Valley Art Asn, 66; Coun Am Artists Award, Hudson Valley, 66; Pauline Law Award, Nat Art Club, 67; plus many others.
Memberships: Assoc Nat Acad Design; Am Watercolor Soc; Allied Artists Am; Audubon Artists; Nat Arts Club; plus others.
Mailing Address: c/o Portraits, Inc, 41 E 57th St, New York, NY 10022.

GREENE, ETHEL MAUD
Painter
Preferred Media: Acrylics.
b Malden, Mass, Nov 11, 12.
Study & Training: Boston Univ Sch Art; Sch Boston Mus; Mass Sch Art.
Work in Public Collections: Calif Western Univ, San Diego; Southwestern Col, Chula Vista, Calif; Calif State Univ, San Diego; Fine Arts Collectors, Inc, San Diego.
Exhibitions: Artists of Los Angeles & Vicinity, Los Angeles Co Mus, 50, 52 & 55; one-man shows, La Jolla Mus, Calif, 56, Feingarten Gallery, Los Angeles, Calif, 70 & Ariz State Univ, Tempe, Ariz, 72; two-man show, Fine Arts Gallery, San Diego, 61.
Awards: San Diego Co Expos Awards, 48, 54, 63 & 72; La Jolla Mus Ann Award, 58; Two Californias Award, Calif Western Univ, 63.
Bibliography: Marilyn Hagberg (auth), The visual puns of Ethel Greene, San Diego Mag, 7/70; Henry Flood Robert, Jr (auth), exhib catalogue, Ariz State Univ, 1/72.
Memberships: San Diego Art Guild (pres, 56); Calif Nat Watercolor Soc.
Publications: Illusr, A dog called bum, 60.
Dealer: Karlebach Gallery, 11-18 Saddle River Rd, Fairlawn, NJ 07410.
Mailing Address: 2940 Helix St, Spring Valley, CA 92077.

GREENE, JENNIE, see MORSE, JENNIE GREENE.

GREENE, STEPHEN
Painter
Preferred Media: Oil.
b New York, N Y, Sept 19, 18.
Study & Training: Art Stud League; State Univ Iowa, BFA, 42, MA, 45; studied with Philip Guston.
Work in Public Collections: Whitney Mus Am Art, New York, N Y; Solomon R Guggenheim Mus, New York; Metrop Mus Art, New York; Tate Gallery, London, Eng; Corcoran Gallery Art, Washington, D C.
Exhibitions: The New Decade, Whitney Mus Am Art, 55; Abstract Expressionists and Imagists, Solomon R Guggenheim Mus, 61; VI Sao Paolo Bienal, Brazil, 61; Internatinale Der Zeichnung, Darmstadt, Ger, 64; L'Art Vivant aux Etats-Unis, Fondation Maeght, France, 71.
Teaching: Artist-in-residence, Princeton Univ, 58-59; instr painting & drawing, Art Stud League, New York, 59-65; from asst prof to prof painting & drawing, Tyler Sch Art, Temple Univ, 65-
Awards: Prix de Rome, Am Acad Rome, 49; grant, Coun Arts & Lett, 66; award, Inst Arts & Lett, 67.
Bibliography: H W Janson (auth), Stephen Greene, Mag Art, 48; Michael Fried (Auth), The Goals of Stephen Greene, Arts Mag, 4 & 5/63; Barbara Rose (auth), Stephen Greene, Art Int, 4/63.
Dealer: William Zierler Gallery, 956 Madison Ave, New York, NY 10021.
Mailing Address: 408A Storms Rd, Valley Cottage, NY 10989.

GREENE-MERCIER, MARIE ZOE
Sculptor, Draftsman
Preferred Media: Bronze, Steel.
b Madison, Wis, Mar 31, 11.
Study & Training: Radcliffe Col, Harvard Univ, AB(fine arts), 33; New Bauhaus, Chicago, Ill, with Moholy-Nagy, Archipenko & Gyorgy Kepes, 37-38.
Work in Public Collections: Mus des Sables, Barcares, France; Ca Pesaro, Mus Mod Art, Venice, Italy; Southwest Mo State Col, Springfield; Roosevelt Univ, Chicago; Hilles Libr, Radcliffe Col, Cambridge, Mass.
Commissions: Portrait in bronze of Rudolph Ganz, Ganz Hall, Roosevelt Univ, Chicago, 52; portrait in bronze, Mr & Mrs Samuel H Nerlove Collection, Santa Monica, Calif, 55; monumental chancel cross, First Baptist Church, Chicago, 67; bronze, penthouse terrace, James W Newell, New York, N Y, 69; steel sculpture, French Govt, Barcares, 71.
Exhibitions: 58th Nat Am Exhib, Art Inst Chicago, 47; Salon d'Automne, Paris, 61, 71 & 72; Salon de Jeune Sculpture, Rodin Mus, Paris, 65; Mus Contemp Art, Chicago, 68; 20th Premio del Fiorino, Palazzo Strozzi, U S Sect, Florence, Italy, 71.
Awards: First hon mention, Nat Arts Club, New York, 45; silver medal for first prize composition, 68 & gold medal for first prize in mod sculpture, 69, Semaines Int de la Femme, Cannes, France.
Bibliography: Italo Mussa (auth), Monograph: Marie Zoe Greene-Mercier, Sifra Editrice, 68; Guido Perocco (auth), Greene-Mercier, Le Arti, 6/70; C L Formals (auth), La femme dans l'art contemporain, Editions Christian Hals, 72.
Memberships: Artists Equity Asn (pres Chicago Chap, 59-62, first nat v pres, 62-64); Arts Club Chicago.
Publications: Auth, Trieste, 101 Disegui, 69, Salzburg, 101 Zeichnungen, 70 & Venezia, 101 Disegni, 70, Edizioni Libreria, Italo Svevo, Trieste.
Dealers: Alinder Associates, 440 W 34th St, New York, NY 10001; Galleria Artivisive, 60 V A Brunetti, Rome, Italy 00186.
Mailing Address: 1232 E 57th St, Chicago, IL 60637.

GREENLEAF, ESTHER (HARGRAVE)
Painter, Serigrapher
Preferred Media: Acrylics, Sand.
b Ripon, Wis.
Study & Training: Univ Minn, BS(archit); Andre L'Hote, Paris, France; Minneapolis Sch Art; Art Stud League New York; also with Rudolf Rey, New York, N Y.
Work in Public Collections: Recreation House Collection in Taylor Park, Millburn, N J; Millburn High Sch Collection.
Exhibitions: N J State Exhib, Montclair Art Mus, 63; Work by New Jersey Artists, Fifth Statewide Triennial, Newark Mus, 64; Nat Asn Women Artists Int Traveling Oil Show, 65; Cambridge Art Asn-Symphony Hall Show in Boston, Mass, 69; N H Art Asn 25th Ann Show, Currier Gallery, Manchester, 71.
Teaching: Instr design & art hist, Minneapolis Sch Art, 27-30; instr hist furniture & decoration, Univ Minn Sch Archit, 28-30; instr art hist, Cooper Union Sch Art, 32-34.
Awards: Zuita Gerstenzang award for oils, Nat Asn Women Artists, 62; first award for oils & Alice Standish Buell Mem Prize for graphics, Pen & Brush, 68.
Memberships: Nat Asn Women Artists; Cambridge Art Asn; N H Art Asn; Artist-Craftsmen N Y; Sharon Art Ctr.

Art Interests: Stoneware ceramics; acrylic on gessoed linen with sand; serigraphy.
Mailing Address: Old Street Rd, Peterborough, NH 03458.

GREENSPAN, GEORGE
Collector
b New York, N Y, May 17, 00.
Collection: Comprehensive collection of impressionist and post-impressionist drawings; contemporary American paintings.
Mailing Address: 885 Park Ave, New York, NY 10021.

GREENWALD, CHARLES D
Collector, Patron
b New York, N Y, Aug 6, 08.
Study & Training: New York Univ.
Collection: American paintings, drawings and etchings after 1900.
Mailing Address: 120 E 81st St, New York, NY 10028.

GREENWALD, DOROTHY KIRSTEIN
Collector
b New York, N Y, Mar 29, 17.
Study & Training: N Y Sch Interior Design; Craft Stud League.
Collection: Twentieth century contemporary & modern American art.
Mailing Address: 120 E 81st St, New York, NY 10028.

GREENWOOD, PAUL ANTHONY
Sculptor, Instructor
Preferred Media: Bronze, Plastic.
b Philadelphia, Pa, Sept 13, 21.
Study & Training: Pa Acad Fine Arts, Philadelphia; Barnes Found, Merion, Pa; Acad Julien, Paris; Temple Univ Sch Fine Arts; also asst to Jo Davidson
Work in Public Collections: Philadelphia Art Mus; N J State Mus, Trenton; Phoenix Art Mus, Ariz.
Commissions: Bronze lion relief, Sons of Italy, Philadelphia, 55; fountains, comn by Mrs William Almy, Malvern, 66 & by Adolph Rosengarten, 70.
Exhibitions: One-man shows, Beryl Lusch Gallery, 54, Pa Acad Fine Arts, 57 & Peale House, Philadelphia, 65; also shows at Pa Acad Fine Arts, Philadelphia Art Mus, Philadelphia Art Alliance & Contemp Club, Trenton.
Teaching: Instr sculpture, Philadelphia Art Mus, 46; instr sculpture, Moore Inst Art & Sci, 47-49; instr sculpture & drawing, Pa Acad Fine Arts, 53-
Awards: Louis Comfort Tiffany grant, 52 & 71; May Audubon Post Prize, 53 & 54; Acad Fel Gold Medal, 55.
Memberships: Life mem Philadelphia Print Club; Peale Club.
Mailing Address: c/o Peale House, 1811 Chestnut St, Philadelphia, PA 19103.

GREER, WALTER MARION
Painter
Preferred Media: Oils.
b Ware Shoals, S C, Aug 11, 20.
Study & Training: The Citadel, BS, 42; Clemson Univ, BS, 47; Atlanta Sch Art, 60; Nat Acad Design, New York, N Y, with Robert Phillipp; also with Ben Shute, Atlanta, 62 & study abroad.
Work in Public Collections: Telfair Acad Arts & Sci, Savannah, Ga; S C State Collection, Columbia Mus Art; paintings, Sea Pines Plantation Co, Hilton Head Island, S C & Home Fed Collection, Charleston, S C; C & S Collection, Atlanta & Greenville, S C.
Commissions: Oil landscape, Gov Mansion, Columbia, 67; three paintings, Phipps Land Co, Hilton Head Island & New York, 70; portrait of pres Emory Univ, 71.
Exhibitions: Mead Paper Show, Atlanta, Ga, 60; Hunter Ann, Chattanooga, Tenn, 62; Savannah Arts Festival, 66; S C Invitational, Columbia, 69; Guild S C Artists, Charleston, 71.
Teaching: Private classes, 63-66; instr spec art classes for Marine Corps, Parris Island, S C, 64-65 & for Savannah Art Asn Sch, 66.
Awards: Savannah Arts Festival Award for Rivers, 66; S C Arts Coun Purchase Award for Pond, 69; S C Archit Award for Pond (Grey Phase), 71.
Bibliography: Virginia Ball (auth), The man that got away, Atlanta Mag, 65; Don Deaton (auth), Island for an artist, Atlanta J, 65; Jack Morris & Robert Smeltz (auth), Contemporary artists of South Carolina, 70.
Memberships: Guild S C Artists (mem bd); hon life mem Beaufort Art Asn.
Publications: Illusr, covers for Islander Mag, 66-
Dealer: Artists' Associates Gallery, 105 Peachtree St N E, Atlanta, GA 30303.
Mailing Address: Firethorn, Hilton Head Island, SC 29928.

GREGG, RICHARD NELSON
Museum Director, Writer
b Kalamazoo, Mich, Sept 4, 26.
Study & Training: Western Mich Univ; Cranbrook Acad Art, BFA & MFA.
Collections Arranged: Inness, 63; Daubigny, 64; Wedgwood, 65; Remington, 67; Dutch Art of the 1600's, 68; Costigan, for the Smithsonian Inst, 68; Antique Steins and Tankards, 69; Contemporary California Art, 70; American Art of the 1930's, 71; The City in American Painting, 72.
Teaching: Instr, Cranbrook Sch for Boys; instr design, Worcester Mus Art.
Positions: Dir, Kalamazoo Inst Art; curatorial asst, Toledo Mus Art; head mus educ, Art Inst Chicago; dir, Paine Ctr & Arboretum; dir, Joslyn Art Mus; dir, Allentown Art Mus, Pa, 72-
Publications: Contribr to Curator, Antiques, Hobbies, Mus News, Midwest Mus Quart, Wis Architect & Connoisseur.
Mailing Address: Box 117, Allentown Art Museum, Allentown, PA 18105.

GREGOR, HELEN FRANCES
Tapestry Artist, Designer
b Prague, Czech, June 28, 21; Can citizen.
Study & Training: Royal Col Art, London, Eng; Sch Am Craftsmen, Rochester, N Y.
Work in Public Collections: Queen's Univ, Kingston, Ont; Univ Toronto, New College, Ont; Can House, London; Can Guild Crafts Collection; plus many others.
Commissions: Works for Labatts Brewery, 69, Music Libr, City of Toronto Libr Bd, 69, YWCA Chapel, Hamilton, 70, New College, 71 & Toronto Star Bldg, 72.
Exhibitions: Fourth Int Biennale Tapestry, Lausanne, 69; Third Stuttgart Int Craft Exhib, 69; Paris Mus Gobelin, 69; Queen's Univ, Kingston, 70; Can House, London, 71.
Teaching: Head textiles, Ont Col Art, 52-
Awards: Can Coun Awards, 64 & 69.
Memberships: Assoc Royal Can Acad; Ont Soc Artists.
Mailing Address: 218 Glen Rd, Toronto, Ont, Can.

GREGOROPOULOS, JOHN
Painter
b Athens, Greece, Dec 16, 21; U S citizen.
Study & Training: In Athens; Univ Conn, BA.
Work in Public Collections: Minn Mus Art, St Paul; Ball State Found, Muncie, Ind; Slater Mus, Norwich, Conn; U S Info Agency.
Exhibitions: Whitney Mus Am Art Ann, New York, N Y, 54; Art U S A, New York, 58; First Biennale Christlicher Kunst Gegenwart, Salzburg, 58; Drawings U S A, Minn Mus Art, 71.
Teaching: Prof art, Univ Conn, 53-
Positions: Pres, Mystic Art Asn, 60-62.
Awards: Small Drawings & Sculpture Purchase Award, Ball State Teachers Col, 55; Grumbacher Award, Chautauqua Art Asn Second Nat, 59; Drawings U S A, St Paul Art Ctr, 63.
Bibliography: F Walkey (auth), John Gregoropoulos, Art Am, 2/55; John Gregoropoulos, Zygos, Athens, 57; Art and the new patron, WEDN TV, 68.
Publications: Auth, Change in art, Nea Estia, Athens, 57.
Mailing Address: R R 3, Box 107, Storrs, CT 06268.

GREGORY, ANGELA
Sculptor, Educator
Preferred Media: Stone, Bronze, Aluminum.
b New Orleans, La, Oct 18, 03.
Study & Training: Art Sch, Newcomb Col, BDesign, Tulane Univ La, MA(archit); Parsons Sch, Paris, France & Italy, Newcomb Col scholar, 25, cert; Acad Grande Chaumière, Paris; N Y State Col Ceramics, summer; also with Charles Keck, New York & Antoine Bourdelle, Paris.
Work in Public Collections: Sculpture of the Western Hemisphere, IBM Collection.
Commissions: John McDonogh Monument, Work Prog Admin, Civic Ctr, New Orleans, La, 38; Bienville Monument, New Orleans, 55; Gen Hy Watkins Allen, State of La, Port Allen, 61; St Louis, Archdiocesan Bldg, New Orleans, 61; panels, aluminum relief on walnut, John XXIII Libr, St Mary's Dominican Col, New Orleans, 67.
Exhibitions: Salon Tuileries, Paris, 28 & 32; Nat Sculpture Soc, at Palace Legion of Honor, San Francisco, 29, Nat Mus, Washington, D C, 32 & Whitney Mus Am Art, New York, N Y, 40; Salon d'Antomme, Paris, 30; one-man show, New Orleans Mus Art, 33-34; Int Exhib Contemp Medals, Numismatic Mus, Athens, Greece, 66.
Teaching: Artist-in-residence, Newcomb Col, Tulane Univ La, 40-41; sculptor-in-residence & prof art appreciation, St Mary's Dominican Col, 62-, Shell Co Found grant, 72.
Positions: State supvr, Work Proj Admin, New Orleans, 41-42; asst engr camouflage, Corps Engrs, New Orleans Dist, 42-43.

Awards: Mary L S Neill Medal, Art Sch, Newcomb Col, 24.
Bibliography: Walter Agard (auth), The new architectural sculpture, 47; Hilda P Hammond & Betsy Peterson (auth), Lady at Dominican, a tribute to a pope, Dixie-Roto, Times-Picayune, 67; Jas Cohen, The birth of a medal, The Numismatist, 72.
Memberships: Fel Nat Sculpture Soc; New Orleans Mus Art.
Mailing Address: 630 Pine St, New Orleans, LA 70118.

GREGORY, JOAN
Educator, Painter
Preferred Media: Collage.
b Montgomery, Ala, Apr 1, 30.
Study & Training: Univ Montevallo, AB, 52; Peabody Col, MA, 53, EdD, 66; Inst Allende, San Miguel Allende, Mex.
Work in Public Collections: Dillard Collection, Weatherspoon Gallery, Univ N C, Greensboro; N C Nat Bank Collection; La State Art Comn Collection; 20th St Bank Collection, Huntington, W Va.
Exhibitions: Exhibs 80 & 180, Huntington Galleries, 56-61; one-woman show, 63 & 13th Dixie Art Ann, Montgomery Mus Fine Arts; Southeastern Painting Show, Gallery Contemp Art, Winston-Salem, N C, 71; Ann N C Artists Exhib & Traveling Show, 71-72.
Teaching: Instr art, Marshall Univ, 55-61; chmn dept art, Bloomsburg State Col, 63-64; assoc prof art & asst head dept, Univ N C, Greensboro, 64-
Awards: Purchase awards, Dillard Collection, 66 & Springs Art Show, Lancaster, S C, 72.
Memberships: Nat Art Educ Asn (mem states assembly, 71-); N C Art Educ Asn (pres, 71-); Southeastern Col Art Conf; Assoc Artists N C (mem bd dirs, 69-71).
Mailing Address: Dept Art, University of North Carolina at Greensboro, Greensboro, NC 27412.

GRESSEL, MICHAEL L
Sculptor
b Wurzburg, Ger, Sept 20, 02; U S citizen.
Study & Training: Art Sch, Bavaria, with Arthur Schleglmünig; Beaux Art Inst Design, New York, N Y.
Work in Public Collections: Bruckner Mus, Albion, Mich; Metrop Mus Art, New York; Nat Theater, Washington, D C; Nat Theater & Acad, New York; County Trust Co, Mount Kisco, N Y.
Commissions: Eagle, Int Motel, Kennedy Airport, New York, 58; two figures, Stepinac High Sch, White Plains, N Y, 60; ivory relief portrait for Gen Eisenhower, 62; City Crest, Town Hall, Greenwich, Conn, 67; bust of Gen V Steuben, 69.
Exhibitions: Hudson Valley Art Asn Ann, White Plains, 46-72; Valhalla High Sch, N Y, 49; Allied Artists Am, Nat Acad Design, 71; Nat Sculpture Soc, New York, 72; Armonk Libr, N Y.
Teaching: Pvt instr.
Awards: Dr Morris Woodrow Award, 51, Mrs John Newington Award for Madonna, 63 & gold medal, 65, Hudson Valley Art Asn; gold medal, Hudson Valley Art Exhib, 72.
Memberships: Hudson Valley Art Asn (dir, 52-); Nat Sculpture Soc.
Mailing Address: N Greenwich Rd, Armonk, NY 10504.

GREY, MRS BENJAMIN EDWARDS
Collector, Patron
b St Paul, Minn.
Study & Training: Vassar Col, BA, 24.
Positions: Mem sch comt, Minneapolis Sch Art, 64-; trustee, Minneapolis Soc Fine Arts, 67-; pres, Ben & Abby Grey Found, 60-
Art Interests: Assembled Minnesota Art Portfolio exhibited in Iran and Mediterranean countries; Iranian contemporary art exhibited in the United States; commissioned American Federation of Arts to assemble sixty contemporary American works and under United States Information Service opened three shows in Turkey, Iran and Pakistan; originated cultural exchange program, Communication through Art; assembled Turkish Art Today, traveling with American print show in Tehran; exhibited Contemporary Art of India and Iran traveling in eastern United States; sponsor of American Section First India Triennial of Contemporary World Art.
Collection: Contemporary art from various countries, specializing on Middle East and South-Asian countries.
Mailing Address: 497 Otis Ave, St Paul, MN 55104.

GRIEGER, (WALTER) SCOTT
Sculptor
b Biloxi, Miss, Aug 27, 46.
Study & Training: Chouinard Art Inst; Otis Art Inst; San Fernando Valley State Col, BA.
Work in Public Collections: Whitney Mus Am Art, New York, N Y.
Exhibitions: Information, Mus Mod Art, New York, 70; Sculpture Ann, Whitney Mus Am Art, New York, 70; Scott Grieger, Los Angeles Co Mus Art, Calif & Reese Palley Gallery, New York, 71; Los Angeles '72, Sidney Janis Gallery, New York, 72.
Teaching: Artist-in-residence, Univ Fla, 71; instr, art ctr, Col Design, 72.

Bibliography: Robert Hughes (auth), Four L A Artists, Time Mag, 2/71; Maurice Tuchman (auth), Scott Grieger (exhib catalogue), 1/71; Jane Livingston (auth), 3 L A Artists, Art in Am, 5-6/71.
Publications: Auth, Impersonations, 70 & Mainstream art, 72.
Dealer: Dave Hickey, 306 E 50th St, New York, NY 10022.
Mailing Address: 48 S Raymond Ave, Pasadena, CA 91101.

GRIESSLER, FRANZ ANTON
Painter
Preferred Media: Charcoal, Oils.
b Vienna, Austria, June 2, 97; U S citizen.
Study & Training: Acad Vienna, 11-15, 19-21.
Work in Public Collections: Portrait of univ prof Dr Otto Pötzl, Gallery Famous Persons Homeland Austria.
Exhibitions: Vienna-Künstlerhaus, 24; Honolulu Acad Arts, 58; 22nd-24th Am Drawing Biennial, Norfolk Mus Arts & Sci, 67-71.
Teaching: Instr portraiture, still-life & life painting, Franz Griessler Private Art Sch, 58-
Positions: Art dir, Munic Vienna (Gewista), 21-45.
Memberships: Artist & Sculptor League Honlulu.
Mailing Address: 2085 Makiki Pl, Honolulu, HI 96822.

GRIFFIN, RACHAEL S
Art Administrator, Writer
U S citizen.
Study & Training: Univ Ore; Portland Mus Art Sch, Ore; Reed Col.
Collections Arranged: Paintings and sculptures of the Pacific Northwest, 59; German Expressionist Painting from the Collection of Morton D May, 67; Selections from the collection of Sterling Holloway, 66; West Coast Now (major regional), 68; also retrospective exhibs of Jack McLarty, 63, Michele Russo, 66 & Charles Voorhies, 72; edited and/or wrote catalogs for these exhibs.
Positions: Dir Educ, Portland Art Mus, 57-60, cur, 60-; art comt, Gifted Child Proj, Ford Found.
Memberships: Am Asn Mus; Nat Comn Humanities in Schs; Contemp Crafts Asn Bd; Catlin Gabel Sch Bd; Northwest Film Study Ctr Bd.
Publications: Auth, Oregon art: distinctive and distinguished, Bookman, 7/54; co-auth, A course in understanding art for secondary schools, Portland Art Mus, 62; auth, Ernst Josephson, Artforum, 12/64; auth, The understanding of art, Mus News, 3/64; auth, Ken Shores, Craft Horizons, 8/70.
Mailing Address: 2327 S W Market Street Dr, Portland, OR 97201.

GRIGGS, MAITLAND LEE
Collector
b New York, N Y, Sept 13, 02.
Study & Training: Christ Church, Oxford Univ.
Collection: Hudson River School of painting (confined to views of and on the Hudson River); old Staffordshire china with Hudson River views; modern paintings; Oriental, African and pre-Columbian artifacts.
Mailing Address: Ardsley-on-Hudson, NY 10503.

GRIGOR, MARGARET CHRISTIAN
Sculptor
Preferred Media: Plasteline, Plaster.
b Forres, Scotland, Mar 2, 12; U S citizen.
Study & Training: Mt Holyoke Col, BA; Pa Acad Fine Arts.
Work in Public Collections: Mt Holyoke Col, South Hadley, Mass; Smithsonian Inst, Washington, D C; Medallic Art Co, New York N Y.
Commissions: Am Med Asn Medal, 48; Rickey Medal, Am Soc Civil Engrs, 49; Alaska-Hawaii Medal, Soc Medalists, 65; Benjamin Franklin Coin, Chase Commemorative Soc, Brooklyn, 66; Alexander Hamilton Medal, Hall of Fame Great Americans, N Y Univ, 71.
Exhibitions: Nat Sculpture Soc Ann, New York, 69 & 72.
Awards: Lindsay Morris Mem Prize, Nat Sculpture Soc, 69.
Memberships: Nat Sculpture Soc; Nat Soc Women Artists; Am Artists Prof League.
Mailing Address: P O Box 326, Steilacoom, WA 98388.

GRILLEY, ROBERT L
Painter, Educator
b Beloit, Wis, Nov 14, 20.
Study & Training: Univ Wis, BS & MS.
Work in Public Collections: Univ Ill, Urbana; Butler Inst Am Art, Youngstown, Ohio; Univ Wis & Wis Union, Madison.
Exhibitions: One-man shows, Univ Wis, 56, Hewitt Gallery, New York, 57, Lane Gallery, Los Angeles, 60-63, Banfer Gallery, New York, 65 & Gilman Gallery, Chicago, 69; plus others.
Teaching: Prof art & chmn grad prog, Univ Wis-Madison, 60-64, chmn dept, 62-64, prof art educ, at present.

Awards: Purchase prizes, Univ Ill, 53; first prize, Milwaukee Art Ctr, 67; awards, Wis Salon, six times.
Mailing Address: Dept Art Education, University of Wisconsin-Madison, Madison, WI 53706.

GRILLO, JOHN
Painter
b Lawrence, Mass, July 4, 17.
Study & Training: Hartford Art Sch, 35-38; Calif Sch Fine Arts, 46, Albert M Bender fel, 47; Hofmann Sch, 49-50.
Work in Public Collections: Los Angeles Co Mus Art, Calif; Newark Mus, N J; Solomon R Guggenheim Mus, New York, N Y; Butler Inst Am Art, Youngstown, Ohio; Wadsworth Atheneum, Hartford, Conn; plus others.
Exhibitions: One-man shows, New Sch Social Res, 67, State Univ Iowa, 67, Simmons Col, 68, Eleanor Rigelhaupt Gallery, Boston, 68 & Benedict Art Ctr, St Joseph, Minn, 69; plus many other group & one-man shows.
Teaching: Southern Ill Univ, 60; Sch Visual Arts, 61; Univ Calif, Berkeley, 62-63; New Sch Social Res, 64-66; Pratt Inst, 64-66; Univ Iowa, 67-; artist-in-residence, Univ Mass, 68-69.
Awards: Prizes, Sacramento State Fair; Ford Found fel to Tamarind Lithography Workshop & Butler Inst Am Art, 64.
Mailing Address: 111 Chestnut St, Amherst, MA 01002.

GRIMLEY, OLIVER FETTEROLF
Painter, Sculptor
Preferred Media: Pen & Ink, Watercolors, Papier-Mâché, Bronze, Wood, Stone.
b Norristown, Pa, June 30, 20.
Study & Training: Pa Acad Fine Arts, Henry J Scheidt traveling scholar, 50 & Univ Pa, BFA & MFA.
Work in Public Collections: Pa Acad Fine Arts; Philadelphia Mus, Pa; Libr Cong, Washington, D C; Woodmere Art Galleries, Philadelphia.
Commissions: Murals, Commonwealth Fed Savings & Loan, Norristown, 63, Continental Bank & Trust, 65 & Am Bank, Lafayette Hills, Pa, 72; papier-mâché eagle, comn by Leonard Tose, Vet Stadium, Philadelphia, 71.
Exhibitions: Whitney Mus Am Art, Libr Cong & Metrop Mus, 52-57; Pa Acad Fine Arts Watercolor Shows, 58-63; Philadelphia Mus.
Teaching: Instr drawing, Hussian Sch Art, 60-; inst drawing, Pa Acad Fine Arts, 65-
Awards: Joseph Pennell Award, Philadelphia Watercolor Club, 66, 68 & 70; Bruce S Marks Prize for Drawing, Woodmere Art Galleries, 71.
Bibliography: Henry Pitz (auth), Oliver Grimley, Am Artist, 71.
Publications: Auth, article, In: Am Artist, 50.
Mailing Address: 16 W Township Line, Norristown, PA 19403.

GRINER, NED H
Educator, Craftsman
Preferred Media: Silver, Bronze, Brass.
b Tipton, Ind, Dec 14, 28.
Study & Training: Ball State Teachers Col, BS; State Univ Iowa, MA; Ind Univ, MFA; Pa State Univ, DEd.
Work in Public Collections: Evansville Mus Art, Ind; Art Gallery, Ball State Univ, Muncie, Ind.
Exhibitions: Craftsmen U S A, Milwaukee Art Ctr, Wis, 66; Wichita Decorative Arts Exhib, Kans, 66; Jewelry 66, State Univ N Y Col Plattsburgh, N Y 66; Midstates Craft Exhib, 66-67; Jewelry Exhib, Purdue Univ, 67.
Teaching: Asst prof art, Ark State Col, 54-60; asst, Pa State Univ, 60-61; prof art, Ball State Univ, 61-, head dept, 70-
Memberships: Nat Art Educ Asn; Ind Art Educ Asn; Col Art Asn Am; Ind Artist Craftsmen (pres, 66-68).
Publications: Auth, Jewelry is sculpture, Palette Mag, spring 62; co-auth, Ned Griner: artist teacher, Sch Arts, 9/63; auth, Individuality in the arts & crafts, Asn Am Women, 12/63; auth, article, In: Quartet Mag, Vol 2, No 10; contribr, Art—search & self discovery, 68.
Mailing Address: Dept of Art, Ball State University, Muncie, IN 47306.

GRIPPE, FLORENCE (BERG)
Painter, Potter
b New York, N Y, Jan 6, 12.
Study & Training: Educ Alliance, 32-34; Works Proj Admin Art Courses, 34-38; pottery with William Soini, 39-41.
Commissions: Portraits commissioned by, Doris Brewer Cohen, Lexington, Mass, 69, Signora Attilio Roveda, Locarno, Switz, 70, Dr Luis Martinez & Julio Farinos Castillo, Valencia, Spain, 70 & Jose Marina Galvao Telles, Lisbon, Portugal, 71.
Exhibitions: Variations on a Theme, Am Mus Nat Hist, 45; Avant Garde Artists Ninth St Exhib, New York, 51; Brooklyn Mus Art Sch, N Y, 51; Contemp Am Art, New Sch Social Res, New York, 57; Lower East Side Independent Artists Third Ann Exhib, 58.

Teaching: Instr drawing, painting, sculpture & puppetry, United Art Workshops Brooklyn Neighborhood Houses, N Y, 47-54; instr design & pottery, Brooklyn Mus Art Sch, 51-57.
Bibliography: Mr & Mrs, Inc, Glamour Mag, 4/42; P O Reilly (auth), Brooklyn Museum ideal place in which to study, Brooklyn Eagle Sun, 11/11/51; S Sheridan (auth), Native handicrafts, N Y Times Mag, 7/52.
Publications: Auth, With the brush, Ceramic Age, 3/56; contribr, Art news from Boston, Art News, 61-63.
Mailing Address: 1190 Boylston St, Newton, MA 02164.

GRIPPE, PETER J
Sculptor, Printmaker
b Buffalo, N Y, Aug 8, 12.
Study & Training: Albright-Knox Art Sch, 23-25; Art Inst Buffalo, 29-35, with Edwin Dickinson; Atelier 17, New York, 44-48, with William Stanley Hayter.
Work in Public Collections: Mus Mod Art, Whitney Mus Am Art & Metrop Mus Art, New York, N Y; Newark Mus, N J; Addison Gallery Am Art, Andover, Mass.
Commissions: Creative arts award medallion, Brandeis Univ, 54; Four Freedoms, Nat Coun U S Art, 55; two sculpture murals, comn by James B Bell & Assoc, Puerto Rican Info Ctr, New York, 58; sculpture, Theodore Shapiro Forum, Brandeis Univ, 63; portrait of Composer Irving Fine, Brandeis Univ, 64; plus one other.
Exhibitions: Painting, Drawing and Sculpture, Am Acad Rome, Italy, 65; Sculptors Guild, New York, 67; The New American Painting & Sculpture: The First Generation, Mus Mod Art, New York, 69; Boston Now (commemorating opening of New City Hall), Inst Contemp Art, Boston, Mass, 69; Whitney Mus Am Art Ann.
Teaching: Instr design, Pratt Inst, 49-50; dir printmaking, Atelier 17, New York, 51-54; prof fine arts, Brandeis Univ, 53-
Awards: Contemp watercolors, drawings & prints award, Metrop Mus Art, 52; Boston Arts Festival Award, Art Comn Boston, 55; Guggenheim fel for sculpture, 64.
Bibliography: Clement Greenberg (auth), Art chronicles, Partisan Rev, 6/49; On sculpture, It Is, autumn 65; W V Anderson (auth), The city of Peter Grippe, Connection, 66.
Publications: Contribr, Credo (Iconograph), 46; ed & contribr, 21 Etchings & poems, Morris Gallery, New York, 58; contribr, Enter Mephistopheles with images, Art News, Vol 59, No 6; contribr, Contemporary American painting & sculpture, Univ Ill Press, 61; auth, Mots Trouvees (collage-poems), Nordness Gallery, New York, 63.
Mailing Address: 1190 Boylston St, Newton, MA 02164.

GRIPPI, SALVATORE WILLIAM
Painter, Educator
b Buffalo, N Y, Sept 30, 21.
Study & Training: Mus Mod Art Sch, 44-45; Art Stud League New York, 45-48; Atelier 17, 51-53; Inst Statale Arte, Florence, Italy, Fulbright scholarships, 53-55.
Work in Public Collections: Whitney Mus Am Art, Metrop Mus Art & New York Publ Libr, New York, N Y; Joseph Hirshhorn Collection, Washington, D C; Milwaukee-Downer Col, Wis.
Exhibitions: 26th & 28th Biennials, Corcoran Gallery Art, Washington, D C, 59 & 63; Whitney Mus Am Art Ann, 60; Recent Painting U S A, The Figure, Mus Mod Art, New York, & through U S, 62; Selected American Painters, Phoenix Art Mus, 67; one-man shows, New York & Los Angeles, 52-72; plus others.
Teaching: Instr painting, drawing & 2-D design, Cooper Union Art Sch, 56-59; instr, Sch Visual Arts, 61-62; assoc prof art, Pomona Col & Claremont Grad Sch, 62-68; prof art, Ithaca Col, 68-
Positions: Invited partic, Ford Found Conf Visual Artists, 61.
Bibliography: Brian O'Dougherty (auth), Variety of exhibitions, New York Times, 3/22/62; Larry Campbell (auth), rev, In: Art News, 10/64; Henry J Seldis (auth), Art walk: a critical guide to the galleries, Los Angeles Times, 5/29/70; plus many others.
Memberships: Life mem Art Stud League New York (treas, 61-62, bd control, 61-64); Col Art Asn Am; Am Asn Univ Prof.
Publications: Auth, Visual impressions of Italy, Inst Int Educ Bull, 56; auth, Turntable kaleidoscope, Mus Mod Art, 56, 57 & 59; contribr, Twenty-one etchings and poems, 58.
Dealer: Feingarten Gallery, 718 N La Cienega Blvd, Los Angeles, CA 90069.
Mailing Address: 423 E Seneca St, Ithaca, NY 14850.

GROAT, HALL PIERCE
Painter
Preferred Media: Acrylics.
b Syracuse, N Y, Dec 31, 32.
Study & Training: Syracuse Univ, BFA, Grad Sch Painting; also spec summer session with Josef Albers.

Work in Public Collections: Berkshire Mus, Pittsfield, Mass;
Philatelic Mus, Geneva, Switz; Syracuse Univ, N Y; State Univ
N Y, Morrisville.
Commissions: Mural, Repub Korea, Third Div, USA, 56; hist murals,
Lemoyne Manor Restaurant, Liverpool, N Y, 60; marine & space
age murals, Naval Ord, Gen Elec Co, Pittsfield, 61; auditorium
murals, Johnstown, N Y, 63.
Exhibitions: Rochester Finger Lakes Exhib, Rochester Mem Art
Gallery, N Y, 59 & 63; Springfield Nat, Mass, 62; Everson Mus
Regional, Syracuse, 64 & 70; Cooperstown Nat, N Y, 67-70; Butler
Inst Am Art, Youngstown, Ohio, 68.
Awards: Best in Show, Assoc Artists Syracuse, 60; Pittsfield Art
League First Prize, Mass, 61; Berkshire Mus Purchase Award,
Berkshire Art Asn, Pittsfield, 62.
Bibliography: 32nd ann midyear show—Butler, La Rev Mod, 2/68;
Review of selected artist, Art Rev, fall 68.
Memberships: Assoc Artists Syracuse (exhib chmn); Sarasota Art
Asn.
Dealer: Priscilla Gallery, 151 Village Rd, Manhasset, NY 11030.
Mailing Address: 8364 Vassar Dr, Manlius, N Y 13104.

GRODENSKY, SAMUEL
Painter
Preferred Media: Oils.
b Brooklyn, N Y, Apr 20, 94.
Study & Training: Nat Acad Design, New York, N Y; Cleveland Inst
Art; Univ Miami.
Work in Public Collections: Joe & Emily Lowe Gallery, Coral
Gables, Fla; Telse Yeshiva, Wickliffe, Ohio; Temple Emanuel,
Cleveland, Ohio; Park Synagogue, New York.
Exhibitions: Chrysler Nat, Provincetown, Mass, 58; Four Arts Soc,
Palm Beach, Fla, 60; three-man show, Fountain Bleau Gallery,
Miami Beach, Fla, 63; one-man show, Kornamm Gallery, Tampa,
Fla, 65; two-man show, The Gallery, Fort Lauderdale, Fla, 67;
Am Artists Prof League Grand Nat, New York, 71-72.
Awards: First prize, 59 & purchase award, 62, Univ Miami.
Memberships: Artists Equity Asn; fel Am Artists Prof League.
Dealer: Wellhausen Gallery, 2427 Rice Blvd, Houston, TX 77005.
Mailing Address: 450 Miller Rd, Coral Gables, FL 33146.

GROELL, THEOPHIL
Painter, Instructor
Preferred Media: Oils.
b Pittsburgh, Pa, Feb 11, 32.
Study & Training: Carnegie Inst Technol, BFA, 53.
Exhibitions: Emerging Talent (selected by Clement Greenberg),
Kootz Gallery, New York, N Y, 54; one-man shows, Tanager Gal-
lery, New York, 56 & Green Mountain Gallery, New York, 70 &
73; Art U S A 59, New York Coliseum, 59; The Contemporary
Figure, Suffolk Mus, Stony Brook, N Y, 71.
Teaching: Adj lectr painting, Queensboro Community Col, 67-
Bibliography: Cindy Nemser (auth), Representational painting in
1971, Arts Mag, 12-1/72.
Dealer: Green Mountain Gallery, 135 Greene St, New York, NY
10012.
Mailing Address: 41 Union Sq W, New York, NY 10003.

GROFF, JUNE
Designer, Painter
b North Lawrence, Ohio, June 26, 03.
Study & Training: Pa Acad Fine Arts, traveling scholar, 35; Barnes
Found; also with Henry McCarter.
Work in Public Collections: Pa Acad Fine Arts, Philadelphia; Mus
Mod Art, New York, N Y; Friends Central Col, Philadelphia; Pa
State Univ; Philadelphia Mus Art; also in pvt collections &
others.
Commissions: Fabric design, Harper's Bazaar, Hattie Carnegie,
Clare Potter & others; design & execution of hanging stained
glass cross for St Barnabas Episcopal Church, Marshallton, Del,
62; stained glass windows & bars for three Philadelphia restau-
rants & lounges.
Exhibitions: One-man show, Little Gallery, Philadelphia, 61; Moore
Col Art, 62-64; Drawing Soc New York Traveling Show, 65-66;
Am Fedn Arts Traveling Exhib, 65-66; one-man show, D'Ascenzo
Studios, Philadelphia, 69.
Positions: Fabric designer, Jack L Larsen Inc, New York, 55-; de-
signer contemporary stained glass, D'Ascenzo Studios, at
present.
Awards: Textile Exhib, Mus Mod Art, New York, 47; prizes, Int Tex-
tile Exhib, Women's Col, Greensboro, 47, 53, 54 & 56.
Memberships: Fellowship Pa Acad Fine Arts.
Mailing Address: 862 N 19th St, Philadelphia, PA 19130.

GROOMS, RED
Painter
b Nashville, Tenn, June 10, 37.
Study & Training: Peabody Col; pvt study with J Van Sickle; New Sch

Social Res; Art Inst Chicago; Hans Hofmann Sch, Provincetown,
Mass; study in Europe & Near East.
Work in Public Collections: Mint Mus Art, Charlotte, N C; Art Inst
Chicago, Ill; Mus Mod Art, New York; N C Mus Art, Raleigh;
Chrysler Mus, Provincetown; plus others.
Commissions: Sets & costumes, Guinevere (play), 64; mural (with
Mimi Gross), Ctr for Mod Cult, Florence, Italy.
Exhibitions: Worcester Art Mus, Mass, 65; Am Fedn Arts, 65-66;
Twenty Americans, Art Inst Chicago, 66; Mus Mod Art, New
York, 66; Venice Biennale, 68; plus many other group & one-man
shows.
Bibliography: Allan Kaprow (auth), Assemblage, environments and
happenings, Abrams, 65; Lucy R Lippard (auth), Pop art,
Praeger, 66; Susan Sontag (auth), Against interpretation, Dell
66; plus others.
Publications: (Movies) Big Sneeze, 65, Before 'n' After, 66, Wash-
ington's Wig Whammed!, 66, Fat Feet, 66 & Meow, Meow!, 67;
plus others.
Mailing Address: 186 Grand St, New York, NY 10012.

GROOMS, REGINALD LESIE
Educator, Painter
b Cincinnati, Ohio, Nov 16, 00.
Study & Training: Cincinnati Art Acad, 17-23; Acad Julien, Paris,
France, 23-25.
Work in Public Collections: Univ Cincinnati; Muncie Art Mus, Ind;
Miami Univ, Oxford, Ohio.
Commissions: Evening Education (mural), Eve Col Off, Univ Cincin-
nati, 48; portraits, Dean Drufngr, 40, Dr Martin Fischer, 60,
Helen Coops, 63 & Joseph Meyer, 69, Univ Cincinnati.
Exhibitions: Soc Artistes Française, Paris Salon, 24 & 25; Century
of Tomorrow, New York World's Fair, 39; San Francisco World's
Fair, 39; Artists of Tomorrow, Carnegie Inst, 42.
Teaching: From instr to assoc prof art, Univ Cincinnati Sch Applied
Arts, 25-55, Albert P Strietmann prof art, head div fine arts &
head dept fine arts, 55-
Memberships: Cincinnati MacDowell Soc (pres, 41-43); Cincinnati
Art Club (pres, 33-35).
Mailing Address: 3436 Lyleburn Pl, Cincinnati, OH 45220.

GROPPER, WILLIAM
Painter, Lithographer
b New York, N Y, Dec 3, 97.
Study & Training: Nat Acad Design; N Y Sch Fine & Applied Arts;
with Robert Henri, George Bellows & Howard Giles; Guggenheim
fel, 37.
Work in Public Collections: Metrop Mus Art, New York; Mus Mod
Art, New York; Phillips Mem Gallery, Washington, D C; Mus
Western Art, Moscow, U S S R; Nat Gallery Prague, Czech, plus
many others.
Commissions: Murals, New Interior Bldg, Washington, D C, Post
Off Bldgs at Freeport, N Y & Detroit, Mich, Wayne State Univ,
Detroit & Schenley Corp.
Exhibitions: One-man shows, ACA Gallery, New York; Los Angeles
Heritage Gallery; Piccadilly Gallery, London, Eng; Manne Mus,
Prague; Retrospective Traveling Show, 67-68, plus many other
group and one-man shows.
Awards: First prize lithography, Artists for Victory, Metrop
Mus Art & John Herron Art Inst, 43; Ford Found artist-in-
residence award, 66; Tamarind Lithographic fel, 67.
Memberships: Nat Inst Arts & Lett.
Publications: Auth, Gropper (collection of drawings); auth, Capri-
chios; auth, The little tailor (portfolio); auth, Twelve etchings
(portfolio); auth, The shtetl (color lithographs); plus others.
Mailing Address: 33 Hickory Dr, Great Neck Estates, NY 11021.

GROSHANS, WERNER (EMIL)
Painter
Preferred Media: Oils, Pastels.
b Eutingen, Ger, July 6, 13; U S citizen.
Study & Training: Newark Sch Fine & Indust Art, with Bernar
Gussow, grad.
Work in Public Collections: Newark Mus, N J; Davenport Munic
Art Gallery, Iowa; D C Ct Gen Sessions Art Trust, Washington,
D C; Newark Pub Libr; New Britain Mus Am Art, Conn.
Exhibitions: Ann Exhib Contemp Am Painting, Whitney Mus Am Art,
New York, N Y, 48; Painting in the United States, Carnegie Inst,
Pittsburgh, Pa, 49; American Painting Today, Metrop Mus Art,
New York, 50; Continuing Tradition of Realism in American Art,
Hirsch-Adler Galleries, New York, 62; 30th Ann Midyear Show,
Butler Inst Am Art, Youngstown, Ohio, 65.
Positions: Chmn dept fine arts, Jersey City Mus, N J, 66-69; mem
adv bd trustees, du Cret Sch Arts, N J, 71.
Awards: Thomas B Clarke prize, Nat Acad Design, 60; Lucy Mc-
Bride Beach Mem first award, Montclair Art Mus, 61; Margaret
Cooper Mem prize, Allied Artists Am, 66.

Bibliography: Philbrook Smith (ed), Avowed champion of realistic art, N J Music & Arts Mag, 11/65; Elizabeth McFadden (auth), Realism in New York show, Newark Sun News, 9/18/66; Margarita Dulac (auth), Werner Groshans, painter of realism & fantasy, Am Artist Mag, 6/70.
Memberships: Nat Acad Design (mem coun, 70-73); Audubon Artists; Allied Artists Am; Assoc Artists N J (dir, 65-67); Conn Acad Fine Arts.
Dealer: Babcock Galleries, 805 Madison Ave, New York, NY 10021.
Mailing Address: 941 Boulevard E, Weehawken, NJ 07087.

GROSS, ALICE (ALICE GROSS FISH)
Sculptor
Preferred Media: Terra-Cotta, Wood, Bronze.
b New York, N Y.
Study & Training: With Ruth Yates.
Work in Public Collections: Berkshire Mus, Pittsfield, Mass.
Exhibitions: Eastern States Exhib, Springfield, Mass, 64; Audubon Artists, 68 & Allied Artists Am, 69, Nat Acad Design, New York, N Y; Knickerbocker Artists, Nat Arts Club, New York, 71; New Rochelle Art Asn, Col New Rochelle, 71.
Awards: Award for Duo, Allied Artists Am, 69; award for Rhythm, Knickerbocker Artists, 70; award for Who's the Fairest of them All, Beaux Arts of Westchester, 71.
Memberships: Silvermine Guild Artists; Audubon Artists; Conn Acad Fine Arts; Allied Artists Am; Knickerbocker Artists.
Mailing Address: 16 Sutton Pl, New York, NY 10022.

GROSS, CHAIM
Sculptor, Instructor
b Kolomea, Austria, Mar 17, 04; U S citizen.
Study & Training: Kunstgewerbe Schulle; Educ Alliance, New York; Beaux-Arts Inst Design, with Elie Nadelman; Art Stud League New York, with Robert Laurent.
Work in Public Collections: Metrop Mus Art, Whitney Mus Am Art & Mus Mod Art, New York, N Y; Newark Mus, N J; Worcester Art Mus, Mass; plus many others.
Commissions: Main Post Off, Washington, D C, 36; Fed Trade Comn Bldg, Washington, D C, 38; Reiss-Davis Child Guidance Clinic, Beverly Hills, Calif, 61; Hadassah Hospital, Jerusalem, 64; Temple Shaaray Tefila, New York, 64; plus others.
Exhibitions: American Painting & Sculpture, Moscow, U S S R, 59; The Making of Sculpture, Mus Mod Art, New York, 61-62; Drawings by Sculptors, Smithsonian Inst, 61-63; New York World's Fair, 64-65; one-man show, Medici II Gallery, Miami Beach, Fla, 71; plus many other one-man & group shows.
Teaching: Instr sculpture, Educ Alliance Art Sch, 27-; instr sculpture, New Sch Social Res, 48-; instr, Mus Mod Art, 52-57.
Awards: Nat Inst Arts & Lett grant, 56; first prize, Boston Arts Festival, 63; award of merit medal, Nat Inst Arts & Lett, 63; plus others.
Bibliography: George A Flanagan (auth), Understanding and enjoying modern art, Thomas Y Crowell, 62; John I H Baur (auth), Revolution and tradition in modern American art, Harvard Univ Press, 65; Wayne Craven (auth), Sculpture in America, Thomas Y Crowell, 68; plus others.
Memberships: Sculptors Guild (mem bd); Educ Alliance Alumni Asn; Fedn Mod Painters & Sculptors; Nat Inst Arts & Lett; Artists Equity Asn.
Publications: Auth, Fantasy drawings, Beechhurst, 56; co-auth, Tree trunk to head & A sculptor speaks (art films), 56; auth, TV prog, Educ Alliance Sch Art, 64; contribr, articles in var art mag.
Mailing Address: 526 W Broadway, New York, NY 10012.

GROSS, EARL
Painter, Lecturer
Preferred Media: Watercolors, Oils.
b Sept 11, 99; U S citizen.
Study & Training: Westminster Col; Carnegie-Mellon Univ.
Work in Public Collections: New Britain Mus Am Art; Atlanta Art Inst, Ga; Reading Mus, Pa; Ill State Mus; Wustum Mus, Racine, Wis; plus others.
Commissions: Off combat artist, U S Air Force, Far East.
Exhibitions: Mac Beth Gallery, New York, N Y, 42; two-man show, Art Inst Chicago, 50; Paintings of Past Decade, Metrop Mus, 52; one-man show, Butler Art Mus, 52; Am Watercolor Soc, New York, 58; plus one other.
Teaching: Prof painting, Longboat Key Art Ctr, Fla; prof painting, New Orleans Acad Art; prof painting, Highland Park Art Ctr; instr, Chicago Acad Fine Art, Ill; instr, Am Acad, Chicago.
Positions: Pres, Stevens-Gross Studios, Chicago, Ill, 26-62.
Awards: First prize, Parkersburg Fine Art Ctr; second prize, Denver Mus, Colo; second prize, Cosmopolitan Mag Competition.
Bibliography: Norman Kent (auth), Sea scapes & landscapes & Wendell Blake (auth), Acrylic watercolor painting, Watson Guptill.

Memberships: Am Watercolor Soc; Philadelphia Watercolor Soc; Washington Watercolor Soc; Arts Club Chicago; Artist Guild Chicago.
Publications: Auth, The watercolor series, 47, Illustrators page, 51, Robert Addison, 58 & Polymer colors in depth, 67, Am Artist Mag.
Dealers: Oehlschlaeger Galleries, 107 E Oak St, Chicago, IL 60611; Frank Oehlschlaeger Gallery, 28 Blvd of the Presidents, Saint Armands Key, Sarasota, FL 33578.
Mailing Address: 1416 Grant Rd, Northbrook, IL 60062.

GROSS, IRENE (IRENE GROSS BERZON)
Painter, Sculptor
Preferred Media: Oils.
U S citizen.
Study & Training: Parson's Sch Design; Am Art Sch.
Work in Public Collections: Springfield Mus Fine Art, Mass; St Vincent's Col, Latrobe, Pa.
Exhibitions: Eastern States, 58-60; Fr Exhib, 66 & Ital Exhib, 72, Nat Asn Women Artists, Florence, Naples; Silvermine Guild New Eng Exhib, New Canaan, Conn.
Awards: Bocour Award, 61 & Goldie Paley Award, 69, Nat Asn Women Artists.
Memberships: Silvermine Guild Artists; Nat Asn Women Artists; Knickerbocker Artists; New Rochelle Art Asn (treas, 69-).
Mailing Address: 87 Disbrow Lane, New Rochelle, NY 10804.

GROSS, MR & MRS MERRILL JAY
Collectors, Patrons
Study & Training: Mr Gross, Univ Pittsburgh, BA, BS; Xavier Univ, MBA; Mrs Gross, Mills Col, BA; Xavier Univ, MEd.
Exhibitions: Paintings by Edward Potthast, Cincinnati Art Mus, 65, Butler Inst Am Art, 65 & Taft Mus, 68.
Collection: Nineteenth & twentieth century American art; Western, genre & impressionist.
Mailing Address: 241 Springfield Pike, Wyoming, OH 45215.

GROSSMAN, MORTON
Painter, Educator
b 26.
Study & Training: Art Stud League New York, scholarships, 44-47; Queens Col (N Y), BA(hons), 48; Louis Comfort Tiffany Found fel, 49-50.
Work in Public Collections: Cleveland Mus Art; Norfolk Mus Art, Va; Ball State Univ, Ind; Birmingham Mus Art, Ala; SS United States; plus many private collections.
Exhibitions: Whitney Mus Am Art; Cincinnati Art Mus; Dallas Mus Fine Arts; Baltimore Mus Art; one-man shows, Tyler Sch Art, Temple Univ, Farnsworth Art Mus, Maine, Kansas City Art Inst, Pub Archit Gallery, Wellington, N Z, Miami Beach Art Ctr & Isaac Delgado Mus Art, New Orleans; plus many others.
Teaching: Instr gen studies, Queens Col (N Y), 55-56; assoc prof art, State Univ N Y Col Buffalo, 56-60; vis faculty, Adelphi Col, summer 60; instr, Cleveland Inst Art, 61-64; asst prof art, Univ Md, 64-69; resident faculty, Haystack Mountain Sch, Maine, summer 65; vis faculty, Tyler Sch Art, Temple Univ, summers 67 & 68; assoc prof painting, Kent State Univ, 69-
Awards: Grand award & gold medal, Am Watercolor Soc, 60; Audubon Artists Medal for Creative Aquarelle, 62; Arches Award, Watercolor, U S A, Springfield Art Mus, 69.
Mailing Address: 217 Crain Ave, Kent, OH 44240.

GROSSMAN, NANCY
Sculptor, Painter
b New York, N Y, Apr 28, 40.
Study & Training: Pratt Inst.
Work in Public Collections: Whitney Mus Am Art, New York; Princeton Univ Art Mus; Univ Mus, Berkeley, Calif; Cornell Col, Ithaca, N Y; Larry Aldrich Mus, Ridgefield, Conn.
Exhibitions: Corcoran Gallery Art Biennial Exhib, Washington, D C, 63; Whitney Mus Am Art Sculpture Ann, 68; Eight + Eight, Riverside Mus, New York, 68; Städtische Kunsthalle Recklinghausen, Ruhrfestspiele, 70; Painting and Sculpture Today, Indianapolis Mus Art, Ind, 70.
Awards: Ida C Haskell Found scholar foreign travel, 62; John Simon Guggenheim Mem Found fel, 65; Inaugural Achievement Award, Pratt Inst, 66.
Bibliography: Von Thomas Schröder & Guido Mangold (auth), Nancy Grossman Ledermonstren, Twen Mag, 5/71.
Dealer: Cordier & Ekstrom, 980 Madison Ave, New York, NY 10021.
Mailing Address: 105 Eldridge St, New York, NY 10002.

GROSSMAN, SHELDON
Museum Curator, Art Historian
b New York, N Y, Aug 30, 40.
Study & Training: Hunter Col, BA, 62; N Y Univ Inst Fine Arts, MA, 66.

Positions: Cur res, Nat Gallery Art, Washington, D C, 71-
Awards: Fulbright-Hays Travel grant, 66; Italian Govt study grant, 66; Chester Dale fel, Nat Gallery Art, 67-69.
Research: Problems in Florentine painting in the late fifteenth and early sixteenth century; analysis of problems of style; archival research.
Publications: Ed, Marsyfas, 65; auth, National Gallery of Art report and studies in the history of art, 68; auth, Mitteilungen des kunst-historischen institutes in Florenz, 69; auth, Master drawings, 72.
Mailing Address: 3051 Idaho Ave N W, Washington, DC 20016.

GROSVENOR, ROBERT
Sculptor
b New York, N Y, 37.
Study & Training: Ecole Beaux-Arts, Dijon, 56; Ecole Nat Arts Decoratifs, 57-59; Univ Perugia, 58; also study & travel in France, Eng, Italy, Ger & Mex.
Work in Public Collections: Walker Art Ctr, Minneapolis, Minn; Mus Mod Art & Whitney Mus Am Art, New York; Mass Inst Technol, Cambridge; Aldrich Mus Art, Ridgefield, Conn; plus others.
Exhibitions: One-man exhib, New York Univ, 67; Minimal Art, The Hague, 58; Whitney Mus Am Art Sculpture Ann, 68-69; Univ Minn, 69; Inst Contemp Art, Chicago, 69; plus many other group & one-man shows.
Teaching: Instr sculpture, Sch Visual Arts, New York.
Awards: Nat Coun on the Arts, 69.
Dealer: Paula Cooper Gallery, 96 Prince St, New York, NY 10012.
Mailing Address: 302 Elizabeth St, New York, NY 10012.

GROSZ, FRANZ JOSEPH
Painter, Designer
Preferred Media: Oils, Glass.
b New York, N Y, Oct 7, 09.
Study & Training: Nat Acad Design, with Kroll, Olinsky & Nielson; Art Stud League New York, with Boardman Robinson & Brackman; also with Hans Hofmann, New York.
Work in Public Collections: Oils, Carnegie Mus, Nat Acad Design, Currier Mus Art, Pa Acad Fine Arts & Corcoran Gallery Art.
Commissions: Glass murals (mixed media), Joseph's Sch Auditorium, Astoria, N Y & Manhasset Congregational Church, Nassau Co, N Y, 60; glass murals, Salem Lutheran Church, Bridgeport, Conn, 61, U S Coast Guard Acad, New London, Conn, 63 & St Anthony Shrine, Boston, Mass, 65; over 350 murals, 41-60.
Exhibitions: Whitney Mus Am Art, New York, 48; one-man show, Galerie Visconti, Paris, France, 71; Oil Paintings, U S Info Serv, currently shown in all maj Europ mus for one year; one-man show sponsored by Fr Embassy, Amsterdam, 73.
Awards: Carnegie Int.
Mailing Address: 43 Pond Rd, Kings Point, NY 11024.

GROTELL, MAIJA
Ceramist, Educator
b Helsingfors, Finland, 99; U S citizen.
Study & Training: Cent Sch Indust Art (Ateneum), Helsingfors, Finland, grad.
Work in Public Collections: Nat Gallery Art, Smithsonian Inst, Washington, D C; Metrop Mus Art, New York, N Y; Cleveland Mus Art, Ohio; Walker Art Ctr, Minneapolis, Minn; plus many others.
Commissions: Numerous vases, Cranbrook Acad Art, Bloomfield Hills, Mich; oblong vase, Cranbrook House, Bloomfield Hills; numerous flower pots, Gen Motors Tech Ctr, Detroit, Mich.
Exhibitions: Metrop Mus Art; Everson Mus Art, Syracuse, N Y; Cleveland Mus Art; Walker Art Ctr; Nat Gallery Art, Smithsonian Inst; plus many others.
Teaching: Instr ceramics, Henry St Crafts Sch, New York, 28-38; instr ceramics & res asst, Rutgers Univ, Sch Ceramic Eng, 36-38; head dept ceramics, Cranbrook Acad Art, 38-66.
Awards: Encycl Britannica Prize & Spec Commendation for Group, 46; Charles Founders Medal, Alfred Univ, 64; hon mem, Nat Coun Educ for Ceramic Arts, 6/72; plus others.
Mailing Address: Cranbrook Academy of Art, Bloomfield Hills, MI 48013.

GROTENRATH, RUTH
Painter
b Milwaukee, Wis, Mar 17, 12.
Study & Training: State Teachers Col, Milwaukee, BA.
Work in Public Collections: Philadelphia Mus Art, Pa; IBM Collection; Madison Union; Milwaukee Art Inst; Wis State Teachers Col.
Commissions: Murals, Post Off, Hart, Mich, Wayzata, Minn & Hudson, Wis; murals, Wis State Teachers Col & Timmerman Field Bldg.
Exhibitions: One-man shows, Wis State Col, Stevens Point, 64, Chapman Gallery, Milwaukee, 65 & Bradley Gallery, 66 & 69; Madison Salon, 67 & 68; Milwaukee Art Ctr; plus others.

Teaching: Instr design, Univ Wis-Milwaukee, 61.
Awards: William & Bertha Clusman Award, 63; Grand Rapids Art Gallery Award; Dayton Co Award, Minneapolis; plus others.
Dealer: Bradley Galleries, 2565 N Downer Ave, Milwaukee, WI 53211.
Mailing Address: 2626A N Maryland Ave, Milwaukee, WI 53211.

GROTH, BRUNO
Sculptor
Preferred Media: Welded Steel, Stainless Steel, Bronze, Wood.
b Stolp, Ger, Dec 14, 05; U S citizen.
Study & Training: Otis Art Inst, Los Angeles, Calif.
Work in Public Collections: Palm Springs Mus, Calif; Humboldt State Col; Joseph H Hirshhorn Collection, New York.
Commissions: Bronze fountain pieces, City of Fresno, Calif & City of Crescent City, Calif; wood sculpture, Humboldt State Col.
Exhibitions: One-man show, De Young Mus, San Francisco, 59; Brussels World Fair; Santa Barbara Mus Art; Portland Art Mus; Mus Contemp Crafts, New York.
Dealer: Ankrum Gallery, 657 N La Cienega Blvd, Los Angeles, CA 90069.
Mailing Address: P O Box 3, Trinidad, CA 95570.

GROTH, JOHN AUGUST
Illustrator, Painter
Preferred Media: Watercolor, Ink.
b Chicago, Ill, Feb 2, 08.
Study & Training: Art Inst Chicago; Art Stud League New York.
Work in Public Collections: Mus Mod Art, New York; Metrop Mus Art, New York; Brooklyn Mus, N Y; Art Inst Chicago; Univ Tex.
Teaching: Instr compos, Art Stud League New York, 46-; artist-in-residence, Univ Tex, 70.
Position: Art dir, Esquire Mag, 33-36; art dir, Parade Mag.
Memberships: Nat Acad Design; Soc Illusr; Am Watercolor Soc.
Publications: Auth, Studio: Europe, 45; auth, Studio: Asia, 52; illusr, Gone with the wind, 68; auth, John Groth's world of sport, 70; illusr, All quiet on the western front, 71.
Mailing Address: 61 E 57th St, New York, NY 10022.

GROTZ, DOROTHY ROGERS
Painter
Preferred Media: Oils.
b Philadelphia, Pa.
Study & Training: Berlin Univ, 29; Columbia Univ, MS, 45; Art Stud League New York, 47.
Work in Public Collections: Rochester Univ Mus Art; Santa Barbara Mus Fine Arts; Norfolk Mus Arts & Sci; Evansville Mus Arts & Sci.
Exhibitions: Columbia Univ Avery Libr, New York, N Y, 50; Van Diemen Lilienfeld Gallery, New York, 62-67; Univ Wis, 67; Bodley Gallery, New York, 72; Columbus Gallery Fine Arts, Ohio, 72.
Publications: Contribr, review, In: Archit Forum, 69; contribr, review, In: Leonardo, 72.
Dealer: Bodley Gallery, 787 Madison Ave, New York, NY 10021.
Mailing Address: 7 St Lukes Pl, New York, NY 10014.

GROVE, EDWARD RYNEAL
Sculptor, Painter
Preferred Media: Oils, Watercolors, Intaglio.
b Martinsburg, W Va, Aug 14, 12.
Study & Training: Nat Sch Art, Washington, D C, 33; Corcoran Sch Art, Washington, D C, with Schuler & Weisz, 34-40; also with Robert Brackman, Noank, Conn, 46.
Work in Public Collections: Univ Pa Grad Sch Med, Philadelphia; Pangborn Corp, Hagerstown, Md; Pa Hist Soc, Philadelphia; Dept of Navy, Off of Chief Naval Opers, Washington, D C; Mil Mus, The Citadel, Charleston, S C.
Commissions: Three etchings, Mount St Alban, Washington Cathedral, D C, 45, 46 & 64; Communion of Saints (mural with Jean Donner Grove), Church of the Holy Comforter, Drexel Hill, Pa, 52-58; U S four cent airmail stamp, Am Air Mail Soc, Cincinnati, Ohio, 54; bronze portrait plaque, Am Bag & Paper Corp, Philadelphia, 66; World War II Medals (30 with Rolf Beck), Pres Art Medals, Inc, Vandalia, Ohio, 66-70.
Exhibitions: Soc Am Etchers Ann, Nat Acad Design, New York, N Y, 45; Watercolor Ann, Pa Acad Fine Arts, Philadelphia, 54; Fourteenth Am Drawing Ann, Norfolk Mus Arts, Va, 58; Second Philadelphia Arts Festival, Philadelphia Mus Arts, 62; Nat Sculpture Soc Ann, Lever House, New York, 67; plus many others.
Positions: Secy, treas & pres, Steel & Copper Engravers League, Philadelphia, 50-62; sculptor-engraver, U S Mint, Philadelphia, 62-65; off sculptor-engraver Order St John of Jerusalem, Knights of Malta Hq, Shickshinny, Pa, 67-
Awards: Grumbacher watercolor award, 65; Lindsey Morris Mem prize, Nat Sculpture Soc, 67; Sculptor of the Yr gold medal, Am Numismatic Asn, 69.

Bibliography: E Williams (auth), The mural, Today Mag, Philadelphia Inquirer, 11/58; T W Becker (auth), Edward R Grove/commitment to America, Franklin Mint Almanac, 11/69; V Culver (auth), The four best, Coins Mag, 6/70.
Memberships: Artists Equity Asn (treas, 57-59, nat first v pres, 65-67); Nat Sculpture Soc; Soc Washington Artists; Philadelphia Sketch Club; Washington Watercolor Asn.
Art Interests: Medallic sculpture & bas-relief.
Publications: Contribr, Design handbook, Nat Philatelic Mus, 54; co-auth & illusr, The communion of saints (brochure), Church of the Holy Comforter, 58; illusr, Our christian heritage, Morehouse-Gorham, 59; auth & illusr, Assignment: Malta, Coin World, 65; auth & illusr, The making of a medal, Am Artist Mag, 1/72.
Mailing Address: Sea-Lake Studio, 3215 S Flagler Dr, West Palm Beach, FL 33405.

GROVE, JEAN DONNER (MRS EDWARD R)
Sculptor
Preferred Media: Bronze, Stone, Wood, Plastics.
b Washington, D C, May 15, 12.
Study & Training: Hill Sch Sculpture; Corcoran Sch Art; Catholic Univ Am; Wilson Teachers Col, BS, 39; Cornell Univ; Philadelphia Mus Art; travel study in Europe; also with Clara Hill, Hans Schuler, Heinz Warneke & Fritz Janschka.
Work in Public Collections: Rosenwald Collection, Philadelphia, Pa; Church of the Holy Comforter, Drexel Hill, Pa; Fine Arts Comn, City Hall, Philadelphia.
Commissions: Many portrait commissions, 40-72; The Communion of Saints (mural with E R Grove), Church of the Holy Comforter, Drexel Hill, 52-58; garden figures, fountains & other works in private collections in Washington, D C, Philadelphia, Pa, N J & N C.
Exhibitions: Pa Acad Fine Arts Ann, Philadelphia, 47, 48 & 51, regional, 53; Allied Artists Am, Nat Acad Design, New York, 49; Philadelphia Mus Art Regional Art Festivals, 55, 59 & 62; Nat Sculpture Soc, Archit League, New York & Topeka, Kans, 57; Art U S A: 58, Madison Square Garden, New York, 58; plus others.
Awards: First prize sculpture, Metrop Regional, Nat Mus, Washington, D C, 46; Morris Goodman Prize, John Herron Art Mus, Indianapolis, Ind, 57; competition prize for design of Artists Equity Asn Philadelphia Award, 60; plus others.
Bibliography: R Hagerty (auth), A Sigma Phi in the chips, Sigma Phi Gamma Int Sorority, 10/51; E Williams (auth), The mural, Today Mag, 11/58.
Memberships: Soc Washington Artists; Artists Equity Asn (dir Philadelphia chap, 64-66); Philadelphia Art Alliance; Soc Four Arts, Palm Beach, Fla; Am Fedn Arts.
Mailing Address: Sea Lake Studio, 3215 S Flagler Dr, West Palm Beach, FL 33405.

GROVE, RICHARD
Art Administrator, Writer
b Lakewood, N J, Feb 7, 21.
Study & Training: Mex City Col, BA, 48; Escuela Universitaria Bellas Artes, San Miguel de Allende, Mex, with David Alfaro Siqueiros; Mex City Col, MA, 50, with Justino Fernandez.
Teaching: Lectr art hist, Wichita State Univ, 59-61.
Positions: Dir, Wichita Art Mus, Kans, 58-64; mus educ specialist, Arts & Humanities Prog, U S Off Educ, Washington, D C, 64-68; assoc dir, Arts Educ Prog, JDR 3rd Fund, New York, 68-70; dep asst secy for hist & art, Smithsonian Inst, Washington, D C, 70-.
Memberships: Am Asn Mus (accreditation comt, 68-70); Int Coun Mus; Nat Art Educ Asn.
Publications: Auth, Mexican popular arts today, 54; auth, articles, In: Am Educ, Mus News & Art Educ, 67-71; auth, The museum and the community: new roles and possibilities for art education, 69; auth, Museums and media: a status report, 70.
Mailing Address: Smithsonian Institution, Washington, DC 20560.

GROVER, VIRGINIA LAURINE, see LAURINE.

GROVES, NAOMI JACKSON
Writer, Lecturer
b Montreal, P Q.
Study & Training: Rannows Art Sch, Copenhagen; Sir George Williams Col: McGill Univ, BA & MA; Heidelberg Univ; Berlin Univ; Munich Univ; Radcliffe Col, AM & PhD; McMaster Univ, DLitt, 72.
Exhibitions: One-man shows, Radcliffe Col, Wheaton Col, McMasters Univ & Montreal Mus Fine Arts.
Teaching: Lect, Ernst Barlach as Sculptor, as Dramatist & Barlach in America, 64; lect, The Group of Seven, Another Look, Nat Gallery Can, 69; lect, McGill Univ, Wheaton Col, Carleton Col; assoc prof in charge fine arts, McMasters Univ.
Positions: Vis comt fine arts, Harvard Univ; mem, Ernst Barlach Gesellschaft; asst to dir, Nat Gallery Can, 42-43, consultant, 63-64.

Awards: Gov Gen's gold medal, McGill Univ, 33; traveling fel, Can Fedn Univ Women, 36-37.
Publications: Auth, The transformations of God, Hamburg, 62; auth, A Y's Canada, Toronto, 68 & 69; auth, Ernst Barlach-Leben im Werk, 72.
Mailing Address: 2896 Highfield Crescent, Ottawa, Ont. K2B 6G5, Can.

GRUBB, PAT PINCOMBE
Painter
Preferred Media: Acrylic Polymers, Gouache.
b Cleveland, Ohio, Nov 29, 22.
Study & Training: Flora Stone Mather Col, Case Western Reserve Univ; Cleveland Inst Art; also with Carl Gaertner.
Work in Public Collections: U S Dept Interior, South Wellfleet, Mass; Massillon Mus, Ohio; Mather Col, Case Western Reserve Univ, Cleveland, Ohio; Maple Heights Regional Libr, Ohio; Akron Med Ctr, Ohio.
Commissions: Painting, Mako Mem, Mather Col Alumnae, Case Western Reserve Univ, 71.
Exhibitions: Cleveland Artists & Craftsmen Show, 66 & Fine Arts Regional Exhib, 67, Massillon Mus; Nat League Am Penwomen Nat Juried Biennial, Washington, D C, 68 & Salt Lake City, Utah, 70; Butler Inst Am Art Mid-Year Nat, Youngstown, Ohio, 70; plus others.
Awards: Baldwin Purchase Award Drawing, Massillon Mus, 63; best in show award, Southgate Ann, Maple Heights Women's Civic League, 65; second prize watercolor field, Nat League Am Penwomen State Biennial, 67; plus others.
Bibliography: Article, In: Repub Steel Mag, Cleveland, 66; Beth Resseger (auth), article, In: Alumnae Folio, Mather Col, Cleveland, 8/69; Ina Keegan (auth), article, In: Southeast Sun Paper, Cleveland, 3/71.
Memberships: Nat League Am Penwomen; Artists Equity Asn; Women's Art Club Cleveland; plus others.
Dealer: Malvina Freedson Gallery, Winton Pl, 12700 Lake Ave, Lakewood, OH 44107.
Mailing Address: 5171 Erwin St, Maple Heights, OH 44137.

GRUBE, ERNST J
Writer, Lecturer
b Tirol, Austria, May 9, 32.
Study & Training: Freie Univ, Berlin, PhD, with Ernst Kuhnel.
Collections Arranged: Muslim Paintings from American Collections, Cini Found, Venice & Asia House, New York, N Y, 62.
Teaching: Lect, Columbia Univ, Univ Mich, Metrop Mus Art, Int Cong Turkish Art, Ankara, 59, Int Cong Persian Art, New York, 61 & Venice, 64; Adj prof, The Art of the Islamic World, Columbia Univ.
Memberships: Am Oriental Soc; Am Res Ctr Egypt.
Publications: Auth, Muslim paintings from the XIII to XIX century from collections in the United States and Canada, Venice, 62; The world of Islam, landmarks of the world's art, 67; The classical style in Islamic painting, 68; contribr to Pantheon, Kunst Orients, Oriental Art, Ars Orientalis & Jour Am Res Ctr Egypt.
Mailing Address: 322 Central Park W, New York, NY 10025.

GRUBER, AARONEL DE ROY
Sculptor, Painter
b Pittsburgh, Pa.
Study & Training: Carnegie-Mellon Univ, BS; studied painting & design with Samuel Rosenberg & Robert Lepper.
Work in Public Collections: Smithsonian Inst, Washington, D C; Rose Art Mus, Brandeis Univ; Chase Manhattan Bank Am, New York, N Y; de Cordova & Dana Mus, Lincoln, Mass; Finch Mus, New York; plus one other.
Commissions: Kinetic acrylic sculpture, Nat Shopping Ctrs, Inc, 70; 32 ft cor-ten steel sculpture, Gen Mills Corp, Minneapolis, Minn, 71; geometric painting, Pittsburgh Nat Bank Pa, 71; kinetic acrylic sculpture, Hillman Libr, Univ Pittsburgh, 71; naval brass & acrylic sculpture in fountain, Grand Cent Mall, Parkersburg, W Va, 72.
Exhibitions: Made of Plastic, Flint Inst Arts, 69; A Plastic Presence, Jewish Mus, New York, 69; Small Sculpture from USA, Smithsonian Inst, 69-72; Transparent and Translucent Art, Mus Fine Arts, Saint Petersburg & Jacksonville Mus, 71; USIA, American Sculpture Acquisitions, Int Tour, 71-73, Far Eastern Tour, 72-75.
Awards: Seven painting & sculpture awards, Fund of Distinction, Carnegie Mus, 61-71; four painting & sculpture awards, Western Pa Sculpture Soc, 69-72.
Bibliography: May O'Hara (auth), Women of the year, Pittsburgh Press, Dec, 68; Patsy Scala (producer), Women in art and technology (film), sponsored by N Y Coun Arts, 72; Donald Miller (auth), Reflections on Plexiglas, Art Int, 73; plus others.

Memberships: Pittsburgh Plan for Art (bd gov, 68-71); Western Pa Soc Sculptors; Assoc Artists Pittsburgh (bd dir, 67-69; Nat Asn Women Artists; Am Fedn Arts; plus others.
Art Interests: Transparent acrylic and metal sculpture (kinetic and stabile).
Dealers: New Bertha Schaefer Gallery, 41 E 57th St, New York, NY 10022; Deson-Zaks Gallery, 226 E Ontario St, Chicago, IL 60611.
Mailing Address: 2409 Marbury Rd, Pittsburgh, PA 15221.

GRUBERT, CARL ALFRED
Cartoonist
b Chicago, Ill, Sept 10, 11.
Study & Training: Chicago Acad Fine Arts, 29-30; Univ Wis, BS, 34.
Exhibitions: Libr Cong, 41; Nat Cartoonists Soc Exhibs, 50 & 51; Metrop Mus Art, 51.
Positions: Staff artist, Great Lakes Bull, 44-45.
Awards: U S Treas Award of Merit, 50; Freedom's Found Medal, 50.
Publications: Auth, The Berrys (int syndicated cartoon), 42-
Mailing Address: Woodlawn Ave, Des Plaines, IL 62216.

GRUEN, SHIRLEY SCHANEN
Painter
Preferred Media: Acrylics, Watercolors.
b Port Washington, Wis, Dec 2, 23.
Study & Training: Univ Wis, BS, 45; Art Ctr Sch, Los Angeles, Calif, 46; Layton Art Sch, Univ Wis-Milwaukee Exten & Cardinal Stritch Col, 50-70.
Work in Public Collections: Port Washington High Sch; Port Washington State Bank; Port Washington First Nat Bank; Phoenix Union Area Voc Ctr, Ariz.
Exhibitions: Westchester Art Soc Exhib, White Plains, N Y, 70; New York Int Art Show, 70; La Watercolor Int, Baton Rouge, La 70 & 71; 13th & 14th Chautauqua Ann, N Y, 70 & 71; Greater New Orleans Exhib, La, 71 & 72.
Teaching: Instr watercolor & portrait, Milwaukee Area Tech Col, Wis, 70-
Awards: Slidell Art League Purchase Award, La, 70; two purchase awards, Port Washington Art Fair, 70; Grumbacher Award for Best Watercolor, Chautauqua 14th Ann, 71.
Bibliography: William F Schanen III (auth), Shirley's Atelier, Ozaukee Press, 71.
Memberships: La Watercolor Soc; Chautauqua Art Asn; Firehouse Fine Arts Asn.
Mailing Address: 6254 N Port Washington Rd, Glendale, WI 53217.

GRUPPE, CHARLES
Painter
Preferred Media: Oils.
b New York, N Y, July 1, 28.
Study & Training: Yale Univ; Nat Univ Mex; Columbia Univ, BFA, 54, Brevoort fel & MFA, 55; Huntington Hartford Found, Pacific Palisades, 56; Fulbright fel Italy, 56-57; Ital Govt Award, 57.
Work in Public Collections: Worth Ave Gallery, Palm Beach, Fla; Shore Galleries, Boston, Mass; Zantman Galleries, Carmel, Calif; Oeschlaeger Galleries, Chicago, Ill.
Commissions: Paintings, Am Presidents Coolidge, Jackson & Wilson, 60; Yale Divinity Sch, New Haven, Conn, 60; Fort Lauderdale Nat Bank, Fla, 64; Dolly O'Brien Estate, Palm Beach, 64; First Nat Bank, New York, 65.
Exhibitions: Allied Artists Am, New York, N Y, 60; Boston Arts Festival, 63; Silvermine Guild Artists, New Canaan, Conn, 65; Provincetown Art Asn, Mass, 65; Rockport Art Asn, Mass, 70.
Mailing Address: 20 Livingston St, New Haven, CT 06511.

GRUPPE, KARL HEINRICH
Sculptor
Preferred Media: Marble, Bronze.
b Rochester, N Y, Mar 18, 93.
Study & Training: Royal Acad, Antwerp, Belg, with Frans Joris; Art Stud League New York; also with Karl Bitter.
Work in Public Collections: U S Vice President, William Rufus King, Clinton, N C; Henry Hudson Monument, Riverdale, N Y; La Joce (marble figure), Brookgreen Gardens, S C; Woman President, Adelphi Col, Long Island, N Y; portrait figure, Andrew Haskell Greene, New York.
Commissions: Bas-relief sculpture, Curtis Inst Music, Philadelphia, Pa.
Exhibitions: Nat Acad Design Ann; Nat Sculpture Soc Ann; Int Bas-Relief Exhib.
Positions: Chief sculpture, Monument Restoration Proj, New York City Dept Parks, 34-37; mem Art Comn, New York, two terms, 44-47; mem bd dirs, Fine Arts Fedn, New York; mem adv bd, Nat Sculpture Rev.
Awards: St Gaudens Prize, Art Stud League New York, 12; Saltus Gold Medal, 52 & Dessie Greer Prize, 56, Nat Acad Design.

Bibliography: Beatrice Gilman (auth), Karl H Gruppe-19th, Nat Sculpture Rev, winter; Proske (auth), President-National Sculpture Society: 1950-51, 67-68.
Memberships: Nat Arts Club; fel Nat Sculpture Soc (pres, 49); academician Nat Acad Design (v pres, 57); Art Comn Assocs, New York; Century Asn.
Mailing Address: Box 926, Southold, Long Island, NY 11971.

GRUSHKIN, PHILIP
Designer, Instructor
b New York, N Y, June 1, 21.
Study & Training: Cooper Union Art Sch.
Exhibitions: Calligraphy, Grolier Club, 58; Art Dirs Club, 60; Int Calligraphy & Lettering Exhib, Nat Libr Scotland, 60; Calligraphy & Handwriting in America, Peabody Inst Libr, Baltimore, 61; Calligraphy & Lettering, Brown Univ, 61; plus many others.
Teaching: Instr lettering, calligraphy & illus, Cooper Union Art Sch, 46-68; dir bk workshop, Radcliffe Publ Procedures Course, Cambridge, Mass, 66-; lectr bk design, New York Univ, 66-; lect, bk arts.
Positions: Cartographer, U S Geol Survey, 42-43; Off Strategic Serv, USA, 43-45; designer, World Publ Co, 55-56; designer, Harry N Abrams, Inc, 57-59, art dir, 59-, v pres, 60-69; pres, Philip Grushkin Inc, Englewood, N J.
Awards: Cert of excellence, Printing for Com Exhib, 50.
Publications: Publ, Calligrapher of Aesop's fables, 46; publ, Christmas carols, 48; contribr, Bouquet for Bruce Rogers, 50 & Calligraphics, 55.
Mailing Address: 86 E Linden Ave, Englewood, NJ 07631.

GRUSKIN, MARY JOSEPHINE
Art Dealer
b Trani, Italy; U S citizen.
Positions: Dir, Midtown Galleries.
Specialty of Gallery: Contemporary American artists.
Mailing Address: 11 E 57th St, New York, NY 10022.

GUERIN, JOHN WILLIAM
Painter, Educator
b Houghton, Mich, Aug 29, 20.
Study & Training: Am Acad Art, Chicago; Art Stud League New York; Escuela Bellas Artes, San Miguel, Mex; Colo Springs Fine Arts Ctr.
Work in Public Collections: Dallas Mus Fine Arts, Tex; Chrysler Mus, Provincetown, Mass; Joslyn Art Mus, Omaha, Nebr; Colo Springs Fine Art Ctr, Colo; Houston Mus Fine Arts, Tex; plus others.
Exhibitions: One-man shows, Kraushaar Gallery, New York, 59, 63, 68; Galeria Realities, Taos, N Mex, 60; Corcoran Gallery Art, 61; Whitney Mus Am Art, New York; retrospective, Fort Worth Art Ctr, 64; plus others.
Teaching: Instr painting, Dallas Mus Fine Arts, 50-52; prof art, Univ Tex, Austin, 53-; artist-in-residence, Skowhegan Sch Painting & Sculpture, 60.
Awards: Ranger Purchase Award, Nat Acad Design, 58; Am Acad Arts & Lett grant, 59; Univ Tex Res Inst grant, 60 & 66; plus others.
Memberships: Tex Fine Arts Asn; life mem Art Stud League New York; assoc Nat Acad Design.
Dealer: Kraushaar Galleries, 1055 Madison Ave, New York, NY 10028.
Mailing Address: 3400 Stoneridge Rd, Austin, TX 78745.

GUERRERO, JOSE
Painter
Preferred Media: Oils.
b Granada, Spain, 14; U S citizen.
Study & Training: Escuela Superior Bellas Artes San Fernando, Madrid, Spain, 40-44; Ecole Beaux-Arts, Paris, France, 45-46.
Work in Public Collections: Solomon R Guggenheim Mus & Whitney Mus Am Art, New York, N Y; Art Inst Chicago, Ill; Carnegie Inst, Pittsburgh, Pa; Mus Span Abstract Art, Cuenca, Spain.
Exhibitions: Younger Americans, Solomon R Guggenheim Mus, 54; Whitney Mus Am Art Ann, 58, 62 & 69; Carnegie Int, Pittsburgh, 58 & 62; Spanish Art Today, traveling exhib to Munich, Berlin, Copenhagen & Amsterdam, 68; Rosc '71, Dublin, Ireland, 71.
Teaching: Instr painting, New Sch Social Res, 62-65.
Awards: Chevalier, Order of Arts & Letters, Fr Govt, 59; Soc Contemp Arts Purchase Prize, Art Inst Chicago, 59; Graham Found Advan Studies in Fine Arts grant, 59.
Bibliography: Alberto Portera (producer), Jose Guerrero painter (film), Madrid, 70; Paintings and sculpture, Crucible Mag, 70.
Dealer: Juana Mordo, Villanueva 7, Madrid, Spain.
Mailing Address: 406 W 20th St, New York, NY 10011.

GUGGENHEIM, PEGGY
Collector, Patron
b New York, N Y, Aug 26, 98.
Positions: Dir (& financed), Gallery Guggenheim Jeune, London, 38-39, Art of This Century, New York, 43-47, Mus Palazzo Venier Leoni, Venice, Italy, 51-
Awards: Hon citizen Venice, 62.
Art Interests: Private collection exhibited through Europe, 51-
Publications: Auth, Out of this century, 46 & 68, Una collezionista ricorda, 56 & Confessions of an art addict, 60; auth, articles & introductions.
Mailing Address: Palazzo Venier dei Leoni, 701 San Gregoria, Venice, Italy.

GUGGENHEIMER, RICHARD HENRY
Painter, Writer
Preferred Media: Oils.
b New York, N Y, Apr 3, 06.
Study & Training: Johns Hopkins Univ, AB; Sorbonne, Paris, France; Acad Grande Chaumière, Paris; also with Picart le Doux, Morrisset, Coubine & Leo Stein.
Work in Public Collections: Baltimore Mus Art Cone Collection, Md; Norfolk Mus Art, Va; Kings Col, Wilkes-Barre, Pa.
Exhibitions: Corcoran Gallery Art Ann, Washington, D C, 38 & 39; six one-man shows, Van Diemen Gallery, 38-50; one-man shows, Georges Seligmann, 56, Kings Col, Wilkes-Barre, 60 & Galerie Zak, Paris, 72; plus many others.
Teaching: Prof art & chmn dept, Briarcliff Col, 42-
Bibliography: Marsden Hartley (auth), Concerning the work of Richard G, 36 & Stephan Bourgeois (auth), Richard G, 41, Van Diemen Gallery.
Publications: Auth, Sight & insight, a prediction of new perceptions in art, Harper, 45 & Kennikat, 70; auth, Creative vision in artist & audience, 50 & Creative vision for art & for life, 60, Harper; auth, New dimensions of destiny, a further measure of man's reach, CSA Press, 72.
Dealer: Van Diemen Gallery, 219 E 57th St, New York, NY 10021.
Mailing Address: 784 Park Ave, New York, NY 10021.

GUION, MOLLY
Painter
Study & Training: Grand Cent Art Sch, with Arthur Woelfle; Art Stud League New York, with George Bridgman; portraiture with Dimitri Romanovsky; also with Grigory Gluckmann.
Work in Private Collections: Brit Royal Navy, Portsmouth; Brit Consulate, New York, N Y; N Y State Capitol, Albany, N Y; many other pub & pvt collections.
Commissions: Portraits of many prominent persons, U S & abroad.
Exhibitions: One-man show, Seattle Art Mus, Wash; Vancouver Art Gallery, B C; Paris Salon, France; Royal Portrait Soc, London; pvt showing, Buckingham Palace; many other exhibs in galleries & mus, U S, Can & abroad.
Awards: Ellerhusen Mem Prize, Allied Artists Am; Catharine Lorillard Wolfe Art Club; gold medals, Nat Art Club & Am Artists Prof League; plus many others.
Memberships: Nat Asn Women Artists; Allied Artists Am; Pen & Brush Club; New Rochelle Art Asn; Hudson Valley Art Asn; plus others.
Mailing Address: 10 Bayberry Lane, Rye, NY 10580.

GUITE, SUZANNE
Painter, Sculptor
Preferred Media: Bronze, Stone, Wood.
b P Q, Dec 10, 27.
Study & Training: Inst Design, Chicago, with Moholy Nagy; Acad Belle Arte, Florence; Mus Romanesque Art, Barcelona; Inst Polytechnico, Mex; also with Archipenko, Chicago & Brancusi, Paris.
Work in Public Collections: Quebec Art Mus; Nat Art Gallery, Ottawa; Jewish Libr, Montreal; Seagram's Art Collection, Montreal; New Carlisle Ct House, P Q.
Commissions: Sandstone mural & granite lintel, Quebec Justice Dept, New Carlisle; granite monument, Can Pavilion, Expo 67, Montreal; wooden monument, Govt Can, Notre Dame Island, Montreal.
Exhibitions: Princeton Univ, 67; Sculpture 67, City Hall, Toronto, 67; Rodin Mus, Paris, 70; Columbia Mus Art, 71; Nat Art Ctr, Ottawa, 72.
Teaching: Dir, Ctr Art Perce, P Q, 57-
Bibliography: Kay Kritzwiser (auth), The timeless and expendable in art, Globe & Mail, Toronto, 3/27/71; Shep Jacobsen (auth), Art from the Gaspe, Ottawa Citizen, 1/29/72; M F O'Leary (auth), Suzanne Guite, sculpteur, Reedition Quebec, 9/72.
Memberships: Quebec Sculpture Soc.
Dealer: Centre D'Art De Perce, P Q, Can.
Mailing Address: Perce Art Center, Perce, P Q, Can.

GUMBERTS, WILLIAM A
Collector, Patron
b Evansville, Ind, May 21, 12.
Study & Training: Harvard Univ; Ohio State Univ.
Positions: Bd dirs, Evansville Pub Mus; critic of art, music & theatre, Evansville Press.
Memberships: Ind Arts Comn; charter mem Evansville Arts & Educ.
Collection: Nineteenth century American oils; etchings of classical periods; moderns.
Mailing Address: 22 Chandler Ave, Evansville, IN 47713.

GUMPEL, HUGH
Painter
Preferred Media: Watercolors.
b New York, N Y, Feb 3, 26.
Study & Training: Columbia Univ; Art Stud League New York.
Commissions: Mural, State of N Y, Pub Works Admin Bldg, 63.
Teaching: Instr painting, Nat Acad Sch Fine Arts, 59-
Awards: Gold medal of honor, Am Watercolor Soc, 59.
Memberships: Nat Acad Design; Am Watercolor Soc.
Mailing Address: 335 Rushmore St, Mamaroneck, NY 10543.

GUMPERT, GUNTHER
Painter
b Krefeld, Ger, Apr 17, 19; U S citizen.
Study & Training: Sch Fine Arts Krefeld; Sch Fine Arts, Wuppertal.
Work in Public Collections: Metrop Mus Art, New York, N Y; Victoria & Albert Mus, London, Eng; Kaiser-Wilhelm Mus, Krefeld; Mus Nat Bellas Artes, Santiago, Chile; Art Mus Princeton Univ.
Commissions: Mural, Inter-Am Develop Bank, Washington, D C, 68.
Exhibitions: Kaiser-Wilhelm Mus, 48, 49 & 52; Salon Réalités Nouvelles, Paris, 58-60 & 62; Int Exhib Abstr Art, Pistoia, 61; Int Exhib Contemp Art, London, 62; Salon Mai, Paris, 62.
Bibliography: Jean Grenier (auth), Gumpert, Preuves, Paris, 60; Victor Summa (auth), Gumpert and the evolution of his art, Educ TV Asn, 63; Willy Huppert (auth), Gunther Gumpert, Kunst-und Kunstgewerbe Verein, Pforzheim, 64.
Dealers: Franz Bader Gallery, 2124 Pennsylvania Ave N W, Washington, DC 20037; Francine Seders Gallery, 6701 Greenwood Ave N, Seattle, WA 98103.
Mailing Address: 3752 McKinley St N W, Washington, DC 20015.

GUNDERSHEIMER, HERMAN (SAMUEL)
Art Administrator, Art Historian
b Würzberg, Ger, Apr 25, 03; U S citizen.
Study & Training: Univ Munich; Univ Würzburg; Univ Berlin; Univ Leipzig, PhD, 26.
Teaching: From asst prof to prof art hist, Temple Univ, 41-70, prof art hist & dir Temple Abroad, Tyler Sch Art, Rome, Italy, 70-
Positions: Cur, Mus Ulm/Danube, Kunstgewerbe Mus, Frankfurt, Ger, 27-33; dir, Rothschild Mus, Frankfurt, 33-39.
Awards: Lindbach award for excellent teaching.
Memberships: Col Art Asn; Am Acad Rome Art Libr; Philadelphia Mus Art; Pa Acad Fine Arts; Renaissance Soc Am.
Research: Renaissance & Baroque art; Jewish ceremonial art.
Collection: Contemporary graphics.
Publications: Publications on fresco painting in the Eighteenth century; contributor to journals & magazines; contributing editor to encyclopedias.
Mailing Address: Tyler School of Art, Temple University, Philadelphia, PA 19126.

GUNN, PAUL JAMES
Painter, Educator
Preferred Media: Oils.
b Guys Mills, Pa, June 21, 22.
Study & Training: Edinboro State Teachers Col, BS, 57; Calif Col Arts & Crafts, MFA, 48; wood block printing with Hideo Hagiwara, Tokyo, Japan, 61-62.
Work in Public Collections: Portland Art Mus, Ore; Seattle Art Mus, Wash; Am Info Serv Collection, Athens, Greece; Bibliotheque Nat, Paris, France; Victoria & Albert Mus, London, Eng.
Exhibitions: Int Bordighera Biennial, Italy; Bay Printmakers Second Ann, Oakland Art Mus, Calif; Ann Northwest Artists, Seattle Art Mus; Western Artists Ann, Denver Art Mus, Colo; Ore Artists Ann, Portland Art Mus.
Teaching: Prof painting & printmaking, Ore State Univ, 48-, chmn dept art, 64-
Positions: Resident dir, Japan Studies Prog, Ore Study Ctr, Waseda Univ, Japan, 72-
Art Interests: Woodcut printmaking.
Dealer: Gallery West, 4836 S W Scholls Ferry Rd, Portland, OR 97225.
Mailing Address: Oregon Study Center, International Division, Waseda University, 1-647 Totsuka-maki, 1 chome Shinjuku-ku, Tokyo 160, Japan.

GURR, LENA
Painter, Graphic Artist
Preferred Media: Oils, Casein
b Brooklyn, N Y, Oct 27, 97.
Study & Training: Educ Alliance, New York, 19; Art Stud League New York, two scholarships & study with John Sloan & Maurice Stern, 20-22; Maxwell Training Sch Teachers, 15-17, dipl.
Work in Public Collections: Metrop Mus Art, New York, N Y; Brasenose Col, Oxford, Eng; Smithsonian Inst & Libr of Cong, Washington, D C; Brooklyn Mus, N Y.
Exhibitions: Painting in the U S A, Carnegie Inst, Pittsburgh, Pa, 45 & 51; Contemp Am Sculpture, Watercolors & Drawings, Whitney Mus Am Art, New York, 53; Am Acad Arts & Lett, 58, 65, 66 & 69; 37 Contemp Americans chosen by Nat Coun Women, IBM Corp, 60; Art in Embassies Prog from ACA Galleries, Athens, Greece, 66-68.
Positions: Rec secy, Nat Soc Painters in Casein, 56-57, bd dirs, 58-67.
Awards: Medal of honor, 54 & 61, & Marcia Brady Tucker Prize, 61, Nat Asn Women Artists; Jersey City Mus Medal, N J Painters & Sculptors Soc, 69.
Bibliography: Elizabeth Lips (auth), Artist Lena Gurr says studio should be neat like office, Brooklyn Eagle, 51; Frank Crotty (auth), Paints big city & Cape Cod scenes, Worcester Sun Telegram, 60.
Memberships: Artists Equity Asn New York (rec secy, 53, bd dirs, 63-65, v pres, 66-); Nat Asn Women Artists; Soc Am Graphic Artists (mem coun, 67-68); Painters & Sculptors Soc N J; Provincetown Art Asn (bd trustees, 65-68).
Dealer: ACA Gallery, 25 E 73rd St, New York, NY 10021.
Mailing Address: 71 Remsen Ave, Brooklyn, NY 11212.

GURSOY, AHMET
Painter
Preferred Media: Oils.
b Turkey, Mar 5, 29; U S citizen.
Study & Training: Tech Univ Istanbul, Turkey, 47-52; Ill Inst Technol, 54-56; Art Stud League New York, 58-63.
Work in Public Collections: Chase Manhattan Collection; Cornell Univ Collection; St Lawrence Univ; Grey Found, Minneapolis, Minn.
Exhibitions: Riverside Mus, 67; Ann New Eng Exhib, Silvermine, Conn, 67-71; State Univ N Y, Binghamton, 70; Univ Chicago, Ill, 71; Minneapolis Col Art & Design, Minn, 71.
Awards: Painting prize, 21st Ann New Eng Exhib, Silvermine, Conn, 70.
Bibliography: Grace Glueck (auth), rev, In: New York Time, 68; C Giuliano (auth), rev, In: Arts Mag, 68 & Gordon Brown (auth), rev, In: Arts Mag, 70.
Memberships: Fedn Mod Painters & Sculptors (v pres, 69-); Silvermine Guild Artists; Music for People (treas, 71-72).
Publications: Auth, Convergence of engineering and art, 70.
Mailing Address: 490 Bellwood Ave, North Tarrytown, NY 10591.

GUSSMAN, HERBERT
Collector, Patron
b New York, N Y, Aug 25, 11.
Study & Training: Cornell Univ, AB, 33.
Collection: French impressionists; American paintings and sculpture; African primitive art; bronzes, Luristan, Africa.
Mailing Address: 4644 S Zunis Ave, Tulsa, OK 74104.

GUSSOW, ALAN
Painter, Writer
Preferred Media: Oils.
b New York, N Y, May 8, 31.
Study & Training: Middlebury Col, BA, 52; Cooper Union, 52-53; Atelier 17 Graphic Workshop, 52-53.
Work in Public Collections: Portland Mus Fine Art, Maine.
Exhibitions: Butler Inst Am Art Ann, 64; Maine—50 Artists of 20th Century, Am Fedn Arts Traveling Show, 64; Pa Acad Fine Arts Ann, Philadelphia, 66; Am Acad Arts & Lett, 66; The American Landscape—A Living Tradition, Peridot Gallery, circulated by Smithsonian Inst, 68-70.
Teaching: Instr painting & drawing, Parsons Sch Design, 56-68, chmn dept, 59-68; instr painting & drawing, Sarah Lawrence Col, 58-59.
Positions: Consult arts, Nat Park Serv, U S Dept Interior, 70-; chmn Rev Comt Artists Environ Conserv, Am Beautiful Fund, 70-; chmn bd, Artists Environ Found, 71-
Awards: Prix de Rome in Painting, Am Acad Rome, Italy, 53-55; artist-in-residence, Cape Cod Nat Seashore, Nat Park Serv, 68; artist-in-residence, Hudson River Valley, Cult Coun Found, 71.
Bibliography: B Barton (auth), The illusion of change, Time, 2/9/62; G Glueck (auth), Artist in residence for mother earth, New York Times, 3/12/72.

Publications: Auth, A sense of place—the artist and the American land, Friends of Earth & Sat Rev Press, 72; auth, The use of artists as artists in the struggle for population control, Population, environment and people, McGraw, 72; auth, We are what we see, Encyclopedia of ecology and pollution, N Am Publ, 72.
Dealer: Peridot-Washburn Gallery, 820 Madison Ave, New York, NY 10021.
Mailing Address: 121 New York Ave, Congers, NY 10920.

GUSSOW, ROY
Sculptor, Educator
Preferred Media: Stainless Steel, Bronze.
b Brooklyn, N Y, Nov 12, 18.
Study & Training: With Archipenko, Chicago & Woodstock, N Y, 46-47; Inst Design, Chicago, BS, 48, with Moholy-Nagy.
Work in Public Collections: Whitney Mus Am Art, New York, N Y; Mus Mod Art, New York; Brooklyn Mus, New York; N C Mus Art, Raleigh; High Mus, Atlanta, Ga.
Commissions: Polished stainless steel sculptures, N C State Col Sch Design, Raleigh, 61, Phoenix Mutual Life Assurance Co, Hartford, Conn, 63, City of Tulsa, Munic Bldg, Civic Ctr, Okla, 68, Xerox Corp, Xerox Sq, Rochester, N Y, 69 & New York City Family Ct Bldg, Manhattan, 72.
Exhibitions: Sculpture 1951, Metrop Mus Art, New York, 51; Pa Acad, Philadelphia, 51-59; N C Artists, N C Mus Art, Raleigh, 52-61; Nat Gold Medal Exhib Bldg Arts, Archit League, New York, 62 & 65; Am Surv Sculpture Biennial, Whitney Mus Am Art, 56, 62, 64, 66 & 68.
Teaching: Instr design & sculpture, Bradley Univ, 48-49; instr design & sculpture, Colo Springs Fine Arts Ctr, Colo, 49-51; prof design & sculpture, Univ N C Sch Design, 51-62; adj prof sculpture, Pratt Inst Sch Archit, 62-68.
Awards: Purchase Awards, N C Mus Art, 52 & 61 & Ford Found, 60 & 62; hon mention, Pa Acad Fine Arts, 58.
Dealer: Borgenicht Gallery, 1018 Madison Ave, New York, NY 10021.
Mailing Address: 4040 24th St, Long Island City, NY 11101.

GUSTAFSON, DWIGHT LEONARD
Art Administrator
b Seattle, Wash, Apr 20, 30.
Study & Training: Bob Jones Univ, BA & MA; Fla State Univ, DMus, with Richard Burgin, Izler Solomon, Carlisle Floyd, John Boda & Elena Nikolaidi.
Teaching: Instr music, Bob Jones Univ, acting dean Sch Fine Arts, 54-56, dean, 56-
Memberships: Music Educ Nat Conf (pres, S C Col Div, 66); Am Choral Dir Asn; Southeastern Composers League.
Publications: Auth, various choral & instrumental compositions.
Mailing Address: Bob Jones University, Greenville, SC 29614.

GUSTEN, THEODORE J H
Art Administrator
Positions: Exec dir, Int Graphic Arts Soc.
Mailing Address: International Graphic Arts Society, 410 E 62nd St, New York, NY 10021.

GUSTON, PHILIP
Painter
Preferred Media: Oils.
b Montreal, P Q, June 27, 13; U S citizen.
Study & Training: Boston Univ, hon DFA, 70.
Work in Public Collections: Solomon R Guggenheim Mus, New York, N Y; Whitney Mus Am Art, New York; Mus Mod Art, New York; Metrop Mus Art, New York; Tate Gallery, London.
Commissions: Murals, facade of WPA Bldg, New York World's Fair, 39, U S Treas Dept, Forestry Bldg, Laconia, N H, 41 & Social Security Bldg, Washington, D C, 42; illus, Art News Ann, 44.
Exhibitions: One-man retrospective exhibs, 5th Bienal, São Paulo, Brazil, 59, 30th Biennale, Venice, 60 & Solomon R Guggenheim Mus, Stedelijk Mus, Amsterdam, Mus Beaux Arts, Brussels, Whitechapel Gallery, London & Los Angeles Co Mus Art, 62; one-man exhibs, Jewish Mus, New York, 66 & Marlborough Gallery, New York, 70.
Teaching: Artist-in-residence, Wash Univ, 45-47; adj prof painting, N Y Univ, 51-58; guest critic painting, Columbia Univ, 69-70 & 72-73.
Positions: Artist-in-residence, Brandeis Univ, spring 66; mem Bd Trustees, Am Acad Rome, 70-, artist-in-residence, 70-71.
Awards: First prize, Carnegie Inst, 45; Guggenheim Found fel, 47 & 68; Ford Found grant, 59.
Bibliography: Dore Ashton (auth), Philip Guston, Grove, 59; H H Arnason (auth), Philip Guston, Solomon R Guggenheim Mus, 62; Philip Guston (film), Blackwood Prod, Inc, 72.

Memberships: Nat Inst Arts & Lett.
Publications: Auth, Statement, Stedelijk Museum catalogue, Amsterdam, 62; auth, Piero della Francesca, Art News, 5/65; co-auth, Dialogue with Philip Guston, Art and literature 7, London, 65; auth, Statement, Art News Ann, 66; contribr, Recent paintings & drawings, Jewish Mus, 66.
Mailing Address: Woodstock, NY 12498.

GUTE, HERBERT JACOB
Painter, Educator
Preferred Media: Watercolors.
b Jeffersonville, N Y, Aug 10, 07.
Study & Training: Pratt Inst; Yale Univ, with Josef Albers & E Savage, BFA.
Work in Public Collections: Atheneum Mus, Hartford, Conn; Yale Univ Gallery, New Haven, Conn; Dept Interior, Washington, D C; Jewish Mus, New York, N Y; IBM Collection, New York.
Commissions: Mural, Submarine Base, New London, Conn, 47; mural at U S Mil Cemetery, Cambridge, Eng, comn by Am Battle Monuments Comt, 53-54.
Exhibitions: Nat Acad Design, 40-; Am Watercolor Soc, 40-; Fifty Foremost American Watercolorists, Boston Art Festival, Mass, 56; Watercolor U S A, 61; 200 Years of American Watercolor, Metrop Mus Art, New York, 65.
Teaching: Asst prof watercolor & orthographic drawing, Yale Univ, 40-
Awards: Muriel Alvord Award, Yale Univ, 35; contemp painting award, State Mass, 51; Int award, Hallmark, 54.
Memberships: Audubon Soc; Am Watercolor Soc; Silvermine Guild Artists; Nat Acad Design; Philadelphia Watercolor Club.
Publications: Illusr, Evacuations at Dura Europos, 36, Man in Western world, 40 & College survey of English literature, 42.
Dealer: Grand Central Gallery, 40 Vanderbilt Ave, New York, NY 10017.
Mailing Address: Yale University School of Art, New Haven, CT 06520.

GUTHMAN, LEO S
Collector
b Chicago, Ill.
Memberships: Gov life mem Art Inst Chicago; Soc Contemp Art, Chicago (dir); Art Collectors Club, New York; Art Club Chicago.
Collection: Contemporary painting, especially by Americans; international sculpture.
Mailing Address: 1040 N Lake Shore Dr, Chicago, IL 60611.

GUTKIN, PETER
Painter
b Brooklyn, N Y, 44.
Study & Training: Tyler Sch Art, Temple Univ, BFA, 66; San Francisco Art Inst, MFA, 68.
Work in Public Collections: Temple Univ, Philadelphia, Pa; collections of Mr & Mrs Ben Wolper, Stanford, Conn; Richard Silver, Stanford, Joseph Munson, Seattle, Wash & Mr & Mrs Gene Estribou, San Francisco, Calif; plus others.
Exhibitions: 15th Sculpture Ann, Richmond Art Ctr, 67; 4 New Artists, Delixi Gallery, San Francisco, 68; Recent Developments In Plastics, Hansen-Fuller Gallery, San Francisco, 68; Ann Exhib Contemp Am Sculpture, Whitney Mus Am Art, New York, N Y, 68; 11 at Ghirardelli, Michael Walls Gallery, San Francisco, 69.
Teaching: Instr, Aspen Sch Contemp Art, Colo, 66.
Positions: Juror, Fourth Ann Fiesta Artes, Los Gatos, Calif, 68.
Publications: Co-auth, The edge of now, KQED TV, San Francisco, 69.
Mailing Address: c/o Hansen-Fuller Gallery, 228 Grant Ave, San Francisco, CA 94108.

GUTMANN, JOHN
Painter, Educator
b Breslau, Ger, May 28, 05.
Study & Training: State Acad Arts & Crafts, Breslau, BA; State Acad Berlin, MA.
Work in Public Collections: San Diego Fine Arts Soc, Calif; M H De Young Mem Mus Art, San Francisco, Calif; Mus Mod Art, New York; Mills Col, Oakland, Calif.
Exhibitions: San Francisco Mus Art, M H De Young Mem Mus Art, New York, N Y, Detroit, Mich & abroad.
Teaching: Prof art, Calif State Univ, San Francisco, 38-
Memberships: Am Asn Univ Prof; Col Art Asn Am.
Publications: Contribr, Life, Time, Asia, Sat Eve Post & other nat mag; producer & photog, two doc films on China, 50.
Mailing Address: 1543 Cole St, San Francisco, CA 94117.

GUY, JAMES M
Painter, Educator
Preferred Media: Oils, Acrylics.
b Middletown, Conn, Feb 11, 10.
Study & Training: Hartford Art Sch.

Work in Public Collections: Wadsworth Atheneum, Hartford, Conn; Olsen Found, Guilford, Conn; Four Arts, Palm Beach, Fla; Mattatuk Mus, Waterbury, Conn; Mass Inst Technol, Boston.
Exhibitions: Whitney Mus Am Art, New York, N Y; Metrop Mus Art, New York; Mus Mod Art, New York; Art Inst Chicago, Ill; plus other int & nat exhibs.
Teaching: Painter & instr painting, Bennington Col, 45-47; head dept art, McMurray Col, 47-54; lectr art, Wesleyan Univ, 61-
Memberships: Essex Art Asn, Conn.
Dealer: Charles Egan Gallery, 41 E 57th St, New York, NY 10022.
Mailing Address: 82 Neptune Ave, Moodus, CT 06469.

GUY, OSMOND SUBLETT
Painter, Educator
Preferred Media: Graphics.
b Springfield, Ill, July 10, 33.
Study & Training: Univ Ill, BFA(advert design); Univ Calif, Los Angeles, summer 58; Art Ctr, Los Angeles, winter 59; Univ Ill, 61-63.
Work in Public Collections: Howard Univ; Purdue Univ.
Commissions: Bldg wall painting, Courier-J & Times, Louisville, Ky, 71.
Exhibitions: Brockport Col Festival Art, 67; 500 Festival Art, Indianapolis, Ind, 70; Downtown Salutes Arts, Louisville, 70; Faculty Shows, Louisville Sch Art, 71; Louisville Sch Art Faculty Show at Georgetown Col, Ky, 71; plus many other group & one-man shows.
Teaching: Instr art, Univ Ill, 60-63; asst prof art, Rochester Inst Technol, 64-69, coordr equip & space, summer 66, coordr & dir art prog Oper Upward Bound, summers 67-69; assoc prof art, Herron Sch Art, Ind Univ-Purdue Univ, Indianapolis, 61-70; prof graphic design & dir, Inst Graphics, Calif Inst Arts, Valencia, 72; assoc prof art, Sangamon State Univ, 72-, graphic design consult, summer 72.
Positions: Art dir, J Walter Thompson Co, Chicago, Ill, summer 57; Wyle Assocs, El Segundo, Calif, 58-59; Chicago Daily Tribune, summer 59; Univ Ill Press, 59-60; v pres & design dir, Jackson-Guy Advert, 63-; design dir, Port Studios, 64; design consult, Louisville Courier-J & Times, 70-71; dir, Louisville Sch Arts, 70-71.
Awards: Award of Excellence, Art Dirs Club Ind, 70; third prize in painting, 500 Festival Art, 70; Best of Show, Downtown Salutes Arts, 70.
Memberships: Art Dirs Club Chicago; Soc Typographic Artists; Int Graphic Arts Educ Asn; Col Art Asn; Nat Conf Artists; plus many others.
Collection: Paintings; prints; posters; calligraphy.
Publications: Auth, Miscellany, Vols I & II, 66 & 69.
Dealer: Riverside Studio, 29 Atkinson St, Rochester, NY 14608.
Mailing Address: Dept Art, Sangamon State Univ, Springfield, IL 62703.

GUZEVICH, KRESZENZ (CYNTHIA)
Painter, Instructor
Preferred Media: Oils.
b Munich, Ger, May 24, 23; U S citizen.
Study & Training: Acad Art, Munich; also with Frank Gervasi, Paul Strisik, Louis Krupp, Helen Van Wyk, Ramon Froman & Ken Gore.
Work in Public Collections: First Nat Bank, Las Cruces, N Mex.
Exhibitions: Overseas Press Club Am, New York, N Y; El Paso Mus Art Exhib, Tex; Grand Nat Exhib, New York; Southwest Intercultural Exhib, El Paso; Artists Equity Show, Albuquerque, N Mex.
Teaching: Instr painting, workshops in var states & pvt studio, 65-
Awards: Artist of yr & best in show award, Black Range Artists, 68; best in show award, N Mex Art League, 69.
Memberships: Am Artists Prof League; El Paso Mus Art Asn; Artists Equity Asn; N Mex Art League; Catharine Lorillard Wolfe Art Club.
Dealer: O'Briens Art Emporium, 7122 Stetson Dr, Scottsdale, AZ 85251.
Mailing Address: 1635 Country Club Circle, Las Cruces, NM 88001.

GWATHMEY, ROBERT
Educator, Painter
Preferred Media: Oil.
b Richmond, Va, Jan 24, 03.
Study & Training: N C State Col, 24-25; Md Inst, 25-26; Pa Acad Fine Arts, 26-30.
Work in Public Collections: Brooklyn Mus, N Y; Carnegie Inst, Pittsburgh, Pa; Los Angeles Co Mus, Los Angeles, Calif; Pa Mus Art, Philadelphia, Pa; Whitney Mus Am Art, New York, N Y.
Exhibitions: Annuals, Whitney Mus Am Art & Carnegie Inst; Metrop Mus Art; biennials, Corcoran gallery Art & Pa Acad Fine Arts.

Teaching: Instr drawing & painting, Carnegie Inst Technol, 38-42; instr drawing, Cooper Union, 42-68; vis prof painting, Boston Univ, 69-70.

Awards: Prize, Carnegie Inst Ann, 43; Rosenwald Fellowship, 44; prize, Corcoran Gallery Art, 57.

Memberships: Artist's Equity N Y (bd mem); Nat Inst Arts & Lett.

Dealer: Terry Dintenfass, Inc, 18 E 67th St, New York, NY 10021.

Mailing Address: Box 108, Amagansett, NY 11930.

GYERMEK, STEPHEN A
Educator
b Budapest, Hungary, Nov 9, 30.
Study & Training: Rijks Akad voor beeldende Kunsten, Amsterdam, Holland, with Heinrich Campendonk; Univ Okla.
Commissions: Murals, Convent at Madrid, Spain, 55 & U S Embassy, Spain, 55; stained glass windows, St Gregory's Abbey, Shawnee, Okla.
Exhibitions: Amsterdam, 52-53, Madrid, 54 & Okla Art Ctr, 60.
Collections Arranged: Archaeology, Europe, Near and Far East, Egypt; American Indians & Central & South American Ethnology; Painting from the Italian Renaissance; 19th Century American Paintings, plus others.
Teaching: Lect, painting methods & religious art; asst prof art hist & art, Univ Okla; instr art hist, San Joaquin Delta Col, 67-
Positions: Dir, Gerrer Mus & Art Gallery, Shawnee, Okla, 57-62; actg dir, Stovall Mus Sci & Hist, Univ Okla, 62-65; dir Pioneer Mus & Haggin Art Galleries, Stockton, Calif, 65-70.
Awards: Prizes & Van Alabbe Award, Amsterdam, Holland, 52.
Memberships: Am Asn Mus; Int Coun of Mus.
Mailing Address: 1870 Douglas Rd, Stockton, CA 95207.

GYRA, FRANCIS JOSEPH, JR
Instructor, Painter
b Newport, R I, Feb 23, 14.
Study & Training: R I Sch Design, dipl; Parsons Sch Design, Paris, France, cert advert illus & X Ital Res Sch; Brighton Col Arts & Crafts, Sussex, Eng; Froebel Inst, Roehampton, Eng; Univ Hawaii; McNeese State Col; Keene State Col, BS.
Work in Public Collections: Providence Art Mus, R I; Tenn Fine Arts Ctr, Nashville.
Exhibitions: Int Watercolor Exhib, Art Inst Chicago, 38 & 40; First Int Ann, Marietta Col, Ohio, 69; First Ann Art Northern New Eng, Canaan, N H, 69; Stratton Arts Festival, Vt, 70; Norwich Univ Eighth Exhib Vt Artists, 71.
Teaching: Supvr, Woodstock Union & Dist Schs, Vt, 49-69; dir art workshops, Vt State Dept Educ, 54-70; art educator, Woodstock Sch Dist, 69-
Positions: Chmn, Vt Educ Asn Prog, 52; adv art & art educ, Aquinas Jr Col, Nashville, 66-
Awards: People's Prize, Art Asn Newport, R I, 38; first prize, Third Ann Norwich Univ Art Exhib, 66; Eva Gebhard-Gourgand Found grants, 66-72.
Memberships: Vt Art Teachers Asn (secy-treas, 57-58); Eastern Arts Asn; Nat Art Educ Asn; life fel, Int Inst Arts & Lett.
Publications: Co-auth, Vermont art guide for the classroom teacher K-6, 69.
Mailing Address: 6 Linden Hall, P O Box A, Woodstock, VT 05091.

H

HAACK, CYNTHIA ROACH
Painter, Printmaker
Preferred Media: Graphics.
b Eagle Bend, Minn.
Study & Training: St Cloud State Col, AA(educ); Univ Wyo; Idaho State Col.
Exhibitions: James River Juried Art Show, Newport News, Va, 68; Ann Print Show, Mint Mus Art, Charlotte, N C, 68; Small Print Show, Albany Inst Hist & Art, N Y, 69; Tidewater Artist's Asn Ann, Norfolk Mus, Va, 70; Wicomico Art League Show, Salisbury, Md, 71 & 72.
Teaching: Instr painting. Walter Cecil Rawls Mus, 71-
Awards: First prize in graphics, Va State Fair Art Show, 68; best in graphics, Thalhimer's Salon des Refuses, 69; second prize in graphics, Norfolk Arts Festival, 70 & 71.
Memberships: Peninsula Art Asn; Tidewater Artists Asn.
Dealer: Seaside Gallery, P O Box 1, Nags Head, NC 27959.
Mailing Address: 509 Virginia Ave, Smithfield, VA 23430.

HAAR, FRANCIS
Photographer, Lecturer
b Csernatfalu, Hungary, July 19, 08; U S citizen.
Study & Training: Nat Acad Decorative Arts, Budapest, Hungary, Master Photog.
Work in Public Collections: Victoria-Albert Mus, London, Eng; Mus Mod Art, New York, N Y.
Commissions: The Arts of Japan (film), U S Info Agency, Tokyo, Japan, 53; Ukiyoe, Japanese print (film), Chicago Art Inst, 59; Hoolaulea (dance film), Honolulu Acad Arts, 60; Japan's Cultural History, Fuji TV Co, Tokyo, 64.
Exhibitions: Ind Univ, Bloomington, 61; one-man shows, Honolulu Acad Arts, 70 & Contemp Arts Ctr, Honolulu, 71.
Teaching: Lectr photog, summer courses, Univ Hawaii, 62-
Awards: First prize, Metrop City Improvement, Chicago, Ill, 59; Golden Eagle Award for Pineapple Country Hawaii, 63 & Hawaii's Asian Heritage, 66, Coun Int Nontheatrical Events, Washington, D C.
Memberships: Painters & Sculptors League; Honolulu Printmakers; Honolulu Acad Arts.
Publications: Auth, Hungarian picture book, 40 & auth, Around Mount Fuji, 41, Benlido Publ Co, Kyoto, Japan; auth, The best of old Japan, 49, co-auth, Japanese theatre in highlights, 51 & Geisha on Pontocho, 53, C Tuttle Publ Co, Tokyo.
Mailing Address: 4236 Carnation Pl, Honolulu, HI 96816.

HAAS, LEZ
Painter, Educator
b Berkeley, Calif, Mar 10, 11.
Study & Training: San Francisco State Teachers Col; Univ Calif, Berkeley, AB & MA; Hans Hofmann Sch Art.
Work in Public Collections: Cedar City, Utah; paintings in pvt collections.
Exhibitions: Roswell Art Mus; Santa Barbara Mus Art; Calif Palace of Legion of Honor; N Mex Fine Arts Mus; Univ Ariz Art Gallery; plus other group & one-man shows.
Teaching: Asst prof, Col Fine Arts, Univ N Mex, 46-47, acting dean, 47-48, dir, Taos Field Sch, 47-48, assoc prof & chmn dept art, 47-53, prof, 53-63, acting dean, 54-55; head art dept, Univ Ariz, 63-69, prof art, 63-
Awards: Mus N Mex Prize, 57.
Memberships: Am Asn Univ Prof; Soc Am Archeol; Prof Photogrs Am.
Mailing Address: Dept of Art, University of Arizona, Tucson, AZ 85721.

HAAS, RICHARD JOHN
Printmaker, Painter
Preferred Media: Intaglio
b Spring Green, Wis, Aug 29, 36.
Study & Training: Univ Wis-Milwaukee, BS, 59; Univ Minn, MFA, 64.
Work in Public Collections: Whitney Mus Am Art, New York, N Y; Yale Univ Art Gallery, New Haven, Conn; Minn Inst Art; Fogg Mus, Cambridge, Mass; Houston Mus Fine Arts, Tex.
Exhibitions: One-man shows, Hundred Acres Gallery & Contract Graphics Gallery in Houston, 72; Copper, Boston Pub Libr, Mass, 72; Contemporary American Art, Herron Mus Art, Indianapolis, Ind, 72; Group Exhib, Whitney Mus Am Art, 72.
Teaching: Instr art Univ Minn, 63-64; asst prof art, Mich State Univ, 64-68; instr printmaking, Bennington Col, 68-
Awards: Ford Found Purchase Prize, 64; first prize, Michigan Printmakers, 66.
Dealers: Brooke Alexander, 24 E 78th St, New York, NY 10021; Hundred Acres Gallery, 453 W Broadway, New York, NY 10013.
Mailing Address: 81 Greene St, New York, NY 10012.

HABER, LEONARD
Collector, Designer
b New York, N Y, Aug 5, 20.
Study & Training: Parsons Sch Design; study in Paris & Italy; Univ Paris; Yale Univ, BFA.
Teaching: Asst prof fine arts, Col William & Mary, 36-40.
Awards: Six medals, Beaux Art Inst Design.
Collection: Contemporary drawings and paintings; Japanese lacquers.
Mailing Address: 8 E 62nd St, New York, NY 10021.

HABERGRITZ, GEORGE JOSEPH
Painter, Sculptor
b New York, N Y, June 16, 09.
Study & Training: Nat Acad Design; Cooper Union, grad; Acad Grande Chaumiere.
Work in Public Collections: Butler Mus, Youngstown, Ohio; Wilberforce Univ, Ohio; Purdue Univ; Safad Mus, Israel; Jewish Mus, London.

Exhibitions: Albright Mus Painting Ann, Buffalo, N Y, 38-40; Va Biennial, Richmond, 40; Am Watercolor Soc Ann, 47-49; Nat Asn Painters Casein, 47-72; Nat Acad Design Drawing & Painting Ann, 48-51.
Teaching: Lectr Artist in Africa, S Pac & India, 57- ; instr painting, Art Stud League New York, 60-64; instr painting, Friend Sch Art, 65- ; instr new media, Workshop Prof Artists, 67-
Positions: Dir, Sch Continuing Art Educ, 68-
Awards: Gold medal for drawing, Nat Acad Design, 38; Grumbacher Awards, Nat Soc Painters Casein, 68 & 70.
Bibliography: G Klotz (auth), Two American artists, Galerie Klotz, Stuttgart, 67.
Memberships: Nat Soc Painters Casein (pres, 63-64).
Mailing Address: 150 Waverly Pl, New York, NY 10014.

HACK, HOWARD EDWIN
Painter
Preferred Media: Oils, Tempera.
b Cheyenne, Wyo, July 6, 32.
Study & Training: Calif Col Arts & Crafts; Mills Col; Univ San Francisco, BA(philos); San Francisco Art Inst; also with Martin Baer, San Francisco, 50-53.
Work in Public Collections: Whitney Mus Am Art, New York, N Y; Sara Roby Found, New York; Oakland Art Mus, Calif.
Exhibitions: Winter Invitational, Calif Palace Legion of Honor, San Francisco, 61; Pittsburgh Int Painting & Sculpture Ann, Carnegie Inst, Pa, 64 & 67; 29th Corcoran Biennial, Corcoran Gallery Art, Washington, D C, 65; San Francisco Mus Art Drawing Nat, 70; Looking West, Joslyn Art Mus Invitational, Omaha, Nebr, 70.
Awards: Neysa McMein Purchase Award, Whitney Mus Am Art, 65; Richard & Hinda Rosenthal Found Award for painting, Nat Acad Arts & Lett, 66; Childe Hassam Found Purchase Award, Am Acad Arts & Lett, 69.
Dealer: Gump's Gallery, 250 Post St, San Francisco, CA 94108.
Mailing Address: 54 Cook St, San Francisco, CA 94118.

HACK, PHILLIP S & PATRICIA Y
Collectors
Mr Hack, b Ill, Dec 8, 16; Mrs Hack, b Los Angeles, Calif, Dec 21, 26.
Study & Training: Univ Ariz; Stanford Univ; Oxford Univ; Ariz State Univ; Wabash Col; Purdue Univ.
Collection: Contemporary paintings, sculpture, prints and drawings.
Mailing Address: P O Box 655, Cave Creek, AZ 85331.

HACKENBROCH, YVONNE ALIX
Museum Curator, Writer
b Frankfurt, Ger, Apr 27, 12; U S citizen.
Study & Training: Univ Frankfurt, 32-33; Univ Rome, 33-34; Univ Munich, PhD(summa cum laude), 36.
Positions: Asst, dept Brit & mediaeval antiq, Brit Mus, London, 36-45; cur, Lee Fareham Collection, Univ Toronto, 45-49; cur, Irwin Untermyer Collection & cur, Western European arts, Metrop Mus Art, 49-
Awards: Ford Found grant, 63; Kress Found grants, 64 & 65.
Research: The decorative arts.
Publications: Auth, seven catalogues of the Irwin Untermyer Collection; contribr to Connoisseur & other mag.
Mailing Address: 7 E 85th St, New York, NY 10028.

HACKLIN, ALLAN DAVE
Painter
b New York, N Y, Feb 11, 43.
Study & Training: Pratt Inst.
Work in Public Collections: Whitney Mus Am Art, New York; Dallas Mus Fine Arts, Tex; Allen Mus, Oberlin, Ohio.
Teaching: Instr painting, Pratt Inst, 69-70; instr painting, Calif Inst Arts, 70-
Dealers: Jos Logiudice Gallery, 59 Wooster St, New York, NY 10012; Betty Parsons Gallery, 24 W 57th St, New York, NY 10019.
Mailing Address: Jefferson, NY 12093.

HADDAD, SAMUEL
Art Dealer
b Willimantic, Conn, May 4, 37.
Study & Training: Univ Conn.
Positions: Dir, Royal Marks Gallery, New York, N Y, 61-
Specialty of Gallery: Twentieth century modern masters; contemporary American sculpture.
Mailing Address: Royal Marks Gallery, 19 E 71st St, New York, NY 10021.

HADEN, EUNICE (BARNARD)
Painter, Illustrator
b Washington, D C, Oct 21, 01.
Study & Training: Oberlin Col, BA; Abbott Sch Art, with Hugo Inden; also with Eliot O'Hara.
Work in Public Collections: In pvt collections only.

Exhibitions: Miniature Painters, Sculptors & Gravers Soc, 46-72; St Augustine Art Asn, 52 & 60; Nat Collection Fine Arts, 53-56; Burr Gallery, New York, 59 & 60; one-man, Payne Gallery, Washington, D C, 64; plus others.
Awards: Prizes, Art Club Washington, 56, 59, 64 & 66.
Memberships: Miniature Painters, Sculptors & Gravers Soc (treas, 54-59, pres, 60-64, corresp secy, 64-66); St Augustine Art Asn; Art Club Washington (exhib comt chmn, 56-57, v chmn 57-58, v chmn prog comt, 56-59, chmn, 61-62, corresp secy, 64-69, bd gov, 65-66).
Publications: Auth & ed, DAR patriot index, first ed, 67, suppl, 69; auth, Yearbks for 68-73, Am Clan Gregor Soc.
Mailing Address: 5112 Connecticut Ave N W, Washington, DC 20008.

HADER, ELMER (STANLEY)
Illustrator, Writer
b Pajaro, Calif, Sept 7, 89.
Study & Training: Calif Sch Design, 07-10; Julien Acad, Paris, France, 12-14.
Work in Public Collections: San Francisco Art Asn.
Exhibitions: Nat Acad Design; Salon Artistes Française, Paris.
Awards: Caldecott medal, 49.
Publications: Auth & illusr, over thirty story & picture bks for children; illusr, McCalls, Pictorial Rev, Good Housekeeping, Century & Christian Sci Monitor.
Mailing Address: 55 River Rd, Grand View-on-Hudson, NY 11227.

HADLOCK, WENDELL STANWOOD
Art Administrator
b Cranberry Isles, Maine, May 11, 11.
Study & Training: Univ Maine, AB(hist & res); Univ Pa, MA(anthrop).
Positions: Admin asst, Peabody Mus Salem, Mass, 49-50; dir, William A Farnsworth Libr & Art Mus, 51-
Mailing Address: P O Box 466, Rockland, ME 04841.

HADZI, DIMITRI
Sculptor, Printmaker
Preferred Media: Bronze.
b New York, N Y, Mar 21, 21.
Study & Training: Cooper Union, cert, 50; Brooklyn Mus Art Sch, 48-50; Polytechnion, Athens, Greece, 50-51.
Work in Public Collections: Mus Mod Art, New York; Solomon R Guggenheim Mus, New York; Whitney Mus Am Art, New York; Fogg Art Mus, Harvard Univ, Cambridge, Mass; Nat Collection Art, Smithsonian Inst, Washington, D C.
Commissions: Elmo (bronze), Mass Inst Technol Art Comt, 62; K-458 (bronze with Max Abramovitz & David Rockefeller), Philharmonic Hall, Lincoln Ctr, New York, 62-66; Helios (bronze), Sun Life Ins Co, Baltimore, Md, 64-65; Thermopylae (bronze with Walter Gropius & Samuel Glaser for U S Govt), John F Kennedy Fed Bldg, Boston, Mass, 66-68; Arcturus (bronze with Gunnar Birkerts), Fed Reserve Bank Bldg, Minneapolis, Minn, 71-72.
Exhibitions: Recent Sculpture U S A, Mus Mod Art, New York, 59; Pittsburgh Int, Carnegie Inst, Pa, 61 & 64; one-man show, Stephen Radich Gallery, New York, 61-62; Two Sculptors: Two Painters, Venice Biennale, Italy, 62; Joseph H Hirshhorn Collection, Solomon R Guggenheim Mus, New York, 62.
Teaching: Artist-in-residence, Dartmouth Col, summer 69.
Awards: Fulbright fel, 50; Guggenheim Found fel, 57; Nat Inst Arts & Lett grant, 62.
Bibliography: Dore Ashton (auth), article, In: Am Sculpture; Peter Hollander (auth), Dimitri works in black wax (film), Kinesis Films, 52.
Memberships: Col Art Asn Am.
Publications: Illusr, Hellas, 71.
Dealer: Alpha Gallery, 121 Newbury St, Boston, MA 02116; Richard Gray Gallery, 620 N Michigan Ave, Chicago, IL 60611.
Mailing Address: Via Eleonora Pimentel, 2, 00195 Rome, Italy.

HAERER, CAROL
Painter
b Salina, Kans, Jan 23, 33.
Study & Training: Doane Col; Univ Nebr, BFA; Chicago Art Inst; Univ Calif, Berkeley, MA.
Work in Public Collections: Whitney Mus Am Art, New York, N Y; Oakland Mus, Calif; Univ Kans Mus Art, Lawrence; Sheldon Mem Art Galleries, Lincoln, Nebr; Kans State Univ, Manhattan.
Exhibitions: Salon des Realities Nouvelles, Paris, France, 55; West Coast Artists, traveling show from San Francisco Art Mus, 58-60; Lyrical Abstraction, Larry Aldrich Mus, Conn, 70; Whitney Mus Am Art Ann, New York, 70 & 72; one-artist show, Max Hutchinson Gallery, New York, 71.
Awards: Fulbright scholar to Paris, 54-55 & Woolley fel, 55-56; Alpha Chi Omega Founders fel, 66.
Bibliography: Larry Aldrich (auth), Young lyrical painters, Art in Am, 11/69.

Dealer: Max Hutchinson Gallery, 127 Greene St, New York, NY 10012.
Mailing Address: Route 2, Hoosick Falls, NY 12090.

HAGAN, (ROBERT) FREDERICK
Printmaker, Painter
b Toronto, Ont, May 21, 18.
Study & Training: Ont Col Art; Art Stud League New York; also with George Miller, New York, N Y.
Commissions: Mural, Oakville Centennial Libr.
Exhibitions: Ont Soc Artists; Can Soc Painters Watercolour; Can Group Painters; Nat Gallery Can; Libr Cong; plus others.
Teaching: Res artist, Pickering Col, Newmarket, Ont, 42-46; instr drawing & printmaking, Ont Col Art, 46-
Memberships: Can Soc Graphic Art; Can Soc Painter-Etchers & Engravers; Ont Soc Artists.
Mailing Address: Ontario College of Art, 100 McCaul St, Toronto, Ont, Can.

HAGEN, ETHEL HALL
Painter
Preferred Media: Watercolors.
b Cleveland, Ohio, Jan 2, 98.
Study & Training: Nat Acad Design; Pratt Inst, with Weiss & Lahey; Corcoran Art Sch, Washington, D C, watercolor with O'Hara; also Eliot O'Hara & Robert Landry, Calif, oil painting with A E R Van de Velde, Calif & watercolor with Lester Boner, Calif.
Commissions: Portrait of Gen Merrit Edson, USS Edson, 58.
Exhibitions: Mus Nat Hist, Washington, D C, 35; San Diego Art Asn Gallery, 50; Laguna Beach Art Gallery, 51; Carlsbad Art Gallery, 52; Escondido Fireside Inn Gallery, 53.
Teaching: Pvt instr watercolor.
Awards: Ten first & eight second awards, Carlsbad, Oceanside, Vista & Escondido Competitions, 50-60.
Memberships: San Diego Art Asn; Carlsbad-Oceanside Art League (treas, secy & pres); Escondido Art Asn; Laguna Beach Art Asn.
Mailing Address: 4407 Highland Dr, Carlsbad, CA 92008.

HAGGART (WINIFRED WATKINS)
Educator, Painter
Preferred Media: Oils.
b Albany, N Y, Nov 19, 11.
Study & Training: Syracuse Univ, BFA; Univ Pa Sch Art, MFA; Pa Acad Fine Arts; Univ Pittsburgh Grad Sch.
Work in Public Collections: Two oils in Collection One Hundred Friends Pittsburgh Art.
Commissions: Portraits of founder of sem, Dr Rowe, comn by alumnae, 44 & Margaret Durham Roby & Dalmation, comn by H Russell Roby, 47, Southern Sem Jr Col & Plato Durham, comn by Robert Lee Durham, Univ N C, 46.
Exhibitions: 11 Assoc Artists Pittsburgh Ann, 36-47, Pittsburgh Artists Exhib Paintings, 38 & Exhib Western Pa Artists, 42, Carnegie Galleries.
Teaching: Head dept art, Southern Sem Jr Col, 42-46, 56-58; asst prof art, Virginia Commonwealth Univ, 47-50; assoc prof art & head dept, Georgetown Col, 50-52.
Positions: Deleg, U S Nat Comn for UNESCO Fourth Nat Conf, Univ Minn, St Paul, 53.
Awards: Purchase awards, One Hundred Friends Pittsburgh Art, 37 & 38; Thouron Prize, Pa Acad Fine Arts, 42.
Memberships: Col Art Asn Am; Ky Guild Artists & Craftsmen.
Mailing Address: 53 Academy Ave, Pittsburgh, PA 15228.

HAGGLUND, IRVIN (ARVID)
Cartoonist
b Holt, Minn, Mar 11, 15.
Work in Public Collections: Cartoons, Syracuse Univ Permanent Collection.
Exhibitions: Cartoon Exhib, San Mateo, Calif, 57; San Diego Co Fair, Del Mar, Calif, 64.
Positions: Assoc cartoon ed, Dow Periodicals, Chicago, Ill, 41.
Publications: Contribr, Best cartoons of the year, 55-72; contribr, Happy holiday, Dodd, 56; contribr, Psychiatry book, Little, 60; contribr, Best of best cartoons, Crown, 61; contribr, Modern composition, Bk 2, Holt, Rinehart & Winston, 69.
Mailing Address: Rte 2, Box 52, Hendersonville, NC 28739.

HAHN, STEPHEN
Art Dealer
Specialty of Gallery: French paintings.
Mailing Address: 960 Madison Ave, New York, NY 10021.

HAINES, RICHARD
Painter, Educator
Preferred Media: Oils.
b Marion, Iowa, Dec 29, 06.
Study & Training: Minneapolis Sch Art; Ecole Beaux Arts, Fontainebleau, France.
Work in Public Collections: Metrop Mus Art, New York, N Y; Corcoran Gallery, Washington, D C; Los Angeles Co Mus; Dallas Mus Art, Tex; Libr Cong, Washington, D C.
Commissions: Murals, Univ Calif, Los Angeles, Schoenberg Hall, 54 & New Physics Bldg, 63, Univ Med Ctr, Lexington, 62, Mayo Diagnostic Clin, Rochester, Minn, 63 & New Fed Bldg, Los Angeles Civic Ctr, 65.
Exhibitions: Am Painting, Metrop Mus Art, New York, 50; Univ Ill, 50, 51 & 61; Corcoran Biennial, 51; Third Biennial, Sao Paulo, Brazil, 55; Pa Ann.
Teaching: Instr painting, Minneapolis Sch Art, 41-42; instr painting & drawing, Chouinard Art Inst, Los Angeles, 45-54; head dept painting, Otis Art Inst, Los Angeles, 54-
Positions: Pres, Calif Watercolor Soc, 50.
Awards: First prize painting for oils, Los Angeles Co Mus, 44 & Los Angeles City Ann, 56; third prize for oils, Corcoran Gallery, 51.
Bibliography: Article, In: Am Artist Mag, 63, Redstone (auth), Art in architecture, McGraw, 68; Mugnaini (auth), Oil painting techniques, Van Nostrand Reinhold, 69.
Memberships: Am Asn Univ Prof.
Dealer: Adele Bednarz Gallery, 902 La Cienega Blvd, Los Angeles, CA 90069.
Mailing Address: 247 Amalfi Dr, Santa Monica, CA 90402.

HALBERS, FRED
Painter
b Berlin, Ger, July 6, 94; U S citizen.
Study & Training: Oberrealschule, Max-Reinhardt Theaterschule, Berlin, 12-14.
Work in Public Collections: New York Pub Libr, Frick Art Ref Libr & Leo Baeck Inst, New York, N Y; Mus Nat Arte Mod, Madrid, Spain; Nat Mus Mod Art, Tokyo, Japan; also in pvt collections.
Exhibitions: La Paz, Sucre, Cochabamba & Potosi, Bolivia, 48-54; Am Artists Prof League, 59 & 60; Abraham Lincoln Gallery, Brooklyn, 60; West Berlin, Ger, 68; Int Platform Asn, 68.
Teaching: Lect, Influence of Religions on the Arts.
Positions: Painter, etcher, art restorer, La Paz, Bolivia, 39-54.
Awards: Am Artist Prof League Gold Medal for etchings, 59, hon mention, 60; Village Travel Awards, 58 & 59.
Memberships: Am Artist Prof League; Int Platform Asn; Am Fedn Arts; Print Coun Am.
Publications: Auth, The sanctified Judas, Ger.
Mailing Address: 23-21 35th St, Astoria, NY 11105.

HALBERSTADT, ERNST
Painter, Sculptor
b Budingen, Ger, Aug 26, 10; U S citizen.
Work in Public Collections: Metrop Mus Art, New York, N Y; Mus Mod Art, New York; New Brit Mus, Conn; Fogg Mus, Harvard Col, Cambridge, Mass; Addison Gallery Am Art, Andover, Mass.
Commissions: Murals, Fortress Monroe, Va, 37, Rockingham Park, Salem, N H, 60 & Irving Trust Co, New York, 65; sculptures, Irving Trust Co, 67 & 72.
Exhibitions: Photog Fine Arts III & IV, 62-63; Art Across Am New Eng Regional Competition, 65; Norfolk Bi-Ann Am Drawings, 69; one-man shows photog, Univ N H, 70 & Traveling Show, D V A Assocs, Fla, 72.
Teaching: Head dept murals, Sch Mus Fine Arts, Boston, Mass, 47-51.
Positions: Dir, New Eng Artists Equity Asn, 49-52.
Awards: Purchase awards, U S Govt, 41; Pepsi Cola Corp New Eng Area fel painting, 46; medals, Art Dirs Club, Boston, 56-57.
Bibliography: H Devree (auth), Newcomber, New York Times, 3/46; T Lyon (auth), E H, double vision—photographer-painter, Prof Photogr, 5/50; P S Hurd (auth), E Halberstadt—expectancy, Christian Sci Monitor, 12/68.
Publications: Illusr, Shore road to Ogunquit, 69.
Dealer: Kendall Art Gallery, Box 742, Wellfleet, MA 02667.
Mailing Address: Sunset Island, Onset, MA 02558.

HALE, NATHAN CABOT
Sculptor, Writer
b Los Angeles, Calif, July 5, 25.
Study & Training: Chouinard Art Inst, Los Angeles; Art Stud League New York.
Work in Public Collections: Bronze madonna, St Anthony of Padua, East Northport, N Y; bronze reliefs, Rose Assoc Bldg, Bronx, N Y; also in mus & pvt collections.
Exhibitions: Many group & one-man shows since 1947.
Teaching: Mem faculty, Pratt Inst, Brooklyn, 63-64; instr anat & drawing, Art Stud League New York, 66-
Positions: Fine arts adv, Wilson & Snibbe, 69-
Memberships: Art Stud League New York.

Publications: Auth, Welded sculpture, 69, Embrace of life—the sculpture of Gustav Vigelund, 70 & Abstraction in art and nature, 72; also contribr to archit & art mags.
Dealer: Midtown Galleries, 11 E 57th St, New York, NY 10022.
Mailing Address: Sheffield Rd, Amenia, NY 12501.

HALE, ROBERT BEVERLY
Art Administrator, Educator
b Boston, Mass, Jan 29, 01.
Study & Training: Columbia Univ Sch Architecture; Fontainebleau, France; Art Stud League New York.
Work in Public Collections: Metrop Mus Art, New York, N Y; Whitney Mus Am Art, New York; Univ Ariz, Tucson.
Collections Arranged: Many collections arranged at the Metrop Mus Art.
Teaching: Lectr & instr drawing & anat, Art Stud League New York, 43-; adj prof anat, Columbia Univ, 45-67; lectr anat, Pa Acad Fine Arts, 69-
Positions: Cur Am art, Metrop Mus Art, 48-66, cur emer, 66-
Memberships: Benjamin Franklin fel Royal Soc Arts; Tiffany Found (pres, 56-66).
Publications: Auth, Drawing lessons from the Great Masters, 64; ed & translr, Dr Paul Richer, Anatomie artistique, 71.
Mailing Address: 2 W 67th St, New York, NY 10023.

HALEY, JOHN CHARLES
Painter, Sculptor
Preferred Media: Oils, Watercolors, Bronze.
b Minneapolis, Minn, Sept 21, 05.
Study & Training: With Cameron Booth, Minneapolis & Hans Hofmann, Munich & Capri.
Work in Public Collections: Phillips Mem Gallery, Washington, D C; Univ Calif, Berkeley; San Francisco Mus Art; Oakland Art Mus; IBM Collection.
Exhibitions: San Francisco Art Asn Ann, 30-60; Contemp Am Painting, Univ Ill, 48 & 51-53; Exhibs Oil Painting, 51 & Drawing, 52, Metrop Mus Art, New York, N Y; Int Biennial, São Paulo, Brazil, 55 & 62; Palace of Legion of Honor Winter Invitationals, 60-64.
Teaching: Prof art, Univ Calif, Berkeley, 30-72, emer prof art, 72-
Positions: Mem bd dirs, San Francisco Art Inst, 59-62; mem, Inst Creative Arts, Univ Calif, 63-64, mem bd dirs, Univ Art Mus Coun, 72-
Awards: Six painting & sculpture awards, San Francisco Art Asn, 36-56; watercolor award, Calif Watercolor Soc, 56; painting award, Richmond Art Ctr, 56 & 58.
Mailing Address: P O Box 31, Point Station, Richmond, CA 94807.

HALFF, ROBERT H
Collector
b San Antonio, Tex, Dec 1, 08.
Study & Training: Wharton Sch, Univ Pa, grad; New Sch Social Res; New York Univ; Univ Calif, Los Angeles Exten.
Collection: American contemporary and European art; Miro, Klee, Dubuffet, Marin, Dove, De Kooning, Kline, Lichtenstein, Oldenburg, Stella, Kelly, Hepworth, Tony Smith, Jasper Johns and others.
Mailing Address: 1659 Waynecrest Dr, Beverly Hills, CA 90210.

HALKIN, THEODORE
Sculptor, Painter
b Chicago, Ill, Mar 2, 24.
Study & Training: Art Inst Chicago, BFA, 50; Southern Ill Univ, MS (art), 52.
Work in Public Collections: Art Inst Chicago; Butler Inst Am Art, Ohio.
Exhibitions: 25th Biennial Contemp Am Oil Painting, Corcoran Gallery Art, Washington, D C, 57; Am Painting & Sculpture Ann, Pa Acad Fine Arts & Detroit Inst Arts, 58; one-man shows, Allan Frumkin Galleries, New York, N Y & Chicago, 61 & Phyllis Kind Gallery, Chicago, 70; Chicago Images Show, Mus Contemp Art, Chicago, 72.
Teaching: Part-time assoc prof art, Art Inst Chicago, 67-; assoc prof art & chmn dept, Elmhurst Col, 69-
Awards: 21st Ann Midyear Show purchase prize, Butler Inst, Ohio, 56; Chicago & Vicinity Show first prize for sculpture, Art Inst Chicago, 65.
Bibliography: Article, In: Art Int, 2/64; Franz Schulz (auth), Fantastic images, Follett, 72.
Mailing Address: c/o Phyllis Kind Gallery, 226 E Ontario, Chicago, IL 60611.

HALL, CARL ALVIN
Painter, Instructor
b Washington, D C, Sept 17, 21.
Study & Training: Meinzinger Art Sch, Detroit, Mich, with Carlos Lopez.

Work in Public Collections: Whitney Mus Am Art, New York, N Y; Boston Mus Art, Mass; Springfield Art Inst, Mass; Swope Art Gallery, Terre Haute, Ind.
Exhibitions: 66th Ann Western, Denver Art Mus, 60; 18th Artists West Miss, Colo Springs, 61; Drawings U S A, St Paul Gallery, Minn & Traveling Show, 61; Century 21, Seattle, Wash, 62; The West, 80 Contemporaries, Univ Ariz, 66.
Teaching: Artist-in-residence, Willamette Univ, 48-; instr adult educ, YWCA, Salem, 57-
Positions: Art critic, Ore Statesman, Salem, 53-68.
Awards: Nat Inst Arts & Lett grant, 49; Newberry Prize, Detroit Inst Art, 49.
Bibliography: Collection of drawings, Northwest Rev, 63.
Memberships: Portland Art Mus.
Mailing Address: 4626 Pettyjohn Rd S, Salem, OR 97302.

HALL, JOHN A
Painter, Educator
b Toronto, Ont, Oct 10, 14.
Study & Training: Ont Col Art.
Work in Public Collections: Art Gallery Toronto.
Commissions: Murals in porcelain enamel on steel panels, Delhi, Port Colborne & Simcoe, Ont & Expo '67, Montreal, P Q.
Exhibitions: Can Group Painters; Ont Soc Artists; Royal Can Acad Arts; New York World's Fair, 39; Rio, 44 & 46; plus others.
Collections Arranged: Design, Can Nat Exhib, Can Furniture Mart & Can Pavilion, Brussels, Belg.
Teaching: Instr, Art Gallery Toronto; instr painting, Ont Dept Educ, summer courses; assoc prof drawing & painting, fac archit, Univ Toronto.
Awards: Can Arts Coun Sr Artists' Award, 63.
Memberships: Can Soc Graphic Art; Ont Soc Artists.
Publications: Illusr, Spirit of Canadian democracy, These English, The grandmothers, Glooscap's country, Nunny-Bay 3 & The road across Can.
Mailing Address: 3 Braemar Ave, Toronto, Ont. M5P 2L1, Can.

HALL, JOYCE C
Collector
b David City, Mo, Aug 29, 91.
Study & Training: Univ Mo, hon LLD, 63, Kans State Univ, 63, Univ Nebr, 68.
Positions: Bd dirs, Am Heritage Found.
Mailing Address: 110th St & State Line, Kansas City, MO 64114.

HALL, LOUISE
Educator, Art Historian
b Cambridge, Mass, July 23, 05.
Study & Training: Wellesley Col, BA, 27; Mass Inst Technol, SB, 30; Univ Paris Inst Art & Archeol, 31; Harvard Univ, PhD(archit), 54.
Teaching: Prof hist art & archit, Duke Univ, 31-
Memberships: Soc Archit Historians (secy-treas, 49, v pres, 51); Soc Archit Historians Gt Brit; Col Art Asn Am.
Mailing Address: Box 6636, College Station, Durham, NC 27708.

HALL, MICHAEL DAVID
Sculptor, Educator
Preferred Media: Steel, Aluminum.
b Upland, Calif, May 20, 41.
Study & Training: Western Wash State Col, 58-60; Univ N C, BA, 62; Univ Iowa, 62; Univ Wash, MFA(sculpture), 64.
Work in Public Collections: Princeton Univ Art Mus, N J; Jacksonville Art Mus, Fla; Univ Iowa Art Mus, Iowa City; J B Speed Art Mus, Louisville, Ky; Univ Wash Conf Ctr, Seattle.
Exhibitions: Whitney Mus Am Art Ann Sculpture Exhib, New York, N Y, 68; Sculpture of the Month, New York City Dept Cult Affairs, 68; Eight American Sculptors, Equitable Life Plaza, Chicago, Ill, 68; Temple Univ Invitational Sculpture Exhib, Ambler, Pa, 69; American Sculpture, Sheldon Mus, Univ Nebr, Lincoln, 70; plus many one-man shows.
Teaching: Instr ceramics & sculpture, Univ Colo, Boulder, 65-66; assoc prof sculpture, Univ Ky, 66-70; resident sculptor, Cranbrook Acad Art, 70-
Awards: Nat Sci Found Study Grant, 64; creative res grant, Univ Ky, 68-69.
Memberships: Mus Am Folk Art; N Y State Hist Asn; New Detroit Arts Div.
Art Interests: American folk art with emphasis on contemporary folk sculpture.
Publications: Auth, American folk sculpture-the personal and the eccentric, 71; auth, articles, In: Cranbrook Mag, 71-72.
Dealer: Gertrude Kasle Gallery, 321 Fisher Bldg, Detroit, MI 48202.
Mailing Address: 500 Lone Pine Rd, Bloomfield Hills, MI 48013.

HALL, REX EARL
Painter, Educator
b Asbury, Mo, Feb 3, 24.
Study & Training: Washburn Univ, AB; Kans City Art Inst; Univ Wichita, MFA.
Work in Public Collections: Wichita Art Mus; Wichita State Univ.
Exhibitions: Kans Ann, 56-63; Kans Biennial, 59-64; one-man shows, Birger Sandzen Gallery, 63, Kansas City Pub Libr, Mo, 63 & Wichita Art Mus, 64; plus others.
Teaching: Prof art, Kans State Teachers Col, 60-68; Emporia State Teachers Col; prof art & chmn dept, Kans State Teachers Col, 69-
Awards: Wichita Air Capital Award, 57 & 58; Living with Art, Wichita, 60; Designer-Craftsmen Show, Lawrence, Kans, 62.
Memberships: Kans Fedn Art (v pres, 62); Kans Art Educ Asn; Col Art Asn; Index Art Group (founder); Wichita Art Guild (v pres, 58-); plus others.
Publications: Auth, A profile, Kans Art Educ Asn J, 61; auth, three booklets for Kans Art Educ Asn, 64-65.
Mailing Address: Art Dept, Kansas State Teachers College, 1200 Commercial, Emporia, KS 66801.

HALLAM, BEVERLY (LINNEY)
Painter, Lecturer
Preferred Media: Acrylics.
b Lynn, Mass, Nov 22, 23.
Study & Training: Mass Col Art, BSEd, 45; Cranbrook Acad Art, 48; Syracuse Univ, MFA, 51-53.
Work in Public Collections: Addison Gallery Am Art, Andover, Mass; Corcoran Gallery Art, Washington, D C; Rose Art Mus, Brandeis Univ, Waltham, Mass; Witte Mem Mus, San Antonio, Tex; Worcester Art Mus, Mass.
Exhibitions: View 1960, Inst Contemp Art, Boston, Mass, circulated throughout U S by Smithsonian Inst, 60-61; New England Contemporary Artists, Northeastern Univ, 63 & 65; Art for U S Embassies, Inst Contemp Art, Boston & State Dept, Washington, D C, 66; Am Watercolor Soc Traveling Exhib, 67; Landscape II, De Cordova Mus, Lincoln, Mass, 71.
Teaching: Chmn art dept, Lasell Jr Col, 45-49; assoc prof painting & teacher educ, Mass Col Art, 49-62; lectr & demonstr, Use of Polyvinyl Acetate as a Painting Medium, throughout Eastern U S, 52-
Awards: Pearl Safir Award for Outstanding Painting by a Woman, Silvermine Guild Artists, 55; Blanche E Colman Found Award, 60; Edwin T Webster Award (first prize), Boston Soc Watercolor Painters, 62.
Bibliography: Christopher C Cook (auth), Beverly Hallam: paintings, drawings and monotypes, 1956-1971, Addison Gallery Am Art, 71.
Memberships: Am Fedn Arts; Ogunquit Art Asn (pres, 64); Barn Gallery Assocs (bd dir, 70-); Archives Am Art; Boston Watercolor Soc.
Publications: Auth, The Saturday morning high school art classes at the Massachusetts School of Art, Art Educ Bull, Vol 13, No 3; auth, Arts and activities, Lineargrams, 57; illusr, Stamping/diemaking (cover designs), Stanger Publ, 69-
Dealer: Fairweather Hardin Gallery, 101 E Ontario St, Chicago, IL 60614.
Mailing Address: Shore Rd, Ogunquit, ME 03907.

HALLEY, DONALD M, JR
Art Administrator, Instructor
b New Orleans, La, Dec 17, 33.
Study & Training: Cornell Univ, BA; Tulane Univ La, MFA.
Collections Arranged: Numerous temporary exhibs for Norfolk Mus Arts & Sci, Va, Des Moines Art Ctr, Iowa & Hudson River Mus, Yonkers, N Y.
Teaching: Instr art educ, Old Dominion Col, summer, 64; adj prof art res, Drew Univ, 71.
Positions: From asst dir to assoc dir, Norfolk Mus Arts & Sci, 58-62; asst dir, Des Moines Art Ctr, 62-68; dir, Hudson River Mus, 68-
Memberships: Am Asn Mus; Assoc mem Int Coun Mus; Northeast Mus Conf (bd gov, 71-72); Gallery Asn N Y State (bd mem, 71-72); Mus Collaborative New York (adv coun, 71-72).
Publications: Auth, Norfolk Mus Bull, 59-62, auth, German expressionism (catalogue), Norfolk Mus, 60; auth, Des Moines Art Ctr Bull, 62-68, auth, Painting: out from the wall (catalogue), Des Moines Art Ctr, 68; auth, Catalogue of the American Republic Insurance Company Collection, 65.
Mailing Address: Hudson River Museum, 511 Warburton Ave, Yonkers, NY 10701.

HALLMAN, (H) THEODORE, (JR)
Craftsman
Preferred Media: Weaving.
Study & Training: Tyler Sch, Temple Univ, Sen scholar, BFA & BSEd; Fontainebleau Fine Arts, Pew scholar, cert, with Jacques Villon; Cranbrook Acad Art, West scholar, MFA(painting) & MFA (textile design); Bundestextilschule, Austria, cert.
Work in Public Collections: Frontispiece to Textile Collection, Smithsonian Inst, Washington, D C; Mus Contemp Crafts, New York, N Y; Victoria & Albert Mus, London; Cooper Hewitt Mus, New York; Oakland Mus Art, Calif.
Commissions: Translucent tapestry, Nieman Marcus, Dallas; room divider, Marshall Field & Co, Chicago; garden divider, Am Chem Soc, Washington, D C; altar hanging, Lutheran Church, Allentown, Pa; window hangings, Ashbourne Country Club, Philadelphia, Pa; plus others.
Exhibitions: Craftsmen U S A, New York, 60; Wall Hangings, Victoria & Albert Mus, 62; Int Kunsthandwerk, Stuttgart, 67; Objects U S A Traveling Show, 69-72; Contemplation Environments, Mus Contemp Crafts, 70.
Teaching: Instr, Haystack Sch, Maine & Penland Sch Crafts, summers 58-69; prof textiles & chmn dept, Moore Col Art, 65-70; assoc prof textile design, San Francisco State Col, spring 71; also lectr, U S & Can.
Positions: Consult, I L O Textiles, Jamaica, summer 68; textile designer, var co.
Awards: Tiffany Found grant, 62; Textile Prize, Int Kunsthandwerk Expos, Stuttgart, 67.
Bibliography: Neuman (auth), Plastics as an art form, Chilten, 68; Regensteiner (auth), The art of weaving, 70 & Willcox (auth), Techniques of Rya knotting, 71, Van Nostrand Reinhold.
Memberships: Am Craftsmen Coun; Philadelphia Coun Prof Craftsmen (treas, 68-70); hon mem Int Soc Arts & Lett.
Mailing Address: Lederach, PA 19450.

HALM, ROBERT JOHN
Painter, Instructor
Preferred Media: Oils.
b Saginaw, Mich, June 9, 22.
Study & Training: Mich State Univ, BA, 48; Univ Iowa, MFA, 50.
Exhibitions: 35th Ann Exhib, Soc Am Etchers, Gravers, Lithographers, Woodcutters, New York, N Y, 51; Terry Nat Art Exhib, Miami, Fla, 52; Sioux Land Watercolor Show, Sioux City, Iowa, 56; Off of the Gov, State Capitol, Des Moines, Iowa, 70; Iowa Arts Coun Drawing & Print Traveling Exhib, 70-71.
Teaching: Artist & instr painting, Iowa Cent Community Col, Fort Dodge, 50-
Positions: Coordr gallery activities, Blanden Art Gallery, Fort Dodge, 53-67, secy bd trustees, 68-
Awards: Third award for oil, Iowa State Fair Art Salon, 50; hon mention for oil, Terry Nat Art Exhib, 52.
Memberships: Artists Equity Asn (v pres, 65-66); Col Art Asn.
Publications: Auth six articles covering work of Moore, Marini, Miro, Chagal, Feininger & Hofmann for Fort Dodge Messenger Newspaper, 65-66.
Mailing Address: 1517 Third Ave N, Fort Dodge, IA 50501.

HALPERN, NATHAN L
Collector
b Sioux City, Iowa, Oct 22, 14.
Study & Training: Otis Art Inst, Los Angeles; Univ Southern Calif, BA, 36; Harvard Univ Law Sch, LLB (cum laude), 39.
Teaching: Lectr, Annenberg Sch Commun, Univ Pa, 66.
Positions: Pres, TNT Commun, Inc.
Collection: Predominantly French impressionist and post-impressionist art.
Mailing Address: 993 Fifth Ave, New York, NY 10028.

HALSEY, WILLIAM MELTON
Painter, Educator
Preferred Media: Oils, Casein, Collage.
b Charleston, S C, Mar 13, 15.
Study & Training: Univ S C; Sch Boston Mus Fine Arts, Paige traveling fel, 39-41, with Alexandre Iacovleff & Karl Zerbe; Acad San Carlo, Mexico City, Mex.
Work in Public Collections: Baltimore Mus Art, Md; S C Arts Comn State Collection, Columbia; Mint Mus Art, Charlotte, N C; Gibbes Art Gallery, Charleston; Greenville Co Mus Art, S C.
Commissions: 3 frescoes, Berkshire Mus Art, Pittsfield, Mass, 39; murals, Beth Elohim Synagogue, Charleston, 50, Baltimore Hebrew Congregation Temple, 52 & Sears Roebuck Co, Charleston, 54; also comns from Container Corp Am & Ford Motor Co.
Exhibitions: Cent S C Exhib Tenn Art League, Parthenon, Nashville, 67; S C State Invitational, Columbia Mus Art, 69; Contemp Artists S C, Columbia Mus, Florence Mus, Greenville Mus & Gibbes Art Gallery, 70; Springs Mills Traveling Exhibs, New York, N Y, 71-72; retrospective, four S C mus, 72-73.
Teaching: Asst prof painting & drawing, Col Charleston, 65-; instr painting & drawing, Newberry Col, 68-70.
Awards: Hughes Found res grants, 50-52; purchase award, Cent S Exhib, 67.

Bibliography: Margaret Harold (auth), Prize-winning oil paintings, 62 & Prize-winning watercolors, 64, Allied Publ; Jack Morris (auth), Contemporary artists of South Carolina, Greenville Co Mus Art, 70; Jack Morris (auth), William M Halsey: retrospective (monogr), Greenville Co Mus Art, 72.

Memberships: Col Art Asn Am; Am Crafts Coun; Guild S C Artists (pres, 58).

Publications: Co-auth, A travel sketch book, 71.

Mailing Address: 38 State St, Charleston, SC 29401.

HALVORSEN, RUTH ELISE
Painter, Writer
Preferred Media: Watercolors, Oils.
b Camas, Wash.
Study & Training: Portland Art Mus Sch, Ore; Pratt Inst, Brooklyn; Columbia Univ; also with Walter Beck, Charles Martin & Albert Heckman.
Work in Public Collections: Reed Col, Portland; Ga-Pac, Portland; Univ Ore, Eugene; Fort Sumner Marine Hosp, N Mex; Portland Art Mus.
Exhibitions: San Francisco World's Fair, Calif, 39; Henry Gallery, Univ Wash, 43; Rockefeller Ctr, New York, N Y, 48; Fifth Army Midwestern Travel Show, 55; Portland Art Mus Show, 71.
Teaching: Instr art, Portland State Col, 40-60; art supvr, Portland Pub Schs, 43-62.
Awards: Pratt Inst Alumni Award for distinguished serv in art educ, 72.
Memberships: Portland Art Mus (mem bd, 47-53); Ore Contemp Crafts Asn (mem bd, 44-71); Nat Art Educ Asn (mem bd, 47-, v pres & pres, 59-63); Pac Art Asn (v pres & pres, 55-57); Mus Contemp Crafts.
Publications: Co-auth, Painting in the classroom, 62; contribr, Art J; also numerous articles for various art mags.
Mailing Address: 422 N E Going St, Portland, OR 97211.

HAMBLETON, BUD
Sculptor
Preferred Media: Steel, Wood
b Jamestown, N Y.
Study & Training: Univ Rochester, with Prof William Ehrich.
Commissions: Busts of Albert Einstein & J Robert Oppenheimer, Atomic Energy Comn & Univ Rochester, 68; Brook Trout Rising, Cerro Corp, Bellefonte, Pa, 68; Genesis (wall sculpture), Brighton Presby Church, Rochester, N Y, 69; The Preacher, Jupiter Corp, Chicago, Ill, 69; large steel owl, Eastman Kodak Co, Rochester, 70.
Exhibitions: Western New York Artists, Albright-Knox Gallery, Buffalo, N Y, 56-57; Rochester Religious Arts Festival, Rochester, 66; Everson Gallery Regional Exhib, Syracuse, 67; Finger Lakes Exhib, Mem Art Gallery, Rochester, 70.
Bibliography: Article, In: Upstate Mag, 68; Link Q Courtney (auth), Salvation (musical using slides of sculpture), David Black-prodocer, 70.
Dealer: Lord & Taylor Gallery, Fifth Ave at 39th St, New York, NY 10016.
Mailing Address: 29 Lynnhaven Ct, Rochester, NY 14618.

HAMBLETT, THEORA
Painter, Illustrator
Preferred Media: Oils.
b Paris, Miss, Jan 15, 95.
Study & Training: Univ Southern Miss; Univ Miss; Famous Artists Sch, Westport, Conn.
Work in Public Collections: Mus Mod Art, New York, N Y; Brooks Mem Art Gallery, Memphis, Tenn; First Nat Bank, Jackson, Miss; also in pvt collections of Gov Nelson Rockefeller, New York & Alec Guiness, Eng; plus many others.
Exhibitions: Atlanta Art Asn, Ga, 65; 50 Artists from 50 States, Am Fedn Arts Traveling Exhib, 66-67; Sixth Nat Biennial Religious Art, Cranbrook Acad Art, Bloomfield Hills, Mich; 17 Naive Painters, Mus Mod Art Traveling Exhib, 66-67; Symbols and Images, Am Fedn Arts, 70-72; plus many others.
Teaching: Asst to beginner's, O'Tuckolota Consolidated High Sch, 24-31.
Bibliography: B Oesterling (auth), Paintings of Theora Hamblett (film), Univ Miss, 67; Guy Northrop (auth), Hamblett's Paintings, Sun Com Appeal, Memphis, 72; Dr L Dollarhide (auth), Hamblett's work, Jackson Daily, 72.
Memberships: Miss Art Asn; Oxford-Lafayette Art Asn; Kate Skipwith Geneal Soc; Miss Folklore Soc.
Publications: Auth, Heaven's descent to earth, 60; auth, Symbols of Faith, 66; co-auth, Dreams can work for you, 70; co-auth, I remember, 71.
Dealer: Parsons Gallery, 24 W 57th St, New York, NY 10019.
Mailing Address: 619 Van Buren Ave, Oxford, MS 38655.

HAMILTON, GEORGE HEARD
Museum Director, Art Historian
b Pittsburgh, Pa, June 23, 10.
Study & Training: Yale Univ, BA, MA, PhD.
Teaching: Mem, hist art dept, Yale Univ, 36-66; Robert Sterling Clark vis prof art, Williams Col, 63-64; Slade prof fine arts, Cambridge Univ, 71-72.
Positions: Curatorial staff, Yale Univ Art Gallery, 36-66; dir Sterling & Francine Clark Art Inst, Williamstown, Mass, 66-; v pres & trustee, Hill-Stead Mus, Farmington, Conn; trustee, Mus Mod Art, New York, N Y; v chmn & trustee, Joseph H Hirshhorn Mus & Sculpture Garden, Washington, D C.
Memberships: Col Art Asn (pres, 66-68).
Research: 19th and 20th century European and American art.
Publications: Auth, Manet and his critics, 54; Russian art and architecture, 54; European painting and sculpture, 1880-1940, 67; co-auth, Raymond Duchamp-Villon, 67; auth, 19th and 20th century art—painting, sculpture, architecture, 70.
Mailing Address: Sterling & Francine Clark Art Institute, Williamstown, MA 01267.

HAMMER, ALFRED EMIL
Painter, Art Administrator
Preferred Media: Oils.
b New Haven, Conn, Jan 11, 25.
Study & Training: R I Sch Design, BFA; Yale Univ, BFA & MFA; also with John R Frazier, Josef Albers, Willem DeKooning, Stuart Davis, Abraham Rattner, Alvin Lustig & John Howard Benson.
Work in Public Collections: Nat J C Mus, Israel; Cleveland Art Asn; R I Sch Design.
Exhibitions: Providence Art Club Ann, R I, 53-67; Columbia Biennial, S C, 58; Newport Ann, R I, 60; Boston Art Festival, Mass, 60; Four Americans, La State Univ, 62.
Teaching: Assoc prof painting, drawing, design & calligraphy, R I Sch Design, 53-69, chmn admis comt, 56-60, dean stud, 60-63, chmn div grad studies, 63-65; vis lectr design & painting, Minneapolis Col Art, 67; dean inst, Cleveland Inst Art, 69-; vis lectr design & painting, Case Western Reserve Univ, 70.
Awards: First prize, R I Artists Ann, 53, Providence Art Club Ann, 54, 55 & 56 & Newport Ann, 60.
Bibliography: Prize winning oil paintings, Allied Fla, 61.
Mailing Address: 3045 Warrington Rd, Shaker Heights, OH 44120.

HAMMER, VICTOR J
Art Dealer
b New York, N Y, Nov 1, 01.
Study & Training: Colgate Univ; Princeton Univ.
Positions: Pres, Appraisers Asn Am, 64; dir, Hammer Galleries.
Specialty of Gallery: Nineteenth and twentieth century Franch art; Western American art, especially Charles M Russell and Frederic Remington; impressionist and post-impressionist paintings; elegant epoch paintings.
Mailing Address: 781 Fifth Ave, New York, NY 10022.

HAMMERSLEY, FREDERICK
Painter, Educator
Preferred Media: Oils.
b Salt Lake City, Utah, Jan 5, 19.
Study & Training: Univ Idaho Southern Br; Chouinard Art Sch, Los Angeles, Calif; Ecole Beaux Arts, Paris, France; Jepson Art Inst, Los Angeles.
Work in Public Collections: Univ Art Mus, Univ Calif, Berkeley; Butler Inst Am Art, Youngstown, Ohio; Santa Barbara Mus Art, Calif; USN, Washington, D C; City of Claremont, Calif.
Exhibitions: Abstract Classicists, San Francisco Mus Art, Los Angeles Co Mus Art & Inst Contemp Art, London, Eng, 59-60; Purist Painting, Am Fedn Arts Traveling Show, 60-61; Responsive Eye, Mus Mod Art, New York, 62; Geometric Abstraction Am, Whitney Mus Am Art, New York, 62; Art Across Am, Mead Corp & Traveling Show, 65-67.
Teaching: Lectr painting, drawing & design, Pomona Col, 53-62; instr painting, drawing & design, Chouinard Art Inst, 64-68; vis assoc prof painting & drawing, Univ N Mex, 68-71.
Awards: Purchase awards, for painting, Butler Inst Am Art, 61 & Los Angeles All City Ann, 64-66 & print, Los Angeles Printmaking Soc, 65.
Bibliography: Jules Langsner (auth), Four abstract classicists, Los Angeles Co Mus Art, 59; Lawrence Alloway (auth), West Coast hard edge, Inst Contemp Art, London, 60; Michel Seuphor (auth), Abstract painting, Abrams, 62.
Publications: Contribr, Classicism or hard-edge?, 60 & Los Angeles letter, 2/61, Art Int; auth, My first experience with computer drawings, 10/69 & My geometrical paintings, 4/70, Leonardo Mag.
Mailing Address: 608 Carlisle S E, Albuquerque, NM 87106.

HAMMON, BILL J
Painter, Sculptor
b Oklahoma City, Okla, Oct 3, 22.
Study & Training: Okla Art Ctr; Colo Springs Fine Arts Ctr; Kansas City Art Inst; Acad San Carlos, Mexico City; also with Boardman Robinson, Arnold Blanch, Edward Laning & Thomas H Benton.
Work in Public Collections: Joslyn Art Mus, Omaha, Nebr; U S Nat Bank, Omaha; Clarkson Hosp & Methodist Hosp, Omaha; Col St Mary's, Omaha.
Commissions: Metal sculpture of hist of flight, Strategic Air Command, Bellevue, Nebr, 70; DNA mosaic, Univ Nebr Med Libr, Omaha, 71; chancel wall mosaic, Mercy Hosp, Council Bluffs, Iowa, 71; concrete sculpture monument to Lewis & Clark, Big Bend, S Dak, 72; metal sculpture, ConAgra, Omaha, 72.
Exhibitions: Many ann, Midwest Biennials; Ford Traveling Exhibs, Nelson Gallery, Denver Mus & Walker Art Ctr.
Positions: Art dir, Omaha Art Sch, 51-58; pres, Cent Area Chap Artists Equity Asn, 60-62.
Awards: McDowell Gold Medal, Southwest Exhib, 54; Midwest Biennial Purchase Award, Joslyn Art Mus, 55; purchase award, Assoc Artists Ann, 60.
Bibliography: Robert Wiener (auth), Bill J Hammon, Channel 12, Shreveport, La; Paul Williams (auth), Who is this Hammon?, Sun Publ, 66; Lee Terry (auth), In the middle of everywhere, KETV, Omaha, 71.
Memberships: Nat Soc Mural Painters; Fla Fedn Art; Purple Isle Art Guild; Assoc Artists (pres & chmn bd, 50-); Am Fedn Art.
Publications: Auth & illusr, articles & stories, In: Ford Times, Omaha World Herald & others.
Mailing Address: Studio 9, Aquila Ct, Omaha, NE 68102.

HAMMOND, NATALIE HAYS
Painter, Museum Director
Preferred Media: Watercolors.
b Lakewood, N J, Jan 6, 04.
Study & Training: Study with Sergei Soudeikine.
Work in Public Collections: The Luxembourg, Paris, France; Pittsfield Mus, Mass; also in pvt collections.
Exhibitions: Royal Miniature Soc, Grieves Gallery, London, Eng, 27-29; one-man shows, Memorial Gallery, Rochester, N Y & Brooklyn Mus, N Y, 27; Pa Acad Fine Arts, Philadelphia, 28; one-man show, Corcoran Gallery Art, Washington, D C, 29 & Philadelphia Art Alliance, 35; also 20 other one-man shows.
Positions: Pres, Natalie Hammond Process Corp, 30-32; dir, Am Arbit Asn, 30; assoc mem, Royal Miniature Soc London, 27-39; founder & dir, Hammond Mus, North Salem, N Y, 57-
Memberships: Mediaeval Acad Am.
Publications: Auth & illusr, Elizabeth of England, Kamin, 36; auth & illusr, Anthology of pattern, Helburn, 49.
Mailing Address: Argaty, Deveaux Rd, North Salem, Westchester, NY 10560.

HAMMOND, RUTH MacKRILLE
Painter
Preferred Media: Watercolors, Oils, Acrylics, Ink.
b West Haven, Conn, Mar 19, 93.
Study & Training: Mt Holyoke Col, BA, 15; Yale Univ Grad Sch; also acrylics with Armen Gasparian, Laguna Beach, 72, and study in Rome, Italy, with Dante Ricci.
Work in Public Collections: Farnsworth Mus, Rockland, Maine; Walker Art Bldg, Brunswick, Maine; Ford Collection, Detroit, Mich.
Commissions: Paintings, Ford Motor Co.
Exhibitions: Allied Artists Am, New York, N Y; Pa Acad Fine Arts; Rockport Art Asn, Mass; Ogunquit Art Asn, Maine; Nat Asn Women Artists.
Collections Arranged: Walker Art Mus, Brunswick, Maine; Farnsworth Mus, Rockland, Maine; Copley Soc, Boston, Mass.
Teaching: Pvt instr watercolors & oils.
Awards: Awards, for The Gurnet & Low Tide, Brick Store Mus & Rain Forest, Rockport, Mass.
Memberships: Ogunquit Art Asn; Laguna Beach Art Asn; Brick Store Mus.
Publications: Auth, The Okefenokee swamp & Trip to Saguenay, Ford Times; auth, bk rev, Portland Press Herald.
Mailing Address: 9 Thompson St, Brunswick, ME 04011.

HAMMONS, VERILY
Painter
Preferred Media: Oils, Acrylics, Pastels.
b Saperton, B C, Apr 12, 18; U S citizen.
Study & Training: Cornish Inst, Seattle, Wash.
Work in Public Collections: Ahmundson Home Savings & Loan Collection, Los Angeles, Calif; Blanchard Mem Libr Collection, Santa Paula, Calif; Walter Foster Publ Gallery Collection, Tustin, Calif.

Exhibitions: Travel Show Selections from Calif Nat Watercolor Soc, Nat Acad Design, 71; California Artists, Long Beach Mus Art, 71; Grand Prix Int de Deauville, France, 72; Grand Prix Int de la Cote D'Azur, Cannes, France, 72; Am Artists Prof League Grand Nat, 72.
Teaching: Instr oil painting, Art League Los Angeles, 69-71.
Awards: Purchase award, All City Art Festival, Los Angeles, 69; gold medal award, Calif Art Club, 71; Watercolor West Award, Calif Nat Watercolor Soc, 71.
Memberships: Fel Am Artists Prof League; life mem Am Inst Fine Arts; Calif Art Club; Calif Nat Watercolor Soc; Laguna Beach Art Asn.
Dealer: Emerson Gallery, 17230 Ventura Blvd, Encino, CA 91316.
Mailing Address: 18632 Vincennes, Northridge, CA 91324.

HAMPTON, PHILLIP JEWEL
Painter, Educator
Preferred Media: Acrylics.
b Kansas City, Mo, Apr 23, 22.
Study & Training: Citrus Jr Col, Glendora, Calif; Kansas State Univ; Drake Univ; Kansas City Art Inst, BFA, 51, MFA, 52; Univ Mo-Kansas City.
Work in Public Collections: Liberty Nat Bank, Savannah, Ga; Lincoln Univ, Jefferson City, Mo; South Co Bank, Clayton, Mo; Tuskegee Inst, Ala; Ga Southern Col, Statesboro, Ga.
Commissions: Epitome of Home Economics, Savannah State Col, 56.
Exhibitions: Nelson Gallery Second Mid-Am Ann, Kansas City, 52; Fourth Coastal Empire Arts Festival, Savannah Art Asn, 64; First Nat Watercolor Competition, Dulin Gallery, Knoxville, Tenn, 64; Southeastern Exhib Prints & Drawings, Jacksonville, Fla, 64; Nat Print & Drawing Competition, 65, Dulin Gallery, Knoxville, Tenn, 65.
Teaching: Assoc prof art & dir, Savannah State Col, 52-69; assoc prof painting & design, Southern Ill Univ, Edwardsville, 69-, coordr Ethnic & Spec Studies Workshop, 71-72.
Positions: Mem bd & chmn educ, Savannah Art Asn, 67-69.
Awards: Teacher of Yr, Stud Nat Educ Asn, 66; award for serv in art to community, Savannah Chap Links & Nat Conf Artists, Savannah Chap, 66.
Bibliography: Alma Thomas (auth), Phillip Hampton, Savannah Morning News & Eve Press, 3/12/67.
Memberships: Col Art Asn Am; Am Fedn Art; Nat Conf Artists.
Research: Investigating synthetic media and their application to painting developments.
Publications: Illusr, brochure, Greenbriar Children's Ctr, Savannah, 61; auth, An approach to art for preadults, 63 & Modern art—the celebration of man's freedom, 66, Savannah State Col Faculty Res Bull; illusr, cover, The Islander, 3/68.
Dealer: Friedman's Art Store, 116 Whitaker, Savannah, GA 31401.
Mailing Address: 832 Holyoake Rd, Edwardsville, IL 62025.

HANAN, HARRY
Cartoonist
b Liverpool, Eng, Dec 14, 16.
Study & Training: Liverpool Sch Art.
Exhibitions: Metrop Mus Art & Mus Mod Art, New York, N Y; Walker Art Gallery, Liverpool, Eng.
Positions: Ed cartoonist, Liverpool Eve Express, 36-40; ed cartoonist, The People, 46-48.
Memberships: Nat Cartoonists Soc.
Publications: Auth & illusr, Louie, daily comic strip, newspapers in U S & abroad, 47-
Mailing Address: 638 Coleman Pl, Westfield, NJ 07090.

HANBURY, UNA
Sculptor
Preferred Media: Bronze, Stone.
b Eng; U S citizen.
Study & Training: Polytech Sch Art; Royal Acad Sch Art, grad; Acad Grande Chaumière & Acad Julien, Paris, France; also with Frank Calderon, March Brothers & Jacob Epstein.
Work in Public Collections: Nat Portrait Gallery, Washington, D C; Corcoran Gallery Art; Bukovička Banja Sculpture Park; Arandjelovac, Yugoslavia.
Commissions: Compassion (stone monument), Arlington Co Junior C of C, Va, 68; Phoenix (polyester wall relief), comn by Julien Redele, Washington, D C, 69; symbolic wall relief (bronze), Med Examiners Bldg, City Baltimore, Md, 69; Dato David Sung (mem bronze bust), Sung family, Kuala Lampus, Malaysia, 71.
Exhibitions: Several exhibs at Royal Acad Art, London, Eng & Salon Automne, Paris, France; Nat Sculpture Soc, Lever House, New York, N Y, 66, 69-72; one-man retrospective exhib, Portrait Heads '60-'70, Folger Shakespearean Libr, Washington, D C, 71; Portraits of the American Stage, Nat Portrait Gallery, Washington, 71; two-man show, Baker Gallery, Lubbock, Tex, 72.
Positions: Art ed, Faith & Storm, 71-

Awards: Best in show, Relig Art Comn, 65; George L Erion Award, Washington Soc Artists, 66; Landsen Prize & gold medal for portrait bust, Royal Acad Art.
Bibliography: Bill Dunning (auth), Una Hanbury, The New Mex, 71; Josephine Novak (auth), Theme in bronze for Baltimore Building, Baltimore Evening Sun, 71; Andrea Cohen (auth), Una Hanbury, Washington D C Gazette, 71.
Memberships: Nat Sculpture Soc; Guild Relig Archit (exhib chmn, 70); Am. Fedn Arts; Artists Equity Asn (v pres, 70).
Mailing Address: 1108 Calle Catalina, Santa Fe, NM 87501.

HANCOCK, WALKER (KIRTLAND)
Sculptor
b St Louis, Mo, June 28, 01.
Study & Training: St Louis Sch Fine Arts; Washington, Univ, 18-20; Univ Wis, 20; Pa Acad Fine Arts, 21-25; Am Acad Rome, fel 28; Washington Univ, hon DFA, 42.
Work in Public Collections: Pa Acad Fine Arts, Philadelphia; John Herron Art Inst, Indianapolis, Ind; Corcoran Gallery Art, Washington, D C; Parrish Art Mus, Southampton, N Y; Nat Gallery Art, Washington, D C; plus many others.
Commissions: Eisenhower Inaugural Medal; Pa RR War Mem; Army & Navy Air Medal; portrait statue of Douglas MacArthur, U S Military Acad; portrait statue of John Paul Jones, Fairmount Park, Philadelphia; plus many other medals, monuments & portrait busts throughout U S & abroad.
Exhibitions: Nat & int museums & galleries.
Teaching: Lect on sculpture; instr sculpture & head dept, Pa Acad Fine Arts, 29-68.
Positions: Sculptor-in-residence, Am Acad Rome, 56-57, 62-63; sculptor-in-charge, Stone Mountain Mem, Ga, 64.
Awards: Adams Mem Award, 54; Proctor prize, Nat Acad Design, 59; Medal of Achievement, Nat Sculpture Soc, 68; plus many others.
Memberships: Nat Acad Design; fel Nat Sculpture Soc; Nat Inst Arts & Lett; Architects League; Smithsonian Art Comn; plus others.
Mailing Address: Lanesville, Gloucester, MA 01930.

HANDELL, ALBERT GEORGE
Painter
Preferred Media: Oils, Pastels.
b Brooklyn, N Y, Feb 13, 37.
Study & Training: Art Stud League New York; Grande Chaumière, Paris, France.
Work in Public Collections: Syracuse Univ, N Y; Bates Col Collection, Lewistown, Maine; Elizabeth T Greenshields Mem Found, Montreal, Can; Salt Lake City Mus Fine Arts, Utah; Art Stud League New York.
Exhibitions: One-man shows, Fitzgerald Gallery, New York, N Y, 61-64, Harbor Gallery, Cold Spring Harbor, N Y, 65, 68 & 70; ACA Gallery, New York, 66 & Eileen Kuhlik Gallery, 72; group shows, Allied Artist Am, New York & Audubon Artist, New York; plus many other group & one-man shows.
Awards: John F & Anna Lee Stacy Scholar Fund, 62-65; Ranger Fund Purchase Prize, Audubon Artist, 68; Elizabeth T Greenshields Mem Found, 72.
Bibliography: Elinor Lathrop Sears (auth), Pastel painting, step by step, Watson-Guptill, 68; Heather-Meredith-Owens (auth), The inner universe of Albert Handell, Am Artist Mag, 4/71; Joe Singer (auth), Pastel portraits, Watson-Guptill (in press).
Memberships: Allied Artist Am; Salmagundi Club; Art Stud League New York.
Dealer: Eileen Kuhlik Gallery, 23 E 67th St, New York, NY 10021.
Mailing Address: 10 Lower Byrdcliffe Rd, Woodstock, NY 12498.

HANDLER, MR & MRS MILTON
Collectors, Patrons
Mr Handler, b New York, N Y, Oct 8, 03.
Study & Training: Mr Handler, Columbia Univ, AB, 24, LLB, 26; Hebrew Univ, hon LLD, 65.
Mailing Address: 625 Park Ave, New York, NY 10021.

HANDVILLE, ROBERT T
Painter, Illustrator
Preferred Media: Watercolors, Acrylics, Ink, Oils.
b Paterson, N J, Mar 23, 24.
Study & Training: Pratt Inst, cert, 48; Brooklyn Mus Art Sch; also painting with Rubentam, 60-64.
Work in Public Collections: J F Kennedy White House Collection; UNICEF; Univ Denver; Syracuse Univ; Univ Okla; plus others.
Commissions: Design of Yellowstone Nat Park Commemorative U S Postage Stamp, Presidential Citizens Adv Stamp Coun, 71-72.
Exhibitions: 200 Yrs Am Watercolor Painting, Metrop Mus Art, New York, N Y, 66; Exhib Olympic Games, Mus Acuarela, Inst Arte Mex, 68; New Eng Silvermine Guild, Conn, 70; Butler Inst Am Art, Youngstown, Ohio; Smithsonian Inst, Washington, D C.

Awards: Anonymous Prize, Audubon Artists; Ranger Fund Purchase Prize; 21st New Eng Exhib Award, Silvermine Guild Artists, 70.
Memberships: Am Watercolor Soc (dir, 62-64); Soc Illusr (treas, 61-62); Westchester Art Soc; Katonah Gallery.
Mailing Address: 99 Woodland Dr, Pleasantville, NY 10570.

HANES, JAMES (ALBERT)
Painter
Preferred Media: Oils.
b Louisville, Ky, Feb 5, 24.
Study & Training: Philadelphia Sch Indust Art; U S Army Univ, France; Pa Acad Fine Arts, with Daniel Garber, Franklin Watkins, Francis Spaeght & Walter Stuempfig.
Work in Public Collections: Pa Acad Fine Arts, Philadelphia; Univ Tampa, Fla; Yale Univ, New Haven, Conn; La Salle Col, Philadelphia; Nat Acad Design, New York, N Y.
Exhibitions: Pa Acad Fine Arts, 49-72; Palazzo Venezia, Rome, Italy, 52; Palazzo Espozione, Rome, 53; Nat Inst Arts & Lett, New York, 56; Univ Pittsburgh, Pa, 72.
Teaching: Instr painting, Pa Acad Fine Arts, 55-58; asst prof painting & artist-in-residence, La Salle Col, 65-
Positions: Art ed, Four Quarters, 70-
Awards: Cresson & Lambert Awards, Pa Acad Fine Arts, 49; Tiffany First Award, Louis Comfort Tiffany Found, 50; Prix de Rome, Am Acad Rome, 51-54.
Bibliography: Valerio Mariani (auth), Un pittore Americano, Idea, 8/16/53.
Memberships: Am Acad Rome; fel Pa Acad Fine Arts.
Mailing Address: 415 W Stafford St, Philadelphia, PA 19144.

HANES, URSULA ANN
Sculptor
b Toronto, Ont, Jan 18, 32.
Study & Training: Cambridge Sch Art, Eng; Art Stud League New York; Columbia Univ; Univ Toronto; also in Italy & Eng.
Commissions: Portrait bust, Stratford Shakespearian Festival Theatre, Ont; fountains, Sheridan Nurseries, Toronto; exterior wall, Welland Co Hosp, Ont; bas-relief murals, lobby of Temple Sinai, Toronto & Cedarbrook Sch, Toronto; plus others.
Exhibitions: Can Nat Exhib, 55-58; Royal Can Acad Arts, 55-64; Sculpture Soc Can, 55, 58 & 65; Ont Soc Artists, 57-64; Stratford Festival Exhib, 64; plus others.
Awards: Prize, New Eng Soc Artists, 53.
Memberships: Ont Soc Artists; Royal Can Acad Arts; Sculptors Soc Can (pres, 64-66).
Mailing Address: c/o J Nadeau, B P 606, Bamako, Republic du Mali, Africa.

HANFMANN, GEORGE M A
Museum Curator, Educator
b Petersburg, Russia, Nov 20, 11; U S citizen.
Study & Training: Univ Berlin, PhD, 34; Univ Jena; Munich Univ; Johns Hopkins Univ, PhD, 35; Harvard Univ, MA, 49.
Teaching: From jr prize fel to asst prof, Harvard Univ, 35-43, asst prof, 45-49, assoc prof fine arts, 49-56, prof, 56-, John E Hudson prof archeol, 71-; vis, classical dept, Mus Fine Arts, Boston; mem managing comt, Am Sch Classical Studies in Athens.
Positions: Cur classical art, Fogg Art Mus, 46-; field dir, archeol exploration, Sardis, 58-; mem Inst Advan Study, Princeton Univ, 71-72; assoc ed, Am J Archaeol; ed bd, Art Bull.
Awards: Soc Antiquaries, London; Inst Studi Etruschi Florence; Ger Archeol Inst; Archeol Inst Am; Am Schs Oriental Res; plus others.
Publications: Auth, bks, monogr, exhib catalogues, articles & rev.
Mailing Address: Fogg Art Museum, Harvard University, Cambridge, MA 02138.

HANNA, BOYD EVERETT
Illustrator, Painter
Preferred Media: Wood, Watercolors, Oils.
b Irwin, Pa, Jan 15, 07.
Study & Training: Univ Pittsburgh, 25-28; Carnegie-Mellon Univ, 28-30.
Work in Public Collections: Metrop Mus Art, New York, N Y; New York Pub Libr; Libr Cong Pennell Collection, Washington, D C; Carnegie Inst, Pittsburgh; Boston Pub Libr.
Exhibitions: Artists For Victory, Metrop Mus Art, 42; Brooklyn Mus Ann, 47; Nat Acad Design 123rd Ann, New York, 49; Soc Am Graphic Artists Ann, New York, 48-56; Colorprint U S A, Lubbock, Tex, 70.
Positions: Graphic designer, Swindell-Dressler Co, Pittsburgh, 50-70.
Awards: Purchase prizes, Calif Soc Etchers, 46 & Print Club Albany, 72; first award, Nat Asn Indust Artists, 67.

Publications: Illusr, Longfellow's poems, Ltd Ed Club, 44; illusr,
The compleat angler, 47, Story of the nativity, 49, Leaves of
grass, 51 & Sayings of Buddha, 57, Peter Pauper Press.
Dealer: Gallerie Sorokin, Fort Lowell Rd, Tucson, AZ 85716.
Mailing Address: 1470 S Palo Verde, J-111, Tucson, AZ 85713.

HANNA, KATHERINE
Art Administrator
b Cleveland, Ohio, Jan 25, 13.
Study & Training: Sweet Briar Col; Oberlin Col.
Collections Arranged: The Taft Art Collection; assembled, arranged
& catalogued spec art & hist exhibs.
Positions: Tech res, NBC TV, Hollywood, Calif, 39-40; assoc to
Harden deV Pratt, architect, Providence, R I & Tidewater, Va,
40-41; cur & dir, The Taft Mus, Cincinnati, Ohio, 52-
Memberships: Asn Art Mus Dirs; Am Asn Mus; Int Coun Mus; Nat
Trust Hist Preserv; Midwest Mus Conf.
Research: History of art and architecture; art appreciation.
Publications: Ed, Taft Museum catalogue, 57; contribr, Let's go to
an art museum, 60; ed, exhib catalogues & brochures; contribr,
art magazines, mus bulletins, newspapers & periodicals.
Mailing Address: 316 Pike St, Cincinnati, OH 45202.

HANSEN, FRANCES FRAKES
Educator, Painter
Preferred Media: Acrylics, Watercolors.
b Harrisburg, Mo.
Study & Training: Univ Denver, BFA; Art Inst Chicago; Univ North-
ern Colo, MA; Univ Southern Calif; Univ Denver; Ecoles Art Am,
Fontainebleau, France.
Commissions: Painting, Alpha Gamma Delta Fraternity, Denver,
Colo, 66.
Exhibitions: Int Textile Exhib, Univ N C, 48 & 49; Nelson Gallery
Mid-Am Ann, Kansas City, 50; Joslyn Mus Biennial, Omaha,
Nebr, 53; Mus N Mex Ann Regional, Santa Fe, 59; Colo State Univ
Centennial Exhib, 70.
Teaching: Prof art, Temple Buell Col, 45-
Awards: Painting Prize for oils, Paradise Cove, 58 & Canyon Pas-
toral, 60, Colo State Fair Prof Show; painting prize for acrylic,
Lights, Univ Northern Colo Centennial Exhib, 70.
Memberships: Delta Phi Delta (Art Inst Chicago Chap); Nat Art Educ
Asn; Colo Art Educ Asn.
Publications: Auth, Native arts in America, U S Cult Bull, 66.
Mailing Address: 700 Pontiac St, Denver, CO 80220.

HANSEN, JAMES LEE
Sculptor
Preferred Media: Bronze.
b Tacoma, Wash, June 13, 25.
Study & Training: Portland Art Mus Sch.
Work in Public Collections: San Francisco Art Mus, Calif; Seattle
Art Mus, Wash; Portland Art Mus, Ore; Mus Art, Univ Ore, Eu-
gene.
Commissions: Talos, City of Fresno Civic Mall, 61; reliefs, Land
Title Bldg, Vancouver, Wash, 63 & St Anns Church, Butte, Mont,
66; Shaman, State Wash Hwy Dept, Olympia, 71.
Exhibitions: Whitney Mus Am Art Ann, 53; Artists Environ, Amon
Carter Mus, Fort Worth, Tex; one-man shows, Fountain Gal-
lery, Portland, 69, Seders Gallery, Seattle, 70 & Portland Art
Mus, 71.
Teaching: Prof sculpture, Portland State Univ, 64-
Awards: Norman Davis Award for Neo Shang, Seattle Art Mus, 58;
Am Trust Co Award, 56 & award for The Ritual, 60, San Fran-
cisco Art Mus.
Bibliography: William Davenport (auth), Art treasures in the West,
Lane, 10/66; J A Schinneller (auth), Art/search & self discovery,
Int Textbk, 12/67; Jinni (auth), Stars in art, N W Art, 6/70.
Dealers: Fountain Gallery, 115 S W Fourth St, Portland, OR 97204;
Polly Friedlander Gallery, 95 Yesler Way, Pioneer Square, Se-
attle, WA 98104.
Mailing Address: 4115 Q St, Vancouver, WA 98663.

HANSEN, ROBERT WILLIAM
Painter
Preferred Media: Lacquer.
b Osceola, Nebr, Jan 1, 24.
Study & Training: Univ Nebr, AB, BFA, 48; Escuela Univ Bellas
Artes, San Miguel Allende, Mex, MFA, 49; also with Alfredo
Zalce, Morelia, Mex, 52-53.
Work in Public Collections: Mus Mod Art, New York, N Y; Whitney
Mus Am Art, New York; Los Angeles Co Mus Art, Calif; San
Diego Gallery Fine Arts, Calif; Long Beach Mus Art, Calif.
Exhibitions: Carnegie Int, Pittsburgh, Pa, 61 & 63; Painting U S A:
The Figure, 62 & Tamarind: Homage to Lithography, 69; Mus
Mod Art, New York; Retrospective, Long Beach Mus Art, Calif,
67; The New Vein, organized & mounted in mus of nat capitols in
Europe & S Am, Smithsonian Inst, 68-70.

Teaching: Prof art, Occidental Col, 56-
Awards: Guggenheim fel, 61; Fulbright sr grant, 61; Tamarind fel,
65.
Dealer: Comara Gallery, 617 N La Cienega Blvd, Los Angeles, CA
90048.
Mailing Address: 1974 Addison Way, Los Angeles, CA 90041.

HANSEN, WANDA
Art Dealer
b Fortuna, Calif, Feb 12, 35.
Study & Training: Univ Calif, Berkeley, BA(polit sci).
Teaching: Elementary sch instr, Oakland Unified Sch Syst, Calif.
Positions: Co-dir, Hansen Fuller Gallery, San Francisco, Calif.
Specialty of Gallery: Contemporary art.
Mailing Address: Hansen Fuller Gallery, 228 Grant Ave, San Fran-
cisco, CA 94108.

HANSON, DUANE
Sculptor, Instructor
Preferred Media: Polyester Resin, Fiberglas.
b Alexandria, Minn, Jan 17, 25.
Study & Training: Macalester Col, BA; Univ Minn; Cranbrook Acad
Art, MFA.
Work in Public Collections: Richmond Mus, Va; Neue Galerie,
Aachen, Ger; Lehmbruck Mus, Duisburg, Ger.
Commissions: Businessman, for Melvin Kaufman, New York, N Y,
71.
Exhibitions: The Grotesque in American Art, Whitney Mus Am Art,
New York, 69; Whitney Mus Am Art Sculpture Ann, 70; Docu-
menta V, Kassel, Ger, 72; Bienale de Colpegar, Medelin, Co-
lumbia, 72; Sharp-Focus Realism, Sidney Janis Gallery, New
York, 72; plus one other.
Teaching: Asst prof art, Miami-Dade Jr Col, Miami, Fla, 65-69.
Awards: Grant for work in sculpture, Ella Lyman Trust, 63; sculp-
ture award, Fla State Fair Fine Arts Exhib, 68.
Bibliography: Kultermann (auth), The new realism, N Y Graphic
Soc, 72; Gerrit (auth), Henry/the soho body snatcher, Art News,
3/72; Sam Hunter (auth), American art since 1960, Abrams, 72.
Publications: Auth, Presenting Duane Hanson, 70.
Mailing Address: c/o Ivan C Karp, 469 W Broadway, New York, NY
10012.

HANSON, JEAN (MRS JEAN ELPHICK)
Painter, Designer
Preferred Media: Oils, Wool.
b Toronto, Ont, Sept 27, 34.
Study & Training: Ont Col Art.
Exhibitions: Smithsonian Inst, 62-63; Art Gallery Hamilton, Ont,
63; Ont Soc Artists, 63-67; Hart House, Univ Toronto, 64; Can
Soc Painters in Watercolour, 68; plus many other group & one-
man shows.
Memberships: Ontario Soc Artists; Can Soc Painters in Water-
colour.
Mailing Address: 523 Valley Dr, Oakville, Ont, Can.

HANSON, PHILIP HOLTON
Painter
Preferred Media: Acrylics.
b Chicago, Ill, Jan 8, 43.
Study & Training: Univ Chicago, BA, 65; Art Inst Chicago, MFA, 69.
Exhibitions: False Image I, 68 & False Image II, 69, Hyde Park Art
Ctr, Chicago; Spirit of the Comic, Univ Pa & Am Fedn of the
Arts Traveling Exhib, 69; Famous Artists, 69 & Chicago Imagist
Art, 72, Mus Contemp Art, Chicago.
Dealer: Phyllis Kind Gallery, 226 E Ontario, Chicago, IL 60611.
Mailing Address: 709 W Buena, Chicago, IL 60613.

HARA, TERUO
Educator, Potter
Preferred Media: Ceramics, Steel.
b Japan, May 26, 29.
Study & Training: Tokyo Univ Educ, 46-52.
Work in Public Collections: Dusseldorf Mus, Ger; Corcoran Gallery
Art, Washington, D C; Houston Mus Fine Arts, Tex.
Commissions: Ceramic murals, Carl M Freeman, Inc, Va, 63 &
Md, 64.
Exhibitions: One-man shows, Yoseido Gallery, Tokyo, Japan, 56,
Design Technics, New York, N Y, 62, Art & Craft Ctr, Pitts-
burgh, Pa, 65 & Corcoran Gallery Art, 68; also shows in Rome,
Italy, São Paulo, Brazil & Brussels, Belg.
Teaching: Assoc prof ceramics, Corcoran Sch Art, 63-69; assoc
prof art, Mary Washington Col, Univ Va, 69-
Awards: Grand Prize, Brussels World's Fair, 58.
Bibliography: Joanna Eagle (auth), Teruo Hara, Craft Horizons, 68;
Paul Richard (auth), The pots of Hara, Potomac Post, 68; G
Lindsey (auth), Three Washington artists, NBC TV, 71.
Mailing Address: 222 East St, Warrenton, VA 22186.

HARBART, GERTRUDE FELTON
Painter, Instructor
b Michigan City, Ind.
Study & Training: Univ Calif; Univ Ill; Art Inst Chicago; Art Stud
League New York; also with Aaron Bohard, Charles Birchfield &
Hans Hofmann.
Work in Public Collections: Purdue Univ; Ind Univ; Ind State Univ;
South Bend Art Inst; Indianapolis Mus Art; plus one other.
Commissions: In many private collections.
Exhibitions: Art Inst Chicago; Corcoran Biennial, Washington, D C;
Butler Inst Am Art, Youngstown, Ohio; Indianapolis Mus Art;
Michiana Biennial, South Bend; plus one other.
Teaching: Instr art, South Bend Art Ctr, 50-; instr art, Dunes Art
Found, 60-; instr art, Michigan City Art League, 60-
Awards: Indianapolis Mus Award, John Herron Mus, 60; Northern
Ind Art Patrons Award, Hammond Art Ctr, 70; Sarasota Art Asn
First Award, 71.
Memberships: Sarasota Art Asn; South Bend Art Ctr; Ind Artists;
Fla Artists; Am Pen Women; plus one other.
Publications: Auth, articles, In: Art News, 6/55 & Sch Arts, 60.
Dealer: Frank J Oehischlaeger, 28 S Blvd of the Presidents, Sara-
sota, FL 33577.
Mailing Address: 2201 Maryben Ave, Long Beach, Michigan City,
IN 46360.

HARDIN, ADLAI S
Sculptor
Preferred Media: Wood, Bronze.
b Minneapolis, Minn, Sept 23, 01.
Study & Training: Art Inst Chicago; Princeton Univ.
Work in Public Collections: Pa Acad Fine Arts; New Brit Mus Am
Art, Conn; Medallic Art Co Collection Bronzes; IBM Collection
Sculptures of Western Hemisphere.
Commissions: Murals, Interchurch Ctr, New York, N Y & Seamen's
Bank Savings, New York; reliefs, McMaster Univ, Hamilton, Ont,
Lutheran Acad Asn, Appleton, Wis & Princeton Univ, N J.
Exhibitions: Nat Acad Design, New York; Pa Acad Fine Arts; Nat
Sculpture Soc; Art Inst Chicago; one-man show, New Brit Mus
Am Art.
Positions: Pres, Nat Sculpture Soc, 57-60.
Awards: Henry O Avery Award, New York Archit League; Saltus
Gold Medal, Nat Acad Design; Lindsey Morris Mem Prize, Nat
Sculpture Soc.
Bibliography: Frederick Whitaker (auth), The sculpture of Adlai
Hardin, Am Artist, 60; Walker Hancock (auth), Adlai S Hardin
past president, Nat Sculpture Rev.
Memberships: Nat Acad Design; fel Nat Sculpture Soc; Old Lyme
Art Asn.
Mailing Address: Cove Rd, Lyme, CT 06371.

HARDIN, SHIRLEY G
Art Dealer
Positions: Co-dir, Fairweather-Hardin Gallery.
Mailing Address: 101 E Ontario St, Chicago, IL 60611.

HARDY, (CLARION) DEWITT
Painter, Art Administrator
Preferred Media: Watercolors.
b St Louis, Mo, June 25, 40.
Study & Training: Syracuse Univ, 58-62.
Work in Public Collections: Bowdoin Col Mus Art, Brunswick,
Maine; Kalamazoo Inst Art, Mich; St Lawrence Univ, Canton, N Y;
Mus Art Ogunquit, Maine; Butler Inst Am Art, Youngstown, Ohio.
Exhibitions: Four New England Artists, Kalamazoo Inst Art, 63; New
England Regional, Drawing Soc, 65; one-man shows, Frank Rehn
Gallery, New York, N Y, 66-71; Butler Inst Am Art, 69-70; one-
man show, Lehigh Univ, Pa, 71.
Collections Arranged: Young American Draughtsmen, Mus Art
Ogunquit, 69.
Positions: Assoc dir, Mus Art Ogunquit, 64-
Awards: First prize for drawing, Summit Art Ctr, N J, 65; purchase
award, Butler Inst Am Art, 69.
Dealer: Frank Rehn Gallery, 655 Madison Ave, New York, NY 10021.
Mailing Address: Oak Woods Rd, North Berwick, ME 03906.

HARDY, THOMAS (AUSTIN)
Sculptor
Preferred Media: Bronze.
b Redmond, Ore, Nov 30, 21.
Study & Training: Ore State Univ, 38-40; Univ Ore, BA, 42, with
Archipenko, summer 51, MFA, 52.
Work in Public Collections: Whitney Mus Am Art, New York, N Y;
Seattle Art Mus, Wash; Springfield Art Mus, Mo; Mus Art, Ogun-
quit, Maine; Portland Art Mus, Ore.
Commissions: Sculptures, Oregon Flora (screens), Portland State
Univ, 62, Diving Birds, Fed Bldg, Juneau, Ala, 64, Duck Fountain,

Univ Ore, Eugene, 64, Flight, Dorothy Chandler Music Ctr, Los
Angeles, Calif, 65 & wall sculpture, State Dept Agr, Salem, Ore,
68.
Exhibitions: Third Biennal, Sao Paulo, Brazil, 55; Am Watercolors,
Drawings & Prints, Metrop Mus Art, 56; Mus Mod Art Sculpture
Exhib, 63; Whitney Mus Am Art Sculpture Ann, 64; Exhib Cand
Grants, Am Inst Arts & Lett, 68.
Teaching: Lectr, Univ Calif, Berkeley, 56-58; instr, Calif Sch Fine
Arts, San Francisco, 56-58; assoc prof sculpture, Tulane Univ
La, 58-59; artist-in-residence, Reed Col, 60-61.
Positions: Mem bd dirs Contemp Crafts Gallery, Portland, 60-71.
Awards: Award For Color Lithography, Soc Am Graphic Artists, 52;
Seattle Art Mus Northwest Ann Sculpture Award, 55; Distin-
guished Serv Award, Univ Ore, 64.
Bibliography: H Wurdemann (auth), Recent art of the West Coast,
Art Am, 2/55; Metal sculptures by Tom Hardy, Am Artist, 4/55;
L Jones (auth), Tom Hardy: sculptor-craftsman, Creative Crafts,
7/62.
Memberships: Portland Art Mus; Contemp Crafts Asn; Friends Mus
Art, Univ Ore; Am Hist Train Asn; Maude Kerns Art Ctr.
Dealer: Kraushaar Galleries, 1055 Madison Ave, New York, NY
10021.
Mailing Address: 1422 S W Harrison St, Portland, OR 97201.

HARE, CHANNING
Painter
b New York, N Y.
Study & Training: Art Stud League New York; also with Robert
Henri, George Bellows & William Zorach.
Work in Public Collections: Boston Mus Fine Arts, Mass; Pa Acad
Fine Arts, Philadelphia; Colo Springs Fine Arts Ctr, Colo; Dav-
enport Munic Art Gallery, Iowa; Va Hist Soc; plus others.
Exhibitions: Metrop Mus Art, New York, 52; Lowe Gallery Art, 55;
Grand Cent Moderns, 56; Findlay Galleries, 62; Palm Beach Gal-
leries, 64-66 & 68; plus others.
Awards: Prizes, Soc Four Arts, 42, 43 & 44.
Memberships: Soc Four Arts (bd dirs).
Mailing Address: 220 Worth Ave, Palm Beach, FL 33482.

HARE, DAVID
Sculptor
b New York, N Y, Mar 10, 17.
Study & Training: Studied in New York, Ariz & Colo.
Work in Public Collections: Long Beach Mus Art; Los Angeles Co
Mus Art; Mus Mod Art, New York; Princeton Univ; Whitney Mus
Am Art; plus others.
Commissions: Sculpture for New York City, States of R I, Mass &
Ill.
Exhibitions: Pittsburgh Bicentennial, Pa, 62; Seattle World's Fair,
62; Dada, Surrealism and Their Heritage, 68 & The New Ameri-
can Painting and Sculpture, 69, Mus Mod Art, New York; retro-
spective, Philadelphia Mus Art, Pa, 69; plus many other group &
one-man shows.
Teaching: Lect extensively.
Positions: Ed, VVV (surrealist mag), 42-44.
Bibliography: Wayne Craven (auth), Sculpture in America, Thomas
Y Crowell, 68; William S Rubin (auth), Dada, surrealism, and
their heritage, Mus Mod Art, 68; Eduard Trier (auth), Form and
space: sculpture in the 20th century, Praeger, 68.
Mailing Address: 34 Leroy St, New York, NY 10014.

HARE, STEPHEN HOPKINS
Painter
b New York, N Y, Dec 1, 21.
Study & Training: Yale Univ.
Work in Public Collections: Boston Mus Fine Arts, Mass; Baltimore
Mus Art, Md; Toledo Mus Art, Ohio; Mus Fine Arts, Houston,
Tex; Norton Gallery Art, West Palm Beach, Fla; plus others.
Exhibitions: Whitney Mus Am Art, New York; Corcoran Gallery Art,
Washington, D C; Pa Acad Fine Arts, Philadelphia; Art Inst Chi-
cago, Ill; Calif Palace of Legion of Honor, San Francisco; plus
others.
Mailing Address: 220 Worth Ave, Palm Beach, FL 33480.

HARI, KENNETH
Painter, Printmaker
Preferred Media: Oils, Graphite.
b Perth Amboy, N J, Mar 31, 47.
Study & Training: Newark Sch Fine & Indust Arts, dipl, 66; Md Inst
Art, BFA, 68; also with Leon Franks, John Delmonte & Donald
Delue.
Work in Public Collections: Newark Mus, N J; Baltimore Mus, Md;
Trenton State Mus, N J; Rutgers Mus, New Brunswick, N J; Nat
Portrait Gallery, London, Eng.
Commissions: Portraits, W H Auden, New York, N Y, M Moore, New
York, 69, Pablo Casals, by Mrs Pablo Casals, Vt, 70, Princess
Gloria Miglionico, New York, 71 & Salvador Dali, New York, 72.

Exhibitions: Md State Coun State Exhib, 67; Union Col, 69; Monmouth Col, 70; Newark Mus, 71; Trenton State Mus, 72.
Positions: Dir, N J Art Festival, 64-69.
Awards: Pulaski Award, Kusiosko Found, 63; Felice Found Award, 69; Trenton State Mus Award, 72.
Bibliography: Art in the Hamptons, New York Times, 69; M Lenson (auth), Portrait of Casals, Newark News, 71; D Brown (auth), Poetess an artist, Home News, 72.
Publications: Illusr, Prophet, 71, Lovers of our time, 71, Vermont, 72, Folk singer, 72 & A time for peace, 72, H S Graphics.
Dealers: C C Price Gallery, 30 W 57th St, New York, NY 10019; H S Graphics, Box 243, Keasbey, NJ 08832.
Mailing Address: 228 Sherman St, Perth Amboy, NJ 08861.

HARKAVY, MINNA
  Sculptor
Study & Training: Art Stud League New York; with Antoine Bourdelle, Paris, France; Hunter Col, BA.
Work in Public Collections: Whitney Mus Am Art & Mus Mod Art, New York, N Y; Mus Munic, St Denis, France; Mus Western Art, U S S R; Ain Harod Mus, Tel-Aviv, Israel; also many pvt collections in U S & abroad.
Commissions: Sculpture, Winchendon Post Off, Mass & Norfolk Mus Art & Sci, Va.
Exhibitions: San Francisco Mus Art, Calif; Art Inst Chicago, Ill; Pa Acad Fine Arts, Philadelphia; Albright-Knox Art Gallery, Buffalo, N Y; Munson-Williams-Proctor Inst, Utica, N Y; plus others.
Awards: Medal of hon, 62 & prizes, 64 & 65, Nat Asn Women Artists; prize, Audubon Artists, 65.
Memberships: Artists Equity Asn; Fedn Mod Painters & Sculptors; Sculptors Guild; assoc mem Int Inst Arts & Lett.
Mailing Address: Hotel Ansonia, 2109 Broadway, New York, NY 10023.

HARLAN, ROMA CHRISTINE
  Painter, Art Administrator
Preferred Media: Oils, Pastels.
b Warsaw, Ind.
Study & Training: Art Inst Chicago, Daughters Ind scholar; Purdue Univ, Lafayette; also with Ralph Clarkson, Chicago, Francis Chapin, Constantine Pougialis & Marie Goth.
Work in Public Collections: U S Supreme Ct Bldg, U S Capitol Bldg, U S Dist Ct, Nat Guard Asn U S & Nat Fedn Bus & Prof Women's Clubs, Washington, D C; plus others.
Commissions: Portraits, Gen Milton A Reckord, Sen Edward Martin & others, Nat Guard Asn U S, 58-65, Sen Kenneth S Wherry, U S Capitol Bldg, 65, Col Mildred I Clark, Walter Reed Army Med Ctr, 68, John Davis, U S Supreme Ct, 71 & Judge Bernita Mathews, U S Dist Ct, 72.
Exhibitions: One-man exhibs, George Washington Univ Gallery, Washington, D C, Lake Shore Club Chicago, Ill & Purdue Univ, Lafayette; Hoosier Salon Ind; All Ill Soc Fine Arts.
Positions: Asst registr, Nat Gallery Art, Washington, D C, 69-; D C State Art Chmn, D C Fedn Women's Clubs, 70-
Bibliography: Eleanor Jewett (auth), article, In: Chicago Tribune; Ruel Tolman (auth), article, In: Portrait; article, In: Washington Eve Star, 67; plus others.
Memberships: Arts Club Washington (election of officers comt, 70, mem comt, 71); Ind Fedn Arts Clubs; Washington Forum Club; D C Fedn Women's Clubs.
Publications: Auth, Rembrandt, Cong Rec, 57.
Mailing Address: 1600 S Joyce St, Apt C-411, Arlington, VA 22202.

HARLEY, HARRY GEORGE
  Cartoonist
b Saint Catharines, Ont, Feb 22, 29.
Study & Training: Ont Col Art; Saint Catharines Col Inst; Univ Toronto.
Publications: Contribr, cartoons in Med Econ, Argosy, Wall St Jour, King Features Syndicate, Cavalier, Med Tribune, Mod Med, & others.
Mailing Address: 5 Grand Ave, Grimsby, Ont, Can.

HARLOW, ROBERT E
  Painter, Instructor
Preferred Media: Oils.
b Philadelphia, Pa, Mar 20, 14.
Study & Training: Pa Acad Fine Arts, Univ Pa, BFA, 36; Columbia Univ; Yale Univ.
Work in Public Collections: Albany Inst Art & Hist; Dunbarton Oaks, Washington, D C; Miami Mus Mod Art; Conn Pub Insts; in collection of John Davis Hatch.
Exhibitions: Artists for Victory, Metrop Mus Arts, New York, N Y, 42; Directions American Art, Carnegie Inst, 42; Artists & Engineers, Brooklyn Mus, 69; one-man shows, Miami Mus Mod Art 69 & Rutgers Univ, 71; N J State Mus Ann, Trenton, 71.

Teaching: Supvr art, Am Sch, Madrid, Spain, 66-67; instr art, Manville, N J Pub Schs, 69-72.
Positions: Supvr & artist, Fed Art Proj, Pa & Conn, 43-44.
Awards: Hon mention, Nat Drawing Ann, Nat Acad Design, 42; cover design award, Nat Drawing Ann, Albany Mus Art & Hist, 43.
Research: Discovery and authentication of Thomas Eakins' painting Pushing for Rail, Stephen Clark Collection.
Dealer: E Van Doren, R F D 3, Princeton, NJ 08540.
Mailing Address: Fernan Gonzoles 64, Madrid, Spain.

HARMAN, JACK KENNETH
  Sculptor, Educator
Preferred Media: Bronze.
b Vancouver, B C, July 31, 27.
Study & Training: Vancouver Sch Art, two yr dipl; Slade Sch Art, Univ Col, Univ London.
Work in Public Collections: Sir George Williams Univ, Montreal, P Q; London Art Mus, Ont; Norman MacKenzie Gallery, Regina, Sask; Univ B C, Vancouver.
Commissions: Cast bronze fountain, Canadian Save the Children, Toronto, Ont, 64; Family (cast bronze), Pac Press, Vancouver, 66; Runners-Bannister & Landy (bronze), Empire Stadium, Vancouver, 67; Mother & Child (bronze), Queens Park, Parliament Bldgs, Toronto, 68; Family Group (bronze), Mus & Archives Bldgs, Victoria, 69.
Exhibitions: 29th Ann, Vancouver Art Gallery, 60, 32nd Ann, 63; 46th Ann, Seattle Art Mus, 60; Nat Outdoor Sculpture Exhib, Quebec, P Q, 60; Montreal Mus Ann, 61; one-man shows, Vancouver Art Gallery, 62; two from Vancouver, D Cameron Gallery, Toronto, 62.
Teaching: Instr sculpture, exten dept, Univ B C, 59-61; instr sculpture & metal casting, Vancouver Sch Art, 70-
Positions: Pres, N W Inst Sculpture, 59-60.
Awards: O'Keefe Art Award, O'Keeffe Breweries, 51; Can Coun grants, 66 & 69.
Bibliography: Articles, In: Arts in Can, 67 & Can Art Mag, summers, 62-64.
Memberships: Assoc mem Royal Can Acad Arts; Soc Sculptors.
Mailing Address: 1190 Kilmer Rd, North Vancouver, BC, Can.

HARMON, CLIFF FRANKLIN
  Painter
Preferred Media: Acrylics, Watercolors, Oils.
b Los Angeles, Calif, June 26, 23.
Study & Training: Bisttram Sch Fine Art, Los Angeles, Calif & Taos, N Mex, with Emil Bisttram; Black Mountain Col, N C, with Joe Fiore; Taos Valley Art Sch, with Louis Ribak.
Work in Public Collections: Mus N Mex, Santa Fe.
Exhibitions: N Mex & Southwest Biennials, N Mex Mus, 66, 70-72; 11th Midwest Biennial, Joslyn Art Mus, Omaha, Nebr, 70; 1st Four Corners Biennial, Phoenix Art Mus, Ariz, 71; Five State Art Exhib, Port Arthur, Tex, 71.
Awards: First premium for abstract painting, N Mex State Fair, 68; hon mention, N Mex Mus & Phoenix Art Mus, 71.
Memberships: Taos Art Asn (first v pres, 68-69).
Dealers: Stables Gallery, Taos, NM 87571; Gallery A, Taos, NM 87571.
Mailing Address: Box 202, Taos, NM 87571.

HARMON, (LOREN) FOSTER
  Art Dealer
b Judsonia, Ark, Nov 5, 12.
Study & Training: Ind Univ; Ohio Univ; State Univ Iowa, BA, 35, MFA, 36.
Collections Arranged: Arrangement & presentation of seven exhibitions annually.
Teaching: Instr drama & dir univ theatre productions, Ind Univ, Bloomington, 36-42.
Positions: Pub rels dir, Ringling Mus Art, Sarasota, Fla, 58-59; dir, Oehlschlaeger Galleries, Sarasota, 61-70; owner-dir, Harmon Gallery, Naples, Fla, 64-
Awards: Award of Merit (for long serv & contrib to art espec in estab Baker Ctr Collection of Am Art), Ohio Univ, 70.
Memberships: Am Fedn Arts; Fla League Arts; Ringling Mus Art (mem coun); Sarasota Art Asn (pres, 59-60).
Specialty of Gallery: Paintings, drawings and sculpture by major American artists of the twentieth century.
Collection: Private collection of American art.
Publications: Auth, Harmon Gallery Publ, including Am artists in the Harmon Gallery, to be internationally distributed by the U S Info Agency.
Dealer: Harmon Gallery, 1258 Third St S, Naples, FL 33940.
Mailing Address: P O Box 6187, St Armands Station, Sarasota, FL 33578.

HARMON, LILY
  Painter, Sculptor
Preferred Media: Oils, Graphics, Constructions.
b New Haven, Conn, Nov 19, 12.
Study & Training: Yale Univ Sch Art; Acad Colorossi; Art Stud League New York.
Work in Public Collections: Whitney Mus Am Art, New York, N Y; Butler Inst Am Art, Youngstown, Ohio; Joseph H Hirshhorn Collection, Washington, D C; Newark Mus, N J; Tel-Aviv Mus, Israel.
Commissions: Mural, Portchester Jewish Ctr, N Y, 49.
Exhibitions: Artists for Victory, Metrop Mus Art, New York, 42; Painting in the United States, Carnegie Inst, Pittsburgh, Pa, 43 & 47; Corcoran Gallery Art, Washington, D C, 47; 37 Contemporary Americans, IBM Gallery, 60; Provincetown Art Asn Golden Anniversary Show, traveling exhib for Am Fedn Arts, 64; plus 16 one-man shows.
Awards: Citation, U S Govt, 42; Silvermine Art Asn Award for best painting, 48; Cape Cod Art Asn Award for best painting, 57.
Bibliography: Grace Pagano (auth), Contemporary American painting, Encycl Britannica, 46; Eleanor Bitterman (auth), Art in modern architecture, Van Nostrand Reinhold, 52; Edmund Burke Feldman (auth), Becoming human through art, Prentice-Hall, 70.
Memberships: Artists Equity Asn; Provincetown Art Asn; Academician Nat Acad Design.
Publications: illusr, Pride & prejudice, 45; illusr, Sounds of a distant drum, 67; illusr, The castle & Metamorphosis, 68; illusr, Buddenbrooks, 68; illusr, Symphonie Pastorale & The Counterfeiters, 70.
Mailing Address: 151 Central Park W, New York, NY 10023.

HARNETT, MR & MRS JOEL WILLIAM
  Collectors
Mr Harnett, b New York, N Y, Dec 3, 25.
Study & Training: Mr Harnett, Univ Richmond, BA; New Sch Social Res.
Memberships: Friends of Whitney Mus Am Art.
Collection: Works by Hopper, Burchfield, Marsh, Greene, Anuszkiewcz, Raphael Soyer, Rosenberg, Seley, Tooker, Jenkins, Pearlstein, Rickey, Francis, Lamis and Fletcher Benton.
Mailing Address: 2 Sutton Pl S, New York, NY 10022.

HAROOTIAN, KHOREN DER
  Painter, Sculptor
b Armenia, Apr 2, 09; U S citizen.
Study & Training: Worcester Art Mus, Mass.
Work in Public Collections: Metrop Mus Art, New York, NY; Whitney Mus Am Art, New York; Worcester Art Mus; Billy Rose Collection, Bezalel Mus, Israel; Armenian Nat Mus, Erevan, Soviet Armenia.
Commissions: Sculptures, Scientist, Fairmount Park Art Asn, 50, Christ, Armenian Cathedral Comt, New York, 58 & Beaver, Baruch Col, 60.
Exhibitions: Whitney Mus Am Art Ann, New York, 45-66; Pa Acad Fine Arts, Philadelphia, 45-66; Fairmount Park Int Exhib, Philadelphia Mus, 48; Am Pavilion Brussels World's Fair, Belg, 58; Royal Acad Arts Summer Exhib, Piccadily, London, Eng, 64 & 65; plus others.
Awards: George D Widener Medal, Pa Acad Fine Arts, 54; Am Acad Arts & Lett & Nat Inst Arts & Lett award & citation, 54; Silver Medal, Gruppo Donatello, Florence, Italy, 62.
Bibliography: Dorothy Grafly (auth), Prophet of man in his eternal battle aginst evil, Am Artist Mag, 11/46; Ralph M Pearson (auth), article, In: Mod Renaissance Am Art, Harper & Row, 54; article, In: Current Biog, 1/55.
Mailing Address: R F D Rte 9-W, Castle Rd, Orangeburg, NY 10962.

HARRILL, JAMES
  Painter
Preferred Media: Acrylics.
b N C, Mar 21, 36.
Study & Training: New York Univ, 52-56; Parsons Sch Design, 52-56; Ogunquit Sch Sculpture & Painting, Maine, with John Laurent.
Work in Public Collections: Mus N Mex, Santa Fe; Colonial Williamsburg Found, Va; Statesville Fine Arts Mus, N C.
Exhibitions: N C Mus Art Ann, Raleigh, 56-68; Southeastern Ann, Atlanta, Ga, 58-68; Zappeion Mus, Athens, Greece, 64; Southwest Biennial, Mus N Mex, Santa Fe, 71 & 72; 30 N C Painters, Shaw Studios, New York, N Y.
Teaching: Instr painting, Int Coun Europe, Greece, 63-64; instr painting & drawing, Proj Newgate, N Mex State Penitentiary, 71-
Awards: Thalhimer Found Award, 60; purchase award, N Mex Biennial, Mus N Mex, 71.
Mailing Address: c/o Janus Gallery, 116 1/2 E Palace Ave, Santa Fe, NM 87501.

HARRIS, ALFRED PETER
  Painter, Art Administrator
Preferred Media: Oils.
b Toronto, Ont, Apr 4, 32.
Study & Training: Ont Col Art, Toronto, hon dipl.
Work in Public Collections: Sir George Williams Univ, Montreal; St Catharines & Dist Arts Coun, Ont; Bronfman Collection, Montreal Mus Fine Art; Brascan Collection, Toronto.
Exhibitions: Mem Gallery, Albright-Knox Gallery, Buffalo, 62; four-man exhib, London Pub Libr & Art Mus, 63-65; two-man exhibs, Dorothy Cameron Gallery, 64-65; two-man show, Roberts Gallery, Toronto, 70; Ann Exhib Contemp Can Art, Hamilton, 70-72.
Collections Arranged: J W Morrice, J Chambers Retrospective & William Kurelec Retrospective, 66; Baker, Boyle & Hollenback, 67; John Newman, 68; Soul of Niagara, 69; John Boyle—Ed Fantinel, 70; Harvey Breverman & Niagara Now, 71; plus earlier exhibs.
Teaching: Art instr, Ont Col Art, 59-60; instr gen art, Ridley Col, Saint Catharines, 63-65; spec lectr mod art, Brock Univ, 66.
Positions: Dir, Saint Catharines & Dist Arts Coun, 59-; pres, Ont Asn Art Galleries, 70-71.
Bibliography: Harry Malcomson (auth), The artist, Toronto Life, 69.
Memberships: Can Soc Graphic Art; Ont Soc Artists.
Publications: Contribr, The nude in Canadian art, 72.
Dealer: Roberts Gallery, 641 Yonge St, Toronto, Ont, Can.
Mailing Address: 109 St Paul Crescent, Saint Catharines, Ont, Can.

HARRIS, JOSEPHINE MARIE
  Educator, Art Historian
b Webster Groves, Mo, Jan 20, 11.
Study & Training: Wash Univ, AB, 31, MA, 32 & PhD, 36; Am Sch Classical Studies, Athens, Greece, 37-39; Dumbarton Oaks, Harvard Univ, Washington, D C, 42-45.
Teaching: Prof fine arts & chmn dept, Wilson Col, 46-
Awards: Award for Distinguished Teaching, Christian R & Mary F Lindback Found, 64.
Memberships: Col Art Asn Am.
Research: A study of Coptic architectural decorative sculpture, with special reference to material found at Oxyrhynohos.
Publications: Contribr, rev, In: Am J Archeol, 60-72.
Mailing Address: Wilson College, Chambersburg, PA 17201.

HARRIS, JULIAN HOKE
  Sculptor, Architect
b Carrollton, Ga, Aug 22, 06.
Study & Training: Ga Inst Technol, BS, 28; Pa Acad Fine Arts, 29-34.
Work in Public Collections: IBM Collection, New York, N Y; High Mus Art, Atlanta, Ga; Univ Va Mus; also in many pvt collections.
Commissions: 50 sculptures for pub & pvt bldgs; 50 portrait & mem comns; 14 commemorative medallions.
Exhibitions: Painting & Sculpture From Sixteen Cities, Mus Mod Art, 33; Pa Acad Fine Arts Mus, 34; three one-man shows, High Mus, Atlanta, 35, 39 & 69; Jewish Mus, New York, N Y, 52; Nat Sculpture Soc Ann, 70-72.
Teaching: Emer prof, Ga Inst Technol Sch Archit, 37-71; prof sculpture, Atlanta Sch Art, 46-52.
Positions: Pres Asn Ga Artists, 39-42; charter mem, Atlanta Citizens Adv Comt Urban Renewal, 58-71; charter mem, Atlanta Civic Design Comn, 65-
Awards: Edgar Tobin Award, Southern States Art League, 39; Fine Arts Gold Medal, Am Inst Architects, 54; Ivan Allen Sr Award, North Ga Chap Am Inst Architects, 62.
Bibliography: Many articles, In: Nat Sculpture Rev, 53-72; Georgia Tech Alumnus, Ga Inst Technol, 53, 71 & 72; Julian Hoke Harris, Am Sculptors Ser, No 16, 54.
Memberships: Fel Nat Sculpture Soc; fel Am Inst Architects; Atlanta Art Asn (sch adv comt, 72).
Publications: Auth, Sculpture can be functional, W Va State Mag, 54; auth, Sculpture in architecture today, J Am Inst Architects, 55; auth, Architectural sculpture, Dixie Contractor, 55; auth, Environment, Atlanta Pub Sch Syst, 60; co-auth, Improving the mess we live in, N Ga Chap Am Inst Architects, 66.
Mailing Address: 177 Fifth St N W, Atlanta, GA 30313.

HARRIS, LAWREN PHILLIPS
  Painter, Educator
b Toronto, Ont, Oct 10, 10.
Study & Training: Boston Mus Fine Arts; also with Lawren S Harris (father), Toronto.
Work in Public Collections: War Records, Nat Gallery Can.
Commissions: Off war artist with Can Army, 43-46; prize, Atlantic awards exhib, 67.

Exhibitions: Ont Soc Arts, 36-; Royal Can Acad Arts, 38-; Can Group Painters, 38-; New York World's Fair, 39; Can Soc Graphic Art, 39-41; plus others.
Teaching: Instr, N Voc Sch, Toronto, 38-40; instr Trinity Col Sch, Port Hope, Ont, 40-41; prof fine arts & head dept, Mount Allison Univ, at present.
Awards: Can Govt Overseas fel, 57-58; hon fel, N S Col Art.
Memberships: Ont Soc Arts; Can Group Painters; Royal Can Acad Arts.
Mailing Address: Fine Arts Dept, Mount Allison University, Sackville, N B, Can.

HARRIS, LEON A, JR
Collector, Patron
b New York, N Y, June 20, 26.
Study & Training: Harvard Col.
Positions: Former trustee, Dallas Mus Fine Arts.
Art Interests: Donor to museums.
Collection: Paintings, drawings and prints.
Publications: Auth, The great picture robbery, Young France, The fine art of political wit & Only to God: the life of Godfrey Lowell Cabot; articles, In: Esquire, Good Housekeeping, McCalls & Encycl Americana.
Mailing Address: 4512 Fairfax, Dallas, TX 45205.

HARRIS, LUCILLE
Painter
b Stockton, Calif.
Study & Training: San Francisco State Col; Univ Calif, Berkeley; San Francisco Art Inst.
Work in Public Collections: Oakland Art Mus, Calif; St Mary's Col, Moraga, Calif; Haggin Mus, Stockton; Playhouse Repertory Theatre, San Francisco; Gamut Theatre, Berkeley.
Exhibitions: Painters & Gravers Ann, Nat Gallery Art, Washington, D C; 2nd-4th Invitationals, Calif Palace Legion of Honor; San Francisco Art Asn Ann, San Francisco Women Artists Ann & Graphics Ann, San Francisco Mus Art; Cult Exchange Exhib, Fukukoa, Japan; Western Mus Travelling Exhib; plus others.
Teaching: Pvt instr painting.
Awards: First award for graphics, San Francisco Art Asn Ann; hon mentions for watercolor & graphics, San Francisco Women Artists Ann & for oil, Oakland Art Mus Ann.
Bibliography: Many rev in newspapers & Artforum.
Memberships: Artists Equity Asn (mem bd); San Francisco Women Artists (mem bd); East Bay Artists Asn (mem bd); Am Fedn Arts; San Francisco Art Asn.
Mailing Address: P O Box 9254, Berkeley, CA 94709.

HARRIS, MARGO LIEBES
Sculptor
Study & Training: Art Stud League New York, N Y; also in Italy.
Work in Public Collections: Portland Mus, Maine; Roseman Collection; Lehman Collection; Zorach Collection; Frank Alt-Schul Collection; plus others.
Commissions: Sheraton Southland Hotel, Dallas; Show Mart, Dallas; portraits, Prince Aziz Elganian, Teheran; Fountains, N P Hildum Interiors; Sheraton Hotel, Chicago; plus others.
Exhibitions: Whitney Mus Am Art; Portland Mus Fine Arts; Detroit Art Inst; Sculpture Ctr, New York; Boston Arts Festival; plus others.
Awards: Nat Acad Design First Prize, Nat Asn Women Artists; Sculpture Medal of Honor Prize, 71; Mr & Mrs Charles Murphy Prize, 72; plus others.
Bibliography: Dona Z Meitach, Contemporary stone sculpture, Crown, 70.
Memberships: New York Soc Women Artists (pres, 67-70, bd dirs & sculpture chmn, 72-74); Am Soc Contemp Artists (bd dirs, juror & v pres); Artists Equity Asn.
Mailing Address: 300 E 74th St, New York, NY 10021.

HARRIS, MARIAN D
Painter, Art Critic
Preferred Media: Oils, Watercolors, Conté, Pastels.
b Philadelphia, Pa, Apr 22, 04.
Study & Training: Pa Acad Fine Arts, 22-26, Cresson traveling scholar, 25; Acad Summer Sch, Chester Springs, Pa, 21-24 & 32; Hugh Breckenridge Summer Sch Art, East Gloucester, Mass, 26; with Wayman Adams, Elizabethtown, N Y, 33, 35 & 38.
Work in Public Collections: Albright-Knox Art Gallery, Buffalo, N Y; Fellowship Pa Acad Fine Arts; Philadelphia Art Alliance; Gov Bacon Hosp, Del; YWCA, Wilmington, Del.
Exhibitions: Pa Acad Fine Arts Ann, 32; Nat Acad Design Ann, New York, N Y, 32; Art Inst Chicago Invitational Int Watercolor Exhib, 35; Am Watercolor Soc Ann, New York, 52; Newark Mus Triennial, N J, 64.

Teaching: Instr painting, Wilmington Acad Art, Del, 27-32, 36-37; instr art, Atlantic City Friends Sch, N J, 56-57; lectr art appreciation, Jewish Community Ctr, Margate, N J, 59.
Awards: George A Rhodes Prize, Wilmington Soc Fine Arts, 30; Best of Show, Atlantic City Art Ctr, 68.
Memberships: Fellowship Pa Acad Fine Arts; Am Watercolor Soc; League South Jersey Artists (pres, 60-61); Atlantic City Art Ctr (pres, 65-66); Cult Arts Ctr, Ocean City, N J.
Dealer: Charles Bertolino Gallery, 406 Harrison Ave, West Berlin, N J 08091.
Mailing Address: 24 N Cornwall Ave, Ventnor, NJ 08406.

HARRIS, MRS MASON DIX
Museum Director
Positions: Dir, Fitchburg Art Mus.
Mailing Address: Fitchburg Art Museum, 25 Merriam Pkwy, Fitchburg, MA 01420.

HARRIS, PAUL
Sculptor
b Orlando, Fla.
Study & Training: With Joy Karen Winslow, Orlando; Univ N Mex; New Sch Soc Res, with Johannes Molzahn; Hans Hofmann Sch.
Commissions: Figures, Univ N Mex Art Bldg Facade.
Exhibitions: Sculpture U S A, 59 & Hans Hofmann & His Students, 64-65, Mus Mod Art, New York, N Y; People Figures, Mus Contemp Crafts, 66-67; Sculpture of the Sixties, Los Angeles Co Mus & São Paulo Biennial, 67; Soft Art, N J Mus, 69; New Vein Show, Vienna, Austria, Cologne, Ger & Mailand, 69-70; plus many one-man shows.
Teaching: Instr art, Univ N Mex, Knox Col, B W I, New Paltz State Col, Calif Art Inst & Cath Univ Chile; prof art, Calif Col Arts & Crafts, presently.
Art Interests: Various media such as plaster and string construction; currently making stuffed figures from cloth.
Dealers: Poindexter Gallery, 24 E 84th St, New York, NY 10028; William Sawyer Gallery, 3045 Clay, San Francisco, CA 94114.
Mailing Address: Box 214, Bolinas, CA 94924.

HARRIS, PAUL STEWART
Art Administrator, Art Historian
b Orange, Mass, Mar 7, 06.
Study & Training: Antioch Col, BS; Harvard Col, SB(hist art); New York Univ Grad Sch Fine Arts.
Collections Arranged: Assisted in installation of the Cloisters and gallery display, Metrop Mus Art; numerous exhibs, Des Moines Asn Fine Arts, Iowa & J B Speed Art Mus, Louisville, Ky 33-62.
Teaching: Lectr Am Art, Univ Minn, 46.
Positions: Curatorial asst & asst cur, Metrop Mus Art, 33-38; dir & secy, Des Moines Asn Fine Arts, 38-40; sr cur, Minneapolis Inst Arts, 41-46; dir & cur, J B Speed Art Mus, 46-62; dep dir, H F du Pont Winterthur Mus, 62-67; dir collections, Henry Ford Mus & Greenfield Village, Mich, 67-71.
Memberships: Am Asn Mus; Col Art Asn Am; Am Fedn Arts (trustee); N H Hist Soc (mus comt); Early Am Indust Asn & League N H Craftsmen.
Research: Mediaeval European art, American art, European decorative arts and paintings and modern art.
Publications: Auth, Fourteen seasons of art accessions, J B Speed Art Mus, 60; auth, 30 early American paintings, Winterthur Mus, (in prep); also var articles in mus bulletins, 34-64.
Mailing Address: R F D Chesham, Marlborough, NH 03455.

HARRIS, ROBERT GEORGE
Painter, Illustrator
Preferred Media: Oils.
b Kansas City, Mo, Sept 9, 11.
Study & Training: Kansas City Art Inst, with Monte Crews; Grand Cent Sch Art, with Harvey Dunn; Art Stud League New York, with George Bridgeman.
Work in Public Collections: Portrait, Phoenix Jr Col; also in many private collections in U S.
Exhibitions: Soc Illusr; Art Dirs Club, 43-46; New Rochelle Art Asn, 49; Westport Artists, 50; one-man show of portraits, Phoenix Art Mus, 62.
Memberships: Soc Illusr; Phoenix Fine Art Asn; Phoenix Art Mus.
Publications: Illusr, McCall's, 39-60, Sat Eve Post, 39-61, Good Housekeeping, 40-60, Ladies' Home J, 40-61 & other nat mags.
Mailing Address: P O Box 1124, 8301 E Serene St, Carefree, AZ 85331.

HARRISON, LAWRENCE VICTOR
Painter, Educator
b Portage la Prairie, Man, Nov 28, 41.
Study & Training: Univ Man, with Ivan Eyre & Don Proch; Tex Christian Univ.

Exhibitions: Wis State Fair, Milwaukee, 68 & 69; Wis Painter & Sculptors, Mem Ctr, 70 & 71.
Teaching: Asst prof art hist, painting, drawing & theory, Univ Wis-Whitewater, 66-
Awards: Can Coun study grant, 64; jury award, Wis State Fair, 69.
Research: Perfection (or possibility of) full color, permanent direct method color printing for studio use.
Mailing Address: 225 Janesville St S, Whitewater, WI 53190.

HARRISON, NEWTON A
Sculptor, Educator
b New York, N Y, Oct 20, 32.
Study & Training: Yale Univ Sch Art & Archit, BFA & MFA.
Work in Public Collections: Los Angeles Co Mus Art, Calif; art gallery, Univ N Mex, Albuquerque; art gallery, Univ Calif, San Diego; Hayward Gallery, London, Eng; Palais des Beaux Arts, Brussels, Belg.
Exhibitions: Explorations: Toward a Civic Art, Smithsonian Inst, Washington, D C, 70; Art & Technology, U S Pavilion, Expo '70, Osaka, Japan, 70 & Los Angeles Co Mus Art, 71; Earth, Air, Fire, Water: Elements of Art, Boston Mus Art, Mass, 71; Eleven Los Angeles Artists, Hayward Gallery, London, Eng, 71.
Teaching: Asst prof art, Univ N Mex, 65-67; assoc prof art, Univ Calif, San Diego, 67-
Awards: Award for E A T:Projects Outside Art; Creative Arts Inst grant, Univ Calif, 71-72.
Bibliography: Jonathan Benthal (auth), Newton Harrison: big fish in a small pool, Studio Int, 12/71; Jack Burnham (auth), Corporate art, Artforum, 10/71; R C Kenedy (auth), London letter: the icon: unmasked or unveiled-Paolozzi, Larry Bell & Newton Harrison, Art Int, Vol 15, No 10.
Art Interests: Conceptual art with reference to lifesystems.
Mailing Address: 8605 Cliffridge Ave, La Jolla, CA 92037.

HARRISON, ROBERT RICE
Educator
b Detroit, Mich, May 5, 08.
Study & Training: Art Inst Chicago; Wayne State Univ, BFA; New York Univ; Univ Iowa, MA & PhD.
Teaching: Prof art & head dept art, Hamline Univ, 54-65; prof art & chmn dept, Calif State Univ, San Bernardino, 65-72, emer prof, 72-
Memberships: Col Art Asn Am; Am Soc Aesthet; Art Historians of the Calif State Cols; Am Asn Univ Prof.
Mailing Address: 25932 18th St, San Bernardino, CA 92404.

HARRISON, TONY
Painter, Educator
b Gt Brit, Aug 18, 31.
Study & Training: Northern Polytech Eng; Chelsea Sch Art, London, Eng; Cent Sch Arts & Crafts, London.
Work in Public Collections: N Y Univ, New York: Achenback Found Legion Hon, San Francisco, Calif; Arts Coun Gt Brit, London; Royal Collection, Stockholm, Sweden; Nat Gallery S Australia; plus many others.
Exhibitions: One-man show, San Francisco Mus Art, 64; Int Exhib, Stockholm, 66; Ohio Mus Art, Columbus, 69; Tenth Anniversary Exhib, Westmoreland Co Mus Art, Greensburg, Pa, 69; Third Kent Invitational Exhib Comtemp Art, Ohio, 69; plus many other group & one-man shows.
Teaching: Asst prof drawing & printmaking, Columbia Univ, 71-72; asst prof painting, N Y Univ, 72-
Awards: Purchase awards, Calif Soc Etchers, 64 & Soc Am Graphic Artists, 65.
Bibliography: Robert Erskine (producer), Artists proof (film), St Georges Gallery, 57; Collectors choice, produced on ITV, London, 62.
Dealer: New Bertha Schaefer Gallery, 41 E 57th St, New York, NY 10022.
Mailing Address: 42 W 30th St, New York, NY 10001.

HARRITON, ABRAHAM
Painter
Preferred Media: Oils.
b Bucharest, Rumania, Feb 16, 93; U S citizen.
Study & Training: Nat Acad Design, 08-15, with Emil Carlsen, Kenyon Cox, George DeForest Brush & Mielatz.
Work in Public Collections: Whitney Mus Am Art, New York, N Y; Addison Gallery Am Art, Phillips Acad, Andover, Mass; Ein Harod Mus, Israel; Syracuse Univ Mus; Abraham Harriton Mss Collection, Syracuse Univ; plus others.
Commissions: Educ, Transp & Indust, U S Govt, Post Off & Agr Bldg, 36.
Exhibitions: 5 Whitney Mus Am Art Ann, 36-41; 15 one-man exhibs,

ACA Galleries, 36-72; Mus Mod Art, 40; Carnegie Inst, 41, 43, 45 & 46; Artists For Victory, Metrop Mus Art, 42.
Teaching: Instr painting & drawing, WPA Art Sch, New York, 32-36; instr painting & drawing, Great Neck Art Asn, N Y, 45-50.
Awards: First hon mention, Audubon Artists, 60; Marine Painting Award, Silvermine Guild Artists, 63; Marjorie Peabody Waite Award, Nat Inst Arts & Lett, 68.
Bibliography: Harry Salpeter (auth), Ex-Picassoid, Esquire Mag, 1/46; Abraham Harriton discusses a system of glazing, Am Artist, 9/51.
Memberships: Audubon Artists (dir, 58); Artists Equity Asn.
Research: Technique of underpainting and glazing as based on Venetian masters.
Dealer: ACA Galleries, 25 E 73rd St, New York, NY 10021.
Mailing Address: 66 W Ninth St, New York, NY 10011.

HARSANYI, CHARLES
Painter
Preferred Media: Oils.
b Tapolza, Hungary, Nov 21, 05; U S citizen.
Study & Training: Royal Acad Fine Arts, Budapest, Hungary, with A Bankhard, 23-28.
Work in Public Collections: Metrop Mus Art, New York, N Y; Washington Co Mus Fine Arts, Hagerstown, Md; Rensselaer Co Mus Art, Troy, N Y; Hungarian Studies Found, Rutgers Univ, Princeton, N J; U S Govt, Washington, D C.
Exhibitions: Pa Acad Fine Arts, Philadelphia, 33-49; Nat Acad Design, New York, N Y, 33-55; four shows, Corcoran Gallery Art Biennial, Washington, D C, 35-51; Art Inst Chicago, Ill, 41-44; Va Mus Fine Arts Biennial, Richmond, 42 & 46.
Awards: Gold medal hon, Washington Co Mus Fine Arts, 46; Allied Artists Am Bronze Medal Hon, 53; William Bradford Green Mem Prize, Conn Acad Fine Arts, 55.
Bibliography: American art today, Am Fedn Art, 39; Monhegan Island, Life Mag, 8/21/50; A wreck at Monhegan, Am Artist, 2/51.
Memberships: Audubon Artists (jury awards dir, 52, chmn admis comt, 53, nominating comt, 55 & 56); Artists Fel; life mem Allied Artists Am (jury awards, 45, jury selection, 54).
Dealer: Doctor Saharunis Art Gallery, 315 Fifth Ave S, Naples, FL 33940.
Mailing Address: 546 Coral Dr, Cape Coral, FL 33904.

HARSH, RICHARD
Painter, Educator
b Feb 6, 40.
Study & Training: Columbia Tech Inst, cert, 61; Univ Northern Iowa, BA, 65; Southern Ill Univ, scholar, 68-69, MFA, 69; also with Siegfried Reinhardt.
Exhibitions: Third Nat Cape Coral, Fla, 69; Third Nat Polymer Exhib, Eastern Mich Univ, Ypsilanti, 70; Second Washington & Jefferson Col Painting Exhib Fine Arts Festival, 70; Am Acad Arts & Lett, Hassam Found, 70; Greater Fall River Art Asn, Mass, 70; plus other group & one-man exhibs.
Teaching: Instr art, Community Unit II High Sch, Greenville, Ill, 66-68; asst to supvr dept painting, Southern Ill Univ, 68, instr art, workshop, summer 69, grad asst, 69; instr art, Univ Northern Iowa, 70-71; asst prof art, Mackinac Col, 72; lectr, var civic, relig & educ orgn.
Positions: Asst, Fed Bur Investigation, Washington, D C, 58-61; illusr, McGregor-Werner Co, 61.
Awards: Hon mention, River Roads Exhib, St Louis, Mo, 68 & Mitchell Gallery Drawing Exhib, Southern Ill Univ, 69; purchase awards, Third Nat Polymer Exhib, Eastern Mich Univ, 70 & Am Acad Arts & Lett, Hassam Found, 70.
Mailing Address: Dept of Art, Mackinac College, Mackinac Island, MI 49757.

HART, AGNES
Painter, Educator
b Conn.
Study & Training: Ringling Col & Sch Art; Iowa State Univ; also with Lucile Blanch, Josef Presser & Paul Burlin.
Work in Public Collections: Metrop Mus Art; Norfolk Mus; Wichita State Univ.
Exhibitions: Am Painting Today, 50 & Watercolors, Drawings & Prints, 52, Metrop Mus Art; Art U S A, 58; Brooklyn Mus; Pa Acad Fine Arts; plus solo exhibs, N Y, Ga & Switz.
Teaching: Instr, Birch Wathen Sch, New York; instr, Dalton Schs, New York, 61-63; instr painting, drawing & compos, Art Stud League New York, 65-
Memberships: Woodstock Artists Asn (mem bd, 55-57); Am Soc Contemp Artists; Art Stud League New York; Phoenix Gallery.
Dealer: Phoenix Gallery, 939 Madison Ave, New York, NY 10022.
Mailing Address: 30 E 14th St, New York, NY 10003.

HART, ALLEN M
Painter, Educator
Preferred Media: Oils, Collage, Mixed Media.
b New York, N Y, June 12, 25.
Study & Training: Art Stud League New York, with Anne Goldthwaite, Frank Vincent Dumond & Jean Liberte; Brooklyn Mus Art Sch, with Vincent Candell.
Work in Public Collections: Butler Inst Am Art, Youngstown, Ohio; Univ Mass, Amherst; Slater Mem Mus, Norwalk, Conn; Children's Aid Soc, New York.
Exhibitions: Art U S A, New York, 58; New York Pub Libr, 61; Cober Gallery, New York, 64-69; The Articulate Subconscious, Am Fedn Arts Traveling Show, 67-68; Visual Arts Ctr, Children's Aid Soc, 70; plus one other.
Teaching: Instr painting, Samuel Field YMHA & YWHA, Littleneck, N Y, 62-68; dir painting, Visual Arts Ctr, 68- ; dean visual arts, Union Am Hebrew Congregations, 70- ; art consult, Bd Coop Educ Serv, 71-
Bibliography: N Y illustrated, NBC-TV, 70; Ned Harris (producer), In the beginning (film), 70 & Shabbat (film), 72; Doris Freedman (auth), Artists in the city, WNYC FM, 10/12/72.
Memberships: Life mem Art Stud League New York.
Publications: Auth, articles, In: Lower Manhattan Twp, 2/20/71 & Herald, 5/1/71.
Dealer: Lerner-Heller Gallery, 789 Madison Ave, New York, NY 10021.
Mailing Address: 34 Jackson Rd, Valley Stream, NY 11581.

HART, BILL
Art Dealer
b Saint Louis, Mo, Oct 17, 39.
Study & Training: Univ Loyola, Los Angeles, BA.
Positions: Dir, Spectrum Gallery, New York, N Y.
Specialty of Gallery: Contemporary American abstract painting and sculpture; some realist work.
Mailing Address: Spectrum Gallery, 464 W Broadway, New York, NY 10013.

HART, MARVELL ALLISON
Museum Curator
Positions: Keeper of collections, Honolulu Acad Arts.
Mailing Address: Honolulu Academy of Arts, 900 S Beretania St, Honolulu, HI 96814.

HART, MORGAN DRAKE
Painter, Instructor
Preferred Media: Oils, Acrylics, Watercolors, Pastels, Crayons.
b Shrub Oak, N Y, Jan 8, 99.
Study & Training: Nat Acad Design, with Charles Webster Hawthorne & Francis C Jones.
Work in Public Collections: Maine Harbor, Hillsborough N J Libr.
Commissions: Portrait in oil of Dr A D Dunbar & landscape mural of George Washington (in auditorium), Peekskill H S, N Y; Frank Dempster Sherman, Poet (portrait), Peekskill Mil Acad, N Y; William R O'Neal (portrait), Rollins Col, Winter Park, Fla.
Exhibitions: Montclair Mus State Show, 53, 59 & 63; Grand Nat Show, Lever House, 60, 65, 71 & 72; Fort Worth Mus, Tex, 65; Am Artists Prof League travelling show, Prince Rainier's Palace, Monaco, 67; one-man show, Ferargi Gallery, New York, N Y, 28.
Teaching: Instr art, Peekskill Eve Schs, 30-35; instr art, Peekskill Mil Acad, 34; instr drawing, Ducret Art Sch, 67-68; instr pvt classes.
Positions: Color technician, Union Carbide Corp, Bound Brook, N J, 48-64.
Awards: Best of show, Union Carbide Corp, 53 & 59; best of show, Raritan Valley Arts Asn, 58, 64 & 68; second prize, N J State Show, Am Artists Prof League, 62 & 70.
Memberships: Am Artists Prof League (secy nat bd, 60-72); hon mem Raritan Valley Arts Asn; Hunterdon Co Art Asn.
Art Interests: Direct landscapes; portraiture.
Dealers: M Knoedler & Co, 21 E 70th St, New York, NY 10021; Swain Gallery, 317 Front St, Plainfield, NJ 07060.
Mailing Address: Hickory Dr, Sunset Lake, Pluckemin, NJ 07978.

HARTELL, JOHN (ANTHONY)
Painter
Preferred Media: Oils.
b Brooklyn, N Y, Jan 30, 02.
Study & Training: Cornell Univ, BArch; Royal Acad Fine Arts, Stockholm, Sweden.
Work in Public Collections: Andrew Dickson White Mus Art, Cornell Univ, Ithaca, N Y; Ill Wesleyan Univ, Bloomington; Munson-Williams-Proctor Inst, Utica, N Y; Univ Nebr, Lincoln; Wake Forest Univ, Winston-Salem, N C.
Exhibitions: Carnegie Inst, Pittsburgh, Pa, 45-47; four exhibs, Whitney Mus Am Art, 45-56; Chicago Art Inst, Ill, 51; Pa Acad Fine Arts, Philadelphia, 53; Walker Art Ctr, Minneapolis, Minn, 58.

Teaching: Prof archit & art, Cornell Univ, 30-68, chmn dept art, 39-59, emer prof archit & art, 68-
Bibliography: Rosamund Frost (auth), Hartell: builder in paint, Art News, 10/15/45; Hartell: visiting artist, Munson-Williams-Proctor Inst Bull, 1/52; John Hartell (catalogue), White Mus, 66.
Dealer: Kraushaar Galleries, 1055 Madison Ave, New York, NY 10028.
Mailing Address: 319 The Parkway, Ithaca, NY 14850.

HARTER, TOM JOHN
Educator, Painter
Preferred Media: Casein.
b Naperville, Ill, Oct 8, 05.
Study & Training: Calif Art Inst, Los Angeles, scholar, 25; Grand Cent Sch Art, New York, N Y, 32-34, with Harvey Dunn; Ariz State Univ, BA, 40; Univ Ore, MFA, 42; Colo Springs Fine Arts Ctr, summer 44.
Work in Public Collections: 12 portraits of notables, Ariz State Univ Portrait Collect, Tempe; Scottsdale Fine Arts Comn, Ariz; Glendale Community Col Fine Arts Collection, Ariz; also in pvt collections.
Exhibitions: Eighth Biennial Exhib Watercolors, American & Foreign Artists, Brooklyn Mus, N Y, 35; Am Watercolor Soc, New York, N Y, 37 & 38; five exhibs, Calif Nat Watercolor Soc, 45-62; one-man show, Phoenix Art Mus, Ariz, 64; one-man retrospective, Matthews Ctr, Ariz State Univ, 72; plus many other group & one-man shows.
Teaching: Prof art, graphic design & painting, Ariz State Univ, 37-
Positions: Designer, Western Litho, Los Angeles, Calif, 22-25; prom artist, Los Angeles Examiner, 25-29; art dir, 29-30; designer, Niagara Lithographic Co, New York, 30-37.
Awards: First prize for oil, 59, first prize for watercolor, 61 & first prize for oil, 62, Ariz State Fair.
Memberships: Calif Nat Watercolor Soc.
Publications: Illusr, Game in the desert, Derrydale Press, 38; illusr, Hunting in the Southwest, 46; illusr, Arizona: the history of a frontier state, Hobson & Herr, 50; also illusr, hist articles, In: Ariz Highways Mag.
Mailing Address: 320 Roosevelt St, Tempe, AZ 85281.

HARTFORD, HUNTINGTON
Collector, Patron
b New York, N Y, Apr 18, 11.
Study & Training: Harvard Univ, AB, 34.
Positions: Patron, Lincoln Ctr for Performing Arts; founder, Huntington Hartford Found, 49; founder & bd dirs, Gallery Mod Art (now New York Cult Ctr), 64; ed-in-chief, Show Mag; mem, Nat Coun on Arts, 69; mem adv coun, dept art hist & archaeol, Columbia Univ.
Awards: Art Man of Year, Nat Art Materials Trade Asn, 62; Am Artists Prof League Award, 64; Orgn Am States Award, 66.
Memberships: Hon fel Nat Sculpture Soc; Nat Arts Club; Salmagundi Club; Am Artists Prof League.
Publications: Auth, Art or anarchy?, 64.
Mailing Address: 420 Lexington Ave, New York, NY 10017.

HARTGEN, VINCENT ANDREW
Painter, Educator
Preferred Media: Watercolors.
b Reading, Pa, Jan 10, 14.
Study & Training: Sch Fine Arts, Univ Pa, BFA & MFA.
Work in Public Collections: Mus Fine Arts, Boston, Mass; Wadsworth Atheneum, Hartford, Conn; Sheldon Swope Art Gallery, Terre Haute, Ind; Walker Art Ctr, Minneapolis, Minn; Wichita Art Mus, Kans.
Exhibitions: One-man shows, Chase Gallery, 62 & 68; Artists of Maine, Am Fedn Arts Traveling Exhib, 64-66; Embassies Art Prog, Dept State, Washington, D C, 66-70; 200 Yrs Watercolor Painting Am, Metrop Mus Art, 67; Landscape I, De Cordova Mus, Lincoln, Mass, 70.
Collections Arranged: Contemp Schs, U S A, Contemp Churches, U S A, 56-57, Ceramics & Dinnerware, 68 & Boxes, Sacks & Bags, 71, Univ Maine Art Gallery.
Teaching: Prof art & dir Art Gallery & Collection, Univ Maine, Orono, 46- , Huddiston Prof Art, 62-
Positions: Trustee, Haystack Sch Crafts, 50-55; comnr, Maine State Comn Arts & Humanities, 65-70.
Awards: Hon mentions, 50 & 66 & Creative Aquarelle Award, 65, Audubon Artists.
Bibliography: H J Seligmann (auth), Vincent Hartgen...artist & teacher, Downeast Mag, 60; Ralph Fabri (auth), Watercolorist for all seasons, Today's Art, 65; Norman Kent (auth), 100 techniques of watercolor painting, 70.
Memberships: Am Asn Univ Prof; Col Art Asn Am; Audubon Artists; Am Watercolor Soc; hon mem Can Soc Painter-Etchers & Engravers.

Publications: Auth, Watercolors, Pen & Brush, 54; auth, Defending the middle ground of the semi abstract, Am Artist, 67.
Dealer: Chase Gallery, 31 E 64th St, New York, NY 10021.
Mailing Address: 109 Forest Ave, Orono, ME 04473.

HARTIGAN, GRACE
Painter
b Newark, N J, Mar 28, 22.
Study & Training: Pvt art classes with Isaac Lane Muse.
Work in Public Collections: Mus Mod Art, Whitney Mus Am Art & Metrop Mus Art, New York, N Y; Carnegie Inst, Pittsburgh, Pa; Walker Art Ctr, Minneapolis, Minn; Art Inst Chicago, Ill; Albright-Knox Art Gallery, Buffalo, N Y; plus many others.
Exhibitions: Carnegie Int, 61; American Vanguard, organized by Solomon R Guggenheim Mus for U S Info Agency, Austria, Eng, Ger & Yugoslavia, 61-62; A Decade of New Talent, Am Fedn Arts Exhib, 64-65; one-man shows, Univ Chicago, 67 & Gertrude Kasle Gallery, Detroit, 68; plus many others.
Teaching: Artist-in-residence, Md Inst Grad Sch Painting, 65-69.
Awards: Mademoiselle Mag Merit Award for Art, 57.
Dealer: Martha Jackson Gallery, 32 E 69th St, New York, NY 10021.
Mailing Address: 1701 1/2 Eastern Ave, Baltimore, MD 21231.

HARTL, LEON
Painter
b Paris, France, Jan 31, 89; U S citizen.
Work in Public Collections: Corcoran Gallery Art, Washington, D C; Wadsworth Atheneum, Hartford, Conn; Whitney Mus Am Art, New York, N Y; Univ Nebr, Lincoln; Phillips Collection, Washington, D C; plus many others.
Exhibitions: Butler Inst Am Art, Youngstown, Ohio; Carnegie Inst, Pittsburgh, Pa; Palazzo del Parco, Bordighera, Italy; Art Inst Chicago, Ill; Nat Inst Arts & Lett; plus others.
Teaching: Instr, Brooklyn Mus Sch Art.
Awards: Marjorie Peabody Waite Award, Nat Inst Arts & Lett, 59; Yaddo fel, 60, 61 & 63; Ingram Merrill Found grant, 68.
Dealer: Zabriskie Gallery, 29 W 57th St, New York, NY 10019.
Mailing Address: 56 Seventh Ave, New York, NY 10011.

HARTMAN, ROBERT LEROY
Painter, Educator
b Sharon, Pa, Dec 17, 26.
Study & Training: Univ Ariz, BFA & MA; Colo Springs Fine Arts Ctr, with Vaclav Vytlacil & Emerson Woelffer; Brooklyn Mus Art Sch.
Work in Public Collections: Nat Collection Fine Arts, Smithsonian Inst, Washington, D C; Colo Springs Fine Arts Ctr; Oakland Mus Art, Calif; Achenbach Found Graphic Arts, San Francisco, Calif; Henry Gallery, Univ Wash, Seattle.
Exhibitions: Contemp Am Painting & Sculpture Biennial, Krannert Mus, Univ Ill, 65; Art Across Am, Traveling Show, 65-67; 4th Int Young Artists Exhib, Am-Japan, Tokyo, 67; Drawings by Americans, Henry Gallery, 67; Artists West of Miss 21st Ann, Colo Springs Fine Arts Ctr, 67.
Teaching: Instr art, Tex Technol Col, 55-58; asst prof art, Univ Nev, Reno, 58-61; assoc prof art, Univ Calif, Berkeley, 61-
Positions: Mem, Univ Calif Inst Creative Arts, 67-68.
Awards: Emanuel Walter Fund First Prize, 85th Ann San Francisco Art Inst, 67; hon mention 4th Int Young Artists Exhib Am-Japan, 67.
Dealer: Bertha Schaefer Gallery, 41 E 57th St, New York, NY 10022.
Mailing Address: 1265 Mountain Blvd, Oakland, CA 94611.

HARTT, FREDERICK
Art Historian, Educator
b Boston, Mass, May 22, 14.
Study & Training: Nat Acad Design; Columbia Col, BA, 35; Princeton Univ, 35-36; New York Univ, MA, 37, PhD, 49.
Teaching: Vis lectr art, Smith Col, 46-47; lectr fine arts, New York Univ, 48-49; from asst prof to prof art hist, Wash Univ, 49-60; prof hist art, Univ Pa, 60-67, chmn dept art, 60-65; vis art historian, Harvard Renaissance Ctr, Florence, Italy, 65-66; McIntire prof hist art & chmn dept art, Univ Va, Charlottesville, 67-
Positions: Asst, Yale Art Gallery, 41-42; actg dir art mus, Smith Col, 46-47; bd dirs, Am Comt for Restoration Ital Monuments, 46-49; mem exec comt, Comt to Rescue Ital Art, 66-
Awards: Guggenheim fel, 48-49, 54-55; Fulbright res grants, 54-55, 65-66; Am Coun Learned Socs fel, 65-66.
Memberships: Col Art Asn Am (dir, 59-62); Am Asn Univ Prof; Renaissance Soc Am (coun, 70); hon academician Acad Arts Design, Florence, Italy.
Research: Italian Renaissance art.
Publications: Auth, Love in baroque art, 64, The paintings of Michelangelo, 64, Michelangelo, the complete sculpture, 69, History of Italian Renaissance art, 69 & Michelangelo's drawings, 71, Abrams; also many articles & rev in art periodicals.
Mailing Address: Old Ordinary Rte 7, Box 164, Charlottesville, VA 22901.

HARTWIG, CLEO
Sculptor
Preferred Media: Stone.
b Webberville, Mich, Oct 20, 11.
Study & Training: Western Mich Univ, AB & hon MA; Int Sch Art, Europe; Art Inst Chicago, summers; also carving with José de Creeft.
Work in Public Collections: Detroit Inst Arts, Mich; Newark Mus, N J; Pa Acad Fine Arts, Philadelphia; Montclair Art Mus, N J; Norfolk Mus Arts & Sci, Va.
Commissions: Family Group (aluminum), Facade of Continental Casualties Bldg, New York, N Y, 52; Wild Ducks (terra-cotta), Cabin Class Lounge, S S United States, 52; bronze kneeling figure with dove, All Faiths Mem Tower, Paramus, N J, 63; two sculpture awards, Columbia Univ Law Sch Alumni, New York, 71.
Exhibitions: Artists for Victory, Metrop Mus Art, New York, 42; American Paintings & Sculpture Ann, Art Inst Chicago, Ill, 42; Pa Acad Fine Arts Ann, 45-54, 58 & 62; Fairmount Park Int Sculpture Exhib, Philadelphia Mus Art, 49; Women Artists of America, Newark Mus, 65.
Teaching: Part-time instr sculpture, Montclair Art Mus, 45-71.
Awards: Audubon Artists First Prize for Sculpture, 52; medal of honor, Nat Asn Women Artists, 67; silver medal, Nat Sculpture Soc Ann, 69.
Bibliography: Enid Bell (auth), The compatibles, Am Artist Mag, summer 68.
Memberships: Sculptors Guild (exec secy, 47-54, 63-65); Nat Sculpture Soc (mem coun, 67-73, exhib chmn, 69-72); Nat Acad Design; Audubon Artists (v pres for sculpture, 70-73); Nat Asn Women Artists (mem sculpture jury, 72-).
Publications: Co-auth, Direct carving in stone, Nat Sculpture Rev, summer 65.
Mailing Address: 5 W 16th St, New York, NY 10011.

HARVEY, DONALD GILBERT
Sculptor, Instructor
Preferred Media: Mixed Media.
b Louisville, Ky, June 25, 47.
Study & Training: Dixie Col, 65; Utah State Univ, BFA, 69; Univ Hawaii, MFA, 71.
Work in Public Collections: Honolulu Acad Arts, Hawaii; State Found Culture & Arts, Honolulu; Utah State Univ Permanent Collection; Advertr Publ Permanent Collection, Hawaii.
Exhibitions: Hawaii Craftsman, 69-70; Artist of Hawaii, 70; Pomona Fair Crafts Exhib, Calif, 70; Easter Art Festival, Honolulu, 70-71; one-man show, Contemp Art Ctr of the Pac, 72.
Teaching: Lectr art, Univ Hawaii, 70-71; instr art, Kamehamea High Sch, 71-
Awards: Outstanding art stud in ceramics award, Dixie Col, 67; outstanding student in sculpture & ceramics, Utah State Univ, 69; Honolulu Acad Arts Purchase Award, 70.
Memberships: Hawaii Painters & Sculptors League; Nat Art Educ Asn.
Mailing Address: Apt 8, 733 Kihapai Rd, Kailua, HI 96734.

HARVEY, JACQUELINE
Painter
Preferred Media: Oils.
b La Madeleine, Lille, France, Feb 2, 27; U S citizen.
Study & Training: High Sch Mus & Art, New York, N Y, 41-45; New Sch Soc Res, 45-46; also silversmith apprentice with Paul Lobel, 45-46 & studio training with Morris Davidson, New York, 45-46, Fernand Leger & Leopold Survage, Paris, 46-47 & William Hayter, New York, 48.
Work in Public Collections: Birla Acad Art & Cult, Calcutta, India; Eggers Partnership, New York.
Exhibitions: One-man shows, Panoras Gallery, New York, 55 & 63 & Eola Gallery, Orlando, Fla, 57; First Ann Metrop Young Artists, Nat Arts Club, New York, 58; Art U S A, Madison Sq Garden, New York, 58; Rose Fried Gallery, New York, 69-70.
Memberships: Am Fedn Arts.
Mailing Address: 279 Park Ave, Manhasset, NY 11030.

HARVEY, ROBERT MARTIN
Painter
b Lexington, N C, Sept 16, 24.
Study & Training: Ringling Sch Art, with Elmer Harmes & Georgia Warren; San Francisco Art Inst, with Nathan Oliveira & Sonia Gechtoff.
Work in Public Collections: Corcoran Gallery Art, Washington, D C; Wichita Art Mus, Kans; Hirshhorn Collection, Washington, D C;

Storm King Art Ctr, Mountainville, N Y; Crown-Zellerbach Found, San Francisco, Calif; plus others.
Exhibitions: American Painting, Va Mus Fine Arts, Richmond, 66; Butler Inst Am Art, Youngstown, Ohio, 66; Univ Ill, 67 & 69; Phoenix Art Mus; Richard White Gallery, Seattle, Wash, 69; plus other group & one-man shows.
Awards: Award of Merit, San Francisco Art Festival, 63; Western Wash State Col Purchase Prize, 65; Mead Painting of the Year, 67; plus others.
Dealers: Oscar Krasner, 1043 Madison Ave, New York, NY 10021; David Stuart Galleries, 807 N La Cienega Blvd, Los Angeles, CA 90046.
Mailing Address: c/o Charles Campbell Gallery, 647 Chestnut, San Francisco, CA 94133.

HASELTINE, JAMES LEWIS
Art Administrator, Painter.
Preferred Media: Oils.
b Portland, Ore, Nov 7, 24.
Study & Training: Portland Mus Art Sch, Ore, 47 & 49; Art Inst Chicago, 47-48; Brooklyn Mus Sch, 50-51.
Work in Public Collections: Portland Art Mus, Ore; Oakland Art Mus, Calif.
Exhibitions: Libr Cong, Washington, D C, 51; Brooklyn Mus, N Y, 51-52; Portland Art Mus, Ore, 51-58; Seattle Art Mus, Wash, 52, 53, 57 & 59; San Francisco Mus Art, Calif, 53-54.
Teaching: Vis lectr art hist, Univ Utah, 64-65.
Positions: Dir, Salt Lake Art Ctr, Salt Lake City, Utah, 61-67; exec dir, Washington State Arts Comn, Olympia, 67-
Awards: Purchase prize, Portland Art Mus, 53; best monogr, Mormon Hist Asn, 65.
Memberships: Western Asn Art Mus (pres, 64-66); Am Asn Mus; Assoc Coun Arts; Nat Assembly State & Prov Arts Agencies (exec comt, 68-70); Nat Endowment Arts (mus panel, 70-72).
Publications: Auth, 100 years of Utah painting, 65; contribr, Mus News, 65; contribr, Utah Hist Quart, Dialogue & The American West, 66.
Mailing Address: Rte 15, Box 570, Olympia, WA 98502.

HASELTINE, MAURY (MARGARET WILSON HASELTINE)
Painter
Preferred Media: Oils, Acrylics.
b Portland, Ore, May 7, 25.
Study & Training: Reed Col; Mus Art Sch, Portland; Eastern N Mex Univ.
Work in Publications: Salt Lake Art Ctr, Salt Lake City, Utah; Univ Ore Mus, Eugene; Snow Col, Ephriam, Utah; Bell Tel Co, Portland; First Nat Bank, Portland.
Commissions: Assemblage collage mural, Donald Lloyd, Assoc Grocers Off, Salt Lake City, 65.
Exhibitions: 12 Shows, Artists Ore, Portland Art Mus, 51-67; Northwest Ann, Seattle Art Mus, 53, 57 & 59; Intermountain Biennial Painting & Sculpture, Salt Lake Art Ctr, 63, 65 & 67; New Accessions U S A, Colo Springs Fine Art Ctr, Colo, 64; Selected Painters 65, Mulvane Art Ctr, Topeka, Kans, 65.
Teaching: Instr oil painting, Salt Lake Art Ctr, 64-65; instr oil & acrylic painting, Creative Activities Ctr, State Capitol Mus, Olympia, Wash, 67-, coordr creative activities, 69-70.
Awards: Southwest Fiesta Biennial Prize, Santa Fe, N Mex, 66.
Bibliography: Charles Miller (producer), Way of art, KUTV, 65; Prize-winning graphics, Allied Publ, 66.
Memberships: Portland Art Mus. State Capitol Mus (chmn hist comt, 68-69, bd mem, 70-72); Ballet Northwest (bd mem, 70-).
Art Interests: Documentation of art forms on pioneer gravestones.
Publications: Contribr, Forms upon the frontier, Utah State Univ Press, 69.
Dealer: Fountain Gallery, 115 S W Fourth Ave, Portland, OR 97204.
Mailing Address: Rte 15, Box 570, Olympia, WA 98502.

HASEN, BURT STANLY
Painter
Preferred Media: Oils, Acrylics.
b New York, N Y, Dec 19, 21.
Study & Training: Art Stud League New York, 40, 42 & 46, with Morris Kantor; Hans Hofmann Sch Fine Arts, 47-48; Acad Grande Chaumiere, Paris, 48-50, with Ossipe Zadkine; Accad Belli Arti, Rome, 59-60.
Work in Public Collections: Walker Art Ctr, Minneapolis, Minn; Worcester Art Mus; Hampton Inst, Va; Crestview Col, Allentown, Pa; Muhlenberg Col, Allentown.
Commissions: Mural, YMHA & YWHA, New York, 47.
Exhibitions: Salon Mai, Mus Art Mod, Paris, 51; Metrop Mus Art, New York, 53; Berlin Acad, W Ger, 56; Whitney Mus Am Art Ann, New York, 63; Walker Art Ctr, 66.
Teaching: Instr painting & drawing, Sch Visual Arts, 53-; instr painting, Col Art & Design, Minneapolis, 66.

Awards: Three purchase prizes, Emily Loew Found, 54; Fulbright grant to Italy, 59-66.
Bibliography: Allen S Weller (auth), Contemporary American painting and sculpture, Krannert Art Mus, 61; The Whitney Annual, Time, 63; Eric Protter (auth), Artists on art, Grosset & Dunlap, 64.
Publications: Illusr, Contes del'inattendu, 59, De la terre a la lune, 61, Voltaire, 61 & Moliere, 61.
Mailing Address: 7 Dutch St, New York, NY 10038.

HASKELL, DOUGLAS
Writer, Critic
b Monastir, Turkey, June 27, 99; U S citizen.
Study & Training: Oberlin Col, AB, 23, hon DFA, 61.
Teaching: Lectr, Pratt Inst, 50-51; adj prof, Sch Archit, Columbia Univ, 60-63; vis lectr & critic at archit schs & var univs & cols.
Positions: Asst ed, Creative Art Mag, 28; asst ed, contribr & sr assoc ed, Archit Record, 29-49; v chmn archit adv comt, Pub Housing Admin, 49-50; archit ed, Archit Forum, 49-51, ed chmn, 52-54, ed, 55-64.
Awards: Order of Southern Cross, Brazil.
Memberships: Nat Arts Club (bd gov, 67-); Soc Archit Historians; Asn Col Schs Archit; fel Am Inst Architects; New York Archit League.
Publications: Ed, Rehousing urban America, 35; ed, Building U S A, 57; contribr, articles to archit publ & popular mag.
Mailing Address: 1 Lexington Ave, New York, NY 10010.

HASKELL, HARRY GARNER, JR
Collector
b Wilmington, Del, May 27, 21.
Study & Training: Princeton Univ, 40-42.
Collection: Andrew Wyeth.
Mailing Address: 1600 Brinckle Ave, Wilmington, DE 19806.

HASLEM, JOHN ARTHUR & JANE N
Art Dealers, Collectors
Mr Haslem, b Saint Louis, Mo, Aug 16, 34; Mrs Haslem b Knoxville, Tenn, Dec 26, 34.
Study & Training: Mr Haslem, Duke Univ, AB; Harvard Univ; Univ N C, MBA & PhD; Mrs Haslem, De Pauw Univ, BA; Ind State Univ.
Teaching: Mrs Haslem, instr art, Mechlenburg Co, N C, East Mecklenburg High Sch & West Mecklenburg High Sch, 58-59.
Positions: Mr Haslem, chmn bd, Haslem Fine Arts, Inc, Jane Haslem Gallery, Washington, D C & Madison, Wis, 60-; Mrs Haslem, pres, Haslem Fine Arts, Inc, Jane Haslem Gallery, Washington, D C & Madison, Wis, 60-
Memberships: Mr Haslem, Corcoran Gallery Art; Am Fedn Arts; Print Coun Am; Washington Print Club. Mrs Haslem, Corcoran Gallery Art; Washington Print Club.
Specialty of Gallery: Contemporary American prints and paintings.
Collection: Twentieth century prints, paintings and sculpture.
Mailing Address: 2121 P St N W, Washington, DC 20037.

HASTIE, REID
Educator, Writer
Preferred Media: Acrylics.
b Donora, Pa, Feb 14, 16.
Study & Training: Edinboro State Col, BS; W Va Univ, MA; Univ Pittsburgh, EdD.
Work in Public Collections: Minneapolis Inst Arts; Minn Mus Arts.
Exhibitions: State Fair Gallery, St Paul, Minn, 66; Northrop Gallery, Univ Minn, 67; Encounters with Artists, 70; Drawings, St Paul, 72.
Teaching: Prof art & art educ, Univ Minn, 49-70; prof art & art educ, Tex Tech Univ, 70-
Awards: Distinguished Art Educator, Minn Art Educ Asn, 66; award of merit, Nat Art Educ Asn, 69.
Memberships: Nat Art Educ Asn (pres, 57-59); Nat Soc Study Educ.
Research: Study of aesthetic theory and sensitivity; the creative process.
Publications: Ed, Art education, 65; auth, Encounter with art, 69.
Mailing Address: 2114-65th Pl, Lubbock, TX 79412.

HASWELL, MR & MRS ANTHONY
Collectors
Mailing Address: 4406 Southern Blvd, Dayton, OH 45429.

HATCH, JOHN DAVIS
Art Consultant, Art Historian
b Oakland, Calif, June 14, 07.
Study & Training: Univ Calif, 26-28; Harvard Univ, 32; Princeton Univ, 38; Yale Univ, 40.
Collections Arranged: Traveling Exhibs for Carnegie Corp, 36-37; pioneer exhib, The Negro Artist Comes of Age, 45.

Teaching: Vis prof, Univ Ore, 48-49; vis prof, Univ Calif, summer 49; coord adv & actg chmn fine arts div, Spelman Col, 64-70; vis prof, Univ Mass, summer 71.
Positions: Exec secy, Seattle Art Mus, 28-29, dir, 29-31; v pres, Western Asn Art Mus, 30-31; asst dir, Isabella Stewart Gardner Mus, 32-35; dir, U S art projs, New Eng States, 33-34; ed, Parnassus, 37-39; founder, Am Art Depository, 38; founder, Am Drawing Ann, 40; dir, Albany Inst Hist & Art, 40-48; ed, Albany Co Hist Asn Record, 41-48; ed, Early Am Indust Chronicle, 42-49; dir, Norfolk Mus Art & Sci, 50-60.
Memberships: Master Drawing Asn (trustee, founder, 62); Am Drawing Soc (adv bd); Berkshire Co Hist Soc (treas, trustee); Col Art Asn Am; MacDowell Colonists.
Art Interests: Life of John VanderLyn and a survey of American drawings and draughtsmen.
Publications: Auth, Reproductions of paintings in the Isabella Stewart Gardner Museum; auth, The Negro artist comes of age & Historic church silver in the Southern Diocese of Virginia; co-compiler, Historic survey of painting in Canada.
Mailing Address: Lenox, MA 01240.

HATCH, JOHN W
Painter, Educator
Preferred Media: Watercolors.
b Saugus, Mass, Nov 1, 19.
Study & Training: Mass Col Art; Sch Fine Arts, Yale Univ, BFA & MFA.
Work in Public Collections: De Cordova & Dana Mus, Lincoln, Mass; Phillips Exeter Acad; Portland Mus Art; Addison Gallery Am Art, Andover, Mass; Pa Acad Art, Philadelphia.
Commissions: Murals, Army Map Service Bldg, Washington, D C, Am Red Cross, Melbourne, Australia & Kingsbury Hall, Univ N H; mem window, Student Union, Univ N H; hist mural, The Ledges, Durham, N H; plus others.
Exhibitions: New Hampshire Art Asn, Currier Gallery Art, 49-65; U S Info Agency Exhib, Russia, 61; Centennial Exhib of Land Grant Cols, Kansas City, Mo, 62; De Cordova & Dana Mus, 62 & 64; Boston Mus Fine Arts, 67-69; plus others.
Teaching: Prof art, Univ N H, at present.
Positions: Visual arts comt, N H Comn on the Arts.
Awards: City of Manchester, N H, Award, 64; New Hampshire Art Asn, 64; Portland Mus Art Festivals; plus others.
Memberships: N H Art Asn (pres, 58-60); Am Asn Univ Prof; Boston Watercolor Soc.
Mailing Address: Paul Creative Arts Center, University of New Hampshire, Durham, NH 03824.

HATCHETT, DUAYNE
Sculptor, Educator
Preferred Media: Metal.
b Shawnee, Okla, May 12, 25.
Study & Training: Univ Mo; Univ Okla, BFA & MFA.
Work in Public Collections: Whitney Mus Am Art; Adison Gallery Am Art, Andover, Mass; Dallas Mus, Tex; Carnegie Inst, Pittsburgh, Pa; Bradley Collection, Milwaukee Art Ctr, Wis.
Commissions: Constructions, Trader's Nat Bank, Kansas City, Mo, 60 & City of Tulsa, Okla, 61.
Exhibitions: Whitney Mus Am Art Ann, 66-68; Am Sculpture of Sixties, Los Angeles Co Mus, 67; Pittsburgh Int, 67-71; 11th Int Biennial Sculpture, Middelheim Mus, Antwerp, Belg.
Teaching: Asst prof sculpture, Univ Tulsa, 54-64; assoc prof sculpture, Ohio State Univ, 64-68; prof sculpture State Univ N Y Buffalo, 68-
Mailing Address: 347 Starin Ave, Buffalo, NY 14216.

HATFIELD, DAVID UNDERHILL
Painter
Preferred Media: Oils.
b Plainfield, N J, July 16, 40.
Study & Training: Miami Univ, BFA, 62; Sch Visual Arts, 63; Art Stud League New York, 64.
Exhibitions: Nat Acad Design Ann, New York, N Y, 70; Nat Arts Club Ann, New York, 71; Am Artists Prof League Grand Nat, New York, 71; Allied Artists Am, New York, 71; Audubon Artists Ann, New York, 71.
Awards: Julius Hallgarten Second Prize, Nat Acad Design, 70; Jane Peterson Mem Prize, Salmagundi Club, 71; Margaret F Dole Mem Prize, Am Artists Prof League, 71.
Memberships: Salmagundi Club; Allied Artists Am; Hudson Valley Art Asn; Am Artists Prof League; Knickerbocker Artists.
Dealer: Grand Central Art Galleries, 40 Vanderbilt Ave, New York, NY 10017.
Mailing Address: 311 E 75th St, New York, NY 10021.

HATFIELD, DONALD GENE
Painter, Educator
Preferred Media: Watercolors.
b Detroit, Mich, May 23, 32.
Study & Training: Northwestern Mich Col, AA; Mich State Univ, BA & MA; Univ Wis, MFA.
Work in Public Collections: Montgomery Mus Art, Ala; Tusgegee Inst, Ala; Univ Wis-La Crosse; Milwaukee Pub Sch, Wis; Opelika Art Asn Collection, Ala.
Exhibitions: 2nd Ann Juried Arts Nat Exhib, Jr League, Tyler, Tex, 63; 7th Ann Nat Exhib, Chautauqua Art Asn, N Y, 64; 8th Ann Nat Exhib, Greater Fall River Art Asn, Mass, 64; 26th Nat Watercolor Exhib, Miss Watercolor Soc, Jackson Munic Art Gallery, 67; 57th Nat Oil Painting Exhib, Miss Art Asn, Jackson, 67.
Teaching: Elem art supvr, Auburndale Elem Sch Syst, Wis; instr jr & sr high art classes, Auburndale High Sch, 62-64; asst prof art, Auburn Univ, 64-71, assoc prof art, 71-; part time instr hist archit & art, Tuskegee Inst, 68-69.
Awards: Purchase award, 49th Ann Exhib Wis Art, Milwaukee Art Ctr, Milwaukee J, 63; purchase award, 11th Dixie Ann, Montgomery Mus Art, 70; Kelly Fitzpatrick Award, 42nd Ann, Montgomery Mus Art, Ala Art League, 71.
Memberships: Ala Art League (first v pres, 69-70, pres, 70-72); Opelika Arts Asn (bd trustees, 71-73); Ala Watercolor Soc; Birmingham Art Asn.
Mailing Address: 550 Forest Park Circle, Auburn, AL 36830.

HATGIL, PAUL
Sculptor
Preferred Media: Plastics.
b Manchester, N H, Feb 18, 21.
Study & Training: Mass Col Art, BFA; Columbia Univ, MFA; Harvard Univ, summer 50.
Work in Public Collections: Fed Aviation Agency, Balboa, C Z.
Commissions: St Paul's Lutheran Church, Austin, Tex; Univ Tex Bus & Admin Bldg, Austin; Our Saviour's Lutheran Church, Victoria, Tex; Design Assocs Bldg, Dallas, Tex; Rio Bldg, Austin; plus others.
Exhibitions: 4th-6th Int Invitational, Smithsonian Inst, Washington, D C; Int Invitational, Gulf-Caribbean Exhib, Houston, Tex; Philbrook Art Ctr Int, Tulsa, Okla; U S World's Fair Pavilion, N Y; Hemisphere 1969, Tex Pavilion, San Antonio, Tex; plus many others.
Teaching: Instr, Columbia Univ; instr, San Antonio Art Inst; instr, Tex Fine Arts Asn, Austin; prof art, Univ Tex, Austin, 51-
Awards: Univ Tex Res Inst grants, 64 & 65.
Memberships: Am Craftsmen Coun; Col Art Asn Am.
Publications: Auth, articles, In: Ceramic Monthly, Sch Arts, Tex Trends Art Educ, La Rev Mod, Ceramic Age & Hellenic Chronicle.
Dealer: Valley House Gallery, 6616 Spring Valley Rd, Dallas, TX 75240.
Mailing Address: 1401 Red Bud Trail, Austin, TX 78746.

HATHAWAY, CALVIN SUTLIFF
Curator
b Lockport, N Y.
Study & Training: Princeton University, AB, 30; Harvard Univ; N Y Univ.
Collections Arranged: (Exhib), Original Designs for French Silversmiths: Work with Examples of the Craft, Nov, 34.
Positions: Asst, decorative arts, Pa Mus Art, 30-31, secy to dir & ed, 31-32, head dept decorative arts & ed, 32-33; asst cur, Cooper Union Mus Arts of Decoration, 33-34, assoc cur, 34-46, cur, 46-51, dir, 51-63; R Wistar Harvey cur decorative arts, Philadelphia Mus Art, 63-72, emer cur decorative arts, 72-
Memberships: Am Inst Interior Designers; Centre International d'Etude des Textiles Anciens (v pres); Int Inst Conservation Hist & Artistic Works; Benjamin Franklin fel Royal Soc Arts.
Research: Research and study continuing throughout most of professional career of equestrian monuments, wallpaper, printed textiles and nineteenth century furniture.
Mailing Address: 2601 Pennsylvania Ave, Apt 125, Philadelphia, PA 19130.

HATHAWAY, JOHN WALLACE
Painter, Printmaker
Preferred Media: Watercolors, Graphics, Mixed Media.
b East Orange, N J, July 7, 05.
Study & Training: Philadelphia Col Art, grad; study in Eng & France; Pa Acad Fine Arts Summer Sch; Barns Found.
Work in Public Collections: Woodmere Art Gallery, Philadelphia, Pa; Yale Univ, New Haven, Conn; Philadelphia Print Club; Beaver Col, Pa; plus many pvt collections.
Commissions: Stained glass windows, Lutheran Church, Philadelphia & Nat Cathedral, Washington, D C, 29-35; designer, studio of Lawrence Saint; also prints & advert art.

Exhibitions: Philadelphia Art Alliance, 28-; Woodmere Art Gallery, Philadelphia, 50-; Nat Acad Design, New York, N Y; Art Asn New Orleans, La; Philadelphia Sketch Club.

Teaching: Instr art, Cheltenham Art Ctr, Philadelphia Col Art, Allens Lane Art Ctr & Graphic Sketch Club; instr art hist, Agnes Irwin Sch Girls, 10 yrs; assoc prof fine arts, Beaver Col, 34-71, instr hist art, Beaver Col London Campus, Eng, 66-67 & 69-70, retired; instr collage & printmaking, Sir John Cass Col Art, London, 69-70.

Positions: Dir, Eugenia Fuller Atwood Libr Art Gallery, Beaver Col.

Awards: Woodmere Art Gallery; Philadelphia Print Club; Philadelphia Art Alliance.

Bibliography: Articles, In: Philadelphia Art Alliance Bull, Beaver Alumni Bull & art sect, Art in Focus, Philadelphia.

Memberships: Philadelphia Art Alliance; Peale Club, Philadelphia Acad Fine Arts; Philadelphia Art Mus; Woodmere Art Gallery; Philadelphia Sketch Club.

Research: Contemporary stained glass in Holland, Germany and France.

Collection: Original contemporary prints, drawings and watercolors.

Mailing Address: 31 W Walnut Lane, Philadelphia, PA 19144.

HAUBERG, MR & MRS JOHN
Collectors
Mailing Address: 1101 McGilvra Blvd E, Seattle, WA 98102.

HAUG, DONALD RAYMOND
Painter, Instructor
Preferred Media: Oils.
b Detroit, Mich, May 12, 25.
Study & Training: Mich State Univ, with Murry Jones & John De Martelly, 46 & 47; Albright Art Sch, with Philip Elliott & Peter Gileran, dipl, 52 & 53; State Univ N Y Col, with Peter Busa, BS & MS, 52-60; Univ Chicago, John Hay Whitney Found fel, with Joshua Taylor & Harold Haydon, 62-63.
Work in Public Collections: Butler Inst Am Art, Youngstown, Ohio; Mem Gallery, Albright-Knox Art Gallery, Buffalo, N Y; also numerous pvt collections.
Exhibitions: Nine shows, Butler Inst Am Art Ann Midyear Show, 56-72; Chautauqua Art Asn Nat Jury Show, N Y, 59, 66 & 72; Cooperstown Art Asn Nat Ann, N Y, 71-72; Drawing & Small Sculpture Ann, Ball State Univ, Muncie, Ind, 72; 62nd Wadsworth Atheneum Ann, Hartford, Conn, 72; plus others.
Positions: Chmn art dept, Eden Cent Schs, N Y.
Awards: Silver medal & patrons award, Buffalo Soc Artists 70th Ann, Albright-Knox Art Gallery, 65; purchase award, 35th Ann Midyear Show, Butler Inst Am Art, 70; first prize still life, Cooperstown Art Asn, 71-72; plus others.
Memberships: Buffalo Soc Artists (past pres, 69, coun mem, 70-72); Patteran Artists (rec secy, 71-72).
Dealer: Marsha More Gallery Without Walls, 460 Franklin, Buffalo, NY 14202.
Mailing Address: 9267 W Lane, Angola, NY 14006.

HAUPT, MRS ENID
Collector
b Chicago, Ill.
Collection: Contemporary art.
Mailing Address: 71 E 71st St, New York, NY 10021.

HAUPT, ERIK GUIDE
Painter
Preferred Media: Oils, Pastels.
b Cassel, Ger, Aug 7, 91; U S citizen.
Study & Training: Md Inst, Baltimore, grad; Royal Acad Munich, Ger; Acad Julien, Paris, France; Acad Colarossi, Paris.
Work in Public Collections: Supreme Ct, Washington, D C; Nat Soc Sons Am Revolution, Washington, D C; Chamber Commerce, New York, N Y; Yale Univ; Johns Hopkins Univ; plus other pub & pvt collections.
Exhibitions: Corcoran Gallery Art, Washington, D C; Philadelphia Acad, Pa; one-man shows, Pittsfield Mus, Mass & retrospective 1913-1971, Nat Arts Club, 72; Nat Acad Design; plus others.
Teaching: Instr drawing & charcoal, Md Inst, 18-25.
Awards: Wyrich Mem Prize, Md Inst; first prize & John Johanson Mem Prize, Nat Arts Club.
Memberships: Nat Arts Club (mem bd, mem exhib comt & chmn house comt); Allied Artists (mem admis comt).
Dealer: Portraits, Inc, 41 E 57th St, New York, NY 10022; Grand Central Galleries, 40 Vanderbilt Ave, New York, NY 10017.
Mailing Address: 1 Gramercy Park, New York, NY 10003.

HAUSER, RICHARD
Painter
Preferred Media: Oils.
b Pittsburgh, Pa, Aug 24, 31.
Study & Training: Carnegie Inst Technol, BA.

Exhibitions: Allied Artist Show; Nat Acad Design; Mainstream's.
Mailing Address: c/o Capricorn Galleries, 8003 Woodmont Ave, Bethesda, MD 20014.

HAUSMAN, FRED S
Painter, Sculptor
Preferred Media: Acrylics.
b Bingen on Rhine, Ger, Apr 27, 21; U S citizen.
Study & Training: Pratt Inst; New Sch Social Res, with Stuart Davis.
Work in Public Collections: Emily Loew Collection, Univ Miami; Mus Mod Art, Bogota, Colombia; Evansville Mus; Rutgers Univ; Fordham Univ.
Exhibitions: N Y Univ, 66; Contemp Art U S A, Norfolk Mus, 67; Columbia Univ, 68; Black & White Show, Smithsonian Inst, 69-70; Second Biennial, Medellin, Colombia, 70.
Dealer: Bodley Gallery, 787 Madison Ave, New York, NY.
Mailing Address: 424 Old Long Ridge Rd, Stamford, CT 06903.

HAUSMAN, JEROME JOSEPH
Educator
b New York, N Y, May 4, 25.
Study & Training: Pratt Inst, 42-43; Cornell Univ, AB, 46; Columbia Univ, 47-48; Art Stud League New York, 48; New York Univ, MA, 51, EdD, 54.
Teaching: Instr art, Elizabeth Pub Schs, N J, 49-53; assoc prof, Sch Fine & Applied Arts, Ohio State Univ, 53-68, actg dir, 58-59, dir, 59-68; vis lectr, Sch Art, Syracuse Univ, 57; vis prof art educ, Pa State Univ, 58; prof div creative arts, New York Univ, 68-.
Positions: Mem arts & humanities panel, U S Off Educ, 64-70; ed bd, J Aesthetic Educ, 68-, consult, John D Rockefeller III Fund, 69-.
Memberships: Nat Art Educ Asn (chmn, res comt, adv, res bd); Nat Comn Art Educ (chmn); Am Soc Aesthetics; Western Arts Asn; Inst for Study Art in Educ (pres).
Publications: Ed, Research in art education (yearbk), Nat Art Educ Asn, 59; ed, Studies in art education, J Issues & Research; contribr, articles in prof journals.
Mailing Address: 212 Rock Creek Lane, Scarsdale, NY 10583.

HAVARD, JAMES PINKNEY
Painter
b Galveston, Tex, June 29, 37.
Study & Training: Sam Houston State Univ, BS; Pa Acad Fine Arts, Cresson scholar to Europe, 64, I J Henry Schiedt scholar, 65.
Work in Public Collections: Philadelphia Mus Art, Pa; also in pvt collections.
Exhibitions: Nat Drawing Exhib, Am Fedn Arts, 65; Nat Inst Arts & Lett, 65; Pa Acad Fine Arts, Philadelphia, 65; Germantown First Ann Exhib & Eastern Cent Exhib, Philadelphia Mus Art, 65; plus others.
Awards: Mabel Wilson Woodrow Award, Pa Acad Fine Arts, 62; purchase prize, Eastern Cent Drawing Exhib, Philadelphia Mus Art, 65; Wechsler Prize, Cheltenham Art Ctr.
Memberships: Fellowship Pa Acad Fine Arts.
Dealer: Atelier Chapman Kelley Galleries, 2526 Fairmount, Dallas, TX 75201.
Mailing Address: 2527 Aspen St, Philadelphia, PA 19030.

HAVELOCK, CHRISTINE MITCHELL
Art Historian
b Cochrane, Ont, June 2, 24; U S citizen.
Study & Training: Univ Toronto, AB; Radcliffe Col, AM; Harvard Univ, Charles Eliot Norton fel, 51-52, PhD.
Teaching: Prof art hist, Vassar Col, 53-.
Awards: Am Asn Univ Women fel, 58-59.
Memberships: Col Art Asn Am; Archeol Inst Am.
Research: Greek sculpture of Hellenistic period.
Publications: Auth, Hellenistic art, New York Graphic Soc, 71.
Mailing Address: Vassar Col, Poughkeepsie, NY 12601.

HAVENS, ELIZABETH CARROLL
Art Historian, Art Dealer
b Bristol, Va, June 29, 44.
Study & Training: Univ Ga; Univ S C, undergrad degree in design; travel in Florence to study Brunelleschi; study of Mayan Archit, Mex, summer, 72.
Teaching: Instr art, Metrop Educ Found, Columbia, S C, summer 68 & 69, supvr art, summer, 70.
Positions: Dir, Havens Gallery, Columbia, 70-
Specialty of Gallery: Modern paintings and graphics.
Mailing Address: Havens Gallery, 2812 Devine St, Columbia, SC 29201.

HAWTHORNE, JACK GARDNER
Educator, Painter
Preferred Media: Watercolors.
b Philadelphia, Pa, May 8, 21.
Study & Training: Philadelphia Col Art, BA, 43; Univ Pa, MSEd, 56, MFA, 58.

Teaching: Dir art educ, Pub Schs, Pa & N J, 43-50; instr drawing,
Philadelphia Col Art, 43-50, registr, 57-60; asst prof educ,
Beaver Col, 60-63; assoc prof art, West Chester State Col, 65-
Awards: Award in Drawing, Pa Acad Fine Arts, 39.
Memberships: Am Asn Univ Prof; Peale Club, Pa Acad Fine Arts;
Philadelphia Art Alliance; life mem Nat Educ Asn; Inst Study Art
Educ.
Publications: Contribr, Course of study in art educ, Commonwealth
Pa, 51.
Mailing Address: 619 W Miner St, West Chester, PA 19380.

HAY, DICK
Sculptor, Educator
Preferred Media: Clay.
b Cincinnati, Ohio, Nov 19, 42.
Study & Training: Ohio Univ, BFA, 64; State Univ N Y Col Ceramics,
Alfred Univ, MFA, 66.
Work in Public Collections: Butler Inst Am Art, Youngstown, Ohio;
J B Speed Art Mus, Louisville, Ky; Sheldon Swope Art Gallery,
Terre Haute, Ind; Alfred Univ, N Y; St Lawrence Univ, Canton,
N Y.
Exhibitions: Craftsmen U S A, Mus Contemp Crafts, New York, N Y,
66; 24th Ann Scripps Col Invitational, Clairmont, Calif, 68;
Forms: Fiber/Clay/Metal, State Univ N Y Col Oneonta, 71;
Twenty Americans, Mus Contemp Crafts, 71; Chicago Plates,
Exhib A Gallery, Chicago, Ill, 72.
Teaching: Asst prof art, Ind State Univ, Terre Haute, 66-; guest
lectr, Univ Iowa, Iowa City, 69, Stout State Univ, Menomonie,
Wis, 70, Purdue Univ, Lafayette, Ind, 72 & State Univ N Y Col
Ceramics, Alfred Univ, 72.
Awards: Nat merit award, Craftsmen U S A, Mus Contemp Crafts,
66; purchase award, Butler Inst Am Art, 69; juror's award,
Boundless Limitations, Fort Wayne Art Mus, Ind, 70.
Bibliography: Portable Mus, Clay '70, 70 & Portable Mus, Twenty
Americans, 71, Am Craftsmen's Coun.
Memberships: Nat Coun Educ Ceramic Arts (bd dirs, 70-); Am
Craftsmen's Coun.
Mailing Address: RR 4, Box 12, Brazil, IN 47834.

HAY, DOROTHY B
Painter, Etcher
Preferred Media: Oils, Watercolors.
b Red Oak, Iowa, Nov 22, 01.
Study & Training: Stanford Univ, BA; Calif Sch Fine Arts; Art Stud
League New York; Acad Andre L'Hote; also sculpture with
Bourdelle, Paris & painting with Eliot O'Hara, Jon Corbino &
F Taubes.
Work in Public Collections: Mus N Mex, Santa Fe; Mus Art, El
Paso, Tex.
Commissions: Decorative murals, Santa Fe R R, Southwest, 40-53;
children's murals, Bishops' Lodge, Santa Fe, 46-55; children's
murals (with Dr B Massey), Children's Wing Thomason Gen
Hosp, El Paso, 60.
Exhibitions: Assoc Am Artists, New York, 37 & Philadelphia Print
Club, 39; Mus N Mex Traveling Shows, 47 & 52; Acad Artists
Asn, Springfield, Mass, 57 & 59; Albany Ann Print Show, N Y, 67
& 68; Southwestern Art Festival, Tucson, Ariz, 69.
Positions: Co-founder, Nat Sun Carnival Exhib, El Paso, 58-59;
judge, Nat Art Exhib, Tubac, Ariz, 65.
Awards: Tex Fine Arts Purchase Prize, 60; Sweepstakes Prize, El
Paso Mus Art Regional, 61; Woman Artist of Yr, Ariz Daily
Star, 64.
Bibliography: J E Reynolds (auth), Featured artist, West, 64; R
Rocsch (auth), Award winning artist, 67.
Memberships: The Group (dir, 72); Southwest Watercolor Guild; El
Paso Art Asn (pres, 58); Cochise Co Art Asn; Black Range Art
Asn.
Mailing Address: 205 Woodland Dr, Tucson, AZ 85711.

HAY, GEORGE AUSTIN
Painter, Writer
Preferred Media: Oils.
b Johnstown, Pa, Dec 25, 15.
Study & Training: Pa Acad Fine Arts; Art Stud League New York;
Nat Acad; Univ Rochester; Univ Pittsburgh, BS & MLitt; Colum-
bia Univ, MA; also with Robert Brackman & Dong Kingman.
Work in Public Collections: New York Pub Libr; Dept Army; Libr
Cong, Washington, D C; Metrop Mus Art; numerous pvt collec-
tions.
Exhibitions: Pittsburgh Playhouse, 37; Rochester Mem Art Gallery,
39; Philharmonic Hall, Lincoln Ctr, 65; Parrish Art Mus, South-
ampton, 69; Riverside Mus, 70.
Awards: Prizes in regional exhibs.
Memberships: Am Artists Prof League; Nat Acad TV Arts & Sci;
Provincetown Art Asn; Allied Artists; Nat Trust for Hist Preser-
vation.

Publications: Auth & illusr, Seven hops to Australia, 45; auth &
illusr, The performing arts experience, 69; auth, MOMA's garden window (film), 72; contribr, Encycl Am, 72.
Dealer: Gallery Madison/90, 1248 Madison Ave, New York, NY
10028.
Mailing Address: National Arts Club, 15 Gramercy Park, New York,
NY 10003.

HAY-MESSICK, VELMA
Painter
Preferred Media: Oils.
b Bloomington, Ill.
Study & Training: Watercolor with Dong Kingman, 44; Chouinard Art
Inst, 47, 48 & 50; Otis Art Inst, 49.
Work in Public Collections: Seton Hall Univ, Newark, N J; City of
Hope, Duarte, Calif; Grumbacher Artists' Palettes, New York,
N Y.
Exhibitions: E B Crocker Gallery Art, Sacramento, Calif, 56 & 57;
Fresno Art Ctr, Calif, 57; Seton Hall Univ, Newark, 58; Nat
League Am Pen Women Southwest Regional, Albuquerque, N Mex,
71.
Positions: Dir, Messick-Hay Studio Gallery, 52-
Awards: Key Award, Seton Hall Univ, 58; first & hon mention for
drawing, Southwest Regional Conf, 71 & second in oils, Calif
State Exhib, 71, Nat League Am Pen Women.
Bibliography: John Oglesby (auth), The lively arts, Sacramento Bee,
57; Vera Williams (auth), Art is a way of life, Southland Mag, 66.
Memberships: Nat League Am Pen Women (Calif S State co-art
chmn, art chmn, Long Beach Br, 72-74).
Specialty of Gallery: Painting, lithographs & drawings.
Mailing Address: Messick-Hay Studio Gallery, 133 St Joseph Ave,
Long Beach, CA 90803.

HAYDON, HAROLD (EMERSON)
Painter, Educator
Preferred Media: Oils, Mosaics, Stained Glass.
b Fort William, Ont, Apr 22, 09; U S citizen.
Study & Training: Univ Chicago, PhB, 30, MA, 31; Sch Art Inst
Chicago, 32-33.
Work in Public Collections: Pickering Col, Newmarket, Ont.
Commissions: Wool ark cover, Temple Beth Am, Chicago, Ill, 58;
glass mosaic murals, Temple Beth El, Gary, Ind, 59-60 & St
Cletus Roman Cath Church, La Grange, Ill, 63; mosaic & stained
glass murals, Sonia Shankman Orthogenic Sch, Univ Chicago, 66.
Exhibitions: Seven Exhibs Artists Chicago & Vicinity, 37-67 & 58th
Ann Am Painting—Abstr & Surrealist Art, 47, Art Inst Chicago;
Options, Mus Contemp Art, Chicago, 68.
Teaching: From instr art to asst prof, George Williams Col, 34-44;
from instr art to prof, Univ Chicago, 44-
Positions: Pres, Renaissance Soc Univ Chicago, 56-65; mem Cult
Adv Comt Mayor's Comt Econ & Cult Develop Chicago, 63-;
art critic, Chicago Sun-Times, 63-; chmn Art Comt, Nat Assess-
ment Educ Progress, 65; accreditation examr, N Cent Asn Schs,
66-
Memberships: Artists Equity Asn, Chicago Chap (pres, 50-52, 55-
57); Chicago Soc Artists (pres, 59-61); Nat Soc Mural Painters.
Publications: Auth, Great art treasures in America's small museums, 67.
Dealer: Richard Feigen Gallery, 226 E Ontario, Chicago, IL 60611.
Mailing Address: 5009 Greenwood Ave, Chicago, IL 60615.

HAYES, BARTLETT HARDING, JR
Art Administrator, Writer
b Andover, Mass, Aug 5, 04.
Study & Training: Phillips Acad, grad, 22; Harvard Col, AB, 26;
studied art in U S, 27-29; study in Europe, 27-33.
Teaching: Instr art, Phillips Acad, 33-; lectr fine arts & res assoc,
Grad Sch Educ, Harvard Univ, 64-68.
Positions: Asst cur, Addison Gallery Am Art, 34-40, dir, 40-69;
trustee, Am Fedn Arts, 40-70; mem ed bd, Art in Am, 44-69;
trustee, Mus Fine Arts, Boston, 49-71; trustee, Old Sturbridge
Village, 50-70; chmn comn to survey role of arts, Mass Inst
Technol, 52-54, 69-70; trustee, Boston Arts Festival, 52-65;
mem art comn, Smithsonian Inst, 54-; bd dirs, Print Coun Am,
57-63; bd ed, John Harvard Libr, 58-61; mem exec comt, Art in
Am Embassies Prog, Dept State, 65-; trustee, St Gaudens Mem,
67-72; trustee, Amon Carter Mus, Fort Worth, 68-; trustee, Inst
Contemp Art, Boston; mem vis comt, Dept Educ, Met Mus Art;
dir, Am Acad Rome, 69-; mem art adv comt, Internal Revenue
Serv, 70-
Memberships: Col Art Asn Am (secy, 59-64); fel Am Acad Arts &
Sci; Colonial Soc Mass.
Publications: Auth, Naked truth and personal vision & American
drawings; auth, Intent of art (TV series), NET; co-auth, Lay-
man's guide to modern art; co-ed, Artist and advocate; plus
others.
Mailing Address: Phillips St, Andover, MA 01810.

HAYES, DAVID VINCENT
Sculptor
Preferred Media: Metal, Ceramics.
b Hartford, Conn, Mar 15, 31.
Study & Training: Ogunquit Sch Painting & Sculpture, with Robert
Laurent; Univ Notre Dame, AB; Ind Univ, MFA, sculpture with
David Smith.
Work in Public Collections: Mus Mod Art, New York, N Y; Guggen-
heim Mus, New York; Mus Arts Decoratif, Paris; Mus Fine Arts,
Houston; Baltimore Mus Art.
Commissions: Ceramics, walls, De Porceleyne Fles, Delft, Holland,
67, Lee Kolker, Stanfordville, N Y, 70 & Elmira Col, 71, mural,
Great Southwest Corp, Atlanta, Ga, 68 & relief, comn by David
Anderson, Ardsley, N Y, 69.
Exhibitions: Salon Jeune Sculpture, Mus Rodin, Paris, 63; Salon
Mai, Mus Art Mod, Paris, 66; Carnegie Int, Pittsburgh, 67;
Smithsonian Organized Drawing Exhib, White House, Washington,
D C, 68; Jewelry 71, Art Gallery Ont, 71.
Teaching: Vis artist, Carpenter Art Ctr, Harvard Univ, 72.
Awards: Fulbright res grant, 61; John S Guggenheim Found fel, 61;
Nat Inst Arts & Lett Award, 64.
Dealers: Willard Gallery, 29 E 72nd St, New York, NY 10021; Agra
Gallery, 1721 DeSalles St, Washington, DC 20037.
Mailing Address: Box 109, Coventry, CT 06238.

HAYES, MARIAN
Educator, Art Historian
b Grand Rapids, Mich, May 23, 05.
Study & Training: Rockford Col, 21-23; Mt Holyoke Col, BA, 25;
N Y Univ Inst Fine Arts, univ fel, 28-29, MA, 29; Radcliffe Col,
MA, 30; Ecole Chartes, Sorbonne, Paris, 30; Harvard Univ, PhD,
44.
Teaching: Instr hist art, Mt Holyoke Col, 32-37, asst prof, 37-44,
assoc prof, 44-54, prof, 54-70; vis prof, Sweet Briar Col, fall 71.
Awards: Mt Holyoke Col fel, 28-29; Carnegie Corp scholar, 29-31.
Memberships: Soc Archit Historians; Int Ctr Medieval Art.
Research: Architecture of Connecticut Valley.
Mailing Address: 106 Woodbridge St, South Hadley, MA 01075.

HAYES, ROBERT T
Painter, Designer
b Bloomfield, Ind, Jan 18, 15.
Study & Training: Miami Univ.
Work in Public Collections: Many pvt & pub collections.
Exhibitions: John Herron Art Inst, Indianapolis, Ind; Butler Inst Am
Art, Youngstown, Ohio; New Orleans Mus Art, La; Philadelphia
Mus Art, Pa; Nat Acad Design; plus more than 100 other nat &
regional juried exhibs.
Positions: Art dir & v pres, Ralph Jones Advert, Inc.
Awards: Nat Watercolor Competition; Knickerbocker Artists, 64-72;
Watercolor U S A; Am Watercolor Soc; plus others; also ten one-
man exhibs.
Memberships: Am Watercolor Soc; Washington Watercolor Soc;
Knickerbocker Artists; Art Dirs Club Cincinnati; Cincinnati Prof
Art Club; plus others.
Mailing Address: 2859 Gilna Court, Cincinnati, OH 45211.

HAYES, TUA
Painter
Preferred Media: Oils, Watercolors.
b Anniston, Ala.
Study & Training: Converse Col, BA; Columbia Univ Teacher's Col;
also with Henry Lee McFee.
Work in Public Collections: Wilmington Soc Fine Arts, Del; Univ
Del, Newark; Chester Co Art Asn, West Chester, Pa; Converse
Col, Spartanburg, S C.
Exhibitions: Nat Jury Show, Chatauqua, N Y, 59; five shows, Univ
Del Regional Exhib, 66-71; Philadelphia Pro-Show, Pa, 67; Nat
Acad Design, New York, N Y, 70; Baltimore Mus Regional Show,
Md.
Awards: First prize, oil painting, 65 & first prize, drawing, 67, Del
Art Mus.
Memberships: Philadelphia Art Alliance; Studio Group, Inc (pres,
54-56); Wilmington Soc Fine Arts (bd dirs, 62-).
Mailing Address: 3 Carriage Rd, Wilmington, DE 19807.

HAYNES, DOUGLAS H
Painter, Educator
Preferred Media: Acrylics, Mixed Media.
b Regina, Sask, Jan 1, 36.
Study & Training: Provincial Inst Technol & Art, Calgary, Alta, with
R Spickett; Royal Acad Fine & Applied Arts, The Hague, Holland.
Work in Public Collections: Edmonton Art Gallery, Alta; Confedera-
tion Art Gallery, Charlottetown, Prince Edward Island; London
Pub Mus & Art Gallery, Ont; Univ Calgary, Alta.

Exhibitions: 5th Biennial Exhib Can Art, London, Eng & Ottawa, Can,
63 & 6th Biennial Exhib, Ottawa, 65; All Alberta '70, Edmonton,
70; West '71 Exhib, Edmonton, 71; Royal Can Acad Arts 91st Ann,
Montreal, 71.
Teaching: Asst prof art, Univ Alta, 70-
Positions: Art adv, Govt Alta, 67-70.
Awards: Govt of Neth scholar, 60; All Alta First Prize, Jacox Gal-
lery, 65; Can Coun Sr Award, Can Govt, 67.
Bibliography: N Yates (auth), Three from Edmonton, Arts Can,
10/69; K Wilkin (auth), Western Canada, a survey, Art in Am,
5-6/72.
Memberships: Assoc Royal Can Acad Arts; Univ Art Asn Can.
Dealer: Terry Burrell, 207-5210 122nd St, Edmonton, Alta, Can.
Mailing Address: 14312 Ravine Dr, Edmonton, Alta, Can.

HAYTER, STANLEY WILLIAM
Painter, Instructor
b London, Eng, Dec 27, 01.
Study & Training: King's Col, Univ London.
Work in Public Collections: Nat Gallery Art, Washington, D C; Mus
Mod Art, New York, N Y; Victoria & Albert Mus, London, Eng;
Bibliot Nat, Paris, France; Bibliot Royale, Brussels, Belg; plus
many others.
Exhibitions: Many exhibs in U S, Eng, France, Ger, Switz, Belg,
Japan, Italy & Mex.
Teaching: Lect, Slade Sch & Royal Col Art, London & in many
univs, cols & art schs in U S.
Positions: Dir, Atelier 17, Paris, France.
Awards: Chevalier, Legion d'Honneur, France; Commander of the
Brit Empire; prize, Tokyo Print Biennale, 60; plus others.
Publications: Auth, New ways of gravure, London, 49; London & New
York, 65; auth, About prints, London, 62; auth, Nature and art of
motion, New York, 65; contribr to Art News, Transformation,
Graphis, Documents & other publ.
Mailing Address: 12 Rue Cassini, Paris 14, France.

HAYWARD, PETER
Painter, Sculptor
Preferred Media: Oils, Bronze.
b Keene, N H, Nov 8, 05.
Study & Training: Middlebury Col, 21-23.
Work in Public Collections: USN Combat Art Collection, Washington,
D C; Hawaii State Found for Culture & the Arts, State of Hawaii;
also in pub collection in Rochester, Miami, Denver & Syracuse.
Commissions: Destroyers on Maneuvers, San Diego to Pearl Harbor,
60; The Proteus, Guam, 66; Apollo 8 Splashdown & Recovery, 68
& Apollo 15 Splashdown & Recovery, Navy Art Cooperation &
Liaison Comt.
Exhibitions: Washington Sq Outdoor Art Show (formerly Hors de
Concours), New York, N Y, 56-63; Salmagundi Fall Show, New
York, 60-70; Four Easter Art Festivals, Honolulu, Hawaii, 63-
71; Nat Acad Design Shows, New York, 66, 68 & 70; Artists of
Hawaii, Honolulu Acad, 68-70.
Teaching: Instr sculpture, Riverdale Country Sch for Girls; instr
oil painting, pvt studio, New York summers & Honolulu winters,
62-67.
Positions: Treas, Am Artists Prof League, 57-58.
Awards: Proctor Prize in portrait sculpture, Nat Acad Design, 48-
49; grand prize all media, Washington Sq Outdoor Art Show, 56-
58; foreign travel prize, Luethansa Air Lines, 59.
Memberships: Salmagundi Club; Asn Honolulu Artists; Windward
Artists Guild (pres, 69-70); Lahaina Art Asn.
Dealers: Grand Central Galleries, 40 Vanderbilt Ave, New York, NY
10017; Royal Hawaiian Gallery, 2259 Kalakaua Ave, Honolulu, HI
96815.
Mailing Address: 53-033 Kamehameha Hwy, Hauula, HI 96717.

HAZEN, JOSEPH H
Collector
b Kingston, N Y.
Collection: Late nineteenth and early twentieth century paintings.
Mailing Address: 1345 Ave of the Americas, New York, NY 10019.

HEAD, GEORGE BRUCE
Painter, Designer
Preferred Media: Acrylics.
b St Boniface, Man, Feb 14, 31.
Study & Training: Univ Man, Dipl(Fine Art), 53.
Work in Public Collections: Nat Gallery Can; London Pub Libr &
Art Mus; Montreal Mus Art; Confedn Centre, P E I; Art Gallery
Hamilton; plus others.
Commissions: Oil on panels, Man Teachers Col, 59; art walls in
enamel, Benson & Hedges, Winnipeg, Can, 60.
Exhibitions: Commonwealth Arts Festival, Carduff Whales, 60;
Nat Gallery, Australian Art Tour, 67-68; Tenth Winnipeg Art
Gallery Biennial, 70; Montreal Spring Exhib; Nat Gallery Can
Biennial; plus others.

Positions: Graphic designer, Can Broadcasting Corp, 56-
Awards: Hon mention & purchase prize, Winnipeg Show, Winnipeg
    Art Gallery; 20th Western Ont Exhib purchase award; Benson &
    Hedges Art Wall Design Award, 72.
Bibliography: H Ochi (auth), article, In: Ideas Mag; W Hertis (auth),
    Graphics annual, Graphic Press; article, In: Art Director Ann;
    plus others.
Dealer: Mixmedia, 61 Gertie St, Winnipeg, Man. R3A 1B5, Can.
Mailing Address: 50 Brewster Bay, Winnipeg, Man. R2C 2X3, Can.

HEAD, ROBERT WILLIAM
    Painter, Educator
Preferred Media: Mixed Media.
b Springfield, Ill, Aug 6, 41.
Study & Training: MacMurray Col, BA(art educ), 63, with Sidman &
    Foresterling; Kent State Univ, MFA, 65, with Shock, Morrow,
    Petersham & Short; Colo Outward Bound Sch, 71.
Work in Public Collections: J B Speed Art Mus, Louisville, Ky; Mint
    Mus, Charlotte, N C; Del Mar Col, Corpus Christi, Tex; Mac-
    Murray Col, Jacksonville, Ill; Massillon Mus, Ohio.
Exhibitions: Ball State Nat Drawing Show, Muncie, Ind; Bucknell Nat
    Drawing Exhib, Lewisburg, Pa; Mainstreams Int Painting Exhib,
    Marietta, Ohio; Brooks Mem Gallery Invitational, Memphis, Tenn;
    Weatherspoon Ann Drawing Exhib, Univ N C.
Teaching: Assoc prof drawing, painting & design, Murray State Univ,
    65-; assoc prof drawing & introd art, World Campus Afloat, Chap-
    man Col, spring, 70 & 72.
Awards: Distinguished alumni award, MacMurray Col, 69; merit
    award for excellence in teaching, Murray State Univ, 70; first
    purchase award, Piedmont Graphic Exhib, Mint Mus.
Memberships: Col Art Asn; Mus Mod Art; Ky Art Educ Asn; Nat
    Audubon Soc; Ky Ornith Soc.
Mailing Address: Box 438, Art Dept, Murray State University, Uni-
    versity Station, Murray, KY 42071.

HEALY, ARTHUR K D
    Painter, Lecturer
Preferred Media: Watercolors.
b New York, N Y, Oct 15, 02.
Study & Training: Princeton Univ, BA, 24, MFA, 26; Ecole Beaux
    Arts, French Govt grant, 25; Princeton Univ, MFA, 26.
Work in Public Collections: Harvard Univ, Mass; Addison Gallery
    Am Art, Andover, Mass; New Britain Mus, Conn; Carnojoharie
    Mus, N Y; Norwich Univ, Northfield, Vt.
Commissions: Many painting comns in U S, Mex & Europe.
Exhibitions: Am Watercolor Soc, New York, 36-70; Philadelphia
    Watercolor Soc, 38-60; Audubon Artists, New York, 40-70; each
    Boston Art Festivals.
Collections Arranged: Many exhibs for Middlebury Col, 44-69; early
    Am Painting By B F Mason 1804-71, Sheldon Mus, Middlebury,
    Vt, 71.
Teaching: Emer prof hist fine arts, Middlebury Col, 44-49; lectr
    am art, Univ Vt; lectr am art, Shelburne Mus, Vt.
Positions: Mem bd, Yaddo Found, 54-; pres & chmn bd, Sheldon
    Mus, 57-; mem Bd Hist Sites Vt, State of Vt, 69-71.
Awards: Zabriski Prize, Am Watercolor Soc, 38; Prizes for water-
    colors, Norwich Univ, 68-70 & Boston Festival Arts.
Memberships: Am Watercolor Soc; Audubon Artists; Boston Water-
    color Soc; Boston Soc Independent Artists; Southern Vt Artists.
Research: Early American painting; subject matter of American
    historical museums.
Publications: Co-auth, Two journeyman painters with Alfred Frank-
    enstein, Art Am; illusr, State of Maine; illusr, Indian folklore;
    auth, many rev & criticisms, Middlebury Col Newslett, Art Am
    & other mags.
Dealers: Deeley Gallery, Manchester, VT 05254; Gallery 7W, Wood-
    stock, VT 05091.
Mailing Address: R D 3, Middlebury, VT 05753.

HEATON, MAURICE
    Designer, Craftsman
b Neuchatel, Switz, Apr 2, 00; U S citizen.
Study & Training: Ethical Cult Schs, 15-19; Stevens Inst Technol,
    20-21.
Work in Public Collections: Metrop Mus Art, New York, N Y; New-
    ark Mus Art, N J; Corning Mus Glass, N Y; Cooper Union Mus
    Art & Mus Contemp Crafts, New York.
Commissions: Glass mural, Polygraphic Co Am; stained glass
    windows, glass murals & lighting fixtures for pvt comns, 23-
Exhibitions: One-man & group shows in over thirty mus & galleries
    in U S & Can plus traveling exhibs.
Teaching: Lect on glass to art & craft orgn.
Awards: Medal, Boston Soc Arts & Crafts, 56; first prize for glass,
    Wichita Art Asn, 60.
Memberships: Artist-Craftsmen New York; York State Craftsmen;
    Rockland Found; Am Crafts Coun; Boston Soc Arts & Crafts.
Mailing Address: Old Mill Rd, Valley Cottage, NY 10989.

HEBALD, MILTON ELTING
    Sculptor, Graphic Artist
Preferred Media: Bronze, Wood, Lithography.
b New York, N Y, May 24, 17.
Study & Training: Art Stud League, 27-28, with Ann Goldwaithe;
    Nat Acad Design, 31-32, with Gordon Samstag; Master Inst
    United Arts, 31-34; Beaux-Arts Inst Design, 32-35.
Work in Public Collections: Whitney Mus Am Art; Philadelphia Mus
    Art; Tel-Aviv Mus, Israel; Va Mus Fine Arts; Joyce Mus, Dub-
    lin, Ireland; plus many others.
Commissions: Bronze frieze, Pan-Am Terminal, Idlewild Airport,
    N Y; Ackland Mem, Univ N C; James Joyce Monument, Zurich,
    Switz, 66; Marshall Field Mem, Sun Times Bldg, Chicago, Ill,
    66; Tempest Group Bronze, Central Park, New York, N Y, 72;
    plus many others.
Exhibitions: Arte Figurativo, Rome, Italy, 64 & 67; Carnegie Inst
    Pittsburgh, Pa, 67; Va Mus Fine Arts, 67; Norton Art Gallery,
    West Palm Beach, Fla, 69; one-man show, Mickelson Gallery,
    Wash, 72; plus many other group & one-man shows.
Teaching: Instr, Brooklyn Mus Sch Art, 46-51; instr, Cooper Union,
    46-53; instr, Univ Minn, 49; instr, Skowhegan Sch Painting &
    Sculpture, summers 50-52; instr, Long Beach State Univ, Calif,
    summer 68.
Awards: Second prize, Pa Acad Fine Arts, 51; first prize New York
    City Dept Pub Works, for E Bronx Tuberculosis Hosp, 52; Prix
    de Rome, 55-58; plus others.
Bibliography: Martha C Cheney (auth), Modern art in America,
    McGraw-Hill, 39; C Ludwig Brumme (auth), Contemporary
    American sculpture, Crown Publ, 48; Frank Getlein (auth), Mil-
    ton Hebald, Viking, 71.
Memberships: Fel Am Acad in Rome: An Am Group.
Mailing Address: Viale Trastevere 60, Rome, Italy.

HEBERLING, GLEN AUSTIN
    Painter, Illustrator
Preferred Media: Oils, Watercolors, Acrylics, Tempera, Pastels,
    Synthetic Resins.
b Ambridge, Pa, Nov 18, 15.
Study & Training: Ad Art Studio Sch, Pittsburgh, Pa, with Ray Sim-
    boli, 36; Art Inst Pittsburgh, with Milan Petrovitz & Vincent Nes-
    bert, scholar, 36-38; Art Stud League New York, with many fa-
    mous Am & European artist instr, 46-51.
Work in Public Collections: Old Economy Hist Mus, Ambridge;
    Ladycliff Col, Highland Falls, N Y.
Commissions: World War II Mem (mural in oil) & portrait in oil,
    for Highland Falls High Sch, comn by 50th Anniversary Comt,
    50; three landscapes & watercol, Marine Midland Bank, High-
    land Falls, 67; plus many pvt comns.
Exhibitions: Assoc Artists Pittsburgh, Pa Ann Regional, Carnegie
    Mus, ten times from 38-47; Am Watercolor Soc Nat Ann, Nat
    Acad Design Galleries, N Y, 44-46; New Year's Show Regional
    Ann, Butler Inst Am Art, Youngstown, Ohio, 45; U S Army Arts
    Contest Nat, Nat Gallery Art, Washington, D C, 45; Artists of the
    Upper Hudson Regional Ann, Albany Inst Art & Hist, N Y, 62.
Teaching: Instr & lectr painting I & II, Ladycliff Col, 61-71.
Positions: Illusr, U S Mil Acad, West Point, N Y, 58-71.
Awards: Hon mention for watercolor, Assoc Artists Pittsburgh Ann,
    Carnegie Mus, 44; first prize & hon mention for watercolors, 2nd
    Serv Comd, Army Arts Contest, Art Stud League New York, 45.
Publications: Illusr, Handbook on physical education, 44; illusr, En
    busco de oro negro, 59; illusr, Assembly, Asn Grads, West
    Point, 66; illusr, Kepler & the discovery of his planetary laws,
    69; illusr, Engineering fundamentals, 70.
Dealer: Hyde Park Art Gallery, Rte 9 at Grandway, Wappinger
    Falls, NY 12590.
Mailing Address: 58 Church St, Highland Falls, NY 10928.

HEBERT, JULIEN
    Sculptor, Designer
b Rigaud, P Q, Aug 19, 17.
Study & Training: Ecole Beaux-Arts, Montreal; Univ Montreal; also
    with Zadkine, Paris, France.
Exhibitions: Int & Can Sect, Milan Trienniale, 54; Design Exhibs,
    Can & abroad.
Teaching: Instr hist art, Ecole Beaux-Arts, Montreal; furniture de-
    sign, Inst Applied Arts, Montreal.
Awards: Design awards, Nat Indust Design Coun & others, 53-58.
Memberships: Asn Can Indust Designers; Interior Decorating Soc
    Quebec; Sculptors Soc Can.
Mailing Address: 4211 Westhill Ave, Montreal, P Q, Can.

HECHT, H HARTMAN
    Collector, Patron
b Baltimore, Md, Mar 12, 37.
Study & Training: Washington & Lee Univ, BA; mus admin at George
    Washington Univ; spec mus tech training, Corcoran Gallery Art
    with Gudmund Vigetl.

Teaching: Lect, Am contemp art, sculpture and Am mus tech, touring Australia, New Zealand, Malaysia, The Philippines, Hong Kong, Taiwan, Japan, Thailand, Ceylon & India.
Positions: Grad asst & admin asst, Corcoran Gallery Art, 62-63; asst dir, Mus African Art, 64-66, chmn mus comt to select & purchase works of contemp Negro artists, 65; chmn art exhib, Capitol Hill Restoration Soc, 65; asst for mus prog, Nat Endowment for the Arts, 66-68; exec dir, Artmongers & Manufactory, Inc, 68.
Awards: John Graham Award for contrib to arts, Washington & Lee Univ, 59.
Art Interests: Established the nucleus collection of graphics for Washington & Lee University, 58, and continuing to enlarge collection. Also, corporation commissions unique designs from contemporary sculptors to be produced in unlimited editions for the American art market.
Collections: Contemporary oils, graphics and sculpture, most recent emphasis on contemporary sculpture. Entire collection exhibited at Washington & Lee University, 59, oils and paintings, 63-65; graphics drawings and sculpture at University of Virginia, 63.
Publications: Auth, articles on art activities in Australia and New Zealand, In: Washington Int Arts Lett, 5/64.
Mailing Address: 9216 Old Mt Vernon Rd, Alexandria, VA 22309.

HEDDEN-SELLMAN, ZELDA
Painter, Instructor
Preferred Media: Acrylics, Watercolors.
b Farmington, Ill.
Study & Training: Bradley Univ, BS & MA; Ohio Univ; Harvard Univ; Western Reserve Univ; also with Ben Shahn, Arnold Blanch & Gladys Rockmore Davis.
Work in Public Collections: Manias Manor, Peoria, Ill; Expos Bldg, Springfield, Ill; Spoon River Col, Canton, Ill.
Exhibitions: Art Schools, U S A, traveling exhib, 50; Old Northwest Territory Show, Springfield, 52; Ohio Valley Watercolor Show, Athens, 53; Ill State Mus, Springfield, 59; three-man show, Kottler Gallery, New York, N Y, 72.
Teaching: Instr art, Ind State Univ, Terre Haute, 53-54; instr art, Ill Cent Col, Peoria, 69-71; instr art, Spoon River Col, 66-
Positions: Dir Peoria Art Ctr Sch, 54-56.
Awards: Cent Ill Artists Award.
Publications: Auth, Treasures in the snow, 64.
Dealer: Upstairs Gallery, Lakeview Center for Arts & Sciences, 1125 W Lake Ave, Peoria, IL 61614.
Mailing Address: 241 Timberlane, Metamora, IL 61548.

HEFLIN, TOM PAT
Painter, Designer
Preferred Media: Oils, Acrylics.
b Monticello, Ark, July 18, 34.
Study & Training: Northeast La State Col; Chicago Art Inst.
Work in Public Collections: Marietta Col, Ohio; Burpee Art Mus, Rockford, Ill; Univ Ill, Champaign; main lobby of Hill Sherman, Meroni, Gross & Simpson Off Bldg, Chicago, Ill.
Exhibitions: Abercrombie & Fitch Nat Sports in Art, New York, N Y, 68; Nat Design Ctr, New York, 69; Mainstreams Int, Marietta Col, 71 & 72; Chicago Art Inst, 71 & 72; House of Congress, Washington, D C, 72.
Teaching: Instr painting, Burpee Art Mus, 69-71; instr painting, Rock Valley Col, 70-
Awards: One-man show award, U S Fine Arts Registry, New York, 69; purchase award, Mainstreams 1/72 Int, 72; first prize for nationwide bicentennial medal design, Franklin Mint, 72.
Bibliography: Article, In: Famous Artists Mag, 70.
Memberships: Rockford Art Asn.
Dealer: Merrill Chase Galleries, Oakbrook Center, Oakbrook, IL 60521.
Mailing Address: 2116 Springbrook Ave, Rockford, IL 61107.

HEIDEL, FREDERICK (H)
Painter, Educator
b Corvallis, Ore, Dec 29, 15.
Study & Training: Univ Ore, BS, with Andrew Vincent, David McCosh & Lance Hart; Art Inst Chicago, Anna Louise Raymond For traveling fel, BFA & MFA, with Boris Anisfeld & Francis Chapin.
Work in Public Collections: World Bk Art Collection, Chicago, Ill; Portland Art Mus, Ore; Hazeltine Collection, Mus Art, Eugene, Ore; Eastern Ore Col, La Grande, Ore; Kaiser Found, Portland.
Commissions: Mural, Lane Co Comn, Lane Co Courthouse, Eugene, 58; fused glass wall, comn by Sally Stafford, Eugene, 70; fused glass Panel, Brock Dixon House, Forest Grove, Ore, 70; laminated glass construction, Portland State Univ, Sci I Bldg, 71; laminated glass window, comn by Mr & Mrs Marvin Witt, Portland.

Exhibitions: Drawing & Watercolor Exhib, Metrop Mus Art, New York, 51; Sao Paulo Third Biennial, Brazil, 56; Second Pac Coast Biennial, West Coast, 57; Vancouver Invitational, B C, 58; The West: 80 Contemporaries, 67.
Teaching: Instr painting, Long Beach City Col, 46-49; instr painting, Univ Ore, 49-53; prof painting, Portland State Univ, 51-, head dept art, 55-
Positions: Chmn artist mem, Portland Art Mus, 52-53; mem bd, Albina Art Ctr, Portland, 64-67.
Awards: Painting award, San Francisco Mus Art, 48; Chapelbrook Found fel, 67.
Bibliography: Rachel Griffin (auth), Painting and sculpture of the Pacific Northwest, Portland Art Mus, 59; painting reproduced, In: World Bk Encycl, 65-72; Nancy McCauley (auth), Article, In: Art Wk, Vol 13, No 15.
Memberships: Portland Art Asn (art comt, 53-55); Col Art Asn Am; Art Ore.
Mailing Address: Dept of Art, Portland State University, Portland, OR 97207.

HEILEMANN, CHARLES OTTO
Designer, Educator
b New York, N Y, May 16, 18.
Study & Training: Parsons Sch Design, dipl; Parsons Paris Atelier, cert; Crondon Sch Art, Eng.
Teaching: Instr interior design, Fashion Inst Technol, 58-69, chmn dept, 69-71, assoc dean art & design div, 71-
Positions: Free lance illusr, Condé-Nast, House & Garden, New York, 47-65; illusr, Skidmore, Owings & Merril, 66-70; designer, Burgin Int, New York, 71-
Mailing Address: 330 E 33rd St, New York, NY 10001.

HEILOMS, MAY
Painter
Preferred Media: Oils, Watercolors, Ink, Casein.
U S citizen.
Study & Training: Hunter Col; Art Stud League New York.
Work in Public Collections: Philadelphia Mus, Pa; Norfolk Mus, Va; Okla Mus; Samuel Fleisher Art Found, Philadelphia; Bat Yam Mus, Israel.
Exhibitions: Pa Acad Fine Arts, Philadelphia; Denver Mus, Colo; Corcoran Gallery, Washington, D C; Okla Mus, Oklahoma City; Butler Inst Am Art, Youngstown, Ohio.
Teaching: Instr art, City Col New York, 60-62; instr art, Fashion Inst Technol, 63-65.
Positions: V pres, Nat Asn Women Artists, 60.
Awards: Medal of honor for oil, Painters & Sculptors Soc N J, 52; Elizabeth Morse Genios Mem Watercolor Prize, Nat Asn Women Artists, 60; Nat Soc Painters Casein Prize, 70; plus others.
Memberships: Painters & Sculptors Soc N J (hon life pres); Audubon Artists (v pres, 56-58); Nat Soc Painters Casein & Acrylics (dir, 65-); Allied Artists (dir); N Y Soc Women Artists (dir & chmn mem).
Mailing Address: 340 W 28th St, New York, NY 10001.

HEINEMAN, BERNARD, JR
Collector
b New York, N Y, Nov 29, 23.
Study & Training: Williams Col, BA.
Collection: Twentieth century American art, including Prendergast, Demuth, Dove, Marin, Sheeler, Tam, Jacob Lawrence and Heliker and sculpture by Lachaise, Cook and Don Russell.
Mailing Address: c/o Heineman & Co, 151 W 40th St, New York, NY 10018.

HEINEMANN, PETER
Painter, Educator
Preferred Media: Oils.
b Denver, Colo, Apr 22, 31.
Study & Training: Black Mountain Col, one year, with Joseph Albers, 48-49.
Commissions: Multi-figure oil mural, New York Coun Arts, N Y, 71-72.
Exhibitions: Nat Inst Arts & Letters, New York, 60, 61, 72 & two in 72.
Teaching: Instr painting & drawing, Sch Visual Arts, New York, 60-
Mailing Address: 229 Grand St, New York, NY 10013.

HEINZ, MR & MRS HENRY J, II
Collectors
Mr Heinz, b Sewickley, Pa, July 10, 08.
Study & Training: Mr Heinz, Yale Univ, AB, 31; Trinity Col, Cambridge Univ, 31-32; Bowling Green State Univ, hon LLD, 43, Allegheny Col, 44, Univ Pittsburgh, 60.
Positions: Mr Heinz, trustee, Carnegie Inst; chmn Agribus Coun, Yale Univ Art Gallery.
Mailing Address: Goodwood, Sewickley, PA 15143.

HEISKELL, DIANA
    Painter, Designer
b Paris, France; U S citizen.
Work in Public Collections: Santa Barbara Mus Art, Calif; Slater
    Mus, Norwich, Conn.
Exhibitions: Whitney Mus Am Art Ann, two yrs; Boston Arts Festi-
    val; Berkshire Art Asn, Pittsfield, Mass; De Cordova & Dana
    Mus, Lincoln, Mass; Southern Vt Art Ctr, Manchester.
Awards: Hon mention, Berkshire Art Asn; Grumbacher Prize,
    Southern Vt Art Ctr.
Memberships: Southern Vt Art Asn (trustee); Berkshire Art Asn.
Mailing Address: Marlboro, VT 05344.

HELCK, (CLARENCE) PETER
    Illustrator, Writer
Preferred Media: Casein, Tempera.
b New York, N Y, June 17, 93.
Study & Training: Art Stud League New York, with Frank Brangwyn,
    Harry Wickey & Lewis Daniel.
Work in Public Collections: Metrop Mus Art, New York; Carnegie
    Inst, Pittsburgh; Mus Am Art, New Britain, Conn; Sheldon Swope
    Galleries, Terre Haute, Ind; Montagu Mus, Beaulieu, Eng.
Exhibitions: Royal Acad, London, 23; Pittsburgh Int, 35; many Nat
    Acad Design Exhibs, 40-50; one-man shows, Art Art Ctr, Little
    Rock, 64 & Sheldon Swope Galleries, 66.
Teaching: Mem faculty illus, Famous Artists Sch, Westport, Conn,
    48-
Positions: Art ed, Bulb Horn, Boston, Mass, 50-; assoc ed, Antique
    Automobile, Hershey, Pa, 50-; artist & auth, Automobile Quart,
    New York, 62-
Awards: Pennell Medal, Philadelphia Acad, 28; five medals, New
    York Art Dirs, 31-51; Hall of Fame Gold Medal, Soc Illusr, 68.
Bibliography: Grace Rogers (auth), The work of C P Helck, The
    Studio, London, 23; Y Inomoto (auth), Auto art, Automobile Illus,
    Tokyo, 71.
Memberships: Nat Acad Design; Am Watercolor Soc; Soc Illusr; Fa-
    mous Artists Sch; Allied Artists Am.
Publications: Illusr, Sat Eve Post, 35-55; illusr, Country Gentle-
    man, 40-50; illusr, Esquire, 40-50; auth & illusr, The checkered
    flag, Scribner, 61; auth & illusr, Automobile Quart, 62-70.
Mailing Address: Boston Corners, R D 2, Millerton, NY 12546.

HELD, AL
    Painter
b New York, N Y, Oct 12, 28.
Study & Training: Art Stud League New York; Acad Grande
    Chaumiere, Paris, France.
Work in Public Collections: Brandeis Univ; Geigy Chem Corp;
    Kunsthalle, Basel, Switz.
Exhibitions: Systemic Painting, Solomon R Guggenheim Mus, 66;
    Jewish Mus, 67; Documenta IV, Kassel, Ger, 68; one-man shows,
    San Francisco Mus Art & Corcoran Gallery Art, 68; plus many
    other group & one-man shows.
Awards: Logan Medal, Art Inst Chicago, 64; Guggenheim Found fel,
    66.
Bibliography: Barbara Rose (auth), American art since 1900, a
    critical history, Praeger, 67; Al Held (exhib catalogue), San
    Francisco Mus Art; Gregory Battcock (ed), Minimal art: a
    critical anthology, E P Dutton, 68.
Dealer: Donald Morris Gallery, 20082 Livernois, Detroit, MI
    48221.
Mailing Address: 435 W Broadway, New York, NY 10012.

HELD, ALMA M
    Painter
Preferred Media: Oils, Watercolors.
b Lemars, Iowa.
Study & Training: State Univ Iowa, BA & MA, with Charles A Cum-
    ming; Nat Acad Design, New York, N Y, with Sydney Dickinson;
    Cape Cod Sch Art, Provincetown, Mass, with Charles Hawthorne
    & Richard Miller.
Work in Public Collections: Waterloo Munic Galleries, Iowa; por-
    trait & landscape paintings, Fort Dodge Pub Schs, Iowa; land-
    scape, YWCA, Waterloo; two paintings, First Congregational
    Church, Waterloo; Garwin Pub Libr, Iowa.
Commissions: Portrait of Jack Logan, Logan Jr High Sch, Waterloo,
    62; portrait, Cedar Falls Woman's Club, Iowa, 71; Flight Into
    Egypt (painting), First Congregational Church, Waterloo, 71.
Exhibitions: Midwest Show, Kansas City Art Inst, Mo, 35; Joslyn
    Mus Art, Omaha, Nebr, 35 & 46; 16th Ann Iowa Artists Exhib,
    Des Moines Art Ctr, Iowa, 64; Ithaca Collects, Ithaca Col Mus
    Art, N Y, 69; 8th Ann Waterloo Munic Galleries Show, 71; plus
    one other.
Teaching: Formerly instr art & later assoc, State Univ Iowa.
Awards: Iowa State Fair Gold Medal, Iowa Art Salon, 26; Purchase
    Prize, First Iowa TV Art Show, Waterloo, 68; first prize, Com-
    petitive Art Show Nat Dairy Cattle Cong, Waterloo, 68.

Memberships: Cent Area Chap Artists Equity Asn; Waterloo Art
    Asn; Cent Iowa Art Asn.
Mailing Address: 623 W Eighth St, Waterloo, IA 50702.

HELD, JULIUS S
    Educator, Writer
b Mosbach, Ger, Apr 15, 05; U S citizen.
Study & Training: Univ Heidelberg, 23; Univ Berlin, 23-24, 27-28;
    Univ Vienna, 25-26, 29; Univ Freiburg, PhD, 30.
Teaching: Lectr, New York Univ, 35-41; Carnegie lectr, Nat Gallery
    Can, 36-37; lectr art, Barnard Col, Columbia Univ, 37-44, asst
    prof, 44-50, assoc prof, 50-54, prof, 54-70, chmn dept art hist,
    67-70, prof emer, 70-; vis lectr Bryn Mawr Col, 43-44; vis prof,
    New Sch Social Res, 46-47; vis prof, Yale Univ, 54, 58; Robert
    Sterling Clark prof art, Williams Col, 69; Andrew W Mellon
    prof, Univ Pittsburgh, 72-73.
Positions: Asst, Staatliche Mus, Berlin, 31-33; mem ed bd, Art
    Bull, 42-; mem ed bd, Art Quart, 59-; consult, Mus Arte Ponce,
    P R, 59-; mem, Inst for Advan Study, Princeton Univ, 67; pres,
    Am Friends Mus Plantin Moretus, Antwerp, 69-
Awards: Belg-Am Educ Found spec advan fel, 47; Fulbright fel, 52-
    53; Guggenheim fels, 52-53, 66-67.
Memberships: Col Art Asn Am (dir, 59-64, mem ed bd); Mediaeval
    Acad Am; Renaissance Soc Am; Soc Hist of Art Francaise;
    Deutscher Verein fur Kunstwissenschaft.
Research: Flemish and Dutch art.
Collection: Old master paintings and drawings.
Publications: Auth, Rubens, selected drawings, Phaidon, 59; auth,
    Rembrandt's Aristotle and other Rembrandt essays, Princeton,
    69; auth, Rubens' leopards, Wittenborn, 71; co-auth, Baroque
    art, 71 & 17th & 18th century art: Baroque & Rococo, 72, Abrams;
    plus many earlier publ; contribr, articles in art periodicals.
Mailing Address: 81 Monument Ave, Bennington, VT 05201.

HELD, PHILIP
    Painter, Instructor
Preferred Media: Oils.
b New York, N Y, June 2, 20.
Study & Training: Art Stud League New York, 38-42 & 46, with
    Kuniyoshi, Fiene, Blanch, Lee & Vytlacil; Sch Art Studies, New
    York, 47-48, with Moses Soyer; Columbia Univ Teachers Col,
    49, serigraphy with Arthur Young.
Work in Public Collections: Berkshire Mus, Pittsfield, Mass; Univ
    Mass, Amherst; Philadelphia Mus Lending Collection; Art Stud
    League New York Collection.
Exhibitions: Woodstock Artists, Riverside Mus, New York, 60;
    U S A Paintings, Pa Acad Fine Arts Ann, 62; Mod Masters,
    Brown Univ, 63; Recent Accessions, Univ Mass, 66; Drawings
    1970, St John's Univ, 70.
Teaching: Instr fine arts, Scarborough Sch, N Y, 47-52; instr fine
    arts, Fieldston Sch, Riverdale, N Y, 52-62; chmn dept, 62-71;
    instr & coordr Fine Arts Prog, Booker-Bay Haven Sch, Sarasota,
    Fla, 71-72.
Awards: Second prize for printmaking, Am Vet Soc Artists, 49;
    Presentation Exhib Award, Woodstock Artists Asn, 64; H Klein-
    ert Found, grant, 66.
Bibliography: V Raynor (auth), Art reviews, Arts Mag, 12/60;
    Gordon Brown (auth), Art voices 1964-65, Art Voices, 65; V
    Donohue (auth), Art reviews, Philadelphia Sun Bull, 10/20/68.
Memberships: Life mem Art Stud League New York; Woodstock
    Artists Asn.
Dealers: Fontana Gallery, 307 Iona Ave, Narberth, Philadelphia, PA
    19072; Polari Gallery, Woodstock, NY 12498.
Mailing Address: 3035 Wood St, Sarasota, FL 33580.

HELIKER, JOHN EDWARD
    Painter, Educator
Preferred Media: Oils, Watercolors.
b Yonkers, N Y, 09.
Study & Training: Art Stud League New York, N Y; hon DFA, Colby
    Col.
Work in Public Collections: Metrop Mus Art, New York; Cleveland
    Mus Art, Ohio; Whitney Mus Am Art, New York; Hirshhorn
    Found; Philadelphia Mus Art.
Exhibitions: Am Painting Today, Metrop Mus Art, 50; Nature in
    Abstraction, 58, Art of the United States 1670-1966, 66 & Retro-
    spective Exhib, 68, Whitney Mus Am Art; World's Fair, Brus-
    sels, 58.
Teaching: Prof painting, Columbia Univ.
Positions: V pres, Am Acad Arts & Lett, 72-
Awards: First W A Clark Prize, Corcoran Gallery Art, 41; Prix de
    Rome, 48; Award of Merit Medal, Am Acad Arts & Lett, 67.
Bibliography: J I H Baur (auth), New decade, 55 & L Goodrich (auth),
    John Heliker, 68, Whitney Mus Am Art; W Nordness (auth), Art
    U S A now, Viking, 62.

Memberships: Nat Inst Arts & Lett.
Dealer: Kraushaar Galleries, 1055 Madison Ave, New York, NY 10028.
Mailing Address: 865 West End Ave, Apt 3C, New York, NY 10025.

HELIOFF, ANNE GRAILE (MRS BENJAMIN HIRSCHBERG)
Painter
Preferred Media: Oils, Acrylics.
b Liverpool Eng; U S citizen.
Study & Training: Art Stud League New York with Nicolaides, Homer Boss & Kuniyoshi; also pvt summer classes; Hans Hofmann Sch.
Exhibitions: Paintings of the Year, all maj mus of the U S; Pa Acad Fine Arts, Philadelphia; Dedication Exhibition, Nat Gallery Art, Washington, D C; Art U S A, New York, N Y & all maj cities of the U S; American Exhibition, Palazzo Uecchio, Florence, Italy & Mus Naples, Italy, 72; plus four solo shows in New York galleries.
Positions: Mem bd control, Art Stud League New York; mem, U S Deleg to 5th Cong, Int Asn Artists, Tokyo, Japan, 66; exec bd, Phoenix Gallery, New York, N Y, 70-72.
Awards: Silver medal & hon mention for oil & watercolor, Albany Mus Hist & Art, 60; oil award, Am Soc Contemp Artists, Riverside Mus, 62; three certificates of merit, Am Soc Contemp Artists, 70.
Bibliography: L Blanch (auth), rev, In: 5 Star & maj New York Newspapers, 5/69 & 5/71; C F Ives (auth), rev, In: Arts Mag, 5/69; Gordon Brown (auth), rev, In: Arts Mag, spec issue, 4/71.
Memberships: Nat Asn Women Artists (dir); Am Soc Contemp Artists (past dir); New York Soc Women Artists (past dir); Artists Equity Asn New York (past dir); life mem Woodstock Artists Asn (past dir).
Dealer: Phoenix Gallery, 939 Madison Ave, New York, NY 10021.
Mailing Address: 340 W 28th St, New York, NY 10001.

HELLER, BEN
Collector
b New York, N Y, Oct 16, 25.
Study & Training: Bard Col, BA.
Positions: Adv, Washington Gallery Mod Art; past trustee or bd mem, Int Coun of Mus Mod Art, Friends of Whitney Mus Am Art & Jewish Mus.
Collection: Contemporary American painting and ancient, Eastern and primitive sculpture.
Mailing Address: 151 Central Park W, New York, NY 10023.

HELLER, DOROTHY
Painter
Preferred Media: Acrylics.
b New York, N Y.
Study & Training: With Hans Hofmann.
Work in Public Collections: Univ Calif Art Mus, Berkeley; Allen Mem Art Mus, Oberlin, Ohio; Mus Mod Art, Haifa, Israel; Greenville Co Mus Art, S C.
Exhibitions: Whitney Mus Am Art, New York, 56; Carnegie Int, Pittsburgh, Pa, 59; Mus Mod Art, New York, 63; Wadsworth Atheneum, Conn, 64; Picadilly Gallery, 67; plus many one-man shows.
Bibliography: Article, In: Arts Mag, 10/72.
Dealer: Betty Parsons, 24 W 57th St, New York, NY 10011.
Mailing Address: 8 W 13th St, New York, NY 10011.

HELLER, GOLDIE (MRS EDWARD W GREENBURG)
Collector
b Salem, Mass.
Study & Training: Mass Sch Art.
Collection: Hans Hartung, Henry Botkin, Ralph Rosenborg, Byron Browne, Noel Rockmore, Andy Warhol, Fransisco Larez, Jose de Creeft, Jean Marie Souverbie (School of Paris), John Ross, Clare Romano and others.
Mailing Address: 440 E 56th St, New York, NY 10022.

HELLER, JULES
Printmaker, Art Administrator
Preferred Media: Graphics.
b New York, N Y, Nov 16, 19.
Study & Training: Ariz State Univ, BA, 39; Columbia Univ, MA, 40; Univ Southern Calif, PhD, 48.
Work in Public Collections: Long Beach Mus Art, Calif; Ariz State Univ, Tempe; Allan R Hite Inst, Univ Louisville, Ky.
Exhibitions: Soc Am Etchers, 50; Second Int Biennial Color Lithography, Cincinnati Art Mus, 52; First Nat Exhib Prints, DePauw Univ, 59; Pa Acad Fine Arts Ann, 59 & 63; Modern Masters of the Print, Queens Col, New York, N Y, 67.
Teaching: Prof printmaking & art hist, Univ Southern Calif, 46-61.
Positions: Dir Sch Arts, Pa State Univ, University Park, 61-63, dean Col Arts & Archit, 63-68; dean Faculty Fine Arts, York Univ, 68-

Memberships: Col Art Asn Am; Univs Art Asn Can.
Publications: Illusr, Canciones de Mexico, 48; contribr, Estampas de la revolucion Mexicana, 48; contribr, Prints by California artists, 54; contribr, Dictionary of art, McGraw, 69; auth, Printmaking today, rev ed, 72.
Mailing Address: 45 Spadina Rd, Toronto 4, Ont, Can.

HELLER, LAWRENCE J
Collector
Mailing Address: 1729 21st St N W, Washington, DC 20009.

HELMAN, PHOEBE
Sculptor
Preferred Media: Steel, Formica.
b New York, N Y.
Study & Training: Art Stud League New York; Wash Univ, with Paul Burlin.
Work in Public Collections: Ciba-Geigy Corp, Ardsley, N Y; Hampton Inst Mus, Va.
Exhibitions: One-woman shows, Village Art Ctr, New York, 63 & Aspen Art Gallery, Colo, 66; two artists show, Wooster Sch, Danbury, Conn, 66; Emily Lowe Gallery, Hofstra Col, N Y, 69.
Teaching: Lectr drawing, Pratt Inst, 72-
Dealer: Max Hutchinson Gallery, 127 Greene St, New York, NY 10012.
Mailing Address: 217 E 23rd St, New York, NY 10010.

HELWIG, ARTHUR LOUIS
Painter, Instructor
Preferred Media: Oils.
b Cincinnati, Ohio.
Study & Training: Art Acad Cincinnati with Herman Wessel & John E Weir; Acad Mod, Paris, France, with Ledger & Ozanfant.
Work in Public Collections: Murals, Nat Hist Mus, Cincinnati & prints, Cincinnati Art Mus; murals, Milcon, Cincinnati, Cincinnati Water Works & Norwood Ohio Pub Schs.
Commissions: Portrait & two murals, Frat House, Miami Univ, 60; backgrounds for Stroll Through Forest, Nat Hist Mus, 65-68; plus many portraits.
Exhibitions: Faculty exhib & 1st-3rd Int Exhib Lithography, 61-63, Cincinnati Art Mus Best Print of Yr Metrop Mus Art, 35 & 36.
Teaching: Instr drawing & supvr painting & graphics, Art Acad Cincinnati, 29-
Positions: Pres, Prof Artist Cincinnati.
Awards: Best print of yr, Metrop Mus Art, 35 & 36; first prize for painting, Cincinnati Womans Club, 50; first prize for print making, Cincinnati Mus Art, 60.
Memberships: Cincinnati Art Club (pres & twice mem bd).
Publications: Auth, Making a lithograph, Cincinnati Mus Asn, 55; auth, Prints by the dozen, produced by WLW-TV.
Mailing Address: 818 Dunore Rd, Cincinnati, OH 45220.

HEMENWAY, NANCY (MRS ROBERT D BARTON)
Painter, Designer
Preferred Media: Bayetage.
b Boothbay Harbor, Maine, June 19, 20.
Study & Training: Wheaton Col, 37-41; with Matheu, Europe, 54-56; Univ Madrid, 56; Art Stud League New York, 57-61; Columbia Univ, with John Heliker, 62-66, MA, 66.
Work in Public Collections: The Net (bayetage), Woodmere Art Gallery, Germantown, Pa; Sea Edge, Chase Manhattan Bank, New York, N Y; plus many works in pvt collections in Europe, Latin Am & U S A.
Commissions: Wool hanging & bayetage, Richard & Neiman Marcus, Dallas, Tex, 71; Monkeys, Crab & Mask (bayetages), Mrs Walter Ford, Detroit, Mich, 72; Tidal (two part screen in silk & velvet), Mr & Mrs Arthur Schultz, Chicago, Ill, 72.
Exhibitions: Nat Gallery Art, La Paz, Bolivia, 68; Smithsonian Mus Art, Washington, D C, 69; Woodmere Gallery Art, Germantown, 71; Copley Soc Boston, Mass, 72; one-woman show, Pan-Am Union, Washington, D C, 70.
Teaching: Prof drawing & painting, U S Mex Cult Inst, 68-70.
Bibliography: Nancy Hemenway & bayetage (film), produced by U S Info Agency, 70.
Memberships: Art Stud League New York; Craftsman's Coun; Maine Hist & Cult Soc; Maine Art Gallery.
Art Interests: Originator of Bayetage, a new art form consisting of wall hangings in collage & stitchery largely on wool.
Mailing Address: Juniper Point, West Boothbay Harbor, ME 04575.

HENDLER, RAYMOND
Painter, Sculptor
Preferred Media: Acrylics, Polystyrene.
b Philadelphia, Pa, Feb 22, 23.
Study & Training: Acad Grande Chaumiere, Paris, France; Contemp Sch Art, Brooklyn, N Y; Tyler Sch, Temple Univ; Pa Acad

Fine Arts; Philadelphia Col Art; Graphic Sketch Club, Philadelphia.
Work in Public Collections: N Y Univ; Walker Art Ctr, Minneapolis; Birla Acad Mus, Calcutta, India; Univ Notre Dame; Geigy Chem Corp, New York; plus others.
Exhibitions: One-man shows, Galerie Huit, Paris, 51, Rose Fried Gallery, New York, since 62, Minneapolis Inst Art, Minn & others; exhibs at major mus, univs & galleries throughout U S, Can & Europe.
Teaching: Dir, Eve Art Sch Pratt Inst; dir, First Yr Prog Sch Visual Arts; head dept painting, Minneapolis Col Art; prof art, Univ Minn, Minneapolis, 68-
Awards: Longview Found Purchase Award, 63.
Bibliography: Orie (auth), Raymond Hendler, Quadrum XVII; Burton (auth), Hendler paintings, Art News, 5/67; Brown (auth), Hendler exhibition, Arts, 6/67.
Memberships: Artists Club, New York; Col Art Asn Am.
Mailing Address: 2212 Seabury Ave S, Minneapolis, MN 55406.

HENDRICKS, BARKLEY LEONNARD
Painter
Preferred Media: Oils, Acrylics.
b Philadelphia, Pa, Apr 16, 45.
Study & Training: Pa Acad Fine Arts, 63-67, William Cresson European Traveling scholar, 66; Yale Univ Sch Fine Arts, 70-72.
Work in Public Collections: Phila Mus Art; Pa Acad Fine Arts, Philadelphia; Cornell Univ, Ithaca, N Y; Wichita State Univ, Kans.
Exhibitions: Fel Exhib, Pa Acad Fine Arts, 67-72; Nat Acad Design Ann, New York, N Y, 70-71; Contemp Black Artist, Whitney Mus Am Art, New York, 71; Childe Hassam Fund Exhib, Am Acad Arts & Lett, 71; Nat Inst Arts & Lett Ann, 71-72.
Teaching: Instr painting & drawing, Pa Acad Fine Arts, 71-72; asst in painting, Yale Univ, 71-72; instr painting & drawing, Conn Col, 72-
Awards: Julius Hallgarten Second Prize, Nat Acad Design, 71; Richard & Hilda Rosenthal Award, Nat Inst Arts & Lett, 72.
Mailing Address: c/o Kenmore Galleries, 122 S 18th St, Philadelphia, PA 19103

HENDRICKS, GEOFFREY
Painter, Educator
Preferred Media: Acrylics, Intermedia.
b Littleton, N H, July 30, 31.
Study & Training: Amherst Col, BA, 53; Norfolk Art Sch, Yale Univ, scholarship, summer 53; Cooper Union Art Sch, 53-56; Columbia Univ, MA, 62.
Work in Public Collections: N J State Mus, Trenton; Mus Mod Art, New York, N Y; Metrop Mus Art, New York; Springfield Art Mus, Mass; Witherspoon Gallery, Univ N C, Chapel Hill.
Exhibitions: Sixth Nat Columbian Festival of Arts, Smithsonian Inst Exhib touring Latin Am, 66; Contemporary American Still Life, Mus Mod Art, New York, Circulating Exhib, 66-68; A Museum of Merchandise, Philadelphia Arts Coun, 67; Ann Art From New Jersey, N J State Mus, 68-70; Happening and Fluxus, Kunstverein, Köln & Stuttgart, Ger, 70-71; Image Bank Post Card Show, Univ Art Gallery, Vancouver, B C & touring, 71; plus many one-man shows.
Teaching: Assoc prof art, Douglass Col, Rutgers Univ, 56-; instr art, New York fine arts winter term prog of Earlham Col, Richmond, Ind, 65-69.
Awards: First prize for watercolors, Champlain Valley Exhib, Vt, 50; MacDowell Colony fel, 55.
Bibliography: K Nobuyuki (auth), The art of trompe l'oeil: Hendricks and Gilardi, Bijutsu-Techo, 4/68; Yosuke Nakahara (auth), Geoffrey Hendricks exhibition (catalog), Tokyo Gallery, 68; Ichiro Haryu (ed), Art as action and concept, Art Now, 72.
Memberships: Col Art Asn Am; Am Asn Univ Prof; Fluxus.
Publications: Contribr, Film Culture - Expanded Cinema (spec issue 43), winter 66; auth, Sky post cards, Vol 1-6, Black Thumb Press, 67-68; contribr, Pop Architektur, Droste Verlag, Dusseldorf, 69; contribr, Notations, Something Else Press, 69; contribr, Space Atlas, Ace Space Co, 71.
Dealer: Galerie Baecker, Berggate 69, D4630 Bochum, West Germany.
Mailing Address: 311 Church St, New York, NY 10013.

HENDRICKS, JAMES (POWELL)
Painter, Educator
Preferred Media: Acrylics, Oils.
b Little Rock, Ark, Aug 7, 38.
Study & Training: Univ Ark, Fayetteville, BA, 63; Univ Iowa, MFA, 64.
Work in Public Collections: Finch Col Mus, New York, N Y; Smithsonian Inst, Washington, D C; Univ Mass, Amherst; Hudson River Mus, Yonkers, N Y; Western Wash State Col, Billingham.
Commissions: Apollo 14 Launch, Nat Gallery Art & NASA, 71.

Exhibitions: Nat Painting Exhib, Soc Four Arts, Palm Beach, Fla, 68; Biennial Contemp Am Painting & Sculpture, Krannert Art Mus, Univ Ill, 69; Nat Drawing Exhib, San Francisco Mus Art, Calif, 70; Nat Gallery Art, 70; Abstr Painting, De Cordova Mus, Lincoln, Mass, 71.
Teaching: Grad instr drawing, State Univ Iowa, 63-64; instr art, Mt Holyoke Col, 64-65; asst prof painting & drawing, Univ Mass, Amherst, 65-
Awards: Top Prize For Painting, Soc Four Arts, 68; painting awards, Purdue Univ Art Gallery, 69 & Silvermine Guild Artists, 69.
Bibliography: H Lester Cooke (auth), Eyewitness to space, Abrams, 71; Ven Deren Coke (auth), The painter & the photograph, Univ N Mex Press, 72.
Publications: Illusr, cover, Time, 71.
Mailing Address: c/o French & Co, 980 Madison Ave, New York, NY 10021.

HENKLE, JAMES LEE
Sculptor, Educator
Preferred Media: Wood, Metals.
b Cedar Rapids, Iowa, Mar 13, 27.
Study & Training: Univ Nebr, BA; Pratt Inst, cert indust design.
Work in Public Collections: Okla Art Ctr, Oklahoma City; Univ Okla Art Mus, Norman; Springfield Art Mus, Mo; Okla State Art Collection, Okla Arts & Humanities Coun, Oklahoma City.
Commissions: Sculpture & fountain, First Fed Savings & Loan Bldg, Fort Smith, Ark, 61; sculpture mural, Numerical Anal Res Ctr, Norman, 63; sculpture mural, Tulsa Pub Libr, Tulsa Hist Soc, Okla, 65; sculpture, Norman Pub Libr, 75th Anniversary Comt, 66; wall sculpture, Dale Hall, Univ Okla, Chi Omega Sorority, 69.
Exhibitions: Nat Col Art Stud Exhib, Andover, Mass, 49; Eight State Art Exhib, Oklahoma City Art Ctr, 61; one-man sculpture exhib, Univ Okla Mus Art, 68 & Philbrook Art Ctr, Tulsa, 70.
Teaching: Prof art, Univ Okla, 53-
Positions: Designer, Dave Chapman Design Firm, 52-53.
Awards: Purchase prize for sculpture, Okla Art Ctr, 65; purchase prize for painting, Springfield Art Mus.
Mailing Address: School of Art, University of Oklahoma, Norman, OK 73069.

HENNING, EDWARD B
Curator, Educator
b Cleveland, Ohio, Oct 23, 22.
Study & Training: Cleveland Art Sch, with Jack Levine, Louis Bosa & Anton Refregier; Western Reserve Univ, BSc(magna cum laude) & MA; Julian Acad, Paris.
Collections Arranged: Paths Abstr Art, 60, Fifty Yrs Mod Art, 66 & many exhibs contemp art, including one-or two-man exhibs Oldenburg, Lichtenstein, Kitaj, Adja Yunkers, Fairfield Porter, Richard Hunt, Cornell, Chamberlain & Lindner.
Teaching: Guest lectr aesthetics, Cleveland Inst Art, 61-67; adj prof mod art, Case Western Reserve Univ, 67-
Positions: Asst & assoc cur educ, Cleveland Mus Art, 55-59, asst to dir, 59-70, cur contemp art, 62-
Memberships: Am Asn Mus; Col Art Asn Am; Am Soc Aesthetics (Cleveland chmn, 65); Cleveland Soc Contemp Art (trustee).
Research: Late nineteenth and twentieth century painting and sculpture connoisseurship, history and aesthetics, especially abstract expressionism.
Publications: Auth, Paths of abstract art, 60; auth, Patronage and style in the arts: a suggestion concerning their relations, 60; co-auth, Analogy in the creative processes and the objects of creation in art and sciences, 64; auth, Fifty years of modern art/ 1916-1966, 66; auth, The art museum and the avant-garde, 70.
Mailing Address: Cleveland Museum of Art, 11150 E Blvd, Cleveland, OH 44106.

HENRICKSEN, RALF CHRISTIAN
Educator, Painter
Preferred Media: Oils, Watercolors.
b Chicago, Ill, June 22, 07.
Study & Training: Art Inst Chicago, BFA; Inst Allende, Mex, MFA, with Boris Anisfeld.
Work in Public Collections: Fed Art Projs; also in private collections.
Commissions: Works, U S Treas Dept, Monroe, Mich Post Off, 38 & Staunton, Ill Post Off, 41.
Exhibitions: Int Exhib Watercolors, Chicago, 42; Contemp Art Exhib, Los Angeles, Calif, 56; Flint Art Inst, Mich, 58; Detroit Artist Mkt, Mich, 68; Cent Mich Univ, 70.
Teaching: Instr drawing, Sch Art Inst Chicago, 41-42; prof painting, Mich State Univ, 46-
Positions: Dir & instr, Leelanau Summer Art Sch, Leland, Mich, 50-71.

Awards: Robert Rice Jenkins Mem Prize, Art Inst Chicago, 33; Mrs
Albert Kahn Watercolor Prize, Art Inst Detroit, 52; first merit
award for oil, South Bend Gallery, Ind, 57.
Memberships: Int Inst Arts & Lett; Alumni Asn Sch Art Inst Chicago.
Mailing Address: Dept of Art, Michigan State University, East
Lansing, MI 48823.

HENRICKSON, PAUL ROBERT
Painter, Writer
b Boston, Mass.
Study & Training: R I Sch Design, BFA; Boston State Col, ME; Univ
Minn, PhD; Clark Univ; Statens Kunst Akademiet, Oslo; Statens
Kunst Industriskole, Oslo.
Work in Public Collections: La Jolla Art Ctr, Calif; Statens Kunst
Industriskole.
Commissions: Canvas panel, Crash, in private collection, N Dak.
Teaching: Prof & head div fine arts, Univ Guam, 64-68; prof research art, Univ North Iowa, 68-
Positions: Exec dir, Insular Arts Coun, Gov Guam, 65-68; owner
creativity workshop, Residence, Santa Fe, N Mex, 71-
Research: Psychology of art.
Publications: Auth, Two primitive micronesian art forms, 68; Lying,
dogmatic and creative persons, 70; The perceptive and silenced
minorities, 72.
Mailing Address: 428 Camino de las Animas, Santa Fe, NM 87501.

HENRY, JEAN
Painter, Instructor
Preferred Media: Oils.
b Oakland, Calif.
Study & Training: Art Acad, Amsterdam, Holland; Am Univ Berlin,
Ger; Maryland Inst, Baltimore.
Work in Public Collections: Triton Mus Art, San Jose, Calif; Palace
of Fine Arts, Chamber of Commerce & Letterman Gen Hosp, San
Francisco, Calif; Schwartz Hall, Presidio, Calif.
Commissions: Portrait of Bernard Maybeck, Palace of Fine Arts,
69; portraits of Gen Letterman, 71 & Gen Schwartz, 72, Letterman Gen Hosp; portrait of Sen Graham, Capitol Bldg, Frankfort,
Ky, 72.
Exhibitions: Soc Western Artists, De Young Mus, 68; De Saisset Gallery, Santa Clara, Calif, 69; one-man show, Triton Mus Art, 70;
Marin Art & Garden Show, 71; Rosicrucian Mus Invitational Show,
71.
Teaching: Instr portrait painting, Maryland Inst, Johns Hopkins
Univ, 58-60; instr painting, Jean Henry Sch Art, San Francisco, 69-; instr painting, Jean Henry Sch Art, Burlingame, 71-
Positions: Dir, Jean Henry Arts & Crafts Ctr, Burlingame, Calif, 72-
Awards: First award, De Young Mus, 68; first award, Antioch Outdoor Festival, 69; first award for portrait, Ann, De Saisset Gallery, 70.
Memberships: Soc Western Artists (publicity dir, 71).
Mailing Address: 5340 Geary Blvd, San Francisco, CA 94121.

HENRY, JOHN R
Illustrator, Painter
b Cleveland, Ohio, Nov 4, 45.
Study & Training: Univ Dayton, BAE; Dayton Art Inst, with Robert
Koepnick; Antioch Col, with Dr Roy Fairfield, MAT.
Exhibitions: All Northwest Painting & Drawing, Bainbridge Island,
Wash, 71; Int Peace Corp Poster Competition, Los Angeles Co
Mus Art, Calif, 72.
Teaching: Instr drawing & design, Univ Dayton, 68-70; vis instr art
educ, Eastern Wash State Col, 70-72.
Positions: Art dir, Dayton North Newspapers, 69-70; art dir, Humanist Mag, 70-; contribr art ed, Rap Mag, 70-71; art dir, Sundance Studios, Cheney, Wash, 71-
Awards: First place layout & design, Weekly Ohio Newspaper Asn,
70; second best painting & jurors award for drawing, All Northwest Painting & Drawing, 71; placement one of forty finalist
posters, Peace Corp, 71; plus one other.
Memberships: Nat Art Educ Asn; Wash Art Asn; Col Art Asn Am;
Dayton Art Asn.
Research: Significance of understanding Indian art education.
Publications: Illusr, There are no hopeless children, 70 & illusr, New
directions for America, 71, Humanist Mag; illusr, Dayton North
Newspaper, 70; illusr, Logo (30 graphic slides), AF-TV, Ramstein, Ger, 71; illusr, Black attitudes, Rap Mag, 72.
Mailing Address: P O Box 213, Sequim, WA 98382.

HENRY, JOHN RAYMOND
Sculptor
Preferred Media: Metals.
b Lexington, Ky, Aug 11, 43.
Study & Training: Univ Ky; Univ Wash; Sch Art Inst Chicago, Edward L Reyerson fel, 69.

Work in Public Collections: Des Moines Register & Tribune, Iowa.
Commissions: Several pvt comns.
Exhibitions: Eight American Sculptors, Chicago, Ill, 68; 22nd Ann
Ill Invitational, Ill State Mus, 69; one-man show, Richard Gray
Gallery, Chicago, 69-71; Painting & Sculpture Exhib, Ind State
Mus, Terre Haute, 70; one-man show, Dorksy Gallery Ltd, New
York, N Y, 72.
Teaching: Vis prof sculpture, Univ Iowa, summer 60; artist-in-residence, Univ Wis-Green Bay, 69-70; vis prof sculpture, Univ
Chicago, summer 70.
Positions: V pres, Chicago Creative Arts Found, 69-
Dealers: Richard Gray Gallery, 620 N Michigan Ave, Chicago, IL
60611; Dorsky Galleries Ltd, 111 Fourth Ave, New York, NY
10003.
Mailing Address: 1017 W Lill Ave, Chicago, IL 60614.

HENRY, ROBERT
Painter, Educator
Preferred Media: Oils.
b Brooklyn, N Y, Aug 3, 33.
Study & Training: Hans Hofmann Sch Fine Art, New York, N Y &
Provincetown, Mass; Brooklyn Col, BA, with Ad Reinhardt &
Kurt Seligmann.
Exhibitions: Hudson River Mus, Yonkers, N Y, 71; Contemporary
Figurative Painting, Suffolk Co Mus, Stony Brook, N Y, 71; one-man show, Green Mountain Gallery, New York.
Teaching: Asst prof art, Brooklyn Col, 60-
Bibliography: L Campbell (auth), Stop, look & look & look, Art
News, 2/72.
Publications: Auth, Horizontally oriented rotating kinetic painting,
Leonardo, 69.
Dealer: Green Mountain Gallery, 148 Greene St, New York, NY
10012.
Mailing Address: 803 Greenwich St, New York, NY 10014.

HENRY, STUART (COMPTON)
Museum Director, Painter
b Tufts College, Mass, 06.
Study & Training: Phillips Acad; Harvard Col, BS.
Work in Public Collections: Fogg Art Mus; also in pvt collections.
Exhibitions: One-man show, Fogg Art Mus; Pittsfield Art League;
Berkshire Mus; Symphony Hall, Boston.
Positions: Dir, Berkshire Mus, at present; trustee, Chesterwood
Studio of Daniel Chester French, Shaker Community, Inc, Hancock, Mass & Berkshire Mus.
Memberships: Am Asn Mus.
Publications: Auth, catalogues of exhibs, collections, guides to
collections & others, Berkshire Mus.
Mailing Address: Berkshire Museum, 39 South St, Pittsfield, MA
01201.

HENSCHE, HENRY
Painter, Instructor
Preferred Media: Oils.
b Chicago, Ill, Feb 20, 01.
Study & Training: Chas W Hawthorne's Cape Cod Sch Art; Art Inst
Chicago; Nat Acad Design; Art Stud League New York; Beaux
Arts Inst Design New York.
Work in Public Collections: Fort Wayne Art Inst, Ind; Chrysler Collection, Norfolk; Mint Mus, N C; Harvard Club, New York; Oklahoma City Mus.
Exhibitions: Pittsburgh Int, Pa, Nat Acad Design, New York, Chicago
Am, Philadelphia Ann & Corcoran Biennial, Washington, D C,
22-33.
Teaching: Instr oils & watercolors, Cape Cod Sch Art, 28-
Awards: Three Hallgarten Prizes, Nat Acad Design, 30.
Memberships: Boston Guild Artist; Provincetown Art Asn.
Dealer: Grand Central Art Gallery, 40 Vanderbilt Ave, New York,
NY 10017.
Mailing Address: Provincetown, MA 02657.

HENSEL, HOPKINS, see, HARE, STEPHEN HOPKINS

HENSELMANN, CASPAR
Sculptor
b Mannheim, Ger, Mar 13, 33; U S citizen.
Study & Training: Art Inst Chicago, BFA; Univ Ill Col Med, MMed-Art; Northwestern Univ; Columbia Univ.
Work in Public Collections: Mus de Locarno, Switz.
Commissions: Lobby sculpture (glass, steel, oil, air), Technicon
Corp, Tarrytown, N Y, 68-69; multiple turbine (aluminum &
stainless), Southridge Shopping Ctr, Milwaukee, Wis, 69-71; wave
piece (stainless), A Clayburgh, Byram, Conn, 71; glass lobby
piece (oil, air), Marshall-Ilsley Bank, Milwaukee, 71.
Exhibitions: Pa Ann Am Art, 64; Kern Co Mus, Bakersfield, Calif,
65; Stamford Mus, Conn, 67; American Abstract Artist, Riverside Mus, New York, N Y, 69; Mus Contemp Crafts, 69.

Awards: Tiffany Award; Ford Found artist-in-residence, Am Fedn Arts.
Mailing Address: 21 Bond St, New York, NY 10012.

HERARD, MARVIN T
Sculptor, Educator
b Puyallup, Wash, July 4, 29.
Study & Training: Burnley Sch Art, Seattle; Seattle Univ; Univ Wash, BA; Cranbrook Acad Art, MFA; Acad Fine Arts, Florence, Italy; Fonderia Artistica Florentina, Italy.
Commissions: Sculpture, Renton Pub Libr; Lemieux Libr, Seattle Univ.
Exhibitions: Palazzo Venezia, Rome, Italy, 62; Seattle Art Mus, 65-67; Gov Invitational, State Capitol Mus, 67-69; Henry Gallery, Univ Wash, 68; Cheney Cowles Mus, Spokane, Wash, 69; plus many others.
Teaching: Instr, Seattle Pub Schs, 56-58; teaching fel sculpture, Cranbrook Acad Arts, 59-60; assoc prof art, Seattle Univ, 60-; instr painting, Pius XII Inst Art, Florence, Italy, 62.
Awards: Am Craftsmen Award, Henry Gallery, 61 & 65; Spokane Pac Northwest Exhib, 63, 64, & 66; Seattle Art Mus, 65; plus others.
Memberships: Nat Art Educ Asn; Am Asn Univ Prof.
Mailing Address: 1131 23rd Ave E, Seattle,WA 98112.

HERBERT, DAVID
Art Dealer, Collector
b Lakewood, N J, Jan 1, 25.
Study & Training: Syracuse Univ, BA; Univ Mich.
Positions: With Betty Parsons Gallery, 51-53, Sidney Janis Gallery, 53-59 & David Herbert Gallery, 59-64; dir, Graham Gallery, 68-
Specialty of Gallery: Nineteenth & twentieth century American art.
Collection: Contemporary American & Latin American art.
Mailing Address: 445 E 86th St, New York, NY 10028.

HERBERT, ROBERT L
Art Historian
b Worcester, Mass, Apr 21, 29.
Study & Training: Wesleyan Univ, BA, 51; Inst Art & Archeol & Ecole du Louvre, Paris, France & Fulbright scholar, 51-52; Yale Univ, MA, 54, PhD, 57; Am Coun Learned Soc grant, 60; Morse fel, London, Eng, 60-61; sr faculty fel, Paris, France, 68-69; Guggenheim fel, Paris & New Haven, Conn, 71-72.
Collections Arranged: Barbizon Revisited, Mus Fine Arts, Boston, 62-63; Neo-impressionists & Nabis in the collection of Arthur G Altschul, Yale Univ Art Gallery, 65; Neo-Impressionism, Solomon R Guggenheim Mus, New York, 68; Retrospective J F Millet, Mus Nat, Paris, France (in prep).
Teaching: Asst art, Wesleyan Univ, 50-51; asst instr art, Yale Univ, 54-55, acting instr art, 55-56, instr art & mem comt hist, arts & letters, 56-60, asst prof hist art, 60-63, assoc prof, 63-66, prof hist art, 66-, undergrad studies, 62-64, mem, Morse Comt, 63-65, interim dir grad studies, spring terms, 65 & 66, acting chmn, 65-66, chmn, 66-68, mem comt teaching & learning, 69-71 & faculty chmn, 70-71.
Awards: Frank Jewett Mather Award for Barbizon Revisited, Col Art Asn, 63; plus others.
Research: Nineteenth and twentieth century French art.
Publications: Auth, Barbizon revisited (book catalogue), Clark & Way, 62; auth, Seurat's drawings, Shorewood, 63; auth, The art criticism of John Ruskin, Doubleday, 64; auth, Neo-impressionism (catalogue), Solomon R Guggenheim Mus, 68 & Van Nostrand-Reinhold, 69; auth, David, Voltaire, Brutus and the French revolution, Penguin (London) & Viking (New York), 72; plus many others.
Mailing Address: Beacon Rd, Bethany, CT 06525.

HERDLE, ISABEL C
Art Administrator
b Rochester, N Y, June 5, 05.
Study & Training: Univ Rochester, AB; Radcliffe Col, MA; Courtauld Inst, Univ London.
Positions: Asst dir, Rochester Mem Art Gallery, 32-
Awards: Carnegie Award for foreign study, 32-33.
Mailing Address: Rochester Memorial Art Gallery, 490 University Ave, Rochester, NY 14607.

HERIC, JOHN F
Sculptor
Preferred Media: Stone, Steel, Plastics, Bronze.
b Reno, Nev, Feb 28, 42.
Study & Training: Ariz State Univ, BFA, 63, with Ben Goo; Southern Ill Univ, Carbondale, MFA, 65.
Work in Public Collections: Ariz State Univ Collections, Tempe; Grossmont Col Collections, El Cajon, Calif; Mesa Community Col, Ariz; Ridgewood High Sch, Norridge, Ill; Glendale Community Col, Ariz.

Commissions: Steel Sculpture, Ridgewood High Sch, 64; complete courtyard, Sopoti Sch, Saguarita Sch Dist, Tucson, Ariz, 71.
Exhibitions: Group Show-1965, St Paul Mus Art, Minn, 65; Sculpture '66 Invitational, Madison, Wis, 66; Wichita Biennial Nat Crafts Exhib, 66; Exhib Chicago, Univ Ill, Chicago Circle, 66; 4th-7th Southwestern Invitational, Yuma, Ariz, 69-72.
Teaching: Instr sculpture, Wis State Univ-Platteville, 65-67; vis lectr sculpture, Ariz State Univ, 67-69; asst prof sculpture, Univ Ariz, 69-
Awards: Best of show, Ariz Crafts, Tucson Art Ctr, 67; first prize sculpture, Ariz Ann, Phoenix Art Mus, 68; purchase award, Yuma Art Asn, 71.
Bibliography: Articles, In: Craft Horizons, 65 & 70.
Memberships: Ariz Designer Craftsmen (rep, 71).
Dealer: Art Wagon Galleries, W Main St, Scottsdale, AZ 85251.
Mailing Address: 3622 Camino Blanco, Rte 5, Tucson, AZ 85718.

HERMAN, LLOYD ELDRED
Art Administrator
b Corvallis, Ore, Mar 19, 36.
Study & Training: Ore State Univ; Univ Ore; Am Univ, BA.
Collections Arranged: Eight exhibs inaugurating the Renwick Gallery, Smithsonian Inst, Washington, D C.
Positions: Prog mgr, off of dir-gen of mus, Smithsonian Inst, 66-71, adminr, Renwick Gallery, Smithsonian Inst, 71-
Memberships: Am Crafts Coun; hon mem Am Inst Interior Designers; Nat Trust for Hist Preserv; Am Asn Mus; Soc Archit Historians.
Art Interests: Twentieth century crafts & industrial design.
Publications: Co-auth, Woodenworks (exhib catalogue), 72.
Mailing Address: Smithsonian Institution, Washington, DC 20560.

HERMAN, VIC
Painter, Writer
Preferred Media: Mixed Media.
b Fall River, Mass.
Study & Training: Yale Puppeteers, Los Angeles, Calif, apprentice, with Harry Burnett; Art Students League New York, with George Bridgman; New York Commercial Illus Sch, with Lu Kimmel; Columbia Univ, with Ed Johnson & Samuel Penchansky.
Work in Public Collection: Vic Herman Collection, Syracuse Univ; Mex-Norteamericano Cult Inst, Guadalajara, Jalisco, Mex; Repub Mex Gallery, Los Angeles; Galeria Zamora, Veracruz, Mex; Galeria Vic Herman, San Diego, Calif; plus others.
Commissions: Many Faces of Mexico, for U S Embassy, Mexico City & Govt Mex, U S & Mex, 60-; Lowrey Pines Bluff (painting), City of Del Mar, 72.
Exhibitions: One-man shows, Munic Gallery, Veracruz, 67, For Corresp Gallery, Mexico City, Mex, 68, Span Monastery Gallery, Miami, Fla, 69, Munic Gallery, St Louis, Mo, 70 & Chicago Press Club Gallery, Ill, 72; plus many others.
Positions: Asst art dir, Warner Bros Studios, New York, 40-43; artist-field corresp, Army News Serv, USA, 43-46; pres & prod chief, Vic Herman Prod, 50-60; freelance illusr & corresp, New York, & Mex, 50-
Awards: USA Army Medal for creation of Winnie the Wac, 46; City Proclamations for Mex paintings, San Diego, Del Mar, Calif, New Rochelle & New York, 50-70; Nat Cartoonists Soc Award Honor, 70.
Bibliography: Cal Whipple (auth), Soldier artist makes a Wac his heroine, Life, 45; Sally Cass (auth), U S artist portrays the Mexican feeling, Mexico City News, 68; Dolly Maw (auth), Herman's hacienda, San Diego Mag, 71; plus many others.
Memberships: Chicago Press Club; Mexico City For Corresp Club; Soc Illusr; La Jolla Art Asn; Graphic Artists Asn (v pres, 62-67).
Publications: Auth & illusr, Winnie the Wac, McKay, 45; illusr, One hundred pounds of popcorn, Scholastic Publ, 60; illusr, My days are made of butterflies, 70 & Language of vision, 72, Holt, Rinehart & Winston; auth & illusr, Sunday in Zamora Park, Holt, Rinehart & Winston, 72; plus others.
Mailing Address: R R 1, M-25 South Lane, Del Mar, CA 92014.

HERNANDEZ-CRUZ, LUIS
Painter, Educator
Preferred Media: Oils, Silkscreen.
b San Juan, P R.
Study & Training: Univ P R, BA; Am Univ, MA, with Ben Summerford.
Work in Public Collections: Chase Manhattan Bank, New York, N Y; Ponce Mus Art, P R; Mus Am, Madrid, Spain; Univ P R Mus; Inst P R Cult Mus.
Commissions: Murals, P R Med Ctr, 64 & 65; mural, Santa Juanita Elem Sch, 68.
Exhibitions: Arte Actual de America y Espana, Madrid, Spain, 63; Esso Salon of Young Artists, Washington, D C, 64; First Salon of Pan-Am Art, Cali, Colombia, 65; Second Biennial, Coltejer-

Medellin, Colombia, 70; First & Second Biennial of Latin Am Prints, San Juan, 70 & 72.
Teaching: Prof painting, Univ P R, Rio Piedras, 68, assoc dir dept fine arts, 68-
Positions: Acting dir univ mus, Univ P R, Rio Piedras, 71.
Awards: First prize in painting, Inst P R Cult, 63; first prize, Esso Art Contest, 64; Nat prize, Second Biennial Latin Am Prints, 72.
Bibliography: Efrain Perez Chanis (auth), El arte abstracto de Luis Hernandez-Cruz, Revista Urbe, 7/64; Pintores Puertorriquenos Hernandez-Cruz, Ediciones Artisticas de P R, 67; Marta Traba (auth), El abstracto que se salva, Artes Visuales, 71; plus others.
Memberships: Ateneo Puertorriqueno (dir plastic arts sect, 67-71).
Mailing Address: Mamey 82, Urb Millaville, Rio Piedras, PR 00928.

HEROLD, DON G
Museum Director
b Brooklyn, N Y, June 8, 27.
Study & Training: State Univ N Y Albany, BA.
Positions: Dir, Davenport Mus; dir, Polk Pub Mus, Lakeland, Fla; dir, Daytona Beach Mus Arts & Sci, Fla; dir, Charleston Mus, at present.
Memberships: Assoc, Am Asn Mus.
Mailing Address: Charleston Museum, 121 Rutledge Ave, Charleston, SC 29401.

HERPST, MARTHA JANE
Painter
Preferred Media: Oils, Watercolors.
b Titusville, Pa.
Study & Training: Pa Acad Fine Arts, 32; Grand Cent Sch Art, New York, N Y, with Wayman Adams, Edmund Greacen, Harvey Dunn & Georg Lober; also with Guy Pene Du Bois.
Work in Public Collections: Nat Arts Club, New York; Titusville Woman's Club; Univ Pittsburgh, Titusville; Gannon Col, Erie, Pa; Titusville Masonic Lodge.
Commissions: Portrait of Charles T Evans, Titusville Masonic Lodge, 43; portraits of Mrs Edgar Doty & Mrs C Burgess, comn by Edgar Doty, Titusville Recreation Ctr, 54; portrait of Archbishop John Mark Gannon, comn by Rev C H Cooper for Gannon Col, 58.
Exhibitions: Nat Arts Club, New York, 33-72; Butler Art Inst, Youngstown, Ohio, 38 & 45; Am Artists Prof League Grand Nat, New York, 46-70; Ogunquit Art Asn, Maine, 51-61; Catherine Lorillard Wolfe Art Club, New York, 54-62.
Teaching: Instr art, St Joseph Acad High Sch, Titusville, 55-69; pvt instr painting, 70-
Awards: Grand Cent Sch Art Medal, 33.
Memberships: Nat Arts Club; Am Artists Prof League.
Mailing Address: 118 W Main St, Titusville, PA 16354.

HERRING, MR & MRS H LAWRENCE
Collectors
Mailing Address: 190 E 72nd St, New York, NY 10021.

HERRING, JAN(ET MANTEL)
Painter, Writer
b Havre, Mont, May 17, 23.
Study & Training: Northern State Teachers Col; also painting with Frederic Taubes.
Work in Public Collections: Grumbacher Collection, New York; Lubbock Art Ctr, Tex; Univ Idaho, Pocatello; Roswell Mus, N Mex.
Exhibitions: One-man shows, El Paso Mus Art, Santa Fe Mus Art, Tulsa Art Ctr, Roswell Mus & Brigham Young Univ.
Teaching: Pvt instr.
Bibliography: F Taubes (auth), article, In: Am Artist Mag, 55; articles, In: La Rev Mod, 61 & House Beautiful, 64.
Publications: Auth, The painters composition handbook, Pool-Henry, 71.
Mailing Address: Box 156, Clint, TX 79836.

HERROLD, CLIFFORD H
Educator, Craftsman
Preferred Media: Metal.
b Luther, Okla.
Study & Training: Cent State Univ(Okla), BA; Univ Northern Colo, MA; Stanford Univ, EdD; Inst Design, Chicago; Sch Am Craftsmen, Rochester, N Y.
Exhibitions: Craftsmen Cent States, Indianapolis, Ind, 62; Fiber-Clay-Metal, St Paul, Minn, 62; Jewelry 1964, Plattsburg, N Y, 64; Craftsmen U S A, Milwaukee, Wis, 66; Six West, Cedar Rapids, Iowa, 70.
Teaching: Prof jewelry, Univ Northern Iowa, 56-
Memberships: Am Crafts Coun; Iowa Designer Craftsmen.
Mailing Address: 2810 Walnut St, Cedar Falls, IA 50613.

HERRON, JASON
Sculptor
b Denver, Colo, Sept 11, 00.
Study & Training: Stanford Univ, BA; Otis Art Inst; Univ Southern Calif, with Merrell Gage & F Tolles Chamberlin.
Work in Public Collections: Los Angeles Mus Art, Calif; Browning Mus, London, Eng; South Pasadena High Sch; Belmont Sch, Los Angeles; Santa Monica High Sch.
Exhibitions: Calif Palace of Legion of Honor, San Francisco; Nat Acad Design, New York, N Y; Corcoran Gallery Art, Washington, D C; Santa Barbara Mus Art, Calif; Art Inst Chicago, Ill; plus others.
Positions: Secy, Civic Comt for Los Angeles Co Art Projects, 45-50; actg dir, Los Angeles Co Art Inst, 52, bd gov, 52, 54-60, hon life mem, 60-; bd gov, Otis Art Inst, 60.
Awards: Prizes, Los Angeles Co Fair, 34; Los Angeles Art Asn; Calif Art Club, 46.
Memberships: Los Angeles Art Asn; Ventura Co Potters Guild; Santa Barbara Mus Asn.
Mailing Address: 1425 Nathan Lane, Ventura, CA 93003.

HERSCHLER, DAVID
Sculptor
Preferred Media: Stainless Steel, Gold.
b Brooklyn, N Y, Mar 1, 40.
Study & Training: Acad Belli Arte, Perugia, Italy, 60; Univ Rome, 60; Cornell Univ, BArch, 62; Claremont Grad Sch, MFA, 67.
Work in Public Collections: Joseph H Hirshhorn Found, Washington, D C; La Jolla Mus Art, Calif; Storm King Art Ctr, Mountainville, N Y; Palm Springs Mus, Calif.
Commissions: Sculptures, comn by Mr & Mrs N S Walbridge, La Jolla, 70, Sigmund Edelstone, Chicago, Ill, 71, Mr & Mrs J W Constance, Santa Barbara, Calif, 72, Mr & Mrs Marvin Smalley, Beverly Hills, Calif, 72 & Storm King Art Ctr, 72.
Teaching: Instr art, San Joaquil Delta Col, Stockton, Calif, 67-69.
Dealers: Percival Gallery, 210 Shops Bldg, Des Moines, IA 50309; Forum Gallery, 1018 Madison Ave, New York, NY 10021.
Mailing Address: c/o Ankrum Gallery, 657 N La Cienega Blvd, Los Angeles, CA 90069.

HERSHMAN, LYNN LESTER
Painter
Study & Training: Ohio Univ; Cleveland Inst Art; Case Western Reserve Univ, BS, 63; Calif Col Arts & Crafts; Otis Art Inst; Univ Calif, Los Angeles; San Francisco State Col, MA, 72.
Work in Public Collections: Nat Collection Fine Arts, Smithsonian Inst; Cleveland Inst Art; City of San Francisco Collection Art; Calif State Cols Collection Art; Richmond Art Ctr; plus other public & private collections.
Commissions: Many private commissions.
Exhibitions: One-woman show, William Sawyer Gallery, 72; Northern Ill Univ Drawing Exhib; Ball State Univ Painting Exhib; San Francisco Mus Ann; Butler Inst Am Art; plus many other one-woman & group shows.
Teaching: Instr art, Cleveland Mus Art, 62-63; asst prof, Calif Col Arts & Crafts, 72-
Positions: Sr cur, Mus Conceptual Art, 71-
Awards: Bates & Springer Award, 62; purchase prize, San Francisco Art Festival, 69; purchase prize, Olive Hyde Drawing Competition, 72.
Bibliography: Thomas Albright (auth), Three women sculptors, San Francisco Chronicle, 3/25/70; Cecille McCann (auth), Lynn Hershman, Artweek, 9/70; Knute Stiles (auth), article, In: Artforum, 11/70; plus many others.
Publications: Art ed of weekly column (under name of Prudence Juris), San Francisco Progress, 71-; art reviewer & critic of weekly column (under name of Herberte Goode), Artweek, 71-; auth, The Newer Art, Studio Int & Interview with Tom Marioni, Umbrella (under name of Prudence Juris), 6/72.
Mailing Address: 3595 Clay St, San Francisco, CA 94118.

HERSTAND, ARNOLD
Painter, Art Administrator
b New York, N Y, Sept 10, 25.
Study & Training: Yale Univ, BFA; Columbia Univ, MA; Art Stud League New York; Pratt Inst; also with Fernand Leger, Paris, France & T Munro.
Work in Public Collections: Gen Mills Corp; Dayton-Hudson Corp; Northwestern Nat Life Ins Corp, Minneapolis, Minn.
Exhibitions: Whitney Mus Am Art Ann, New York, N Y, 48; Everson Mus Art Ann, Syracuse, N Y, 55-62; Munson-Williams-Proctor Inst Ann, Utica, N Y, 55-62; Walker Art Ctr Biennial, Minneapolis, 64; Minneapolis Inst Arts Biennial, 66-68.
Teaching: Lectr, City Col New York, 52-54; instr, Colgate Univ, 54-57, asst prof, 57-62; assoc prof music & visual art, 62-63; vis artist, Cornell Univ, 63.

Positions: Dir, Minneapolis Col Art & Design, 63-69, pres, 69-; consult, Danforth Regional Conf; consult, Univ Wash & Art Inst Chicago Bd Trustees.
Awards: Grants, Littauer Found, 57-58 & Danforth Found, 60; Ford Found fel, Harvard Univ, 58-59.
Memberships: Ben & Abby Grey Found, St Paul (bd dirs); Union Independent Cols Art (v pres exec comt, 71-72); Col Art Asn Am; assoc Am Asn Univ Prof; Nat Asn Schs Art (bd dirs, 71-72).
Publications: Auth, articles, In: Art J, Eastern Arts Quart, Art News & J Gen Educ.
Mailing Address: 200 E 25th St, Minneapolis, MN 55404.

HERTZBERG, ROSE
Painter, Printmaker
Preferred Media: Oils, Watercolors.
b Passaic, N J, Dec 17, 12.
Study & Training: With Ben Benn; Hans Hofmann Art Sch; Art Stud League New York, with Vaclav Vytlacil & Will Barnet; New York Graphics Workshop; Rockland Community Col; Fairleigh Dickinson Univ Art Seminars.
Work in Public Collections: Edward Williams Col, Hackensack, N J; Rockland Community Col, Suffern, N Y; Bloomfield Col, N J; Broadway Bank & Trust Co, Paterson, N J; Hackensack Pub Libr & Ramsey Pub Libr, N J.
Commissions: Many pvt commissions.
Exhibitions: Am Watercolor Soc, New York, N Y, 67, 69 & 71; Trenton State Mus, N J, 69-71; Painters & Sculptors Soc N J, Jersey City, 69-72; N J Watercolor Soc, Morristown, 71; Nat Asn Women Artists, 71 & 72; plus many one-woman shows.
Awards: Mary S Litt Award, Am Watercolor Soc, 67; Freylinghuysen Award, N J Watercolor Soc, 70; Putnam Mem Award, Nat Asn Women Artists, 71.
Memberships: Life mem Art Stud League New York; Nat Asn Women Artists; Mod Artists Guild; Painters & Sculptors Soc N J.
Dealer: Cramer Gallery, Glen Rock, NJ 07452.
Mailing Address: 27 Buckingham Dr, Ramsey, NJ 07446.

HESKETH
Sculptor
b Maine.
Study & Training: Wellesley Col, BA; also with John Flannagan & Ahron Ben-Schmuel.
Work in Public Collections: San Francisco Mus Art, Calif; Addison Gallery Am Art, Andover, Mass; Atlanta Mus Art, Ga.
Exhibitions: Detroit Inst Art, Mich; Whitney Mus Am Art, New York; Art Inst Chicago, Ill; Carnegie Inst, Pittsburgh, Pa; Pa Acad Fine Arts, Philadelphia; plus others.
Memberships: Artists Equity Asn.
Mailing Address: Bluehills Studio, R D 1, Kempton, PA 19529.

HESS, EMIL JOHN
Painter, Sculptor
Preferred Media: Oils, Metal.
b Willock, Pa, Sept 25, 13.
Study & Training: Duquesne Univ, 38-39; Art Inst Pittsburgh, 46-49; Brooklyn Mus Art Sch, 50-51; N Y Univ, 59.
Work in Public Collections: Smithsonian Inst, Washington, D C; Pa State Mus, Harrisburg, Pa; Earle Ludgins Col, Chicago, Ill; Eliah Root Col, N Y; Phillip Johnson Collection, N Y.
Exhibitions: Nat Acad Design, New York, N Y, 50; one-man show, Betty Parsons Gallery, 51, 52, 68 & 70; Metrop Mus Art, New York, 53; Stable Gallery, New York, 53 & 55; Mus Mod Art Traveling Exhibs, 59.
Bibliography: New means for moderns, Life, 54; Emily Genauer (auth), Beatnik sculp in big museum show, New York Herald Tribune, 59; Sounds of Hess sculpture, WBAI, New York, 70.
Memberships: Life mem Art Stud League New York; Am Fedn Arts; Int Platform Asn.
Dealer: Betty Parsons Galleries, 24 W 57th St, New York, NY 10019.
Mailing Address: 130 W 10th St, New York, NY 10014.

HESS, THOMAS B
Art Critic, Writer
b Rye, N Y, July 14, 20.
Study & Training: Yale Univ, BA.
Collections Arranged: De Kooning, 68 & Newman, 71, Mus Mod Art, New York, N Y.
Positions: Assoc ed, Art News, 46-50, managing ed, 50-65, ed, 65-72.
Research: Modern painting and sculpture.
Publications: Auth, Abstract painting, background and American phase, 51; auth, Willem de Kooning, 59; auth, Willem de Kooning retrospective, 68; auth, Barnett Newman, 69 & 71; ed, Woman as sex object, 72.
Mailing Address: 19 Beekman Pl, New York, NY 10022.

HESSE, DON
Cartoonist
b Belleville, Ill, Feb 20, 18.
Study & Training: Saint Louis Sch Fine Arts, Wash Univ, 36-37.
Work in Public Collections: Libr Cong, Washington, D C; also in pvt collections.
Positions: Artist-photog, Belleville Daily News-Democrat, 35-40; mem art staff, Saint Louis Globe-Democrat, 46-, ed cartoonist, 51-; nat syndicated cartoonist, Los Angeles Times Syndicate.
Awards: Freedoms Found Awards, 54 & 64; Christopher Award, 55; Nat Headliners Award, 60; plus others.
Memberships: Nat Cartoonists Soc; Asn Am Ed Cartoonists.
Mailing Address: 30 Hemlock Dr, Belleville, IL 62221.

HESSING, VALJEAN McCARTY
Painter
Preferred Media: Watercolors.
b Tulsa, Okla, Aug 30, 34.
Study & Training: Philbrook Art Ctr, Tulsa, 45-47; Mary Hardin-Baylor Col, 52-54; Univ Tulsa, 54-55.
Work in Public Collections: Philbrook Art Ctr; Heard Mus, Phoenix, Ariz; Anadarko Southern Plains Mus, Okla; Five Civilized Tribes Mus, Muskogee, Okla; Bur Indian Affairs, Washington, D C.
Exhibitions: Indian Ann, Philbrook Art Ctr, 66-72; Cowboy Hall of Fame, Oklahoma City, Okla, 67; Five Civilized Tribes Mus, 67-72; Scottsdale Nat Indian Art Exhib, Ariz, 68-72; Heard Mus, 72.
Awards: Spec award for traditional Indian art, Scottsdale Nat Indian Art Exhib, 69 & 71; first place for Choctaw div, Five Civilized Tribes Mus, 70 & 71; second place award for Woodland div, Philbrook Art Ctr.
Mailing Address: Box 613, Route 1, Owasso, OK 74055.

HEUSSER, ELEANORE ELIZABETH
Painter
Preferred Media: Ink, Oils.
b North Haledon, N J.
Study & Training: Cooper Union, dipl; Columbia Univ Sch Painting & Sculpture, Sch fel, 45-46; Innsbruck Univ, Fulbright fel, 52-55.
Work in Public Collections: Newark Mus; Lending Libr Mus Mod Art, New York.
Exhibitions: Kunsthitorisches Inst, Innsbruck, Austria, 54; Konzerthaus Gallery, Vienna, Austria, 54; Fulbright Grantees Show, Duveen-Graham Gallery & mus throughout U S, 57-58; Pa Acad Fine Arts Ann, Philadelphia, 59 & 65; N J Artists 1972, N J State Mus, Trenton, 72.
Teaching: Instr fundamentals art, Columbia Univ Sch Painting & Sculpture, 46-52; instr drawing, City Col New York, 60-62; instr painting, private studio, New York, 60-
Awards: Private grant study in Mex, George Grebe, 43.
Bibliography: M Finkelstein (auth), Artist in the Alps, Inst Int Educ New Bull, 6/55.
Mailing Address: 60 Roosevelt Ave, North Haledon, NJ 07508.

HEWITT, FRANCIS RAY
Painter, Educator
Preferred Media: Acrylics.
b Rutland, Vt, May 12, 36.
Study & Training: Carnegie-Mellon Univ, BFA, with Balcomb Greene; Oberlin Col, MA, with Wolfgang Stechow & Charles Parkhurst; Case Western Reserve Univ, with Thomas Munro.
Work in Public Collections: Cleveland Mus Art, Ohio; Martha Jackson Galleries, New York, N Y; Lodz Mus Fine Art, Poland; Caracas Mus Mod Art, Venezuela.
Exhibitions: Movement II, Denise Rene Gallery, Paris, France, 64; Responsive Eye, Mus Mod Art, New York, 65; 1 + 1 = 3, Univ-Tex, 65; Plus & Minus, a Review of Constructivism, Knox-Albright Mus, Buffalo, N Y, 67; The Square in Painting, Am Fedn Arts Traveling Exhib, 68.
Teaching: Instr painting, Cleveland Inst Art, Ohio, 60-64; lectr design, Bath Acad Art, Corsham, Eng, 64-65; assoc prof drawing & design, Cooper Union, New York, 65-70.
Positions: Trustee, Vt Coun Arts, Montpelier, 70-74.
Mailing Address: Flanders Brook Rd, East Corinth, VT 05040.

HEYMAN, MR & MRS DAVID M
Collectors
Collection: Paintings.
Mailing Address: 3 E 76th St, New York, NY 10021.

HIBEL, EDNA
Painter, Lithographer
Preferred Media: Oils.
b Boston, Mass, Jan 13, 17.
Study & Training: Boston Mus Fine Arts Sch.
Work in Public Collections: Mus Fine Arts, Boston; Detroit Art Inst, Mich; De Saisset Mus, Santa Clara, Calif; Flint Inst Art, Mich; Crocker Art Gallery, Sacramento, Calif.

Exhibitions: Pa Acad Fine Arts, Philadelphia; Art Inst Chicago, Ill; Oehlschlaeger Gal, Sarasota, Fla; Galerie de Tours, San Francisco & Carmel, Calif; Main St Gallery, Rockport; plus many other group & one-man shows.
Memberships: Artists Equity Asn.
Dealer: Harmon Gallery, 125 S Third Ave, Naples, FL 33940.
Mailing Address: 2923 Lake Dr, Riviera Beach, FL 33404.

HICKEN, PHILIP BURNHAM
Painter, Educator
Preferred Media: Acrylics.
b Lynn, Mass, June 27, 10.
Study & Training: Mass Col Art.
Work in Public Collections: Metrop Mus Art, New York, N Y; Philadelphia Mus Fine Art, Pa; Brooklyn Mus, N Y; Libr of Cong, Washington, D C; U S Dept Mil Hist.
Commissions: Mural, Fed Art Proj, Fort Warren, Mass, 41; combat art, European Theatre, U S Army, 42-45; combat art assignment, U S Dept Mil Hist, 70.
Exhibitions: Boston Arts Festival, Mass, 54; Nat Acad, Rome, Italy, 54; Brooklyn Ann, N Y, 59; Eastern States Expos, Springfield, Mass, 60; Boston Soc Watercolors, Mass, 60-72.
Teaching: Instr painting, Harvard Univ Grad Sch Design, 50-53; instr painting, Boston Univ, 56-57; chmn dept fine arts, Art Inst Boston, 57-
Awards: Brooklyn Mus purchase award, 58; Boston Soc Watercolor Painters Award, 60; Yankee Mag award, Copley Galleries, 69.
Bibliography: Patricia Wilson (auth), article, In: Christian Sci Monitor, 66.
Memberships: Boston Soc Watercolor Painters; Boston Printmakers; Cambridge Art Asn; fel Royal Soc Art; Nantucket Art Asn.
Dealer: Eric Galleries, 61 E 57th St, New York, NY 10022.
Mailing Address: 108 Morse St, Watertown, MA 02221.

HICKEN, RUSSELL BRADFORD
Art Administrator, Lecturer
b Jacksonville, Fla, Dec 24, 26.
Study & Training: Fla State Univ, BS; Univ Fla.
Teaching: Instr art, Duncan Fletcher High Sch, Jacksonville, 51-57.
Positions: Dir, Jacksonville Art Mus, 57-63; dir, Tampa Art Inst, 63-66; dir, Mint Mus Art, Charlotte, N C, 66-68; dir, Jacksonville Art Mus, 68-
Memberships: Southeastern Mus Conf (pres, 68-70); Am Asn Mus (Southeastern Regional Rep, 70-)
Mailing Address: 4160 Boulevard Center Dr, Jacksonville, FL 33207.

HICKS, HAROLD JON (JACK)
Sculptor
Preferred Media: Steel, Aluminum, Wood
b Dubuque, Iowa, Nov 18, 39.
Study & Training: Univ Ariz, BFA; Univ Utah.
Work in Public Collections: Utah Mus Fine Arts, Salt Lake City; Salt Lake City Art Ctr; Tucson Art Ctr, Ariz; Univ Utah, Salt Lake City.
Exhibitions: Phoenix Ann, Ariz, 67; 73rd Western Ann Invitational, Denver, Colo, 71; three-man show, Salt Lake City Art Ctr, 72; 11th Biennial Utah Painting & Sculpture, Salt Lake City, 72; Mainstreams '72, Marietta, Ohio, 72.
Positions: Mgr gallery, Tucson Art Ctr, 63-67; asst to dir, Utah Mus Fine Arts, 68-
Mailing Address: 440 E 200 South, Centerville, UT 84014.

HIGA, (YOSHIHARU)
Painter, Photographer
b Okinawa, Japan, Jan 15, 38.
Study & Training: Tama Art Univ, Tokyo, Japan, BFA; Art Stud League New York, N Y; Pratt Graphic Ctr, New York.
Work in Public Collections: Mus Mod Art, New York; Brooklyn Mus, N Y; Philadelphia Mus, Pa; Los Angeles Co Mus, Calif; also at the Am Embassy.
Exhibitions: Contemp Japanese Art Exhib, Mus Tokyo, 64; 50th Ann Exhib, Soc Am Graphic Artists, 69; New Talent Printmaker, Assoc Am Artists, New York, 70; Int Engraving Biennial, Buenos Aires, Arg, 70; Am Graphics Artists traveling show to tour the East, U S Info Agency, 70.
Teaching: Instr drawing, painting & printmaking, Upsala Col, 69-; photographer, Mt St Vincent Col, 72-
Awards: Best print in show, 50th Ann Exhib, Soc Am Graphic Artists, 69; mus purchase award, Int Print Exhib, Seattle Art Mus, Wash, 70; mus purchase award, Nat Print Exhib, Boston, Mass.
Bibliography: Original art, hot off the presses, Life, 6/23/70; Famous artist ann, a treasury of contemp art, Famous Art Sch, 70.
Mailing Address: 135 Wooster St, New York, NY 10013.

HIGA, CHARLES EISHO
Painter, Instructor
Preferred Media: Watercolors, Clay.
b Honolulu, Hawaii, Feb 1, 33.
Study & Training: Univ Hawaii, BFA; N Y Univ, MA.
Work in Public Collections: Honolulu Acad Arts; work at state capitol bldg, State Found on Cult & Arts, Honolulu.
Commissions: Clay sculptures, Honolulu Int Airport & Chem Bldg, Univ Hawaii, 72.
Exhibitions: Watercolor U S A, Springfield, Mo, 63, 65 & 67; Crafts IV, Southwest Regional, Oakland, Calif, 68; The Excellence of the Object: Tour Exhib U S A, Am Crafts Coun, 69; Northern Ill Crafts Invitational, Oakbrook, 70.
Teaching: Instr art, Radford High Sch, Honolulu, 60-65; instr art educ, Univ Victoria, summer, 65; instr art, McKinley High Sch, Honolulu, 65-
Awards: Purchase prize, Honolulu Acad Arts, 67; purchase prize, Hawaii State Found on Cult & Arts, 69; teacher of yr, State Dept Educ, Hawaii, 70.
Memberships: Hawaii Painters & Sculptors League (v pres, 63); Hawaii Craftsmen (v pres, 70); Am Craftsmen.
Dealer: Daisy, Contemporary Crafts Gallery, 463 Kapahulu Ave, Honolulu, HI 96815.
Mailing Address: 3055 Pualei Circle, Apt 306, Honolulu, HI 96815.

HIGGINS, (GEORGE) EDWARD
Sculptor
b Gaffney, S C, Nov 13, 30.
Study & Training: Univ N C, BA, 54.
Work in Public Collections: Mus Mod Art, Solomon R Guggenheim Mus & Whitney Mus Am Art, New York, N Y; Albright-Knox Art Gallery, Buffalo, N Y; Dallas Mus Fine Arts, Tex; plus others.
Commissions: Sculpture, Cameron Bldg, New York, 62 & N Y State Theatre, Lincoln Ctr for Performing Arts, New York, 64.
Exhibitions: New York World's Fair, 64-65; Contemporary American Sculpture, Selection 1, Whitney Mus Am Art, 66; Flint Invitation, Flint Inst Art, Mich, 66; Documenta IV, Kassel, Ger, 68; Duke Univ, 69.
Teaching: Instr sculpture, Parsons Sch Design, 61-62; Philadelphia Mus Sch, 63.
Awards: Louis C Tiffany grant, 62; purchase prize, Flint Institute Art, 66.
Bibliography: Harriet Janis & Rudi Blesh (auth), Collage: Personalities—Concepts—Techniques, Chilton, 62; Sam Hunter (ed), New art around the world: painting and sculpture, Abrams, 66; Eduard Trier (auth), Form and space: sculpture in the 20th century, Praeger, 68.
Mailing Address: Old Philadelphia Rd, R F D 4, Easton, PA 18042.

HIGGINS, THOMAS J, JR
Cartoonist
b Far Rockaway, N Y, Nov 21, 22.
Study & Training: Cartoonists & Illusrs Sch, New York, with Jack Markow, Burne Hogarth & Dan Koerner.
Work in Public Collections: IBM Corp Collection.
Publications: Contribr cartoons, In: Sat Eve Post, Argosy, Theatre Arts, Extension, Parade & others, ed, Cartoon Markets, 59; publ The cartoon collector.
Mailing Address: 20-58 Crescent Ave, Astoria, NY 11102.

HIGHTOWER, JOHN B
Art Administrator
b Atlanta, Ga, May 23, 33.
Study & Training: Yale Univ, BA, 55.
Positions: Asst to pub, Am Heritage Publ Co, 61-63; exec asst, N Y State Coun on the Arts, 63-64, exec dir, 64-70, mem, 70-; cult adv, Rockefeller Mission to Latin Am for Pres Nixon, 69; Am rep, UNESCO Conf on Performing Arts, Canberra, Australia, 69; dir Mus Mod Art, New York, 70-72; pres, Assoc Councils of the Arts, 72-; chmn, Planning Corp for Arts; bd dirs, Urban Arts Corps, MacDowell Colony & Cunningham Dance Found; vis critic, Sch Drama, Yale Univ; mem, Comt for John & Yoko.
Awards: New York State Award, 70.
Memberships: Century Asn; Buffalo Acad Fine Arts.
Mailing Address: 333 Central Park W, New York, NY 10025.

HILDEBRAND, JUNE MARY ANN
Printmaker, Painter
b Eureka, Calif, Nov 2, 30.
Study & Training: Calif Col Arts & Crafts; Art Stud League New York, scholar; Queens Col, BFA; Hochschule Bildende Kunste Berlin; Hunter Col, MA; Pratt Graphic Ctr.
Work in Public Collections: Philadelphia Mus Art, Pa; Univ Wisconsin, Madison; N Y Pub Libr; Everson Mus Art; Univ Minn; plus others.

Exhibitions: Am Color Print Soc, 64-69; Pratt Int Miniature Print Exhib, 66 & 68; Oneonta State Univ, 67; Montclair State Col, 68; Gotham Bk Mart, New York, 69.
Publications: Contribr graphics, Artists Proof Mag.
Mailing Address: 229 E 12th St, Apt 2, New York, NY 10003.

HILDEBRANDT, WILLIAM ALBERT
Painter, Educator
Preferred Media: Oils.
b Philadelphia, Pa, Oct 1, 17.
Study & Training: Tyler Sch Art, Temple Univ, BFA, BSEd & MFA; Philadelphia Col Art, cert advert design.
Work in Public Collections: Glen-Croft Baptist Church, Folcroft, Pa.
Exhibitions: One-man shows, Philadelphia Art Alliance, 62 & Widener Col, Chester, Pa, 65; Am Drawing Biennial, Norfolk Mus Arts & Sci, Va, 67; Nat Drawing Soc Eastern Cent Regional Drawing Exhib, Philadelphia Mus Art, 65 & 70; Pennsylvania 71, William Penn Mem Mus, Harrisburg, 71.
Teaching: Supvr art educ, Philadelphia Pub Schs, 54-
Awards: Philip Klein Award, Tyler Sch Art Ann Alumni Show, 65; Francis Homer Award, Woodmere Gallery Earth-Sky-Water Exhib, 66; Best of Show Ann Award, Philadelphia Art Teachers Asn, 70.
Memberships: Philadelphia Art Teachers Asn (pres, 50-52); Tyler Sch Art Alumni Asn (pres, 47-48); Woodmere Art Gallery.
Publications: Illusr, The keystone state, 53; auth, Authur Graeff, John C Winston Co; illusr, Humanities curriculum, 68 & Echoes from Mount Olympus, 70, Instrnl Serv, Sch Dist of Philadelphia.
Mailing Address: 417 Turner Rd, Media, PA 19063.

HILDRETH, JOSEPH ALAN
Printmaker, Painter
Preferred Media: Intaglio
b Bowling Green, Ky, Sept 2, 47.
Study & Training: Western Ky Univ, BFA, 69; Pratt Inst, MFA, 71, with Walter Rogalski
Work in Public Collections: Mint Mus, Charlotte, N C.
Exhibitions: Western Ill Nat Print & Drawing Exhib, 70; St John's First Ann Drawing Show, 70; 6th Ann Piedmont Graphics, 70; Mercyhurst Nat Graphics Exhib, 70; 24th American Drawing Biennial, Norfolk Mus, 71.
Teaching: Instr painting, design & drawing, State Univ N Y Col Potsdam, 71-
Mailing Address: Route 1, Madrid, NY 13660.

HILL, CLINTON J
Painter
Preferred Media: Acrylics.
b Payette, Idaho, Mar 8, 22.
Study & Training: Univ Ore, BS, 47; Brooklyn Mus Art Sch, 49-51; Acad Grande Chaumiere, Paris, France, 51; Inst Arte Statale, Florence, Italy, 51-52.
Work in Public Collections: Mus Mod Art, New York, N Y; Philadelphia Mus Art, Pa; Brooklyn Mus, N Y; Phoenix Art Mus, Ariz; Hampton Inst, Va.
Exhibitions: Drawing U S A, Mus Mod Art, New York, 56; Collage in America, Am Fedn Arts Circulating Exhib, 58; Two Decades of America Prints, Brooklyn Mus, 68; five one-man exhibs, Zabriskie Gallery, New York, 55-71; Recent American Painting, Chicago Art Inst, Ill, 72.
Teaching: Instr design, Queens Col (N Y), 68-
Awards: Fulbright grant to India, 56.
Bibliography: Harriet Janis & Rudi Blesh (auth), Collage: personalities, concepts, techniques, Chilton, 62; Lawrence Campbell (auth), Reviews & previews, Art News, 3/71; Robert Pincus-Witten (auth), New York, Artforum, 5/71.
Dealer: Zabriskie Gallery, 29 W 57th St, New York, NY 10019.
Mailing Address: 178 Prince St, New York, NY 10012.

HILL, DALE LOGAN
Painter, Instructor
Preferred Media: Oils.
b Boise, Idaho, July 23, 09.
Study & Training: Minneapolis Inst Art, scholar; Am Acad Art, Chicago, Ill; Frederick Mizen Sch Art; also with Pruett Carter, Stanley Parkhouse, Harry Timmins, Haddon Sundlom & other prominent instructors.
Commissions: Many pvt commissions of prominent personalities.
Exhibitions: Village Gallery, Taos, N Mex; Jamison Gallery, Santa Fe, N Mex; Desert Southwest Gallery, Palm Desert, Calif; Desert Art Mus, Palm Springs, Calif; Laguna Art Asn Gallery, Laguna Beach, Calif; plus others.
Teaching: Instr art, Orange Co Art Inst; instr art, pvt classes.
Positions: Owner, dir & instr, South Coast Acad Art, Santa Ana & Newport Beach, Calif; owner, D Logan Hill Fine Art Gallery, Carmel, Calif.

Memberships: Am Inst Fine Arts; Allied Artists Am; Los Angeles Art Dir Club.
Art Interests: Paintings in oil of antique silver, cut glass and crystal; palette knife westerns.
Mailing Address: Lincoln between Fifth & Sixth, P O Box 4381, Carmel, CA 93921.

HILL, DOROTHY KENT
Museum curator
b New York, N Y, Feb 3, 07.
Study & Training: Vassar Col, AB; John Hopkins Univ, PhD.
Positions: Res assoc, Walters Art Gallery, Baltimore, Md, 34-37, assoc cur ancient art, 37-40, cur ancient art, 40-69, cur Greek & Roman art, 70-
Memberships: Archaeol Inst Am; Am Oriental Soc; corresp mem, Deutsches Archäologisches Institut, Istituto di Studi Etruschi ed Italici.
Publications: Auth, Catalog of classical bronze sculpture, Walters Art Gallery, 49; ed, book rev, Old World, Am J Archaeol, 58-; ed, Bull, Walters Art Gallery, 48-71; auth, articles in Am J Archaeol, Hesperia & others.
Mailing Address: 259 W 31st St, Baltimore, MD 21211.

HILL, (JAMES) JEROME
Painter
b St Paul, Minn, Mar 2, 05.
Study & Training: Yale Univ, BA, 27; Brit Acad Painting, Rome, 27-28; Scandinavian Acad Art, Paris, 28-32.
Work in Public Collections: Mus Mod Art, New York, N Y; Minneapolis Inst Art, Minn; St Paul Art Ctr, Minn.
Commissions: Frescoes, St Paul Acad, 21-22, murals, 65; stations of the cross & windows, Chapel Our Lady of Mercy, Boca Grande, Fla.
Exhibitions: Santa Barbara Mus Art, 57; Carstairs Gallery, New York, 61; Babcock Galleries, 64-; St Paul Art Ctr, 65.
Awards: Acad Award for Albert Schweitzer (motion picture), 38.
Publications: Dir of motion pictures incl Grandma Moses, 53, Merry Christmas, 68, Anti Corrida, 68, The artist's friend, 69 & The canaries, 69.
Dealer: Babcock Galleries, 805 Madison Ave, New York, NY 10021.
Mailing Address: Hotel Algonquin, 59 W 44th St, New York, NY 10036.

HILL, JIM
Sculptor, Art Dealer
Preferred Media: Plexiglass, Metals.
b Albuquerque, N Mex, Mar 24, 44.
Study & Training: Univ N Mex, BFA & MA, with Charles Mattox.
Work in Public Collections: Fine Arts Mus, Univ N Mex, Albuquerque; Mus N Mex, Santa Fe.
Exhibitions: Tri-Culture Show, Mus N Mex, 69; Light Sculpture, Esther Robles Gallery, Los Angeles, Calif, 70; Art Multiples, Univ Md Art Mus, Baltimore, 71; Light Sculpture, Hill's Gallery, Santa Fe, 71; Scheid-Hill, Deson-Zaks Gallery, Chicago, 71.
Positions: Owner, Hill's Gallery, Santa Fe.
Bibliography: Jim Hill, light sculpture, Art Int spec summer issue, 70; Light sculpture (Jim Hill), Southwest Art Gallery Mag, 1/72.
Memberships: N Mex Mus Found.
Specialty of Gallery: Fine arts.
Publications: Auth, My plexiglas and light sculptures, Leonardo, 3: 9-17.
Mailing Address: Rte 2, Box 3, Santa Fe, NM 87501.

HILL, JOAN (CHEA-SE-QUAH)
Painter, Illustrator
Preferred Media: Oils, Gouache, Acrylics, Collage, Tempera.
b Muskogee, Okla.
Study & Training: Northeastern State Col, BA Educ, 52; Famous Artists Course, 53-; spec study Indian art, with Dick West, 58-63; pvt study with int artists, 58-72; extensive air-travel-study on T H Hewitt Painting Workshops, 64-72, with Dong Kingman, Millard Sheets, Rex Brandt & George Post.
Work in Public Collections: Heard Mus, Phoenix, Ariz; Dept Interior, Arts & Crafts Bd, Washington, D C; Mus of the American Indian, Heye Found, New York, NY; Fine Arts Mus of N Mex, Santa Fe; Philbrook Art Ctr Mus, Tulsa, Okla.
Commissions: 14 portraits (pastel), Hardin Nelson Co, Muskogee, Okla, 59; two mural-type oil paintings of Cherokee Nation through Dept Interior, Tahlequah, Okla, 67; portrait (gouache) for book, Sam Houston with the Cherokees, comn by Rennard Strickland & Jack Gregory Collection, Tulsa, Okla, 67; portrait & ten illus for book poetry, Five Civilized Tribes Mus, Muskogee, Okla, 68; two mural-type oil paintings, comn by U S Dept Interior Designer for Govt Bldgs, Albuquerque, N Mex, 69.
Exhibitions: Five Ann Center Arts Indian America, Dept Interior, 64, 67-70; American Embassies Overseas, Dept Interior Traveling Exhibition, 65-66; America Discovers Indian Art, Smithsonian Inst, Washington, D C, 67; Outstanding Indian Painters &

Sculptors' Hon Exhib, Princeton Univ, 70; Hon Exhib sponsored by Am for Indian Opportunity, Washington Gallery of Art, 71; plus others.
Teaching: Instr art, Tulsa Secondary Pub Schs, 52-56; instr art, adult art educ, Muskogee Art Guild, 59-60.
Positions: Art dir & publicity dir, Muskogee Art Guild, 58-64; career day art consult, Am Asn Univ Women, 62-63.
Awards: Three first awards, Philbrook Art Ctr Mus, 66, 68 & 71; Walter Bimson Grand Award, Scottsdale Nat Indian Arts Exhib, Ariz, 68; grand spec award, All Am Indian Art Exhib, Sheridan, Wyo, 71; plus over 100 major awards, 52-
Bibliography: Bill Harmon (auth), Not bound by tradition, Orbit Mag, 7/21/63; Joan Bucklew Hale (auth), A critic views Indian art in general and painting in particular, New Dimensions in Indian Art, 65; Marion Gridley (auth), Indians of Today, Indian Coun Fire Publ, 71.
Memberships: Nat League Am Pen Women; Int Platform Asn; Southwestern Art Asn; Muskogee Art Students Guild (art dir & publicity dir, 58-64); Intercontinental Biog Asn.
Publications: Illusr, A history of the Baird-Scales family, 60; contribr, Look to the mountain top, 72; constrib & illusr, The American way, Am Airlines, 72.
Mailing Address: Rte 3, Box 151, Harris Rd, Muskogee, OK 74401.

HILL, MARVIN WILLIAM
Painter
Preferred Media: Sumi Ink, Tempera.
b Akron, Ohio, Nov 18, 15.
Study & Training: Akron Univ, with Malcolm Dashiell; Art Stud League New York.
Work in Public Collections: Canton Art Inst, Canton, Ohio; Massillon Mus, Massillon, Ohio.
Exhibitions: Jewish Ctr Art Show, Canton, 65; Akron Art Inst Ann Spring Show, 65; Ohio State Fair, Columbus, 66; one-man shows, Massillon Mus, 66 & Canton Art Inst, 67.
Awards: First prize watercolor, Jewish Ctr, second prize graphics, Ohio State Fair, Columbus, 66; first prize print, Canton Art Inst, 66.
Mailing Address: 1000 Third St S W, Canton, OH 44707.

HILL, MEGAN LLOYD
Sculptor, Art Dealer
Preferred Media: Leather, Ceramics, Beads, Feathers.
b Chicago, Ill, Sept 22, 42.
Study & Training: Ind Univ, BA, 65; Univ Chicago, with Max Kuhn; Univ N Mex, with Charles Mattox, MA, 69.
Work in Public Collections: Univ N Mex Fine Arts Mus, Albuquerque; Mus N Mex, Santa Fe.
Exhibitions: Five-State Invitational, Port Arthur, Tex, 71; Intrinsic Art, Friends of Contemp Art, Denver, Colo, 71; Southwest Biennial, Mus N Mex, Santa Fe, 72; 1972 Fall Invitational, Roswell Mus, N Mex, 72; one-man show, Hill's Gallery, Santa Fe, 71 & 72; plus other one-man shows.
Positions: Owner, Hill's Gallery.
Awards: Two hon mentions, Five-State Invitational, Port Arthur, 71; hon mention, Southwest Biennial, Mus N Mex, 72.
Bibliography: Donna Meilack (auth), Leather book, 71; article, In: Art in Am, 8/72; article, In: Southwest Art Gallery Mag, 12/72.
Memberships: Mus N Mex Found.
Specialty of Gallery: Contemporary New Mexico art.
Publications: Contribr, Aiming at the creative environment, Southwest Art Gallery Mag, 11/71.
Mailing Address: 121 Lincoln Ave, Santa Fe, NM 87501.

HILL, PETER
Painter, Educator
Preferred Media: Acrylics, Oils.
b Detroit, Mich, Nov 29, 33.
Study & Training: Albion Col, AB, 56; Cranbrook Acad Art, Bloomfield Hills, Mich, MFA, 58.
Work in Public Collections: Joslyn Art Mus, Omaha, Nebr; Sheldon Mem Gallery, Lincoln, Nebr; Springfield Art Mus, Mo; Sioux City Art Ctr, Iowa; Spiva Art Gallery, Joplin, Mo.
Exhibitions: Nelson Gallery Mid-Am Ann, Kansas City, Mo, 68; Max Nat Painting Exhib, Purdue Univ, Lafayette, Ind, 69; Springfield Art Mus Ann, Mo, 70; Northern Ill Univ Nat Drawing Exhib, De Kalb, 71; Twelfth Midwest Biennial, Joslyn Art Mus, Omaha, 72.
Teaching: From instr to chmn dept, Univ Nebr, Omaha, 58-
Awards: Ford Found Purchase Award, Twelfth Ann Mid-Am Exhib, 62; Springfield Art Mus Purchase Awards, Ann, 63 & Watercolor U S A, 67.
Dealer: Gallery at the Market, 1102 Howard St, Omaha, NE 68102.
Mailing Address: 11734 Shirley St, Omaha, NE 68144.

HILL, POLLY KNIPP
Etcher, Painter
b Ithaca, N Y, Apr 2, 00.
Study & Training: Univ Ill; Syracuse Univ, BP; Acad Colarossi, Paris; also painting with George Snow Hill, Paris.
Work in Public Collections: Syracuse Mus Fine Arts, N Y; Libr Cong, Washington, D C; Metrop Mus Art, New York, N Y; J B Speed Mem Mus, Louisville, Ky; New York Pub Libr.
Commissions: Gift print for Printmakers Soc Calif, 62.
Exhibitions: Nat Acad Design; Soc Am Graphic Artists; Chicago Soc Etchers; Libr Cong; one-man show, Smithsonian Inst.
Teaching: Instr art, George S Hill Studios, 40-50.
Awards: Nathan I Bijur Award, Brooklyn Soc Etchers, 29; Libr Cong Purchase Prizes, Philadelphia Print Club, 41, Nat Acad Design, 43 & Soc Am Etchers, 47; plus others.
Bibliography: Fine prints of the year, 30, 32 & 33; Contemporary American prints, 31; Albert Reese (auth), Prize prints of the twentieth century, 49.
Memberships: Soc Am Graphic Artists; Mus Fine Arts St Petersburg; Ringling Mus Art.
Publications: Illusr, Woodpile poems, 36, Bible chillun, 39, Dark windows, 42 & Rainbow through the web, 44.
Dealer: R&R Robinson Galleries, Naples, FL 33940; Contemporary Galleries, St Petersburg, FL 33730.
Mailing Address: 2233 Green Way S, St Petersburg, FL 33712.

HILLES, SUSAN MORSE
Collector, Patron
b Simsbury, Conn, July 4, 05.
Study & Training: Mus Fine Arts Sch, Boston, 24-25; Sacker Sch Design, Boston, 26-29; Kings Col, Halifax, N S, DCL, 58; Wheaton Col, LittD, 67.
Positions: Trustee, Yale Art Gallery Assocs, 57-; trustee, Mus Fine Arts Boston, 68-; trustee, Larry Aldrich Mus, 69; trustee, Whitney Mus Am Art, 70; hon trustee, Wadsworth Athcneum, 71; trustee, Am Acad in Rome, 72.
Collection: Contemporary sculpture and painting.
Mailing Address: P O Box 525, Old Lyme, CT 06371.

HILLMAN, ARTHUR STANLEY
Printmaker, Educator
Preferred Media: Photo Silk-screen.
b Brooklyn, N Y, Feb 21, 45.
Study & Training: Philadelphia Col Art, with Jerome Kaplan & Benton Spruance, BFA; Univ Mass, Amherst, MFA.
Exhibitions: 4th Print & Drawing Nat, Dulin Gallery Art, Knoxville, Tenn, 68; 21st & 22nd Nat Exhib, Libr Cong, Washington, D C, 69 & 71; Prize Winning Am Prints, Pratt Graphics Ctr, New York, N Y, 69; one-man show, Philadelphia Art Alliance, Pa, 70.
Teaching: Instr printmaking & chmn dept, Mass Col Art, Boston, 68-
Awards: Univ Mass fel, 67; Pennell Fund Purchase Award, Libr Cong, 69; Northern Ill Univ Purchase Award, 70.
Memberships: Col Art Asn Am; Philadelphia Print Club; Pratt Graphics Ctr.
Mailing Address: 53 Fairview Ave, Nashua, N H 03060.

HILLSMITH, FANNIE
Painter
b Boston, Mass, Mar 13, 11.
Study & Training: Boston Mus Fine Arts Sch; Art Stud League New York, with Alexander Brook, Kuniyoshi, Zorach & Sloan; Atelier 17, with Stanley Hayter.
Work in Public Collections: Mus Mod Art, New York, N Y; Boston Mus Fine Arts, Mass; Currier Gallery Art, Manchester, N H; Fogg Mus Art, Cambridge, Mass; Newark Mus Art, N J; plus others.
Exhibitions: Boston Arts Festival, 50-54 & 56-61; Berkshire Art Asn, 56-58 & 64; Cornell Univ, 64; one-man retrospective, Brockton Mus, Mass, 71 & Bristol Mus, R I, 72; plus many others.
Teaching: Vis critic, Cornell Univ, 63-64.
Awards: Alumni traveling scholar, Boston Mus Fine Arts Sch, 58; Tour Gallery Award, 64; Berkshire Mus Award, 64; plus many others.
Memberships: Art Educ Asn.
Mailing Address: 915 Second Ave, New York, NY 10017.

HILTON, JOHN WILLIAM
Painter, Illustrator
Preferred Media: Oils, Wax.
b Carrington, N Dak, Sept 9, 04.
Study & Training: With Maynard Dixon, Clyde Forsythe & Nicolai Fechin; Int Inst Arts & Lett fel; Am Inst Fine Arts fel.
Work in Public Collections: Desert Southwest Art Gallery, Palm Desert, Calif; La Verne Col; Nat Park Visitor Ctrs; San Diego Mus Nat Hist; Palm Springs Desert Mus; plus many others.

Commissions: Murals, Desert Southwest Gallery, 37 & Saddleback Western Gallery, Santa Ana, Calif, 62; diorama, Living Desert Reserve, Palm Desert, Calif, 72.
Exhibitions: Hundreds of group & one-man shows in U S & abroad, 35-72.
Bibliography: Dave Packwood (auth), An artist looks at Baja California, Westways, 3/56; Mason Sutherland (auth), Californians escape to the desert, Nat Geog, 57; Ed Ainsworth (auth), Painters of the desert (bk), Desert Mag, 60; plus many others.
Memberships: Grand Cent Art Gallery; Salmagundi Club; life mem Laguna Beach Art Asn; Lahaina Art Asn; life mem Twentynine Palms Artists Guild (pres, 52-55).
Publications: Auth & illusr, What makes the jumping bean jump, Sat Eve Post, 42; auth & illusr, Sonora sketchbook, Macmillan, 47; auth & illusr, This is my desert, Ariz Hwys, 64; auth & illusr, Hilton paints the desert, Desert Mag; plus many articles.
Dealers: Grand Central Galleries, 40 Vanderbilt Ave, New York, NY 10017; Desert Southwest Galleries, Palm Desert, CA 92260.
Mailing Address: P O Box 357, Lahaina Maui, HI 96761.

HILTS, ALVIN
Sculptor
Preferred Media: Wood, Stone.
b Newmarket, Ont, Apr 2, 08.
Study & Training: In Mex & Can.
Work in Public Collections: Churches, Kirkland Lake, Welland & Newmarket; also in schs.
Commissions: Mem, Newmarket, 36; Univ Guelph, 61; Univ Lennoxville, 70; also private comns, Vancouver, Toronto, Ottawa, Oshawa & Saint Louis.
Exhibitions: Sculpture Soc, 31-72; Royal Can Acad; Ont Soc Artists.
Memberships: Sculpture Soc Can (pres, 57, 58 & 61).
Mailing Address: 605 Oshawa Blvd N, Oshawa, Ont, Can.

HINDS, PATRICK SWAZO, see SWAZO.

HINKHOUSE, FOREST MELICK
Art Consultant
b West Liberty, Iowa, July 7, 25.
Study & Training: Coe Col, AB; Univ Mex; res at Fogg Art Mus, Harvard Univ; New York Univ Inst Fine Arts, MA; Univ Madrid, PhD.
Collections Arranged: Industrial Gouaches of John Hultberg, 57; Paintings & Portraits by Frank Mason, 58; Contemporary Arizona Painting, 58; Festival of Arts, 58; One Hundred Years of French Painting 1860-1960, 61; English Landscape Painting, 61.
Teaching: Asst prof art, Albright Art Sch, Univ Buffalo, 56-57; lects, Spanish Painting, Mediaeval Art, Art of the Far East & Contemporary Art.
Positions: Pub relations, Int House Asn, New York; art critic, Buffalo Eve News, Ariz Repub & Phoenix Gazette; dir, Phoenix Art Mus & Phoenix Fine Arts Asn, 57-67; co-founder, Hinkhouse Gallery, Coe Col, 65; consult & adv, Phoenix Art Mus, 67-; consult, Calif Art Comn, 68-; co-founder, Hinkhouse Collection, Melick Libr, Eureka Col, Ill, 69.
Memberships: Claustro Extraordinario, Madrid; Col Art Asn Am; Am Asn Mus.
Mailing Address: 1815 Jones St, San Francisco, CA 94109.

HINMAN, CHARLES B
Painter, Sculptor
Preferred Media: Acrylics.
b Syracuse, N Y, Dec 29, 32.
Study & Training: Syracuse Univ, BFA, 55; Art Stud League New York, with Morris Kantor.
Work in Public Collections: Mus Mod Art, New York, N Y; Larry Aldrich Mus Contemp Art, Conn; Los Angeles Co Mus, Calif; Detroit Inst Art, Mich; Mus Mod Art, Nagaoka, Japan; plus many others.
Exhibitions: Retrospective, Philharmonic Hall, Lincoln Ctr, New York, 69; Opening Exhib, Contemp Art Ctr, Cincinnati, Ohio, 70; Contemporary Painting and Sculpture from New York Galleries, Wilmington Soc Fine Arts, Delaware Art Ctr, 70; Selections from Chase Manhattan Bank Collection, Finch Col, 71; Sculpture and Shapes of the Last Decade, Aldrich Mus, Ridgefield, Conn; plus many others.
Mailing Address: 231 Bowery, New York, NY 10002.

HIOS, THEO
Painter, Graphic Artist
Preferred Media: Oils, Acrylics.
b Sparta, Greece, Feb 2, 10; U S citizen.
Study & Training: Am Artists Sch; Art Stud League New York; Pratt Inst; Nat Univ Athens.
Work in Public Collections: Griffiths Art Ctr, St Lawrence Univ, Canton, N Y; Parrish Art Mus, Southampton, N Y; Guild Hall Mus,

Easthampton, N Y; Rose Art Mus, Brandeis Univ, Waltham, Mass; Tel Aviv Mus, Israel; plus others.
Exhibitions: Int Watercolor Exhib, 47 & Long Island Artists, 58, Brooklyn Mus, N Y; Fedn Mod Painters & Sculptors, traveling exhib sponsored by Am Fedn Arts, 54 & 55; Carnegie Inst Int Exhib, 61; Guild Hall Mus Regional, 61, 63 & 69; Pa Acad Fine Arts Nat, 62; plus fourteen one-man shows in galleries & museums.
Teaching: Instr painting & drawing, City Col New York, 58-61; instr painting & drawing, Dalton Sch, 62-; instr painting & drawing, New Sch Soc Res, 62-
Awards: First prize, New Eng Exhib, Silvermine Guild Artists, 48; purchase prize, Riverside Mus, 62; one-man show award, Guild Hall Mus, 69; plus one other.
Bibliography: Lawrence Campbell (auth), article, In: Art News, 11/63; Marshall Matusow (auth), article, In: Art Collector's Almanac, 65.
Memberships: Fedn Mod Painters & Sculptors (v pres, 57-62, 66-).
Mailing Address: 136 W 95th St, New York, NY 10025.

HIRSCH, DAVID W (DAVE)
Cartoonist
b New York, N Y, Dec 26, 19.
Study & Training: Brooklyn Col; Art Stud League New York; Grand Cent Art Sch; Cartoonist & Illustrators Sch.
Publications: Contribr cartoons, Sat Eve Post, Look, Christian Sci Monitor, Argosy, Am Legion Mag, U S Info Agency Russian publ, America, Am Weekly, Wall St Jour, King Features Syndicate & MacNaught Syndicate; plus others.
Mailing Address: 627 Second Ave, New York, NY 10016.

HIRSCH, HORTENSE M
Patron
b Chicago, Ill, Aug 25, 87.
Study & Training: Smith College, BA; Mus Mod Art; also pvt classes.
Mailing Address: Hotel Pierre, 2 E 61st St, New York, NY 10021.

HIRSCH, JOSEPH
Painter
b Philadelphia, Pa, Apr 25, 10.
Study & Training: Philadelphia Mus Sch, 27-31; also with Henry Hensche, Provincetown & George Luks, New York, N Y.
Work in Public Collections: Whitney Mus Am Art & Mus Mod Art, New York; Corcoran Gallery Art, Washington, D C; Boston Mus Fine Arts, Mass; Metrop Mus Art, New York; plus many others.
Commissions: Murals, Benjamin Franklin High Sch, Philadelphia, Amalgamated Clothing Workers Bldg, Philadelphia & Philadelphia Munic Court Bldg; documentary paintings for U S Govt.
Exhibitions: Paintings exhibited in principal mus & galleries of U S, 34-; one-man shows, major cities of the U S, 34-
Teaching: Instr painting sem, Univ Utah, summer 59; instr painting, Art Stud League New York, 59-67; vis artist, Dartmouth Col, 66; instr, Brigham Young Univ, 71.
Awards: Altman Prize, Nat Acad Design, 59 & 67; purchase prize, Butler Inst Am Art, 64; Carnegie Prize, 68; plus many others.
Memberships: Artists Equity Asn (founder); Nat Acad Design (first treas); Nat Inst Arts & Lett; Philadelphia Watercolor Club.
Mailing Address: 90 Riverside Dr, New York, NY 10024.

HIRSCH, RICHARD TELLER
Museum Curator, Writer
b Denver, Colo, Sept 12, 14.
Study & Training: Ecole Louvre, Acad Grande Chaumiere & Inst Art Contemp, Paris, France.
Collections Arranged: Four Centuries of Still Life, 59; Great Periods of Tapestry, 60; The World of Benjamin West, 62; James A Michener Foundation Collection, 63 & 65; Chalres Sheeler Retrospective, 63; Arms and Armor, 64; 17th Century Painters of Haarlem, 65; The History of Glass, 66; Charles Dent Collection of Bronzes, 67; Eugène Carrière, Seer of the Real, 68.
Teaching: Lect on art hist.
Positions: Publ graphics, Paris, 37-39, 45-46; art critic, Palm Beach Times, 54-56; dir, Pensacola Art Ctr, 56-59; dir, Allentown Art Mus, 59-68; spec cur, The Michener Collection, Univ Tex, Austin, 68-71; dir, Auckland City Art Gallery, N Z, 72-
Awards: Samuel H Kress Found museology study grant, 67.
Memberships: Am Asn Mus; Am Fedn Arts; Col Art Asn Am; Am Soc Aesthet; Int Coun Mus; plus others.
Mailing Address: 10 Shortland Flats, Auckland, N Z.

HIRSCH, WILLARD NEWMAN
Sculptor
b Charleston, S C, Nov 19, 05.
Study & Training: Nat Acad Design; Beaux Arts Inst Design.
Work in Public Collections: Gibbes Art Gallery, Charleston, S C; Columbia Mus Art, S C; Florence Mus Art, S C; S C State Art

Collection, Columbia; Sculpture of Western Hemisphere, IBM Collection.

Commissions: Stainless steel works, Clemson Univ, 49-55 & Charleston Co Libr, 61; Pulpit Sculpture, Woodsdale Temple, Wheeling, W Va, 65; steel & brass sculpture, Porter-Gaud Sch, Charleston, 66; bronze fountain figure, Home Fed Savings & Loan, Charleston, 70.

Exhibitions: Nat Acad Design, New York, N Y, 35-42; Pa Acad Fine Art, Philadelphia, 42; Syracuse Mus Art, N Y, 48; Fairmont Park Third Int, Philadelphia, 49; Whitney Mus Am Art, New York, 50.

Teaching: Pvt instr.

Bibliography: Jack Morris, Jr (auth), Contemporary artists of South Carolina, S C Tricentennial Comn, 70.

Memberships: Charleston Artists Guild; S C Artists Guild (pres).

Mailing Address: 2 Queen St, Charleston, SC 29401.

HIRSCHFELD, ALBERT
Caricaturist

Preferred Media: Ink.

b St Louis, Mo, June 21, 03.

Study & Training: Nat Acad Design, New York, N Y; Julien's, Paris; London Co Coun; Art Stud League New York.

Work in Public Collections: Whitney Mus Am Art, New York; Mus Mod Art, New York; Metrop Mus Art, New York; Brooklyn Mus Art, N Y; St Louis Mus Art.

Commissions: Hist of Cinema, Fifth Ave Playhouse, New York, 45; Personalities, Eden Roc Hotel, Miami, Fla, 55; Am Theatre, Brussels World's Fair, 59; Opening Night, Playbill Room, Manhattan Hotel, N Y, 60.

Exhibitions: One-man shows, Staten Island Mus, N Y, 61; Hammer Gallery, New York, 67 & Mus Performing Arts, Lincoln Ctr, New York, 68.

Positions: Theatre caricaturist, New York Times, 23-

Awards: Specialist grant, U S State Dept.

Publications: Auth, Harlem, Hyperion, 41; auth, Show business is no business, Simon & Schuster, 51; auth, The American theatre George Braziller, 61; auth, The world of Hirschfeld, Abrams, 71.

Mailing Address: 122 E 95th St, New York, NY 10028.

HIRSCHL, NORMAN
Art Dealer

Positions: Co-owner & dir, Hirschl & Adler Galleries.

Mailing Address: 21 E 67th St, New York, NY 10021.

HIRSHHORN, JOSEPH H
Collector

b Latvia, Aug 11, 99; U S citizen.

Positions: Trustee, George Washington Univ, Washington, D C, Friends of Whitney Mus, Arch Am Art & Palm Springs Mus, Calif.

Bibliography: Jay Jacobs & Jean Lipman (auth), The collector in America, Viking Press, 71.

Art Interests: Donated Hirshhorn Museum and Sculpture Garden, Smithsonian Institution, Washington, D C.

Collection: American nineteenth and twentieth century painting; European twentieth century painting; sculpture from antiquity to the present.

Mailing Address: Round Hill, John St, Greenwich, CT 06830.

HITCH, JEAN LEASON
Painter

Preferred Media: Oils.

b Sydney, Australia, Oct 18, 18; U S citizen.

Study & Training: Melbourne Tech Art Training Sch, Australia; Leason Sch Painting; Wayman Adams Sch Painting, Adirondacks, N Y.

Exhibitions: Allied Artists Am, New York, N Y; Am Artist Prof League, New York; Catharine Lorillard Wolfe Art Club, New York; Hudson Valley Art Asn, White Plains, N Y; Audubon Artists, New York.

Positions: Art curator, Staten Island Inst Arts & Sci, 45-51.

Awards: Kathleen Grumbacher Award, 66; Coun Am Artists Soc Award, 69; Anna Hyatt Huntington Horse-Head Award, 72.

Memberships: Allied Artists Am; Catharine Lorillard Wolfe Art Club (first v pres, 71); Hudson Valley Art Asn; Am Artist Prof League.

Mailing Address: 2187 Clove Rd, Staten Island, NY 10305.

HITCH, ROBERT A
Painter

Preferred Media: Oils.

b Brooklyn, N Y, May 12, 20.

Study & Training: Art Career Sch, New York, N Y; also painting with Wilford S Conrow, Percy Leason & Douglas Grant.

Work in Public Collections: Hickory Art Mus, N C; Tamassee D A R Sch, S C.

Exhibitions: Allied Artists Am, New York; Am Artists Prog League, New York; Hudson Valley Art Asn, White Plains, N Y; Staten Island Mus Arts & Sci, N Y; Nat Arts Club, New York.

Awards: Henry Ward Ranger Prize, Nat Acad Design, 54; Grand Nat Award, Am Artists Prof League, 54.

Memberships: Allied Artists Am (pub relations, 69-); Hudson Valley Art Asn; Am Artists Prof League.

Mailing Address: 2187 Clove Rd, Staten Island, NY 10305.

HITCHCOCK, HENRY RUSSELL
Art Historian, Art Critic

b Boston, Mass, June 3, 03.

Study & Training: Harvard Univ, AB, 24, MA, 27.

Teaching: Asst prof art, Vassar Col, 27-28; asst prof art, Wesleyan Univ, 29-41, assoc prof, 41-47, prof, 47-48; instr, Conn Col, 34-42; prof art, Smith Col, 48-61, Sophia Smith prof art, 61-68; prof art Univ Mass, Amherst, 68; adj prof, Inst Fine Arts, New York Univ, 69-; lectr, Mass Inst Technol, 46-48, vis lect, Yale Univ, 52-53, 59-60, 69; vis lect, Cambridge Univ, 62, Harvard Univ, 65, Columbia Univ, 71.

Positions: Dir, Smith Col Mus Art, 49-55.

Awards: Soc Archit Historians Book Award, 55; Col Art Asn Book Award, 58; Am Coun Learned Soc Prize, 61; plus others.

Memberships: Franklin fel Royal Soc Arts; Soc Archit Historians (dir, pres, N Y chap, 70-); Victorian Soc Am (pres, 69-); Col Art Asn Am; Royal Inst Brit Architects.

Publications: Auth, In the nature of materials, the buildings of Frank Lloyd Wright, 42 & 69; auth, Architecture: 19th and 20th centuries, 58, 69 & 72; auth, Rococo architecture in Southern Germany, 69; co-auth, Architecture in England, Arno, 70; auth, Modern architecture: romanticism & reintegration, Hacker, 71; plus others.

Mailing Address: 152 E 62nd St, New York, NY 10021.

HNIZDOVSKY, JACQUES
Painter, Printmaker

Preferred Media: Oils, Woodcuts.

b Pylypcze, Ukraine, Jan 27, 15; U S citizen.

Study & Training: Acad Fine Arts, Warsaw; Acad Fine Arts, Zagreb, Yugoslavia.

Work in Public Collections: Mus Fine Arts, Boston, Mass; Philadelphia Mus Art, Pa; Cleveland Mus, Ohio; Nelson Rockefeller Collection; Mus Mod Art, Spain.

Exhibitions: Boston Printmakers Ann, Mus Fine Arts, Boston, 61-; Contemporary U S Graphic Arts, U S S R, 63; Contemporary U S Printmakers, Tokyo, Japan, 67; one-man shows, Lumley-Cazalet, London, Eng, 69 & 72; one-man retrospective, Ten Years of Woodcuts, Assoc Am Artists, New York, N Y, 71.

Awards: Tiffany fel, 61; first prize for woodcut, Mus Fine Arts, Boston, 62; MacDowell Colony fel, 63.

Bibliography: Slavko Nowytski (auth), Sheep in wood (film), Am Film Festival, New York, 71.

Memberships: Soc Am Graphic Artists; Audubon Artists; Boston Printmakers; Int Platform Asn.

Publications: Illusr (woodcuts), Poems of John Keats, Crowell-Collier, 64; illusr (woodcuts), Poems of Samuel Taylor Coleridge, Crowell-Collier, 67; illusr, Tree tails in Central Park, 71; co-auth & illusr, Flora exotica, D Godine, Boston, 72.

Dealer: Associated American Artists, 663 Fifth Ave, New York, NY 10017.

Mailing Address: 5270 Post Rd, Riverdale, NY 10471.

HOARE, TYLER JAMES
Sculptor, Printmaker

Preferred Media: Wood, Metals.

b Joplin, Mo, June 5, 40.

Study & Training: Univ Colo; Sculpture Ctr, New York, N Y; Univ Kans, BFA, 63; Calif Col Arts & Crafts, Oakland.

Work in Public Collections: U S Info Agency, Washington, D C; State Univ N Y Albany; Oakland Mus, Calif; plus many private collections.

Exhibitions: One-man shows, Univ Calif, Berkeley, 66 & 67; John Bolles Gallery, San Francisco, Calif, 69 & 71 & Camberwell Sch Art, London, Eng, 71; 4th Int Print Exhib, Pratt Graphics Ctr, New York, 71, 22nd Nat Print Exhib, Libr of Cong, Washington, D C, 71; plus many other one-man & group shows.

Teaching: Guest lectr Xerox prints, San Francisco Art Inst, 72.

Awards: Merit award, 22nd Ann San Francisco Art Festival, San Francisco Art Comn, 68; jurors choice award, West Art Graphic '70; merit award, 2nd Ann Graphic Exhib, Olive Hyde Art Ctr, 72.

Bibliography: Thomas Albright (auth), Funk refinement, San Francisco Chronicle, 3/69; New American sculpture, U S Info Agency, 71; Robert Cartmell (auth), Xerox is okay-but will it last?, Albany Times Union, 2/72.

Art Interests: Development of a techno-art form using xerographic processes.
Dealer: John Bolles Gallery, 10 Gold St, San Francisco, CA 94601.
Mailing Address: 30 Menlo Pl, Berkeley, CA 94707.

HOBBIE, LUCILLE
Painter, Illustrator
Preferred Media: Watercolors.
b Boonton, N J, June 14, 15.
Work in Public Collections: Montclair Art Mus, N J; Newark Pub Libr, N J; Colonial Williamsburg, Va; Seeing Eye, Morristown; N J; Prudential Life Ins, Newark.
Exhibitions: N J State Ann, 50-72; N J Watercolor Soc Ann, 50-72; Audubon Soc Ann, 53-72; Am Watercolor Soc Ann, Nat Acad Design Gallery, 56; 50 Artists, N J State Mus, Trenton, 56.
Positions: Admin asst, Newark Sch Fine & Indust Art, 63-
Awards: First prize, N J State Exhib Award for lithography, 51 & watercolor, 52 & 62; Agnes Noyes Award, N J Watercolor Soc, 56 & 63.
Memberships: N J Watercolor Soc (pres, 50-52); Asn Artists N J (bd dirs, 70-72); Nat Soc Arts & Lett.
Publications: Illusr, A calendar for Dinah, 69 & Ecliptecs, 70.
Dealers: Grand Central Galleries, 40 Vanderbilt Ave, New York, NY 10017; Fine Art Center, 10 De Hart St, Morristown, NJ 07960.
Mailing Address: Talmadge Rd, Mendham, NJ 07945.

HOBBS, (CARL) FREDRIC
Sculptor, Film Maker
Preferred Media: Steel, Fiber Glass, Acrylics.
b Philadelphia, Pa, Dec 30, 31.
Study & Training: Cornell Univ, BA; Acad San Fernando Belles Artes, Madrid, Spain.
Work in Public Collections: Mus Mod Art, New York, N Y; Metrop Mus Art, New York; Finch Col Mus, New York; Oakland Mus Art, Calif; Spencer Mem Church, Brooklyn, N Y; plus others.
Commissions: Big Sur Redwoods, Episcopal Church, 62-; Hall of Spirits, monumental environ sculpture for motion pictures, 72-73.
Exhibitions: Concurso Int, Palacio Virreina, Barcelona, Spain, 60; Biennial Exhib Am Art, Pa Acad Fine Arts, Philadelphia, 64; Nat Fine Arts Collection, Smithsonian Inst, Washington, D C, 64; The Highway (traveling exhib to U S mus), Inst Contemp Art, Philadelphia, 70; one-man show, Paintings by Fredric Hobbs, Calif Palace Legion of Hon, San Francisco.
Positions: Pres, Fredric Hobbs Films, Inc, 70-; distinguished speaker, Progs Int Syst.
Bibliography: John W McCoubrey (auth), Art & the road, Highway, 70; Thomas Albright (auth), Visuals, Rolling Stone Mag, 71; plus other maj publs, 60-
Publications: Auth five original screenplays, 69-72.
Dealers: John Bolles Gallery, 10 Gold St, San Francisco, CA 94133; Heritage Gallery, 718 N La Cienega Blvd, Los Angeles, CA 90069.
Mailing Address: P O Box 334, Los Altos, CA 94022.

HOBSON, KATHERINE THAYER
Sculptor
b Denver, Colo, Apr 11, 89.
Study & Training: Art Stud League New York; also in Europe; sculpture with Walter Sintenis, Dresden, Ger.
Commissions: Statue, Bahnhofs Platz, Goettingen; busts, Univ Goettingen & Univ Koenigsberg; bust, Sch Technol, Dresden & univ libr, Goettingen; war mem, St James Episcopal Church, New York, N Y.
Exhibitions: Nat Acad Design, Allied Artists Am, Am Artists Prof League, Hudson Valley Art Asn & Catharine Lorrilard Wolfe Art Club, New York, 66-; also many earlier exhibs.
Teaching: Lect, Roman, Greek, Renaissance and Gothic Sculpture.
Positions: Secy, Fine Arts Fedn, New York, 52-69.
Awards: Prizes, Allied Artists Am, Am Artists Prof League & Hudson Valley Art Asn, 68; plus others.
Memberships: Fel Nat Sculpture Soc; Hudson Valley Art Asn; Pen & Brush Club; Allied Artists Am; Am Artists Prof League; plus others.
Mailing Address: 27 W 67th St, New York, NY 10023.

HODGE, G STUART
Museum Director
b Worcester, Mass.
Study & Training: Sch Fine Arts, Yale Univ, BFA; Cranbrook Acad Arts, MFA; Univ Iowa, PhD.
Positions: Dir, Flint Inst Arts, at present.
Memberships: Col Art Asn Am; Am Asn Mus; Am Fedn Arts.
Mailing Address: Flint Institute of Arts, 1120 E Kearsley St, Flint, MI 48503.

HODGE, ROY GAREY
Painter, Instructor
Preferred Media: Acrylics, Watercolors.
b Moweaqua, Ill, July 27, 37.
Study & Training: Eastern Ill Univ, BS(educ), 61; Harvard Univ Summer Sch, with William Georgenes.
Commissions: Private commissions.
Exhibitions: Tri-State Exhib, Evansville Mus, Ind, 59; Miss Valley Invitational, Ill State Mus, Springfield, 64; Ill Bell Tel Exhib, Chicago, 67; two-man exhib, McMurray Col, 69; River Roads Exhib, St Louis, Mo, 69, 70 & 72.
Teaching: Instr painting, graphics & design, Lanphier High Sch, Springfield, 62-; artist-in-residence painting, Springfield Art Asn, 68-70.
Positions: V pres, Lahonton Valley Art Asn, Fallon, Nev, 61-62.
Awards: Runner up, New York World's Fair Sculpture Design, Int Fair Consults, 63; second in painting, Northside Art Asn, St Louis, 69.
Bibliography: I see Chicago, Ill Bell Tel TV Spec, 67.
Memberships: Ill Art Educ Asn(exec coun, 69-71); Ill State Mus Soc; Northside Art Asn.
Publications: Contribr, La Rev Mod, 60.
Mailing Address: 1133 N 14th St, Springfield, IL 62702.

HODGELL, ROBERT OVERMAN
Printmaker, Painter
b Mankato, Kans, July 14, 22
Study & Training: Univ Wis, BS & MA; Dartmouth Col; Univ Iowa; Univ Ill; Univ Michoacana, Mex; also with John Steuart Curry.
Work in Public Collections: Joslyn Art Mus; Dartmouth Col; Libr Cong; Des Moines Art Ctr; Metrop Mus Art; plus others.
Teaching: Artist-in-residence & instr, Des Moines Art Ctr, 49-53; asst prof art, Fla Presby Col (now Eckerd Col), 62-67, artist-in-residence, 67-
Positions: Asst art dir in charge illus, Our Wonderful World, Champaign, Ill, 53-56; art dir, ed & commun serv, Univ Wis Exten Div, Madison, 57-59; bk illusr for UNESCO in Pakistan, 61.
Memberships: Soc Typographic Art; Fla Craftsmen; Soc Am Graphic Artists.
Dealer: Contemporary Gallery, 110 First Ave N E, Saint Petersburg, FL 33701.
Mailing Address: Art Dept, Eckerd College, Saint Petersburg, FL 33733.

HODGES, STEPHEN LOFTON
Painter, Art Administrator
Preferred Media: Acrylics.
b Port Arthur, Tex, Oct 9, 40.
Study & Training: Univ Tex; Lamar Univ, BS; Univ Ark, MFA.
Work in Public Collections: Isaac Delgado Mus, New Orleans, La; Atlanta Artist's Club, Ga.
Exhibitions: Biennial Artists of Southeast & Texas, Isaac Delgado Mus, 71; 12th Ann Piedmont Painting & Sculpture Exhib, Mint Mus Art, Charlotte, N C, 72; one-man shows, Isaac Delgado Mus, 72, Galerie Simonne Stern, New Orleans, 72 & Southwest Mo State Col, Springfield, 73.
Positions: Asst dir gallery, Univ Fla, 68-
Awards: Purchase awards, Atlanta Artist's Club, 70 & Isaac Delgado Mus, 71.
Memberships: Am Asn Mus; Southeastern Mus Conf.
Dealer: Galerie Simonne Stern, 516 Royal St, New Orleans, LA 70130; Trend House Gallery, 3629 Henderson Blvd, Tampa, FL 33609.
Mailing Address: 1901 N W 55 Terrace, Gainesville, FL 32601.

HODGSON, TREVOR
Painter, Photographer
Preferred Media: Mixed Media.
b Bradford, Eng, Apr 27, 31.
Study & Training: Lancaster Col Art; Univ London.
Work in Public Collections: Oxford Univ, Eng; Accrington City Art Gallery, Eng; Birmingham Univ, Eng; J B Speed Art Mus, U S A; Agnes Etherington Art Ctr, Can.
Commissions: Mural, First Nat Lincoln Bank, Louisville, Ky, 66; mural, York Univ, Eng, 69; fiber glass relief mural, Queen's Univ, Kingston, Ont, 71; Art & Environment (film), 71 & colour-slide collection, 72, Ont Educ Commun Auth.
Exhibitions: One-man shows, Artist's Int Asn Gallery, London, 61 & 68, Merida Gallery, U S A, 66 & Oxford Univ, 67; Six British Artists, U S A, 67; one-man show, York Univ, 68.
Teaching: Asst prof found studies & art educ, Queen's Univ, 69.
Awards: Fulbright scholar to U S A, 65; best work award, State of Ky, 66; Teron Prize, Agnes Etherington Art Ctr, Can, 71.
Memberships: Can Artists' Rep; Can Soc Artists; Int Soc Educ through Art.
Mailing Address: 206 Frontenac St, Kingston, Ont, Can.

HOEHN, HARRY
Painter, Printmaker
Preferred Media: Graphics.
b New York, N Y, Sept 30, 18.
Study & Training: San Miguel Univ, Mex; Atelier 17, New York.
Work in Public Collections: Victoria & Albert Mus, London, Eng; Rosenwald Collection, Nat Gallery Fine Arts; Philadelphia Mus Fine Arts; Brooklyn Mus.
Exhibitions: Whitney Mus Am Art, New York, 63; Young American Printmakers, Mus Mod Art, New York, 53-54; Drawings U S A, Saint Paul, Minn, 61; American Art Today, N Y World's Fair, 64-65; U S Pavillion, Expo 67, Osaka, Japan, 70.
Teaching: Co-dir intaglio graphics, S W Hayter's Atelier 17, New York, 51-52; assoc prof graphics, C W Post Ctr, L I Univ, 66-
Positions: Co-dir, Creative Litho Workshop, New York, 50-51; co-dir, Pipers Graphic Workshop, Huntington, N Y, 51-
Awards: Purchase award, Brooklyn Mus, 53; Charles M Lee Award, Print Club, Philadelphia, 54; purchase award, Assoc Am Artist, 59.
Memberships: Soc Am Graphic Artist (coun, 72).
Publications: Auth, What is a fine print, Pipers Press, 62; auth, Workshop: a new planographic printing process, Craft Horizons, 2/72; auth, Dry lithography, Am Artist, 1/73; auth, Dry lithography—the new graphic medium—an instruction book (in press).
Dealer: Associated American Artist, 663 Fifth at 52nd, New York, NY 10022.
Mailing Address: 42 Oakland St, Huntington, NY 11743.

HOENIGAN, HENRY
Painter
Preferred Media: Oils, Gouache, Watercolors, Pastels, Acrylics.
b Zarnowiec, Poland; Can citizen.
Study & Training: Acad Fine Arts, Cracow, Poland, with W Weiss.
Work in Public Collections: Doon Sch Fine Arts, Ont; Univ Toronto Faculty Pharm; Katz Art Gallery, Tel-Aviv, Israel.
Commissions: Portraits, Lt Gen Sikorski, Free Polish Force, Egypt, 44 & sch pres, Assoc Hebrew Schs, Toronto, 66.
Exhibitions: One-man shows, Palace Fine Arts, Cracow, Poland, 38, Katz Art Gallery, Tel-Aviv, Israel, 47, Eglinton Gallery, Toronto, 55, Tygesen Gallery, 64 & Lamton Gallery, Toronto, 71.
Awards: Hon mention, Univ Buffalo, 63.
Bibliography: Henry Hoenigan, Can Family Tree, 67; A Wolodkowicz (auth), Henry Hoenigan, Polish Contrib to Arts & Sci in Can, 69.
Memberships: Palestine Artists & Sculptors Asn; Soc Can Artists.
Mailing Address: 36 Shelborne Ave, Toronto 12, Ont, Can.

HOFER, INGRID (INGEBORG)
Painter, Instructor
Preferred Media: Watercolors, Graphics.
b New York, N Y.
Study & Training: Meisterschule Fuer Mode, Hamburg, Ger, BA, 48; Univ Hamburg. Traphagen Sch Design, New York, 51; with A Odefey, Goettingen, Ger; also with Albert Bross Jr, Pauline Lorentz, John R Grabach, Adolf Konrad & Nicholas Reale.
Work in Public Collections: Fairleigh Dickinson Univ.
Commissions: Many private commissions in Ger, Switz, Middle & Eastern U S, 56-71.
Exhibitions: Art Exhibs Coun, Newark, N J, 70-72; Painters & Sculptors Soc N J, Jersey City Mus, 70-72; Hudson Valley Art Asn, White Plains, N Y, 70 & 71; Catharine Lorillard Wolfe Art Club, Nat Acad Design, New York, 70 & 71; Am Artist Prof League Grand Nat, Lever House, New York, 70-72.
Teaching: Sr instr mixed media, adult educ, YWCA, Summit, N J, 67-73; instr mixed media, Acad Artists, Trailside Mus, Mountainside, N J, 68-70.
Awards: Award for Milkweed Pods, N J Chapter, 68, award for Lily, Lever House, 72, Am Artists Prof League; award for Iris, Catharine Lorillard Wolfe Art Club, 71.
Memberships: Am Artists Prof League (dir, Am Art Week, N J, 68-70, trustee, 69-71); Catharine Lorillard Wolfe Art Club; Summit Art Ctr; Westfield Art Asn; Morris Co Art Asn.
Dealer: Gallery 9, 9 N Passaic Ave, Chatham, NJ 07928.
Mailing Address: 79 Deep Dale Dr, Berkeley Heights, NJ 07922.

HOFF, (SYD)
Cartoonist, Writer
Preferred Media: Washes, Ink.
b New York, N Y, Sept 4, 12.
Study & Training: Nat Acad Design.
Positions: Cartoonist, Laugh it off.
Publications: Contribr, New Yorker, Esquire Mag, Playboy Mag & others; auth & illusr, children's bks.
Mailing Address: 4335 Post Ave, Miami Beach, FL 33140.

HOFF, MARGO
Painter, Printmaker
Preferred Media: Acrylics, Collage.
b Tulsa, Okla.
Study & Training: Tulsa Univ; Art Inst Chicago; Pratt Graphics Ctr; St Marys Col, Notre Dame, hon DFA, 69.
Work in Public Collections: Whitney Mus Am Art, New York, N Y; Brooklyn Mus, N Y; Art Inst Chicago, Ill; Krannert Mus, Univ Ill, Champaign; Rosenwald Found Collection; plus others.
Commissions: Wall design (75 canvases), Home Fed Bank, Chicago, 66; Mirror Toman (mural), Mayo Clinic, Rochester, Minn, 68; portrait of S Fairweather, Fairweather Hardin Gallery, Chicago, 67; stage set & costumes for Murray Louis Dance Co, 69; portrait of S Madeleva, St Marys Col, Notre Dame, Ind, 70; plus others.
Exhibitions: One-man shows, UNESCO Palace, Beirut, Lebanon, 57, Wildenstein Gallery, Paris, France, 58, Banfer Gallery, New York, 64, 66 & 68, four shows, Fairweather Hardin Gallery, 64-72 & Bednarz Gallery, Los Angeles, 67.
Teaching: Teaching grant, Am Univ, Beirut, 56-57; artist-in-residence, Univ Southern Ill, 66-67; artist-in-residence, St Marys Col, Notre Dame, 69-70; teaching grant, Goretti Sch, Fort Portal, Uganda, E Africa, 71.
Awards: Armstrong Prize, 54 & Campana Award, 55, Art Inst Chicago.
Memberships: Am Asn Univ Prof; Whitney Mus Am Art; Mus Mod Art, New York.
Publications: Illusr, Christmas House, Coachhouse Press, 65; illusr, 4 seasons & 5 senses, 66 & Christmas cupboard, 67, Funk & Wagnall.
Dealer: Fairweather Hardin Gallery, 101 E Ontario St, Chicago, IL 60610.
Mailing Address: 114 W 14th St, New York, NY 10011.

HOFFA, HARLAN EDWARD
Educator
b Kalamazoo, Mich, June 23, 25.
Study & Training: Wayne Univ, BSc & MEd; Pa State Univ, EdD; Sch Am Craftsmen; Ohio State Univ.
Teaching: Assoc prof art educ, Boston Univ, 59-64; prof art educ & chmn prog, Ind Univ, Bloomington, 67-70; prof art educ & head dept, Pa State Univ, University Park, 70-
Positions: Art specialist, Arts & Humanities Prog, U S Off Educ, 64-67.
Memberships: Nat Art Educ Asn (pres, 71-).
Mailing Address: Dept of Art Education, Pennsylvania State University, University Park, PA 16802.

HOFFMAN, EDWARD FENNO, III
Sculptor
Preferred Media: Bronze.
b Philadelphia, Pa, Oct 20, 16.
Study & Training: Pa Acad Fine Arts.
Work in Public Collections: Philadelphia Art Mus; Pa Acad Fine Arts; Brookgreen Gardens, S C; Huntington Galleries, W Va; Grand Cent Art Galleries, New York, N Y.
Commissions: Bronzes, Girl with Basin, Philadelphia Chap Herb Soc Am, 60, figures, Weightlifters Hall of Fame, York, Pa, 60-72; Winnie the Pooh, Children's Libr, Hanover, Pa, 66 & Fawn, Lima, Pa, 72; Holy Family (marble), St Matthew's Roman Cath Church, Philadelphia, 66.
Exhibitions: Allied Artists Am Ann, New York, 71; Mainstreams 72, Marietta Col, Ohio, 72; Nat Sculpture Soc Ann, New York, 72; Am Artists Prof League Ann, 72; Nat Acad Design Ann, New York, 72.
Awards: Artists Prize, 69 & Watrous Gold Medal, 72, Nat Acad Design; gold medal of honor, Am Artists Prof League, 72.
Bibliography: Proske (auth), Brookgreen Gardens sculpture, Brookgreen Gardens.
Memberships: Assoc Nat Acad Design; Nat Sculpture Soc (mem coun, 67-); Am Artists Prof League; Allied Artists Am.
Dealer: Grand Central Art Galleries, 40 Vanderbilt Ave, New York, NY 10017.
Mailing Address: 353 Oak Terr, Wayne, PA 19087.

HOFFMAN, ELAINE JANET
Painter
Preferred Media: Watercolors.
b Oak Park, Ill.
Study & Training: Averett Col; Portland Art Mus, with Eunice Jensen; also with Charles Mulvey, Perry Acker & George Hamilton; Northwest Watercolor Sch, with Irving Shapiro.
Exhibitions: Watercolor Soc Ore Traveling Tours, 68-72; Artists of Ore, Portland Art Mus, 70; Am Artists Prof League, New York, N Y, 71; George Fox Col Invitational, Newberg, Ore, 72; Seventh Prof Ore Artists Invitational Exhib, Coos Bay Mus, Ore, 72.

Teaching: Pvt classes in watercolor landscapes, 65-
Positions: Bd dirs, Lake Oswego Art Guild, Ore, 65-68.
Awards: Grand award, Soc Wash Artists, 68; spec merit award,
 Watercolor Soc Ore, 69 & 70; Ecology Award, Lake Oswego Gar-
 den Club, 71.
Memberships: Fel Am Artist Prof League; Portland Art Mus; Ore
 Watercolor Soc; Lake Area Artists (pres, 67-68, 71-72); Ore Soc
 Artists.
Dealers: The Art Factory, 5500 Macadem Rd, Portland, OR 97201;
 Lake Area Artist Gallery, Second St, Lake Oswego, OR 97034.
Mailing Address: 16695 Glenwood Ct, Lake Oswego, OR 97034.

HOFFMAN, HARRY ZEE
 Painter
Preferred Media: Acrylics.
b Baltimore, Md, Dec 5, 08.
Study & Training: Univ Md, 28; Md Inst Fine Arts, 37; Pratt Inst, 47;
 also with Robert Brackman, 30-40 & Aldro T Hibbard, 40.
Work in Public Collections: Community Col Baltimore; Baltimore
 Mus Art; Enoch Pratt Libr, Baltimore.
Exhibitions: Pa Acad Fine Arts, Philadelphia, Pa, 41, 46 & 53;
 Audubon Nat Gallery, New York, N Y, 45; Laguna Beach Art Asn,
 Calif, 45; Albany Inst Hist & Art, N Y, 45, 47 & 49; Galerie Inter-
 nationale, New York, 67.
Teaching: Private lessons, all media, in Baltimore.
Awards: Prizes, Water Color Show, Washington Co Art Mus, 59,
 Jewish Community Ctr Show, 61 & Baltimore Water Color Club
 Show, 68.
Bibliography: G W Johnson (auth), Three pictures, Baltimore Evening
 Sun, 54.
Memberships: Baltimore Water Color Club; Washington Water
 Color Soc; Artists Equity Asn; Am Artists Prof League.
Dealer: Galerie Internationale, 1095 Madison Ave, New York, NY
 10028.
Mailing Address: 3910 Clarks Lane, Baltimore, MD 21215.

HOFFMAN, HELEN BACON
 Painter
Preferred Media: Oils.
b San Antonio, Tex, July 14, 30.
Study & Training: Ogontz Col, Philadelphia, Pa; Parsons Sch Design.
Work in Public Collections: N Am-Mex Inst Cult Relations, Mexico
 City, Mex; Wichita Art Asn, Kans.
Exhibitions: Smithsonian Inst Regional, Washington, D C, 64;
 Corcoran Gallery Art Regional, Washington, 65; three one-man
 shows, North Star Gallery, San Antonio, Tex, 66-70; one-man
 shows, Grand Cent Art Galleries, New York, N Y, 69 & 71; Pa
 Acad Fine Arts 164th Ann, Philadelphia, 69; plus others.
Awards: Three Pentagon Art Show Awards, 64-68; Soc Wash Artists
 Award, 66; Philadelphia Award, Pa Acad Fine Arts, 69; plus
 others.
Memberships: Artists Equity Asn; Soc Wash Artists; Nat Soc Arts &
 Lett.
Dealers: Veerhoff Galleries, 1512 Connecticut Ave, Washington, DC
 20036; Grand Central Art Galleries, Biltmore Hotel, 40 Vander-
 bilt Ave, New York, NY 10017.
Mailing Address: U S Delegation I M S, NATO Military Committee,
 APO New York 09667.

HOFFMAN, LARRY GENE
 Art Administrator
b Paola, Kans, Mar 12, 33.
Study & Training: Drake Univ, BFA, MSE(comprehensives); Des
 Moines Art Ctr, with Thomas S Tibbs.
Collections Arranged: Lascaux, Birth of the Painter, 63; Parade
 into Athens, 65; West Virginia Arts & Humanities Exhibitions,
 67-69; Appalachia Regional Exhibition 180, 68; Authur S Dayton
 Collection, 69; Henri Dourif Memorial, 69; Mid-Mississippi Val-
 ley Annual, 71-72; Grant Wood, 72; Nicholas Marsicano, 72.
Teaching: Mem & administr vis guest artist prog, Des Moines Art
 Ctr, 52-67; instr art, Des Moines Pub Sch Syst, 55-60.
Positions: Consult art, Des Moines Pub Sch Syst, 60-62; dir educ,
 Des Moines Art Ctr, 62-67; consult art, W Va Arts & Humanities
 Coun; collaborator, Walter Gropius mus bldg addition, Hunting-
 ton, W Va, 67-69; dir, Huntington Galleries, 67-71; dir, Daven-
 port Munic Art Gallery, 71-
Awards: Model jr mus, Saint Louis Conf, Am Asn Mus, 67.
Memberships: Am Asn Mus; Am Fedn Arts; Delta Phi Delta (past
 pres); Iowa State Art Educ Asn (past pres).
Publications: Contribr to Sch Arts & Mus News & auth exhib cata-
 logues.
Mailing Address: Davenport Municipal Art Gallery, 1737 W Twelfth
 St, Davenport, IA 52804.

HOFFMAN MARTIN (JOSEPH)
 Painter, Illustrator
b St Augustine, Fla, Nov 1, 35.
Work in Public Collections: Miami Mus Mod Art.
Commissions: Numerous pvt comns, Fla, 60-72; numerous paintings
 & illus, Playboy Mag, 66-72; cover, Art Direction Mag, 4/72.
Exhibitions: Three one-man shows, Miami Mus Mod Art, 60-67; Re-
 cent Am Painting & Sculpture, Mus Mod Art, New York, N Y, 64-
 66; Erotic Art, Sidney Janis Gallery, New York, 66; Miami 33,
 Miami Art Ctr, 71.
Teaching: Instr grad painting & drawing, Univ Miami, 69-71.
Positions: Art dir, numerous Miami advert Agencies, 57-70;
 designer-illusr, Graphic Arts, Inc, 60-70.
Awards: Numerous painting awards in var regional shows, 60-70;
 art dir awards, Miami Art Dirs Club, 60-70; illus awards, Chi-
 cago advert clubs, 71-72.
Bibliography: Doris Reno (auth), var rev, 57-65 & article, In: Miami
 Herald, 8/23/70; Griffin Smith (auth), article, In: Tropic Mag,
 9/71.
Memberships: Kooter Buggers Am (pres, 72).
Publications: Illusr, Evergreen Rev & Redbook, 67, Playboy Mag &
 Tropic Mag, 67-72 & Art Direction, 4/72.
Mailing Address: 241 W 97th St, New York, NY 10025.

HOFFMAN, RICHARD PETER
 Painter
b Allentown, Pa, Jan 10, 11.
Study & Training: Mercersburg Acad, grad, 29; Parsons Sch De-
 sign, grad, 33.
Work in Public Collections: Butler Inst Am Art, Youngstown, Ohio;
 Moravian Col, Bethlehem, Pa; Pa Power & Light Co, Allentown;
 Call-Chronicle Newspapers, Allentown; Liberty High Sch, Beth-
 lehem, Pa.
Exhibitions: Philadelphia Watercolor Exhibs, Pa; Am Watercolor
 Soc; Nat Soc Painters in Casein, New York; Audubon Artists
 Exhibs; Woodmere Art Gallery, Philadelphia; plus one-man
 shows.
Awards: Gertrude Rowan Capolino prize, Woodmere Art Gallery,
 Philadelphia, 52; Grumbacher prize for casein, Knickerbocker
 Artists, 55; Com Mus Civic Ctr award, 65.
Memberships: Int Platform Asn; Philadelphia Watercolor Soc; Wood-
 mere Art Gallery; Allentown Art Mus; Lehigh Art Alliance.
Art Interests: Photographer & lecturer.
Publications: Article, In: Am Artist, 11/48; article, In: La Rev Mod,
 3/53.
Mailing Address: 1035 N 30th St, Allentown, PA 18104.

HOFFMANN, ARNOLD, JR
 Painter, Designer
b New York, N Y, Jan 16, 15.
Study & Training: Nat Acad Design; Art Stud League New York.
Work in Public Collections: Chrysler Mus, Provincetown; Corcoran
 Art Gallery, Washington, D C.
Exhibitions: Many ann, Allied Artists Am & Am Watercolor Soc;
 Stuttman Gallery, New York, 63; Angeleski Gallery, 65; Osgood
 Gallery, 68.
Positions: Art dir, New York Times Mag, 43-; dir, silk screen fine
 art workshop, East Hampton, 72-
Mailing Address: 144 Water Hole Rd, East Hampton, NY 11937.

HOFFMANN, LILLY ELISABETH
 Weaver, Instructor
Preferred Media: Textiles.
b Strassburg, Alsace, Nov 8, 98; U S citizen.
Study & Training: With Florence House.
Work in Public Collections: Mus Mod Art, New York, N Y; Currier
 Gallery Art, Manchester, N H.
Commissions: Hanging, Andover-Harvard Theol Sch, Cambridge,
 Mass; curtains, Temple Beth Abraham, Nashua, N H; 32 pieces,
 Holy Trinity Methodist Church, Danvers, Mass.
Exhibitions: Designer Craftsmen U S A, Brooklyn Mus, N Y, 53; Nat
 Gold Medal Exhib Archit League New York; Fabrics Int, U S A &
 Can, 61-63.
Teaching: Instr weaving, N H Asn for Blind, Concord; instr weaving,
 League N H Craftsman, Concord, 49-; lect, Exploring the Crafts:
 Weaving, channel 11, 67.
Awards: Grand Award, Designer Craftsmen U S A, 53.
Memberships: League N H Craftsmen.
Mailing Address: Rte 2, Concord, NH 03301.

HOGUE, ALEXANDRE
 Painter, Writer
Preferred Media: Oil, Watercolor, Lithography.
b Memphis, Mo, Feb 22, 98.
Work in Public Collections: Mus Nat Art Mod, Paris, France; Nat
 Collection Fine Arts, Washington, D C; Dallas Mus Fine Arts,
 Tex; Okla Art Ctr, Oklahoma City; Springfield Mus Art, Mo.

Exhibitions: Int Exhib, Jeu de Paume, Paris, 38; Carnegie Int Exhibs, 38 & 39; Tate Gallery, London, Eng, 46; Mus Mod Art, New York, several years; Wilderness, Corcoran Gallery Art, Washington, D C, 71.

Teaching: Instr life drawing & painting, Tex State Col Women, summers, 31-42; prof & hd dept art, Univ Tulsa, 45-68, emeritus prof, 69-

Awards: Purchase award, Ninth Southwest Prints & Drawings, Dallas Mus Fine Arts, 59; grand award, Philbrook Art Ctr, Tulsa, Okla, 61; purchase award, Springfield Mus Art, Mo, 65.

Bibliography: Albert Reese (auth), American prize prints of the 20th Century, Am Artists Group, 49; staff article, Nouvelles acquisitions, La Revue Du Louvre, 61; Ralph K Andrist (editor), History of the 20's and 30's, Am Heritage Publishing Co, 70.

Publications: Auth, Cathedral Voices (poem), Southwest Rev, Autumn, 31; Ignorance (poem), Nimrod Mag, Winter, 59-60; A portrait of Pancho Dobie, Southwest Rev, Spring, 65; Six directions, Out of reach, Silence, Observed (poems), New Mex Quart, Spring, 65; To a young artist (poem), Alumni Mag, Univ Tulsa, Spring, 68.

Mailing Address: 4052 E 23rd St, Tulsa, OK 74114.

HOIE, CLAUS
Painter, Etcher
Preferred Media: Watercolors, Graphics.
b Stavanger, Norway, Nov 3, 11; U S citizen.
Study & Training: Pratt Inst; Art Stud League New York; Ecole Beaux Arts, Paris, France.
Work in Public Collections: Brooklyn Mus, N Y; Norfolk Mus, Va; Butler Inst Am Art, Youngstown, Ohio; Okla Mus Art; Guild Hall Mus, East Hampton, N Y.
Exhibitions: Am Watercolor Soc Ann, New York, N Y, 60-71; Brooklyn Mus Watercolor Biennial, 63; Mus Watercolor Painting, Mexico City, Mex, 68; Pa Acad Fine Arts Ann, 69; Long Island Painters, Guild Hall, East Hampton, N Y, 70.
Awards: Am Artist Mag Medal, 56, gold medal of hon, 62 & prize, 65, Am Watercolor Soc.
Memberships: Am Watercolor Soc (v pres, 60-62).
Publications: Auth, Technique of watercolor, Am Artist Mag, 57; auth, My views on watercolor painting, North Light Mag, 70.
Mailing Address: 20 W 12th St, New York, NY 10011.

HOKIN, GRACE E
Art Dealer, Collector
b Chicago, Ill.
Study & Training: Sch Design, Chicago, cert; Northwestern Univ, BFA.
Specialty of Gallery: Contemporary painting; sculpture; graphics; primitive art.
Collection: Twentieth century painting & sculpture; African & other primitive art.
Mailing Address: 245 Worth Ave, Palm Beach, FL 33480.

HOLADAY, WILLIAM H, JR
Educator, Painter
b Wheeling, W Va, June 03, 07.
Study & Training: Ohio State Univ, BA; Franklin Univ; Omaha Univ, MA; Univ Chicago; Dakota Wesleyan Univ; Univ Iowa.
Exhibitions: Dakota Wesleyan Univ, 53; Little Gallery, Spearfish, S Dak, 56; Northern State Col, 58; Univ S Dak, 60-64; Dakota State Univ, 64.
Teaching: Assoc prof art & head dept, Dakota Wesleyan Univ, 48-58; assoc prof art, Northern State Col, 58-, chmn dept, 58-71.
Awards: S Dak State Fair, 51-62.
Memberships: Kappa Pi; Assoc Omaha Artists; Nat Art Educ Asn; Delta Phi Delta.
Mailing Address: Art Dept, Northern State College, Aberdeen, SD 57401.

HOLBROOK, ELIZABETH BRADFORD
Sculptor
Preferred Media: Clay, Wax, Stone, Bronze.
b Hamilton, Ont, Nov 7, 13.
Study & Training: Hamilton Tech Inst; Ont Col Art, Toronto; Royal Col Art, London; also with Emanuel Hahn & Carl Milles.
Work in Public Collections: Nat Gallery Can, Ottawa, Ont; Parliament Bldgs Gallery, Ottawa; Art Gallery Hamilton; McMaster Univ.
Commissions: Girl with dove in stone, Bird Protection Soc, Royal Bot Gardens, Hamilton, 37; archit decoration Canadiana in stone (with Husband, Robertson & Wallace, Architects), Fed Bldg, Hamilton, 53; centennial fountain in stone, Dunnville, Ont, 67; bronze portrait, Roy G Cole, Hamilton, 69; Rabbi Bernard Baskin bronze portrait, Anshe Sholom Temple, Hamilton, 70; plus others.
Exhibitions: Art Gallery Hamilton Ann, 42-; Ont Soc Artists Ann, Toronto, 45-71; Art Gallery Hamilton Ann, 45-; Sculptor's Soc Can Ann, 60-; Nat Sculpture Soc New York Ann, 62 & 69; Int Fedn Medallists, Cologne, Ger, 71.

Teaching: Instr sculpture, Dundas Valley Sch Art, 65-70.
Awards: Lt Gov Medal, Ont Col Art-Govt Ont, 36; Nat Sculpture Soc New York Gold Medal Award, 69.
Bibliography: E Wyn Wood (auth), Canadian sculpture, 48; Charles Comfort (auth), Observations on a decade 1938-48, Royal Archit Inst Can J; John Bryden (auth), Art, Hamilton Spectator, 70, 71 & 72.
Memberships: Sculptor's Soc Can; Ont Soc Artists; Royal Can Acad Art; life mem Art Gallery Hamilton (benefactor, 45-); Art Gallery Ont.
Mailing Address: 1177 Mineral Springs Rd, R R 3, Dundas, Ont, Can.

HOLBROOK, HOLLIS HOWARD
Educator, Painter
Preferred Media: Acrylics.
b Natick, Mass, Feb 7, 09.
Study & Training: Mass Sch Art, dipl, 34; Yale Univ, BFA, 36; Univ Michoacan, Morelia, Mex, 50-51.
Work in Public Collections: Norfolk Mus Arts & Sci, Va; Southern Col, Lakeland, Fla; Sheldon Swope Art Gallery, Terre Haute, Ind; Natick Pub Libr, Mass; Univ Fla, Gainesville.
Commissions: John Eliot & Indians (egg tempera mural), Natick Post Off Bldg, 37; frescoes, Morelia Libr, Michoacan, Mex, 51; History of Florida (egg tempera), Univ Fla Libr, 53; Life in the World (collage panels with Harrison Covington), Col R I, Providence, 59; Ocala Industries (collage panels), U S Post Off, Ocala, 61.
Exhibitions: Contemporary Painting and Sculpture, Univ Ill Biennial, 61; Pa Acad Fine Arts Painting & Sculpture Ann, 64; 29th Biennial Contemp Am Painting, Corcoran Gallery Art, 65; 21st Am Drawing Biennial, Norfolk Mus Arts & Sci, 65; 22nd Southeastern Ann, High Mus Art, Atlanta, Ga, 67.
Teaching: Prof art, Univ Fla, 38-
Positions: Designer-illusr, Dennison Mfg Co, Framingham, Mass, 29-30; designer-illusr, Assoc Press, New York, 41; designer, Warren Telechron Co, Ashland, Mass, 42.
Awards: Award & purchase prize for Winter, Walter Chrysler, Jr, 8th Ann Nat, Sarasota, Fla, 58; purchase prize for Protest (drawing), Norfolk Mus Arts & Sci, 65; top award for Figure with Blue Patch, 22nd Southeastern Ann, High Mus Art, 67.
Bibliography: Jacqueline Barnitz (auth), Holbrook exhibit, New York City, Arts Mag, 12/65.
Memberships: Nat Soc Mural Painters.
Publications: Auth, Fresco painting, Design Mag, summer 51; auth, A media laboratory, Am Artist Mag, 9/60; auth, Development of the plastic arts of Central America, Univ Fla Press, 61; auth, Painting for non-majors, Art J, summer, 70.
Dealers: Nordness Gallery, 236 E 75th St, New York, NY 10021; Chase Gallery, 31 E 64th St, New York, NY 10021.
Mailing Address: 1710 S W 35th Pl, Gainesville, FL 32601.

HOLBROOK, VIVIAN NICHOLAS
Painter, Art Administrator
Preferred Media: Oils, Inks.
b Mount Vernon, N Y, Mar 31, 13.
Study & Training: Yale Univ, BFA.
Work in Public Collections: Univ Ga.
Exhibitions: Butler Art Inst Ann, Youngstown, Ohio, 52; Patronato Belles Artes y Mus Nat, Havana, Cuba, 56; Columbia Mus Art, S C, 59; Purdue Univ Small Painting Show, Lafayette, Ind, 64; Ball State Univ Ann, Muncie, Ind, 72.
Teaching: Instr painting & drawing, Colby Jr Col, New London, N H, 36-39; interim instr painting & drawing, Univ Fla, 42-44; instr painting, Ctr Mod Art, Micanopy, Fla, 69-70.
Positions: Dir, Ctr Mod Art, 69-; designer exhibs, Fla State Mus, summer 70.
Awards: Second Award, Harry Rich Competition, Miami, 57; Top Award, 58 & Atwater Kent Award, 66, Soc Four Arts.
Mailing Address: 1710 S W 35th Pl, Gainesville, FL 32601.

HOLCOMBE, BLANCHE KEATON
Painter, Educator
Preferred Media: Oils.
b Anderson, S C, July 19, 12.
Study & Training: Anderson Col, AA, 34; Furman Univ, BA, 58; Univ S C, Charleston; Clemson Univ Sch Archit, 63.
Work in Public Collections: Mayor's Off, Anderson City Hall; S C Employment Off, Anderson; Anderson Savings & Loan Co; Town House, Anderson; Steak Gallery, Anderson.
Exhibitions: Florence Art Gallery, S C, 53; Columbia Mus Art, S C, 53 & 68; Gibbes Art Gallery, Charleston, S C, 54; Winston-Salem Art Gallery, N C, 59; Int Platform Exhib, Washington, D C, 67.
Teaching: Chmn art, design & art appreciation, Anderson Col, 56-
Awards: First prize, Watson Village Art Show, Watson Village Merchants Asn, 64 & 65; first prize in prof div, Christian Art Festival, Baptist Church, Seneca, S C, 65.

Memberships: Anderson Art Asn (first pres, 66, historian, 71, treas, 72); Guild S C Artists; Am Fedn Arts; Am Asn Univ Women.
Publications: Illusr, Anderson College cook book, 68; illusr, Anderson County sketches, 69; illusr, Ivy leaves, 72.
Mailing Address: Dept of Art, Anderson College, Anderson, SC 29621.

HOLCOMBE, R GORDON, JR
Collector, Patron
b Lake Charles, La, Oct 28, 13.
Study & Training: Vanderbilt Univ; Tulane Univ, BS; Sch Med, MD.
Positions: Past pres Art Assocs Lake Charles; past pres, Calcasieu Parish Med Soc; past pres, La Chap Am Col Surgeons; mem bd gov Am Col Surgeons.
Collection: Paintings, including works by Bernard, Derain, Buffet, Levier & Courbet; early nineteenth century American paintings.
Mailing Address: 1607 Foster St, Lake Charles, LA 70601.

HOLDEN, RAYMOND JAMES
Painter, Illustrator
b Wrentham, Mass, May 2, 01.
Study & Training: R I Sch Design, 23.
Work in Public Collections: Children's Mus, West Hartford, Conn; Mus Am Art, New Britain, Conn.
Exhibitions: Jones Libr, Amherst, Mass, 69; Providence Pub Libr, R I, 70.
Memberships: Providence Watercolor Club.
Publications: Illusr, Thoreau's Cape Cod, 69; & others.
Mailing Address: R F D, Box 130, Sterling, CT 06377.

HOLDER, CHARLES ALBERT
Painter
b Miami, Fla, June 15, 25.
Study & Training: Univ Fla, BFA; Art Inst Chicago; Jerry Farnsworth Sch Art; Henry White Taylor Scholar, 49.
Commissions: Many portraits, 48-58.
Exhibitions: Fla Fedn Arts, Winter Haven Artists Asn, Lakeland Art Guild & New Smyrna Beach, Fla, 63; Grand Cent Art Galleries, 64.
Teaching: Instr, Fla Gulf Coast Art Ctr, Clearwater; Auburndale Art Asn, Fla; Lakeland Art Guild, 64; summer sch dir, Fla Fedn Arts, 64; instr, Fla Gulf Coast Art Ctr, Belleair, 67-71.
Positions: Dir, Holder Gallery, Miami, 60.
Awards: Prize, Coral Gables Art Asn, 54; Sarasota Art Asn, 54; Harry Rich Competition, Miami, 55; plus others.
Memberships: Salmagundi Club; Artist's & Craftsmen Assoc, Dallas, Tex; Allied Artists Am.
Mailing Address: 4610 98th Ave, Tampa, FL 33617.

HOLGATE, EDWIN HEADLEY
Painter
b Allandale, Ont, Aug 19, 92.
Study & Training: Art Asn Montreal; Paris, France, with Lucien Simon & others.
Work in Public Collections: Nat Gallery Can; Sarnia Art Gallery; Art Asn Montreal; Le Havre, France; Montreal, P Q.
Commissions: Murals, Chateau Laurier Hotel, Ottawa; off war artist, RCAF, 43-44.
Exhibitions: Group of Seven Exhib, 36; Coronation, 37; Tate Gallery, London, 38; New York World's Fair, 39; UNESCO, 46; plus others.
Teaching: Instr, Art Asn Montreal; instr wood engraving, Ecole Beaux-Arts, Montreal.
Memberships: Can Group Painters; Fedn Can Artists; Royal Can Acad Arts.
Publications: Illusr, Other days, other ways.
Mailing Address: Morin Heights, P Q, Can.

HOLLADAY, HARLAN H
Painter, Educator
Preferred Media: Oils, Acrylics.
b Greenville, Mo, Dec 10, 25.
Study & Training: Southeast Mo State Col, BS(educ); Wash Univ; State Univ Iowa, MA; Cornell Univ, PhD.
Work in Public Collections: Munson-Williams-Proctor Inst, Utica, N Y; St Lawrence Univ Collection, Canton, N Y; Des Moines Art Ctr, Iowa; Sioux City Art Ctr, Iowa.
Exhibitions: Corcoran Gallery Art Biennial, Washington, D C, 51; Whitney Mus Am Art Ann, New York, N Y, 52; Pa Acad Fine Arts Oils Exhib, Philadelphia, 52, Watercolor Exhib, 53 & 59; 61st Nat Watercolor Ann, Washington, 58.
Teaching: Asst prof drawing & painting, Univ Nev, Reno, 55-58; prof art & artist-in-residence, Am Col Switz, 68-69; prof fine arts, St Lawrence Univ, 61-, head dept, 65-71.

Awards: First prize for other media, Nat Art Roundup, Las Vegas, Nev, 58; hon mention, 61st Nat Watercolor Ann, Washington, 58; Reynolds Award, Cooperstown Art Asn, N Y, 67.
Memberships: Col Art Asn; Soc Archit Historians; Am Asn Univ Prof; Northeast Mus Asn; Cooperstown Art Asn.
Art Interests: Fifteenth century art, especially Northern European painters and sculptors; American art of the nineteen thirties.
Publications: Auth, Art in the liberal arts curriculum, 64 & auth, The value of a teaching collection, St Lawrence Univ Bull, 70; auth, A collection of contemporary art (catalogue for McGinnis Collection, St Lawrence Univ), 70.
Mailing Address: Dept of Fine Arts, St Lawrence University, Canton, NY 13617.

HOLLAND, DANIEL E
Cartoonist
b Guthrie, Ky, Feb 2, 18.
Study & Training: David Lipscomb Col, 36-38; Chicago Acad Fine Arts, 38-39.
Teaching: Instr ed cartooning, Chicago Acad Fine Arts, 46-
Positions: Directorial cartoonist, Nashville Banner, 39-41; cartoonist, Chicago Tribune, 45-50; cartoonist, Washington Times-Herald, 50-54; cartoonist, Chicago Tribune, 54-72, chief ed cartoonist, 72-
Awards: Freedom Found cert of merit, 49, medals, 50, 51 & 58.
Mailing Address: 412 Laurel Ave, Libertyville, IL 60048.

HOLLAND, TOM
Painter
b Seattle, Wash, 36.
Study & Training: Willamette Univ; Univ Calif, Santa Barbara; Univ Calif, Berkeley.
Work in Public Collections: Stanford Univ; St Louis City Mus; San Francisco Mus Art; Mus Mod Art, New York; Art Inst Chicago; plus many others.
Exhibitions: Kid Stuff, Albright-Knox Art Gallery, Buffalo, N Y, 71; New Options in Painting, Walker Art Ctr, Minneapolis, Minn, 72; California Prints, Mus Mod Art, New York, N Y, 72; U S A-West Coast, Hamburg, Hanover & Cologne, Ger, 72; Works in Progress, San Francisco Mus Art, 72; plus many other group & one-man shows.
Teaching: Instr art, San Francisco Art Inst, at present.
Awards: Fulbright grant, Santiago, Chile, 59-60.
Mailing Address: c/o Hansen Fuller Gallery, 228 Grant Ave, San Francisco, CA 94108.

HOLLERBACH, SERGE
Painter, Illustrator
Preferred Media: Casein, Acrylics, Inks.
b Pushkin, Russia, Nov 1, 23; U S citizen.
Study & Training: Acad Fine Arts, Munich, Ger, 46-49; Art Stud League New York, with Ernst Fiene, 50; Am Art Sch, with Gordon Samstag, 51.
Work in Public Collections: St Paul Gallery Art, Minn; Bridgeport Mus Art, Sci & Indust, Conn; Ga Mus Art, Athens; Seton Hall Univ Art Gallery, South Orange, N J; Norfolk Mus Art & Scis, Va.
Exhibitions: Am Watercolor Soc Ann Exhib, 55-72; Nat Acad Design Ann Exhib, 56-71; Drawings U S A, St Paul, Minn, 61; 200 Yrs of Watercolor Painting in Am, Metrop Mus Art, New York, 66; Am Acad Arts & Letters, New York, 67-69.
Awards: Childe Hassam purchase award, Am Acad Arts & Letters, 68-69; N J Soc Painters & Sculptors medal of hon, 69; Adolph & Clara Obrig Prize, Nat Acad Design, 71.
Memberships: Am Watercolor Soc (dir, 72); Audubon Artists (v pres, 71); Allied Artists Am; N J Soc Painters & Sculptors; Nat Soc Painters in Casein & Acrylics.
Publications: Illusr, Westaway, 68 & illusr, Gunnar scores a goal, 68, Harcourt; illusr, They flew alone, Warne, 69.
Dealer: Eileen Kuhlik Gallery, 23 E 67th St, New York, NY 10021.
Mailing Address: 894 Riverside Dr, New York, NY 10032.

HOLLINGER, (HELEN WETHERBEE)
Painter, Lecturer
Preferred Media: Oils, Pastels, Acrylics.
b Indianapolis, Inc.
Study & Training: Herron Sch Art, fine arts dipl; also with Donald Mattison, Henrik Mayer & Emile Gruppé.
Work in Public Collections: First Fed Savings & Loan Asn, Miami, Fla; Herron Sch Art, Indianapolis, Ind.
Exhibitions: Invitational one-man exhib, Bacardi Gallery, Miami, 68; Grand Nat Exhib, Am Artists Prof League, New York, N Y, 69-72; Nat Biennial Art Exhib, Nat League Am Pen Women, Salt Lake City, Utah, 70; invitational one-man exhib, Gables Art Gallery, Coral Gables, Fla, 70.
Teaching: Instr art, Miami Shores Community Ctr, Fla, 71-72.

Awards: Nat League Am Pen Women First prize for portraiture, Fla State Art Exhib, 69; first place art achievement award, Wometco Enterprises, Miami, 71; Poinciana Art Exhib Best in Show, Burdine's, Miami, 72.

Memberships: Am Artists Prof League (pres, Miami Chap, 69-70, dir, 71-73); Nat League Am Penwomen (art chmn, Fla State Orgn, 66-68, nat art bd, 72-74); Blue Dome Art Fel; Miami Art League (pres, 66-67, dir, 71).

Dealer: Mirell Gallery, 3421 Main Highway, Coconut Grove, FL 33133.

Mailing Address: 80 N E 97th St, Miami Shores, FL 33138.

HOLLINGSWORTH, ALVIN CARL
Painter, Educator
Preferred Media: Acrylics, Collage.
b New York, N Y, Feb 25, 30.
Study & Training: Music & Art H S; City Univ New York, BA, 56, MA, 59; Art Stud League New York, with Kunioshi, Ralph Fabri & Dr Bernard Myers, 50-52.
Work in Public Collections: Chase Manhattan Bank, New York; Brooklyn Mus Permanent Collection, N Y; IBM Collection, White Plains, N Y; Williams Col Art Collection; Johnson Publ Permanent Art Collection, Chicago, Ill; plus others.
Commissions: Don Quijote limited ed lithographs, Orig Lithographs Inc, 67; Don Quijote murals, Don Quijote Apts, Bronx, N Y, 69; mural, Rutgers Univ, New Brunswick, N J, 70.
Exhibitions: Art U S A, Madison Square Garden, New York, 57; Emily Lowe Award Exhib, 63; Traveling Exhib Black Painters America, Univ Calif, Los Angeles, 66; 15 New Voices, Hallmark Gallery, New York & traveling, 69; Am Black Painters, Whitney Mus Am Art, New York, 71; plus three one-man shows.
Teaching: Instr graphics, H S Art & Design, 61-70; instr painting, Art Stud League New York, 69-; asst prof painting, Hostos Community Col, 71-
Positions: Consult art & art coord, Harlem Freedom Sch, Off Econ Opportunity, 66-67; dir, Lincoln Inst Gallery, Lincoln Inst Psycho-Ther, 66-68; supvr art, Proj Turn-On, New York, 68-69.
Awards: Award, Emily Lowe Art Competition, 63; award, Whitney Found, 64; award of distinction, Smith Mason Gallery, 71.
Bibliography: Cedric Dover (auth), American Negro art, 61; Samella Lewis (auth), Black artist on art, privately pub, 71.
Research: Aesthetic use of fluorescent materials in the fine arts.
Publications: Auth & illusr, I'd like the Goo-gen-heim, Regnery, 69; co-auth, Art of acrylic painting, Grumbacher, 69; illusr, The sniper, McGraw, 69; illusr, Black out loud, Macmillan, 70; illusr, Journey, Scholastic, 70.
Dealers: Lee Nordness Gallery, 236 E 75th St, New York, NY 11724; Harbor Gallery, 43 Main St, Cold Spring Harbor, NY 11724.
Mailing Address: 614 W 147th St, New York, NY 10031.

HOLLISTER, PAUL
Painter
b New York, N Y.
Study & Training: Harvard Col, BS.
Exhibitions: Riverside Mus, N Y; Whitney Mus Am Art, New York; New York City Ctr; New Sch Social Res, New York; Silvermine Guild Artists; plus others.
Memberships: Silvermine Guild Artists; Old Sturbridge Village; Nat Early Am Glass Club; Soc for Preserv New Eng Antiquities.
Publications: Auth & illusr, Fine tooth comb, 47; auth, Outstanding French and American paperweights in The Wells Collection, 66, New light on Gilliland, Cambridge and Gillinder paperweights, 68 & The Kahila Dig at Mt Washington, 9/72, Antiques Mag; auth, The encyclopedia of glass paperweights, 69.
Mailing Address: c/o Harmon Gallery, 1258 Third St S, Naples, FL 33940.

HOLLISTER, VALERIE (DUTTON)
Painter
Preferred Media: Acrylics.
b Oakland, Calif, Dec 29, 39.
Study & Training: Stanford Univ, AB, 61, MA, 65; San Francisco Art Inst; Col Art Study Abroad, Paris, France.
Exhibitions: Corcoran Biennial Contemp Am Painting & Corcoran Gallery Area Show, Washington, D C, 67; Whitney Mus Ann Contemp Am Painting, 67-68; plus other one-woman & group shows.
Dealer: Jefferson Place Gallery, 2144 P St N W, Washington, DC 20037.
Mailing Address: c/o Swarthmore College, Swarthmore, PA 19081.

HOLM, MILTON W
Painter
Preferred Media: Oils.
b Rochester, N Y.
Study & Training: With Edward S Siebert, Rochester.

Work in Public Collections: Mem Art Gallery, Rochester; Rochester Inst Technol; Univ Rochester; Greenville Pub Libr, S C.
Exhibitions: Mem Art Gallery, 24-71; Nat Acad Design Ann, New York, N Y, 35-68; Allied Artists Am, New York, 38-71; Currier Art Gallery, Manchester, N H, 40; Cincinnati Art Gallery, Ohio, 45.
Awards: Ranger Purchase Award, Nat Acad Design, 40; James Hogarth Dennis Award, Mem Art Gallery, 58-62, Rochester Art Club Award, 69-71.
Memberships: Allied Artists Am; Rochester Art Club (pres, 57-59); Genesee Group (pres).
Dealer: Wolfard Galleries, 9 S Goodman St, Rochester, NY 14607.
Mailing Address: 30 Hathaway Rd, Rochester, NY 14617.

HOLMAN, ARTHUR (STEARNS)
Painter
Preferred Media: Oils.
b Bartlesville, Okla, Oct 25, 26.
Study & Training: Univ N Mex, BFA, 51; Hans Hofmann Sch Art, Provincetown, Mass, 51; Calif Sch Fine Arts, San Francisco, 53.
Work in Public Collections: San Francisco Mus Art; Oakland Mus, Calif; Stanford Univ Mus, Palo Alto, Calif; Eureka Col, Ill.
Exhibitions: One-man shows, Esther Robles Gallery, Los Angeles, 60, M H De Young Mem Mus, San Francisco, 63 & William Sawyer Gallery, San Francisco, 71; Fifty California Artists, Whitney Mus Am Art, New York, N Y, 62; 19th Artists West of the Mississippi, Colorado Springs Fine Arts Ctr, 63.
Awards: Purchase award, invitational show, Stanford Univ, 62; public vote prize, Bay Area Art, First Savings Bank of San Francisco, 64.
Dealer: William Sawyer Gallery, 3045 Clay St, San Francisco, CA 94115.
Mailing Address: Box 72, Lagunitas, CA 94938.

HOLMBOM, JAMES WILLIAM
Painter
Preferred Media: Acrylics.
b Monson, Maine, Mar 3, 26.
Study & Training: Portland Sch Art, with Alexander Bower; Univ Maine, BSA; Inst Allende, Mex, MFA, with James Pinto & Fred Samuelson.
Work in Public Collections: Inst Allende, San Miguel Allende, Mex; also in the corporate collections of Union Mutual Life Ins Co, Portland, Maine, Andover Inst Bus, Mass, Beverly Trust Corp, Mass, Casco Bank & Trust Corp, Portland, Maine & Maine Savings Bank, Portland.
Exhibitions: Three-man invitational show, Inst Allende, 67; Mainstreams U S A, 70; UNICEF Invitational Exhib, 71; Bridgton Art Show, Maine, 71; Searsport Marine Mus, Maine, 72.
Teaching: City art dir, Montpelier, Vt, 56-59; city art dir, Marblehead, Mass, 59-71; pvt classes, Essex, Mass, 56-71; instr landscape & studio painting, Inst Allende, 66-67.
Awards: Purchase prizes, Portland Art Festival, 69, 70 & 71.
Mailing Address: Box 52, Hancock, ME 04640.

HOLMES, DAVID BRYAN
Painter, Instructor
Preferred Media: Tempera.
b London, Eng, Aug 8, 36; Can citizen.
Study & Training: Twickenham Tech Col, Eng; Harrow Sch Art, London; Queen's Univ Ont; Art Stud League New York, with Robert Beverley Hale.
Work in Public Collections: Willistead Art Gallery, Windsor, Ont.
Commissions: Many private commissions in Eng & N Am.
Exhibitions: Queen's Univ Ont Ann Spring Exhib, 64-71; two-man exhib, Queen's Univ Ont, 67; Soc Can Artists Ann, Toronto, 68-71; Country Scenes in Quebec, City of Montreal, P Q, 69; one-man exhibs, Galerie Gauvreau, Montreal, 69 & 70.
Teaching: Instr art, St Lawrence Col Applied Arts & Technol, Kingston, Ont, 68-
Awards: Ann Nat Spring Exhib, Queen's Univ Ont, 67, 69 & 71; award for Country Scenes in Quebec, City of Montreal, 69.
Memberships: Soc Can Artists; Art Stud League New York.
Dealer: Wally F Findlay Galleries Inc, 17 E 57th St, New York, NY 10022.
Mailing Address: 434 Johnson St, Kingston, Ont, Can.

HOLMES, PAUL JAMES & MARY E
Collectors
Mr Holmes, b North Henderson, Ill, Jan 28, 96; Mrs Holmes, b Chicago, Ill, Sept 12, 00.
Study & Training: Mr Holmes, Univ Mich, BS; Univ Toulouse; Mrs Holmes, Art Inst Chicago; also with Sadie M Hess, Gary, Ind.
Collection: Eighteenth century porcelains and figurines; miniatures; patch and snuff boxes; Russian enamels, porcelains and Faberge; Russian icons; rare items in porcelain, art glass and graphics;

Medieval and eighteenth century enamels of England and the Continent; wax portraits and groups; silhouettes; Verre de Nevers; momentos mori.

Mailing Address: 836 Du Shane Ct, South Bend, IN 46616.

HOLMES, REGINALD
Painter, Photographer
Preferred Media: Acrylics.
b Calgary, Alta, Oct 4, 34.
Study & Training: Vancouver Sch Art.
Work in Public Collections: Larry Aldrich Mus, Ridgefield, Conn; Art Gallery Ont, Toronto; Chase Manhattan Bank, New York, N Y; New York Bank Savings; Port Auth, Kennedy Airport, New York.
Exhibitions: Vancouver Art Gallery, B C, 65; Isaacs Gallery, Toronto, 67, 69 & 71; Can Biennial, Ottawa, 69; Gallery 99, Fla, 70; Whitney Exp Sch, New York, 70.
Teaching: Instr painting, Vancouver Art Sch, 59-68; instr design, N Y Univ, 70.
Awards: Can Coun Awards, 69, 70 & 72.
Bibliography: Walter Klepac (auth), The contingencies of colour and form, Artscan, 2-3/72.
Dealer: Isaacs Gallery, Young St, Toronto, Ont, Can.
Mailing Address: 59 E Broadway, New York, NY 10002.

HOLMES, RUTH ATKINSON
Painter, Sculptor
b Hazlehurst, Miss.
Study & Training: Miss State Col Women; Tulane Univ; Miss Col & Southwest Jr Col.
Work in Public Collections: Univ La, Alexandria & Baton Rouge; Miss State Col Women, Columbus; Miss State Univ, Starkville.
Commissions: Mural (with Bess Dawson), Church of God, McComb, Miss; mural (with Bess Dawson & Halcyone Barnes), Progressive Bank, Summit, Miss; mural (with Bess Dawson & Halcyone Barnes), First Nat Bank, Mc Comb; 14 Stations of the Cross, Church of Mediator, McComb, 72.
Exhibitions: One-man shows, Ahda Artzt, New York, N Y, 64, Mary Chilton Gallery, Memphis, Tenn, 66, Brooks Mem Gallery & Mus, Memphis, 69, Univ La, Alexandria, 69 & Bryant Gallery, Jackson, Miss, 71.
Awards: First prize pastel, Chautauqua Art Asn, N Y, 62; first prize, Miss Art Asn Nat Oil Show, Jackson, 66; first prize, La Font Workshop, S Cent Bell Tel Co, Pascagoula, Miss, 68.
Memberships: Miss Art Asn (bd mem, 69); Miss Art Colony; LeFonte Art Colony.
Publications: Co-auth, Camellia magic, 50.
Dealer: McComb Gallery, McComb, MS 39648.
Mailing Address: P O Box 543, McComb, MS 39648.

HOLT, CHARLOTTE SINCLAIR
Medical Illustrator, Sculptor
b Springfield, Mass, June 11, 14.
Study & Training: Mass Normal Art Sch & Boston Mus Fine Arts, 29-34; Walker Sch Fine Arts & Crafts, Boston, 32-34,dipl; Boston Univ, 33-34, Col Med, 34-35; also portraits with Bernard Keyes, Boston, 34; Sch Med Illus, cert, 37; med photog, with Laurence Toriello & Anthony Kuzma, 36-37; also with Willard C Shepard, 37-38, watercolor with Elliot O'Hara, Maine, 41, sculpture with Malvina Hoffman, New York, plaster casting with John Pletinkx & plastic carving with Joseph Krstolich; Marquette Univ Med Col, 71.
Work in Public Collections: Miracle of Growth (permanent exhib), Mus Sci & Indust, Chicago, Ill.
Exhibitions: Med, sci, res, educ & lay exhibs, local, state & nat med meetings, 37-70.
Positions: Chief med illusr & sculptor, Visual Educ Prog, Univ Ill Col Med in coop with Ill State Dept Health, instr,Sch Med Illus, col, 37-45; free lance med illusr sculptor & graphic artist for advert agencies & pharmaceut co & illusr jour & med bk publ, 36-; adv ed, J Am Med Illusr, 59-70, assoc ed, 70-; med artist, Am Med Asn, 61-63; dir Med Audio/Visual Communications, Akron Med Ctr, 72-
Awards: Distinguished Serv Awards, 66 & 70 & Presidential Award, 71, Asn Med Illusr; plus others.
Memberships: Asn Med Illusr (v pres, 60-61, bd gov, 61-66 & 71-76, corresp secy, 65-69, pres, 70-71 & mem many comts); fel Med Artists Asn Gt Brit; Royal Photog Soc; assoc Inst Med & Biol Illus; Allied Artists Am; plus many others.
Publications: Co-auth & illusr, Obstetric and gynecologic nursing, Mosby, 37, rev ed 41; co-auth & illusr, Atlas of obstetric complications, Lippincott, 62; illusr, many jour.
Mailing Address: 738 Keystone Ave, River Forest, IL 60305.

HOLTON, LEONARD T
Cartoonist
b Philadelphia, Pa, Sept 6, 06.
Commissions: Script writer, TV, stage & screen productions; de-

signer & writer TV commercials for Bert Lahr, Nat Cleo Festival & New York Advert Club.
Memberships: Soc Illustrators; Writers Guild Am.
Publications: Illusr, leading magazines & newspaper syndicates; co-auth &/or illusr, bks publ by Schribners, Simon & Schuster & others.
Mailing Address: 129 E 82nd St, New York, NY 10028.

HOLTY, CARL ROBERT
Painter, Writer
Preferred Media: Oils.
b Freiburg, Ger, June 12, 00; U S citizen.
Study & Training: Art Inst Chicago, 19; Nat Acad Design, with E Bolton Jones, 20-21; Hans Hofmann Sch, Munich, Ger, 26.
Work in Public Collections: Whitney Mus Am Art, New York, N Y; Solomon R Guggenheim Mus, New York; Addison Gallery Am Art, Andover, Mass; J B Speed Art Mus, Louisville, Ky; James A Michener Collection, Univ Tex, Austin.
Exhibitions: American Painting Today: 1950, Metrop Mus Art, New York, 50; Abstract Painting & Sculpture in America, Mus Mod Art, New York, 51; The 1930's: Painting in New York, Poindexter Gallery, New York, 57; The 1930's: Painting & Sculpture in America, Whitney Mus Am Art, 68; Carl Holty: Fifty Years, City Univ New York, 72; plus others.
Teaching: Instr art, Art Stud League New York, 39 & 50; artist-in-residence, Univ Ga, 48-50; artist-in-residence, Univ Calif, summer 51; artist-in-residence, Univ Fla, 52-53; artist-in-residence, Univ Louisville, 62-63; prof art, Brooklyn Col, 64-70, emer prof fine arts, 70-
Awards: Krannert prize, Univ Ill, 48; Ford Found Award, 62.
Bibliography: Lawrence Campbell (auth), The other side of freedom, Art News, summer 65; Patricia Kaplan (auth), Carl Holty: fifty years (catalogue of retrospective exhibition), City Univ New York, 9-10/72.
Publications: Auth, A memoir of Mondrian, Arts Mag, 9/57; auth, The mechanics of creativity: a memoir, Leonardo, 68; co-auth, The painters mind, Grove, 69.
Dealer: Poindexter Gallery, 24 E 84th St, New York, NY 10028.
Mailing Address: 327 Central Park W, New York, NY 10025.

HOLVEY, SAMUEL BOYER
Sculptor, Designer
Preferred Media: Metal Direct Construction, Lumia.
b Wilkes Barre, Pa, July 20, 35.
Study & Training: Syracuse Univ, BFA, 57; Am Univ, MA, 69.
Commissions: Bas-relief mural, Wyo Valley Country Club, Wilkes Barre, 62.
Exhibitions: Corcoran Area Show, Corcoran Gallery, Washington, D C, 68.
Teaching: Asst prof design, Corcoran Sch Art, Washington, 65-; instr design, Univ Md, College Park, 67-71.
Positions: Designer, William Fertig Interiors, Kingston, Pa, 57-58, 63-64; art dir, WFM TV, Eatontown, N J, 60-61; designer display exhibs, The Displayers Inc, New York World's Fair Pavilions, 61-63; designer, Robert Kayton Assocs, New York, 62.
Dealer: Franz Bader Gallery Inc, 2124 Pennsylvania Ave N W, Washington, DC 20037.
Mailing Address: 1423 N Nash St, Arlington, VA 22209.

HOMAR, LORENZO
Printmaker, Painter
Preferred Media: Silk-screen.
b Puerta de Tierra, P R, Sept 10, 13.
Study & Training: Pratt Inst, 40-42; Brooklyn Mus, with Peterdi, Tamayo & Osver, 46-50; Inter-Am Univ P R, hon DFA; also with Gabor Peterdi.
Work in Public Collections: Libr Cong, Washington, D C; Mus Mod Art, New York, N Y; Metrop Mus Art, New York; Klingspor Mus, Offenbach, W Ger; Poster Mus, Warsaw, Poland.
Commissions: Mural of olympic swimming pool, Dept Parks, San Juan, 67-68; mural of pub sch,Dept Educ,San Juan, 71; portafolio, Blanco-Casals-Homar, Galeria Colibri, San Juan, 71.
Exhibitions: Leipzig Bk Festival, 65; Tokyo Biennale, 68; Poster Biennale, Warsaw, 70; San Juan Biennale, 70; Havana Exhib Prints, Cuba, 72.
Collections Arranged: First San Juan Print Biennale; Retrospective Exhib, Mus Int P R Cult, San Juan, 70.
Teaching: Master printing silkscreen, Inter-Am Univ P R, summer 72; Cali, Colombia; Sch Plastic Arts, Inst P R Cult, presently.
Positions: Jewelry designer, Cartier Inc, New York, N Y, 38-50; dir graphic workshop, Div Community Educ, 50-56; dir graphic workshop, Inst P R Cult, 58-72.
Awards: Guggenheim fel, 57; hon mention, Leipzig Bk Exhib, 65.

Bibliography: Lorenzo Homar & Fritz Eichenberg (auth), Posters in Puerto Rico, Artist Proof, 6: 9-10; Jose Gomez Sicre (auth), 6 Puerto Rican artists (film), Pan-Am Union, 68; Marta Traba (auth), Proposed polemics on Puerto Rican art, Libr Int Rio Piedras, P R, 71.
Publications: Auth, Los Renegados, 62; illusr, children's bk, Harcourt Brace & World, N Y, 69; auth, Aqui en la lucha, 70.
Dealer: Galeria Santiago, Calle Del Cristo, San Juan, PR 00901.
Mailing Address: Calle Cuevillas 607, Miramar, PR 00907.

HOMER, WILLIAM INNES
Art Historian, Educator
b Merion, Pa, Nov 8, 29.
Study & Training: Princeton Univ, BA; Harvard Univ, MA, PhD.
Teaching: Asst prof art & archaeol, Princeton Univ, 61-64; assoc prof hist art, Cornell Univ, 64-66; prof hist art, Univ Del, 66-
Positions: Cur, Mus Art, Ogunquit, Maine, 55-58; acting asst dir, Princeton Univ Art Mus, 56-57.
Awards: Jr fel, coun humanities, Princeton Univ, 62-63; Am Coun Learned Soc fel, 64-65; Guggenheim fel, 72-73.
Memberships: Col Art Asn; Soc Archit Historians; Royal Soc Arts; Wilmington Soc Fine Arts; Nat Arts Club.
Publications: Auth, Seurat and the science of painting, 64; auth, Robert Henri & his circle, 69.
Mailing Address: Dept of Art History, University of Delaware, Newark, DE 19711.

HONEYMAN, ROBERT B, JR
Collector
Collection: Contemporary art.
Mailing Address: Rancho Los Serritos, San Juan Capistrano, CA 92675.

HONIG, MERVIN
Painter, Painting Conservator
Preferred Media: Oils.
b New York, N Y, Dec 25, 20.
Study & Training: Art studies with Francis Criss, 39-41, Amadee Ozenfant, 46 & Hans Hofmann, 47-50; conservation studies at Brooklyn Mus, with Caroline & Sheldon Keck, 56-58.
Work in Public Collections: Okla Mus Art, Oklahoma City; Colby Col Mus Art, Waterville, Maine; also in many private collections.
Exhibitions: Portrait of America, Metrop Mus Art, New York, 44 & Carnegie Inst Fine Arts, 45; Whitney Mus Am Art Artists Ann, 49; Brooklyn & Long Island Artists, Brooklyn Mus, 60; Wadsworth Atheneum Artists Ann, 65; plus many others.
Teaching: Lectr life drawing, New York City Community Col, 68-70; lectr conservation of painting, Hofstra Univ, 72-
Awards: Gold medal for best in show, Am Vet Soc Artists, 66; first prize for oil painting, Locust Valley Art Show, 66; award of excellence, Mainstreams '70, Marietta Col, Ohio, 70.
Bibliography: Margaret Harold (auth), Prize winning paintings, 66; Amy Pett (auth), Beneath suburban exterior are two dedicated artists (husband & wife), Port Washington News & other newspapers, 70.
Memberships: Audubon Artists; Col Art Asn Am; assoc Int Inst Conserv Artistic & Hist Works.
Research: The use of polyurethane foam in the process of transfer.
Dealer: Frank Rehn Gallery, 655 Madison Ave, New York, NY 10021.
Mailing Address: 64 Jane Ct, Westbury, NY 11590.

HOOD, DOROTHY
Painter
Preferred Media: Oils, Ink.
b Bryan, Tex.
Study & Training: R I Sch Design, grad; Art Stud League New York, N Y.
Work in Public Collections: Mus Mod Art, New York; Whitney Mus Am Art, New York; Brooklyn Mus, N Y; Philadelphia Mus, Pa; Everson Mus, Syracuse, N Y.
Exhibitions: First Salon Int Exp Art, Mexico City, 55; U S Artists Latin Am, Pan Am Union, Washington, D C, 55; Golden Yrs Am Drawing, Brooklyn Mus, 56; State Univ N Y Col Potsdam; Drawing Soc Nat Am Fedn Arts Circulating Exhib, 70-72; plus one-man shows, Tex, N Y & Mexico City.
Teaching: Instr painting & drawing, Mus Fine Art, Houston, 62-72.
Awards: Nat Scholastic scholar, 40.
Bibliography: Bartlett Hayes, Jr (auth), Drawings of the masters, Am Vol, Shorewood Publ, 65; James Harithas (auth), Dorothy Hood (monogr), Contemp Arts Mus, 5/70; Philippe de Montebello (auth), Dorothy Hood, Haiti, a surrealist abstraction, Mus Fine Arts Bull, 6/71.
Dealer: Houston Galleries, 2323 San Felipe, Houston, TX 77006.
Mailing Address: 1408 Missouri St, Houston, TX 77006.

HOOD, ETHEL PAINTER
Sculptor
b Baltimore, Md, Apr 9, 08.
Study & Training: Art Stud League New York, N Y; Acad Julian, Paris.
Work in Public Collections: St Francis of the Curbs, Brookgreen Gardens, S C.
Exhibitions: Baltimore Mus Art; Corcoran Gallery Art, Washington, D C; Nat Acad Design, New York; Whitney Mus Am Art, New York; Pa Acad Fine Arts, Philadelphia; also four one-man exhibs, New York.
Memberships: Fel Nat Sculpture Soc; Nat Asn Women Artists.
Mailing Address: 15 E 61st St, New York, NY 10021.

HOOD, (THOMAS) RICHARD
Printmaker, Designer
Preferred Media: Graphics
b Philadelphia, Pa.
Study & Training: Univ Pa Sch Fine Arts; Philadelphia Mus Sch Art, BFA, 53.
Work in Public Collections: Philadelphia Mus Art; New York Pub Libr, N Y; Mus Mod Art, New York; Smithsonian Inst Nat Portrait Gallery, Washington, D C; Libr Cong, Washington, D C.
Exhibitions: New Horizons, Mus Mod Art, New York, 36; Am Art Today, New York World's Fair, 39; Art Dirs Ann, Philadelphia, 52-72; Fabulous Decade, Smithsonian Inst, 64; Color Prints of Americas, N J State Mus, Trenton, 70.
Teaching: From instr to assoc prof, Philadelphia Col Art, 51-
Positions: Assoc dir advert design, Philadelphia Col Art, 57-60, dir exhibs, 67-; design consult, 67-
Awards: Art Dirs Club Philadelphia Gold Medal, 66; Franklin Gold Medal, Printing Industs Philadelphia, 70; Nat Graphic Arts Design Award, 70.
Bibliography: Gertrude Benson (auth), Tradition versus innovation, Pa Traveler, 5/59; Sam Gamburg (auth), Professor Hood and award winning invitation, Centennial News, spring 71; Victoria Donohoe (auth), Dick Hood's timeless, abstract, balancing act, Philadelphia Inquirer, 2/25/72.
Memberships: Philadelphia Art Alliance (print comt, 60-); Mus Mod Art; Print Club Philadelphia; Am Color Print Soc (pres, 56-); fel Int Inst Arts & Lett.
Dealer: Marion Locks Gallery, 1524 Walnut St, Philadelphia, PA 19102.
Mailing Address: 1452 E Cheltenham Ave, Philadelphia, PA 19124.

HOOK, WALTER
Painter, Educator
Preferred Media: Watercolors.
b Missoula, Mont, Apr 25, 19.
Study & Training: Univ Mont, BA, 42; Univ N Mex, MA, 50, with Kenneth Adams & Randall Davey.
Work in Public Collections: Cheney Cowles Mem Mus, Spokane, Wash; Butler Inst Am Art, Youngstown, Ohio; Springfield Art Mus, Mo; Richmond Art Mus, Va; Yellowstone Art Ctr, Billings, Mont.
Commissions: Sculptures, Sta of Cross, 63 & mosaic, 64, St Anthony's Parish, Missoula, Mont; mosaic, St Vincent de Paul Parish, Fed Way, Washington, 65; lower relief, Newman Ctr, Missoula, 65.
Exhibitions: Butler Inst Am Art Ann, 64, 67 & 68; Pac Northwest Watercolor Soc Ann, Seattle, 68-71; Calif Nat Watercolor Soc Ann, Los Angeles, 68-71; Pa Acad Fine Arts Ann, Philadelphia, 69; Am Watercolor Soc Ann, New York, 71.
Teaching: Prof painting & drawing, Univ Mont, 55-
Positions: Sci illusr, Western Elec Atomic Energy Comn Prog, Albuquerque, N Mex, 51-54; art dir, Gen Elec Atomic Energy Comn Prog, Richland, Wash, 54-55.
Awards: Philadelphia Watercolor Club Award, 69; Watercolors U S A Purchase Award, Springfield Art Mus, 71; Fred Marshall Watercolor Award, Northwest Watercolor Soc, Seattle, 71.
Memberships: Ala Watercolor Soc; Calif Nat Watercolor Soc; Philadelphia Watercolor Soc; Artists Equity Asn.
Dealer: Pearl Fox, 103 Windsor Ave, Melrose Park, Philadelphia, PA 19126.
Mailing Address: 400 Pattee Canyon Dr, Missoula, MT 59801.

HOOKER, MRS R WOLCOTT
Collector, Patron
b Missoula, Mont, Sept 28, 08.
Study & Training: Col William & Mary; Art Stud League New York, drawing with Robert Beverly Hale; Albright Art Sch, Buffalo.
Positions: Dir, Int Coun Mus Mod Art; trustee, Am Fedn Arts.
Awards: First prize, painting award, Garrett Club, Buffalo.
Collection: Contemporary painting and sculpture.
Mailing Address: 563 Park Ave, New York, NY 10021.

HOOPES, DONELSON FARQUHAR
Museum Curator, Art Historian
b Philadelphia, Pa, Dec 3, 32.
Study & Training: Pa Acad Fine Arts, 50-53; Univ Pa, AB, 60; Univ Firenze, 58-59.
Collections Arranged: The Private World of John Singer Sargent, 64; 300 Years of American Art, New York World's Fair, 64; The Triumph of Realism, 67; The Beckoning Land: Nature and the American Artist, 71; The Düsseldorf School and the Americans, 72.
Positions: Dir, Portland Mus Art, Maine, 60-62; cur, Corcoran Gallery Art, 62-64; cur painting & sculpture, Brooklyn Mus, 65-69; cur American Art, Los Angeles Co Mus Art, 72-
Awards: Notable Bk of 1969 (Homer Watercolors), Am Libr Asn, 69.
Memberships: Col Art Asn Am; Am Asn Mus.
Research: Relating the cultural history of the nineteenth century America to its artists.
Publications: Co-auth, Maine and its role in American art, 63; auth, Winslow Homer watercolors, 69; auth, Sargent watercolors, 70; auth, Eakins watercolors, 72; auth, American impressionist painting, 72.
Mailing Address: Los Angeles County Museum of Art, 5905 Wilshire Blvd, Los Angeles, CA 90036.

HOOTON, BRUCE DUFF
Art Administrator, Writer
b Waukegan, Ill, Dec 11, 28.
Study & Training: Southwestern Col, 46-50; Memphis Acad Arts, 48-50; Harvard Univ, scholar, 51-52.
Collections Arranged: Sculptors Guild Bryant Park Exhibition, in association with New York Cultural Affairs, N Y, 67; Niezvestny (modern Russian sculpture), Sculptors Guild, New York, 68; Drawing Society Regional Drawing Exhibition (8 museums), American Federation Arts, 70-72.
Positions: Ed & auth, Drawing Mag, 57-60; art critic, ed & reviewer, New York Herald Tribune, 62-65; head New York off, Archives Am Art, New York, 65-66; ed, Art News, 68-69; acting chmn, Venice Comt, New York, 71; assoc, Lee Ault & Co, 71-
Memberships: Drawing Soc (v pres, 72); Stravinsky Diaghilev Found (v pres, 72); Charles Burchfield Ctr (adv bd, 72); New York State Coun Arts (consult, 72); Cooper-Hewitt Mus (Friends of Prints & Drawings, 71-72).
Specialty of Gallery: Twentieth century paintings, sculpture & drawings; French & European masters; South American masters; young masters.
Publications: Ed, Drawings of Edwin Dickinson, Yale Univ Press, 60; ed, Mother & child in modern art, Duell, Sloan & Pearce, 64; ed, American paintings in Reynolda House, Reynolda House, 70.
Mailing Address: Lee Ault & Co, 25 E 77th St, New York, NY 10021.

HOOVER, F HERBERT
Art Dealer, Writer
b Atlanta, Ga, June 16, 29.
Study & Training: Maryville Col, BA(cum laude); sculpture with Michael Von Meyer.
Teaching: Instr hist art, Am Inst Banking, San Francisco, Calif, fall 69; instr art collecting, Univ Calif, Santa Cruz, fall 71-; lectr & instr, Univ Calif Exten.
Positions: Dir, Pomeroy Galleries, San Francisco, 65-69; owner, Hoover Gallery, 69-
Memberships: Calif Arts Comn (appointed three times by Gov Reagan, 66-); Am Soc Appraisers.
Research: Life of American sculptress Patience Lovell Wright & French painter Marie Laurencin.
Specialty of Gallery: Nineteenth century American & European painters & contemporary American painters & sculptors.
Publications: Auth, Taste in the arts, 65; auth, Brushstrokes, 71.
Mailing Address: Hoover Gallery, 710 Sansome St, San Francisco, CA 94111.

HOOVER, FRANCIS LOUIS
Collector, Educator
b Sherman, Tex, Mar 12, 13.
Study & Training: N Tex State Univ, BS, 33; Columbia Univ, MA, 35; N Y Univ, DEd, 41; Art Stud League New York, 40-41; New Sch Soc Res, 40-41.
Teaching: Asst prof art, N Tex State Univ, 36-40; asst prof art, Eastern Ill State Univ, 41-44; prof art, Ill State Univ, 44-, dir Univ Mus, 72-
Positions: Dir, LaSalle Art Gallery, 33-36; ed, Arts & Activities Mag, 52-67; dir, Fairway Gallery, 62-67.
Awards: Award of Merit for Ed Excellence, Indust Mkt Sixth Ann, 54.
Memberships: Appraisers Asn Am; Am Soc Appraisers; Int Platform Asn.
Collection: Art of the Cuna Indians; pre-Columbian ceramics and jade; primitive arts of Africa and Oceania; folk arts of Middle America; works are in permanent collections of Philadelphia Museum of Art, Cleveland Museum of Art, Art Institute of Chicago, Field Museum of Natural History, Peabody Museum, Honolulu Academy of Art and others.
Publications: Auth, Guide for teaching art, 56, Art activities for the very young, 62, Young printmakers I, 63, Young printmakers II, 64 & Young sculptors, 67.
Mailing Address: 305 N University Ave, Normal, IL 61761.

HOOVER, (SIDNEY) TODD
Printmaker, Instructor
Preferred Media: Graphics.
b South Bend, Ind, May 26, 45.
Study & Training: Ind Univ, BS(art educ), 68; Univ Notre Dame, MA, 72.
Work in Public Collections: N Dak State Univ; Univ Notre Dame.
Exhibitions: Olivet Nat Print & Drawing Show, Mich, 71; 14th Ann N Dak Exhib Prints & Drawings, Univ N Dak, 71; Dulin Nat Print & Drawing Competition, Knoxville, Tenn, 71; Regional Fine Art Biennial, J B Speed Art Mus, Louisville, Ky, 71; Works on Paper, Indianapolis Mus Art, 72.
Teaching: Head dept art, Riley High Sch, South Bend, 68-
Awards: Purchase award, 14th Nat N Dak Exhib Prints & Drawings, 71; award, Regional Fine Art Biennial, J B Speed Art Mus, 71; second prize for prints, 7th Biennial Mich Regional Art Competition, South Bend, 71.
Publications: Auth, Correlation of art ability and intellectual ability, Phi Delta Kappan Mag, 70.
Dealer: Radecki's Art Gallery, Jefferson St, South Bend, IN 46614.
Mailing Address: 1336 E Cambridge Dr, South Bend, IN 46614.

HOOWIJ, JAN
Painter
Preferred Media: Oils, Acrylics, Tempera.
b Hengelo, Holland, Sept 13, 07.
Study & Training: Acad Fine Arts, The Hague, Holland, BA; Acad Grande Chaumiere, Paris; also painting with Henk Meyer, Holland.
Work in Public Collections: Paintings, Brooklyn Mus, N Y, Joslyn Mem Mus, Omaha, Nebr, Witte Mem Mus, San Antonio, Tex, Art Ctr, Tulsa, Okla & Acad Art, Honolulu, Hawaii.
Commissions: Portraits, of Mayor Wagner, New York, N Y, 55, Gov Allred, Fed Courthouse, Corpus Christi, Tex, 59 & Neil Jacoby, Sch Bus Admin, Univ Calif, Los Angeles, 71; mosaic murals, Ardmore Develop Co, Phoenix, Ariz, 61 & Hollywood, Calif, 62.
Exhibitions: Rijksmuseum Nat Show, Amsterdam, Holland, 35; Brooklyn Mus Regional Show, 42; Int Marine Art Show, Palais Chaillot, Paris, 46; Carnegie Inst Nat Ann, Pittsburgh, Pa, 47; Los Angeles Co Art Mus Regional Ann, 56.
Teaching: Instr figure, Acad Fine Arts, The Hague, 31-34; pvt instr painting, 52-57.
Awards: Royal Subsidy For Artists, Holland, 31-34; Therese Van Duyl Schwartz Prize for Best Portrait in Holland, 36; Purchase prize, Witte Mem Mus, 59.
Bibliography: Janice Lovoos (auth), The paintings of Jan Hoowij, Am Artist Mag, 8/65.
Dealer: Emerson Gallery, 17230 Ventura Blvd, Los Angeles, CA 91316.
Mailing Address: 16614 Chaplin Ave, Encino, CA 91316.

HOPE, HENRY RADFORD
Art Historian
b Chelsea, Mass, Dec 15, 05.
Study & Training: Harvard Univ, PhD.
Teaching: Chmn dept fine arts, Ind Univ, 41-67, dir art mus, 60-71.
Positions: Ed, Art J.
Mailing Address: 1 Las Olas Circle, Fort Lauderdale, FL 33310.

HOPKINS, BUDD
Painter
Preferred Media: Oils, Acrylics.
b Wheeling, W Va, June 15, 31.
Study & Training: Oberlin Col, BA, 53; Columbia Univ, 53-54, with Meyer Schapiro.
Work in Public Collections: Whitney Mus Am Art, New York, N Y; Solomon R Guggenheim Mus Art, New York; San Francisco Mus Art, Calif; Joseph Hirshhorn Collection, Washington, D C; Williams Col Mus, Mass.
Commissions: Oil painting, W Va State Humanities Coun, 72.
Exhibitions: Five Ann Whitney Mus Am Art, 58-72; Festival Two Worlds, Spoleto, Italy, 58; Young Am, Whitney Mus Am Art, Baltimore Mus Art, City Art Mus St Louis & others, 60; Benjamin Collection, Yale Univ Art Gallery, 67; Young New Eng Painters, Ringling Mus Art, Portland Mus Art & Currier Gallery, 69.
Teaching: Docent, Mus Mod Art, summers 55-56; docent, Whitney Mus Am Art, 57-60.

Bibliography: Brian O'Doherty (auth), Budd Hopkins, master of a
movement manque, Object & Idea, 67; April Kingsley (auth), An
interview with Budd Hopkins, Art Am, 72; Ward Jackson (auth),
Art now—New York, Univ Galleries, Vol 4, No 2.
Memberships: Provincetown Art Asn (hon v pres, 68-70).
Publications: Contribr, Three young Americans, Allen Mem Art
Mus Bull, 57; contribr, Young America, 1960, Whitney Museum
catalogue, 60; contribr, First person singular, Art Gallery Mag,
4/72; co-auth, Concept vs art object, Arts Mag, 4/72.
Dealer: William Zierler Gallery, 956 Madison Ave, New York, NY
10021.
Mailing Address: 246 W 16th St, New York, NY 10011.

HOPKINS, JOHN FORNACHON
Painter, Educator
b Peking, China, June 30, 20.
Study & Training: Cornell Univ, BFA & MFA, with John Hartell,
Norman Daly & Joseph Hanson.
Work in Public Collections: Cornell Univ; Hofstra Univ;
Sewanahaka High Sch.
Exhibitions: Miami Univ; Cornell Univ; Addison Gallery Am Art,
Andover, Mass; Denver Art Mus, Colo; Munson-Williams-
Proctor Inst, Utica, N Y; plus others.
Teaching: Prof art & art hist & chmn dept fine arts, Hofstra Univ,
at present.
Positions: Asst dir, Arts Around Us & American Art Today (two
26-week series), WOR TV, 56.
Awards: Emily Lowe Award, 56.
Memberships: N Y Art Teachers Asn; Long Island Art Teachers
Asn; Am Asn Univ Prof.
Publications: Illusr, art hist bks.
Mailing Address: 30 Vineyard Rd, Huntington, NY 11743.

HOPKINS, KENDAL COLES
Painter
Preferred Media: Oils.
b Haddonfield, N J, Jan 6, 08.
Study & Training: Pa Acad Fine Arts; Acad Grande Chaumière.
Work in Public Collections: Woodmere Art Gallery, Philadelphia,
Pa; plus many private collections.
Commissions: Many private portrait commissions.
Exhibitions: Pa Acad Fine Arts Ann, Philadelphia; Philadelphia Mus
Art, Pa; Nat Acad Design, New York, N Y; Ivan Spence Gallery,
Ibiza, Spain; one-man show, Farnsworth Mus, Rockland, Maine;
plus 15 other one-man shows.
Teaching: Instr painting, Bryn Mawr Col, Pa; head dept art, Baldwin
Sch, Bryn Mawr, Pa; instr art, Fieldston Sch, New York.
Memberships: Pa Acad Fine Arts; Philadelphia Mus; Peal Club,
Philadelphia.
Dealer: Vendo Nubes Gallery, 1929 Chestnut St, Philadelphia, PA
19103.
Mailing Address: Maisfield Rd, Phoenixville, PA 19460.

HOPKINS, PETER
Painter, Educator
Preferred Media: Oils.
b New York, N Y, Dec 18, 11.
Study & Training: Art Stud League New York, 27 & 45-50, with
George Bridgman, Reginald Marsh, Kenneth H Miller, Robert B
Hale & sculpture with William Zorach.
Work in Public Collections: Mus City of New York.
Commissions: Landscapes, 49 & portraits, 50, Theatre Guild, New
York; mural, comn by Stewart Chaney, New York, 54; mural,
comn by Gino di Grandi, 55; illus, RCA Victor Corp, New York,
56.
Exhibitions: Paintings in the Maroger Medium, Lyman Allyn Mus,
New London, Conn, 47; Art Stud League New York, Nat Acad De-
sign Galleries, 49; Am Acad Arts & Lett, 50; Artists Equity,
51 & Contemp Painting, 52, Whitney Mus Am Art.
Teaching: Instr drawing & painting, Moore Inst Art, Sci & Indust,
49-50; instr art, New York-Phoenix Schs Design, 61-, chmn dept
fine art, 67-; dean mem, 62-67.
Positions: Supvr libr, N Y Univ, 53; asst dir, Mortimer Brandt Gal-
lery, 53-58.
Awards: Art grants, Am Acad Arts & Lett, 50 & Nat Inst Arts &
Lett, 50.
Bibliography: The artist & the Copa girls, See, 53; C B (auth), Art
exhibition notes, New York Herald Tribune, 1/25/58.
Memberships: Life mem Art Stud League New York; assoc Am Mus
Nat Hist.
Publications: Contribr, Town & Country Mag, 44 & Family Circle
Mag, 45; auth, The essentials of perspective, Resley, 64; illusr,
The American heritage history of the 1920s and 1930s, 70; auth,
Population & geonomics, New York-Phoenix Sch Design, 70.
Dealer: Grand Central Art Galleries, 40 Vanderbilt Ave, New York,
NY 10017.
Mailing Address: 36 Horatio St, New York, NY 10014.

HOPKINS, RUTH JOY
Painter
b Fremont, Nebr, Aug 17, 91.
Study & Training: Colo Springs Fine Arts Ctr; Col Fine Arts,
Morelia, Mex; Inst San Miguel, Mex.
Work in Public Collections: Holdrege Mus, Nebr; Wyoming State
Capitol, Cheyenne; Fort Casper Mus; St Francis Boys' Home,
Salina, Kans; Kans State Col; plus others.
Exhibitions: Retrospective, Midland Col, Fremont, 61-64; Fort
Riley, Kans, 63; Gov Exhib, Omaha, 64; Beta Sigma Phi Sorority,
Casper, 65; two-man show, Casper Art Guild, 66; plus others.
Awards: Prizes, Natrona Co Fair, 53 & Wyoming State Fair, 55.
Memberships: Casper Art Guild; Wyoming Art Asn; Fremont Art
Asn.
Mailing Address: 78 South C St, Fremont, NE 68025.

HOPPES, LOWELL E
Cartoonist
b Alliance, Ohio, July 1, 13.
Publications: Created over 20,000 cartoons in Colliers, Post, Amer-
ican, Esquire, New Yorker, Farm Jour, Parade Family Weekly,
King Features Syndicate & others.
Mailing Address: 642 Calle del Otono, Sarasota, FL 33561.

HOPPS, WALTER
Art Administrator
Collections Arranged: Organizer & comnr United States contribution
to Venice Biennale, sponsored by Nat Collection Fine Arts,
Smithsonian Inst, 72.
Positions: Former dir, Corcoran Gallery Art; vis cur contemp art,
Nat collection Fine Arts, Smithsonian Inst, at present.
Bibliography: Grace Glueck (auth), U S photos & movies for bien-
nale, New York Times, 4/72.
Art Interests: Current American art, especially wall-space exper-
ience.
Mailing Address: 2222 Q St N W, Washington, DC 20008.

HORIUCHI, PAUL
Painter
b Yamanashiken, Japan, Apr 12, 06.
Study & Training: Univ Puget Sound, hon LHD, 68.
Work in Public Collections: Harvard Univ; Denver Art Mus, Univ
Ore, Eugene; Wadsworth Atheneum, Hartford, Conn; Santa Bar-
bara Mus Art; plus others.
Commissions: Free-standing mural, Seattle World's Fair, 62.
Exhibitions: American Painting, Va Mus Fine Arts, Richmond, 66;
one-man shows, San Francisco, Calif, 66 & 68 & Tacoma, Wash,
67; retrospective, Univ Oregon & Seattle Art Mus, 68.
Awards: Ford Found, 60; Seattle World's Fair, 62; Burpee Mus,
Rockford, Ill, 66; plus many others.
Dealer: Gordon Woodside Gallery, 803 E Union St, Seattle, WA
98122.
Mailing Address: 9773 Arrowsmith Ave S, Seattle, WA 98118.

HORN, MILTON
Sculptor, Writer
Preferred Media: Bronze, Wood, Stone.
b Russia, Sept 1, 06; U S citizen.
Study & Training: Beaux Arts Inst Design, New York, N Y; also with
Henry H Kitson.
Work in Public Collections: Brookgreen Gardens, S C; Olivet Col,
Mich; Smithsonian Inst Div Numismatics; Bernard Horwich Ctr,
Chicago, Ill.
Commissions: Three symbolic bronze groups on facade of hq bldg,
Nat Cong Parents & Teachers, Chicago, 53-54; eight marble re-
liefs, W Va Univ Med Ctr, 54-59; symbolic bronze on facade &
holy ark in sanctuary, B'nai Israel Temple, Charleston, W Va,
59-60; bronze Hymn to Water, Central Water Filtration Plant,
Chicago, 65; bronze, Nat Bank Commerce, Charleston, W Va, 68-
69.
Exhibitions: American Art Today, New York World's Fair, 39 & 40;
Third Int Exhib Sculpture, Philadelphia Mus Fine Arts, Pa, 49;
American Sculpture—1951, Metrop Mus, New York, 51; Chicago
& Vicinity Exhib, Art Inst Chicago, 52; Nat Inst Arts & Lett, New
York, 53 & 55.
Teaching: Artist-in-residence & prof art, Olivet Col, 39-49.
Awards: Award for excellence in the fine arts allied with archit,
Chicago Chap, Am Inst Architects, 55; Nat Citation Hon, Nat
Conf, Am Inst Architects, Washington, D C, 57; Henry Hering
Mem Medal, Nat Sculpture Soc, New York, 72.
Bibliography: Avram Kampf (auth), Contemporary synagogue art,
Union Am Hebrew Congregations, 61; Cecil Roth (auth), History
of Jewish art, 61 & 71 & Louis Redstone (auth), Art in architec-
ture, 68, McGraw-Hill.
Memberships: Founding mem Sculptors Guild; founding mem Art-
ists Equity Asn; Col Art Asn Am; fel Nat Sculpture Soc.

Publications: Contribr, Proceedings of teachers seminar, Col Schs Archit, Aspen, Colo, 57; contribr, The Christian century, 2/59; contribr, New city-men in metropolis, Chicago, 3/1/64; contribr, Indland architect, Chicago, 65; contribr, Nat Sculpture Rev, 72.
Mailing Address: 1932 N Lincoln Ave, Chicago, IL 60614.

HORNE, (ARTHUR EDWARD) CLEEVE
Painter, Sculptor
b Jamaica, B W I, Jan 9, 12.
Study & Training: Ont Col Art, AOCA, also study with D Dick, Eng & in Europe.
Work in Public Collections: Nat Gallery Can.
Commissions: Alexander Bell Mem, Brantford, Ont; War Mem, Law Soc Upper Can; Shakespeare Mem; Stratford, Ont; plus other portrait painting, archit sculpture & memorials.
Exhibitions: Nat Gallery Can; Royal Can Acad Arts, 28- ; Ont Soc Artists, 39; Sculptors' Soc Can, 35-
Positions: Art adv, Ont Hydro-elec Power Comn, St Lawrence Seaway Power House Proj, 57-58; art consult, Imperial Oil Bldg, Toronto; art consult, Can Imperial Bank Com, 61-63; mem art consult comt, York Univ, 63- ; art consult, Queen's Park Proj, Ont Govt, 66-69.
Awards: Allied Arts Medal, Royal Archit Inst Can, 63.
Memberships: Ont Soc Artists (past pres); Arts & Lett Club (pres, 55-57); Royal Can Acad Arts.
Mailing Address: 181 Balmoral Ave, Toronto, Ont, Can.

HORNUNG, CLARENCE PEARSON
Designer, Writer
b New York, N Y, June 12, 99.
Study & Training: Cooper Union; Art Stud League New York; City Col New York, BS, 20.
Work in Public Collections: New York Pub Libr; Springfield Mus, Mass; Newark Pub Libr, N J; N Y State Mus, Albany; Nat Gallery Art, Washington, D C.
Memberships: Am Inst Graphic Artists; Typophiles.
Publications: Auth, Handbook of design & devices, 32; auth, Early American advertising art, 47; auth, Wheels across America, 59; auth & illusr, Portraits of early automobiles, 65; auth, Treasury of American design, 72.
Mailing Address: 12 Glen Rd, West Hempstead, NY 11552.

HORNUNG, GERTRUDE SEYMOUR
Educator, Lecturer
b Boston, Mass.
Study & Training: Wellesley Col, AB; Case Western Reserve Univ, MA, PhD(visual arts), 49.
Teaching: Lectr art hist, Cleveland Mus Art, 37-45, supvr, 45-60; free lance writer & lectr, 60-
Positions: Founder & chmn Jr Coun, Cleveland, 41-42; deleg, White House Conf Educ, Washington, D C, 55; pres, Adult Educ Coun Greater Cleveland, 56-58; founder & chmn Greater Cleveland Educ TV Comt, 58-60; trustee, Cleveland Area Arts Coun, 72.
Awards: Ital Ministry For Affairs res grant, 62-
Memberships: Assoc Int Coun Mus; Am Asn Mus; life mem Cleveland Mus Art; Mus Mod Art; Metrop Mus Art.
Research: History of Italian art; art of the South Seas, especially Polynesia & Melanesia; contemporary American art.
Collection: Contemporary Italian and American paintings.
Publications: Auth & ed, Cultural directory of greater Cleveland, 47; contribr, several articles on art history in mags & jours, 50-72.
Mailing Address: 2240 Elandon Dr, Cleveland, OH 44106.

HOROWITZ, NADIA
Painter, Designer
b Warsaw, Poland; U S citizen.
Study & Training: Warsaw Acad Fine Art, with Pruszkowski & Schultz; Acad Grande Chaumière, Paris, France, with L Lefèvre; Ecole Superieure Art Graphiques, Belg, with Paul Van Maas & Tilla Vandervelde; Rheiman Sch, Berlin, Ger; silver sculpture, with Prof Sliwniak.
Commissions: Painting in Colina medium, commissioned by Dr Harrison-Pollock for Gerard Croisset, Holland, 68; painting in Colina medium, commissioned by Vincent Lopez, 69; painting in oil commissioned by M Elkin for Tel-Aviv Mus; plus murals in pvt houses in Fr Riviera, Israel, U S A & Holland.
Exhibitions: One-man shows, New York Jewish Mus, New York Anthrop Soc Am, La Petite Galerie, Brussels, Belg, Sophie Ryback Gallery, Paris, France & Hilton Hotel, Cascais, Portugal; plus many other group & one-man shows.
Teaching: Asst instr art, Adam Rychtarski Art Sch, 37-38; instr pvt studio, 52-
Positions: Asst stylist, M & Avon, 53-61; art exhib dir, Israeli 20th Anniversary Traveling Exhib, 68.
Awards: First prize for The Colours of my Homeland (oil), Polish Art Asn, 57; first prize for Meditation & second prize for Sanguina, M Loewenstein Inc, 57.

Bibliography: J Lefevre (auth), article, 32 & A Werner (auth), article, 67, In: Grande Chaumière; BMurphy (auth), article, In: E S Sentinel, Art Mag, 66.
Memberships: Artist Equity Asn New York; Polish Artist Equity (v pres, 68); Nat Asn Women Artists; Artist 72 Group 8.
Art Interests: Originator of Colina media.
Mailing Address: 205 W 89th St, Apt 6 E, New York, NY 10024.

HOROWITZ, MR & MRS RAYMOND J
Collectors
Mr Horowitz b New York, N Y, May 7, 16.
Study & Training: Mr Horowitz, Columbia Univ, AB, 36, LLB, 39.
Mailing Address: 930 Fifth Ave, New York, NY 10022.

HOROWITZ, SAUL
Collector
b New York, N Y.
Collection: French Impressionists & Post Impressionists.
Mailing Address: 35 E 76th St, New York, NY 10021.

HORTER, ELIZABETH LENTZ
Painter
b Philadelphia, Pa, Jan 4, 00.
Study & Training: Westchester State Teachers Col; Temple Univ, BS Educ; Tyler Sch Fine Arts, Temple Univ, MFA; Cornell Univ; Univ Pa; Moore Inst Art; Philadelphia Mus Sch Art, with Earle Horter.
Work in Public Collections: Woodmere Art Gallery.
Exhibitions: Libr Cong, Washington, D C; Pa Acad Fine Arts, Philadelphia; Carnegie Inst, Pittsburgh, Pa; Brooklyn Mus, N Y; Print Club Philadelphia; plus others.
Teaching: Supvr art intern prog, Temple Univ, 64.
Mailing Address: 310 W Hortter St, Philadelphia, PA 19119.

HORTON, JAN E
Painter, Writer
Preferred Media: Oils.
b Tecumseh, Nebr.
Study & Training: Univ Nebr, BFA; Millsaps Col; Univ Miss.
Work in Public Collections: Miss Art Asn; Miss Auth Educ TV Libr; Eastern Educ Network Videotape Libr; WNET Videotape Libr, NIT Videotape Libr.
Exhibitions: Tri-State Exhib, Cheyenne, 55; Gulf Coast Arts Festival, Biloxi, 65; Frontal Images, Jackson, Miss, 65-70; Nat Watercolor Exhib, Jackson, 66 & 68; Monroe Competition, La, 69.
Teaching: Instr art hist, Miss Col, 62-64 & summer 67; instr, Murrah High Sch, 66-67; instr watercolor & art, Univ Miss Exten.
Positions: Writer, Miss Educ TV, 70- , TV producer art films, 71-
Awards: First award for watercolor, Buffalo For Sale, Shreveport, 69; best in show for Pyrocantha, Cleveland, 70; Peabody Award in Film/TV for Art For The Day, 72.
Bibliography: Bettersworth (auth), Mississippi history, 68.
Memberships: Civic Arts Coun; Miss Art Asn.
Publications: Auth & ed, Art for the day (educ TV ser).
Mailing Address: 3965 Peachtree Ct, New Orleans, LA 70114.

HORWITT, WILL
Sculptor
b New York, N Y, Jan 8, 34.
Study & Training: Art Inst Chicago, 52-54.
Work in Public Collections: Boston Mus Fine Arts, Mass; Chase Manhattan Bank, New York & Tokyo; Collection N Y State, Albany; Wadsworth Atheneum, Hartford, Conn; Yale Univ Art Gallery, New Haven, Conn.
Awards: John Simon Guggenheim fel, 65; Louis Comfort Tiffany Found Purchase Grant, 68-69.
Dealer: Lee Ault & Co, Inc, 25 E 77th St, New York, NY 10021.
Mailing Address: 131 E 15th St, New York, NY 10003.

HOSTETLER, DAVID
Sculptor, Instructor
Preferred Media: Wood.
b Beach City, Ohio, Dec 27, 26.
Study & Training: Ind Univ, BS; Ohio Univ, MFA.
Work in Public Collections: Speed Mus, Louisville, Ky; Butler Inst Am Art, Youngstown, Ohio; Fort Lauderdale Mus, Fla; Miami Mus Mod Art, Fla.
Commissions: Head of William McGuffey, Massillon Mus, Ohio, 65; bronze figure, One Erieview Plaza, Cleveland, Ohio, 68; wood carved head, Solon Pub Libr, Cleveland, 69.
Exhibitions: Parke-Bernet Galleries, Bernard Davis Col, New York, N Y, 62; one-man show, Sculpture Ctr Gallery, New York, 65-72; Pa Acad Fine Arts, Philadelphia, 66; one-man shows, Downey Mus Art, Calif, 69 & Speed Mus, 71.
Teaching: Instr ceramics, Ind Univ, Bloomington, summer 48; instr sculpture, Ohio Univ, 50- ; instr, San Miguel Allende, Mex, summer 58.

Positions: Mem adv panel, Ohio Arts Coun, Columbus, 69-73.
Awards: First prize, Mainstreams '69', Marietta Col, 69; purchase prize, Butler Art Inst, 70; Ohio Arts Coun Award, 71.
Bibliography: Phillip Adams (auth), The Carver from Coolville Ridge, Western Mich Univ Press, 67; Eye on art (film), CBS TV, 67; Joseph Slate (auth), The heavy folk thing, Kenyon Rev, 69.
Dealer: James Hunt Barker Galleries, One Pleasant St, Nantucket, MA 02554 & 336 Worth Ave, Palm Beach, FL 33480.
Mailing Address: Box 989, Athens, OH 45701.

HOTVEDT, KRISTINE J
Printmaker, Instructor
b Wautoma, Wis, Jan 29, 43.
Study & Training: Layton Sch Art, Milwaukee, Wis, 61-64; San Francisco Art Inst, BFA, 65; Inst Allende, San Miguel de Allende, Mex, MFA, 67; teaching asst with Diederich Kortlang.
Work in Public Collections: Centre House, Swannanoa, N C.
Exhibitions: N Mex Biennial Printing, Traveling Exhib, Santa Fe, 69; Southwest Fine Arts Biennial, Santa Fe, 70 & 72; one-woman show, Ariz State Univ, Tempe, 72; one-woman show, Univ Sonora, Hermosillo, Mex, 72; Bertrand Russell Peace Found Art Exhib, Rotunda Gallery, London, Eng, 72; plus others.
Teaching: Instr painting & printmaking, Pembroke State Univ, 67-69; head art dept, Los Llanos Sch Arts & Crafts, Santa Fe, 70-72; substitute art instr, Inst Am Indian Arts, Santa Fe, fall, 71.
Awards: First prize purchase award, Ctr House Ann Print Show, Swannanoa, N C, 68.
Publications: Illusr, Southwest arts & crafts, Tom Vinegar Press, 70; illusr, Pembroke Mag, 71; illusr, Christ and the poets, Ausburg Publ House, 72; illusr & ed, Pembroke Mag, 72; illusr, Tierra Amarilla Calendar, Craft Coop Northern N Mex, 72.
Dealers: Gallery of Modern Art, Taos, NM 87571; Janus Gallery, Palace Ave, Santa Fe, NM 87501.
Mailing Address: 120 Mesa Verde, Santa Fe, NM 87501.

HOTZ, HENRY, JR
Art Administrator
b Lansdowne, Pa, June 27, 12.
Study & Training: Haverford Col, BS(econ), 34; Pa Acad Fine Arts, Philadelphia, 34-38, Cresson European traveling scholar, 37; Barnes Found, 38-39.
Positions: Curator Pa Acad Fine Arts Sch, 38-42; mfg qual admin & mgr engraving dept, Curtis Publ, 56-59; adminr Pa Acad Fine Arts Sch, 69-
Memberships: Fellowship Pa Acad Fine Arts.
Mailing Address: Pennsylvania Academy of the Fine Arts, Broad & Cherry Sts, Philadelphia, PA 19102.

HOUGH, RICHARD
Photographer, Designer
b Roanoke, Va, Mar 1, 45.
Study & Training: Roanoke Col, BBA, 67; Rochester Inst Technol, summer 69; Hotchkiss Workshop, with Minor White, summer 71; Sch Design, Calif Inst Arts, 71-
Exhibitions: Virginia Photographers 1969 & 1971, Va Mus, Richmond, 69 & 71; 23rd Irish Int, Dublin, Ireland, 70; New Photographics, Cent Washington State Col, 71; Soc Photog Educ Exhib, Univ Ill, Chicago Circle, 71.
Teaching: Asst prof photog, Va Western Community Col, Roanoke, 68-71; grad teaching asst photog, Calif Inst Arts, 72-
Memberships: Soc Photog Educ.
Publications: Contribr, Mill Mt Rev, 70 & Networks, 72.
Mailing Address: 23933 Avenida Crescenta, Valencia, CA 91355.

HOUGHTON, ARTHUR A, JR
Art Administrator
b Corning, N Y, Dec 12, 06.
Study & Training: Harvard Univ, 25-29; Lehigh Univ, hon LHD, 50, Univ Md, 63; Univ Rochester, hon LLD, 52, Alfred Univ, 54, Wesleyan Univ, 63; Washington Col, hon LittD, 53, Hofstra Col, 56, Trinity Col, 55, St John's Univ, 66; Beaver Col, hon DLit, 57; Hobart & William Smith Col, hon DSc, 58, Bucknell Univ, 68; Washington & Jefferson Col, hon DFA, 71; MacMurray Col, 71.
Positions: Pres, Steuben Glass, 33-; cur rare books, Libr Cong, 40-42, mem trust fund bd & hon consult, Eng bibliog; dir, Corning Glass Works, 30-; v pres, Corning Mus of Glass & Pierpont Morgan Libr; trustee, past chmn & past pres, Metrop Mus Art; hon trustee & past chmn, Parsons Sch Design; trustee & past chmn, Cooper Union; hon cur, Keats Collection, Harvard Univ; hon trustee, Inst Contemp Art, Boston.
Awards: Comdr, l'Ordre des Arts et des Lettres; Michael Friedsam Medal in indust art; Gertrude Vanderbilt Whitney Award, Skowhegan Sch Painting & Sculpture; plus others.
Memberships: Fel Royal Col Art; Royal Soc Arts.
Mailing Address: 715 Fifth Ave, New York, NY 10022.

HOUSE, JAMES CHARLES, JR
Sculptor, Educator
Preferred Media: Wood.
b Benton Harbor, Mich, Jan 19, 02.
Study & Training: Univ Mich, 19-21 & Law Sch, 21-23; Pa Acad Fine Arts, 23-27; Univ Pa, BSEd, 41, MA, 72.
Work in Public Collections: Whitney Mus Am Art; Woodmere Art Gallery, Germantown, Pa.
Commissions: Mem tryptic (birch wood), Swartmore Presby Church, Pa, 56-57; large head of John Dewey (oak), Penniman Libr, Univ Pa, 56-57; St Christopher & Jesus (oak lunette), St Clements Episcopal Church, Philadelphia, Pa, 58; med emblem, Norfolk Med Tower, Va, 60; teak wall relief, Philadelphia Br Libr, Bustleton, Pa, 65-66.
Exhibitions: Whitney Mus Am Art Sculpture Biennials, 34 & 36; Kansas City Art Inst, 35; Int Sculpture Shows, Philadelphia Mus Art, 40 & 50; Artists For Victory, Metrop Mus Art, 42; Nineteen Cities, Mus Mod Art, New York, 47.
Teaching: Assoc prof sculpture & drawing, Univ Pa Grad Sch Fine Arts, 27-; assoc prof, Philadelphia Mus Art Eve Class, 49-50; assoc prof, San Diego State Col, summer 56.
Positions: Freelance caricaturist, New York Eve Post, Philadelphia Pub-Ledger, New Yorker & others, 25-32; caricaturist, Philadelphia Eve Bull, 47-54.
Awards: John Frederick Lewis First Prize For Caricature, Pa Acad Fine Arts, 27.
Bibliography: Dorothy Grafly (auth), article, In: Am Artist, 55.
Publications: Illusr, Fifty drawings, 30.
Mailing Address: 810 Crum Creek Rd, Media, PA 19063.

HOUSER, JAMES COWING, JR
Painter, Educator
Preferred Media: Acrylics.
b Jacksonville, Fla, Nov 12, 28.
Study & Training: Ringling Sch Art; Fla Southern Col, BS; Art Inst Chicago; Univ Fla, MFA; Johns Hopkins Univ.
Work in Public Collections: Univ Notre Dame, South Bend, Ind; Cornell Univ, Ithaca, N Y; N Y Univ; Bethlehem City Ctr, Pa; Syracuse Univ Art Collection, N Y.
Exhibitions: Soc Four Arts, Palm Beach, Fla, 64-72; one-man shows, Grand Cent Mod, New York, 67 & Lehigh Univ, Bethlehem, 68; Peter Rudolph Galleries, Woodstock, N Y & Coral Gables, Fla, 67-72; Mainstreams U S A, Ohio, 68.
Teaching: Asst prof painting, Ky Wesleyan Col, 54-60; prof painting, Palm Beach Jr Col, 60-, chmn dept, 64-70.
Awards: Atwater Kent Award, Soc Four Arts, 64; Hors de Concours, Contemp Am Painting Exhib, 66-69; best in show award, Hortt Mem Show, 69.
Bibliography: Margaret Harold (auth), Prize-winning paintings, Allied Publ, 67 & 68.
Dealers: Peter Rudolph Galleries, 22 Mill Hill Rd, Woodstock, NY 12498; Peter Rudolph Galleries, 338 Sevilla Ave, Coral Gables, FL 33134.
Mailing Address: 693 Jog Rd, West Palm Beach, FL 33406.

HOUSER, VIC CARL
Sculptor, Painter
b Los Angeles, Calif, Mar 6, 95.
Study & Training: Art Inst Chicago; Carl Werntz Sch Fine Arts, Chicago; also with Lorado Taft.
Commissions: Six First award medals for Calif Art Club, 58; monument to Joe Frisco, Del Mar Racetrack; Anita Metz trophy for Calif Yacht Club; Mem to combat flyers of all U S wars, U S Air Force Acad; wood sculpture, Cathedrals in Los Angeles, Sacramento & Fresno, Calif; portraits, heraldic arms & figureheads for pvt comns.
Exhibitions: Worcester Mus Art, Mass; City Art Mus St Louis, Mo; All-City Show, Los Angeles; one-man shows, Cath Women's Club Los Angeles & Whittier Art Asn; plus many others.
Collections Arranged: All Sculpture Show, Laguna Beach Art Asn, 62.
Teaching: Lect, demonstrations, TV & radio talks.
Positions: Mem adv bd & nominating jury, Calif State Fair Art Show; ed, Calif Art Club Bull; dir & ed, monthly bull, Am Inst Fine Arts; adv to exec dir, Calif State Art Comn; juror, Calif State Fair Art Show, 64; judge, Madonna Art Festival, Los Angeles, 65; plus many other art positions.
Awards: Citation & award, Blakeman-Florence, Calif, 56; Southland Art Asn, 56; Laguna Beach Art Asn, 56 & 57.
Memberships: Calif Art Club (pres); Laguna Beach Art Asn; Vinculum Fine Arts (founder & pres); Prof Artists Roost (founder).
Mailing Address: 3200 Durand Dr, Hollywood, CA 90028.

HOUSMAN, RUSSELL F
Painter, Educator
b Buffalo, N Y, Jan 13, 28.
Study & Training: Albright Art Sch, Buffalo, dipl; State Univ N Y Col

Buffalo, BS; N Y Univ, MA & PhD; also with Hale Woodruff &
Revington Arthur.
Work in Public Collections: Human Resources Ctr Collection;
Forum Gallery Collection; N Y Univ; State Univ N Y.
Commissions: Mural, USA, Kansas Munic Auditorium, 52; painting,
L Goodyear Collection, 57; Discovery Ctr, Human Resources
Ctr, 72.
Exhibitions: State Univ N Y; Tri-State Invitational, Chautauqua, N Y;
one-man show, Silvermine Guild Art, Albany Inst Hist & Art &
Wellons Gallery, New York; plus others.
Collections Arranged: Arms & Armor, 60 & Civil War Centennial,
60, Decatur Art Ctr, Ill; George Crosz Retrospect, Firehouse
Gallery, Garden City, N Y, 64.
Teaching: Prof art, Adelphi Univ, 56-59; prof art & chmn dept, Mil-
liken Univ, 59-61; prof art, Nassau Community Col, 63-, dir
Firehouse Gallery, 63-70.
Positions: Dir, Decatur City Art Ctr, 59-61; art consult, Human Re-
sources Ctr, Albertson, N Y, 61-
Awards: Purchase award, State Univ N Y, 68; prizes, Silvermine
Art Guild & Chautauqua Art Ctr.
Bibliography: Viscardi (auth), The school, Eriksson, 64; 21 paint in
hyplar, Grumbacher, 68; Watson (auth), The artist as a cook,
Country Art Gallery, 72.
Memberships: Am Fedn Art; Silvermine Art Guild; N Y State Art
Teachers (ed, 69); Long Island Art Teachers.
Research: Core humanities curriculum for disabled children; artist
in psychological warfare; the child as artist.
Publications: Auth, Psychological warfare capabilities and vulnera-
bilities as found in Soviet art, 54; The design of an art room, 55,
Utilization of artist personnel in psychological warfare, 63, Tele-
phone assisted teaching devices, 69 & Core humanities curricu-
lum for disabled children, 70.
Mailing Address: 38 Hampshire Rd, Great Neck, NY 11023.

HOUSSER, YVONNE McKAGUE
Painter, Designer
Preferred Media: Oils, Acrylics, Mixed Media, Collage, Water-
colors.
b Toronto, Ont, Aug 4, 98.
Study & Training: Ont Col Art, scholar; Acad Grande Chaumiere &
Acad Ranson, 21, 22 & 24, with Prinet; Univ Vienna; also with
Hans Hofmann & Emile Bistram.
Work in Public Collections: Nat Gallery Can; Art Gallery Ont; Lon-
don Art Gallery, Ont; Robert McMichael Collection Art; Univ To-
ronto; plus many others.
Commissions: Mural, The Canadian, Can Pac Rwy.
Exhibitions: Royal Can Ann, Ont Soc Artists; Can Group of Painters,
Nat Gallery Can; Contemporanea, Rio de Janeiro; Century of Can
Art, Tate Gallery, London, Eng; plus many others.
Teaching: Instr art, Ont Col Art, 20-41; also instr at Doon Sch Fine
Art & Ryerson Inst.
Awards: Can Nat Purchase Award; Baxter Award, Ont Soc Artists,
65.
Memberships: Royal Can Acad; Ont Soc Artists.

HOVELL, JOSEPH
Sculptor
b Kiev, Russia.
Study & Training: Cooper Union Art Sch, with Brewster; Nat Acad
Design, with Robert Aitken.
Commissions: Portrait busts & bas-reliefs of many prominent per-
sons in pvt collections; plaques & busts, Carnegie Hall, N Y; Na-
than Sachs bronze mem plaque; mem plaque, Hebrew Union Col &
Jewish Inst Relig, Cincinnati.
Exhibitions: Nat Acad Design; Brooklyn Mus; Whitney Mus Am Art;
Carnegie Hall Gallery; Jewish Mus, New York; plus others.
Awards: Agnon Gold Medal, Am Friends of Hebrew Univ, Jerusalem,
67.
Mailing Address: 130 W 57th St, New York, NY 10019.

HOVEY, WALTER READ
Art Historian, Lecturer
b Springfield, Mass, July 21, 95.
Study & Training: Yale Univ, AB; Harvard Univ, AM; Wooster Col,
hon PhD.
Teaching: Head Dept Fine Arts Univ Pittsburgh, 36-68, retired.
Positions: Dir, Henry Clay Frick Art Mus, Univ Pittsburgh, retired.
Collection: Chinese ceramics.
Mailing Address: Cedar St, Chatham, MA 02633.

HOVING, THOMAS
Museum Director
b New York, N Y, Jun 15, 31.
Study & Training: Princeton Univ, BA(summa cum laude), 53, Grad
Sch Art & Archaeol, Nat Coun Humanities fel, 55, study & travel
in Europe, 56-57, Grad Sch Fine Arts, Kienbusch & Haring fel,
57, MFA, 58, PhD(art hist), 59; Pratt Inst, hon LLD, 67; Hofstra
Univ, hon LHD; New York Univ, DFA, 68; Princeton Univ, DH, 68;
Middlebury Col, LittD, 68.
Positions: Curatorial asst, Dept Medieval Art & The Cloisters,
Metrop Mus Art, 59-60, asst cur, 60-63, assoc cur, 63-65, cur,
65-66, dir, 67-; parks comnr (title officially changed to adminr
recreation & cult affairs), City of New York, 66-67; mem, N Y
State Coun on the Arts; mem adv coun, dept art hist & archaeol,
Columbia Univ; mem bd dirs, Int Ctr Medieval Art; mem bd dirs,
Brooklyn Arts & Cult Asn; mem, Partnership for the Arts; mem
U S comt, Int Coun Mus; mem ed bd, Pantheon, Int Zeitschrift
für Kunst.
Awards: Distinguished achievement award, Advert Club Am, 66;
Elsie de Wolfe Award, Am Inst Interior Designers, 67; Park Asn
New York City Award for distinguished contribs to parks, 67;
plus others.
Memberships: Asn Art Mus Dirs; Asia Soc; Am Asn Mus; Assoc
Coun of the Arts; hon mem Am Inst Architects; plus others.
Publications: Auth, Guide to the Cloisters, 62; auth, The face of St
Juliana, 1/63, The Bury St Edmunds Cross, 6/64 & Italian
Romanesque sculpture, 6/65; auth, Branch out, Mus News, 9/68;
plus many others.
Mailing Address: Metropolitan Museum of Art, Fifth Ave & 82nd
St, New York, NY 10028.

HOVSEPIAN, LEON
Painter, Designer
b Bloomsburg, Pa, Nov 20, 15.
Study & Training: Worcester Art Mus Sch, cert; Yale Univ, Alice
Kimball traveling fel, 41-42, BFA; Fogg Mus.
Work in Public Collections: Worcester Art Mus, Mass; Fitchburg
Art Mus, Mass; Fine Arts Collection, Washington, D C; Spring-
field Mus, Mass.
Commissions: Fresco, Immaculata Retreat House, Willimantic,
Conn, 60; mosaics, Oblate Fathers Retreat House, Willimantic,
61; stained glass, Holy Cross Col, Worcester, 65; portraits,
Leiceister Jr Col, Mass, 68-69; mural, Springfield Post Off,
Mass.
Exhibitions: Art Inst Chicago, 41; Albright Art Gallery, 46; Nat
Gallery Art, 47; R I Sch Design, 48; Worcester Art Mus Am
Biennial, 48.
Teaching: Instr art, Bancroft Sch, 36-38; prof art, Woman's Col
New Haven, 38-40; instr art, Worcester Art Mus Sch, 40-, instr,
Pub Educ Div, 41-56.
Positions: Dir, Boylston Summer Art Sch, Mass, 41-
Awards: St Wulstan Soc Art Award, 38-40; painting prize, Fitchburg
Art Mus.
Bibliography: Adlow (auth), Stuart gallery, Christian Sci Monitor,
46; Sandrof (auth), Artist in his studio, Feature Parade, 53;
Browne (auth), Leon Hovsepian, Art News, 11/66.
Memberships: The Bohemians.
Publications: Illusr, Worcester fedral, past—present—future, 52;
illusr, Androck, 58.
Dealer: Triart Studios, 90 Pocasset Ave, Worcester, MA 01606.
Mailing Address: 96 Squantum St, Worcester, MA 01606.

HOWARD, CECIL RAY
Painter, Sculptor
Preferred Media: Collage, Assemblage.
b Wichita, Kans, Jan 25, 37.
Study & Training: Kans State Teachers Col, BS; Wichita State Univ,
MFA.
Work in Public Collections: Wichita Art Mus; Amarillo Col Gallery,
Tex; Wichita State Univ; Glendale Community Col, Ariz; Kans
State Teachers Col, Emporia.
Commissions: Collage mural, Western N Mex Univ, Silver City, 69;
tympanum ceramic sculpture, Church Good Shepherd, Silver City,
71.
Exhibitions: One-man invitationals, Marion Koogler McNay Gallery,
San Antonio, Tex, 60 & Wichita Art Mus, 67; Mid-America Show,
Nelson Gallery, Atkins Mus, Kansas City, Mo, 62; Mainstreams
'68 Int Exhib, Marietta, Ohio, 68; Int Designer-Craftsmen Exhib,
El Paso Art Mus, Tex, 69.
Teaching: Instr ceramics & sculpture, Western N Mex Univ, 63-
Positions: Dir, McCray Gallery, Western N Mex Univ, 63-
Awards: Purchase awards, Wichita Art Mus, 60 & 62; juror's
award for distinction, Mainstreams '68 Int Exhib, 68; first place
award in ceramics, El Paso Art Mus, 69.
Memberships: N Mex Designer-Craftsmen
Publications: Illusr, A voyage to America, Univ Nebr Press, 67;
auth, An assemblage, Western Rev, 68.
Dealer: Hill's Gallery, 121 Lincoln Ave, Santa Fe, NM 87501.
Mailing Address: Rt 10, Box 138, Glenwood, NM 88039.

HOWARD, DAN F
Painter, Art Administrator
Preferred Media: Oils.
b Iowa City, Iowa, Aug 4, 31.
Study & Training: Univ Iowa, BA, 53, MFA, 58.
Work in Public Collections: Joe & Emily Lowe Art Mus, Univ Miami, Fla; Parthenon Mus, Nashville, Tenn; Ark Arts Ctr, Little Rock, Masur Mus Art, Monroe, La; Fort Smith Art Mus, Ark.
Exhibitions: Nat Painting Exhib, Lowe Art Mus, 63; Contemporary Americans, Ark Arts Ctr, 67; Ark Pavilion Invitational, Hemis-Fair '68, San Antonio, Tex, 68; Contemp Am Painting Exhib, Palm Beach, Fla, 70; Regional Artists Invitational, Nelson Gallery, Kansas City, Mo, 72.
Teaching: From instr to assoc prof painting & drawing, Ark State Univ, 58-71, chmn div art, 65-71; prof painting & drawing & head dept art, Kans State Univ, 71-
Positions: Dir art gallery, Ark State Univ Fine Arts Ctr, Jonesboro, 67-71; exec dir, Friends of Art, Kans State Univ, Manhattan, 71-
Awards: First prize, Nat Painting Exhib, Miami, 63; top award, Ark-La-Miss Show, Monroe, La, 65; top award, Cent South Exhib, Nashville, 68.
Bibliography: Dan Howard, artist, The Changing Middle South, 67; Weathersby (auth), Art in Arkansas, Ark State Mag, 67; Margaret Harold (auth), Prize-winning paintings, Allied Fla, 64-66.
Memberships: Col Art Asn Am; Am Fedn Arts; Mid-Am Col Art Asn; Kans State Fedn Art (bd dirs, 72-); Manhattan Cult Arts Coun (bd dirs, 72-).
Dealer: Oliva Associates Ltd, 818 Madison Ave, New York, NY 10021.
Mailing Address: 1809 Cassell Rd, Manhattan, KS 66502.

HOWARD, HUMBERT L
Painter
b Philadelphia, Pa, July 12, 15.
Study & Training: Univ Pa; Howard Univ Sch Fine Arts; Int Acad Arts & Lett, Rome, Italy, hon degree.
Work in Public Collections: Howard Univ; Pa Acad Fine Arts, Philadelphia; Philadelphia Civic Center Mus; Libr Cong; Stanley Bernstein Collection & numerous other pvt collections.
Exhibitions: City Col New York, 67; Grabar Gallery, 68; Howard Univ; Int Acad Arts & Lett, 70; William Penn Mem Mus Exhib, 71; plus others.
Teaching: Former fac mem, Allens Lane Art Ctr, Philadelphia.
Positions: Am Found for Negro Affairs Comn on Cult & Performing Arts.
Awards: Silver medal for painting, Int Acad Arts & Lett, Rome, 70.
Memberships: Pyramid Club (former art dir); Artists Equity Asn; Peale Club; Philadelphia Art Alliance.
Mailing Address: 3411 Hamilton St, Philadelphia, PA 19104.

HOWARD, LEN R
Craftsman, Designer
b London, Eng, Aug 2, 91; U S citizen.
Study & Training: Camberwell Sch Arts & St Martin's Sch, London; Copley Soc; Pratt Inst Art Sch; Art Stud League New York.
Commissions: Stained glass windows for churches & schs, Eastern & Southern U S.
Teaching: Lect, stained glass techniques.
Awards: Meriden Arts & Crafts prize.
Memberships: Kent Art Asn (v pres); Salmagundi Club; Meriden Arts & Crafts.
Mailing Address: Kent, CT 06757.

HOWARD, RICHARD FOSTER
Art Administrator
b Plainfield, N J, July 26, 02.
Study & Training: Harvard Col, BS, 24; Harvard Univ Grad Sch, 27-29.
Collections Arranged: For Tex Centennial, Dallas Mus, Des Moines Art Ctr & Birmingham Mus Art.
Positions: Dir, Dallas Mus Fine Arts, 35-41; chief, Monuments, Fine Arts & Arch, Ger, 46-49; dir, Des Moines Art Ctr, 49-51; dir, Birmingham Mus Art, 51-
Awards: Stella Solidarieta, Repub Italy; Order of White Lion, Czech.
Memberships: Southeastern Mus Conf (pres, 73-74).
Mailing Address: 2000 Eighth Ave N, Birmingham, AL 35203.

HOWARD, ROBERT A
Sculptor, Educator
Preferred Media: Welded Steel, Fiberglas.
b Sapulpa, Okla, Apr 5, 22.
Study & Training: Phillips Univ; Univ Tulsa; with Ossip Zadkine, Paris, France.
Work in Public Collections: N C Mus Art, Raleigh; Ackland Art Ctr, Chapel Hill, N C; N C Nat Bank, Chapel Hill, N C.

Exhibitions: 153rd Ann Exhib, Pa Acad Fine Arts, Philadelphia, 58; Art 65—Young American Sculpture, New York World's Fair, N Y, 65; Sculpture of the Sixties, Los Angeles Co Mus, Calif, 67; Ann Contemp Sculpture, Whitney Mus Art, New York, 68; Contemp Am Painting & Sculpture, Univ Ill, 69.
Teaching: Prof sculpture, Univ N C, 51-72; prof sculpture, Univ Southern Calif, 72-
Awards: Coop Prog in Humanities, Duke Univ, Univ N C & Ford Found, 65 & Univ N C, 71; Nat Endowment for the Arts, 72.
Publications: Auth, Space as form, Col Art J, 51.
Dealer: Royal Marks Gallery, 29 E 64th St, New York, NY 10021.
Mailing Address: 831 Second St, Santa Monica, CA 90403.

HOWARD, ROBERT BOARDMAN
Sculptor
b New York, N Y, Sept 20, 96.
Study & Training: Calif Sch Arts, Berkeley, 15-16; Art Stud League New York, 16-17; also in Europe, 20-22.
Work in Public Collections: Acad Sci, San Francisco, Calif; San Francisco Mus Art, Calif; Oakland Mus Art, Calif; Univ Calif, Santa Cruz; Bank Am, Head Off Bldg, San Francisco.
Commissions: Sculpture murals, San Francisco Stock Exchange, 30 & Yosemite Park Co, Calif, 36; Whale fountain, City of San Francisco, Golden Gate Park, 40; two reliefs, P G & E Elec Sta, San Francisco, 48; Hydro Gyro, IBM Res Ctr, San Jose, Calif, 58.
Exhibitions: San Francisco Art Inst Ann, 22-72; six Whitney Mus Am Art Ann, 48-55; Sao Paulo, Brazil, 51-55; Salon Mai, Paris, France, 62-64; San Francisco Art Comn, 71; plus others.
Teaching: Instr sculpture, San Francisco Art Inst, 45-54; instr sculpture, Mills Col, Oakland, 46.
Positions: Comnr, San Francisco Art Comn.
Awards: Awards, for Eyrie, San Francisco Art Asn, 46, Night Watch, San Francisco Art Comn, 51 & Rocket, San Francisco Art Inst, 55.
Bibliography: Alfred Frankenstein (auth), many articles, In: San Francisco Chronicle, San Francisco Art Inst; San Francisco Mus Art; plus others.
Memberships: San Francisco Art Inst; San Francisco Mus Art; Univ Calif Art Mus, Berkeley; Mus Mod Art.
Mailing Address: 521 Francisco St, San Francisco, CA 94133.

HOWAT, JOHN KEITH
Art Museum Curator, Art Historian
b Denver, Colo, Apr 12, 37.
Study & Training: Harvard Univ, BA, 59, MA, 62.
Collections Arranged: David Smith, Hyde Collection, 64; John F Kensett, Am Fedn Art, 68; 19th Century America: Paintings and Sculpture, 70 & American Paintings and Sculpture, 71, Metrop Mus Art.
Positions: Cur, Hyde Collection, 62-64; asst cur Am painting, Metrop Mus Art, 67-68, assoc cur, 68-70, cur Am painting & sculpture, 70-
Awards: Ford Found fel, 65; Chester Dale fel, Metrop Mus Art, 65-67.
Memberships: Am Fedn Arts; Arch Am Art (adv comt).
Research: American paintings of eighteenth and nineteenth centuries, especially the Hudson River School.
Publications: Auth, John F Kensett (catalogue), 68; co-auth, 19th century America: paintings and sculpture (catalogue), 70; auth, The Hudson River and its painters, 72.
Mailing Address: Metropolitan Museum of Art, New York, NY 10028.

HOWE, NELSON S
Designer, Lecturer
b Lansing, Mich, Nov 5, 35.
Study & Training: Univ Mich, BA, 57, MA, 61.
Work in Public Collections: New Orleans Mus Fine Arts, La; Libr Collections, Mus Mod Art, New York, N Y; Finch Col Mus Art, New York; Chase Manhattan Bank Collection, New York; Univ Calif, Berkeley.
Commissions: Wall I (fabric wall), Mr & Mrs Keith Waldrof, Providence, R I, 68; Fur Music (installation unit), Mus Contemp Crafts, New York, 71; Fur Score (fur wall), New Orleans Mus Fine Arts, 72.
Exhibitions: One-man show, Little Gallery, Minneapolis Inst Art, Minn, 67; N J Artists Triennial, Newark Mus, 68; 50 Best Books of the Year, Am Inst Graphic Arts, 69; Fur and Feathers Show, Mus Contemp Crafts, 71; Experimental Sound, I C E S Festival, London, Eng, 72; plus others.
Positions: Artist mem, Participation Proj Found.
Awards: 50 Best Books of the Year Award, Am Inst Graphic Arts, 69; Intermedia Found grant for lab serv, 72.
Bibliography: Rose De Neve (auth), Art - notation - art, Print Mag, Vol XXV, No 1.

Publications: Illusr, To the sincere reader, Wittenborn, 68; illusr, Body image, Wittenborn, 70; co-auth, Job art, Wittenborn, 71; illusr & auth, Daily translating systems, Circle Press (London), 71.
Mailing Address: 307 W Broadway, New York, NY 10013.

HOWE, OSCAR
Painter, Educator
Preferred Media: Casein.
b Joe Creek, S Dak, May 13, 15.
Study & Training: Dakota Wesleyan Univ, BA, 52; Univ Okla, MFA, 54.
Work in Public Collections: Denver Art Mus, Colo; Joslyn Art Mus, Omaha, Nebr; Mus N Mex, Santa Fe, Philbrook Art Ctr, Tulsa, Okla; Smithsonian Inst, New York Br; plus others.
Commissions: Murals, Mitchell Libr, S Dak, 40, Nebraska City, Nebr, City of Mobridge, S Dak, auditorium, 41 & high sch, Hillside, Ill, 56.
Exhibitions: Mus Mod Art, New York, 36; Collectors Choice Exhib, Denver Art Mus, 63; one-man shows, Philbrook Art Ctr, Tulsa, 64, Joslyn Art Mus, 67 & Heard Mus, Phoenix, Ariz, 71.
Teaching: Artist-in-residence, Dak Wesleyan Univ, 48-52; prof art & artist-in-residence, Univ S Dak, 57-
Positions: Dir art, Pierre High Sch, S Dak, 53-57.
Awards: Dorothy Field Award, Denver Art Mus, 52; Mary Benjamin Rogers Award, Mus N Mex, 58; Waite Phillips Trophy, Philbrook Art Ctr, Tulsa, 66.
Bibliography: Robert Pennington (auth), Oscar Howe, artist of the Sioux, Dakota Territory Cent Co, 61; Panorama for Pakistan, U S Info Serv, 71; John Milton (auth), Oscar Howe, the story of an American Indian, Dillon, 72.
Memberships: Delta Phi Delta; fel Int Inst Arts & Lett.
Mailing Address: University of South Dakota, Vermillion, SD 57069.

HOWE, THOMAS CARR
Museum Director
b Kokomo, Ind, Aug 12, 04.
Study & Training: Harvard Univ, AB(magna cum laude), 26, Sch Archit, 27-28, MFA, 29; Calif Col Arts & Crafts, hon DFA, 69.
Teaching: Tutor & instr fine arts, Harvard Univ, 27-28.
Positions: Asst dir, Calif Palace Legion of Honor, 31-39, dir, 39-68, dir emer, 68-; v chmn, Comt Pub Works of Art Proj, San Francisco, 34; dep chief monuments, fine arts & arch sect, U S Forces, Ger & Austria, 45-46; spec art comnr, Golden Gate Int Expos, 58; mem, Fine Arts Comt for White House; mem, Smithsonian Art Comn; art adv, Hearst Castle; adv coun, Princeton Univ Art Mus, 69; chmn, Nat Collection Fine Arts, Smithsonian Inst, 70.
Awards: Chevalier, Legion of Honor, Fr Govt; Off, Order of Orange-Nassau, Dutch Govt.
Memberships: Asn Am Art Mus Dirs (pres, 60-61); Am Fedn Arts (trustee); Western Asn Art Mus Dirs (pres, 41-42).
Publications: Auth, Salt mines and castles, 46; contribr to var art periodicals.
Mailing Address: 2709 Larkin St, San Francisco, CA 94109.

HOWELL, CLAUDE FLYNN
Painter, Educator
Preferred Media: Oils, Watercolors.
b Wilmington, N C, Mar 17, 15.
Study & Training: With Charles Rosen, Woodstock, N Y, Bernard Karfiol & Jon Corbino.
Work in Public Collections: N C Mus Art, Raleigh; Weatherspoon Gallery, Univ N C, Greensboro; N C Nat Bank, Charlotte; Wake Forest Univ, Winston-Salem, N C; IBM Collection, New York.
Commissions: Illus, John F Blair Publ Co, Winston-Salem, 58; mosaics, N C Dept Arch & Hist, Mus Old Brunswick, 65 & State Ports Maritime Bldg, Wilmington, 66.
Exhibitions: Am Watercolors 1952, Metrop Mus Art, New York, N Y, 52; Fifth Ann Painting Yr, Atlanta Art Asn Galleries, Ga, 59; Piedmont Purchase Award Show, Mint Mus Art, Charlotte, 63; Art on Paper, Weatherspoon Gallery, 67; N C Artists Ann, N C Mus Art, 70.
Teaching: Assoc prof painting & art hist & chmn dept art, Univ N C, Wilmington, 58-
Awards: Rosenwald Found fel, 48; purchase awards, N C Mus Art, 54 & N C Col Durham, 68.
Bibliography: Senta Bier (auth), Notes on a North Carolina artist, Longview J, 71.
Memberships: Asn Artist N C (v pres & bd dirs, 61-69); N C State Art Soc (adv coun, 69-).
Publications: Illusr, The hatterasman, 58, Exploring the seacoast of North Carolina, 70 & The beachcombers handbook of seafood cookery, 71.
Mailing Address: Box 214, Wilmington, NC 28401.

HOWELL, DOUGLASS (MORSE)
Painter, Art Historian
Preferred Media: Watercolors, Graphics.
b New York, N Y, Nov 30, 06.
Study & Training: Study in Europe.
Work in Public Collections: Handmade papers, Boston Mus Fine Art; Brooklyn Mus; handpress printing bks, New York Pub Libr; Huntington Mus, San Marino, Calif; plus other work in pvt collections.
Exhibitions: Phillips Exeter Acad; Huntington Mus, Long Island, N Y; Univ Tex, Austin, 61; N Y State Art Teachers Asn Convention, Corning, N Y, 61; Univ Western Ont, London & Sheridan Col, Oakville, 72; plus other group & one-man shows.
Collections Arranged: Recovery studies of Two Albrecht Dürer Woodcuts.
Teaching: Lectr, Off Cult Develop, Nassau Co Pub Schs, 71 & 72; artist-in-residence, C W Post Col, Long Island Univ, 72.
Positions: Dir, Handmade Paper Workshop Fine Arts & Handpress of Douglass Howell, 46-
Awards: Ford Found fel res papers, 61.
Bibliography: Many.
Memberships: Int Inst Conserv Hist & Artistic Works.
Art Interests: A correct metrology for research in the fine arts.
Mailing Address: 625 Bayville Rd, Locust Valley, NY 11560.

HOWELL, ELIZABETH ANN
Painter, Illustrator
Preferred Media: Watercolors, Acrylics.
b Hartselle, Ala, Feb 27, 32.
Study & Training: Birmingham Southern Col, BA; Famous Artists Sch; watercolor & advan tech with John G Kramer.
Work in Public Collections: Birmingham Mus Art, Ala; Montclaire Gallery, Birmingham.
Commissions: Illus & cover for bk of sermons, Rev Ralph K Bates, United Methodist Church, Hartselle, 67; portrait class mem, Morgan Co High Sch, Hartselle, 69; children's portraits, Mr & Mrs Thomas Caddell, Decatur, Ala, 70; children's portraits, Dr & Mrs William Sims, Decatur, 71; illus & cover for cook bk, Decatur Jr Serv League, Inc, 72.
Exhibitions: Southeastern Art Exhib, Panama City, Fla, 68; Birmingham Art Asn Jury Show, 69; Williamsburg Art Exhib, Va, 70; Charleston Art Exhib, S C, 70; Int Platform Asn Art Exhib, Washington, D C, 71.
Teaching: Pvt Studio Instr Fine Art, 63-68; dept head fine art, Morgan Co High Sch, 64-66.
Positions: Dept head, Hubert Mitchell Industs, Inc, Hartselle, 49-55.
Awards: Hannah Elliott Award, Lovemans of Birmingham, 69; second pl award, Decatur Art Guild Jury Show, Decatur Art Guild, 69; second pl award, Rickwood Park, Richter Bros, Cullman, Ala, 70.
Bibliography: France-Amerique, Courrier Etats-Unis, New York, 69; Huida G Lawrence (auth), article, In: Park East News, New York, 69; article, In: Aufbau, New York, 69.
Memberships: Life mem Kappa Pi (pres, col chap, 53-54); founding mem Decatur Arts Coun (v pres & mem bd dirs); Decatur Art Guild (founder, actg pres, publ chmn & v pres, 67-); charter mem Birmingham Mus Asn; Birmingham Art Asn.
Publications: Illusr, Emmanuel-God with us, 67 & Cotton country cooking, 72.
Dealers: Lynn Kottler Gallery, 3 E 65th St, New York, NY 10021; Sovereign Exhibits Ltd, P O Drawer R, Hampton, VA 23366.
Mailing Address: P O Box 585, Hartselle, AL 35640.

HOWELL, FRANK
Painter, Art Dealer
Preferred Media: Egg Tempera, Oils, Watercolors, Acrylics, Ink.
b Sioux City, Iowa, July 31, 37.
Study & Training: Univ Northern Iowa, BA.
Commissions: Two paintings, Breckenridge Co, Colo, 70; portrait, Sioux City Pub Libr.
Exhibitions: 17th Ann Mich Outstanding Artists Exhib, Ann Arbor, 69; 26th Ann Scarab Club Watercolor Show, Detroit, Mich, 69; plus many one-man shows, 69-
Teaching: Instr art, W Del High Sch, Manchester, Iowa, 60-68; instr art, Detroit Pub Schs, 68-69.
Positions: Owner, Breckenridge Galleries; partner, Breckenridge Galleries, Inc; owner, Breckenridge Bronze Corp.
Awards: Critic's Choice, 17th Ann Outstanding Mich Artists, 69; first hon mention, 26th Ann Scarab Club Watercolor Show, 69.
Specialty of Gallery: Realism.
Mailing Address: Box 687, 121 S Main, Breckenridge, CO 80424.

HOWELL, HANNAH JOHNSON
Art Librarian
b Oskaloosa, Iowa, June 22, 05.
Study & Training: Penn Col, Oskaloosa; Univ Chicago, PhD; Columbia Univ Sch Libr Serv, BLS.

Positions: Head librn, Frick Art Ref Libr, New York, N Y, 47-70, consult librn, 70-
Mailing Address: 151 E 83rd St, New York, NY 10028.

HOWELL, MARIE W
Designer, Instructor
b Milwaukee, Wis, July 30, 31.
Study & Training: Conn Col Women, 49-50; Philadelphia Mus Sch Art, 51; R I Sch Design, BFA, 54.
Exhibitions: New Eng Craft Show; Haystack Retrospective Craft Show; Decorative Arts & Ceramic Exhib, Women's Int Expos; Contemporary Am Textiles, 65-67 & Threads of History, 65-67, Int Traveling Exhibs; plus many others.
Teaching: Instr, R I Sch Design, 55-61, asst prof textile design, 61-65; mem fac, Pa Guild Craftsmen, summer 58; mem fac weaving, Haystack Mountain Sch Crafts, 58-59; vis scholar, Univ Del, 60; mem fac, Parsons Sch Design, 65-
Positions: Spec consult, Alliance for Progress in Colombia, S Am, 65; des assoc, Larson Design Corp, 65-68; designer, Carson, Lundin & Shaw, Architects, 68-70; designer, United Textile Corp, 70-
Awards: Prizes, Women's Int Expos, 59 & R I Arts Festival, 60 & 61.
Memberships: Nat Home Fashions League.
Publications Contribr to Design (India), Upholstering, Handweaver & Craftsmen, Cross Country Craftsman, Decorative Art (Eng), Am Fabrics & Casa y Jardines (Arg).
Mailing Address: 298 Elizabeth St, New York, NY 10012.

HOWELL, RAYMOND
Painter, Photographer
b Oakland, Calif, Sept 27, 27.
Work in Public Collections: Oakland Art Mus; Anna Warden Br, San Francisco Pub Libr, Calif; Fine Am Art Calendar Collection; Julius Fleischmann Collection, Cincinnati, Ohio; also in private collection of Harold Zellerbach.
Exhibitions: Negro in Am Art, Kaiser Ctr, Oakland; Univ N C, Chapel Hill; Mich State Univ; Black Am Artists/71, Ill Bell Tel, Chicago; Los Angeles Int Black Art Show, Oakland Art Mus.
Awards: First prize for photograph, 68 & first prize for graphics, 69, City of Berkeley Art Festival; first prize for oil painting, Univ Calif, Berkeley Black Art Festival, 70.
Bibliography: Articles, In: Black Artists on Art, Artforum & San Francisco Mag.
Dealer: Gilbert Galleries, 590 Sutter St, San Francisco, CA 94102.
Mailing Address: 55 Colton St, San Francisco, CA 94103.

HOWETT, JOHN
Art Historian
b Kokomo, Ind, Aug 7, 26.
Study & Training: John Herron Inst, BFA; Univ Chicago, MA & PhD.
Collections Arranged: Collection of Mr & Mrs Joseph R Shapiro, 64, Circa 1300: Paintings, Sculpture, Illum & Textiles, 65 & Mod Image, 72; also catalogue, Kress Study Collection Notre Dame, 62.
Teaching: Asst prof Renaissance & mod, Univ Notre Dame, 61-66; assoc prof Renaissance & mod, Emory Univ, 66-
Research: Italian and Northern Renaissance painting and sculpture; contemporary art and culture.
Publications: Auth, The Kress Study Collection at Notre Dame, 62, The University of Notre Dame Art Gallery, Art J, 62, Handbook of the University of Notre Dame Collections, 67 & The art museum, New York Element, 72; co-auth, The modern image, 72.
Mailing Address: 325 Hertford Circle, Decatur, GA 30030.

HOWLAND, RICHARD HUBBARD
Art Historian, Writer
b Providence, R I, Aug 23, 10.
Study & Training: Brown Univ, AB, 31, hon DArts; Harvard Univ, AM, 33; Johns Hopkins Univ, PhD, 46.
Teaching: Instr, Wellesley Col, 39-42; organizer dept hist art, Johns Hopkins Univ, 47, chmn dept, 47-56; chmn managing comt, Am Sch Class Studies, Athens.
Positions: Fel Agora excavations, Athens, Greece, 36-38; chief pictorial records sect, OSS, 43-44; pres, Nat Trust for Hist Preserv, 56-60; chmn dept civil hist, Smithsonian Inst, 60-67; spec asst to secy, 68-; mem bldg comt, Nat Cathedral; founding mem, Am Comt Int Comn Hist Sites & Monuments; trustee, L A W Fund, Sotterley Found & Evergreen Found.
Memberships: Fel in Am Studies; Soc Archit Historians (dir); Irish Georgian Soc (trustee); Archaeol Inst Am.
Publications: Co-auth, Architecture of Baltimore, 54; auth, Greek Lamps and their survivals, 58 & 66.
Mailing Address: Smithsonian Institution, Washington, DC 20560.

HOWLETT, CAROLYN SVRLUGA
Educator, Designer
b Berwyn, Ill, Jan 13, 14.
Study & Training: Art Inst Chicago, BAE, 37, MAE, 52; Northwestern Univ, MA, 53.
Commissions: Stained glass windows, State Ill Host House, Chicago World's Fair, 33.
Exhibitions: Art Inst Chicago Ann, 45, 46, 52 & 55; Am Fedn Arts Print Show, 48; Newspaper Critics Shows, Findlay Galleries, Chicago, 49 & 50; Assoc Am Artists Galleries, Chicago, 50; two-man shows, Chicago Press Club, 66 & 68.
Teaching: Instr art educ, Oak Park & Libertyville Pub Schs, 34-37; instr design & crafts, Sch Art Inst Chicago, 37-70, prof art educ, 52-70; tech consult, Arts & Skills Prog, Am Red Cross, 42-45; lectr fine art & crafts, Univ Ill Exten, 67-69.
Positions: Head dept art educ & Jr Sch, Sch Art Inst Chicago, 43-63, assoc dean & educ consult, 63-68; dir Gallery Studio, Coonley Estate, 70-
Awards: Gov Art Award, Ill State Fair, 31; Gen Excellence Award, 32 & Conf Club Pres Award, 33 & 34, Sch Art Inst Chicago.
Bibliography: Louis Hoover (ed), Leaders in art education, Arts & Activities, 57; Edwin Ziegfield (auth), Research in art education, Nat Art Educ Asn Yearbook, 59.
Memberships: Arts Club Chicago; Nat Art Educ Asn (coun mem, 47-51, mem prof develop comt, 69-); Ill Art Educ Asn (pres, 62-63); Around Chicago Art Educ Asn (pres, 38-39); Marquis Biog Soc (adv mem, 69-).
Publications: Contribr, Arts & Activities, Sch Arts, House Beautiful & Design, 42-70; auth, The need for art, Related Arts Serv Bull, 49; contribr, World Bk Encycl & Childcraft Encycl, 49-59; contribr, Research in art education, Nat Art Educ Asn Yearbooks, 54 & 59; ed, Art education bibliography, Art Inst Chicago, 60.
Mailing Address: Gallery Studio, 336 Coonley Rd, Riverside, IL 60546.

HOWZE, JAMES DEAN
Educator, Painter
Preferred Media: Charcoal, Metal, Mixed Media.
b Lubbock, Tex, Apr 8, 30.
Study & Training: Austin Col, BA; Art Ctr Col Design; Univ Mich, MS.
Exhibitions: Fifth Nat Biennial Relig Art Exhib, Cranbrook Acad, Bloomfield Hills, Mich, 66; Southwest Biennial Exhib, Mus N Mex, Santa Fe, 66; Pavillion Texan Cult, Hemisfair World's Fair, San Antonio, 68; Tex Fine Arts Asn Nat, Laguna Gloria Mus, Austin, 69 & 71; Third Ann Drawing & Small Sculpture Exhib, Del Mar Col, Corpus Christi, Tex, 70.
Teaching: Assoc prof, dept archit & allied arts, Tex Tech Univ, 58-68, prof studio art, dept art, 68-
Awards: Purchase award, Nat Drawing & Small Sculpture Exhib, Del Mar Col, 70; best in exhib, Nat Mensa Mem Exhib, 71; cert recognition, Art Ctr Soc of Alumni Int Competition, 72.
Memberships: Hon mem Dallas-Fort Worth Soc Visual Commun.
Publications: Contribr, cartoons & humorous verse, Sports Car Graphic, 65-66; designer & illusr, var advert publ.
Mailing Address: 2503 45th St, Lubbock, TX 79413.

HOYT, DOROTHY (DOROTHY HOYT DILLINGHAM)
Painter
Preferred Media: Oils, Watercolors.
b East Orange, N J, Aug 11, 09.
Study & Training: Cornell Univ, BS & MA; Art Stud League New York, N Y; New Sch Soc Res, New York; Graphic Arts Workshop, Pratt Inst.
Exhibitions: Whitney Mus Am Art, New York; Nat Asn Women Artists, Kyoto, Japan; Pa Acad Fine Arts, Philadelphia; one-man show, Riverside Mus, New York; Mem Art Gallery, Rochester, N Y; plus many other group & one-man shows.
Awards: Medal of honor for Graphics, Nat Asn Women Artists, 58; Mary Kelner Award for Graphics, Brooklyn Soc Artists, 58; first prize, Cent Adirondack Art Asn, 66.
Mailing Address: Box 125, Myers, NY 14866.

HOYT, WHITNEY F
Painter, Collector
Preferred Media: Oils, Watercolors, Acrylics, Pastels.
b Rochester, N Y, July 7, 10.
Study & Training: New York Sch Fine & Appl Arts; Ecole Beaux Arts, Fontainebleau, with Camille Liausu, Paris & Fritz Trautman, Rochester.
Work in Public Collections: Springfield Mus Fine Arts, Mass; Munson-Williams Proctor Inst, Utica, N Y; Rochester Mem Art Gallery, N Y.
Exhibitions: Five From Rochester, 40 & Juror's Show, 46, Rochester Mem Art Gallery; Fifty Oncoming Americans, Inst Mod Art,

Boston, 41; Railroad in Painting, Dayton Art Inst, 49; Iron Horse In Art, Fort Worth Art Ctr, 58.
Awards: Rochester Finger Lakes Exhib Award, 46 & George L Herdle Mem Award, Rochester Mem Art Gallery; Allied Artists Prize, 51.
Bibliography: Ernest Watson (auth), The paintings of Whitney Hoyt, Am Artist, 11/52; David P Morgan (auth), The railroad in painting, Trains, 6/61.
Memberships: Artists Equity Asn; Allied Artists Am; Conn Acad Fine Arts; Artists Fel.
Art Interests: Gift of art studio building to independent co-educational school; financial support to museums.
Collection: Old master drawings of the seventeenth century; contemporary paintings.
Mailing Address: 39 E 79th St, New York, NY 10021.

HSIAO, CHIN
Painter, Sculptor
Preferred Media: Metal Constructions, Acrylics.
b Shanghai, China, 35.
Study & Training: Taipei Normal Col, BA; with Li Chun-Sen, Taipei, Taiwan.
Work in Public Collections: Mus Mod Art, New York, N Y; Metrop Mus Art, New York; Nat Gallery Mod Art, Rome, Italy; Philadelphia Mus Art, Pa; Detroit Inst Art, Mich.
Commissions: Mural, Mr S Marchetta, Messina, Sicily, 71.
Exhibitions: Carnegie Int, Pittsburgh, Pa, 61; Int Malerei 1960/61, W Eschenbach, 61; Art Contemporain, Grand Palais Paris, France, 63; Seventh Biennial São Paulo, Brazil, 63; Fourth Salon Galeries-Pilotes, Lausanne, Switz & Paris, 70.
Teaching: Instr art, Southampton Col, Long Island Univ, 69; prof visual communication, Inst Europeo Design, Milan, Italy, 71-72; vis artist, La State Univ, Baton Rouge, 72-
Awards: City of Capo d'Orlando, Italy prize, 70.
Bibliography: K Leonhard (auth), Hsiao Chin (portfolio of eight prints), 63 & Hsiao Chin, V Scheiwiller, 65; W Schönenberger (auth), Hsiao, Prearo, 72.
Dealer: Giorgio Marconi, 15 Via Tadino, Milan, Italy 20124.
Mailing Address: 30 E 70th St, New York, NY 10021.

HUBBARD, EARL WADE
Painter
b Bradford, Pa, Feb 3, 24.
Study & Training: Amherst Col, BA, 49.
Exhibitions: Mystic Art Asn, 58; Sharon Art Gallery, Conn, 58-60; Rehn Gallery, New York, N Y, 58, 60-62; Pa Acad Fine Arts, Philadelphia, 62; Gallery Mod Art, New York, 65; plus others.
Bibliography: Aline Saarinen (auth), One-man show from Rehn Gallery, CBS TV, 62.
Publications: Auth, One step two step & Challenge is freedom.
Mailing Address: Wells Hill Rd, Lakeville, CT 06039.

HUBBARD, ROBERT
Sculptor
b New York, N Y, Mar 27, 28.
Study & Training: Lafayette Col, BA; R I Sch Design, BFA.
Work in Public Collections: Lafayette Col; Sara Roby Found.
Exhibitions: Ravinia Festival, Chicago, 63 & 69; Whitney Mus Am Art, New York, 66 & 72; R I Art Mus, 67; Newport Art Asn, R I, 67; Providence Art Club, 69; plus others.
Awards: R I Art Festival, 60; Providence Art Club, 69; Howard fel, 69.
Mailing Address: West Rd, Little Compton, RI 02837.

HUBBARD, ROBERT HAMILTON
Art Historian, Art Administrator
b Hamilton, Ont, June 7, 16.
Study & Training: McMaster Univ, BA; Univ Wis, MA & PhD; Univ Paris, cert.
Collections Arranged: Can Painting, Tate Gallery, London, 64; 300 Yrs Can Art, 67 & Scottish Painting, 68, Nat Gallery Can; plus many others.
Teaching: Lectr hist art, Univ Toronto, 45-46.
Positions: Cur Can art, Nat Gallery Can, 47-54, chief cur, 54-
Memberships: Fel Royal Soc Can; Col Art Asn Am; Can Hist Soc; Can Mus Asn; Royal Can Geog Soc.
Research: History of Canadian art.
Publications: Auth, National Gallery of Canada catalogue, Univ Toronto Press, Vols I-III, 56-60; auth, The development of Canadian art, Queen's Printer, 63; auth, Rideau Hall, a history of Government House, 67; auth, Thomas Davies, Oberon Press, 72.
Mailing Address: National Gallery of Canada, Ottawa, Ont. K1A 0M8, Can.

HUBENTHAL, KARL SAMUEL
Cartoonist
b Beemer, Nebr, May 1, 17.
Study & Training: Chouinard Art Inst, Los Angeles.
Work in Public Collections: State Hist Soc Wis; Syracuse Univ; Truman Mem Libr; Eisenhower Mem Libr; Lyndon B Johnson Libr.
Exhibitions: Am Ed Cartoonists Traveling Exhib, U S, Can & Eng, 62-72; Int Salon Caricature, Montreal, 65-72; Univ Minn, 68; Los Angeles Co Mus, 69; Madison Sq Garden Gallery Sport, 71.
Positions: Political cartoonist, Hearst Newspapers, 55-
Awards: Nat Headliners Award For Outstanding Achievement In Jour, 59; Nation's Best Ed Cartoonist, Nat Cartoonists Soc, 62, 67 & 70; Helms Athletic Found Medal Contrib Sport in Art, 64.
Memberships: Marine Corps Newsmens Asn; Nat Cartoonists Soc (dir, 63-69); Los Angeles Soc Illusr (pres, 58-59); Asn Am Ed Cartoonists (pres, 63-64).
Mailing Address: 16863 Marmaduke Pl, Encino, CA 91316.

HUDSON, KENNETH EUGENE
Painter, Educator
b Xenia, Ohio, Dec 28, 03.
Study & Training: Ohio Wesleyan Univ, 21-23; Acad Royale, Brussels, Belgium; Yale Univ, BFA, 27; Fontainebleau, France.
Commissions: Murals, Univ Ore, Munic Bldg, Columbia, Mo & Hendrix Hall, Univ Mo triptychs, Citizens Comt for Army & Navy.
Teaching: Asst prof & head drawing & painting dept, Univ Ore, 27-29; prof & chmn fine arts dept, Sch Fine Arts, Univ Mo, 29-38; dean, St Louis Sch Fine Arts, Wash Univ, 38-69, dean, Schs Archit & Fine Arts, 52-53, dean emer, 69-
Positions: Pres, Nat Asn Schs Design, 53-55.
Memberships: Fel, Belgian-Am Educ Found; fel Nat Asn Schs Art.
Mailing Address: 7900 Stanford Ave, St Louis, MO 63130.

HUDSON, RALPH MAGEE
Art Historian, Educator
Preferred Media: Watercolors.
b Fields, Ohio, Dec 18, 07.
Study & Training: Ohio State Univ, BA, BSc & MA; Univ Ala, EdD.
Work in Public Collections: Univ Ark, Fayetteville; Mus Fine Arts, Little Rock, Ark.
Exhibitions: Ark Watercolor Soc, 37-40; Grumbacher Aquarelle Travel Exhib, 38; one-man show, Hendrix Col, Conway, Ark, 40-41; Meridian Art Asn, Miss, 46-50; Miss State Col Women, Columbus, 46-68.
Teaching: Instr art & acting head dept, Morehead State Col, 31-36; head dept art, Univ Ark, Fayetteville, 36-46; prof & chmn dept, Miss State Col Women, 46-69; vis prof art, Blue Mountain Col, summers 58-60; vis prof art, Miss Valley State Col, fall 68; prof art & chmn dept, Univ Ala, Huntsville, 69-
Awards: Univ Ala & Nat Endowment Humanities res grants Afro-Am art.
Memberships: Southeastern Col Art Conf (pres, 66-67, treas, 71-); Col Art Asn Am; Nat Art Educ Asn (Ala chmn bldg fund, 71-); Kappa Pi (int historian, 48-); Ala Art Educ Asn.
Research: Nineteenth century American art, architecture and furnishings; Afro-American art.
Publications: Auth & illusr, Art in Arkansas, Ark Hist Quart, winter 44; ed, Ida Kohlmeyer, 68; auth, Afro-American art: a bibliography, Nat Art Educ Asn, 70.
Mailing Address: 7102 Criner Rd S E, Huntsville, AL 35802.

HUDSON, ROBERT H
Sculptor
b Salt Lake City, Utah, Sept 8, 38.
Study & Training: San Francisco Art Inst, BFA, 62, MFA, 63.
Work in Public Collections: Los Angeles Co Mus, Calif; San Francisco Mus Art, Calif; Oakland Mus Art, Calif.
Exhibitions: Five Whitney Mus Am Art Ann, New York, N Y, 64-72; Los Angeles Co Mus Art, 67; Philadelphia Mus Art, Pa, 67; Art Inst Chicago, Ill, 67; Walker Art Ctr, Minneapolis, Minn, 69.
Teaching: Instr, San Francisco Art Inst, 64-65, chmn sculpture & ceramic dept, 65-66; asst prof art, Univ Calif, Berkeley, 66-
Awards: Purchase prize, San Francisco Art Festival, 61; San Jose State Col, 64; Nealie Sullivan Award, San Francisco, 65; plus others.
Bibliography: Peter Selz (auth), Funk, Univ Calif Press, 67; Maurice Tuchman (auth), American sculpture of the sixties, Los Angeles Co Mus Art, 67.
Dealers: Allan Frumkin Gallery, 41 E 57th St, New York, NY 10022; Nicholas Wilder Gallery, 8225 Santa Monica Blvd, Los Angeles, CA 90028.
Mailing Address: P O Box 153, Stinson Beach, CA 94970.

HUDSON, WINNIFRED
Painter
Preferred Media: Oils, Acrylics, Collage.
b Sunderland, Eng, May 21, 05; U S citizen.
Study & Training: Honolulu Acad Arts; Univ Hawaii; with Joseph Feher, Wilson Y Stamper, John Hultberg & Norman Ives; also with James Pinto, Mex.
Work in Public Collections: Honolulu Acad Arts; State Fedn Cult & Arts; Contemp Arts Ctr; Castle & Cooke Ltd.
Exhibitions: One-man shows, Recent Paintings, 67 & Winnifred Hudson Paintings, 72, Contemp Arts Ctr; Three Plus One, Ala Moana Art Ctr, 69; Honolulu Acad Arts Ann; Honolulu Printmakers Ann.
Teaching: Private classes, five years.
Awards: Purchase award for print, Watumull Found, 67; first prize for painting, Ala Moana Festival.
Bibliography: Nell Hutton (auth), The techniques of collage, Batson/Watson-Guptill (London), 68.
Memberships: Hawaii Painters & Sculptors League; Honolulu Printmakers.
Dealer: Downtown Gallery, Merchant St, Honolulu, HI 96813.
Mailing Address: 426-B Kekau St, Honolulu, HI 96817.

HUETER, JAMES WARREN
Sculptor, Painter
Preferred Media: Wood, Oils.
b San Francisco, Calif, 25.
Study & Training: Pomona Col, BA; Claremont Grad Sch, MFA, with Henry Lee McFee, Albert Stewart & Millard Sheets.
Work in Public Collections: Pasadena Art Mus; Scripps Col, Claremont, Calif; Nat Orange Show, San Bernardino, Calif; Long Beach State Col.
Exhibitions: San Gabriel Valley Artists, Pasadena Art Mus, 50-56 & 58 & one-man show, 55; Artists Los Angeles & Vicinity, Los Angeles Co Mus, 52 & 54-59; Denver Mus Art Ann, 54 & 59; Butler Inst Am Art Midyear Ann, 55, 57-59 & 62; Long Beach Mus Art Drawing Invitational, 60.
Teaching: Instr painting & drawing, Mt San Antonio Col Eve Div, Walnut, Calif, 51- ; instr sculpture, Pomona Col, 59-60; instr drawing, Claremont Grad Sch, summer 63; lectr art, Pitzer Col, 72.
Awards: First prize & purchase award for painting, Pasadena Art Mus, 52; first prize for sculpture, Los Angeles Co Mus, 55; first prize for painting, Frye Mus, Seattle, Wash, 57.
Bibliography: A Segunda (auth), Reviews, Vol 1, No 8 & Delores Yonker (auth), James Hueter, Vol 2, No 2, Artforum.
Mailing Address: 190 E Radcliffe Dr, Claremont, CA 91711.

HUGGINS, (LEONARD) VICTOR, (JR)
Painter, Educator
Preferred Media: Acrylics.
b Durham, N C, July 23, 36.
Study & Training: Univ N C, Chapel Hill, AB & MA.
Work in Public Collections: Ackland Art Ctr, Univ N C, Chapel Hill; B Carroll Reece Mus, E Tenn State Univ, Johnson City; Brooks Mem Gallery Art, Memphis, Tenn; Vanderbilt Univ, Nashville, Tenn; Weatherspoon Art Gallery, Univ N C, Greensboro.
Exhibitions: One-man shows, Bertha Schaefer Gallery, New York, N Y, 70, Jane Haslem Gallery, Washington, D C, 71; Twentieth Century Gallery, Williamsburg, Va, 71; D Carroll Reece Mus, Johnson City, Tenn, 72; group show, Gallery Contemp Art, Winston-Salem, N C, 71.
Teaching: Asst prof art, Vanderbilt Univ, 68-69; assoc prof painting & drawing, Va Polytech Inst & State Univ, 69-
Awards: First purchase awards, N C Nat Bank, 67, Springs Art Contest, Springs Mills, 67 & Ann Southern Contemp Painting Exhib, 68.
Dealer: Bertha Schaefer Gallery, 41 E 57th St, New York, NY 10022.
Mailing Address: 206 Wilson St, Blacksburg, VA 24060.

HUGHES, EDWARD JOHN
Painter
Preferred Media: Oils.
b North Vancouver, B C, Feb 17, 13.
Study & Training: Vancouver Sch Art.
Work in Public Collections: Nat Gallery Can, Ottawa; Art Gallery Ont, Toronto; Vancouver Art Gallery; Montreal Mus Fine Art; Greater Victoria Art Gallery.
Exhibitions: Retrospective, Vancouver Art Gallery, 67.
Positions: War artist, Can Army, 40-42, off war artist, 42-46.
Awards: Emily Carr scholar, Lawren Harris, 47; Can Coun fels & awards, 58, 63 & 67 & short term grant, 70.
Bibliography: Doris Shadbolt (auth), E J Hughes, Can Art Mag, spring 53.
Memberships: Royal Can Acad Art.
Dealer: Dr Max Stern, 1438 Sherbrooke St W, Montreal 109, P Q, Can.
Mailing Address: Chapman Rd, R R 1, Cobble Hill, B C, Can.

HULL, MARIE (ATKINSON)
Painter
Preferred Media: Oils, Watercolors, Acrylics, Casein.
b Summit, Miss.
Study & Training: Pa Acad Fine Arts; Art Stud League New York, N Y; also with John F Carlson, Robert Reid, Robert Vonnoh & George Elmer Browne.
Work in Public Collections: Witte Mus, San Antonio Tex; Birmingham Mus, Ala; Miss Art Asn Permanent Collection; Univ Miss; plus others.
Commissions: Portraits, Univ Miss, Oxford, Tulane Univ La, New Orleans, Miss State Univ, Starkville, Miss Col, Clinton; plus others.
Exhibitions: Salon Paris, 31; Art Inst Chicago Am Ann; Butler Art Inst Ann, Youngstown, Ohio; New York World's Fair, 39; Golden Gate Expos, 39; Atlanta Southeastern Ann, Ga; plus many others.
Positions: Pres, Miss Art Asn.
Awards: First Award, Montgomery Mus Ann, 60; First Award, Birmingham Mus Ann, 63; First Award, Ala Watercolor Soc Nat, 65.
Memberships: Am Watercolor Soc; Miss Art Asn; Ala Art League.
Mailing Address: 825 Belhaven St, Jackson, MS 39202.

HULSEY, WILLIAM HANSELL
Collector
b Carbon Hill, Ala, May 2, 01.
Positions: Mem bd dirs, Birmingham Mus Art.
Collection: Paintings including works by Laurencin, Modigliani, Rouault, Degas, Vlaminck, Buffet, Bezombes and Corbellini.
Mailing Address: 2980 Cherokee Rd, Birmingham, AL 35223.

HULTBERG, JOHN PHILLIP
Painter
Preferred Media: Oils.
b Berkeley, Calif, Feb 8, 22.
Study & Training: Fresno State Col, BA, 43; Calif Sch Fine Arts, 47-49; Art Stud League New York, 49-51.
Work in Public Collections: Metrop Mus Art, New York, N Y; Mus Mod Art, New York; Solomon R Guggenheim Mus Art, New York; Albright-Knox Mus, Buffalo, N Y; Stedlijk Mus, Eindhoven.
Commissions: Paintings of Newport News Shipyard, Fortune Mag, 57.
Exhibitions: One-man shows, Martha Jackson Gallery, New York, 55-72, Corcoran Gallery Art, Washington, D C, 56, ICA Gallery, London, Eng, 56, Galerie Dragon, Paris, France, 56-71 & Oakland Mus, Calif, 60.
Teaching: Instr painting, Art Stud League New York, summer 60; instr painting, San Francisco Art Inst, 63-64; artist-in-residence, Honolulu Art Acad, 66-67.
Awards: First prize, Corcoran Biennial, Washington, D C, 55; Am Fedn Arts-Ford Found grant, 64; Benjamin Altman Prize (landscape), Nat Acad Design, 72.
Bibliography: Emily Genauer (auth), article, In: New York Herald Tribune Mag, 55; article, In: Int Studio (London), 66.
Mailing Address: c/o Martha Jackson Gallery, 32 E 69th St, New York, NY 10021.

HUMES, RALPH H
Sculptor
Preferred Media: Bronze.
b Philadelphia, Pa, Dec 25, 02.
Study & Training: Md Inst Art, with Rhinhart; Pa Acad Fine Arts.
Work in Public Collections: Brookgreen Gardens, S C; Children's Zoo, Lincoln, Nebr; Pa Acad Fine Art, Philadelphia; plus others.
Commissions: Mahogany Comanche figurehead, J Price Yacht, Miami, Fla; Fountain of the Sea, Coral Gables Libr, Fla; Tony Janus Mem, Saint Petersburg, Fla; Padre Kino Statue, Nogales, Ariz; bird panel fountain, Fairchild Tropical Garden, Miami.
Exhibitions: Nat Acad Design, New York, N Y; Nat Sculpture Soc Shows; Art Inst Chicago, Ill; Rosequist Galleries, Tucson, Ariz; Conn Acad Fine Arts.
Bibliography: Article, In: Brookgreen Gardens Publ Sculptors.
Memberships: Assoc nat academician, Nat Acad Design; fel Nat Sculpture Soc; Soc Medalists; fel Pa Acad Fine Arts; Soc Washington Artists; plus others.
Mailing Address: 2616 Azalea Pl, Coachwood Colony, Leesburg, FL 32748.

HUMPHREY, DONALD GRAY
Art Administrator, Lecturer
b Hutchinson, Kans, May 3, 20.
Study & Training: Univ Kans, BFA; State Univ Iowa, MFA & PhD.
Collections Arranged: Albert Bloch Retrospective, 61; Our Ancient Heritage, 63; Magic Realism, 64; Medieval Art, 65; French and American Impressionism, 67; The American Sense of Reality, Contemporary Latin American Painting, 69; Texas Collects 20th Century American Art, 71.

Teaching: Instr art hist, State Univ Iowa, 50-51; asst prof art hist, Okla Univ, 51-57; instr art hist, State Univ Iowa, 57-58; adj prof art hist, Tulsa Univ, 67-72.
Positions: Dir, Philbrook Art Ctr, 59-
Memberships: Southwestern Art Asn (pres, 72-); Am Asn Mus; Am Fedn Arts; Okla Mus Asn; Okla Arts & Humanities Coun.
Publications: Contribr, Mus News.
Mailing Address: Philbrook Art Center, 2727 S Rockford Rd, Tulsa, OK 74114.

HUNT, JULIAN COURTENAY
    Painter, Instructor
Preferred Media: Oils, Pastels.
b Jacksonville, Fla, Sept 17, 17.
Study & Training: Ringling Sch Art; Farnsworth Sch Painting.
Commissions: Portraits, Univ Fla, Gainesville; Jacksonville Univ, Fla; Jacksonville City Hall; Duval Co Ct House, Jacksonville; Shrine Mem, Washington, D C.
Exhibitions: Allied Artists Am, 52-56; Sarasota Art Asn, Fla, 52-56; Audubon Artists Am, 53-57; Norton Gallery, West Palm Beach, Fla, 60-65; Soc Four Arts, Palm Beach, Fla, 65-.
Memberships: Portraits, Inc; Cummer Gallery Art; St Augustine Art Asn.
Mailing Address: P O Box 247, Orange Park, FL 32073.

HUNT, KARI
    Sculptor, Writer
b Orange, N J, Jan 29, 20.
Study & Training: Mt Holyoke Col, 37-39; Univ Buffalo, summer 38; Cornell Univ, summer 39; maskmaking with Doane Powell, New York, N Y, 50-51.
Commissions: Produced mask advertisements for Remington Rand, 54, Geritol Corp & Worthington Corp, 55.
Exhibitions: Montclair Art Mus, N J; Jersey City Mus Asn, N J; N J Col for Women; ANTA & in numerous libr.
Teaching: Lect & demonstrations, art of mask making, clubs, orgn, libr & on TV.
Art Interests: Sculptured masks of the world.
Collection: The late Doane Powell collection of portrait masks, books, masks of Java, Bali, Tibet, Siam, Japan & others; collection is widely exhibited.
Publications: Co-auth, Masks and mask makers, Abingdon, 61; co-auth, Pantomine—the silent theater, Atheneum, 65; co-auth, The art of magic, Atheneum, 67.
Mailing Address: R D, Box 358, Glen Gardner, NJ 08826.

HUNT, RICHARD HOWARD
    Sculptor
Preferred Media: Metals.
b Chicago, Ill, Sept 12, 35.
Study & Training: Art Inst Chicago, BAE.
Work in Public Collections: Mus Mod Art, New York, N Y; Cleveland Mus Art, Ohio; Art Inst Chicago; Nat Mus Israel, Jerusalem; Mus 20th Century, Vienna, Austria.
Exhibitions: Whitney Mus Am Art Ann, New York, 70; American Sculpture, Univ Nebr Art Gallery, Lincoln, 70; Large Scale Sculptures, Ravinia Park, Highland Park, Ill, 71; The Sculpture of Richard Hunt, Mus Mod Art, New York & Art Inst Chicago, 71; one-man exhib, Dorsky Gallery, New York, 71.
Bibliography: Lieberman (auth), The sculpture of Richard Hunt, Mus Mod Art, New York, 71.
Memberships: Nat Coun Arts; Ill Arts Coun; Col Art Asn Am (bd dirs, 70-).
Dealer: Dorsky Gallery, 111 Fourth Ave, New York, NY 10003.
Mailing Address: 1503 N Cleveland Ave, Chicago, IL 60610.

HUNT, ROBERT JAMES
    Painter, Educator
b Fargo, N Dak, Apr 5, 21.
Study & Training: Univ Iowa, BA, 47, MFA, 50.
Work in Public Collections: Univ Iowa; Mulvane Art Mus; Des Moines Art Ctr; Kans State Teachers Col; Wichita Art Mus.
Exhibitions: Wichita Art Mus; Mid-America Artists; Kansas Free Fair; Am Fedn Arts; Colo Springs Fine Arts Ctr; plus others.
Teaching: Prof art & chmn art dept, Washburn Univ, 50-
Positions: Dir, Mulvane Art Ctr, Washburn Univ, 50-
Awards: Purchase prizes, Wichita Art Mus & Kansas State Univ.
Memberships: Mid-West Col Art Asn; Col Art Asn Am.
Mailing Address: Art Dept, Washburn University, Topeka, KS 66621.

HUNTER, EDMUND ROBERT
    Art Administrator
b Toronto, Ont, June 4, 09.
Study & Training: Ont Col Art; Royal Ont Mus Archaeol, with Dr C T Currelly; Courtauld Inst, Univ London, grad, 35.

Positions: Tech Adv, Montreal Art Asn, 38-40; dir, Norton Gallery & Sch Art, 43-49; dir, Atlanta Art Asn, 49-54; consult dir, Pensacola Art Asn, 54-56; dir, Jacksonville Art Mus, 55-57; dir, Vizcaya, Dade Co Art Mus, 57-60; dir, Art Gallery, McCormick Pl, Chicago, 60-62; dir, Norton Gallery & Sch Art, 62-
Memberships: Am Asn Mus; Southeastern Mus Conf; Southeastern Art Mus Dirs Asn; Fla Art Mus Dirs Asn.
Publications: Auth, J E H MacDonald, a biography and catalogue of his work, 40; auth, Thoreau MacDonald, 42.
Mailing Address: P O Box 2300, West Palm Beach, FL 33402.

HUNTER, GRAHAM
    Cartoonist
b La Grange, Ill.
Study & Training: Landon Sch Cartooning, Cleveland, Ohio; Art Inst Chicago; Art Instr, Inc, Minneapolis, Minn.
Work in Public Collections: Ed cartoons in permanent J Edgar Hoover FBI Collection; Peter Mayo Editorial Cartoon Collection, State Hist Soc, Columbia, Mo.
Exhibitions: Editorial Cartoon Exhibit, Wayne State Univ, Detroit, 64.
Positions: Cartoonist, Nat Asn Mfrs, 52-, Indust Press syndicated features, 54- & Nation's Agr, 64-
Awards: Distinguished Serv Citation, U S Treas, 43; George Washington Honor Medal, Freedoms Found, 59 & 62; Hon Cert Award for Cartoon, Freedoms Found, 60 & 61.
Publications: Auth, Creating the busy scene cartoon (cartoon course lesson), Art Instr, Inc; cartoons for Chicago Sun Tribune & McClure Syndicate, Farm & Ranch, Motor Mag, Curtis Publ Co, Banking Mag & others.
Mailing Address: Lindenshade, 42 Clonavor Rd, Silver Spring Park, West Orange, NJ 07052.

HUNTER, JOHN H
    Painter, Educator
Preferred Media: Collage, Mixed Media.
b Pa, Sept 26, 34.
Study & Training: Pomona Col, BA, 56; Claremont Grad Sch, MFA, 58.
Work in Public Collections: Mus Mod Art, New York, N Y; Los Angeles Co Mus, Los Angeles; Pasadena Art Mus, Calif; Amon-Carter Mus, Fort Worth, Tex; Scripps Col, Claremont, Calif.
Commissions: Poster for Tamarind Exhib, Mus Mod Art, Tamarind Lithography Workshop, Los Angeles, 69.
Exhibitions: Western Painters Under 35, Univ Calif, Los Angeles, 58; Fulbright Artists Show, U S Info Serv, Florence, Italy, 65; Painters Behind Painters, Calif Palace of Legion of Honor, San Francisco, 67; Drawings, Fort Worth Art Ctr Mus, 69; A Decade of Accomplishment, Ill Bell Tel Co, Chicago, 70.
Teaching: Instr fine art, Ohio State Univ, 60-63; guest artist, Ind Univ, Bloomington, summer 63; assoc prof art, Calif State Univ, San Jose, 65-; guest artist, Tamarind Lithography Workshop, 69.
Awards: Fulbright fel painting, Florence, 63-64, renewal grantee, 64-65.
Bibliography: Peter Plagens (auth), The possibilities of drawing, Artforum, 10/69; also rev in New York Times, Los Angeles Times, Rome Daily Am, Art News & others.
Mailing Address: Dept of Art, California State University, San Jose, 125 S Seventh St, San Jose, CA 95114.

HUNTER, ROBERT DOUGLAS
    Painter, Instructor
Preferred Media: Oils.
b Boston, Mass, Mar 17, 28.
Study & Training: Cape Sch Art, Provincetown, Mass, with Henry Hensche; Vesper George Sch Art, Boston; also with R H Ives Gammell, Boston.
Work in Public Collections: Maryhill Mus, Goldendale, Wash; Chrysler Mus, Norfolk, Va; Northeastern Univ, Boston; Tufts Univ, Boston; Boston Univ Med Ctr.
Commissions: Epiphany mural, Church St Mary of the Harbor, Provincetown, 56; altar frontal, Emmanuel Church, West Roxbury, Mass, 62.
Exhibitions: Acad Artists Show, Springfield, Mass, 61; Am Artists Prof League Show, New York, N Y, 66, 67 & 70; New Eng Artists Exhib, Boston, 70.
Teaching: Instr fine arts, Vesper George Sch Art, 55-; instr fine arts, Worchester Art Mus, 70-
Positions: Mem adv comt, Art Ctr, Ogunquit, Maine, 65-
Awards: 14 Richard Milton Gold Medals, New Eng Artists Exhib, 54-70; Gold Medal, 62 & Newington Prize, 66 & 67, Am Artists Prof League.
Bibliography: Richard Goets (auth), The sight sized method, Am Artist, 70.

Memberships: Guild Boston Artists (v pres, 68-); Am Artists Prof
League (dir, 60-70); Acad Artists Asn; Copley Soc Boston; Grand
Cent Art Gallery.
Dealer: Grand Central Art Gallery, 40 Vanderbilt Ave, New York,
NY 10017.
Mailing Address: 30 Ipswich St, Boston, MA 02215.

HUNTER, ROBERT HOWARD
Painter, Sculptor
Preferred Media: Mixed Media.
b Auburn, Wash, May 17, 29.
Study & Training: Ore State Univ, 47-49; Univ Ore, BS & MFA, 49-
53; Univ S C, 55-56.
Work in Public Collections: Ackland Art Ctr, Univ N C, Chapel Hill;
Duke Univ, Durham, N C; Greenville Co Mus Art, S C; Beaufort
Art Mus, S C; Lee Gallery, Clemson Univ, S C.
Exhibitions: 159th Ann Painters & Sculptors, Philadelphia, Pa, 64;
7th Nat Show Art, Brockton, Mass, 64; Art on Paper, Weather-
spoon Art Gallery, N C, 65; 16th Ann Drawing & Small Sculpture
Show, Ball State Univ, 70; one-man show, Ackland Art Ctr, Univ
N C, Chapel Hill, 68.
Teaching: Instr figure drawing, Univ Ore, 52-53; prof printmaking,
painting & basic design, Clemson Univ, 56-, head dept visual
studies, 67-
Positions: Gallery dir, Rudolph Lee Gallery, Clemson Univ, 58-68;
Ford Found fel, Univ N C, Chapel Hill, 66-67.
Awards: Guild of S C Artists awards, 56-63; Springs Art Contest,
S C, 61; eighth ann painting of yr, Atlanta Art Asn, 62.
Memberships: Col Art Asn Am; S C Arts Comn (subcomt state art
collection, 69-71, subcomt environ art, 71-73).
Publications: Auth, Twenty lithographs by Robert Hunter, 61; con-
tribr, Prize winning art-book 6, 66; auth, The shape of, R Hun-
ter, 66; illusr, The binnacle, R Peterson, 67; contribr, Con-
temporary artists of South Carolina, Jack Morris, 70.
Dealer: McDonalds Art Gallery, 753 Providence Rd, Charlotte, NC
28207.
Mailing Address: 11 Farrs Bridge Rd, Greenville, SC 29611.

HUNTER, SAM
Art Historian
b Springfield, Mass, Jan 5, 23.
Study & Training: Williams Col, AB; Univ Florence, cert.
Collections Arranged: Many exhibs at Mus Mod Art, New York,
Minneapolis Inst Arts, Rose Art Mus, Jewish Mus, New York &
Princeton Art Mus.
Teaching: Former instr, Harvard Univ, Univ Calif, Los Angeles,
Barnard Col, Columbia Univ, Cornell Univ & Brandeis Univ;
prof art hist, Princeton Univ, 69-
Positions: Art critic, New York Times, 47-49; cur, Mus Mod Art,
56-58; dir, Minneapolis Inst Arts, 58-60; dir, Rose Art Mus,
Brandeis Univ, 60-65; dir, Jewish Mus, 65-68; consult ed, Harry
N Abrams, Inc, 68-; fac cur mod art, Princeton Art Mus, 69-
Awards: Guggenheim fel, 71-72.
Memberships: Col Art Asn Am.
Publications: Auth, Hans Hofmann, 63; auth, New art around the
world, 66; auth, Larry Rivers, 69; auth, Avant-garde painting in
America, 70; auth, Josef Albers, 71; plus many others.
Mailing Address: 151 West End Ave, New York, NY 10024.

HUNTINGTON, JIM
Sculptor
b Elkhart, Ind, Jan 13, 41.
Study & Training: Ind Univ, Bloomington, 58-59; El Camino Col, 59-
60.
Work in Public Collections: Addison Gallery Am Art, Andover,
Mass; Rose Art Mus, Brandeis Univ, Waltham, Mass; Mass Inst
Technol, Cambridge; Everson Mus Art, Syracuse, N Y; Whitney
Mus Am Art, New York, N Y; plus many others.
Exhibitions: Corcoran Gallery Art Biennial, Washington, D C &
Traveling Exhib, 65 & 67; Whitney Mus Am Art Painting Ann, 68
& Sculpture Ann, 69; one-man shows, Hayden Gallery, Mass Inst
Technol, 68, Max Hutchinson Gallery, New York, 71 & Parker St
470, 72; plus many others.
Awards: Grand prize award, Sheraton-Boston Invitational Competi-
tion & Blanche Colman Award, Boston, 65.
Dealers: Max Hutchinson Gallery, 127 Greene St, New York, NY
10012; Parker St 470, Boston, MA 02115.
Mailing Address: 29 Park Row, New York, NY 10038.

HUNTINGTON, JOHN W
Collector, Patron
b Hartford, Conn, Oct 19, 10.
Study & Training: Yale Col, BA, 32; Sch Archit, Columbia Univ,
BArch, 36.

Positions: Trustee & v pres, Wadsworth Atheneum, Hartford; bd
trustees, Children's Mus, Hartford.
Collection: Contemporary paintings, drawings and graphic arts.
Mailing Address: 159 Bloomfield Ave, Hartford, CT 06105.

HUNTLEY, DAVID C
Painter, Educator
b Lenoir, N C, Oct 17, 30.
Study & Training: Univ N C, AB & MA.
Exhibitions: City Art Mus St Louis, Mo, 66; Raymond Ducan Gallery,
Paris, 66; Ligoa Duncan Gallery, New York, N Y, 67; Peoria Art
Ctr, 68; Wesleyan Col, Macon, Ga, 69; plus many other group &
one-man shows.
Teaching: Instr children's art, Univ N C; instr hist art, design &
art, Limestone Col; prof art, Ala Col, Montevallo; prof & chmn
fine arts div, Southern Illinois Univ, Edwardsville, at present.
Awards: Johnson Award, Birmingham Mus Art, 58; N C Mus Award,
Raleigh, 60; Soc Independent Artists St Louis, 66; plus others.
Memberships: Col Art Asn Am; Ill Art Asn; Ala Watercolor Soc;
S C Art Asn; Am Asn Univ Prof; plus others.
Mailing Address: Fine Arts Div, Southern Illinois University, Ed-
wardsville, IL 62025.

HUPP, FREDERICK DUIS
Painter, Educator
Preferred Media: Acrylics.
b Streator, Ill, Dec 21, 38.
Study & Training: Univ Ariz, BFA, 62, MFA, 66.
Work in Public Collections: Tucson Art Ctr, Ariz.
Exhibitions: Am Fedn Arts Painting Exhib, 70-72; 15th Ann Sun
Carnival, El Paso, Tex, 71; Festival Painting Competition,
Tucson, 72; Western Ann, Denver, 72; Nat Small Painting Exhib,
Albuquerque, N Mex, 72.
Teaching: Instr design, Univ Ariz, 68-; instr drawing & painting,
Tucson Art Ctr Sch, 68-, dir educ, 69-70.
Positions: Cur, Univ Ariz Art Mus, 60-61; instr, Fenster Ranch
Sch, Tucson, 64-65.
Awards: Helene Wurlitzer Found residence painting grant, Taos,
N Mex, 67-68; first prize for painting in Ariz Ann, Phoenix Art
Mus, 69; Festival Painting Award, Tucson Art Ctr, 72.
Mailing Address: 323 N Main, Tucson, AZ 85705.

HURD, JUSTIN G (JUD)
Cartoonist
b Cleveland, Ohio, Nov 12, 12.
Study & Training: Cleveland Inst Art; Case Western Reserve Univ,
AB, 34; Chicago Acad Fine Arts, 35-36; Spencerian Bus Col,
Cleveland, 40-42.
Positions: Cartoonist, Charles Mintz Animated Cartoon Studio, 36-
37; cartoonist, comic bk cartoons, Dell Publ & others, 40-42; U S
Army weekly cartoon bull, 42-46; dir, Jud Hurd Cartoon Studio,
46-58; founder & owner Ticker Toons Syndicate, 59-; ed, The
Cartoonist, Nat Cartoonists Soc Mag, 65-69; publ, Cartoonist
Profiles, 69-
Memberships: Nat Cartoonists Soc (Ohio regional chmn, 57-64, re-
gional coordr, 65, ed newsletter, 65-66); Newspaper Comics
Coun; Advert Club New York.
Publications: Health Capsules (daily cartoon), syndicated by United
Features Syndicate, in U S newspapers & in Turkey, E Pakistan,
Argentina, The Philippines, Chile, Brazil & other countries, 61-
Mailing Address: 281 Bayberry Lane, Westport, CT 06880.

HURD, PETER
Painter, Writer
b Roswell, N Mex, Feb 22, 04.
Study & Training: U S Mil Acad, 21-23; Haverford Col, 23-24; Pa
Acad Fine Arts, 24-26, with N C Wyeth; Tex Tech Univ, DFA;
N Mex State Univ, LLD, 68.
Work in Public Collections: Metrop Mus Art, New York; Nat Gallery,
Edinburgh, Scotland; Delaware Art Mus, Wilmington; Dallas Art
Mus, Tex; Roswell Mus, N Mex; plus many others.
Commissions: 16 fresco panels, Mus of Tex Tech Univ; fresco mu-
rals, Big Spring Post Off Bldg, Tex; mural panel, Prudential Ins
Co Bldg, Houston, Tex; portrait of Pres Johnson for White House
Hist Asn (now in Nat Portrait Gallery); murals, Alamogordo Post
Off Bldg, N Mex; plus others.
Exhibitions: Retrospective, Amon Carter Mus Art, Ft Worth, Tex,
64 & Calif Palace of Legion of Honor, 65.
Positions: War corresp, Life Mag & USAAF, 42-45, artist, Life mag,
46-; Mem, Nat Fine Arts Comn, 58-63.
Awards: Wilmington Soc Fine Arts, 41 & 45; medal, Pa Acad Fine
Arts, 45; Isaac Maynard prize, Nat Acad Design, 54.
Memberships: Academician Nat Acad Design; Wilmington Soc Fine
Arts; Am Watercolor Soc; Century Asn.

Publications: Illusr, The last of the Mohicans, 26, Great stories of the sea and ships, 33 & Habit of empire, 38, plus others; auth, Count-down at Canaveral, Art in Am, 63; auth, Peter Hurd-the lithographs, Baker Gallery, 69 & Sketch book, Swallow, 71.
Mailing Address: Sentinel Ranch, San Patricio, NM 88348.

HURST, RALPH N
Sculptor, Educator
Preferred Media: Alabaster, Wood.
b Decatur, Ind, Sept 4, 18.
Study & Training: Ind Univ, Bloomington, BS & MFA; Ogunquit Sch Painting & Sculpture, Maine, with Robert Laurent; Fla State Univ faculty res grant, summer 61; instrnl grant, summer 67; faculty develop grant in Italy, 71.
Work in Public Collections: Evansville Mus Arts & Sci, Ind; Columbus Mus Arts & Crafts, Ga; Mobile Art Asn Gallery, Ala; Gulf Life Ins Co, Jacksonville, Fla; LeMoyne Art Found Gallery, Tallahassee, Fla.
Commissions: Relief sculpture, Fla State Univ Col Educ, 57; wall relief sculptures (with Leon Mead), Fla State Univ Union Bldg, Tallahassee, 63; sculpture-Madonna, St Thomas More Cath Church, Tallahassee, 71.
Exhibitions: Am Sculpture 1951, Metrop Mus, New York, N Y, 51; Contemp Sculptors Drawings, Ohio State Univ, 54; Art U S A, Madison Square Garden, New York, N Y, 58; Nat Liturgical Art Exhib, San Francisco, Calif, 60; Southeastern Art Exhib, High Mus, Atlanta, Ga, 67.
Teaching: Prof art educ & construct design, Fla State Univ, 53-
Positions: Cur, Mus Art of Ogunquit, summer 53.
Awards: Purchase award, Assoc Fla Architects Art Exhib, Jacksonville, Fla, 59; Ball Gallery Award, Nat Small Sculpture Exhib, Ball State Univ, Muncie, Ind, 60; community purchase award, Mobile Art Gallery, Ala, 71.
Memberships: Nat Art Educ Asn; Am Craftsmen.
Dealers: Harmon Gallery, 1258 Third St S, Naples, FL 33940; Le Moyne Art Foundation, 125 N Gadsden, Tallahassee, FL 32301.
Mailing Address: 1801 Skyland Dr, Tallahassee, FL 32303.

HURT, SUSANNE M
Painter
Preferred Media: Oils.
b New York, N Y.
Study & Training: Duke Univ; Art Stud League New York, with Frank V Dumond & Kenneth Hayes Miller; Corcoran Sch Art; also Wayman Adams & A Ginsburg.
Commissions: In private collections.
Exhibitions: One-man show, Cayuga Mus Hist & Art, Auburn, N Y, 71; Catharine Lorillard Wolfe Art Club, Nat Acad Design, New York, 71; Hudson Valley Art Asn, Westchester Co Ctr, White Plains, N Y, 72; Am Artists Prof League, Lever House, New York, 72; Nat Art League, Long Island, N Y, 72.
Teaching: Pvt classes & demonstrations.
Awards: Special award for oil, Art League of Long Island, 68; Anna Hyatt Huntington First Prize for Painting, Catharine Lorillard Wolfe Art Club, 70; first prize for oil, Composers, Authors & Artists Am, 72.
Memberships: Catharine Lorillard Wolfe Art Club (corresp secy, 71-); Am Artists Prof League; Hudson Valley Art Asn; Composers, Authors & Artists Am (nat rec secy, 71-); Acad Artists Asn.
Art Interests: Portraits & still lifes.
Mailing Address: 299 Riverside Dr, New York, NY 10025.

HURTIG, MARTIN RUSSELL
Painter, Sculptor
b Chicago, Ill, Aug 11, 29.
Study & Training: Inst Design Chicago, BS, 52; Atelier 17, Paris, 55; Inst Design Chicago, MS, 57.
Work in Public Collections: Bibliot Nat, Paris, France; Philadelphia Free Libr; Carroll Reese Mus, Johnson City, Tenn; Honolulu Acad Art.
Commissions: Stained glass windows & mural wall, Union Church Lake Bluff, Ill, 63; outdoor ct sculpture, Waukegan Pub Libr, Ill, 64; lobby relief sculpture, Midwest Iron Works, Chicago, 67.
Exhibitions: 11th & 16th Nat Print Exhib, Brooklyn Mus, 58 & 68; one-man shows, Flint Inst Arts, 61 & 68, Alonzo Gallery, 66 & 67 & Ecole Spec Archit, Paris, 69; 6th Am Artists Traveling Show, Paris & 12 French cities, 69-70.
Teaching: Asst prof drawing & design, Mich State Univ, 57-62; prof painting & printmaking, Univ Ill, Chicago Circle, 62-
Awards: Purchase awards, Carroll Reese Mus, 67 & Honolulu Acad Arts, 71.
Bibliography: F Schulze (auth), Art News in Chicago, Art News, 11/71; A Goldin (auth), Vitality vs greasy kids stuff, Art Gallery

Mag, 4/72; D Guthrie & J Allen (auth), Waging polemical warfare, Chicago Tribune, 4/30/72.
Dealer: Alonzo Gallery, 26 E 63rd St, New York, NY 10021.
Mailing Address: 1727 Wesley St, Evanston, IL 60201.

HURTUBISE, JACQUES
Painter
Preferred Media: Acrylics.
b Montreal, P Q, Feb 28, 39.
Study & Training: Beaux Art Sch, Montreal.
Work in Public Collections: Mass Inst Technol, Boston; Peter Stuyvesant Art Found, Amsterdam; Galerie Nat Can, Ont; Art Gallery Ont, Toronto; Vancouver Art Gallery.
Commissions: Murals, Ottawa Univ, 69, Place Radio Can, Montreal, 72 & Ministry of Defense, Ottawa, 72.
Exhibitions: 9th Int Biennial, Sao Paolo, Brazil, 67; 300 Ans d'Art Canadien, Galerie Nat Can, Ottawa, 67; Canada Art d'Aujourd'hui, Paris, France, Rome, Italy & Lauzanne, Switz, 68; 7 Canadians, Mass Inst Technol, Boston & Gallery Mod Art, Washington, D C, 68; Edinburgh Festival, Scotland, 68.
Awards: First prize, Concours Artistique Quebec, P Q govt, 65.
Bibliography: Laurent Lamy (auth), Hurtubise, Lidec, 71.
Memberships: Royal Can Acad Art.
Dealer: Marlborough-Godard Ltd, 1490 Sherbrooke St W, Montreal, P Q, Can.
Mailing Address: 1226 Rue St Louis, Terrebonne, P Q, Can.

HUSEBY, ARLEEN
Painter, Instructor
Preferred Media: Oils.
b Park Ridge, Ill.
Study & Training: Art Inst Chicago, with Stanley Woodward; Chicago Acad Fine Arts, with Bennett Bradbury; also with ReVeau Bassett, Dallas, Tex.
Work in Public Collections: Works in pvt collections.
Exhibitions: Dallas Mus Fine Arts; Am Artists Prof League, New York; one-man show, Laguna Beach Art Asn; All Calif Show, 68; San Gabriel Fine Arts, 69.
Teaching: Instr oil painting, Monrovia High Sch Adult Educ, 59-
Awards: Gold medal for Blue Fog, San Gabriel Fine Arts, 69; award for Calle Padre Hidalgo, Glendale Art Club; award for Oahu Sea, Arcadia Libr Exhib, 72.
Memberships: Artists & Craftsmen Asn; San Gabriel Fine Arts; Desert Art Asn; Laguna Beach Art Asn; Mid Valley Art Asn.
Mailing Address: 1215 Oakglen Ave, Arcadia, CA 91006.

HUSTED-ANDERSEN, ADDA
Craftsman, Designer
Preferred Media: Metal.
b Denmark.
Study & Training: Thyra Vieth's Sch, Copenhagen; Tech State Sch, Copenhagen; Badishe Kunstgewerbe Schule, Pforzheim, Ger; also with Jean Dunand, Paris.
Work in Public Collections: Newark Mus Art.
Exhibitions: Brussels World's Fair, 58; plus nat exhibs.
Teaching: Head jewelry & enameling, Craft Stud League, New York, N Y.
Positions: Mem ed staff, Craft Horizons.
Awards: Gold & Silversmith Guild Medal, Copenhagen.
Memberships: Artist-Craftsmen New York; Am Craftsmen Coun; World Crafts Coun.
Mailing Address: 887 First Ave, New York, NY 10022.

HUTCHINSON, JANET L
Museum Director, Collector
b Washington, D C, May 2, 17.
Collections Arranged: William Grant Sherry; Gene Klebe; Carmen Z Simpkins; Kan Man Shu (Diana Kan); Richard Tucker; Harry Stump, sculptor; George Curtis, sculptor; Alfred van Loen, sculptor; Scott Croft; Bruce Elliott Roberts; Harriet Arnold, photographer; Vincent Hartgen; Eda Kassel, sculptor; African sculpture on loan from Carlebach Gallery, New York, N Y.
Positions: Owner-dir, Broadlawn Gallery, Camden, Maine, 57-64; cur, Old Merchants House, New York, 61-62; dir, Martin Co Hist Soc: Elliott Mus & House of Refuge, 65-
Mailing Address: Martin County Historical Society, Elliott Museum, Hutchinson Island, Stuart, FL 33494.

HUTCHINSON, MAX
Art Dealer
b Melbourne, Australia, Aug 25, 25.
Study & Training: Royal Melbourne Inst Technol.
Positions: Dir, Max Hutchinson Gallery, New York, NY.
Specialty of Gallery: Contemporary painting and sculpture.
Mailing Address: 127 Greene St, New York, NY 10012.

HUTCHINSON, PETER ARTHUR
Painter
Preferred Media: Mixed Media.
b London, Eng, Mar 4, 30.
Study & Training: Univ Ill, BFA, 60.
Work in Public Collections: Mus Mod Art, New York, N Y; Mönchengladbach Mus, W Ger; Krefeld Mus, W Ger; Rose Mus, Boston, Mass; Chrysler Mus, Norfolk Va.
Exhibitions: The Artists Viewpoint, Jewish Mus, New York, 69; Landscapes & Paricutin Project, John Gibson Gallery, 69-70; Images: 2 Ocean Projects, 69 & Information, 70, Mus Mod Art; Nature & Art, Krefeld Mus, Haus Lange, W Ger, 72.
Awards: Outstanding grad painter, Univ Ill, 60.
Bibliography: Robbins (auth), Images two ocean projects, Arts Mag, 11/69; Scheldahl (auth), Breadworks as earth works, N Y Times, 69; Back to nature, Time, 6/70.
Publications: Auth, The fictionalization of the past, 68 & auth, Earth in upheaval, 68, Arts Mag; auth, Science fiction: an aesthetic for science, Art Int, 68; auth, Is there life on earth, 68 & auth, Foraging: being an account of a hike through the snow mass wilderness as a work of art, 72, Art in Am.
Mailing Address: c/o John Gibson, 120 E 89th St, New York, NY 10028.

HUTCHISON, ELIZABETH S
Painter
Study & Training: Otis Art Inst; also with Joseph Mugnaini & Aimee Bourdieu.
Work in Public Collections: Rice Univ Permanent Collection, Houston, Tex; Utah State Univ Permanent Collection; Chaffey Col Permanent Collection, Alta Loma, Calif; Am Fedn Social Settlements Permanent Collection, New York, N Y; plus many others in pvt collections.
Exhibitions: Calif Nat Watercolor Soc Ann, 66-72; Watercolor U S A, Springfield, Mo, 69, 70 & 72; Old Bergen Art Guild, 70-72; Nat Acad Design, New York, 70-72; Sacramento State Fair, 71-72; plus many other group & one-man shows.
Awards: Purchase award, Watercolor U S A, 69; hon mention, Southern Calif Art for 1970, Del Mar, Calif; purchase prize, Fifth Ann St Raymond's Art Show, Thousand Oaks, Calif, 71; plus many others.
Memberships: Calif Nat Watercolor Soc (bd mem, 4 yrs, pres, 71-72, juror, 72-73); Women Painters West (juror, 69-72, first v pres, 71-73); Laguna Beach Art Mus Asn; Los Angeles Art Asn; Westwood Art Asn.
Dealer: Albert J Kramer Gallery, 710 N La Cienega Blvd, Los Angeles, CA 90069.
Mailing Address: 3611 Sapphire Dr, Encino, CA 91316.

HUTCHISON, MILBURN ROBERT
Painter, Illustrator
b Morrill, Nebr, June 27, 17.
Study & Training: San Diego Sch Arts & Crafts, La Jolla, Calif; also with Herbert Turner, Del Mar, Calif & Harvey Adams, San Diego.
Exhibitions: Two shows, Chriswood Gallery Rancho Calif Art Show, Temecula, Calif, 71; Lake San Marcos Calif, 71; 20th Ann Old Town Art Fiesta, San Diego, 72.
Teaching: Instr perspective drawing, San Diego Sch Arts & Crafts, 47-49.
Positions: Tech illusr, Consol Vultee Aircraft Corp, San Diego, 40-45; art dir, Gordan Eby & Assocs-Advert, San Diego, 45-49; art supvr & ed, Gen Dyn Convair, San Diego, 50-67; sr engr illusr, Rohr Corp, Chula Vista, Calif, 67-70.
Memberships: San Dieguito Art Guild; San Diego Art Inst.
Art Interests: Western Americana; boats and sandcasting.
Dealer: La Galeria, 2161 Avenida de la Playa, La Jolla, CA 92037.
Mailing Address: Studio M Stratford Square, 1442 Camino Del Mar, Del Mar, CA 92014.

HUTH, HANS
Art Historian, Art Administrator
b Halle, Ger, Nov 11, 92; U S citizen.
Study & Training: Univ Vienna; Univ Berlin, PhD, 22.
Collections Arranged: Relig Show, Art Inst Chicago, 54.
Teaching: Lectr mus training, N Y Univ, 38-39; lectr mus training, Univ Calif, Los Angeles, 68-69.
Positions: Asst cur, State Mus, Munich & Berlin, 24-26; cur admin, Royal Palaces, Prussia, 27-36; consult, Nat Park Serv Br Hist, 39-50; cur, Art Inst Chicago, 44-63; consult & ed, Encycl Britannica, 54-
Memberships: Charter mem Nat Trust Hist Preserv; Col Art Asn Am; Int Coun Mus.
Research: Decorative arts; preservation; conservation.

Publications: Auth, Künstler und werkstatt der Spätgotik, 23 & rev ed, 67, auth, Abraham und David Roentgen, 28 & rev ed, 73; auth, Der park von Sanssouci, 22 & rev ed, 29; auth, Nature and the American, 59 & 72; auth, Lacquer of the West, 71; plus others.
Mailing Address: P O Box 4414, Carmel, CA 93921.

HUTH, MARTA
Painter, Photographer
b Munich, Ger, Dec 25, 98; U S citizen.
Study & Training: State Sch Photog, Munich, Master; Acad Munich.
Work in Public Collections: Städtisches Mus, Munich; Monterey Peninsula Mus Art.
Exhibitions: Art Inst Chicago Regionals, 48-60; one-man shows, Calif Palace Legion of Honor, 54 & Chicago Pub Libr, 54; Naval Postgrad Sch Relig Ann, Monterey, 64-72; Interiors of Berlin (photos), Berlin Mus, 70.
Bibliography: Painting on glass, Craft Horizon, 2/54; Gisland Ritz (auth), Hinterglas malerei, München, 72.
Publications: Co-auth, Baroness von Riedesel and the American Revolution, J, 65.
Mailing Address: P O Box 4414, Carmel, CA 93921.

HUTSALIUK, LUBO
Painter
Preferred Media: Oils, Watercolors.
b Lvov, Ukraine, Apr 2, 23; U S citizen.
Study & Training: Cooper Union Art Sch, 54.
Work in Public Collections: Palm Springs Mus, Calif; Vt Art Ctr, Manchester.
Exhibitions: One-man shows, Juster Gallery, New York, N Y, 57, Jacques Norval Gallery, Paris, 59, Hilde Gerst Gallery, New York, 61 & 67 & Angle Du Faubourg Gallery, Paris, 63.
Awards: First prize fine arts, Cooper Union Art Sch, 54; silver medal, Acad T Campanella, Rome, 70.
Bibliography: Pierre Imbourg (auth), La reve d'Hutsaliuk, J Amateur Art, 66; J Hess Michel (auth), The vibrant paintings of Hutsaliuk, Am Artist, 69.
Memberships: Salon Independents Paris; Salon Automne; Audubon Artists.
Dealer: Burrell Galleries, Madison Ave at 75th St, New York, NY 10021.
Mailing Address: 260 Riverside Dr, New York, NY 10025.

HUTTON, DOROTHY WACKERMAN
Designer, Printmaker
Preferred Media: Graphics.
b Cleveland, Ohio, Feb 9, 99.
Study & Training: Minneapolis Sch Art, cert; Univ Minn, with Vytlacil, Earl Horter & Hobson Pittman; Acad Andre L'Hote, Paris.
Work in Public Collections: Smithsonian Inst, Washington, D C; Harvard Univ; plus others.
Exhibitions: Five Pennell Exhibs, Libr Cong, Washington, D C; Corcoran Gallery Art, Washington, D C; Philadelphia Print Club, Pa; Carnegie Exhib, Pittsburgh; Grand Cent Art Gallery, New York, N Y.
Memberships: Philadelphia Art Alliance (print comt, 50-); Am Colorprint Soc (corresp secy, 65-); Philadelphia Watercolor Club (dir, 65 & 68); Plastic Art Club Women.
Mailing Address: 42 Rosedale Rd, Philadelphia, PA 19151.

HUTTON, HUGH McMILLEN
Cartoonist
Preferred Media: Crayon, Ink.
b Lincoln, Nebr, Dec 11, 97.
Study & Training: Minneapolis Art Inst Sch; Beaux Arts, Paris; Univ Minn.
Work in Public Collections: Libr Cong; Smithsonian Inst; White House; Dept Justice; U S Supreme Ct; plus others.
Positions: Ed cartoonist, New York World, 30-32; ed cartoonist, United Features Syndicate, 32-33; ed cartoonist, Philadelphia Pub Ledger, 33-34; ed cartoonist, Philadelphia Inquirer, 34-70.
Awards: Awards, Nat Safety Coun, Freedoms Found & Christophers.
Publications: Auth & illusr, Paul Bunyan, Mead Paper Co, 50-52.
Mailing Address: 42 Rosedale Rd, Overbrook Hills, Philadelphia, PA 19151.

HUTTON, LEONARD
Art Dealer
Positions: Owner & dir, Leonard Hutton Galleries.
Specialty of Gallery: Russian avant-garde art and the expressionists.
Mailing Address: 967 Madison Ave, New York, NY 10021.

HUTTON, WILLIAM
Museum Curator
b New York, N Y, Oct 2, 26.
Study & Training: Williams Col, BA, 50; Harvard Univ, MA, 52.

Positions: Asst cur, Toledo Mus Art, 52-65; dir, Currier Gallery
  Art, 65-68; res staff, Victoria & Albert Mus, London, Eng, 68-
  71; chief cur, Toledo Mus Art, 71-
Research: Eighteenth century Meissen porcelain.
Mailing Address: Toledo Museum of Art, Box 1013, Toledo, OH
  43697.

HUXTABLE, ADA LOUISE
  Critic
b New York, N Y.
Study & Training: Hunter Col, AB(magna cum laude); New York Univ;
  Fulbright fel for advan study in archit & design, Italy, 50 & 52;
  Guggenheim fel for studies in Am archit, 58; hon degrees, Yale
  Univ, Oberlin Col, Smith Col, Skidmore Col, Mt Holyoke Col,
  Trinity Col, Pratt Inst, Pace Col, La Salle Col & others.
Positions: Asst cur archit & design, Mus Mod Art, New York, N Y,
  46-50; contrib ed, Progressive Archit Art in Am, 50-63; archit
  critic, New York Times, 63-; bd dirs, Munic Art Soc New York &
  Soc Archit Historians.
Awards: Elsie de Wolfe Award, Am Inst Interior Designers, 69;
  Strauss Mem Award, New York Soc Architects, 70; Pulitzer
  Prize for distinguished criticism, 70; plus others.
Memberships: Am Soc Archit Historians; Nat Trust Hist Preserv;
  Victorian Soc Am.
Publications: Auth, Pier Luigi Nervi, Braziller, 60; auth, Four walk-
  ing tours of modern architecture in New York City, Mus Mod Art,
  61; auth, Classic New York, 64; auth, Will they ever finish Bruck-
  ner Boulevard?, Macmillan, 70.
Mailing Address: New York Times, 229 W 43rd St, New York, NY
  10036.

HYDE, ANDREW CORNWALL
  Art Administrator, Art Consultant
b Detroit, Mich, Apr 25, 41.
Collections Arranged: Many exhibs, 69-72.
Positions: Dir, Inst Contemp Art, Boston, 68-71; spec adv visual
  arts, Mass Bay Transit Auth; dir Vis Ctr, Children's Mus,
  Boston, 71-72; assoc publ, Boston Rev Arts, 72-
Memberships: Metrop Cult Alliance (exec comt, 70-); Inst Contemp
  Art (trustee, 71-); Boston Film Ctr (trustee, 69-); Music & Art
  Develop (trustee, 70-); Gov Task Force Arts Educ.
Research: Art for public places; community involvement in the arts;
  government's role in the arts.
Mailing Address: 80 Chilton St, Cambridge, MA 02138.

HYDE, LAURENCE
  Painter, Designer
b London, Eng, June 6, 14.
Study & Training: Cent Tech Sch, Toronto.
Work in Public Collections: Nat Gallery Can; Art Gallery Vancouver,
  B C; Art Gallery Toronto; Libr Cong, Washington, D C.
Commissions: Design of seven stamps for Can Postal Dept.
Exhibitions: Ont Soc Artists; Can Soc Painter-Etchers & Engravers;
  Can Soc Graphic Art; New York World's Fair, 39; Rio, 46.
Positions: Producer & dir, Nat Film Bd Can.
Memberships: Can Soc Graphic Art.
Publications: Auth, Southern cross, 52; illusr, The Ottawa, 61; auth,
  Under the pirate flag, Houghton Mifflin, 65; illusr, History of the
  Bank of Montreal, 2 vols, 67; auth, Captain Deadlock, Houghton,
  Mifflin, 68; contrib to Can Arts & Can Geog Mag.
Mailing Address: 15 Crichton St, Ottawa, Ont, Can.

HYSLOP, ALFRED JOHN
  Sculptor, Educator
b Castle-Douglas, Scotland, Apr 10, 98.
Study & Training: Edinburgh Col Art, DArt; Royal Col Art, London,
  Assoc.
Work in Public Collections: In pvt collections.
Commissions: Murals, Buckham Mem Libr & Faribault, Minn.
Positions: Chmn art dept, Carleton Col, Northfield, Minn, 23-63,
  emer, 63-
Mailing Address: 6912 Big Bear Dr, Tucson, AZ 85715.

HYSLOP, FRANCIS EDWIN
  Art Historian
b Philadelphia, Pa, Jan 7, 09.
Study & Training: Princeton Univ, BA, 31, MA, 33, MFA, 34.
Teaching: Prof art hist, Pa State Univ, 34-
Memberships: Col Art Asn.
Research: Nineteenth century French art and literature.
Publications: Translr, Le Corbusier, When the cathedrals were
  white, Reynal & Hitchcock, 47; co-auth, Baudelaire as a critic,
  64; Henri Evenepoel à Paris, 72.
Mailing Address: 229 Arts Bldg, University Park, PA 16802.

I

IACURTO, FRANCESCO
  Painter, Instructor
Preferred Media: Oils, Pastels, Charcoal, Watercolors.
b Montreal, P Q, Sept 1, 08.
Study & Training: Fine Arts Sch Montreal; Grande Chaumiére Cola-
  rossi, Paris, France, govt scholar; also with Charles Maillard,
  Ed Dyonnet, John Y Johnstone & others.
Work in Public Collections: Prov Mus Que; Can House, London, Eng;
  House of Senate, Ottawa, Ont; Rideau Hall, Gov Gen Can; Klincoff
  Gallery, Montreal.
Commissions: Portraits, Lord Rothermere & Lord Cromer, Eng, 53;
  portraits, Price Bros & Anglo Paper Que, 63; fall landscapes,
  Bank Montreal, London, 71; painting, Janin Construct, Que, 71;
  pastel, Can Govt, Ottawa, 71.
Exhibitions: Royal Can Acad, Toronto, Ont, 48 & 51 & Montreal, 60;
  Spring Exhib, Montreal Mus Art, 52 & 53.
Teaching: Instr drawing, Cath Sch Comn, 29-33; instr drawing, Art
  & Trades Montreal, 29-38; instr painting, Libr Ste Foy, P Q, 66-
Awards: First medal for art, 28 & scholar to Europe, 29, Govt P Q;
  silver medal, Ministry exterior, France, 29.
Memberships: Assoc Royal Can Acad Arts; Soc Artists Profes-
  sionels Que; Independent Art Asn.
Dealer: Klincoff, Sherbrooke St W, Montreal, P Q, Can.
Mailing Address: 1232 La Vigerie, Quebec 10, P Q, Can.

ICAZA (FRANCISCO DE ICAZA)
  Painter, Sculptor
Preferred Media: Oils, Acrylics, Woods, Bronzes.
b Mexico, Oct 5, 30.
Study & Training: Univ Madrid, BA, BC.
Work in Public Collections: Mus Mod Art, Mex; La Jolla Mus Art,
  Calif; Mus Art, San Diego, Calif; Phoenix Art Mus, Ariz.
Commissions: In Mex Pavilion, Expo '67, Can, 67; in Mex Pavilion,
  Hemisphere U S; at Osaka '70, Japan, 70; mural for Hotel Casino
  de la Selva, Cuernavaca, Mex; sculpture in bronze, Unidad Cle-
  mente Orozco, Guadalajara, Mex.
Exhibitions: 4th Int Exhib, Guggenheim Mus, New York, N Y, 64;
  Phoenix Art Mus, Ariz, 67; Long Beach Mus Art, Calif, 68; Ariz
  State Mus, 68; Second Exhib Salon Independiente, Nat Univ Mex,
  69.
Awards: First prize for Nuevos Valores, 57, second prize for Na-
  tional Landscape, 60 & first prize for Salon de la Plastica Mex,
  62, Mus Mod Art, Mex.
Bibliography: Margarita Nelken (auth), El expresionismo en Mexico,
  Bellas Artes; Luis C y Aragon (auth), Mexico pintura de hoy,
  Fondo Cult Econ; Raquel Tibol (auth), Historia de la pintura
  moderna Mexicana.
Memberships: Frente Nac Artes Plasticas (treas, 56); Nueva
  Presencia (founder, 63); Salon Independiente (founder, 68).
Mailing Address: Adolfo Prieto No 601, Col del Valle, Mexico DF,
  Mexico.

IDEN, SHELDON
  Painter, Educator
Preferred Media: Oils, Graphics, Charcoal, Pastels.
b Detroit, Mich, Sept 29, 33.
Study & Training: Art Inst Chicago; Wayne State Univ, BFA; Cran-
  brook Acad Art, MFA, with Zoltan Sepeshy.
Work in Public Collections: Detroit Inst Arts; Cranbrook Acad Art,
  Bloomfield Hills, Mich; Ball State Univ, Muncie, Ind; Wayne State
  Univ, Detroit; Macomb Community Col, Warren, Mich.
Exhibitions: 2nd Biennial, Pa Acad Fine Arts & Detroit Mus Art, 60;
  Mich Artists Ann, 60-70 & 72 & Other Ideas, 69, Detroit Inst
  Arts; Drawing & Sculpture Ann, Ball State Univ, 62; All Mich
  Show, Flint Mus Art, 72.
Teaching: Instr drawing & painting, Wayne State Univ, 63-68; asst
  prof drawing & painting, Eastern Mich Univ, 68-
Positions: Artist-in-residence, Mich Coun Arts, 69.
Awards: Fulbright fel to India, 62; mus purchase award, 70 &
  Gertrude Kasle Award for painting, 71, Detroit Inst Arts.
Bibliography: Hakanson (auth), Made in Detroit, Art Scene, 67;
  Hakanson (auth), critical rev, In: Detroit News, 71; Tall (auth),
  critical rev, In: Detroit Free Press, 71.
Mailing Address: 24711 Rosewood, Oak Park, MI 48237.

IERVOLINO, JOSEPH ANTHONY
  Art Dealer, Collector
b Brooklyn, N Y, Aug 4, 20.
Study & Training: City Col New York; Univ Miami Law Sch, LLB;
  Americana Art Ctr.
Positions: Owner & pres, Americana Galleries, 61-
Memberships: Assoc Int Inst Conserv of Hist & Artistic Works; Am
  Soc Appraisers.

Specialty of Gallery: American contemporary painting, sculpture and prints.
Collection: Contemporary paintings of North and South America and Europe; nineteenth century American and European.
Mailing Address: Americana Galleries, Inc, 271 Waukegan Rd, Northfield, IL 60093.

IERVOLINO, PAULA
Art Dealer, Collector
Preferred Media: Oils, Metal.
b N Dak.
Study & Training: Art Inst Chicago; Northwestern Univ.
Positions: Com artist, Advertisers Art Serv, Chicago, 39-40; com artist (catalog), Furniture Mfg, Chicago, 41-61; gallery dir, Americana Galleries, 61-
Memberships: Art Inst Chicago Alumni Asn; Munic Art League Chicago; Am Fedn Arts; Am Soc Appraisers.
Specialty of Gallery: Contemporary American artists.
Collection: Contemporary artists of America; paintings, sculpture and graphics.
Mailing Address: 271 Waukegan Rd, Northfield, IL 60093.

IGLEHART, ROBERT L
Educator
b Baltimore, Md, Feb 2, 12.
Study & Training: Md Inst Art, scholar for European study; Johns Hopkins Univ; Columbia Univ, BS Educ; New Sch Social Res.
Teaching: Instr, Sch Art, Univ Wash, 38-41; chmn dept art educ, New York Univ, 46-55; prof art, Univ Mich, 55-, chmn dept art, 55-71.
Awards: Nat Gallery Art Medal for distinguished serv to art educ, 66.
Memberships: Mus Mod Art, New York; John Dewey Soc; Col Art Asn Am; Nat Art Educ Asn.
Publications: Auth, numerous articles for prof mag.
Mailing Address: 117 Dixboro Rd, Ann Arbor, MI 48105.

INDIANA, ROBERT
Painter, Sculptor
Preferred Media: Oils, Steel.
b New Castle, Ind, Sept 13, 28.
Study & Training: John Herron Sch Art; Munson-Williams-Proctor Inst; Art Inst Chicago, BFA; Skowhegan Sch Painting & Sculpture; Univ Edinburgh & Edinburgh Col Art, Scotland.
Work in Public Collections: Mus Mod Art & Whitney Mus Am Art, New York, N Y; Carnegie Inst Arts, Pittsburgh, Pa; Stedelijk Mus, Amsterdam, Neth; Detroit Inst Arts, Mich.
Commissions: Electric mural, New York World's Fair, 64-65.
Exhibitions: Americans 1963, Mus Mod Art, New York, 63; Dunn Int, Tate Gallery, London, Eng, 63; New Realism, Gemeentemuseum, The Hague, Neth, 64; White House Festival of Arts, Washington, D C, 65; Ninth São Paulo Bienal, Brazil, 67.
Bibliography: Brattinga (auth), Robert Indiana, Gebrauchsgraphik, 64; Swenson (auth), Horizons of Robert Indiana, Art News, 66; McCoubrey (auth), Robert Indiana, Univ Pa, 68.
Memberships: Royal Soc Arts.
Publications: Illusr, Numbers, 68.
Dealer: Galerie Denise René, 6 W 57th St, New York, NY 10019.
Mailing Address: 2 Spring St, New York, NY 10012.

INDIVIGLIA, SALVATORE JOSEPH
Painter, Instructor
Preferred Media: Watercolors.
b New York, N Y, Nov 16, 19.
Study & Training: Leonardo da Vinci Art Sch; Sch Indust Arts; Pratt Inst, BA; fresco & mural painting with Alfred D Crimi; also with Buck Ulrick, Nicholas Volpe, Earl Winslow & George Harrington, Jr.
Work in Public Collections: USN Combat Art Collection, Washington, D C; Grumbacher & Sons Collection, New York; Mutual Benefit Life Ins Co, N J; Annin Flag Co, New York; Morris Davis Collection, Emily Lowe Found, New York.
Commissions: Assisted Alfred D Crimi with hist mural for Northampton, Mass, 40, Gen Anthony Wayne Mural for Wayne, Pa, 41 & Bowery Mission Mural for Bowery Mission, New York, 42.
Exhibitions: American Watercolor Soc Ann, New York, 53-72; Audubon Artists Ann, New York, 53-72; Joe & Emily Lowe Foundation Show, 55 & 60; Operations Palette, USN Combat Art, Smithsonian Inst, Washington, D C, 66; Nat Acad Design, New York, 65.
Teaching: Asst & instr, City Col New York & pvt classes, 46-69; instr watercolors, East Williston Libr, New York & pvt classes, 60-72; instr fine & applied arts, Mechanics Inst, New York, 62-66.
Positions: Off USN combat artist, 61-; art dir & acct exec prod mgr, Vogue Wright Studios, 64-; dir art, Electrographic Corp, 69-71.
Awards: Gold medal for watercolor, Knickerbocker Artists, 53 & 60; Emily Lowe Award for watercolor & oil, 55 & 60; gold medal for oil, Nat Art League, 66.

Memberships: Artists Fellowship (pres, 60-63); Am Watercolor Soc (dir, chmn, 53-72); Allied Artists Am (secy, 59-62); Knickerbocker Artists (v pres, 57-59); Audubon Artists (jury watercolor awards, 71).
Publications: Contribr, Direction, Int Rels Div, Off Info, 66; contribr, The Watch, USNR, 67; contribr, Naval Aviation News, 68; contribr, All Hands, Bur Naval Personnel, 69; auth, The watercolor page, Am Artist Mag, 71.
Mailing Address: 974 Lorraine Dr, Franklin Square, NY 11010.

INGLE, TOM
Painter, Lecturer
b Evansville, Ind, Mar 31, 20.
Study & Training: Princeton Univ, BA; also with Robert Lahr & Fran Soldini.
Work in Public Collections: Evansville Pub Mus; Wadsworth Atheneum, Hartford, Conn; Lyman Allyn Mus Art, New London, Conn.
Exhibitions: One-man shows, Univ Hartford, 65 & Leone Kahl Assoc, Dallas, Tex, 66; Cinema I and II, New York, 65; New York World's Fair, 65; Eastern States Exhib, Springfield, Mass, 67; plus others.
Teaching: Lect on Philosophy of Art & Art History; lectr art, Conn Col, 61-
Positions: Mem adv coun, Lyman Allyn Mus Art, 55-
Awards: Silvermine Guild, 56; Norwich Art Asn, 60 & 69; Mystic Art Asn, 64 & 07.
Memberships: Essex Art Asn (pres, 49-57); Mystic Art Asn (pres, 64-65).
Mailing Address: R R 1, Box 369, Old Lyme, CT 06371.

INGRAHAM, ESTHER PRICE
Painter
Preferred Media: Watercolor
b Needham, Mass.
Study & Training: Mt Holyoke Col, BA; Cleveland Sch Art; Montana State Univ; Famous Artists Sch, Westport, Conn, cert; also with Taubes, Earl Cordrey, John Pike, Jade Fon & Tadeshi Sato.
Exhibitions: Maui Art Shows, Hawaii, 64-68; Easter Art Festival, Honolulu & Windward Artists Shows, Hawaii, 68-71.
Teaching: Instr painting, Seabury Hall, Makawao, Maui, 64-65; pvt classes on Maui & Oahu, 65-71.
Awards: Watercolor prize, Maui Art Soc, 66.
Memberships: Windward Artists Guild (bd dirs, 68-71); Artists of Hawaii.
Collection: Hawaiian landscapes.
Dealer: Royal Hawaiian Art Gallery, Royal Hawaiian Hotel, Honolulu, HI 96815.
Mailing Address: C-1 Pohai Nani, Kaneohe, HI 96744.

INGRAM, JERRY CLEMAN
Painter, Designer
Preferred Media: Tempera.
b Battiest, Okla, Dec 13, 41.
Study & Training: Inst Am Indian Arts; Okla State Univ Sch Tech Training, BA, 66.
Work in Public Collections: Nat Gallery Art, Washington, D C; Heard Mus, Phoenix, Ariz; R C Gorman Navajo Gallery, Taos, N Mex; also in the collections of Jerry Bregman, New York, N Y & Dr Byron Butler, Phoenix.
Commissions: Mural of dancers, Okla State Univ Sch Tech Training, Okmulgee, 65.
Exhibitions: Philbrook Art Ctr Indian Art Ann, Tulsa, Okla, 66; two-man show, 70, Indian Art Ann, 71 & one-man show, 72, Heard Mus; Scottsdale Indian Art Ann, Ariz, 71 & 72; Charles W Bowers Mem Mus, Santa Ana, Calif, 72; Gallup Ceremonial & N Mex State Fair, 72.
Awards: Hon mention for Vision, Heard Mus, 71; spec award for Buffalo Dancer, Scottsdale Indian Art Ann, 72; first prize for Buffalo Woman Dancing, Gallup Ceremonial, 72.
Bibliography: Jean Snodgrass (auth), Catalog of American Indian artists, Philbrook Art Ctr, 67; Tom Bahti (auth), Southwest Indian ceremonials, K C Publ, 70; Doris Monthan (auth), Indian individualists, Northland, (in press).
Mailing Address: 1801 La Poblana Rd N W, Albuquerque, NM 87104.

INGRAM, JUDITH
Printmaker, Painter
Preferred Media: Acrylics, Wood Block Printing.
b Philadelphia, Pa, Oct 12, 26.
Study & Training: Philadelphia Col Art; printmaking with Carol Summers.
Work in Public Collections: Del Mus Art, Wilmington; Free Libr Philadelphia, Pa; Univ Pa Law Sch, Philadelphia; Drexel Inst, Philadelphia; RCA Corp, Eastern U S A & P R.
Exhibitions: Philadelphia Print Club Exhib; Boston Printmakers Ann, 70; Philadelphia Women in Fine Arts, Moore Col Art; Phil-

adelphia Art Alliance; N J State Mus, Trenton; solo exhibs, Gallery 252, Philadelphia, 67, 69 & 71.
Teaching: Artist-in-residence, Pa Title 3 Prog, Springfield Sch Dist, Pa, 68-69.
Memberships: Am Color Print Soc; Artists Equity Asn.
Dealer: Gallery 252, 252 S 16th St, Philadelphia, PA 19102.
Mailing Address: 5 Kenny Circle, Broomall, PA 19008.

INMAN, PAULINE WINCHESTER
Printmaker, Illustrator
b Chicago, Ill, Mar 3, 04.
Study & Training: Smith Col, AB; also with Allen Lewis.
Work in Public Collections: Carnegie Inst, Pittsburgh, Pa; Libr Cong, Washington, D C; Metrop Mus Art, New York, N Y; Montclair Art Mus, N J; Boston Pub Libr, Mass.
Exhibitions: Nat & int exhibs incl Exchange Italian Exhib, Contemp Print Exhib, Tokyo, Japan & London, Eng.
Memberships: Boston Printmakers; Soc Am Graphic Artists (coun, 54-56, corresp secy, 59-61, 65-66); Conn Acad Fine Arts; Acad Artists Asn.
Publications: Illusr, How to know American antiques, 51, New world writing number 2, 52 & Down east reader, 62; contribr, articles, In: Antiques, 60 & 69 & Artists Proof, 64; illusr, The antiques guide to decorative arts in America, Dutton, 72.
Mailing Address: 4 Currituck Rd, Newtown, CT 60470.

INOKUMA, GUENICHIRO
Painter
Preferred Media: Oils, Acrylics.
b Takamatsu, Japan, Dec 14, 21.
Study & Training: Tokyo Acad Fine Arts, Ueno; also with Prof Takeji Fujushima in Japan & Matisse in France.
Work in Public Collections: Nat Mus, Tokyo, Japan; Baltimore Mus Art, Md; Institute Contemp Art, Boston, Mass; Bridgestone Mus, Tokyo; San Francisco Mus Art, Calif; plus one other.
Commissions: Murals, Keio Univ, 47, Maruei Hotel, Nagoya, 52, Tokyo Cent Sta, 53; Takashimaya Dept Store, 58 & ceramic mural, Munic Bldg, Kagawa Prefecture, 59.
Exhibitions: Imperial Art Exhib, 27-30; Tokyo Munic Art Mus, 37; São Paulo Biennale, 54 & 59; Mus Mod Art, Tokyo, 64; Int Art Festival, Saint Louis, Mo & Maline City, Ill, 67; plus one other.
Teaching: Prof oil painting, Japanese Acad Fine Arts, 37-40; estab art sch in Japan, 45; lect mod art to Crown Prince before world tour, 53.
Awards: Mainichi Cult & Artistic Prize for murals, 52; first prize, Japanese Contemp Artists Exhib, 64; first prize, Japanese Govt, Tokyo Biennale, 69.
Memberships: Dainibuki.
Dealer: Willard Gallery, 29 E 72nd St, New York, NY 10021.
Mailing Address: 33 E 22nd St, New York, NY 10010.

INSEL, PAULA
Art Dealer, Art Administrator
b Paris, France, Jan 13, 03; U S citizen.
Study & Training: City Col New York, cert, 54; New York Univ, cert, 55; New York Sch Interior Design, cert, 57.
Positions: Dir, Artravelrama, N Y State 20 Shows in Tex, 58; dir, Stuyvesant Outdoor Art Festival, Union Square Savings Bank, New York, 59; dir, Galerie Paula Insel, New York, 60-; dir, Coney Island Art Show, C of C, Brooklyn, NY, 70.
Awards: Grumbacher Art Co Award of Merit for Var Nat Exhibs, 57; citation for original art exhibs, Murray Hills, New York, 57; citation, State Mus City of New York by Police Athletic League Comnr, 59.
Memberships: Am Fedn Art; Mod Mus Art.
Specialty of Gallery: Mostly contemporary.
Publications: Auth, column, In: Art World, 54-55; auth, New York galleries, Arts Mag, 4/71; plus others.
Mailing Address: Galerie Paula Insel, 987 Third Ave, New York, NY 10022.

INSLEE, MARGUERITE T
Painter, Collector
Preferred Media: Oils.
b Grand Rapids, Mich, June 17, 91.
Study & Training: Univ Mich Exten, Grand Rapids Art Mus; Colo Springs Fine Arts Ctr, with Emerson Woelfer; Inst Allende, San Miguel de Allende, Mex, West Mich Show grant, 59; Escuela Bellas Artes, Taxco, Mex; Int Summer Acad Fine Arts, Salzburg, Austria, with Oscar Kokashka.
Exhibitions: Grand Rapids Art Mus, 59; Sch Fine Arts, Taxco, Mex; one-woman shows, Steel Case, Inc, Women's Club & Fountain Street Church, Grand Rapids.
Awards: Prize for oil, Grand Rapids Art Mus, 59.
Memberships: Grand Rapids Art Mus; Mus Mod Art, New York; Smith Col Mus Art; Grand Rapids Print Club.

Collection: Les Yeux Clos, Redon; Peasant Girl with Kerchief, Picasso; Vienna, Oskar Kokaschka; Young Bather Standing (bronze), Maillol.
Mailing Address: 909 Floral Dr S E, Grand Rapids, MI 49506.

INSLEY, WILL
Painter, Instructor
b Indianapolis, Ind, Oct 15, 29.
Study & Training: Amherst Col, BA; Harvard Univ Grad Sch Design, MArch.
Commissions: Great Southwest Indust Park, Atlanta, Ga, 68.
Exhibitions: One-man shows, Stable Gallery, 68 & John Gibson Gallery, 69, New York, N Y; Will Insley: Space Diagrams, Inst Contemp Art, Univ Pa, Philadelphia, 69; Will Insley: Ceremonial Space, Mus Mod Art, New York, 71; Documenta 5, Kassel, W Ger, 72.
Teaching: Artist-in-residence, Oberlin Col, 66; art critic, Univ N C, 67-68; art critic, Cornell Univ, 69; instr art, Sch Visual Art, 69-.
Awards: Nat Found Arts & Humanities Award, 66; Guggenheim fel, 69.
Bibliography: S Prokopoff (auth), Will Insley: space diagrams (catalog), Inst Contemp Art, Univ Pa, 69; A Drexler (auth), Will Insley: ceremonial space (catalog), Mus Mod Art, 71.
Dealer: Paul Maenz, Lindenstrasse 32, 5 Köln 1, West Germany.
Mailing Address: 2 Spring St, New York, NY 10012.

INUKAI, KYOHEI
Painter, Sculptor
Preferred Media: Oils, Acrylics, Metals.
b Chicago, Ill, July 13, 13.
Study & Training: Art Inst Chicago; Nat Acad Design; Art Stud League New York.
Work in Public Collections: Brandeis Univ Mus Fine Art, New York, N Y; Portland Mus, Maine; Wichita Univ Mus Art, Kans; Atlantic Richfield Collection, New York, Chase Manhattan Bank Collection, New York; plus many others.
Commissions: Sculpture for shopping mall, Robert Kahn Assocs, Architects, Knoxville, Tenn.
Exhibitions: U S Info Agency Print Exhib, Osaka Worlds Fair, 70; White House Rotating Exhib; Screenprints 1970, Int Silk Screen Asn, 70; Dixon White Art Ctr, Cornell Univ, 70; ann print exhib, Brooklyn Mus, N Y, 71; Am Fedn Arts Traveling Print Show.
Mailing Address: 884 West End Ave, New York, NY 10025.

INVERARITY, ROBERT BRUCE
Designer, Museum Director
b Seattle, Wash, July 5, 09.
Study & Training: Univ Wash, BA, 46; Fremont Univ, MFA, 47, PhD, 48; also with Kazue Yamagishi, Blanding Sloan & Mark Tobey.
Work in Public Collections: Univ Washington, Seattle; U S Naval Collection, Washington, D C; Also paintings in pvt collections.
Commissions: Two mosaics, Univ Washington, 40; cut aluminum decorations, U S Naval Airstation, Seattle, 40; six panels, Wash State Mus.
Exhibitions: One-man shows & numerous group exhibs, U S & Can, 29-39.
Teaching: Dir, sch creative art, Vancouver, Can, 31-33; instr, Univ Wash, 33-37; asst dir, Fred Archer Sch Photography, 47-49; assoc, Sch Am Res, 49-54; res asst, Yale Univ, 51-53.
Positions: State dir, Works Progress Admin Art Proj, Seattle, 37-41; off war artist, USN, 43-45; art dir, Boeing Aircraft Co, Seattle, 46-47; dir Mus Int Folk Art, 49-54; dir, Adirondack Mus, 54-65; dir, Philadelphia Maritime Mus, 69-.
Awards: Meritorious Civilian Serv Award, USN, 45; Wenner-Gren Found grant for anthrop res, 51.
Publications: Auth & illusr, Art of the Northwest Coast Indians, 50; ed, Winslow Homer in the Adirondacks, 59; auth & illusr, Visual files coding index, 60; auth, Accessioning and cataloguing, 65; co-auth, Early Chinese art and its possible influence in the Pacific Basin, 72.
Mailing Address: 210 Locust St, Philadelphia, PA 19106.

IOLAS, ALEXANDRE
Art Dealer
Positions: Owner & dir, Alexandre Iolas Gallery.
Mailing Address: 15 E 55th St, New York, NY 10022.

IPPOLITO, ANGELO
Painter, Educator
Preferred Media: Oils.
b S Arsenio, Italy, Nov 9, 22; U S citizen.
Study & Training: Ozenfant Sch Fine Arts, New York; Brooklyn Mus Art Sch, with John Ferren; Meschini Inst, Rome, Italy; also with Afro, Rome.

Work in Public Collections: Whitney Mus Am Art, New York, N Y; Munson-Williams-Proctor Inst, Utica, N Y; Phillips Gallery, Washington, D C; Norfolk Mus Arts & Sci, Va; Milwaukee Mus, Wis.
Commissions: Mural (oil painting), comn by Singer & Sons, now in collection of Montreal Trust Co, P Q, 67.
Exhibitions: Carnegie Int, Carnegie Inst, Pittsburgh, Pa, 56-59; Young America, Whitney Mus Am Art, 57; Abstract Impressionism, Arts Coun, London, Eng, 58; São Paulo Bieñal, Brazil, 61; American Collages, Mus Mod Art, New York & Beuningen Mus, Rotterdam, 66.
Teaching: Instr painting, Cooper Union, 56-66; artist-in-residence, Mich State Univ, 66-71; assoc prof painting, State Univ N Y Binghamton, 71-
Awards: Fulbright fel to Florence, Italy, 58; Ford Found artist-in-residence to Arnot Gallery, 65.
Bibliography: Dore Ashton (auth), Arte Americana contemporanea, Commentari, Lionello Venturi Rome, 55; Irving Sandler (auth), Angelo Ippolito Landscapes, Provincetown Advocate, 7/4/57; Alfred Frankenstein (auth), Professors tell a story at Bolles, San Francisco Chronicle, 10/1/61.
Publications: Contribr, Italy rediscovered (catalog), Munson-Williams-Proctor Inst, 55; contribr, It Is, spring 58; contribr, Nature in abstraction, Whitney Mus.
Dealer: Grace Borgenicht Gallery, 1018 Madison Ave, New York, NY 10021.
Mailing Address: Friendsville Stage, Binghamton, NY 13903.

IRELAND, RICHARD WILSON (DICK)
Painter, Instructor
b Marion, Ind, Mar 31, 25.
Study & Training: Ind Univ, BA & MA; Art Stud League New York.
Work in Public Collections: Mus Mod Art, New York, N Y.
Exhibitions: John Herron Art Inst, 48, 51 & 53; Ind Printmakers, 52; one-man show, Ind Univ, 52; Mus Mod Art, New York, 56; Baltimore Mus Art, Md; plus others.
Teaching: Instr fine arts, Md Inst Art, at present, former dean, Exten Div.
Mailing Address: Maryland Institute, College of Art, 1300 Mt Royal Ave, Baltimore, MD 21217.

IRIZARRY, CARLOS
Painter, Printmaker
Preferred Media: Mixed Media.
b Santa Isabel, P R, Aug 26, 38.
Study & Training: Sch Art & Design, New York, N Y.
Work in Public Collections: Mus Mod Art, New York, N Y; Ponce Mus, P R; Inst P R Culture, San Juan, P R; Assoc Am Artists, New York; also in collection of Harry N Abrams, New York.
Exhibitions: Artists as Adversary, Mus Mod Art, New York, 71; Int Exhib Prints, Tokyo, Japan & Yugoslavia, 70, Cracow, Poland & Norway, 72; Drawings, Int Riejka, Yugoslavia, 72.
Awards: Hon mention, Primera Bienal de Grabado Latino Americano, San Juan, 70; prize, Print Biennale, Vienna, Austria.
Dealers: Harry N Abrams Editions, 110 E 59th St, New York, NY 10022; Galeria Colibri, San Juan, PR 00901.
Mailing Address: 208 Cristo St, San Juan, PR 00901.

IRVIN, MARY FRANCIS, S C
Painter, Educator
b Canton, Ohio, Oct 4, 14.
Study & Training: Seton Hill Col; Carnegie-Mellon Univ, BFA; Art Inst Chicago; Cranbrook Acad Art, MFA.
Work in Public Collections: Carnegie Inst; St Charles Borromeo Church, Twin Rocks, Pa; Peabody, Cent Catholic & Elizabeth Seton High Schs, Pittsburgh, Pa.
Exhibitions: Libr Cong, Washington, D C, 44; Greensburg Art Club, 44-64; Relig Art Ctr Am, 60; Westmoreland Co Mus Art, 64; Pittsburgh Nat Bk, 64; plus others.
Teaching: Prof art & dir develop, Seton Hill Col, 65-72.
Positions: Mem bd, Relig Art Ctr Am.
Awards: Assoc Artists Pittsburgh; four awards, Greensburg Art Asn.
Memberships: Assoc Artists Pittsburgh; Greensburg Art Club; Col Art Asn Am; Cath Art Asn; Pa Art Educ Asn; plus others.
Mailing Address: Seton Hill College, Greensburg, PA 15601.

IRVIN, REA
Painter
b San Francisco, Calif, Aug 26, 81.
Study & Training: Hopkins Art Inst, San Francisco.
Work in Public Collections: Mus of City of New York; Annapolis; Booth Libr, Newtown, Conn.
Positions: Former artist & art ed, New Yorker.
Mailing Address: 1031 St Croix, Frederiksted, VI 00840.

IRWIN, GEORGE M
Patron, Collector
b Quincy, Ill, May 2, 21.
Study & Training: Univ Mich, BA, 43.
Positions: Chmn bd, Assoc Coun Arts, 62-; chmn bd, 63-71 & mem, Ill Arts Coun; mem, Am Fedn Arts Nat Exhib Comt; mem bd, Ill State Mus; mem bd, Mus Contemp Art; Chicago, Ill.
Memberships: Am Craftsmen Coun; Am Fedn Arts; Am Film Inst; Am Symphony Orchestra League; Mus Mod Art, New York; plus others.
Collection: Primarily twentieth century American artists, with interest in German expressionists and oceanic carvings and crafts.
Mailing Address: 428 Maine St, Quincy, IL 62031.

IRWIN, JOHN N, II
Collector
b Keokuk, Iowa, Dec 31, 13.
Study & Training: Princeton Univ, 37; Balliol Col, Oxford Univ, BA, 39, MA, 44; Fordham Univ, LLB, 41; Parsons Col, hon LLD, 60, Union Col, 63.
Positions: Trustee, John S Guggenheim Mem Found; trustee, Metrop Mus Art.
Mailing Address: 2510 Virginia Ave N W, Washington, DC 20037.

IRWIN, ROBERT
Painter
b Long Beach, Calif, 28.
Study & Training: Otis Art Inst, 48-50; Jepson Art Inst, Los Angeles 51; Chouinard's Art Inst, Los Angeles, 51-53.
Work in Public Collections: Mus Mod Art, New York, N Y; Los Angeles Co Mus Art, Calif; Whitney Mus Am Art, New York, N Y; Walker Art Ctr, Minneapolis, Minn; Albright-Knox Art Gallery, Buffalo, N Y.
Exhibitions: Los Angeles Co Mus Art, 67; one-man show, Jewish Mus, New York, 68; Vancouver Art Ctr, B C, 68; Stedelijk Mus, Amsterdam, Holland, 70; Fogg Mus, Harvard Univ, Cambridge, Mass, 72.
Teaching: Chouinard Art Inst, 57-58; Univ Calif, Los Angeles, 62; Univ Calif, Irvine, 68-69.
Bibliography: Jan Butterfield (auth), article, In: Arts Mag.
Mailing Address: 13327 Beach Ave, Venice, CA 90291.

ISAACS, AVROM
Art Dealer, Art Administrator
b Winnipeg, Can, 26.
Study & Training: Univ Toronto, BA (polit sci & econ).
Positions: Dir & owner, Isaacs Gallery, 56-; owner, Innuit Gallery, 70-; assoc fel, Calumet Col, York Univ, 70-
Specialty of Gallery: (Isaacs Gallery) Contemporary Canadian art; (Innuit Gallery) art of the Eskimo.
Mailing Address: 832 Yonge St, Toronto 285, Ont, Can.

ISELIN, LEWIS
Sculptor
Preferred Media: Bronze.
b New Rochelle, N Y, June 22, 13.
Study & Training: Art Stud League New York, 34-38, with Mahonri Young, John Stuart, Curry, George Bridgman & Gleb Derujunshy.
Work in Public Collections: Columbus Gallery Fine Arts, Ohio; Fogg Art Mus, Cambridge, Mass; Colby Col Mus, Waterville, Maine; Yale Univ, New Haven, Conn.
Commissions: Sculpture, U S Mil Cemetery, Suresnes, France, 50; portraits of John Wanamaker & Marshall Field, Merchandise Mart, 54; figure of Gen Nathaniel Greene, City of Philadelphia, 60; figure of St Vincent de Paul, Vincent Astor Found, 65; sculpture mural, Midland Mutual Life Ins, 71.
Exhibitions: Metrop Mus Art, 45; Pa Acad Fine Arts, 40-60; Whitney Mus Am Art, 40-60.
Awards: Helen Foster Badnet Prize, Nat Acad Design, 38; Guggenheim fel, 52.
Dealer: Larcada Gallery, 23 E 67th St, New York, NY 10021.
Mailing Address: Belfast Rd, Camden, ME 04843.

ISEN, HAROLD BERNARD
Sculptor, Printmaker
Preferred Media: Bronze, Polyester Resins, Fiberglass, Clay.
b Washington, D C, Dec 8, 40.
Study & Training: Am Univ, BA, 62; Pratt Inst, MFA, 64.
Work in Public Collections: Libr Cong, Washington, D C; Nat Collection Fine Arts, Washington, D C; Nat Libr Med, Bethesda, Md; San Francisco Mus Art, Calif; Corcoran Gallery Art, Washington, D C.
Commissions: Acrobats resinated bronze outdoor sculpture, Bucher-Myers, Baltimore, Md, 70; Daedalus aluminum-leafed polyester resin bas-relief, Montgomery Ctr Bldg, Bucher-Myers, Silver Spring, Md, 71.

Exhibitions: Self-Portraits, Smithsonian Inst Traveling Exhib, 65; Soc Graphic Artists Print Nat, Allied Artists Am Gallery, New York, N Y, 65; Bucknell Second Ann Drawing Nat, Bucknell Univ, 66; one-man show, Corcoran Gallery Art, 67; 5th Ann Exhib Artists, Baltimore Mus Art, 71.

Teaching: Instr drawing & design, Corcoran Sch Art, Washington, D C, 64-66; asst prof printmaking & drawing, Univ Md, College Park, 66-

Awards: Soc Washington Printmakers Purchase Award, Smithsonian Inst, 68; creative & performing arts award, Univ Md, 70; anonymous donor's award for sculpture, Baltimore Mus Art, 71.

Bibliography: Artists Equity (auth), Washington artists today, Acropolis Press, Washington, D C, 67; Ed Brohel (auth), The prints of Harold Isen (TV series), WNTC TV, New York, N Y, 12/3 & 5/68.

Memberships: Soc Washington Printmakers; Artists Equity Asn.

Publications: Illusr, Spellbinders in suspense, 67; illusr, Potomac Mag, Washington Post, 68-72; illusr, Physical movement for the theater, Richards-Rosen, 71.

Mailing Address: 11400 Monticello Ave, Silver Spring, MD 20902.

ISENBURGER, ERIC
Painter
Preferred Media: Oils.
b Frankfurt am Main, Ger, May 17, 02; U S citizen.
Study & Training: Frankfurt Art Sch.
Work in Public Collections: Mus Mod Art, New York, N Y; Corcoran Gallery Art, Washington, D C; Pa Acad Fine Arts, Philadelphia, Pa; M H De Young Mem Mus, San Francisco, Calif; John Herron Art Inst, Indianapolis, Ind.
Exhibitions: Art of Today, 1951, Metrop Mus Art, New York; Pa Acad Fine Arts, Philadelphia; Art Inst Chicago, Ill; Carnegie Inst, Pittsburgh, Pa; eight one-man shows, Knoedler's, New York.
Teaching: Instr painting, Nat Acad Sch Fine Arts, 59-
Awards: Third prize, Carnegie Inst, 47; first prize & gold medal, Corcoran Gallery Art, 49; Edwin Palmer Mem Prize, Nat Acad Design, 57 & 70.
Memberships: Academician Nat Acad Design; Audubon Artists.
Publications: Auth, article, In: Am Artist, 48.
Mailing Address: 140 E 56th St, New York, NY 10022.

ISHAM, SHEILA EATON
Painter
b New York, N Y, Dec 19, 27.
Study & Training: Bryn Mawr Col, BA(cum laude), 50; Hochschule Fiü Bildende Künste, Berlin, Ger, 50-54.
Work in Public Collections: Mus Mod Art, New York; Nat Collection Fine Arts, Washington, D C; Philadelphia Mus Art, Pa; Corcoran Gallery Art, Washington, D C; San Francisco Mus Art, Calif.
Exhibitions: One-man shows, Jefferson Place Gallery, 68-70 & French & Co Gallery, New York, 70; Washington Painting, Baltimore Mus Art, 70 & Hayden Gallery, Mass Inst Technol, 71; one-man show, Brockton Art Ctr, Mass, 72; Dorthea Speyer, Paris, 72; Fischbach Gallery, New York, 73.
Teaching: Instr art hist & graphics, Chinese Univ Hong Kong, 63-65.
Awards: Print award, Corcoran Gallery Art, 58; print award, Libr Cong, Pennell Comt, Wash Soc Printmakers, 60 & 61.
Bibliography: New images, Arts Mag, summer 70; Sidra Stich (auth), Five new Washington artsts, Art Int, 12/71; Edward Fry (auth), Sheila Islam (catalog), Brockton Art Ctr, 72.
Publications: Co-auth, I Ching (portfolio of 8 lithographs with poems).
Dealers: Fischbach Gallery, 29 W 57th St, New York, NY 10019; Jefferson Place Gallery, 2144 P St, Washington, DC 20037.
Mailing Address: 5126 Albermarle St, Washington, DC 20016.

ISHIKAWA, JOSEPH
Art Administrator, Lecturer
b Los Angeles, Calif, July 29, 19.
Study & Training: Univ Calif, Los Angeles, AB, 42; Univ Nebr.
Collections Arranged: Beloit & Vicinity Exhibition, annually, 62-; Nathan Cummings Collection of Ancient Peruvian Ceramics, 63; Figure in the 60's, 69; The Art Beyond, 69; The Black Experience, 70; Harvey Littleton: Glass, 71.
Positions: From asst cur to cur, Univ Nebr Art Galleries, 43-51; from cur to asst dir, Des Moines Art Ctr, 51-58; dir, Sioux City Art Ctr, 58-61; dir, Wright Art Ctr, Beloit Col, 61-
Awards: Scandinavian Sem, Am Asn Mus & Fulbright, 65; Beloit Col & Ford Found Humanities grant, 69.
Memberships: Int Coun Mus; Am Asn Mus; Midwest Mus Conf (v pres, 70), Wis Fedn Mus (chmn, 70-).
Research: Influence of Puvis de Chavannes on twentieth century painting.

Publications: Auth, The university as tastemaker, Palette, 58; auth, Puvis de Chavannes: moderne Malgre Lui, Art J, 68.
Mailing Address: Wright Art Center, Beloit College, Beloit, WI 53511.

ISSERSTEDT, DOROTHEA CARUS
Art Dealer, Art Historian
Study & Training: Univ Munich; Univ Freiburg, PhD(art hist); Wheaton Col.
Positions: Dir, Carus Gallery.
Research: Medieval art, mainly twelfth & thirteenth century sculpture.
Specialty of Gallery: Art of the German Expressionists & art of the twenties.
Mailing Address: 243 E 82nd St, New York, NY 10028.

ITCHKAWICH, DAVID MICHAEL
Printmaker
b Westerly, R I, Aug 18, 37.
Study & Training: R I Sch Design, BFA.
Work in Public Collections: John Sloane Study Collection, Univ Del; Charles Dana Mus, Colgate Univ.
Exhibitions: Nat Print Exhib, Brooklyn Mus, N Y, 70 & 72; one-man show, Horizon Gallery, New York, N Y, 71; two-man show, Michael Wyman Gallery, Chicago, Ill, 72.
Bibliography: The visions of David Itchkawich, Intellectual Digest, 2/72.
Dealer: Horizon Gallery, 45 Christopher St, New York, NY 10014.
Mailing Address: c/o Rogovin, Apt 4B, 1428 Lexington Ave, New York, NY 10028.

ITTLESON, HENRY, JR
Collector
b Saint Louis, Mo, Oct 25, 00.
Study & Training: Colgate Univ, 19-21; Univ Mich, 21-22.
Collection: French impressionists.
Mailing Address: Hotel Pierre, 2 E 61st St, New York, NY 10021.

IVES, GLEN PALMER
Museum Director
b Saint Charles, Ill, Aug 9, 33.
Study & Training: Northern Ill Univ, BS Educ & MS Educ.
Positions: Dir, Evansville Mus Arts & Sci, 72-
Memberships: Am Asn Mus; Southeastern Mus Conf; Midwest Mus Conf.
Mailing Address: Evansville Museum of Arts & Science, 411 S E Riverside Dr, Evansville, IN 47713.

IVEY, JAMES BURNETT
Cartoonist, Collector
Preferred Media: Ink.
b Chattanooga, Tenn, Apr 19, 25.
Study & Training: Univ Louisville; George Washington Univ; Nat Art Sch.
Work in Public Collections: Libr Cong, Washington, D C; Syracuse Univ, N Y; Albert T Reid Collection, Univ Kans, Lawrence; Mo State Hist Soc; State Hist Soc Wis, Madison.
Collections Arranged: Cartoons from Gillray to Goldberg, San Francisco Mus Art, 62; The Cartoon Museum, Madeira Beach, Fla, 67-68; Cartoon from Hogarth to Herblock, Lock Haven Art Ctr, Orlando, Fla, 71.
Positions: Political cartoonist, Washington (D C) Star, 50-53, St Petersburg Times, 53-59, San Francisco Examiner, 59-66, Orlando Sentinel, 67-; cur & dir, Cartoon Mus, Madeira Beach, Fla, 67-68; ed & publ, Cartoon, 71-
Awards: Reid Found fel, 59.
Bibliography: John Chase (auth), Today's cartoon, Haiser Press, 63; Dorothy MacGreal (auth), World of comic art, 66.
Memberships: Nat Cartoonist Soc (Chmn, Fla Chap, 72-); Asn Am Ed Cartoonists.
Collection: Original cartoon art, approximately 2000 cartoons representing entire history of the art in twenty countries.
Publications: Contribr, Freedom & union: European cartoonists, 61; contribr, Freedom & union: U S and European cartoon compared, 62; contribr, Cartoonist profiles, 70; contribr, Cartoon: pen mightier than suit, 71.
Mailing Address: 561 Obispo Ave, Orlando, FL 32807.

IVY, GREGORY DOWLER
Educator, Painter
b Clarksburg, Mo, May 7, 04.
Study & Training: Cent Mo State Col, BS; Saint Louis Sch Fine Arts, Wash Univ; Columbia Univ, MA; New York Univ.
Exhibitions: Art Inst Chicago; Brooklyn Mus, N Y; Metrop Mus Art, New York, N Y; High Mus Art, Atlanta, Ga; Mint Mus Art, Charlotte, N C; plus others.

Teaching: Instr art, State Teachers Col, Indiana, Pa, 32-35; prof art & head dept, Woman's Col, Univ N C, Greensboro, 35-61, dir, Burnsville Sch Fine Arts, 52-53; dir, summer session fine arts, Beaufort, N C, 54; chmn dept art, Calif State Univ, Fullerton, 65-67, prof, 65-

Positions: Bd dirs & exec comt, N C Mus Art, 56-58; mem policy comt, Col Art Asn, 56-58; v pres, Southeastern Col Artists Conf, 57-58; mem policy comt, Nat Art Educ Asn, 57-59; mem exec comt, Assoc Artists N C, 59-60; bd mem, N C State Artists Soc, 60-62.

Publications: Auth & illusr, An approach to design (monogr).

Mailing Address: Dept of Art, California State University, 800 N State College Blvd, Fullerton, CA 92634.

IZACYRO (ISAAC JIRO MATSUOKA)
Painter
b Honolulu, Hawaii, Mar 17, 30.
Study & Training: Baker Univ; Univ Hawaii, BFA; Art Stud League New York; hon DFA, Saint Olav's, Malmo, Sweden, 69.
Work in Public Collections: Saint Paul Art Ctr Mus, Minn; Galerie Int, New York, N Y; Duncan Gallery, New York.
Exhibitions: Gima's Art Gallery, Honolulu, 53-63; Drawings U S A, Saint Paul, 63; Galerie Int, New York, 64-69; Am Artists, Salon de Prix Paris, 71; two-man show, East-West Art Cult Ctr, 68.
Awards: Award for Ink-Painting, Artists of Hawaii, 60; cert merit, Int Biog, Eng, 68.
Dealer: Galerie Internationale, 1095 Madison Ave, New York, NY 10028.
Mailing Address: 1111 14th Ave, Honolulu, HI 96816.

J

JACHMANN, KURT M
Collector
Collection: Pre-Columbian and Oceanic art; French abstract-expressionist; calligraphic paintings; German expressionists.
Mailing Address: 215 E 68th St, New York, NY 10021.

JACKOVICH, ANTHONY
Painter
Preferred Media: Oils, Watercolors.
b Cummings, Iowa, Dec 6, 23.
Study & Training: Art Stud League New York, 46-47, with Reginald Marsh; Chicago Art Inst, 47-48; Ecole Superieur Nat Beaux Arts, Paris, France, 49-50; Acad Julian, Paris, 50-51; Acad Grande Chaumière, 51-53.
Exhibitions: Am Watercolor Soc, 71; Nat Acad Design, 72.
Dealer: Round Pond Art Gallery, Round Pond, ME 04564.
Mailing Address: Round Pond, ME 04564.

JACKSON, A B
Educator, Painter
b New Haven, Conn, Apr 18, 25.
Study & Training: Yale Norfolk summer fel, 52, with Josef Albers, Nicholas Marsicano & Gabor Peterdi; Yale Univ Sch Art & Archit, BFA, 53, MFA, 55.
Work in Public Collections: Yale Univ, New Haven, Conn; Dartmouth Col, Hanover, N H; Univ Mass, Amherst, Mint Mus, Charlotte, N C; Chrysler Mus, Norfolk, Va.
Exhibitions: Int Figure Painting Invitational Traveling Show, 69-70; Smithsonian American Drawing Traveling Show, 69-72; Black Artists in Review (Invitational), Cleveland State Univ, 72; Va Mus Traveling Exhibs.
Teaching: Instr art, Southern Univ, 55-56; asst prof art, Norfolk State Col, 56-67, prof art, Old Dominion Univ, 67-
Positions: Artist-in-residence, Living Arts Ctr, Dayton, Ohio, summer, 69; artist-in-residence, Dartmouth Col, spring 71; vis artist, Humanities Ctr, Richmond, Va, 71; vis artist, Roanoke Fine Arts Ctr, Va, spring 72.
Awards: Purchase award, Va Biennial, Va Mus Fine Arts, 64; purchase award, Graphics Ann, Mint Mus, Charlotte, 67; purchase award, Am Drawing Exhib, Chrysler Mus, Norfolk, 71.
Bibliography: Sidney Hurwitz (auth), A B Jackson: his porch people, Am Artist, 2/68.
Publications: Illusr several issues of Red Clay Reader, 65-70; illusr, Randolph Bourne, legend & reality, 66.
Dealer: Eric Schindler Gallery, Broad St, Richmond, VA 23233.
Mailing Address: Dept of Art, Old Dominion University, Norfolk, VA 23508.

JACKSON, ALEXANDER YOUNG
Painter
b Montreal, P Q, Oct 3, 82.
Study & Training: Monument Nat, Montreal; Art Inst Chicago; Acad Julian, Paris, with J P Laurens; Queen's Univ, LLD.
Work in Public Collections: Tate Gallery, London, Eng; Nat Gallery Can; Wellington Gallery, New Zealand; Art Gallery Toronto; Vancouver Art Museum, B C; also in McMichael Can Collection; plus others.
Commissions: Official war artist with Can Army in France, 17-18.
Exhibitions: Can War Mem, 23 & 24; West Coast Exhib, Nat Gallery Can, 27; Paris, 27; Group of Seven Exhibs, 36; Coronation, 37; Tate Gallery, 38; plus many others.
Awards: Companion, Order of St Michael & St George; Companion, Order of Can.
Memberships: Royal Can Acad Art; Can Group Painters; Group of Seven (original); Ont Soc Artists; Arts & Letters Club Toronto.
Publications: Auth & illusr, The Far north, 28, Banting as an artist, 43 & A painter's country, 58; contribr, Can Art Mag.
Mailing Address: Kleinburg, Ont, Can.

JACKSON, BEATRICE (BEATRICE JACKSON HUMPHREYS)
Painter
Preferred Media: Oils.
b London, Eng, Dec 25, 05; U S citizen.
Study & Training: Art Stud League New York; Grand Cent Art Sch, 26; Smith Col, 27; Colorossi Acad, Paris, France, 28; also with Wayman Adams, George Elmer Browne & Andre L'Hote.
Work in Public Collections: Southern Vt Art Ctr, Manchester.
Exhibitions: Paris Salon des Artistes Francais, Salon d'Automne, 28-39; Nat Acad Design, New York, N Y, 41, 55 & 64; Conn Acad Fine Arts, Hartford, 54-59 & 62; Art U S A, 58; Audubon Artists, New York, 62-71.
Awards: Bronze medal of honor, Allied Artists Am, 55; Conn Acad Fine Arts, 56; Nat Asn Women Artists, 70.
Memberships: Audubon Artists (rec secy, 70-73); Allied Artists Am; Nat Asn Women Artists (exec bd); Conn Acad Fine Arts; Royal Soc Arts, London.
Dealer: Grand Central Art Galleries, Hotel Biltmore, Madison Ave & 43rd St, New York, NY 10017.
Mailing Address: 450 E 63rd St, New York, NY 10021.

JACKSON, BILLY MORROW
Painter
b Kansas City, Mo, Feb 23, 26.
Study & Training: Wash Univ, BFA; Univ Ill, Urbana, MFA.
Work in Public Collections: Metrop Mus Art, New York, N Y; Calif Palace Legion of Honor, San Francisco, Calif; Springfield Mus Art, Mo; Butler Inst Am Art, Youngstown, Ohio; Evansville Mus Art, Ind; plus many others.
Exhibitions: McClung Mus, Univ Tenn, 65 & 66, two-man show, 67; Fine Arts Gallery San Diego, Calif, 66; Lehigh Univ, Bethlehem, Pa, 66; Decatur Art Ctr, Ill, 66; 4 Arts Gallery, Evanston, Ill, 67; plus many other group & one-man shows.
Teaching: Prof art, Univ Ill, Urbana, at present.
Awards: Purchase prize, Evansville Mus Arts & Sci, 66; Butler Inst Am Art, 66; Union League Club, Chicago, 67; plus many others.
Memberships: Soc Am Grahic Artists; Boston Printmakers; Philadelphia Watercolor Soc.
Dealer: Jane Haslem Gallery, 1669 Wisconsin Ave, N W, Washington, DC 20007.
Mailing Address: Dept of Art, University of Illinois, Urbana, IL 61801.

JACKSON, EVERETT GEE
Painter, Illustrator
Preferred Media: Oils.
b Mexia, Tex, Oct 8, 00.
Study & Training: Tex A&M Univ; Art Inst Chicago; San Diego State Col, BA; Univ Southern Calif, MA; also study in Mex.
Work in Public Collections: Houston Mus Art, Tex; Fine Arts Gallery, San Diego, Calif; Los Angeles Co Mus Art, Calif; Pa Acad Fine Arts, Philadelphia.
Exhibitions: Exhib Am Painting, Art Inst Chicago, Ill, 27; Whitney Mus Am Art, New York, N Y; Pa Acad Fine Arts, Philadelphia; Los Angeles Co Mus Art; San Francisco Mus Art, Calif; plus others.
Teaching: Prof art, Calif State Univ, San Diego, 30-63; prof art, Univ Costa Rica, 62.
Positions: Bd trustees, Fine Arts Soc, San Diego, 35-, chmn Latin-Am Arts Comt, 65-70, acquisitions comt; mem adv bd, Calif State Univ, San Diego, 63-70.
Awards: First Anne Bremer Prize, San Francisco Art Asn, 29; first prize, 30 & Leisser Farnham Prize, 30, Fine Arts Gallery, San Diego; award, Los Angeles Co Mus Art, 34.

Memberships: San Diego Art Guild; Am Asn Univ Prof.
Research: Maya sculpture.
Publications: Illusr, Wonderful adventure of Paul Bunyon, The ugly
    duckling, Popol Vuh, Ramona & American Indian legends, Limited
    Ed Club & Heritage.
Mailing Address: 1234 Franciscan Way, San Diego, CA 92116.

JACKSON, HARLAN CHRISTOPHER
    Painter
Preferred Media: Acrylics.
b Cleburne, Tex, Apr 21, 18.
Study & Training: Kans State Teachers Col, 38; Calif Sch Fine Arts,
    45-48, Abraham Rosenberg traveling fel, 48; Hans Hoffman Sch
    Fine Arts, 51.
Work in Public Collections: IBM Collection; Guild Hall Collection;
    Howard Univ Collection; Southampton Col Collection.
Exhibitions: Calif Palace Legion of Hon, San Francisco, Calif, 48;
    San Francisco Mus, 48; Int Expos, Palais des Beaux, Port-au-
    Prince, Haiti, 50; Cincinnati Art Mus Int Biennial, 54; Howard
    Univ Col Art, Washington, D C, 70.
Positions: Art dir, Boys Harbor, Inc, East Hampton, N Y, 54-60.
Mailing Address: 129 Neck Path, East Hampton, NY 11937.

JACKSON, HARRY ANDREW
    Painter, Sculptor
Preferred Media: Oils, Bronze.
b Chicago, Ill, Apr 18, 24.
Study & Training: Chicago Art Inst, 31-38; with Ed Grigware, Cody,
    Wyo, 38-42; Brooklyn Mus Art Sch, with Hans Hofmann, 46-48;
    Fulbright & Ital Govt grants, 57.
Work in Public Collections: Whitney Gallery Western Art, Cody;
    Amon Carter Mus, Fort Worth, Tex; Fort Pitt Mus, Pittsburgh,
    Pa; Woolarac Mus, Bartlesville, Okla; Am Mus Gt Brit, Bath,
    Eng.
Commissions: Oil murals, Stampede, 60 & Range Burial, 66, Whitney
    Gallery Western Art; Sor Capanna (monument), Piazza dei Mer-
    canti, Rome, 62; painted sculpture of John Wayne (for cover),
    Time Mag, 8/8/69; Mem Bronze of Adm Lord Cochrane, comn by
    Douglas Cochrane, Plaza Cochrane, Valdivia, Chile, 70; River,
    Road and Point (mosaics, bronzes & mural), Fort Pitt Mus, Pitts-
    burgh, Pa (almost completed).
Exhibitions: Tate Gallery, London, Eng, 45; Nat Collection Fine
    Arts, Washington, D C, 64; Nat Acad Design, New York, N Y, 64
    & 68; XVII Nostra Int Arte, Premio Fiorino, Florence, Italy, 66;
    Nat Cowboy Hall of Fame, Oklahoma City, Okla, 66.
Positions: Off combat artist, USMC, 44-45.
Awards: Interstate gold medal, Pennational Artists Ann, 67; Samuel
    Finley Breese Morse Gold Medal, Nat Acad Design, 68; silver
    medal, Nat Cowboy Hall of Fame, 71.
Bibliography: D Seiberling (auth), Painter striving to find himself,
    Life Mag, 56; D G Lowe (auth), Death on the range, Am Heritage,
    67; J McGuire (auth), Harry Jackson a man and his art, Barbre
    Prod, 72.
Memberships: USMC Combat Corresp Asn; Nat Sculpture Soc; Cow-
    boy Artists Am; fel Am Artists Prof League.
Publications: Contribr, monograph catalogue, Kennedy Galleries,
    69; auth, Lost wax bronze casting, Northland Press, 72.
Dealer: Kennedy Galleries, 20 E 56th St, New York, NY 10022.
Mailing Address: Lost Cabin, Lysite, WY 82642.

JACKSON, HAZEL BRILL
    Sculptor
b Philadelphia, Pa.
Study & Training: Boston Mus Fine Arts; Scuola Rosatti, Florence,
    Italy; also with Angelo Zanelli, Rome, Italy & with Bela Pratt &
    Charles Grafly.
Work in Public Collections: Concord Art Mus; Wellesley Col; Vas-
    sar Col; Dartmouth Col; Calgary, Mus, Can.
Exhibitions: Nat Acad Design; Nat Acad Rome; Nat Acad, Firenze,
    Italy; one-man shows, Boston Guild Artists & Corcoran Gallery
    Art, Washington, D C.
Art Interests: Animal sculpture, especially horses and dogs.
Mailing Address: Twin Oaks, Old Balmville Rd, Newburgh, NY 12550.

JACKSON, HERB
    Painter, Educator
Preferred Media: Acrylics, Graphics.
b Raleigh, N C, Aug 16, 45.
Study & Training: Davidson Col, BA; Phillips Univ, Marburg, W Ger;
    Univ N C, MFA.
Work in Public Collections: Calif Palace of Legion of Honor, San
    Francisco, Calif; Libr Cong, Washington, D C; Philadelphia Mus
    Art, Pa; Smithsonian Inst, Washington, D C; Whitney Mus Am Art,
    New York, N Y.

Exhibitions: N C Artists Exhib, N C Mus Art, Raleigh, 62 & 69-71;
    Piedmont Graphics Exhib, Mint Mus, Charlotte, N C, 68 & 70-71;
    Artists of the Southeast & Tex, Isaac Delgado Mus, New Orleans,
    La, 71; Western Ill Univ Drawing & Print Show, 72; Drawings
    U S A, Minn Mus Art.
Teaching: Asst prof studio art, Davidson Col, 69-
Memberships: Col Art Asn Am; Southeastern Col Art Conf.
Dealer: Lakeside Studio, 150 S Lakeshore Rd, Lakeside, MI 49116.
Mailing Address: Box 2495, Davidson, NC 28036.

JACKSON, LEE
    Painter
Preferred Media: Oils.
b New York, N Y, Feb 2, 09.
Study & Training: N Y Univ, one yr; Art Stud League New York; also
    with John Sloan & George Luks.
Work in Public Collections: Metrop Mus Art, New York; Corcoran
    Gallery Art, Washington, D C; Walker Art Ctr, Minneapolis,
    Minn; Nebr Art Asn, Lincoln; Los Angeles Co Mus Art, Calif.
Exhibitions: 56th Ann Paintings, Art Inst Chicago, 46; Whitney Mus
    Am Art, New York, 49-50; Am Painting Today 1950, Metrop Mus
    Am, 50; 23rd Biennial, Corcoran Gallery Art, 53; 140th Ann, Nat
    Acad Design, New York, 65.
Teaching: Instr painting & drawing, Sch Art Studies, 47-48; instr
    painting & drawing, City Col New York, 48-54.
Awards: Guggenheim fel, 41; Univ Nebr Art Gallery purchase prize,
    43; Thomas B Clarke prize, Nat Acad Design, 51.
Memberships: Art Stud League New York; Audubon Artists Am (dir,
    chmn ways & means); Am Watercolor Soc; Artists Equity Asn;
    Nat Soc Painters in Casein.
Publications: Contribr, Drawings by American artists, 47; contribr,
    Am Artist Mag, 9/53.
Mailing Address: Strong's Lane, Water Mill, NY 11976.

JACKSON, NIGEL LORING
    Painter, Art Administrator
Preferred Media: Oils.
b Kingston, Jamaica, W I, Jan 23, 40.
Study & Training: Manhattan Community Col; New Sch Social Res,
    New York, N Y; Art Stud League New York, three yr scholar, 71.
Work in Public Collections: New York Harlem Music Ctr; Ministe-
    rial Interfaith Asn, New York; also in collections of Jack Royce,
    New York & Hon & Mrs Bruce Wright.
Commissions: Sounds, New York Harlem Music Ctr, 72.
Exhibitions: Art in Black America, Interracial Coun Bus Opportu-
    nity, New York, 70; New York Int Art Show, 70; Black Art Festi-
    val, Riverside Church, New York, 70; Rebuttal to Whitney Mus
    Exhib, 71 & one-man show, Acts of Art, Inc, New York, 72.
Positions: Pres & art dir, Acts of Art, Inc, 69-
Awards: Silver award, New York Int Art Show, 70.
Bibliography: Oakley N Holmes Jr (auth), Black artists in America-
    part II (film), 71; John Canaday (auth), Black artists on view in 2
    exhibitions, 4/7/71 & David Shirrey (auth), Gallery in the village
    seeks to inspire black artists, 2/5/72, New York Times.
Memberships: Art Stud League New York.
Mailing Address: c/o Acts of Art, Inc, 15 Charles St, New York, NY
    10014.

JACKSON, SUZANNE (FITZALLEN)
    Painter, Writer
Preferred Media: Acrylics.
b Saint Louis, Mo, Jan 30, 44.
Study & Training: San Francisco State Col, BA; Otis Art Inst, Los
    Angeles, with Charles White.
Work in Public Collections: Joseph Hirshhorn Collection, Palm
    Springs Desert Mus, Calif; Mafundi Inst, Watts, Calif; DMJM Co,
    Los Angeles, Calif.
Exhibitions: Joseph Hirshhorn Collection, Palm Springs Desert Mus,
    70; Two Generations of Black Artists, Calif State Col, Los Ange-
    les, 70; Black Untitled II/Dimensions of the Figure, Oakland Mus,
    Calif, 71; U S A? 1971-1972, Carnegie Inst, Pittsburgh, Pa, 71-
    72; Black Expo' 72 Nat, San Francisco, Calif, 72.
Collections Arranged: Coordr art exhibs & ed catalogue, Nat, Afri-
    can, Children's, Hist & Calif Art Exhibs for San Francisco Bay
    Area Black Expo' 72.
Teaching: Art instr, St Stephens Sch, San Francisco, 65-66; dance
    & crafts instr, Watts Towers Art Ctr, 70; lectr art, Stanford
    Univ, summer 72.
Positions: Owner-dir, Gallery 32, Los Angeles, 68-70; bd dirs, Los
    Angeles Black Arts Coun, 69-70; art exhibs coord, San Francisco
    Bay Area Black Expos 1972; mem, Mayor Alioto's Screening
    Comt for St Artists, San Francisco Art Comt, 72-74.
Awards: Int Latham Found Humane Kindness & World Peace scholar,
    61.
Bibliography: Samella Lewis (auth), African American artists,
    Harcourt-Brace, 72; Alfred Frankenstein (auth), Wide contrasts

in Black Expo' 72 Art Exhibition, San Francisco Chronicle, 9/72; Henry J Seldis (auth), Art walk, Los Angeles Times, 9/72.
Memberships: Nat Conf of Artists, Int Art Manifesto for the Defense of Political Prisons, San Franciso.
Art Interests: Organizing exhibitions of contemporary black artists, historical black artists, African art and black folk art of America, also documentation of exhibitions.
Publications: Contribr, Black artists on art, Vol 2, 71 & auth & illusr, What I love, 72, Contemp Crafts; contribr, Third world women's book, Pocho-Che Publ, 72; ed & contribr, Statements Mag, 72.
Dealer: Ankrum Gallery, 657 N La Cienega Blvd, Los Angeles, CA 90069.
Mailing Address: 132 Southwood Dr, San Francisco, CA 94112.

JACKSON, VAUGHN L
Painter, Illustrator
Preferred Media: Watercolors, Acrylics, Inks.
b Raymond, Ohio, Jan 7, 20.
Study & Training: Am Univ, AA, BA, 69; Corcoran Sch Art, with Richard Lahey, 47-50; Ohio State Univ, 42-43; Columbus Art Sch, 39-40; with Hans Hofmann, Provincetown, summer 55; also with Eliot O'Hara.
Work in Public Collections: Many in private collections.
Commissions: Over 900 design & illus in advert, tech & mil publ, displays, visual presentations for art studios, advert agencies, govt & com accts, including Gen Elec Supply Corp, Hotpoint, Allegheny Airlines, Hot Shoppes, Wilkins Coffee, Am Hosp Asn & others.
Exhibitions: Am Artists Prof League, 50-52 & 57; Washington Watercolor Club Ann Nat Exhibs, 54-58; Am Art League, 58; Soc Tech Writers & Publ Ann, 71; one-man show, Washington, D C, 56 & 58; plus others.
Positions: Advert artist, Kal, Ehrlich & Merrick Advert Agency, 47-52; artist-illusr, Opers Res Off, Johns Hopkins Univ, 52-55, asst art dir, 55-63, publ art dir, Res Anal Corp, 63-67, visual & graphics mgr, 67-72; visual & graphics mgr, Gen Res Corp, 72-.
Awards: Silver medal for best in ann show, Landscape Club Washington, D C, 55; award for outstanding achievement in tech commun, Soc Tech Writers & Publs, 71.
Memberships: Soc Tech Commun; Am Inst Graphic Arts; Art Dirs Club Metrop Washington (charter mem, bd dirs); Washington Watercolor Asn (bd mgrs, v pres).
Publications: Work in Ed & Publ, Printers Ink, Aviation Age, Electronics Mag, Agr Chemicals, point of sale & direct mail campaigns, Washington Post, Evening Star & other newspapers.
Mailing Address: Ten Penny Studio, P O Box 54, Fairfax Station, VA 22039.

JACKSON, VIRGIL V
Cartoonist, Illustrator
b Peoria, Ohio, Sept 17, 09.
Study & Training: Columbus Art Sch, scholarships.
Commissions: Murals, U S Govt, Marysville High Sch, Ohio; portrait comns in Ohio.
Exhibitions: Columbus Art Gallery.
Teaching: Instr drawing & cartooning, Columbus Art Sch.
Positions: Com artist & dir, Columbus Citizen & Washington Post; v pres & treas, Com Art Studios, Inc & Graphic Craftsmen, Inc, Washington, D C.
Memberships: Art Dir Club, Washington, D C; Advert Club, Washington, D C.
Publications: Contribr, cartoons & illus, Columbus Dispatch, Columbus Citizen, Nat Educ Asn, Signs of the Times, Ohio State J & Washington Post.
Mailing Address: 611 F St N W, Washington, DC 20004.

JACKSON, WARD
Painter, Editor
b Petersburg, Va, Sept 10, 28.
Study & Training: Richmond Prof Inst of Col William & Mary, BFA, MFA; Hans Hofmann Sch Fine Arts, scholar, 52.
Work in Public Collections: Nat Collection Fine Arts, Smithsonian Inst, Washington, D C; N Y Univ Art Collection, New York; Riverside Mus Collection, Rose Art Mus, Brandeis Univ, Waltham, Mass; Elvehjem Art Ctr, Univ Wis-Madison; Va Mus Fine Arts, Richmond.
Exhibitions: One-man shows, Fleischman Gallery, New York, 58-60, Univ Wis-Madison, 67; Va Mus Fine Arts, Richmond, 71 & Graham Gallery, New York, 72; three-man exhib, Atrium Gallery, Seattle, Wash, 65.
Teaching: Instr art hist, Rollins Col, Winter Park, Fla, 54-55.
Awards: Fel, Va Mus Fine Arts, 48 & 49; first prize for painting, New York City Ctr Gallery, 56.
Memberships: Col Art Asn Am; New Art Asn.
Publications: Co-ed, Folio, 49-51; auth, Art in glass (works of art

by Louis Comfort Tiffany), Rollins Col Lit Mag, 55; co-ed, Art now: New York, 69-72; auth, George L K Morris: forty years of abstract art, Art J, 72.
Dealer: Graham Gallery, 1014 Madison Ave, New York, NY 10021.
Mailing Address: 65 Rivington St, New York, NY 10002.

JACOBS, DAVID (THEODORE)
Sculptor, Educator
Preferred Media: Aluminum, Rubber, Sound.
b Niagara Falls, N Y, Mar 1, 32.
Study & Training: Orange Coast Col, AA; Los Angeles State Col, AB, MA.
Work in Public Collections: Guggenheim Mus, New York, N Y; Mus Art, Richmond, Va; Otterbein Col, Ohio; Hofstra Univ, New York; Assyrian Embassy, New York.
Exhibitions: The Art of Assemblage, Mus Mod Art, New York, 61; 68th Am Exhib, Art Inst Chicago, 66; Sound, Light, Silence, Art that performs, W R Nelson Gallery, Atkins Mus, Kansas City, Kans, 66; Options, Milwaukee Art Ctr, 68; Inflatable Sculpture, Jewish Mus, New York, 69; plus many one-man shows, 61-71.
Teaching: Assoc prof sculpture, Hofstra Univ, 62-; vis critic sculpture, Cornell Univ, New York Prog, 69 & 70.
Mailing Address: 51 Eighth Ave, Sea Cliff, NY 11579.

JACOBS, HAROLD
Painter, Sculptor
Preferred Media: Mixed Media, Multi-Media.
b New York, N Y, Oct 29, 32.
Study & Training: Cooper Union, 53; N Y Univ; New Sch Social Res; Sorbonne, Fulbright scholar, 61.
Work in Public Collections: Whitney Mus Am Art, New York; Portland Art Mus, Ore; Kalamazoo Art Ctr; McCory Corp.
Teaching: Assoc prof painting & chmn dept, Moore Col Art, 66-
Dealer: Gimpel & Weitzenhoffer, 1040 Madison, New York, NY 10021.
Mailing Address: 1628 Pine St, Philadelphia, PA 19103.

JACOBS, TED SETH
Painter
Preferred Media: Oils.
b Newark, N J, June 11, 27.
Study & Training: Art Stud League New York, 43-47.
Work in Public Collections: Mus Mod Art, New York, N Y; Finch Col Mus, New York.
Commissions: Portraits in oil, Dr Theodor Reik, 62, Jane Fonda, 64 & Mrs Mary Ellen Fahs, 71; portrait drawing, Thomas Hoving, 66; plus over two hundred portrait commissions & many murals.
Exhibitions: One-man shows, St Vincents Col, Latrobe, Pa, 65, Drawing Exhib, The Drawing Shop, New York, 65 & 66, paintings, Noah Goldowsky Galleries, New York, 66 & Drawing Exhib, Adelson Galleries, Boston, Mass, 67 & 68; Reyn Galleries, New York, 72.
Awards: Bridgeman prize, Art Stud League New York, 44; first prize, John F & Anna Lee Stacey Award, 52.
Dealer: Reyn Galleries, 64th St & Madison Ave, New York, NY 10021.
Mailing Address: 523 E 83rd St, New York, NY 10028.

JACOBS, WILLIAM KETCHUM, JR
Collector
b Brooklyn, N Y, Mar 17, 08.
Collection: Late nineteenth and twentieth century paintings.
Mailing Address: 895 Park Ave, New York, NY 10021.

JACOBSEN, RAY (EUGENE)
Painter
Preferred Media: Oils.
b Englewood, Colo, Jan 19, 38.
Work in Public Collections: Southern Calif Carton Co, Los Angeles.
Exhibitions: Northern Calif Arts Ann, 67; Winter Ann, Richmond Art Ctr, 67; San Francisco Art Festival, 67-69; Cabrillo Col Gallery, 69; Chabot Col, 71.
Collections Arranged: John Bolles Gallery, 67 & 69; Crocker Gallery, 69; Emerson Gallery, Encino, Calif, 70.
Awards: First prize, painting, Northern Calif Arts Ann, 67; second prize, painting, Artrium, Santa Rosa, Calif, 67; hon mention, painting, San Francisco Arts Festival, 68.
Memberships: Richmond Art Ctr; Oakland Art Asn; Artrium.
Dealer: Vorpal Gallery, 1168 Battery St, San Francisco, CA 94111.
Mailing Address: 17323 Hillside Ave, Sonoma, CA 95476.

JACOBSON, ARTHUR ROBERT
Painter, Printmaker
Preferred Media: Oils.
b Chicago, Ill, Jan 10, 24.
Study & Training: Univ Wis, BS, MS(art); Madrid Print Workshop, Spain; London, Eng, 72.

Work in Public Collections: Dallas Mus Art, Tex; Pa Acad Fine
Arts, Philadelphia; Mus N Mex, Santa Fe; Ariz State Univ, Tempe;
Hastings Col, Nebr.
Commissions: Exterior mural in marblecrete, Phoenix Jewish Com-
munity Ctr, Ariz, 62.
Exhibitions: Corcoran Biennial of Painting, Corcoran Gallery Art,
Washington, D C, 57; Libr of Cong Print Exhib, Washington, D C,
65; Minn Mus Art Exhib Drawings, St Paul, 71; Graphics U S A,
Clarke Col, Iowa, 71.
Teaching: Prof painting & printmaking, Ariz State Univ, 56-; guest
prof painting, Univ Wis, 67-68.
Awards: Purchase awards, Pa Acad Fine Arts & Dallas Mus Art, 65;
first prize for painting, Phoenix Art Mus, 71.
Memberships: Phoenix Art Mus.
Mailing Address: 5618 E Montecito, Phoenix, AZ 85018.

JACOBSON, YOLANDE (MRS J CRAIG SHEPPARD)
Sculptor
Preferred Media: Bronze, Wood.
b Norman, Okla, May 28, 21.
Study & Training: Univ Okla, BFA; also study in Norway, France &
Mex.
Work in Public Collections: Gilcrease Mus Art, Tulsa, Okla; Jacob-
sen Mus Art, Norman; State Hist Soc, Reno, Nev; Hist Mus, Car-
son City, Nev.
Commissions: Sen Patrick McCarran (bronze statue), Statuary Hall,
Washington, D C, 61; President's portrait bust, Univ Nev, Reno,
62; bronze sculpture, Governor's Mansion, Carson City, 65.
Exhibitions: Denver Mus Art, 41; Okla Ann, Tulsa, 42-45; Mid-West
Ann, Kansas City, 51; Oakland Mus Art, 56; Silver Centennial,
Virginia City, Nev, 61.
Positions: Asst ed & bk designer, Univ Nev Press, 63-66.
Awards: Mid-West Ann, Kansas City, 41; Denver Mus Art, 41; Sil-
ver Centennial, Virginia City, 61.
Mailing Address: 1000 Primrose St, Reno, NV 89502.

JACQUEMON, PIERRE
Painter, Illustrator
Preferred Media: Oils.
b Lyon, France, Aug 6, 35; U S citizen.
Work in Public Collections: Gotesborg Mus, Sweden; Magdalene Col,
Cambridge, Eng; Mus d'Art Mod, Paris, France; St Paul Sch,
N H; Ika-Shika Nat Univ, Tokyo, Japan.
Exhibitions: Autagouismes, Palais du Louvre, Paris, 60; Fort
Worth Art Ctr, Tex, 63; Charleroy Mus, Belg, 65; Inst Contemp
Art, Boston, 70; one-man show, Berkshire Mus, Mass, 63.
Dealer: Phoenix Gallery, 939 Madison Ave, New York, NY 10021.
Mailing Address: 62 E Seventh St, New York, NY 10003.

JAFFE, IRMA B
Art Historian
b New Orleans, La.
Study & Training: Columbia Univ, BS, MA, PhD.
Teaching: Prof art hist, Fordham Univ, 66-
Positions: Res cur, Whitney Mus Am Art, New York, N Y, 64-65.
Memberships: Col Art Asn Am; Am Studies Asn.
Research: American art.
Publications: Auth, Joseph Stella, Harvard Univ Press, 70; auth,
Cubist elements in the painting of Marsden Hartley: a phenomeno-
logical view, Art Int, 70; auth, Fordham's Trumbull drawings,
Am Art J, 71; ed, Art, In: Main Currents, 71-; ed, Baroque art:
the Jesuit contribution, Fordham Univ Press, 72.
Mailing Address: Dept of Fine Arts, Fordham University, Bronx,
NY 10458.

JAFFE, MRS WILLIAM B
Collector
Collection: Paintings, contemporary art.
Mailing Address: 640 Park Ave, New York, NY 10021.

JAGGER, GILLIAN
Painter, Lecturer
b London, Eng, Oct 27, 30.
Study & Training: Carnegie Inst Technol, BFA; Colo Springs Fine
Arts Ctr, scholar, 52, with Vytlacil; Univ Buffalo; Columbia Univ;
New York Univ, MA.
Work in Public Collections: Finch Col Mus, New York; Brompton's,
Montreal, P Q; Carnegie Inst, Pittsburgh, Pa.
Commissions: Portrait comns, 47-51.
Exhibitions: Assoc Artists Pittsburgh, 52 & 53; Abstract Artists
Pittsburgh, 53; two-man & group shows, Loft Gallery, 55-57; one-
man shows, Ruth White Gallery, New York, 61, 63 & 64; Finch
Col Mus, 64.
Teaching: Lect art, Radio Free Europe, cols & prof art schs; instr
painting, New York Univ, Post Col & New Rochelle Acad; for-
merly asst prof hist & philos art, Post Col.

Positions: Display artist, 53-55; textile designer, Wamsutta Mills,
Fruit of the Loom, 55-57.
Mailing Address: 418 Central Park W, New York, NY 10025.

JAGMAN, EDWARD
Painter
Preferred Media: Watercolors.
b Chicago, Ill, Nov 29, 36.
Study & Training: Am Acad Art, Chicago.
Work in Public Collections: Park Forest Pub Libr, Ill.
Exhibitions: One-man show, Chicago Pub Libr, 66; Ill State Fair,
Springfield, 67; Nat Watercolor exhib, Erie, 69; Painters &
Sculptors N J 28th Ann, 69; Am Watercolor Soc 102nd Ann, 69;
plus others.
Awards: Purchase award, Park Forest Libr, 63-64; hon mention, Ill
Festival Arts, 64; Am Watercolor Soc 102nd Ann Traveling
Award, 69.
Dealer: Baehlers, P O Box 247, Georgetown, CO 80444.
Mailing Address: 1911 S Marion, Denver, CO 80210.

JAGOW, ELLEN T
Painter
Preferred Media: Acrylics.
b Wisconsin Rapids, Wis, Sept 21, 20.
Study & Training: Concordia Teachers Col, BS; Art Inst Chicago.
Work in Public Collections: Butler Inst Am Art, Youngstown, Ohio;
Riverview Sch, Milwaukee, Wis; Fox-Richmond Gallery, Keuka
Park, N Y; Lincoln Col, Ill.
Exhibitions: Cent Ill Exhib, Peoria, 65; Miss Valley Artists, Ill
State Mus, Springfield, 66; Butler Inst Am Art, Youngstown, 69;
Massillon Mus Show, Ohio, 69.
Awards: Purchase award, Midyear Show, Butler Inst Am Art, 69.
Memberships: Am Fedn Art; Galesburg Civic Art Ctr (hon life mem,
pres, 64); Cleveland Mus Art; Butler Inst Am Art; Artists Equity
Asn.
Dealer: Bonfoey Gallery, 1710 Euclid Ave, Cleveland, OH 44115.
Mailing Address: Box 7, Garfield Rd, Hiram, OH 44234.

JAMEIKIS, BRONE ALEKSANDRA
Designer, Instructor
Preferred Media: Stained Glass.
b Vilnius, Lithuania; U S citizen.
Study & Training: Univ Vilnius, dipl; Ecole Arts et Métiers, Freiburg, Ger, dipl; Art Inst Chicago, BFA & MFA; Univ Hawaii, MA.
Commissions: Mosaic, Holy Cross Church, Chicago, Ill, 52; leaded
stained glass, St Philomena Church, Chicago, 60; mosaic &
faceted slab glass, Holy Cross Church, Dayton, Ohio, 64; faceted
slab glass windows, Springdale Mausoleum, Peoria, Ill, 66; leaded
& faceted slab glass, O'Hare Int Airport, Chicago, 68.
Exhibitions: Artists of Lithuania, Windsor Mus, Can, 57; Artists of
United States, Denver Mus Art, 57; Nat Biennial Relig Art Exhib,
Cranbrook Acad, Detroit, Mich, 60-69; Artists of Hawaii, Hono-
lulu Acad Arts, 61 & 72; Ecumenical Art Show, St Benet Gallery,
Chicago, 65.
Teaching: Instr art, Univ Hawaii, 58-61.
Positions: Art dir, Valeska Art Studios, Chicago, 51-58 & 62-71;
keeper, AV educ, Honolulu Acad Arts, 71-
Awards: Award for leaded stained glass, Relig Art Exhib, Chicago,
56; award for stained & slab glass, Am Inst Designers, 60;
award for faceted slab glass, Madonna Theme in Art Exhib,
Honolulu, 61.
Bibliography: David Asherman (auth), Rare gift from Europe to
Hawaiian art, Honolulu Advertiser, 60; J Dainauskas (auth),
Brone Jameikis-stained glass artist, Aidai-Echoes, Brooklyn,
N Y, 69; D J Anderson (auth), An artist brings light to dark
corners, Vol 9, No 4, Chicago.
Memberships: Inst Lithuanian Artists.
Mailing Address: P O Box 4212, Honolulu, HI 96813.

JAMES, CATHERINE, see CATTI

JAMES, FREDERIC
Painter
b Kansas City, Mo, Sept 28, 15.
Study & Training: Col Arch, Univ Mich, BDes; Cranbrook Acad Art.
Work in Public Collections: Nelson Gallery Art, Kansas City, Mo;
Denver Art Mus, Colo; Univ Mo, Columbia; Cranbrook Acad Art,
Bloomfield Hills, Mich.
Commissions: Murals, Trinity Lutheran Church, Mission, Kans,
Overland Park State Bank, Kans & Consumer's Coop Asn, Kansas
City; Wildflowers in America (print series), New York Botanical
Garden.
Exhibitions: Milch Gallery, New York, N Y; Nelson Gallery Art; Mid-
Am Ann; Springfield Mus Art, Mass; Maynard Walker Gallery,
New York; plus others.

Awards: Prizes, Denver Art Mus & Nelson Gallery Art.
Memberships: Am Watercolor Soc.
Dealers: Graham Gallery, 1014 Madison Ave, New York, NY 10021; Kachina Gallery, 112 Shelby St, Santa Fe, NM 87501.
Mailing Address: 850 W 52nd St, Kansas City, MO 64112.

JAMESON, DEMETRIOS GEORGE
Painter, Printmaker
Preferred Media: Oils.
b St Louis, Mo, Nov 22, 19.
Study & Training: Corcoran Sch Art, Washington, D C, 46; Wash Univ Sch Fine Arts, BFA, 49; Univ Ill Sch Fine & Appl Arts, Urbana, MFA, 50.
Work in Public Collections: Portland Art Mus, Ore; Seattle Art Mus, Wash; Denver Art Mus, Colo; Victoria & Albert Mus, London, Eng; Am Embassy, Athens, Greece; plus others in pub & pvt collections.
Exhibitions: Younger Am Painters, Guggenheim Mus, New York, N Y, 54; Fourth Int Print Show, Bordighera, Italy, 58; Northwestern Art Today, Seattle World's Fair, Wash, 62; one-man show, Portland Art Mus, 52 & 60; plus many other group & one-man shows.
Teaching: Prof art, Ore State Univ, 50-
Awards: J T Millican foreign travel award, Wash Univ, 50; Coos Art Mus, Ore; Rogue Valley Art Asn, Medford, Ore; plus many others.
Memberships: Portland Art Asn (pres, 57-58); Corvallis Art Ctr.
Mailing Address: 735 N W 28th St, Corvallis, OR 97330.

JAMIESON, MITCHELL
Painter
b Kensington, Md, Oct 27, 15.
Study & Training: Washington, D C & Mexico City, Mex.
Work in Public Collections: White House, Washington, D C; Whitney Mus Am Art & Metrop Mus Art, New York, N Y; Brooklyn Mus, N Y; Seattle Art Mus, Wash; Fort Worth Art Ctr, Tex; plus others.
Commissions: Murals, Interior Bldg, Washington, D C, Comptroller Gen Suite, Washington, D C, Post Off Bldgs, Upper Marlboro, Laurel, Md & Willard, Ohio; paintings for Life Mag, 57.
Exhibitions: One-man shows, Santa Barbara Mus Art, Calif, Des Moines Art Ctr, Iowa, Calif Palace of Legion of Honor, San Francisco, Norton Gallery Art, West Palm Beach, Fla & Corcoran Gallery Art, Washington, D C; plus many other nat exhibs.
Teaching: Head painting dept, Cornish Sch, Seattle, 49-51; instr painting, Madeira, Sch, Greenway, Va, 52-55; vis instr, Norton Gallery & Art Sch, 52-53, 56-57.
Awards: Bronze Star for work as Navy Combat Artist, 46; Guggenheim fel, 46; Am Acad Arts & Lett grant, 47.
Mailing Address: 1108 Prince St, Alexandria, VA 22314.

JAMISON, PHILIP (DUANE, JR)
Painter
Preferred Media: Watercolors.
b Philadelphia, Pa, July 3, 25.
Study & Training: Philadelphia Mus Sch Art, grad.
Work in Public Collections: Pa Acad Fine Arts, Philadelphia; Wilmington Soc Fine Arts, Del; Nat Acad Design, New York, N Y; Flint Inst Art, Mich; Frye Art Mus, Seattle, Wash.
Exhibitions: Pa Acad Fine Arts, 49-69; Nat Acad Design, 56-71; Am Watercolor Soc, New York, 56-; 200 Yrs of Watercolor Painting in Am, Metrop Mus Art, New York, 67; one-man shows, Hirschl & Adler Galleries, New York, 59-71.
Teaching: Instr watercolor, Philadelphia Col Art, 61-63.
Awards: Dana Medal, Pa Acad Fine Arts, 61; gold medal of honor, Allied Artists Am, 64; Nat Acad Design prize, 67.
Memberships: Nat Acad Design; Am Watercolor Soc; Philadelphia Watercolor Club; Wilmington Soc Fine Arts.
Publications: Contribr, Am Artist Mag, 62.
Dealer: Hirschl & Adler Galleries, Inc, 21 E 67th St, New York, NY 10021.
Mailing Address: 104 Price St, West Chester, PA 19380.

JANICKI, HAZEL (MRS WM SCHOCK)
Painter, Instructor
Preferred Media: Tempera.
b London, Eng, Feb 9, 18; U S citizen.
Study & Training: Cleveland Inst Art, dipl.
Work in Public Collections: Cleveland Mus Art, Ohio; Chicago Art Inst, Ill; Univ Ill, Champaign; Detroit Inst Fine Arts, Mich; Melbourne Art Inst, Australia.
Commissions: Painted & sculptured door for children's story room, Akron Pub Libr, Ohio, 69.
Exhibitions: Five one-man shows, Durlacher Bros Gallery, New York, N Y, 52-67; two-man show, Fairweather Hardin Gallery,

Chicago, 70; Am Painting & Sculpture 1948-1969, Univ Ill, Champaign, 71; one-man show, Distinguished Alumni Series, Cleveland Inst Art, 72; 36th Midyear Show, Butler Inst Am Art, Youngstown, Ohio, 72.
Teaching: Part-time instr painting, Kent State Univ Sch Art, 55-70.
Awards: Louis Comfort Tiffany Found Award, 49; Nat Inst Arts & Lett grant, 55; third medal, 36th Midyear Show, Butler Inst Am Art, 72.
Memberships: Artists Equity Asn.
Dealer: Fairweather Hardin Gallery, 101 E Ontario St, Chicago, IL 60611.
Mailing Address: 3390 Verner Rd, Kent, OH 44240.

JANIS, CONRAD
Art Dealer, Collector
b New York, New York, Feb 11, 28.
Collections Arranged: Participated in arranging all exhibitions at Sidney Janis Gallery from New Realism, 62 through Sharp Focus Realism, 72.
Positions: Co-dir, Sidney Janis Gallery.
Specialty of Gallery: All historic movements in twentieth century art to the present.
Collection: Contemporary American art.
Mailing Address: Sidney Janis Gallery, 6 W 57th St, New York, NY 10019.

JANIS, SIDNEY
Art Dealer, Writer
b Buffalo, N Y, July 8, 96.
Collections Arranged: Les Fauves, 50; Futurism, 54; Analitical Cubism, 56; New Realists (Pop Art), 62; Sharp Focus Realism, 72; plus many one-man shows, including Henri Rousseau, Dada, Delaunay, Kandinsky, Mondrian, deKooning, Pollock, Rothko & Kline; plus many others.
Positions: Owner, Sidney Janis Gallery.
Memberships: Art Dealers Asn Am (bd dir, 69-71).
Specialty of Gallery: Presentation of work by three generations in twentieth century art from cubism to pop art and sharp-focus realism.
Collection: The Sidney and Harriet Janis Collection given to The Museum of Modern Art, New York.
Publications: Auth, School of Paris comes to U S, Decision, 11-12/41; auth, They taught themselves, XXth century American primitive painting, Dial Press, 42; auth, Abstract & surrealist art in America, Reynal Hitchcock, 44; co-auth, Picasso: the war years 1939-46, Doubleday, 46; auth, Aims of the Janis Gallery, Arts Mag, 4/71; plus others.
Mailing Address: 6 W 57th St, New York, NY 10019.

JANKOWSKI, JOSEPH P
Painter, Educator
b Cleveland, Ohio, Jan 12, 16.
Study & Training: St Mary's Col, Mich; John Huntington Polytech Inst; Art Stud League New York; Cleveland Inst Art, BFA.
Work in Public Collections: Akron Art Inst, Ohio; Univ Ala; Cleveland Print Club; USAF Collection; Cleveland Mus Art; plus others.
Commissions: Stations of the Cross, St Mary's Church, McKeesport, Pa; mural, Jewish Community Ctr, Cleveland; St Mary's Col, Orchard Lake, Mich.
Exhibitions: Art Inst Chicago; Albright-Knox Art Gallery, Buffalo, N Y; Audubon Artists, New York, N Y; Isaac Delgado Mus Art, New Orleans, La; High Mus Art, Atlanta, Ga; plus others.
Teaching: Assoc prof art, Univ Ala, 49-53; instr art, Notre Dame Col, Ohio, 54; instr painting, Cleveland Inst Art, 53-, dir, eve sch, 55-
Awards: Prizes, Albright-Knox Art Gallery, Akron Art Inst, Butler Inst Am Art & Cleveland Mus Art; plus many others.
Memberships: Col Art Asn Am; Mid-Am Col Art Asn; Art Stud League New York.
Mailing Address: The Cleveland Institute of Art, 11141 East Blvd, Cleveland, OH 44106.

JANOWSKY, BELA
Sculptor, Instructor
b Budapest, Hungary, 00.
Study & Training: Ont Col Art; Pa Acad Fine Arts; Cleveland Sch Art; Beaux-Arts Inst Design.
Commissions: Bust, Queens Univ, Kingston, Ont; gold medal, Royal Soc Can; bronze reliefs, U S Dept Com Bldg, Washington, D C; bronze mem, Post Off, Cooperstown, N Y; bronze 150th anniversary plaque, Naval Shipyard, Brooklyn, N Y.
Exhibitions: Allied Artists Am Ann, 39-; Am Artists Prof League; Nat Acad Design; Nat Sculpture Soc; Pa Acad Fine Arts, Philadelphia; plus others.

Positions: Instr sculpture, Craft Stud League, YWCA, New York, 52-
Awards: Lindsey Morris Mem Prize, Allied Artists Am, 51 & 64.
Memberships: Allied Artists Am; Nat Sculpture Soc.
Mailing Address: 52 W 57th St, New York, NY 10019.

JANSON, HORST WOLDEMAR
Art Historian
b Leningrad, U S S R, Oct 4, 13; U S citizen.
Study & Training: Univ Hamburg, 32-33; Univ Munich, 33-34; Univ
Hamburg, 34-35; Harvard Univ, MA, 38, PhD, 42.
Teaching: Asst fine arts, Harvard Univ, 36-38; docent & lectr fine
arts, Worcester Art Mus, 36-38; instr fine arts, State Univ Iowa,
38-41; asst prof fine arts, Washington Univ, 41-48; prof fine arts
& chmn dept, New York Univ, 49-
Awards: Guggenheim fel, 48-49 & 55-56; Charles Rufus Morey
Award, Col Art Asn Am, 52 & 57.
Memberships: Col Art Asn Am (pres, 70-72).
Research: Italian renaissance sculpture; iconography; nineteenth
and twentieth century art.
Publications: Auth, Apes and ape lore in the middle ages and the
renaissance, 52; co-auth, The story of painting for young people,
52; auth, The sculpture of Donatello, 57; auth, Key monuments of
the history of art, 59; auth, History of art, 62.
Mailing Address: 29 Washington Sq W, New York, NY 10011.

JANSS, EDWIN, JR
Collector
Collection: Painting, contemporary art.
Mailing Address: 100 E Thousand Oaks Blvd, Thousand Oaks, CA
91360.

JANUSAS, CESLOVAS
Painter
Preferred Media: Oils, Watercolors.
b Krimea, Russia, July 18, 07; U S citizen.
Study & Training: Acad Art Lithuania, with M V Doboujinsky &
others; study in Ger, Austria, Switz & other European countries.
Work in Public Collections: Art Mus Vilnius; Vytautas the Gt Mus
Kaunas; Marine Mus, Hamburg, W Ger; Ciurlionis Gallery, Chi-
cago, Ill; Franciscan Fathers Collections, Maine.
Commissions: Horses on the Shore, Mus Vilnius, Lithuania, 34;
opera & drama stage, Lithuania State Opera, 37; Ocean (painting),
Marine Mus, Hamburg, 45; Winter (painting), Frankfurt, W Ger,
45; On the Beach (watercolor), U S Army Serv Protection Art &
Monuments, Washington, D C, 45.
Exhibitions: Am Artists Prof League, New York, N Y, 50-72 &
Smithsonian Inst, Washington, D C, 63; Art League Long Island,
N Y, 50-72; Hudson Valley Artists Asn, 60; one-man shows,
Lithuanian Artists Asn, Kaunas, Lithuania, 35 & 37 & Am Lith-
uanian Artists Asn, Chicago.
Teaching: Instr art, various schs in Europe & Lithuania, 31-40;
lectr appl art, Sch Appl Arts, Lithuania, 33-44; instr & dir, Sch
Appl Art & Design, Lithuania, 40-43; instr & dir, Appl Arts
Studio, Wuerzburg, Ger, 43-45.
Awards: First in oil for Ocean, Art League Long Island, 58; first in
watercolors for Moonlight, St Luke's Art Guild, 59; grand nat ex-
hib award, Am Artists Prof League, 65.
Bibliography: Articles in various mags & papers, 31-72; M Harold
(auth), Prize winning oil paintings, Allied, 60.
Memberships: Am Artists Prof League; Art League Long Island
(second v pres, 53); Am Lithuanian Artists Asn.
Mailing Address: 101-55 107th St, Ozone Park, New York, NY 11416.

JARAMILLO, VIRGINIA
Painter
Preferred Media: Acrylics.
b El Paso, Tex, Mar 21, 39.
Study & Training: Otis Art Inst, 58-61.
Work in Public Collections: Long Beach Mus Art, Calif; Pasadena
Art Mus, Calif; Aldrich Mus Contemp Art, Ridgefield, Conn.
Exhibitions: Los Angeles Co Mus Art Ann, Calif, 59 & 61; South-
west Regional Painting-Sculpture Show, Mus Fine Arts, Hous-
ton, Tex, 62; Deluxe Show, Houston, 71; Whitney Mus Am Art
Ann, New York, N Y, 72; Contemporary Reflections 1971-72,
Adlrich Mus Contemp Art, Ridgefield, 72.
Positions: Assoc dir & aesthetic adv, Hybrid Inc, 72-
Awards: Ford Found grant, 62; Nat Endowment Arts, 72-73; N Y
State Coun Arts award, 72-73.
Bibliography: F Bowling (auth), Outside the galleries: four artists,
Arts Mag, 11/70; Deluxe show, Houston Chronicle, 8/71; C Rat-
cliff (auth), The Whitney annual, part I, Artforum, 4/72.
Research: Religious architecture throughout Europe.
Mailing Address: Box 101 Prince St, New York, NY 10012.

JARETZKI, MR & MRS ALFRED, JR
Collectors
Mailing Address: 895 Park Ave, New York, NY 10021.

JARKOWSKI, STEFANIA AGNES
Painter, Educator
Preferred Media: Oils, Watercolors.
b Gdansk, Poland; U S citizen.
Study & Training: Liberal Col, Torun, Poland, dipl; Acad Fine Arts,
Warsaw, Poland; art study in Paris, France; restoration study,
Nat Mus Poland, with Dr J Burshe.
Work in Public Collections: George Washington Carver Mus, Tuske-
gee, Ala; Bochnia Mus, Poland; Argonne Nat Lab; Chicago, Ill;
Milenium Art Gallery, Warsaw.
Commissions: (Restoration of works) Yucca Gloriosa, 66 & Still Life,
67 (oils by George Washington Carver), Tuskegee Inst; Nobleman
(fourteenth century oil), Nat Mus, Warsaw, 67; oil by Roederstein,
Alice Pike Barney Collection, Smithsonian Inst/Tuskegee Inst, 69;
oil portrait by Shieffelin, Tuskegee Inst, 71.
Exhibitions: One-man shows, George Washington Carver Mus, 63,
Polish Artists Asn Zacheta, Warsaw, 65 & Polish Ctr, Hamilton,
Can, 67; Burr Artists Group Show, New York, N Y; Ala Water-
color Soc Traveling Exhib.
Teaching: Lectr & instr art, Tuskegee Inst, 62-
Positions: Dir art gallery, George Washington Carver Mus, Tuske-
gee Inst, 62-
Awards: Hon mention, Kalamazoo Art Festival, 61 & Milenium Art
Show, Warsaw, 65; Nat Art Festival Award, Beaux Arts Guild, 64.
Memberships: Am Asn Univ Prof; Art Educ Asn; Ala Watercolor
Burr Artists; Polish Artists Asn.
Mailing Address: 410 Parker Ave, Tuskegee Institute, AL 36088.

JARMAN, WALTON MAXEY
Collector
b Nashville, Tenn, May 10, 04.
Study & Training: With Philip Perkins & Gus Baker.
Collection: Abstracts in oils, acrylics & collages.
Mailing Address: Box 941, Nashville, TN 37202.

JARVAISE, JAMES J
Painter
b Indianapolis, Ind, Feb 16, 31.
Study & Training: Carnegie Inst Technol; Ecolue Art, Biarritz,
France, with Leger; Univ Southern Calif, BFA, 53, MFA, 55.
Work in Public Collections: Larry Aldrich Mus, Ridgefield, Conn;
Mus Mod Art, New York, N Y; Albright-Knox Art Gallery, Buf-
falo, N Y; Los Angeles Mus Art, Calif; Butler Inst Am Art,
Youngstown, Ohio; plus others.
Exhibitions: Carnegie Int, Pittsburgh, Pa, 59 & 65; Va Mus Fine
Arts, Richmond, 61 & 67; Director's Choice, New York World's
Fair, 64; Calif Inst of the Arts, Los Angeles, 66 & 67; plus many
other group & one-man shows.
Teaching: Instr, Univ Southern Calif, 55-62; instr, Pa State Univ,
summer 63; instr, Univ Madrid (Int Art Expos), 63; instr, Occi-
dental Col, 65, 66 & 67; instr, Calif Inst of the Arts, 65-68; instr,
Univ Southern Calif, summers 66 & 67.
Mailing Address: 233 E Islay, Santa Barbara, CA 93101.

JAUSS, ANNE MARIE
Painter, Illustrator
Preferred Media: Wash, Oils, Watercolors, Linoleum, Dry Point.
b Munich, Ger, Feb 3, 07; U S citizen.
Study & Training: Art Sch State Munich.
Work in Public Collections: New York Pub Libr Print Rm, N Y.
Exhibitions: Group shows, Ger, before 32; one-man shows, UP,
Portugal, Lisbon, 38, Secretariado da Propagande Nacional, Lis-
bon, 40, 43 & 45, Portraits of Pets, Portraits Inc, New York, 47,
Old Custom House, Philadelphia, Pa, 51 & graphics, Netherwood
Arts, Hyde Park, N Y, 71.
Awards: Author's award for The Pasture, N J Asn Teachers Eng,
68.
Bibliography: R C (auth), Anne Marie Jauss, Panorama, 42; Eugen
Guerster (auth), Anne Marie Jauss, Am-Ger Rev, 6/51; Bruno
Werner (auth), Anne Marie Jauss, Die Kunst, 1/52.
Publications: Auth, Legends of saints & beasts, 54; Discovering
nature the year round, 55, The river's journey, 57, Under a green
roof, 60 & The pasture, 68; co-auth, The little horse of seven
colors & other Portuguese folk tales, 70; illusr of over 60 bks,
mostly for children.
Dealers: Portraits Inc, 41 E 57th St, New York, NY 10019; Gaston
Art Studio, 1010 Pearl, La Jolla, CA 92037.
Mailing Address: R D 1, Box 82h, Stockholm, NJ 07460.

JECT-KEY, ELSIE
Painter
Preferred Media: Oils, Watercolors.
b Koege, Denmark; U S citizen.
Study & Training: Art Stud League New York, with Bridgman; Nat
Acad Art Sch, with Olinsky; Beaux Arts Inst.
Work in Public Collections: Butler Inst Am Art, Youngstown, Ohio;
Norfolk Mus, Va.

Exhibitions: Glassboro State Col, N J, 60; Fairleigh-Dickinson Univ, Rutherford, N J, 61; Butler Inst Am Art, 71; Nat Acad Design Ann, 71; Am Watercolor Soc Ann, 72.
Awards: Salmagundi Club prize, Allied Artists Am, 67; medal of honor, Nat Asn Women Artists, 71; William Church Osborne Mem award, Am Watercolor Soc, 72.
Memberships: Nat Asn Women Artists (first v pres, 67-69, finance chmn); Allied Artists Am (corr secy, 61-64, treas, 67-68); Knickerbocker Artists (corr secy, dir, 70); Am Watercolor Soc (treas, 70).
Mailing Address: 333 E 41st St, New York, NY 10017.

JEFFERY, CHARLES BARTLEY
   Educator, Art Administrator
b Paducah, Ky, July 6, 10.
Study & Training: Cleveland Inst Art, BS; Case Western Reserve Univ, MA.
Work in Public Collections: Cleveland Mus Art, Ohio; Butler Inst Am Art, Youngstown, Ohio; Syracuse Mus Art, N Y.
Exhibitions: Am Craftsmen Exhib, Expos Int, Paris, France, 37 & Brussels World's Fair, Belg, 57; Nat Exhib Am Crafts, Wichita Art Asn, Kans, 60; Enamels '70, Art Alliance, St Louis, Mo, 70; Nine Distinguished American Enamelists, Memphis Acad, Tenn, 72.
Teaching: Mem educ dept staff, Cleveland Mus Art, 35-40; coord art educ, Shaker Heights Schs, Ohio, 46-69; instr enamels, Cleveland Inst Art, 69-
Positions: Conductor enamel workshops in art schs, cols & craft ctrs in U S A, 53-
Awards: Bronze medal, Expo Int, Paris, 37; Horace Potter Mem Award, Cleveland Mus Art, 56; first prize for prize for enamels, Nat Decorative Arts Exhib, Wichita Arts Asn, 60.
Bibliography: Enamels of Charles B Jeffery, Ceramics Monthly, 12/70; one-man show rev, In: Crafts Horizon, 7/71.
Publications: Contribr, Enamels '70 (catalogue), 70.
Mailing Address: 1865 Nela Ave, East Cleveland, OH 44112.

JELINEK, HANS
   Graphic Artist, Educator
b Vienna, Austria; U S citizen.
Study & Training: Acad Appl Arts, Vienna; Univ Vienna.
Work in Public Collections: Metrop Mus Art, New York, N Y; Victoria & Albert Mus, London, Eng; Libr of Cong, Washington, D C; Philadelphia Mus Art, Pa; Boston Mus Fine Arts, Mass.
Commissions: Prints in color, Int Graphic Art Soc, 53 & 61 & Soc Am Graphic Artists, 56.
Exhibitions: Am Watercolors, Drawings & Prints, Metrop Mus Art, New York, 52; First Int Exhib Woodcuts XYLON, Kunsthaus Zurich, Switz, 53; First Expos Int Gravure, Gallery Mod Art, Lubljana, Yugoslavia, 55; Art from the U S, De Beyerd Cult Ctr, Breda, Holland, 57; Contemp Am Prints, Tokyo, Japan, 67.
Teaching: Prof graphic art, City Col New York, 48-; instr graphic art, New Sch Soc Res, 45-50.
Awards: First prize for woodcut, Artists for Victory, Nat Graphic Art Exhib, 43; Pennell prize, Third Nat Exhib Current Am Prints, Libr of Cong, 45; Paul J Sachs prize, 15th Ann Exhib, Boston Printmakers, 62.
Bibliography: A Reese (auth, American prize prints of the 20th century, Assoc Am Artists; H C Pitz (auth), A treasury of American book illustration; Lynn Ward (auth), Hans Jelinek, Soc Am Graphic Artists, 56.
Memberships: Academician Nat Acad Design (mem comt, 53); Royal Soc Arts, London (Benjamin Franklin fel); Soc Am Graphic Artists (mem coun, treas); Audubon Artists (dir, v pres).
Art Interests: Woodcuts.
Mailing Address: Dept of Art, Eisner Hall, City College New York, 133 Convent Ave, New York, NY 10031.

JELLICO, JOHN ANTHONY
   Art Administrator, Writer
b Koehler, N Mex, June 26, 14.
Study & Training: Art Inst Pittsburgh, dipl; Univ Pittsburgh, teaching cert; Phoenix Sch Design; Grand Cent Sch Art, New York.
Commissions: Seven relig murals, St Patricks Cath Church, Raton, N Mex, 37; sixty two chapel murals, Third Air Force, Tampa, Fla, 43-45.
Exhibitions: Raton Ann Art Show, N Mex, 37; Phoenix Art Inst Ann, New York, N Y, 38; Art Inst Pittsburgh Exhib, Pa, 40; Taos Art Colony Ann Show, N Mex, 41; Gallery Santa Fe, N Mex.
Teaching: Head illus, Art Inst Pittsburgh, 46-56; dir drawing, Colo Inst Art, 56-
Positions: Asst dir, Art Inst Pittsburgh, 50-56; dir, Colo Inst Art, 56-62, pres, 62-72.
Memberships: Hon mem Eugene Fields Soc; Mark Twain Soc.

Publications: Auth, How to draw horses for commercial art, 46; co-auth, Land of the southwest, Naylor, 50; auth, textbks, Int Correspondence Schs, 59-60; auth, articles, 59-68, contribr ed, 68-, Am Artist Mag; auth, articles, In: Westerner Mag, 72.
Mailing Address: 1 Martin Lane, Englewood, CO 80110.

JENKINS, PAUL
   Painter
b Kansas City, Mo, July 12, 23.
Study & Training: Kansas City Art Inst & Sch Design, 38-41; Art Stud League New York, 48-51.
Work in Public Collections: Mus Mod Art, Whitney Mus Am Art & Solomon R Guggenheim Mus, New York, N Y; Tate Gallery, London, Eng; Mus Art Mod, Paris; Stedelijk Mus, Amsterdam, Holland; Mus Western Art, Tokyo, Japan; plus many others.
Exhibitions: Art Inst Chicago; Carnegie Inst, Pittsburgh; Corcoran Gallery Art, Washington, D C; Arthur Tooth Gallery, London; Tokyo Gallery; plus many other group & one-man shows.
Awards: Silver Medal, Corcoran Biennial, 67; Golden Eagle Award for film, The Ivory Knife, 67.
Bibliography: Kenneth Sawyer (auth), The paintings of Paul Jenkins, Ed Two Cities, Paris, 61; Allen S Weller (auth), The joys and sorrows of recent American art, Univ Ill Press, 68.
Publications: Co-ed, Observations of Michael Tapie, Wittenborn, 56.
Dealer: Martha Jackson Gallery, 32 E 69th St, New York, NY 10021.
Mailing Address: 31 E 72nd St, New York, NY 10021.

JENKINS, PAUL RIPLEY
   Sculptor, Painter
Preferred Media: Wood, Watercolors.
b Torrington, Wyo, May 29, 40.
Study & Training: Art Inst Chicago, BFA; Univ Mich, MFA; Univ Wash, res awards.
Work in Public Collections: Many in private collections.
Commissions: Sculpture, Sea-Tac Int Airport, 72.
Exhibitions: Art Across America, San Francisco Art Inst, 65; Northwest Ann Exhib, 65-68 & Prospect Northwest, 72, Seattle Art Mus; 35 Seattle Artists, Seattle & Kobe, Japan Tour, 66; American Drawings National Exhibition, Erie, Pa, 66.
Teaching: Assoc prof drawing, painting & sculpture, Univ Wash, 64-
Awards: Award for painting, 65 & 67 & wood sculpture, 72, Agnes Anderson.
Bibliography: Review, In: Artforum, 70.
Dealers: Francine Seders Gallery, 6701 Greenwood Ave N, Seattle, WA 98103; Allan Stone Gallery, 48 E 86th St, New York, NY 10028.
Mailing Address: 711 N 60th St, Seattle, WA 98103.

JENNEWEIN, C PAUL
   Sculptor
b Stuttgart, Ger, Dec 2, 90; nat U S.
Study & Training: With Buhler & Lauter & Art Stud League New York, 07-09; with Clinton Peters, 10.
Work in Public Collections: Metrop Mus Art, New York, N Y; Pa Acad Fine Arts, Philadelphia; Corcoran Gallery Art, Washington, D C; Cincinnati Mus Art, Ohio; Houston Mus Art, Tex; plus many others.
Commissions: Tomb of the Unknowns (coin medal), Nat Commemorative Soc, 66; portrait plaques of Donald Wood Gilbert, 67 & Louis A Alexander, 68, Univ Rochester; ten portrait models of astronauts, Tex C of C, 69; Hall of Fame medals of Horace Mann & John Lothrop Motley, 69-70; John F Kennedy Medal (portrait), Kennedy Ctr Performing Arts, Washington, D C, 71; plus many others.
Awards: Benjamin Clinedinst Mem medal for achievement exceptional artistic merit in sculpture, 67; Am Numismatic Asn art award, 70; Daniel Chester French Award Medal, Nat Acad Design, 72; plus many others.
Memberships: Fel Am Acad Rome; Nat Inst Arts & Lett; Nat Acad Design (past v pres); fel Nat Sculpture Soc (past pres); Am Inst Architects; plus many others.
Mailing Address: 538 Van Nest Ave, Bronx, NY 10460.

JENNINGS, FRANCIS
   Sculptor, Painter
b Wilmington, Del, Feb 27, 10.
Study & Training: Wilmington Acad Art; Fleischer Mem Sch Art.
Work in Public Collections: Mural, Del Indust Sch for Boys.
Exhibitions: One-man show, Phoenix Gallery, New York, N Y, 62; Brandt Gallery, New York, 62; Whitney Mus Am Art, New York, 62; Baltimore Mus Art, Md, 63; four shows, Makler Gallery, Philadelphia & Rose Fried Gallery, New York, 60-66; plus others.

Teaching: Lect, Nat Art Teachers Asn Conv, 4/69.
Publications: Contribr, The artist in New York (radio series), 67; contribr, You and the artist (TV series), 69.
Mailing Address: 55 Greene St, New York, NY 10013.

JENNINGS, FRANK HARDING
Painter, Instructor
Preferred Media: Watercolors.
b Can, Oct 26, 05; U S citizen.
Study & Training: Phoenix Art Inst, New York, N Y, grad; with Norman Rockwell eight mos; also grad from three schs of com art.
Work in Public Collections: In many private collections.
Commissions: Many private commissions.
Exhibitions: One-man show, Bacardi Gallery, Miami, Fla, 69; Blue Dome Art Fel, Miami, 70-71; Coral Gables Art Club, Fla, 70-71; Miami Art League, 71; Am Artists Prof League, New York, 71-72.
Teaching: Lectr at numerous regional organizations, 64-; instr fine art, Miami-Dade Jr Col, 64-67; instr fine art, Merrick Demonstration Sch, 68-
Positions: Art dir, Platt-Forbes Inc, Hartford, Conn, 42-45; com artist, New York & Miami, 45-60; art dir, Miami Herald, Fla, 60-
Awards: Best in show for watercolor, Mirell Gallery, Coconut Grove, Coral Gables, Fla, 71; first prize in watercolor, Seven Lively Arts, Hollywood, 71; first prize in watercolor, Burdines Poincianna Festival, Miami, 72.
Memberships: Blue Dome Art Fel (treas, 71); Am. Artists Prof League (pres, Miami chap, 71); Coral Gables Art Club (dir, 71-); hon mem Aetna Art Guild.
Dealer: Robinson Art Gallery, 627 S Miami Ave, Miami, FL 33130.
Mailing Address: 29 Palermo Ave, Coral Gables, FL 33134.

JENSEN, ALFRED
Painter
b Guatemala City, Guatemala, Dec 11, 03.
Study & Training: San Diego Fine Arts Sch, 25; Hofmann Sch, Munich, Ger, 27-28; Ecole Scandinave, Paris, France, 29-34; also with Charles Despiau, Charles Dufresne, Othon Firesz, Marcel Gromaire & Andre Masson.
Work in Public Collections: Solomon R Guggenheim Mus & Mus Mod Art, New York, N Y; Dayton Art Inst, Ohio; Rose Art Mus, Brandeis Univ; Galerie Beyeler, Basel, Switz; plus others.
Commissions: Mural, Time, Inc.
Exhibitions: Venice Biennale, 64; Post Painterly Abstraction, Los Angeles Co Mus Art, Calif, 64; Int Biennial Exhib Paintings, Tokyo; Plus by Minus, Albright-Knox Art Gallery, Buffalo, N Y, 68; Documenta IV & V, Kassel, Ger, 68 & 72; plus many other group & one-man shows.
Teaching: Maryland Inst, 58.
Awards: Tamarind fel, 65.
Mailing Address: 152 Hawthorne Ave, Glen Ridge, NJ 07028.

JENSEN, EVE
Painter
Preferred Media: Oils.
b Chicago, Ill.
Study & Training: Art Inst Chicago; also with Sergei Bongart & Leon Franks.
Work in Public Collections: San Fernando Valley State Col, Northridge, Calif.
Exhibitions: Laguna Art Asn Gallery; Los Angeles Press Club; All City Festival, Los Angeles, Calif, 57; Old Town Gallery, San Diego, Calif, 64; Orange Show, San Bernardino, Calif, 64.
Teaching: Instr art, pvt classes, 71-72.
Positions: Taurine artist, Pena Taurina Seda Sangre y Sol, 56-72.
Awards: Greek theatre gold trophy, San Fernando Valley Art Club, 62; gold medal, Valley Artists Guild, 71; figure, Fri Morning Club, 72.
Bibliography: Elaine Lynn (auth), Fashion for living, produced by KCOP TV.
Memberships: Valley Artists Guild (pres, 72); hon life mem San Fernando Valley Art Club; Affil Coun Traditional Artists; Laguna Art Asn.
Mailing Address: 4170 Vanetta Dr, Studio City, CA 91604.

JENSEN, HANK
Sculptor
Preferred Media: Steel, Wood, Fiber Glass.
b Pittsburgh, Pa, Apr 29, 30.
Study & Training: Carnegie Inst Technol; Pratt Inst, BID; also with Hans Hoffmann.
Work in Public Collections: Joseph H Hirshhorn Collection, Washington, D C; Roswell Mus & Art Ctr, N Mex.
Commissions: Stage construct for dance theater piece Sanctum, Nikolais Dance Co, Henry St Playhouse, New York, 64; abstract plywood sculpture, Tuttie Art Gallery, Waitsfield, Vt, 67; steel

sculpture, Vt State Cols & Vt Coun Arts, Lyndon State Col, Lyndonville, Vt, 69; two abstract plywood & fiber glass sculptures, Roswell Mus, 72.
Exhibitions: Southern Asn Sculptors Nat, 67-68; Traveling Exhibs Proj of Vt Coun Arts, 68; one-man shows, Lyndon State Col, 69 & Roswell Mus & Art Ctr, 72; Laguna Beach Festival Arts, Laguna Beach Art Gallery, Calif, 72; plus others.
Teaching: Art dir, Goddard Exp Prog in Further Educ, Goddard Col, Plainfield, Vt, 69-71.
Positions: Artist-in-residence, Roswell Mus & Art Ctr, 72-73.
Awards: First Prize, Gymnasium One-Man Show, New York, 64; Fulbright award to Florence, 64-65; hon mention, Southern Asn Sculptors, 67-68.
Memberships: Col Art Asn Am.
Dealer: Doris Meltzer Gallery, 783 Madison Ave, New York, NY 10021.
Mailing Address: Rte 1, Box 244, Roswell, NM 88201.

JENSEN, JOHN EDWARD
Painter, Designer
Preferred Media: Watercolors.
b New London, Conn, June 12, 21.
Study & Training: McLane Art Inst, New York, N Y, scholar, 40-42; Art Stud League New York, 45-47.
Work in Public Collections: Bergen Mall, Bergen Co Mus; painting of Paterson Falls, Passaic Co Courthouse; Riveredge Boro Hall; also in permanent collection of Broadway Bank, Paterson, N J.
Exhibitions: Am Watercolor Soc, 68, 70 & 72; Nat Arts Club Show, 72; Knickerbocker Art Show, 72; Painters & Sculptors N J Show, 72; Mystic Outdoor Art Show, 72.
Awards: Best in Show Award, Mystic Outdoor Art Festival, 71; purchase award, Art in the Park, Paterson, 71; award for watercolor, Painters & Sculptors N J, 72.
Memberships: Am Artists Prof League; Knickerbocker Art Asn; N J Watercolor Soc; Painters & Sculptors N J; Ridgewood Art Asn.
Mailing Address: 44 Roosevelt Ave, Westwood, NJ 07675.

JENSEN, LAWRENCE N
Painter
Preferred Media: Watercolors.
b Orange, N J, Feb 5, 24.
Study & Training: Art Stud League New York; Columbia Univ, BS, MA & EdD.
Work in Public Collections: Springfield Mus Art; Frye Mus, Seattle, Wash.
Exhibitions: Am Watercolor Soc, 60-65; Soc Four Arts, 61-63; Silvermine Guild Art, 62-64; Watercolors: U S A, 63 & 64.
Teaching: Instr painting & design, Swain Sch Design; New York Univ; chmn art dept, Castleton State Col, Vt, 62-65; chmn art dept, Southern Conn State Col, 65-71.
Awards: Prizes, Am Watercolor Soc, Watercolors: U S A & Silvermine Guild Art, 64.
Bibliography: Work included in Prize winning watercolors, Bk III, 65.
Memberships: Am Watercolor Soc; Nat Art Educ Asn; Eastern Art Asn.
Publications: Auth, Synthetic painting media, Prentice-Hall, 64.
Mailing Address: 239 Winthrop Ave, New Haven, CT 06511.

JENSEN, LEO (VERNON)
Sculptor, Painter
Preferred Media: Bronze, Polychrome Wood.
b Montevideo, Minn, July 10, 26.
Study & Training: Walker Art Ctr, scholar, 46-47.
Work in Public Collections: Rose Art Mus, Brandeis Univ, Mass; New Britain Mus Am Art, Conn; Phillip Morris Traveling Collection; U S Info Agency, Washington, D C; Walker Art Ctr Sch, Minneapolis.
Commissions: Mural, Sheraton Hotels, Minneapolis, 63; bronze musicians, United Artists Corp, New York, N Y, 67; construction, Macmillan Publ Co, New York, 68; polychrome relief, Gulf & Western Corp, New York, 69; polychrome relief, Med World News, New York, 70.
Exhibitions: Pop Art & American Tradition, Milwaukee Art Ctr, Wis, 65; Contemporary Art U S A, Norfolk Mus, Va, 66; Phillip Morris Int, Am Fedn Arts, 66-67; Artist & the Athlete, Nat Art Mus Sport, New York, 68; one-man show, The Sculpture of Leo Jensen, New Britain Mus, 67.
Awards: First prize for wood carving, Silvermine Guild Artists Ann, 58; first prize for sculpture, John Slade Ely House Invitational, 63.
Bibliography: L Lippard (auth), Pop art, Praeger, 66; M B Scott (auth), The art & the sportsman, Renaissance, 68; D Z Meiloch (auth), Contemporary art with wood, Crown, 68.
Art Interests: Direct metal bronze and polychrome wood sculpture.
Dealer: FAR Gallery, 746 Madison Ave, New York, NY 10021.
Mailing Address: P O Box 264, Ivoryton, CT 06442.

JENSEN, MARIT
Painter, Serigrapher
Preferred Media: Oils.
b Buffalo, N. Y.
Study & Training: Carnegie Inst Technol Sch Painting; Hans Hofmann Sch Fine Art, Provincetown.
Work in Public Collections: Va Mus Fine Arts, Richmond; Pittsburgh Bd Pub Educ; Univ of the South, Sewanee, Tenn; cult div, U S Info Agency; Unity Ctr of Pittsburgh.
Exhibitions: Corcoran Gallery Art, Washington, D C, 47; Serigraph Int, Riverside Mus, 59; Int Cult Ctr, New Delhi, 67; Traveling Exhib, Nat Asn Women Artists, 69-71; Invitational Exhib, Provincetown Art Asn, 72.
Positions: Dir bd, Assoc Artists Pittsburgh, 45-47; trustee bd, Nat Serigraph Soc, 51-59; dir bd, Arts & Crafts Ctr, Pittsburgh, 60-61; dir bd, Provincetown Art Asn, 71-74.
Awards: Carnegie Inst prize, 45; purchase prize, Va Mus Fine Arts, 47; Grumbacher Prize, Nat Asn Women Artists, 60.
Bibliography: Frances Walker (auth), Artist paints space about us, 5/7/56 & Jeannette Jena (auth), Marit Jensen's recent work, 5/9/56, Pittsburgh Post Gazette; Eleanor Meldahl (auth), One man show opens in Provincetown, Cape Cod Standard Times, 6/28/69.
Memberships: Provincetown Art Asn; Nat Asn Women Artists; Provincetown Group Gallery.
Dealer: Group Gallery, The Mews, Provincetown, MA 02657.
Mailing Address: 7 Anthony St, Provincetown, MA 02657.

JENSEN, PAT
Painter
b Montevideo, Minn, Mar 17, 28.
Study & Training: Pasadena City Col, 49-50; with Leo Jensen, 54-57; Univ Ga & Aberham Baldwin Col, 57-59.
Work in Public Collections: Gertrude Herbert Inst Art, Ga; plus many others in pvt collections.
Exhibitions: Print show, Ward Nasse Gallery, Boston, Mass, summer 68; Reese Palley, New York & Atlantic City, N J, 69-70; O K Harris Gallery, New York, 71; Beth El Temple, Hartford, Conn, 72; Far Gallery, New York, 72; plus many other group & one-man shows.
Awards: First prize for oil & watercolor & second prize for watercolor, Fifth Ann Mystic Outdoor Art Festival, 62; first prize for oil painting, Mitchel Pappas Mem Award, Beth El Temple, 72.
Bibliography: Ralo T Coe (auth), Popular art, Nelson Gallery, 4/63; B Brooks (auth), article, In: Saybrook Pictorial, 3/72.
Mailing Address: P O Box 264, Ivoryton, CT 06442.

JERGENS, ROBERT JOSEPH
Painter, Educator
b Cleveland, Ohio, Mar 18, 38.
Study & Training: Cleveland Inst Art; Skowhegan Sch Painting & Sculpture; Yale Univ, BFA & MFA; Am Acad in Rome.
Work in Public Collections: Cleveland Mus Art; North Am College, Rome, Italy; Newman Relig Art Gallery; Skowhegan Sch Painting & Sculpture; Sem Archivescovile, Bari, Italy.
Exhibitions: Cleveland Mus Art, 57-64; Exhibs by Cleveland Mus & U S Info Agency; Mus Mod Art, New York, N Y; Corcoran Gallery Art, Washington, D C; Mostra Univ, Rome; plus others.
Teaching: Instr design, Cooper Union; instr drawing, Sch Art & Archit, Yale Univ; instr design, Cleveland Inst Art, at present.
Awards: Mary C Page grant, 61; Johnson Award for Printmaking, 61; prize, Cleveland Mus Art, 61; plus others.
Mailing Address: 2324 Brookdale Ave, Parma, OH 44134.

JESWALD, JOSEPH
Painter
b Leetonia, Ohio, May 17, 27.
Study & Training: Acad Julian, Paris, France; with Fernand Leger, Paris; Columbia Univ.
Work in Public Collections: Hirschhorn Collection; Addison Gallery Am Art; Colby Col; Simmons Col; Rockefeller Univ.
Exhibitions: Anna Herb Mus, Augusta, Ga, 54; Grippi Gallery, New York, N Y, 59 & 60; Cober Gallery, New York, 63; Art Galleries, Ltd, Washington, D C, 63; Gallery 7, Boston, Mass, 64-65; plus many other group & one-man shows.
Positions: Bd dirs, Land's End Cult Ctr, Rockport, Mass; chmn dept fine arts, New England Sch Art, Boston; dir, Montserrat Sch Visual Art, Beverly, Mass, 70-
Awards: Prize, Beverly Farms Regional, 61.
Memberships: Rockport Art Asn.
Mailing Address: Revere St, Gloucester, MA 01930.

JEWELL, KESTER DONALD
Museum Curator
b Terre Haute, Ind, Sept 1, 09.
Study & Training: John Herron Art Inst; Nat Acad Design, with

Authur Covey; Art Stud League New York, with Dumond & Bridgman; mus training, Newark Mus Assocs.
Collections Arranged: Ancient Treasures of Peru, 60; catalogued Worcester Art Mus collection.
Teaching: Head adult workshop, gen art courses, Newark Mus Art, Sci & Indust, 35-38.
Positions: Dir, Fitchburg Art Mus, 38-41; adminr, Worcester Art Mus, 41-71, cur pre-Columbian art, 71-
Awards: Carnegie Found grant for Europ studies, 38.
Memberships: Am Asn Mus; Nat Soc Arts & Lett.
Research: Museum administration and pre-Columbian art.
Publications: Ed, Ancient treasures of Peru, 60.
Mailing Address: 528 Main St, Shrewsbury, MA 01545.

JIMENEZ, LUIS ALFONSO, JR
Sculptor
Preferred Media: Fiberglass, Epoxy.
b El Paso, Tex, July 30, 40.
Study & Training: Univ Tex, BS Art & Archit, 64; Ciudad Univ, 64; asst to Seymorc Lipton, 66.
Work in Public Collections: Beacon St Collection, Boston, Mass; Giovanni Agnelli Collection, Turin, Italy; Long Beach Mus, Calif; also in collections of Richard Brown Baker & Alfonso Ossorio, New York, N Y.
Commissions: Southwest monument, D Anderson & Roswell Mus, Roswell, N Mex, 71; glass goggles (swimmer), Steuben Glass, New York, 71.
Exhibitions: Alliance in Art, Brandeis Univ for UNESCO, Washington, D C, 68; Human Concern/Personal Torment, Whitney Mus Am Art, New York, 69; Recent Figure Sculpture, Fogg Art Mus, 71; Battery Park, New York, 71; Whitney Mus Biennial, 71.
Bibliography: Hilton Kramer (auth), Sculpture emphasising poetry, New York Times, 5/2/70; Chris Homer (auth), Toward the year 2000 (spec on art for 50 U S cities & Can), Nat Can TV, 71; Barry Schwartz (auth), Humanist art in the U S, Praeger, 71.
Dealer: O K Harris Gallery, 465-69 W Broadway, New York, NY 10012.
Mailing Address: c/o Electric & Neon, Inc, P O Box 3458, Sta A, El Paso, TX 79902.

JOACHIM, HAROLD
Museum Curator
Positions: Cur prints & drawings, Art Inst Chicago.
Mailing Address: Art Institute of Chicago, Michigan Ave at Adams St, Chicago, IL 60603.

JOCDA (JOSEPH CHARLES DAILEY)
Painter, Art Administrator
Preferred Media: Oils, Acrylics.
b Reynoldsville, Pa, Mar 4, 26.
Study & Training: Youngstown Univ, AB, with Margaret Evans, David P Skeggs, John Naberezny & Robert Elwell.
Work in Public Collections: Youngstown Col; Westmar Col; Sioux City Art Ctr; Mo Synod; Des Moines Art Ctr; plus others.
Exhibitions: Butler Inst Am Art, 52 & 53; Siouxland Watercolor Exhib, 55-57; Six State Exhib, 55-58; Life of Christ Show, Iowa, 57 & 58; Laas-George Gallery, San Francisco, 61; plus others.
Positions: Designer, Crest Johnson Studios, Youngstown, Ohio, 53; staff artist, Warren, Ohio, 54; asst dir, Sioux City Art Ctr, 57-61 & designer & ed; arts & crafts coordr, Cent Community Ctr, Columbus, Ohio, 64-68; freelance artist, 69-
Awards: Awards, Trumble Co, 50 & Mahoning Co, 51; Youngstown Col Purchase Award, 52; 11th Iowa Artist Ann Purchase Award, 59.
Memberships: Midwest Mus Conf; fel Inst Arts & Lett.
Mailing Address: 2431 N High St, Columbus, OH 43202.

JOFFE, BERTHA
Designer
Preferred Media: Watercolors, Tempera.
b Leningrad, Russia; U S citizen.
Study & Training: N Y Phoenix Sch Design; City Col New York, BS (educ); Teachers Col, Columbia Univ, MA; N Y Univ Inst Fine Arts; Art Stud League New York, with William Zorach, Winold Reiss & Oronzo Malderelli.
Work in Public Collections: Drapery designs in leading hotels; design on drapery fabric, UN Staff Dining Rm.
Exhibitions: Provincetown Art Asn, Mass, 40; Artists for Victory, Metrop Mus Art, New York, N Y, 42; Art in Business Exhib, New York, 42; Int Textile Exhib, New York, 44.
Teaching: Docent art hist, Metrop Mus Art, 41; instr textile design, City Col New York, 40-43.
Positions: Free lance textile designer, 42-
Mailing Address: 77 Parker Ave, Maplewood, NJ 07040.

JOHANSEN, ANDERS DANIEL
Painter
Preferred Media: Oils, Watercolors.
b Denmark; nat U S.
Study & Training: Pratt Inst, 22; also with Charles Hawthorne & Daniel Garber.
Work in Public Collections: Yale Univ, New Haven, Conn; J H Vanderpoel Mus Collection, Chicago, Ill; Reading Pub Mus, Pa; Tiffany Found, Long Island, NY; plus many private collections.
Exhibitions: Pittsfield Mus; Nat Acad Design; Allied Artists Am; Nat Arts Club.
Awards: Pratt Alumnae award.
Memberships: Berkshire Artists Asn; Allied Artists Am; Nat Arts Club; Columbia Co Arts & Crafts.
Mailing Address: 50 Hudson St, Chatham, NY 12037.

JOHANSON, GEORGE E
Painter, Instructor
b Seattle, Wash, Nov 1, 28.
Study & Training: Portland Mus Sch, Ore; Atelier 17, New York, N Y.
Exhibitions: Northwest Printmakers; Henry Gallery, Seattle, Wash; Int Printmakers Exhib.
Teaching: Instr, Painting & Printmaking, Portland Mus Art Sch, 55-
Awards: Purchase prizes, Northwest printmakers, 55 & 63; Seattle Art Mus, 63.
Mailing Address: 2237 S W Market St, Portland, OR 97501.

JOHANSON, PATRICIA (MAUREEN)
Sculptor, Painter
b New York, N Y, Sept 8, 40.
Study & Training: Art Stud League New York; Bennington Col, Vt, BA, with Paul Feeley, Tony Smith & E C Goossen; Hunter Col, MA; City Col Sch Archit, New York.
Commissions: Stephen Long sculpture, Buskirk, N Y, 68; Ixion's Wheel, State Univ N Y, Albany, 69; comn to design gardens for House & Garden Mag, 69; Cyrus Field landscape sculpture, Buskirk, 70-71; var projs for Mitchell/Giurgola Assocs Architects, 72.
Exhibitions: One-man shows, Tibor de Nagy Gallery, New York, 66, 67 & 68; Cool Art, Aldrich Mus, Ridgefield, Conn, 68; Art of the Real, Mus Mod Art, New York, Grand Palais, Paris, France, Kunsthaus, Zurich, Switz & Tate Gallery, London, Eng, 68-69; Concept, Vassar Col, Poughkeepsie, N Y, 69; Projected Art: Artists at Work, Finch Col Mus, New York, 71; plus others.
Teaching: Vis prof art, State Univ N Y, Albany, 69.
Awards: Guggenheim fel, 70-71.
Bibliography: Stephen Long (film), CBS TV, distrib by Mus-at-Large, New York, 68; T H Littlefield (auth), Line is her thing, Albany Times-Union, 10/13/68; E C Goossen (auth), The art of the real, Mus Mod Art, New York, 68.
Mailing Address: 14 Rose Lane, Merrick, NY 11566.

JOHNS, JASPER
Painter
b Augusta, Ga, 30.
Study & Training: Univ S C.
Work in Public Collections: Tate Gallery Art, London, Eng; Mus Mod Art & Whitney Mus Am Art, New York, N Y; Albright-Knox Art Gallery, Buffalo, N Y; Wadsworth Atheneum, Hartford, Conn; Mod Mus, Stockholm, Sweden.
Exhibitions: New York 13, Vancouver Art Gallery, B C, 69; The Development of Modernist Painting: Jackson Pollock to the Present, Washington Univ, St Louis, Mo, 69; Rose Art Museum Collection, Scudder Gallery, Univ N H, Durham, 69; New York: The Second Breakthrough, 1959-1964, Univ Calif, Irvine, 69; Robert Hull Fleming Museum, Univ Vt, Burlington, 69; plus many other group and one-man shows.
Mailing Address: c/o Leo Castelli Gallery, 4 E 77th St, New York, NY 10021.

JOHNSEN, MAY ANNE
Painter, Etcher
Preferred Media: Silver Point, Oil.
b Port Chester, N Y.
Study & Training: With John Carroll.
Work in Public Collections: St Mary's Church, Hudson, N Y; also in collection of Philip Schyler, Albany, N Y.
Commissions: Painting, Fire Equipment 1890's, Tsaawassa Fire Dept, Brainard, N Y, 53.
Exhibitions: Nat Art Exhib, Oqunquit, Maine, 59; Drawing Int, Barcelona, Spain, 60; Knickerbocker Artists Nat, New York, N Y, 61; Miniature Painters, Sculptors & Gravers Soc of Washington Nat, 62-72; Catharine Lorillard Wolfe Nat Art Show, New York, 64.
Awards: Silvermine Guild Marine Award, 59; first prize, Columbia Co Fair, 59; Ohio Marine Award, Ohio Miniature Soc, 69.

Bibliography: Article, In: La Rev Mod, 68.
Memberships: Miniature Art Soc N J.
Dealer: Squillaci Gallery, 524 Summit Ave, Schenectady, NY 12307.
Mailing Address: Box 5, Brainard, NY 12024.

JOHNSON, AVERY FISCHER
Painter, Instructor
Preferred Media: Watercolors.
b Wheaton, Ill, Apr 3, 06.
Study & Training: Wheaton Col, BA, 28; Art Inst Chicago, grad, 33.
Work in Public Collections: Newark Mus, N J; Montclair Art Mus, N J; Philbrook Mus, Tulsa, Okla; Holyoke Mus, Mass; Libr Cong, Washington, D C.
Commissions: Post Off murals, North Bergen, N J, Bordentown, N J, Catonsville, Md, Lake Village, Ark & Liberty, Ind.
Exhibitions: 200 Years of Watercolor Painting in America, Metrop Mus Art, New York, N Y, 67; Mus Aquarelle, Mexico City, Mex, 68; also numerous ann exhibs at Am Watercolor Soc, New York, Montclair Art Mus, N J & N J Watercolor Soc.
Teaching: Instr painting, Montclair Art Mus, 40-70; instr painting, Newark Sch Fine & Indust Arts, 47-60.
Awards: First watercolor award, Montclair Art Mus, 60; Sen George Hammond Watercolor Award, Mus Fine Arts, Springfield, Mass, 64; Winsor-Newton Award, Am Watercolor Soc, 65.
Memberships: Assoc Nat Acad Design; Am Watercolor Soc; Audubon Artists; N J Watercolor Soc.
Publications: Auth, Suburban life (art column), N J, 66-68; auth, Watercolor page, Am Artist, 10/67; illusr, Factory & Mod Mfg, 67-71.
Dealer: Grand Central Art Galleries, 40 Vanderbilt Ave, New York, NY 10017.
Mailing Address: R F D 1, Cooper Rd, Dover, NJ 07801.

JOHNSON, BUFFIE
Painter, Lecturer
Preferred Media: Oil on Canvas.
b New York, N Y, Feb 20, 12.
Study & Training: Art Stud League New York; Atelier 17, Paris, France, engraving with S W Hayter; Univ Calif, Los Angeles, MA.
Work in Public Collections: Boston Mus Fine Arts, Mass; Yale Univ Art Gallery; Nat Collection Fine Arts, Washington, D C; Whitney Mus Am Art, New York, N Y; Walker Art Ctr, Minneapolis, Minn; plus many others.
Commissions: Murals, Astor Theatre, New York, 59; Knox Murals, St James, N Y, 69-70.
Exhibitions: Peggy Guggenheim's Art of this Century; Carnegie Int; Gedok Am Women Artist Show, Hamburg, Ger, 72; Women Choose Women, New York Cult Ctr, 73: one-man show, Betty Parsons Gallery & many others.
Teaching: Lectr, U S Dept State, in Rome, Italy, Nürnberg, Ger & Univ of Bologna, Münster, Zagreb, Athens & others: instr, Parsons Sch Design, 46-50; Univ Calif, Los Angeles.
Awards: Yaddo fel; Bollingen Found Award; second prize, Salon Int Femme, Nice, France, 70.
Bibliography: Dr Ernest Harms (auth), On becoming an abstract artist, Am Artist, 6/59; Parker Tyler (auth), On Buffie Johnson: the city as cosmic mural, 10/60 & Horace Gregory (auth), The transcendentalism of Buffie Johnson, 11/65, Art Int.
Memberships: Group Espace, Paris; Women in the Arts, New York.
Mailing Address: 231 E 77th St, New York, NY 10021.

JOHNSON, CECILE RYDEN
Painter
Preferred Media: Watercolors.
b Jamestown, N Y.
Study & Training: Augustana Col, AB; Pa Acad Fine Arts; Art Inst Chicago; Am Acad Fine Arts.
Work in Public Collections: Chicago Mus Sci & Indust; Davenport Munic Mus; Augustana Col; Ford Motor Co Collection; Bank of Bermuda.
Exhibitions: Am Watercolor Soc; Washington Watercolor Soc; Art Dirs Ann, Chicago; U S Info Agency & State Dept Traveling Exhib to Europe, Asia, Africa & S Am; one-man shows, Davenport Munic Mus & Hudson River Mus; plus many others.
Awards: Catharine Lorillard Wolfe Art Club Gold Medal; prizes, Am Watercolor Soc, Knickerbocker Artists & others.
Memberships: Am Watercolor Soc; Nat League Am Pen Women; Am Asn Univ Women; Westchester Art Soc; Scarsdale Art Asn.
Mailing Address: Apt 4D, 340 Riverside Dr, New York, NY 10025.

JOHNSON, CHARLOTTE BUEL
Art Historian, Educator
b Syracuse, N Y, July 21, 18.
Study & Training: Barnard Col, BA, 41; Inst Fine Arts, New York Univ, MA, 51.

Teaching: Instr art hist, Hollins Col, 47-48; asst prof art & art hist, Maryville Col, 48-52; mus instr, Worcester Art Mus, 52-57; lectr & res asst, Albright-Knox Art Gallery, 57-58, cur educ, 58-
Positions: Contrib ed, Sch Arts Mag, 63-70.
Memberships: Am Asn Mus.
Research: Nineteenth century American art; contemporary European and American art.
Publications: Auth, Alvan Fisher and the European tradition, Art in Am, Vol 41, No 2; auth, Man from Eden by Walt Kuhn & Two contemporary French abstractionists, Gallery Notes, Vol 21, No 2; auth, Optical illusion & Antonio Tapies, Gallery Notes, Vol 27, No 2; auth, New Art, Instr, 9-10/69; auth, articles for prof journals, 53-
Mailing Address: 710 Potomac Ave, Buffalo, NY 14222.

JOHNSON, CLIFFORD LEO
Cartoonist
b Minneapolis, Minn, Sept 30, 31.
Study & Training: Art Instr, Inc, Minneapolis; Am Acad Art, Chicago.
Awards: Cartooning Award, Nat Competition, Art Instr, 51.
Publications: Contribr, cartoons to True, Sports Afield, Golf Digest, Boy's Life & King Features.
Mailing Address: 157 W 106th St, New York, NY 10025.

JOHNSON, CROCKETT
Painter, Writer
b New York, N Y, Oct 20, 06.
Study & Training: N Y Univ; Cooper Union.
Exhibitions: One-man show, Glezer Gallery, New York, 67.
Memberships: Silvermine Guild Artists; Writers Guild Am.
Art Interests: Mathematical abstractions in oils.
Publications: Auth, A geometric look at pi, Mathematical Gazette, 70; auth, Mathematics of geometric abstractions, Leonardo, 72.
Mailing Address: 24 Owenoke, Westport, CT 06880.

JOHNSON, DANIEL LaRUE
Sculptor, Painter
b Los Angeles, Calif, Feb 18, 38.
Study & Training: Chouinard Art Inst, BFA.
Work in Public Collections: Mus Mod Art, New York, N Y; Bathome Tower, New York; Martin Luther King Park; Robert Hastings, Detroit, Mich; Smith Haven Mall.
Commissions: Some Am Hist, De Menil Found, 70; Peace Form One Monument, UN for Ralph Bunche, 72.
Awards: Statan Art fel, 60, John Hay Whitney fel, 63; Guggenheim Found fel, 65.
Bibliography: Article, In: Look Mag, 1/7/69; articles, In: Time Mag, 4/6/70 & 4/12/71.
Mailing Address: P O Box 101, Prince St Station, New York, N Y. 10012.

JOHNSON, DORIS MILLER (MRS GARDINER JOHNSON)
Painter
Preferred Media: Oils, Gouache, Acrylics, Watercolors, Inks, Pencils.
b Oakland, Calif, Dec 8, 09.
Study & Training: Calif Col Arts & Crafts, 32-33; Univ Calif, Berkeley, BA, 34, grad study, 34-36.
Work in Public Collections: Piedmont H S Art Gallery & Collection, Calif.
Exhibitions: 13th & 14th Int Watercolor, Art Inst Chicago, 34-35; Golden Gate Int Expos, Fine Arts Bldg, Calif, 39-40; Portland Art Mus Invitational, Ore, 40; Carnegie Traveling Show from San Francisco Mus Art, 40-41; Nat Drawing Exhib, San Francisco Mus Art, 70.
Teaching: Instr art, Oakland Art Mus, 39-52.
Positions: Founder children's art classes, Art League East Bay, 39; dir, Oakland Art Mus, 39-52, chmn art rental gallery, 56-59; chmn acquisitions comt of activities bd, San Francisco Mus Art, 57-64; mem bd trustees, Calif Col Arts & Crafts, 70-
Awards: First prize, Nat Watercolor Exhib, Colorado Springs, 36; pres purchase prize, 13th Ann San Francisco Women Artists, 38 & artists fund prize, San Francisco Art Asn Ann, 40, San Francisco Mus Art.
Memberships: San Francisco Women Artists (pres, 46-48, mem artists coun, 70-); hon life mem Art League East Bay.
Mailing Address: 329 Hampton Rd, Piedmont, CA 94611.

JOHNSON, EDVARD ARTHUR
Painter, Educator
b Chicago, Ill, Dec 18, 11.
Study & Training: Chicago Acad Fine Arts; Art Inst Chicago; Univ Ga, BFA; Inst Design, Ill Inst Technol, with L Moholy-Nagy & Alexander Archipenko, also MS.

Work in Public Collections: Nat Mus, Vaxiö, Sweden; Ga Mus Art, Univ Ga, Athens; Univ Rochester Mem Art Mus, N Y.
Exhibitions: Eastern States Ann, Springfield, Mass, 59; New Eng Exhib, New Canaan, Conn, 61; Watercolor U S A, Springfield, Mo, 66; Nat Acad Design, New York, N Y, 70; New Haven Festival, Conn, 71.
Teaching: Asst prof advan design, illus & drawing, Univ Ga, 47-51; instr visual fundamentals, Inst Design, Ill Inst Technol, 52; instr painting & drawing, Famous Artists Schs, 60-
Positions: Art dir for mags, Holt, Rinehart & Winston, New York, 53-58.
Awards: Nat Swed-Am Art Asn purchase award, 41; Miss Art Asn watercolor prize, 50; Rockefeller fel, 51-52.
Memberships: Arts Club Chicago; Conn Watercolor Soc; Silvermine Guild Artists; Col Art Asn Am.
Publications: Designer, American sculptor series, Univ Ga Press, 49; designer, Israel re-visited, Ralph McGill, 50.
Dealer: Silvermine Guild of Artists, 1037 Silvermine Rd, New Canaan, CT 06840.
Mailing Address: 33 Otter Trail, Westport, CT 06880.

JOHNSON, EVERT ALFRED
Art Administrator, Painter
Preferred Media: Oils, Watercolors.
b Sioux City, Iowa, Mar 2, 29.
Study & Training: Morningside Col, BA, 53; Univ Iowa, MA, 54.
Collections Arranged: National Drawing Invitational, 71 & WPA Revisited, 72, Southern Ill Univ, Carbondale.
Teaching: Asst prof art & head dept, Westmar Col, 56-61; instr painting, Hampton Inst, 65-66; lectr art hist & mus technol, Southern Ill Univ, Carbondale, 66-
Positions: Dir, Sioux City Art Ctr, 61-65; dir, Col Mus, Hampton Inst, 65-66; cur, Univ Galleries, Southern Ill Univ, Carbondale, 66-
Publications: Auth, Animal sculpture, Sch Arts Mag, 59; auth, Unfired clay, Craft Horizons Mag, 70.
Mailing Address: University Galleries, Southern Illinois University at Carbondale, Carbondale, IL 62901.

JOHNSON, IVAN EARL
Educator, Designer
Preferred Media: Fabrics, Wood.
b Denton, Tex, Sept 23, 11.
Study & Training: N Tex State Univ, BA; Columbia Univ, MA; N Y Univ, PhD.
Teaching: Dir art, Ind Sch Dist, Dallas, Tex, 46-52; prof art educ & head dept, Fla State Univ, 52-
Awards: Founders Day Award, N Y Univ, 60; Fla State Univ grant for study in Denmark, 71.
Memberships: Nat Art Educ Asn (Western regional v pres & pres, 48-52, nat pres, 55-57); Fla Art Educ Asn (mem bd, 60-61); Fla Coun Arts (mem bd, 65-66); Am Inst Designers.
Research: Investigation of performance objectives & evaluation instruments on basic color knowledge.
Publications: Co-auth, Design for living, Laidlow, 52; auth, Preparation of art teachers (report of comn of art in educ), Nat Art Educ Asn, 69; auth, Relevance in art education, J Art Educ, 71.
Mailing Address: Arts Education Dept, Florida State University, Tallahassee, FL 32304.

JOHNSON, MRS J LEE, III
Collector, Patron
b Fort Worth, Tex, Oct 19, 23.
Study & Training: Sarah Lawrence Col, BA, 45.
Positions: Chmn bd, Amon Carter Mus Western Art; trustee emer, Fort Worth Art Ctr Mus; founder, Ft Worth Art Coun; trustee, Nat Trust Hist Preservation; v pres, Int Coun Mus Mod Art, 67-72.
Memberships: Nat Endowment of the Arts; Fort Worth City Art Comn.
Art Interests: Trinity River beautification program with Lawrence Halprin and Robert Zion, Fort Worth; commissioned Philip Johnson for Fort Worth Water Gardens.
Collection: French nineteenth century; European and American sculpture and graphics; modern and ancient art.
Mailing Address: 1200 Broad Ave, Fort Worth, TX 76107.

JOHNSON, J STEWART
Museum Curator
b Baltimore, Md, Aug 31, 25.
Study & Training: Swarthmore Col, BA; Univ Delaware, MA, Winterthur Prog in Early Am Cult.
Positions: Cur decorative arts, Newark Mus, 64-68; cur decorative arts, Brooklyn Mus, 68-, v dir for collections, 70-72.

Memberships: Victorian Soc Am (pres, 66-69); Am Friends of Attingham Park (dir); Lockwood-Mathews Mansion, Norwalk, Conn (adv).
Mailing Address: The Brooklyn Museum, Eastern Pkwy, Brooklyn, NY 11238.

JOHNSON, KATHERINE KING
Art Administrator, Painter
Preferred Media: Oils.
b Lincoln, Nebr.
Study & Training: Univ Nebr Col Fine Arts, with Dwight Kirsh, Francis Colburn, Darwin Dunkin & Marshel Merritt.
Work in Public Collections: Lyndon B Johnson Mem Libr, Austin, Tex; Bennington Mus Art & Hist, Vt; Fleming Mus, Burlington, Vt; Southern Vt Art Ctr, Manchester; Rutland Hosp Mem Collection, Vt.
Exhibitions: Southern Vt Artists Nat Traveling Show, 56; Nat League Am Pen Women Regional, 65-71; Indio Date Festival, Calif, 68; Hale Galleries Invitational, Palm Springs, Calif, 70; Stratton Art Festival, Vt, 70.
Collections Arranged: Loan exhibition of Currier & Ives Prints; traveling exhibit of prints & drawings by Kay Cassill, 70; Humor in Art, commemorating the 75th year of the comicstrip & Honduras Art Loan Exhib, 71; Gottlob Briem Memorial Exhibit, 72.
Positions: Pres & founder, Rutland Area Art Asn Inc, 61-; exec dir, Chaffee Art Ctr, Rutland, 61-; parlimentarian, Shadow Mountain Palette Club, Palm Desert, Calif, 71; Vt state pres, Nat League Am Pen Women.
Bibliography: M Farnsworth (auth), article, 62 & Doris Goodhue (auth), article, 68, Pen Women; article, In: Restorer, 71.
Memberships: Nat League Am Pen Women (br pres & state art chmn, 65); Rutland Area Art Asn Inc, Vt; Southern Vt Artists Asn Inc; Shadow Mountain Palette Club.
Mailing Address: 40 Piedmont Pkwy, Rutland, VT 05701.

JOHNSON, LESTER F
Painter, Educator
b Minneapolis, Minn, Jan. 27, 19.
Exhibitions: Carnegie Int, Pittsburgh, Pa, 64, 68 & 72; Rosc '67, Dublin, Ireland; L'Art Vivant aux Etats-Unis Fondation, Maeght, France, 71; 10 Independents, Solomon R Guggenheim Mus, New York, N Y, 72; Chicago Biennial, 72.
Teaching: Prof painting & dir grad painting, Yale Univ, 65-
Awards: Guggenheim fel, 72.
Mailing Address: 294 Gulf St, Milford, CT 06460.

JOHNSON, LESTER L
Painter, Instructor
Preferred Media: Acrylics.
b Detroit, Mich, Sept 28, 37.
Study & Training: Wayne State Univ.
Work in Public Collections: Detroit Inst Arts; Nat Bank Detroit; Johnson Publ Co, Chicago, Ill; Sonnenblick-Goldman Corp, New York, N Y; City of Hope Med Ctr, Los Angeles, Calif; plus one other.
Commissions: Urban Wall Mural, New Detroit, Living With Art Comt, 73.
Exhibitions: One-man exhib, Gallery 7, Detroit, 70 & Detroit Artists Mkt, 72; Contemp Black Artists Am, 71 & Contemp Am Painting, 72, Whitney Mus Am Art; Nat Afro-Am Exhib, Carnegie Inst, Pittsburgh, Pa, 71-72.
Teaching: Instr drawing & painting, Summer Workshop, Neighborhood Youth Corps, Detroit, 66; instr drawing, Genesee Community Col, Flint, Mich, 71-
Awards: John S Newberry Purchase Prize, 54th Exhib Mich Artists, Detroit Inst Arts, 64; first prize painting, Mich State Fair Art Exhib, 69; gallery purchase award, Harlem Gallery Sq, 72.
Bibliography: Margaret Harold (auth), Award winning art, 65 & Prize-winning watercolors, 65, Allied.
Memberships: Calif Nat Watercolor Soc; Mich Watercolor Soc; Founders Soc, Detroit Inst Arts; Arts Extended Gallery; hon mem Laguna Beach Art Asn.
Publications: Contribr, Seven Black artists, 69 & Misalliance, 69, Detroit Artists Mkt; contribr, Black reflections, Flint Community Schs, 69-70.
Mailing Address: 8350 E Morrow Circle, Detroit, MI 48204.

JOHNSON, LOIS MARLENE
Printmaker, Educator
Preferred Media: Intaglio, Silk-screen.
b Grand Forks, N Dak, Nov 17, 42.
Study & Training: Univ N Dak, BS, 64; Univ Wis-Madison, MFA, 66.
Work in Public Collections: Philadelphia Mus Art, Pa; Eluehjem Art Ctr, Madison; McCray Gallery, Univ N Mex, Albuquerque; Univ N Dak, Grand Forks; Adolph Behn Mem Collection, New York, N Y.

Commissions: Poster, Philadelphia Mus Art, 72.
Exhibitions: Soc Am Graphic Artists, New York, 65-67, 70 & 71; Northwest Printmakers Int, Seattle, Wash, 68; Am Color Print Soc, 68-72; Silk Screen, Philadelphia Mus Art, 72; 18th Biennial Exhib, Brooklyn Mus, N Y, 72; plus many others.
Teaching: Asst prof printmaking & chmn dept, Philadelphia Col Art, 67-
Awards: Abraham Hankins Award, Am Color Print Soc, 68; award, Prints in Pa, 69; Eyre Medal, Philadelphia Watercolor Club, 71.
Memberships: The Print Club (prints in progress, 67-72); Am Color Print Soc (coun, 68-72); Philadelphia Watercolor Club (bd dirs, 72); Soc Am Graphic Artists; Philadelphia Art Alliance (print comt), 72.
Publications: Contribr, Artist proof, Pratt Graphic Ctr, 67.
Dealer: The Print Club, 1614 Latimer St, Philadelphia, PA 19102.
Mailing Address: 29 S 19th St, Philadelphia, PA 19103.

JOHNSON, (LEONARD) LUCAS
Painter, Illustrator
Preferred Media: Oils.
b Hartford, Conn, Oct 24, 40.
Work in Public Collections: Mus Mod Art, New York, N Y; Mus Art, San Francisco, Calif; Mus Mod Art, Tel-Aviv, Israel; Nat Mus, Warsaw, Poland; Ponce Mus, P R.
Commissions: Four color lithograph, Masonite Co, Fibracel S A, Mexico City, Mex, 72.
Exhibitions: Salon Independiente, Mexico City, 68 & 70; Galeria Arte Misrachi, Mexico City, 70 & 72; Gotham Gallery, New York, 71; Image of Mexico, traveling exhib, Gen Motors Permanent Collection; Pratt Inst Lithography Collection, traveling.
Bibliography: Tom Cranfield (auth), article, In: Tex Quart, 70; Ann Holmes (auth), Fantastic artists, Southwest Arts Mag, 72.
Publications: Illusr, Loss of rivers, Azazel, 67; illusr, Moonshots, 67 & Pablo Neruda-early poems, 69, New Rivers; illusr, Master of knives, Harmon, 70; illusr, various works, Antaeus.
Dealer: Galeria de Arte Misrachi, Genova 20, Mexico 6, D F, Mex.
Mailing Address: c/o Janus Gallery, 116 1/2 E Palace Ave, Santa Fe, NM 87501.

JOHNSON, MARIAN WILLARD
Art Dealer
b New York, N Y, Apr 20, 04.
Positions: Founder, East River Gallery, 36-38; assoc, Neumann-Willard Gallery, 38-40; owner & dir, Willard Gallery, 40-; chmn ad comt, Mus Mod Art, New York, 44-46, bd trustees & acquisitions comt, 44-46; chmn, Asia House Gallery, 59-, trustee, 61-, exec comt, 63-67; v pres, Mus Am Folk Art, 62-69, trustee, 62-, secy, 71-; bd overseers, Rose Art Gallery, Brandeis Univ, 65-69.
Specialty of Gallery: Contemporary American art.
Mailing Address: Willard Gallery, 29 E 72nd St, New York, NY 10021.

JOHNSON, PATRICIA PAUL
Painter
Preferred Media: Oils.
b Camden, Ark, July 24, 46.
Study & Training: La Tech Univ, BFA; Skowhegan Sch Painting & Drawing, with James McGarrell, Phillip Pearlstein & Jacob Lawrence; Univ Ariz, MFA.
Work in Public Collections: La Tech Univ, Ruston; Tucson Art Ctr, Ariz.
Exhibitions: Monroe Ann, Masur Mus, Monroe, La, 69; one-man show, El Dorado Art Ctr, Ark, 69; Painting & Sculpture Biennial, Phoenix Art Mus, Ariz, 71; Tucson Festival Exhib, Tucson Art Ctr, Ariz, 72; Fraser-Gifford Gallery, Tucson, 72.
Teaching: Instr painting, Univ Ariz, 72-

JOHNSON, PAULINE B
Educator, Writer
Preferred Media: Watercolors.
b Everett, Wash.
Study & Training, Columbia Univ, MA; Moore Col, hon DFA.
Exhibitions: Calif Palace Legion of Honor, 33; Oakland Art Gallery; Ann Watercolor, Seattle Art Mus, 37; Henry Art Gallery, 66; Art Louie Gallery, 72.
Teaching: Prof art, Univ Wash, 41-
Positions: Mem ed bd, Art Educ J, 62-73; mem ed bd, Sch Arts Mag, 63-67.
Awards: First prize for watercolor painting, Seattle Art Mus, 37.
Bibliography: Reproduction of ink painting, Argus, 6/66.
Awards: Award, 71 & purchase award, 72, Tucson Art Ctr; George Bright Mem Award, Phoenix Art Mus, 71.
Mailing Address: 2120 E Hampton St, Tucson, AZ 85719.
Memberships: Nat Art Educ Asn (mem coun, 56-60); Pac Arts Asn (v pres, 58-60); Wash Art Asn (pres, 54-55).

Publications: Auth, Creating with paper, 58; co-auth, Crafts design, 62; auth, creative bookbinding, 63; contribr, 64th Yearbook N S S E, Nat Soc Study Educ, 65; contribr, Christ & the modern mind, 72.
Mailing Address: Dept of Art, University of Washington, Seattle, WA 98195.

JOHNSON, PHILIP CORTELYOU
Collector, Architect
b Cleveland, Ohio, July 8, 06.
Study & Training: Harvard Univ, AB, Grad Sch Design, BArch.
Commissions: Design of Mus Mod Art Annex & Sculpture Ct, N Y State Theatre, Lincoln Ctr, New York, Glass House, New Canaan, Conn & Plaza of Seagram Bldg; plus many others.
Teaching: Design critic, Cornell Univ & Yale Univ; instr, Pratt Inst; vis comt, Sch Design, Harvard Univ, 50-51; coun comt, Sch Art & Archit, Yale Univ, 59-
Positions: Dir dept archit & design, Mus Mod Art, 30-36, 46-54, trustee, 58-
Awards: First prize, São Paulo Bienal, 54; Progressive Architecture Design Award, 64; Elsie DeWolfe Award, N Y Chap, Am Inst Interior Designers, 65; plus many others.
Memberships: Nat Inst Arts & Lett (coun).
Collection: Young Americans.
Publications: Co-auth, The international style, 32, rev 66; auth, Machine art, 34; auth, Mies van der Rohe, 47, rev 53; auth, Architecture, nineteen forty-nine to nineteen sixty-five, 66.
Mailing Address: Ponus St, New Canaan, CT 06840.

JOHNSON, RAY
Painter
b Detroit, Mich, Oct 16, 27.
Study & Training: Art Stud League New York; Black Mountain Col, 45-48, with Josef Albers, Robert Motherwell, Mary Callery & Ossip Zadkine.
Work in Public Collections: Art Inst Chicago, Ill; Dulin Gallery; Houston Mus Fine Arts; De Cordova Mus, Lincoln, Mass; Mus Mod Art, New York, N Y.
Exhibitions: Chicago Mus Contemp Art, 67; Finch Col, 67; Am Fedn Arts Circulating Exhib, 67; Hayward Gallery, London, 69; two-man show, Univ B C, 69; plus other group & one-man shows.
Positions: Founder, New York Corresp Sch Art, 62-
Awards: Nat Inst Arts & Lett Award, 66.
Bibliography: Becker et al (auth), Happenings, fluxus, pop, nouveau realism, Rowohlt Verlag GMBH, 65; Al Hansen (auth), A primer of happenings and time/space art, Something Else Press, 65; John Russell & Suzi Gablik (auth), Pop art redefined, Praeger, 69; plus others.
Publications: Auth, The paper snake, 65.
Mailing Address: c/o Richard Feigen Gallery, 27 E 79th St, New York, NY 10021.

JOHNSON, ROBERT LEWIS
Painter, Photographer
Preferred Media: Watercolors.
b Springfield, Mo, Apr 27, 31.
Study & Training: Southwest Mo State Col, BS(educ).
Work in Public Collections: Springfield Art Mus, Mo; Spiva Art Ctr, Joplin, Mo.
Exhibitions: Watercolor U S A, Springfield Art Mus, 67-70; Wichita Watercolor Centennial, 71.
Teaching: Educ cur painting, Springfield Art Mus, 57-71; instr art, Stetson Univ, 71-
Awards: Watercolor U S A Sargent Award, 67, purchase award, 68 & California Award, 70, Springfield Art Mus.
Mailing Address: 11 Sunshine Blvd, Deland, FL 32720.

JOHNSON, SELINA (TETZLAFF)
Museologist, Photographer
b New York, N Y.
Study & Training: Hunter Col, AB; City Col New York, MS(educ); Ctr Human Relations Studies, New York Univ, PhD.
Work in Public Collections: Bronze portrait bas-relief, Bergen Mall, Paramus, N J; mus plans, Bergen Community Mus Art & Sci; nature photographs, Mus Natural Sci, Nantucket Island, Mass.
Commissions: Mem plaque for Hans Christian Andersen Madison, Bergen Mall, 59; Report on Mus Needs & Resources, Bd Chosen Freeholders, Bergen Co, 68.
Exhibitions: Nat Tour Nature Photog, Photog Soc Am, 52; Fine Arts in Commercial Art, Third Ann Exhib, Freedom House, New York, 59; Painting & Sculpture Ann, Bergen Co Artist's Guild, 60; Photographic Art of Selina Johnson & Louis Davidson, Art Asn, Nantucket Island, Mass, 61; Books Illustrated by N J Artists, Johnson Libr, Hackensack, N J, 69.
Collections Arranged: Prints & Printmakers of Bergen County, N J, 56; 350th Year: Henry Hudson Here 1609-1959; County Craftsmen Create Stained Glass, 60; Driftwood Designs, Flower Paintings &

Fresh Arrangements, 60; The Fine Art of Color Photography, 61; Excavating our Hackensack Mastodon, 62-64; First N J Junior Historians' Fair, Celebrating Our State Tercentenary, 64-69; New Arts in Old County Home: Bergen Community Museum Opens B Spencer Newman Gallery, 70.
Teaching: Instr kinesiology & phys educ, Hunter Col; instr comp anat & biol, N Y Univ & City Col New York; guest lectr landscape archit, Columbia Univ.
Positions: Biol staff artist, City Col New York, seven yrs & biol & med illusr; founder, dir & trustee, Youth Mus Leonia, 50-56; founder, dir & first pres, Bergen Community Mus, 56-70, trustee, 70-; biol & med illus, Harvard Univ & physicians; archit consult hist hall, Bd Freeholders, 68-69; chmn, Bergen Co Cult & Heritage Comn, 72-77.
Awards: First prize in art for Silver Orchid, 51, first prize for photog, 65, 67 & 69, N J State Fedn Women's Clubs.
Bibliography: Editorials & articles, In: New York Times, Bergen Bull, The Record & Press J, 50-72; Clifford Mische (auth), Museum in Overpeck Park, Bergen Co Park Comn, 56; Georgianne Ensign (auth), The hunt for the Mastodon, Watts, 71.
Memberships: Nat Trust Hist Preservation; Mus Coun N J (chmn standards comt, 65-67); North Jersey Cult Coun; Bergen Co Artist's Guild; North Jersey Opera Theatre (founding trustee & pres, 69-).
Research: Museology as practiced in developing museums, including study of their origins, relationships & cultural effects.
Publications: Illusr, Adventures with living things, Heath, 38; illusr, Angina Pectoris, Williams & Wilkins, 39; auth, Creating a community museum, 54; auth & illusr, Museums for youth in the United States, Univ Microfilms, 62; illusr, The hunt for the Mastodon, 71.
Mailing Address: 24 Hawthorne Terrace, Leonia, NJ 07605.

JOHNSON, WESLEY E
Painter, Instructor
b Ojai, Calif, June 15, 34.
Study & Training: Ventura Col; Univ Calif, Santa Barbara; also with Andre L'Hote in Paris, France.
Work in Public Collections: U S Dept State; Forum of the Arts.
Exhibitions: San Francisco Mus Art, Calif, 60, 65 & 66; one-man show, Santa Barbara Mus Art, 63; Calif Nat Watercolor Soc, 63, 65-68; Calif State Fair, 65-68; M H De Young Mem Mus, San Francisco, 66; plus others.
Teaching: Instr painting, Ventura Col.
Awards: Purchase prize, Forum of the Arts, 64; Calif Nat Watercolor Soc, 66; Calif State Fair, 66 & 68; plus others.
Memberships: Calif Nat Watercolor Soc; San Francisco Art Inst.
Mailing Address: 291 Avenida de la Vereda, Ojai, CA 93023.

JOHNSTON, RICHARD M
Sculptor, Educator
Preferred Media: Metals.
b Kankakee, Ill, Sept 22, 42.
Study & Training: El Camino Jr Col; Calif State Col, Long Beach, BA; Cranbrook Acad Art, MFA.
Work in Public Collections: Utah Mus Fine Art; Salt Lake Art Ctr.
Commissions: Steel wall sculpture, Western Airlines, Los Angeles, Calif, 69; bronze wall sculpture, Telemation Inc, Salt Lake City, Utah, 71; gold leaf/steel sculpture, Sun Valley Ski Corp, Idaho, 71.
Exhibitions: Craftsman U S A, Los Angeles Co Mus Art, 66; Nat Invitational Crafts, Univ N Mex, 68; Inter-Mountain Biennial, Salt Lake Art Ctr, 70; 73rd Western Ann, Denver Art Mus, 71; Nat Small Sculpture & Drawing Show, San Diego State Col, 72.
Teaching: Asst prof metal & basic design, Univ Utah, 68-
Awards: First prize, Sterling Silversmiths, 68; purchase award, Utah Mus Fine Art, 69; purchase award, Salt Lake Art Ctr, 70.
Memberships: Col Art Asn; Am Crafts Coun.
Mailing Address: c/o Brena Gallery, 313 Detroit, Denver, CO 80206.

JOHNSTON, YNEZ
Painter, Printmaker
b Berkeley, Calif.
Study & Training: Univ Calif, Berkeley, MA, 46.
Work in Public Collections: Whitney Mus Am Art, New York, N Y; Wadsworth Atheneum, Conn; Metrop Mus Art, New York; Mus Mod Art, New York; Philadelphia Mus Art, Pa.
Commissions: Etchings, Int Graphic Arts Soc, New York, 58-60, 62 & 64; etchings, Roten Galleries, Baltimore, Md, 66-67; drawings, Washington Gallery Mod Art, D C, 65.
Exhibitions: One-man show, Retrospective-Graphics, San Francisco Mus Art, 67; The West-80 Contemporaries, Univ Ariz, Tucson, 67; U S Painting Invitational, Pa Acad Fine Arts, 68; Mostra Internazionale della Grafica, Unione Fiorentina, Florence, Italy, 68-69; Four Printmakers, Calif Inst Technol, 69.
Awards: Guggenheim grant, 52; first award, Am Ann Watercolor, Metrop Mus Art, 52; Louis Comfort Tiffany award in painting & graphics, 55 & 56.

Bibliography: Henry Seldis (auth), Woman of the year in art, Los Angeles Times, 59; Gerald Nordland (auth), review-exhibit, In: Art News, 62; review-exhibit, In: Art Int, 70.
Art Interests: Painting & etching.
Dealer: Jodi Scully Gallery, 651 N La Cienega, Los Angeles, CA 90069.
Mailing Address: 569 Crane Blvd, Los Angeles, CA 90065.

JOLLEY, JERRY (GERALDINE HAZEL JOLLEY)
Painter, Sculptor
Preferred Media: Oils.
b Rochester, N Y, June 14, 11.
Study & Training: Rochester Inst Technol, watercolor with Margaret Weston & sculpture with Ehrich; Rochester Mem Art Mus, ceramics with Francis Denny; Univ Wash; also plastics with Cora Scofield Johnson, New York, watercolor with Richard Yip & with Eliot O'Hara.
Work in Public Collections: Rochester Inst Technol.
Commissions: Four oils & two watercolors, Marcus Glaser Co, San Francisco, 63.
Exhibitions: Rochester Mem Mus N Y State Sculpture Exhib, 39; Western Painters Show, 54 & Alameda Art Asn 11th Ann, 55, Oakland Art Mus; Henry Gallery, Univ Wash, Seattle, 55; New York Int Art Exhib, New York, 70.
Teaching: Pvt instr beginning art.
Positions: Display designer, Sibley Lindsey & Curr Co, Rochester, 36-38; packaging & children's game designer, E E Fairchild Co, Rochester, 38-41; art dir, Fleishhacker Paper Box Co, San Francisco, 46-51; free lance indust designer, San Francisco, 52-55.
Awards: Awards for Tribulation (sculpture), Rochester Mem Art Mus, 33, Alameda Art Asn 11th Ann, 54 & for Carriage Ride In Central Park (painting), 55, Oakland Art Mus.
Bibliography: A J Bloomfield (auth), Art previews in San Francisco, News-Call Bull, 60; Felice T Ross (auth), Gallery previews in New York, Pictures Exhib, 67; Interesting personalities, WROC-TV, Rochester, 6/67.
Memberships: Artists Equity Asn (nat mem chmn, 69-71, mem bd Northern Chap, 70); Marin Soc Artists Ross Calif (publicity chmn, 65-66); Soc Western Artists; Eight Women Watercolorists of West (pres, 53-57).
Art Interests: Oil painting palette knife technique.
Publications: Auth, Palette knife painting instruction (rec), 68.
Mailing Address: 2257 Washington St, San Francisco, CA 94115.

JONES, AMY (AMY JONES FRISBIE)
Painter, Educator
Preferred Media: Oils, Watercolors.
b Buffalo, N Y, Apr 4, 99.
Study & Training: Pratt Inst, scholar; also with Peppino Mangrarite, Xavier Gonzales, Ippolito, Carlus Dyer, Roger Prince & Bryan Kay.
Work in Public Collections: Norfolk Mus Arts & Sci, Va; New Britain Mus Am Art, Conn; Wharton Sch Finance, Univ Pa, Philadelphia; Standard Oil Co N J presented to State of Md; 34 works in New York Hosp, N Y.
Commissions: Mural (oil on canvas), Winsted, Conn, 39, mural (underpainted & glazed), Painted Post, N Y, 40 & mural (egg tempera on canvas), Scotia, N Y, 41, Fine Arts Sect, U S Treas Dept.
Exhibitions: Brighton Mus Invitational, Eng, 59; Royal Soc Painters in Watercolor Invitational, London, Eng, 60; one-man shows, Philadelphia Art Alliance, 62, New Britain Mus Am Art, Conn, 63 & Norfolk Mus Arts & Sci, Va, 67; Galleria S Stefano, Venice, 72.
Teaching: Instr art, Bedford Art Ctr, 62-; instr printmaking, Col New Rochelle, summer 72.
Awards: Purchase award, Ranger Fund, Nat Acad Design, 56; purchase award, Wash Co Mus, Hagerstown, Md, 58; first prize for graphics, Northern Westchester Artists, 61.
Bibliography: Norman Kent (auth), Amy Jones, Am Artist Mag, 54 & Amy Jones, Watson-Guptill, 56.
Memberships: Silvermine Guild Artists; Katonah Gallery; Philadelphia Watercolor Club; Audubon Artists; Am Watercolor Soc.
Art Interests: Printmaking & lost wax sculpture.
Mailing Address: Byram Lake Rd, Mount Kisco, NY 10549.

JONES, BENJAMIN FRANKLIN
Painter, Sculptor
b Paterson, N J, May 26, 42.
Study & Training: Sch of Visual Arts; New York Univ, MA; Pratt Inst; Univ Sci & Technok, Kumasi, Ghana.
Work in Public Collections: Newark Mus, N J; Howard Univ; Studio Mus, New York, N Y; Mid Block Gallery, Newark; Johnson Publ, Chicago, Ill.
Exhibitions: Mus Mod Art; Studio Mus in Harlem; Boston Mus, Mass; Princeton Mus, N J; Cleveland Mus, Ohio; plus one other.
Teaching: Prof fine arts, Jersey City State Col, 68-
Positions: Art dir, Urban League Essex Co Exhib, 72.

Bibliography: Articles, In: Art in Am, 71 & New York Times, 72; included in: Black perspectives & Black contemporary artists.
Research: African art and culture in W Africa and Paris, France.
Mailing Address: 15 Goldsmith Ave, Newark, NJ 07112.

JONES, (CHARLES) DEXTER (WEATHERBEE), III
Sculptor
b Ardmore, Pa, Dec 17, 26.
Study & Training: Pa Acad Fine Arts & Chester Springs Art Sch, with Charles Rudy & Walker Hancock; Accad Belli Arti, Florence, Italy.
Work in Public Collections: Pa Acad Fine Arts, Philadelphia; Woodmere Art Gallery.
Commissions: Clinical Meeting Gold Medal, Am Med Asn, 60; A C Storz Tribute Tablet, Omaha Airport, 61; two hist relief panels, New Bradford Nat Bank Bldg, 61; Newcomb Cleveland Medal, Am Asn Advan Sci, 64; Great Seal of Philadelphia, Munic Serv Bldg, Philadelphia, 65; plus many other portraits, plaques & medals.
Exhibitions: Pa Acad Fine Arts, Nat Acad Design, Nat Sculpture Soc, Allied Artists Am & Nat Art Club, many exhibs, 49-65.
Awards: Silver medal, DaVinci Alliance, 60; Gregory Award, 61; Art Dir Club Philadelphia Award, 66; plus many others.
Memberships: Fel Nat Sculpture Soc; Allied Artists Am; Nat Art Club; Academician Nat Acad Design; Fellowship Pa Acad Fine Arts; plus others.
Mailing Address: 2124 Lombard, Philadelphia, PA 19146.

JONES, DOUGLAS McKEE (DOUG)
Painter, Art Dealer
Preferred Media: Oils, Pastels.
b Sewell, Chile, Oct 16, 29; U S citizen.
Study & Training: San Diego Fine Arts & Crafts; San Diego State Col; Los Angeles Art Ctr Col Design, grad; spec study with Lorser Feitelson, Audubon Tyler, Leon Franks & Sergei Bongart.
Commissions: Portraits of Mayor Charles Dail, San Diego & Mayor Kiyoshi Nakarai, Yokahama, comn by San Diego Chapter, Am Inst Architects, 63; 33 portraits, Int Aerospace Hall of Fame, San Diego, 64-72; portrait of Gen Claire Chenault, Flying Tigers Asn, 71; portrait of Mrs Marie Winzer, addition to Scripps Hospital; also many portraits of prominent people and children.
Positions: Owner & dir, The Jones Gallery, 64-
Specialty of Gallery: Paintings, sculpture and ceramics by distinguished nineteenth and twentieth century American artists.
Mailing Address: The Jones Gallery, 1262 Prospect St, La Jolla, CA 92037.

JONES, EDWARD POWIS
Painter, Sculptor
Preferred Media: Oils, Watercolors, Bronze.
b New York, N Y, Jan 8, 19.
Study & Training: Harvard Univ; Art Stud League New York; Acad Ranson, Paris, France.
Work in Public Collections: Mus Mod Art, New York; Libr Cong, Washington, D C; Riverside Mus, New York; Philadelphia Mus Art, Pa; Brooklyn Mus, N Y; plus others.
Exhibitions: Libr Cong; Brooklyn Mus; Tokyo Print Bienale, Japan, 68; Modern Religious Prints, Mus Mod Art Circulating Exhib, 63; Sci Workshop, 68; plus others.
Teaching: Lectr, The Modern Illustrated Book; instr art, Loyola Sch, New York, 70-72.
Memberships: Philadelphia Print Club; Century Asn; Munic Art Soc; Artists Equity Asn; Fels Pierpont Morgan Libr (chmn coun, 72).
Publications: Contribr, Art in Am; illusr, Liturgical Arts.
Dealer: Graham Gallery, 1014 Madison Ave, New York, NY 10021.
Mailing Address: 925 Park Ave, New York, NY 10028.

JONES, ELIZABETH
Sculptor, Medalist
Preferred Media: Wax, Plaster, Silver, Gold, Bronze.
b Montclair, N J, May 31, 35.
Study & Training: Vassar Col, BA, 57; Art Stud League New York, 58-60; Scuola Arte Medaglia, The Mint, Rome, Italy, 62-64.
Work in Public Collections: Portrait plaque, Creighton Univ.
Commissions: Portrait of Albert Schweitzer, Franklin Mint, Pa, 66; Ann Prize Medals, St Stephen's Sch Rome, 67-72; four gold sculptures with precious stone, Govt Italy, 68; portrait of Picasso, Stefano Johnson, Milan, Italy, 72; Gold Medal Award for Archeol, Univ Mus, Univ Pa, 72; plus many others.
Exhibitions: Five shows, Tiffany & Co, New York, N Y, Houston, Los Angeles, Chicago & San Francisco, 66-68; Montclair Art Mus, N J, 67; many int medallic art shows, in Rome, Madrid, Paris, Athens, Prague & Cologne; Smithsonian Inst & Nat Sculpture Soc, New York, 72.

Awards: Hon dipl, Acad Brasileira Belas Artes, Rio de Janeiro, 67; Outstanding Sculptor of the Year, Am Numismatic Asn, Colorado Springs, Colo, 72.
Bibliography: Mario Valeriana (auth), Medalists in Italy, Editalia, Rome, 72; plus various articles in Women's Wear Daily, Coin World & other mags & newspapers in the U S & Italy.
Memberships: Nat Sculpture Soc; Am Numismatic Asn; Fedn Int Medaille; Ital Soc Medalists.
Mailing Address: Via Lazio 20, Rome, Italy 00187.

JONES, ELIZABETH ORTON
Illustrator, Writer
b Highland Park, Ill, June 25, 10.
Study & Training: Univ Chicago, PhB, 32; Ecole Beaux Arts, Paris, France, dipl, 32; Art Inst Chicago, 32; Wheaton Col, hon MA, 55.
Commissions: Murals, Crotched Mountain Ctr, Greenfield, N H; panel, Univ N H Libr.
Exhibitions: O'Brien Galleries, Chicago; Smithsonian Inst; plus others.
Awards: Charles Muller Prize, Chicago Soc Etchers, 39; Caldecott Medal for illus for Prayer for a Child, 44; Lewis Carroll Shelf Award, Univ Wis, 58.
Publications: Auth & illusr, Maminka's children, Twig, Big Susan & How far is it to Bethlehem?; illus, The peddler's clock, Small rain, Prayer for little things, & others.
Mailing Address: Mason, NH 03244.

JONES, FRANCES FOLLIN
Museum Curator
b New York, N Y, Sept 8, 13.
Study & Training: Bryn Mawr Col, AB, 34, MA, 36, PhD, 52; Am Sch Class Studies at Athens, 37-38.
Positions: Secy & asst cur class art, Art Mus, Princeton Univ, 43-46, asst to dir & cur class art, 46-60, chief cur & cur class art, 60-71, cur collections & cur class art, 71-
Publications: Contribr to prof journals & publ.
Mailing Address: Art Museum, Princeton University, Princeton, NJ 08540.

JONES, HOWARD WILLIAM
Painter, Sculptor
b Ilion, N Y, June 20, 22.
Study & Training: Toledo Univ; Columbia Univ; Syracuse Univ, BFA; Cranbrook Acad Art.
Work in Public Collections: Jewish Mus, New York, N Y; Walker Art Ctr, Minneapolis, Minn; Knox-Albright Mus, Buffalo, N Y; Milwaukee Art Inst, Wis; St Louis Art Mus, Mo.
Commissions: Time Columns: The Sound of Light (wall of light & sound), Whitney Mus Am Art, New York, 68; Sonic Games Chamber (sound environ), Nelson-Atkins Mus & Performing Arts Coun, Kansas City, Mo, 68; Terminator (sound environ for pub entry way), Northland Bank, St Louis, 71.
Exhibitions: Light, Motion, Space, Walker Art Ctr, Minneapolis, 67 & Mus Contemp Art, Chicago, Ill, 68; Magic Theater, Nelson-Atkins Mus, Kansas City, Automation House, New York, Montreal, Can & others, 68-70; Art of the 60's, Princeton Univ, N J, 70; Kinetic Art, Arts Coun Gt Brit & Hayward Gallery, London, Eng, 70; one-man shows, Nelson-Atkins Mus, Kansas City, Mo, 65, Royal Marks Gallery, New York, 66 & Howard Wise Gallery, 68 & 70.
Teaching: Instr painting & design, Tulane Univ La, 51-54; asst prof painting & design, Fla State Univ, 54-57; prof multi-media, Wash Univ, 57-
Awards: Graham Found fel & grant, 66-67; New Talent: U S A, Art in Am Mag, 66-67.
Bibliography: Ralph Coe (auth), Post pop possibilities: Howard Jones, Art Int, 1/66 & Breaking the sound barrier, Art News Mag, summer 71; Nat Endowment Arts (producer), Artist in America: Howard Jones (film), KETC TV, 71.
Memberships: Col Art Asn Am.
Mailing Address: 12 N Newstead St, St Louis, MO 63108.

JONES, JACOBINE
Sculptor
Preferred Media: Stone, Bronze.
b London, Eng.
Study & Training: Regent St Polytech; also with H Brownsword, London & in Denmark.
Work in Public Collections: Kelvin Mus, Glasgow, Scotland; Confederation Life Bldg, Toronto, Ont; Nat Gallery Can; Hamilton Art Gallery, Ont; plus many others.
Commissions: Seven figures in bronze, Facade of Bank of Can, Ottawa, Ont; four figures in stone, Facade of Sigmund Samuel Mus, Toronto; mural in stone, Confederation Life Bldg, Toronto; Facade of Gen Hosp, Toronto; mural in marble, N Wall of Main Banking Rm, Bank of N S, Toronto.

Exhibitions: Paris Salon, 32; Royal Can Acad Arts, 32-; Tate Gallery, London, Eng, 38; Hamilton, Ont, 66-69; one-man show, Rodman Hall Art Ctr, St Catharines, 69; plus others.
Teaching: Lect on sculpture; former dir sculpture & ceramics, Ont Col Art, 51-58.
Awards: Gold medal, Regent St Polytech, London.
Memberships: Royal Can Acad Art; Sculptors' Soc Can; Am Soc Animal Artists.
Dealer: Laing Galleries, 194 Bloor W, Toronto, Ont, Can.
Mailing Address: 209 Davey St, Niagara-on-the-Lake, Ont, Can.

JONES, JOHN PAUL
Painter, Printmaker
b Indianola, Iowa, Nov 18, 24.
Study & Training: State Univ Iowa, BFA, 49, MFA, 51, with Mauricio Lasansky.
Work in Public Collections: Mus Mod Art, New York, N Y; Brooklyn Mus, N Y; Libr Cong, Washington, D C; Los Angeles Co Mus Art, Calif; Nat Gallery Art, Washington, D C.
Exhibitions: Art of America in Spain, Madrid, 63; Pittsburgh Int, Carnegie Inst, 64-67; chmn, N Y State Hist Trust, 66-72; American Painting, Va Mus Arts & Sci, Richmond, 66-70; Tamarind: Homage to Lithography, Mus Mod Art, New York, 69; The New Vein—Europe, toured in Europe by Smithsonian Inst, 69-70.
Teaching: Asst prof prints, Univ Calif, Los Angeles, 53-63; lectr prints & drawings, Univ Calif, Irvine, 70-
Awards: Graphics award, Louis Comfort Tiffany Found, 51; creative printmaking award, Guggenheim Found, 60.
Bibliography: Una Johnson (auth), John Paul Jones, prints & drawings 1948-1963 (monogr), Brooklyn Mus, 63; Henry Hopkins (auth), John Paul Jones, painting & sculpture 1955-1965 (monogr), Los Angeles Co Mus Art, 65; Eugene Anderson (auth), John Paul Jones (monogr), Felix Landau Gallery, Los Angeles, 67.
Dealer: Margo Leavin Gallery, 812 N Robertson Blvd, Los Angeles, CA 90069.
Mailing Address: 22370 Third Ave, South Laguna, CA 92677.

JONES, LOUIS C
Museum Director
b Albany, N Y, June 28, 08.
Study & Training: Hamilton Col, AB, 30; Columbia Univ, AM, 31, PhD, 41; Hamilton Col, hon LHD, 62.
Teaching: Instr, State Univ N Y Albany, 34-46.
Positions: Exec dir, N Y State Hist Asn & Farmers Mus, 46-72, emer dir, 72-; chmn, N Y State Hist Trust, 66-72; mem N Y State Coun on Arts, 60-72; state liaison off, Nat Regist Hist Places; mem ed bd, Am Heritage; ed, N Y Hist, 47-52.
Awards: Guggenheim fel, 46; Award of Distinction, Am Asn State & Local Hist, 69; Rochester Mus Fel; plus others.
Memberships: Fel Am Folklore Soc; Am Asn Mus (coun, 52-70); Am Asn State & Local Hist (exec coun, 50-58); N Y State Hist Asn (trustee, exec dir); Folklore Soc (co-founder, ed quart, 45-50); plus others.
Art Interests: American folk art.
Publications: Auth, Cooperstown, 49; co-auth, American folk art, 52; auth, Things that go bump in the night, 59; co-auth, New found folk art of the young republic, 60; auth, Growing up in the Cooper Country, 65; plus others.
Mailing Address: Pomeroy Pl, Cooperstown, NY 13326.

JONES, NELL CHOATE
Painter
b Hawkinsville, Ga.
Study & Training: Adelphi Acad; Fountainebleau Sch Art, 29; also with John Carlson & Frederick K Boston.
Work in Public Collections: Represented in many pub & pvt collections.
Exhibitions: Nat Acad Design; Allied Artists Am; Audubon Artists; N Y Watercolor Soc; exhib in mus throughout the U S & Europe, 46-
Awards: First prize, 46 & founders prize, 51, Pen & Brush Club N Y; medal of honor, Nat Asn Women Artists, 55; Lena Newcastle Watercolor Prize, 58; plus others.
Memberships: Fel Swiss Int Inst Arts & Lett; hon life mem Nat Asn Women Artists (pres, 51-55); Brooklyn Soc Artists (pres, 49-52); Studio Traveling Guild; Southern States Art Asn Clubs; plus others.
Mailing Address: 296 Clermont Ave, Brooklyn, NY 11205.

JONES, ROBERT CUSHMAN
Painter
Preferred Media: Oils.
b West Hartford, Conn, Oct 15, 30.
Study & Training: R I Sch Design, BFA, 53, MS, 59.
Exhibitions: Drawings U S A, Saint Paul Mus, 61-71; 17th Ann Exhib Am Painting & Sculpture, Pa Acad Fine Arts, 62; 82nd Ann

Exhib, 63 & Far West Regional Exhib of Art Across Am, 65, San Francisco Mus Art; The West—80 Contemporaries, Univ Ariz, 67.

Teaching: Instr drawing & painting, R I Sch Design, 56-60; instr drawing & painting, Univ Wash, 60-; instr drawing & painting, Univ B C, summers 66 & 71.

Dealer: Francine Seders Gallery, 6701 Greenwood Ave N, Seattle, WA 98103.

Mailing Address: 5412 21st St N E, Seattle, WA 98105.

JONES, RUSSELL
Painter

Preferred Media: Acrylics.

b Vineland, N J, Jan 13, 10.

Study & Training: Swarthmore Col.

Exhibitions: Del Valley Artists Asn, Milford, N J, 67-69; Phillips Mill Ann Art Exhib, New Hope, Pa, 67-70; N J State Exhib, Clinton, 68-70; Salmagundi Club, New York, 68-70; Multiple Sclerosis Art Show, Trenton, N J, 68-70.

Awards: Award, 69 & first prize, 72, Yardley Art Ctr, Pa; Grumbacher Award, N J State Exhib, Hunterdon Art Ctr, 67; Pearl Van Sciver Mem Award, Woodmere Gallery Exhib, Philadelphia, 67; plus others.

Memberships: Salmagundi Club; Woodmere Art Gallery; Del Valley Artists Asn.

Mailing Address: Paxson & Sugan Rds, Solebury, PA 18963.

JONES, RUTHE BLALOCK
Painter

Preferred Media: Watercolors, Acrylics, Oils.

b Claremore, Okla, June 8, 39.

Study & Training: Bacone Col, with Dick West, AA; Univ Tulsa, with Carl Coker, BFA.

Work in Public Collections: Mus Am Indian, Heye Found, New York, N Y; Indian Arts & Crafts Bd, U S Dept Interior, Washington, D C; Heard Mus, Phoenix, Ariz; Philbrook Art Ctr, Tulsa, Okla; Five Civilized Tribes Mus, Muskogee, Okla.

Exhibitions: U S Dept Interior Invitational Indian Exhib, Washington, D C, 65; Indian Ann, 68 & 72 & Okla Ann, 72, Philbrook Mus, Tulsa; Indian Ann, Five Civilized Tribes Mus, Muskogee, 69 & 70; Scottsdale Indian Nat Art Exhib, Ariz, 72.

Awards: First for traditional Indian painting, Philbrook Mus, 68; spec award, U S Dept Interior, Okla State Soc; second for watercolor painting, Scottsdale Nat Indian Art Exhib, 72.

Bibliography: J Snodgrass (auth), Handbook American Indian artists, Mus Am Indian, 67; Forum, Christian Sci Monitor, 6/67; Ruth B Jones—something a bit different, Ariz Repub, 7/67.

Research: Delaware Indian big house ceremony.

Art Interests: Lithography, serigraphy & drawing.

Publications: Illusr, Nimrod (Am Indian issue), Univ Tulsa J, spring 72.

Mailing Address: 618 E 15th St, Okmulgee, OK 74447.

JONES, TOM DOUGLAS
Designer, Educator

b Kansas City, Mo.

Study & Training: Kansas City Art Inst; Teachers Col, Columbia Univ; New York Univ; Ecole Beaux-Arts, Fountainebleau, France, dipl, 35; Univ Kans, BFA, 36; Univ Iowa, MA, 43; Bethany Col, hon DFA, 60.

Teaching: Asst prof design, Univ Kans, 36-44; res prof, Long Island Univ, Brooklyn, 64-71.

Positions: Artist & designer, Kansas City Star, Brooklyn Eagle & New York World, 26-34; dir, IBM Gallery Arts & Scis, 52-62.

Awards: Nat Acad Sci grant, 43.

Memberships: Am Soc Aesthetics; Soc Illustrators; Salmagundi Club.

Research: Color and light; inventor of Chromaton (color organ) and other devices.

Mailing Address: 25 Clark St, Brooklyn, NY 11201.

JONES, W LOUIS
Painter, Sculptor

Preferred Media: Acrylics, Wood.

b Durham, N C, Feb 22, 43.

Study & Training: Pa Acad Fine Art; E Carolina Univ, BS; Cranbrook Acad Art, MFA.

Work in Public Collections: Butler Inst Am Art, Youngstown, Ohio; Kalamazoo Inst Art, Mich; N C Mus Art, Raleigh; Mint Mus Art, Charlotte, N C; Univ Omaha, Nebr.

Exhibitions: U S Art in Embassies, 67; Butler Inst Am Art, 67; Nat Soc Painters in Casein, Washington, D C, 68; Northwest Artists Ann, Seattle, Wash, 68; Nat Realists Invitational; Gallery Contemp Art, Winston-Salem, N C, 71.

Teaching: Instr painting, Atlanta Sch Art, Ga, summer, 65; instr painting, Univ Idaho, 67-69; instr painting, Skidmore Col, 69-

Awards: Purchase awards, N C Mus Art, 63, Butler Inst Am Art, 67 & Mint Mus Art.

Memberships: Nat Soc Painters in Casein; Am Asn Univ Prof.

Dealer: Arwin Galleries, 222 Grand River W, Detroit, MI 48226.

Mailing Address: 11 Fifth Ave, Saratoga Springs, NY 12866.

JONNIAUX, ALFRED
Painter

Preferred Media: Oils.

b Brussels, Belg; U S citizen.

Study & Training: Acad Beaux Arts, Brussels; Calvin Coolidge Col Lib Arts, hon DFA, 58.

Work in Public Collections: De Young Mem Mus, San Francisco, Calif; Palais des Beaux Arts, Brussels; Royal Soc Portrait Painters, London, Eng; U S Capitol, Washington, D C; Brandeis Univ; plus others.

Commissions: Many portrait commissions of personalities.

Exhibitions: Smithsonian Inst Invitational, Washington, D C, 46.

Bibliography: Loring Hilmes Dodd (auth), Alfred Jonniaux, portrait painter.

Mailing Address: 1155 Jones St, San Francisco, CA 94109.

JONSON, RAYMOND
Painter, Art Administrator

Preferred Media: Acrylic polymer, Oil, Watercolor, Casein Tempera, Pencil.

b Chariton, Iowa, July 18, 91.

Study & Training: Portland Mus Art Sch, Ore; Chicago Acad Fine Arts; Chicago Art Inst.

Work in Public Collections: Rose Art Mus, Brandeis Univ, Waltham, Mass; William Rockhill Nelson Gallery Art, Kansas City, Mo; Dallas Mus Fine Arts, Tex; Cincinnati Art Mus, Ohio; Jonson Retrospective Collection of 545 works, Univ New Mex, Albuquerque.

Commissions: Six mural panels, A cycle of science, Univ New Mex, 34; murals, Art & Science, East New Mex Univ, Portales, 36.

Exhibitions: Critics Choice, Cincinnati Art Mus, 45; 58th Ann Am Exhibit, Abstract and Surrealist American Art, Chicago Art Inst, 47 & 48; Internationale Graphik, Salzburg & Vienna, Austria, 52; Golden Years of American Drawing, Brooklyn Mus, 57; Cubism: Its Impact in the U S A, Albuquerque, San Antonio, San Francisco, Los Angeles, 67.

Teaching: Prof, painting, Univ New Mex, 34-54.

Positions: Dir, Jonson Gallery, Univ New Mex, 50-

Awards: Laureate, Delta Phi Delta, 46; hon fel, Sch Am Res, 56; Dr Humane Lett, Univ New Mex, 71.

Bibliography: Chas Morris (auth), Search for a life of significance, Tomorrow I, No 2, 41; Ben Wolf (auth), Raymond Jonson, New Mex Artists, 52; Ed Garman (auth), The art of Raymond Jonson, El Palacio 63, Nos 5 & 6, 56.

Mailing Address: 1909 Las Lomas Rd, NE, Albuquerque, NM 87106.

JONYNAS, VYTAUTAS K
Painter, Designer

b Alytus, Lithuania, Mar 16, 07.

Study & Training: Nat Art Col, Kaunas, Lithuania; Conservatoire Nat Arts et Metiers & Ecole Boulle, Paris, France.

Work in Public Collections: Nat Mus in Lithuania, Latvia, Estonia, Weimar & Hamburg, Ger, Antwerp, Belg, Amsterdam City Mus, Metrop Mus Art, New York, N Y, Libr Cong, Washington, D C & others.

Commissions: Stained glass windows for numerous churches in U S; designed & executed front entrance sculpture, cross & altar in Vatican Pavilion, N Y World's Fair, 64-65; mosaics in chapel, Nat Shrine of the Immaculate Conception, Washington, D C; design of chapel of Our Lady of Vilnius in St Peter's Basilica, Rome; redecoration of a number of Catholic churches in Northeastern U S.

Exhibitions: Am Watercolor Soc Traveling Exhib, 56-58; Am Fedn Arts Traveling Exhib, 58-60; Conn Acad Fine Arts, 61; Fordham Univ, 63; Int Art Gallery, Cleveland, Ohio, 64; plus many others.

Teaching: Instr drawing, painting & graphic arts, cols & insts in Europe, 35-51; instr, Catan-Rose Inst Fine Arts, 52-57; instr, Fordham Univ, 56-70.

Awards: Gold medal, Paris World's Fair, 37; purchase prize, Calif Soc Etchers, 61; winner, Int Stained Glass Window Competition, Wilton, Conn; plus many others.

Publications: Contribr, illus, In: Das Kunstwerk, 47, 50 & 57 & Am Artist Mag, 52.

Mailing Address: 85-52 168th St, Jamaica, NY 11432.

JORDAN, BARBARA SCHWINN
Painter, Illustrator

b Glen Ridge, N J, Oct 20, 07.

Study & Training: Parsons Sch Design; Grand Cent Art Sch; Art Stud League New York, with Frank DuMond, Luigi Lucioni & others; Grande Chaumiere & Acad Julian, Paris, France.

Exhibitions: Two one-man exhibs, Soc Illustrators; one-man exhib, Barry Stephens Gallery; Nat Acad Design, 55; Royal Acad, London, Eng, 56; Guild Hall, 69.
Teaching: Lect illus & portrait painting; instr illus, Parsons Sch Design, 52-54; adv coun, Art Instr Schs, 56-70.
Positions: Founder & chmn art comt, UNICEF, 50-61.
Awards: Prizes, Guild Hall & Art Dirs Club.
Memberships: Soc Illustrators.
Publications: Auth, The technique of Barbara Schwinn & Fashion illustration, past and present, Art Instr Schs, 68.
Mailing Address: 1 W 67th St, New York, NY 10023.

JORN, ASGER
Painter, Writer
b Vejrum, Denmark, 1914.
Study & Training: With Fernand Leger, 36-37.
Work in Public Collections: Mus Mod Art, New York, N Y; Guggenheim Mus, New York; Tate Gallery, London, Eng; Mus Mod Art, Paris, France; Louisiana Mus, Denmark; plus other leading mus Europe & U S.
Commissions: Ceramic murals, State Denmark for high sch, Aarhus, 59 & Randers, Denmark, 71.
Exhibitions: Art Since 1950, Seattle World's Fair, 62; Guggenheim Int, New York, 64; Int Jorn Retrospective, Kunsthalle, Basel, Stedelijk Mus, Amsterdam & Louisiana Mus, Denmark, 64-65; Jorn Retrospective, Kestner-Gesellschaft, Hannover, Ger, plus five other Europ Mus, 73.
Bibliography: Werner Haftmann (auth), Asger Jorn, Quadrum Brussels, 62; Larence Alloway (auth), Guggenheim international award (preface to catalogue), Guggenheim Found, New York, 64; Guy Atkins (auth), Asger Jorn in Scandinavia, Wittenborn, 68.
Publications: Auth, Memoires, 52; auth, Pour la forme, Ed Int Situationniste, 58; auth, Gedanken eines kuenstlers, Van de Loo, Munich, Ger, 67; auth, La langue verte et la cuite, Jean-Jacques Pauvert, Paris, 68; auth, Indfald og udfald, Bongens Forlag, Denmark, 72.
Mailing Address: c/o Lefebre Gallery, 47 E 77th St, New York, NY 10021.

JOSIMOVICH, GEORGE
Painter, Designer
Preferred Media: Oil
b Mitrovica, Srem, Yugoslavia, May 2, 94; U S citizen.
Study & Training: Art Inst Chicago, Ill, 14-19; also with George Bellows & Randall Davey; studied with Herman Sachs, craftsman, 19-20 & worked in Paris, France, 26-27.
Work in Public Collections: Joslyn Art Mus, Omaha, Nebr.
Exhibitions: One-man, Galerie d'Art Contemporain, Paris, France, 27; 28th Int Exhib, Carnegie Inst, Pittsburgh, Pa, 29; Selected Paintings by Contemp Am Artists, Toledo Mus Art, Ohio, 30; ann exhibs by artists of Chicago & vicinity, Art Inst Chicago, 33, 34, 36, 38, 39, 41, 42, 44 & 49; Three Rivers Art Festival, Carnegie Inst, 68, 70.
Teaching: Supvr craft shop, Dayton Mus Art, Ohio, 21; instr parents' ceramic class, Pine Grove Pre-school, Chicago, 53-55.
Positions: V pres, Chicago Soc Artists, 42-43, pres, 43-44.
Awards: Silver medal, Chicago Soc Artists, 29.
Bibliography: J Z Jacobson (auth), The Chicago independent, The Arts, June, 31; J Z Jacobson (auth), Art of today, L M Stein, 33; C J Bullict (auth), Six Chicagoans, Art Digest, May, 50.
Mailing Address: 113 Lexington Ave, Aspinwall, Pittsburgh, PA 15215.

JOSTEN, PETER
Collector
Mailing Address: 161 E 61st St, New York, NY 10021.

JOSTEN, MRS WERNER E
Collector
Collection: Contemporary paintings.
Mailing Address: 944 Fifth Ave, New York, NY 10021.

JOSUS (JOSEPHINE HUTSON GRAHAM)
Painter, Educator
Preferred Media: Plastic Resin Paints; Watercolors.
b Newport, Ark.
Study & Training: Univ Ark, BA; Univ Colo, with Max Beckman, Richard Diebenkorn & Ralston Crawford; Parsons Sch Design, with Stephen Greene; Columbia Univ, MA; Art Stud League New York, N Y, with Jose de Creeft; also watercolor with Dong Kingman.
Work in Public Collections: Main Gallery, Little Rock, Ark; Ark Col, Batesville; Univ Ark, Little Rock; Jacksonport Mus, Ark.
Commissions: City scene, Commercial Nat Bank, Little Rock, 70.

Exhibitions: Am Watercolor Soc Exhib, Nat Acad Design Galleries, New York, 62; Nat Asn Women Artists, New York, 63; Hemisfair Art Exhib, San Antonio, Tex, 68; Ark Invitational Exhibs, First Am Nat Bank, 71 & 72.
Teaching: Asst prof art, Little Rock Univ, 62-67; asst prof art educ, Univ Ark, Little Rock, 67-70; asst prof art educ, State Col Ark, 70-
Positions: Art chmn, Pen Women, Little Rock, 65-66; pres, Suggin Soc, Newport, 72.
Awards: Iris Clark Art Award, 63; Sears Roebuck Art Award, 65; Midsouthern Watercolorists Award, 72.
Memberships: Assoc Am Watercolor Soc; Midsouthern Watercolorists (v pres, 70-72, pres, 72); Nat Asn Women Artists; Nat Art Educ Asn; Ark Art Educ Asn.
Dealer: Heirloom House, 2521 Fairmount St, Dallas, TX 75201.
Mailing Address: 101 Normandy Rd, Little Rock, AR 72207.

JOY, NANCY GRAHAME
Illustrator, Educator
Preferred Media: Ink.
b Toronto, Ont, Jan 15, 20.
Study & Training: Ont Dept Educ, sr matriculant, 38; Ont Col Art, assoc, dipl & hon grad, 42; Univ Toronto Faculty Med, spec stud with Dr J C B Grand & Dr William Boyd, 42-44; Univ Ill, spec stud med illus & asst to Prof Tom Jones.
Exhibitions: Contrib to permanent exhib human growth & develop, Mus Sci & Indust, 45-48.
Teaching: Prof, dept med illus, Univ Man, 56-62; prof art appl to med & dir BSc Art Appl to Med, 68-
Awards: Hughes Owens Grad Prize, 42; Biocommun '70 Mcd Educ Film Award & Asn Med TV Broadcasters Second Film Award, 70.
Memberships: Asn Med Illusr (bd gov, 56-61); Can Asn Med Illusr (bd gov, 71); Acad Med, Toronto, Can.
Publications: Auth, Pictured fact and fancy in current medical literature, Ann of Surg, Vol 156, No 3; auth, Dean's reports, BSc Art Appl to Med, 68-; auth, Medical illustrations and copyright, Med & Biol Illus, 4/64; ed, Medical illustration (cumulative bibliog), Asn Med Illusr, 67.
Mailing Address: Dept of Art as Applied to Medicine, Rm 304, 256 McCaul St, University of Toronto, Toronto 5, Ont, Can.

JOYNER, HOWARD WARREN
Painter, Art Historian
Preferred Media: Oils, Watercolors.
b Chicago, Ill, July 12, 00.
Study & Training: Kansas City Art Inst; Univ Mo, BFA, Univ Calif, AM; Ecole des Beaux Arts, Fontainebleau, France; Univ Iowa, MFA; also with Ross Braught, Jean Despujols & Hans Hofmann.
Exhibitions: Mich Ann, Lansing Art Asn, 30; Detroit Inst Art Ann, 31; New York Invitational, Rockefeller Ctr, 36; Joslyn Mem Art Mus Ann, 36; Tex Gen, 41-42.
Teaching: Asst prof art, Mich State Univ, 27-33; asst prof art & head dept, Univ S Dak, 35-37; prof art & head dept, Univ Tex, Arlington, 37-69.
Positions: Registrar, Kansas City Art Inst, 33-35.
Awards: First prize for figure painting, Lansing Art Asn, 30; first prize for watercolor, Arlington Art Asn, 56.
Memberships: Arlington Art Asn (pres & founder, 52); Fort Worth Art Asn (bd dirs, 41-66).
Research: Ancient, medieval, Mexican & modern art.
Art Interests: Restoration.
Publications: Auth, A prize winning poster, Everyday Art, 47.
Mailing Address: 1611 W Second, Arlington, TX 76013.

JU, I-HSIUNG
Painter, Educator
Preferred Media: Ink, Acrylics, Watercolors.
b Kiangyin, China, Sept 15, 23.
Study & Training: Nat Univ Amoy, China, AB(Chinese art), 47; Univ Santo Tomas, Manila, BFA, 55, MA(hist), 68.
Work in Public Collections: Philippine Cult Ctr, Manila; Art Asn Philippines, Manila; Nat Mus Hist, Taipei, Taiwan, Int Ctr, Univ Conn, Storrs; Du Pont Art Gallery, Washington & Lee Univ, Lexington, Va.
Commissions: Lotus & Blue Birds, House of Puyat, Manila, 61; Willow Trees, The Willow Ct, Makati, Rizal, Philippines, 66; Benedicite Montes Domino, R E Lee Mem Church, Lexington, Va, 70; 14 paintings, Gulf States Paper Corp Nat Hq, Tuscaloosa, Ala, 70-71.
Exhibitions: South-East Asian Art Contest, Manila, 57; Asian Arts Festival, Univ Philippines, Manila, 65; Philippine & Japan Joint Art Exhib, Nat Mus Hist, Taipei, 66; 10th Japan Nan-ga-in Exhib, Tokyo, Kyoto & Osaka Mus, 70; Nat Painting & Calligraphy Exhib, Nat Gallery, Taipei, 70.
Teaching: Lectr Chinese arts, Univ Maine, Univ N H, Univ Vt & Univ Conn, 68-69; lectr Chinese arts, Va Mus Fine Arts, Richmond, 69-71; prof art, Univ Va & Washington & Lee Univ, 69-

Awards: Nan-ga-in Awards, Japan Nan-so-ga Soc, 66-67; Ring-Tum-Phi Award, Washington & Lee Univ, 71.

Memberships: Va Mus Fine Arts; Col Art Asn Am; Nat Mus Philippines (hon curator, 64-); Art Asn Philippines (pres, dir & other positions, 55-68).

Publications: Illusr, The children of light, 56; auth, About art, 59 & Book of Bamboo, 68, Philippine Cult Publ Co; ed, Selection of short plays, 59; ed, Sorrows of my homeland, 59.

Dealer: Roanoke Fine Arts Center, Cherry Hill, Roanoke, VA 24014.

Mailing Address: Washington & Lee University, Lexington, VA 24450.

JUDD, DONALD CLARENCE
Sculptor
Preferred Media: Metals, Wood, Concrete, Plexiglass.
b Excelsior Springs, Mo, June 3, 28.
Study & Training: Art Stud League New York, 47-53; Columbia Univ, BS(philos), 53, grad study, 58-61.
Work in Public Collections: Mus Mod Art, New York, N Y; Whitney Mus Art, New York; Walker Art Ctr, Minneapolis, Minn; Los Angeles Co Mus, Calif; Albright-Knox Art Gallery, Buffalo, N Y.
Exhibitions: One-man shows, Whitney Mus Am Art, 68, Stedelijk Van Abbemuseum, Eindhoven, Holland, 70, White Chapel Gallery, London, Eng, 70 & Pasadena Art Mus, Calif, 71; New York Painting & Sculpture: 1940-1970, Metrop Mus Art, New York, 69-70.
Positions: Contrib ed, Arts Mag, 59-65.
Awards: U S Govt grant, 67; Guggenheim grant, 68.
Bibliography: William Agee (auth), Don Judd, Whitney Mus Am Art, 68; John Coplans (auth), Don Judd, Pasadena Art Mus, 71.
Mailing Address: c/o Leo Castelli Gallery, 4 E 77th St, New York, NY 10021.

JUDKINS, SYLVIA
Painter
Preferred Media: Watercolors, Ink, Acrylics.
b New York, N Y.
Study & Training: Pratt Inst, Brooklyn, N Y; Sch Visual Arts, New York; China Inst, New York; also painting tours with Edgar Whitney & Barse Miller; Nat Acad Fine Arts, scholar, 68-70.
Exhibitions: Am Artists Prof League Grand Nat Exhib, Lever House, New York, 67 & 70; Knickerbocker Artists Ann Exhib, Nat Art Club, New York, 68, 70 & 71; Am Watercolor Soc Ann, Nat Acad Design, New York, 68, 71 & 72; Parrish Mus Ann Exhib, Southampton, N Y, 70; Nat Art League Spring Exhib, Adelphi Univ, Garden City, N Y, 71.
Positions: Display artist, three dept store & display firms, 50-60; tech illusr for four different corporations, 60-65.
Awards: Award, Am Watercolor Soc, 69; award, Am Artists Prof League Grand Nat Exhib, 70; first prize watercolor, Huntington Art League, 70.
Memberships: Am Artists Prof League; Nat Art League (recording secy, 70, gallery chmn, 71-); Island Art Guild (asst prog chmn); Jackson Heights Art Club (exhib chmn, 69, publicity chmn, 70 & ed, newsletter, 71-).
Dealer: Art Collectors, 322 Bleeker St, New York, NY 10014.
Mailing Address: 35-36 76th St, Jackson Heights, NY 11372.

JUDSON, JEANNETTE ALEXANDER
Painter
Preferred Media: Oils, Acrylics.
b New York, N Y, Feb 23, 12.
Study & Training: Nat Acad Design, with Robert Phillip & Leon Kroll; Art Stud League New York, with Vaclav Vytlacil, Charles Alston, Carl Holty & Sidney Gross.
Work in Public Collections: Joseph H Hirshhorn Collection; N Y Univ Collection; Brandeis Univ, Waltham, Mass; Syracuse Univ, N Y; Fordham Univ, New York; plus many other pub & pvt collections.
Exhibitions: One-man shows, Fairleigh-Dickinson Univ, Rutherford, N J, 65, Bodley Gallery, New York, 67, 69 & 71, Laura Musser Mus Art, Muscatine, Iowa, 69, Pa State Univ, 69 & N Y Univ, 69.
Awards: Grumbacher award, Nat Asn Women Artists, 67.
Memberships: Nat Asn Women Artists (exten comt, 69); League Present Day Artists; N Y Soc Women Artists; Artists Equity New York.
Dealer: Bodley Gallery, 787 Madison Ave, New York, NY 10021.
Mailing Address: 1130 Park Ave, New York, NY 10028.

JUDSON, SYLVIA SHAW
Sculptor
Preferred Media: Bronze, Stone.
b Chicago, Ill, June 30, 97.
Study & Training: Art Inst Chicago, with Albin Polasek; Acad Grande Chaumière, Paris, France, with Antoine Bourdelle.
Work in Public Collections: Fountain, Art Inst Chicago; Nat Acad Design, New York; First Lady's Garden, White House, Washington, D C; Brookgreen Gardens, Ga; Kosciaseo Park, Milwaukee, Wis.
Commissions: Mem fountain to Theodore Roosevelt, Brookfield Zoo, 54; Violinist, Norman Ross Mem, Ravinia Park, Chicago, 55; monument to Mary Dyer, State House, Boston, Mass Art Comn, 59; group of granite animals, Fairmount Park Asn, Philadelphia, Pa, 65; gate posts & drinking fountain, Morton Arboretum, Lisle, Ill, 70.
Exhibitions: One-man shows, Art Inst Chicago, 38, Arden Gallery, New York, 40 & Sculpture Ctr, New York, 57; Int Sculpture Exhib, Philadelphia Mus; American Shows, Art Inst Chicago, Mus Mod Art, New York & Whitney Mus Am Art, New York.
Teaching: Instr sculpture, Am Univ, Cairo, 63.
Positions: Pres, Chicago Pub Sch Art Soc, 48-50; v pres women's bd, Art Inst Chicago, 53-54; clerk, Lake Forest Friends Meeting, 56-57; mem humanities vis comt, Univ Chicago, 62-.
Awards: Logan prize, Art Inst Chicago, 29; purchase prize, Int Sculpture Show, Philadelphia Mus, 49; Millbrook Garden Club Medal, 57.
Bibliography: What is good sculpture, House Beautiful, 57.
Memberships: Nat Acad Design; fel Nat Sculpture Soc; hon mem Nat Acad Interior Decorators; Art Club Chicago; Cosmopolitan Club, New York.
Publications: Auth, The quiet eye, 54 & For gardens & other places, 68, Regnery.
Mailing Address: 1230 N Green Bay Rd, Lake Forest, IL 60045.

JULES, MERVIN
Painter, Educator
b Baltimore, Md, Mar 21, 12.
Study & Training: Baltimore City Col; Md Inst Fine & Applied Arts; Art Stud League New York.
Work in Public Collections: Metrop Mus Art, New York, N Y; Art Inst Chicago, Ill; Mus Fine Arts, Boston, Mass; Portland Art Mus, Ore; Libr Cong, Washington, D C; plus many other pub & pvt collections.
Exhibitions: Carnegie Int, Pittsburgh, Pa; San Francisco World's Fair, Calif; Artists for Victory, sent to Eng; Corcoran Gallery Art, Washington, D C; Whitney Mus Am Art; plus many other group & one-man shows.
Teaching: Fieldston Sch, Mus Mod Art, War Vet Art Ctr & Peoples Art Ctr, New York; Highfield Art Workshop, Falmouth, Mass, summer 50; Univ Wis, 51; George Walter Vincent Smith Art Mus, 53; Univ Mass; Univ Mich, summer 62; vis artist, Smith Col, 45-46, assoc prof, 46-63, prof, 64-69; prof art & chmn dept, City Col New York, 69-
Positions: Adv ed, Sch Arts Mag; trustee, Cummington Sch Music & Art & Provincetown Art Asn; gov bd, Inst for Study of Art in Educ.
Awards: Hon mention, 19th Ann Exhib Boston Printmakers, 67; Asian-African Study Prog grant to Japan, 67; Alfred Vance Churchill Found grant, 67; plus others.
Publications: Auth, many articles in nat art publ.
Mailing Address: Dept of Art, City College of New York, New York, NY 10031.

JULIO, PAT T
Educator, Craftsman
b Youngstown, Ohio, Mar, 1, 23.
Study & Training: Wittenberg Col, BFA, with Ralston Thompson; Univ N Mex, MA, with Raymond Jonson & Lez Haas; Univ Colo, with Robert Lister; Ohio State Univ, with Edgar Littlefield; Tex Western Col, with Wiltz Harrison.
Work in Public Collections: Pvt collections only.
Commissions: Stained glass windows, Episcopal Good Samaritan Church, Community Church & pvt collections.
Exhibitions: Denver Art Mus, Colo, 50 & 63; Pueblo Art Mus, 60, one-man, 64; Pueblo Col, 60 & 69; one-man show, Western State Art Gallery, 69.
Teaching: Lect, Indian Art, American Art & The Kachina Doll; assoc prof art, Western State Col, 56-71, prof, 71-
Positions: Ed, Colo Art Educ Asn Bull.
Memberships: Col Art Asn Am; Western Art Asn; Am Ceramic Soc; Am Crafts Coun; Inst Indian Studies; plus others.
Mailing Address: Art Dept, Western State College, Gunnison, CO 81230.

JUNGWIRTH, IRENE GAYAS
Painter, Designer
Preferred Media: Egg Tempera, Oils.
b McKee's Rocks, Pa.
Study & Training: Cass Tech, Detroit, Mich; Marygrove Col, BFA; Wayne State Univ; Mich State Univ; also study abroad.
Work in Public Collections: Detroit Inst Arts, Mich; Marquette Univ Art Collection, Milwaukee, Wis; Marygrove Col Art Collection, Detroit, Mich; CSSP Seminary Collection, Ann Arbor, Mich.
Commissions: Stations of Cross (with Leonard D Jungwirth), Churches, Detroit, 55-62; crown in gold, topaz & diamonds, St Mary's Church, Detroit, 57-58; crucifixion (with Leonard D Jung-

wirth), St John's Church, East Lansing, Mich, 60; stained glass windows, YMCA-children's chapel, Methodist Church, 60-63; mural painting, dept hort, Mich State Univ, 67.
Exhibitions: Michigan Artists, Detroit Art Inst, 43-63; Flint Art Inst, 51; Int Ecclesiastical Show, 55-62; Va Biennial; Butler Inst Am Art, Youngstown, Ohio.
Awards: Painting of child, 43 & nocturne with figure & peacocks, 57, Detroit Inst Arts; Whitcomb Prize, Spring Nocturne, Butler Art Inst, 52.
Mailing Address: Route 1, Box 153-A, Mountain View Rd, Emmitsburg, MD 21727.

JUNKIN, MARION MONTAGUE
Painter, Educator
b Chunju, Korea, Aug 23, 05; U S citizen.
Study & Training: Washington & Lee Univ, AB, 27; Art Stud League New York, 27-30; also with Luks, Locke & McCartan, 30-32; Washington & Lee Univ, hon Arts D, 49.
Work in Public Collections: Va Mus Fine Arts; IBM Corp Collection.
Commissions: Murals, HQ Va State Police Dept, Richmond, McCormick Libr, Lexington, Stonewall Jackson Hosp, Lexington & Fed Savings & Loan Asn, Memphis; frescoes, Memphis, Tenn, Richmond & Roanoke, Va.
Exhibitions: Art Inst Chicago, Ill; Pa Acad Fine Arts, Philadelphia; Corcoran Art Gallery, Washington, D C; Carnegie Inst, Pittsburgh, Pa; Whitney Mus Am Art, New York, N Y; plus others.
Teaching: Prof fine arts & assoc dir, Richmond Sch Arts, 33-42; prof & head dept fine arts, Vanderbilt Univ, 41-49; prof & head dept fine arts, Washington & Lee Univ, 40-
Awards: Prizes, Va Mus Fine Arts, 46, Butler Inst Am Art, 46 & Richmond Acad Fine Arts; plus others.
Mailing Address: 801 Stonewall St, Lexington, VA 24450.

JUSTUS, ROY BRAXTON
Cartoonist
b Avon, S Dak, May 16, 01.
Study & Training: Morningside Col, 20-23, hon LLD, 56.
Work in Public Collections: Syracuse Univ, N Y.
Positions: Political cartoonist, Sioux City Tribune, 24-26, 27-41; ed cartoonist, Sioux City Jour, 41-44; ed cartoonist, Minneapolis Star & Tribune, 44-
Awards: Nat Headliner's Club Award, 44; Freedoms Found Awards, 49-56; Christopher Award, 55; plus others.
Memberships: Asn Am Ed Cartoonists (pres, 58-59).
Mailing Address: 19 S First St, Minneapolis, MN 55401.

K

KABAK, ROBERT
Painter, Educator
Preferred Media: Oils.
b New York, N Y.
Study & Training: High Sch Music & Art, New York, N Y; Brooklyn Col, BA(cum laude); Yale Univ Sch Fine Art, MFA.
Work in Public Collections: Mus Mod Art Permanent Collection, New York.
Exhibitions: New Talent, Mus Mod Art, 56; Whitney Mus Am Art Painting Ann, New York, 56 & 58; one-man show, Betty Parsons Gallery, New York, 67; Carnegie Int, Carnegie Mus Art, Pittsburgh, 67; one-man traveling show, Western Asn Art Mus, 68-71; plus many other one-man shows.
Teaching: Instr art, Brooklyn Co, 60-62; asst prof design, Univ Calif, Berkeley, 62-67; assoc prof art, Northern Ill Univ, 68-
Awards: Painting fels, seven grants, MacDowell Colony, 56-67; H Hartford Found, 60, 61 & 63 & H Wurlitzer Found N Mex, 69, 70 & 73.
Bibliography: J S Pierce (auth), Robert Kabak's big landscapes, Art Int, 3/69.
Mailing Address: Dept of Art, Northern Illinois University, De Kalb, IL 60115.

KACERE, JOHN C
Painter
b Walker, Iowa, June 23, 20.
Study & Training: Mizen Acad Art, Chicago, 38-42; Univ Iowa, BFA, 49, MFA, 51.
Work in Public Collections: Wadsworth Atheneum, Hartford, Conn; Mt Holyoke Col, Mass; Yale Univ, New Haven, Conn; Brandeis Univ, Waltham, Mass.

Exhibitions: Walker Art Ctr & circulated through U S, Can & S Am, 49-51; Mus Mod Art, New York, N Y; Art Inst Chicago, Ill; Philadelphia Mus Art, Pa; Joslyn Mus Art, Omaha, Nebr; plus others.
Teaching: Instr, Univ Manitoba, 50-53; instr, Univ Fla, 53-65; Cooper Union; Parsons Sch Design.
Mailing Address: 100 W 14th St, New York, NY 10011.

KACHADOORIAN, ZUBEL
Painter, Educator
Preferred Media: Oils, Charcoal, Inks, Watercolors, Gold, Silver.
b Detroit, Mich, Feb 7, 24.
Study & Training: Meinzinger Art Sch Detroit, 43-44; Saugatuck Summer Art Sch, Mich, 44-45; Skowhegan Sch Painting & Sculpture, Maine, 46; Colo Springs Fine Arts Ctr, summer 47.
Work in Public Collections: Detroit Inst Art; Art Inst Chicago; Worcester Mus, Mass; Smithsonian Inst, Washington, D C; Nelson Gallery Art, Mo.
Commissions: Gold leaf & oil altar painting, St John's Amenian Church Greater Detroit, 67.
Exhibitions: Univ Ill, Urbana, 61; Am Ann, Art Inst Chicago, 61; Art U S A Now, Johnson Wax Collection, 62; Butler Inst Am Art Ann, Youngstown, Ohio, 64; Flint Invitational, Mich, 66.
Teaching: Artist-in-residence, Sch Art Inst Chicago, 60-61; instr painting & drawing, Skowhegan Sch Painting & Sculpture, summer 64; prof drawing, Wayne State Univ, 67-
Positions: Adv, Common Grounds Detroit, 65-66.
Awards: Pepsi-Cola Midwest fel, 46; Prix-de-Rome, Am Acad Rome, 56-59; Richard & Hinda Rosenthal Award, Nat Inst Arts & Lett, 61.
Bibliography: A S Weller (auth), Art-U S A-now, C J Bucher, 62.
Memberships: Fel Am Acad Rome.
Mailing Address: 1214 Beaubien, Detroit, MI 48226.

KACHERGIS, GEORGE JOSEPH
Painter, Educator
Preferred Media: Oils, Acrylics.
b Waterbury, Conn, Apr 11, 17.
Study & Training: Art Inst Chicago Sch, MFA; also with Boris Anisfeld.
Work in Public Collections: High Mus, Atlanta, Ga; N C Mus Art, Raleigh; Ackland Art Mus, Chapel Hill, N C; Terry Art Inst, Miami, Fla.
Exhibitions: 21st Int Exhib Watercolors, Art Inst Chicago, 41; 145th Ann, Pa Acad Fine Arts, Philadelphia, 41-42; Am Painting Today, 50 & Am Watercolors, Drawings & Prints, 52, Metrop Mus Art, New York, N Y; Ann Exhib Contemp Painting, Whitney Mus Am Art, New York, 52.
Teaching: Instr art, Francis W Parker Sch, 46-47; instr drawing & painting, Bradley Univ, 47-49; prof drawing & painting, Univ N C, Chapel Hill, 49-
Awards: Tiffany fel in painting, 51; Terry Nat Art Exhib, 52; Eighth Southeastern Ann, 53.
Mailing Address: Rte 1, Box 131-A, Pittsboro, NC 27312.

KAEP, LOUIS JOSEPH
Painter
Preferred Media: Watercolors.
b Dubuque, Iowa, Mar 19, 03.
Study & Training: Loras Col; Art Inst Chicago; Julian Acad, Paris, France.
Work in Public Collections: Loras Col, Dubuque; City of Chicago, Ill; Kalamazoo Inst Arts, Mich; Soc New York Hosps, N Y; Am Acad Arts & Lett, New York.
Commissions: With 6th Fleet in Mediterranean, 60 & with Seabees in S Pac & Far East, 61, U S Navy, Washington, D C.
Exhibitions: Royal Watercolor Soc, London, Eng, 62; 200 Years of Watercolor Painting in America, Metrop Mus, New York, 66; Am Watercolor Soc 100th Ann, New York, 67; 50 Am Watercolor Soc Watercolors, Mus Aquarelle, Mexico City, Mex, 68; Nat Acad Design 147th Ann, New York, 72.
Teaching: Instr painting, Art Inst Chicago, 24-26; instr watercolors, Chicago Acad Fine Arts, 36-42.
Positions: V pres, Vogue Wright Studios, New York, 52-56; pres, 56-65; pres, Electrographic Corp, New York, 65-71, v chmn, 71-
Awards: Olsen award for Sampans & Junks, Hong Kong, Am Watercolor Soc 95th Ann, 62; assoc mem award for The Old Quarry, Allied Artists Am, 69; gold medal for Fiesta, Toledo, Spain, Hudson Valley Art Asn, 70.
Bibliography: Developing paintings from sketches (film), 71.
Memberships: Am Watercolor Soc (first v pres, 62); Salmagundi Club (bd dirs, 65); Artists & Writers Asn; Nat Acad Design; Allied Artists Am.
Publications: Contribr, Fairfield watercolor group, Am Artists Mag, 7/72.
Mailing Address: 14 Anderson Rd, Greenwich, CT 06803.

KAHANE, ANNE
Sculptor
Preferred Media: Wood.
b Vienna, Austria, Mar 1, 24; Can citizen.
Study & Training: Cooper Union Art Sch, 45-47.
Work in Public Collections: Nat Gallery Can, Ottawa; Montreal Mus Fine Arts, P Q; Winnipeg Art Gallery, Man; Art Gallery Hamilton, Ont; Vancouver Art Gallery, B C.
Commissions: Exterior mural (mahogany), Mount Allison Univ, Sackville, N B, 62; interior sculpture (mahogany), Winnipeg Int Airport, Man, 63; interior sculpture (mahogany), Place des Arts, Montreal, P Q, 65; exterior sculpture (mahogany), Expo 67, Montreal, 67; interior mural (pine), Can Chancery, Islamabad, Pakistan, 72.
Exhibitions: Can Pavilion, Brussels Worlds Fair & Venice Biennial, Italy, 58; Pittsburgh Int, Carnegie Inst, Pa, 59; 30 Years of Can Art, Nat Gallery Can, 67; Sculpture 67, Toronto, Ont, 67.
Awards: Unknown Political Prisoner, Eng, 53; Grand Prix for sculpture, Concours, Que, 56; Can Coun Arts fel, 61.
Bibliography: Malcolm Ross (auth), The arts in Canada, Macmillan, 58; Charles Spencer (auth), Ann Kahane, The Studio, Vol 160, No 807; Dorothy Cameron (auth), People in the park, Art & Artists, Vol 4, No 8.
Memberships: L'Association Sculpteurs du Que.
Dealer: Isaacs Gallery, 832 Yonge St, Toronto, Ont, Can.
Mailing Address: 3794 Hampton Ave, Montreal 261, PQ, Can.

KAHANE, MELANIE (MELANIE KAHANE GRAUER)
Designer
b New York, N Y, Nov 26, 10.
Study & Training: Parsons Sch Design, grad, 31; Paris, France, 32.
Commissions: Designer, Reid Hall, Paris, France, 48, Children's Mus, Fort Worth, Tex, 55, Gov Shriver, s Mansion, Austin, Tex, 57, Playbill Restaurant, New York, 58 & Ziegfield Theatre, New York, 63; plus others.
Teaching: Lectr, Parsons Sch Design, 50-
Positions: Illusr, Tobias Green Advert Co, 31-32; designer, Lord & Taylor, 33-34; founder & pres, Melanie Kahane, Inc, 35-52; founder & pres, Melanie Kahane Assocs, Interior & Indust Design, 52-; designer, Charles of Ritz Beauty Salons throughout U S, 57-; dir styling & design, Sprague & Carleton Furniture Co, 62-
Awards: Decorator of the Year Award, 53; Career Key Award, Girls' Clubs Am, 61; one of 100 Am Women of Accomplishment, Harper's Bazaar, 67; plus others.
Memberships: Fel Am Inst Interior Designers (past nat secy, bd dirs, past pres, N Y Chap, nat treas, 71-); Munic Art Soc; Decorator's Club New York; Inter-Soc Color Coun; Inst Practising Designers, Eng; plus others.
Publications: Producer, Decorating, a way of life (doc film), 49; auth, There's a decorator in your doll house, 68; also contribr to bks & encycls.
Mailing Address: 29 E 63rd St, New York, NY 10022.

KAHN, ANNELIES RUTH
Ceramist, Instructor
Preferred Media: Clay, Metal, Plastics.
b Dresden, Ger, Aug 17, 27; U S citizen.
Study & Training: R I Sch Design, BFA; Tex Woman's Univ, MA.
Exhibitions: 7th Int Exhib Ceramic Art, Smithsonian Inst, Washington, D C, 58; Ann Area Competition, Corcoran Gallery, Washington, D C, 59; 22nd Ceramic Nat, Everson Mus, Syracuse, N Y & Traveling Show, 62 & 68; Am Craftsmen's Coun Exhib, Oakland, Calif, 63; Form and Quality, Int Exhib, Munich, Ger, 64-69.
Teaching: Instr ceramics, Md Art Inst, Baltimore, 57-59; instr ceramics, Southern Methodist Univ, 64-69; instr ceramics & sculpture, Mountain View Col, Dallas, Tex, 70-
Positions: Designer & glaze analyst, Calif Art Tile Co, Richmond, 51-52; asst to dir, Gump's Gallery, San Francisco, Calif, 52-53; asst to dir, Fine Art Gallery, Dallas, 64-66.
Awards: Craft Horizons Award, Smithsonian Inst, 58; first prize, Corcoran Gallery, 59 & Southern Area Command, Munich, 61.
Bibliography: Creation in clay, KERA TV, 68.
Memberships: Tex Designer Craftsmen (secy, 71), Dallas Craft Guild; World Crafts Coun; Am Craftsmen Coun.
Dealer: Contemporary Gallery, 2800 Routh St, Dallas, TX 75201.
Mailing Address: 10808 Snow White Dr, Dallas, TX 75229.

KAHN, PETER
Painter, Designer
Preferred Media: Graphics.
b Leipzig, Ger, July 5, 21; U S citizen.
Study & Training: With Hans Hofmann, 47-49; N Y Univ, 48-51, BS, MA.
Work in Public Collections: Utica Mus; Va Mus; White Mus; Cornell Univ; Univ Notre Dame Gallery.

Exhibitions: Art U S A 1954, Va Mus, 54; Artists of Central New York, Utica, 59-61; New Graphic Art, travelling in Holland, 65; Natural Vision, Columbia Univ, 68; Retrospective, Hobart Col, Geneva, N Y.
Teaching: Asst prof graphic design, La State Univ, Baton Rouge, 51-53; assoc prof graphic design & chmn dept, Hampton Inst, Va, 53-57; prof graphics & paintings, Cornell Univ, 57-68, lectr art hist, 69-72, prof art hist, 72-
Awards: Gov award, Va Mus, 56; first prize for graphics, Binghamton Mus, 58; first prize, Utica Mus, 59 & 60.
Mailing Address: Dept of Art History, Cornell University, Ithaca, NY 14850.

KAHN, RALPH H
Art Dealer, Lecturer
b Trier, Ger, Aug 17, 20; U S citizen.
Study & Training: Spec study with W Baumeister.
Collections Arranged: Ten exhibs annually, Contemp Gallery, 65-
Teaching: Guest lectr twentieth century art, art collecting & art processes, for mus, cols & private art groups.
Positions: Dir, Contemp Gallery, Dallas, Tex, 65-
Memberships: Terra Linda Art Asn (asst dir, 63); Tex Fine Arts Asn (pres, 72); Am Soc Appraisers.
Research: W Baumeister and other twentieth century contemporary artists.
Specialty of Gallery: Twentieth century contemporary paintings, prints & sculpture.
Collection: Baumeister, Braque, Chagall, Klee, Miro & Picasso.
Mailing Address: Contemporary Gallery, 2800 Routh, Dallas, TX 75201.

KAHN, SUSAN B
Painter
Preferred Media: Oils.
b New York, N Y, Aug 26, 24.
Study & Training: Parsons Sch Design; also with Moses Soyer.
Work in Public Collections: New York Cult Ctr; Montclair Mus, N J; Butler Inst Am Art, Youngstown, Ohio; Reading Mus, Pa; Joslyn Art Mus, Omaha, Nebr.
Exhibitions: City Ctr, New York, 68; Nat Arts Club, 69; Springfield Mus, Mass, 69; Audubon Artists, New York, 69; Nat Acad Design, 70.
Awards: Knickerbocker Artists Medal of Honor, 64; Nat Arts Club Award, 67; Famous Artist Sch Award, Nat Asn Women Artists, 67.
Bibliography: Margaret Harold (auth), Award winning art, Allied Publ, 65; Marshall Matusow (auth), Art Collectors almanac, Jerome E Treisman, 65.
Memberships: Artists Equity Asn; Nat Asn Women Artists; Knickerbocker Artists.
Publications: Contribr, How to paint a prize winner, 65.
Dealer: ACA Gallery, 25 E 73rd St, New York, NY 10021.
Mailing Address: 870 United Nations Plaza, New York, NY 10017.

KAHN, WOLF
Painter
Preferred Media: Oils, Pastels.
b Stuttgart, Ger, Oct 4, 27.
Study & Training: New Sch Social Res, with Stuart Davis; Hans Hofmann Sch; Univ Chicago, BA.
Work in Public Collections: Whitney Mus Am Art, New York, N Y; Mus Mod Art, New York; Brooklyn Mus, N Y; Houston Mus Fine Arts, Tex; City Art Mus, St Louis, Mo.
Exhibitions: Whitney Mus Am Art Ann, 58 & 59; Univ Ill Biennial, 58-60; Young America, Whitney Mus Am Art, 61; Americans in Europe 11E, circulated by Am Fedn Arts, 71-72; New England Art, Inst Contemp Art, Boston, 72.
Teaching: Vis assoc prof painting, Univ Calif, Berkeley, 60-61; adj asst prof painting, Cooper Union Art Sch, 60-
Awards: Purchase award, Ford Found 63; Fulbright scholar to Italy, 63-65; Guggenheim fel, 66.
Bibliography: L Campbell (auth), In the mist of life, Art News, 2/69; Gussow (auth), Sense of place, Friends of the Earth, 72.
Publications: Auth, Uses of painting today, Daedalus Mag, 69.
Dealers: Grace Borgenicht, 1018 Madison Ave, New York, NY 10021; Meredith Long Gallery, 2323 San Felipe, Houston, TX 77027.
Mailing Address: 813 Broadway, New York, NY 10003.

KAINEN, JACOB
Painter, Printmaker
Preferred Media: Oils.
b Waterbury, Conn, Dec 7, 09.
Study & Training: Art Stud League New York, with Nicolaides; New York Univ Eve Sch Archit; Pratt Inst, grad.
Work in Public Collections: Metrop Mus Art, New York, N Y; Phillips Collection, Washington, D C; Corcoran Gallery Art, Washington, D C; Carnegie Inst, Pittsburgh, Pa; Bezalel Nat Mus, Israel.

Exhibitions: Painting Retrospective, Catholic Univ, Washington, D C, 52; Corcoran Gallery Art Painting Biennial, 57; U S Info Agency Contemp Am Painting Tour of Latin Am, 61-62; one-man show, Roko Gallery, New York, 64-66; one-man show, Pratt Manhattan Ctr, New York, 72.
Memberships: Artists Equity Asn; Soc Washington Printmakers.
Mailing Address: 27 W Irving St, Chevy Chase, MD 20015.

KAISER, CHARLES JAMES
Painter
Preferred Media: Oils, Acrylics, Watercolors.
b Milwaukee, Wis, Mar 10, 39.
Study & Training: Layton Sch Art, Milwaukee; Univ Wis-Milwaukee, BFA, MS & MFA, painting with John Colt & Robert Burkert.
Work in Public Collections: Wustum Mus, Racine, Wis; Union Art Gallery, Univ Wis-Milwaukee; Civic Art Collection, Munic Bldg, Springfield, Ill; Marquette Univ, Milwaukee.
Exhibitions: Five shows, Watercolor U S A, Springfield, Mo, 62-72; Northwest Miss Valley Artists Invitational, Ill State Mus, Springfield, 66; Calif Nat Watercolor Soc, Laguna Beach, 70 & 72; Exhib Contemp Am Painting, Palm Beach, Fla, 70; Chicago & Vicinity, Chicago Art Inst, Ill, 71.
Positions: Wis hon rep for Calif Nat Watercolor Soc, 70-
Awards: Calif Nat Watercolor Soc Purchase Award, Butrijamp Found, 70; Madison Salon Graphic Art Drawings & Prints Award, Wis State J & others, 70; Wis Watercolor Soc Award for Excellence, 71.
Memberships: Calif Nat Watercolor Soc; Wis Watercolor Soc.
Dealer: Bradley Galleries, 2565 N Downer Ave, Milwaukee, WI 53211.
Mailing Address: 2952 N Maryland Ave, Milwaukee, WI 53211.

KAISER, VITUS J
Painter, Instructor
Preferred Media: Acrylics, Watercolors.
b Erie, Pa, May 3, 29.
Study & Training: N C State Col; Veterans Sch, Erie, with Joseph Plavcan; Univ Pittsburgh.
Work in Public Collections: Erie Pub Libr.
Exhibitions: Pa Watercolor Show, Edinboro, Pa, 59; Nat Watercolor Competition, Galerie 8, Erie, 69; Chautauqua Nat Juried Show, N Y, 69; Am Drawing Biennial XXIV, Norfolk Mus, Va, 71; Albright-Knox Art Gallery, Mem Gallery, Buffalo, N Y, 72.
Teaching: Instr art, Tech Mem High Sch, 70-
Memberships: Erie Art Ctr (adv bd, 70); Chautauqua Art Asn.
Dealer: Galerie 8, 421 W Eighth St, Erie, PA 16402.
Mailing Address: 551 W 26th St, Erie, PA 16508.

KAISH, LUISE
Sculptor
Preferred Media: Metals, Stone.
b Atlanta, Ga.
Study & Training: Syracuse Univ, BFA & MFA, with Ivan Mestrovic & Taller Grafico; Escuela Pinture y Escultura, Mexico City, Mex.
Work in Public Collections: Whitney Mus Am Art, New York, N Y; Jewish Mus, New York; Rochester Mem Art Gallery, N Y; St Paul Art Ctr, Minn; High Mus Art, Atlanta, Ga.
Commissions: Ark of Revelations (bronze), Temple B'rith Kodesh, Rochester; Great Ideas of Western Man & Walter Paepke Award Sculpture, Container Corp Am; Christ in Glory (bronze), Holy Trinity Mission Sem, Silver Spring, Md; spice container (bronze), Jewish Mus; ark doors, menorahs, eternal light (bronze), Temple Beth Shalom, Wilmington, Del.
Exhibitions: Sculpture U S A, Metrop Mus Art, New York; Recent Sculpture U S A, Mus Mod Art, New York; Int Biennial Relig Art, Europ tour; Synagogue Art & Architecture in America, Jewish Mus; Art in Embassies, U S State Dept.
Awards: Guggenheim fel creative sculpture; Louis Comfort Tiffany grant creative sculpture; Rome prize fel in sculpture.
Memberships: Sculptors Guild.
Mailing Address: c/o Staempfli Gallery, 47 E 77th St, New York, NY 10021.

KALB, MARTY JOEL
Painter
Preferred Media: Oils, Acrylics.
b Brooklyn, N Y, Apr 13, 41.
Study & Training: Mich State Univ, BA, 63; Yale Univ, BFA, 64; Univ Calif, Berkeley, MA, 66.
Work in Public Collections: J B Speed Mus, Louisville, Ky; Univ Mass.
Exhibitions: 23rd Am Drawing Biennial, Norfolk Mus, 69; Regional Fine Art Biennial, J B Speed Mus, 69; Ohio Artists, Dayton Art Inst, 70; Small Paintings, Purdue Univ, 70; Ohio Artists, Canton Art Inst, 72.

Teaching: Instr, Univ Ky, 66-67; asst prof painting, Ohio Wesleyan Univ, 67-
Memberships: Col Art Asn Am.
Dealer: Alonzo Gallery, 26 E 63rd St, New York, NY 10021.
Mailing Address: 79 Richards Dr, Delaware, OH 43015.

KALINOWSKI, EUGENE M
Painter, Sculptor
b Pittsburgh, Pa, Jan 19, 29.
Study & Training: Carnegie-Mellon Univ, BFA, 52, MFA, 65.
Work in Public Collections: In pvt collections only.
Exhibitions: Inst Contemp Art, Boston, 62; Albright-Knox Art Gallery, Buffalo, N Y, 62; Butler Inst Am Art, Youngstown, Ohio; Carnegie Inst, Pittsburgh; one-man show, Slippery Rock State Col, Pa, 66.
Teaching: Instr painting & drawing, Pittsburgh Pub Sch System; instr, Arts & Crafts Ctr, Pittsburgh, 68.
Awards: Second prize for sculpture, 58, jury award for distinguished painting, 60 & award for distinguished work in watercolor, 61, Assoc Artists Pittsburgh; first prize, Pittsburgh Playhouse Show, 60.
Memberships: Assoc Artists Pittsburgh (bd dirs, 62-64); Pittsburgh Watercolor Soc; Soc Sculptors; Pittsburgh Plan for Art; Centro Studi e Scambi Int, Rome.
Mailing Address: 5356 Rosetta St, Pittsburgh, PA 15224.

KALLEM, HERBERT
Sculptor, Instructor
b Philadelphia, Pa, Nov 14, 09.
Study & Training: Nat Acad Design; Pratt Inst; Hans Hofmann Sch Fine Arts.
Work in Public Collections: Whitney Mus Am Art, New York, N Y; Wadsworth Atheneum, Hartford, Conn; New York Univ Loeb Collection, N Y; Newark Mus Art, N J; Chrysler Mus, Provincetown, Mass; also in pvt collections.
Exhibitions: Whitney Mus Am Art, New York; Carnegie Inst, Pittsburgh, Pa; Univ Ill, Urbana; plus others.
Teaching: Former instr sculpture, Sch Visual Arts & New York Univ.
Memberships: Sculptors Guild; Am Abstract Artists.
Dealers: Contemporary Arts Gallery, 566 La Guardia Pl, New York, NY 10012; Roko Gallery, 90 E 10th St, New York, NY 10003.
Mailing Address: 45 W 28th St, New York, NY 10001.

KALLER, ROBERT JAMESON
Art Dealer
Study & Training: Columbia Univ; Harvard Univ; New York Univ.
Positions: Owner, Galerie de Tours, San Francisco, Carmel & Beverly Hills, Calif, 60-; art critic; art consult to mus & corps; cert appraiser; pres, Arts & Humanities Coun, Monterey, Calif, 63-64.
Specialty of Gallery: Nineteenth and twentieth century American art; German expressionists; French impressionists; seventeenth century Dutch.
Mailing Address: P O Box 413, Pebble Beach, CA 93953.

KALLIR, OTTO
Art Dealer, Art Historian
b Vienna, Austria, Apr 1, 94; U S citizen.
Study & Training: Univ Vienna, PhD, 31.
Positions: Dir art dept, Rikola Verlag, Vienna, 20-22; founder-owner, Neue Galerie, Vienna, 23-72; founder-owner, Johannes Press, Vienna & New York, N Y, 23-; founder-owner, Galeries St Etienne, Paris, France, 38-39, New York, 39-; pres, Grandma Moses Properties, Inc, New York, 50-
Awards: Grosses Ehrenzeichen (grand medal of honor for merit in the field of art), Repub of Austria, 60; Silbernes Ehrenzeichen (silver medal of honor for fostering relations in art between Austria & the U S A), City of Vienna, 68.
Memberships: Art Dealers Asn Am.
Research: Austrian Expressionist art, especially Egon Schiele; Kaethe Kollwitz; American Primitive art, especially Grandma Moses; history of aeronautics.
Specialty of Gallery: Austrian & German Expressionists; American Primitive art.
Collection: Austrian nineteenth & twentieth century art; American Primitive art; history of aeronautics.
Publications: Auth, Egon Schiele (catalogue raisonne of the paintings), 30, rev & enlarged ed, 66; auth, Grandma Moses: American primitive, 46 & 47; ed, My life's history by Grandma Moses, 52; ed, A sketchbook by Egon Schiele, 67; auth, Egon Schiele (catalogue raisonne of the graphic work), 70.
Mailing Address: 24 W 57th St, New York, NY 10019.

KALLWEIT, HELMUT G
Painter, Sculptor
b Ger, Sept 18, 06.
Exhibitions: Riverside Mus; Art: U S A, 58; Parrish Mus Art; Guild Hall, East Hampton, N Y; New York Times Gallery; plus others.
Mailing Address: 90 Columbia St, New York, NY 10002.

KALTENBACH, STEPHEN JAMES
Painter, Sculptor
b Battlecreek, Mich, May 5, 40.
Study & Training: Univ Calif, Davis, BA & MA.
Work in Public Collections: Allen Art Mus, Oberlin Col, Ohio.
Exhibitions: When Attitudes Become Form, Kuntshalle, Berne, Switz, 69; Information, Mus Mod Art, New York, N Y, 70; Conceptual Art, Conceptual Aspects, New York Cult Ctr, 70; Tokyo Bienale, Japan, 70; Sacramento Sampler, E B Crocker Art Gallery, Calif, 72; plus many others.
Bibliography: Germano Celant (auth), Art povera, 70; Cindy Nemser (auth), An interview with Stephen Kaltenbach, Artforum, 11/70; Article, In; Art Now, 3/72.
Mailing Address: 1640 Sherman Ave, Madison, WI 53704.

KAMIHIRA, BEN
Painter
b Yakima, Wash, Mar 16, 25.
Study & Training: Art Inst Pittsburgh; Pa Acad Fine Arts, 48-52, J Henry Schiedt traveling scholar, 52.
Work in Public Collections: Whitney Mus Am Art, New York, N Y; Pa Acad Fine Arts, Philadelphia; Ringling Mus, Sarasota, Fla; Colo Springs Fine Arts Ctr, Colo; Dallas Mus Fine Arts, Tex; plus others.
Exhibitions: Nat Acad Design; Pa Acad Fine Arts; Corcoran Gallery Art, Washington, D C; Butler Inst Am Art, Youngstown, Ohio; Mus Mod Art, New York; plus many others.
Teaching: Instr drawing & painting, Pa Acad Fine Arts & Pa State Univ.
Awards: Johnson Prize, New Eng Ann, 61; first Altman Prize, Nat Acad Design, 62; first prize, Chatauqua Nat Exhib, 62; plus many others.
Memberships: Fellowship Pa Acad Fine Arts; Acad Nat Acad Design.
Dealer: Atelier Chapman Kelley, 2526 Fairmount St, Dallas, TX 75201.
Mailing Address: Cheyney Rd, Cheyney, PA 19319.

KAMMERER, HERBERT LEWIS
Sculptor
Preferred Media: Bronze, Stone, Terra-Cotta, Steel.
b New York, N Y, July 11, 15.
Study & Training: Apprentice to Charles Keck & C Paul Jennewein; asst to Paul Manship; Nat Acad Design; Art Stud League New York; Yale Univ, BFA, 41; Am Acad Rome, 49-52.
Work in Public Collections: Va Mil Inst; Eisenhower Collection; HRH Queen Elizabeth, Eng.
Commissions: Many medals, portraits & archit sculpture.
Exhibitions: Pa Acad Design Ann, 41, 48 & 52-; Fairmont Int Show, 49; Nat Acad Design, 49, 51 & 52; Palazzo Venezia Int, 50 & 51; plus many others.
Teaching: Prof sculpture, State Univ New York Col New Paltz, 62-
Awards: George D Widener Gold Medal, Pa Acad Design Ann, 48; Prix d'Rome, Am Acad Rome, 49; grant in sculpture, Nat Inst Arts & Lett, 52.
Memberships: Nat Sculpture Soc (pres, 63-65); Century Asn.
Mailing Address: 64 Plains Rd, New Paltz, NY 12561.

KAMROWSKI, GEROME
Painter, Educator
Preferred Media: Mixed Media.
b Warren, Minn, Jan 29, 14.
Study & Training: St Paul Sch Art; Art Stud League New York; New Bauhaus; Hans Hofmann Sch, New York, N Y.
Work in Public Collections: Flint Inst Arts, Mich; Detroit Inst Art, Mich; Solomon R Guggenheim Mus, New York; Phillips Mem Gallery; Albion Col, Mich; plus others.
Exhibitions: Blood Flames, Hugo Gallery, New York, 45; Int Expos Surrealism, Gallerie Maegt, Paris, France, 46; Surrealism & Abstract Art, Sydney Janis Gallery; one-man shows, Betty Parsons, New York, 42 & Galerie Creuze, Paris, 51; plus many other group & one-man shows.
Teaching: Prof art, Univ Mich Col Art & Archit, Ann Arbor, 46-
Positions: Mentor, Hylozoist Group, Detroit, Mich, 57-67; mentor, Ann Arbor Group, 63.
Awards: Founders prize, Detroit Inst Art; Guggenheim fel, 37; Racknam fel, 72.
Bibliography: Andre Breton (auth), Surrealisme et la peinturu, Brentano's; Manupilii (auth), Celestial rythms (film); Nicolas Calas (auth), Blood flames (catalogue), Hugo Gallery, 46.
Mailing Address: 1501 Beechwood Dr, Ann Arbor, MI 48103.

KAMYS, WALTER
Painter, Educator
b Chicago, Ill, June 8, 17.
Study & Training: Art Inst Chicago, 43, with Hubert Ropp & Brois Anisfeld; pvt study with Gordon Onslow-Ford, Mex, 44.

Work in Public Collections: Yale Univ; Mt Holyoke Col; Smith Col; Fogg Art Mus; Regional Contemp Art Collection, Fargo, N D; plus others.
Exhibitions: Silvermine Guild Artists, 54, 55 & 67; Art for U S Embassies, Inst Contemp Art, Boston, 66; Smithsonian Inst, 68; Amherst Col, 68; one-man show, Ward-Nasse Gallery, Boston, 68; plus other group & one-man shows.
Teaching: Instr art, Putney Sch, Vt, 45; instr art, G W V Smith Art Mus, Springfield, Mass, 47-60; prof painting & drawing, Univ Mass, 60-, dir, Art Acquisition Prog, 62-
Awards: Boston Art Festival, 55; Amherst, Mass, 57 & 58; Westfield State Col Purchase Prize, 68; plus others.
Bibliography: Harriet Janis & Rudi Blesh (auth), Collage: personalities—concepts—techniques, Chilton Co, 62.
Mailing Address: Cave Hill Farm, Montague, MA 01351.

KAN, DIANA
Painter
Preferred Media: Watercolors.
b Hong Kong, Mar 3, 26; U S citizen.
Study & Training: With Chang Dai Chien, China, 46; Art Stud League New York, with Robert Johnson & Robert B Hale, 49-51; École Beaux Arts, Paris, France with Paul Lavelle, 52-54.
Work in Public Collections: Nat Hist Mus, Taiwan; St John's Univ, Shanghai, China; Dalhousie Univ, Halifax, N S; Elliott Mus, Fla; Bruce Mus, Conn.
Commissions: Lotus painting, Nat Hist Mus, Taiwan, 71.
Exhibitions: Royal Acad Arts, London, Eng, 64; Royal Soc Painters, London, 64; one-man shows, Elliott Mus, 67; Nat Hist Mus, Taiwan, 71 & New York Cult Ctr, 72; plus others.
Awards: Am Watercolor Soc Traveling Award, 68; Barbara Vassillieff Mem Award, Allied Artists Am, 69; Anna Hyatt Huntington Bronze Medal, Catharine Lorillard Wolfe Art Club, 70.
Bibliography: Robert Harris (auth), Pictures by a Chinese artist, London Times, 64; Barbara Wright (auth), Diana Kan, Arts Rev, London, 64; Daniel Su (auth), Chinese paintings, Cosmorama Pictorial, 72.
Memberships: Am Watercolor Soc; Allied Artists Am; Catharine Lorillard Wolfe Art Club; Pen & Brush (mem bd dirs, 68); Nat League Am Pen Women.
Publications: Auth, White cloud.
Dealer: Christopher Gallery, 766 Madison Ave, New York, NY 10021. Lord & Taylor Art Gallery, Fifth Ave, New York, NY 10018.
Mailing Address: 26 W Ninth St, New York, NY 10011.

KAN, MICHAEL
Art Historian, Art Administrator
b Shanghai, China, July 17, 33; U S citizen.
Study & Training: Columbia Col, BA(art hist & archeol), 53; State Univ N Y Agr & Tech Col Alfred, MFA(ceramics & sculpture), 57; Columbia Univ, MA(art hist), 69.
Collections Arranged: African Art & Simpson Collection, Brooklyn Mus, 70; Ancient Art of West Mexico, guest cur, Los Angeles Co Mus Art, 70; African Art Tribal Art from West Africa, curatorial consult, Portland Mus, 71; Pre-Columbian Art in the Collection of Jay C Leff, curatorial consult, Allentown Mus, 72.
Teaching: Lectr art hist, Univ Calif, Berkeley, 64-66; lectr art Eastern Asia, Finch Col, 66-67; lectr African art, N Y Univ, 70-
Positions: Assoc cur primitive art, Brooklyn Mus, 68-70, cur, 70-
Memberships: African Civilization Studies Orgn (trustee, 72); Am Asn Mus.
Research: The art of early cultures of pre-Columbian Peru and pre-Columbian Mexico; African art education.
Publications: Contribr, Early Chinese art and the Pacific Basin, 68; auth, African sculpture, 70; co-auth, Ancient art of West Mexico, 70; auth, The feline motif in northern Peru, In: The Dumbarton Oaks conference on the feline, (in press).
Mailing Address: Brooklyn Museum, 188 Eastern Pkwy, Brooklyn, NY 11238.

KANE, BOB PAUL
Painter
Preferred Media: Oils.
b Cleveland, Ohio, July 11, 37.
Study & Training: Cornell Univ; Art Stud League New York, with Will Barnet; Pratt Inst.
Work in Public Collections: Cincinnati Art Mus, Ohio; Mus Munic St Paul de Vence, France; Joseph H Hirshhorn Collection; Palm Springs Desert Mus.
Exhibitions: Lytton Mus, Los Angeles, 67; Joslyn Art Mus, Nebr, 68; Collector's Choice, Okla Art Ctr, 68; American Painting on the Market Today, Cincinnati Art Mus, 68; 20 Painters of Southern California, Palm Springs Desert Mus, 70; plus many other group & one-man shows.
Teaching: Instr painting & art hist, Mt Clair Col, 69-70; instr painting & art hist, N Y Univ, 69-70.

Bibliography: Richard Boyle (auth), Bob Kane, Mus Munic St Paul de Vence, 72.
Dealers: Bertha Schaefer Gallery, 41 E 57th St, New York, NY 10022; Ankrum Gallery, 657 N La Cienega Blvd, Los Angeles, CA 90069.
Mailing Address: 125 Riverside Dr, New York, NY 10024.

KANE, MARGARET BRASSLER
Sculptor
b East Orange, N J, May 25, 09.
Study & Training: Syracuse Univ; Art Stud League New York, N Y; also with John Hovannes.
Work in Public Collections: U S Maritime Comn; Limited Ed Lamp Co; plaque, for Burro Monument, Fairplay, Colo.
Exhibitions: Argent Gallery Nat Tour, 58; Lever House, New York, 59-70; Mattatuck Mus, Conn, 67; Lamont Gallery, Exeter, N H, 67-70; New York Bank Savings, 68; plus others nationally.
Teaching: Lectr, Creative Approach to Sculpture.
Positions: Juror, Am Mach & Foundry Co, 57.
Awards: Awards, Brooklyn Mus, 46 & 51, Greenwich Soc Art, 52, 54, 58 & 60 & Silvermine Guild Artists, 54-56 & 63; plus others.
Memberships: Sculptors Guild; Nat Asn Women Artists; Pen & Brush Club; Greenwich Art Soc; Silvermine Guild Artists; fel Int Inst Arts & Lett.
Publications: Auth, article, In: Am Artist, 1/70; reproductions, In: Contemporary stone sculpture, Crown, 71; reproductions of wood carvings, McGraw-Hill, 73.
Mailing Address: 30 Strickland Rd, Cos Cob, CT 06807.

KANEE, BEN
Collector
b Melville, Sask, Oct 12, 11.
Positions: Former chmn permanent collection comt & former v pres, Vancouver Art Gallery.
Memberships: Hon life mem Vancouver Art Gallery.
Collection: Contemporary West Coast artists; British works including drawing by Augustus John and drawing and oil by R Dunlop; sculpture by Rodin, Valentine and Maillol; Canadian art including works by Turner, Cox and Osterle; graphics including works by Picasso, Chagall, Miro, Renoir, Bonnard, Vlaminck, Villon, Moore, Dali, Uchima, Braque and Albers; Canadian Eskimo carvings and prints, Haida Indian carvings including a totem pole by Bill Reid; Etruscan antiquities, Luristan bronze, early Hebrew art, pre-Columbian and early Peruvian art.
Mailing Address: 6449 Cedarhurst, Vancouver, B C, Can.

KANEGIS, SIDNEY S
Art Dealer
b Winthrop, Mass, Sept 6, 22.
Study & Training: Boston Mus Fine Art Sch.
Positions: Owner & dir, Kanegis Gallery, Boston, Mass, 50-
Specialty of Gallery: Contemporary art; modern master graphics.
Mailing Address: 244 Newbury St, Boston, MA 02116.

KANEMITSU, MATSUMI
Painter, Lecturer
Preferred Media: Oils, Acrylics, Duco, Watercolors.
b Ogden, Utah, May 28, 22.
Study & Training: Painting with Fernand Leger, Paris, France; Art Stud League New York, with Kuniyoshi, Sternberg, Auston & Browne; also sculpture with Karl Metzler, Baltimore, Md.
Work in Public Collections: Galleria Civica Arte Mod, Turin, Italy; Honolulu Acad Arts, Hawaii; Mus Mod Art, New York, N Y; San Francisco Mus Art, Calif; Corcoran Gallery Art, Washington, D C.
Commissions: Watercolor, Shinwa Bowl, Kawasaki City, Japan, 72.
Exhibitions: In Memory of My Feelings, Mus Mod Art, New York, 67; Tamarind: An Homage to Lithography, Mus Mod Art, New York, 69; Trends in 20th Century Art, Univ Calif, Santa Barbara, 70; Black & White Drawings & Watercolors, San Francisco Mus Art, 71; one-man show, Michael Smith Gallery, Los Angeles, 71; plus many other group & one-man shows.
Teaching: Instr art, Chouinard Art Sch, 65-72; artist-in-residence, Univ Calif, Berkeley, 66; artist-in-residence, Honolulu Acad Arts, 67-68; Calif State Col, Los Angeles, 69; Art Ctr Col Design, Los Angeles, 70; Univ Calif, Berkeley, 70-71; Otis Art Inst, 71; Calif Inst Arts, Valencia, 71-72.
Awards: Ford Found Awards, 61 & 64; Longview Found Award, 62; Japan Cult Forum Award, Fourth Int Young Artists Exhib, 67.
Dealer: Michael Smith Gallery, 936 N La Cienega Blvd, Los Angeles, CA 90069.
Mailing Address: 854 S Berendo St, Los Angeles, CA 90005.

KANGAS, GENE
Sculptor, Collector
Preferred Media: Metal, Mixed Media.
b Painesville, Ohio, May 22, 44.
Study & Training: Miami Univ, BFA; Bowling Green Univ, MFA; Univ Ky, sculpture sem with Mike Hall.
Work in Public Collections: Butler Inst Am Art, Ohio; Univ N C, Chapel Hill; Bowling Green Univ, Ohio; Ackland Art Ctr, Chapel Hill.
Exhibitions: Toledo Glass Nat II, Ohio, 68; N C Sculpture Invitational, 69; Young Americans 1969, Am Crafts Coun, New York, 69-71; one-man show, Royal Marks Gallery, New York, N Y, 70; Ohio Sculpture Invitational, 72.
Teaching: Instr sculpture, Univ N C, 68-71; asst prof sculpture, Cleveland State Univ, 71-
Awards: Fulbright-Hays scholar, 68; univ res grant, 68-70 & Smith Fund grant, 70, Univ N C.
Collection: Patchwork quilts; carved wooden decoys.
Mailing Address: 6852 Painesville-Ravenna Rd, Painesville, OH 44077.

KANOVITZ, HOWARD
Painter
Preferred Media: Acrylics.
b Fall River, Mass, Feb 9, 29.
Study & Training: Providence Col, BS, 49; R I Sch Design, 49-51; also with Franz Kline, 51-52.
Work in Public Collections: Whitney Mus Am Art, New York, N Y; Wallraf-Richartz Mus, Cologne, Ger; Neue Galerie Stadt Aachen, Ger; Mus Contemp Art, Utrecht, Holland; Göteborgs Konstmuseum, Göteborg, Sweden.
Commissions: The Opening, 180 Beacon Corp, Boston, Mass, 67; A Death in Tremé, Florists Transworld Delivery Collection, Detroit, Mich, 71; Collector's Wall, F K Johnssen, Essen, Ger, 71.
Exhibitions: Mus Contemp Art, Chicago, Ill, 71; Hayward Gallery, London, Eng, 71; Am Inst Arts & Lett, 72; Whitney Mus Am Art Ann, New York, 72; Dokumenfa 5, Kassel, Ger, 72.
Teaching: Instr painting & design, Brooklyn Col, 61-64; instr 2-D design, Pratt Inst, 64-66.
Bibliography: B H Friedman (auth), Focus on physical reality, Art News, 10/66; Rosalind Constable (auth), Style of the year: the inhumanists, New Yorker Mag, 12/16/68; Peter Sager (auth), Neve formen des realismus, Mag Kunst, 71.
Dealer: Galerie M E Thelen, Lindenstrasse 20, Cologne, West Germany.

KANTOR, MORRIS
Painter
b Minsk, Russia, Apr 15, 96.
Study & Training: Independent Sch Art, New York, N Y, with Homer Boss.
Work in Public Collections: Whitney Mus Am Art, Metrop Mus Art & Mus Mod Art, New York; Carnegie Inst, Pittsburgh, Pa; Newark Mus, N J; Art Inst Chicago, Ill; plus many others.
Exhibitions: Int Biennial Exhib Prints, Tokyo, Japan, 62; Smithsonian Inst, & White House, Washington, D C, 66; Univ N Mex Traveling Exhib, 67; Nat Collection Fine Arts, Washington, D C, 68; plus many others.
Teaching: Instr fine arts, Art Stud League New York, 34-; Univ Mich, 58, Michigan State Univ, 60; Univ Colo, 62; Univ Ill, 63; Univ Minn, Duluth, 63; Univ N Mex, 64.
Awards: Third Clark Prize, Corcoran Gallery Art, 39; Temple Medal, Pa Acad Fine Arts, 40; purchase prize, Univ Ill, 51; plus others.
Dealer: Bertha Schaefer Galleries, 41 E 57th St, New York, NY 10022.
Mailing Address: 45 S Mountain Rd, New City, NY 10956.

KAPLAN, ALICE MANHEIM
Patron, Collector
b Budapest, Hungary, Nov 27, 03; U S citizen.
Study & Training: Teachers Col, Columbia Univ, BS, 24, MA (art hist), 66; Cedar Crest Col, hon DFA, 68.
Positions: Trustee, J M Kaplan Fund, 44-, v pres, 58-; trustee, Am Fedn Arts, 58-; pres, 67-; co-chmn, 50th anniversary exhib, Armory Show, 63; mem adv bd, Mus Am Folk Art, 63; mem creative arts awards comn, Brandeis Univ, 64-; mem adv coun, dept art & archaeol, Columbia Univ, 65-, chmn, 72-; mem adv coun, Inst Fine Arts, New York Univ, 65-; mem Fine Arts Comn, New York City, 69-; chmn adv comt, Cooper-Hewitt Mus, Smithsonian Inst, 68-; coun fels, Morgan Libr.
Awards: Ford Found grant, 66.
Memberships: Munic Arts Soc; Nat Trust Club.

Collection: Diversified with emphasis on drawings; nineteenth and twentieth century American paintings and sculpture; Oriental, pre-Columbian and African.
Mailing Address: 760 Park Ave, New York, NY 10021.

KAPLAN, JACQUES
Collector
b Paris, France, Oct 24, 22.
Study & Training: Sorbonne, Paris, PhL; St Cyr.
Collection: Contemporary American art.
Mailing Address: 4 E 70th St, New York, NY 10021.

KAPLAN, JEROME EUGENE
Printmaker
Preferred Media: Intaglio, Lithography.
b Philadelphia, Pa, July 12, 20.
Study & Training: Philadelphia Col Art, dipl; also with Paul Froelich & Benton Spruance.
Work in Public Collections: Libr of Cong, Washington, D C; Philadelphia Mus Art, Pa; Nat Gallery Art, Washington, D C; New York Pub Libr, N Y; Rosenwald Collection.
Exhibitions: Fourth Int of Prints, Ljubjana, Yugoslavia, 61; Am Prints Today, Print Coun Am at 24 various mus, 62; 164th Ann Watercolors & Prints, Pa Acad Fine Arts, Philadelphia, 69; Soc Am Graphic Artists 51st Ann, New York, 71; First Biennial Int l'Estampe, Epinal, France, 71.
Teaching: Prof printmaking, Philadelphia Col Art, 48-, chmn dept, 64-72.
Awards: Guggenheim fel, 61; fel, Tamarind Lithography Workshop, 62.
Memberships: Print Coun Am (artists adv comt, 72); Print Club Philadelphia; Soc Am Graphic Artists.
Publications: Illusr, The ballad of the Spanish civil guard, 64; illusr, The bucket rider, 72.
Dealer: The Print Club, 1614 Latimer St, Philadelphia, PA 19103.
Mailing Address: 7029 Clearview St, Philadelphia, PA 19119.

KAPLAN, JOSEPH
Painter
Preferred Media: Oils, Gouache.
b Minsk, Russia, Oct 3, 00; U S citizen.
Study & Training: Educ Alliance, New York, N Y; Nat Acad Design, New York.
Work in Public Collections: Butler Inst Am Art, Youngstown, Ohio; Decatur Art Ctr; Newark Mus; Univ Ky, Lexington; Tel Aviv Mus.
Exhibitions: Nat Acad Design; Carnegie Inst; Corcoran Gallery Art; Audubon Artists; Pa Acad Fine Arts.
Collections Arranged: Traveling Show, five Midwest mus; also exhibs for Art Alliance, Philadelphia & Cape Cod Art Asn, Hyannis, Mass.
Awards: Awards, for oil, Cape Cod Art Asn, 62, Interior, Audubon Artists, 67 & Self Portrait, Nat Acad Design, 69.
Bibliography: Carl Fortes (interviewer), taped interview, Mus Arch, 68.
Memberships: Provincetown Art Asn (hon v pres & trustee, 55-); Audubon Artists.
Mailing Address: 638 Commercial St, Provincetown, MA 02657.

KAPLAN, RHODA B
Painter, Instructor
Perferred Media: Oils, Charcoal, Pastels.
b Newark, N J, June 23, 16.
Study & Training: Newark Sch Fine & Indust Arts; Hull Art Sch, Union, N J; also pvt study with John R Grabach.
Exhibitions: Exposition Inter-Continentale, Monaco, Deuville & others; Am Artists Prof League Grand Nat, New York, N Y; Catharine Lorillard Wolfe Art Club, Nat Arts Club & Nat Acad Design, New York; N J State Mus, Trenton; Newark Mus, N J; plus other group & one-man shows.
Teaching: Instr art, Sloan Sch, South Orange, N J, YMHA & YWHA, Northfield, N J, YWCA, Summit, N J & pvt classes.
Memberships: Am Artists Prof League; Artists Equity Asn; Acad Artists; Westfield Art Asn; South Orange-Maplewood Art Gallery (pres).
Mailing Address: 10 Archbridge Lane, Springfield, NJ 07081.

KAPLINSKI, BUFFALO
Painter
b Chicago, Ill, May 25, 43.
Study & Training: Art Inst Chicago; Am Acad Art.
Exhibitions: 140th Ann, Nat Acad Design, New York, N Y; 98th Ann, Am Watercolor Soc, New York; 162nd Ann, Pa Acad Fine Arts, Philadelphia; 27th Exhib, Audubon Artists, New York; 15th-18th Ann, Nat Soc Painters in Casein; plus many other group & one-man shows.
Awards: Hon mention, 15th Ann Exhib, Nat Soc Painters in Casein; purchase award, Southwestern Watercolor Soc, Southern Methodist Univ Fine Arts Ctr; hon mention, Southwestern Biennial, N Mex Arts Mus, Santa Fe.
Bibliography: Article, In: Am Artist Mag, 8/72.
Mailing Address: Star Route 2, Box 171, Evergreen, CO 80439.

KAPROW, ALLAN
Painter, Educator
b Atlantic City, N J, Aug 23, 27.
Study & Training: Hans Hofmann Sch Fine Arts, 47-48; New York Univ, BA, 49, postgrad, 49-50; Columbia Univ, MA, 52; also with John Cage, New York, 56-58.
Exhibitions: Inst Contemp Arts, Boston, Mass, 66; Central Park, New York, 66; Westchester Art Soc, White Plains, N Y, 66; State Univ N Y Stony Brook, 67; retrospective, Pasadena Art Mus, Calif, 67; one-man show, John Gibson Gallery, 69; plus many others.
Teaching: Instr fine arts, Rutgers Univ, 53-56, asst prof, 56-61; lectr aesthetics, Dept Fine Arts, Pratt Inst, 60-61; assoc prof fine arts, State Univ N Y Stony Brook, 61-66; prof, 66; assoc dean sch art, Calif Inst Arts, 66-
Positions: Co-founder, Hansa Gallery, New York, 52, Reuben Gallery, New York, 59; dir, Judson Gallery, New York, 60, co-dir, 61; dir criticism & exp res, Inst Contemp Arts, Boston, 65-66.
Awards: Copley Found Award, 62; Off For Area Studies, State Univ N Y, 65; Guggenheim Found fel, 67; plus many others.
Publications: Auth, Assemblage, environments and happenings, Abrams, 65; auth, var bks & articles.
Dealer: John Gibson Gallery, 120 E 89th St, New York, NY 10028.
Mailing Address: 270 Wigmore Dr, Pasadena, CA 91105.

KAPSALIS, THOMAS HARRY
Painter, Sculptor
Preferred Media: Oils.
b Chicago, Ill, May 31, 25.
Study & Training: Sch Art Inst Chicago, BAE, 49, MAE, 57; also Fulbright grant, Ger, with Willie Baumeister, Otto Baum & Hans Warneke, 53-54.
Exhibitions: Pa Acad Fine Arts Ann Watercolor & Print Exhib, Philadelphia, 46; Contemp Drawings From 12 Countries, Art Inst Chicago, 52; Barone Gallery Group Show, New York, N Y, 56; 27th Biennial Exhib Contemp Painting, Corcoran Gallery Art, Washington, D C, 61; Ill Art Coun Traveling Exhib, 71.
Teaching: Assoc prof drawing & painting, Sch Art Inst Chicago, 54-; lectr painting, Northwestern Univ, Chicago & Evanston, 58-71.
Awards: Huntington Hartford Found grant, 56 & 59; Pauline Palmer Prize, 60 & Jule F Brower Prize, 69, Art Inst Chicago.
Bibliography: Meilach & Seiden (auth), Direct metal sculpture, Crown, 66.
Mailing Address: 5204 N Virginia Ave, Chicago, IL 60625.

KARABERI, MARIANTHE
Sculptor, Painter
b Boston, Mass.
Study & Training: Pa Acad Fine Arts; Univ Pa, BFA; Barnes Found; Art Stud League New York, with John Hovannes; Corcoran Sch Art, with Heinz Warnecke.
Commissions: Many portrait busts of prominent persons incl Luther H Hodges, U S Secy Com, Andreas Ioanou, Prefect of Dodecanese, Rhodes & George P Kournoutos, Dir Fine Arts, Greece.
Exhibitions: Corcoran Gallery Art Ann, 55-; Nat Acad Design, 58; one-man show, Mint Mus Art, 58; Pen & Brush Club, 60; one-man show, French Inst, Athens, Greece, 61; plus many group shows in New York, Philadelphia, Washington, D C & Athens.
Awards: Prizes, Corcoran Gallery Art, 57 & Pen & Brush Club, 60.
Memberships: Nat Arts Club; Pen & Brush Club; Philadelphia Art Alliance.
Mailing Address: 2990 Newcastle Ave, Silver Spring, MD 20910.

KARAWINA, ERICA (MRS SIDNEY C HSIAO)
Designer, Painter
Preferred Media: Stained Glass.
b Ger; U S citizen.
Study & Training: Study in Europe, also in Boston, Mass, with Frederick W Allen & Charles J Connick.
Work in Public Collections: Metrop Mus Art, New York; Mus Mod Art, New York; Boston Mus Fine Arts, Mass; Libr of Cong, Washington, D C; Honolulu Acad Arts, Hawaii.
Commissions: Sea Pattern (leaded glass), Commissioned Off Club, Pearl Harbor, Hawaii, 61; 20 lancets of faceted glass in concrete, Robert Shipman Thurston, Jr Mem Chapel, Punahou Sch, Honolulu, 67; Crux Gemmata (glass in concrete) Manoa Valley Church, Honolulu, 67; six windows of sculptured glass, St Anthony's Church, Kailua, Oahu, Hawaii, 68; sculptured glass, This Earth is Ours, News Bldg Foyer, Honolulu Advertiser, 72; plus many others.
Exhibitions: Dance Int, Rockefeller Ctr, New York, 37; competition of State of Mass, New York's Fair, 39; Protestant Orthodox Ctr,

New York World's Fair, 64; one-man show, China Inst Int, Taipei, Taiwan, 56, plus over 20 other one-man shows.
Teaching: Draftsman stained glass, Co Studios, Boston, 30-33; designer stained glass, Burnham Studios, Boston, 35-38.
Awards: John Poole Mem Prize, Honolulu Acad Arts, 52; James C Castle Award, Narcissus Art Festival, Honolulu, 61.
Bibliography: Jean Charlot (auth), Exhibition of stained glass, 5/53, Harriet Ghee (auth), Island artist Erica Karawina, 7/55 & Joanne Shaw (auth), Echoes of universality, Vol 72, No 9, Paradise of Pac.
Memberships: Honolulu Print Makers; Hawaii Painters & Sculptors League; fel Int Inst Arts; Nat League Am Pen Women.
Art Interests: Leaded & faceted sculptured glass.
Publications: Contribr, From Maui to Mainz, 56-57 & From Hawaii to Holland, 63, Stained Glass.
Mailing Address: 3529 Akaka Pl, Honolulu, HI 96822.

KARESH, ANN BAMBERGER
Painter, Sculptor
Preferred Media: Acrylics.
b Bamberg, Ger; U S citizen.
Study & Training: Willesden Tech Col, London, Eng; Hornsey Col Art, London.
Work in Public Collections: Gibbes Art Gallery, Charleston, S C; Home Fed Savings & Loan Asn Collection, S C; Jewish Community Ctr Collection, Charleston.
Exhibitions: Watercolor U S A, Nat Watercolor Exhib, 62; 23rd Ann Contemp Am Painting, Palm Beach, Fla, 62; Directors Choice, 10 S C Artists (traveling exhib), 65; Contemp Artists, S C Invitational, 70-71; 18th Ann Nat Watercolor Exhib, Jackson, Miss.
Awards: First prize in painting, S C Artists Ann, 63; best in enamel, 68 & best in metal, 70, S C Craftsmen.
Bibliography: Jack A Morris, Jr (auth), Contemporary artists of South Carolina, S C Tricentennial Comn, 70.
Memberships: Guild of S C Artists (v pres, 65-66, pres, 66-67); S C Craftsmen; Carolina Art Asn (exhib comt, 55-59).
Dealer: Metarco Galleries, 957 Madison Ave, New York, NY 10021.
Mailing Address: 1 Chalmers St, Charleston, SC 29401.

KARN, GLORIA STOLL
Painter, Instructor
Preferred Media: Oils.
b New York, N Y, Nov 13, 23.
Study & Training: Art Stud League New York; also with Eliot O'Hara & Samuel Rosenberg.
Work in Public Collections: Yale Univ, Conn; Carnegie Inst Mus, Pittsburgh, Pa; Brooklyn Mus, N Y; Pittsburgh Pub Schs.
Exhibitions: Assoc Artists Pittsburgh Ann, 49-; Butler Inst Am Art Ann, 61; one-man shows, Pittsburgh Plan for Art, 65 & Carnegie Inst Mus, 66; Sacred Arts Show, St Stephens, Pittsburgh, 66.
Teaching: Instr painting & collage, North Hills Artists' & Craftsmen's Guild, 65-
Awards: Purchase prize, Brooklyn Mus Nat Print Ann, 49; Carnegie Inst Purchase Prize, 60; Westinghouse Purchase Prize, 66.
Memberships: Assoc Artists of Pittsburgh; Group A, Pittsburgh (pres, 66-70); Arts & Crafts Ctr, Pittsburgh (bd mem, 69-72); North Hills Artists' & Craftsmen's Guild (bd mem, 70-72).
Mailing Address: 151 Louise Rd, Pittsburgh, PA 15237.

KARNIOL, HILDA
Painter, Instructor
Preferred Media: Oils.
b Vienna, Austria, Apr 28, 10; U S citizen.
Study & Training: With Olga Konetzny-Maly & A F Seligman, Vienna, 25-28; Acad for Women, 26-30.
Work in Public Collections: St Vincent Abbey, Latrobe, Pa; Del Art Ctr, Wilmington; Lycoming Col, Williamsport, Pa; Lincoln Sch, Honesdale, Pa; U S Dept Health, Educ & Welfare.
Commissions: Dr Gustave Weber, Pres of Susquehanna Univ, bd dirs, Susquehanna Univ, Selinsgrove, Pa, 68; plus many other pvt portrait commissions.
Exhibitions: Pa State Mus, Harrisburg, 54; Adha Artzt Gallery, New York, N Y, 60; Drexel Inst Technol, Philadelphia, Pa, 60; La Salle Col, Philadelphia, 64; La State Univ, New Orleans, 71; plus over 100 one-man shows.
Teaching: Instr painting, Susquehanna Univ, 58-
Positions: Artist-in-residence, Fed Govt Cult Enrichment Prog for Clearfield, Clinton, Centre & Lycoming Cos, 67.
Awards: Recipient first prize in portraiture, Berwick Art Ctr, Pa, 65.
Bibliography: L E L (auth), Art & artists, gallery guide, New York-J Am, 11/5/60; Sigmund Stoler (auth), Upstate artist's 14th show, Harrisburg Patriot, 67; Michael Lenson (auth), The realm of art, culture mirror, Newark Sun News, 11/67.
Memberships: Midstate Artists; Nat Forum Prof Artists; Art Alliance Cent Pa; Soroptimist, Sunbury, Pa.

Publications: Illusr, Melusine & illusr, The nose, 29, Adolf Synek; auth, From the sketchbook of Hilda Karniol, Standard, 70.
Dealers: Rembrandt Art Gallery, Inc, 1051 Madison Ave, New York, NY 10028; Millbrook Art Gallery, Mill Hall, PA 17751.
Mailing Address: 960 Race St, Sunbury, PA 17801.

KAROLY, ANDREW B
Painter
b Varanno, Hungary, May 5, 93.
Study & Training: Univ Art & Archit, Budapest, BA & MAA.
Work in Public Collections: Nat Mus, Budapest; Art Mus, Helsinki, Finland.
Commissions: (Murals) The Romantic Past of the New York University in 1860 & Mr Abraham Lincoln Addressing in Cooper Union University in 1860, 66-68; George Washington's Inauguration in the Vanderbilt Era, Vanderbilt Bank, 68-69; Light in the Wilderness, City Community Ctr; easel painting, Rouen Cathedral; interior of St Peter's & others.
Memberships: Budapest Art Club; Royal Acad Art, Budapest.
Mailing Address: 54 W 74th St, New York, NY 10023.

KAROLY, FREDRIC
Painter, Sculptor
Preferred Media: Oils, Acrylics.
U S citizen.
Study & Training: Berlin, Ger.
Work in Public Collections: Whitney Mus Am Art, New York, N Y; Mus Fine Arts, St Petersburg, Fla; Mus Bellas Artes, Buenos Aires, Arg; Wash Univ, St Louis, Mo; N Y Univ; plus others.
Exhibitions: Three Whitney Mus Am Art Ann; Sao Paulo Biennale, 51; Tokyo Int Independent Exhib.
Awards: Nat Coun Arts Award, 68.
Bibliography: Christian Zervos (auth), article, In: Cahiers Art, 49; Bardi (auth), Sao Paulo, Habitat, Brazil, 51.
Mailing Address: 3 Crosby St, New York, NY 10013.

KARP, IVAN C
Art Dealer, Lecturer
b June 4, 26; U S citizen.
Teaching: Instr art hist, Finch Col, 66-67; instr art hist, Sch Visual Arts, 70-71; lectr.
Positions: Pres, Anonymous Arts Recovery Soc, 60-; dir, OK Harris Gallery.
Memberships: Nat Trust Hist Preservations; Soc Indust Archeol.
Specialty of Gallery: Contemporary painting & sculpture.
Publications: Auth, articles, In: Artforum & Arts Mag.
Mailing Address: 465 W Broadway, New York, NY 10012.

KARSH, YOUSUF
Photographer
b Armenia, Dec 23, 08; Can citizen.
Study & Training: Study in Boston with John H Garo; hon degrees from seven univs.
Work in Public Collections: Metrop Mus Art, New York, N Y; Mus Mod Art, New York; Nat Portrait Gallery, London, Eng; St Louis Art Mus, Mo; Nat Gallery Can, Ottawa, Ont.
Exhibitions: One-man show, Men who make our world, Expo 67, Montreal, P Q, 67; Boston Mus Fine Arts, Mass, 68, Corcoran Gallery Art, Washington, D C, 69, Seattle Art Mus, Wash, 70, Mus Mod Art, Tokyo, 71-72 & all over Europe; plus many other group & one-man shows.
Teaching: Vis prof photog & fine arts, Ohio Univ, 68-70; vis prof photog & fine arts, Emerson Col, 72-73.
Positions: Photog adv, Expo 70, Osaka, Japan, 69-70; trustee, Photog Arts & Sci Found, 65-72.
Awards: Can Coun Medal, 65; Order of Can, Can Govt, 68; Rochester Sci Mus fel, 72.
Bibliography: Faces of our time, telescope diary of a portraitist, Can Broadcasting Co, 68; Liptak (auth), Interview with Karsh, Honolulu Mag, 70; Forsee (auth), Yousuf Karsh, In: Five famous photographers, 70.
Memberships: Hon fel Royal Photog Soc; Prof Photog Asn Can; Century Club; hon fel Prof Photog Am.
Publications: Auth, Faces of destiny (photos & text), 46; auth, Portraits of greatness (photos & text), 59; auth, In search of greatness (memoirs), 62; auth, Karsh portfolio (photos & text), 67; auth, Faces of our time (photos & text), 71.
Mailing Address: 130 Sparks St, Ottawa, Ont. K1P 5B6, Can.

KARSHAN, DONALD H
Museum Director, Collector
b New York, N Y, Jan 17, 29.
Study & Training: Art Stud League New York, with Bridgman, Kuniyoshi & Liberte; Columbia Univ, with Seong Moy; New York Univ.

Positions: Trustee, Am Fedn Arts; trustee, New York Studio Sch; adv bd, Pratt Ctr Contemp Printmaking; mem coun, Whitney Mus Am Art; prints ed, Art in Am; founder & pres, Mus of Graphic Art; dir, New York Cult Ctr.
Memberships: Art Collectors Club.
Research: American graphic art history.
Collection: Extensive graphic art collection covering five centuries, shown in its entirety in several museums in the United States.
Publications: Auth, Language of the print, a selection from the Donald H Karshan Collection, Random, 68; auth, Picasso linocuts, 1958-1963, Tudor; auth, Archipenko: international visionary, Smithsonian, 70; auth, Archipenko: content and continuity; auth, Three centuries of American printmaking; also many articles on graphic arts for art periodicals & introductions for mus exhib catalogs.
Mailing Address: 245 W 19th St, New York, NY 10011.

KASAK, NIKOLAS
Sculptor, Painter
b Lushtcha, Russia, Sept 24, 17; U S citizen.
Study & Training: City Col Arts, Warsaw, BFA; Acad Fine Art, Vienna, MFA; Acad Fine Art Sch Advan Study, Rome, dipl.
Work in Public Collections: Mus Fine Art, Minsk; Mus Fine Art, Baranowicze; Arte Madi Collection, Buenos Aires, Arg; Denis Rene Gallery, Paris; Numero Gallery, Florence.
Commissions: Sgraffito, City Hall Warsaw; mural, City Hall, Baranowicze.
Exhibitions: Quadrienale Arte Rome Rassegna Naz, Galleria Naz Arte Moderna, Rome, 49; Mus Mod Art, Dallas, Houston & San Antonio, Tex, 51; Solomon R Guggenheim Mus, New York, N Y; Arte Madi Int, Mus Mod Art, Buenos Aires 61 & Denis Rene Gallery, Paris, four shows, Riverside Mus, N Y, 58-68.
Awards: First prize for Warsaw Emblem, City Hall Warsaw; first prize for mural, City Hall Baranowicze; prize for painting-construct, Art Club Rome.
Bibliography: The world of abstract art, Wittenborn, 57.
Memberships: Am Abstr Artists.
Research: Originator of physical art concept based on action of primary positive and negative elements of reality; painted wood constructions of positive and negative space.
Publications: Auth, Physical art—action of positive & negative elements, Manifesto, 46-47; contribr, Storia de pitture contemporanee, Domani, Rome, 48; contribr, Negative and positive space, Arte Madi, Buenos Aires, 51 & Arte fisico-constructivo, 52, Arte Madi, Buenos Aires; auth, The art of Kasak (monogr), 68 & The figurative art of Kasak, 69, October House.
Mailing Address: 5648 Delafield Ave, Riverdale, New York, NY 10471.

KASLE, GERTRUDE
Art Dealer, Collector
b New York, N Y, Dec 2, 17.
Study & Training: With John Barber, Art Stud League, New York, N Y; New York Univ; Univ Mich; Soc Arts & Crafts, Detroit; Wayne State Univ, BS(art educ).
Positions: Assoc dir & partner, Franklin Siden Gallery, 64-65; pres, Gertrude Kasle Gallery, 65-
Awards: Distinguished alumni award, Wayne State Univ, 68.
Memberships: Art Dealers Asn Am; Mich Coun Arts (comt visual arts & mus, 71); Detroit Art Dealers Asn (v pres, 71-72); Mus Mod Art & Whitney Mus Am Art, New York; patron, Detroit Inst Arts (Founders' Soc).
Specialty of Gallery: Contemporary paintings, sculpture and graphics with emphasis on living American artists.
Mailing Address: Gertrude Kasle Gallery, 310 Fisher Bldg, Detroit, MI 48202.

KASSOY, BERNARD
Painter, Printmaker
Preferred Media: Oils, Watercolors, Pastels.
b New York, N Y, Oct 23, 14.
Study & Training: City Col New York, BSS(cum laude), MSE(fine arts); Cooper Union Art Sch, grad, 37; also with John Ferren, Isaac Soyer & Arthur Osver.
Work in Public Collections: Workmans Circle Community House, Bronx, N Y.
Commissions: Birdiness (film photography & editing), Bd Educ, High Sch Music & Art, New York, 57.
Exhibitions: Art U S A 1958, New York, 58; Nat Acad Design, New York, 68; Showcase, Bronx Coun Arts, New York, 68 & 69; 28 Contemporaries-Bronx Museum Arts, New York, 71; one-man show, United Fedn Teachers Gallery Invitational, 65, plus one other.
Teaching: Instr fine arts, High Sch Music & Art, 39-; instr lithography, City Col New York, 66-67.

Memberships: Artists Equity Asn New York (bd dirs & ed, Newsletter, 62-); League Present Day Artists (bd dirs, 70-).
Mailing Address: 130 Gale Pl, Bronx, NY 10463.

KASSOY, HORTENSE
Sculptor, Painter
Preferred Media: Wood, Marble, Bronze, Watercolors.
b Brooklyn, N Y, Feb 14, 17.
Study & Training: Pratt Inst, grad; Columbia Univ Teachers Col, BS & MA, with Oronzo Maldarelli; Am Artists Sch, with Chaim Gross.
Commissions: Maternal Force, marble sculpture, Amalgamated Housing Coop Towers, Dickenson & Sedgewick Ave, Bronx, N Y, 71.
Exhibitions: Sculpture Today, Toledo Mus & Toronto Mus, 47; Art: USA:58, Madison Sq Garden, New York, N Y, 58; Nat Acad Design, New York, 71; 28 Contemporaries, 71 & Ann, 72, Bronx Mus Art; plus others.
Teaching: Instr sculpture, painting & 3D design, Evander Childs High Sch, Bronx, 61-72.
Awards: Grumbacher first prize in watercolor, Painters Day at World's Fair, 40.
Memberships: Artists Equity Asn New York; Cooperstown Art Asn.
Mailing Address: 130 Gale Pl, Bronx, NY 10463.

KASTEN, KARL ALBERT
Painter, Printmaker
b San Francisco, Calif, Mar 5, 16.
Study & Training: Marin Col; Univ Calif, AB & MA; Univ Iowa, with Lasansky; Hans Hofmann Sch Art.
Work in Public Collections: Victoria & Albert Mus, London, Eng; Mus Mod Art, New York, N Y; Auckland City Mus, New Zealand; Mus Beaux-Arts, Rennes, France; Los Angeles Co Art Mus, Calif.
Exhibitions: American Painting & Graphics Exhib, Metrop Mus Art, New York, 50; Fifth Contemporary Printmakers, Univ Ill, Champaign, 56; Int Biennial, São Paulo, Brazil, 55; Art Inst Chicago Am Painting Ann, 60; Contemporary American Painting & Sculpture, Univ Ill, 69.
Teaching: Instr painting & drawing, Univ Mich, 46-47; asst prof painting & drawing, San Francisco State Col, 47-50; prof painting & graphics, Univ Calif, Berkeley, 50-
Awards: Artists Coun Purchase Prize, San Francisco Art Asn, 39; Oakland Art Mus Women's Bd Purchase Prize, Western Painters Exhib, 54; Tamarind Lithography fel, 68.
Bibliography: R Bethers (auth), How paintings happen, Norton, 51; Shiply & Weller (auth), Contemporary American painting & sculpture, Univ Ill, 69; S Minamora (auth), On collography, Educ Films, 69.
Memberships: Calif Soc Printmakers (coun mem, 72); San Francisco Art Inst (bd dirs, 50).
Dealers: John Bolles Gallery, 10 Gold St, San Francisco, CA 94133; Julie Dohan Gallery, 746 N La Cienega Blvd, Los Angeles, CA 90069.
Mailing Address: 1884 San Lorenzo Ave, Berkeley, CA 94707.

KASUBA, ALEKSANDRA
Sculptor
b Lithuania, Jan 10, 23; U S citizen.
Study & Training: Art Inst Kaunas, Lithuania, 41-42; Acad Fine Arts, Vilnius, Lithuania, 42.
Work in Public Collections: Atlanta Univ Collection, Ga; Delgado Mus Art, New Orleans, La; Mus Contemp Crafts, New York, N Y; Johnson's Wax Collection.
Commissions: Mural (cement), New York Hilton Hotel, 63; four brick walls, Rochester Inst Technol, N Y, 67-69; marble wall, Bank of Calif, Portland, Ore, 69; white marble wall, Container Corp Am, Chicago, Ill, 69; marble walls, City of Baltimore, Md, 71.
Exhibitions: One-man show, Waddell Gallery, New York, 66; Experiments in Art & Technology, Brooklyn Mus Art, N Y, 68; Objects: U S A, 69-72 & Europe, 72-74; Contemplative Environments, Mus Contemp Crafts, New York, 70; Space Shelters for Senses, New York, 71-72.
Teaching: Instr creative processes & elements art in archit scale, Sch Visual Arts, 71-72.
Awards: Am Inst Archit citation, Artist-Archit Collab, 71; citation for inovative space treatment, Women's Archit Auxiliary & New York Chap Am Inst Archit, 72.
Bibliography: Rita Reif (auth), article, In: New York Times, 5/11/71; James D Morgan (auth), article, In: Archit Rec, 8/71; Gloria Campisi (auth), Philadelphia Daily News, 6/16/72; plus many others.
Art Interests: Architectural materials.

Publications: Contribr, Report on art & technology program of the Los Angeles County Museum of Art, 71; contribr, Acrylic for sculpture & design, Van Nostrand, 72.
Mailing Address: 43 W 90th St, New York, NY 10024.

KATO, KAY
Cartoonist, Illustrator
b Budapest, Hungary
Study & Training: Art Acad, Budapest; Pa Acad Fine Arts; also with Janos Vaszary.
Commissions: Cover, Am Tel & Tel Mag, 54; book jacket for The television-radio audience and religion, 55; cover, Today's living, New York Herald-Tribune, 57; also covers for Christian Sci Monitor, Sat Eve Post & others.
Exhibitions: White Mountains Art Festival, 63; one-man shows at Pa Acad Fine Arts, Montclair Art Mus, Boston Pub Libr & Newark Pub Libr; plus others.
Teaching: Lect on The Art of Cartooning & other subjects, women's clubs, prof groups, cruises & others; instr, Cambridge Ctr Adult Educ, Mass, 44-47; instr, South Orange & Maplewood Adult Sch, fall 63.
Positions: Cartoonist, Am Cyanamid Co; cartoonist, Nat Asn Home Economists Convention, 63; spec featured appearance, New York World's Fair, 64.
Awards: Best Cartoons of the Year, 43; second prize, Am Art Wk, 55; Foremost Woman in Commun, 70.
Memberships: Essex Watercolor Club; Overseas Press Club Am (chmn graphic arts comt, mem bull comt).
Publications: Contribr to This Week, Nation's Bus, New York Times Mag, Am Weekly & others; auth, weekly cartoon column, Star Ledger, Newark; guest cartoonist on NBC TV & other nat shows.
Mailing Address: 60 Chapman Pl, Glen Ridge, NJ 07028.

KATZ, ALEX
Painter
Preferred Media: Oils.
b New York, N Y, July 24, 27.
Study & Training: Cooper Union.
Work in Public Collections: Mus Mod Art, New York; Art Inst Chicago, Ill; Whitney Mus Am Art, New York; Detroit Inst Arts, Mich; Wadsworth Atheneum, Hartford, Conn.
Exhibitions: Twenty Years of American Painting, Mus Mod Art, New York, 66; Figures and Environments, Walker Art Ctr, Minneapolis, Minn, 70; Retrospective Exhib, Wadsworth Atheneum, 71; 32nd Biennial Exhib Contemp Am Painting, Corcoran Gallery Art, Washington, D C, 71; American Collage, Mus Mod Art, New York.
Awards: Guggenheim fel, 72.
Bibliography: Nicol Calas (auth), Art in the age of risk, Dutton, 68; Sam Hunter (auth), American art since 1945, Abrams, 69; Irving Sandler & William Berkson (ed), Alex Katz, Praeger, 71.
Mailing Address: 435 W Broadway, New York, NY 10012.

KATZ, A(LEXANDER) RAYMOND
Painter, Lecturer
Preferred Media: Casein, Oils.
b Hungary; U S citizen.
Study & Training: Art Inst Chicago; Acad Fine Arts, Chicago.
Work in Public Collections: Butler Inst Am Art; Evansville Mus, Ind; Caravan France, New York, N Y; Ghent Mus Collection, Oak Park Temple.
Commissions: Off Mural of Century of Progress, 33-34; History of the Immigrant, Madison Post Off, Ill, 36; Ten Commandments Frescoes, 36; exterior murals, Temple Beth-El, Baltimore; stained glass windows (with Alfonso Ianelli & Don Benardon), Vaughn Army Hosp, Ill.
Exhibitions: Carnegie Inst Int, 41; 11 exhibs, Art Inst Chicago & one-man show, 46; one-man shows, Jewish Mus, New York, 56 & Mus Sierkunst, Ghent, Belg, 63; Mus Contemp Crafts, 62.
Teaching: Lettering asst to Fayerweather Babcock, 24-26; master craftsman, Ninth Naval Dist; instr painting, Evanston Art League, 46.
Positions: Dir poster dept, Paramount, Chicago, 26-31; mem art staff, Chicagoan Mag, 28-31; dir posters, Chicago Civic Opera, 30-33; asst dir posters, Century of Progress, 33-34.
Awards: First prize for poster, Century of Progress, 34; first prize, Miss Art Asn.
Bibliography: Robert Andrews (auth), Corner of Chicago; Alfred Werner (auth), Adventures in casein; Mar Dulac (auth), A Raymond Katz, master of mixed techniques, Am Artist, 69.
Memberships: Nat Soc Mural Painters (bd dirs); Artists Equity Asn (bd dirs); hon mem Hudson Valley Art League.
Publications: Auth, A new art for an old religion, third ed, L M Stein, 46; auth, Adventures in casein, Bks Int, 51; auth, Holidays

and festivals, Crown, 60; auth, Seven names, 69 & Song of songs, 70-71, A R Fine arts.
Dealer: Caravan De France, 121 E 57th St, New York, NY 10022.
Mailing Address: 260 Riverside Dr, New York, NY 10025.

KATZ, ETHEL
Painter, Instructor
b Boston, Mass, July 12, 00.
Study & Training: Boston Mus Fine Arts Sch; Mass Normal Art Sch; Art Stud League New York; also with Randall Davey, Howard Giles, & Samuel Halpert.
Work in Public Collections: Riverside Mus; Collection of Rose Mus, Brandeis Univ; Norfolk Mus Art & Sci; Art Stud League New York.
Exhibitions: New York Soc Women Artists, 37-65; Nat Asn Women Artists Traveling Exhibs, 42, 43, 49-52 & 63-65; High Mus Art, 44; Brooklyn Soc Art, 49-52; Riverside Mus, 54 & 56; plus other exhibs in U S & Europe.
Teaching: Instr, Art Stud League New York, 43-
Awards: Prizes, Nat Asn Women Artists, 39, 47 & 63 & medals, 50 & 54; Brooklyn Soc Art Award.
Memberships: Nat Asn Women Artists; New York Soc Women Artists.
Mailing Address: 45 Grove St, New York, NY 10014.

KATZ, HILDA
Painter, Graphic Artist
b June 2, 09; U S citizen.
Study & Training: Nat Acad Design; New Sch Soc Res, scholar, 40 & 41.
Work in Public Collections: Nat Gallery Art, Washington, D C; Metrop Mus Art, New York, N Y; Libr of Cong, Washington, D C; Nat Collection Fine Arts, Washington, D C; Nat Air & Space Mus, Washington, D C; plus others.
Exhibitions: Venice Biennial, U S Pavilion, Italy, 40; Corcoran Gallery Art Biennial, Washington, D C; Boston Pub Libr Invitations to Turin, Venice, Florence & Naples, Italy also France & Israel; U S Info Agency Exhibs to Europe, Asia, Middle East & Africa; Soc Am Graphic Artists-Japan Invitational Exchange; plus others.
Teaching: Lectr demonstrations in painting & graphics for art asns, until 51.
Awards: Six purchase awards, Libr of Cong; Am Artists Graphic prize, Soc Am Graphic Artists; two awards for watercolors, Nat Asn Women Artists; plus others.
Bibliography: Article, In: Metrop Mus Art Bull, 66; Report & studies in history of art, Nat Gallery Art, 67-69; article, In: Nat Air & Space Catalogue, 71.
Memberships: Soc Am Graphic Artists (jury-award selection bd); Nat Asn Women Artists (jury-award selection bd); Int Platform Asn; Philadelphia Watercolor Club; Am Color Print Soc.
Mailing Address: 915 West End Ave, Apt 5D, New York, NY 10025.

KATZ, JOSEPH M
Collector, Patron
b Iampol, Russia, July 8, 13.
Study & Training: Univ Pittsburgh, 31-34.
Collection: Nineteenth and twentieth century paintings and sculpture; gold and enamel snuff boxes of seventeenth, eighteenth and nineteenth centuries; ancient glass of the Roman era; French and English porcelain; eighteenth century French furniture.
Mailing Address: Gateway Towers, Pittsburgh, PA 15222.

KATZ, LEO
Painter, Writer
Preferred Media: Watercolors, Tempera, Fresco, Acrylics, Intaglio, Graphics, Lithography.
b Roznau, Austria, Dec 30, 87; U S citizen.
Study & Training: Acad Fine Arts, Vienna, grad, 08; Acad Fine Arts, Munich, 09.
Work in Public Collections: Whitney Mus Am Art, New York, N Y; Print Dept, Metrop Mus Art, New York; Print Dept, Mus Mod Art, New York; Print Dept, Lessing Rosenwald Collection, Nat Gallery, Washington, D C; Bibliot Nat, Paris; plus others.
Commissions: Murals, comn by Baron W Von Gutmann, Tobitschau Castle, Czech, 13-15, Give Us This Day Our Daily Light, Century Prog Expos, Johns-Manville Bldg, Chicago, 33-34, Crossroads, Works Prog Admin, Frank Wiggins Trade Sch, Los Angeles, Calif, 35-36 & Metamorphosis 1942, comn by Dr & Mrs Bela Schick, Garrison, N Y; sect of Orozco frescoes, Dartmouth Col, N H, 32.
Exhibitions: One-man shows, Old Nat Gallery, Smithsonian Inst, Washington, D C, 24 & Fine Arts Mus, San Diego, Calif, 27; Nat Print Shows, Long Beach, Calif, 38 & Cong Libr, Washington, D C, 46; U S Embassy-Cult Attaché Exhib, Paris, 51 & Traveling Exhib New York, France, Italy, Egypt, India, Pakistan & others, 51-52.
Teaching: N Y Univ lectr, Metrop Mus Art, 27-33; vis lectr, New Sch Soc Res & Univ Calif, Los Angeles, 29-33; lectr, Cooper

Union Art Sch, 36-46; assoc prof hist art, painting, photog, graphics & design, Brooklyn Col, 42-45.

Positions: Chmn dept art, Hampton Inst, 46-53; dir, Atelier 17, New York, 46 & 50-55; pres & trustee, Va Art Alliance, Richmond, 51-52; Whitney prof artist-in-residence, Spelman Col, 55-57.

Awards: First prize for lithography, Nat Print Soc, Long Beach, 38; Pennell Purchase Prize For Engraving & Etching, Libr Cong Print Dept, 46; MacDowell fel, 60-62.

Bibliography: F E Washburn Freund (auth), Leo Katz: Freud of the easel, Int Studio, 4/23; Meyer Levin (auth), Myth and cosmos & Adolph Rosenberg (auth), Leo Katz, Southern Israelite, 11/27/59; Stanley & Lelie Krippner (auth), Dreams, creativity and prophetic art, Psychic, 7/72; plus one other.

Memberships: Soc Am Graphic Artists; Found Mind Res (adv bd); Am Soc Psychical Res; Metrop Mus Art, Whitney Mus Am Art & Mus Mod Art; plus others.

Research: Pre-Columbian art and mythology; comparative religions, parapsychology; astro-mythological psychology; competitive and creative thinking; dimensional dynamics.

Publications: Contribr, chap, In: Encycl Social Sci, Columbia Univ Press, 30; auth, Understanding modern art, Vols I-III, 36-40; contribr, Miniature camera work, Morgan & Lester, 38; contribr, four chapters, In: Encycl Photog, 42-72; contribr, Art & archeology in the Aztec figure of Coatlicue, Mag Art, 4/45.

Dealer: Allan Stone Gallery, 48 E 86th St, New York, NY 10028; Lotte Jacobi Studio of Art & Photography, Hillsboro, NH 03244.

Mailing Address: 1125 Grand Concourse, Bronx, NY 10452.

KATZ, THEODORE (HARRY)
Educator, Painter

Preferred Media: Watercolors, Pencil, Ink.

b Philadelphia, Pa, July 29, 37.

Study & Training: Franklin & Marshall Col, AB, 59; Philadelphia Col Art, 59-60; Sch Dent, Univ Pa, 60-61; Colo Col, 61, with Hanya Holm; Art Stud League New York, N Y, 61-65, with John Groth & Mario Cooper; Martha Graham Sch Mod Dance, 61-65; Metrop Opera Sch Ballet, New York, 61-65; Mia Slavenska Sch Ballet, New York, 61-65, with Mia Slavenska; Matt Mattox Sch Jazz Dance, New York, 61-65, with Matt Mattox; Acad Grande Chaumiere, Paris, 64-65; Boston Mus Sch Arts, 68-71, with Jason Berger & George Dergalis; Carpenter Ctr, Harvard Univ, 69, with Mirko Baseldella, Grad Sch Educ, Experienced Teacher fel, 68-70, EdM, 69, EdD, 72.

Exhibitions: Fleisher Art Mem, Philadelphia, 68; Meeting House Gallery, Boston, Mass, 68-70; Wessell Libr, Tufts Univ, Boston, 69; Jewish Community Ctr, Wilmington, Del, 70.

Teaching: Master instr & curriculum developer, N C Advan Sch, Winston-Salem, 65-67; dir commun prog, Pa Advan Sch, Philadelphia, 67-68; lectr & consult classroom Renaissance arts, Humanities Leadership Inst, State of N J, 68-70.

Positions: Master instr & curriculum developer, Skidmore Col, 67; field reader, Off Educ, Arts & Humanities, Dept Health, Educ & Welfare, 67-71; res asst, proj, Grad Sch Educ, Harvard Univ, 69-71; dir, Ford Found Proj, Inst Am Indian Arts, Santa Fe, N Mex, 72-73.

Awards: Best in show, 68 & 69 & first prize for painting, 70, Meeting House Gallery.

Bibliography: The Advancement School for boys who could do better, Carnegie Quart, Vol 14, No 3; Howard Taubman (auth), Awakening the defeated, New York Times, 11/12/66; Henry S Resnik (auth), Turning on the system: war in the Philadelphia Public Schools, Pantheon, 70.

Memberships: Cambridge Art Asn; Copley Soc.

Dealer: Meeting House Gallery, Charles St, Boston, MA 02109.

Mailing Address: Institute of American Indian Arts, Cerrillos Rd, Santa Fe, NM 87501.

KATZEN, LILA (PELL)
Sculptor, Educator

Preferred Media: Steel, Plastics, Other Metals.

b New York, N Y.

Study & Training: Art Stud League New York; Cooper Union; also with Hans Hofmann, New York & Provincetown, Mass.

Work in Public Collections: Nat Collection Fine Arts, Smithsonian Inst, Washington, D C; Ga Mus Art, Athens; Milwaukee Art Ctr, Wis; Santa Barbara Mus, Calif; Chrysler Mus, Norfolk, Va.

Commissions: Light-floors, Archit League New York, 68; Universe as Environment, State Univ N.Y Stony Brook, 69; Laterna Magika, Czech Theatre Facade, Expo '70, Eurofilm Ltd, 70; Moon-Marker Print Series, Irwin Hollander Workshop, New York, 70; media-wall (with James R Edmunds, III, Architect), Chesapeake & Potomac Tel Co, Baltimore, Md, 72.

Exhibitions: Options, Milwaukee Art Ctr, Wis, 68; Painting & Sculpture Today, Indianapolis Mus, Ind, 70; Explorations '70 (Sao Paulo Biennale), Smithsonian Inst, Washington, D C, 70; Highlights of the Season, Larry Aldrich Mus, Ridgefield, Conn, 71; Gedok, Kunsthaus, Hamburg, Ger, 72.

Teaching: Instr 3-D design, 2 & 3-D media-sculpture & art & perception, Md Inst Col Art, 62-

Awards: Tiffany Found grant, 64; Lannan Found grant, 66; Archit League New York grant, 68.

Bibliography: Lawrence Alloway (auth), Directions I: options (catalog), Milwaukee Art Ctr, 68; William Paul (auth), Lila Katzen (catalogue), Ga Mus Art, 69; Cindy Nemser (auth), Lila Katzen defines environment, Arts Mag, 6/72.

Memberships: Archit League New York.

Dealer: Max Hutchinson Gallery, 127 Greene St, New York, NY 10028.

Mailing Address: 345 W Broadway, New York, NY 10013.

KATZENBACH, WILLIAM E
Designer, Lecturer

b Summit, N J, Aug 30, 04.

Study & Training: Princeton Univ; Oxford Univ; apprentice to Norman Bel Geddes.

Commissions: Organized mural scroll program & published three editions of mural scrolls by Calder, Matisse, Matta & Miro; supervised production of the approved Williamsburg Wallpaper Reproductions.

Exhibitions: Wallpaper & Wall Decoration Exhibs, Metrop Mus Art, Corcoran Gallery Art, Baltimore Mus Art, Cleveland Mus Art, Philadelphia Art Alliance & many others.

Collections Arranged: Modern Wallpaper, circulated by Am Fedn Arts, 48-49; Today's American Wallcoverings, circulated by Smithsonian Inst, 63-65.

Teaching: Critic & lectr, Parsons Sch Design, 46-64; lect, Am Inst Interior Designers, Inter Soc Color Coun, Drexle Inst, Moore Inst, Pratt Inst, New York Sch Design, Carnegie Inst & others.

Positions: Design assoc mem, Am Inst Interior Designers; dir, Rockland Found, 53-54; mem adv bd, Cooper-Hewitt Mus Design; mem bd mgrs, Moore Inst; coordr, decorative arts exhib prog & trustee, Am Fedn Arts, 64-

Awards: Justin Allman Award, 51; Trail Blazer Award, Home Fashion League, 54.

Publications: Co-auth, Practical book of American wallpaper, 51.

Mailing Address: Woods Rd, Palisades, NY 10964.

KAUFFMAN, (CAMILLE) ANDRENE
Painter, Sculptor

Preferred Media: Acrylics, Ceramic Glaze, Oils, Watercolors.

b Chicago, Ill, Apr 19, 05.

Study & Training: Art Inst Chicago, BFA; Univ Chicago, MFA; Ill Inst Technol; Univ Ill, Chicago; also with André Lhôte, Paris, France.

Work in Public Collections: Art Inst Chicago; Vanderpoel Gallery, Beverly Art Ctr, Chicago; Rockford Col, Ill; Mt Mary Col, Milwaukee, Wis; also many easel paintings in schs throughout midwest.

Commissions: 20 murals in oil on canvas, Works Progress Admin & U S Treas Dept, Burbank & Hirsch High Sch, Cook Co Hosp, Ida Grove & Iowa Post Off Bldgs, 34-42; 12 bas reliefs in wood or stone, Works Progress Admin, schs & field houses, Oak Park & Evanston, Ill, 34-42; two murals in ceramic tile, Sci Bldg, Rockford Col, 51-52; 19 murals in ceramic & stained glass window, Third Unitarian Church Chicago, 55-69; acrylic mural, Forest Park Pub Libr, Ill, 72.

Exhibitions: Two one-woman shows, San Diego Mus & La Jolla Fine Arts Gallery, Calif, 50; two one-woman shows, Bernard Gallery, Chicago, early 60's; one-woman show, Mt Mary Col, 64; one-woman retrospective (350 works), Third Unitarian Church Chicago, 67; one-woman show, Vanderpoel Gallery, 70.

Teaching: Prof, Art Inst Chicago, 27-67, prof emer, 67-

Awards: John Quincy Adams fel to Europe, Art Inst Chicago, 27; hon mention for drawing, Chicago & Vicinity Exhib, Art Inst Chicago, 46; second prize, Block Print Calendar, 73, Chicago Soc Artists, 72.

Bibliography: Robert B Johnson (auth), Sermon results in murals, Unitarian Register, 1/59; Prof John Hayward (narrator), Third Church trilogy (TV prog), Channel 11, Chicago, 8/59; Donald Key (auth), Kauffman show rich in color, Milwaukee J, 9/17/61.

Memberships: Arts Club Chicago; Nat Soc Mural Painters; Chicago Soc Artists.

Dealer: Art Rental & Sales Gallery, The Art Institute of Chicago, Michigan Blvd at Adams St, Chicago, IL 60603.

Mailing Address: 411 N West Ave, Elmhurst, IL 60126.

KAUFFMAN, ROBERT CRAIG
Painter, Sculptor

Preferred Media: Acrylics, Plastic.

b Los Angeles, Calif, Mar 31, 32.

Study & Training: Univ Southern Calif Sch Archit, 50-52; Univ Calif, Los Angeles, MA, 56.

Work in Public Collections: Mus Mod Art & Whitney Mus Am Art,
New York, N Y; Tate Gallery Art, London, Eng; Art Inst Chicago,
Ill; Los Angeles Co Mus Art, Calif.
Exhibitions: The New Aesthetic, Washington Gallery Mod Art, 67;
V Paris Biennale, Paris, France & Pasadena, Calif, 67; The
1960's, Mus Mod Art, New York, 67; Kompas IV, Holland, Ger &
Switz, 69; California Prints, Mus Mod Art, New York, 72.
Teaching: Instr painting & sculpture, Univ Calif, Irvine, 67-72;
instr painting & sculpture, Univ Calif, Berkeley, 69; instr paint-
ing & sculpture, Sch Visual Arts, New York, 70-71.
Awards: U S Govt fel for the arts, 67; first prize, 69th Am Exhib,
Art Inst Chicago, 70.
Bibliography: Barbara Rose (auth), Craig Kauffman (catalog for New
Aesthetic), 67; Jane Livingston (auth), Recent works by Craig
Kauffman, Artforum, 69; Review of Kauffman show, Artforum, 70.
Publications: Auth, foreword statement for A New Aesthetic, 67;
co-auth, Transparency, Reflection, Light, Space, 71.
Dealer: Pace Gallery, 32 E 57th St, New York, NY 10022.
Mailing Address: 160 La Brea, Laguna Beach, CA 92651.

KAUFMAN, EDGAR, JR
Designer, Writer
b Pittsburgh, Pa, Apr 9, 10.
Study & Training: Painting in New York, Vienna, Florence & London; apprentice with Frank Lloyd Wright.
Collections Arranged: Dir, Good Design, thrice-yearly exhibs spon-
sored by Merchandise Mart, Chicago & Mus Mod Art, New York;
dir, two exhibs, U S Consumer Wares, circulated by U S Govt
in Europe, 50-55; dir, Int Competition for Low-Cost Furniture
Design, 54-55; dir exhib, Textiles & Jewelry from India, 54-55;
U S Coordr, The Arts of Denmark Exhib, Metropolitan Mus Art,
60; traveling exhibs organized for Smithsonian Inst on work of
Fulbright designers & for U S Info Agency on Am designers.
Teaching: Bemis Lectr, Mass Inst Technol, 56; lectr, New York
Univ, Inst Fine Arts, 61; lectr, Mus Mod Art & others.
Positions: Dir dept indust design, Mus Mod Art, 46-50; adv dept de-
sign in indust, Parson's Sch Design, 55-61; mem comt on 20th
century painting & sculpture, Art Inst Chicago; dept ed applied
arts, Encycl Britannica, 58-; chmn design comt & adminr Kauf-
man Int Design Award, 59-
Memberships: Fel Royal Soc Arts; Int Design Inst; Am Inst Interior
Designers; Chicago Art Club.
Publications: Auth, Prize designs for modern furniture, What is
modern design?, What is modern interior design & Taliesin
drawings, Mus Mod Art; ed, An American architecture; auth,
Drawings for a living architecture, 59 & Frank Lloyd Wright,
writings and buildings, 60.
Mailing Address: 278 First Ave, New York, NY 10009.

KAUFMAN, IRVING
Painter, Educator
b New York, N Y, Oct 4, 20.
Study & Training: Art Stud League New York; N Y Univ, BA, MA.
Work in Public Collections: Univ Mich Mus Art; Saginaw Mus Art;
Ohio State Univ; Parke-Davis Co; Columbia Univ Law Libr.
Exhibitions: Pa Acad Fine Arts, Philadelphia, 49, 53 & 60; Detroit
Inst Art, 57-61; Art Inst Chicago, Ill, 60; Butler Inst Am Art,
Youngstown, Ohio, 60; Nat Acad Design, 62.
Teaching: Assoc prof art, Univ Mich, Ann Arbor, 56-64; prof art,
City Col New York, 64-
Memberships: Inst Study Art in Educ (pres, 72); Col Art Asn Am;
Univ Coun Art Educ.
Publications: Auth, Art & education in contemporary culture, 66;
contribr, Concepts in art education, 70; contribr, Confronting
curriculum reform, 70; contribr, New ideas in art education,
72.
Dealer: Rehn Gallery, 655 Madison Ave, New York, NY 10021.
Mailing Address: 34 Corell Rd, Scarsdale, NY 10583.

KAUFMAN, JANE A
Painter, Instructor
Preferred Media: Acrylics.
b New York, N Y, May 26, 38.
Study & Training: Cornell Univ; N Y Univ, BA; Hunter Col, MA.
Work in Public Collections: Whitney Mus Am Art, New York;
Aldrich Mus, Ridgefield, Conn; Corcoran Gallery, Washington,
D C.
Exhibitions: One-man shows, A M Sachs Gallery, New York, 58 &
70 & Whitney Mus Am Art, 71; The Structure of Color, Whitney
Mus Am Art, 71; Paley & Lowe Gallery, New York, 71.
Teaching: Instr art, Lehman Col, 69-70; instr art, Bard Col, 71-
Dealer: Paley & Lowe Gallery, 59 Wooster St, New York, NY 10012.
Mailing Address: 262 Bowery St, New York, NY 10013.

KAUFMAN, JOE
Illustrator
b Bridgeport, Conn, May 21, 11.
Study & Training: Lab Sch Indust Design; also with Herbert Bayer.
Work in Public Collections: Mus Mod Art, New York, N Y.
Exhibitions: Art Dirs Club, 43-60; Soc Illustrators, 45; one-man
show, Fleisher Art Mem, Philadelphia, 50.
Memberships: Soc Illustrators.
Publications: Auth & illusr, Christmas Tree Book, Words, 68 &
What makes it go, work, fly, float?, 71, Western Publ; illusr,
Eddie's moving day, Western Publ, 69 & I spy with my little eye,
McGraw, 70; plus other bks and illus incl in leading nat mag.
Mailing Address: 18 W 70th St, New York, NY 10023.

KAUFMAN, MICO
Sculptor, Writer
Preferred Media: Bronze, Stainless Steel, Plastics.
b Romania, Jan 3, 24; U S citizen.
Study & Training: Acad Fine Arts, Rome & Florence, Italy, 47-51.
Work in Public Collections: Bas relief, Rivier Col, Nashua, N H;
Andover Gallery Fine Arts, Mass; Kiski Acad, Saltburg, Pa;
Weltman, Weltman Conserv Music, Malden, Mass.
Commissions: Galactic, bas relief, Geophys, Inc, Burlington, Mass,
65; Samuel F Morse Coin Medal, Nat Commemorative Soc, Phil-
adelphia, Pa, 71; Aristotelian Award, AHEPA, Lowell, Mass, 71;
Maggie L Walker Coin Medal, Am Negro Commemorative Soc,
Philadelphia, 72; Lincoln Mint, Chicago, Ill; plus others.
Exhibitions: Rockport Artists Asn, 67; Prudential Art Fesitval, New
Eng Sculpture Soc, 69; Nat Sculpture Soc, New York, 70-71;
Audubon Artists, 71; Allied Artists Am, 71.
Teaching: Instr sculpture, Boston Ctr Adult Educ, 59-62; instr
sculpture, New Eng Sch Art, Boston, 69-70; instr sculpture,
Nashua Arts & Sci, 70-71.
Awards: Alma & Ulysses Ricci Award for best conservative sculp-
ture or painting, 67 & R V T Steeves Award for most outstanding
work in sculpture, 69 & 72, Rockport Artists Asn; Bronze Medal
of Honor, Concord Art Asn, 69; first prize, N Shore Art Asn,
Gloucester.
Bibliography: Ann Schecter (auth), Vivid sculptural works, 11/19/67
& Pertinax (auth), Maggie Walker Medal, 11/11/71, Lowell Sun,
Mass; Brenda Badolato (auth), The sculpture of Mico Kaufman,
Lawrence Eagle Tribune, Mass, 6/18/68.
Memberships: Nat Sculpture Soc; New Eng Sculpture Asn; Cambridge
Art Asn; Rockport Artists Asn.
Publications: Auth, The making of mold block and case, 60; contribr,
Your most penetrating portrait ever, Nat Sculpture Rev, 72.
Mailing Address: 23 Marion Dr, North Tewksbury, MA 01876.

KAULITZ, GARRY CHARLES
Painter, Printmaker
Preferred Media: Acrylics, Serigraphy.
b Rapid City, S Dak, Oct 6, 42.
Study & Training: Rochester Inst Technol, BFA & MFA.
Work in Public Collections: Brockport State Col, N Y; Gallery Today
Collection, Indianapolis, Ind.
Exhibitions: Springfield Nat Print Show, Mass, 68; Images on Paper,
Int Print Show, S C, 69; one-man shows, J B Speed Art Mus,
Louisville, Ky, 71 & Gallery Today, 71; Corp Collections, Citi-
zens Fidelity Bank, Louisville, 72.
Teaching: Assoc prof printmaking, Louisville Sch Art, 68-
Awards: Brockport State Col Purchase Award, 67; Evansville Mus
Ann Exhib Award, 68; Arthur D Allen Mem Award, Regional Fine
Arts Biennial, 71.
Bibliography: New printmaker, 68 & Sarah Lansdell (auth), Review of
work, 2/71, Courier-J & Times.
Mailing Address: P O Box 23322, Anchorage, KY 40223.

KAUPELIS, ROBERT JOHN
Painter, Educator
Preferred Media: Acrylics, Oils.
b Amsterdam, N Y, Feb 23, 28.
Study & Training: State Univ N Y Col Buffalo, BS; Albright Art Sch,
cert; Teachers Col, Columbia Univ, MA & DEd.
Work in Public Collections: Univ Mass, Amherst; Mich State Univ,
E Lansing; State Univ N Y Col Potsdam; New York Univ Art Col-
lection, N Y; Montclair State Col, N J.
Exhibitions: New Eng Ann, Silvermine Guild, Conn, 68, 70 & 71;
Crosscurrents U S A, Detroit Inst Art, Mich, 69-70; one-man
shows, Bertha Schaefer Gallery, New York, 69, 70 & 72, Galleria
Arvil, Mexico City, 71 & Circle Gallery, New Orleans, La, 72.
Teaching: Prof art, New York Univ, 56-
Awards: First prize int drawing competition, State Univ N Y Col
Potsdam, 60; prize for sculpture, New Eng Ann, 69; first prize,
Artists of Northern Westchester, Pace Col, 68.

Bibliography: Ellen Zeifer (auth), Robert Kaupelis teaches a
personal approach to drawing, Am Artist, 3/72.
Memberships: Nat Art Educ Asn; N Y State Art Teachers Asn.
Publications: Auth, Learning to draw, Watson-Guptill, 66.
Dealer: Bertha Shcaefer Gallery, 41 E 57th St, New York, NY 10022.
Mailing Address: 988 Barberry Rd, Yorktown Heights, NY 10598.

KAWA, FLORENCE KATHRYN
Painter
Preferred Media: Oils.
b Weyerhauser, Wis, Feb 24, 12.
Study & Training: Minneapolis Sch Art, Minn, 30-32 & 33-34; Univ
Wis-Milwaukee, BS, 40; La State Univ, Baton Rouge, MA, 44;
summers, Black Mountain Col, 44, Columbia Univ, 46-48, Cran-
brook Acad Art, 51, Mass Inst Technol, 56 & Leeds Col Art,
England, 70.
Work in Public Collections: Oil painting, Univ Wis-Madison; water-
color, La Art Comn, Baton Rouge; three watercolors & three
drawings, by U S Info Agency for permanent collections in Am
Embassies abroad; watercolors by Pub Bldgs Admin for Marine
Hosps.
Exhibitions: Int Watercolor Biennial, Brooklyn Mus, N Y, 51, 55,
57 & 59; Ann Exhib Contemp Am Sculpture, Watercolor & Draw-
ings, Whitney Mus Art, New York, N Y, 53; Nat Competition Wa-
tercolors, Drawings & Prints, Metrop Mus Art, New York, 53;
Contemp Watercolor in the U S, sponsored by U S Embassy Cult
Div, Paris & major mus, France, 53; Twentieth Century Am
Graphic Arts, U S Info Agency Touring Foreign Mus, 56-57.
Teaching: Asst prof painting & design, Fla State Univ, 46-62; assoc
prof painting & design, Drake Univ, 64-
Awards: Sculpture award, Milwaukee Art Inst, 38; Edith & Esther
Younker prize for creative painting, 69 & Edmundson Award for
best work in any medium, 70, Des Moines Art Ctr.
Mailing Address: 1545 29th St, Des Moines, IA 50311.

KAYE, GEORGE
Educator, Painter
Preferred Media: Watercolors, Pastels, Mixed Media.
b Malden, Mass, Nov 21, 11.
Study & Training: Swain Sch Design; Brooklyn Mus Art Sch; Brook-
lyn Col, BA; City Col New York Grad Sch; N Y Univ, MA.
Work in Public Collections: Philathea Col Mus, London, Ont; dept
educ film libr, Mus Mod Art, New York, N Y.
Exhibitions: One-man shows, Artzt Gallery, New York, 66, Bronx
Community Col, N Y, 67-69, Community Ctr, Newark, Del, 71,
Univ Del, Newark, 71 & Philadelphia Art Alliance, 72.
Teaching: Instr art, New York City Pub Schs, 34-53; chmn dept art,
High Sch Music & Art, New York, 53-59; lectr art educ, N Y
Univ, 60-62; lectr hist art, Pratt Inst, 65-66; lectr hist art,
Bronx Community Col, 67-68.
Positions: Asst dir art, Bd Educ, New York, 59-68; dir art, 68-;
consult art, Mayors Off, New York, 65-66; consult art, Dept Pub
Events, New York, 66-
Awards: Cert commendation, Park Asn New York, 66; cert apprecia-
tion, New York City Soc Osteopathic Physicians & Surgeons, 70;
citation, N Y State Educ Dept, 72.
Bibliography: J M McCormick (auth), Gallery reviews in New York,
Pictures on Exhib, 3/66; J Gollin (auth), Reviews & previews,
Art News, 3/66.
Memberships: Nat Art Educ Asn (local chmn, 72); N Y State Art
Teachers Asn (New York City Liaison, 59-72); N Y State Coun
Adminstr Art Educ (v pres, 63-72); New York City Art Dir Asn
(chmn, 60); N Y Soc Exp Study Educ (chmn art sect, 63-72).
Publications: Contribr, Color in education, Color Eng, 64; contribr,
N Y Soc Exp Study Educ Yearbook, 65; ed, Art & the young child,
68; ed, Creative crafts for today, 70; co-auth, A child's story of
Vincent Van Gogh, 70.
Mailing Address: 645 W 239th St, Bronx, NY 10463.

KAYSER, STEPHEN S
Educator, Writer
b Karlsruhe, Ger, Dec 23, 00.
Study & Training: Class State Sch, Karlsruhe; Univ Heidelberg,
PhD.
Teaching: Lect, Univ Calif, Berkeley, 41-44; prof hist art, San Jose
State Col, 45-62; prof art, Univ Judaism, Los Angeles, 62-; vis
prof art, Univ Calif, Los Angeles, 66-70; lect, History of Painting
& Synagogue Art & Architecture.
Positions: Former cur & dir exhibs, Jewish Mus, New York.
Publications: Auth, Jewish ceremonial art, 55 & The book of books
in art, 56; contribr, Parnassus, Rev of Relig, Pacific Art Rev,
Art Quart & Art News.
Mailing Address: Dept of Art, University of Judaism, 6525 W Sun-
set Blvd, Los Angeles, CA 90028.

KAZ (LAWRENCE KATZMAN)
Designer, Cartoonist
b Ogdensburg, N Y, June 14, 22.
Study & Training: Univ Pa, BS; Art Stud League New York, with
Reginald Marsh.
Positions: Pres & chmn bd, Kaz Mfg Co, 47-; spec proj chmn &
mem comt, Overseas Tours, Nat Cartoonists Soc; bus mgr, Car-
toonist; chmn, Int Cong Comics.
Awards: Silver Cup of City of Bordighera, Italy, 59; Palma d'Oro,
66; Silver T-Square, Nat Cartoonists Soc.
Memberships: Art Stud League New York; Nat Cartoonists Soc;
Mag Cartoonists Guild.
Publications: Auth & illusr, Nellie the nurse, 58, For doctors only,
Eng, 60, Prima y dopo i pasti, Italy, 60, Calling nurse Nellie, 61
& Nellie's laff-in, 68; plus other bks & cartoons in mags & news-
papers in U S, France, Eng, Belg, Holland, Italy, Spain, Mex,
Denmark, Sweden & others.
Mailing Address: 101 Central Park W, New York, NY 10023.

KAZ, NATHANIEL
Sculptor, Instructor
b New York, N Y, Mar 9, 17.
Study & Training: Art Stud League New York, with George Bridgman.
Work in Public Collections: Brooklyn Mus, N Y; Whitney Mus Am
Art & Metrop Mus Art, New York; also in pvt collections.
Commissions: Limestone carving, Fine St Temple, Nashville, Tenn;
bronze sculpture, Pub Sch 59, Brooklyn; two colored aluminum
reliefs to Thespians Tragedy & Comedy, Jr High Sch 164, Queens;
sculpture, Temple Beth Emeth, Albany, N Y, 65; plus others.
Exhibitions: Whitney Mus Am Art, Metrop Mus Art & Mus Mod Art,
New York; Art Inst Chicago, Ill; Philadelphia Mus Fine Arts, Pa;
plus others.
Teaching: Instr sculpture, Art Stud League New York.
Awards: Prize, 47 & medal of honor, 60, Audubon Artists; Brooklyn
Soc Artists, 48 & 52; Nat Inst Arts & Lett grant, 57.
Memberships: Sculptors Guild; Woodstock Soc Art; Brooklyn Soc
Art; Audubon Artists; Archit League.
Mailing Address: 160 W 73rd St, New York, NY 10023.

KEANE, BIL
Cartoonist
b Philadelphia, Pa, Oct 5, 22.
Work in Public Collections: Bil Keane Original Cartoon Collection,
Syracuse Univ.
Positions: Staff artist, Philadelphia Eve Bull, 45-59; creator & nat
syndicated cartoonist, The Family Circus.
Memberships: Nat Cartoonists Soc; Newspaper Comics Coun; Mag
Cartoonists Guild.
Publications: Auth, The family circus, 67, I need a hug, 68 & Wanna
be smiled at?, 69, Fawcett Gold Medal Bks; auth, Through the
year with the family circus, Judson, 69; auth, It's apparent
you're a parent, Doubleday, 71.
Mailing Address: 5815 E Joshua Tree Lane, Paradise Valley, AZ
85253.

KEANE, LUCINA MABEL
Painter, Educator
b Gros, Nebr, 04.
Study & Training: Ashland Col, Ohio; Ohio State Univ, BS Educ;
Teachers Col, Columbia Univ, MA; Pa State Univ; Temple Univ;
New York Univ.
Exhibitions: Allied Artists W Va; Clarksburg Art Ctr, W Va; Cen-
tennial Exhib, Huntington Art Gallery, W Va.
Teaching: Lect, Sculpture & Art Appreciation; instr art, Univ N Dak,
26-29; instr art, Ill State Normal Univ, 30-31; assoc prof art, &
head dept, Morris Harvey Col, 36-72.
Positions: Pres bd & mem steering comt, Charleston Art Gallery,
63-66; mem, Centennial Art Comt W Va, 63; U S Govt Post Off
art consult.
Awards: Five prizes, Allied Artists W Va, 36-59.
Memberships: Col Art Asn Am; Nat Art Educ Asn; Eastern Art
Educ Asn; Allied Artists W Va; plus others.
Collection: Print collector, Europe, South America & Japan.
Mailing Address: 2908 Noyes Ave, Charleston, WV 25304.

KEARL, STANLEY BRANDON
Sculptor
Preferred Media: Cast Bronze.
b Waterbury, Conn, Dec 23, 13.
Study & Training: Yale Univ, BFA, 41, MFA, 42; Univ Iowa, PhD,
48; study in Rome, Italy, nine yrs.
Work in Public Collections: Univ Iowa, Ames; Univ Minn, Duluth;
Naz Galeria, Rome, Italy; Nat Mus, Stockholm, Sweden; Mus
Goteborgs, Sweden; plus others.

Exhibitions: Whitney Mus Am Art Ann, New York, N Y, 62; Hudson River Mus, Yonkers, 63, one-man show, 64; Grand Cent Mod, New York, 65 & 68; Inst Int Educ, Graham Gallery, New York, 69; plus others.
Teaching: Univ Minn, Duluth, 47-48; Pratt Inst, 67.
Awards: Fulbright exchange prof to Univ Rome, Italy, 49-50; Inst Contemp Arts, Florence, Italy, 52; Conn Acad Sculpture Prize, 58; plus others.
Bibliography: Torsten Bergmark (auth), Palettes, Swed Art J, 52; Michel Seuphor (auth), The sculpture of this century, dictionary of modern sculpture, A Swemmer, Ltd, London, 59.
Memberships: Col Art Asn Am.
Dealer: Graham Galleries, 1014 Madison Ave, New York, NY 10021.
Mailing Address: 344 Sprain Rd, Scarsdale, NY 10583.

KEARNEY, JOHN (W)
Sculptor, Educator
Preferred Media: Bronze, Silver, Gold, Steel.
b Omaha, Nebr, Aug 31, 24.
Study & Training: Cranbrook Acad Art, Bloomfield Hills, Mich, 45-48; Fulbright grant Italy & Ital Govt grant sculpture, 63-64, Univ Stranieri, Perugia, 63.
Work in Public Collections: Norfolk Art Mus, Va; Detroit Children's Mus, Mich; Mundelein Col, Chicago; St Paul Gallery & Sch Art; Roosevelt Univ, Chicago.
Exhibitions: Corcoran Biennial, Washington, D C, 55; Am Fulbright Artists, Palazzo Venezia, Rome, 64; Painting & Sculpture Today, John Herron Mus, Indianapolis, 65; Soc Contemp Am Art Exhib, Art Inst Chicago, 66 & many shows, Chicago & Vicinity, Art Inst Chicago.
Teaching: Dir, Contemp Art Workshop, Chicago, 51-; instr sculpture, Mundelein Col, 70-71.
Awards: S J Wallace Truman Prize, Nat Acad Design, 53; Man of Yr, Adult Educ Coun Chicago, 62.
Bibliography: Numerous articles & discussions in mags, newspapers & bks.
Memberships: Provincetown Art Asn (v pres, 62-70); Arts Club Chicago.
Dealers: ACA Gallery, 25 E 73rd St, New York, NY 10021; Galleria Schneider, Rampa Mignanelli, Rome, Italy.
Mailing Address: 830 Castlewood Terr, Chicago, IL 60640.

KEARNS, JAMES JOSEPH
Sculptor, Painter
Preferred Media: Bronze, Fiberglass.
b Scranton, Pa, Aug 7, 24.
Study & Training: Art Inst Chicago, BFA, 51.
Work in Public Collections: Mus Mod Art, New York, N Y; Whitney Mus Am Art, New York; Newark Mus Art, N J; N J State Mus, Trenton; Nat Collection Fine Arts, Smithsonian Inst, Washington, D C.
Exhibitions: Nat Inst Arts & Lett, 59; Whitney Mus Am Art Ann, 59-61; Johnson Wax Collection, World Tour, 62-67; Pa Acad Fine Arts, Philadelphia, 64-65; San Diego Nat Invitational Print Show, Calif, 64, 66 & 69.
Teaching: Instr drawing, painting & sculpture, Sch Visual Arts, 60-; instr sculpture, Fairleigh-Dickinson Univ, 62-63; instr painting & sculpture, Skowhegan Sch Painting & Sculpture, summers 62-65.
Positions: Mem bd gov, Skowhegan Sch Painting & Sculpture, 64-70.
Awards: Nat Inst Arts & Lett grant, 59.
Bibliography: Selden Rodman (auth), Conversations with artists, Devin Adair, 57; Selden Rodman (auth), The insiders, La State Univ Press, 60; Lee Nordness (auth), Art U S A Now, Viking Press, 63.
Publications: Illusr, Can these bones live, New Directions, 60; illusr, The heart of Beethoven, Shorewood Press, 62.
Dealer: Sculpture Ctr, 167 E 69th St, New York, NY 10021.
Mailing Address: 452 Rockaway Rd, Dover, NJ 07801.

KECK, SHELDON WAUGH
Educator, Art Conservator
b Utica, N Y, May 30, 10.
Study & Training: Harvard Univ, BA, 32; apprentice in restoration, Fogg Art Mus, 32-33.
Teaching: Dir art conserv, New York Univ Conserv Ctr, 61-65, prof fine arts, 64-66; prof art conserv, Cooperstown Grad Progs, State Univ N Y Col Oneonta, 69-
Positions: Conservator, Brooklyn Mus, 34-61.
Awards: Fulbright fel, 59; Guggenheim fel, 59-60.
Memberships: Brooklyn Mus (gov comt); Cooperstown Art Asn (bd dirs); Int Inst Conserv Hist & Artistic Works (mem coun); Int Conf Mus (conserv comt).
Publications: Auth, numerous articles in prof journals & art periodicals on exam & conserv of paintings.
Mailing Address: River St, Cooperstown, NY 13326.

KEELING, HENRY CORNELIOUS
Painter, Educator
Preferred Media: Watercolors, Collage.
b St Albans, W Va, Sept 4, 23.
Study & Training: Pratt Inst, BFA(interior design); N Y Univ; Hans Hofmann Sch Fine Art, New York, with Hans Hofmann; Art Stud League New York; Marshall Univ, MA(fine art); also with Bernard Klonis, Reuben Tam, Leo Manso & Victor Kandell.
Work in Public Collections: Huntington Galleries, W Va; Charleston Art Gallery of Sunrise, W Va; W Va Arts & Humanities Coun Permanent Collection, Charleston; gift to Herbert M Rothchild Collection, New York, N Y.
Commissions: Three paintings & mural, Consolidated Gas Corp, Clarksburg, W Va, 67; two paintings, Roanoke Indust Savings & Loan Corp, Va, 68.
Exhibitions: Brooklyn Mus Art Sch Ann, 54 & 55; New York City Ctr Gallery Monthly Shows, 55-57; Exhibs 180, 65-68 & one-man show, 72, Huntington Galleries; Three West Virginia Artists, Charleston Art Gallery, 68.
Teaching: Instr design & art appreciation, Marshall Univ, 67-69; asst prof art hist & painting & drawing, Morris Harvey Col, 69-, acting head dept, 72-
Awards: First prize, W Va Allied Artist Ann, 70; purchase awards for graphics, Charleston Art Gallery, 71 & W Va Arts & Humanities, 71.
Memberships: Provincetown Art Asn; W Va Allied Artists.
Mailing Address: 406 Park St, St Albans, WV 25177.

KEEN, HELEN BOYD
Painter, Collector
Preferred Media: Oils.
b Tacoma, Wash.
Study & Training: Calif Sch Fine Arts, with Mark Tobey, 8 yrs; Art Stud League New York, with Cobino, Hale & Vytlacil, 4 yrs.
Work in Public Collections: Seattle Art Mus, Wash; Addison Gallery Am Art, Andover, Mass; Art Gallery Greater Victoria, B C; Tacoma Art Mus.
Exhibitions: U S State Dept Show (selected by Mus Mod Art), Paris & France, 56-57; Pa Acad Fine Arts, 57; Brooklyn Mus, 57; Norfolk Mus Arts & Sci, 63; Avanti Gallery, New York, N Y, 72; plus one other.
Awards: First award, Tacoma Art Mus, 45.
Memberships: Art Stud League New York; Art Gallery Greater Victoria; Tacoma Art Mus; Asia House, New York.
Collection: Mark Tobey, Pehr Vytlacil, John Ford, Mario Bambagini, Judith Rothschild, Toko Shinoda & Ethel Schwabacher.
Dealer: Avanti Galleries, 145 E 72nd St, New York, NY 10021.
Mailing Address: 201 E 79th St, New York, NY 10021.

KEENE, MAXINE M
Sculptor, Educator
Preferred Media: Bronze.
b Cleveland, Ohio, Apr 7, 39.
Study & Training: Kent State Univ, BFA, grad study; Cranbrook Acad Art, Bloomfield Hills, Mich, MFA.
Work in Public Collections: Ball State Univ Gallery Art, Muncie, Ind.
Commissions: Bronze bas reliefs, Am United Life, Muncie, 70 & D Doctors Accounting Serv Co, Indianapolis, Ind, 71.
Exhibitions: Mid States Art Exhib, Evansville Mus Art, Ind, 69; 150 Yrs Ind Art Invitational, Anderson Fine Arts Ctr, 69; Presenting Seven Sculptors, Sculptors Gallery, Washington, D C, 70; 23rd Ann Ceramic & Sculpture Show, Butler Inst Am Art, Youngstown, Ohio, 72; 53rd Ann May Show, Cleveland Mus Art, Ohio, 72.
Teaching: Assoc prof art, Ball State Univ, 65-; artist-in-residence, Hiram Col, 72-73.
Awards: Contemp Art Soc Award & Morris-Goodman Talbot Gallery Award, Herron Mus Art.
Memberships: Col Art Asn Am; Muncie Art Asn.
Publications: Contribr, articles, In: La Rev Mod, Paris, France, 67.
Mailing Address: 13 Center Dr, Burlington Park, Muncie, IN 47302.

KEENE, PAUL
Painter, Sculptor
b Philadelphia, Pa, Aug 24, 20.
Study & Training: Phila Mus Sch & Univ Pa, 39-41; Tyler Sch Art, Temple Univ, 45-48; Acad Julien, Paris, France, 49-51; Whitney fel, 52-54.
Work in Public Collections: Pa Acad Fine Arts, Philadelphia; Phila delphia Mus; Howard Univ, Washington, D C; Morgan State Col, Baltimore, Md; Bowdoin Col, Maine.
Commissions: History of University (mural), Johnson C Smith Univ, Charlotte, N C; Garden of Martyrs (sculpture with Neil Lieberman), 59th St Baptist Church, Philadelphia; Dancers (sculpture with Neil Lieberman), Moylon Recreation Ctr, Philadelphia; medal for Am Negro Commemorative Soc, Philadelphia; play sculpture (with Neil Lieberman), Beckett Proj, Philadelphia.

Exhibitions: Salon de Jeunes Pientres, Paris, France, 51; Pa Acad Fine Arts Ann, Philadelphia, 52-53 & 68-69; Lagos Mus, Nigeria, 61; San Jose State Col, Calif, 69; Master Series, Carnegie Libr, Pittsburgh, Pa, 70.
Teaching: Prof painting & dir course, Centre D'Art, Port-au-Prince, Haiti, 52-53; assoc prof drawing & painting, Philadelphia Col Art, 54-68, chmn basic art prog, 63-66; prof drawing & design, Bucks Co Community Col, Newton, 68-, chmn dept art, 70-, area coordr art dept, 68-70.
Awards: Alumni award in art, Temple Univ.
Bibliography: Briskin (auth), New talent art in America, Art in Am, 54; Lewis/Waddy (auth), Black artists on art, Contemp Crafts, 71.
Mailing Address: 2843 Bristol Rd, Warrington, PA 18976.

KEENER, ANNA ELIZABETH
Painter, Educator
Preferred Media: Acrylics, Graphics.
b Flagler, Colo, Oct 16, 95.
Study & Training: Bethany Col (Kans), BFA & BA; Art Inst Chicago; Kansas City Art Inst; Univ N Mex, MA; also graphics with George Miyasake & mural painting with James Pinto.
Work in Public Collections: Rare Bk Sect, N Mex State Univ Libr; Mus N Mex Fine Arts; Birger Sandzen Mem Gallery, Lindsborg, Kans; U S Nat Monument, Los Alamos, N Mex; current seals for Sul Ross State Univ, Alpine, Tex & Eastern N Mex Univ, Portales.
Commissions: Zuni Pottery Making (mural), McKinley Co Courthouse, Gallup, N Mex; Baptistry, Bd Dirs, Baptist Church, Portales.
Exhibitions: Mus N Mex Biennial, Santa Fe, 68; Rocky Mountain States Print Collection, 69; Southwestern Art Festival, Tucson, Ariz, 70; 47th Ann, Springville, Utah, 71; 5 State Exhib, Port Arthur, Tex, 71.
Teaching: Supvr art, Ariz Pub Schs, Globe; instr art, Kansas City High Sch; head dept art, Eastern N Mex Univ.
Positions: Bd Dirs, N Mex Art Educators Asn; juror, Mus N Mex Art Exhibs; juror, N Mex Pub Schs Exhibs, State Fair; State Chmn Fine Arts Prog, Am Asn Univ Women; State Chmn Fine Arts, N Mex Fed Women's Clubs.
Awards: Bronze Medal for Barn on the Hill, Kansas City Art Inst; Poorbough Press Award for Giraffes, 56; award for collagraph, Mus N Mex Fine Art, 62; plus one other.
Bibliography: Roy S Dunn (auth), Archives for the American Southwest, Tex Tech Univ, 65-72.
Memberships: Artists Equity Asn (pres Santa Fe Chap, 64-65).
Dealer: Kachina Gallery, 112 Old Santa Fe Trail, Santa Fe, NM 87501.
Mailing Address: 312 Cadiz Rd, Santa Fe, NM 87501.

KEITH, DAVID GRAEME
Museum Curator
b Toronto, Ont, Sept 21, 12.
Study & Training: Western Reserve Univ, BA & MA; Harvard Univ; New York Univ.
Positions: Cur decorative arts, M H de Young Mem Mus, at present.
Mailing Address: M H de Young Memorial Museum, Golden Gate Park, San Francisco, CA 94118.

KELEMEN, PAL
Art Historian
b Budapest, Hungary, Apr 24, 94; U S citizen.
Study & Training: Univ Budapest; Univ Munich; Univ Paris; mus res in Budapest, Vienna, Florence, London, Madrid & Seville.
Teaching: Lectr, Nat Gallery Art, Metrop Mus Art & other mus & univs; spec lect tour, U S Dept State, Europe & the Near East.
Positions: Survey trips, U S Dept State, Mex, Cent Am & Europe, 33-; mem comn for protection & salvage of artistic & hist monuments in war areas, World War II.
Awards: Comdr, Order of Merit, Ecuador.
Memberships: Fel Royal Anthrop Inst; mem var sci socs in U S, Latin Am & Europe.
Research: Early Christian art; pre-Columbian and colonial art in Latin America.
Publications: Auth, Ancient, colonial art of the Americas, Dutch, 62, Ger, 64, Fr, 65, Span, 67, Port, 69; auth, Art of the Americas, 69 & 70; auth, Peruvian colonial painting, 71; contribr, Encycl Britannica; contribr, Stauffacher's World Art History & other leading periodicals in the U S, Europe & Latin Am.
Mailing Address: Box 447, Norfolk, CT 06058.

KELLEHER, DANIEL JOSEPH
Painter, Instructor
Preferred Media: Acrylics, Collage.
b Erie, Pa, Nov 15, 30.
Study & Training: Edinboro State Col, BS, 53; Syracuse Univ.

Work in Public Collections: Washington & Jefferson Col, Washington, Pa; Hemingway Collection, New York, N Y; First Nat Bank, Erie; Erie Pub Libr.
Exhibitions: Nat Soc Painters in Casein, New York, 67; Butler Inst Am Art, Youngstown, Ohio, 67 & 68; Audubon Artists 26th Ann, New York, 68; Mainstream 69, Marietta Col, Ohio, 69; Watercolor U S A, Springfield, Mo, 71.
Teaching: Art educator, Erie Sch Dist, 61-
Awards: Hon mention, Four Arts Soc, Palm Beach, Fla, 67; purchase award, Washington & Jefferson Col, 68; award of excellence, Mainstream 69, 69.
Bibliography: Clyde Singer (auth), Butler midyear show, 67; Connie Kienzle (auth), Washington & Jefferson show, Pittsburgh Press, 68; Group show Erie artist, Cleveland Plain Dealer, 69.
Memberships: Erie Art Ctr (mem bd dirs, 68-); Chautauqua Inst Art, N Y; Pa Art Educ Asn.
Publications: Contribr, articles, In: Sch Arts Mag, 68 & 72.
Dealer: Galerie 8, 2594 W Eighth St, Erie, PA 16505.
Mailing Address: 427 E Eighth St, Erie, PA 16502.

KELLEHER, PATRICK JOSEPH
Art Administrator, Art Historian
b Colorado Springs, Colo, July 26, 17.
Study & Training: Colo Col, AB, 39; Princeton Univ, MFA, 42, PhD, 47; Am Acad Rome, fel, 47-49; fine arts specialist off, Ger, 45-46.
Collections Arranged: Art Mus, Princeton (new bldg), 66 & numerous spec exhibs, incl European & American Painting & Sculpture in Princeton Alumni Collections, 72.
Teaching: Lectr art hist, Univ Buffalo, 50-51; res prof art hist, Univ Mo, 56-59; prof art hist, Princeton Univ, 60-
Positions: Chief cur art, Los Angeles Co Mus, 49; cur collections, Albright-Knox Art Gallery, 50-54; cur European art, Nelson Gallery-Atkins Mus, 54-59; dir, Art Mus, Princeton Univ, 60-; juror, regional exhibs.
Memberships: Asn Art Mus Dirs.
Publications: Auth, The holy crown of Hungary, Am Acad Rome, 50; auth, Expressionism in American art, Albright-Knox Art Gallery, 53; co-auth, The century of Mozart, Nelson Gallery, 56; contribr, European & American painting & sculpture in Princeton Alumni Collection, 72; auth, John White Alexander (in prep).
Mailing Address: 176 Parkside Dr, Princeton, NJ 08540.

KELLER, DEANE
Educator, Painter
Preferred Media: Oil.
b New Haven, Conn, Dec 14, 01.
Study & Training: Art Stud League, New York, N Y, with George Bridgman; Yale Univ Sch Fine Arts; with Eugene F Savage & E C Taylor; Am Acad Rome (Prix de Rome 3 yrs), 26.
Work in Public Collections: Hq, U S Post Office, Washington, D C; portrait of Sen Robert Taft, Senate Reception Chamber, Capitol Bldg, Washington, D C; Conn Ct Errors (Supreme Ct), Hartford, Conn; Yale Univ, New Haven; N Y Hospital, Cornell Univ, New York.
Commissions; Two murals, Shriver Hall, Johns Hopkins Univ, Baltimore, Md, 57; mural (with Baurel LaFarge), Pub Libr, New Haven.
Exhibitions: Portraits, Inc, New York, several exhibs in 60's; Yale Univ; Hartford, Conn; Harrisburg, Pa; others.
Teaching: Prof art, Yale Univ Sch Art & Archit, 30-70; prof art, Paier Sch Art, 55-
Positions: Chief, fine arts sect, Fifth Army, Italy, 43-46.
Memberships: New Haven Paint & Clay Club (pres, 36-39).
Dealer: Portraits, Inc, 41 E 57th St, New York, NY 10022.
Mailing Address: 18 Brookhaven Rd, Hamden, CT 06517.

KELLEY, CHAPMAN
Painter, Art Dealer
Preferred Media: Oils, Pastels.
b San Antonio, Tex, Aug 26, 32.
Study & Training: Hugo D Pohl Art Sch San Antonio; Trinity Univ; Pa Acad Fine Arts, with Franklin Watkins, Hobson Pittman, Walter Steumpfig, Abraham Rattner, Morris Blackburn, Julius Bloch, Harry Rosin, Francis Speight & Roswell Weidner.
Work in Public Collections: Mulvane Art Ctr, Topeka, Kans; Okla Art Ctr, Oklahoma City; Witte Mem Mus, San Antonio; Dallas Mus Fine Arts, Tex; Tex Instruments, Inc, Dallas; Colo Springs Fine Arts Ctr.
Exhibitions: Southwestern Art Invitational, Dallas Mus Fine Arts, nat circulation Am Fedn Art, 57; 157th Ann Am Painting & Sculpture, Pa Acad Fine Arts, Philadelphia, 62; Childe Hassam Fund Exhib, Am Acad Arts & Lett, New York, N Y, 63; Butler Inst Am Art Midyear Shows, 64 & 66-67; 11th Midwest Biennial, Joslyn Mus, Omaha, Nebr, 70; Artists Southeast & Tex Biennial, Delgado Mus, New Orleans, 71; plus many other group & one-man shows.

Teaching: Pvt instr, Dallas, 57-68; instr painting & drawing, Dallas Mus Fine Arts, 59-67; sem instr, Univ Northern Ill, 71.
Positions: Partic Matrix For Arts Symp, Ctr Advan Studies, Urbana, Ill, 67; panelist, Nat Sculpture Conf, Univ Kans, 70; dir, Atelier Chapman Kelley.
Awards: Top Purchase Award, Okla Art Ctr, 65; El Paso Mus Art Purchase Prize, Sun Carnival Nat, 69.
Bibliography: Sold out art, Life Mag, 9/20/63; article, In: Burlington Mag, 64; Past jurors invitational (catalogue), Okla Art Ctr, 69.
Specialty of Gallery: Contemporary, major twentieth century and impressionist works.
Collection: Twentieth century and contemporary works.
Mailing Address: 2526 Fairmount St, Dallas, TX 75201.

KELLEY, RAMON
Painter
Preferred Media: Oils, Watercolors, Pastels.
b Cheyenne, Wyo, Feb 12, 39.
Study & Training: Colo Inst Art.
Work in Public Collections: George Amos Mem Libr, Gillette, Wyo.
Exhibitions: One-man show, Oklahoma City Mus Art, Redridge, Okla, 71; Beaux Arts Ball, Dallas Mus Fine Art, Tex, 71; 104th Ann Exhib, 71 & 105th Ann Exhib, 72, Am Watercolor Soc; Mainstreams '72, Marietta, Ohio, 72; Southwestern Drawing Biennial, Tucson, Ariz; plus many others.
Awards: Helen Gapen Ohler Award, 104th Ann Exhib, 71, 104th Ann Traveling Exhib, 71 & 105th Ann Traveling Exhib, 72, Am Watercolor Soc.
Publications: Contribr, Am Artist Mag, 3/69.
Dealer: Canyon Rd Art Gallery, 710 Canyon Rd, Santa Fe, NM 87501.
Mailing Address: 1180 Detroit St, Denver, CO 80206.

KELLY, ELLSWORTH
Painter, Sculptor
b Newburgh, N Y, May 31, 23.
Study & Training: Boston Mus Sch, 46-48.
Work in Public Collections: Metrop Mus Art; Mus Mod Art; Guggenheim Mus; Whitney Mus Am Art, New York, N Y; Tate Gallery, London, Eng.
Commissions: Sculpture, Penn Ctr Transp Bldg Lobby, Philadelphia, 56; lobby mural, Eastmore House, New York, 56; wall sculpture, comn by Philip Johnson, New York World's Fair, New York Pavilion, 64; mural, UNESCO, Paris, France, 69.
Exhibitions: 16 Americans, 59 & Art of the Real, 68, Mus Mod Art, New York; Paintings, Sculpture & Drawings by Ellsworth Kelly, Washington Gallery Mod Art, 63; Venice Biennale Int Art, 66; New York Painting & Sculpture, 1940-1970, Metrop Mus Art, 69.
Awards: Carnegie Int Prizes, 62 & 64; Brandeis Creative Arts Award, 63; Tokyo Int Educ Ministry Award, 63.
Bibliography: Eugene Goossens (auth), Derriere le miroir, Paris, Maeght Ed, 58; Diane Waldman (auth), Ellsworth Kelly drawings, collages, prints, New York Graphic Soc, 71; John Coplans (auth), Ellsworth Kelly, Abrams, 72.
Mailing Address: 1 West 67th St, New York, NY 10023.

KELLY, JAMES
Painter
b Philadelphia, Pa, Dec 19, 13.
Study & Training: Pa Acad Fine Arts, Philadelphia; Barnes Found, Merion, Pa; Calif Sch Fine Arts, San Francisco.
Work in Public Collections: San Francisco Mus Art; Mus Mod Art, New York, N Y; Los Angeles Mus Art, Calif; Univ Mass, Boston; Westinghouse Corp, Salem, N C & Pittsburgh, Pa.
Exhibitions: San Francisco Mus Art Painting Ann, 55-58; Minneapolis Inst Art, Minn, 57; Am Fedn Arts Traveling Exhib, 58-59; Los Angeles Co Mus Art, 68; one-man shows, Westbeth Galleries, New York, 71-72.
Teaching: Lectr painting, Univ Calif, Berkeley, summer 56.
Awards: Ford Found grant lithography, 63.
Dealer: G W Einstein Co, 23 E 67th St, New York, NY 10021.
Mailing Address: 463 West St, New York, NY 10014.

KELLY, LEE
Sculptor
Preferred Media: Metals.
b McCall, Idaho, May 24, 32.
Study & Training: Mus Art Sch, Portland, Ore.
Work in Public Collections: Univ Houston, Tex; Portland Art Mus; Seattle Art Mus, Wash; Candlestick Park, San Francisco, Calif; Univ Ore Mus, Eugene.
Commissions: Welded steel play piece, Unthanr Park, Portland, 68; welded steel fountain, Milwaukee Ore Libr, 69; welded stainless steel wall piece, Pac Northwest Bell, Portland, 71; welded stainless steel water piece, Univ Houston, 72; welded steel gateway, Candlestick Park, San Francisco, 72.

Exhibitions: Ore Centennial Invitational, 60; Denver Mus Ann Invitational, 61 & 71; Pacific Profile, Pasadena Mus, Calif, 62; West Coast Now, Portland Art Mus, Ore.
Teaching: Instr art, Mt Angel Col, 68-71.
Awards: Seattle Art Mus purchase award, 60-61; Ford Found purchase award, 63; Art Advocates Proj award, 70.
Dealers: Sally Judd Gallery, 212 S W Stark St, Portland, OR 97204; John Bolles Gallery, 10 Gold St, San Francisco, CA 94133.
Mailing Address: 13099 S Warnock Rd, Oregon City, OR 97045.

KELLY, LEON
Painter
Preferred Media: Oils.
b Perpignan, France, Oct 21, 01; U S citizen.
Study & Training: Pa Acad Fine Arts, traveling scholar, 24; Acad Grande Chaumiére, Paris; also with Jean Auguste Adolphe, Alexandre Portinoff, Arthur Carles & Earl Horter.
Work in Public Collections: Mus Mod Art, New York, N Y; Whitney Mus Am Art; Wadsworth Atheneum, Conn; Metrop Mus Art, New York; Tel Aviv Mus, Israel; plus many others.
Exhibitions: Retrospective 1920-65, Int Gallery, Baltimore, Md, 65, Pa Acad Fine Arts, 67; Long Beach Found, N J, 68; Exhibs, Richard Feigen Gallery, Chicago, 68 & 70; Newark Mus, N J, 69; plus many other one-man & group shows.
Teaching: Instr, Pa Acad Fine Arts.
Awards: William & Nora Copley Award, 58.
Mailing Address: 268 Pompano Dr, Loveladies, NJ 08008.

KELLY, WALTER W
Art Dealer
b Chicago, Ill, Jan 14, 41.
Study & Training: Roosevelt Univ, BA, 63.
Positions: Dir, Walter Kelly Gallery.
Specialty of Gallery: Contemporary American painting and sculpture.
Mailing Address: 620 N Michigan Ave, Chicago, IL 60611.

KELPE, PAUL
Painter
Preferred Media: Oils, Watercolors.
b Minden, Ger, 02; U S citizen.
Study & Training: Art Sch, Hanover, Ger; Univ Chicago, MA & PhD.
Work in Public Collections: Detroit Inst Arts, Mich; Howard Univ, Washington, D C; Md State Teachers Col, Towson; Univ Ill, Urbana; Dept Labor, Washington, D C.
Exhibitions: Am Abstr Artists, Betty Parsons Gallery, New York, N Y, 59; Am Abstr Artists, Riverside Mus, New York, 66; Citation Exhib, Tex Fine Arts Asn, 71; Geometric Abstraction of 1930s, Zabriskie Gallery, New York, 72; plus many others.
Bibliography: Jacobson (auth), Art of today, Stein Publ, 33; M Candler Cheney (auth), Modern art in America, McGraw, 39; The world of abstract art, Wittenborn, 57.
Memberships: Am Abstr Artists (treas, 36-39, secy, 39-41); Tex Fine Arts Asn.
Mailing Address: 705 Texas Ave, Austin, TX 78705.

KELSEY, MURIEL CHAMBERLIN
Sculptor
Preferred Media: Stone.
b Milford, N H.
Study & Training: Univ N H, BS, 19; Univ Vt, 21; Teachers Col, Columbia Univ, 33; New Sch Soc Res, 34; Sculpture Ctr New York, with Dorothea Denslow.
Commissions: Dancing Pickaninny (bronze statuette), Brookgreen Gardens Mus, S C, 37; plus many others in pvt commissions.
Exhibitions: Sculpture Ctr New York, N Y, 34-; Audubon Artists, New York, 58-62; Nat Acad Design, New York, 59-62; Harmon Gallery, Naples, Fla, 64-; Third Sculpture Int, Fairmount Park Art Asn, Philadelphia, Pa.
Teaching: Asst zool lab, Univ N H, 20; asst zool lab, Univ Vt, 21.
Awards: Sarasota Festival Arts, 53; Art League Manatee Co, 59; first prize, Longboat Key Art Ctr, 65.
Memberships: Sculpture Ctr New York.
Dealers: Harmon Gallery, 1258 Third St S, Naples, FL 33940; Oehlschlaeger Galleries, 107 E Oak St, Chicago, IL 60611.
Mailing Address: Mira Mar Hotel, 63 S Palm Ave, Sarasota, FL 33578.

KEMOHA (GEORGE W PATRICK PATTERSON)
Painter, Art Historian
Preferred Media: Oils.
b Centralia, Ill, Dec 29, 14.
Study & Training: Univ Okla.
Commissions: Murals, Our Lady of Guadalupe, Dewey, Okla, 50; murals, St John's Cath Church, Bartlesville, Okla, 60; murals,

St Charles Borromeo, Oklahoma City, Okla, 70; plus hundreds of pvt portrait commissions.
Positions: Dir, Woolaroc Mus, 38-70.
Mailing Address: 418 Texas Ave, Woodward, OK 73801.

KEMP, PAUL ZANE
Printmaker
Preferred Media: Intaglio, Metal.
b Apache Creek, N Mex, Nov 6, 28.
Study & Training: N Mex Highlands Univ, BA, 50, MA, 54; Cranbrook Acad Art, MFA, 60.
Exhibitions: Third Ann Prints, Drawings & Crafts, Ark Arts Ctr, Little Rock, 69; Am Graphics 69, Col of the Pac, 69; Nat Graphic Arts & Drawing Show, Wichita Art Asn, Kans, 69; Northwest Printmaker's Int, Seattle, Wash, 69; Tex Fine Arts Asn Ann Citation Show, Austin, 69 & 70.
Teaching: Asst prof art, Baylor Univ, 61-64, assoc prof, 64-69, prof, 69-
Awards: Jurors Choice, Tex Fine Arts Asn Citation Show, 69 & 70; purchase entry, Ark Art Ctr, 69.
Memberships: Tex Designer-Craftsmen; Print Coun Am; Tex Fine Arts Asn; Am Crafts Coun; Col Art Asn Am.
Publications: Contribr & illusr, Tex Trends Art Educ, spring 69.
Dealer: Ed Hill, 5736 Trobridge Dr, El Paso, TX 79925.
Mailing Address: 2812 Cole, Waco, TX 76707.

KEMPER, JOHN GARNER
Educator, Designer
Preferred Media: Graphics, Oils.
b Muncie, Ind, June 3, 09.
Study & Training: Ohio State Univ, BFA; Columbia Univ, MA; Chicago Acad Fine Arts.
Exhibitions: Ann Exhibs Mich Artists, 44 & 46 & Relig Christmas Card Competition, 55, Detroit Inst Arts; 11th Ann New Yr Show, Butler Inst Am Art, Youngstown, Ohio, 46; Ogunquit Art Ctr, Maine, 58-62.
Teaching: Prof art, Western Mich Univ, 42-70.
Positions: Designer, Ohio Wax Paper Co, 34-36; designer, Dell Publ Co, 36-41.
Awards: Awards, for Three Houses (serigraph), Friends Am Art, Grand Rapids, 46 & The Experiment Station (oil), Ohio Valley Oil & Water Show, 54; Report of Pres, Am Col Pub Rel Asn, 69.
Publications: Illusr, var articles & covers, Design Mag, 31-33; auth & illusr, A portable marionette stage, Indust Arts & Voc Educ Mag, 43; auth & illusr, Marionettes, Sch Arts Mag, 46; co-auth, Art consciousness comes to Kalamazoo, Design Mag, 47.
Mailing Address: 605 W Lovell St, Kalamazoo, MI 49007.

KEMPTON, GRETA
Painter
b Vienna, Austria, Mar 22, 03.
Study & Training: Nat Acad Design; Art Stud League New York.
Work in Public Collections: The White House, The Pentagon, U S Treas Dept, U S Supreme Court, Nat Portrait Gallery, Apostolic Delegation & Georgetown Univ, Washington, D C; plus many other mus & pvt collections in U S & abroad.
Exhibitions: One-woman shows, Corcoran Gallery Art, Washington, D C, Canton Art Inst, Ohio, Col Wooster, Ohio, Art Asn Harrisburg, Pa, Akron Art League, Ohio & Circle Gallery, Cleveland, Ohio; plus many others.
Memberships: Fel Royal Soc Arts; Burr Artists.
Mailing Address: 14 E 75th St, New York, NY 10021.

KENDA, JUANITA ECHEVERRIA
Painter, Educator
b Tarentum, Pa, Nov 12, 23.
Study & Training: Stephens Col; Art Stud League New York; Temple Univ, BFA; Univ Hawaii; also with Jon Corbino, Sam Hershey, Boris Blai, Raphael Sabatini, Jean Charlot, George Bridgman & others.
Commissions: Murals, Straub Clinic & Children's Hosp, Honolulu.
Exhibitions: The Gallery, Honululu, 60; Honolulu Painters & Sculptors, 60 & 61; Moorestown Friends Sch, 61; Univ Hawaii, 65; Galeria Santiago, San Juan, P R, 67; plus many others.
Collections Arranged: Organized Exhib, Art of Hawaii Children, circulated by Smithsonian Inst, 60-64.
Teaching: Lect, art educ; instr workshop, Hawaii Summer Sch, 51; chmn art teaching conf, 51-52, 53, 55, 56 & 58; instr, Univ Hawaii Sch Educ, 65-66.
Positions: Adv, Art Teachers Asn, 50-; chmn sch art exhib, Honolulu Acad Arts, 50-, head creative art sect, 49-63; state prog spec, State Dept Educ, Honolulu, 63-64; community relations off, East-West Ctr, 68-70; pres, Downtown Gallery Ltd, 69-; Hon Consul of Mex in Hawaii.
Memberships: Honolulu Printmakers; Hawaii Painters & Sculptors League; Asn Art Mus; Pacific Art Asn; Nat Art Educ Asn; plus others.

Publications: Auth & illus, Art education in Hawaii, Hawaii's children exhibit their art, Art & art education in Hawaii & Art guide for Hawaii, Sch Arts Mag; auth & illusr, Curriculum outline—elementary art & curriculum outline—secondary art, Dept Educ, State of Hawaii; contribr to Paradise of the Pacific; auth, Art guide for pre-school and kindergarten, San Diego Schs, Calif, 71.
Mailing Address: 3708 Lurline Dr, Honolulu, HI 96816.

KENDALL, VIONA ANN
Painter, Printmaker
b Berkeley, Calif, Aug 28, 25.
Study & Training: Occidental Col; Lukets Acad Fine Arts; also with T N Lukets, Sam Hyde Harris, Leon Franks, Sergei Bongart & Joe Mungnaini.
Work in Public Collections: In pvt collections only.
Exhibitions: Long Beach Mus Art, 66; Montana State Univ, 67; Butler Inst Am Art, 67; Nevada Art Gallery, 67; Long Beach City Col, 67; plus many others.
Teaching: Lect & demonstrations, women's clubs, art galleries & on TV.
Positions: Bd gov, Hollywood Art Asn, 54; pres, Burbank Art Asn, 54, dir, 55; corresp secy & bd dirs, Valley Art Guild, 54 & 55.
Awards: All-City Art Festival, 62; All-Calif Exhib, 63; Frye Mus, 63; plus others.
Bibliography: Work reproduced in La Rev Mod, 61; also in Prize winning oil paintings.
Memberships: Nat Soc Arts & Lett; fel Int Inst Arts & Lett; Calif Art Club; Los Angeles Art Asn; Am Artists Prof League; plus others.
Mailing Address: 4808 Brewster Dr, Tarzana, CA 91356.

KENNEDY, DORIS WAINWRIGHT
Painter
Preferred Media: Watercolors.
b Bernice, La, Jan 26, 16.
Study & Training: La Polytech Inst, BA.
Work in Public Collections: Springfield Mus Art, Mass; Butler Inst Am Art, Youngstown, Ohio; Birmingham Mus Art, Ala; Springfield Mus Art, Mo; Univ Tenn, Nashville; plus others.
Exhibitions: Art Collectors Gallery, Mexico City, Mex, 61 & 65; Fort Worth Art Mus, Tex, 67; Univ Tenn, 67; Univ S C, 68; Birmingham Mus Art, 68; plus many others.
Teaching: Instr art, Birmingham Pub Schs, 36-41.
Awards: Prizes, Birmingham Mus Art, 53-69; Butler Inst Am Art, 61 & 63; Southeastern Ann, 66; plus others.
Memberships: Philadelphia Watercolor Club; Audubon Artists; Ala Watercolor Soc; Birmingham Art Asn.
Mailing Address: 19 Pine Ridge Lane, Birmingham, AL 35213.

KENNEDY, J WILLIAM
Painter, Educator
Preferred Media: Oils.
b Cincinnati, Ohio, Aug 17, 03.
Study & Training: Art Acad Cincinnati; Carnegie Inst Technol, AB; Univ Ill, MFA.
Work in Public Collections: Portraits, Ind Univ, Bloomington & Univ Ill, Champaign; A E Stoley Co, Decatur, Ill; Withrow High Sch, Cincinnati.
Commissions: Portraits, of pres Herman B Wells, 62, v pres Joseph Franklin, 63 & dean Edmundson, 64, Ind Univ, Bloomington & dean Carl Brandley, 67 & Col Leslie A Bryan, 69, Univ Ill, Champaign.
Exhibitions: First, second & third Nat Exhibs, Rockefeller Ctr, New York, N Y; San Francisco World's Fair; Corcoran Biennial; two Pa Acad Fine Arts Ann; Richmond Biennial, Va.
Teaching: Prof art, Univ Ill, Champaign, 26-70.
Awards: Award of merit, Fla Gulf Coast Art Ctr, 72; hon mention, Milwaukee Art Gallery; first prize in painting, Decatur Art Ctr.
Memberships: Provincetown Art Asn; Fla Gulf Coast Art Ctr; Midwest Col Art Conf.
Dealer: Secrest Gallery, Wellfleet, MA 02667.
Mailing Address: 1414 Monte Carlo Dr, Clearwater, FL 33516.

KENNEDY, LETA MARIETTA
Educator, Craftsman
b Pendleton, Ore, July 4, 95.
Study & Training: Mus Art Sch, Portland, Ore; Columbia Univ Teachers Col, BS; Colo Springs Art Ctr; also with Arthur Wesley Dow, Herman Rosse, Hans Hofmann, Maholy-Nagy, Arthur Baggs, Dorothy Wright Liebes, Frances Senska, Marian Hartwell & Minor White.
Work in Public Collections: Portland Art Mus; Seattle Art Mus.
Exhibitions: Northwest Printmakers, Seattle Art Mus, 38; Philadelphia Art Alliance, Pa, 39; Contemp Crafts Asn, Portland, 62; 10 Artists Ore, Portland Art Mus, 67; Univ Ore, Eugene.

Teaching: Head dept, Mus Art Sch, Portland, 22-71.
Memberships: Portland Art Asn; Contemp Crafts Asn.
Mailing Address: 2545 S W Terwilliger, Portland, OR 97201.

KENNY, BETTIE ILENE (BIK)
Painter, Writer
Preferred Media: Oil on Linen Canvas, Lead Glass.
b Longmont, Colo, June 5, 31.
Study & Training: Pac Lutheran Univ, with George Roskos; design with James Marca; Univ Wash, BA(Eng, with hons); with Norman Lundin, Everett Du Pen, Edward L Praczukowski & George Tsutakawa; also with Florence Gould, Jack Cady & E H Smith.
Work in Public Collections: Commemorative portraits on glass of President Nixon & Tricia Nixon & Edward Finch Cox, The White House; commemorative portrait of President J F Kennedy on glass, Smithsonian Inst; pictures & slides of diamond-point work, Corning Mus Glass, N Y; Henry Art Gallery Arch of Artists, Seattle, Wash.
Commissions: Oil painting award for Nazarene Church, Longmont, 47; Joan French (oil portrait), Gilbert & Sullivan Operetta Co, Seattle, 58; Anniversary Commemorative (drawing in diamond-point), Church of God, 71; diamond-point drawing (32 percent glass lead), Baptist Church, Seattle, 72; Ski Scene (drawing in diamond-point), for State of Wash to be presented at Heavenly Valley Ski Races, 72.
Exhibitions: Boeing Art Shows, Seattle, 58-60; Bellevue Arts & Crafts Shows, Wash, 59-62; 10th Ann Puget Sound Area Exhib, Charles & Emma Frye Art Mus, Seattle, 68; Lambda Rho Art for Collectors' Sale, 71 & Women in Art, 72, Henry Art Gallery, Seattle.
Awards: Creative thinking merit awards, Boeing Co, Seattle, 58-59; letter of commendation from Gov Daniel J Evans, State of Wash, 72; commendation for portrait on glass, Lawrence Welk, 72.
Bibliography: Guest artist demonstration of diamond-point engraving on full percent lead glass, Channel 5, King TV Telescope Prog, 5/31/72.
Research: Techniques of diamond-point engraving and techniques of the masters in glass work of the seventeenth, eighteenth and nineteenth centuries.
Publications: (Written under pseudonym, Bik Kenny) Birches to brag about, Organic Gardening & Farming, 63; Science in music, 63, The Baroque organ, 64 & Opening the piano to play it like a harp, 65, Keyboard Jr; Apricots by the bushelful, Organic Gardening & Farming, 70.
Mailing Address: P O Box 1503, Seattle, WA 98103.

KENNY, THOMAS HENRY
Painter
b Bridgeport, Conn, Jan 12, 18.
Study & Training: Knox Col; Ohio Christian Univ, MA.
Work in Public Collections: Metrop Mus Art, New York, N Y; Philadelphia Mus Art, Pa; Stedelijk Mus, Amsterdam, Netherlands; Mus Mod Art, Mexico City, Mex; plus 347 mus collections in 27 countries.
Exhibitions: Kenny-Retrospect, Mus Mod Art, Miami, Fla, 70; 246 Years of Am Art, New Brit Mus, 70; Int Graphics, Neue Galerie der Stadt Linz, Austria, 70; New Acquisitions, Mus Arte Moderna, Rio de Janeiro, Brazil, 71; plus 177 exhibs in 14 countries.
Memberships: Life fel Royal Soc Arts, London; Col Art Asn Am; Am Fedn Arts; Inst Contemp Arts, London.
Art Interests: Lithography.
Mailing Address: Oak Ridge Lane, North Hills, Roslyn, NY 11576.

KENT, CORITA, I H M
Serigrapher, Educator
b Fort Dodge, Iowa, Nov 20, 18.
Study & Training: Immaculate Heart Col, BA; Univ Southern Calif, MA; Chouinard Art Inst.
Work in Public Collections: Victoria & Albert Mus, London; Art Inst Chicago, Ill; Metrop Mus Art, New York, N Y; Libr Cong & Nat Gallery Art, Washington, D C; plus others.
Exhibitions: Vatican Pavilion, New York World's Fair, 64-65; IBM Bldg, 66; Morris Gallery, 67; Sala Gaspar Gallery, Spain.
Teaching: Prof art, Immaculate Heart Col, at present.
Publications: Auth & illusr, Footnotes and headlines: a play-pray book, 67 & Sister Corita, 68; co-auth, City, uncity, Doubleday, 69; auth & illusr, Damn everything but the circus, Holt, Rinehart & Winston, 70; co-auth & illusr, To believe in things, Harper & Row 71; plus others.
Mailing Address: Dept of Art, Immaculate Heart College, 2021 N Western Ave, Los Angeles, CA 90027.

KENT, FRANK WARD
Painter, Art Administrator
b Salt Lake City, Utah, Feb 16, 12.
Study & Training: Univ Utah, 30; Art Inst Chicago, 31; Art Stud

League New York, 31-32; pvt study in Paris, France, 34; Syracuse Univ, BFA, 37, MFA, 38; pvt study in Mex, 46 & 52.
Work in Public Collections: Iowa State Univ; Bradley Univ; Univ Ill; Art Inst Chicago; Syracuse Mus Fine Arts.
Exhibitions: Syracuse Mus Fine Arts, 44-55; Rochester Mem Art Gallery, Utica, N Y; Pan-Am Union; New Georgetown Gallery, Washington, D C; Mex Embassy, Washington, D C; plus others.
Teaching: Instr art, Bradley Univ, 38-44; prof fine art, Syracuse Univ, 44-58; educ dir, Mex Art Workshop, 49-55; lectr, Postiano Art Workshop, Italy, 56.
Positions: Dir publ prog & exhibs, Syracuse Univ, 50-; dir, Crocker Art Gallery, Sacramento, 58-68; fine arts appraiser, researcher, restorer, Hunter Gallery, San Francisco, 68-
Awards: Prizes, Syracuse Mus Fine Arts, Rochester Mem Art Gallery & Univ Utah.
Memberships: Am Soc Appraisers.
Mailing Address: Apartado Postal 283, Chapala, Jalisco, Mex.

KEPALAITE, ELENA, see KEPALAS.

KEPALAS (ELENA KEPALAITE)
Sculptor, Painter
Preferred Media: Bronze.
b Vilnius, Lithuania; U S citizen.
Study & Training: Ont Col Art, Toronto; Brooklyn Mus Sch Art.
Work in Public Collections: Pa Acad Fine Arts, Philadelphia; Univ Mass Art Gallery, Amherst; M K Ciurlionis Lithuanian Art Gallery, Chicago, Ill; Lithuanian Mus, Adelaide, Australia; Mus Mod Art Lending Serv, New York, N Y.
Commissions: Bronze bust, Mr Louis Horst, New York, 62; bronze bust, Mrs Gunilla Kessler, New York, 71.
Exhibitions: Pa Acad Fine Arts Invitational, Philadelphia, 68; Silvermine Guild Artists Ann, New Canaan, Conn, 69; Jersey City Mus, N J, 69-71; Phoenix Gallery, New York, 70 & 72; one-man show, Brooklyn Mus, N Y, 64.
Awards: 1970 Sculpture House Award, Jersey City Mus, 70.
Memberships: Am Soc Contemp Artists.
Mailing Address: c/o Phoenix Gallery, 939 Madison Ave, New York, NY 10021.

KEPES, GYORGY
Painter, Educator
b Selyp, Hungary, Oct 4, 06.
Study & Training: Royal Acad Fine Arts, Budapest, MFA, 28.
Work in Public Collections: Univ Ill; Dallas Mus Fine Arts, Tex; Albright-Knox Art Gallery, Buffalo, N Y; Mus Mod Art & Whitney Mus Am Art, New York, N Y; plus many others.
Commissions: Murals, Grad Ctr, Harvard Univ, Travelers Ins Co, Los Angeles, Sheraton Hotel, Dallas & Chicago, Children's Libr, Fitchburg, Mass & Church of Redeemer, Baltimore, Md; plus many others.
Exhibitions: Art Inst Chicago, Ill; San Francisco Mus Art, Calif; Mus Fine Arts, Houston, Tex; Whitney Mus Am Art, New York; Carnegie Inst, Pittsburgh, Pa; plus others in mus in the U S & Rome, London, Copenhagen, Amsterdam & other cities.
Collections Arranged: Designed exhib, Arts of the United Nations, Art Inst Chicago, 64; designer sect of Triennale de Milano, 68.
Teaching: Head light & color dept, New Bauhaus, 37-38; Inst Design, 38-43; prof visual design, Mass Inst Technol, 46-, dir Ctr Advan Visual Studies, 67-, Inst prof, 70.
Awards: Guggenheim fel, 60-61; Medaglia d'Oro, Convegno Int Artisti Critici e Studiosi d'Arte, 66; fine arts award, Am Inst Architects, 68.
Memberships: Nat Inst Arts & Lett; fel Am Acad Arts & Sci.
Publications: Auth, Language of Vision, 44 & The new landscape, 56; ed, Visual arts today, 60; ed, Vols I-VII, In: Vision & value series, Braziller.
Mailing Address: 90 Larchwood Dr, Cambridge, MA 02138.

KEPETS, HUGH MICHAEL
Painter
b Cleveland, Ohio, Feb 6, 46.
Study & Training: Carnegie-Mellon Univ, with Joanne Maier & Robert Gardner, BFA; Fontainebleau Sch Art; Art Stud League New York, with Sidney Gross; Ohio Univ, with Harvey Daniels, MFA.
Work in Public Collections: Cleveland Mus Art; Pittsburgh Nat Bank, Pa; Utah State Univ, Logan.
Commissions: Painting, Determined Prod, San Francisco, Calif, 69.
Exhibitions: Four shows, Artists Western Reserve May Show, Cleveland Mus Art, 66-72; Appalachian Corridors Exhib 3, Charleston, Va, 72; 36th Midyear Show, Butler Inst Am Art, Youngstown, Ohio, 72; 18th Nat Print Show, Brooklyn Mus, 72.
Teaching: Instr design, San Francisco Art Acad Col, spring 70; instr painting & drawing, Ohio Univ, 70-72.
Awards: Cleveland Mus Art Purchase Award, 72; Appalachian Corridors 3 Achievement Award, 72.

Publications: Illusr, Washington DC guide, 69.
Dealers: Michael Wyman Gallery, 233 E Ontario St, Chicago, IL 60611; Associated American Artists, 663 Fifth at 52nd, New York, NY 10022.
Mailing Address: Rte 183, Stockbridge, MA 01262.

KERFOOT, MARGARET (MRS M W JENNISON)
Painter, Educator
b Winona, Minn, July 4, 01.
Study & Training: Hamline Univ, BA, 23; Art Inst Chicago, 25; Paris Atelier of Parsons Sch Art, 28; Univ Iowa, with Grant Wood & MA, 37; Harvard Univ, Carnegie grant, 40; Univ Ore, Carnegie grant, 41.
Work in Public Collections: Denver Pub Schs, Colo.
Exhibitions: Chicago Artists, Art Inst Chicago, Ill, 34; Midwestern Artists, Kansas City Art Inst, Mo, 42; Everson Mus Art Regional, Syracuse, N Y, 55-71; Artists of Central New York, Munson-Williams-Proctor Mus, Utica, N Y, 58-71; Finger Lakes Exhib, Rochester Mem Art Gallery, N Y, 60-63.
Teaching: Asst prof art & acting chmn dept, Carleton Col, 37-45; asst prof art, Hood Col, 46-48; prof art & chmn dept, Hamline Univ, 48-52; lectr art, sch art, Syracuse Univ, 52-66.
Awards: Purchase prize for Red Landscape, First Trust Bank, Syracuse, 72.
Memberships: Assoc Artists Syracuse; Everson Mus Art.
Mailing Address: 307 Standish Dr, Syracuse, NY 13224.

KERKOVIUS, RUTH
Painter
Preferred Media: Intaglio.
b Berlin, Ger, June 9, 21; U S citizen.
Study & Training: In Munich, Ger, 46-49; New Sch Soc Res; Art Stud League New York; Pratt Graphic Art Ctr, scholar; Sch Visual Arts.
Work in Public Collections: New York Pub Libr; Mus Fine Arts, Boston; Mus Western Art, Fort Worth, Tex; White House; Ford Found; plus others.
Exhibitions: Print Club Philadelphia, 67; Asheville Art Mus, N C, 68; Assoc Am Artists, New York, 69; Tenn Fine Arts Ctr, Nashville, Tenn, 68; C Troup Gallery, Dallas, 70; plus others.
Awards: Second prize for intaglios, Jersey City Mus, 62, DePauw Univ, 66 & Wesleyan Univ, 67.
Memberships: Print Club Philadelphia; Soc Am Graphic Artists (past coun mem).
Mailing Address: Mas Le Paladium, Quartier Villevieille, Pont de Crau, 13200, Arles, France.

KERMES, CONSTANTINE JOHN
Painter, Printmaker
Preferred Media: Oils, Acrylics.
b Pittsburgh, Pa, Dec 6, 23.
Study & Training: Carnegie-Mellon Univ, BFA; also with Victor Candell, Leo Manso & Frank Lloyd Wright.
Work in Public Collections: Storm King Art Ctr, Mountainville, N Y; Notre Dame Art Mus, South Bend, Ind; Shaker Heights Hist Soc, Cleveland, Ohio; Ind Univ Pa; Pa State Univ, University Park.
Commissions: Icon paintings, Holy Cross Greek Orthodox Church, Pittsburgh, 55; two murals, Pa Hist & Mus Comn, Cornwall Mus, 68; assemblage panels, Hain Wolf Assocs, Harrisburg, Pa, 70.
Exhibitions: One-man exhibs, eight exhibs, Jacques Seligmann Gallery, 50-70; Des Moines Art Ctr, Iowa, 53 & Pa State Univ, University Park, 71; Butler Inst Am Art Ann, Youngstown, Ohio, 64; Design Rev, Smithsonian Inst, Washington, D C, 69.
Teaching: Instr printmaking, Millersville State Col, summer 69.
Positions: Prof art adv, Lancaster Co Tech Schs, 70-
Awards: Ann Design Rev Awards, Indust Design Mag, 62, 64 & 68; design award, Am Iron & Steel Inst, 65 & 69; Traveling Exhib Painting Prize, Petrol Industs, 71.
Bibliography: Emily Genauer (auth), Icons of American saints, This Wk, 5/17/53; D Yoder (auth), Painter of the Amish, Pa Folklife, summer 66; George Swetnam (auth), Search for simplicity, Pittsburgh Press, 9/6/70.
Publications: Illusr, Shaker cookbook, 68; auth & illusr, There is a season, 69; painting reproduced, In: 1972 UNICEF Art Calendar.
Dealer: Jacques Seligmann Gallery, 5 E 57th St, New York, NY 10022.
Mailing Address: 981 Landis Valley Rd, Lancaster, PA 17601.

KERN, ARTHUR (EDWARD)
Educator, Sculptor
b New Orleans, La, Oct 27, 31.
Study & Training: Tulane Univ La, BA, 53, MFA, 55.
Teaching: Asst prof drawing, Univ Southwestern La, 67-69; assoc prof painting & sculpture, Tulane Univ La, 69-, assoc chmn dept art, 72-

Dealer: Diane Rauch, 4636 Pontchartrain Blvd, New Orleans, LA 70118.
Mailing Address: 1730 Pine St, New Orleans, LA 70118.

KERNS, ED (JOHNSON, JR)
Painter
Preferred Media: Acrylic Polymer.
b Richmond, Va, Feb 22, 45.
Study & Training: Va Commonwealth Univ, BFA; with Grace Hartigan, Md Inst, Col Art, Baltimore, MFA.
Work in Public Collections: Aldrich Mus Art, Ridgefield, Conn; Chase Manhattan Bank Collection, New York, N Y; A M Sachs Collection, New York; Univ Mass Art Collection, Amherst.
Exhibitions: Today, Md Inst, Col Art, 71; New Talent, 71 & one-man show, A M Sachs Gallery, 72; Contemporary Reflections, Aldrich Mus Art, 72; Art Acquisitions, Univ Mass, 72.
Awards: Artist of the Year, Larry Aldrich Assoc, New York, 71; art achievement key, Va Commonwealth Univ, 67.
Bibliography: Rev of 72 show at A M Sachs Gallery, A Mikotajuk in Arts Mag, 4/72, B Schwartz in Art News Mag, 4/72 & H Gerard, Art Int Mag, 5/72.
Dealer: A M Sachs Gallery, 29 W 57th St, New York, NY 10019.
Mailing Address: 92 Reade St, New York, NY 10013.

KERR, BERTA BORGENICHT
Art Dealer, Collector
b New York, N Y, Nov 27, 43.
Study & Training: Boston Univ, BA.
Positions: Asst dir, Grace Borgenicht Gallery, New York, 65-
Specialty of Gallery: Contemporary American painting and sculpture.
Collection; Picasso, Klee, Seurat, Avery, Marsden Hartley, José de Rivera, Valladon, Bolotowsky & Vasarely.
Mailing Address: c/o Borgenicht Gallery, 1018 Madison Ave, New York, NY 10021.

KERR, E COE
Art Dealer
b New York, N Y, Sept 3, 14.
Study & Training: Yale Univ, BA.
Positions: Pres, M Knoedler & Co, 57-69; pres, Coe Kerr, Inc, 69-
Memberships: Art Dealers Asn.
Specialty of Gallery: Contemporary American art.
Mailing Address: 49 E 82nd St, New York, NY 10028.

KERR, JAMES WILFRID
Painter, Lecturer
Preferred Media: Oil.
b New York, N Y, Aug 7, 97.
Study & Training: Poppenhusen Inst, College Point, N Y, 14; New York Sch Fine & Applied Art, 20-23, dipl-cert; New Sch Social Res, 33-34; study with Howard Giles, Camilio Egas, Ecuador, Jacques Maroger, Louvre, Paris, France.
Work in Public Collections: Mus City New York, N Y; Joslyn Art Mus, Omaha, Nebr; Masonic Home, Burlington, N J; N M State Fair Permanent Art Collection, Albuquerque; Fla Southern Col Fine Art Collection, Lakeland.
Exhibitions: Painting in the United States, Carnegie Inst, Pittsburgh, Pa, 49; Art U S A, Madison Sq Garden, New York, 58; Allied Artists Am Ann, New York, 61, 62 & 63; Albuquerque Invitational, Mus New Mex, Santa Fe, 61; 47th Ann Nat Art Exhib, Mus Art, Springville, Utah, 71.
Teaching: Asst instr art, N Y Sch Fine & Applied Art, summer 21; dir art educ, Kerr Summer Sch Art, Detroit, Mich, summers, 23-24; spec lect art educ, Syracuse Univ, summer 32.
Positions: Founder & owner, Fairbairn Publishers, New York, 25-40; art dir, Harry Doehla Co, Fitchburg, Mass, 45-50.
Awards: First Altman Prize, Nat Acad Design, New York, 45; purchase prize, N Mex State Fair, Albuquerque, 63; silver medal, Am Vet Soc Artists, New York, 63.
Memberships: Salmagundi Club; Allied Artists Am (treas, 52-55); Am Vet Soc Artists (pres, 58-60); Artists Equity Asn (nat treas, 59-61); Mus Albuquerque Asn (pres & mem bd trustees, 67).
Publications: Contrib, Art recovery, Sch Arts Mag, 33; co-auth, Historic design for modern use, 38; auth, Modern lettering, 39.
Dealer: Grand Central Galleries, 40 Vanderbilt Ave, New York, NY 10017.
Mailing Address: 7017 Bellrose Ave NE, Albuquerque, NM 87110.

KERR, JOHN HOARE
Art Administrator, Art Historian
b Newport, R I, Apr 19, 31.
Study & Training: Art Stud League New York; Yale Univ & Sch Fine Arts; Boston Mus Sch Fine Arts.
Collections Arranged: Planned exhibs on American Art Collection for Nat Collection Fine Arts; planned extensive exhibs on American & Europ Art at Huntington Galleries.

Positions: Dir interpretation, Sleepy Hollow Restorations, 61-63; spec consult, Am art & mus collection planning, Nat Collection Fine Arts, 63-64; dir, Huntington Galleries, 64-67; cult consul, U S Consulate Gen, Madras, India, 67-69; dir educ, Nat Endowment for the Arts, 69-
Memberships: Am Asn Mus; Nat Trust for Hist Preserv; Soc Archit Historians; Am For Serv Asn.
Research: American art from earliest days through 1540's; South Indian bronzes (India).
Collection: Small personal specimen collection of European, American and Asian (Indian) paintings, sculpture, prints and decorative arts with emphasis on the nineteenth and twentieth centuries.
Publications: Auth, Museum collections of the Trirandrum Museum, Kerala, South India, 68; auth, South Indian bronzes in the Madras Government Museum, Tamilnadu, 70.
Mailing Address: 2804 P St, Washington, DC 20007.

KERR, KENNETH A
Painter, Designer
Preferred Media: Watercolors.
b Pittsburgh, Pa, Feb 10, 43.
Study & Training: San Diego City Col, AA; Art Ctr Col, BA; also with Rex Brandt & Robert E Wood.
Commissions: Paintings, U S Financial Corp, San Diego, 72.
Exhibitions: Calif 200th, 70; Del Mar Fair, 71; Watercolor West, 71; Calif-Hawaii Regional, 71; Art Inst 14th Ann, 71.
Teaching: Instr life drawing & watercolor, San Diego Community Cols, 70-
Positions: Illusr, Gen Dynamics, San Diego, 61-64; designer, Collage Studios, Los Angeles, 66-68; art dir, Art Assocs, San Diego, 68-69; art dir & owner, Daisy Studio, San Diego, 69-
Awards: Firsts for watercolors, San Diego Art Inst Ann, 71 & Southern Calif Expo, 71; distinctive merit, Soc Communicating Age, 71.
Memberships: San Diego Watercolor Soc (v pres, 70, pres, 71); San Diego Art Inst (pres, 70-71); Am Inst Fine Art; Artists Equity Asn; Nat Soc Communicating Arts.
Dealer: San Diego Art Institute, Balboa Park, San Diego, CA 92013.
Mailing Address: 3628 Front St, San Diego, CA 92103.

KERR, LESLIE
Painter
b Detroit, Mich, Mar 26, 34.
Study & Training: Univ Calif, Los Angeles, BA & MA.
Work in Public Collections: San Francisco Mus Art, Calif.
Exhibitions: One-man shows, Dilexi Gallery, San Francisco, 60, 62-64 & 67; Calif Palace Legion of Honor, 62 & 63; Stanford Univ, 62 & 65; Whitney Mus Am Art, New York, 62 & 67; Odyssia Gallery, New York, 68; plus others.
Teaching: Instr art, Univ Calif, Los Angeles, 57-58; instr art, New York Univ, 66-67.
Awards: Schwabacher-Frey Award, San Francisco Mus Art, 61.
Mailing Address: 909 Madison, Albany, CA 94706.

KERSLAKE, KENNETH ALVIN
Printmaker, Educator
Preferred Media: Intaglio.
b Mount Vernon, N Y, Mar 8, 30.
Study & Training: Pratt Inst, 50-53, with Calvin Alberts & Philip Guston; Univ Ill, Urbana, BFA, 55, MFA, 57, with Lee Chesney.
Work in Public Collections: Libr Cong, Washington, D C; Boston Mus Fine Arts, Mass; De Cordova Mus, Lincoln, Mass; Seattle Art Mus, Wash; Univ Nebr, Lincoln; plus others.
Exhibitions: Second & Third Brit Int Print Biennial, Bradford, Eng, 70; Four Printmakers, Sheldon Mem Gallery, Univ Nebr, Lincoln, 70; Intag One Exhib, San Fernando Valley State Col, Calif, 71; Photo/graphics, George Eastman House, Rochester, N Y, 71; one-man traveling exhib, Ringling Mus, Sarasota, Fla, 72.
Teaching: Assoc prof printmaking, Univ Fla, 58-
Awards: State Fair Graphics Award, 69; award, Fla Mus Dirs & Fla Gas Co, 71; Intag One Best of Show, San Fernando Valley State Col, 71.
Bibliography: H Williams (auth), Notes for a young painter, Prentice-Hall, 63.
Memberships: Col Art Asn Am; Boston Printmakers; Print Coun Am.
Dealers: Associated American Artists, 663 Fifth Ave, New York, NY; C & D Editions, 939 Madison Ave, New York, NY 10022.
Mailing Address: 1114 N W 36th Dr, Gainesville, FL 32601.

KERSWILL, J W ROY
Painter
Preferred Media: Watercolors, Oils.
b Bigbury, Eng, Jan 17, 25; U S citizen.
Study & Training: Plymouth Col Art, Eng; Bristol Col Art, scholar.
Work in Public Collections: Wyo State Art Gallery; Mus Mountain Man; Grand Teton Natural Hist Asn Nat Park, Wyo.

Commissions: Hist murals, Alpenhof Teton Village, Wyo, First Nat Bank Englewood, Colo & Cheyenne Nat Bank, Wyo.
Exhibitions: Am Artists Prof League Ann, New York, N Y, 50-
Memberships: Am Artists Prof League; Artist Equity Asn.
Dealer: May Gallery, P O Box 1972, Jackson, WY 83001.
Mailing Address: Teton Village, Jackson Hole, WY 83025.

KERTESS, KLAUS D
Art Dealer, Art Historian
b New York, N Y, July 16, 40.
Study & Training: Yale Univ, BA(art hist, magna cum laude), 62, MA (art hist), 64; Univ Bonn & Univ Cologne, 62-63.
Positions: Dir, Bykert Gallery, New York.
Mailing Address: Bykert Gallery, 24 E 81st St, New York, NY 10028.

KESKULLA, CAROLYN WINDELER
Painter, Printmaker
Preferred Media: Watercolors.
b Farmingdale, N J, Jan 20, 12.
Study & Training: Art Stud League New York, with Benton Robinson; Pratt Inst, dipl; N Y Univ, BS(art educ).
Work in Public Collections: Newark Pub Libr, N J; plus many in pvt collections.
Exhibitions: Print Exhib, Libr of Cong, Washington, D C, 42; May Show, Cleveland Art Mus, Ohio, 45; Montclair Art Mus, 50-72; Newark Mus, N J, 60; Morris Mus Arts & Sci, Morristown, 72.
Teaching: Instr art, Port Richmond High Sch, Staten Island, N Y, 32-38; instr art, Basking Ridge Elem Sch, N J, 68-
Awards: First prize for watercolor, 65 & second prize for mixed media, 72, Am Asn Univ Women Exhib; Grumbacher award, Hunterdon Co Art Ctr, Clinton, N J, 69.
Memberships: Assoc Artists N J (secy, 60-68, pres, 70-72); Artists Equity Asn N J (v pres, 68-72); N J Watercolor Soc; Hunterdon Co Art Ctr.
Mailing Address: Stone House Rd, Millington, NJ 07946.

KESSLER, ALAN
Painter
Preferred Media: Oils.
b Philadelphia, Pa, Oct 15, 45.
Study & Training: Philadelphia Col Art, BFA; Yale Univ Summer Sch, Norfolk, Conn, Yale fel, 66; Md Inst Col Art, Baltimore, Hoffberger fel painting, 68-69, MFA; also with Grace Hartigan.
Work in Public Collections: Am Fedn Arts, New York, N Y; N Y Univ Collection, New York; Brockton Art Mus, Mass; Rose Art Mus, Brandeis Univ; State Univ N Y Col Cortland.
Exhibitions: One-man show, Dove Galleries, Philadelphia, Pa, 66; Md Invitational Exhib, Baltimore Mus Art, 69; Ten Downtown, New York, 70; Aspects of Realism, Danenberg Galleries, New York, 71; Still Life Today, Am Fedn Arts Traveling Exhib, 72.
Teaching: Instr painting & drawing, Md Inst Col Art, 68-69.
Awards: First prize in painting, Acad Arts, Easton, Md, 68.
Bibliography: Jay Jacobs (auth), Pertinent and impertinent, Art Gallery Mag, 4/70; Ruth Bowman (host), One to one—ten downtown exhib, WNYC TV, New York, 4/70; Fred McDarrah (photogr), Ten downtown artists exhib, Village Voice, 4/16/70.
Dealer: Bernard Danenberg Galleries, 1020 Madison Ave, New York, NY 10021.
Mailing Address: 45 Bond St, New York, NY 10012.

KESSLER, EDNA LEVENTHAL
Painter, Instructor
Preferred Media: Oils, Watercolors, Graphics.
b Kingston, N Y.
Study & Training: Parsons Sch Design, teaching cert; N Y Univ; Columbia Univ; Queens Col; Inst San Miguel, Mex; also with Joseph Margulies, Paul Puzinas, Edgar A Whitney, Charles Kinghan, Dong Kingman & Victor D'Amico.
Exhibitions: Hudson Valley Art Asn, White Plains, N Y, 64-69; Travel Show U S A, Am Watercolor Soc-Nat Acad Design, New York, N Y, 65; Am Artists Prof League Grand Nat, New York & Dallas, Tex, 62-69; Fine Arts Festival, Parrish Mus, Southampton, N Y, 65-69; La Biennale Int, Vichy & Clermont-Ferrand, France, 66-68.
Teaching: Instr costume design & illus, Parsons Sch Design, 29-31; instr oils & watercolors, Temple Sholom, Glen Oaks, N Y, 60-69; instr pvt classes, Hallandale & Hollywood, Fla, 69
Positions: Pres, Edna L Kessler-Interior Designs, N Y, 46-69, Fla, 69-; free lance artist, New York & Miami Beach, Fla, 58-
Awards: Gold medal, Nat Art League, 61; Arbogast Mem Award, Fine Arts Festival, Parrish Mus, 65; Grand Prix d'Aquerelle, La Biennale Int, 66.
Memberships: Nat Art League (dir, 58-69); Am Artist Prof League; Catharine Lorillard Wolfe Art Club; Hudson Valley Art Asn; Allied Arts North Miami (dir, 71-72).

Publications: Contribr, Prize winning art, 65-67, La Rev Mod, 65-67, Prize winning watercolors, 66-67, Exhibit No 26 & No 34, 68-69 & Rev des Beaux Arts, 70.
Dealer: Deligny Art Galleries, 709 E Las Olas Blvd, Fort Lauderdale, FL 33301.
Mailing Address: 1170 NE 191 St, North Miami Beach, FL 33162.

KESSLER, SHIRLEY
Painter, Instructor
Preferred Media: Oils, Watercolors.
b New York, N Y.
Study & Training: Art Stud League New York, with Frank Vincent Du Mond, Raphael Soyer, Jon Corbino, Kunyoshi & Harry Sternberg.
Work in Public Collections: Iowa State Mus, Iowa City; Nashville Mus Art, Tenn; Asheville Mus Art, N C; Norfolk Mus Art, Va.
Exhibitions: Museo Nacional Bellas Artes, Buenos Aires, Arg, 63; Am Watercolor Soc Ann, 64 & Audubon Artists, 65, Nat Acad Design, New York; First Int Exhib Women Painters, Cult Ctr, Cannes, France, 66; Int Peinture de Saint Germaine-des-Pres, Paris, France, 70.
Teaching: Instr painting, adult div, Bd Educ, New York, 48-
Awards: Medal of honor, Nat Asn Women Artists, 70; art laureate, dipl & rosette, medal of hon, Soc D'Encouragement au Progress, Paris, France, 70; exhib award, Nat Soc Painters Casein & Polymer, 70.
Bibliography: Vallobra (auth), Man & the arts, Paul Verlaine Ed, 69 & article, In: Apollo Defenseur des Arts, 69-70; Archives of American art, Smithsonian Inst, 70.
Memberships: Nat Asn Women Artists (pres, 67-70, permanent adv bd, 71-); Nat Soc Painters Casein & Polymer (bd dirs, 70-); N Y Soc Women Artists (bd dirs, 69-); Soc D'Encouragement au Progress (U S A permanent off, 70-); N J Painters & Sculptors Soc.
Mailing Address: 185 E 85th St, New York, NY 10028.

KESTER, LENARD
Painter
Preferred Media: Oils, Watercolors, Gouache.
b New York, N Y, May 10, 17.
Work in Public Collections: Brooklyn Mus, N Y; Toledo Mus, Ohio; Denver Mus, Colo; Boston Mus Fine Arts, Mass; Everson Mus Art, Syracuse, N Y.
Commissions: First Nowell (painting), Life, 47; Pictorial Record of Pacific Northwest, Louis Comfort Tiffany Found, 49; Man's Musical Heritage (mural), Mayo Clin, Rochester, Minn, 53; stained glass windows, Billy Rose Estate, Billy Rose Mausoleum, N Y, 67.
Exhibitions: Five exhibs, Los Angeles Mus, Calif, 43-55; Art Inst Chicago, Ill, 47; Carnegie Inst, Pittsburgh, Pa, 47-49; six exhibs, Nat Acad Design, New York, 51-66; Corcoran Gallery Art, Washington, D C, 57.
Teaching: Pvt instr & pub lect.
Awards: First prize, Storm in the Canyon, Los Angeles Mus, 43; Saltus Gold Medal For Merit, November 7th, Nat Acad Design, 58; first prize, Venice Reflections, Calif State Expos, 71.
Bibliography: Janice Lovoos (auth), The art of Lenard Kester, Am Artist, 2/59.
Memberships: Assoc Nat Acad Design; Am Watercolor Soc; Soc Western Artists.
Dealer: William V O'Brien, 7122 Stetson Dr, Scottsdale, AZ 85251.
Mailing Address: 1117 N Genesee Ave, Los Angeles, CA 90046.

KESTNBAUM, GERTRUDE DANA
Collector
b Boston, Mass.
Study & Training: Wellesley Col, BA, 16; Simmons Col, BS, 19.
Collection: Contemporary painting & sculpture; antique silver, porcelain & furniture; Chinese & Japanese porcelain, jade.
Mailing Address: 209 E Lake Shore Dr, Chicago, IL 60611.

KETCHAM, HENRY KING (HANK)
Cartoonist
b Seattle, Wash, Mar, 14, 20.
Study & Training: Univ Wash, 38.
Work in Public Collections: Albert T Reid Collection; William Allen White Found, Univ Kans; Achenbach Found for Graphic Arts, Calif Palace of Legion of Honor; Boston Univ Libr.
Positions: Animator, Walter Lantz Prod, 38-39, Walt Disney Prod, 39-42; co-designer, Dennis the Menace Playground, Monterey, Calif; founder, Playart Found, 69.
Awards: Billy De Beck Award as outstanding cartoonist, 52; cert for best comic mag, Boys' Club Am, 56.
Memberships: Nat Cartoonists' Soc.
Art Interests: Donor, Hank Ketcham Collection to Boston University Libraries.

Publications: Auth & illusr, Dennis the Menace ann book collection, 54-; auth & illusr, daily syndicated cartoon, Dennis the Menace, U S & Foreign newspapers, 51-; contribr, Cartoons to nat newspapers; auth, I wanna go home, McGraw-Hill, 65; creator, Half Hitch daily & Sun syndicated comic strip to U S Newspapers.
Mailing Address: 14, parc du Chateau Banquet, 1202 Geneva, Switz.

KEY, DONALD D
Art Critic, Writer
b Iowa City, Iowa, Jan 30, 23.
Study & Training: Univ Iowa.
Positions: Ed asst, Daily Iowan, Iowa City, Iowa, 48-50; asst to ed, Cedar Rapids Gazette, 50-59.
Awards: Cert of merit for bk on multiple sclerosis, Multiple Sclerosis Soc, 72.
Memberships: Cedar Rapids Jaycees (bd dirs, 56); Milwaukee Press Club.
Publications: Auth, Future unknown, Views & Rev; auth, Printmaking impressions (booklet); art ed, Milwaukee J, 59-
Mailing Address: 7519 N Crossway Rd, Milwaukee, WI 53217.

KEY, TED
Cartoonist
b Fresno, Calif.
Study & Training: Univ Calif, Berkeley.
Publications: Auth & illusr, 17 Hazel bks, The biggest dog in the world, Phyllis, Many happy returns & Squirrels in the feeding station; auth, Million dollar duck, Walt Disney Prod.
Mailing Address: 1694 Glenhardie Rd, Wayne, PA 19087.

KEY-OBERG, ELLEN BURKE
Sculptor
Preferred Media: Wood, Stone, Terra-cotta.
b Marion, Ala, Apr 11, 05.
Study & Training: Cooper Union, grad.
Work in Public Collections: Norfolk Mus, Va; Univ Wis.
Exhibitions: Nat Acad Design, New York, N Y, 43; Nat Ceramic Ann, Syracuse Mus & Traveling Shows, 43-54; Pa Acad Fine Arts Ann, Philadelphia, 53; Whitney Mus Am Art Ann, 53.
Teaching: Instr painting & sculpture, Chapin Sch, 37-70, head dept art, 65-70; instr sculpture, Arts Workshop, Newark Mus, N J, 55-65.
Awards: First prize & hon mentions, Audubon Artists, 44; Pauline Law Prize, Nat Asn Women Artists, 59.
Bibliography: Jacques Schnier (auth), Sculpture in modern America, Univ Calif Press, 48; John B Kenny (auth), Ceramic sculpture, Greenberg, 53 & Ceramic design, Chilton, 63.
Memberships: Sculpture Guild; Sculpture Ctr; Audubon Artists; Nat Asn Women Artists.
Mailing Address: Chateau Girard, 935 Genter St, La Jolla, CA 92037.

KEYES, BERNARD M
Painter
b Boston, Mass, Aug 27, 98.
Study & Training: Boston Mus Fine Arts Sch; Fogg Mus Art.
Work in Public Collections: Harvard Univ; Brown Univ; Tufts Col; Mt Holyoke Col; Holyoke Pub Libr, Mass; plus others.
Teaching: Instr, Boston Mus Sch Fine Arts; instr, Boston Univ; instr, Scott Carbee Sch; instr, Boston YMCA.
Awards: Paige traveling scholar, 21-22; prizes, Corcoran Gallery Art, 37; Nat Acad Design, 38.
Mailing Address: 30 Oakley Lane, Waltham, MA 02154.

KEYSER, ROBERT GIFFORD
Painter, Educator
Preferred Media: Oils, Watercolors.
b Philadelphia, Pa, July 27, 24.
Study & Training: Univ Pa, 42-47; Atelier Fernand Leger, 49-51, cert.
Work in Public Collections: Munson-Williams-Proctor Inst, Utica, N Y; Lyman Allyn Mus, New London, Conn; Phillips Gallery, Washington, D C; Vassar Col Art Gallery, N Y.
Exhibitions: Salon Mai, 50; Salon Automno, 50; Salon Realities Nouvelles, 51; Pa Acad Fine Arts Ann, 51-70; Collage Am, 58-60; Am Fedn Arts Traveling Show.
Teaching: Assoc prof painting & drawing & chmn dept, Philadelphia Col Art, 63-
Dealer: Paul Rosenberg & Co, 20 E 79th St, New York, NY 10021.
Mailing Address: Box 258, R D 4, Quakertown, PA 18951.

KIDDER, ALFRED, II
Art Administrator
Positions: Cur Am Sect, Univ Pa Mus.
Mailing Address: University of Pennsylvania Museum, 33rd & Spruce Sts, Philadelphia, PA 19104.

KIELKOPF, JAMES ROBERT
Painter
Preferred Media: Oils, Graphite.
b Saint Paul, Minn, July 13, 39.
Study & Training: Minneapolis Sch Art, 61-65, BFA; Grand Marias Art Colony, summer 63; Skowhegan Sch Painting, summer 64.
Work in Public Collections: Walker Art Ctr, Minneapolis, Minn.
Exhibitions: Walker Art Ctr Biennial, 64 & 66; Minneapolis Inst Art Biennial, 67; Interchange, Dallas Mus Fine Arts, Tex, 72.
Dealer: Martin Gallery, 2116 Second Ave S, Minneapolis, MN 55408.
Mailing Address: 1963 Ashland, Saint Paul, MN 55104.

KIENBUSCH, WILLIAM AUSTIN
Painter
Preferred Media: Casein, Oils.
b New York, N Y, Apr 13, 14.
Study & Training: Princeton Univ, BA(magna cum laude), with Henry Varnum Poor, Abe Rattner, Anton Refregier & Stuart Davis.
Work in Public Collections: Metrop Mus Art, New York; Mus Mod Art, New York; Whitney Mus Am Art, New York; Philadelphia Mus, Pa; Boston Mus Fine Arts, Mass.
Exhibitions: New Decade, Whitney Mus Am Art, 55; Brussels World's Fair, 58; Masters Am Watercolors, 60-62, Six Int Tokyo, 62-63 & Maine Artists, 64-66, Am Fedn Arts.
Teaching: Instr art, Brooklyn Mus Art Sch, 48-69.
Awards: Metrop Mus Art Prize for Drawing, 52; Guggenheim Found fel, 58; Ford Found Purchase Award, 61.
Bibliography: E Eliot (auth), 300 years of American painting, New York Times, 57; Maine and its role in American art 1740-1963, Viking Press, 63; Alan Gussow (auth), A sense of place—the artist and the American land, Sat Rev Press, 72.
Dealer: Kraushaar Galleries, 1055 Madison Ave, New York, NY 10028.
Mailing Address: 120 E 80th St, New York, NY 10021.

KILIAN, AUSTIN FARLAND
Painter, Educator
Preferred Media: Collage.
b Lyons, S Dak, Sept 19, 20.
Study & Training: Augustana Col (S Dak), BA, 42; Univ Iowa, MFA, 49; Acad Montmartre, Paris, France, 51, with Fernand Leger; Mexico City Col, 52; Ohio State Univ, 55; Univ Calif, Los Angeles, 66.
Work in Public Collections: D D Feldman Collection, Dallas, Tex; Univ Iowa Galleries, Iowa City.
Exhibitions: Terry Nat Art Exhib, Miami, Fla, 52; Laguna Gloria Mus Citation Regional, Austin, Tex, 58; Art Asn New Orleans, Delgado Mus, 59; Made in Tex By Texans, Dallas Mus Contemp Arts, 59; San Diego Art Instrs Show, Art Ctr La Jolla, Calif, 61.
Collections Arranged: Waco Art Forum Mus Regional Shows, 59; San Diego Art Guild Shows, Fine Arts Gallery, 61; Art In All Media, Southern Calif Expos, Del Mar, 63-70.
Teaching: Instr photog, Univ Idaho, 49-50; head dept art, Dillard Univ, 50-53; asst prof, Baylor Univ, 53-59; chmn dept art, Calif Western Univ, 59-64; assoc prof, Col of the Desert, 70-
Awards: Art Asn New Orleans Third Award, Delgado Mus, 52; Sons of Herman Award, San Antonio, Tex, 55; purchase award, D D Feldman Exhib, 68.
Memberships: San Diego Art Guild (pres, 60-61); Palm Springs Desert Mus; Fine Arts Soc San Diego; Col Art Asn Am.
Publications: Auth, Catalog loan exhibition of notable works from the Metropolitan, 52, Culture makes a face, KABC TV, Hollywood, 62, The two Californias (catalog), 63, Southern California exposition, art in all media (catalogs), 63-70 & article, In: San Diego Eve Tribune, 6/14/64.
Mailing Address: 3720 Wawona Dr, San Diego, CA 92107.

KILLAM, WALT
Painter, Art Dealer
Preferred Media: Oils, Gouaches.
b Providence, R I, June 18, 07.
Study & Training: R I Sch Design.
Work in Public Collections: Millbrook Sch, N Y; Lyman-Allen Mus, New London, Conn; South Co Art Asn; plus many in pvt collections.
Commissions: Many pvt commissions.
Exhibitions: U S A, Mex, Hawaii & Can, 32-70.
Teaching: Instr art, Millbrook Sch; guest instr advan drawing & painting, Minneapolis Sch Fine Art.
Positions: Head supvr projs, Works Proj admin, New York, N Y, owner, Fine Oriental Arts, Chester, Conn, 65-
Awards: First Prize, First H₂O Exhib, Hartford Art Asn, Conn, 34; award, Silvermine Guild Artists, 54; award, Essex Art Asn, 56.
Memberships: Hon mem South Co Art Asn; hon mem Essex Art Asn (past pres); hon mem Mystic Art Asn (past pres).

Specialty of Gallery: Oriental porcelains & allied arts.
Collection: Small art objects of world-wide arts.
Mailing Address: 71 Middlesex Pike, Chester, CT 06412.

KILLMASTER, JOHN H
Painter, Educator
Preferred Media: Acrylics, Resins.
b Allegan, Mich, Dec 2, 34.
Study & Training: Soc Arts & Crafts, Detroit, Mich; Hope Col, BA; Univ Guanajuato, Mex, with Jesus Gillardo; Cranbrook Acad Art, MFA, with Zolton Sepeshy, Estaban Vicente, Don Willet & Clement Greenburg.
Work in Public Collections: Hope Col Harrington Mem Collection, Holland, Mich; Ferris State Col Collection, Big Rapids, Mich; Boise Cascade World Hq Collection Fine Art, Boise, Idaho; Gen Motors Bldg, Detroit.
Exhibitions: First Nat Acrylic Show, Eastern Mich Univ, 67; Mainstreams '68, Int Art Exhib, Marietta, Ohio, 68; Juried Arts Nat Exhib, Tyler, Tex, 68; 31st Ann Northwest Watercolor Exhibs, Seattle Art Mus, 71; one of five Idaho painters in Rocky Mt States Traveling Exhib, 72.
Teaching: Instr drawing & painting, Troy Pub Schs, Mich, 68-69; asst prof painting, Ferris State Col, 69-70; asst prof art, Boise State Col, 70-
Positions: Artist designer, Ladriere Art Studio, Detroit, 58-61; designer illusr, Format Studio, Detroit, 61-62.
Awards: Jurors award of distinction, Marietta Col Mainstreams '68 Exhib; purchase award, 35 Idaho Artists Ann, Boise Art Mus, 70; second prize drawing award, Idaho Drawing & Print Exhib, Col Idaho, 71.
Bibliography: George Roberts (auth), Idaho landscape painter (film), Idaho Arts Coun, 72.
Memberships: Am Asn Univ Prof; Col Art Asn Am; Idaho Art Asn.
Publications: Illusr, Gen Motors Stockholders Publ, 59.
Dealer: Tuesdays Child Gallery, 3018 Overland Rd, Boise, ID 83705.
Mailing Address: 2723 N 36th St, Boise, ID 83703.

KIM, ERNIE
Ceramist, Art Administrator
Preferred Media: Stoneware
b Manteca, Calif, Sept 2, 18.
Study & Training: Los Angeles City Col, 40-42; also design with Marian Hartwell, 50-53.
Work in Public Collections: Smithsonian Inst, Washington, D C; Everson Mus Art, Syracuse, N Y; St Paul Art Ctr, Minn; Utah State Univ; San Francisco Arts Comn.
Exhibitions: Cannes Festival, France, 55; Fiber Clay & Metal Nat, St Paul, 57 & 58; Wichita Ceramic Nat, 59 & 62; Buenos Aires Invitational, Arg, 62; Syracuse Ceramic Nat, 62, 64 & 66.
Collections Arranged: Multi-Media Exhibition: Featuring Black Artists and Craftsmen, Richmond Art Ctr.
Teaching: Ceramic instr, Palo Alto Adult Educ, Calif, 52-56; instr ceramics & head dept, San Francisco Art Inst, 57-62; ceramics instr & supv art instr, Richmond Art Ctr, 62-70.
Positions: Dir, Richmond Art Ctr, 70-
Awards: First award, Sixth Int Exhib Ceramic Art, Washington Kiln Club, 57; purchase awards, Wichita Nat Ceramic Exhib, 59 & 62; Helen S Everson Mem Award, Syracuse Nat Ceramic Exhib, 66.
Memberships: Asn San Francisco Potters; Am Crafts Coun.
Mailing Address: 265 Washington Ct, Richmond, CA 94801.

KIMBALL, WILFORD WAYNE, JR
Lithographer
b Salt Lake City, Utah, July 15, 43.
Study & Training: Southern Utah State Col, BA, 68; Univ Ariz, MFA, 70; Tamarind Inst, Albuquerque, N Mex, fel printing, 70-71, Master Printer, 71.
Work in Public Collections: Southern Utah State Col, Cedar City; Tamarind Collection.
Exhibitions: Marion Locks Gallery, Philadelphia, Pa, 71; Univ N Mex Art Mus, 71; Fourth Ann Nat Print Show, San Diego, Calif, 71; Sixth Ann Southwest Area Art Show, Midland, Tex, 72.
Teaching: Lectr lithography, Univ N Mex, fall 71; vis lectr lithography, Univ Wis-Madison, 72-73.
Positions: Artist-in-residence, Roswell Mus & Art Ctr, N Mex, 72.
Mailing Address: 6120 Century Ave, Apt 205, Middleton, WI 53562.

KIMBALL, YEFFE
Painter
b Mountain Park, Okla, 14.
Study & Training: Art Stud League New York, 35-39; study & work in France & Italy, 36-39; also with Léger in Paris, France & New York, N Y.
Work in Public Collections: Nat Gallery Art, Washington, D C; Boston Mus Fine Arts, Mass; Dayton Art Inst, Ohio; Portland Art Mus, Ore; Norfolk Mus Arts & Sci, Va; plus many others in pub & pvt collections.

Exhibitions: National Gallery Art, 70; Smithsonian Inst, Washington, D C, 70; Princeton Univ, N J, 70; Northern Va Fine Arts, Alexandria, 71; Trinity Col, Hartford, Conn, 71; plus many other group & one-man shows.
Collections Arranged: Expertised & catalogued 6000 art objects of Pac Northwest Coast Indians, Portland Art Mus, Ore, 49; Am Indian Exhib, Mattuck Mus, Waterbury, Conn, 50; asst on Northwest Indian Art Exhib, Brooklyn Mus, N Y, 51; selected Am Indian art objects for U S Dept State Exhib Tour abroad, 53; exhib asst, Am Indian Exhib, Isaac Delgado Mus, New Orleans, La, 64; plus others.
Teaching: Am Forum Int Study, spec Am Indian prog Inst Am Indian Arts, Santa Fe, 70; panel mem, Convocation Am Indian Scholars, Princeton Univ, 70.
Positions: Tech adv, Americana Found, New York, 51-56; Juror, Nat Am Indian Exhib, Scottsdale, Ariz, 70; consult & adv to mus, publ, & U S govt on Indian hist & art.
Awards: First hon mention, Nat Exhib Am Ind Painting, Philbrook Art Ctr, 47 & 51; first prize, Nat Indian Exhib, Philbrook Art Ctr, 59.
Memberships: Nat Cong Am Indian; Artists Equity Asn New York; Nat Acad Design; Audubon Artists; Native North Am Artists.
Publications: Illusr, Story of the totem pole, 51, Some people are Indians & The world of Manaboze, 65, Vanguard Press; illusr, The story of the Pueblo Indians, Caedmon Records, 55; co-auth & illusr, The art of American Indian cooking, Doubleday, 65 & Avon Press, 70.
Dealer: Frank Rehn Gallery, 655 Madison Ave, New York, NY 10021.
Mailing Address: 11 Bank St, New York, NY 10014.

KIMBROUGH, (SARA) DODGE
Painter
Preferred Media: Oils, Pastels, Conté, Watercolors.
b New York, N Y.
Study & Training: Cooper Union; Grand Cent Art Sch, scholar; also with William DeLeftwich Dodge, Henry Lee McFee, Jerry Farnsworth & Frederick MacMonnies.
Work in Public Collections: Phoenix Pub Libr, Ariz; Leflore Co Courthouse, Greenwood, Miss; U S Sen Pat Harrison Libr, Univ Miss; Mem Rm, Davison Speech Sch, Atlanta, Ga; Beauvoir, Jefferson Davis Shrine, Biloxi, Miss; plus others.
Commissions: Many portrait commissions of prominent persons, 30-72.
Exhibitions: Mellon Gallery, Washington, D C; Ariz State Fair, Phoenix, 51-57; Nat Asn Women Painters & Sculptors; Am Artists Prof League; one-man shows, Phoenix Art Ctr & Meridian Mus Art, Miss; plus many others.
Awards: League Am Pen Women, 36; grand nat finalist, Am Artists Prof League, 53; award, Ill Valley Art Exhib, 60.
Memberships: Miss Art Asn; Gulf Coast Art Asn; Am Fedn Arts; regional mem Portraits, Inc.
Art Interests: Portraits in oils, pastels, watercolors & conté crayon; still lifes & landscapes.
Dealers: Downtown Gallery, 532 Chartres St, New Orleans, LA 70130; Vztop Gallery, E Zaragossa, Pensacola, FL 32503.
Mailing Address: 806 North Beach, Bay Saint Louis, MS 39520.

KIMBROUGH, VERMAN
Educator
b Rockford, Ala, Apr 6, 02.
Study & Training: Birmingham-Southern Col, AB; Univ Fla; also in France & Italy.
Positions: Pres, Ringling Sch Art, 31-70, emer pres, 70-
Memberships: Sarasota Art Asn; Ringling Mus Guild; Friends of Ringling Mus Art (v pres).
Mailing Address: 1874 Wisteria St, Sarasota, FL 33579.

KIMMELMAN, HAROLD
Sculptor
Preferred Media: Stainless Steel, Bronze.
b Philadelphia, Pa, Feb 20, 23.
Study & Training: Cape Sch Art, Provincetown, Mass; Pa Acad Fine Art, Philadelphia.
Commissions: Giraffe, Philadelphia Dept Recreation, 68; Decline & Rise, Westmill Creek Greenway, Philadelphia, 69; Wind Chime, Crawford Mem Park, Norristown, Pa, 70; Free Flight, West Park Plaza, Philadelphia, 71; Butterfly, Penn Tower Corp, 71.
Exhibitions: Pa Acad Fine Arts, 68; Philadelphia Civic Ctr Show, 71.
Awards: Braverman Karp Prize for sculpting, 68; May Audubon Prize for sculpting, 69.
Memberships: Artists Equity Asn (v pres Philadelphia Chap, 71); fel Pa Acad Fine Arts.
Mailing Address: 538 W Carpenter Lane, Philadelphia, PA 19119.

KIMURA, SUEKO M
Painter, Educator
b Hawaii.
Study & Training: Univ Hawaii, BA & MFA; Chouinard Art Inst, with Rico Lebrum; Columbia Univ, with Dong Kingman; Brooklyn Mus Sch Art, with Arthur Osver & John Ferren; Art Stud League New York, with Kuniyoshi.
Work in Public Collections: Honolulu Acad Arts.
Commissions: Fresco mural, Univ Hawaii Bilger Hall
Exhibitions: Artists of Hawaii, 60-64; State Art Show, 61-64; one-man show, Gima Art Gallery, 63; IBM Exhib, New York, 64; Kyoto Mus Mod Art, 67; plus others.
Teaching: Lect, Communication in Magazine Layout & Princess Kaiulani; prof art, Univ Hawaii, at present.
Awards: Honolulu Printmakers, 62; Easter Art Show, 62, 65 & 68; purchase prizes, State Found Cult & Arts, 68, 69 & 72; plus others.
Memberships: Hawaii Painters & Sculptors League; Honolulu Printmakers.
Publications: Illusr, cover design & drawings, Philosophy and culture, East and West, 62.
Mailing Address: 2567-B Henry St, Honolulu, HI 96817.

KIMURA, WILLIAM YUSABURO
Painter, Instructor
b Seattle, Wash, June 28, 20.
Study & Training: Hollywood Art Ctr, 39; Cornish Sch Art, Seattle, 40; also with Adolph Kronengold, Danny Pierce, Junichiro Sekino, Bill Richie & Evan Phoutrides.
Work in Public Collections: Anchorage Fine Art Mus, Alaska; Alaska Methodist Univ, Anchorage; Color Ctr Gallery, Anchorage.
Exhibitions: Ann Exhib Northwest Artists, Seattle, 53, 58, 62 & 63; Smithsonian Traveling Exhib, U S A & Europe, Washington, D C, 62; one-man shows, Alaska Methodist Univ, 63, Mel Kohler Gallery, 64 & Anchorage Fine Art Mus, 71; Ann All Alaska Exhib Artists & Craftsmen, 65-72; Wenatchee Apple Blossom Festival, Wash, 71.
Teaching: Instr painting, Anchorage Community Ctr, 59-60; instr painting, Anchorage Community Col, 61-63; artist-in-residence, Alaska Methodist Univ, 66.
Positions: Mem coun, Alaska Coun Arts, 64-68; chmn exhibs, Ann All Alaska Art Exhib, 65-
Awards: First award in painting, Fur Rendezvous Exhib, 60; best of show, South Cent Alaska Exhib, 62; Mel Kohler Award in Painting, Ann All Alaska Exhib, 66.
Bibliography: Paintings and prints, Alaska Methodist Univ, 63; Woodcuts & prints, Mel Kohler Gallery, 64; Paintings and prints, Anchorage Fine Art Mus, 71.
Memberships: Life mem Alaska Artist Guild (pres, 63-65).
Dealer: Color Center Gallery, 111 Fireweed Lane, Anchorage, AK 99503.
Mailing Address: 1025 W 11th Ave, Anchorage, AK 99501.

KIND, PHYLLIS
Art Dealer
b New York, N Y.
Study & Training: Univ Pa, AB; Univ Chicago, MA.
Positions: Dir, Phyllis Kind Gallery.
Specialty of Gallery: Representing major Chicago artists; acquiring prints and drawings by modern and old masters; introducing exhibitions and selected works by other major contemporary American artists.
Mailing Address: 226 E Ontario, Chicago, IL 60611.

KING, EDWARD S
Art Administrator
b Baltimore, Md, Jan 27, 00.
Study & Training: Johns Hopkins Univ; Princeton Univ, AB & MFA; Harvard Univ.
Teaching: Lect, Art History.
Positions: Assoc cur paintings & Far Eastern art, Walters Art Gallery, 34-41, cur, 41-51, actg adminr, 45-46, adminr, 46-51, dir, 51-69, res assoc, at present.
Memberships: Am Asn Mus.
Publications: Contribr, Art Bull & Walters Art Gallery Jour.
Mailing Address: 4520 N Charles St, Baltimore, MD 21210.

KING, ETHEL MAY
Collector, Patron
b New York, N Y.
Study & Training: Columbia Univ.
Memberships: Mus Primitive Art; life fel Metrop Mus Art.
Collection: Religious art and Americana.
Publications: Auth, Darley, the most popular illustrator of his time.
Mailing Address: 50 E 79th St, New York, NY 10021.

KING, HAYWARD ELLIS
Art Dealer, Instructor
b Little Rock, Ark, Mar 28, 28.
Study & Training: San Francisco Art Inst, BFA, 55; Fulbright
scholar, 55, Sorbonne, 55-57; also lithography with Gaston
Dorfinant, Paris, 55-57.
Exhibitions: Many ann, San Francisco Art Asn & San Francisco Mus
Art; two Winter Invitationals, Calif Palace Legion of Honor; Ful-
bright Painters Traveling Show; Rolling Renaissance; Under-
ground Arts of San Francisco, 1945-68.
Collections Arranged: Solo & Group exhibs, including drawings of
Richard Diebenkorn & Elmer Bischoff, paintings of Richard
Fiscus, John Kalamaras, Fred Martin & Theodore Polos, ce-
ramics of Howard Whalen & others, Richmond Art Ctr; exhibs,
Karl Kasten, Peter Shoemaker, John Battenberg, Lee Kelly,
Gurdon Woods, & others, John Bolles Gallery.
Teaching: Lectr gallery design & mus training, Calif State Univ,
San Francisco.
Positions: Grad eve sch registr, San Francisco Art Inst, 58-62;
registr, San Francisco Mus Art, 63-66; cur dir, Richmond Art
Ctr, Calif, 66-70; cur, John Bolles Gallery, San Francisco, 70-
Memberships: Int Child Art Ctr (mem adv bd, 68-69); Univ Art Mus
Coun, Berkeley (mem bd dirs, 69-70); Western Asn Art Mus
(second v pres, 68-70).
Specialty of Gallery: Contemporary painting, sculpture and graphics.
Mailing Address: c/o John Bolles Gallery, 10 Gold St, San Fran-
cisco, CA 94133.

KING, JOSEPH WALLACE (VINCIATA)
Painter
b Spencer, Va, May 11, 12.
Study & Training: Corcoran Sch Art; also in Italy & France.
Work in Public Collections: Wake Forest Col; N C Mus Art, Raleigh;
Va Mil Inst; Gov Mansion, Raleigh, N C; Lotos Club, New York;
also in pvt collections.
Commissions: Mural, Community Ctr Bldg, Winston-Salem, N C;
portrait of Pres Nixon, Duke Univ; portrait of Queen Elizabeth,
London, 71.
Exhibitions: Corcoran Gallery Art, Washington, D C; Fra Angelico
Salon, Rome, Italy; Royal Soc Brit Art Exhib, London; one-man
show, Bernheim-Jeune, Dauberville, Paris, France; five shows,
Hammer Galleries, New York, 60-68; plus others.
Memberships: Am Int Acad New York; Int Fine Arts Coun, Paris;
Lotos Club, New York.
Publications: Contribr, Newsweek, 2/72, Time & Tide Mag, 3/72,
Town & Country, 10/72, The Connoisseur, London, 10/72 & Visi-
tors East, N Y, 11/72.
Mailing Address: 1201 Arbor Rd, Winston-Salem, NC 27104.

KING, WARREN THOMAS
Cartoonist
b New York, N Y, Jan 3, 16.
Study & Training: Fordham Univ, BS, 38; Grand Cent Sch Fine Arts,
38, with Ivan Olinsky, Grelian, Maura & Biggs; Phoenix Art Inst,
38-41, with Franklin Booth & others.
Work in Public Collections: The Pentagon, Washington, D C; Air
Force Acad, Colorado Springs, Colo; Metrop Mus Art (ed car-
toons), New York.
Exhibitions: Collection of ed cartoons toured in nat mus; int exhibs.
Teaching: Lect, Fundamentals of Art & Editorial Cartooning, schs,
art orgn & clubs.
Positions: Ed cartoonist, Nat Asn Mfrs, New York, 51-; ed car-
toonist, Daily News, New York, 55-
Awards: Nat Headliners Club Award, 68; Nat Art Dirs Club Award,
68; Overseas Press Club Citation, 68; plus others.
Memberships: Soc Illustrators; Nat Cartoonist Soc; Soc Silurians;
Am Asn Ed Cartoonists.
Publications: Contribr, Chicago Tribune News Syndicate & nat news-
papers & magazines.
Mailing Address: 12 W 69th St, New York, NY 10023.

KING, WILLIAM ALFRED
Painter, Educator
Preferred Media: Oils, Watercolors.
b Tulsa, Okla, Nov 11, 25.
Study & Training: Univ Tulsa, BA & MA; Okla State Univ; 1st Statale
Arte, Florence, Italy; Univ Int Arte, Florence.
Work in Public Collections: Univ Wis-Green Bay; Univ Tulsa, Okla;
Volkhochschule, Erlangen, Ger; U S Consulate, Stuttgart, Ger;
Vrije Acad, Amsterdam, Holland.
Exhibitions: One-man shows, Gallerie Dom, Frankfurt, Ger, 57,
Vrije Acad, Amsterdam, 59, Galleria Vigna Nuova, Florence &
Univ Wis-Madison, 64; Univ Erlangen, 58; plus many others.
Collections Arranged: Four nat invitational exhibs, 68-
Teaching: Assoc prof painting & cur art, Univ Wis-Green Bay, 64-

Positions: Dir arts & crafts, USA, Ger & Italy, 56-64.
Awards: Ten Best Award, Painters in Wis, Marquette Univ, 68.
Memberships: Col Art Asn Am; Midwest Col Art Conf.
Publications: Auth, Toward design in the vernacular, Transactions,
69; auth, The museum as anti environment, University of Wiscon-
sin monogr art educ, 72.
Mailing Address: 1132 S Quincy, Green Bay, WI 54301.

KING, WILLIAM DICKEY
Sculptor
b Jacksonville, Fla, Feb 25, 25.
Study & Training: Univ Fla, 42-44; Cooper Union Art Sch, 45-48;
Brooklyn Mus Art Sch, 49; Skowhegan Sch Painting & Sculpture,
48; also in Rome, Italy.
Work in Public Collections: Addison Gallery Am Art, Andover,
Mass.
Commissions: SS United States; Bankers Trust Co, New York, N Y.
Exhibitions: Whitney Mus Am Art, Mus Mod Art & Solomon R Gug-
genheim Mus, New York; Philadelphia Mus Art, Pa; Los Angeles
Co Mus Art, Calif; plus other group & one-man shows.
Teaching: Instr sculpture, Brooklyn Mus Sch Art, 53-59; lectr
sculpture, Univ Calif, Berkeley, 65-66; instr sculpture, Art Stud
League New York, 68-69.
Awards: Fulbright fel, 49; Brooklyn Mus, 49; St Gaudens Medal,
Cooper Union, 64; plus others.
Dealer: Terry Dintenfass, Inc, 18 E 67th St, New York, NY 10021.
Mailing Address: 17 E 96th St, New York, NY 10028.

KINGHAN, CHARLES ROSS
Painter
Preferred Media: Watercolors.
b Anthony, Kans, Jan 18, 95.
Study & Training: Am Acad Art; Art Inst Chicago.
Work in Public Collections: Philadelphia Mus Art, Pa; Nat Acad De-
sign, New York, N Y; Smithsonian Inst, Washington, D C.
Exhibitions: Wichita Art Asn, Kans, 56; Allied Artists Am, New
York, 57-; Am Watercolor Soc, 57-; Nat Acad Design, New York,
57-
Teaching: Instr art, Am Acad Art; instr watercolor, pvt classes,
37-; instr oil & watercolor, Huguenot Sch Art, 45-51.
Positions: Sketch man, Maxon Advert Agency, New York, 51-53;
sketch man, Batton Barton Durstin Advert Co, New York, 53-62.
Awards: Gold medal, 56 & gold medal for portrait, 64, Allied Art-
ists Am; gold medal, Hudson Valley Art Asn, 60.
Bibliography: Rendering techniques, 58 & Ted Kautzky, master of
pencil & watercolor, 59, Reinhold.
Memberships: Academician Nat Acad Design; Am Watercolor Soc
(v pres, 69); Hudson Valley Art Asn (v pres, 68); Allied Artists
Am; Acad Artists Asn; plus one other.
Art Interests: Portraits.
Dealers: Blair Gallery Ltd, Santa Fe, NM 87501; Grand Central
Galleries, 40 Vanderbilt Ave, New York, NY 10017.
Mailing Address: 1177 Skyline Dr, Laguna Beach, CA 96251.

KINGMAN, DONG M
Painter, Illustrator
Preferred Media: Watercolors, Lacquer.
b Oakland, Calif, Mar 31, 11.
Study & Training: Lingnan Sch, Hong Kong, with Sze-To-Wai, 26;
Fox & Morgan Art Sch, Oakland, Calif.
Work in Public Collections: Metrop Mus Art, Mus Mod Art & Whit-
ney Mus Am Art, New York, N Y; Boston Mus Fine Arts, Mass;
M H De Young Mus, San Francisco, Calif.
Commissions: Murals for Works Progress Admin Proj, San Fran-
cisco, 42, Hilton Hotel, New York, 63, (mosaic) Pres Hotel, Hong
Kong, 64, Bank Calif, San Francisco, 68 & Boca Raton Hotel, Fla,
70.
Exhibitions: Am Watercolor Soc; San Francisco Art Asn; Metrop
Mus Art Watercolor Exhib; Whitney Mus Am Art Ann; Columbus
Mus Arts & Crafts, Ga.
Teaching: Instr art, Columbia Univ, 46-54; instr watercolor & hist
Chinese art, Hunter Col, 48-53; instr watercolor, Famous Art-
ists Sch, Westport, Conn, 54-
Positions: Art dir, Greatest Amusements Mag, presently.
Awards: Prizes at San Francisco Art Asn Ann Exhib, 36, Metrop
Mus Art Watercolor Exhib & Am Watercolor Soc Ann.
Bibliography: Dong Kingman, U S A, Life Mag, 5/15/51; Dong King-
man (film), directed by James Wong Howe, 54; Alan D Gruskin
(auth), The watercolors of Dong Kingman, Thomas Y Crowell Co,
58.
Memberships: Am Watercolor Soc; West Coast Watercolor Soc.
Publications: Illusr, The bamboo gate, 46; illusr, China's Story, 46;
illusr, Johnny Hong in Chinatown, 52; illusr, City on the golden
hill, 67; illusr, The effect of gamma rays on man-in-the-moon
marigolds, 71.
Dealer: Hammer Gallery, 51 E 57th St, New York, NY 10022.
Mailing Address: 21 W 58th St, New York, NY 10019.

KINGMAN, EUGENE
Painter, Art Administrator
Preferred Media: Tempera, Acrylics.
b Providence, R I, Nov 10, 09.
Study & Training: Yale Univ, BA, 32; Yale Univ Sch Fine Arts, BFA, 35; Creighton Univ, hon DFA, 68.
Work in Public Collections: Crater Lake Mus, Sinott Mem, Ore; Joseph Pennell Collection, Libr Cong, Washington, D C; Philbrook Art Ctr, Tulsa, Okla; Joslyn Art Mus, Omaha, Nebr; Bur Reclamation Collection, Washington, D C.
Commissions: Paintings of Crater Lake, Carnegie Inst Washington, 35; Geological Excavations (mural), comn by U S Govt for Kemmerer Post Off, Wyo, 38; mural of local subjects, comn by U S Govt for East Providence Post Off, R I, 39; Western Hemisphere (mural with Richard Edes Harrison, Cartogr), New York Times Lobby, 49; Missouri River Mainstem Dams (six paintings), USA Corps Engrs, Omaha, Nebr, 68.
Exhibitions: Colo Springs Fine Arts Ctr Invitational, 40; 48th Ann, Denver Art Mus, Colo, 42; Artists of the Missouri Valley, Mulvane Art Mus, Topeka, Kans, 52; Okla Ann Invitational, Tulsa, 53; 17th Ann Region 20 Exhib, Tex Fine Arts Asn, 72.
Collections Arranged: Time, Space and Maps, Joslyn Art Mus, 48; Beginnings of Modern Painting, 51, Life on the Prairie: The Artists Record, 54 & Artist-Explorers of the 1830's: Catlin, Bodmer & Miller, 63, Joslyn Art Mus.
Teaching: Instr mural painting, R I Sch Design, 35-39; Joslyn prof art, Univ Omaha, 48-57.
Positions: Dir, Philbrook Art Ctr, 39-42; dir, Joslyn Art Mus, 47-69; dir exhibs & cur art, Tex Tech Univ Mus, 69-
Awards: First prize in graphic arts, Okla Artists Ann, 40; Jr League Topeka First Purchase Prize, Mulvane Art Mus, 52; first prize for oil painting, Providence Art Club, 57.
Bibliography: Ted Landale (auth), His light under a bushel, Omaha World-Herald, 6/21/53; Rosemary Madison (auth), Easterner Kingman plants his roots in prairie, Omaha Sun, 3/11/65; A day in the life of a museum director (TV program), KMTV, 66.
Memberships: Life mem Providence Art Club; Audubon Artists; Col Art Asn Am; Asn Art Mus Dirs (secy-treas, 65-66, v pres, 67); Am Fedn Arts.
Publications: Illusr, 13 paintings for article, In: Nat Geog Mag, 3/37; illusr, Physiographic provinces of North America, 38; auth, Painters of the plains, Am Heritage, 12/54; contribr, article on plains art, In: Heritage of the middle west, Univ Okla Press, 56; auth, Mus focus on heritage, Panhandle-Plains Hist Rev, 70.
Dealer: The Baker Co, 1301 13th St, Lubbock, TX 79401.
Mailing Address: 3714 68th St, Lubbock, TX 79413.

KINGREY, KENNETH
Designer, Educator
b Santa Ana, Calif, Dec 23, 13.
Study & Training: Univ Calif, Los Angeles, BE & MA.
Exhibitions: 50 Best Books, Am Inst Graphic Arts, 58; Traveling Exhib, U S, Europe, Cent Am, Russia; Univ Hawaii, annually; Ann State Fair; plus others.
Teaching: Prof advert art, Univ Calif, Los Angeles, 40-53; prof art, Univ Hawaii, 50-51, 53-
Awards: 50 Best Books Award, Am Inst Graphic Arts, 58 & 61; Western Books Awards, 58-63.
Memberships: Los Angeles Art Dirs Club; Hawaii Painters & Sculptors League; Nat Art Dirs Club; Nat Art Educ Asn.
Publications: Ed, Design Quart, Walker Art Ctr, 60; contribr, Idea, 61; contribr, Graphic design, Eur-Asian Graphics.
Mailing Address: 5959 Kalanianaole Hwy, Honolulu, HI 96816.

KINGSBURY, ROBERT DAVID
Sculptor, Craftsman
b Detroit, Mich, Oct 19, 24.
Study & Training: Univ Mich, BDes; Konstfackskolan, Stockholm, Sweden.
Commissions: Frieze, Domus Hotel, Stockholm; font, Hope Lutheran Church, Colma, Calif; Grace Cathedral, San Francisco, Calif.
Exhibitions: San Francisco Mus Art, 63; Galerie de Tours, San Francisco, 63; Calif State Univ, Hayward, 64; Pasadena Art Mus, Calif, 65 & 68; Mus Contemp Art, New York, 68; plus others.
Memberships: Artists Equity Asn.
Mailing Address: 760 Wisconsin St, San Francisco, CA 94107.

KINGTON, LOUIS BRENT
Sculptor, Educator
Preferred Media: Iron, Steel, Silver, Gold.
b Topeka, Kans, July 26, 34.
Study & Training: Univ Kans, BFA, 57; Cranbrook Acad Art, MFA, 61.
Work in Public Collections: Mus Contemp Crafts, New York, N Y; Johnson Collection, Racine, Wis; St Paul Art Ctr, Minn; Krannert Art Mus, Univ Ill, Urbana; Univ Wis-Milwaukee.
Exhibitions: Objects U S A, Racine, 69; Goldsmith 70, St Paul, 70; Wichita Nat, Kans, 70; Design in Steel, New York, 71; Acquisitions, New York, N Y.
Teaching: Prof metal smithing, Southern Ill Univ, Carbondale, 61-
Awards: Spec recognition, St Paul Art Ctr, 65; Nat Merit Award, Am Craftsmen Coun, 65; Design in Steel Award for Excellence, Am Iron & Steel Inst, 71.
Memberships: Soc N Am Goldsmiths (pres, 70-); Am Craftsmen Coun.
Dealer: Gilman Galleries, 103 E Oak, Chicago, IL 60611.
Mailing Address: School of Art, Southern Illinois University, Carbondale, IL 62901.

KINIGSTEIN, JONAH
Painter, Designer
b New York, N Y, June 26, 23.
Study & Training: Cooper Union Art Sch, 41-43; Grande Chaumiere, Paris, France, 47-51; Belle Arte, Rome, Italy, 53-54.
Work in Public Collections: Mus Mod Art, New York; Albright-Knox Art Gallery, Buffalo, N Y; Nelson Gallery Art; Washington Mus; Ain Herod Mus, Tel-Aviv, Israel; plus others in pvt collections.
Exhibitions: Butler Inst Am Art, Youngstown, Ohio, 56; Young Americans, Whitney Mus Am Art, New York, 57; Nat Acad Arts & Lett, 68; one-man show, Grippi Gallery, New York & Kinematic Art at Nordness Gallery, 64; plus others.
Awards: First prize, Silvermine Guild, 59; Louis Comfort Tiffany Found Award, 62; Perkins-Elmer Prize, 62; plus others.
Mailing Address: 123 Second Ave, New York, NY 10003.

KINSTLER, EVERETT RAYMOND
Painter
b New York, N Y, Aug 5, 26.
Study & Training: Nat Acad Design, New York; Art Stud League, New York, with DuMond; and with Wayman Adams & John Johansen.
Work in Public Collections: Metrop Mus Art, New York; Carnegie Inst, Pittsburgh, Pa; Brooklyn Mus, N Y; Smithsonian Inst, Washington, D C; Players Club, New York.
Commissions: Portraits of Astronaut Scott Carpenter, USN Combat Art, Washington, D C, 63 & Astronaut Alan Shepard, 65; Orville Freeman, Secy Agr, U S Dept Agr, Washington, D C, 69; N Y Gov Herbert Lehman, Sch Int Affairs, Columbia Univ, 71; Ambassador David Kennedy, U S Dept Treas, Washington, D C, 72.
Exhibitions: One-man shows, Grand Cent Art Galleries, New York, 58 & Columbia Mus Art, S C, 70; Am. Watercolor Soc Ann, New York, 67; Nat. Acad Design Ann, New York, 70; one-man exhib, Lotos Club, New York, 72.
Teaching: Inst painting & drawing, Art Stud League, New York, 70-
Awards: Gold medal for painting, Nat Arts Club, New York, 64; purchase prize, Ranger Fund, Nat Acad Design, 71; gold medal, Lotos Club, New York, 72.
Bibliography: H Rogoff (auth), The pro's nest, Palette Talk, M Grumbacher Inc, 70; Norman Kent (auth), The artists studio, Am Artist Mag, 1/70; Wendon Blake (auth), Acrylics, Am Artist Mag, 1/72.
Memberships: Nat Acad Design; Am Watercolor Soc; Century Club (trustee); Nat Arts Club (v pres); Audubon Artists (v pres).
Publications: Illusr, Opera companion, Dodd, 61 & Verdi, 63; auth, Painting portraits, Watson-Guptill, 71.
Mailing Address: 15 Gramercy Park, New York, NY 10003.

KIPNISS, ROBERT
Painter
Preferred Media: Oils.
b New York, N Y, Feb 1, 31.
Study & Training: Art Stud League New York; Wittenberg Col; Univ Iowa, BA & MFA.
Work in Public Collections: Whitney Mus Am Art, New York; New York Pub Libr; Ohio Univ, Athens; Univ Iowa, Iowa City.
Exhibitions: Butler Inst Am Art Ann, Youngstown, Ohio, 53; Am Fedn Arts Traveling Show, 63-65; one-man show, Allen R Hite Inst, Univ Louisville, Ky, 65; Recent Acquisitions, Whitney Mus Am Art, 72.
Awards: Purchase prize, Ohio Univ, 65.
Publications: Illusr, Poems of Emily Dickinson, Thomas Y Crowell, 64; illusr, Collected poems of Robert Graves, Anchor Doubleday, 66.
Dealers: Merrill Chase Galleries, 620 N Michigan Ave, Chicago, IL 60611; FAR Gallery, 746 Madison Ave, New York, NY 10021.
Mailing Address: 49 Cedar Dr, Great Neck, NY 11021.

KIPP, LYMAN
Sculptor
b Dobbs Ferry, N Y, Dec 24, 29.
Study & Training: Pratt Inst, 50-52; Cranbrook Acad Art, 52-54.

Work in Public Collections: Whitney Mus Am Art, New York, N Y; Albright-Knox Art Gallery, Buffalo, N Y; State of N Y Albany Mall.
Exhibitions: Four Whitney Mus Am Art Sculpture Ann, 64-70; Primary Structures, Jewish Mus, New York, 66; Sculpture in Environment, New York, 67; Art of the Real, Mus Mod Art, New York, 68; plus many others.
Teaching: Instr sculpture, Bennington Col, 60-63; asst prof sculpture, Hunter Col, 63-66; prof sculpture & chmn dept, Lehman Col, 66-
Awards: Guggenheim fel, 66; Fulbright grant, 66.
Memberships: Sculptors Guild.
Mailing Address: North Salem, NY 10560.

KIPP, ORVAL
Painter, Educator
b Hyndman, Pa, May 21, 04.
Study & Training: Stetson Univ; Carnegie Inst, AB; Teachers Col, Columbia Univ, AM; Univ Pittsburgh, PhD.
Work in Public Collections: Latrobe High Sch, Aspinwall High Sch, Greensburg Pub Schs, Indiana Pub Schs & Uniontown High Sch, Pa.
Exhibitions: Provincetown Art Asn; Assoc Artists Pittsburgh; Am Fedn Arts Traveling Exhib; Kottler Gallery, New York; Am Artists Prof League Grand Nat, 72; plus others.
Teaching: Instr art, Indiana Univ Pa, 36-41; dir art dept, 41-60; chmn, 60-64, prof, 60-69, prof emer, 69-; lect, Trick or Treat in Art Education, Ind State Art Teachers, Indianapolis; lect & demonstrations, The Mystery of The Masters.
Awards: Prizes, Indiana Art Asn, 47-57; spec jury award, Pittsburgh Soc Art, 68.
Memberships: Eastern Art Asn; Assoc Artists Pittsburgh (bd dirs, v pres, 55, pres, 57-58); Indiana Art Asn; Pa Art Educ Asn (coun); Artists Equity Asn; plus others.
Mailing Address: 635 Church St, Indiana, PA 15701.

KIRKBY, PAULA ZOLLOTO
Art Dealer
b Lynn, Mass, Apr 3, 34.
Study & Training: Mus Sch, Boston, Mass; Lesley Col; Harvard Sch Design.
Positions: Dir, Galerie Smith-Andersen, 69-
Specialty of Gallery: Contemporary drawings and paintings.
Mailing Address: 200 Homer St, Palo Alto, CA 94301.

KIRKLAND, VANCE HALL
Painter, Collector
Preferred Media: Oils, Watercolors.
b Convoy, Ohio, Nov 3, 04.
Study & Training: Cleveland Sch Art, BEA; Cleveland Col Educ, Western Reserve Univ, with Henry Keller, Frank Wilcox, William Joseph Eastman & Albert Olson; also study in Europe, Africa & Asia.
Work in Public Collections: Denver Art Mus, Colo; Art Inst Chicago, Ill; Nelson Gallery Art, Kansas City, Mo; Columbus Gallery Fine Arts, Ohio; Norton Gallery Fine Arts, West Palm Beach, Fla.
Commissions: Ceiling In Drawing Room, comn by Mrs Gerald Hughes, Denver, 36; Hist of Costume (five murals), Neusteter's, Denver, 37; mural room & ranch bar, Albany Hotel, Denver, 37; Cattle Round-Up, U S Treas Dept, Eureka, Kans, 38 & Land Rush, U S Treas Dept, Sayre, Okla, 40.
Exhibitions: Int Watercolors, Art Inst Chicago, 30-46; Contemp Am Painting, Univ Ill, 52; Artists West of Miss, Colo Springs Fine Arts Ctr, 65; 73rd Western Ann, Denver Art Mus, 71; Color Exp Space Retrospective, Denver Art Mus, 72.
Teaching: Prof art & dir Sch Art, Univ Denver, 29-32; instr art & dir, Kirkland Sch Art, Denver, 32-45; prof art & dir Sch Art, Univ Denver, 46-69.
Awards: Awards for watercolors, Mountain Climbers, Friends Art, Nelson Gallery, 41 & Gwydenmanders, Denver Art Mus, 45.
Collection: Contemporary art; Oriental art.
Mailing Address: 1311 Pearl St, Denver, CO 80203.

KIRKWOOD, MARY BURNETTE
Painter
Preferred Media: Oils.
b Hillsboro, Ore, Dec 21, 04.
Study & Training: Univ Mont, BA; Univ Ore, MFA; Harvard Univ Sch Fine Arts, art hist with Prof Paul J Sachs; Royal Art Sch, Stockholm, Sweden, with Prof Otte Sköld; Art Stud League New York, with Reginald Marsh; also with Joseph Stefanelli & Robert Goldwater, Paris, France.
Work in Public Collections: Cheney Cowles Mus, Spokane, Wash; Boise Art Gallery, Idaho; IBM Corp; Bank of Idaho; Boise Cascade Corp.

Commissions: Murals for agr sci bldg, 48 & libr, 52, Univ Idaho.
Exhibitions: West Coast Juried, Seattle Art Mus, 62; West of the Mississippi Invitational, Colorado Springs, Colo, 63; Intermountain Invitational, Salt Lake City Art Ctr, 63 & 65; Fifty States Exhib Invitational, Burpee Art Mus, Rockford, Ill, 66; Western States Exhib, Denver Art Mus Invitational, 71; plus others.
Teaching: Prof art, Univ Idaho, 30-70.
Awards: Third prize for Miercoles Santo, Pac Coast Ann, Wenatchee, Wash, 63; best of show for El Cristo de la Columna, 63 & second prize for Trampoline, 66, Cheney Cowles Mus, Spokane, Wash.
Memberships: Nat Art Educ Asn (Idaho chmn, 68-72); Portland Art Asn; Idaho Art Asn; Boise Art Asn.
Mailing Address: 812 Apple Lane, Moscow, ID 83843.

KIRSCHENBAUM, JULES
Painter, Educator
Preferred Media: Acrylics.
b New York, N Y, Mar 25, 30.
Study & Training: Brooklyn Mus Art Sch.
Work in Public Collections: Butler Inst Am Art, Youngstown, Ohio; Whitney Mus Am Art, New York; Weatherspoon Art Gallery; Univ N C; Des Moines Art Ctr, Iowa; Everhardt Mus, Scranton, Pa.
Commissions: Hist of Iowa, Cent Nat Bank, Des Moines, 64.
Exhibitions: Drawings U S A, 34 & Painting U S A The Figure, 63, Mus Mod Art, New York; Whitney Mus Am Art Ann, 55; Artists Abroad, Paintings from Whitney Collection, 69; Gov Exhib Nine Iowa Artists, 71.
Teaching: Artist-in-residence, Des Moines Art Ctr, 63-67; prof painting, Drake Univ, 67-; vis prof art, Temple Univ, 72-73.
Awards: Fulbright fel, 56; first prize for figure painting, Nat Acad Design, 57; first prize for oils, Butler Inst Am Art, 60.
Bibliography: The figure, Time, 62.
Dealer: Forum Gallery, 1018 Madison Ave, New York, NY 10021.
Mailing Address: 3908 Grand Ave, Des Moines, IA 50312.

KIRSTEIN, MR & MRS LINCOLN
Collectors
Mr Kirstein, b Rochester, N Y, May 4, 07.
Study & Training: Mr Kirstein, Harvard Univ, BS, 30.
Publications: Auth, Pavel Tchelitchew drawings, 47; auth, Elle Nadelman drawings, 49.
Mailing Address: 128 E 19th St, New York, NY 10003.

KIRSTEN, RICHARD CHARLES
Painter, Printmaker
Preferred Media: Watercolors.
b Chicago, Ill, Apr 16, 20.
Study & Training: Art Inst Chicago; Univ Wash; also study in Japan, 58-69.
Work in Public Collections: Seattle Art Mus, Wash; Libr Cong, Washington, D C; Metrop Mus Art, New York, N Y; Tokyo Mus Mod Art, Japan; also in pvt collections.
Exhibitions: Seattle Art Mus, numerous shows, 45-69; Frye Mus, Seattle, 60-65 & 69; Gov Invitational, 67; Collector's Gallery, Bellevue, Wash, 67; Richard White Gallery, Seattle, 68; plus many others.
Positions: Art ed, Seattle Post-Intellingencer, 48-
Awards: Bellevue Arts & Crafts Exhib, 56 & 57; purchase prize, Univ Ore, 68; purchase prize, Seattle First Nat Bank, 69; plus others.
Memberships: Am Fedn Arts; Northwest Watercolor Soc (pres, 68 & 69); Northwest Printmakers.
Mailing Address: 900 N 102nd St, Seattle, WA 98133.

KISCH, GLORIA
Painter
Preferred Media: Mixed Media.
b New York, N Y, Nov 14, 41.
Study & Training: Sarah Lawrence Col, BA, 63; Boston Mus Sch, 64-65; Otis Art Inst, Los Angeles, BFA & MFA, 69.
Work in Public Collections: Palm Springs Desert Mus, Calif; Otis Art Inst; Downey Mus Art, Calif.
Exhibitions: Long Beach Mus Art Seventh Ann, 69; one-woman show, Ankrum Gallery, Los Angeles, 69 & 72; Introductions 70, Downey Mus Art, 70; Spec Exhib (honoring Joseph Hirshhorn), Palm Springs Desert Mus, 70; Calif-Hawaii Regional, Fine Art Mus San Diego, 72.
Teaching: Instr drawing & design, Southwestern Col, 70.
Awards: Second prize for painting, Nat Orange Show, 68.
Memberships: Artists Equity Asn.
Dealer: Ankrum Gallery, 657 N La Cienega Blvd, Los Angeles, CA 90069.
Mailing Address: 4621 Ocean Front Walk, Venice, CA 90291.

KISELEWSKI, JOSEPH
Sculptor
b Browerville, Minn, Feb 16, 01.
Study & Training: Minneapolis Sch Art, 18-21; Nat Acad Design, 21-23; Beaux-Arts Inst Design, 23-25; Am Acad in Rome; Acad Julian, Paris, France.
Commissions: Harold Vanderbilt (statue), Nashville, Tenn, 65; Moses (statue), Law Col, Syracuse Univ, 66; Sylvanus Thayer bronze bust for Hall of Fame for Great Americans, New York Univ, 66; groups, Bronz Co Court House, N Y; fountain, Huntington Mus, S C; plus others.
Awards: Beaux Arts Paris Prize, 25-26; Prix de Rome, 26-29; Elizabeth N Watrous Gold Medal, 37; plus others.
Memberships: Nat Acad Design; assoc fel Am Acad Rome; Nat Sculpture Soc; Archit League New York.
Mailing Address: 433 E 82nd St, New York, NY 10028.

KISH, MAURICE
Painter
Preferred Media: Oils.
b Russia; U S citizen.
Work in Public Collections: Hermitage Mus, Leningrad, Russia; Brooklyn Mus, N Y; Ein Horod Mus, Israel; Mus City of New York, N Y; Springville Mus, Utah.
Exhibitions: Nat Acad Design, since 32; Corcoran Gallery Art, 37; Pa Acad Fine Arts, 38; Carnegie Inst Fine Arts, 41; Detroit Inst Fine Arts, 59.
Awards: Prize for outstanding painting, Coal Towers, 45; gold medal for Hills of Sorrow, Am Vet Soc Artists, 63; Minnie R Stern Medal for Street of Forgotten Men, Audubon Artists, 64; plus many others.
Memberships: Allied Artists Am; Audubon Artists; Painters & Sculptors Soc N J; Conn Acad Fine Arts; Am Vet Soc Artists (pres, 62).
Art Interests: Creative, original & representational art.
Publications: Auth, The world is my song, Ykuf, 68.
Mailing Address: 417 Brightwater Ct, Brooklyn, NY 11235.

KISKADDEN, ROBERT MORGAN
Painter, Educator
Preferred Media: Oils, Watercolors.
b Tulsa, Okla, Dec 6, 18.
Study & Training: Univ Kans, BFA; Ohio Wesleyan Univ, MA.
Work in Public Collections: Wichita Art Mus, Kans; Birger Sandzen Mem Gallery, Lindsborg, Kans; Bloomfield Collection, Wichita State Univ; Univ Tex, El Paso Gallery; Kans State Univ Gallery, Manhattan; also in many pvt collections.
Commissions: City scape, Mid-Kans Fed Savings & Loan, Wichita, 62
Exhibitions: Many local, regional & nat exhibs, 48-72.
Teaching: Prof art, Wichita State Univ, 49-, asst dean Col Fine Arts, 71-72, Nat Endowment Arts grant to collect art for McKnight Art Ctr, 72-73.
Mailing Address: 301 N Old Manor, Wichita, KS 67208.

KISSEL, WILLIAM THORN, JR
Sculptor
Preferred Media: Bronze, Marble.
b New York, N Y, Feb 6, 20.
Study & Training: Harvard Univ, BA, 44; Pa Acad Fine Arts, 51-53; Barnes Found, Menon, Pa, grad, 53; Rinehart Grad Sch Sculpture, grad, 58, with Sidney Waugh, Cecil Howard & Bruce Moore.
Commissions: Granite mem, Montclair, N J, 56; many bronze animal sculptures, eastern U S, 65-70.
Exhibitions: Mass Sculptor's Exhib, Beverly, Mass, 58; Am Artists Prof League Grand Nat, Lever House, New York, 64 & 66; Nat Acad Design Exhibs, New York, 65-68 & 71; Nat Sculpture Soc Exhibs, Lever House, 67 & 70; Md Arts Coun Exhib & State Tour, 71 & 72.
Awards: Speyer Awards, Nat Acad Design, 66 & 68; Am Artists Prof League Award, 66.
Bibliography: Article, In: Am Art Stone, 59; article, In; La Rev Mod, Paris, France, 66.
Memberships: Nat Sculpture Soc; fel Am Artists Prof League; fel Pa Acad Fine Arts; N Shore Arts Asn; Munic Art Soc New York.
Mailing Address: Owings Mills, MD 21117.

KISSNER, FRANKLIN H
Collector
b Pa, 09.
Study & Training: Harvard Univ, grad, 30.
Mailing Address: 24 Gramercy Park S, New York, NY 10003.

KITAJ, RONALD
Painter, Printmaker
b Chagrin Falls, Ohio, 32.
Study & Training: Ruskin Sch, Univ Oxford, dipl, 60; Royal Col Art, grad, 62.

Work in Public Collections: Mus in the U S & Europe.
Exhibitions: One-man shows, Los Angeles Co Mus Art, 65, Stedelijk Mus, Amsterdam, 67, Cleveland Mus, 67, Whitney Mus Am Art, 67 & Univ Calif, Berkeley, 68; plus others.
Teaching: Vis lectr, Slade Sch, Univ London; vis prof, Univ Calif, Berkeley & Univ Calif, Los Angeles.
Mailing Address: c/o Marlborough Gallery, 41 E 57th St, New York, NY 10022.

KITNER, HAROLD
Educator
b May 18, 21; U S citizen.
Teaching: Prof painting & drawing, Kent State Univ, 47-, chmn dept, 50-67, chmn Sch Art, 64-65.
Positions: Art critic, Akron Beacon Jour, 48-61; dir, Blossom-Kent Art Prog, 67.
Mailing Address: 531 Stonewood Dr, Akron, OH 44313.

KITZINGER, ERNST
Art Historian
b Munich, Ger, Dec 27, 12; U S citizen.
Study & Training: Univ Rome, 31-32; Univ Munich, PhD, 34.
Teaching: A Kingsley Porter univ prof, Harvard Univ, 67-
Positions: Asst, Brit Mus, London, Eng, 35-40; with Dumbarton Oaks Ctr for Byzantine Studies, Washington, D C, 41-67; mem, Inst Advan Study, Princeton Univ, 66-67.
Memberships: Medieval Acad Am; Col Art Asn Am; Archeol Inst Am; Ger Archaeol Inst; Am Philos Soc; plus others.
Research: Early Christian, Byzantine and medieval art.
Publications: Auth, Early medieval art in the British Museum, 40 & The mosaics of Monreale, 60.
Mailing Address: 7 Waterhouse St, Cambridge, MA 02138.

KIVA, LLOYD, see NEW, LLOYD H.

KIZER, CHARLOTTE ELIZABETH
Designer, Craftsman
Preferred Media: Gold, Silver.
b Lincoln, Nebr.
Study & Training: Univ Nebr, BFA; Columbia Univ Teachers Col, MA; also jewelry & enameling with Adda Husted Andersen, silversmithing with Rudolph Schumacher & enameling with Margaret Seeler.
Exhibitions: Am House, 44 & Mus Contemp Crafts, 63; Designer Craftsmen U S A, Brooklyn Mus & Am Fedn Arts Tour, 53-55; Artist Craftsmen New York, Cooper Union, New York Design Ctr & Chase Manhattan Bank, 58-72; Craftsmen of Eastern States, Smithsonian Inst & Tour, 64.
Teaching: Instr jewelry, Westchester Workshop, White Plains, N Y, 41-56.
Positions: Supvr art, Lincoln Pub Schs, 26-36; dir arts & crafts, Westchester Workshop, Westchester Co, N Y, 39-66; pres, New York Soc Craftsmen, 52-55.
Awards: Awards for jewelry, Westchester Arts & Crafts Guild, 54 & 56; Spec Award For Silversmithing, Artist Craftsmen New York, 68.
Bibliography: Winebrenner (auth), Jewelry making, Int Textbook Co, 53.
Memberships: Artist Craftsmen of New York.
Mailing Address: Eton Lodge, 117 Garth Rd, Scarsdale, NY 10583.

KJARGAARD, JOHN INGVARD
Painter, Printmaker
Preferred Media: Acrylics.
b Denmark, Sept 13, 02; U S Citizen.
Study & Training: Cooper Union; Calif Sch Fine Arts, San Francisco; Univ Calif, Berkeley; Univ Hawaii, with Joseph Albers.
Work in Public Collections: Mint Mus Art, Charlotte, N C; Honolulu Acad Arts, Hawaii; Libr of Cong, Washington, D C; Hawaii State Found Cult & Arts.
Commissions: Glass mosaic mural, Honolulu Int Airport, Hawaii State Dept Transportation, 72.
Exhibitions: One-man shows, 58 & 69 & First Hawaii Nat Print Exhib, 71, Honolulu Acad Arts, Hawaii; juried print exhib, Rochester, N Y, 62; Mex-Hawaii Invitational Exchange Exhib, 68; Pac Cities Loan Exhib, Auckland City Art Gallery, New Zealand, 71.
Awards: Watumull Found Purchase Award, 58; Elsie Das Mem Award, 63; Honolulu Printmakers, 66.
Memberships: Hawaii Painters & Sculptors League (pres, 60); Honolulu Printmakers (pres, 53 & 58); Honolulu Acad Arts.
Publications: Contribr, mag sect, Los Angeles Times, 54 & 56; contribr, Paradise of the Pacific, 12/58 & 59; contribr, Design Quarterly, 60; contribr, The Hawaii book, Ferguson, 61; contribr, The technique of collage, 68.
Dealer: Downtown Gallery, 125 Merchant St, Honolulu, HI 96813.
Mailing Address: 2080 Mauna Pl, Honolulu, HI 96822.

KLARIN, WINIFRED ERLICK
Painter
Preferred Media: Acrylics.
b Portland, Maine, Dec 8, 12.
Study & Training: Portland Mus Fine Art, Hayloft scholar, 30; Vesper George Sch Art, grad, 33; Soc Arts & Crafts, Detroit, 58-60; Wayne State Univ, 58-62; Cranbrook Grad Sch Art, 63.
Work in Public Collections: U S Libr, State Dept, Washington, D C; Owens-Corning Fiberglass Corp, Toledo, Ohio; Steel Case Corp, Grand Rapids, Mich; First Fed Savings & Loan, Detroit, Masco Corp, Ypsilanti, Mich.
Exhibitions: One-woman shows, Pace Gallery, 66, J P Speed Mus, Louisville, Ky, 69, Forsythe Gallery, Ann Arbor, Mich, 67, 69 & 71 & Clossons Gallery, Cincinnati, Ohio, 69-71; Henry Ford Col, 66; Rackham Gallery & Univ Mich, Ann Arbor, 66-67; plus others.
Awards: Outstanding Mich Artist, Nat Bank Detroit, 65; two Top Awards— Best In Show, Scarab Club & Palette & Brush, 67.
Bibliography: Figueras (auth), Aux Etas-Unis 30 Midyear Show, La Rev Mod, Paris, France, 66; Ellen Goodman (auth), Hylozoists create way-out designs, Detroit Free Press, 1/26/67; Jean Paul Susser (auth), Art in review, Ann Arbor News, 4/7/67.
Dealer: Forsythe Gallery, 201 Nickels Arcade, Ann Arbor, MI 48108.
Mailing Address: 1027B Grand Ave, Cincinnati, OH 45204.

KLAVANS, MINNIE
Painter, Sculptor
b Garrett Park, Md, May 10, 15.
Study & Training: Wilson Teachers Col, BSEd, 35; private instr in silversmithing, 51-55; painting with Laura Douglas, 58-60; Am Univ, 60-64; with Luciano Penay, 60-70; Corcoran Gallery Art, plastics with Ed McGowin, 70-71.
Work in Public Collections: Nat Collection Fine Arts, Smithsonian Inst, Washington, D C; White House, Washington, D C; Voc-Tech High Sch, La Plata, Md; Corcoran Gallery Art, Washington, D C.
Exhibitions: Corcoran Gallery Art, 65 & 67; Dedication Nat Bur Standards, Washington, D C, 66; Baltimore Mus Art, Md, 67; Inst Hispanic Cult, Madrid, Spain, 68; Mus Mod Art, Bilbao, Spain, 69.
Awards: First prize for silversmithing, Smithsonian Inst, 53 & 55; spec award, Baltimore Mus Art, 67.
Memberships: Artists Equity Asn.
Dealer: Mickelson Gallery, 707 G St N W, Washington, DC 20001.
Mailing Address: 2134 Bancroft Pl N W, Washington, DC 20008.

KLEBE, GENE (CHARLES EUGENE)
Painter, Writer
Preferred Media: Watercolors.
b Philadelphia, Pa, Sept 18, 07.
Study & Training: Philadelphia Col Art; Univ Pa.
Work in Public Collections: U S Navy & Marine Art Gallery, Washington, D C; Farnsworth Mus, Rockland, Maine; Nat Acad Design, New York, N Y; Univ Maine, Orono; Maine Nat Bank, Portland.
Commissions: Combat art, U S Navy, 59-72; Maine State series, Maine Nat Bank, Portland, 60-72; Expo '67 mural, State of Maine, 67; sesquicentennial seal, Maine Sesquicentennial Comn, 70.
Exhibitions: Salmagundi Club, 45-72; Am Watercolor Soc, 50-72; Allied Artists Am, 50-72; Acad Artists Asn, 64-72; Nat Acad Design, 69-72.
Positions: Pres, Pemaquid Group Artists, 55-; mem, Gov Coun Art & Cult, 65-69; chmn, Maine State Art Comn, 66-71.
Awards: Wu-Ject-Key Award, Am Watercolor Soc, 69; watercolor award no 1, Salmagundi Club, 71; Baltimore Watercolor Club Mem Award, 72.
Bibliography: Lew Deitz (auth), Gene Klebe-Maine artist, Down East Mag, 69.
Memberships: Acad Artists Asn; Am Watercolor Soc (juror, 63); Allied Artists Am; Salmagundi Club; Nat Acad Design.
Publications: Co-auth, Penguin family, 64; contribr, Maine through the eyes of her artists, 65; contribr, U S Navy combat art, 69; auth, Gene Klebe watercolor page, Am Artists Mag, 3/72.
Mailing Address: Pemaquid Rd, Bristol, ME 04539.

KLEIN, DORIS
Painter, Sculptor
Preferred Media: Oils.
b New York, N Y, Nov 10, 18.
Study & Training: Art Stud League New York, with Sidney Gross; Works Prog Admin Sch, with James Leschay & Anton Refregier; also sculpture with Maurice Glickman.
Work in Public Collections: Univ Maine Permanent Collection.
Exhibitions: Mus Belles Artes, Arg, 63; Alley Gallery, Houston, Tex, 66; Maxwell Gallery, San Francisco, 67; Audubon Artists, 68; Roko Gallery, New York, 68-72.

Awards: Best of Show, Jersey City Mus, 63-66; Marion K Haldenstein Mem Prize, Nat Asn Women Artists, 68; Grumbacher Award, Mamaroneck Artists Guild, 69.
Bibliography: Hilton Kramer (auth), Review of Roko show, New York Times, 68; Betty Chamberlain (auth), Philharmonic Hall program, 72.
Memberships: Nat Asn Women Artists; Mamaroneck Artists Guild.
Dealer: Hartley Gallery, 50 E 73rd St, New York, NY 10021.
Mailing Address: 235 W 76th St, New York, NY 10023.

KLEIN, ESTHER M
Patron, Collector
b Philadelphia, Pa, Nov 3, 07.
Study & Training: Temple Univ, BS; Univ London.
Positions: Ed, Philadelphia Art Alliance Bull; art critic, WPEN daily radio prog; founding dir, Long Beach Island Found Arts & Sci, N J.
Awards: Award for art talks on radio, Artists Equity Philadelphia.
Memberships: Life mem Pa Acad Fine Arts; life mem Philadelphia Print Club; Philadelphia Art Alliance (comt mem); Color Print Soc (v pres); contrib mem Art Inst Chicago; plus others.
Art Interests: Donor of annual prizes to Print Club and Clothesline Exhibit to encourage young Philadelphia artists.
Collection: Philadelphia artists.
Mailing Address: 1530 Spruce St, Philadelphia, PA 19102.

KLEIN, MEDARD
Painter
Preferred Media: Oils, Casein, Watercolors, Gouache, Pastels, Pencil, Ink.
b Appleton, Wis, Jan 6, 05.
Study & Training: Var art schs, Chicago.
Work in Public Collections: Private collections in Chicago, New York, Boston, Detroit, Mexico City & others.
Exhibitions: Int Watercolor Show, Art Inst Chicago; Salon Realites Nouvelles; Joslyn Mem Mus, Omaha, Nebr; San Francisco Mus Art; Ill State Mus, Springfield; plus many other group & one-man shows.
Mailing Address: 1159 N Dearborn St, Chicago, IL 60610.

KLEIN, SANDOR C
Painter, Sculptor
Preferred Media: Oils.
b New York, N Y, Oct 27, 12.
Study & Training: Nat Acad Design; Acad Julien, Paris, France; Beaux-Arts, Paris; Acad Fine Arts, Vienna; Royal Acad Art, Budapest; Am Acad Rome, fel, 31.
Work in Public Collections: Nat Gallery Art, Washington, D C; Albany State Mus, N Y; Luxembourg Mus; Coast Guard Acad, New London, Conn; Pentagon, Washington, D C.
Commissions: Portraits of Hon Schuyler Otis Bland, Chmn Maritime & Fisheries Comn, 46, Gen Nathan F Twining, Chmn Joint Chiefs of Staff, 61 & Gen Curtis E LeMay, USAF Chief of Staff, 62, comn by U S Govt; portrait of Eleanor Roosevelt, comn by Am Cancer Soc, 63; portrait of Pres Armand Hammer, Occidental Petrol Co, 67.
Exhibitions: Paris Salon; Carnegie Int; plus others in the U S & abroad.
Teaching: Instr painting, Nat Acad, New York, Beaux Arts & Acad Julien, Paris.
Awards: Pulitzer Prize for Painting, 31; Silver Medal, Paris Salon; medal, Int Biennale, Venice, 32.
Mailing Address: 33 W 67th St, New York, NY 10023.

KLEINHOLZ, FRANK
Painter, Writer
Preferred Media: Oils.
b Brooklyn, N Y, Feb 17, 01.
Study & Training: Fordham Univ, LLB, 23; Colby Col, hon DFA; also with Alexander Dobkin, Yasuo Kuniyoshi & Sol Wilson.
Work in Public Collections: Metrop Mus Art, New York, N Y; Brooklyn Mus, N Y; Marquette Univ, Milwaukee, Wis; Mus Mod Art, Tel-Aviv, Israel; Fine Arts Mus, Moscow, U S S R.
Commissions: Outdoor mural, Blankman Found, Sands Point, N Y, 58.
Exhibitions: Directions in American Painting, Carnegie Inst, Pittsburgh, Pa, 41; Artists for Victory, Metrop Mus Art, 42; first one-man show, Assoc Am Artists, New York, 42; American Painting Today, Metrop Mus Art, 50; one-man show, ACA Gallery, Rome, Italy, 65.
Awards: Sixth purchase prize for Back Street, Hearn Fund, Metrop Mus Art, 42; first prize for Bright Lights, Manhasset Art Asn, 53; first prize for prints for Sunflower, YMHA, Miami, Fla, 72.
Bibliography: Edwin Alden Jewell (auth), Frank Kleinholz holds art show, New York Times, 42; Donald Bear (auth), Contemporary American painting, Encycl Britannica, 46; August L Freundlich (auth), Frank Kleinholz, the outsider, Univ Miami Press, 69.

Publications: Auth, Frank Kleinholz, a self portrait, Shorewood Press, 64; auth, Abstract art is dead, Am Dialog, 7/64; auth & illusr, Ile de Bréhat—the flowering rock, Univ Miami Press, 71.
Dealer: ACA Galleries, 25 E 73rd St, New York, NY 10021.
Mailing Address: P O Box 65, Perrine, FL 33157.

KLEINMAN, SUE
Painter
Preferred Media: Oils.
b New York, N Y, Nov 12, 17.
Study & Training: Pratt Inst, Brooklyn, N Y, BFA; Caton-Rose Inst Fine Arts; New Sch Soc Res, New York; Mus Mod Art, New York, with Zoltan Hecht & Donald Stacey; also with Raphael Soyer & Anthony Toney.
Work in Public Collections: Brown Univ, R I; Fairleigh Dickinson Univ, Rutherford, N J; Maimonides Hosp, Brooklyn.
Commissions: Privately comn portraits only.
Exhibitions: Knickerbocker Art, New York, 59; Audubon Art, Weiner Gallery, New York, 60; one-man shows, Crown Gallery, New York, 62, Ctr Gallery, New York, 65 & 69 & Int Hotel, New York, 67.
Positions: Chmn mem comt, 54-58 & treas, 58-60, Kew Forest Art Asn.
Awards: Bronze medal, Village Art Ctr, 58; hon mention, Rockport Art Asn, 60; silver medal, Trade Bank New York.
Bibliography: Jane Jaffe (auth), article, In: Manhattan E, 65; Dorothy Hall (auth), article, In: Park E, 69; Saint-Evermond (auth), article, In: France-Amerique, 69.
Memberships: Artists Equity Asn; Nat Womens Art Asn.
Dealer: Center Art Gallery, 49 W 57th St, New York, NY 10019.
Mailing Address: 111-14 76th Ave, Forest Hills, NY 11375.

KLEP, ROLF
Museum Director, Illustrator
b Portland, Ore, Feb 6, 04.
Study & Training: Univ Ore, BA; Art Inst Chicago; Grand Cent Sch Art.
Work in Public Collections: Baseball Hall of Fame; Univ Ore Mus Art; Haseltine Collection of Northwest Art; Mariner's Mus, Newport; Maritime Mus, City Hall & Pub Libr, Astoria, Ore; plus others.
Teaching: Lect with slide illus throughout Ore, incl Univ Ore Mus Art, 60.
Positions: Bd dirs, Friends of the Mus, Univ Ore; bd dirs, Univ Ore Develop Fund, 59-65; founder, pres & present dir, Columbia River Maritime Mus, Astoria, Ore, 62-
Publications: Auth & illusr, Album of the great, 37 & The children's Shakespeare, 38; illusr, Beowulf, 41; contribr & illusr, Across the space frontier, 52 & Conquest of the moon, 53; also illusr for nat mag & advert agencies.
Mailing Address: Columbia River Maritime Museum, Astoria, OR 97103.

KLINE, ALMA
Sculptor
b Nyack, N Y.
Study & Training: Radcliffe Col, AB; also sculpture with Jose De Creeft.
Work in Public Collections: Cronkhite Grad Ctr, Cambridge, Mass; Norfolk Mus Arts & Sci, Va; St Lawrence Univ, N Y.
Exhibitions: Women's Int Art Club, London, 55; Nat Asn Women Artists, Mus Bellas Artes, Buenos Aires, 63; 10 one-man shows, Travel Art Guild, 64; one-man show, Thomson Gallery, New York, N Y, 69; Soc Animal Artists, Nat Hist Mus, Smithsonian Inst, 71.
Awards: Grumbacher Purchase Award, Audubon Artists, 60; medal of honor, Knickerbocker Artists, 64; Patrons of Art Award, Painters & Sculptors Soc N J, 69.
Memberships: Audubon Artists (chmn ways & means, 72); Nat Asn Women Artists (adv, 72); Soc Animal Artists (treas, 72); Knickerbocker Artists; Silvermine Guild Artists.
Publications: Contribr, Prize Winning Sculpture, 64, Nat Wildlife, 67 & Nat Sculpture Rev, 69.
Mailing Address: 225 E 74th St, New York, NY 10021.

KLITGAARD, GEORGINA
Painter, Writer
Preferred Media: Oils, Watercolors.
b New York, N Y, July 3, 93.
Study & Training: Barnard Col, Columbia Univ; Nat Acad Design; Art Stud League New York.
Work in Public Collections: Metrop Mus Art, New York; Whitney Mus Am Art, New York; Newark Mus, N J; New Britain Mus Art, Conn; Dayton Art Mus, Ohio.
Commissions: Old Poughkeepsie, Poughkeepsie Post Off, N Y; painting, Goshen Post Off, N Y; landscape, Pelham Post Off, Ga; two landscapes, Chesapeake & Ohio RR.

Exhibitions: Six one-man shows, Rehn Galleries, New York, 29-61, Woodstock, N Y, 56-60 & one-man traveling show, Col Art Asn Am, 45; Pan-Am Exhib, San Francisco, Calif, 33; Pa Acad Fine Arts, 33-45.
Teaching: Instr painting, Durham Sch Painting, 45-46.
Awards: Guggenheim fel, 35; Huntington fel, 65-66; Wirlitzer Found, 68-70; plus others.
Bibliography: J P Slusser (auth), G K, 38; Ray Bethers (auth), How paintings happen, Norton, 51; Kay Klitgaard (auth), Through the American landscape, Univ N C Press.
Memberships: Audubon Artists; Woodstock Artists Asn; MacDowell Colony.
Publications: Contribr, Meet the artist, The art of the artist, Through the American landscape & How paintings happen.
Dealer: Rehn Galleries, 655 Madison Ave, New York, NY 10021.
Mailing Address: Bearsville, NY 12409.

KLITZKE, THEODORE ELMER
Educator, Art Historian
b Chicago, Ill, Nov 4, 15.
Study & Training: Art Inst Chicago, BFA, 40; Univ Chicago, BA, 41, PhD, 53.
Teaching: Instr art hist, Univ Chicago, 46-47; asst prof art hist, State Univ N Y Col Ceramics, Alfred Univ, 53-59; prof art hist & chmn dept art, Univ Ala, Tuscaloosa, 59-68.
Positions: V pres acad affairs & dean, Md Inst Col Art, 68-; chmn dean's comt Union Independent Cols Art, Kansas City, Mo, 71-; bd dirs, Nat Asn Schs Art, 71-
Memberships: Am Studies Asn; Col Art Asn Am; Soc Archit Historians; Southeastern Col Art Conf (pres, 61-62).
Research: Social history of American art; nineteenth century French art; history of prints & drawings.
Publications: Contribr, reviews, In: Col Art J & Art Bull, 59-; contribr, The arts in America, Southwest La J, 59; contribr, Alexis de Tocqueville & the arts in America, Festschrift Ulrich Middeldorf, 68; auth, Melville Price retrospective: 1920-1970, Frame House Gallery, 70; contribr, Hermann Wilhelm (catalog), 72.
Mailing Address: 1300 Mount Royal Ave, Baltimore, MD 21217.

KLONIS, STEWART
Painter, Educator
Preferred Media: Watercolors.
b Naugatuck, Conn, Dec 24, 01.
Study & Training: Art Stud League New York.
Work in Public Collections: IBM Collection & many pub & pvt collections.
Exhibitions: Am Watercolor Soc; Century Asn.
Teaching: Instr Queens Col, 40-45; exec dir, Art Stud League New York, 46-
Memberships: Munic Art Soc; Nat Arts Mus Sports (trustee, 63-); Benjamin Franklin fel Royal Soc Arts; MacDowell Colony (bd dirs); Inst Int Educ (adv comt for arts, 61-).
Mailing Address: 215 W 57th St, New York, NY 10019.

KLOSS, GENE (ALICE GENEVA GLASIER)
Etcher, Painter
Preferred Media: Oils, Watercolors
b Oakland, Calif, July 27, 03.
Study & Training: Univ Calif, Berkeley, AB(hon in art), 24; Calif Sch Fine Arts, 24-25; Calif Sch Arts & Crafts.
Work in Public Collections: Libr of Cong, Washington, D C; Metrop Mus Art, New York, N Y; Carnegie Inst, Pittsburgh, Pa; Pa Acad Fine Arts, Philadelphia; Mus Tokyo, Japan.
Commissions: Prints, Soc Print Connoisseurs, New York, 49; prints, Print Club Albany, N Y, 52; prints, Soc Am Graphic Artists, New York, 53; prints, Print Makers Calif, Los Angeles, 56.
Exhibitions: Three Centuries of Art in United States (in collab with Mus Mod Art, New York), Paris, France, 38; Nat Acad Design Ann, New York, 50-; Embassy Bldg, New Delhi, India, 61; Soc Am Graphic Artists, yearly; The West by Members of the National Academy of Design, Phoenix Art Mus, Ariz, 72; plus one-man shows.
Awards: Eyre Gold Medal, Pa Acad Fine Arts, 36; purchase award, Libr of Cong, 53; anonymous prize, Nat Acad Design, 61.
Memberships: Academician Nat Acad Design; Soc Am Graphic Artists; Philadelphia Watercolor Club; Albany Print Club.
Mailing Address: Box 33, Taos, NM 87571.

KNAPP, SADIE MAGNET
Painter, Sculptor
Preferred Media: Enamels.
b New York, N Y, July 18, 09.
Study & Training: N Y Training Sch Teachers, lic; City Col New York; Brooklyn Mus Art Sch; Atelier 17; Sculpture Ctr.
Work in Public Collections: Ga Mus Art, Athens; Norfolk Mus Art, Va; Riverside Mus, New York.

Exhibitions: Corcoran Gallery Art, Washington, D C; Baltimore Mus, Md; Pa Acad Fine Arts, Philadelphia; Butler Inst Art, Youngstown, Ohio; plus others in Can, Eng, France, Switz, Arg, Mex, Japan, India, Scotland & Italy.

Teaching: Instr enamels, Worcester Crafts Ctr, 63.

Awards: Awards for paintings, Baltimore Mus, 56, 58 & 61; award for painting, Silvermine Guild Artists, 65; Grumbacher award for painting, Nat Acad Design, 68.

Memberships: Nat Asn Women Artists (v pres, 61-65, pres, 65-67); Nat Soc Painters in Casein & Acrylics (treas); Am Soc Contemp Artists; Artists Craftsmen New York; Artists Equity Asn.

Mailing Address: 106 82nd Dr, Kew Gardens, NY 11415.

KNECHT, KARL KAE
Editorial Cartoonist
Preferred Media: India Ink.
b Iroquois, S Dak, Dec 4, 83.
Study & Training: Art Inst Chicago.
Work in Public Collections: Art Inst Chicago; plus others.
Exhibitions: Many exhibs.
Memberships: Cartoonists Rotary Clubs; Am Asn Ed Cartoonists.
Mailing Address: Continental Apts, Evansville, IN 47715.

KNEE, GINA (MRS ALEXANDER BROOK)
Painter, Etcher
Preferred Media: Watercolors, Oils.
b Marietta, Ohio, Oct 31, 98.
Work in Public Collections: Guild Hall, East Hampton, N Y; Johnson Collection, Univ N Mex, Albuquerque; Denver Art Mus, Colo; Phillips Art Gallery, Washington, D C; Buffalo Fine Arts Acad, N Y.
Exhibitions: Guild Hall Ann, 50-71; Willard Gallery, New York & Pyramid Gallery, Washington, D C, 55; Metrop Mus Art, New York, 59; Newark Mus, N J, 65.
Awards: First prize, Calif Watercolor Soc, 38; first prize, Nat Oil Exhib, New Orleans, La, 47; first prize, Guild Hall Exhib, 63.
Bibliography: Sidney Janis (auth), Abstract & surrealist art in America, Reynal & Hitchcock, 44; Van Deren Coke (auth), Taos and Santa Fe, 1882-1942, Amon Carter Mus, 63.
Memberships: Artists Equity Asn; Guild Hall.
Dealer: Larcada Gallery, 123 E 67th St, New York, NY 10021.
Mailing Address: Box 1092, Sag Harbor, NY 11963.

KNERR, SALLIE FROST
Painter, Printmaker
Preferred Media: Watercolor, Serigraph, Lithograph.
b Plattsburg, Mo, Apr 7, 14.
Study & Training: Univ Mo; Cincinnati Acad Com Art; Corcoran Sch Art; Canal Zone Jr Col; Nat Acad Design; Am Univ; George Washington Univ, BA, 64; scholarship for travel-study in Mexico & Guatamala, Univ Ga, 67, MFA, 68.
Work in Public Collections: Biblioteca Nac, Panama; Greenville News Piedmont, S C.
Exhibitions: Contemporary Artists of South Carolina, Greenville Co Mus Art, Columbia Gallery Art & Gibbes Gallery Art, Charleston, S C, 70; La Watercolor Soc 3rd Int Show, 71; 13th Dixie Ann Montgomery Mus Fine Arts, Ala, 72.
Teaching: Asst prof art, Baptist Col Charleston, 68-70; instr, Gibbes Gallery Sch.
Awards: First in watercolor, Marshall Award Show, Art League Northern Va, 62; hon mention for woodcut, S C Guild Artists Show, Greenville, 65.
Bibliography: Jack Morris (auth) & Robert Smeltzer (auth), Contemporary artists of South Carolina, Greenville Co Mus Art, 70; Louise & Paul Trescott (auths), Sallie Frost Knerr, printmaker, Sandlapper Mag, 2/70; John D Morse (auth), Prints in and out of America to 1850, Winterthur Mus, 70.
Memberships: Guild S C Artists (awards comt, 68-69, secy, 70-71); S C Craftsmen's Guild; Carolina Art Asn; Charleston Artists Guild.
Research: Exploration of relief printing and its combination with other printmaking media.
Publications: Illusr, The student pilot's training primer, Knerr, 41.
Dealer: Turtle Shop, Gibbes Gallery Art, 135 Meeting St, Charleston, SC 29401.
Mailing Address: Box 335, Isle of Palms, SC 29451.

KNIGHT, FREDERIC CHARLES
Painter, Educator
Preferred Media: Oils.
b Philadelphia, Pa, Oct 29, 98.
Study & Training: Pa Mus Sch Indust Art, State of Pa scholar, 16, cert grad, 20; also in France & Italy, 26.
Work in Public Collections: Dartmouth Col, Hanover, N H; Everhart Mus, Scranton, Pa; Univ Ariz Mus, Tucson; Berkshire Mus, Pittsfield, Mass; Montclair Mus, N J.

Commissions: Murals in lobby of post off of Johnson City, N Y, Treasury Art Project, Washington, D C, 38.
Exhibitions: Contemp Am Art, Whitney Mus Am Art, New York, N Y, 33-48; Biennial Exhib Contemp Am Oil Paintings, Corcoran Gallery Art, Washington, D C, 35-51; Pa Acad Fine Arts Ann, 38-62; Painting in the U S, Carnegie Inst, Pittsburgh, Pa, 41-45; one-man shows, Berkshire Mus, Pittsfield, Mass, 67 & 72 & Albany Inst Hist & Art, N Y, 68; plus others.
Teaching: Asst prof drawing & painting, Newcomb Sch Art, Tulane Univ La, 43-46; from lectr to asst prof drawing & painting, Columbia Univ, 46-64.
Positions: Pres, An Am Group, Inc, New York, 33-40; chmn, Artists Coord Comt, New York, 37-40; chmn exhib comt, Columbia Univ, 54-64.
Awards: First prize for drawing & spec award for gen excellence, Pa Mus Sch Indust Art, 20; first prize for painting, Woodstock Artists Asn, 33.
Bibliography: Edward Bruce (auth), & Forbes Watson (auth), Art in federal buildings, Vol I, Art Fed Bldgs, 36.
Publications: Contribr, The art of the artist, Crown, 51.
Dealer: Boyer Gallery, 2540 E Sixth St, Tucson, AZ 85719.
Mailing Address: P O Box 17616, Tucson, AZ 85710.

KNIGHT, HILARY
Illustrator, Designer
Study & Training: Art Stud League New York.
Publications: Illusr, When I have a son, 67 & Sunday morning, 68, Harper & Row; auth & illusr, Sylvia the sloth, Harper & Row, 69; illusr, Child's book of natural history, Platt, 69; illusr, Angie, Harper & Row, 71; plus many others.
Mailing Address: 300 E 51st St, New York, NY 10022.

KNIGIN, MICHAEL JAY
Painter
b Brooklyn, N Y, Dec 9, 42.
Study & Training: Tyler Sch Art, BFA.
Work in Public Collections: Whitney Mus Art, New York, N Y; Nat Collection Fine Arts, Washington, D C; New York Univ; Albright-Knox Art Gallery, Buffalo, N Y; Mus Graphic Arts, New York.
Exhibitions: Smithsonian Inst, Washington, D C, 69; Osaka World's Fair, Japan, 70; Albright-Knox Art Gallery, Buffalo, 70; Mus Mod Art Lending Serv, New York, 71; Recent Acquisitions, Whitney Mus Am Art, New York, 71.
Teaching: Instr graphics, Pratt Inst, 68-
Awards: Ford Found grant, Tamarind Lithography Workshop, 64; MLA-ALA Lithographic Tech Inst, 69.
Bibliography: A note on the frontispiece, Artists Proof, 71.
Publications: Co-auth, The technique of fine art lithography, 70; auth, Local choice, Pratt Graphics Ctr, 72.
Mailing Address: 831 Broadway, New York, NY 10003.

KNIPSCHILD, ROBERT
Painter, Educator
Preferred Media: Oils.
b Freeport, Ill, Aug 17, 27.
Study & Training: Univ Wis, BA, 49; Cranbrook Acad Art, MFA, 51.
Work in Public Collections: Pa Acad Fine Arts, Philadelphia; Baltimore Mus Art, Md; Phillips Gallery, Washington, D C; Libr Cong, Washington, D C; Cranbrook Mus, Bloomfield Hills, Mich.
Exhibitions: American Painting Today, Metrop Mus Art, New York, N Y, 51; Pa Acad Fine Arts Ann, 51; Carnegie Int, Pittsburgh, Pa, 52; Container Corp Am, 63; 50 Artists from 50 States, Am Fedn Arts, 65.
Teaching: Vis artist, Am Univ, 52; instr painting, Univ Conn, 54-56; asst prof, Univ Wis-Madison, 56-60; assoc prof, Univ Iowa, 60-66; prof painting, Univ Cincinnati, 66-
Awards: Purchase awards, Libr Cong, 51, Pa Acad Fine Arts, 51 & Am Fedn Arts, 63.
Bibliography: Patricia Boyd (auth), Exhibition of Robert Knipschild, Christian Sci Monitor, 11/3/69.
Memberships: Mid Am Col Art Asn; Nat Asn Schs Art.
Dealer: Sneed Gallery, 2024 Harlem Blvd, Rockford, IL 61103.
Mailing Address: 3346 Jefferson Ave, Cincinnati, OH 45220.

KNOBLER, LOIS JEAN
Painter
b New York, N Y, Feb 2, 29.
Study & Training: Syracuse Univ Col Fine Arts, BFA; Fla State Univ, MA.
Exhibitions: New England Regional Drawing Exhib, Smith Col Mus, Northampton, Mass, 65; New England Art Today, Northeastern Univ, Boston, Mass, 65; Art for U S Embassies, Inst Contemp Art, Boston, 66; Contemp Women Artists, Skidmore Col, Saratoga Springs, N Y, 70; one-man show, Jorgensen Gallery, Univ Conn, Storrs, 70.
Mailing Address: R F D 1, Mansfield Center, CT 06250.

KNOBLER, NATHAN
Sculptor, Educator
Preferred Media: Stone, Wood, Bronze, Woodcut, Lithography.
b Brooklyn, N Y, Mar 13, 26.
Study & Training: Newark Sch Fine & Indust Art; Ohio State Univ;
Syracuse Univ, BFA, 50; Fla State Univ, MA, 51.
Work in Public Collections: U S Info Agency; Smith Col Mus, North-
ampton, Mass; Munson-Williams-Proctor Mus, Utica, N Y; Fla
State Univ; Slater Mus, Norwich, Conn.
Commissions: Silver Award Sculpture, Int Silver Co, Meriden, Conn;
Bronze Award Sculpture, G Fox & Co, Hartford, Conn.
Exhibitions: Pa Acad Fine Arts Nat Print Show, Philadelphia; Brook-
lyn Mus Nat Print Show, N Y; Drawing Soc Traveling Nat; Selec-
tion 1964, Inst Contemp Art, Boston, Mass; Surreal Images, De
Cordova Mus, Lincoln, Mass.
Teaching: Prof art, Univ Conn Sch Fine Arts.
Memberships: Col Art Asn Am.
Research: Art appreciation; drawing.
Publications: Auth, The visual dialogue, 67, rev ed, 70; auth, El
dialogo visual, 70.
Mailing Address: Dept of Art, University of Connecticut School of
Fine Arts, Storrs, CT 06268.

KNORR, JEANNE BOARDMAN
Craftsman, Educator
b Chambersburg, Pa.
Study & Training: Ind Univ Pa, BS; Columbia Univ Teachers Col,
MA; Art Stud League New York, N Y, scholar; Ohio State Univ,
PhD(painting).
Work in Public Collections: Dallas Theol Sem, Tex; Lakeview Ctr
Arts, Peoria, Ill; Ohio State Univ Mus Collections, Columbus.
Commissions: Fabric wall hanging, St Paul's Episcopal Cathedral,
Peoria, 69; plus many fabric wall hangings in pvt collections in
Ill & N Y.
Exhibitions: Fifth Biennial Nat Relig Art Exhib, Cranbrook Acad
Art, Mich, 66; Madison Art Asn Regional Crafts Exhib, 68; Ind
Univ Nat Craft Exhib, 69; Nat Drawing Biennial, Chrysler Mus,
Norfolk, Va, 70; one-man exhib, Robinson House, Va Mus, Rich-
mond, 72.
Teaching: Assoc prof art, Norfolk State Col, 69-
Awards: Artist of Distinction in crafts, 70 & in sculpture, 71, Va
Mus.
Bibliography: Craftsmen U S A part one, 3/66 & Dona Meilach
(auth), Creative stitchery, 8/71, Craft Horizon Mag; Cornelia
Justice (auth), Review of exhibitions at Studio Gallery, 4/66;
plus others.
Memberships: Am Craftsmen Coun.
Publications: Contribr, Directions, Ill Art Educ Asn, 70.
Mailing Address: 730 Maury Ave, Norfolk, VA 23517.

KNORR, LESTER
Sculptor, Painter
b Wilder, Idaho, May 1, 16.
Study & Training: San Jose State Col, AB; Ohio State Univ, MA &
PhD.
Work in Public Collections: Decorator Ctr, Dallas, Tex; Ohio State
Univ; also in pvt collections.
Exhibitions: Kohl Gallery, Dallas, 65; Sherman Gallery, Chicago,
Ill, 65; Knox Col, Galesburg, Ill, 68; Sherbeyn Gallery, Chicago,
67; Studio Gallery, Virginia Beach, Va, 71.
Teaching: Prof art, Norfolk State Col.
Positions: Art publicity for gallery, Southwest Tex State Col, 56-59.
Awards: Prize, Am Vet Soc Am, 52; Irene Leach Mem Prize for
sculpture, Norfolk Mus, 71.
Mailing Address: 730 Maury Ave, Norfolk, VA 23517.

KNOWLES, DOROTHY ELSIE (DOROTHY ELSIE PEREHUDOFF)
Painter
Preferred Media: Oils, Acrylics, Watercolors, Charcoal.
b Unity, Sask, Apr 7, 27.
Study & Training: Univ Sask, BA, with Eli Bornstein & Reta Cowley;
workshops, Emma Lake, with Will Barnet, Clement Greenberg,
Ken Noland, Jules Olitski, Lawrence Alloway & Michael Steiner.
Work in Public Collections: Edmonton Art Gallery; Kitchener-
Waterloo Art Gallery; Winnipeg Art Gallery; Willisted Art Gal-
lery at Windsor, Ont; Norman MacKenzie Art Gallery, Regina,
Sask.
Exhibitions: Nat Gallery Biennial, 68; Sask Art & Artists, Norman
MacKenzie Art Gallery, 71; 22nd Ann Exhib Paintings, Hamilton,
Ont, 71; West 71, Edmonton, Alta, 71; Watercolour Painters from
Saskatchewan, Nat Gallery Traveling Show, 71-72.
Bibliography: Karen Wilkin (auth), Canada—a report from the West,
Art Am, 6/72; Terrence Heath (auth), Dorothy Knowles, Arts
Can, autumn 72.
Dealer: Waddington Galleries, 1456 O Sherbrooke W, Montreal 109,
P Q, Can.
Mailing Address: 1131 Second St E, Saskatoon, Sask S7H 1R4, Can.

KNOWLES, RICHARD H
Painter
Preferred Media: Oils.
b Evanston, Ill, June 29, 34.
Study & Training: Grinnell Col; Northwestern Univ, Evanston, BA,
56; Ind Univ, MA, 61.
Work in Public Collections: Ind Univ, Bloomington; Ark State Univ;
State of Tenn Collection, Reece Mus, Nashville; Burpee Mus,
Rockford, Ill.
Exhibitions: 1st Nat, Tyler Tex, 62; 22nd Artists West Miss Ann,
Colo Springs, Colo, 63; 6 Americans, Ark Art Ctr, Little Rock,
64; 50 States Exhib & Tour, Rockford Art Asn & Am Fedn Arts,
65-67; 40 Tenn Artists Exhib & Tour, 68-69; plus other group &
one-man shows.
Teaching: Asst prof art, Univ Ark, 61-65; assoc prof art, Memphis
State Univ, 66-
Awards: Best entry for Ark artist, Delta Ann, 61 & 62; painting
prize, Mid-South Exhib, 72.
Mailing Address: 3610 Watauga, Memphis, TN 38111.

KNOWLTON, DANIEL GIBSON
Bookbinder
b Washington, D C, Nov 14, 22.
Study & Training: With Marian U M Lane, Washington, D C; Boston
Arts & Crafts, grad.
Work in Public Collections: Univ Chicago Libr, Ill; Brown Univ
Libr, Providence R I; Dumbarton Oaks Libr, Washington, D C;
Harvard Univ Libr, Boston, Mass; Cornell Univ Libr, Ithaca,
N Y.
Commissions: Epistle (gold & leather binding), Grace Church,
Providence, 56; The Anguish of the Jews (gold & leather binding),
comn by Ciro Scotti, Vatican Libr, 68.
Exhibitions: Hand bookbinding exhibs, Corcoran Gallery Art, 58;
one-man shows, Ann-Mary Brown Mem Libr, Providence, 67 &
R I Sch Design, 71, Handicrafts Club, Providence, 68 & Bristol
Hist Soc R I, 69.
Teaching: Instr bookbinding, Brown Univ Exten Div, 58-
Positions: Owner & bookbinder, Longfield Studio, 47-; bookbinder,
Brown Univ, 56-
Bibliography: Lawrence Thompson (auth), article, In: Libri, 55;
Yankee Damon (auth), article, In: Yankee Mag, 62; Ann Banks
(auth), article, In: Brown Alumni Monthly, 71.
Memberships: Miniature Painters, Sculptors & Gravers Soc Wash-
ington, D C.
Mailing Address: 1202 Hope St, Bristol, RI 02809.

KNOWLTON, GRACE FARRAR
Sculptor
Preferred Media: Clay.
b Buffalo, N Y, Mar 15, 32.
Study & Training: Smith Col, BA; Corcoran Sch Art; Am Univ;
painting with Kenneth Woland & Vatclav Vitlacil; drawing &
sculpture with Lothar Brabanski.
Work in Public Collections: J Patrick Lannan Mus, Palm Beach,
Fla; Lloyds of London, Washington, D C.
Commissions: Pottery prototypes for Appalachian Workshops, Am
Fedn Arts, New York, N Y, 71.
Exhibitions: Smithsonian Inst, Washington, D C, 67; one-man shows,
Hinckley & Brohel Gallery, Washington, D C, 69 & Spectrum Gal-
lery, New York, 71; Western Highlands Hudson First Ann, 71;
Ninth Ann Southern Tier Show, Corning, N Y, 72.
Teaching: Instr art, Arlington Co Pub Schs, 57-60.
Positions: Asst to cur graphic arts dept, Nat Gallery Art, Wash-
ington, D C, 54-57.
Awards: First prize, Sculptor's Studio, Washington, D C, 68; jury
award, Ninth Ann Southern Tier Show, Corning, N Y, 72.
Bibliography: E Brohel (auth), Midnight Raku (film), Hinckley &
Brohel Gallery, 69.
Memberships: Am Fedn Art (trustee, 72).
Dealers: Spectrum Gallery, 464 W Broadway, New York, NY 10012;
Henri Gallery, 1500 21st St N W, Washington, DC 20036.
Mailing Address: Ludlow Lane, Sneden's Landing, Palisades, NY
10964.

KNOWLTON, JONATHAN
Painter
Preferred Media: Acrylics.
b New York, N Y, Feb 22, 37.
Study & Training: Yale Univ, BA; Univ Calif, Berkeley, MA.
Work in Public Collections: Mus Mod Art, New York; Los Angeles
Co Mus Art, Calif; Victoria & Albert Mus, London, Eng; Univ
Calif Art Mus, Berkeley; La Jolla Mus Fine Art, Calif.
Exhibitions: Survey '68, Montreal Mus Fine Arts, 68; 17th Nat
Print Exhib, Brooklyn Mus, N Y, 70.

Teaching: Asst prof fundamentals design & painting, Univ Alta, 66-
Awards: Purchase award, Los Angeles Co Mus Art, 61; Fulbright grant, 64-65; Can Coun grant, 68-69.
Dealer: John Bolles Gallery, 10 Gold St, San Francisco, CA 94133.
Mailing Address: 14358 Park Dr, Edmonton, Alta, Can.

KNOX, GEORGE
Art Historian
b London, Eng, Jan 1, 22.
Study & Training: Courtauld Inst Art, Univ London, BA, MA & Ph D.
Collections Arranged: Tiepolo Bicentenary Exhib, Fogg Art Mus, Cambridge, Mass, 70; Tiepolo Drawings, Staatsgalerie, Stuttgart, 70.
Teaching: Instr Slade Sch Art, Univ London, 50-52; instr, King's Col, Newcastle, Univ Durham, 52-58; instr, Queen's Univ (Ont), 69-70; prof fine arts & head dept, Univ B C, 70-
Art Interests: Venetian eighteenth century art, particularly the drawings of the Tiepolo family.
Publications: Auth, Catalogue of the Tiepolo drawings in the Victoria & Albert Museum, 60; auth, Domenico Tiepolo: raccolta di teste, Udine, 70.
Mailing Address: Dept of Fine Arts, University of British Columbia, Vancouver, B C, Can.

KNOX, KATHARINE McCOOK
Art Historian, Collector
b Washington, D C.
Collections Arranged: (Voluntary Services) Chmn, Washington Loan Exhibition of Early American Paintings, Miniatures & Silver, Nat Mus, 25; chmn of portrait comt, Robert E Lee Memorial Foundation Loan Exhibition, 31 & Primarily American Exhibitions, 59, Textile Mus; chmn of portrait comt, The George Washington Bicentennial Commission Exhibition of Portraits, 32 & The George Washington Sesquicentennial Commission Exhibition of Portraits, 39, Corcoran Gallery Art; co-chmn, Privately Owned Exhibition, Corcoran Gallery Art, 52; chmn, Mus Mod Art Loan Exhibition, Washington, D C, 38; spec consult, American Processional, 50 & Our Town, 56, Alexandria, Va; spec consult, Profiles of the Time of James Monroe, Smithsonian Inst, 58; plus many others.
Positions: (Voluntary Services) Honorary mem, Lincoln Sesquicentennial Comn; adv coun, Civil War Centennial Comn; mem, Pres Adv Comt on Arts, John F Kennedy Ctr for Performing Arts; D C comt, R E Lee Mem Found; trustee, Frick Art Ref Libr, New York.
Awards: Bronze Medallion, Lincoln Sesquicentennial Comn, 60; Bronze Medal of Merit, Corcoran Gallery Art, 66.
Bibliography: Helen Cooke & Evelyn Dent Boyer (auth), Distinguished Women of Washington, 64; plus many acknowledgments & comments in other publ.
Art Interests: During the Hoover Administration the Director of the Frick Art Reference Library, New York, suggested that Mrs Knox list and describe the paintings then in the White House. This was accomplished without remuneration and with the cordial cooperation of Mrs Hoover.
Collection: Extensive collection of Washingtoniana and Lincolniana, as well as modern paintings and sculpture.
Publications: Auth, The Sharples: their portraits of George Washington and his contemporaries, Yale Univ Press 30 & Da Capo Press, 72; auth, Portraits of Adams-Clement Collection and their painters, Smithsonian Inst, 51; auth, Healy's Lincoln No 1, 56, rev ed, 59 & Surprise personalities in Georgetown, D C, 58 & 59, privately pub; contribr, 1861-1865, Vol III, In: Lincoln day by day: a chronology 1809-1865, Lincoln Sesquicentennial Comn, 60; plus others.
Mailing Address: 3259 N St N W, Washington, DC 20007.

KNOX, SEYMOUR H
Patron
b Buffalo, N Y, Sept 1, 98.
Study & Training: Yale Univ, BA, 20; Univ Buffalo, hon DFA, 62; Syracuse Univ, hon LHD, 66; St Lawrence Univ, hon DFA, 67.
Positions: Chmn, N Y State Coun on the Arts; pres & dir, Buffalo Fine Arts Acad; fel Rochester Mus & Sci Ctr.
Awards: Buffalo & Erie Co Hist Soc Red Jacket Medal, 62; Buffalo Club Medal, 62; Michael Friedsam Archit Award, 66; plus others.
Mailing Address: 57 Oakland Pl, Buffalo, NY 14222.

KO, ANTHONY
Printmaker, Educator
Preferred Media: Lithography.
b Hong Kong, Dec 8, 34; U S citizen.
Study & Training: Nat Taiwan Univ, BA; Univ Nev, with James McCormick, Charles Ross & Craig Sheppard; Univ Calif, Davis, MA, with Ralph Johnson, Roland Petersen & William Wiley; Univ N Mex & Tamarind Lithography Workshop, with Garo Antreasian.

Work in Public Collections: Mus Mod Art, New York, N Y; Art Inst Chicago, Ill; Los Angeles Co Mus Art, Calif; Achenbach Found for Graphic Arts, San Francisco, Calif; Hong Kong City Mus Art Gallery.
Commissions: 6 Impressions (suite of six lithographs), Univ Nev, Reno, 68; Return to Harmony (edition of 50 multicolor lithographs, Erie Art Ctr, 69.
Exhibitions: Nat Lithography Exhib, Fla State Univ, Tallahassee, 69; Brooklyn Mus 17th Ann Print Exhib, New York, 70; Color Print U S A, Tex Tech Univ, Lubbock, 70 & 71; Soc Am Graphic Artists, Kennedy Gallery, New York, 71; 20 American Printmakers, State Univ N Y, Col Oneonta, 72.
Teaching: Asst prof undergrad & grad printmaking, Edinboro State Col, 68-
Awards: Ford Found fel, Tamarind Lithography Workshop, 66.
Bibliography: Margaret Harold (auth), Prize-winning graphics, Allied Publ, 66; Six Impressions, Univ Nev Press, 68; Color Print U S A (film slides), Art Libr, Tex Tech Univ, 72.
Memberships: Col Art Asn Am; Pittsburgh Print Group (co-chmn adv & res comt, 72-).
Dealers: Richard Feigen Graphics, 25 E 77th St, New York, NY 10021; Associated American Artists, 663 Fifth Ave, New York, NY 10022.
Mailing Address: R D 2, Box 620, Edinboro, PA 16412.

KOBAYASHI, KATSUMI PETER
Painter, Lecturer
Preferred Media: Oils, Watercolors, Pastels.
b Hiroshima, Japan, Feb 5, 35.
Study & Training: Univ Hawaii, BFA, 64, MFA, 66.
Commissions: Oil paintings, Cent Pac Bank, Honolulu, Hawaii, 71 & Manoa, C S Wo & Sons, Honolulu, 71.
Exhibitions: Two-man show, Libr Hawaii, 65; Artist Hawaii Exhib Acad Arts, Honolulu, 65, 66, 69 & 71; one-man shows, Gateway House, Honolulu, 66 & Advertiser Contemp Arts Ctr, Hawaii, 72; Hawaii Painters & Sculptors Exhib, 69-72.
Teaching: Instr oil painting, Adult Educ, Farrington High Sch, Honolulu, 64-71; instr oil painting, Unitarian Church, Honolulu, 66.
Positions: Visual Aid Media Specialist, Univ Hawaii, 66-
Awards: Found Cult & Arts Purchase Award, 70-72 & Dept Educ Award, 71-72, State of Hawaii; purchase award, Honolulu Advertiser, 72.
Memberships: Hawaii Painters & Sculptors League (v pres, 70-72; Hawaii Art Educ Asn.
Dealer: Downtown Gallery, 125 Merchant St, Honolulu, HI 96813.
Mailing Address: 4894-3, Kilauea Ave, Honolulu, HI 96816.

KOBLICK, FREDA
Sculptor
Preferred Media: Plastics
b San Francisco, Calif.
Study & Training: San Francisco City Col; San Francisco State Col; Plastic Indust Tech Inst, plastics engr, 43.
Commissions: Cast acrylic doors, Sheraton Dallas Hotel, Tex, 61; prismatic construct of acrylic, comn by Anshen & Allen, Int Bldg, San Francisco, 63; cast acrylic relief, Rohm & Haas Co, Independence Hall, Philadelphia, Pa, 64; cast acrylic fountain, comn by Robert Royston, City of Vallejo, Calif, 66.
Exhibitions: One-woman shows, Mus Contemp Crafts, New York, N Y, 68, Ariz State Univ, Tempe, 70 & Fountain Art Gallery, Portland, Ore, 71; invitational group shows, Pierres de Fantasie, Oakland Mus, Calif, 70 & Object U S A, int tour at present.
Teaching: Sr res fel, Royal Col Art, London, Eng, 65-67; lectr in sculpture, Calif State Univ, Hayward, at present; also int lect & workshops.
Awards: Louis Comfort Tiffany Found grant-in-aid, 69; Guggenheim Found fel, 70-71.
Bibliography: Chamberlain (auth), An interview with Freda Koblick, Craft Horizons, 3/63; article, In: Western Plastics, 12/64; Charles Spencer (auth), article, In: Art & Artists Eng, 10/67.
Memberships: Artists Equity Asn; Plastics Inst Gr Brit.
Publications: Auth, The plastics age, Vogue (Eng), 66.
Mailing Address: 401 Francisco St, San Francisco, CA 94133.

KOCH, ARTHUR ROBERT
Painter, Educator
Preferred Media: Wood, Plastics.
b Meriden, Conn, Feb 20, 34.
Study & Training: Wesleyan Univ; R I Sch Design, BFA, 57, with John Frazier; Univ Wash, MFA, 61.
Exhibitions: Art: U S A:59, New York, N Y, 59; U S Info Agency Painting Show, Europe, 62-66; Tex Painting and Sculpture of the 20th Century, 70-71.
Teaching: Instr studio, Univ N H, 57-59; instr studio, El Centro Col, Dallas, Tex, 66-70; asst prof studio, Southern Methodist Univ, 70-

Positions: Chmn Acad Standards Comt, Tex Asn Schs Art, 70-71.
Awards: Fort Worth Art Ctr Award, 70.
Memberships: Dallas Area Artists Equity Asn (pres, 70-71); Artists Equity Asn (v pres, 71); Blue Bonnets Anonymous (chmn, 71-72).
Dealer: Atelier Chapman Kelly Gallery, 2526 Fairmount, Dallas, TX 75201.
Mailing Address: 11149 Lanewood Circle, Dallas, TX 75218.

KOCH, GERD (HERMAN)
   Painter, Educator
Preferred Media: Oils, Acrylics.
b Detroit, Mich, Jan 30, 29.
Study & Training: Wayne State Univ, BFA; Univ Calif, Los Angeles; Univ Calif, Santa Barbara, MFA.
Work in Public Collections: Los Angeles Co Mus Art; La Jolla Art Mus; Pasadena Art Mus; Univ N C; Santa Barbara Art Mus.
Commissions: Design of Ash Grove (folk music cabaret), 58.
Exhibitions: Los Angeles Co Mus Art Ann, 59; La Jolla Art Mus Ann, 60-62; three-man Traveling Show, Western Asn Mus, 62-65; Calif State Fair, 63; Art or Anti Art, Occidental Col, 65.
Teaching: Prof painting & drawing, Ventura Col, 60-61; 67-; instr painting & drawing, Univ Calif Exten, 67-
Awards: Purchase & first award, Los Angeles Co Mus Art, 59; Calif State Fair First Award, 63; Calif Nat Watercolor Soc Purchase Award, 67.
Bibliography: Prize winning oil paintings, Allied Publ, 60.
Memberships: Calif Nat Watercolor Soc (juror, 67 & 71); Ventura Art Asn.
Mailing Address: 444 Aliso, Ventura, CA 93001.

KOCH, IRENE MABEL
   Painter, Lecturer
Preferred Media: Oils.
b Detroit, Mich, Nov 5, 29.
Study & Training: Wayne State Univ.
Work in Public Collections: Newport Beach Mus; Long Beach Mus; Pasadena Mus.
Commissions: Screen, comn by Eugene Anderson, Santa Barbara.
Exhibitions: Pac Coast Biennial, 55-57; Artists South Calif, 58; Artists Southern Calif, 58-60; Pac Profile Traveling Exhib, 62-63; one-man show, Pasadena Mus.
Teaching: Summer instr still life & painting, Ventura Art Asn.
Positions: Judge, Calif Art Asn.
Awards: Awards, Newport Beach Art Ctr, 59, Long Beach Art Mus, 63 & Jewish Community Ctr, Los Angeles, 67 & 69.
Bibliography: Ed Reef (auth), Watercolor, Van Nostrand Reinhold, 71.
Memberships: Calif Nat Watercolor Soc (juror, 60); life mem Ventura Art Asn.
Mailing Address: 444 Aliso, Ventura, CA 93001.

KOCH, JOHN
   Painter, Collector
Preferred Media: Oils.
b Toledo, Ohio, Aug 18, 09.
Work in Public Collections: Metrop Mus Art, New York, N Y; Brooklyn Mus, N Y; Boston Mus Fine Arts, Mass; Nelson Gallery Art, Kansas City, Mo; Detroit Inst Fine Arts, Mich.
Exhibitions: Carnegie Inst, Pittsburgh, Pa, 43; one-man show, Suffolk Mus, Long Island, N Y, 51; one-man show, Va Mus Arts & Sci, Richmond & Mus of City of New York, 63; one-man show, Speed Mus, Louisville, Ky, 71.
Teaching: Instr painting, Art Stud League New York, 44-45.
Awards: Benjamin Altman Prize, 59, Saltus Gold Medal, 62 & Benjamin Altman Prize, 64, Nat Acad Design.
Bibliography: Dorothy Parker (auth), John Koch and his glorious people, Esquire, 11/19/64; Douglas Davis (auth), Art doesn't have to be new, Nat Observer, 4/22/48; Emily Genauer (auth), Miracles without trickery, New York Post, 3/11/72.
Memberships: Nat Inst Arts & Lett; Academician Nat Acad Design; Benjamin Franklin fel Royal Soc Arts.
Collection: Works by Tintoretto, Rubens, El Greco, Ingres, Gainsborough, Guardi, Steen, Magnasco, Solimena, Vuillard, Marsh & Burchfield.
Dealer: Kraushaar Gallery, 1055 Madison Ave, New York, NY 10028.
Mailing Address: 300 Central Park W, New York, NY 10024.

KOCH, ROBERT
   Art Historian, Writer
b New York, N Y, Apr 7, 18.
Study & Training: Harvard Univ, AB, 39; N Y Univ, MA, 53; Yale Univ, PhD, 57.
Teaching: Prof art hist, Southern Conn State Col, 56-
Research: Art nouveau in France, Spain, Latin America & the U S A.

Publications: Auth, articles, In: Gazette des Beaux Arts, 57 & 59; auth, articles, In: Art in Am, 62, 64 & 65; auth, Louis C Tiffany, rebel in glass, 64; contribr, Artistic America, Tiffany glass & art nouveau, 70; auth, Louis C Tiffany's glass-bronzes-lamps, 71.
Mailing Address: 9 Outer Rd, Norwalk, CT 06854.

KOCH, VIRGINIA GREENLEAF
   Painter
Preferred Media: Acrylics.
b Chicago, Ill.
Study & Training: Yale Univ Sch Fine Arts; Am Univ; also with Ivan Olinsky, Robert Brackman & Gene Davis.
Exhibitions: Mariners Mus, Newport News, Va, 70 & 71; Phillips Collection, Washington, D C, 71; one-man shows, Art League Northern Va, 71, Studio Gallery, Washington, D C, 71 & World Bank, Washington, D C, 71.
Memberships: Artists Equity Asn.
Dealer: Studio Gallery, 1735 Connecticut Ave, Washington, DC 20009.
Mailing Address: 2510 Virginia Ave N W, Washington, DC 20037.

KOCHER, ROBERT LEE
   Painter, Art Administrator
Preferred Media: Dye.
b Jefferson City, Mo, Dec 19, 29.
Study & Training: Univ Mo-Columbia, AB, MA, also with Fred Shane & Paul Brach.
Commissions: Religious Feasts, Culver-Stockton Col Dining Hall, 57.
Exhibitions: Mid-Am Ann, Kansas City, Mo, 60; All Iowa Artists, Des Moines Art Ctr Ann, 63-71.
Teaching: Prof art, Coe Col, 59-
Positions: Bd dirs, Cedar Rapids Art Ctr, 61-; Cedar Rapids, Marion Coun Arts, 71-
Awards: First prize for painting, All Iowa Artists, Des Moines Art Ctr, 69; Yonkers Award.
Mailing Address: 1955 Park Ave S E, Cedar Rapids, IA 52403.

KOCHERTHALER, MINA
   Painter
Preferred Media: Acrylics.
b Munich, Ger; U S citizen.
Study & Training: Columbia Univ; Art Stud League New York, N Y, with Mario Cooper; Nat Acad Design Sch Fine Art, with Ralph Fabri.
Work in Public Collections: Norfolk Mus Arts & Sci; also in many pvt collections.
Exhibitions: Royal Soc Painters Watercolours, London, 62; 200 Yrs Watercolor Painting Am, Metrop Mus Art, New York, 66-67; Mus Acuarela, Mexico City, Mex, 68; Butler Inst Am Art, 70; Can Soc Painters Watercolour, 71-72.
Positions: Deleg U S Comt Int Asn Arts, New York, 60-62.
Awards: John J Karpick Mem Medal, Audubon Artists, 62; Gramercy Prize, Nat Soc Painters Casein, 64; Grumbacher Polymer Award, Catharine Lorillard Wolfe Art Club, 71.
Memberships: Am Watercolor Soc (rec secy & coordr chmn, 62-); Audubon Artists (corresp secy, 60-62); Nat Soc Painters Casein & Acrylic (v pres, 62-); Allied Artists Am; Catharine Lorillard Wolfe Art Club.
Mailing Address: 124 W 79th St, New York, NY 10024.

KOCHTA, RUTH (MARTHA)
   Painter
Preferred Media: Oils.
b Ridgewood, N Y.
Study & Training: Art Stud League New York, with Rudolf Baranik & Julian Levi; also with E B Whitaker & Leo Manso.
Work in Public Collections: Philathea Col Mus, Ont, Can; Art Garden, Forest Hills, N Y; Scarsdale Gallery Contemp Art, N Y.
Exhibitions: Nat Acad Design Ann, New York, N Y, 68; Heckscher Mus, Huntington, N Y, 69 & 71; Wadsworth Atheneum, Hartford, Conn, 71; Elizabeth Ney Mus, Austin, Tex, 71; New Britain Mus, Conn, 72.
Awards: Best in show, Manhasset Art Festival, 70; first in oils, Bedford Art Show & Armonk Art Festival, 71.
Memberships: Conn Acad Fine Arts; Queens Coun Arts.
Dealer: Scarsdale Gallery of Contemporary Art, 20 Garth Rd, Scarsdale, NY 10583.
Mailing Address: 156-09 45th Ave, Flushing, NY 11355.

KOCSIS, ANN
   Painter
b New York, N Y.
Study & Training: Nat Acad Design, New York.
Work in Public Collections: Fla South Col; Seton Hall Univ; Am Hungarian Inst; Sq & Compass Crippled Children's Clin; Sonora Desert Mus, Ariz.

Exhibitions: Allied Artists Am, New York; Audubon Artists, New York; Am Artists Prof League Grand Nat, New York; Fairleigh-Dickinson Univ Exhib, N J; European Tour & Japan Exchange Exhib.
Awards: Hon mention & merit citation, Fla Int Art Exhib, Fla Southern Col, 52; gold key & Grambacher Award, Seton Hall Univ, 58; hon mention, Am Artists Prof League, 62.
Bibliography: Reproductions paintings & revs in newspapers & art magazines.
Memberships: Life mem Nat Arts Club (chmn, arts comt); Nat Asn Women Artists (nominating comt); Knickerbocker Artists (corresp secy & 2nd v pres, 66); life fel Royal Soc Arts, London, Eng; life fel Int Inst Arts & Lett, Switz.
Mailing Address: 327 W 76th St, New York, NY 10023.

KOENIG, JOHN FRANKLIN
Painter
Preferred Media: Oils, Acrylics.
b Seattle, Wash, Oct 24, 24.
Study & Training: U S Army Univ, France, 45; Univ Wash, grad, 48.
Work in Public Collections: Mus Art Mod, Paris, France; Ctr Nat Art Contemporain, Paris; Mus Western Art, Tokyo; Seattle Art Mus; Mus Art Contemporain, Montreal.
Commissions: Mural & glass windows (with Wogenscky), CHU Hosp, St-Antoine, Paris, 65.
Exhibitions: Collage & Objects, ICA Gallery, London, 54; First Biennale Paris, 59; Ecole Paris, Tate Gallery, London, 62; Carnegie Int, Carnegie Inst, Pittsburgh, 64; Aventure Art Abstrait, var French mus, 67-69.
Positions: Ballet critic, Cimaise, Paris, 68-; ballet critic, Art Vivant, Paris, 70-71.
Awards: Stud Show Prize, Univ Wash, 48; Third Prix Artistes Etrangers, Mus Art Mod, Paris, 59; Prix Critiques Art de Presse Parisienne, First Biennale Paris, 59.
Bibliography: Pierre Restany (auth), John Franklin Koenig, Galerie Arnaud, Paris, 60; Rene Deroudille (auth), John Franklin Koenig, Tête d'Or, Lyon, 61; Sylvie Nikitine (auth), Le regard du peintre, TV Scolaire, Paris, 68.
Publications: Co-auth, John Franklin Koenig, 65 & 70.
Mailing Address: c/o Galerie Arnauld, 212 Blvd St-Germain, Paris, France.

KOEPNICK, ROBERT CHARLES
Sculptor, Educator
b Dayton, Ohio, July 8, 07.
Study & Training: Dayton Art Inst, dipl; Cranbrook Acad Art; also with Carl Milles.
Commissions: Facade sculpture, St Michael Church, Houston, Tex; portrait of Max Rudolf (bronze sculpture) plus screen, St John's Chapel, Dayton, 67; sculpture, St James of the Valley Church, Wyoming, Ohio, 67; aluminum panel, Valentine Match Plate Co, Dayton, 68; Johnny Appleseed Mem, Springgrove Cemetery, Cincinnati, Ohio, 68; plus many others.
Exhibitions: Pa Acad Fine Arts, Philadelphia; Art Inst Chicago, Ill; Metrop Mus Art, New York, N Y; Nat Acad Design, New York; Syracuse Mus Fine Arts, N Y; plus others.
Teaching: Instr sculpture, Dayton Art Inst, 36-41, 46-; vis sculptor, Mt St Joseph Col, 51-55; vis sculptor, Antioch Col, 53-54.
Positions: Tech adv, Ohio Art Coun, 68-
Memberships: Dayton Soc Painters & Sculptors; Cincinnati Liturgical Art Group.
Mailing Address: Dayton Art Institute, Forest & Riverview Ave, Dayton, OH 45401.

KOERNER, DANIEL
Painter, Cartoonist
b New York, N Y, Nov 16, 09.
Study & Training: Art Stud League New York; Educ Alliance Art Sch.
Work in Public Collections: Metrop Mus Art, New York; Queens Col, New York; City Art Mus Saint Louis, Mo.
Commissions: Textbook illus; illus for var co & Encycl Am.
Teaching: Pvt instr, 38-41; cartoon instr, Cartoonist & Illustrators Sch, 48-52.
Publications: Contribr cartoons, Colliers, New York Times, Sat Rev, Nation's Bus, King Features, This Week & other nat mag.
Mailing Address: 408 E Tenth St, New York, NY 10009.

KOERNER, HENRY
Painter, Designer
Preferred Media: Ink, Watercolors, Oils.
b Vienna, Austria, Aug 28, 15; U S Citizen.
Study & Training: Acad Appl Art, Vienna; also with Victor Theodore Slama, Vienna.
Work in Public Collections: Whitney Mus Am Art; Mus Mod Art; Art Inst Chicago; Munson-Williams-Proctor Inst, Utica, N Y.

Exhibitions: Nat Cancer Poster Competition, 39; Nat War Poster Competition, Mus Mod Art, 42; Philadelphia Mus Art, 50; Artist of Yr, Pittsburgh, Pa, 63; Westmoreland Co Mus Art, Greensburg, Pa.
Teaching: Instr art, Munson-Williams-Proctor Inst, 47-48; artist-in-residence, Chatham Col, 52-53; instr art & head dept, Wash Univ, 56.
Positions: Head Graphic Div, Off Mil Govt, Berlin, Ger, 45-47.
Awards: First prize Nat Cancer Asn, 39 & first & second prize Nat War Poster Competition, 42, Mus Mod Art; Temple Award, Art Inst Philadelphia, 50.
Bibliography: His own tragedy spurs artist to paint moving post war paintings, Life, 48; Alexander Eliot (auth), Story Teller, 3/27/50 & 300 years of American painting, 59, Time.
Memberships: Nat Acad Design; Assoc Artists Pittsburgh; Pittsburgh Watercolor Soc.
Publications: Illusr, Tracy's tiger, 49, A sense of purpose, Col Art J, 51, The living god, Jewish Commentary, 59 & CBS yearbook, 59; auth & illusr, University of Pittsburgh in drawings, 65; plus others.
Mailing Address: 1055 S Negley Ave, Pittsburgh, PA 15217.

KOESTNER, DON
Painter
Preferred Media: Oils.
b Saint Paul, Minn, Nov 28, 23.
Study & Training: Minneapolis Sch Art, four yrs.
Commissions: Mural, St Olaf's Church, Minneapolis, Minn, 50; diorama-mural, Goodhue Co Hist Soc, Red Wings, Minn, 66.
Exhibitions: Twin Cities Show, Minneapolis Inst Art, 48-56; Red River Regional Show, Minn, 60; Ogunquit Art Ctr Nat Art Exhib, 64; Minn State Fair Fine Arts Ann, 66; Am Artists Prof League, 68.
Teaching: Instr painting, art instr schs, Minneapolis, 60-69; instr oil painting & drawing, Minn Mus Art Sch, 70-
Awards: Grumbacher Award, Ogunquit Art Ctr Nat Exhib, 64; first prize for oil painting, Minn State Fair, 66; award, Am Artists Prof League, 68.
Mailing Address: 9501 123rd St E, Rte 2, Hastings, MN 55033.

KOHLER, MEL (OTTO)
Art Dealer
b Wilcox, Sask, Dec 7, 11; U S citizen.
Study & Training: Univ Wash, BA, 35; Calif Sch Fine Arts, 36, with Maurice Sterne; Columbia Univ Teachers Col, MA, 42.
Collections Arranged: Western Wash Fair, Puyallup, 40, 46 & 51; Fur Rondezvous Exhibs, Anchorage, Alaska, 58-66; Alaska Music Festival, Anchorage, 65-66.
Teaching: Instr & asst prof art & head dept & galleries, Univ Puget Sound, 34-37; assoc prof art & head dept art & galleries, Alaska Methodist Univ, 58-66.
Positions: Founder & dir, Tacoma Art Asn, 34-37; cur & dir, Henry Gallery, Univ Wash, 48-52; cur, Eastern Wash State Hist Soc, 67-69; dir, Mel Kohler Gallery, Seattle & Anchorage, 69-
Specialty of Gallery: Contemporary artists, especially local artists.
Mailing Address: 800 First Ave N, Seattle, WA 98109.

KOHLHEPP, NORMAN
Painter, Printmaker
b Louisville, Ky.
Study & Training: Univ Cincinnati; Grande Chaumiere, Paris, France; Acad Colorossi; Andre L'Hote Acad, Paris, France.
Work in Public Collections: J B Speed Art Mus; Univ Louisville; Seagram Collection; Devoe & Raynolds Collection; print collection throughout U S.
Exhibitions: Mid-States Exhib, 65-67; Cincinnati Mus, Ohio, 67; J B Speed Art Mus, 68; Pa Acad Fine Arts, 66; Latin-Am Festival, 69; plus others.
Positions: Treas, Louisville Art Ctr Asn, 58-59, secy, 60-61, bd mem, 62-72, hon bd mem, 72-; co-chmn, Downtown Salutes the Arts, Louisville, 64 & 65; Jr Art Gallery, 71-72.
Awards: Va-Intermont Exhib, 58; first prize, Women's Club, 61 & 64; Ky State Fair, 67 & 68; plus others.
Dealer: J B Speed Art Museum, 2035 S Third, Louisville, KY 40208.
Mailing Address: 2116 Lauderdale Rd, Louisville, KY 40205.

KOHLMEYER, IDA (R)
Painter
Preferred Media: Oils.
b New Orleans, La, Nov 3, 12.
Study & Training: Newcomb Col, BA, 33, MFA, 56; also with Hans Hofmann, 56.
Work in Public Collections: Rochester Mem Art Gallery, N Y; Addison Gallery Am Art, Phillips Acad, Andover, Mass; Mus Fine Arts, Houston, Tex; High Mus Art, Atlanta, Ga; Corcoran Gallery Art, Washington, D C; plus many others.

Exhibitions: Biennial Contemp Am Painting, Corcoran Gallery Art, Washington, D C, 63 & 67; Art Across America, Knoedler Galleries, New York, 65; An Anthology of Modern American Painting, from collections of High Mus, Atlanta & Whitney Mus Am Art, New York, 66; Third Bienal de Arte Coltejer, Medellin, Colombia, 72; American Women: 20th Century, Lakeview Ctr Arts & Sci, Peoria, Ill, 72; plus many other group & one-man shows.
Teaching: Instr drawing & painting, Newcomb Col, 56-64.
Awards: First prize, Chautauqua Nat Exhib Am Painting, 62; Ford Found purchase award, 28th Corcoran Biennial Am Art, 63; mus purchase award, High Mus, Atlanta, 63 & 66; plus many others.
Dealer: Galerie Simonne Stern, 516 Royal St, New Orleans, LA 70130.
Mailing Address: 11 Pelham Ave, Metairie, LA 70005.

KOHN, GABRIEL
Sculptor
b Philadelphia, Pa, June 12, 10.
Study & Training: Cooper Union Art Sch, 29; Beaux-Arts Inst Design, 30-34; Zadkine Sch Sculpture, Paris, France, 46.
Work in Public Collections: Mus Mod Art & Whitney Mus Am Art, New York, N Y; Ringling Mus Art, Sarasota, Fla; Albright-Knox Art Gallery, Buffalo, N Y; Cranbrook Mus, Bloomfield Hills, Mich; also in pvt collections.
Exhibitions: Aspects of American Sculpture, Claude Bernard, Paris, France, 60; Four Whitney Mus Am Art Ann, 60, 62, 64 & 72; Seattle World's Fair, Wash, 62; Mus Mod Art, 63-64; Ringling Mus Art, 64; Int Sculpture Symposium, Calif State Col Long Beach; plus many others.
Teaching: Instr sculpture, Brooklyn Mus Art Sch, 59; La Jolla Art Ctr, 62; San Francisco Art Inst, 63; Univ Wash, 64; Univ Calif, Santa Barbara, 67; Calif Inst Fine Arts, 68.
Awards: Ford Found fel, 60; Tamarind Lithography Workshop fel, 63; Guggenheim Found fel, 67-68.
Bibliography: Sam Hunter (ed), New art around the world: painting and sculpture, Abrams, 66; Barbara Rose (auth), American art since 1900, a critical history, Praeger, 67; Maurice Tuchman (auth), American sculpture of the sixties, Los Angelees Co Mus Art, 67; plus others.
Mailing Address: c/o Marlborough Gallery, Inc, 41 E 57th St, New York, NY 10022.

KOHN, MISCH
Painter, Printmaker
b Kokomo, Ind, Mar 26, 16.
Study & Training: John Herron Art Inst, BFA, 39; also with Jose Clemente Oroszco & Leopoldo Mendez, Mexico City, Mex, 43.
Work in Public Collections: Bezalel Nat Mus, Jerusalem; Bibliot Nat, Paris, France; Victoria Mus, Melbourne, Australia; Mus Mod Art & Metrop Mus Art, New York, N Y; Nat Gallery Art, Libr Cong & Smithsonian Inst, Washington, D C; plus many others.
Exhibitions: Art Inst Chicago, 51 & 60; Los Angeles Co Mus Art, Calif, 58-60; Mus Nat Art Mod & Bibliot Nat, Paris, France, 59; Retrospective, Ford Found & Am Fedn Arts, 61; plus many others.
Teaching: Assoc prof art, Ill Inst Technol, 53-65, prof art, 65-70.
Awards: Tamarind fel, 61; prizes, Brooklyn Mus, 68; prize, Philadelphia Print Club, 69; plus many others.
Bibliography: Gabor Peterdi (auth), Printmaking: methods old and new, Macmillan, 59; S W Hayter (auth), About prints, Oxford Univ Press, London, 62.
Memberships: Soc Am Graphic Arts; Acad Florence; Print Coun Am; Philadelphia Print Club.
Mailing Address: 1200 E Madison Park, Chicago, IL 60615.

KOKINAS, GEORGE
Painter
b Chicago, Ill, Nov 17, 30.
Study & Training: Art Inst Chicago; Univ Chicago.
Work in Public Collections: In pvt collections only.
Exhibitions: Art Inst Chicago, Ill, 60-65; Denver Mus Art, Colo, 63; Whitney Mus Am Art, 63; Purdue Univ, 65; Walker Art Ctr, Minneapolis, Minn, 65; plus others.
Teaching: Instr advan painting, Northwestern Univ, summer 65.
Awards: Frank C Logan Award, Art Inst Chicago, 61.
Memberships: Chicago Art Club.
Mailing Address: 4716 N Sawyer Ave, Chicago, IL 60625.

KOLLIKER, WILLIAM AUGUSTIN
Painter, Graphic Artist
Preferred Media: Acrylics.
b Bern, Switz, Oct 12, 05; U S citizen.
Study & Training: Berner Secundar Schule, Bern; Nat Acad Design, Md Inst; Boston Sch Art, Grand Cent Art Sch; Art Stud League New York; Univ Tex, El Paso.

Work in Public Collections: El Paso Mus Art, Tex; Johnson Libr, Austin, Tex.
Commissions: Mosaic mural, El Fed Savings & Loan, El Paso, 64; design of bronze eagles, Amistad Dam, Del Rio, Tex, 68; gold medal, 69 & bronze plaques, 70, Chamisal Settlement.
Exhibitions: El Paso Mus Art, 64; 25th & 26th Ann Tex Painting & Sculpture Exhib, Dallas Mus Art, 64 & 65; Witte Mem, San Antonio, Tex, 64 & 65; Univ Tex, Austin, 64 & 65; Hemisfair, San Antonio, 68.
Teaching: Instr com art, Univ Tex, El Paso, 60-63.
Positions: Dir art, Cunningham & Walsh Advert Agency, New York, 52-54; dir art, White & Shuford, El Paso, 54-65.
Collection: Pre-Columbia artifacts & graphic collection.
Publications: Illusr, Street & Smith Publs, 40-45; illusr, Aesop's fables, 40; illusr, Adventures in puddle muddle, 41; illusr, Coronet, 42; illusr, 34-44, art dir & art ed, 44-52, Am Weekly.
Dealer: Ojo del Sol, 612 N Oregon, El Paso, TX 79902.
Mailing Address: 3812 Hillcrest Dr, El Paso, TX 79902.

KOMODORE, BILL
Painter, Sculptor
Preferred Media: Acrylics, Watercolors, Ink.
b Athens, Greece, Oct 23, 32; U S citizen.
Study & Training: Tulane Univ La, BA, 55, MFA, 57; Hans Hofmann Sch, Provincetown; also with George Rickey, Mark Rothko & David Smith.
Work in Public Collections: Whitney Mus Am Art, New York, N Y; Des Moines Art Ctr, Iowa.
Exhibitions: The Responsive Eye, Mus Mod Art, 64; Art in Motion, Cincinnati Art Mus, 65; Young America, 1965, Whitney Mus Am Art, 65; Plus by Minus: Today's Half Century, Albright-Knox Gallery, 68; The Square in Painting, Am Fedn Arts Show, assembled by Anuszkiewics, 68-69; plus many others.
Teaching: Vis artist, Northwood Inst, Cedar Hill, Tex, spring 69.
Awards: Bausch & Lomb Sci Award, 50; Houston Mus Award, 60.
Bibliography: Robert Trout (interviewer), Op art, CBS News with Walter Cronkite, 64; Douglas McAgy (auth), Plus by minus: today's half century (catalogue), Albright-Knox Gallery, 68; Cyril Barrett (auth), An introduction to optical art, Studio Vista, 71.
Publications: Illusr, Fishes of Lake Pontchartrain, Tulane Univ Press, 54; contribr, Contemporary American painting and sculpture, Univ Ill Press, 65; contribr, Young America, 1965, Whitney Mus Am Art, 65.
Dealer: Associated American Artists, 663 Fifth Ave, New York, NY 10022.
Mailing Address: 175 E Broadway, Apt 403, New York, NY 10002.

KOMOR, MATHIAS
Art Dealer
b Jan 24, 09; U S citizen.
Study & Training: Univ Grenoble, Dr Univ, 29.
Specialty of Gallery: Antiquities, Greek, Egyptian, Far East and others.
Mailing Address: 19 E 71st St, New York, NY 10021.

KONI, NICOLAUS
Sculptor, Painter
Preferred Media: Wood, Marble, Bronze, Jade, Gold.
b Hungary, May 6, 11; U S citizen.
Study & Training: Acad Fine Art, Vienna, Austria, dipl anat fine art; Masters Sch, Paris, France; Masters Sch, Florence, Italy.
Work in Public Collections: Bronze sculptures, Fountain of the Night, Okla Art Ctr, Oklahoma City, Secy Defense James Forrestal, Annapolis Naval Mus, bust of Marian Anderson, Metrop Opera, Lincoln Ctr, New York, N Y; Seminole Club, Palm Beach, Fla & Nat Mus Jerusalem, Israel.
Commissions: Bronze sculpture of C Walter Nichols, N Y Univ Bus Admin Sch.
Exhibitions: Whitney Mus Am Art, New York; Birmingham Mus Fine Art, Ala; Perrish Art Mus, South Hampton, N Y; Milch Galleries, New York.
Teaching: Instr sculpture, Graham-Eckes Sch, Palm Beach; lectr, Univ Bridgeport; instr fine art, Univ Mo-Columbia.
Awards: First prize in art, 8th Ann Art Festival, Perrish Art Mus.
Bibliography: Nicolaus Koni; a sculptor bringing out the spirit asleep in matter (film), N Y Fine Arts Coun; Classical influence and values in modern art (slide prog).
Memberships: Nat Sculpture Soc; Quilleis Art Soc (past chmn).
Dealer: Milch Art Gallery, 1014 Madison Ave, New York, NY 10021.
Mailing Address: 41 E 60th St, New York, NY 10022.

KONOPKA, JOSEPH
Painter
b Philadelphia, Pa, Oct 6, 32.
Study & Training: Cooper Union, grad, 54; Columbia Univ, 55.
Work in Public Collections: N J State Mus, Trenton; Newark Mus, N J; Cult Arts Ctr Ocean City, N J; Ct Gen Sessions Art Trust, Washington, D C; Atlantic City Art Collection, N J.

Exhibitions: Corcoran Gallery Art 30th Biennial, Washington, D C, 67; Am Fedn Art Traveling Exhib, 67-69; Newark Mus, 68; N J State Mus, 68, 70 & 71; Monmouth Col, West Long Branch, N J, 69-72.
Awards: Purchase awards, Newark Mus, 68 & N J State Mus, 70; Medal of honor, N J Painters & Sculptors Soc, 71.
Memberships: Am Fedn Art; Assoc Artists N J (mem bd trustees, 72); N J Painters & Sculptors Soc.
Dealer: Spectrum Gallery, 464 W Broadway, New York, NY 10012.
Mailing Address: 26 Snowden Pl, Glen Ridge, NJ 07028.

KONRAD, ADOLF FERDINAND
Painter
Preferred Media: Oils.
b Bremen, Ger; U S citizen.
Study & Training: Newark Sch Fine & Indust Art, N J; Cummington Sch, Mass; Newark State Col, hon DFA.
Work in Public Collections: Newark Mus; Springfield Mus Fine Art, Mass; Montclair Art Mus, N J; Nat Acad Design, New York, N Y; N J State Mus, Trenton.
Exhibitions: Am Painting Today, Metrop Mus Art, New York, 50; Whitney Mus Am Art Ann, New York, 52; Butler Inst Am Art, Youngstown, Ohio, 56; Pa Acad Fine Arts Painting Exhib, 64; Mainstream 70, Marietta Col, Ohio, 70.
Teaching: Adj instr painting, Newark State Col, 72.
Awards: Louis Comfort Tiffany Found fel creative painting, 61; Andrew Carnegie Prize, Nat Acad Design, 67; N J Symphony Ann Arts Award, 69.
Bibliography: An artist looks at Newark, Newark Mus, 66; Henry Gasser (auth), Adolf Konrad, painter of the American scene, Am Artist, 11/68.
Memberships: Nat Acad Design; Audubon Artists; Artists Equity Asn (pres, N J Chap, 54-60); Assoc Artists N J (pres, 58-60).
Mailing Address: Box 268E, Asbury, NJ 08802.

KONZAL, JOSEPH
Sculptor
Preferred Media: Metals, Wood, Constructions.
b Milwaukee, Wis, Nov 5, 05.
Study & Training: Beaux-Arts Inst of Design, New York; Art Stud League New York, with Max Weber & Robert Laurent, 26-31.
Work in Public Collections: Tate Gallery Art, London, Eng; Whitney Mus Am Art, New York, N Y; New Sch Social Res, New York; Storm King Art Ctr, Mountainville, N Y; N J State Mus, Trenton.
Commissions: Sculpture comn awarded by Nassau Co Court House, John F Kennedy Mem Cult Ctr, 68; sculpture, comn by Blossom-Kent Univ Comt, Blossom Music Ctr, Cuyahoga Falls, Ohio, 72.
Exhibitions: Six Whitney Mus Am Art Ann, 48-68; Recent Sculpture U S A, 1959, Mus Mod Art, New York, 59; Carnegie Int, Pittsburgh, Pa, 62; Geometric Abstraction in America, Whitney Mus Am Art, 62; May Show for Ohio Artists, Cleveland Mus Art, 72.
Teaching: Part-time instr sculpture, Brooklyn Mus Art Sch, 49-69; adj assoc prof sculpture, Adelphi Univ, 54-69; part-time lectr sculpture, Queens Col, 67-69; asst prof sculpture, Kent State Univ Sch Art, 71-
Awards: Guggenheim fel for creative work in sculpture, 65-66.
Memberships: Life mem Art Stud League New York.
Publications: Auth, Who are the tastemakers, Art J, spring 69; auth, Art, technology and liberal art colleges, Art J, winter 70-71.
Dealer: Bertha Schaefer Gallery, 41 E 57th St, New York, NY 10022.
Mailing Address: 428 Park Ave, Kent, OH 44240.

KOONS, DARELL J
Painter, Instructor
Preferred Media: Watercolors, Polymers.
b Albion, Mich, Dec 18, 24.
Study & Training: Bob Jones Univ, BS, 51; Western Mich Univ, MA, 55; Eastern Mich Univ.
Work in Public Collections: Butler Inst Am Art, Youngstown, Ohio; Mint Mus Art, Charlotte, N C; Gibbes Gallery, Charleston, S C; Greenville Co Mus Art, S C; Florence Mus Art, S C.
Commissions: Hist mural of Homer, Mich, Homer Community Schs, 55.
Exhibitions: Southeastern Exhibs, Atlanta, Ga, 63-65; Acquarella Galleries, New York, 64 & 66; Springfield Mus Art Nat, Mass, 65; Soc Four Arts Nat, Palm Beach, Fla, 67; Chico State Col Invitational, Calif, 72.
Teaching: Instr art, Homer Community Schs, 52-54; instr art, Bob Jones Univ, 55-
Awards: Purchase Awards, Guild S C Artists, 63, Davis Assocs, Chattanooga, Tenn, 65 & Wake Forest Univ Gallery Contemp Art, 65.
Bibliography: Steve Yates (auth), Greenville's noted barn painter, Sandlapper, 3/68.

Memberships: Greenville Art Asn & Guild; Guild S C Artists (mem bd); Int Platform Asn.
Mailing Address: 20 Prof's Pl, Bob Jones University, Greenville, SC 29614.

KOOTZ, SAMUEL M
Art Dealer, Writer
b Portsmouth, Va, Aug 23, 98.
Study & Training: Univ Va, LLB, 21.
Positions: Owner, Kootz Gallery, 44-66.
Specialty of Gallery: Modern American and European painting and sculpture.
Publications: Auth, Modern American painters, 28, Puzzle in paint, 43, New frontiers in American painting, 44, Puzzle in petticoats, 44 & Home is the hunter (play), 46.
Mailing Address: 480 Park Ave, New York, NY 10022.

KOPLIN, NORMA-JEAN
Painter
Preferred Media: Pencil.
b Chicago, Ill.
Study & Training: R I Sch Design; Yale Univ, with Joseph Albers, BFA; Fontainebleau Ecolé Beaux Arts.
Work in Public Collections: Finch Col Mus.
Exhibitions: One-man show, David Herbert, 62; Mus Mod Art Penthouse, 62-69; Philadelphia Mus Art, 67; one-man shows, Graham Gallery, 68 & Benson Gallery, 72.
Teaching: Instr drawing & color, Columbia Univ Sch Archit, 66-67.
Memberships: Women in Arts.
Mailing Address: 525 E 86th St, New York, NY 10028.

KOPMANIS, AUGUSTS A
Sculptor
b Riga, Latvia, Mar 17, 10.
Study & Training: Acad Fine Arts, Riga.
Exhibitions: Colour & Form Soc, 53-64; Nat Gallery Can, 63; Confederation Art Gallery & Mus, Charlottetown, P E I, 64; Hamilton, Ont, 64 & 65; Albert White Gallery, Toronto, 65; plus others.
Memberships: Sculptors Soc Can; Ont Soc Arts; fel Int Inst Arts & Lett.
Publications: Illusr, Season in Latvian folk songs, 56.
Mailing Address: 19 Millbrook Crescent, Toronto, Ont, Can.

KOPPE, RICHARD
Painter, Educator
Preferred Media: Oils, Acrylics, Watercolors, Ink.
b St Paul Minn, Mar 4, 16.
Study & Training: St Paul Acad & Sch Art, with Cameron Booth, Le-Roy Turner & Nicolai Cikovsky; New Bauhaus, Chicago, with Moholy-Nagy, Archipenko, Gyorgy Kepes, Hin Bredendieck, Ralph W Gerard, Carl Eckart & Charles W Morris.
Work in Public Collections: Whitney Mus Am Art, New York, N Y; Brooklyn Mus, N Y; Richard Koppe Paintings & Mss Collection, Syracuse Univ; Smith Col Mus Art, Northampton, Mass.
Commissions: Well of the Sea (seven murals & four sculptures), Hotel Sherman Restaurant, Chicago, Ill, 48-49; scale paintings for geodesic dome model, comn by R Buckminster Fuller, Chicago, 49; textile design, Blanch Martin & Assocs, Chicago, 50; three panels on glass mirrors, Med Bldg, Chicago, 51; metal sculpture panel, Club Lido, South Bend, Ind, 54.
Exhibitions: Pittsburgh Int Exhib Contemp Paintings, Carnegie Inst, Pa, 52; 53 Painters from Chicago, U S Info Agency, France, Ger & Holland, 57-59; one-man retrospective, Crown Hall, Ill Inst Technol, 61; 50 Yrs Bauhaus-Kunstgebaude, Stuttgart, Royal Acad Art, London, Stedelijk Mus, Amsterdam, Mus Art Mod, Paris, Crown Hall, Chicago Pasadena Art Mus, Mus Nac Bellas Artes, Buenos Aires & Nat Mus Mod Art, Tokyo, 68-71; one-man show, Mus Contemp Art, Chicago, 70; plus others.
Teaching: Instr prod illus, Univ Tex Exten, Fort Worth, 43-45; assoc prof & head visual design & fine art, Inst Design, Ill Inst Technol, 46-63; prof painting & sculpture, Univ Ill, Chicago Circle, 63-
Positions: Painter & designer, Ill Arts & Crafts, Work Projs Admin, 38-41; camouflage & res auth, War Serv, Chicago, 41-42; free lance artist, Chicago, 42-; group leader & prod illusr Consol Vultee Aircraft Co, Fort Worth, 43-46.
Awards: Martin B Cahn Prize, 58th Ann Am Abstr & Surrealist Show, Art Inst Chicago, 47-48; Old Northwest Territory Exhib First Award, Ill State Fair, Springfield, 50; Pauline Palmer Prize, 63rd Ann Chicago & Vicinity, 60.
Bibliography: Bitterman (auth), Art in modern architecture, Van Nostrand Reinhold, 52; Frank J Roos, Jr (auth), An illustrated handbook of art history, Macmillan, 59; Wingler (auth), Das Bauhaus, Rasch Dumont, Ger, 68 & The Bauhaus, Mass Inst Technol Press, 69.
Memberships: Mus Contemp Art; Artists Equity Asn.

Publications: Auth, The sources of contemporary painting, Arts &
Archit, 62; auth, Laszlo Moholy-Nagy and his visions, 69 & Re-
cent paintings, construction and reflections, 69, Art Int; contribr,
Bauhaus and Bauhaus people, Van Nostrand Reinhold, 69; con-
tribr, Bauhaus und Bauhausler, Hallwag Verlag, 71.
Mailing Address: 5256 N Rockwell St, Chicago, IL 60625.

KOPPELMAN, CHAIM
Printmaker, Educator
b New York, N Y, Nov 17, 20.
Study & Training: Am Artists Sch; Art Col Western Eng, Bristol;
Ozenfant Sch Fine Arts; also with Eli Siegel.
Work in Public Collections: Victoria & Albert Mus, London, Eng;
Mus Fine Arts, Caracas, Venezuela; Mus Mod Art, Metrop Mus
Art & Whitney Mus Am Art, New York; Libr Cong, Washington,
D C; Los Angeles Co Mus, Calif; plus others.
Exhibitions: 17th Nat Print Exhib, Brooklyn Mus, N Y, 70; The Kind-
est Art, Terrain Gallery, New York, 71; 2nd Nat Print Invita-
tional, Purdue Univ, 72; 2nd Ann Print Int, Utah State Univ, 72;
plus many others.
Teaching: New York Univ, 47-55; Brooklyn Col, 50-60; State Univ
N Y Col New Paltz, 52-58; head printmaking dept, Sch Visual
Arts, 59-
Positions: Consult, Aesthetic Realism Consultations, 71-
Awards: Tiffany Found grant, 56 & 59; prize, Soc Am Graphic Art-
ists, 66; 3rd Int Miniature Print Exhib Prize, 68; plus others.
Bibliography: Ralph Shikes (auth), The indignant eye, Beacon Press,
69.
Memberships: Soc for Aesthetic Realism; Soc Am Graphic Artists
(former pres).
Publications: Contribr, Liberation Mag, 69; co-auth, Aesthetic
realism: we have been there, 69; auth, This is the way I see
aesthetic realism, 69; illusr, Damned welcome, Definition, 72.
Mailing Address: 498 Broome St, New York, NY 10012.

KOPPELMAN, DOROTHY
Painter, Gallery Director
b New York, N Y, June 13, 20.
Study & Training: Brooklyn Col; Am Artists Sch; Art Stud League
New York; also with Eli Siegel.
Work in Public Collections: Yale Univ, New Haven, Conn; Hampton
Inst, Va.
Exhibitions: Mus Mod Art, New York, 62; San Francisco Mus Art,
Calif; Pratt Graphics Traveling Exhib, 62-63; two-man show,
Terrain Gallery, 69; three-man exhib, The Kindest Art, Terrain
Gallery, 70; plus many others.
Teaching: Instr art, adult educ, Brooklyn Col, 52; consult,
Aesthetic Realism, 71-
Positions: Dir, Terrain Gallery, 55-; dir, Visual Arts Gallery,
63-64.
Awards: First prize for painting, City Ctr Gallery, 57; prize for
painting, Brooklyn Soc Artists, 60; Tiffany Found grant, 65-66.
Memberships: Soc Aesthetic Realism.
Publications: Co-auth, Aesthetic realism: we have been there, 69;
illusr, Children's guide to parents and other matters, 71.
Mailing Address: 498 Broome St, New York, NY 10012.

KORAS, GEORGE
Sculptor
Preferred Media: Bronze.
b Florina, Greece, Apr 1, 25; U S citizen.
Study & Training: Sch Fine Arts, Athens, Greece, dipl, 55; study in
Paris, France & Rome, Italy, 55; Art Stud League New York, 55;
with Jacques Lipchitz, 55-59.
Work in Public Collections: W P Chrysler Collection; Provincetown
Mus, Mass; Norfolk Mus, Va; Pnevmatikon Centron Florinis,
Greece.
Commissions: Cast bronze sculpture, G Moffett, Edgartown, Mass,
69-70; cast bronze sculpture, Bd Educ, Queen's, N Y, 71; cast
bronze sculpture, Bd Educ, Bronx, N Y, 72; cast bronze sculp-
ture, Marcus Asn, Hauppauge, N Y, 72.
Exhibitions: Panhellenios Zapeion, Athens, Greece, 49; Brooklyn
Mus, N Y, 60; Pa Acad Fine Arts, Philadelphia, 64; Silvermine
Guild Artists, New Canaan, Conn, 67; Art Inst, New York, 68.
Teaching: Assoc prof art, State Univ N Y Stony Brook, 66-
Awards: Brooklyn Mus, 60; Pa Acad Fine Arts, 64; Hofstra Univ, 65.
Bibliography: Radio interview, produced on Voice of Am, New York,
72 G Koras sculptor (TV film), produced by N Y State Coun
Arts, 72.
Memberships: Audubon Artists (dir sculpture, 63-66, 68-71).
Mailing Address: 43-44 149th St, Flushing, NY 11355.

KORJUS, VERONICA MARIA ELISABETH
Painter, Lecturer
Preferred Media: Oils, Pastels.
b Tallinn, Estonia; U S citizen.
Study & Training: Prof Women's Col, Higher State Acad Art,

Estonia, dipl, 42; Univ Stockholm, 43-45; Columbia Univ, MA, 52;
Phoenix Sch Art, 53-56; Nat Acad Design, New York, N Y, 60-61;
La Grande Chaumiére, Paris, France, 61; 69-70; also private
studies in Mus Louvre, Mus Jeu Paume & other mus.
Work in Public Collections: Three comn portraits, World Coun
Churches.
Commissions: Portraits, UN Ambassador Dr Jan Papanek, Scars-
dale, N Y, 63; Dr Richard Fafara, 69, Susan Bell, 70, Countess
Maria Thérèse Pérez de Cavanillas, 70 & Ingrid Bergman, 72.
Exhibitions: Ctr Art Gallery, New York, 64; Int Art Gallery, To-
ronto, 64-66; one-man shows, IBM Country Club, Poughkeepsie,
N Y, 64 & 69 & Las Mimosas, Tangier, Morocco, 66; Barnard
Col Art Asn, New York, 69.
Teaching: Lectr & demonstr portraits, IBM Country Club, 64, River-
side Arts, New York, 65-67, Mus Louvre & Mus Jeu Paume, 70
& Cape Coral Art League, Fla, 72.
Awards: Two Thousand Women of Achievement Award, London, Eng,
72.
Memberships: Am Artists Prof League; Fraternitas Artis; Int Plat-
form Asn.
Mailing Address: 5350 Del Monte Ct, Cape Coral, FL 33904.

KORMAN, HARRIET R
Painter
b Bridgeport, Conn, Dec 10, 47.
Study & Training: Skowhegan Sch Painting & Sculpture, summer 68;
Queens Col (N Y), BA, 69.
Work in Public Collections: Solomon R Guggenheim Mus, New York,
N Y.
Exhibitions: Solomon R Guggenheim Mus, New York, 71; Whitney
Ann Exhib Painting, Whitney Mus Am Art, New York, 72.
Awards: Theodoron Found award, 71.
Dealer: Joe LoGuidice, 59 Wooster St, New York, NY 10012.
Mailing Address: c/o Dick Bellamy, Noah Goldowsky Gallery, 1078
Madison Ave, New York, NY 10028.

KORN, ELIZABETH P
Painter, Educator
Preferred Media: Mixed Media.
U S citizen.
Study & Training: Inst Fine & Applied Arts, Univ Breslau, Berlin,
Ger; Mus Fine & Applied Arts, Masterclass, Berlin; also study in
Rome, Italy & Madrid, Spain; Columbia Univ; New Sch Social Res;
New York Univ Inst Fine Arts; Art Stud League New York, with
Maurice Kantor.
Work in Public Collections: Plimpton, Dale & Smith Libr, Columbia
Univ, New York, N Y; Newark Mus, N J; Drew Univ, Madison,
N J; Prudential Ins Co Am, Newark, N J; Stevens Inst Technol,
Hoboken, N J; plus others.
Exhibitions: Galleria Bragaglia, Rome, Italy, 65; Theol Sem, Drew
Univ, 69; Cols & Univs Traveling Exhib, Emory & Henry Col, Va
& King Col, Bristol, Tenn, 69; one-man shows, Roko Gallery,
New York, 69-71; Genesee Community Col, Batavia & Cornell
Univ, Ithaca, N Y, 70; plus many other group & one-man shows.
Collections Arranged: Collections for exhibs for Drew Univ.
Teaching: Fla Presby Col, St Petersburg; artist-in-residence & vis
scholar, Emory & Henry Col & King Col, Tenn; prof art & chmn
dept, Drew Univ, 58-65; artist-in-residence, 66; vis prof art,
Newark Col Eng; fac studio, Stevens Inst Technol; vis prof, Sac-
red Heart Acad; Summit Art Ctr, N J; also lect art, cols, univs,
clubs & groups in Eastern & Southern U S.
Awards: Grumbacher Award; prize for oil, Six-State Eastern Col
Exhib; Windsor & Newton Award; plus others.
Memberships: Col Art Asn Am; Nat Asn Women Artists; Am Asn
Univ Prof; life mem Art Stud League New York; plus others.
Publications: Co-auth & illusr, At home with children, Henry Holt;
co-auth & illusr, Trailblazer to television, Scribner; co-auth &
illusr, Apple pie for Lewis, Aladin Bks; co-auth & illusr, Nando
of the beach, Bruce Publ; also reports, reviews & articles, var
publ in U S & abroad.
Dealer: Roko Gallery, 90 E Tenth St, New York, NY 10003.
Mailing Address: 1500 Manhattan Ave, Union City, NJ 07087.

KORNER, JOHN (JOHN MICHAEL ANTHONY KOERNER)
Painter
Preferred Media: Oils, Acrylics.
b Novy Jicin, Czech, Sept 29, 13; Can citizen.
Study & Training: With F Kausek, Prague & Othon Friesz, Paul
Colin & Victor Tischler, Paris.
Work in Public Collections: Nat Gallery Can, Ottawa; Montreal Mus
Fine Arts; Vancouver Art Gallery; Seattle Art Mus; Toronto Art
Gallery; plus others.
Commissions: Murals, comn by D J Simpson, Vancouver, 66, King's
Daughters Hosp, Duncan, B C, 67, A B Cliff, Palm Springs,
Calif, 68, CHQM Radio Sat, Vancouver, 69 & H B McDonald, Van-
couver, 70; plus others.

Exhibitions: Nat Gallery Can Biennials, 54-64; World's Fair, Seattle, 62; Art Inst, Minneapolis, 63; San Francisco Mus Art, 65; Commonwealth Inst, London, Eng, 68; plus others.
Teaching: Instr painting, Vancouver Sch Art, 53-58; instr painting, Univ B C, 58-62.
Awards: Winnipeg Show Awards, 55, 57 & 61; Vancouver Art Gallery Centennial Award, 59; Govt Can Centennial Medal, 67.
Dealer: Bau-Xi Gallery, 3003 Granville St, Vancouver, B C, Can.
Mailing Address: 5816 Kingston Rd, Vancouver 8, B C, Can.

KORPELA, EDWARD S
    Painter, Educator
Preferred Media: Watercolors, Acrylics.
b Eveleth, Minn, May 29, 14.
Study & Training: Eveleth Jr Col; Winona State Col, BS; Art Inst Chicago; Colo State Col; Univ Minn; Inst Allende, Mex; Ariz State Univ; also with Yasuo Kuniyoshi.
Work in Public Collections: Mason City Pub Libr, Iowa; Col St Teresa, Winona, Minn; First Nat Bank, Winona; med clin, Rapid City, S Dak; plus numerous private collections in U S, Can & foreign countries.
Commissions: Mural, YMCA, Winona, 65; archit renderings, archit firms in Minn & Wis, 70-
Exhibitions: Col St Teresa, 63; Witte Mem Mus, San Antonio, Tex, 65; Gulf Coast Art Ctr, Clearwater, Fla, 65; Banff Sch Fine Arts, Alta, Can, 66-71; Mason City Pub Libr, 71.
Teaching: Head dept art, Winona Pub Schs, 46-; instr watercolors, Banff Sch Fine Arts, 66-72, acting head painting div, 69-70.
Positions: Dir & instr, Winona Art Group; free-lance archit delineator.
Awards: Award, Northwestern Bell Tel Calendar, Omaha, Nebr, 67; first pl, Mesa Art League, 69; merit award, Rochester, Minn Art Ctr.
Bibliography: Work discussed in numerous resumes & critiques.
Publications: Auth, article, in: The Illusr, 63.
Dealers: Peter's Art Barn, 6051 Hidden Valley Dr, Cave Creek, AZ 85331; Seven Rays Gallery, Taos, NM 87571.
Mailing Address: 203 W Mill St, Winona, MN 55987.

KORTHEUER, DAYRELL
    Painter
b New York, N Y, July 25, 06.
Study & Training: Art Stud League New York, with Frank DuMond, George Bridgman & John Carroll; Nat Acad Design, with Charles Hawthorne.
Work in Public Collections: Portraits, Merchant's Asn, New York; Mint Mus Art; Emory Univ; Univ N C; Davidson Col; plus others.
Exhibitions: Asheville Mus Art, 53; Blowing Rock Art Asn, 55; Statesville, N C, 57 & 64; Hickory, N C, 58; Carson-McKenna Gallery, Charlotte, N C, 69.
Teaching: Instr painting, Mint Mus Art.
Awards: Prizes, Nat Arts Club, 28; awards, Mint Mus art, 41 & 42; gold medal, 54 & award, 55, Blowing Rock Art Asn.
Memberships: Portraits, Inc; Int Inst Conserv Hist & Artistic Works; N C State Art Soc; Mint Mus Art.
Mailing Address: 1924 Sharon Lane, Charlotte, NC 28211.

KORTLANDER, WILLIAM (CLARK)
    Painter, Educator
Preferred Media: Acrylics, Oils, Watercolors.
b Grand Rapids, Mich, Feb 9, 25.
Study & Training: Mich State Univ, BA; Univ Iowa, MA & PhD.
Work in Public Collections: Columbus Gallery Fine Arts, Ohio; Huntington Galleries, W Va; Otterbein Col, Westerville, Ohio; W Va State Col; Zanesville Art Inst, Ohio.
Exhibitions: Art Across Am, Knoedler Gallery, New York, N Y, 65; Pa Acad Fine Arts 180th Ann, 65; one-man shows, A M Sachs Gallery, New York, 67 & 68; Am Drawings of Sixties, New Sch Art Ctr, New York, 70.
Teaching: Instr art hist, Lawrence Univ, 54-56; asst prof art hist, Univ Tex, Austin, 56-61; vis asst prof art hist, Mich State Univ, summer 61; prof painting, Ohio Univ, 61-, Baker Award, 67.
Awards: Painting of Yr, Mead Corp, 65.
Dealer: A M Sachs Gallery, 29 W 57th St, New York, NY 10019.
Mailing Address: Angel Ridge, Rte 4, Athens, OH 45701.

KOSCIELNY-PARKER, MARGARET
    Painter, Sculptor
Preferred Media: Ink, Plexiglass.
b Tallahassee, Fla, Aug 13, 40.
Study & Training: Tex Woman's Univ, with Toni Lasalle; Univ Ga, BA(art hist) & MFA, with Irving Marantz.
Work in Public Collections: Jacksonville Art Mus, Sch Art Ctr, Fla.
Commissions: Plexiglass sculpture, John Portman, Atlanta, Ga, 69; plexiglass sculpture, Maurice D Alpert, First Nat Bank Towers, Atlanta, 72.

Exhibitions: Southeastern Print & Drawing Competition, Jacksonville, 64, 66 & 67; Fla State Fair, Tampa, 65; American Drawing 1968, Philadelphia, Pa, 68; Drawing U S A, Saint Paul, Minn, 69.
Teaching: Instr printmaking, Jacksonville Art Mus, 68; guest instr printmaking, Jacksonville Pub Sch Teachers Art Dept Workshop, Jacksonville Art Mus, 70 & 71.
Mailing Address: 2105 River Blvd, Jacksonville, FL 32204.

KOSTER, MARJORY JEAN
    Printmaker
Preferred Media: Wood.
b Grand Rapids, Mich, Feb 9, 26.
Study & Training: Univ Mich Exten Night Sch, 47-64; Pratt Graphic Workshop, New York, N Y, summer 64.
Work in Public Collections: Metrop Mus Art, New York; Brooklyn Mus Art, N Y; Chicago Art Inst, Ill; Grand Rapids Art Mus; Kalamazoo Inst Art, Mich.
Exhibitions: 9th Ann Exhib Prints & Drawings, Oklahoma City Art Ctr, Okla, 67; 7th Ann Mercyhurst Col Nat Graphics Exhib, Erie, Pa, 67; 3rd Nat Print & Drawing Exhib, Western Mich Univ, Kalamazoo, 68; 16th Nat Print Exhib, Brooklyn Mus, 68; 1st Nat Print Exhib, Honolulu, Hawaii, 71.
Dealer: Associated American Artists, 663 Fifth Ave, New York, NY 10022.
Mailing Address: 940 Maynard N W, Grand Rapids, MI 49504.

KOTALA, STANISLAW WACLAW
    Painter, Art Historian
Preferred Media: Watercolors, Oils
b Boleslawiec, Poland, Sept 27, 09; U S citizen.
Study & Training: Inst Design, Poland, dipl, 37; Acad Fine Arts, Cracov, Poland, with K Sichulski & P Dadlez, 38-39; Acad Fine Arts, Dusseldorf, Ger, with T Champion & W Heuser, BA, 49; Rutgers Univ, New Brunswick, MLS, 65.
Work in Public Collections: Dom Wojska Polskiego, Warszawa, Poland; Mus Slaskie, Katowice, Poland.
Exhibitions: Int Festival, Polish Arts Exhib, Edinburgh, Gt Brit, 47; Polish-Am Artist Exhib, Kosciuszko Found, New York, N Y, 50; Nat Exhib Paintings by Am Artists of Polish Descent, Alliance Col, Cambridge Springs, Pa, 51; Plastyka za Drutami, Warszawa, 63; one-man show, Samuel Fleisher Art Mem, Philadelphia, Pa, 60.
Teaching: Dir art hist, Inst Art Teachers, Dossel, Ger, 43-44; instr com art, Com H S, Lippstadt, Ger, 46-47.
Positions: Artist-painter, Cordey China Art Studio, Philadelphia, 52-59; art ref librarian, Free Libr Philadelphia, 59-
Awards: First award, Off Club, 45; first prize, Acad Fine Arts, Dusseldorf, 48.
Bibliography: W Borzecki (auth), W zwierciadle sztuki, Nowy Swiat, 10/15/50; W Denkowski (auth), S W Kotala lecture, Gwiazda, 2/6/69.
Memberships: Am Libr Asn.
Publications: Illusr, Nasz Plomyczek, 46; illusr, Wiadomosci, 46.
Mailing Address: 8147 Revere St, Philadelphia, PA 19152.

KOTIN, ALBERT
    Painter, Educator
Preferred Media: Oils, Acrylics.
b Russia, Aug 7, 07; U S citizen.
Study & Training: Art Stud League New York; Nat Acad Design; with Charles Hawthorne, Provincetown, Mass, 24-29; Acad Julian & Acad Grande Chaumiére, Paris, France, 29-32; Atelier de Fresque, with Paul Baudouin; also with Hans Hofmann, New York & Provincetown, 46-50.
Work in Public Collections: Syracuse Mus Fine Art, N Y; Kalamazoo Inst Art, Mich; Brooklyn Pub Libr; Newark Bd Educ, N J; Long Island Univ.
Commissions: Mural sociol dept, N Y Univ, 34; two murals, U S Treas Dept, Arlington, N J, 37; mural, Ada Post Off, Ohio, 38.
Exhibitions: Libr of Cong Print Exhib, 47; 9th St Show, New York, 51; New York Artists Ann, Stable Gallery, 52-57; Galerie Iris Clert, Paris, 60; one-man show, Grand Cent Mod, N Y, 58; plus many other group & one-man shows.
Teaching: Distinguished vis artist, Southern Ill Univ, Carbondale, 61; artist-in-residence, Stout State Univ, 64-66; assoc prof art, Long Island Univ, 66-
Positions: Juror of murals, New York Art Exhib, N Y, 38; color consult, Cult Comn Mex Olympic Orgn, 68.
Awards: First prize, N J Post Off Competition, U S Treas Dept, 37; purchase award, Longview Fund, 62.
Bibliography: Friedeberg (auth), Kotin, Art Supplement, Archit Mag, 62; Prampolini (auth), El arte contemporaneo editorial pormaca, Macmillan, 64; Rodriguez (auth), Que ha pasado con la pintura? Inst Investigaciones Esteticas, 68.
Publications: Contribr, It is, 60.
Mailing Address: 210 E 34th St, New York, NY 10016.

KOTTLER, LYNN
Art Dealer
b New York, N Y.
Study & Training: Columbia Univ; New York Univ; City Col New
York; New Sch Social Res.
Positions: Founder, Acad Galleries, 40-44; founder, Portrait
Painters Guild, 45-48; dir, Lynn Kottler Galleries, 49-
Specialty of Gallery: Paintings, sculpture and all media by leading
contemporary artists, both American and foreign.
Mailing Address: 3 E 65th St, New York, NY 10021.

KOUWENHOVEN, JOHN A
Writer, Educator
b Yonkers, N Y, Dec 13, 09.
Study & Training: Wesleyan Univ, AB; Columbia Univ, AM & PhD.
Collections Arranged: Backgrounds of Modern Design, For Modern
Living Exhib, Detroit Inst Arts, 49; Art out of the Attic Exhib,
Vt Coun Arts, Johnson Art Ctr, Middlebury, Vt, 70.
Teaching: Prof vernacular in Am arts of design, Barnard Col, Co-
lumbia Univ, 46-
Positions: Trustee, Vt Coun Arts, Montpelier; mem adv bd, Arch
Am Art, Smithsonian Inst.
Publications: Auth, Made in America: the arts in modern civiliza-
tion, 48; auth, The Columbia historical portrait of New York, 53;
auth, The beer can by the highway: essays on what's American
about America, 61; auth, Design and chaos, Shaping of art &
architecture in nineteenth century America, Metrop Mus, 72.
Mailing Address: Dorset, VT 05251.

KOWAL, DENNIS J
Sculptor
Preferred Media: Stone, Wood, Metal, Plastic.
b Chicago, Ill, Sept 9, 37.
Study & Training: Art Inst Chicago; Southern Ill Univ, BA, 61, MFA,
62.
Work in Public Collections: A Robbins Off, Chicago; N Dehann
Archit Off, Chicago.
Commissions: Monuments, comn by Dr N Giarretta, Md, 69, Sacred
Heart Hosp, Md, 70, Allegheny Col, Md, 71 & Krannert Perform-
ing Arts Ctr, Univ Ill, 71.
Exhibitions: 66th Artists Chicago Ann, 63 & Soc Contemp Am Art,
64; Art Inst Chicago; Ill Sculptors, Arts Coun, Ill State Mus, 68;
Smithsonian Traveling Exhib, Washington, D C, 69-70; Plastics
in Sculpture, Boston Univ Galleries, 72.
Teaching: Asst prof sculpture, Columbus Col Art, Ohio, 63-64;
asst prof sculpture, Univ Ill, Champaign, 66-70; asst prof sculp-
ture, Mass Col Art, Boston, 71-72.
Awards: Artist-in-residence fel, MacDowell Colony, N H, 65 & 72,
Yaddo, N Y, 70 & Dartmouth Col, N H, 71.
Bibliography: J Kind (auth), Chicago sculptors, Art News, summer
66; Sculpture, The Art Gallery, 71; D Kowal—sculptor, Channel
Five TV, Boston, 72.
Memberships: Art Inst Chicago; Boston Visual Artists Union; New
Eng Sculptors Asn, Boston; Mus Mod Art, New York.
Publications: Contribr, Contemporary wood sculpture, 68, Con-
temporary stone sculpture, 69 & auth, Casting sculpture, 72,
Crown.
Mailing Address: 600 Jerusalem Rd, Cohasset, MA 02025.

KOWALKE, RONALD LEROY
Painter, Printmaker
b Chicago, Ill, Nov 8, 36.
Study & Training: Univ Chicago, 54-56; Art Inst Chicago, 54-56;
Rockford Col, BA, 59; Cranbrook Acad Art, MFA, 60.
Work in Public Collections: Mus Mod Art, New York, N Y; Metrop
Mus Art, New York; Libr Cong, Washington, D C; Nat Gallery,
Washington, D C; Rockford Col, Ill.
Exhibitions: Seven American Printmakers, Amsterdam, Holland, 67.
Teaching: Instr design, Northern Ill Univ, 60-61; instr drawing, de-
sign & printmaking, Swain Sch Design, New Bedford, Mass, 61-64;
assoc prof drawing & printmaking, Univ Hawaii, 69-, faculty res
grant, 70 & 71.
Bibliography: Sidney Horowitz (auth), White ground etchings of Ron
Kowalke, Am Artist Mag, 1/66.
Memberships: Honolulu Printmakers (mem bd adv, 70-).
Dealers: Associated American Artists, Inc, 663 Fifth Ave, New
York, NY 10022; Ferdinand Roten, Inc, 123 W Mulberry, Balti-
more, MD 21201.
Mailing Address: 2947 Al Phonse Pl, Honolulu, HI 96816.

KOWALSKI, RAYMOND ALOIS
Painter
Preferred Media: Acrylics, Collage.
b Erie, Pa, June 21, 33.
Study & Training: Pa State Teachers Col, Edinboro; Cleveland Inst
Art.

Work in Public Collections: State of Pa Educ System.
Exhibitions: Chautauqua Nat, N Y, 67; Watercolor U S A, 68; May
Show, Cleveland Mus Art, 69-71; one-man show, Bluffton Col,
Ohio, 70; Preview 71, Mt St Joseph's Col, Cincinnati, Ohio, 71;
plus many other group & one-man shows.
Teaching: Instr design, Cooper Sch Art, Cleveland, 69-70; instr
painting, local art groups, 70-
Positions: Designer, Am Greetings Corp, Cleveland, 59-65, art
dir, 65-
Awards: Cleveland Inst Art Stud Show Award, Am Greetings Corp;
Excellence in Painting, Chagrin Valley Art Asn, 70.
Bibliography: Helen Brosick, article, In: Cleveland Plain Dealer
Suppl, 68; Ray Kowalski—painter of houses, Wonderful World
Ohio, 10/69.
Mailing Address: 12000 Fairhill Rd, Cleveland, OH 44120.

KOZLOFF, ALEXANDER IVAN
Painter, Printmaker
Preferred Media: Oils, Watercolors, Wood.
b New York, N Y, Sept 14, 26.
Study & Training: Pratt Inst; Acad Allied Arts; Educ Alliance Sch;
Moses Soyer Art Sch, with David Burluik & Moses Soyer.
Work in Public Collections: Print, Metrop Mus Art, New York, N Y;
also in pvt collection of Mrs Jacqueline Kennedy.
Commissions: Oil paintings, Dell Publ Co, 48, Int Paper Co, 48, E R
Squibb & Sons, 48-50, Life Mag, 49 & portrait of v pres, Bank of
Metuchen, N J, 53.
Exhibitions: 1939 New York World's Fair Exhib, 39; Brooklyn Mus
Ann, 45-48; 13th Int Ann Knickerbocker Artists, 60; Salmagundi
Club Art Ann, 60-63; 19th Ann Audubon Artists, New York, 61.
Awards: Hon mention for oils, Educ Alliance Art Sch, 57; gold medal
& hon mention for oils, Ahda Artzt Gallery, 67 & 68.
Bibliography: Alexander Z Kruse (auth), At the art galleries, Brook-
lyn Eagle, 45-46 & 47-48; Ray Nash (auth), Print on International
Paper Co, Print, Quart J Graphic Arts, 49; Mabel M Carver
(auth), Artist should bend in many directions, 8/2/62 & Local art,
7/9/64, The Villager.
Memberships: Artists Equity Asn New York; League Present Day
Artists; Contemp Artists Brooklyn; Burr Artists (v chmn ex-
hibs, 69-).
Publications: Ed, Dorothy Scott, Time, 7/17/39; illusr, Print, 49.
Mailing Address: 1857 85th St, Brooklyn, NY 11214.

KOZLOFF, JOYCE
Painter
Preferred Media: Acrylics.
b Somerville, N J, Dec 14, 42.
Study & Training: Carnegie Inst Technol, BFA, 64; Columbia Univ,
MFA, 67.
Exhibitions: One-woman exhibs, Tibor de Nagy Gallery, New York,
N Y, 70, 71 & 72; GEDOK Am Woman Artist Show, Kunsthaus, Ham-
burg, Ger, 72; Colorforum, Univ Tex, Austin, 72; Whitney Mus
Am Art Painting Ann, 72.
Teaching: Instr ACE prog, Queens Col, Flushing, N Y, 72-
Awards: Grant, Tamarind Lithography Inst, Albuquerque, N Mex,
72.
Memberships: Los Angeles Coun Women Artists; Ad Hoc Comt
Women Artists; Women in the Arts.
Dealer: Tibor de Nagy Gallery, 29 W 57th St, New York, NY 10019.
Mailing Address: 225 W 106th St, Apt 16 K, New York, NY 10025.

KOZLOFF, MAX
Art Critic
b Chicago, Ill, June 21, 33.
Study & Training: Univ Chicago, BA, 53, MA, 58; Inst Fine Arts, New
York Univ; Fulbright scholar, France, 62-63.
Teaching: Instr, Cooper Union, 60-61; instr, Wash Square Col, New
York Univ, 61-62.
Positions: Art critic, The Nation, 61-; New York corresp, Art Int,
62-64; assoc ed, Artforum, 64-
Awards: Pulitzer fel in critical writing, 62-63; Frank Jewett Mather
Award in art criticism, 66; Guggenheim fel, 68-69.
Publications: Auth, Renderings: essays on a century of modern art,
68 & Jasper Johns, 69; contribr, art & film criticism to major
journals.
Mailing Address: 225 W 106th St, New York, NY 10025.

KOZLOW, RICHARD
Painter, Lecturer
Preferred Media: Acrylics.
b Detroit, Mich, May 5, 26.
Study & Training: Cass Tech High Sch, Detroit; Soc Arts & Crafts,
Detroit.
Work in Public Collections: Detroit Inst Arts; Butler Art Inst,
Youngstown, Ohio; Int Nickel Corp, New York, N Y; Miami
Herald, Fla; Art Gallery of Windsor, Ont.

Commissions: Mural, Am Savings & Loan.
Exhibitions: Contemporary Art U S A, Los Angeles, 56; Group Teix, Palma de Mallorca, Spain, 62; Transatlantics, U S Embassy, London, Eng, 66; 20th Century Am Art Invitational, San Diego, Calif, 68; Hudson River Mus Exhib Lithographs from Mourlot Graphics, New York, N Y, 70; plus 15 one-man exhibs in New York, Los Angeles, Detroit, Palm Beach & Mex.
Teaching: Instr design, Soc Arts & Crafts, Detroit, 50-60; instr painting, Inst Allende, San Miguel de Allende, Mex, 61; instr advan acrylic painting, Bloomfield Art Asn, Mich, 66-71.
Awards: Purchase award, Butler Art Inst, 50; Founders Award, Detroit Inst Arts, 63.
Bibliography: Louise Brunner (auth), The landscape painting of Richard Kozlow, Am Artist Mag, 5/56; Jose Gutierrez & Nicholas Roukes (auth), Painting with acrylics, 65 & Wendon Black (auth), Complete guide to acrylic painting, 71, Watson-Guptill.
Publications: Auth & illusr, Of man's inhumanity to man, Lark Publ, 65.
Dealer: Kennedy Gallery, 20 E 56th St, New York, NY 10022. Arwin Gallery, 222 W Grand River, Detroit, MI 48226.
Mailing Address: 176 Suffield, Birmingham, MI 48009.

KOZLOW, SIGMUND
Painter, Instructor
Preferred Media: Oils, Pastels.
b New York, N Y, Dec 7, 13.
Study & Training: Nat Acad Design; Fontainbleau Sch Fine Arts, France.
Work in Public Collections: State Teachers Col, Indiana, Pa; Munson-Williams-Proctor Inst, Utica, N Y; Univ Ga; Mus Fine Arts, Springfield, Mass.
Exhibitions: Nat Acad Design 146th Ann, New York, 71; Audubon Artists 30th Ann, New York, 72; Allied Artists Am 58th Ann, New York, 72; Rockport Art Ann, Mass, 72; Springfield Mus Nat Ann, Mass, 72.
Teaching: Instr painting, Summit Art Ctr, 65-
Positions: Pres, Delaware Valley Artists Asn, 52-60; trustee, Hunterdon Art Ctr, Clinton, N J, 71.
Awards: Pulitzer Prize, 36-37 & S J Wallace Truman Award, 45, Nat Acad Design; Marine award, Silvermine Guild Artists, 60.
Memberships: Audubon Artists; Allied Artists Am; Rockport Art Asn; N J Watercolor Soc; Allied Artists N J.
Dealer: Grand Central Art Galleries, 40 Vanderbilt Ave, New York, NY 10017.
Mailing Address: Mountain Rd, Finesville, NJ 08865.

KRAMARSKY, MRS SIEGFRIED
Collector
Collection: Paintings.
Mailing Address: 101 Central Park W, New York, NY 10023.

KRAMER, HILTON
Art Critic
b Gloucester, Mass, Mar 25, 28.
Study & Training: Syracuse Univ, BA; Columbia Univ; New Sch Social Res; Harvard Univ; Ind Univ.
Teaching: Lect, Art Today.
Positions: Assoc ed & feature ed, Arts Digest, 54-55; managing ed, Arts Mag, 55-64; art critic, New York Times, at present.
Publications: Contribr, Arts Mag, Partisan Rev, Commentary, New Repub, The Progressive, Western Rev, Indust Design & other publ.
Mailing Address: New York Times, 229 W 43rd St, New York, NY 10036.

KRAMER, JACK N
Painter, Educator
Preferred Media: Oils.
b Lynn, Mass, Feb 24, 23.
Study & Training: Sch Mus Fine Arts, Boston, dipl, 49, with Karl Zerbe, Albert H Whittin Traveling fel; Univ Reading, 50, with J Anthony Betts; with Oskar Kokoschka, London, 50; R I Sch Design, BFA, 54.
Work in Public Collections: Addison Gallery Am Art; Phillips Acad, Andover, Mass; William Gurlitt Mus, Linz, Austria.
Exhibitions: Nat Acad Design, New York, N Y, 56; Univ Ill, Urbana, 57; Inst Contemp Art, Boston, 60-61; Boston Univ, 63, 66 & 69; Kunst Salon-Wolfberg, Zurich, 69.
Teaching: Prof art, Boston Univ, 57-
Bibliography: Portfolio of drawings, Audience Mag, 61; Portfolio of drawings, Liberal Context, 65.
Publications: Auth, Human anatomy and figure drawing, 72.
Mailing Address: 67 Thatcher St, Brookline, MA 02146.

KRAMER, MARJORIE ANNE
Painter
Preferred Media: Oils, Watercolors.
b Engelwood, N J, Apr 21, 43.
Study & Training: Cooper Union, BFA, 66; New York Studio Sch, with M Matter & C Cajori.
Exhibitions: Painterly Realism, Am Fedn Arts Traveling Exhib, 69-71; Green Mountain Gallery, New York, N Y, 69-72; Smith Col Mus Christmas Invitational, 70; New England Landscapes, Fleming Mus, Burlington, Vt, 71; Drawing Each Other & Fence Show Award Winners, Brooklyn Mus, 72.
Positions: Ed, Women & Art Quart, New York, 71-72.
Memberships: Alliance Figurative Artists (mem steering comt, 71-72).
Mailing Address: c/o Green Mountain Gallery, 135 Greene St, New York, NY 10012.

KRAMER, REUBEN
Sculptor
Preferred Media: Bronze.
b Baltimore, Md, Oct 9, 09.
Study & Training: Rinehart Sch Sculpture, Europ Traveling Scholarships, 31 & 33; Am Acad Rome; Acad Grand Chaumiere.
Work in Public Collections: Baltimore Mus Art, Md; Corcoran Gallery Art, Washington, D C; Walters Art Gallery, Baltimore; Portland Art Mus, Ore; Western Md Col, Westminster.
Commissions: Many portrait comns.
Exhibitions: Prix Rome Exhib, 36; Nat Art Wk, IBM Corp, Md, 41; Int Sculpture Show, Philadelphia, Pa, 49; Nat Inst Arts & Lett, 64; one-man show, Baltimore Mus Art, 66.
Teaching: Pvt instr sculpture, 39-; instr sculpture, Adult Educ, Baltimore City Col & Polytech Inst; head dept sculpture, Am Univ.
Awards: Prix de Rome, Am Acad Rome, 34; Nat Inst Arts & Lett grant, 64.
Bibliography: Alton Balder (auth), Six Maryland artists, Balboa Publ, 55; Man the maker, WMAR TV, Baltimore, 61; Theodore L Low (auth), The art of Reuben Kramer, Walters Art Gallery, 63.
Memberships: Artists Equity Asn(v pres, 68).
Mailing Address: 121 Mosher St, Baltimore, MD 21217.

KRAMOLC, THEODORE MARIA
Painter, Designer
Preferred Media: Oils, Pastels.
b Ljubljana, Yugoslavia, Mar 27, 22; Can citizen.
Study & Training: Univ Ljubljana, with Prof J Plečnik; Ont Col Art, dipl, 51; graphic art with N Hornyansky & painting with Jock McDonald.
Work in Public Collections: Nat Gallery Can, Ottawa; Art Gallery Ont, Toronto; Art Gallery Hamilton, Ont; Art Gallery Windsor, Ont; Nat Assembly Slovenia, Ljubljana.
Exhibitions: Exhib Mod Sacred Art, Buenos Aires, Arg, 54; Nat Exhib Prints, Libr of Cong, Washington, D C, 55; Can Nat Exhib, Sports Hall Fame, Toronto, 56 & 57; Biennial, Minneapolis, Minn, 58; Can Graphic Art Biennial, Nat Gallery Can, 62.
Bibliography: Pearl/McCarty (auth), articles, In: Toronto Globe & Mail, 52-57; M Marolt (auth), Slovenian painters in exile, SKA, Buenos Aires, 59; Robert Fulford (auth), articles, In: Toronto Daily Star, 61 & 62.
Memberships: Can Soc Graphic Art; Soc Can Painters, Etchers & Engravers.
Mailing Address: 40 Bucksburn Rd, Rexdale, Ont, Can.

KRAMRISCH, STELLA
Curator, Educator
b Vienna, Austria; U S citizen.
Study & Training: Univ Vienna, PhD, hon PhD.
Collections Arranged: Art of Nepal, Asia House, New York, N Y; Unknown India, Tribal and Ritual Art, Philadelphia Mus Art.
Teaching: Prof Indian art, Univ Calcutta, 23-50; lectr Indian art, Courtauld Inst, Univ London, 37-40; prof South Asian art, Univ Pa, 50-69; prof Indian art, New York Univ Inst Fine Arts, 64-
Positions: Ed, J of Indian Soc Oriental Art, 32-50; cur Indian & Himalayan art, Philadelphia Mus Art, 56-; ed, Artibus Asiae, 60-
Awards: Bollingen Found fel; Am Philos Soc; Rockefeller Fund grant.
Publications: Auth, Indian sculpture, 32; auth, The Hindu temple, 46; auth, Dravida & Kerala, 46; auth, The art of Nepal, 64; auth, Unknown India: ritual art in tribe & village, 68.
Mailing Address: R R 1, Box 111, Malvern, PA 19355.

KRANER, FLORIAN G
Painter, Educator
Preferred Media: Watercolors, Acrylics, Oils.
b Vienna, Austria, June 7, 08; U S citizen.
Study & Training: Kunstgewerbeschule Oesterreichischen Mus Kunst & Indust, Vienna, cert, 34.

Work in Public Collections: Watercolor painting, Norfolk Mus Permanent Collection; illus works, Libr Univ Minn.
Commissions: Pictorial murals & maps (with Richard Erdoes), Jamestown Festival, Richmond Mus Fine Arts, 57.
Exhibitions: Audubon Soc Ann, 52, 56 & 65, Am Watercolor Soc Ann, 67 & 68 & Allied Artists Nat, 68-71, Nat Acad Design Gallery; UN Travel Show, 61-62; 21 one-man shows watercolors, 65-66.
Teaching: Assoc prof art, City Col New York, 52-
Positions: Art dir, Erle Racy Advert Agency, Dallas, Tex, 35-36; art dir, Baron Colliers Street & Rwy Advert Agency, 36-37.
Awards: J J Newman Medal & First Award, 12th Ann Nat Soc Painters Casein, 66; first award for watercolor, Ringwood Manor Art Asn State Ann, 67; Digby Award For Watercolor, Nat Soc Painters & Sculptors Soc Ann, 67.
Bibliography: Article, In: Am Graphics Artist, 52.
Memberships: Nat Soc Painters Casein & Acrylic (pres, 64 & 65); Am Watercolor Soc; Nat Soc Painters & Sculptors; Allied Artists Am; Ringwood Manor Art Asn (pres, 66-70, dir, 70-).
Publications: Illusr, covers, Time, 42 & 43; illusr, Wonder tales of giants and dwarfs, 47 & Famous myths of the golden age, 49, Random; illusr, King Arthur and his knight of the round table, Dunlap & Grosset, 50.
Mailing Address: Dept of Art, City College of New York, 133rd & Convent Ave, New York, NY 10031.

KRASNER, LEE
Painter
b Brooklyn, N Y.
Study & Training: Woman's Art Sch, Cooper Union, 26-28; Nat Acad Design, 29-32; City Col New York, 33; also with Hans Hofmann, 38-40.
Work in Public Collections: Philadelphia Mus Art, Pa; Whitney Mus Am Art, New York, N Y; also in pvt collections.
Exhibitions: White House traveling exhib, organized by Smithsonian Inst, 67; Mus Mod Art, New York, 69; Marlborough Galleria Art, Rome, Italy, 71; one-man shows, Marlborough Gallery, New York, 69 & Gallery Reese Palley, San Francisco, Calif, 69.
Mailing Address: The Springs, East Hampton, NY 11937.

KRASNER, OSCAR
Art Dealer
Positions: Dir, Krasner Gallery, 54-
Specialty of Gallery: Contemporary American painting and sculpture.
Mailing Address: 1043 Madison Ave, New York, NY 10021.

KRATINA, K GEORGE
Sculptor
b New York, N Y, Feb 12, 10.
Study & Training: Syracuse Univ, BS & MS; Yale Univ, BFA.
Commissions: Heroic pioneer monument, Chattanooga, Tenn; relief, Bonaventure Univ, N Y; statues, St Paul Cathedral, Los Angeles; sanctuary sculptures for Fac Chapel, Fr Judge Sem, Va; steel sculpture, Adath Israel Temple, Merion, Pa; plus many other works from 39-
Teaching: Prof design, Sch Archit, Rensselaer Polytech Inst, 63-64; former prof, div art & archit, Cooper Union; lect, Art and Architecture, Collaboration in the Arts & New Horizons for Sculpture, sculpture seminars & forums, mus, univs, insts & others.
Awards: Prix de Rome, 38; Nat Prize for sculpture competition for Cath Welfare Bldg, Washington, D C, 40; Awards for collaborative excellence, Am Inst Architects, 41, 58 & 60.
Memberships: Fel Nat Sculpture Soc.
Mailing Address: R D 1, Old Chatham, NY 12136.

KRATZ, MILDRED SANDS
Painter
Preferred Media: Watercolors.
b Pa.
Work in Public Collections: Philadelphia Mus Fine Art, Pa; Wayne Art Ctr; Reading Pub Mus, Pa; Brandywine Gallery, West Chester, Pa.
Exhibitions: Pottstown Area Artists Guild; Philadelphia Art Alliance; Nat Forum Prof Artists; Nat League Am Pen Women; Am Watercolor Soc Exhibs, New York, 67-72; plus many others.
Awards: First prize, Motorola Nat; popular vote, Nat Exhib, Cape May; Gold Medal, Catharine Lorillard Wolfe Art Club, 72.
Bibliography: George Michael (auth), Contemporary corner, Nat Antiques Rev, 5/70; plus many others.
Memberships: Am Watercolor Soc; Philadelphia Art Alliance; Nat League Am Pen Women; Nat Forum Prof Artists; Chester Co Art Asn.
Specialty of Gallery: Nineteenth and twentieth century American art.
Publications: Illusr, cover, Nat Antiques Rev, 1/72.
Mailing Address: c/o Gallery Madison 90, 1248 Madison Ave, New York, NY 10028.

KRAUSE, LaVERNE ERICKSON
Painter, Printmaker
Preferred Media: Acrylics, Oils, Woodcuts.
b Portland, Ore, July 21, 24.
Study & Training: Univ Ore, BS, 46; Mus Art Sch, Portland, 52-58; Pratt Graphic Ctr, New York, summer 66.
Work in Public Collections: Seattle Art Mus; Portland Art Mus; Salt Lake Art Ctr, Utah; La State Univ Union, Baton Rouge; Bank Calif.
Exhibitions: Several Northwest Ann, Seattle Art Mus, 47-; every ann, Artists Ore, Portland Art Mus, 49-; six shows, Int Printmakers, Seattle Art Mus, 60-71; Northwest Art Today, Seattle World's Fair, 62; West Coast Graphics, Univ Ky, circulated by Smithsonian Inst, 71-72.
Teaching: Vis artist, Mt Angel Col, Ore, summer 65; from asst prof to assoc prof painting & printmaking, Univ Ore, 66-, faculty summer & res award, 71; vis assoc prof, La State Univ, Baton Rouge, summer 70.
Positions: Juror, Int Printmakers, Seattle Art Mus, 62; mem gov Planning Coun Arts, 65-67; juror, Ninth Ann Exhib Redwood Art Asn, 67.
Awards: Ford Found Purchase Prize for painting, 64; Painting Artists Ore Award, Portland Art Mus, 69.
Memberships: Artists Equity Asn (pres, Ore Chap, 54-55 & 67-68, nat pres, 69-70); Col Art Asn Am; Portland Art Asn (secy, 52, chmn exhibs, 54 & 61).
Publications: Illusr, Clouded sea (etchings), Press 22, 71.
Dealer: Fountain Gallery of Art, 115 S W Fourth Ave, Portland, OR 97204.
Mailing Address: 3295 W 16th Ave, Eugene, OR 97402.

KRAUSER, JOEL
Instructor, Printmaker
Preferred Media: Intaglio, Oils.
b Bronx, N Y, June 17, 36.
Study & Training: Harvard Col, BA, 57; Cooper Union Art Sch, 60-62; N Y Univ, MA, 65; Art Stud League New York, N Y, with Frank Reilly & Lennart Anderson; Pratt Graphics Ctr, 71-72.
Work in Public Collections: Washington & Jefferson Col, Washington, Pa.
Commissions: Oil, Spirit of WEVD, WEVD Radio Sta, New York, 71; intaglio ed for Artists Proof Mag, Pratt Graphics Ctr, New York, 72.
Exhibitions: American Realist Painters, Edelstein Gallery, Philadelphia, Pa, 71; Artists Pratt Graphic Ctr, 72; Washington & Jefferson Nat Painting Exhib, 72; Painters & Sculptors Soc N J Nat Exhib, Jersey City Mus, 72; Nat Arts Club Print & Drawing Show, New York, 72.
Collections Arranged: Washington & Jefferson Col Permanent Collection; one-man show for Bergen Community Mus, fall 72.
Teaching: Chmn dept art, Northern Valley Regional High Sch, Demarest, N J, 64-, instr life drawing, Adult Educ, Dist, 70-; instr calligraphy, Art Ctr Northern N J, June 71.
Awards: Nat Arts Club Award, 72; Bienfang Paper Co Award for Graphics, 72; Bradlow Prize for Graphics, Pratt Graphics Ctr, 72.
Memberships: Italic Soc; Painters & Sculptors Soc N J.
Publications: Auth, Learning to see through drawing, Sch Arts, 68; auth, Focusing on the group in art education, Design Mag, 70.
Mailing Address: 139 Jefferson Ave, Tenafly, NJ 07670.

KRAUSHAAR, ANTOINETTE M
Art Dealer
b New York, N Y.
Positions: Dir, Kraushaar Galleries.
Specialty of Gallery: Twentieth century American art.
Mailing Address: 1055 Madison Ave, New York, NY 10028.

KRAUSZ, LASZLO
Painter
Preferred Media: Ink, Oils.
b Pécs, Hungary, Apr 4, 03; U S citizen.
Study & Training: Univ Basel; Cooper Sch Art, Cleveland; Inst Art, Cleveland; Skowhegan Sch Painting; Pratt Inst; Western Reserve Univ, MA.
Work in Public Collections: Mus Art, Safed, Israel.
Commissions: 115 drawings, comn by Sam Miller, Cleveland, 61; portraits of mem Cleveland Orch, U S Info Agency Cult Exchange Prog, 64-65.
Exhibitions: One-man shows, Jewish Community Ctr, Cleveland, Severance Hall, Friedson Gallery, Art Inst Akron, Carnegie Hall, U S Embassy, London, Case Inst & Cooper Sch Art.
Teaching: Instr, Cooper Sch Art; spec lectr & head, Exp Art Studio, Case Inst Technol.
Awards: Award, Cleveland Chap Mil Order of World War I & II, 54.

Bibliography: Amerika, U S Info Agency, 66; R Breuer (auth), biog,
In: Delphian Quart, 67; Edith Carter (auth), Drawings for stereo,
Am Artists, 60 & 69.
Publications: Contribr, numerous articles in art mags.
Mailing Address: 1741 Middlehurst Rd, Cleveland, OH 44118.

KRAUTHEIMER, RICHARD
Educator
b Fuerth, Bavaria, July 6, 97; U S citizen.
Study & Training: Univ Munich; Univ Berlin; Univ Marburg; Halle
Wittenberg Univ, PhD, 23; Univ Louisville, DHL, 59; Frankfurt
Univ, hon Dr, 65, Rome Pontifical Inst Christian Archeol, 68.
Teaching: Privatdozent, Marburg Univ, 28-35; asst prof, Univ
Louisville, 35-37; prof hist art, Vassar Col, 37-52; prof hist
art, Inst Fine Arts, New York Univ, 52-65, Jayne Wrightsman
prof, 65-
Positions: Sr res analyst, OSS, 42-44.
Awards: Guggenheim fel, 50 & 63.
Memberships: Fel Am Jewish Acads Arts & Sci; Medieval Acad
Am; Brit Acad; Col Art Asn Am; Pontifical Acad Archeol;
plus others.
Publications: Auth, Corpus of the early Christian basilicas in Rome,
37; auth, Lorenzo Ghiberti, 56 & 70; auth, Early Christian and
Byzantine architecture, 65; auth, Collected essays, 69.
Mailing Address: 28 Via Gregoriana, Rome, Italy.

KREBS, ROCKNE
Sculptor
b Kansas City, Mo, Dec 24, 38.
Study & Training: Univ Kans, BFA.
Work in Public Collections: Corcoran Gallery Art, Washington, D C;
Nat Collection Fine Art, Washington, D C; New Orleans Mus Fine
Art, La; Witte Mus, San Antonio, Tex; Larry Aldrich Mus, Ridge-
field, Conn.
Commissions: Hemisfair '68 (transparent plastic sculpture), comn
by Gilbert Denman, San Antonio, 68; laser beams, Stern Line,
comn by Phillip Stern, Washington, D C, 70, Day Passage, Night
Passage, Albright-Knox Art Gallery, Buffalo, N Y, 71, Rite de
Passage, comn by Mrs Edgar B Stern, New Orleans, 71, & Light
is the City at Night, comn by Shepard Latter, New Orleans, 72.
Exhibitions: Ann Exhib Contemp Sculpture, Whitney Mus Am Art,
New York, N Y, 66 & 68; 69th Am Exhib, Art Inst Chicago, Ill, 70;
New Arts, U S Pavilion, Expo 70, Osaka, Japan, 70; Art and Technology, Los Angeles Co Mus Art, Los Angeles, Calif, 71; Works
for New Spaces, Walker Art Ctr, Minneapolis, Minn, 71.
Awards: Artist fel, Washington Gallery Mod Art Workshop, 68; art
fel, Nat Endowment Arts, 70; Guggenheim Found fel, 72.
Bibliography: Walter Hopps & Nina Felshin (auth), Three Washington
artists, Art Int, 5/70; James N Wood (auth), Rockne Krebs, Albright-Knox Art Gallery, 71; Jane Livingston (auth), Art and technology, Los Angeles Co Mus Art, 71.
Publications: Auth, Artists on their art, Art Int, 4/68.
Mailing Address: 3523 16th St N W, Washington, DC 20010.

KREDEL, FRITZ
Illustrator
Preferred Media: Watercolors, Inks.
b Michelstadt, Ger, Feb 8, 00; U S citizen.
Study & Training: Realgymnasium, Darmstadt, 18; Kunstgewerbe-
schule, Offenbach, 22.
Work in Public Collections: Libr of Cong, Washington, D C; New
York Pub Libr, N Y; Kerlan Collection, Univ Minn, Minneapolis.
Exhibitions: Hessischl Landesbibliothek, Darmstadt, Ger, 60;
Klingspor Mus, Offenbach, Ger, 61; Kunsthalle, Mannheim, Ger,
62; Goethe House, New York, 69.
Awards: Golden medal for bk illus, World Exhib, Paris, France, 38;
Goethe medallion, State of Hesse, 60; Johann Heinrich Merck
Ehrung, City of Darmstadt, 60.
Bibliography: Paul Standard (auth), Fritz Kredel, artist, woodcutter
& illustrator, Motif, 59 & Kredel, renaissance man among illus-
trators, Publications Weekly, 67.
Memberships: Grolier Club; Maximilian Gesellschaft, Hamburg;
Verein deutsche Buchkünstler, Offenbach.
Mailing Address: 180 Pinehurst Ave, New York, NY 10033.

KREEGER, DAVID LLOYD
Patron, Collector
b New York, N Y, Jan 4, 09.
Study & Training: Rutgers Univ, AB; Harvard Law Sch, LLB.
Memberships: Corcoran Gallery Art (trustee); Baltimore Mus Art
(trustee); Int Coun Mus Mod Art; Am Fedn Arts Art; Collectors
Club.
Art Interests: Donor of Kreeger Annual Purchase Awards at Cor-
coran Gallery Biennial and area shows, Kreeger Annual Art
Prize at American University and prizes in painting, sculpture
and art history at George Washington University.

Collections: Painting and sculptures, especially from mid-nineteenth
century to the contemporary period.
Mailing Address: 2401 Foxhall Rd N W, Washington, DC 20007.

KREINDLER, DORIS BARSKY
Painter, Lithographer
Preferred Media: Oil, Watercolor, Intaglio.
b Passaic, N J, Aug 12, 01.
Study & Training: N Y Sch Applied Design for Women; Nat Acad De-
sign; Pratt Graphic Ctr; with Hans Hofmann, Ivan Olinsky, Char-
les Hinton & Emil Carlsen.
Work in Public Collections: Mus Mod Art, New York, N Y; Metrop
Mus Art, New York; Nat Collection Art, Washington, D C; Brook-
lyn Mus, N Y; Boston Mus Fine Arts, Mass.
Exhibitions: Eight Brooklyn Artists with Eight Paintings, Brooklyn
Mus, 35; graphics, Smithsonian Inst, 35 & miniatures, 55; Nat
Asn Women Artists, 36-72; one-man exhibs, oils & graphics,
Silvermine Guild, 60; Butler Inst, Youngstown, Ohio, 63; plus
others in U S, Europe & India.
Teaching: Private lessons to gifted children, 48-54.
Positions: Juror of casein exhib, Nat Painters in Casein, 67 & 70;
graphics exhib, Audubon Soc, 70; oils exhib, Nat Asn Women Art-
ists, 71-73.
Awards: Award for oils, Brooklyn Soc Artists, 58 & Sarasota Soc
Artists, 60; award for Silhouette (engraving), Am Soc Contemp
Artists, 70.
Bibliography: Reproduction of prints in Prize Winning Prints, N Y
Graphics, 63; reproduction of paintings in Peters edition Music
Calendar, 64.
Memberships: Audubon Soc Artists; Am Soc Contemp Artists (bd dir,
36-); Nat Soc Painters in Casein (bd dir, 60-); Nat Asn Women
Artists; Soc Am Graphic Artists.
Art Interests: Support of all art organizations with donations of art
and money.
Collection: Contemporary artists' work in all media, sculpture,
painting & prints.
Publications: Cover for Yankee Mag, 61.
Dealer: Jacques Seligmann & Co, 5 E 57th St, New York, NY 10022.
Mailing Address: 75 Central Park W, New York, NY 10023.

KREITZER, DAVID MARTIN
Painter
Preferred Media: Oils.
b Ord, Nebr, Oct 23, 42.
Study & Training: Concordia Teachers Col, BS, 65; San Jose State
Col, MA, 67.
Work in Public Collections: Santa Barbara Mus, Calif; Joseph
Hirshhorn Found, Washington, D C.
Commissions: Woman's Place & U S Army Corps of Engineers,
covers for Atlantic Mag, 70; California and the War, cover for
Motorland Mag, 70.
Exhibitions: One-man show & American Art Since 1850, 68, Max-
well Gallery, San Francisco, Calif; Benedictine Art Awards, New
York, N Y, 69; Sixth Mobile Ann, Ala, 71; one-man show, Ankrum
Gallery, Los Angeles, Calif, 71.
Teaching: Instr painting, San Jose State Col, 68.
Awards: Ciba-Geigy Award, 71.
Dealers: Maxwell Galleries Ltd, 551 Sutter St, San Francisco, CA
94102; Ankrum Gallery, 657 N La Cienega, Los Angeles, CA
90069.
Mailing Address: 378 Scenic Rd, Fairfax, CA 94930.

KRENECK, LYNWOOD
Printmaker
b Kenedy, Tex, June 11, 36.
Study & Training: Univ Tex, BFA, 58, MFA, 65.
Work in Public Collections: Fine Arts Gallery San Diego, Calif;
Wichita Art Asn Galleries, Kans; Northern Ill Univ, De Kalb, Ill;
Springfield Art Mus, Mo; Bucknell Univ, Lewisburg, Pa.
Exhibitions: Seattle Print Int, Wash, 71; Second Nat Invitational
Show, Fine Arts Gallery, San Diego, 71; Invitational Graphics,
Minot, N Dak, 72; An Exhibition of Prints, Univ R I, 72; 20 Amer-
ican Printmakers Invitational, Oneonta, N Y, 72.
Teaching: Assoc prof printmaking, Tex Tech Univ, 65-
Awards: Purchase awards, 34th Nat Graphic Arts & Drawing Exhib,
Wichita Art Asn, 69, Third Ann Nat Prints & Drawing Competi-
tion, Northern Ill Univ, 70 & Fine Arts Gallery, San Diego, 71.
Memberships: Tex Printmakers; Tex Watercolor Soc (dir at large,
72-73); Boston Printmakers.
Mailing Address: 5224 14th St, Lubbock, TX 79416.

KRENTZIN, EARL
Sculptor, Silversmith
Preferred Media: Silver.
b Detroit, Mich, Dec 28, 29.
Study & Training: Wayne State Univ, BFA, 52; Cranbrook Acad Art,
MFA, 54; Royal Col Art, London, Fulbright fel, 57-58.

Work in Public Collections: Detroit Inst Art, Mich; Cranbrook Galleries, Bloomfield Hills, Mich; St Paul Art Ctr, Minn; Jewish Mus, New York, N Y; Sumner Found, N J.
Commissions: Enamel plaque, Gloria Dei Lutheran Church, Detroit, 54; Menorah, Temple Israel, Detroit, 63; metal sculpture, Westland Shopping Ctr, Detroit, 65; plus many private commissions of silver sculptures, 54-
Exhibitions: Mich Artists & Artists-Craftsmen's Exhib, Detroit Inst Art, 52-68; Fibre-Clay-Metal, St Paul Art Ctr, 57, 62 & 64; Mus Contemp Crafts, New York, 63 & 65; N J State Mus, Trenton, 70; one-man shows, Kennedy Galleries, New York, 68-71.
Teaching: Instr art, Univ Wis-Madison, 56-60; vis prof silversmithing, Univ Kans, 65-66; vis prof metalwork, Fla State Univ, 69.
Awards: Tiffany grant, 66; Nat Decorative Arts Exhib, Wichita Art Ctr, Kans, 66.
Publications: Auth, Centrifugal casting, Craft Horizons Mag, 11/54.
Dealer: Kennedy Galleries, 20 E 56th St, New York, NY 10022.
Mailing Address: 412 Hillcrest, Grosse Pointe Farms, MI 48236.

KRESS, MRS RUSH H
    Collector
Mailing Address: 1020 Fifth Ave, New York, NY 10028.

KREVOLIN, LEWIS
    Designer, Craftsman
b New Haven, Conn, June 21, 33.
Study & Training: Alfred Univ, BFA; also with Kja Franck, Finland.
Commissions: Bethlehem Steel Corp, Travelers Ins Co & pvt clients; terra cotta mural for Bethesda-Bradley Bldg, Md, 64.
Exhibitions: Young America Exhibit, 58 & 62; Cooper Union, 61; Silvermine Guild, 63; Craftsmen of the Northeast, 63 & The Craftsmen Designs, 64, circulated by Am Fedn Arts & Smithsonian Inst; Archit League New York, 65.
Teaching: Instr ceramics, Brooklyn Mus Sch Art & Dutchess Community Col.
Positions: Design consult, numerous mfrs, 55-; chief designer, Russell Wright Assocs, 59-61; co-owner, Krevolin & Constantine, designers.
Awards: Fulbright grant in glass & ceramics to Finland, 61.
Memberships: Am Crafts Coun; York State Craftsmen; Artist-Craftsmen New York.
Publications: Auth & illusr, Poland, Craft Horizons, 10/62; co-auth & illusr, Ceramics, 65.
Mailing Address: 61 W 74th St, New York, NY 10023.

KREZNAR, RICHARD J
    Painter, Sculptor
b Milwaukee, Wis, May 1, 40.
Study & Training: Univ Wis, BFA; Brooklyn Col, MFA; Inst Allende, Mex.
Work in Public Collections: Walker Art Ctr, Minneapolis, Minn; Milwaukee Art Ctr, Wis; Univ Wis, Madison; Wis Nat Bank, Milwaukee; Colgate Univ, Hamilton, N Y.
Exhibitions: Pa Acad Fine Arts, 63; Butler Inst Am Art, Youngstown, Ohio, 65; Milwaukee Art Ctr, 66; Southampton Col, New York, 65-66; Paley & Lowe Inc, New York, N Y, 72.
Teaching: Instr beginning art courses, Brooklyn Col, 64-70, lectr art, 71-
Awards: Prizes Milwaukee Art Ctr & Walker Art Ctr, 62 & 64; Wis Salon of Art, 63; Ford Found Purchase Award, 64.
Dealer: Paley & Lowe Inc, 59 Wooster St, New York, NY 10012.
Mailing Address: 104 Franklin St, New York, NY 10013.

KRIENSKY (MORRIS) (E)
    Painter, Sculptor
Preferred Media: Oils.
b Glasgow, Scotland, July 27, 17; U S citizen.
Study & Training: Boston Mus Fine Arts, 36-40, with Alma O Lebrecht; Art Stud League New York, N Y, 48-49; Escuela Tech Mex, 50-51.
Work in Public Collections: Pushkin Mus, Moscow, U S S R; Alfred Khouri Mem Collection, Norfolk Mus, Va; Lincoln Ellsworth Collection; also many pvt collections in U S, China, U S S R & Mex.
Exhibitions: Am Watercolor Soc; Nat Acad Design; Inst Mex-Norte Am Relac Cult; one-man shows, Knoedler Gallery, White House, Art Inst Chicago, Frick Art Libr, Univ Conn (15 yr retrospective) & many others.
Awards: First prize, Inst Mex-Norte Am Relac Cult, 50.
Bibliography: Many mag articles & rev.
Publications: Auth, The way is . . . , book of drawings, painting & poems, Gibson, 73.
Mailing Address: 463 West St, New York, NY 10014.

KRIGSTEIN, BERNARD
    Painter, Illustrator
Preferred Media: Oils, Watercolors, Pastels.
b New York, N Y, Mar 22, 19.
Exhibitions: Am Watercolor Soc Ann, 65, 68 & 72, traveling exhib,

68; Painters & Sculptors Soc N J, 69; Anchorage Mus, Alaska, 69; Knickerbocker Artists Ann, 70 & 72; Audubon Artists Ann, 72; plus many other group & one-man shows.
Teaching: Instr painting & drawing, High Sch Art & Design, New York, 62-70; asst prof fine art, painting & drawing, Fashion Inst Technol, State Univ N Y, 70-71; instr painting & drawing, High Sch Art & Design, 71-
Awards: First prize for graphic arts, Brooklyn Soc Artists 33rd Ann; Jersey City Mus Award, Painters & Sculptors Soc N J 31st Ann, 72.
Bibliography: Bhob Stewart (auth) & John Benson (auth), Talk with B Krigstein, privately pub, 63.
Memberships: Painters & Sculptors Soc N J (treas, 72).
Publications: Illusr, Manchurian candidate, McGraw, Various fables from various places, Capricorn-Putnam, Buccaneers & pirates of our coasts, Random, Boy's Life Mag & Harpers Mag; plus many other bks & mag.
Dealer: Alexander Gallery, 117 E 39th St, New York, NY 10016.
Mailing Address: 140-21 Burden Crescent, Jamaica, NY 11435.

KRIMS, LESLIE ROBERT
    Painter, Photographer
b New York, N Y, Aug 16, 43.
Study & Training: Cooper Union, New York, BFA; Pratt Inst, Brooklyn, N Y, MFA.
Work in Public Collections: Mus Mod Art, New York; Nat Gallery Can, Ottawa; Bibliot Nat, Paris, France; George Eastman House, Rochester, N Y; Minneapolis Inst Art, Minn.
Exhibitions: One-man exhibs, George Eastman House, 69 & 71 & Fictions, Galerie Prisma IV, Lund, Sweden, 70; Photographs of Women, Mus Mod Art, 71; two-man show, Witkin Gallery, New York, 72; 60's Continuum, 72.
Teaching: Asst prof art, State Univ N Y Col Buffalo, 69-
Awards: State Univ N Y Res Found grant & grant-in-aid, 70 & 71, Nat Endowment Arts fel & N Y State Coun Arts grant, 71.
Bibliography: Leslie Krims, Photo Image, Japan, 70; Leslie Krims, Camera, Switz, 71.
Memberships: Soc Photog Educ; Patteran Artists.
Publications: Auth & illusr, Eight photographs: Leslie Krims, Doubleday, 70; auth & illusr, The incredible case of the stack o wheat murders, 72; auth & illusr, The little people of America 1971, 72; auth & illusr, The deerslayers, 72; auth & illusr, Making chicken soup, 72.
Dealer: Witkin Gallery, 243 E 60th St, New York, NY 10022.
Mailing Address: 298 Fargo Ave, Buffalo, NY 14213.

KRODY, BARRON J
    Designer, Instructor
b Cincinnati, Ohio, Feb 7, 36.
Study & Training: Art Acad Cincinnati, cert; also design with Noel Martin.
Work in Public Collections: Cincinnati Art Mus; Mus Mod Art, New York, N Y; Carl Solway Gallery.
Commissions: Urban Walls: Cincinnati & Fed Reserve Bank, Carl Solway Gallery; Model Cities, Bd Educ & Model Cities Prog, Cincinnati.
Exhibitions: Art Dirs Club Ann Exhib, Cincinnati, 62-71; Communication Through Typography, Harvard Univ, 64; Laser Art Exhib, Cincinnati Art Mus, 69; Urban Walls: Cincinnati Traveling Exhib Silk Screen Prints, 71-72; Communication Graphics 1971/72, Am Inst Graphic Arts, 72.
Teaching: Instr graphic design, Mt St Joseph Col, Cincinnati, 64-65; instr graphic design, Art Acad Cincinnati, 66-, actg dean, 72.
Awards: Cert excellence, Art Dirs Club, Cincinnati, 67 & Am Inst Graphic Design, 71-72.
Memberships: Contemp Arts Ctr.
Mailing Address: 222 E Central Pkwy, Cincinnati, OH 45202.

KROLL, LEON
    Painter, Lithographer
b New York, N Y, Dec 6, 84.
Study & Training: Art Stud League New York, with John Henry Twachtman; Nat Acad Design; Acad Julian, Paris, France, with Jean Paul Laurens.
Work in Public Collections: Metrop Mus Art & Mus Mod Art, New York; Art Inst Chicago, Ill; Corcoran Gallery Art, Washington, D C; San Francisco Mus Art, Calif; plus many others.
Commissions: Murals, Justice Bldg, Washington, D C; war mem, Worcester, Mass; mosaic dome, U S Mil Cemetery, Omaha Beach, France; murals, Johns Hopkins Univ Auditorium.
Exhibitions: Whitney Mus Am Art, New York; Detroit Art Inst, Mich; Cleveland Mus Art, Ohio; Baltimore Mus Art, Md; City Mus of St Louis, Mo; plus many others.
Teaching: Nat Acad Design & Art Stud League New York, 11-; Md Inst, 19-21; Art Inst Chicago, 24-25; Pa Acad Fine Arts, 29-30.
Positions: Hon pres, U S Comn, Int Asn Plastic Arts, 54-

Awards: Chevalier, Legion of Honor, France; Benjamin Altman Award for landscape painting, 65; many other nat & int awards.
Bibliography: Van Deren Coke (auth), Taos and Santa Fe: the artistic environment, Univ N Mex Press, 63; William H Gerdts, Jr (auth), Painting and sculpture in New Jersey, Van Nostrand, 64.
Memberships: Nat Inst Arts & Lett; Am Acad Arts & Lett (dir & chmn art comt); life mem Nat Arts Club; Nat Acad Design.
Publications: Auth, Leon Kroll (catalogue), Cleveland Print Club, 45; auth, Leon Kroll (monogr), Am Artists Group, 46.
Mailing Address: 15 W 67th St, New York, NY 10023.

KRUEGER, JACK
Sculptor
b Appleton, Wis, Aug 3, 41.
Exhibitions: Hemisfair, San Antonio, Tex, 68; Moore Col Art, Philadelphia, Pa, 68; Wash Univ, St Louis, Mo, 69; Krannert Art Mus, Univ Ill, 69; one-man show, Leo Castelli Gallery 68 & Leo Castelli Warehouse Exhib, 69; plus others.
Mailing Address: 310 Spring St, New York, NY 10013.

KRUG, HARRY ELNO
Printmaker, Educator
b Oshkosh, Wis, Aug 20, 30.
Study & Training: Univ Wis-Milwaukee, BFA; Univ Wis-Madison, MS; Nat Art Acad, Stuttgart, Ger, with Erich Monch.
Work in Public Collections: Libr Cong, Washington, D C; Nelson-Atkins Art Gallery, Kansas City, Mo; U S Info Agency; Springfield Art Mus, Mo; Ohio Univ Galleries.
Exhibitions: 22nd Am Color Print Exhib, Am Color Print Soc, 63; 6th Nat Print Exhib, Silvermine Guild Artists, New Canaan, Conn, 67; 19th Ann Exhib, Boston Mus Fine Arts, Mass, 68; Teacher-Artist Today, State Univ N Y, Oswego, 69; Hopman, Krug, Ecker, Galerie Feursee, Stuttgart, 70.
Teaching: Assoc prof printmaking, Kans State Col, 58-
Positions: Crafts dir, spec serv, Baumholder, Ger, 62-64; crafts dir, spec serv, Stuttgart, 68-71.
Awards: Mid-Am Ann Purchase Award, Nelson-Atkins Art Mus, Kansas City, 60; Sonia Watter Award, Am Color Print Soc, Pa, 62; prize for graphics, Jersey City Mus, N J, 68.
Memberships: Boston Printmakers; Philadelphia Print Club.
Mailing Address: Rte 3, Box 182, Pittsburg, KS 66762.

KRUGER, LOUISE
Sculptor
Preferred Media: Wood, Bronze.
b Los Angeles, Calif.
Study & Training: Scripps Col, Calif; Art Stud League New York; Opoku Dwumfuor, Kumasi, Ghana.
Work in Public Collections: Mus Mod Art, New York, N Y; New York Libr Print Collection; Mod Mus, Sao Paulo; Brooklyn Mus, N Y.
Exhibitions: Metrop Mus, New York; Whitney Mus Am Art, New York; Mus Mod Art, New York; Art Inst Chicago, Ill; Kunsthaus, Zurich.
Dealer: Robert Schoelkopf Gallery, 825 Madison Ave, New York, NY 10021.
Mailing Address: 30 E Second St, New York, NY 10003.

KRUKOWSKI, LUCIAN
Painter, Educator
b Brooklyn, N Y, Nov 22, 29.
Study & Training: Brooklyn Col, BA, 52; Yale Univ, BFA, 55; Pratt Inst, MS, 58.
Work in Public Collections: St Louis Art Mus, Mo.
Commissions: Outdoor wall painting, Nat Endowment Arts, St Louis, 72.
Exhibitions: Staempfli Gallery, New York, N Y, 58 & 62; Cee-je Gallery, New York, 67; Loretto Hilton Gallery, St Louis, 70.
Teaching: Prof art, Pratt Inst, 55-69, chmn dept fine arts, 67-69; prof art & dean Sch Fine Arts, Wash Univ, 69-
Memberships: Nat Asn Schs Art; Col Art Asn Am.
Mailing Address: 24 Washington Terr, St Louis, MO 63112.

KRUPP, LOUIS
Painter, Designer
Preferred Media: Oils, Watercolors, Charcoal.
b Miesenbach, W Ger, Nov 26, '88; U S citizen.
Study & Training: Chicago Art Inst, Ill; Art Stud League New York, with Wellington J Reynolds, Karl A Buehr, Charles Schroeder, Elmer Forsberg & George D Bridgman.
Work in Public Collections: Inst Zacatecano Bellas Artes, Mex.
Exhibitions: El Paso Sun Carnival Exhib, 61; El Paso Mus Art, 65, 68 & 71; Am Artists Prof League Grand Nat, 71.
Awards: Hon mention, Chicago Art Inst, 16; first in oil, El Paso Mus Art, 68; first pl, El Paso Art Asn, 69.
Memberships: Am Artists Prof League; El Paso Art Mus Asn; El Paso Art Asn; Nat Soc Arts & Lett; Tex Fine Arts Soc.
Mailing Address: 2609 Silver Ave, El Paso, TX 79930.

KRUSHENICK, NICHOLAS
Painter, Lecturer
b New York, N Y, May 31, 29.
Study & Training: Art Stud League New York, 48-50; Hans Hofmann Sch, New York, 50-51.
Work in Public Collections: Metrop Mus Art, New York; Mus Mod Art, New York; Los Angeles Co Mus Art; Folkwang Mus, Essen, W Ger; Stedelijk Mus, Amsterdam, Holland.
Commissions: Large painting, State of N Y, Albany, 69.
Exhibitions: Post Painterly Abstraction, Los Angeles, Toronto & Minn, 64; Systemic Painting, Guggenheim Mus, New York, 66; New Forms & Shapes of Color, Amsterdam & Basel, 66; 1960 Mus Mod Art, 66; Documenta IV, Kassel, W Ger, 68.
Teaching: Vis artist, Univ Wis, 69; critic art, Yale Univ, 69-70; artist, Cornell Univ, 70.
Awards: Tamarind Lithography grant, 65; Guggenheim Found fel, 67.
Dealer: Pace Gallery, 32 E 57th St, New York, NY 10022.
Mailing Address: 61 Studio Rd, Stamford, CT 06903.

KRUSHENICK, JOHN
Painter, Educator
b New York, N Y, Mar 18, 27.
Study & Training: City Col New York; Art Stud League New York, with Johnson, Hale, Browne & Vytlacil; Hans Hofmann Sch Fine Arts, New York, with Hans Hofmann.
Work in Public Collections: Mus Mod Art Permanent Collection, New York; Bank St Col Educ, New York.
Exhibitions: Mus Mod Art Tokyo, Hiroshima & Kyoto, 59; Homage to Camus, Esther Stuttman, 60; Martha Jackson Gallery; Green Camp, Cooper Union, 71; New York Civil Liberties Show, Leo Castelli-Downtown, 72.
Teaching: Adj instr studio crafts & procedures, Cooper Union, 68-69; assoc prof mus & gallery procedures & dir Fine Arts Gallery, Univ Wis-Milwaukee, 72.
Positions: Owner-dir, House of Brata Frames & Brata Gallery Coop, 57-64; framing consult, Dain/Schiff, 65-67; dir-cur, Dorsky Gallery, 70-71.
Bibliography: Fred McDarrah (auth), Artists world; John Canady (auth), Embattled critic.
Publications: Contribr, Voice of America, 59; co-auth, Dorsky Gallery statement, Arts, 4/71.
Mailing Address: Dept of Fine Art, University of Wisconsin-Milwaukee, Milwaukee, WI 53201.

KRUSKAMP, JANET ELAINE
Painter
Preferred Media: Oils, Egg Tempera.
b Grants Pass, Ore, Dec 10, 34.
Study & Training: Chouinard Art Inst, Los Angeles, scholarships; also with Viona Ann Kendall, N Hollywood, Calif.
Work in Public Collections: Rosicrucian Egyptian Mus, San Jose, Calif; Triton Mus Art, Santa Clara, Calif.
Commissions: Private comns only.
Exhibitions: Soc Western Artists Ann, M H De Young Mus, San Francisco, 71; Artistes U S A, Salon Prix Paris, France, 71; Frye Mus Art, Seattle, Wash, 71; Am Artists Prof League Grand Nat, 72; Soc Western Artists Invitational, Rosicrucian Egyptian Mus, 72; plus others.
Teaching: Private instr oils, 66-
Awards: Best of Show, Santa Clara Co Hist Landmarks Exhib, 69; Soc Western Artists Ann first pl oils, 70; trustees' award & Andy Trophy, Grand Galleria Art Competition, Seattle, 72; plus others.
Bibliography: Marcia Wells (auth), Art is all around you (film), Campbell Sch Dist, 71; Gerald A Bailey (auth), Gallery Page, Rosicrucian Digest, 71; Bernard Gauthron (auth), Salon Prix de Paris and artistes U S A, La Rev Mod, 71.
Memberships: Fel Am Artists Prof League; Soc Western Artists; Los Gatos Art Asn (pres, 69).
Dealers: Gallery de New Almaden in Los Gatos, 110 N Santa Cruz Ave, Los Gatos, CA 95030; Raymond Phillips Gallery, 2517 Fairmount, Dallas, TX 75201.
Mailing Address: 1627 Hyde Dr, Los Gatos, CA 95030.

KUBLER, GEORGE ALEXANDER
Art Historian, Writer
b Los Angeles, Calif, July 26, 12.
Study & Training: Yale Univ, BA, 34, MA, 36, PhD, 40.
Teaching: Prof hist art, Yale Univ, 38-
Research: Pre-Columbian and colonial Latin American art; art of Spain and Portugal.
Publications: Auth, Religious architecture of New Mexico, 40; auth, Mexican architecture of the sixteenth century, 48; co-auth, Art and architecture of Spain and Portugal, 59; auth, Art and architecture of ancient America, 62; auth, The shape of time, 62.
Mailing Address: 56 High St, New Haven, CT 06520.

KUBLY, DONALD R
Designer, Art Administrator
b Los Angeles, Calif, Nov 14, 17.
Study & Training: Pasadena Jr Col, AA; Art Ctr Col Design, BPA.
Exhibitions: N Y Art Dirs Ann Exhib, 56 & 71.
Positions: Sr art dir, N W Ayer & Son, Advert, 49-63; dir, Art Ctr Col Design, Los Angeles, 63-, pres, 65-
Awards: Gold medal, N Y Art Dirs Ann Exhib, 56 & 71.
Memberships: Am Inst Graphic Arts (dir, 72); Los Angeles Art Asn; Soc Typographic Arts.
Publications: Contribr, Graphics & Creative Arts, 56-71.
Mailing Address: 5353 W Third St, Los Angeles, CA 90020.

KUEHN, EDMUND KARL
Curator, Lecturer
b Columbus, Ohio, Aug 18, 16.
Study & Training: Columbus Art Sch, cert, 38; Art Stud League New York, cert, 39.
Work in Public Collections: Columbus Gallery Fine Arts.
Collections Arranged: Paintings from Columbus Homes, 63; Jean Crotti in Retrospect, 65; The Gordian Knot, 67; Works by David Blythe, 68.
Teaching: Asst prof drawing & painting, Ohio State Univ, 46-47; assoc prof drawing & painting, Columbus Col Art & Design, 52-62.
Positions: Cur, Columbus Gallery of Fine Arts, 39-43, asst dir, 62-67, cur collections, 67-
Memberships: Columbus Art League; Am Asn Mus.
Mailing Address: 480 E Broad St, Columbus, OH 43215.

KUEHN, FRANCES
Painter
Preferred Media: Acrylics.
b New York, N Y, Feb 16, 43.
Study & Training: Douglass Col, Rutgers Univ, BA, Rutgers Univ, New Brunswick, MFA.
Work in Public Collections: J B Speed Art Mus, Louisville, Ky.
Commissions: Portrait for private collection, 72.
Exhibitions: Whitney Ann, New York, 72; Phases of New Realism, Lowe Art Mus, Coral Gables, Fla, 72.
Dealer: Max Hutchinson Gallery, 127 Greene St, New York, NY 10012.
Mailing Address: R D 4, Box 550, Princeton, NJ 08540.

KUEKES, EDWARD D
Cartoonist
b Pittsburgh, Pa, Feb 2, 01.
Study & Training: Baldwin-Wallace Col, hon LHD, 57; Cleveland Inst Art; Chicago Acad Fine Arts.
Work in Public Collections: Five thousand original cartoons in collection at Syracuse Univ.
Teaching: Lect, So you can't draw a straight line, either, art groups nationally.
Positions: Cartoonist, Cleveland Plain Dealer, 22-49; chief ed cartoonist, 49-66, cartoonist emer, 66-; cartoonist, Metro Newspapers, Inc, Cleveland, 68-
Awards: Pulitzer Prize, cartoon div, 53; three first prize awards, Freedom Found; plus many others.
Memberships: Asn Am Ed Cartoonists; Nat Cartoonist Soc.
Publications: Auth, Funny fables, 38; co-auth, Alice in wonderland & Knurl the gnome (cartoon features), United Features Syndicate; creator, All in the Week, Along the Road, Cartoonists Looks at The News & other featured cartoons.
Mailing Address: 1280 Medfield Dr, Rocky River, OH 44116.

KUH, KATHARINE
Art Critic, Art Consultant
b Saint Louis, Mo, July 15, 04.
Study & Training: Vassar Col, BA; Univ Chicago, MA(art hist); New York Univ.
Positions: Owner & dir, Katharine Kuh Gallery, Chicago, 36-42; cur mod art, Art Inst Chicago, 42-59; art ed, Sat Rev, 59-71; art ed, World Mag, 72-; art consult, First Nat Bank Chicago, 68-
Publications: Auth, Art has many faces, Harper & Row, 51; auth, Léger, Univ Ill Press, 58; auth, The artist's voice, Harper & Row, 61; auth, Break-up: the core of modern art, N Y Graphic, 65; auth, The open eye, Harper & Row, 70.
Mailing Address: 140 E 83rd St, New York, NY 10028.

KUHN, BRENDA
Art Administrator
b New York, N Y, June 13, 11.
Study & Training: Friends Sem, New York; also art estate mgt with Walt & Vera Kuhn.
Positions: Co-mgr, Kuhn Estate, 49-56, mgr, 56-66; mgr, Collection of Brenda Kuhn, 66-; pres, Kuhn Mem Corp, 68-

Memberships: Arch Am Art; assoc, Copley Soc Boston; Am Asn Mus; Am Fedn Arts.
Mailing Address: Kuhnhouse, Cape Neddick Park, Cape Neddick, ME 03902.

KUHN, MARYLOU
Educator, Painter
Preferred Media: Encaustic.
b South Bend, Ind, Oct 18, 23.
Study & Training: Layton Sch Art; Univ Wis; Art Inst Chicago; Ohio State Univ, univ fel, 53, BSc & PhD; Teachers Col, Columbia Univ, MA.
Exhibitions: LeMoyne Art Found, 65-
Teaching: Prof art educ, Fla State Univ, 51-; guest lectr art educ, Inst Educ, Univ London, 66-67.
Positions: Ed, Fla Art News, 60-62; ed, Southeastern Arts Bull, 62-64; mem ed bd, Studies in Art Educ, Nat Art Educ Asn, 62-66, regional ed, Art Educ J, 64-66, co-ed Studies in Art Educ, 70-
Memberships: Int Soc Educ Through Art (del, 57-); Nat Art Educ Asn (nat comts, 60-); Adult Educ Asn U S A; Assoc Coun Arts; Am Fedn Arts.
Research: Community & adult art education, curriculum & teacher education in art, philosophy & theory.
Publications: Auth, Art education in a world context, Southeastern Arts Bull, 63; ed & auth, Continuing art education for adults, 12/65, auth, Means & meaning in art education, 3/65, The relevance of art education to the future, 6/67 & INSEA XVIII, Prague, Czechoslovakia, 68, Art Educ; auth, Standards & criteria, Adult & Extension Art Educ, 66.
Dealer: LeMoyne Art Foundation, 125 N Gadsden St, Tallahassee, FL 32303.
Mailing Address: 1403 Betton Rd, Tallahassee, FL 32303.

KULICKE, ROBERT M
Painter, Craftsman
b Philadelphia, Pa, Mar 9, 24.
Study & Training: Philadelphia Mus Sch Art; Tyler Sch Fine Arts, Temple Univ; Atelier Fernand Leger, 46-50.
Work in Public Collections: Philadelphia Mus Art, Pa.
Exhibitions: Silvermine Guild, 64; Art Inst Chicago, Ill; Dayton Art Inst, Ohio; 100 Years of American Realism, Am Fedn Arts, 65; Whitney Mus Am Art, New York, N Y, 69; plus others.
Teaching: Instr, Univ Calif, 64 & 70; Kulicke Cloisoone Workshop, New York, 64-
Awards: Int Design Award, Am Inst Interior Designers, 68.
Mailing Address: Orchard Crest Farm, R D 2, Box 840, Newton, NJ 07860.

KUNIE
Painter, Photographer
b Nagoya, Japan.
Study & Training: Art Inst Chicago, BFA, 67; Sch Visual Arts.
Work in Public Collections: Rose Mus, Brandeis Univ, Mass; Va Mus Fine Arts; Ryerson Inst, Toronto, Can; George Eastman House, Rochester, N Y; Larry Aldrich Mus, Ridgefield, Conn.
Exhibitions: 1972 Ann Contemp Am Painting, Whitney Mus Am Art, New York, N Y, 72.
Bibliography: J Scully (auth), CKO, Modern Photography, 2/68; M Brown (auth), Ten hour color print, U S Camera, 11/68.
Dealer: Warren Benedek Gallery, 380 W Broadway, New York, NY 10012.
Mailing Address: 168 W 86th St, New York, NY 10024.

KUNTZ, ROGER EDWARD
Painter, Sculptor
Preferred Media: Oils, Bronze.
b San Antonio, Tex, Jan 4, 26.
Study & Training: Pomona Col, BA; Claremont Grad Sch, MFA, 50; Guggenheim fel, 56-57.
Work in Public Collections: Denver Art Mus; Scripps Col Collection; Los Angeles Co Mus; Am Acad Design; Univ Ill.
Commissions: Three bronze figures, Gibraltar Savings, San Marino, Calif, 66; plus many comns for portraits in Southern Calif.
Exhibitions: Am Acad Design, 52; Denver Art Mus, 52 & 53; Los Angeles Co Mus Ann, 53-55 & 57; Third Biennial, São Paulo, Brazil, 55; Carnegie Int, Pittsburgh, 55.
Awards: Carnegie & Purchase Prizes, Am Acad Design, 52; Purchase Awards, Denver Art Mus, 52 & 53; Purchase Prizes & Awards, Los Angeles Co Mus, 53-55 & 57.
Mailing Address: 483 Jasmine St, Laguna Beach, CA 92651.

KUP, KARL
Art Historian
b Haarlem, Holland, May 7, 03.
Study & Training: Univ Munich, with Wolfflin; Univ Berlin, with Goldschmidt; also with Diehl, Paris; Lakeside Press Sch Printing, Chicago.

Teaching: Lect, Book Illustration, Illuminated Manuscripts & Books of the Orient; instr graphic arts, Princeton Univ Libr.
Positions: Contrib ed, Juvenile Dept, Oxford Univ Press, 28-34; cur Spencer Collection, New York Pub Libr, 34-68, cur prints, 41-68, dir exhibs, 47-55, chief art & archit div, 56-65; trustee, Corning Mus Glass, Print Coun Am, Pratt Inst Print Ctr; fel Pierpont Morgan Libr; contrib ed, Publishers Weekly, 41-52 & Am Artist, 41-49.
Memberships: Bibliog Soc Am; Grolier Club; China Inst; Asia Soc.
Publications: Auth, The council of Constance, 1414-1418; auth, The girdle book; co-auth, Books and printing; auth, The Christmas story in medieval manuscripts; contribr, New York Pub Libr Bull, Am Artist, Artist's Proof, Libr J, Publishers Weekly & other publ.
Mailing Address: 136 E 36th St, New York, NY 10016.

KUPFERMAN, LAWRENCE
Painter
Preferred Media: Acrylics, Tempera.
b Boston, Mass, Mar 25, 09.
Study & Training: Sch Mus Fine Arts, Boston, 29-31; Mass Col Art, Boston, BScEd, 35.
Work in Public Collections: Boston Mus Fine Arts; Mus Mod Art, New York, N Y; Whitney Mus Am Art, New York; Wadsworth Atheneum, Hartford, Conn.
Commissions: Murals, Am Export Lines, S S Constitution, 48 & S S Independence, 48.
Exhibitions: Whitney Mus Am Art Sculpture, Painting & Watercolor Ann, 57; 62nd Ann Art Inst Chicago, 57; Contemp Am Painting & Sculpture Biennial, Univ Ill, 61; 22nd Int Watercolor Biennial Brooklyn Mus, 63; 160th Watercolors Ann, Pa Acad Fine Arts, Philadelphia, 65.
Teaching: Prof painting, Mass Col Art, 41-68.
Awards: Saratoga Springs Victorian Purchase Prize, Assoc Am Artists, 47; Purchase prize for Tempest, Krannert Art Mus Biennial, 53; first prize for painting, Odysseus, R I Arts Festival, Providence, 61.
Bibliography: John I H Baur (auth), Revolution and tradition in American art, Harvard Univ Press, 51; Bartlett H Hayes (auth), The naked truth and personal vision, Addison Gallery Am Art, 55; Nathaniel Pousette-Dart (auth), American painting today, Hastings House, 56.
Memberships: Assoc Nat Acad Design.
Dealer: Horizon Gallery, 43 Glendale Rd, Newton Centre, MA 02159; Horizon West, 10345 W Olympic Blvd, Los Angeles, CA 90064.
Mailing Address: 38 Devon Rd, Newton Centre, MA 02159.

KUPFERMAN, MURRAY
Painter, Sculptor
Preferred Media: Casein.
b Brooklyn, N Y.
Work in Public Collections: St Vincent Col, Latrobe, Pa; Brooklyn Mus; New Rochelle Col, N Y; Smithsonian Inst, Washington, D C; Univ Conn; plus others.
Commissions: Underseas mural, Caravelle Hotel, St Croix, V I.
Exhibitions: Smithsonian Inst, 72; Nat Soc Painters Casein, 72; Am Watercolor Soc, 72; Allied Artists Am, 72; Wash Co Mus Fine Arts, Hagerstown, Md, 72; plus many others.
Teaching: Instr art appreciation & painting, Brooklyn Tech, 27-65; instr painting, Educ Alliance, 65-70.
Awards: Numerous awards.
Bibliography: Many articles & rev.
Memberships: Am Watercolor Soc; Allied Artists Am; Nat Soc Painters Casein; League Present Day Artists; Maine Art Asn.
Dealers: Grand Central Art Galleries, 40 Vanderbilt Ave, New York, NY 10017; Center Art Gallery, 49 W 57th St, New York, NY 10036.
Mailing Address: 1270 E 19th St, Brooklyn, NY 11230.

KURDIAN, HAROUTIUN HARRY
Writer, Collector
b Aug 9, 02; U S citizen.
Collection: Armenian manuscripts; Irish silver; pre-Columbian art.
Publications: Auth, Armenian Keutahia pottery, 43, History of rug weaving in Armenia, 47, Armenian silver smithing, 49, Armenian wood carving IX-XIV centuries, 66 & Armenian brocades until XVII century, 68.
Mailing Address: 2924 E Douglas, Wichita, KS 67214.

KURELEK, WILLIAM
Painter
b Alta, 27.
Study & Training: Univ Man, BA, 49; Inst Allende, San Miguel, Mex.
Work in Public Collections: Mus Mod Art, New York, N Y; Montreal Mus Fine Arts; Philadelphia Mus Art; Nat Gallery Can, Ottawa; Art Gallery Ont, Toronto; plus other pub & private collections.
Exhibitions: Can Art, J B Speed Art Mus, Louisville, Ky, 62; Re-

ligious Art, Regis Col, 62 & 66; Invitation Show, Rochester Mem Art Gallery, New York, N Y, 63; Biennial Can Painting, Nat Gallery Can, 63, 65 & 68; Images of the Saints, Montreal Mus Fine Arts, 65; plus many others.
Awards: Sr Can Coun fel, 69.
Bibliography: Kurelek, Nat Film Bd, 67.
Publications: Illusr, The Passion according to St Matthew, 160 tempera paintings reproduced in slides.
Mailing Address: 175 Balsam Ave, Toronto, Ont, Can.

KURHAJEC, JOSEPH A
Sculptor
b Racine, Wis, Oct 13, 38.
Study & Training: Univ Wis, BS, 60, MFA, 62.
Work in Public Collections: New Sch Soc Res, New York, N Y; Español Mus Contemp Art, Madrid, Spain; Mus Mod Art, New York; Chicago Art Inst, Ill; Walker Art Ctr, Minneapolis, Minn.
Commissions: Bronze cone, comn by Allan Stone, Purchase, N Y, 71; bronze sculpture, Norman Shaifer, Brooklyn Heights, N Y, 71.
Exhibitions: Am Fedn Art Traveling Exhib, 64; Sculpture Ann, 64 & Young America, 65, Whitney Mus Am Art, New York; Español Mus Contemp Art, 69; Ten Independents, Guggenheim Mus, New York, 72.
Teaching: Asst prof, Cornell Univ, 65-66; asst prof, Newark Sch Indust & Fine Art, 67-69; asst prof, Univ Wis-Stout, 71-
Dealer: Allan Stone Gallery, 48 E 86th St, New York, NY 10028, Bienville Gallery, New Orleans, LA 70130.
Mailing Address: 37 Crosby St, New York, NY 10013.

KUSHNER, DOROTHY BROWDY
Painter, Instructor
b Kansas City, Mo.
Study & Training: Kans City Teachers Col, BS, 37; Columbia Univ, MA, 38; Art Stud League New York; Art Inst Chicago; Kans City Art Inst.
Work in Public Collections: Pasadena Art Mus; Univ Ill; Va Mus Fine Arts; Camino Grove Sch, Arcadia.
Exhibitions: Libr Cong, 60; Boston Mus Fine Arts, 65; Calif State Fair, 69; Nat Acad Design, 71; Calif Nat Watercolor Soc, 72.
Teaching: Instr art, Kans City Pub Schs; instr art, Grover Cleveland High Sch, New York, N Y, 40-46; instr art, Pasadena City Col, 69-
Awards: Awards, Laguna Beach Art Asn, 69, Calif Nat Watercolor Soc, 70 & Pasadena Soc Artists, 70.
Memberships: Am Color Print Soc; Calif Nat Watercolor Soc; Los Angeles Art Asn; Laguna Beach Art Asn; Pasadena Soc Artists.
Mailing Address: 3121 Monroe Way, Costa Mesa, CA 92626.

KUSHNER-WEINER, ANITA MAY
Painter, Art Administrator
Preferred Media: Watercolors.
b Philadelphia, Pa, Nov 30, 35.
Study & Training: Univ Pa, BA; Temple Univ, MA; New Sch Social Res, with Egas & Poussette d'Arte; Pa Acad Fine Arts.
Work in Public Collections: Mus Mod Art, Haifa, Israel; B'nai Brith Mus, Washington, D C; Univ Amsterdam, Holland; Picadilly Galleries, London, Eng; Grabar Galleries, Philadelphia.
Exhibitions: Pa Acad Fine Arts Biannual Drawing & Watercolor, 67; New Talents, Whitney Mus Am Art, New York, 68; Okla Mus Traveling Art Show, 68; one-man show, B'nai Brith Int Mus, 71; Anita Weiner, Debra Sprude-Dual Show, Philadelphia Art Alliance, 71.
Teaching: Art supvr elem educ, Pennsauken Bd Educ, N J, 63-65; instr, drawing, T-Square Atelier Architects, 63-68; instr voc art, Philadelphia Bd Educ, 65-71; instr studio art & art hist, Oakton Community Col, 72-
Positions: Demonstr, Print Club Philadelphia, 66-68; art dir, Jewish Community Ctr, Skokie, Ill, 71-72.
Awards: First prize graphics, 68 & first print painting, 69, Philadelphia Civic Mus; critics choice list, New York Times, 67.
Bibliography: Contemporary art in America, La Rev Mod, 67; Sara Wilkinson (auth), An artist in a Tel-Aviv Show, Jerusalem Post Mag, Israel, 69.
Memberships: Artists Equity Asn; Ill Comt Arts; organizing mem Artists Mkt Chicago; Drawing Soc New York; Print Club Philadelphia.
Dealers: Piccadilly Gallery, 16A Cork St, London W1, England; Wanamakers Artists Gallery, 137 Chestnut, Philadelphia, PA 19106.
Mailing Address: c/o Maass, 320 E Gowan St, Philadelphia, PA 19119.

KUSSOY, BERNICE (HELEN)
Sculptor
b Brooklyn, N Y, 34.
Study & Training: Art Stud League New York; Cooper Union; Western Reserve Univ, BS; Cleveland Inst Art, MFA.

Work in Public Collections: Butler Inst Am Art, Youngstown, Ohio;
Kalamazoo Art Inst, Mich; Univ Calif, Santa Barbara; Mex-Am
Inst Cult Relations, Mexico City; Bundy Art Gallery, Waitsfield,
Vt; plus other pub & pvt collections.
Commissions: Brancusi Marble Co, Los Angeles, Calif; United Res
Serv, Burlingame, Calif; Temple Beth Israel, Pomona, Calif.
Exhibitions: Laguna Beach Art Asn, 64; Otis Art Inst, Los Angeles,
64; Pioneer Mus & Haggin Galleries, Stockton, Calif, 64; Mexico
City, 65; Judah L Magnes Jewish Mus of the West, Berkeley,
Calif, 68; plus others.
Awards: Prizes, Butler Inst Am Art, 58 & Cincinnati Mus Asn, 58.
Mailing Address: 3169 Washington St, San Francisco, CA 94115.

KUTKA, ANNE (MRS DAVID McCOSH)
Painter
Preferred Media: Oils.
b Danbury, Conn.
Study & Training: Art Stud League New York, with Kenneth Hays
Miller, Kimon Nicolaides & Eugene Fitsch.
Work in Public Collections: Portland Art Mus, Ore; Am Red Cross,
Washington, D C.
Exhibitions: New York World's Fair, N Y, 39; Seattle Art Mus, 45;
Exhib of Watercolors, Drawings & Prints, Metrop Mus Art, New
York, 52; Portland Art Mus, 70; Pac Northwest Art Ann, Eugene,
Ore, 72.
Teaching: Instr painting & drawing, M I Kerns Art Ctr, Eugene, 60-
Awards: Tiffany fel, 30; G R D Traveling Scholar, 34.
Memberships: Art Stud League New York; Portland Art Mus; Mus
Art, Eugene.
Mailing Address: 1870 Fairmount Blvd, Eugene, OR 97403.

KUWAYAMA, TADAAKI
Painter
Preferred Media: Acrylic.
b Nagoya, Japan, Mar 4, 32.
Study & Training: Tokyo Univ Art, BFA, 56.
Work in Public Collections: Albright-Knox Art Gallery, Buffalo, N Y;
Worcester Art Mus, Mass; Wadsworth Atheneum, Hartford, Conn;
Larry Aldrich Mus, Ridgefield, Conn; Herron Art Mus, Indianap-
olis, Ind.
Exhibitions: Carnegie International, Pittsburgh, Pa, 61-67; Formalist
Show, Washington Gallery Mod Art, Washington, D C, 63; Sys-
temic Show, Solomon R Guggenheim Mus, New York, N Y, 66;
New Forms and Shapes of Color, Sredelijk Museum, Amsterdam,
Netherlands, 67; Plus by Minus, Today's Half-Century, Albright-
Knox Art Gallery, 68.
Awards: Nat Coun Arts Grant, 69.
Dealer: Richard Bellamy, 1078 Madison Ave, New York, NY 10028.
Mailing Address: 725 Ave of the Americas, New York, NY 10010.

KYRIAKOS, ALEKO
Sculptor
Preferred Media: Bronze.
b Berlin, Ger, Dec 9, 22; U S citizen.
Study & Training: Sch Fine Arts, Polytechnium, Athens, Greece.
Work in Public Collections: Philadelphia Mus Art, Pa; Allentown Art
Mus, Pa; Kutztown State Col, Pa; St Francis De Sales Col, Allen-
town; Wellesley Col, Mass.
Commissions: Evangelist, plastic relief, Albright Col, Reading, Pa,
63; Plylax, bronze figure, 66 & bronze double relief, 69, Franklin
& Marshall Col, Lancaster, Pa; St John, bronze figure, St John
Lutheran Church, Allentown, 66; Sappho, bronze figure, Swarth-
more Col, Pa, 67.
Exhibitions: One-man shows, Allentown Art Mus, 63 & 70; Pa Acad
Fine Arts, 66.
Mailing Address: R D 1, Alburtis, PA 18011.

L

LABINO, DOMINICK
Sculptor, Writer
Preferred Media: Glass.
b Fairmount City, Pa, Dec 4, 10.
Study & Training: Carnegie Inst Technol, 29-32; Toledo Mus Art
Sch Design, 47-49; Bowling Green State Univ, hon D F A, 70.
Work in Public Collections: Toledo Mus Art, Ohio; Corning Mus
Glass, N Y; Smithsonian Inst, Washington, D C; Pilkington Mus
Glass, St Helens, Eng; Leerdam Mus Glass, Holland.
Commissions: Hot-cast panels, Vitrana, entrance to Glass Gallery,
Toledo Mus Art, 69, Columbus Gallery Fine Arts, 71 & Riverside
Hosp, Toledo, 72.

Exhibitions: Toledo Glass Nat & Traveling Exhib, 66, 68 & 70; 20th-
24th Ceramic & Sculpture Show, Butler Inst Am Art, Youngstown,
Ohio, 68-72; Dominick Labino—a retrospective exhibition, Corn-
ing Mus Glass, 69; Objects U S A, Johnson Wax Co Collection,
Mus Contemp Crafts, New York, 69; one-man exhib, Columbus
Gallery Fine Arts, Ohio, 70 & 71.
Teaching: Instr hot glass, Toledo Mus Art, 66 & 67; vis prof hot
glass, Bowling Green State Univ, 72-73.
Positions: Hon cur glass, Toledo Mus Art, 68-; pres, Early Am
Glass Club Toledo, 69-70.
Awards: First award for glass, Toledo Mus Art, 66, 68 & 70; Ohio
Arts Coun Award for glass, 71; Toledo Glass & Ceramic Award,
Am Ceramic Soc, 72.
Memberships: Am Crafts Coun; World Crafts Coun; Toledo Fedn Art
Socs (v pres, 51 & 52; pres, 53 & 54); Craft Club Toledo (pres,
52 & 53).
Research: Technical and creative aspects of glass-making in earli-
est times; technique of Eighteenth Dynasty Egyptian hollow glass
vessels.
Publications: Auth, The Egyptian sand-core vessels, Corning J
Glass Studies, 66; auth, Visual art in glass, Wm C Brown Publ,
68.
Mailing Address: Box 154, Grand Rapids, OH 43522.

LABRIE, ROSE
Painter, Writer
Preferred Media: Oils.
b Boston, Mass, Aug 31, 16.
Study & Training: Univ N H, 44-45; with Robert Grant & Carroll
Towle, 54-56; Univ Wis, 58-59.
Work in Public Collections: Strawbery Banke Colonial Preserv Mus,
Portsmouth, N H; Richard Morton Collection, Portsmouth; Univ
N H Colonial Heritage Film Ser, Durham; John F Barker Collec-
tion, Cambridge, Eng.
Commissions: Mural, USS Thresher, comn by George Bergeron,
New Market, N H; Earl of Halifax (signpost), comn by Richard
Morton.
Exhibitions: Copley Soc, Boston, Mass; Crest Gallery; one-man
shows, Shapely Towne House Gallery, Portsmouth & ann, John
Sedgley Homestead, York, Maine.
Awards: First prize for mem painting of USS Thresher; awards
from var local art groups.
Bibliography: Article, In: Nat Antiques Rev, 7/72.
Memberships: Copley Soc; York Art Asn; S Street Seaport Mus;
Armed Forces Writers League; Piscataqua Pens.
Art Interests: Contemporary primitive paintings.
Publications: Illusr, Story of pemaguid light & History of Cape Ned-
dick light station; contribr, Yankee, N H Profiles, 58-68 & Nat
Antiques Rev, 71; plus many other articles & illus.
Dealers: Crest Galleries, 40 S Main St, Yardley, PA 19067; Copley
Society Gallery, 158 Newbury St, Boston, MA 02116.
Mailing Address: 127 Middle Rd, Portsmouth, NH 03801.

LACHMAN, MR & MRS CHARLES R
Collectors
Mailing Address: 645 Madison Ave, New York, NY 10022.

LACK, RICHARD FREDERICK
Painter, Instructor
Preferred Media: Oils.
b Minneapolis, Minn, Mar 26, 28.
Study & Training: Minneapolis Sch Art, Minn; R H Ives Gammell
Studios, Boston, Mass.
Work in Public Collections: Maryhill Mus Fine Arts, Wash; Eliza-
beth T Greenshields Mem Found Collection, Montreal, P Q.
Commissions: Six portraits of Joseph P Kennedy, Sr, comn by Am-
bassador Kennedy & the Kennedy Found, New York, N Y.
Exhibitions: Allied Artists Am, 53; Boston Arts Festival, 53 & 54;
Nat Acad Design Ann, 55; Twin City Biennial, Minneapolis Inst
Arts, 62; five Am Artists Prof League Nat, 67-72.
Teaching: Dir & instr painting & drawing, Atelier Lack, Minne-
apolis, 69-
Awards: Popular prize, Ogunquit Art Ctr, Maine, 58 & 64; first
prize, Copley Soc, Boston, 62; gold medal, Am Artists Prof
League, 67,
Bibliography: D Jardine (auth), Richard Lack's atelier system of
training painters, Am Artist Mag, 6/71.
Memberships: Am Artists Prof League.
Mailing Address: 5827 Louis Ave, Minnetonka, MN 55343.

LACROIX, RICHARD
Painter, Sculptor
Preferred Media: Acrylics.
b Montreal, P Q, July 14, 39.
Study & Training: Montreal Inst Graphic Arts, dipl; Paris Atelier
17; Montreal Sch Fine Art, cert pedagog.

Work in Public Collections: Montreal Mus Fine Arts; Nat Gallery Can; Cabinet Estampes, Paris; Mus Mod Art, New York, N Y; Victoria & Albert Mus, London.
Commissions: Several print albums, Montreal Graphic Guild, 66-72; kinetic sculptures, Can Pavilion & Youth Pavilion, Expo 67, 67 & Montreal Int Airport, 68; murals, Montreal Sch Bd, 71.
Exhibitions: Color Prints Am, 70; Second Int Bienal Engraving, Paris, 70; Quebec Pavilion, Osaka, Japan, 70; Fourth Am Bienal Engraving, Chile, 70; Second Brit Int Print Bienal, 70.
Teaching: Instr etching, Montreal Sch Fine Art, 60-61; vis instr art hist, Univ Que, 69-70.
Positions: Co-founder, Fusion Arts.
Awards: Can Graphic Asn Prize, 64; prize, Int Biennal, Lugano, Switz, 64; prize for painting, Montreal Hadassah, 65.
Bibliography: Lacroix, 65 & S Raphael (auth), Richard Lacroix, 71, Vie Arts; Deroussan (auth), Richard Lacroix, Lidec, 66.
Memberships: Soc Prof Artists Quebec; Graphic Guild (pres, 66-); Atelier Libre Recherches Graphiques (dir, 64-).
Mailing Address: 4677 Rue St Denis, Montreal 176, P Q, Can.

LADERMAN, GABRIEL
Painter, Educator
b Brooklyn, N Y, Dec 26, 29.
Study & Training: Brooklyn Mus Sch; Brooklyn Col, BA; Hans Hofmann Sch Fine Arts; Cornell Univ, MFA; Atelier 17, fel, 52.
Exhibitions: Vassar Col, 68; Milwaukee Art Ctr, 69; State Univ N Y New Paltz & traveling, 69; Ind Univ, 69; Corcoran Gallery of Art, 69; plus others.
Teaching: Grad lectr, Yale Univ; Lect, univs, art schs, cols in N Y, Mass, Iowa, Ind, Ohio & other states; asst, Cornell Univ, 55-57; asst prof, State Univ N Y New Paltz, 57-59; asst prof, Pratt Inst, 59-69; asst prof art, Queens Col, 69-
Awards: Tiffany Found Award, 59; Fulbright fel to Italy, 62-63; Yaddo fels, 60, 61 & 65.
Dealer: Schoelkopf Gallery, 825 Madison Ave, New York, NY 10021.
Mailing Address: 760 West End Ave, New York, NY 10025.

LAESSIG, ROBERT
Painter, Illustrator
Preferred Media: Watercolors.
b N J, 20.
Study & Training: Art Stud League New York; also study in Ger.
Work in Public Collections: Cleveland Mus Fine Arts, Ohio; Butler Inst Am Art, Ohio; Norfolk Mus, Va; Springfield Inst Fine Arts, Ohio; Akron Art Inst, Ohio.
Commissions: Official White House Christmas card, comn by President & Mrs Johnson, 64-68.
Exhibitions: Am Watercolor Soc Exhibs, New York, N Y, 60-72; Audubon Artists, New York, 60-72; Nat Acad Design, New York, 60-72; Philadelphia Watercolor Soc, 64-70; Allied Artists, New York, 70-72.
Memberships: Nat Acad Design; Am Watercolor Soc.
Mailing Address: c/o Gallery Madison 90, 1248 Madison Ave, New York, NY 10028.

LAFAYE, NELL MURRAY
Painter, Educator
Preferred Media: Oils.
b Columbia, S C, Nov 9, 37.
Study & Training: Sullins Col, with Alvin Sella; Cranbrook Acad Art, BFA, 58, with Fred Mitchell, MFA, 59, with Zolton Sepeshy & Marianne Strengall.
Work in Public Collections: S C State Art Collection; Univ S C.
Exhibitions: Spring Mills Traveling Art Show, Lancaster, S C, 61-69; Mint Mus Crafts Exhib, Charlotte, N C, 65 & Painting Exhib, 66 & 67; Mainstreams Int, Marietta, Ohio, 68 & 69; Gardens Art Festival, Pine Mountain, Ga, 72.
Teaching: Asst prof art, Univ S C, 68-
Awards: First prize, Spring Mills, 68.
Bibliography: Jack Morris (auth), Contemporary South Carolina artists, S C Tricentennial Comn, 70.
Memberships: S C Art Educ Asn (pres, 67-69); Nat Art Educ Asn (rep to nat assembly, 67-70); Am Craftsmen Coun; S C Artist Guild.
Mailing Address: 2630 Stratford Rd, Columbia, SC 29204.

LAFON, DEE J
Painter, Sculptor
Preferred Media: Oils, Mixed Media.
b Ogden, Utah, Apr 23, 29.
Study & Training: Weber State Col; Univ Utah, BFA, 60, MFA, 62; also with Francis de Erdley, Phil Paradise & Marguerite Wildenhain.
Work in Public Collections: Utah State Fine Art Collection, Salt Lake City; Okla Art Ctr, Oklahoma City; Philbrook Art Mus, Tulsa, Okla; Univ Okla, Norman; Dillard Collection, Univ N C, Greensboro.

Commissions: Wood sculpture, Univ Okla, 72; copper fountain, E Cent State Col, 72.
Exhibitions: Watercolor U S A, Springfield, Mo, 68; Nat Oil Painting Exhib, Jackson, Miss, 68; Am Drawing Bienniale, Norfolk, Va, 69; Int Miniature Prints Show, Pratt Graphic Ctr, New York, 70; Midwest Bienniale, Omaha, Nebr, 72.
Teaching: Instr ceramics & drawing, Weber State Col, 62-64; prof painting & drawing, E Cent State Col, 64-
Positions: Dir, Contemp Art Found, Okla, 68-; consult, Okla Art Ctr, 70-71.
Awards: Eight State Exhib Purchase Award, 70; hon mention, Midwest Biennale, 72; Tulsa Regional Painting & Drawing Award, 72.
Memberships: Okla Designer Craftsman.
Dealer: Sam Stone, 5800 S Lewis, Tulsa, OK 74101.
Mailing Address: 2027 Woodland Dr, Ada, OK 74820.

LaFRENIERE, ISABEL MARCOTTE
Painter
b Providence, R I.
Study & Training: R I Sch Design, grad; R I Univ; also private study in Paris, France.
Exhibitions: Knickerbocker Artists, New York, N Y, 70; Catharine Lorillard Wolfe Art Club, New York, 70; Nat Art League, New York, 70; Springfield Acad Artists, Mass, 70; Jordan Marsh Ann, Boston, Mass, 70.
Awards: Figure Award, Rockport Art Asn, Mass, 70; Grumbacher Award, Nat Art League, 70; Best in Show, Medford, Mass, 70.
Memberships: Nat Art League; Springifeld Acad Artists; Rockport Art Asn; N Shore Art Asn.
Mailing Address: 5B Smith St Ct, Rockport, MA 01966.

LAGING, DUARD WALTER
Educator
b Spring Valley, Minn, Nov 7, 06.
Study & Training: Univ Minn, BA, 37, MA, 45; Minneapolis Art Inst, 31; Univ Iowa, 45.
Teaching: Instr, Univ Minn, 40-45; asst prof art hist, Mich State Univ, 45-47; mem art fac, Univ Nebr, 47-, prof art hist, 54-72, chmn dept art, 62-72, emer prof, 72-
Positions: Dir, Univ Nebr Art Galleries, 51-56; art consult, Fed Land Bank, Saint Paul; chmn, Vreeland awards comt; mem consult comt, Sheldon Gallery; mem bd, Community Arts Coun.
Memberships: Nebr Art Asn; Minn Art Asn; Col Art Asn Am; Lincoln Artists Guild; Am Asn Univ Prof.
Publications: Auth, The methods used in making the bronze doors of Augsburg Cathedral, Art Bull, 67; plus other articles in art periodicals.
Mailing Address: 1140 S 20th St, Lincoln, NE 68502.

LAGORIO, IRENE R
Sculptor, Painter
b Oakland, Calif, May 2, 21.
Study & Training: Calif Col Arts & Crafts, Oakland, 38-39; Univ Calif, Berkeley, AB & MA, 42; Columbia Univ, 45.
Work in Public Collections: San Francisco Mus Art Collection, Calif State Libr Collection, Sacramento; Va Mus Fine Arts, Richmond; La State Fine Arts Comn, Baton Rouge; Libr of Cong, Washington, D C; plus others.
Commissions: Mosaic mural, S S Pres Roosevelt, Am Pres Lines, 61; jewel painted mural, Lloyd Ctr, Portland, Ore, 60 & metal sculpture mural, Seaside, Ore, U S Bancarp, 64; mosaic mural, Soc Nat Bank, Cleveland, Ohio, 69; mosaic mural design, Episcopal Condominium, Los Gatos, Calif, 70.
Exhibitions: Third Int Biennial, Sao Paulo, Brazil; Metrop Mus Art Watercolor Exhib, 53; Seventh Monterey Peninsula Competitive, Monterey Mus Art, Calif, 70; Am Color Print Soc Ann, Philadelphia, Pa, 72; U S Info Serv Traveling Color Print Exhib Throughout Europe, 72.
Teaching: Spec lectr, Univ Calif Exten Courses, 60-
Positions: Cur educ dept, Calif Palace Legion of Honor Mus, 50, dir, Achenbach Found Graphic Arts, 51-55.
Awards: Grant for graphic project, Chapelbrook Found, Boston, Mass, 69; best in show, Monterey Peninsula Mus Art Seventh Competitive, 71.
Bibliography: E Loran (auth), The San Francisco scene, Art News, 53; G Dorfles (auth), Modern painters in U S A, Domus Mag, 54; Exposition de San Francisco, La Rev Mod, 60.
Memberships: Am Color Print Soc; Carmel Art Asn (pres, 72-); Ars Assoc Found (dir, 61-).
Publications: Illusr, This open zoo-a bestiary, Salamander, 71.
Mailing Address: First & Mission Sts, Box 153, Carmel, CA 93921

LAGUNES, MARIA (MARIA LAGUNES HERNANDEZ)
Sculptor, Painter
b Veracruz, Mex.
Study & Training: Univ Femenina, Veracruz, 51-53; sculpture with Francisco Zuniga & Tomas Chavez Morado & wood & linoleum

engraving with Arturo Garcia Bustos, 58-61; metal engraving with Guillermo Silva Santamaria, 60-63; with Yukio Fukasawa & Isamu Ishikawa, 63; painting & drawing with Antonio Rodriguez Luna, 61-65; Fr scholar to study sculpture, archit & urban integration with Andre Bloc, Paris, France, 66.
Work in Public Collections: Gen Motors Mex Collection.
Exhibitions: Mexico City, Mex, 61; Buenos Aires, Arg, 63; Conception Univ, Chile, 64; Mod Art Mus III & IV Biennial, Mexico City, 67-69; Solar, Fine Arts Palace, Mex, 68; one-woman shows, Misrachi Art Gallery, Mexico City, 69 & 72; plus many other group & one-woman shows.
Teaching: Instr sculpture, Univ State Mex, 69-
Awards: Second prize of the press for Ciudad No 6; third prize, Salon Pintores Veracruz.
Bibliography: Article, In: Tex Quart; article, In: Image of Mex II.
Memberships: Salon Plastica Mex; Inst Nac Bellas Artes.
Dealer: Galeria de Arte Misrachi, Genova No 20, Mexico 6, DF, Mex.
Mailing Address: Felix Cuevas No 318-35, Mexico 12, DF, Mex.

LAHEY, RICHARD (FRANCIS)
Painter, Lecturer
Preferred Media: Oils, Watercolors.
b Jersey City, N J, June 23, 93.
Study & Training: Art Stud League New York, with Robert Henri, Max Weber & John Sloan, 13-17; also traveled & studied abroad, summers 20-27.
Work in Public Collections: Carlotta also watercolors & etchings, Corcoran Gallery Art, Washington, D C; Head of Joan, Compote with Fruit & Main Inlet, Whitney Mus Am Art, New York, N Y; Pop Hart, Mus Mod Art, New York; Fourteenth of July, Detroit Inst Art, Mich; Pont Neuf, Brooklyn Mus Art, N Y; plus many other mus.
Commissions: Over the Alleghenies to the West (mural), Brownsville Post Off, Pa; mural (with Carlotta Gonzales), Am Battle Monuments Comn, Honolulu, Hawaii; portraits for U S Treas Dept, U S Supreme Ct & Elks Club Washington, D C; drawing for Alexander Woollcott, New York Times, 25; Seeing N Y (drawing with verse by John Farrar), Sun Mag New York World.
Exhibitions: Metrop Mus Art, New York; Art Inst Chicago, Ill; Carnegie Int, Pittsburgh, Pa; one-man shows, Corcoran Gallery Art, Washington, D C; Richmond Mus Art, Va; plus many other group & one-man shows.
Teaching: Instr painting & drawing, Art Stud League New York, 22-34; prof fine arts, Goucher Col, 35-60; from prin to emer painting & drawing, Corcoran Sch Art, 35-64; prof painting & drawing, Ga Univ, 68.
Positions: Artist, camouflage corps, U S Navy, Washington, D C & overseas, 18 mos; lectr art subjects, Lee Keedick Bur, 32-72.
Awards: William H Tuthill Prize, Art Inst Chicago, 25; Beck Gold Medal for portraiture, Pa Acad Fine Arts, 29.
Bibliography: Richard Lahey, portrait instructor, Art Stud League, New York, 33; Herman W Williams, Jr (auth), Richard Lahey, a retrospective exhibition, Corcoran Gallery Art, 4/63.
Memberships: Hon mem Art Stud League New York; Century Asn; Am Soc Painters, Sculptors & Gravers; Am Fine Arts Soc.
Dealer: Franz Bader Inc, 2124 Pennsylvania Ave N W, Washington, DC 20037.
Mailing Address: 9530 Clark Cross Rd, Vienna, VA 22180.

LA HOTAN, ROBERT L
Painter
Preferred Media: Oils, Watercolors.
b Cleveland, Ohio, 1927.
Study & Training: Columbia Univ, Brevoort-Eickmeyer fel, 50-53.
Work in Public Collections: Lehigh Univ, Bethlehem, Pa; Northern Trust Co, Kansas City, Mo.
Exhibitions: Corcoran Biennial, 56; Dallas Mus Contemp Art, 58; Rochester Mem Art Gallery, 66; one-man show, Lehigh Univ, 69; Kraushaar Galleries, 72.
Awards: Fulbright fel to Ger, 53-55.
Dealer: Kraushaar Galleries, 1055 Madison Ave, New York, NY 10028.
Mailing Address: 865 West End Ave, New York, NY 10025.

LAI, WAIHANG
Painter, Instructor
Preferred Media: Watercolors.
b Hong Kong, Jan 7, 39; U S citizen.
Study & Training: Chinese Univ Hong Kong, BA, 64; Claremont Grad Sch & Univ Ctr, MA, 67.
Exhibitions: Watercolor U S A, Springfield Art Mus, Mo, 69; The Best in the West, Edward-Dean Mus, Calif, 70; Philadelphia Watercolor Club Exhib, Philadelphia Civic Ctr Mus, 72; one-man shows, Phoenix Art Mus, Ariz, 67 & Kauai Mus, Hawaii, 71.

Teaching: Vis prof art, Ariz State Univ, Tempe, summer 67; asst prof art, Maunaolu Col, Maui, Hawaii, 68-70; instr art, Kauai Community Col, 70-
Awards: Hon mention, Hong Kong Art Exhib, Univ Hong Kong, 59-61; first award for watercolor, First Ann Apring Festival Fine Arts, Rowland Heights, Calif, 68; first place for watercolor, Maui Co Creative Arts Exhib, Hawaii, 68.
Memberships: Am Watercolor Soc; Philadelphia Watercolor Club.
Publications: Auth, The Chinese landscape paintings of Waihang Lai, 66; auth, The watercolors of Waihang Lai, 67.
Mailing Address: P O Box 363, Lihue, HI 96766.

LAINE, LENORE
Painter
Preferred Media: Acrylics, Oils, Watercolors.
b Philadelphia, Pa.
Study & Training: Philadelphia Col Art.
Work in Public Collections: Nat Mus Mod Art, Tokyo, Japan; Miami Mus Mod Art, Fla; Finch Col, New York, NY; Ohio State Univ; Phoenix Art Mus, Ariz; plus others.
Exhibitions: Eight Americans in Paris, Am Libr, Paris; Americans in France, Mus Lyons, St Etienne; Optical Art, Am Fedn Art Traveling Show.
Dealer: East Hampton Gallery, 450 W 27th St, 10D, New York, NY 10001.
Mailing Address: 116 Central Park S, New York, NY 10019.

LALIBERTE, NORMAN
Painter
b Worcester, Mass, Nov 24, 25.
Study & Training: Mus Fine Arts, Montreal; Ill Inst Technol, BS, 51, MS, 54; Cranbrook Acad Arts, 52.
Work in Public Collections: In numerous pvt collections.
Exhibitions: Tucson Art Ctr, Ariz, 67; Int Festival Arts, New York, N Y, 67; LaMonte Gallery, Tampa, Fla, 67; Mint Mus Art, Charlotte, N C, 67; Newton Col, 67; plus many others.
Teaching: Instr, Kansas City Art Inst, 60-61; artist-in-residence, St Marys Col, Notre Dame, 60-62; lectr, Webster Col, 64; assoc prof, R I Sch Design, 65; artist-in-residence, Newton Col, 67-
Positions: Design consult, Vatican Pavilion, New York World's Fair, 63; design consult, Sol Productions, 63 & 66.
Publications: Auth, The history of the cross, 60, Banners and hangings, 66, Wooden images, 66, Painting with crayon, 67 & Silhouettes, 67; plus articles.
Mailing Address: Newton College of the Sacred Heart, 885 Center St, Newton, MA 02159.

LAM, JENNETT (BRINSMADE)
Painter, Educator
Preferred Media: Oils.
b Ansonia, Conn, May 2, 11.
Study & Training: Yale Univ, BFA & MFA, with Josef Albers.
Work in Public Collections: Mus Mod Art, New York, N Y; Whitney Mus Am Art, New York; Brooklyn Mus, N Y; Philadelphia Mus Fine Arts, Pa; Yale Art Gallery.
Exhibitions: Carnegie Inst, Pittsburg, 64; Painting Ann, 65 & Women in Permanent Collection, 71, Whitney Mus Am Art; U S A Group 67, U S Embassy, Paris & Mus France, 67; Selections From Chase Manhattan Collection, Finch Col Mus, 71.
Teaching: Prof art, Univ Bridgeport, 72-
Awards: MacDowell Colony fel, 60 & 61.
Bibliography: Hubert Damisch (auth), Les chaises de Jennett Lam aux couleurs de l'absence, Cahiers Art Ann XXe siecle, 6/65; Patrick Waldberg (auth), Jennett Lam, Quadrum XIX, 65.
Dealer: Cordier & Eekstrom, 980 Madison Ave, New York, NY 10021; Le Point Cardinal, 3 Rue Jacob, Paris 6, France.
Mailing Address: 2340 North Ave, Bridgeport, CT 06604.

LA MALFA, JAMES THOMAS
Sculptor, Educator
Preferred Media: Iron.
b Milwaukee, Wis, Nov 30, 37.
Study & Training: Univ Wis-Madison, BS, 60, MS, 61, MFA, 62; sculpture with Leo Steppat; printmaking with Alfred Sessler.
Work in Public Collections: Memphis Acad Art; Univ Wis-La Crosse.
Commissions: Large relief sculpture, Phillips Hall, Univ Wis-Eau Claire, 66; sacred sculpture, Wittenberg Univ, Springfield, Ohio, 68.
Exhibitions: The States 1st Ann, Neville Pub Mus, Green Bay, Wis, 65; Springfield Art Ctr, Ohio, 67; Print & Drawing Nat, Minot State Teachers Col, N D, 70; 29th Northeastern Wis Art Ann, Green Bay, 70; 23rd Ohio Ceramic & Sculpture Ann, Butler Inst Art, Youngstown, Ohio, 71.

Teaching: Instr visual arts, Univ Wis-Eau Claire, 63-66; instr visual arts, Wittenberg Univ, 66-69; asst prof visual arts, Univ Wis-Green Bay, 69-72; assoc prof visual arts, Univ Wis Ctr-Marinette, 72-
Bibliography: J J (auth), rev, In: Art News, 4/64; Pierre Mornand (auth), Expositions diverses review, La Rev Mod, 11/71.
Memberships: Wis Acad Sci, Arts & Lett.
Mailing Address: Univ of Wisconsin Center-Marinette, Bay Shore Rd, Marinette, WI 54143.

LAMANTIA, JAMES
Painter, Collector
Preferred Media: Oils.
b New Orleans, La, Sept 22, 23.
Study & Training: Tulane Univ La, BSArch, 43; Harvard Univ Grad Sch Design, BArch, 47; Skowhegan Sch, 47.
Work in Public Collections: New Orleans Mus Fine Art.
Awards: Prix de Rome, 48-49; Fulbright fel, 49-50.
Bibliography: Equal arts of James Lamantia, Archit Forum, 52.
Memberships: Corp mem Am Inst Architects.
Collection: English drawings and paintings of the second half of the nineteenth century.
Mailing Address: 539 Bienville St, New Orleans, LA 70130.

LaMARCA, HOWARD J
Designer, Museum Director
Preferred Media: Graphics.
b Teaneck, N J, July 11, 34.
Study & Training: Cooper Union Art Sch, scholarship, 52-56, cert graphic arts, 56; Columbia Univ, BFA, 60; Syracuse Univ, grad asstship, 60-62, MFA, 62.
Collections Arranged: Charles Shedden, Sculptor-Ralph Didriksen, painter, 71; Anita Friend, Paintings-Ruth Cowell, Gravestone Rubbings, 71; New Jersey Designer-Craftsmen, 71; George Fish, Painting-Shirley Yudkin, Painting, 72; Marion Lane, Painting Retrospective, 72; Arts in Parts (group show), 72; Paul Burns, Painting Retrospective, 72.
Positions: Advert art dir, New York City, 57-71; dir, Bergen Community Mus, 71-
Memberships: Col Art Asn Am.
Publications: Auth, An analysis of Gauguin's 'What are we? Where do we come from? Where are we going?', Artist Mag, London, 3/62; auth, An analysis of the facade of San Marco, Eleven Mag, spring 72.
Mailing Address: 3 Crescent Ave, Cliffside Park, NJ 07010.

LAMB, ADRIAN
Painter
Preferred Media: Oils.
b New York, N Y, Mar 22, 01.
Study & Training: Art Stud League New York; Julian Sch, Paris, France.
Work in Public Collections: Nat Portrait Gallery, Washington, D C; Capitol Bldg, Washington, D C; Harvard Law Sch, Boston, Mass; Supreme Court, Tallahassee, Fla; Rockefeller Found, New York.
Commissions: Portraits of Stillmans, Chauncey Stillman, Stillman Mem, Brownsville, Tex, 58; portrait of Charles Merrill, Merrill Lynch, Fenner & Smith, co Bd Rm, Wall St, New York, 60; founder of Buford Col, Carnation Co, Buford, S C, 65; portrait of Mr Duke, Duke Endowment, New York, 68; portrait of Gheen, father & son, Mrs Richard Hill, Baptist Sem, Louisville, Ky, 72.
Exhibitions: Westchester, White Plains, N Y; Salmagundi Club, New York; Sculpin Gallery, Edgartown, Mass; New Canaan Libr, Conn.
Memberships: Salgamundi Club (v pres); Nat Arts Club; Art Stud League New York.
Dealers: Portraits, Inc, 41 E 57th St, New York, NY 10022; M Knoedler & Co, 21 E 70th St, New York, NY 10021.
Mailing Address: Des Artists Hotel, 1 W 67th St, New York, NY 10023.

LAMB, KATHARINE, see TAIT, KATHARINE LAMB

LAMIS, LEROY
Sculptor, Educator
Preferred Media: Plastics.
b Eddyville, Iowa, Sept 27, 25.
Study & Training: N Mex Highlands Univ, BA, 53; Columbia Univ Teachers Col, MA, 56.
Work in Public Collections: Albright-Knox Mus; Des Moines Art Ctr; Whitney Mus Am Art; Joseph H Hirshhorn Collection, Washington, D C; Larry Aldrich Mus.
Exhibitions: Whitney Mus Am Art Sculpture Ann, New York, N Y, 64, 66 & 68; Responsive Eye, Mus Mod Art, New York, 65; one-man

shows, Staempfli Gallery, New York, 66 & traveling show, 69, J B Speed Mus, Louisville, John Herron Mus, Indianapolis, Des Moines Art Ctr, La Jolla Mus Art, Calif & Tacoma Mus, Wash; Plastic Presence, Jewish Mus, New York, 70; Constructivists Tendencies, U S, 70-72.
Teaching: Asst prof Cornell Col, 56-60; prof sculpture, Ind State Univ, Terre Haute, 61-
Awards: Artist-in-residence, Dartmouth Col, 70; N Y State Coun Arts Award, 70.
Dealer: Staempfli Gallery, 47 E 77th St, New York, NY 10021.
Mailing Address: 3101 Oak, Terre Haute, IN 47803.

LAMONT, FRANCES (KENT)
Sculptor
b Lawrence Park, N Y.
Study & Training: Bennett Sch; also with Solon Borglum, Mahonri Young, Boardman Robinson & Anna Hyatt.
Work in Public Collections: Metropolitan Mus Art, New York; Cranbrook Mus, Bloomfield Hills, Mich; Denver Art Mus, Colo; Colo Springs Art Ctr, Colo; Ogunquit Mus Art, Maine; plus others.
Commissions: New Canaan War Mem; Mellon Garden, comn by Ailsa & Paul Mellon for their mother.
Exhibitions: 10 Ann, Whitney Mus Am Art; Salon Tuileries; one-man sculpture show, Bermuda, Denver & Kansas City; Artists for Victory, Metrop Mus Art.
Bibliography: Article, In: Life.
Memberships: Nat Sculpture Soc.
Dealer: Far Gallery, 765 Madison Ave, New York, NY 10021.
Mailing Address: 21 W Tenth St, New York, NY 10011.

LA MORE, CHET HARMON
Painter, Sculptor
Preferred Media: Acrylics, Watercolors, Steel, Bronze.
b Dane Co, Wis, July 30, 08.
Study & Training: Colt Sch Art, 26-28; Univ Wis, BA, 28, MA, 32.
Work in Public Collections: Libr Cong, Washington, D C; Nat Collection, Smithsonian Inst, Washington, D C; Syracuse Mus, N Y; Olsen Found, Conn; Colo Springs Mus, Colo.
Commissions: History of Sports (mural), comn by U S Treas Dept, Polytech Inst, Baltimore, Md, 33-34.
Exhibitions: Chicago Print Int, Ill, 37; Whitney Mus Am Art Ann, 43-48, 50; Calif Palace of Legion of Honor, San Francisco, 45; Int Arte Mod, UNESCO & U S State Dept, Paris, France, 47; Carnegie Inst Ann, Pittsburgh, Pa, 49.
Teaching: Prof art, Univ Mich, 47-
Awards: Fine prints of the Year Award, Int Selection, 38; purchase prize, serigraph, Mus Mod Art, 41; Rackham creative res grants, 56, 60 & 68.
Dealer: Forsythe Gallery, Nickels Arcade, Ann Arbor, MI 48104.
Mailing Address: 503 S First St, Ann Arbor, MI 48103.

LAND, ERNEST ALBERT
Painter
Preferred Media: Oils.
b Hamilton, Ont, Sept 21, 18; U S citizen.
Work in Public Collections: NASA Space Mus, Washington, D C; Grumbacher Collection Fine Art; IBM Collection Fine Art, New York, N Y; Butler Inst Am Art, Youngstown, Ohio.
Commissions: Mural, USA Corps Engrs, Seattle World's Fair, 60; nine murals on hist solid propellants, USN Mus, Indian Head, Md, 62-63; exhib, Work of Dr Leakey, Olduvai Gorge, Africa (with Robert Widder & Ken Hopkins), Nat Geog Explorers Hall, 63-64.
Exhibitions: Butler Inst Am Art Ann, Youngstown, Ohio, 70; Mainstreams Int, Marietta Col, Ohio, 70 & 72; Allied Artists Am 58th Ann, Nat Acad Design Galleries, 71; Am Artists Prof League Grand Nat, 71.
Teaching: Lectr, Chase Manhattan Bank, New York, 54-55; lectr, Am Tel & Tel, New York, 55-62.
Awards: Grand Nat Arts Award, Am Artists Prof League, 56 & Grumbacher Purchase Award, 57; Best in Show, St Peter's Episcopal Third Relig Art Ann, 68; John J McDonough Award, Butler Inst Am Art, 72.
Bibliography: Joseph Grumbacher (auth), Twenty-one paint in polymer, M Grumbacher, 65; Gutierrez & Roukes (auth), Painting with acrylics, Watson-Guptill, 65; Joseph Giacalone (auth), Leonardo would have use polymer, Syndicate Mag, 66.
Memberships: Life fel, Royal Soc Art, London; fel Am Artists Prof League; Art League Northern Va (pres, 62).
Publications: Illusr, U S Senate Comt Aeronaut & Space Sci, U S Govt Printing Off, 63.
Dealers: Capricorn Galleries, 8003 Woodmont Ave, Bethesda, MD 20014; Grand Central Art Galleries, 40 Vanderbilt Ave, New York, NY 10017.
Mailing Address: 517 W Great Falls St, Falls Church, VA 22046.

LANDAU, FELIX
Art Dealer
b Vienna, Austria, Oct 24, 24.
Memberships: Art Dealers Asn Am.
Specialty of Gallery: Twentieth century American and European art.
Mailing Address: 706 N La Cienega Blvd, Los Angeles, CA 90069.

LANDAU, JACOB
Painter, Printmaker
Preferred Media: Watercolors, Wood, Lithography.
b Philadelphia, Pa, Dec 17, 17.
Study & Training: Philadelphia Col Art, cert, 38, with Earl Horter & Franklin Watkins; New Sch Soc Res, 48-49 & 52-53, with Erich Fromm, Rudolf Arnheim & Eugene O'Neill, Jr.
Work in Public Collections: Mus Mod Art, New York, N Y; Whitney Mus Am Art; Metrop Mus Art; Libr Cong; Philadelphia Mus Art.
Commissions: Print For Peace, Smithsonian Inst, 67; suite lithographs illus work of E T A Hoffman, Univ Chicago Press, 69; 10 stained glass windows, Keneseth Synagogue, Israel, 71.
Exhibitions: The Figure, Recent Paintings U S A, 62 & Tamarind—Homage to Lithography, 69, Mus Mod Art; Smithsonian Print Show, White House, Washington, D C, 66; Three Artists View The Human Condition, N J State Mus, Trenton, 68; Human Concern/Personal Torment, Whitney Mus Am Art, 69.
Teaching: Instr, Pratt Inst, 57-62, asst prof, 62-65, assoc prof, 65-68, prof, graphic art, 68-, learning coordr, Univ-Without-Walls Proj.
Awards: Tamarind Lithography Workshop fel, 65; Nat Arts Endowment sabbatical grant, 66; Guggenheim Found fel, 68; plus others.
Bibliography: H C Pitz (auth), Jacob Landau, Am Artist, 10/56; Jacob Landau, Current Biog, 12/64; Barry Schwartz (auth), Tiger of wrath—Jacob Landau, Arts Soc, spring-summer, 71.
Memberships: Soc Am Artists.
Publications: Illusr, Charades, Tamarind Lithography Workshop, 65; auth, Yes-no, art-technology, Wilson Libr Bull, 9/66; illusr, Out of the whirlwind, Union Am Hebrew Congregations, 68 & Selected writings of Hoffmann, Univ Chicago Press, 69; plus others.
Dealers: Associated American Artists, 663 Fifth Ave, New York, NY 10022; Lerner-Heller Gallery, 789 Madison Ave, New York, NY 10021.
Mailing Address: 2 Pine Dr, Roosevelt, NJ 08555.

LANDAU, ROM
Sculptor, Writer
Preferred Media: Bronze.
b Eng, Oct 17, 99.
Study & Training: Sculpture with George Kolbe, Berlin, Ger; study in Florence, Italy; Univ of the Pac, hon LHD.
Exhibitions: In Eng & the continent.
Teaching: Prof Islamic arts, Am Acad Asian Studies, San Francisco, Calif, 51-53; prof Islamic art, philos & sci, Univ of the Pac, 52-67; vis prof North African studies & lit, Harvard Univ, Princeton Univ, Yale Univ, Columbia Univ, Stanford Univ, Cornell Univ & Univ Chicago, 52-66.
Positions: Art critic, Brit & continental rev & newspapers, 24-38; dir native studies, Peace Corps I, Morocco, 62-63.
Awards: Comdr, Royal Moroccan Order, Ouissam Al Aouite, awarded by HM King Muhammad V, 56.
Research: Islamic & Moorish architecture & arts.
Publications: Auth, Minos the incorruptible, 25, An outline of Moroccan culture, 53, The Arabesque, the abstract art of Islam, 55, The Arab heritage of western civilization, 62 & Morocco, Marrakesh, Fez, Rabat, 67.
Mailing Address: Marrakesh, Morocco.

LANDAU, SAMUEL DAVID, see LEV-LANDAU.

LANDECK, ARMIN
Painter, Engraver
b Crandon, Wis, June 4, 05.
Study & Training: Columbia Univ, BArch, 27.
Work in Public Collections: Mus Mod Art, Metrop Mus Art & New York Pub Libr, New York, N Y; Toledo Mus Art, Ohio; Libr Cong, Washington, D C; Swedish Nat Mus, Stockholm; Kaiser Friedrich Mus, Berlin, Ger; plus others.
Exhibitions: Libr Cong; Soc Am Graphic Arts; Nat Acad Design; Pa Acad Fine Arts; Int Graphic Exhib, Yugoslavia.
Awards: S F B Morse Gold Medal, Nat Acad Design, 62; Wiggin Award, Boston Printmakers, 69; purchase prize, So Am Graphic Arts, 69.
Memberships: Soc Am Graphic Arts; Am Inst Arts & Lett; Nat Acad Design; fel Int Inst Arts & Lett.
Mailing Address: R D 1, Litchfield, CT 06759.

LANDIS, LILY
Sculptor
Preferred Media: Bronze, Stone, Epoxy.
b New York, N Y.
Study & Training: Sorbonne, France; sculpture with De Creeft; Art Stud League New York.
Work in Public Collections: Lobby, Merck, Sharpe & Dohme Bldg, New York.
Exhibitions: Art Inst Chicago; Mus Mod Art, New York; Pa Acad Fine Arts; Whitney Mus Am Art; Corcoran Gallery Art.
Awards: Peabody Award, 68; Tiffany grant.
Dealer: Miriam Redein, 50 E 78th St, New York, NY 10021.
Mailing Address: 400 E 57th St, New York, NY 10022.

LANDON, EDWARD AUGUST
Printmaker, Painter
b Hartford, Conn, Mar 13, 11.
Study & Training: Hartford Art Sch; Art Stud League New York, N Y; also with Carlos Merida, Mex.
Work in Public Collections: Bibliot Nat, Paris; Mus Mod Art, New York; Metrop Mus Art, New York; San Francisco Mus; Nat Mus, Stockholm.
Exhibitions: Nat Serigraph Soc, 40-60; Am Color Print Soc Ann, 45-65; Northwest Printmakers Ann, 50-60; U S Info Agency Int Circulating Exhib, 52; Boston Printmakers Ann, 55-70.
Positions: Pres, Artists Union Western Mass, 34-38; pres, Nat Serigraph Soc, 52-53.
Awards: First prize for prints, Springfield Art League, 45; purchase prize, Boston Printmakers, 54; first prize, Nat Serigraph Soc, 59; plus others.
Bibliography: Making a serigraph (film), Harmon Found, 47.
Memberships: Am Color Print Soc; Boston Printmakers; Print Coun Am; Philadelphia Print Club.
Dealer: Doris Meltzer Gallery, 783 Madison Ave, New York, NY 10019.
Mailing Address: Lawrence Hill Rd, Weston, VT 05161.

LANDRY, ALBERT
Art Dealer
b New York, N Y, Oct 9, 19.
Study & Training: Columbia Univ, MA (art hist); Nat Acad Design; Atelier Leger, Paris, France.
Positions: Dir, Galerie Villard-Galanis, Paris, 50-54; dir, Assoc Am Artists, 54-58; dir, Albert Landry Galleries, New York, 58-64; dir, J L Hudson Co Art Gallery, Detroit, 64-; dir, Landry-Bonino Gallery, at present; dir, New York Art '73, at present.
Specialty of Gallery: Contemporary American and European art.
Mailing Address: 7 W 57th St, New York, NY 10019.

LANDSMAN, STANLEY
Sculptor
b New York, N Y, Jan 23, 30.
Study & Training: Univ N Mex, 47-50, 54-55, BFA, 55, with Randall Davey, Adja Yunkers & Agnes Martin.
Work in Public Collections: Mus Mod Art & Whitney Mus Am Art, New York; Larry Aldrich Mus, Ridgefield, Conn; Mus Mod Arte, Paris, France; Walker Art Ctr, Minneapolis, Minn; Milwaukee Art Mus, Wis; plus others.
Exhibitions: First World Triennial, New Delhi, India, 68; Cleveland Mus Art, Ohio, 68; Whitney Mus Am Art Sculpture Ann & Light, Object and Image, 68; Electric Art, Univ Calif, Los Angeles, 69; Univ Ill, Urbana, 69; plus other group & one-man shows.
Teaching: Instr sculpture, Adelphi Col, Sch Visual Arts & Pratt Inst; artist-in-residence, Aspen Inst & Univ Wis.
Bibliography: Tracy Atkinson (auth), Directions I: options 1968 (catalog), Milwaukee Art Ctr, 68.
Mailing Address: 45 Downing St, New York, NY 10014.

LANDWEHR, WILLIAM CHARLES
Art Administrator, Sculptor
Preferred Media: Mixed Media.
b Milwaukee, Wis, Sept 19, 41.
Study & Training: Univ Wis-Stevens Point, BS, 63; Univ N Dak, MA, 68.
Work in Public Collections: Albion Col, Mich; Kenosha Pub Mus, Wis; Milwaukee Art Ctr, Wis; Tyler Mus Art, Tex; Whitney Mus Am Art, New York, N Y.
Commissions: Murals, Univ N Dak, 68; mural/construction (with Robert A Nelson), State of N Dak, Hwy Dept Bldg, Bismarck, 68.
Exhibitions: New York Corresp Sch Exhib, Whitney Mus Am Art, 70; Selection Contemp Am Prints, State Univ N Y Col Oneonta, 70; Graphics U S A, Clark Col, Dubuque, Iowa, 70; one-man exhibs, Minneapolis Inst Arts Minneapolis, 70 & Tyler Mus Art, Tex, 71.
Collections Arranged: Barry Le Va: Six Blown Lines (Accumulation Drift), Art Ctr Gallery, Stout State Univ, 69; Peter Max; New Graphics, S Dak Mem Art Ctr, Brookings, 70; Richard Hunt:

Small Sculpture/Drawings/Lithographs, Quincy Art Ctr, Ill &
Civic Fine Arts Asn, Sioux Falls, S Dak, 72.
Teaching: Instr art, Univ N Dak, 66-68; instr art, S Dak State Univ,
69-71; lectr art, Western Ill Univ, 72-
Positions: Cur, Art Ctr Gallery, Stout State Univ, 68-69; dir, S Dak
Mem Art Ctr, 69-71; artist & dir, Quincy Art Ctr, 71-
Awards: Wis Painters & Sculptors 50th Anniversary Award, Mil-
waukee Art Ctr, 64; purchase award, Albion Col Nat Print &
Drawing Exhib, 68.
Memberships: Am Asn Mus; Ill Art Educ Asn; Assoc Coun Arts;
Midwest Mus Conf.
Publications: Auth, Melvin F Spinar: figure & fantasy, S Dak Mem
Art Ctr, 71; auth, Richard Hunt: small sculpture/drawings/
lithographs, Quincy Art Ctr, 72.
Mailing Address: 2631 Maine St, Quincy, IL 62301.

LANDY, JACOB
Art Historian, Educator
b New York, N Y, Apr 18, 17.
Study & Training: City Col New York, BSS & MsEd; N Y Univ, MA &
PhD.
Teaching: Prof art hist, City Col New York, 45-
Memberships: Col Art Asn Am; Soc Archit Historians; Victorian Soc
Am; Nat Trust Hist Preserv; Arch Am Art.
Research: American architecture in the nineteenth century.
Publications: Auth, History of art, 65, Introduction, The modern
builder's guide, 69 & The architecture of Minard Lafever, 70;
also articles, In: Archeol, Enciclopedia Spettacolo & J Soc
Archit Historians.
Mailing Address: 11 Gardenia Lane, Hicksville, NY 11801.

LANE, ALVIN SEYMOUR
Collector
b Englewood, N J, June 17, 18.
Study & Training: Univ Wis, PhB; Harvard Univ Law Sch, LLB; New
Sch Social Res with Seymour Lipton.
Positions: Chmn comt on art, New York Bar Asn, 63-65; mem bd
overseers fine arts, Brandeis Univ, 66; mem adv bd to New York
Atty Gen on Art Legis, 66-; secy, Aldrich Mus Contemp Art,
68, trustee, 69, mem acquisitions comt, 72.
Research: Problems on authentication of sculpture and the documen-
tation regarding authenticity.
Collection: Contemporary sculpture and sculptors' drawings.
Publications: Auth, How the bar can assist the art community, New
York Bar Asn, 65; auth, The case of the careless collector, Art
in Am, 65.
Mailing Address: 60 E 42nd St, New York, NY 10017.

LANE, BENT
Painter
Preferred Media: Oils.
b Chicago, Ill.
Study & Training: Univ Calif, Berkeley, AB, 24; Radcliffe Col, 25;
Art Stud League New York, 49; Am Univ, 51-53.
Work in Public Collections: Univ Vt; Simpson Col; also in pvt col-
lections.
Exhibitions: Argent Gallery, New York, N Y; one-man shows,
Manatee Art League, 66, Sarasota Art Asn, 66, Stetson Univ, 67,
Longboat Key Art Ctr, 69 & Friends Gallery, 69; plus others.
Teaching: Artist-in-residence, St John's Col, Annapolis, 54-55;
artist-in-residence & asst prof, Simpson Col, 55-60; instr art,
Manatee Art League, 65-66
Positions: Art adv comt, Iowa Fedn Womens Clubs, 56; summer
colonist, MacDowell Colony, 57; owner, Bent Lane Studio-Gallery,
Burlington, Vt, 60-61; v pres & prog chmn, Nat League Am Pen
Women, Sarasota Br, 64-69; bd, Sarasota Art Asn, 69-71.
Awards: Ursell Award, Soc Washington Artists, 61; Aileen Vander-
bilt Webb Award, Nat Asn Women Artists, 61; Sarasota Art Asn,
72; plus others.
Memberships: Longboat Key Art Ctr; Nat League Am Pen Women;
Sarasota Art Asn (rec secy, 69).
Mailing Address: 421 Cleveland Dr, Sarasota, FL 33577.

LANE, CHRISTOPHER
Painter
b New York, N Y, June 7, 37.
Study & Training: Goddard Col; Sch Painting & Sculpture, Mexico
City, Mex.
Exhibitions: Mus Mod Art, New York, 64-65; Salon Jeune Peinture,
Paris, 65; New Art Centre, London, 65; Mus Mod Art Traveling
Exhib, Mus Mod Art, Mexico City, 67; Karmanduca Gallery, San
Francisco, Calif, 68; plus others.
Mailing Address: 229 E Fourth St, New York, NY 10009.

LANG, DANIEL S
Painter
Preferred Media: Acrylics, Oils.
b Tulsa, Okla, Mar 17, 35.
Study & Training: Northwestern Univ, Evanston; Univ Tulsa, BFA,
with Alexander Hogue; Univ Iowa, MFA, 59, with Mauricio
Lasansky.
Work in Public Collections: Mus Mod Art, New York, N Y; Art Inst
Chicago; Libr Cong, Washington, D C; Nelson-Atkins Mus Fine
Art, Kansas City; Boston Pub Libr.
Exhibitions: Boston Mus Fine Arts, 61; Art Inst Chicago, 64 & 67;
Arthur Tooth & Sons Gallery, London, Eng, 70; Fairweather
Hardin Gallery, 71; French & Co, New York, 72 & 73.
Teaching: Asst prof painting, Art Inst Chicago, 62-64; asst prof
painting, Wash Univ, 64-65; vis artist, Ohio State Univ, 68-69;
vis artist, Univ S Fla, fall 72.
Mailing Address: c/o French & Co, 980 Madison Ave, New York,
NY 10021.

LANG, MARGO TERZIAN
Painter
Preferred Media: Watercolors, Oils.
b Fresno, Calif.
Study & Training: Fresno State Col; Stanford Univ; Arizona State
Univ; Prado Mus, Madrid, Spain; also spec study with Edgar
Whitney, Dong Kingman & Rex Brandt.
Work in Public Collections: 30 Paintings in U S Embassies in Brus-
sels, Tripoli, Bulgaria, Malta, Iceland, Laos, Guatemala, Iran &
others; Pepsi Cola Co, Dean Witter & Co, Am Collection Fine
Art; N Y Life Ins Co Fine Art Calendars.
Commissions: Sunrise Tomorrow (cross superimposed on desert
sunrise), comn by J Parker Nicholson, Glass & Garden Church,
Scottsdale, Ariz, 71; Arizona Scenes, Pepsi-Cola Bldg.
Exhibitions: Inst Cult, Guadalajara, Mex, 68; Grand Cent Galleries
Ann, New York, N Y, 68 & 69; one-man show, New York, 69; Int
Platform Asn Art Exhib, Washington, D C, 70 & 71; Phoenix Art
Mus, Ariz, 70 & 71; Arizona State Fair, Phoenix, 71.
Awards: Ann competition award, Grand Cent Galleries, 68 & 69; best
of show award, 70 & silver medal of excellence, 71, Int Platform
Asn.
Memberships: Int Platform Asn; Nat Soc Arts & Lett (nat bd mem).
Am Artists Prof League; Ariz Watercolor Asn; Phoenix Art Mus.
Publications: Voice of Am & Radio Liberty broadcasts, 69.
Dealer: Grand Central Galleries, 40 Vanderbilt Ave, New York, NY
10017.
Mailing Address: 6127 Calle del Paisano, Scottsdale, AZ 85251.

LANGLAIS, BERNARD
Sculptor, Painter
Preferred Media: Wood
b Old Town, Maine, July 23, 21.
Study & Training: Corcoran Sch Art, with Ben Shahn; Skowhegan Sch
Painting & Sculpture, with Henry Varnum Poor; Brooklyn Mus
Art Sch, with Max Beckmann; Acad Grande Chaumiere, Paris,
France; Acad Art, Fulbright grant, Oslo, Norway.
Work in Public Collections: Whitney Mus Am Art, New York, N Y;
Art Inst Chicago, Ill; Philadelphia Mus Art, Pa; Chrysler Mus,
Provincetown, Mass; Mus Art Ogunquit, Maine.
Commissions: Wood wall reliefs, Dryden Assocs, Pittsburgh, Pa,
68; Indian (wood sculpture), Town of Skowhegan, Maine, 69; Jun-
gle (wood relief mural), Philadelphia Zool Gardens, Pa, 70; wood
sculpture, Munic Park, Kansas City, Mo, 70; Barn Interior (wood
relief mural), Robert Montgomery, North Haven, Maine, 71.
Exhibitions: Art Inst Chicago, 60, 61 & 64; Carnegie Int, Pittsburgh,
61-62; Mus Mod Art, New York, N Y, 61-63; Whitney Mus Am Art
Ann, New York, 61, 63 & 66; Inst Int Educ Show, traveled around
the world, 69.
Awards: Ford Found Purchase Award, 62; Nat Acad Arts & Lett
Purchase Award, 69; Guggenheim fel, 72.
Bibliography: Edith Dugmore (auth), Bernard Langlais, Craft Hori-
zons, 3-4/66; Jay Molishever (auth), Big stuff, the wood sculp-
tures of Bernard Langlais, Boston Sun Globe Mag, 5/9/71; Isabel
Currier (auth), Maine's Bernard Langlais and his gigantic art,
Down East Mag, 6/72.
Dealer: Lee Ault & Co, Inc, 25 E 77th St, New York, NY 10021.
Mailing Address: Star Rte, Cushing, ME 04861.

LANGSDORF, MARTYL SCHWEIG, see MARTYL.

LANGSTON, MR & MRS LOYD H (MILDRED J)
Art Dealers, Collectors
Mr Langston, b Bowers Mill, Mo, Jan 28, 91; Mrs Langston, b
Passaic, N J, Mar 3, 02.
Study & Training: Mr Langston, Columbia Univ, PhD; Mrs Langston,
Simmons Col, AB; Columbia Univ, MA.
Teaching: Mrs Langston, instr bus, Simmons Col, 25-27; prof bus,
Long Island Univ, 29-36; acad dean, Katherine Gibbs Sch, 37-67.

Memberships: Mr Langston, Monmouth Mus (trustee, 65-); N J State Mus Asn for Arts (trustee, 65-). Mrs Langston, charter mem Monmouth Mus; Chinese Snuff Bottle Asn; Maryville Col (bd mem, 60-).
Specialty of Gallery: French paintings; art of the Orient; Chinese handstones and porcelains.
Art Interests: Mr Langston, supporter of Frick Collection.
Mailing Address: 2 Third St, Rumson, NJ 07760.

LANING, EDWARD
Painter
b Petersburg, Ill, Apr 26, 06.
Study & Training: Univ Chicago; Art Inst Chicago; Art Stud League New York, with Max Weber, John Sloan, Thomas Hart Benton & Kenneth Hayes Miller.
Work in Public Collections: Metrop Mus Art & Whitney Mus Am Art, New York, N Y; William Rockhill Nelson Gallery, Kansas City, Mo; Pentagon Gallery, Dept Defense, Washington, D C; New York Pub Libr.
Commissions: Ellis Island, N Y, 37; Rockingham Post Off, N C, 37; Bowling Green Post Off, Ky, 41; New York Pub Libr, 42; Sheraton-Dallas Hotel, Dallas, Tex, 60.
Exhibitions: Many Whitney Mus Ann; Corcoran Gallery Art, Washington, D C, 38; Art Inst Chicago, Ill, 40; American Drawings, Metrop Mus Art, 52; Nat Acad Design, New York, 72.
Teaching: Instr painting & drawing, Cooper Union, 40-43; head dept painting & drawing, Kansas City Art Inst, 45-50; instr painting & drawing, Art Stud League New York, 52-
Positions: Dir, Beaux Arts Inst Design, 40-42.
Awards: Kohnstamm Prize, Art Inst Chicago, 40; Guggenheim fel, 45; Fulbright fel, 50-52.
Memberships: Nat Soc Mural Painters (pres, 68-); Nat Acad Design (rec secy, 68-); life mem Art Stud League New York.
Publications: Auth, Perspective for artists, 69; auth, Memoirs of a WPA artist, Am Heritage, 10/70; auth, Spoon River revisited, Am Heritage, 6/71; auth, The new deal mural projects, Smithsonian Anthology, 72; auth, The act of drawing, 72.
Mailing Address: 30 E 14th St, New York, NY 10003.

LA NOUE, TERENCE DAVID
Sculptor
Preferred Media: Latex, Wood, Tobacco Cloth.
b Hammond, Ind, Dec 4, 41.
Study & Training: Ohio Wesleyan Univ, BFA; Hochschule für Bildende Künste, W Berlin; Cornell Univ, MFA.
Work in Public Collections: Roy Neuberger Mus, Purchase, N Y; Cornell Univ; Univ Hartford; Wadsworth Atheneum; Whitney Mus Am Art.
Exhibitions: Art Inst Chicago; Dayton Art Inst; Albright-Knox Gallery, 71; Indianapolis Mus Art, 72; Newark Mus Art, 72.
Teaching: Asst prof art, Trinity Col, 67-72; assoc prof art & head dept, La Guardia Col, 72-
Awards: Fulbright scholar, 64-65; Nat Endowment for Arts, 72-73.
Bibliography: Will Groamann (auth), Nachliches a la pop, Frankfurter Allegemeine, 65; Rolf Gunter-Dienst (auth). Terence La Noue, Kunstwerk, 69; Robert Pincus-Witten (auth), New York, 71 & 72, Artforum.
Mailing Address: c/o Paley & Lowe, 59 Wooster St, New York, NY 10012.

LANSNER, FAY
Painter
b Philadelphia, Pa.
Study & Training: Tyler Sch Fine Art, 45-47; Art Stud League New York, 47-48; Hans Hofman Sch, 48-50; also with Leger, Lhote, Paris, 50-51.
Work in Public Collections: Weatherspoon Art Mus, Greensboro, N C; New York Univ Art Collection, N Y; Kenton Corp, New York; Newsweek, Washington Post Co, New York; Rutgers Univ Art Mus, Newark, N J; plus others.
Exhibitions: Corcoran Gallery, Washington, D C, 67; Albright-Knox Mus, Buffalo, N Y, 67; Mus Mod Art, New York, 68, 69 & 71; 17th Brooklyn Mus Print Ann, N Y, 70; Women in the Arts, Stamford Mus, Conn, 72.
Bibliography: Barbara Guest (auth), Contradictory opposites, Art News Mag, 12/12/63; Harold Rosenberg (auth), Hofman students, Art News Ann, 63; Doris Reno (auth), Lansner paintings show, Times Herald Post, Miami, Fla, 66.
Memberships: Women in the Arts.
Publications: Auth, Barbara Riboud, Craft Horizons Mag, 4/72.
Dealers: Marlborough Graphics, 41 E 57th St, New York, NY 10022; La Demeure, 6 Place St Sulpice, Paris, France.
Mailing Address: 317 W 80th St, New York, NY 10024.

LANTZ, MICHAEL F
Sculptor
Preferred Media: Bronze, Limestone, Marble.
b New Rochelle, N Y, Apr 6, 08.
Study & Training: Nat Acad Design, 24-26; also with Lee Lawrie, 26-35; Beaux Arts Inst Design, 28-31.
Commissions: Spring Hill Ave Synagogue, Mobile, Ala, 56; Battle Monument, St Avold, France, 59; Nat Guard Mem Bldg, Washington, D C, 59; Sculptural Outlines, Architect's Bldg, Albany, N Y, 68; Pan Am World Health Ctr, Washington, D C, 69.
Exhibitions: Philadelphia Mus, Pa, 40; Silver Medal Int Exhib, Madrid, Spain, 59; many exhibs, Nat Acad Design & Lever House, New York.
Teaching: Prof sculpture, Adult Educ, New Rochelle, 36-38; instr, Nat Acad Design, 61-
Positions: Ed, Nat Sculpture Rev, 50-55, ed adv, 69-
Awards: Medal of the City of New York, 48; J Sanford Saltus Medal, 69; Elizabeth Watrous Gold Medal, Nat Acad Design, 70.
Memberships: Nat Sculpture Soc (pres, 69-); Nat Acad Design (coun mem, 70-); Fine Arts Fedn New York (v pres, 70).
Publications: Auth, articles, In: Nat Sculpture Rev.
Mailing Address: 979 Webster Ave, New Rochelle, NY 10804.

LANYON, ELLEN
Painter, Printmaker
Preferred Media: Acrylics, Lithography.
b Chicago, Ill, Dec 21, 26.
Study & Training: Art Inst Chicago, BFA, 48, with Joseph Hirsch; State Univ Iowa, MFA, 50, with M Lasansky; Courtauld Inst, Univ London, with Helmut Reuhman.
Work in Public Collections: Art Inst Chicago; Denver Art Mus, Colo; Libr Cong, Washington, D C; Finch Col, New York, N Y; Krannert Art Mus, Univ Ill, Champaign.
Commissions: Mural, Mr Kelly's, Chicago, 67; lithograph, Ravinnia Asn, 68; painting, Florists' Tel Delivery Asn Traveling Exhib, 70; painting, Ill Bell for dir cover, 71.
Exhibitions: Art Inst Chicago Am Biennials, 46-61 & Vicinity Anns, 46-71; Young Printmakers, Metrop Mus Art, 53; Recent Painting U S A: The Figure, Mus Mod Art, New York, 62; The Painter & The Photograph, Am Fedn Arts Traveling Exhib, 65-66; The Chicago School, Imagist Art, Mus Contemp Art, Chicago, 72.
Teaching: Instr painting & dir, Ox Bow Summer Sch of Painting, Saugatuck, Mich, 60-; vis instr drawing, Sch Art Inst Chicago, 64-65; lectr drawing, Univ Ill, Chicago Circle, 66, artist-in-residence, 71.
Positions: Adv Adult Educ Coun, Chicago, 69-72; adv visual arts, Ill Art Coun, 69-
Awards: Pauline Palmer Prize, Art Inst Chicago, 62 & 64; Fulbright stud grant, 50-51; Cassandra Found Award, 71.
Bibliography: Dennis Adrian (auth), Ellen Lanyon, Art Scene, 2/68; Van Deren Coke (auth), The painter & the photograph (1965), Univ New Mex Press, 12/71; Franz Schulze (auth), Ellen Lanyon (fantastic images - Chicago art since 1945), Follett, 5/72.
Memberships: Am Fedn Arts; Art Inst Chicago Alumni Asn.
Publications: Contribr, Art Scene, 9/68; auth & illusr, Wonder production, Vol I, 71.
Dealers: Richard Gray, 620 N Michigan Ave, Chicago, IL 60611; Zabriskie Gallery, 29 W 57th St, New York, NY 10019.
Mailing Address: 412 N Clark St, Chicago, IL 60610.

LA PIERRE, THOMAS
Painter, Printmaker
Preferred Media: Oils, Watercolors
b Toronto, Ont, Dec 28, 30.
Study & Training: Ont Col Art, AA; Ecole Beaux Arts; Atelier 17.
Work in Public Collections: Montreal Mus Fine Art, P Q; Sir George Williams Univ.
Exhibitions: São Paulo Biennial, 63; Focus on Drawing, Art Gallery Ont, 65; Price Fine Art Awards Exhib, 70.
Teaching: Instr drawing & painting, Ont Col Art, 58-
Awards: Can Coun grant, 66 & 71; Ont Soc Artists Award, 68; Price Fine Art Award, 70.
Bibliography: William McElcheran (auth), Dialogue with demons, Arts Can, 70.
Memberships: Can Soc Graphic Art; Ont Soc Artists; Can Soc Painters in Watercolour; assoc Royal Can Acad.
Mailing Address: 2067 Proverbs Dr, Mississauga, Ont, Can.

LAPINER, ALAN C
Art Dealer
b Palma de Mallorca, Spain, Aug 30, 33; U S citizen.
Study & Training: Antioch Col, BA.
Positions: Owner-dir, Arts of the Four Quarters, Ltd, New York, N Y.

Specialty of Gallery: Pre-Columbian art, specializing in art of ancient Peru and ancient textiles.
Mailing Address: Arts of the Four Quarters, Ltd, 111 W 13th St, New York, NY 10011.

LARCADA, RICHARD KENNETH
Art Dealer
b Brooklyn, N Y, Sept 11, 35.
Study & Training: N Y Univ, BA, 56.
Positions: Assoc dir, Maynard Walker Gallery, New York, N Y, 61-65; dir, Larcada Gallery, New York.
Specialty of Gallery: Neo-Romantics; artists of the twenties and thirties.
Mailing Address: 23 E 67th St, New York, NY 10021.

LARIAR, LAWRENCE
Cartoonist, Writer
b Brooklyn, N Y, Dec 25, 08.
Study & Training: New York Sch Fine & Applied Arts, 26-29; Acad Julien, Paris, France; Art Stud League New York.
Teaching: Dir, Prof Sch Cartooning.
Positions: Com advert artist, 30-33; illustr & polit cartoonist, 33-; cartoon ed, Liberty Mag, 41-48; ed, Best Cartoons of Year, 42-; cartoon ed, Parade Mag, 57-
Memberships: Am Soc Mag Cartoonist (past pres, mem war comt); Author's League Am.
Publications: Auth, You've got me from 9 to 5, 56, You've got me on the rocks, 56, The real lowdown, 56, Girl running, 56, Boat and be damned, 57; contribr, cartoons in leading nat mags & New York daily newspapers; also auth & ed, many other books.
Mailing Address: 248 Mount Joy Ave, Freeport, NY 11520.

LARK, RAYMOND
Painter, Draftsman
Preferred Media: Oil, Pencil.
b Philadelphia, Pa, June 16, 39.
Study & Training: Philadelphia Mus Sch Art; Pa, Dobbins Voc, Philadelphia, Temple Univ, BS; Los Angeles Tech Col.
Work in Public Collections: Dalzell Hatfield Galleries, Los Angeles, Calif; Nader's Art Gallery, Port-au-Prince, Haiti; Blue Cross Ins Co, Los Angeles, plus others.
Exhibitions: Exec Mansion of Gov Nelson A Rockefeller, N Y, 67; Dalzell Hatfield Galleries, Los Angeles, Calif, 68-70; Cape Cod Art Asn Gallery, Hyannis, Mass, 69; Phillip E Freed Gallery Fine Art, Chicago, Ill, 70; N J State Mus, Trenton, 72; plus over 30 other exhibs.
Teaching: Lect art, First Unitarian Church Los Angeles, 69; lect art, Nat Secretaries Asn (Int), Hollywood, Calif, 70; lect art, EYOA of Greater Los Angeles, 71; also lect at many cols & asns.
Awards: U S rep, Art Event of the Year (Int), 66; best in show, Immanuel's Art Exhib, Calif, 67, 68, two addn prizes, 68; best in show, Florenz's Art Exhib, Calif, 69; many others.
Bibliography: Dr Samella S Lewis & Ruth G Waddy, Black artist on art, vol 1, 69; Dave Larsen, Artist pines for acclaim at bowl festival, Los Angeles Times, 7/66; articles in nat art mags, 67-70.
Memberships: Art West Assoc, Inc (pres, 68-70); Int Platform Asn.
Publications: Auth, A portfolio of 6 prints by Raymond Lark (ed ltd to 500 portfolios), Contemp Crafts, Los Angeles, 72.
Mailing Address: P O Box 0990, Los Angeles, CA 90008.

LARKIN, EUGENE
Printmaker, Educator
b Minneapolis, Minn, June 27, 21.
Study & Training: Univ Minn, BA & MA.
Work in Public Collections: Mus Mod Art, New York, N Y; Nat Gallery Art & Libr Cong, Washington, D C; Art Inst Chicago, Ill; Addison Gallery Am Art, Andover, Mass; Nelson Gallery Art, Kansas City; plus others.
Commissions: Int Graphic Arts Soc; Gen Mills Corp; Bus Wk; Minneapolis Soc Fine Arts; U S Info Agency.
Exhibitions: U S Info Agency Traveling Exhib to Iran, Italy, France, Spain & Ger; one-man shows, Minneapolis Inst Art, 68 & Hamline Univ, 68; State Univ N Y Albany, 69; Univ Calif, Long Beach, 69; plus others.
Teaching: Instr, Kans State Col, Pittsburgh, 48-54; head printmaking dept & chmn fine arts div, Minneapolis Sch Art, 54-69; prof design, Dept Related Arts, Univ Minn, 69-
Awards: Walker Art Ctr, 60; Washington Watercolor & Print Exhib, 63; plus thirty other awards.
Memberships: Artists Equity Asn.
Mailing Address: 64 Groveland Terr, Minneapolis, MN 55403.

LARKIN, WILLIAM
Painter, Printmaker
b Washington, D C, Dec 8, 02.
Study & Training: Univ Va; George Washington Univ; Art Stud League New York.

Work in Public Collections: Metrop Mus Art, New York, N Y; Brandeis Univ; M H de Young Mem Mus, San Francisco, Calif; Seattle Art Mus, Wash; Denver Art Mus, Colo; plus others.
Exhibitions: Libr Cong, Washington, D C; Pa Acad Fine Arts, Philadelphia; Boston Printmakers, 54-68; Am Color Print Soc, 55 & 68; Loan-Own Art Serv, Va Mus Fine Arts, 63-69; plus others.
Awards: Hon mentions, Springfield Art League, 55; Northwest Printmakers, 56; Audubon Artists, 57.
Memberships: Am Color Print Soc; Boston Printmakers; Artists Equity Asn.
Mailing Address: 516 W 162nd St, New York, NY 10032.

LARRINAGA, MARIO
Painter, Designer
Preferred Media: Oils.
b Las Flores, Mex, Jan 19, 95; U S citizen.
Study & Training: Chouinard Sch Art, Los Angeles, Calif, with Purett Carter; also with E J Bisttram, Taos, N Mex, Walter Hall & Arthur Hurtt.
Work in Public Collections: Mus N Mex, Santa Fe; N Mex State Fair.
Commissions: Scenic designs, Shrine Temple, Los Angeles, 25; paintings, This is Cinerama, Seven Wonders, Search for Paradise & Marco Polo Club, New York, N Y, by Lowell Thomas.
Exhibitions: One-man shows, Taos Art Asn, 56-58 & Allied Artists N Mex, 64-72; N Mex Art Mus Traveling Shows, 62 & 70.
Positions: Scenic artist, Flagg Scenic Studios, Los Angeles, 14-20; scenic & set design, Universal Studios, Hollywood, Calif, 20-25; art dir, First Nat R K O, Warner Bros, 25-36, spec effects design, Warner Bros, 36-50.
Memberships: Taos Art Asn (art comt); Allied Artists N Mex (pres); Art Comt Univ N Mex.
Mailing Address: P O Box 221, Taos, NM 87571.

LARSEN, ERIK
Art Historian, Educator
b Vienna, Austria, Oct 10, 11; U S citizen.
Study & Training: Inst Supérieur Hist Art & Archeol, Brussels, Belg, BA; Cath Univ Louvain, MA & PhD; restoration with Jef Lammens, Ghent & Jules Defort, Brussels.
Teaching: Lectr, Belg; res prof art, Manhattanville Col Sacred Heart, 47-55; instr, Sch Gen Studies Exten Div, City Col New York, 48-55; from lectr to vis prof, Georgetown Univ, 55-58, assoc prof fine arts, 58-63, prof fine arts, 63-67, head dept fine arts, 60-67; prof hist art, Univ Kans, 67-, dir, Ctr Flemish Art & Cult, 70-
Positions: Dir & ed-in-chief, Pictura; Belg Govt Cult Mission in Brazil, 46-47; Am ed, Artis.
Awards: Knight's Cross, Order of Leopold & Order of the Crown, Belg; laureate, Inst France, Prix Thorlet, 62; mem, Jury Taras Shevshenko Mem, Washington, D C.
Memberships: Col Art Asn Am; Am Appraisers Asn Am; Am Asn Univ Prof; Asn Dipl Hist Art & Archeol, Cath Univ Louvain; plus others.
Research: History of northern Baroque and northern renaissance art.
Publications: Auth, P P Rubens, with a complete catalogue of his works in America, 52; auth, Les primitifs flamands au Musee Metropolitain de New York, 60; auth, Frans Post, interprete du Bresil, 62; auth, Rembrandt and the Dutch school, Tudor, 67; contribr, McGraw-Hill dictionary of art, McGraw-Hill, 69; plus others.
Mailing Address: 3103 Trail Rd, Lawrence, KS 66044.

LARSEN, JACK LENOR
Designer
b Seattle, Wash, Aug 5, 27.
Study & Training: Univ Washington, BFA, 50; Cranbrook Acad Art, MFA, 51.
Work in Public Collections: Mus Mod Art, New York, N Y; Victoria & Albert Mus, London, Eng; Stedelijk Mus, Amsterdam, Holland; The Am Archive, Detroit, Mich; Cooper-Hewitt, New York.
Commissions: Wall panels, comn by Louis Khan for Unitarian Church, Rochester, N Y, 66; act curtain for Filene Ctr, comn by Mrs Jouett Shouse for Wolf Trap Farm Found, 71; theatre curtain, comn by Charles Luckman Assocs, Phoenix Civic Plaza, Concert Hall, Ariz, 72.
Exhibitions: One-man shows, Cranbrook Acad Art, Bloomfield Hills, Mich, 63 & Mus Bellerive, Zurich, Switz, 70; retrospectives, Ft Wayne Mus Art, Ind, 69, Mus Fine Arts, Boston, Mass, 71 & Renwick Gallery, Washington, D C, 72.
Collections Arranged: Co-dir, Wall Hangings, Mus Mod Art, New York, 70.
Teaching: Dir fabric design dept, Philadelphia Col Art, 61-63.
Positions: Chmn, U S Sect, World Crafts Coun, 70-71.
Awards: Gold medal for design dir of U S Pavilion, Triennale, Milan, Italy, 57; gold medal award for craftsmanship, Am Inst Architects, 68; Elsie DeWolfe Award, Am Inst Interior Designers, 71.

Memberships: Haystack Mountain Sch (bd trustees, 54-, v pres, 70); Am Crafts Coun (bd trustees, 54-).
Publications: Co-auth, Elements of weaving, Doubleday, 67; co-auth, Beyond craft: the art fabric, Van Nostrand Reinhold.
Mailing Address: 41 E 11th St, New York, NY 10012.

LARSEN, OLE
Painter, Illustrator
Preferred Media: Oils, Pastels.
b Manistee, Mich.
Study & Training: Chicago Acad Fine Arts; Art Inst Chicago; Am Acad Art; also landscapes with Edward Timmons.
Work in Public Collections: Michigan City Pub Libr, Ind; Riveredge Found, Calgary, Alta; Am Saddle Horse Mus, Lexington, Ky.
Exhibitions: Ill State Fair Prof Art Exhib, Springfield, 55-58; West Suburban Fine Arts Alliance, Oakbrook, Ill, 64-69; Nat Artists Exhib, Ill State Mus, Springfield, 67; West Suburban Artists Guild, Hillside, Ill, 72.
Awards: Awards, for Sir Dudly, Ky State Fair Animal Artists Exhib, 37 & Early Days of a Thoroughbred, Ill State Fair, 56.
Bibliography: Articles, In: Globe Democrat Tempo Mag, 51, Chicago Tribune, 51 & 52 & State J Regist, 67.
Memberships: Soc Animal Artists; Hinsdale Community Artists.
Dealer: Findlay Galleries, 320 S Michigan Ave, Chicago, IL 60604; Abercrombie & Fitch Co, 9 N Wabash Ave, Chicago, IL 60602.
Mailing Address: 441 S Adams, Hinsdale, IL 60521.

LARSON, SIDNEY
Painter, Sculptor
b Sterling, Colo, June 16, 23.
Study & Training: Univ Mo, AB & MA; Univ Okla; also with Thomas Hart Benton & Fred Shane.
Work in Public Collections: Baker Gallery, Lubbock, Tex.
Commissions: Life Along the Missouri River, Mo State Training Sch Boys, Boonville, 50, Social History of Phelps Co, Rolla Daily News, Mo, 52; Social History of Insurance, MFA Ins Co, Columbia, Co, 59; Social History of Ceramics and Metal, Riback Industs, Columbia, 67; Historical Architecture, First Bank Commerce, Columbia, 71.
Exhibitions: St Louis People's Art Ctr, 64; Mo Pavilion, New York World's Fair, 65; one-man & invitational exhibs, Oklahoma City, Univ Mo, Columbia Col, Spiva Art Ctr & others.
Collections Arranged: Mo Masters, Mo Pavilion, New York World's Fair, 64-65; George Caleb Bingham Exhibs, 65; Thomas Hart Benton Drawings & Lithographs, 69; Arrow Rock, 70.
Teaching: Instr, Oklahoma City Univ, 50-51; instr, Univ Mo-Columbia, summers; dir art, Columbia Col, 51-
Positions: Mus cur, State Hist Soc Mo, 61-; dir Cult Exhib, New York World's Fair, 64 & 65.
Awards: Ittner Fine Arts Prize, Univ Mo, 50; Okla Ann Award, Philbrook Art Mus, 51; Huntington Hartford Found, 62.
Memberships: Nat Soc Mural Painters; Am Asn Univ Prof; Columbia Art League; (mem bd); Mo Mus Assocs.
Research; Conservation of art, especially of the nineteenth and twentieth centuries.
Publications: Auth, Introduction to Fred Shane drawings, 64; auth, articles on Thomas Hart Benton, In: Mo Hist Rev, 69 & Conservation of a Bingham, Mo Hist Rev, 72.
Dealer: Columbia Art League Gallery, Columbia, MO 65201.
Mailing Address: 2025 Crestridge Dr, Columbia, MO 65201.

LASANSKY, MAURICIO
Printmaker
b Buenos Aires, Arg, 14; U S citizen.
Study & Training: Super Sch Fine Arts, Arg; Iowa Wesleyan Col, hon DA, 59; Pac Lutheran Univ, hon DFA, 69.
Work in Public Collections: Art Inst Chicago, Ill; Seattle Mus, Wash; Libr Cong, Washington, D C; Uffizi Gallery, Florence, Italy; Mus Arte Contemp, Madrid, Spain; plus many others in the U S & abroad.
Exhibitions: First Int Biennial, Honolulu, Hawaii, 71; Int Graphic Art, 1945-1970, Albertine Mus, Vienna, 71; Third Biennial of Graphic Art, Palazzo Strozzi, Florence, Italy, 72; Second San Juan Biennial, Puerto Rico, 72; Int Print Biennale, Fredrikstad, Norway; plus many others in the U S & abroad.
Teaching: Dir, Free Fine Arts Sch, Villa Maria Cordoba, Arg, 36; dir, Taller Manualidades, Cordoba, 39; vis lectr, Univ Iowa, 45, asst prof art, 46, assoc prof art, 47, prof art, 48-65, res prof, 65-67, Virgil M Hancher distinguished prof art, 67-71, res prof art, 71-72; Lucas lectr, Carleton Col, 65.
Positions: Mem fine arts jury, John S Guggenheim Mem Found, 65.
Awards: Guggenheim fels, 43-44, to Spain & France, 53, to Spain & Latin Am, 65; Bertha von Moschzisker Prize, Philadelphia Print Club Ann, 71; purchase awards, Ga State Univ, 71; plus many others.
Bibliography: L Edmondson (auth), Etching, Van Nostrand Reinhold, 72; Barry Schwartz (auth), Humanism in 20th century art, Prae-

ger, 72; Jules Heller (auth), Printmaking today, Holt, Rinehart & Winston, 72; plus many other books & periodicals.
Memberships: Col Art Asn Am (bd dirs, 70-).
Mailing Address: Dept of Art, University of Iowa, Iowa City, IA 52240.

LASKER, MRS ALBERT D
Collector
b Watertown, Wis.
Study & Training: Radcliffe Col, AB (cum laude); Oxford Univ; Univ Wis, hon LLD; Univ Southern Calif, hon LHD, Bard Col, Womens Med Col, New York Univ, New York Med Col, Jefferson Med Col.
Positions: Former art dealer, Reinhardt Galleries.
Awards: Chevalier, Legion of Honor, Fr Govt; Presidential Medal Freedom, 69.
Collection: Paintings.
Mailing Address: 29 Beekman Pl, New York, NY 10022.

LASKER, JOSEPH (L)
Painter, Illustrator
Preferred Media: Oils.
b Brooklyn, N Y, June 26, 18.
Study & Training: Cooper Union Art Sch, cert, 39.
Work in Public Collections: Whitney Mus Am Art, New York, N Y; Philadelphia Mus Art, Pa; Springfield Mus, Mass; Joseph H Hirshhorn Collection, Washington, D C; Calif Palace Legion of Honor, San Francisco.
Commissions: Murals, U S Pub Works Admin, Post Off, Calumet, Mich, 41 & Milbury, Mass, 42 & Henry St Settlement Playhouse, New York, 48.
Exhibitions: Pa Acad Fine Arts Ann, 47-53; Whitney Mus Am Art Ann, 47-58; Nat Acad Design Ann, New York, 47-72; plus many others.
Teaching: Assoc prof painting, Univ Ill, 52-53.
Awards: Prix de Rome fel, Am Acad Rome, 50 & 51; Guggenheim Found fel, 54; Nat Inst Arts & Lett grant, 68.
Bibliography: 19 young Americans, Life, 3/20/50; An American painter looks at art boom, Parade, 9/1/63.
Memberships: Nat Acad Design.
Publications: Contribr, Fortune Mag, 55; illusr, Christopher Columbus, Scholastic Mag, 60; contribr, UNICEF calendar, 66; illusr, What do I say, 67 & auth & illusr, Mothers can do anything, 72, Albert Whitman & Co.
Dealer: Kraushaar Galleries, 1055 Madison Ave, New York, NY 10028.
Mailing Address: 20 Dock Rd, Norwalk, CT 06854.

LASKEY, DR & MRS NORMAN F
Collectors
Collection: Twentieth century primitives, fauve-non objective, op; American primitive sculpture.
Mailing Address: Croton Lake Rd, Mount Kisco, NY 10549.

LASLO, PATRICIA LOUISE
Sculptor, Instructor
Preferred Media: Bronze, Aluminum.
b Park Ridge, Ill, Feb 22, 30.
Study & Training: De Paul Univ; Univ Ill; Univ Wis; also with David Packard.
Commissions: Sculpture, Landsmiths, Lake Zurich, 72.
Exhibitions: One-man shows, Janus Gallery, New York, N Y, Benjamin Gallery, 70; New Horizons in Art, Chicago, 67, 68, 70 & 71; Old Orchard Invitational, Chicago, 67, 68 & 70; 51st Ann Show Wis Artists, Milwaukee Art Ctr, 68; Woman's Art Show, Kohler Art Ctr, Wis, 71.
Teaching: Instr sculpture & painting, Countryside Art Ctr, 66-70, gallery dir, 67-68; instr life drawing & 3D design, Chicago Acad Fine Art, 68-70; instr art, Maine N High Sch, 70-
Awards: Awards, Countryside Art Ctr, 68, for War God, Milwaukee Art Ctr, 68 & for Cyrano, Evanston Art Ctr, 69.
Bibliography: H Haydon (auth), Review of show, Chicago Sun Times, 70-72; D Anderson (auth), Review of show, Chicago Today, 72; F Schultz (auth), Review of show, Chicago Daily News, 72.
Memberships: Art Inst Chicago; Mus Contemp Art; Countryside Art Ctr; N Shore Art League.
Dealer: Benjamin Galleries, 900 N Michigan, Chicago, IL 60611.
Mailing Address: 150 E Northwest Hwy, Des Plaines, IL 60016.

LASSAW, IBRAM
Sculptor
b Alexandria, Egypt, May 4, 13.
Study & Training: Sculpture Ctr, 26-30; Beaux Arts Inst Design, 30-31; City Col New York.
Work in Public Collections: Albright-Knox Art Gallery, Buffalo, N Y; Baltimore Mus Art, Md; Whitney Mus Am Art, New York, N Y; Mus Mod Art, New York, N Y; Mus Mod Art, Rio de Janeiro, Brazil; plus many others.

Commissions: Sculpture, comn by Percival Goodman for Beth El Temple, Springfield, Mass; Baldachin & altar screen, House of Theology of Franciscan Fathers, Centerville, Ohio; hanging sculpture for lobby, Hilton Hotel, New York; sculpture for Beth El Temple, Providence, R I, Temple of Aaron, St Paul, Minn & Temple Anshe Chesed, Cleveland, Ohio, plus others.

Exhibitions: One-man show, Drawings, Vanderbilt Univ, Nashville, Tenn, 70; Modern Sculpture, Sheldon Mem Art Gallery, Univ Nebr, Lincoln, Nebr; Parrish Art Mus, Southampton, N Y; Recent Acquisitions, Whitney Mus Am Art, New York; Artists of Suffolk County, The Abstract Tradition, Hecksher Mus, Huntington, N Y; plus many others.

Teaching: Instr sculpture, YMHA, 92nd St, New York, 35-36; instr sculpture, Am Univ, 50; artist-in-residence, Duke Univ, 62-63; vis artist, Univ Calif, Berkeley, 65-66; also pvt classes in studio.

Positions: Fed Arts Proj, Public Works Admin, 33-42.

Bibliography: Dore Ashton (auth), Modern American sculpture, Abrams, 70; George M Cohen (auth), A history of American art, Laurel-Dell, 71; Bazin (auth), A history of world sculpture, Graphic Arts Soc; plus many others.

Memberships: Am Abstract Artists (founder, pres, 46-49); Artists Club.

Dealer: Kennedy Galleries, 20 E 56th St, New York, NY 10022.

Mailing Address: 678 Fireplace Rd, The Springs, East Hampton, NY 11937.

LASSITER, VERNICE (Vernice Lassiter Brown)
Painter
Preferred Media: Mixed Media.
b Millry, Ala, Nov 6, 27.
Study & Training: Univ Ala, with August Trovoahe; Famous Artist Sch; Art Stud League New York; also with Joseph Hirsch, Robert Brackman & Valdi Maris.
Exhibitions: Southeastern Ann Exhib, Atlanta, Ga, 57; 26th & 27th Miniature Painters, Sculptors & Gravers Soc, Washington, D C, 59 & 60; Mobile's Cult Exchange Prog, Malagna, Spain, 65; Sears Vincent Price Traveling Show, 70; plus many other one-man and group shows.
Teaching: Pvt classes, lects & demonstrations in painting.
Awards: First & best of show & gold cup, Mobil Art Asn Azales Trail Exhib, 61; first & best of show & gold cup, Mobile Art Asn Outdoor Art Exhib, first watercolor gold plaque, Alabama State Fair, 65.
Bibliography: Donald A Burrows (auth), rev, In: Fort Worth Art Mus catalog; Sterling McIlhany (auth), article, In: Am Artist.
Memberships: Mobile Art Asn; Birmingham Art Asn; Eastern Shore Art Asn.
Mailing Address: 4951 Winslow Dr, Mobile, AL 36608.

LASTRA, LUIS
Art Dealer, Art Critic
b Cuba, May 5, 30.
Study & Training: Univ Havana.
Positions: Art ed Visual Arts Bull, Orgn Am States, 63-69; art dealer, Pyramid Galleries, Washington, D C, 69-
Specialty of Gallery: Contemporary art; Latin American art.
Mailing Address: 2121 P St N W, Washington, DC 20037.

LATHAM, BARBARA
Painter, Illustrator
Preferred Media: Oils.
b Walpole, Mass, June 6, 96.
Study & Training: Norwich Art Sch, Conn; Pratt Inst; Art Stud League New York; also with Andrew Dasburg.
Work in Public Collections: Metrop Mus Art Print Collection; Libr Cong, Washington, D C; Santa Fe Mus; Philadelphia Mus; var Tex mus.
Exhibitions: Three Whitney Mus Am Art Ann; Brooklyn Mus Watercolor Int, 40; Prints, Carnegie Inst, 44; Prints, Nat Acad Design, 46, 48 & 49; Chicago Mus Watercolor Int; plus others.
Awards: Several purchase prizes.
Publications: Illusr, Pedro, Nina and Perrito, Harper & Row, 39, Calling South America, Ginn, 45, Perrito's pup, Knopf, 46, Tales of old time Texas, Little, 55 & Flying Horseshoe Ranch, Viking Press, 55.
Dealer: Allied Artists Gallery A, Taos, NM 87571.
Mailing Address: Box 73, Rancho de Taos, NM 87557.

LATHROP, CHURCHILL PIERCE
Educator, Gallery Director
b New York, N Y, Aug 26, 00.
Study & Training: Rutgers Univ, LittB, with John C Van Dyck; Princeton Univ, AM, with Rufus Morey; Dartmouth Col, hon AM, 37.
Teaching: Prof medieval, renaissance & mod art, Dartmouth Col, 28-70, chmn dept art, 37-47, 64-68.

Positions: Dir, Art Galleries, Dartmouth Col, 40-66, dir emer, 66-, art consult, Dartmouth Col, 68-
Memberships: Am Asn Mus; Col Art Asn Am; Mus Mod Art, New York; Soc Archit Historians; Am Asn Univ Prof.
Publications: Co-auth, The individual and the world, 42; auth, Paul Sample, 48; auth, The story of art at Dartmouth, 51.
Mailing Address: 7 Sargent St, Hanover, NH 03755.

LATHROP, DOROTHY P
Illustrator, Writer
b Albany, N Y, Apr 16, 91.
Study & Training: Teachers Col, Columbia Univ; Pa Acad Fine Arts; Art Stud League New York; also with Henry McCarter & F Luis Mora.
Work in Public Collections: Libr Cong, Washington, D C; Albany Inst Hist & Art; Woodmere Art Gallery, Philadelphia, Pa; Holyoke Mus, Mass.
Exhibitions: Nat Acad Design & Soc Am Graphic Artists, New York, N Y; Pa Acad Fine Arts, Philadelphia; Libr Cong, Washington, D C; Woodmere Art Gallery.
Awards: Caldecott Medal for Animals of The Bible, 38; Eyre Medal, Philadelphia Watercolor Exhib, 39; Pennell Purchase Prize, Libr Cong, 46; plus others.
Memberships: Assoc Nat Acad Design; Soc Am Graphic Artists; Albany Print Club; Philadelphia Watercolor Club; Kent Art Asn; plus others.
Publications: Illusr, Puppies for keeps, 43; auth & illusr, Who goes there, 63 & Let them live, 66, Macmillan; illusr, Bells and grass, Viking Press, 64 & Animals of the Bible, Lippincott, 69; plus many others.
Mailing Address: Undermountain Rd, Falls Village, CT 06031.

LATHROP, GERTRUDE K
Sculptor
b Albany, N Y, Dec 24, 96.
Study & Training: Art Stud League New York; Sch Am Sculpture; also with Solon Borglum & Charles Grafly.
Work in Public Collections: Houston Pub Libr, Tex; Albany Pub Libr, N Y; N Y State Teachers Col; Smithsonian Inst, Washington, D C; Brookgreen Gardens, S C.
Commissions: War mem, Mem Grove, Albany, N Y; commemorative half-dollar, Albany & New Rochelle, N Y; medals, Garden Club Am, 42, 50, Hispanic Soc Am, 50, Mariners' Mus, 54, N Y State Univ Hall of Fame, 62, 66 & Nat Steeplechase & Hunt Asn, 64; plus others.
Exhibitions: One-man shows, Albany Inst Hist & Art, 57 & 66 & Woodmere Art Gallery, Philadelphia, Pa, 63.
Awards: Medal of honor, Allied Artists Am, 64; silver medal, Pen & Brush Club, 67; Saltus Gold Medal for merit, Nat Acad Design, 70; plus others.
Memberships: Nat Acad Design; Nat Inst Arts & Lett; Nat Sculpture Soc; Soc Medalists; Am Numismatic Soc; plus others.
Mailing Address: Under Mountain Rd, Falls Village, CT 06031.

LATNER, ALBERT J
Collector, Patron
b Can.
Memberships: Ont Art Gallery, Toronto; Royal Ont Mus, Toronto.
Collection: Twentieth century masters; specialty sculpture; German Expressionists; Cubist & Contemporary art.
Mailing Address: 245 Warren Rd, Toronto 195, Ont, Can.

LAUCK, ANTHONY JOSEPH, CSC
Sculptor, Art Administrator
Preferred Media: Wood, Stone, Watercolors.
b Indianapolis, Ind, Dec 30, 08.
Study & Training: John Herron Art Sch; Corcoran Sch Art; Art Stud League New York; Univ Notre Dame; spec study with Heinz Warneke, Hugo Robus, Ivan Mestrovic, Carl Milles & Oronzio Maldarelli.
Work in Public Collections: Visitation (terra-cotta), Indianapolis Mus Art; Judas (limestone), Corcoran Gallery Art, Washington, D C; Beside the Cross (walnut), Pa Acad Fine Arts, Philadelphia; Street Crash (cherrywood carving), Ball State Univ Art Mus, Muncie, Ind; The Wife of Lot (terra-cotta), Grand Rapids Mus Art, Mich.
Commissions: Facet glass screen, Congregation of Holy Cross, Moreau Chapel, Notre Dame, 55; Image of the Virgin (stone), Univ Notre Dame, 58; facet glass walls, Sisters St Ursula, Chapel at Chatham, Ont, 67; Image of St Angela (stone), Sisters St Ursula, col grounds, Chatham, 70.
Exhibitions: 143rd Pa Acad Fine Arts Ann, 48; Third Sculpture Int, Philadelphia Mus Art, 49; Nat Acad Design Nat, 51; 148th Pa Acad Fine Arts Ann, 53; Indiana Artists' Ann, Indianapolis Mus Art, ten yrs.
Collections Arranged: Ashanti Goldweights: Eric de Kolb Collection, 71, The Graphic Work of Georges Rouault, 72 & 18th Century

France: A Study of Its Art and Civilization, 72, Univ Notre Dame Art Gallery.
Teaching: Prof sculpture, Univ Notre Dame, 50-
Positions: Dir, Univ Notre Dame Art Gallery; mem jury of selection, State Bicentennial Medal, State of Ind, 72.
Awards: Fairmount Park Art Asn Prize, Philadelphia Mus Art, 59; George D Widener Mem Medal, Pa Acad Fine Arts, 53; Leonard Cantor Mem Award for sculpture, Indianapolis Mus Art, 53 & 58.
Bibliography: Norman Kent (auth), Anthony Lauck, priest and artist, Am Artist, 6/61; Dean A Porter (auth), Preface to Exhibition at Art Gallery, Notre Dame (exhib catalogue), 3-4/68; Martin Harrison (auth), Lauck sculpture in Canada, Today's Art, 10/70.
Memberships: Audubon Artists; Am Asn Mus; Col Art Asn Am.
Publications: Auth, articles in nat art mag.
Dealer: Jacques Seligmann & Co, Inc, 5 E 57th St, New York, NY 10022.
Mailing Address: Moreau Seminary, Notre Dame, IN 46556.

LAUFMAN, SIDNEY
Painter
Preferred Media: Oils.
b Cleveland, Ohio, Oct 29, 91.
Study & Training: Cleveland Sch Art; Art Inst Chicago; Art Stud League New York.
Work in Public Collections: Metrop Mus Art, Mus Mod Art & Whitney Mus Am Art, New York, N Y; Art Inst Chicago, Ill; Corcoran Gallery Art, Washington, D C; plus others.
Exhibitions: One-man shows, Galerie Devambez, Paris, France, 22, Marie Sterner Gallery, New York, 22, Arts Club Chicago, 27, Galerie Katia Grahoff, Paris, 29 & De Haucke Gallery, New York, 31; plus over 30 others.
Teaching: Instr painting, Art Stud League New York, 38-50; vis lectr painting, Brandeis Univ, 59-60.
Awards: Mr & Mrs Frank S Logan Prize, Art Inst Chicago, 32; third prize, Carnegie Int, 34; first Altman prize, Nat Acad Design, 37.
Memberships: Nat Acad Design; Woodstock Artists Asn.
Dealer: Forum Gallery, 1018 Madison Ave, New York, NY 10021.
Mailing Address: 62 Glasco Turnpike, Woodstock, NY 12498.

LAURENT, JOHN LOUIS
Painter, Educator
Preferred Media: Acrylics, Oils.
b Brooklyn, N Y, Nov 27, 21.
Study & Training: With Walt Kuhn, 46-48; Syracuse Univ, BFA, 48; Acad Grande Chaumiere, Paris, 48-49; Ind Univ, MAT, 54.
Work in Public Collections: Univ Nebr; Univ Ill; First Nat Bank Boston, Mass; Exeter Acad, N H; De Cordova & Dana Mus, Lincoln, Mass.
Commissions: Great Bay Area Mural, Univ N H, two panels, Dove & Fish, St George's Church, York, Maine, 68.
Exhibitions: One-man exhibs, Kraushaar Galleries, New York, N Y, 67-69, Mus Art, Ogunquit, Maine, 68 & Addison Gallery Am Art, Andover, Mass, 72; Father & Son, Sweat Mus, Portland, Maine, 69; Am Paintings & Sculpture, Univ Ill, Champaign, 71.
Teaching: Asst dir drawing & painting, Ogunquit Sch Painting & Sculpture, summers 46-60; asst prof drawing & painting, Va Polytech Inst, 50-53; prof drawing & painting, Univ N H, 54-
Awards: Louis Comfort Tiffany Found grant, 62; Nat Coun Arts Award, 66-67; City of Manchester Prize, Currier Gallery, N H, 70.
Bibliography: Rev, In: Time, 67; Peter Cox (auth), A talk with John Laurent, 69 & The best of Maine at Frost Gallery, 69, Maine Times.
Memberships: Barn Gallery (bd dirs, 68-71); York Art Asn; N H Art Asn.
Dealer: Hobe Sound Galleries, 739 Bridge Rd, Hobe Sound, FL 33455.
Mailing Address: Mill Lane Rd, York, ME 03909.

LAURER, ROBERT A
Educator
b Rochester, N Y, Mar 10, 21.
Study & Training: Univ Rochester, BA; Harvard Univ, MA.
Teaching: Asst prof art, Univ Colo, 49-53; asst prof art, Univ Ark, 54-55; asst prof art, Skidmore Col, 55-56; asst prof & actg chmn art dept, Fairleigh Dickinson Univ, 62-68; assoc prof art, 68-
Positions: Asst dir, Mus Contemp Crafts, 56-60, assoc dir, 60-62.
Mailing Address: Fine Arts Dept, Fairleigh Dickinson Univ, Rutherford, NJ 07070.

LAURINE (VIRGINIA LAURINE GROVER)
Painter
Preferred Media: Oils.
b Durham, Maine, Sept 15, 20.
Study & Training: Famous Artists Sch, dipl fine arts; also with Alicia Stonebreaker & Lillian Hale.

Work in Public Collections: St Joseph's Col; RCA Distributors, Portland, Maine; Jean O Mamin, Paris, France.
Commissions: Oil painting, Dr & Mrs Donald Cowing, Dresden, Maine, 71; oil painting, Judge Charles J Luke II, Daytona Beach, Fla, 72.
Exhibitions: Harlow Gallery, Hallowell, Maine, 67-70; Ogunquit Gallery, Maine, 69-71; Berkshire Mus, Pittsfield, Mass, 71; Decatur Art Guild Nat Show, Ala, 72; Benedictine Art Awards, New York, N Y, 72.
Awards: Best in Show, Decatur Art Guild, 71; Benedictine Award of Merit, 72; purchase prize award, RCA Distributors.
Bibliography: C L Dinsmore (auth), Profile of a state of Mainer, Portland Press Herald, 68.
Memberships: Kennebec Valley Art Asn; Lincoln Co Cult & Hist Soc; Kennebec Art Club; Am Artists Prof League; Berkshire Mus Art Asn.
Publications: Contribr, Artist/ U S A, 71-72 & 72-73.
Mailing Address: Birch Point Rd, Wiscasset, ME 04578.

LAURITZ, PAUL
Painter
b Larvik, Norway, Apr 18, 89.
Work in Public Collections: Vanderpoel Col; Univ Chicago; San Diego Fine Arts Gallery; Joslyn Mus Art, Omaha, Nebr; Los Angeles City Col; plus other pub & pvt collections.
Exhibitions: Nat exhibs in mus & art galleries.
Awards: Ebell Club Los Angeles, 60; purchase award, Cedar City, Utah, 62; Sacramento Expos, 62 & 64; plus many others.
Memberships: Soc Western Artists; Calif Art Club; Royal Soc Arts.
Mailing Address: 3955 Clayton Ave, Los Angeles, CA 90027.

LAURY, JEAN RAY (JEAN RAY BITTERS)
Designer, Writer
Preferred Media: Fabric.
b Doon, Iowa, Mar 22, 28.
Study & Training: Northern Iowa Univ, BA; Stanford Univ, MA.
Work in Public Collections: Crocker Gallery, Sacramento, Calif; Fresno Arts Ctr, Calif.
Commissions: Wood panel, Fresno Redevelop Agency, 70; mural, stitchery & wood panels, Fresno State Univ Stud Union, 70; mural, stitchery, United Calif Bank, Fresno, 70 & 72.
Exhibitions: Five Craftswomen, Fresno State Univ, 71; Quilts & Dolls, Egg & Eye Gallery, Los Angeles, Calif, 71; also numerous one-man & group shows.
Teaching: Instr art, Fresno State Univ; instr art, Univ Calif, Davis; lect & workshops throughout the country.
Publications: Auth, Applique stitchery, 68, Quilts & coverlets, 70, Dollmaking: a creative approach, 70 & Cut and painted wood, 72, Van Nostrand-Reinhold; co-auth, Handmade rugs, Doubleday, 71.
Mailing Address: 25090 Auberry Rd, Clovis, CA 93612.

LAVENTHOL, HANK
Painter, Etcher
Preferred Media: Casein, Oils, Aquatint, Bronze, Marble.
b Philadelphia, Pa, Dec 22, 27.
Study & Training: Yale Univ, with Robert Georges Eberhard, BA (sculpture); Acad Belli Arti, Florence, Italy.
Work in Public Collections: Yale Univ Art Mus, New Haven, Conn; Evansville Mus, Ind; Pepsico Corp, New York, N Y.
Commissions: Island Mists (five-color lithograph), 69 & Image du Rose (etching), 72, Assoc Am Artists, New York; Deer Park (color etching), New York Graphic Soc, Greenwich, Conn, 70; Ruth (four-color etching), Commentary Bk Soc, New York, 71; seven color etchings, George Visat, Paris, France, 72.
Exhibitions: Salon de Otono, Palmade Mallorca, 63-65; Festival Cult, Pollensa, Mallorca, 64; Philadelphia Mus Art, Pa, 68; Print Club Philadelphia, 69; Westchester Art Soc, 72; plus many other group & one-man shows in U S & Europe.
Memberships: Artists Equity Asn New York; Circulo Bellas Artes, Palma Mallorca.
Dealer: Bodley Gallery, 1063 Madison Ave, New York, NY 10028.
Mailing Address: 85 Campfire Rd, Chappaqua, NY 10514.

LAW, PAULINE ELIZABETH
Painter
Preferred Media: Oils, Watercolors.
b Wilmington, Del, Feb 22, 03.
Study & Training: Art Stud League New York; Grand Cent Art Sch; with John F Carlson, Henry Snell, Margery Ryerson, Aldro Hibbard, John Pike, Wayman Adams, John Conaway & George Bridgman.
Work in Public Collections: Norfolk Mus Arts & Sci, Va; Mus Athens, Greece; Ringwood Mus, N J.
Commissions: Amon Carter Peak, Big Bend Nat Park, Tex, 61.
Exhibitions: Allied Artists Am, 72; Nat Asn Women Artists, 72; Nat Arts Club, 72; Am Artists Prof League, 72; Knickerbocker Artists, 72.

Awards: Allied Artists Am Prize, 60; Lawrence Dorothy McCoy Prize, 60; Southern Vt Art Asn Prize, 62.
Memberships: Allied Artists Am; Knickerbocker Artists; Nat Asn Women Artists (first v pres, 55-57); Nat Arts Club; Catharine Lorillard Wolfe Art Club (chmn finance comt).
Mailing Address: Lindy's Lake, Butler, NJ 07405.

LAWRENCE, JACK
Collector
Mailing Address: 369 Lexington Ave, New York, NY 10017.

LAWRENCE, JACOB
Painter, Educator
Preferred Media: Gouache, Casein, Tempera.
b Atlantic City, N J, Sept 7, 17.
Study & Training: Harlem Art Workshop, 34-39; Am Artists Sch, 38; Denison Univ, hon DFA, 70, Pratt Inst, 72.
Work in Public Collections: Metrop Mus Art, New York, N Y; Mus Mod Art, New York; Phillips Mem Gallery, Washington, D C; Am Acad Arts & Lett, New York; Whitney Mus Am Art, New York.
Commissions: Three paintings, comn by Fortune Mag, 8/48; painting, Container Corp Am, 53; lithograph, Benrus Watch Co, 67; portrait of Jesse Jackson for cover, Time Mag, 4/70; olympic poster, Ed Olympia 1972 (Munich, Ger), 72; plus others.
Exhibitions: Migration Series (sixty paintings), Mus Mod Art, New York, 44; John Brown Series, Am Fedn Arts Traveling Exhib, 47; retrospective, Brooklyn Mus, N Y, 61; Migration Series, M'Bari Artists & Writers Club, Lagos, Nigeria, 62; Toussaint L'Overture Series, Fisk Univ, Nashville, Tenn, 68.
Teaching: Instr painting, Black Mountain Col, summer 47; instr painting, Pratt Inst, 56-71; prof painting, Univ Wash, 71-
Awards: Guggenheim fel, 46; Nat Inst Arts & Lett grant, 53; Brooklyn Art Bks Children Citation for Harriet and the promised land, 73.
Bibliography: Alain Locke (auth), And the migrants kept coming, Fortune Mag, 41; Aline B Saarinen (auth), Jacob Lawrence, Am Fedn Arts, 60; Bearden & Henderson (auth), 6 black masters of American art, Zenith Bks, 72.
Memberships: Artists Equity Asn New York (past pres); Nat Inst Arts & Lett; Black Acad Arts & Lett.
Publications: Illusr, One way ticket, 49; illusr, Harriet and the promised land, 68; illusr, Aesops fables, 70.
Dealer: Terry Dintenfass Gallery, 18 E 67th St, New York, NY 10021.
Mailing Address: 4316 37th Ave N E, Seattle, WA 98105.

LAWRENCE, MARION
Art Historian, Educator
b Longport, N J, Aug 25, 01.
Study & Training: Bryn Mawr Col, AB, 23; Radcliffe Col, AM, 24, PhD, 32.
Teaching: Asst art, Wellesley Col, 24-25; instr art hist, Bryn Mawr Col, 27-28; from instr to prof art hist, Barnard Col, Columbia Univ, 29-67, emer prof, 67-
Awards: Radcliffe, Carnegie Corp, Fulbright & Inst Advan Study fels, 25-50.
Memberships: Col Art Asn Am (dir, 40); Archaeol Inst Am (var comts); Mediaeval Acad Am.
Research: Late antique and early Christian sarcophagi.
Publications: Auth, The sarcophagi of Ravenna, Col Art Asn, 45, republ, Brettschneider, Rome, 70; also numerous articles in jours, 28-
Mailing Address: 88 Morningside Dr, New York, NY 10027.

LAWSON, EDWARD PITT
Art Administrator
b Newton, Mass, Sept 12, 27.
Study & Training: Bowdoin Col, BA; Inst Fine Arts, New York Univ, AM.
Teaching: Instr, Toledo Mus Art Sch of Design, 54-56; vis lectr, Sir George Williams Univ, 63-67; lectr, Univ Ariz, 68-69.
Positions: Curatorial asst, Toledo Mus Art, 56-57; supvr art educ, 57-59; asst cur, The Cloisters, 59-62; asst dir, Montreal Mus Fine Arts, 62-67; dir, Tucson Art Ctr, 67-69; admin asst, Int Exhibs Found, 69-70; asst dir, Am Asn Mus, 70-72.
Awards: Belg-Am summer fel, 56; Metrop Mus Art travel grant, 61; Montreal Mus travel grant, 65.
Memberships: West Mus League (v pres, 68-69); Am Asn Mus; Can Mus Asn (coun mem, 63-67); Province of Quebec Mus Asn (v pres, 63-65, pres, 65-67).
Mailing Address: 1216 Raymond Ave, McLean, VA 22101.

LAX, DAVID
Painter
Preferred Media: Oils, Polymers, Pastels, Ink.
b Peekskill, N Y, May 16, 10.
Study & Training: Ethical Cult Sch, painting scholar, 24-28, CFA,

with H R Kniffen, Victor D'Amico & Victor Frisch; Archipenko Art Sch, with Alexander Archipenko.
Work in Public Collections: Gallery Mod Art, New York, N Y; Clearwater Mus, Fla; Laguna Gloria Mus, Austin, Tex; Pentagon War Art Collection; State Univ N Y Collection; plus others.
Commissions: Several hundred genre paintings, Irving Mills Collection, 32-42; combat paintings, USA, Pentagon, 42-45; Denunciation (paintings), Grossman Mem, N Y, 45-50; murals, Vet Admin Regional Off Bldg, New York, 50-52; paintings of New York in the 50s, comn by group of New Yorkers, Dutchess Community Col, 52-57.
Exhibitions: Grand Cent Founders Show, New York, 39-46; Corcoran Gallery 18th Biennial, 43; Painting in the U S, Carnegie Inst, Pittsburgh, Pa, 46; Nat Arts Club 20th Ann, New York, 70; Tex Fine Arts Asn 60th Anniversary Exhib, 71.
Teaching: Chmn dept art, Dutchess Community Col, 58-
Awards: Mills Artists fel, 32-42; silver medal for painting, Int Inst Arts & Lett, 60.
Bibliography: Swerdlow (auth), Denunciation series, Laurel Hill, 49; Valente (auth), 60 paintings since denunciation, Hamilton Reproductions, 70; Brass (auth), Raunchy dogs of defeat, J Am Med Asn, 72.
Memberships: Grand Cent Art Galleries; Assoc Am Artists; Dutchess Co Art Asn; Int Inst Arts & Lett.
Publications: Co-auth, David Lax, painting and sculpture, 41, Lax paintings, TC in the battle of Europe, 45, Denunciation, paintings concerning man's fate, 49, David Lax, portraits, 51 & David Lax, paintings of New York in the fifties, 72.
Dealer: Washington Irving Gallery, 126 E 16th St, New York, NY 10003.
Mailing Address: Box 94, Red Hook, NY 12571.

LAYCOX, (WILLIAM) JACK
Painter, Designer
Preferred Media: Oils, Watercolors.
b Auburn, Calif, Mar 11, 21.
Study & Training: Univ Calif, Berkeley; San Francisco State Univ, BA, 48.
Work in Public Collections: Keith Gallery, St Mary's Col Calif; Holy Names Col Gallery, Oakland, Calif; Gen Tire Int Collection, Akron, Ohio; Naval Hosp Collection, Oakland; Latter Day Saints Collection, Salt Lake City, Utah.
Commissions: Paintings for calendars, Zellerbach Paper Co, San Francisco, 63 & Gen Tire Int Corp, 71 & 72; 10 paintings, Thompson Aircraft Corp, San Francisco, 65 & 66; oil paintings, White Weld & Co, San Francisco, 67; watercolor ser, Williamhouse-Regency, Van Nuys, Calif, 69-71.
Exhibitions: Contemp Am Art, Kyoto & Tokyo, Japan, 65; Am Watercolor Soc Ann, 65-66; Rosicrucian Egyptian Mus, San Jose, Calif, 70; Wichita Centennial Nat, Kans, 70; Calif State Fair Art Exhib, Sacramento, Calif, 71.
Teaching: Instr watercolor, Jade Fon Watercolor Workshop, Asilomar, Calif, summers 71 & 72.
Positions: Tech illusr, Atomic Energy Comn, Oak Ridge, Tenn, 43-46; art dir, Bacon Am Corp, Muncie, Inc, 49-56; designer, Mission-Regency Cards, Van Nuys, 66-
Awards: Best of Show, Diabolo Pageant Arts, 61; second awards, for watercolor, Soc Western Artists, 63 & oils, Calif State Fair, 65.
Bibliography: Wilson (auth), Jack Laycox: painter, Christian Sci Monitor, 66; P Mornand (auth), Review of American watercolors La Rev Mod, 66; Alexander (auth), A visit to Jack Laycox' studio, Contra Costa Times, 68.
Memberships: Soc Western Artists.
Publications: Auth, Dramatic paintings from familiar scenes, Walter Foster Bks, 72.
Mailing Address: P O Box 5054, Carmel, CA 93921.

LAYTON, RICHARD
Painter
b Wilmington, Del, Apr 15, 29.
Study & Training: With Frank E Schoonover & Carolyn Wyeth; Philadelphia Mus Col Art.
Work in Public Collections: In many bus & pvt collections in U S & abroad.
Commissions: Ten murals, incl Univ Del & E I Du Pont de Nemours & Co.
Exhibitions: Corcoran Gallery Art, Washington, D C; Am Watercolor Soc; Audubon Artists; Pa Acad Fine Arts, Philadelphia; Del Art Mus; plus many others.
Collections Arranged: Sixteen regional & nat exhibs incl N C Wyeth Exhib, Pa State Mus, Harrisburg, 65, Brandywine Heritage, 71 & N C Wyeth Exhib, 72, Brandywine River Mus.
Positions: Former cur, Brandywine River Mus, Chadds Ford, Pa; pres, Del Arts Soc, at present; pres, Brandywine Editions, Ltd.

Memberships: Wilmington Soc Fine Arts; Nat Soc Mural Painters; Int Platform Asn.
Publications: Auth, article, In: Del Today Mag, 5/71; auth, introd to N C Wyeth, Crown, 72.
Mailing Address: 2600 W 19th St, Wilmington, DE 19806.

LAZARD, ALICE ABRAHAM
Painter
Preferred Media: Oils, Watercolors, Acrylics, Casein.
b New Orleans, La, Nov 1, 93.
Study & Training: Art Inst Chicago; also with Archipenko, Briggs Dyer and others.
Work in Public Collections: Miami Mus Mod Art, Fla; Vanderpool Art Mus, Chicago, Ill; Strassel Co Art Galleries, Louisville, Ky; Sinai Temple Ctr, Chicago.
Exhibitions: Pan-Am Exhib, 59; Ravinia Art Festival, 59; Old Orchard Art Fairs; Avant-Gard'e Gallery, New York, N Y, 59; one-woman shows, Mason City, Iowa, 59 & 60.
Awards: Second prize oil, Northshore Art League, 55; silver medal, Chicago Soc Artists, 66; second prize watercolor, Suburban Art Ctr, 69.
Memberships: N Shore Art League; Artists Equity Asn; Suburban Art Ctr.
Mailing Address: 1610 Linden Ave, Highland Park, IL 60035.

LAZZARI, PIETRO
Sculptor, Painter
Preferred Media: Concrete, Bronze, Mixed Media.
b Rome, Italy, May 15, 98; U S citizen.
Study & Training: Ornamental Sch Rome, Master Artist, 22.
Work in Public Collections: Art Inst Chicago, Ill; Miami Mus Mod Art, Fla; Nat Collection Fine Arts, Washington, D C; San Francisco Mus Art, Calif; Whitney Mus Am Art, New York, N Y.
Commissions: Bronze bust of Eleanor Roosevelt, pvt comn & in collection of FDR Libr, Hyde Park, N Y, 65; frieze in high relief, Watergate West, Washington, D C, 69; bronze monument to Ed M Gallaudet, Gallaudet Col Alumni, Washington, D C, 69; bronze monument to Walter Reuther, United Auto Workers, Washington, D C, 70; polychrome concrete murals & bronze fountain, Embassy Row Hotel, Washington, D C, 71.
Exhibitions: Venetian Biennial, Venice, Italy, 47; Baltimore Mus, Md, 52; Corcoran Gallery Art, Washington, D C, 59; Whitney Mus Am Art, New York, 65; Nat Collection Fine Arts, Washington, D C, 70.
Teaching: Instr sculpture & drawing, Am Univ, 48-50; head dept art, Col Holy Cross, 48-50; instr sculpture, Corcoran Sch Art, 65-69.
Awards: Fulbright scholar, 50; Baltimore Mus Lord Prize in Sculpture, 52; first prize for sumi drawing, Washington Watercolor Asn, 64.
Bibliography: Seuphor (auth), A dictionary of abstract painting, Paris Bk Ctr, 58; Margaret Harold (auth), Award-winning art, 65; Washington artists today, Acropolis, 67.
Memberships: Washington Watercolor Soc; Artists Equity Asn.
Art Interests: Archeology; sculpture in polychrome concrete; engravings.
Publications: Auth & illusr, I Carbonizzati (series of 42 plates), 67 & Adam & Eve (series of 12 plates), 70.
Dealer: Hom Gallery, 7315 Wisconsin Ave, Bethesda, MD 20014.
Mailing Address: 3609 Albemarle St N W, Washington, DC 20008.

LEA, TOM
Painter, Illustrator
b El Paso, Tex, July 11, 07.
Study & Training: Art Inst Chicago, 24-25; study in Italy, 30 & New Mex, 33-35; Baylor Univ, hon LittD, 67; Southern Methodist Univ, hon LHD, 70.
Work in Public Collections: Dallas Mus Fine Art, Tex; El Paso Mus Art, Tex; State Capitol, Austin, Tex; Pentagon War Art Collection; also in pvt collections.
Commissions: Murals, Court House & Pub Libr, El Paso, U S Post Off Bldg, Pleasant Hill, Mo, Odessa, Tex & Washington, D C.
Exhibitions: One-man shows, Fort Worth Art Ctr, Tex, 61 & El Paso Mus Art, 63.
Positions: Artist & war corresp, Life Mag, 41-46.
Publications: Auth & illusr, The wonderful country, 52, The King Ranch, Vols I & II, 57, The primal yoke, 60, The hands of Cantu, 64 & A picture gallery, 68, Little; plus others.
Mailing Address: 2401 Savannah St, El Paso, TX 79930.

LEACH, FREDERICK DARWIN
Painter, Art Historian
Preferred Media: Oils, Acrylics, Bronze, Steel.
b Arkansas City, Kans, Sept 19, 24.
Study & Training: James Millikin Univ, BA; Univ Wis, with Carlos Lopez; State Univ Iowa, MA, MFA & PhD.

Work in Public Collections: State Univ Iowa; Ball State Univ; Minn Mus Art.
Exhibitions: Old Northwest Territory, Springfield, Ill, 46-57; Ohio State Fair, Columbus, 56 & 57; Ball State Drawing & Small Sculpture, Muncie, Ind; Exhibition 180, Huntington, W Va, 56-62; Encounter, Minn Mus Art, Saint Paul.
Collections Arranged: National Print & Drawing Exhibition: Ultimate Concerns, Ohio Univ, 60.
Teaching: From instr to asst prof art hist, State Univ Iowa, 48-56, actg head dept, 55; prof art hist & drawing & dir, sch art, Ohio Univ, 56-68; prof art hist & drawing, Hamline Univ, 68-, actg head dept art, 71-72, chmn fine arts div, 72-73.
Awards: Juror's exhib award, Huntington, W Va, 57; drawing prize, Ball State Univ, 63.
Memberships: Col Art Asn Am; Midwest Col Art Asn; Minn Art Historians.
Publications: Auth, Hogarth's distressed poet: the riddle of the garret, Ohio Univ Rev, 60; auth, Speculation on an artistic common denominator, Topic: 5, 63; auth, The found object, State Univ N Y Col Buffalo, 65; auth, Review of Nathan Lyons', photographers on photography, Aperture, 67; auth, Paul Manship: an intimate view (monogr), Minn Mus, 72.
Mailing Address: Dept of Art, Hamline University, Saint Paul, MN 55104.

LEAF, JUNE
Painter, Sculptor
b Chicago, Ill, Aug 4, 29.
Work in Public Collections: Art Inst Chicago; Mus Mod Art, New York, N Y; Carbondale Mus, Ill.
Exhibitions: Contemp Am Artists, Chicago Art Inst, 69.
Teaching: Instr visual fundamentals, Art Inst Chicago, 52-58, instr painting & drawing, 54-58; instr drawing, Parsons Sch Design, New York, N Y, 67-69.
Awards: Fulbright scholar, 59.
Bibliography: Franz Schulze (auth), Fantastic art, Follett, 72.
Dealer: Gallery Bernard, 235 E Ontario, Chicago, IL 60611.
Mailing Address: Box 18, Mabou, Inverness County, N S, Can.

LEAF, RUTH
Printmaker, Instructor
Preferred Media: Graphics.
b New York, N Y.
Work in Public Collections: Libr Cong; N Y Univ; U S Info Agency; Bowdoin Col Mus Art; Colgate Univ.
Exhibitions: Sala Exposiciones, Escuela Nac Artes Plasticas, 67; Boston Mus, 70; De Cordova Mus, Mass, 71; Soc Am Graphic Artists, New York, 71; Galerie Art & Gravure, Paris, 72.
Teaching: Dir, Ruth Leaf Studio, Douglaston, N Y, 63-; instr intaglio, N Shore Community Art Ctr, 69-
Awards: Purchase awards, Lib Cong, 46, Hofstra Univ, 63 & Olivet Col, 67.
Bibliography: Ron Perkins (auth), Artists at work—filmstrip 4, Jam Handy Sch Serv, 70.
Memberships: Soc Am Graphic Artists; Boston Printmakers; Silvermine Artists Guild; Print Club, Philadelphia; Am Color Print Soc.
Mailing Address: c/o Bermond Art Ltd, 3000 Marcus Ave, Lake Success, NY 11040.

LEAKE, EUGENE W
Painter, Art Administrator
b Jersey City, N J, Aug 31, 11.
Study & Training: Yale Univ Sch Art & Archit.
Work in Public Collections: Baltimore Mus Art; J B Speed Art Mus, Louisville, Ky.
Teaching: Instr painting, Univ Louisville, 49-59; instr painting, Yale Univ, 60-61.
Positions: Pres, Md Inst Col Art, Baltimore, 61-
Mailing Address: 1300 Mt Royal Ave, Baltimore, MD 21217.

LEAKE, GERALD
Painter
b London, Eng, Nov 26, 84; U S citizen.
Work in Public Collections: Nat Arts Club.
Exhibitions: Royal Acad, London; Walker Art Ctr, Minneapolis, Minn; Art Inst Chicago, Ill; Corcoran Gallery Art, Washington, D C; Pa Acad Fine Arts, Philadelphia; plus many others.
Positions: Bd dirs, Island City Art Sch & Key West Art & Hist Soc.
Awards: Prizes, Nat Acad Design, Salmagundi Club, Allied Artists Am & others.
Memberships: Academician Nat Acad Design; Soc Illustrators; Nat Arts Club; Royal Soc Arts; Lakeland Fine Arts Soc; plus others.
Mailing Address: 1000 15th St, Marathon, FL 33050.

LEAVITT, THOMAS WHITTLESEY
Art Administrator, Art Historian
b Boston, Mass, Jan 8, 30.
Study & Training: Middlebury Col, AB, 51; Boston Univ, MA, 52; Harvard Univ, PhD, 58.
Collections Arranged: New Renaissance in Italy, Pasadena, Calif, 58; Piet Mondrian, Santa Barbara, Calif, 65; American Portraits in California Collections, Santa Barbara, 66; Brucke, Cornell Univ, 70; George Kolbe, Cornell Univ, 72.
Teaching: Lectr Am art, Univ Calif, Santa Barbara, 64-65; prof hist art, Cornell Univ, 68-
Positions: Asst to dir, Fogg Art Mus, 54-56; dir, Pasadena Art Mus, 57-63; dir, Santa Barbara Mus Art, 63-68; exec dir, Fine Arts Comn, People to People Prog, 67; dir Andrew Dickson White Mus Art, Cornell Univ, 68-72; dir mus prog, Nat Endowment for Arts, 71-72; trustee, Am Fedn Arts, 72-; dir, Herbert F Johnson Mus Art, Cornell Univ, 73-
Memberships: Col Art Asn Am; Am Asn Mus; assoc Asn Art Mus Dirs.
Research: American 19th century painting.
Publications: Auth, New renaissance in Italy (catalogue), 58; auth, Mondrian (catalogue), 65; auth, American portraits in California collections (catalogue), 66; auth, Brucke (catalogue), 70; auth, The crisis in museums, 71; plus many other catalogues.
Mailing Address: 27 East Ave, Ithaca, NY 14850.

LEBEDEV, VLADIMIR
Painter
Preferred Media: Oils.
b Moscow, Russia, June 17, 10; U S citizen.
Study & Training: Tech Indust Art, grad; Acad Arts, Leningrad, grad, with Bernstein & Filanov; also with V Favorski & El Lisitski, Moscow.
Work in Public Collections: Acad Arts, Leningrad; Kunstkabinett Keterer, Stuttgart, Ger; Berry Hill Gallery, New York, N Y; Far Gallery, New York; also mus in Moscow & Khazan, Russia.
Commissions: Interior decoration, U S S R Bldg, World's Fair, New York, 39.
Exhibitions: Expos Artistes Exile, Paris, 48; Expos Stedelijk Mus Amsterdam, 49; Expos Artistes, Mus Nat Belg, 49; one-man show, Charles Barzansky Gallery, New York, 57; Nat Acad Design, New York, 65-66.
Awards: Hon mention, World's Fair, 39; first prize, Art Exhib, Block Island, R I, 61.
Bibliography: Articles, In: Herald Tribune, 3/7/53 & France Amerique, 3/3/57; Picture on exhibition, 2/57.
Memberships: Artists Equity Asn; Am Fedn Arts; Int Inst Conserv.
Publications: Auth, article, In: Life, 58.
Dealer: Far Gallery, 746 Madison Ave, New York, NY 10021.
Mailing Address: 144 E 36th St, New York, NY 10016.

LEBER, ROBERTA (ROBERTA LEBER McVEIGH)
Ceramist, Instructor
b Hoboken, N J.
Study & Training: N Y State Col Ceramics, Alfred Univ, BS; Columbia Univ.
Exhibitions: Five Nat Ceramic Shows, Everson Mus, Syracuse, N Y; Vision, George Jensen New York, 60; Environ Gallery, New York, N Y; Contemp Crafts, Worcester Mus, Mass; Rockland Found-Craft Award Show, 72.
Teaching: Instr ceramics, N Y Art Workshop, New York, 34-47; head ceramic dept, Craft Stud League, New York, 35-; instr ceramics, Rockland Found, West Nyack, N Y, 57-
Positions: Art coordr, Community Resources Pool-South Orangetown Cent Sch, 62 & 63.
Awards: Ceramic stoneware vase award of merit, Rockland Found, 72.
Memberships: Artist Craftsmen N Y (bd dirs, 68-70 & 72); Rockland Found (bd dirs, 68-69, chmn bd, 71 & 72); Worlds Craft Coun; Mus Am Folk Art.
Mailing Address: 117 Leber Rd, Blauvelt, NY 10913.

LEBKICHER, ANNE ROSS
Painter, Art Administrator
Preferred Media: Oils, Gouache, Watercolors, Conté.
b New York, N Y.
Study & Training: Univ Wash; Univ Mont; Columbia Univ; Chouinard Art Sch; Univ Wis; Univ Southern Calif; Otis Art Inst; Marymount Col; Palos Verdes Peninsula, Calif; also with Ejnar Hansen & Robert Frame, Pasadena, Calif, Joseph Mugnaini & Kero Antoyan, Los Angeles, Calif, Leonard Edmundson, Claremont, Calif & Francis De Erdley.
Commissions: Portraits & other types of work.
Exhibitions: Palos Verdes Community Arts Asn Ann, Palos Verdes Estates, Calif, 50-67; South Bay, Los Angeles Co, Calif, 55-60; Los Angeles Regional, 60-66; Mont Inst Arts at Kalispell, 69; Flathead Co Art Asn Int Art Festival, 70.

Collections Arranged: Several hundred exhibs, including G Rouault, Francis De Erdley, Paul Darrow, Douglas Parshal, Edgar Ewing, Amen, Connor Evarts, Keith Crown, Ted Gilien & Frederic Taubes.
Bibliography: June Lee Roddan (auth), Silhouette, Palos Verdes Soc Rev, 6/66; Alan Garrett (auth), Meet our artists, Gallery Manual, 70; Neva D Baker (auth), Art in action, Golden Days Reporter, 8/71.
Memberships: Flathead Co Art Asn (exhib chmn, 69-72, bd dirs, 70-, v pres, 73-75); Nat League Am Pen Women; Mont League Prof Women Artists; Palos Verdes Community Arts Asn (exhib chmn, 45-65, pres, 55-56); Mont Inst Arts.
Dealer: Hockaday Art Gallery, Second Ave at Third St, Kalispell, MT 59901.
Mailing Address: Methodist Camp Rd, Rollins, MT 59931.

LECHAY, JAMES
Painter
b New York, N Y, July 5, 07.
Work in Public Collections: Art Inst Chicago, Ill; Brooklyn Mus, N Y; Des Moines Art Ctr, Iowa; Pa Acad Fine Arts, Philadelphia; Mus Art, Univ Iowa.
Exhibitions: Metrop Mus Art, New York; Art Inst Chicago; Pa Acad Fine Arts; Carnegie Inst, Pittsburgh, Pa; Toledo Mus Art, Ohio.
Teaching: Instr art, Stanford Univ, summer 51; instr art, Skowhegan Sch Painting & Sculpture, summer 63; prof art, Univ Iowa, 45-72.
Awards: Norman Waite Harris Medal, Art Inst Chicago, 42; purchase awards, Pa Acad Fine Arts & Des Moines Art Ctr.
Dealer: Kraushaar Galleries, 1055 Madison Ave, New York, NY 10028.
Mailing Address: 1191 Hotz Ave, Iowa City, IA 52240.

LECHTZIN, STANLEY
Designer, Educator
Preferred Media: Metals, Plastics.
b Detroit, Mich, June 9, 36.
Study & Training: Wayne State Univ, BFA; Cranbrook Acad Art, Bloomfield Hills, Mich, MFA.
Work in Public Collections: Mus Contemp Crafts, New York, N Y; Detroit Inst Arts; Schmuckmuseum Pforzheim, Ger; Minn Mus Art, Saint Paul; Objects U S A, Johnson Collection Contemp Crafts.
Commissions: Silver mace, Temple Univ, Philadelphia, Pa, 66; silver Christmas ornament, Adina Corp, Philadelphia, 71.
Exhibitions: Int Exhib Design in Stainless Steel, Nat Gallery Can, 60; Int Exhib Mod Jewelry, Goldsmiths Hall, London, Eng, 61; Form & Quality, Int Invitational, Munich, Ger, 65-72; Int Jewelry Exhib, Tokyo, Japan, 70; Jewelry-Objects, Int Invitational, Mus Bellerive, Zurich, Switz, 71.
Teaching: Prof metalsmithing, Tyler Sch Art, Temple Univ, 62-, chmn craft dept, 65-
Awards: Wichita Arts Asn First Prize in Jewelry & Medal of Hon, 58; highest award for creation of most outstanding design, Cult Pearl Asn Am & Japan, 66; Louis Comfort Tiffany Found Award in Crafts, 67.
Bibliography: Graham Hughes (auth), The renaissance of the artist jeweler, Optima, 70; Lee Nordness (auth), Objects U S A, Viking Press Inc, 70; film by Gazelle Film Prod Ltd (in prep), 72.
Memberships: Philadelphia Coun Prof Craftsmen (pres, 71-); Soc N Am Goldsmiths (mem bd dirs, 70-); Am Crafts Coun.
Publications: Auth, Electrofabrication of metal, Craft Horizons, 64; contribr, Metal techniques for craftsmen, 68; auth, Museum of contemporary crafts (brochure), 69; contribr, Contemporary jewelry, 70; auth, rev of occupational brief, Chronicle Guid Publ, Inc, 72.
Dealer: American Crafts Council Gallery, 44 W 53rd St, New York, NY 10019.
Mailing Address: 6540 N 11th St, Philadelphia, PA 19126.

LECKY, SUSAN
Painter
Preferred Media: Acrylics, Watercolors.
b Los Angeles, Calif, July 19, 40.
Study & Training: Univ Southern Calif, BFA; also European travel.
Work in Public Collections: Los Angeles Co Mus.
Exhibitions: Los Angeles Vicinity, 61 & 62; Midwest Ann, Decatur, Ill, 68 & 69; Univ Southern Calif, 70; Joslyn Mus, Omaha, Nebr, 72; one-man show, Urbana, Ill, 66.
Memberships: WEB-Women's Art Registry.
Mailing Address: 306 S Orchard St, Urbana, IL 61801.

LE CLAIR, CHARLES
Painter, Educator
Preferred Media: Oils, Acrylics, Watercolors.
b Columbia, Mo, May 23, 14.
Study & Training: Univ Wis, BS & MS, 35; Acad Ranson, Paris, 36; Columbia Univ, 40-41.

Work in Public Collections: Beaver Col; Temple Univ; Chatham Col; Albright-Knox Art Gallery; Pittsburgh Hundred Friends of Art.
Exhibitions: Butler Art Inst, Youngstown, Ohio, 51, 56 & 71; Whitney Mus Am Art, New York, N Y, 51-56; Int Watercolor Exhib, Brooklyn Mus, N Y, 59; Nat Acad Design Ann, 60; Pa Acad Fine Arts, Philadelphia, 63 & 65.
Teaching: Assoc prof painting, Chatham Col, 46-52, chmn art dept, 46-60, prof painting, 52-60; prof painting & dean Tyler Sch Art, Temple Univ, 60-
Awards: Ten awards, Assoc Artists Pittsburgh, 46-; Ford Found fel advan educ, 52-53; Pennell Mem Award, Pa Acad Fine Arts, 65.
Memberships: Nat Asn Schs Art; Int Coun Fine Arts Deans; Col Art Asn Am; Am Fedn Arts; Consortium Univ Art Schs.
Publications: Co-auth, Integration of the arts, Harper, 54; co-auth, Meeting student needs through the humanities, Current Issues in Higher Educ, Asn Higher Educ, Washington, D C, 55; auth, A salute to William Pitt (catalog), Chatham Col, 58; auth, Humanities, Principles of Eval & Measurement for Higher Educ, Rochester Inst Technol, 61; auth, Education of the artist, Alumni Rev, Temple Univ, 1/62.
Dealer: Galleria 88, Via Margutta, Rome, Italy.
Mailing Address: 7614 Lafayette Ave, Philadelphia, PA 19126.

LECOQUE
Painter, Writer
Preferred Media: Oils, Tempera.
b Prague, Czech, Mar 21, 91; U S citizen.
Study & Training: Acad Beaux Arts, Zagreb, with Crnic; Acad Julian, Paris, with Baschett & Emile Bernard; also with Auguste Renoir.
Work in Public Collections: Mus Old Montmartre, Paris; Collection Beaux-Arts Ville Paris; Mus Prague; Mus Davenport, Iowa; Mus Mod Art, Haifa, Israel.
Commissions: Rooftops of Prague, by President Jan Masaryk for President Eisenhower, 45; portrait, Adlai Stevenson, Chicago, Ill, 52.
Exhibitions: Gallery Charpentier, Paris, 12; Anglo-Ger Exhib, Crystal Palace, London, Eng, 13; Int Sect, Biennale Venice, 26 & 28; Galleries Bergen, Oslo, 35; Munic Tower Gallery, Los Angeles, Calif, 58.
Awards: First prize of Architect Turek, Prague, 14; Soc Arts, Sci, Lett, Paris Gold Medal, 66.
Bibliography: H Adam (auth), article, In: Lett Françaises, 61; Maximillien Gauthier (auth), Paris, 61; Pierre Cailler (auth), Documents, Cahiers Art, 66; plus others.
Memberships: Soc Arts, Sci, Lett, Paris; Club Culturel Français, Los Angeles.
Publications: Auth, La ragazza dalla gamba di legno, 51, Tragic weekend, 65, Renoir my friend—Renoir mon ami, 68, Capri unfinished portrait, 68 & Monography, 72.
Dealer: Alred Loeb, 11, Rue Chauchat, Paris 9e, France.
Mailing Address: 8079 Selma Ave, Los Angeles, CA 90046.

LEDERER, WOLFGANG
Designer, Educator
b Mannheim, Ger, Jan 16, 12.
Study & Training: Akad Graphische Kuenste und Buchgewerbe, Leipzig, Ger; Acad Scandinave, Paris, France, with Othon Friesz; Officina Pragensis, Prague, Czech, with H Steiner-Prag.
Work in Public Collections: San Francisco Mus Art, Calif.
Commissions: Bk design, Univ Calif Press & others.
Exhibitions: One-man show, Vienna, Austria, 37; Elder Gallery, San Francisco, 41; San Francisco Mus Art, 42; San Francisco Art Asn, 43.
Teaching: Lect, Design, Illustrations & The Work of H Steiner-Prag, to mus & art socs; prof graphic design & illus & chmn dept design, Calif Col Arts & Crafts, 45-, dir, div design, 70.
Mailing Address: Dept of Design, California College of Arts & Crafts, Oakland, CA 94618.

LEDYARD, WALTER WILLIAM
Sculptor
Preferred Media: Marble, Alabaster, Wood.
b Rockford, Ill, Mar 6, 15.
Study & Training: Rockford Col, with Marquis Reitzel; Univ Ill, AB, Univ Ill Col Med, MD; also with Gil Petroff.
Work in Public Collections: S C State Art Collection; Columbia Mus Art, S C.
Exhibitions: S C Artists Guild Ann, 62-71; S C Invitational, 69.
Positions: Mem bd trustees, Columbia Mus Art, 63-66, v pres, 66-68, pres, 68-70.
Awards: S C State Art Comn Purchase Prize, 69.
Memberships: S C Artists Guild (exec bd).
Collection: Etchings & lithographs from seventeenth century to contemporary & contemporary sculpture.
Mailing Address: 3900 MacGregor Dr, Columbia, SC 29206.

LEE, AMY FREEMAN
Painter, Lecturer
Preferred Media: Watercolors.
b San Antonio, Tex, Oct 3, 14.
Study & Training: St Mary's Hall, San Antonio, grad, 31; Univ Texas, Austin, 31-34; Incarnate Word Col, 34-42, hon LittD, 65; critiques from Charles Rosen, Ralph Pearson & Edward John Stevens.
Work in Public Collections: D D Feldman Collection, Univ Tex Mus, Austin; Smith Col Mus Fine Arts, Northampton, Mass; Ft Worth Art Ctr, Tex; Norfolk Mus Arts & Sci, Va; San Antonio Art League, HemisFair Plaza, Tex.
Commissions: Camellia Award Painting, Joskes of Texas, San Antonio, 71.
Exhibitions: Drawings by Contemporary Americans, Cult Relations Sect, U S For Serv, France, 56-58; Mex-Am Cult Exchange Inst Invitational, OPIC Gallery, Mexico City, 65; Contemporary American Drawings II, 21st Am Drawing Biennial, Smithsonian Inst Traveling Exhib, 65-67; Am Watercolor Soc Ann, Nat Acad Design, New York, N Y, 59, 65 & 69; Calif Nat Watercolor Soc Ann, Otis Art Inst, Los Angeles & Western Asn Art Mus, 67, 68 & 70.
Teaching: Lectr comp cult, Trinity Univ, 54-57; lectr contemp art, San Antonio Art Inst, 55-57; lectr expansion of perception, Our Lady of the Lake Col, 69-
Positions: Art critic, San Antonio Express, 39-42; art critic, KONO Radio Sta, San Antonio, 47-52 .
Awards: A Grumbacher Award of Merit & hon mention, Fla Southern Col Int Art Exhib, 52; Walker Award, 8th Ann New Eng Exhib, Silvermine Guild, 57; Purchase prize, 15th Ann Tex Watercolor Soc Exhib, Witte Mus, 64.
Bibliography: Dorothy Adlow (auth), Amy Freeman Lee Exhib, Christian Sci Monitor, 59 & 63; Fearing et al (auth), Our expanding vision, 59 & Art & the creative teacher, 71, Benson.
Memberships: Mex-Am Cult Exchange Inst (int consult, 72); Tex Watercolor Soc (founder, pres, 71-72); Texas Fine Arts Asn (adv coun, 71-72); San Antonio Art League (adv bd pres, 71-72).
Research: Equine ballets of the baroque period.
Publications: Auth, Morris Graves, the mystical realist, Witte Mus, 69; auth, Twenty questions, mineral, vegetable, animal or man?, Philos Soc Tex, 69; auth, Juan O'Gorman, a man & his magic rocks, Mex Quart Rev, 69; auth, Eco or echo?, Humane Soc U S, 70; auth, Creativity & the human spirit, Tex Quart, 72.
Dealers: L & L Gallery, 1107 N Fourth St, Longview, TX 75601; Shook-Carrington Gallery, 6700 N, New Braunfels, San Antonio, TX 78209.
Mailing Address: 127 Canterbury Hill, San Antonio, TX 78209.

LEE, DORIS
Painter, Illustrator
b Aledo, Ill, Feb 1, 05.
Study & Training: Rockford Col, AB, 27; Kansas City Art Inst, 28-29; study in Europe, 31; Calif Sch Fine Arts, San Francisco, 31, with Arnold Blanch; also with Andre Lhote, Paris, France; Rockford Col, LLD, 48, Russell Sage Col, 54.
Work in Public Collections: Art Inst Chicago, Metrop Mus Art, New York, N Y; Libr Cong, Washington, D C; Albright-Knox Art Gallery, Buffalo, N Y; Cranbrook Mus, Bloomfield Hills, Mich; plus others.
Commissions: Mural, U S Post Off Bldg, Washington, D C; designed curtain for Oklahoma (play); design & illus for Rodgers & Hart Songbook, Tough Blue & Gone is my Goose; paintings for Life Mag.
Exhibitions: Carnegie Mus, Pittsburgh, Pa; Whitney Mus Am Art, New York; New York & San Francisco World's Fairs; Asn Am Artists; World House, New York; plus others.
Teaching: Guest artist, Univ Hawaii, 57.
Positions: Mem fine arts adv bd, Famous Artists Schs.
Awards: Gold medal, Art Dirs Club New York, 57; Berkshire Painting Prize, New Eng Show, 64; first prize, Art & Sci Exhib, 66; plus others.
Bibliography: Paintings presented in Metro-Goldwyn-Mayer picture, The Pirate; monogr of paintings, Am Artists Group, 46.
Memberships: An Am Group; Woodstock Art Asn; Am Soc Painters, Sculptors & Gravers; Am Artists Cong.
Publications: Illusr, The great Quillon, Hired man's elephant, St John's River & Mr Benedict's lion; co-auth, Painting for enjoyment.
Mailing Address: R D 496, Woodstock, NY 12498.

LEE, ELEANOR GAY
Painter
Preferred Media: Oils, Pastels.
b Atlanta, Ga, Jan 15.
Study & Training: Nat Acad Design Sch Fine Art.
Work in Public Collections: Mus City of New York, N Y; Mus Fine Art, Hickory, N C; Mus Fine Art, Greenville, S C; River Edge Mus, Can; Tamassee Daughters Am Revolution, S C.

Exhibitions: Parrish Mus, Southampton, N Y, 60; Guild Hall, E Hampton, N Y, 63; Burr Galleries, New York, 71; Nat Biennial Composers, Authors & Artists Am, 71; Catharine Lorillard Wolfe Art Club Open, 71.
Positions: Dir one-man shows, Burr Galleries, 57-64; attendant, Thompson Gallery, New York, 66-69.
Awards: First prize for oils, N Y Co Fair, 55 & Composers, Authors & Artists, 71.
Memberships: Burr Artists (founding pres, 71); Catharine Lorillard Wolfe Art Club (pres, 50); Composers, Authors & Artists Am (v pres, 71); Nat League Am Pen Women, New York Br (rec secy, 55); Gotham Painters (rec secy, 68).
Mailing Address: Nat Arts Club, 15 Gramercy Park S, New York, NY 10003.

LEE, GEORGE J
Art Administrator, Photographer
b Boston, Mass, July 14, 19.
Study & Training: Harvard Univ, AB, 40, AM, 47.
Collections Arranged: Many oriental art exhibs, Brooklyn Mus, N Y, 49-59 & Yale Univ Art Gallery, New Haven, Conn, 59-
Positions: Cur oriental art, Brooklyn Mus, 49-59; cur oriental art, Yale Univ Art Gallery, 59-
Bibliography: M Domit (auth), George Lee, recent color photography, Corcoran Gallery, Washington, D C, 10/69.
Memberships: Asia Soc (ed bd, 50-); Oriental Ceramic Soc London.
Research: Far Eastern art and Chinese ceramics.
Publications: Auth, Selected Far Eastern art in the Yale University Art Gallery, 70.
Mailing Address: Yale University Art Gallery, 1111 Chapel St, New Haven, CT 06520.

LEE, MANNING DE VILLENEUVE
Illustrator, Painter
Preferred Media: Oils, Watercolors, Inks.
b Summerville, S C, Mar 15, 94.
Study & Training: Pa Acad Fine Arts, Europ Traveling scholar, 21.
Work in Public Collections: Six Marine Paintings, U S Naval Acad, Annapolis; William S Hart Co Mus, Los Angeles, Calif; Cranbrook Acad, Birmingham, Mich; Presidential Palace, Monrovia, Liberia; also in pvt collections.
Commissions: Portraits, of Jacob H Lowrey, 22, F Styers, Supt U S Mint, Philadelphia, 22 & Lawrence Lafore, 23; Sea Plane PN9, Adm Rodgers, 23 & five paintings, Philadelphia Wk Engraving Co, U S Naval Acad Yearbook, 25; plus others.
Exhibitions: Gribbs Art Gallery, Charleston, S C, 20; Pa Acad Fine Arts Watercolor Show, 31; N W Ayer & Co, Philadelphia, 45.
Awards: Gold Medal, Charleston Expos, 07; second Toppan Prize, Pa Acad Fine Arts, 21.
Memberships: Fel Royal Soc Arts, London; Philadelphia Art Alliance.
Publications: Illusr, From star to star, 44, Cadmus Henry, 49, Colt of destiny, 50, Night watch, 52 & Buffalo trace, 55; plus 195 others.
Mailing Address: Boxwood Farm, Ambler, PA 19002.

LEE, RENSSELAER WRIGHT
Art Historian
b Philadelphia, Pa, June 15, 98.
Study & Training: Princeton Univ, AB, 20, PhD, 26.
Positions: Prof hist art, Northwestern Univ, Evanston, 31-40; prof hist art, Smith Col, 41-48; prof hist art, Columbia Univ, 48-54; prof hist art, Princeton Univ, 55-66.
Memberships: Col Art Asn Am (pres, 44-46); Am Acad Rome (pres, 70-72); vis comt Dept Art, Columbia Univ; adv comt, N Y Univ Inst Fine Arts; adv comt, Mellon Ctr Brit Art, Yale Univ.
Research: Theory of art, especially in its relation to literature; influence of Italian Renaissance literature on painting.
Publications: Auth, An English Gothic embroidery in the Vatican, 30, Ut Pictura Poesis: the humanistic theory of painting, 40 & 67 & Poetry into painting: Tasso and art, 70; contribr, articles & rev to var learned journals.
Mailing Address: 120 Mercer St, Princeton, NJ 08540.

LEE, RICHARD ALLEN
Painter, Collector
Preferred Media: Acrylics.
b Warren, Pa, June 22, 49.
Study & Training: Pa Acad Fine Arts, cert, Cresson traveling scholar, 71; Philadelphia Col Art, BFA.
Work in Public Collections: In pvt collections in Pa, Ohio, N Y, N J, Calif, Tenn & London, Eng.
Exhibitions: Cresson Exhib, 71; Fellowship Pa Acad Fine Arts, 71 & 72; Woodmere Gallery, Philadelphia, 72.
Awards: Hallmark Prize, 69; first prize, Fellowship Pa Acad Fine Arts, 71.

Memberships: Fellowship Pa Acad Fine Arts.
Collection: American and European sculpture and porcelain antiques; American and European twentieth century painting.
Dealer: Gallery by the Hill, 8139 German Town Ave, Philadelphia, PA 19102.
Mailing Address: c/o Pennsylvania Academy of Fine Arts, Broad & Cherry Sts, Philadelphia, PA 19103.

LEE, ROBERT J
Painter, Educator
b Oakland, Calif, Dec 26, 21.
Study & Training: Acad Art, San Francisco, with Richard Stephens, Hamilton Wolf & Richard Guy Walton.
Work in Public Collections: U S Air Force Hist Soc; Mt Holyoke Mus, Mass; Springfield Mus Fine Arts, Mass; Evanston Mus, Ill; Columbia Mus Art, S C.
Exhibitions: Palace Legion of Honor, San Francisco, Calif, 46; Art Inst Chicago, 47-49; Butler Inst Am Arts, Youngstown, Ohio; Conn Acad Fine Arts, Hartford; Smithsonian Inst, Washington, D C, 71.
Teaching: Instr illus, Pratt Inst, 55-57; assoc prof painting & design, Marymount Col (N Y), 62-
Awards: Purchase award, Springfield Mus Fine Art, 55; first prize gold medal of honor, Allied Artists, 60; award of excellence, Soc Illusr, 67.
Bibliography: N Kent (auth), The artist speaks out, Am Artist, 68.
Publications: Illusr, Heroes of the Bible, 65 & The science of man, 68, Western Publ; Men and women, the poetry of love, Am Heritage, 70 & Old devil wind, 70 & Exploring music, 71, Holt Rinehart & Winston.
Dealer: Christopher Gallery, 766 Madison Ave, New York, NY 10021.
Mailing Address: Seminary Hill, Carmel, NY 10512.

LEE, SHERMAN EMERY
Art Museum Director
b Seattle, Wash, Apr 19, 18.
Study & Training: Am Univ, BA & MA; Case Western Reserve Univ, PhD.
Teaching: Lectr art hist, Univ Wash, 48-52; lectr art hist, Case Western Reserve Univ, 58, prof art, 62-
Positions: Cur Far Eastern art, Detroit Inst Art, 41-46; with dept arts & monuments div, civil info & educ sect, gen hq, Supreme Comdr, Allied Powers, Tokyo, 46-68; asst dir to assoc dir, Seattle Mus Art, 48-52; cur Oriental art, Cleveland Mus Art, 52-, asst dir, 57, assoc dir, 58, dir, 58-; consult comt, Artibus Asiae.
Awards: Legion of Honor; Order of the North Star.
Memberships: Am Asn Mus; Asn Art Mus Dirs (past pres); Nat Humanities Coun; Am Acad Arts & Sci.
Publications: Auth, Chinese Landscape painting, 54, rev ed, 62; co-auth, Streams and mountains without end, 55; auth, Japanese decorative style, 61; auth, History of Far Eastern art, 64; co-auth, Chinese art under the Mongols, 68.
Mailing Address: 2536 Norfolk Rd, Cleveland, OH 44106.

LEE-SMITH, HUGHIE
Painter, Lecturer
Preferred Media: Oils, Watercolors, Pencil, Charcoal.
b Eustis, Fla, Sept 20, 15.
Study & Training: Art Sch Detroit Soc Arts & Crafts, Scholastic Mag scholar; Cleveland Inst Art, cert, 38; Wayne State Univ, BS(art educ), 53.
Work in Public Collections: Detroit Inst Arts, Mich; Parrish Mus, Southampton, N Y; Lagos Mus, Nigeria; USN Art Ctr, Washington, D C; Univ Mich, Ann Arbor.
Exhibitions: Cleveland Mus Art Regional, Ohio, 35-40; Detroit Inst Arts Regional, 48-57; Nat Acad Design Nat, New York, N Y, 57-72; Boston Mus Nat, Mass, 70; Whitney Mus Am Art Nat, New York, 71.
Teaching: Instr painting, Grosse Pointe War Mem, Mich, 56-66; instr drawing & painting, Princeton Country Day Sch, N J, 63-65; instr painting, Vt Acad, summer 68; artist-in-residence, Howard Univ, 69-71; instr, Art Stud League New York, presently.
Awards: Emily Lowe Award, 57; Allied Artists Am Prize, 58; Clarke Prize, Nat Acad Design, 58.
Memberships: Nat Acad Design; Artists Equity Asn New York; The Players, New York.
Dealer: Grand Central Art Galleries, 40 Vanderbilt Ave, New York, NY 10017.
Mailing Address: 253 W 72nd St, Apt 1706, New York, NY 10023.

LEEBER, SHARON CORGAN
Sculptor
Preferred Media: Steel, Aluminum, Marble.
b St Johns, Mich, Oct 1, 40.
Study & Training: Univ Wyo; Trinity Univ.

Work in Public Collections: Shreveport Mus, La; Del Mar Col, Corpus Christi, Tex; Las Cumbres, Acapulco, Mex.

Commissions: Six welded steel pieces, Stemmons Inn, Dallas, Tex, 72; large welded male, John Higenbothim, III Collection, Dallas, 72.

Exhibitions: Tex Fine Arts Nat, Austin, Tex, 69; one-man retrospective show, Elizabet Ney Mus, Austin, 71; Tex Sculpture & Painting, Dallas, 71; Okla Painting & Sculpture, Oklahoma City, 71; Tex Ann Erotic Show, San Antonio, Tex, 71 & 72.

Teaching: Instr sculpture, El Centro Col, Dallas, 72-

Awards: Purchase award, Shreveport Mus, 69; purchase award, Del Mar Col.

Bibliography: J Kutner (auth), Surprise in art, Dallas Morning News, 4/30/71; L Haacke (auth), Bumpers form Leeber sculpture, Dallas Times Herald, 5/2/71; Sculptures by Sharon Leeber, Austin Am Statesman, 7/11/71.

Memberships: Nat Sculptor's Asn; Artists Equity Asn (secy, Dallas Chap, 71-72); Engrs, Artists & Technologists; Tex Fine Arts Asn.

Dealer: Contemporary Gallery, 2800 Routh St, The Quadrangle, Dallas, TX 75201.

Mailing Address: 6410 Dykes Way, Dallas, TX 75230.

LEECH, HILTON
Painter, Instructor
Preferred Media: Watercolor.
b Bridgeport, Conn.
Study & Training: Grand Cent Art Sch; Art Stud League New York.
Work in Public Collections: High Mus Art, Atlanta, Ga; Dallas Mus Fine Art, Tex; Hickory Mus Art, N C; John Herron Art Inst, Indianapolis, Ind; Hamilton Art Gallery, Ont; plus others.
Commissions: Murals, Court House, Chattanooga, Tenn & U S Post Off, Bay Minette, Ala.
Teaching: Guest instr, John Herron Art Inst, 53; guest instr, Southern Artists, Hot Springs, Ark; dir & instr, Madison Art Sch, Virginia City, Mont, summers; guest instr, Springfield Art Mus, Mo, 65.
Awards: Morse Award, Nat Acad Design, 65; prizes, Audubon Artists, Knickerbocker Artists & others.
Memberships: Am Watercolor Soc; Philadelphia Watercolor Club; Salmagundi Club; Sarasota Art Asn; Fla Artists Group; plus others.
Mailing Address: 2362 Pine Terr, Sarasota, FL 33581.

LEEDS, ANNETTE
Painter
Preferred Media: Oils.
b Boston, Mass, May 2, 20.
Study & Training: Mass Col Art, grad; Art Stud League New York, N Y; Brooklyn Mus, with Moses Soyer; also with Paul Puzinas & Howard Beesendahl.
Exhibitions: Community Arts Coun S Shore 69, Green Acres, N Y, 69; N Y State Biennial, Nat League Am Pen Women, N Y, 71; Catharine Lorillard Wolfe Art Exhib, Nat Acad Design Galleries, New York, 71; Long Island Art 72, Abraham & Straus Gallery, Hempstead, N Y, 72; Brooklyn Mus Fence Show, N Y, 72.
Teaching: Private instr, 68-
Awards: First prize & gold medal, 63 & spec award, 64, Art League Long Island; third prize, Art League Nassau Co, 65.
Memberships: Nat League Am Pen Women (art chmn, 71); Catharine Lorillard Wolfe Art Club (chmn publicity, 69-, exhib chmn, 72); Burr Artists (chmn publicity, 69-); Art League Nassau Co.
Mailing Address: 116-17 Union Turnpike, Forest Hills, NY 11375.

LEEPA, ALLEN
Painter, Educator
Preferred Media: Acrylics on canvas.
b New York, N Y, Jan 9, 19.
Study & Training: Am Art Sch New York, scholarship; Art Stud League New York; New Bauhaus, Chicago, scholarship; Columbia Univ, scholarship, dean's fel, 47, BS, MA & EdD; Sorbonne & Grande Chaumiere, Paris, France; Fulbright award to France, 50-51; Ford Found grant, Brazil, 70.
Work in Public Collections: South Bend Mus Art, Ind; Royal Acad, Scotland; Grand Rapids Mus, Mich.
Exhibitions: Mus Mod Art, New York, N Y, 53; Sao Paulo Biennale, Brazil, 63; one-man show, Galerie Cour Ingres, Paris, 63; Mus Art Mod, Paris, 64 & 65; Retrospective, Hofstra Univ, 65; plus many others.
Teaching: Instr art, Brooklyn Art Ctr, 39-41; instr art, Brooklyn Mus & Metrop Mus Art, 40-41; instr art, Mus Mod Art, New York, 40-41; prof art, Mich State Univ, 45-; instr art Hull Sch, Chicago, 47-48.
Awards: Grand Rapids Mus Award, 58 & 65; Am Fedn Arts Printmakers Award, 67; Childe Hassam Award, Am Acad Arts & Lett, 69; plus others.

Bibliography: Michael Seuphor (auth), Abstract painting, 62 & Dictionary of abstract art, 63, Abrams.
Memberships: Am Asn Univ Prof; Mich Acad Arts, Sci & Lett.
Research: Creative problems in contemporary painting.
Publications: Auth, The challenge of modern art, 49 & 61; auth, The humanities in contemporary life, 60; auth, Abraham Rattner, 72; contribr, articles, In: New Art, 66, Minimal Art, 68 & New Ideas in Art Educ, 72; plus others.
Dealer: Detroit Artists Market Gallery, 1452 Randolph St, Detroit, MI 48226.
Mailing Address: 540 E South St, Mason, MI 48854.

LEEPER, DORIS MARIE
Painter, Sculptor
Preferred Media: Metal, Wood, Fiberglass.
b Charlotte, N C, Apr 4, 29.
Study & Training: Duke Univ, BA, 51.
Work in Public Collections: Nat Collection Fine Arts, Washington, D C; Hunter Gallery Art, Chattanooga, Tenn; Mint Mus Art, Charlotte; Loch Haven Art Ctr, Orlando, Fla; Cummer Gallery Art, Jacksonville, Fla.
Commissions: Fiberglass sculpture, comn by patron for Jacksonville Art Mus, 70; enamel painting, Tupperware Int Hq, Kissimmee, Fla, 71; fiberglass sculpture, Alpert Investment for Forum 303, Arlington, Tex, 71; three-sect fiberglass sculpture, Alpert Investment Corp for Park 436, Orlando, Fla, 72; fiberglass sculpture, First Nat Bank, Tampa, Fla, 72-73.
Exhibitions: Painting: Out from the Wall, Des Moines Art Ctr, Iowa, 68; Recent Trends in American Art, Westmoreland Co Mus Art, Greensburg, Pa, 69; N C Sculpture Invitational, Duke Univ & Ackland Art Ctr, Chapel Hill, N C, 69; Contemporary Women Artists, Nat Arts Club, New York, N Y, 70; Color as Form, Jacksonville Civic Auditorium, Fla, 72.
Awards: Purchase award, Southeastern Ann, Mint Mus Art, Charlotte, 68; purchase award, Frontal Images Nat, Miss Art Asn, Jackson, 69; Nat Endowment for the Arts grant, 72.
Bibliography: Edith Neely (auth), The world of Doris Leeper, Jacksonville Fine Arts Illus, 69.
Dealer: Bertha Schaefer Gallery, 41 E 57th St, New York, NY 10022.
Mailing Address: P O Box 2093, New Smyrna Beach, FL 32069.

LEEPER, JOHN P
Painter
Preferred Media: Acrylics.
b Dandridge, Tenn, Apr 23, 09.
Study & Training: Los Angeles Co Art Inst.
Work in Public Collections: IBM Collection; Long Beach Mus; Calif State Fair Collection.
Commissions: Mural, Ariz State Univ, Tempe.
Exhibitions: Calif Watercolor Soc; Los Angeles Mus Art; Calif & Can Traveling Exhib; Santa Barbara Mus Art; Long Beach Mus Art; plus others.
Awards: Calif State Fair Purchase Prize, 64; Los Angeles Festival Arts Purchase Prize, 64; Nat Orange Show, San Bernardino, 64.
Memberships: Calif Watercolor Soc.
Dealer: Adele Bednarz Gallery, 902 N La Cienega Blvd, Los Angeles, CA 90069.
Mailing Address: 624 W 46th Ave, Los Angeles, CA 90065.

LEEPER, JOHN PALMER
Museum Director
b Denison, Tex, Feb 4, 21.
Study & Training: Southern Methodist Univ, BS, 42; Harvard Univ, MA.
Teaching: Instr art hist, Dexter Sch, Boston, 46; instr art hist, Univ Southern Calif, 51; instr art hist, Pasadena Sch Fine Arts, 52; instr art hist, Trinity Univ, 56-57.
Positions: Keeper W A Clark Collection, Corcoran Gallery Art, 48-49, asst dir, 49-50; dir, Pasadena Art Mus, 50-53; dir, McNay Art Inst, 54-
Memberships: Am Asn Mus; Asn Art Mus Dirs.
Publications: Auth, Everett Spruce, 59; auth, Otis Dozier, 60; ed, The autobiography of Jose Clemente Orozco, 62; auth, A caribbean sketchbook by Jules Pascin, 64.
Mailing Address: 6000 N New Braunfels, San Antonio, TX 78209.

LEET, RICHARD EUGENE
Art Administrator, Painter
Preferred Media: Watercolors, Oils.
b Waterloo, Iowa, Sept 11, 36.
Study & Training: Univ Northern Iowa, BA, 58; Univ Iowa, 61-64, with Stuart Edie & Robert Knipschild; Univ Northern Iowa, MA, 65, with Ansei, Uchima, Ted Egri, Paul R Smith & John Page.
Work in Public Collections: Mus Art, El Paso, Tex; Hamline Univ, St Paul, Minn; Luther Col, Decorah, Iowa; Iowa State Fair Asn Ann Purchase Award Collection, Des Moines, Iowa; Iowa Artist Collection, Salisbury Labs, Charles City, Iowa.

Exhibitions: Seven Ann Iowa Artists Exhib, Des Moines Art Ctr, 58-72; Ann Nat Watercolor Exhib, Miss Art Ctr, Jackson, 67 & 68; Ann Midyear Show, Butler Inst Am Art, Youngstown, Ohio, 69; Ann Sun Carnival Exhib, Mus Art, El Paso, 71; Midwest Biennial, Joslyn Art Mus, Omaha, Nebr, 72.
Teaching: Art instr, Oelwein Community Schs, Iowa, 58-65; instr painting & drawing, C H MacNider Mus, Mason City, Iowa, 65-
Positions: Mus dir & founding dir, Chas H MacNider Mus, Mason City, 65-
Awards: Purchase award for watercolor & first award in graphics, Iowa State Fair Art Salon, 70; purchase award, Mus Art, El Paso, 71.
Bibliography: George Shane (auth), Visual arts, Des Moines Regist, 11/12/67; Nick Baldwin (auth), Visual arts, Des Moines Regist, 8/24/69; Milton S Koslow (auth), Art review, Charleston Gazette, 6/5/72.
Memberships: Am Asn Mus; Midwest Mus Conf (v pres from Iowa, 69-71, exec v pres & prog coord, 71-72, pres 72-); Iowa Arts Coun (mem coun, 70-).
Publications: Auth, Art with Leet, monthly column in Mason City Globe Gazette, 68-
Mailing Address: 1149 Manor Dr, Mason City, IA 50401.

LEETE, WILLIAM WHITE
Painter
Preferred Media: Acrylics.
b Portsmouth, Ohio, June 12, 29.
Study & Training: Yale Univ, BA, 51, BFA, 55, MFA, 57.
Work in Public Collections: De Cordova Mus, Lincoln, Mass; Cleveland Mus, Ohio; Worcester Mus, Mass; Univ Mass.
Exhibitions: New Eng Contemp Artists, Boston, 63 & 65; Silvermine Guild, Conn, 66; Art in Embassies, Inst Contemp Arts, Boston, 66; Structured Art, De Cordova Mus, 69; Young New England Painters, John & Mabel Ringling North Mus, Fla, Portland Mus & Currier Gallery, Manchester, 69.
Teaching: Assoc prof art, Univ R I, 57-, actg chmn art dept, spring 68 & 69-70.
Positions: Comt mem, R I Arts Festival, 61-68; bd trustees, R I Gov Sch, 69-
Dealers: Lenore Grey, 15 Meeting St, Providence, RI 02903; Ward-Nasse Gallery, 178 Prince St, New York, NY 10013.
Mailing Address: 50 Silver Lake Ave, Wakefield, RI 02879.

LEFEBRE, JOHN
Art Dealer
b Berlin, Ger; U S citizen.
Study & Training: Univ Berlin, with Prof Deri.
Positions: Dir, Lefebre Gallery.
Specialty of Gallery: Contemporary European artists.
Mailing Address: 47 E 77th St, New York, NY 10021.

LE FEVRE, RICHARD JOHN
Painter, Educator
Preferred Media: Acrylics, Watercolors, Oils.
b Rochester, N Y, Feb 11, 31.
Study & Training: Rochester Inst Technol, BS, 55, MFA, 67.
Work in Public Collections: State of Tenn, Nashville; Fall Creek Falls State Park, Tenn; E Tenn State Univ, Johnson City; Univ Tenn, Knoxville; Nat Bank N C, Charlotte.
Commissions: Oil, St Stephen's Church, Rochester, 60; acrylic on plexiglas, Church of Epiphany, Rochester, 65; polymer, Marine Midland Bank, Rochester, 65; acrylic on plexiglas, Capital Cadillac Corp, Atlanta, Ga, 70; acrylic on plexiglas altarpiece, Tyson Episcopal Ctr, Knoxville, Tenn, 71.
Exhibitions: Appalachian Corridors Exhib 1, Va, 68; Experiments in Art and Technology, High Mus, Atlanta, 69; Midsouth Competition, Parthenon Mus, Nashville, 70; Art U S A 2, Univ Northern Ill, De Kalb, 71; Tenn Arts Comn, Dulin Gallery, Knoxville, 72.
Teaching: Dir arts & graphic arts, Rochester Inst Technol, 65-67; asst prof design, Univ Tenn, Knoxville, 67-
Positions: Designer, Todd Co, Rochester, 54-55; designer, S M Crossette, Rochester, 55-58; pres, Le Fevre Studios, Rochester, 58-65.
Awards: First pl for mixed media, Huntsville Art League & Mus Asn, Ala, 68; purchase awards, Carroll Reece Mus, 71 & Mint Mus, 71.
Memberships: Knoxville Watercolor Soc.
Dealer: Gallerie Illien, 123 14th St, Atlanta, GA 30309.
Mailing Address: Rte 18, Lancelot Dr, Knoxville, TN 32921.

LEFF, JAY C
Collector
b Brownsville, Pa, Jan 7, 25.
Collections Arranged: Exotic Art from Ancient and Primitive Civilizations, Carnegie Inst, Pittsburgh, Pa, 59-60; African Sculpture from the Collection of Jay C Leff, Mus Primitive Art, New York, N Y, 64-65; Faces and Figures: Pacific Island Art, Am Mus Nat-

ural Hist, New York, 65; Ancient Art of Latin America from the Collection of Jay C Leff, Brooklyn Mus, N Y, 66-67; The Art of Black Africa: Collection of Jay C Leff, Carnegie Inst, 69-70.
Memberships: Pa Coun on the Arts (chmn, 71-); Carnegie Inst Art Comt.
Collections: Art from Ancient Latin America, sculpture from Africa and Oceania, and objects from the Far and Near East.
Publications: Auth, The art of black Africa, Carnegie Inst, 69.
Mailing Address: Fayette Bank and Trust Co, Uniontown, PA 15401.

LEFF, RITA
Printmaker, Painter
b New York, N Y.
Study & Training: Art Stud League New York; Brooklyn Mus; Parsons Sch Design; also with Abraham Rattner, Louis Shanker, Adja Yunkers, Worden Day & Louis Calapai.
Work in Public Collections: Metrop Mus Art, New York; Libr Cong, Washington, D C; Brooklyn Mus; Pa Acad, Philadelphia; Dallas Mus, Tex.
Exhibitions: Metrop Mus Art, 59; Brooklyn Mus Print Exhibs, 59, 61 & 63; Butler Mus Painting Ann, 66-67; Libr Cong Print Ann; Pa Acad Design Print & Watercolor Ann.
Awards: Four medals of honor, Nat Asn Women Artists, 64, 66, 68 & 69; Grand Prix, Salon Int De Femme, Cannes, France, 69; First Prize Norton Gallery, Palm Beach, Fla, 71 & 72.
Memberships: Soc Am Graphic Artists (coun mem); Audubon Artists (juror); Nat Asn Women Artists (chmn prints); Boston Printmakers.
Publications: Contribr, Prize winning paintings, How to win a prize winning painting & Prize winning watercolors.
Mailing Address: 106 Somerset-F, Century Village, West Palm Beach, FL 33401.

LEHMAN, IRVING
Painter, Sculptor
Study & Training: Cooper Union, 20-24; Nat Acad, 25-30.
Work in Public Collections: St Edmund's Hall, Oxford Univ, Eng; Ein Harod, Israel; Nat Mus Bezalel, Israel; John H Vanderpoel Mem Collection, Chicago; Mus Art Populaire Juif, Paris; plus others.
Exhibitions: Albany Inst Hist & Art; Ala Watercolor Soc; Brooklyn Mus; Charleston Art Gallery; Art Inst Chicago; plus others.
Teaching: Instr, Brooklyn Col Adult Educ; instr, New York Bd Educ; instr, studio workshops.
Awards: Kellner Award, Brooklyn Soc Artists 42nd Ann, 59; Am Soc Contemp Artists 44th Ann Distinctive Merit Award, 61; Lafayette Nat Bank Award, Am Soc Contemp Artists 47th Ann, 64; plus others.
Bibliography: Articles, In: Am Abstr Art, 36-66, Univ Syracuse Libr Mss & House & Garden Decorating Guide, fall/winter, 68-69; plus others.
Memberships: Am Abstr Artists; Audubon Artists Am; Am Soc Contemp Artists.
Mailing Address: 70 La Salle St, New York, NY 10027.

LEHMAN, LOUISE BRASELL
Painter
b Orwood, Miss, Oct 15, 01.
Study & Training: Miss State Col Women; George Washington Univ; Corcoran Sch Art; Teachers Col, Columbia Univ, BS.
Work in Public Collections: Montgomery Mus Fine Arts; Miss State Col Women; Brooks Mem Art Gallery.
Exhibitions: Southern Art Festival, 67; Brooks Mem Art Gallery, 68; Miss Art Asn, 68; Tenn Art Comn Traveling Exhib, 68; Smithsonian Inst Traveling Exhib to Europe, 68; plus others.
Awards: Prizes, Brooks Mem Art Gallery, 68; Tenn All-State Art Exhib, Nashville, 68; Tenn Art Comn Purchase Prize, 68; plus others.
Memberships: New Orleans Art Asn; Artist's Registry (bd dirs).
Mailing Address: 476 N Willett St, Memphis, TN 38112.

LEHRER, LEONARD
Painter, Educator
Preferred Media: Oils.
b Philadelphia, Pa, Mar 23, 35.
Study & Training: Philadelphia Col Art, BFA, 56; Univ Pa, MFA, 60.
Work in Public Collections: Mus Mod Art, New York, N Y; Philadelphia Mus Art; Libr Cong, Washington, D C; Yale Univ Art Gallery, New Haven, Conn; Lessing J Rosenwald Collection, Jenkintown, Pa.
Exhibitions: One-man shows, Larcada Gallery, New York, 67 & Sindelir Gallery, Coral Gables, Fla, 68; New Realism, St Cloud Col, Minn, 70; Denver Mus Inaugural 73rd Western Exhib, 71; Brooklyn Mus Print Show, 72.
Teaching: Assoc prof, Philadelphia Col Art, 56-70; prof art & chmn dept, Univ N Mex, 70-
Positions: Pres Phila Chap, Artists Equity Asn, 60-62.

Awards: George Roth Prize, Philadelphia Print Club, 66; print
award, Cheltenham Art Ctr Exhib, 67; faculty summer grant,
Union Independent Cols Art, 69.
Bibliography: V D Coke (auth), The painter and the photograph, Univ
N Mex Press, 72.
Memberships: Col Art Asn Am.
Dealer: Marian Locks Gallery, 1524 Walnut St, Philadelphia, PA
19102.
Mailing Address: 829 Adams N E, Albuquerque, NM 87110.

LEIBER, GERSON AUGUST
Painter, Printmaker
Preferred Media: Graphics.
b Brooklyn, N Y, Nov 12, 21.
Study & Training: Art Stud League New York; Brooklyn Mus Art Sch.
Work in Public Collections: Metrop Mus Art & Whitney Mus Am Art,
New York; Nat Gallery Art, Washington, D C; Libr Cong, Wash-
ington, D C; Boston Mus Fine Arts, Mass.
Commissions: Print eds, Assoc Am Artists & Int Graphic Arts Soc.
Exhibitions: Am Prints Today, U S A, New York, 59; Cincinnati Int
Biennial, 60; American Prints, in Russia, Rome, Italy, Mexico
City, Mex & Salzburg, Ger; Libr Cong Exhibs; plus many others.
Teaching: Instr graphics & illus, Newark Sch Fine & Indust Art, 61-
68.
Awards: Tiffany fels, 57 & 60; Audubon Medals of Honor for graph-
ics, 63-65; prize for Am Nat Print Exhib, Assoc Am Artists Gal-
lery.
Bibliography: Margaret Harold (auth), Prize-winning graphics, Al-
lied Publ, Vols II & VII, 64 & 67; Frank Getlein (auth), Bite of
the print, Potter, 63; Hooten & Kaiden (auth), Mother and child in
modern art, Meredith Corp.
Mamberships: Soc Am Graphic Artists (treas, 69-72, coun mem);
Audubon Artists; Calif Soc Printmakers; Boston Printmakers.
Publications: Illusr, Crisis (poem), Oxhead Press, 69.
Mailing Address: 120 E 34th St, New York, NY 10016.

LEICHMAN, SEYMOUR
Painter
Preferred Media: Oils.
b New York, N Y, Apr 26, 33.
Study & Training: Cooper Union, with Morris Kantor.
Work in Public Collections: Butler Inst Am Art, Youngstown, Ohio;
Marine Midland Bank, New York.
Commissions: Murals, State of N J, Oakland, 63-64 & Ministry of
Justice, Jamaican Govt, 68.
Exhibitions: One-man shows, Vanderbilt Univ, 62, Griffin Gallery,
New York, 63, David Gallery, Houston, Tex, 68 & 69 & Kennedy
Gallery, New York, 72.
Teaching: Instr painting, Art Stud League, Woodstock, summer 71.
Awards: Certs of merit, Type Dirs Club New York, 56, Am Inst
Graphic Arts, 56-58 & 60 & Art Dirs Club New York, 60.
Bibliography: Selden Rodman (auth), The Rodman collection, Van-
derbilt Univ Press, 62 & The collector, Status Mag, 69.
Publications: Illusr, Death of the hero, Shorewood Publ, 63; auth &
illusr, The boy who could sing pictures, Doubleday, 68.
Dealer: Kennedy Galleries, 20 E 56th St, New York, NY 10022.
Mailing Address: 276 Riverside Dr, New York, NY 10025.

LEIFERMAN, SILVIA W
Painter, Sculptor
Preferred Media: Oils, Acrylics, Hot Wax.
b Chicago, Ill.
Study & Training: Univ Chicago, 60-61; extensive study Chicago, Ill,
Provincetown, Mass, Mex, Rome, Italy & Madrid, Spain.
Work in Public Collections: Miami Mus Mod Art; Lowe Art Mus,
Univ Miami; Roosevelt Univ, Chicago; in collections of Jack
Benny & Gov Haydon Burns; also in pvt collections throughout the
world.
Exhibitions: Int Platform Asn, 67; Hollywood Mus Art, 68; Lowe Art
Mus; Beau Art Gallery, Univ Miami; one-man show, Miami Mus
Mod Art, 72; plus others.
Positions: Co-founder & v pres, Silvia & Irwin Leiferman Found;
founder, Mt Sinai Hosp Greater Miami; founder, Greater Technion
Inst Technol Israel; pres, Active Accessories by Silvia, Chicago,
64-
Awards: Woman of Valor, State of Israel, 63; awards & citations,
U S Govt & Treasury Dept; citation, Community Leaders Am;
plus others.
Memberships: Int Platform Asn; Int Coun Mus; Am Fedn Arts; Art-
ists Equity Asn; life mem Miami Mus Mod Art; plus others.
Dealer: Hall Galleries Inc, 2325 Collins Ave, Miami Beach, FL
33139.
Mailing Address: 5255 Collins Ave, Miami Beach, FL 33140.

LEIGH, DAVID I
Collector
b New York, N Y, June 27, 33.
Study & Training: Pratt Inst, BA.
Memberships: Am Inst Graphic Arts; Package Designers Coun.
Collection: Sculpture, graphics, icons, African art, and paintings—
fourteenth century to present.
Mailing Address: 1245 Park Ave, New York, NY 10028.

LEIGHTON, CLARE
Engraver, Writer
b London, Eng, Apr 12, 01.
Study & Training: Slade Sch, Univ London, 21-23; Colby Col, hon
DFA, 40.
Work in Public Collections: Prints in leading mus in U S & Eng.
Commissions: Designed 33 stained glass windows, St Paul's
Cathedral, Worcester, Mass; mosaic, Convent Holy Family of
Nazareth, Monroe, Conn; 6 windows, Lutheran Church, Water-
bury, Conn; 2 windows, Methodist Church, Wellfleet, Mass.
Exhibitions: Represented Gt Brit in Venice Biennale.
Memberships: Royal Soc Painters, Etchers & Engravers, London;
Nat Acad Design; Soc Am Graphic Artists (v pres); Soc Wood
Engravers, London; Nat Inst Arts & Lett (v pres).
Publications: Auth, The music box, Woodcuts and wood engravings,
Sometime-never, Give us this day & Where land meets sea.
Mailing Address: Woodbury, CT 06798.

LEIGHTON, DAVID S R
Art Administrator
b Regina, Sask, Feb 20, 28.
Positions: Dir, Banff Ctr, Sch Fine Arts, 70-
Mailing Address: Box 1020, Banff, Alta, Can.

LEIGHTON, THOMAS CHARLES
Painter, Instructor
Preferred Media: Pastels.
b Toronto, Ont, Sept 3, 13; U S citizen.
Study & Training: London, New York & Chicago; with John Russell,
Toronto; also gallery study in Paris, Rome, Madrid, Athens, Am-
sterdam, Vienna, Florence & Venice.
Work in Public Collections: Portraits, still-life & flowers repre-
sented in pub & pvt collections in Can, Eng, U S & Denmark.
Exhibitions: Royal Can Acad Arts; Nat Gallery Art, Ottawa, Ont;
Nat Acad Design, New York, N Y; Am Watercolor Soc, New York;
Smithsonian Inst, Washington, D C; plus many others.
Teaching: Asst, Russell Acad, Toronto, 33-35; dir fine arts, Ridley
Col, Ont, 36-42; dir voc art, Niagara Falls Inst, 38-42; dir fine
art, Arts & Lett Club Toronto, 48; instr drawing & painting &
lectr anat & art hist, Art League Calif, San Francisco, 48-55;
dir, Leighton Studio, San Francisco, 55-; lectr, art & art hist,
TV, radio & forums; also guide lectr on tours of Europe.
Positions: Pres, Niagara Art Asn, 36-42.
Awards: Soc Western Artists Dipl Honor, 59; Klumke Award, De
Young Mus, San Francisco, 64; first award, Coun Am Artist Socs
Ann, New York, 64; plus others.
Bibliography: Articles, In: Prize-Winning Graphics, La Rev Mod,
Paris & Les Images, Cairo, 66; plus others.
Memberships: Soc Western Artists (dir & bd trustees, 51-, pres,
52-); Bohemian Club San Francisco; Am Artists Prof League (nat
bd dirs, 57-); fel Int Inst Arts & Lett.
Mailing Address: 471 Buena Vista Ave E, San Francisco, CA 94117.

LEIN, MALCOLM EMIL
Art Administrator, Designer
b Havre, Mont, July 19, 13.
Study & Training: Univ Minn, BArch.
Collections Arranged: Fiber, Clay & Metal Biennial, 52-; Drawings
U S A, Biennial, 61-; Goldsmith, 70; The Introspective Italian, 71.
Positions: Dir, Minn Mus Art, 47-
Memberships: Am Asn Mus.
Mailing Address: 361 Summit Ave, St Paul, MN 55102.

LEITH-ROSS, HARRY
Painter
Preferred Media: Watercolor.
b Mauritius, Jan 27, 86.
Study & Training: Nat Acad Design, with C Y Turner; Art Stud
League New York, with Birge Harrison & J F Carlson; Acad
Julian, Paris, France, with Jean Paul Laurens; also with Stan-
hope Forbes, Eng.
Work in Public Collections: Pa Acad Fine Arts, Philadelphia; Nat
Acad Design, New York, N Y; Philadelphia Watercolor Club.
Commissions: Mural, U S Post Off, Masontown, Pa.
Exhibitions: Numerous exhibs at Nat Acad Design, Pa Acad Fine
Arts, Corcoran Gallery Art, Washington, D C, Art Inst Chicago,
Ill, & Carnegie Inst, Pittsburgh, Pa; plus others.
Teaching: Vis instr, Univ Buffalo, 41; vis instr, Univ Utah, 55; vis
instr, Col Southern Utah, 55.

Awards: Prizes from Baltimore Watercolor Club, Salmagundi Club, Nat Acad Design & others.
Memberships: Nat Acad Design; Salmagundi Club; Am Watercolor Soc; Philadelphia Watercolor Club; Baltimore Watercolor Club.
Publications: Auth, The landscape painter's manual, 56, 2nd ed, 61.
Mailing Address: c/o Golden Door Gallery, Parry Barn, New Hope, PA 18938.

LEITMAN, NORMAN
Art Dealer
b New York, N Y, June 24, 33.
Study & Training: H S Mus & Art; Cornell Univ, BA; New York Univ Inst Fine Arts, 54-57.
Collections Arranged: Old Master Drawings, 60 Anonymous Drawings, The Neglected 19th Century & 17th Century Dutch Paintings, H Shickman Gallery.
Positions: Dir, H Shickman Gallery, New York.
Memberships: Art Dealers Asn; Col Art Asn.
Specialty of Gallery: Old master paintings & drawings.
Mailing Address: 325 E 77th St, New York, NY 10021.

LEITMAN, SAMUEL
Painter
Preferred Media: Watercolors.
b New York, N Y, Feb 12, 08.
Study & Training: Art Stud League New York, with Anne Goldthwaite & Bernard Klonis; Nat Acad Design, with John Pellew; also with Edgar Whitney.
Work in Public Collections: West Point Mus; Norfolk Mus, Va; Charles & Emma Frye Mus, Seattle, Wash.
Exhibitions: Am Watercolor Soc Ann, 60-; Salmagundi Club Ann, 61-; Am Artists Prof League, 65-; Allied Artists Ann, 67-, Knickerbocker Artists, 71-72.
Teaching: Instr watercolor, Salmagundi Club.
Positions: Owner, Leitman Studios, 45-
Awards: Gold medal of honor, Am Artists Prof League, 67; Painting Holidays Award, 70 & John Young Hunter Mem Award, 72, Am Watercolor Soc.
Memberships: Am Watercolor Soc (corresp secy, 70-); Salmagundi Club (chmn art comt, 72); Knickerbocker Artists (dir, 70-).
Mailing Address: 31-22 56th St, Woodside, NY 11377.

LEKAKIS, MICHAEL NICHOLAS
Sculptor
b New York, N Y, 07.
Work in Public Collections: Mus Mod Art, Whitney Mus Am Art & Guggenheim Mus, New York; Dayton Art Mus, Ohio; Portland Art Mus, Ore; plus many others.
Exhibitions: Seven Sculptors, Guggenheim Mus, 58; Mus Mod Art, New York; Dayton Art Mus, Ohio; plus others.
Awards: Ford Found Sculpture Purchase grant for Mus Mod Art, New York.
Mailing Address: 57 W 28th St, New York, NY 10001.

LEKBERG, BARBARA HULT
Sculptor
Preferred Media: Bronze, Steel.
b Portland, Ore, Mar 19, 25.
Study & Training: Univ Iowa, BFA & MA, with Humbert Albrizio; Simpson Col, hon DFA, 64.
Work in Public Collections: Montclair Mus Art, N J; Des Moines Art Ctr, Iowa; Knoxville Art Ctr, Tenn; Simpson Col, Indianola, Iowa.
Commissions: Three interior sculptures, Beldon-Stratford Hotel, Chicago, Ill, 53; three interior sculptures, Socony-Mobil Co, New York, N Y, 55; lobby relief, Riedl & Freede Advert, Clifton, N J, 64; life-size figure, Bayfield Clark, Bermuda, 71.
Exhibitions: Five Pa Acad Fine Arts Ann, Philadelphia, 50-62; New Talent, Am Fedn Arts Traveling Show, 59-60; Recent Sculpture U S A, Mus Mod Art, New York, 59; one-man shows, Sculpture Ctr, New York, 59, 65 & 71; traveling one-man show, Birmingham Mus Art, Ala & Columbia Mus Art, S C, 73.
Awards: Am Inst Arts & Lett grant, 56; Guggenheim Found fels, 57 & 59.
Dealer: Sculpture Ctr, 167 E 69th St, New York, NY 10021.
Mailing Address: 911 Stuart Ave, Mamaroneck, NY 10543.

LELAND, WHITNEY EDWARD
Painter, Educator
Preferred Media: Acrylics, Watercolors.
b Washington, D C, Apr 12, 45.
Study & Training: Memphis Acad Arts, BFA; Univ Tenn, Knoxville, MFA.
Work in Public Collections: Montgomery Mus Arts, Ala; Dulin Gallery Art, Knoxville, Tenn; Memphis Acad Art, Tenn.

Exhibitions: 25th Ann Nat Watercolor Exhib, Jackson, Miss, 69; Box Top Art, Univ Ill, 71; Dixie Ann, Montgomery, 71; Tennessee Printmakers, Knoxville, 72.
Teaching: Asst prof painting, Univ Tenn, Knoxville, 70-
Awards: Purchase prize, Montgomery Mus Arts, 71; purchase award, Dulin Gallery Art, 72; hon mention, Montgomery Mus Arts, 72.
Dealer: Gilman Galleries, Oak St, Chicago, IL 60611.
Mailing Address: 1840 Terrace Ave, Knoxville, TN 37916.

LEM, RICHARD DOUGLAS
Painter
Preferred Media: Oils.
b Los Angeles, Calif, Nov 24, 33.
Study & Training: Univ Calif, Los Angeles, BA; Calif State Col, Los Angeles, MA; Otis Art Inst; Calif Inst Arts; also with Rico Le-Brun & Herbert Jepson.
Work in Public Collections: San Diego Fine Arts Gallery.
Exhibitions: Third Ariz Ann, Phoenix Art Mus, 61; Nat Orange Show, San Bernardino, Calif, 65; Calif: South, San Diego Fine Arts Gallery, 65; one-man show, Gallery 818, 65; two-man show, Palos Verdes Art Gallery, 68.
Awards: Los Angeles Fine Arts Soc & Art Guild award for painting, 65.
Mailing Address: 1861 Webster Ave, Los Angeles, CA 90026.

LEMBECK, JOHN EDGAR
Painter, Art Dealer
b Saint Louis, Mo, Dec 25, 42.
Study & Training: Univ Kans, BFA, 66; Yale Univ, univ scholar, 68 & 69, State Conn scholar, 69, MFA, 70.
Exhibitions: United Gallery, New Haven, Conn, 69; New Talent Show, Alpha Gallery, Boston, Mass, 71; Joseloff Gallery, Univ Hartford, 72; Monotypes, Pratt Graphics Ctr, 72; one-man show, Spectrum Gallery, New York, N Y, 72; plus others.
Teaching: Asst lectr art, Saint Louis Art Mus, 69, lectr art, 70; instr design & drawing, Yale Univ Sch Art & Archit, 70-, instr drawing, Yale Summer Sch Music & Art, 71 & 72, dir, gallery, 71.
Positions: Printer, Setlich Sign Co, 61-62; printer, Hallmark Cards, 64-65; pres, Spectrum Gallery, New York, 71-
Awards: Prize, Wash Univ, 62; award, Univ Kans, 65.
Specialty of Gallery: Contemporary American painting & sculpture.
Mailing Address: Spectrum Gallery, 464 W Broadway, New York, NY 10012.

LEMIEUX, JEAN PAUL
Painter
b Quebec, P Q, Nov 18, 04.
Study & Training: Beaux-Arts, Montreal; Acad Colarossi, Paris, France; Laval Univ, Quebec, hon Dr, 69.
Work in Public Collections: Collection of Queen Elizabeth; Art Gallery Toronto, Ont; Mus Prov Quebec.
Exhibitions: Warsaw, 62; Tate Gallery, London, Eng, 63; Mus Mod Art Traveling Exhib through Can, 63; Mus Galliera, Paris, France, 63; Retrospective Exhib, Montreal & Ottawa, 67; plus others.
Teaching: Instr, Beaux-Arts Montreal, 33-34 & Ecole du Meuble, Montreal, 35-36; instr, Beaux-Arts, Quebec.
Awards: Prize, Quebec Prov Painting; Govt Overseas Award, 54-55; Companion, Order of Can, 68; plus others.
Memberships: Royal Can Acad Arts.
Mailing Address: 2008 Dickson, Sillery, P Q, Can.

LENNEY, ANNIE
Painter
Preferred Media: Oils, Watercolors.
b Potsdam, N Y.
Study & Training: Art Stud League New York; Grand Cent Art Sch, New York; N Y Univ; Fordham Univ; Syracuse Univ; St Lawrence Univ; Col St Elizabeth, BA; also with Haley Lever.
Work in Public Collections: Butler Inst Am Art, Youngstown, Ohio; Munson-Williams-Proctor Inst, Utica, N Y; Newark Mus, N J; Oklahoma City Art Ctr, Okla; Brook Mem Art Gallery, Memphis, Tenn; plus many others.
Exhibitions: Audubon Artists, Allied Artists Am & Nat Asn Women Artists, Nat Acad Design, New York; Assoc Artist Exhibs & Mus Ann, Montclair Mus, N J; plus ten one-man shows in New York City & many throughout U S.
Teaching: Art instr, Sch Fine & Indust Arts, Newark, 46-63; supvr, Sat Jr Art Sch, Newark, 53-55; art instr, Newton Pub Sch Syst, N J, 63-71.
Awards: Awards, Mus Ann, 48 & 52 & first in oil, Montclair Mus; Samuel Karasick Mem Prize, 62nd Ann Nat Asn Women Artists, 54.
Bibliography: Gerry Turner (auth), The magic of a home town, Design Mag, 1-2/60; M J R Arthur (auth), Blairstown's Annie Lenney is renowned artist, Family Form, 3/30/71.

Memberships: Audubon Artists (dir oils, 71, rec secy, 72-); Allied Artists Am; Nat Asn Women Artists; Assoc Artists N J; Painters & Sculptors Soc N J.
Publications: Auth, American watercolor, Am Artist, 2/51.
Mailing Address: Gaisler Rd, Blairstown, NJ 07825.

LENNIE, BEATRICE E C
Sculptor, Designer
b B C.
Study & Training: Vancouver Sch Art; Calif Sch Fine Art; pvt study in Rome & Florence; also with Frederick H Varley, J W G Macdonald, Ralph Stackpole, Carlo Marega & Harry Tauber, Vienna.
Work in Public Collections: Winnipeg Art Gallery; pvt collections, Can & U S A.
Commissions: Vancouver Labor Temple, Dom Construct Stone; Shaughnessy Mil Hosp, Fed Govt, Mercer & Mercer; Ryerson Mem Ctr United Church Can, P Underwood; Acad Med Libr, B C Med Soc; St John's Mem Church, C Thornton Sharp; plus others.
Exhibitions: Many shows, Royal Can Acad, Toronto, Ont & Montreal, Que, Can Nat Exhib, Sculptor's Soc Can & Seattle Art Mus, Wash; one-man show, Toronto Picture Loan, Queen's Univ; plus others.
Teaching: Head dept sculpture, B C Col Art, Vancouver; instr sculpture & theatre arts & creative puppetry, Univ B C; spec art lectr, Crofton House Sch, Vancouver.
Positions: Dir, Child Art Ctr, Vancouver Art Gallery; broadcaster art subj, Can Broadcasting Corp Trans Can.
Awards: Award, Sculptor's Soc Can.
Bibliography: Archit rev, In: Can Rev Mus & Art, Vancouver Prov, Toronto Sat Night & others.
Memberships: Life mem B C Soc Art; Sculptor's Soc Can; Vancouver Art Gallery.
Mailing Address: 4011 Rose Crescent, West Vancouver, B C, Can.

LENSKI, LOIS
Writer, Illustrator
b Springfield, Ohio, Oct 14, 93.
Study & Training: Art Stud League New York, N Y; Boyes Sch Art, London.
Publications: Auth, Shoo-fly girl, 63, The life I live: collected poems, 65, To be a logger, 67, Deer Valley girl, 68, Christmas stories, 68; also auth & illusr many other juvenile bks.
Mailing Address: Tarpon Springs, FL 33589.

LENSSEN, HEIDI (MRS FRIDOLF JOHNSON)
Painter, Lecturer
b Frankfurt, Ger; U S citizen.
Study & Training: Uffizi, Florence, Italy, copy degree, 25; Berlin State Acad Fine Arts, cert, 29; pvt study in Paris, France; also with Count Merveldt, Rome, 32-33; Acad Rossi, Florence; Ecole Arts et Metiers, Paris.
Work in Public Collections: Berlin Mus; Kunsthalle Mannheim.
Commissions: More than 100 portrait comns, U S A & Europe.
Exhibitions: Kunsthalle, Mannheim, 31; Pavillion of Today, New York World's Fair, 39; Schoneman Gallery, 40; Audubon Artists, 44 & 45; one-man show, Lynn Kottler Gallery, 54 & 70; plus others.
Teaching: Instr art & co-dir, Am Sch Design, New York, 37-42; lectr art, City Col Adult Educ, 45-58, instr art & lectr, Hunter Col, 49-51; lectr art, Franklin Sch Prof Arts, 52-57.
Bibliography: Marthe Davidson (auth), article, In: Art News, 37; Emily Grauer (auth), article, In: World Telegram New York, 40.
Publications: Auth & illusr, Art and anatomy, J J Augustin, Inc, Publ & Barnes & Noble, 44-; auth, Hands in nature and art, Studio Publ.
Mailing Address: 34 Whitney Dr, Woodstock, NY 12498.

LENT, BLAIR
Illustrator, Writer
Preferred Media: Acrylics.
b Boston, Mass, Jan 22, 30.
Study & Training: Boston Mus Sch, grad (hons), Cummings Mem traveling fel, to Switz & Italy, one yr, Bartlett traveling fel for res to U S S R.
Work in Public Collections: Wiggin Gallery, Boston Pub Libr.
Commissions: Why the Sun and the Moon Live in the Sky (animated film), ACI Films, New York, 71.
Exhibitions: Children's Books, Am Inst Graphic Arts, New York, N Y, 68; The Work of Blair Lent 1965-1970 (retrospective), Wiggin Gallery, Boston, 70; Work by Five Major American Illustrators, Univ Art Gallery, Albany, N Y, 72.
Awards: Silver medal, Bienal Int Arte Grafice, Sao Paulo, Brazil, 65; Caldecott Medal Honor Book, Am Libr Asn, 65, 69 & 71; bronze medal, Bienale Illustrators, Bratislava, Czech, 69.
Bibliography: William Sleator (auth), An illustrator talks, Publ Weekly, 69; Lee Hopkins (auth), Books are by people, Citation, 69; Selma Lanes (auth), Down the rabbit hole, Atheneum, 71.

Publications: Auth & illusr, Pistachio, 63 & John Tabor's ride, 66, Little; auth (pseud Ernest Small) & illusr, Baba Yaga, Houghton Mifflin, 66; auth & illusr, From King Boggen's Hall to nothing-at-all, Little, 67; illusr, The funny little woman, Dutton, 72.
Mailing Address: 10 Dana St, Cambridge, MA 02138.

LEON, DENNIS
Sculptor
b London, Eng, July 27, 33; U S citizen.
Study & Training: Temple Univ, BSc (educ), 56; Tyler Sch Art, MFA, 57.
Exhibitions: Pa Acad Fine Arts, 56, 64 & 68.
Teaching: Prof sculpture, Philadelphia Col Art, 60-72; prof sculpture, Calif Col Arts & Crafts, 72-
Awards: Guggenheim fel, 67; Nat Inst Arts & Lett, 67.
Publications: Auth, Paul Harris, 73.
Dealer: Antoinette Kraushaar, 80th & Madison Ave, New York, NY 10016.
Mailing Address: 3143 Eton Ave, Berkeley, CA 94705.

LEONARDI, HECTOR
Painter, Instructor
b Waterbury, Conn, Jan 18, 30.
Study & Training: R I Sch Design, BFA; Yale Univ, MFA.
Work in Public Collections: Univ Notre Dame; Univ Bridgeport.
Exhibitions: New York World's Fair, 64; Albright-Knox Art Gallery, Buffalo, N Y, 66; The Contemporaries, New York, 66 & 67; Critics Choice Invitational Exhib, Tokyo, Japan, 67; Obelisk Gallery, Boston, Mass, 68 & 69; plus others.
Teaching: Instr color, design, drawing & painting, Univ Bridgeport; instr color, Parsons Sch Design, at present.
Mailing Address: 254 E 53rd St, New York, NY 10022.

LEONG, JAMES CHAN
Painter
Preferred Media: Mixed Media.
b San Francisco, Calif, Nov 27, 29.
Study & Training: Calif Col Arts & Crafts, BFA & MFA; San Francisco City Col, MA; Univ Oslo.
Work in Public Collections: Princeton Art Mus, N J; Harvard Univ, Cambridge, Mass; Dallas Mus Fine Arts, Tex; New York Univ Mus, N Y; Univ Tex, Austin.
Commissions: Mural, Chung Mei Home for Boys, El Cerrito, Calif, 51; mural, Ping Yuen Housing Proj, San Francisco, 52; mural, San Francisco State Col, 52; prologue sequence, John Huston's Movie Freud, 62.
Exhibitions: Univ Ga, Athens, 71; Middle Tenn State Univ, Murfreesboro, 71; Pa State Univ, 71; Inverse Illusionism, Am Fedn Arts Traveling Exhib, 71-72; U S Info Serv, Rome, Italy, 72.
Teaching: Vis prof painting, Univ Ga, 71.
Bibliography: Robert Craft & Igor Strawinsky (auth), Themes and episodes, Doubleday.
Mailing Address: Piazza del Biscione 95, Rome 00186, Italy.

LEONID (LEONID BERMAN)
Painter
Preferred Media: Oils.
b St Petersburg, Russia, 96; U S citizen.
Study & Training: Acad Rancon, Paris, France, 19-22; also with Vuillard, Bounard, Serusier, Maurice Desnis & Valloton.
Work in Public Collections: Metrop Mus Art, New York, N Y; Mus Mod Art, New York; Kansas City Mus; Hartford Mus, Conn; murals, Nat Collection Fine Arts, Washington, D C.
Exhibitions: Julian Levy Gallery, 46-; Durlacher Gallery, 46-; Larcada Gallery, 66-; also exhibs in London, Eng, Rome, Italy & Paris, France.
Mailing Address: c/o Larcada Gallery, 23 E 67th St, New York, NY 10021.

LEPPER, ROBERT LEWIS
Educator, Sculptor
Preferred Media: Mixed Media.
b Aspinwall, Pa, Sept 10, 06.
Study & Training: Carnegie Inst Technol, BA; Harvard Univ Grad Sch Bus Admin, cert.
Work in Public Collections: Butler Mus Am Art, Youngstown, Ohio; Carnegie Mus Art, Pittsburgh, Pa; Ind Univ, Bloomington; Mus Mod Art, New York, N Y; Stedelijk Mus, Amsterdam, Holland.
Commissions: Mural, W Va Univ, Morgantown, 40; mural, airport, Charleston, W Va, 50; sculpture, Pittsburgh Hilton Hotel, Pa, 59; windows, Convent Immaculate Conception, Washington, Pa, 61; sculpture, New York World's Fair, 64.
Exhibitions: Pittsburgh Int, 61; Artist-teacher today—U S A, State Univ N Y Col Oswego, 69; Blossom, Kent Third Invitational, 70.
Teaching: Prof design, Carnegie-Mellon Univ, 30-

Awards: Medal, Pa Soc Architects, 61; purchase award, Carnegie
  Mus Art, 63; Honored Artist, Assoc Artists Pittsburgh, 70.
Bibliography: Student projects, Indust Design, 2/57; T R Newman
  (auth), Plastics as an art form, Chilton, 64; N Roukes (auth),
  Sculpture in plastics, Reinhold, 69.
Memberships: Assoc Artists Pittsburgh (mem bd, 64).
Publications: Auth, The problem of the creative artist in America
  today, Col Art J, 54; auth, Signs & symbols, Archit Record, 56;
  co-auth, Transit vehicle design & rider satisfaction, Urban &
  Social Change Rev, 70; co-auth, Ride on, Indust Design, 71.
Mailing Address: 5732 Kentucky Ave, Pittsburgh, PA 15232.

LERMAN, LEO
  Writer, Art Historian
b New York, N Y, May 23, 14.
Teaching: Lectr, TV & radio; lect art of biog & writing of children's
  bks, New York Univ.
Awards: Lotus Club Award for the Museum—100 years of the Met-
  ropolitan Museum of Art, 69.
Research: Italian renaissance; international nineteenth century art
  especially 1830-1914; art of the 1920's.
Publications: Auth, Leonardo da Vinci: artist & scientist, Bobbs-
  Merrill, 40; auth, Michelangelo: a renaissance profile, Knoff, 47;
  auth, The museum—100 years of the Metropolitan Museum of
  Art, Viking Press, 69; auth, many articles, In: Vogue, New York
  Times, Atlantic Mo, Sat Rev & others.
Mailing Address: c/o Conde Nast Publications, Inc, 420 Lexington
  Ave, New York, NY 10017.

LERNER, ABE
  Book Designer, Art Director
b New York, N Y, Sept 14, 08.
Exhibitions: Cooper Union, 48.
Collections Arranged: Exhib of art bks, Every Home a Museum, Assoc Am Art Gallery, Am Inst Graphic Arts, 51.
Teaching: Lect series on design problems & their solution for young
  bk designers, Am Inst Graphic Arts; instr bk design & prod, Am
  Inst Graphic Arts, 41-42; instr bk design & prod, Columbia Univ,
  53-64.
Positions: Chmn, trade bk clinic, Am Inst Graphic Arts, 53-54, exec
  comt, trade bk clinic, 41-42; chmn, 50 Bks of Yr Comt, 55; art
  dir & prod mgr, World Publ Co, Cleveland & New York; dir de-
  sign & prod, The Macmillan Co, 64-71, ed art books, 71-
Awards: Bks included in Fifty Books of the Year, 8 yrs, 38-54;
  Trade Bk Clinic mo selections, 38-
Memberships: Am Inst Graphic Arts (bd dirs, 59-60, 60-61).
Publications: Contribr, articles on typography & bk prod to Publish-
  er's Weekly & Bk Prod; also articles, In: The Writer.
Mailing Address: 69 W Ninth St, New York, NY 10011.

LERNER, ABRAM
  Museum Director
b New York, N Y, Apr 11, 13.
Study & Training: N Y Univ, BA; also var art schs, New York &
  Florence.
Exhibitions: One-man exhib, Davis Gallery, New York; Brooklyn
  Mus; Pa Acad Fine Arts, ACA Gallery, New York; Peridot Gal-
  lery, New York.
Positions: Asst dir, ACA Gallery, 45-55; asst dir, Artists Gallery,
  55-56; cur, Hirshhorn Collection, 56-67, dir, Hirshhorn Mus &
  Sculpture Garden, Smithsonian Inst, 67-
Memberships: Arch Am Art (adv bd).
Mailing Address: 135 E 65th St, New York, NY 10021.

LERNER, ALEXANDER
  Collector
Collection: Impressionist thru hard edge avant garde art.
Mailing Address: 785 Fifth Ave, New York, NY 10022.

LERNER, MARILYN ANN
  Painter
Preferred Media: Acrylics.
b Milwaukee, Wis, Sept 19, 42.
Study & Training: Univ Wis, BS, 64; Pratt Inst, 66.
Exhibitions: One-man show, Zabriskie Gallery, 69; two-man show,
  70 & Gallery Selections, 72, Kasle Gallery, Detroit, Mich; Whit-
  ney Mus Am Art Ann, New York, N Y, 71; American Women Art-
  ists, Gedok, Ger, 72.
Teaching: Instr printmaking, Brooklyn Mus, summer 69; instr en-
  viron sculpture, Newark Sch Fine & Indust Art, 69-71; adj lectr
  art, Hunter Col, 71-72.
Dealer: Kasle Gallery, 310 Fisher Bldg, Detroit, MI 48202.
Mailing Address: 262 Bowery, New York, NY 10012.

LERNER, RICHARD J
  Art Dealer
b New York, N Y, Feb 23, 29.
Study & Training: Univ Denver, BA.
Positions: Dir, Lerner-Heller Gallery.
Specialty of Gallery: Twentieth century art.
Mailing Address: 789 Madison Ave, New York, NY 10021.

LERNER, SANDY R
  Painter, Lithographer
Preferred Media: Oils, Mixed Media.
b Pa, May 13, 18.
Study & Training: Pratt Inst; Art Stud League New York; Nat Univ
  Mex; Wash Univ; also with Diego Rivera, Orosco, Fred Conway,
  Frank Reilly, Hans Hofmann & Zorach.
Work in Public Collections: Smithsonian Inst, Washington, D C; Navy
  Mus, Washington, D C; Brooklyn Navy Yard, N Y; Tel Aviv,
  Israel; Pratt Inst, Brooklyn; plus others.
Exhibitions: Nat Arts Club; Burr Artists; Audubon Artists; Salma-
  gundi Artists; N J Prof Artists; plus others.
Memberships: Salmagundi Club (v chmn, 70-); Burr Artists (house
  comt co-chmn, 71-); Col Art Asn Am (v pres, 69-70); Art Stud
  League New York; NACAL.
Dealer: Schuster Gallery, 536 Third Ave, New York, NY 10016.
Mailing Address: Pratt Institute, Brooklyn, NY 11205.

Le ROY, HAROLD M
  Painter, Lecturer
Preferred Media: Oil, Serigraph.
b New York, N Y, Dec 12, 05.
Study & Training: Columbia Univ, BA; Brooklyn Mus Art Sch; Art
  Stud League; Hans Hofmann Art Sch.
Work in Public Collections: Butler Inst Am Art, Youngstown, Ohio;
  Mint Mus Art, Charlotte, N C; Miami Mus Mod Art, Fla; Philathea
  Col Mus Mod Art, London, Ont; Safad Munic Mus, Israel.
Exhibitions: Societe de L'Ecole Francaise, Mus Artes Mod, Paris,
  France, 69 & 70; Audubon Artists 28th Ann Exhib, Nat Acad Gal-
  leries, New York, 70, 29th Ann Exhib, 71, 30th Ann Exhib, 72;
  Spring Arts Festival, Elec Indust Ctr, Flushing, N Y, 72.
Awards: Thomas Jefferson Silver Medal, Thomas Jefferson High
  Sch, 24.
Bibliography: Eleanor Marko (auth), The palette of Le Roy, Daily
  Register of N J, 66; Barbara Consolas (auth), Harold M Le Roy,
  artist, Plotinus Press, 66 & Le Roy & the world of art, 72.
Memberships: Artists Equity Asn N Y (bd dir, 67-); Metrop Painters
  & Sculptors; Group Three (v pres); Soc N Am Artists.
Dealer: Gallery Royel, 1474 Coney Island Ave, Brooklyn, NY 11230.
Mailing Address: 1916 Ave K, Brooklyn, NY 11230.

LESCH, ALMA WALLACE
  Textile Craftsman, Educator
Preferred Media: Textiles.
b McCracken Co, Ky.
Study & Training: Murray State Univ, BS, 41; Louisville Sch Art, 59-
  61; Univ Louisville, MEd, 62.
Work in Public Collections: Objects: U S A, The Johnson Collection;
  J B Speed Art Mus, Louisville, Ky; Mint Mus, Charlotte, N C;
  Flint Inst Art, Mich; Joseph Heil Collection, New York, N Y.
Commissions: Draperies, Bernheim Forest Nature Mus, Clermont,
  Ky, 62; wall hangings, First Nat Bank, Louisville, Ky, 67, First
  Presby Church, Columbus, Ind, 70, Educ Bldg, Okla Christian
  Col, Oklahoma City, 71 & Citizens Fidelity Bank, Louisville, 72.
Exhibitions: Nat Decorative Arts Wichita, Kans, 62, 66 & 70; Fabric
  Collage, Mus Contemp Crafts, New York, 65; First Surv Contemp
  Am Crafts, Univ Tex, Austin, 67; The Fine Art of Collage,
  Kunstegewerbemus, Zurich, Switz, 68; Objects: U S A, Smith-
  sonian Inst, 70.
Teaching: Assoc prof textiles & chmn dept, Louisville Sch Art, 61-;
  instr vegetable dyeing, Haystack Mountain Sch Crafts, Deer Isle,
  Maine, summers 66 & 70, Philadelphia Col Textiles & Memphis
  Acad Art, summer 67 & Indian Sch, Santa Fe, N Mex, 72; plus
  other workshops.
Awards: Craft Horizon's Merit Award, 65; Best of Show, Mint Mus,
  67; Merit Award & many other craft awards, J B Speed Art Mus,
  68.
Bibliography: Nik Krevitsky (auth), Stitchery: art and craft, Van
  Nostrand Reinhold, 66; Rose Slivka (auth), Craftsmen of the mod-
  ern world, Horizon, 68; Lee Nordness (auth), Objects: U S A,
  Viking Press, 70.
Memberships: World Crafts Coun; Am Crafts Coun (Ky State Rep,
  64-69); Ky Guild Artists & Craftsmen; Louisville Craftsmen
  Guild.
Publications: Auth, Vegetable dyeing, Watson-Guptill, 70.
Mailing Address: P O Box 67, Shepherdsville, KY 40165.

LESH, RICHARD D
Painter, Instructor
b Grand Island, Nebr, May 3, 27.
Study & Training: Univ Nebr; Univ Denver, BA, MA; Mexico City
Col.
Exhibitions: Midwest Biennial, 58; Nebraska Centennial, Joslyn Mus,
Omaha, 67 & Sheldon Gallery, Lincoln, 68.
Teaching: Instr painting & head dept art, Wayne State Col, 51-
Positions: Pres, Nebr Art Coun, 68-69.
Awards: Second prize for painting, Midwest Biennial, Joslyn Mus,
55; first prize for painting, May Show, Sioux City Art Mus, 58.
Memberships: Col Art Asn Am; Nebr Art Teachers Asn (v pres, 56-
58); Kappa Pi (sponsor, 51-).
Mailing Address: 505 E 10th St, Wayne, NE 68787.

LESLEY, PARKER
Art Historian, Educator
b Baltimore, Md, Aug 31, 13.
Study & Training: Stanford Univ, AB, 34; Univ Paris, cert, 35;
Princeton Univ, MFA, 37; Univ Brussels, cert, 37; New York
Univ, 47-48; with C R Morey, Erwin Panofsky & Marcel Aubert.
Collections Arranged: Assembled, catalogued & arranged numerous
exhibs, Cooper Union Mus Arts of Decoration, 50-54.
Teaching: Asst prof art & archit, Univ Minn, 39-42; from asst prof
to prof art, Old Dom Univ, 59-
Positions: Cur Europ art, Detroit Inst Arts, 38-39; keeper, Dept
Exhibs, Cooper Union Mus Arts of Decoration, 50-54.
Awards: Chevalier Order Polonia Restituta, Poland, 46; Hon Medal
Art & Sci of House-Order of Orange-Nassau, Netherlands, 47.
Memberships: Col Art Asn Am.
Publications: Auth, Early Christian, Byzantine and Romanesque art,
Detroit Inst Arts, 39; auth, Handbook and catalogue of the Lillian
Thomas Pratt collection of Russian imperial jewels, Va Mus Fine
Arts, 60; auth, Renaissance jewels and jeweled objects, Balti-
more Mus Art, 68.
Mailing Address: 732 Yarmouth St, Norfolk, VA 23510.

LESLIE, ALFRED
Painter
b New York, N Y, Oct 29, 27.
Study & Training: Study with Tony Smith, William Baziotes, Hale
Woodruff & John McPherson; New York Univ, 56-57.
Work in Public Collections: Mus Mod Art & Whitney Mus Am Art,
New York; Mus Mod Art, São Paulo, Brazil; Nat Mus, Stockholm,
Sweden; Kunsthalle, Basel, Switz; Walker Art Ctr, Minneapolis,
Minn; plus others.
Exhibitions: White Mus, Cornell Univ; Am Fedn Arts Traveling Ex-
hib; Univ Nebr; Jewish Mus; Carnegie Int, Pittsburgh, Pa; plus
others.
Teaching: Great Neck Adult Educ Prog, New York, 56-57; San Fran-
cisco Art Inst, summer, 64.
Awards: Guggenheim fel, 69.
Publications: Ed, The hasty papers, 60; co-dir, co-producer, ed &
publ, Pull my daisy (film).
Dealer: Noah Goldowsky Gallery, 1078 Madison Ave, New York, NY
10028.
Mailing Address: 8 W 13th St, New York, NY 10011.

LESNICK, STEPHEN WILLIAM
Painter, Instructor
Preferred Media: Oils.
b Bridgeport, Conn, Mar 22, 31.
Study & Training: Silvermine Col Art; Art Career Sch; also with
Revington Arthur, Jon McCleand, Jack Wheat & Gail Symon.
Work in Public Collections: Burndy Libr Arts & Sci, Comn; State
Capitol Bldg, Carson City, Nev; Elks Lodge, Las Vegas, Nev;
Boulder City Hosp Art Collection, Nev.
Commissions: Indust paintings, Burndy Libr Art & Sci, 59; portrait
of Gov mansion, comn by Gov Paul Laxalt, Carson City, 68; com-
memorative coin for Boulder Dam, Elks Lodge, Las Vegas, 71-
73.
Exhibitions: All New Eng Art Exhib, Conn, 55; Layout & Design Int
Art Competition, Japan, 63; Ann Conn Relig Art Exhib, 63 & 64;
Ann Am Watercolor Soc Show, 68; Helldorado Western Art
Exhib, Nev, 68.
Teaching: Art instr, Desert Art League, Boulder City, 65-66; art
instr, Las Vegas Art League, 65-68; art instr, Artists & Crafts-
mans Guild, Nev, 65-68; owner & instr, Lesnick Art Studio, Las
Vegas, 65-
Positions: Layout designer, Vacart Art Studio, Stamford, Conn, 60-
65; art dir, Kelley & Reber Advert, Las Vegas, 65-66; illusr, E G
& G, Inc, Las Vegas, 66-; art ed, Las Vegas Sun, 70-
Awards: Int Design Show, Japan, 63; Conn Relig Show, Hallmark
Greeting Cards, 63 & 64; first prize, Nev Bicentennial Com-
memorative Medallion, Franklin Mint, 72.

Bibliography: Articles, In: Desert Scope, 69-71.
Memberships: Nev State Watercolor Soc.
Dealer: Art Dealer, 700 E Sahara Ave, Las Vegas, NV 89114.
Mailing Address: 1127 Westminster Ave, Las Vegas, NV 89119.

LETENDRE, RITA
Painter
Preferred Media: Acrylics.
b Drummondville, Que, Nov 1, 28.
Study & Training: Ecole Beaux Arts, Montreal; P E Borduas, Mon-
treal.
Work in Public Collections: Mus Art Contemporain, Montreal; Mus
Beaux-Arts, Montreal; Long Beach Mus Fine Arts, Calif; Rose
Art Mus, Brandeis Univ, Waltham, Mass; Mus Que.
Commissions: Wall painting, Calif State Col, Long Beach, 65; mural,
Greenwin of Toronto, 71; wall painting, Benson & Hedges, Neil-
Wyick Col, Toronto, 71; mural, J D S Investment, Sheridan Mall,
Pickering, Ont, 72.
Exhibitions: Internationalism des Arts, Mus Beaux-Arts, 60; 5 Fes-
tival di due Mondi, Spoleto, Italy, 62; IV Biennale Can Painting,
Tate Gallery, London, Eng, 63; Can Pavillion Expo 67, Montreal,
67; Que Pavillion, Worlds Fair, Osaka, Japan, 70.
Awards: Le Prix de Peinture, Concours Artistique Que, 61; P Q
Bourse de Recherche, 67; Can Arts Coun sr grant award, 71.
Bibliography: C Delloye (auth), Rita Letendre, Art Aujourdhui, 62;
D Travers (auth), Rita Letendre wall painting, Arts & Archit, 66;
Jules Heller (auth), Printmaking today, Holt, Rinehart & Winston,
71.
Mailing Address: 61 W 74th St, Apt 2C, New York, NY 10023.

LEV-LANDAU (SAMUEL DAVID LANDAU)
Painter
Preferred Media: Oils, Casein.
b Warsaw, Poland, Apr 17, 95; U S citizen.
Study & Training: Graphic Sketch Club, Philadelphia; also with Sol
Wilson & Phil Reisman.
Work in Public Collections: Butler Inst Am Art, Youngstown, Ohio;
Norfolk Mus Arts & Sci, Va; Adelphi Univ, Garden City, N Y;
Meninger Mus, Topeka, Kans; Mus Tel Aviv, Israel; plus others
including pvt collections.
Exhibitions: Carnegie Inst, Pittsburgh, Pa; Pa Acad Fine Arts,
Philadelphia; Corcoran Gallery Art, Washington, D C; Nat Acad
Design, New York, N Y; Dayton Art Inst, Ohio; plus many other
group & one-man shows.
Awards: First prize for oil, Brooklyn Soc Artists Ann, 54; second
purchase prize, Abraham Lincoln H S, 64; Albert Dorn Prize,
Audubon Artists, 65.
Memberships: Artists Equity Asn (mem bd, 71-72); Am Soc Con-
temp Art.
Dealer: Gallery Royel, 1474 Coney Island Ave, Brooklyn, NY 11230.
Mailing Address: Hotel Chelsea, 222 W 23rd St, New York, NY
10011.

LE VA, BARRY
Painter
b Long Beach, Calif, 41.
Exhibitions: Art in Mind, Oberlin Col, Ohio, 69; 955,000, Vancouver
Art Gallery, B C, 70; Anti-Materialism, La Jolla, Calif, 70; Pro-
cedure & Materials, 69 & Whitney Ann, 70, Whitney Mus Am Art,
New York, N Y; one-man show, Minneapolis Inst Art, Minn, 70;
plus other group & many one-man shows.
Mailing Address: c/o Reese Palley, 93 Prince St, New York, NY
10012.

LEVAL, MRS FERNAND
Collector
b New York, N Y, Apr 5, 11.
Positions: Partner, Jacques Schiffrin & Co, publ; dir, Pantheon
Bks, 45-60.
Collection: Impressionists, post-impressionists; contemporary
painting, drawing and sculpture.
Mailing Address: 660 Park Ave, New York, NY 10021.

LEVEE, JOHN H
Painter, Sculptor
Preferred Media: Acrylics, Plexiglass.
b Los Angeles, Calif, Apr 10, 24.
Study & Training: Art Ctr Sch & Chenard Sch, Los Angeles; Univ
Calif, Los Angeles, BA, 48; New Sch Soc Res, with Stuart Davis,
Abe Rattner & Kunyoshi, 48-49; Acad Julian, Paris, France, 49-
51; Grand Prix, 51.
Work in Public Collections: Mus Mod Art, New York, N Y; Whitney
Mus Am Art, New York; Guggenheim Mus, New York; Corcoran
Gallery Art, Washington, D C; Walker Art Ctr, Minneapolis,

Minn; plus many others in major U S A & European mus; also many in pvt collections.
Commissions: Wall, Architects, Chateau Vaudreuil, Paris, 71-72; walls, Bank Credit Com, Paris, 72-73.
Exhibitions: Salon de Mai, Paris, 54-; Salon Realities, Paris, 54-; Carnegie Int, 55-58; Corcoran Gallery Art, 56-58; New Acquisitions, 57 & Young Am Painters, 57-58, Mus Mod Art, New York; Whitney Mus Am Art, 57, 58 & 66; plus many other group & one-man shows.
Teaching: Vis prof art, Univ Ill, 64-65, Wash Univ, 67, N Y Univ, 67-68 & Univ Southern Calif, 70.
Awards: Grand Prix, First Biennial Paris, 59; purchase award, Commonwealth Va, 66; Ford fel, Tamarind Workshop, 69.
Bibliography: Seuphor (auth), Dictionary of abstract art, 57; Reed (auth), A concise history of modern art, 60; Ragon (auth) & Seuphor (auth), History of modern painting, 69.
Collection: African, Pre-Columbian & contemporary painting & sculpture.
Dealers: Andre Emmerich Gallery, 41 E 57th St, New York, NY 10022; Leavin, Margo Gallery, 812 N Robertson Blvd, Los Angeles, CA 90035.
Mailing Address: 119 rue Notre Dame des Champs, Paris 6, France.

LEVENTHAL, ETHEL S
Painter
Preferred Media: Watercolors, Oils.
b Brooklyn, N Y, Dec 20, 11.
Study & Training: Brooklyn Mus Art Sch; Art Stud League New York; New Sch Soc Res; also with Abraham Rattner, George Picken, Paul Buclin & Charles Seide.
Exhibitions: Nat Asn Women Artists, New York; Woodstock Art Asn, N Y; Parnassus Square Gallery, Woodstock; Ann Leonard Gallery, Woodstock.
Awards: Awards for prints, 62, watercolors, 65 & oils, 67, Nat Asn Women Artists.
Memberships: Nat Asn Women Artists; Woodstock Art Asn.
Mailing Address: 47 Plaza St, Brooklyn, NY 11217.

LEVENTHAL, RUTH LEE
Painter, Sculptor
Preferred Media: Bronze.
b New York, N Y, Oct 5, 23.
Study & Training: Art Stud League New York; Nat Acad Design; also with John Terken, Robert Tompkins & Maxim Bugaster.
Work in Public Collections: Fedn Jewish Philanthropies, New York; YMHA & YWHA, Brooklyn, N Y; Riverside Mem Chapel, New York.
Commissions: Three paintings, World's Fair, New York, 64-65; sculpture, 70 & six sculptures, 72, Riverside Mem Chapel; portrait of Golda Meir, privately comn, 72.
Exhibitions: Six shows, Nat Acad Design, New York; World's Fair, New York, 64-65; five shows, Nat Arts Club, New York; one-man shows, Kottler Galleries, New York, 70 & Temple Sinai, Roslyn, Long Island, N Y, 71; Sculptured Gold Jewelry, Bergdorf-Goodman, New York, 72.
Awards: Nat 3M Award, 69; Catharine Lorillard Wolfe Art Club Gold Medal, Nat Acad Design, 70.
Bibliography: Ruth Lee Leventhal, Newsweek, 5/70; article, In: Art News.
Memberships: Fel Royal Soc Arts; Nat Soc Arts & Lett (co-chmn lit, 72); Catharine Lorillard Wolfe Art Club; Allied Artists Am; Am Soc Composers, Authors & Publ.
Publications: Co-auth, Take one of my pills, 65 & Our romance is over, 66, New Recording; illusr, cover, NATA Quart, fall/winter 70.
Mailing Address: 440 E 57th St, New York, NY 10022.

LEVERING, ROBERT K
Painter, Illustrator
b Ypsilanti, Mich, May 22, 19.
Study & Training: Univ Ariz, AB; Art Inst Chicago; Brooklyn Mus Sch Art; Art Stud League New York; Pa Acad Fine Arts; New Sch Social Res.
Work in Public Collections: Paintings, USAF Collection, Washington, D C; also in pvt collections.
Commissions: Portraits of Kennedy, Eisenhower, U Thant & Martin Luther King.
Exhibitions: Seven exhibs, New York City Ctr Gallery; Soc Illustrators Gallery, New York; Mikelson Gallery, Washington, D C, 68; Art Dirs Exhib, 69.
Teaching: Guest lectr & critic, Parsons Sch Design, 65, 66, 68, 71 & 72.
Awards: Citations from Soc Illustrators, 62-64, gold medal, 69; citation, N J Art Dirs Club, 69; Soc Publ Designers, 69.

Publications: Contribr, illus to McCalls, Good Housekeeping, Cosmopolitan, Sat Eve Post, Redbook Woman's Day, Reader's Digest & other leading nat mag & bks.
Mailing Address: 330 E 79th St, New York, NY 10021.

LEVI, JOSEF
Painter
b New York, N Y, Feb 17, 38.
Study & Training: Univ Conn, BA, 59; Columbia Univ, 60.
Work in Public Collections: Mus Mod Art, New York; Albright-Knox Gallery, Buffalo, N Y; Aldrich Mus Contemp Art, Ridgefield, Conn; Krannert Art Mus, Univ Ill, Urbana; Des Moines Art Ctr, Iowa.
Exhibitions: Highlights of the 65-66 Art Season, Aldrich Mus Contemp Art, 66; Sound, Light, Silence, Art that Performs, Nelson Atkins Gallery, Kansas City, Mo, 67; Light, Motion, Space, Walker Art Ctr, Minneapolis, Minn, 67; Whitney Mus Am Art Ann, New York, 68; Smithsonian Inst Near East & S Asia Traveling Exhib, 71.
Awards: Purchase award, Univ Ill, Urbana, 66; selected for New Talent U S A, Art in Am, 66.
Bibliography: William Wilson (auth), In the eye of the beholder, Art News, 2/70; J Patrice Marander (auth), Preface for silkscreen portfolio, Domberger, 71.
Mailing Address: 171 W 71st St, New York, NY 10023.

LEVI, JULIAN (E)
Painter, Educator
Preferred Media: Oils.
b New York, N Y, June 20, 00.
Study & Training: Pa Acad Fine Arts.
Work in Public Collections: Metrop Mus Art, New York; Mus Mod Art, New York; Whitney Mus Am Art, New York; Detroit Inst Arts, Mich; Pa Acad Fine Arts, Philadelphia; plus many others.
Exhibitions: Venice Biennial; Pittsburgh Int; Krannert Art Mus, Univ Ill, 61; Art: U S A, Smithsonian Inst, 61; Whitney Mus Am Art Ann, 64.
Teaching: Instr painting, New Sch Soc Res, 45-66; instr painting, Art Stud League New York, 46-; instr painting, Pa Acad Fine Arts, 64-
Positions: Dir art workshops dept, New Sch Soc Res, 60-
Awards: Hon mention, Carnegie Inst, 45; grant in art, Nat Inst Arts & Lett, 55; Temple Gold Medal, Pa Acad Fine Arts, 62.
Memberships: Nat Inst Arts & Lett (mem coun, 68-71).
Art Interests: Color lithography.
Publications: Auth, Modern art: an introduction, Pitman, 61.
Dealer: Frank Rehn Gallery, 655 Madison Ave, New York, NY.
Mailing Address: 79 W 12th St, New York, NY 10011.

LEVICK, MR & MRS IRVING
Collectors
Collection: Contemporary American and European artists, including Gatch, Weber, Dove, Hartley, Rivers, Levine, Marin, Weinberg, King, Knaths, Shahn, Roth, Tam, Greene, Guerero, Avery, Soutine, Matisse, Dubuffet, Matta, Marchand, Levee, Nikos, Nicolson, Sutherland, Marini, Fraser, Francis, Wiley, Buggiani, Kinley, Lawrence, Appel, Corneille, Severini, Kingstein, Katzman, Rouault, Graves, Brice, Heerup, Wols, Bauermeister, Jimmy Ernst, James Wines, Lynn Chadwick, Georgia O'Keeffe, Saul Steinberg, Davies, Seymour Drumlevitch, Harriet Grief and others.
Mailing Address: 227 Nottingham Terr, Buffalo, NY 14216.

LEVIN, JEANNE
Painter, Collector
b Cleveland, Ohio, Dec 13, 01.
Study & Training: Cleveland Sch Art; Wells Col, BA; Cranbrook Acad Art; Soc Arts & Crafts, Detroit; Norton Gallery & Sch Art; pvt study with Gerald Brockhurst, Ernest Fiene, Bruce Mitchell & Zubel Katchadoorian.
Exhibitions: One-man shows, Contemp Gallery, Palm Beach, Fla, 63, 65 & 68 & Norton Gallery, 67; Benson Gallery, Bridgehampton, N Y, 67; Compass Gallery, Nantucket, Mass, 67; Am Contemp Exhib, Soc Four Arts, Palm Beach.
Positions: Assoc trustee, Friends of Modern Art, 58-63, chmn, 58-63; chmn, Futurists Exhib, Detroit Inst Arts, chmn, Acquisition Comt Mod Art; founding mem, Gallery Contemp Art, Palm Beach; trustee, New York Studio Sch, 65-
Awards: Hon mention, Mich Artists Exhib, Detroit Inst Arts, 46; Paley Award, Norton Gallery, 62 & 66; Four Arts Soc, Palm Beach, 68.
Collection: Post-impressionists paintings and sculpture; contemporary paintings and sculpture; primitive sculpture, Greek, African and pre-Columbian; The complete collection was exhibited at Cranbrook Academy of Art, Detroit Institute of Arts and Norton Gallery of Art.
Mailing Address: 316 Garden Rd, Palm Beach, FL 33480.

LEVIN, KIM (KIM PATEMAN)
Painter, Art Critic
U S citizen.
Study & Training: Vassar Col, AB; Yale-Norfolk Summer Sch Art; Columbia Univ, MA.
Exhibitions: One-man shows, Suffolk Mus, Stony Brook, L I, 63, Poindexter Gallery, N Y, 64 & 67 & Vassar Col Art Gallery, 65.
Teaching: Lectr drawing, Philadelphia Col Art, Pa, 67-70; lectr drawing & painting, Parsons Sch Design, New York, N Y, 69-
Positions: Ed assoc, Art News, New York, 64-
Bibliography: Jane Holtz Kay (auth), For art's sake, Mademoiselle, 68.
Publications: Contribr, Am J Archaeol, 64; contribr, Art News, 64-; co-auth, Light in art, Collier, 69; auth, Lucas Samaras (monogr), (in prep).
Mailing Address: 52 W 71st St, New York, NY 10023.

LEVINE, JACK
Painter
b Boston, Mass, Jan 3, 15.
Study & Training: Study with Dr Denman W Ross, 29-31; also with Harold Zimmerman; Colby Col, hon DFA, 46.
Work in Public Collections: Metrop Mus Art & Mus Mod Art, New York, N Y; Addison Gallery Am Art, Andover, Mass; Univ Nebr; Portland Mus Art, Ore; Walker Art Ctr, Minneapolis, Minn; Art Inst Chicago, Ill.
Exhibitions: Retrospectives, Inst Contemp Art, Boston, 53, Whitney Mus Am Art, New York, 55 & Palacio Bellas Artes, Mexico City, Mex, 60; annually, Carnegie Inst, Pittsburgh, Pa & Art Inst Chicago; plus many others.
Teaching: Lect, Art Inst Chicago, Skowhegan Sch Painting & Sculpture, Univ Ill, Pa Acad Fine Arts, Am Art Sch, New York & Cleveland Mus Art Sch.
Awards: Guggenheim fel, 45 & 46; Pa Acad Fine Arts, 48; Corcoran Gallery Art, 59.
Memberships: Nat Inst Arts & Lett; Artists Equity Asn; Am Acad Arts & Sci.
Dealer: Kennedy Galleries, 20 E 56th St, New York, NY 10022.
Mailing Address: 68 Morton St, New York, NY 10014.

LEVINE, LES
Sculptor, Museum Curator
Preferred Media: Gold.
b Dublin, Ireland, Oct 6, 35; Can citizen.
Study & Training: Cent Sch Arts & Crafts, London, Eng.
Work in Public Collections: Nat Gallery Can, Ottawa, Ont; Whitney Mus Am Art & Mus Mod Art, New York, N Y; Philadelphia Mus Art, Pa.
Commissions: Iris (sculpture), Mr & Mrs Robert Kardon, 67; Contact (sculpture), Gulf & Western Indust, 69.
Exhibitions: Sao Paolo Biennale, Brazil, 68; Biennale Paris, France, 69.
Teaching: Artist-in-residence, Aspen Inst, Colo, 67 & 69; assoc prof commun, New York Univ, spring 72.
Positions: Pres, Mus Mott Art, Inc, 71-
Awards: Can Coun Arts fel, 65 & 66; first prize for The Star Machine, Sculpture Biennale, Art Gallery Ont, 68.
Bibliography: John Perreault (auth), Plastic man strikes, Art News, 3/68; David Bourdon (auth), Plastic art's biggest bubble, Life Mag, 8/69; Van Schley (auth), Les Levine movie, E Vander Schley (producer), 69.
Memberships: Archit League New York (v pres, 68-70, exec comt, presently).
Publications: Auth & ed, Culture hero, 70; contribr, Collected essays, Dutton, 72; contribr, Newsday, Village Voice & Studio Int.
Dealer: Fischbach Gallery, 29 W 57th St, New York, NY 10019.
Mailing Address: 181 Mott St, New York, NY 10012.

LEVINE, MARILYN ANNE
Sculptor
Preferred Media: Ceramics.
b Medicine Hat, Alta, Dec 22, 35.
Study & Training: Univ Alta, BSc, 57, MSc, 59; Univ Calif, Berkeley, MA, 70, MFA, 71.
Work in Public Collections: Nat Mus Mod Art, Kyoto & Tokyo; Univ Art Mus, Berkeley; Montreal Mus Fine Arts; Int Mus Ceramics, Faenza, Italy; Confedn Art Gallery & Mus, Charlottetown.
Exhibitions: Survey 70 (Realisms), Montreal Mus Fine Arts, 70; San Francisco Art Inst Centennial Exhib, De Young Mus, 71; Clayworks; 20 Americans, Mus Contemp Crafts, New York, 71; Contemp Ceramic Art, Nat Mus Mod Art, Tokyo & Kyoto, 71-72; Sharp Focus Realism, Sidney Janis Gallery, New York, 72; plus many others.
Teaching: Instr ceramics, Univ Sask, 66-; vis instr art, Univ Calgary, summers 68 & 71; vis lectr art, Univ Calif, Davis, spring 72.
Awards: Arts Bursary, Can Coun, 69; gold medal, 27th Concorso Int

Ceramica D'Arte, 69; Louise & Adolphe Schwenk Mem Prize for Sculpture, 69.
Memberships: Can Craftsmen Asn (coun, 72); Can Artists Representation; Col Art Asn Am.
Dealer: Bernard Danenberg Galleries, 1000 Madison Ave, New York, NY 10021. Hansen Fuller Gallery, 228 Grant Ave, San Francisco, CA 94108.
Mailing Address: 1506 College Ave, Regina, Sask S4P 1B5, Can.

LEVINE, REEVA (ANNA) MILLER
Painter, Instructor
Preferred Media: Oils, Acrylics, Watercolors.
b Hollywood, Calif, Nov 23, 12.
Study & Training: With Emil Bistrom & Alexander Rosenfeld.
Work in Public Collections: Temple Israel, Long Beach, Calif; E Madison YMCA, Seattle, Wash; Mt Zion Baptist Church, Seattle.
Commissions: Stained glass windows, Temple Beth Sholom, Santa Monica, Calif, 44; stained glass windows, Temple Sinai Wedding Chapel, Oakland, Calif, 48; ceiling of dome, Al Jolson Mem, Los Angeles, Calif, 51; mosaic, Temple Beth Sholom, Anchorage, Alaska, 66; relig arks, Temple Beth Israel, Aberdeen, Wash, 66; plus others.
Exhibitions: One-man show, Santa Monica Art Asn, 48; Calif Art Asn Greek Theatre, 50; Seattle World's Fair Liturgical Conf, 62; Seattle Art Mus, 67; one-man show, Olympia Art League, Wash, 70.
Teaching: Instr art, Calif & Seattle, Wash, 48-; instr art, Temple de Hirsch, Seattle, 62-69.
Positions: Art dir, Camp Ben Swig, Saratoga, Calif, 53-58.
Awards: First in drawing, 45 & second in watercolor, 48, Santa Monica Art Asn; artist of yr, Music & Art Found, Seattle, 70.
Memberships: Artists Equity Asn (news lett ed, Wash State Chap, 72).
Publications: Illusr, Holy mountain, 53.
Mailing Address: 2830 Cascadia Ave S, Seattle, WA 98144.

LEVINE, SEYMOUR R
Collector
b Russia, May 28, 06.
Study & Training: Wash Square Col, New York Univ, Sch Law, JD.
Collection: Includes works by de Creeft, Elkan, Rubin, Blum, Neujean and others.
Mailing Address: Carhart Ave, Peekskill, NY 10566.

LEVINE, SHEPARD
Painter, Educator
b New York, N Y, June 21, 22.
Study & Training: Univ N Mex, BA & MA; Univ Toulouse, France.
Work in Public Collections: Prints in Parnassus Hall, Athens, Greece, sponsored by U S Info Serv Collection of U S Embassy in 1960; Univ Ore; Ore State Univ; Arkia Airlines, Israel.
Exhibitions: Am Graphic Arts Asn; Brooklyn Mus; Henry Gallery, Univ Wash; San Francisco Mus Art; Portland Art Mus, Ore; Spokane Art Mus; plus others.
Teaching: Lect, Roots of Contemporary Expression, The Artists Vision, Motif in the Work of Three American Jewish Artists, Icons of Jewish Art, The Mind Symbol & Reflections in the Presence of Medusa; to mus & pvt groups; sem, movement & style in art & mus; prof art, Oregon State Univ, at present.
Awards: Purchase award, Univ Ore.
Memberships: Am Asn Univ Prof.
Mailing Address: Dept of Art, Oregon State University, Corvallis, OR 97331.

LEVINSON, FRED (FLOYD)
Designer, Cartoonist
b New York, N Y, May 23, 28.
Study & Training: Syracuse Univ, BFA.
Exhibitions: Cartoon Exhib, Eng, 53, Italy, 54 & France, 54; all N Y state exhibs; Cannes Film Festival, 60; New York Film Festival; Edinburg Film Festival, 60.
Positions: Pres, Wylde Productions.
Awards: Hollywood Film Festival, 60; Edinburgh Film Festival, 60; New York Film Festival, 61.
Art Interests: Industrial films, live and animated TV commercials.
Publications: Contribr cartoons, Best cartoons from True, Cartoon cavalcade, & Best cartoons of the year, 54; contribr, cartoons, In: Sat Eve Post, Colliers, Look, True, This Week & many others.
Mailing Address: Wylde Films, Inc, 53 E 25th St, New York, NY 10010.

LEVINSON, MON
Sculptor
b New York, N Y, Jan 6, 26.
Work in Public Collections: Whitney Mus Am Art, New York; Joseph H Hirshhorn Collection, Washington, D C; New York Univ Art Collection; Rose Art Gallery, Brandeis Univ, Waltham, Mass; Columbia Broadcasting System, New York.

Commissions: Objects, Mus Mod Art, New York, 64, 66 & 69; sculpture, Astor Found grant, P S 166, New York, 67; mural-sculpture, Great Southwest Atlanta Corp, Atlanta, Ga, 68; mural-sculpture, Housing & redevelop bd, Demountable Vest Pocket Parks, New York, 69.
Exhibitions: The Responsive Eye, Mus Mod Art, New York, 65; Plus by Minus, Albright-Knox Gallery, Buffalo, N Y, 68; A Plastic Presence, Milwaukee Art Ctr, Milwaukee, Wis, New York & San Francisco, Calif, 69-70; Whitney Mus Am Art Sculpture Ann, New York, 70; Maeght Found, Art Vivant aux Etats Unis, France, 70.
Teaching: Vis artist, C W Post Col, 70-72.
Mailing Address: 309 W Broadway, New York, NY 10013.

LEVIT, HERSCHEL
Painter, Illustrator
b Shenandoah, Pa, May 29, 12.
Study & Training: Pa Acad Fine Arts, Cresson traveling scholar, 33; Barnes Found.
Commissions: Murals, Rowan Sch, Philadelphia, Recorder of Deeds Bldg, Washington, D C, U S Post Off Bldg, Leisville, Ohio & Jenkintown, Pa; 33 portrait drawings of Red Seal Artists, RCA Victor, 58; photographs for Mus Mod Art.
Exhibitions: Pa Acad Fine Arts, 66-69; Art Inst Chicago, Ill; Springfield Art Mus, Ill; Brooklyn Mus, N Y; Metrop Mus Art & Whitney Mus Am Art, New York, N Y; plus others.
Teaching: Prof art & advan design, Pratt Inst, at present.
Publications: Illus, Horizon book of ancient Rome, 66, Horizon book of the Elizabethan world, 67, Horizon book of great cathedrals, 68 & Master builders of the middle ages, 69; auth & illusr, Just point, 72; plus others.
Mailing Address: 220 W 93rd St, New York, NY 10025.

LEVITAN, ISRAEL (JACK)
Sculptor, Lecturer
b Lawrence, Mass, June 13, 12.
Study & Training: Arts & Crafts, Detroit, Mich; Chicago Art Inst; also with Amédée Ozenfant & Hans Hofmann, New York, N Y, Ossip Zadkine, Paris, France & Rammurti S Mishra, San Francisco, Calif.
Work in Public Collections: Guild Hall Mus, East Hampton, Long Island, N Y; Temple Beth El, Great Neck, Long Island; Mus Mod Art Lending Libr, New York, N Y.
Commissions: Merle Armitage sculpture, Yucca Valley, Calif, 59; dancing figures, Forest Hills Apt Lobby, New York, 60; abstr ceiling narthex of chapel, Interchurch Ctr, New York, 62; head of Ben Gurion, Maurice Dershowitz, 64; bronze of Moses' hands, Murray Reiter, 65.
Exhibitions: Realites Nouvelle, Mus Art Mod, Paris; Am Abstr Artists, Mus Mod Art, Tokyo, Japan; retrospective, Barone Gallery, 60; Am Sculptors, Galerie Claude Bernard, Paris, 62; retrospective, Univ Calif, Berkeley, 62.
Teaching: Sculpture class & lectr, Brooklyn Mus, N Y, 55-59; sculpture class & lectr, Greenwich House, New York, 58; sculpture class & lectr, Cooper Union, 59; instr sculpture, Univ Calif, Berkeley, 62; instr sculpture, Philadelphia Mus Col Art, 67-68; instr sculpture, New York Univ, 68; sculpture class & lectr, Guild Hall Mus, 71.
Awards: First prize, Guild Hall Mus, 58.
Bibliography: A baker's dozen in sculpture, CBS Camera Three, 62; Fred McDarrah (auth), chap, In: Artists' world, 64; Michel Seuphor (auth), chap, In: Sculpture of the 20th century, 66.
Publications: Contribr, Life Mag, 58, portfolio, Art News Ann, 64, Evergreen Rev, 65, Das Kunst, 66 & Look Mag, 67.
Dealer: Jane Wade, 46 E 66th St, New York, NY 10021.
Mailing Address: 45 Alewive Brook Rd, East Hampton, Long Island, NY 11937.

LEVITINE, GEORGE
Educator, Art Historian
b Kharkoff, Russia, Mar 17, 16; U S citizen.
Study & Training: Univ Paris, PCB, 38; Boston Univ, MA, 46; Harvard Univ, Edward R Bacon scholar & PhD, 52.
Teaching: From instr to prof hist art, Boston Univ, 49-64; prof hist art, Harvard Univ Exten, 59-64; prof & head dept art, Univ Md, 64-
Awards: Am Coun Learned Socs grant, 61.
Memberships: Col Art Asn Am (chmn Porter Prize comt, bk rev ed, Col Art J); Am Soc Aesthetics.
Research: European art of the eighteenth and nineteenth century, particularly romanticism.
Publications: Auth, The influence of Lavater & Girodet's Expression des sentiments de l'âme, Art Bull, 54; auth, Some emblematic sources of Goya, J of Wartburg & Courtauld Inst, 59; auth, Vernet tied to a mask in a storm: the evolution of an episode of art historical romantic folklore, Art Bull, 67; auth, The 18th century rediscovery of Alexis Grimou and the emergence of the Proto-Bohemian Image of the French artist, Eighteenth Century Studies, Vol

21, No 1; auth, The sculpture of Falconet, New York Graphic Ltd, 72.
Mailing Address: Dept of Art, University of Maryland, College Park, MD 20742.

LEVITT, ALFRED
Painter
b New York, N Y, Aug 15, 94.
Study & Training: Columbia Univ; Art Stud League New York; with Hans Hofmann, New York; also Acad Grande Chaumière, France.
Work in Public Collections: Neveh-Sha'anan Mus, Haifa, Israel; plus many other pvt collections in Europe & U S A.
Exhibitions: Butler Inst Am Art, Youngstown, Ohio, 46; Pa Acad Fine Arts, Philadelphia, 48; Brooklyn Mus, New York, 47, 51, 53, 55 & 59; Whitney Mus Am Art, New York, 49, 53 & 55; one-man shows, Babcock Galleries, New York, 45 & 46, Art Alliance Philadelphia, 47; plus many other group & one-man shows.
Teaching: Lectr cave art—the birth of painting, N Y Univ, Cooper Union, Archaeol Inst Am at Wagner Col, North Shore Soc Archaeol Inst Am, New York Pub Libr, Philadelphia Art Alliance & also in France.
Positions: Coord chmn Mod Artists Cape Ann, Mass, 47; lectr mod art; founder, dir & instr, Ecole Mod de Provence, St Remy de Provence, France, 49-50 & 59-62.
Bibliography: Artist returns from fifth trip to prehistoric caves, Villager, 11/5/70.
Memberships: Fel MacDowell Colony; Archaeol Inst Am; Soc Prehistorique L'Ariege; Soc Amis Mus Chateau Saint Germain-en Laye; Soc Prehistorique L'Ardeche; life mem Archaeol Soc Staten Island.
Research: Various researches of cave art & prehistory; extended visits & studies of the drawing, engraving, painting & sculpture of the Stone Age artists.
Publications: Contribr articles on art to prof periodicals.
Mailing Address: 505 W Broadway, New York, NY 10013.

LEVY, BEATRICE S
Painter
b Chicago, Ill, Apr 3, 92.
Study & Training: Art Inst Chicago; also with Charles Hawthorne & Vojtech Preissig.
Work in Public Collections: Chicago Munic Collection; Bibliot Nat, Paris, France; Libr Cong, Washington, D C; Fine Arts Gallery San Diego; Smithsonian Inst, Washington, D C; plus others.
Exhibitions: Art Inst Chicago; Carnegie Inst, Pittsburgh, Pa; Pa Acad Fine Arts, Philadelphia, Pa; Nat Acad Design; Ceramic Traveling Exhib, Yokohama, Japan, 63-64; plus many other group & one-man exhibs.
Awards: Art Inst Chicago, Coronado Art Asn & San Diego Fine Arts Guild; plus others.
Memberships: San Diego Fine Arts Guild; Renaissance Soc, Univ Chicago; La Jolla Mus Art; plus others.
Mailing Address: c/o Trust Dept, Southern California First National Bank, P O Box 1907, La Jolla, CA 92037.

LEVY, DAVID CORCOS
Photographer, Educator
b New York, N Y, Apr 10, 38.
Study & Training: Columbia Col, BA, 60; New York Univ, MA, 67.
Work in Public Collections: Guggenheim Mus, New York.
Teaching: Dean, Parsons Sch Design, New York, 70-
Research: Photographic essays in Gothic Architecture.
Mailing Address: Parsons School of Design, 66 Fifth Ave, New York, NY 10011.

LEVY, HILDA
Painter
b Pinsk, Russia.
Study & Training: Univ Calif, Berkeley, AB; Pasadena City Col; Jepson Art Inst; Univ Calif, Los Angeles; also with Adolph Gottlieb.
Exhibitions: Nat Gallery Can, Ottawa, Ont; Libr Cong, Washington, D C; Butler Inst Am Art, Youngstown, Ohio; San Francisco Mus Art & M H de Young Mem Mus, San Francisco, Calif; plus many others.
Awards: 27 local & nat awards.
Memberships: Calif Watercolor Soc; Bay Printmakers; San Francisco Art Inst.
Mailing Address: 2411 Brigden Rd, Pasadena, CA 91104.

LEVY, TIBBIE
Painter
Preferred Media: Oil.
b New York, N Y, Oct 29, 08.
Study & Training: Cornell Univ with Arshile Gorky, AB; Art Stud League, New York; Acad Grande Chaumière & Acad André Lhote, Paris, France; New York Univ, JD.

Work in Public Collections: Contemp Art Soc Great Britain; Mus Mod Art, Madrid, Barcelona & Bilbao, Spain; Princeton Univ Mus; Cornell Univ Mus; Brandeis Univ; plus 21 other Mus.
Exhibitions: Bodley Gallery, New York, 60, 62, 64, 65, 66 & 70; Galerie Ror Volmar, Paris, 61; Sala Nebli, Madrid, 62; Galeria Forum, Madrid, 63; Portal Gallery, London, Eng, 63 & 65.
Teaching: Lect on art.
Dealer: Bodley Gallery, 787 Madison Ave, New York, NY 10021.
Mailing Address: 2 Sutton Pl S, New York, NY 10022.

LEW, WEYMAN MICHAEL
Painter
Preferred Media: Ink, Watercolors, Acrylics.
b San Francisco, Calif, Feb 17, 35.
Study & Training: Univ Calif, Berkeley, BS, 57; San Francisco Art Inst, 65-66, with Jay deFeo.
Work in Public Collections: M H de Young Mem Mus, San Francisco; Univ Calif Mus, Berkeley; Inst Arte Contemporaneo, Lima, Peru; Santa Barbara Mus Art, Calif; Oakland Art Mus, Calif.
Exhibitions: One-man shows, M H de Young Mem Mus, 70, Inst Arte Contemporaneo, 70, Western Asn Art Mus Circulating Exhib, 70-71, Santa Barbara Mus Art, 71 & Art Gallery Greater Victoria, B C, 72.
Teaching: Guest instr painting, drawing & serigraphy, M H de Young Mem Mus Art Sch, 70-71.
Positions: Dir, Kelley Galleries, San Francisco, 68.
Dealer: John Bolles Gallery, 10 Gold St, San Francisco, CA 94133.
Mailing Address: 2505 Pacific Ave, San Francisco, CA 94115.

LEWANDOWSKI, EDMUND D
Painter, Educator
b Milwaukee, Wis, July 3, 14.
Study & Training: Layton Sch Art, 32-35.
Work in Public Collections: Addison Gallery Am Art, Andover, Mass; Brooklyn Mus, N Y; Boston Mus Fine Arts, Mass; Mus Mod Art, New York, N Y; Mus Fine Arts, Krakow, Poland; plus many others.
Exhibitions: Art Inst Chicago, Ill; Carnegie Inst, Pittsburgh, Pa; Corcoran Gallery Art, Washington, D C; Pa Acad Fine Arts, Philadelphia; Phillips Collection, Washington, D C; plus others.
Teaching: Prof, Layton Sch Art, 45-49; prof painting, Fla State Univ, 49-54, head dept, 52-54; dir, Layton Sch Art, 54-
Awards: Awards, Gimbel Centennial, Hallmark Int Competition & Milwaukee Art Inst; plus many others.
Bibliography: Andrew C Ritchie (auth), Abstract painting and sculpture in America, Mus Mod Art, 51; Nathaniel Pousette-Dart (ed), American painting today, Hastings House, 56; John I Baur (auth), Revolution and tradition in modern American art, Harvard Univ Press, 59.
Memberships: Wis Painters & Sculptors; Polish-Am Artists; Chicago Fine Arts Club.
Publications: Contribr, covers & reproductions to Fortune Mag.
Mailing Address: 1360 N Prospect Ave, Milwaukee, WI 53202.

LEWICKI, JAMES
Illustrator, Educator
b Buffalo, N Y, Dec 13, 17.
Study & Training: Albright Art Sch; Art Sch Detroit Soc Arts & Crafts, scholar; Pratt Inst, cert.
Exhibitions: Audubon Artists Ann; Am Watercolor Soc Ann; Pop Prints, Adelphi Univ, New York, N Y, 64; Christmas Paintings, Dartmouth Col, Hanover, N H, 64; one-man show, Golden Bough Paintings, C W Post Col, 70.
Teaching: Instr art, Pratt Inst, 46-52; prof art, C W Post Col, Long Island Univ, 63-, chmn grad prog art, 69-
Awards: Second prize, Christmas card competition, Am Artists, 43; New Masters award for Sunflowers (painting), Audubon Artists 25th Anniversary Exhib, 67.
Bibliography: Articles, In: Am Artist Mag, 62 & North Light Mag, 71.
Memberships: Am Watercolor Soc; Audubon Artists.
Publications: Ed & illusr, Christmas tales, Golden Press, 56; ed & illusr, Life treasury of American folklore, 61; illusr, Tales of old Russia, Garrard, 64; illusr, Little Christmas, Houghton Mifflin, 64; illusr, The golden bough, Vols I & II, 68 & 69; illusr for nat mags, 39-
Mailing Address: 5 Hawthorne Ct, Centerport, NY 11721.

LEWIN, BERNARD
Art Dealer, Collector
b Ger; U S citizen.
Study & Training: With Kurt Wagner, Berlin.
Positions: Art dir, B Lewin Galleries, Beverly Hills, Calif, 60-
Memberships: Art Dealers Asn.
Specialty of Gallery: Mexican masters, Tamayo, Siqueiros, Merida, R Martinez, R Coronel and others.

Collection: Mexican masters, American and European.
Mailing Address: B Lewin Galleries, 260 N Beverly Dr, Beverly Hills, CA 90210.

LEWIS, DOUGLAS
Art Historian, Art Curator
b Centreville, Miss, Apr 30, 38.
Study & Training: Lawrenceville Sch, N J, dipl, 56; Yale Col, BA, 59 & 60; Clare Col, Cambridge Univ, BA, 62; Yale Univ, MA, 63; Am Acad Rome, Pris de Rome fel, 64; Clare Col, Cambridge Univ, MA, 66; Am Acad Rome, dipl, 66; Yale Univ, PhD, 67.
Collections Arranged: African Sculpture, 70, The Art of Wilhelm Lehmbruck, 72 & Native Art of the American Arctic, 73, Nat Gallery Art.
Teaching: Asst prof baroque & romantic art, Bryn Mawr Col, 67-68; asst prof renaissance & baroque art, Univ Calif, Berkeley, spring 70; sem leader renaissance archit, Folger-Shakespeare Renaissance Sem, Washington, D C, spring 72.
Positions: David E Finley fel Venetian art, Nat Gallery Art, Washington, D C, 65-67; guest juror, Las Vegas Sem, Yale Univ Sch Archit, 68; curator sculpture, Nat Gallery Art, 68-
Memberships: Fel Am Acad in Rome; Soc Archit Historians; Col Art Asn Am; John Marshall House, Richmond (trustee, 72-); Belg-Am Educ Found (Am fel comt, 72-).
Research: Art and architecture and their patronage in Renaissance Venice; monographic studies on Baldassare Longhena, Andrea Palladio & Paolo Veronese.
Publications: Auth, The late baroque churches of Venice, 67; auth, Notes on XVIII century venetian architecture, 67 & auth, Sanmicheli, Sansovino, e il mecenatismo artistico di Vettor Grimani, 72, Bollettino Mus Civici Veneziani; auth, Two lost renaissances of venetian architecture, J Warburg & Courtauld Insts (in press); auth, Titian's portraits of the Corner family, Studies in Hist Art, Nat Gallery, Washington, D C (in press).
Mailing Address: National Gallery of Art, Washington, DC 20565.

LEWIS, ELMA INA
Art Administrator
b Boston, Mass, Sept 16, 21.
Study & Training: Emerson Col, BLI, 43; Boston Univ, MEd, 44; Emerson Col, hon LHD, 68; Anna Maria Col, hon LHD, 71; Boston Col, hon LHD, 71; Colby Col, hon DFA, 72; Harvard Univ, hon ArtD, 72.
Teaching: Founder & dir, Elma Lewis Sch Fine Arts, Boston, 50-
Positions: Founder & dir, Nat Ctr Afro-Am Artists, Boston, 68-
Awards: Outstanding Woman's Award, Campfire Girls Am, 70; Mayors Citation, City of Boston, 70; Henry O Tanner Award, Black Arts Coun Calif, 71; plus others.
Bibliography: Margo Miller (auth), Black Boston's Miss Lewis: art czarina with a needle, Boston Globe, 4/18/68; Caryl Rivers (auth), Black America's Barnum, Hurok and Guthrie, New York Times, 11/17/68; editorial, in: Vogue, 5/69.
Memberships: Fel Black Acad Arts & Lett; Gov's Task Force on Arts & Humanities, Boston Int Platform Artists; Metrop Cult Alliance, Boston; Mass State Dept Educ Adv Bd.
Publications: Contribr, Who took the weight, Little, 72; auth, At the crossroads: doom or bloom, Forum Mag, 72; auth, Celebrating us little people, Boston Rev of Arts, 9/72; auth, Black Dance in America, Doubleday (in prep).
Mailing Address: National Center of Afro-American Artists, 122 Elm Hill Ave, Dorchester, MA 02121.

LEWIS, GOLDA
Painter, Sculptor
Preferred Media: Compages.
b New York, N Y.
Study & Training: With Vaclav Vytacil, Hans Hofmann & Jack Tworkov; woodblock with Seong Moy & papermaking with Douglass Howell.
Work in Public Collections: Ciba-Geigy Chem Co, Ardsley, N Y; Madden Corp, New York, N Y; Hercules Powder Co, Wilmington, Del; Dome Labs, West Haven, Conn.
Exhibitions: One-woman shows, Balin-Traube Gallery, New York, 63, XXth Century West Galleries, New York, 67, Benedicta Arts Ctr Gallery, Saint Joseph, Minn, 67, Court Gallery, Copenhagen, Denmark, 70 & Alonzo Gallery, New York, 71; Art on Paper (group show), Weatherspoon Ann, Greensboro, N C, 69; plus many others.
Teaching: Ballard Sch, New York, 61-71; lectr, Marymount Manhattan Col, fall 71.
Awards: N Y State Coun Arts grant, 71.
Bibliography: Edith Dugmore (auth), Compages by Golda Lewis, Craft Horizons, 11/66; Paper as work of art (interview), Berlingske Tidende, Copenhagen, 70; Henk Voorn (auth), Papierwereld, Holland, 70.

Memberships: Women in the Arts.
Art Interests: Painting and reliefs in paper, handmade by the artist, called compages.
Dealer: Alonzo Gallery, 26 E 63rd St, New York, NY 10021.
Mailing Address: 140 E 40th St, New York, NY 10016.

LEWIS, JEANNETTE MAXFIELD
Painter, Etcher
Preferred Media: Oils.
b Oakland, Calif.
Study & Training: Sch Fine Arts, San Francisco; also with Armin Hansen, Monterey, Calif.
Work in Public Collections: Oakland Art Gallery.
Exhibitions: Am Soc Graphic Artists, New York; Calif Soc Etchers; Am Artists Prof League; Philadelphia Print Club; Soc Western Artists; plus many other group & one-man shows.
Awards: Group award, Am Artists.
Bibliography: Article, In: Am Artist Mag, 4/62.
Memberships: Nat Asn Women Artists; Am Soc Graphic Artists; Calif Soc Etchers; Philadelphia Print Club; Print Club Albany.
Mailing Address: P O Box 352, Pebble Beach, CA 93953.

LEWIS, MICHAEL H
Painter, Educator
Preferred Media: Oils, Film.
b Brooklyn, N Y, Aug 10, 41.
Study & Training: State Univ N Y Col New Paltz, BS, 63, painting with Ilya Bolotowsky & George Wexler; Mich State Univ, MA, 64, printmaking with John DeMartelly.
Work in Public Collections: Mich State Univ Art Dept Collection.
Exhibitions: Artists of Upper Hudson, Albany Inst Hist & Art Ann, N Y, 66; N J Soc Painters & Sculptors Ann, Jersey City Mus, 67; Drawings by Young Americans, Mus Art Ogunquit, Maine, 69; New York Int Art Competition, 70; one-man show of paintings & drawings, Gallery I, Carnegie Hall & Univ Maine, Orono, 72.
Teaching: Art instr, Kingston City Pub Schs, N Y, 64-66; assoc prof painting, drawing & filmmaking, Univ Maine, Orono, 66-, faculty res award for work of art film designed for TV, summer 71.
Positions: Mem Maine Comn Arts & Humanities, 72-
Awards: Coughtry Prize for Representational Painting, Albany Inst Hist & Art, 66; silver medal, New York Int Art Show, 70.
Bibliography: Rob Ellowitch (auth), Films: Michael Lewis, Maine's leader, Maine Times, 9/26/69; Toby Mussman (auth), The artist as filmmaker 9/28/69 & Lynn Franklin (auth), Life at 30 is a painting, 6/18/72, Maine Sun Telegram.
Mailing Address: 104 Bennoch Rd, Orono, ME 04473.

LEWIS, NAT BRUSH
Painter, Instructor
Preferred Media: Watercolors.
b Boston, Mass, Dec 17, 25.
Study & Training: Pembroke Col, Brown Univ & R I Sch Design, AB; Art Stud League New York; watercolor with Maria Cooper; also with Henry Gasser & Ray Ellis.
Work in Public Collections: Am Asn Univ Women, Somerset Hills, N J; Bloomfield Art League, N J.
Exhibitions: N J Watercolor Soc, Morris Mus, Morristown, N J, 67-71; Am Watercolor Soc, Nat Acad Design Galleries, 68 & 72 & Traveling Exhib, 72; Nat Arts Club Open Watercolor Exhib, New York, N Y, 69-71; Art Ctr Oranges Regional Exhib, E Orange, N J, 69, 71 & 72
Teaching: Instr watercolor, Studio Four, Roseland, N J, 68-
Awards: Agnes B Noyes Award, N J Watercolor Soc, 68; Garden State Art Ctr Award, Federated Art Asns N J, 70; first award in watercolor, Ringwood Manor State Exhib, 71.
Memberships: N J Watercolor Soc (corresp secy, 69-71, v pres, 71-); Am Artists Prof League, N J Chap (third v pres, 71-); W Essex Art Asn; Port Clyde Arts & Crafts Soc.
Mailing Address: 51 Overlook Rd, Caldwell, NJ 07006.

LEWIS, NORMAN WILFRED
Painter, Instructor
Preferred Media: Oils.
b New York, N Y.
Study & Training: Columbia Univ.
Work in Public Collections: Art Inst Chicago, Ill; Munson-Williams-Proctor Inst, Utica, N Y; Mus Mod Art, New York; IBM Collection; John D Rockefeller Collection; plus others.
Exhibitions: Venice Biennale, Italy; São Paulo, Brazil; Pa Acad Fine Arts, Philadelphia; Grenoble, France; Libr Cong, Washington, D C; plus many other group & one-man exhibs.
Teaching: Instr art, Jr High Sch 139, New York; instr art, Fed Art Proj, New York; supvr art ctr, A & T Col & Bennett Col, N C; instr art, Harlem Art Ctr & Thomas Jefferson Sch, New York; instr art, Indian Hill Music Sch, Stockbridge, Mass; supvr, Haryou-Act, Inc; instr art, Art Stud League New York, 71-

Positions: Bd dirs, Cinque Gallery, New York.
Awards: Carnegie Int Exhib Award, 55; Am Acad Arts & Lett Award, 70; Nat Inst Arts & Lett Award, 71.
Mailing Address: 64 Grand St, New York, NY 10013.

LEWIS, PHILLIP HAROLD
Museum Curator
b Chicago, Ill, July 31, 22.
Study & Training: Art Inst Chicago, BFA, 47; Univ Chicago, MA, 53; Fulbright grant to Australian Nat Univ, 53-54; Univ Chicago, PhD, 66.
Collections Arranged: Anthrop, geol & hist exhibs, Grout Hist Mus, Waterloo, Iowa, 55; What is Primitive Art?, 58; estab Hall of Primitive Art, 61 with exhibs Primitive Artists Look at Civilization and The Human Image in Primitive Art & Australian Aboriginal Art: Arnhem Land of the collection of Louis A Allen, Palo Alto, Calif, Field Mus Natural Hist.
Teaching: Lectr dept anthrop, Univ Chicago, 67-
Positions: Field res proj primitive art, New Ireland, 53-54 & 70; asst cur primitive art, Field Mus Natural Hist, 57-59, assoc cur, 60, cur, 61-67, cur primitive art & Melanesian ethnol, 68-
Awards: Chicago Natural Hist Mus fel, 50-51, 54-55.
Memberships: Am Anthrop Asn; fel Royal Anthrop Inst Gt Brit & Ireland; fel Am Authors Asn.
Publications: Auth, A definition of primitive art, Vol 36, 61 & The social context of art in Northern New Ireland, Vol 58, 69, In: Fieldiana, Field Mus Natural Hist.
Mailing Address: Field Museum of Natural History, Roosevelt Rd & Lake Shore Dr, Chicago, IL 60605.

LEWIS, SAMELLA SANDERS
Painter, Art Historian
b New Orleans, La, Feb 27, 24.
Study & Training: Hampton Inst, BS; Ohio State Univ, MA & Ph D; Tunghai Univ, Taiwan, Fulbright fel, 62; Univ Southern Calif, Nat Defense Educ Act grant, 64-66; N Y Univ Inst Fine Arts, 65.
Work in Public Collections: Oakland Mus, Calif; Baltimore Mus Fine Arts; Va Mus Fine Arts, Richmond; High Mus, Atlanta, Ga; Atlanta Univ Mus Contemp Art.
Commissions: Mural Fla hist, comn by pres, Fla A&M Univ, 55; paintings, comn by dean, Hampton Inst, 67.
Exhibitions: Joseph Hirshhorn Collection, Palm Springs Mus, 69; Dimensions of Black, La Jolla Mus Art, 70; Two Generations of Black Artists, Calif State Univ, Los Angeles, 70.
Collections Arranged: Five Black Artists, 70 & The Renaissance in Harlem, 71, Lang Art Gallery, Scripps Col.
Teaching: Prof fine arts & head dept, Fla A&M Univ, 53-58; prof humanities & art hist, State Univ N Y, 58-68; assoc prof art hist, Scripps Col, 69.
Positions: Coord educ, Los Angeles Co Mus Art, 69-70; pres, Contemp Crafts Publ, 69; owner, Multi-Cul Gallery, 71.
Awards: N Y State-Ford Found grant, 65.
Bibliography: The black artists (film), Afrographics, 68; Focus, KNBC-TV, 68; article, In: Los Angeles Times, 70.
Memberships: Col Art Asn Am; Nat Conf Artists (co-chairperson, 70-73); Am Soc Aesthetics.
Research: African, Asian and African-American art.
Collection: Rare African works, including Bakuba in the 1890's; sand paintings of the American Indian; contemporary Asian and African-American works.
Publications: Co-ed, Black artists on art, Vols I & II, 69 & 71.
Dealer: Ankrum Gallery, 657 N La Cienega Blvd, Los Angeles, CA 90019.
Mailing Address: 1237 Masselin Ave, Los Angeles, CA 90019.

LEWIS, STANLEY
Sculptor, Printmaker
b Montreal, Que, Mar 28, 30.
Study & Training: Montreal Mus Fine Arts, 48-51; Inst Allende, San Miguel, Mex, scholars, 52-55; Elizabeth T Greenshields Mem Found grant, Florence, Italy, 56-59.
Work in Public Collections: Que Prov Mus; Nat Gallery Can, Ottawa; Montreal Mus Fine Arts; Jerusalem Mus, Israel; Samuel Zacks Collection.
Commissions: Sleeping Spirit, lava boulder, 53, standing nude, white marble, 53 & The Corngrinder, gray marble, 54, Inst Allende; late Samuel Bronfman, Can Jewish Cong, 66.
Exhibitions: One-man shows, Montreal Mus Fine Arts, 52 & 59, Israel Art Auction Gallery, Tel-Aviv, Israel, 65 & Nat Gallery Can, 71; Celestial Lights Exhib, Man & His World, Montreal, 71.
Teaching: Instr modeling, McGill Univ Sch Archit, 52; instr sculpture, Montreal Mus Fine Arts, 61-63; instr sculpture, Saidye Bronfman Art Ctr, Montreal, 68-

Awards: Prize, Concours Artistiques, Que, 59; prize for sculpture, 60 & prize for stone-cut prints, 62, Nat Art & Photog Exhib, Que.
Bibliography: Peter Olwyer (auth), article, In: Can Art, fall 55; Earle Birney (auth), article, In: Sat Night, 55; Folch (auth), article, In: Vie Arts, summer 55.
Memberships: Founding mem Que Sculptors' Asn.
Research: Contributed original research on Michelangelo's childhood and marble carving techniques to writing of Irving Stone's, The Agony and the Ecstasy.
Art Interests: Developed a unique technique in multi-coloured stone-cut printing.
Publications: Auth, The stone speaks, 53, Hands to create wonders, 61 & Space, man and stone, 69.
Mailing Address: 4131 Cote des Neiges Rd, Apt 4, Montreal 109, Que, Can.

LEWIS, VIRGINIA ELNORA
Art Administrator, Art Historian
b Sault Ste Marie, Ont, Apr 7, 07; U S citizen.
Study & Training: Wellesley Col, 26-28; Univ Pittsburgh, AB, 31, with Walter Read Hovey, AM, 35; Carnegie Inst Technol, cert, 32-33; Harvard Univ, with Jacob Rosenberg, summer 37, with Kenneth Conant, summer 40; Brit Mus Dept Prints, with Arthur M Hind, summer, 38.
Collections Arranged: Exhibitions organized, arranged & catalogued independently & in collaboration with Dr Walter Read Hovey, Henry Clay Frick Fine Arts Gallery & other museums & galleries, 37-67.
Teaching: Lectr & instr fine arts, Univ Pittsburgh, 34-50, instr eng compos & civil air regulations, ASTP Prog, 42-43, instr eng, 44-46, asst prof fine arts, 50-54, assoc prof fine arts, 54-57, prof fine arts, 57-67, emer prof, 67-
Positions: Proofreader, Carnegie Inst Press, 31-33; cur slides & photographs, Univ Pittsburgh, 34-43, cur exhibs, 46-47, acting head Frick Fine Arts Dept, 40-63, head librarian, Frick Fine Arts Libr, 63-65, asst dir, Frick Fine Arts Bldg, 65-67, res, Frick Found, 68-69, dir, Frick Art Mus, 70-; dir, Dennis Art Gallery, Raymond Moore Found, Mass, summer 53; consult dir, Westmoreland Co Mus Art, Woods Marchand Found, Greensburg, Pa, 54-56.
Memberships: Am Asn Mus (Pittsburgh comt, 59); Int Coun Mus; Col Art Asn Am (local chmn Pittsburgh meeting, 56); Soc Archit Hist (bd dirs, nat secy, chmn Pittsburgh chap, local Pittsburgh meeting, 56, chmn session, Washington, D C, 58); Nat Trust Hist Preservation (chmn 14th ann session, 60).
Research: Jean Antoine Houdon, French 18th century sculptor.
Mailing Address: Frick Art Museum, 7227 Reynolds St, Pittsburgh, PA 15208.

LEWIS, WILLIAM ARTHUR
Painter, Art Administrator
Preferred Media: Watercolors.
b Detroit, Mich, Mar 20, 18.
Study & Training: Col Archit & Design, Univ Mich, BDesign, 48.
Work in Public Collections: Butler Inst Am Art, Youngstown; St Paul Art Ctr; Grand Rapids Mus Art; Univ Mich Grad Sch; Grinnell Col.
Commissions: Two groups of watercolors, Detroit Bank & Trust Co, Detroit & London, 63 & 69; watercolor series, Bohn Aluminum Co, Detroit, 70; oil painting, Grand Rapids City Hall, 71; acrylic painting, Soc Mfg Engrs, Dearborn, Mich, 71.
Exhibitions: Five ann, Butler Inst Am Art, 54-65; Drawing U S A, Mus Mod Art, 56; Corcoran Gallery Biennial, Washington, D C & Am Fedn Art Tour, 57; one-man show, The Last Year of the Civil War, Univ Mich, Detroit Hist Soc, Mint Mus, Madison Col(Va), Eastern Mich Univ, Dearborn Hist Mus & others, 62-65; Drawing U S A, St Paul Art Ctr, 63 & 66.
Teaching: Prof art, Col Archit & Design, Univ Mich, Ann Arbor, 64-, Rackham Sch Grad Studies faculty res grants, Last Year of the Civil War, 60-62 & J M W Turner, 64.
Positions: Assoc dean, Col Archit & Design, Univ Mich, Ann Arbor, 66-; mem Comn Accreditation & v pres, Nat Asn Schs Art, 70-
Awards: St Paul Art Ctr Purchase Award, Drawing U S A, 63.
Bibliography: Hazen Schumacher (auth), The painting professor, Univ Mich TV Studios, 62; Louise Bruner (auth), Feelings of an artist, Toledo Blade, 64.
Memberships: Col Art Asn; Mich Watercolor Soc.
Publications: Auth & illusr, The Civil War—a contemporary approach, Dimension, spring 62; illusr, cover & article, Limnos, summer 69.
Dealers: Arwin Galleries, 222 Grand River, Detroit, MI 48226; Forsythe Gallery, 201 Nickels Arcade, Ann Arbor, MI 48104.
Mailing Address: 1106 S Forest Ave, Ann Arbor, MI 48104.

LEWIS, WILLIAM R
Instructor, Painter
Preferred Media: Watercolors.
b Osceola, Iowa, Sept 23, 20.
Study & Training: Drake Univ, BFA, 49; Univ Wash; Ariz State Univ, MA, 52.
Work in Public Collections: Ariz Western Col, Yuma; Glendale Community Col, Ariz; Scottsdale Civic Ctr, Ariz.
Exhibitions: Ariz Ann, Phoenix Art Mus, 61-68; Butler Art Mus Ann Midyear Show, 62; Am Watercolor Soc Ann, 63-65; Southwestern Invitational, Yuma, 67-72; Watercolor U S A Traveling Show, 68.
Teaching: Chmn art dept, S Mountain High Sch, Phoenix, 64-
Awards: Ariz Ann First in Watercolor, Phoenix Art Mus, 62.
Bibliography: Margaret Harold (auth), Prize winning watercolors, Vol II, Allied Fla, 62.
Memberships: Ariz Watercolor Asn (pres, 63-64).
Mailing Address: 313 E 15th St, Tempe, AZ 85281.

LEWISON, FLORENCE (MRS MAURICE GLICKMAN)
Writer, Art Dealer
b Jersey City, N J.
Study & Training: Sch Art Studies, 45-49, art hist & criticism with Maurice Glickman; also study in Eng, France & Italy, 56 & 61.
Positions: Art critic, feature writer & art news ed, Design Mag, 49-51; founder & dir, Florence Lewison Gallery, 61-
Research: Revival and reevaluation of nineteenth and early twentieth century American artists.
Specialty of Gallery: A program of exhibitions devoted solely to the reintroduction and reevaluation of nineteenth and early twentieth century American artists.
Publications: Theodore Robinson: America's first impressionist, 2/63, The uniqueness of Albert Bierstadt, 9/64, John Frederick Kensett: a tribute to man and artist, 10/68 & G P A Wealy: a success at home and abroad, 12/68, Am Artist Mag; auth, Theodore Robinson and Claude Monet, Apollo Mag, London, Eng, 9/63.
Mailing Address: 30 E 60th St, New York, NY 10022.

LEWITT, SOL
Sculptor
b Hartford, Conn, 28.
Study & Training: Syracuse Univ, BFA, 49.
Work in Public Collections: Mus Mod Art, New York, N Y; work also in Ger mus.
Exhibitions: Minimal Art, The Hague, 68; Prospect '68, Dusseldorf, 68; Stadtische Kunsthalle, Dusseldorf, 69; Univ B C, 69; plus many others.
Teaching: Instr, Mus Mod Art Sch, 64-67; instr, Cooper Union, 67.
Bibliography: Gregory Battcock (ed), Minimal art: a critical anthology, Dutton, 68; E C Goosen (auth), The art of the real U S A 1948-1968, Mus Mod Art, 68; Lucy R Lippard (auth), Minimal art, Haags Gemeentemuseum, 68; plus others.
Dealer: John Weber Gallery, 420 W Broadway, New York, NY 10012.
Mailing Address: 117 Hester St, New York, NY 10022.

LIBBY, WILLIAM C
Painter, Writer
Preferred Media: Oils.
b Pittsburgh, Pa.
Study & Training: Univ Pittsburgh; Carnegie-Mellon Univ, BA; Univ Tex; Colorado Springs Fine Arts Ctr; Acad Grande Chaumière; Atelier 17, with Stanley W Hayter.
Work in Public Collections: Pennell Collection, Libr of Cong, Washington, D C; Brooklyn Mus, N Y; Carnegie Mus Art, Pittsburgh; Butler Inst Am Art, Youngstown, Ohio; Metrop Mus Art, New York, N Y.
Commissions: Presentation print, Print Club, Rochester, N Y, 56; bicentennial dir cover, Bell Tel Co Pa, Pittsburgh, 57; commemorative hist painting, Pa Railroad, Pittsburgh, 58; History of Pittsburgh (hist illus), 60; altar piece, Carnegie-Mellon Chapel, Pittsburgh, 63.
Exhibitions: Painting in the U S, Carnegie Mus Art, 48; Nat Acad Design, New York, 51; USIA Overseas Exhib Am Graphic Art, 61; Sixth Int Graphics Exhib, Ljubljana, Yugoslavia, 65; First Biennial Graphic Art, Krakow, Poland, 68.
Teaching: Prof drawing & painting, Carnegie-Mellon Univ, 45-
Awards: Purchase award, Nat Print Exhib, Brooklyn Mus, 52; jury award of distinction, Assoc Artists Pittsburgh, 66; purchase award, Nat Print Exhib, Kutztown, Pa, 66.
Bibliography: Norman Kent (auth), William Libby, Am Artist Mag, 59.
Memberships: Soc Am Graphic Artists; Assoc Artists Pittsburgh (pres, 55-57); Nat Acad Design.
Publications: Illusr, The story of an American city, Doubleday, 59; auth, They know what they like, Eastern Arts Asn Bull, 59;

auth, A look at printmaking, Carnegie Mag, 60; auth, Offset lithography as a fine art, 67 & auth, Marco de Marco, 70, Am Artist Mag.
Mailing Address: Box 135, Carnegie-Mellon University, Pittsburgh, PA 15213.

LIBERI, DANTE
Painter, Sculptor
Preferred Media: Oils.
b New York, N Y, Oct 15, 19.
Work in Public Collections: Acad Fine Arts, Montecatini, Italy; Country Art Gallery, Locust Valley, N Y.
Exhibitions: Audubon Artists, New York, 50; Knickerbocker Artist, New York, 52; one-man shows, Norlyst Gallery, New York, 48, Vera Lazuk Gallery, Cold Spring Harbor, N Y, 61, 67 & 68, Galleria Vannucci, Pistoia, Italy, 70 & Galleria Ghelfi, Montecatini, Italy, 72; plus many other group & one-man shows.
Awards: First prize for sculpture, Oper Democracy.
Publications: Illusr, New Yorker Mag, 43.
Dealer: Country Art Gallery, The Plaza, Locust Valley, NY 11560.
Mailing Address: 15 Ardis Lane, Palinview, NY 11803.

LIBERMAN, ALEXANDER
Painter, Sculptor
b Kiev, Russia, 12; U S citizen.
Study & Training: Painting with Andre Lhote, Paris, France, 29-31; archit with August Perret & at Ecole Beaux-Arts, Paris, 30-32.
Work in Public Collections: Addison Gallery Am Art, Andover, Mass; Albright-Knox Art Gallery, Buffalo, N Y; Art Inst Chicago, Ill; Mus Mod Art & Whitney Mus Am Art, New York, N Y; Tate Gallery, London, Eng; Nat Collection Fine Arts, Washington, D C; plus many others.
Exhibitions: HemisFair '68, San Antonio, Tex, 68; Betty Parsons Private Collection, Finch Col Traveling Exhib, 68-69; The Art of the Real: 1948-1968, 68 & The New American Painting and Sculpture, 69, Mus Mod Art, New York; Contemp Am Sculpture Ann, Whitney Mus Am Art, 69; Pure and Clear, Philadelphia Mus Art, 69; plus many other group & one-man shows.
Positions: Ed dir, Conde Nast Publ, 62-
Publications: Auth, The artist in his studio, 60 & Greece, Gods and art, 68, Viking Press.
Dealer: Andre Emmerich Gallery, 41 E 57th St, New York, NY 10028.
Mailing Address: 173 E 70th St, New York, NY 10021.

LICHTENBERG, MANES
Painter
Preferred Media: Oils.
b New York, N Y.
Study & Training: Art Stud League New York; with F Léger, Paris, France; Acad Grande Chaumière, Paris.
Exhibitions: Philadelphia Acad Fine Arts, Pa; Nat Acad Design, New York; Mus Mod Art, Paris; Allied Artists Am, New York; Mus I'lle de France, Paris.
Awards: Prix Othon Friesz, Paris, 61; Gold medal of honor, Allied Artists Am, 64; Prix Maurice Utrillo, Utrillo Found Int, Paris, 64.
Memberships: Allied Artists Am; Am Watercolor Soc.
Dealer: Maxwell Galleries, 551 Sutter St, San Francisco, CA 94102.
Mailing Address: 26 Adele Rd, Cedarhurst, NY 11516.

LICHTENSTEIN, ROY
Painter, Sculptor
b New York, N Y, Oct 27, 23.
Study & Training: Ohio State Univ, BFA, 46, MFA, 49.
Work in Public Collections: Solomon R Guggenheim Mus & Whitney Mus Am Art, New York, N Y; Pasadena Mus Art, Calif; Tate Gallery, London, Eng; Stedelijk Mus, Amsterdam, Holland, Albright-Knox Art Gallery, Buffalo, N Y; plus others.
Commissions: Outside wall for Circarama, N Y State Pavilion, New York World's Fair, 63; billboard for Expo '67, Montreal.
Exhibitions: Retrospective, Pasadena Art Mus, 67; Tate Gallery, London, 68, Documenta IV, Kassel, Ger, 68; Print Biennial, Brooklyn Mus, 68; Solomon R Guggenheim Mus, 69; plus many other group & one-man shows.
Teaching: Instr, Ohio State Univ, 46-51; State Univ N Y Col Oswego, 57-60; Douglass Col, Rutgers Univ, 60-63.
Bibliography: William Beeren (auth), Roy Lichtenstein, Stedelijk Mus, 67; John Coplans (auth), Roy Lichtenstein, Pasadena Art Mus, 67; plus many others.
Mailing Address: 190 Bowery, New York, NY 10012.

LIEB, LEONARD
Painter, Educator
Preferred Media: Oils.
b Poland, Dec 27, 12; U S citizen.
Study & Training: Irene Kaufmann Settlement Art Sch; Univ Pitts-

burgh; also with Samuel Rosenberg, Armondo Del Cimmuto & Phil Elliot.
Work in Public Collections: Carville Marine Hosp, La; Carnegie Mus, Pittsburgh, Pa; Bd Pub Educ, Pittsburgh; Indiana Univ Pa; Point Park Col, Pittsburgh.
Exhibitions: Assoc Artists Pittsburgh, Carnegie Mus, Pittsburgh, 36-72; Carville Marine Hosp Competition, Nat Gallery Art, Washington, D C, 41; Nat Watercolor Show, Art Inst Chicago, 46; Nat Exhib, Pa Acad Fine Art, Philadelphia, 52; Drawing Soc Regional Show, Philadelphia Mus, 65.
Teaching: Instr drawing & painting, Arts & Crafts Ctr, Pittsburgh, 48-70.
Awards: Nat watercolor award, U S Treas Dept, 41; purchase award, Carnegie Inst, 58; award for distinguished drawing, Assoc Artists Pittsburgh, 62.
Memberships: Assoc Artists Pittsburgh (v pres, 53-55); A Group; Pittsburgh Watercolor Soc; South Oakland Arts Coun (pres, 70-71).
Mailing Address: 409 Cato St, Pittsburgh, PA 15213.

LIEBERMAN, HARRY
Painter
Preferred Media: Oils.
b Gnieveshev, Poland, Nov 15, 77; U S citizen.
Work in Public Collections: Joseph H Hirshhorn Collection, Washington, D C; Mus Boymans-Van Beuningen, Rotterdam, Holland; Seattle Mus Art, Wash; Palm Springs Desert Mus, Calif; Judah Magnes Mem Jewish Mus, Berkeley, Calif.
Exhibitions: American Primitive Painting Today, Los Angeles Art Asn, 58; Of Time and the Image, Phoenix Art Mus, 66; one-man shows, Botolph Gallery, Ctr Contemp Art, Boston, 68, Judah Magnes Mem Mus, 69 & St Andrew's Priory, Valyermo, Calif, 71.
Awards: William Mordecai Kramer (auth), Harry Lieberman, KCOP TV; The holidays (greeting card), Jewish Bk Club Commentary Mag.
Publications: Illusr, cover design, Moise, Mont-Blanc, Geneva, Switz; illusr, Great Ideas Western Man Series, Container Corp Am, 65; The holidays (full color lithograph), Commentary Libr/Jewish Bk Club Ltd Ed, 72.
Dealer: Ankrum Gallery, 657 La Cienega Blvd, Los Angeles, CA 90069.
Mailing Address: 9 Birch St, Great Neck, NY 11023.

LIEBERMAN, MEYER FRANK
Painter, Printmaker
Preferred Media: Watercolors.
b New York, N Y, Aug 28, 23.
Study & Training: Art Stud League New York, with Reginald Marsh; Pratt Graphics Ctr, with Andrew Stasik.
Work in Public Collections: Jewish Mus, New York; Flatbush Jewish Ctr, Brooklyn, N Y.
Exhibitions: Coney Island, Mus City New York, 55; Drawing U S A, Mus Mod Art, New York, 56; one-man shows, Jewish Mus, New York, 55, Herzl Inst, New York, 69 & La Salle Col, Philadelphia, Pa, 70.
Teaching: Instr drawing, painting & composition, Art Life Craft Studios, New York, 64-68; instr drawing, painting & composition, Temple Emanu-El, Yonkers, N Y, 66-; instr drawing, painting & composition, Flatbush Jewish Ctr, Brooklyn, 67-
Memberships: Artists Equity Asn (dir, 68-71).
Mailing Address: R F D 421, Zena Rd, Woodstock, NY 12498.

LIEBERMAN, WILLIAM S
Art Administrator
b Paris, France, Feb 14, 24.
Study & Training: Swarthmore Col, BA(hons), 43; Harvard Univ, with Paul J Sachs, 44-45.
Collections Arranged: Amedeo Modigliani, 51; Picasso: 75th Anniversary Exhibition, 57; German Art of the 20th Century, 58; Joan Miro, 59; Max Ernst, 61; The New Japanese Painting and Sculpture, 66; Jackson Pollock, 67; Jean Dubuffet, 68; Julio Gonzalez, Kandinsky Watercolors, Tamarind: Homage to Lithography, George Grosz: Drawings and Watercolors, Archipenko: The Parisian Years & The Sculpture of Richard Hunt, 69-71; plus many other exhibitions & permanent collections at the Mus Mod Art.
Positions: Mem staff, Dept Exhibs & Publ, Mus Mod Art, New York, 43, asst to dir mus collections, 45-49, assoc cur prints & illus bks, 49-53, cur prints, 53-66, dir drawings & prints, 66-, cur painting & sculpture, 67-71; staff adv, Jr Coun, 54-64.
Awards: Chevalier de l'Ordre des Arts et des Lettres, Repub France.
Memberships: Grolier Club; Am Fedn Arts (trustee); Cassandra Found (trustee); Drawing Soc (trustee); Int Graphic Arts Soc (trustee); plus others.

Collection: Eighteenth century silver boxes, Japanese prints of the Meiji ear and first editions of one British and two American authors.
Publications: Auth, Picasso: blue and rose periods, Abrams, 54; auth, Matisse: 50 years of his graphic art, Braziller, 56; auth, Edvard Munch, Los Angeles Co Mus Art, 69; Redon: prints and drawings & Jacques Villon, Mus Mod Art; plus many other books & catalogues, bulletins & articles in the U S & abroad.
Mailing Address: Museum of Modern Art, 11 W 53rd St, New York, NY 10019.

LIGARE, DAVID H
Painter
Preferred Media: Oils, Watercolors.
b Oak Park, Ill, 45.
Study & Training: Art Ctr Col Design.
Work in Public Collections: Ga Mus Art, Athens; Univ Kans Mus Art, Lawrence; Sara Roby Found Collection; Birmingham Mus Art, Ala; Weatherspoon Art Gallery, Greensboro, N C.
Exhibitions: Am Watercolor Soc Ann, 67-72; Calif Portraits, Civic Art Ctr, Walnut Creek, 71; Three Young Realists, ACA Gallery, New York, N Y, 71; Drawings U S A & Traveling Exhib, Minn Mus Art, St Paul, 71-73; Realism, Cleveland Inst Art, Ohio, 72.
Awards: Mary S Litt Award, Am Watercolor Soc, 69; Monterey Peninsula Mus Art Award, 70.
Memberships: Am Watercolor Soc.
Dealer: ACA Gallery, 25 E 73rd St, New York, NY 10021.
Mailing Address: Big Sur, CA 93920.

LILES, RAEFORD BAILEY
Painter, Sculptor
b Birmingham, Ala, July 20, 23.
Study & Training: Birmingham-Southern Col; Auburn Univ, BSEE, 49; Atleir, Fernand Leger, Paris, France, 49-51.
Work in Public Collections: Musee d'Art Mod, Eliat, Israel; Andrew Dickson White Mus Art, Cornell Univ; Corcoran Gallery Art, Washington, D C; Amos Andersons Konstmuseum, Helsingfors, Finland; Alfred Khouri Collection, Norfolk Mus, Va; plus others.
Commissions: Silk screen series, East Hampton Gallery, N Y, 67; fomaca sculpture series, Miss Silvia Pizitz, New York, N Y, 70; collage series, Mrs D O'Kennedy, Long Island, 71; painted plastic series, Dr Bill Lipscomb, Boston, Mass, 72.
Exhibitions: Salon d'Art Independent & Art Libre, Paris, 51; Salon Nouvelle Reality, Moma, Paris, 55; Mirco Salon d'Avril, Iris Clert, Paris, 56; Carroll Reece Mus 11 Ann Purchase Exhib, Johnson City, Tenn, 68; Art for Peace, New York, 70; plus other group & one-man shows.
Awards: Prize, Students of Leger, 51; first prize, Alpine Gallery, 58.
Bibliography: Turpin (auth), L'Orleanais dans les art, 52; Orinese (auth), Tour d'expositions combat, 55; Brown (auth), Review of expositions, Art Mag, 68.
Memberships: Birmingham Art Asn; Ala Watercolor Soc.
Dealers: East Hampton Gallery, 450 W 27th St, New York, NY 10001.
Mailing Address: 446 W 38th St, New York, NY 10018.

LILIENTHAL, MR & MRS PHILIP N, JR
Collectors
Collection: Paintings and contemporary art.
Mailing Address: 2275 Summit Dr, Burlingame, CA 94010.

LILJEGREN, FRANK
Painter, Educator
Preferred Media: Oils.
b New York, N Y, Feb 23, 30.
Study & Training: Art Stud League New York, with John Groth, Dean Cornwell & Frank J Reilly.
Work in Public Collections: Manhattan Savings Bank, New York; Am Educ Publ Inst, New York.
Exhibitions: Hudson Valley Art Asn, White Plains, N Y, 62-68; Allied Artists Am, Nat Acad Design, New York, 62-72; Coun Am Artists Soc, Lever House, New York, 64 & 67; Salmagundi Club, New York, 64-68; Acad Artists Asn, Springfield Fine Arts Mus, Mass, 66-70.
Teaching: Instr painting, Westchester Co Art Workshop, White Plains, N Y, 66-
Awards: Frank V Dumond Award, Salmagundi Club, 65 & 67; gold medal of honor, Hudson Valley Art Asn, 67; Today's Art Medal of Merit for oil painting, Today's Art Mag, 11/71.
Bibliography: Jo Mary McCormick-De Guyton (auth), Frank Liljegren & his old friends, Am Artist Mag, 2/72; Ralph Fabri (auth), Medal of merit winner in 58th A A A annual, Today's Art Mag, 3/72.
Memberships: Allied Artists Am (exhib chmn, 68-74, pres, 70-74); Artists Fellowship; Salmagundi Club; life mem Art Stud League New York.
Mailing Address: 64 Lispenard Ave, New Rochelle, NY 10801.

LINCOLN, RICHARD MATHER
Potter, Educator
Preferred Media: Ceramics.
b Ann Arbor, Mich, Mar 1, 29.
Study & Training: Potters Guild, Ann Arbor, with Rhoda Le Blanc Lopez & J T Abernathy.
Work in Public Collections: Dallas Mus Fine Arts, Tex; Witte Mus, San Antonio, Tex; Univ Mich Mus, Ann Arbor; Detroit Inst Arts, Mich; Davenport Art Ctr, Iowa.
Commissions: Murals, Apparel Mart, Dallas & Fort Worth Children's Hosp, Tex; light fixtures, The Quadrangle, Dallas.
Exhibitions: Eight Ceramic Nat & Int, Everson Mus, Syracuse, N Y, 54-68; Young Americans, New York, N Y, 56; Fiber, Clay & Metal, St Paul, Minn, 60; Miami Ceramic Nat, Fla, 60; five S-Cent Regional Exhibs, Santa Fe, N Mex, 62-71.
Teaching: Assoc prof ceramics, Tex Christian Univ, 63-
Awards: Third Pottery Prize, Young Americans, 56; purchase award, Univ Mich Mus, 56; First Pottery Award, S-Cent Regional Exhib, 62.
Bibliography: Texas potter—Richard Lincoln, Designers W, 11/70.
Memberships: Am Craftsmen Coun.
Mailing Address: 4759 Westcreek, Fort Worth, TX 76133.

LIND, VICTOR
Painter, Educator
Preferred Media: Graphics.
b Lunner, Norway, Dec 15, 40.
Study & Training: Nat Col Arts & Crafts, Oslo, Norway; Nat Acad Fine Art, Oslo.
Work in Public Collections: Nat Gallery Fine Arts, Oslo; Statens Konstråd, Stockholm; Ore State Univ; Gladsaxe Kunstbibliotek, Denmark.
Commissions: Relief, oil & tempera, Meirerienes Fallesfabrikk, Brevik, Norway, 65; relief, metal & glass, Christiania Bank Creditkasse, Oslo, 68; work, comn by Holtan Ungdomsskole, Horten, Norway, 69.
Exhibitions: One-man exhibs, Oslo, 66, 68, 69 & 71; Int Jugend-Festspieltreffen, Bayreuth, Ger, 69; Northwest Printmakers Int Exhib, Seattle, 70; Brit Int Print Biennale, Bradford, Eng, 70; Premio Int Biella L'Incisione, Italy, 71.
Teaching: Prof graphics, Royal Acad Fine Arts, Oslo, 72-
Positions: V pres bd, Kunstnernes Hus, Oslo, 71-
Awards: Finnes Legat, 67, Houens Fond, 68 & Houens Legat, 70, Norweg Govt.
Memberships: Norweg Young Artists Asn; Asn Norweg Painters; Asn Norweg Printmakers.
Publications: Auth, Reorganizing the art organizations, 69; auth, What's on in the Nordic Youth Biennale 1970, 70; auth, Television and politics, 71; auth, Norwegian artists and the Common Market, 72; auth, Art and artists in the Common Market, 72.
Dealer: Alonzo Gallery, 26 E 63rd St, New York, NY 10021.
Mailing Address: Haugveien 12, 1838 Flateby, Norway.

LINDEN, FRED
Painter, Instructor
Preferred Media: Oils, Watercolors.
b Vienna, Austria; U S citizen.
Study & Training: Oesterr Gewerbemuseum Art Sch Children, Vienna, with Csisek; Acad Visual Art, Univ Vienna, with Franz Windhager, Adolf Curry & Karl V Mayer, PhD.
Commissions: Portrait & miniatures, Empress Zita, Austria, 18; portraits, Joseph Schmidt, 37, L E Visser, 39, Cordell Hull, 42 & Frederick M E Schaefer, 42.
Exhibitions: Competition for Grand Austrian State Award, Kuenstlerhaus, Vienna; one-man show, Eland Gallery, The Hague, 39; Portraits, Inc, New York, N Y, 46-52; Schoneman Gallery, New York, 49; Am Artists Prof League, New York, 68-72.
Teaching: Owner, adminr & instr painting & drawing, Linden Art Sch, Forest Hills, N Y, 45-
Memberships: Am Artists Prof League.
Publications: Contrib, Am Artist Mag.
Mailing Address: 75-40 Austin St, Forest Hills, NY 11375.

LINDGREN, CHARLOTTE
Weaver
Preferred Media: Fibers.
b Toronto, Ont, Feb 1, 31.
Study & Training: Univ Mich, BS; with Jack Lenor Larsen; Can Coun studies in Finland, Sweden & Eng.
Work in Public Collections: Can High Comnr, London, Eng; York Univ, Toronto; Winnipeg Art Gallery; Confedn Ctr Art Gallery, Charlottetown, P E I; Can Dept External Affairs, Ottawa.
Commissions: Shaped wall tapestry, IBM Hq, Toronto, 67; ten woven cylinders, Queen's Col, Saint John's, Nfld, 68; tabernacle veil, St Michael's Church, Spryfield, N S, 68; woven sculpture, Expo '70, Can Dept External Affairs, Osaka, Japan, 69; shaped wall tapestry, Dalhousie Univ, Halifax, 70.

Exhibitions: Nat Gallery, Ottawa, 66; Am Fedn Arts Threads of History, toured major U S Galleries, 66-69; Competition Perspective 67, Art Gallery Ont, Toronto, 67; Expo '67, Can Art Gallery Pavilion, Montreal, 67; Int Biennial Tapestry, Lausanne, Switz, 67 & 69.
Positions: Juror arts bursaries, Can Coun, 70, consult arts panel, 71-72.
Awards: Haystack Sch scholar award, 64; Can Coun Arts Award, 65; major prize award, Perspective Competition Centennial Comn, Govt Can, 67.
Bibliography: C Fraser (auth), article, In: Arts Can, 6/66 & J Graham (auth), article, In: Arts Can, 7/71; L Rombout (auth), article, In: Vie Art, winter 67.
Memberships: Assoc Royal Can Acad Artists; Can Artists' Representation (rep, 69-72); Winnipeg Art Gallery.
Mailing Address: 6A Fairmount Rd, Halifax, N S, Can.

LINDMARK, ARNE
Painter, Lecturer
Preferred Media: Watercolors.
b Poughkeepsie, N Y, Oct 26, 29.
Study & Training: Pratt Inst; also watercolor with Edgar Whitney.
Work in Public Collections: Huntington Gallery, W Va.
Exhibitions: Am Watercolor Soc & Traveling Exhibs, 66-72; Nat Arts Club Ann, 69-71; 50 American Watercolorists, Mexico City Olympics, 70; Allied Artists Am, 71-72; Mainstreams 72, Marietta, Ohio, 72.
Teaching: Instr painting & watercolor, Huntington Gallery, summer 71 & Beckley Art Group, W Va, summer 72.
Awards: Herb Olsen Award, 68 & William Church Osborne Award, 70, Am Watercolor Soc; silver medal of honor, Nat Arts Club, 71.
Bibliography: Wendon Blake (auth), Acrylic watercolor painting, Watson-Guptill, 70; Margit Malmstrom (auth), Arne Lindmark, master of the watercolor scene, Am Artist Mag, 1/71.
Memberships: Am Watercolor Soc; Allied Artists Am (jurist, 72); Hudson River Art Asn; Duchess Co Art Asn.
Publications: Contribr, Acrylic watercolor painting, 70; contribr, Am Artist Mag, 71.
Mailing Address: 101 Forbus St, Poughkeepsie, NY 12603.

LINDNER, ERNEST
Painter
b Vienna, Austria, May 1, 97; Can citizen.
Work in Public Collections: Nat Gallery Can, Ottawa; Art Gallery Ont, Toronto; Winnipeg Art Gallery, Man; Mendel Art Gallery, Saskatoon; Beaver Brook Art Gallery, Fredericton, N B; plus others.
Exhibitions: One-man show, Banfer Gallery, New York, N Y, 64; Seventh Biennial of Can Painting, Nat Gallery, Ottawa, 68.
Teaching: Dir art dept, Saskatoon Tech Inst, 31-62; free lance artist, 62-
Awards: Hon LLD, Univ Sask, 72.
Bibliography: Article, In: Time Mag, 7/19/68.
Memberships: Can Artists Representation.
Mailing Address: 414 Ninth St E, Saskatoon, Sask, Can.

LINDNER, RICHARD
Painter
Preferred Media: Oils, Watercolors.
b Hamburg, Ger, Nov 11, 01; U S citizen.
Study & Training: Acad Munich.
Work in Public Collections: Mus Mod Art, New York, N Y; Whitney Mus Am Art, New York; Mus Nat Arte Mod, Paris, France; Tate Gallery Art, London, Eng; Kunst Halle, Hamburg.
Teaching: Prof painting, Pratt Inst, 52-64; vis artist, Yale Univ, 62-63.
Awards: Lichtwerk Award, Hamburg, 70.
Bibliography: Dore Ashton (auth), R Lindner, Abrams, 70; R G Dienst (auth), R Lindner, Thames & Hudson, London, 70; S Tillim (auth), R Lindner, William & Noma Copley Found, Chicago.
Memberships: Nat Inst Arts & Lett.
Mailing Address: 333 E 69th St, New York, NY 10021.

LINDSAY, KENNETH C
Art Historian, Writer
b Milwaukee, Wis, Dec 23, 19.
Study & Training: Univ Wis, PhB, 41, scholar, 47, MA, 48; Ecole Louvre, Fulbright fel, 49; Univ Wis, PhD, 51.
Collections Arranged: Marshall Glasier, An Exhibition of Paintings & Drawings, 59; Jean Lappier, Paintings, Watercolors, Graphic Works, 64; Architectural Process, Works of James Mowry, 67; The Works of John Vandelyn, 70.
Teaching: Asst surv, Univ Wis, 47-49; instr, Williams Col, 50-51; prof, State Univ N Y, Binghamton, 51-
Positions: Mem, N Y State Comn Arts, 66-67; coun archit & urban design, Binghamton, 67-68.

Awards: N Y State Res Found grants, 67, 69 & 72.
Research: American painting, modern.
Publications: Auth, DBR cover design, Art Bull, 35: 47-52; co-auth, Method in Breughel's paintings, J Aesthet & Art Criticism, 15: 376-386; auth, Kandinsky in 1914 New York, Art News, 55: 32-33, 58; auth, Kandinsky in Russia (catalog), Guggenheim Mus, 63; auth, Les themes de l'inconscient, XX⁰ Siecle, 27: 46-52.
Mailing Address: Art Dept, State University of New York at Binghamton, Binghamton, NY 13901.

LINDSTROM, GAELL
Painter, Educator
b Salt Lake City, Utah, July 4, 19.
Study & Training: Univ Utah, BS; Calif Col Arts & Crafts, MFA; also with Roy Wilhelm, Gloucester, Mass.
Work in Public Collections: Utah State Univ; Southern Utah State Col.
Commissions: Murals, Southern Utah State Col & Cedar City Pub Libr; mosaic mural, Utah State Univ Forestry Bldg, 61.
Exhibitions: Am Watercolor Soc, 53 & 57; Calif Watercolor Soc, 57.
Collections Arranged: Maynard Dixon Exhib, Southern Utah State Col, 55; Nat Ceramic Exhib, 57 & 58 & Nat Painting Exhib, 58, Utah State Univ.
Teaching: Prof art, Southern Utah State Col, 53-56; prof art, Utah State Inst Fine Arts, 57-61; prof art, Utah State Univ, 57-
Awards: Prizes & purchase awards, Utah State Fair, 52-54; Utah State Art Inst, 54; Am Watercolor Soc, 57.
Memberships: Am Watercolor Soc; Calif Watercolor Soc.
Mailing Address: Dept Art, Utah State University, Logan, UT 84322.

LINNELL-FFRENCH, PHYLLIS MARJORIE, see FFRENCH

LINSKY, MR & MRS JACK
Collectors
Mr Linsky b Russia, Jan 1, 97; U S citizen.
Collection: Ancient art and paintings.
Mailing Address: 927 Fifth Ave, New York, NY 10028.

LIONNI, LEO
Sculptor, Painter
Preferred Media: Bronze, Oils.
b Amsterdam, Holland, May 5, 10; U S citizen.
Study & Training: Univ Genoa, Italy, PhD(econ).
Work in Public Collections: Philadelphia Mus Art, Pa; Mus Mod Art & Metrop Mus Art, New York, N Y.
Exhibitions: Four American Graphic Artists, Mus Mod Art, New York, 53; one-man shows, Worcester Mus, Mass, 58 & Portland Mus, 59; Galleria Del Milione, 72; Venice Biennale, 72.
Positions: Art dir, N W Ayer & Son, Philadelphia, 39-48; art dir, Fortune, 48-60.
Awards: Art Dir of the yr, Nat Soc Art Dirs, 55.
Bibliography: Ben Shahn (auth), catalog, 64; Manuel Gasser (auth), catalog, 71; Franco Russoli (auth), Brera Mus Catalog, Milan, 72.
Publications: Auth & illusr, Little blue and little yellow, 59; auth & illusr, Swimmy, 63; auth & illusr, Frederick, 66; auth & illusr, Alexander and with wind-up mouse, 69; auth & illusr, Taccuino di Lionni, 72.
Dealer: Il Milione, Via Bigli 21, Milano, Italy.
Mailing Address: Via San Bernardo, Lavagna, Italy.

LIPCHITZ, JACQUES
Sculptor
b Druskieniki, Lithuania, Aug 22, 91.
Study & Training: Ecole Beaux-Arts, Paris, 09-11, with Jean Antonine Ingalbert & Dr Richet; Acad Julian, Paris, with Raoul Verlet; Acad Colarossi, Paris; Columbia Univ, hon LHD, 68.
Work in Public Collections: Mus Arte Mod, Paris; Mus Grenoble; Mus Mod Art & Metrop Mus Art, New York, N Y; Albright-Knox Art Gallery, Buffalo, N Y; Philadelphia Mus Art, Pa; plus many others.
Commissions: Five bas-reliefs, Dr Albert Barnes, 22; Prometheus, Paris World's Fair, 37; sculpture, Fairmount Park Asn, Philadelphia, 64; Presidential Scholars Medallion, 64; statue of Sieur Duluth, Univ Minn, Duluth, 64; plus many others.
Exhibitions: Many exhibs, nat & int; retrospective, Metrop Mus Art, 72.
Awards: Gold Medal for sculpture, Am Acad Arts & Lett & Nat Inst Arts & Lett, 66.
Bibliography: Maurice Raynal (auth), Jacques Lipchitz (monogr, Fr text), Ed Jeanne Bucher, Paris, 47; Henry R Hope (auth), The sculpture of Jacques Lipchitz, Mus Mod Art, 54; Bert Van Bork (auth), Jacques Lipchitz: the artist at work, Crown, 66.
Memberships: Am Acad Arts & Lett; Nat Inst Arts & Lett (coun mem).
Dealer: Marlborough Gallery, 41 E 57th St, New York, NY 10022.
Mailing Address: c/o Hanno D Mott, 60 E 42nd St, New York, NY 10017.

LIPINSKY DE ORLOV, LINO S
Painter, Illustrator
Preferred Media: Etching, Oils.
b Rome, Italy, Jan 14, 08; U S citizen.
Study & Training: Brit Acad Arts, Rome; Lipinsky Art Acad, Rome; Accad Belle Arti, Rome.
Work in Public Collections: Metrop Mus Art, New York, N Y; New York Pub Libr; Detroit Inst Art; Galleria Naz Arte Mod, Rome; Mus Revoltella, Trieste, Italy.
Commissions: Mosaic, The Grenadier, Hq Second Regiment, Rome, 37; Christ the King, Christ the King Church, Saint Louis, Mo, 41; etchings, Libr Cong, Washington, D C; diorama, Verrazzano's Landing in New York Bay in 1524, 57 & mural, New Amsterdam, 1660, 66, Mus City New York.
Exhibitions: Int Biennale, Venice, Italy, 34-36; Libr Cong, Washington, D C, 42-54; Cleveland Art Mus, 43; Nat Acad Design, New York, 43-49; Am Watercolors, Drawings & Prints, Metrop Mus Art, 52.
Teaching: Prof graphic arts, Lipinsky Art Acad, 25-39.
Positions: Founder & dir, Garibaldi & Meucci Mem Mus, Staten Island, N Y, 56; exhibs dir, Mus City New York, 59-67; admis comt, Huntington Hartford Found, 62-65; cur hist, John Jay Homestead, Katonah, N Y, 67-
Awards: Grand Prix & Gold Medal, Int Exhib, Paris, France, 37; Order of Merit, Italy, 58; gold medal & cert of merit, Order Sons of Italy Am, 61.
Bibliography: Jeff Straw (auth), The masterly art of Lipinski, Polish Rev, Vol 6, No 5; Elena Canino (auth), Clotilde tra due guerre, Longanesi & Co, Milan, Italy, 57; Rita Reif (auth), To the state, it's a historic trust; to two young boys, it's home, New York Times, 9/22/70.
Memberships: Audubon Artists (chmn exhib, 52); Soc Am Graphic Artists; N Y State Asn Mus; Bedford Hist Soc (bd dirs, 68-); Coun Arts Westchester; plus others.
Publications: Auth, Pocket anatomy in color for artists, Int House Publ, 47; auth, Giovanni da Verrazzano, the discoverer of New York Bay, 1524, 58; illusr, Roman people, Houghton Mifflin Co, 59; illusr, The ghost of Peg-leg Peter, Vanguard, 65; contribr, Giovanni da Verrazzano, Yale Univ Press, 70.
Dealer: James St L O'Toole, 667 Madison Ave, New York, NY 10021.
Mailing Address: Jay St, John Jay Homestead, P O Box AH, Katonah, NY 10536.

LIPMAN, HOWARD W
Collector
b Albany, N Y, July 11, 05.
Positions: Trustee, Aldrich Mus Contemp Art, 65-; trustee, Whitney Mus Am Art, 67-; pres, Arch Am Art, 70-; trustee, Phoenix Art Mus, Ariz.
Memberships: Smithsonian Inst; Solomon R Guggenheim Found; Mus Mod Art, New York; Whitney Mus Am Art; Am Fedn Arts.
Collection: Sculpture through the Howard and Jean Lipman Foundation for the Whitney Museum of American Art; sculpture of the 1960's with special accent on Alexander Calder and Louise Nevelson.
Mailing Address: 120 Broadway, New York, NY 10005.

LIPMAN, JEAN
Art Editor, Writer
b New York, N Y, Aug 31, 09.
Study & Training: Wellesley Col, BA; New York Univ, MA.
Positions: Ed-in-chief, Art in Am, 41-71; ed publ, Whitney Mus Am Art, 71-
Memberships: Mus Am Folk Art (trustee).
Collection: American folk art and contemporary American sculpture.
Publications: Auth, American primitive painting, 42 & American folk art, 48; co-auth, Primitive painters in America, 50, American folk decoration, 51 & American folk painting, 66; auth, Rufus Porter, Yankee pioneer, 68; co-auth, Calder's circus, 72.
Mailing Address: 226 Cannon Rd, Wilton, CT 06897.

LIPMAN-WULF, PETER
Sculptor, Printmaker
b Berlin, Ger, Apr 27, 05; U S citizen.
Study & Training: State Acad Fine Arts, Berlin, with Ludwig Gies.
Work in Public Collections: Metrop Mus Art, New York, N Y; Whitney Mus Am Art, New York; Nat Gallery Art, Washington, D C; Brit Mus, London, Eng; Nat Mus, Berlin.
Commissions: Stone fountains, Berlin, 32; Mem (bronze), First Presby Church, Stamford, 62; bronze busts of Bruno Walter & Karl Böhm, Metrop Opera, New York, 58 & 72; St Andrew (ceramic), St Andrew Lutheran Church, Chicago, 67; Joy of Life (ceramic relief), Mill Lane High Sch, Farmingdale, Conn, 68.
Exhibitions: Pa Acad Fine Arts Ann, 50-64; Whitney Mus Am Art Ann, 50-68; Int Sculpture Exhib, Philadelphia, Pa, 52; Ceramics Int, Syracuse Mus, N Y, 59; Jewish Mus, N Y, 60.

Teaching: Prof sculpture, Adelphi Univ, 61-
Awards: Gold medal, World Exhib, Paris, France, 37; Guggenheim fel, 49-50; Olivetti Award, Silvermine Guild Artists, 62.
Memberships: Artists Equity Asn; Am Soc Contemp Artists; Silvermine Guild Artists.
Publications: Auth, Dance in my sculpture, 70, Wall & space, 71 & Artist as teacher in America, 72, Leonardo.
Dealer: Harbor Gallery, Cold Springs Harbor, Long Island, NY 11724.
Mailing Address: 361 Bleeker St, New York, NY 10014.

LIPOFSKY, MARVIN B
Sculptor, Glass Blower
Preferred Media: Glass.
b Barrington, Ill, Sept 1, 38.
Study & Training: Univ Ill, Urbana, BFA; Univ Wis-Madison, MS & MFA.
Work in Public Collections: Mus Art Contemporain, Skopje, Yugoslavia; Mus Contemp Crafts, New York, N Y; Mus Boymans-Van Beuningen, Rotterdam, Holland; Stedelijke Mus, Amsterdam, Holland; Oakland Art Mus, Calif.
Commissions: Glass, plastic, metal twin panels, Metro Media Bldg, Los Angeles, Calif, 69.
Exhibitions: One-man shows, San Francisco Mus Art, Calif, 67, Hansen Gallery, San Francisco, 68, Mus Contemp Crafts, New York, 69 & Stedelijke Mus, Amsterdam, Holland, 70; Glass Today, Mus Bellerive, Zurich, Switz.
Teaching: Asst prof glassblowing, Univ Calif, Berkeley, 64-72; lectr glassblowing, Calif Col Arts & Crafts, Oakland, 67-; vis prof glassblowing, Bazalel Acad Art, Jerusalem, Israel, 71.
Awards: Top award, Milwaukee Art Ctr, 63; purchase award, Toledo Mus Art, 68 & Northern Ill Univ, 69.
Bibliography: John Coney(producer), Marvin Lipofsky blows glass (film), KQED, San Francisco, 68; E Marc Treib (auth), Marvin Lipofsky—just doing his thing, Craft Horizon Mag, 69.
Memberships: Int Comt Artists in Glass.
Mailing Address: 1012 Pardee, Berkeley, CA 94710.

LIPPARD, LUCY ROWLAND
Writer
b New York, N Y, Apr 14, 37.
Study & Training: Smith Col, BA, 58; New York Univ Inst Fine Arts, MA, 62; Moore Col Art, hon PhD, 72.
Teaching: Sem, Word & Image, Sch Visual Arts, 69-72.
Awards: Guggenheim fel, 68; Nat Endowment grant, 72-73.
Memberships: Ad Hoc Women Artists Comt; West-East Bag.
Publications: Auth & ed, Pop Art, 66; auth, Changing: essays in art criticism, 70; ed, Dades on art, 71; ed, Surrealists on art, 71; auth, Ad Reinhardt (in prep); plus others.
Mailing Address: 138 Prince St, New York, NY 10012.

LIPPINCOTT, JANET
Painter
Preferred Media: Oils, Acrylics.
b New York, N Y, May 16, 18.
Study & Training: Colo Springs Fine Art Ctr; Art Stud League New York; San Francisco Art Inst, Calif; also with Emil Bisttram, Taos, N Mex.
Work in Public Collections: Utah Fine Arts Mus, Salt Lake City; N Mex Fine Arts Mus, Santa Fe; Columbia Fine Arts Mus, S C; Denver Art Mus, Colo; Roswell Mus & Art Ctr, N Mex.
Exhibitions: Denver U S Nat Ctr, Colo, 63; Colo State Col, Greeley, 61; St John's Col, Santa Fe, 68; Columbia Fine Arts Mus, S C, 72; Arts & Crafts Mus, Columbus, Ga, 72, plus many others.
Awards: Atwater Kent Award, Palm Beach, Fla, 63; Southwestern Biennial Award, Santa Fe, 66; arts-in-residence, Durango, Colo, 68.
Bibliography: Margaret Harold (auth), Prize winning paintings, 63; Artist of the month, Southwest Art Gallery Mag, 5/72.
Memberships: Friends of Art, Albuquerque, N Mex (mem bd).
Dealers: Jamison Gallery, 111 San Francisco St, Santa Fe, NM 87501; Gallery of Contemporary Art, Taos, NM 87571.
Mailing Address: P O Box 1412, Santa Fe, NM 87501.

LIPPOLD, RICHARD
Sculptor
Preferred Media: Wire, Metals.
b Milwaukee, Wis, May 3, 15.
Study & Training: Art Inst Chicago, BFA, 37; Univ Chicago; Univ Mich.
Work in Public Collections: Metrop Mus Art, New York, N Y; Mus Mod Art, New York, N Y; Va Mus Fine Arts, Richmond; Des Moines Mus Fine Arts, Iowa; Mus Vin, Cauillac, Gironde, France.
Commissions: Outdoor sculpture, comn by Walter Gropius, Architect, Harvard Univ, Cambridge, Mass, 50; lobby sculpture comn by Walter Gropius, Pan-Am Bldg, New York, 61; lobby sculpture,

comn by Max Abramowitz, Philharmonic Hall, Lincoln Ctr, New York, 61; lobby sculpture, comn by Jesse Jones Found, Jesse Jones Hall, Houston, Tex, 66; Baldacchino, Cathedral of St Mary, San Francisco, 70.

Exhibitions: Origins of Modern Sculpture, St Louis Mus, Mo & Detroit Art Inst, Mich, 45; Unknown Political Prisoner (competition finalists), Tate Gallery Art, London, Eng, 52; Fifteen Americans, Mus Mod Art, New York, 52; Salute to France, Mus Arte Mod, Paris, France, 55; The New Decade, Whitney Mus Am Art, New York, 55.

Teaching: Head art dept, Trenton Jr Col, 47-52; prof art, Hunter Col, 52-65.

Positions: V pres, Nat Inst Arts & Lett, 63.

Awards: Creative arts award, Brandeis Univ, 58; silver medal, Architects League New York, 60; fine arts medal, Am Inst Architects, 70.

Bibliography: Dorothy Miller (auth), Fifteen Americans, Mus Mod Art, New York, 52; Brian O'Dougherty (producer), Richard Lippold (TV film), Boston Educ TV, 60; The sun and Richard Lippold (TV film), New York TV, 69.

Mailing Address: c/o Willard Gallery, 29 E 72nd St, New York, NY 10021.

LIPSKY, PAT
Painter
Preferred Media: Acrylics, Oils.
b New York, N Y, Sept 21, 41.
Study & Training: Brooklyn Mus Art Sch, summers 60 & 61; Cornell Univ, BFA, 63; Art Stud League New York, 64; Hunter Col, MA, 68, with Tony Smith.
Work in Public Collections: Whitney Mus Am Art, New York; Aldrich Mus, Ridgefield, Conn.
Exhibitions: Lyrical Abstraction, 69, Highlights 1969-70 & exhibs, 72, Aldrich Mus; Pat Lipsky Recent Paintings, Everson Mus, 70; Lyrical Abstraction, Whitney Mus Am Art, 71.
Dealer: André Emmerich Gallery, 41 E 57th St, New York, NY 10022.
Mailing Address: Wilson Hill Rd, Hoosick Falls, NY 12090.

LIPTON, SEYMOUR
Sculptor
b New York, N Y, Nov 6, 03.
Study & Training: City Col New York, 21-22; Columbia Univ, 23-27.
Work in Public Collections: Mus Mod Art & Metrop Mus Art, New York; São Paulo Mus, Brazil; Franklin Inst, Philadelphia, Pa; Albright-Knox Art Gallery, Buffalo, N Y; Toronto Art Gallery, Ont; plus many others.
Commissions: Lincoln Ctr for the Performing Arts, New York; Dulles Int Airport, Washington, D C; Milwaukee Ctr for Performing Arts, Wis, 69; City of Philadelphia, Pa.
Exhibitions: One-man shows, Milwaukee Art Ctr, Wis, 70, Mass Inst Technol, 71 & Va Mus Fine Arts, 72.
Teaching: Instr sculpture, Cooper Union, 42-44; instr sculpture, New Sch Social Res, 40-64.
Positions: Vis art critic, Yale Univ, 56; mem art curriculum adv bd, New York Univ; sculptor chmn, Art Comn New York City, 67.
Awards: Ford Found grant, 62; Archit League Award, 63; Widener Gold Medal, Pa Acad Fine Arts, 68; plus many others.
Bibliography: Barbara Rose (auth), American art since 1900, a critical history, Praeger, 67; Allen S Weller (auth), The joys and sorrows of recent American art, Univ Ill Press, 68; Albert E Elsen (auth), Seymour Lipton (monogr), Abrams, 69; plus many others.
Dealer: Marlborough Gallery, 41 E 57th St, New York, NY 10022.
Mailing Address: 302 W 98th St, New York, NY 10025.

LISSIM, SIMON
Painter, Educator
Preferred Media: Gouache.
b Kiev, Russia, Oct 24, 00; U S citizen.
Study & Training: In Russia & Paris, France.
Work in Public Collections: Mus Nat du Leu de Paume, Paris; Metrop Mus Art, New York, N Y; Nat Collection Fine Arts, Washington, D C; Victoria & Albert Mus, London, Eng; Albertina Mus, Vienna, Austria; plus 57 other mus in U S A, Can & Europe.
Exhibitions: Int Exhibs, Paris, 25 & 37; Int Exhib, Barcelona, Spain, 28; Theatre Exhib, Vienna, 33 & Mus Gallerie, Paris, 33; plus over 60 group & one-man shows.
Teaching: From asst prof to prof painting & design, City Col New York, 44-71, emer prof, 71-
Positions: Chmn, Nat Selecting Comt Fulbright Awards in Painting, Sculpture & Graphic Arts, 56.
Awards: Silver medal, 25 & two diplomes d'honneur, 37, Int Exhib, Paris; gold medal, Int Exhib, Barcelona, 28.
Memberships: Societe de Salon d'Autonme, Paris; Societe des

Artistes Decorateurs Francais; Audubon Artists; Soc Miniature Painters, Eng; Royal Soc Arts Eng (sr hon corresp mem in U S A, v pres coun).
Publications: Monogrs & many forewords for exhibs & articles published in Paris, England & U S A, 28-58.
Mailing Address: 55 Magnolia Dr, Dobbs Ferry, NY 10522.

LIST, VERA G
Patron, Collector
b Boston, Mass, Jan 6, 08.
Study & Training: Simmons Col.
Positions: Chmn, art ctr comt & trustee, New Sch Social Res; hon chmn bd gov, Jewish Mus; dir, List Art Posters, New York.
Awards: Solomon Schechter Medal, Jewish Theol Sem Am, 59; Louise Waterman Wise Award, 64; N Y State Coun on the Arts Award to Albert A List Found for List Art Poster Prog, 69.
Art Interests: Financed establishment of New School Art Center, 1960, and purchase fund, 1962, for purchase of art for Lincoln Center, New York; established List Art Posters Program; many gifts of art to New York museums and others.
Collection: Contemporary sculpture and painting.
Mailing Address: Byram Shore Rd, Byram, CT 10573.

LISZT, MARIA VERONICA
Painter, Designer
Preferred Media: Oils.
b Boston, Mass.
Study & Training: Scott Carbee Sch Art, grad; Boston Mus Sch Fine Art, grad; Art Stud League New York; landscape painting with Aldro Hibbard, Rockport, Mass, Carl Nordstrom, Ipswich, Mass, Emile Gruppe, Gloucester, Mass & Lester Stevens, Conway, Mass.
Commissions: Murals for hotels in Boston, N Y & Fla, commissioned by Carl Abbott; murals commissioned by Carl Gundlach & Emile Coulon, Boston for leading hotels, ballrooms, dining rooms & foyer entrances; also many portrait commissions.
Exhibitions: North Shore Arts Asn Exhibs, Gloucester; Nat Asn Women Painters, Acad Design, New York; Acad Artists, Springfield, Mass; Grand Central Art Galleries, New York; N J Art Asn.
Teaching: Instr pvt classes.
Awards: Elizabeth T Greenshield's Mem Award, 61.
Memberships: North Shore Art Asn; Acad Artists Asn; Nat Asn Women Painters.
Dealer: Grand Central Art Galleries, 40 Vanderbilt Ave, New York, NY 10017.
Mailing Address: 12 Wonson St, East Gloucester, MA 01930.

LITAKER, THOMAS (FRANKLIN)
Painter
Preferred Media: Watercolors.
b Concord, N C, Apr 26, 06.
Study & Training: Ga Inst Technol, BS; Mass Inst Technol, MS; also with John Whorf, John Frazer & Hans Hofmann.
Work in Public Collections: Honolulu Acad Arts, Hawaii; Mint Mus Art, Charlotte, N C.
Commissions: Fort St Mall Mural (with Howard L Cook), Wilcox Develop Corp, Honolulu, 69.
Exhibitions: One-man exhibs, Morton Galleries, 44, Honolulu Acad Arts, 51, Country Art Gallery, Westbury, N Y, 56, Retrospective, Royal Hawaiian Art Gallery, Honolulu, 68 & Downtown Gallery, Honolulu, 71.
Teaching: Instr, Univ Hawaii, 46-61.
Memberships: Hawaii Painters & Sculptors League; Am Inst Architects; Nat Soc Arts & Lett; Hawaii Art Educ Asn.
Dealer: Downtown Gallery, 125 Merchant St, Honolulu, HI 96813.
Mailing Address: 3913 Gail St, Honolulu, HI 96815.

LITTLE, JOHN
Painter, Sculptor
Preferred Media: Oils, Bronze.
b Sanford, Ala, Mar 18, 07.
Study & Training: Buffalo Fine Arts Acad; Art Stud League New York, with George Grosz; Hans Hofmann Sch Fine Art, New York, N Y & Provincetown, Mass.
Work in Public Collections: Ball State Univ, Muncie, Ind; Guild Hall, East Hampton, N Y; Berkeley Art Mus, Calif; Dillard Univ, New Orleans, La.
Exhibitions: Major one-man shows, Calif Palace of Legion of Honor, San Francisco, 46 & Betty Parsons Gallery, New York, 48; Osaka Festival (Gutai Group), Japan, 58; G David Thompson Collection, exhibited Kunstmuseum, Duseldorf, Ger, Munic Mus, The Hague, Holland & Guggenheim Mus, New York, 59; Panorama, Gallerie Beyeler, Basle, Switz, 61.
Teaching: Lectr painting, Univ Calif, Berkeley, spring 63 & Long Island Univ, summer 67.
Positions: Treas, Signa Gallery, East Hampton, N Y, 57-61.

Awards: Anne Bremer Mem Prize, San Francisco Mus Ann, 48; purchase prize, Longview Found, 62.
Bibliography: Hans Namuth (auth), Image from the sea, Film Images, New York, 54-55.
Memberships: Smithsonian Inst.
Publications: Auth, Statement of the artist, It Is, 59.
Dealer: A M Sachs Gallery, 29 W 57th St, New York, NY 10019.
Mailing Address: 367 Three Mile Harbor Rd, East Hampton, NY 11937.

LITTLE, NINA FLETCHER
Collector, Art Historian
b Brookline, Mass, Jan 25, 03.
Positions: Trustee & mem art comt, N Y State Hist Asn; trustee, consult & chmn curatorial comt, Old Sturbridge Village; cataloger & res consult, Abby Aldrich Rockefeller Folk Art Collection, 54-57.
Awards: Art Res Award, Hist Soc Early Am Decoration, 53; Rotary Club Brookline for distinguished pub serv, 56; Crowninshield Award, Nat Trust for Hist Preserv, 64.
Research: New England painting, architecture and decorative arts.
Collection: American decorative arts, especially folk paintings and furniture.
Publications: Auth, New England on land & sea, Peabody Mus, American decorative wall painting, 52, Abby Aldrich Rockefeller Folk Art Collection (catalog), 57, Maine's role in American art (1700-1865 sect), 63 & 72 & Country art in New England, 65; also var articles in mag.
Mailing Address: 305 Warren St, Brookline, MA 02146.

LITTLETON, HARVEY K
Sculptor, Educator
Preferred Media: Glass.
b Corning, N Y, June 14, 22.
Study & Training: Univ Mich, BDesign; Brighton Sch Art, Eng; Cranbrook Acad Art, MFA.
Work in Public Collections: Toledo Mus Art, Ohio; Victoria & Albert Mus, London; Mus Mod Art, New York, N Y; Milwaukee Art Ctr, Wis; Mus Contemp Crafts, New York.
Exhibitions: 13th Triennale Exhib Archit & Decorative Art, 64; Form and Qualitat, Handwerkskammer, Munich, W Ger, 68-69; Vrij Glas, Boymans Mus, Rotterdam, Netherlands, 69; Objects U S A, Johnson Wax Collection, 69-72; Artist Produced Glass, Bellerive Mus, Zurich, Switz, 72.
Teaching: Instr ceramic art, Toledo Mus Art Sch Design, 49-51; prof art & ceramics, Univ Wis-Madison, 51-, chmn dept art, 64-67 & 69-71, univ res grants, 54, 57, 62 & 72.
Awards: Toledo Mus Art res grant, 62; Louis Comfort Tiffany Found grant, 70-71.
Bibliography: Colescott (auth), Harvey Littleton, 59 & Dido Smith (auth), Off hand glassblowing, 64, Craft Horizons; Hot glass, WTMJ TV & Milwaukee Art Ctr, 66.
Memberships: Am Crafts Coun (trustee, 57, 59-64).
Publications: Auth, Erwin Eisch, 63, Craft Horizons; auth, Glassblowing—a search for form, Van Nostrand Reinhold, 72.
Dealer: Lee Nordness Galleries, 236-238 E 75th St, New York, NY 10021.
Mailing Address: Rte 1, Littleton Rd, Verona, WI 53593.

LITTMAN, FREDERIC F
Sculptor
Preferred Media: Bronze.
b Hidegszamos, Hungary, Feb 17, 07; U S citizen.
Study & Training: Nat Sch Fine Arts, Budapest, Hungary, 24-25; Acad Julien & Ecole Beaux-Arts, Paris, 25-27; Acad Ranson, Paris, 32-34.
Work in Public Collections: Portland Art Mus, Ore; Univ Ore Mus; Reed Col, Portland.
Commissions: Doors (with Belluscal architect), Zion Lutheran Church, 50; Franklin D Roosevelt Mem, U S Bur Reclamation, Coulee Dam, Wash, 52; Laberee Mem Fountain, City of Portland, Coun Crest Park, 54; Marion Co War Mem (with Belluscal architect), Marion Co, Salem, Ore, 55; bronze doors of the ark, Temple Beth Israel, Portland, 60.
Exhibitions: Art Inst Chicago, 40; Fairmount Park, Philadelphia, 50; two-shows, Art Inst San Francisco; Portland Art Mus Show, 50 & retrospective, 66; one-man show, Fountain Gallery, 70.
Teaching: Instr sculpture, Acad Ranson, 34-40; instr sculpture, Reed Col, 41-45; instr sculpture, Portland Mus Art Sch, 45-61; instr sculpture, Portland State Univ, 61-
Awards: Cert of recognition, Ore Chap Am Inst Architects, 52.
Bibliography: Numerous articles in newspapers & mags.
Memberships: Ore Guild Painters & Sculptors (pres, 48-50); Northwest Inst Sculpture (pres, 55-56); Artists Equity Asn.
Dealer: Fountain Gallery of Art, 115 S W Fourth Ave, Portland, OR 97204.
Mailing Address: 445 N W Skyline Blvd, Portland, OR 97229.

LITTMAN, ROBERT R
Art Administrator, Art Historian
b New York, N Y.
Study & Training: Antioch Col, BA (hist); N Y Univ Inst Fine Arts, MA (art hist).
Collections Arranged: Art Around the Automobile, 71, Ornaments from New York's Lost Buildings, 71, The Art of the American Indian, 71, The Green Gallery Revisited, 72, 11 American Photographers, 72, Eats—An Exhibition of Food in Art, 72 & Jasper Johns, Decoy: the Print & the Painting, 72, Emily Lowe Gallery, Hofstra Univ.
Positions: Dir, Emily Lowe Gallery, Hofstra Univ, 69-; consult, Asn Better New York, 70-
Publications: Auth, Hanging & leaning (catalogue), 70; co-auth, Universal limited art editions in Long Island collections (catalogue), 70; ed, The art of the American Indian (catalogue), 70; auth, Art around the automobile (catalogue), 71; co-auth, Jasper Johns, decoy: the print & the painting (catalogue), 72.
Mailing Address: 188 E 75th St, New York, NY 10021.

LIVINGSTON, CHARLOTTE (MRS FRANCIS VENDEVEER KUGHLER)
Painter, Art Administrator
Preferred Media: Watercolors.
b New York, N Y.
Study & Training: Nat Acad Design; Art Stud League New York; Columbia Univ.
Work in Public Collections: Ford Mus, Dearborn, Mich; Jumel Mansion, New York; Tamassee DAR Schs, S C; Hickory Mus Art, N C; Greenville Mus, N C.
Exhibitions: Am Artist Prof League, 66; Hotel Monmouth, Spring Lake, N J, 72; Nat Arts Club, 72; Authors, Artists & Writers Invitational, Pacem in Terris, 72; Bronx Mus, 72; plus one other.
Positions: Dir, Kingsbridge Hist Soc, 59-72; pres, Bronx Artists Guild; pres, Gotham Painters.
Awards: Mary Yates Medal, 70; Eva Rappleye Medal, 71; Anna Morse Medal, 72; plus other hon mentions.
Memberships: Nat Arts Club; Staten Island Inst Arts & Sci; Bronx Mus.
Mailing Address: 2870 Heath Ave, New York, NY 10463.

LIVINGSTON, SIDNEE
Painter
Preferred Media: Oils, Watercolors.
b New York, N Y.
Study & Training: Nat Acad Design.
Work in Public Collections: Princeton Univ; Everhart Mus, Pa; Univ Miami, Fla; Univ Miss; Columbus Mus, Ga.
Exhibitions: Art Inst Chicago, 50; Butler Art Inst; Philadelphia Acad Fine Arts; St Louis Mus, Mo; Libr of Cong, Washington, D C.
Awards: Fel, MacDowell Colony, 60 & 63; first prize for watercolor, Painters & Sculptors N J, 65; Mildred Tommy Atkins prize, Nat Asn Women Artists, 71.
Memberships: Artists Equity Asn New York.
Mailing Address: 14 Minetta St, New York, NY 10012.

LIVINGSTON, VIRGINIA (MRS HUDSON WARREN BUDD)
Painter, Illustrator
Preferred Media: Watercolors.
b Baltimore, Md
Study & Training: Md Inst Art; Cooper Union Art Sch; Art Stud League New York; Nat Acad Design; Beaux Art Am, Fontainbleau, France; with Ferdinand Leger, Paris Acad, France; also with Brackman, Ryerson, Kroll, O'Hara & Phillip, New York.
Work in Public Collections: Draped Figure, Home Fed Bank Bldg, Charleston, S C.
Exhibitions: Salon de L'Arte Libre, Paris, 51; Miniature Painters, Sculptors & Gravers Soc, Smithsonian Inst, Washington, D C, 52; Am Watercolor Soc Ann & Allied Artists Am Ann, Nat Acad Art, New York, 54-60; Corcoran Gallery Art, Washington, D C, 55; one-man show, Mus City New York, 60; plus many others.
Awards: First prize for Banjo Player, Ann Studio Club, YWCA, New York, 52; hon mention, Smithsonian Inst, 52; medal of honor for Jeanie, Ann Artists Prof League, New York, 56; plus others.
Bibliography: Article, In: La Rev Mod, Paris, 56.
Memberships: Carolina Art Asn; Charleston Artists Guild (planning comt chmn, 69-).
Art Interests: Organized new gallery, LaPetite Louve, to promote young artists.
Publications: Illusr fashions & by-line, Chicago Tribune Synd, 24-26; illusr, textbooks, Scribners, 24-25; co-auth & illusr, ann calendar for Am Cyanamid Co, 59-60.
Dealer: Blue Knight Gallery, 82 Broad St, Charleston, SC 29401.
Mailing Address: 138 Tradd St, Charleston, SC 29402.

LIVINGSTONE, BIGANESS
Painter
Preferred Media: Charcoal, Acrylics.
b Cambridge, Mass, May 17, 30.
Study & Training: Mass Col Art, BFA, 51; Boston Univ, drawing with Walter Murch, 66; Newton Col of the Sacred Heart, MPhEd, 72.
Work in Public Collections: Chase Manhattan Bank, New York, N Y; Cranwell Sch, Lenox, Mass; Radcliffe Col, Cambridge; Sheraton Corp, Boston; S Shore Equip Corp, Mass.
Exhibitions: De Cordova Mus, Lincoln, Mass, 58 & 63; Carl Siembab Gallery, Boston, 60; Mus Mod Art, New York, 62; Ward-Nasse Gallery, Boston, 71; Harvard Univ, Cambridge, 72.
Teaching: Asst prof art, Newton Col, 70-, artist-in-residence, 72; lectr studio art & dir exhibs, Colby Jr Col, N H, 69-70.
Awards: Radcliffe Inst fel paintings, 63-65.
Bibliography: Ted Farah (auth), Art collecting for pleasure and profit.
Memberships: Am Asn Univ Prof; Col Art Asn Am.
Dealer: Ward-Nasse Gallery, 178 Prince St, New York, NY 10012.
Mailing Address: Sunapee, NH 03782.

LLOYD, MRS H GATES
Collector, Patron
b Devon, Pa, July 19, 10.
Positions: Trustee, Philadelphia Mus Art, Am Fedn Arts & Washington Gallery Mod Art.
Collection: Contemporary painting and sculpture.
Mailing Address: Darby Road, Haverford, PA 19401.

LLOYD, TOM
Sculptor
b New York, N Y, Jan 13, 29.
Study & Training: Pratt Inst, with Gottlieb, McNeil, Guston & Nakian; Brooklyn Mus scholar, 61 pvt study with Peter Agostini.
Work in Public Collections: In pvt collections only.
Exhibitions: Studio Mus in Harlem, 68; Dr Martin Luther King Benefit Exhib, 68; C W Post Col, Greenvale, N Y, 69; Univ Calif, Los Angeles, 69; Phoenix Art Mus, Ariz, 69; plus many others.
Teaching: Dir painting & sculpture, adult creative arts workshop, Dept Parks, New York City, 67-70; instr light media, Sarah Lawrence Col, 69-71; instr three dimensional design, Cooper Union, 69-71.
Positions: Art consult, group serv agencies & educ div, Lincoln Hosp, New York, 66.
Mailing Address: 154-02 107th Ave, Jamaica, NY 11433.

LOBDELL, FRANK
Painter
b Kansas City, Mo, 21.
Study & Training: Saint Paul Sch Fine Art, Minn; Calif Sch Fine Art; Acad Grande Chaumière, Paris, France.
Work in Public Collections: Pasadena Art Mus, Calif; Los Angeles Co Mus, Calif; Stanford Mus, Calif; San Francisco Mus Art, Calif; Oakland Mus Art, Calif.
Exhibitions: Salon du Mai, Paris, France, 50; Third Biennial of São Paulo, Brazil, 55; International Art of a New Era, Osaka, Japan, 58; Kompas 4, West Coast U S A, Van Abbemuseum, Eindhoven, 70; 32nd Biennial Am Painting, Corcoran Gallery Art, Washington, D C, 71.
Teaching: Prof art, Stanford Univ, 66-
Bibliography: Michel Tapie (auth), Frank Lobdell, David Anderson (Paris), 66; Walter Hoppe (auth), Frank Lobdell 1948-1965, Pasadena Art Mus, 66; Gerald Nordland (auth), Frank Lobdell, San Francisco Mus Art, 69.
Dealer: Martha Jackson Gallery, 32 E 69th St, New York, NY 10021.
Mailing Address: 340 Palo Alto Ave, Palo Alto, CA 94301.

LOBERG, ROBERT WARREN
Painter, Instructor
b Chicago, Ill, Dec 1, 27.
Study & Training: City Col San Francisco, AA; Univ Calif, Berkeley, BA & MA; San Francisco State Univ; Hans Hofmann Sch Art, Provincetown, Mass.
Work in Public Collections: Art Inst Chicago, Ill; San Francisco Art Comn; Portland Art Mus, Ore; Oakland Art Mus, Calif; Gallery Mod Art, Washington, D C; plus others.
Exhibitions: Richmond Art Ctr, Oakland Art Mus & San Francisco Mus Art, annually, 55-; U S Info Agency Exhib, Paris, France, 64; Ithaca Col Art Mus, N Y, 68; Henry Gallery, Univ Wash, 68; Calif Col Arts & Crafts, Oakland, 69; plus others.
Teaching: Art lect; instr painting & drawing, Calif Col Arts & Crafts, 61-63; instr art, San Francisco Art Inst, 63-66; instr art, Univ Calif, Berkeley, 65; vis fac, dept art, Univ Wash, 67-68.
Awards: Yaddo Found scholar, 57; MacDowell Colony scholar, 59, 60; La Jolla Art Mus Prize, 62; plus others.
Mailing Address: c/o Berkeley Gallery, 370 Brannan St, San Francisco, CA 94107.

LOCHHEAD, KENNETH CAMPBELL
Painter, Educator
b Ottawa, Ont, May 22, 26.
Study & Training: Pa Acad Fine Arts; Barnes Found.
Work in Public Collections: Numerous pub collections throughout Can.
Commissions: Mural decoration for Regina Br, Can Legion & Gander Int Airport, Nfld.
Exhibitions: In major Can art galleries through Nat Gallery Can & Western Can Art Circuit Exhibs; Contemp Can Painters Exhib, circulated Australia, 57; Can Pavilion, World's Fair, 58; Utrecht Cent Mus & Groningen Mus, 58; Fine Arts Mus, Mexico City, Mex, 60; Los Angeles Co Mus, Calif, 64; plus numerous one-man shows.
Teaching: Dir, Sch Art, Univ Sask, Regina, 50-64; prof art, Sch Art, Univ Man, 64-
Awards: O'Keefe Award, 50; Dow Award, 63; Robinson Award, Montreal Mus, 64.
Mailing Address: School of Art, University of Manitoba, Winnipeg, Man, Can.

LOCHRIE, ELIZABETH DAVEY
Painter, Sculptor
b Deer Lodge, Mont, July 1, 90.
Study & Training: Pratt Inst, life cert, normal art, 11; study with Weinold Reiss, summers 43 & 44; secco with Dorothy Pucinneli, summer 46; fresco with Victor Arnitoff, 46.
Commissions: 18 murals, State of Montana for Galen Hosp, 24-25; murals, comn by U S Treas Dept for Post Off Bldgs, Burley, Idaho, 37, St Anthony, Idaho, 38 & Dillon, Mont, 39; bronze Mem portrait panel, Cummerford-Walker family, Washington, D C, 48; Indian portraits, five Butte schs, Mont, 50-72; bronze bas-relief portrait, James Finlen, Fort Lauderdale, Fla, 70.
Exhibitions: One-man shows, State Hist Gallery, Helena, Mont, 44, Arthur Newton Gallery, New York, N Y, 59, Stadtler Hotel Gallery, Los Angeles, Calif, 60 & Marquette Nat Bank Gallery, Minneapolis, Minn, 63; Whitney Mus Art, Cody, Wyo, 68.
Teaching: Pvt classes in studio art, 32-39.
Bibliography: Local watercolor scenes, IBM Ann, 44; Gamers confectionary, Ford Motor Co Cookbook, 72; Dale Burk (auth), Modern interpretation, Bk Mont Artists, 72.
Memberships: Life fel, Int Inst Arts & Lett; Mont Inst Arts; Mont Hist Soc.
Art Interests: All things pertaining to the West.
Collection: Indian and mining artifacts covering 150 years.
Mailing Address: 1102 W Granite St, Butte, MT 59701.

LOCK, CHARLES K
Art Dealer
Positions: Dir, Lock Galleries.
Mailing Address: 20 E 67th St, New York, NY 10021.

LOCKE, CHARLES WHEELER
Painter, Printmaker
b Cincinnati, Ohio, Aug 31, 99.
Study & Training: Ohio Mechanics Inst; Cincinnati Art Acad; Art Stud League New York, with Joseph Pennell; study in Paris, 28.
Work in Public Collections: (Prints) Metrop Mus Art & Whitney Mus Am Art, New York, N Y; Nat Gallery, London, Eng; (paintings) Corcoran Gallery Art & Phillips Collection, Washington, D C; Dartmouth Col; plus others; also in pvt collections.
Teaching: Lect on lithography; instr lithography, Art Stud League New York, 22-37.
Awards: Tiffany Found award, 20; Logan Award, 36; Am Acad Arts & Lett grant.
Memberships: Nat Acad Design; Century Club.
Publications: Illusr, Tale of a tub, Walden & Capt Stormfield's visit to heaven; contribr, illus to Freeman Mag.
Mailing Address: Old Post Rd, Garrison, NY 10524.

LOCKER, THOMAS
Painter
Preferred Media: Oils.
b New York, N Y, June 26, 37.
Study & Training: Univ Chicago, with Joshuah Taylor; Am Univ.
Work in Public Collections: John Herron, Indianapolis; Chicago Arts Coun.
Exhibitions: Banfer, N Y, 64; Gilman Galleries, Chicago, Ill, 64, 67 & 68; Rex Evans, Los Angeles, 70; Vincent Price Gallery, Chicago, Ill, 70 & 71; R S Johnson Int Gallery, Chicago, 72.
Bibliography: J C Taylor (auth), Introd to catalogue.
Dealer: R S Johnson International Gallery Inc, 645 N Michigan Ave, Chicago, IL 60605.
Mailing Address: R R 1, Elizabeth, IL 61028.

LOCKHART, JAMES LELAND
Illustrator, Painter
b Sedalia, Mo, Sept 26, 12.
Study & Training: Univ Ark; Am Acad Art; Art Inst Chicago, with Edmund Giesbert.
Commissions: Container Corp Am; Baseball Hall of Fame Mus, Cooperstown, N Y; Ferry Hall Sch; Lincoln Rm, Gettsburg Mus, Pa; R R Donnelley Co; plus others.
Exhibitions: One-man shows, Art Guild Chicago, 58, Ferry Hall Sch, 58, Great Lakes Naval Base, 58, Lake Forest Pub Libr, 58 & 61 & Lake Forest Acad, 68.
Teaching: Lect, Wild Life Painting & Magazine Illustration.
Awards: Nat Graphic Arts Awards, 68 & 70; Printing Indust Award, 70-71.
Memberships: Art Guild Chicago; fel Int Inst Arts & Lett; Arts Club Chicago.
Publications: Portfolio of Upland Game Bird Prints, 60; Portfolio of Cats, 61; Prints of Waterfowl and Game Birds, 64; auth & illusr, Portrait of Nature, Crown, 67; illusr, Sat Eve Post, Colliers, Coronet, Sports Afield & others.
Mailing Address: 980 E Walden Lane, Lake Forest, IL 60045.

LOEB, MR & MRS JOHN L
Collectors
Collection: Paintings.
Mailing Address: 730 Park Ave, New York, NY 10021.

LOEHR, MAX
Museum Curator, Educator
b Chemnitz, Ger, Dec 4, 03; U S citizen.
Study & Training: Univ Berlin, 33-34; Univ Munich, PhD, 36; Harvard Univ, hon MA.
Teaching: Assoc prof, Tsinghua Univ, Peking, 47-48; lectr, Far Eastern art, Univ Munich, 50-51; prof Far Eastern art, Univ Mich, 51-60; Abby Aldrich Rockefeller prof Oriental art, Harvard Univ, 60-
Positions: Asst cur, Mus Volkerkunde, 36-40; dir, Sino-Ger Inst, Peking, 41-45; ed, Sinologische Arbeiten, Peking, 43-45; cur, Mus Volkerkunde, 50-51; hon res assoc, Freer Gallery Art, 52-60; Far Eastern ed, Arts Orientalis, 54-60; cur Oriental art, Fogg Art Mus, Harvard Univ, 60-; co-ed, Harvard Jour Asian Studies.
Awards: Guggenheim Found grant, 57-58.
Memberships: Fel Am Acad Arts & Sci; Col Art Asn Am; Am Oriental Soc; Chinese Art Soc Am.
Research: Chinese art and archaeol.
Publications: Auth, Chinese bronze age weapons, 56, Relics of ancient China, 65, Chinese art: symbols and images, 67; Chinese landscape woodcuts, 68 & Ritual vessels of bronze age china, 68; also contribr, articles to Artibus Asiae, Ars Orientalis, Oriental Art, Jour Asian Studies & others.
Mailing Address: Fogg Art Museum, Harvard University, Cambridge, MA 02138.

LOEW, MICHAEL
Painter, Educator
Preferred Media: Oils.
b New York, N Y, May 8, 07.
Study & Training: Art Stud League New York, 26-29, with Richard Lahey & Boardman Robinson; Acad Scandinave, Paris, France, 29, with Dufresne; Hans Hofmann Sch Fine Arts, New York, 46-49; Atelier Leger, Paris, 50, with F Leger.
Work in Public Collections: Whitney Mus Am Art, New York; Philadelphia Mus Fine Arts, Pa; Sheldon Swope Mem Mus, Lincoln, Nebr; Univ Art Mus, Univ Calif, Berkeley; Joseph H Hirshhorn Mus, Washington, D C.
Commissions: Evolution of Textile Making (mural), Works Progress Admin, Stradehuller High Sch, New York, 33; mural (with Wilhelm DeKooning), Hall of Pharm, New York World's Fair, 39; murals, U S Post Off Bldgs, Amherst, Ohio 41 & Belle Vernon, Pa, 42, U S Treas Dept Sect Fine Arts.
Exhibitions: American Drawings, Watercolors & Prints, Metrop Mus Art, New York, 52; Classic Tradition in American Painting, Walker Art Ctr, Minn, 53; Geometric Abstraction in America, Whitney Mus Am Art, New York, 62; 67th Ann Contemp Painting & Sculpture, Art Inst Chicago, 64; American Painting & Sculpture, Pa Acad Fine Arts, Philadelphia, 66; plus many other group and one-man shows.
Teaching: Sr instr painting, Sch Visual Arts, 58-, co-chmn fine arts dept, 62-70; vis prof painting, Univ Calif, Berkeley, 60-61, vis lectr painting, 65-66.
Positions: Pres & secy, Artists Union, New York, 34-35; mem, Mayor LaGuardia's Art Comt of 100, 35-36; selecting juror, Int Asn Plastic Arts European Touring Exhib, 57.
Awards: Sadie A May fel, 29; hon mention for murals, Treas Dept, 41 & 42; Ford Found Purchase Award, Art Inst Chicago Exhib, 64.

Bibliography: Stuart Preston (auth), Abstract quartet, New York Times, 11/27/49; Dore Ashton (auth), About art and artists, New York Times, 11/29/55; Natalie Edgar (auth), Art review, Art News, 2/65.
Memberships: Am Abstract Artists; Fedn Mod Painters & Sculptors.
Publications: Contribr, statement, In: Realities Novelles, Paris, 50 & It Is, autumn 58; contribr, Josef Albers, impersonalization in perfect form, 56 & Academy, 59, Art News; contribr, Artists and critics, a letter, Arts Mag, 10/62.
Mailing Address: 280 Ninth Ave, New York, NY 10001.

LOGAN, FREDERICK MANNING
Educator, Writer
b Racine, Wis, July 18, 09.
Study & Training: Milwaukee State Teachers Col, BE, 32; Art Inst Chicago, 33; Columbia Univ Teachers Col, MA, 39.
Teaching: Head div art educ, Milwaukee State Teachers Col, 43-46; prof art, Univ Wis-Madison, 46-; vis lectr, Sch Art Educ, Birmingham, Eng, summer 64.
Positions: Pres, Wis Artists Fedn, 34-41; mem bd, Madison Art Asn, 52-67; coun mem, Comt Art Educ, Mus Mod Art, New York, 53-63; mem bd, Western Arts Asn, 54-57.
Memberships: Inst Study Art Educ; Nat Art Educ Asn; Wis Acad Sci, Arts & Lett; Int Soc Educ Art.
Research: Aesthetics of the environment.
Publications: Auth, Growth of art in American schools, 55; contribr, Report of commission on art education, 65; contribr & ed, A report for urban America, Educ Aesthetic Awareness Environ, 66; ed, Geography and psychology of urban cultural centers, Arts & Soc, 67; auth, A challenge to art education, J Nat Art Educ, 70.
Mailing Address: 2913 Waunona Way, Madison, WI 53713.

LOGAN, MAURICE
Painter, Illustrator
Preferred Media: Watercolors, Oils.
b San Francisco, Calif, Feb 21, 86.
Study & Training: Partington Art Sch, San Francisco; Mark Hopkins Art Inst, with Theodore Wores & Frank Van Sloan; Chicago Art Inst, with Reynolds; Calif Col Arts & Crafts, DFA, 56.
Work in Public Collections: Nat Acad Design, New York, N Y; Calif State Fair Permanent Collection, Sacramento; Oakland Mus, Calif; Reading Pub Mus & Art Gallery, Pa; Charles & Emma Frye Pub Art Mus, Seattle, Wash.
Exhibitions: Nat Acad Design, New York, 54-67; Am Watercolor Soc, 54-68; one-man show, M H de Young Mem Mus, San Francisco, 57; Two Hundred Years of American Watercolor, Metrop Mus Art, 66; Society of Six, Oakland Mus, 72.
Teaching: Instr figure painting, Calif Col Arts & Crafts, 35-44.
Positions: Trustee, Calif Col Arts & Crafts, 35-72.
Awards: Grand prize & gold medal, Am Watercolor Soc, 58; cert of merit, Nat Acad Design, 58; first place purchase award, Calif State Fair, Sacramento, 62.
Bibliography: Articles, In: Am Artist Mag, 6/62 & 5/68; Society of six (catalogue), Oakland Mus Art Dept, 72.
Memberships: Nat Acad Design; Am Watercolor Soc; Soc Illustrators Calif; Oakland Art Asn; Soc Western Artists.
Mailing Address: 7117 Chabot Rd, Oakland, CA 94618.

LOGEMANN, JANE MARIE
Painter
Preferred Media: Mixed Media.
b Milwaukee, Wis, Nov 12, 42.
Study & Training: Layton Sch Art, Milwaukee, summers; Aspen Sch Contemp Art, Colo, summers; Univ Wis-Milwaukee, BA.
Work in Public Collections: James Michener Collection, Univ Tex, Austin.
Exhibitions: Kornblee Gallery, New York, N Y, 68; Richard Feigen Gallery, New York, 69; Parker Street 470 Gallery, Boston, Mass, 70; LoGiudice Gallery, New York, 71.
Mailing Address: 144 Wooster St, New York, NY 10012.

LOGGIE, HELEN A
Printmaker, Painter
b Bellingham, Wash.
Study & Training: Smith Col, 16-17; Art Stud League New York; study in France & Italy, 26-27; also pvt study with John Taylor Arms & Mahonri Young.
Work in Public Collections: Univ Nebr; Libr Cong; Mus Fine Arts Houston; Seattle Art Mus, Nat Mus Stockholm; plus many others.
Exhibitions: Nat Acad; Soc Am Etchers; Am Fedn Arts; Carnegie Inst; Whitney Mus Am Art; plus many others.
Awards: Gold Medal, Am Artists Prof League, 60; Acad Artists, 60; S F B Morse Medal, Nat Acad Design, 69; plus many others.
Bibliography: Article & portfolio of drawings, In: Am Artist Mag, 69.

Memberships: Assoc Nat Acad Design; Soc Am Graphic Artists;
Calif Printmakers; Northwest Printmakers; Audubon Artists;
plus many others.
Mailing Address: 2203 Utter St, Bellingham, WA 98225.

LOMAHAFTEWA, LINDA (LINDA JOYCE SLOCK)
Painter, Educator
b Phoenix, Ariz, July 3, 47.
Study & Training: Inst Am Indian Arts, Santa Fe, N Mex; San
Francisco Art Inst, Calif, BFA & MFA.
Work in Public Collections: Ctr Arts Indian Am, Washington, D C.
Exhibitions: Riverside Mus, New York, N Y, 65; Mus N Mex, Santa
Fe, 65-66; Ctr Arts Indian Am, 67-68; San Francisco Art Inst
Spring Show, 70-71; Scottsdale Nat Indian Art Exhib, Ariz, 70-71.
Teaching: Asst drawing, San Francisco Art Inst, 70; painting instr,
Assoc Am Indian Arts, San Francisco, summer 72; asst prof
native Am studies, Calif State Col, Sonoma, 72-73.
Awards: Hon mention for oil painting, Mus N Mex, 65; first place in
graphic arts purchase award, Ctr Arts Indian Am, 67; third place
in drawing, Scottsdale Nat Indian Art Exhib, 70.
Bibliography: Lloyd E Oxendine (auth), 23 contemporary Indian
artists, Art Am, 7-8/72.
Publications: Illusr, Indian Mag, 71; illusr, Weewish tree, Am
Indian Historian Press, 71; contribr, article, In: Art Am, 72.
Mailing Address: 2082 Golden Gate Ave, San Francisco, CA 94115.

LOMBARDO, JOSEF VINCENT
Art Historian, Educator
b New York, N Y, Nov 6, 08.
Teaching: Prof fine arts, Queens Col, City Univ New York, 38-
Awards: Columbia Univ res grant spec study of Michelangelo, 68.
Memberships: Renaissance Soc Am; Soc Archit Historians; Metrop
Mus Art.
Research: Michelangelo; the Pietà and other masterpieces; Italian
culture in the twentieth century.
Publications: Co-auth, Italian culture in the twentieth century, 52;
auth, Michelangelo: the Pietà and other masterpieces, Simon &
Schuster, 65.
Mailing Address: 100-11 70th Ave, Forest Hills, NY 11375.

LO MEDICO, THOMAS GAETANO
Sculptor, Designer
b New York, N Y, July 11, 04.
Study & Training: Beaux Arts Inst Design.
Work in Public Collections: Sculpture, New York Pub Schs, 60; three
heraldic medallions, Deerfield Acad, 61; Seal for City of Rye,
N Y, 64; Alice Freeman Palmer Medal for Hall of Fame, N Y,
64; sculpture, Jr High Sch, Staten Island, N Y, 64.
Commissions: Family Group, Metrop Life Ins Co, New York World's
Fair, 39-40.
Exhibitions: Metrop Mus Art; Whitney Mus Am Art; Pa Acad Art;
Nat Acad Design; plus many others.
Teaching: Instr, Nat Acad Design Sch Fine Arts, New York.
Awards: J Sanford Saltus Medal, Am Numismatic Soc, 56; Mrs
Louis Bennett Prize & Lindsey Morris Mem Prize, Nat Sculp-
ture Soc.
Memberships: Fel Nat Sculpture Soc (coun); fel Am Numismatic
Soc; Archit League New York; Allied Artists Am.
Mailing Address: 61 Main St, Tappan, NY 10983.

LONDON, ALEXANDER
Collector, Illustrator
b Paris, France; U S citizen.
Study & Training: Lycee Mantaigne, Paris; Univ Pa, MS (chem
eng); Columbia Univ.
Positions: Pres, Marstin Printing Corp, 69-; publ, Electronic &
Appliance Co, 70-; exec dir, Imprimerie Centrale Commer-
ciale, Paris, 70-
Awards: Seven typographical awards, 56-71; award for illustra-
tions in Kelavala, 54.
Memberships: Sustaining mem New York Acad Sci; assoc fel Am
Inst Aeronaut & Astronaut.
Collection: French Impressionists; French Montparnasse; Ameri-
can Contemporary.
Publications: Illusr, Kalevala, 54; contribr & illusr for various
catalogs & art mag.
Mailing Address: 350 Central Park W, New York, NY 10025.

LONDON, JEFF
Sculptor, Lecturer
Preferred Media: Mixed Media.
b New Haven, Conn, Dec 11, 42.
Study & Training: Philadelphia Mus Col Art.
Work in Public Collections: Off Secy State, Captiol Bldg, Hartford,
Conn; Berkeley Divinity Sch, New Haven.
Commissions: People that talk too much (centerpiece), Nat Soc In-
terior Designers for Home Show, Hartford, 69; New Methods

(demonstration), Assoc Coun Arts Convention, St Louis, Mo, 71;
A Parentally Prescribed Children's Playground (experience
structure), Conn Comn Arts, Wadsworth Atheneum, Hartford, 71.
Exhibitions: Jeff London...Caustic Merriment T M, John Slade Ely
House, New Haven, 67; Under 35, New Brit Mus Am Art, 69;
people furniture, U S Plywood Corp, New York, N Y, 71; Artist
Save Face, Parish House Gallery, New Haven, 72; people
chairs...Unusual-ity, Stamford Mus.
Teaching: Vis artist caustic merriment, Conn State Grade Schs, 69-
70; vis artist caustic merriment, Conn Grade & High Schs, 69-;
resident artist caustic merriment, North Haven High Sch, Conn,
71; Nat Endowment Fund resident artist, Choate Sch, Wallingford, Conn, 72-73.
Bibliography: Robert Holland (auth), The merry man from Stony
Creek, Regist Pictorial, 71; A parentally prescribed children's
playground...re Jeff London, WTIC TV, 71; Jeff London...
Caustic Merriment T M, Conn Pub TV, 72.
Art Interests: Caustic Merriment, a trademarked, kind of hard
humored therapeutic form of art that lets you laugh at things
you most ordinarily don't.
Mailing Address: 180 Thimble Islands Rd, Stony Creek, CT 06405.

LONEY, DORIS HOWARD
Painter
b Everett, Wash, Jan 24, 02.
Study & Training: Univ Wash, BA; Art Stud League New York, with
Robert Brackman & Yasuo Kuniyoshi; Farnsworth Sch Art;
Scripps Grad Art Sch, with Henry McFee & Millard Sheets;
watercolor with Dong Kingman.
Commissions: Portraits, three pres, Univ Wis-Superior, bd dirs,
First Nat Bank, Superior, pres, Univ Ariz, Dr & Mrs Richard
Harvill, Columbia Univ, Dr Robert Terry; plus other outstanding
persons.
Exhibitions: One-man show, Rosequist Gallery, Tucson, 56; two-man
show, Fine Arts Gallery, Univ Ariz, 60; three-man show, Tucson
Art Ctr, 62; Nat League Am Pen Women Nat Biennial, 62, 64 &
70; Tucson Festival Six State Show, 62 & 70; plus seven one-man
shows in U S.
Positions: Mem bd Tucson Coun Art, 65-69; pres, Nat League Am
Pen Women, 66-68, state art chmn, 69-71.
Awards: First for figure painting, Sally, Seattle Art Mus, 50; first
prize for portrait, Papago Today, Nat Biennial, Nat League Am
Pen Women, 70; hon mention for watercolor, Hong Kong Harbor,
Southwest Watercolor Guild, 71.
Memberships: Life mem Art Stud League New York; Nat League Am
Pen Women; New York Pen & Brush; Tucson Palette & Brush;
Tucson Art Ctr.
Dealers: Rosequist Art Galleries, 2843 Campbell Ave, Tucson, AZ
85719; Portraits, Inc, 41 E 57th St, New York, NY 10022.
Mailing Address: 2200 N Alvernon Way, Tucson, AZ 85712.

LONG, C CHEE
Sculptor, Painter
Preferred Media: Wood, Casein, Oils.
b Smith Lake, N Mex, Dec 5, 42.
Study & Training: Inst Am Indian Arts, cert; Univ Ariz, two yrs.
Work in Public Collections: Inst Am Indian Arts Mus, Santa Fe,
N Mex; Indian Arts & Crafts Collection, C of C, Gallup, N Mex;
Navajo Tribal Mus, Window Rock, Ariz.
Commissions: Navajo History (mural), Ariz State Fair Comn, 65;
mural of chapel altar, design, St Michael High Sch, 68.
Exhibitions: Scottsdale Indian Art Nat, Ariz, 66 & 71; Guild Am In-
dian Arts & Crafts Exhib, Heard Mus, Phoenix, Ariz, 70 & 71;
Arts & Crafts Exhib, Inter-Tribal Indian Ceremonial, 71 & 72.
Collections Arranged: Navajo Centennial Exhib, Navajo Tribal Mus,
Window Rock, 68.
Positions: Asst cur, Navajo Tribal Mus, 65-68, staff artist, 68-70.
Awards: Merit award for paintings, 70 & first, second, third & merit
awards for sculpture, 71 & 72, Inter-Tribal Indian Ceremonial
Asn.
Collection: Indian and western artifacts.
Publications: Contribr poems & design, Four directions, Inst Am
Indian Arts, 63; illusr cover & article, Long walk 1868, Window
Rock, 68; contribr, Navajo Indian (poem), Univ Chicago Mag, 68;
contribr ten poems, Blue Cloud Quart, 69; contribr poems, Rob-
erts English Series, 71.
Dealer: Woodards Indian Arts, 224 W Coal Ave, Gallup, NM 87301.
Mailing Address: Box 22, Continental Divide, NM 87312.

LONG, GWEN
Painter, Instructor
Preferred Media: Oils.
b Tuttle, Okla, Mar 31, 26.
Study & Training: Abilene Christian Col; Univ Okla; with Henry
Hensche, Cape Cod, Richard Goetz, Oklahoma City & Betty War-
ren, Albany, N Y.

Work in Public Collections: KOTV Sta, Tulsa, Okla; Deutsch Collection, New York, N Y; Bus Admin Bldg, Okla State Univ, Stillwater; Decorlite Imports, Ltd, McLean, Va.
Exhibitions: Tulsa Regional, Tulsa Cent Libr, Okla, 68; Red Ridge Mus, Oklahoma City, Okla, 68; Big Bend's Nat, Tallahassee, Fla, 68; Philbrook Art Ctr, Tulsa, 68; Fort Smith Art Ctr 19th Ann, Ark, 69.
Teaching: Private instr oils, 57-
Positions: Pres, Stillwater Art Guild, 65-66.
Awards: Second pl for Cloak Room, Tulsa Regional, 68; first pl for Spring Collage, Red Ridge Mus, 68; Sweepstakes Award for Silver Pitcher, Tulsa State Fair, 70.
Memberships: McLean Art Club.
Mailing Address: 3095 Covington St, Fairfax, VA 22030.

LONG, MEREDITH J
    Art Dealer
b Joplin, Mo, Sept 14, 28.
Study & Training: Univ Tex, BA, 50, Law Sch, 50-51, 53-54.
Positions: Pres, Meredith Long & Co, 57-
Memberships: J F K Ctr Performing Arts (President's Adv Bd); Contemp Art Mus, Houston (bd dir, 70-, v pres, 71); Am Asn Mus; Am Fedn Arts.
Research: Nineteenth and twentieth century American art.
Publications: Ed, Americans at home and abroad catalogue, 71.
Mailing Address: 2323 San Felipe, Houston, TX 77019.

LONG, SANDRA TARDO
    Printmaker, Lecturer
b Hodge, La, Apr 2, 36.
Study & Training: La State Univ, BS & MA, with Caroline Durieux, Paul Dufour & Tom Cavanaugh.
Work in Public Collections: La State Univ Libr, Baton Rouge; Jonesboro State Bank, La.
Exhibitions: Sixth Delta Exhib, Ark Art Ctr, Little Rock, 63; Birmingham Festival Art Graphics Competition, Ala, 63; Old Testament Nat Art Competition, Inst Art, St Louis, Mo, 63; Piedmont Graphics Ann, Mint Mus, 68 & 69.
Teaching: Asst art, La State Univ, 61-63, dir arts & crafts, Stud Union, 63-65; instr art, Va Polytech Inst & State Univ, 71-72.
Positions: Cur, Va Polytech Inst & State Univ Col Archit, 68-69.
Memberships: Philadelphia Print Club; Blacksburg Regional Art Asn (chmn mem, 71-72).
Mailing Address: 404 Progress St N E, Blacksburg, VA 24060.

LONG, WALTER KINSCELLA
    Museum Director, Painter
b Auburn, N Y, Feb 2, 04.
Study & Training: Syracuse Univ, BFA & MFA.
Work in Public Collections: Paintings, Syracuse Univ Collection Fine Arts; sculpture, Univ Fla Bldgs & New York World's Fair, 39; mural painting, Lansing Cent Sch; soldiers & sailors monument, Shotwell Park, Skaneateles, N Y.
Commissions: Church murals; portraits for pvt comns; City of Auburn Civic Award Medal; Syracuse Univ Sch Journalism.
Exhibitions: Syracuse Mus Fine Arts; Rochester Mem Art Gallery; New York City Galleries.
Collections Arranged: Homespun Art; Shoes Thru the Ages; Cayuga County Inventions; plus others.
Teaching: Instr basic art & art appreciation, Auburn Community Col; lect, Art Appreciation, World Art, History of Art & others to civic groups, mus, schs & study groups.
Positions: Ed, Archaeol Soc Cent N Y Bull; Cayuga Co Historian; secy-treas, Northeast Mus Conf; dir, Finger Lakes Art Asn; dir, Instrument Res Inst; mem, Int Coun Mus, UNESCO; dir, Cayuga Mus Hist & Art, at present.
Awards: Mus Asn fel, Rochester Mus Arts & Sci; citizen of the year, 63; Honor Teacher of the Year, 64.
Memberships: Fel Royal Soc Arts; fel Int Inst Arts & Lett; Nat Acad TV Arts & Sci; Int Platform Asn.
Mailing Address: Cayuga Museum of History and Art, 203 Genesee St, Auburn, NY 13021.

LONGACRE, MARGARET GRUEN
    Printmaker, Lecturer
Preferred Media: Aquatint, Drypoint
b Cincinnati, Ohio, Nov 21, 10.
Study & Training: Les Allières, Lausanne, Switz; with Miss Heywood in Paris, France; Univ Cincinnati, BA; Art Acad Cincinnati; also with E T Hurley.
Work in Public Collections: Pennell Collection, Libr Cong, Washington, D C; Cleveland Mus Art, Ohio; North Shore Artists, Gloucester, Mass; Nat Acad Design, New York, N Y; Strietmann Collection, Cincinnati.

Exhibitions: Ohio Printmakers, circulated in cities in Ohio, 38-71; Miniature Printers & Gravers, Corcoran Gallery Art, Washington, D C, 40-63; North Shore Art Exhib, Gloucester, Mass, 40-71; Pennell Exhib, Libr Cong, 41-71; Cincinnati Artists, Nat Acad Design, New York, 41-71.
Teaching: Lectr graphic arts, on radio & in person, 50-
Positions: Judge for exhibs, St Louis & Cincinnati, 55-69.
Awards: Pennell Fund Award for Texas & Matterhorn in Moonlight, Libr Cong, 43; Streitman prize & others for San Juan Capistrano, 45-48; purchase prize for Waikiki Hawaii, Cleveland Mus, 51.
Memberships: North Shore Arts Asn; Cincinnati Woman's Art Club; Washington Watercolor Club; Cincinnati Woman's Club (chmn art dept, 63-65); Art Club Cincinnati.
Dealer: A B Closson, Jr Co Galleries, Fourth & Race Sts, Cincinnati, OH 45202.
Mailing Address: 3460 Oxford Terr, Cincinnati, OH 45220.

LONGLEY, BERNIQUE
    Painter
Preferred Media: Oils, Acrylics.
b Moline, Ill.
Study & Training: Art Inst Chicago, grad, Byron Lathrop foreign traveling fel, 45.
Work in Public Collections: Mus N Mex, Santa Fe; Dallas Mus, Tex.
Commissions: Murals commissioned by Alexander Girard, Santa Fe, 59 & La Fonda Del Sol, N Y, 60.
Exhibitions: Int Watercolor Show, Art Inst Chicago, 48; Denver Mus Art Regional Show Sculpture, 48; Mus N Mex Biennial Show, 53 & 65; N Mex Mus Fine Arts Invitational Show, 68.
Awards: Hon mention, Art Inst Chicago, 48; purchase prize, Mus N Mex, 53.
Memberships: Alumni Asn Art Inst Chicago; Int Liaison Network Women Artists.
Art Interests: Lithography.
Publications: Auth, Suite of lithographs, Tamarind Inst, 72.
Mailing Address: 427 Camino del Monte Sol, Santa Fe, NM 87501.

LONGMAN, LESTER DUNCAN
    Art Historian
b Harrison, Ohio, Aug 27, 05.
Study & Training: Oberlin Col, AB, MA; Princeton Univ, Carnegie fel, 28-30, MFA, 30, Am Coun Learned Socs fel, 30-32, PhD, 34; Fulbright fel, 52-53; Iowa Wesleyan Col, hon LHD, 55; Simpson Col, hon DFA, 61.
Teaching: Prof hist art, McMaster Univ, 33-36; prof art & head dept, Univ Iowa, 36-58; prof art, Univ Calif, Los Angeles, 58-, chmn dept, 58-63.
Positions: Pres, Midwestern Col Art Conf, 39, 49 & 58; ed, Parnassus, 40 & 41; bd dirs, Col Art Asn Am, 40-42; pres, Am Soc Aesthetics, 53-55.
Mailing Address: 718 Enchanted Way, Pacific Palisades, CA 90272.

LONGO, VINCENT
    Painter, Educator
b New York, N Y, Feb 15, 23.
Study & Training: Cooper Union Art Sch, 42-46; Brooklyn Mus Art Sch, 49-51; Fulbright schol to Italy, 51.
Work in Public Collections: Mus Mod Art, New York; Whitney Mus Art, New York; Libr Cong, Washington, D C; Detroit Inst Arts, Mich; Corcoran Gallery Art, Washington, D C.
Exhibitions: Whitney Mus Am Art Painting Ann, 51; Young Printmakers, Mus Mod Art, 54; Two Decades of American Prints, Brooklyn Mus, 69; one-man, Print Retrospective, 1954-1970, Corcoran Gallery & Detroit Inst Arts, 70; Whitney Mus Am Art Painting Ann, 72.
Teaching: Instr art, Bennington Col, 57-67; prof art, Hunter Col, 67-
Positions: Dir, Yale Univ Summer Sch Art, 69; contrib ed, Arts Mag, 55-59.
Awards: Guggenheim fel painting, 71.
Bibliography: Hilton Kramer (auth), The woodcuts of Vincent Longo, Arts Mag, 59; Gene Baro (auth), catalog notes for print retrospective, Corcoran Gallery, 70; Judith Goldman (auth), Print criteria, Art News, 1/72.
Memberships: Soc Am Graphic Artists (coun, 70-).
Dealer: Harry Lunn, 3243 P St N W, Washington, DC 20007.
Mailing Address: 105 E 63rd St, New York, NY 10021.

LONGSTAFFE, JOHN RONALD
    Collector, Patron
b Toronto, Ont, Apr 6, 34.
Positions: Pres, Vancouver Art Gallery, 66-68; v chmn, Nat Mus Can, 68-69.
Art Interests: Aid to young Canadian painters and sculptors; aid to Vancouver Art Gallery's Permanent Collection.

Collection: Contemporary Canadian art; contemporary international graphics.
Mailing Address: 15th Floor, 505 Burrard St, Vancouver, B C, Can.

LONGSTREET, STEPHEN
Painter, Art Historian
Preferred Media: Oils.
b New York, N Y, Apr 17, 07.
Study & Training: N Y Sch Fine & Appl Art, 27; also in Paris, 27-29 & 33-38, with Mattise & Bonnard & sketching with Pascin, Grosz, Arp & Feitelson.
Work in Public Collections: San Francisco Mus; Yale Univ; Jazz Mus New Orleans; Los Angeles Art Asn; drawings, Mus Mod Art.
Exhibitions: Nu-World Shows, Balbac Gallery, Paris, 40-60; San Francisco Mus Show, 65; Santa Barbara Mus Show, 67; Southern Calif Ann, 70; Paideia Galleries, Los Angeles, 71; plus others.
Teaching: Lectr, Los Angeles Art Asn, 50-; prof art, Viewpoints Inst, 65-; lectr mod art, Univ Calif, Los Angeles, 69; lectr, Los Angeles Co Mus; instr at large, Univ Southern Calif, 73-
Positions: Ed-in-chief, The great draftsmen (30 vols), 65-72.
Awards: Winader Found first prize for watercolor, 30; first prize for oils, Am Art Festival, 46; second prize for drawings, Midwest Antiwar Soc, 69.
Memberships: Los Angeles Art Asn (pres, 72); Viewpoints Inst (mem bd dir); Writers Guild Film Soc; Los Angeles Mus Art Graphic Soc; Paris-Am Arts.
Collection: Daumier prints; Rowlandson; Goya; Japanese prints.
Publications: Auth, A treasury of the world's great prints, 62; auth, Man of Montmartre, 66; auth, Yoshiwara, 70; illusr, We all went to Paris, 72.
Dealer: Paideia Gallery, 765 La Cienega Blvd, Los Angeles, CA 90069.
Mailing Address: 1133 Miradero Rd, Beverly Hills, CA 90210.

LOOMER, GIFFORD C
Educator, Painter
Preferred Media: Acrylics, Oils.
b Millard, Wis, Nov 29, 16.
Study & Training: Northern Iowa Univ, BA; Univ Wis-Whitewater, BEd; Teachers Col, Columbia Univ, MA; Univ Wis-Madison, PhD.
Exhibitions: Eighteen one-man painting shows in eleven states, 66-
Teaching: Instr, high sch, Iowa, 39-41; asstship, Columbia Univ, 47; instr art, Ball State Univ, 47-49; asst prof art, Eastern Ill Univ, 51-54; prof & head dept art, Western Ill Univ, 54-
Positions: Dir or instr, five foreign art tours, Mexico & Europe; jurist, several regional & area art shows.
Awards: Cert of merit for distinguished serv in studio art, London, Eng; Alpine Medal of Tourism, Vienna, Austria; awards in painting, photography, sculpture & com art.
Memberships: Ill Art Educ Asn; Nat Art Educ Asn; Western Arts Asn; Nat Educ Asn; life fel Int Asn Arts & Lett.
Publications: Auth, Learning experiences in art, 52 & Evaluations in drawings, 53, Univ Wis Press; auth, Arts & crafts of Mexico, Int Sketchbook, 63; auth, Award winning art, 65; auth & illusr, Rubens & Rembrandt, Int Sketchbook, spring 72.
Mailing Address: 227 Western Ave, Macomb, IL 61455.

LOPEZ, DOMINGO
Painter, Sculptor
Preferred Media: Graphics.
b Gurabo, P R, Dec 9, 42.
Study & Training: Univ P R.
Exhibitions: Cisneros Gallery, New York, N Y, 69; First San Juan Biennial Latin Am Graphic Art, 70; Second Bienal Arte Coltejer, Medellin, Columbia, 70; Drawing & Graphics Exhib, Cali, Columbia, 70; Salon Bache, San Juan, 70.
Mailing Address: Calle Cristo No 208, San Juan, PR 00902.

LOPEZ, RHODA LE BLANC
Sculptor, Instructor
Preferred Media: Clay.
b Detroit, Mich, Mar 16, 12.
Study & Training: Detroit Art Acad, Wayne State Univ; Cranbrook Acad Art, with Maija Crotell.
Work in Public Collections: Detroit Inst Arts; Univ Wis-Madison; Scripps Col, Claremont, Calif.
Commissions: Figure of Christ incised in concrete, Claremont Lutheran Church, 67; two sculpted brick fireplaces, 69 & one high relief fireplace, 70, Sim Bruce Richards; baptismal fountain, University City Lutheran Church, 70; wall fountain, Med Ctr, Dr Larry Fine, 71.
Exhibitions: Syracuse Nat, 49-55; Mich Craftsmen Ann, 49-58; five shows, Scripps Invitational, 53-66; Allied Craftsmen Ann, San Diego, 60-72; Design 8-11, Pasadena, 65, 68 & 71.

Teaching: Instr ceramics, Ann Arbor Potters Guild, Mich, 50-59; instr ceramics, Univ Calif Exten, San Diego, 56-; instr ceramics, La Jolla Mus Art Ctr, 60-65; lectr, Pac Arts Conf, 67; lectr series, San Diego Co Pub Schs, 72.
Positions: Med artist, Univ Mich Med Sch, 53-59.
Bibliography: Rhoda Le Blanc Lopez, Designers West, 71; Valerie Hatch (auth), article, In: Art West, 71; Marie Stanton (auth), A visit into Rhoda Lopez world of clay, San Diego Union, 1/72.
Memberships: Allied Craftsmen (pres, 65-68); Fine Arts Gallery San Diego; Southern Calif Designers Craftsmen; Am Craftsmen's Coun; Calif State Crafts Coun (secy).
Mailing Address: 1020 Pacific Beach Dr, San Diego, CA 92109.

LOPEZ-REY, JOSE
Art Historian
b Madrid, Spain, May 14, 05.
Study & Training: Univ Madrid, PhD, 35; Univ Florence; Univ Vienna.
Teaching: Asst prof Italian art & Spanish painting, Univ Madrid, 32-39.
Positions: Res fel hist art, Centro Estudios Historicos, Madrid, 32-39; adv fine arts, Ministry Pub Educ, Madrid, 33-39; v pres, Int Found Art Res, New York, 70-
Awards: Guggenheim fel, 47-48, 60-61 & 67-68.
Research: History of Spanish painting; nineteenth & twentieth century art.
Publications: Auth, Antonio del Pollaiuolo y el fin del Quattrocento, Hauser y Menet, 35; auth, Goya's Caprichos: beauty, reason & caricature, Princeton Univ Press, 53; Auth, A cycle of Goya's drawings: the expression of truth & liberty, 56, Velazquez: a catalogue raisonne of his oeuvre, 63 & Velazquez' work & world, 68, Faber & Faber.
Mailing Address: Institute of Fine Arts, New York University, 1 E 78th St, New York, NY 10021.

LORAN, ERLE
Painter, Writer
Preferred Media: Acrylics, Oils, Gouache.
b Minneapolis, Minn, Oct 3, 05.
Study & Training: Univ Minn, 22-23; Minneapolis Sch Art, grad, 26; Chaloner Found scholar for study in Europe, 26-30; also with Hans Hofmann, New York, N Y, 54.
Work in Public Collections: Univ Art Mus, Univ Calif, Berkeley; Krannert Art Mus, Univ Ill, Champaign; Smithsonian Inst, Washington, D C; San Francisco Mus Art, Calif; Denver Art Mus, Colo.
Exhibitions: Sixteen American Cities, Mus Mod Art, New York, 33; Five Shows, Contemporary American Painting, Whitney Mus Am Art, New York, 37-52; American Painting & Sculpture, 38 & Four Int Exhibs Watercolors, 39-46, Art Inst Chicago; Carnegie Inst, Pittsburgh, Pa, 41; Six Shows, Krannert Art Mus, Univ Ill, 49-69.
Teaching: Prof art, Univ Calif, Berkeley, 36-, chmn dept art, 52-56.
Awards: Bronze medal, Pepsi-Cola Nat, New York, 48; Artists' Coun Prize, San Francisco Mus Art, 56; purchase prize for Imago in Reds, Krannert Art Mus, 65.
Bibliography: Forbes Watson (auth), American painting today, Am Fedn Arts, 39; Allen S Weller (auth), Contemporary American painting, Univ Ill, 49-69; Nathaniel Pousette-Dart (auth), American painting today, Hastings House, 56.
Memberships: Univ Calif, Berkeley, Arts Club.
Publications: Auth, Cézanne composition, Univ Calif Press, 43 & 70; contribr, Cézanne, les peintres celebres, Ed Art Lucien Mazenod, Geneva & Paris, 48; contribr, Trial by juries, Art News, 12/52; auth, Cézanne in 1952, Art Inst Chicago Quart, 2/52; contribr, Cézanne and Lichtenstein; problems of transformation, Artforum, 9/63.
Dealers: New Bertha Schaefer Gallery, 41 E 57th St, New York, NY 10022; William Sawyer Gallery, 3045 Clay St, San Francisco, CA 94115.
Mailing Address: 10 Kenilworth Ct, Berkeley, CA 94707.

LORBER, STEPHEN NEIL
Painter
b Brooklyn, N Y, Aug 30, 43.
Study & Training: Pratt Inst, BFA; Brooklyn Col, MFA; Yale Univ, Stoeckel fel, 64.
Exhibitions: First Nat Lithography Exhib, Fla State Univ, 64; Soc Am Graphic Artists, New York, N Y, 66; Pa Acad Fine Arts Ann, 69; Newport Art Asn, R I, 69; Brooklyn Mus, 71.
Awards: Yaddo fel, 71.
Mailing Address: 310 Spring St, New York, NY 10013.

LORCINI, GINO
Sculptor
Preferred Media: Aluminum, Stainless Steel.
b Plymouth, Eng, July 7, 23; Can citizen.
Study & Training: Montreal Mus Sch Art
Work in Public Collections: Nat Gallery Can, Ottawa; Mus Art
Contemporain, Montreal; Chase Manhattan Bank, New York, N Y;
Aluminum Co Can, Montreal; Fleming-Hull Mus, Burlington, Vt.
Commissions: Murals, Nat Arts Ctr, Ottawa, 68 & Montreal Forum,
P Q, 69; fountain sculpture, Ste Anne's Hosp, P Q, 70; sculpture,
Nat Defence Bldg, Ottawa, 72.
Exhibitions: Op from Montreal, Fleming-Hull Mus, 66; Sculpture
67, Toronto, 67; Surv 68, Montreal, 68; one-man traveling exhib,
Atlantic Provinces Mus, Can, 69; 3D Into the 70s, Art Gallery
Ont, Toronto, 70.
Teaching: Asst prof painting & sculpture, McGill Univ, 60-68; resi-
dent artist, Univ Western Ont, 69-
Awards: Jessie Dow Award, Montreal Mus Fine Arts, 65; Arts
Award, Can Coun, 68.
Bibliography: M Gaulin (auth), Sculptor Lorcini, Time, 68; D
Sanders (auth), Gino Lorcini, Bus Quart, 71.
Memberships: Assoc Royal Can Acad Arts; Nat Sculpture Conf,
Univ Kans (mem adv bd).
Publications: Co-auth, Creative response, McGill J Educ, 67.
Dealer: Marlborough Godard Gallery, 22 Hazleton Ave, Toronto,
Ont, Can.
Mailing Address: 282 Ramsay Rd, London 75, Ont, Can.

LORENTZ, PAULINE
Painter, Instructor
Preferred Media: Oils, Charcoal.
b Newark, N J.
Study & Training: Newark Sch Fine & Indust Arts, N J, grad; Art
Stud League New York, N Y; also with John R Grabach.
Exhibitions: Expos Intercontinentale, Monaco & Dieppe, France, 67-
68; Am Artist Prof League Grand Nat, New York, 69; 24th Am
Drawing Biennial, Norfolk Mus Arts & Sci, Va, 71; 22nd Ann
Nat Exhib, Mus Fine Arts, Springfield, Mass, 71; Smithsonian
Traveling Exhib, U S A, 71-73.
Teaching: Instr, Summit Art Ctr, N J, 62-; instr, Heritage Arts,
S Orange, N J, 67-
Awards: Gold medals for drawing, Catharine Lorillard Wolfe Art
Club, 67 & 69, Am Artists Prof League, 67 & 70 & Arts Atlantic,
Gloucester, Mass, 72.
Bibliography: Philbrook Smith (auth), article, In: N J Mus & Arts
Mag, 2/64.
Memberships: Am Artists Prof League; Catharine Lorillard Wolfe
Art Club; Hudson Valley Art Asn; Knickerbocker Artists; Nat
Arts Club.
Dealer: Heritage Arts, 24 First St, South Orange, NJ 07079.
Mailing Address: 20 Southview Dr, Berkeley Heights, NJ 07922.

LORENZANI, ARTHUR EMANUELE
Sculptor
Preferred Media: Bronze, Marble.
b Carrara, Italy, Feb 12, 86; U S citizen.
Study & Training: Acad Belle Arti, Carrara, grad, 04; Rome Prize
& three yr pension.
Work in Public Collections: Acad Gallery, Carrara; Golden Age,
bronze, Brookgreen Gardens; Young Mather, bronze; Kinney Di-
rect bronze, Kansas City, Mo.
Commissions: John F Kennedy (bronze portrait), M Labetti Post Vet
For Wars, Staten Island, 64.
Exhibitions: Nat Acad Design, New York, N Y; Pa Acad Fine Arts,
Philadelphia; Albright-Knox Gallery, Buffalo, N Y; Nat Sculpture
Soc, New York.
Teaching: Instr sculpture, Staten Island Mus, 51-53.
Awards: First prize, City of Parma, Italy; hon mention, Garden Club
Am, 29; spec silver medal, Nat Sculpture Soc, 68.
Bibliography: B G Proske (auth), Brookgreen Gardens sculpture.
Memberships: Fel Nat Sculpture Soc; Allied Artists Am.
Publications: Auth & illusr, article, In: Nat Sculpture Rev, summer,
62.
Mailing Address: 273 McClean Ave, Staten Island, NY 10305.

LORING, CLARICE
Painter, Muralist
Preferred Media: Oils, Mixed Media.
b Vancouver, B C.
Study & Training: Vancouver Art Sch, Can; Johannesburg Art Sch,
S Africa; Art Stud League New York; Univ Calif, Santa Barbara,
BA (art); Univ Calif, Berkeley, MA (art); Univ Michoacan,
Morelai, with Alfredo Salze.
Work in Public Collections: Victoria Art Gallery, Can; Ottawa Art
Gallery, Can; State Hawaii.

Commissions: Ceramic tile & aluminum, for admin bldg, Aloha Air-
lines, 61; acrylic wall mural, Unity Bldg, Honolulu, Hawaii, 66;
illuminated plexiglass (3 units), Ala Moana Hotel, Honolulu, 70.
Exhibitions: Artists of Hawaii, Honolulu, 71; Hawaii Painters &
Sculptors League, Honolulu, 72; Art Festival, Honolulu, 72.
Memberships: Honolulu Acad Arts; Hawaii Painters & Sculptors
League (past pres, 65); Honolulu Printmakers.
Mailing Address: 1867 Vancouver Dr, Honolulu, HI 96822.

LOTHROP, KRISTIN CURTIS
Sculptor
Preferred Media: Bronze, Wood, Stone.
b Tucson, Ariz, Feb 8, 30.
Study & Training: Bennington Col, BA; also four yrs with George
Demetrios, sculptor.
Exhibitions: Nat Sculpture Soc, 67-71; Hudson Valley Art Asn, 68;
Nat Acad Design, 68-71; Allied Artists Am, 69.
Awards: Mrs Louis Bennett Award, Nat Sculpture Soc, 67; Thomas
R Proctor Award, 68 & Daniel Chester French Award, 70, Nat
Acad Design.
Memberships: New Eng Sculptors Asn; Nat Sculpture Soc.
Mailing Address: Bridge St, Manchester, MA 01944.

LOTTERMAN, HAL
Painter, Educator
Preferred Media: Oil, Lacquer.
b Chicago, Ill, Sept 29, 20.
Study & Training: Univ Ill, BFA, 45, Univ Iowa, MFA, 46.
Work in Public Collections: Butler Inst Am Art, Youngstown, Ohio;
Akron Art Inst, Ohio; Ohio Univ, Athens; Ball State Univ, Muncie,
Ind; Mulvane Art Ctr, Topeka, Kans.
Exhibitions: Metrop Mus Art, New York, N Y, 50; Carnegie Int,
Pittsburgh, Pa, 52; Pa Acad Fine Arts Ann, Philadelphia, 53; Nat
Acad Design Ann, New York, 54; Art U S A 58, New York, 58.
Teaching: Instr art, Univ Iowa, 47-50; instr art, Toledo Mus Art, 50-
56; prof art, Univ Wis-Madison, 65-
Awards: Tiffany Found painting scholar, 51; Univ Iowa Purchase
Award, 57.
Art Interests: Video tape.
Mailing Address: 125 S Randall Ave, Madison, WI 53715.

LOTTON, IWAN LEROY
Painter, Illustrator
Preferred Media: Oils.
b Rising Sun, Ind, Feb 12, 13.
Study & Training: Art Inst Chicago; Chicago Acad Fine Art; Am
Acad Art; also with Gillette Elvgren, Earl Gross, William Mosby,
Wellington J Reynolds, Anton Sterba, Herb Olson, Andrew Loomis
& Merlin Enabnit.
Work in Public Collections: Am Field Publ Co Gallery of Field Trial
Hall of Fame Paintings, Chicago, Ill; Am Kennel Club Gallery
Fine Art Canine Paintings, New York, N Y; Thoroughbred Record
Hall, Lexington, Ky.
Commissions: Portraits of all dogs elected to Field Trial Hall of
Fame, 52-; also many pvt comn.
Teaching: Instr oil painting, adult eve classes, Roselle Schs, Ill, 60-
Positions: Owner, Lotton's Studio Gallery.
Memberships: Artists Guild Chicago; Elmhurst Artist Guild; Soc
Animal Artists.
Art Interests: Original oil paintings of dogs and horses.
Mailing Address: P O Box 246, 17 Howard St, Roselle, IL 60172.

LOUGHLIN, JOHN LEO
Painter, Lecturer
Preferred Media: Watercolors.
b Worcester, Mass, Apr 11, 31.
Study & Training: Worcester Art Mus Sch; Clark Univ, AB, 57;
Bridgewater State Col, EdM, 64; also with Eliot O'Hara, Edgar
Whitney & Barse Miller.
Work in Public Collections: M & M Karolik Collection, Boston Mus
Fine Art; Cumberland R I Housing for Elderly; Old Colony Sav-
ings Bank, Providence, R I; U S Naval War Col, Newport, R I.
Exhibitions: Boston Arts Festival, Mass, 55; Acad Artists Show,
Springfield, Mass, 59; Bristol Art Mus Show, R I, 70; Am Water-
color Soc, Nat Acad Design Galleries, New York, 71; Providence
Art Club Open Watercolor Show, 72.
Teaching: Private instr, 69-; vis lectr watercolor, Providence Col,
70-72.
Positions: Illusr cartogr, Nat Geog Mag, 58-59; head dept art, U S
Naval War Col, 61-68; art dir, WSBE-TV, Providence, 68-
Awards: W Alden Brown Mem Award, Providence Watercolor Club,
69; C Gordon Harris Award, 71; Dr Edwin Dunlop Award, 72.
Bibliography: Watercolor, WSBE-TV, 69.
Memberships: Assoc Am Watercolor Soc; Providence Art Club;
Providence Watercolor Club (v pres, 70-72, pres, 72); artist
mem Rockport Art Asn.

Publications: Illusr, Nat Geog Mag, 58; illusr, Mass Wildlife Mag, 59; contribr & illusr, Salt Water Sportsman Mag, 59; illusr, Naval Rev, 67; illusr, New Eng Sch Develop Coun Publ.
Dealer: The Galleries, Wellesley Hills, MA 02181.
Mailing Address: 124 Angell Rd, Lincoln, RI 02865.

LOURIE, HERBERT S
Painter, Educator
b Boston, Mass, Dec 26, 23.
Study & Training: Ind Univ; Yale Univ, BFA & MFA.
Work in Public Collections: Munson-Williams-Proctor Inst, Utica, N Y.
Exhibitions: Wadsworth Atheneum; Farnsworth Mus; Fitchburg Art Mus; Currier Gallery Art; Inst Contemp Arts, Boston; plus many others.
Teaching: Asst prof art, Nasson Col, 52-55; vis lectr, Univ N H, 53-54; instr, Univ R I, 56-58; asst prof art, Elmire Col, 58-61; assoc prof art, Keene State Col, 66-
Awards: Prize, Currier Gallery Art, 55; purchase prize, Arnot Art Gallery, 61.
Memberships: Col Art Asn Am; N H Art Asn.
Mailing Address: Art Dept, Keene State College, Keene, NH 03431.

LOVATO, CHARLES FREDRIC
Painter
Preferred Media: Acrylics.
b Santa Fe, N Mex, May 23, 37.
Work in Public Collections: Heard Mus, Phoenix, Ariz; Philbrook Art Ctr, Tulsa, Okla.
Exhibitions: Scottsdale Nat, Ariz, 68; Heard Mus Invitational, Phoenix, 69; Washington D C Biennial, 69; Gallup Inter-Tribal Ceremonial, N Mex, 72.
Awards: Most outstanding painting, Dr Avery, Pecos, Tex, 70 & 71; best artist-best painting, Philbrook Art Ctr, 71.
Mailing Address: Sile Star Rte 72, Pena Blanca, NM 87041.

LOVE, IRIS CORNELIA
Art Historian
b New York, N Y, Aug 1, 33.
Study & Training: Smith Col, BA; Univ Firenze, Italy; Inst Fine Arts, New York Univ; Dowling Col, Hon LittD, 71.
Teaching: Instr Greek & Roman art, Cooper Union, 63 & Smith Col, 64-65; asst prof art hist & archaeol, Long Island Univ, 66-67; res asst prof, 67-; instr & coordr, three lect series, New York Univ Sch Continuing Studies, 68-70; instr community educ, Hofstra Univ, 69; distinguished Fromer prof, Russell Sage Col, 72; Robert Sterling Clark lectr art hist, Williams Col, 73.
Positions: Staff mem, Archaeol Exped to Island of Samothrace, New York Inst Fine Arts, 55-65; collabr with Dir Brit Sch in Rome, excavation of Quattro Fontanile, Isola Farnese, Italy, 61; dir, Archaeol Exped to Knidos, Turkey, Long Island Univ, 67-
Memberships: Archaeol Inst Am; Am Asn Univ Prof; Turkish-Am Soc.
Research: Archaeology; Greek and Roman art; art history.
Publications: Auth, Greece, Gods and art, Viking Press, 68; contribr to Bollingen Series, Marsyas, Am Jour Archaeol, Anatolian Studies & others.
Mailing Address: R F D 1, Box 301, Bristol, VT 05443.

LOVE, JIM
Sculptor
b Amarillo, Tex, 27.
Exhibitions: Dallas Mus Contemp Art, Tex; Mus Mod Art, New York, N Y; Mus Fine Arts, Houston, Tex; Univ St Thomas, Houston; Whitney Mus Am Art, New York; plus others.
Dealer: Louise Ferrari, 3711 San Felipe, Houston, TX 77027.
Mailing Address: 906 Truxillo St, Houston, TX 77002.

LOVE, JOSEPH
Painter
b Worcester, Mass, 29.
Study & Training: Col of the Holy Cross; Boston Col, MA; Sophia Univ, Japan; Columbia Univ.
Work in Public Collections: Metrop Mus Art, New York, N Y; Art Inst Chicago, Ill; Allentown Art Mus, Pa; New York Pub Libr; Southern Ill Univ.
Exhibitions: One-man shows, Saint Louis Univ, 63 & Alonzo Gallery, 67; Japan Print Asn Ann, 63 & 64; Hijiyama Hall, Hiroshima, Japan, 65; Col of the Holy Cross, Worcester, Mass, 65.
Teaching: Instr art, Sophia Univ, Japan, 56-
Publications: Contribr, Art Int.
Mailing Address: c/o Alonzo Gallery, 26 E 63rd St, New York, NY 10021.

LOVE, PAUL VAN DERVEER
Gallery Director, Art Historian
b Long Branch, N J, Aug 1, 08.
Study & Training: Princeton Univ, BA; Univ Pa, Am Inst Architects scholar, 45; New York Univ, scholar, 48; Columbia Univ, fel, 48, PhD, 50.
Exhibitions: Mich Watercolor Soc, 52-53; Baltimore Mus Art, Md, 53; Ala Watercolor Soc, 53; Kresge Art Ctr Gallery, East Lansing, Mich, 71; 15th Nat Exhib, Fall River, Mass, 72.
Collections Arranged: The Turn of the Century; American Nineteenth Century Painting, 66; Earl Kerkam: Paintings and Drawings, 72.
Teaching: Prof Am, mod & pre-Columbian art, Mich State Univ, 53-66.
Positions: Dir, Kresge Art Ctr Gallery, 63-; ed, Kresge Art Ctr Bull, 67-
Memberships: Col Art Asn Am; Am Asn Mus; Midwestern Mus Asn.
Publications: Auth, Modern dance terminology, 53; co-auth, An introduction to literature and fine arts, 53; auth, Patterned brickwork in Southern New Jersey, 55.
Mailing Address: 3891 Okemos Rd, Okemos, MI 48864.

LOVE, ROSALIE BOWEN
Painter, Instructor
Preferred Media: Oils.
b Jamestown, N Y.
Study & Training: Jepson Art Sch; also with Karl Seethaler, Hayward Veal, Will Foster, J Thompson Pritchard, Bennett Bradbury & Paul Puzinas.
Work in Public Collections: De Grimm Gallery, Detroit, Mich; Chautauqua Art Inst, N Y; Fri Morning Club, Severance Salon, Los Angeles, Calif.
Commissions: Christ mural, Come unto Me, Christ Church, Unity, Los Angeles, 72.
Exhibitions: Nat Orange Show, San Bernardino, Calif, 67; Frye Mus, Seattle, Wash, 68, Chautauqua, N Y, 68; Tucson, Ariz, 69; Wilshire Ebell, Los Angeles, 72.
Teaching: Free-lance art instr portraiture, 55-
Awards: Popular award, Nat Orange Show, 67; first award, City Hall Gallery, Los Angeles, 68; first award, Wilshire Fed Gallery, Beverly Hills, 69.
Memberships: Life mem Am Inst Fine Arts (bd dirs, 67-68); Calif Art Club; Valley Artist Guild (bd dirs, 65-67); Laguna Beach.
Mailing Address: 15635 Vandorf Pl, Los Angeles, CA 91316.

LOVELL, TOM
Painter, Illustrator
Preferred Media: Oils
b New York, N Y, Feb 5, 09.
Study & Training: Syracuse Univ, BFA.
Work in Public Collections: New Britain Mus, Conn; Explorers Club, New York; U S Marine Corps Hq, Washington, D C; Va Mil Inst; U S Merchant Marine Acad, King's Point, N Y.
Commissions: Series of hist paintings, U S Marine Corps, 45; painting of civil war, Life Mag, 61; series of hist paintings, Nat Geog Soc, Washington D C, 65-68; series of hist paintings, Abell-Hanger Found, 69-73.
Exhibitions: Soc Illustrators, New York, 63; one-man show, Syracuse Univ Centennial, Lubin House, 70.
Awards: Gold medal, Soc Illustrators, 63; gold medal, Syracuse Univ Centennial, 70; Westbury Artists Award, 71.
Bibliography: Norman Kent (auth), Tom Lovell & his work, Am Artist.
Memberships: Soc Illustrators; Westport Artists.
Publications: Auth, North Light Book Club (article), Westport, Conn, 72.
Mailing Address: 3 Skytop Dr, Norwalk, CT 06855.

LOVET-LORSKI, BORIS
Sculptor
b Lithuania, Dec 25, 94; U S citizen.
Study & Training: Acad Art, St Petersburg, Russia.
Work in Public Collections: Luxembourg Mus & Petit Palais, Paris, France; Brit Mus, London, Eng; Metrop Mus Art, New York, N Y; Seattle Art Mus, Wash; San Francisco Mus Art, Calif; plus others.
Commissions: Franklin D Roosevelt (heroic head in bronze), City of Paris, 49; monumental busts of Charles DeGaulle, Dwight D Eisenhower & John Foster Dulles, Paris, 59; sculpture for U S War Mem, Manila, Philippines, 54-56; John Foster Dulles (heroic bronze head), Washington Int Airport, 63; John F Kennedy (heroic bronze bust), Brandeis Univ, 65.
Exhibitions: One-man exhibs, Caracas, Venezuela, London, Philadelphia, New York, Manila & other major cities.
Awards: Chevalier, Legion of Honor, France, 48.
Memberships: Nat Acad Design; fel Nat Sculpture Soc; Lotos Club.
Publications: Auth, Lithographs of Lovet-Lorski, 29; illusr, Tribute to woman; auth, Sculpture, Lovet-Lorski, 30.
Mailing Address: 131 E 69th St, New York, NY 10021.

LOW, JOSEPH
Designer, Printmaker
Preferred Media: Graphics.
b Coraopolis, Pa, Aug 11, 11.
Study & Training: Univ Ill, 30-32; Art Stud League New York, 35, with George Grosz.
Work in Public Collections: Princeton Univ; Harvard Univ; Libr Cong; Va Mus Fine Arts; San Francisco Pub Libr; plus many others.
Exhibitions: Boston Mus Fine Arts, Mass; New York Pub Libr, N Y; Metrop Mus Art, New York; Herron Inst Art, Indianapolis, Ind; Philadelphia Mus Art, Pa; plus many others.
Mailing Address: Cruz Bay, Saint John, VI 00830.

LOWE, HARRY
Art Administrator, Designer
b Opelika, Ala, Apr 9, 22.
Study & Training: Auburn Univ, BA, 43, MFA, 49; Cranbrook Acad Art, 51 & 53.
Collections Arranged: Stuart Davis Memorial, Nat Collection Fine Arts, Washington, D C, Art Inst Chicago, Ill, Univ Calif Art Galleries, Los Angeles & Whitney Mus Am Art, New York, N Y, 65; The Charles Sheeler Exhibition, Philadelphia Mus Art, Pa & Whitney Mus Am Art, 69.
Teaching: Prof art, Auburn Univ, 49-59; fac, Sem for Hist Adminrs, Williamsburg, Va, 65, 67-71.
Positions: Dir, Tenn Fine Arts Ctr, Nashville, 59-64; cur, Dept Exhib & Design, Nat Collection Fine Arts, 64-72, asst dir opers, 72-
Memberships: Am Asn Mus; Nat Trust Hist Preserv; Soc Archit Historians; Col Art Asn Am.
Mailing Address: National Collection of Fine Arts, Ninth & G Sts, Washington, DC 20560.

LOWE, J MICHAEL
Sculptor, Educator
Preferred Media: Welded Metal.
b Cincinnati, Ohio, Aug 18, 42.
Study & Training: Ohio Univ, BFA; Cornell Univ, MFA.
Work in Public Collections: Butler Inst Am Art, Youngstown, Ohio; Tyler Mus Art, Tex; State Univ N Y Col Potsdam; Cornell Univ, Ithaca, N Y; St Lawrence Univ, Canton, N Y.
Exhibitions: Butler Inst Am Art Ann, 64, 71 & 72; Finger Lakes Regional, Rochester Mem Art Gallery, 65 & 66; Artists of Central New York, Munson-Williams-Proctor Inst, Utica, N Y, 65, 67-69 & 71; Tyler Mus Art, 67, 69 & 70; Ball State Univ, Muncie, Ind, 67 & 72.
Teaching: Instr fine arts, St Lawrence Univ, 66-67, asst prof, 67-72, chmn dept, 71-, assoc prof, 72-
Awards: Inez D'Amanda Barnell Award for Sculpture, Rochester Mem Art Gallery, 66; purchase awards, Tyler Mus Art, 70 & Butler Inst Am Art, 72.
Memberships: Col Art Asn Am.
Mailing Address: Dept of Fine Arts, St Lawrence University, Canton, NY 13617.

LOWE, JOE HING
Painter, Instructor
Preferred Media: Oils, Pastels, Watercolors, Charcoal.
b Canton, China, Sept 15, 34; U S citizen.
Study & Training: With Lajos Markos & Dan Greene.
Work in Public Collections: U S Navy Combat Artist Gallery, Washington, D C; U S Navy Air Sta, Lakehurst, N J; Switlik Parachute Co, N J.
Commissions: Portraits, comn by Rep John M Murphy, 65, Adm C E Rosendahl, 67, Adm Arleigh Burke, 70 & Adm Arnold Frederic Schade, 71.
Exhibitions: Springfield Mus, 68; Am Watercolor Soc, Nat Acad Design Galleries, 69; Hudson Valley Art Asn, 72; Am Artists Prof League, 72; Salmagundi Club, 72.
Teaching: Instr, Metrop Portrait Studio, 64-; instr Big Six Art League. 70-
Awards: Dumont Mem Fund Award for pastel portrait, Salmagundi Club, 69; Sterling Silver Award for The Rice Bowl, Nat Art Club, 69; Mary Spreadling Mem Award for Oriental Myth, 70.
Bibliography: Rep John M Murphy, J Am, Brooklyn Sect, 5/12/65; Jack Besterman (auth), article, In: Big Six Chapel & Pensioners News, 2/72.
Memberships: Salmagundi Club; Am Artists Prof League; Hudson Valley Art Asn; Artists Fel; Knickerbocker Artists; plus one other.
Publications: Contribr, How to do portraits in pastel, 72; contribr, Palette talk, 72.
Dealer: C C Price Gallery, 30 W 57th St, New York, NY 10019.
Mailing Address: 150 Columbus Ave, New York, NY 10023.

LOWE, MARVIN
Printmaker, Painter
b Brooklyn, N Y, May 19, 27.
Study & Training: Juillard Sch Mus; Brooklyn Col, BA, 54; Univ Iowa, with Mauricio Lasansky, MFA.
Work in Public Collections: Libr Cong, Washington, D C; Philadelphia Mus Art, Pa; Brooklyn Mus, N Y; Columbia Univ, New York, N Y; New York Pub Libr.
Exhibitions: 19th Nat Exhib Prints, Libr Cong, 63; America-Japan Contemporary Print Exhib, Tokyo, 67; Brooklyn Mus Nat Print Exhib, 67; Graphics, 1968; Recent American Prints, Univ Ky, 68; 1st Hawaii Nat Print Exhib, Honolulu, 71.
Teaching: Asst prof printmaking, Bucknell Univ, 63-68; instr, Bottega Arte Grafica, Florence, Italy, 67; assoc prof printmaking, Ind Univ, Bloomington, 68-
Awards: Paul J Sachs Purchase Award, Boston Printmakers, 65; Lessing J Rosenwald Purchase Prize, Philadelphia Print Club, 66; first prize in prints, Springfield Col, Mass, 67.
Memberships: Soc Am Graphic Artists; Boston Printmakers; Philadelphia Print Club; Soc Washington Printmakers.
Dealer: Weyhe Gallery, 794 Lexington Ave, New York, NY 10021.
Mailing Address: Dept Fine Arts, Indiana University, Bloomington, IN 47401.

LOWENTHAL, MILTON
Collector
Mailing Address: 1035 Fifth Ave, New York, NY 10028.

LOWNEY, BRUCE STARK
Printmaker
Preferred Media: Oils, Lithography.
b Los Angeles, Calif, Oct 16, 37.
Study & Training: N Tex State Univ, BA; San Francisco State Col, MA; Univ N Mex, asst to Garo Antreasian.
Work in Public Collections: Minneapolis Inst Art, Minn; Art Inst Chicago, Ill; Art Mus Univ N Mex, Albuquerque; Roswell Mus & Art Ctr, N Mex; Oklahoma City Art Ctr, Okla.
Exhibitions: Whitney Mus Am Art Print Exhib, New York, N Y, 70; Northwest Printmakers 41st Int Exhib, Seattle, Wash, 70; 22nd Nat Exhib Prints, Libr Cong, Washington, D C, 71; San Francisco Art Inst Centennial Exhib, Calif, 71; one-man show, Martha Jackson Gallery, New York, 71.
Awards: Louis Comfort Tiffany Found graphics art award, 69; artist-in-residence grant, Roswell Mus & Art Ctr, 70.
Dealer: Martha Jackson Gallery, 32 E 69th St, New York, NY 10021.
Mailing Address: P O Box 505, Placitas, NM 87043.

LOWRY, BATES
Art Historian, Art Critic
b Cincinnati, Ohio, June 21, 23.
Study & Training: Univ Chicago, PhB, 44, MA, 53, PhD, 56.
Teaching: Asst prof art, Univ Calif, Riverside, 54-57; asst prof art, Inst Fine Arts, New York Univ, 57-59; prof art & chmn art dept, Pomona Col, 59-63; prof art & chmn art dept, Brown Univ, 63-67; mem, Inst Advan Study, 71; prof art & chmn dept art, Univ Mass, Boston, 71-
Positions: Ed, monogr series, Col Art Asn, 59-62, 64-67; ed, Art Bull, 64-68; dir, Mus Mod Art, New York, 68-69.
Awards: R I Gov's Award for contrib to arts, 67; Grand Off, Star of Solidarity, Italy, 68.
Memberships: Col Art Asn (bd dirs, 63-66); Soc Archit Historians (bd dirs, 60-62, 64-66); Art Historians Southern Calif (pres, 61-63); Comt to Rescue Italian Art (co-founder, chmn nat exec comt, 66-); Am Fedn Arts (trustee, 69-71).
Research: Renaissance architecture.
Publications: Auth, The visual experience, 61; auth, Renaissance architecture, 62; auth, articles, In: Art Bull & Col Art J.
Mailing Address: Essex, NY 12936.

LOWRY, W McNEIL
Art Administrator
b Columbus, Kans, Feb 17, 13.
Study & Training: Univ Ill, AB & PhD.
Positions: Dir, humanities and the arts, The Ford Foundation, 57-64, v pres, 64-
Mailing Address: The Ford Foundation, 320 E 43rd St, New York, NY 10017.

LOY, JOHN SHERIDAN
Painter
Preferred Media: Oils.
b St Louis, Mo, Nov 4, 30.
Study & Training: Colo Springs Fine Art Ctr, Colo; Wash Univ Sch Fine Arts, BFA, 54; Cranbrook Acad Art, Bloomfield Hills, Mich, MFA, 58.
Work in Public Collections: Munson-Williams-Proctor Inst, Utica,

N Y; Utica Col, N Y; Hayes Nat Bank, Clinton, N Y; Savings Bank Utica.
Exhibitions: Mo Show, St Louis City Art Mus, 59; Artists Cent N Y, Munson-Williams-Proctor Inst, 60-70; Albany Inst Hist & Art Regional, N Y, 69; Everson Mus Regional, Syracuse, N Y, 70; Cooperstown Art Asn Ann, N Y, 71.
Teaching: Instr drawing, Wash Univ, 59; instr drawing & painting, Munson-Williams-Proctor Inst, 60-
Positions: Prog dir, Peoples Art Ctr, St Louis, 59.
Awards: Painting Award, St Louis City Art Mus, 59; first painting prize, Cooperstown Art Asn, 71.
Mailing Address: 602 Tracy St, Utica, NY 13502.

LOZOWICK, LOUIS
Painter, Printmaker
b Kiev, Russia, Dec 10, 92; U S citizen.
Study & Training: Nat Acad Design, 12-15; Ohio State Univ, BA, 18; study in Paris, France, 22 & Berlin, Ger, 23.
Work in Public Collections: Whitney Mus Am Art & Mus Mod Art, New York, N Y; Walker Art Gallery, Minneapolis, Minn; Newark Mus, N J; Libr Cong, Washington, D C.
Commissions: Two panels for Main Post Off, New York, N Y.
Exhibitions: Carnegie Int, Pittsburgh, Pa, 30; Corcoran Biennial, Washington, D C, 32-33; Pa Acad Fine Arts, Philadelphia, 34; Realists & Magic Realists, Mus Mod Art, New York, 43; Butler Inst Am Art, Youngstown, Ohio, 60.
Awards: Award for City on a Rock, Cleveland Print Club, 31; award for Nuns in Wall Street, Rochester Print Club, 48; award for Fishing Village, N J Painters & Sculptors Soc, 65.
Bibliography: Bruno W Reimann (auth), Louis Lozowick, Jarbuch der Jungen Kunst, 23; Milton W Brown (auth), American art from the Armory Show to the depression, 55; William H Gerdts, Jr (auth), Painting & sculpture in New Jersey, 64.
Memberships: Nat Soc Painters in Casein; Nat Acad Design; Soc Am Graphic Artists; Audubon Artists; Associated Artists N J.
Publications: Auth, Modern Russian art, 25; co-auth, Voices of October, 30; contribr, U S S R: a concise handbook, 47; contribr, Understanding the Russians, 47; auth, A treasury of drawings from prehistory to Picasso, 48.
Dealer: Zabriskie Gallery, 29 W 57th St, New York, NY 10019.
Mailing Address: 62 Massel Terr, South Orange, NJ 07079.

LUBBERS, LELAND EUGENE
Sculptor, Educator
Preferred Media: Metals.
b Stoughton, Wis, June 6, 28.
Study & Training: St Louis Univ, AB, MA, PhL & STL; Univ Paris, Docteur de l'Universite de Paris; Acad Grande Chaumière, Paris, France.
Work in Public Collections: Duchesne Col, Omaha, Nebr; Sheldon Gallery, Univ Nebr, Lincoln; Seattle Opera Asn, Wash; Art in Embassies Prog, U S State Dept; Jacksonville Art Mus, Fla.
Commissions: Sculpture sets for Fidelio, Seattle Opera Co, Opera House, Seattle Ctr, Wash, 68; outdoor fountain, City of Omaha, 69; sculptured constructions (with Larry Austin), for centennial exhib at Albright-Knox Art Gallery for Canisius Col, Buffalo, N Y, 70.
Exhibitions: One-man shows, Automated Junk Sculpture Exhib, Sheldon Gallery, Univ Nebr, Lincoln, 65, Jacksonville Art Mus, 67 & Frye Art Mus, Seattle, 68; group shows, Ninth-Eleventh Midwest Biennial, 66-70 & Nebraska Art Today Centennial Invitational, 67, Joslyn Art Mus, Omaha.
Teaching: Instr Latin, speech & English, Creighton Prep Sch, Omaha, 53-56, instr French, German & art, 63-65; assoc prof fine arts, founder & head dept, Creighton Univ, 65-
Positions: Dir, Nebr Arts Coun, Omaha, 66-72; pres, Omaha Civic Ballet Asn, 68-70, dir, 70-; pres, Omaha Acad Ballet Bd, 69-72.
Bibliography: Robert Reilly (auth), Jesuit junkman, Critic Mag, 2-3/68; John Wain (auth), To Lee Lubbers in Omaha, In: Letters to five artists, Viking, 70; Larry Austin (auth), Caritas: symphony of the gigantic hammered welded aluminum imitation earth volumes, Source, 11/70.
Memberships: Asn Int des Docteurs (lettres) de l'Universite de Paris; Nebr Art Educ Asn; Assoc Artists Omaha.
Art Interests: Welded metals.
Publications: Auth, L'image publicitaire actuelle et ses origines, Univ Paris 63; auth, Phenomene du xxe siecle, l'affiche a change la rue, Galerie des Arts, 6/64.
Dealer: Ward-Nasse Gallery, 178 Prince St, New York, NY 10012.
Mailing Address: Fine Arts Dept, Creighton University, 2400 California St, Omaha, NE 68131.

LUBNER, MARTIN PAUL
Painter
b New York, N Y, Dec 26, 29.
Study & Training: Univ Calif, Los Angeles, BA, 52, MA, 53, with Clinton Adams, Gordon Nunes & Jan Stussy.

Work in Public Collections: Tate Gallery, London, Eng; Los Angeles Co Mus Art, Los Angeles; Mus Mod Art, Israel; Albany Jr Col Mus, N Y; Kettering Mus, Eng.
Exhibitions: Los Angeles Co Mus Art Ann, 56, 57 & 59; Spoleto Int, Italy, 63-64.
Teaching: Instr painting & drawing, Univ Calif Exten, 56-, Los Angeles, 64; instr painting & drawing, Univ Southern Calif, 68.
Dealers: Gallery Z, 1634 Tower Grove Dr, Beverly Hills, CA 90210; Crane Kalman Gallery, 178 Brompton Rd, London S W 3, Eng.
Mailing Address: c/o Black, 6420 Moore Dr, Los Angeles, CA 90048.

LUCAS, CHARLES C, JR
Collector
b Charlotte, N C, Mar 4, 39.
Study & Training: Duke Univ, BA.
Positions: Trustee, Mint Mus Art, Charlotte, 67-68; controller, Juilliard Sch, New York, N Y, 68-
Memberships: Am Asn Mus.
Collection: American art—Ashcan School, abstract and realist contemporary painting and sculpture; pre-Columbian.
Mailing Address: 80 East End Ave, New York, NY 10028.

LUCCHESI, BRUNO
Sculptor
b Lucca, Italy, July 31, 26; U S citizen.
Study & Training: Inst Arte, Lucca, MFA, 53.
Work in Public Collections: Pa Acad Fine Arts, Philadelphia; Dallas Mus Fine Arts, Tex; Ringling Mus, Sarasota, Fla; Cornell Univ, N Y; Univ Utah.
Commissions: Sculpture for Trade Bank, New York, N Y & Willard Strait Hall, Cornell Univ.
Exhibitions: Whitney Mus Am Art, New York; Pa Acad Fine Arts; Corcoran Gallery Art, Washington, D C; Nat Inst Arts & Lett; Brooklyn Mus, N Y; plus others.
Teaching: Instr, Acad Fine Arts, Univ Florence, Italy, 52-57; instr, New Sch Social Res, 62-
Awards: Watrous Gold Medal, Nat Acad Design, 61; gold medal, Nat Arts Club, 63; S F B Morse Medal, Nat Acad Design, 65; plus others.
Memberships: Sculptors Guild; Artists Equity Asn; Nat Acad Design; Am Asn Univ Prof.
Dealer: Forum Gallery, 1018 Madison Ave, New York, NY 10021.
Mailing Address: 14 Stuyvesant St, New York, NY 10003.

LUCIONI, LUIGI
Painter, Etcher
b Malnate, Italy, Nov 4, 00; U S citizen.
Study & Training: Cooper Union Eve Sch, 16-20; Nat Acad Design, 20-25; also with William Starkwether, 18-25.
Work in Public Collections: Pears with Pewter, Metrop Mus Art, New York, N Y; Two Willows & Jo, Whitney Mus Am Art; Rose Hobart, Pa Acad Fine Arts, Philadelphia; Vermont Pastoral, Carnegie Inst, Pittsburgh, Pa.
Exhibitions: Carnegie Int, Pittsburgh; Art Inst Chicago, Ill; Venice Biennale, Italy; Pa Acad Fine Arts, Philadelphia; Corcoran Gallery Art Biennial, Washington, D C.
Teaching: Instr portrait painting, Art Stud League New York, 32-33.
Awards: First popular prize, Carnegie Int, 39; first popular prize, Corcoran Biennial, 47-49; popular prize, Nat Acad Design, 57.
Bibliography: The art of Luigi Lucioni (film), Vt Educ TV, 68, shown throughout the U S, 69-72.
Dealer: Milch Gallery, 1014 Madison Ave, New York, NY 10021.
Mailing Address: 33 W 10th St, New York, NY 10011.

LUCK, ROBERT
Art Administrator, Art Critic
b Tonawanda, N Y, Oct 31, 21.
Study & Training: Univ Buffalo, BFA, 47; Harvard Univ, MA, 49; Inst Meschini, Rome, Italy, cert in painting, 50.
Teaching: Instr, Toledo Mus Art, 52-54.
Positions: Cur, Cincinnati Art Mus, 54-55; dir, Akron Art Inst, 55-56; dir, Telfair Acad Arts & Sci, Savannah, Ga, 56-57; asst dir, Am Fedn Arts, 58-72.
Memberships: Am Asn Mus; Col Art Asn Am.
Mailing Address: 152 E 94th St, New York, NY 10028.

LUDEKENS, FRED
Painter, Illustrator
b Hueneme, Calif.
Exhibitions: Contemp Am Illus, Int Gallery, New York.
Teaching: Co-founder, chmn bd & mem faculty, Famous Artists Schs, Westport, Conn.
Memberships: Soc Illustrators; Art Dir Club, New York & San Francisco.

Publications: Illusr, Ghost town & The ranch book; contribr, Sat
Eve Post, This Wk & Fawcett Publ.
Mailing Address: P O Box 348, Belvedere, CA 94920.

LUDGIN, EARLE
Collector
b Chicago, Ill, July 22, 98.
Positions: Former trustee, Am Fedn Arts; former pres, Soc Con-
temp Art; life trustee, Art Inst Chicago; life trustee, Univ Chi-
cago.
Memberships: Arts Club Chicago.
Collection: Contemporary American art.
Mailing Address: 1127 Sheridan Rd, Hubbard Woods, IL 60093.

LUDINGTON, WRIGHT S
Collector, Patron
b New York, N Y, June 10, 00.
Study & Training: Yale Univ; Pa Acad Fine Arts; Art Stud League
New York.
Positions: Pres, Santa Barbara Mus Art, 50-51.
Collection: Paintings and sculptures, early twentieth century;
classical Greek and Roman sculpture and vases; Gothic,
Romanesque, Egyptian sculpture.
Mailing Address: 1097 Buckthorn Rd, Montecito, CA 93103.

LUDWIG, EVA
Sculptor
Preferred Media: Wood, Ceramics.
b Berlin, Ger, May 25, 23; U S citizen.
Study & Training: Greenwich House Pottery, 58-62, with Lu Duble;
Sculptor's Workshop, 64, with Harold Castor; Craft Stud League,
68, wood sculpture with Domenico Facci.
Exhibitions: Exhib Contemp Liturgical Art, Philadelphia, 63; Own
Your Own, Denver Art Mus, 68; Rochester Festival Religious Art,
N Y, 71; Cooperstown Art Asn Ann, N Y, 71; Nonmem Exhib, Nat
Sculpture Soc, New York, 72.
Awards: Best in wood, 69 & Bert Wangler Mem Award, 72, Wood-
stock Guild Craftsmen; first prize in sculpture, Cooperstown
Art Asn, 71.
Memberships: Woodstock Guild Craftsmen; Cooperstown Art Asn;
Burr Artists, N Y.
Mailing Address: 57-44 164th St, Flushing, NY 11365.

LUEDERS, JIMMY C
Painter, Educator
Preferred Media: Acrylics.
b Jacksonville, Fla, July 4, 27.
Study & Training: Pa Acad Fine Arts, Philadelphia, William Emlen
Cresson Mem traveling scholar, 50, Henry Schiedt Mem scholar,
51.
Work in Public Collections: Pa Acad Fine Arts; Philadelphia Mus
Art; Sch Pharm, Temple Univ, Philadelphia; Moore Col Art,
Philadelphia; Tyler Sch Art, Temple Univ.
Exhibitions: Butler Art Inst, Youngstown, Ohio; Am Fedn Art
Traveling Exhib Art Schs, 56; Metrop Young Artist Show, Nat
Arts Club, New York, N Y, 60; Nat Acad Design, New York, 60;
Nat Inst Arts & Lett, New York, 69.
Teaching: Instr painting, Cheltenham Twp Art Ctr, 52-; instr paint-
ing, Pa Acad Fine Arts, 57-; instr painting, Philadelphia Mus
Art, 67-
Awards: Third Hallgarten Prize, Nat Acad Design, New York, 60.
Memberships: Artists Equity Asn, Philadelphia Chap.
Dealer: McCleaf Gallery, 1713 Walnut St, Philadelphia, PA 19103.
Mailing Address: 547 Carpenter Lane, Philadelphia, PA 19119.

LUKIN, PHILIP
Collector
b New York, N Y, June 25, 03.
Study & Training: New York Univ, 21-22; Brown Univ, PhB, 24.
Memberships: Fel Metrop Mus Art.
Collection: Catholic in scope and representative.
Mailing Address: 328 El Vedado, Palm Beach, FL 33480.

LUKIN, SVEN
Painter
b Riga, Latvia, Feb 14, 34.
Study & Training: Univ Pa.
Work in Public Collections: Albright-Knox Art Gallery, Buffalo,
N Y; Los Angeles Co Mus Art, Calif; Larry Aldrich Mus, Ridge-
field, Conn; Univ Tex, Austin; Whitney Mus Am Art, New York,
N Y; plus others.
Exhibitions: Univ Ill, Urbana, 65; Torcuato di Tella, Buenos Aires,
Arg, 65; New Shapes of Color, Stedelijk Mus, Amsterdam, Hol-
land, 66; Univ Colo, Denver, 67; Painting: Out From the Wall,
Des Moines Art Ctr, Iowa, 68; plus others.

Awards: Guggenheim fel, 66.
Bibliography: Sam Hunter (ed), New art around the world, Abrams,
66; Allen S Weller (auth), The joys and sorrows of recent American art, Univ Ill Press, 68; Gregory Battcock (ed), Minimal art:
a critical anthology, Dutton, 68.
Mailing Address: 807 Ave of the Americas, New York, NY 10001.

LUKOSIUS, RICHARD BENEDICT
Painter, Educator
Preferred Media: Acrylics.
b Waterbury, Conn, Oct 26, 18.
Study & Training: Yale Univ, BFA & MFA, with Josef Albers.
Exhibitions: New Eng Art Today, Northeastern Univ, Boston, Mass,
65; Conn Artist-Educator Invitational, Trinity Col, Hartford,
Conn, 65; one-man show, Lyman Allyn Mus, New London, Conn,
68; New Eng Artists, Slater Mus, Norwich, Conn, 68; Contemp
Drawings, Univ Conn, Storrs, 71.
Teaching: Assoc prof painting, drawing & graphic design, Conn Col,
54-
Mailing Address: Connecticut College, New London, CT 06320.

LUND, DAVID
Painter
b New York, N Y, Oct 16, 25.
Study & Training: Queens Col, N Y, BA.
Work in Public Collections: Toronto Art Gallery; Whitney Mus Am
Art; Chase Manhattan Bank, N Y; Finch Col Mus; Univ Mass.
Exhibitions: Four one-man shows, Grace Borgenicht Gallery, N Y,
60-69; Mich State Univ Group & Traveling, 62; Washington Gal-
lery Mod Art, 63; R I Sch Design, 64-65; Pa Acad Fine Arts,
Philadelphia, 65, 66 & 69.
Teaching: Instr painting, Cooper Union Art Sch, 55-57 & 59-; instr
painting Haystack Sch, Deer Isle Maine, summer 63; instr paint-
ing, Parsons Sch Design, N Y, 63-69; instr painting, Columbia
Univ, 69-
Awards: Fulbright grant to Italy, 57-59; Ford Found Purchase Prize,
Whitney Mus Am Art, 61.
Mailing Address: 470 West End Ave, New York, NY 10024.

LUNDE, KARL ROY
Art Historian, Writer
b New York, N Y, Nov 1, 31.
Study & Training: Columbia Univ, BA, MA & PhD.
Teaching: Instr art hist, Sch Gen Studies, Columbia Univ, 58-70;
prof art hist, William Paterson Col N J, 70-
Positions: Dir, The Contemporaries (art gallery), New York, 56-65.
Research: Italian renaissance bronzes; nineteenth century romantic
art in Scandinavia.
Publications: Contribr, Slavic Rev, 70-71; contribr, Art & Artists,
72; auth, Monograph on Nathaniel Neujean, 72; auth, Monograph
on Richard Anuszkiewicz & Monograph on Isabel Bishop, Abrams
(in press).
Mailing Address: 440 Riverside Dr, New York, NY 10027.

LUNDEBERG, HELEN (HELEN LUNDEBERG FEITELSON)
Painter
Preferred Media: Acrylics.
b Chicago, Ill, June 24, 08.
Study & Training: With Lorser Feitelson.
Work in Public Collections: Los Angeles Co Mus Art, Calif; San
Francisco Mus Art, Calif; Joseph H Hirshhorn Collection; La
Jolla Mus Contemp Art, Calif; Xerox Corp, New York, N Y.
Exhibitions: Fantastic Art, Dada, Surrealism, Mus Mod Art, New
York, 36-37; São Paulo Biennial, Brazil, 55; Geometric Abstrac-
tion in America, 62 & Contemp Am Painting Ann, 67, Whitney Mus
Am Art, New York; Lundeberg Retrospective Exhib, La Jolla Mus
Contemp Art, 71.
Bibliography: Joseph E Young (auth), Helen Lundeberg: an American
independent, Art Int, 9/20/71.
Memberships: Los Angeles Art Asn.
Mailing Address: 8307 W Third St, Los Angeles, CA 90048.

LUNGE, JEFFREY (ROY)
Painter
Preferred Media: Watercolors.
b London, Eng, July 20, 05; U S citizen.
Study & Training: Art Ctr, Los Angeles; also with James Couper
Wright.
Work in Public Collections: Palm Springs Desert Mus; Mus North-
ern Ariz, Flagstaff; Joseph Hirshhorn Collection; Ariz Bank,
Phoenix.
Commissions: Mural, George Beadle, Calif Inst Technol Biol Bldg,
Pasadena, Calif, 56.
Exhibitions: Pasadena Soc Artists Ann, 52-65; San Gabriel Valley
Artists Asn, Pasadena, 58; San Diego Bicentennial Celebration,
67-68; Dealer's Choice, Northern Ariz Univ, Flagstaff, 69; Sixth
Southwestern Invitational, Yuma, Ariz, 71.

Memberships: Phoenix Art Mus; Mus Northern Ariz.
Dealer: Art Wagon Galleries, 7120-7156 Main St, Scottsdale, AZ 85251.
Mailing Address: Box 853, Sedona, AZ 86336.

LUNTZ, IRVING
Art Dealer, Writer
b Milwaukee, Wis, Jan 9, 29.
Positions: Pres & dir, Irving Galleries, Inc, Milwaukee, Wis & Palm Beach, Fla, 59-
Memberships: Art Dealers Asn Am; Appraisers Asn Am.
Research: Nineteenth & twentieth century American & European painting; sculpture & graphics.
Mailing Address: 404 E Wisconsin Ave, Milwaukee, WI 53202.

LUPPER, EDWARD
Painter
Preferred Media: Casein, Oils.
b N J, Jan 4, 36.
Study & Training: With Wesley Lea, Frenchtown, N J; Trenton Jr. Col; Parsons Sch Design, New York, N Y; Calif Col Arts & Crafts, Oakland; San Francisco Art Inst, Calif; San Francisco State Col.
Work in Public Collections: Works in private collections only.
Exhibitions: Baltimore Mus Art, Md, 55; Tucson Art Ctr, Ariz, 59; Fort Worth Art Ctr, Tex, 60; San Francisco Mus Art, 60.
Awards: Huntington Hartford Found fel, 64.
Bibliography: Articles, In: San Francisco Chronicle, 60, San Francisco Examr, 62 & 65 & Seattle Times, 71.
Publications: Auth, articles, In: San Francisco Exam Pictorial Living, 65, Sunset Mag, 67 & Am Home Mag, 71.
Dealers: Lord & Taylor Gallery, Fifth Ave, New York, NY 10018; Pantechnicon, 1849 Union St, San Francisco, CA 94123.
Mailing Address: 1251 Pacific, San Francisco, CA 94109.

LURIA, GLORIA
Art Dealer
b New York, N Y.
Study & Training: Pratt Inst; Art Stud League New York; Skidmore Col, BS.
Positions: Dir, Gloria Luria Gallery, Miami, Fla.
Specialty of Gallery: Master graphics; contemporary painters and sculptors.
Mailing Address: 14700 Biscayne Blvd, Miami, FL 33161.

LUSKER, RON
Painter, Educator
Preferred Media: Acrylics.
b Chicago, Ill, Jan 28, 37.
Study & Training: Sch Art Inst Chicago, 54-60; Univ Ill, Chicago Circle, Ill State Gen Assembly scholar, 57-62; Univ Chicago, 62-63; Southern Ill Univ, Carbondale, BA, 65, MFA, 66.
Exhibitions: 14th Ann Painting & Sculpture Exhib, Peoria Art Ctr, Ill, 66; 70th Ann Midwest Painting Exhib, Art Inst Chicago, 67; Convocation Arts, Sculpture, State Univ N Y Albany, 68; 4th Ann Art Exhib, Sculpture, Staten Island, 69; Eastern Seaboard Regional 3rd Ann Sculpture Exhib, 70; plus others.
Teaching: Instr art, Southern Ill Univ, Carbondale, 65-67; asst prof art, State Univ N Y Stony Brook, 68-72; Grad Sch for Sculpture fel & grant-in-aid, 69 & 70; assoc prof art, Kingsborough Community Col, 72-
Bibliography: Malcolm Preston (auth), Assemblages display intellectual fantasy, Newsday, 5/21/69; Claire White (auth), Exhibition review, Craft Horizons, 6/70; Albert Boime (auth), Cosmic artifacts: the work in lucite of Ron Lusker, Art J, winter 72.
Memberships: Am Craftsmen Coun; Col Art Asn Am; Ctr Study Democratic Insts; Mus Mod Art; Whitney Mus Art; Am Asn Univ Prof.
Publications: Auth, New York: the season in sculpture, 8/70, The green meadow school, 8/70, The jewelry of Marci Zelmanoff, 12/70 & Attitudes, Brooklyn Museum, 70, Craft Horizons Mag.
Dealer: Alonzo Gallery, 26 E 63rd St, New York, NY 10021.
Mailing Address: 492 Broome St, New York, NY 10013.

LUST, HERBERT
Art Historian, Collector
b Chicago, Ill, Oct 31, 26.
Study & Training: Univ Chicago, MA, 49; Fulbright scholar to France, 50.
Research: Giacometti; Surrealism.
Collection: Giacometti drawings; also Bellmer, Leaf, Baj & Calder.
Publications: Auth, The twelve principles for art investment, 69; auth, Giacometti: the complete graphics and fifteen drawings, Tudor, 71; auth, Enrico Baj, dada impressionist with catalogue raisonné, 72.
Mailing Address: 2340 Orrington, Evanston, IL 60201.

LUST, VIRGINIA
Art Dealer
b Chicago, Ill, July 23, 30.
Study & Training: Art Inst Chicago, 46; Mundelein Col, grad, 52.
Collections Arranged: Paintings, Drawing, Early Prints (first Am show of Hans Bellmer); The Complete Graphics (first world show of Delvaux).
Positions: Dir, Gallery Bernard, Chicago, 68-; sales dir, Collectors Press.
Specialty of Gallery: Surrealism; Giacometti, paintings and drawings.
Mailing Address: 235 E Ontario St, Chicago, IL 60611.

LUTZ, DAN S
Painter
Preferred Media: Oils, Watercolors, Acrylics.
b Decatur, Ill, July 7, 06.
Study & Training: Millikin Univ; Art Inst Chicago, James Nelson Raymond European travel fel & dipl, 31; Univ Southern Calif, BFA, 34; also painting under Boris Anisfeld.
Work in Public Collections: Phillips Mem Art Gallery, Washington, D C; Fine Arts Gallery, San Diego, Calif; Los Angeles Co Mus Art, Calif; Philadelphia Mus Art, Pa; Santa Barbara Mus Art, Calif; plus others.
Commissions: Portrait, Fac of Westhampton Col, Richmond, Va, 55.
Exhibitions: Four Am Painting Exhibs, Art Inst Chicago, 38-46; Five Biennial Exhibs, Va Mus Art, 40-48; Am Painting, Watercolor & Drawing Exhibs, Metrop Mus Art, New York, 42, 50 & 52; Painting in the United States, 43-49 & Int Painting Exhib, 50, Carnegie Inst, Pittsburgh, Pa; Contemporary American Painting, Whitney Mus Am Art, New York, 44 & 50.
Teaching: Instr painting, Univ Southern Calif, 32-42; instr painting, Chouinard Art Inst, 44-52; instr painting (guest artist), Univ Ga, 55.
Positions: Mem Men of Art Guild, San Antonio, 55.
Awards: Thomas B Clark Prize for oils, Nat Acad Design, 41; third hon mention for oil, Carnegie Inst, 43; Wheelwright Prize for watercolors, Pa Acad Fine Arts, 45.
Bibliography: Donald Bear (auth), Recent pictures by Dan Lutz, Mag of Art, 12/43; Arthur Millier (auth), Dan Lutz-a painter with a compelling gift for lyric expression, Am Artist, 12/51; Janice Lovoos (auth), Dan Lutz, Christian Sci Monitor, 67.
Memberships: Calif Nat Watercolor Soc; Am Watercolor Soc; Philadelphia Watercolor Club; Santa Barbara Art Asn; Art Inst Chicago Alumni Asn.
Dealer: Dalzell-Hatfield Galleries, Ambassador Hotel, P O Box K, Los Angeles, CA 90070.
Mailing Address: 369 Hot Springs Rd, Santa Barbara, CA 93108.

LUX, GLADYS MARIE
Painter
Preferred Media: Watercolors, Oils.
b Chapman, Nebr.
Study & Training: Kearney State Col, SS, 18; Univ Nebr, BFA, 25, AB, 33, MA, 35; Sch Art Inst Chicago, SS, 29.
Work in Public Collections: Peru State Teachers Col, Nebr; Doane Col, Crete, Nebr; Pub Schs, Kearney, Nebr; Artists Guild Collection, Lincoln, Nebr.
Exhibitions: Regional shows, Omaha, Nebr, Minneapolis, Minn, Kansas City, Wichita & Topeka, Kans, 27-67; Art Inst Chicago, 36; Rockefeller Ctr, 36-38; World's Fair, New York, N Y, 39; Joseph Pennell Mem Print Exhib.
Teaching: Instr art methods, Univ Nebr Summer Schs, Lincoln, 23-25; instr art methods, Sioux City Pub High Sch, Iowa, 25-27; chmn art dept, Nebr Wesleyan Univ, 27-33, asst prof drawing, painting, art hist & appreciation art methods & chmn art dept, 36-66.
Awards: Nebr Art Teachers Asn Serv Award, 69.
Bibliography: Rev, In: Art Digest, 36-38; World's fair exhibit, New Yorker, 39; articles in local & regional newspapers over the yrs.
Memberships: Lincoln Artist Guild (past pres, secy); hon mem Nebr Art Teachers Asn (past pres, v pres).
Publications: Auth, Symbols of good neighbors, Christ of the Andes, Candle Beam, 43; auth, European arts seen internationally, Western Arts Asn Bull, 55; auth, Students exhibs, 59; illusr, In a tall land, 63; auth, The baby doll, an evolution, United Fedn Doll Clubs Bk, 72.
Mailing Address: 5203 Garland St, Lincoln, NE 68504.

LUX, GWEN (GWEN LUX CREIGHTON)
Sculptor
Preferred Media: Polyester Resin, Concrete, Metals.
b Chicago, Ill.
Study & Training: Maryland Inst Arts; Boston Mus Fine Arts Sch; also study in Paris, France & with Ivan Mestrovic, Yugoslavia.
Work in Public Collections: Detroit Mus, Mich; Hawaii State Found Cult & the Arts.

Commissions: Totem pole, bird pole (metal & wood), Northwood Shopping Ctr, Detroit, 52; chrome abstraction, Gen Motors Tech Ctr, Detroit, 56; stainless steel abstraction, Aviation Trades High Sch, New York City, 58; bronze & concrete abstraction, KRON TV Bldg, San Francisco, Calif, 65; concrete abstraction, State Off Bldg, Kauai, Hawaii, 71.
Exhibitions: Whitney Mus Am Art, New York, N Y, 35; Detroit Mus, 48; World House Galleries, New York, 62; Pomeroy Galleries, San Francisco, Calif, 68; Contemp Arts Ctr, Honolulu, Hawaii, 70; plus others.
Teaching: Instr sculpture, Arts & Crafts Soc; Detroit, 45-48.
Awards: Guggenheim Found fel, 33; Detroit Inst Award, 45 & 46; Nat Indust Arts Coun Can Award, 65.
Bibliography: C Ludwig Brumme (auth), Contemporary American sculpture, Crown, 48.
Memberships: Hawaii Artists & Sculptors League.
Dealers: Hoover Gallery, 710 Sansome St, San Francisco, CA 94111; Downtown Gallery, 125 Merchant St, Honolulu, HI 96813.
Mailing Address: 4340 Pahoa Ave, Honolulu, HI 96816.

LUZ, VIRGINIA
Painter
b Toronto, Ont, Oct 15, 11.
Study & Training: Cent Tech Sch.
Work in Public Collections: Huron Col; Can Dept External Affairs; J S McLean Collection; London Art Mus; also in many pvt collections.
Exhibitions: Ont Soc Artists, 45-70; Can Soc Painters in Watercolour, 47-72; Can Tours; Can Group Painters; Art Gallery Hamilton, 52-65; plus others.
Teaching: Instr illus & head art dept, Cent Tech Sch, Toronto.
Memberships: Ont Soc Artists (exec coun, 65-66); Can Soc Painters in Watercolour.
Mailing Address: 113 Delaware Ave, Toronto, Ont, Can.

LYE, LEN
Sculptor, Kinetic Artist
b Christchurch, New Zealand, July 5, 01; U S citizen.
Study & Training: Wellington Tech Col; Canterbury Col Fine Arts.
Work in Public Collections: Albright-Knox Art Gallery, Buffalo, N Y; Whitney Mus Mod Art; Art Inst Chicago; eight films in libr of Mus Art, New York.
Commissions: New York films for Brit Govt.
Exhibitions: One-man show, Motion Sculpture, Mus Mod Art, New York, 61; Cinema Art Ctr; Art in Motion, Stedelijk Mus, Amsterdam, Holland, 61-62; Whitney Mus Am Art Ann, 62; On the Move, Howard Wise Gallery, New York, 63.
Teaching: Instr film technique, City Col New York; instr creative imagination, Sch Performing Arts, New York Univ, 66-
Awards: Int Film Festival for Colour Box, Brussels, Belg; experimental film competition, World's Fair Int, Brussels, 58.
Art Interests: Invented direct film technique of painting or etching image on film itself, no camera used.
Publications: Auth, No trouble, Paris, 30; contribr to Life & Lett, London & Tiger's Eye, 49.
Mailing Address: 801 Greenwich, New York, NY 10014.

LYFORD, CABOT
Sculptor, Educator
Preferred Media: Stone, Metal, Watercolor.
b Sayre, Pa, May 22, 25.
Study & Training: Skowhegan Sch Art, summer, 47; Cornell Univ, BFA, 50; Sculpture Ctr, New York, N Y, 50-51.
Work in Public Collections: Lamont Gallery, Exeter, N H; Addison Gallery Am Art, Andover, Mass; Wichita Mus, Wichita, Kans; N Eng Ctr Continuing Educ, Durham, N H; over fifty private collections.
Commissions: Wild Geese (cypress wood), Summit Lodge, Mt Sunapee, N H, 64; brass mobile, State N H exhib, N Y World's Fair, 65; granite Christ head, Christ Church, Exeter, N H, 69; candelabra, 70 & black granite & brass flower holder, 71.
Exhibitions: Maine Art Gallery, Wiscassett; Rhode Island Festival, Providence; N H Art Asn, Manchester; Addison Gallery, Andover, Mass; Fitchburg Art Mus; plus others.
Teaching: Instr sculpture & chmn art dept, Phillips Exeter Acad, N H, 63-
Awards: Prizes, City Manchester, 70 & N H Architects Asn, 71.
Memberships: Boston Visual Artists Union.
Publications: Contribr, Contemporary stone sculpture, 71.
Dealer: Joan Peterson Gallery, Copley Sq, Boston, MA 02116.
Mailing Address: 9 Center St, Exeter, NH 03833.

LYNCH, JAMES BURR, JR
Art Historian
b Miona, Va, Aug 23, 19.
Study & Training: Harvard Univ, AB, AM & Ph D.

Teaching: Assoc prof art hist, Boston Univ, 55-66; prof art hist, Univ Md, College Park, 66-
Memberships: Col Art Asn Am.
Research: Latin American painting and architecture, especially Mexican and Cuban; Italian art of the sixteenth century.
Publications: Auth, History of Raphael's small St George in the Louvre, 4/62 & G P Lomazzo's self-portrait in the Brera, 10/64, Gazette Beaux-Arts; auth, Lomazzo and the Accademia della Valle de Bregno, Art Bull, 6/66; auth, Siqueiros, Encycl World Art, Vol XIII; auth, An unsung artist of the Mexican renaissance, Américas, 6/70.
Mailing Address: 1325 Dale Dr, Silver Spring, MD 20910.

LYNCH, JAMES O'CONNOR
Collector
Mailing Address: 240 W 98th St, New York, NY 10025.

LYNDS, CLYDE WILLIAM
Sculptor
b Jersey City, N J, June 22, 36.
Study & Training: Art Stud League New York, N Y; Frank J Reilly Sch, New York.
Exhibitions: N J State Mus, Trenton, 67; Drawings of Young Americans, Mus Art Ogunquit, Maine, 69; Contemp Am Painting & Sculpture, Krannert Mus, Univ Ill, 69; McNay Art Inst, San Antonio, Tex, 69; Ind State Univ Centennial, 70.
Awards: Frist prizes, Monmouth Col(N J), 68 & Union Col, Cranford, N J, 68; first prize & medal of honor, Jersey City Mus, 68.
Dealer: Babcock Gallery, 805 Madison Ave, New York, NY 10021.
Mailing Address: 237 Innes Rd, Woodridge, NJ 07075.

LYNES, RUSSELL
Writer, Critic
b Great Barrington, Mass, Dec 2, 10.
Study & Training: Yale Univ, BA; Union Col, hon DFA.
Positions: Managing ed, Harper's Mag, 47-67, contrib ed, 67-; pres, Arch Am Art, 64-71, trustee, presently; pres, Bd Dirs, MacDowell Colony; trustee, New York Hist Soc; v-chmn, New York Found for Arts; vis comt, Am Dept, Metrop Mus Art, vis comt, Costume Inst; mem New York City Art Comn.
Publications: Auth, The tastemakers, 54; auth, The domesticated Americans, 63; auth, Confessions of a dilettante, 66; The artmakers of 19th century America, Atheneum, 70; also auth many articles for Harpers Mag, Life, Look, Yale Rev, Vogue & others, 45-
Mailing Address: 427 E 84th St, New York, NY 10028.

LYSUN, GREGORY
Painter, Restorer
Preferred Media: Oils.
b Yonkers, N Y, Oct 24, 24.
Study & Training: Art Stud League New York, N Y, with Louis Bouche, Edwin Dickinson, John Groth, Robert Beverly Hale & Reginald Marsh, 47-53.
Work in Public Collections: Art Stud League New York; Berkshire Mus, Pittsfield, Mass; Butler Inst Am Art, Youngstown, Ohio.
Commissions: Portraits of M D Safanie, Shearson, Hammill & Co, New York, 65 & Wilmer Wright, Wright Assocs, New York, 67; restoration work of The Whistle, 71 & Simon Stevens, 71, comn by Mrs D E Kastner, Chatham, Mass.
Exhibitions: 56th Ann Allied Arts Am, 69; 22nd Ann Nat Realist Art, Acad Artists Asn, Mus Fine Arts, Springfield, Mass, 71; 35 Years in Retrospect, 1936-1970, Butler Inst Am Art Midyear Show, 71; Am Artists Prof League Grand Nat, 72; Conn Acad Fine Arts Exhib, New Brit Mus Am Art, 72.
Teaching: Instr painting & drawing, Westchester Art Workshop, Co Ctr, White Plains, N Y, 69-; instr painting & drawing, New Brit Art League, 69-; instr painting & drawing & chmn dept arts, Fairview-Greenburgh Community Ctr, Greenburgh, N Y, 72-
Awards: Purchase prize, 31st Ann Nat, Butler Inst Am Art, 66; Coun Am Art Socs Award for best figurative or traditional painting, Miniature Painters & Sculptors Soc N J Nat, 71; Gen Tel & Electronics Corp Award, Silvermine Guild Artists, 72.
Bibliography: R Stevens (auth), Gregory Lysun, La Rev Mod, 64 & 69; Margaret Harold (auth), Self-portrait and things by Gregory Lysun, Prize winning art, 67; Winifred B Bell (auth), Paintings by Gregory Lysun, Berkshire Eagle, 71.
Memberships: Life mem Art Stud League New York; Allied Artists Am; Am Artists Prof League; Conn Acad Fine Arts; Hudson Valley Art Asn.
Dealer: Capricorn Galleries, 8003 Woodmont Ave, Bethesda, MD 20014.
Mailing Address: 481 Winding Rd N, Ardsley, NY 10502.

LYTLE, RICHARD
Painter, Educator
Preferred Media: Oils.
b Albany, N Y, Feb 14, 35.
Study & Training: Cooper Union; Yale Univ, BFA, MFA, also with Josef Albers.
Work in Public Collections: Mus Mod Art, New York, N Y; Yale Art Gallery, New Haven, Conn; Nat Collection Art, Washington, D C; Columbia Univ Int House, New York; Cincinnati Art Mus, Ohio.
Commissions: Concrete relief mural, Fairfield Univ, Conn, 65.
Exhibitions: 16 Americans, Mus Mod Art, New York, 59; Seattle World's Fair, Wash, 62; Whitney Mus Am Art Ann, New York, 63; Art: U S A: Now, S C Johnson Collection World Tour, 63-; Contemp Am Painting, Krannert Art Mus, Champaign, Ill, 67.
Teaching: Instr art, Yale Univ, 60-63; dean, Silvermine Col Art, 63-66; assoc prof art, Yale Univ, 66-
Awards: Fulbright grant to Italy, 58.
Dealer: Grace Borgenicht Gallery, 1018 Madison Ave, New York, NY 10021.
Mailing Address: Sperry Rd, Woodbridge, CT 06525.

M

MacAGY, DOUGLAS GUERNSEY
Art Administrator
b Winnipeg, Man, July 8, 13; U S citizen.
Study & Training: Univ Toronto; Barnes Found; Courtauld Inst, Univ London; Univ Pa; Cleveland Sch Art; Case Western Reserve Univ.
Collections Arranged: Cleveland Mus Art, San Francisco Mus Art, New York Mus Comt for UNESCO, Mus Mod Art, New York, Dallas Mus Contemp Arts, Contemp Arts Mus, Houston, Houston Mus Fine Arts, Albright-Knox Art Gallery, Buffalo, Corcoran Gallery Art, Washington, D C & Others, 40-
Teaching: Tutor classical & mediaeval art, Univ Toronto, 35-36; dir aesthet & mod art, Calif Sch Fine Arts, 45-50; guest lectr contemp art, Univ Pa, 65-66.
Positions: Curatorial asst, Cleveland Mus Art, 39-41; cur, San Francisco Mus Art, 41-43; spec consult to dir, Mus Mod Art, New York, 51-55; dir, Dallas Mus Contemp Arts, 59-63; dep chmn, Nat Coun on the Arts/Nat Endowment for the Arts, 68-72; dir exhibs, Hirshhorn Mus & Sculpture Garden, Washington, D C, 72-
Bibliography: Alfred Frankenstein (auth), The intellectual climate of San Francisco, Harper's Bazaar, 2/47; Dore Ashton (auth), An Eastern view of the San Francisco School, Evergreen Rev, Vol 1, No 2; Mary McChesney (auth), Was there a San Francisco School?, Oakland Mus, 72.
Memberships: Int Found for Art Res (trustee, 69-); Nat Coun Churches of Christ (cult comt, 67-); Tamarind Lithography Workshop (trustee, 60-); Four Winds Theatre, New York (trustee, 68-); also var prof asns.
Research: Twentieth century art.
Publications: Contribr, Zeitschrift für aesthetik und allgemeine Kunst-Wissen Shaft—Index 1906-1939, Cleveland Mus Art, 40; ed, Western round table on modern art: modern artists in America, Wittenborn & Schulz, 51; auth, The museum looks in on TV, Mus Mod Art, 55; co-auth, Going for a walk with a line, Doubleday, 59; auth, The art that broke the looking-glass, Dallas Mus Contemp Arts, 61.
Mailing Address: Smithsonian Institution, 1000 Jefferson Dr, Washington, DC 20560.

MacALISTER, PAUL RITTER
Designer, Collector
b Camden, N J, Oct 15, 01.
Study & Training: Pa Acad Fine Arts, Philadelphia; Sch Indust Design; Yale Univ Sch Archit; Ecole Beaux Arts, Fontainebleau, France, with Bourdelle & Carlu.
Work in Public Collections: Astrasphere (celestial globe), Maritime Mus, Greenwich, Eng & White House Libr; Capellini glassware, Mus Arts Decoratifs et Metiers, Paris, France.
Commissions: Plan-A-Rm (3-D planning device), 40-72; Amtico Showrooms, Am Biltrite Rubber Co, U S, Can & Europe, 54-67; Decorama (slide film), Libbey-Owens-Ford Glass Co, Toledo, Ohio, 55.
Exhibitions: Miniature TV Rm Settings, Art Inst Chicago, 50.
Positions: Dir, Paul MacAlister, Inc, 26-42; designer & dir, Permanent Exhib Decorative Arts & Crafts, 33-40; comdr, USN Spec Devices Div & Navy Exhibs, 42-46; dir, Bureaus Indust & Interior Design, Montgomery Ward & Co, 46-48; dir & sr partner, Paul MacAlister & Assocs, Lake Bluff, Ill, 48-, dir, Americana Hayloft Mus, 50-
Awards: Beaux Arts Medal, 24; silver medal, Indust Designers Inst, 56; Dorothy Dawes Award, Am Furniture Mart Press Ann, 55.
Bibliography: Articles, In: House & Garden, 7/66 & Interior Design, 4/68, 10/68 & 9/72.
Memberships: Fel Indust Designers Soc Am (pres, 50 & 51, chmn design award prog, 50-60); fel Royal Soc Arts, London; Early Am Industs Asn; Midwest Tool Collectors Asn.
Collection: American eagle in art form; early hand tools; early scientific instruments; rare books on perspective, architecture and the arts; collections exhibited Chicago Pub Libr, Lake Forest Libr, Lake Forest Acad Antiques Show & Art Inst Chicago.
Publications: Auth, Display for better business, 54; auth, articles, In: Lake Forest Acad Antiques Show Catalog, 69-71; contribr, var newspapers, mags & TV shows.
Mailing Address: Box 157, Lake Bluff, IL 60044.

McALLISTER-KELLY, (ROSANA)
Painter
Preferred Media: Acrylics.
b Buenos Aires, Arg.
Study & Training: Munic Sch Art, Buenos Aires; Beaux Art Asn, Buenos Aires.
Work in Public Collections: Fla State Supreme Court, Tallahassee; Miami Mus Mod Art, Fla; Clairol Collection, U S A.
Exhibitions: Brandeis Univ Pan Am Union for Latin Am Art & Contemp Painting, Washington, D C, 65; Hortt Mem Exhib, Mus Arts, Fort Lauderdale, Fla, 65-71; Nat Sch Plastic Arts, Nat Comt Cult & Fine Arts, Guatemala City, Guatemala, 68; Arg Group Exhib, Miami Mus Mod Art, 71; Beaux Arts, Lowe Art Mus, Univ Miami, 71.
Awards: Atwater Kent Award, Soc Four Arts, Palm Beach, Fla, 69; hon mention, Hortt Mem Exhib, Fort Lauderdale Mus Arts, 71; second prize, YM-YWHA Greater Miami, 72.
Bibliography: Marta De Castro (auth), El arte en Cuba, Ed Universal, 70.
Memberships: Hon mem Miami Mus Mod Art; Miami Art Ctr.
Dealer: Gloria Luria Gallery, 14700 Biscayne Blvd, Miami, FL 33161.
Mailing Address: 4279 S W 9 Terr, Miami, FL 33134.

McALPIN, DAVID H
Collector
Mailing Address: Pretty Brook Rd, Princeton, NJ 08540.

McANDREW, JOHN
Art Historian, Educator
b New York, N Y, May 4, 04.
Study & Training: Harvard Univ, BS(magna cum laude), 24, MArch, 40.
Teaching: Instr art hist, Vassar Col, 31-36; prof art hist, Wellesley Col, 44-68.
Positions: Cur archit, Mus Mod Art, New York, 36-40.
Awards: Alice Davis Hitchcock Award, Soc Archit Historians, 65; Comdr, Order of Merit, Repub Italy, 70.
Memberships: Soc Archit Historians (dir, 65-68); Inst Veneto Sci, Lett & Arti (corresp & hon, 70-); Venice Comt, Int Fund for Monuments (chmn, 68-70); Save Venice, Inc (pres, 71-).
Publications: Auth, Open-air churches of sixteenth century Mexico, Harvard Univ Press, 65.
Mailing Address: 282 Beacon St, Boston, MA 02116.

McANINCH, BETH
Painter
Preferred Media: Watercolors, Pencil.
b Corn, Okla, Nov 23, 18.
Study & Training: Southwestern State Col, grad; also with Jack Valle, Millard Sheets, Edgar Whitney, John Pike & others.
Work in Public Collections: Okla Art Ctr, Oklahoma City; Okla Christian Col, Oklahoma City; Liberty Nat Bank, Oklahoma City; Westinghouse Corp, Oklahoma City; Okla Arts Coun.
Exhibitions: Okla Nat Printmakers & Watercolor Show, 61; Southwestern Watercolor Soc Regional & Open, Dallas, Tex, 67, 69 & 71; 8 State Exhib Painting & Sculpture Ann, Okla Art Ctr, 71; Watercolor U S A, Springfield, Mo, 72; Okla Artists Ann, Phillbrook, Tulsa, Okla, 61-72.
Teaching: Instr painting & drawing, pvt classes, 60-70; instr painting & drawing, Okla Sci & Art Found, 62-66.
Awards: Southwestern Watercolor Soc Award, 67; first painting award, 7th Ann Artists Salon, Okla Mus Art, 68; first award, 7th Ann Southwestern Watercolor Soc, 71.
Bibliography: Numerous articles in newspapers.

Memberships: Oklahoma City Arts Coun Bd; Southwestern Water-
color Soc.
Dealers: Norman Wilks Interiors, 3839 NW 63rd St, Oklahoma City,
OK 73116; Oklahoma Art Center, 3113 General Pershing, Okla-
homa City, OK 73107.
Mailing Address: 1409 Dorchester Dr, Oklahoma City, OK 73114.

MACARAY, LAWRENCE RICHARD
Painter, Educator
Preferred Media: Oils.
b Elsinore, Calif, May 8, 21.
Study & Training: Whittier Col, BA, 51; Calif State Univ, Long
Beach, MA, 55.
Work in Public Collections: Bowers Mus, Santa Ana, Calif; Thomp-
son Industs, Los Angeles, Calif; Torrance High Sch, Calif.
Exhibitions: College Art Professors Traveling Exhibition, Western
Asn Mus Art, 70-71; New Talent, New Work, Los Angeles Co
Mus Art, 71; Long Beach Mus Art Group Exhib, Calif, 71; 11th
Ann Juried Show, Palos Verdes Mus Art, Calif, 71; All California
Art Exhibition, Nat Orange Show, San Bernardino, Calif, 72; plus
many other group & one-man shows.
Teaching: Prof drawing & painting, El Camino Col, 62-
Positions: Art & travel ed, Torrance Press-Herald, Calif, 63-70.
Mailing Address: 628 Buttonwood St, Anaheim, CA 92805.

MacBETH, JEROME RUSSELL
Art Administrator
b Washington, D C, May 19, 33.
Study & Training: Cath Univ Am, AB; Univ Florence, Italy.
Collections Arranged: Carroll Cloar, 69; Art of China-3000 Years,
71; George Catlin-Artist Historian, 71.
Positions: Asst to dir, Cummer Gallery Art, Jacksonville, Fla, 65-
66; dir, Tenn Fine Arts Ctr, Nashville, Tenn, 68-72; dir, Gibbes
Art Gallery, Charleston, S C, 72-
Memberships: Am Asn Mus; Southeastern Mus Conf; Col Art Asn;
Southeastern Col Art Conf.
Publications: Auth, Ralph E W Earl, Antiques, 71.
Mailing Address: 135 Meeting St, Charleston, SC 29401.

McBRIDE, JAMES JOSEPH
Painter, Illustrator
Preferred Media: Watercolors.
b Fort Wayne, Ind, May 19, 23.
Study & Training: Fort Wayne Art Inst; Cape Cod Sch Art, Province-
town, Mass; Pa Acad Fine Art, Philadelphia & summer sch;
Barnes Found Mod Art, Merion, Pa.
Work in Public Collections: Fort Wayne Art Inst, Ind; Ind Tri Kappa
Collection, Nashville; Wabash Col, Ind.
Commissions: Murals, Key Largo Motel, Howards Gift Shop,
Olympic Club & St Joseph Hosp, Fort Wayne.
Exhibitions: Hoosier Salon, Indianapolis, Ind, 50- & one-man show,
69; four exhibs, Watercolor U S A, Springfield, Mo, 62-72; Xmas
Art Nat, Marymount Col, 67; Nat Soc Casien Painters, New York,
70; Am Watercolor Soc, New York, 72.
Teaching: Instr watercolor, Fort Wayne Art Inst, 64-65; instr water-
color, St Francis Col, Ind, 69-70; instr creative watercolor, Ind
Univ-Purdue Univ, Fort Wayne Campus, 71-
Positions: Art dir, WKVG TV, Fort Wayne, 53-59; art dir, Our Sun-
day Visitor, Huntington, Ind, 59-69; pres, Graphics, Inc, Fort
Wayne, 69-
Awards: Nat Cath Press Asn Award, 66; Hoosier Salon Award, Ind
Nat Bank, 71; Robert Stahl Purchase Award, Watercolor U S A,
72.
Memberships: Hoosier Salon Asn; Ind Artists Club; Fort Wayne
Artists Guild.
Publications: Illusr, Family Digest, 69 & Schema XIII, 71.
Dealer: Larry Williamson, 308 S Seminole Circle, Fort Wayne, IN
46807.
Mailing Address: 6220 Rolling Hills Dr, Fort Wayne, IN 46804.

McBRIDE, WALTER HENRY
Art Administrator
b Waterloo, Ind, Apr 20, 05.
Study & Training: John Herron Art Sch & Ind Univ, BAE; Oakland
Sch Arts & Crafts, Calif; Harvard Grad Sch Fine Arts; also
study abroad.
Collections Arranged: Painting, sculpture, prints & crafts on local,
state & nat level.
Teaching: Instr design & watercolor, John Herron Art Sch, 29-53.
Positions: Dir, Fort Wayne Art Sch & Mus, Ind, 33-34; dir, Grand
Rapids Art Mus, Mich, 54-70; retired.
Memberships: Am Asn Mus Dirs; Midwest Mus Dirs (pres, 59);
Am Asn Mus (accrediting comt).
Mailing Address: 2738 Elmwood Dr S E, Grand Rapids, MI 49506.

McCALLUM, CORRIE (MRS WILLIAM HALSEY)
Painter, Instructor
Preferred Media: Oils.
b Sumter, S C, Mar 14, 14.
Study & Training: Univ S C, cert fine arts, 36; Boston Mus Sch, with
Karl Zerbe.
Work in Public Collections: La State Univ, Baton Rouge; Gibbes Art
Gallery, Charleston, S C; S C Arts Comn, State Collection; Mint
Mus Art, Charlotte, N C; Columbia Mus Art, S C.
Commissions: Mural, state competition sponsored by Home Fed
Bank, 63.
Exhibitions: Dixie Ann, Montgomery Mus, Ala, 68; First South
Carolina State Invitational, Columbia Mus Art, 69; Contemporary
Artists of South Carolina, Greenville Mus, Columbia Mus Art,
Gibbes Art Gallery & Florence Mus, 70; one-man shows, Kunst-
salon Wolfsberg, Zurich, Switz, 69 & Concourse Gallery, State
St Bank, Boston, Mass, 71.
Teaching: Pvt art sch to 60; cur art educ for Charleston Co, Gibbes
Art Gallery, 60-69; instr painting & drawing, Newberry Col, S C,
69-71; instr painting, drawing & printmaking, Col Charleston, 71-
Awards: Purchase prize for drawing, Mint Mus Graphics Ann, 64;
painting award, Guild S C Artists Ann, 65; Scientific Educ Found
grant for travel & study around the world, 68.
Bibliography: J A Morris, Jr (auth), Contemporary artists of South
Carolina, Greenville Co Mus Art, 70.
Memberships: Guild S C Artists (pres, 61); Col Art Asn Am; Copley
Soc, Boston.
Publications: Illusr, Dutch Fork farm boy & 50 years along the way,
Univ S C Press, 68; co-auth, A travel sketchbook, R L Byran Co,
71.
Dealer: Kunstsalon Wolfsberg, Bederstrasse 109, Zurich, Switz.
Mailing Address: 38 State St, Charleston, SC 29401.

McCANNEL, MRS MALCOLM A
Collector
b Minneapolis, Minn, Nov 20, 15.
Study & Training: Smith Col, BA; Minneapolis Sch Art.
Positions: Bd mem, Walker Art Ctr, Minneapolis.
Collection: Contemporary American sculpture and painting.
Mailing Address: 58 Groveland Terr, Minneapolis, MN 55403.

McCARTHY, DENIS
Painter
b New York, N Y, Feb 21, 35.
Study & Training: Cooper Union, 59-64; Yale Univ, BFA & MFA,
64-66.
Work in Public Collections: Work in pvt collections only.
Exhibitions: Group Exhib, 69 & one-man show, 70, Stable Gallery,
New York; Whitney Mus Am Art Painting Ann, New York, 70;
Group Exhib, O K Harris, New York, 72.
Teaching: Instr drawing, Sch Visual Arts, New York, 67-72; instr,
art workshop, Hunter Col, 71-
Mailing Address: 147 Spring St, New York, NY 10012.

McCARTHY, DORIS JEAN
Painter, Instructor
Preferred Media: Oils, Watercolors.
b Calgary, Alta, July 7, 10.
Study & Training: Ont Col Art, assoc, 30; Cent Sch Arts & Crafts,
London, Eng, with John Farleigh & John Skeaping.
Work in Public Collections: Art Gallery Ont, Toronto; London Art
Gallery, Ont; Imp Oil Collection; Seneca Col, Willowdale, Ont;
Pickering Col, Newmarket, Ont.
Commissions: Mural, Toronto Pub Libr, 33; mem bk, Malvern Col,
Toronto, 48; creche figures, Church of St Aldan, Toronto, 48;
fabric banner Trinity, St James Cathedral, Toronto, 55.
Exhibitions: Ont Soc Artists Ann, 33-; Royal Can Acad Ann, 34-;
Canadian Women Artists, Riverside Mus, New York, N Y, 47;
Can Nat Exhib, 48; Ont Centennial Art Exhib, 67.
Teaching: Instr drawing, painting & hist art, Central Tech Sch To-
ronto, 33-, asst head mss mus study, 68-72.
Memberships: Assoc Royal Can Acad; Ont Soc Artists (exec v pres,
64-65, pres, 65-68); Can Soc Painters in Watercolor (secy & pres,
56-57); Fedn Can Artists (secy); Prof Artists Can (chmn, 67-69).
Mailing Address: 1 Meadowcliff Dr, Scarborough, Ont, Can.

McCARTIN, JAN
Painter
Preferred Media: Oils, Casein.
b Vancouver, B C, July 6, 09; U S citizen.
Study & Training: Art Stud League New York, with Robert Laurent
& Boardman Robinson.
Exhibitions: Nat Soc Casein Painters, 59-62; Audubon Artists Ann,
63; Maine Coast Artists, Rockport, Maine, 70; 7 from Monhegan,

Exeter Acad, Lamont Gallery, 70; Artist & the American Landscape, A M Sachs Gallery, 71; plus other group & also one-man shows.
Mailing Address: 381 Bleeker St, New York, NY 10014.

McCARTIN, WILLIAM FRANCIS
Painter
Preferred Media: Acrylics.
b New York, N Y, Dec 9, 05.
Study & Training: Art Stud League New York, with Richard Lahey, five yrs; New Sch Soc Res, one yr.
Exhibitions: Gallery Contemp Arts, Pittsburgh, Pa; Maine Coast Artists, Rockport, 70; 7 from Monhegan, Phillips Exeter Acad, N H, 70; Joseph De Meers Ltd, Hilton Head, S C, 71; one-man show, Beaumont Art Mus, Tex, 71; plus other group & one-man shows.
Awards: Tiffany Found grant, 25; John Newman Medal, Casein Soc, 60.
Dealer: Alonzo Gallery, 26 E 63rd St, New York, NY 10021.
Mailing Address: 381 Bleeker St, New York, NY 10014.

McCHESNEY, ROBERT PEARSON
Painter
b Marshall, Mo, Jan 16, 13.
Study & Training: Washington Univ Art Sch, with Fred Conway; Otis Art Inst, Los Angeles.
Work in Public Collections: San Francisco Art Comn; Whitney Mus Am Art; Oakland Art Mus; San Francisco Mus Art.
Commissions: Wall decoration, USS Monterey.
Exhibitions: Six shows, De Young Mem Mus, San Francisco, 47-61; four shows, Art Inst Chicago Ann, 47-61; one-man shows, San Francisco Mus Art, 49 & 53; Corcoran Gallery Art, 57; Calif Palace of Legion of Honor, 62; plus many other group & one-man shows.
Awards: Purchase prizes, San Francisco Art Comn, 50 & 69; purchase prize, Whitney Mus Am Art, 55; prize San Francisco Mus Art, 60.
Bibliography: San Francisco Art Inst (bd trustees).
Mailing Address: 2955 Mountain Rd, Petaluma, CA 94952.

McCHRISTY, QUENTIN L
Painter, Designer
Preferred Media: Transparent Watercolor, Ink, Oils.
b Cushing, Okla, Jan 24, 21.
Study & Training: Okla State Univ, with Doel Reed, BA; Cincinnati Acad Art, with Helwhig & Crawford.
Work in Public Collections: Philbrook Art Ctr, Tulsa, Okla; Joslyn Mus Art, Omaha, Nebr; Butler Inst Am Art, Youngstown, Ohio; Pa State Univ, State College; Dean Weller, Col Fine Arts, Univ Ill, Urbana.
Commissions: Murals, Fort Worth Children's Mus & Wesley Found, Methodist Church, Stillwater, Okla; designed decorations glassware, Bartlett Collins, mfrs domestic & export glassware; plus others.
Exhibitions: 26th Biennial, Corcoran Gallery, Washington, D C, 59; Contemporary American Art, Oklahoma City, Okla, 60; All City Arts Festival, Los Angeles, Calif, 60-; Audubon Artist Nat Galleries, New York, N Y, 62; Pa Acad Fine Arts, Philadelphia, 63; plus others.
Teaching: Instr drawing, Okla State Univ; instr art, Fort Worth Children's Mus.
Positions: Art dir, Fort Worth Children's Mus, 50; Nat Artist Show judge, 65; Las Vegas Revolving Show judge, 69.
Awards: Purchase award, 47, prize, 48 & Ruskin Award, 62; Philbrook Art Ctr; painting exhib awards, Wind River Valley Nat Show, Dubois, Wyo, 61 & 65; Butler Mus Art Friends of Art Award, 69; plus others.
Bibliography: Article, In: Encycl Interazionale Degli Artisti, 70-71.
Memberships: Int Platform Asn.
Publications: Four pen drawings, Am Artist Mag, 6-8/64.
Mailing Address: 1301 N McKinley, Oklahoma City, OK 73106.

McCLELLAN, ROBERT JOHN
Painter, Illustrator
Preferred Media: Oils, Watercolors.
b Hopewell, N J, May 19, 06.
Study & Training: Fliesman Sch Art; Newark Indust Sch Art, Pratt Inst; Art Stud League New York, N Y; also with John L Carlson, Frank B A Linton, Paul Remmy & Harry Leith-Ross.
Work in Public Collections: Thompson Neely House Hist Mus.
Commissions: Pvt comns.
Exhibitions: Painters & Sculptors Soc Jersey City, N J; Allied Artists Am, Nat Acad Design Galleries; Fla Int, Lakeland; Salmagundi Club; Ogunquit Art Summer Show, Maine.
Teaching: Instr fine arts & owner, New Hope Sch Art, Pa, 47-52; instr art, New York Sch Crafts & Printing.
Positions: Retouch artist, var newspapers & mags, 27-71.

Awards: Medal of honor for best in show, N J Painters & Sculptors Soc, 50; first award for watercolor, Plainfield Art Asn N J, 57; Auth Award, N J Asn Teachers English, 68.
Memberships: Life mem Art Stud League New York.
Publications: Auth, Contemporary thinking, Am Photo-engraver, 58 & The Delaware Canal, Rutgers Univ Press, 67; contribr, var newspapers.
Mailing Address: Box 202, Lakeview St, Vinalhaven, ME 04863.

McCLELLAND, JEANNE C
Printmaker
b Edmeston, N Y.
Study & Training: Albright-Knox Sch Fine Arts, Buffalo, N Y, dipl; State Univ N Y Col Buffalo, BS(art educ).
Work in Public Collections: Mus Fine Arts, Springfield, Mass; St John Fisher Col, Rochester, N Y; Holyoke Mus, Mass.
Exhibitions: Cooperstown Art Asn, N Y, 53-71; Rochester Festival Relig Arts, N Y, 63-72; Artists of Central New York, Munson-Williams-Proctor Inst, Utica, N Y, 64, 68 & 69; Academic Artists, Springfield Art Mus, Mass, 65-72; Soc Am Graphic Artists, New York, N Y, 66.
Memberships: Munson-Williams-Proctor Inst; Acad Artists; Cooperstown Art Asn; Roberson Ctr-Arts & Sci.
Art Interests: Relief prints.
Dealer: Munson-Williams-Proctor Institute, 310 Genesee St, Utica, NY 13502.
Mailing Address: 17 Sharon St, Sidney, NY 13838.

McCLOSKEY, EUNICE LonCOSKE
Painter, Writer
Preferred Media: Oils, Watercolors.
b Johnsonburg, Pa, May 25, 04.
Study & Training: Columbia Univ.
Work in Public Collections: Thiel Col, Greenville, Pa; Pa State Univ; Ridgway Area Schs.
Exhibitions: Carnegie Mus, Pittsburgh, Pa, 50-70; Chautauqua Art Gallery, New York, N Y, 57; Langenheim Gallery, Greenville, 60; Ind Univ Art Gallery, Pa, 60; ten one-man shows, Upstairs Gallery, Pittsburgh, 62-72; plus many others.
Teaching: Lectr, Pa, N Y & Ohio, 40-70; instr watercolor, YMCA Art Classes, 67-69.
Positions: Judge, Nat League Am Pen Women, Philadelphia, 62; chmn Clothesline Exhib, Elk Co & Potter Co, Pa.
Awards: Assoc artists Pittsburgh Prize, 50 & Henry Posner Award, 53, Carnegie Mus; Aimee Jackson Short Award, Philadelphia, 62; first prize, Nat League Am Pen Women.
Bibliography: Douglas Naylor (auth), Fame beats a path to her door, 56 & Connie Kienzee (auth), Poet and painter, 69, Pittsburgh Press; Betty Lawrence (auth), Woman in love with life, Lutheran Nat Mag, 59.
Memberships: Assoc Artists Pittsburgh (dir, 59-60); Nat League Am Pen Women (nat poetry & short story ed); Philadelphia Art Alliance; fel Int Inst Art & Lett; Prof & Artistic Hall Fame.
Publications: Auth & illusr, six poetry bks, 38-70; auth, two biog & two novels, 52-72; auth & illusr, six art bks, 59-69.
Mailing Address: 403 Oak St, Ridgway, PA 15853.

McCLOSKEY, ROBERT
Painter, Illustrator
b Hamilton, Ohio, Sept 15, 14.
Study & Training: Vesper George Sch Art, Boston; Nat Acad Design, New York; Miami Univ, LittD; Mount Holyoke Col, LittD.
Work in Public Collections: May Massee Collection, William Allen White Libr, Emporia State Teachers Col, Kans.
Awards: Caldecott Medal, Am Libr Asn, 42 & 58.
Bibliography: Marc Simont (auth), Robert Mc Closkey, inventor, Horn Bk, 58; Robert McCloskey (film), Weston Woods Studio, 65.
Memberships: Fel Am Acad in Rome; Author's League; PEN.
Publications: Auth & illusr, Make way for ducklings, 41, Homer Price, 42, Blueberries for Sal, 47, Time of wonder, 57 & Burt Dow, deep water man, 63.
Mailing Address: Scott Islands, Harborside, ME 04642.

McCLOY, WILLIAM ASHBY
Painter, Sculptor
Preferred Media: Collage, Steel.
b Baltimore, Md, Jan 2, 13.
Study & Training: State Univ Iowa, BA, 33, MA, 36, MFA, 49 & PhD, 58.
Work in Public Collections: Walker Art Ctr, Minneapolis, Minn; Joslyn Art Ctr, Omaha, Nebr; Winnipeg Art Gallery; Libr Cong, Washington, D C.
Commissions: Three figure group sculpture, Conn Col, New London, 70.

Teaching: Asst prof drawing & painting, Univ Wis-Madison, 39-48; prof drawing & art hist & dir sch art, Univ Man, 50-54; prof studio & art hist, Conn Col, 54-
Mailing Address: 430 Kitemaug Rd, Uncasville, CT 06328.

McCLURE, THOMAS F
Sculptor, Educator
Preferred Media: Metals.
b Pawnee City, Nebr, Apr 17, 20.
Study & Training: Univ Nebr, BFA, 41; Washington State Col, 41; Cranbrook Acad Art, MFA, 47.
Work in Public Collections: Seattle Art Mus, Wash; Syracuse Mus Fine Arts, N Y; Detroit Inst Arts, Mich; Wright Mem Ctr, Beloit Col, Wis; DeWaters Art Mus, Flint, Mich.
Commissions: Large welded sculptural screen, comn by Skidmore Owings & Merrill, Ford Motor Co Cent Staff Off Bldg, Dearborn, Mich, 55; welded bronze relief, comn by Victor Gruen Assocs, Eastland Shopping Ctr, Detroit, Mich, 56; cast bronze relief, DeWaters Art Ctr, 58; welded bronze free standing sculpture, comn by Albert Kahn Assocs, Univ Mich Undergrad Libr, Ann Arbor, Mich, 59; cast bronze relief sculptures (ten), comn by Congregation Shaarey Zedek, Detroit, 69.
Exhibitions: Momentum Midcontinental, Chicago, Ill, 55; Pa Acad Fine Arts Ann, Philadelphia & Detroit, 58; 20th Ceramic Int, Syracuse, 58; Contemporary Sculpture 1961, Cincinnati Art Mus & John Herron Art Inst, 61; Drawings U S A, St Paul, Minn, 61.
Teaching: Instr design, Sch for Am Craftsmen, Alfred, N Y, 47-48; asst prof drawing & design, Univ Okla, 48-49; prof sculpture, Univ Mich, 49-
Awards: First prize for painting, Northwest Artists Ann, Seattle, 43; prize in sculpture, 12th Nat Ceramics Ann, Syracuse, 47; founders prize in sculpture, 45th Mich Artists Ann, Detroit, 54.
Dealer: Gilman Galleries, 103 E Oak St, Chicago, IL 60611.
Mailing Address: 3361 N Maple Rd, Ann Arbor, MI 48103.

McCORMICK, HARRY
Painter
Preferred Media: Oils, Graphics, Watercolors, Pastels.
b Bayonne, N J, June 12, 42.
Work in Public Collections: Newark Mus Art, N J; Ark Art Ctr, Little Rock; Wichita State Univ Collection, Kans; Canton Art Inst, Ohio; Univ Wyo Mus Art, Laramie.
Exhibitions: Selected Works by Contemp N J Artists, Newark Mus Art, 65-66; Meticulous Realism, Univ Md, 66-67; 20th Century Americans, ACA Galleries, New York, N Y, 70; Windows & Doors, Weckscher Mus, Huntington, N Y, 72; Trends in Realism, McCormick-Chase-Dobbs-Cigare-Sarsony, St Mary's Col, Md, 72.
Dealer: ACA Galleries, 25 E 73rd St, New York, NY 10021.
Mailing Address: 69 Gansevoort St, New York, NY 10014.

McCORMICK, JO MARY (JO MARY McCORMICK-SAKURAI)
Painter, Art Critic
b New York, N Y, Mar 6, 18.
Study & Training: Nat Acad Design, 47; Art Stud League New York, work scholar, 48; Columbia Univ, 55.
Commissions: Painting, Msgr Le Roy McWilliams, Highland Falls, N J, 64; Mus Mod Art; Yale Univ; Columbia Univ.
Exhibitions: Burr Gallery, 62; Graphics show, Nat Arts Club, 63; Barzansky Art Gallery, 65.
Positions: Art critic, Pictures on Exhib Mag, 59-; writer, Am Artist Mag, 72.
Memberships: Women's Press Club; life mem Art Stud League New York.
Publications: Illusr, Art: U S A now, 64; auth, Wings of thought and art, column in New York Column Newspaper, 71-72; contribr, Am Artist Mag, 71.
Mailing Address: 444 Second Ave, New York, NY 10010.

McCOSH, DAVID J
Painter
Preferred Media: Oils.
b Cedar Rapids, Iowa, July 11, 03.
Study & Training: Coe Col; Art Inst Chicago.
Work in Public Collections: Univ Ore Mus Art, Eugene; Portland Art Mus, Ore; Seattle Art Mus, Wash; IBM Corp; Portland State Univ, Ore.
Commissions: Murals, Chicago World's Fair for Century of Progress, 33, Pub Bldgs Admin Sect Fine Arts, Washington, D C for Post Off Kelso, Wash 36, Dept Interior Nat Parks, 40 & Beresford Post Off, S D, 42; paintings, U S Nat Bank, Eugene, 60.
Exhibitions: Golden Gate Int Expos & N Y World's Fair, 39-40; one-man show, Seattle Art Mus, 51; Seattle World's Fair, 62; one-man shows, Portland Art Mus, 64 & Univ Ore Mus Art, 67.

Teaching: Instr lithography, Art Inst Chicago, 33-34; prof art, Univ Ore, 34-70; vis prof, Art Inst Chicago, 36; vis prof, Mont State Univ, 47 & 53; vis prof, San Jose State Univ, 57.
Positions: Juror, nat & regional exhibs.
Awards: Seattle Art Mus Purchase Award; Portland Art Mus Watercolor Award, 70; Erb Mem Oil Painting Award, Univ Ore, 72.
Bibliography: Edward B Rowan (auth), article, In: Am Mag Art, 11/37.
Memberships: Portland Art Mus; Univ Ore Mus Art.
Publications: Illusr, The rainbow serpent, 62.
Mailing Address: 1870 Fairmount Blvd, Eugene, OR 97403.

McCOY, JASON
Art Dealer
b Middletown, Conn, Jan 26, 48.
Study & Training: Boston Univ.
Positions: Mgr, Marlborough Graphics Gallery, New York, N Y, 68-69; asst dir, Reese Palley Gallery, New York, 69-70; dir, Tibor de Nagy Gallery, New York, 70-72.
Specialty of Gallery: Twentieth century American & European painting.
Mailing Address: 16 W 16th St, New York, NY 10011.

McCOY, JOHN W, (II)
Painter, Educator
Preferred Media: Mixed Media.
b Pinole, Calif, May 11, 10.
Study & Training: Cornell Univ, BFA, 33; Am Sch, Fontainebleau, France, 30-32; also with N G Wyeth.
Work in Public Collections: Pa Acad Fine Arts, Philadelphia; Farnsworth Mus, Rockland, Maine; Montclair Mus, N J; Brandywine River Mus, Chadds Ford, Pa; Del Art Mus, Wilmington.
Commissions: Portrait of Gov Reed, State of Maine, State Capitol, Augusta, Maine, 70.
Exhibitions: Pa Acad Fine Arts Ann, 40-68; Carnegie Int, 50; Metrop Mus; Whitney Mus Am Art; Nat Acad Design, 72.
Teaching: Instr painting, Pa Acad Fine Arts, 47-
Awards: Whitmer Prize, Am Watercolor Soc, 55; Philadelphia Watercolor Club Award, Pa Acad Fine Arts, 55; W F B Morse Medal, Nat Acad Design, 72.
Memberships: Philadelphia Watercolor Club (v pres, 50-58); Nat Acad Design; Am Watercolor Soc; Audubon Artists; Wilmington Soc Fine Arts (trustee, 45-, v pres, 60-68).
Dealer: Coe Kerr Gallery, 49 E 82nd St, New York, NY 10028.
Mailing Address: R F D 1, Chadds Ford, PA 19317.

McCOY, WIRTH VAUGHAN
Painter, Educator
Preferred Media: Oils.
b Duluth, Minn, Dec 16, 13.
Study & Training: Univ Minn, BA, 37; Univ Iowa, MFA, 48; Acad Grande Chaumiere, cert painting & design, 51; Calif Sch Fine Art, 49; Acad Montmartre, 50; also with James Lechay, Maurice Lasansky, Mark Rothko, Yasuo Kunioshi & others.
Work in Public Collections: Portland Art Mus, Ore; Seattle Art Mus; Mineral Industs Mus, Pa State Univ; Univ Iowa; Wash State Univ.
Exhibitions: San Francisco Ann; Northwest Artists, Seattle; Artists Ore, Portland, 54; Centennial Exhib, Kansas City Art Inst, 62; Spokane Int Art Exhib, 64.
Teaching: Asst prof painting & drawing, Ore State Univ, 48-53; prof painting & drawing, resident artist & dir, Wash State Univ Ctr, 53-64; head dept art, Pa State Univ, 64-71; prof art, 71-
Memberships: Am Fedn Arts; Col Art Asn Am; Peale Club Philadelphia; Pa Acad Fine Arts; Art Alliances Cent Pa.
Mailing Address: 932 E McCormick, State College, PA 16801.

McCRACKEN, HAROLD
Art Administrator, Art Historian
b Colorado Springs, Colo, Aug 31, 94.
Study & Training: Hope Col, Hon Dr Lit, 57; Univ Alaska, Hon Dr Lit, 66; Colo State Univ, Hon Dr Humane Lett, 72.
Positions: Dir, Whitney Gallery Western Art & Buffalo Bill Hist Ctr, Cody, Wyo, 59-
Publications: Auth, Frederic Remington-artist of the old West, The Frederic Remington book, The Charles M Russell book, George Catlin and the old frontier & Portrait of the old West.
Mailing Address: Whitney Gallery of Western Art, Cody, WY 82414.

McCRACKEN, JOHN HARVEY
Sculptor, Painter
Preferred Media: Fiberglass, Wood.
b Berkeley, Calif, Dec 9, 34.
Study & Training: Calif Col Arts & Crafts, BFA, 62, grad work, 62-65.
Work in Public Collections: Mus Mod Art, New York, N Y; Whitney Mus Am Art, New York; Solomon R Guggenheim Mus, New York; Los Angeles Co Mus, Calif; Pasadena Art Mus, Calif.

Exhibitions: Primary Structures, Jewish Mus, New York, 66; American Sculpture of the Sixties, Los Angeles Co Mus Art, 67; 5th Guggenheim Int Exhib, Guggenheim Mus, 67; Art of the Real, Mus Mod Art, New York, 69; 69th Am Exhib, Art Inst Chicago, Ill, 70.
Teaching: Asst prof sculpture & painting, Univ Calif, Irvine & Los Angeles, 65-68; asst prof sculpture, Sch Visual Arts, New York, 68-69; asst prof sculpture & painting, Hunter Col, 71-
Awards: Nat Endowment for the Arts Award, 68.
Bibliography: Dennis Young & James Monte (auth), John McCracken: sculpture 1965-1969, Art Gallery Ont, Toronto, 69; John McCracken, Sonnabend Gallery, Paris, 69.
Mailing Address: c/o Nicholas Wilder Gallery, 8225½ Santa Monica Blvd, Los Angeles, CA 90046.

McCRACKEN, PHILIP
Sculptor
b Bellingham, Wash, Nov 14, 28.
Study & Training: Univ Wash, BA.
Work in Public Collections: Seattle Art Mus; Henssler Mem, Mount Erie, Wash; Weyerhaeuser Corp, Tacoma; Detroit Inst Art; Univ Ore Mus; also in pvt collections.
Exhibitions: One-man shows, Seattle Art Mus, 61 & Victoria Mus, B C; Corcoran Gallery Art, 66; Rutgers Univ, 68; Grand Rapids Art Mus, 69; plus many other group & one-man shows.
Awards: Norman Davis Award, 57; Artists of the Year, 64; Irene Wright Mem Award, Seattle Art Mus, 65.
Dealers: Williard Gallery, 29 E 72nd St, New York, NY 10021; Art Gallery of Greater Victoria, 1040 Moss St, Victoria, B C, Can.
Mailing Address: Guemes Island, Anacortes, WA 98221.

McCRAY, DOROTHY M
Printmaker, Educator
Preferred Media: Intaglio.
b Madison, S Dak, Oct 13, 15.
Study & Training: State Univ Iowa, BA, 37, MA, 39; Calif Col Arts & Crafts, MFA, 55; Tyler Sch Art, Temple Univ; Univ Florence; independent Europ study.
Exhibitions: Chicago Int Watercolor Exhib, Art Inst Chicago, Ill, 40-41; Fourth & Fifth Int Exhib Color Lithography, Cincinnati Art Inst, 56-57; Northwest Printmakers Int, 57; Grenchen Print & Drawing Triennial, Switz, 67; U S Off Info Traveling Show, Europe, 71-72; plus others.
Teaching: Assoc prof art, Western N Mex Univ.
Positions: Dir, Western N Mex Univ Art Study Prog in Italy, 69.
Memberships: Am Color Print Soc; Print Coun Am; Col Art Asn Am; Mus N Mex (artist's adv coun, 59-60); Am Fedn Arts.
Mailing Address: 802 N Cheyenne St, Silver City, NM 88061.

McCRAY, PORTER A
Art Administrator
Positions: Dir Asian Cult Prog, The JDR 3rd Fund.
Mailing Address: 50 Rockefeller Plaza, New York, NY 10020.

McCULLOUGH, JOSEPH
Art Administrator, Painter
Preferred Media: Acrylics.
b Pittsburgh, Pa, July 6, 22.
Study & Training: Cleveland Inst Art, dipl, 48; Yale Univ, with Lewis York, 49-50, BFA, 50, with Josef Albers, 50-51, MFA, 51.
Work in Public Collections: Cleveland Mus Art, Ohio; Dayton Art Inst, Ohio; Ohio Univ, Athens; Syracuse Univ, N Y; Youngstown Pub Schs, Ohio.
Commissions: Stained glass windows, St Edmund R C Church, Warren, Mich, 69.
Exhibitions: Corcoran Biennial Exhib, Washington, D C, 55; Audubon Artists Ann Exhib, New York, 56; Contemp Am Painting & Sculpture, Univ Ill, 57; All Ohio Painting & Sculpture Show, Dayton Art Inst, 67; Cleveland Arts Prize Exhib, 71.
Positions: Dir, Cleveland Inst Art, 55-; secy, Cleveland Art Asn, 55-; pres, Nat Asn Schs Art, 62-65; chmn fine arts adv comt, Cleveland City Planning Comn, 65-
Awards: Spec award for painting, Cleveland Mus Art, 58; purchase award for painting, Dayton Art Inst, 67; Cleveland Arts Prize for visual arts, Women's City Club Cleveland, 71.
Memberships: Col Art Asn (bd dirs, 63-68).
Publications: Contribr, Art in Cleveland architecture, AIA handbook to Cleveland architecture, Reinhold, 58; contribr, The enamelist, Kenneth Bates, World, 66.
Mailing Address: 2223 Delaware Dr, Cleveland, OH 44106.

MACDONALD, GRANT
Painter, Illustrator
b Montreal, P Q, June 27, 09.
Study & Training: Ont Col Art, Toronto; Art Stud League New York; Heatherley's Art Sch, London, Eng.

Work in Public Collections: Redpath Libr, McGill Univ; Hart House, Univ Toronto; Art Gallery Toronto; Queen's Univ; Kingston Coll Inst; also in galleries, schs, univs, libr & pvt collections, Can, U S A & Eng.
Exhibitions: Nine shows, Art Asn Montreal, 41-68; Art Asn Kingston, 48-55, 67 & 68; Royal Can Acad, 49, 51-55 & 67; Ont Soc Artists, 49, 51-55, 66 & 67; seven shows, Art Gallery Hamilton, 49-68; plus many others.
Teaching: Instr figure drawing, summer sch, Queen's Univ, Kingston, 48, 52, 53, 64 & 65.
Awards: Medal, Art Dirs Club, Toronto, 52.
Memberships: Royal Can Acad; Ont Soc Artists.
Publications: Illusr, Shakespeare for young players, 42, Haida, 46, Behind the log, 47, Sunshine sketches of a little town, 48 & A masque of Aesop, 52; plus others.
Mailing Address: Tarquin, 32 Lakeshore Rd, Kingston, Ont, Can.

MacDONALD, THOMAS REID
Art Administrator, Painter
Preferred Media: Oils.
b Montreal, P Q, June 28, 08.
Study & Training: With Adam Sherriff Scott & Edmond Dyonnet.
Work in Public Collections: Nat Gallery Can, Ottawa; Montreal Mus Fine Arts, P Q; Art Gallery Windsor, Ont; Art Gallery Hamilton, Ont; Father's Confederation Art Gallery, Charlottetown, Prince Edward Island.
Exhibitions: New York World's Fair, N Y, 39; London World's Fair, Eng; Royal Can Acad.
Teaching: Instr life drawing & painting, Art Asn Montreal.
Positions: Head dept fine arts, Mount Allison Univ, Sackville, N B, 45-46; dir, Art Gallery Hamilton, Ont, 47-
Memberships: Royal Can Acad.
Mailing Address: 175 Dufferin St, Hamilton, Ont, Can.

MacDONALD, THOREAU
Illustrator, Painter
b Toronto, Ont, Apr 21, 01.
Study & Training: With J E H MacDonald.
Work in Public Collections: Nat Gallery Can; Art Gallery Toronto.
Exhibitions: Wembley; Paris; Coronation; Tate Gallery, London, Eng; N Y World's Fair.
Publications: Illusr, Maria Chapdelaine, Macmillan, 21 & 38; auth, The group of seven, McGraw, 44; illusr, Thornhill: an Ontario village, 64 & Old time Thornhill, 70, FitzGerald; plus over 200 others.
Mailing Address: Box 197, Thornhill, Ont, Can.

MacDONALD, WILLIAM ALLAN
Art Historian, Educator
b Lorain, Ohio, July 28, 11.
Study & Training: Oberlin Col, AB; Johns Hopkins Univ, AM & PhD.
Teaching: Prof hist art, Western Md Col; prof art & archaeol, George Washington Univ, 59-
Positions: Former asst dir, Baltimore Mus Art, Md.
Memberships: Archaeol Inst Am.
Publications: Contribr, Hellenistic Art, New Cath Encycl.
Mailing Address: Dept of Art & Archaeology, George Washington University, Washington, DC 20006.

MACDONALD-WRIGHT, STANTON
Painter
Preferred Media: Oils.
b Charlottesville, Va, July 8, 90.
Study & Training: Sorbonne, with Focillon, Ecole Beaux-Arts, Colorossi & Acad Grande Chaumiere, Paris, France.
Work in Public Collections: Large mus in the U S, Eng, France, Poland, Italy, Japan & others; also in many pvt collections.
Commissions: Murals for many schs, libr & pub bldgs.
Exhibitions: Neue Kunst Salon, Munich, Ger; Bernheim Jeune, Paris; Carrol Galleries, New York; Smithsonian Inst; Los Angeles Mus Art; retrospective, Univ Calif, Los Angeles; plus others.
Teaching: Prof Oriental art & Iconography, Univ Calif, Los Angeles, Scripps Col, Univ Southern Calif, Univ Hawaii, Art Stud League New York & others.
Bibliography: Lloyd Goodrich & John Baur (auth), American art of our century, Praeger, 61; Giov Micheli (auth), La sincromia, Libr Editrice Baroni, Lucca, 63; Michel Seuphor (auth), L'art abstrait, Galerie Maeght, Paris, Vols I & II, 71-72.
Art Interests: Oriental art.
Publications: Auth, Blueprint for a textbook on art, Col Art J, 45; auth, Beyond aesthetics (Japanese), Tokyo, 55; auth, Treatise on color (reprint), Smithsonian Press, 67.
Mailing Address: 336 Bellino Dr, Pacific Palisades, CA 90272.

McDONNELL, JOSEPH ANTHONY
Sculptor
Preferred Media: Bronze, Steel, Marble.
b Detroit, Mich, Oct 20, 36.
Study & Training: Univ Notre Dame, with Ivan Mestrovic, BFA & MFA; Acad Belli Arte, Florence, Italy.
Work in Public Collections: Milwaukee Pub Mus, Wis.
Commissions: Play sculptured tumblers, Nanuet Mall, Homart Develop Co, N Y, 69; nine fabricated sculptures, E & W Towne Malls, Madison, Wis, 70; stainless steel suspended sculpture, Lakehurst Shopping Ctr, Waukegan, Ill, 71; stainless steel fountain, Janesville Mall, Wis, 72; lunarscape sculpture, Fashion Square Mall, Saginaw, Mich, 72.
Exhibitions: U S Info Serv Am Artists in Florence, 63; Mostra Mercato Nat Arte Contemporanea, Florence, 63; one-man shows, McNay Art Inst, San Antonio, Tex, 64; Flint Art Inst, Mich, 64 & John Wanamaker Fine Arts Gallery, Philadelphia, Pa, 70.
Bibliography: Glen Tucker (auth), rev, In: San Antonio Light, 2/16/64; rev, In: Philadelphia Inquirer, 11/1/70; Harriet Schiff (auth), article, In: Detroit News, 9/17/71.
Mailing Address: Guard Hill Rd, Bedford, NY 10506.

McDONOUGH, JOHN JOSEPH
Collector, Patron
b Carbondale, Pa.
Study & Training: St John's Col, Toledo, Ohio, BS; Loyola Univ Med Sch, MD.
Positions: Bd trustees, Friends Am Art, 63-66; gen chmn, Youngstown Fine Arts Festival for Proj Hope, 63-72; trustee, Butler Inst Am Art, Youngstown, Ohio, 68-71.
Memberships: Art Collectors Club Am.
Collection: Eighteenth, nineteenth and twentieth century American art.
Mailing Address: 1005 Belmont Ave, Youngstown, OH 44504.

MC ELCHERAN, WILLIAM HODD
Designer, Sculptor
b Hamilton, Ont, July 9, 27.
Study & Training: Ont Col Art, Toronto.
Work in Public Collections: Art Gallery Hamilton, Ont; Art Gallery London, Ont; York Univ, Toronto, Ont; sch archit, Univ Toronto.
Commissions: Archit design & sculpture, McMaster Divinity Col, Hamilton, Ont, 60; wood sculpture, Briarcliff Col, Sioux City, Iowa, 62; mahogany stations of the cross, St Augustines Col, Scarboro, Ont, 66; plastic relief, Walkerton Fed Bldg, Ont, 70; sculpture, St Michael's Libr, Univ Toronto, 72.
Exhibitions: Sculpture '67, Toronto, 67; one-man shows, Roberts Gallery, Toronto & Art Gallery Hamilton, 69; People in the Park, Stratford, Ont, 70; Fed Int Medaille, Cologne, Ger, 71.
Teaching: Instr carving, Ont Col Art, 63-66; artist-in-residence, sch archit, Univ Toronto, 71-72.
Positions: Art dir & designer, Valley City Mfg Co, Dundas, 52-56; designer, Brown, Brisley & Brown, Architects, Toronto, 56-60.
Awards: Lt Gov Medal, Lt Gov Ont, 49; Can Coun Sr Arts Award, 69; Aviva Sculpture Prize, Aviva Chap, Hadassah, 69.
Bibliography: Paul Duval (auth), William McElcheran, The Hamilton Spectator, 11/69; Kay Kritzwizer (auth), article, In: Toronto Globe & Mail, 5/71; Eric Freifeld (auth), William McElcheran, Artscan Mag, 4-5/71.
Memberships: Assoc Royal Can Acad; Sculptors Soc Can; Arts & Letters Club Toronto.
Publications: Auth, The revolution in liturgical art, brief to the bishops, Longmans Green, 65; illusr, By the circus sands, 67.
Dealer: Roberts Gallery, 641 Yonge St, Toronto, Ont, Can.
Mailing Address: 191 Balsam Ave, Toronto 13, Ont, Can.

McEWEN, JEAN
Painter
b Montreal, P Q, Dec 14, 23.
Work in Public Collections: Mus Mod Art; Walker Art Ctr, Minneapolis, Minn; Albright-Knox Art Gallery; Ottawa Mus; Toronto Mus; plus others.
Commissions: Stained glass window, Sir George Williams Univ, 66; murals, Toronto Airport & Plase Arts, Montreal, 67.
Exhibitions: Four one-man shows, Gallery Godart-Lefort, Montreal, 62-69; Dunn Int Exhib, Tate Gallery, London, Eng, 63; one-man show, Gallery, Montreal, 63; four one-man shows, Gallery Moos, Toronto, 63-69; one-man show, Mayer Gallery, Paris, France, 64; plus others.
Awards: Quebec Art Competition, 62; Jessie Dow Award, Montreal Spring Show, 64.
Memberships: Academician Royal Can Acad Arts.
Publications: Illusr, La pain quotidien, 64.
Dealer: Marlborough-Godard Ltd, 1490 Sherbrooke St W, Montreal 109, P Q, Can.
Mailing Address: 580 Davaar St, Montreal 153, P Q, Can.

McFEE, JUNE KING
Educator, Writer
b Seattle, Wash, June 3, 17.
Study & Training: Whitman Col, 35-37; Univ Wash, BA, 39; Cent Wash Col, MEd, 54; Stanford Univ, EdD, 57; Archipenko Sch Art; Cornish Sch Art; also with Amede Ozenfant.
Exhibitions: Seattle Art Mus; Seattle Artists Summer Shows; Wash State Invitational; Stanford Art Gallery Faculty Exhibs.
Teaching: From instr to asst prof art educ, Stanford Univ, 55-63; vis assoc prof, Ariz State Univ, 64-65; from assoc prof to prof art educ & dir, Inst Community Studies, Univ Ore, 65-.
Positions: Pres, Pac Regional, Nat Art Educ Asn, 67-69; ed, Studies in Art Educ.
Memberships: Nat Art Educ Asn; Soc Res in Art Educ.
Research: Study of the creative potential of academically superior adolescents, supported by a Ford Foundation grant to a secondary education project at Stanford University; study of the City for Children supported by the American Institute of Architects.
Publications: Auth, Creative problem solving abilities in art of academically superior adolescents, Nat Art Educ, 68, Visual communication in educational media: theory into practice, 69 & Preparation for art, Wadsworth Publ, 70; auth, Art for academically talented, Encycl Educ, Macmillan, 72; contribr, articles, In: Res in Art Educ & Western Arts Bull; plus many others.
Mailing Address: Institute for Community Studies, School of Architecture & Allied Arts, University of Oregon, Eugene, OR 97403.

McGARRELL, JAMES
Painter, Educator
b Indianapolis, Ind, Feb 22, 30.
Study & Training: Indiana Univ, AB, 53; Skowhegan Sch Painting & Sculpture, 53; Univ Calif, Los Angeles, MA, 55; Stuttgard Acad Fine Arts, Ger, Fulbright fel, 56.
Work in Public Collections: Whitney Mus Am Art & Mus Mod Art, New York, N Y; Mus Mod Art, Paris, France; Mus Hambourg, Ger; San Francisco Inst Art, Calif.
Exhibitions: Dokumenta III, Kassel, Ger; Americans, Art Inst Chicago, Ill; Salons Galeries Pilotes, Lausanne, Switz, Venice Biennale, Italy, 68; Carnegie Int, Pittsburgh, Pa.
Teaching: Vis artist, Reed Col, 56-59; prof fine arts, Ind Univ, 59-
Awards: Nat Inst Arts & Lett citation & grant, 63; Guggenheim Found fel, 64; Nat Endowment on the Arts Award for artists who teach, 66.
Bibliography: Peter Selz (auth), New images of man, Mus Mod Art, New York, 59; Giovanni Testori (auth), McGarrell, Claude Bernard (Paris), 67; Norman Geske (auth), Venice 34, the figurative tradition in recent American art, Smithsonian, 68.
Memberships: Col Art Asn Am (bd dirs, 70-).
Dealers: Allan Frumkin Galleries, 41 E 57th St, New York, NY 10022; Galerie Claude Bernard, 5 Rue des Beaux Arts, Paris, France.
Mailing Address: Dept of Fine Arts, Indiana University, Bloomington, IN 47401.

McGARVEY, ELSIE SIRATZ
Curator, Lecturer
b Bethlehem, Pa, May 25, 12.
Study & Training: Philadelphia Col Art, Pa.
Collections Arranged: Facts and Fads of Fashion—Exhibition of Period Costumes and Accessories, Beaver Col, 65; The Bride in Fashion—Three Centuries of Wedding Gowns, 66 & The Story of Samplers (display of samplers and embroideries from 1662 to the present), 71, Philadelphia Mus Art.
Teaching: Instr-lectr fashion illus, Beaver Col Fine Art Dept, 39-68; instr-lectr fashion design, Philadelphia Col Art, 42-63.
Positions: Artist, Vogue-Vogue Pattern Serv, Conte Nast Publ, Greenwich, Conn, 34-39; cur costume & textiles, Philadelphia Mus Art, 56-
Awards: Citizen of week, Willow Grove Guide, 65; personality of week, Times Chronicle, 67; Temple Univ Woman of Achievement, 70.
Bibliography: Portrait of a professor, Beaver Col Alumni J, 2/66.
Memberships: Am Asn Univ Prof; Fashion Group Philadelphia; Philadelphia Art Alliance; Acad Fine Arts & Peale Club; Am Asn Mus.
Publications: Auth, The fashion wing, Philadelphia Mus Art Bull, autumn 61.
Mailing Address: Philadelphia Museum of Art, P O Box 7646, Philadelphia, PA 19101.

McGEE, OLIVIA JACKSON
Painter, Illustrator
Preferred Media: Watercolors.
b S C, Nov 19, 15.
Study & Training: Limestone Col, BA; Clemson Univ Sch Visual

Arts; Rex Brandt's Sch Painting, Europe & Corona del Mar, Calif; Whitney Sch Watercolor, Maine; painting with Eliot O'Hara.
Work in Public Collections: Sandlapper Gallery, Columbia, S C; Red Piano Gallery, Hilton Head Island, S C; Chemstrand Corp, Empire State Blvd, New York, N Y; People's Nat Bank & Trust Co, Greenville, S C; Gov Mansion, Columbia, S C.
Exhibitions: Greenville Co Mus Art, Greenville, S C, 69; Contemp S C Artists, 70; Picken's Co Artists, Rudolf E Lee Gallery, Clemson Univ, S C, 71 & 72; Guild S C Artists, Columbia; Greenville Arts Festival.
Teaching: Instr watercolor, Clemson Univ Continuing Educ Ctr, 63-; instr watercolor McGee Sch Painting, Clemson, 72.
Positions: Illusr, Clemson Univ Exten Serv, 50-56; state pres, Nat League Am Pen Women, 66-68; mem, Pickens Co Arts Comn, 71-72.
Awards: Best in show awards, Greenville Arts Festival, 68, Watson Village Arts Festival, 69 & Anderson Co Fair, 69.
Bibliography: Jack Morris (auth), Contemporary artists of South Carolina, Greenville Co Mus Art, 70; Charles M Israel (auth), Artist Olivia McGee, Sandlapper Mag, 71.
Memberships: Greenville Co Artists Guild; Anderson Co Art Asn; Guild S C Artists; assoc mem Am Watercolor Soc.
Mailing Address: 221 Riggs Dr, Clemson, SC 29631.

McGEE, WILLIAM DOUGLAS
Painter, Educator
Preferred Media: Acrylics, Oils, Watercolors.
b Syracuse, N Y, May 11, 25.
Study & Training: Black Mountain Col; Univ N Mex, BFA; Ind Univ, MFA; also with Franz Kline, Jack T Workov & Adja Yunkers.
Work in Public Collections: Dallas Mus Fine Arts, Tex; Baltimore Mus Fine Art, Md; Albright-Knox Mus, Buffalo, N Y; Jonson Mus, Albuquerque, N Mex, Tate Gallery, London, Eng.
Exhibitions: Metropolitan Artists, Nat Arts Club, New York, N Y, 59; American Abstract Art, Chrysler Mus, Provincetown, Mass, 59-60; Younger American Painters, Am Acad Arts & Lett, New York, 59-61; Seymour Knox Collection, Yale Univ, 61; Wit & Whim in 20th Century Art, Am Fedn Arts, 62-63.
Teaching: Asst prof painting, Brown Univ, 56-60; asst prof painting, Hunter Col, 62-68; assoc prof painting, Lehman Col, 68-
Awards: First pruchase prize for prints, Dallas Mus Fine Arts, 49; res awards, 68 & 69, City Univ New York.
Dealer: Max Hutchinson Gallery, 127 Greene St, New York, NY 10012.
Mailing Address: Titicus Lake Rd, Purdy Station, NY 10578.

McGEE, WINSTON EUGENE
Painter, Art Administrator
Preferred Media: Oils, Acrylics.
b Salem, Ill, Sept 4, 24.
Study & Training: Univ Mo, BJ, 48, MA, 49; Univ Wis; Ecole Superieure Beaux-Arts, 50-51; Atelier-M Jean Souverbie, French Nat Acad, 51.
Work in Public Collections: Whitney Mus Am Art, New York, N Y; Calif Palace of Legion of Honor, San Francisco, Calif; Philadelphia Mus Art, Pa; Smithsonian Inst, Washington, D C; Indianapolis Mus Art, Ind.
Commissions: Wall tapestry, Inst Esthetique, Paris, France; mural, Lincoln Commons, Lake Erie Col, Painesville, Ohio.
Exhibitions: Am Artists in Europe, Paris, 53; 11 Artists in Europe, Int Cult Exhib, Paris, 58; one-man show, Trabie Gallery, New York, 61; 50th Yr Anniversary Traveling Show, Cleveland Mus, 68; Lincoln Fine Arts Ctr Dedication Exhib, 70.
Positions: Head dept art, Lake Erie Col, 52-69; new mkt design rev bd, Lake County, Ohio, 68-72; actg chmn art, Cleveland State Univ, 69-
Awards: Fulbright scholar to Paris, 51; Cleveland Mus May Show Jury Award, 68; Annie McEntree Norton Award Painting & Graphic, Univ Mo.
Bibliography: Dedication catalogue, Lincoln Fine Arts Ctr, 70; article, In: Graphic Artists, 72.
Memberships: Cleveland Coun Arts; Col Art Asn Am; Cleveland Art Community.
Mailing Address: 3336 Maynard Rd, Shaker Heights, OH 44122.

McGEOCH, LILLIAN JEAN
Painter, Sculptor
Preferred Media: Oils, Bronze.
b Sundridge, Ont, Jan, 03.
Study & Training: Cent Tech Commercial Art Course; Ont Col Art; sculpture with Alfred Howell & Emmanuel Hahn; painting with William J Beatty.
Work in Public Collections: Halifax Art Asn.

Exhibitions: Maritime Art Asn, Halifax, N S, 65; N S Soc Artists, Halifax, 66; Douglas Art Gallery, Toronto, 66; Etobicoke Artists, Islington, 67-68; Lambton Gallery, Toronto, 70-71.
Teaching: Instr drawing & painting, Burnamthorpe Col, 52-; instr drawing & painting, Scarlett Heights Col, 60-
Positions: Commercial artist, Brigden's Ltd, Toronto, 20-26; fashion designer, Photo Engravers, Toronto, 26-28.
Awards: Etobicoke Art Group award of merit, 62 & 63.
Memberships: Womens Art Asn Toronto (v pres, 64-66); N S Soc Artists (v pres & secy, 61-63); Sculptors Nine Toronto; Etobicoke Art Group (v pres & secy, 52-); Women's Art Asn Hamilton.
Dealers: Lambton Gallery, Dundas St, Toronto, Ont, Can; Fine Art Gallery Eatons, Yonge St, Toronto, Ont, Can.
Mailing Address: 15 King Georges Rd, Toronto 18, Ont, Can.

MAC GILLIS, ROBERT DONALD
Painter, Illustrator
Preferred Media: Watercolors.
b Bayonne, N J, June 30, 36.
Study & Training: Mech Inst, New York, N Y; Newark Sch Fine Arts, N J.
Work in Public Collections: Grover M Hermann Fine Arts Ctr, Marietta Col, Ohio.
Exhibitions: Allied Artists Am, New York; Knickerbocker Artists, New York; Acad Artists, Springfield, Mass; Mainstreams 72, Marietta, Ohio; Salmagundi Club, New York.
Positions: Indust artist, Gen Dynamics Elec Boat Div, Groton, Conn, 60-
Awards: Hon mention, Acad Artists, 71; Salmagundi Award, Salmagundi Club, 72; best in show, Nat Minature Art Soc, 72.
Memberships: Salmagundi Club; Providence Watercolor Soc; Mystic Art Asn; Am Artists Prof League.
Mailing Address: 71 Blueberry Hill Rd, Groton, CT 06340.

McGINNIS, CHRISTINE
Painter
Preferred Media: Acrylics, Graphics.
b Philadelphia, Pa.
Study & Training: Pa Acad Fine Arts.
Work in Public Collections: Mus Nat Sci, Philadelphia; Civic Ctr Mus, Philadelphia; Free Libr Philadelphia; Am Embassy, Dublin, Ireland; Pa Acad Fine Arts.
Exhibitions: Pa Acad Fine Art Nat Ann, 59; Philadelphia Art Mus Regional Exhib, 64; Brooklyn Art Mus 14th Nat Exhib, New York, 65; Am Express Pavillion, New York World's Fair, 66; Libr of Cong 20th Nat, Washington, D C, 67.
Awards: Thomas Eakins Prize, 58 & H S Morris Mem Drawing Prize, 61, Pa Acad Fine Arts; Cresson traveling scholar, 60.
Publications: Illusr for Mademoiselle Mag, 61, Chelsea Rev No 12, 62 & Ctr City Mag, 63.
Dealer: Gallery Madison 90, 1248 Madison Ave, New York, NY 10028.
Mailing Address: 5929 Devon Pl, Awbury Arboretum, Philadelphia, PA 19138.

McGONAGLE, WILLIAM ALBERT
Art Administrator
b Duluth, Minn, Dec 23, 24.
Study & Training: Univ Minn, BS(art educ & soc studies), 48; Univ Mich, MFA, 51; Buffalo Mus Sci, N Y, 48-49; Albright-Knox Art Gallery, Buffalo, 48-49.
Collections Arranged: Mary Cassatt Among the Impressionists, 69; The Thirties Decade: American Artists and their European Contemporaries, 71.
Positions: Cur, Detroit Inst Arts, Mich, 51-61; cur, Honolulu Acad Arts, Hawaii, 61-65; cur, Joslyn Art Mus, Omaha, Nebr, 65-71, dir, 72-
Memberships: Asn Art Mus Dir; Am Asn Mus; Nebr Arts Coun (bd dirs); Historic Gen Dodge House, Council Bluffs, Iowa (trustee).
Publications: Ed & auth, Mary Cassat among the Impressionists (catalogue), 69; ed & auth, The thirties decade: American artists and their European contemporaries (catalogue), 71.
Mailing Address: Joslyn Art Museum, 2200 Dodge St, Omaha, NE 60102.

McGOUGH, CHARLES E
Printmaker, Educator
Preferred Media: Graphics.
b Elmhurst, Ill, Aug 2, 27.
Study & Training: Southwestern Univ; Ray Vogue Commercial Art

Sch, dipl; Univ Tulsa, BA & MA; N Tex State Univ; also with Hardin Simmons.
Work in Public Collections: Boston Mus; Philbrook Mus; Dallas Mus Fine Arts; Little Rock Mus Fine Arts; Mus Mod Art.
Commissions: Genre mural, Southern Hills Country Club, Tulsa, Okla, 56; mural, E Tex State Univ, Commerce, Tex, 63; mural, Goodfellow AFB, San Angelo, Tex, 64; several graphic works, First Nat Bank, Dallas, Tex, 65; several graphic works, Southwestern Life Ins Co, Dallas, 67.
Exhibitions: Nat Serigraph Ann, Brooklyn Mus Art; Drawing U S A, Walker Art Ctr, 63 & 66; Nat Print Ann, Boston Mus Fine Arts, 65 & 67; Southwest Print & Drawing Ann, Dallas Mus Fine Arts, 67, 68 & 70; Nat Print & Drawing Ann, Okla Art Ctr, 69-72.
Teaching: Instr art, N R Crogier Tech High Sch, Dallas, 52-56; head art dept, E Tex State Univ, 56-
Positions: Owner, McGough Advert Co, 45-50; art dir, Crane Advert, Tulsa, 50-52.
Awards: Graphic purchase award, Boston Univ Mus Show, 65; Southwest Print & Drawing Ann Award, Dallas Mus Fine Arts, 67; graphic purchase award, Nat Print Ann, Okla Art Ctr, 71.
Memberships: Southwest Print & Drawing Soc; Tex Asn Schs Art.
Publications: Auth, Print painting, Dallas Morning News, 67; auth, Serigraphy, Dallas Times Herald, 68; auth, Serigraph and the total image, Tex Trends Art Educ, 68.
Dealer: Troup Gallery, 2211 Cedar Springs, Dallas, TX 75428.
Mailing Address: 1603 Walnut, Commerce, TX 75428.

McGOWIN, WILLIAM ED
Sculptor, Painter
Preferred Media: Plexiglass, Urethane Foam.
b Hattiesburg, Miss, June 2, 38.
Study & Training: Miss Southern Col, BS; Univ Ala, MA.
Work in Public Collections: Whitney Mus Am Art, New York, N Y; Corcoran Gallery Art, Washington, D C; Addison Mus Art, Andover, Mass; Philadelphia Mus Art, Pa; State Univ N Y, Potsdam.
Exhibitions: Whitney Ann Am Sculpture, 68; Plastic Presance, Jewish Mus, New York, 69; Gilliam Krebs McGowin, Corcoran Gallery, 69; Washington 20 Years, Baltimore Mus Art, 70; New Washington Painting, Hayden Gallery, Mass Inst Technol, Cambridge, 71; plus one other.
Teaching: Chmn sculpture, Corcoran Sch Art, 69-
Awards: Nat Endowment for the Arts Award, 67; Casandra Found Award, 71.
Bibliography: Rose (auth), Gallery without walls, Art in Am, 68; Footlick (auth), Careers, Dow Jones & Co, Princeton, N J, 69; Hopps & Osnos (auth), 3 Washington artists Gilliam Krebs McGowin, Art Int, 70.
Mailing Address: 1884 Columbia Rd, Washington, DC 20009.

McGRATH, JAMES ARTHUR
Art Administrator, Painter
Preferred Media: Oils, Earth Pigments, Mixed Media.
b Tacoma, Wash, Sept 2, 28.
Study & Training: Cent Wash State Col, 45-48; Univ Ore, BS, 50; Montana State Univ, summer 51; Univ Wash, 52; Staatliche Akademie den Bildenden Kunste, Karlsruhe, Ger, 58-59, with H A P Grieshaber.
Work in Public Collections: Mus N Mex, Santa Fe; Marjorie Weiss Gallery, Belleview, Wash; Hills Gallery, Santa Fe; New Westinghouse Bldg, Oklahoma City, Okla; Panelette Corp, Skokie, Ill.
Commissions: Hopi (painting), Bur Indian Affairs, Washington, D C, 70.
Exhibitions: Seattle Art Mus, Wash, 51; Zimmer Galerie Franck, Frankfurt am Main, Ger, 56; Galerie Dorothea Loehr, Frankfurt am Main, 61; Five Shows, Mus N Mex, 64-71; Butler Inst Am Arts, Youngstown, Ohio, 66.
Collections Arranged: Am Indian exhibs & catalogs, Ctr for Arts of Indian Am, Washington, D C, 63-70; Am Indian Dance Prog, The White House, Washington, D C, 65; American Indian Arts, Riverside Mus, 65; Spec Am Indian Exhibs, U S Dept State, 66-69; American Indian Arts, Edinburgh Festival, 66, Berlin Festival, 66, Ankara, Turkey, 66, Alaskan Centennial, 67, Mus Bellas Artes, Buenos Aires, Arg, 67, Bibliot Nac, Santiago, Chile, 68 & Mexican Olympics, Mexico City, 68; 50 Years with Laura Gilpin, Photographer, 69; Dance and Indian children & Native American Musical Instruments, Ctr for Arts of Indian Am, Washington, D C, 70-
Teaching: Instr art, Richland Pub Schs, Wash, 52-55; instr & dir art, U S Dept Defense Schs in Ger, France, Italy & Ethiopia, 55-62; instr written & visual arts, Inst Am Indian Arts, Santa Fe, 62-
Positions: Exhib consult & designer, Ctr for Arts of Indian Am, 63-70; Am Indian spec, exhibs & projs, U S State Dept, 66-69; dir arts, U S Dept Interior, Bur Indian Affairs, Inst Am Indian Arts, 64-72, dir spec projs, 72-

Awards: First prize for Spawning Salmon (stone sculpture), Bellevue Fair, Wash, 52; first prize for Sequafnehma (painting), Mus N Mex, 64; hon mention for Bear Hunter (bronze sculpture), Mus N Mex, 69.
Bibliography: H Remschardt (auth), Den kräften der erde nah, Frankfurter Rundschau, 5/7/62; Sally Hayman (auth), Shadow of Indian spirits by sun, lamp and fire, Seattle Post Intelligencer, 11/19/67; Albie Muldavin & John Noel Chandler (auth), Correspondence, Arts Can, 6-7/71.
Memberships: Int Soc Educ through the Arts; UNESCO Conf on Creativity, Hamburg, Ger; Smithsonian Inst; plus others.
Research: Native American cultures (Indian, Aleut, Eskimo) and their contributions to contemporary life styles.
Art Interests: Intercultural arts specialist.
Publications: Auth, Powhoge: the Martinez family of San Ildefonso Pueblo, 67; auth, Quilaut: the art of getting in touch with the spirits, 67; auth, Art and Indian children, 70; auth, Dance and Indian children, 72; auth, Native American musical instruments, 72; plus others.
Dealer: Hills Gallery, 121 Lincoln Ave, Santa Fe, NM 87501.
Mailing Address: 948 Acequia Madre, Santa Fe, NM 87501.

McGRATH, KYRAN MURRAY
Art Administrator
b Chicago, Ill, Aug 24, 34.
Study & Training: Georgetown Univ, BSS(cum laude), 56, LLB, 59.
Positions: Dir, Am Asn Mus, 68-
Memberships: Am Soc Asn Exec; Am Asn State & Local Hist; Nat Trust for Hist Preserv; Int Coun Mus.
Publications: Auth, numerous articles, In: Mus News, Compact & Art in Am, 68-; auth, 1971 Financial & salary survey, Am Asn Mus, 71.
Mailing Address: American Association of Museums, 2233 Wisconsin Ave N W, Washington, DC 20007.

McGREGOR, JACK R
Museum Director
b Coffeyville, Kans, Mar 17, 30.
Study & Training: Univ Kans, BA(chem), 52; Brown Univ, 52-53; Univ Ital per Stranieri, Perugia, Italy, summer 56; Harvard Univ, 57-58; New York Univ, Metrop Mus Art fel, 57-58; also independent study in Europe.
Collections Arranged: Assisted in formation & cataloging Wrightsman Collection, 63.
Positions: Admin asst, Metrop Mus Art, 57-62; dir, M H de Young Mem Mus, 63-69; dir, San Antonio Mus Asn, 69-
Awards: Order of the North Star, King of Sweden, 68.
Mailing Address: 3801 Broadway, San Antonio, TX 78209.

McGREW, RALPH BROWNELL
Painter
Preferred Media: Oils, Charcoal.
b Columbus, Ohio, Sept 6, 16.
Study & Training: Otis Art Inst, Los Angeles, Calif, four yrs with full scholarship & spec faculty awards; also with Edouard Vysekal, Ralph Holmes & E Roscoe Shrader.
Work in Public Collections: Cowboy Hall Fame Permanent Collection, Oklahoma City, Okla; DeSaisset Gallery, Univ Santa Clara, Calif; Read Mullan Gallery Western Art, Phoenix, Ariz; Mus Northern Ariz Permanent Collection, Flagstaff, Ariz; Diamond M Mus, Snyder, Tex.
Exhibitions: Cowboy Artists Am, Cowboy Hall Fame, Oklahoma City; Death Valley Invitational, Calif; All-California Invitational, Laguna Beach, 59-62; Charles Russell Rendezvous Invitational, Helena, Mont, 72; Springville Utah Invitational.
Teaching: Asst instr art, Otis Art Inst.
Positions: Chmn, Stacey Scholar Found.
Awards: Five first prizes, Death Valley Invitational, 61-68; gold medal for drawing & silver medal for painting, 70 & gold medal for drawing, 72, Cowboy Hall Fame.
Bibliography: Ed Ainsworth (auth), Painters of the desert, Desert Mag Press, 60 & 61; Dorothy Harmsen (auth), Harmsen's Western Americana, Northland Press, 71; The West & Walter Bimson, Univ Ariz Mus Art, 71.
Memberships: Cowboy Artists Am; fel Am Inst Fine Arts.
Publications: Auth, Artist on the Colorado, 61 & auth, Tewa-quap-tewa, Hopi Chief, 61, Desert Mag; auth, Water of life for God's red children, This Day Mag, 65; auth, The art of R Brownell McGrew, Ariz Hwys, 7/69.
Dealer: O'Brien's Art Emporium, 72 W Stetson, Scottsdale, AZ 85251.
Mailing Address: P O Box 987, Cottonwood, AZ 86326.

MACHETANZ, FRED
Painter
Preferred Media: Oil.
b Kenton, Ohio, Feb 20, 08.
Study & Training: Ohio State Univ, AB, 30, MA, 35; Chicago Art Inst, 30-32; Am Acad, Chicago, Ill, 30-32; Art Stud League, 45.
Work in Public Collections: Heritage Libr, Anchorage, Alaska; Rasmuson Libr, Univ Alaska, College; Glenbow Found, Alberta Mus, Calgary; Anchorage Fine Arts Mus; Northwest Indian Ctr, Gonzaga Univ, Spokane, Wash.
Commissions: Paintings, Arctic Explorer, Explorers Club New York, N Y, 63; Capt Cook in Arctic, Scripps Inst for res ship, Alpha Helix, 63; Capt Cook at Cook Inlet, Capt Cook Hotel, Anchorage, 64; Eskimo Whalers, Dept Interior, Washington, D C, 69; Dr Irving on Ice Field, Laurence Irving Bldg, Univ Alaska, Inst Arctic Biol, 71.
Exhibitions: Anchorage Fur Rendezvous, 60-72; Mainstreams, Marietta Col, Ohio, 68; one-man shows, Univ Alaska, 64-72, Anchorage Fine Arts Mus, 68 & Frye Mus, Seattle, Wash, 72.
Teaching: Instr portrait painting, Univ Alaska, summers 64-71.
Positions: Distinguished assoc art, Univ Alaska, 64-
Bibliography: Sara Machetanz, Where else but Alaska, Scribner, 54; K Lawton (auth), Fred Machetanz, Alaska Review, Alaska Methodist Univ, 65; W Jones (auth), Fred M—artist of Alaska, Am Artist Mag, 4/68.
Memberships: Anchorage Fine Arts Mus Asn (bd mem, 60-).
Publications: Auth & illusr, Panuck, Eskimo sled dog, Scribner, 39 & On arctic ice, 41; illusr, A puppy named Gih, Scribner, 57.
Mailing Address: Box S-885, Palmer, AK 99645.

MACHLIN, SHELDON M
Sculptor, Printmaker
b New York, N Y, Sept 6, 18.
Work in Public Collections: Mus Mod Art, New York, N Y; Whitney Mus Am Art, New York; Va Mus Fine Arts, Richmond; Aldrich Mus Contemp Art, Ridgefield, Conn; Fogg Art Mus, Cambridge, Mass.
Exhibitions: Hardedge & Geometric Painting & Sculpture, Mus Mod Art, 63 & The Responsive Eye, 65, Mus Mod Art; Whitney Mus Am Art Contemp Am Sculpture Ann, 64, 66 & 68; Options, Milwaukee Art Ctr & Mus Contemp Art, Chicago, Ill, 68; Aldrich Fund Acquisitions for Mus Mod Art, 59-69 at Aldrich Mus Contemp Art, 71.
Memberships: Fedn Mod Painters & Sculptors.
Mailing Address: 39 Columbia Pl, Brooklyn Heights, New York, NY 11201.

McILHENNY, HENRY PLUMER
Collector
b Philadelphia, Pa, Oct 7, 10.
Study & Training: Harvard Univ, AB(magna cum laude), 33, grad study, 33-34.
Collections Arranged: Degas; Daumier; Philadelphia Silver; Connelly and Haines; Tucker China; Shaker Furniture.
Positions: Cur decorative arts, Philadelphia Mus Art, 35-64, trustee, 64-, v pres, 68-; mem vis comt art mus, Harvard Col; mem Comn for Nat Collection Fine Arts, Washington, D C.
Mailing Address: 1914 Rittenhouse Sq, Philadelphia, PA 19103.

McIVER, JOHN KOLB
Painter
Preferred Media: Watercolors, Acrylics.
b Jacksonville, Fla, Oct 20, 30.
Study & Training: Trinity Col, Hartford, Conn, AB, 53.
Work in Public Collections: Okla Mus, Oklahoma City; Jacksonville Art Mus, Fla; Cummer Gallery Art, Jacksonville; Hunter Gallery, Chattanooga, Tenn.
Exhibitions: Am Watercolor Soc, New York, N Y, 64-68; Allied Artists Am, New York, 66; Nat Acad Design, New York, 67; Watercolor U S A, Springfield, Mo, 70; Mainstreams '71, Ohio, 71.
Awards: John Marin Mem Award, Watercolor U S A, 70.
Memberships: Am Watercolor Soc; Copley Soc, Boston, Mass.
Publications: Contribr, Acrylic watercolor painting, Watson Guptill, 70.
Mailing Address: Box 6202, Evansville, IN 47712.

MacIVER, LOREN
Painter
b New York, N Y, Feb 2, 09.
Study & Training: Art Stud League New York, 19.
Work in Public Collections: Mus Mod Art; Metrop Mus Art; Detroit Inst Art; Addison Gallery Am Art, Andover, Mass; Whitney Mus Am Art; plus others.
Exhibitions: Venice Biennale, 67; Tolouse Mus Fine Arts, 67; Mus Beaux Arts, Lyons, France, 68; Mus Art Mod Ville de Paris, 68; Mus Ponchettes, Nice, France, 68; plus others.

Awards: Ford Found grant, 60; first prize, Art Inst Chicago, 61; purchase prize, Kranner Art Mus, Univ Ill, 63; plus others.
Memberships: Nat Inst Arts & Lett.
Dealer: Pierre Matisse Gallery, 41 E 57th St, New York, NY 10022.
Mailing Address: 61 Perry St, New York, NY 10014.

McIVOR, JOHN WILFRED
Printmaker, Painter
b Henderson, Ky, July 17, 31.
Study & Training: Murray State Univ, 49-50; Univ Ill, BFA (summa cum laude), 57, fel, 57-59, MFA, 59.
Work in Public Collections: Albright-Knox Art Gallery, Buffalo, N Y; Am Fedn Arts, New York, N Y; Libr of Cong, Washington, D C; State Univ N Y Albany; Jacksonville Mus, Fla.
Commissions: Exterior (with David Hatchett), Buffalo Rehab Comn, 71.
Exhibitions: 100th Anniversary Show of Land Grant Colleges, Kansas City Art Inst, 68; Master Drawings & Watercolors Since the 15th Century, Albright-Knox Art Gallery, 69; North of the Penn Line, traveling show to mus of northeast, 69-71; Am Fedn Arts Traveling Exhib, 70-71; Watercolors Since 1900, Birmingham Mus Art, Ala, 72.
Teaching: Asst prof art, Auburn Univ, 59-63; prof art, State Univ N Y Buffalo, 63-; vis prof, Southern Ill Univ, spring 70.
Positions: Founder, Team Workshop, Buffalo.
Awards: Faculty fel, State Univ N Y Res Found, 70 & 72.
Bibliography: Edward Reep (auth), The content of watercolor, Reinhold, 69.
Mailing Address: 663 Lafayette Ave, Buffalo, NY 14222.

MACK, RODGER ALLEN
Sculptor, Educator
Preferred Media: Cast Metals, Stone, Wood, Plastics.
b Barberton, Ohio, Nov 8, 38.
Study & Training: Cleveland Inst Art, BFA, 61; Cranbrook Acad Art, Bloomfield Hills, Mich, MFA, 63; Acad Belle Arti, Florence, Italy, 63-64.
Work in Public Collections: Ark Arts Ctr, Little Rock, Ark; Munson-Williams-Proctor Inst, Utica, N Y.
Commissions: Plaza sculpture, City of North Little Rock, Ark, Mkt Plaza, North Little Rock, 68; Syra cast bronze, Syracuse Univ, Dellplain Hall, 69.
Exhibitions: One-man show, Galleria Arte, Florence, 64; Nat Coun Award Winning Artists, Witte Mem Mus, San Antonio, Tex, 68; Cross Currents in American Art, Humboldt State Col, Arcada, Calif, 69; Everson Region, Everson Mus Art, Syracuse, N Y, 70-71; one-man shows, Krasner Gallery, New York, N Y, 70-72.
Teaching: Instr sculpture, Arks Sch Art/Drama, Little Rock, 64-68; assoc prof sculpture, Syracuse Univ, 68-
Awards: A Kahn Assoc Artists Award, Detroit Inst Arts, Mich, 63; Fulbright grant study in Italy, 63-64; Nat Endowment for the Arts Award, Nat Coun Arts, Washington, D C, 67.
Bibliography: John Canaday (auth), rev, In: New York Times, 1/70, 1/71 & 1/72.
Dealer: Oscar Krasner Gallery, 1043 Madison Ave, New York, NY 10021.
Mailing Address: 2400 Euclid Ave, Syracuse, NY 13224.

MACKAY, DONALD CAMERON
Painter, Art Historian
Preferred Media: Oils.
b Fredericton, N B, Mar 30, 06.
Study & Training: N S Col Art, assoc, 28, fel, 29, DFA, 70; Dalhousie Univ, cert fine arts; Chelsea Col Art; Acad-Colorossi, Paris; Univ Toronto, with Arthur Lismer; also with Prof Jowett & Graham Sutherland.
Work in Public Collections: Nat Gallery Can, Ottawa; New York Pub Libr; N S Mus Fine Arts; Prov N S & Pub Arch N S; Teachers Col N B.
Commissions: Three murals, Halifax Mem Libr, 51; first pres, Dalhousie Univ, Thomas MacCulloch, Dalhousie Senate, 53; Jacques Cartier at Stadacona, HM Can Ship Stadacona Wardroom, Halifax, 55.
Exhibitions: Can Soc Graphic Arts, 30-40; Art of the Western Hemisphere, IBM, 40; First Post War Can Bienniele, 46; Can Sect N Y World's Fair; Royal Can Acad.
Collections Arranged: Halifax Bicentennial-200 Years of Art in Halifax, 49; Development of Canadian Art, Halifax Mem Libr, 51; A Century of Painting in Nova Scotia 1800-1900, N S Col Art, 65.
Teaching: Instr graphic arts, Northern Voc Sch Toronto, Art Gallery Toronto, 31-35; instr, N S Col Art, Halifax, 35-39; spec lectr art hist, Dalhousie Univ, 37-71; prof art & prin, N S Col Art, Halifax, 45-71.
Positions: War artist, RCN, 41-43.
Awards: Bronze medal, Art of the Western Hemisphere, IBM, 40; silver medal, Allied Arts, Royal Archit Inst Can, 53.
Memberships: Fel Royal Soc Arts; Can Soc Educ through Art (pres,

57-58); Maritime Art Asn (pres, 51-53); Can Soc Graphic Art (v pres, 34-40); Can Arts Coun (v pres, 56-58); plus others.
Research: Topographical and portrait painters of the Atlantic Provinces; silver and silversmith of the Atlantic Provinces; Tsuba and sword furniture of Japan.
Publications: Auth & illusr, High lights of Nova Scotia history, 30; co-auth, Master goldsmiths and silversmiths of Nova Scotia, 48; illusr, Halifax warden of the North, 49; illusr, Tales of the sea, 52; auth & contribr, many articles, 40-71.
Mailing Address: 5883 Inglis St, Halifax, N S, Can.

MacKAY, HUGH
Art Dealer
b New York, N Y, July 4, 36.
Positions: Pres, Nabis Fine Arts Inc, New York, 70-
Memberships: Am Fedn Arts.
Specialty of Gallery: Publisher of graphics; art consultants to architects, design groups, corporations and galleries in all media.
Mailing Address: 276 Park Ave S, New York, NY 10010.

McKAY, JOHN SANGSTER
Art Administrator, Educator
b Farmers City, Ill, May 30, 21.
Study & Training: Univ Ill, Urbana-Champaign, BFA, 47; Inst Design, Chicago, Ill, cert, 48; Univ Buffalo, 50.
Teaching: Instr design, Albright Art Sch, Buffalo, 47-54; asst dean design, Sch Fine Arts, Wash Univ, 54-68; prof & assoc dean visual arts, Sch Fine Arts, Univ Kans, 68-
Memberships: Fel Nat Asn Schs Art (secy, 61-62, v pres, 66-68, pres, 69-72); Am Coun Arts Educ (bd dirs, 69-72); Int Coun Fine Arts Deans; Lawrence Community Arts Coun (chmn).
Publications: Co-auth, Nat Asn Schs Art Bull, 72.
Mailing Address: 742 Indiana, Lawrence, KS 66044.

McKEAN, HUGH FERGUSON
Painter, Educator
b Beaver Falls, Pa, July 28, 08.
Study & Training: Pa Acad Fine Arts; Art Stud League New York, N Y; Ecole Beaux-Arts, Fontainebleau, France; Rollins Col, BA & DFA; Williams Col, MA; Stetson Univ, LHD; Brevard Col, DSpaceEd; Univ Tampa, LLD.
Work in Public Collections: Toledo Mus Art; Univ Va.
Exhibitions: Soc Four Arts, 48; Allied Artists Am, 49; exhib, Atlanta, Ga, 49.
Teaching: Prof art, Rollins Col, 52-69.
Positions: Dir, Morse Gallery Art, Rollins Col, acting pres Col, 51-52, pres, 52-69, chancellor & chmn bd, 69-; trustee, Ringling Mus State of Fla; mem Fla Arts Coun, 69-
Awards: Prizes, Fla Fedn Art, 31 & 49; Cervantes Medal, Span Inst; Decoration of Honor, Rollins Col.
Memberships: Fla Fedn Art (pres, 51-52); Louis Comfort Tiffany Found (trustee); N H Art Asn; Orlando Art Asn; Am Fedn Arts; plus others.
Mailing Address: Rollins College, Winter Park, FL 32789.

McKEEBY, BYRON GORDON
Printmaker, Educator
Preferred Media: Lithography, Intaglio.
b Humboldt, Iowa, Feb 27, 36.
Study & Training: Coe Col, BA, 59; Art Inst Chicago, BFA, 63; Tulane Univ La, MFA, 65; Univ N Mex, Tamarind Artist-Teacher fel, with Garo Antresian, summer 65.
Work in Public Collections: Dallas Mus Fine Arts, Tex; Philadelphia Mus, Pa; Brooklyn Mus, N Y; Norfolk Mus Arts & Sci, Va; Ark Art Ctr, Little Rock.
Exhibitions: Four exhibs, Northwest Printmakers, Seattle, Wash, 65-69; four exhibs, Okla Printmakers, Oklahoma City, 65-71; Potsdam Print Ann, State Univ N Y Col Potsdam, 68 & 69; Print & Drawing Nat, North Ill Univ, De Kalb, 68, 69 & 71; Nat Print Ann, Ga State Univ, Athens, 70 & 71.
Teaching: Assoc prof printmaking, Univ Tenn, Knoxville, 65-
Bibliography: Edward Brohel (auth), New American printmakers (TV prog), N Y Educ TV, 66.
Dealers: Associated American Artists, Inc, 663 5th at 52nd, New York, NY 10022; Vorpal Gallery, 1168 Battery St, San Francisco, CA 94111.
Mailing Address: Art Dept, University of Tennessee, Knoxville, TN 37916.

MacKENDRICK, LILIAN
Painter
Preferred Media: Oils, Pastels, Watercolors, Charcoal, Ink.
b New York, N Y.
Study & Training: Sculpture with Louis Keila, drawing & painting

with Dorothy Block; lithography at Art Stud League New York; Washington Sq Col, New York Univ, BS.
Work in Public Collections: Metrop Mus Art, New York; Hirshhorn Collection, Washington, D C; Wadsworth Atheneum Hartford, Conn; Walker Art Ctr, Minneapolis, Minn; Mus Fine Arts Houston, Tex.
Exhibitions: Audubon Artists, New York, 51 & 53; New York Dealers' Show, Witte Mus Art, San Antonio, Tex, 52; Third Biennial of American Painting, Bordighera, Italy, 55; Eleven Americans, touring Fr Mus, 56-57.
Awards: Hon mention, Brooklyn Soc Artists, 53; gold medal, Third Biennial American Painting, Bordighera, Italy, 55; award for pub serv, Northside Ctr for Child Develop, 61.
Bibliography: C Roger Marx (auth), Deux femmes peintures Americaines, Jardin Arts, Paris, 7/56; Joan Hess (auth), Lilian MacKendrick, Am Artist, 1/59; Dian Buchman (auth), Last of the great lady painters, Show, 4/70.
Memberships: Artists Equity Asn.
Publications: Illusr, Cat in my mind, Putnam's (Eng), 58; illusr, cover mag sect, New York Herald Tribune, 2/9/59.
Dealer: Hammer Galleries, 51 E 57th St, New York, NY 10021.
Mailing Address: 230 Central Park S, New York, NY 10019.

McKENNIS, GAIL COLLINS
Printmaker, Painter
Preferred Media: Graphics.
b Wilmington, N C, May 12, 39.
Study & Training: Richmond Prof Inst, Va Commonwealth Univ, BFA; 63, MFA, 64; Royal Col Art, London, 71.
Work in Public Collections: Victoria & Albert Mus, London; Mint Mus Art, Charlotte, N C; Dillard Collection, Weatherspoon Gallery, Univ N C, Greensboro; Rawls Mus, Courtland, Va; Va Commonwealth Univ, Richmond, Va.
Exhibitions: One-man show, Va Mus Fine Arts, Richmond, 68; 24th Southeastern Ann, High Mus, Atlanta, Ga, 70; Northern Young Contemporaries, Whitworth Gallery, Manchester, Eng, 71; 4th Int Print Biennale, Cracow, Poland, 72; 3rd Brit Int Print Biennale, Bradford, Eng, 72.
Teaching: Instr painting, printmaking & drawing, Va Commonwealth Univ, 65-69; instr printmaking & drawing, Univ N C, Wilmington, 69-71; instr silkscreen, Univ Reading, 72-
Awards: Va Mus Fine Arts Biennial Exhibs Awards, 67-69; Eighth Ann Piedmont Graphics Award, Mint Mus Art, Charlotte, 71; Third Brit Int Print Biennale Award, Gratham Warehouses, 72.
Mailing Address: 1417 Brookland Pkwy, Richmond, VA 23227.

MacKENZIE, HUGH SEAFORTH
Painter
Preferred Media: Tempera, Watercolors.
b Toronto, Ont, June 19, 28.
Study & Training: Ont Col Art; Mt Allison Univ, BFA.
Work in Public Collections: Montreal Mus Fine Arts, P Q; Art Gallery Ont, Toronto; London Art Gallery, Ont; House of Commons, Ottawa.
Commissions: Portrait of L B Pearson, Ottawa Dept State, 68.
Exhibitions: Five one-man shows, Morris Gallery, Toronto, 63-72; Realism in Canadian Art, Montreal Mus Fine Arts, P Q & Art Gallery Ont, Toronto, 70.
Teaching: Instr art, Ont Col Art, 68-
Awards: J W G Forster Award, Ont Soc Artists, 61; Can Coun Award, 70.
Bibliography: Mendes (auth), Hugh MacKenzie, 12/69 & Dauct (auth), review, spring 72, Arts Can; Hale (auth), review, Arts Mag, 2/70.
Memberships: Assoc Royal Can Acad.
Mailing Address: c/o Jerrold Morris Gallery, 15 Prince Arthur Ave, Toronto, Ont, Can.

McKESSON, MALCOLM FORBES
Painter, Sculptor
Preferred Media: Watercolors, Wood, Wood Constructions, Oils, Ink.
b Monmouth Beach, N J, July 24, 09.
Study & Training: Harvard Col, AB(art), 33; Art Career Sch, 51-53; Art Stud League New York, 55; N Y Univ, MA(art educ), 56; N Y State Teachers Col, New Paltz.
Exhibitions: Composers, Authors & Artists Am, 59-72; Pen & Brush Club, New York, N Y, 65; Burr Artists, 66-72; Nat Arts Club, 65-69; Lynchburg Art Ctr, 69; plus others.
Teaching: Instr art, New York City Pub Schs, 56-60.
Memberships: Composers, Authors & Artists Am (pres, 65-66); Burr Artists.
Art Interests: Architectural & landscape subjects.
Mailing Address: 22 E 29th St, New York, NY 10016.

McKIBBEN, TEAL
Painter
Preferred Media: Oils.
b Ames, Iowa, Dec 15, 28.
Study & Training: Stephens Col; Univ N Mex.
Work in Public Collections: Addison Gallery Am Art, Andover, Mass; Worcester Art Mus, Mass; Univ Mass, Amherst; Commerce Trust Co, Kemper Found, Kansas City, Mo; Bradford Jr Col, Haverhill, Mass.
Exhibitions: Boston Arts Festival, Mass, 59; View 1961, Inst Contemp Arts, Boston, 61; American Painting 62, Va Mus, Richmond, 62; 16 Women Painters, Fitchberg Mus, 65; Landscape 2, DeCordova Mus, Lincoln, Mass, 72.
Dealer: Joan Peterson Gallery, 561 Boyl, Boston, MA 02129.
Mailing Address: 34 University Rd, Brookline, MA 02146.

McKIM, WILLIAM WIND
Printmaker, Painter
Preferred Media: Tempera, Acrylics.
b Independence, Mo, May 13, 16.
Study & Training: Kansas City Art Inst, with Thomas Hart Benton & John S DeMartelly.
Work in Public Collections: William Rockhill Nelson Gallery; Kansas City Art Inst.
Commissions: Wildlife panorama, Kansas City Mus, 62.
Exhibitions: Mo Pavilion, New York World's Fair, 64-65; Art of Two Cities, Kansas City & Minneapolis, 66; one-man show, Kansas City Art Inst & Albrecht Gallery, Saint Joseph, Mo, 67-68; 10 Missouri Painters Traveling Exhib, 68-69; Mid Am Artists Exhib, Saint Louis & Kansas City, 68 & 70.
Teaching: Instr drawing, Kansas City Art Inst, 45-48, instr lithography, 48-58, prof lithography, 58-
Awards: D M Lighton Award, Midwestern Ann, Kansas City, 40; New York State Fair Award.
Mailing Address: 8704 E 32nd St, Kansas City, MO 64129.

McKININ, LAWRENCE
Educator, Painter
Preferred Media: Oils, Acrylics.
b Yukon, Pa, Aug 24, 17.
Study & Training: Wayne State Univ, BS, 39; Soc Arts & Crafts, Detroit, Mich, with John Carroll, 39-40; Univ Wis, summer 41; Cranbrook Acad Art, with Zoltan Sepeshy, 46-48, MFA, 48; Inst Design, Chicago, summer 49; Handy & Harman Silversmithing Workshop, Sch Am Craftsmen, Rochester, N Y, summer 50.
Work in Public Collections: Friends of Art, Nelson Gallery, Kansas City, Mo; Springfield Mus Art, Mo; Vera Mott Mem Collection, Columbia, Mo.
Commissions: Portrait of O M Stewart & H M Reese, Univ Mo Physics Dept, Columbia, 67.
Exhibitions: Mid-Am Ann, Nelson Gallery, 50 & 51; seven shows, Springfield Art Mus Ann, 50-72; Midwest Exhib, Joslyn Mus, Omaha, Nebr, 51 & 52; American Jewelry and Related Objects, circulated by Smithsonian Inst, 55-57; 10 Missouri Painters II, Mo Arts Coun Circulation Exhib, 68-69.
Teaching: Instr art, Univ Mo-Columbia, 48-50, asst prof art, 50-55, assoc prof art & chmn dept, 55-59, prof art, 59-
Positions: Art ed, Archaeol Mag, 53-54.
Awards: Purchase prize for painting Exodus, Mid-Am Exhib, Friends of Art, Nelson Gallery, 50; purchase prize for painting White Lake, Springfield Art Mus, 50; award for design of bk, Fred Shane drawings, Chicago Bk Clin 16th Ann Exhib, 65.
Memberships: Mid-Am Col Art Asn.
Publications: Designer & ed, Fred Shane drawings, 65.
Mailing Address: A126 Fine Arts Bldg, University of Missouri-Columbia, Columbia, MO 65201.

McKINNEY, DONALD
Art Dealer
b New York, N Y.
Positions: Dir, Marlborough Gallery.
Specialty of Gallery: Nineteenth and twentieth century European and American art.
Mailing Address: c/o Marlborough Gallery, 41 E 57th St, New York, NY 10021.

McKNIGHT, ELINE
Printmaker
Preferred Media: Graphics.
b Yokohama, Japan, 1910.
Study & Training: Barnard Col & Teachers Col, Columbia Univ; Art Stud League New York; Yale Sch Fine Arts.
Work in Public Collections: Libr Cong; New York Hilton Hotel, Rockefeller Ctr; Univ Tenn.

Exhibitions: U S Info Agency Traveling Exhib, Europe, 60-62; Soc Am Graphic Artists Traveling Exhib, 60-62; Brooklyn Mus, 60, 64 & 66; Am Haus, Stuttgart, 65; Corcoran Gallery Art, 67; plus many other nat & int exhibs.
Positions: Conducted discussion groups on looking at mod art, Ford Fund Adult Educ; mem ed staff, New York Arts Calendar, 64; assoc ed, Collectors Almanac, 65.
Awards: Purchase prize, prints for U S Embassies abroad, U S Info Agency.
Mailing Address: 100 Riverside Dr, New York, NY 10024.

McLANATHAN, RICHARD B K
Art Consultant, Writer
b Methuen, Mass, Mar 12, 16.
Study & Training: Harvard Univ, AB, 38, grad sch, 41-43, Soc Fels, 43-46, PhD, 51.
Collections Arranged: The M & M Karolik Collection of American Paintings, 1815-1865, Mus Fine Arts, Boston, 49; Art Across America, Munson-Williams-Proctor Inst, Utica, 60.
Positions: Secy mus, Mus Fine Arts, Boston, 52-56, ed publ, 52-57, cur decorative arts, 54-57; dir mus art, Munson-Williams-Proctor Inst, 57-61; cur art exhib, Am Nat Exhib, Moscow, 59; mem N Y State Coun on the Arts, 60-64; mem N Y State Comnr Comt Art & Mus Resources, 60-66.
Awards: Prix de Rome, Am Acad Rome, 48; distinguished serv award, U S Info Agency, 59.
Memberships: Am Asn Mus; Northeast Conf Am Mus Asn (pres, 61); N Y State Mus Asn; Asn of Fels of Am Acad Rome (pres, 64).
Research: Medieval art; renaissance art, especially Italian; American arts; modern art.
Publications: Co-auth, The M & M Karolik collection of American paintings, 1815-1865, 49; auth, Images of the universe: Leonardo da Vinci, The artist as scientist, 66; auth, The pageant of medieval art and life, 66; contribr, U S philanthropic foundations, their history, structure, management and record, 67; auth, The American tradition in the arts, 68.
Mailing Address: 439 E 51st St, New York, NY 10022.

McLAREN, NORMAN
Painter, Art Administrator
b Stirling, Scotland, Apr 11, 14; Can citizen.
Study & Training: Glasgow Sch Art, Scotland.
Work in Public Collections: Nat Gallery Can, Ottawa.
Positions: Film dir, Nat Film Bd Can, 41-
Awards: Motion Picture Acad Oscar for Neighbors, 52; award for Blinkity Blank, Grand Prix, Cannes, France, 55; outstanding achievement award, Can Govt, 72.
Bibliography: Gavin Miller (auth), The eye hears & the ear sees (film), BBC-TV, Eng; M.E Cutler (auth), Unique genius of Norman McLaren, Can Art, 5 & 6/65; Laurence Elliott (auth), Norman McLaren, gentle genius of the screen, Reader's Digest, 8/71.
Memberships: Academician Royal Can Acad Art.
Publications: Auth, Cameraless animation, 58; illusr, Six musical forms, Jeunesses Musicales, Montreal, 67; illusr, Interplay, Graphic Guild, Montreal, 71.
Mailing Address: 3590 Ridgewood Ave, Apt 305, Montreal 247, Que, Can.

McLARTY, WILLIAM JAMES (JACK)
Painter, Instructor
b Seattle, Wash, Apr 24, 19.
Study & Training: Mus Art Sch, Portland, Ore; Am Art Sch, N Y; also with Anton Refregier & Joseph Solman.
Commissions: Murals, Collins-View Sch, Laurelhurst Sch, Riverdale Sch, Ridgewood Sch, Portland, & Portland Civic Auditorium.
Exhibitions: One-man show, Bush House Mus, Salem, Ore, 61; Recent Paintings: U S A, Mus Mod Art, 62-63; 20 yr retrospective, Portland Art Mus, 63; First & Second Int Miniature Print Exhib, Pratt Graphic Art Ctr, N Y, 64; Multiform, Ore State Univ Invitational, 68; plus many other group & one-man shows.
Teaching: Instr painting, drawing & compos, Portland Mus Art Sch, presently.
Awards: Prize, Cheney Cowles Mus, Spokane, Wash, 65; purchase prize, Lewis & Clark Col Invitational, Portland, 65; prize, Northwest Printmakers, Seattle, 66; plus others.
Memberships: Portland Art Asn.
Publications: Auth, 17 love poems, 67; contribr, Prize-winning graphics, 67 & Northwest rev, Univ Ore, 67.
Mailing Address: Portland Museum Art Sch, Portland, OR 97205.

McLAUGHLIN, JOHN D
Painter
Preferred Media: Oils, Acrylics.
b Sharon, Mass, May 21, 98.
Work in Public Collections: Los Angeles Co Mus Art, Calif; Bowdoin Col Mus Art, Brunswick, Maine; Metrop Mus Art, New York,

N Y; Nat Collection Fine Arts, Smithsonian Inst, Washington, D C; Univ Art Mus, Univ Calif, Berkeley.

Exhibitions: Painting & Sculpture Ann, 49, Contemporary Painting in the United States, 51 & Four Abstract Classicists, 59-60, Los Angeles Co Mus; Sphere of Mondrian, Inst Contemp Art, Houston, Tex, 57; Purist Painting, Toured by Am Fedn Art, 60-61.

Awards: Corcoran Bronze Medal, Corcoran Gallery, Washington, D C, 66; William A Clark Prize, 66; Nat Found Arts & Humanities grant, 67.

Bibliography: Jules Langsner (auth), Summer in Los Angeles, Art News, 53; Gerald Nordland (auth), Paintings at the Felix Landau Gallery, Arts, 62; John Coplans (auth), West Coast art: three images, Artforum, 63.

Memberships: Los Angeles Co Mus Art; Mus Mod Art, New York; life mem Laguna Beach Mus Art.

Dealer: Nicholas Wilder, Los Angeles, CA 90069.

Mailing Address: Dana Point, CA 92629.

MacLEAN, ARTHUR
Painter, Lithographer
b New York, N Y.
Study & Training: Nat Acad Design, New York; Art Stud League New York; Grand Cent Art Sch.

Exhibitions: Nat Acad Design, 60-70; Allied Artists Am, 60-72; Hudson Valley Art Asn, 60-72; Knickerbocker Artists, 60-72; Acad Artists, 60-68; plus others.

Positions: Free-lance commercial artist.

Awards: Medal of hon, Knickerbocker Artist, 63; silver medal, Am Artist Prog League, 63; Jane Peterson Prize, Hudson Valley Art Asn, 71; plus others.

Memberships: Allied Artists; Knickerbocker Artists; Am Artists Prof League; Hudson Valley Art Asn; plus others.

Dealer: Gallery Madison/90, 1248 Madison Ave, New York, NY 10028.

Mailing Address: 249 Hamilton Ave, Stamford, CT 06902.

McLEAN, DORIS PORTER
Painter
Preferred Media: Oils, Watercolors.
b Norfolk, Va.
Study & Training: With Hans Hofmann, Capri, Italy, 28; Pa Acad Fine Arts, 33; Wayne State Univ, BA & MA(art educ), 37; Univ Mich, MFA, 42; also with Zoltan & Vaclav Vytlacil.

Work in Public Collections: Pa Acad Fine Arts, Philadelphia; Cranbrook Mus, Bloomfield Hills, Mich; Univ Mich.

Commissions: Mural, St Mary's Hall, Burlington, N J, 33; mural, Ford Sch, Highland Park, Mich, 35; Sweitzer (bust), Sweitzer Sch, Wayne, Mich, 65.

Exhibitions: Pa Acad Fine Arts, 33; Nat Acad Design, 33; Corcoran Gallery Art, 40; Michigan Artists, Toledo, 49 & Detroit Mus, 50; plus one other.

Positions: Consult art, Wayne Pub Schs, 50-56; owner & dir, Olde Towne Gallery, Portsmouth, Va, 70; former head, Frederick Col, Dartsmouth, Va; free lance artist.

Awards: Lambert Award, Pa Acad Fine Arts, 33; Grosse Pointe Artists Award, 34 & 50; Women Painter's Award, Detroit Soc Women Painters & Sculptors, 49.

Bibliography: Articles in newspapers & Mich Acad Arts, Sci & Lett reports.

Memberships: Life mem Detroit Soc Women Painters & Sculptors (v pres, 41); Women Painters of Ann Arbor (pres & hon founder, 50); Palette & Brush, Detroit (founder & hon pres, 34); Mich Acad Arts, Sci & Lett (chmn art sect, 62 & 63); Tidewater Artists (publicity, 70-72).

Mailing Address: 7726 Castleton Ave, Norfolk, VA 23505.

McLEAN, RICHARD THORPE
Painter, Educator
Preferred Media: Oils.
b Hoquiam, Wash, Apr 12, 34.
Study & Training: Calif Col Arts & Crafts, BFA, 58; Mills Col, MFA, 62.

Work in Public Collections: Oakland Art Mus, Calif; Valparaiso Univ, Ind; Whitney Mus Am Art, New York, N Y; Va Mus Fine Arts, Richmond.

Exhibitions: Expo '70, Osaka, Japan, 70; 22 Realists, Whitney Mus Am Art, 70; Radical Realists, Mus Contemp Art, Chicago, Ill, 71; Sharp Focus Realism, Sidney Janis Gallery, New York, 72; Documenta 5, Kassel, Ger, 72.

Teaching: Asst prof painting & drawing, San Francisco State Col, 63-

Dealer: O K Harris Works of Art, 465 W Broadway, New York, NY 10012.

Mailing Address: 6471 Oakwood Dr, Oakland, CA 94611.

MacLEAN-SMITH, ELIZABETH
Sculptor, Lecturer
Preferred Media: Wood, Stone, Clay, Bronze, Plastics.
b Springfield, Mass, Feb 18, 16.
Study & Training: Wellesley Col, AB; Belgian-Am Educ Found traveling fel, Belgium, 37; Boston Mus Sch, with Frederick Warren Allen & Sturdivant traveling fel, Mex, 41.

Work in Public Collections: Mus Fine Arts, Boston, Mass; Mus Fine Arts, Springfield, Mass; Williams Col, Williamstown, Mass.

Commissions: Polyester murals, Dini's Sea Grill, Boston, 62-70; fountain & garden sculptures & portraits in private collections.

Exhibitions: New Eng Sculptor's Asn juried exhibs at most New Eng mus, 48-72; seven juried Boston Arts Festivals, 55-65; New Eng Sculptor's Asn Invitational, Prudential Ctr, Boston, Mass, 68 & 70; one-man shows, G W V Smith Mus, Springfield, 50, Tufts Col, Medford, Mass, 52, Crane Mus, Pittsfield, Mass, 56 & McIver-Ready Gallery, Boston, 68.

Teaching: Instr sculpture, Boston Mus Sch, 40-53; instr sculpture, Bradford Jr Col, 3 yrs.

Memberships: Fel Nat Sculpture Soc; New Eng Sculptor's Asn (five terms as pres).

Mailing Address: 92 Russell St, Charlestown, MA 02129.

McMAHON, JAMES EDWARD
Art Dealer
b New York, N Y, Jan 1, 37.
Study & Training: Hofstra Col, BA.
Positions: Owner, Gallery Madison 90.
Specialty of Gallery: American art of the nineteenth and twentieth centuries; American illustrators.
Mailing Address: Gallery Madison 90, 1248 Madison Ave, New York, NY 10028.

McMILLAN, CONSTANCE
Painter
Preferred Media: Oils, Acrylics.
b Millinocket, Maine, Mar 10, 24.
Study & Training: Bennington Col, painting with Karl Knaths & sculpture with Simon Moselsio, BA, 46; Colorado Springs Fine Arts Ctr, with Boardman Robinson, 46; Mills Col, fel, 53-55, art hist with Alfred Neumeyer & ceramic sculpture with Antonio Prieto, MA, 55.

Exhibitions: Am Fedn Arts Travelling Show, 66; Rackham Gallery Invitational, Univ Mich, Ann Arbor, 68; Artists Market Gallery, Detroit, Mich, 72; one-man shows, Morris Gallery, New York, N Y, 56 & Panoras Gallery, New York, every two yrs, 59-

Teaching: Instr painting, design & art hist, San Luis Sch, Colorado Springs, 49-51; instr painting, design & art hist, Emma Willard Sch, Troy, N Y, 52-53; instr painting & design, Angel Sch, Ann Arbor, 62-63.

Awards: First prize, Morris Gallery, 56; first & hon mention awards, Mich Watercolor Soc Ann, 67 & 68.

Memberships: Am Fedn Arts; Detroit Soc Women Painters; Ann Arbor Art Asn (bd mem, 64-68).

Publications: Illusr, Chikka, 62 & Ponies for a king, 63, Reilly & Lee; illusr, Memory of a large Christmas, Norton, 62.

Dealer: Panoras Gallery, 62 W 56th St, New York, NY 10019.

Mailing Address: 2760 Heather Way, Ann Arbor, MI 48104.

McMILLAN, ROBERT W
Painter, Educator
b Belleville, Ill, Jan 22, 15.
Study & Training: Southern Ill Univ, BEd, 37; Columbia Univ, MA, 40; Wash Univ, 48; Univ Iowa, PhD, 58.

Exhibitions: Brooklyn Mus, 40; Joslyn Mem Mus, Omaha, Nebr, 44; Saint Louis City Mus, 47; Cincinnati Mus, 56; Des Moines Art Ctr, 64; plus others.

Teaching: Instr art, Univ Kansas City, 46-48; prof art, Southern Ill Univ, Carbondale, 50-60; prof art, Grinnell Col, 60-69, chmn dept, 61-68; prof art & head dept, Univ Ariz, 69-

Positions: Dir, Schaeffer Gallery, Grinnell Col, 60-69.

Memberships: Am Asn Univ Prof; Col Art Asn Am; Midwestern Col Art Conf; Int Platform Asn.

Mailing Address: Dept of Art, University of Arizona, Tucson, AZ 85721.

McNAB, ALLAN
Painter, Printmaker
b Swaythling, Eng, May 27, 01; U S citizen.
Study & Training: Royal Col Art, London, MA, 29; Ecole Beaux-Arts, Paris, France, 29-30.

Work in Public Collections: Brit Mus; also in galleries, Australia, Italy, France & Holland.

Exhibitions: Royal Acad, London; Royal Scottish Acad; Royal Soc Painters & Etchers; New Eng Art Club; Art Inst Chicago; plus others.

Positions: Design dir, Norman Bel Geddes, 38-45; art dir, Life Mag, 45-50; dir, Lowe Gallery, 50-55; chmn, Southern Art Mus Dirs Asn, 53-54; dir, Soc Four Arts, Palm Beach, Fla, 55-56; adv, Nat Mus, Havana, Cuba, 55-59; asst dir, Art Inst Chicago, Ill, 56-57, assoc dir, 57-59, dir admin, 59-66; consult, bldg new mus, City of Oakland, Calif, 62-; mem art adv panel, Internal Revenue Serv, 66-69; art consult, Mayo Found, 67-; trustee, Minn Mus Art, Saint Paul; trustee, Allentown Mus Art, Pa; dir, Telfair Acad Arts & Sci, Inc, Savannah, Ga.
Awards: Chicago Lighting Inst Award mus lighting, 63.
Memberships: Royal Geog Soc; Chelsea Art Club, London; Archit League, N Y; Arts Club Chicago; Tavern Club Chicago.
Mailing Address: Telfair Academy of Arts & Sciences, Inc, Telfair Sq, P O Box 10081, Savannah, GA 31402.

McNAMARA, RAYMOND EDMUND
Printmaker, Painter
Preferred Media: Graphics.
b Chicago, Ill, Sept 25, 23.
Study & Training: Sch Art Inst Chicago, BAE; Univ Mich, MA; Wayne State Univ; also with Max Kahn, William Woodward, Peter Gilleran & Stanley Hayter.
Work in Public Collections: Charleston Art Gallery, W Va; State House, Charleston; Huntington Galleries, W Va; Concord Col, Athens, W Va; Gallery Akep, New York, N Y.
Exhibitions: Six shows, Exhibition 180, Huntington Galleries, 64-69; Charleston Art Gallery Exhibs, 64-72; Appalation Corridors, Charleston, 68; Ball State Drawing & Small Sculpture Nat, Ball State Univ, Muncie, Ind, 68; Am Drawing Biannual, Norfolk Mus Arts & Sci, Va, 69.
Teaching: Assoc prof printmaking, W Va State Col, 64-
Awards: First award painting, Huntington Galleries, 66; five purchase awards, W Va Arts & Humanities Coun, 66-70; award, Am Drawing Biannual, Norfolk Mus Arts & Sci, 69.
Memberships: Am Asn Univ Prof; Alumni Asn Art Inst Chicago.
Mailing Address: 306 Ruffner Ave, Charleston, WV 25311.

McNEAR, EVERETT C
Painter, Designer
b Minneapolis, Minn, Sept 30, 04.
Study & Training: Minneapolis Sch Art, with Cameron Booth; also with Edmund Kinzinger & Louis Marcoussis.
Commissions: Mosaic panels, Skiles Sch, Evanston, Ill, 59; mural, Perkins & Will Partnership.
Exhibitions: Art Inst Chicago; Pa Acad Fine Arts; one-man shows, San Francisco Mus Art, 46; Walker Art Ctr, Minneapolis, 48; Gallery, Univ Notre Dame, 61; plus others.
Positions: Chmn exhib comt, Chicago Art Club, 53-; design consult, Art Inst Chicago, 58-; mem adv coun, Art Gallery, Univ Notre Dame.
Awards: Medal, Art Dirs Club, Chicago, 50 & 55; prizes, Art Guild, 51, 55, 57 & 58 & Ill State Mus, 60; plus others.
Memberships: Chicago Art Club; 27 Designers.
Publications: Illusr, Many a green isle, 41 & Young eye seeing, 56; contribr, articles, In: Bull Atomic Scientists & Am Artist Mag.
Mailing Address: 1448 Lake Shore Dr, Chicago, IL 60610.

McNEIL, GEORGE J
Painter, Educator
b New York, N Y, Feb 22, 08.
Study & Training: Pratt Inst, Brooklyn, 27-29; Art Stud League New York, 30-31 & 32-33; Hans Hofmann Sch Fine Art, 33-36; Teachers Col, Columbia Univ, MA, 43, EdD, 52.
Work in Public Collections: Mus Mod Art; Nat Mus, Havana, Cuba; Newark Mus Art; Walker Art Ctr, Minneapolis, Minn; Whitney Mus Am Art; plus others.
Exhibitions: Whitney Mus Am Art Ann, 53, 57, 61 & 65; U S Info Agency Pan-Am Exhib, circulated Latin Am, 61-62; Yale Univ Art Gallery, 61-62; Pa Acad Fine Arts, 62; Wadsworth Atheneum, Hartford, Conn, 62; plus many other group and one-man shows.
Teaching: Prof art, grad dept art & design, Pratt Inst, presently.
Awards: Ford Found purchase award, 63; Nat Coun Arts Award, 66; Guggenheim fel, 69.
Mailing Address: 226A Willoughby Ave, Brooklyn, NY 11205.

MacNELLY, JEFFREY KENNETH
Cartoonist
Preferred Media: India Ink, Watercolors.
b New York, N Y, Sept 17, 47.
Study & Training: Univ N C.
Positions: Mem staff, Richmond News Leader.
Awards: Pulitzer Prize as editorial cartoonist, 72.
Publications: Auth, MacNelly, the Pulitzer Prize winning cartoonist: a specially selected collection, Westover, 72.
Mailing Address: 333 E Grace St, Richmond, VA 23219.

McNETT, ELIZABETH VARDELL
Painter, Illustrator
Preferred Media: Oils, Tempera.
b New Bern, N C, Nov 17, 96.
Study & Training: Flora McDonald Col, 15; Art Stud League New York; Nat Acad Design, 17-19; Johns Hopkins Med Sch, cert med art; Charcoal Club, Baltimore; Pa Acad Fine Arts, Univ Pa, Pa Acad Fine Arts scholar, BFA, 43, MFA, 45.
Commissions: Murals, Lankenau Hosp, Philadelphia, Pa, Col Pharm, Philadelphia & other med ctrs.
Exhibitions: Pa Acad Fine Arts; Art Alliance, Philadelphia; Artists Union, Philadelphia; Plastic Club, Philadelphia; Allied Arts, Durham, N C.
Teaching: Head dept painting, Andrew Col, Cuthbert, Ga, 19-23; instr painting & drawing, Fleischer Mus Sch; dir sch art, Allied Arts, Durham, N C, 54-58.
Positions: Staff artist, Lankenau Hosp, 30-50; staff artist, WTVD, Durham, N C, 56.
Publications: Illusr, many med bks.
Mailing Address: Chestnut Circle, Blowing Rock, NC 28605.

McQUILLAN, FRANCES C
Painter, Instructor
Preferred Media: Watercolors, Oils, Acrylics.
b Chicago, Ill, Dec 1, 10.
Study & Training: New York Sch Fine & Applied Art, grad; Art Stud League New York; Fairleigh Dickinson Univ; Montclair Art Mus Adult Sch.
Exhibitions: Conn Acad Fine Arts, 59 & 72; Allied Artists Am, 67; Expos Intercontinental Invitational, Dieppe, France, 67 & Monaco, 68; Am Artists Prof League, 66-69 & 72; Montclair Art Mus Invitational, 68.
Teaching: Instr drawing, watercolors & oils, Montclair Art Mus, N J, 50-; instr drawing, Montclair Adult Sch, 67-70; instr oil painting, Yard Sch Art, Montclair, 67-70.
Positions: Illusr, Peerless Fashions, New York, N Y, 32-37.
Awards: Silver medal for oil painting, Knickerbocker Artists, 53; first prize in watercolors, Am Artists Prof League, 70; first prize in oils, Art Centre Oranges, 72.
Memberships: N J Watercolor Soc (secy, treas, v pres & pres); Conn Acad Fine Arts; Am Artists Prof League (treas, 68-69); Essex Watercolor Club; Art Centre Oranges.
Mailing Address: 3 Godfrey Rd, Upper Montclair, NJ 07043.

MacRAE, EMMA FORDYCE (EMMA FORDYCE SWIFT)
Painter
Preferred Media: Oils.
b Vienna, Austria; U S citizen.
Study & Training: New York Sch Art; Art Stud League New York, N Y; Nat Acad Design.
Work in Public Collections: Wesleyan Col; Cosmopolitan Club; Nat Acad Design; also in pvt collections.
Exhibitions: Carnegie Inst; Art Inst Chicago; Joslyn Mus Art; Mus Fine Arts Houston; Newport Art Asn; plus others.
Awards: Awards, Allied Artists Am, 42; prizes, Pen & Brush Club, 46, 50 & 55; Medal of Merit, Royal Acad Art, Eng, 63.
Memberships: Nat Acad Design; Nat Asn Women Artists; Allied Artists Am, N Shore Art Asn; Cosmopolitan Club; plus others.
Mailing Address: 888 Park Ave, New York, NY 10021.

McVEIGH, MIRIAM TEMPERANCE
Painter
Preferred Media: Oils, Acrylics.
b Wabash, Ind.
Study & Training: Calif Col Arts & Crafts, BFA; Acad Goetz, Paris, France; also with Elmer Tafflinger, Clifton Wheeler & Eugen Neuhaus.
Work in Public Collections: Mus Monbart, Dijon, France.
Exhibitions: Butler Inst Am Art, Youngstown, Ohio, 51; Hoosier Salon, Indianapolis, Ind, 54; Am Vet Soc Artists, New York, N Y, 61; one-man show, St Petersburg Jr Col, Fla, 61; Artistes U S A, Galeries Raymond Duncan, Paris, 72.
Dealer: Ligoa Duncan, 825 Madison Ave, New York, NY 10021.
Mailing Address: 8200 14th St N, Saint Petersburg, FL 33702.

McVEY, LEZA
Sculptor, Designer
Preferred Media: Clay.
b Cleveland, Ohio, May 1, 07.
Study & Training: Cleveland Sch Art, grad; Cranbrook Acad Art.
Work in Public Collections: Cleveland Mus Art; Craft Mus, New York, N Y; Smithsonian Inst, Washington, D C; Syracuse Mus, N Y; Butler Inst Am Art, Youngstown, Ohio.
Commissions: Ceramic mural (with William McVey), Fine Art Ctr, Flint, Mich, 61.

Exhibitions: Syracuse Mus & Nat Circuit, 45-66; Smithsonian Inst, 51-61; Int Cong Contemp Ceramics, Ostend, Belg, 60; one-man show, Ceramic Pieces, Cleveland Inst Art, 65; one-man show, Albright-Knox Art Gallery, 65.
Awards: Ceramic form 33 award, Harshaw Chem Co, 51; spec awards & group awards, Cleveland Mus Art, 54-67; ceramic form 39 award, Grand Prix des Nations, Ostend, Belg, 60.
Bibliography: Louis G Farber (auth) Leza McVey profile, Ceramic Mo, 53; Meg Torbert (auth), Leza McVey, Every Day Art Quart, 53; Joe McCullough (auth), Leza McVey, Cleveland Inst Art, 65.
Mailing Address: 18 Pepper Ridge Rd, Cleveland, OH 44124.

McVEY, WILLIAM M
Sculptor, Educator
Preferred Media: Stone.
b Boston, MA, July 12, 05.
Study & Training: Rice Univ; Cleveland Inst Art; Acad Colarossi, Acad Grande Chaumiere & Acad Scandinave, Paris, 29-31; pupil of Despiau.
Work in Public Collections: Heroic head of Winston Churchill, Smithsonian Inst, Washington, D C & Chartwell, Eng; Sister Ann (hollow built ceramic), Ariana Mus, Geneva, Switz; L'Ecrivain (bronze), Houston Mus, Tex; Rumination (Ga marble), Cleveland Mus Art, Ohio, Beached Whale (cement fondu), Lincoln Center, Univ Ill, Urbana.
Commissions: San Jacinto Monument, Tex Centennial Comt, 35; Berry Monoment, Hopkins Airport, Cleveland, 61; Long Road (aluminum relief), Jewish Community Ctr, 64; U S Seals, Fed Bldg, Cleveland, 66; St Margaret of Scotland; Jan Hus, St Olga of Russia for Washington Cathedral.
Exhibitions: Grand Salon; Salon d'Automne; Pa Acad Fine Arts; Tex Ann; Cleveland May Shows.
Teaching: Instr, Cleveland Mus, 32; instr, Houston Mus, 36-38; instr, Univ Tex, 39-46; instr, Ohio State Univ, summer 46; instr, Cranbrook Acad Art, 46-53; head sculpture dept, Cleveland Inst Art, 53-68; vis sculptor, Sch Fine Arts, Ohio State Univ, 63-64.
Positions: Chmn, Nat Fulbright Screening Comt, four yrs; juror for most Midwest shows.
Awards: Award, Nat Syracuse Ceramic Show, 54; 11 spec awards, Cleveland May Shows; purchase award, Butler Inst Am Art, Youngstown, Ohio, 67.
Bibliography: Helen Borsick (auth), Story of a statue (Winston Churchill at the British Embassy in Washington), Plain Dealer Mag, 66; Sculptor for today, Ohio Mag; Animals, animal sculpture and animal sculptors, Nat Sculpture Rev, 71.
Memberships: Col Art Asn Am; fel Nat Sculpture Soc; Int Platform Asn (bd gov).
Mailing Address: 18 Pepper Ridge Rd, Cleveland, OH 44124.

McVICKER, J JAY
Painter, Educator
Preferred Media: Acrylics.
b Vici, Okla, Oct 18, 11.
Study & Training: Okla State Univ, BA & MA.
Work in Public Collections: Libr Cong, Washington, D C; Dallas Mus Fine Arts, Tex; Joslyn Art Mus, Omaha, Nebr; Okla Art Ctr; Philbrook Art Ctr, Tulsa, Okla.
Exhibitions: Am Japan Contemp Print Exhib, Tokyo, 67; Rockhill-Nelson Gallery, Kansas City, Mo, 69; Dallas Mus Fine Arts, 69; Audubon Artists, New York, N Y, 71; one-man show, Fred Jones Mem Gallery, Norman, Okla, 71.
Teaching: Mem art faculty, Okla State Univ, 41-, prof printmaking, 59-
Awards: Painting purchase award, Okla Art Ctr, 67; print purchase award, Dallas Mus Fine Arts, 69; painting purchase award, Longview Jr Serv League, Tex, 71.
Memberships: Audubon Artists; Soc Am Graphic Artists; Philadelphia Print Club.
Mailing Address: 4212 N Washington, Stillwater, OK 74074.

McWHINNIE, HAROLD JAMES
Printmaker, Educator
Preferred Media: Intaglio.
b Chicago, Ill, July 15, 29.
Study & Training: Art Inst Chicago, BAE; Univ Chicago, MFA; Stamford Univ, EdD.
Work in Public Collections: Los Angeles Mus Art, Calif; Pasadena Art Mus, Calif; Borg-Warner Collection, Chicago, Ill; Ohio State Univ Col Fine Arts.
Exhibitions: Libr Cong Print Show, 55; Pratt Graphic Workshop, 69; Philadelphia Art Alliance Show, 71; Laguna Beach Art Asn Show, 71; Frostburg State Col, 71.
Teaching: Asst prof art educ, Ohio State Univ, 65-70; assoc prof ceramics, Univ Md, College Park, 70-
Awards: Huntington Hartford fel, 56; Fulbright fel, 60; Ohio State Univ faculty fel, 65.

Memberships: Nat Art Educ Asn; Am Soc Aesthet; Brit Soc Aesthet; Washington Print Club; Print Club Philadelphia.
Dealer: Jane Haslem Gallery, 1669 Wisconsin Ave N W, Washington, DC 20007; Jane Haslem Gallery, 638 State St, Madison, WI 53703.
Mailing Address: 10111 Frederick Ave, Kensington, MD 20795.

McWHORTER, ELSIE JEAN
Painter, Sculptor
b Laurel, Miss, Apr 5, 32.
Study & Training: Univ Ga, BFA, 54, MFA, 56, with Lamar Dodd, Howard Thomas, Abbott Patterson, Joseph Di Martini, Ulfert Wilkie & Dan Lutz; Brooklyn Mus Art Sch, Max Beckmann scholar, 56-57, with Reuben Tam & Yonia Fain.
Work in Public Collections: Gibbes Art Gallery, Charleston, S C; Brooks Art Gallery, Memphis, Tenn; Greenville Co Mus Art, S C; Arts Comn S C, Columbia; Miss Art Asn, State Coliseum, Jackson; plus others.
Commissions: Seal for Sumter Co, S C, 65; welded bronze fountain, Tom Jenkins Realty Co, Columbia, 66; mural, U S Post Off, Camden, S C, 67; mural, Baker Bldg, Southern Bell Tel Co, Columbia, 68; plus others.
Exhibitions: U S Info Agency Show-Europe & Near East, 56-57; Mid-South Exhib, Memphis, Tenn, 62; Butler Inst Am Art Ann, Youngstown, Ohio, 63; Drawing U S A, Saint Paul 2nd Biennial Competition, Saint Paul Art Ctr, Minn, 63; 23rd Ann Nat Watercolor Exhib, Miss Art Asn, 64; plus others.
Teaching: Asst prof art, Morningside Col, 58-61; instr drawing, painting & sculpture, Richland Art Sch, Columbia Mus Art, 61-; instr sculpture & design, Univ S C, 66-67.
Awards: First prize, 5th Ann All-State Show, Knoxville, Tenn, 55; first prize, 24th Nat Watercolor Show, State Coliseum, Jackson, Miss, 65; first prize, Flower Festival, Greenwood, S C, 71; plus others.
Bibliography: Prize winning sculpture, 63 & Prize winning watercolors, 65, Allied Fla; Jack Morris (auth), article, In: Contemp S C Artist, 70.
Memberships: Guild S C Artist; Artist Guild Columbia; S C Craftmen.
Mailing Address: 5419 Sylvan Dr, Columbia, SC 29206.

MACIEL, MARY OLIVEIRA
Illustrator, Educator
b New Bedford, Mass.
Study & Training: With Alva Glidden; Swain Sch Art; Vesper George Sch Art; Md Inst Art; Marjorie Martinett Sch Art; Art Stud League New York, N Y, with George Bridgeman; Johns Hopkins Univ, with Max Brödel.
Commissions: Illus for 14 textbooks, Univ Cincinnati & Vet Admin; illus for many U S & foreign sci jour.
Exhibitions: Med Illus, Cincinnati, 48 & Med Illusr as Scientist, Columbus, 55, Ohio State Med Asn; Med Visual Aids, Univ Helsinki, Finland, 58; Med Illus: A Select Career, Cincinnati Pub Libr, 62; Artist In Operating Rm, Cincinnati Woman's Club, 65,
Teaching: Prof med illus & dir, Col Med, Univ Cincinnati, 47-
Awards: Six first awards for best sci exhibs, Ohio State Med Asn, 48-65; Fulbright prof, Univ Strasbourg, 56; Abbott Lab Award for illus in S Africa, 69.
Memberships: Asn Med Illusr (bd dirs, 55-59); Cincinnati Speakers Forum (bd dirs, 46-); McDowell Soc.
Publications: Auth & illusr, Modern prostheses for human defects, Graphics, 55; auth, Rapport sur la realization d'une preparation a l'illustration medicale, Arch U S Educ Comn France, 56; auth, The broad field of medical illustration, Cincinnati Post, 57; auth & illusr, Twenty points for creating good visual teaching aids, Univ Helsinki Arch, 58; auth, Importance of adequate medical visual teaching aids, Univ Cape Town, 69.
Mailing Address: 3317 Bishop St, Cincinnati, OH 45220.

MADDEN, BETTY I
Art Historian, Lecturer
b Chicago, Ill, Nov 15, 15.
Study & Training: Am Acad Art, Chicago; Northwestern Univ; Univ Ill, BFA; Inst Design, Chicago; with Herb Olson, Spain & Italy; also with John Pellew, Ireland & England.
Work in Public Collections: Ill State Hist Libr, Springfield.
Exhibitions: Ill State Fair Prof Artists Exhib, 57; Ill State Mus Invitational, 59.
Collections Arranged: Annual Mississippi Valley Artists Exhibitions, 63-67; Arts & Crafts in Old Illinois, 65; Artists & Sculptors in Illinois: 1820-1945, 72.
Positions: Com artist & illusr, Consolidated Bk Publ, Chicago, 44-46; fashion illusr, Evans, Work & Costa Advertising, Springfield, Ill, 55-59; fashion illusr, S A Barker Co, Springfield, 59-61; tech asst art dept, Ill State Mus, 61-63, cur art, 63-

Memberships: Am Asn Mus; Clayville Folk Arts Guild; Soc Archit Historians; Springfield Art Asn.
Research: Art, architecture & crafts in Illinois.
Mailing Address: 1145 S First St, Springfield, IL 62704.

MADSEN, VIGGO HOLM
Printmaker, Instructor
b Kaas, Denmark, Apr 21, 25; U S citizen.
Study & Training: Anderson Col, Syracuse Univ, BFA & MFA; New York Univ; Columbia Univ Teachers Col; Adelphi Univ; Inst Allende, San Miguel, Mex; Det Danske Selskab, Denmark.
Work in Public Collections: Philadelphia Ctr Older People, Pa; Nassau Community Col, Garden City, N Y; Anderson Col, Ind; C W Post Col, Brookville, N Y; N Shore Community Art Ctr, Great Neck, N Y.
Exhibitions: Drawings U S A, Saint Paul Art Ctr, Minn, 66; Triennial Exhib Graphics, Grenchen, Switz, 67; Xylon IV, Geneva, Switz, 68; U S Senate Chambers, Washington, D C, 68; Heckscher Mus Fine Arts, Huntington, N Y, 72.
Teaching: Instr art, Roslyn High Sch, N Y, 60-; instr art, Nassau Community Col, 66-
Positions: Ed, Newsletter, L I Art Teachers Asn, 62-64.
Awards: Second prize in graphics, Port Washington Art Adv Coun, 65-68; award of excellence, L I Craftsmen's Guild, 66-68; first prize graphics, Nat Art League, 72.
Bibliography: Jeanne Paris (auth), rev, In: L I Press, 7/71; Malcolm Preston (auth), rev, In: Newsday, 2/72; Dona Z Meilach (auth), chap, In, Creating art with textiles, Reilly & Lee.
Memberships: Prof Artists Guild (v pres, 69-70); L I Craftsmen's Guild; N Y State Art Teachers Asn (pres, 64-65); Am Crafts Coun; L I Art Teachers Asn (pres, 57-58).
Publications: Contribr, Art in action, 61, J Nat Art Educ Asn, 63 & J Eastern Arts Asn, 64; auth & publ, three demonstration booklets: Batik, Silk screening & Woodcut prints, 70-72.
Dealer: Marcos Baiter, 339 New York Ave, Huntington, NY 17743.
Mailing Address: 5 Meldon Ave, Albertson, NY 11507.

MAEHARA, HIROMU
Painter, Designer
b Nawiliwili, Hawaii, Nov 1, 14.
Study & Training: N Y Sch Design.
Exhibitions: Honolulu Artists, 41-61.
Teaching: Instr drawing & painting, Honolulu, Hawaii.
Positions: Former art dir advan art.
Awards: 9 prizes, Honolulu Artists, 55-69; prizes, 50th State Exhib, 60 & Hawaii Home Builders, 66; plus others.
Memberships: Asn Honolulu Artists.
Mailing Address: 2885 Kalili Valley Rd, Honolulu, HI 96814.

MAGAFAN, ETHEL
Painter
Preferred Media: Egg Tempera.
b Chicago, Ill.
Study & Training: Colo Springs Fine Arts Ctr with Frank Mechau, Boardman Robinson & Peppino Mangravite.
Work in Public Collections: Metrop Mus Art, New York, N Y; Munson-Williams-Proctor Inst, Utica, N Y; Butler Inst Am Art, Youngstown, Ohio; Memorial Library, Univ Notre Dame, Ind; Evansville Mus, Ind.
Commissions: Murals, Cotton Pickers, Post Office Lobby, Wynne, Ark, 39; Prairie Fire, Post Office Lobby, Madill, Okla, 40; Mountains in Snow (with Jenne Magafan), Bd Rm, Social Security Bldg, Washington, D C, 41; Horse Corral, Post Office Lobby, S Denver Br, Colo, 42; Battle of New Orleans, Main Foyer, Recorder of Deeds Bldg, Washington, D C, 43.
Exhibitions: American Painting Today, Metrop Mus Art, New York, 50; Am. Acad Arts & Lett, New York, 61, 64 & 69; Pa Acad Design, Philadelphia, 61, 62, 64, 67 & 69; Butler Inst Am Art, 63-66, 68-70; Nat Acad Design, New York, 65-72.
Awards: Benjamin Altman Prize, Nat Acad Design, 56 & 64; Juror's Choice Award, Albany Art Inst, 69; Childe Hassam Purchase Award, Am Acad Arts & Lett, 70.
Bibliography: Ernest W Watson (auth), Magafan & mountains, Am Artist Mag, 12/57; Jean Lipman & Cleve Gray (auth), The amazing inventiveness of women painters, Cosmopolitan Mag, 10/61.
Memberships: Nat Acad Design (mem coun, 72-75); Am Watercolor Soc; Audubon Artists; Philadelphia Watercolor Club; Woodstock Artist's Asn.
Dealer: Midtown Galleries, 11 E 57th St, New York, NY 10022.
Mailing Address: RFD Box 284, Woodstock, NY 12498.

MAGAZZINI, GENE
Painter
Preferred Media: Oils.
b New York, N Y, Nov 5, 14.
Study & Training: Siena, Italy, with pvt tutors; Brooklyn Col; Art Stud League New York, with Ivan Olinsky.

Work in Public Collections: Sloan-Kettering Inst, New York.
Exhibitions: State Capitol, Albany, N Y, 62; Allied Artists Am, Nat Acad Design, New York; Palais Congres, Expos Intercontinentale, Monaco; Nat Arts Club, New York; Salmagundi Club, New York.
Awards: First prize, Salmagundi Club, 69; best in show & purchase prize, Salmagundi Club, 70; best in show & gold medal, Nat Art League, 71.
Memberships: Salmagundi Club (cur, 70-72); Artists' Fel; Nat Art League; Art Stud League New York; Am Artists Prof League.
Dealer: Marcoleo, Ltd, 1295 First Ave at 70th St, New York, NY 10021.
Mailing Address: 249 Euclid Ave, Brooklyn, NY 11208.

MAGLEBY, FRANCIS R (FRANK)
Painter, Educator
Preferred Media: Oils.
b Idaho Falls, Idaho, Mar 22, 28.
Study & Training: Brigham Young Univ, BA, MA, 52; Art Stud League New York; Am Art Sch, New York; Columbia Univ, EdD, 67.
Commissions: Historical paintings for various church bldgs, Mormon Church, Salt Lake City, Utah & New York, N Y, 58-59; Heleman (mural), Brigham Young Univ, 65.
Exhibitions: One-man shows, Southern Vt Art Ctr, 55-59, Grand Cent Art Gallery, 57 & Brigham Young Univ, Utah, 68.
Teaching: Assoc prof painting, Brigham Young Univ, 59-
Positions: Dir, B F Larson Gallery, Brigham Young Univ, 62-69.
Memberships: Am Fedn Arts; Southern Vt Art Ctr; Grand Cent Art Gallery; Western Asn Mus; Art Stud League New York.
Mailing Address: 464 E 2200 North, Provo, UT 84601.

MAGRIEL, PAUL
Collector
b Mar 12, 16.
Study & Training: Columbia Univ.
Positions: Cur, dance arch, Mus Mod Art, N Y, 39-42.
Collection: Sport in art; American still life paintings, numismatics, drawings, watercolors; has been exhibited in 84 American museums.
Mailing Address: 85 East End Ave, New York, NY 10028.

MAGUIRE, CHARLES
Art Dealer
b Calcutta, India
Study & Training: Univ Calcutta; L'acad Maurice Testard, Paris, France; Univ Bradford; with Georges Benda & Andrew Shunney, Paris.
Positions: Mem admin staff, Hammer Galleries, New York, N Y, 66-67; dir, Wiener Galleries, New York, 67-68; v pres & dir, Vestart Inc, New York, 68-70; dir, Nantucket Gallery, Inc, Mass, 71-
Specialty of Gallery: Paintings & sculpture from Impressionists to present.
Mailing Address: Nantucket Gallery, Inc, Nantucket, MA 02554.

MAHAFFEY, MERRILL DEAN
Painter, Instructor
Preferred Media: Acrylics.
b Albuquerque, N Mex, Aug 12, 37.
Study & Training: Calif Col Arts & Crafts; Sacramento State Col, BA; Ariz State Univ, MFA, 67.
Work in Public Collections: Ariz State Univ, Tempe.
Exhibitions: Joslyn Mus Biennial, Omaha, Nebr, 61; one-man exhib, Fort Worth Art Ctr, Tex, 62; Mus N Mex Biennial, Santa Fe, 67; one-man exhib, Phoenix Art Mus, Ariz, 69; Ace Space Co Notebook Number One, Victoria Sch Visual Arts, Can, 70.
Teaching: Instr painting & art hist, Phoenix Col, 67-; fac art, Fat City Sch Finds Art, 72.
Positions: Dir, Southern Colo Long-haired Trout Fishermen's Asn, 68-; assoc, Ace Space Co, 70-
Dealer: Art Wagon Galleries, 7156 Main St, Scottsdale, AZ 85251.
Mailing Address: Art Dept, Phoenix College, 1202 W Thomas Rd, Phoenix, AZ 85013.

MAHAFFEY, NOEL A
Painter
Preferred Media: Acrylics.
b Saint Augustine, Fla, Apr 23, 44.
Study & Training: Dallas Mus Fine Arts, Tex; Pa Acad Fine Arts, Philadelphia.
Work in Public Collections: Okla Art Ctr, Oklahoma City; Philadelphia Mus Art; Pa Acad Fine Arts.
Exhibitions: Painting & Sculpture Show, Univ Ill, Urbana, 67; one-man show, Hundred Acres, New York, N Y, 71; Sharp Focus

Realism, Sidney Janis Gallery, New York, 72; Whitney Painting Ann, Whitney Mus Am Art, New York, 72.
Mailing Address: c/o Hundred Acres, 456 W Broadway, New York, NY 10012.

MAHEY, JOHN A
Art Administrator
b Du Bois, Pa, Mar 30, 32.
Study & Training: Columbia Col, 50-52; Pa State Univ, BA, MA (art hist).
Collections Arranged: Sarah Miriam Peale, Peale Mus, Baltimore, Md, 68; Master Drawings from Sacramento, E B Crocker Art Gallery, Calif, 71.
Positions: Asst dir, Peale Mus, Baltimore, 64-69; dir, E B Crocker Art Gallery, Sacramento, 69-72; dir, Cummer Gallery Art, Jacksonville, 72-
Research: James McNeil Whistler & Rembrandt Peale.
Publications: Auth, Letters of James McNeil Whistler to George Lucas, 67, Sarah Miriam Peale, portraits & still life, 68, The lithographs of Rembrandt Peale, 69, The studio of Rembrandt Peale, 69 & Master drawings from Sacramento: the Crocker Collection, 71.
Mailing Address: Cummer Gallery of Art, 829 Riverside Ave, Jacksonville, FL 32204.

MAHMOUD, BEN
Painter
Preferred Media: Acrylics.
b Charleston, W Va, Oct 6, 35.
Study & Training: Columbus Art Sch, prof cert; Ohio Univ, BFA & MFA.
Work in Public Collections: Ill State Mus, Springfield, Ill; Krannart Mus, Univ Ill, Urbana; Ball State Univ, Muncie, Ind; Josyln Mus, Omaha, Nebr; Columbus Gallery Fine Arts, Ohio.
Commissions: Bas-relief, Wurlitzer Co, 67; serigraph, Quincy Found, Ill, 72.
Exhibitions: First Flint Int Invitational, Flint Art Inst, 66; Violence Exhib, Mus Contemp Art, Chicago, Ill, 67; Contemp Art in the Midwest, Notre Dame Univ, South Bend, Ind, 68; Art Today, Indianapolis Mus Art, Ind, 70; New Horizons in Painting, Chicago, 72.
Awards: Purchase award, Ball State Univ, 70; purchase award, Images on Paper '70, Miss, 70; best of show, New Horizons in Painting, Chicago, 71.
Bibliography: Frans Schultze (auth), review, Chicago Daily News Panorama, 67; Joshua Kind (auth), review, Art News, 67; Kulterman (auth), New painting, Praeger, 70.
Publications: Auth, article, In: Prize Winning Paintings, Allied Fla, 61 & 64; contribr, Chicago Omnibus, Chicago Midwest Art & Art Gallery Mag, 67; illusr, Motive Mag, 68.
Dealer: Phyllis Kind Gallery, E Ontario St, Chicago, IL 60611.
Mailing Address: 222 W Church St, Genoa, IL 60135.

MAHONEY, JAMES OWEN
Painter, Educator
b Dallas, Tex, Oct 16, 07.
Study & Training: Southern Methodist Univ, BA, 29; Yale Sch Fine Arts, BFA, 32; Prix de Rome, Am Acad in Rome, 32-35.
Commissions: Murals, Hall of State, Tex Centennial Expos, Dallas, 36, Hall of Judiciary, Fed Bldg & Commun Bldg, N Y World's Fair, 38, pres suite, Adolphus Hotel, Dallas, 50 & Shriver Hall, Johns Hopkins Univ, 57; altar piece, All Saints Episcopal Church, Chevy Chase, Md, 58.
Exhibitions: Pa Acad Fine Arts; Grand Cent Art Gallery; Mace Gallery, Dallas; Archit League.
Teaching: Prof art, Cornell Univ, 54-, chmn dept, 63-68.
Memberships: Nat Soc Mural Painters.
Mailing Address: 45 Twin Glens Rd, Ithaca, NY 14850.

MAINARDI, PATRICIA M
Painter, Writer
Preferred Media: Oils.
b Paterson, N J, Nov 10, 42.
Study & Training: Vassar Col, AB, 59-63; Columbia Univ, with John Heliker, 63-64; New York Studio Sch, with Mercedes Matter, Charles Cajori & Estaban Vicente, 65-66.
Exhibitions: Painterly Realism, Am Fedn Arts Nat Traveling Exhib, 69-71; The Representational Spirit, Univ Gallery, State Univ N Y Albany, 70; Drawing Each Other, Brooklyn Mus, N Y, 71; New England Landscapes, Fleming Mus, Burlington, Vt, 71; one artist show, Green Mountain Gallery, New York, N Y, 71.
Teaching: Vis lectr, Moore Col, 69, N Y Univ, 69, Pratt Inst, 71, Univ R I, 71 & State Univ N Y Buffalo, 72.
Positions: Ed, Coccatrice, 61-63; ed, Women & Art, 71-72; ed, Feminist Art J, 72-

Bibliography: Reviews, In: Art News, 10/69 & 11/71; Sara Whitworth (auth), Pat Mainardi, The Ladder, 72; Cindy Nemser (auth), Changes, Male Nude, 6/72.
Memberships: Women in Arts; Figurative Artists Alliance.
Publications: Contribr, Sisterhood is powerful, 70; contribr, Notes from second year, N Y Rev Bks, 70; contribr, Woman's World, 72.
Dealer: Green Mountain Gallery, 135 Greene St, New York, NY 10012.
Mailing Address: 602 Carlton Ave, Brooklyn, NY 11238.

MAITIN, SAMUEL (CALMAN)
Printmaker, Designer
Preferred Media: Graphics.
b Philadelphia, Pa, Oct 26, 28.
Study & Training: Philadelphia Mus Sch Art, dipl, 49; Univ Pa, BA, 51; printmaking with Ezio Martinelli.
Work in Public Collections: Libr Cong, Washington, D C; Mus Mod Art, New York, N Y; Philadelphia Mus Art, Pa; Victoria & Albert Mus, London, Eng; Nat Gallery Art, Washington, D C.
Commissions: 47 posters, Major Poster Proj, Philadelphia YM/YWHA Arts Coun, 61-68; color etching still life, Nude & Oscar Wilde, Philadelphia Print Club, 62; Androcles and the Lion (film), NBC TV film, 63; Laird-God, Tamarind Lithography Workshop, Calif, 69; French Primitive Photographers, Aperture, 70.
Exhibitions: Brooklyn Mus Ann, N Y, 51-66; 3 Graphic Artists: Feldman, Maitin, Mavignier, Philadelphia Mus Art, 66; Yoseido Gallery, Tokyo, Japan, 67, 69 & 70; 3rd Int Graphic Biennale, Poland, 70; Klingspor-Mus, Offenbach, Ger, 72.
Teaching: Instr design, Moore Col Art, 49-51; instr printmaking & drawing, Philadelphia Col Art, 49-59; head visual graphic commun, Annenberg Sch Commun, Univ Pa, 64-70.
Awards: John Simon Guggenheim Found fel graphics, 68; Am Color Print Soc Purchase Prize, 70; 50 Best Bks of Yr, Minor White, 70; plus others.
Bibliography: Ruth Rotko (auth), The style of Sam Maitin, Ctr City Philadelphian, 71; Sam Maitin—his work—1956-1971 (catalog), Philadelphia Mus Art, 71.
Art Interests: Book design, murals.
Publications: Designer, Minor white—mirrors, messages, manifestations, 69 & The Appalachian photographs of Doris Ulmann, 71, Aperture; illusr, Turning of the year, 70, Gentle gentle Thursday, 71 & A love story, 72, Holt, Rinehart & Winston.
Mailing Address: 704 Pine St, Philadelphia, PA 19106.

MAJDRAKOFF, IVAN
Painter, Educator
b New York, N Y, June 19, 27.
Study & Training: Cranbrook Acad Art, with Wallace Mitchell.
Work in Public Collections: Univ Gallery, Univ Minn; Minneapolis Inst Art.
Commissions: Black & white photographic collage, Bronx State Hosp, N Y, 71; Masonite outdoor mural, San Francisco Art Comn.
Exhibitions: Pa Acad Art, Philadelphia; Detroit Art Inst, Mich; Walker Art Ctr, Minneapolis; San Francisco Mus Art; Drawing Exhib, Mus Mod Art, New York, N Y.
Teaching: Instr drawing & painting, San Francisco Art Inst, 57-; instr drawing, Stanford Univ, 57-58 & 68-69.
Positions: Actg dir, univ art gallery, Univ Minn, 52-55; dir, Stanford Univ Gallery, 62.
Bibliography: Al Wong (auth), Portrait of Ivan (film), 68.
Mailing Address: 70 Zoe St, San Francisco, CA 94107.

MAKARENKO, ZACHARY PHILIPP
Painter, Sculptor
Preferred Media: Tempera, Oils, Watercolors, Acrylics, Granite, Marble, Wood.
b North Caucasus, Russia, Feb 20, 00; U S citizen.
Study & Training: State Univ Acad Fine Arts, Kiev; also study in Ger & Italy.
Work in Public Collections: Many pub & pvt collections worldwide.
Exhibitions: Angelicum, Regional Italian IV Relig Exhib, Milan, 47; U S A Relig Exhib, Burr Gallery, New York, N Y, 58; Am Artists Prof League Grand Nat, New York, 66; Painter & Sculptor Soc Exhib, Jersey City Mus, N J, 71; Nat Acad Design Galleries, New York, 71.
Teaching: Instr pvt studio, 20-
Awards: Ann Hyatt Huntington Award, Am Artists Prof League, 66; medal of hon, Painter & Sculptor Soc Exhib, Jersey City Mus, 71; Allied Artists Am Gold Medal of Hon for sculpture, Nat Acad Design Galleries, 71.
Bibliography: Article, In: La Rev Mod, Paris, France, 64; article, In: City East, New York, 71.
Memberships: Fel Am Artists Prof League.
Mailing Address: 7332 Kennedy Blvd, North Bergen, NJ 07047.

MAKI, ROBERT RICHARD
Sculptor
b Walla Walla, Wash, Sept 15, 38.
Study & Training: Western Wash State Col, BA, 62; Univ Wash, MFA, 66; San Francisco Art Inst Summer Workshop, 67.
Work in Public Collections: Henry Gallery, Univ Wash, Seattle; Wash Univ, Saint Louis, Mo; State Hwy Admin Bldg, Olympia, Wash.
Commissions: Cent plaza sculpture, comn by Port of Seattle, Seattle-Tacoma Int Airport, 72.
Exhibitions: One-man show, Richmond Art Ctr, Calif, 67; West Coast Now, Portland Art Mus, Seattle Art Mus Pavilion, De Young Mus, San Francisco, Calif & Los Angeles Munic Mus, Calif, 68; Robert Maki-Construction, Michael Walls Gallery, San Francisco, 69; Doane Col Nat, Crete, Nebr, 69; Uses of Structure, Michael Walls Gallery, San Francisco, 70; plus others.
Awards: Nat Endowment for the Arts Award, 68.
Bibliography: Sally Hayman (auth), Design defies classification, Northwest Today Mag, Seattle Post Intel, 9/22/68; Peter Selz & Tom Robbins (auth), West Coast report: the Pacific Northwest today, Art in Am, 11-12/68; Palmer D French (auth), San Francisco, Artforum, 9/69.
Mailing Address: 14341 Interlake Ave N, Seattle, WA 98133.

MAKLER, HOPE WELSH
Art Dealer
b Philadelphia, Pa, Mar 24, 24.
Study & Training: Drexel Univ, BS; Bryn Mawr Col & Univ Pa, MA; Barnes Found.
Positions: Owner & dir, Makler Gallery.
Specialty of Gallery: Twentieth century painting, sculpture and graphics; Indian and African art.
Mailing Address: 1716 Locust St, Philadelphia, PA 19103.

MALBIN, LYDIA WINSTON
Collector
Positions: Comnr, trustee & chmn collection comt, Detroit Inst Arts; mem int coun, Mus Mod Art, New York.
Art Interests: Collection was exhibited as a whole in Detroit Institute of Arts, in part in other museums in the United States and Europe.
Collection: Twentieth century art—futurism, cubism, deStill, Dada, colorists, constructionists; also large collection of graphics of the twentieth century including drawings by Picasso, Gris, Leger, Boccioni, Severini, Balla and others; numerous prints.
Mailing Address: 483 Aspen Rd, Birmingham, MI 48009.

MALICOAT, PHILIP CECIL
Painter
Preferred Media: Oils, Pencil.
b Indianapolis, Ind, Dec 9, 08.
Study & Training: John Herron Art Inst; Cape Cod Sch; Cape Sch Art; also with Charles W Hawthorne & E W Dickinson.
Work in Public Collections: Rochester Mus Art, N Y; Chrysler Mus, Norfolk, Va; Provincetown Art Asn, Mass; Joseph H Hirshhorn Collection, Washington, D C.
Exhibitions: Provincetown Art Asn, 32-72; Pa Acad Fine Arts, Philadelphia, 33; Corcoran Gallery Art, Washington, D C, 38; Nat Acad Design, New York, N Y, 54; Art U S A, New York, 59.
Awards: Prizes from Cape Cod Art Asn & Falmouth Artists Guild.
Memberships: Provincetown Art Asn (trustee, 66-69, hon v pres, 69-72); Beachcombers (pres).
Dealer: Provincetown Group Gallery, 359 Commercial St, Provincetown, MA 02657.
Mailing Address: 320 Bradford St, Provincetown, MA 02657.

MALKASIAN, GREGOR
Sculptor
Preferred Media: Stone.
b New York, N Y, 43.
Study & Training: Sch Visual Arts; Soc Illustrators.
Exhibitions: Silvermine Guild Artists, Conn, 71; Allied Artists Am 58th Ann, New York, 71; 10th Ann Sculpture House Exhib, 71; Nat Acad Design 147th Ann, New York, 71 & 148th Ann, 72.
Awards: 10th Ann Sculpture House Award, 71.
Mailing Address: c/o Gallery Madison 90, 1248 Madison Ave, New York, NY 10020.

MALLARY, ROBERT
Sculptor, Educator
b Toledo, Ohio, Dec 2, 17.
Study & Training: Escuela Artes Libro, Mexico City, 38-39.
Work in Public Collections: Mus Mod Art & Whitney Mus Am Art, New York, NY; Los Angeles Co Mus, Calif; Albright-Knox Art Gallery, Buffalo; Univ Calif, Berkeley.
Commissions: Glass & plastic mosaic (with Dale Owen), Beverly Hills Hotel, 54; N Y State Pavilion, New York World's Fair, 64; welded steel mural, Albany Mall Proj, 67.
Exhibitions: 16 Americans, 59 & The Art of Assemblage, 61, Mus Mod Art, New York; Carnegie Int, Pittsburgh, Pa, 62; Ten American Sculptors, Seventh São Paulo Biennial, Brazil, 63; Cybernetic Serendipity, Inst Contemp Art, London, Eng, 68.
Teaching: Asst prof art, Univ N Mex, 55-59; adj prof art, Pratt Inst, 59-67; prof sculpture, Univ Mass, Amherst, 67-
Positions: Dir, Arstecnica: Interdisciplinary Ctr for Art & Technol, Univ Mass, 72-
Bibliography: Art crashes through the junk pile, Life Mag, 51: 60-64; Collage: personalities, concepts, techniques, Janis & Plesh, 62; Harris Rothenstein (auth), Ideologue in lotus land, Art News, 10/66.
Publications: Auth, Self interview, Location, Spring 63; auth, The air of art is poisoned, Art News, 10/63; co-auth, Interview, Artforum, 1/64; auth, computer sculpture: six levels of cybernetics, Artforum, 5/69.
Dealer: Allan Stone Gallery, 86th St at Madison, New York, NY 10028.
Mailing Address: P O Box 48, Conway, MA 01341.

MALLINSON, CONSTANCE (CONSTANCE MALLINSON ALTER)
Painter
Preferred Media: Acrylics.
b Washington, D C, May 10, 48.
Study & Training: Univ Ga, BFA.
Exhibitions: Atlanta First Nat, Ga, 71; Piedmont Art Exhib, Atlanta, 71; Group Show, Illien Gallery, Atlanta, 71; Northern Va Fine Arts Exhib, Alexandria, 72; one-woman show, Atheneum, Alexandria, Va, 72.
Positions: Art dir, Film Group, Inc, Alexandria, 71-
Awards: Best in show, Northern Va Fine Arts Asn, 72.
Mailing Address: 131 N Washington St, Alexandria, VA 22304.

MALLORY, LARRY RICHARD
Painter, Instructor
Preferred Media: Pencil.
b Punxsutawney, Pa, June 18, 49.
Study & Training: Ind Univ Pa, BS & grad work.
Exhibitions: Indiana, Pa, 70; Johnstown War Mem Exhib, 71; Am Artists Prof League Ann, Pa Chap, Ebensburg, 71; Am Artists Prof League Grand Nat, New York, N Y, 72; One-man show, Carnegie-Mellon Univ, Pittsburgh, Pa, 72.
Teaching: Asst art, Ind Univ Pa, 70-71; instr art, Moskannon Valley Sch Dist, 71-
Awards: First prize, Am Artists Prof League Fair Show, Ebensburg, 72; first drawing award, Indiana Art Asn.
Memberships: Am Artists Prof League; Indiana Art Asn.
Mailing Address: R D 1, Glen Campbell, PA 15742.

MALLORY, MARGARET
Collector
b Brooklyn, N Y, Oct 30, 11.
Positions: Pres, Falcon Films, Inc; trustee, Santa Barbara Mus Art; trustee, Marine Hist Asn, Mystic, Conn; chmn affil art, Univ Calif, Santa Barbara.
Collection: Nineteenth and twentieth century European and American paintings, drawings, sculpture; Baroque sculpture.
Mailing Address: 305 Ortega Ridge Rd, Santa Barbara, CA 93103.

MALLORY, RONALD
Sculptor
b Los Angeles, Calif, June 17, 35.
Study & Training: Univ Colo, BA, 51; Univ Fla, BArch, 52; Sch Fine Arts, Rio de Janeiro, with Roberto Burle Marx, 56; Acad Julian, Paris, 58.
Work in Public Collections: Mus Mod Art; Whitney Mus Am Art; Univ Mus, Berkeley, Calif; Inst Contemp Art, Boston, Mass; Inst Contemp Art, Philadelphia, Pa; plus others.
Exhibitions: Mus Mod Art, 66 & 68; Worcester Mus Art, Mass, 67; Univ Ill, 67 & 68; Larry Aldrich Mus, Ridgefield, Conn, 67 & 68; Torcuato di Tella, Buenos Aires, Arg, 69; plus others.
Mailing Address: 333 E 69th St, New York, NY 10021.

MALONE, JAMES WILLIAM
Art Administrator
b Savannah, N Y, Apr 12, 43.
Study & Training: State Univ N Y Col Oswego, BA.
Work in Public Collections: Dallas Mus Fine Arts, Tex.
Exhibitions: Invitational Drawing Show, Southern Ill Univ, 70; Project S/SW II, Fort Worth Art Ctr Mus, Tex, 71; Whitney Mus Am Art Ann, New York, N Y, 72.
Positions: Registrar, Fort Worth Art Ctr Mus, 70-
Mailing Address: 1204 15th Pl, Fort Worth, TX 76106.

MALONE, LEE H B
Art Administrator
b Las Cruces, N Mex, May 28, 13.
Study & Training: Univ Sch, Cleveland, Ohio; Sch Fine Arts, Yale
Univ, BA; Chillon Col, Switz; also with Henri Focillon.
Collections Arranged: Art in Colonial Mexico, 52.
Teaching: Instr hist art, Notre Dame Col, Staten Island, 40.
Positions: Dir, Columbus Gallery Fine Arts; dir, mus fine arts,
Houston, 53-59; exec dir, Nat Develop Comn, Pierpont Morgan
Libr, 60-61; dir, Mus Fine Arts, St Petersburg, 68-
Awards: W L Ehrich Mem Prize for research, Yale Univ, 39.
Publications: Auth, Spiritual values in art, Abrams, 53.
Mailing Address: 255 Beach Drive N E, St Petersburg, FL 33701.

MALONE, ROBERT R
Painter, Printmaker
Preferred Media: Mixed Media.
b McColl, S C, Aug 8, 33.
Study & Training: Furman Univ; Univ N C, AB; Univ Chicago, MFA;
State Univ Iowa.
Work in Public Collections: Whitney Mus Am Art, New York, N Y;
Calif Palace of Legion of Hon, San Francisco; Philadelphia Mus
Art, Pa; Smithsonian Inst, Washington, D C; Libr of Cong, Wash-
ington.
Commissions: Color etching (edition of 200), Int Graphic Arts Soc,
New York, 66; several editions of intaglio & relief prints,
Ferdinand Roten Galleries, Baltimore, Md, 66-69; two editions
intaglio & relief prints, De Cinque Gallery, Hollywood, Fla, 67;
three editions mixed media prints, Eye Corp, Chicago, Ill, 72.
Exhibitions: 15th Nat Print Exhib, Brooklyn Mus Art, N Y, 66;
Decade .7, Contemporary American Art (invitational), Southern
Ill Univ, 67; New Talent in Printmaking, 1968 (invitational), AAA
Gallery, New York, 68; Invitational Biennial Print Exhib, Calif
State Col, Long Beach, 69; Bienniale Int L'Estampe 1970, Mus
Mod Art, Paris, France, 70.
Teaching: Assoc prof painting & printmaking, Wesleyan Col, Macon,
Ga, 61-68; assoc prof printmaking, W Va Univ, Morgantown, 68-
70; assoc prof printmaking, Southern Ill Univ, Edwardsville, 70-
Awards: Philips award, 85th Ann Exhib, San Francisco Art Inst, 66;
purchase award, 1st Ann Print Am Exhib, Peabody Col, 67;
purchase award, Colorprint U S A, Tex Tech Univ, 71.
Memberships: Silvermine Guild Artists; Mid-Am Col Art Conf; Col
Art Asn Am.
Dealer: Associated American Artists, 663 Fifth Ave, New York,
NY 10022.
Mailing Address: 600 Chapman St, Edwardsville, IL 62025.

MALSCH, ELLEN L
Painter, Instructor
Preferred Media: Watercolors.
b Copenhagen, Denmark; U S citizen.
Study & Training: Art Inst Chicago.
Work in Public Collections: Univ Wis-Madison; Luther Col, Dec-
orah, Iowa; Univ Wis-La Crosse; Waukesha Co Tech Inst, Pe-
waukee, Wis; Univ Wis, Rockcount Campus, Janesville.
Exhibitions: Wis Painters & Sculptors Show, Milwaukee Art Ctr,
62; three-man show, Wright Art Ctr, Beloit Col, Wis, 64; Draw-
ings U S A, Nat Biennial Show, St Paul, Minn, 66; Ill State Fair
Prof Show, Springfield, Ill, 69; Watercolor U S A, Springfield,
Mo, 71; plus others.
Teaching: Private classes, 60-72; instr watercolor, Burpee Art
Mus, Rockford, Ill, 67-70; lectr, watercolor techniques.
Awards: First prize, Rockford Vicinity Show, Burpee Art Mus, 63;
purchase prize, Beloit Vicinity Show, Beloit Col, 65; purchase
prize, Univ Wis-La Crosse, 69.
Bibliography: Margaret Harold (auth), Prize winning watercolors,
Allied Publ, 63 & 64; article, In: La Rev Mod, 67.
Memberships: Wis Painters & Sculptors.
Dealer: Art Independent Gallery, Main St, Lake Geneva, WI 53147.
Mailing Address: Walker Rd, Rte 1, Box 298, Beloit, WI 53511.

MALTZMAN, STANLEY
Printmaker, Painter
Preferred Media: Charcoal, Graphics.
b New York, N Y, July 4, 21.
Work in Public Collections: Eisenhower Col, Salem, N Y; Pleasant-
ville Mid Sch, N Y.
Exhibitions: Am Acad Arts & Letters, New York, 69; Nat Acad De-
sign, New York, 70; Norfolk Mus Arts & Sci, Va, 71; Smithsonian
Inst Traveling Exhib, 71-72; Acad Artists Asn, Mus Fine Arts,
Springfield, Mass, 72.
Awards: Childe Hassam Fund purchase award, Am Acad Arts &
Letters, 69; gold medal, Am Artists Prof League, 70; gold medal,
Hudson Valley Art Asn, 71.

Memberships: Hudson Valley Art Asn (dir, 72); Am Artists Prof
League; Yonkers Art Asn; Acad Artists Asn.
Dealers: Weyhe Gallery, 794 Lexington Ave, New York, NY 10021;
Frank Rehn Gallery, 655 Madison Ave, New York, NY 10021.
Mailing Address: 8 Armstrong Ave, Yonkers, NY 10701.

MANAREY, THELMA ALBERTA
Printmaker, Painter
Preferred Media: Graphics.
b Edmonton, Alta, May 2, 13.
Study & Training: Inst Technol & Art, Calgary; Univ Alta; Univ Wash
Summer Workshops; Banff Sch Fine Arts, with Charles Stegeman;
Univ Calgary, with Shane Weare & Andrew Stasik; also with
Emma Lake, John Ferren & Ken Noland.
Work in Public Collections: Edmonton Pub Sch Bd; Can Painter-
Etchers & Engravers; ERB Mem Union, Univ Ore; Manisphere,
Winnipeg.
Commissions: Portrait of Roberta MacAdams, Women of Alta, Prov
Legis, 67.
Exhibitions: Can Landscape Painters, Stratford, 64; Tenth Winnipeg
Show, 66; Can Graphics, 70; West '71; Design, 72; Canpex, 72.
Awards: Manisphere Award, 65; Centennial Visual Arts Award, 67;
award, Pac Northwest Art Ann, 69.
Memberships: Alta Soc Artists (prov v pres, 65, 67 & 68); Can
Painter-Etchers & Engravers.
Dealer: Framecraft, 7711 85th St, Edmonton, Alta, Can.
Mailing Address: 12026 93rd St, Edmonton, Alta T5G 1E8, Can.

MANCA, ALBINO
Sculptor
b Tertenia, Italy, Jan 1, 98.
Study & Training: Acad Fine Arts, Rome, with Ferrari & Zanelli.
Commissions: Pieta Medallion in gold, off medal Vatican Pavillion,
N Y World's Fair, 64-65; Pope Paul VI Peace Medallion in gold,
Treasury of St Peter, The Vatican, 65; The Diving Eagle, 2nd
World War E Coast Mem, Battery Park, New York, N Y; The
Gate of Life, entrance gate, Queens Zoo, New York, N Y, 68;
Robert Moses Bronze Medallion, Fordham Univ, 70; plus others.
Exhibitions: Many nat & int exhibs.
Teaching: Former prof, Acad Fine Arts, Rome.
Awards: Ellin P Speyer Prize for Lady Gazelle, 64 & Mahonry
Young Mem Prize, 66, Nat Acad Design; winner competition for
Hodgkins Medal, Smithsonian Inst, 65; plus others.
Memberships: Nat Acad Design; fel Nat Sculpture Soc; Am Artists
Prof League; Allied Artists Am.
Mailing Address: 131 W 11th St, New York, NY 10011.

MANCUSO, LENI (LENI MANCUSO BARRETT)
Painter, Instructor
Preferred Media: Watercolor, Casein.
b New York, N Y.
Study & Training: Brooklyn Mus Art Sch, with Reuben Tam & Wil-
liam Kienbusch; Art Stud League New York; Pratt Inst, N Y.
Work in Public Collections: Newberry Collection, Detroit, Mich;
First Nat Bank Boston, Mass; Portland Mus Art, Maine; St Paul's
Sch, Concord, N H.
Exhibitions: Maine Art Gallery, Wiscasset, 70; New Eng Landscape
Paintings, De Cordova Mus, Lincoln, Mass, 71; Lyman Allen
Mus, Conn; Wadsworth Athenaeum, Hartford, Conn; New Eng Col,
Henniker, N H; plus others.
Teaching: Instr painting & head art dept, Proctor Acad, Andover,
N H, 55-60; instr painting & watercolor, Currier Gallery Art Sch,
Manchester, N H, 62-70; instr painting & compos, St Paul's Sch,
Concord, N H, 67-
Awards: Watercolor prize, Portland Mus Art, Maine, 61 & Currier
Gallery Art, N H, 68.
Memberships: N H Art Asn; Boston Visual Artists Union.
Dealer: Klein-Vogel, 8104 E Jefferson, Detroit, MI 48214.
Mailing Address: St Paul's School, Concord, NH 03301.

MANDEL, HOWARD
Painter, Sculptor
Preferred Media: Acrylics, Oils, Watercolors.
b Bayside, N Y, Feb 24, 17.
Study & Training: Pratt Inst, New York; New York Sculpture Ctr;
Art Stud League New York; Atelier Fernand Léger, Paris,
France; Atelier André L'Hôte, Paris; Ecole Beaux Arts, Sor-
bonne, France.
Work in Public Collections: Whitney Mus Am Art, New York, N Y;
Butler Inst Am Art, Youngstown, Ohio; Norfolk Mus Arts & Sci,
Va; State Univ Teachers Col Mus, Oswego, N Y; San Antonio Mus,
Tex.
Commissions: Three-dimensional mural, Zenith Radio Corp, for
Refregier Studio, Woodstock, N Y, 58.
Exhibitions: Whitney Mus Am Art Ann, 48-59; American Painting
Today 1950, Metrop Mus Art, New York, 50; & Am Watercolors,

Drawings & Prints, Metrop Mus Art, New York; Nat Inst Arts & Lett, Acad Art Gallery, New York 55 & 61; Fulbright Painters, Whitney Mus Am Art & Smithsonian Inst, Washington, D C, 59.
Positions: Graphic artist, film design, CBS TV Studio One, 54-57; graphic artist, film design, NBC TV Amahl & the Night Visitors, 55; art dir, Heath de Rochemont, D C Heath & Co, Boston, Mass, 63-68; art dir, Roemer-Young Assocs, New York, 69; art dir, Film Group, Inc, Cambridge, Mass, 71.
Awards: Louis Comfort Tiffany fel, 39 & 49; Hallmark Int Awards, 49, 52 & 55; Fulbright scholar to Paris, 51-52.
Bibliography: Zaidenberg (auth), The art of the artist, Crown, 51; Ralph M Pearson (auth), The modern renaissance in American art, Harper & Row, 54; Herdeg & Rosner (auth), article, In: Graphics Ann, 55.
Memberships: Am Watercolor Soc; Nat Soc Mural Painters; Nat Soc Painters in Casein & Acrylic (corres secy, 64-67, v pres, 68); Audubon Artists; Allied Artists Am.
Mailing Address: 285 Central Park W, New York, NY 10024.

MANDEL, JOHN
Painter
b New York, N Y, Dec 6, 41.
Study & Training: Pratt Inst, BFA, 64.
Work in Public Collections: Nat Gallery Australia; Pa State Univ.
Exhibitions: Whitney Mus Am Art Painting Ann, 69 & 72; The Contemp Figure, A New Realism, Suffolk Mus & Carriage House at Stony Brook, N Y, 71; In Sharp Focus, Sidney Janis Gallery, New York, 72; Indianapolis Mus Ann, Ind, 72.
Teaching: Instr painting, grad & undergrad sch, Pratt Inst, 71-; instr painting, Calif Inst Arts, 72-
Bibliography: John Canaday (auth), Art: the figure as defined by Mandel, New York Times, 11/21/71.
Mailing Address: c/o Max Hutchinson Gallery, 127 Greene St, New York, NY 10012.

MANDELBAUM, DR & MRS ROBERT A
Collectors
Dr Mandelbaum, b New York, N Y, Feb 11, 22; Mrs Mandelbaum, b New York, N Y, Dec 20, 20.
Study & Training: Dr Mandelbaum, Wesleyan Univ; New York Univ Col Med; Mrs Mandelbaum, Mt Holyoke Col.
Collection: African sculpture; modern sculpture, including works by Moore, Marini, Calder, Lipton, Stanckiewicz, Arp, Nojuchi, Smith and Caro; modern painting including works by Knaths, O'Keefe, Avery, Davis, Sutherland, Gatch, Burchfield, Pearlstein, Hoffman, Bannard, Stella, Noland, Olitski, Katz, Rothko, Rauschenberg, Motherwell, Ron Davis, Vasarely and Frankenthaler; modern graphics.
Mailing Address: 571 Ocean Ave, Brooklyn, NY 11226.

MANDLE, EARL ROGER
Art Administrator, Art Historian
b Hackensack, N J, May 13, 41.
Study & Training: Williams Col, BA, 63; Art Stud League New York; Inst Fine Arts, New York Univ, mus training cert & MA, 67; Metrop Mus Art; Victoria & Albert Mus.
Collections Arranged: 30 Contemporary Black Artists, 68; Catalogue of European Paintings, Minneapolis Inst Arts, 70; Dutch Masterpieces from the Eighteenth Century, 71-72.
Teaching: Instr art, Phillips Acad, Andover, Mass, 63-64; instr art, McBurney Sch, New York, N Y, 64-65.
Positions: Cur, Inst Fine Arts Photog Arch, New York, 67; asst dir, Minneapolis Inst Arts, 67-71, assoc dir, 72-
Awards: Andover teaching fel, Phillips Acad, 63; Ford Found mus fel, 66-67.
Bibliography: J Woelm (auth), Dutch Masterpieces from the 18th century (film), Woelm-Polister Prod, 72; J Canaday (auth), Dutch masterpieces from the 18th century, New York Times, 72.
Memberships: Col Art Asn Am; Achtiendse Eeuw Werkgroep, Holland; Am Soc 18th Century Studies; Hendrik De Keyser Hist Soc, Holland; Am Asn Mus.
Research: Eighteenth century Dutch art and nineteenth centure English art.
Publications: Contribr, A new drawing by Jacques De Gheyn, 68, Lamentation, 69 & Peace concluded, 70, Minneapolis Inst Arts Bull; contribr, The shepherd's dream, Albertina-Studien, 72; contribr, Jacob De Wit and the Amsterdam Town Hall, Apollo, 8/72.
Mailing Address: Minneapolis Institute of Art, 201 E 24th St, Minneapolis, MN 55404.

MANDZUIK, MICHAEL DENNIS
Painter, Printmaker
Preferred Media: Acrylics, Ink.
b Detroit, Mich, Jan 14, 42.
Work in Public Collections: Numerous pvt collections.

Exhibitions: New York Int Art Show, 70; Tex Fine Arts Asn Ann Traveling Show, 71 & 72; J L Hudson 4 in One Show, Detroit, 71; Boston Printmakers 24th Nat, 72.
Teaching: Lectr, Univ Mich Sch Med Creativity Sem, 69 & Psychiat J, 70.
Positions: Artist-craftsman juror, Ann Arbor St Art Fair, 71; indust illusr, Ford Motor Co.
Awards: Merit award, Detroit Artist Mkt, 71 & 72; purchase award, Park Forest Ill Art Ctr, 72.
Mailing Address: 17994 Ruth St, Melvindale, MI 48122.

MANGIONE, PATRICIA ANTHONY
Painter
Preferred Media: Oils, Acrylics.
b Seattle, Wash.
Study & Training: Fleisher Art Mem, Philadelphia; Barnes Found, Merion, Pa.
Work in Public Collections: Inst Contemp Art, Dallas, Tex; Fleisher Art Mem; Moore Col Art, Philadelphia, Pa; Westchester State Mus, Pa; Rochester Mem Art Gallery, N Y.
Commissions: Acrylic on wood mural, Continental Bank & Trust Co, Philadelphia, 69.
Exhibitions: Four one-man shows, Frank Rehn Gallery, 60-68; one-man shows, Univ Pa, 64, U S Govt Gallery, Palermo, Italy, 65; Rosemont Col, Pa, 67 & McCleaf Gallery, Philadelphia, 71.
Teaching: Instr painting, Fleisher Art Mem, 48-61; instr painting, Suburban Art Ctr, Bryn Mawr, Pa, 59-61.
Awards: Philadelphia Art Teachers Asn First Prize, 57 & 64; five Yaddo resident fels, 62-72; Saratoga Springs Oil Prize, 66.
Bibliography: Burton Wasserman (auth), The art of Patricia Mangione, Sims Press, Inc, 71 & Painter with flair, Courier-Post, Camden, 71.
Memberships: Artists Equity Asn; Philadelphia Art Alliance; Inst Contemp Art, Univ Pa.
Publications: Illusr, Sicilia, Ital Govt Quart, 66 & 68; auth, Some observations on the experience of painting, Parapsychol Found, Inc, 70; auth, Exercise in magic, Sunday Bull, Philadelphia, 71.
Dealer: Frank Rehn Gallery, 655 Madison Ave, New York, NY 10021.
Mailing Address: 1939 Panama St, Philadelphia, PA 19103.

MANGOLD, ROBERT PETER
Painter
b North Tonawanda, N Y, Oct 12, 37.
Study & Training: Cleveland Inst Art; Yale Univ, BFA & MFA.
Work in Public Collections: Solomon R Guggenheim Mus, Mus Mod Art & Whitney Mus Am Art, New York, N Y; Los Angeles Co Mus Art, Calif.
Exhibitions: Robert Mangold, Solomon R Guggenheim Mus, 71.
Teaching: Instr art, Sch Visual Arts, Hunter Col, Cornell Univ, Skowhegan Summer Art Sch & Yale-Norfolk Summer Art Sch.
Awards: Nat Coun on the Arts Award, 66; Guggenheim Mem grant, 69.
Bibliography: Harris Rosenstein (auth), To be continued, Art News, 10/70; Diane Waldman (auth), Robert Mangold (catalogue), Solomon R Guggenheim Mus, 71; Lucy R Lippard (auth), Silent art: Robert Mangold, In: Changing essays in art criticism, Dutton, 71.
Dealer: Fischbach Gallery, 29 W 57th St, New York, NY 10019.
Mailing Address: P O Box 71, Callicoon Ctr, NY 12724.

MANGOLD, SYLVIA PLIMACK
Painter
Preferred Media: Acrylics
b New York, N Y, Sept 18, 38.
Study & Training: Cooper Union, cert, 59; Yale Univ Art Sch, BFA, 61.
Exhibitions: Realism Now, Vassar Col, Poughkeepsie, N Y, 68; Direct Representation, Fischbach Gallery, 69; Twenty Six Contemporary Women Artists, Aldrich Mus, Conn, 71; New Realism, Potsdam, N Y, 71; Whitney Mus Am Art Ann, New York, 72.
Teaching: Instr drawing, Sch Visual Arts, New York, 70, instr painting, 70-71.
Dealer: Fischbach Gallery, 29 W 57th St, New York, NY 10019.
Mailing Address: P O Box 71, Callicoon Center, NY 12724.

MANGRAVITE, PEPPINO GINO
Painter, Lecturer
Preferred Media: Acrylics.
b Lipari, Italy, June 28, 96; U S citizen.
Study & Training: Scuole Techniche; Belle Arti, Italy; Cooper Union, cert, 24, citation, 56; Art Stud League New York.
Work in Public Collections: Metrop Mus Art, New York, N Y; Whitney Mus Am Art, New York; Phillips Gallery Art, Washington, D C; Art Inst Chicago, Ill; Calif Palace of Legion of Honor, San Francisco.

Commissions: History of Transportation (two murals) comn by U S Treas Dept, Hempstead Post Off, N Y, 33; American at Rest & Play (two murals), comn by U S Treas Dept, Atlantic City Post Off, N J, 35.
Exhibitions: Venice Biennale, Italy, 38; most nat & int exhibs, 30-65; 48 one-man exhibs, New York, Washington, D C, Chicago, Colo, Calif & others.
Teaching: Dir art dept, Sara Lawrence Col, 30-35; instr drawing, Cooper Union, 37-42; prof painting, Columbia Univ, 42-65.
Awards: Guggenheim fel, 32 & 35; purchase prize for painting, Golden Gate Int Expos, 39; silver medal for mosaic design, Archit League New York, 55.
Bibliography: Helen Appleton Read (auth), Peppino Mangravite, Parnassus, 34; Harry Salpeter (auth), Mangravite: music in art, Esquire, 39; Ralph M Pearson (auth), Peppino Mangravite: the modern renaissance in American art, Harper & Row, 54.
Memberships: Century Asn.
Publications: Auth, The American painter and his environment, 35; auth, Aesthetic freedom and the Artists' Congress, 36; auth, Relation of creative design to an education in the humanities, 52; auth, The art of the war poster—an index to American taste, 57; auth, Dante through three artists' eyes, 65.
Dealer: Frank Rehn Gallery, 655 Madison Ave, New York, NY 10021.
Mailing Address: Old Town Rd, West Cornwall, CT 06796.

MANGUM, WILLIAM (GOODSON)
Sculptor, Painter
Preferred Media: Oils, Bronze.
b Kinston, N C.
Study & Training: Corcoran Sch Art, Washington, D C; Art Stud League New York; Univ N C, Chapel Hill, BA & MA.
Work in Public Collections: Carl Sandburg Mem Mus, Flat Rock, N C.
Commissions: Lamp of Learning Monument, Dunning Indusrs, Greensboro, N C, 67; portrait bust of Carl Sandburg, Greensboro C of C, 68.
Exhibitions: Galerie Paula Insel Invitational, New York, NY; Bodley Gallery Nat, New York; Mass Mus Nat, Springfield; Isaac Delgado Mus, New Orleans, La; Va Mus Fine Art Invitational.
Teaching: Assoc prof art history & sculpture, Salem Col.
Awards: Cert of distinction, Va Mus Fine Art; award, Isaac Delgado Mus; award, N C Mus Art.
Memberships: Southern Asn Sculptors.
Publications: Auth, Marino Marini as portraitist, 70.
Dealer: Gallery of Contemporary Art, S Main St, Winston-Salem, NC 27108.
Mailing Address: Dept of Art, Salem College, Winston-Salem, NC 27108.

MANHOLD, JOHN HENRY
Sculptor
Preferred Media: Marble, Bronze.
b Rochester, N Y, Aug 20, 19.
Study & Training: Univ Rochester, BA; New Sch, with Chaim Gross & Manolo Pasqual; also with Ward Mount.
Work in Public Collections: City of West Orange, N J; Mem Sloan-Kettering Hosp, New York, N Y; Pyrofilm Corp, Whippany, N J; A J Levera Assocs, Madison, N J; Jacques Piccard Inst, Bern, Switz; plus others.
Commissions: Numerous bronze & stone figures; Fred Collins, 67-; bronze bust, Kallman Assocs, Jersey City, N J; three bronze busts, Col Med & Dent N J, Newark, 69 & 70; bronze figure, Bernard Koven, 71.
Exhibitions: Allied Artists Am, 66; Audubon Artists Am, 67-69; Mainstreams '68 & '71, Grover M Hermann Fine Arts Ctr, Ohio, 68 & 71; Nat Sculpture Soc, 69; Am Artists Prof League, 70-72; plus others.
Positions: Dir sculpture, Ringwood Manor Asn Arts, 68-70, first v pres, 70-71.
Awards: Medal of hon for sculpture, State of N J, 68; second prize patrons award, Painters & Sculptors Soc N J, 71; John Subkis Award, Nat Arts Club, 71; plus others.
Bibliography: David Leis (auth), pictures, In: Life Mag, 69; Pierre Morand (auth), La section Americaine de la Salon del'arte Française, La Rev Mod, 70; Ruth Ann Williams (auth), Art of the oranges, N J Music & Art, 72.
Memberships: Acad Artists Asn; fel Am Artists Prof League; Painters & Sculptors Soc N J; Nat Arts Club; Knickerbocker Artists.
Mailing Address: 83 Cranford Pl, Teaneck, NJ 07666.

MANIATTY, STEPHEN GEORGE
Painter
Preferred Media: Oils.
b Norwich, Conn, Sept 5, 10.
Study & Training: Mass Sch Art, grad, 33.
Work in Public Collections: Holyoke Mus, Mass.

Commissions: Historical murals, Franklin Co Trust Co, Greenfield, Mass, 53-54.
Exhibitions: Conn Acad Fine Arts Nat, Hartford, 70; Hudson Valley Art Asn Nat, White Plains, N Y, 72; Am Artists Prof League Nat, New York, N Y, 72; Acad Artists Asn Nat, Springfield, Mass, 72; Jordon Marsh Regional Show, 72.
Teaching: Supvr art, Deerfield Union Pub Schs, Mass, 36-45; artist-in-residence, Deerfield Acad, 45-50; supvr art, Orange Pub Schs, Mass, 51-62; plus private classes for adults.
Positions: Coun mem, Acad Art Asn, 40-, pres, 45-49.
Awards: Jasper Cropsey Award, Hudson Valley Art Asn, 62; gold medal of hon, Rockport Art Asn, 68; gold medal of hon, Am Artists Prof League, 70.
Memberships: Salmagundi Club; Guild of Boston Artists; Rockport Art Asn; Hudson Valley Art Asn; Am Artists Prof League.
Mailing Address: Main St, Deerfield, MA 01342.

MANILLA, TESS (TESS MANILLA WEINER)
Painter
Preferred Media: Oils, Collages.
b Poland; U S citizen.
Study & Training: Educ Alliance, New York, with Abbo Ostrowsky; Brooklyn Mus Art Sch, with Reuben Tam, Victor Candell, Manfred Schwartz & Louis Finkelstein; Art Stud League New York, with Morris Kantor, Sidney Gross & Morris Davidson; Pratt Graphics Ctr, with Walter Ragolsky; Provincetown Workshop, with Leo Manzo.
Work in Public Collections: Long Island Univ.
Exhibitions: Audubon Artists, from 61-70; Prospect Park Centennial, 66; Nat Asn Women Artists Travel Show, 70-72; Silvermine Guild Artists, New Canaan, Conn; one-man shows, Long Island Univ, 65 & Contemp Arts, Inc, New York, 66.
Teaching: Instr pvt classes, children & adults.
Awards: Award, Village Art Ctr, 58; Helen Hurzberger scholar, Art Stud League New York, 61; award, Nat Asn Women Artists, 72.
Memberships: Artists Equity Asn New York; Nat Asn Women Artists (mem exten comn, 71); Metrop Painters & Sculptors (pres, 68-72); Brooklyn Arts & Cult Asn (art chmn, 70-72); Avant VI (pres, 70-72).
Mailing Address: 50 Lenox Rd, Brooklyn, NY 11226.

MANKOWSKI, BRUNO
Sculptor
b Ger, Oct 30, 02; U S citizen.
Study & Training: Munic Art Sch, Berlin, Ger; State Art Sch, Berlin; Beaux Arts Inst, New York, N Y.
Work in Public Collections: Am Numismatic Soc, New York; Smithsonian Inst Div Numismatics, Washington, D C; Metrop Mus Art, New York; Nat Acad Design, New York; Soc Medalists, New York.
Commissions: Sculptured panel, by U S Govt-Soc Fine Arts, Chesterfield, S C, 39; mem plaque, Macombs Jr High Sch, N Y, 49; carvings, architect of capitol, Washington, D C, 50 & 60; designs for Steuben Glass, Steuben Glass, Corning, N Y, 54-55; medal-Asa Gray, Hall Fame Great Am, New York Univ, 72.
Exhibitions: Nat Acad Design Ann, 40-71; Pa Acad Fine Arts Ann, 47-54; Nat Sculpture Soc Ann, 47-71; Am Acad Arts & Lett, 49-50; Allied Artists Am Ann, 52-71.
Awards: Am Inst & Acad Arts & Lett grant creative work in art, 50; J Sanford Saltus Silver Medal, Am Numismatic Soc, 60; Daniel Chester French Award, Allied Artists Am, 64.
Bibliography: Articles, In: Am Artists Mag, 49-59; rev, In: Nat Sculpture Soc, 53-70; Works of art in United States Capitol, U S Govt Printing Off, 65.
Memberships: Nat Acad Design (mem comt, 71-73); fel Nat Sculpture Soc (coun mem, 53-58 & 71-73, chmn exhib comt, 56-58); life fel Am Numismatic Soc; Allied Artists Am; Archit League.
Mailing Address: 2231 Broadway, New York, NY 10024.

MANN, DAVID
Art Dealer
b N J, July 23, 18.
Positions: Dir, Bodley Gallery.
Memberships: Art Dealers Asn Am.
Specialty of Gallery: Surrealist work, modern master drawings and exhibits of contemporary paintings and sculpture.
Mailing Address: Bodley Gallery, 1063 Madison Ave, New York, NY 10021.

MANN, KATINKA
Painter, Printmaker
Preferred Media: Polymers.
b New York, N Y, June 28, 25.
Study & Training: Univ Hartford Art Sch; Pratt Graphic Arts, New York.

Work in Public Collections: Nassau Community Col, Garden City, N Y.

Exhibitions: Soc Am Graphic Artists-Assoc Am Artists 50th Ann, 69; Light Happening, Suffolk Mus, Stony Brook, N Y, 70; U S Info Agency, Washington, D C, 71-73; Nat Asn Women's Artists Ital Exhib, Florence, Naples & Milan, Italy, 72; Int Miniature Print Exhib, Assoc Am Artists Gallery, New York, 72-73.

Awards: Judith Leiber Co Purchase Award, Soc Am Graphic Artists, 69; purchase award, Nassau Community Col, 71.

Bibliography: David Shapiro (auth), 50 years in American print-making, Soc Am Graphics, 69; Ruth Solomon (auth), Artists of Suffolk County, Heckscher Mus, 7/72; June Blum (auth), Unmanly art, Suffolk Mus, 10/72; plus others.

Memberships: Nat Asn Women Artists; Prof Artists Guild (v pres-prog chmn, 69-71, mem jury co-chmn & bd mem, 72-73); Mus Mod Art; Artists Equity Asn; Women in the Arts.

Dealer: Glass Gallery, 315 Central Park W, New York, NY 10025.

Mailing Address: 294 Pidgeon Hill Rd, Huntington Station, NY 11746.

MANN, VAUGHAN (VAUGHAN GRAYSON)
Painter, Printmaker
b Moose Jaw, Sask.
Study & Training: Columbia Univ, BS.
Work in Public Collections: Royal Ont Mus.

Exhibitions: Can Soc Painter-Etchers & Engravers, 54, 55 & 57; Moose Jaw, Sask, 56, 61 & 67; one-man shows, Kelowna, B C, 56 & Nelson, B C, 60; Vancouver Art Gallery; plus others.

Teaching: Lectr, exten div, Univ B C & Univ Sask Summer Sch.

Positions: Dir art, Teacher's Col; Moose Jaw Fine Arts Guild; Vernon Art Soc, B C.

Memberships: Can Soc Painter-Etchers & Engravers; Nat Serigrapher Soc, N Y.

Publications: Auth, Picture appreciation—elementary school & Picture appreciation—junior high school, J M Dent & Sons, London.

Mailing Address: Box 1, R R 1, Oyama, B C, Can.

MANNEN, PAUL WILLIAM
Painter, Educator
Preferred Media: Oils, Watercolors.
b Topeka, Kans, June 22, 06.
Study & Training: Univ, Kans, with, Albert Bloch, Karl Mattern & Raymond J Eastwood, BFA, 33; Ohio State Univ, with Hoyt Sherman & Erwin F Frye, MA, 39.

Work in Public Collections: Thayer Art Mus, Univ Kans, Lawrence; Jr High Sch, Lawrence; Elem Sch, Lawrence.

Commissions: Murals, Univ Kans, Pub Libr, Lawrence & cmndg gen off, Fort Riley, Kans.

Exhibitions: Kans Artists, 36-41; Prairie Watercolor Painters Traveling Exhibs, 37-42 & 59-64; 55th Ann, Denver, Colo, 49; six shows, Sun Carnival, El Paso, Tex, 49-62; plus others.

Teaching: Instr painting, Topeka Art Ctr, Kans, 39-41; prof art & head dept, Okla Col Women, 45-48; prof art & head dept, N Mex State Univ, 48-59, prof painting & art hist, 59-69, emer prof, 69-

Positions: Ed, Air Force films, Wright Field, Ohio, 42-45.

Awards: First prize oil paintings, Dayton Art Inst, 42; several Kans State Fair Prizes.

Bibliography: C J Bulliet (auth), rev, In: Chicago Daily News, 7/11/36; Felipe Beraza (auth), Interview on Orozco murals, Excelsior, Mexico City, 9/8/47; Richard C Green (auth), Image in contemporary art (catalog) Jr Col, Decatur, Ala, 1/71.

Memberships: Kans Fedn Art; MacDowell Fine Arts Soc; Am Asn Univ Prof.

Mailing Address: 1700 S Luna St, Las Cruces, NM 88001.

MANNING, JO
Printmaker
b Sydney, B C, Dec 11, 23.
Study & Training: Ont Col Art, Toronto, grad, 45, spec stud printmaking, 60.

Work in Public Collections: Nat Gallery Can, Ottawa; Montreal Mus Fine Art; London Libr & Art Mus, Ont; Willistead Gallery, Windsor; Univ Calgary, Alta.

Exhibitions: Biennale Int Graphica, Florence, Italy, 70; Fourth Am Biennale Engravings, Santiago, Chile, 70; Cracow Poland Biennale, 70 & 72; Expos Int Dessins, Rijeka, Yugoslavia, 70 & 72; Venice Biennale, 72.

Teaching: Assoc master printmaking, Sheridan Col, Brampton, Ont, 71-

Awards: Nicholas Hornyansky Award, Can Soc Painter-Etchers & Engravers, 70; gold medal, Florence, Italy, 70; Presidente Frei, Fourth Am Biennale, Santiago, Chile, 70.

Memberships: Can Soc Graphic Art (past pres, 68-69); Can Soc Painter-Etchers & Engravers (exec, 63-65).

Mailing Address: 15 Binscarth Rd, Toronto 5, Ont, Can.

MANNING, REG (WEST)
Cartoonist, Writer
b Kansas City, Mo, Apr 8, 05.
Study & Training: Phoenix Union High Sch Art Classes.

Work in Public Collections: Cartoon Collection, Syracuse Univ; Lyndon Johnson Libr, Austin, Tex; Presidential Mus, Odessa, Tex; Univ Southern Miss, Hattiesburg.

Exhibitions: One-man show, Phoenix Art Mus, 61.

Positions: Ed cartoonist, Ariz Republic, 26-

Awards: Pulitzer Prize, Columbia Univ, 51; Abraham Lincoln Award, Freedoms Found, 70 & 71.

Bibliography: Alan D Covey (auth), Southwestern authors, Ariz Librn, fall 66.

Memberships: Asn Am Ed Cartoonists; Nat Cartoonists Soc; Phoenix Fine Arts Asn.

Publications: Auth & illusr, Cartoon guide of Arizona, 38, What kinda cactus izzat?, 41, Little itchy itchy, 44, From tee to cup, 54 & What is Arizona really like ?, 68.

Mailing Address: 5724 E Cambridge, Scottsdale, AZ 85257.

MANSHIP, JOHN PAUL
Painter, Sculptor
Preferred Media: Oils, Gouache, Watercolors, Mosaics.
b New York, N Y, Jan 16, 27.
Study & Training: Harvard Univ, AB, 48; with George Demetrios; Brera Acad, Milan.

Work in Public Collections: Nat Collection Fine Arts, Washington, D C; Louisville Art Mus, Ky; Long Beach Art Mus, Calif.

Commissions: Baptism of Christ, Baptistry, St John Martyr, New York, 63; Pentecost (fresco), Chapel Sisters of St Joseph, Pawtucket, R I, 65; stations of cross, St Clements Church, Warwick, R I, 66; Resurrection (with Margaret Cassidy), St Anthony's Church, Springfield, Mass, 71; portrait of Judge O'Connor, Worcester Co Courthouse, 72.

Teaching: Instr drawing & painting, Marymount Col, New York, 63.

Positions: Dir, Burr Artists, New York, 69-

Awards: Childe Hassam purchase award, Am Acad Arts & Letters, 55; watercolor prize, Nat Arts Club, 62; Ranger Fund purchase award, Nat Acad Design, 65.

Memberships: Am Watercolor Soc; Nat Soc Mural Painters (secy, 72-); Am Fine Arts Fedn; Rockport Art Asn; North Shore Art Asn (dir, 70-).

Publications: Auth, Paul Claudel, Commonweal, 55; auth, Raphael, Catholic Encycl Youth, 64.

Dealer: Grand Central Art Galleries, Madison Ave & 43rd St, New York, NY 10017.

Mailing Address: 463 West St, New York, NY 10014.

MANSO, LEO
Painter, Educator
Preferred Media: Oils, Acrylics, Collage, Assemblage.
b New York, N Y, Apr 15, 14.
Study & Training: Nat Acad Design; New Sch Social Res.

Work in Public Collections: Mus Mod Art & Whitney Mus Am Art, New York; Mus Fine Arts, Boston, Mass; Worcester Mus, Mass; Corcoran Gallery Art, Washington, D C.

Commissions: Mural, Lincoln Pub Libr, Nebr, 65.

Exhibitions: Nat Inst Arts & Lett, 61 & 69; Mus Mod Art Collage Exhib, 65; Whitney Mus Am Art Ann, 47-66; Pa Acad Fine Arts, Philadelphia, 68; New England Arts Festival, 71.

Teaching: Co-founder, Provincetown Workshop, Mass, 59-; prof painting & drawing, New York Univ, 50-

Awards: Award for Aspects of the Harbor (oil), Urbana Ann, Ill, 50; purchase award for Seasons (oil), Ford Found, 63; Childe Hassam Purchase Award for Juggernaut (construct), Am Acad Arts & Lett, 69.

Dealer: Frank Rehn Gallery, 655 Madison Ave, New York, NY 10021.

Mailing Address: 460 Riverside Dr, New York, NY 10027.

MANTON, JOCK (ARCHIMEDES ARISTIDES GIACOMANTONIO)
Sculptor, Art Administrator
Preferred Media: Bronze, Marble.
b Jersey City, N J, Jan 17, 06.
Study & Training: Leonardo da Vinci Art Sch, New York, N Y; Royal Acad Fine Arts, Rome, Italy; also with Onorio Ruutolo & Vincenzo Gemito.

Work in Public Collections: Truman (sculpture), Truman Libr, Independence, Mo; Vincenzo Gemito (sculpture), Galleria di Arte Moderna, Rome, Italy; Grandma (sculpture), Royal Palace, Rome; Mediterranean Flower (sculpture), Mus Capitoleum, Rome.

Commissions: Spanish American War Soldier (sculpture), Union City, 42; Eisenhower (sculpture), West Point Mil Acad, N Y, 45; Wounded Soldier (sculpture), Lincoln H S, Jersey City, 46; Chris-

topher Columbus (sculpture), Hoboken Citizens, Columbus Park, 48; Christopher Columbus (sculpture), Jersey City Columbus Mall, 50.
Exhibitions: Montclair Art Mus, 38; Metrop Mus Art, New York, N Y, 43; Nat Acad Design; Allied Artists Am; Nat Sculpture Soc.
Positions: Trustee, Mus Jersey City, N J; reviewer arts, Am Broadcasting Co, 51-71; exec dir, Sussex Co Arts Coun, Inc, 71-
Awards: Maynard prize, Nat Acad Design; first prize for sculpture, Montclair Mus; first prize for bust of Beethoven, Radio Sta WEAF, 26.
Bibliography: Truman poses for Giacomantonio (film), produced on ABC-TV.
Memberships: Nat Sculpture Soc; Lotos Club; Allied Artists Am.
Mailing Address: 42 W 67th St, New York, NY 10023.

MANVILLE, ELSIE
Painter
Preferred Media: Oils, Pastel.
b Philadelphia, Pa, May 11, 22.
Study & Training: Tyler Sch Fine Arts, Temple University, with Boris Blai, Franklin Watkins, Rafael Sabatini & Alexander Abels; also work with Leon Karp.
Work in Public Collections: Temple Univ, Philadelphia.
Exhibitions: Pa Acad Annuals, 48, 49, 51 & 53; Butler Inst Am Art, 56; Walker Art Ctr, 58; one-man exhibs, Kraushaar Galleries, 58, 66 & 69; Dallas Mus, 63.
Awards: Carol Beck Medal for best portrait & Mary Smith Prize, Pa Acad, 53; Tyler Award, Tyler Sch Fine Arts, 56.
Mailing Address: c/o Kraushaar Galleries, 1055 Madison Ave, New York, NY 10028.

MAPES, DORIS WILLIAMSON
Painter
Preferred Media: Watercolors, Acrylics.
b Russellville, Ark, June 25, 20.
Study & Training: Little Rock Jr Col; Hendrix Col, Conway, Ark; Ark Arts Ctr, Little Rock, Ark; Rex Brandt's Sch Painting, cert, Corona del Mar, Calif; also with George Post; John C Pellew, Louis Freund, Edgar A Whitney, Robert E Wood, John Pike & Robert Andrew Parker, 72.
Work in Public Collections: Winthrop Rockefeller Gallery, Petit Jean, Ark; Ark Col Mus, Batesville; Am Found Life Ins Co, Little Rock, Ark; First Nat Bank, Little Rock; Worthen Bank & Trust Co, Little Rock.
Exhibitions: Mid-South Exhib, Brooks Mem Mus, Memphis, Tenn, 68; Delta Exhib, 69 & Mid-Southern Watercolorists, 71 & 72, Ark Arts Ctr, Little Rock; Nat League Penwomen, Salt Lake Palace, Salt Lake City, Utah, 70; Southwestern Watercolor Soc, Dallas, Tex, 68, 69 & 71 & Albuquerque, N Mex, 72.
Awards: Top of show, Ark State Festival Arts, 68 & Grand Prairie Festival Arts, 71; first award, Southern Artists Asn, 72; plus many others.
Memberships: Mid-Southern Watercolorists (pres, 70-72); Southwestern Watercolor Soc; Am League Penwomen (v pres, Little Rock Br, 66-70); assoc mem Am Watercolor Soc; Southern Artists Asn.
Dealer: Sketch Box Gallery, 5606 R St, Little Rock, AR 72207.
Mailing Address: 622 N Bryan, Little Rock, AR 72205.

MARAIS (MARY RACHEL BROWN)
Painter
Preferred Media: Oils.
b New York, N Y.
Work in Public Collections: J Aberbach Collection, Long Island, N Y; Theodora Settele Collection, New York.
Exhibitions: Galerie St Placide, Paris, France, 61; New Masters Gallery, New York, 64; Pe Mena Gallery, New York, 67 & 68; Panoras Gallery, New York, 71; Community Temple Gallery, Long Island, 72.
Mailing Address: 33 W 67th St, New York, NY 10023.

MARANS, MOISSAYE
Sculptor, Instructor
Preferred Media: Wood, Stone.
b Chişinau, Romania, Oct 11, 02; U S Citizen.
Study & Training: Cooper Union Inst, 25-27, with Brewster; Nat Acad Design, New York, N Y, 27, with Robert Aitken; Pa Acad Fine Arts, 28-29, with Charles Grafly; Beaux Arts Inst Design, New York, 32-33.
Work in Public Collections: Norfolk Mus Fine Arts; San Jose Mus; Smithsonian Inst & Mus Natural Hist, Washington, D C; West Baden Col, West Baden Springs, Ind; Rodeph Shalom Congregation, Pittsburgh, Pa.
Commissions: Family at Prayer, Temple Emanu-El, Houston, Tex, 56; Moses, First Presby Church, Beloit, Wis, 58; Story Time, Linden Pub Libr, N J, 60; Isaiah, Community Church New York, 61; Prince of Peace, Church Ctr UN, New York, 67.

Exhibitions: Los Angeles Mus Ann, 38 & 56; Whitney Mus Am Art Sculpture Festival, 40; Pa Acad Fine Arts Ann, 41-58; Philadelphia Mus Art Sculpture Int, 40 & 49; Detroit Inst Arts, 58.
Teaching: Lectr sculpture, Brooklyn Col, 55-
Positions: Mem artists panel, Union Am Hebrew Congregations, 58-
Awards: 1953 Medal for Reflection, Archit League New York, 53; Henry Hering Award, Nat Sculpture Soc, 63; Daniel Chester French Medal, Nat Acad Design, 67.
Bibliography: Lee E Dirks (auth), Religion in action, Nat Observer, 64; Frederic Whitaker (auth), The sculpture of Moissaye Marans, Am Artist, 2/64; Baker's pictorial introduction to The Bible (illus), 68.
Memberships: Nat Acad Design; Archit League New York (v pres, 54-55); Nat Sculpture Soc (secy, 49-50); Audubon Artists (treas, 55-56); Allied Artists Am.
Mailing Address: 93 Court St, Brooklyn, NY 11202.

MARCA-RELLI, CONRAD
Painter
b Boston, Mass, June 5, 13.
Work in Public Collections: Mus Mod Art; Whitney Mus Am Art; Wadsworth Atheneum; Metrop Mus Art; Michener Found; plus many others.
Exhibitions: Carnegie Inst; retrospective, Whitney Mus Am Art, 67; Art Inst Chicago; Am Fedn Arts, 67-68; The New American Painting & Sculpture, Mus Mod Art, 69; plus many other group & one-man shows.
Teaching: Former vis critic, Yale Univ, Univ Calif, Berkeley & New Col, Sarasota, Fla.
Awards: Logan Medal & purchase prize, 54 & Kohnstamm Prize, 63, Art Inst Chicago; Ford Found award, 59; purchase prize, Detroit Inst Art, 60.
Bibliography: Parker Tyler (auth), Marca-Relli (monogr), fall 60; H Harvard Arnason (auth), Marca-Relli (monogr), Abrams, 62; William C Agee (auth), Marca-Relli (catalogue), Whitney Mus Am Art, 67; plus many others.
Mailing Address: c/o Marlborough-Gerson Gallery, 41 E 57th St, New York, NY 10022.

MARCUS, EDWARD S
Collector
b Dallas, Tex, Oct 13, 10.
Positions: Bd trustees, Contemp Art Mus Houston, Tex, 55; pres, Dallas Mus Contemp Art, 59-62; bd trustees, Dallas Mus Fine Arts, 63-64; educ comt, 69-71.
Collection: Contemporary and pre-Columbian Art.
Mailing Address: 4007 Stonebridge, Dallas, TX 75204.

MARCUS, IRVING E
Painter, Graphic Artist
b Minneapolis, Minn, May 17, 29.
Study & Training: Univ Minn, BA; Univ Iowa, MFA.
Work in Public Collections: Minneapolis Inst Art; Allen Art Mus, Oberlin Col; Temple Israel, Saint Louis; State Univ Iowa; also in many pvt collections.
Exhibitions: San Francisco Inst Art, 60, 63 & 64; Los Angeles Mus Art, 63; La Jolla Mus Art, 63; Luz Mus, Manila, Philippines, 64; Univ Wis, 64; plus many other group & one-man shows.
Teaching: Instr art, Oberlin Col, 55-56; instr, Univ Hawaii, 56-57; instr, Blackburn Col, 57-59; prof painting & printmaking, Sacramento State Col, 59-, chmn dept art, 66-
Awards: Prizes, Denver Mus Art, 52 & 58, Jacksonville Art Ctr, Ill, 58 & Crocker Art Mus, 63; plus others.
Memberships: San Francisco Art Asn.
Publications: Contribr, A handbook for the development of art in small colleges, Col Art Asn.
Dealers: Candy Store Gallery, Folsom, CA 95630; William Sawyer Gallery, 3045 Clay, San Francisco, CA 94115.
Mailing Address: 601 Shanri Lane, Sacramento, CA 95825.

MARCUS, MARCIA
Painter
Preferred Media: Oil, Acrylics on canvas.
b New York, N Y, Jan 11, 28.
Study & Training: New York Univ, BA, 47; Art Stud League, 54, with Edwin Dickinson; Fulbright fel to France, 62-63.
Work in Public Collections: Whitney Mus Art, New York; Newark Mus, N J; R I Sch Design, Providence; Phoenix Art Mus, Ariz; Randolph-Macon Jr Col, Lynchburg, Va.
Exhibitions: Young Artists, 60, Whitney Mus Art, 60; 4 Women, Kansas City, 63; Carnegie Inst, Pittsburgh, Pa, 64; Butler Inst Art, Youngstown, Ohio, 65; Flint Inst. Arts, Mich, 70.
Teaching: Adj instr painting, Cooper Union Sch Art, New York, 70-71; assoc prof painting & drawing, La State Univ, Baton Rouge, spring, 72; instr painting & drawing, New York Univ, summer, 72.

Awards: Ingram Merrill Award, 64; artist-in-residence, R I Sch Design, Ford Found, 66.
Mailing Address: 703 E 6th St, New York, NY 10009.

MARCUS, STANLEY
Collector
b Dallas, Tex, Apr 20, 05.
Study & Training: Harvard Univ, BA, 25, Bus Sch, 26; Southern Methodist Univ, hon HHD, 65.
Positions: Dir, Dallas Symphony Soc; adv dir, Fort Worth Art Asn; trustee, Eisenhower Exchange Fellowships; Bus Comt for the Arts; former pres, Dallas Art Asn; pres, Neiman-Marcus Co, 50-
Collection: Paintings, contemporary art.
Mailing Address: Neiman-Marcus Co, Main & Ervay Sts, Dallas, TX 75201.

MARDEN, BRICE
Painter, Educator
Preferred Media: Oils.
b Bronxville, N Y, Oct 15, 38.
Study & Training: Boston Univ, BFA, with Reed Kay, Arthur Hoerner & Hugh Townley; Yale-Norfolk Summer Sch Music & Art with Bernard Chaet & Jon Schueler; Sch Art & Archit, Yale Univ, MFA, with Esteban Vicente & Alex Katz.
Work in Public Collections: Mus Mod Art, New York, N Y; Whitney Mus Am Art, New York; Walker Art Ctr, Minneapolis, Minn; Fort Worth Art Ctr, Tex; San Francisco Mus Mod Art, Calif.
Exhibitions: Whitney Mus Am Art Ann, New York, 69; Modular Painting, Albright-Knox Art Gallery, Buffalo, N Y, 70; Painting—New Options, Walker Art Ctr, 72; 17th Am Exhib, Art Inst Chicago, Ill, 72; Documenta 5, Kassel, Ger, 72.
Teaching: Instr painting, Sch Visual Arts, New York, 70-; instr painting, Skowhegan Sch Painting & Sculpture, summer 71-72.
Positions: Bd Govs, Skowhegan Sch Painting & Sculpture, 72.
Bibliography: Harris Rosenstein (auth), Total & complex, Art News, 5/67; John Ashberry (auth), Grey eminence, Art News, 3/72; Robert Pincus-Witten (auth), Manzoni, Ryman & Marden, Art-forum, summer 72.
Dealer: Klaus Kertess, Bykert Gallery, 24 E 81st St, New York, NY 10028.
Mailing Address: 26 Bond St, New York, NY 10012.

MARDER, DORIE
Painter
b Poland; U S citizen.
Study & Training: Sorbonne; Art Stud League New York; New Sch Social Res; also with Harry Shoulberg & Morris Kantor.
Work in Public Collections: Norfolk Mus, Va; Idaho; State Dept for Europ Embassies; Safed Mus, Israel.
Exhibitions: Riverside Mus, 46-50; Northwest Printmakers, Seattle Art Mus, 50; Wichita Art Asn, Kans, 51; Audubon Artists, 64-70; Lehigh Univ, Pa, 71.
Awards: Award for oil painting, Clendenen, 61; award for serigraph, Montag, 65.
Memberships: League of Present Day Artists (dir, 71-72); Nat Asn Women Artists; Artists Equity Asn New York; Nat Serigraph Soc.
Mailing Address: 223 W 21st St, New York, NY 10011.

MAREMONT, ARNOLD H
Collector
b Chicago, Ill, Aug 24, 04.
Study & Training: Univ Mich, Ann Arbor; Univ Chicago, PhB, 24, JD, 26.
Positions: Trustee, Am Fedn Arts, 58-64; trustee, Lyric Opera of Chicago, 59-65; trustee, City Ctr Music & Drama, New York, N Y, 59-65.
Memberships: Gov life mem Art Inst Chicago.
Collection: Twentieth century art.
Mailing Address: Maremont Corp, 168 N Michigan, Ave, Chicago, IL 60601.

MARGO, BORIS
Painter, Sculptor
b Wolotschisk, Russia, Nov 7, 02; U S citizen.
Study & Training: Polytechnik Art, Odessa, U S S R, cert; Futemas (workshop for art of the future), Moscow, U S S R; Pavel Filonov Sch, Leningrad, U S S R.
Work in Public Collections: Metrop Mus Art & Mus Mod Art, New York, N Y; Nat Collection Fine Arts, Washington, D C; Art Inst Chicago, Ill; São Paulo Mus Art, Brazil.
Exhibitions: Abstract & Surrealist Art in the United States, Cincinnati Art Mus, San Francisco Mus Art & others, 44; several São Paulo Bienales, 52-; Carnegie Int, Pittsburgh, Pa, 52; Japan Print Asn 30th Anniversary Int, 62; Venice Biennales, 56 & 70.

Teaching: Vis artist, Am Univ, 46-48; vis prof painting, Art Inst Chicago, 57-59; vis prof printmaking & drawing, Sch Art, Syracuse Univ, 66-67; artist-in-residence, Acad Art, Honolulu, 72.
Positions: Res assoc (on the creative process), Psychiatric Inst, Univ Md, 57-
Awards: Watson F Blair Purchase Prize for watercolor, Art Inst Chicago, 47; purchase award for oil painting, Portland Mus Art, Maine, 60; six purchase awards, Brooklyn Mus Print Exhibs, 47-68.
Bibliography: Laurence Schmeckebier (auth), Boris Margo, graphic work, 1932-1968, Syracuse Univ Press, 68.
Memberships: MacDowell Colony Fels; Soc Am Graphic Artists.
Publications: Auth, Boris Margo: my theories and techniques, Mag Art, 11/47; auth, Margo: is there an American school of art?, The Tiger's Eye, 12/47.
Dealer: Associated American Artists, 663 Fifth Ave, New York, NY 10017.
Mailing Address: 749 West End Ave, New York, NY 10025.

MARGOLIES, ETHEL POLACHECK
Painter, Art Administrator
Preferred Media: Oils, Collage.
b Milwaukee, Wis, Aug 1, 07.
Study & Training: Smith Col, AB, 29; Silvermine Guild Artists; Umberto Romano Sch, East Gloucester, Mass; Univ Vt Summer Sch.
Work in Public Collections: Burndy Libr, Norwalk, Conn; Gen Time Corp, Stamford, Conn; Springfield Mus, Mass; Int Petroleum Corp; New Haven Paint & Clay Club, Conn.
Exhibitions: Silvermine Guild Artists, New Eng Exhib, New Canaan, Conn, 54-57, 60-68; Int Petroleum Art Festival, Tulsa, Okla, 66; Conn Acad Fine Arts, Hartford; Conn Watercolor Soc, Hartford; Audubon Artists, New York, N Y.
Positions: Gallery dir, Larry Aldrich Mus Contemp Art, 64-66; gallery dir, Silvermine Guild Artists, 54-
Awards: Awards for indust painting, Silvermine Guild, 54, 57, 60 & 64; purchase award, Springfield Mus, Mass, 57; award for painting, Int Petrol Corp, 66.
Memberships: Artists Equity Asn New York; Silvermine Guild Artists (bd trustees, 54-73); Conn Acad Fine Arts; Conn Watercolor Soc; New Haven Paint & Clay Club.
Mailing Address: 103 Jelliff Mill Rd, New Canaan, CT 06840.

MARGOLIES, JOHN SAMUEL
Photographer, Educator
b New York, N Y, May 16, 40.
Study & Training: Univ Pa, AB, Annenberg Sch Commun, MA.
Work in Public Collections: Pasadena Art Mus, Calif; Vancouver Art Gallery, B C; Baltimore Mus Art, Md; Art Galleries, Univ Calif, Santa Barbara.
Exhibitions: Morris Lapidus: Architecture of Joy, Archit League New York, 70; The Television Environment, 21st Aspen Design Conf, Colo, 71; The Television Environment, simultaneously in Pasadena Art Mus, Univ Art Mus, Univ Calif, Berkeley, Baltimore Mus Art, Vancouver Art Gallery & Fla State Univ Art Gallery, Tallahassee, 71; The Television Environment, Art Galleries, Univ Calif, Santa Barbara & Colo State Univ, Fort Collins, 72.
Teaching: Instr, Workshop in Commun, Doc & Environ, Calif Inst Arts, 71; instr 20th century archit, Univ Calif, Santa Barbara, 72.
Positions: Asst ed, Archit Record, 64-68; chmn current work, Archit League New York, 66-68; resident thinker, Am Fedn Arts, 69-70.
Awards: Graham Found archit journalism grant, Walker Art Ctr Prog, 70; J Clawson Mills scholar, Archit League New York, 70; Nat Endowment for Arts photog grant, 71.
Bibliography: Ada Louise Huxtable (auth), Show offers joy of hotel architecture, New York Times, 10/15/70; Pop art, Time Mag, 11/1/71; Maureen Koch (auth), Recapturing the TV environment, Coast Mag, 3/72.
Memberships: Archit League New York (exec comt, 68-70).
Publications: Auth, TV—the next medium, Art in Am, 9-10/69; ed, Design Quart spec issue on conceptual architecture, 11/70; auth, Now, once and for all, know why I did it: Morris Lapidus, Progressive Archit, 10/70; auth, Art machine for the 70's, Archit Forum, 1-2/70; co-auth & illusr, A side order of Los Angeles, West Mag, 9/26/71.
Mailing Address: 2622 Second St, Santa Monica, CA 90405.

MARGULIES, JOSEPH
Painter, Etcher
Preferred Media: Oils, Watercolors, Graphics.
b Austria, July 7, 96; U S citizen.
Study & Training: Cooper Union; Nat Acad Design; with Maynard; Art Stud League New York, with Joseph Pennell; also study abroad.

Work in Public Collections: Nat Portrait Gallery, Smithsonian Inst, Washington, D C; Metrop Mus Art, New York, N Y; Cleveland Mus Art, Ohio; New York Pub Libr; Libr Cong, Washington, D C; Judiciary, House Representatives, Washington, D C.

Commissions: Portrait of John F Brosnan, regent & chancellor, Univ of State of N Y, 61; portrait of Sen Jacob K Javitts, comn by Atty Gen, N Y State Capitol, Albany; portrait of Congressman Emannuel Celler, comn by chmn Judiciary Staff, 63; portrait of Dr Bela Schick, Nat Portrait Gallery, 69; portrait of John Dewey, comn by Dr Corlis Lamont for Dewey Ctr, Carbondale, Ill.

Exhibitions: Graphics, Univ Maine, Orono, 65; also yearly exhibs, Provincetown Art Asn, Audubon Artists, Allied Artists Am & Am Watercolor Soc.

Awards: Louis E Seeley Purchase Prize for Riviera Wine Grower (oil), 59; Grand Nat Award for Flemish Mother with a Jug (etching), Am Artists Prof League, 65; Seas of World Award for Along the Mediterranean (oil), The Gortons of Gloucester, 71.

Bibliography: B F Morrow (auth), The art of aquatint, Putman, 35; Norman Kent (auth), 100 watercolor techniques, Watson-Guptill, 69.

Memberships: Audubon Artists (mem coun & secy); Allied Artists Am (mem jury); Salmagundi Club (mem jury); Am Watercolor Soc; Rockport Art Asn.

Publications: Auth, Joseph Margulies paints a portrait in watercolor, Am Artist Mag, 60.

Dealer: Associated American Artists, 663 Fifth Ave, New York, NY 10022.

Mailing Address: 27 W 67th St, New York, NY 10023.

MARIANO, ANNE
Painter
Preferred Media: Acrylics.
b Rochester, N Y, Oct 16, 34.
Work in Public Collections: Brown Univ, Providence, R I; Nat Bank Geneva, N Y.
Exhibitions: Chatauqua Nat, N Y, 63 & 64; Rochester Festival Religious Arts Nat, 63-65 & 70-72; Western New York Nat, Albright-Knox Art Gallery, 64; N Y State Exhib, 67; Provincetown Art Asn, 67 & 68.
Awards: Schuler-Pierce design award, 68; award, Rochester Relig Arts Comt, 68; McAlpine Relig Art Award, 69.
Memberships: Arena Group, Rochester (publicity-steering comt, 72); Hochstein Group (co-orig, 65-66, dir, 67).
Dealer: Kendall Art Gallery, Box 742, E Main St, Wellfleet, MA 02667.
Mailing Address: 344 Westminster Rd, Rochester, NY 14607.

MARIL, HERMAN
Painter, Educator
Preferred Media: Oils, Casein, Acrylics.
b Baltimore, Md, Oct 13, 08.
Study & Training: Md Inst Fine Arts, grad.
Work in Public Collections: Whitney Mus Am Art & Metrop Mus Art, New York, N Y; Baltimore Mus Art, Md; San Francisco Mus Art, Calif; Nat Collection Fine Arts, Smithsonian Inst, Washington, D C; plus others.
Commissions: Murals, West Scranton Post Off, Pa, 39 & Alta Vista Post Off, Va, 40, Pub Bldgs Admin, U S Treas Dept.
Exhibitions: San Francisco Golden Gate Expos, 39; Carnegie Inst Ann, Pittsburgh, Pa, 40-45; Retrospective, Baltimore Mus Art, 67; Pa Acad Fine Arts, Philadelphia & Corcoran Gallery Art Biennials, Washington, D C, many yrs; plus others.
Teaching: Vis instr painting, Philadelphia Mus Col Art, 55-56; prof painting, Univ Md, 47-
Awards: First award, Silvermine Guild, 63; Univ Md grant for creative & performing arts, 66; Stefan Hirsch Mem Award, Audubon Artists, 72.
Bibliography: Eliot O'Hara (auth), Restraint (film), 61; Emery Grossman (auth), Art & tradition, Yoseloff, 67; Frank Getlein (auth), Herman Maril, Baltimore Mus Art, 67.
Memberships: Baltimore Mus Art (hon trustee, 72); Provincetown Art Asn (hon v pres, 72); Col Art Asn Am; Artists Equity Asn.
Dealer: Forum Gallery, 1018 Madison Ave, New York, NY 10021.
Mailing Address: 5602 Roxbury Pl, Baltimore, MD 21209.

MARIN, KATHRYN GARRISON
Painter, Printmaker
Preferred Media: Oils, Pencil, Mixed Media.
b Birmingham, Ala, July 14, 36.
Study & Training: Hollins Col, BA, 58; Univ Iowa, MFA, 64.
Work in Public Collections: Ga Comn Arts, Atlanta; Ga State Univ; Mint Mus Art, Charlotte, N C; Columbia Mus Art, S C; Dreher High Sch, Columbia; Waccamaw Arts & Crafts Guild, Myrtle Beach, S C.
Commissions: Illustrations, This Issue Mag, Atlanta, 70-71.

Exhibitions: 4th Dulin Nat Print & Drawing Competition, Knoxville, Tenn, 68; 23rd Am Drawing Biennial, Norfolk, Va, 69; 10th Hunter Gallery Ann, Chattanooga, Tenn, 69; 10th Ann Piedmont Painting & Small Sculpture Exhib, Charlotte, N C, 70; 3rd Nat Print Exhib, Atlanta, 72.
Awards: Alice Collins Dunham Prize, 58th Conn Acad Fine Arts Exhib, 68; three-man show award, Columbia Artist Guild, 69; purchase award, Ga Comn Arts, 72.
Mailing Address: 6122 N Trenholm Rd, Columbia, SC 29206.

MARINELLI, EVA, see MARTINO, EVA E.

MARINO, ALBERT JOSEPH
Collector
b Pittsburgh, Pa, June 30, 99.
Memberships: Am Asn Mus.
Collection: 275 original oil paintings and other medias, all subjects and also sculptures to be contributed to the community as a public art gallery.
Mailing Address: 472 Ohio Ave, Rochester, PA 15074.

MARIS, VALDI S
Painter, Instructor
Preferred Media: Oils, Acrylics, Mixed Media.
b Riga, Latvia, Sept 4, 19; U S citizen.
Study & Training: Acad Fine Arts, Riga, Latvia; Univ Heidelberg.
Work in Public Collections: East Brunswick Pub Libr, N J; in collection of R S Pierrepont, Princeton, N J; also in pvt collection throughout U S A, Can, Australia & Europe.
Exhibitions: Five shows, Montclair Mus, N J, 54-63; Jersey City Mus, 56 & 57; Maris U S A Traveling one-man show nationwide, 63-65; Int Platform Asn Convention Art Shows, Washington, D C, 67, 68 & 71; one-man shows, Bresler-Eitel Gallery, Milwaukee, Wis, 70 & Monmouth Co Libr, 71.
Teaching: Instr painting, pvt studio, 50-; instr painting, Shrewsbury Guild Creative Art, 63-; lectr-demonstr, Art Youth Festival, Trenton Mus, 72.
Positions: Art critic, Home News, New Brunswick, N J, 57-65; expert in color fidelity, for reprod in exclusive collection med illus, 72.
Awards: First, second & third prizes oil paintings, N J State Shows, 59-64; hon dipl & silver medal, Acad Tommaso Campanella, Rome, 70; Nat Starch & Chem Award, 72.
Bibliography: Abandoned mill(film), M Grumbacher Co, New York, 67.
Memberships: Int Platform Asn; Artists Equity Asn (bd dirs, 67-69); Guild Creative Art.
Mailing Address: Maris House, Gates Ave, East Brunswick, NJ 08816.

MARISOL, ESCOBAR
Sculptor
b Paris, France, 1930.
Study & Training: Ecole Beaux Arts, 49; Art Stud League New York, 50; New Sch, 51-54; Hans Hoffman Sch; Moore Col Art, Philadelphia, Pa, hon Dr, 70.
Work in Public Collections: Mus Mod Art, New York, N Y; Whitney Mus Am Art, New York; Albright-Knox Art Gallery, Buffalo, N Y; Mus Bellas Artes, Caracas, Venezuela; Nat Portrait Gallery, Washington, D C; plus others.
Exhibitions: Painting and Sculpture of a Decade, Tate Gallery, London, 64; New Realism, Munic Mus, The Hague, 64; Whitney Sculptures & Prints Ann, Whitney Mus Am Art, 66; Soc Contemp Art 28th Ann, Art Inst Chicago, Ill, 68; Image of Man Today, Inst Contemp Arts, London, 68; plus others.
Bibliography: Barbara Gold (auth), Portrait of Marisol, Interplay, 1/68; Don Cyr (auth), A conversation with Marisol, Arts & Activities, Vol 63, No 1; Lawrence Campbell (auth), Marisol, Art News, 11/67; plus others.
Publications: Contribr, The art of assemblage, Doubleday; contribr, Pop art, Praeger; contribr, The new American Arts, Collier, 67; contribr, In memory of my feelings, Crafton Graphic Co, 67; contribr, Stamps indelibly, Multiples, Inc, 67; plus others.
Mailing Address: c/o Sidney Janis Gallery, 6 W 57th St, New York, NY 10019.

MARK, BENDOR
Painter
b New York, N Y, June 5, 12.
Study & Training: Cooper Union.
Work in Public Collections: Denver Art Mus, Colo; Nat Collection Fine Arts, Washington, D C; Butler Inst Am Art, Youngstown, Ohio; Ga Mus Art, Athens; also in many pvt collections.
Exhibitions: ACA Nat Competition, New York, 36; American Art To-Day, New York World's Fair, 39; Art Inst Chicago, Ill, 40; Am Fedn Art Traveling Show, 40-41; Pepsi Cola Nat Competition,

Metrop Mus, New York, 45; plus others.
Awards: Second prize, Cooper Union, 29; second prize, ACA Nat
Competition, 36.
Mailing Address: 5727 Chelsea Ave, La Jolla, CA 92037.

MARK, PHYLLIS
Sculptor
b New York, N Y.
Study & Training: Ohio State Univ; New Sch Soc Res, sculpture
study with Seymour Lipton.
Work in Public Collections: Dickerson-White Mus, Cornell Univ;
permanent collection, Syracuse Univ; Lowe Art Mus, Fla; R C A
Corp Collection.
Exhibitions: New Acquisitions, Lowe Art Mus, Fla, 70; Kaleido-
scope, Morris Mus, N J, 70; Light Sound Motion, Hudson River
Mus, Yonkers, N Y, 71; Critic's Choice, Sculpture Ctr, 72; Fon-
tana Gallery, Pa, 72.
Memberships: Sculptors League; Archit League New York; New
York Soc Women Artists.
Art Interests: Kinetic sculpture; a leading exponent of large-scale
multiple sculpture and editions of sculpture.
Publications: Auth, On art, New Leader, 59; auth, Art Galleries,
New York Independent, 63; a mini multiple incl in Art Gallery
Mag, 11/72.
Dealer: Editions available from Gimpel-Weitzenhoffer Ltd, 1040
Madison Ave, New York, NY 10021.
Mailing Address: 803 Greenwich St, New York, NY 10014.

MARKELL, ISABELLA BANKS
Painter, Graphic Artist
b Superior, Wis, Dec 17, 91.
Study & Training: Fountainbleau, France, 30; Md Inst, 33-34; Pa
Acad Fine Arts, 35; O'Hara Sch, 38; Brackman Sch, 42, 43 & 46;
also with Farnsworth.
Work in Public Collections: N Y Pub Libr; N Y Hist Soc; Mus City
of New York; Northwest Printmakers; Metrop Mus Art; plus many
others.
Exhibitions: Newark Mus Art; Northwest Printmakers; Metrop Mus
Art; Baltimore Mus Art; Birmingham Mus Art; plus many other
group & one-man shows.
Awards: Prizes, Pen & Brush Club, 53, 55 & 64 & Nat Asn Women
Artists, 56, 58-60 & 64; three gold medals, 60 & prize, 64, Am
Artists Prof League; plus many others.
Memberships: Soc Am Graphic Artists; Pen & Brush Club; Philadel-
phia Print Club; Washington Printmakers; Miami Art Asn; plus
many others.
Mailing Address: 10 Gracie Square, New York, NY 10028.

MARKOW, JACK
Cartoonist, Painter
Preferred Media: Oils.
b London, Eng, Jan 23, 05; U S citizen.
Study & Training: Art Stud League New York, with Boardman Robin-
son, Richard Lahey & Walter Jack Duncan, 22-29.
Work in Public Collections: Metrop Mus Art, New York, N Y; Libr
Cong, Washington, D C; Brooklyn Mus, N Y; Univ Ga; Hunter Col,
New York.
Exhibitions: One-man show drawing & lithographs, ACA Gallery,
New York, 37; Pa Acad Art, Philadelphia, 38; Corcoran Gallery,
Washington, D C, 39; Whitney Mus Am Art, New York, 40; one-
man show paintings, Hudson Guild Gallery, New York, 58.
Teaching: Instr drawing & cartooning, Sch Visual Arts, New York,
47-53.
Positions: Cartoon ed, Argosy Mag, New York, 51-53.
Memberships: Life mem Art Stud League New York; Nat Cartoonists
Soc; Mag Cartoonists Guild (mem exec bd, 68-72).
Publications: Auth & illusr, Drawing and selling cartoons, 55, Draw-
ing funny pictures, 70 & Drawing comic strips, 72, Pitman; con-
tribr, monthly column Artists and cartoonists Q's, In: Writer's
Digest, 63-72; auth & illusr, Cartoonists and gag writers hand-
book, Writer's Digest, 67.
Mailing Address: 2428 Cedar St, Manasquan, NJ 08736.

MARKS, MR & MRS CEDRIC H
Collectors, Patrons
Art Interests: Donated works to various museums and colleges in the
United States and Israel.
Collection: Far eastern, near eastern, pre-Columbian medieval and
classical antiquities.
Mailing Address: 880 Fifth Ave, New York, NY 10021.

MARKS, MRS LAURENCE M
Trustee
Positions: Bd trustees, Sch Art League, N Y.
Mailing Address: School Art League, 131 Livingston, Brooklyn, NY
11201.

MARKS, ROYAL S
Art Dealer, Collector
b Detroit, Mich, Sept 11, 29.
Study & Training: Wayne Univ.
Positions: Owner & dir, Royal Marks Gallery, New York, N Y.
Specialty of Gallery: Works by Kupka, Tobey, Torres Garcia; also
Delaunay, Robert, Villon, Jacques, Braque; contemporary sculp-
tors, Robert Howard, Duayne Hatchett, David Weinrib & Richard
Randell; contemporary painters, Fred Martin & Landes Levitin;
also oceanic art and antiques.
Mailing Address: 29 E 64th St, New York, NY 10021.

MARKS, STANLEY A
Collector
Mailing Address: 950 Fifth Ave, New York, NY 10021.

MARKUS, MRS HENRY A
Collector
Collection: Picasso, Henry Moore, Chagall, Giocometti, Miro &
Max Ernst paintings and sculptures; Manzu sculpture, Jean Arp
sculptures and Renee Magritte paintings. Can be seen at Art
Inst Chicago, Notre Dame Univ, Evansville Mus & Brandeis Univ.
Mailing Address: 1300 Lake Shore Dr, Chicago, IL 60610.

MARLIN, HILDA VAN STOCKUM
Painter
Preferred Media: Oils.
b Rotterdam, Holland, Feb 9, 08; U S citizen.
Study & Training: Dublin Sch Art; Amsterdam Acad Art, cert;
Corcoran Sch Art; also with Andre L'Hote, Paris.
Exhibitions: Corcoran Biennial, Washington, D C, 37; one-man
shows in Dublin, 54, Holland, 64, Geneva, 64 & Washington, D C,
66, 69 & 72; Montreal Acad, Can, 58; Royal Acad, London, 59;
New York, 72.
Teaching: Instr oil painting & creative writing, Inst Lifetime Learn-
ing, 65-
Publications: Auth & illusr, A day on skates, Kersti and St Nicholas,
40, The winged watchman, 62, Lille old bear, 62 & Penengro, 72.
Mailing Address: 3630 Patterson St N W, Washington, DC 20015.

MAROZZI, ELI RAPHAEL
Sculptor, Instructor
Preferred Media: Marble, Synthetic Stone.
b Montegallo, Italy, Aug 13, 13; U S citizen.
Study & Training: Univ Wash, BA; Univ Hawaii, MA; also with Mark
Tobey.
Work in Public Collections: St Andrew's Cathedral, Honolulu, Ha-
waii.
Commissions: Figure-group in marble, Ramakrishna Vedanta Ctr,
Seattle, Wash, 49; stone sun-dial with figure, Hanahauoli Sch,
Honolulu, 53; stone bas-relief, Tennent Art Found, Honolulu, 55;
stone lion, State Found Cult & Arts, Honolulu, 71; stone figure
portrait, Vedanta Soc Sacramento, Carmichael, Calif, 72.
Exhibitions: Seattle Art Mus Ann, 47 & 48; Artists of Hawaii Ann,
Honolulu Acad Arts, 50-69; Assoc Artists Hawaii, Honolulu, 52-
55; Hawaii Painter's & Sculptor's League, Honolulu, 55-70; two-
man show, Contemp Art Ctr.
Teaching: Art instr, Honolulu Acad Arts, 50-55; art instr, YWCA
Adult Educ, Honolulu, 50-; art instr, Univ Hawaii Exten, Honolulu,
51-53.
Awards: Hon mention for etching, Honolulu Acad Arts, 51; first
prize in sculpture, Honolulu Assoc Artists, 55.
Memberships: Hawaii Painters & Sculptors League; hon mem Wind-
ward Artists Guild; hon mem Honolulu Assoc Artists.
Publications: Auth, The influence of material & technique on sculp-
tural form, 52; contribr, Times of India Mag, 53; contribr, Es-
says in philosophy, 62; contribr, Swami Vivekananda in East and
West, 68; contribr, Prabuddha Bharata Mag, 69.
Mailing Address: 1081 Young St, Honolulu, HI 96814.

MARROZZINI, LUIGI
Art Dealer, Lecturer
b Rome, Italy, July 30, 33.
Study & Training: Univ Leonardo Di Vince, Rome, grad.
Teaching: Lectr.
Positions: Secy & tech adv, San Juan Bienal Latin Am Graphic Art,
70 & 72; jury mem, Third Int Miniature Print Show, Pratt Graph-
ics Ctr, 68; dir, Galeria Colibri, San Juan, P R.
Memberships: Am Fedn Arts.
Specialty of Gallery: Original graphics by old and modern masters;
publisher of the most outstanding Latin American artists.
Publication: Auth, Catalog raisonné of the complete Orozco graph-
ics, 69.
Mailing Address: Box 1734, San Juan, PR 00903.

MARSH, ANNE STEELE
Painter, Printmaker
b Nutley, N J, Sept 7, 01.
Study & Training: Cooper Union Art Sch.
Work in Public Collections: Newark Pub Libr; Brooklyn Mus; New
York Pub Libr; N J State Mus, Trenton; Metrop Mus Art; plus
others.
Exhibitions: Metrop Mus Art; Nat Acad Design; Art Inst Chicago;
Am Watercolor Soc; Soc Am Graphic Artists; plus others.
Memberships: New York Soc Women Artists; Asn Art N J; Nat Asn
Women Artists; Del Valley Art Asn; Boston Soc Printmakers;
plus others.
Mailing Address: Fiddlers Forge, Pittstown, NJ 08867.

MARSH, (EDWIN) THOMAS
Potter, Educator
Preferred Media: Ceramics.
b Winchester, Ky, Feb 11, 34.
Study & Training: Univ Louisville, BS(fine arts), 60; apprentice to
Totaro Sakuma, Mashiko, Japan & Kei Fujiwara, Imbe, Bizen,
61-63; Ind Univ, MAT(ceramics), 70, also with Kark Martz.
Work in Public Collections: Ashland Oil Collection, Louisville, Ky;
Akino Collection, Oiso, Japan; Nogeyama Kyokai, Yokohama,
Japan; Ind Univ, Bloomington.
Commissions: 14 holy water fonts & other ceramic pieces (with
David Day, architect), Abbey of Gethsemani, Trappist, Ky, 66;
holy water font (with David Day), St Margaret of Cortona Church,
Columbus, Ohio, 68.
Exhibitions: One-man exhibs, Shingei Gallery, Tokyo, Japan, 64,
Togei Gallery, Kyoto, Japan, 64; Art Ctr, Louisville, Ky, 68 &
69 & The Gallery, Bloomington, Ind, 71.
Teaching: Assoc prof ceramics, sculpture & design, Univ Louis-
ville, 70-; vis prof ceramics, Purdue Univ, summers, 70 & 72.
Awards: First Nat Bank Award & Aetna-Ashland Oil Purchase
prize, 60; merit award, Gen Elec Co, 72.
Memberships: Nat Coun Educ Ceramic Arts; Am Asn Univ Prof;
Am Craftsmen's Coun.
Publications: Auth, The folk potters of Mashiko, Ceramics Monthly,
10/61.
Mailing Address: Marsh Pottery, R R 1, Box 221-B, Borden, IN
47106.

MARSHALL, ALICE LORD
Painter
Preferred Media: Watercolors.
b East Orange, N J, Oct 1, 95.
Study & Training: New York Sch Fine & Appl Art; with William B
Schimmel, Ariz, Douglas Greenbow & Rex Brandt, Calif & Rob-
ert Ewood, Spain & Portugal.
Work in Public Collections: Ariz Bank, Phoenix; Yuma Art Asn,
Ariz.
Exhibitions: Am Watercolor Soc, New York, N Y; Ariz State Fair,
Phoenix; Nat League Am Pen Women; Am Soc Arts & Lett; plus
many others.
Awards: Gold Cup, Mesa, Ariz; scholar, New York; plus many
others.
Memberships: Assoc Am Watercolor Soc; Ariz Watercolor Asn
(secy); Ariz Artists Guild; Am Soc Arts & Lett; Nat League Am
Pen Women.
Mailing Address: 7345 N 15th Ave, Phoenix, AZ 85021.

MARSHALL, JOHN CARL
Craftsman
Preferred Media: Gold, Silver.
b Pittsburgh, Pa, Feb 25, 36.
Study & Training: Cleveland Inst Art, BFA; Syracuse Univ, MFA.
Work in Public Collections: Everson Mus, Syracuse, N Y; Objects
U S A.
Commissions: Cruets & lavabo bowl, Cathedral of Immaculate Con-
ception, Syracuse, 67; chancellors bowl, Syracuse Univ, 69; gold
bowl, Hendricks Chapel, Syracuse, 69; mace, State Univ N Y Col
Cortland, 71; cross, standing candle holders & baptismal bowl,
Our Redeemers Lutheran Church, Seattle, Wash, 72.
Exhibitions: 45th Ceramic Nat, 68; Objects U S A, 69; Goldsmiths
'70; Jewelry & Holloware Nat, Iowa State Univ, 72; Nat Enamel &
Glass Show, Tex Tech Univ, 72.
Teaching: Asst prof metalworking, design & enamel, Syracuse Univ,
65-70; assoc prof metalworking, Univ Wash, 70-
Awards: Nat merit award, Am Craftsmen Coun, Craftsmen U S A,
66; Thomas C Thompson Prize 45th Ceramic Nat Competition, 68;
Am Metalcraft Award, Nat Enamels Exhib, 70.
Memberships: Northwest Designer Craftsmen; Am Craftsmen's
Coun; Soc N Am Goldsmiths.
Mailing Address: 23312 Robinhood Dr, Edmonds, WA 98020.

MARSICANO, NICHOLAS
Painter, Educator
b Shenandoah, Pa, Oct 1, 14.
Study & Training: Pa Acad Fine Arts & Barnes Found, 31-34.
Work in Public Collections: Mus Mod Art; Hallmark Collection;
Michener Found, Pipersville, Pa; Larry Aldrich Mus; Dallas
Mus Fine Arts; plus many others.
Exhibitions: Whitney Mus Am Art, 60-62; Mus Mod Art, 61 & 62;
Larry Aldrich Mus, Ridgefield, Conn, 64; Univ Tex, Austin, 64,
66 & 68; The New American Painting & Sculpture, Mus Mod Art,
69; plus many other group & one-man shows.
Teaching: Assoc prof art, Cooper Union, 48-; instr, Univ Mich,
summer 50; instr, Yale Univ, summers 51-54; instr, Brooklyn
Mus Sch, 51-58; instr, Pratt Inst, 57-60; instr, Cornell Univ,
summer 59.
Awards: Cresson fel & Barnes Found scholar to Europe, Pa Acad
Fine Arts, 33-36; second prize, Fifth Hallmark Int Competition,
60.
Publications: Contribr, It Is Mag; contribr, print of painting on
cover, In: Art News, 60; contribr, color print, In: Man and his
image, 68.
Mailing Address: Dept of Art, Cooper Union, Cooper Square, New
York, NY 10003.

MARSTELLER, WILLIAM A
Collector
b Champaign, Ill, Feb 23, 14.
Collection: Modern American art.
Mailing Address: 866 Third Ave, New York, NY 10022.

MARTELL, BARBARA BENTLEY
Painter
Preferred Media: Oils, Acrylics, Mixed Media.
b Trenton, N J.
Study & Training: Philadelphia Col Art, Pa.
Exhibitions: Philadelphia Sketch Club Ann, 68-; Philadelphia Plas-
tic Club, 71-72; Long Beach Island Found Arts & Sci; plus many
other local & regional shows.
Awards: Hon for pastel portrait, Long Beach Island Found Arts &
Sci, 69; hon for mixed media, Philadelphia Plastic Club, 72;
second best show in oils, Willingboro Pa Art Alliance, 72.
Mailing Address: 1514 Pine St, Philadelphia, PA 19102.

MARTIN, BERNARD MURRAY
Painter
Preferred Media: Oils.
b Ferrum, Va, June 21, 35.
Study & Training: Wake Forest Col, N C; Richmond Prof Inst, Va,
BFA; Hunter Col, MA.
Work in Public Collections: Va Mus Fine Arts, Richmond; Walter
Rawls Mus, Courtland, Va; Wachovia Nat Bank, Winston-Salem,
N C.
Exhibitions: Nostalgia and the Contemporary Artist, Am Fedn Arts
Traveling Exhib, 68; Am Painting 1970, Va Mus Fine Art, 70;
Friends of the Corcoran, Corcoran Gallery Art, Washington,
D C, 71; one-man show, Gallery Marc, Washington, D C, 71; 32nd
Southeastern Exhib, Gallery Contemp Art, Winston-Salem, 72.
Teaching: Assoc prof painting, Va Commonwealth Univ, 61-
Awards: Cert distinction, Va Artists Exhib, Va Mus Fine Arts, 64,
66, 68 & 70; first prize, Southeastern Exhib, Gallery Contemp
Art, 70 & 71.
Dealer: Gallery Marc, 2121 P St N W, Washington, DC 20037.
Mailing Address: 3329 Hanover Ave, Richmond, VA 23221.

MARTIN, BERNICE FENWICK
Painter, Printmaker
Preferred Media: Oils, Graphics.
b Shelbourne, Ont, July 7, 12.
Study & Training: Toronto Tech Schs; Ont Col Art, Univ Toronto,
with J W Beatty & Frank Carmichael; McMaster Univ; Univ Alta,
with Toshi Yoshida.
Work in Public Collections: In collections of Hon Mitchell Sharpe,
Ottawa, Ont, Harold Smythe & Glen Bannerman; also pub bldgs,
schs & many pvt collections Can & int.
Exhibitions: Soc Can Painter-Etchers & Engravers' Ann & Traveling, 54-71; Can Expo' 1967, Montreal, Que, 67; Centennial Oper
Ont Art '67, City Hall, Toronto, 67; one-man show & pub demonstration color block prints, Can Nat Exhib, Toronto, 68-69; exhibs across Can, art galleries, mus & pub libr, 47-71; also
many one-man exhibs.
Memberships: Soc Can Painter-Etchers & Engravers (chmn, presentation graphic arts print comn, 56-57); fel Int Inst Arts & Lett.
Mailing Address: 150 Millwood Rd, Toronto 7, Ont, Can.

MARTIN, CHARLES E
Designer, Painter
Preferred Media: Watercolors, Acrylics, Oils, Ink.
b Chelsea, Mass, Jan 12, 10.
Work in Public Collections: Mus City New York; Metrop Mus, N Y.
Exhibitions: One-man shows, Brooklyn Mus Art Sch, 54 & Rockland Found, 56-57; Ruth White Gallery, 60.
Teaching: Instr watercolor paintings, Brooklyn Mus Art Sch, 63-65.
Positions: Cartoonist designer, New Yorker Mag, 35-; illusr, eve newspaper, 39-42; art dir, air drop newspapers, New York, London, Naples & Paris, 42-45.
Memberships: Mag Cartoonist Guild Am (exec comt).
Publications: Contribr, New Yorker Mag, New York Times, Playboy, Sat Rev, Life & Time Mags, 35-
Mailing Address: 45 E 85th St, New York, NY 10028.

MARTIN, FLETCHER
Painter
Preferred Media: Oils, Watercolors, Print Media.
b Palisade, Colo, Apr 29, 04.
Work in Public Collections: Metrop Mus Art & Whitney Mus Am Art, New York, N Y; William Rockhill Nelson Gallery, Kansas City, Kans; Los Angeles Mus Art, Calif; Pa Acad Fine Arts, Philadelphia.
Commissions: True fresco, Works Progress Admin, Hollywood High Sch, 35; oil on canvas, U S Secy Fine Art, Fed Bldg, San Pedro, Calif, 37; oil on canvas, U S Secy Fine Art, Post Off Bldg, Lamesa, Tex, 38; bas relief sculpture, U S Secy Fine Art, Co Court House, Bonner's Ferry, Idaho, 39; oil on canvas, U S Secy Fine Art, Post Off Bldg, Kellogg, Idaho, 40.
Exhibitions: Los Angeles Mus Ann, 35; Americans 1942, Mus Mod Art, New York, 42; Pa Acad Fine Arts, 47; Nat Acad Design Ann, New York, 49; Retrospective, Roberson Mem Ctr, Binghamton, N Y, 68.
Teaching: Artist-in-residence, Univ Iowa, 40-41; head dept painting, Kansas City Art Inst, 41-43; vis artist, Univ Fla, 50-52; artist-in-residence, Roberson Mem Ctr, 67-68.
Positions: Nat committeeman, Artists Equity Asn, 49-55.
Awards: Van Rensselaer Wilbur Prize, Los Angeles Mus, 35; Lippincott Prize for Figure painting, Pa Acad Fine Arts, 47; Altman Prize, Nat Acad Design, 49.
Bibliography: Barbara Ebersole (auth), Fletcher Martin, Univ Fla Press, 54; H Lester Cooke (auth), Fletcher Martin, Abrams, 73.
Memberships: Woodstock Artists Asn (chmn, 53-55).
Publications: Illusr, Tales of the gold rush, 44; illusr, Mutiny on the bounty, 47; illusr, The sea wolf, 61; illusr, The jungle, 65; illusr, Of mice and men, 69.
Dealers: Eve Loring Gallery, 661 Central Ave, Cedarhurst, NY 11516; Rudolph Galleries, Woodstock, NY 12498.
Mailing Address: Apartado 73, Guanajuato, Guanajuato, Mex.

MARTIN, FRED THOMAS
Painter
b San Francisco, Calif, June 13, 27.
Study & Training: Univ Calif, Berkeley, BA, 49, MA, 52; San Francisco Art Inst, with David Park, Clifford Still & Mark Rothko.
Work in Public Collections: Whitney Mus Am Art, New York, N Y; San Francisco Mus Art; Oakland Art Mus, Calif.
Exhibitions: San Francisco Mus Art Ann, 50-60; Whitney Ann, 70; one-man shows, M H DeYoung Mus, San Francisco, Richmond Art Ctr, Calif & Royal Marks Gallery, New York; plus others.
Teaching: Dir col, San Francisco Art Inst, 66-
Awards: Nat Found Arts Artists grant, 70-71.
Mailing Address: 232 Monte Vista, Oakland, CA 94611.

MARTIN, G W
Painter, Educator
Preferred Media: Oils.
b Tacoma, Wash, Apr 19, 13.
Study & Training: Herron Art Sch, Millikan Europ travel scholar & BFA, 38; State Univ Iowa, with Philip Guston, Fletcher Martin & Emil Ganso, MFA; Boston Mus Art Sch, with Karl Zerbe.
Work in Public Collections: Lithograph Libr Cong, Washington, D C; Watercolor Wadsworth Atheneum, Hartford, Conn; Conn Printers, Hartford.
Commissions: Mural, U S Post Off, Danville, Ind; mural, Gengras Campus Ctr, Univ Hartford; portrait Chancellor Coffin, Univ Hartford.
Exhibitions: Mus Mod Art, New York, N Y, 42; Color Print Soc, Philadelphia, Pa, 42; Carnegie Inst, 42 & 43; Conn Acad Fine Arts, 47-57 & 62; Mus Am Art, New Brit, Conn, 68.
Teaching: Prof art & head dept, Lindenwood Col, 41-43; assoc prof art, Hartford Art Sch, Univ Hartford, 57-
Awards: New Eng Drawing Exhib Award, 58; mural competition, Gengras Campus Ctr, Univ Hartford, 68.
Mailing Address: 618 Willard Ave, Newington, CT 06111.

MARTIN, KEITH
Museum Director, Painter
b Perth Amboy, N J, Jan 22, 10.
Study & Training: Harvard Univ, BA; also with Wayman Adams.
Collections Arranged: Exhibition of Art of the Americas, Int Expos, Port-au-Prince, Haiti, 50; Models of Inventions of Leonardo da Vinci, 52.
Teaching: Head art dept, Syracuse Univ, 46-48.
Positions: Dir, Kansas City Art Inst & Sch Design, 39-43; dir, fine arts dept, IBM, 46-53; dir, Roberson Ctr Arts & Sci, Binghamton, N Y, 54-
Memberships: Am Asn Mus; N Y State Asn Mus; Northeast Asn Mus; Assoc Couns Arts; Eastern Regional Inst Educ (trustee).
Mailing Address: Roberson Center for the Arts & Sciences, Binghamton, NY 13905.

MARTIN, KEITH MORROW
Painter
b Lincoln, Nebr, Jan 27, 11.
Study & Training: Univ Nebr; Art Inst Chicago.
Work in Public Collections: Art Inst Chicago; Denver Mus; Baltimore Mus Art; Munson-Williams-Proctor Inst; Butler Inst Am Art; plus others.
Exhibitions: Norfolk Mus Am Drawing Ann, Va, 62; 159th Ann Am Painting & Sculpture, Pa Acad Fine Arts, 65; Ball State Ann, Muncie, Ind, 65, 67, 69 & 70; Embassy Art Prog, State Dept, Washington, D C, 67 & 69; Art On Paper, Weatherspoon Ann, Greensboro, N C, 68 & 69; plus many other group & one-man exhibs.
Teaching: Instr, Baltimore Mus Art, 58-68.
Awards: 2nd Md Exhib Acad Arts Award, Easton, 66; Benedictine Art Purchase Prize, 67; WCBM Area Exhib Prize, Baltimore, 69; plus others.
Bibliography: A Breeskin (auth), New talent U S A, Art Am, 2/55; A Balder (auth), Six Maryland artists, Balboa Publ, 55; article, In: Baltimore Mus Art News, 67.
Publications: Auth, Keith Martin remembers Gertrude Stein, Baltimore Mus Art Rec, Vol 1, No 8.
Mailing Address: 3208 St Paul St, Baltimore, MD 21218.

MARTIN, KNOX
Painter, Sculptor
b Barranquilla, Colombia, Feb 12, 23; U S citizen.
Study & Training: Art Stud League New York, four years.
Work in Public Collections: Loeb Stud Ctr, New York Univ, N Y; Univ Miami, Fla; Whitney Mus Am Art, New York, N Y; Mus Art, Austin, Tex; Univ Calif, Berkeley.
Commissions: Nineteen story wall painting, City Walls, Inc, West Side Hwy, New York, 71; wall painting, Mercor, Inc, Merritt Complex, Fort Lauderdale, Fla, 72.
Exhibitions: Stable Gallery, New York, 52; Gallery Mod Art, Washington, D C, 63; Santa Barbara Mus Art, Calif, 64; Concrete Expressionism, Loeb Stud Ctr, New York Univ, 65; Yale Univ Art Gallery, 66.
Teaching: Asst prof drawing & painting, Yale Univ, 65-70.
Awards: Longview fel, 56; balloonist award, Matt Wiedekehr, St Paul, Minn, 72; Nat Endowment for the Arts, 72.
Bibliography: Knox Martin super creation (collage/film, color), Yale Univ Art Dept, 67; George Parrino (auth), Knox Martin, The Deadalian Work, 72.
Dealer: Galeria Bonino, 7 W 57th St, New York, NY 10019.
Mailing Address: 128 Fort Washington Ave, New York, NY 10032.

MARTIN, LANGTON
Painter, Printmaker
Preferred Media: Graphics.
b Toronto, Ont, May 15, 13.
Study & Training: Ont Col Art, Univ Toronto, with J W Beatty; Toronto Tech Schs; McMaster Univ.
Exhibitions: Soc Can Painter-Etchers & Engravers; Ann & Traveling Exhibs across Can, art galleries, mus & pub libr, 54-71; Can Expo' 1967, Montreal, Que, 67; Can Nat Exhib, Toronto, 68-69.
Memberships: Soc Can Painter-Etchers & Engravers (keeper of the prints, 56-60, historian, 61-72); Arts & Lett Club; fel Int Inst Arts & Lett.
Mailing Address: 150 Millwood Rd, Toronto 7, Ont, Can.

MARTIN, LUCILLE CAIAR (LUCILLE MARTIN HAMPTON)
Painter
Preferred Media: Oils.
b Carlsbad, N Mex, June 7, 18.
Study & Training: With La Vora Norman; Frederic Taubes Workshops, Cloudcroft & Ruidoso; Merlin Enabnit Art Sch, Chicago, dipl.
Work in Public Collections: Carlsbad Libr & Mus, N Mex; Houston Med Ctr, Tex; Collier-Miller Gallery, Saint Joseph, Mo; Western Tradition Gallery, Boulder, Colo; Winters Gallery, Tucson, Ariz.

Commissions: Jordan River (mural), Hillcrest Baptist Church, Carlsbad, 62; Sacred River (mural), First Baptist Church, McCrory, Ark, 63; El Capitan (mural), Security Savings & Loan, Carlsbad, 64; N Mex State Bird-Roadrunner, Young Democrats for Gov Off, State Capitol, Santa Fe, 64; roadrunner painting, comn by Gov Campbell for aircraft carrier Constellation, 64.
Exhibitions: Fla Int Art Exhib, Lakeland, 52; Nat Polo Duro Art Show, W Tex State Univ, Canyon, 64; Nat Sun Carnival Art Exhib, El Paso Mus Art, Tex, 64; Boulder City Art Festival, Nev, 70; one-man show, N Mex State Univ, Las Cruces, 65.
Awards: Grand sweepstakes, Tri-State Invitational Art Exhib, El Paso, 57; Artists Choice, Am Asn Univ Women, 63; first place, Carlsbad Area Art Asn Exhibs, 64, 65 & 66.
Bibliography: Articles, In: N Mex Newspaper & El Paso Times, 64 & 65; Elena Montes (auth), Lucille Martin of Carlsbad, N Mex Mag, 4/65.
Memberships: Charter mem Carlsbad Area Art Asn.
Publications: Contribr, Ariz Highways Mag, 3/70.
Mailing Address: 5901 E Third St, Tucson, AZ 85711.

MARTIN, ROGER
Painter, Graphic Artist
b Gloucester, Mass, Sept 3, 25.
Study & Training: Boston Mus Fine Arts Sch.
Commissions: Brochure, Cambridge Electron Accelerator, Harvard Univ & Mass Inst Technol, 64; graphic art, D C Heath & Co, Allyn & Bacon, Beacon Press, 65-68 & United Teaching Pictures; designed cases & executed carvings, C B Fisk Pipe Organs, Harvard Univ & Pohick Church, Lorton, Va, 65-69.
Exhibitions: Boston Art Festival, 56 & 61; Rockport Art Asn, 57-72; Cape Ann Art Festival; Portland Art Festival, Maine; DeCordova Mus, 66, 67, 69 & 72; plus others.
Teaching: Instr design & drawing & head freshman dept, New Eng Sch Art, Boston, Mass, 67-69; instr design & painting, Montserrat Sch Visual Art, Beverly, Mass, 69-72.
Memberships: Rockport Art Asn.
Publications: Contribr, illus, In: New Yorker Mag, Atlantic Monthly & New York Times; contribr, articles & illus, In: Child Life Mag & textbks.
Mailing Address: Mt Locust Ave, Rockport, MA 01966.

MARTIN, WILLIAM HENRY (BILL)
Painter, Sculptor
Preferred Media: Oils.
b South San Francisco, Calif, Jan 22, 43.
Study & Training: San Francisco Art Inst, BFA, 68, MFA, 70; Acad Art Col, San Francisco.
Exhibitions: Stockton Art Mus, Calif, 70; San Francisco Art Inst Centennial, Calif, 71; Univ Southern Calif, Los Angeles, 71; Inst Contemp Art, Philadelphia, Pa, 72; Whitney Mus Am Art Painting Ann, New York, N Y, 72.
Teaching: Instr painting, Acad Art Col, San Francisco, 70-71; instr painting, Univ Calif, Berkeley, 72; instr painting, San Francisco Art Inst, 72-
Awards: Tiffany Found grant, 70.
Bibliography: David Kolodney (auth), Paintings by Bill Martin, Ramparts Mag, 10/70; Tom Albright (auth), Visuals, Rolling Stone Mag, 9/2/71.
Mailing Address: 946 Greenwich, San Francisco, CA 94133.

MARTINELLI, EZIO
Sculptor
b West Hoboken, N J, Nov 27, 13.
Study & Training: Acad Fine Arts, Bologna, Italy, 31; Nat Acad Design, 32-36; Barnes Found, Merion, Pa, 40.
Work in Public Collections: Whitney Mus Am Art & Solomon R Guggenheim Mus, New York, N Y; Newark Mus, N J; Seattle Mus, Wash; Art Inst Chicago, Ill.
Commissions: Aluminum sculpture, Gen Assembly Bldg, UN, 60.
Exhibitions: Salon for Younger Artists, Art of this Century Gallery, New York, 42; Abstract and Surrealist Art in America, Art Inst Chicago, 47; Survey of American Sculpture, Newark Mus, 62; Whitney Mus Am Art Sculpture, Drawings & Prints Ann, 66; Modern Sculptors, Their Drawings, Watercolors and Prints, Storm King Art Ctr, Mountainville, N Y, 71.
Teaching: Prof sculpture, Sarah Lawrence Col, 47-; artist-in-residence, Ford Found, Ringling Mus, Sarasota, Fla, 64; sculptor-in-residence, Am Acad Rome, 64-65; instr sculpture, Skowhegan Sch Painting & Sculpture, summer 69.
Awards: Guggenheim Found fel, 56-62; Tiffany Found fel, 64; Nat Inst Arts & Lett award, 66.
Bibliography: G Carandente (auth) Dictionary of modern sculpture (Rome), 57; D Ashton (auth), Modern American sculpture.
Mailing Address: 121 W 85th St, New York, NY 10024.

MARTINET, MARJORIE D
Painter
b Baltimore, Md, Nov 3, 86.
Study & Training: Md Inst, 04; Rhinehart Sch Sculpture, 04-05; Pa Acad Fine Arts, Thouron prize & Cresson Europ scholar, 05-10; also with William M Chase & Cecelia Beaux & in Europe.
Work in Public Collections: Asn Jewish Charities Bldg, Baltimore.
Exhibitions: Peabody Inst; Pa Acad Fine Arts; Philadelphia Plastic Club; one-man show, Baltimore Mus Art; Nat Asn Women Artists, 60-62; plus others.
Positions: Dir, Martinet Sch Art, Baltimore, 12-69; chmn art comt, Lizette Woodworth Reese Mem Tablet for Pratt Libr, Baltimore; art consult, Oldfields Sch, Glencoe, Md, 62.
Memberships: Philadelphia Art Alliance; Nat Asn Women Artists; Am Fedn Arts; fel Pa Acad Fine Arts.
Mailing Address: 621 Westview St, Philadelphia, PA 19119.

MARTINEZ-MARESMA, SARA (SARA SOFIA MARTINEZ)
Painter, Instructor
Preferred Media: Oils.
b Havana, Cuba; U S citizen.
Study & Training: San Alejandro Art Sch, Havana, with Leopoldo Romanach & Armando Menocal, prof drawing & painting (summa cum laude).
Work in Public Collections: Cardinal's Arteaga (portrait), Cardinal's Palace, Havana; St Jose Pignatelli (painting), Church Sagrado Corazon, Havana; Holy Family (painting), Noviciado de St Stanislao's Col, Havana; John F Kennedy (portrait), White House, Washington, D C; Stephen P Clark (portrait), City Hall, Miami, Fla.
Exhibitions: Havana Univ Gallery, 48; Cuban Mus, Daytona Beach, Fla, 63; Miami-Dade Jr Col, Fla, 64; Am Artists Prof League, New York, N Y, 71 & 72; one-man show, Bacardi Gallery, Miami, 70.
Teaching: Prof drawing & painting, Havana's Superior Sch, 48-59; prof drawing & painting, Apostolado Teacher's Sch, Havana, 49-59; vis prof painting, Havana Univ, 50-51.
Awards: First prize, Am Cancer Soc, 67; hon mention, Jordan Marsh, 69; prestige award, Am Artists Prof League, 69.
Bibliography: Maria Elena Saavedra (auth), Sara Maritnez Maresma, great Cuban painter, Diario Las Americas, 68; Frank Soler (auth), Artist's output fills her home: roses favorite, Miami Herald, 69.
Memberships: Am Artists Prof League; Fla Fedn Art; Miami Palette Club.
Mailing Address: 2632 S W 30th Ct, Miami, FL 33133.

MARTINO, ANTONIO P
Painter
Preferred Media: Oils.
b Philadelphia, Pa, Apr 13, 02.
Study & Training: Philadelphia Mus Col Art; La France Art Inst; also with Albert Jean Adolphe.
Work in Public Collections: Nat Acad Design, New York, N Y; Pa Acad Fine Arts, Philadelphia; Butler Art Inst, Youngstown, Ohio; Springville Art Mus, Utah; IBM Collection.
Commissions: Portraits & landscapes, Jud & Mrs O'Neill, Chestnut Hill, Pa, 47, Joseph Harris, Philadelphia, 55, Mr & Mrs Alex Manos, Thousand Oaks, Calif, 60, Misericordia Hosp, Philadelphia, 62 & Mr & Mrs A Ricci, Philadelphia, 65.
Exhibitions: Sesqui-Centennial, Philadelphia, 26; Nat Acad Design Ann, 26-; Golden Gate Int Expos, San Francisco, Calif, 40; Carnegie Inst, Pittsburgh, Pa, 40-44; Corcoran Gallery, Washington, D C, 40-47.
Awards: Jennie Sesman Gold Medal, Pa Acad Fine Arts, 38; Nat Arts Club Gold Medal, 58; Saltus Gold Medal Merit, Nat Acad Design, 64.
Bibliography: Joseph Finigan (auth), article, In: Am Artist Mag, 25; Henry Pitz (auth), Antonio P Martino, G Alan Chidsey, N Y, 1/53; Ernest Watson (auth), Composition, landscape & still life, Watson-Guptill, 59.
Memberships: Nat Acad Design; life mem Nat Arts Club; Am Watercolor Soc; Philadelphia Watercolor Club; Woodmere Art Gallery.
Publications: Auth, Prize winning watercolors, Allied Fla, 63 & Prize winning paintings, Margaret Harold Publ, 64.
Mailing Address: 1864 Rutgers Dr, Thousand Oaks, CA 91360.

MARTINO, EVA E
Painter, Sculptor
Preferred Media: Oils, Woods.
b Philadelphia, Pa.
Study & Training: Gwynedd Mercy Col; Montgomery Co Community Col; also with Giovanni Martino.
Exhibitions: Reading Mus, Pa, 62; Nat Acad Design, New York, N Y, 65; Pa Acad Fine Arts, Philadelphia, 66; Edinboro Teacher's Col, Pa, 67; Butler Inst Am Art, Youngstown, Ohio, 70.

Awards: Bronze medal, Da Vinci Alliance, 53; first prize, Plymouth Meeting Hall, 67; third prize, Philadelphia Sketch Club, 72.
Memberships: Nat Forum Prof Artists; Woodmere Art Gallery; Artists Equity Asn.
Mailing Address: 1435 Manor Lane, Blue Bell, PA 19422.

MARTINO, GIOVANNI
Painter
Preferred Media: Oils, Watercolors.
b Philadelphia, Pa, May 1, 08.
Study & Training: Spring Garden Inst, Pa; La France Inst, Pa; Philadelphia Graphic Sketch Club.
Work in Public Collections: Nat Acad Design, New York, N Y; Pa Acad Fine Arts, Philadelphia; Va Mus Fine Art; Springfield Art Mus, Mo; Butler Art Inst, Youngstown, Ohio.
Exhibitions: Royal Acad in Eng; Carnegie Inst, Pa; Whitney Mus Am Art, New York; San Francisco Int Expos, Calif; Nat Acad Design.
Teaching: Instr painting, Lehigh Univ, 57-58.
Awards: Pratt Prize, Am Watercolor Soc, 53; Elmer Fox Purchase Award, Springfield Art Mus, 72; Hallmark Award, Nat Acad Design, 72.
Memberships: Nat Acad Design; Am Watercolor Soc; Woodmere Art Gallery (exhib comt, 69-).
Mailing Address: 1435 Manor Lane, Blue Bell, PA 19422.

MARTINSEN, IVAR RICHARD
Painter, Educator
b Butte, Mont, Dec 9, 22.
Study & Training: Mont State Col; Univ Wyo.
Exhibitions: Wyo Artists Traveling Exhib, Sheridan & Laramie, Wyo; Scottsbluff, Nebr.
Teaching: Prof art, Sheridan Col.
Awards: Prizes, Wyo-Nebr Exhib, 58 & 59 & Wyo State Fair, 60.
Memberships: Sheridan Artist Guild; Wyo State Art Asn.
Mailing Address: Dept of Art, Sheridan College, Sheridan, WY 82801.

MARTMER, WILLIAM P
Painter, Photographer
Preferred Media: Oils.
b Detroit, Mich, Sept 25, 39.
Study & Training: Art Sch of Soc Arts & Crafts; Cranbrook Acad Art; Wayne State Univ.
Work in Public Collections: Cranbrook Acad Mus; Gen Motors Corp.
Exhibitions: Cranbrook Acad Art Gallery; Northern Ill Univ Art Dept; Brooklyn Mus Print Show; Wayne State Univ Alumni Invitational; Raven Gallery, Detroit, Mich.
Teaching: Instr art, Detroit Inst Arts; instr art, Wayne State Univ.
Awards: Lewis Art Prize, Huntington Woods Ann; popular prize, Kalamazoo Art Ctr & Scarab Club Detroit.
Dealer: Alan Rubiner, 621 S Washington, Royal Oak, MI 48067.
Mailing Address: Bundy Rd, Route 2, Coloma, MI 49038.

MARTYL (MARTYL SCHWEIG LANGSDORF)
Painter
b Saint Louis, Mo, Mar 16, 18.
Study & Training: Washington Univ, AB; Colorado Springs Fine Arts Ctr, with Arnold Blanch & Boardman Robinson.
Work in Public Collections: Whitney Mus Am Art, New York, N Y; Art Inst Chicago, Ill; Pa Acad Fine Arts, Philadelphia; Colorado Springs Fine Arts Ctr, Colo; Los Angeles Co Mus, Calif.
Commissions: Mural comn by Sect Fine Arts, Russell Post Off, Kans, 41; mural, comn by Sect Fine Arts, St Genevieve Post Off, Mo, 42; Recorder of Deeds (mural), comn by Sect Fine Arts, Washington, D C, 43; Darkness into Light (mural), Unitarian Church, Evanston, Ill, 62; 22 projections for Arnold Schoenberg's Pierrot Lunaire, Fine Arts Quartet, Chicago, Ill, 62.
Exhibitions: Painting in the U S A, Carnegie Inst, Pittsburgh, Pa, 43-45; five Univ Ill Am Art Biennials, 51-61; Chicago Artists Exhib, circulated by U S Info Serv to seven Fr cities, 58; New Accessions, Ninth Biennial Exhib Contemp Paintings, Colorado Springs Fine Arts Ctr, 62; American Drawing Biennial XXIV, Norfolk Mus Arts, 71.
Teaching: Instr painting, Univ Chicago, 65-70.
Positions: Mem artists comt, Art Inst Chicago, 69; exec comt, Artists Equity Asn Chicago, 58-60.
Awards: Logan Award & Award, 50 & William Bartels Award, 57, Art Inst Chicago; Am Inst Architects Honor Award, 62.
Bibliography: Allen Weller (auth), Mural dedication, Unitarian Church, Evanston, 61; H W Janson (auth), Martyl, Kovler Gallery Publ, 67; George McCue (auth), Martyl, Oriental Inst Mus, 69.
Memberships: Arts Club Chicago; Renaissance Soc, Univ Chicago (pres, 70-72).
Publications: Illusr, Atomic Scientists Bull, 45-71; contribr, Methods and techniques of gouache painting, 46; co-ed, Atomic Scien-

tists Bull, Art & Sci Issue, 2/59; auth, Cliches, old and new, Saint Louis Post-Dispatch, 67; auth, Art scene—Fred Sweet, 68.
Mailing Address: Box 228, Meacham Rd, Schaumburg, IL 60172.

MARX, ROBERT ERNST
Painter, Printmaker
Preferred Media: Intaglio
b Northeim, Ger, 25.
Study & Training: Univ Ill, 47; study & travel in Ger, Austria, Italy, Switz & France, one yr; Univ Ill, BFA, 51, MFA, 53.
Work in Public Collections: Mus Mod Art, New York, N Y; Philadelphia Mus Art, Pa; Dallas Mus Art, Tex; Seattle Art Mus, Wash; Munson-Williams-Proctor Inst, Utica, N Y; plus many others.
Exhibitions: U S Info Agency Graphics Traveling Exhib, U S S R, 63-64, Rumania & Poland, 65, India, 65, Czech, 65, Eastern Asia, 66; one-man shows, Ohio State Univ, 68, Univ Maine, Orono, 71, Red Hedgehog Gallery, Binghamton, N Y, 71 & Optik Gallery, Amherst, Mass, 73; plus many others.
Teaching: Instr, Univ Wis, 53; chmn art dept, Flint Jr Col, 56; instr sch art, Syracuse Univ, 58; assoc prof art, State Univ N Y Binghamton, 66-69, prof, 69-70; assoc prof, State Univ N Y Col Brockport, 70-72, prof, 72-
Positions: Artist attached to exhib in Prague & Bratislava, Czech, 65; dir, Flint Inst Art, 57; dir, Impressions Workshop, Boston, 69.
Mailing Address: 457 Moscow Rd, Hamlin, NY 14464.

MARYAN, MARYAN S
Painter
Preferred Media: Oils.
b Nowy-Sacz, Poland, Jan 1, 27; U S citizen.
Study & Training: L'Ecole Nat Beaux Arts, Paris, three yrs.
Work in Public Collections: Carnegie Inst, Pittsburgh, Pa; Art Inst Chicago, Ill; Mus Mod Art, New York, N Y.
Commissions: Tapestry for Tomb of Unknown Martyred Jew, Fr Govt, Paris.
Exhibitions: Salon des Surindependants, 51-52; Biennale de Paris, 57 & 59; Festival de Bayreuth, Denmark, 58; Carnegie Int, Pittsburgh, 61 & 64; Am Exhib, Art Inst Chicago, 64 & 65.
Awards: Prix des Critiques d'Art Paris, Biennale Paris, 59.
Publications: Illusr, The trial, 53; illusr, Legend of the golem, 55; auth, La menagerie humaine, Ed Tisne, Paris, 62.
Dealer: Allan Frumkin Gallery, 41 E 57th St, New York, NY 10022.
Mailing Address: 301 E 63rd St, New York, NY 10021.

MARZANO, ALBERT
Painter, Designer
Preferred Media: Acrylics, Oils, Watercolors.
b Philadelphia, Pa, Aug 22, 19.
Study & Training: Philadelphia Graphic Sketch Club; Philadelphia Plastic Club.
Commissions: Mural for pub health, 67 & mural, air pollution theme, 69, Dept Pub Health, Philadelphia.
Exhibitions: Chautauqua Art Asn Ann Juried Show, N Y, 59; 25th Ann Mid-Year Show, Butler Inst Am Art, Youngstown, Ohio, 60; 7th Ann Exhib, Nat Soc Painters in Casein, New York, N Y, 61; one-man shows, St Joseph's Col, Philadelphia, Pa, 70 & La Salle Col, Philadelphia, 71; plus other group & one-man shows.
Teaching: Instr drawing & painting, Sons Italy in Am, Philadelphia, 65-70.
Positions: Designer-consult, Philadelphia Asn Blind, 53-56; art dir-consult, J Cunningham Cox Agency, Bala-Cynwyd, Pa, 58; art consult & graphic designer, Philadelphia Pub Health Dept, 58-60; art dir-consult, Benn Assocs, Philadelphia, 60.
Awards: Gold medals, Philadelphia Art Dirs Club, 54, 55 & 56; gold medal, Haddonfield Art Ctr, N J, 59; gold medal, Nat Soc Painters in Casein, 61.
Memberships: Watercolor Club Philadelphia; Philadelphia Art Alliance; Woodmere Art Gallery.
Mailing Address: 1809 Delancey Pl, Philadelphia, PA 19103.

MASER, EDWARD ANDREW
Art Historian, Educator
b Detroit, Mich, Dec 23, 23.
Study & Training: Univ Mich, 41-43; Univ Chicago, MA, 49, PhD, 58.
Collections Arranged: (exhibs) German & Austrian 18th Century Painting, Sculpture and Graphics, 56, Benton, Curry, Woods Retrospectives 57, 58 & 59 & The Pre-Raphaelites, 60, Univ Kans Mus Art.
Teaching: Assoc prof art hist, Univ Kans, 53-61; prof art hist, Univ Chicago, 61-, chmn dept art, 61-64.
Positions: Dir, David & Alfred Smart Gallery, Univ Chicago, 72-
Awards: Fulbright res fel, 50-52, Fulbright sr res scholar, 65-66; Guggenheim res fel, 69-70.

Memberships: Col Art Asn Am; Renaissance Soc Am; Am Asn Univ Prof.

Research: Italian, German and Austrian art of the seventeenth and eighteenth centuries.

Publications: Co-auth, Il Museo del Opificio delle Pietre Dure, 53; auth, Giovan Domenico Ferretti, Florence, Marchi & Bertolli, 68; ed & auth, Baroque and Rococo pictorial imagery, Dover Press, 71; auth, Disegni inediti di Johann Michael Rottmayr, Monumenta Bergomensia Bergamo, 71.

Mailing Address: 5318 Hyde Park Blvd, Chicago, IL 60615.

MASON, ALDEN C
Painter, Educator
Preferred Media: Oils, Watercolors.
b Everett, Wash, July 14, 19.
Study & Training: Univ Wash, MFA.
Work in Public Collections: Seattle Art Mus, Wash, Henry Art Gallery, Seattle; Cent Wash State Col; Univ Wash Henry Suzzallo Libr.
Exhibitions: Spirit of the Comics, Inst Comtemp Art, Univ Pa, 69, circulated by Am Fedn Arts, N Y, 71-72; Invitational Drawing Soc Nat Exhib, circulated by Am Fedn Arts, 70-72; Pacific Cities Invitational, Auckland, N Z, 71; Gerrard John Hayes Gallery, 71-72; one-man show, Denver Art Mus, Colo, 73; plus others.
Teaching: Prof art, Univ Wash, 47-
Awards: Purchase award, 44th Northwest Ann, 63 & 54th Northwest Ann, 68, Seattle Art Mus; Northwest Watercolor Soc Ann Award, Seattle Art Mus Pavillion, 71.
Dealers: Gerard John Hayes Gallery, 722 N La Cienega, Los Angeles, CA 90069; Polly Friedlander Gallery 95 Yesler Way, Seattle, WA 98102.
Mailing Address: 1916 N E 73rd St, Seattle, WA 98115.

MASON, ALICE FRANCES
Lithographer, Painter
Preferred Media: Lithography.
b Chicago, Ill, Jan 16, 95.
Study & Training: Northwestern Univ, BS; Art Inst Chicago, BFA, MFA, Summer Sch Painting, Saugatuck, Mich, with Chapin, Kahn & others; Univ Chicago; study in Vienna; also with Maroger of the Louvre, Paris, France and others.
Work in Public Collections: Metrop Mus Art, New York, N Y; Pa Acad Fine Arts, Philadelphia; Univ Chicago, Ill; Libr Cong, Washington, D C; & others.
Commissions: Lithographs for print of the year, Chicago Soc Artists, 49.
Exhibitions: Lithography Show & Vicinity Shows, Art Inst Chicago Int, 12 shows, 37-56; Metrop Mus Art, 42 & 52; Soc Am Graphic Artists, New York, 52-55, 57; New Britain Art Mus, Conn, 52-53; one-man, Chicago Pub Libr, 61, others by invitation, 65-71.
Teaching: Instr lithography.
Awards: Hon mention, Print Club Philadelphia, 52; hon mention, Soc Am Graphic Artists, 53; first prize, New Britain Mus, 53.
Memberships: Conn Acad Fine Arts; Chicago Soc Artists (v pres, 53, pres, 54-58); Renaissance Soc, Univ Chicago (formerly bd dir, hon, 70-); Cordon Club Chicago (pres, 3 yrs); Arts Club Chicago.
Art Interests: Subjects relating to nature.
Collection: Paintings and lithographs, mainly nature related.
Dealers: I F A Gallery, 2623 Connecticut Ave, NW, Washington, DC 20008; Art Institute of Chicago, Michigan Ave & Adams St, Chicago, IL 60603.
Mailing Address: 9775 W Huron River Dr, Box 21, Dexter, MI 48130.

MASON, BETTE
Painter
Preferred Media: Acrylics, Oils.
b Tex.
Study & Training: Trinity Univ; Syracuse Univ; Art Stud League New York; Mus Mgt Sem, Mus Mod Art, New York, N Y.
Exhibitions: Westchester Art Soc Juried Exhib Painting & Sculpture, Tarrytown, N Y, 70-72; one-man show, Christopher Gallery, New York, 71; Union Carbide Co Invited Artists Exhib, New York, 72; one-man show, Scarsdale Gallery Contemp Art, N Y, 72; Galerie Int Group Exhib, New York, 72.
Teaching: Dir art dept, Westchester Learning Ctr, Fleetwood, N Y, 71-72.
Positions: Dir, Assoc Artists Gallery, Syracuse, 66-68.
Awards: First award, Scarsdale Art Soc, 70; Beaux-Arts Award, Federated Woman's Clubs, New York, 71; merit award, Westchester Art Soc, 72.
Memberships: Women in the Arts, New York; Artists Equity Asn New York; Westchester Art Soc (former pres); Scarsdale Art Soc; Greenwich Art Barn; plus others.
Dealer: Galerie Internationale, 1095 Madison Ave, New York, NY 10028.

MASON, FRANK HERBERT
Painter, Educator
Preferred Media: Oils.
b Cleveland, Ohio, Feb 21, 21.
Study & Training: Nat Acad Design, New York, N Y, with George Nelson, 37-38; Art Stud League New York, with Frank Vincent DuMond, 37-49.
Work in Public Collections: Eureka Col Mus, Ill; Butler Inst Am Art, Youngstown, Ohio; Am Embassy, London, Eng; Hall of Governors, State Capitol, Albany, N Y; U S War Dept, Washington, D C.
Commissions: Life of St Anthony of Padua (eight large canvases), Eleventh Century Church of San Giovanni di Malta, Venice, Italy, 64; Resurrection, Old St Patrick's Cathedral, New York, 72.
Exhibitions: Assoc Artists Pittsburgh, Carnegie Inst Mus Art, Pittsburgh, Pa, 46; Nat Acad Design, New York, 63; Exposition Intercontinentale, Palais des Congres, Monaco, 68; Penn-National, Ligonier, Pa, 68; Butler Inst Am Art, Youngstown, 69.
Teaching: Instr fine arts, Art Stud League New York, 50-
Awards: Popular prize, Assoc Artists Pittsburgh, Carnegie Inst Mus Art, Pittsburgh, 46; figure composition-St Anthony, Penn-National, Ligonier, 68; Prix d'Amerique du Nord, Expos Intercontinentale, Monaco, 68.
Bibliography: Condon Riley (auth), Frank Mason, painter, Am Artist, 6/64; Alexander Eliot (auth), Manzu, Mason & God, Art in Am, 65.
Memberships: Art Stud League New York; Nat Soc Mural Painters; Int Inst Conserv of Hist & Artistic Works; academician Nat Acad Design.
Dealer: Grand Central Galleries, 40 Vanderbilt Ave, New York, NY 10017.
Mailing Address: 385 Broome St, New York, NY 10013.

MASON, JOHN
Sculptor
Preferred Media: Ceramics.
b Madrid, Nebr, Mar 30, 27.
Study & Training: Otis Art Inst, Los Angeles, 49-52; Chouinard Art Inst, Los Angeles, 53-54.
Work in Public Collections: Art Inst Chicago, Ill; Los Angeles Co Mus Art, Calif; San Francisco Mus Art, Calif; Mus Contemp Crafts, New York, N Y; Nat Mus Mod Art, Kyoto, Japan; plus others.
Commissions: Ceramic relief, Palm Springs Spa, Calif, 59; ceramic relief, Tishman Bldg, Los Angeles, 61; ceramic doors, Sterling Holloway, South Laguna, Calif; plus others.
Exhibitions: One-man show, Pasadena Art Mus, Calif, 60; Whitney Mus Am Art, 64; one-man show, Los Angeles Co Mus Art, 66; Kompas 4, Van Addemuseum Eindhoven, Netherlands, 69; Nat Mus Mod Art, Kyoto, Japan, 71; plus others.
Teaching: Assoc prof art, Univ Calif, Irvine, 67-
Awards: Ford Found Award, 67th Am Exhib, Art Inst Chicago, 64; Univ Calif Award, Creative Arts Inst, 69-70; plus others.
Bibliography: John W Mills (auth), The technique of sculpture, Reinhold Corp, N Y, 65; John Coplans (auth), John Mason—sculpture, Los Angeles Co Mus Art, 66; Glenn C Nelson (auth), Ceramics, Holt, Rinehart & Winston, 71.
Dealer: Hansen-Fuller Gallery, 228 Grant Ave, San Francisco, CA 94108.
Mailing Address: 1521 S Central Ave, Los Angeles, CA 90021.

MASSE, GEORGES SEVERE
Painter, Lecturer
Preferred Media: Oils, Watercolors, Mixed Media.
b Montreal, Que, Aug 10, 18.
Study & Training: Montreal Mus Fine Arts, with Harold Beament & A Sheriff-Scott, 37-39; Banff Sch Fine Arts, with Frederic Taubes, 48.
Exhibitions: Four one-man shows, 42-47 & spring show, 55, Montreal Mus Fine Arts; six shows, Art Gallery Hamilton, 48-55; Royal Can Acad, 48-58; Que Art Festival, 51; Victoria Art Gallery, 57-58.
Teaching: Instr creative art, Montreal Mus Fine Arts, 42-44; lectr.
Positions: Sci illusr, Univ Montreal, 40-41; ex-pres, Indust Art Asn, Montreal, 69-71.
Awards: MacPherson Prize, 38; award, painting, Montreal Mus Fine Arts, 39.
Bibliography: Article, In: Encycl Int Degli Artisti, 72.
Mailing Address: 1593 Marie Claire, LaSalle, Montreal 660, Que, Can.

MASSEY, ROBERT JOSEPH
Painter, Educator
Preferred Media: Egg Tempera.
b Fort Worth, Tex, May 14, 21.
Study & Training: Okla State Univ, 39-47, BA, with Doel Reed; Univ

Havana, 47-48; Univ Mich, fall 48; Syracuse Univ, MFA, 52; Univ Tex, Austin, PhD, 62.
Work in Public Collections: Permanent Collections of Dallas Mus Fine Art, Syracuse Univ, Soc Am Graphic Artists, El Paso Mus Art & Univ N Mex; plus others.
Commissions: Enamel mosaic, State Nat Bank El Paso; applique hanging (with Sally Bishop), 69 & polyester-coated polyeurathane sculpture, 69, Univ Tex, El Paso Union Bldg.
Exhibitions: Nat Small Painting Exhib, Univ of the Pac, Stockton, Calif, 70; 5th Ann Gulf Coast Art Exhib, Mobile, Ala, 70; 11 State Small Painting Show, Albuquerque, N Mex, 70; 12th, 13th & 14th Ann Invitational Painting Exhib, Longview, Tex, 70-72; 5 State Art Exhib, Port Arthur, Tex, 71; plus many others.
Teaching: Asst, Okla State Univ, 47; instr, Inst Cult Cubano-Norte-americano, 48; teaching fel, Univ Mich, 48-49; vis prof art, Fla State Univ, 49-50; instr, Syracuse Univ, 52-53; prof art, Univ Tex, El Paso, 53-
Positions: Juror, N Mex State Fair Art Exhib, 58, Ariz Fine Arts Asn Exhib, State Fair, 69, El Paso Art Asn Ann, El Paso Art Mus, 69 & Ninth Ann Art Exhib, Carlsbad, N Mex, 72.
Awards: Hon mentions for painting & graphics, El Paso Artists Ann, 61; purchase award for painting, 6th Nat Arts Exhib, Tyler, Tex, 69; 3rd award, 11 State Small Painting Show, 70.
Publications: Auth, Formulas for painters, 67 & Notes for American readers, In: Notes on the technique of painting, 69, Watson-Guptill; auth, Formulas for artists, B T Batsford, London, 68; auth, Painting, drawing and printmaking supports, 9/70 & The artist's ideal studio, 1/71, Am Artist.
Dealer: Two-Twenty-Two Gallery, 222 Cincinnati Ave, El Paso, TX 79902.
Mailing Address: 708 McKelligon St, El Paso, TX 79902.

MASSIN, EUGENE MAX
Painter, Educator
Preferred Media: Acrylic Sheet.
b Galveston, Tex, Apr 10, 20.
Study & Training: Art Inst Chicago; Univ Chicago, BFA, 48; Escuela Univ Bellas Artes, Mex, MFA, 49; 1st asst to David Alfara Sequeiros, Mexican muralist.
Work in Public Collections: Brandeis Univ, Boston, Mass; Lowe Mus, Univ Miami, Fla; Escuela Univ Bellas Artes, Mex; Ringling Mus, Fla; Norton Gallery, Palm Beach, Fla.
Commissions: Mural, acrylic on acrylic sheet, Cafritz Co, Washington, D C, 65-66; mural, acrylic/canvas, City Nat Bank of Miami, Fla, 66; mural, acrylic sheet (with Julia Busch), City Nat Bank of Miami Beach, Fla, 72; mural, acrylic, Southern Gen Builders Inc, 72; painting of Fla, World Book Encyclopedia, 72.
Exhibitions: Metrop Mus Art, New York, N Y, 53; Whitney Ann, New York, 55; Art U S A Invitational, 59; Am Fedn Art traveling exhib, 62; Southeastern Ann, Atlanta, Ga, 64.
Teaching: Instr art, Univ Wis, 49-50; instr art, Univ S C, 52; prof art, Univ Miami, Fla, 54-
Positions: Pres, Artist Equity Asn, 55-58, founder, Fla Chap; adv, Arts Coun, 60-64; adv, Cafritz Found for Arts, Washington, D C, 66; juror, Nat Scholastic Art Awards, 71.
Awards: Humanities award, Univ Miami, Fla, 64 & 71; artist-in-residence, Univ W Va, 66; research award, Esso, 71.
Bibliography: Biographical movie developed for educ TV, Miami, Fla, 67-68; Julia Busch (auth), A painter's plastic sculpture, Art J, 70; Thelma Newman (auth), Plastics as design form, Chilton, 72.
Publications: Contribr, Art techniques, Reinhold, 65; Lucite spectrum, Du Pont Co Mag, 67-68.
Mailing Address: 3891 Little Ave, Coconut Grove, FL 33133.

MASSON, HENRI
Painter
Preferred Media: Oils.
b Spy, Belg, Jan 10, 07; Can citizen.
Study & Training: Ottawa Art Asn; Windsor Univ, LLD, 54.
Work in Public Collections: Nat Gallery Can; Art Gallery Ont; Nat Gallery Caracas, Venezuela; Mus P Q; Bezalel Mus, Jerusalem.
Exhibitions: Aspects of Contemporary Painting in Canada, Andover, Mass, 42; Rio de Janeiro, Brazil, 46; Can Painting, Washington, D C, 50; Biennale, São Paulo, 51; Colombon Int Exhib Mod Art, New Delhi, 53.
Teaching: Instr painting, Queen's Univ, Kingston, Ont, 48-52.
Bibliography: Painters of Quebec (film), Nat Film Bd, 42; M Barbeau, Henri Masson, Ryerson Press, 45; Graham McInnes (auth), Canadian art, Macmillan, 50.
Memberships: Can Group Painters; Can Soc Painter in Watercolor; Can Soc Graphic Arts.
Publications: Illusr, Quebec in revolt, Fortune Mag, 66.
Dealer: Walter Klinkhoff Gallery, 1200 Sherbrooke S W, Montreal, Que, Can.
Mailing Address: 1870 Ferncroft Crescent, Ottawa, Ont, Can.

MASUROVSKY, GREGORY
Printmaker, Illustrator
Preferred Media: Ink, Graphics.
b Bronx, N Y, Nov 26, 29.
Study & Training: Black Mt Col, N C, with Ilya Bolotowsky, 47-48; Art Stud League New York, with Will Barnet, 52-53; Sorbonne, ESPPPE, 54-61.
Work in Public Collections: Mus Mod Art, New York, N Y; Fogg Art Mus, Cambridge, Mass; Minneapolis Inst Arts, Minn; Carnegie Mus, Pittsburgh, Pa; Ctr Nat Art Contemporain, Paris, France; plus others.
Exhibitions: IIe & IIIe Biennale Paris, 61 & 63; Documenta, Kassel, Ger, 64; 1st Int Biennial Graphic Art, Cracow, Poland, 66; 5th Minn Artists Biennial, Minneapolis Inst Arts, 67; plus others.
Teaching: Vis prof drawing, Minneapolis Sch Art, 66-67.
Positions: Graphics monitor, Art Stud League New York, 52-53; artist-in-residence, Tamarind Lithography Workshop, Los Angeles, Calif, 69.
Awards: Critics prize for drawing, IIe Biennale Paris, 61; William & Noma Copley Found Award, 63; Prix special, 1st Int Bienniel Graphic Art, Cracow, Poland, 66.
Bibliography: M C Lacoste (auth), Masurovsky-an American in Paris, Studio Int, 3/65; G Boudaille (auth), Masurovsky, Cimaise, 5/65; H Kramer (auth), Art: poetic drawings by Masurovsky, New York Times, 2/27/71.
Memberships: Club Laureats-Biennale Gravure, Cracow, Poland.
Publications: Illusr, Litanie d'eau, Ed La Hune, Paris, 64; illusr, Western duo, Tamarind Lithography Workshop, 69; illusr, Seven poems, Assoc Am Artists, New York, 70.
Dealer: Betty Parsons Gallery, 24 W 57th St, New York, NY 10019.
Mailing Address: 43, rue Liancourt, 75 Paris XIVe, France.

MATHESON, DONALD ROY
Printmaker, Educator
b Honolulu, Hawaii, Jan 30, 14.
Study & Training: U S Mil Acad, West Point, BS; Univ Mich, AM; Ecole Louvre, Paris, France.
Work in Public Collections: Detroit Inst Art; Cincinnati Mus Asn; Libr Cong; South Bend Art Ctr; Univ Okla.
Exhibitions: Detroit Inst Art, 54, 55 & 57; Libr Cong, 55-57; Boston Printmakers, 55, 57 & 58; Cincinnati Mus Asn, 56 & 58; Am Color Print Soc, 58; plus others.
Teaching: Instr art & dir mus, Univ Okla, 56-57; prof art, Univ Mass, Amherst, 58-
Positions: Dir, West Point Mus, 52-53.
Awards: Prize, Detroit Inst Art, 55; Scarab Club Award, 57; Yankee Mag Award, Boston Printmakers Nat Print Show, 63; plus others.
Memberships: Col Art Asn Am; Mich Acad Sci, Arts & Lett; Print Coun Am.
Mailing Address: Dept of Art, University of Massachusetts, Amherst, MA 01002.

MATISSE, PIERRE
Art Dealer
Positions: Owner & dir, Pierre Matisse Gallery Corp.
Mailing Address: 41 E 57th St, New York, NY 10022.

MATSON, ELINA
Weaver
b Vaasa, Finland, Dec 12, 92; U S citizen.
Study & Training: Norfolk Mus Art Sch; Penland Sch Handicrafts, N C.
Work in Public Collections: Va Mus Fine Arts, Richmond; Norfolk Mus Fine Arts, Va.
Exhibitions: Delgado Mus Art, New Orleans, La, 53; Chesapeake Craftsmen, Norfolk Mus Fine Arts, 54 & 56; Va Mus Fine Arts, 55, 57 & 59; Pen & Brush Club, New York, N Y, 56; Women's Int Exhib, New York, 56 & 57.
Awards: Cert distinction, Va Mus Fine Arts, 55; purchase prize, Norfolk Mus Fine Arts, 55; weaving prize, Pen & Brush Club, 56.
Memberships: Tidewater Weavers Guild (treas, 52-56, librn, 56-59, pres, 59-61); Tidewater Arts Coun; Pen & Brush Club.
Mailing Address: 8750 Old Ocean View Rd, Norfolk, VA 23503.

MATSON, GRETA (GRETA MATSON KHOURI)
Painter
Preferred Media: Oils, Watercolors.
b Claremont, Va.
Study & Training: Grand Cent Sch Art, New York; also with Jerry Farnsworth, Cape Cod.
Work in Public Collections: New Britain Mus Am Art, Conn; Va Mus Fine Arts, Richmond; Little Rock Mus, Ark; Tex Technol Col, Lubbock; Longwood Col, Farmville, Va.
Commissions: Portraits, Dean Grace Landrum, William & Mary Col, Williamsburg, Va, 46 & Mary Calcott, Calcott Sch, Norfolk, Va, 53.

Exhibitions: Nat Drawing Ann, Albany Inst Hist & Art, N Y, 40 & 45; Oil Nat, Carnegie Inst, Pittsburgh, Pa, 41, 44 & 45; Oil & Watercolor Nat, Art Inst Chicago, Ill, 42, 43 & 46; Oil Nat, Butler Art Inst, Youngstown, Ohio, 43, 45, 57 & 59; Oil Nat, Va Mus Fine Arts, Richmond, 53 & 57.

Awards: Altman Figure Prize, Nat Acad Design, 45; Am Artist Mag Medal, Am Watercolor Soc, 55; Allied Artists Am Gold Medal, 62.

Memberships: Nat Asn Women Artists (pres, 61-65); Audubon Artists (corres secy, 61-62); Allied Artists; Am Soc Contemp Artists (1st v pres, 61); Am Watercolor Soc.

Publications: Auth, Painting in watercolor at the seashore, Am Artist Mag, 56.

Mailing Address: 8750 Old Ocean View Rd, Norfolk, VA 23503.

MATSON, VICTOR (STANLEY)
Painter
b Salt Lake City, Utah, Mar 18, 95.
Study & Training: Univ Utah, BS; spec art training with McDermitt, Jack W Smith, Frans Feritz & Trude Hanscom.
Work in Public Collections: City of Los Angeles Collection; City of Eilat Israeli Collection.
Exhibitions: Five shows, Painters & Sculptors Club, 53-64; City of Los Angeles Art Festival, 53-68; Valley Art Guild, 55-64; Artists of the Southwest, 57-65; Calif Art Club Ann, 61-69; plus others.
Awards: Prizes, Artists of the Southwest, 57, 66 & 68; Fri Morning Club, 65, 66 & 69 & San Gabriel Fine Arts Asn, 68; plus others.
Memberships: Calif Art Club; Painters & Sculptors Club, Los Angeles (pres, 64); Am Inst Fine Arts (chmn adv bd, 64-65); life mem Laguna Beach Art Asn; Artists of the Southwest (treas, 65); plus others.
Mailing Address: 2038 Stratford Ave, South Pasadena, CA 91030.

MATSUOKA, ISAAC JIRO, see IZACYRO.

MATTHEWS, GENE (EUGENE EDWARD)
Painter, Educator
Preferred Media: Acrylics.
b Davenport, Iowa, Mar 22, 31.
Study & Training: Bradley Univ, 48-51; Univ Iowa, BFA, 53, MFA, 57.
Work in Public Collections: Nat Collection Fine Arts, Smithsonian Inst, Washington, D C; Butler Inst Am Art, Youngstown, Ohio; Denver Art Mus, Colo; Norfolk Art Mus, Va; Joslyn Art Mus, Omaha, Nebr.
Exhibitions: Am Watercolors, Drawings & Prints, Metrop Mus Art, New York, N Y, 52; 1st Festival of Two Worlds Exhibition, Spoleto, Italy, 58; Antagonismes, Int Painting Exhib, Louvre, Paris, France, 60; Contemp Am Watercolors, Cleveland Art Inst, 68; 50 American Drawings, Smithsonian Inst Traveling Exhib, 72.
Teaching: Prof fine arts, Univ Colo, Boulder, 61-
Awards: Prix di Rome Fel Painting, Am Acad Rome, Italy, 57-60; faculty fel for creative res, Univ Colo, Boulder, 66; gold medal of hon for watercolor, Nat Arts Club, New York, 69.
Bibliography: Wendon Blake (auth), Acrylic watercolor painting, Watson-Guptill, 70.
Dealer: Brena Gallery, 313 Detroit St, Denver, CO 80210.
Mailing Address: 2865 Jay Rd, Boulder, CO 80301.

MATTIELLO, ROBERTO
Painter, Sculptor
Preferred Media: Oils, Mixed Media.
b Montebelluna, Italy, Feb 13, 34.
Study & Training: Pvt study, Treviso, Italy; Inst Design, Buenos Aires, Arg, with Hector Cartier; Ikebana, Buenos Aires, with Tazko Niimura.
Work in Public Collections: Mus Mod Art, Buenos Aires; Kliner & Bell Art Fund, Los Angeles, Calif; Am Fedn Art, New York, N Y; Galerie B Bischofberger, Zurich, Switz.
Commissions: Mural & interior design, Olivetti Arg, Buenos Aires, 58; Roads, mural, C I D A R - Ford, Buenos Aires, 60; Cosmic Voyage, mural, Varig Airline, Arg, 61; Ballad, mural on fiber glass, Jack Parker Co, New York, N Y, 64; Fusion, wall sculpture, Parker 72nd St Bldg, New York, 65.
Exhibitions: Primera Expos Int Arte Mod Buenos Aires, Mus Arte Mod, Arg, 61; Art Artists, Riverside Mus, New York, 63; one-man show, New York Hilton Hotel, 66; 1, 2, 3 Infinity, Contemp Gallery, New York, 67; Psychedelic Art, Galerie Boschofberger, Zurich & Dussendorf, 68.
Awards: Hon mention, Segunda Bienal Arg Arte Sagrado Mod, Hist Mus of the Church, Arg, 56.
Bibliography: Kevin Sanders (auth), Surrealism, ABC-TV Eyewitness News, 2/72.
Publications: Contribr, Mandala, Shambala Publ, 7/72.
Mailing Address: 243 E 31st St, New York, NY 10016.

MATTIL, EDWARD L
Educator, Writer
b Williamsport, Pa, Oct 25, 18.
Study & Training: Pa State Univ, BS, 40, MA, 46, DEd, 53; also with Viktor Lowenfeld & Hobson Pittman.
Teaching: From asst prof to assoc prof, Pa State Univ, 48-60, prof art educ & head dept, 60-70; prof art & chmn dept, N Tex State Univ, 71-
Positions: Ed, Everyday Art, 57-
Awards: Distinguished serv award, Nat Gallery Art, 65.
Memberships: Nat Art Educ Asn (pres, 63-65).
Publications: Auth, Meaning in Crafts, Prentice-Hall, Inc, 59, 65 & 71; co-auth, Providing for individual differences in the elementary schools, 60 & The arts in higher education, 69; ed, A seminar in art education for research and curriculum development.
Mailing Address: Dept of Art, North Texas State University, Denton, TX 76203.

MATTISON, DONALD MAGNUS
Painter
Preferred Media: Oils.
b Beloit, Wis, Apr 24, 05.
Study & Training: Yale Sch Fine Arts, BFA; Am Acad in Rome, fel, also with Eugene Francis Savage.
Work in Public Collections: Art Inst Chicago, Ill, Indianapolis Mus Art, Ind; Princeton Univ, N J.
Commissions: Portraits, Emil Schram, pres, New York Stock Exchange, N Y, 57, Gov Harold Handley, Ind Hist Soc, 60, Frank McHale, Nat Bank Logansport, Ind, 70, Elvis Stahr, pres, Ind Univ, Bloomington, 71 & Judge Wilbur F Pell, Jr, Seventh Dist Bar Asn, U S Court Appeals, Chicago, 72.
Exhibitions: Nat Acad Design Ann, New York, 33; San Francisco Golden Gate Expos, 39; Rockefeller Ctr First Nat Exhib Am Art; Critics Choice Contemp Am Painting, Cincinnati, Ohio, 45; American Painting Today, Metrop Mus, New York, 50.
Teaching: Instr painting & design, New York Univ, 31-33; instr painting & drawing, Columbia Univ, 31-33; dir painting & dean, Herron Sch Art, Ind Univ, Indianapolis, 33-70.
Positions: Trustee, Indianapolis Mus Art, 69-
Awards: Prix de Rome, Am Acad in Rome, 28; art asn prize, John Herron Art Inst, 35; hon mention, Delgado Mus Art, New Orleans, La, 49.
Bibliography: Ernest W Watson (auth), Twenty painters and how they work, Watson-Guptill, 50.
Memberships: Contemp Art Soc, Indianapolis Mus Art; Ind Artists Club (chmn exhib comt, 71-72); Ind Mus Art; Nat Asn Schs Art (bd mem, 66-67); Midwestern Col Art Asn (mem bd control, 49-50).
Mailing Address: 4821 Buttonwood Crescent, Indianapolis, IN 46208.

MAULDIN, BILL
Cartoonist, Writer
b Mountain Park, N Mex, Oct 29, 21.
Study & Training: Chicago Acad Fine Arts; Conn Wesleyan Univ, hon MA, 46; Albion Col, LittD, 70; Lincoln Col, LHD, 70.
Positions: Cartoonist, Chicago Sun-Times, Chicago, Ill, 62-
Awards: Pulitzer Prize, 44 & 58; Sigma Delta Chi Award, 64.
Memberships: Nat Cartoonists Soc.
Publications: Auth, What's got your back up?, 61 & I've decided I want my seat back, 65, Harper-Row; auth, Up front, 68 & Brass ring, 71, Norton; auth & illusr, articles, In: Life, Sat Eve Post, Sports Illus, Atlantic Monthly, New Repub & many others.
Mailing Address: Chicago Sun-Times, 401 N Wabash Ave, Chicago, IL 60611.

MAURER, EVAN MACLYN
Art Historian, Art Administrator
b Newark, N J, Aug 19, 44.
Study & Training: Amherst Col, BA, 66; Univ Minn, MA, 68; Univ Pa.
Collections Arranged: MIA Portraits, Rochester & Red River, Minn, 71; Landscape Masterpieces, Grand Rapids, Minn, 72; The Human Image, 72 & Observations: The Female Image, 72, Minneapolis Inst Arts.
Teaching: Head teaching fel intro art hist, Univ Pa, 70-71.
Positions: Cur & asst to dir, Minneapolis Inst Arts, 71-; chmn Vanderlip Award Jury, Minneapolis Col Art & Design, 72.
Memberships: Col Art Asn; Am Asn Mus.
Research: Relationships between Surrealism & Primitivism.
Mailing Address: Minneapolis Institute of Arts, 201 E 24th St, Minneapolis, MN 55404.

MAURICE, ALFRED PAUL
Printmaker, Educator
b Nashua, N H, Mar 11, 21.
Study & Training: Univ N H, 40-42; Mich State Univ, BA, 47, MA, 49.

Commissions: Murals (with Raymond Pinet), Nat Youth Admin, Jr High Sch, Hudson, N H & Community Chest Bldg, Nashua, 39-40.
Exhibitions: Brooklyn Mus 3rd & 5th Print Nat, 49 & 51; Philadelphia Print Club Print Nat, 54; 15th Audubon Artists Ann, 57; 54th Mich Artists Exhib, 64.
Collections Arranged: 20th Century American Artists, 62, Four Artists in New England, 63, Three Mid-Atlantic Seaboard Artists, 63, George Rickey/Ulfert Wilke, 64, Miklos Suba, 64 & Oliver Chaffee, 64, Kalamazoo Art Ctr.
Teaching: Instr printmaking, calligraphy & drawing, Macalester Col, 47-49; asst drawing, Mich State Univ, 49-50; from asst prof to assoc prof drawing, painting, printmaking & design, State Univ N Y, New Paltz, 50-57, actg chmn art dept, 55-56; exec dir, Md Inst Col Art, Baltimore, 57-59; chmn art dept, Univ Ill, Chicago Circle, 65-67, prof printmaking design & drawing, 65-, assoc dean faculties, 69-
Positions: Dir, Art Ctr, Kalamazoo Inst Arts, Mich, 59-65.
Memberships: Col Art Asn.
Collection: Extensive collection of American prints of all periods and in all print media.
Publications: Auth, Four Printmakers, 62, Miklos Suba, 64 & Oliver Chaffee, 64.
Mailing Address: 2725A S Michigan Ave, Chicago, IL 60616.

MAUZEY, MERRITT
Painter, Illustrator
b Clifton, Tex, Sept 16, 97.
Work in Public Collections: Brooklyn Mus Mem Collection; John Van Wicht Pub Libr, Boston; print, Philadelphia Mus; Warren Mack Collection; Benton Spruce Mem, Pa State Univ; plus many others.
Exhibitions: Local, state, regional & nat exhibs & one-man shows, 36-; work in six overseas tours & represented in exchange exhibs with Brit & Japanese artists.
Awards: Guggenheim Found fel creative lithography, 46.
Memberships: Soc Am Graphic Artists; Audubon Artists; Nat Print Coun.
Publications: Auth & illusr, Texas ranch boy, 55, Oilfield boy, 57, Rice boy, 58, Rubber boy, 62 & Salt boy, 63, Abelard; plus other bks & mag covers.
Mailing Address: 3424 Stanford St, Dallas, TX 75225.

MAVIAN, SALPI MIRIAM
Painter
Preferred Media: Oils.
b Mar 27, 08; U S citizen.
Study & Training: Sch Practical Arts, Boston, Mass; Art Stud League New York; also with Robert Brackman, Joseph Hirsch & Robert Philipp.
Work in Public Collections: Three mus, Armenia, U S S R.
Commissions: St John the Baptist & St Gregory the Illuminator, St John Church of Detroit, Mich, 68; Archbishop Garigin, Diocese of Armenian Church N Am, New York, N Y, 63; plus commissions for portraits.
Exhibitions: Hudson Valley Art Asn, N Y, 59; Knickerbocker Artists, New York, 59-60; Allied Artists Am, New York, 63; one-man show, Armenia, U S S R; Artists Equity Asn, 65; one-man show, Panaras Gallery.
Memberships: Art Stud League New York.
Mailing Address: 435 E 57th St, New York, NY 10022.

MAWICKE, TRAN
Painter, Illustrator
Preferred Media: Oils, Watercolors.
b Chicago, Ill, Sept 20, 11.
Study & Training: Art Inst Chicago, with Louis Ritman; Am Acad Art, Chicago; Acad Fine Art, Chicago.
Work in Public Collections: USAF Collection, Washington, D C; Williamsburg Corp, Va; Schenectady Mus, N Y; Garrott Collection, Los Angeles, Calif.
Commissions: Portraits, Gen Elec Corp Knolls Lab, 48 & N Y Nat Guard, Schenectady, 53.
Exhibitions: Am Watercolor Soc, 48 & 69-72; Audubon Artists; Soc Illusrs; Am Watercolor Traveling Exhib, 70.
Bibliography: S Meyer (auth), Fairfield watercolor group, Am Artist, 7/72.
Memberships: Am Watercolor Soc (dir, 70 & 72); life mem, Soc Illusrs (pres, 60-61); Fairfield Watercolor Group; life mem Joint Ethics Comn (chmn, 55-60).
Publications: Illusr, South America illustrated, G & D, 60; illusr, Little britches, Norton, 62; co-auth, Famous horses, World Publ, 72.
Dealers: Cross Roads of Sport, 11 E 47th St, New York, NY 10017; Blair Gallery, Santa Fe, NM 87501.
Mailing Address: 10 Brooklands, Bronxville, NY 10708.

MAX, PETER
Designer, Illustrator
Preferred Media: Mixed Media.
b Berlin, Ger, Oct 19, 37; U S citizen.
Study & Training: Art Stud League New York, N Y; Pratt Inst; Sch Visual Arts.
Commissions: Non-commercial art show, Metro Transit Advert Co, local buses across U S, 68; zodiac poster ser, New York Daily News, Chicago Tribune, Detroit Free Press & other newspapers, 71.
Exhibitions: Riverside Gallery, Shreveport, La; Munic Art Gallery, Los Angeles, Calif; The World of Peter Max, M H De Young Mem Mus, San Francisco, Calif & U S Tour, 70; London Arts Gallery Peter Max Exhib, 12 major world cities, 70; two Smithsonian Inst Peter Max Exhibs, U S, 72-74; plus many others.
Positions: Dir, Daly-Max Design Studio; designer, Gen Foods, Elgin Nat Industs, Takashimaya Ltd Japan, Van Heusen, UN & other major orgns.
Awards: Awards, Am Inst Graphic Arts, Soc Illusr & Int Poster Competition Poland; plus many others.
Publications: Auth, Peter Max posterbook & Peter Max superposterbook, Crown; auth, Peter Max astrological calendar, Grosset & Dunlap; auth, The new age organic vegetarian cookbook & Peter Max crochet book, Pyramid Publ; plus many others.
Dealer: London Arts Gallery, 321 Fisher Bldg, Detroit, MI 48202.
Mailing Address: 325 E 75th St, New York, NY 10021.

MAXON, JOHN
Associate Museum Director
b Salt Lake City, Utah, 1916.
Study & Training: Cooper Union, 34-38; Univ Mich, BDesign, 41; Harvard Univ, MA, 45, PhD, 48.
Positions: Dir, mus art, R I Sch Design, 52-59; dir fine arts, Art Inst Chicago, 59-66, assoc dir, 66-72, v pres, collections & exhibs, 72-
Memberships: Am Asn Mus Dirs; Am Asn Mus; Col Art Asn Am.
Mailing Address: Art Institute of Chicago, Chicago, IL 60603.

MAXWELL, JOHN R
Painter
b Rochester, N Y, Nov 3, 09.
Study & Training: Rochester Athenaeum (now Rochester Inst Technol); Univ Rochester; Provincetown Workshop, with Victor Candell & Leo Manso; also with other nationally known instrs.
Work in Public Collections: Lehigh Univ; Butler Inst Am Art, Youngstown, Ohio; Philadelphia Mus Art, Pa; Woodmere Art Gallery; galleries in New York, Philadelphia, Cleveland, Ohio, Palm Beach & Bay Harbor, Fla; also in many pvt collections.
Exhibitions: Contemporary American Drawings, Smithsonian Inst; Pa Acad Fine Arts; Toledo Mus Art; Am Watercolor Soc Traveling Exhibs, Butler Inst Am Art; Nat Acad Design; plus others.
Awards: First prize, Pa 71 Statewide Exhib, 1971; Dana Medal, Pa Acad Fine Arts; two awards, Am Watercolor Soc, New York; plus others.
Bibliography: Articles, In: Am Artist Mag, New York Times & Art News; plus others.
Memberships: Am Watercolor Soc; Nat Acad Design; Pa Acad Fine Arts; Philadelphia Art Alliance; Woodmere Gallery.
Dealers: Piccolo Mondo D'Arte, Worth Ave, Palm Beach, FL 33480; Fontana Gallery, 307 Iona Ave, Norberth, PA 19072.
Mailing Address: 415 Holly Lane, Wynnewood, PA 19096.

MAY, E M (ELIZABETH M MESSITER)
Painter, Illustrator
Preferred Media: Watercolors, Mixed Media, Ceramics.
b Chicago, Ill, 13.
Study & Training: Univ Ill, BArt; Vogue Sch Design, Chicago; Am Acad Art, Chicago; Univ Miami; San Miguel de Allende, Mex; also with William Billmeyer, Eugene Massin, watercolor with Eliot O'Hara & oils with Byron Newton.
Work in Public Collections: Norton Gallery, Palm Beach, Fla.
Commissions: Watercolor, Lyford Cay Gallery, 71.
Exhibitions: Soc Four Arts, Palm Beach, 58; Hortt Mem, Palm Beach, 60; Design Derby, Miami, Fla, 60; Columbia Mus Art, S C, 61; Lowe Gallery, Univ Miami, Coral Gables, Fla, 69.
Awards: Am Artist Award Cert, State of Fla, 50; Best of Show Awards, Miami Art League, 58-60; Wilfred Beattie Award for best Fla Painting, 65.
Memberships: Miami Art League (secy-treas, 50); Lowe Gallery; Blue Dome Art Fel (secy-treas, 50-55); Bahamas Art Soc, Miami Art Ctr.
Dealers: Nassau Art Gallery, Nassau, Bahamas; Kolean Gallery, Del Ray Beach, FL 33444.
Mailing Address: P O Box 1301, Coral Gables, FL 33134.

MAY, MORTON DAVID
Collector, Patron
b Saint Louis, Mo, Mar 25, 14.
Study & Training: Dartmouth Col, BA, 36.
Awards: Great Cross of Ger Govt for interest in Ger painting in U S A, 63.
Collection: German expressionism; oceanic and pre-Columbian Collections; other primitive sculpture; twentieth century painting and sculpture.
Mailing Address: 12 Brentmoor Park, Saint Louis, MO 63105.

MAY, WILLIAM L
Collector
b La Grange, Ga, Apr 4, 13.
Study & Training: Columbia Univ, BS; Spencer Bus Col, art hist with Robert E Day.
Positions: Prof photog participation, New York, N Y, 45-48; photog stud art work via contract, art dept, Columbia Univ; bd dirs, La Interior Design Inst, 69.
Awards: Nomination for Pulitzer Prize in Jour, 55; Int Patron Art, Boston Mus Fine Arts, 69.
Collection: Graphic prints by old masters; works by contemporary artists; oils, watercolors, gouache, polymer, including works by Moore, Rockmore.
Publications: Auth, A businessman looks at art, Register, 68; auth, brochures for artists & galleries, New Orleans, La, 68.
Mailing Address: 10022 E Coronado Dr, Baton Rouge, LA 70815.

MAYEN, PAUL
Designer
b La Linea, Spain, May 31, 18.
Study & Training: Cooper Union Art Sch; Art Stud League New York; Columbia Univ; New Sch Social Res.
Work in Public Collections: Mus Mod Art.
Exhibitions: Brooklyn Mus; Mus Mod Art; Nelson Gallery Art; Ann Advert Art.
Teaching: Lectr; instr advert design, Cooper Union Art Sch; former instr advert design, Parsons Sch, New York, N Y.
Positions: Asst art dir, F W Dodge-Sweet's Catalog; design consult, var indust orgns; bk designer, leading publ, ads, booklets & others; art dir, Agfa, Inc, Orradio & N Am Philips Co; design coordr, Cadre Industs & Habitat, Inc; designer, for exhibs, U S Info Agency; staff designer, Intrex, Inc.
Awards: Art Dirs Club Award, N Y.
Publications: Contribr, articles, In: Indust Design, Interiors, Progressive Archit, Art News Ann, Arts & Archit & others.
Mailing Address: 61 Cedar Rd, Cresskill, NJ 07626.

MAYER, BENA FRANK
Painter
Preferred Media: Oils, Watercolors.
b Norfolk, Va, May 31, 00.
Study & Training: Cooper Union; Hunter Col; Art Stud League New York; portrait painting with Cecelia Beaux; also with George Luks & Kenneth Miller.
Work in Public Collections: Norfolk Mus Arts & Sci, Va; Whitney Mus Am Art, New York, N Y; Huntington Hartford Collection, New York; in collections of Mrs Charles Love, Rochester, N Y & Mrs David Levy, New York; plus others.
Commissions: Portraits, comn by Mrs Edward Rohr, Norfolk, 24, World Med Asn, New York, 59; Dr Nachtigall, New York, 59, Dr William M Hitzig, New York, 70 & Katharine Trenchard, New York, 70; plus others.
Exhibitions: Carnegie Int, 40; New York Soc Women Artists Ann, 47-; Nat Asn Women Artists Ann, 50-; Am Soc Contemp Artists Ann, 50-; New York Watercolor Soc, 53.
Awards: Silver & bronze medals for drawing, Cooper Union Art Sch, 20's; Marcia Brady Tucker Prize, 51 & Lena Newcastle Prize, 59, Nat Asn Women Artists.
Bibliography: Helen Worden (auth), The artist in her studio, 49 & Ann Geracimos (auth), An odessey for art, 61, New York World Telegram, 61; J Harvey Rosenthal (auth), Bena Frank Mayer, Travel in Fashion, spring, 59.
Memberships: Am Soc Contemp Artists (chmn various comts, 50-, bd gov, 65-); Nat Asn Women Artists (const comt, 69-); New York Soc Women Artists (pres, 52 & 53); Artists Equity Asn; Artists Tech Res Inst (admin asst, 59-).
Mailing Address: 207 W 106th St, New York, NY 10025.

MAYER, GRACE M
Museum Curator, Collector
b New York, N Y.
Study & Training: Pvt schs & tutors in the U S & abroad.
Collections Arranged: Currier & Ives and the New York Scene, 39, Philip Hone's New York, 40, New York Between Two Wars, 44, Stranger in Manhattan, 50, Charles Dana Gibson's New York, 50 & Currier & Ives Printmakers to the American People, 57-58, Mus of City of New York; 70 Photographers Look at New York (with Edward Steichen), 57-58, The Sense of Abstraction, 60, Steichen, The Photographer, 61 & others, Mus Mod Art, New York.
Positions: Cur, New York Iconography, Mus of City of New York, 31-59; spec asst to dir, Dept Photog, Mus Mod Art, New York, 59-60, assoc cur, Dept Photog, 61-62, cur, Dept Photog, 62-68, cur, The Edward Steichen Archive, Dept of Photog, Mus Mod Art, 68-
Memberships: Print Coun Am (now treas); Cosmopolitan Club New York (resident mem).
Research: New York subjects; history of photography.
Collection: Posters and lithographs and autograph letter signed Toulouse-Lautrec; photographs, especially those of Edward Steichen; books on photography.
Publications: Auth, articles, In: Mus of City of New York Bull, Mus Mod Art Bull & var photog mags; auth, Once upon a city, Macmillan, 58.
Mailing Address: The Museum of Modern Art, 11 W 53rd St, New York, NY 10019.

MAYER, RALPH
Painter, Writer
Preferred Media: Oils.
b New York, N Y, Aug 11, 95.
Study & Training: Rensselaer Polytech Inst (chem); Art Stud League New York, with Hayley Lever.
Exhibitions: Ann Faculty Exhibs, Columbia Univ Sch Painting & Sculpture, 44-65; Portrait of Am, Metrop Mus Art & Traveling Show, 45; Am Soc Contemp Artists Ann, 50-72; Ann Faculty Exhibs, New Sch Social Res, 58-65; one-man retrospective, Firehouse Gallery, Nassau Community Col, 67.
Teaching: Instr, Columbia Univ, 44-64; instr New Sch Social Res, 58-65; instr, Silvermine Col, Conn, 61-62; lectr, Art Stud League New York & other art schs in East & Midwest.
Positions: Tech ed, Art Digest & Arts, 50-55; dir, Artists Tech Res Inst, 52-; tech ed, Am Artist, 62-
Awards: J S Guggenheim Found fel, 52; Grumbacher Award, 49th Ann Am Soc Contemp Artists, 66; Am Art Award, Man of Yr in Art, Nat Art Mat Trade Asn, 69.
Memberships: Am Soc Contemp Artists (first v pres); fel Int Inst Conserv Hist & Artistic Works; fel Am Inst Chemists.
Publications: Auth, The artists handbook of materials and techniques, 40, 57 & 70; auth, The painter's craft, 48 & 67; auth, A dictionary of art terms and techniques, 70.
Mailing Address: 207 W 106th St, New York, NY 10025.

MAYER, ROBERT BLOOM
Collector
b Chicago, Ill, Sept 10, 10.
Study & Training: Univ Chicago, BA & PhD.
Positions: Treas, Gallery Contemp Art, Chicago, 64-65; mem comt 20th century painting & sculpture, Art Inst Chicago, 64-
Memberships: Art Collectors Club.
Collection: Contemporary art; oriental art; antiques.
Mailing Address: 915 Sheridan Rd, Winnetka, IL 60093.

MAYERS, JOHN J
Collector
b New York, N Y, Aug 16, 06.
Study & Training: Univ Fla; Sch Dent & Oral Surg, Columbia, DDS & cert proficiency orthodont.
Awards: Univ alumni medal conspicuous serv, Columbia Univ, 49.
Collection: Oils, watercolors, drawings and sculpture, including works by Braque, Picasso, Matisse, Chagall, Laurens, Maillol, Renoir, Utrillo, Prendergast, Marin & Kuniyoshi.
Mailing Address: 64 Metropolitan Oval, New York, NY 10462.

MAYHALL, DOROTHY A
Art Administrator, Sculptor
Preferred Media: Wood.
b Portland, Ore, May 31, 25.
Study & Training: Univ Iowa, BFA, 48, MFA, 50; Ecole Beaux-Arts, Paris, France, Fulbright scholar, 50.
Exhibitions: Westchester Art Soc, 67; Silvermine Guild New Eng Exhib, 68 & 69; one-woman show, Painted Forms, A M Sachs Gallery, New York, 72.
Collections Arranged: Five exhibs, Highlights of the Art Season, 66-71, Rev Contemp Art Scene, 1964-1968, 69, Young Artists From Collection of Charles Cowles, 69, Lyrical Abstraction, 70, Aldrich Fund Acquisitions For Mus Mod Art 1959-1969, 71, plus others, Aldrich Mus Contemp Art; Painting & Sculpture 1972, 72 & Outdoor Sculptors Indoors 72, Storm King Art Ctr.

Positions: Exec secy Jr Coun, Mus Mod Art, 61-65; dir, Aldrich Mus Contemp Art, 65-71; dir, Storm King Art Ctr, Mountainville, N Y, 71-
Dealer: A M Sachs Gallery, 29 W 57th St, New York, NY 10019.
Mailing Address: Old Pleasant Hill Rd, Mountainville, NY 10953.

MAYHEW, EDGAR DE NOAILLES
Educator, Museum Director
b Newark, N J, Oct 1, 13.
Study & Training: Amherst Col, BA, 35; Yale Univ, MA, 39; Johns Hopkins Univ, Carnegie fel, 39-41, PhD, 41.
Collections Arranged: Contents of Lyman Allyn Mus, check list published.
Teaching: Instr art hist, Wellesley Col, Mass, 44-45; prof art hist, Connecticut Col, New London, 45-
Positions: Dir, Lyman Allyn Mus, New London, 50-
Awards: Am Philos Soc grant for res, 68.
Memberships: New London Co Hist Soc (bd mem, 60-); Conn Antiqn & Landmarks Soc, (furnishings chmn, 68-); Conn Comn Arts (chmn, 71); mem, many hist soc & preservation groups.
Research: Working on a documentary history of the American interior at present.
Collection: Approximately one hundred Old Master drawings.
Publications: Co-auth, The book of the courtier, 58; auth, Sketches by Thornhill in the Victoria and Albert Museum, 67.
Mailing Address: 613 Williams St, New London, CT 06320.

MAYHEW, RICHARD
Painter, Illustrator
b Amityville, N Y, Apr 3, 24.
Study & Training: Brooklyn Mus Art Sch, with Edwin Dickinson & Reuben Tam, 48.
Work in Public Collections: Whitney Mus Am Art; Olsen Found; Brooklyn Mus; Mus Mod Art; Nat Acad Design; also in pvt collections.
Exhibitions: Butler Art Inst, Youngstown, Ohio, 61; Carnegie Inst, 61; Brooklyn Mus, 61; Whitney Mus Am Art Ann; Univ Ill, 63; plus others.
Teaching: Instr art, Brooklyn Mus Art Sch & Art Stud League New York; instr, Smith Col, 69-70.
Awards: Tiffany Found fel, 63; Am Acad Arts & Lett grant, 65; Benjamin Altman award, Nat Acad Design, 70; plus others.
Memberships: Nat Acad Design; Macdowell Colony Asn.
Dealer: Midtown Galleries, 11 E 57th St, New York, NY 10022.
Mailing Address: 541 S Mountain Rd, New York, NY 10956.

MAYORGA, GABRIEL HUMBERTO
Painter, Sculptor
Preferred Media: Oils, Pastels, Watercolors, Epoxy Plastics, Polyester Plastics.
b Colombia, S Am, Mar 24, 11; U S citizen.
Study & Training: Nat Acad Design, painting with Leon Kroll & Ivan Olinsky, etching with Aerobach-Levi & sculpture with Robert Aikin; Art Stud League New York, with Brackman; Grand Cent Art Sch, New York, with Harvey Dunn.
Work in Public Collections: Inst Ingenieros, Bogota, Colombia, 37; Art Gallery of Barbizon-Plaza, New York, 55; West Point Mus, N Y.
Commissions: Many painting & portrait commissions, 55-
Exhibitions: Inst Ingenieros, Bogota, Colombia, 37; Art Gallery of Barbizon Plaza, New York, 55; Mayorga Art Gallery, 60; Int Expos, Paris, France, 62; Int Art Show, New York, N Y, 70.
Teaching: Instr painting & fashion, Pan-Am Art Sch, New York, 60-72.
Positions: Art dir, Revista Estrellas, Bogota, 37-38; art dir, Mannequins by Mayorga Inc, New York, 40-65; art dir-illusr, Revista Temas, 53-54.
Bibliography: Morton Cooper (auth), How to be an artist & still eat, Art & Photography, 57; Morton Cooper (auth), Gabriel Mayorga, New York angry artist, Figure, 60; J Rothschild (auth), Artists create with plastics, By Gum, 70.
Publications: Illusr, Revista Estrellas, 37-38; illusr, Theory & practice of fencing, 37; illusr, Popular Publications, 38; illusr, Revista Temas, 53-54; illusr, Don Mag.
Mailing Address: Mayorga Art Gallery, 331 W 11th St, New York, NY 10014.

MAYTHAM, THOMAS NORTHRUP
Art Administrator, Lecturer
b Buffalo, N Y, July 30, 31.
Study & Training: Williams Col, BA, 54; Yale Univ, MA, 56.
Collections Arranged: Ernst Ludwig Kirchner Retrospective (148 works), Seattle Art Mus, Pasadena Art Mus & Boston Mus, 68-69; Great American Paintings from the Boston and Metropolitan Museum (100 paintings), Nat Gallery Art, City Art Mus St Louis & Seattle Art Mus, 70-71; also numerous smaller exhibs, some with publ catalogues.

Teaching: Lectr, mus, clubs, groups & art asns in Boston & Seattle areas.
Positions: Assistantship, Wadsworth Atheneum, summer 55; res asst, Prof Carroll L V Meeks, Yale Univ, summer 56; asst in dept paintings, Mus Fine Arts, Boston, 56-57; head dept paintings, Boston Mus, 57-67, asst cur paintings, 67; assoc dir, Seattle Art Mus, 67-; juror, nat & regional exhibs; mem airport art adv comt, Port of Seattle; mem agency coun, United Arts Coun.
Memberships: Am Asn Mus; Int Coun Mus.
Publications: Auth, articles, In: Boston Mus Bull, Antiques & Can Art; ed, American painting in the Boston Museum (catalog), Vols I & II, 68; auth, Great American paintings from the Boston and Metropolitan Museums (catalog), Seattle Art Mus & Viking Press, 70; auth, TV prog for Nat Educ TV, produced by Boston Mus.
Mailing Address: Seattle Art Museum, Volunteer Park, Seattle, WA 98102.

MAZUR, MICHAEL B
Painter, Printmaker
b New York, N Y, Nov 2, 35.
Study & Training: Amherst Col, BA, 57; Sch Art & Archit, Yale Univ, BFA & MFA, 61.
Work in Public Collections: Mus Mod Art & Whitney Mus Am Art, New York; Art Inst Chicago, Ill; Libr Cong, Washington, D C; Philadelphia Mus Art, Pa; plus many other pub & pvt collections.
Exhibitions: Homage to Tamarind, Mus Mod Art, New York, 70; Human Concern, Whitney Mus Am Art, 70; New Acquisitions, Boston Mus Fine Arts, Mass, 70; one-man exhibs, Finch Col Mus, New York, 71 & Univ Conn, Storrs, 72; plus many other group & one-man exhibs.
Teaching: From instr to asst prof, R I Sch Design 61-64; Yale-Norfolk Summer Art Sch, 63; asst prof, Brandeis Univ, 65-; vis artist, Sch Art & Archit, Yale Univ, spring 72; lect & vis criticism, Tyler Sch Art, Yale Univ, Harvard Univ, Vassar Col, Detroit Inst Art, Pratt Inst & Cleveland Inst Art.
Positions: Juror shows, Libr Cong Print Biennial, 71, Currier Gallery, Manchester, N H, Southeastern Printmakers, Mint Mus, Charlotte, N C & Silvermine Print Invitational, 72.
Awards: Nat Inst Arts & Lett grant, 64; Guggenheim fel, 64-65; Tamarind artist fel in lithography, 68.
Bibliography: Artists proof, Pratt Graphic Ctr, 70; John Canaday (auth), Reviews, In: New York Times, 3/66, 4/68 & 11/27/71; reviews, In: Art News, Arts Mag & Artforum; plus others.
Dealer: Terry Dintenfass Gallery, 18 E 67th St, New York, NY 10021.
Mailing Address: 5 Walnut Ave, Cambridge, MA 02140.

MAZZONE, DOMENICO
Sculptor, Painter
b Rutigliano, Italy, May 16, 27.
Work in Public Collections: Mus Foggia, Italy; monument in Rutigliano; monument in Barletta, Italy; S Fara, Temple, Bari, Italy; UN Bldg, New York, N Y.
Exhibitions: Nat Exhib Marble, Carrara, Italy, 62; Nat Exhib, San Remo, Italy, 63; Int Exhib Metal, Gubbio, Italy, 65; Exhib Tree State, Silvermine Conn, 66; Ital Club Exhib, UN Bldg, 67.
Awards: Silver medal, Carrara Exhib, 62; gold medal, Exhib Int Viareggio, 72.
Bibliography: M Pescara (auth), Mazzone sculptor, Mario Pescara Enterprise, New York, 69; Dino Campini (auth), Arte Italiana, Soc Ed Nuova Torino, 71; J Passantino (auth), Mazzone, Passantino Ed, New York, 71.
Dealer: Nechimia Glezer Gallery, 870 Madison Ave, New York, NY 10021.
Mailing Address: 44 Lembeck Ave, Jersey City, NJ 07305.

MEADMORE, CLEMENT L
Sculptor
Preferred Media: Steel.
b Melbourne, Australia, Feb 9, 29.
Study & Training: Royal Melbourne Inst Technol.
Work in Public Collections: Art Inst Chicago, Ill; Nat Gallery Australia; J B Speed Mus, Ky; Atlantic Richfield Collection; Chase Manhattan Bank Collection.
Commissions: Large outdoor sculptures, Australian Mutual Provident Soc, 68, Mexico City, 68, Columbia Univ, 68, N Y State, Albany, 71 & Princeton Univ, 71.
Exhibitions: Guggenheim Int, New York, N Y, 67; Riverside Mus, New York, 68; Aldrich Mus, Ridgefield, Conn, 68; Rockefeller Collection, Mus Mod Art, New York, 69; Whitney Mus Am Art Ann, New York, 69.
Positions: Dir, Gallery A, Melbourne, Australia, 59-60; v pres of sculpture, Archit League New York, 70-72.

Bibliography: McCaughey (auth), article, In: Art Int, 11/70; Hughes (auth), article, In: Time Mag, 4/71; Segal (auth), Clement Meadmore: circling the square, Art News, 2/72.
Dealer: Max Hutchinson Gallery, 127 Green St, New York, NY 10012.
Mailing Address: 317 W 99th St, New York, NY 10025.

MEADOWS, ALGUR H
Patron
b Vidalia, Ga, Apr 24, 99.
Study & Training: Centenary Col Law Sch, grad, 26, hon LLD, 69; Southern Methodist Univ, DHL, 65.
Memberships: Dallas Art Asn.
Mailing Address: 6601 Turtle Creek Blvd, Dallas, TX 75205.

MEDEARIS, ROGER
Painter
Preferred Media: Tempera, Acrylics.
b Fayette, Mo, Mar 6, 20.
Study & Training: Kansas City Art Inst, with Thomas Hart Benton.
Exhibitions: American Painting Today, Metrop Mus Art, New York, N Y, 50; West Coast Exhibition, Frye Art Mus, Seattle, Wash, 66; Midyear Show, Butler Inst Am Art, Youngstown, Ohio, 69-72; Mainstreams International, Grover Hermann Fine Arts Ctr, Marietta, Ohio, 70-72.
Awards: Mihaly Munkacsy Award, Frye Art Mus, Seattle, 66; first award for painting, 71 & grand prize award, 72, Mainstreams Int, Marietta, Ohio.
Dealer: Capricorn Galleries, 8003 Woodmont Ave, Bethesda, MD 20014.
Mailing Address: 213 Barranca Dr, Monterey Park, CA 91754.

MEDRICH, LIBBY E
Sculptor
Preferred Media: Bronze.
b Hartford, Conn.
Study & Training: New York Univ, 31; Vassar Col, 49 & 54; Silvermine Guild Sch, 51; Art Stud League New York, 52-55; White Plains Co Ctr, 57 & 58; also with John Hovannes, Clara Fasano, Albert Jacobson, Helen Beling, Domenico Facci, George Koras, Harold Castor & others.
Work in Public Collections: Univ Chicago, Ill; First Church Christ, Wethersfield, Conn.
Exhibitions: Allied Artists Am Ann, Nat Acad Design, New York, N Y, 65 & 66; Prix de Paris, Galerie Raymond Duncan, Paris, France, 67; Painters & Sculptors Soc N J, Jersey City Mus, 69, 71 & 72; New York Int Art Show, New York Coliseum, 70; Union Carbide Invitational, New York, 72; plus in over 100 other shows.
Awards: Hon mention for sculpture, Nat Arts Club, 68 & 72; first prize for sculpture, Mamaroneck Woman's Club, 70.
Bibliography: Stevens (auth), L'art a l'etranger, La Rev Mod, 11/66; Mary Brett-Surman (auth), Everything is grist to sculptor's mill, Daily Times, Mamaroneck, 11/4/68; Betsy Powell (auth), Art & artists, Park East News, New York, 3/16/72.
Memberships: Artists Equity Asn New York; Mamaroneck Artists Guild (pres, 68-70); Westchester Art Soc.
Dealers: Roko Gallery, 90 E Tenth St, New York, NY 10003; Charles Z Mann Gallery, 1226 Third Ave, New York, NY 10021.
Mailing Address: 88 Carleon Ave, Larchmont, NY 10538.

MEEHAN, WILLIAM DALE
Painter, Designer
Preferred Media: Oils.
b Decatur, Ill, Oct 23, 30.
Study & Training: Sch Art Inst Chicago, BFA; Bradley Univ, MA.
Work in Public Collections: Ohio Univ; Bradley Univ; Evansville Mus Arts & Sci; DePauw Univ.
Commissions: Mural design (with Richard Peeler & students), DePauw Univ Art Ctr, 72.
Exhibitions: Artists Ill Exhibs, Peoria Art Ctr, Ill, 59-60; Syracuse Regional Exhibs, Everson Mus Art, N Y, 61-63; Mid-States Art Exhib, Evansville Mus Arts & Sci, Ind, 64; Ind Artists Exhibs, Herron Mus, Indianapolis, 64-65 & 67-69; Works on Paper, Indianapolis Mus Art, 71.
Teaching: Instr design & drawing, Syracuse Univ, 60-64; assoc prof design & painting, DePauw Univ, 64-, dir, summer art tour to Europe, 68-70.
Positions: Art dir, Southwestern Press, Fort Smith, Ark, 55-56; advert designer, Caterpillar Tractor Co, Peoria, Ill, 56-60; art dir, Nichols Advert, Decatur, summer 61; design consult, DePauw Univ, 64-
Awards: Purchase award, Ohio Valley Oil & Watercolor Show, Athens, 59; first prize, 22nd Ann Cent Ill Exhib, Decatur, 66; first prize watercolor, 62nd Ind Artists Exhib, Indianapolis, 67.
Mailing Address: 411 E Seminary, Greencastle, IN 46135.

MEEKER, BARBARA MILLER
Educator, Painter
Preferred Media: Watercolors, Collage, Acrylics.
b Peru, Ind, Dec 31, 30.
Study & Training: DePauw Univ, BA; also with Robert Weaver, Harriet Rex Smith & Gertrude Harbart.
Work in Public Collections: DePauw Univ Art Ctr Print Collection, Greencastle, Ind; Purdue Univ, Calumet Campus, Hammond, Ind; Tri-State Col, Angola, Ind; Oak Park River Forest High Sch, Ill; Hammond Pub Schs.
Commissions: Many portraits, in pastels, acrylics & oils.
Exhibitions: Fort Wayne Art Mus, Ind, 62; DePauw Univ Printmakers Exhib, Greencastle, 68; Ind Artists Club Ann, Indianapolis, Ind; Michiana Regional, South Bend, Ind; Hoosier Art Salon, Indianapolis.
Teaching: Asst prof freehand drawing & painting, Purdue Univ, Calumet Campus, 65-
Awards: Purchase & merit award, Ind Artists Club; award for The Gold Pitcher (collage), Northern Ind Art Salon; hon mention, outstanding teacher award, Purdue Univ, Calumet Campus, 71.
Bibliography: Hawkins & McClarren (auth), Indiana lives, Hist Rec Asn, 67.
Memberships: Ind Artists Club; Gary Artists League; Hammond Art Ctr (adv).
Publications: Auth, Freehand drawing, 72.
Mailing Address: 8314 Greenwood Ave, Munster, IN 46321.

MEEKER, DEAN JACKSON
Printmaker, Painter
b Orchard, Colo, May 18, 20.
Study & Training: Art Inst Chicago, BFA & MFA; Northwestern Univ; Univ Wis.
Work in Public Collections: Boston Mus Fine Arts; Seattle Art Mus; San Francisco Mus Art; Dallas Mus Fine Arts; Denver Art Mus; plus others.
Exhibitions: Seattle Art Mus, 53-55; Munic Mus, The Hague, 54; Boston Mus Fine Arts, 54-56; La Gravure, 59; Los Angeles Mus Art, 59; plus others.
Teaching: Assoc prof art educ, Univ Wis-Madison, 46-70, prof, 70-
Awards: Medal of hon, Milwaukee Art Inst, 52 & 56; Guggenheim fel, 58.
Bibliography: S W Hayter (auth), About prints, Oxford Univ Press, 62.
Dealer: Jane Haslem Gallery, 1669 Wisconsin Ave NW, Washington, DC 20007.
Mailing Address: Dept of Art, University of Wisconsin-Madison, Madison, WI 53706.

MEGARGEE, LAWRENCE ANTHONY (LAWRIE)
Illustrator
Preferred Media: Watercolors, Pastels, Inks.
b Philadelphia, Pa, July 10, 00.
Study & Training: Pa Acad Fine Arts; Nat Acad Design; Art Stud League New York; Pratt Inst Art Sch; Cooper Union Art Sch; Grand Cent Art Sch.
Work in Public Collections: Grand Cent Art Gallery, New York, N Y; Cross Roads of Sport, New York; Ackerman Gallery, New York; Harlow Gallery, New York.
Publications: Illusr, The Spur, Town & Country, Country Life & The Sportsman Mag.
Mailing Address: 208 Bloomingdale Ave, Wayne, PA 19087.

MEGREW, ALDEN FRICK
Art Historian, Educator
b Plainfield, N J, Aug 30, 08.
Study & Training: Harvard Univ, BS & MA.
Teaching: Lectr art hist, confs & pub audiences; instr, Lawrence Col, 34-40; instr, Univ Iowa, 40-47; head dept fine arts, Univ Colo, Boulder, 47-64, prof, 47-, faculty fel Romanesque archit & sculpture, 65; vis prof, Am Col, Paris, 68.
Memberships: Col Art Asn Am; Colo Educ Asn (coun mem, 47-); Midwestern Col Art Conf (secy, v pres & pres); Southwestern Col Art Conf (pres).
Publications: Auth, Outline of northern renaissance art, 47 & Outline of medieval art, 47; contribr, articles, In: Col Art J & Gesta.
Mailing Address: Dept of Fine Arts, University of Colorado, Boulder, CO 80302.

MEHRING, HOWARD WILLIAM
Painter
Preferred Media: Acrylics.
b Washington, D C, Feb 19, 31.
Study & Training: Wilson Teachers Col, BS(educ), 53; Cath Univ Am, Nat Inst Arts & Lett scholar, 53-55, MFA, 55; also with Kenneth Noland.

Work in Public Collections: Solomon R Guggenheim Mus, Mus Mod Art, Whitney Mus Am Art & Chase Manhattan Bank Collection, New York, N Y; Corcoran Gallery Art, Washington, D C.
Exhibitions; Carnegie Int, Pittsburgh, Pa, 62; Post Painterly Abstraction, Los Angeles Co Mus, Calif, 64; Systemic Painting, Solomon R Guggenheim Mus, 66; The Abrams Family Collection, Jewish Mus, New York, 66; Whitney Mus Am Art Painting Ann, 67.
Teaching: Instr art, George Washington High Sch, Alexandria, Va, 59; instr art, Montgomery Jr Col, 62-64.
Awards: First prize purchase award for painting, 65 & artist fel, 72, Corcoran Gallery Art.
Dealer: A M Sachs Gallery, 29 W 57th St, New York, NY 10019.
Mailing Address: 735 Tenth St S E, Washington, DC 20003.

MEIGS, JOHN LIGGETT
Painter, Art Historian
Preferred Media: Egg Tempera, Watercolors.
b Chicago, Ill, May 10, 16.
Study & Training: Univ Redlands; Acad Grande Chaumière, Paris.
Work in Public Collections: Roswell Mus, N Mex; Univ Tex, Austin; W Tex Mus, Lubbock; Mus N Mex, Santa Fe.
Commissions: Pioneer frescoes (with Peter Hurd), Tex Tech Univ, Holden Hall, Lubbock, 51-54; murals, Nickson Hotel, Roswell, 51, F O Masten Farms, Tex, 60, N Jr HS, Abilene, Tex, 61 & Weatherford First Nat Bank, Tex, 71.
Exhibitions: One-man shows, Honolulu Acad Fine Arts, Hawaii, Palace Legion of Honor, San Francisco, Dayton Art Inst, Ohio, Mus N Mex & Ball State Mus, Muncie, Ind.
Awards: Awards, Tex Watercolor Soc, Mus N Mex Biennial & El Paso Sun Carnival Exhib.
Bibliography: James Baker (auth), catalogue, Baker Gallery; Paul Horgan (auth), catalogue, Roswell Mus; W C Holden (auth), catalogue, W Tex Mus.
Research: American graphics, especially 1930-1950.
Collection: American graphics and drawings; Peter Hurd; Henriette Wyeth; American Realists.
Publications: Ed, Peter Hurd—the lithographs, Baker Gallery, 70; ed, Peter Hurd—sketchbook, 71, ed, The cowboy in American prints, 72 & auth, American graphics—Bellows to Baskin, 73, Swallow; contribr, N Mex Mag, Ford Times, Southwest Art Gallery Mag & Ariz Highways.
Dealer: Baker Gallery, 13th & Ave L, Lubbock, TX 79401.
Mailing Address: San Patricio, NM 88348.

MEIGS, WALTER
Painter
Preferred Media: Plastic Paints.
b New York, N Y, Sept 21, 18.
Study & Training: Syracuse Univ, BFA; Ecole Beaux-Arts, Fontainebleau, France, dipl; Univ Iowa, MFA.
Work in Public Collections: Amherst Col, Mass; Denver Art Mus, Colo; Va Mus Fine Arts, Richmond; Smithsonian Inst, Washington, D C; Ohio Univ, Athens.
Exhibitions: Boston Fine Arts Festival, 56; Carnegie Int, Pittsburgh, Pa, Whitney Mus Am Art Ann, New York, Univ Ill, Champaign & Univ Iowa, Iowa City, several yrs.
Teaching: Asst prof art, Univ Nebr, 49-53; prof oil painting & chmn art dept, Univ Conn, 53-61.
Awards: Purchase prize, Birmingham Art Mus, 54; best exhib, Springfield Art Mus, Mass, 57; first prize for drawing, Boston Fine Arts Festival, 59.
Bibliography: Lee Nordness (auth), Distinguished exhibition of American Art 7, 60; A J Weller (auth), Art: U S A: now, C J Bucher, 62.
Dealer: Nordness Gallery, 236-238 E 75th St, New York, NY 10021.
Mailing Address: Candelaria, Tenerife, Canarias, Spain.

MEISS, MILLARD
Art Historian, Writer
b Cincinnati, Ohio, Mar 25, 04.
Study & Training: Princeton Univ, AB, 26; Harvard Univ, 28; New York Univ, MA, 31, PhD, 33; Univ Florence, hon LittD.
Teaching: Prof hist art, Inst Advan Study, 58-
Positions: Mem ed bd, Art Bull, 43-
Awards: Decorated Stella della Solidarieta, Italy, 49 & grande ufficiale, 68; Morey Award, Col Art Asn Am, 69; plus others.
Memberships: Metrop Mus Art (hon trustee); corres mem Accad Senese degli Intronati; Col Art Asn Am (dir exec comt, 40-47, secy, 43, dir exec comt, 52-57, v pres, 54-56); fel Mediaeval Acad Am; Comité Int Hist Art (pres, 61-64, v pres, 64-); plus others.
Publications: Auth, Giovanni Bellini's St Francis, Princeton Univ Press, 64; auth, French painting in the time of Jean de Bary, 2 Vols, 67 & French painting in the time of Jean de Bary: the

Boucicaut master and his workshop, 69, Phaidon; auth, Giotto & Assisi, Norton, 67; auth, Great age of Fresco discoveries, recoveries, & survivals, Braziller, 70; plus others.
Mailing Address: Institute for Advanced Study, Princeton, NJ 08540.

MEISSNER, BERNIECE CRAM-GILL
Collector
b Scarborough, Maine, Nov 30, 03.
Study & Training: Portland Sch Fine & Appl Art; Boston Mus Art, with Dorothy Adlow; also with Eliot O'Hara & Alexander Bower.
Positions: Auth, weekly column, Portland Sun Telegram, 40-66.
Memberships: Portland Sch Fine & Appl Art Alumni; Lincoln Co Cult & Hist Asn; life fel William A Farnsworth Libr & Art Mus.
Collection: Graphics; large collection given to Farnsworth Mus, Rockland, Maine, included were six Rembrandt etchings, plus others.
Mailing Address: Avon Rd, Shore Acres, Cape Elizabeth, ME 04107.

MEISSNER, LEO J
Painter, Engraver
Preferred Media: Oils, Mixed Media, Wood.
b Hamtramck, Mich, June 28, 95.
Study & Training: Sch Fine Arts, Detroit, Mich, with John P Wicker; Art Stud League New York, scholar; also with George Luks & Robert Henri.
Work in Public Collections: Metrop Mus, New York, N Y; Libr Cong, Washington, D C; Boston Pub Libr, Mass; Farnsworth Mus, Rockland, Maine; Okla Mus Art, Oklahoma City.
Exhibitions: Nat Print Shows, Libr Cong; Mem Ann, Nat Acad, New York; Boston Printmakers Ann; Acad Artists Ann, Springfield, Mass; plus many others.
Positions: Art ed, Motor Boating Mag, New York, 26-50.
Awards: Two Canon Prizes, Nat Acad Design; ten purchase prizes, Libr Cong; Smith & Giern Prizes, Detroit Inst Arts.
Bibliography: Article, In: Fine prints of the year, 37; Albert Reese (auth), article, In: American prize prints of the twentieth century, 49; Isabel Currier (auth), The Maine direction of Leo Meissner's art, Down East Mag, 69.
Memberships: Nat Acad Design; Soc Am Graphic Artists; Audubon Artists; Boston Printmakers; Print Club Albany.
Mailing Address: Avon Rd, Shore Acres, Cape Elizabeth, ME 04107.

MEITZLER, (HERBERT) NEIL
Painter, Designer
Preferred Media: Acrylics, Tempera, Watercolors.
b Pueblo, Colo, Sept 14, 30.
Study & Training: With Kenneth Callahan.
Work in Public Collections: Seattle Art Mus, Wash; Memphis Acad Art, Tenn.
Exhibitions: Art in U S A, New York, N Y, 59; one-man show, Seattle Art Mus, Wash, 59; Seattle World's Fair, Wash, 62; Pac Coast Invitational, Santa Barbara Mus Art, Calif, plus five other mus, 62-63; Artists of the Northwest, Japanese World's Fair, 71.
Positions: Designer, Seattle Art Mus, 57-
Awards: Katharine Baker Award, Seattle Art Mus, 58; Nat Coun Theatres Award, U S Govt, 67.
Dealer: Woodside Gallery, 803 E Union, Seattle, WA 98102.
Mailing Address: 16841 Newport Way, Issaquah, WA 98027.

MEIXNER, MARY LOUISE
Painter, Educator
Preferred Media: Oils, Acrylics.
b Milwaukee, Wis, Dec 7, 16.
Study & Training: Milwaukee-Downer Col, BA; State Univ Iowa, MA; Art Stud League New York with Hale; Univ Minn & Bowling Green Univ, with Max Weber; Mills Col, with Yasuo Kuniyoshi; Am Sch at Fontainebleau, France; Carpenter Ctr Visual Arts, Harvard Univ.
Work in Public Collections: Nat Am Home Econ Asn, Washington, D C; Des Moines Art Ctr, Iowa; Denison Arts Asn Gallery, Iowa.
Commissions: Private comn for child portrait, 63.
Exhibitions: Des Moines Art Ctr Ann, 54, 55 & 62; Mid Am Ann, Kansas City, Mo, 55; one-man show, Nat Design Ctr, New York, N Y, 69; MacNider Mus Ann, Mason City, Iowa, 70-71; Red River Ann, Moorhead, N Dak, 71.
Teaching: Prof art hist, Milwaukee-Downer Col, 45-52; prof color, design process & painting, Iowa State Univ, Ames, 53-
Awards: Regional small exhibs awards.
Memberships: Col Art Asn Am; Intersoc Color Coun; Mid Am Art Asn; Delta Phi Delta; Milwaukee Art Ctr.
Research: Experiments in light and color—additive light box; after-image; animation.
Publications: Auth, articles, In: Sch Arts, 40 & 42, Am Camping Mag, 53, 55 & 66, Art J, 53-71, Lyrical Iowa Poetry Mag, 62-68 & Design Mag, 67 & 68.
Mailing Address: 2521 N 32nd St, Milwaukee, WI 53210.

MEIZNER, PAULA
Sculptor
Preferred Media: Fieldstone, Aluminum.
b Belchatow, Poland; U S citizen.
Study & Training: Westchester Workshop, White Plains, N Y.
Exhibitions: Pa Acad Fine Arts, Philadelphia, 60; Detroit Inst Fine
Arts, Mich, 60; Juried Arts, Tyler, Tex, 62; Competitive Art
Exhib, Art & Home Ctr, N Y State Fair, Syracuse, 67; New Eng
Exhibs, New Canaan, Conn, 72.
Teaching: Instr, adult groups, privately.
Awards: E C K Finch Award, 59 & Caludia & Maurice L Stone Mem
Award, 72, New Eng Exhib, New Canaan; Charles N Whinston
Mem Award, Nat Asn Women Artists, New York, 72.
Memberships: Audubon Artists; Silvermine Guild Artists; Nat Asn
Women Artists; Conn Acad; Knickerbocker Artists.
Mailing Address: 126 Seacord Rd, New Rochelle, NY 10804.

MEJER, ROBERT LEE
Painter, Instructor
b South Bend, Ind, Nov 8, 44.
Study & Training: South Bend Art Ctr, with Joseph Wrobel; Notre
Dame Univ, with Ivan Mestrovic & Ted Golubic; Ball State Univ,
BS, with John Cavanaugh & Ronald Penkoff; Miami Univ, MFA,
with Robert Wolfe, Jr.
Work in Public Collections: Ball State Univ, Muncie, Ind; Quincy Art
Ctr, Ill; Radecki Art Galleries, South Bend; Int Arts League of
Youth, New York, N Y; State Univ N Y Buffalo.
Commissions: Archit design, Future City, Muncie Redevelopment
Show, Ball State Univ, 65; illus prog, Am grand premiere, School
pal (play), Quincy Col, 69; billboard, Progressive Playhouse, 71.
Exhibitions: Eighth Ann Dunes Arts Found, Mich, 66; Dayton Art
Inst Traveling Drawing Show, 67; one-man shows, St Mary's Col,
Notre Dame, Ind, 70 & Culver-Stockton Col, Mo, 71; Three points
of view-Bell, Bradshaw, Mejer, Ill State Mus, Springfield, 72;
Limestone Col, Gaffney, S C, 72; plus others.
Collections Arranged: Byron Burford Circus, 2/71, In Search of an
Ideal Landscape-Syed J Iqbal Geoffrey, 10-11/71, Ben Mahmoud,
9/71 & Don Crouch, American West Series, 1/73, Quincy Col.
Teaching: Instr painting & drawing, Pace Proj Title III, Ball State
Univ, summers 66 & 67; instr drawing, Miami Univ, 66-68; asst
prof art & gallery dir, Quincy Col, 68-
Positions: Vis artist, Muncie Artist Guild, spring 63; vis artist,
Twin Rivers Art League, Pittsfield, Ill, fall 71; gallery asst, Ball
State Art Gallery, 62-66; Quincy Art Ctr, Ill, 70-; recognition
visitation team, Off Supt Pub Instr, Ill, 71-; vis artist, Culver-
Stockton Col, Canton, Mo, summer 72.
Awards: Best painting in show, Biennial Exhib, Strawn Art Gallery,
Ill, 69; first in graphics, 20th Ann Regional Exhib, Sinnock Gal-
lery, Ill, 69; purchase award, 22nd Ann Art Exhib, Quincy Art
Ctr, 71; plus one other.
Bibliography: Thomas Carbol (auth), article, In: The printmaker in
Ill, 71-72; Robert Evans (auth), The living museum-three points
of view, Ill State Mus, 1/72.
Memberships: Delta Phi Delta; Nat Art Educ Asn; St Joe Valley
Watercolor Soc; Ill Art Educ Asn (exec coun, 70-72); Col Art
Asn Am.
Publications: Auth, Quincy happening, 68; illusr, Salt-Lick Mag, 68-
71; contribr, Barnes' works provide exciting art show, 71; con-
tribr, Geoffrey, 71; contribr, The magic world of imagination—
Marc Chagall, 71.
Mailing Address: Fine Arts Dept, Quincy College, Quincy, IL 62301.

MELAMED, ABRAHAM
Collector, Patron
b Chicago, Ill, Nov 19, 14.
Positions: Mem, Gov Coun Arts, Wis, 63-65; bd dirs, Wis Art Fedn
& Coun, 65-71; trustee, Arch Am Art, Smithsonian Inst, 66-
Bibliography: Cubist prints in collection of Dr and Mrs Abraham
Melamed, Univ Wis Press, 72.
Art Interests: Visual arts; contributor to art organizations and in-
stitutions.
Collection: Contemporary and modern works-graphics, paintings,
sculpture.
Mailing Address: 1107 E Lilac Lane, Milwaukee, WI 53217.

MELCARTH, EDWARD
Painter, Sculptor
b Louisville, Ky, Jan 31, 14.
Study & Training: Harvard Col, 32-36; Acad Ranson, Atelier 17,
Paris, France; also with Karl Zerbe.
Work in Public Collections: Wadsworth Atheneum; Boston Mus Fine
Arts; Detroit Inst Art; Univ Louisville; Bradford, Eng; plus
others.
Commissions: Lobby & auditorium, Rooftop Theatre, N Y, 57;
ceiling, Lunt Fontanne Theatre, 58 & Time Life, 58; painting &
sculpture, walls & ceiling, Oval Rm, Hotel Pierre, New York,
N Y & IBM, 58; plus others.

Exhibitions: Whitney Mus Am Art; Corcoran Gallery Art; Pa Acad
Fine Arts; Art Inst Chicago; Am Fedn Arts Traveling Exhib;
plus others.
Teaching: Instr painting & drawing, Univ Louisville; instr, Parsons
Sch Design, 46-48; instr, Columbia Univ, 48-50; instr, Univ
Wash, 50-51; instr, Art Stud League New York, 65-71.
Awards: Ranger Prize, 64 & Thomas B Clarke Award, 69, Nat Acad
Design; Childe Hassam Purchase Award, Inst Arts & Lett, 65;
plus others.
Memberships: Nat Acad Design; Nat Soc Mural Painters; Archit
League.
Publications: Illusr, Fortune, Harper's, Life, The Lamp, Town &
Country & others.
Dealers: Galleria 88, via Margutta 88, Rome, Italy; Sculpture
House, 38 E 30th St, New York, NY 10016.
Mailing Address: San Trovaso 1374, Calle del Magazeh, Venice,
Italy.

MELCHERT, JAMES FREDERICK
Sculptor, Educator
Preferred Media: Clay.
b New Bremen, Ohio, Dec 2, 30.
Study & Training: Princeton Univ, AB; Univ Chicago, MFA; Univ
Calif, Berkeley, MA; ceramics with Peter Voulkos.
Work in Public Collections: San Francisco Mus Art, Calif; Mus Mod
Art Kyoto, Japan; Victoria & Albert Mus, London; Oakland Mus
Art, Calif; R I Sch Design, Providence.
Exhibitions: Abstr Expressionist Ceramics, Univ Calif, Irvine, 66;
Contemp Am Sculpture, Whitney Mus Am Art, New York, N Y, 66,
68 & 70; Documenta 5, Kassel, Ger, 72.
Teaching: Chmn dept ceramics, San Francisco Art Inst, Calif, 61-64;
assoc prof sculpture, Univ Calif, Berkeley, 64-; vis sculptor,
Univ Wis-Madison, spring 71.
Awards: Louis Comfort Tiffany Found grant, 63; Nealie Sullivan
Award, San Francisco Art Inst, 70; Nat Found Arts grant, 72.
Mailing Address: 6077 Ocean View Dr, Oakland, CA 94618.

MELIKIAN, MARY
Painter
Preferred Media: Watercolors, Oils.
b Worcester, Mass.
Study & Training: R I Sch Design, Providence, BFA, 55; Columbia
Univ Teachers Col.
Work in Public Collections: Worcester Mus Art, Mass; Mint Mus,
Charlotte, N C; Yerevan Mus, Armenia; Vassar Col Art Mus; Art
for U S Embassies, State Dept.
Exhibitions: One-man shows, Burr Galleries, New York, N Y, 62,
Myers Gallery, New York, 64, Casdin Gallery, Worcester, 69;
Nat Arts Club, New York, 69 & 70; one-man show, Stable Art
Gallery, Scottsdale, Ariz, 70.
Teaching: Instr art, Nutley High Sch, 57-60.
Positions: Asst designer, Fuller Fabrics, N Y, 56; asst dir, Grand
Cent Moderns, New York, 60-61; dir pub rels, Grand Cent Art
Galleries, New York, 61-67.
Awards: First prize, Kit Kat Club, 61, Armenian Stud Asn, 61 & 62
& Women's Nat Repub Club, 70 & 72.
Bibliography: Stan Haste (auth), Mary Melikian, R I Sch Design Mag,
9/68; Colette Roberts (auth), rev, In: France-Am; N Stepanian
(auth), Paintings of Mary Melikian, Voice of Am, 68.
Memberships: R I Sch Design (alumni bd gov, 67-70, trustee, 70-72);
Burr Artists.
Publications: Auth, articles, In: Ararat Mag.
Mailing Address: 338 E 55th St, New York, NY 10022.

MELLON, JAMES
Printmaker, Painter
b New York, N Y, Feb 14, 41.
Study & Training: Creative Graphic Workshop, with Chaim Koppie-
man, 56-59; Art Stud League New York, 57-58.
Work in Public Collections: Everson Mus Art, Syracuse, N Y; Pen-
nell Collection, Libr Cong; Smithsonian Inst; Univ Pa.
Exhibitions: Sch Visual Arts Gallery, N Y, 62; Soc Am Graphic
Artists Traveling Exhib, S Am, 62; Everson Mus Art, 68; Int
Miniature Print Exhib, Pratt Inst, 67 & 68; Cranbrook Acad Art,
Bloomfield Hills, Mich; plus others.
Teaching: Instr media, adult educ dept, Brooklyn Col, 64-67; instr
graphics, Sch Visual Arts, 65-
Awards: Pennell Purchase Prize, Libr Cong, 58 & 61; Warren
Mack Mem Award, 65; purchase prize, Everson Mus Art.
Memberships: Soc Am Graphic Artists (coun mem).
Mailing Address: 498 Broome St, New York, NY 10012.

MELLON, PAUL
Collector, Art Administrator
b Pittsburgh, Pa, June 11, 07.
Study & Training: Choate Sch, Wallingford, Conn, 19-25; Yale Univ,

BA, 29; Clare Col, Cambridge Univ, BA, 31, MA, 38; Oxford Univ, hon LittD, 61, Carnegie Inst Technol, hon LLD, 67; Yale Univ, hon LHD, 67.
Positions: Trustee Nat Gallery Art, 38-39, 45-, pres, 38-39, 63-; trustee, Va Mus Fine Arts, Richmond, Va, 38-
Awards: Nat Inst Arts & Lett Award for distinguished service to the arts, 62; Benjamin Franklin Medal, Royal Soc Arts, 65; Gertrude Vanderbilt Whitney Award, Skowhegan Sch Painting & Sculpture, 72.
Collection: (Mr & Mrs Paul Mellon) English paintings, 1700-1850; impressionist and post-impressionist paintings.
Mailing Address: 1729 H St N W, Washington, DC 20006.

MELLOR, GEORGE EDWARD
Educator, Sculptor
b Bronxville, N Y, Sept 13, 28.
Study & Training: Oberlin Col, AB(fine arts), 54; Atelier Zadkine, 52-53; Tyler Sch Fine Arts, MFA, 65.
Work in Public Collections: Nat Collection Fine Art, Smithsonian Inst; Danvers Security Nat Bank, Lynn, Mass; Southeastern Mass Univ.
Exhibitions: Regional Exhib, Pa Acad Fine Arts, Philadelphia, 64; one-man shows, Lamont Gallery, Exeter, N H, 68, Tufts Univ, Medford, Mass, 69 & Kangeis Gallery, Boston, Mass, 70; plus many others.
Teaching: Instr art, Solebury Sch, New Hope, Pa, 57-65; asst prof sculpture & ceramics, Southeastern Mass Univ, 68-
Positions: Dir art gallery, Exeter Acad, N H, 65-68.
Bibliography: Directed by Fred Stein, Sketches-some American sculpture (film), U S Info Agency, 70.
Art Interests: Metal fabrication; casting.
Dealer: Kanegis Gallery, 244 Newbury St, Boston, MA 02116.
Mailing Address: 298 Front St, Marion, MA 02738.

MELLOW, JAMES R
Art Critic
b Gloucester, Mass, Feb 28, 26.
Study & Training: Northwestern Univ, BS, 50.
Positions: Ed, Arts Mag, 61-65; regular art critic, The New Leader, 65-; art critic, Art Int, 65-69; art critic, New York Times, 70-
Publications: Ed, The best in arts, 62; ed, New York: the art world, 64.
Mailing Address: 298 Eighth Ave, Sea Cliff, NY 11579.

MELTZER, ANNA E
Painter, Instructor
Preferred Media: Oils, Graphics.
b New York, N Y, Aug 6, 96.
Study & Training: Cooper Union Art Sch; Art Stud League New York; also with Vincent Dumond & Alexander Brook.
Work in Public Collections: Brooklyn Mus, N Y; Berkshire Mus, Pittsfield, Mass; Joslyn Mem Mus, Omaha, Nebr; Calif Palace of Legion of Honor, San Francisco, Calif; Ga Mus Fine Arts, Athens.
Exhibitions: Audubon Artists, Nat Acad, New York, 42, 44 & 45; one-man shows, Francis Taylor Gallery, Beverly Hills, Calif, 47, Marie Sterner Gallery, French & Co, New York, 48, Collector's Gallery, New York, 59 & Peter Cooper Gallery, New York, 64.
Teaching: Instr painting & graphics, Anna Meltzer Sch Art, 42-; instr painting & graphics, City Col New York Exten Div, 52-64.
Awards: Audubon Artist's Award, 42; citation for contrib to contemp Am painting & fine arts educ, Fla Southern Col, 50.
Bibliography: Dorothy Grafly (auth), The art of Anna Meltzer, Design Mag, 48; Dan Daniels (auth), An adventure in casein painting (film), Grumbacher, 51; Bess Barzansky (auth), 44 colographs from realism to prismatism, Lumas-Nakle-Art Publ, 69.
Memberships: Audubon Artists; Cooper Union Alumni; Artists Equity Asn; Kappa Pi; fel Royal Soc Encouragement Arts.
Mailing Address: 315 West End Ave, New York, NY 10023.

MELTZER, ARTHUR
Painter, Instructor
Preferred Media: Oils.
b Minneapolis, Minn, July 31, 93.
Study & Training: Minneapolis Sch Fine Art; Pa Acad Fine Arts, Cresson traveling scholar, 21, fel prize, 25.
Work in Public Collections: Pa Acad Fine Arts, Philadelphia; Moore Inst; Woodmere Art Gallery, Columbus Gallery Fine Art; Art Alliance, Philadelphia.
Commissions: Budd Trains, murals & Stephen Girard, murals, Girard Fed, Philadelphia.
Exhibitions: Pa Acad Fine Arts; Nat Acad Design, New York, N Y; Art Inst Chicago, Ill.

Teaching: Head fine arts dept, Moore Col, Philadelphia, 25-49.
Awards: Gold medal, Ligonier Art League, 61.
Memberships: Fel Pa Acad Fine Arts; Philadelphia Mus; Woodmere Art Gallery; Artists Equity Asn.
Mailing Address: 1521 Welsh Rd, Huntingdon Valley, PA 19006.

MELTZER, DORIS
Art Dealer, Printmaker
b Ulster Co, N Y, Jan 1, 08.
Study & Training: New York Univ, BS(art educ), 33; Art Stud League New York, 39.
Work in Public Collections: Pennell Collection, Libr Cong, Washington, D C; Flower Hosp, New York, N Y; plus others.
Exhibitions: Nat juried exhibs & traveling exhibs abroad, U S Info Agency, 41-58.
Positions: Easel painter, Fed Art Proj, Works Progress Admin, 36-38; dir & v pres, Nat Serigraphy Soc, 45-62; dir, Meltzer Gallery, 55-62; owner & dir, Doris Meltzer Gallery, 63-
Memberships: Am Art Conserv Soc; Oriental Ceramic Soc, London; Am Fedn Arts.
Specialty of Gallery: Ukiyoe master prints and pottery; American, European and Oriental art; drawings and prints.
Collection: Japanese pottery from the fifteenth to the nineteenth century; miscellaneous art objects of various periods and places.
Mailing Address: 783 Madison Ave, New York, NY 10021.

MELVILLE, GREVIS WHITAKER
Painter, Printmaker
Preferred Media: Oils.
b Damariscotta, Maine, Dec 23, 04.
Study & Training: Yale Sch Art & Archit; Art Stud League New York; also with Will Barnet & William C Palmer.
Work in Public Collections: William A Farnsworth Libr & Art Mus, Rockland, Maine; Pierson Col, Yale Univ, New Haven, Conn; Damariscotta Region Info Bur.
Exhibitions: Pa Acad Fine Art, Philadelphia; one-man show, Bowdoin Col Mus, Brunswick, Maine; Maine State Art Festival, Augusta; Maine Artists Shows, Portland Mus Art; one-man show, Smith Col Mus, Northampton, Mass; plus others.
Teaching: Artist-in-residence, Hackley Sch, Tarrytown, N Y, 41-42.
Memberships: Maine Art Gallery (bd dirs, 68-69); Pemaquid Group Artists (dir, 66-72).
Publications: Illusr, Windswept, Macmillan, 42 & Maine memories, Greene, 68.
Dealer: Jacques Seligmann Galleries, 5 E 57th St, New York, NY 10022.
Mailing Address: 38 Main St, Damariscotta, ME 04543.

MELVIN, GRACE WILSON
Painter, Illustrator
Preferred Media: Watercolors, Mixed Media, Acrylics, Collage.
b Glasgow, Scotland; Can citizen.
Study & Training: Glasgow Sch Art, grad, with Robert Anningbell.
Work in Public Collections: Victoria Art Gallery, B C; Winnipeg Art Gallery; Charlottetown Art Gallery, P E I.
Commissions: Two bks of remembrance, Can engrs World Wars I & II, St Pauls Cathedral; illuminated address to Elizabeth II, Can Govt.
Exhibitions: Victoria Gallery Exhib, Glasgow, Paris, Vancouver & Winnipeg; one-man exhibs, Victoria, Vancouver & B C; retrospective exhib, now circulating art mus of Can.
Teaching: Instr design, Glasgow Sch Art, 20-24; head dept design, Vancouver Sch Art, 32-52.
Awards: Var traveling & maintenance scholarships, Glasgow Sch Art; painting award, Winnipeg Show.
Memberships: Royal Soc Artists; Can Group Painters; Can Soc Graphic Arts.
Publications: Auth, Lettering for art schools, Longmans Green, London; co-auth, The Indian speaks.
Mailing Address: 6212 Balaclava St, Vancouver 13, BC, Can.

MENDELOWITZ, DANIEL MARCUS
Painter, Writer
Preferred Media: Watercolors.
b Linton, N Dak, Jan 28, 05.
Study & Training: Stanford Univ, BA, 26, MA, 27; Art Stud League New York, scholar, 29.
Commissions: Mural, U S Govt Post Off, Oxnard, Calif, 40.
Exhibitions: New York Watercolor Soc, N Y; Corcoran Biennial, Washington, D C; San Francisco Art Asn, Calif; Palace of Legion of Honor, San Francisco; Toledo Art Mus, Ohio.
Teaching: Prof art, Stanford Univ, 34-70.
Positions: Secy-treas, Pac Arts Asn, 22-28.
Research: Field of American art.

Publications: Auth, Children are artists, Stanford Univ Press, 53; auth, History of American art, 60, rev ed, 70 & Drawing, 67, Holt, Rinehart & Winston.
Mailing Address: 800 Lathrop Dr, Stanford, CA 94305.

MENIHAN, JOHN CONWAY
Painter, Designer
b Rochester, N Y, Feb 14, 08.
Study & Training: Wharton Sch, Univ Pa, 30.
Work in Public Collections: Libr Cong, Washington, D C; Carnegie Inst, Pittsburgh, Pa; Mem Art Gallery, Rochester.
Commissions: Polyester mural, Xerox, Rochester, 60; glass mural, Nazareth Col Libr, 62; polyester murals, Security Trust, Rochester, 65; Rochester Tel Co, 67 & R T French, Rochester & Fresno, Calif, 68.
Exhibitions: Finger Lakes Show, Mem Art Gallery, Rochester, 30 & 71; Art Inst Chicago, Ill, 39; World's Fair, New York, 39; Nat Acad Design, New York, 48; Am Watercolor Soc, New York, 54.
Teaching: Asst prof drawing & painting, Univ Rochester, 46-65.
Awards: Lillian Fairchild Award, Univ Rochester, 40; Marion Stratton Gould Award, Univ Rochester Mem Art Gallery, 46.
Bibliography: Norman Kent (auth), John C Menihan/lithographer, Am Artist, 45.
Memberships: Fel Rochester Mus & Sci Ctr; Nat Acad Design; Am Watercolor Soc; Asn Am Inst Architects.
Publications: Illusr, How scientists find out, Little, 65.
Mailing Address: 208 Alpine Dr, Rochester, NY 14618.

MENKES, SIGMUND
Painter
b Lwow, Poland, May 7, 96; U S citizen.
Study & Training: Higher Inst Art Decorative, Lwow, 14; Acad Fine Art, Crncov, Poland, 19.
Work in Public Collections: Metrop Mus Art; Wichita Art Asn; Cranbrook Acad Art; Encycl Britannica Collection; Pa Acad Fine Arts; plus many others.
Exhibitions: Carnegie Inst; Art Inst Chicago; Corcoran Gallery Art; Pa Acad Fine Arts; Univ Nebr; plus many other group & one-man shows.
Awards: Award, Nat Inst Arts & Lett, 55; medal of hon, 65 & silver medal, 67, Audubon Artists; prize, Polish Inst Arts & Sci, 68; plus others.
Bibliography: Emily Genauer (auth), Best of art, Doubleday, 48; Arthur Zaidenberg (ed), The art of artists, Crown, 51; Nathaniel Pousette-Dart (ed), American painting today, Hastings, 56.
Memberships: Life fel Int Inst Arts & Lett; Fedn Mod Painters & Sculptors (pres, 42-43); Assoc Nat Acad Design.
Mailing Address: 5075 Fieldstone Rd, Riverdale, NY 10471.

MENSES, JAN
Painter
Preferred Media: Tempera.
b Rotterdam, Netherlands, Apr 28, 33; Can citizen.
Work in Public Collections: Mus Mod Art, New York, N Y; Solomon R Guggenheim Mus, New York; Art Inst Chicago, Ill; Brooklyn Mus, N Y; Munic Mus, Amsterdam, Holland.
Exhibitions: 5th & 7th Biennial Can Painting, 63 & 68 & 1st & 2nd Biennial Can Watercolours, Drawings & Prints, 64 & 66, Nat Gallery Can, Ottawa; 20 New Acquisitions, Mus Mod Art, New York, 66; 9th & 11th Int Exhib Drawings & Engravings, Lugano, Switz, 66 & 72.
Awards: Grand Prize Concours Artistiques P Q, 65; award, Ninth Int Exhib Drawings & Engravings, City Lugano, Switz, 66; prize, Perspective 67, Prov of Ont, 67.
Bibliography: The arts, Time Mag (Can ed), 7/19/68; Francois Gagnon (auth), La serie des k'lipoth de Jan Menses, Vie Arts, spring 72.
Memberships: Assoc mem Royal Can Acad Arts; Soc Artistes Professionnels Que.
Dealer: Galerie Martal, 1110 Sherbrooke St W, Montreal, P Q, Can.
Mailing Address: 6284 De Vimy, Montreal, P Q, Can.

MEREDITH, DOROTHY LAVERNE
Weaver, Educator
Preferred Media: Fibers.
b Milwaukee, Wis, Nov 17, 06.
Study & Training: Layton Sch Art, Milwaukee; Wis State Col, BAE; Cranbrook Acad Fine Art, Bloomfield Hills, Mich, MFA.
Work in Public Collections: Objects U S A, Johnson Found; Milwaukee Art Ctr; Cranbrook Acad Art; Fedn Handweavers Gallery, Wellington, N Z; Univ Wis-Milwaukee.
Exhibitions: 22 Wis Designer Craftsmen, 46-72; Nippon Gendai Kogei Bijutgu Int, Japan, 67 & 68; 6 Midwest Designer Crafts-

men; Am Crafts Coun Craftsmen of Midwest; Fiber Clay Metal; plus others.
Teaching: Prof weaving, Univ Wis-Milwaukee, 53-
Awards: Miss River Crafts Award, 62; Nippon Gendai Kogei Bijutso Award, Japan, 66; Nine Wis Designer Craftsmen Award, Milwaukee Art Ctr, 71.
Memberships: World Crafts Coun; Am Crafts Coun (trustee, 58-61, state rep, 62-63); Am Crafts Coun N Cent Regional; Midwest Designer Craftsmen; Wis Designer Craftsmen (secy & pres).
Mailing Address: 2932 N 69th St, Milwaukee, WI 53210.

MEREDITH, JOHN
Painter
b Fergus, Ont, 33.
Work in Public Collections: Art Gallery, Ont; Nat Gallery Can; Univ Waterloo, Ont; Mus Mod Art, New York, N Y; Montreal Mus Fine Arts; plus many other pub & pvt collections.
Exhibitions: Canada 101, Edinburgh Festival, Scotland, 68; 10th Int Black & White Exhib, Lugano, Switz, 68; Winters Col, York Univ, Toronto, 69; Rothmans Art Gallery, Stratford, Ont, 70; 8 Artists from Canada, Tel-Aviv Mus, Israel, 70; plus many other group & one-man shows.
Dealer: Isaacs Gallery, 832 Yonge St, Toronto 285, Ont, Can.
Mailing Address: 531 Yonge St, Apt 1, Toronto, Ont, Can.

MERIDA, CARLOS
Painter
b Guatemala City, Guatemala, Dec 2, 91.
Work in Public Collections: Mus Mod Art, New York, N Y; Mus Mod Art, San Francisco, Calif; Mus Dallas, Tex; Mus Mod Art, São Paulo, Brazil; Mus Arte Mod, Caracas, Venezuela.
Commissions: Murals, (colored concrete), Apts Juarez, Mexico City, 51, Champion Bougies (enameled tiles), Mexico City, 68, Hemisfair, San Antonio, Tex, 68 & enamel on copper, Banco Guatemala, 69.
Bibliography: Luis Cardoza (auth), Carlos Merida, Ministry Educ, 35; Margarita Nelken (auth), Carlos Merida, Nat Univ Mex, 61; Mus Mod Art (monogr), Mexico City, 70.
Publications: Imagenes de Guatemla (10 stencils), Quatre Chemins, Paris, France, 28; Tres motivos huacograbados (portfolio), Mex, 36; Dances of Mexico (portfolio of 10 lithographs), Far Ed, New York, 37; Mexican costumes (portfolio of 25 serigraphs), Pocahontas Press, Chicago, 41; Estampas del popol vuh (portfolio of lithographs), Mexico City, 43.
Dealer: Galeria de Arte Mexicano, Milan 18, Mexico City 6, Mex.
Mailing Address: Manuel M Ponce 138, Mexico City 20, Mex.

MERKIN, RICHARD MARSHALL
Painter, Printmaker
b Brooklyn, N Y, Oct, 1938.
Study & Training: Syracuse Univ Sch Art, BFA; R I Sch Design, MFA.
Work in Public Collections: Mus Art, R I Sch Design; Mus Mod Art; Finch Col, N Y; Rose Art Mus, Brandeis Univ; Mass Inst Technol.
Exhibitions: Whitney Mus Am Art, 69 & 72; Chicago Inst Contemp Art; Finch Col Mus; one-man shows, Obelisk Gallery, Boston & Mass Inst Technol, Cambridge, Mass.
Teaching: Teaching fel, R I Sch Design, asst prof painting, presently.
Awards: Tiffany Found fel painting.
Mailing Address: 500 West End Ave, New York, NY 10024.

MERMIN, MILDRED (SHIRE)
Painter
Preferred Media: Oils, Watercolors.
b New York, N Y.
Study & Training: Nat Acad Design; Art Stud League New York, with Boardman Robinson & George Grosz; also with Charles W Hawthorne & Philip Evergood.
Work in Public Collections: Israel Mus, Jerusalem; Norfolk Mus Arts & Sci, Va; Springfield Mus Fine Arts, Mass.
Exhibitions: Pa Acad Fine Arts, Philadelphia: Japanese-Am Exchange Exhib, Nat Mus, Tokyo, Japan, 61; Silvermine Guild Artists Nat Exhib, New Canaan, Conn, 62; Nat Acad Design, New York, 63; New Haven Festival Art, Conn, 69.
Awards: Am Art Mag Award, 57 & Ziuta Gerstenzang Award, 64, Nat Asn Women Artists; Grumbacher Award, Am Soc Contemp Artists, 68.
Memberships: Fel MacDowell Colony; Artists Equity Asn New York; Am Soc Contemp Artists; Nat Asn Women Artists; Silvermine Guild Artists.
Mailing Address: 100 Colony Rd, New Haven, CT 06511.

MERRIAM, JOHN F
Trustee
b Constableville, N Y, July 1, 04.
Study & Training: Univ Chicago, PhB, 25; Chicago Kent Col Law, LLB, 30.
Positions: Chmn bd trustees, Joslyn Art Mus, Omaha, Nebr.
Mailing Address: 8405 Indian Hills Dr, Omaha, NE 68114.

MERRIAM, RUTH
Conservator, Collector
b Denver, Colo, May 15, 09.
Study & Training: Bryn Mawr Col, BA & MA.
Positions: Asst cur, class sect, Univ Mus, 32-40; rec photog, conserv dept, assisting in cleaning, relining & in-painting & asst to conservator, Philadelphia Mus Art, 54-
Collection: From old masters to contemporary art.
Publications: Auth, History of the deanery, Bryn Mawr Col.
Mailing Address: Maybrook, Wynnewood, PA 19096.

MERRICK, JAMES KIRK
Painter
Preferred Media: Watercolors.
b Philadelphia, Pa, Oct 8, 05.
Study & Training: Philadelphia Col Art, dipl; Cape Sch Art, Provincetown, Mass, with Henry Hensche.
Work in Public Collections: Philadelphia Mus Art; State Mus Art, Harrisburg, Pa; State Mus N J, Trenton; Lehigh Univ, Bethlehem, Pa; Du Pont Collection, Wilmington, Del.
Exhibitions: Pa Acad Fine Arts, Philadelphia, 35-; Philadelphia Mus Art, 40-; Nat Acad Design Watercolor Shows, New York, Audubon Artists, New York & Art Inst Chicago, Ill, 40-49.
Teaching: From instr to prof art, Philadelphia Col Art, 29-60.
Positions: Exec dir, Philadelphia Art Alliance, 60-70.
Awards: Gold medal, Philadelphia Col Art Alumni Asn, 54; gold medal award of merit, Philadelphia Watercolor Club, 55; Dawson Medal, Pa Acad Fine Arts, 64.
Memberships: Hon life mem Philadelphia Art Alliance (secy bd dirs); Philadelphia Watercolor Club (hon life pres, 60-); Am Nat Theater Acad (founding mem); Philadelphia Col Art Alumni Asn (pres, 48-52).
Publications: Auth & illusr, Brian; illusr, Those were actors.
Mailing Address: 341 S Hicks St, Philadelphia, PA 19102.

MERRILL, DAVID KENNETH
Painter, Instructor
Preferred Media: Acrylics.
b Bridgeport, Conn, Oct 18, 35.
Commissions: The entrance, Univ Maine, Gorham, 71; Monroe Green, town of Monroe, Conn, 72.
Exhibitions: Kent Art Asn, Conn, 69; Northern Vt Artists Asn, 71; Sacopee Valley Art League, Maine, 71; Burlington Garden Show, Vt, 72.
Teaching: Instr art, Southbury Training Sch, Conn, 63-67.
Awards: Medal of merit, Kent Art Asn, 69; first place, Burlington Garden Show, 72; first place, Northern Vt Artists Asn, 72.
Memberships: Kent Art Asn; Washington Art Asn; Northern Vt Art Asn.
Dealer: Raymond Farrell, Jr, Silver Hammer Studio, P O Box 781, Sandy Hook, CT 06482.
Mailing Address: Pine Meadow, Hiram, ME 04041.

MERRITT, FRANCIS SUMNER
Painter, Designer
b Danvers, Mass, Apr 8, 13.
Study & Training: Vesper George Sch Art; San Diego Acad Fine Art; Mass Sch Art; Boston Mus Sch; Yale Univ Sch Fine Arts; hon DFA, Colby Col, 71.
Commissions: Murals, Bd Educ, New London High Sch, N H, 43 & Knox Co Med Ctr, Rockland, Maine, 52.
Exhibitions: Directions in American Art, Am Fedn Arts Traveling Unit, Carnegie Inst, 42; Int Watercolor Show, Art Inst Chicago, 42-43; Artists for Victory, Metrop Mus Art, 42; Butler Art Inst Ann, Youngstown, Ohio, 47; Greetings Exhib, Mus Mod Art, New York, N Y, 47; plus others.
Teaching: Instr painting & drawing, Abbot Acad, Andover, Mass, 37-39; instr painting & drawing, Colby Jr Col, New London, 40-44; instr painting & drawing, Kingswood, Cranbrook, Bloomfield Hills, Mich, 46-47; instr painting & drawing, Bradford Jr Col, Mass, 53-57.
Positions: Cur, John Esther Art Gallery, Andover, 37-39; dir, Flint Inst Art, Mich, 47-51; dir, Haystack Mt Sch Crafts, Deer Isle, Maine, 51-
Awards: First award painting, Flint Inst Art Ann, 47.
Bibliography: Haystack Mountain Sch of Crafts, Handweaver & Craftsman, 12/51; An unusual school, Dansk Kunst Haandvaerk, 4/60; Haystack-Hinckley, Craft Horizons, 5/70.

Memberships: Artists Equity Asn (regional bd mem, 47-48); Am Crafts Coun (trustee, 56-62); State of Maine Comn Arts & Humanities (v chmn, 67-); fel Royal Soc Arts.
Mailing Address: Deer Isle, ME 04627.

MESCHES, ARNOLD
Painter, Educator
b New York, Aug 11, 23.
Study & Training: Art Ctr Sch; Chouinard's Art Inst; Jepson's Art Inst.
Work in Public Collections: Los Angeles Mus Art, Calif; Joseph Hirshhorn Found, New York; Philadelphia Mus Art, Pa; San Francisco Mus Art, Calif; Brooklyn Mus Art, N Y.
Commissions: Murals, Hotel Newhouse, Salt Lake City, Utah, 50 Dr & Mrs August, Maymudes, La, 70 & Temple Isaiah, La, 72.
Exhibitions: One-man shows, Pasadena Mus Art, Calif, 53, Santa Barbara Mus Art, Calif, 66, Carroll Reece Mus Art, Johnson City, Tenn, 69, Long Beach Mus Art, Calif, 69 & Univ Buffalo Art Gallery, N Y, 69 & 72.
Teaching: Instr beginning painting & drawing, Univ Southern Calif, summer 50; instr advan painting, drawing & compos & dir, New Sch Art, Los Angeles, 54-57; instr advan drawing & compos, Otis Art Inst, Los Angeles, 63-67; instr advan painting, Univ Calif Exten, Los Angeles, 72.
Awards: Purchase awards, Philadelphia Art Mus, 68, Home Savings & Loan, Los Angeles Munic Exhib, 69 & San Francisco Mus Art, 69.
Bibliography: Arthur Secunda (auth), Mesches, McMenamin & Pederson Bros, Art Voices Mag, 65; Thomas Leavitt (auth), preface to catalog, Santa Barbara Mus Art, 66; Bea Mego (auth), Arnold Mesches and his paintings, Jewish Voice, 67.
Memberships: Los Angeles Printmaking Soc; Screen Actor's Guild.
Publications: Illusr, Frontier Mag, 54-60; auth, Red, white and Rosie, 72; contribr, A search for form & A book on painting.
Dealer: Jacqueline Anhalt Gallery, 750 N La Cienega Blvd, Los Angeles, CA 90069.
Mailing Address: 9507 Santa Monica Blvd, Beverly Hills, CA 90210.

MESIBOV, HUGH
Painter, Educator
Preferred Media: Acrylic, Watercolor.
b Philadelphia, Pa, Dec 29, 16.
Study & Training: Fleischer Memorial Art Sch, Philadelphia, 34-35; Pa Acad Fine Arts, Philadelphia, 35-37; Albert C Barnes Found, Merion, Pa, 36-40.
Work in Public Collections: Metrop Mus Art, New York, N Y; Philadelphia Mus Art; Albert C Barnes Found; Pa Acad Fine Arts; N Y Univ Collection Contemp Am Art, New York.
Commissions: Mural design, Benjamin Franklin High Sch, 37-40; mural, WPA art project, Bennet Hall, Univ Pa, 37-40; mural, Steel Industry, U S Treas, U S Post Office, Hubbard, Ohio, 41; color lithograph, New York Hilton Art Collection, 62; mural, acrylic/canvas, Job, Temple Beth El, Spring Valley, N Y 72.
Exhibitions: Pa Acad Fine Arts, 40, 58 & 67; Whitney Mus Am Art, New York, 46, 56 & 59; Hallmark Int Water Color Show, New York, 52; Corcoran Gallery Art, Washington, D C, 59; Am Acad Arts & Lett, New York, 67.
Teaching: Art therapist, Wiltwyck Sch for Boys, N Y, 57-66; assoc prof art, Rockland Community Col, Suffern, N Y, 66-
Awards: Lambert Purchase Fund Award for oil, Pa Acad Fine Arts, 52; May Audobon Post Prize for oil, Fellowship of Pa Acad Fine Arts, 58; first prize, oil painting, Tappan Zee Bank, Rockland Found Award Show, 64.
Memberships: Philadelphia Water Color Club; fel Pa Acad Fine Arts.
Mailing Address: 377 Saddle River Rd, Monsey, NY 10980.

MESSEGUER, VILLORO BENITO
Painter, Sculptor
b Mora de Ebro, Spain, Oct 27, 30.
Study & Training: Escuela Pintura y Escultura, Inst Nac Bellas Artes, 46-51 & 56; Escuela Estudiantes Extranjeros, Univ Mex, 56; Trinity Univ, 69-70.
Work in Public Collections: Inst Nac Bellas Artes Mex; Mus Veersjeva, Israel; Mus Arte Mod Mex, Mexico City; Mus Chilpancingo, Guerrero, Mex.
Commissions: Acrilico sobre asbesto, Hotel Casino La Selva, Cuernavaca, Morelos, Mex, 61; acrilico sobre asbesto, Escuela Nac Economía, Univ Mex, 63; acrilico sobre base tipo Fresco, Inst Mex Audicion y Lenguage, Mexico City, 66; sobrerelieve de plástico, Inst Mex Protec a Infancia, Mexico City, 70; revestimiento de un muro lateral de edificio, Soldominio Conjunto Habitacional, Mexico City, 70.
Exhibitions: Second Salon Nac Paisaje, Mexico City, 61; Bienal Jovenes Paris, France, 63 & 65; Bienal Tokyo, Japan, 65; Gilbert Salerie, San Francisco, Calif, 67.

Bibliography: Alfonso Newvillete (auth), Pintura actual de México 1966, Artes Mex, 66; Antonio Rodriguez (auth), Der mensch in flamman, VEB Verlag der Kunst, 67; Antonio Rodriguez (auth), El hombre en llamas, Thomas & Hudson, 70.
Memberships: Salón Plástica Mex.
Dealers: Merle Kupper Mooliere, Mexico City, Mex; José María Tasende Costera Miguel Alemán, Acapulco, Mex.
Mailing Address: Privada Josefa Ortíz de Domínguez 18, Tizapán, México City 20, Mex.

MESSER, THOMAS M
Museum Director, Art Historian
b Bratislava, Czech, Feb 9, 20; U S citizen.
Study & Training: Exchange stud, Inst Int Educ, Thiele Col, 39; Boston Univ, BA, 42; Sorbonne, Paris, France, 47; Harvard Univ, MA, 51; spec fel, Brussels, Belg, 53; Univ Mass, hon DFA, 62.
Collections Arranged: For The Solomon R Guggenheim Mus: Hirshhorn Collection, 62; one-man show, Vasily Kandinsky, 62; Thannhauser Collection, 65 & 72; one-man shows, Edward Munch, 66 & Paul Klee, 68; Permanent Collection, specially arranged, 70; also first U S mus shows, Egon Schiele & New Departures: Latin America, Inst Contemp Art.
Teaching: Sr fel advan studies, Wesleyan Univ Ctr Advan Studies, 66; vis prof mod art, Barnard Col, 66 & 71.
Positions: Dir, Roswell Mus, 49-52; asst dir, Am Fedn Arts, 52-53, dir exhibs & dir, 53-56; dir, Inst Contemp Arts, Boston, 57-61; dir, Solomon R Guggenheim Mus, 61-
Awards: Knight First Class, Order of St Olaf.
Memberships: Am Asn Mus Dir; Int Coun Mus (secy-treas, U S nat comt); Czech Soc Arts & Sci (v pres); Century Asn; Studio Int Mag Adv Panel.
Publications: Auth, Egon Schiele, 1890-1918: work on paper, Galerie St Etienne, 65; auth, Paul Klee exhibition at the Guggenheim Museum: a post-scriptum, Guggenheim Found, 68; auth, Julius Bissier, 1893-1965: a retrospective exhibition, Guggenheim Found, 68.
Mailing Address: The Solomon R Guggenheim Museum, 1071 Fifth Ave, New York, NY 10028.

MESSERSMITH, FRED LAWRENCE
Painter, Educator
Preferred Media: Watercolors.
b Sharon, Pa, Apr 3, 24.
Study & Training: Ohio Wesleyan Univ, BFA, 48, MA, 49.
Work in Public Collections: Addison Gallery Am Art, Andover, Mass; Cummer Gallery, Jacksonville, Fla; Butler Inst Am Art, Youngstown, Ohio; Springfield Art Mus, Mo; Huntington Galleries, W Va.
Exhibitions: Am Watercolor Soc, 57-; Mid-Year Show, Butler Inst Am Art, 65; Ringling Mus Art, Sarasota, Fla, 67; one-man show, Arno Gallery, Florence, Italy, 70; Yale Univ, 71.
Teaching: Chmn dept art, W Va Wesleyan Col, 49-59; chmn dept art, Stetson Univ, 59-
Awards: Spec watercolor award, Mead Packaging, Atlanta, 60; first award, Fla State Fair, 67.
Bibliography: Norman Kent (auth), Fred Messersmith paints on rice paper, Am Artist Mag, 12/60.
Memberships: Am Watercolor Soc; Fla Artist Group (pres, 64-66); Ala Watercolor Soc.
Publications: Auth, Pottery of Gene Bunker, 62 & Francis Chapin, 65, Am Artist Mag; contribr, 100 watercolor techniques, 68, Acrylic watercolor painting, 70 & Eyewitness to space, 71.
Mailing Address: Dept of Art, Stetson University, Deland, FL 32720.

MESSICK, BEN (NEWTON)
Painter, Instructor
Preferred Media: Oils.
b Strafford, Mo, Jan 9, 01.
Study & Training: Los Angeles Sch Art & Design, 23; Chouinard Art Inst, 25-32; anatomy with F Tolles Chamberlain.
Work in Public Collections: San Francisco Mus Art, Calif; Springfield Mus Art, Mo; Los Angeles Co Mus Art, Calif; Long Beach Mus Art, Calif; Nat Mus, Washington, D C.
Commissions: Three murals, U S Treasury Dept, 35-40.
Exhibitions: U S Nat Mus, 44; Two Yr Travel Exhib Midwest & Southwest Mus & Galleries, 50-51; E B Crocker Gallery, 57; Long Beach Art Mus, 57; Springfield Art Mus, 67.
Teaching: Instr life drawing, Chouinard Art Inst, Los Angeles, 43-51; instr drawing & painting, San Diego Sch Arts & Crafts, La Jolla, Calif, 48-53; instr drawing & painting, Messick-Hay Studio, Long Beach, 52-
Positions: Sketch artist, Disney Studios, Los Angeles, 40; sketch artist, Metro-Goldwyn-Mayer, Culver City, Calif, 42.
Awards: Calif Graphics Award, Fla Southern Col, 51; Seton Hall Univ Key Award, 58.

Bibliography: Janice Penny Lovoos (auth), Ben Messick, Am Artist, 50; Michael M Engel (auth), Sketching the spec, Design Mag, 56; Vera Williams (auth), Art is a way of life, Southland Mag, 66.
Memberships: Fel Royal Soc Arts.
Dealer: Messick-Hay Studio Gallery, 133 St Joseph Ave, Long Beach, CA 90803.
Mailing Address: 133 St Joseph Ave, Long Beach, CA 90803.

METCALF, JAMES
Sculptor
b New York, N Y, Mar 11, 25.
Study & Training: Dayton Art Inst Sch; Pa Acad Fine Arts, 44-46; Cent Sch Arts & Crafts, London, Eng, 50-53.
Work in Public Collections: Univ Ariz; Mus 20 Jahrhunderts; New York Hilton Hotel; Yale Univ.
Commissions: War mem, Middletown, Ohio, 49.
Exhibitions: Goldsmith's Hall, London, 52; Third Biennial Span-Am Art, Barcelona, 55; Expos Int Sculpture, Paris, France, 61; Actualite Sculpture, Paris, 63; Documenta III, Kassel, Ger, 64; plus others.
Awards: William & Noma Copley Found grant, 57; Clark Found grant.
Bibliography: Michel Seuphor (auth), The sculpture of this century, dictionary of modern sculpture, A Zwemmer Ltd, London, 59; Herbert Tead (auth), A concise history of modern sculpture, Praeger, 64; Sam Hunter (auth), James Metcalf (monogr), William & Noma Copley Found.
Mailing Address: Springfield Pike, Yellow Springs, OH 45387.

METCALF, ROBERT M
Designer, Instructor
Preferred Media: Stained Glass.
b Springfield, Ohio, Dec, 02.
Study & Training: Columbus Art Sch; Wittenberg Col; Pa Acad Fine Arts.
Commissions: Windows, St James Chapel Cathedral of St John the Divine, New York, by Stephan Clark, 33; hist of med window, Mayo Clin, Rochester, Minn, 40; windows, Trinity Lutheran Church, Rochester, 48; windows, Nat Masonic Mem Bldg, Alexandria, Va, 50; windows, Christ Church, Cincinnati, Ohio, 55.
Teaching: Chmn painting & design, decorative arts dept, Dayton Art Inst, 34-45; chmn painting & design, art dept, Antioch Col, 45-68.
Positions: Pres, Robert M Metcalf & Assocs, 45-70.
Awards: Cresson Europ traveling scholar, Pa Acad Fine Arts, 23; Great Lakes Col Asn Award, funded by Carnegie Corp to photograph pre-Columbian sites and mus works in Mex & Guatemala, 67; Kress Found Award, 68.
Memberships: Col Art Asn Am.
Publications: Co-auth, Making stained glass, McGraw, 72.
Mailing Address: 573 Ridgecrest Dr, Yellow Springs, OH 45387.

METZ, FRANK ROBERT
Painter, Art Director
Preferred Media: Oils.
b Philadelphia, Pa, July 3, 25.
Study & Training: Philadelphia Mus Sch, with Ezio Martinelli; Art Stud League New York, with Will Barnet.
Work in Public Collections: Olsen Found, Guilford, Conn; Ball State Teachers Col, Muncie, Ind.
Exhibitions: Painting & Sculpture Ann, Pa Acad Fine Arts, 48, 52 & 53; Watercolor-Drawings Ann, Metrop Mus Art, 52; Ann Drawing & Small Sculpture, Ball State Teachers Col, 62-63 & 64-65; Am Acad Arts & Lett, Childe Hassem Fund, 66; The American Landscape—A Living Tradition, Peridot Gallery, New York, N Y, 68.
Positions: Art dir, Simon & Schuster, 50-
Awards: Elisabeth Ball Purchase Award, Ball State Teachers Col, 64.
Bibliography: Jules Perel (auth), Landscape drawings of Frank Metz, Am Artist, 5/62.
Dealer: Joe De Mers Gallery Ltd, 5 Harbour House, Light House Rd, Hilton Head Island, SC 29928.
Mailing Address: 800 West End Ave, New York, NY 10025.

MEYER, MR & MRS ANDRE
Collectors
Mr Meyer b Paris, France, Sept 3, 98.
Positions: Mr Meyer, trustee, Metrop Mus Art.
Collection: Paintings and contemporary art.
Mailing Address: 35 E 76th St, New York, NY 10021.

MEYER, FRED (ROBERT)
Sculptor, Painter
Preferred Media: Bronze, Gouache.
b Oshkosh, Wis.
Study & Training: Univ Wis; Harvard Grad Sch Bus Admin; Cranbrook Acad Art, BFA & MFA.

Work in Public Collections: New York State Theatre, Lincoln Ctr Performing Arts; Everson Mus, Syracuse, N Y; Munson, Williams, Proctor Inst, Utica, N Y; Cranbrook Mus, Bloomfield Hills, Mich; Little Rock Mus Art, Ark.
Commissions: Murals, Schrafft's Motor Inn, Binghamton, N Y, 58, Exec Motel, Buffalo, N Y, 59 & Holiday Inn, Niagara Falls, N Y, 60; two bronze sculptural groups, Lazarus Mall, Columbus, Ohio, 67; two murals, Sarah Coventry Int Hq, Newark, N J, 71.
Exhibitions: One-man shows, Midtown Galleries, New York, N Y, 47, 48 & 69; one-man shows, Philadelphia Art Alliance, 64 & Everson Mus, Syracuse, N Y, 65; Scripps Col Ceramic Invitational, 66; Ann Arbor Film Festival Tour, 68.
Teaching: Prof & chmn grad prog, Col Fine & Appl Arts, Rochester Inst Technol, 55-
Awards: Ford Found fel, 55; Carburundum Award, Western N Y State Exhib, 64.
Memberships: Nat Soc Interior Designers.
Publications: Auth, Sculpture in ceramic, Watson-Guptil, 71.
Dealer: Midtown Galleries, 11 E 57th St, New York, NY 10022.
Mailing Address: 17 Church St, Scottsville, NY 14546.

MEYER, SEYMOUR W
Sculptor
Preferred Media: Bronze.
b Brooklyn, N Y.
Study & Training: With Louise Nevelson.
Work in Public Collections: C W Post Col, Long Island Univ, Brookville, N Y; Temple Beth-El, Great Neck, N Y; Arlen Industs, New York; Lester Avnet Collection, N Y; Mus Mod Art, Rio de Janeiro, Brazil.
Exhibitions: Sculpture House Gallery, N Y, 66; Curator's Choice, C W Post Col, Long Island Univ, N Y, 66; Crane-Kochin Gallery, Manhasset, N Y, 68-70; Wiener Gallery, N Y, 70-72; State Univ N Y Col Plattsburg Ann Show, 71.
Memberships: Am Fedn Arts; Mus Mod Art New York, Solomon R Guggenheim Mus.
Dealer: George Wiener Gallery, 963 Madison Ave, New York, NY 10021.
Mailing Address: 495 E Shore Rd, Great Neck, NY 11024.

MEYER, URSULA
Sculptor, Photographer
Preferred Media: Metal.
b Hannover, Ger.
Study & Training: New Sch Social Res, BA, 60; Columbia Univ Teachers Col, MA, 62.
Work in Public Collections: Brooklyn Mus; Finch Col Mus; Newark Mus; Larry Aldrich Mus; Grad Ctr, City Univ New York.
Exhibitions: Schemata 7, Finch Col Mus, 67; Listening to Pictures, Brooklyn Mus, 68; Cool Art of 1967, 68 & Highlights of 1967-1968 Art Season, Larry Aldrich Mus; Cool Art, Abstractions Today, Newark Mus, 68.
Teaching: Asst prof, Hunter Col, 66-68; assoc prof sculpture, Lehman Col, 68-, City Univ res grant, 70.
Awards: Estelle Goodman Award for best sculpture at Nat Design Ctr, 66.
Bibliography: Christopher Andreae (auth), Exhibition by Ursula Meyer at A M Sachs Gallery, Christian Sci Monitor, 2/26/68; Gregory Battcock (auth), Minimal art, 68; Al Rogers (auth), Ursula Meyer, Alre-Films, 70.
Memberships: Women's Interart Ctr; Women in Arts.
Publications: Auth, De-objectification of the object, Arts Mag, summer 69; auth, Conceptual art, 70 & The eruption of anti-art, In, Idea-art, 73, Dutton; auth, How to explain pictures to a dead hare, Art News, 1/70; auth, Towards feminist art, Women & Art, summer-fall 72.
Mailing Address: 260 Riverside Dr, New York, NY 10025.

MEYEROWITZ, WILLIAM
Painter
Preferred Media: Oil.
b Ekaterinoslav, Ukraina, July 15, 98.
Study & Training: Nat Acad of Design.
Work in Public Collections: Metrop Mus Art, New York, N Y; Brooklyn Mus, Smithsonian Inst, Washington, D C; Duncan Phillips Mus, Washington, D C; Columbus Mus Arts & Crafts, Ga; plus others.
Exhibitions: Carnegie Int, Pittsburgh, Pa; Metrop Mus Art; Corcoran Gallery Art, Washington, D C; Pa Acad Fine Arts.
Teaching: Instr painting & etching, E 105th St Settlement House, New York, 30-40; instr painting & etching, Mod Sch Self-Expression, 40-45, dir summer art course, 45-68.
Positions: Mem Arts Coun, Gloucester, Mass, 67-70.
Awards: Clair Layton Prize for painting, Audubon Soc Artists, 58; Speyer Prize for painting, Nat Acad Design, 65; gold medal of honor for painting, Rockport Art Asn, Mass, 70.

Bibliography: Royal Cortissoi (auth), Contemporary American art, Am Art Dealers Asn, 31; Susan Hutchinson (auth), American fine prints of the year, London Minton Balchulo 33; Duncan Phillips (auth), A collection in the making, Phillips Publ no 5, 36.
Memberships: Nat Acad Design; hon life mem North Shore Arts Asn, Gloucester (v pres, 68-69); Rockport Art Asn; Audubon Soc Artists (dir, 60-67); Allied Artists Am (dir, 73).
Publications: Contribr, Col Art Asn, 37; Menoran J, 44; auth, On the need of art, Menoran J 55; contribr, Encycl Am Art, 70-71.
Dealer: Chase Gallery of Art, 31 E 64th St, New York, NY 10021.
Mailing Address: 54 W 74 St, New York, NY 10023.

MEYERS, DALE (MRS MARIO COOPER)
Painter, Instructor
Preferred Media: Watercolors.
b Chicago, Ill, Jan 24, 22.
Study & Training: Corcoran Gallery Sch Art; Art Stud League New York; also watercolor with Mario Cooper, graphics with Seong Moy.
Work in Public Collections: Nat Acad Design, New York, N Y; NASA, Washington, D C; Mus Acuarela, Mexico City, Mex; Univ Utah, Logan; Schumacher Gallery, Capital Univ, Columbus, Ohio.
Commissions: Apollo 11 Moon Flight (painting), Nat Gallery Art for NASA, Washington, D C, 69; ecology subjects (paintings), Environ Protection Agency, Washington, D C, 72.
Exhibitions: Smithsonian Inst, Washington, D C, 62-63; 200 Years of Watercolor Painting in America, Metrop Mus Art, New York, 66; Nat Acad Design, 68-71; Butler Inst Am Art, Youngstown, Ohio, 69-70; Eyewitness to Space, Nat Gallery Art, 70.
Teaching: Instr watercolor, Kefauver Sch Art, Washington, D C, 61-62; asst instr watercolor, Art Stud League New York, 65-; workshops in N Mex, Calif & Maine, 70-72.
Positions: Ed newsletter, Am Watercolor Soc, 62-
Awards: Bronze medal of honor, Am Watercolor Soc, 68; Anna Hyatt Huntington Bronze Medal, Catharine Lorillard Wolfe Art Club, Nat Acad Galleries, 71; Paul B Remmey Award, Am Watercolor Soc, 72.
Memberships: Assoc Nat Acad Design; Am Watercolor Soc (dir, 70-71); Allied Artists Am (asst treas, 70-). fel Royal Soc Arts; Art Stud League New York.
Publications: Auth, articles, In: Am Artist Mag, 69 & Today's Art Mag, 70; contribr, Eyewitness to space, Abrams, 71.
Mailing Address: 1 W 67th St, New York, NY 10023.

MEYERS, ROBERT WILLIAM
Illustrator
b New York, N Y, June 17, 19.
Study & Training: Nat Acad Design, with Ivan Olinsky; Grand Cent Art Sch; Traphagen Sch Fashion.
Exhibitions: One-man shows, Soc Illusr, 55-56, Whitney Mus Western Art, Cody, Wyo, 67, Desert Southwest Gallery, Palm Desert, Calif, 69, Gallery 85, Billings, Mont, 69 & Golden Eagle Gallery Western Art, Cody, 69; plus others.
Awards: Prize, one of 100 best posters for 1955, Art Dirs Club, Chicago, 55.
Memberships: Grand Cent Art Gallery.
Art Interests: Western paintings.
Publications: Illusr, The winning dive, 50, The base stealer, 51, The mysterious caboose, 50, The haunted hut, 50, Jockie, 51 & others; also contribr, illus, In: True, Argosy, Reader's Digest & others.
Mailing Address: Circle M Ranch, South Fork Rte, Cody, WY 82414.

MICHAELS, GLEN
Sculptor, Painter
b Spokane, Wash, July 21, 27.
Study & Training: Yale Sch Music, 50-52; Eastern Wash Col Educ, BA, 57; Cranbrook Acad Art, with Zoltan Sepeshy, 57-58, MFA, 58.
Work in Public Collections: Detroit Inst Arts; Johnson's Wax Collection.
Commissions: Brick terrace, W Hawkins Ferry, Grosse Pointe, Mich, 64; pillar, J Walter Thompson, New York, 65; tile, wood & bronze mural, Int Monetary Fund, Vincent Kling, Washington, D C, 65; tile, wood & bronze, Cent Penn Nat Bank—Vincent Kling, Philadelphia, 70; tile, wood & brass bas relief, Shaarey Zedek Synagogue, Southfield, Mich, 71.
Exhibitions: Thirteenth Trienale, Milan, Italy, 64; Archit League New York Gold Medal Exhib, 65; Plastic as Plastic, Mus Contemp Crafts, 68; Objects: U S A, 69-70; Smithsonian Plastic Exhib, 69-70.
Teaching: Supvr art for children, Cranbrook Acad Art, 59-65; asst prof sculpture, Wayne State Univ, 67-69; asst prof sculpture, Univ Windsor, 70-71.

Awards: Stutgart Handcraft Exhib Award, 66.
Bibliography: Slivka (auth), The crafts in the modern world, Horizon, 68; Redstone (auth), Art in architecture, McGraw, 68; Nordness (auth), Objects: U S A, Viking Press, 70.
Dealer: Little Gallery, 915 E Maple, Birmingham, MI 48010.
Mailing Address: 763 Lakeview, Birmingham, MI 48009.

MICHELI, JULIO
Painter, Printmaker
Preferred Media: Assemblage.
b Ponce, P R, Aug 14, 37.
Study & Training: Univ Miami, BA, 62; Claremont Grad Sch, MFA, 65.
Work in Public Collections: Mus Art Ponce; Ateneo Puertorriqueño, San Juan, P R; Mus San Juan.
Commissions: Serigraphs (three ed), Hotel San Juan, 69 & (five ed), Hotel Caribe Hilton, San Juan, 71.
Exhibitions: South Calif Second Ann, Long Beach Mus Art, 63; First Nat Painting Exhib, Joe & Emily Lowe Art Gallery, Coral Gables, Fla, 64; Expos Pan-Am Art Gráficas, Cali, Colombia, 70; Primera Bienal San Juan Grabado Latin Am, San Juan, 70 & Segunda Bienal, 72.
Teaching: Assoc prof art, Cath Univ P R, 65-, chmn dept, 71-
Awards: First prize in painting, IBEC Corp, San Juan, 65; first prize in painting, Ateneo Puertorriqueño, San Juan, 66 & first prize in prints, 69.
Bibliography: Nine artists of Puerto Rico (film), Orgn of Am States, 68.
Memberships: Col Art Asn Am.
Publications: Contribr, How to make your own greeting cards, 68.
Dealer: Helene Santiago-Galería Santiago, 207 Calle del Cristo, San Juan, PR 00901.
Mailing Address: 14 Baldorioty St, Ponce, PR 00731.

MICHELSON, ANNETTE
Art Critic, Writer
b New York, N Y.
Study & Training: Brooklyn Col, BA; Columbia Univ; Univ Paris.
Teaching: Assoc prof cinema studies, New York Univ, 67-
Positions: Art ed, N Y Herald Tribune, int ed, Paris, France, 57-61; Paris corresp, Arts Mag, 57-65 & Art Int, Lugano, Switz, 61-65; contrib ed, Art Forum Mag, N Y, 65-; film ed, Praeger Publ, N Y, 69-72.
Memberships: Soc Cinema Studies (coun woman, 67-).
Research: Contemporary painting and sculpture, film aesthetics, new American cinema, the Soviet cinema.
Publications: Auth, Robert Moris, an aesthetics of transgression, 70; contribr, The future of art, Viking Press, 70; contribr & ed, The film culture reader, Praeger, 71; ed, The writings of Jean Dubuffet, Praeger, 72.
Mailing Address: 101 W 80th St, New York, NY 10024.

MIDDLETON, DAVID V
Painter, Ceramist
b Sheffield, Ala, Dec 15, 22.
Study & Training: Centenary Col La, BS, with Don Brown; Northwestern State Univ; La State Univ, MEd, with Armin Scheler & Tom LaDousa.
Exhibitions: State Art Comn, Baton Rouge, La; Dallas Southwest Drawing & Print Show; Masur Mus, Monroe, La; Southwest Art Inst, Lafayette, La; one-man show, La State Univ, Shreveport; plus others.
Teaching: Instr crafts, Eve Div, Centenary Col La; instr crafts, Exten, La Tech Univ.
Awards: Awards, La State Forestry Show, Shreveport Art Club Regional & Hodges Gardens Art Festival; plus others.
Memberships: La Crafts Coun; Shreveport Contemp Art Group; La Artists; Men's Art Guild.
Mailing Address: 942 Drexel Dr, Shreveport, LA 71106.

MIDENER, WALTER
Sculptor, Instructor
Preferred Media: Metal, Wood, Clay, Bronze.
b Ger, Oct 11, 12; U S citizen.
Study & Training: Vereinigten Staats Schulen Fine & Appl Art; Berlin Acad, 32-36; Wayne State Univ, MA, 50.
Work in Public Collections: Whitney Mus Am Art, New York, N Y; Detroit Inst Art, Mich; Flint Inst Art, Mich; House Living Judaism, New York.
Commissions: Portrait bust Justice Butzel, Mich Supreme Court, 62; monument, Temple Bethel Mem Park, 62; sculpture, Bundy Corp, Detroit, 63; carved wood relief, Detroit Pub Libr, 64; hammered metal screen, Pontiac Motor Div, Gen Motors Corp, 68-69.
Exhibitions: Mich Artists Shows, 46-61; Modellers, Carvers, Welders, Mus Mod Art, New York, 49-50; American Sculpture,

Metropolitan Mus, New York, 51; Pa Acad, Philadelphia, 59; Friends of Whitney Collection, Whitney Mus Am Art, 64.
Teaching: Instr sculpture, Henry St Settlement, 39-41; head sculpture dept, Soc Arts & Crafts Art Sch, 46-66, asst dir, 58-61, actg & assoc dir, 61-67, dean faculty, 67-68, dir, 68.
Awards: Mus Purchase Prize, Mich Artists Show, 50 & Founders Prize, 52, Founders Soc; Scarab Club Gold Medal, 60.
Memberships: Scarab Club.
Mailing Address: Society of Arts & Crafts Art School, 245 E Kirby, Detroit, MI 48202.

MIDGETTE, WILLARD FRANKLIN
Painter
Preferred Media: Oils, Acrylics.
b Baltimore, Md, July 9, 37.
Study & Training: Skowhegan Sch Painting & Sculpture, with J Levine & Shahn, 53-56 & 59; Boston Univ Sch Fine & Appl Art, with David Aronson, 56-58; Harvard Col, AB, 58; Pratt Graphic Art Ctr, with Walter Rogalski, 59-60; Ind Univ, MFA, 62, with James McGarrell.
Work in Public Collections: Reed Col, Portland, Ore; Mt Hood Community Col, Portland; Roswell Mus & Art Ctr, N Mex.
Commissions: Illusionistic mural, Donald B Anderson, Roswell, 69; illusionistic hallway, H J Szold, New York, N Y, 72; illusionistic portraits, Edward Elson, Atlanta, Ga, 72.
Exhibitions: Northwest Int, Seattle Art Mus, 68; one-man shows, Fountain Gallery, Portland, 70, Clean Well Lighted Place, Austin, Tex, 71 & Allan Franklin Gallery, New York & Chicago, 71; Sharp Focus Realism, Sidney Janis Gallery, New York, 72.
Teaching: From artist-in-residence to assoc prof painting, drawing & printmaking, Reed Col, 63-70; lectr, Univ Wis & Univ Ill, Chicago Circle, 71; lectr, Moore Col Art & La State Univ, 72; artist-in-residence & chmn dept painting, drawing & printmaking, St Ann's Episcopal Sch, Brooklyn, N Y, 72-
Awards: Reed-Rockefeller faculty grant, 69; Roswell Mus residence grant, 69-71.
Bibliography: David Rosand (auth), Portrait of the artist as portrait of the artist, Art News, 3/71; David Hickey (auth), Review of Sidney Janis sharp focus show, Art in Am, 3-4/72; Judson Hand (auth), Realism returns in a tough new form, Sunday News Mag, New York, 6/72.
Publications: Auth, The naked truth, the work of Philip Pearlstein, Art News, 11/67.
Dealer: Allan Frumkin Gallery, 41 E 57th St, New York, NY 10022.
Mailing Address: 124 Pierrepont St, Brooklyn, NY 11201.

MIECZKOWSKI, EDWIN
Painter
b Pittsburgh, Pa, 1929.
Study & Training: Cleveland Inst Art, BFA; Carnegie Inst, MFA.
Work in Public Collections: Cleveland Mus Art.
Exhibitions: Anonima Gallery, 66-69; Albright-Knox Art Gallery, 68.
Memberships: Founding mem Anonima Group.
Mailing Address: 268 Bowery, New York, NY 10012.

MIELZINER, JO
Designer, Lecturer
b Paris, France, Mar 19, 01; U S citizen.
Study & Training: Nat Acad Design; Art Stud League New York; Pa Acad Fine Arts; also in Paris & Vienna; Fordham Univ, hon DFA, 47; Otterbein Col, hon HHD, 67; Univ Mich, hon DFA, 71; Univ Utah, hon LHD, 72.
Commissions: Setting & lighting for UN Conf, San Francisco, 45; Michelangelo's Pieta, Vatican Pavilion, New York World's Fair.
Exhibitions: One-man shows of paintings, Libr & Mus Performing Arts, Lincoln Ctr, Brandeis Univ & Coffee House Club, 66, Va Mus Fine Arts, Richmond, 67 & Int Exhibs Found tour, 68-69; Century Asn Exhib, 71; Mielziner Theatrical Designs, Toneelmuseum, Amsterdam, Holland, 72.
Teaching: Lectr stage design, Fordham Univ & many others.
Positions: Designer stage settings for operas, ballets, musical comedies, 24-, incl Winterset, Glass Menagerie, Death of a Salesman, Street Scene, Summer and Smoke, Guys and Dolls, A Streetcar Named Desire, The King and I, Gypsy, The Innocents, Can-Can & many others; collaborating designer, Repertory Theatre, Lincoln Ctr; consult designer, The Forum, Los Angeles Music Ctr; co-designer & consult, Univ Mich Theatre, Ann Arbor, theatre, Univ Ill Krannert Ctr & Southern Ill Univ, Edwardsville theatre; designer, spec portable stage, East Room, The White House; plus many others.
Awards: Oscar for color art dir on Picnic, Acad Motion Pictures, 55; five Antoinette Perry Awards & five Donaldson awards for set design; Ford Found award for Theatre Design, 60; plus others.
Memberships: Benjamin Franklin fel Royal Soc Arts; U S Inst Theatre Technol (bd dirs); Am Theatre Planning Bd (chmn); Brit Theatre Lighting Designers; Century Asn.

Publications: Contribr, The theatre of Robert Edmond Jones; auth, Designing for the Theatre; auth, Shapes of our theatre, 70.
Mailing Address: 1 W 72nd St, New York, NY 10023.

MIHICH, VASA VELIZAR, see VASA

MIKUS, ELEANORE
Painter, Instructor
b Detroit, Mich, July 25, 27.
Study & Training: Art Stud League New York; study in Cent Europe; Univ Denver, BFA & MA.
Work in Public Collections: Mus Mod Art & Whitney Mus Am Art, New York, N Y; Cincinnati Mus, Ohio; Los Angeles Co Mus Art, Calif; Indianapolis Mus Art, Ind.
Exhibitions: One-woman shows, Pace Gallery, Boston, Mass, 63, Pace Gallery, New York, 64 & 65, O K Harris Gallery, New York, 71 & 72.
Teaching: Asst prof painting, Monmouth Col, 66-70; vis instr painting, Cooper Union, 70-
Awards: Guggenheim Found fel in painting, 66-67; Ford Found Tamarind fel in lithography, 68.
Dealer: O K Harris Gallery, 469 W Broadway, New York, NY 10012.
Mailing Address: 429 Broome St, New York, NY 10013.

MILCH, HAROLD CARLTON
Art Dealer
b New York, N Y, Jan 2, 08.
Study & Training: City Col New York, BA; Sch Art, Columbia Univ.
Positions: Pres, Milch & Vogel Art Gallery, New York, 29-34; assoc of Milch Galleries, 35-51; pres, E & A Milch, Inc (Milch Galleries), 51-
Memberships: Art Dealers Asn Am (pres, 68-70; bd dirs, presently); Friends of Whitney Mus Am Art; Metrop Mus Art; Am Fedn Arts; Arch Am Art.
Specialty of Gallery: American painting.
Art Interests: Assisted in formulating some of the great American collections, both with museums and privately.
Mailing Address: 1014 Madison Ave, New York, NY 10021.

MILES, CYRIL
Painter, Instructor
Preferred Media: Acrylics, Collage.
b Boston, Mass, June 13, 18.
Study & Training: Wayne State Univ, BS, 42, MA, 43.
Work in Public Collections: IBM Bldg, Southfield, Mich; Metrop Fed Savings Bank, Detroit, Mich; Mfrs Bank, Detroit; Mich Acad Arts & Sci, Ann Arbor.
Commissions: Happening: Italian, Bloomfield Art Asn, Mich, 65; Happening: U S A, Northamerican, Mex Cult Inst, Mexico City, Mex, 67; Happening: U S A, Detroit Artist Mkt, 67; Happening: U S A, Downing Mus Art, Calif, 67.
Exhibitions: Int Watercolor Exhib, Art Inst Chicago, 42; Drawing U S A, Saint Paul, Minn, 65; one-man shows, Northamerican Mex Cult Inst, 67 & Downey Mus Art, 68; Premier Invenaire Int Poesie Elementaire, Paris, 68.
Teaching: Instr painting, Detroit Inst Art, 42-67; supvr art, Highland Park Pub Schs, 50-64; instr art, Highland Park Community Col, 42-; ed, African Art Coloring Book, 71-
Awards: Mich Watercolor Soc Award; Mich Acad Art & Sci; one of ten best films at Rochester, N Y, 67.
Bibliography: Jean Paul Slusser (auth), Art in review, Ann Arbor News, 10/1/64; Marie De Larson (auth), Cyril Miles, Manana/ S A Lago Rasna 37, 7/29/67; Jean-Francois Bory (auth), Once again (poetry anthology), New Directions, 68.
Memberships: Mich Acad Arts & Sci; Mich Watercolor Soc (chmn, 55); Mus Mod Art; Detroit Inst of Art Founders Soc; hon mem Detroit Soc Women Painters.
Publications: Auth, Knee-deep in poetry, Rubiner Art Gallery, Royal Oak, Mich, 66; auth, Environment or happening thing, single issue newspaper, 67; contribr, Critical review of Moholy Nagy, 6/71 & Book review, Hans Richter, 6/72, J Aesthet & Art Criticism.
Dealer: Arts Extended Gallery, Inc, 1549 Broadway, Detroit, MI 48226.
Mailing Address: 17711 Hamilton Rd, Detroit, MI 48203.

MILES, JEANNE PATTERSON
Painter, Sculptor
Preferred Media: Oils.
b Baltimore, Md.
Study & Training: George Washington Univ, BFA; Grande Chaumiere, Paris, France; also with Marcel Gromaire, Paris.
Work in Public Collections: Guggenheim Mus, New York, N Y; New York Univ Collection; William Munster Proctor Mus, Utica, N Y; Andrew C White Mus, Cornell Univ; Santa Barbara Mus, Calif.
Commissions: Mural designs for Kentile Co, Kansas City, 60, Los Angeles, 62, Atlanta, Ga, 63, mural symbolic design, Chicago, Ill, 64 & rm divider in geometric design, N Y, 65.

Exhibitions: Ten Years at Betty Parsons Gallery, New York, 54; Mysticism in Art, Rome-New York Found, Rome 57; Geometric Art, Whitney Mus Am Art, New York, 63; The Square in Art Traveling Show, Am Fedn Art, 68-69; Gedok, Am Woman Artists Show, Hamburg, Ger, 72.
Teaching: Docent, Mus Non Objective Art, New York, 45-50; dir art dept, Moravian Col Women, 48-51; docent, Guggenheim Mus, New York, 51-52; asst dir painting & life drawing, Oberlin Col, 52-53; instr painting, N Y Inst Technol, 68-69.
Awards: C C Ladd study scholar, 39-40; Am Inst Arts & Lett emergency grant, 69; Mark Rothko Found grant, 71.
Bibliography: Patricia Wilson (auth), Sculptor by Jeanne Miles, Christian Sci Monitor, 68; Collette Roberts (auth), tape, New York Univ Arch, 68; article, In: Art Now, New York, 69.
Memberships: Am Abstr Artists.
Mailing Address: 463 West St, Apt A 1103, New York, NY 10014.

MILETTI, CLEMENCE M
Painter, Instructor
Preferred Media: Watercolors, Oils, Woods.
b New York, N Y.
Study & Training: Pratt Inst, cert teacher training; New York Univ, BS(educ), MS(educ); Columbia Teachers Col; Art Stud League New York; Univ Wis; also with Dong Kingman, William Zorach & Pietro Montana.
Exhibitions: Knickerbocker Artists, New York, 54; Mexican Paintings, Burr Gallery, 56; Grand Nat, Am Artists Prof League, Nat Arts Club, New York, 57 & Lever House, New York, 72; Art Chmns Asn Exhib, New York, 72.
Teaching: Instr fine arts, Newton H S, New York, 36-55, chmn dept fine arts, 55-
Memberships: Am Artists Prof League; Art Chmns Asn, New York; Art Teachers Asn; Nat Art Educ Asn.
Publications: Auth, Museum atmosphere in school, Art Educ J, Vol 15, No 2.
Mailing Address: 3743 90th St, Jackson Heights, New York, NY 11372.

MILLER, BARBARA DARLENE
Painter, Instructor
Preferred Media: Acrylics, Intaglio.
b Jarbidge, Nev.
Study & Training: Univ Wash, BA; Univ Hawaii, MEd; etching with Rudy Pozzatti & Gabor Peterdi; design with Clayton Rippey; painting with Tadashi Sato.
Work in Public Collections: Lahaina Art Gallery, Maui, Hawaii; State Found Cult & Arts, Honolulu, Hawaii; Village Gallery, Kaanapali, Maui; Univ Hawaii Art Dept Etching Collection.
Commissions: Acrylic mural, KPOI Radio, Waikiki, Honolulu, 68; acrylic painting Christ with thorns, Church of Good Shepherd, Kahului, Maui, 70; acrylic painting Buddah, Kahului Hongwanji Mission, Maui, 72; Mosaics (film), State Found & Maui Arts Coun, 72.
Exhibitions: Volunteer Park Art Mus, Seattle, Wash, 49; Regional Hawaii Painting & Sculpture Exhib, Fort Ruger, Honolulu & State Tour, 62; Nat Walker Art Ctr, Minneapolis, Minn, 65; Painters of Hawaii Circulating Exhib, 69; Etchings, Hawaii State Libr, 70; Regional Ethel Baldwin Mem, Wailuku, 72; plus others.
Teaching: Art instr Hilo High Sch, 57-60; elem art specialist, Kahului Elem Sch, 64-68; art instr, Maui Community Col, 68-
Positions: Artist, Logos layouts, KPOI Radio, 65-67; art dir, KHVH Radio-TV, Honolulu, 67-68; free-lance muralist.
Awards: Awards & prizes, Hawaii Artists Exhibs, 65-72; State Found Cult & Art Purchase Award, 72.
Bibliography: Eileen Webster (auth), Milady of the week—Barbara Miller & Darrell Neilson (auth), Works of Mrs Miller, 68, Maui News; Tim Mitchell (auth), Art news—Barbara Miller painter, Honolulu Mag, 69.
Memberships: Maui Arts Coun (visual arts chmn, 68-72); Hui Noeau Art Soc (past pres, bd mem & mem bd dir); Nat Art Educ Asn.
Publications: Illusr, Festival of arts (cover design), 69; co-auth, Grass roots, Poetry & Art (20 page bk), 70; illusr, cover of Our changing times, Univ Hawaii Div Continuing Educ, 70.
Dealer: Village Gallery-Whalers Village, Kaanapali, Maui, HI 96753.
Mailing Address: Maui Community College, 3100 Kaahumanu Ave, Kahului, Maui, HI 96753.

MILLER, DANIEL DAWSON
Painter, Sculptor
Preferred Media: Watercolors.
b Pittsburgh, Pa, July 7, 28.
Study & Training: Lafayette Col, BFA, 51; Pa State Univ, summers with Hobson Pittman; Pa Acad Fine Arts, 55-59; Univ Pa, MFA, 58.

Work in Public Collections: Pa Acad Fine Arts, Philadelphia; Philadelphia Mus Art, Pa; Rutgers Mus, New Brunswick, N J; Wilmington Soc Fine Arts, Del; Dickinson Col, Carlisle, Pa.
Exhibitions: 11 Modern American Artists, Rahr Mus, Manitowoc, Wis, 63; 158th-162nd Ann Exhib, Pa Acad Fine Arts, Philadelphia, 63-67.
Teaching: Instr life & still life painting, Philadelphia Mus Art, 62-; instr life painting, Pa Acad Fine Arts, 64-; instr art & head fine arts dept, Eastern Col, St Davids, Pa, 64-
Positions: Mem bd, Fellowship of Pa Acad Fine Arts, 62-
Awards: Prize for oil, Del Ann, Del Soc Fine Arts, 60; May Audubon Post Prize, 61 & Bertha M Goldberg Mem Award, 70, Fellowship of Pa Acad Fine Arts.
Memberships: Philadelphia Watercolor Club.
Dealer: Gallery by the Hill, 8139 Germantown Ave, Philadelphia, PA 19118.
Mailing Address: Box 108, Christiana, PA 17509.

MILLER, DONALD
Art Critic, Writer
b Pittsburgh, Pa, Dec 21, 34.
Study & Training: Univ Pittsburgh, AB; Am Fedn Artists Critics Workshop, with Barbara Novak, 70.
Teaching: Lectr Rebels Mod Art, Community Col Allegheny Co, Pittsburgh, winter 72; lectr Rebels Mod Art, Westmoreland Co Mus Art, Greensburg, Pa, spring 72.
Positions: Art critic, Pittsburgh Post-Gazette, 66-
Publications: Auth, Vasarely's dream, 70, auth, The imaginative art of Jean Ipousteguy, 70, auth, Ernest Trova as Neo-Surrealist, 70 & auth, The 1970 Pittsburgh International, Art Int, 71; auth, One man's search for outstanding African art (Jay C Leff Collection), Connoisseur, 71.
Mailing Address: Pittsburgh Post-Gazette, Pittsburgh, Pa 15222.

MILLER, DONALD RICHARD
Sculptor
Preferred Media: Bronze, Stone, Wood, Terra Cotta.
b Erie, Pa, June 30, 25.
Study & Training: Dayton Art Inst, 47-52; Pratt Inst, 55-57; Art Stud League New York, 58-61; also with Ulysses A Ricci, 56-60.
Work in Public Collections: Dayton Art Inst, Ohio; William Farnsworth Art Mus, Rockland, Maine; Medallic Art Co, New York, N Y; Div Numismatics, Smithsonian Inst.
Commissions: Bookcase with four relief panels, Dr Gerd Fenchel, New York, 59; two gargoyles, Washington Cathedral, 60; music stand with relief, private collection, Philadelphia, Pa, 63; Tex O'Rourke (portrait), Lamb's Club, New York, 64; Thoreau Medal, Soc Medalists, 67.
Exhibitions: Pa Acad Fine Arts, Philadelphia, 53; Mus Fine Arts, Springfield, Mass, 63-70; Allied Artists Am, 63-72; Nat Acad Design, 67-72; Nat Sculpture Soc, 67-72.
Awards: Mrs Louis Bennett Prize, Nat Sculpture Soc, 68; Miriam B Beline Mem Award, Allied Artists Am, 69; Springfield Acad Artists Asn Award, 72.
Memberships: Fel Nat Sculpture Soc (chmn exhib comn; ed bd, Nat Sculpture Rev, 67); Soc Animal Artists (exhib comt, 67); fel Am Artists Prof League (bd dirs, 67); Allied Artists Am (mem comt, 63); Acad Artists Asn, Springfield, Mass.
Dealer: Gallery Madison 90, 1248 Madison Ave, New York, NY 10028.
Mailing Address: 900 Riverside Dr, New York, NY 10032.

MILLER, DOROTHY CANNING
Museum Curator
b Hopedale, Mass.
Study & Training: Smith Col, BA, LHD, 59.
Collections Arranged: Many exhibs, Mus Mod Art, 36-69.
Positions: Asst to dir, Mus Mod art, 34, assoc cur painting & sculpture, 35-43, cur painting & sculpture, 43-47, cur mus collections, 47-67, sr cur painting & sculpture, 67-69; art adv, var collectors, cols & corp, 69-
Publications: Ed, 12 Americans, 56, The new American painting, 58, 16 Americans, 59, Americans 1963 & 20th century art from the Nelson Aldrich Rockefeller Collection, 69; plus many others.
Mailing Address: Museum of Modern Art, 11 W 53rd St, New York, NY 10019.

MILLER, EVA-HAMLIN
Painter, Educator
Preferred Media: Acrylics, Oils.
b Brooklyn, N Y.
Study & Training: Pratt Inst, BFA; Columbia Univ, MA; New York Univ, with Hale Woodruff; Art Stud League New York, with Charles Austin; Villa Schifanoia Sch Art, Florence, Italy; Univ Ibadan.

Work in Public Collections: N C Cent Univ, Durham; Am Fed Savings & Loan Bldg, Greensboro, N C; Johnson Publ Co, Chicago, Ill; Greensboro Nat Bank.
Commissions: Stained glass window, St James Presby Church, Greensboro, 61; four stained glass windows, St Mathews Methodist Church, Greensboro, 71; stained glass window, Shilo Baptist Church, Greensboro, 72.
Exhibitions: Links-Nat Assembly, Prudential Ctr, Boston, Mass, 67; Gallery Contemp Art, Winston-Salem, N C, 69 & 70; Int Art Exhib, New York Coliseum, 70; 15 Afro-American Women, N C Taylor Gallery, Greensboro, 70; Eva-Hamlin Miller, Washington & Lee Univ, Lexington, Va, 71; plus one other.
Teaching: Dir art, Tuskegee Inst, Ala, 33-36; dir art, Bennett Col, Greensboro, 37-41; supvr art, Greensboro City Schs, 42-53; chmn art dept, Winston-Salem Teachers Col, 59-63; assoc prof art, N C A&T State Univ, 63-, curator, Taylor Art Gallery, 67-
Awards: Southern area award, Links Inc, 67 & 72; Greensboro Artists League, 71.
Bibliography: Lewis & Waddy (auth), Black artists on art, Contemp Crafts, 69; Afro-American women in art, Alpha Kappa Alpha Sorority, 69.
Memberships: Am Fedn Arts; Int Soc Educ through Art; N C State Art Soc; Am Asn Mus; Greensboro Artists League (bd mem, 70-72); plus others.
Mailing Address: 1412 Benbow Rd, Greensboro, NC 27406.

MILLER, MRS G MACCULLOCH
Collector
Collection: Contemporary art.
Mailing Address: 10 Gracie Sq, New York, NY 10028.

MILLER, H McRAE
Sculptor, Painter
b Montreal, P Q, Nov 3, 95.
Study & Training: Art Stud League New York, with John Sloan; Beaux-Arts, Montreal, with Alfred Laliberte; also with C W Simpson & F S Coburn.
Work in Public Collections: Nat Gallery Can.
Commissions: Portrait sculpture, Que Prov Mus.
Exhibitions: Montreal Mus Fine Arts, 27-30 & 35-45; Royal Can Acad Art, 27-59; Nat Gallery Can, 50; Royal Can Acad, Quebec & Winnipeg, 60.
Positions: Sculptors' Soc Can, pres, 55-56.
Awards: Sculptors' Soc Can Award, 58; Royal Can Acad Art Award, 55.
Memberships: Assoc Royal Can Acad Art; fel Int Inst Arts & Lett.
Publications: Auth, Poems for Peggy, 66.
Mailing Address: R R 2, Range 6, Sainte Agathe des Monts, P Q, Can.

MILLER, HAROLD GEORGE
Painter, Designer
Preferred Media: Oils.
b Newport, Ky.
Study & Training: Cincinnati Acad Art; Nat Acad Design, with Dean Cornwell; Art Stud League New York, with Pruitt Carter.
Exhibitions: Allied Artists, Knickerbocker Artists, Burr Artists & Composers, Authors & Artists Am, New York, 60-; N J State Mus, 60-
Teaching: Private classes, 63-
Positions: Art dir, Fed Aviation Agency, New York, 46-49; chief art dir & v pres, Humphrey, Alley & Richards, New York, 49-57; art dir, Reach, McClinton, New York, 59-61; free lance artist, 61-
Awards: First prize for oil, 67 & 69, first prize for design, 69 & second prize for watercolor, 67, Composers, Authors & Artists Am.
Memberships: Allied Artist; Burr Artists (first v pres, 67-72); Composers, Authors & Artists Am; Salmagundi Club; Ridgewood Art Asn.
Mailing Address: c/o Thomson Gallery, 19 E 75th St, New York, NY 10021.

MILLER, LEON GORDON
Designer, Sculptor
b New York, N Y, Aug 3, 17.
Study & Training: N J State Teachers Col, BS; Art Stud League New York; Newark Sch Fine & Indust Art, CFA; Fawcett Art Sch, with Bernar Gussow; Baldwin Wallace Col, hon DFA, 71.
Work in Public Collections: Libr Cong, Washington, D C; Gertrude Stein Collection, Yale Univ.
Commissions: Stained glass windows, ceremonial sculpture & tapestries, Fairmont Temple, Cleveland, Ohio, Temple Israel, Gary, Ind; Temple Israel, Columbus, Ga; Temple Adath Jeshurun, Louisville, Ky & others, 60-68; metal wall sculpture, Avis Rent-A-Car Systs, Inc, New York, 67.

Exhibitions: 12 one-man shows, Paintings, Drawings, Prints & Photographs, 47-72; 4 shows, Nat Gold Medal Exhib, N Y Archit League, 55-60; Am Inst Architects Allied Arts Exhib, 58; Am Iron & Steel Inst Design in Steel Awards Prog, 63; Art in Worship Exhib, Am Craftsman's Coun, Mus Contemp Craft, 67.
Teaching: Instr indust design, Cleveland Inst Art, 47-50.
Positions: Pres, Leon Gordon Miller & Assocs, Inc, 47-; U S del, Int Coun Socs Indust Design, 59, 62 & 68, bd chmn, K V Design Int, Ltd, 71-; bd mem, fine arts adv bd, Rose Art Mus, 72-
Awards: Ann Awards Prog, 59, 62 & 68; silver medal outstanding design award, Indust Designers' Inst, 62; design/planning first award, Inst Bus Designer, 69 & 71.
Bibliography: Victoria Ball (auth), The art of interior design, Macmillan, 60; Western Reserve University firsts, Western Reserve Univ Sch Med Bull, 5/62; Avram Kamph (auth), Contemporary synagogue art, Union Am Hebrew Congregations, 66.
Memberships: Fel Indust Design Soc Am; Am Craftsman's Coun; Am Inst Architects Guild for Relig Archit; Stained Glass Asn Am; World Craft Coun.
Publications: Auth, The industrial designer—new member of the team, Cur, 63; co-auth, Lost heritage of Alaska, World Publ, 67; auth, Light by design, Gen Elec Co, 71.
Mailing Address: 1220 Huron Rd, Cleveland, OH 44115.

MILLER, MITCHELL
Collector
Mailing Address: 146 Central Park W, New York, NY 10023.

MILLER, NANCY
Sculptor, Painter
Preferred Media: Plexiglas, Paper.
b Lancaster, Ohio, Mar 31, 27.
Study & Training: Bennett Col; Md Inst Col Art.
Work in Public Collections: Small Sculpture, U S A & Graphics U S A, U S Info Agency.
Exhibitions: May Show, Columbus Gallery Fine Arts, Ohio, 62-71; All Ohio Painting & Sculpture, Dayton Art Inst, Ohio, 65-70; Midyear Show, Butler Inst Am Art, Youngstown, Ohio, 66; one-man shows, Huntington Trust Gallery, Columbus, 68 & Environ Gallery, New York, 70-72; Gilman Galleries, Chicago, Ill, 72.
Awards: Gallery prize, 67, purchase prize, Wittenberg Univ, 70 & sculpture award, 71, Columbus Gallery Fine Arts.
Memberships: Columbus Art League; Am Soc Contemp Artists.
Dealers: Gilman Galleries, 103 E Oak St, Chicago, IL 60611; Environment Gallery, 205 E 60th St, New York, NY 10022.
Mailing Address: 300 Scioto St, Urbana, OH 43078.

MILLER, RALPH RILLMAN
Painter, Designer
Preferred Media: Oils.
b Wayne, Pa, Dec 12, 15.
Study & Training: Columbia Univ, BS; study with Alexander Archipenko, U S & Nerina Simi, Florence, Italy.
Work in Public Collections: Mus of City of New York, N Y.
Exhibitions: Audubon Artists, New York, 64; Festival San Lorenzo, Florence, Italy, 70.
Collections Arranged: Many exhibs incl The Dutch Gallery, 66 & New York, the Scene, 67, Mus of City of New York.
Positions: Dir, Mus of City of New York, 60-70.
Awards: Gold medal, Festival of San Lorenzo, 70.
Memberships: Benjamin Franklin fel Royal Soc Arts; Am Asn Mus (exec comt, 66-70, treas, 67-71); N Y State Maritime Mus (trustee, 67-73).
Research: Technical property of painting with emphasis on seventeenth century Dutch and sixteenth century Italian technique.
Publications: Auth, They are coming (educ film), 70-71.
Mailing Address: 11 E 92nd St, New York, NY 10028.

MILLER, RICHARD KIDWELL
Painter
Preferred Media: Oils, Acrylics.
b Fairmont, W Va, Mar 15, 30.
Study & Training: Pa Acad Fine Arts; Am Univ, BA; Columbia Univ, MFA.
Work in Public Collections: Phillips Collection, Washington, D C; Edward Joseph Gallagher, III, Memorial Collection, Univ Ariz, Tucson; Columbia Univ; Rochester Mus Art, N Y; Albrecht Gallery, St Joseph, Mo.
Commissions: Painting, Plessey Corp, Gen Motors Bldg, New York, 71.
Exhibitions: Pa Acad Fine Arts Ann, Philadelphia, 56-62; Salon Nat Paris, France, 58; Whitney Mus Am Art Ann, New York, 60; Carnegie Int, Pittsburgh, Pa, 62; Tokyo Int, Japan, 66.
Teaching: Asst prof painting, Kansas City Art Inst, 68-69.

Awards: Gertrude Vanderbilt Whitney Scholar, Nat Inst Arts & Lett, 48-56; Washington Times-Herald scholar, 47; Fulbright fel, 53.
Dealer: Peter Rose Gallery, 320 W 52nd St, New York, NY 10019.
Mailing Address: 222 W 83rd St, Apt 8C, New York, NY 10024.

MILLER, RICHARD McDERMOTT
Sculptor
Preferred Media: Wax, Bronze.
b New Philadelphia, Ohio, Apr 30, 22.
Study & Training: Cleveland Inst Art, 40-42, 49-51, grad 51.
Work in Public Collections: Sheldon Mem Art Gallery, Lincoln, Nebr; Univ Houston, Tex; Butler Inst Am Art, Youngstown, Ohio; Canton Art Inst, Ohio; Massillon Mus, Ohio.
Exhibitions: Five one-man shows, Peridot Gallery, New York, N Y, 64-71; one-man shows, Holland Gallery, Chicago, Ill, 65, Feingarten Gallery, Los Angeles, Calif, 66 & Alwin Gallery, London, Eng, 68; group show, American Sculpture, Univ Nebr, Lincoln, 70.
Teaching: Instr sculpture, Queens Col, 67-
Awards: Page scholar, Cleveland Inst Art, 52; purchase award, Butler Inst Am Art, 70.
Bibliography: Sidney Tillim (auth), Richard Miller, primary realist, Artforum, summer 67; Gabriel Laderman (auth), Unconventional realists, Artforum, 3/71; Grace Glueck (auth), A new realism in sculpture?, Art in Am, 12/71.
Memberships: Alliance of Figurative Artists (prog chmn, 70-72).
Publications: Auth, Figure sculpture in wax & plaster, Watson-Guptill, 71.
Dealer: Washburn Gallery, 820 Madison Ave, New York, NY 10021.
Mailing Address: 53 Mercer St, New York, NY 10013.

MILLER, MRS ROBERT WATT
Patron
b Oakland, Calif, July 20, 98.
Positions: Sponsor, Harry Lehman Show, Maxwell Gallery, San Francisco; chmn, Van Gogh Show; chmn, Faberge Show; chmn, San Francisco Opera Guild, 50-52; chmn, Ital Festival, San Francisco, 59; chmn, De Young Mem Mus Soc, 61-63; former mem bd trustees, Childrens Hosp, San Francisco; co-chmn, Golden Anniversary, United Bay Area Crusade; mem bd trustees, United Bay Area Crusade; hon chmn, Golden Anniversary, San Francisco Opera Asn.
Awards: Ital Cross Solidarity, San Francisco, 59.
Art Interests: Presentation of shows in museums.
Mailing Address: 1021 California St, San Francisco, CA 94108.

MILLER, SAMUEL CLIFFORD
Museum Director
b Roseburg, Ore, May 6, 30.
Study & Training: Stanford Univ, BA; Inst Fine Arts, New York Univ, grad study; also in Japan, Europe & Mex.
Positions: Asst to dir, Nat Serigraph Soc & Meltzer Gallery, N Y, 56-61; asst to dir, Albright-Knox Art Gallery, Buffalo, N Y, 64-67; asst dir, Newark Mus Asn, 67, mus dir, 68-
Memberships: Am Asn Mus; Northeast Mus Conf; Mus Coun N J; Am Fedn Arts; Asn Art Mus Dirs; plus others.
Mailing Address: Newark Museum Association, 49 Washington St, Newark, NJ 07101.

MILLIKEN, GIBBS
Painter, Educator
b Houston, Tex, Dec 15, 35.
Study & Training: Scheiner Inst; Univ Colo; Trinity Univ, BSc; Cranbrook Acad Art, MFA.
Work in Public Collections: Cranbrook Acad Art; Montgomery Mus Fine Arts, Ala; Serv League, Longview, Tex; Butler Inst Am Art.
Exhibitions: Trinity Univ, 60, 61 & 68; San Antonio Artists, Witte Mus, 60-68; Tex Ann Painters & Sculptors, Witte Mus, Corpus Christi, Beaumont Mus & Dallas Mus Fine Arts, 62-66; Bucknell Univ, 67; Tex Fine Arts Comn, Hemisfair, San Antonio, 68; plus many other group & one-man shows.
Teaching: Instr painting & drawing, Cranbrook Acad Art, Bloomfield Hills, Mich, 64 & 65; instr art, Univ Tex, Austin, 65-69, asst prof, 69-
Positions: Asst, Univ Colo Mus; former artist, photographer, asst cur, cur & head dept exhibs, Witte Mem Mus, San Antonio.
Awards: Grumbacher Award, 64, Naylor Award, 66 & Freeman Purchase Prize, 67, Tex Watercolor Soc, Witte Mem Mus; plus many others.
Memberships: Am Fedn Arts; Am Asn Univ Prof; Men of Art Guild; Contemp Artists Group.
Mailing Address: Dept of Art, University of Texas at Austin, Austin, TX 78712.

MILLONZI, VICTOR
Sculptor
Preferred Media: Neon.
b Buffalo, N Y.
Study & Training: Albright Art Sch, BA; Univ Buffalo, BA(art educ); Columbia Univ, MA.
Work in Public Collections: Nat Collection Fine Arts, Washington, D C; Corcoran Gallery Art, Washington, D C; Albright-Knox Art Gallery, Buffalo; State Mus N J, Trenton; Mus Mod Art, New York, N Y.
Commissions: Mural, Nat Broadcasting Co, Rockefeller Ctr, New York, 70.
Exhibitions: Art in Process, Finch Col Mus, New York, 66; Stedelijk Van Abbemuseum, Eindhoven, Holland, 66; Light, Motion, Space, Walker Art Ctr, Minneapolis, Minn, 67; Sculpture: The New York Scene, Riverside Mus, New York, 68; Focus on Light, N J State Mus, 69.
Bibliography: Light Art, Art in Am, 67.
Dealer: Bertha Schaefer Gallery, 41 E 57th St, New York, NY 10022.
Mailing Address: Box 232, Stone Ridge, NY 12484.

MILLS, FREDERICK VAN FLEET
Art Administrator, Educator
b Bremen Fairfield, Ohio, June 5, 25.
Study & Training: Ohio State Univ, BS, 49; Ind Univ, MS, 51, EdD, 56.
Teaching: Prof art & art educ & chmn dept art educ, Ind Univ, Bloomington, 59-66; chmn dept related arts, crafts, & interior design, Univ Tenn, Knoxville, 66-68; prof art & chmn dept, Ill State Univ, 68-; vis prof art, Univ Tex.
Positions: Pres, Ind Art Educ Asn, 56; ed, Western Arts Bull, 58-62.
Memberships: Nat Art Educ Asn (bd dirs, 64-66); Col Art Asn Am; Western Arts Asn (v pres, 62-64, pres, 64-66); Ill Art Educ Asn; Tenn Arts Coun.
Publications: Contribr, Western Arts Bull, 59 & 60; contribr, Sch Arts Mag, 59, 60, 69 & 70; contribr, Civil defense, Off President U S, 60; contribr, Arts & Activities Mag, 61, 66, 68 & 69; educ co-auth, As an artist sees, Ind Univ AV Ctr, 65.
Mailing Address: Dept of Art, Illinois State University, Normal, IL 61761.

MILLS, GEORGE THOMPSON
Educator, Writer
b East Cleveland, Ohio, May 8, 19.
Study & Training: Dartmouth Col, BA; Harvard Univ, MA & PhD.
Collections Arranged: Saints and Kachinas, 53; Penitentes of New Mexico and Colorado (with Richard Grove), 55.
Teaching: Prof sociol & anthrop, Lake Forest Col, presently.
Positions: Former cur, Taylor Mus; former asst dir, Colorado Springs Fine Arts Ctr, Colo.
Memberships: Am Asn Mus; Am Soc Aesthet; fel Am Anthrop Asn; AAAS; Soc Appl Anthrop.
Art Interests: Educational role of the art museums and with the relations of art and culture.
Publications: Auth, Navaho art and culture; contribr, articles, In: Col Art J, Am Anthropologist, Brand Bk & others.
Mailing Address: 705 S Green Bay St, Lake Forest, IL 60045.

MILLS, PAUL CHADBOURNE
Museum Curator
b Seattle, Wash, Sept 24, 24.
Study & Training: Reed Col, 45-48; Univ Wash, BA, 53; Univ Calif, Berkeley, MA, 61; Calif Col Arts & Crafts, hon PhD, 71.
Positions: Reporter, Bellevue Am, Wash, 48-51; asst cur, Henry Gallery, Univ Wash, 52-53; cur art, Oakland Mus, Calif, 53-70; v pres, Western Mus Conf, 56 & 59; dir, Santa Barbara Mus Art, 70-
Awards: Ford Found fel, 60-61.
Memberships: Western Asn Art Mus (v pres, 56-57, treas, 71-72); Am Asn Mus (prog chmn); Am Asn Art Mus Dirs (trustee, 71-72).
Publications: Auth, Early paintings of California, 56, An introduction to the art of William Keith, 56 & Contemporary bay area figurative paintings, 58; co-auth, The California missions of Edwin Deakin, 66.
Mailing Address: 1470 San Leandro Park Lane, Santa Barbara, CA 93103.

MILLS, ROBERT JAMES
Painter, Designer
Preferred Media: Watercolors.
b Columbia, S C, Oct 10, 20.
Study & Training: Univ S C; Booth Bay Harbor Art Colony, Maine.
Work in Public Collections: State House, Columbia, S C; S C State Arts Comn, Columbia; Seibels Bruce Ins Co; S C Nat Bank.
Commissions: Oil painting, Shakespeare Co, Columbia, 67; seascape oil painting, Charleston Savings & Loan Co, 71.

Exhibitions: Univ S C Faculty; S C Artist Guild, Columbia; Charleston Mus Art; Butler Inst Am Art, Youngstown, Ohio, 55; Southeastern Art Exhib, Atlanta, Ga, 64.
Teaching: Instr watercolor, drawing & grafic design, Univ S C, 66-
Awards: Southeastern Art Exhib Award; Columbia Mus Art Award, S C Arts Comn; S C Artist Guild Award.
Memberships: Columbia Mus Art; S C Artist Guild; Columbia Artist Guild.
Mailing Address: Rt 1, Box 246 A, Chapin, SC 29036.

MILLSAPS, DANIEL
Painter, Writer
Preferred Media: Watercolors.
b Darlington, S C, June 30, 29.
Study & Training: Univ S C, AB; Art Stud League New York, with Kuniyoshi, Sternberg, Martin Lewis & Nahum Tchbasov.
Work in Public Collections: Va Mus Fine Arts, Richmond; U S State Dept, Washington, D C; Columbia Mus Art, S C; Libr Cong, Washington, D C; Berkshire Mus, Pittsfield, Mass.
Exhibitions: Va Mus Fine Arts, 47; Delgado Mus, New Orleans, La, 48; Am Inst Graphic Arts, New York, N Y, 48; Univ Colo, Denver, 58; 10 yr retrospective, Columbia Mus Art, 66.
Positions: Ed & publ, Washington Int Arts Lett, 62-
Awards: Best woodcut & Va Mus Fine Arts Purchase Prize, 48; Am Inst Graphic Arts Award for 50 best, 48; Anthony Hampton Award, 50.
Research: Patronage of the arts; critic of government and arts relationships.
Publications: Auth & illusr, Sounds pretty, Harper & Row, 48; auth & illusr, Millsaps, first portfolio, Int Publ, 51; ed, Grants and aid to individuals in the arts, 70; ed, Private foundations active in the arts, Vol I, 71.
Mailing Address: 115 Fifth St S E, Washington, DC 20003.

MILTON, PETER WINSLOW
Printmaker
b Lower Merion, Pa, Apr 2, 30.
Study & Training: Yale Univ, BFA, 54, MFA, 62 with Josef Albers.
Work in Public Collections: Mus Mod Art New York, N Y; Philadelphia Mus Art, Pa; Metrop Mus, New York; Nat Collection Fine Arts, Washington, D C; Libr of Cong, Washington.
Exhibitions: Am Prints of the Sixties, Nat Collection Fine Arts, Washington, 65; American Graphic Workshops: 68, Cincinnati Art Mus, Ohio; 28 Amerikaanse Grafici, Rijkakademie, Amsterdam, Holland, 68; Primera Bienal Americana de Artes Graficas, 71 & one-man show, 72, Mus La Tertulia, Cali, Colombia; Nat Mus Mod Art Biennial, Seoul, Korea, 72; one-man show, 72, Corcoran Gallery Art, Washington, 72; plus 27 other one-man shows.
Teaching: Instr drawing & basic design, Maryland Inst Col Art, Baltimore, 61-68; instr printmaking, Yale Univ Summer Sch Music & Art, 70.
Awards: Louis Comfort Tiffany Found Grant in graphics, 64; first prize in graphics, 9th Columbian Festival de Arte, Mus La Tertula, 69; grand prize, Int Biennial Exhib Prints, Seoul, Korea, 72.
Bibliography: Irving Finkelstein (auth), Julia passing: the world of Peter Milton, Artist's Proof, 72; Harriet Shapiro (auth), All realism is visionary: a reach into the ambiguous realm of Peter Milton, Intellectual Digest, 11/72.
Dealers: Franz Bader Gallery, 2124 Pennsylvania Ave N W, Washington, DC 20037; Associated American Artists, 663 Fifth Ave, New York, NY 10022.
Mailing Address: P O Box 137, Francestown, NH 03043.

MINA-MORA, DORISE OLSON
Painter
Preferred Media: Watercolors, Acrylics.
b New York, N Y, June 8, 32.
Study & Training: Art Stud League New York, with Mr Hale & Louis Bosa; Salmagundi Club scholar & study with Daniel Greene.
Work in Public Collections: Six works at Southampton High Sch.
Exhibitions: Brooklyn Mus Community Galleries, 68-71; Nat Arts Club Watercolor Ann, 68-72; Catharine Lorillard Wolfe Art Club Exhib, Nat Acad Design, 70 & 71; Nat Acad Design, Allied Artists Am, 70-72; Parrish Art Mus Spring Watercolor Show, 72.
Awards: Gold medal of hon, Knickerbocker Artists, 68 & Nat Art League, 70; Grumbacher Award for watercolor, Nat Arts Club, 70.
Memberships: Nat Arts Club; Nat Art League; Allied Artists Am; Catharine Lorillard Wolfe Art Club; Am Artists Prof League.
Mailing Address: 106-20 Shore Front Parkway, Rockaway Park, NY 11694.

MINA-MORA, RAUL JOSE
Painter, Illustrator
b Santa Anna, El Salvador, Mar 13, 15; U S citizen.
Study & Training: San Francisco Acad Advan Arts; Art Stud League New York, with Howard Traffton; also with Daniel Gree, Harte, Austria.
Work in Public Collections: South Hampton High Sch Permanent Collection, N Y; Freid Corp.
Exhibitions: Brooklyn Mus, N Y, 71; Nat Art Club, 71; Nat Soc Casein Painters; Salmagundi Club, 71; Parrish Art Mus, N Y, 71 & 72.
Teaching: Archit design & visual archit, Rudolp Shapher Sch Design; instr design, San Francisco Sch Design.
Positions: Creative dir, Hanna Advert Co, 47-48.
Awards: Guldi Award, Parrish Art Mus, 71; first prize for abstr, Brooklyn Art Mus, 71; silver medal, Nat Art Club, 71.
Memberships: Salmagundi Art Club; Am Artist Prof League; Nat Soc Casein & Acrylic Painters; Knickerbocker Artists New York; Nat Art League.
Publications: Illusr for, Fortune Mag, 65, Rutledge, 69, Macmillan, 69, Cronwell-Colliers, 69 & Holt, Rinehart & Winston, 71.
Mailing Address: 106-20 Shore Front Parkway, Rockaway Park, NY 11694.

MINER, DOROTHY EUGENIA
Museum Curator, Art Historian
b New York, N Y, Nov 4, 04.
Study & Training: Columbia Univ, BA, 26; 28-31; Bedford Col, Univ London, 26-27.
Collections Arranged: Illuminated Books of the Middle Ages & Renaissance, Baltimore, 49; The World Encompassed, 52 (in collab); The History of Bookbinding 525-1950, 57; The International Style, 1962 (in collab); 2000 Years of Calligraphy, 1965 (in collab); plus many smaller ones.
Teaching: Asst medieval art, Barnard Col, New York, 31-32; vis lectr medieval art, Johns Hopkins Univ, Baltimore, Md, 47, 51, 60, 63, 64 & 66; adj prof medieval mss, N Y Univ summer session in Brussels, 62.
Positions: Asst, Pierpont Morgan Libr, New York, 33-34; libr & keeper of mss, Walters Art Gallery, Baltimore, 34-
Awards: Rosenbach fel bibliography, Rosenbach Found, Philadelphia, 55; H P Kraus lectureship in ms illum, Yale Univ, 70.
Memberships: Col Art Asn Am (dir, 59-62); Int Ctr Medieval Art (adv coun, 67-); Mediaeval Acad Am; Renaissance Soc Am; Soc Scribes & Illuminators, London (hon).
Research: Present concerns with Jean Pucelle & his atelier; fifteenth-century Paris and Dutch illumination; early bookbinding; medieval atelier methods.
Publications: Co-auth, Proverbes en rimes, 37; auth, Illuminated books of the Middle Ages & Renaissance, 49; History of bookbinding 525-1900 A D, 57; ed, Studies in art & literature for Belle da Costa Greene, 54; co-auth, International style, 62.
Mailing Address: Walters Art Gallery, Charles & Centre St, Baltimore, MD 21201.

MINNICK, ESTHER TRESS
Painter
Preferred Media: Watercolors.
b Chicago, Ill.
Study & Training: Art Stud League New York, N Y; also with Edgar Whitney, Wong Suiling & Barbara Vassilioff.
Work in Public Collections: Va State Col; Mem Hosp, New York; also many pvt collections.
Exhibitions: Nat Women's Republican Club, New York, 67; Nat Soc Painters Casein & Travel Exhib, New York, 68; Garden State Watercolor Soc, Princeton, N J, 70; Princeton Art Asn, 71; Am Artists Prof League, New York; plus others.
Awards: First award, Larchmont, 60; first & third prizes, Nat Women's Republican Club, 67; award, Princeton Bank, 70.
Memberships: Knickerbocker Artists; Catharine Lorillard Wolfe Art Club.
Mailing Address: 95 Gloucester Way, Jamesburg, NJ 08831.

MINTICH, MARY RINGELBERG
Sculptor, Craftsman
Preferred Media: Metals, Plastics, Clay.
b Detroit, Mich.
Study & Training: Albion Col; Ind Univ, BA; Queens Col; Univ Tenn; Univ N C, Greensboro, MFA.
Work in Public Collections: Everson Mus Art, Syracuse, N Y; Mint Mus Art, Charlotte, N C; N C Nat Bank, Charlotte; Sea Islands Develop Corp, Ga; Sacred Heart Col, Belmont, N C.
Exhibitions: 24th Ceramics Nat, 66 & 25th Ceramics Nat, 68, Everson Mus, Syracuse; Piedmont Painting & Sculpture & Piedmont Craft Expos (11 state regionals), Mint Mus, Charlotte, 71; Spring Mills Traveling Exhib.
Teaching: Asst prof sculpture, painting & ceramics, Sacred Heart

Col, 67-; instr enameling, Penland Sch Crafts, 72; instr, Winthrop Col, 72-
Awards: Ferro Corp Purchase Award; purchase award, Mint Mus Art.
Memberships: Am Crafts Coun (state rep, 69-71); Piedmont Craftsmen (standards comt, 72-); Nat Art Educ Asn.
Publications: Illusr, Red clay reader, 68.
Dealers: McDonald Art Gallery, 753 Providence Rd, Charlotte, NC; 28207; Gallery 501, 501 Hempstead Pl, Charlotte, NC 28207.
Mailing Address: P O Box 913, 515 Dogwood Lane, Belmont, NC 28012.

MINTZ, HARRY
Painter
Preferred Media: Oils.
b Sept 27, 09; U S citizen.
Work in Public Collections: Art Inst Chicago, Ill; New Evansville Mus, Ind; Whitney Mus Am Art, New York; Tel-Aviv Mod Mus Art, Israel; Rio de Janeiro Mus Art, Brazil; plus others.
Exhibitions: Art Inst Chicago, 34-63; Whitney Mus Am Art, New York, N Y; Venice Biennale, Italy; Denver Art Mus, Colo, 63; Corcoran Gallery Art, Washington, D C; plus many other group & one-man shows.
Teaching: Assoc prof, Art Inst Chicago.
Awards: Hon mentions, 38 & 53, Jules F Brower Prize, 52 & 54 & Silver's Prize, 62, Art Inst Chicago.
Mailing Address: 429 W Briar Pl, Chicago, IL 60657.

MIRVISH, DAVID
Art Dealer
b Toronto, Ont, Aug 29, 44.
Positions: Dir, David Mirvish Gallery.
Specialty of Gallery: Twentieth century art.
Mailing Address: David Mirvish Gallery, 596 Markham St, Toronto 4, Ont, Can.

MISS, MARY
Sculptor
b New York, N Y, May 27, 44.
Study & Training: Univ Calif, Santa Barbara, BA, 66; Rinehart Sch Sculpture, Md Art Inst, Baltimore, MFA, 68.
Exhibitions: Whitney Mus Am Art Sculpture Ann, New York, 70; Twenty-six Contemporary Women Artists, Larry Aldrich Mus, Ridgefield, Conn, 71; Thirteen Women, 117 Prince St, New York, 72; GEDOK - Am Women Artists, Hamburg, Ger, 72.
Teaching: Instr, Univ Colo, Colorado Springs Ctr, summer 70; instr, Sch Visual Arts, New York, spring 72; vis artist, Univ R I, summer 72.
Bibliography: Marjorie Wellish (auth), Material extensions in new sculpture, Arts Mag, summer 71; Germano Celant (auth), Informazione negata, Domus, 1/72; Lawrence Alloway (auth), Art, The Nation, 3/27/72.
Memberships: Women's Ad Hoc Comt.
Dealer: 55 Mercer Gallery, 55 Mercer, New York, NY 10013.
Mailing Address: Box 304, Canal St Sta, New York, NY 10013.

MITCHELL, BRUCE KIRK
Painter
Preferred Media: Oils.
b Salt Lake City, Utah, July 31, 33.
Study & Training: Univ Utah, BS.
Exhibitions: Am Artist Prof League, Lever House, N Y, 71 & 72; Mainstreams, Marietta Col Int, 72.
Memberships: Am Artist Prof League.
Mailing Address: c/o Heritage Gallery, 9N, Keene, NY 12942.

MITCHELL, CLIFFORD
Painter, Architect
Preferred Media: Oils, Watercolors, Graphics.
b Birmingham, Ala, Sept 22, 25.
Study & Training: Tuskegee Inst, BS, 49; Univ Hartford Art Sch, BFA, 58.
Work in Public Collections: New Britain Mus Am Art, Conn; Low Haywood Sch, Stamford, Conn; Univ Conn Sch Pharm, Storrs, Conn; James E Cook Elem Sch, Saint Louis, Mo; Stamford Mus & Nature Ctr, Stamford; plus others.
Exhibitions: Silvermine Guild Artists New Eng Exhib, New Canaan, Conn, 64; Twelve New England Artists, Slater Mem Mus, Norwich, Conn, 68; Am Watercolor Soc Ann, New York, N Y, 69; Audubon Artists Ann, New York, 70; Galerie-8 Watercolor, Print & Drawing Nat, Erie, Pa, 70; plus others.
Teaching: Instr interior design, eve course, Univ Hartford Art Sch, 68-69.
Positions: Painter, studio, Hartford, 59-; architect, Golden-Thornton-La Bau Architects, Hartford, 72-

Awards: Two best in show awards for oil & watercolor paintings, New Haven Arts Festival, 59; Larry Aldrich Award, Silvermine Guild Artists, 60; past pres prize, Conn Watercolor Soc, 70; plus others.

Bibliography: Janet Gaston (auth), Aux etats-unis/a New York salon audubon, La Rev Mod, 60; J V W B (auth), Works by Mitchell at local mus, New Britain Herald, 68; Jolene Goldenthal (auth), Look at art/an architect turns artist, Hartford Courant, 71.

Memberships: Conn Acad Fine Arts; Conn Watercolor Soc (pres, 70-72); Silvermine Guild Artists; Nat Soc Interior Designers (pres, Conn Chap, 69-72); Am. Inst Architects.

Dealer: Silvermine Guild of Artists, Silvermine, New Canaan, CT 06840.

Mailing Address: 105 W Euclid St, Hartford, CT 06112.

MITCHELL, DANA COVINGTON, JR
Collector
b Bluefield, W Va, Feb 22, 18.
Study & Training: Univ W Va, BA & MD.
Positions: Pres bd trustees, Columbia Mus Art, 60-61.
Collection: Contemporary American art.
Mailing Address: 600 Spring Lake Rd, Columbia, SC 29206.

MITCHELL, ELEANOR
Fine Arts Specialist, Librarian
b Orange, N J, Apr 4, 07.
Study & Training: Douglass Col, New Brunswick, N J, BA, 28; Columbia Univ Sch Libr Serv, BS, 29; Carnegie summer scholar, Inst Art & Archaeol, Univ Paris, 32; Harvard Univ, 34; Smith Col, MA, 36; additional studies art, languages & music, Univ Florence, Carnegie Inst, Univ Pittsburgh & George Washington Univ; Douglass Col, LittD, 68.
Positions: Asst cur bks & photog, art dept, Smith Col, 29-36; asst, Grad House, Florence, Italy, 36-37; librn, dept fine arts, Univ Pittsburgh, 37-42; asst to dir, Bibliot Pub Estado Jalisco, Guadalajara, Mex, 42-43; chief art div, N Y Pub Libr, 43-52; prog specialist, cult activities dept, UNESCO, Paris, France, 48-49; dir libr serv, U S Info Serv, Italy, 51-54; consult fine arts, Libr Cong, Washington, D C, 54-55; consult, Montclair Free Pub Libr, 55; U S specialist, Int Educ Exchange Serv, Bibliot Pub Dept, Cali, 55-56; U S specialist, Dept State, Univ Antioquia, Medellín, Columbia, 56-57; exec dir fine arts comt, People-to-People Prog, Corcoran Gallery, 57-61; specialist, Bks for the People Fund, Inc, Pan Am Union, Washington, D C, 61-62; bibliog asst, Rockefeller Found, Proj Int Rice Res Int-Philippines, Washington, D C, 62-63; consult, Hisp Found, Libr Cong, 63; libr consult, Univ Católica, Quito, Ecuador, under Saint Louis Univ-Agency Int Develop contract, 63-68; proj off, Int Rels Off, Am Libr Asn, Washington, D C, 69-72.
Memberships: Am Libr Asn; Soc Int Develop; Soc Women Geogr; Am Asn Mus.
Publications: Contribr, articles, In: Gazette Beaux-Arts, Col Res Libr, N Y Pub Libr Bull, Art Educ Bull & Douglass Alumnae Bull, 37-61.
Mailing Address: 730 24th St N W, Washington, DC 20037.

MITCHELL, (MADISON) FRED
Painter
b Meridian, Miss, Nov 24, 23.
Study & Training: Carnegie Inst Technol; Accad Belle Arti, Rome, Italy; Cranbrook Acad Art, BFA & MFA.
Work in Public Collections: Cranbrook Acad Mus, Bloomfield Hills, Mich.
Commissions: Archit screen, Miss State Col Women.
Exhibitions: Dallas Mus Fine Arts, 55; Cranbrook Acad Art, 57; Rome-New York Found, Rome, Italy, 58; Carnegie Int, 61; one-man show, White Art Mus, Cornell Univ, 69; plus many other group & one-man shows.
Teaching: Instr, adult classes Riverdale Neighborhood House, N Y, 53; instr design, Finch Col, N Y, 54; instr painting, Positano Art Workshop, Italy, summer 56; instr drawing & painting, Cranbrook Acad Art, 55-59; instr drawing & painting, New York Univ, 61; artist-in-residence, Columbia Mus Art, S C.
Positions: Critic, Pictures on Exhib, N Y, 52-53; vis critic art, Cornell Univ, 69.
Awards: Pepsi-Cola fel painting, 48.
Mailing Address: 92 Hester St, New York, NY 10002.

MITCHELL, HENRY (WEBER)
Sculptor
b Canton, Ohio, Aug 27, 15.
Study & Training: Princeton Univ, AB; Tyler Sch Fine Arts, Temple Univ, MFA; Acad Brera, Milan, Italy, with Marino Marini.
Work in Public Collections: Philadelphia Mus Art; Pa Acad Fine Arts; Wilmington Soc Fine Arts; Provident Nat Bank, Philadelphia, Pa; John Wanamaker, King of Prussia, Pa; plus others.

Commissions: Fountain, Philadelphia Mus Art; Impala fountain, Philadelphia Zoo; two sculptures, Philadelphia Free Libr; reliefs, Philadelphia Zoo & Cobbs Creek Park; Logos Mem to Adlai Stevenson, Ill State Univ, Normal; plus others.

Exhibitions: Philadelphia Art Alliance, 54; Philadelphia Mus Art, 55; Munson-Williams-Proctor Inst, 56; Pa Acad Fine Arts, 56; Wilmington Soc Fine Arts; plus many other group & one-man shows.

Teaching: Instr design & sculpture, Philadelphia Mus Art; instr, Wilmington Soc Fine Arts.

Awards: Fulbright fel, 50-51; gold medal, N Y Show, Philadelphia Flower Show, 64.

Memberships: Artists Equity Asn; Philadelphia Art Alliance; Franklin Inn Club, Philadelphia.

Mailing Address: Valley House, Level & Arcola Rd, Arcola, PA 19420.

MITCHELL, JAMES E
Illustrator, Painter
Preferred Media: Casein, Oils.
b New York, N Y, Jan 1, 26.
Study & Training: Pratt Inst, Brooklyn, N Y, cert; Acad Grande-Chaumiere, Paris, France; also with Edouard Goerg.
Work in Public Collections: Submarine Mus, New London, Conn; U S Merchant Marine Acad, Kings Point, N Y; U S Navy Art Collection, Washington, D C; Mariners Mus, Newport News, Va.
Commissions: Operation sea orbit, Mariners Mus, Newport News, Va, 65; DASO-Cape Kennedy, U S Navy, 69.
Exhibitions: One-man shows, Lord & Taylor Gallery, New York, 66-69.
Publications: Auth & illusr, Hydrofoils: a sketchbook of the future, MotorBoating, 62; illusr, History in the making, Boating Mag, 67; illusr, Shell Oil Diary, 69-70; auth & illusr, Pirates of Guadeloupe, Sail Mag, 71; auth & illusr, Sketchbook: SORC '72, Rudder Mag, 72.
Dealers: Lord & Taylor Gallery, 424 Fifth Ave, New York, NY 10016; Bay Harbor Galleries, 1007 Kane Concourse, Bay Harbor Island, Miami, FL 33154.
Mailing Address: Hill & Dale Country Club, P O Box 236, Carmel, NY 10512.

MITCHELL, JOAN
Painter
b Chicago, Ill, 26.
Study & Training: Smith Col, 42-44; Columbia Univ; Art Inst Chicago, BFA, 47; New York Univ, MFA, 50.
Work in Public Collections: Basel Mus, Switz; Albright-Knox Art Gallery, Buffalo, N Y; Art Inst Chicago, Ill; Mus Mod Art, New York, N Y; Phillips Collection, Washington, D C; plus others.
Exhibitions: Pa Acad Fine Arts, Philadelphia, 66; Two Decades of American Painting, Mus Mod Art, circulated in Japan, India & Australia, 67; Univ Ill, 67; Jewish Mus, 67; one-man show, Galerie Fournier, Paris, 67; plus many other group & one-man shows.
Bibliography: Michel Seuphor (auth), Abstract painting: 50 years of accomplishment, from Kandinsky to the present, Dell, 64; Int Dir Contemp Art, Metro, Milan, 64; San Hunter (ed), New art around the world: painting and sculpture, Abrams, 66; plus others.
Mailing Address: c/o Martha Jackson Gallery, 32 E 69th St, New York, NY 10021.

MITCHELL, JOHN BLAIR
Painter, Educator
b Brooklyn, N Y, Jan 30, 21.
Study & Training: Pratt Inst, cert, with Edmondson, Rogalski & Ponce de Leon, 39-43, Pratt Inst Sch Educ, 46-47; Columbia Univ Teachers Col, BS, 48, Columbia Univ, MA, 49; New York Univ Sch Educ, PhD, 63.
Work in Public Collections: Metrop Mus Art, New York, N Y; Libr Cong, Washington, D C; Silvermine Guild Artists, Conn; Baltimore Mus Art, Md; Notre Dame Col, Baltimore.
Commissions: Mural, Baltimore City Hosp, 72.
Exhibitions: Six shows, Corcoran Gallery Art, Washington, D C, 54-63; Libr Cong 19th Nat Exhib Prints, 63; Silvermine Guild Artists 5th Nat, 64; one-man show, Baltimore Mus Art, 64; Hochschild Kohn Maryland Artists Today Anniversary Invitational, 72.
Teaching: Prof graphics & painting & coord grad art prog, 49-; instr art, Columbia Univ Teachers Col, summers 50, 53 & 54; chmn art dept, Towson State Col, 51-57 & 63-65; instr graphics, Baltimore Mus Art, 63-
Positions: Bk reviewer, Art Educ, 59-60.
Awards: First award, Corcoran Gallery Art, 55; purchase award, Silvermine Guild Artists, 64; Maryland Artists Today First Award, Hochschild Kohn Co, 72.
Bibliography: Lincoln Johnson (auth), rev Baltimore Hebrew Cong Art one-man show, The Sun, Baltimore, 12/71.

Memberships: Artists Equity Asn (past pres, Md Chap, 65); Baltimore Print Club (bd mem).
Publications: Auth, Art education, 52; co-auth, Art in our Maryland schools, State Manual, State Dept Educ, 53; auth, School arts, 2/57; auth, Eastern Arts Quart, 1-2/63.
Mailing Address: 9918 Finney Dr, Baltimore, MD 21234.

MITCHELL, PETER TODD
 Painter
Preferred Media: Oils.
b New York, N Y, Nov 16, 29.
Study & Training: Acad Bellas Artes, Mexico City, Mex, with Lozano & Galvan; Groton; Yale Art Sch.
Work in Public Collections: Metrop Mus Art, New York.
Commissions: Murals, Van Wrangell, Malaga, Spain, 55 & Thomas Murphy, St Tropez, France, 70.
Exhibitions: Am Painters in Philadelphia Collections, 62; Smithsonian Traveling Show Graphics, 71; London Bridge Show, Guildhall-London, 72.
Awards: First Tiffany Found Award for Painting, 52.
Bibliography: Berg (auth), L'oeuvre de P T Mitchell, Jardin Arts, 69.
Dealer: Tratford Gallery, 119 Mount St, London W1, England.
Mailing Address: 116 E 57th St, New York, NY 10022.

MITCHELL, WALLACE (MacMAHON)
 Museum Director, Painter
b Detroit, Mich, Oct 9, 11.
Study & Training: Hamilton Col, 30-33; Northwestern Univ, BA, 34; Cranbrook Acad Art, 35; Columbia Univ, MA, 36.
Work in Public Collections: Cranbrook Acad Art Mus; Detroit Inst Art; Guggenheim Mus; Kalamazoo Art Ctr.
Commissions: Murals, Gen Motors Tech Ctr & Univ Ky Med Ctr.
Exhibitions: Art Inst Chicago, 38-41; Detroit Inst Art Ann; Albright Art Gallery, 39; Univ Nebr; Old Northwest Territory Exhib; plus others.
Teaching: Instr, Cranbrook Acad Art, 36-55.
Positions: Registr, Cranbrook Acad Art, 44-64, dir galleries, 54-71, pres, 70-
Mailing Address: Cranbrook Acad Art, Bloomfield Hills, MI 48013.

MITTLEMAN, ANN
 Painter
Preferred Media: Oils.
b Jan 15, 98; U S citizen.
Study & Training: New York Univ; New Sch Social Res; also with Tchac Basov, Robert Laurent & Philip Evergood.
Work in Public Collections: Univ Minn; Jewish Mus; New York Univ Mus; Miami Mus; Birmingham Mus; plus 26 other mus.
Exhibitions: Bodley Gallery; Wickersham Gallery; Traveling Mus Show; retrospective exhib, Univ Minn.
Memberships: Nat Asn Women Artists; Am Soc Contemp Artists; Artists Equity Asn; fel Royal Soc Arts London; Arch Am Art.
Dealer: Madison Avenue Gallery, 981 Madison Ave, New York, NY 10021.
Mailing Address: 710 Park Ave, New York, NY 10021.

MIYASAKI, GEORGE JOJI
 Printmaker, Painter
b Kalopa, Hawaii, Mar 24, 35.
Study & Training: Calif Col Arts & Crafts, BFA & BAEd, 57, MFA, 58.
Work in Public Collections: San Francisco Mus Art, Calif; Brooklyn Mus Art, N Y; Mus Mod Art, New York, N Y; Art Inst Chicago, Ill; Pasadena Art Mus, Calif.
Teaching: Assoc prof painting & printmaking, Univ Calif, Berkeley, 64.
Awards: John Simon Guggenheim fel, 63-64.
Memberships: Soc Am Graphic Artists.
Mailing Address: c/o Associated American Artists, 663 Fifth Ave, New York, NY 10022.

MIYASHITA, TAD
 Painter
b Puukolii, Hawaii, May 10, 22.
Study & Training: Corcoran Sch Art, Washington, D C; Art Stud League New York.
Work in Public Collections: State Found Cult & Arts, Honolulu, Hawaii; Honolulu Acad Arts; New York Times, N Y; Solomon R Guggenheim Mus, New York; Whitney Mus Am Art, New York.
Exhibitions: Pa Acad Fine Arts Ann, Philadelphia, 52; Nebr Art Asn Ann, 54; One Hundred Works on Paper, Salzburg, Austria, 59; Whitney Mus Am Art Ann, 67 & 68; Collages by American Artists, Ball State Univ, Muncie Ind, 71.

Bibliography: J Canaday (auth), article, In: New York Times, 66; J R Mellow (auth), article, In: Art Int, 68; W Anderson (auth), article, In, Honolulu Star-Bull, 71.
Mailing Address: 121 E 23rd St, New York, NY 10010.

MOCHI, UGO
 Sculptor
Preferred Media: Graphics.
b Firenze, Italy, Mar 11, 89; U S citizen.
Study & Training: Accad Belle Arti, Akad Kunste, Berlin; also sculpture with August Gaul.
Work in Public Collections: Metrop Mus Art, New York, N Y; Mus Natural Hist, New York; Franklin Inst, Philadelphia; Cranbrook Mus Art, Mich; Queen Mary Windsor Castle Collection, Eng; plus others.
Commissions: Transparent windows, St Regis Hotel, New York, 28 & Am Mus Natural Hist, New York, 70.
Exhibitions: Exhibs, London, Eng, 23, New York Mus Sci & Indust, McGill Univ, Montreal; Columbia Univ & Col New Rochelle, N Y, 66; plus others.
Awards: First prizes for graphics, Fedn Westchester Art Clubs, 52 & Beaux Arts, White Plains, N Y, 71; award for mus work, New York Zool Soc, 69.
Bibliography: E Watson (auth), article, In: Am Artist, 51; article, In: Natural Hist Mag, 53; Bugatti (auth), entry, In: Enciclopedia internazionale degli artisti, 70-71; plus others.
Memberships: Hon mem New Rochelle Art Asn (past pres); Asn Animal Artists (second v pres); New York Zool Soc; Audubon Artists; hon mem Music Teachers Asn New Rochelle.
Publications: Auth, L'ombra delle bestie, Italy, 23, African shadows, 34, Hoofed mammals of the world, Scribner, 53 & 71, Theodore Roosevelt's America, 55 & American water and game birds, Rand, 56; illusr, A natural history of giraffes, Scribner, 73.
Mailing Address: 26 Orchard Pl, New Rochelle, NY 10801.

MOCHIZUKI, BETTY AYAKO
 Painter
Preferred Media: Watercolor.
b Vancouver, B C.
Study & Training: Ont Col Art.
Work in Public Collections: Art Gallery Ont, Toronto; Victoria Col, Univ Toronto.
Exhibitions: One-man shows, Picture Loan Soc, Toronto, 55, 58 & 60; Victoria Col, Univ Toronto, 67.
Awards: C W Jeffery Award, 62.
Memberships: Can Soc Painters in Watercolour; Can Soc Graphic Art.
Mailing Address: 175 Livingstone Ave, Toronto 10, Ont, Can.

MOCHON, DONALD
 Painter, Educator
b Troy, N Y, Mar 20, 16.
Study & Training: Rensselaer Polytech Inst, MArch, 38.
Exhibitions: San Francisco Mus Art; Pa Acad Fine Arts; Berkshire Mus; Everson Mus Art; Munson-Williams-Proctor Inst, Utica, N Y; plus others.
Teaching: Adj prof archit, Rensselaer Polytech Inst, 46-67; prof art & dir art gallery, State Univ N Y Albany, 67-
Positions: Vis critic archit, Williams Col, 59-
Awards: Stud medal, Am Inst Architects, 36.
Memberships: Am Asn Univ Prof; Am Inst Graphic Arts.
Mailing Address: Dept of Art, State University of New York at Albany, 1400 Washington Ave, Albany, NY 12203.

MOCK, GLADYS (GLADYS MOCK WETTER)
 Painter
Preferred Media: Graphics.
b New York, N Y.
Study & Training: Art Stud League New York, scholar, also with Kenneth Hayes Miller & William Stanley Hayter.
Work in Public Collections: Todd Mus, Kalamazoo, Mich; Metrop Mus Art, New York; Pa Acad Fine Arts, Philadelphia; Smithsonian Inst, Washington, D C; New York Pub Libr; Libr Cong.
Commissions: Paul Spoke Here, for Rev William Ward Ayers, 37; portrait of John B Gambling, 38; portrait of Dean Alexander Klemin, N Y Univ, 50; portrait of J David Stern, publisher, 68; Mrs John Tulenko comn by Mr John Tulenko, 69.
Exhibitions: Soc Am Graphic Artists Ann; Audubon Artists Ann; U S Info Agency tour overseas, 60; Pa Acad Fine Arts, 61; Nat Acad Design, 63-70.
Positions: Rep in New York for Am Fedn Arts, 18-28; del for Audubon to U S Comt Int Art Asn, 69-72.
Awards: John Taylor Arms Mem Medal, Audubon Artists, 68; purchase prize, Hunterdon Art Ctr, 68; Kathryn Colton Prize, Nat Asn Women Artists, 71.

Memberships: Soc Am Graphic Artists (pres, 59-62, past pres on
    coun, 72); Audubon Artists (v pres graphics, 64-66, mem bd, 72);
    Hunterdon Art Ctr; Pen & Brush Club; Nat Asn Women Artists.
Dealer: Associated American Artists, 663 Fifth Ave, New York,
    NY 10022.
Mailing Address: 24 Washington Square N, New York, NY 10011.

MOCSANYI, PAUL
    Art Administrator
Positions: Dir, art ctr, New Sch Social Res, New York, N Y.
Mailing Address: 130 E 72nd St, New York, NY 10021.

MOE, HENRY ALLEN
    Art Administrator
b Monticello, Minn, July 2, 94.
Study & Training: Hamline Univ, BS, 16; Oxford Univ, Rhodes
    scholar, 20-23, Brasenose Col, BA, 22, BCL, 23, MA, 33, hon
    DCL, 50; Hamline Univ, hon LHD, 29; Kenyon Col, 41, Southern
    Ill Univ; Johns Hopkins, LLD, Yale Univ, Columbia Univ, Wes-
    leyan Univ, Univ Calif, 58, Brown Univ, Swarthmore Col, Rocke-
    feller Univ, Dartmouth Col, 66; New Sch Social Res, LittD,
    Princeton Univ, Emory Univ.
Positions: V chmn, N Y State Coun on Arts; chmn, Nat Endowment
    for Humanities, 65-66; trustee & v pres, Maude E Warwick Fund;
    trustee & emer pres, John Simon Guggenheim Mem Found;
    trustee, Mus Mod Art, New York (v chmn trustees); Inst Modern
    Art, New York (chmn trustees); trustee, Am Acad Rome; trustee,
    Farmers' Mus, Cooperstown, N Y (pres); trustee, Louis Comfort
    Tiffany Found.
Awards: Distinguished Service to the Arts Award, Nat Inst Arts &
    Lett, 55; Pub Serv Medal, Nat Acad Sci, 58; Award of Merit, Phil-
    adelphia Mus Col Art, 65; plus others.
Memberships: Benjamin Franklin fel Royal Soc Arts; N Y State Hist
    Asn (chmn bd trustees, pres); Asn Am Rhodes Scholars (asst
    treas, dir); hon fel Brasenose Col; Am Philos Soc (pres, 59-70).
Mailing Address: 30 Wall St, New York, NY 10005.

MOELLER, ROBERT CHARLES, III
    Art Historian, Art Administrator
b Providence, R I, Jan 22, 38.
Study & Training: Washington & Lee Univ, BA (hist art), 59; Har-
    vard Univ, with John Beckwith, Dr Hanns Swarzenski, J M Del-
    aisse & J H Plummer, MA (art hist), 63.
Collections Arranged: Brummer Collection, Duke Univ Art Mus.
Teaching: Teaching fel hist art, Harvard Univ, 64-65; instr art,
    Duke Univ, 68, asst prof art, 68-69; instr seminar medieval
    sculpture, Univ N C, Chapel Hill, spring 68.
Positions: Res assoc dept art, Duke Univ, 67-68, dir Duke Univ
    Art Mus, 68-69; asst cur dept decorative arts & sculpture, Mus
    Fine Arts, Boston, 70-71, cur decorative arts & sculpture, 71-
Memberships: Mediaeval Acad Am; Col Art Asn Am; Soc Française
    d'Archeologie; Int Coun Mus; Am Asn Mus.
Research: Study of mid-twelfth century sculpture in Burgundy con-
    centrating on Narthex sculpture of Charlieu, seventeenth century
    sculpture and decorative arts.
Publications: Contribr, Le second ange de Terret (appendix to 2nd
    Fr ed), Trianon, 66; auth, Sculpture—decorative art (Brummer
    Collection catalogue), Duke Univ Press, 67; contribr, The Brum-
    mer Collection at Duke University, Art J, 68; auth foreword, The
    graphic art of Edvard Munch, Duke Univ Art Mus Exhib, 12/69;
    auth, Sculpture from Brive & Sculpture from Savigny, R I Sch De-
    sign, 7/69.
Mailing Address: Dept of European Decorative Arts & Sculpture,
    Museum of Fine Arts, Boston, MA 02115.

MOGLIA, LUIGI (JOHN)
    Painter, Educator
Preferred Media: Watercolors.
b Dover, N J, Feb 12, 99.
Study & Training: Pratt Inst, grad(interior design); Berkshire Sum-
    mer Sch Art; also with Ernest Watson, Edgar Whitney, John
    Rogers & Rutledge Bate.
Exhibitions: Am Watercolor Soc, Audubon Artists & Allied Artists,
    Nat Acad Galleries, New York, N Y; Knickerbocker Artists 3/4,
    Nat Arts Club, New York; Am Artists Prof League, Lever House,
    New York.
Teaching: Instr interior design, Pratt Inst, Brooklyn, N Y, 10 yrs.
Positions: Interior designer, W & J Sloane, New York; private
    practice, 26 yrs.
Awards: Nat Art League; Manhasset Art Asn; Port Washington Art
    Coun.
Memberships: Audubon Artists; Knickerbocker Artists; Am Artists
    Prof League; Nat Art League; Manhasset Artists Asn.
Mailing Address: 14 Baker Hill Rd, Great Neck, NY 10023.

MOHN, CHERI (ANN)
    Painter
b Akron, Ohio, Aug 12, 36.
Study & Training: Akron Art Inst, Ohio; Youngstown State Univ, BA.
Work in Public Collections: Butler Inst Am Art, Youngstown, Ohio;
    Paintin' Place Gallery Inc, Columbiana, Ohio; Gallerie des
    Champignons, Youngstown; Phoenix Gallery, Philadelphia, Pa;
    Johnny Artcher's Ghost Town Gallery, Mogollon, N Mex.
Exhibitions: Mademoiselle Mag Contest, New York, N Y, 61; Peter
    Hurd Water Color Show, Artesia, N Mex, 68; Butler Inst Am Art
    Midyear Show, Youngstown & Guest Artist at Studio 09, Cleve-
    land, Ohio, 70; John Young Invitational, Youngstown, 72.
Teaching: Dir/instr fine arts, Cheri Mohn Sch Arts, Youngstown,
    63-67; instr fine arts, Paintin' Place Gallery Inc, Columbiana,
    71-
Awards: Mademoiselle Mag Top Ten Women Artists in U S A, 60;
    Gallerie des Champignons Purchase Award, 68; Butler Inst Am
    Art Purchase Prize, 70.
Bibliography: Rakocy (auth), Artist of the Month, Pigment & Form,
    67; Feature artist, Paintin' Place News, 71-72.
Memberships: Soc N Am Artists; Cleveland Mus Art; Friends of Am
    Art, Butler Inst Am Art.
Publications: Auth & illusr, articles, In: Pigment & Form, 67-68;
    asst ed-feature writer & illusr, Paintin' Place News Inc, 72;
    illusr, Village Life Inc, 72; ed, Niles Times, 58.
Mailing Address: 12691 South Ave, North Lima, OH 44452.

MOIR, ALFRED
    Art Historian
b Minneapolis, Minn, Apr 14, 24.
Study & Training: Harvard Univ, AB, 48, AM, 49; Univ Rome, 50-
    51; Harvard Univ, PhD, 53.
Teaching: From instr to assoc prof hist art, Newcomb Col, Tulane
    Univ, 52-62; from assoc prof to prof hist art, Univ Calif, Santa
    Barbara, 62-, chmn dept art, 63-69.
Memberships: Col Art Asn Am; Soc Archit Historians; Renaissance
    Soc; Medieval Acad Am; Southern Calif Art Historians.
Research: Italian baroque art, particularly Caravaggio and his
    followers; also drawings.
Publications: Ed, Eighteenth century drawings, 55; contribr, Art
    in Italy 1600-1700, 65; auth, The Italian followers of Caravaggio.
Mailing Address: 103 Mesa Lane, Santa Barbara, CA 93109.

MOL, LEO
    Sculptor
Preferred Media: Bronze.
b Ukraine, Jan 15, 15; Can citizen.
Study & Training: Kunst Akad, Berlin, Ger; Acad Art, The Hague,
    Netherlands.
Work in Public Collections: Hamilton Art Gallery, Ont, Can; Mc-
    Michael Conserv Art, Kleinberg, Ont; Toronto Art Gallery, Ont;
    Winnipeg Art Gallery, Man, Can; Vatican, Rome, Italy.
Commissions: Monument to a poet, T Shevchenko, Citizen's Comt,
    Washington, D C, 64; bust of Right Hon J G Diefenbaker, Senate,
    Ottawa, Can, 64; bust of Gen Dwight D Eisenhower, Gettysburg,
    Pa, 65; bust of Pope Paul VI, St Clements Univ, Rome, Italy, 67;
    monument to T Shevchenko, Citizen's Comt, Buenos Aires, Arg,
    71.
Exhibitions: Winnipeg Art Gallery, Man, 50-71; Royal Can Acad
    Arts, Montreal, Ottawa, Toronto & Winnipeg, 56-70; Art Gal-
    lery Hamilton, Ont, 56-71; Mus Fine Arts, Montreal, 59; Allied
    Artists Am, Nat Acad Galleries, New York, N Y, 63-64.
Awards: Allied Artists Medal, Royal Archit Inst Can, 60; first
    prize in competition for monument in Washington, D C, 62;
    Jacob C Stone Prize, Allied Artists Am, 63.
Bibliography: Leo Mol, sculptor, Royal Archit Inst Can J, 60;
    Clement Greenburg (auth), View of art on the prairies, Can Art,
    63; Anna Tillenius (auth), The lost wax casting, Winnipeg Free
    Press, 1/2/71.
Memberships: Royal Can Acad Arts.
Mailing Address: 104 Claremont Ave, Winnipeg, Man R2H 1V9,
    Can.

MOLDROSKI, AL R
    Painter, Educator
b Terre Haute, Ind, Aug 27, 28.
Study & Training: Ind State Univ, BSc; Mich State Univ, MA; South-
    ern Ill Univ, grant.
Exhibitions: Pa Acad Fine Arts; Detroit Mus Art; City Art Mus,
    Saint Louis; De Waters Art Ctr; Boston Festival Arts; plus many
    other group & one-man shows.
Teaching: Lectr art, Southern Ill Univ; asst prof art, Glenville
    State Col; from instr to asst prof art, Eastern Ill Univ, 63-

Awards: Tiffany Found grant; purchase award, Pa Acad Fine Art; Mary Richart Mem Award in painting & Art Directors Award, Detroit Mus Art; plus many others.
Mailing Address: Dept of Art, Eastern Illinois University, Charleston, IL 61920.

MOLIN, BRITA
Painter, Printmaker
Preferred Media: Oils, Acrylics.
b Skara, Sweden, June 12, 19.
Study & Training: Isaac Grünewald Art Sch, Stockholm, Sweden, 46-47; Acad Libre, Stockholm, 48-51; Swedish State Sch Art & Design, Stockholm, 54-56; Royal Acad Art Graphic Sch, Stockholm; Atelier 17, Paris, France, with Stanley William Hayter, 63-64.
Work in Public Collections: Mus Mod Art, New York, N Y; Metrop Mus Art, New York; Cleveland Mus Art, Ohio; Smithsonian Inst, Washington, D C; Bibliot Nat, Paris; plus many others.
Commissions: Stone ware composition, HSB, Bldg Firm, Sweden, 66; tapestry, Swedish State Bd Art, Stockholm, 70; tapestry, Coop Asn Sweden, 71; tapestries, City of Stockholm & Ersta Hosp, 72.
Exhibitions: Six Swedish Graphic Artists, Civic Ctr Mus, Philadelphia, Pa, 68; Royal Acad, Stockholm, 69; one-man shows, Galleri Heland, Stockholm, Sweden, 69, Alonzo Gallery, New York, 69 & Art Design Corner, Cleveland, Ohio, 69; plus many other group & one-man shows.
Positions: Mem, Art Purchase Bd Schs, Stockholm, 66-70; mem bd, Exhibs Swedish Art Abroad, 72-
Awards: Painters prize, Orgn Swedish Women Artists, 58; grants, Swedish Govt, 70 & 71.
Bibliography: G Hellman (auth), article, In: Storstaden, 71; Hökby (auth), article, In: New Swedish Artists.
Memberships: Philadelphia Print Club; Swedish Artist Orgn, KRO (mem bd, 65-66); Graphic Soc, Stockholm (mem bd, 72-).
Mailing Address: c/o Alonzo Gallery, 26 E 63rd St, New York, NY 10021.

MOLINA, ANTONIO J
Painter, Art Critic
b Cuba, Sept 2, 28; U S citizen.
Study & Training: Univ Havana; Univ P R; Acad Eicholz, Bonn, Ger.
Work in Public Collections: Mus Bellas Artes, Havana; Libr Cong; Mus Ponce, P R; Mus Mod Art, New York, N Y; Mus Mod Art Miami; Columbia Univ; Inter-Am Univ.
Commissions: Mural, Racquet Club Hotel.
Exhibitions: Pan Am Union, Washington, D C, 64; Festival via Margutta, Rome, Italy; Galeria Aprag, New York, 66; Mus Mod Art Miami, Fla, 68; Int Exhib Drawings, Mayaguez, 68; plus many others.
Teaching: Lectr, Mus Ponce, Cath Univ P R & Inter-Am Univ P R.
Positions: Art critic, El Mundo, 69-; art critic, Artes Visuales, 70-
Bibliography: Rosa Oliva (auth), Arte de Molina, El Mundo, Havana, 60; E Perez Chanis (auth), Pintura de Molina, Urbe, 70; Exhibition de Molina, El Imparcial, 71.
Memberships: Inst Internac Castillos Hist; Am Fedn Arts; Ateneo Puertorriqueño; Soc Escritores P R; Club Gente Prensa.
Collection: Ex-libris and antique engravings; pre-Columbian ceramics.
Publications: Auth, Pintura en Cuba, 60; auth, Mis versos son asi, Havana, 61; auth, Diccionario biographico de Ciudad de Sancti Spiritus, Cuba, 61; auth, Criticas de arte, El Mundo, 69-72; plus others.
Dealer: Gallery Santiago, 207 Cristo St, San Juan, PR 00902.
Mailing Address: P O Box 1361, San Juan, PR 00902.

MOLINARI, GUIDO
Painter, Sculptor
b Montreal, Que, Oct 12, 33.
Study & Training: Ecole Beaux-Arts, Montreal; Sch Art & Design, Montreal Mus Fine Arts.
Work in Public Collections: Kuntsmuseum, Basel, Switz; Mus Mod Art, New York, N Y; Simon Guggenheim Mus, New York; Chase Manhattan Bank, New York; Nat Gallery Art, Ottawa, Ont.
Commissions: Murals, comn by Dept of Pub Works, Ottawa for Vancouver Int Airport, B C, 68 & Dept Nat Defence Hq Bldg, Ottawa, 72.
Exhibitions: 4th Guggenheim Int Exhib, New York, 64; The Responsive Eye, Mus Mod Art, 65; Canada: Art Aujourdui, Rome, Paris, Lausanne, Bruxelles, 68; Venice 34th Biennial, Italy, 68; Can 101, Edinburgh, Scotland, 68.
Teaching: Head painting sect, Sir George Williams Univ, 70-
Positions: Founder & pres, L'Actuelle, 55-57.
Awards: Robertson Award, Montreal Mus Fine Arts, 65; John S Guggenheim Mem Found fel, 66; Bright Found Award Painting, 68.

Bibliography: B Teyssédre (auth), Seven Montreal painters (catalog), Mass Inst Technol, Cambridge, 67; David Silcox (auth), article for Can 101, Can Coun, Ottawa, 68; Gros plan (film), Radio-Can, Montreal, 71.
Memberships: Academician Royal Can Acad Arts; Soc Esthétique Expérimentale, Paris; Soc Color Res, Nat Coun Res (dir, 72).
Publications: Auth, 19th statement, Norman Mackenzie Art Gallery, Regina, Sask, 67; auth, Sculpture 67 statement, Nat Gallery, Ottawa, 67; co-auth, Débats sur la peinture Québecoise, Univ Montreal Press, 71.
Mailing Address: 1611 rue de la Visitation, Montreal 133, Que, Can.

MOLLER, HANS
Painter
Preferred Media: Oils, Watercolors.
b Wuppertal, W Ger, Mar 20, 05; U S citizen.
Study & Training: Kunstgewerbeschule Wuppertal-Barmen, 19-27; Acad Fine Arts, Berlin, 27-28.
Work In Public Collections: Mus Mod Art & Whitney Mus Am Art, New York, N Y; Detroit Inst Art, Mich; Phillips Mem Gallery, Washington, D C; Walker Art Ctr, Minneapolis, Minn.
Commissions: Stained glass window, comn by Am Fedn Arts & stained glass indust of the U S, 53; tapestry (executed in Aubusson, France), comn by Mr & Mrs Lawrence Buttenwieser, New York, 66; seven stained glass windows, comn by Mr & Mrs Neil Carothers III for Christ Church, Georgetown, Washington, D C, 69.
Exhibitions: Seven Shows, Contemporary American Painting, Univ Ill, Urbana, 49-59; Third Art Int, Japan, 55; One-man shows, Allentown Art Mus, Pa & Norfolk Mus, Va, 69; Contemporary Painting, Sculpture & Graphics, 69.
Teaching: Instr painting, Cooper Union Sch Art, 44-56.
Awards: First purchase prize, Nat Relig Art Exhib, Sacred Heart Sem, Detroit, 64; Palmer Mem Prize for marine painting, Nat Acad Design, 68; Samuel F B Morse Medal, 144th Ann Exhib, Nat Acad Design, 69.
Bibliography: John I H Baur (auth), Nature in abstraction, Whitney Mus Am Art, 58; Abram Kampf (auth), Contemporary synagogue art, Union Am Hebrew Congregation, 66.
Memberships: Nat Acad Design; Fedn Mod Painters & Sculptors.
Dealer: Midtown Galleries, 11 E 57th St, New York, NY 10022.
Mailing Address: 2207 Allen St, Allentown, PA 18104.

MONAGHAN, EILEEN (MRS FREDERIC WHITAKER)
Painter
Preferred Media: Watercolors.
b Holyoke, Mass, Nov 22, 11.
Study & Training: Mass Col Art, Boston.
Work in Public Collections: Hispanic Mus, New York, N Y; Atlanta Art Mus, Ga; Norfolk Art Mus, Va; Springfield Mus Fine Arts, Mass; Okla Mus Art, Oklahoma City.
Exhibitions: Am Watercolor Soc Ann Juried Shows, New York, 49-; Nat Acad Design Ann, New York, 57-; Childe Hassam Show, Am Acad Arts & Lett, New York, 63; Calif Watercolor Soc Juried Show, Los Angeles, Calif, 66; Watercolor U S A, Springfield, Mo, 68-70.
Awards: Adolph & Clara Obrig Prize for watercolor, Nat Acad Design, 64; silver medal, 65 & Charles R Kinghan Award, 72, Am Watercolor Soc.
Bibliography: Norman Kent (auth), 100 watercolor techniques, 68; Wendon Blake (auth), Acrylic watercolor painting, 70 & Susan Meyer (auth), 24 watercolorists, 72, Watson-Guptill.
Memberships: Assoc Nat Acad Design; Am Watercolor Soc; Soc Western Artists; West Coast Watercolor Soc.
Dealer: O'Brien's Art Emporium, 82 W Stetson Dr, Scottsdale, AZ 85251.
Mailing Address: 6453 El Camino del Teatro, La Jolla, CA 92037.

MONAGHAN, KEITH
Painter, Educator
b San Rafael, Calif, May 15, 21.
Study & Training: Univ Calif, Berkeley, BA & MA.
Work in Public Collections: In pvt collections only.
Exhibitions: San Francisco 12th Ann Watercolor, San Francisco Mus, Calif, 48; Contemp Am & Can Painting, Vancouver Art Gallery, B C, 58; Western Art, Seattle World's Fair, 62; 29th Ann Butler Inst Am Art, Youngstown, Ohio, 64; one-man show, Fountain Gallery Art, Portland, Ore, 66.
Teaching: Lectr art, Univ Calif, Berkeley, 46-47; prof art, Wash State Univ, 47-
Awards: San Francisco Art Asn Award, 48; Seattle Art Mus Award, Northwest Watercolor Soc, 51; Frye Mus Casein Exhib Award, 56.
Mailing Address: N E 1705 Lower Dr, Pullman, WA 99163.

MONGAN, AGNES
Art Administrator, Art Historian
b Somerville, Mass.
Study & Training: Bryn Mawr Col, AB; Smith Col, AM, hon LHD, 41; Wheaton Col, hon LittD, 54; Univ Mass, hon DFA, 70.
Teaching: Lectr fine arts, Harvard Univ; vis lectr fine arts, Mt Holyoke Col, 66-67; vis lectr fine arts, Oberlin Col, 67-
Positions: Res asst, Fogg Art Mus, Harvard Univ, 28-37, cur drawings, 37-, assoc dir, 64-69, dir, 69-71; vis dir, Timken Art Gallery, San Diego, Calif, 71-72.
Awards: Palms d'Academie, Fr Govt, 47; Cavaliere, Order of Merit, Repub Italy, 71.
Memberships: Col Art Asn Am; Asn Art Mus Dirs; hon fel Morgan Libr; Benjamin Franklin fel Royal Soc Arts.
Research: Relation to drawings by the Masters, especially Tiepolo, Fragonard, Watteau, Ingres, Daumier and Degas.
Publications: Co-auth, Drawings in the Fogg Museum, 41; co-auth, Ingres drawings, 67; co-auth, Tiepolo drawings, 70; auth, articles, In: Burlington Mag, Art Quart, Art News, Gazette Beaux-Arts, Master Drawings & others.
Mailing Address: Fogg Art Museum, Harvard University, Cambridge MA 02138.

MONROE, GERALD
Painter, Educator
Preferred Media: Oils.
b New York, N Y, Aug 17, 26.
Study & Training: Art Stud League New York, N Y; Cooper Union; N Y Univ, EdD.
Work in Public Collections: N Y Univ Collection; Finch Col Mus Art; Glassboro State Col Collection.
Positions: Asst prof art, Glassboro State Col, 68-
Research: History of the Artists Union of New York.
Mailing Address: 463 West St, New York, NY 10014.

MONSEN, DR & MRS R JOSEPH
Collectors
Dr Monsen, b Payson, Utah, Mar 13, 31.
Study & Training: Dr Monsen, Univ Utah, BS, 53; Stanford Univ, MA, 54; Univ Calif, Berkeley, PhD, 60.
Mailing Address: Dept of Business Administration, Graduate School of Business, University of Washington, Seattle, WA 98105.

MONT, FREDERICK
Art Dealer
Positions: Pres, Frederick Mont, Inc.
Specialty of Gallery: Old European masters.
Mailing Address: 465 Park Ave, New York, NY 10022.

MONTAGUE, JAMES L
Art Administrator, Painter
Preferred Media: Oils, Graphics.
b New Rochelle, N Y, May 6, 06.
Study & Training: Dartmouth Col, AB, 28; Art Stud League New York, with Kimon Nicolaides; also with Leger, Ozenfant & Galanis, Paris, France.
Work in Public Collections: U S Mil Acad; Southern Vt Artists Permanent Collect.
Commissions: Private portrait commissions.
Exhibitions: Various group shows & one-man exhibitions throughout the New England States & New York.
Positions: Dir, Sharon Art Ctr, N H, 61-63; dir, Southern Vt Art Ctr, 64-
Awards: Fitchburg Mus Award, 62; Print Club Albany Award, 70; award, Norwich Univ, 71.
Memberships: Art Stud League New York, Nat Arts Club; Print Club Albany; Northern Vt Artists.
Specialty of Gallery: Living New England artists.
Mailing Address: P O Box 105, Manchester Center, VT 05255.

MONTAGUE, RUTH DuBARRY, see CRIQUETTE

MONTANA, BOB
Cartoonist
Preferred Media: Ink.
b Stockton, Calif, Oct 23, 20.
Study & Training: Mus Fine Arts, Boston, Mass; Phoenix Art Inst, N Y; Art Stud League New York.
Work in Public Collections: Libr Cong, Washington, D C; Truman Libr, Mo; Syracuse Univ, N Y.
Positions: Cartoonist, syndicated comic strip, Archie, 46-
Memberships: Nat Cartoonists Soc.
Mailing Address: R F D 1, Meredith, NH 03253.

MONTANA, PIETRO
Sculptor, Painter
b Alcamo, Italy; U S citizen.
Study & Training: Cooper Union Art Sch, dipl; also with George T Brewster.
Work in Public Collections: Am Numismatic Soc, New York, N Y; Brookgreen Gardens, S C; Mus Risorgimento Italiano, Turin, Italy; Ga Mus Art, Athens; Hickory Mus Art, N C.
Commissions: The Dawn of Glory (war Mem), commissioned by people of district, Highland Park, Brooklyn, N Y, 24; Mem to Jose de Diego, gift of Oscar Bravo, Mayaguez, P R, 35; Stations of the Cross, Fordham Univ, New York, 47-52; garden sculpture in bot garden, Norrvikens Tragardar, Basted, Sweden, 54; four saints for Shrine Immaculate Conception, Washington, D C, commissioned by Kennedy, Walsh & Kennedy, Architects, 59.
Exhibitions: Nat Acad Design Ann, New York, 21 & 31 plus others; Nat Sculpture Soc Ann, New York, 23-; one-man show, Rome, Italy, 30; Allied Artists Am Ann, New York, 32-; Hudson Valley Art Asn Ann, White Plains, N Y, 37-
Teaching: Instr sculpture, Master Inst Arts, New York, 31-34; instr painting & sculpture, Fordham Univ, 47-52.
Awards: Elizabeth M Watrous Gold Medal for sculpture, Nat Acad Design, 31; Herbert Adams Mem Medal & Citation for serv to soc, Nat Sculpture Soc, 62; gold medal & citation for attainment in sculpture & painting, Hudson Valley Art Asn, 62.
Bibliography: The work of Pietro Montana, Nat Sculpture Rev, summer 70.
Memberships: Nat Acad Design; fel Nat Sculpture Soc (mem coun); Allied Artists Am (treas, 12 yrs); Artist's Fellowship (treas, 4 yrs); Hudson Valley Art Asn.
Mailing Address: Via Pompeo Magno 1, 00192 Rome, Italy.

MONTE, JAMES K
Associate Curator
Positions: Assoc cur, painting & sculpture, Whitney Mus Am Art.
Mailing Address: Whitney Museum of American Art, 945 Madison Ave, New York, NY 10021.

MONTENEGRO, ENRIQUE E
Painter
Preferred Media: Oils.
b Valparaiso, Chile, Dec 7, 17; U S citizen.
Study & Training: Univ Fla, BFA, 44; Art Stud League New York, out-of-town scholar, 44-45; Colorado Springs Fine Arts Ctr, summer 43; also with Morris Kantor, Kunioshi & Boardman Robinson.
Work in Public Collections: Denver Mus Art, Colo; N C Mus Art, Raleigh; Colorado Springs Fine Arts Ctr; Issac Delgado Mus, New Orleans, La; Mt Holyoke Col Mus, South Hadley, Mass.
Exhibitions: New Talent in the U S A, Art in Am Mag Traveling Show, 55; one-man shows, N C Mus Art, 57 & Parma Gallery, New York, N Y, 59; Landau Gallery, Los Angeles, Calif, 60; The Painter and the Photograph, Art News Ann Traveling Show, 65.
Teaching: Instr art, Univ N Mex, Brown Univ, Pa State Univ, Colorado Springs Fine Arts Ctr, Mt Holyoke Col, Univ Fla & N C State Col, 46-
Awards: Denver Mus Art Purchase Prize, 53; Catherwood Award study in Europe, 56.
Bibliography: Fred Bartlett (auth), New talent in the U S A, Art in Am Mag, 2/55; Dorothy Seiberling (auth), New painters of the West, Life Mag, 11/4/57; Hiram Williams (auth), Notes for a young painter, Prentice-Hall, Inc, 63.
Mailing Address: 701 W Joppa Rd, Baltimore, MD 21204.

MONTGOMERY, CHARLES FRANKLIN
Art Administrator, Educator
b Austin Township, Ill, Apr 14, 10.
Study & Training: Harvard Univ, AB, 32; Univ Del, hon MA, 54; Yale Univ, hon MA, 70.
Collections Arranged: Henry Francis du Pont Winterthur Mus & Mabel Brady Garvan Collection, Yale Univ Art Gallery.
Teaching: Lectr & adj prof Am arts, Univ Del, 52; prof Am arts, Yale Univ, 70-
Positions: Assoc cur, Henry Francis du Pont Winterthur Mus, 51-54, dir, 54-61, sr res fel, 61-70; cur, Mabel Brady Garvan & Related Collection Am Arts, Yale Univ Art Gallery, 70-
Memberships: Walpole Soc (secy, 58-64); fel Am Studies; Col Art Asn Am; Pewter Club Am (v pres, 54-60); Soc Archit Historians.
Research: American arts and crafts.
Publications: Ed, Prints pertaining to America, 62; auth, American furniture, the Federal Period, 66; ed, Arts crafts and trades series, 71.
Mailing Address: 232 Bradley St, New Haven, CT 06510.

MONTLACK, EDITH
Painter
Preferred Media: Oils.
b New York, N. Y.
Study & Training: Metrop Mus Art Sch, scholar, with Michael Jacobs; Nat Acad Design, with Louis Bouché; Art Stud League New York.
Exhibitions: Parrish Mus; Riverside Mus, New York; Hall of Art, New York; Knickerbocker Artists, New York; Nat Arts Club Gallery, New York; plus many others.
Awards: Emil Kohn Medal; St Gaudens Medal; first prize for watercolors, Nat Asn Women Art.
Memberships: Life fel Royal Soc Art, London; Nat Asn Women Artists.
Mailing Address: 90 Taymil Rd, New Rochelle, NY 10804.

MONTOYA, GERONIMA CRUZ (PO-TSU-NU)
Painter, Instructor
b San Juan Pueblo, N Mex, Sept 22, 15.
Study & Training: Santa Fe Indian Sch; Claremont Col; Col St Joseph, Albuquerque, BS; also with Dorothy Dunn, Kenneth Chapman & Alfredo Martinez; Univ N Mex; Col Santa Fe.
Work in Public Collections: De Young Mus Art; Hall of Ethnol; Mus N Mex; Indian Arts & Crafts Mkt, Washington, D C.
Exhibitions: Mus N Mex, Santa Fe; Indian Art Exhib, 54 & 55; Mus N Mex Traveling Exhib Indian Paintings; one-man shows, Hall of Ethnol, Santa Fe, 59 & Philbrook Art Ctr, 65; plus others.
Teaching: Lectr Indian design & painting; instr, adult educ, San Juan Day Sch, N Mex adult educ, eight northern pueblos.
Awards: Spec award Indian art, N Mex State Fair, 60; purchase prize, N Mex Mus, 61; ceremonial for mod Indian painting, Gallup, N Mex, 61; plus others.
Memberships: N Mex Educ Asn.
Mailing Address: 1008 Calle de Suenos, Santa Fe, NM 87501.

MOORE, BEVERIDGE
Painter
Preferred Media: Oils.
b Richmond, Va, July 25, 15.
Study & Training: Univ Va, BA; Art Stud League New York with Yasuo Kuniyoshi, Morris Kantor & William Zorach.
Work in Public Collections: Beveridge Moore Collection, Valentine Mus, Richmond, Va; Fordham Univ, New York; Rutgers Univ, New Brunswick, N J; Evansville Mus Arts & Sci, Ind; Phoenix Art Mus, Ariz; plus many others.
Exhibitions: Nat Acad Design, New York, 48; Va Mus Fine Arts, Richmond, 57; four one-man shows, Bodley Gallery, New York, 62-70; Art Alliance, Philadelphia, Pa, 65; Butler Inst Am Art, Youngstown, Ohio, 67.
Dealer: Bodley Gallery, 787 Madison Ave, New York, NY 10021.
Mailing Address: Star Route, New Hope, PA 18938.

MOORE, E BRUCE
Sculptor
b Bern, Kans, Aug 5, 05.
Study & Training: Pa Acad Fine Arts, with Albert Laessle & Charles Grafly.
Work in Public Collections: Whitney Mus Am Art; Wichita Art Mus; Pa Acad Fine Arts; Brookgreen Gardens, S C; Wichita Art Asn; plus others.
Commissions: Monumental sculpture, Nat Mem Cemetery of the Pac, Honolulu, Hawaii, 60-61; Osgood Hooker Doors, Grace Cathedral, San Francisco, Calif; Walter H Beech Mem Doors, Wichita Art Asn; two bronze tigers, Princeton Univ; portraits & animal sculptures also in pvt collections.
Exhibitions: Whitney Mus Am Art, 42; Meriden Arts & Crafts, 40 & 42; Whitney Mus Am Art, 42; Nat Inst Arts & Lett, 43; Va Mus Fine Arts, 58; Mostra Art Mod, Camaiore, Italy, 68; plus others.
Awards: Nat Inst Arts & Lett grant, 43; medal, Am Numismatic Soc, 52; Henry Hering Mem Medal, Nat Sculpture Soc, 68; plus others.
Memberships: Academician Nat Acad Design; Nat Inst Arts & Lett; Nat Sculpture Soc; fel Am Numismatic Soc.
Mailing Address: Hotel Gralyn, 1745 N St N W, Washington, DC 20036.

MOORE, ETHEL
Art Administrator, Writer
b Chicago, Ill.
Study & Training: Vanderbilt Univ, BA; Col William & Mary, BFA; Art Stud League New York; State Univ Iowa, Yaddo Found fel, 63.
Positions: Ed publ & admin off, Albright-Knox Art Gallery, Buffalo, N Y.
Publications: Ed, Gallery notes, 66, Letters from 31 artists, 68 & Contemporary art: 1942-72, Albright-Knox Art Gallery; auth, articles, In: Arts Mag & others.
Mailing Address: Albright-Knox Art Gallery, Buffalo, NY 14222.

MOORE, FANNY HANNA
Collector, Patron
b Cleveland, Ohio, June 29, 85.
Positions: Chmn, Assocs in Fine Arts, Yale Univ, 55-65.
Awards: Award, Nat Audubon Soc, 54; Assoc Dame, Venerable Order of Hosp of St John of Jerusalem, 63; George McAneny Medal Hist Preservation, Am Scenic & Hist Preservation Soc; plus others.
Memberships: Cleveland Mus Art; Friends of Whitney Mus; Metrop Mus Art; Am Fedn Arts; Assocs in Fine Arts, Yale Univ (trustee & benefactor); plus others.
Collection: Eighteenth and nineteenth century English horse paintings.
Mailing Address: Canfield, Convent, NJ 07961.

MOORE, INA MAY
Instructor, Painter
Preferred Media: Watercolors.
b Hayden, Ariz, Feb 20, 20.
Study & Training: Univ Ariz, BA(educ, art & music); Ariz State Univ, MA(art educ).
Work in Public Collections: Phoenix Col, Ariz; Valley Nat Bank, Ariz; Ariz Bank, Phoenix; Western Savings & Loan Asn, Yuma, Ariz; First Fed Savings & Loan Asn, Yuma.
Exhibitions: Phoenix Art Mus; Ariz Watercolor Asn Traveling Exhib Ann; Nat Art Exhib, Tubac, Ariz; Invitational Exhib, Univ S Dak, 68; Nat League Am Pen Women, Salt Lake City, Utah, 71.
Teaching: Part-time instr art, elem pub schs, 40-50; private classes, 50-64; instr watercolor, Phoenix Art Mus, 65-
Awards: Purchase prizes, Valley Nat Bank, 66, Ariz Bank, 68 & Phoenix Col, 69.
Memberships: Ariz Watercolor Asn (pres, 66-68); Nat League Am Pen Women; Ariz Artist's Guild; Ariz Art Educ Asn; Phoenix Art Coun.
Mailing Address: 5718 N Tenth Ave, Phoenix, AZ 85013.

MOORE, MARTHA E (MRS LOUIS A BURNETT)
Painter
Preferred Media: Oils, Acrylics.
b Bayonne, N J.
Study & Training: Art Stud League New York.
Work in Public Collections: Harvard Univ, Boston, Mass; Norfolk Mus Art, Va; Merchant Marine Acad, Kings Point, Long Island; St Vincent's Hosp, New York, N Y; Tyler Art Mus, Tex.
Commissions: Portrait of Mr Wyatt Jackson, Tyler Art Mus, 59; portrait of Mr Aldrich, Harvard Univ, 60; portrait of Bishop Weldon, West Springfield Monastery, Mass, 62; portrait of Mr J L Reiss, St Vincent's Hosp, 63.
Exhibitions: Butler Art Inst, Ohio, 64; Nat Acad Design, New York, 65; Brooklyn Mus, N Y, 66; Audubon Artists, New York, 72; Allied Artists Am, New York, 72.
Teaching: Pvt instr, Rockport, Mass, at present; demonstr portrait painting throughout U S A.
Awards: Issac Hayward Portrait Award, Nat Acad Design, 62; gold medal of honor, Nat Asn Women Artists, 63; gold medals of honor, Catharine Lorillard Wolfe Art Club, 63 & 66.
Memberships: Life mem Art Stud League New York; Allied Artists Am (treas, 63-65); Audubon Artists (corresp secy, 64-66); Nat Asn Women Artists; Rockport, Mass Art Asn.
Dealers: Portraits, Inc, 41 E 57th St, New York, NY 10022; Doll & Richards, 172 Newbury St, Boston, MA 02116.
Mailing Address: 4 Hoffman Rd, High Bridge, NJ 08829.

MOORE, ROBERT JAMES
Painter, Instructor
Preferred Media: Oils, Graphics.
b San Jose, Calif, July 24, 22.
Study & Training: USAAF Photo Sch, Lowry Field, Colo, grad; San Jose State Col, BA; N Y Inst Fine Arts, with Salmony, Schoenberger, Panofsky & Offner; Columbia Univ Teachers Col, MFA; also with Brackman, Miller Barnet & others.
Exhibitions: Pa Acad Fine Arts, Philadelphia, 50; James D Phelan Awards Competition, San Francisco Art Mus, 51; 11 yr Retrospective of Prizewinners, Village Art Ctr, Whitney Mus Am Art, New York, N Y, 54; Audubon Artists, Nat Acad Design, New York, 62; Berkshire Mus, Pittsfield, Mass, 66.
Teaching: Assoc prof art, Goddard Col, 54-57; instr art & photog, Battin High Sch, Elizabeth, N J, 60-64; instr art, Julia Richman High Sch, New York, 64-
Awards: Second prize, Village Art Ctr Seventh Ann Graphic Art Show, Village Art Ctr, New York, 52; blue ribbon, New Talent Show, Ruth Sherman Gallery, New York, 64; award, Berkshire Mus, 66.
Memberships: Artists Equity Asn New York; life mem Art Stud League New York; Nat Art Educ Asn.
Publications: Auth, The other side of the coin, League, spring 51.
Mailing Address: 246 E 51st St, New York, NY 10022.

MOOS, WALTER A
Art Dealer
b Karlsruhe, Ger, Sept 6, 26.
Study & Training: Ecole Superieure Com, Geneva, Switz, BA; New Sch Soc Res, with Paul Zucker & Meyer Shapiro.
Positions: Dir, Gallery Moos Ltd.
Memberships: Prof Art Dealers Asn Can (pres, 71 & 72).
Specialty of Gallery: Contemporary Canadian, European & American paintings, sculptures & graphics.
Mailing Address: Gallery Moos Ltd, 138 Yorkville Ave, Toronto 185, Ont, Can.

MOOSE, PHILIP ANTHONY
Painter, Illustrator
Preferred Media: Oils, Acrylics.
b Newton, N C, Jan 16, 21.
Study & Training: Nat Acad; Columbia Univ; Skowhegan Sch Painting; Taxco Sch Arts, Mex; Acad Fine Arts, Munich, Ger.
Work in Public Collections: Atlanta Mus Art, Ga; Norfolk Mus, Va; N C State Mus Art, Raleigh; Colchester Mus, Eng; Mint Mus Art, Charlotte, N C.
Commissions: Mural, Montreat-Anderson Col, N C, 72.
Exhibitions: Am Watercolors, Metrop Mus, New York, N Y; Corcoran Biennial, Washington, D C; Southeastern Ann, Atlanta, Ga; Fulbright Artists, W Ger; Piedmont Ann, Charlotte.
Teaching: Assoc prof art, Davidson Col, 51-53; assoc prof art, Queens Col, N C, 56-67.
Awards: Pulitzer Award, 48; Tiffany Found Award, 49; Fulbright Award, 53-63.
Publications: Illusr, History of Catawba County, 52 & Exploring the mountains, 72.
Mailing Address: Linville Rd, Blowing Rock, NC 28605.

MOQUIN, RICHARD ATTILIO
Sculptor, Instructor
Preferred Media: Clay, Plastic, Fiberboard.
b San Francisco, Calif, July 1, 34.
Study & Training: City Col San Francisco, AA; San Francisco State Col, BA & MA, with Seymour Locks.
Work in Public Collections: Sacramento State Col; Sacramento State Fair.
Exhibitions: 24th Ceramic Nat, Everson Mus, Syracuse, N Y, 66; 23rd Scripps Col Invitational, Claremont, Calif, 67; Col Marin Invitational, Kentfield, Calif, 69; M H De Young Mus Show, San Francisco, 70; Stanford Univ Sculpture Invitational, 71 & 72.
Teaching: Instr sculpture, City Col San Francisco, 69-
Positions: V pres, Asn San Francisco Potters, 67-68.
Awards: Purchase awards, Sacramento State Fair, 68, San Francisco Art Fair, 69 & M H De Young Mus, 70.
Bibliography: Albright (auth), Ceramic sculpture, San Francisco Chronicle, 68 & 70; A Meisel (auth), Ceramic sculpture, Craft Horizons, 72.
Dealer: Quay Gallery, 2 Jerome Alley, San Francisco, CA 94124.
Mailing Address: 3 Herbing Lane, Kentfield, CA 94904.

MORADO, CHAVEZ JOSE
Painter, Educator
Preferred Media: Fresco, Oils, Tempera.
b Silao, Mex, Jan 4, 09.
Study & Training: Self-taught except for brief study at Art Sch, Mex Univ.
Work in Public Collections: Nat Mus Mod Art, Mexico City; Varsovia Art Mus, Poland; Mus Mod Art, New York, N Y; Haifa Mus, Israel; Mus Nat de Historia, Mexico City.
Commissions: Glass mosaics (exteriors), University City, Mexico City, 52; stone mosaics (exteriors), Ministry of Public Works, Mexico City, 54; frescoes & mixed mosaics, CIBA Labs, Mexico City, 55; oil mural & bronze pilar (with Tomas Chavez Morado in sculptural works), Mus Anthrop, Mexico City, 64; fresco & acrylic murals, Mus Alhondiga de Granaditas, Guanajuato, 55, 66 & 67.
Exhibitions: Mus Nat d'Art Mod, Paris, France, 52; Fifth Int Art Exhib, Tokyo, Japan, 59; Portrait of Mexico Traveling Exhib, several countries, 60-70; Mus Nac Arte Mod, Mexico City, 61; Biennal of Sao Paulo, Brazil.
Collections Arranged: Designing the Museo de la Alhondiga de Granaditas, History, Arquelogia, Etnography.
Teaching: Prof painting, Escuela Nat Artes Plasticas, Mexico City, 42-52; dir-founder, Taller de integracion Plastica, Mexico City, 50-60; dir-founder, Escuela de Diseno y Artesanias, Mexico City, 60-66.
Positions: Inspector of art teaching, Inst Nac Bellas Artes, Mexico City, 34-36, head art educ, 36-40, dir art schs, 40-66; dir, Mus Hist, Inst Nac Antropologia e Historia, Guanajuato, 70-
Awards: Medalla de Prata, 10th Salao Pan Americano, Inst Bellas Artes Rio Grande, Brazil, 58; Medalla Colalaboration Gran Premio, 8th Biennal Sao Paulo, Brazil, 65.

Bibliography: Julio Prieto (auth), Jose Chavez Morado, Ed Mexicanas, Mex, 51; Luis Cardosa y Aragon (auth), Pintura Mexicana, Fondo de Cultura Economica, Mex, 64; Antonio Rodriguez (auth), A history of Mexican mural painting, Thames & Hudson, London, 69.
Collection: Pre-hispanic, Mexican colonial and folk art.
Publications: Illus, Rin-Rin Renacuajo (children's book), 50.
Dealers: Ines Amor, Galeria Arte Mexicano, Milan 18, Mexico City, Mex; Lurdes Chumacero, Salon de La Plastica Mexicana, Havre 7, Mexico City, Mex.
Mailing Address: Pastita 158, Torre del Arco, Guanajuato, Guanajuato, Mex.

MORALES, ARMANDO
Painter
Preferred Media: Oils.
b Granada, Nicaragua, Jan 15, 27.
Study & Training: Sch Fine Arts, Managua, Nicaragua; Pratt Graphic Art Ctr, New York, N Y.
Work in Public Collections: Mus Mod Art, New York; Guggenheim Mus, New York; Inst Art, Detroit, Mich; Mus Art, Philadelphia, Pa; Mus Fine Arts, Houston, Tex.
Exhibitions: Bienal Mod Art, São Paulo, Brazil, 53, 55 & 59; Carnegie Int, Pittsburgh, Pa, 58, 64 & 67; Arte Am y España, Madrid, Barcelona, Rome & Berlin, 61; Guggenheim Int, New York, 60; The Emergent Decade, Cornell Univ & Guggenheim Mus, 66.
Teaching: Prof painting, Cooper Union, 71-
Awards: Ernest Wolf Award, V Bienal, São Paulo, Brazil, 59; award, Arte Am y España, Madrid, Spain, 63; J L Hudson Award, Carnegie Int, 64.
Bibliography: Dore Ashton (auth), Visual pleasure from austerity, Studio Int, London, 2/65; Heinz Ohff (auth), Anleitnung zum optimismus: begegnung mit Armando Morales in Berlin, Der Taggespiegel, Berlin, 6/19/65; Esperanza Brault (auth), Armando Morales, El Sol Mex, Mexico City, 10/4/68.
Dealer: Lee A Ault & Co, 25 E 77th St, New York, NY 10021.
Mailing Address: 33 Bond St, New York, NY 10012.

MORDVINOFF, NICOLAS
Painter, Illustrator
b Saint Petersburg, Russia, Sept 27, 11; U S citizen.
Study & Training: Univ Paris; also with Fernand Leger & Amedee Ozenfant.
Work in Public Collections: N Y Pub Libr; Metrop Mus Art.
Exhibitions: One-man shows, Luyber Gallery, N Y, 49, Philadelphia Art Alliance, 52 & N Y Pub Libr, 52; Wickersham Gallery, 70; Galerie 9, Paris, 70; plus others.
Awards: Caldecott Award, 52; Herald Tribune Award, 54; Am Inst Graphic Arts Cert Excellence, 55-57.
Publications: Auth, illusr & designer, Bear's land, 55 & Coral Island, 57; illusr & designer, Evangeline, 59; illusr, Russet & the two reds, 62 & The boy and the forest, 64; plus many others.
Mailing Address: Rte 1, Hampton, NJ 08827.

MORETON, RUSSELL
Painter
Preferred Media: Oils.
b Feb 20, 29; U S citizen.
Study & Training: Art Inst Chicago.
Work in Public Collections: Gen Serv Admin, Western White House, San Clemente, Calif.
Exhibitions: Ebell Salon Art, Los Angeles, Calif, 67-71; Lake San Marcos Invitational, Calif, 68-70; Showcase 21, Los Angeles, 68-72; 14th Ann Nat Art Round-up, Las Vegas, Nev, 70; Southern Calif Art Expos, Del Mar, Calif, 71.
Awards: First place, Lake San Marcos Invitational; 68 & second place, 71, second place, Ebell of Los Angeles, 71.
Publications: Note paper & Christmas cards of paintings in reproduction, Western Tradition, Boulder Colo, nine yrs; three seascapes, Donald Art Co, New York, 71; four landscapes, Bernard Picture Co, Chicago & New York.
Dealer: Showcase Gallery, 1420 S Coast Hwy, Laguna Beach, CA 92651.
Mailing Address: P O Box 622, Laguna Beach, CA 92652.

MOREZ, MARY
Painter, Illustrator
b Tuba City, Ariz.
Study & Training: Univ Ariz, Rockefeller Found scholar; Ray-Vogue Schs Commercial Art, Chicago, Ill; Maricopa Tech Col, Phoenix, Ariz.
Exhibitions: 5 exhibs, Scottsdale Nat Indian Art Show, Ariz, 67-72; Nat Indian Art Shows, Sheridan, Wyo, 68-70; Heard Mus Ann Indian Arts & Crafts, 69-71; Red Cloud Indian Art Shows, Pine Ridge, S D, 69-71; Trail of Tears, Cherokee Nat Hist Soc, 72.

Positions: V pres, Phoenix Indian Med Ctr, 70-72; res asst, Mus Navajo Ceremonial Arts, Santa Fe, N Mex, 70-; mem Phoenix Civic Plaza Indian Cult Comt, 71-
Awards: Best of show for Navajo Creation, Red Cloud Indian Art Show, 69; awards, for Changing Woman & Her Weaving Loom, Nat Indian Art Show, Sheridan, 69 & Father Sky & Mother Earth, Heard Mus Ann Ind Arts & Crafts, 72.
Research: Navajo baskets.
Publications: Illusr, Death of an elder Klallm, Baleen Press, 69; illusr, jacket covers, Canyon Rec, 69-71; illusr, N Mex Rev & Legis J, Santa Fe, 70, Navajo Times, Window Rock, Ariz, 71 & health care pamphlets, U S Pub Health Serv, 72; plus others.
Dealers: Hunter's Trading Post, Town & Country Shopping Ctr, 2035 E Camelback Rd, Phoenix, AZ 85016; Covered Bridge Art Gallery, R R 2, Box 99, Flagstaff, AZ 86001.
Mailing Address: P O Box 1762, Gallup, NM 87301.

MORGAN, ARTHUR C
Sculptor
Preferred Media: Bronze, Marble.
b Riverton Plantation, La, Aug 3, 04.
Study & Training: Beaux Arts Inst Design; also with Gutzon Borglum, Mario Korbel and others.
Work in Public Collections: Centenary Col, Shreveport, La; Shreve Mem Libr, Shreveport; Civic Theater, Shreveport; Civic Ctr & Hist Libr, Thibodaux, La; plus numerous pvt collections.
Commissions: Heroic figure, Chief Justice Edward Douglass White, Edward Douglass White Mem Comn, U S Capitol, Washington, D C, 55; Earl K Long Monument, State Parks & Recreation Comn, Winnfield, La, 63; Paul Geisler Mem, Comt Friends of Paul Geisler, Stadium Grounds, High Sch, Burwick, La, 65; Henry Miller Shreve Monument, City of Shreveport & Pub Subscription, River Pkwy, Shreveport, 66; A J Hodges Commemorative Bust, Trustees of Hodges Gardens, Hodges Gardens, Many, La, 72.
Exhibitions: One-man shows, La State Univ, Baton Rouge, 27, La State Exhib Mus, Shreveport, 40 & 50; Philbrook Art Ctr, Tulsa, Okla, 52 & Centennial Mus, Corpus Christi, Tex, 57; Mem Exhib, Nat Arts Club, New York, 60-
Teaching: Instr drawing, painting, sculpture & art hist & dir dept art, Centenary Col La, 28-34; dir sculpture & drawing, Southwestern Inst Arts, 34-
Bibliography: Patsi Farmer (auth), Biographer in bronze, Shreveport Mag, 12/58; Mary Gray Morris Walker (auth), Portrait of an artist, N La Hist Asn J, 7/65; Edwin Adams Davis (auth), Louisiana, the pelican state, La State Univ Press.
Memberships: Nat Arts Club.
Mailing Address: 657 Jordan St, Shreveport, LA 71101.

MORGAN, BARBARA BROOKS
Painter, Photographer
b July 8, 00.
Study & Training: Univ Calif, Los Angeles, 19-23.
Work in Public Collections: Mus Mod Art, New York, N Y; Int Mus Photog, Rochester, N Y; Hist Photog, Smithsonian Inst, Washington, D C; Amon Carter Mus, Fort Worth, Tex.
Exhibitions: One-woman show, Modern American Dance, Inter-Am Off, Nat Gallery Art for tour in Latin Am, Span & Portuguese versions; George Eastman House, Rochester, N Y, 64; Smithsonian Inst, 70; Mus Mod Art, 72; Amon Carter Mus, 72; plus others.
Teaching: Instr, art dept, Univ Calif, Los Angeles, 25-30; Ansel Adams Photog Workshop, Yosemite, summers; also lect & sem.
Publications: Auth, photographer & designer, Martha Graham: sixteen dances in photographs, 41-42; auth, photographer & designer, Summer's children: a photographic cycle of life at camp, 51; ed, photographer & designer, Barbara Morgan Monograph, 72.
Mailing Address: 120 High Point Rd, Scarsdale, NY 10584.

MORGAN, CHARLES H
Writer, Educator
b Worcester, Mass, Sept 19, 02.
Study & Training: Harvard Univ, AB, 24, AM, 26, PhD, 28.
Teaching: Instr fine arts, Harvard Univ, 24-27; lectr class archaeol, Bryn Mawr Col, 29-30; prof fine arts, Amherst Col, 30-68, dir, Mead Art Bldg, 48-68.
Positions: Dir, Am Sch Class Studies, Athens, Greece, 35-38.
Publications: Auth, Corinth XI, the Byzantine pottery, 42, The life of Michelangelo, 60, George Bellows, 65 & The Amherst College art collection, 72.
Mailing Address: 22 Snell St, Amherst, MA 01002.

MORGAN, DARLENE
Painter
Preferred Media: Ink, Oils.
b Salt Lake City, Utah, Feb 1, 43.
Study & Training: With Merle Olson.
Work in Public Collections: Pac Northwest Indian Ctr.

Exhibitions: Flathead Int Art Festival & Show, 71; Pac Northwest Indian Ctr Art Auction Ann, 71-72; Charles Russell Exhib & Auction Ann, 72; Nat Parks Centennial Exhib, Glacier Park, Mont, 72.
Awards: Best in show, Pac Northwest Indian Art Auction, 72.
Bibliography: Dave Crowell (auth), Montana's own, Gateway, 70.
Mailing Address: Woodsbay, Bigfork, MT 59911.

MORGAN, FRANCES MALLORY
Sculptor
Preferred Media: Bronze, Marble, Wood.
b Memphis, Tenn.
Study & Training: Art Stud League New York; Nat Acad Design; Pa Acad Fine Arts; also with John Hovannes & Alexander Archipenko.
Work in Public Collections: Brooks Mem Art Gallery, Memphis; IBM Corp.
Commissions: Neely Grant, bronze, Mrs Neely Grant, Memphis, 34; Sen Gilbert Hitchcock, 45 & bronze fountain, 49, Mrs Gilbert Hitchcock, Washington, D C; bronze fountain, Vance Norfleet, Memphis, 52; many portraits of children.
Exhibitions: World's Fair, New York, N Y, 39-40; Whitney Mus Am Art, New York, 40; Artists for Victory, Metrop Mus, New York, 42; Philadelphia Art Alliance, 46; Pa Acad Fine Arts, 47.
Awards: Anna Hyatt Huntington Award, Nat Asn Women Artists for Olympia, 41; Nat Asn Women Artists Prize for Peace Again, 44; Audubon Artists Award for Fish, 61.
Memberships: Nat Asn Women Artists; Sculptors Guild; Audubon Artists.
Mailing Address: Sunset Lane, Rye, NY 10580.

MORGAN, GLADYS B
Painter, Instructor
Preferred Media: Watercolors.
b Houma, La, Mar 24, 99.
Study & Training: Randolph-Macon Women's Col, BA; Columbia Univ, grad work; spec study with Will H Stevens & Arthur C Morgan.
Work in Public Collections: Centenary Col, Shreveport, La; La State Univ, Shreveport.
Exhibitions: Regional Exhib Painting & Sculpture, Delgado Mus, New Orleans, 41; one-man shows, Old Capitol Mus, Baton Rouge, La, 42 & Montgomery Mus Art, Ala, 46; Shreveport Art Club Regional, Barnwell Garden & Art Ctr, Shreveport, 70; one-man show, Centenary Col Libr Gallery, 71.
Teaching: Instr & lectr hist art, drawing & painting, Centenary Col, 27-34; instr drawing, painting & graphics, Southwestern Inst Arts, Shreveport, 34-
Awards: Blanche Bailey Wilde (auth), Gladys B Morgan: water colorist, N La Hist Asn J, 1/66.
Dealer: Charles Russell's Southern Gallery, 717 Milam St, Shreveport, LA 71101.
Mailing Address: 657 Jordan St, Shreveport, LA 71101.

MORGAN, HELEN BOSART
Sculptor
Preferred Media: Bronze, Plastic, Lead, Stone.
b Springfield, Ohio, Oct 17, 02.
Study & Training: Wittenberg Univ, AB; Dayton Art Inst; Sch Art Inst Chicago.
Work in Public Collections: Snyder Park, Springfield, Ohio; Springfield Art Ctr; Warder Libr, Springfield; Ohio Univ Libr, Athens, Ohio.
Exhibitions: Nat Acad Design; Nat Asn Women Artists; Cincinnati Mus Art; Columbus Gallery Fine Art; Butler Art Inst, Youngstown, Ohio; plus one other.
Awards: Least imitative in concept & execution award, Columbus Gallery, 63; sculpture prize, Ohio Liturgical Arts Guild, 71; first prize-sculpture, Springfield Art Asn, 71.
Memberships: Nat Asn Women Artists; Artists Equity Asn; Columbus Art League.
Dealer: Gallery 200, 200 W Mound St, Columbus, OH 43215.
Mailing Address: 845 E High St, Springfield, OH 45505.

MORGAN, LUCY CALISTA
Craftsman, Instructor
b Franklin, N C, Sept 20, 89.
Study & Training: Cent Teachers Col, Mount Pleasant, Mich; Univ Chicago; Cent Mich Col Educ, hon HHD, 52; Women's Col, Univ N C, DHL, 55; also with Edward F Worst.
Positions: Founder & bd mem, Penland Sch Handicrafts, N C, 29-; dir, Penland Weavers & Potters, 36-46; appointed by Gov Sanford, N C, to organize & work with a state proj of finding, collecting & selecting photographs of the past, 65.
Memberships: Southern Highland Handicraft Guild; Bus & Prof Women's Club, Spruce Pine, N C.

Publications: Co-auth, Gift from the hills: Miss Lucy Morgan's story of her unique Penland School, Univ N C Press, 58 & 71; contribr, The Weaver.
Mailing Address: Webster, NC 28788.

MORGAN, MARITZA LESKOVAR
Painter, Illustrator
b Zagreb, Yugoslavia, Nov 20, 21; U S citizen.
Study & Training: Cornell Univ, 42; Art Stud League New York, 43.
Work in Public Collections: Wilson Mus, Dartmouth Col, Hanover, N H; All Souls Unitarian Church, Tulsa, Okla; First Presby Church, Warren, Pa; St Luke's Chapel, Chautauqua, N Y; Hurlbut Mem Church, Chautauqua.
Commissions: Murals, Smith-Wilkes Mem Libr, Chautauqua Inst, 70.
Exhibitions: Nat Jury Show, Chautauqua, 66; Festival Arts Northwest Pa, 72.
Teaching: Supvr art, Warren Co, Pa, 51-57; instr pvt classes, Chautauqua, N Y, 66-
Positions: Artist-in-residence, Chautauqua Inst, 66-
Memberships: Chautauqua Art Asn (secy, 70-).
Dealer: Contemporary Christian Art Gallery, Madison Ave & 77th St, New York, N Y, 10021.
Mailing Address: Box 168, Chautauqua, NY 14722.

MORGAN, NORMA GLORIA
Painter, Engraver.
Preferred Media: Acrylics, Watercolor, Engraving on copper.
b New Haven, Conn.
Study & Training: Art Stud League New York, N Y, with Julian Levi; Hans Hofmann Sch Fine Art, New York; Atelier 17, New York, with Stanley W Hayter.
Work in Public Collections: Nat Gallery Art, Washington, D C; Mus Mod Art, New York; Victoria & Albert Mus, London, Eng; Philadelphia Mus Art, Pa; Pennell Collection, Libr Cong, Washington, D C.
Commissions: Moor Lodge, engraving on copper, Assoc Am Artists, New York, 54; Granite Tor, engraving on copper, Int Graphic Arts Soc, New York, 55; Moorland Sanctuary, oil mural, Old White Lion Inn, Haworth, Eng, 63; Carolina Paraquets, engraving on copper, Wildlife Int, Cincinnati, Ohio, 69; Moorland Sanctuary, engraving on copper, Assoc Am. Artists, 72.
Exhibitions: Print Coun Am, New York, 62; The Graven Image, London, Eng, 62; New York World's Fair, N Y, 65; Soc Am Graphic Artists, 67; Assoc Am Artists; two solo shows.
Awards: Gold medal for graphics, Am Artists Prof League, Smithsonian Inst, 63; gold medal for graphics, Painters & Sculptors Soc N J 26th Ann, 67; blue ribbon (first prize), graphics, Composers, Authors & Artists Conv, 69.
Bibliography: Janet Kalmine (auth), Above the crowd (monogr), Travel in Fashion, 58.
Memberships: Int Graphic Arts Soc; Print Coun Am; Soc Am Graphic Artists; Assoc Am Artists; Knickerbocker Artists.
Publications: Auth-illusr, Engraving, The Artist, 9/63, Imaginative Painting, 3/64.
Mailing Address: 239 W 63rd St, New York, NY 10023.

MORGAN, RANDALL
Painter
b Knightstown, Ind, Feb 24, 20.
Study & Training: Ind Univ; Cincinnati Univ; Teachers Col, Columbia Univ.
Work in Public Collections: Whitney Mus Am Art; Barnes Found; Detroit Inst Art Toledo Mus Art; City Art Mus Saint Louis; plus others.
Exhibitions: Mus Mod Art; Whitney Mus Am Art; Corcoran Gallery Art; Pa Acad Fine Arts; one-man show, Galleria 88, Rome, Italy; plus many others.
Teaching: Instr ceramics, Teachers Col, Columbia Univ, 48; instr painting, Sch Fine Arts, Wash Univ, 62-63.
Positions: Art dir, Positano Art Workshop, Italy, 53-60; dir, Randall Morgan Sch Art, Sant' Agata, Due Golfi, Naples, Italy, 67-
Awards: Ind Univ fel painting in Italy, 49-51; artist-in-residence, Festival of Two Worlds, Spoleto, Italy, 64; Ingram Merrill Found fel, 65-66.
Mailing Address: c/o Roko Gallery, 90 E Tenth St, New York, NY 10003.

MORIN, THOMAS EDWARD
Sculptor, Educator
Preferred Media: Metals.
b Malone, N Y; Sept 22, 34.
Study & Training: Mass Col Art, 52-56, BS(educ); Cranbrook Acad Art, MFA, 57; Brown Univ, basic metal cert, 66, plastics technol cert, 67.
Work in Public Collections: Richmond Mus Art, Va; Brown Univ, Providence, R I; Barn Gallery Assoc, Ogunquit, Me; Am Tube Gallery, West Warwick, R I; New York Univ, Oneonta.
Commissions: Cast aluminum high relief, Brown Univ, 64; bronze sculpture & bronze screen, Am Tube, 72.
Exhibitions: Inst Contemp Art Invitational, Boston, Mass, 60; Whitney Mus Am Art Ann, New York, N Y, 61; Eleven New Eng Sculptors, Wadsworth Atheneum, Hartford, Conn, 63; Contemp Box & Wall Sculpture Invitational, R I Sch Design Mus Art, 65; Univ Conn Mus Art, Storrs, 70.
Teaching: Head dept sculpture, Silvermine Guild Artists Col Art, 58-60; assoc prof sculpture & head sculpture grad prog, R I Sch Design, 61-
Awards: First prize & best in show, Silvermine Guild Artists, 60; first prize, R I Art Festival, 63; first prize, New Haven Art Festival, 66.
Memberships: Union Independent Cols Art (dept head, 69); Am Foundrymens Soc.
Art Interests: Cast metal sculpture with multi-media fabrication.
Mailing Address: 62 Waterman St, Providence, RI 02906.

MORLEY, GRACE L McCANN
Museum Director, Writer
b Berkeley, Calif, Nov 3, 00.
Study & Training: Univ Calif, AB & MA; Univ Paris, Dr; Mills Col, hon LLD, 37; Smith Col, DHL, 57; Calif Col Arts & Crafts, DFA, 57; Univ Calif, Los Angeles, LLD, 58; also in Grenoble, France.
Teaching: Lectr Latin Am & contemp art; instr Fr & art, Goucher Col, Baltimore, Md, 27-30.
Positions: Cur, Cincinnati Mus Asn, 30-33; dir, San Francisco Mus Art, 35-58; dir, Pac House, Golden Gate Expos, San Francisco, 39; consult, art comt, Off Inter-Am Affairs, 41-43; adv, mus, UNESCO, 46, head mus, 47-49; head, Regional Agency in Asia of Int Coun Mus, 47-; mem ed bd, Mus; mem nat comt, UNESCO, 50-56; asst dir, Solomon R Guggenheim Mus, New York, N Y, 59; dir, Nat Mus, New Delhi, India, 60-; adv mus, Govt India, 66-68.
Awards: Chevalier Legion of Hon, 49; Wattamul Award, 63.
Memberships: Col Art Asn Am; Am Fedn Arts; Am Asn Mus; Am Asn Mus Dirs.
Publications: Auth, Le sentiment de la nature en France dans la premiére moitié du 17e siecle, B Franklin, 26; auth, Carl Morris, Am Fedn Arts, 59; auth, Art in museums, 63; auth, Museums today, Univ Baroda, 67; auth, Pre-Columbian Art (introduction to the Heeramoneck Collection), Nat Mus, New Delhi, India, 67; also contribr, prof periodicals, encycl & mus publ.
Mailing Address: National Museum, New Delhi, India.

MORRELL, WAYNE (BEAM)
Painter
Preferred Media: Oils.
b Clementon, N J, Dec 24, 23.
Study & Training: Philadelphia Sch Indust Art; Drexel Inst.
Work in Public Collections: Sloan Kettering Cancer Res Ctr, New York, N Y.
Exhibitions: Nat Acad Design, New York; Allied Artist Am, New York, 72; Knickerbocker Artists, New York; Rockport Art Asn, Mass, 72; Expos Intercontinentale, Monoco, France; plus one other.
Teaching: Instr, pvt classes, 61-66.
Positions: Art dir, John Oldham Studios, Conn, 58-61; designer, Paris & Brussels World's Fairs.
Awards: Jane Peterson Prize, 69 & Coun Am Art Socs Award, 71, Allied Artist Am; gold medal, Rockport Art Asn, 70.
Bibliography: R Kolby (auth) A stand for nature, Am Artist, 3/72.
Memberships: Allied Artist Am (jury mem, 72); Springfield Acad Artist (coun, 60-61); Salmagundi Club; Rockport Art Asn.
Publications: Illusr, Readers Digest, 69.
Dealers: Newman Galleries, 1625 Walnut, Philadelphia, PA 19103; Grand Central Galleries, 40 Vanderbilt Ave, New York, NY 10017.
Mailing Address: 153 Main St, Rockport, MA 01966.

MORRIS, CARL
Painter
Preferred Media: Oils.
b Calif.
Study & Training: Art Inst Chicago; Kunstgewerbeschule, Vienna; Akademie Bildenden Kuenste, Vienna; Inst Int Educ fel for study in Paris, France.
Work in Public Collections: Solomon R Guggenheim Mus & Metropolitan Mus Art, New York, New York; Nat Gallery Art & Joseph Hirshhorn Collection, Washington, D C; Mus Mod Art & Whitney Mus Am Art, New York.
Commissions: Murals, U S Treas Dept, for Post Off Bldg, Eugene, Ore, 41; murals, Ore Centennial Comn for Hall of Relig Hist, 59.
Exhibitions: Carnegie Int, Pittsburgh, Pa; Rome-New York Art Found Exhib; Pittsburgh Int; San Francisco Mus Art, Calif; Art U S A Int.
Awards: Ford Found Award, Retrospective Exhib, 60-62; purchase award, Nat Inst Arts & Lett; purchase award, Ford Found, 60.

Bibliography: P Colt (auth), Carl Morris: a decade of painting in Portland, Portland Art Mus, 52; G L M Morley (auth), Ford Found, 60; H Seldis (auth), Pacific heritage, Art in Am, 65.
Memberships: Portland Art Asn.
Publications: Illusr, covers & drawings for Poetry Northwest, summer 61 & summer 63; illusr, cover and drawings for Five poets of the Pacific Northwest, Univ Wash Press, 64.
Dealers: Kraushaar Galleries, 1055 Madison Ave, New York, NY 10021; Fountain Gallery, 115 S W Fourth Ave, Portland, OR 97204.
Mailing Address: 919 N W Skyline Blvd, Portland, OR 97229.

MORRIS, DONALD FISCHER
Art Dealer
b Detroit, Mich, Apr 12, 25.
Positions: Owner & dir, Donald Morris Gallery, Inc, Detroit.
Memberships: Art Dealers Asn Am; Mich Coun Arts; Detroit Art Dealers Asn (pres, 71-).
Specialty of Gallery: Twentieth century American and European painting and sculpture; African art.
Mailing Address: Donald Morris Gallery, Inc, 20082 Livernois, Detroit, MI 48221.

MORRIS, EDWARD A
Painter, Illustrator
b Philadelphia, Pa, July 28, 17.
Study & Training: Philadelphia Col Art, with Henry C Pitz & W Emerton Heitland.
Work in Public Collections: In many pvt collections.
Exhibitions: Am Watercolor Soc Ann; also in numerous eastern galleries & mus.
Awards: Fed Migratory Duck Stamp Design Award, 61-62 & 62-63.
Memberships: Asn Prof Artists: Ducks Unlimited.
Publications: Contribr, Northwestern Banks Hunting Guide, 62, Gopher Historian, Naturalist, Linn's Weekly Stamp News & others.
Mailing Address: 822 Plymouth Bldg, Minneapolis, MN 55402.

MORRIS, GEORGE L K
Painter, Sculptor
Preferred Media: Oils, Marble.
b New York, N Y, Nov 14, 05.
Study & Training: Yale Univ, BA; Art Stud League New York, with John Sloan & K H Miller; Galerie Mod, Paris, France, with Léger and Ozenfant.
Work in Public Collections: Metrop Mus Art, New York; Whitney Mus Am Art, New York; Philadelphia Mus Art, Pa; Corcoran Gallery Art, Washington, D C; N C Mus Art, Raleigh.
Commissions: Mosaic mural, Elementary Sch, Lenox, Mass, 62; large painting, Madison Sq Garden Corp, 65.
Exhibitions: Whitney Mus Am Art Ann, 40; Artists for Victory, Metrop Mus Art, 46; Abstract Painting & Sculpture in America, Mus Mod Art, 51; Younger American Artists, Guggenheim Mus, New York, 54; Pa Acad Fine Arts, Philadelphia, 64.
Collections Arranged: For Mus Living Art, New York Univ, 36, Corcoran Gallery Art, 66 & Montclair Mus Art, N J, 71.
Teaching: Instr painting, Art Stud League New York, 45-46; artist-in-residence, St John's Col, Annapolis, Md, 61-62.
Positions: Trustee, New York City Ctr Music & Drama, 66-
Awards: Achievement award, Pepsi-Cola Competition, 48; Temple Gold Medal, Pa Acad Fine Arts, 64; Berkshire Hills Award, 66.
Bibliography: Ilya Bolotowsky, art film, 62; Donelson Hoopes (auth), The art of George L K Morris, Corcoran Gallery, 65; W W Jackson (auth), George L K Morris: forty years of his art, Col Art Asn Am, 72.
Memberships: Am Abstract Artists (pres, 47-50); Fedn Mod Painters & Sculptors; Century Asn.
Publications: Auth, articles, In: Plastique (Paris), 37-39, Partisan Rev, 37-42, Mag of Art, 53, Art News, 54 & The World of Abstract Art, 56.
Dealer: Hirschl & Adler Galleries, 21 E 67th St, New York, NY 10021.
Mailing Address: 1 Sutton Pl S, New York, NY 10022.

MORRIS, HILDA
Sculptor, Painter
Preferred Media: Bronze, Cement, Sumi.
b New York, N Y.
Study & Training: Art Stud League New York; Cooper Union Sch Art & Archit.
Work in Public Collections: Chase-Manhattan Bank; Calif Palace of Legion of Honor, San Francisco, Calif; Munson-Williams-Proctor Inst Mus; Walter P Chrysler, Jr Collection, Va Mus; San Francisco Mus Art.
Commissions: Sculpture, Seattle Opera House, Wash, 63; bronze, Standard Plaza Bldg, Portland, Ore, 67; bronze, Pac Nat Bldg, Tacoma, Wash, 71.

Exhibitions: American Sculpture, Metrop Mus Art, 51; Third Pac Coast Biennial, Santa Barbara Mus Art, 60; Northwest Art Today, Seattle World's Fair, 62; Nat Print Show, Brooklyn Mus, 64; many exhibs, San Francisco Mus Art.
Awards: Ford Found fel, 60.
Bibliography: New talent, 3/57 & Regional accent: Pacific Northwest, 65, Art in Am; Robin Skelton (auth), Sculpture as metaphor: five bronzes by Hilda Morris, Malahat Rev, 7/69.
Memberships: Portland Art Asn.
Publications: Illusr, cover drawings, Poetry Northwest, spring 68, summer 68 & spring 69.
Dealer: Fountain Gallery of Art, 115 S W Fourth, Portland, OR 97212.
Mailing Address: 919 N W Skyline Blvd, Portland, OR 97229.

MORRIS, JACK AUSTIN, JR
Art Administrator, Writer
b Macon, Ga, Sept 29, 39.
Study & Training: Univ S C, AB, with Edmund Yaghjian, Augusta Wittkowski & Catherine Rembert; Univ S C; Harvard Univ Inst Arts Admin.
Collections Arranged: Arnold H Maremont Collection (20th Century American & European Painting & Sculpture), 65; Ida Kohlmeyer (one-man exhibition), 67; Jasper Johns Prints, Harbor Town Mus, Hilton Head Island, S C, 71.
Teaching: Lectr, Kress Collection, Columbia Mus Art, S C, 62-65; instr drawing & painting, Richland Art Sch, Columbia, 64-65.
Positions: Curatorial assoc, Columbia Mus Art, 62-63, asst to dir, 63-65; exec dir, Greenville Co Mus Art, 65-
Memberships: Am Asn Mus; Guild S C Artists (pres, 68); S C Fedn Mus (founder, v pres, 71-72); S C Arts Comn (chmn exec comt, 72-73); Southeastern Mus Conf.
Research: Contemporary American art.
Publications: Ed, Museum news, 64-65 & illusr, Two-hundred years of the arts of France, 65, Columbia Mus Art; auth, Contemporary artists of South Carolina (catalogue), 70; contribr, Jasper Johns: recent prints, Harbor Town Mus, 71; auth, William M Halsey: retrospective (catalogue), 72.
Mailing Address: 106 DuPont Dr, Greenville, SC 29607.

MORRIS, KATHLEEN MOIR
Painter
b Montreal, P Q, Dec 2, 93.
Study & Training: Art Asn Montreal; also with Maurice Cullen.
Work in Public Collections: Nat Gallery Can; Montreal Mus Fine Arts; Hart House, Univ Toronto; Art Gallery, Hamilton; Mackenzie King Mus; Can Legation, Paris, France; plus others.
Exhibitions: One-man show, Montreal Mus Fine Arts, 39; N Y World's Fair, 39; Can Club, N Y, 50; Festival of Brit, 51; Royal Can Acad Exhib, Toronto, Ottawa & Halifax, 57; plus many others.
Awards: Willingdon Art Competition, 30.
Memberships: Can Group Painters; Assoc Royal Can Acad Art.
Mailing Address: 79 Windsor Ave, Westmount, Montreal 217, P Q, Can.

MORRIS, KYLE RANDOLPH
Painter
Preferred Media: Oils, Acrylics.
b Des Moines, Iowa, Jan 17, 18.
Study & Training: Art Inst Chicago, 35-40; Northwestern Univ, BA 39, MA, 40; Cranbrook Acad Art, MFA, 47.
Work in Public Collections: Albright-Knox Gallery, Buffalo, N Y; Detroit Inst Arts, Mich; Guggenheim Mus, N Y; San Francisco Mus Art, Calif; Whitney Mus Am Art, New York, N Y; plus others.
Exhibitions: Younger American Painters, Guggenheim Mus, 54; Nature in Abstraction, Whitney Mus Am Art, 58; American Painting, Am Pavilion, Brussels World's Fair, Belg, 58; American Painting, New York-Rome Found, Rome, Italy, 58; Pittsburgh Int Exhib, Carnegie Inst, Pa, 61; plus others.
Teaching: Instr art hist & painting, Stephens Col, Columbia, Mo, 40-41; asst prof art hist & painting, Univ Tex, Austin, 45-46; assoc prof painting, Univ Minn, Minneapolis, 47-51; assoc prof painting, Univ Calif, Berkeley, 52-54; lectr art hist, Cooper Union, 58; vis critic, Yale Grad Sch, 65; guest artist & critic, Carnegie Mellon Univ, 70.
Awards: Purchase award, Six States Second Biennial Exhib, Walker Art Ctr, Minneapolis, 49; purchase award, American Painting, San Francisco Mus Art, 53; hon mention, II Biennial, Belles Artes, Mexico City, Mex, 60; plus others.
Mailing Address: 243 E 17th St, New York, NY 10003.

MORRIS, ROBERT
Sculptor
b Kansas City, Mo, Feb 9, 31.
Study & Training: Kansas City Jr Col; Kansas City Art Inst, 48-50;

Univ Kansas City; San Francisco Art Inst; Reed Col, 53-55; Hunter Col, MA, 66.
Commissions: Earth Proj, Nat Planning Comn, Ottawa.
Exhibitions: Guggenheim Int, Solomon R Guggenheim Mus, 67; Minimal Art, The Hague, 68; The Art of the Real, Mus Mod Art, 68; Philadelphia Mus Art, 68; Whitney Mus Am Art, 72; plus many others.
Awards: Prizes, Guggenheim Mus, 67 & Torcuato di Tella, Buenos Aires, Arg, 67; Guggenheim Found fel, 69; plus others.
Bibliography: Gregory Battcock (ed), Minimal art: a critical anthology, Dutton, 68; E C Goosen (auth), The art of the real U S A 1948-1968, Mus Mod Art, 68; Max Kozloff (auth), Renderings, Simon & Schuster, 68; plus others.
Mailing Address: c/o Castelli Gallery, 4 E 77th St, New York, NY 10021.

MORRISON, BOONE M
Photographer, Designer
b Berkeley, Calif, Jan 28, 41.
Study & Training: Stanford Univ, BA(hist), 62, BA(commun), 63; Yosemite Photog Workshops, with Ansel Adams, 71.
Work in Public Collections: Honolulu Acad Art, Hawaii; Bishop Mus, Honolulu; State of Hawaii Collection.
Commissions: Portfolio of portraits, Hawaiian Music Found, Honolulu, 70; mural photographs, Kauai Mus, Lihue, 71; photo document, State Found Cult & Art, Hawaii, 71; Project Documerica, Fed Govt Sponsored Doc Environ, 72; photo arch, C Brewer Co, 72.
Exhibitions: Four Photographers, Foundry, Honolulu, 70; Artists of Hawaii Ann, Honolulu Acad Art, 70 & 72; Hawaii State Found Cult & Arts Exhib, 71 & 72; one-man show, Foundry, 72; Easter Art Ann, Honolulu, 72.
Teaching: Instr photog, Univ Hawaii, Manoa Campus, 69-71, instr archit, 70-72; instr photog, Fed Model Cities Prog, Kalihi-Palama, 70.
Positions: Co-dir, Art-Park Pub Festival Arts, State Hawaii, 69; owner-founder, Foundry Art Gallery, Honolulu, 69-71; dir-designer, Statewide Photog Exhib, 70.
Awards: Purchase award, Hawaii State Found Cult & Art, 72; purchase award, Easter Arts Ann, 72.
Bibliography: C Eyre (auth), How they found the foundry, Honolulu Mag, 70; The eye of the camera (film), KHET-TV, Hawaii, 71; Tomi Knaffler (auth), Fine arts photography in Hawaii, Honolulu Star Bull, 72.
Memberships: Friends of Photog.
Publications: Contribr, Beautiful Hawaii, Lane, 72; illusr, Keki'o'ka aina, Mind's Eye Press, Honolulu (in prep); illusr, Hawaii legends, Bishop Mus Press (in prep).
Mailing Address: 3349 A Anoai Pl, Honolulu, HI 96822.

MORRISON, KEITH ANTHONY
Painter, Educator
Preferred Media: Oils, Watercolors, Acrylics.
b Jamaica, W I, May 20, 42; U S citizen.
Study & Training: Art Inst Chicago, BFA, 63, MFA, 65; Univ Ill; DePaul Univ; Loyola Univ.
Work in Public Collections: Jamaica Inst, W I; Nat Collection Liberia, W Africa; Fisk Univ; Art Inst Chicago; Dusable Mus Afro-Am Hist.
Commissions: Painting for Liberian Govt, 64 & Dusable Mus Afro-Am Hist, 71; mural commissioned by Phyllis Kind Gallery for Main Bank, Chicago, Ill, 72.
Exhibitions: Black & White, Kovler Gallery, 69; Chicago Prints, Allan Frumkin Gallery, 69; Nat Exhib Black Artists, Smith-Mason Gallery, Washington, D C, 71; Black American Artists 71, Ill Bell/Ill Arts Coun, 71; Biennial Chicago & Vicinity, Art Inst Chicago, 71; plus one other.
Collections Arranged: Toussaint L'ouverture, paintings of Jacob Lawrence, organized for DePaul Univ, Chicago, 69; Black Experiences in Art, exhibition of painting & sculpture, Bergman Gallery Univ Chicago, 71.
Teaching: Instr art, Hyde Park Art Ctr, Chicago, 65-67; asst prof drawing, Fisk Univ, Nashville, Tenn, 67-68; assoc prof printmaking & chmn dept, DePaul Univ, 68-71; assoc prof painting, Univ Ill, Chicago-Circle, 69-.
Awards: Second prize, Jamaica Inst, 59.
Bibliography: Doris Sanders (auth), Morrison's panel, Defender, 5/69; Robin Glauber (auth), Keith Morrison at Black Hawk, Skyline, 9/70; Kitty Kingston (auth), Keith Morrison, Gleaner, 2/71.
Memberships: Col Art Asn; Nat Conf Artists; Chicago Soc Artists.
Publications: Auth, The probing line, Fisk Univ, 68; auth, The art of Jacob Lawrence, DePaul Univ, 69; auth, Jacob Lawrence's Toussaint L'ouverture, Art Scene, 69; auth, Meaningful concept of art in humanities, Musart, 70; auth, Black experiences, Univ Chicago, 71.
Mailing Address: 5007 S Dorchester, Chicago, IL 60615.

MORRISON, ROBERT CLIFTON
Printmaker, Painter
Preferred Media: Wood, Acrylics.
b Billings, Mont, Aug 13, 24.
Study & Training: Carleton Col, BA; Univ N Mex, MA.
Work in Public Collections: Harvard Univ Libr Print Collection, Cambridge, Mass; Ministry Art & Cult, Ghana; Rocky Mt Col, Billings; Int Col Copenhagen, Denmark.
Commissions: Mosaic mural, Mont State Unemployment Comn, Helena, 61; mosaic mural, Lucerne Pub Schs, Wyo; mural, Lockwood Pub Schs, Billings.
Teaching: Dir art educ, Billings Pub Schs, 57-67; assoc prof art, Rocky Mt Col, 67-
Positions: Ed, Rocky Mt Rev, 63-69; pres, bd dirs, Yellowstone Art Ctr, Billings, 64-65.
Awards: Mont Artist-Teacher of Yr, Am Artists Prof League, 64.
Publications: Auth & illusr, Maxims of LaRochefoucauld, 67.
Dealer: Gallery '85, Emerald Dr, Billings, MT 59101.
Mailing Address: 2815 Woody Dr, Billings, MT 59102.

MORSE, A REYNOLDS
Collector
b Denver, Colo, Oct 20, 14.
Study & Training: Univ Colo, BA, 38; Harvard Bus Sch, MBA, 39.
Positions: Pres, Salvador Dali Mus, Cleveland, Ohio, 70.
Collection: 93 oils, 117 drawings watercolors, over 500 prints all by Salvador Dali.
Publications: Auth, Dali, a study of his life and works, N Y Graphic Soc, 58, A Dali primer, 70, The draftsmanship of Dali, 70, Dali, the masterworks, 71 & Dali, a collection, 72.
Mailing Address: 24050 Commerce Park Rd, Cleveland, OH 44122.

MORSE, JENNIE GREENE
Designer, Educator
Preferred Media: Pastels, Watercolors, Gouache.
b New York, N Y, Mar 19, 08.
Study & Training: N Y Sch Appl Design for Women, Art scholar, 26-27; Berkshire Summer Sch Art; State Univ N Y, cert teacher training; Columbia Univ; Fashion Inst Technol, New York, AAS.
Exhibitions: Am Mus Natural Hist, New York; Metrop Mus Art, New York; Grand Cent Art Gallery, New York; var schs & cols.
Teaching: High Sch instr textile design, Bd Educ, New York, 29-45; prof textile design, Fashion Inst Technol, 45-, chmn dept, 55-71; asst examr, Bd Examr, Bd Educ, New York.
Positions: Free-lance artist-designer, Cyrus Clark-Waverly Fabrics, New York, 27-36; artist-designer, J A Migel, New York, 28-29; artist-designer, C K Eagle, New York, 29-30; artist-designer-stylist, United Textile Print Works, New York, 31-36.
Awards: Sch Art League art scholar, 25-26; five awards best designs, var firms in textile indust.
Bibliography: M D C Crawford (auth), Textiles, Ann Am Design, 31; Travaux decoratifs, La Rev Mod, 6/32; Honoring educators, N Y State Jr Col News Bull, 1/68.
Memberships: Sch Art League; N Y State Asn Jr Cols.
Mailing Address: 1327 Shore Pkwy, Brooklyn, NY 11214.

MORSE, JOHN D
Art Editor
b Gifford, Ill, Sept 26, 06.
Study & Training: Univ Ill, AB & MA; Wayne Univ; New York Univ.
Teaching: Lectr gen art hist & interpretation; instr, Univ Ill, 34-35; instr art hist, Kent Sch, 54-56.
Positions: Asst ed, Am Boy Mag, 28-29 & 30-31; mus instr, Detroit Inst Art, 35-41; managing ed, Art Quart, 38-41; assoc in radio, Metrop Mus Art, New York, N Y, 41-42; ed, Mag of Art, 42-47; art ed, '47 Mag of the Year, 47-48; dir publ, Art Stud League New York, 48-50; assoc ed, Am Artist Mag, 51-53; conductor, Am Artist Mag Europ Tours, 50-52; exec dir, Amateur Artists Asn Am, 51-53; exec secy, Kent Sch, 54-56; chief commun, Detroit Inst Arts, 59-62; head nat exten prog, Henri Francis du Pont Winterthur Mus, Del, 62-70; ed, Am Art J, 72-
Memberships: Century Asn, N Y.
Publications: Auth, Old masters in America, 55; producer, Flanders in the fifteenth century (film), 60, The gardens of Winterthur (film), 64 & Winterthur in bloom (film), 69; ed, Prints in and of America to 1850 (Winterthur conf report), Univ Press Va, 70; ed, Ben Shahn, Praeger, 72; contribr, Mag of Art, London Eve Standard & other mags.
Mailing Address: 215 E 80th St, New York, NY 10021.

MORTON, RICHARD H
Painter, Art Administrator
Preferred Media: Watercolors.
b Dallas, Tex, Aug 8, 21.
Study & Training: Pratt Inst, cert; Oklahoma City Univ, BA; Univ Tulsa, MA; Inst Allende, Mexico City, MFA.

Work in Public Collections: Oklahoma Art Ctr, Oklahoma City; Am Petrol Co, Oklahoma City; Univ Tulsa, Okla.
Exhibitions: Watercolor U S A, Springfield Art Mus, Mo, 66 & 70; Past Jurors Invitational, 69 & Eight State Exhib, 70, Okla Art Ctr; Southwestern Watercolor Soc, Brandywine Galleries, Albuquerque, N Mex, 71.
Teaching: Instr design, Southern Ill Univ, Carbondale, 55-59; asst dean, Columbus Col Art & Design, Ohio, 59-60; asst prof design, Cent State Univ, 61-65; assoc prof painting, Northeast Mo State Univ, Kirksville, 65-72.
Positions: Dir, Door B Art Sch, El Paso, Tex, 72-
Awards: Purchase award in Southwest Am Art Exhib, Okla Art Ctr, 62; transparent watercolor award, Watercolor U S A, W Coast Watercolor Soc, 70; first hon mention in Southwestern Watercolor Soc Exhib, 72.
Memberships: Col Art Asn Am; Southwestern Watercolor Soc.
Publications: Contribr, G I sketchbook, Penguin, 44 & Prize-winning watercolors, Allied Fla, 63.
Dealer: New West Gallery, 5908 Lomas N E, Albuquerque, NM 87110.
Mailing Address: 4800 N Stanton 22, El Paso, TX 79902.

MOSCATT, PAUL N
Painter, Instructor
Preferred Media: Oils, Acrylics.
b Brooklyn, N Y, July 9, 31.
Study & Training: Cooper Union Art Sch; Yale Univ Sch Fine Arts, BFA & MFA.
Work in Public Collections: Univ Bridgeport, Conn; Yale Univ Art Dept; Earlham Col, Richmond, Ind; Cincinnati Art Mus; Allegheny Col, Meadville, Pa.
Exhibitions: One-man shows, Aspects Gallery, New York, N Y, 62 & 63, Earlham Col, 65, Peter Cooper Gallery, New York, 68, Univ Md, Baltimore, 70 & Towson State Col, Md, 70.
Teaching: Instr painting & drawing, Univ Bridgeport, 62-64; instr painting & drawing, Art Acad Cincinnati, 64-66; instr painting & drawing, Md Inst Col Art, 67-
Mailing Address: Maryland Institute College of Art, 1300 Mount Royal Ave, Baltimore, MD 21217.

MOSE, CARL C
Sculptor, Lecturer
Preferred Media: Bronze, Stone, Ceramic.
b Copenhagen, Denmark; U S citizen.
Study & Training: Art Inst Chicago, apprenticeship with Lorado Taft; Midway Studio Group, Chicago, Ill; Art Stud League New York; Beaux Arts Acad, New York; independent study, Copenhagen & Paris.
Work in Public Collections: Corcoran Gallery Art, Washington, D C; Smithsonian Inst; Tenn Fine Arts Ctr, Cheekwood, Nashville; Evansville Mus Art & Sci, Ind; Carleton Col, Northfield, Minn.
Commissions: Bronze statue of Gen J J Pershing, for State Capitol Grounds, State of Mo, now in Laclede, Mo, 57; bronze eagle & fledglings monument, U S Air Force Acad, Colo, 58; statue of St Francis, Turner Mem, Forest Park, Saint Louis, Mo, 62; statue of Stan Musial, Plaza, Busch Mem Stadium, Civic Ctr, Saint Louis, 68; numerous archit carvings in stone & medals.
Exhibitions: Am Paintings & Sculpture & Artists of Chicago & Vicinity Ann, Art Inst Chicago, 23-24 & 28-31; Royal Acad Int Exhib, Copenhagen, Denmark, 27; Twin City Art Exhibs, Minneapolis Art Inst, Minn, 30-31; New York Worlds Fair Exhib, N Y, 39; Nat Sculpture Soc, Lever House, New York, 72.
Teaching: Head sculpture dept, Corcoran Sch Art, Washington, D C, 27-30; head sculpture dept, Minneapolis Art Inst Sch Art, 30-33; head sculpture dept, Wash Univ Sch Fine Arts, 36-47; lectr.
Positions: Chief medalist, Inst Heraldry, USA, Alexandria, Va, 62-65.
Awards: Two first prizes, Soc Washington Artists, 35-36; first, regional competition, U S Treasury, Fed Bldg, Salina, Kans, 39; two first prizes & hon mention, Saint Louis Artists' Guild, Mo, 48, 49 & 55.
Bibliography: Educ TV Series (11), The sculpture, Ann Arbor, Mich, 58; George McCue (auth), A sculptor's imprint on Saint Louis, Saint Louis Post-Dispatch, 8/12/62; Bev Conolly (auth), Carl Mose—sculptor of minds as well as images, The Art Scene, Washington, D C, winter 70-71.
Memberships: Fel Nat Sculpture Soc; Artists' Equity Asn.
Dealer: Agra Gallery, 1721 DeSales St N W, Washington, DC 20036.
Mailing Address: Rte 1, Box 74-B, New Windsor, MD 21776.

MOSELEY, RALPH SESSIONS
Painter
Preferred Media: Acrylics.
b Kingston, N Y, June 5, 41.
Study & Training: Williams Col, BA; Hunter Col, MA.
Work in Public Collections: Whitney Mus Am Art, New York, N Y; Aldrich Mus, Ridgefield, Conn.

Exhibitions: Ann, 69 & Lyrical Abstraction, 70, Whitney Mus Am Art; Aldrich Mus, 70.
Mailing Address: 438 Broome St, New York, NY 10013.

MOSELEY, SPENCER ALTEMONT
Painter, Educator
Preferred Media: Oils.
b Bellingham, Wash, July 18, 25.
Study & Training: Univ Wash, BA, 48, MFA, 51; Ecole Fernand Leger, Paris, 49.
Work in Public Collections: Seattle Art Mus, Wash; Henry Art Gallery, Univ Wash.
Exhibitions: Kobe Exchange Show, Japan, 65; Art Across America, San Francisco Mus Art, 65; The West—80 Contemporaries, Univ Ariz Art Gallery, Tucson, 67; 73rd Western Ann, Denver Art Mus, 71; Pac Cities Loan Exhib, Auckland Art Mus, N Z, 71; plus others.
Teaching: Prof art hist & painting, Univ Wash, 49-, dir, sch art, 66-
Awards: First prize, Pac Northwest Arts & Crafts Fair, 65; Ford Found Purchase Award, 66; purchase prize, 54th Ann Northwest Painting & Sculpture, 68; plus others.
Bibliography: Carraher (auth), Optical illusions and the visual arts, 66 & Proctor (auth), Principles of pattern, 69, Reinhold; Westphal (auth), Textiles (catalog), Mus Contemp Crafts, New York, 67.
Publications: Co-auth, Crafts design, Wadsworth Publ, 52; auth, History of painting in the western world, Frontier Press Co, 64.
Mailing Address: School of Art, University of Washington, Seattle, WA 98195.

MOSER, JULON
Painter
Preferred Media: Watercolors.
b Schenectady, N Y.
Study & Training: Binghamton Fine Arts, 25, with Frank Taylor Bowers; Chouinard Sch Art, 29-30, with Pattie Patterson; Univ Calif, Berkeley, 43-44, with Wessels; Scripps Col, 47, with Millard Sheets; also pvt study with Nicolai Fechin.
Work in Public Collections: Over 250 paintings in pvt collections.
Exhibitions: Golden Gate International, Treasure Island, San Francisco, 39; Calif Nat Watercolor Soc Current Exhib, Nat Acad Design, 72 & Ann Exhib, Laguna Beach Gallery, 72; Invitational Exhib touring Sweden, 72-73; one-woman shows, Pomoroy Galleries, 62 & Oxnard Art Gallery, 72.
Awards: 12 awards for still life & others, Women Painters of the West, 38-55; award for Morning, Taos, N Mex, Clearwater High Sch, 41; award for Shades of Prometheus, Oxnard Art Gallery, 72.
Memberships: Calif Nat Watercolor Soc (rec secy, 72-73); Women Painters of the West (pres, 56-58, corresp secy, 72-73); Los Angeles Art Asn; Oxnard Art Asn; hon mem Ventura Art Club.
Dealer: Milk House Art Galleries, Pacific Coast Hwy & Washington St, Marina del Rey, CA 90291.
Mailing Address: 10790 Wilshire Blvd, Los Angeles, CA 90024.

MOSES, ED
Painter
b Long Beach, Calif, 1926.
Study & Training: Univ Calif, Los Angeles, MA; Tamarind Lithography grant.
Work in Public Collections: Art Inst Chicago, Ill; Corcoran Gallery Art, Washington, D C; Pasadena Mus, Calif; Walker Art Ctr, Minneapolis, Minn; San Francisco Mus Art.
Exhibitions: Int Graphics Exhib, Florence, Italy, 69; Tamarind Prints, Mus Mod Art, New York, N Y, 69; Corcoran Gallery Art Biennial, Washington, D C, 71; Current Am Artists, Art Inst Chicago Ann, 72; Documenta 5, Kassel, W Ger, 72; plus others.
Teaching: Instr art, Univ Calif Irvine, 68-71.
Mailing Address: c/o Ronald Feldman Fine Arts Gallery, 33 E 74th St, New York, NY 10021.

MOSES, FORREST (LEE), (JR)
Painter
Preferred Media: Oils.
b Danville, Va, May, 34.
Study & Training: Washington & Lee Univ, BA, 56; Pratt Inst, 60-62; Houston Mus Sch Fine Arts, 63-64.
Exhibitions: Beaumont Art Mus Ann Show, Tex, 65; Monterey Peninsula Mus Competition, Carmel, Calif, 67; Southwest Biennial, Mus N Mex, Santa Fe, 70 & 72; Artists' Choice Traveling Show, Mus N Mex, 70-72.
Teaching: Instr drawing, Pratt Inst, 61-62; instr drawing & watercolor, Univ Houston, 69.
Mailing Address: c/o Janus Gallery, 116 1/2 E Palace Ave, Santa Fe, NM 87501.

MOSES, FORREST KING
Painter
Preferred Media: Oils.
b Verona, Va, May 17, 93.
Study & Training: With Grandma Moses.
Work in Public Collections: Ft Stanwix Mus, Rome, N Y; Rensselaer Co Hist Soc, Rome; Acad Arts, Easton, Md; Bennington Mus, Vt; Robert F Kennedy Collection, Syracuse, N Y.
Commissions: Siege of Ft Stanwix, Ft Stanwix Mus, 67; Erie Canal, Erie Canal Sequi Celebration Comt, Rome, 67; Battle of Bennington, Bennington Mus, 69; plus many other hist scenes of Mohawk Valley Region.
Exhibitions: Int Naive Art Exhibs, Art Wagon Galleries, Scottsdale, Ariz, 71-72.
Dealer: Raymond J Poppelman, P O Box 352, Oxford, MD 21654.
Mailing Address: Eagle Bridge, NY 12057.

MOSHIER, ELIZABETH ALICE
Painter, Educator
b Utica, N Y, Dec 24, 01.
Study & Training: Skidmore Col, BS, 22; Columbia Univ, MA, 31; Andre L'Hote Studio, Paris, France, 37; Kunstgewerbe Schule, Vienna, Austria, 38; with Moholy-Nagy, Chicago, Ill, 42; Black Mt Col, with Joseph Albers, 46; Mirko Studio, Rome, Italy, 48; Skidmore Col, hon LHD, 72.
Exhibitions: Albany Inst Hist & Art; Syracuse Mus Fine Arts; Ind Univ Gallery; Rochester Mem Art Gallery; Skidmore Col.
Teaching: Lectr mod painting, India & contemp design; instr art, Skidmore Col, 25-41, prof art, 41-68, chmn dept art, 59-68, emer prof art, 68-
Awards: Outstanding alumnae award, Skidmore Col, 72.
Memberships: Col Art Asn Am; Am Asn Univ Prof.
Mailing Address: 8 Watson Pl, Utica, NY 13502.

MOSKOWITZ, ROBERT S
Painter
b New York, N Y, June 20, 35.
Work in Public Collections: Mus Mod Art & Whitney Mus Am Art, New York, N Y; Albright-Knox Art Gallery, Buffalo, N Y; Rose Art Mus, Brandeis Univ, Waltham, Mass.
Exhibitions: Art of Assemblage, Mus Mod Art, New York, 61; Whitney Mus Am Art Ann, 69; one-man shows, Leo Castelli Gallery, New York, 62, French & Co, New York, 70 & Hayden Gallery, Mass Inst Technol, Cambridge, Mass, 71.
Awards: Guggenheim fel, 67.
Mailing Address: 81 Leonard St, New York, NY 10013.

MOSKOWITZ, SHIRLEY (MRS JACOB W GRUBER)
Painter, Sculptor
Preferred Media: Acrylics, Woods.
b Houston, Tex, Aug 4, 20.
Study & Training: Mus Sch Art, Houston; Rice Univ, BA, 41; Oberlin Col, MA, 42; also with Morris Davidson, New York, N Y.
Work in Public Collections: Allen Mus Art, Oberlin, Ohio; Congregation Beth Yeshuren, Houston; Har Zion Temple, Philadelphia, Pa.
Exhibitions: Ann Oil & Ann Watercolor, Pa Acad Fine Arts, Philadelphia, 53, 57 & 69; Am Watercolor Soc, Nat Acad Design, 63; one-man shows, Allen Art Mus, Oberlin, 46, Sullivan Libr, 48 & 56 & Paley Libr, 70, Temple Univ & Woodmere Art Gallery, Philadelphia, 68.
Teaching: Instr art hist, Univ Tex, Austin, spring 43; lectr art, Houston Pub Schs, 43-46; dir art, Oberlin Pub Schs, 46-47.
Positions: Art prog for grade schs, Oberlin Pub Schs, 47; pres, Norristown Art League, 65-66.
Awards: Prize for oil painting, Houston Artists Exhib, Mus Fine Arts, Houston, 44; second prize for sculpture, regional show, Cheltenham Art Ctr, Pa, 62; Charles Smith Sculpture Prize, Woodmere Art Gallery, 70.
Memberships: Pa Acad Fine Arts; Artists Equity Asn; Woodmere Gallery Art Centre; Philadelphia Watercolor Club (secy, 68-70).
Dealer: Gallery 500, 500 Germantown Pike, Lafayette Hills, PA 19444.
Mailing Address: 2211 Delancey Pl, Philadelphia, PA 19103.

MOSLEY, ZACK T
Illustrator, Cartoonist
b Hickory, Okla, Dec 12, 06.
Study & Training: Chicago Acad Fine Arts, 26-27; Art Inst Chicago, 27-28.
Positions: Creator, syndicated comic strip Smilin' Jack, Chicago Tribune-New York News.
Memberships: Nat Cartoonists Soc.
Mailing Address: 114 Edgewood Dr, Stuart, FL 33494.

MOSS, IRENE
Painter
Preferred Media: Oils.
b Eperjes, Czech; U S citizen.
Study & Training: Brooklyn Mus Sch Art; also with Moses Soyer & Dmitri Romanofsky, New York, N Y.
Work in Public Collections: Akron Art Inst, Ohio; Finch Col Mus, New York; Rose Art Mus, Brandeis Univ, Mass; New Britain Mus Am Art, Conn; Norfolk Mus, Va.
Exhibitions: Albright-Knox Art Gallery, Buffalo, N Y, 68; Fort Worth Art Ctr, Tex, 68; Rochester Mem Art Gallery, N Y, 68; one-woman show, Suffolk Mus, Stony Brook, N Y, 71; Stamford Mus, Stamford, Conn, 72.
Positions: Co-ed, Feminist Art Jour, at present.
Bibliography: John Gruen (auth), Friday tour of art, World Jour Tribune, 66; Jacqueline Barnitz (auth), Images, Arts Mag, 68; Cindy Nemser (auth), Focus, Arts Mag, 69.
Dealer: Haller Gallery, 979 Third Ave, New York, NY 10022.
Mailing Address: 214 West End Ave, Brooklyn, NY 11235.

MOSS, JOE (FRANCIS)
Sculptor, Painter
Preferred Media: Plastics, Metal, Wood.
b Kincheloe, W Va, Jan 26, 33.
Study & Training: W Va Univ, AB, 51, MA, 60.
Work in Public Collections: Huntington Galleries, W Va; Arts & Humanities Coun, Charleston, W Va; State Capitol, Charleston; Urban Coalition, Washington, D C.
Commissions: Kinetic sculpture, W Va Univ, Morgantown, 65; decorative sculpture, First Presby Church, Morgantown, 66; hanging sculpture, Floradora Shop, Morgantown, 66.
Exhibitions: Watercolor U S A, Springfield, Mo, 64; Drawing Nat, Bucknell Univ, Lewisburg, Pa, 65; Mem Exhib, Mus Mod Art, New York, N Y, 66; 50 States of Art, Am Fedn Art Traveling Exhib, 66-67; one-man show, Washington Gallery Mod Art, Washington, D C, 67.
Teaching: Assoc prof art, W Va Univ, 60-70; vis prof art, Univ Md, College Park, summer 67; assoc prof art, Univ Del, 70-
Positions: Artist-in-residence, Bethany Col, W Va, 67.
Awards: Painting award, Huntington Galleries, 63; prize for environ design, Three Rivers Arts Festival, Pittsburgh, Pa, 68; sculpture award, Appalachian Corridors Exhib, Charleston, 70.
Bibliography: Article In: Time Mag, 63; George Richey (auth), Constructivism, George Braziller, 67; taped interview, On: Voice of Am, 67.
Dealer: Max Hutchinson Gallery, 127 Green St, New York, NY 10012.
Mailing Address: 7 Woodsman Dr, Newark, DE 19711.

MOSS, JOEL C
Painter, Educator
b U S A.
Study & Training: Ft Hays Kans State Col, BS, 38; George Peabody Col, MA, 42; Columbia Univ, EdD, 53.
Work in Public Collections: Wichita Art Mus, Kans; Wichita Asn Gallery; Gallery Art, Hastings Col, Nebr; Hutchinson Art Asn, Kans; over 250 paintings in pvt collections.
Exhibitions: Nelson Gallery Mid Am Exhib, Kansas City, Mo, 55; San Francisco Art Mus, Calif, 56; Joslyn Mus, Omaha, Nebr, 65; Watercolor U S A, Springfield, Mo, 68; Wichita Art Mus Artist Ann, 70.
Teaching: Instr art, Parsons Jr Col, Kans, 39-42; prof art, Ft Hays Kans State Col, 46-, chmn dept, 50-
Awards: First prize watercolor, 15 Kans Artist Ann, 67; first purchase prize, Wichita Art Asn Statewide Watercolor, 69 & 70; Amsden Award & Cult Arts Award, Kans Watercolor Soc, 71.
Memberships: Kans Watercolor Soc (bd dirs, 68-); Kans Cult Arts (adv, 64-); Outstanding Educators U S A.
Dealer: Raven Gallery, Twin Lakes Shopping Center, Wichita, KS 67303.
Mailing Address: 408 W Fourth, Hays, KS 67601.

MOSS, MILTON
Painter, Lecturer
Preferred Media: Oils.
b New York, N Y.
Study & Training: Cooper Union; Ecoles Beaux Arts, Paris.
Work in Public Collections: Phoenix Mus Fine Arts, Ariz; Norfolk Mus Art & Sci, Va; Miami Mus Mod Art, Fla; Univ Maine; Houston Mus, Tex.
Exhibitions: Butler Inst Am Art, Youngstown, Ohio, 63; one-man shows, Gallery Die Drie Hendricken, Amsterdam, Netherlands, 65, Harry Salpeter Gallery, New York, N Y, 67, Wickersham Gallery, New York, 69 & Syosset Pub Libr, New York, 71.
Dealer: Harbor Gallery, 43 Main St, Cold Spring Harbor, NY 11724.
Mailing Address: 189 Forest Dr, Jericho, NY 11753.

529 / 09 pixel

MOSS, MORRIE ALFRED
Collector
b Chicago, Ill, June 2, 07.
Collection: Paul Storr silver, over 1000 pieces; 66 old master paintings; 75 jades; 100 ivories; 16 Faberges; 48 pairs Dorothy Doughty bird models. Exhibited in Brooks Mem Art Gallery, Memphis, Tenn & currently at Indianapolis Mus Art & Dayton Art Inst.
Mailing Address: 41 N Perkins Rd, Memphis, TN 38117.

MOTHERWELL, ROBERT
Painter, Printmaker
Preferred Media: Collage, Ink, Aquatint.
b Aberdeen, Wash, Jan 24, 15.
Study & Training: Stanford Univ, BA, 36; Harvard Univ Grad Sch Arts & Sci, 37; Columbia Univ, 40, with Meyer Schapiro.
Work in Public Collections: Mus Mod Art, Metrop Mus Art & Whitney Mus Am Art, New York, N Y; San Francisco Art Mus, Calif; Tate Gallery Art, London, Eng.
Commissions: Mural, J F Kennedy Fed Bldg, Boston, Mass, 66; diptych, S Edelstone, Chicago, Ill, 71; A la Pintura (suite of aquatints), comn by Rafael Alberti, Universal Art Ed, Long Island, 72; tapestry, Westinghouse Broadcasting Co, Philadelphia, 72; mural, Univ Iowa Art Mus, Iowa City, 73.
Exhibitions: Collage Exhib, Gallery Berggruen, Paris, France, 61; Retrospective, Mus Mod Art, New York & other galleries & mus, U S & Europe, 65; Collage Exhib, Whitney Mus Am Art, 68; Recent Paintings, with Matisse Sculpture, Walker Art Ctr, Minneapolis, Minn, 72; Robert Motherwell's A la Pintura: The Making of a Book, Metrop Mus, New York, 72; plus many others, including The Collages of Robert Motherwell.
Teaching: Instr painting, Black Mountain Col, 45, 51; instr painting, Hunter Col, 50-58; distinguished prof, Hunter Col, 71-72.
Positions: Conroy fel, St Paul's Sch, N H, 70; educ adv, J S Guggenheim Found; adv ed, Am Scholar, Washington, D C, 68-75; ed, Documents of 20th Century Art, 68-; art ed, Viking Press, 68-
Awards: Am rep, São Paulo VI Biennale, Mus Mod Art, 61; Am prize, Guggenheim Int, 64; Belgian Art Critics Prize, Brussels, 66.
Bibliography: Frank O'Hara (auth), Motherwell, Mus Mod Art, 65; Bryan Robertson & Octavio Paz (auth), Robert Motherwell paintings & collages 1967-70, Galerie I M Erker, 71.
Memberships: Smithsonian Inst (counr); Nat Collection Fine Arts (counr); J S Guggenheim Found (adv); fel Royal Soc Arts; fel in perpetuity Metrop Mus Art.
Dealers: Lawrence Rubin Gallery, 49 W 57th St, New York, NY 10019; David Mirvish Gallery, 596 Markham St, Toronto 174, Ont, Can.
Mailing Address: 909 North St, Greenwich, CT 06830.

MOULD, LOLA FROWDE
Painter
Preferred Media: Watercolors, Oils, Pastels.
b Sydney, N S, Dec, 08.
Study & Training: Mt Allison Univ; Boston Sch Design; New York Sch Design.
Work in Public Collections: Bank Montreal, Sydney Br; Miners Mus, Glace Bay, C B; also in many pvt collections, Can, U S A & Europe.
Exhibitions: Many one-man shows in Sydney, Halifax, Lord Beauebrooke, Art Gallery, Frederickton, N B, Boston & New York, Montreal & exhibited in traveling shows across Can.
Teaching: Instr painting, dept educ & pvt classes; lectr hist art, I O D E, Sydney, N S.
Memberships: N S Soc Artists (v pres); Maritime Asn Artists; Int Inst Arts & Lett.
Mailing Address: 15 Amelia St, Sydney, N S, Can.

MOUNT, CHARLES MERRILL
Painter
b New York, N Y, May 19, 28.
Study & Training: Columbia Univ; Univ Calif, Los Angeles; Art Stud League New York.
Exhibitions: Dublin, Ireland; Newman Galleries, Philadelphia, Pa; Hotel Barbizon, New York; plus others.
Teaching: Guest lectr numerous mus & univs.
Awards: Guggenheim fel, 56; grant, Arch Am Art, 62.
Memberships: Irish Portrait Soc (founder & first pres); Burr Artists (rec secy); Pacem in Terris Gallery, New York (mgt comt).
Publications: Auth, John Singer Sargent, Norton, 55; auth, John Singer Sargent, Cresset Press, London, 57; auth, Gilbert Stuart, Norton, 64; auth, Claude Monet, Simon & Schuster, 67; John Singer Sargent, Kraus Reprint, 69.
Dealers: Grand Central Galleries, 40 Vanderbilt Ave, New York, NY 10017; Capricorn Galleries, 8003 Woodmont Ave, Bethesda, MD 20014.
Mailing Address: 308 Beach 145 St, Neponsit, NY 11694.

MOUNT, (PAULINE) WARD
Painter, Sculptor
b Batavia, N Y.
Study & Training: Art Stud League New York; N Y Univ; also with Albert P Lucas & Joseph P Pollia.
Work in Public Collections: Jersey City Mus; Roosevelt Mus, Hyde Park, N Y; Palm Beach Hotel, Fla.
Commissions: Silver bell for Bell of America, comn by Carlebach Galleries, New York, N Y; bronze medal, Painters & Sculptors Soc, Jersey City Mus; holiday card for 1971 (casein), Am Heart Asn, 71.
Exhibitions: Audubon Artists, New York, 40-42; Nat Acad Design, New York, 44; Nat Sculpture Soc, New York, 45-48; Pa Acad Fine Arts, Philadelphia, 49; Smithsonian Inst, Washington, D C, 51.
Teaching: Head dept painting & casting sculpture, N J State Teachers Col, 41-45.
Positions: Former founder & head painting & sculpture, Jersey City Med Ctr, N J; dir, Ward Mount Art Classes, Jersey City, 39-
Awards: First prize for painting, N J Artists, 45; Clayton F Freeman Award for sculpture, Montclair Art Mus, 45; first prize for sculpture, Kearney Mus, 47.
Bibliography: Peyton Boswell (auth), article, In: Arts Digest; article, In: Cue Mag; article, In: Revue Mod Francaise.
Memberships: Artists Equity Asn New York (founding mem); Painters & Sculptors Soc N J (founder & pres, 12 yrs, hon pres); fel Royal Soc Art in England.
Art Interests: Contributor of collection of Louis C Tiffany to museums.
Mailing Address: 74 Sherman Pl, Jersey City, NJ 07307.

MOY, SEONG
Painter, Graphic Artist
b Canton, China, Oct 20, 21; U S citizen.
Study & Training: Saint Paul Sch Art, with Cameron Booth, 36-40; Art Stud League New York, with Vaclav Vytacil, 41-42; Hofmann Sch, with Hans Hofmann, 41-42; Atelier 17, New York, 48-50.
Work in Public Collections: Mus Mod Art; Brooklyn Mus; Metrop Mus Art; Pa Acad Fine Arts; N Y Pub Libr; plus others.
Commissions: Three ed, Int Graphic Arts Soc; New York Hilton Hotel.
Exhibitions: Metrop Mus Art, 50; Whitney Mus Am Art, 50; Univ Ill, 51, 53 & 54; Carnegie Inst, 52 & 55; New York World's Fair, 64-65; plus many other group & one-man shows.
Teaching: Instr, Univ Minn, 51; instr, Ind Univ, 52-53; instr, Smith Col, 54-55; dir, Seong Moy Sch Painting & Graphic Arts, Provincetown, Mass, summers 54-; instr, Univ Ark, 55; instr, Vassar Col, 55; instr, Cooper Union Art Sch, 57-70; instr, Columbia Univ, 59-70; instr, Art Stud League New York, 63-; assoc prof, City Col New York, 70-
Awards: John Hay Whitney Found grant, 50-51; Guggenheim fel, 55-56.
Memberships: Art Stud League New York; Am Fedn Arts; Artists Equity Asn; Col Art Asn Am; Fedn Mod Painters & Sculptors.
Mailing Address: 100 La Salle St, New York, NY 10027.

MOYER, ROY
Painter, Art Administrator
Preferred Media: Oils.
b Allentown, Pa, Aug 20, 21.
Study & Training: Columbia Col, BA, Columbia Univ, MA.
Work in Public Collections: Rochester Mem Art Gallery, N Y; Brandeis Univ Art Gallery, Waltham, Mass; Wichita Art Mus, Kans; Sara Roby Found, New York, N Y; Rockford Art Asn, Ill.
Exhibitions: Audubon Artists, New York, 71; Nat Acad Design, New York, 72.
Collections Arranged: Inverse Illusionism, traveling exhib; numerous others for the Am Fedn Arts.
Teaching: Lectr art hist, Univ Toronto, 53-55.
Positions: Dir, Am Fedn Arts, 63-72; chief art & design, UNICEF, 72-
Memberships: Nat Coun on the Arts (exec comt, 65-72); Audubon Artists.
Research: Byzantine art and architecture; sixteenth century painting and sculpture.
Dealer: Midtown Galleries, 15 E 57th St, New York, NY 10022.
Mailing Address: 440 Riverside Dr, New York, NY 10027.

MUDGE, EDMUND WEBSTER, JR
Collector
b Pittsburgh, Pa, Nov 29, 04.
Study & Training: Harvard Univ, AB.
Collection: Impressionist and post-impressionist paintings; English, French and German antique porcelain and pottery; antique Chinese snuff bottles and Chinese export porcelains; porcelain birds of Dorothy Doughty and Edward Marshall Boehm.
Mailing Address: 5926 Averill Way, Dallas, TX 75225.

MUELLER, EARL GEORGE
Art Historian, Educator
b Harvard, Ill, Feb 12, 14.
Study & Training: Univ Rochester, BMusic; State Univ Iowa, MFA & PhD.
Teaching: Prof art & chmn dept, Duke Univ, 64-
Research: Northern renaissance art; graphics.
Mailing Address: Dept of Art, Duke University, College Station 6605, Durham, NC 27701.

MUELLER, HENRIETTA WATERS
Painter, Sculptor
Preferred Media: Oils, Watercolors, Acrylics, Steel, Aluminum.
b Pittsburgh, Pa, Apr 13, 15.
Study & Training: Sch Art Inst Chicago, with Helen Gardner, BFA, 38; Univ Wyo, MA, 48, MEd, 60; Art Stud League New York, with Will Barnet; Univ Colo, Boulder, with Wendell Black; also with George McNeil & Ilya Bolotowsky.
Work in Public Collections: Joslyn Mus, Omaha, Nebr; New York Pub Libr, N Y; William Rockhill Nelson Gallery, Kansas City, Mo; Mills Col Collection, New York; Univ Wash, Seattle.
Commissions: Stainless steel monument, Commemorative Wyo Women's Rights 1890-1970, Albany Co Courthouse, Laramie, Wyo, 72.
Exhibitions: Six shows, Print Club Philadelphia, Philadelphia Mus, 52-61; Western Art Ann, 52-55 & Own Your Own Exhibs, 67, Denver Art Mus; 22nd Drawing & Print Ann, San Francisco Mus Art, 58; 11th Art Ann, Pioneer Mus, Stockton, Calif, 71.
Teaching: Asst prof art & design, Univ Wyo, 50-61; asst prof art, Univ Nebr, 56-57; asst prof art, Univ Pac, 70-71.
Awards: Int Textile Exhib Award, Univ N C, Greensboro, 48; Wilson Daly Prize, 50 Ind Prints, John Herron Art Inst, Indianapolis, Ind, 52; color drawing award, Poudre Valley Tenth Ann, Colo State Univ, Fort Collins, 70.
Memberships: Wyo Artists' Asn (conf ann lectr); Artists Equity Asn (secy-treas, Wyo Chap, 50-65); Laramie Art Guild.
Dealer: Overland Art Gallery, 2111 Grand Ave, Laramie, WY 82070.
Mailing Address: 1309 Steele St, Laramie, WY 82070.

MUELLER, M GERARDINE, OP
Sculptor, Educator
b Newark, N J.
Study & Training: Caldwell Col, BA; Univ Notre Dame, MA & MFA, with A Lauck & K Milonadis; also with W Otto, Berlin; Inst Cult, Guadalajara, Mex.
Commissions: Portrait of pres, Fordham Univ, Bronx, N Y, 55; wood high relief sculpture, St Dominic Acad, Jersey City, N J, 62; iluminated ceremonial bk, Sisters of St Dominic, Caldwell, N J, 59; six-panel mosaic mural, 70, Caldwell Col, N J; windows, Sisters Chapel, Caldwell, 62.
Exhibitions: Nat Sculpture Soc Show, N Y, 62; N J Col Art Teachers Show, N J State Mus, Trenton, 66; Joy in Religion, Old Bergen Art Guild Three Yr Tour, 68; Miniature Art Soc N J, Paramus, 71; New Jersey Artists, Bergen Art Guild Nat Two Yr Tour, 72.
Teaching: Lectr lettering & crafts, Fordham Univ, 61; prof & chmn art dept, Caldwell Col, 63-
Positions: Pres, Cath Fine Arts Soc, 69-71.
Awards: First pl award for lettering & illumination, Miniature Art Soc N J, 71; outstanding educator of yr, Outstanding Educators of Am, Chicago, Ill, 72.
Bibliography: Williams (auth), article, In: N J Music & Arts, 6/71; Buckley (auth), article, In: Newark Advocate, 12/71; article, In: Newark Eve News, 4/72.
Memberships: Cath Fine Arts Asn (pres); Nat Art Educ Asn; Col Art Asn Am; N J Art Educ Asn; Brit Soc Italic Handwriting.
Publications: Auth, Yearbook production, Photolith Mag, 61; auth, Art in Latin America & Art in Indian missions of U S, Cath Youth Encycl, McGraw-Hill, 62; auth, New mosaic evolvement, Cath Fine Arts Soc, 68.
Mailing Address: Caldwell College, Caldwell, NJ 07006.

MUENCH, JOHN
Painter, Graphic Artist
b Medford, Mass, Oct 15, 14.
Study & Training: Art Stud League New York; Acad Julian, Paris, France.
Work in Public Collections: Metrop Mus Art, New York, N Y; Victoria & Albert Mus, London, Eng; Bibliot Nat, Paris, France; Nat Collection & Smithsonian Inst, Washington, D C; Nat Mus, Jerusalem; plus others.
Exhibitions: Nine shows, Libr Cong, 45-56; Soc Am Graphic Artists, 47 & 50-52; Audubon Artists, 47, 48 & 56; Pa Acad Fine Arts, 49, 50 & 53-55; Cincinnati Mus, 54 & 56; plus many others.
Teaching: Dir, Portland Sch Fine & Appl Arts, Maine, 58-65; assoc prof art, R I Sch Design, 65-

Awards: Prizes, 56, 59 & 60 & John Taylor Arms Award & Medal, 65, Audubon Artists; vis fel Tamarind Lithography Workshop, Los Angeles, 62; U S Dept State specialist grant, 66; plus others.
Memberships: Philadelphia Watercolor Club; Soc Am Graphic Artists; Audubon Artists; Am Color Print Soc; Nat Acad Design.
Dealer: Associated American Artists, 663 Fifth Ave, New York, NY 10019.
Mailing Address: Dept of Fine Arts, Rhode Island School of Design, 2 College St, Providence, RI 02903.

MUENSTERBERGER, HELENE COLER
Art Dealer.
b Montreal, P Q, Oct 10, 21.
Study & Training: Smith Col; Columbia Univ; N Y Univ Inst Fine Arts.
Positions: Asst dir, Van Dieman-Lilienfeld Galleries, 56-58; dir, Seiferheld & Co, 58-
Memberships: Art Dealers Asn Am.
Specialty of Gallery: Old Master drawings.
Mailing Address: 160 E 65th St, New York, NY 10021.

MUENSTERBERGER, WERNER
Collector, Writer
Teaching: Assoc prof psychiat, State Univ N Y Downstate Med Ctr, 49-
Positions: Res assoc, Royal Inst Tropics, Amsterdam, 39-45; cur asst, Stedeljk Mus, Amsterdam, Holland, 45-47.
Awards: Guggenheim fel, 69.
Memberships: Fel Pierpont Morgan Libr.
Research: Primitive art of oceanic and Africa; relationship between artist, artistic themes & personality development.
Collection: West African & oceanic sculpture.
Publications: Auth, The creative process..., The Psychoanalytic Study Soc II, 62; auth, Sculpture of primitive man, Thames & Hudson, London-Abrams (N Y), 55; auth, Roots of primitive art, Psychoanal & Cult, 51; auth, Some elements of artistic creativity among primitive peoples, 50; auth, Vincent Van Gogh: drawings, sketches, watercolors, 47.
Mailing Address: 166 E 61st St, New York, NY 10021.

MUGNAINI, JOSEPH ANTHONY
Painter, Writer
Preferred Media: Graphics.
b Viareggio, Italy, July 12, 12; U S citizen.
Study & Training: Otis Art Inst.
Work in Public Collections: Los Angeles Co Mus Art; Pasadena Mus; Libr of Cong, Washington, D C; Bradley Univ; Univ Hawaii.
Commissions: Icarus (film), for Format Films & United Artists, Los Angeles, 64.
Exhibitions: Los Angeles Co Mus Art, Calif, 50; Pasadena Mus, Calif, 57; Calif State Fair, Sacramento, 64 & 65; Traveling Graphics Exhib, sponsored by Am Soc Graphic Artists, U S State Dept throughout Europe & Middle East, 67; Cedar City Invitational, Utah, 72.
Teaching: Prof drawing, Otis Art Inst, 46-; prof drawing & painting, San Fernando Valley State Col, 63; prof drawing & painting, Temple Univ, 68; instr, Utah State Univ, 70.
Awards: First prize for drawing, Regional Art City Los Angeles, 50; Penner award for graphics, Libr of Cong, Soc Am Graphic Artists, 55, 66 & 67; first prize for graphics, Cedar City Invitational, Cedar City Col, 72.
Bibliography: The drawings of Joseph Mugnaini (film), produced by St Ives Prod, 69; Vanis Loovis (auth) & Sterling Mackhany (auth), The drawings of Joseph Mugnaini, Am Artist Mag, 70.
Memberships: Asn Am Prof.
Publications: Illusr, Age of fable & illusr, War of the worlds, Limited Ed; auth, Drawing a search for form & auth, Oil painting, Reinhold.
Mailing Address: Dept of Drawing, Otis Art Institute, 2401 Wilshire Blvd, Los Angeles, CA 90057.

MUHLSTOCK, LOUIS
Painter
b Narajow, Poland, Apr 23, 04.
Study & Training: Montreal, P Q; Paris, France, with L-F Biloul.
Work in Public Collections: Nat Gallery Can; Art Gallery Toronto; Mus P Q; Art Mus, London, Ont; Montreal Mus Fine Arts; plus others.
Exhibitions: Nat Gallery Art, Washington, D C, 50; one-man show, Montreal Mus Fine Arts, 51 & 54; Int Graphic Exhib, Lugano, 54; Nat Gallery Can, 55; Carnegie Inst, 55; plus many others.
Memberships: Can Soc Graphic Art; Can Group Painters; Fedn Can Artists; Contemp Arts Soc, Montreal.
Mailing Address: 3555 St Famille St, Montreal, P Q, Can.

MUIR, EMILY LANSINGH
Painter, Designer
Preferred Media: Oils.
b Chicago, Ill.
Study & Training: Art Stud League New York, with Richard Lahey & Leo Lentelli; Univ Maine, LHD, 69.
Work in Public Collections: Brooklyn Mus, N Y; U S Govt; Univ Maine.
Commissions: Design of contemp summer homes, year-round homes, portraits & portrait busts for pvt owners.
Exhibitions: Int Watercolor; U S Govt; Maine Art Gallery; Univ Maine.
Teaching: Lectr art, Asn Am Cols, 50-60.
Positions: Mem, Comn Fine Arts, Washington, D C, 55-59; mem adv comt, Kennedy Ctr Performing Arts, Washington, D C, 69-
Awards: Outstanding achievement in commercial venture, contrib to visual arts, Maine Comt Skowhegan Sch, 72.
Bibliography: Martin Dibner (auth), People of the Maine Coast, Doubleday; William Caldwell (auth), article, In: Portland Press Herald; J R Wiggins (auth), article, In: Bangor Daily News.
Publications: Auth, Small potatoes, Scribner, 40.
Mailing Address: Muir Studios, Stonington, ME 04681.

MULCAHY, FREDA
Painter, Art Administrator
Preferred Media: Acrylics, Pastels.
b Staten Island, N Y.
Study & Training: Am Art Sch; Nat Acad Design; New Sch Social Res; also with Jack Tworkov.
Work in Public Collections: Staten Island Mus.
Exhibitions: City Ctr Gallery, New York, N Y, 55; Art U S A, 58; Corcoran Gallery, Washington, D C, 60; Washington & Regional Artists Show, Smithsonian Inst, 60.
Positions: Educ cur, Staten Island Inst Arts & Sci, 64-
Awards: Hon mention, ACA Gallery Int Show, 55; Staten Island Mus Awards, 55, 56 & 57; hon mention, City Ctr Gallery, 58 & 59.
Mailing Address: Staten Island Institute of Arts & Sciences, Staten Island, NY 10301.

MULLEN, BUELL
Painter
Preferred Media: Stainless Steel, Epoxy, Stained Glass.
b Chicago, Ill.
Study & Training: Tyler Sch, Chicago; Brit Acad, Rome; also with Petrucci, Rome & Cucguier, Belg.
Work in Public Collections: Libr Cong Hisp Rm, Washington, D C; Simon Fraser Univ; Bowling Green State Univ; Houston Art Ctr, Temple Buell Col; Lake Erie Col.
Commissions: Mural, Volta Redonda, Brazil, 60; mural, Western Elec Foyer, 63; mural, Int Nickel Corp, exec floor, New York Plaza, 65; mural, Int Minerals-Chem, Libertyville, Ill, 69; four panels, Paul Wolfe Chapel, Inter-Am Univ, P R, 70.
Exhibitions: One-man shows, Smithsonian Inst, Washington, D C; Findlay Chicago & Dayton Art Inst, Ohio; Salon, Paris, All-Ill Soc Arts, Chicago.
Positions: Jury mem, N Y Fedn Fine Arts Competition, 72.
Awards: All-Ill Soc Arts Gold Medal.
Memberships: Archit League; Nat Soc Mural Painters (bd mem, 67 & secy); fel Royal Soc Arts; N Y Fedn Fine Arts (bd mem, 67- & rep muralists); U S Nat Comn UNESCO (rep for Int Asn Art, 67-).
Publications: Auth, Carnegie Inst; co-auth, article, In: Design Mag; auth, article, In: Am Soc Testing & Mat Tech Publ; contribr, Zie & Er, Switz, Die Architekt, Ger & Archit Record, U S & Can.
Mailing Address: 222 Central Park S, New York, NY 10019.

MULLEN, PHILIP EDWARD
Drawer
Preferred Media: Pencil, Pastels.
b Akron, Ohio, Oct 10, 42.
Study & Training: Univ Minn, BA, with Peter Buza; Univ N Dak, MA, with Robert A Nelson; Ohio Univ, PhD.
Work in Public Collections: Columbia Mus Art, S C; Art Inst Zanesville, Ohio; Mint Mus Art, Charlotte, N C; Carroll Reece Mus, Johnson City, Tenn; Univ of the South, Sewanee, Tenn.
Exhibitions: 1970 Nat Drawing Exhib San Francisco, Calif, 70; 24th Am Drawing Biennial, Norfolk, Va, 71; First Contemp Int, Chico, Calif, 71; Drawings U S A Traveling Exhib, 71-73; Fifth Contemp Am Drawings, Smithsonian Traveling Exhib, 71-73.
Teaching: Asst prof & chmn studio art, Univ S C, 69-
Awards: First prize, Guild of S C Artists, 69; purchase award, Mint Mus Art, 71; juror's choice, 24th Am Drawing Biennial, Norfolk Mus Arts & Sci, 71.
Mailing Address: Dept Art, University of South Carolina, Columbia, SC 29201.

MULLICAN, LEE
Painter, Educator
Preferred Media: Oils.
b Chickasha, Okla, Dec 2, 19.
Study & Training: Abilene Christian Col; Univ Okla; Kansas City Art Inst.
Work in Public Collections: San Francisco Mus Art, Calif; Santa Barbara Mus Art, Calif; Mus Mod Art, New York, N Y; Oklahoma Art Ctr, Oklahoma City; Univ Calif, Los Angeles.
Exhibitions: Sao Paulo Biennial, Brazil, 49; Art Inst Chicago, 51; California Artists, Whitney Mus Am Art, 62; Carnegie Int, Pittsburgh, Pa, 67; Pa Acad Fine Arts, Philadelphia, 68.
Teaching: Prof painting & drawing, Univ Calif, Los Angeles, 61-
Awards: Guggenheim fel, 60; Tamarind fel, 66.
Bibliography: W Paalen & G Onslow Ford (auth), Dynaton, San Francisco Mus Art, 51; Langsner (auth), Mullican paints a picture, Art News, 52; Lee Mullican (catalogue), Univ Calif, Los Angeles, 69.
Dealers: Willard Gallery, 29 E 72nd St, New York, NY 10021; Scully Gallery, 651 N La Cienega Blvd, Los Angeles, CA 90069.
Mailing Address: 370 Mesa Rd, Santa Monica, CA 90402.

MUNDT, ERNEST KARL
Sculptor, Educator
b Bleicherode, Ger, Oct 30, 05; U S citizen.
Study & Training: Berlin Inst Technol, dipl archit, 30; Univ Calif, PhD, 61.
Work in Public Collections: San Francisco Mus Art.
Commissions: Steel sculpture, Westmoor High Sch, Daly City, Calif.
Exhibitions: Detroit Inst Art, 44; San Francisco Mus Art, 46; Calif Palace of Legion of Honor, 49; Metrop Mus Art, 50; Whitney Mus Am Art, 51; plus others.
Teaching: Asst prof, Univ Mich, 41-44; instr, Brooklyn Col, 45-46; instr, Calif Sch Fine Art, 47-50, dir, 50-55; asst prof art, Calif State Univ, San Francisco, 55-59, chmn dept, 58-61, assoc prof, 59-64, prof, 64-
Memberships: Col Art Asn Am.
Publications: Auth & illusr, A primer of visual art, 50, Art, form, and civilization, 52 & Birth of a cook, 56; contribr, Arts & Archit, Col Art J, Art Quart & J Aesthet Mags.
Mailing Address: Dept of Art, California State University, San Francisco, 1600 Holloway Ave, San Francisco, CA 94132.

MUNOZ, FREDDY MARCEL
Painter
Preferred Media: Mixed Media.
b Algiers, N Africa, Apr 18, 31; U S citizen.
Study & Training: Nat Sch Fine Arts, Algiers; Nat Sch Fine Arts, Paris, with R Legueult; Univ Minn, MFA, 61.
Work in Public Collections: Walker Art Ctr, Minneapolis, Minn; Mus Algiers; Santa Barbara Art Mus, Calif; Univ Art Galleries, Omaha, Nebr.
Commissions: Oil painting, Mann Theater, Minneapolis.
Exhibitions: First Nat Bank Exhib, Minneapolis, 60; Nat Small Painting Show, Univ Omaha, 60; Second Ann Invitational Show, San Diego, Calif, 68; Drawings U S A Fourth Biennial Traveling Exhib, 68; Drawings, Ten Minnesota Artists, Walker Art Ctr, 71.
Teaching: Instr painting, Univ Minn, Minneapolis, 60-64, assoc prof painting, Univ Minn, Duluth, 64-
Awards: First prize painting, First Nat Bank Show, 60; Ford Found Purchase Award, 64.
Bibliography: Gus Baker (auth), Prize winning paintings critical commentary, Margaret Harold Publ, 62; Suzanne Foley (auth), Introduction to one man show (catalog), 63 & Philip Larson (auth), Introduction ten Minnesota artists (catalog), 71, Walker Art Ctr.
Mailing Address: 417 E Buffalo, Duluth, MN 55811.

MUNSTERBERG, HUGO
Art Historian, Educator
b Berlin, Ger, Sept 13, 16; U S citizen.
Study & Training: Harvard Col, AB, 38, Harvard Univ, PhD, 41.
Teaching: Asst prof fine arts, Mich State Univ, 46-49, assoc prof, 49-52; prof art hist, Int Christian Univ, Tokyo, 52-56; prof, Hunter Col; prof art hist, State Univ N Y Col New Paltz, 58-, chmn dept, 68-71.
Positions: Art critic, Arts Mag, 57-60.
Memberships: Col Art Asn Am; Oriental Ceramic Soc London; Chinese Art Soc; Japan Soc.
Research: Oriental art (China and Japan).
Collections: Oriental art, especially ceramics.
Publications: Auth, Art of the Far East, 68 & India & Southeast Asia, 70, Abrams; auth, Arts of China, C E Tuttle; auth, The sculpture of the Orient, Dover, 72; as well as other bks, articles & rev.
Mailing Address: 48 Elting Ave, New Paltz, NY 12561.

MUNZER, ARIBERT
Painter, Educator
b Mannheim, Ger, Jan 9, 30.
Study & Training: Syracuse Univ, BFA; Cranbrook Acad Art, MFA.
Exhibitions: Nat & regional shows, 53-63.
Teaching: Instr painting & design, Minneapolis Sch Art, 55-68, assoc prof painting, div fine arts, 68-
Mailing Address: 5575 B N Pineview Lane, Minneapolis, MN 55442.

MURCHISON, JOHN D
Collector
b Tyler, Tex, Sept 5, 21.
Study & Training: Yale Univ.
Collection: Contemporary American art.
Mailing Address: 2300 First National Bank Bldg, Dallas, TX 75202.

MURPHY, CATHERINE E
Painter
Preferred Media: Oils.
b Cambridge, Mass, Jan 22, 46.
Study & Training: Pratt Inst, BFA, 67; Skowhegan Sch Painting & Sculpture, summer 66, with Elmar Bichoff.
Exhibitions: One-man show, First Street Gallery, New York, N Y, 70; Group Landscape Show, De Cordova & Dana Mus, Lincoln, Mass, 70; Group Figure Show, Suffolk Mus, Stony Brook, N Y, 71; Whitney Mus Am Art Ann, New York, 71; Am Fedn Arts Group Traveling Landscape Show, 71-72.
Awards: Purchase Award, Am Fedn Arts, 71.
Dealers: Fourcade & Droll, 36 E 75th St, New York, NY 10021; First Street Gallery, 118 Prince St, New York, NY 10012.
Mailing Address: 35 Poplar St, Jersey City, NJ 07307.

MURPHY, CHESTER GLENN
Painter
Preferred Media: Oils.
b Harper, Kans, May 28, 07.
Study & Training: With Clyde Keller, Portland, Ore.
Commissions: Mural, Little World's Fair, Damascus, Ore, 62; two murals, Lake Oswego Shopping Ctr, Ore, 67; mural, Safeco Ins, Portland, 68; Ore scene in oils, U S S Sperry, 69; two Ore scenes in oil, Western Elec, Vancouver, Wash, 72.
Exhibitions: Four-man group invitational show, Maryhill Mus Fine Arts, Wash, 60; three-man invitational, dedication, Anna Hyatt Huntington Statue, Lincoln City, Ore, 65; Coun Am Artist Soc Invitational, 66; Visiting Exhib of Ore Art, N Mex State Capitol Bldg, 69; Am Artists Prof League Grand Nat, 71 & 72.
Teaching: Instr oil painting, Willamette View Manor, 69-72; instr oil painting, summer workshops, Ore; guest lectr oil painting, pub schs, Ore & Wash.
Awards: First prize, Motorola Nat Art Contest, Ore, 61; first prize, Lake Oswego Ann Arts & Flowers Festival; first in prof div, All-Ore Art Show, State Fair.
Memberships: Fel Am Artists Prof League (pres Ore chap, 71); Ore Soc Artists; Lake Area Artists (pres, 72); Coun Am Artist Soc.
Publications: Contribr, Art is for everybody, 60; co-auth, An artist paints the Northwest, 71.
Dealer: Old West Gallery, 312½ E Second St, The Dalles, OR 97058.
Mailing Address: 19076 Midhill Dr, West Linn, OR 97068.

MURPHY, EUGENIE MUELHAUSER, see EUGENIE.

MURPHY, GLADYS WILKINS
Painter, Craftsman
b Providence, R I, Apr 15, 07.
Study & Training: R I Sch Design.
Exhibitions: Am Watercolor Soc; Nat Acad Design; Libr Cong; Philadelphia Print Club; Philadelphia Art Alliance; plus others.
Positions: Dir, Art Gallery Rockport, Mass, 46-
Memberships: Providence Art Club; Providence Watercolor Club; Rockport Art Asn.
Mailing Address: The Old Mill, 19 King St, Rockport, MA 01966.

MURPHY, HERBERT A
Architect, Painter
b Fall River, Mass, June 13, 11.
Study & Training: R I Sch Design, 32.
Exhibitions: Rockport Art Asn; N Shore Art Asn; Providence Art Club; Providence Watercolor Club; R I Sch Design; plus others.
Positions: Architect, pvt practice, 41-; co-dir, Art Gallery & Craft Studio, Rockport, Mass, 44-; mem graphics jury, Rockport Art Asn, 61-62.
Memberships: Rockport Art Asn (v pres, 60-62, pres, 63-65); Providence Art Club; Boston Architects Club; Providence Watercolor Club.
Mailing Address: 19 King St, Rockport, MA 01966.

MURPHY, ROWLEY WALTER
Painter, Designer
Preferred Media: Oils, Watercolors, Tempera.
b Toronto, Ont, May 28, 91.
Study & Training: Ont Col Art; Pa Acad Fine Art, Philadelphia, Cresson Europ traveling scholarships, 13 & 14.
Work in Public Collections: Art Gallery Toronto; Art Gallery Hamilton; Art Gallery Montreal.
Commissions: Design & construction of several grisaille windows, Bryn Athyn, Pa.
Teaching: Instr, Ont Col Art; instr, Artists' Workshop, Toronto.
Memberships: Royal Can Acad Art.
Research: Yacht designs.
Publications: Auth & illusr, Inland seas (ser).
Mailing Address: 230 Glen Rd, Toronto, Ont, Can.

MURRAY, ALBERT (KETCHAM)
Painter
Preferred Media: Oils, Watercolors.
b Emporia, Kans, Dec 29, 06.
Study & Training: Cornell Univ; Syracuse Univ, BFA(cum laude), 30; Eng & France, 31; also with Wayman Adams, N Y & Mex, 34-38.
Work in Public Collections: Nat Gallery Art, Washington, D C; Nat Portrait Gallery, Washington, D C; Smithsonian Inst, Nat Fine Arts Collection, Washington, D C; U S Naval Acad Mus, Annapolis, Md; Combat Art Collection, Navy Dept, Washington, D C.
Commissions: Portrait of Alfred P Sloan, Mem Hosp, New York, N Y, 65; portrait of Rush Kress, Kress Found, New York, 54; portrait of Laurance Rockefeller, N Y Zool Soc, New York, 60; portrait of Arthur Ochs Sulzberger, New York Times, 63; portrait of R K Mellon, Pittsburgh, Pa, 64.
Exhibitions: Carnegie Inst Int, Pittsburgh, 37; Corcoran Gallery Biennial, Washington, D C, 37; Your Navy, Metrop Mus Art, 48; American War Paintings, Salon Marine, Paris, 48; Men Who Made Washington, Nat Gallery Art, 51.
Dealers: Grand Central Art Galleries, Hotel Biltmore, 40 Vanderbilt Ave, New York, NY 10017; Portraits Inc, 41 E 57th St, New York, NY 10022.
Mailing Address: 33 W 67th St, New York, NY 10023.

MURRAY, FLORETTA MAY
Painter, Educator
Preferred Media: Watercolors, Acrylics.
b Minn.
Study & Training: Winona State Col, BEd; Univ Minn, MA; Minneapolis Col Art & Design; Univ Chicago; also in France, Belg & Italy.
Work in Public Collections: Minn Sch Art; Univ Chicago.
Commissions: Mural, History of Winona County, Winona Co Hist Mus; pres medallion, Winona State Col.
Exhibitions: Grand Cent, 59; Saint Paul Gallery Art, 60; Northrup Gallery, Univ Minn, 62; Nat League Am Pen Women, 68; Smithsonian Inst, 69; Minn Mus Art, 71; plus others.
Teaching: Prof art & chmn dept, Winona State Col, 40-; prof art & acting head dept, Bemidji State Col, 49-50; instr painting, Univ Minn, Minneapolis, 58; prof, Col St Teresa, Winona, 55-58; lectr, St Mary's Col(Minn), 70.
Awards: Merit Award, Minn State Fair, 38 & Rochester Art Ctr; purchase award, 62.
Memberships: Am Asn Univ Prof (secy-treas, 69-71); Nat Art Educ Asn; Minn Sculpture Soc; Col Art Asn Am; Int Platform Asn; plus others.
Mailing Address: 501 Harriet St, Winona, MN 55987.

MURRAY, JOHN MICHAEL
Painter
b Tampa, Fla, May 28, 31.
Study & Training: Univ Tampa, BA, 63; Ohio Univ, MFA, 65.
Work in Public Collections: Staten Island Mus, N Y; Bundy Art Mus, Watefield, Vt; N S Col Art, Halifax.
Exhibitions: Dorsky Gallery, New York, N Y, 70; The Apple Cut Five Ways, Univ Chatanooga, 72; New Prints, New York Cult Ctr, 72; one-man shows, Dorsky Gallery, 72 & N S Col Fine Arts, Halifax, 72.
Teaching: Assoc prof fine arts, New York Inst Technol, 66-
Awards: First prize in painting, Fla State Ann, 63.
Memberships: Am Asn Univ Prof.
Publications: Contribr, Art work—no commercial value, Grossman, 72.
Dealer: Dorsky Galleries, Ltd, 111 Fourth Ave, New York, NY 10003.
Mailing Address: 124 W Houston St, New York, NY 10012.

MURRAY, RICHARD DEIBEL
Painter, Sculptor
Preferred Media: Ink, Acrylics, Stone.
b Youngstown, Ohio, Dec 25, 21.
Study & Training: Univ Notre Dame, BS, 42.

Work in Public Collections: Am Col Surgeons, Chicago, Ill; Staatsoper, Vienna, Austria; Medart Collection, Youngstown; Archduke Otto Von Habsburg, Starnbergsee, Ger.
Commissions: Four limestone sculptures on four seasons, Mill Creek Park, Youngstown, 62; four murals & three limestone sculptures, Youngstown Symphony Ctr, 69.
Exhibitions: Several exhibs, Butler Inst Am Art, Youngstown; several exhibs, Canton Art Inst, Ohio; several exhibs, Ohio State Fair, Columbus; Int, Galerie Int, New York, N Y, 72.
Dealers: Galerie Internationale, 1095 Madison Ave, New York, NY 10028; Clyde Gallery, 222 Boardman St, Youngstown, OH 44503.
Mailing Address: 2125 Glenwood Ave, Youngstown, OH 44511.

MURRAY, ROBERT (GRAY)
Sculptor
Preferred Media: Steel, Aluminum.
b Vancouver, B C, Mar 2, 36.
Study & Training: Univ Sask Sch Art, 55-58; Mex, 59; Emma Lake Artist's Workshops.
Work in Public Collections: Whitney Mus Am Art, New York, N Y; Nat Gallery Can, Ottawa; Walker Art Ctr, Minn; Everson Mus, Syracuse; Aldrich Mus, Ridgefield, Conn; plus others.
Commissions: Sculpture, Expo (Montreal), 67, Fredonia State Col, N Y, 69, Vancouver Int Airport, 69, Dept Nat Defense, Ottawa, 72 & Dept External Affairs, Ottawa, 72.
Exhibitions: Whitney Mus Ann Exhib Contemp Sculpture, 64, 66, 68 & 70; Guggenheim Int Exhib, Guggenheim Mus, N Y, 67; American Sculpture of the Sixties, Los Angeles Co Mus, 67; 14 Sculptors: The Industrial Edge, Walker Art Ctr, Minn, 69; X São Paulo Biennial, Brazil, 69.
Teaching: Instr, art dept, Hunter Col; instr, Sch Visual Art; lectr, cols throughout U S.
Awards: Can Coun bursary, 60 & sr grant, 69; second prize, X São Paulo Biennial, Brazil, 69.
Bibliography: Brydon Smith (auth), Robert Murray/Canada, Queen's Printer, Ottawa, 69; D Shadbolt (auth), Ronald Bladen/Robert Murray, Art Gallery Vancouver, 70; Krainin-Sage (auth), ArtIs (film), N Y State Coun Arts, 71.
Dealers: Lippincott Inc, 400 Sackett Point Rd, North Haven, CT 06473; David Mirvish Gallery, 596 Markham St, Toronto, Ont, Can.
Mailing Address: First Floor, 66 Grand St, New York, NY 10013.

MURRAY, WILLIAM COLMAN
Collector, Patron
b Dunkirk, N Y, Mar 15, 99.
Study & Training: Cornell Univ, AB, 21; Hamilton Col, hon LHD, 63.
Positions: Trustee, Munson-Williams-Proctor Inst, Utica, N Y, 49-, pres & secy, 55-; trustee, Am Fedn Arts, 55-63; trustee & v pres, Root Art Ctr, 59-; pres & dir, Cent N Y Community Arts Coun, 67-
Awards: Colgate Univ Civic Award, 58.
Memberships: Collectors Club.
Art Interests: Substantial donations to Munson-Williams.
Collection: Primarily contemporary American; ancestral portraits and some French.
Mailing Address: 1603 Sherman Dr, Utica, NY 13501.

MUSGRAVE, SHIRLEY H
Educator, Photographer
b Lexington, Ky, Nov 28, 35.
Study & Training: Miss State Col Women, BFA, 57; Colorado Springs Fine Arts Ctr, summer 56; Univ Kans, scholar, 57-58, MS, 63; Univ Ark, 64-65; Univ Iowa, 66-67; Fla State Univ, univ fel, 67-69, PhD, 70.
Exhibitions: 15th & 18th Ann Nat Watercolor Shows, Miss Art Asn, Jackson, 56 & 59; Kans Painters & Printmakers Show, Kans State Col, Pittsburgh, 59; 28th Ann Am Graphic Arts Exhib, Wichita Art Asn, Kans, 59; one-artist photog exhib, Iowa City Civic Ctr, 65; two-artist photo show, Memphis State Univ Gallery, Tenn, 72.
Teaching: Art supvr, Linwood Pub Schs, Kans, 58-60; assoc prof art educ, Memphis State Univ, 70-72; asst prof art educ, Fla Int Univ, 72-
Awards: First prize in graphics, Ark Artists Ann, Little Rock Mus Fine Arts, 56.
Memberships: Nat Art Educ Asn; Southeastern Col Art Conf; Fla Art Educ Asn.
Research: Reaction to pattern & content in creative photography by subjects with & without training in art; the development & testing of instructional modules for photographic art ciriticism.
Mailing Address: 10710 S W 43rd Lane, Miami, FL 33165.

MUSSELMAN, DARWIN B
Painter, Educator
Preferred Media: Oils, Tempera.
b Selma, Calif, Feb 16, 16.
Study & Training: Fresno State Col, AB, 38; Art Ctr Col Design, Los Angeles, 38-39; Calif Col Arts & Crafts, MFA, 50; Univ Calif, Berkeley, MA, 52; also with Lyonel Feininger, 37 & Yasuo Kuniyoshi, 49.
Work in Public Collections: Oakland Art Mus, Calif; Fresno Arts Ctr, Calif; Reedley Jr Col, Calif; Vallejo Jr High Sch, Calif; Pittsburg Jr High Sch, Calif.
Commissions: Mural of cotton indust, Prod Cotton Oil Co, Fresno, 54.
Exhibitions: Third Ann Legion of Honor Exhib, San Francisco, 48; Calif Watercolor Soc Exhib, Riverside Gallery, N Y, 48; Calif Artists Exhib, Los Angeles Mus, 49; Denver Mus Ann, Colo, 54; Butler Inst Art Nat, Youngstown, Ohio, 56.
Teaching: Assoc prof painting & art educ, Calif Col Arts & Crafts, 48-53; prof painting & commercial art, Fresno State Col, 53-
Positions: Artist & art dir, Thomas Advert, Fresno, 39-41 & 45-46; free-lance artist, 54-63.
Awards: First prize painting, San Joaquin Valley Art Contest, Rouze Gallery, Fresno, 47, Northern Calif Arts, Crocker Gallery, Sacramento, Calif, 56 & Ann Show, Fresno Arts Ctr, 61.
Bibliography: Emil Kosa Jr (auth), California painters, Am Artist Mag, 3/50; Barbara Cott (auth), Darwin Musselman, Fresno Arts Ctr, 62.
Memberships: Am Watercolor Soc; Calif Nat Watercolor Soc.
Publications: Illusr, Valley of the Yokuts, 40.
Dealers: Conacher Galleries, 134 Maiden Lane, San Francisco, CA 94108; Contemporary Arts, 2273 Shattuck Ave, Berkeley, CA 94704.
Mailing Address: 5161 N Sequoia Dr, Fresno, CA 93705.

MYER, PETER LIVINGSTON
Sculptor, Painter
b Ozone Park, N Y, Sept 19, 34.
Study & Training: Brigham Young Univ, BA, 56; Univ Utah, MFA, 59; summers with Harry Sternberg & Joseph Hirsch.
Work in Public Collections: Colorado Springs Fine Arts Ctr, Colo; Denver Art Mus, Colo; Phoenix Art Mus, Ariz.
Exhibitions: Lights in Orbit, Howard Wise Gallery, New York, N Y, 67; Light, Motion, Space, Walker Art Ctr, Minneapolis, Minn, 67; Some More Beginnings, Brooklyn Mus, N Y, 68; Art & Technology, High Mus Art, Atlanta, Ga, 69; Art of the 60's, Denver Art Mus, 70.
Teaching: Assoc prof art & chmn dept, Univ Nev, Las Vegas, 62-72; assoc prof art, Brigham Young Univ, 72-
Awards: Sweepstakes award for Ranch Ride, 65 & first prize for Orb I, 66, Nat Art Roundup; best in show for Ars Moriendi, Spring Art Roundup, 65.
Bibliography: Articles, In: Prize Winning Paintings, 64 & 66; Art for tomorrow (film), The 20th Century, CBS; Light is the medium, Time Mag, 4/28/67.
Mailing Address: Art Dept, Brigham Young University, Provo, UT 84601.

MYERS, C STOWE
Designer
b Altoona, Pa, Dec 7, 06.
Study & Training: Univ Pa, BFA; Grand Cent Sch Art, New York, N Y; Chouinard Sch Art, Los Angeles, Calif.
Exhibitions: Int Exhib Indust Design, Mus Mod Art, Buenos Aires, Arg, 63; Int Exhib Indust Design, Salle Arts Decoratif, Louvre, Paris, 64; var design exhibs, U S A & abroad, 64-
Teaching: Lectr design, Sch Design & Ill Inst Technol.
Positions: Designer, Norman Bel Geddes, 33-35; partner, Walter Dorwin Teague, 35-49; assoc, Raymond Loewy, 49-53; owner, Stowe Myers Design, 54-72; Design Planning Group/Chicago, Ill, 72-
Memberships: Indust Designers Soc Am; Caxton Club; Am Watercolor Soc.
Mailing Address: 3180 N Lake Shore Dr, Chicago, IL 60657.

MYERS, DENYS PETER
Art Historian, Lecturer
b Boston, Mass, Apr 23, 16.
Study & Training: Harvard Col, BS, 40; Columbia Univ, MA, 48; Fogg Art Mus, 49-50.
Collections Arranged: Zanesville Sesquicentennial Exhib, 47; Adorations of the Magi, 48; The Grand Manner, Baroque Exhib, 49; Romanticism, Columbus Gallery Fine Arts.
Teaching: Lectr medieval, Baroque, romantic & contemp subjects; lectr, Johns Hopkins Univ, 60-64; lectr, Cath Univ Am, 66-67.

Positions: Dir, Art Inst Zanesville, Ohio, 47-55; dir, Philbrook Art Ctr, Tulsa, Okla, 55-58; dir, Des Moines Art Ctr, Iowa, 58-59; asst dir, Baltimore Mus Art, 59-64; dir, Northern Va Fine Arts Asn, 64-66; historian, Nat Park Serv, U S Dept Interior, Washington, D C, 66-68, prin archit historian, hist Am bldgs surv, 68-
Memberships: Col Art Asn Am; Soc Archit Historians (bd dirs, 62-65); Am Asn Mus; Steamship Hist Soc Am.
Publications: Contribr, Soc Archit Historians J.
Mailing Address: 201 N Columbus St, Alexandria, VA 22302.

MYERS, FORREST WARDEN
    Sculptor
b Long Beach, Calif, Feb 14, 41.
Study & Training: San Francisco Art Inst.
Work in Public Collections: Mus Mod Art; Patric Lannon Mus, Palm Beach, Fla; Great S W Corp, Atlanta, Ga; Am Embassy, Mexico City, Mex.
Exhibitions: Calif Sch Fine Arts, San Francisco, 59; Jewish Mus, 67; Philadelphia Mus Art, 68; Los Angeles Co Mus, 68; Whitney Mus Am Art, 68 & 72; plus others.
Teaching: Instr sculpture, San Francisco Art Inst, 67; instr, Sch Visual Art, N Y, 68; lectr art & indust, IBM Corp, 68.
Positions: Dir art res, Art Res, Inc, 64-69; pres, Dynamite Lite Aura Co, 68-69.
Awards: Am Steel Inst Award, 68; Aero Space Industs Design Award, 68.
Memberships: Exp in Art & Technol.
Mailing Address: 238 Park Ave S, New York, NY 10003.

MYERS, FRANCES
    Printmaker
b Racine, Wis, Apr 16, 36.
Study & Training: Univ Wis, MFA; San Francisco Art Inst.
Work in Public Collections: Libr of Cong, Washington, D C; Victoria & Albert Mus, London, Eng; Metrop Mus Art, New York, N Y; Philadelphia Mus Art; Cincinnati Mus Art.
Commissions: Limited ed print, Wis Arts Coun, 71.
Exhibitions: Prints of the 60's, Kovler Gallery, Chicago, Ill, 69; Biennial of Prints, Mus d'Art Mod, Paris, France, 70; U S Pavilion, World's Fair, Osaka, Japan, 70; Potsdam Prints, State Univ N Y Col Potsdam, 72; Women Artists, Jane Haslem Gallery, Washington, D C, 72.
Teaching: Lectr printmaking, St Martin's Sch Art, London, Eng, 66-67; lectr printmaking, Col Art & Design, Birmingham, Eng, 66.
Positions: Co-dir, Mantegna Press, Hollandale, Wis, 71-.
Awards: Purchase prize, Philadelphia Print Club, 71 & Univ N Dak, 72.
Memberships: Philadelphia Print Club.
Dealer: Gallery of Graphic Arts, 1603 York Ave, New York, NY 10028.
Mailing Address: Hollandale, WI 53544.

MYERS, FRED A
    Art Administrator
b Lancaster, Pa, Dec 21, 37.
Study & Training: Harvard Univ, BA, 59, MA, 62.
Positions: Asst to dir, Mus Art, Carnegie Inst, Pittsburgh, Pa, 62-70; dir, Grand Rapids Art Mus, Mich, 70-
Mailing Address: Grand Rapids Art Museum, 230 E Fulton, Grand Rapids, MI 49502.

MYERS, JOHN
    Art Dealer, Collector
b London, Eng, Sept 1, 95; U S citizen.
Study & Training: Sch Dent, Paris, France.
Positions: Owner & pres, John Myers Gallery, N Y; pres, John Myers Found.
Awards: Key to city, Perth Amboy, N J; spec feature award, Great Neck Tribune, N Y.
Memberships: Mus Mod Art; Metrop Mus Art.
Art Interests: Donor of art scholarships to New School for Social Research annually.
Collection: Far Eastern art.
Publications: Auth, Old masters come to life, 64.
Mailing Address: 45 Sutton Pl S, New York, NY 10022.

MYERS, JOHN B
    Art Dealer
Positions: Former dir, Tibor de Nagy Gallery, New York, N Y; dir, John Bernard Myers Gallery, New York, presently.
Mailing Address: John Bernard Myers Gallery, 50 W 57th St, New York, NY 10019.

MYERS, LEGH
    Sculptor
Preferred Media: Marble.
b Ventnor, N J, Nov 11, 16.
Study & Training: Pa State Univ, 35-36; Lehigh Univ, 36-39; also with J Wallace Kelly, 52-54.
Work in Public Collections: In numerous pvt collections, New York, Philadelphia & Atlantic City.
Exhibitions: Ten shows, Knickerbocker Artists Ann, Nat Arts Club, New York, N Y, 57-72; seven shows, Audubon Artists Ann, Nat Acad, New York, 60-72; Allied Artists Ann, Nat Acad, 61 & 62; Ann Arts Festival, Cleveland Mus, 66; Sculptors Guild Ann Mem Show, Lever House, New York, 71 & 72; plus three one-man shows in New York.
Awards: Audubon Artists Medal Creative Sculpture, 28th Ann Exhib, Nat Acad, 70 & Margaret Hirsch Levine Mem Prize Sculpture, 30th Ann Audubon Artists Exhib, Nat Acad, 72.
Bibliography: R Stevens (auth), Expositions diverses, La Rev Mod, 9/61; Ruth White (auth), Legh Myers—sculpture in marble, 4/65; Ralph Fabri (auth), The 28th Audubon annual, Todays Art, 7/70; plus others.
Memberships: Sculptors Guild (dir & exec comt, 72-); Audubon Artists; Knickerbocker Artists.
Dealer: Van der Straeten Galleries, 981 Madison Ave, New York, NY 10021.
Mailing Address: 9 S Mansfield Ave, Margate, NJ 08402.

MYERS, MALCOLM HAYNIE
    Printmaker, Painter
b Lucerne, Mo, June 19, 17.
Study & Training: Wichita State Univ, BFA; Univ Iowa, MA & MFA.
Work in Public Collections: Libr Cong, Washington, D C; Saint Louis Art Mus, Mo; Walker Art Ctr, Minneapolis, Minn; Seattle Art Mus, Wash; Brooklyn Art Mus, N Y; plus others.
Exhibitions: Salon Mai, Paris, France, 51; Int Color Print Soc, Grenchen, Switz, 55; Ford Found Award, U S A, 57; Am Prints Today, Print Coun; New York World's Fair Art Exhib; plus others.
Teaching: Instr art, Univ Iowa, 45-47; prof art, Univ Minn, Minneapolis, 48-, chmn dept art, 65-70.
Positions: Pres, Twin City Chap Artists Equity Asn, 53-55; mem bd trustees, Minn Mus Art, Saint Paul, 72-
Awards: John Simon Guggenheim fels, 50-51 & 54-55; Ford Found Award, 57.
Bibliography: Article, In: Artists Proof, 60; Kenneth Campbell (auth), Malcolm Myers (film), Wis State Univ-Eau Claire, 69.
Mailing Address: Dept of Studio Arts, 208 Art Bldg, University of Minnesota, Minneapolis, MN 55455.

MYHR, DEAN ANDREW
    Art Administrator
b Swea City, Iowa, Mar 16, 30.
Study & Training: Lake Forest Col; Univ Northern Iowa, Cedar Falls.
Positions: Dir, Waterloo Munic Galleries, 58-61; dir educ, Minneapolis Inst Arts, 61-64; dir, Rochester Art Ctr, Minn, 64-66; exec dir, Minn State Arts Coun, Minneapolis, 66-
Mailing Address: 3750 Blackhawk Rd, Saint Paul, MN 55122.

N

NADALINI, (LOUIS) (ERNEST)
    Painter
Preferred Media: Oils, Acrylics, Ink.
b San Francisco, Calif, Jan 21, 27.
Study & Training: City Col San Francisco; Art Stud League New York, N Y, with George Grosz; also with Martin Baer, San Francisco, 58-60.
Work in Public Collections: Oakland Art Mus, Calif; Univ Calif, Berkeley; San Francisco Pub Sch, Calif; Wells Fargo Bank, San Francisco, Calif.
Exhibitions: One-man shows, Village Art Ctr, New York, 53 & Am Stud & Artist Ctr, Paris, France, 54; San Francisco Mus Art Painting Ann, 57-59 & 66; Calif Palace Legion of Honor, San Francisco, 63-67; Pa Acad Fine Arts 161st Ann, 66; Oakland Art Mus Painting Ann, 66-69.
Teaching: Instr art, San Francisco Pub Sch, 69-70.
Awards: YMCA All City Art Exhib First Prize, San Francisco, 39; James D Phelan Award, Palace Legion of Honor, 65 & 67.
Bibliography: A Fried (auth), article, In: San Francisco Examr, 58; A Frankenstein (auth), article, In: San Francisco Chronicle, 66; W Ramsey (auth), Paintings, KPIX TV, San Francisco, 1/66.

Memberships: Am Fedn Arts; Artists Equity Asn; East Bay Artists
Asn.
Publications: Auth, Catalogue of the Art Bank, San Francisco Art
Inst Sch, 59-60; auth, From the West, San Francisco Art Inst, 64;
auth, articles & reviews, In: Artforum, 3/66 & 5/71 & San Fran-
cisco Arts, 6/67.
Dealer: Esther Bear Gallery, 1125 High Rd, Santa Barbara, CA
93108.
Mailing Address: 1230 Grant Ave, No 295, San Francisco, CA 94133.

NAEVE, MILO M
Art Administrator, Art Historian
b Ness Co, Kans, Oct 9, 31.
Study & Training: Univ Colo, BFA; Univ Del, Winterthur Prog Am
Studies & MA.
Positions: Mem staff, Winterthur Mus, Del & Colonial Williamsburg,
Va; dir, Colorado Springs Fine Arts Ctr, Colo.
Memberships: Col Art Asn Am; Am Asn Mus; Nat Trust for Hist
Preservation; Asn Art Mus Dirs.
Research: American painting, sculpture, architecture, and decora-
tive arts from the seventeenth to the twentieth century.
Publications: Contribr, Art Quart, 59, New Eng Quart, 60 &
Antiques Mag; ed, Winterthur Portfolio, Vols I, II & III, 64-66.
Mailing Address: 41 W Cache La Poudre St, Colorado Springs, CO
80903.

NAGANO, PAUL TATSUMI
Painter, Designer
Preferred Media: Watercolors, Oils.
b Honolulu, Hawaii, May 21, 38.
Study & Training: Columbia Col, BA, 60; Pa Acad Fine Arts, Phila-
delphia, 63-67.
Exhibitions: Providence Art Club Ann, R I, 69; Springfield Art
League Ann, Mass, 69; Cambridge Art Asn Group Exhib, Mass,
71; Pa Acad Fine Arts 75th Ann Fel Exhib, 72; Cambridge Art
Asn Jurors' Exhib, 72.
Awards: First prize landscape with figures, Popular Photog, 63;
Packard Prize Drawing, 64 & Lewis S Ware traveling scholar,
67, Pa Acad Fine Arts.
Memberships: Fel Pa Acad Fine Arts.
Dealer: Pucker/Safrai Gallery, 171 Newbury St, Boston, MA 02116.
Mailing Address: 1720 Beacon St, Brookline, MA 02146.

NAGANO, SHOZO
Painter
Preferred Media: Acrylics.
b Kanazawa, Japan.
Study & Training: Kanazawa Fine Arts Univ, AB; Art Stud League
New York, N Y, with Julian Levi; Pratt Inst, New York.
Work in Public Collections: Allentown Art Mus, Pa; Berkshire
Mus, Pittsfield, Mass; Hudson River Mus, Yonkers, N Y; James
Michener Collection, Univ Tex, Austin; State Univ N Y Albany.
Commissions: It is Finished (painting), comn by Richard Hirsch,
cur James Michener Collection, 71.
Exhibitions: One-man shows, Sato Gallery, Tokyo, Japan, 55-63,
Berkshire Mus, 69, State Univ N Y Albany, 70 & Alonzo Gallery,
71-72; Dir's Choice, Fourth Anniversary Show, Community Gal-
lery, Brooklyn Mus, 72.
Teaching: Instr painting, Seibu Gakuen, Tokyo, 60-65.
Bibliography: Alvin Smith (auth), article, In: Art Int, 5/72.
Memberships: Yonkers Art Asn.
Publications: Illusr, Kiristo-Kyo-Hoiku, 61-72; contribr, Haha no
Hikari, 69-72.
Dealer: Alonzo Gallery, 26 E 63rd St, New York, NY 10021.
Mailing Address: 332 E 93rd St, New York, NY 10028.

NAGLER, EDITH KROGER
Painter
Preferred Media: Oils, Watercolors.
b New York, N Y.
Study & Training: Nat Acad Design, with Douglas Volk, Francis
Jones & George Deforest Brush; Art Stud League New York, with
Frank Vincent DuMond, Kenneth Hayes Miller & Robert Henri.
Work in Public Collections: Mus Fine Arts, Springfield, Mass;
George Walter Vincent Smith Art Mus, Springfield; Wadsworth
Atheneum, Hartford, Conn; Highland Park Mus, Dallas, Tex; Fed
Ct House, Boston, Mass.
Exhibitions: Corcoran Gallery Art, Washington, D C, 23; Nat Acad
Design, New York, 28; Art Inst Chicago, 30; Philadelphia Arts
Club; Pa Acad Fine Arts.
Positions: Mem bd control, Art Stud League New York.
Awards: Crowninshield Prize, Stockbridge, Mass; first watercolor
purchase prize, Springfield.
Memberships: Am Watercolor Soc; Am Artists Prof League; Audu-
bon Artists; Bronx Artists Guild.

Dealers: Cornell Galleries, Springfield, MA 01101; Grand Central
Art Galleries, 40 Vanderbilt Ave, New York, NY 10017.
Mailing Address: 5742 Berkshire Lane, Dallas, TX 75209.

NAGLER, FRED
Painter
Preferred Media: Oil.
b West Springfield, Mass.
Study & Training: Art Stud League New York, also with Henri, Du-
mond & Bridgman.
Work in Public Collections: Va Mus Fine Arts, Richmond; Metrop
Mus Art, New York, N Y; Dwight Chapel, Yale Univ, New Haven,
Conn; Nat Acad Design, New York; Temple Univ, Pa.
Exhibitions: Carnegie Inst, Pittsburgh, Pa; Corcoran Gallery Art,
Washington, D C; Art Inst Chicago, Ill; Pa Acad Fine Arts, Phila-
delphia; Nat Acad Design, New York.
Awards: Clark Medal & award, Corcoran Gallery Art; Payne Medal
& purchase prize, Va Mus Fine Arts; Altman prize, Nat Acad
Design; plus many others.
Dealer: Midtown Galleries, 11 E 57th St, New York, NY 10022.
Mailing Address: 5742 Berkshire Lane, Dallas, TX 75209.

NAHA, RAYMOND
Painter
Preferred Media: Acrylics.
b Polacca, Ariz.
Work in Public Collections: Dept Interior, Washington, D C.
Exhibitions: Scottsdale Indian Arts & Crafts Exhib, Ariz; Indian Art-
ists Exhib, Tulsa, Okla; Gallup Arts & Crafts Show, N Mex; Al-
buquerque Art Show, N Mex.
Awards: Grand award, Scottsdale Indian Arts & Crafts Show; first
pl, Southwest Category, Tulsa, Okla.
Mailing Address: Box 602, San Carlos, AZ 85550.

NAKAMURA, KAZUO
Painter
Preferred Media: Oils, Watercolors.
b Vancouver, B C, Oct 13, 26.
Study & Training: Cent Tech Sch, Toronto.
Work in Public Collections: Nat Gallery Can, Ottawa; Art Gallery
Ont, Toronto; Mus Mod Art, New York, N Y; Winnipeg Art Gal-
lery; R McLaughlin Art Gallery, Oshawa.
Commissions: Two sculptures, Toronto Int Airport, 63; mural panel,
Queen's Park Complex, Toronto.
Exhibitions: 20th Biennial Int Watercolor, Brooklyn Mus, 59; 5th Int
Hallmark Art Award Exhib, New York, 61; 2nd Bienniale Mus Art
Mod, Paris, 61; Recent Acquisitions, Mus Mod Art, New York, 63;
Can Artists 68, Art Gallery Ont, Toronto, 68.
Awards: Prizewinner, Fourth Int Exhib Drawings & Engravings,
Lugano, Switz, 56.
Bibliography: Andrew Bell (auth), The art of Nakamura, Can Art,
8/59; J M Careless (ed), The Canadians, MacMillan Co Can, 67.
Dealer: Morris Gallery, 15 Prince Arthur Ave, Toronto, Ont, Can.
Mailing Address: 3 Langmuir Crescent, Toronto 325, Ont, Can.

NAKIAN, REUBEN
Sculptor
b College Point, N Y, Aug 10, 97.
Study & Training: Robert Henri Sch, with Homer Boss & A S Baylin-
son; Art Stud League New York, 12; also with Paul Manship &
Gaston Lachaise.
Work in Public Collections: Mus Mod Art; New Sch Art Ctr.
Commissions: Sculpture, New York Univ, 60.
Exhibitions: Whitney Mus Am Art; Art Inst Chicago; Pa Acad Fine
Arts; retrospective, 66 & The New American Painting & Sculp-
ture, 69, Mus Mod Art; 34th Venice Biennial, 68; plus others.
Awards: Guggenheim Found fel, 30; Ford Found grant, 59; prize,
São Paulo, 60.
Bibliography: Sam Hunter (ed), New art around the world: painting
and sculpture, Abrams, 66; Frank O'Hara (auth), Nakian (cata-
logue), Mus Mod Art, 66; Wayne Craven (auth), Sculpture in
America, Crowell, 68; plus others.
Mailing Address: c/o Egan Gallery, 1005 Second Ave, New York,
NY 10022.

NAMA, GEORGE ALLEN
Printmaker, Painter
Preferred Media: Intaglio.
b Pittsburgh, Pa, Feb 23, 39.
Study & Training: Carnegie Mellon Univ, BFA & MFA; Atelier 17,
Paris, with Stanley William Hayter.
Work in Public Collections: Philadelphia Mus Art; Smithsonian Inst,
Washington, D C; Libr Cong, Washington, D C; Brooklyn Mus;
Butler Inst Am Art, Youngstown, Ohio.
Exhibitions: Original Prints, Palace Legion of Honor, San Fran-
cisco, Calif, 64; Pratt Graphic Art Ctr Serigraph Exhib, 65;

Northwest Printmakers Int Exhib, 65-67; Contemp Am Prints, Gt Brit, 69-71; U S Info Agency Exhibs, Japan Expo, 70.
Awards: David Berger Mem Prize, Mus Fine Arts, Boston, 67; Stuart M Egnal Prize, Philadelphia Print Club, 68; Stella Drabkin Mem Award, Am Color Print Soc, 71.
Bibliography: Leonard Slatkes (auth), Printmakers on exhibit, Art Scene, 68; Richard Shelton (auth), Journal of return, Kayak, 69; S Hazo (auth), Poets and prints, Artist Proof Mag, 71.
Memberships: Soc Am Graphic Artists.
Publications: Illusr, Longjaunes his periplus, Kayak, 68; illusr, Journal of return Kayak, 69; illusr, Twelve poems with twelve prints, 70; illusr, Monuments, 71; illusr, Seascript, 71.
Dealer: Associated American Artists, 663 Fifth Ave, New York, NY.
Mailing Address: 209 S Craig St, Pittsburgh, PA 15213.

NAMUTH, HANS
Photographer, Film Maker
b Essen, Ger, Mar 17, 15; U S citizen.
Work in Public Collections: Mus Mod Art & Metrop Mus Art, New York, N Y; Tulane Univ, New Orleans, La; Cleveland Mus Art, Ohio; Va Mus Fine Arts, Richmond; plus others.
Exhibitions: U S Pavilion, Brussels, Belg, 58; Jackson Pollock, Mus Mod Art, 67; New York Cult Ctr, 70; Philadelphia Col Art, Pa, 72; one-man show, Artists: U S A, U S Dept State.
Positions: Founder & secy, Museum-at-Large, New York, 70-
Awards: Citation in recognition of pub serv, U S Dept State, 58; Grand Prix de Bergamo, 58.
Collection: Prints drawings and lithographs by Rauschenberg, J Johns, Albers, Robert Indiana, Lee Bontecou, George Segal, Constantine Nivola, Richard Lindner, Robert Morris, Robert Motherwell and W de Kooning; paintings by de Kooning, Jackson Pollock, Josef Albers, Joseph Cornell, Mary Bauermeister, Kenzo Okada, Ludwig Sander and others.
Publications: Co-auth (films), Jackson Pollock, 51, Willem de Kooning, 58, Homage to the square (Josef Albers), 69, Brancust at the Guggenheim, 70, Matisse at the Grand Palais, 71 & The architect Louis Kahn, 72; co-auth, Eight American masters, Random House (in press); co-auth, Fifty artists (portfolio of photographs), 4/73.
Dealer: Charles Byron, 25 E 83rd St, New York, NY 10021.
Mailing Address: 125 E 78th St, New York, NY 10021.

NARDIN, MARIO
Sculptor
Preferred Media: Bronze.
b Venice, Italy, Mar 17, 40.
Study & Training: Acad Belle Arti, Venice, with Guido Manarin.
Work in Public Collections: Hudson River Mus, Yonkers, N Y; Fordham Univ; also works in private collections.
Exhibitions: One-man shows, Hudson River Mus, 67 & 72, Atelier Gallery, New York, 68, Fordham Univ, 69 & Lesnick Gallery, 70; State Univ N Y Col Plattsburgh, 71.
Positions: Asst to Jacques Lipchitz, 64-71; asst mgr, Avent-Shaw Art Foundry, 64-
Awards: New Rochelle Art Asn Award, 67; Greenburgh Arts & Cult Comt Award, 71.
Memberships: Am Soc Contemp Artists; Sculptors League; Yonkers Art Asn; Hudson River Mus.
Publications: Noel Frackman (auth), Nardin at the Hudson River Museum, Arts Mag, 3/72; Louisa Kreisberg (auth), Young artist brings collection to museum & Nardin: sculpture in bronze, Rockland & Westchester Newspapers, 3-4/72; Successo a Nuova York di uno scultore Veneziano, Gazzetino Venice, 72.
Dealer: Solomon & Co Fine Art, 959 Madison Ave, New York, NY 10021.
Mailing Address: 184 Warburton Ave, Hastings-on-Hudson, NY 10706.

NAROTZKY, NORMAN DAVID
Painter, Printmaker
Preferred Media: Acrylics, Oils.
b Brooklyn, N Y, Mar 14, 28.
Study & Training: High Sch Mus & Art, N Y; Brooklyn Col, BA(cum laude), with Ad Reinhardt & Alfred Russell; Art Stud League New York, N Y, with Robert Ward Johnson & Howard Trafton; Cooper Union, dipl, with Morris Kantor, Charles Seide & Nicholas Marsicano; Atelier 17, Paris, with S W Hayter; Kunstakademie, Munich; N Y Univ Inst Fine Arts; also with Moses Soyer.
Work in Public Collections: James A Michener Found Collection, Univ Tex Art Mus, Austin; Philadelphia Mus Art, Pa; Mus Contemp Art, Madrid, Spain; Mills Col Art Gallery, Oakland, Calif; Mus Arte Contemporaneo, Barcelona, Spain.
Commissions: Mural, Banco de Guipuzcoa, San Sebastian, 63.
Exhibitions: Sixth Bienal São Paulo, Brazil, 61; Recent Painting U S A: The Figure, Mus Mod Art & others, 62; Whitney Mus Am Art Ann, New York, 62; Arte Am Y España, Madrid, Barcelona, Naples, Rome, Berne & Berlin, 63-64; Grosse Kunstler Ausstellung, Haus der Kunst, Munich, 71; plus 22 one-man shows.

Awards: Wooley Found fel, Paris, 54-55; French Govt fel, Paris, 55-56; Fulbright fel, Ger, 57-58.
Bibliography: M Molleda (auth), Narotzky, Ateneo, Madrid, 62; F J Quirk (auth), Introduction to catalog, Lehigh Univ, 65; A del Castillo (auth), Narotzky, Diario Barcelona, 71.
Memberships: Art Stud League New York.
Publications: Auth, Spain: a disenchantment with materia, 9-10/65, Conversation with Cuixart, 3/66 & The Venice Biennale: pease porridge in the pot nine days old, 9-10/66, Arts Mag; auth, Ibiza—from art refuge to art center, Art Voices, fall 65; auth, Form and communication in my art work, Leonardo Mag, 7/69.
Mailing Address: Córcega 198-6, Barcelona 11, Spain.

NASH, KATHERINE E
Sculptor, Educator
Preferred Media: Metals.
b Minneapolis, Minn.
Study & Training: Univ Minn, BS; Minneapolis Sch Art; Univ N Mex, computer graphics with Richard Williams; Doane Col, hon DFA.
Work in Public Collections: Walker Art Ctr, Minneapolis; U S Arts & Humanities Coun, Washington, D C; Joslyn Art Mus, Omaha, Nebr; Nebr Art Asn, Univ Nebr, Lincoln; Univ Minn, Minneapolis.
Commissions: Works, welded steel, Wright Co Ct House foyer, Buffalo, Minn, 60 & Stud Union, Doane Col, 64, welded copper, steel & brass, Epworth Church, Council Bluffs, Iowa, 66, welded copper & brass, Edina Village Coun, Edina Libr, Minn, 69 & welded copper, Fed Land Bank, Saint Paul, Minn, 70.
Exhibitions: Walker Art Ctr, 50-72; Joslyn Art Mus, 50-65; Brussels World's Fair, 58; U S Embassy exhibs, 66-69; Nebr Centennial, 67.
Teaching: Asst prof sculpture, Univ Nebr, Lincoln, 47-53; vis assoc prof sculpture, San Jose State Col, 61-62; prof sculpture/computer graphics, Univ Minn, 64-, univ grant, 65-71.
Awards: Minn State Arts Coun Artists Award, 69-70; McMillan Award travel grant, 69 & 72.
Bibliography: Marcel Brion (auth), Art fantastique, Albin Michel, 61; Paul Vogt (auth), Stand plastiken aus stahl, Herausgeber & Verlag, 62; Reichardt (auth), The computer in art, Van Nostrand Reinhold, 71.
Memberships: Artists Equity Asn (regional dir exec bd, 57-61; Mid-Am Col Art Asn (secy, 67-68); Sculptors Guild; Int Computer Arts Soc; Am Asn Univ Prof.
Art Interests: Computer-generated graphics.
Dealer: Seligman Galleries, 5 E 57th St, New York, NY 10022.
Mailing Address: Rte 3, Box 784, Excelsior, MN 55331.

NASH, RAY
Art Historian
b Milwaukie, Ore, Feb 27, 05.
Study & Training: Univ Ore, BA, 28; Harvard Univ, MA; Summer Art Sch, Belg, 37; Dartmouth Col, hon MA; New Eng Col, hon ArtD, 57.
Teaching: Instr art, New Sch Soc Res, 32-34; lectr art hist, Dartmouth Col, 37-, asst prof, 41-49, prof, 49-70, emer prof, 70-; vis lectr bibliog, Oxford Univ, 66.
Awards: Gold medal, Am Inst Graphic Arts, 56.
Memberships: Int PEN; fel Am Acad Arts & Sci; Royal Acad Sci, Lett & Fine Arts, Belg; fel Soc Antiquaries London; Am Antiquarian Soc; plus others.
Publications: Auth, Calligraphy and printing in the sixteenth century, 40, rev ed, 64; Printing as an art, 55, American writing masters and copybooks, 59, American penmanship 1800-1850, 69 & calligraphy article, In: Encycl Britannica, 70; plus many contrib to journals.
Mailing Address: Hanover, NH 03755.

NATKIN, ROBERT
Painter
b Chicago, Ill, Nov 7, 30.
Study & Training: Art Inst Chicago, BA, 52.
Work in Public Collections: Guggenheim Mus, N Y; Whitney Mus Am Art; Los Angeles Mus Art; Carnegie Inst; Hartford Atheneum; plus others.
Exhibitions: Young America, 60 & Ann, 66 & 68, Whitney Mus Am Art; Carnegie Inst, 63; Int Biennale, Japan, 63; Mus Fine Arts Houston, Tex, 63; retrospective, San Francisco Mus Art, 69; plus many other group & one-man shows.
Teaching: Former Ford Found artist-in-residence, Kalamazoo Inst Arts.
Dealer: Fairweather Hardin Gallery, 101 E Ontario St, Chicago, IL 60611.
Mailing Address: 924 West End Ave, New York, NY 10025.

NATZLER, OTTO
Ceramist, Sculptor
b Vienna, Austria, Jan 31, 08; U S citizen.
Work in Public Collections: Mus Mod Art & Metrop Mus Art, New

York, N Y; Art Inst Chicago, Ill; Kunstgewerbemuseum, Zürich, Switz; Victoria & Albert Mus, London, Eng.
Exhibitions: One-man exhibs, Kunstgewerbemuseum, Zürich, 59, Art Inst Chicago, 63 & San Francisco Mus Art, Calif, 63; retrospective exhibs, Los Angeles Co Mus Art, Calif, 66 & M H De Young Mem Mus, San Francisco, 71.
Bibliography: R Henderson (auth), Natzler ceramics, The Studio, 1/57; B Johnson (auth), A civilized expression in ceramics, Los Angeles Times, 6/12/66; E Penney (auth), The ceramic art of the Natzlers, Film Assocs, Los Angeles, 67.
Publications: Auth, The Natzler glazes, Craft Horizons, 64; co-auth, Gertrud & Otto Natzler, retrospective exhibition (catalog), Los Angeles Mus Art, 66; auth, Gertrud & Otto Natzler ceramics, Sperry collection, Los Angeles Mus Art, 68; co-auth, The ceramic work of Gertrud & Otto Natzler (catalog), De Young Mem Mus, 71.
Mailing Address: 7837 Woodrow Wilson Dr, Los Angeles, CA 90046.

NAUMER, HELMUTH
Painter
b Ger, Sept 1, 07; U S citizen.
Study & Training: Frank Wiggins Art Sch; Otis Art Inst, Los Angeles, Calif.
Work in Public Collections: Permanent Collections of N Mex State Art Mus; Bandelier Nat Monument; Univ Wyo; Univ N Mex; Mus Sci & Hist, Fort Worth, Tex; plus many others in U S & Venezuela, Guatemala, Mex, Can, Africa, Australia & Europe.
Exhibitions: Am Asn Mus & Can Mus Asn Meeting, Toronto, 67.
Bibliography: Articles, In: Am Ger Rev, N Mex Mag & El Palacio.
Memberships: Inst Fine Arts, Los Angeles.
Mailing Address: Rancho de San Sebastian, Santa Fe, NM 87501.

NAVAS, ELIZABETH S
Collector, Patron
b Coffeyville, Kans, June 29, 95.
Study & Training: Teachers Col, Columbia Univ; spec art study.
Positions: Trustee, Louise C Murdock Estate, 15-; adminr, Roland P Murdock Collection, Wichita Art Mus, 39-
Awards: Resolution of honor & commendation for outstanding cult contrib & serv to Wichita Art Mus & city & citizens of Wichita in compiling Roland P Murdock Collection at Wichita Art Mus, City of Wichita, 65.
Memberships: Life mem Am Fedn Arts (hon trustee & var offices); Munic Art Soc; Metrop Mus Art; Natural Hist Mus; Nat Coun Women.
Publications: Auth, Louise C Murdock, In: Notable American Women 1607-1950, Harvard Univ Press, 71.
Mailing Address: 250 E 63rd St, New York, NY 10021.

NAY, MARY SPENCER
Painter, Educator
b Crestwood, Ky, May 13, 13.
Study & Training: Art Ctr Asn Sch, Louisville, Ky, 34-40; Cincinnati Art Acad, 41; Univ Louisville, BA, 41; Art Stud League New York, 42; study with Boris Margo, Provincetown, Mass, 50-51; Univ Louisville, MA, 60.
Work in Public Collections: Speed Art Mus, Louisville; Evansville Mus Arts & Sci, Ind; Ky Wesleyan Col, Owensboro; Univ Louisville; Ohio Univ, Athens.
Commissions: Mural for children's room, Louisville Pub Libr, Fed Art Proj, 34.
Exhibitions: IBM Exhib, New York World's Fair, 40; Artists for Victory, Metrop Mus Art, 41; Contemporary Color Lithography Int Biennials, 50, 52 & 54; 60th Ann Am Exhib, Art Inst Chicago, Ill, 51; Terry Nat Exhib, Miami, Fla, 52.
Teaching: Instr painting & printmaking, Art Ctr Asn Sch, 40-59, dir, 44-49; prof art educ & painting, Univ Louisville, 59-
Positions: Supvr, Puppet Proj, Nat Youth Admin, 37-39.
Awards: Ashland Oil Co Purchase Awards, Art Ctr Asn Regional, 45, 50 & 58; Evansville Mus Purchase Awards, Tri-State Ann, 52, 56 & 58; Kentucky State Fair Bd Purchase Awards, 54, 56 & 58.
Memberships: Ky Arts & Crafts Guild (bd dirs, 67-70); Art Ctr Asn (libr & bd dirs, 71-72); J B Speed Art Mus; Provincetown Art Asn; Ky Art Educ Asn.
Mailing Address: 207 S Galt Ave, Louisville, KY 40206.

NAYLOR, ALICE STEPHENSON
Painter
Preferred Media: Acrylics, Watercolors.
b Columbus, Tex.
Study & Training: Univ N Mex; San Antonio Art Inst, with Andrew Dasburg, Leonard Brooks, Charles Rosen, Xavier Gonzalez, Millard Sheets & Doug Kingman.
Work in Public Collections: Beaumont Art Mus, Tex; San Antonio Art League Mus, Hemisfair; Columbus Art Mus.

Exhibitions: Critics Choice, Cincinnati Art Mus; Libr Cong Print Show, 47; many Tex Fine Arts Asn Exhibs, Laguna, Gloria, Austin; many Tex Watercolor Soc Exhibs, 50-72; Corpus Christi Art Mus, Tex.
Teaching: Instr painting & lithography, San Antonio Art Inst, 42-58; head dept art, Incarnate Word Col, 58-64.
Awards: Witte Mem Mus Award for Spring Motif, 50; award, Beaumont Art Mus, 58; Tex Watercolor Soc Award for Nosegay, McNay Mus, 72.
Memberships: San Antonio Art League; Tex Fine Arts Asn (past v pres); Contemp Artists Group (past pres); San Antonio Craft Guild (past pres); Hill Country Arts Found (mem bd).
Publications: Illusr, D'Hanes, 61 & San Pedro Springs Park, 67.
Dealer: Shook-Carrington Gallery, N New Braunfels, San Antonio, TX 78209.
Mailing Address: 125 Magnolia Dr, San Antonio, TX 78212.

NAYLOR, JOHN GEOFFREY
Sculptor, Educator
Preferred Media: Aluminum.
b Morecambe, Eng, Aug 28, 28; U S citizen.
Study & Training: Leeds Col Art, nat dipl in design; Hornsey Col Art, ATD; Univ Ill, MFA.
Commissions: Relief, Fla Gas Co, Gainesville, 68; fountain, Alpert Investment Co, Cocoa Beach, Fla, 69; relief, Great Southwest Corp, Atlanta, Fla, 69; kinetic relief, Gulf Life Ins Co, Jacksonville, Fla, 69; relief, First Nat Bank, Tampa, Fla, 72.
Exhibitions: Isaac Delgado Mus Art Bi-Annual, New Orleans, La, 63-64; Contemporary Southern Sculpture, 68; Chapman Kelley Gallery, Dallas, Tex, 68-69; Kinetic Sculpture, Cummer Gallery, Jacksonville, Fla, 70.
Teaching: Instr drawing, Fla Southern Col, 67-69; assoc prof sculpture, Univ Fla, 69-
Positions: Cur, Fort Wayne Art Mus, Ind, 65-66.
Awards: Fulbright travel grant, 54; Nat Found of the Arts Award, 67.
Dealer: Art Sources, Lobby Universal Marion Bldg, Church St, Jacksonville, FL 32202.
Mailing Address: 104 N W Seventh St, Gainesville, FL 32601.

NAZARENKO, BONNIE COE
Painter
Preferred Media: Oils.
b San Jose, Calif, Oct 26, 33.
Study & Training: San Jose State Col; Carmel Art Inst, under John Cunningham.
Work in Public Collections: Mint Mus, Charlotte, N C.
Exhibitions: Gallery Contemp Art, Winston-Salem, N C, 70; Am Artists Prof League, New York, N Y, 72; Soc Animal Artists, Grand Cent Art Gallery, New York, 72.
Awards: Beaufort Art Festival Award, S C, 66; Mint Mus Purchase Award, 68.
Memberships: Soc Animal Artists; Am Artists Prof League.
Dealer: Anne Metcalf, 3937 W Kennedy Blvd, Tampa, FL 33609.
Mailing Address: 8314 Pocahontas St, Tampa, FL 33615.

NEAL, (MINOR) AVON
Writer, Printmaker
b Indiana, July 16, 22.
Study & Training: Long Beach Col; Escuela Bellas Artes, Mex, MFA, with Siquieros.
Work in Public Collections: Metrop Mus Art, New York, N Y; Libr Cong, Washington, D C; Smithsonian Inst, Washington, D C; Abby Aldrich Rockefeller Mus Am Folk Art, Williamsburg, Va; Winterthur Mus, Wilmington, Del.
Commissions: 500 original rubbings, 70 & 250 original rubbings, 71 (all with Ann Parker), Am Heritage.
Exhibitions: One-man & two-man shows, New Eng Gravestone Rubbings, Am Embassy, London, 65, Know Ye The Hour, Hallmark Gallery, New York, 68, Amon Carter Mus, Fort Worth, Tex, 68 & 71, Ephemeral Image, Mus Am Folk Art, 70 & Mus Fine Arts, Springfield, Mass, 72.
Positions: Mem adv bd, Mus Am Folk Art, 68-71.
Awards: Ford Found grants, 62, 63 & 64.
Bibliography: M J Gladstone (auth), New art from early American sculpture, Collector's Quart Report, 63 & Pedestrian art, Art Am, 4/64; Stephen Chodorov (auth), Know ye the hour, Camera Three, CBS, 11/68.
Publications: Co-auth, Archaic art of New England gravestones, Art Am, 63; A portfolio of rubbings from early American stone sculpture, 64 & Rubbings as a print technique, Artists Proof, 64; auth, Ephemeral folk figures, Potter, 69 & When shall we three meet again, Am Heritage, Vol 11, No 3.
Dealer: Gallery of Graphic Arts, 1603 York Ave, New York, NY 10028.
Mailing Address: Thistle Hill, North Brookfield, MA 01535.

NEAL, REGINALD H
Painter, Educator
b Leicester, Eng, May 20, 09.
Study & Training: Yale Univ, 29-30; Bradley Univ, BA, 32; State Univ Iowa, summer 36; Univ Chicago, MA, 39; Colorado Springs Fine Arts Ctr, summer 41.
Work in Public Collections: Libr Cong; Mus Mod Art; Queen's Col, Kingston, Ont; Brigham Young Univ; Brooks Mem Gallery; plus many others.
Commissions: Two ed lithographs, AAA Gallery, New York, N Y.
Exhibitions: Metrop Mus Art, 52; Cincinnati Mus Asn, 54; Mus Mod Art, 65; Des Moines Art Ctr, 66; N J State Mus, 67; plus many other group & one-man shows.
Teaching: Lectr, Asn Am Cols, 53 & 54; Univ Miss; instr, Southern Ill Univ, 58-59; univ prof art & chmn dept, Douglass Col, Rutgers Univ, New Brunswick, 59-; instr, Yale Univ, 66; instr, Southern Ill Univ, 66 & 67.
Awards: Golden Reel Award, Film Coun Am, 56.
Bibliography: Albert Reese (auth), American prize prints of the 20th century, Am Artists Group, 49; Oto Bihalji-Merin (auth), Adventures of modern art, Abrams, 66.
Memberships: Col Art Asn Am.
Mailing Address: Dept of Art, Douglass College, Rutgers University, New Brunswick, NJ 08903.

NEDDEAU, DONALD FREDERICK PRICE
Painter, Designer
b Toronto, Ont, Jan 28, 13.
Study & Training: Ont Col Art; also with J W Beatty, Franklin Carmichael & Archibald Barnes.
Exhibitions: 11 shows, Royal Can Acad, 36-61; 20 shows, 42-65 & traveling exhibs, 44-48 & 51-65, Ont Soc Artists; group shows, 43 & 48-65 & traveling exhibs, 49-65, Can Soc Painters in Water Colour; Can Soc Painters in Water Colour & Calif Watercolor Exhib, 50-58; Can Group Painters, 55, 56, 58 & 61; plus others.
Teaching: Head dept art & prin art summer sch, Cent Tech Sch, Toronto, Ont, 48-72.
Positions: Past pres, Can Soc Painters in Water Colour.
Awards: Scholar, 36 & Rous & Mann Award, 36, Ont Col Art.
Memberships: Ont Soc Artists; Can Soc Painters in Water Colour; Can Guild Potters; Arts & Lett Club, Toronto; fel Int Inst Arts & Lett; plus others.
Mailing Address: 21 Sherwood Ave, Toronto 12, Ont, Can.

NEEL, ALICE
Painter
Preferred Media: Oils.
b Merion Square, Pa, Jan 28, 00.
Study & Training: Philadelphia Sch Design for Women, 21-25; Moore Col Art, hon Dr, 71.
Work in Public Collections: Mus Mod Art, New York, N Y; Whitney Mus Am Art, New York; Robert Mayer Collection, Winetka; Dillard Inst, New Orleans, La; Graham Gallery, New York.
Exhibitions: Retrospective, Moore Col Art, 71.
Teaching: Lectr painting sem, Univ Pa Grad Sch, 71-72; lectr, Skowhegan Sch Painting & Sculpture, summer 72.
Positions: Easel painter, Fed Works Agency, 35-42.
Awards: Longview Found Award, 62; Am Acad Arts & Lett Award, 69; Benjamin Altman Figure Prize, Nat Acad Design, 71.
Bibliography: H Crehan (auth), Introducing the portraits of Alice Neel, 10/62 & Ted Berrigan (auth), Double portraits, 1/66, Art News; Jack Kroll (auth), Curator of souls, Newsweek, 1/31/66.
Memberships: Artists Equity Asn.
Dealer: Graham Gallery, 1014 Madison Ave, New York, NY 10021.
Mailing Address: 300 W 107th St, Apt 3A, New York, NY 10025.

NEFF, JOHN A
Painter, Designer
Preferred Media: Watercolors.
b Lebanon, Pa, May 5, 26.
Study & Training: Whitney Sch Art, New Haven, Conn, cert; Paier Sch Art, Hamden, Conn, with Herbert Gute.
Work in Public Collections: New Brit Mus Am Art, Conn; Mus Fine Arts, Springfield, Mass; Greater Hartford Arts Coun, Conn; Mus Art, Sci & Indust, Bridgeport, Conn; First Nat Bank Boston, Mass.
Exhibitions: New Eng Exhib, Silvermine, Conn, 65; Landscape I, De Cordova Mus, Lincoln, Mass, 70; Allied Artists, New York, N Y, 71; Am Watercolor Soc, New York, 72; Hudson Valley Nat Exhib, White Plains, N Y, 72.
Positions: Sr graphic designer, Muirson Label Co, North Haven, Conn, 50-71; partner, Crossmark Assocs, Wallingford, Conn, 72.
Awards: Watercolor prize, Acad Artists, Springfield, 65; watercolor award, Hudson Valley Art Asn, 66; Salmagundi Club Award, New York, 72.

Bibliography: T F Potter (auth), A proxy visit, Meriden Rec-J, Conn, 69.
Memberships: Am Watercolor Soc; Allied Artists Am; Salmagundi Club; Silvermine Artists Guild; Conn Watercolor Soc (bd dirs, 71-72).
Mailing Address: 17 Parkview Rd, Wallingford, CT 06492.

NEHER, FRED
Cartoonist
b Nappanee, Ind, Sept 29, 03.
Study & Training: Chicago Acad Fine Arts.
Work in Public Collections: Syracuse Univ; Butler Inst Am Art; Albright Col, Reading, Pa.
Exhibitions: Humor Festival, World Cartoon Exhib, Knokke, Heist, Belg, 70 & 71.
Teaching: Instr cartooning, Univ Colo, Boulder, 64-
Positions: Cartoonist, Life's Like That, 34-
Memberships: Nat Cartoonist Soc; Soc Illustrators.
Publications: Auth, Will-yum, Hi-teens & Some punkins.
Mailing Address: One Neher Lane, Boulder, CO 80302.

NEIKRUG, MARJORIE
Art Dealer
b New Rochelle, N Y.
Study & Training: Sarah Lawrence Col.
Positions: Owner & dir, Neikrug Galleries, Inc.
Memberships: Am Soc Appraisers; Am Arbitration Soc; Am Soc Mag Photogr; Fairleigh Dickinson Univ (fine arts comt).
Specialty of Gallery: Photography: pre-Columbian art; fine art.
Mailing Address: 224 E 68th St, New York, NY 10021.

NEILL, T JOSEPH
Sculptor, Educator
Preferred Media: Wood, Plastics.
b New Eagle, Pa, Aug 29, 44.
Study & Training: Westminster Col, BA; Bowling Green Univ, MFA.
Work in Public Collections: Mem Gallery Univ Rochester, N Y; Tyler Mus, Tex; Westminster Col, New Wilmington, Pa; Univ Conn.
Exhibitions: 31st Midyear Show, Butler Mus Art, Youngstown, Ohio, 66; The Dominant Woman, Finch Col Mus, New York, N Y, 68; one-man exhib, Hemingway-Bendrat, New York, 70; two-man exhib, Wadsworth Atheneum, Hartford, Conn, 71; 22nd New Eng Exhib, Silvermine Guild, New Canaan, Conn, 71.
Teaching: Asst prof art, Univ Conn, 69-
Awards: First Award for Sculpture, Sharon Creative Arts Found, Conn, 71; 22nd New Eng Award for Sculpture, Silvermine Guild, 71; Mr & Mrs Chesman Daly Award, 71.
Memberships: Conn Acad Fine Arts.
Mailing Address: 858 Capitol Ave, Hartford, CT 06106.

NEILSON, KATHARINE B
Educator, Lecturer
b New York, N Y, Apr 8, 02.
Study & Training: Bryn Mawr Col, AB; Radcliffe Col, AM & PhD.
Teaching: From instr to assoc prof art, Wheaton Col, 33-43; assoc prof art, Hartford Col, 55-68.
Positions: Cur educ, Albright Art Gallery, Buffalo, N Y, 43-49; actg dir educ & pub rels, Mus Art, R I Sch Design, Providence, 49-52; dir educ & ed, mus publ, 52-55; educ dir, Wadsworth Atheneum, Hartford, Conn, 55-68; ed assoc, Yale Univ Art Gallery, 68-72.
Memberships: Col Art Asn Am.
Publications: Auth, Filippino Lippi: a critical study, Harvard Univ Press, 38 & Greenwood, 72; contribr, articles & rev, In: art periodicals.
Mailing Address: 460 Middlesex Rd, Darien, CT 06820.

NEIMAN, LeROY
Painter, Printmaker
Preferred Media: Oil, Enamel.
b Saint Paul, Minn, June 8, 26.
Study & Training: Inst Chicago; Univ Chicago; Univ Ill.
Work in Public Collections: Minneapolis Inst Art; Ill State Mus; Joslyn Art Mus; Wodham Col, Oxford, Eng; Mus Sport in Art, New York, N Y; plus one other.
Commissions: Murals, Continental Hotel, Chicago, Ill, 63; Mercantile Nat Bank, Hammond, Ind, 65; Swedish Lloyd Ship "Patricia", Stockholm, Sweden, 66; Madison Sq Garden, New York, 69.
Exhibitions: Chicago Artists and Vicinity Show, 54-60; Carnegie Int, Pittsburgh, Pa, 56; Corcoran American Exhibition of Oil Painting, Washington, D C, 57; Chicago American Exhibit of Painting and Sculpture, Art Inst Chicago, 60; Museo de Bellas Artes, Caracas, Venezuela, 72; plus one other.
Teaching: Instr figure drawing, Sch Art, Inst Chicago, 50-60; instr painting, Winston-Salem Art Ctr, 64; instr painting, Atlanta Poverty Art Prog, 67-68.

Positions: Resident artist, New York Jets Prof Football Team, 68-; artist reporter, ABC TV Wide World of Sports, 69-; official artist, Major League Baseball Promotions, 71-; ABC-TV official artist, XX Olympiad, Munich, Ger, 72.
Awards: 1st prize, Twin-City Exhibit, Minneapolis Inst Art, 53; municipal prize, Chicago Show, Art Inst Chicago, 58; gold medal, Salon d'art Moderne, Paris, France, 61.
Publications: Illusr-contribr, Miami Notebook (with George Plimpton), Harpers Mag, 6/64; Paris Review, fall, 65; Time Mag covers, 3/1/68 & 1/17/72; Countdown to Superbowl, (with Dave Anderson), Random, 69; This Great Game, Prentice-Hall, 71; plus one other.
Dealers: Hammer Galleries, 51 E 57th St, New York, NY 10022; Félicie, Inc, 1411 E 56th St, New York, NY 10022.
Mailing Address: 1 W 67th St, New York, NY 10023.

NELSON, CAREY BOONE
Sculptor
Preferred Media: Bronze, Marble.
b Lexington, Mo.
Study & Training: Wellesley Col, BA; Northwestern Univ; Univ Mo; Wagner Col, MSEd; Art Stud League New York, with John Hovannes, Arturo Lorenzani & John Terken.
Work in Public Collections: Wagner Col, Staten Island, N Y; R F Shelare Libr, St Joseph Hill Acad, Staten Island; Sheldon Swope Mus, Terre Haute, Ind.
Commissions: Mother Holding Child, comn by Dr Hugo Cimber, Zurich, Switz, 68; Portrait of Martin Luther, Wagner Col, 69; Portrait of Barry, comn by Hix Green, Atlanta, Ga, 70; Discovered Grotto, comn by John Fischer, Ridgewood, N J, 71; Richard, comn by Gabriel Cucolo, Brooklyn, N Y, 71.
Exhibitions: Allied Artists Am, Nat Acad Design Galleries, 57-69; Int Art Exchange, Monte Carlo, Monaco, Paris & Cannes, 66-68; Hudson Valley Art Asn, Westchester Community Ctr, N Y, 68 & 70-72; Am Artists Prof League Grand Nat, 68 & 70-72; Burr Artists, New York, N Y, 70 & 71; plus 33 other group & one-man shows.
Awards: George Salzman Mem Award, Staten Island Mus, 68; first pl for sculpture, Composers, Auth & Artists Biennial Expos, 70; Anna Hyatt Huntington First Pl for Sculpture, Catharine Lorillard Wolfe Art Club, 71.
Bibliography: Articles, In: The Key, spring 69 & fall 71; article, In: Art News, 11/70; article, In: Small Talk, 10/71.
Memberships: Catharine Lorillard Wolfe Art Club (chmn ann exhib, 69, co-chmn sculpture, 69-71, chmn sculpture, 71-, chmn pub rel, 72); Am Artists Prof League; Composers, Auth & Artists Am (chmn sculpture shows New York).
Mailing Address: 282 Douglas Rd, Staten Island, NY 10304.

NELSON, DONALD RICHARD
Painter
b Hackensack, N J, Jan 20, 27.
Study & Training: Univ Southern Calif; Univ Calif, Los Angeles; Sch Fine Art, Los Angeles.
Exhibitions: One-man shows, Long Beach Mus Art, Calif, 71, Quay Gallery, San Francisco, Calif, 71 & Anhalt Gallery, Los Angeles, 71; Nat Orange Show, San Bernardino, Calif, 72; Am Portraits New & Old, Long Beach Mus Art, 72.
Dealer: Anhalt Gallery, 750 N La Cienega Blvd, Los Angeles, CA 90069.
Mailing Address: 11436 Dona Evita, Studio City, CA 91604.

NELSON, GEORGE LAURENCE
Painter, Art Restorer
Preferred Media: Oils.
b New Rochelle, N Y, Sept 26, 87.
Study & Training: Buffalo Art Stud League; Art Stud League New York, N Y; Nat Acad Design Sch, New York; Julian Acad, Paris, with J P Laurens.
Work in Public Collections: Lithograph, Metrop Mus Art; oil & lithograph, New Britain Art Mus, Conn; portraits, Am Acad Arts & Lett; Peace Palace, Geneva, Switz & New York Hosp.
Commissions: Portraits, New York Acad Med, 50, Canterbury Sch, New Milford, Conn, 50, Cochran House Fairfield State Hosp, 56, Shipley Sch, Bryn Mawr, Pa, 66 & Middlesex Nursing Sch, Middletown, Conn, 71.
Exhibitions: Paris Salons, 12-13; Corcoran Gallery Art, Washington, D C, 25; Pa Acad Fine Arts, Philadelphia, 28; Venice Int, 41; Nat Acad Design, New York, 71; plus many other ann & exhibs.
Teaching: Instr drawing, Nat Acad Design Sch, 10-41; instr painting, Cooper Union, 16-26; instr painting, 30-
Positions: Pres, Kent Art Asn, 54-68.
Awards: Isidor Gold Medal, Nat Acad Design, 21; first prize for print, Meriden Arts & Crafts, 64; first prize for oils, Kent Art Asn, 69.

Bibliography: Portraits, Grand Cent Art Galleries; Contemporary American portrait painters, Cuthbert Lee, 29.
Memberships: Nat Acad Design; Am Watercolor Soc; Allied Artists Am (pres, 41-43); emer mem, Salmagundi Club; life mem Nat Arts Club.
Dealer: Grand Central Art Galleries, 40 Vanderbilt Ave, New York, NY 10017; D Matt, 223 E 80th St, New York, NY 10021.
Mailing Address: P O Box 91, Kent, CT 06757.

NELSON, HARRY WILLIAM
Painter, Printmaker
Preferred Media: Oils.
b New York, N Y, June 9, 08.
Study & Training: Yale Univ Sch Fine Arts, 31-32, Yale Univ, BA, 33; New London Art Stud League, with Harve Stein, 49-59; with Katherine Howe, 53; with Clarence Brodeur, 63-70; Lyman Allyn Mus, New London, Conn, with Beatrice Cuming, 64-67.
Work in Public Collections: Lyman Allyn Mus; also in many pvt collections.
Exhibitions: One-man show, Lyman Allyn Mus, 68; Lyme Art Asn 68th Ann, Old Lyme, Conn, 69; Essex Art Asn 35th Ann, Conn, 70; Slater Mus 28th Ann Conn Artists, Norwich, 71; Mystic Art Asn 15th Ann, Conn, 71; plus many others.
Teaching: Spec demonstrations monotypes, Mystic Art Asn, 68 & 70.
Positions: Pres, New London Art Stud League, Conn, 65-68.
Awards: Silver trophy, 68 & spec prize design & graphics, 71, Am Cancer Soc Show, Mitchell Col, New London; first prize tech excellence, Univ Conn, Avery Point, 69.
Bibliography: Tom Ingle (auth), One man show is delight, New London Day, 3/15/68; Leslie Pfeil (auth), Groton's award-winning multi-media man, Groton News, 7/27/71; Diane Santangelo (auth), Impressionistic artist reveals value of personal creativity, Scarlet Tanager, 4/6/72.
Memberships: Mystic Art Asn; Essex Art Asn; Lyman Allyn Mus; Lyme Art Asn.
Publications: Illusr, The moon is near, 44.
Mailing Address: 213 Pleasant Valley Rd, Groton, CT 06340.

NELSON, LEONARD
Painter, Educator
Preferred Media: Oils, Metal.
b Camden, N J, Mar 5, 12.
Study & Training: Philadelphia Acad Fine Arts, 36-40; Barnes Found, 36-41; Philadelphia Col Art, BFA, 52.
Work in Public Collections: Mus Mod Art; Philadelphia Mus Art; Dallas Mus Mod Art; Walker Mus Art; Portland Mus; plus many others.
Exhibitions: 3 one-man shows, New York; 26 one-man shows, Philadelphia; many exhibs, Pa Acad Fine Art; Mus Mod Art; Art Inst Chicago.
Teaching: Prof printmaking, Moore Col Art, 52-, head dept, 69-
Awards: European fel, Bd Fine Art, 39; Nat Wood Block award, 42.
Memberships: Am Asn Univ Prof; Print Club (mem bd trustees, 52-57); fel Pa Acad Fine Arts; Am Fedn Teachers.
Mailing Address: 825 N 27th St, Philadelphia, PA 19130.

NELSON, LUCRETIA
Painter, Educator
b Nashua, N H, Feb 19, 12.
Study & Training: Univ Calif, AB & MA; Calif Inst Technol.
Exhibitions: Pa Acad Fine Arts, 38; one-man show, Seattle Art Mus, 47; De Young Mem Mus; San Francisco Art Asn.
Teaching: Instr design, Univ Calif, Berkeley, 38-42, asst prof, 42-46, assoc prof, 46-52, chmn dept decorative art, 54-61, prof design, 56-
Awards: Taliesin fel, 34-35; Europ scholar, Univ Calif, 36-37; prize, San Francisco Soc Women Artists, 44.
Memberships: San Francisco Art Asn; Col Art Asn Am; Am Asn Univ Prof.
Publications: Illusr, Textile of the Guatemala highlands, 45.
Mailing Address: 1641 Grand View Dr, Berkeley, CA 94705.

NELSON, RICHARD L
Painter, Educator
b Georgetown, Tex, Feb 27, 01.
Study & Training: Art Inst Chicago; Stevens Inst Technol; Univ Calif, Berkeley, BA & MA; Ecole Beaux-Arts, Paris.
Exhibitions: San Francisco Mus Art, 50, 51, 53 & 54; Oakland Art Mus, 54; De Young Mem Mus, 56 & 58; Calif State Fair, 53 & 55-57; & in Can; plus others.
Teaching: Lectr contemp art & aesthet; prof art, Wash State Col, 48-52; chmn art dept, Univ Calif, Davis, 53-66, prof art, 53-70, dir lab res in fine arts & museology, 66-69, emer prof art, 70-
Awards: Prizes, San Francisco Art Asn, 50, San Francisco Mus Art, 53 & Crocker Mus Art, Sacramento, 53.

Memberships: Pac Art Asn; Col Art Asn Am; Am Soc Aesthet; Western Art Dirs Asn.
Mailing Address: Rte 1, Box 2561, Davis, CA 95616.

NELSON, ROBERT ALLEN
Painter, Printmaker
Preferred Media: Stone, Oils.
b Milwaukee, Wis, Aug 1, 25.
Study & Training: Sch Art Inst Chicago, BAE, 50, MAE, 51, lithography with Max Kahn; John Herron Sch Art, Indianapolis, Ind, 64, lithography with Garo Antresian, N Y Univ, EdD, 71.
Work in Public Collections: Walker Art Inst, Minneapolis, Minn; Joslyn Mus, Omaha, Nebr; Sheldon Mus, Lincoln, Nebr; Butler Inst Am Art, Youngstown, Ohio; Addison Gallery Am Art, Phillips Acad, Andover, Mass.
Commissions: Murals, outdoor mosaics, Viking Sch, Grand Forks, N D, 58 & Bridston Savings & Loan, Grand Forks, 59, Univ N Dak, Chester Fritz Libr, Grand Forks, 60 & State of N Dak Hwy Dept Bldg, Bismarck, 68.
Exhibitions: Figure Painting U S A, Mus Mod Art, New York, N Y, 61; Butler Inst Ann, Youngstown, Ohio, 63; Artists West of Miss, Colo Springs Fine Arts Ctr, Colo, 65; New Vein, Smithsonian Inst Invitational, Washington, D C, 68; Watercolors U S A, Springfield, Mo, 72.
Teaching: Instr drawing, Sch Art Inst Chicago, 52-53; asst prof lithography & painting, Univ Man Sch Art, 53-56; prof painting & drawing, Univ N Dak, 56-72; prof printmaking, Cleveland State Univ, 72-
Awards: Frist prizes for painting, Univ Wis Salon Art, Madison, 65 & Manisphere Exhib Can & U S, 68; purchase prize for drawing & painting, Davidson Col, 72.
Bibliography: Garo Antreasian & Clinton Adams (auth), The Tamarind book of lithography: art and techniques, Abrams, 72.
Memberships: Boston Printmakers; Soc Am Graphic Artists.
Publications: Illusr, cover, Rec, 71 & Supertooth, 72.
Dealers: Graphics Gallery, 1 Embarcadero Center, San Francisco, CA 94111; Rourke Gallery, 523 S Fourth St, Moorhead, MN 56560.
Mailing Address: 3185 Warrington Rd, Shaker Heights, OH 44120.

NELSON, SIGNE (SIGNE NELSON STUART)
Painter
b New London, Conn, Dec 3, 37.
Study & Training: Univ Conn, BA, 59; Yale-Norfolk Summer Art Sch, 59; Univ N Mex, MA, 60.
Work in Public Collections: Tacoma Art Mus, Wash; Roswell Mus & Art Ctr, N Mex; Univ N Mex Art Mus, Albuquerque; Johnson Gallery, Albuquerque; Salt Lake City Pub Libr, Utah.
Exhibitions: 50th Ann Exhib Northwest Art, Seattle Art Mus, Wash, 64; Intermountain Biennial, Salt Lake City, Utah, 71; two-man exhibs, Yellowstone Art Ctr, Billings, Mont, 67, Johnson Gallery, 69 & Univ Ariz, Tucson, 70; one-man show, Sheldon Mem Art Gallery, Lincoln, Nebr, 72.
Awards: Ford Found purchase award, 64.
Bibliography: Jan Vander Marck (auth), The chromatic waves of Signe Nelson, ArtsCan, 71.
Mailing Address: 719 Eighth St, Brookings, SD 57006.

NEMEC, NANCY
Printmaker
b Pinehurst, N C, Nov 30, 23.
Study & Training: Colby Jr Col, New London, N H; Vesper George Sch Arts, Boston, Mass, grad, 44; Columbia Univ Sch Gen Studies, winter 48.
Work in Public Collections: Libr Cong; New York Pub Libr; Philadelphia Free Libr; Greenville Mus, S C; Hudson River Mus; Ga Mus Art; New Britain Mus Am Art; plus others.
Commissions: Print ed, Collectors Am Art, Silvermine Guild Artists, Hudson River Mus, Print Club Albany & New York Graphic Soc.
Exhibitions: One-man shows, Hudson River Mus, 59, 62 & 65; Albany Inst Hist & Art, 62 & 63, Silvermine Guild Artists; Westfield Atheneum, Jasper Rand Mus & Fremont Found; plus many others.
Teaching: Former instr, Westchester Art Workshop, White Plains, N Y, Hudson River Mus & Manhattanville Col.
Awards: Awards, Knickerbocker Artists, 60, 65 & 71; medal of honor, Audubon Artists Ann, 68; Miniature Art Soc N J, 71 & 72.
Memberships: Am Color Print Soc; Silvermine Guild Artists; Print Coun Am; Nat Asn Women Artists; Washington Watercolor Asn; plus others.
Mailing Address: Kearsarge Mountain Rd, Warner, NH 03278.

NEMSER, CINDY
Art Critic, Lecturer
b Brooklyn, N Y, Mar 26, 37.
Study & Training: Brooklyn Col, BA, 58, MA(Eng lit), 64; Inst Fine Arts, New York Univ, MA(art hist), with Walter Friedlander, Charles Sterling & Donald Posner.
Teaching: Guest lectr, Pratt Inst, Md Inst, R I Univ, New York Univ & others.
Positions: Curatorial interne, New York State Coun on the Arts, Mus Mod Art, 67; contrib ed, Arts Mag, 71-; co-ed, Feminist Art J, 71-
Awards: Am Fedn Arts tuition grant, Art Critics Workshop, 68.
Memberships: Women in the Arts (founding mem, 72); Col Art Asn Am (coordr, three sessions on women artists, 72-73); Am Soc Aesthetics.
Research: Position of women in the art world.
Publications: Auth, Art criticism and perceptual research, Art J, spring 70; auth, Stereotypes and women artists, Feminist Art J, 4/72; auth, Louise Nevelson: an interview, Feminist Art J, fall 72; auth, Art criticism and gender prejudice, Arts Mag, 3/72; auth, The Washington Women's Conference, Art in Am, 1/73; plus many others.
Mailing Address: The Feminist Art Journal, 41 Montgomery Pl, Brooklyn, NY 11215.

NEPOTE, ALEXANDER
Painter, Educator
b Valley Home, Calif, Nov 6, 13.
Study & Training: Calif Col Arts & Crafts, BA, 39; Mills Col; Univ Calif, MA, 42.
Work in Public Collections: San Francisco Mus Art; Oakland Art Mus; Metrop Mus Art; Pasadena Art Mus; Calif Palace of Legion of Honor; plus others.
Exhibitions: Metrop Mus Art, 52; San Francisco Mus Art, 55; Art: U S A, 58; Am Fedn Arts Traveling Exhib, 58-59; Americans, Va Mus Fine Arts, 62; plus many others.
Teaching: Prof art & dean faculty, Calif Col Arts & Crafts, 45-50; prof art, Calif State Univ, San Francisco, 50-
Awards: Prizes, Jack London Square Exhib, 65 & Rio Hondo, Calif, 68; first award, San Mateo Art Fiesta, 69; plus many others.
Memberships: Calif Nat Watercolor Soc; Peninsula Art Asn.
Mailing Address: 410 Taylor Blvd, Millbrae, CA 94030.

NESBITT, ALEXANDER JOHN
Educator, Designer
b Paterson, N J, Nov 14, 01.
Study & Training: Art Stud League New York, N Y; Cooper Union; also with Harry Wickey.
Work in Public Collections: Cooper Union Mus, New York; Houghton Libr, Boston; Providence Pub Libr, Klingspor Mus, Offenbach am Maine, Ger; Deutche Bucherei, Leipzig.
Commissions: Mem tablets, comn by Col Truman Smith, St John's Church, Stamford, Conn, 52 & comn by John D Skilton, Trinity Chapel, Southport, Conn, 56; mem doc, Pilgrim John Howland Soc, presented to Lady Churchill, 66; designs for four gravestones, comn by John D Skilton, Monroeville, Ohio, 66.
Exhibitions: Working Calligrapher & Lettering Artist, Brown Univ, Providence, 61; Calligraphy & Handwriting, 63 & 2000 Yrs Calligraphy, Peabody Inst; Alexander Nesbitt—lettering, Calligraphy, Typographic Design, Crapo Gallery, New Bedford, 66; Int Buchkunst-Ausstellung, Leipzig, 71.
Collections Arranged: Working Calligrapher & Lettering Artist, Brown Univ, 61.
Teaching: Instr typography & lettering, Cooper Union, 50-57; assoc prof graphic design & chmn dept, R I Sch Design, 57-65; Travel & Study grant, 59; prof dept design, Southeastern Mass Univ, 65-
Positions: Tech art dir, Jordanoff Aviation Co, 42-44; art dir, Technographic Publ, 44-45; owner, Third & Elm Press, 65-
Awards: Graphic Excellence Award, Fox River Paper Corp, 63; bronze medal, Int Buchkunst-Ausstellung, 71.
Bibliography: Leo Joachim (auth), Nesbitt reviews recent European graphics safari, Printing News, 3/5/60; Leona G Rubin (auth), Nesbitt calligraphy exhibit praised, New Bedford Standard-Times, 2/20/66; Walter Plata (auth), Alexander Nesbitt, Polygraph 1972, 72.
Memberships: Am Inst Graphic Arts; Providence Art Club (mem jury panels, 59); Type Dirs Club New York (mem bd gov, 55); Inter-Soc Color Coun.
Research: Calligraphy, book design and design history.
Publications: Auth, Lettering—the history and technique of lettering as design, 50; ed, Decorative alphabets and initials, 59; ed, 200 decorative title-pages, 64; ed, Color—order and harmony, 64; co-auth, Weathercocks and weathercreatures, 70.
Mailing Address: 29 Elm St, Newport, RI 02840.

NESBITT, LOWELL (BLAIR)
Painter, Lecturer
Preferred Media: Oils.
b Baltimore, Md, Oct 4, 33.
Study & Training: Tyler Sch Fine Arts, Temple Univ, BFA; Royal Col Art, London, Eng.

Work in Public Collections: Nat Collection Fine Arts, Smithsonian Inst, Washington, D C; Mus Mod Art, New York, N Y; NASA, Washington, D C; Peter Ludwig Collection, Aachen Mus, Ger; Nat Gallery Art, Washington, D C.

Commissions: Oil of Northern Trust Co, comn by Mr & Mrs Solomon Smith, Chicago, Ill, 67; poster, comn by List Found, New York City Ctr, 68; Apollo 9 & 13 (oils), NASA, 69 & 70; poster of Renwick Mus, Smithsonian Inst, 71; Clearing Sky 72 (oil), Environ Protection Agency, Washington, D C, 72.

Exhibitions: Tokyo Biennale, Japan, 67; São Paulo Biennale, Brazil, 67; Whitney Mus Am Art Ann, New York, 67; Int Art Fair, Basel, Switz, 70; New American Realism, Gallerie Gestlo, Bremen, W Ger, 71.

Teaching: Instr printmaking, Towson State Col, 66-67; instr printmaking, Baltimore Mus Art, 67-68; honorarium lect, Univ Miami, Univ Richmond & Baltimore Mus Art, 68, 69 & 71; instr painting, Sch Visual Arts, 70-71.

Positions: Asst set designer, Ogunquit Playhouse, Maine, 53 & 54; art dir TV, Walter Reed Med Ctr, 56-60.

Awards: Purchase awards for oils & prints, Baltimore Mus Art, 56; award for Ben Berns Studio (oil), 69 & Baker Brush Co (drawing), 71, Nat Collection Fine Arts.

Bibliography: Coverage of Studio series, Time Mag, 69; reprod of Vab Bay (oil), Eyewitness to Space, NASA & Abrams, 71; The Ruins (film), John Huzar Prod, 71.

Dealer: Gimpel & Wetizenhoffer, 1040 Madison Ave, New York, NY 10021.

Mailing Address: 59 Wooster St, New York, NY 10013.

NESLAGE, OLIVER JOHN, JR
Art Dealer
b Joplin, Mo, Mar 8, 25.
Study & Training: Univ Pittsburgh, AB, 50; Oxford Univ, 51; Univ Pittsburgh, Grad Sch, 51-52, Sch Law, 52-53.
Positions: Pres & managing dir, Venable Neslage Galleries, Washington, D C, 63-; pres, Neslage Assocs, Washington, D C, 68-
Memberships: Nat Press Club; Direct Mail Advert Asn; Am Soc Pub Rels.
Specialty of Gallery: Contemporary European and American artists in oil, graphics and drawings.
Mailing Address: 1625 Connecticut Ave N W, Washington, DC 20009.

NESS, (ALBERT) KENNETH
Painter, Educator
Preferred Media: Oils.
b Saint Ignace, Mich, June 21, 03.
Study & Training: Univ Detroit, 23-24; Detroit Sch Appl Art, 24-26; Wicker Sch Fine Art, 26-28; Sch Art Inst Chicago, dipl, 32, with Boris Anisfeldt.
Work in Public Collections: N C State Art Mus, Raleigh; Ackland Art Ctr, Chapel Hill, N C.
Exhibitions: Int Watercolor Exhibs, 34-39 & Am Painting Ann, 35 & 37, Art Inst Chicago; Golden Gate Int Expos, San Francisco, 39; Am Painting Ann, Butler Inst Am Art, Youngstown, Ohio, 51; Pa Acad Fine Arts Ann, 53 & 54.
Teaching: Resident artist & assoc prof, Univ N C, Chapel Hill, 41-49; resident artist & prof art, 49-
Positions: Dir, Univ N C War Art Ctr, Chapel Hill, 42-44, acting head dept art & acting dir, Person Hall Art Gallery, 44, 45, 55, 57 & 58.
Awards: Robert Rice Jenkins Mem Prize, Chicago Artists Ann, Art Inst Chicago, 34; purchase award, N C State Art Mus Ann, 54.
Memberships: Hon assoc N C Chap Am Inst Architects; life fel Int Inst Arts & Lett.
Publications: Ed, Student art at the University of North Carolina, Chapel Hill, 64; producer, Mona Lisa rides again (film), 69 & Art is where you mind it (film), 71-72.
Mailing Address: P O Box 14, Chapel Hill, NC 27514.

NEUBERGER, ROY R
Collector, Patron
b Bridgeport, Conn, July 21, 03.
Study & Training: N Y Univ & Univ Sorbonne.
Teaching: Lect art, Wadsworth Atheneum, Vassar Col, Brooklyn Mus, Detroit Inst Art, Mass Inst Technol Alumni Assocs, plus others.
Positions: Bd dir, City Ctr Music & Drama, Inc, 57-, finance chmn, 71-, exec comt; pres, Am Fedn Arts, 58-67, hon pres, 68-; Friends of Whitney Mus Am Art, 60-62; chmn, adv coun arts, New York City Housing Authority, 60-; adv coun, Inst Fine Arts, N Y Univ, 61-; trustee, Whitney Mus Am Art, 61-68, trustee emer, 69-; fine arts gifts comt, Nat Cultural Ctr, 62; art ctr comt, New Sch Social Res, 62-69, 70-, trustee, 67-; adv comt art, Mt Holyoke Col, 63-; fine arts adv comt, Amherst Col, 63-70; nat adv comt, Washington Gallery Mod Art, 63-65; adv comt, Mus Am Folk Art, 65-; hon trustee, Metrop Mus Art, 67-; pres coun, Mus City New York, 71-

Awards: Art in America, 59; N Shore Community Arts Ctr, 61.
Memberships: Benjamin Franklin fel, Royal Soc Arts; fel in perpetuity, Nat Acad Design.
Collection: Primarily American art, substantial part being given to the Roy R Neuberger Museum of the State University of New York College at Purchase; parts of private collection have been exhibited in museums, universities and galleries in the United States and abroad.
Publications: Contribr to Art in America and various art catalogues.
Mailing Address: 120 Broadway, New York, NY 10005.

NEUBERT, GEORGE WALTER
Sculptor, Art Administrator
b Minneapolis, Minn, Oct 24, 42.
Study & Training: Hardin-Simmons Univ, BS, 65; San Francisco Art Inst, 67; Mills Col, MFA, 69.
Work in Public Collections: Oakland Mus, Calif; Richmond Art Ctr, Calif.
Exhibitions: Contemporary Sculpture, San Francisco Art Inst, Calif, 67; Invisible Painting & Sculpture, 69 & one-man show, 70, Richmond Art Ctr; 11 Bay Area Sculptors Under 35, Michael Walls Gallery, San Francisco, 69.
Collections Arranged: Pierres de Fantaisie, 70, Color and Scale, 71 & Off the Stretcher, 72, Oakland Mus; Tropical, Oakland Mus & Santa Barbara Mus, 72.
Positions: Cur art, Oakland Mus, 70-
Awards: Trefethen Found fel, Mills Col, 68.
Bibliography: D Robbeloth (auth), Art scene, Coast FM & Fine Arts, 6/60; T Albright (auth), Object and illusion, San Francisco Chronicle, 6/70; C McCann (auth), Six, six, six, artweek, 6/71.
Memberships: Am Asn Mus; Western Asn Art Mus (regional rep, 72).
Publications: Auth & ed, Pierres de fantaisie, 70; auth & ed, Color and scale, 71; ed & contribr, Tropical (trop scenes by 19th century painters of Calif), 71.
Mailing Address: Oakland Museum, 1000 Oak St, Oakland, CA 94607.

NEUMAN, ROBERT S
Painter, Lecturer
b Kellogg, Idaho, Sept 9, 26.
Study & Training: Calif Col Arts & Crafts; Calif Sch Fine Arts; Univ Idaho; Mills Col; also in Stuttgart, Ger.
Work in Public Collections: San Francisco Mus Art; Boston Mus Fine Arts; Worcester Mus Art, Mass; Mus Mod Art; Addison Gallery Am Art, Andover, Mass; plus others.
Exhibitions: De Cordova & Dana Mus, 60-65; Seattle World's Fair, 62; New Eng Art Today, 63 & 65; Mus Mod Art, 64; Art Across America, Boston, 65; plus others.
Teaching: Instr, Calif Cols Arts & Crafts, 51-53; instr, Brown Univ, 61-63; instr, Carpenter Ctr for Visual Arts, Harvard Univ, 64-65, lectr drawing on Osgood Hooker Endowment, presently.
Awards: Fulbright grant, 53-54; Guggenheim fel, 56-57; prize, San Francisco Mus Art; plus others.
Mailing Address: Carpenter Center for Visual Arts, Harvard University, 19 Prescott St, Cambridge, MA 02138.

NEUMANN, HANS
Collector
Collection: Modern paintings; antique sculpture and modern sculpture; antique jewelry and watches.
Mailing Address: Apartado 5475, Caracas, Venezuela.

NEUSTADT, BARBARA (MRS GUNTHER MEYER)
Graphic Artist, Lecturer
Preferred Media: Intaglio.
b Davenport, Iowa, June 21, 22.
Study & Training: Smith Col, BA; Univ Chicago; Ohio Univ Sch Fine Arts; Art Stud League New York; also with Ben Shahn & Arnold Blanch.
Work in Public Collections: Metrop Mus Art, New York, N Y; Philadelphia Mus Art, Pa; Libr of Cong, Washington, D C; Nat Gallery Art, Washington, D C· Permanent Collection Am Prints, Bonn, Ger.
Commissions: Ed of etchings, Collectors of Am Art, New York, 56, 58 & 61; ed of etchings, Int Graphic Arts Soc, 60; ed of etchings, New York Hilton, 61; ed of etchings, Woodstock Artists Asn, N Y, 70.
Exhibitions: Brooklyn Mus Nat Print Exhib, New York, 54, 58 & 60; one-man shows, Ruth White Gallery, 58 & Philadelphia Art Alliance, 59; Int Exchange Exhib, Soc Am Graphic Artists Invitational, Europe & S Am, 60 & 61; one-man exhib, Portland Mus Art, 65.
Positions: Art dir, Shepherd Cards, Inc, 56-63; acquisition comt, Portland Mus Art, Maine, 65-66; dir-instr, Studio Graphics Workshop, Woodstock, 70-

Awards: Scholar, Art Stud League New York, 52; Lady Black prize, Boston Printmakers, 57; Joseph Pennell Mem medal, Philadelphia, 72.
Bibliography: A Zaidenberg (auth), Prints & how to make them, Harper, 64; K Marsh (producer), Woodstock community video (interview & demonstration), 72.
Memberships: Soc Am Graphic Artists; Philadelphia Watercolor Club; Hunterdon Co Art Ctr; Woodstock Artists Asn (bd mem, 63-64).
Publications: Illusr, The first Christmas, Crowell, 60.
Dealer: Polari Gallery, Woodstock, NY 12498.
Mailing Address: California Quarry Rd, Woodstock, NY 12498.

NEUSTADTER, EDWARD L
Collector, Patron
b New York, N Y, Mar 29, 28.
Study & Training: Ohio State Univ, BSC.
Collection: Twentieth century American sculpture and oils; French, German and Spanish sculpture and oils.
Mailing Address: Woodlands Rd, Harrison, NY 10528.

NEVELL, THOMAS G
Designer
b London, Eng, Sept 16, 10.
Study & Training: Col Fine Arts, New York Univ; Columbia Univ.
Positions: Partner, Cushing & Nevell, New York, N Y, 33-, secy-treas, subsidiary co, New York, Los Angeles, Toronto, Ont & Cushing & Nevell Tech Design Corp, New York.
Awards: Elec Mfg Award, 40; Indust Designers Inst Award, 51; N Y Employing Prints Asn Awards, 60, 61 & 64; plus others.
Memberships: Indust Designers Soc Am; Assoc Am Soc Mech Eng; Indust Designers Inst.
Publications: Contribr, articles indust design, In: leading trade mags.
Mailing Address: Cushing & Nevell, 101 Park Ave, New York, NY 10017.

NEVELSON, LOUISE
Sculptor
b Kiev, Russia, 00; U S citizen.
Work in Public Collections: Mus Mod Art & Whitney Mus Am Art, New York, N Y; Princeton Univ, N J; Tate Gallery Art, London, Eng; Art Inst Chicago, Ill.
Commissions: Aluminum sculpture, South Mall Proj, Albany, N Y, 68; wood sculpture, Temple Beth-El, Great Neck, N Y, 70; Corten steel sculpture, Binghamton, N Y, 72; Cor-ten steel sculpture, Scottsdale, Ariz, 72; monumental wood sculpture, World Trade Ctr, New York, 72.
Exhibitions: One-man & group exhibs all over the world, regularly for many years.
Bibliography: Glimcher (auth), Louise Nevelson, Praeger, 72.
Memberships: Artists Equity Asn (pres, 63).
Dealer: Pace Gallery, 32 E 57th St, New York, NY 10022.
Mailing Address: 29 Spring St, New York, NY 10012.

NEVELSON, MIKE
Sculptor
Preferred Media: Metals.
b New York, N Y, Feb 23, 22.
Work in Public Collections: Colby Col; Wadsworth Atheneum; Whitney Mus Am Art.
Exhibitions: Whitney Mus Am Art; Silvermine Guild Art; Grand Central Moderns; Herron Art Mus; Expo 68, Montreal; plus others.
Mailing Address: 3 Milltown Rd, New Fairfield, CT 06810.

NEW, LLOYD H (LLOYD KIVA)
Art Administrator, Designer
b Fairland, Okla, Feb 18, 16.
Study & Training: Okla State Univ; Univ N Mex; Art Inst Chicago; Univ Chicago, BAE, 38; Harvard Univ; textile printing & dyeing with D D & Leslie Tillett.
Work in Public Collections: Indian Arts & Crafts Bd Collection, Washington, D C.
Exhibitions: First & Second Int Fashion Shows, Philadelphia Mus, Pa, 51 & 52; Textile Exhib, Mus Mod Art, New York, N Y; Am Craftsmen Coun Exhibs; World Crafts Coun Exhib, Peru; Int Touring Exhib, U S Dept Interior; plus others.
Teaching: Dir arts & instr arts & crafts, Int Am Indian Arts, Santa Fe, N Mex, 62-67.
Positions: Chmn, Indian Arts & Crafts Bd, U S Dept Interior; owner-operator, Lloyd Kiva, Inc, Scottsdale, Ariz, 46-62; dir, Inst Am Indian Arts, 67-
Awards: Cult serv medal, Univ Ariz, 59; merit award, Mus Mod Art, New York, 62.
Bibliography: Articles, In: Sat Eve Post, Life Mag & Nat Geog.

Memberships: Am Coun Arts Educ (chmn Intercult Comt); Heard Mus, Phoenix, Ariz (bd trustees); N Mex Arts Comn; Am Crafts Coun; World Crafts Coun.
Research: Indian arts research; history of architecture, crafts & performing arts; contemporary expression of the Indian artist.
Art Interests: Textile design.
Publications: Auth, The crafts of the Indian, House Beautiful, 6/71; auth, Performing arts & the American Indian, Am Way, 7/72; auth, Arts & minorities, Arts in Soc, 8/72.
Mailing Address: Institute of American Indian Arts, Cerrillos Rd, Santa Fe, NM 87501.

NEWBILL, AL JAMES
Painter, Instructor
b Springfield, Mo, Jan 13, 21.
Study & Training: Detroit Soc Arts & Crafts, with John Carroll; Brooklyn Mus Sch, with John Ferren; Hofmann Sch, with Hans Hofmann.
Work in Public Collections: Southern Ill Univ; Olson Found; Univ Kans; Mus Mod Art; Marist Col, Poughkeepsie, N Y; plus others.
Exhibitions: Detroit Inst Art; Cleveland Mus Fine Arts; Rose Fried Gallery, N Y, 57; one-man shows, Leo Castelli Gallery, N Y, 59 & Parma Gallery, N Y, 60; plus others.
Teaching: Instr painting, Queens Col, N Y, 58; vis artist, Southern Ill Univ, 60-61; former vis artist, Univ Calif, Berkeley.
Publications: Contribr, art criticisms, In: Arts Mag.
Mailing Address: c/o Benson Gallery, Bridgehampton, NY 11932.

NEWER, THESIS
Painter
Preferred Media: Oils.
b New York, N Y.
Study & Training: Acad Delle Belle Arte, Florence, Italy, four yrs; Pratt Inst Interior Design, grad.
Work in Public Collections: Pvt collections only.
Exhibitions: Allied Artists Am; Knickerbocker Artists; Jersey City Mus; Hudson Valley Art Asn; Painters & Sculptors Soc N J.
Awards: Best in show, Catharine Lorillard Wolfe Art Club, 68; top award for polymer, Am Artists Prof League, 68; gold medal, Nat Art League, Nat Arts Club, 69; plus others.
Bibliography: Article, In: La Rev Mod, Paris, 70-71.
Memberships: Hudson Valley Art Asn; Am Artists Prof League; Catharine Lorillard Wolfe Art Club; Nat Art League; Painters & Sculptors Soc N J.
Mailing Address: 876 Adams Ave, Franklin Square, NY 11010.

NEWHALL, BEAUMONT
Art Historian, Writer
b Lynn, Mass, June 22, 08.
Study & Training: Harvard Col, AB(cum laude fine arts), 30; Grad Sch Arts & Sci, Harvard Univ, MA, 31; Inst Art & Archeol, Univ Paris, 33; Courtauld Inst Art, Univ London, Eng, 34.
Collections Arranged: Permanent collections of photog in Mus Mod Art, 37-45 & George Eastman House, 48-71; also collection of Exchange Nat Bank, Chicago, Ill (with Nancy Newhall).
Teaching: Lectr, Philadelphia Mus Art, 32-33; lectr photog hist, Univ Rochester, 54-56; lectr photog hist, Rochester Inst Technol, 56-68; vis prof, State Univ N Y Buffalo, 68-71; vis prof, Univ N Mex, 71-
Positions: Asst in dept decorative arts, Metropolitan Mus Art, 33-34; libr, Mus Mod Art, 35-42, cur photog, 40-45; cur, Int Mus Photog, George Eastman House, 48-52, dir, 52-71.
Awards: Guggenheim Mem Found fel, 46; Kulturpresiträger, Deutsche Gesellschaft für Photographie, 70.
Bibliography: Bibliography (of over 600 titles), Trustees of George Eastman House, 71.
Memberships: Hon fel Royal Photog Soc; hon master of photog, Prof Photogr Am; corresp mem Deutsche Gesellschaft für Photographie; fel Photog Soc Am; fel Am Acad Arts & Sci.
Research: History of photography.
Publications: Auth, Frederick H Evans, 64; auth, Latent image, 67; auth, The daguerreotype in America, 2nd ed, rev 68; auth, Airborne camera, 69; auth, The history of photography, 4th ed, rev 71.
Mailing Address: 20 Link N W, Albuquerque, NM 87120.

NEWHOUSE, BERTRAM MAURICE
Art Dealer
b St Louis, Mo, Oct 15, 88.
Study & Training: Smith Acad, St Louis, grad, 06.
Positions: Pres, Newhouse Galleries, New York, 28-; v pres, Art & Antique League Am, 33-38.
Awards: Capital Order Alphonso X, Govt Spain, 64.
Memberships: Lotus Club New York (art comt, 70); Royal Soc Arts Gt Brit.
Publications: Auth, Paintings by William Merritt Chase, 27.
Mailing Address: 19 E 66th St, New York, NY 10021.

NEWMAN, ARNOLD
Photographer
b New York, N Y, Mar 3, 18.
Study & Training: Univ Miami.
Work in Public Collections: Metrop Mus Art, New York; Mus Mod
Art, New York; Art Inst Chicago, Ill; Philadelphia Mus Art, Pa;
Smithsonian Inst, Washington, D C.
Exhibitions: One-man shows, Artists Look Like This, Philadelphia
Mus Art, Pa, 45-46, Arnold Newman Retrospective, Art Inst Chi-
cago, 53 & Faces In Am Art, Metrop Mus Art, 57; Arnold New-
man Portraits, Fourth Int Biennale Fotografia, Venice, Italy, 63;
Camera & Human Facade, Smithsonian Inst, 70; retrospective,
George Eastman House, Rochester, N Y, 72.
Teaching: Instr advan photog, Cooper Union, 69-
Positions: Acting cur & adv photog dept, Israel Mus, Jerusalem, 67-
Awards: Photokina Award, Cologne, Ger, 51; Newhouse Citation,
Syracuse Univ, 61; gold medal, Fourth Biennale Int Fotografia,
63.
Bibliography: H M Kinzer (auth), Arnold Newman biography, In: The
encyclopedia of photography, Hawthorn, 64; Peter Pollack (auth),
Arnold Newman, In: The picture history of photography, Abrams,
69; Paul Cunningham, two taped interviews, Arch Am Art, 71.
Memberships: Am Soc Mag Photogr (trustee).
Publications: Auth, Bravo Stravinsky, World Publ, 67.
Dealer: Light Gallery, 1018 Madison Ave, New York, NY 10021.
Mailing Address: 33 W 67th St, New York, NY 10023.

NEWMAN, (JOHN) CHRISTOPHER
Sculptor, Educator
Preferred Media: Aluminum.
b Boston, Mass, Jan 23, 43.
Study & Training: Harvard Col, BA(cum laude), 65; Univ Pa, BFA,
66, MFA, 68.
Work in Public Collections: Univ Mass, Amherst.
Exhibitions: 10th Regional Award Sculpture Exhib, Philadelphia Civic
Ctr Mus, 70; 23rd New England Exhib, Silvermine Guild Artists,
72; one-man shows, Ruth White Gallery, New York, N Y, 70 &
Philadelphia Art Alliance, 71.
Teaching: Asst prof art & sculpture, Bucks Co Community Col, 69-
Memberships: Artists Equity Asn.
Dealer: Ruth White Gallery, 401 E 74th St, New York, NY 10021.
Mailing Address: 28 N Lincoln Ave, Newtown, PA 18940.

NEWMAN, ELIAS
Painter, Writer
Preferred Media: Encaustic, Casein, Watercolors.
b Stashow, Poland, Feb 12, 03; U S citizen.
Study & Training: Nat Acad Design, 18-20; Educ Alliance Art Sch,
20-25; Acad Grande Chaumiere, Paris, France, 29.
Work in Public Collections: Everson Mus Art, Syracuse, N Y; Bos-
ton Mus Fine Arts, Mass; Brooklyn Mus, N Y; San Francisco Mus
Art, Calif; Tel Aviv Mus, Israel.
Exhibitions: Juden in der Kunst, Salon Brendle', Zurich, Switz, 29;
Art: U S A, New York, N Y, 58; Am Acad Arts & Lett, New York,
59; Butler Inst Am Art, Youngstown, Ohio, 60; New Accessions
U S A, Colorado Springs Fine Arts Ctr, Colo, 62.
Teaching: Instr painting, Educ Alliance Art Sch, 46-48; instr paint-
ing, YMHA 92nd St Art Sch, New York, 49-51; instr painting,
Elias Newman Sch Art, Rockport, Mass, 51-64; exten lect on Art
of Israel.
Positions: Art dir, Palestine Pavilion, New York World's Fair, 38-
40; art consult, Palestine Sect, Int Expos, Cleveland, 47; ed, Im-
provisations, 50-52; art consult, Am Fund for Israel Inst, 54-55.
Awards: Stern Mem Medal & Prize, Audubon Artists 18th Ann, 60;
Beatrice S Katz Award for Graphics, Am Soc Contemp Artists,
71; medal of merit, Nat Soc Painters in Casein, Today's Art
Mag, 71.
Bibliography: Stephen S Kayser (auth), Elias Newman exhibition,
Jewish Mus, 49; Henry A La Farge (auth), Elias Newman exhibi-
tion, Art News, 2/49; Ralph Fabri (auth), Medal winner in casein
annual, Today's Art, 7/71.
Memberships: Artists Equity Asn New York (pres, 70-); Conf Am
Artists (chmn, 71-); Audubon Artists (dir, 71-); Nat Soc Painters
in Casein (pres, 66-70, hon pres, 71-); Am Soc Contemp Artists
(dir, 71).
Research: Art of Israel; economic and cultural problems of Ameri-
can artists.
Publications: Auth & illusr, Art in Palestine, 39; auth, Art in
Israel, Reconstructionist Mag, 6/29/56; ed, Directory of open
exhibitions, 57.
Dealer: Agra Gallery, 1721 De Sales St N W, Washington, DC 20036.
Mailing Address: 215 Park Row, New York, NY 10038.

NEWMAN, RALPH ALBERT
Cartoonist, Illustrator
Preferred Media: Ink.
b Newberry, Mich, June 27, 14.
Study & Training: Albion Col, BA.
Positions: Illusr, Old Timer (weekly cartoon panel), Indust Press
Serv, 54-; comic bk writer, Harvey, 56-
Mailing Address: P O Box 1047, Darien, CT 06820.

NEWMARK, MARILYN (MARILYN NEWMARK MEISELMAN)
Sculptor
Preferred Media: Bronze.
b New York, N Y, July 20, 28.
Study & Training: Adelphi Col; Alfred Univ; also with Paul Brown,
Garden City, N Y.
Commissions: Cormac, Edward McVitty, New York, 54; Elkridge,
Kent Miller, S C, 55; Peggy Augustus on Waiting Home, Mrs
Augustus, Va, 61; Hacking Home Trophy, Prof Horseman's Asn,
71; Hobson Perpetual Trophy, Liberty Bell Race Track, Pa, 72.
Exhibitions: Allied Artists Am, New York, 70-72; Nat Sculpture
Soc, New York, 70-72; Nat Art Mus Sport, New York, 71; James
Ford Bell Mus Natural Hist, Minneapolis, Minn, 71; Nat Acad
Design, New York, 71 & 72.
Awards: Anna Hyatt Huntington Award, Am Artists Prof League, 71;
Anna Hyatt Huntington Award, Hudson Valley, 72; award, Coun
Am Artists Soc Nat Sculpture Show, 72.
Bibliography: Margit Malmstrom (auth), The bronze horses of M
Newmark, Am Artist, 71; Molly Marks (auth), Life interest ex-
pressed in sculpture, Horsemen's Yankee Peddlar, 72; Horses in
sculpture, Am Horseman, 72.
Memberships: Fel Nat Sculpture Soc; Am Artists Prof League; Cath-
arine Lorillard Wolfe Art Club; Nat Art League; Soc Animal
Artists.
Publications: Contribr, Sculpturing horses, Morning Telegraph, 71.
Dealer: Arthur Ackermann & Son Inc, 50 E 57th St, New York, NY
10022.
Mailing Address: Woodhollow Rd, East Hills, NY 11577.

NEWPORT, ESTHER, S P
Painter, Art Administrator
b Clinton, Ind, May 17, 01.
Study & Training: Art Inst Chicago, BA; Saint Mary-of-the-Woods
Col, AB; Syracuse Univ, MFA; St Mary's Col, Notre Dame, LLD,
56.
Exhibitions: Lakeside Press Gallery; five shows, Hoosier Salon, 33-
42; John Herron Art Inst, 38; Metrop Mus Art, 44; Contemp Relig
Art, Tulsa, Okla, 49; Int Expos Sacred Art, Rome, Italy, 50.
Collections Arranged: U S Sect, Int Expos Sacred Art, Rome, 50.
Positions: Founder, Cath Art Asn, 36, dir, 36-40, bd adv, 40-58;
head art dept, Saint Mary-of-the-Woods Col, 37-64; founder & ed,
Cath Art Quart, 37-40; chmn, U S comn, Holy Yr Exhib, 49-51;
mem staff, Cath Univ, 52-57; dir art workshop, 54, 58 & 59; mem
collection comt, Children's Art Exhib, Vatican Pavillion, Brus-
sels World Fair, 58; dir art sect, Nat Cath Charities Jubilee
Prog, 58-60; founder & gen chmn, Conf Cath Art Educ, 58-61,
permanent exec secy, 60-63; art supvr, Bd Educ, 62-68; art
supvr, Sisters of Providence, 62-; dir, Summer Inst Art Educ,
Chicago, 65; speaker & consult elem art educ, Nat Cath Educ
Asn Convention, New York, N Y, 65.
Awards: Prizes, Hoosier Salon, 37, 39 & 42.
Publications: Auth, Nat Liturgical Wk, 57; ed, Catholic art educa-
tions, new trends, 59 & Reevaluating art in education, 60; auth,
Art teaching plans (3 bks), 60 & Art appreciation and creative
work, 61; plus many others.
Mailing Address: Foley Hall, Saint Mary-of-the-Woods College,
Saint Mary-of-the-Woods, IN 47876.

NEWTON, DOUGLAS
Art Administrator
b Malacca, Malaysia, Sept 22, 20.
Collections Arranged: Art Styles of the Papuan Gulf, 61; Art of the
Massim Area, New Guinea, 64; Art of Africa, Oceania and the
Americas, Metrop Mus Art, 69.
Positions: Cur, Mus Primitive Art.
Research: Relationships of art and oral traditions in New Guinea.
Publications: Auth, Art styles of the Papuan Gulf, 61; auth, New
Guinea art in the Museum of Primitive Art, 67; auth, Crocodile
and cassowary, 72; auth, Art of the Massim area, 72.
Mailing Address: 15 W 54th St, New York, NY 10019.

NEWTON, EARLE WILLIAMS
Art Administrator, Collector
b Cortland, N Y, Apr 10, 17.
Collections Arranged: British Painting 17th-18th Centuries, 57, 62,
69 & 70; Jacob Eicholtz: Pennsylvania Painter, 58; Hogarth & His
Sch, 59.

Positions: Mem ed bd, Art in Am, 53-55; dir, Pa State Mus, 56-59; dir, Mus Art, Sci & Indust, Conn, 59-62; dir, Saint Augustine & Pensacola Hist Preserv Bd, 62-

Awards: Award of merit, Am Inst Graphic Arts, 50-52; Comdr, Order of Isabel la Catholica, Spain, 65; comdr, Order of Merit, Spain, 68.

Memberships: Am Asn Mus; Soc Archit Historians; Am Asn State & Local Hist (secy-treas, 47-53); Soc Am Historians (secy, 48-50); Nat Trust Hist Preserv.

Research: Anglo-American art.

Collection: Anglo-American art of the seventeenth and eighteenth centuries; pre-Columbian art; Latin American folk art; American maps; Americana.

Publications: Auth, Before Pearl Harbor, 42; ed, Vermont Life, 46-50; auth, The Vermont story, 1749-1949, 49; ed, Am Heritage, 49-54; ed, Gulf Coast Conf Proceedings, 70-72.

Mailing Address: 105 Gonzalez St, Pensacola, FL 32501.

NEWTON, FRANCIS JOHN
Museum Director
b Butte, Mont, Dec 27, 12.
Study & Training: Univ Idaho, BA, 36, MA, 39; Univ Iowa, PhD, 51.
Teaching: Vis prof art hist, Univ Ore, summer 59; vis prof, Portland State Col, summer 61.
Positions: Cur asst, Worcester Mus Art, Mass, 51-53; cur, Portland Art Mus, Ore, 53-60, dir, 60-; chief consult art, Portland Curric Study, 59; mem, Gov Planning Coun Arts & Humanities.
Awards: Order of N Star, Sweden, 65.
Memberships: Col Art Asn Am; Am Asn Mus; Western Asn Art Mus (pres, 60-61); Asn Art Mus Dirs; hon assoc mem Am Inst Architects (Ore chap).
Mailing Address: 6805 S E 31st Ave, Portland, OR 97202.

NICHOLAS, DONNA LEE
Potter, Educator
Preferred Media: Clay.
b South Pasadena, Calif, Mar 30, 38.
Study & Training: Pomona Col, BA(cum laude), 59; apprentice with Kako Morino, Kyoto, Japan, 60-62; Claremont Grad Sch & Univ Ctr, with Paul Soldner & MFA, 66.
Work in Public Collections: Flint Inst Arts, Mich.
Exhibitions: Sixteen Michigan Ceramists, Cranbrook Acad Art, Bloomfield Hills, Mich, 67; one-man show, Sherbeyn Gallery, Chicago, Ill, 70; For Men Only, Lee Nordness Gallery, New York, N Y, 71; Appalachian Corridors, Exhibition 3, Charleston Art Gallery, W Va, 72; Salt Glaze Ceramics, Mus Contemp Crafts, New York, 72.
Teaching: Instr ceramics, Genesee Community Col, Flint, Mich, 66-69; assoc prof ceramics, Edinboro State Col, Pa, 69-
Positions: Vis artist/instr, Penland Sch Crafts, N C, summer 71.
Memberships: Am Craftsmen's Coun; Nat Coun Educ Ceramic Arts.
Mailing Address: Box 150, Edinboro, PA 16412.

NICHOLAS, THOMAS ANDREW
Painter
Preferred Media: Oils, Watercolors.
b Middletown, Conn, Sept 26, 34.
Study & Training: Sch Visual Arts, N Y, scholar, 53-55.
Work in Public Collections: Butler Inst Am Art, Youngstown, Ohio; Ga Mus, Athens; Univ Utah; Adelphi Univ; Greenshields Mus, Montreal; plus others.
Exhibitions: Major exhibs, New York, N Y, New Eng, & Washington, D C, 59-
Teaching: Instr, Famous Artists Schs, Westport, Conn, 58-61.
Awards: Elizabeth T Greenshields Mem Found grants, 61 & 62; gold medal hon, Allied Artists Am, 68; gold medal hon, Am Watercolor Soc; plus many others.
Bibliography: Articles, In: Am Artist, 3/60 & 8/72 & North Light Mag, fall 70; John L Cooley (auth), article, In: The Old Watercolor Soc, Eng, 71; plus others.
Memberships: Nat Acad Design; Am Watercolor Soc; Allied Artists Am; Salmagundi Club; Knickerbocker Artists; plus others.
Mailing Address: 7 Wildon Heights, Rockport, MA 01966.

NICHOLS, ALICE W
Painter, Educator
Preferred Media: Collage.
b Saint Joseph, Mo, June 15, 06.
Study & Training: Tex Woman's Univ; Pratt Inst; Univ Tex, Austin, BA & MA; Teachers Col, Columbia Univ.
Work in Public Collections: Ball State Univ Art Gallery, Muncie, Ind.
Collections Arranged: 18 Ann Drawing & Small Sculpture Shows, 55-; Crafts 1967, 67 & Collages by American Artists, 71, Ball State Univ Art Gallery.
Teaching: Prof art, W Tex State Teachers Col; prof art, Univ Denver; prof art, Ball State Univ, 47-72, head art dept, 47-69.

Positions: Dir art gallery, Ball State Univ, 67-72; pres, Nichols Assocs, Design Consults.
Awards: Gibson Award outstanding contrib to Ind archit, Ind Soc Architects, 72.
Memberships: Am Asn Mus; Delta Phi Delta; Am Asn Univ Prof; Ind State Arts Comn.
Art Interests: Contemporary art.
Collection: European graphics including Braque, Picasso, Burri and others; also contemporary American unknowns.
Publications: Auth, Art Vol for Jr Britannica; auth, articles, In: Palette; auth, articles, In: Hoosier Schoolmaster, 66, 69 & 70; auth, 7 outside (brochure), Indianapolis Mus Art, 70; also numerous mus catalogs.
Mailing Address: 402 N Calvert, Muncie, IN 47303.

NICHOLS, DONALD EDWARD
Designer, Educator
b Buffalo, N Y, Nov 20, 22.
Study & Training: Albright Art Sch, grad graphic design, 47; Univ Buffalo, BFA, 49; Mass Inst Tech, summer design prog, 67.
Commissions: Graphics for ann catalog, N Y State Coun on Arts, Albany, 62; cover design, J Creative Behavior, Creative Educ Found, 69; logotype creation, Humanist Mag, Amherst, N Y, 69; commun graphics, Am Acad Arts & Sci, Cambridge, Mass, 69; corp graphic prog, Amarillo Art Ctr Asn, Tex, 70-72.
Exhibitions: Four Western N Y Exhibs, Albright-Knox Gallery, Buffalo, 54-67; N Y State Fair, 63 & 67; University Artists 67, Albright-Knox Gallery, 67; Convocation on the Arts, State Univ N Y Albany, 69; Int IONALES Design Zentrum, Berlin, Ger, 70.
Teaching: Instr art, Albright Art Sch, 49-54; prof art & head commun design option, State Univ N Y Buffalo, 54-
Awards: Lyman Prize, Kittinger Award, Western New York Exhib, Albright-Knox Gallery, 54; N Y State Expos Award, Art Today Exhib, Syracuse, 67; State Univ N Y, fac res fels & grants, 68 & 69.
Publications: Illusr, CA J of Commun Arts, 59; illusr, Sch Arts Mag, 59 & 67; illusr, J Creative Behavior, 69; illusr, Humanist Mag, 69.
Mailing Address: 530 Mt Vernon Rd, Buffalo, NY 14226.

NICHOLS, JEANNETTIE DOORNHEIN
Painter, Instructor
Preferred Media: Acrylics, Oils, Watercolors.
b Holland, Mich, July 27, 06.
Study & Training: Art Inst Chicago, BA; Ill Inst Technol; Univ Chicago; lithography with Francis Chapin; painting with Carl Hoeckner; mural painting with Peppino Mangravite.
Work in Public Collections: Univ Ind, Gary; Wash Pub High Sch, Chicago; Portage Clin, Ind; Portage Pub Schs.
Exhibitions: Pa Acad Fine Arts, Philadelphia, 37; one-man show, Crespi Gallery, New York, N Y, 59; Minneapolis Art Mus Invitational, Minn, 63; Ann Ceramic Show, South Bend, Ind, 66; one-man show, Kreig Art Gallery, Lombard, Ill, 71-72.
Teaching: Art supvr, Belvedere Pub Sch System, Ill, 29-33; com art instr (adult classes), Chicago Eve Schs, 33-35; chmn art, Hyde Park High Sch, Chicago, 45-57; chmn art, Wash High Sch, Chicago, 57-72; retired.
Awards: Second award for Macatawa Bay, Peaceful Harbor (watercolor), Southern Shores Ann, 56; first, second & third purchase awards for three Christs (enamel on copper), South Bend Ceramic Show, 56; award for Washington School Playground of 1959 (oil), Tri-Kappa, 67.
Bibliography: Charles A Wagner (auth), World of art, New York Mirror, 9/20/59; Helen Ruth Huber (auth), Outstanding area artists, Gary Post Tribune, 61; Nikki Hollwager (auth), Painting is her life, Chicago Tribune.
Memberships: Assoc Artists & Craftsmen of Porter Co (former pres); Art Inst Chicago Alumni Asn; Artists Equity Asn; life fel, Int Inst Arts & Lett.
Publications: Auth, Arts and activities, In: Mural painting in high school, 56.
Dealers: Krieg Art Gallery, 9-E Ash St, Lombard, IL 60148; Lynn Kotler Galleries, 3 E 65th St, New York, NY 10021.
Mailing Address: 2 Frederick Dr, Gower, MO 64454.

NICHOLS, WARD H
Painter, Printmaker
Preferred Media: Oils.
b Welch, W Va, July 5, 30.
Work in Public Collections: N C Nat Bank Collection, Raleigh; Huntington Gallery Art, W Va; Springfield Mus Art, Mass.
Exhibitions: Acad Artists Exhibs, Mus Fine Arts, Springfield, 66-70; Allied Artists Am, Nat Acad Design Galleries, New York, N Y, 68; Mainstreams, Fine Arts Ctr, Marietta Col, Ohio, 69, 70 & 72, Frontal Images Exhib, Miss Mus Art, Jackson, 70.
Teaching: Instr oil painting, Wilkes Community Col, Wilkesboro, N C, 72-; also guest lectr, many cols in eastern U S.

Awards: Hon mention, Huntington Mus Art, 69; Grumbacher Award of Merit, El Paso Mus Art, 70; jurors merit award, Miss Mus Art, 71.
Bibliography: Of heart and hand (doc film), W Va Dept Commerce, 69; Matter of communication, Huntington Mag Sect, 69; articles, In: La Rev Mod, 70, 71 & 72.
Memberships: Acad Artists Asn; W Va Artist & Craftsman Guild; Wilkes Art Guild; Northwest N C Artists; Soc N Am Artists.
Dealer: Northwest Gallery, Hwy 115 at Armory Rd, North Wilkesboro, N C 28659.
Mailing Address: Rte 5, Box 638, North Wilkesboro, NC 28659.

NICK, GEORGE
Painter, Educator
Preferred Media: Oils.
b Rochester, N Y, Mar 28, 27.
Study & Training: Cleveland Inst Art, with Frank Wilcox; Brooklyn Mus Art Sch; Art Stud League New York, with Edwin Dickinson; Yale Univ, BFA & MFA.
Work in Public Collections: Rose Art Gallery, Brandeis Univ, Waltham, Mass; Galleria Sant' Onofrio, Rome, Italy.
Exhibitions: Md Artists Ann Exhib, Baltimore, 66; Pa Artists Ann, Philadelphia Acad Fine Arts, 67.
Teaching: Assoc prof drawing, Carnegie-Mellon Inst, 64-65; assoc prof painting, Univ Pa, 66-69; assoc prof painting, Mass Col Art, Boston, 69-
Awards: Elizabeth Canfield Hicks Award, 62 & E Stanton Griggs Award Excellence in Drawing, 63, Yale Univ; four jury awards, Baltimore Mus Art, Md Artists Ann Exhib, 66.
Dealer: 100 Acres Gallery, 456 W Broadway, New York, NY 10012.
Mailing Address: 76 Batterymarch St, Boston, MA 02110.

NICKERSON, RUTH (RUTH NICKERSON GREACEN)
Sculptor
Preferred Media: Stone.
b Appleton, Wis, Nov 23, 05.
Study & Training: Simcoe Col Inst, Ont; Nat Acad Design; also with Ahron Ben-Smuel, New York, N Y.
Work in Public Collections: Brooklyn Pub Libr, Arlington Br, Brooklyn, N Y; Cedar Rapids Art Asn, Iowa; Montclair Art Mus, N J; Interchurch Ctr, New York.
Commissions: Many portrait comns for pvt collectors, 32-; Learning (stone group), Fed Art Proj, Brooklyn, 34; Tympanum, Fed Govt, New Brunswick Post Off, N J, 36; American Oriental Rug Weaving (ceramic mural), Fed Art Proj, Leaksville Post Off, N C; mem plaque, New Rochelle Art Comt for City Hall, 60.
Exhibitions: Nat Acad Design Ann, New York, N Y, 32-; Whitney Mus Am Art, New York, 34; Mus Mod Art, New York, 39; Artists for Victory, Metrop Mus Art, New York, 42; Pa Acad Fine Arts, Philadelphia, 48.
Teaching: Instr sculpture, Roerich Mus, New York, 34-35; instr sculpture, Westchester Art Workshop, 45-47 sporadically, 48-69.
Positions: Charter mem & secy pro tem, White Plains Civic Art Comn, 48-60.
Awards: Saltus Gold Medal, Nat Acad Design, 33; Montclair Mus Art Medal, 39; Guggenheim fel, 46-47.
Bibliography: Jacques Schneir (auth), Art in modern America.
Memberships: Nat Sculpture Soc (mem coun, 60-63, rec secy, 62-63); assoc Nat Acad Design; Audubon Artists (dir & bd mem, 55); Scarsdale Art Asn (treas, 43-44); Hudson Valley Art Asn.
Mailing Address: 106 Woodcrest Ave, White Plains, NY 10604.

NICKFORD, JUAN
Sculptor, Educator
Preferred Media: Metals, Mixed Media.
b Havana, Cuba, Aug 8, 25; U S citizen.
Study & Training: Acad Art, Havana, MFA, 46; Sch Archit, Univ Havana.
Work in Public Collections: Smith Col Mus Art, Northampton, Mass; Spaeth Found, New York, N Y; also in collections of Roy Neuberger, New York & Phil Berg, Los Angeles, Calif.
Commissions: Three welded metal sculptures, Socony Oil Bldg, New York, 56; metal mural, Trade Show Bldg, New York, 56; free standing group, Philco Corp Trade Mart, Chicago, Ill, 57; two screens, Grace Line, SS Santa Rosa, 60; outdoor sculpture, Tappan Town Soc, Tappan, N Y, 72.
Exhibitions: American Sculpture, Metrop Mus Art, New York, 51; Whitney Mus Am Art Ann, 50-57; God and man in art, Am Fedn Arts Traveling Show, 59; Junior Council, Mus Mod Art, New York, 61; Man Came This Way, Los Angeles Co Mus Art, Calif, 71.
Teaching: Vis artist, Univ Hartford, 65-66; vis artist, Smith Col, 66-69; asst prof sculpture, City Col New York, 70-
Positions: Mem exhib comt, Sculpture Ctr New York, 70-; mem exhib comt, City Col New York, 71-

Awards: Hon mention, Pa Acad Fine Arts, 58; bronze medal, N Y State Expos, 64; Inst Int Educ grant for creative sculpture, Cintas Found, 71.
Bibliography: Frank & Dorothy Getlein (auth), Christianity in modern art, Bruce Publ Co, 61; Meilach & Seiden (auth), Direct metal sculpture, George Allen & Unwin Ltd, (London), 66; Nathan Cabot Hale (auth), Welded sculpture, Watson-Guptill, 68.
Memberships: Sculptor's Guild; Rockland Found Art.
Publications: Contribr, New talent, Art in Am, 56.
Dealer: Sculpture Center, Inc, 167 E 69th St, New York, NY 10021.
Mailing Address: 161 Old Tappan Rd, Tappan, NY 10983.

NICKLE, ROBERT W
Painter, Educator
b Saginaw, Mich, May 22, 19.
Study & Training: Univ Mich, BD; Inst Design, Chicago.
Work in Public Collections: Art Inst Chicago.
Exhibitions: Carnegie Inst, 59; Mus Mod Art, 61; Univ Ill, Urbana-Champaign, 69; Purdue Univ, 69; Art Inst Chicago; plus others.
Teaching: Prof drawing & design, Univ Ill, Chicago Circle, 55-
Awards: Purchase prize, Art Inst Chicago.
Mailing Address: Dept of Art, University of Illinois at Chicago Circle, Chicago, IL 60680.

NICODEMUS, CHESTER ROLAND
Sculptor, Designer
Preferred Media: Ceramics, Bronze.
b Barberton, Ohio, Aug 17, 01.
Study & Training: Cleveland Sch Art, grad, 25; Univ Dayton; Ohio State Univ.
Work in Public Collections: Portrait, Dayton Art Inst, Ohio; ceramic jug, Columbus Gallery Fine Arts, Ohio; ceramic figure, Capital Univ, Columbus.
Commissions: Wright Bros Tablet, Wilbur Wright High Sch, Dayton, 28; Francis C Sessions Tablet, Columbus Gallery Fine Arts, 32; Columbus Art League Medal, 47; Edward Orton Tablet, Unitarian Church, Columbus, 63; Butler Inst Am Art Medal, Youngstown, Ohio, 72.
Exhibitions: Ceramic Nat, Syracuse, N Y, 54; Ceramic Int, 58; Columbus Art League, 63; Butler Inst Am Art, 65.
Teaching: Instr sculpture, Dayton Art Inst, 25-30; instr sculpture, Columbus Art Sch, 30-43, dean, 31-43.
Memberships: Nat Sculpture Soc; Columbus Art League (pres, 33-36).
Mailing Address: 447 Clinton Heights Ave, Columbus, OH 43202.

NIEMANN, EDMUND E
Painter
b New York, N Y.
Study & Training: Nat Acad Design; Art Stud League New York.
Work in Public Collections: Norfolk Mus Arts & Sci, Va; Springfield Art Mus, Mass; Storm King Art Mus, Mountainville, N Y; Syracuse Univ Art Mus, N Y; Swarthmore Col, Pa.
Exhibitions: Directions Am Painting, Carnegie Inst, Pa, 41; Pa Acad Fine Arts Watercolor & Drawing Ann, 64; Butler Inst Am Art Painting Nat, 68; Nat Acad Design Ann, 68; Watercolor U S A, 72.
Awards: Emily Lowe Found, 55; Ball State Univ Drawing Ann Purchase Award, 60; Allied Artists Am Award, 71.
Memberships: Audubon Artists; Am Watercolor Soc; Conn Acad; Allied Artists Am; Nat Soc Painters Acrylic & Casein.
Publications: Auth, Drawing with unusual tool, Am Artists, 1/70.
Mailing Address: 38-15-208th St, Bayside, NY 11361.

NIEMEYER, ARNOLD MATTHEW
Collector, Patron
b Saint Paul, Minn, Mar 7, 13.
Positions: Trustee, Minn Mus Art.
Collection: All media, especially fine graphics.
Mailing Address: 1364 Summit Ave, Saint Paul, MN 55105.

NIERMAN, LEONARDO M
Painter, Sculptor
Preferred Media: Acrylics, Onyx, Bronze.
b Mexico City, Mex, Nov 1, 32.
Study & Training: Nat Univ Mex, BA.
Work in Public Collections: Boston Mus Fine Arts, Mass; Santa Barbara Mus, Calif; Mus Arte Mod, Mexico City; Atlanta Mus, Ga; Mus Mod Art, Haifa, Israel.
Commissions: Murals Sch Commerce, Univ City, Mex, 56 & Golden West Savings, San Francisco, Calif, 65; stained glass windows, two temples, Mexico City, 66-67; Cosmic Meditation (mural), Physics Bldg, Princeton Univ, N J, 68; Eagle (bronze sculpture), Toronto, Can, 72.
Exhibitions: Paris Biennale, Mus Mod Art, France, 61; Marlborough-Gerson Gallery, New York, N Y, 64; Pittsburgh Int, Carnegie Inst, Pa, 64 & 67; El Paso Mus Art, Tex, 64 & 71; Mus Arte Mod, 72.

Awards: First prize, Art Inst Mex, 64; Palm D'Or Beaux Arts, Monaco, 69; gold medal, Tomasso Campanella Found, Italy, 72.
Bibliography: Enrique Gual (auth), Leonardo Nierman, Ed Monterrey, 64; Carlos Pellicer (auth), Leonardo Nierman, 67 & Jose Gomez Sicre (auth), Nierman, 71, Artes Mex.
Memberships: Royal Soc Arts, London; Int Biog Asn: U K; Int Arts Guild, Monte Carlo; Salon Plastica Mex.
Dealer: Wally F Findlay Galleries, 17 E 57th St, New York, NY 10022.
Mailing Address: Ave Nuevo Leon 160, Mexico City 11, Mex.

NIESE, HENRY ERNST
Painter, Film Maker
Preferred Media: Acrylics.
b Jersey City, N J, Oct 11, 24.
Study & Training: Cooper Union, cert, with Robert Gwathmey & Morris Kantor; Acad Grande Chaumiere, cert, with Othon Friesz; Columbia Univ, BFA, with Leo Manso, John Heliker & Meyer Schapiro.
Work in Public Collections: Whitney Mus Am Art, New York, N Y; Chrysler Mus, Norfolk, Va; Albright-Knox Mus; N J State Mus, Trenton; Filmkundliches Arkiv, Cologne, W Ger.
Exhibitions: Corcoran Biennials, 55, 57 & 59; Young America 62 & 40 Artists Under 40, 64, Whitney Mus Am Art; 4th Int Exp Film Festival, Brussels, Belg, 67; 7th-9th New York Avant Garde Festivals, 69, 71 & 72.
Teaching: Spec lectr grad humanities, N Y Univ, 65-69; asst prof studio art, Ohio State Univ, 66-69; asst prof studio art, Univ Md, 69-, Creative & Performing Arts grant, 71.
Awards: Pulitzer Found Traveling fel, 55; Int Cinema Prize, Mus Arte Mod, Vitoria, Brasil, 69.
Dealer: Frank Rehn Gallery, 655 Madison Ave, New York, NY 10019.
Mailing Address: Rte 2, Box 12924, Ellicott City, MD 20742.

NIGROSH, LEON ISAAC
Designer, Instructor
Preferred Media: Ceramics.
b Cambridge, Mass, Aug 7, 40.
Study & Training: Carnegie Inst Technol, 58-59; R I Sch Design, BFA, 63; Rochester Inst Technol, MFA, 65.
Commissions: Ceramic mural, Waltham Supermarket, Mass, 63; ceramic, metal & glass panels, Mr & Mrs Benjamin Cooperstein, Belmont, Mass, 64; ceramic wall panels, Mr & Mrs Sanford Bomstein, Washington, D C, 69; ceramic & acrylite sculpture, Mr & Mrs George Klomberg, L I, N Y, 70; ceramic wall panel, Mr & Mrs Robert Massey, Holden, Mass, 70.
Exhibitions: One-man show, B'nai B'rith Bldg, Washington, D C, 69; Mass Asn Craftsmen Invitational, Boston, 71; Worcester Relig Art Festival, Mass, 71; one-man show, Lawrence Acad, Groton, Mass, 71.
Teaching: Instr ceramics, Auburn Community Col, 64-65; instr ceramics & studio mgr, Greenwich House Pottery Sch, New York, N Y, 65-66; instr ceramics & dept head, Craft Ctr, Worcester, 67-
Memberships: Am Craftsmen's Coun; Mass Asn Craftsmen.
Publications: Auth, article & rev, In: Craft Horizons, 71-
Mailing Address: Craft Center, 25 Sagamore Rd, Worcester, MA 01605.

NIIZUMA, MINORU
Sculptor
Preferred Media: Marble.
b Tokyo, Japan, Sept 29, 30.
Study & Training: Tokyo Univ Arts, BFA.
Work in Public Collections: Mus Mod Art, New York; Nat Mus Mod Art, Tokyo; Albright-Knox Gallery, Buffalo, N Y; Rockefeller Univ, New York; Des Moines Art Ctr, Iowa; plus others.
Commissions: Stone monuments, Metrop Tokyo, 56, Asia House, Tokyo, 58; Int Sculpture Symp, Vt, 68, St Margarethen, Austria, 69 & New York, 71.
Exhibitions: Mus Mod Art, New York, 65 & 66; Whitney Mus Am Art Sculpture Ann, New York, 66 & 68; one-man shows, Howard Wise Gallery & Gimpel & Weitzenhoffer Gallery, New York, 66, 68 & 72 & Rockefeller Univ, 71; Pittsburgh Int, Carnegie Inst, 67.
Teaching: Instr sculpture, Brooklyn Mus Art Sch, 64-69; guest critic, Columbia Univ, 72-
Awards: Mod Art Asn Award, Japan, 55 & 56.
Memberships: Mod Art Assoc Japan (permanent juror, 57-); Sculptors Guild.
Dealer: Gimpel & Weitzenhoffer Gallery, 1040 Madison Ave at 79th, New York, NY 10021.
Mailing Address: 463 West St, New York, NY 10014.

NIVOLA, CONSTANTINO
Sculptor
b Orani, Sardinia, July 5, 11.
Study & Training: Inst Superiore Arte, Monaz, Italy, with Marino Marini & Marcello Nizzoli, 30-36, MA, 36.
Work in Public Collections: Mus Mod Art; Whitney Mus Am Art.
Commissions: Murals, Motorola Bldg, Chicago, Ill, 60; 35 sculpture, Saarinen Dormitories, Yale Univ, 62; designed a mem plaza, Nuoro, Italy, 66; sculpture, P S 320, Brooklyn, N Y, 67; sculpture, 19th Olympiad Nac, Mexico City, Mex, 68; plus many others.
Exhibitions: Whitney Mus Am Art, 57; Carnegie Inst, 58; Mus Contemp Crafts, 62; Nat Gold Medal Exhib Bldg Arts, New York, 62; American Drawing Traveling Exhib, Am Fedn Arts, 64; plus many other group & one-man shows.
Teaching: Instr, Columbia Univ, 61-63.
Positions: Dir, design workshop, Harvard Univ Grad Sch, 53-57.
Awards: Gold medal, Regional Exhib Figurative Art, Cagliari, Italy; cert commendation, Park Asn New York, 65; fine arts medal, Am Inst Architects, 68; plus many others.
Bibliography: Michel Seuphor (auth), The sculpture of this century, dictionary of modern sculpture, A Zwemmer Ltd, London, 59; Fred Licht (auth), Sculpture, 19th and 20th centuries, N Y Graphic Soc, 67; Eduard Trier (auth), Form and space: sculpture in the 20th century, Praeger, 68; plus others.
Memberships: Archit League New York.
Mailing Address: 47 W Eighth St, New York, NY 10011.

NOBLE, JOSEPH VEACH
Art Administrator
b Philadelphia, Pa, Apr 3, 20.
Study & Training: Univ Pa.
Collections Arranged: Drug Scene, 71; Cityrama, 72.
Teaching: Instr filmmaking, City Col New York, 46-49.
Positions: V dir, Metrop Mus Art, 56-70; dir, Mus of City of New York, 70-
Awards: Scientific documentary medal, Venice Film Festival, 48.
Memberships: N Y State Hist Trust (chmn, 72-); N Y State Asn Mus (pres, 70-72); Archaeol Inst Am (treas, 63-70); Brookgreen Gardens (v pres, 70-); Corning Mus Glass (trustee, 69-).
Publications: Auth, The historical murals of Maplewood, 61; co-auth, An inquiry into the forgery of the Etruscan Terra-cotta Warriors, 61; auth, The techniques of painted attic pottery, 65.
Mailing Address: Museum of the City of New York, Fifth Ave at 103rd St, New York, NY 10029.

NOCHLIN, LINDA (LINDA POMMER)
Art Historian, Educator
b New York, N Y, Jan 30, 31.
Study & Training: Vassar Col, BA; Inst Fine Arts, New York Univ, PhD.
Teaching: Mary Conover Mellon prof art, Vassar Col, 63-
Awards: Kingsley Porter Prize, best article in Art Bull, 67; E Harris Harbison Award gifted teaching, 72; Am Coun Learned Soc fel, 72-73.
Research: Painting and sculpture of nineteenth and twentieth century.
Publications: Auth, Mathis at Colmar, Red Dust, 63; auth, Realism and tradition in art, eighteen forty-eight-nineteen hundred, 66 & Impressionsim and post-impressionism, 1874-1904, 66, P-H; auth, Realism, Penguin, 72; contribr, Art Bull, Art News, Art News Ann & Artforum.
Mailing Address: Dept of Art, Vassar College, Poughkeepsie, NY 12601.

NODEL, SOL
Illuminator, Designer
Preferred Media: Stained Glass.
b Washington, D C, 12.
Study & Training: Wash Univ Sch Fine Arts; Grand Cent Sch Art; also with Edmund Wuerpel, Gustav Goetsch, Harvey Dunn & Leo Dubson.
Work in Public Collections: Collections of Presidents Johnson, Kennedy, Eisenhower, Truman & Hoover; windows, Saint Louis, Mo, Hopatcong, N J & others; plus many others in U S, Europe & Far East.
Exhibitions: Saint Louis Bicentennial Celebration, Pius XII Mem Libr, Saint Louis Univ; also many exhibs in U S mus, univs & libr.
Positions: Chmn Art Comn, Int Synagogue, Mus & Libr, John F Kennedy Int Airport; mem Nat Arts Comn, Mary McLeod Bethune Mem Monument, Washington, D C.
Awards: Many awards for illuminations.
Bibliography: Steinmetz & Rice (auth), chap, In: Vanishing crafts and their craftsmen, Rutgers Univ Press.

Memberships: Hon mem Law Sci Found & Law Sci Acad; Soc Jewish Bibliophiles; Nat Coun Art In Jewish Life; life fel Brit Royal Soc Arts.
Mailing Address: 55 W 42nd St, New York, NY 10036.

NOGUCHI, ISAMU
Sculptor
b Los Angeles, Calif, Nov 17, 04.
Study & Training: With Onorio Ruotolo & Brancusi.
Work in Public Collections: Metrop Mus Art; Mus Mod Art; Whitney Mus Am Art; Guggenheim Mus; Brooklyn Mus; plus many others.
Commissions: Relief sculpture, A P Bldg, Rockefeller Ctr, New York, N Y, 38; fountain, Ford Expos Bldg, N Y World's Fair, 39; fountain & sculpture, John Hancock Bldg, New York & Chase Manhattan Bank, New York; fountains & entrance sculpture, Mus Mod Art, Tokyo, 69; plus many others.
Exhibitions: Cordier & Ekstrom, N Y, 63 & 68; Paris, 64; Claude Bernard Gallery, Paris, 64; Gulbenkian Exhib, Tate Gallery, London, 64; retrospectives, Whitney Mus Am Art, 66 & 68; plus many other group & one-man shows.
Awards: Guggenheim fel; Bollingen fel, 50-51; Logan Medal, Art Inst Chicago.
Bibliography: Shuzo Takiguchi (auth), Noguchi (monogr), Bijutsu Shippan-Sha, Tokyo, 53; Eduard Trier (auth), Form and space: sculpture in the 20th century, Praeger, 68; John Gordon (auth), Isamu Noguchi (catalogue), Whitney Mus Am Art, 68; plus many others.
Memberships: Archit League; Nat Inst Arts & Lett; Nat Sculpture Soc.
Publications: Auth, A sculptor's world (autobiog), Harper & Row, 68.
Mailing Address: 33-38 Tenth St, Long Island City, NY 11106.

NOLAND, KENNETH
Painter
b Asheville, N C, 24.
Study & Training: Black Mountain Col, 46-48; also with Ossip Zadkine, Paris, France, 48-49.
Work in Public Collections: Mus Mod Art, New York, N Y; Tate Gallery Art, London, Eng; Mus Fine Arts, Boston, Mass; Art Inst Chicago, Ill; Los Angeles Co Mus Art, Calif.
Exhibitions: Kenneth Noland, Jewish Mus, New York, 64; Three American Painters: Noland, Olitski, Stella, Fogg Art Mus, Cambridge, Mass & Pasadena Art Mus, Calif, 65; Morris Louis, Anthony Caro, Kenneth Noland, Metrop Mus Art, New York, 68; New York Painting & Sculpture: 1940-1970, Metrop Mus Art, 70; Selections from the Guggenheim Museum Collection 1900-1970, New York, 70.
Bibliography: Clement Greenberg (auth), Louis and Noland, Art Int, 5/60; Michael Fried (auth), Recent work by Kenneth Noland, Artforum, summer 69; Kenworth Moffett (auth), Noland vertical, Art News, 10/71.
Dealer: Andre Emmerich Gallery, 41 E 57th St, New York, NY 10022.
Mailing Address: Shaftsbury, VT 05262.

NONAY, PAUL
Painter, Instructor
Preferred Media: Oils, Watercolors, Collage.
b Simeria, Rumania, May 1, 22; U S citizen.
Study & Training: Royal Acad Fine Arts, Budapest, with Istvan Szönyi; Acad Fine Arts, Munich, with Hans Gött; Ludwig Maximilian Univ, Munich.
Work in Public Collections: Larry Aldrich Mus, Ridgefield, Conn; Springfield Mus Fine Arts, Mass; Loeb Collection, New York Univ, New York, N Y; Univ Bridgeport Permanent Collection, Conn; Southern New Eng Teacher's Col, New Haven, Conn.
Commissions: Hist mural, Hotel Utica, Utica, N Y, 51; bas-reliefs, Nat Bank of Westchester, New Rochelle, N Y, 69.
Exhibitions: Art U S A 1958, New York, 58; Conn Acad Fine Arts, Wadsworth Atheneum, Conn Watercolor Soc, Hartford, 58-64 New Eng Ann, Silvermine, Conn, 58-70; Nat Acad Design, Am Watercolor Soc, Audubon Artists Ann, New York, 61-66; Univ Fairfield, Univ Bridgeport & Quinnipiac Col Invitational Shows, 61-71.
Teaching: Lectr art, Silvermine Guild Artists, 60-61; lectr art, Univ Bridgeport, 60-71; vis prof art, Trinity Col, 72.
Awards: Conn Acad Fine Arts Prize, 62; Ford Found Purchase Prize 65 & Springfield Mus Purchase Prize, 66; New Haven Arts Festival Prizes, 66-68.
Memberships: Silvermine Guild Artists (bd mem, 64-70); Springfield Art League; Rowayton Art Ctr (co-dir, 60-68); Int Art Guild; Am Asn Univ Prof.
Publications: Illusr, cover designs for Grade Teacher, 55-56, The Reporter, 55 & 60, Today's Living, 57, La Rev Mod, Paris, France, 59 & Science and Technology, 63.
Mailing Address: Hillside Rd, Weston, CT 06880.

NOORDHOEK, HARRY CECIL
Sculptor
Preferred Media: Stone.
b Moers, Ger, Feb 10, 09; Can citizen.
Study & Training: Gemealde Galerie, Kassel, Ger, 27-28.
Work in Public Collections: Quebec Prov Mus, Quebec City; Elmwood Corp, Montreal; Mus Arte Mod, Milan, Italy; Buerdeke Galerie, Zurich, Switz; Mus Giorgi, Florence, Italy.
Commissions: Serenite Deux (sculpture), City of Alma, P Q, 65.
Exhibitions: Confrontation 65, City of Montreal, P Q & Stratford, Ont, 65; solo exhib, Mus Art Contemporain, Montreal, 66; 89th Ann, Royal Can Acad Arts, Hamilton & Edmonton, 68; 6th Int Open Air Sculpture Exhib, Milan, 70; 1st Int Sculpture Show, Carrara, Italy, 72.
Awards: Sir Otto Beit Medal for Sculpture of Spec Merit in Brit Commonwealth, Royal Soc Brit Sculptors, 65; acquisition prize, Second Concours Artistiques, P Q, 66; Renato Colombo Gold Medal, Ital Nat Prize, 72.
Bibliography: M Ballantyne (auth), A sculptor of cool serenity, Montreal Star, 2/27/65; T Krieber (auth), Violence at serenite s'opposent, Progres-Dimanche, Chicoutimi, P Q, 8/8/65; R Montbizon (auth), Harry C Noordhoek, sculptor, The Gazette, Montreal, 5/21/66.
Memberships: Asn Sculpteurs Quebec; Royal Can Acad Arts.
Publications: Ed, Enciclopedia universale seda dell' arte moderna, Milan, 72.
Mailing Address: P O Box 263, Carrara 54033, Italy.

NORDHAUSEN, A HENRY
Painter
Preferred Media: Oils.
b Hoboken, N J, Jan 25, 01.
Study & Training: N Y Sch Fine & Appl Art; Royal Acad Fine Art, Munich, Ger; Kunst Geverve Schule, Munich; Mass Inst Technol; New Sch Soc Res.
Work in Public Collections: Cleveland Mus Fine Art; Columbus Art Mus, Ga; New Brit Mus, Conn; Syracuse Univ; Pentagon, Washington, D C; plus many others.
Commissions: Several portraits, Syracuse Univ, Pentagon, Royal Crown Cola Co, Columbus, Ga, Ga Inst Technol, Atlanta, Ga Power Co, plus many others.
Exhibitions: Metrop Mus Art; Nat Acad Design, New York, N Y; Glass Palace, Munich; Art Inst Chicago; Corcoran Gallery, Washington, D C; plus many others.
Teaching: Instr portraits, Roerich Mus; instr art, New York High Schs; instr art, Musemont, Columbus.
Positions: Lectr, Metrop Mus Art & Brooklyn Mus Art; art demonstr, Columbus Mus Art.
Awards: MacDowell Colony fel; Trask Found fel; Tiffany Found fel; plus many others.
Memberships: Am Watercolor Soc; Salmagundi Club (pres, 59-63); Artist Fel (v pres); Dutch Treat Club; Explorers Club; plus others.
Dealer: Capricorn Gallery, 8003 Woodmont Ave, Bethesda, MD 20014.
Mailing Address: 1 W 67th St, New York, NY 10023.

NORDLAND, GERALD JOHN
Museum Director, Art Critic
b Los Angeles, Calif, July 10, 27.
Study & Training: Univ Southern Calif, AB & JD.
Collections Arranged: Gaston Lachaise, Los Angeles Co Mus Art & Whitney Mus Am Art, 63-64; Richard Diebenkorn Retrospective, Washington Gallery Mod Art, Washington, D C, 64; Anthony Caro, Piet Mondrian, Josef Albers & The Washington Color Painters, Washington Gallery Mod Art; John Altoon, Julius Bissier (with Guggenheim Mus), Robert Natkin, Al Held, Fritz Glarner & others, San Francisco Mus Art.
Positions: Dean, Chouinard Art Sch of Calif Inst Arts, 60-64; dir, Washington Gallery Mod Art, 64-66; dir, San Francisco Mus Art, 66-72; dir, Art Galleries, Univ Calif, Los Angeles, 73-
Memberships: Nat Endowment for the Arts (mus adv panel, 70-73); Asn Art Mus Dirs.
Research: More than thirty museum publications on twentieth century artists and movements, emphasizing American painting, science and photography.
Publications: Auth, Gaston Lachaise, Los Angeles Co Mus Art, 63; auth, Richard Diebenkorn, Washington Gallery Mod Art, 64; auth, Washington color painters, Washington Gallery Mod Art, 65; auth, John Altoon retrospective, San Francisco Mus Art, 67; auth, Paul Jenkins retrospective, San Francisco Mus Art, 71.
Mailing Address: 3965 Sacramento, San Francisco, CA 94118.

NORDNESS, LEE
Art Dealer
b Olympia, Wash, Dec 24, 24.
Study & Training: Univ Wash, 40-42; Stanford Univ, 43; Uppsala Univ, 47-48.

Collections Arranged: Art: U S A: 58, Madison Square Garden; Art: U S A: 59, New York Coliseum; Art: U S A, The Johnson Collection of Contemporary American Paintings; Objects: U S A, The Johnson Collection of Contemporary Crafts.
Positions: Dir, Lee Nordness Galleries, New York, N Y, 58-
Publications: Auth, Art: U S A Now, 63 & Objects: U S A, 70, Viking Press.
Mailing Address: Lee Nordness Galleries, 236-238 E 75th St, New York, NY 10021.

NORDSTRAND, NATHALIE JOHNSON
Painter
Preferred Media: Watercolors, Oils.
b Woburn, Mass.
Study & Training: Bradford Jr Col; Barnard Col; Columbia Univ; with Jay Connaway, Roger Curtis, Paul Strisik & Don Stone.
Work in Public Collections: First Nat Bank Boston, Mass; Am Mutual Ins Co, Wakefield, Mass.
Exhibitions: Acad Artists Am, 67-72; Am Watercolor Soc Ann, 69-72; Allied Artists Am, 69-72; Mainstreams 71, Ohio, 71; Hudson Valley Art Asn.
Awards: Grumbacher Purchase Awards, Allied Artists Am, 69; bronze medal, Catharine Lorillard Wolfe Art Club, 70; gold medal, Am Artists Prof League, 71.
Bibliography: Robert Kolbe (auth), Nathalie J Nordstrand poetry of the sea, Am Artist Mag, 9/72.
Memberships: Am Watercolor Soc; Allied Artists Am; Am Artists Prof League; Acad Artists; Guild Boston Artists.
Publications: Contribr, La Rev Mod, Paris, France, 72.
Mailing Address: 384 Franklin St, Reading, MA 01867.

NORMAN, DOROTHY (S)
Writer, Photographer
b Philadelphia, Pa, Mar 28, 05.
Study & Training: Smith Col; Univ Pa.
Work in Public Collections: Philadelphia Mus Art; Mus Mod Art, New York, N Y.
Exhibitions: Captions, Family of Man, Mus Mod Art & Tour, 55 & Forms of Israel, Am Fedn Arts & Tour, 58-60; 60 Photographs & New Workers, Mus Mod Art; Selections From Dorothy Norman Collection, Philadelphia Mus Art, 68.
Positions: Ed & publ, Twice a Yr, 37-48.
Bibliography: William Wasserstrom (auth), Introduction, In: Civil liberties and the arts, Syracuse Univ Press, 64.
Collection: Contemporary and ancient symoblical art.
Publications: Co-ed, America and Alfred Steiglitz, 34; ed, Selected writings of John Marin, 49; auth, Alfred Stieglitz—introduction to an American seer, 60; auth, The hero: myth/image/symbol, 69; auth, Alfred Stieglitz—an American seer, winter 73.
Mailing Address: 124 E 70th St, New York, NY 10021.

NORMAN, EMILE
Painter, Sculptor
Preferred Media: Oils, Acrylics, Wood, Bronze, Gold, Silver, Concrete.
b El Monte, Calif, Apr 22, 18.
Work in Public Collections: Oakland Mus.
Commissions: Mosaic window & marble relief, Calif Masonic Mem Temple, San Francisco, 56-58; Horse (wood sculpture), Crown Zellerbach Bldg, San Francisco, 59; St Francis (bronze sculpture), 67 & wood inlay mural, 68, Bank Calif Bldg, San Francisco.
Exhibitions: Archit Art Exhib, Pasadena Art Inst, 49; Relig Art Show, De Young Mus, San Francisco, 53; 20th Ann Soc Contemp Art, Art Inst Chicago, 60; Contemp Am Painting & Sculpture, Krannert Art Mus, Univ Ill, 61; Design & Esthetics in Wood, Lowe Art Ctr, Syracuse Univ, 67.
Positions: Owner-dir, Emile Norman Gallery, Carmel, Calif.
Bibliography: Eliz Gordon (auth), The flowering of our times, House Beautiful, 10/58; Janice Lovoos (auth), The art of Emile Norman, Am Artist Mag, 11/61.
Memberships: Carmel Art Asn; Nat Soc Mural Painters.
Mailing Address: P O Box 4268, Carmel, CA 93921.

NORRIS, (ROBERT) BEN
Painter, Educator
Preferred Media: Watercolors, Oils.
b Redlands, Calif, Sept 6, 10.
Study & Training: Pomona Col; Harvard Univ; Inst Art & Archeol Sorbonne, Paris; also with Stanton MacDonald Wright, Jean Charlot, Max Ernst & Josef Albers.
Work in Public Collections: Honolulu Acad Arts, Hawaii; Nat Collection Fine Arts, Washington, D C; Am Fedn Arts Mus Collection; U S State Dept Art In Embassies Prog; Ore State Univ Mus.
Commissions: Murals, First Hawaiian Bank, Honolulu, Royal Hawaiian Hotel, Honolulu & Royal Lahaina Hotel, Maui, Hawaii.

Exhibitions: Regional & local exhibs, West Coast & Hawaii, 36-; Chicago Int Watercolor Exhib, 38-42; Metrop Mus Mid-century Exhib, 51.
Teaching: From instr to prof art, Univ Hawaii, 37-
Dealer: Saxon Gallery, 750-C Palani Ave, Honolulu, HI 96816.
Mailing Address: 2009-B, Makiki St, Honolulu, HI 96822.

NORTON, ANN
Sculptor
Preferred Media: Stone, Wood, Bronze, Charcoal, Pastels, Watercolors.
U S citizen.
Study & Training: Nat Acad Design; Cooper Union Art Sch.
Work in Public Collections: Detroit Art Inst; Art Inst Chicago; Los Angeles Co Mus Art; High Mus, Atlanta, Ga.
Exhibitions: Mus Mod Art, 30; Schneider Gallery, Rome; Galleria XXII, Venice; one-man shows, Bodley Gallery, New York, N Y, 68 & 70.
Mailing Address: 253 Barcelona Rd, West Palm Beach, FL 33401.

NORTON, PAUL FOOTE
Art Historian, Educator
b Newton, Mass, Jan 23, 17.
Study & Training: Oberlin Col, BA, 38; Princeton Univ, MFA, 47, PhD, 52.
Teaching: From asst prof hist art to assoc prof, Pa State Univ, University Park, 47-58; from assoc prof hist art to prof, Univ Mass, Amherst, 58-, chmn dept, 58-71.
Awards: Fel, Am Coun Learned Socs, 51-52; Fulbright sr res fel, 53-54; Nat Endowment Humanities sr fel, 71-72.
Memberships: Soc Archit Historians (dir, ed j, 59-64); Col Art Asn Am; Soc Française Archeol; Archeol Inst Am; fel Royal Soc Arts.
Research: History of architecture; England and America in the eighteenth and nineteenth centuries.
Publications: Co-auth, Arts in America: the nineteenth century, 69; auth, articles, In: J Soc Archit Historians, Art Bull, Encycl Britannica & Encycl World Biog.
Mailing Address: Dept of Art, University of Massachusetts, Amherst, MA 01002.

NORWOOD, MALCOLM MARK
Painter, Educator
Preferred Media: Watercolors.
b Drew, Miss, Jan 21, 28.
Study & Training: Miss Col, BA & Med; Univ Ala, MA; Univ Colo, painting with Mark Rothko.
Work in Public Collections: Munic Art Gallery, Jackson, Miss; Miss Collection, First Nat Bank, Jackson; Miss Col, Clinton; Belhaven Col, Jackson; Jackson Country Club.
Commissions: Portrait, Southwestern Theol Sem, New Orleans, 63; landscapes & watercolors, First Nat Bank, Cleveland, Miss, 64 & 66; pottery, People's Bank, Indianapolis, Miss, 70.
Exhibitions: SMU Invitational, Fort Worth, Tex, 62; Washington Watercolor Asn, Smithsonian Inst, 63; Contemp Southern Art Exhib, Weatherspoon Art Gallery, Univ N C, 66; Artists Registry Exhib, Brooks Art Gallery, Memphis, Tenn, 69; La State Art Comn, Baton Rouge, 69.
Teaching: Head dept art, Delta State Col, 62-
Awards: First prize, Nat Oil Exhib, Miss Power & Light Co, 63; painting award, Holiday Inns Am Arts Festival, 69; first prize in drawing, Edgewater Merchants Asn Ann, 71.
Memberships: Miss Art Asn (v pres, 54 & 60); Cleveland Arts Coun (projs chmn, 70-); Miss Arts Comn (educ adv bd, 71-); Greater Greenwood Arts Festival (adv bd, 71-72); Miss Art Colony (bd dirs, 63-66).
Publications: Auth, article, In: Jackson Daily News/Clarion Ledger, 64; illusr, 64 & cover, 68, Delta Rev.
Mailing Address: 600 Canal Ave, Cleveland, MS 38732.

NOTARBARTOLO, ALBERT
Painter
Preferred Media: Acrylics, Mixed Media.
b New York, N Y, Jan 12, 34.
Study & Training: High Sch Mus & Art, New York; Nat Acad Fine Arts, scholar, 50; apprenticeship to mural painter Ignacio La Russa, 51-53.
Work in Public Collections: Fort Bragg, N C; Aldrich Mus Contemp Art, Ridgefield, Conn.
Commissions: Portraits, U S Army, 57-59; series of paintings, comn by Larry Aldrich, New York, 67; painting, Radio Corp Am, New York, 71; drawing, Newsweek, New York, 72.
Exhibitions: Albright-Knox Gallery, N Y, 68; Corcoran Gallery Art, Washington, D C, 68; Mus Mod Art, New York, 68-70; 21 Am Artists, Del Art Mus, 70; Aldrich Mus Contemp Art, 72.
Teaching: Private instr, 67-; instr painting & compos, YMHA, New York & Riverdale, N Y, 72.
Awards: First prize, New York Intercult Soc, 53.
Mailing Address: 215 W 98th St, New York, NY 10025.

NOTARO, ANTHONY
Sculptor
Preferred Media: Bronze, Marble, Wood.
b Italy, Jan 10, 15; U S citizen.
Study & Training: Rinehart Sch Sculpture, Md Inst, Baltimore; also with Harry Lewis Raul, Hans Schuler, Herbert Adams & William Simpson.
Work in Public Collections: Hall of Fame for Great Am; Stud Ctr, Seton Hall Univ; Nat Commemorative Soc.
Commissions: Sarah Josepha Hale Award Medal, 57; anniversary medallion, Geiger Eng & Mfg Co, 57; Hemerocallis Soc Medal, 60; N J Tercentenary Medallion, 62; Univ Iowa Medal, 63; plus others.
Exhibitions: Nat Acad Design; Nat Sculpture Soc; Providence Art Club; Allied Artists Am; Audubon Artists; plus many others.
Awards: Ellen P Speyer Prize, Nat Acad Design, 56; Louis Comfort Tiffany Award, 57; Coun Am Artist Socs Award, 67; plus others.
Memberships: Nat Sculpture Soc; Allied Artists Am.
Mailing Address: Box 224, Brookfield Way, Mendham, NJ 07945.

NOVAK, BARBARA (MRS BRIAN O'DOHERTY)
Art Historian, Educator
b New York, N Y.
Study & Training: Barnard Col, Columbia Univ, BA; Radcliffe Col, MA & PhD.
Teaching: Prof art hist & chmn dept, Barnard Col, Columbia Univ, 58-
Awards: Belg-Am Educ Found fel, 53; Fulbright Award to Belg, 53-54.
Memberships: Col Art Asn Am.
Research: Nineteenth century American painting.
Publications: Auth, American painting of the nineteenth century, Praeger, 69; contribr, Metropolitan Museum symposium on 19th century American art, 72; contribr to numerous art hist periodicals.
Mailing Address: Dept of Art History, Barnard College, New York, NY 10027.

NOVINSKI, LYLE FRANK
Painter, Educator
Preferred Media: Leather, Acrylics.
b Montfort, Wis, June 23, 32.
Study & Training: Wis State Univ, BA; Univ Wis, MS & MFA; Marquette Univ.
Commissions: Thomas Aquinas Chapel, 69 & Albert the Great Priory, 72, Univ Dallas.
Exhibitions: Riverside Invitational, 61; Tex Gen, 64 & 72; Okla Eight State Exhib, 68; Okla Invitational, 70; Fort Worth Art Ctr, 71.
Teaching: Assoc prof painting, art hist & design & chmn dept, Univ Dallas, 60-
Awards: Purchase award, Okla Eight State, 68; top award, Tex Gen, 72.
Bibliography: Articles, In: Christian Arts, 68, Liturgical Arts, 70, Art Gallery, 71-72 & many catalogues.
Memberships: Dallas Mus Fine Arts; Western Arts Asn; Col Art Asn Am; Tex Art Asn; Fort Worth Art Ctr.
Dealer: Contemporary Fine Arts Gallery, 2800 Routh, Dallas, TX 75201.
Mailing Address: 1101 Owenwood, Irving, TX 75061.

NOVOTNY, ELMER LADISLAW
Painter, Educator
Preferred Media: Oils, Polymers, Watercolors.
b Cleveland, Ohio, July 27, 09.
Study & Training: Cleveland Sch Art, dipl; Case Western Reserve Univ, BA; Kent State Univ, MA; Slade Sch, Univ London; Acad Zagreb, Yugoslavia; Yale Univ.
Work in Public Collections: Cleveland Mus Art; Butler Inst Am Art, Youngstown, Ohio; Akron Art Inst, Ohio; Canton Art Inst, Ohio; Cleveland Munic Collection.
Commissions: Mural for game room, John Sherwin, Jr, Waite Hill Village, Ohio, 37; History of Kent (mural), Portage Nat Bank, Kent, Ohio, 49; portrait of Gov Martin L Davey, comn by family, Kent, 50; portrait of Robert Carr, Oberlin Col, Ohio, 70; portrait of James A Michener for Michener Collection, Kent State Univ, 71.
Exhibitions: Cleveland Mus Ann May Show, 29-71; Butler Inst Am Art Ann Nat, 35-71; Canton Art Inst Ann Show, 37-65; Akron Art Inst Ann May Show, 37-71; Directions in American Painting, Carnegie Mus, Pittsburgh, Pa, 42.
Teaching: Instr portraiture, Cleveland Inst Art, 33-43; prof painting & drawing, Kent State Univ, 36-46, dir sch art, 46-

Awards: First prize for Nancy (portraiture), Cleveland Mus Art, 37; purchase award for Wingaersheer Beach, Butler Inst Am Art, 60; jurors award for Chateaux, Akron Art Inst, 69.
Memberships: Hon life mem Akron Soc Artists; life fel Int Inst Arts & Lett; Cleveland Soc Artists.
Publications: Auth, Byways of Southern Europe, Kent State Univ Press, 69.
Mailing Address: 7317 Westview Rd, Kent, OH 44240.

NOYES, ELIOT
Architect, Designer
b Boston, Mass, Aug 12, 10.
Study & Training: Harvard Univ, AB, 32, MArch, 38.
Teaching: Assoc prof & critic indust design, Yale Univ, 48-53.
Positions: Cur exhibs, Yale Univ Art Gallery, 48-50; pres, Int Design Conf, Aspen, Colo, 65-70.
Awards: Top ann award, Am Inst Architects; Homes for Better Living Award, 57; indust arts medal, 66.
Memberships: Fel Am Inst Architects; Royal Soc Arts; Indust Designers Soc Am.
Publications: Contribr, articles in publ.
Mailing Address: Eliot Associates, 96 Main St, New Canaan, CT 06840.

NUALA (ELSA DE BRUN)
Painter
Preferred Media: Pastels.
b Stockholm, Sweden, Oct 11, 96; U S citizen.
Study & Training: Anna Sanstrom Sch, Stockholm; also with W S Hayter.
Work in Public Collections: Stained glass window, Carnegie Hall, New York, N Y; 43 paintings to James Joyce's Finnegans Wake, Univ Tex, Austin; Carnegie Endowment Peace Bldg, New York; Benedictine Abbey, Glenstol Co, Limerick, Ireland; Mus Irish Art Hq, New York.
Exhibitions: Whitney Mus Am Art Ann, New York, 49, 50 & 55; Int Watercolor Exhib, Brooklyn Mus, N Y, 52; Am Acad Arts & Lett, New York, 61, 63 & 65; Art of Organic Form, Smithsonian Inst, Washington, D C, 69; The Organic Vision, Hobart/William Smith Cols, N Y, 71; plus many other group & one-man shows.
Bibliography: John Marin (auth), Illuminations (catalogue), Kleeman Gallery, 56; Abram Lerner (auth), Nuala (catalogue), Hirshhorn Mus Dir, 71; Leif Sjoberg (auth), Art of Elsa de Brun, Am Scand Rev, 71.
Memberships: James Joyce Soc.
Dealer: Betty Parsons Gallery, 24 W 57th St, New York, NY 10019.
Mailing Address: 161 E 81st St, New York, NY 10028.

NUGENT, ARTHUR WILLIAM
Cartoonist, Illustrator
b Wallingford, Conn, Feb 20, 91.
Study & Training: Fawcett Art Sch, Newark; Soc Illusr Art Sch, N Y.
Positions: Creator, syndicated puzzle-page feature Funland, Bell-McClure, U S & abroad; cartoonist & illusr, Puzzle Cart, Bell-McClure Syndicate, 32-72; cartoonist & illusr, United Feature Syndicate, 72-
Memberships: Soc Illusr.
Publications: Auth, cartoonist & publ, comic bks & contest puzzles; auth & illusr, numerous children's puzzle & game bks.
Mailing Address: 12 Tuxedo Pkwy, Newark, NJ 07106.

NULF, FRANK ALLEN
Painter, Educator
b Lima, Ohio, Sept 23, 31.
Study & Training: Ariz State Univ, BS, 59; Mich State Univ, MA, 60; Ohio Univ, PhD, 69.
Exhibitions: 4th Nat Exhib Contemp Am Art, Oklahoma City, 62; Soc Washington Printmakers 24th Int, 62; Boston Printmakers Ann, Boston Mus Fine Arts, Mass, 65; Int Miniature Print Exhib, Assoc Am Artists Gallery, 71; Can Printmakers Showcase, Ottawa, Ont, 72.
Teaching: Assoc prof art, State Univ N Y Col Potsdam, 60-69; prof art & dean Fine Arts, Univ Sask, 69-
Awards: Fulbright grant painting, Madrid, Spain, 62-63.
Memberships: Fel Royal Soc Arts; Col Art Asn Am; Univ Art Asn Can; Int Coun Fine Arts Deans.
Research: Film history and film criticism.
Publications: Auth, Report on the Bergamo film festival, Vol 5, No 3, ed, Network television and the personal documentary, Vol 6, No 1 & ed, The intensification of reality, Vol 6, No 1, Film Comment; auth, Luigi Pirandello and the cinema, Film Quart, winter 70-71.
Mailing Address: University of Saskatchewan, Regina, Sask, Can.

O

OBERHUBER, KONRAD J
Art Historian
b Linz, Austria, Mar 31, 35.
Study & Training: Univ Vienna, DrPhil, Dozent; Univ Cologne.
Teaching: Instr art hist, Smith Col, 64-65; instr art hist, Cambridge Univ, Eng, winter 68; instr art hist, Univ Vienna, fall 70 & spring 72.
Positions: Cur, Albertina, Vienna, 61-71; cur, Nat Gallery Art, Washington, D C, 71-
Awards: Kress fel, Itatti, Florence, Italy, 65-66.
Research: Prints, drawings & paintings of the sixteenth century in Italy & the Netherlands.
Publications: Auth, Parmigianino und sein kreis (catalogue), 63, auth, Die kunst der graphik III, renaissance in Italien, 66 & auth, Die kunst der graphik IV, zwischen renaissance und Barock, 68, Albertina; co-auth, The famous Italian drawings of the Albertina, New York-Milan, 72; auth, Raphaels zeichnungen, Berlin, 72.
Mailing Address: 3511 Idaho Ave N W, Washington, DC 20016.

O'BRIEN, JOAN
Painter, Designer
b New York, N Y, 40.
Study & Training: Hunter Col, BA; Art Stud League New York, N Y; Fulbright award, Aubusson & Angers, France, 62.
Work in Public Collections: Aubusson Collection; Piccolo Mondo, Palm Beach, Fla.
Exhibitions: Nat Acad Design, 72; Audubon Artists, 72.
Mailing Address: c/o Gallery Madison 90, 1248 Madison Ave, New York, NY 10028.

OCEJO, (JOSE GARCIA)
Painter
b Cordoba, Mex, June 14, 28.
Study & Training: Nat Univ Mex; painting workshop with Diego Rivera, Mex; Bellas Artes, Madrid, dipl honor; Sommer Acad, Salzburg, Austria, dipl honor, with Oskar Kokoschka.
Commissions: Murals, Ciudad Universitaria, Inst Cult Hispanica, Madrid, 50, Casino Arte, Mexico City, 52, El Potrero, Ingenio El Potrero, Mexico City, 53, Inst Madera, Direccion Gen Montes, Madrid, 58 & Basilica Nazareth (mosaic), Inst Nac Bellas Artes Mex & Comt Tierra Santa Milan, 68.
Exhibitions: Pinturas G Ocejo, Inst Nac Bellas Artes, Madrid, 61; Ocejo, 66 & Estancias Del Placer, 72, Palacio Nac Bellas Artes, Mexico City; Obra De Ocejo, Kaigado Gallery, Tokyo, Japan, 66; Ocejo, Louisiana Gallery, Houston, Tex, 68; plus many other group & one-man shows.
Awards: Medallas de honor, Inst Cult Hispanica, Madrid, 50 & Sommer Acad, 64; Primer Premio Olimpiada Cult, Inst Elias Sourasky, Mex, 68.
Bibliography: Alfonso Neuvillate (auth), Pintura actual, Artes Mex, 66; Ida Rodriguez (auth), Surrealismo y arte fantastico, 69 & Alfonso Neuvillate (auth), Jose Garcia Ocejo, 69, Nat Univ Mex; plus others.
Memberships: Inst Cult Hispanica, Madrid; Inst Cult Hispano, Mex, Mex; Inst Cult Mex-Norte Am, Mex; Mus Arte Mod, Mex; Inst Nac Bellas Artes, Mex.
Collection: Art nouveau; pieces from China and Thailand.
Publications: Auth, Panorama art visuais, Brasil J, 65; auth, Artes visuales, Union Pan Am, Washington, 66.
Dealer: Galeria Arvil, Hamburgo 241, Mexico City 6, Mex.
Mailing Address: Colima 230, Mexico City 7, Mex.

OCHIKUBO, TETSUO
Painter, Designer
Preferred Media: Oils.
b Waipahu, Hawaii, July 29, 23.
Study & Training: Syracuse Univ, MFA; Art Stud League New York; Art Inst Chicago.
Work in Public Collections: Munson-Williams-Proctor Inst; Honolulu Acad Art; Albright-Knox Art Gallery; Chrysler Mus; Los Angeles Co Mus Art.
Commissions: Sculpture-painting, State Hawaii, Hilo, 72.
Exhibitions: Over 100 exhibs.
Teaching: Vis prof painting, Mary Washington Col, Fredericksburg, Va, 61-63; assoc prof design, Syracuse Univ, 64-; instr printmaking, Art Stud League New York, 71.
Awards: John Hay Whitney Found fel, 57-58; Guggenheim fel, 58-59; Tamarind Lithography Workshop fel, Ford Found, 61.
Dealer: Krasner Gallery, 1061 Madison Ave, New York, NY 10021.
Mailing Address: 582 Kukuau St, Hilo, HI 96720.

O'CONNELL, GEORGE D
Printmaker, Educator
Preferred Media: Drypoint.
b Madison, Wis, Oct 16, 26.
Study & Training: Univ Wis, BS, 50, MS, 51; Ohio State Univ; Fulbright fel, Rijksakademie Van Beeldende Kunsten, Amsterdam, Netherlands, 59-60.
Work in Public Collections: Baltimore Mus Art, Md; Smithsonian Inst, Washington, D C; Libr of Cong, Washington; Gemeentemuseum Van Schone Kunsten, The Hague, Netherlands; Nat Collection Fine Arts, Washington.
Commissions: Volunteer artist prog, Dept Hist of Army, 71.
Exhibitions: Am Embassy, Dublin, Ireland; Baltimore Mus, Md; John & Mabel Ringling Mus Art; Contemporary American Graphic Art, Corcoran Gallery Art, Washington; U S I A Traveling Exhib Contemp Prints, U S Info Agency.
Teaching: Assoc prof printmaking, Univ Md, 61-68; prof printmaking, State Univ N Y Col Oswego, 69-, chmn dept art, 71-
Awards: Creative Arts & Crafts, Univ Md, 68.
Dealer: Franz Bader Gallery, Pennsylvania Ave, Washington, DC 20176.
Mailing Address: 39 Baylis St, Oswego, NY 13126.

O'CONNOR, THOM
Printmaker
b Detroit, Mich, June 26, 37.
Study & Training: Fla State Univ, BA; Cranbrook Acad Art, MFA.
Work in Public Collections: Mus Mod Art, New York, N Y; Whitney Mus Am Art, New York; Brooklyn Mus, N Y; Philadelphia Mus Art, Pa.
Commissions: Witches of Salem (suite), State Coun Arts, N Y, 72.
Exhibitions: Brooklyn Print Ann, 68; San Diego Print Invitational, 72.
Teaching: Prof lithography, State Univ N Y Albany, 62-; vis artist, Williams Col, 70; vis artist, Vassar Col, 71 & 72.
Awards: Tamarind Printer fel, 64; State Univ N Y Res Found fel, 65 & 72.
Dealer: Associated American Artists, 663 Fifth Ave, New York, NY 10002.
Mailing Address: Moss Rd, Voorheesville, NY 12186.

ODATE, TOSHIO
Conceptual Artist, Instructor
b Tokyo, Japan, July 9, 30.
Study & Training: Art Sch, Tokyo, 50-54; Nat Chiba Univ, 57-58.
Work in Public Collections: Rochester Mem Art Gallery, N Y; Bundy Art Gallery, Waitsfield, Vt; Great Southwest Atlanta Corp, Atlanta, Ga; Brooklyn Mus, N Y.
Exhibitions: Waning Moon & Rising Sun—Japanese Artists, Houston Mus Art, Tex, 59; Joseph H Hirshhorn Collection, Solomon R Guggenheim Mus, New York, 63; The Artists Reality, New Sch Social Res, New York, 64; Whitney Mus Am Art Sculpture Ann, 65-66; Attitudes, Brooklyn Mus, 70.
Teaching: Instr sculpture, Brooklyn Mus Art Sch, 61-; instr sculpture, Pratt Inst, 68-; guest lectr, Denver Mus Art, 67, Univ Wis, Wausa, 68 & Univ Ky, 69.
Publications: Contribr, Modern sculpture from the Joseph H Hirshhorn Collection, 62; contribr, Modern American sculpture, 67.
Dealer: Stephen Radich Gallery, 56 E 11th St, New York, NY 10021.
Mailing Address: 263 Eastern Parkway, Brooklyn, NY 11238.

O'DOHERTY, BRIAN
Sculptor, Writer
b Ballaghaderrin, Ireland, 34.
Exhibitions: One-man shows, Betty Parsons Gallery.
Positions: Dir visual arts progs, Nat Endowment Arts, 69-; ed, Art in Am, 71-
Publications: Auth, Object & idea: a critic's journal, Simon & Schuster, 67.
Mailing Address: 15 W 67th St, New York, NY 10023.

ODORFER, ADOLF
Sculptor, Educator
Preferred Media: Ceramics, Wood.
b Vienna, Austria, Dec 6, 02; U S citizen.
Study & Training: With Prof Friedrich Thetter & Prof Robert Obsieger, Vienna, 18-23; Wienerberger Workshop Sch Ceramics, Vienna, 20-23; Fresno State Col, BA; also study in Brazil & Mex, 23-35.
Work in Public Collections: Syracuse Mus Fine Arts, N Y.
Commissions: Outdoor sculpture for mall by Fed Bldg, City Fresno, Calif, 72.
Exhibitions: 12 ceramic nat exhibs, Syracuse Mus Fine Arts, 37-52; ceramic exhibs, Scripps Col, Claremont, Calif, 47, 49 & 53; ceramic exhib, Cranbrook Acad Fine Arts, Bloomfield Hills, Mich, 49; 61st Western Ann, Denver Art Mus, Colo, 55; 8th Ann Exhib Creative Art, Portland Art Mus, Ore, 58.

Teaching: Vis instr ceramics, Teacher's Col, Columbia Univ, summer 45; assoc prof ceramics, Fresno State Col, 47-66.
Positions: Ceramic technician, Ceramica Jundiaiense, Jundiai, Sao Paulo, Brazil, 23-26; ceramic technician, El Arte Azteca, Tlaquepaque, Jalisco, Mex, 30-35.
Awards: Six sculpture awards in ceramic nat exhibs, Syracuse Mus Fine Arts, 37-51; first prize in sculpture, Eighth Ann Pac Coast Ceramic Exhib, 49.
Memberships: Fresno Arts Ctr.
Publications: Contribr, articles, In: Sch Arts Mag, 11/46 & 1/47.
Mailing Address: 4715 N Thorne Ave, Fresno, CA 93705.

OEHLER, HELEN GAPEN
Painter, Lecturer
Preferred Media: Oils, Watercolors.
b Ottawa, Ill, May 30, 93.
Study & Training: Art Inst Chicago, honor grad; also with Elmer Browne, Provincetown, Mass & New York, N Y.
Work in Public Collections: Ryerson Libr, Art Inst Chicago; Chrysler Art Mus, Provincetown.
Commissions: Many pvt commissions.
Exhibitions: Salon D'Automne, Paris, France, 38; Nat Acad Design, New York, 39; Salon des Artistes Francais, 39; Am Fedn Arts traveling, 42; five exhibs, de Young Mus, San Francisco, Calif, 62-72; plus many other group & one-man shows.
Teaching: Instr Sat juvenile summer normal, Art Inst Chicago, 14-15; instr art, supvr grade & high schs, Dixon, Ill, 15-18; instr ancient art hist, high sch, Evanston, Ill, 18-20.
Positions: Dir, Art Coun N J, 41-52; pres, Ridgewood Art Asn, N J, 46-48; chmn, Artist Assoc Gallery, Mill Valley, Calif, 58-62.
Awards: Award for September, Flax Mase, de Young Mus, 66; degree of honor, Soc Western Artists, 68; award for Dated, Northern Calif Painting Competition, 72.
Memberships: Am Watercolor Soc (bd control, 44-); Am Artists Prof League (N J State pres, 46-48, nat dir, Am Art Wk, 48-49, nat secy, 50-51); Soc Western Artists; Century Travel Club.
Publications: Art ed, Pen Women, 51.
Mailing Address: Box 5397, Carmel, CA 93921.

OEHLSCHLAEGER, FRANK J
Art Dealer
b Paducah, Ky, Sept 8, 10.
Study & Training: Cornell Univ, grad, 33.
Positions: Dir, Chicago Galleries of Assoc Am Artists, 45-47; dir, Marshall Fields & Co Art Gallery, Chicago, Ill, 47-49; dir & owner, Oehlschlaeger Gallery, Chicago, 49-, Sarasota, Fla, 62-
Specialty of Gallery: Contemporary American & European art.
Mailing Address: 28 S Blvd of Presidents, Sarasota, FL 33577.

OENSLAGER, DONALD MITCHELL
Stage Designer
b Harrisburg, Pa, Mar 7, 02.
Study & Training: Harvard Univ, AB, 23; Sachs fine arts traveling fel; also with George Pierce Baker, Denman Ross & Maurice Sterne; Colo Col, hon DFA, 53.
Work in Public Collections: Metrop Mus Art & Mus Mod Art, New York, N Y; Boston Mus Fine Arts, Mass; Detroit Inst Arts, Mich; Mus of City of New York.
Commissions: Designed over 250 theatrical productions in New York, 26-; consult on 15 new theatres incl Lincoln Ctr, Kennedy Ctr & Albany South Mall.
Exhibitions: One-man exhibs, Marie Sterner Galleries, 36, Feragil Galleries, 49, Yale Gallery Fine Arts 49, Detroit Inst Arts, 56 & Am Fedn Arts Traveling Exhib, 57.
Teaching: Prof stage design, Sch Drama, Yale Univ, 25-70; lectr theatre, Salzburg Sem in Am Studies, 68 & 71; prof theatre, Grad Ctr, City Univ New York, 71-72.
Positions: Trustee, Brooklyn Mus & Pratt Inst; pres, Art Comn City New York, 65-; trustee, Mus of City of New York, 64-
Awards: Pa Ambassador Award, State of Pa, 50; Antonette Perry Award, Am Theatre Wing, 58-59.
Memberships: Am Fedn Arts (trustee, 66-); Brooklyn Inst Arts & Sci (trustee); Benjamin Franklin fel Royal Soc Arts; Int Exhibs Found (trustee, 72-).
Collection: Books, drawings and manuscripts of the sixteenth to twentieth century American theatre.
Publications: Auth, Scenery, then and now, 36; ed, Notes on scene painting, 52.
Mailing Address: 1501 Broadway, Suite 1915, New York, NY 10036.

OESTERLE, LEONHARD FRIEDRICH
Sculptor, Educator
Preferred Media: Stone, Bronze.
b Bietigheim, Ger, Mar 3, 15; Can citizen.
Study & Training: With Fritz Wotruba, Otto Huller, Hans Aeschbacher & Kunst Gewerbeschule, Zürich, Switz.

Work in Public Collections: Staats Gallery, Stuttgart, Ger; Württembergischer Kunstverein, Stuttgart; Nat Gallery, Ottawa, Can; London Art Gallery, Ont, Can; Kitchener Waterloo Art Gallery, Can.
Commissions: Playground sculpture, City of Berlin, 51; four figure group in bronze, Col McLaughlin Collegiate, Oshawa, 63; bronze statuary (religious), St Augustin Chapel, Scarborough, Can, 64; wall sculpture & mural, Cent Labs, Toronto, 67; sculpture in lobby, Can Trust Bldg, London, Ont, 69.
Exhibitions: Young Sculptor's Exhib, Helmhaus, Zürich, 49; Schwäbische Maler und Bildhauer, Zürich, 51.
Teaching: Instr sculpture, Ont Col Art, 63-68, 70-
Awards: Ont Soc Artists spec award, 68.
Bibliography: John Sommer (auth), Leonhard Oesterle, Peter Shore, 11/71.
Memberships: Sculptor's Soc Can (v pres, 58 & 70-72); Ont Soc Artists; Royal Can Acad Arts.
Dealer: Dunkelman Art Gallery, 15 Bedford Rd, Toronto 5, Ont, Can.
Mailing Address: 27 Alcina Ave, Toronto 4, Ont, Can.

OFFIN, CHARLES Z
Collector, Art Critic
b New York, N Y, Feb 5, 99.
Study & Training: City Col New York; Nat Acad Design; Art Stud League New York; Ecole Beaux-Arts, Fontainebleau, France.
Work in Public Collections: Etchings, Metrop Mus Art, New York & New York Pub Libr.
Exhibitions: One-man exhibs, Paris, Barcelona, Spain & New York.
Teaching: Instr City Col New York, 32-35.
Positions: Art critic, Brooklyn Eagle, 33-36; ed & publ, Pictures on Exhibit, 37-; pres & treas, Charles Z Offin Art Fund.
Collection: Twentieth century European art.
Mailing Address: 30 E 60th St, New York, NY 10022.

OFFNER, ELLIOT
Sculptor, Calligrapher
Preferred Media: Wood, Bronze.
b Brooklyn, N Y, July 12, 31.
Study & Training: Cooper Union; Yale Univ, BFA, with Josef Albers & MFA.
Work in Public Collections: Brooklyn Mus; De Cordova Mus, Lincoln, Mass; Lowe Art Mus, Syracuse Univ, N Y; Metrop Mus Art, New York, N Y; Joseph Hirshhorn Found.
Commissions: Eight hammered bronze sculptures, Rehilleth Israel, Brookline, Mass, 59; Ten Commandments (bronze facade sculpture), B'Nai Israel, Northampton, Mass, 63.
Exhibitions: Nat Inst Arts & Lett, 65; Pa Acad Fine Arts Ann, 68; Humanism in New England, De Cordova Mus, 70; one-man shows, Forum Gallery, New York, 64, 67 & 72 & Int Fedn Arts Galleries, Washington, D C, 68 & 72.
Teaching: Instr art, Univ Mass, 59-60; prof art, Smith Col, 60-
Positions: Dir, Rosemary Press, 67-
Awards: Tiffany Found grants, 64 & 65; Nat Inst Arts & Lett grant, 65; Nat Environ for Arts & Humanities grant, 67.
Memberships: Printing Hist Soc; Pvt Libr Asn; William Morris Soc; Wynkyn de Worde Soc.
Publications: Auth & illusr, The Granjon arabesque, 69.
Dealer: Forum Gallery, 1018 Madison Ave, New York, NY 10021.
Mailing Address: 74 Washington Ave, Northampton, MA 01060.

OGDEN, RALPH E
Collector, Patron
Positions: Founder, Storm King Art Ctr, 60, v chmn bd, at present.
Mailing Address: c/o Storm King Art Center, Mountainville, NY 10953.

OGILVIE, WILL (WILLIAM ABERNETHY)
Painter
b Cape Province, S Africa, Mar 30, 01; Can citizen.
Study & Training: With Erich Mayer, Johannesburg, S Africa; Art Stud League New York, with Nicolaides.
Work in Public Collections: Nat Gallery Can, Ottawa; Art Gallery, Toronto; Art Gallery, London; Art Gallery, Hamilton; Winnipeg Art Gallery.
Commissions: Mural, Chapel of Hart House, 36, stained glass windows in Massey Mem, 69, Univ Toronto.
Exhibitions: Nat Gallery Can, Ottawa; Art Gallery Ont, Toronto; Tate Gallery, London, 38; War Art, Nat Gallery, London, 44; UNESCO, 46.
Teaching: Dir drawing & painting, Montreal Mus Fine Arts, 37-41; instr painting & murals, Ont Col Art, Toronto, 47-55; spec lectr hist techniques painting, dept art & archaeol, Univ Toronto, 59-68.
Awards: Can Coun fel, Italy, 57-58.
Memberships: Assoc Royal Can Acad; Can Group Painters; Can Soc Painters in Watercolour.
Mailing Address: c/o Roberts Art Gallery, 641 Yonge St, Toronto, Ont, Can.

O'HANLON, RICHARD E
Sculptor, Educator
Preferred Media: Stone, Bronze, Copper, Brass, Aluminum.
b Long Beach, Calif, 06.
Study & Training: Santa Barbara Art Sch, Calif; Calif Col Arts &
Crafts; Calif Sch Fine Arts; pvt study in Europe, Near East,
India, Japan & Mex.
Work in Public Collections: Addison Gallery Am Art, Andover,
Mass; Worcester Mus Art, Mass; Walker Art Ctr, Minneapolis,
Minn; San Francisco Mus Art, Calif; Denver Mus Art, Colo.
Commissions: Centennial hist monument, State of Calif, San Fran-
cisco, 50; two steel & concrete reliefs, IBM Corp, W Coast Hq,
55; bronze sculpture, music bldg, Univ Calif, Berkeley, 61;
bronze relief, San Francisco Art Comn Civic Bldg, 66; black
granite sculpture, Mill Valley Pub Libr, 66.
Exhibitions: Whitney Mus Am Art Ann, New York, N Y, 48; Critics
Choice Exhib, New York, 50; San Francisco Art Asn Ann, 50-71;
São Paulo Biennial, Brazil, 55; one-man shows, Carnegie Inst,
Pittsburgh, Pa, 67 & Santa Barbara Mus Art, 69.
Teaching: Prof sculpture, Univ Calif, Berkeley, 48-
Positions: Consult archit rev comt, San Francisco Redevelopment
Agency, 65-68.
Awards: First prize for sculpture, San Francisco Art Asn, 58.
Bibliography: A Frankenstein (auth), Sculpture of Richard O'Hanlon,
Mag Art, 48.
Memberships: San Francisco Art Inst (bd dirs, 50-62).
Research: Repoussé sculpture.
Dealer: Willard Gallery, 29 E 72nd St, New York, NY 10021.
Mailing Address: 616 Throckmorton Ave, Mill Valley, CA 94941.

O'HARA, (JAMES) FREDERICK
Printmaker, Educator
b Ottawa, Ont, Aug 16, 04; U S citizen.
Study & Training: Mass Sch Art, 22-26, dipl; Sch Mus Fine Arts,
Boston, 26-29; Inst Bellas Artes, Toledo, Spain, Paige traveling
scholar, 29-31.
Work in Public Collections: Lessing J Rosenwald Collection, Nat
Gallery Art, Washington, D C; Metrop Mus Art, New York, N Y;
Cincinnati Mus Art, Ohio; Stadtmuseum, Karlsruhe, W Ger;
Achenbach Found Graphic Art, San Francisco, Calif.
Commissions: Four limited editions of prints, Int Graphic Art Soc,
New York, 53-59.
Exhibitions: Int Print Exhib Biennial, Cincinnati Mus Art, 58-62;
Prints of the World, London Art Gallery, Camberwell, Eng, 62;
Alliance for the Visual Arts, Utah State Univ Galleries, Logan,
72; one-man shows, Yoseido Gallery, Tokyo, Japan & Stadtmu-
seum, Karlsruhe, W Ger, 56.
Teaching: Vis prof art, Univ N Mex, 48-50, Highlands Univ, 58 &
Coronado Sch Fine Arts, 53 & 62.
Positions: Art adv comt, Sch Am Res, Archaeol Inst Am, Santa Fe,
N Mex, 54-57.
Awards: Fel & print purchase awards, Tamarind Lithography
Workshop, Los Angeles, 62.
Bibliography: Lez Haas (auth), Frederick O'Hara, N Mex Quart, 51;
Kiyoshi Saito (auth), Frederick O'Hara, Japanese Art Mag, 56;
Rolf Stubbe (auth), work, In: Graphic Arts in the Twentieth Cen-
tury, 62.
Art Interests: Woodcuts, lithography & monoprints.
Publications: Auth, Modern art today: El Palacio, Sch Am Res, 56;
auth, Toward technical excellence in printmaking, Artists Mag,
61.
Dealer: Jones Gallery, Prospect St, La Jolla, CA 92037.
Mailing Address: 846 Forward St, La Jolla, CA 92037.

OHASHI, YUTAKA
Painter, Sculptor
Preferred Media: Collage.
b Kure City, Japan, Aug 19, 23.
Study & Training: Tokyo Acad Fine Art, Japan, 41-46, BFA; Sch
Mus Fine Arts, Boston, Mass, 50-55.
Work in Public Collections: Mus Fine Arts, Boston; Solomon R
Guggenheim Mus, New York, N Y; Nat Mus Mod Art, Tokyo;
Addison Gallery Am Art, Andover, Mass; Art Gallery, Yale
Univ, New Haven, Conn.
Exhibitions: American Painting 1958, Va Mus Fine Arts, Richmond,
58; Carnegie Int, Pittsburgh, Pa, 59; Summer Selection, 1962,
Solomon R Guggenheim Mus, New York, 62; Japanese Artists
Abroad, Nat Mus Mod Art, Tokyo, 65; A Painter-A Potter, Mont-
clair Art Mus, N J, 70.
Teaching: Vis lectr critics, painting & design, col archit, Cornell
Univ, fall 61 & col human ecol, spring 67 & 69.
Awards: William Page traveling scholar, Mus Fine Arts, Boston, 56-
57; Guggenheim fel, 59-60.
Dealer: Lee Nordness Gallery, 236 E 75th St, New York, NY 10021.
Mailing Address: 5 Great Jones St, New York, NY 10012.

OHLSON, DOUGLAS DEAN
Painter
b Cherokee, Iowa, Nov 18, 36.
Study & Training: Univ Minn, BA, 61.
Work in Public Collections: Corcoran Gallery Art, Washington, D C;
Weatherspoon Gallery, Univ N C, Greensboro; Mus Purchase
Fund Collection, Am Fedn Arts; Beacon Collection, Boston, Mass.
Exhibitions: Color, Image, Form, Detroit Inst Arts, Mich, 67; The
Art of the Real: U S A 1948-1968, Mus Mod Art, New York, N Y,
68-69; Whitney Ann, 69 & The Structure of Color, 71, Whitney
Mus Am Art, New York; American Art Since 1960, Art Mus,
Princeton Univ, 70.
Teaching: Asst prof art, Hunter Col, 64-
Awards: Guggenheim fel, 68.
Bibliography: S Burton (auth), Doug Ohlson: in the wind, Art News,
5/68; T Littlefield (auth), When walls matter, Times-Union,
9/8/68; G Battcock (ed), Minimal art (critical anthology), Dutton,
68.
Dealer: Fischbach Gallery, 29 W 57th St, New York, NY 10019.
Mailing Address: 35 W 26th St, New York, NY 10010.

OHRBACH, JEROME K
Collector
b New York, N Y, Dec 17, 07.
Study & Training: Cornell Univ, AB, 29.
Collection: Impressionist and post-impressionist art and sculpture.
Mailing Address: 5 W 34th St, New York, NY 10001.

OKADA, KENZO
Painter
Preferred Media: Oils.
b Yokohama, Japan, Sept 28, 02; U S citizen.
Work in Public Collections: Metrop Mus Art & Mus Mod Art, New
York, N Y; Art Inst Chicago, Ill; Solomon R Guggenheim Mus &
Whitney Mus Am Art, New York; plus many others.
Commissions: Murals & paintings for Hilton Hotel, Tokyo, Japan,
Dunn Int, Ford Found, UNESCO & Venice Biennial.
Exhibitions: São Paolo Biennial, Brazil (representing the U S), 55;
Venice Biennial (representing Japan), 58; Albright-Knox Art Gal-
lery, Buffalo, N Y, 65; Retrospective Traveling Exhib, Asahi-
Shimbun Press, Tokyo, Nat Mus Mod Art, Kyoto, Honolulu Acad
Arts, Hawaii, M H De Young Mem Mus, San Francisco, Calif &
Univ Art Mus, Univ Tex, Austin, 66-67; one-man shows, Betty
Parsons Gallery, 53-71; plus many others.
Awards: First prize, Columbia Biennial, S C, 57; Mainichi Art
Award, 66; Award Poster, New York Coun of the Arts, 69.
Bibliography: Gordon B Washburn (auth), Retrospective traveling
show (catalogue), 66-67; J Canaday (auth), Okada's figurative
style, New York Times, 3/15/69; Grace Clueck (auth), Early
light, Art in Am, 3-4/69.
Mailing Address: 51 W 11th St, New York, NY 10011.

OKAMURA, ARTHUR
Painter
b Long Beach, Calif, Feb 24, 32.
Study & Training: Art Inst Chicago, scholar, 50-54; Univ Chicago,
51 & 53; Yale Univ Summer Art Sem, 54; Edward L Ryerson for
travel fel, 54; Univ Chicago, 57.
Work in Public Collections: Kalamazoo Col, Mich; Nat Collection
Fine Arts; Smithsonian Inst; Ill Bell Tel, Chicago, Ill; Stanford
Univ Collection; plus many others.
Exhibitions: Painters Behind Painters, Calif Palace of Legion of
Honor, San Francisco, 67; Pittsburgh Int, Carnegie Inst, 67; one-
man show drawings, San Francisco Mus Art, 68; Takashima 1970
Expos, Osaka, Tokyo, Japan, 70; Asian Artists, Oakland Mus, 71;
plus many other group & one-man shows.
Teaching: Instr, Cent YMCA Col, Chicago, 56 & 57; instr, Evanston
Art Ctr, Ill, 56 & 57; instr, Sch Art Inst Chicago, 57; instr, N
Shore Art League, Winnetka, Ill, 57; instr, Acad Art, San Fran-
cisco, 57; instr, Calif Sch Fine Arts, San Francisco, 58; instr,
Calif Col Arts & Crafts, 58, 59 & 66-71; instr, Saugatuck Summer
Art Sch, Mich, 59 & 62; guest lectr, Univ Utah, 64.
Positions: Dir, San Francisco Studio Art, 58.
Awards: Schwabacher-Frey Award, 79th Ann, San Francisco Mus,
60; Neysa McMein Purchase Award, Whitney Mus Am Art, 60;
purchase award, Nat Soc Arts & Lett; plus many others.
Bibliography: Lee Nordness (ed), Art: U S A: Now, C J Bucher, 62.
Memberships: Am Fedn Arts.
Dealer: Hansen Fuller Gallery, 228 Grant Ave, San Francisco, CA
94108.
Mailing Address: P O Box 21, Ocean Pkwy, Bolinas, CA 94924.

O'KEEFFE, GEORGIA
Painter
b Sun Prairie, Wis, Nov 15, 87.
Study & Training: Art Inst Chicago, with John Vanderpoel, 05-06;
Art Stud League New York, with William M Chase, 07-08; Univ

Va, with Alon Bement, summer 12; Columbia Univ, with Arthur Dow & Alon Bement, 14-16; William & Mary Col, hon DFA, 38; Univ Wis, hon LittD, 42, Mills Col, 52; Univ N Mex, hon DFA, 64, Randolph-Macon Women's Col, 66; Columbia Univ, hon LHD, 71; Brown Univ, hon DFA, 71; Mount Holyoke Col, hon LittD, 71; Minneapolis Col Art & Design, hon DFA, 72.

Work in Public Collections: Metrop Mus Art; Mus Mod Art; Whitney Mus Am Art; Brooklyn Mus; Art Inst Chicago; plus others in most maj mus throughout the country.

Exhibitions: One-man retrospectives, Art Inst Chicago, 43, Mus Mod Art, 46, Worcester Mus Art, 60, Amon Carter Mus, Fort Worth, Tex, 66 & Mus Fine Arts Houston, 66; plus many other one-man & group shows starting with Alfred Stieglitz's 291, 16.

Teaching: Supvr art, Amarillo Pub Schs, Tex, 13-16; instr art, Univ Va, summers 13-16; head art dept, West Tex Normal Col, Canyon, 16-18.

Awards: Creative arts award, Brandeis Univ, 63; Gold Medal for Painting, Nat Inst Arts & Lett, 70; M Carey Thomas Award, Bryn Mawr Col, 71 & Edward MacDowell Medal, 72.

Bibliography: Daniel Catton Rich (auth), Georgia O'Keeffe (catalogue), Art Inst Chicago, 43; Lloyd Goodrich & Doris Bry (auth), Georgia O'Keeffe (catalogue), Whitney Mus Am Art, 70; Barbara Rose (auth), Georgia O'Keeffe's late paintings, Artforum, 11/70; plus many others.

Memberships: Nat Inst Arts & Lett; Am Acad Arts & Lett; Am Acad Arts & Sci.

Publications: Auth, The work of Georgia O'Keeffe (portfolio of 12 paintings), 37; auth, Georgia O'Keeffe drawings (ltd ed of 10 drawing reproductions signed & numbered by artist), 68.

Dealer: Doris Bry, 11 E 73rd St, New York, NY 10021.

Mailing Address: Abiquiu, NM 87510.

OKOSHI, EUGENIA SUMIYE
Painter.
Preferred Media: Oils, Acrylics, Graphics.
b Seattle, Wash.
Study & Training: St Margaret & Futaba Col, Tokyo, Japan; Seattle Univ, with Fay Chang & Nicholas Damascus; Henry Frye Mus Sch & New Sch Workshop.
Work in Public Collections: Miami Mus Mod Art; Lowe Gallery, Univ Miami.
Exhibitions: Bohman Art Gallery, Stockholm, Sweden, 68 & 69; Miami Mus Mod Art, Fla, 70; Japanese Artists, N Y, 72; Westbeth Gallery, N Y, 72.
Mailing Address: c/o Westbeth Studio G226, 463 West St, New York, NY 10014.

OLDENBURG, CLAES THURE
Sculptor
b Stockholm, Sweden, Jan 28, 29.
Study & Training: Yale Univ, BA, 51; Art Inst Chicago, 52-54.
Work in Public Collections: Albright-Knox Art Gallery, Buffalo, N Y; Allen Art Mus, Oberlin Col, Ohio; Art Gallery Ont, Toronto; Art Inst Chicago, Ill; City Art Mus, Saint Louis, Mo; plus many others.
Exhibitions: Metrop Mus Art, New York, N Y, 69; one-man shows, Mus Mod Art, New York, 69, Pasadena Art Mus, Calif, 71 & Philadelphia Mus Art, 72; plus many other group & one-man shows.
Bibliography: Barbara Rose (auth), Claes Oldenburg, Mus Mod Art, 70; Ellen Johnson (auth), Claes Oldenburg, Penguin, 71.
Publications: Auth, Store days, Something Else Press, 68; auth, Notes in hand, Dutton & Petersburg, 71; auth, Object into monument, Pasadena Art Mus, 71.
Mailing Address: c/o Sidney Janis Gallery, 6 W 57th St, New York, NY 10019.

OLDENBURG, RICHARD ERIK
Art Administrator
b Stockholm, Sweden, Sept 21, 33; U S Citizen.
Study & Training: Harvard Col, AB, 54.
Positions: Dir publ, Mus Mod Art, New York, N Y, 69-72, dir mus, 72-
Mailing Address: 11 W 53rd St, New York, NY 10019.

OLDS, ELIZABETH
Painter, Printmaker
b Minneapolis, Minn, Dec 10, 96.
Study & Training: Univ Minn, 2 yrs; Minneapolis Sch Art, 3 yrs; Art Stud League New York, 2 yrs; also with George Luks, Paris, France, 4 yrs.
Work in Public Collections: (Prints) Metrop Mus Art, New York, N Y; Brooklyn Mus, N Y; Baltimore Mus Art, Md; Philadelphia Mus Art, Pa; San Francisco Mus Art, Calif; plus one other.

Commissions: Drawings on World War II years & Pa Coal Country, New Repub, 40-49; war material paintings, Fortune Mag, 42; series of paintings on Lykes Indust, Fortune Mag, 54.

Exhibitions: Artists for Victory, Metrop Mus Art, 42; Whitney Mus Am Art Watercolors & Drawings, 45-47; Prints & Books for Children, Mus Mod Art, New York; Brooklyn Mus Int Watercolor Exhibs, 49, 53 & 55; one-woman show, Staten Island Mus, 69; also one-man shows.

Teaching: Pvt classes in silk-screen printmaking.

Awards: Guggenheim fel for painting in Europe, 26-27; first prize for lithograph, Philadelphia Print Club, 37 & Art Alliance, 38; first prize for Mexican Village (watercolor), Baltimore Mus Art, 44.

Publications: Auth & illusr, The big fire, 45, Riding the rails, 48, Feather mountain, 51 & Deep treasure, 58, Houghton Mifflin Co; auth & illusr, Plop plop ploppie, Scribner, 62.

Mailing Address: Brown Hill Rd, Tamworth, NH 03886.

OLINSKY, TOSCA (MRS CHARLES F BARTEAU)
Painter
b Florence, Italy.
Study & Training: Nat Acad Design; Art Stud League New York.
Exhibitions: One-man show, Lyman Allyn Mus, New London, Conn, 58; Nat Acad Design; Allied Artists Am; Audubon Artists; Am Watercolor Soc; plus others.
Awards: Jane Peterson Prize, 57 & Lamont Prize, 59, Audubon Artist Ann; Gloria Layton Prize, Allied Artists Am, 60; plus others.
Memberships: Academician Nat Acad Design; Audubon Artists; Am Watercolor Soc; Allied Artists Am; Lyme Art Asn.
Mailing Address: Beckwith Lane, Old Lyme, CT 06371.

OLITSKI, JULES
Painter
Preferred Media: Acrylics.
b Gomel, Russia, Mar 27, 22.
Study & Training: Nat Acad Design, 39-42; Acad Grande Chaumière, Paris, France, 49; N Y Univ.
Work in Public Collections: Art Inst Chicago; Corcoran Gallery Art, Washington, D C; Whitney Mus Am Art, New York, N Y; Mus Mod Art, New York; Chrysler Mus, Provincetown.
Exhibitions: Olitski, Paintings 1963-67, Corcoran Gallery Art & Pasadena Mus, 63-67; Post Painterly Abstraction, Los Angeles Co Mus Art, 64-65; Whitney Mus Am Art Ann, 64, 68 & 72; The Sculpture of Jules Olitski, Metrop Mus Art, New York, 69; Abstract Painting in the 70's, Boston Mus Fine Arts, Mass, 72.
Teaching: Prof art, Bennington Col, 63-67.
Awards: Second prize for painting, Pittsburgh Int Painting & Sculpture, 61; first prize for painting, Corcoran Gallery Art, 67.
Bibliography: Gregory Batcock (auth), Minimal art—a critical anthology, 68 & Henry Geldzahler (auth), New York painting & sculptures 1940-1970, 69, Dutton; Kenworth Moffett (auth), Jules Olitski's sculpture, Artforum, 4/69.
Dealer: Lawrence Rubin Gallery, 49 W 57th St, New York, NY 10019.
Mailing Address: 831 Broadway, New York, NY 10003.

OLIVER, HENRY, JR
Collector
Mailing Address: Blackburn Rd, Sewickley, PA 15143.

OLKINETZKY, SAM
Painter, Museum Director
Preferred Media: Collage.
b New York, N Y, Nov 22, 19.
Study & Training: Brooklyn Col; Inst Fine Arts, New York Univ.
Work in Public Collections: Philbrook Art Ctr, Tulsa, Okla; Okla Art Ctr, Oklahoma City; Mus Art, Univ Okla, Norman; Sch Bus, Okla State Univ, Stillwater; Lawton Munic Collection, Okla.
Exhibitions: Philbrook Art Ctr Ann, 50-70; Int Painting & Sculpture Exhib, Mus Non-Objective Art, New York, 51-52; Recent Drawings, U S A, Mus Mod Art, New York, 55; Momentum Midcontinental, Chicago Inst Design, Ill, 55; Southwestern Painting and Sculpture Ann, Okla Art Ctr, 60-70.
Teaching: Asst prof art, Okla State Univ, 47-57; prof art, Univ Okla, 57-; vis prof art & humanities, Univ Ark, 62, 63-67; lectr humanities, Langston Univ, 69-70.
Positions: Art consult, Kerr-McGee Indust, 04-; dir, Mus Art, Univ Okla, 59-; art consult, Okla Art Ctr, 72-
Awards: St Gaudens Medal for draughtsmanship, City New York, 37; purchase award for painting, Philbrook Art Ctr, 51; purchase award for drawing, Okla Art Ctr, 65.
Memberships: Am Asn Mus; Okla Mus Asn; Am Asn Univ Prof.
Publications: Contribr, Review of Oklahoma Designer Craftsmen Exhibition, Craft Horizons, 71.
Mailing Address: Rte 1, Box 151B, Norman, OK 73069.

OLMSTED, PAT
Painter, Photographer
Preferred Media: Watercolors, Mixed Media.
b New York, N Y.
Study & Training: Brearly Sch, New York; Spence Sch, New York; also with Betty Esman, New York.
Work in Public Collections: Int Watercolor Biennial, Brooklyn Mus, 61 & 63; N Y State Expos, Syracuse, N Y, 64; one-man show, Art Asn, Harrisburg, Pa, 65; Nat Asn Women Artists Exhib, New York, 68 & Traveling Exhib, Can & France, 70.
Memberships: Nat Asn Women Artists.
Dealer: Roko Gallery, 90 E Tenth St, New York, NY 10003.
Mailing Address: Lodge Point, Bacolet, Tobago, West Indies.

OLSEN, DON
Painter
Preferred Media: Oils, Acrylics.
b Provo, Utah, Dec 3, 10.
Study & Training: Brigham Young Univ, BA, 35; Univ Utah, 50; Hans Hofmann Sch Fine Arts, 57.
Work in Public Collections: Utah State Inst Fine Arts, Utah State Capitol Bldg, Salt Lake City; Salt Lake Art Ctr, Salt Lake City; Salt Lake City Pub Libr.
Exhibitions: San Francisco Art Asn, 57; Art U S A 1958, Nordness Gallery, New York, N Y, 58; Salt Lake Art Ctr Biennial Intermountain Exhib, 60-66; Colorado Springs Fine Art Ctr, 64; Fifty Artists-Fifty States, Rockford Ill Art Asn, 66; plus many other group & one-man shows.
Awards: Purchase award, Utah State Inst Fine Arts, 58; first prize, 60, 62 & 64 & purchase prizes, 64 & 69, Salt Lake Art Ctr Intermountain Exhib; Ford Found award, Salt Lake Art Ctr, 63.
Dealer: Phillips Gallery, 444 E 200 S, Salt Lake City, UT 84115.
Mailing Address: 77 W 7065 S, Midvale, UT 84047.

OLSEN, FREDERICK L
Potter, Sculptor
Preferred Media: Ceramics.
b Seattle, Wash, Feb 25, 38.
Study & Training: Univ Redlands, BA; Univ Southern Calif, MFA; Kyoto City Col Fine Art, Japan; also three yr apprenticeship with Tomimoto Kenkichi & Kondo Yuzo, Kyoto.
Work in Public Collections: Gallery New South Wales, Sydney, Australia; Contemp Craft Mus, Denmark; Sturt Collection, Mittigong, Australia.
Exhibitions: Nat Shinsho-Ten, Japan, 61-63; Kyo-Ten, Kyoto Mus Mod Art, 62; Nat Asahi-Ten, Tokyo, Japan, 62; also one-man exhibs in Sydney, 63, 64 & 69, Melbourne, 63 & 69, Adelaide, 69, Copenhagen, 65, Seattle, 71, Portland, Ore, 71 & Los Angeles, Calif, 71.
Teaching: Lectr kiln bldg, Univ Southern Calif, 66-68; asst prof kiln bldg, Univ Puget Sound, summer 71.
Positions: Owner, Pinyon Crest Pottery, 67-
Bibliography: American potter in Japan, Asahi TV Corp, 63.
Publications: Auth, Kiln building—principles in kiln design and methods of construction, Keramos Bks, 72.
Dealers: Serisawa Gallery, 8320 Melrose Ave, Los Angeles, CA 90069; Northwest Craft Center-Seattle Center, Seattle, WA 98101.
Mailing Address: Star Rte Box 205, Mountain Center, CA 92361.

OLSEN, HERB
Painter, Writer
Preferred Media: Watercolors.
b Chicago, Ill, July 12, 05.
Study & Training: Am Acad Art; Art Inst Chicago.
Work in Public Collections: Reading Mus, Pa; Springville Mus, Utah; Jacksonville Mus, Fla; Norfolk Mus, Va; Cayuga Mus, N Y.
Exhibitions: Nat Acad Design, New York, N Y, 70; Am Watercolor Soc, New York, 72; South Cent, Tenn, 72; plus many others.
Awards: First prize, 51 & Edwin Palmer Award, 64, Nat Acad Design; two gold medals, Hudson Valley Art Asn, 53 & 62.
Memberships: Nat Acad Design; Am Watercolor Soc; Philadelphia Watercolor Club; Artists & Writers; Authors Guild.
Publications: Auth, Watercolor made easy, Painting the figure in watercolor, Painting children in watercolor, Herb Olsen's guide to watercolor landscape & Painting the marine scene in watercolor, Van Nostrand.
Mailing Address: Box 446, Westport, CT 06880.

OLTEN, CAROL (CAROL MIRABILE)
Writer
b Washington, Mo, Feb 19, 42.
Study & Training: Univ Mo, BJ, 64.
Positions: Art writer, San Diego Union, Calif.
Mailing Address: San Diego Union, 940 Third Ave, San Diego, CA 92112.

O'MEILIA, PHILIP JAY
Painter, Illustrator
b Tulsa, Okla, July 17, 27.
Study & Training: Art Stud League New York; Cape Sch Art, Provincetown, Mass; Chicago Acad Fine Arts; George Washington Univ; Univ Tulsa.
Work in Public Collections: Ford Motor Co; Okla Art Mus; Gilcrease Mus, Tulsa; Tower Life Ins Co, Springfield, Mo; Philbrook Mus, Tulsa.
Commissions: Murals, United Founders Life Ins Co, Oklahoma City, Assembly of God Church, Tulsa & C Engrs.
Exhibitions: Philbrook Art Ctr, 49-64; Okla Art Ctr, 56-65; Am Watercolor Soc, 62-64, 65 & 67; Watercolor: U S A, 64 & 67; Southwestern Watercolor Soc, 67; plus many others.
Awards: Purchase prize, Watercolor: U S A, Springfield, Mo, 64; prizes, Nat Sports Exhib, 66 & Southwestern Watercolor Exhib, Dallas Mus Fine Arts; plus many others.
Memberships: Am Watercolor Soc; hon life mem Assocs in Art of Tulsa.
Mailing Address: 1108 Sunset Dr, Tulsa, OK 79114.

OMWAKE, LEON, JR
Painter, Sculptor
Preferred Media: Acrylics.
b New Rochelle, N Y, June 14, 46.
Study & Training: Pa Acad Fine Arts, 64-68.
Work in Public Collections: Whitney Mus Am Art, New York, N Y; Pa Acad Fine Arts, Philadelphia; Philadelphia Mus Art.
Exhibitions: Philadelphia Mus Art, 70; Fischbach Gallery, New York, 72; Whitney Ann Am Painting, New York, 72; Cheltenham Ann Painting Exhib, 72; one-man show, Marian Locks Gallery, 72; plus others.
Teaching: Instr painting, Pa Acad Fine Art; instr painting, Cheltenham Art Ctr, Pa; instr painting, Chaddsford Art Sch.
Awards: H M Williams Biddle Cadwalder Prize, Pa Acad Fine Arts, 68; Cheltenham Ann Netsky-Sernaker Prize, 72; Philadelphia Mus Art Purchase Prize, 72; plus others.
Dealer: Marion Locks Gallery, 1524 Walnut St, Philadelphia, PA 19102.
Mailing Address: 2419 Aspen St, Philadelphia, PA 19130.

O'NEIL, JOHN
Painter, Educator
Preferred Media: Acrylics, Pastels.
b Kansas City, Mo, June 16, 15.
Study & Training: Univ Okla, BFA, MFA; Colorado Springs Arts Ctr, with Boardman Robinson, Paul Burlin & Henry Varnum Poor; Taos Sch Art, with Emil Bisttram; Studio Hinna, Rome, Italy.
Work in Public Collections: Denver Art Mus, Colo; Dallas Mus Fine Arts, Tex; Libr of Cong, Washington, D C; Univ Mich Mus Art; Seattle Art Mus, Wash.
Exhibitions: Directions in American Painting, Carnegie Inst, Pittsburgh; Abstract & Surrealist Art, Art Inst Chicago; Contemporary American Painting, Univ Ill; Troisieme Salon Int des Realites Nouvelles, Paris, France; M-59 Exhib, Copenhagen, Denmark.
Teaching: Prof painting, Univ Okla, 39-65; prof painting, Rice Univ, 65-
Awards: 23 awards in regional & national exhibitions.
Memberships: Col Art Asn Am.
Publications: Contribr, Oklahoma: a guide to the Sooner State, Art & Archit, 57; contribr, Thoughts on light, Kunst, 63; contribr, On color, Cimarron Rev, 72.
Dealer: Louisiana Gallery, Houston, TX 77013.
Mailing Address: 2224 Wroxton Rd, Houston, TX 77005.

ONLEY, TONI
Painter
Preferred Media: Oils, Watercolors, Intaglio.
b Douglas, Isle of Man, Eng, Nov 20, 28.
Study & Training: Douglas Sch Art; Inst Allende, Mex.
Work in Public Collections: Tate Gallery, London, Eng; Nat Gallery Can; Victoria & Albert Mus, London; Mus Mod Art, New York, N Y; Seattle Mus, Wash.
Commissions: Oil mural, Queen Elizabeth Playhouse, Vancouver, B C, 62.
Exhibitions: Seattle World Fair, 62; Contemporary Canadian Art, Nat Gallery Can & Africa, 62-63; Fifteen Canadian Artists, Mus Mod Art & U S A, 63-64; Two Canadians, Commonwealth Inst, London, 64; 36 Venice Biennale, Italy, 72.
Teaching: Asst prof fine arts, Univ B C, 67-
Awards: Jessie Dow Award, Montreal Spring Exhib, 60; Sam & Ayala Zacks Award, 83rd Ann, Royal Can Acad, 63; Sr Can Coun fel, 63.
Dealer: Ban-Xi Gallery, 3003 Granville St, Vancouver, B C, Can.
Mailing Address: 3506 W 28th Ave, Vancouver, B C, Can.

OPPENHEIM, DENNIS A
Sculptor
b Mason City, Wash, Sept 6, 38.
Study & Training: Calif Col Arts & Crafts, BA; Univ Hawaii; Stanford Univ, MA.
Work in Public Collections: Mus Mod Art, New York, N Y; Whitney Mus Am Art, New York; Oakland Art Mus, Calif; Stedelijk Mus, Amsterdam, Holland; Ont Art Mus, Toronto.
Commissions: Ocean projs, De Menil & List Founds, Tobago, W I, 69; ground mutations, Armand & Celeste Bartos, Aspen, Colo, 70.
Exhibitions: Earthworks, Dwan Gallery, New York, 68; When Attitude Becomes Form, Kunsthalle, Bern, Switz, 69; A Report Two Ocean Projects, 69 & Information, 70, Mus Mod Art, New York; Documenta, Kassel, Ger, 72.
Teaching: Guest artist sculpture, Yale Univ, 69; guest artist, Pratt Inst Art, Brooklyn, 69; guest artist, Calif Col Arts & Crafts, 70; guest artist, R I Col Design, 70; guest artist, Univ Wis-Whitewater, 70; guest artist, Art Inst Chicago, 71-72; guest artist sculpture, N S Col Art, 71-72.
Awards: Newhouse Found grant, Stanford Univ, 65; John Simon Guggenheim Found fel, 71-72.
Dealer: Sonnabend Gallery, 420 W Broadway, New York, NY 10012.
Mailing Address: 85 Franklin St, New York, NY 10013.

OPPENHEIM, SAMUEL EDMUND
Painter
Preferred Media: Oils.
Study & Training: Nat Acad Design; Art Stud League New York.
Work in Public Collections: Chrysler Mus Art, Va; White House, Washington, D C; West Point Mil Acad, N Y; Nat Acad Design, New York, N Y; Grand Cent Art Gallery, New York; plus many others.
Exhibitions: Nat Acad Design; Audubon Artists; Allied Artists Am; Hudson Valley Art Asn; Grand Cent Art Galleries; plus many others.
Teaching: Instr art, Art Stud League New York, 67-
Awards: Prizes, Allied Artists Am, Hudson Valley Art Asn & Am Artists Prof League.
Memberships: Salmagundi Club; Allied Artists Am; Grand Cent Art Gallery; Artists Fel; Hudson Valley Art Asn.
Mailing Address: 580 E Lake Dr, Naples, FL 33940.

OPPENHEIMER, SELMA L
Painter
Preferred Media: Oils.
b Baltimore, Md, Jan 13, 98.
Study & Training: Goucher Col, AB; Maryland Inst Col Art.
Work in Public Collections: Baltimore Pub Schs; Loyola Col.
Exhibitions: Baltimore Mus Art Ann & Invitational, 68; Corcoran Gallery Art Biennials, Washington, D C; Art Inst Chicago, Ill; Va Mus Art, Richmond; Mus Mod Art, New York, N Y.
Awards: Wilson Levering Smith Medals, Baltimore Mus Art, 35-38; Lillian Cotton & Susan Kahn Awards, Nat Asn Women Artists, 52, 60 & 65; purchase award, Loyola Col, 67.
Memberships: Artists Equity Asn (past pres Baltimore Chap); Nat Asn Women Artists; Baltimore Watercolor Club; Am Fedn Art; Baltimore Mus Art (bd trustees, 61-72).
Mailing Address: 7121 Park Heights Ave, Baltimore, MD 21215.

OPPER, JOHN
Painter
b Chicago, Ill, Oct 29, 08.
Study & Training: Cleveland Sch Art; Case Western Reserve Univ, BS; Columbia Univ, MA & EdD; also with Hans Hofmann.
Work in Public Collections: Mus Mod Art, New York, N Y; James Michener Found Mus, Austin, Tex; Guild Hall Mus, East Hampton, N Y; High Mus Art, Atlanta, Ga; New York Univ Collection.
Exhibitions: Int Watercolor Exhib, Art Inst Chicago, Ill, 60; Int Watercolor Exhib, Brooklyn Mus, N Y; Int Exhib Paintings, Carnegie Inst, Pittsburgh, Pa, 61; American Drawings, Moore Inst, 68; Recent Acquisitions, Mus Mod Art, New York.
Teaching: Assoc prof art, Univ N C, 52-57; prof art, New York Univ, 57-
Awards: First prize for oil painting, High Mus Art, 55; Guggenheim fel, 69.
Memberships: Col Art Asn; Am Asn Univ Prof.
Dealer: Borgenicht Gallery, 1018 Madison Ave, New York, NY 10021.
Mailing Address: 110 Bleecker St, New York, NY 10012.

ORDONEZ, EFREN
Painter, Sculptor
Preferred Media: Oils, Acrylics, Watercolors, Concrete, Iron.
b Chihuahua, Mex, Aug 20, 27.
Study & Training: Univ Nuevo Leon.
Work in Public Collections: Mus Mod Art, Mexico City.
Commissions: Cristo Rey (stained glass), 63, Maria Reina (mural), 64 & 12 Apostles, 65, Sem Sch, Monterrey, Mex; Morelos, Govt Montemorelos, Mex, 68; Sagrado Corazon (fiber glass), Sagrado Corazon Church, Mexico City, 70.
Exhibitions: One-man show, Dreyer Gallery, Houston, Tex, 65; Confrontacion 66 & Solar Show, 68, Palacio Bellas Artes, Mexico City; 6 Mexican Artists, Ariz State Univ, 68; 50 Ordoñez Works, Govt Palace, Monterrey, 72.
Teaching: Instr drawing, Univ Nuevo Leon, 53-55; instr watercolor, Monterrey Inst Technol, Mex, 55-57.
Positions: Juror, Chapultepec Gallery, Inst Nat Bellas Artes, Mexico City, 67.
Awards: Medal of honor for oil painting, Mex, 59.
Publications: Illusr, Soc Artistica Technol (covers), 57-70; illusr, Esther M Allison Poetry, 69; illusr (cover), Soc & Trabajo Soc, 70.
Mailing Address: Rio Nazas, 106 Col Mexico, Monterrey, Nuevo Leon, Mex.

ORDORICA, HILDA TRULL
Painter
Preferred Media: Watercolors
b Portland, Maine, Aug 31, 08.
Study & Training: Douglas Col, AB; Cooper Union; Montclair Art Mus, with Avery Johnson, Tom Vincent & E Ingersol Maurice.
Exhibitions: Audubon Artists, 70, Allied Artists Am, 70 & Am Watercolor Soc, 70, Nat Acad Design Galleries, New York, N Y; Nat Arts Club Ann, New York, 70 & 71; Art Ctr Oranges Ann Regional Art Exhib, East Orange, N J, 71 & 72.
Awards: Spec prize for Hydrangea, Morris Co Art Asn, 69; First prize for Crefeld's Sunflowers, Summit Art Ctr, 70; second prize for Churchyard, Hudson Artists, 70.
Memberships: N J Watercolor Soc (rec secy, 71 & 72); Montclair Art Mus; Essex Watercolor Club; Art Ctr Oranges (chmn hospitality comt, 70).
Mailing Address: 310 Valley Rd, Montclair, NJ 07042.

ORKIN, RUTH (MRS MORRIS ENGEL)
Photographer, Film Maker
b Boston, Mass.
Work in Public Collections: Still photos, Mus Mod Art & Metrop Mus Art, New York, N Y.
Exhibitions: Little Fugitive, Edinburgh Film Festival, 54, Montevideo Film Festival, 55 & Melbourne Film Festival; Lovers & Lollipops, Venice Film Festival, 55; Kodak's New York World's Fair Int Color Exhib, 63 & 64.
Awards: Silver Lion of San Marco, for direction of Little Fugitive, Venice Film Festival, 53; Academy Nomination for writing Little Fugitive, 53; third prize winner, Life's Young Photographer's Contest, 51.
Bibliography: The incredible Ruth Orkin, Photog Workshop, winter 53; America's interesting people, Woman's Home Companion, 11/56; Saul Bellow (auth), Movies, Horizon Mag, 9/62.
Memberships: Acad Motion Picture Arts & Sci; Soc Mag Photographers.
Art Interests: Still photos of classical musicians, New York views, children, photo-reportage and personalities.
Publications: Contribr, Tanglewood Souvenir Guidebook, 47 & 48; contribr, Family of Man; contribr, Ruth Orkin's New York, Horizon, 3/59; plus many other leading publ, 47-57.
Mailing Address: 65 Central Park W, New York, NY 10023.

ORR, ELLIOT
Painter
Preferred Media: Oils.
b Flushing, Long Island, June 26, 04.
Study & Training: Grand Cent Art Sch, with George Luks & Charles W Hawthorne.
Work in Public Collections: Brooklyn Mus, N Y; Whitney Mus Am Art, New York; Addison Gallery, Andover, Mass; Detroit Inst Arts, Mich; Chrysler Mus, Norfolk, Va.
Exhibitions: Romantic Painting in America, Mus Mod Art, New York, 43; Painting in the United States, Carnegie Inst, Pittsburgh, Pa, 48; American Painting Today, 50 & Am Watercolors Drawings & Prints, 52, Metrop Mus Art, New York; Golden Anniversary, Provincetown Art Asn, 64.
Awards: Joseph Lewis Weyrich Mem Prize, Baltimore Mus, 30; Crossett First Prize, Cape Cod Art Asn, 48.
Bibliography: F F Sherman (auth), Notes on Elliot Orr, Art in Am, 40; Rosamund Frost (auth), Contemporary art, Crown, 42; John I H Baur (auth), Revolution & tradition in modern American art, Harvard Univ Press, 51.
Memberships: Life mem Provincetown Art Asn.
Mailing Address: 733 Main St, Chatham, MA 02633.

ORSINI (GWENDOLYN ORSINGER ANDERSON)
  Enamelist, Art Dealer
Preferred Media: Enamels, Watercolors.
b Chicago, Ill, May 31, 12.
Study & Training: Univ Calif, Los Angeles, 34-35; Univ Ill, BS, 37;
  Univ Va, 55.
Work in Public Collections: Va Mus Fine Arts, Richmond; Balti-
  more Mus, Md; Corcoran Gallery Art, Washington, D C; Thomas
  C Thompson Collection Contemp Am Enamelists, Chicago.
Exhibitions: Fifth Creative Craft Biennial, 62, Ninth Int Ceramic
  Exhib, 63 & Nat League Am Pen Women 22nd Biennial Art Ex-
  hib, 64, Smithsonian Inst, Washington, D C; Seventh Creative
  Craft Biennial, Norfolk Mus, Va, 66; 14th Ann Rochester Festi-
  val Religious Arts, 72; plus eight one-man shows.
Teaching: Instr enameling, 1,000 Island Mus Craft Sch, Clayton,
  N Y, 66-67; instr enameling, Am Art Assocs, 67-; instr enamel-
  ing, Cross Creek Ceramics, 72.
Positions: Dir-partner, Artist's Mart, 54-
Awards: Outstanding craftsmanship award, Smithsonian Inst, 56;
  first prize in ceramics, Corcoran Gallery Art, 57; first prize in
  enamels, Nat League Am Pen Women, 69.
Memberships: Kiln Club, Washington, D C (v pres, 68-69); Nat
  League Am Pen Women (v pres, 56-58, pres, 58-60); Va Crafts-
  mens Coun; Md Crafts Coun; World Craft Coun.
Specialty of Gallery: Contemporary American artists paintings,
  sculpture & ceramics.
Dealers: Artist's Mart, 1361 Wisconsin Ave, Washington, DC 20007;
  Galerie Santiago, San Juan, PR 00936.
Mailing Address: 6520 Ivy Hill Dr, McLean, VA 22101.

ORTIZ, RALPH
  Sculptor
Preferred Media: Mixed Media.
b New York, N Y, Jan 30, 34.
Study & Training: Brooklyn Mus Art Sch; Art Stud League New
  York; Pratt Inst, BS, MFA; Columbia Univ.
Work in Public Collections: Mus Mod Art, New York; Whitney Mus
  Am Art, New York; Finch Mus, New York; Chrysler Mus Fine
  Art, Provincetown, Mass; Oxford Mus Mod Art, Eng.
Exhibitions: Traveling Assemblage Exhib, Mus Mod Art, New York,
  63; Young America Exhibition, Whitney Mus Am Art, New York,
  65; The Destruction in Art Symposium, London, Eng, 66; Celebra-
  tion-Eros-Thanatos, Youth Pavilion, Expo '67, Montreal, Can,
  67; Theater Ritual, Am Educ Theater Asn Conf, Temple Univ,
  Philadelphia, Pa, 70.
Teaching: Instr graphic plastic forms, mixed media, intermedia,
  color & design, Columbia Univ Teachers Col, 67; asst prof art,
  Livingston Col, Rutgers Univ, 72-
Positions: Dir & cur, El Museo del Barrio, New York, 69-70; comt
  mem, Ghetto Arts Panel, N Y State Coun Arts, 70-71; v chmn,
  Planning Corp Arts, New York, 71-
Awards: John Hay Whitney fel grant, 65.
Bibliography: Barry Farrell (auth), The other culture, Life Mag,
  2/17/67; Kurt Von Meier (auth), Violence art & the American
  way, Arts Can, 4/68; Charlotte Willard (auth), Violence & art,
  Art in Am, 1-2/69.
Publications: Auth, Disassemblage, Art & Artists, 66; ed & auth,
  Ritual theatre, Aspen Mag, 69; auth, Culture & the people, Art
  in Am, 71.
Mailing Address: Box 44, Village Post Office, New York, NY 10014.

ORTLIP, PAUL DANIEL
  Painter
Preferred Media: Oils, Mixed Media.
b Englewood, N J, May 21, 26.
Study & Training: Houghton Acad; Art Stud League New York, N Y;
  with Louis Bouche, 47, Reginald Marsh, 48, Robert Brackman &
  Edwin Dickinson, 49; Acad Grande Chaumiere, 50.
Work in Public Collections: U S Navy Art Collection, Pentagon,
  Washington, D C; Bergen Community Mus, Paramus, N J; Fair-
  leigh Dickinson Univ, Rutherford, N J; Bergen Co Court House,
  Hackensack, N J; N J Col Med, Newark.
Commissions: Mem portrait of JFK, Fairleigh Dickinson Univ
  Libr, 64; Gemini 5 Astronauts, 65, Vietnam (painting), 67 &
  Apollo 12 Astronauts, 69, Off Info, USN; Historic Fort Lee
  (mural), comn by Arthur Bruni, 71.
Exhibitions: Salon L'Art Libre Ann, Paris, France, 50; Nat Acad
  Design Ann, New York, N Y, 52; Allied Artists Am Ann, 60-71;
  Salmagundi Club Ann, 60-71; Collection of Fine Arts, Smith-
  sonian Inst, Washington, D C.
Teaching: Instr painting, Montclair Acad, N J, 57-58; artist-in-
  residence, Fairleigh Dickinson Univ, 57-67; instr painting, Mont-
  clair Mus, 58-59.
Positions: Off U S Navy artist, Off Info, Washington, D C, 63-; art
  cur, Fairleigh Dickinson Univ, 67-

Awards: First prize in oils, N J State Am Artists Prof Award, 60;
  Franklin Williams Award, Salmagundi Club, 67; Artist of the
  Year Award, Hudson Artists, Jersey City Mus, 70.
Bibliography: Marg Dulac (artist), Odyssey of an artist, N J Mus &
  Arts, 5/71.
Memberships: Life mem Art Stud League New York; Allied Artists
  Am; Salmagundi Club; U S Navy Liaison Comt (off artist); N J
  Watercolor Soc.
Dealer: Portraits, Inc, 41 W 57th St, New York, NY 10022.
Mailing Address: 95 Main St, Fort Lee, NJ 07024.

ORTMAN, GEORGE EARL
  Painter, Sculptor
Preferred Media: Constructions.
b Oakland, Calif, Oct 17, 26.
Study & Training: Ariz State Univ; Calif Col Arts & Crafts; Atelier
  17, New York, N Y; Acad Andre Lhote, Paris, France; Hans Hof-
  mann Sch, New York.
Work in Public Collections: Mus Mod Art & Whitney Mus Am Art,
  New York; Walker Art Ctr, Minneapolis, Minn; Albright-Knox
  Art Gallery, Buffalo, N Y; Milwaukee Art Ctr, Wis.
Commissions: Relig banners, Christian Theol Sem Indianapolis, Ind,
  66; mural, comn by Bd Educ, P S 192, New York, 67; Reredo,
  Unitarian Church, Princeton, N J, 68; banners, Indiana Univ
  Opera House, 71; Oracle (three panels), Mfrs Hanover Trust, 71.
Exhibitions: Carnegie Int, Pittsburgh, Pa, 60, 64 & 70; Toward a New
  Abstraction, Jewish Mus, New York, 63; Tokyo Biennial, Japan,
  64; 100 Years of American Art, 64 & Two Decades of Geometric
  Abstraction, 65, Whitney Mus Am Art.
Teaching: Sr fel painting, Princeton Univ, 66-69; head painting dept,
  Cranbrook Acad Art, 70-
Awards: Guggenheim fel, 65; first prize for Religion in Art, Bir-
  mingham Mus Art, 66; first prize, N J State Mus Second Ann, 67.
Bibliography: J Borgzinger (auth), Analytical art, Time Mag, 4/64;
  Martin Friedman (auth), Symbols, Art News, 10/65; J Brown
  (auth), Introduction for catalog to one-man show, Indianapolis
  Mus Art, 4/71.
Dealer: Gimpel-Weitzenhoffer Galleries, 1040 Madison Ave, New
  York, NY 10021.
Mailing Address: Box 192, Castine, ME 04421.

ORTMAYER, CONSTANCE
  Sculptor, Educator
Preferred Media: Wood, Ceramic.
b New York, N Y, July 19, 02.
Study & Training: Royal Acad Fine Arts & Royal Acad Master Sch,
  Vienna, Austria, MFA.
Work in Public Collections: Am Numismatic Soc, New York;
  Brookgreen Gardens, S C.
Commissions: Bronze group, State of S C, Brookgreen Gardens, 34;
  U S Half Dollar, Stephen Foster Commemorative, 36; bas reliefs
  U S Post Off, Arcadia, Fla, 39 & Scottsboro, Ala, 41; Award
  Medals, Fla Acad Sci & Rollins Col, 52-62.
Exhibitions: Vienna Secession, 32; Nat Asn Women Painters &
  Sculptors, New York, 35; Allied Arts, Brooklyn Mus, 36; Nat
  Sculpture Soc, Whitney Mus Am Art, New York, 40; Pa Acad
  Fine Arts, Philadelphia, 41.
Teaching: Prof sculpture, Rollins Col, 37-68, emer prof, 68-
Positions: Head dept art, Rollins Col, 60-68.
Awards: Anna Hyatt Huntington Prize, Nat Asn Women Painters &
  Sculptors, 35; Henry O Avery Archit Prize, Nat Sculpture Soc,
  40; Award of Merit, Fla Fedn Art, 48.
Memberships: Nat Sculpture Soc; Fla Fedn Art; hon mem Orlando
  Ceramic Soc.
Mailing Address: 773 Antonette Ave, Winter Park, FL 32789.

OSBORN, ELODIE C
  Art Administrator
b Brooklyn, N Y, Dec 6, 11.
Study & Training: Packer Col Inst; Wellesley Col, BA; Sch Fine
  Arts, New York Univ; Sorbonne, Paris, France, cert.
Collections Arranged: Many exhibs at Mus Mod Art, New York, for
  tour to other mus, cols & schs; Klee Memorial Exhibition, Mus
  Mod Art, New York, 41.
Positions: Dir traveling exhibs, Mus Mod Art, New York, 33-48;
  dir, Salisbury Film Soc, 51-
Memberships: Am Fedn Arts (adv comt, 41-56); Mus Mod Art; Int
  Film Seminars (bd trustees, 68-); MacDowell Colony (trustee,
  70-, secy bd, 72-); Am Fedn Film Socs (v pres, 57-58).
Publications: Auth, Modern sculpture (portfolio), Mus Mod Art, 47;
  auth, Texture and pattern (portfolio), Mus Mod Art, 49; auth, Man-
  ual of traveling exhibitions, UNESCO, 53; contribr, Art in Am, 66
  & Film Quart, 68; contribr, Film Libr Quart, 72.
Mailing Address: Salisbury, CT 06068.

OSBORN, ROBERT
Painter, Drawer
b Oshkosh, Wis, Oct 26, 04.
Study & Training: Yale Univ; Brit Acad, Rome; Acad Scandinav, Paris, France; also with Friesz, Varoquier & Despiau; Md Inst Art, hon DFA, 63.
Work in Public Collections: Mus Mod Art, New York, N Y; Addison Gallery Art, Andover, Mass; Paine Art Mus, Oshkosh, Wis; Corcoran Gallery Art, Washington, D C; Wadsworth Atheneum, Hartford, Conn.
Commissions: Mural, Quinta da Bacalhoa Azeitao, Port, 38-39; mural, Am Mus Natural Hist, New York, 55; mural, comn by Stonoroff for Planning Comn Philadelphia, 56; two murals, comn by Ivan Chermayeff for Puerto Rico Planning Comn, 70; three murals, comn by Ivan Chermayeff for Smithsonian Exhib on Productivity, 72.
Exhibitions: Wartime Posters, Art Inst Chicago, Ill, 46; Va Mus Fine Arts, Richmond, 52; Wadsworth Atheneum, Hartford, Conn, 58; Whitney Mus Am Art, New York, 60; Brooklyn Mus, N Y, 61.
Teaching: Founder & head art dept, Hotchkiss Sch, Lakeville, Conn, 29-35; chmn Yale Coun, Sch Art & Archit, Yale Univ, 60-65, alumni exec coun, 70-
Positions: Presented first show of Edward Weston in the East, Hotchkiss Sch, 31.
Awards: Gov medal, Wis.
Bibliography: Leo Lionni (auth), Osborn, Print, Vol 5; Russell Lynes (auth), Osborn's Americans, Horizon, 9/60; Fritz Eichenberg (auth), Osborn, Am Graphic Artist, 65; plus others.
Memberships: Elizabethan Club; Scroll & Keys; Century Asn.
Collection: (With Elodie C Osborn) Despiau, Miros, Klees, Calders, Marinni, MacIver, Hartley, Picasso, Dubuffets, Friedmans, Shahns and others.
Publications: Auth & illusr, War is no damn good, Leisure, The vulgarians, Low and inside & An Osborn festival of phobias.
Dealer: Edith Halpert, 57th St & Park Ave, New York, NY 10022.
Mailing Address: Salisbury, CT 06068.

OSBORNE, ROBERT LEE
Painter, Instructor
b Chandler, Ind, June 24, 28.
Study & Training: Ind Univ, with Pickens, Marx, Engel, Ballinger & Hope, MA; Univ Iowa, with Lechay, Hecksher, Longman, Ludens & Tomasini, MA.
Exhibitions: Cincinnati Mus Asn, 55; John Herron Art Inst, 55-60; Tri-State Exhib, 50-60; one-man shows, Evansville Col, 55 & 58; Art: U S A.
Teaching: Lectr, Evansville Mus; asst prof art & head dept, Evansville Col; instr, Evansville Mus; instr, Ringling Sch Art, Sarasota, Fla, presently.
Positions: Former designer, Olszewski Art Glass Co, Saint Louis.
Awards: Gold key award, Evansville, Ind, 46; prize, Ind Univ, 52.
Memberships: Artists Equity Asn; Evansville State Teachers Asn; Nat Educ Asn; Evansville Mus; Tri-State Art Guild (pres, 58-61).
Publications: Illusr, Organization of aquatic clubs, 55.
Mailing Address: Ringling School of Art, Sarasota, FL 33580.

OSBY, LARISSA GEISS
Painter
b Artemowsk, Russia, June 7, 28; U S citizen.
Study & Training: Lyceum & Univ Goettingen, Ger; Univ Munich; Acad Fine Arts, Munich, Ger.
Work in Public Collections: Carnegie Inst, Pittsburgh, Pa; Univ Pittsburgh; Pittsburgh Bd Educ; Westinghouse Electric Corp Collection; U S Steel Corp Collection; plus others.
Commissions: Koppers Co & First Fed Savings & Loan Asn, Pittsburgh, Pa, 72.
Exhibitions: One-man shows, Pittsburgh Plan for Art Gallery, 63, 68 & 71; Walker Art Ctr Biennial, Minneapolis, Minn, 66; Pennsylvania 71, William Penn Mem Mus, Harrisburg, Pa, 71; one-man show, Carnegie Inst Mus Art, Pittsburgh, 72; plus others.
Awards: Jury award of distinction, Mainstreams Int, 68; first prize, Pittsburgh Watercolor Soc, 68; jury award of distinction, Assoc Artists of Pittsburgh Ann, 69.
Memberships: Arts & Crafts Ctr Pittsburgh; Pittsburgh Plan for Art; Assoc Artists of Pittsburgh; Pittsburgh Watercolor Soc; Group A.
Mailing Address: Glasgow Rd, Valencia, PA 16059.

O'SICKEY, JOSEPH BENJAMIN
Painter, Educator
Preferred Media: Oils.
b Detroit, Mich, Nov 9, 18.
Study & Training: Cleveland Sch Art, cert, with Paul Travis, Henry G Keller, Carl Gaertner, Frank N Wilcox & Hoyt L Sherman.
Work in Public Collections: Cleveland Mus Art, Ohio; Pepsi Cola Collection, New York, N Y; Cleveland Arts Asn; Mus Mod Art Poster Collection 1949-50 Exhib.

Exhibitions: Fourteen juried exhibs, Cleveland Mus Art, 38-72; Pa Acad Fine Art, Philadelphia; Columbus Gallery Art Invitational; Akron Art Inst; Blossom Invitational; plus other group shows & many one-man shows.
Teaching: Instr art, Ohio State Univ, 46-47; instr art, Akron Art Inst, 49-52; lectr art, Case Western Reserve Univ, 56-64; prof art, Kent State Univ, 64-, coord painting & sculpture, 68-
Positions: Art dir & graphic designer, pvt co, 49-64.
Awards: Spec jury mention & awards, Cleveland Mus Art, 62-67; spec jury mention, Akron Art Inst.
Mailing Address: Dept of Art, Kent State University, Kent, OH 44240.

OSSORIO, ALFONSO A
Painter, Sculptor
b Manila, Philippines, Aug 2, 16; U S citizen.
Study & Training: Harvard Col, AB, 38; R I Sch Design, 38-39.
Work in Public Collections: Philadelphia Mus Art; New York Univ Art Collection; Guggenheim Mus, New York; Mus Mod Art; Whitney Mus Am Art; plus many others.
Commissions: Murals, Church St Joseph, Victorias, Negros, Philippines, 50-51 & Washington Square Village, New York, N Y, 54; large circular assemblage, New York Hilton Hotel, 64.
Exhibitions: Whitney Mus Am Art Painting & Sculpture Ann, 53-; Osaka Art Festival, Japan, 58 & 60; Structure & Style, Turin, Italy & Bochum, W Ger, 62; Documenta, Kassel, W Ger, 64; The New American Painting & Sculpture, Mus Mod Art, 69; plus many other group & one-man shows.
Positions: Dir exhibs, Exec House, New York, 56-57; co-founder & dir, Signa Gallery, East Hampton, N Y, 57-60.
Bibliography: Jean Dubuffet (auth), Peintures initiatiques d'Ossorio (monogr), La Pierre Volante, Paris, 52; Michel Tapie (auth), Ossorio (monogr), Ed Arte Fratelli Pozzo, Turin, 61; B H Friedman (auth), Ossorio (monogr), Abrams, 72.
Collection: Contemporary painting and sculpture; art brut, primitive and oriental.
Dealer: Cordier & Ekstrom, 980 Madison Ave, New York, NY 10021.
Mailing Address: The Creeks, East Hampton, NY 11937.

OSTENDORF, (ARTHUR) LLOYD, JR
Painter, Instructor
Preferred Media: Watercolors, Inks, Oils.
b Dayton, Ohio, June 23, 21.
Study & Training: Dayton Art Inst; Lincoln Mem Univ, Lincoln Dipl Hon, 66; Lincoln Col (Ill), LittD, 68.
Work in Public Collections: Gov William Lee D Ewing (oil portrait), Hall of Gov, Ill State Capitol, Springfield; Msgr Harry Ansbury (oil portrait), Parish Recreation House, Corpus Christi; Msgr Joseph D McFarland (oil portrait), Holy Angels Sch, Dayton, Ohio; President elect Lincoln 1860 (oil) & Lincoln christening site of town, Lincoln, Ill (oil), lobby, Lincoln Savings & Loan Asn; Speaker W Robert Blair (oil portrait), Ill State Capitol, Springfield, 72.
Commissions: The Jesuit Martyrs (oil), Jesuit Retreat Chapel, Milford, Ohio, 49; six religious oil paintings, Hoyne Funeral Chapel, Dayton, 55.
Exhibitions: Dayton Art Inst, 41.
Teaching: Instr com art & painting & dir, Ostendorf Art Acad, 69-
Awards: Winner in design for Chicago Lincoln (statue), Lincoln Square C of C, Chicago, 58.
Memberships: Montgomery Co Hist Soc (v pres, 56); Civil War Round Table of Dayton, Ohio (pres, 55-56, 58-59).
Publications: Art ed, Lincoln Herald, 57-; auth, Mr Lincoln came to Dayton, 59; auth & illusr, A picture story of Abraham Lincoln, 62; co-auth, Lincoln in photographs, an album of every known pose, 63; auth, The photographs of Mary Todd Lincoln, 69.
Mailing Address: 225 Lookout Dr, Dayton, OH 45419.

OSTER, GERALD
Painter, Craftsman
b Providence, R I, Mar 24, 18.
Study & Training: Brown Univ, ScB; Cornell Univ, PhD.
Work in Public Collections: Milwaukee Art Ctr; San Francisco Mus Art.
Exhibitions: Mus Mod Art, 64; Albright-Knox Art Gallery, Buffalo, N Y, 65; Walker Art Ctr, Minneapolis, Minn, 67; Milwaukee Art Ctr, Wis, 68; Inst Contemp Art, Chicago, Ill, 68; plus others.
Publications: Auth, The science of Moire patterns, 64 & 69; contribr, Art Int.
Mailing Address: 241 W 11th St, New York, NY 10014.

OSTROW, STEPHEN EDWARD
Art Historian, Art Administrator
b New York, N Y, May 7, 32.
Study & Training: Oberlin Col, BA, 54; N Y Univ Inst Fine Arts, MA 59, PhD, 66.

Collections Arranged: Baroque Painting: Italy and Her Influence, 68; Visions and Revisions, 68; Raid the Icebox I, with Andy Warhol, 69-70; Days Gone By, 71.
Teaching: Lectr art hist, Rutgers Univ, New Brunswick, 58-62; asst prof art hist, Univ Mo-Columbia, 62-66; vis lectr art hist, Brown Univ, 71-
Positions: Cur collections, Herron Mus Art, 66-67; chief cur, Mus Art, R I Sch Design, 67-71, dir, 71-
Memberships: Col Art Asn Am; Am Asn Mus; Asn Art Mus Dirs.
Publications: Auth, Annibale Carracci and the Jason frescoes: toward an internal chronology, Art Bull, 64; auth, Diana or Bacchus in the Palazzo Riario, Marsyas, 65; auth, Baroque painting, Italy and her influence, 68; auth, Visions and revisions, 68; auth, A drawing by Annibale Carracci for the Jason frescoes and the S Gregorio baptism, Master Drawings, 70.
Mailing Address: 224 Benefit St, Providence, RI 02903.

OSTUNI, PETER W
Painter
Preferred Media: Oils, Vitreous Enamel, Glass, Metals.
b New York, N Y, Oct 9, 08.
Study & Training: Cooper Union Sch Art & Archit, cert.
Commissions: Vitreous enamel mural, in lounge of S S United States, U S Steamship Lines, 51; enamel murals, Children's Mus, Fort Worth, Tex, 52; laminated stained glass, Prudential Life Ins Main Off, Newark, N J, 59; seven cast stone bas-reliefs, for Grace Lines SS Santa Maria, 65; six windows in laminated plastics, Phipps Plaza, Atlanta, Ga, 70.
Exhibitions: New Work in Stained Glass, Am Fedn Arts, 53; Craftsmen U S A, 63 & Enamels U S A, 65, Mus Contemp Crafts, New York; New York State Artists, Munson-Williams-Proctor Inst, 70; Retrospective, List Arts Ctr, Kirkland Col, 70.
Teaching: Instr painting, Cooper Union Sch Art & Archit, 37-38; instr painting & sculpture, Simon's Rock Col, 66-68; prof painting & sculpture, Kirkland Col, 68-
Bibliography: Eugene Clute (auth), Murals in vitreous enamels, 12/52 & Priscilla Ginsberg (auth), Peter Ostundi, 1/61, Craft Horizons.
Art Interests: Architectural art.
Publications: Contribr, Dimensions of design, 58 & The craftsmans world, 59.
Mailing Address: Dept of Art, Kirkland College, Clinton, NY 13323.

OSVER, ARTHUR
Painter
b Chicago, Ill, July 26, 12.
Study & Training: Northwestern Univ, 30-31; Art Inst Chicago, with Boris Anisfeld, 31-36.
Work in Public Collections: Mus Mod Art; Whitney Mus Am Art; Davenport Munic Art Gallery; Peabody Mus, Salem, Mass; plus many others.
Commissions: Cover, Fortune Mag, 60.
Exhibitions: Whitney Mus Am Art, 44, 45 & 63; one-man show, Univ Fla, 52; Art: U S A: Now, 64-65; one-man show, Coe Col, Cedar Rapids, Iowa, 66; retrospective, Iowa State Col, Ames, 68; plus many other group & one-man shows.
Teaching: Instr painting, Brooklyn Mus Art Sch, 49-51; instr, Columbia Univ, 52; instr, Univ Fla, 54-55; instr painting, Cooper Union Art Sch, 55 & 58; vis critic painting, Yale Univ, 56-57; painter-in-residence, Am Acad in Rome, 57-58; instr, Wash Univ, 60-
Awards: Medal, Art Dirs Club, Chicago, 61; J Henry Schiedt Mem Prize, Pa Acad Fine Arts, 66; sabbatical grant, Nat Endowment Arts, Washington, D C, 66; plus many others.
Bibliography: Ray Bethers (auth), How paintings happen, Norton, 51; Lee Nordness (ed), Art: U S A: Now, C J Bucher, 62.
Mailing Address: 465 Foote Ave, Saint Louis, MO 63119.

OTTIANO, JOHN WILLIAM
Educator, Sculptor
Preferred Media: Bronze, Gold, Silver.
b Medford, Mass, July 23, 26.
Study & Training: Mass Col Art, BS, 54; Boston Univ, MFA, 60; Pa State Univ, DEd, 63.
Work in Public Collections: Painting, Viktor Lowenfeld Mem, Pa State Univ; sculptures, Univ Western Ill, Gloucester Co Col & Glassboro State Col.
Commissions: Four marble murals, Mimosa, The Age of Miracles & two other large exterior murals, Glassboro State Col, 67; Art Educator Award, Sculpture, N J Art Educ Asn, 69.
Exhibitions: Pa Acad Fine Arts, Philadelphia, 64; Nat Acad Galleries, New York, 65; N J State Mus, Art From N J, 66-70; Sculpture in the Park, Van Suan Park, Paramus, N J, 71; Artists Equity, Philadelphia Civic Ctr, 72.
Teaching: Instr, three-dimensional design & jewelry, Boston Univ, 54-60; asst prof, Mass Col Art, 61-62; prof, Pa State Univ, University Park, 62-63; prof, Glassboro State Col, 63-

Awards: First for sculpture, N J Tercentenary, 64.
Bibliography: Artist/Educator, Sch Arts, 2/66; article, In: La Rev Mod, 3/1/66.
Memberships: Am Asn Univ Prof; N J Art Educ Asn (pres, 70-); N J Designer-Craftsmen Asn (pres, 70-72); Artists Equity Asn; Nat Art Educ Asn (N J state rep, 63-).
Research: The relationship between surface texture preference, personality characteristics, and three-dimensional art performance.
Art Interests: Cire Perdue method of casting.
Mailing Address: 1115 Glen Lake Blvd, Pitman, NJ 08071.

OWENS, WINIFRED (WHITEBERGH)
Painter, Lecturer
b Colorado Springs, Colo, July 21, 11.
Study & Training: Colo Col; Taos Sch Art, N Mex; also pvt study.
Commissions: Murals, Bethany Baptist Church, Press Club & Stratton Estate, Colorado Springs; theatre murals, Taos, N Mex.
Exhibitions: Smithsonian Inst; Artists' Mart; one-man shows, Mus N Mex, Santa Fe, Colorado Springs Fine Arts Ctr & Lee Gallery, Alexandria, Va, 65; plus others.
Awards: Prizes, Colorado Springs Fine Arts Ctr & Canon City Art Festival.
Memberships: Artists Equity Asn; Taos Art Colony.
Publications: Contribr, articles, In: Colorado Springs Gazette & Denver Post.
Mailing Address: 3405 Cypress Dr, Falls Church, VA 22042.

OWSLEY, DAVID THOMAS
Museum Curator
b Dallas, Tex, Aug 20, 29.
Study & Training: Harvard Col, AB, 51; Inst Fine Arts, New York Univ, MFA, 62.
Collections Arranged: Decorative Arts Collection & Ailsa Mellon Bruce Collection, Carnegie Inst Mus Art.
Positions: Fel, Am Wing, Metrop Mus Art; asst cur decorative arts & sculpture, Mus Fine Arts, Boston; visitor, Victoria & Albert Mus, London, Eng; cur decorative arts, Carnegie Inst Mus Art, presently.
Mailing Address: Carnegie Institute Museum of Art, 4400 Forbes Ave, Pittsburgh, PA 15213.

OWYANG, JUDITH FRANCINE
Art Critic
b Sacramento, Calif, Feb 9, 40.
Study & Training: Univ South Calif, BA, with Edward S Peck & jour with Jack C Searles.
Positions: Art ed & columnist, Santa Monica Eve Outlook, 70-
Memberships: Kappa Pi.
Mailing Address: 3827 Beethoven St, Los Angeles, CA 90066.

P

PABLO (PAUL BURGESS EDWARDS)
Painter, Art Administrator
b Moulton, Iowa, Feb 18, 34.
Study & Training: Iowa Wesleyan Col, BA, with S Carl Fracassini; Wichita State Univ, MA.
Work in Public Collections: Wichita Art Mus, Kans; Miami Beach Pub Libr, Fla; Iowa Wesleyan Col, Mount Pleasant; Wichita State Univ; Citizen's Libr, Washington, Pa.
Exhibitions: 29th Ann Nat Graphics Art Show, Wichita Art Asn, 60; Ann Juror's Award Show, Huntington Gallery, W Va, 65; 19th Ann Nat Decorative Arts Show, Wichita Art Asn, 66; Max 24, Nat Small Painting Show, Purdue Univ, Lafayette, Ind, 66; 2nd Nat Polymer Exhib, Eastern Mich Univ, Ypsilanti, 68.
Teaching: Instr ceramics, Wichita State Univ, summer 62; asst prof sculpture & design, West Liberty State Col, 63-65; chmn, dept art, Washington & Jefferson Col, 65-
Positions: Pres, Wichita Artists Guild, 61-62; chmn, Washington & Jefferson Nat Painting Show, 68-; pres Arts Coun Washington Co, Pa, 69-72.
Awards: First prize in painting, Bethany Col Ann Show, 64; first prize in summer show, Oglebay Inst, 64; Juror's Best of Show Award, Huntington Gallery, 65.
Mailing Address: Dept of Art, Washington & Jefferson College, E Lincoln St, Washington, PA 15301.

PACE, MARGARET BOSSHARDT
Designer, Painter
b San Antonio, Tex, Dec 9, 19.
Study & Training: Newcomb Col, BFA; Trinity Univ; also with Will Stevens, Etienne Ret & Xavier Gonzalez.
Work in Public Collections: In pvt collections.
Commissions: Murals, recreation rm, Victoria Plaza, Golden Age Ctr, 60; mosaic murals, St Lukes Episcopal Church, San Antonio, 59, Episcopal Diocesan Ctr, Diocese of W Tex, 61 & Episcopal Cathedral, 65; designed & executed chalice, pattern & pix, ordination of Father Braun, Pinckneyville, Ill, 69.
Exhibitions: Tex Ann, 58, 59 & 69; Invitational Contemp Artists Group, Mexico City Consulate, 65 & 68; Religious Art, Hemisfair, 68; Trinity Univ, San Antonio, 69; Artists Inst Tex Cult, 69; plus many other group & one-man shows.
Teaching: Instr, Incarnate Word Col, 64-65; asst prof art, San Antonio Col, 65-72.
Positions: Bd mem & v pres, San Antonio Art Inst; bd mem, Friends of McNay Mus, San Antonio, 67-72; Southwest Craft Ctr, 69-73.
Awards: Henry Steinbomer Award, Tex Watercolor Soc, 49 & 66; Grumbacher Purchase Award, 60; Richard Kleberg Purchase Award, 60; plus many others.
Memberships: San Antonio Art League (bd mem, 67-68); Tex Fine Arts Asn; Tex Watercolor Soc; Contemp Artists Group; San Antonio Craft Guild; plus others.
Mailing Address: 208 Morningside Dr, San Antonio, TX 78209.

PACE, STEPHEN S
Painter
Preferred Media: Oils, Watercolors.
b Charleston, Mo, Dec 12, 18.
Study & Training: Inst Allende, San Miguel Allende, Mex; Acad Grande Chaumiere, Paris, France; Inst Arte Statale, Florence, Italy; Art Stud League New York, with Cameron Booth & Morris Cantor; Hans Hofmann Sch.
Work in Public Collections: Whitney Mus Am Art, New York, N Y; Univ Calif, Berkeley; James Michener Found, Univ Tex, Austin; Walker Art Ctr, Minneapolis, Minn; Des Moines Art Ctr, Iowa.
Exhibitions: Carnegie Int, Pittsburgh, Pa, 55; Int Biennial, Japan, selected by Mus Mod Art, New York, 57; one-man show, Howard Wise Gallery, New York, 64; Abstract Watercolors by 14 Americans, Mus Mod Art, toured Europe, Asia & Australia, 64-66; 10 Year Retrospective, Des Moines Art Ctr, 70.
Teaching: Artist-in-residence, Washington Univ, spring-summer 59; instr art, Pratt Inst, 61-68; instr art seminars, Univ Calif, Berkeley, spring, 68.
Awards: Dolia Lorian Award to promising painters, 54; Hallmark Co Purchase Award, 61.
Bibliography: Hubert Crehan (auth), A change of pace, Art News, 4/64; Russell Arnold (auth), Paintings by Stephen Pace, Crucible, fall 65; Denver Lindley (auth), In a landscape (film), 69-71.
Mailing Address: 345 W 29th St, New York, NY 10001.

PACHNER, WILLIAM
Painter
Preferred Media: Oils, Watercolors, Ink.
b Brtnice, Czech, Apr 7, 15; U S citizen.
Study & Training: Acad Arts & Crafts, Vienna, Austria.
Work in Public Collections: Whitney Mus Am Art, New York, N Y; Rose Gallery, Brandeis Univ, Waltham, Mass; Butler Inst Am Art, Youngstown, Ohio; Fort Worth Art Ctr, Tex; Iowa State Teacher's Col, Ames.
Exhibitions: Carnegie Int, Pittsburgh, Pa; Whitney Mus Am Art Ann; Corcoran Gallery Art Biennial, Washington, D C; Pa Acad Fine Arts, Philadelphia; U S Fine Arts Pavilion, New York World's Fair, 65.
Teaching: Instr painting & drawing, Art Stud League New York, 69-70.
Awards: Am Acad Arts & Lett & Inst Arts & Lett Award, 49; Ford Found Awards, 59-64; Guggenheim fel, 60.
Bibliography: Kenneth Donahue (auth), William Pachner, Am Fedn Arts, 59.
Mailing Address: 962 Ohayo Mountain Rd, Woodstock, NY 12498.

PACKER, CLAIR LANGE
Painter, Writer
Preferred Media: Watercolors, Oils, Inks, Crayons.
b Geuda Springs, Kans, Aug 27, 01.
Study & Training: Univ N Mex, Taos, with Millard Sheets & Barse Miller; also with Harry Anthony De Young, San Antonio, Tex & Paul Barr, Grand Forks, N Dak.
Work in Public Collections: Gilcrease Mus, Tulsa, Okla; Davis Gallery, Tulsa; Alley Gallery, Houston, Tex; Glasser Gallery, San Antonio; Seven Rays Gallery, Taos.
Exhibitions: Philbrook Mus, Tulsa; Houston Mus; Gilcrease Mus, Tulsa; Elizabet Ney Mus, Austin, Tex; Dallas Mus, Tex.

Teaching: Instr pvt classes art in San Antonio & Tulsa.
Positions: Artist, San Antonio Express, 46-48; instr art, Littlehouse Gallery, San Antonio, 47-48; artist, Tulsa World, 48-65.
Awards: Hon mention for watercolor, Houston Mus; purchase prize for watercolor, Gilcrease Mus, Fourth Nat Bank, Tulsa.
Art Interests: Action sketches of rodeo contestants; landscapes, Indians, cowboys & marines.
Publications: Auth & illusr, articles, In: Western Publ; auth & illusr, articles, In: Tulsa World Sunday Mag; auth & illusr, articles, In: Tulsa World Ranch & Farm World; auth, articles, In: Lapidary J; auth, articles, In: Gun Report Mag.
Mailing Address: 3307 E Fifth Pl, Tulsa, OK 74112.

PADDOCK, DENIS EMIL
Collector
U S citizen.
Collection: Surrealist and geometric works.
Mailing Address: Grumman Aerospace Corp, Bethpage, NY 11714.

PADOVANO, ANTHONY JOHN
Sculptor, Lecturer
Preferred Media: Metal, Concrete.
b Brooklyn, N Y, July 19, 33.
Study & Training: Carnegie Inst Technol; Pratt Inst; Columbia Univ, with Oronzio Maldarclli.
Work in Public Collections: Whitney Mus Am Art, New York, N Y; Nat Collection Fine Arts, Washington, D C; Univ Ill; John Herron Art Inst; Storm King Art Ctr, N Y.
Commissions: Sculpture In The Park, Parks Dept, New York, 68; design, N Y State Art Awards, N Y State Coun Arts, 69; sculpture, World Trade Ctr, Port Auth N Y & N J, 70; three arcs, donated by Trammel & Crow Co for City of Dallas, 72.
Exhibitions: Third Mostra Arte Figurative Int, Rome, Italy, 61; Young Am, Whitney Mus Am Art, 65; Am Sculpture, Mus Mod Art, 66; Am Express Pavilion, New York World's Fair, 66; Inauguration of Nat Collection Fine Arts, Washington, D C, 67.
Teaching: Asst prof sculpture, Columbia Univ, 64-; asst prof sculpture, Univ Conn, 72; adj asst prof sculpture, Queens Col (N Y), 72.
Positions: Adv mem N J State Coun Arts, 65-67.
Awards: Prix de Rome, Am Acad Rome, 60; Guggenheim Found fel, 64; Ford Found Purchase Award, 66.
Bibliography: Young talent, Art Am, 65; James Mellow (auth), article, In: New York Times Sun Rev, 4/70.
Memberships: Sculptors Guild (v pres, 68-69); Silvermine Guild Artists.
Publications: Contribr, Young America, 65.
Dealer: James Graham Gallery, 1014 Madison Ave, New York, NY 10021.
Mailing Address: Box 64, Ancram, NY 12502.

PAEFF, BASHKA (BASHKA PAEFF WAXMAN)
Sculptor
Preferred Media: Bronze, Marble.
b Minsk, Russia, Aug 12, 93.
Study & Training: Boston Mus Sch Fine Arts, with Bela Pratt, 14; also in Paris, France.
Work in Public Collections: Mass Inst Technol; Grad Ctr, Radcliffe Col, Cambridge, Mass; Boston Mus Fine Arts; Harvard Univ; Rockefeller Inst, N Y; plus others.
Commissions: Life size bas-relief, Justice Oliver Wendell Holmes, Harvard Law Libr; bas-relief, Jan Addams, Addams House, Philadelphia, Pa; bronze reliefs, Dr Southard, Harvard Med Libr, Dir Augusta Bronner, Judge Baker Found, Boston & Dr Martin Luther King, Jr, Boston Univ, 69; plus others.
Exhibitions: One-man show, Boston Guild Artists, 59; Nat Acad Design; Nat Sculpture Soc; Johns Hopkins Art Ctr.
Positions: Mem bd, Cambridge Art Asn.
Awards: Medal, Tercentenary Expos, Boston, 33; Daniel Chester French Medal, Nat Acad Design, 69.
Memberships: Guild Boston Artists; fel Nat Sculpture Soc.
Mailing Address: 21 Foster St, Cambridge, MA 02138.

PAGE, ADDISON FRANKLIN
Art Administrator
b Princeton, Ky, Oct 9, 11.
Study & Training: Wayne State Univ, BFA & MA.
Collections Arranged: 19 Canadian Painters, 62; Reg Butler: A Retrospective Exhibition, 63; Treasures of Chinese Art, 65; The Figure in Sculpture 1865-1965, 65; Treasures of Persian Art, 66; Indian Buddhist Sculpture, 68; The Sirak Collection, 68; Ciechanowiecki Collection of Gilt and Gold Medals and Plaquettes, 69; 19th Century French Sculpture: Monuments for the Middle Class, 71.
Teaching: Instr sculpture, Wayne State Univ, 47-55, instr hist sculpture, 55-58; instr hist mod art, Cranbrook Acad Art, 58-62.
Positions: Jr cur educ, Detroit Inst Arts, 47-58, cur contemp art, 58-62; dir, J B Speed Art Mus, 62-

Memberships: Mich Sculpture Soc (chmn, 50); Mich Watercolor Soc (bd mem, 60); Asn Art Mus Dirs.
Publications: Auth, Modern sculpture: a handbook, 50 & Diego Rivera's Detroit frescoes: a handbook, 55, Detroit Inst Arts.
Mailing Address: J B Speed Art Museum, 2035 S Third St, Louisville, KY 40208.

PAGE, JOHN HENRY, JR
Printmaker, Painter
b Ann Arbor, Mich, Jan 18, 23.
Study & Training: Minneapolis Sch Art; Art Stud League New York; Univ Mich, BDesign; Univ Iowa, MFA.
Work in Public Collections: Libr Cong, Washington, D C; Walker Art Ctr, Minneapolis, Minn; Des Moines Art Ctr, Iowa; Joslyn Art Mus, Omaha, Nebr; Carnegie Inst, Pittsburgh, Pa.
Commissions: Memberships Print, Des Moines Art Ctr, 69.
Exhibitions: Young American Printmakers, Mus Mod Art, New York, N Y, 53; 10th Nat Print Show, Brooklyn Mus, N Y, 56; 23rd Ann Iowa Artists Show, Des Moines Art Ctr, 71; Art U S A, Northern Ill Univ, DeKalb, 71; Nine Iowa Artists, Gov Exhib, 71-72.
Teaching: Prof printmaking, Univ Northern Iowa, 54-; chmn art dept, Univ Omaha, 60-61.
Awards: Pennell Purchase Prize, Libr Cong, 64; purchase prize for prints, Sioux City Art Ctr, 71; Younker Prize for Prints, Des Moines Art Ctr, 71.
Memberships: Col Art Asn Am.
Dealer: Percival Galleries, Inc, Shops Bldg, Des Moines, IA 50321.
Mailing Address: 1615 Tremont, Cedar Falls, IA 50613.

PALADIN, DAVID CHETHLAHE, see CHETHLAHE.

PALAU, MARTA
Painter, Weaver
b Albesa, Lerida, Spain, July 17, 34.
Study & Training: La Esmeralda, Inst Nat Bellas Artes, Mex; San Diego State Col, spec study with Paul Lingren; Barcelona Escuela Artes Y Oficios, weaving with Grau Garriga.
Work in Public Collections: Univ San Diego Med Sch, La Jolla, Calif; Hebrew Home for Aged, San Francisco, Calif; Club Indust, Mexico City; Ctr Arte Mod, Guadalajara, Mex.
Commissions: Mural, comn by Miguel Aldana, Ctr Arte Mod, Guadalajara, 71.
Exhibitions: La Jolla Art Mus, 64; San Diego Fine Arts, 69; Univ Tex Art Mus, 70; Bienal Cali, Colombia, 70; Bienal Santiago de Chile, Chile, 70.
Dealers: Wenger Gallery, Box 37, San Ysidro, CA 92073; Galeria Pecanins, Hamburgo 103, Mexico City, Mex.
Mailing Address: 20 de Noviembre 485, Zapopan, Jalisco, Mex.

PALEY, JEFFREY
Art Dealer
b Chicago, Ill, Aug 11, 38.
Study & Training: Harvard Col, BA, 60.
Positions: Co-dir, Paley & Lowe Gallery.
Specialty of Gallery: Contemporary American.
Collection: Contemporary American and Nepalese; Indian and Tibetan painting and sculpture.
Mailing Address: 59 Wooster St, New York, NY 10012.

PALEY, MR & MRS WILLIAM S
Collectors
Mr Paley, b Chicago, Ill, Sept 28, 01.
Study & Training: Mr Paley, Univ Chicago, 18-19; Univ Pa, BS, 22, LLD, 67; Bates Col, hon LLD, 63.
Positions: Mr Paley, trustee, Mus Mod Art, New York, pres, 68-
Collection: Contemporary paintings.
Mailing Address: Kiluna Farm, Manhasset, NY 11030.

PALITZ, MRS CLARENCE Y
Collector
Mailing Address: 895 Park Ave, New York, NY 10028.

PALL, DR & MRS DAVID B
Collectors
Dr Pall b Ft William, Ont, Apr 2, 14; U S citizen.
Study & Training: Dr Pall, McGill Univ, BSc, 36; Brown Univ, 36-37; McGill Univ, PhD, 39.
Collection: Contemporary art.
Mailing Address: 5 Hickory Hill, Roslyn Estates, NY 11576.

PALLEY, REESE
Art Dealer
b Atlantic City, N J, Jan 26, 22.
Study & Training: London Sch Economics, Eng; New Sch Social Res.
Positions: Owner, Reese Palley Gallery, New York, San Francisco, Atlantic City & Paris, France.

Specialty of Gallery: Avant-garde American art plus porcelain objet d'art.
Publications: Auth, The Boehm experience, Syracuse Univ Press & Grosset & Dunlap, 72.
Mailing Address: 40 Fifth Ave, New York, NY 10011.

PALMER, FRED LOREN
Collector, Patron
b Richmond Hill, N Y, Sept 12, 01.
Study & Training: Hamilton Col, AB.
Positions: Trustee, Am Fedn Arts, 55-63, mem exec comn, 57-63; chmn bd adv, Edward W Root Art Ctr, Hamilton Col, 58-; mem adv coun, State Mus N J, 60-63; trustee, Summit Art Ctr, N J, 70-
Collection: Watercolors by Robert Parker, Kingman, Fredenthal and others; drawings by Baskin, Kuniyoshi, Tam, Shahn, Hirsch, Liberman, Thomas George and others; oils by William Palmer, Rattner, Kerkam, Venard, Meigs and others; prints and etchings by Isabel Bishop, Matisse, Picasso and Beckmann; sculpture by Maldarelli & Hardy.
Mailing Address: 10 Woodcroft Rd, Summit, NJ 07901.

PALMER, HERBERT BEARL
Art Dealer, Art Critic
b New York, N Y, June 23, 15.
Study & Training: New York Univ, Carnegie scholar, 38, Michael Friedsam scholar, 39, Charles Hayden scholar, 40, BA & MA, with A P McMahon, Inst Fine Arts; Univ Southern Calif; Univ Calif, Los Angeles.
Collections Arranged: The Film and Modern Art (designed, arranged & catalogued), Munic Art Gallery, Los Angeles, 69.
Teaching: Lects, Contemporary Art, Collecting and Investing in Art & Photography in the Arts, Univ Calif, Los Angeles Exten.
Positions: Western & contrib ed, Minicam Photog, 46-50; owner-consult, Herbert Palmer Assocs, 50-58; art consult, Kalimar Inc, 58-63; dir, Feigen-Palmer Gallery, 63-68; pvt dealer, 68-
Memberships: Ethnic Arts Coun Los Angeles (bd dirs, 69-71). Col Art Asn Am; Am Asn Mus; Mayor's Radio & TV Comt, St Louis (chmn, 58-63); Int Soc Gen Semantics.
Research: Problems in museum management and development.
Specialty of Gallery: Twentieth century Masters and contemporary art.
Collection: Contemporary art.
Publications: Auth, Art Museums face crisis of identity, Los Angeles Times; auth, Anti-educational influence of pictorial communication, J Sec Educ; auth, Perspective and optical illusions, Design; auth, The company museum, Boston Bus Mag; auth, The mollusk in art, Nature Mag.
Mailing Address: 2252 Mandeville Canyon Rd, Los Angeles, CA 90049.

PALMER, LUCIE MACKAY
Painter, Lecturer
b Saint Louis, Mo, May 23, 13.
Study & Training: Boston Mus Fine Arts Sch; Saint Louis Sch Fine Arts, Wash Univ; Art Stud League New York, with Rapheal Soyer, J N Newell & Robert Brackman.
Exhibitions: One-man shows, Am Mus Natural Hist, 43 & 58-59, Nat Asn Women Artists, 44-46, Rochester Mus Arts & Sci, 59, Chicago Nat Hist Mus, 60 & Calif Acad Sci, San Francisco, 61; plus others.
Teaching: Lectr painting above & below the sea.
Awards: Prize, Nat Asn Women Artists, 44; hon mention, Art League Orange County, 61.
Memberships: Nat Asn Women Artists; Saint Louis Art Guild; Orlando Art Asn; Art League Orange County (corres secy).
Research: Underwater painting.
Mailing Address: 5399 Lindell Blvd, Saint Louis, MO 63108.

PALMER, WILLIAM C
Painter, Educator
b Des Moines, Iowa, Jan 20, 06.
Study & Training: Art Stud League New York; Ecole Beaux-Arts, Fontainebleau, France.
Work in Public Collections: Whitney Mus Am Art & Metrop Mus Art, New York, N Y; Des Moines Art Ctr; Munson-Williams-Proctor Inst, Utica, N Y; Cranbrook Acad Art, Bloomfield Hills, Mich; plus others.
Commissions: Murals, Post Off Bldg, Washington, D C, First Nat City Bank New York, Queens Gen Hosp, Jamaica, N Y & Homestead Savings & Loan Asn, Utica, N Y.
Exhibitions: Corcoran Gallery Art, Washington, D C; Va Mus Fine Arts, Richmond; Carnegie Inst, Pittsburgh, Pa; four one-man shows, Midtown Galleries, New York, 63-69; one-man exhib, Two Decades of Painting, Munson-Williams-Proctor Inst & Cummer Art Gallery, Jacksonville, Fla, 71; plus others.

Teaching: Dir, Munson-Williams-Proctor Inst Sch Art, 41-
Awards: Prize, Nat Acad Design, 46; medal, Audubon Artists, 47; Am Acad Arts & Lett grant, 53; plus others.
Memberships: Nat Acad Design; Architects League; Art Educ Asn; Am Asn Mus; Audubon Artists.
Publications: Contribr, Am Artist Mag.
Mailing Address: Munson-Williams-Proctor Institute School of Art, 310 Genesee St, Utica, NY 13502.

PALMER-PORONER, MARGOT
Art Dealer
b P Q; U S citizen.
Study & Training: Montreal Art Sch, P Q.
Positions: Dir, East Hampton Gallery, New York, N Y.
Mailing Address: 450 W 27th St, Apt 10D, New York, NY 10001.

PANABAKER, FRANK S
Painter
b Hespeler, Ont.
Study & Training: Ont Col Art, Toronto; Grand Cent Sch Art; Art Stud League New York.
Work in Public Collections: Art Gallery Toronto; Art Gallery, Hamilton; Art Gallery, London, Ont.
Exhibitions: Royal Can Acad; Ont Soc Artists; Can Nat Exhib, Toronto; Salmagundi Club, N Y; Can Painting Exhib, London, Eng, 55; plus others.
Positions: Trustee, Nat Gallery Can, 59-66.
Awards: Jessie Dow Prize, Art Asn Montreal, 30.
Memberships: Assoc Royal Can Acad.
Publications: Auth, Reflected lights, 57.
Mailing Address: 375 Wilson St, Ancaster, Ont, Can.

PAONE, PETER
Printmaker, Painter
b Philadelphia, Pa, Oct 2, 36.
Study & Training: Philadelphia Col Art, BFA, 53.
Work in Public Collections: Libr Cong; Philadelphia Mus Art; Mus Mod Art; Fort Worth Art Ctr Mus; Victoria & Albert Mus, London, Eng; plus others.
Exhibitions: Brooklyn Mus, 62 & 64; Butler Inst Am Art, 65; Contemp Art Overseas; N Y World's Fair, 65; Otis Art Inst, Los Angeles, Calif, 64 & 66; plus many others.
Teaching: Instr, Philadelphia Col Art, 59; instr, Pratt Inst, 59-66; instr art hist, Positano Art Sch, Italy, 61.
Awards: Tiffany Found grant, 62 & 64; purchase prize, Syracuse Univ, 64; Guggenheim fel, 65-66; plus others.
Bibliography: Selden Rodman (auth), The insiders, La State Univ Press, 60.
Memberships: Soc Am Graphic Artists.
Publications: Auth & illusr, Paone's zoo, 61, Five insane dolls, 66 & My father, 68; plus others.
Mailing Address: 845 West End Ave, Apt 14F, New York, NY 10025.

PAPASHVILY, GEORGE
Sculptor, Writer
Preferred Media: Stone.
b Kobiantkari, Georgia, Aug 23, 98; U S citizen.
Work in Public Collections: Woodmere Gallery, Philadelphia, Pa; Reading Pub Mus & Art Gallery, Pa.
Commissions: Sculptures, Cascades Conf Ctr, 65 & walkway, 67, Colonial Williamsburg, Va; sculptures, Fox Chase Br Libr, 69 & West Oak Lane Br Libr, 70, Free Libr Philadelphia; sculpture, Baltimore Co Pub Libr, Catonsville Md Br, 70; sculpture, Friends of Beverly Hills Libr for Beverly Hills Pub Libr, Calif, 71.
Exhibitions: One-man shows, Allentown Art Mus, Pa, 51, Lehigh Univ Art Gallery, Bethlehem, Pa, 57, Scripps Col Art Gallery, Claremont, Calif, 66, Reading Pub Mus & Art Gallery, Pa, 70 & William Penn Mem Mus, Harrisburg, Pa, 71.
Bibliography: D Grafly (auth), Sculpture of George Papashvily, Am Artist Mag, 10/55; A Stenius (auth), Beauty in stone (film), Wayne State Univ, 59.
Memberships: Artists Equity Asn; Audubon Artists; Philadelphia Art Alliance (sculpture comt, 52-59).
Publications: Co-auth, Anything can happen, 45, Yes & no stories, 46, Thanks to Noah, 50, Dogs & people, 54 & Russian cooking, 69.
Mailing Address: R D 4, Quakertown, PA 18951.

PAPPAS, MARILYN
Craftsman, Educator
Preferred Media: Collage.
b Brockton, Mass, Jan 1, 31.
Study & Training: Mass Col Art, BSEd; Pa State Univ, MEd.
Work in Public Collections: Objects U S A, Johnson Collection; Viktor Lowenfeld Mem Collection, Pa State Univ; Krannert Art Mus, Univ Ill; Dayton Traveling Mus, Ohio.

Commissions: Wall covering, comn by Lee Nordness, New York, N Y, 67; theater curtain, Temple Israel, Miami, 68; fabric collage, Pan Am Int, 70.
Exhibitions: Young Americans, 62, Craftsmen of the Eastern States, 63, Fabric Collage, 65 & Craftsmen U S A, 66, Mus Contemp Crafts; History of Collage, Kunstgewerbemus, Zurich, Switz, 68.
Teaching: Asst prof art educ, Pa State Univ, 59-64; assoc prof art, Miami-Dade Jr Col, 65-
Awards: Young Americans Award, Mus Contemp Crafts, 62; Fla Craftsmen Ann Awards, 66, 67 & 71; Miami Art Ctr Award, 71 & 72.
Bibliography: Bartlett Hayes (auth), Drawings of the masters: American drawings, Shorewood Publ, 65; Nik Krevitsky (auth), Stitchery: art and craft, Art Horizons, 66; Lee Nordness (auth), Objects U S A, Viking Press, 70.
Memberships: Am Crafts Coun; Fla Craftsmen.
Publications: Contribr, Sch Arts Mag, 62-67.
Mailing Address: 8825 S W 64th Ct, Miami, FL 33156.

PARADISE, PHIL (HERSCHEL)
Painter, Sculptor
Preferred Media: Graphics.
b Ontario, Ore, Aug 26, 05.
Study & Training: Chouinard Art Inst, grad; also with F Tolles Chamberlain, Rico Lebrun & Leon Kroll.
Work in Public Collections: Libr of Cong, Washington, D C; Philadelphia Watercolor Club, Pa; San Diego Fine Arts Soc, Calif.
Exhibitions: Los Angeles Co Mus Art, Calif, 40; San Francisco Art Asn, Calif, 41; Art Inst Chicago, Ill, 43; Carnegie Int, Pittsburgh, Pa, 43-44; Whitney Mus Am Art, New York, N Y, 45.
Teaching: Prof painting, Chouinard Art Inst, 31-40; lectr painting & drawing, Univ Tex, El Paso, 52; lectr painting & drawing, Scripps Col, 56-57.
Positions: Dir fine arts, Chouinard Art Inst, 36-40; art dir & prod designer, Sol Lesser Prod, Paramount Studios, 41-48; dir, Greystone Galleries, 62-
Awards: Purchase award for Goleta, 39 & Dana Medal for Suburban Supper, 43, Philadelphia Watercolor Club; purchase award for Landscape, San Francisco Int Exhib, 41.
Bibliography: Janice Lovos (auth), Guatemala journey, 50 & Phil Paradise serigraphs, 69, Am Artist Mag; Beverly Johnson (auth), Phil Paradise & his works, Los Angeles Times Home Mag, 67.
Memberships: Assoc Nat Acad Design.
Publications: Illusr, Fortune Mag, Westways Mag, True Mag & others, 40-60.
Mailing Address: c/o Greystone Galleries, Greystone Way, P O Box 416, Cambria, CA 93428.

PARDON, EARL B
Craftsman, Educator
b Memphis, Tenn, Sept 6, 26.
Study & Training: Memphis Acad Art, BFA; Syracuse Univ, MFA.
Work in Public Collections: Mus Contemp Crafts; Saint Paul Mus & Sch Art; Lowe Art Ctr, Syracuse; Memphis Acad Art; Skidmore Col.
Commissions: Mus Contemp Crafts & Prudential Life Ins Co, Newark, N J.
Exhibitions: Mus Contemp Crafts; Wichita Craft Biennial; Syracuse Ceramics Nat; Skidmore Col; Schenectady Mus Art; plus others.
Teaching: Lectr painting, jewelry & design, art schs, craftsmens orgns & col alumni groups; prof art & chmn dept, Skidmore Col, presently.
Mailing Address: Dept of Art, Skidmore College, Saratoga Springs, NY 12866.

PARIS, DOROTHY
Painter
Preferred Meida: Oil.
b Boston, Mass, Oct 14, 99.
Study & Training: Columbia Univ Exten, 20; Am Acad Dramatic Art, 21; Acad Grande Chaumiere, Paris, France, 26; Honolulu Acad Art, 45; Univ Hawaii, 45; Art Stud League, 47; also with Hans Hoffman, 48.
Work in Public Collections: Mus Cognac & Mus Cannes, France; Purdue Univ; Butler Inst Am Art; Tufts Col Art Collection; plus many others.
Exhibitions: Mus des Belles Arts, Argentina; Mus Fine Arts, Mexico; Sheldon Swope Mus Art, 64; World's Fair, 65; Nat Asn Women Artists Foreign Exhib, Palazzo Vecchio, Florence, Italy, 72; plus many others.
Teaching: Instr, Ceramic Workshop & Sch, New York, N Y, 39-41.
Positions: Dir, two art galleries, New York, 32-36; Ceramic Coop, Puerto Rico, 36-38; chmn, art benefits, Vis Nurse Serv, New York; Treas, Conf Am Artists, 71.
Awards: Jersey City Mus, 57; Brooklyn Soc Artists, 58; Am Soc Contemp Artists, 70; plus three others.

Memberships: Nat Asn Women Artists (chmn traveling oil exhib, 61-63, 1st v pres, 72-74); Am Soc Contemp Artists (chmn ways & means comt, 64-66, treas, 65-66, 1st v pres, 65-67, pres, 67-69, chmn publicity, 69-72); Int Asn Art (deleg, U S comt & VI cong, 69, treas, Florence flood fund, 67, secy, 69-72); fel, Albert Gallatin Assoc, New York Univ.
Mailing Address: 88 Seventh Ave S, New York, NY 10014.

PARIS, HAROLD PERSICO
Sculptor
Preferred Media: Plastics, Bronze, Graphics.
b Edgemire, Long Island, Aug 16, 25.
Study & Training: Akademie Bildenden Kunst, Munich, Ger; Atelier 17, New York, N Y.
Work in Public Collections: Philadelphia Mus Art, Pa; Mus Mod Art, New York, N Y; Univ Art Mus, Univ Calif, Berkeley, Calif; Milwaukee Art Ctr, Wis; Art Inst Chicago, Ill.
Commissions: Fountain, Southridge, Taubman Industs, Milwaukee, Wis, 72.
Exhibitions: American Sculpture in the Sixties, Los Angeles Co Mus Art, Calif, 67; Human Concern & Personal Torment, Whitney Mus Am Art, New York, N Y, 69; L'Art Vivant aux Etats-Unis, Fondation Maeght, Saint Paul, France, 70; 3ᵉ Salon Int de Galeries-Pilotes, Lausanne, Switz, 70; The California Years, Harold Paris 12 yr Retrospective, Univ Art Mus, Univ Calif, Berkeley, 72.
Teaching: Prof sculpture, Univ Calif, Berkeley, 60-
Awards: Guggenheim fel, 53-55; Creative Arts Inst award, Univ Calif, Berkeley, 67; Linus Pauling Peace Prize, 70.
Bibliography: Peter Selz (auth), The final negation, 3-4/69 & John Fitzgibbons (auth), Paris in Berkeley, 5-6/72, Art in Am; Robert Hughes (auth), Souls in Aspic, Time, 5/22/72.
Mailing Address: 326 Athol Ave, Oakland, CA 94606.

PARIS, JEANNE C
Art Critic, Writer
b Newark, N J.
Study & Training: Newark Sch Fine Arts; Tyler Sch Art, Temple Univ; Columbia Univ; N Y Univ.
Collections Arranged: Organized & directed The Artist of the Month, providing lecturers & demonstrators in all the arts for organizations & schools; organized exhibs of American art for Latin America, Italy & U S A.
Teaching: Lectr art, univs, cols, art leagues, women's clubs, mus asns, radio & NBC TV series, You're a Part of Art.
Positions: Assoc dir, Valente Gallery, New York; art critic, Long Island Press, 63-
Memberships: New York Reporters Asn; Newspaper Women's Club; Friends of Hofstra Mus (bd dirs); Friends of Whitney Mus Am Art; Art Inst Chicago.
Collection: Twentieth century painting & sculpture.
Publications: Auth articles for Weekly Newspaper Chain, Record Pilot & Newsday; auth, Art feature, In: Cue Mag, 7/72.
Mailing Address: 21 Whitney Circle, Glen Cove, NY 11548.

PARIS, LUCILLE M (LUCILLE M BICHLER)
Painter
b Cleveland, Ohio, Apr 8, 28.
Study & Training: Univ Calif, Berkeley, BA, Taussig traveling fel, 50-51, McEnerney grad fel, 52 & MA; Atelier 17, Paris, France.
Work in Public Collections: Butterfield Collection; Newark Mus Collection of Contemp Art.
Exhibitions: Artist-Bay Area Graphics, 64; Monmouth Col, 64, 65, 68 & 72; Univ Minn Art Gallery, 65; one-man show, Aegis Gallery, New York, N Y, 65; N J State Mus, Trenton, 68 & 72; plus others.
Teaching: Prof painting & graphics, Ball State Univ, 55-57; prof art, William Paterson Col, 59-
Awards: Purchase award, Ball State Univ, 56; Bainbridge Award, Argus Gallery, N J, 63; Monmouth Col Award, 65.
Mailing Address: Dept of Art, William Paterson College, Wayne, NJ 07470.

PARISH, BETTY WALDO
Painter, Writer
b Dec 6, 10; U S citizen.
Study & Training: Art Stud League New York, with Kenneth Hays Miller & John Sloan; Acad Julian, Paris, France; Grand Cent Sch, New York; Chicago Acad Fine Arts.
Work in Public Collections: Metrop Mus Art, New York, N Y; Libr of Cong, Washington, D C; Brit Mus, London, Eng; Mus d'Art, Burssels, Belg; Pa Acad Fine Arts, Philadelphia; plus others.
Commissions: Pvt comn, 42.
Exhibitions: Pa Acad Fine Arts Ann, 39-41; Nat Asn Women Artists, 39-45; Libr of Cong; Nat Acad Design, New York; Nat Arts Club, 68-72; plus many others including one-man shows.
Awards: Second prize, Am Artists Prof League, 64; Nat Arts Graphic Prize, 70; David Humprys Mem Prize, Allied Artists Am, 72; plus many others.

Memberships: Audubon Artists (bd dirs, 60-); Allied Artists Am (bd dirs, 65); Nat Asn Women Artists (exec bd, 37-40, bd dirs, 54-56); Art Stud League New York (bd dirs, 38-40); Pen & Brush (chmn oil sect, 43-47, 60-61, bd dirs, 60-63); plus many others.
Publications: Auth, Rome, 58, England again, 59 & Paris, 60.
Mailing Address: 41 Union Square, New York, NY 10003.

PARISH, JEAN E
Painter, Educator
b Oneonta, N Y.
Study & Training: Ohio State Univ, BS; Parsons Sch Design; Art Stud League New York, N Y, with Kunyoshi, Zorach & Sidney Gross; Drake Univ, MFA; Arrowmont Sch Crafts, Univ Tenn; Mass Inst Technol, summer scholar & cert.
Work in Public Collections: Munson-Williams-Proctor Inst, Utica; Fox Hosp, Oneonta.
Commissions: Paramonts and Cloths, United Methodist Church, Oneonta, 71; murals, Goldman Theater, Philadelphia & Ritz Carleton, Montreal.
Exhibitions: Art Today, 67 & Graphics Nat, 69, N Y State Fair; 19th Ann New Eng Exhib, Silvermine Guild Artists, 68; Nat Exhib Contemp Am Painting, Soc Four Arts, Palm Beach, 69; Miss Nat Ann Art Asn, Jackson, 70.
Teaching: Assoc prof design & color, State Univ N Y Col Oneonta, 66-
Positions: Designer, various interior design firms, New York, 50-
Awards: Purchase award, Munson-Williams-Proctor, 67; Juror's Choice Award, 33rd Regional Artists Upper Hudson, 68; first prize drawing, Roberson Ctr Ann, 71.
Memberships: Oneonta Community Art Ctr (gallery chmn, 68); Upper Catskill Community Coun Arts (exec v pres, 72); Col Art Asn Am; Cooperstown Art Asn; Berkshire Art Asn.
Mailing Address: 71 Maple St, Oneonta, NY 13820.

PARKE, WALTER SIMPSON
Painter, Illustrator
Preferred Media: Oils.
b Little Rock, Ark, Dec 30, 09.
Study & Training: Art Inst Chicago; Am Acad Art; also with Wellington Reynolds.
Work in Public Collections: Univ Ill Col Dentistry; Union League Civic & Arts Found; plus others in private collections.
Exhibitions: Union League Club Art Show, Chicago, Ill; Allied Artists Am 52nd Ann, New York, N Y; Munic Art League, Chicago; Am Artists Prof League, New York; Denver Art Mus; plus many other group & one-man shows.
Teaching: Instr portrait painting, Palette & Chisel Acad, 66-
Awards: Five purchase awards, Union League Club Exhib, 55-69; gold medal, Chicago Asn Painters & Sculptors, 57; gold medal, Munic Art League, 71.
Memberships: Brown Co Art Guild; Am Artists Prof League (local pres, 68-); Palette & Chisel Acad; Munic Art League; Oak Park Art League.
Mailing Address: 30 W 225 Argyll Lane, Naperville, IL 60540.

PARKER, ALFRED
Illustrator
b Saint Louis, Mo, Oct 16, 06.
Study & Training: Saint Louis Sch Fine Arts, Wash Univ, 23-28.
Commissions: Creator mother & daughter covers, Ladies Home J, 38-51.
Exhibitions: Exhibs in major cities of U S & Can.
Teaching: Lectr, major cities U S & Can.
Positions: Founder & mem, Famous Artists Schs, Westport, Conn, 47-
Awards: Citation, Wash Univ, 53; award of hon, Philadelphia Art Dirs Club, 62; named to Hall of Fame, Soc Illusr, 65; plus others.
Memberships: Fel Int Inst Arts & Lett; hon mem Soc Illusr; Saint Louis Art Dirs Club; Art Dirs & Artists Club San Francisco; Westport Artists Group (founder & past pres).
Publications: Contribr, illus, In: Ladies Home J, Good Housekeeping, Town & Country, McCalls & Cosmopolitan; plus others.
Mailing Address: 56 Rancho Rd, Carmel Valley, CA 93924.

PARKER, ANN (ANN PARKER NEAL)
Photographer, Printmaker
b London, Eng, Mar 6, 34; U S citizen.
Study & Training: R I Sch Design; Yale Univ, BFA.
Work in Public Collections: Metrop Mus Art, New York, N Y; Libr of Cong, Washington, D C; Smithsonian Inst, Washington, D C; Mus Mod Art, New York; Mus Int Folk Art, Santa Fe, N Mex.
Commissions: Ed of 500 original rubbings (with Avon Neal), 70 & ed of 250 original rubbings (with Avon Neal), 71, Am Heritage.
Exhibitions: Rubbings of New England Gravestones, Am Embassy, London, 65; Fenimore House, Cooperstown, N Y, 66; Know ye the Hour, Hallmark Gallery, New York, 68; Ephemeral Image, Mus

Am Folk Art, 70; Mus Fine Arts, Springfield, Mass, 72; plus many other group & one-man exhibs.
Awards: 50 Best Bks Award, Am Inst Graphic Artists, 57; grant in arts & humanities, Ford Found, 62-63 & 63-64.
Bibliography: M J Gladstone (auth), New art from early American sculpture, Collector's Quart Report, 63 & Pedestrian art, Art in Am, 4/64; Stephen Chodorov (auth), Know ye the hour, produced on Camera Three, CBS-TV, 11/68.
Memberships: Friends of Photog.
Art Interests: Stone rubbings.
Publications: Auth, Eleven international dinners, 56; co-auth, What is American in American art, archaic art of New England gravestones, 63; co-auth, A portfolio of rubbings from early American stone sculpture, 64; photogr, Ephemeral folk figures, Potter, 69; photogr, When shall we three meet again, Am Heritage, Vol 21, No. 3.
Dealer: Gallery of Graphic Arts, 1603 York Ave, New York, NY 10028.
Mailing Address: Thistle Hill, North Brookfield, MA 01535.

PARKER, BILL
Painter
Preferred Media: Acrylics.
b Josephine, Tex, Mar 2, 24.
Study & Training: San Francisco Sch Fine Arts; Acad Grande Chaumiére, Paris, France; also Fred Hocks, La Jolla, Calif & Hans Hoffman, New York, N Y.
Work in Public Collections: Mus Mod Art, Paris; Stedelijk Mus, Amsterdam; Whitney Mus Am Art, New York; Moscow Mus, U S S R; Univ Maine, Orono Art Collection.
Exhibitions: Five American Painters, Stedelijk Mus, Amsterdam, 55; Salon Mai, Paris, 56; Nat Exhib Contemp Am Painting & Sculpture, Univ Ill, 57; Summer Arts Festival Int Exhib, Univ Maine, 63.
Awards: Burhle Prize, Gallery Kaganovitch, Paris, 52.
Bibliography: R Nacenta (auth), School of Paris, New York Graphic Soc, 57; L Durand (auth), article, In: Newsweek, 3/31/58; Y Taillandier (auth), American in Paris, Connaissance Arts, 3/58.
Dealer: Chase Gallery, 31 E 64th St, New York, NY 10021.
Mailing Address: 5 rue Juge, Paris, 15, France.

PARKER, HARRY S, III
Museum Educator
b Saint Petersburg, Fla, Dec 23, 39.
Study & Training: Harvard Univ, BA; Inst Fine Arts, New York Univ, MA.
Teaching: Lectr mus educ.
Positions: Asst to dir, Metrop Mus Art, New York, N Y, 63-67, v dir educ, 68-
Memberships: Am Asn Mus; Am Fedn Arts; Int Coun Mus.
Publications: Contribr, Metrop Mus Art Bull.
Mailing Address: 333 E 43rd St, New York, NY 10017.

PARKER, JAMES
Painter
Preferred Media: Acrylics, Pencil, Pastels.
b Butte, Mont, Oct 20, 33.
Study & Training: Columbia Col, BA, 55; independent study, Spain, 60-62.
Work in Public Collections: Whitney Mus Am Art, New York, N Y; Aldrich Mus, Ridgefield, Conn; Carnegie Inst, Pittsburgh, Pa.
Exhibitions: Salt Lake City Mus Biennial, Utah, 67; Structure of Color, Whitney Mus Am Art, 71; New Acquisitions, 71 & Whitney Ann, 72, Whitney Mus Am Art; Aldrich Mus Show, 72.
Teaching: Instr art hist, drawing, painting & design, Metrop State Col, Denver, Colo, 65-67.
Positions: Part-time mem dean's staff, Columbia Univ Sch Eng, 67-
Publications: Auth, Pop's ancestors, Denver Quart, 67.
Mailing Address: 547 Riverside Dr, New York, NY 10027.

PARKER, JAMES VARNER
Art Administrator, Designer
Preferred Media: Collage.
b Senath, Mo, Aug 27, 25.
Study & Training: Phoenix Community Col, AA; Ariz State Univ, BFA & MA.
Work in Public Collections: Southeast State Teachers Col, Mo; City of Phoenix Civic Art Collection, Ariz; Cent High Sch Art Collection, Mo; Alhambra High Sch Art Collection, Ariz; Heard Mus, Phoenix.
Commissions: Carl Hayden High Sch Stud Body, Phoenix, 60; Mr & Mrs Eugene Pulliam, Phoenix; Dr & Mrs Dean Nichols, Phoenix; Greater Ariz Savings Bank, Tucson, Ariz; Heard Mus.
Exhibitions: Tucson Art Ctr, 66; Phoenix Art Mus, 66; Stanford Res Inst, Palo Alto, Calif, 66; Yuma Art Asn, Ariz, 70; State Teachers Col, Mo, 70.

Collections Arranged: African Art, Heard Mus, 6 & 9/72; Indian Art Collection, 68 & 72.
Teaching: Art instr, Phoenix Col, 68-70; art instr, Glendale Community Col, 71-72.
Positions: Curator educ, Heard Mus, 58-68, curator art, 68-
Awards: Nat Vet Award, Santa Monica Recreation Dept, 53; O'Brien Art Award, Ariz State Fair, 60; UNICEF Award, 68.
Bibliography: Design/crafts/education (film), NAET TV, Ariz State Univ, 60.
Memberships: Ariz Art Asn (secy, 60); Nat Art Educ Asn; Ariz Watercolor Asn (founder & pres, 59); Ariz Art Asn (pres, 60).
Publications: Illusr, Heard Mus, 58 & 71; illusr, The story of Navaho weaving, 61; illusr, Pima basketry, 65; illusr, Women in 1970, 70.
Dealer: Thompson Gallery, 2020 N Central Ave, Phoenix, AZ 86004.
Mailing Address: 2433 W Sweetwater Ave, Phoenix, AZ 85029.

PARKER, RAYMOND
Painter
Preferred Media: Oils.
b Beresford, S Dak, Aug 22, 22.
Study & Training: Univ Iowa, BA, 46, MFA, 48.
Work in Public Collections: Solomon R Guggenheim Mus, Mus Mod Art & Whitney Mus Am Art, New York, N Y; Tate Gallery, London, Eng; Los Angeles Co Mus, Calif.
Exhibitions: One-man exhibs, Walker Art Ctr, Minneapolis, Minn, 50, Kootz Gallery, New York, 60-66, Solomon R Guggenheim Mus, 61, Dayton Art Inst, Ohio, 65 & San Francisco Mus Art, Calif, 67.
Teaching: Prof art, Hunter Col, 55-
Awards: Ford Found Purchase Award, Corcoran Biennial, 63; Nat Coun on the Arts Award, 67; Guggenheim fel, 67.
Bibliography: L Campbell (auth), Parker paints a picture, Art News, 11/62; G Nordland (auth), exhib catalogue, San Francisco Mus Art, 67.
Publications: Contribr, Student, teacher, artist, Col Art J, 53; contribr, Direct painting, spring 58 & Intent painting, fall 58, It is.
Dealer: Fischbach Gallery, 29 W 57th St, New York, NY 10019.
Mailing Address: 101 Prince St, New York, NY 10012.

PARKER, ROBERT ANDREW
Painter
b Norfolk, Va, May 14, 27.
Study & Training: Art Inst Chicago, BAE, 52; Skowhegan Sch Painting & Sculpture; Atelier 17, New York, 52-53.
Work in Public Collections: Los Angeles County Mus; Metrop Mus Art; Morgan Libr, New York, N Y; Mus Mod Art; Whitney Mus Am Art; plus others.
Commissions: Designer sets, William Shuman Opera, Mus Mod Art, 61.
Exhibitions: Brooklyn Mus, 55; Mus Mod Art, 57; Laon Mus, Aisne, France, 56; New Sch Social Res, N Y, 65; Sch Visual Arts, N Y, 65; plus many others.
Awards: Rosenthal Found grant, Nat Inst Arts & Lett, 62; Tamarind Lithography Workshop fel, 67; Guggenheim fel, 69-70; plus others.
Publications: Illusr, hand colored ltd ed poems, Mus Mod Art, 62; illusr poetry, The days of Wilfred Owen (film), 66.
Dealers: Terry Dintenfass, Inc, 18 E 67th St, New York, N Y 10021; Katonah Gallery, 28 Bedford Rd, Katonah, NY 10536.
Mailing Address: Kent Cliffs Rd, Carmel, NY 10512.

PARKER, ROY DANFORD
Painter
Preferred Media: Oils.
b Raymond, Iowa, Feb 23, 82.
Work in Public Collections: Berkshire Mus, Pittsfield, Mass; Minisink Gallery, Wallpack, N J; Grout Hist Mus, Waterloo, Iowa; Everhart Mus, Scranton, Pa; Bridgeport Mus, Conn; plus other pub & pvt collections.
Exhibitions: One-man shows, three times at New York, N Y, 56-57, Berkshire Mus, Pittsfield, 58, Grout Hist Mus, Waterloo, 60, Minisink Gallery, Wallpack, 61 & Hall of Fame, Goshen, N Y, 62.
Awards: Forty six prizes.
Memberships: Middletown Art Group; Pocono Mountain Art Group.
Mailing Address: 88 Highland Ave, Middletown, NY 10940.

PARKHURST, CHARLES
Art Administrator, Writer
b Columbus, Ohio, Jan 23, 13.
Study & Training: Williams Col, BA, 35; Oberlin Col, MA, 38; Princeton Univ, MFA, 41.
Collections Arranged: Good Design is Your Business, Albright-Knox Art Gallery, 47; Gorky & Watercolors by Max Beckmann, Princeton Art Mus, 48; several exhibs, Oberlin Col, 49-62; several exhibs, Baltimore Mus Art, 62-71.
Teaching: Asst prof art & archaeol, Princeton Univ, 47-49; prof hist & appreciation of art & head dept art, Oberlin Col, 49-62.

Positions: Dir, Allen Mem Art Mus, Oberlin Col, 49-62; dir, Baltimore Mus Art, 62-70; asst dir, Nat Gallery Art, 71-
Awards: Chevalier, Legion of Honor, Fr Govt, 47; Ford Found fel, 52-53; Fulbright res fel, Univ Utrecht, 56-57.
Memberships: Col Art Asn Am (pres); Intermus Conserv Asn Bd (co-founder & past pres); Asn Art Mus Dirs (v pres); Am Asn Mus (pres).
Research: Sixteenth and seventeenth century scientific color theories and their relationship to visual arts.
Publications: Co-auth, French Painting from the Chester Dale Collection (catalogue), Nat Gallery Art, 41; auth, Light and color (art treasures of the world, New York and Toronto), Abrams, 55; auth, America's Museums: prices and priorities (the Belmont report), Cult Affairs, 69; auth, A color theory from Prague: Anselm de Boodt, 1609, Allen Mem Art Mus Bull, 71; auth, Red-yellow-blue/a color triad in 17th century painting, Baltimore Mus Art Ann IV, 72.
Mailing Address: 3125 Chain Bridge Rd, Washington, DC 20016.

PARKINSON, ELIZABETH BLISS
Patron, Collector
b New York, N Y, Sept 25, 07.
Positions: Trustee, Mus Mod Art, New York, 39-, pres int coun, 57-65, pres mus, 65-68.
Collection: Paintings and modern art.
Mailing Address: 215 E 72nd St, New York, NY 10021.

PARKS, CHARLES CROPPER
Sculptor
b Va, June 27, 22.
Study & Training: Pa Acad Fine Arts.
Commissions: Joseph with the body of Christ, Hockessin Methodist Church, Del, 68; boy & dogs, H B Du Pont, Wilmington, Del, 69; James F Byrnes, Byrnes Found, Columbia, S C, 70; father & son, Mother A U M P Church, Wilmington, 71; The Family, Philadelphia Redevelop Auth, 72.
Exhibitions: Nat Sculpture Soc Ann, 62-71; Nat Acad Design, 65-71; Allied Artists Am, 67-71.
Positions: Mem adv comt, John F Kennedy Ctr, 68-
Awards: Wemys Found travel grant, Greece, 65; Am Artists Prof League Gold Medal, 70; Nat Sculpture Soc Gold Medal, 71.
Bibliography: Wayne Craven (auth), A biography mid way (catalog), Del Art Mus, 71; Nancy Mohr (auth), The Parks family, Del Today Mag, 72.
Memberships: Fel Nat Sculpture Soc; Allied Artists Am; assoc Nat Acad Design; Del State Arts Coun.
Publications: Contribr, Sights & sounds of Easter, TV film produced by Wilmington Coun Churches, 64.
Mailing Address: R D 1, Box 214, Southwood Rd, Hockessin, DE 19707.

PARKS, CHRISTOPHER CROPPER
Sculptor, Painter
b Wilmington, Del, July 29, 49.
Study & Training: With Charles Parks.
Exhibitions: Nat Acad Design, New York, N Y, 68; Allied Artists Am, New York, 71; Nat Sculpture Soc, 72; plus others.
Awards: Helen Foster Barnett Prize, Nat Acad Design, 68; Lindsey Morris Mem Prize, Allied Artists Am, 71; C Percival Dietsch Prize, Nat Sculpture Soc, 72.
Memberships: Nat Sculpture Soc.
Mailing Address: R D 1, Box 214, Hockessin, DE 19707.

PARKS, ERIC VERNON
Sculptor
Preferred Media: Bronze, Steel.
b Wilmington, Del, Mar 8, 48.
Study & Training: Cornell Univ, BS; Pa Acad Fine Arts; also sculpture with Charles Parks.
Commissions: Bronze portrait, pvt comn, Wilmington, 69; bronze heron, pvt comn, Wilmington, 71; two bronze equestrians, pvt comn, Chadds Ford & Unionville, Pa, 72.
Exhibitions: Allied Artists Ann, New York, N Y, 70 & 71; Nat Acad Design Ann, New York, 72; Nat Sculpture Soc Ann, 72; Three Sculptors of American Realism, Hewlett-Packard Instrument Div Ann, Avondale, Pa, 72.
Awards: Hon mention, Allied Artists Ann, 70; silver medal with patrons prize, Arts Atlantic Nat Exhib, Gloucester, Mass, 72.
Memberships: Brandywine Valley Art Asn (mem planning comt, spring 72).
Mailing Address: Box 528A, R D 1, Chadds Ford, PA 19317.

PARRISH, DAVID BUCHANAN
Painter
Preferred Media: Oils.
b Birmingham, Ala, June 19, 39.
Study & Training: Univ Ala, with Melville Price & Richard Brough, BFA.

Work in Public Collections: Brooks Mem Art Gallery, Memphis, Tenn; Parthenon, Nashville, Tenn; Monsanto Chem Co, Decatur, Ala.
Exhibitions: Documenta & No Documenta Realists, Galerie Gestlo, Hamburg, Ger, 72; Sharp Focus Realism, Sidney Janis Gallery, New York, N Y, 72; Painting & Sculpture Today, Indianapolis Mus Art, Ind, 72; Phases of New Realism, Lowe Mus, Coral Gables, Fla, 72; Realists Revival, Am Fedn Arts Traveling Show, 72-73.
Awards: Award of merit, 23rd Southeastern Ann Exhib, High Mus, Atlanta, Ga, 68; top award, 61st Ann Jury Exhib, Birmingham Mus Art, 69; top award, Mid-South Ann, Brooks Mem Art Gallery, 70.
Dealer: French & Co, Inc, 980 Madison Ave, New York, NY 10021.
Mailing Address: 700 Cleermont Dr, Huntsville, AL 35801.

PARSHALL, DOUGLASS EWELL
Painter
Preferred Media: Oils, Watercolors.
b New York, N Y, Nov 19, 99.
Study & Training: Art Stud League New York; Santa Barbara Sch Arts.
Work in Public Collections: De Young Mus, San Francisco, Calif; Santa Barbara Mus Art, Calif; Richmond Mus Fine Arts, Va; Springfield Art Mus, Mo; Detroit Mus, Mich; plus others.
Exhibitions: Carnegie Inst Mus Art, Pittsburgh, Pa, 24-34; Pa Acad Fine Arts, Philadelphia, 24-41; Chicago Inst World's Fair, Ill, 35; San Diego Expos, Calif, 35; San Francisco World's Fair, 40.
Teaching: Instr portraits, Santa Barbara Art Inst, 67-
Awards: Hallgarten Prize, Nat Acad Design, 24-27; Calif Watercolor Soc purchase awards, 62, 64 & 65; purchase awards, Watercolor U S A, 69.
Memberships: Nat Acad Design; Calif Nat Watercolor Soc; West Coast Watercolor Soc; Soc Western Artists.
Publications: Contribr, Am Artist Mag.
Dealers: Gallery de Silva, 1470 E Valley Rd, Santa Barbara, CA 93108; Challis Galleries, 1390 S Coast Blvd, Laguna Beach, CA 92651.
Mailing Address: 245 Santa Rosa Lane, Santa Barbara, CA 93108.

PARSONS, BETTY BIERNE
Painter, Art Dealer
Preferred Media: Acrylics.
b New York, N Y.
Study & Training: Study with Bourdelle, Paris, France; sculpture with Archipenko & Zadkine; summers in Brittany studying watercolor with Arthur Lindsey.
Work in Public Collections: Montclair Art Mus, N J; Nat Collection Fine Arts, Washington, D C; Whitney Mus Am Art, New York; plus many pvt collections.
Exhibitions: Pa Acad Fine Arts Jury Meeting, 57; Nat Coun Women of the U S, 59; Am Abstract Artists, 62; Soc Four Artists, 64; Artists of Suffolk County, Part II: Abstract Tradition, Heckscher Mus, 70; plus many other group & one-woman exhibs.
Teaching: Creativity sem, Sarah Lawrence Col, spring 72.
Positions: Owner & dir, Betty Parsons Gallery.
Bibliography: E Glazebrook (auth), One of the early birds, The Times (London), 12/16/68; N Gosline (auth), Not a time to worship, The Observer Rev, 11/24/68; Dora Z Meilach (auth), Creating Art from Anything, 68; plus many others.
Specialty of Gallery: Exclusively contemporary art.
Collection: Predominantly contemporary art.
Mailing Address: 24 W 57th St, New York, NY 10019.

PARSONS, KITTY (KITTY PARSONS RECCHIA)
Painter, Writer
Preferred Media: Watercolors.
b Stratford, Conn.
Study & Training: With Richard Recchia; also life classes, Rockport Art Asn.
Work in Public Collections: Syracuse Univ.
Exhibitions: Rockport Art Asn Ann, 31-; Nat Asn Women Artists, 31 & 60; North Shore Arts Asn, Gloucester, Mass, 31-40 & 71; two-man show, Bennington Mus, Vt, 39; one-man show, Berkshire Mus, Pittsfield, Mass, 42.
Awards: Hon mention, Ogunquit Art Ctr, 35; prize, Nat League Am Pen Women, 55 & 56.
Bibliography: Beethold (auth), Kitty Parsons watercolors share sense of beauty, Gloucester Times, 4/6/65; If on some distant day, Prudential Ctr News, 1/15/66; Virginia Bright (auth), Art, mutual respect bind talented Recchias closer, Boston Sunday Globe, 8/30/70.
Memberships: Rockport Art Asn (bd mem, 27-60, chmn arts & exhibs & entertainment, 28-30, chmn publicity, 61-62); North Shore Arts Asn; Nat Asn Women Artists; Nat League Am Pen Women.
Publications: Ed, Artists of the Rockport Art Association, 40.
Mailing Address: Hardscrabble, Rockport, MA 01966.

PARTCH, VIRGIL FRANKLIN, II
Cartoonist, Illustrator
b St Paul Island, Alaska, Oct 17, 16.
Study & Training: Chouinard Art Inst, Los Angeles.
Positions: Illusr, syndicated comic strip & daily panel Big George.
Awards: First prize, Brussels Cartoon Exhib, 64.
Publications: Auth, It's hot in here; auth & illusr, Hanging way over; auth & illusr, VIP tosses a party, S&S, 59; auth & illusr, New faces on the bar room floor, 61; contribr, cartoons, In: Look & True Mags; plus others.
Mailing Address: Box 725, Corona Del Mar, CA 92014.

PARTIN, ROBERT (E)
Painter, Educator
Preferred Media: Oils, Acrylics.
b Los Angeles, Calif, June 22, 27.
Study & Training: Univ Calif, Los Angeles, with Clinton Adams, Gordon Nunes, S Macdonald-Wright & BA, 50; Yale-Norfolk Art Sch, fel & study with Conrad Marca-Relli, 55; Columbia Univ, with Andre Racz, John Heliker, Meyer Shapiro, Paul Tillich & MFA, 56; Tamarind Lithography Workshop, Herron Art Sch, fel & study with Garo Antreasion, 63.
Work in Public Collections: Solomon R Guggenheim Mus Art, New York, N Y; N C Mus Art, Raleigh; Picker Art Gallery, Dana Arts Ctr, Colgate Univ, Hamilton, N Y; Jonson Gallery, Univ N Mex, Albuquerque; Weatherspoon Art Gallery, Univ N C, Greensboro.
Exhibitions: Whitney Mus Am Art Ann, New York, 63; 84th Ann San Francisco Art Inst, San Francisco Mus Art, Calif, 65; California South 7, Fine Arts Gallery San Diego, Calif, 69; San Francisco Art Asn Centennial Exhib, De Young Mus, 71; Viewpoints 5, Dana Arts Ctr, Colgate Univ, Hamilton, 71; plus one other.
Teaching: Assoc prof art, Univ N C, Greensboro, 57-66; vis assoc prof art, Univ N Mex, 63-64; prof art, Calif State Univ, Fullerton, 66-
Awards: Ford Found purchase prize, Whitney Mus Am Art Ann, 63; purchase prize, N C Mus Art Ann, 64 & 65; purchase award, Viewpoint 5, Colgate Univ, 71.
Bibliography: Mortimer Guiney (auth), The art of Robert Partin, In: Vol 1, 63, Analects, Univ N C Press; Van Deren Coke (auth), Robert Partin, The Painter & Photograph, 65; William Wilson (auth), Review of one-man show, Orlando Gallery, Encino, Calif, Art Walk, 11/71.
Dealer: Orlando Gallery, 17037 Ventura Blvd, Encino, CA 91316.
Mailing Address: Dept of Art, California State University, 800 N State College Blvd, Fullerton, CA 92631.

PARTON, NIKE
Painter, Sculptor
Preferred Media: Watercolors.
b New York, N Y, June 23, 22.
Study & Training: Ringling Sch Art, fine art cert; also sculpture with Lesley Posey & painting with Jay Connaway.
Work in Public Collections: Univ Fla; Stetson Univ.
Exhibitions: One-man shows, Southern Vt Art Ctr, 63, Westport Womens Club, Conn, 65, Tampa Prof Artist, 68, Sarasota Art Asn, 69 & Longboat Art Ctr, 72.
Teaching: Instr painting, Art League Manatee Co, 54-62; instr pvt studio, 63-
Awards: Award for Thru the Trees (watercolor), Sarasota Art Asn, 67; award for Manatee (watercolor), DeSoto Comt, 68; award for Ducks (woodcut), Art League Manatee Co, 70.
Memberships: Fla Artist Group; Sarasota Art Asn; Art League of Manatee Co; Longboat Key Art Ctr.
Dealer: Ralph Wells, 1322 Fourth Ave W, Bradenton, FL 33505.
Mailing Address: 840 Edgemere Lane, Sarasota, FL 33581.

PASCAL, DAVID
Painter, Cartoonist
Preferred Media: Inks.
b New York, N Y.
Study & Training: Am Artists Sch.
Exhibitions: Mus Decorative Arts, Paris, France, 67; Mus Arte, São Paulo, Brazil, 70; one-man show, Libr Le Kiosque, Paris, 65.
Teaching: Instr graphic journalism, Sch Visual Arts, 55-58.
Positions: Int rep, Newspaper Comics Coun, New York, 69-; U S rep of Phenix Mag, France, Comics, Italy & RanTanPlan, Belg, 70-
Awards: Dattero d'oro, Salone Internazionale dell Umorismo, Italy, 63; award for illus excellence, 69 & silver t-square, 72, Nat Cartoonists Soc.
Bibliography: Sergio Trinchero (auth), Visit to funland, Sgt Kirk Mag, 68; Rinaldo Traini (auth), Incontro con David Pascal (slide prog), Immagine, 3/15/69; Claude Moliterni (auth), David Pascal, Phenix Mag, 70.
Memberships: Nat Cartoonists Soc (foreign affairs secy, 64-); Mag Cartoonists Guild; Int Comics Orgn (U S A rep, 70-).

Publications: Illusr, The art of inferior decorating, 63; illusr, Fifteen fables of Krylov, 65; auth & illusr, The silly knight, 67; auth, Comics: an American expressionism, Mus Arte, Brazil, 70; ed, Graphis Mag, 72.
Dealer: Graham Gallery, 1014 Madison Ave, New York, NY 10024.
Mailing Address: P O Box 31, Village Station, New York, NY 10014.

PASILIS, FELIX
Painter
b Batavia, Ill, 22.
Study & Training: Am Univ, 46-48, with William H Calfee; Hans Hofmann Sch, 49-52.
Work in Public Collections: Mint Mus, Charlotte, N C; Mass Inst Technol, Cambridge; Tex A&M Univ.
Exhibitions: Richard Brown Baker Collection, Staten Island, 59; Yale Univ, 61; one-man show, RJ Gallery, New York, N Y, 62, Greer Gallery, New York, 63 & Great Jones Gallery, New York, 66; plus other group & one-man shows.
Positions: Co-founder, Hansa Gallery, New York.
Awards: Longview Found grant; Walter K Gutman Found grant.
Mailing Address: 95 E Tenth St, New York, NY 10003.

PASSUNTINO, PETER ZACCARIA
Painter, Sculptor
b Chicago, Ill, Feb 18, 36.
Study & Training: Art Inst Chicago Schs, scholarships, 54-58; Oxbow Sch Painting, summer 58; Inst Art Archeologie, Paris, France, 63; Fulbright fel, 63-64; Guggenheim fel, 71.
Work in Public Collections: Walter P Chrysler Mus, Provincetown, Mass; Norfolk Mus, Va.
Exhibitions: Sherman Gallery, Chicago, 60-61; Zabriskie Gallery, New York, N Y, 62; New Sch Social Res, New York, 70; Sonraed Gallery, New York, 71; Galerie B, Paris, 72.
Positions: Chmn, Momentum, Chicago, 57-58.
Bibliography: Articles, In: Art News, 1/71, Artforum, 2/71, Arts Mag, 1/72 & Humanism, 72.
Dealers: Gallery Marc, Alexandria, VA 22313; Gallery Bienville, 539 Bienville, New Orleans, LA 70130.
Mailing Address: 530 La Guardia Pl, New York, NY 10012.

PATERNOSTO, CESAR PEDRO
Painter
Preferred Media: Acrylic Paint on Canvas.
b La Plata, Buenos Aires, Arg, Nov 29, 31.
Study & Training: Nat Univ La Plata, Sch Fine Arts, 57-59, Inst Philos, 61.
Work in Public Collections: Mus Mod Art, New York, N Y; Nat Fine Arts Mus, Buenos Aires; Plastic Arts Mus, La Plata; Mus Mod Art, Buenos Aires; Albright-Knox Gallery, Buffalo, N Y.
Exhibitions: Latin American Art Since Independence, Yale Univ, Conn, 65; Third Biennial Am Art, Cordoba, Arg, 66; The 1960's, Mus Mod Art, New York, 67; Second Biennial Coltejer, Medellin, Colombia, 70; First Biennial Am Graphic Arts, Cali, Colombia, 71.
Awards: First prize, 3rd Biennial Am Art, Cordoba, 66; acquisition award, 15th Exhib, Mar Del Plata, Arg, 66.
Bibliography: Sam Hunter (auth), The Cordoba bienal, Art Am, 4/67; J R Mellow (auth), New York letter, Art Int, 11/68; K Kline (auth), Reviews, Art News, 1/70.
Dealer: Galerie Denise René, 6 W 57th St, New York, NY 10019 & Galerie Denise René, Hans Mayer, Dusseldorf, W Ger.
Mailing Address: 248 Lafayette St, Fifth Floor, New York, NY 10012.

PATRICK, GENIE H
Painter
Preferred Media: Oils.
b Fayetteville, Ark, Nov 25, 38.
Study & Training: Miss State Col Women, 56-58; Univ Ga, BFA; Univ Ill, Urbana-Champaign, 60-61; Univ Colo, MA, 62.
Exhibitions: Mid-South Ann, Memphis, Tenn, 59, 60 & 64; Walker Ann, Minneapolis, Minn, 66; Iowa Artist Exhib, Des Moines Art Ctr, 66, 70 & 71; Invitational Drawing Exhib, Benedicta Arts Ctr Gallery, Saint Joseph, Minn, 70; two-man exhib, Drawing & Painting, Coe Col Galleries, Cedar Rapids, Iowa, 71.
Teaching: Instr art, Northeast Miss Jr Col, Booneville, 62-64; instr art, Radford Col, Va, 64-65; instr children's art classes, Cedar Rapids Art Ctr, 65-70.
Positions: Fel-in-residence, Huntington Hartford Found, Pacific Palisades, Calif, summer 64.
Mailing Address: 1190 E Court St, Iowa City, IA 52240.

PATRICK, JOSEPH ALEXANDER
Painter, Educator
Preferred Media: Oils.
b Chester, S C, Feb 10, 38.
Study & Training: Univ Ga, BFA, 60; Univ Colo, Boulder, MFA, 62.

Work in Public Collections: Univ Colo, Boulder; Univ Nebr, Omaha; Davenport Munic Art Gallery & Coe Col, Cedar Rapids, Iowa; Fairfield Co Hist Soc, Winnsboro, S C; State Univ N Y Col Plattsburgh.

Exhibitions: Midwest Biennial, Joslyn Art Mus, Omaha, 65; Nat Small Painting Show, Univ Nebr, Omaha, 66; Container Corp Sixth Ann Fine Arts Exhib, Rock Island, Ill, 67; Dedication Exhib, Fine Arts Ctr, State Univ N Y Col Plattsburgh, 70; Drawing Exhib, Benedicta Arts Ctr Gallery, St Joseph, Minn, 71.

Teaching: Asst art, Univ Colo, Boulder, 60-62, instr drawing & painting, 61-62; instr drawing & painting & head dept, Northeast Miss Jr Col, Booneville, 62-64; instr drawing & painting, Radford Col, 64-65; instr drawing & painting, Univ Iowa, 65-68, asst prof drawing & painting, 68-71, assoc prof drawing, 71-

Positions: Mus asst, Univ Ga Mus Art, Athens, 58-60; instr art, Davenport Art Ctr, Iowa, 68, 69 & 72; instr art, Keokuk Art Asn, Iowa, 72.

Awards: Residence fel, Huntington Hartford Found, 64; summer faculty fel, 69 & faculty grant, 73, Univ Iowa Found.

Memberships: Mid-Am Art Asn; Col Art Asn Am.

Mailing Address: 1190 E Court St, Iowa City, IA 52240.

PATTERSON, GEORGE W PATRICK, see KEMOHA.

PATTERSON, PATTY (MRS FRANK GRASS)
Painter, Craftsman
b Oklahoma City, Okla, Jan 16, 09.
Study & Training: Univ Okla, BFA; Ecole Beaux-Arts, Fontainebleau, France; Taos Sch Art; Art Stud League New York; Okla State Univ; Univ Okla; also with Emil Bisttram, Robert E Woods, Milford Zarnes, George Post & Edgar Whitney.
Exhibitions: One-man show, YWCA, Oklahoma City; Mass Inst Technol; Okla Art Asn, 32-58; Tulsa Art Asn; Oklahoma City Art Ctr, 62-64; plus others.
Teaching: Lectr art trends, art & geneal, clubs & art orgns; instr art, Oklahoma City Schs & Oklahoma City Univ, 34-
Positions: V pres & secy, Okla Art Asn.
Awards: Medal, McDowell Club, 40 & 44; prize, Okla Art League, 42.
Memberships: Okla Art Asn; Okla Art League; Okla Writers; Okla Conserv Artists; Southwest Watercolor Soc; plus others.
Mailing Address: 2506 N W 66th St, Oklahoma City, OK 73116.

PATTISON, ABBOTT
Sculptor, Painter
b Chicago, Ill, May 15, 16.
Study & Training: Yale Col, BA, 37, Yale Sch Fine Arts, BFA, 39.
Work in Public Collections: Whitney Mus Am Art; Israel State Mus, Jerusalem; San Francisco Mus; Buckingham Palace, London, Eng; Art Inst Chicago; plus others.
Commissions: Sculpture, Cent Nat Bank, Cleveland, Mayo Clin, St Thomas Acad, Saint Paul, Minn, New Trier W High Sch, Chicago, Ill & U S State Dept; plus others.
Exhibitions: Art Inst Chicago, 40-69; Metrop Mus Art, 51 & 52; four shows, Whitney Mus Am Art, 53-59; one-man shows, Holbrook Mus, Univ Ga, 54 & Sculpture Ctr, N Y, 56; plus many other group & one-man shows.
Teaching: Instr, Art Inst Chicago, 46-52; sculptor-in-residence, Univ Ga, 54; instr, Skowhegan Sch Art, 55-56.
Awards: First Logan Prize, Art Inst Chicago, 42; prize, Metrop Mus Art, New York, 50; prize, Bundy Mus, Vt, 67.
Memberships: Chicago Art Club.
Mailing Address: 334 Woodland Ave, Winnetka, IL 60093.

PAUL, BERNARD H
Craftsman
b Baltimore, Md, Apr 22, 07.
Study & Training: Md Inst, Baltimore.
Commissions: Christmas shows, Colonial Williamsburg, 56-57 & 60-; marionettes for opera, Peabody Conservatory Music, 57; miniature model sets, Hutzler's Dept Store's 100th Anniversary, 58; puppets used by U S Dept Health, Educ & Welfare for series of motion pictures for Social Security TV spots.
Teaching: Instr puppetry, Md Inst Col Art, 29-47 & 58-; puppet shows, Hutzler's Br Store, 58-
Positions: Dir TV prog, Paul's Puppets, WBAL-TV, Baltimore, 48-57, WMAR-TV, 57-58.
Awards: Prizes, Md Inst, 29, 33 & 37.
Mailing Address: 414 Hawthorne Rd, Linthicum Heights, MD 21091.

PAUL, WILLIAM D, JR
Museum Director, Painter
b Wadley, Ga, Sept 26, 34.
Study & Training: Atlanta Art Inst, BFA; Univ Ga, AB & MFA; Emory Univ; Ga State Col; Univ Rome, Italy.

Work in Public Collections: General Mills, Inc, Minneapolis, Minn; Hallmark Cards, Kansas City, Mo; Little Rock Art Ctr, Ark; Ga Mus Art, Atlanta; Univ Ga, Athens; plus others.
Exhibitions: Southeastern Ann, Atlanta; Va Intermont Col, Bristol; Birmingham Ann, Ala; Corcoran Gallery Art, Washington, D C; Art of Two Cities, Nat Traveling Exhib, Am Fedn Arts; plus many others.
Collections Arranged: Sixty small original exhibs, Charlotte Crosby Kemper Gallery, Kansas City Art Inst, 61-65; Art of Two Cities, Am Fedn Arts Traveling Exhib, 65; The Visual Assault, 67, Drawings by Richard Diebenkorn, Selections: The Downtown Gallery, Drawing and Watercolors by Raphael Soyer, Recent Collages by Samuel Adler, Twentieth Anniversary Exhibition & Art of Ancient Peru, The Paul Clifford Collection, Ga Mus Art; American Painting: the 1940's, 68; American Painting, the 1950's, 68; American Painting: the 1960's, 69; Philip Pearlstein, Retrospective Exhibition, 70.
Teaching: Instr art & art hist, Kansas City Art Inst, Park Col & Univ Ga.
Positions: Dir exhibs & cur study collections, Kansas City Art Inst, 61-65; cur, Ga Mus Art, 67-69; dir, Ga Mus Art, 69-
Awards: Macy's Ann, Kansas City, 59, 61, 63 & 64; Atlanta Paper Co Ann, 61; Hallmark Award, Mid-Am Ann, 62; plus others.
Memberships: Am Fedn Arts (trustee); Col Art Asn; Am Asn Mus.
Mailing Address: Georgia Museum of Art, University of Georgia, Athens, GA 30601.

PAULIN, RICHARD CALKINS
Museum Director, Craftsman
b Chicago, Ill, Oct 25, 28.
Study & Training: DePauw Univ, BA; Univ Denver, MA; Inst Fine Arts, New York Univ; also in Guadalajara, Mex.
Exhibitions: Univ Ill, 60; Rockford Art Asn, 61; Beloit Col, 61-63 & 65; two-man show, Nat Col Educ, Evanston, Ill, 64.
Collections Arranged: Teachers Who Paint, 59; Chicago Painters, 60; Six Chicago Painters, 61; Picasso Preview, 62; George Rouault-His Aqua Tints and Wood Engravings, 63; Collectors Showcase, 64; 30 Contemporary Living American Painters, 64; First National Invitational Painting Exhibition: Fifty States of Art, 65; Swedish Handcraft, 61.
Teaching: Instr arts & crafts, Roosevelt Jr High Sch, Rockford, Ill; former instr basic & intermediate art courses, Rockford Art Asn.
Positions: Former dir, Harry & Della Burpee Art Gallery, Rockford, Ill; asst dir art educ, Mus Art, Univ Ore, presently.
Awards: Canfield Award, Rockford Art Asn, 61.
Memberships: Nat Educ Asn; Nat Coun Art Educ; Mus Dirs Asn N Am; Western Art Asn; Mid-Western Mus Dirs Asn; plus others.
Mailing Address: Museum of Art, University of Oregon, Eugene, OR 97403.

PAYSON, MR & MRS CHARLES S
Collectors
Mr Payson, b Portland, Maine, Oct 16, 98.
Study & Training: Mr Payson, Yale Univ, grad, 21; Harvard Univ, LLB, 24.
Collection: Contemporary art.
Mailing Address: Manhasset, NY 11030.

PEABODY, AMELIA
Sculptor
Preferred Media: Stone, Bronze, Ceramics.
b Marblehead, Mass, July 3, 90.
Study & Training: Boston Mus Fine Arts Sch, with Charles Grafly; hon DFA, Northeastern Univ.
Work in Public Collections: End of an Era (marble), Mus Fine Arts, Boston, Mass; Boy with Cat (stone), Children's Med Ctr, Boston; plastic fox, Audubon Soc Laughing Brook Reservation.
Commissions: Victory Medal, Joslin Clin, Boston; baptismal font, church in Oxford, Mass; portrait plaque of Dr Hsein Wu, Harvard Med Sch, Cambridge, Mass; Woodchucks & Pheasants, cast stone for entrance gate of Groton Mem Park, Mass; granite setter in animal graveyard for Mrs Frank C Paine, Wayland, Mass.
Exhibitions: New York World's Fair, N Y, two yrs; Whitney Mus Am Art, New York, 40; Carnegie Inst, 41; Nat Asn Women Artists, 53.
Teaching: Chmn arts & skills, Am Red Cross, Boston.
Awards: Mrs Oakleigh Thorne Medal, Garden Club Am.
Memberships: Guild Boston Artists; Nat Asn Women Artists; Nat Sculpture Soc; New England Sculptors' Asn; Copley Soc.
Dealer: Guild Boston Artists, 162 Newbury St, Boston, MA 02116.
Mailing Address: 120 Commonwealth Ave, Boston, MA 02116.

PEAKE, CHANNING
Painter
b Marshall, Colo, Oct 24, 10.
Study & Training: Calif Col Arts & Crafts, 28; Santa Barbara Sch Art, 29-31; Art Stud League New York, with Rico Lebrun, 35-36.

Work in Public Collections: Santa Barbara Mus Art.
Commissions: Murals (with Louis Rubenstein), Germanic Mus, Harvard Univ, 36 (with Rico Lebrun), Pa Sta, New York, N Y, 36-38 (with Howard Warshaw), Santa Barbara Pub Libr, 58.
Exhibitions: Pa Acad Fine Arts; Univ Ill, 53 & 55; three-man show, Santa Barbara Mus Art, 53 & 56; Colorado Springs Fine Arts Ctr, Colo; Los Angeles Co Mus Art; plus others.
Positions: Founder, Santa Barbara Mus Art.
Mailing Address: c/o Felix Landau Gallery, 706 N La Cienega Blvd, Los Angeles, CA 90069.

PEARLMAN, HENRY
Collector
b New York, N Y, Mar 25, 95.
Memberships: Art Collectors Club.
Collection: Impressionist and post-impressionist paintings, including works by Cezanne, Van Gogh, Lautrec, Modigliani, Soutine and Lipchitz.
Mailing Address: 993 Park Ave, New York, NY 10028.

PEARLSTEIN, PHILIP
Painter, Educator
b Pittsburgh, Pa, May 24, 24.
Study & Training: Carnegie Inst, with Sam Rosenberg, Robert Lepper & Balcomb Greene, BFA, 49; Inst Fine Arts, New York Univ, MA, 55.
Work in Public Collections: Whitney Mus Am Art; New York Univ, Milwaukee Art Ctr, Wis; Hirshhorn Collection, James Michener Found; Art Inst Chicago; also in pvt collections.
Exhibitions: Eight ann group shows, 55-72 & 22 Realists, 70, Whitney Mus Am Art; Univ Ill, 65, 67 & 69; Vassar Col, 68; Smithsonian, circulated Latin Am, 68-70; Aspects of A New Realism, Milwaukee Art Ctr, 69; plus many other group & one-man shows.
Teaching: Instr, Pratt Inst, 59-63; from asst prof to prof art, Brooklyn Col, 63-
Awards: Fulbright fel to Italy, 58-59; Nat Endowment Arts grant, 69; Guggenheim fel, 71 & 72.
Bibliography: Allen S Weller (auth), The joys and sorrows of recent American art, Univ Ill Press, 68; Udo Kultermann (auth), The new painting, 69 & Radical realism, 72, Praeger; Ellen Schwartz (auth), A conversation with Philip Pearlstein, Art in Am, 9-10/71; plus others.
Dealer: Allan Frumkin Gallery, 41 E 57th St, New York, NY 10022.
Mailing Address: 163 W 88th St, New York, NY 10024.

PEARSON, HENRY C
Painter
Preferred Media: Acrylics, Oils.
b Kinston, N C, Oct 8, 14.
Study & Training: Univ N C, BA, 35; Yale Univ, MFA, 38; Art Stud League New York, 53-56.
Work in Public Collections: Mus Mod Art, Metrop Mus Art & Whitney Mus Am Art, New York, N Y; Albright-Knox Art Gallery, Buffalo, N Y; N C Mus Art, Raleigh.
Commissions: World University Service (poster), List Art Posters, 65; Sixth New York Film Festival—Lincoln Center (poster), List Art Posters, 68; Five Psalms (book), Women's Comt, Brandeis Univ, 69.
Exhibitions: The Responsive Eye, Mus Mod Art, New York, 65; 29th Biennial Exhib, Corcoran Gallery Art, Washington, D C, 65; Contemporary Selections, Birmingham Mus Art, Ala, 71; Drawings U S A 71, Minn Mus Art, Saint Paul, 71; Color Painting, Amherst Col, Mass, 72.
Teaching: Instr painting, New Sch Social Res, at present; gen critic, Pa Acad Fine Arts.
Awards: Tamarind Lithography Workshop, Ford Found, 64; Kreeger Purchase Prize, Corcoran Gallery Art, 65; J Henry Scheidt Award, Pa Acad Fine Arts, 69.
Bibliography: Lippard (auth), Henry Pearson, Art Int, 65.
Memberships: Am Abstract Artists.
Dealer: Betty Parsons Gallery, 24 W 57th St, New York, NY 10019.
Mailing Address: 58 W 58th St, New York, NY 10019.

PEARSON, JAMES EUGENE
Instructor, Painter
b Woodstock, Ill, Dec 12, 39.
Study & Training: Northern Ill Univ, BS (educ), 61, MS (educ), MFA, 64; Tyler Sch Art, Temple Univ; Ithaca Col.
Work in Public Collections: Northern Ill Univ, DeKalb; Palais des Beaux Arts, Charleroi, Belg; Taft Field Campus, Northern Ill Univ, Oregon, Ill; Dixon State Sch, Ill; Sch Dist 15, McHenry, Ill.
Commissions: Lorado Taft (bronze relief plaque), Taft Field Campus, Northern Ill Univ, 67; Vicki Unis (oil portrait), Sarasota, Fla, 69; Mae Stinespring (oil portrait), comn by Harry Stine-

spring, McHenry, Ill, 69; portraits in oils of Mr & Mrs Francis Hightower & Mrs Nancy Langdon, Algonquin, Ill, 71.
Exhibitions: 21st Am Drawing Biennial, Norfolk Mus Arts & Sci, Va, 65; 54th Ann Exhib, Art Asn Newport, R I, 65; 2 eme Salon Int de Charleroi, Palais des Beaux Arts, Belg, 69; Fifth Int Grand Prix Painting & Etching, Palais de la Scala, Monte Carlo, Monaco, 69; 29th Ill Invitational Exhib, Ill State Mus, Springfield, 71.
Teaching: Instr art, Woodstock High Sch, Ill, 61-; instr art, McHenry Co Col, Crystal Lake, Ill, 70-
Awards: Best of show award, William Boyd Andrews, 61; purchase prize, Mr & Mrs Allen Leibsohn, 63; Mary E Just art award contest, Waukegan News-Sun, 69.
Bibliography: F Tramier (auth), James E Pearson, La Rev Mod, 65; Sally Wagner (auth), Volume tells McHenry history, Chicago Tribune, 69.
Memberships: Col Art Asn Am; Ill Art Educ Asn; Ill Craftsmen's Coun; Am Fedn Arts; Centro Studi E Scambi Internazionali, Rome.
Publications: Illusr, McHenry County 1832-1968, 68; auth, A dream never realized, 69 & auth, Eagle's nest colony, 70, Outdoor Ill; auth, Perspective: outdoor education from an artists point of view, J Outdoor Educ, 71; illusr, The rectangle, 72.
Mailing Address: 5117 Barnard Mill Rd, Ringwood, IL 60072.

PEARSON, JOHN
Painter, Instructor
b Boroughbridge, Yorkshire, Eng, Jan 31, 40.
Study & Training: Harrogate Col Art, Yorkshire, nat dipl design, 60; Royal Acad Schs, London, Eng, cert, 63, with Ernst Geitlinger; Northern Ill Univ, MFA, 66.
Work in Public Collections: Mus Mod Art, New York, N Y; Bochumer Mus, Stuttgart, W Ger; Pasadena Mus Fine Art, Calif; Kleye Collection, Doertmund, W Ger; Kunstverien, Hannover, W Ger.
Exhibitions: Four Young Artists, Inst Contemp Art, London, 63; one-man shows, Galerie Muller, Stuttgart, 64, Gray Gallery, Chicago, Ill, 67-68, Paley & Lowe Gallery, New York, 71 & Pollock Gallery, Toronto, Can, 71.
Teaching: Instr painting, Univ N Mex, 66-68; assoc prof painting & head dept, N S Col Art & Design, Halifax, 68-70; int artist-in-residence, Cleveland Inst Art, Ohio, 70-72; assoc prof art, Oberlin Col, 72-
Awards: Austin Abbey traveling fel, Brit Arts Coun, 63; Can Coun grant, 70; first prize for painting, Cleveland Mus Art, 72.
Bibliography: Jock Wittet (auth), Editorial, Studio Int, 3/68; Harry Bouras (auth), John Pearson, Chicago Omnibus, 5/68; Lizzie Borden (auth), John Pearson, Artforum, 2/72.
Publications: Contribr, Art: the measure of man, Directions 66/67, 66; contribr, article, In: Mus Educ J, 66.
Dealer: Paley & Lowe Gallery, 59 Wooster St, New York, NY 10012.
Mailing Address: Dept Art, Oberlin Col, Oberlin, OH 44074.

PEARSON, LOUIS O
Sculptor
Preferred Media: Stainless Steel.
b Wallace, Idaho, Apr 28, 25.
Work in Public Collections: Storm King Art Ctr, Mountainville, N Y; Univ N Mex, Albuquerque.
Exhibitions: Crocker Art Gallery, Sacramento, Calif, 66, Joslyn Art Mus, Omaha, Nebr, 66; Northern Ariz Univ Art Gallery, 66.
Mailing Address: 224 12th St, San Francisco, CA 94103.

PEARSON, MARGUERITE STUBER
Painter
Preferred Media: Oils.
b Philadelphia, Pa.
Study & Training: Sch Mus Fine Arts, Boston, Mass, figure painting & portraiture with William James & Frederick Bosley, landscape with Aldro T Hibbard & Harry Leith-Ross, design with Henry Hunt Clark & Howard Giles & illus with Harold N Anderson & Chase Emerson.
Work in Public Collections: Springville Art Mus, Utah; Beach Mem Art Mus, Storrs, Conn; Case Inst Technol, Cleveland, Ohio; Salem Ct House Portrait Collection, Mass; Somerville City Hall Portrait Collection, Mass.
Exhibitions: Nat Acad Design, New York, N Y, 34; Corcoran Biennial Exhib, Washington, D C, 35; Pa Acad Fine Arts Ann, Philadelphia, 36; Allied Artists Am, New York, 71; Jordan Marsh Co Ann Exhib of New Eng Artists, Boston, 72.
Awards: Gold medal for best oil painting, Am Artists Prof League, New York, 61; award for best painting in any medium, Catharine Lorillard Wolfe Art Club, Coun Am Artists Soc, 70; Mem prize award, North Shore Arts Asn, Gloucester, Mass, 72.
Memberships: Allied Artists Am; Guild Boston Artists; North Shore Arts Asn; Rockport Art Asn; Acad Artists Soc.
Mailing Address: 47 Marmion Way, Rockport, MA 01966.

PEASE, DAVID G
Painter, Educator
Preferred Media: Acrylics.
b Bloomington, Ill, June 2, 32.
Study & Training: Univ Wis-Madison, BS, 54, MS, 55, MFA, 58.
Work in Public Collections: Whitney Mus Am Art, New York, N Y; Philadelphia Mus Art, Pa; Pa Acad Fine Arts, Philadelphia; Power Gallery, Univ Sydney, Australia; Des Moines Art Ctr, Iowa.
Exhibitions: Carnegie Int Exhib Painting & Sculpture, Carnegie Inst, Pittsburgh, 61; Corcoran Biennial Painting, Corcoran Gallery Art, Washington, D C, 61 & 63; Whitney Ann Exhib Painting, Whitney Mus Am Art, New York, 63; Nat Drawing Exhib, San Francisco Mus Art, Calif, 69; Drawings U S A, Minn Mus Art, Saint Paul, 71.
Teaching: Prof painting & chmn dept painting & sculpture, Tyler Sch Art, 60-
Awards: William A Clark Award, Corcoran Gallery Art, 63; Guggenheim fel, 65-66; Childe Hassam Fund purchase award, Am Acad Arts & Lett, 70.
Memberships: Col Art Asn Am.
Dealer: Terry Dintenfass Inc, 18 E 67th St, New York, NY 10021.
Mailing Address: 611 65th Ave, Philadelphia, PA 19126.

PEASE, ROLAND FOLSOM, JR
Art Critic, Collector
b Boston, Mass, Dec 11, 21.
Study & Training: Dartmouth Col; Columbia Univ, BS.
Positions: Reporter, United Press Int, 52-55; exec ed, Art Voices, 52, assoc ed, 62-63, contributing ed, 63; managing ed, Harry N Abrams, Inc, 63-64; mem, Denhard & Stewart, Inc, New York, N Y.
Collection: Works by Grace Hartigan, Larry Rivers, Robert Goodnough, Fairfield Porter, Jane Wilson, Sherman Drexler, Red Grooms, Gorchov, Jane Freilicher, George L K Morris and Diego Rivera.
Publications: Contribr, art criticisms, In: Art Int, Metro, Pictures on Exhib & Auth Guild Bull.
Mailing Address: 11 E 71st St, New York, NY 10021.

PECHE, DALE C
Painter
Preferred Media: Gouache.
b Long Beach, Calif, Nov 28, 28.
Study & Training: Long Beach City Col; Art Ctr Col Design of Los Angeles; also with Reckless, Tyler, Legakes, Feitelson, Polifka, Williamaoski & Kramer.
Commissions: Paintings of San Francisco & Fishermans Wharf, Lezius Hiles Collection, Cleveland, Ohio, 72.
Exhibitions: Indust Graphics Int, 56 & 71; New York Art Dir Show, 62; Los Angeles Art Dirs Show, 62 & 70; West Coast American Realists, Muckenthaler Cult Ctr, Fullerton, Calif, 72; one-man show, Challis Galleries, Laguna Beach, Calif, 72.
Positions: Graphic designer, N Am Aviation, Inc, 56-60; art dir-owner, Graphic Directions, 60-68; art dir, Publ Serv Ltd, 68-71; art dir, Design Vista Inc, 71-
Awards: 25 awards, Indust Graphics Int, 58-71; award, New York Art Dirs Show, 62; 2 awards, Los Angeles Art Dirs Show, 63 & 70.
Mailing Address: c/o Challis Galleries, 1390 S Coast Hwy, Laguna Beach, CA 92651.

PECK, JAMES EDWARD
Painter, Designer
Preferred Media: Watercolors, Enamels, Woods.
b Pittsburgh, Pa, Nov 07, 07.
Study & Training: Cleveland Inst Art, cert.
Work in Public Collections: Cleveland Mus Art, Ohio; U S Govt, Carville, La; Dayton Art Inst, Ohio; Am Acad Arts & Lett, New York, N Y; Seattle Art Mus, Wash.
Exhibitions: Cleveland Mus Art May Shows, 33-49; Am Watercolor Soc, New York; Seattle Art Mus Northwest Ann; Pepsi-Cola Drawing & Watercolor Exhib, Metrop Mus Art, New York.
Teaching: Head dept art, Cornish Sch, Seattle, 47-52; Instr painting & graphic design, Burnley Sch Art, Seattle, 66-
Positions: Illusr, Fawn Art Studios, Cleveland, 36-46; art dir, Miller, McKay, Hoeck & Hartung, Seattle, 54-60; graphic designer, 60-66; graphic designer, Boeing Co, 66-70.
Awards: Awards for watercolors, May Show, Cleveland Mus Art, 37-49; awards for watercolors, Dayton Art Inst, 42-45; award for painting, Guggenheim Found, 42 & 46.
Memberships: Puget Sound Group Northwest Painters (past pres); Art Studio Owners Asn.
Publications: Illusr, Ford Times Mag.
Mailing Address: 1917 Broadway E, Seattle, WA 98102.

PEDERSON, MOLLY FAY
Painter, Sculptor
Preferred Media: Oils, Acrylics, Brass, Copper.
b Waco, Tex, Apr 26, 41.
Study & Training: Pvt study with Carl Cogar, Las Cruces, New Mex, James Woodruff, Houston, Mary Berry, McKinney, Tex, Ramon Froman, Dallas, Tex, Ken Gore, Mass, Stewart Matthews, Arnold Vail & H E Fain, Dallas.
Exhibitions: Richardson Civic Arts Soc Ann, Tex, 68-70; Artists Market, Dallas, 68-72; Bond's Alley Art & Craft Show, Hillsboro, Tex, 69-70; Texas Fine Arts Asn Exhib, Dallas, 70; Temple Emanu-El Ann Brotherhood Art Festival, Dallas, 70-72.
Teaching: Instr oil painting, Richardson Recreation Ctr, 72; art instr, Air Am Sch, Udorn, Thailand, 72-73.
Positions: Com artist, Goldstein-Migel Co, Waco, Tex, 58-59; layout artist, Sun Printing Co, El Paso, Tex, 60-64.
Awards: Award for Manarola, Texans Asn Art Show, 68; Richardson Community Fair Award, 69; award for black & white abstract, Bond's Alley Arts & Crafts Show, 70.
Bibliography: Articles, In: Dallas Morning News, 4/5/69, Waco Citizen, 5/30/70 & Richardson Daily News, 12/3/71.
Memberships: Texas Fine Arts Asn; Richardson Civic Arts Soc (v pres, secy, treas, 68-70); Arlington 200 (bd mem, show chmn); Texas Starving Artists.
Mailing Address: 1228 Briarcove, Richardson, TX 75080.

PEELER, RICHARD
Potter, Sculptor
Preferred Media: Ceramics.
b Indianapolis, Ind, Aug 8, 26.
Study & Training: De Pauw Univ, AB, 49; Ind Univ, MA, 60.
Work in Public Collections: Int Minerals, Skokie, Ill; Armstrong Cork Co; Ind State Univ; Taylor Univ; Ind Cent Univ; plus others.
Commissions: Sculpture in stone, Gobin Methodist Church, Greencastle, Ind, 63; portrait busts in stone, Pres & Mrs William Kerstetter, Greencastle, 65; sculpture in fiberglass & epoxy, First Christian Church, Greencastle, 68; portrait bust in ceramic, Harrison Johnson, Cleveland, Ohio, 71; ceramic mural, De Pauw Univ, 72; plus one other.
Exhibitions: Syracuse Nat Ceramic Show, 64; Ceramics U S A 1966, Int Minerals Corp, 66; one-man shows, Ind Cent Col, Goshen Col & Univ Evansville.
Teaching: Instr art, Indianapolis Pub Schs, 51-58; assoc prof art, De Pauw Univ, 58-72; vis lectr, Kyoto City Col Fine Arts, Japan, 66.
Memberships: Nat Coun Educ Ceramic Arts (v pres & dir, 66-70, pres, 70-71); Ind Art Educ Asn; Ind Artist Craftsmen.
Publications: Auth, 13 articles, In: Ceramics Monthly Mag, 62-65; film maker 8 films on ceramic art, McGraw, 66-68.
Mailing Address: Rte 1, Box 320, Reelsville, IN 46171.

PEERS, GORDON FRANKLIN
Painter, Educator
b Easton, Pa, Mar 17, 09.
Study & Training: R I Sch Design; Art Stud League New York; Beaux-Arts Inst Design; also with John R Frazier.
Work in Public Collections: R I Sch Design.
Exhibitions: Provincetown Art Asn, 58; Dept Interior, Washington, D C; Univ Ill; Rockford Art Asn, Ill; Boston Art Festival, 58; plus many others.
Teaching: Head dept painting, R I Sch Design, 34-36 & 38-69, prof painting & chmn div fine arts, 69-
Positions: Chief critic, R I Sch Design Europ Hons Prog, Rome, Italy, 61-62.
Awards: Prizes, Boston Art Festival, 55 & Newport Art Asn, 58.
Mailing Address: 65 Halsey St, Providence, RI 02906.

PEHAP, ERICH K
Painter, Graphic Artist
b Viljandi, Estonia, Apr 10, 12.
Study & Training: State Sch Arts & Handicrafts, Tallinn, Estonia, 32-33; Estonia Acad Fine Arts, Tartu, grad painting, 37, grad graphic art, 39; Didactic-Methodical Teaching Col, Tartu Univ, grad, 38; Montreal Inst Mech Draughting, dipl, 52.
Work in Public Collections: Estonian Nat Mus; Art Gallery Hamilton.
Exhibitions: Estonian Art Exhib, Montreal, 51-55, 60, 62 & 65-71; four shows, Royal Can Acad, 54-68; Exhib Estonian Art, Cleveland, 68; Laurentian Univ Art Gallery, 68; Toronto Nat Exhib Art Gallery, 68; also exhib numerous group shows, U S, Can & abroad.
Awards: Estonian Govt Ministry Educ Award, 40 & 41; Int Acad Award, Rome, Italy, 72.
Memberships: Fel Int Inst Arts & Lett; Soc Estonian Artists in Toronto (pres, 61-); Estonian Artist Soc (pres, 61-67); Can Soc Graphic Art.

Publications: Illusr, Selected poems, 42; illusr, The country life (album 12 linoleum engravings), 43; illusr, album 10 prints, In: New Direct Method, 61; illusr, album 9 linoleum cuts, Memories from Estonia, 72; illusr, Erich Pehap selected prints 1932-1972, 72.
Mailing Address: 14 Ozark Crescent, Toronto 6, Ont, Can.

PEIPERL, ADAM
Sculptor
Preferred Media: Light, Water, Plastics.
b Sosnowiec, Poland, June 4, 35; U S citizen.
Study & Training: George Washington Univ, BS, 57; Pa State Univ, 57-59.
Work in Public Collections: Nat Mus Hist & Technol, Washington, D C; Nat Collection Fine Arts, Washington, D C; John F Kennedy Ctr Performing Arts, Washington, D C; Pa Acad Fine Arts, Philadelphia; Boymans-Van Beuningen Mus, Rotterdam, Holland.
Exhibitions: Corcoran Gallery Art, 68; one-man shows, Marlborough-Gerson Gallery, New York, N Y, 69, Baltimore Mus Art, 69, Pa Acad Fine Arts, 69 & Nat Mus Hist & Technol, 72-73.
Bibliography: Frank Getlein (auth), He defied tradition and made it work, Sun Star, Washington, 7/21/68; Victoria Donohoe (auth), Two one-man shows look off into space, Philadelphia Inquirer, 11/23/69; Diane Chichura & Thelma Stevens (auth), New directions in kinetic sculpture, Van Nostrand-Reinhold, 73.
Dealer: Marlborough Gallery, 41 E 57th St, New York, NY 10022.
Mailing Address: 1135 Loxford Terr, Silver Spring, MD 20901.

PELLAN (ALFRED)
Painter
Preferred Media: Oils.
b Quebec City, Can, May 16, 26.
Study & Training: Ecole des Beaux Arts, Quebec City, grad, 20.
Work in Public Collections: Mus Nat d'Art Mod, Paris, France; Mus Grenoble, France; Que Mus, Quebec City; Nat Gallery Can, Ottawa; Montreal Mus Fine Arts, P Q.
Commissions: Painting, Winnipeg Airport, Man, 63; stained glass, La Place des Arts, Montreal, 63; stained glass, Church Saint Theophile, Laval-Quest, P Q, 64; two paintings, Nat Libr & Archives, Ottawa, 67; polychromy of bldgs, Vt Constructions Inc, Laval City, 68.
Exhibitions: Galerie Jeanne Bucher, Paris, 39; one-man shows, Pellan, retrospective, Mus Nat d'Art Mod, Paris, 55, Pellan, retrospective, Hall of Hon, Montreal, P Q, 56; Alfred Pellan, retrospective, Nat Gallery Can, Art Gallery Toronto & Montreal Mus Fine Arts, 60-61; Voir Pellan, Mus d'Art Contemporain, Montreal, 69.
Teaching: Instr painting, Ecole Beaux Arts, Montreal, 43-52; instr painting, Art Centre Sainte Adele, P Q, summer 57.
Awards: First prize, First Gt Exhib Mural Art Paris, 35; first prize for painting, 65th Ann Spring Exhib, Montreal Mus Fine Arts, 48; first prize for painting, P Q Competition, 48.
Bibliography: Donald W Buchanan (auth), Alfred Pellan, McClelland & Stewart, 62; Guy Robert (auth), Pellan, Centre Psychologie Pedagogie, Montreal, 63; Voir Pellan, Nat Film Bd Can, 69.
Memberships: Soc Artistes Prof Que; assoc Royal Can Acad Arts.
Publications: Contribr, Les iles de la nuit, Parizeau Ed, 44; contribr, Le voyage d'Arlequin, Cahiers File Indienne, 46.
Mailing Address: 649 Des Mille Iles Blvd, Auteuil, Laval City, PQ, Can.

PELLEW, JOHN CLIFFORD
Painter
Preferred Media: Watercolor, Oil.
b Heamoor, Eng, Apr 9, 03; U S citizen.
Study & Training: Penzance Sch Art, Eng.
Work in Public Collections: Metrop Mus Art, New York, N Y; Butler Inst Am Art, Youngstown, Ohio; Ga Mus Fine Arts, Athens; Adelphi Col, Garden City, N Y; New Britain Mus Am Art, Conn.
Exhibitions: Nat Acad Design, New York, N Y. 48-72; Butler Inst Am Art, Youngstown, Ohio, 64; 200 Years of Watercolor Painting in America, Metrop Mus Art, New York, 67; Landscape 1, De Cordova & Dana Mus, Lincoln, Mass, 70; Am Watercolor Soc Exchange Exhib, Canada, 72.
Awards: Adolph & Clara Obrig Prize, Nat Acad Design, 61; first award for watercolor, Butler Inst Am Ar, 64; silver medal, Am Watercolor Soc, 70.
Bibliography: Norman Kent (auth), Watercolor methods, Watson-Guptill, 55; Wendon Blake (auth), Complete guide to acrylic painting, Watson-Guptill, 71.
Memberships: Nat Acad Design; Am Watercolor Soc; Allied Artists Am; Southwestern Watercolor Soc; Salmagundi Club.
Publications: Auth, Acrylic landscape painting, 68; Painting in watercolor, 69; Oil painting outdoors, 71.
Dealer: Grand Central Art Galleries, 40 Vanderbilt Ave, New York, NY 10017.
Mailing Address: 123 Murray St, Norwalk, CT 06851.

PELLICONE, WILLIAM
Painter
Preferred Media: Oil.
b Philadelphia, Pa, Apr 12, 15.
Study & Training: Pa Acad Fine Arts, Philadelphia; Barnes Found, Merion, Pa.
Work in Public Collections: Boston Mus, Mass; Smithsonian Inst, Washington, D C; Allan Stone Galleries, New York & Purchase, N Y; Philip Desind, Capricorn Gallery, Bethesda, Md; Am Broadcasting Co, N Y.
Commissions: Murals, Abraham & Strauss, Brooklyn, N Y, 69, 70.
Exhibitions: Pa Acad Fine Arts, 39; Nat Acad Design, New York, 39; Woodmere Art Gallery, Philadelphia; Art Alliance, Philadelphia; group show, Baltimore Mus, Md, 71.
Dealers: Capricorn Gallery, 8003 Woodmont Ave, Bethesda, MD 20014; Allan Stone Gallery, 48 E 86th St, New York, NY 10028.
Mailing Address: 47 Bond St, New York, NY 10012.

PELS, ALBERT
Painter, Art Administrator
Preferred Media: Oils, Watercolors, Graphics.
b Cincinnati, Ohio, May 7, 10.
Study & Training: Art Acad Cincinnati; Univ Cincinnati; Beaux Arts Sch; Art Stud League New York, six scholarships, also with Thomas Hart Benton, Kenneth Hayes Miller & Bridgeman.
Commissions: The Landing of the Swedes, Courthouse, Wilmington, Del, 42; Early History of Normal, Ill, in post off; Africa scene for ship, North African Line, 50; History of Norfolk, Va, for naval base; gen hist of Anniston, Alabama area, YMCA.
Exhibitions: Whitney Mus Am Art Ann, 40-50; Carnegie Int Exhib, 42-48; Nat Acad Design, 45-52; Butler Inst Am Art Ann, 45-55; Chicago Ann, 49; plus many other group & one-man shows.
Teaching: Instr art, Jones Mem Sch & Hessian Hills Sch; instr fine art, Albert Pels Sch Art, Inc, 46-
Positions: Dir, Albert Pels Sch Art, Inc, 72-; demonstr oil painting on educ TV.
Awards: Cincinnati Art Mus scholar, 32; first prize for Sea Disaster, Butler Inst Am Art, 46; Schackenberg scholar, 49.
Research: Techniques of the old masters.
Art Interests: Traditional art of the old masters.
Collection: Late nineteenth & early twentieth century.
Publications: Contribr, Art News, 46; illusr, Easy puppets, 52 & Water pets, 56.
Dealer: Gorwit Galleries, Roslyn, NY 11576.
Mailing Address: 2109 Broadway, New York, NY 10023.

PEN, RUDOLPH
Painter
Preferred Media: Oils, Watercolors.
b Chicago, Ill, Jan 1, 18.
Study & Training: Art Inst Chicago, BFA; also Europe, S Am, Mex & N Africa.
Work in Public Collections: Davenport Mus, Iowa; Libr of Cong, Washington, D C; Philadelphia Mus, Pa; Vincent Price Collection; Art Inst Chicago.
Exhibitions: Carnegie Inst, Pittsburgh, Pa, 46; Contemp Artists Exhib, Art Inst Chicago, 61-; Watercolor Print Exhib, Pa Acad Fine Arts, Philadelphia; Am Watercolor Soc, Nat Acad Design, New York; Corcoran Gallery Art, Washington, D C.
Teaching: Asst prof painting, Art Inst Chicago, 48-63; dir pvt sch, 63-
Positions: Pres, Alumni Asn, Art Inst Chicago, 60-62; dir, Summer Sch Painting, 64-65.
Awards: Huntington Hartford Found grant, 58; Ryerson traveling fel, 63; plus many other awards.
Bibliography: Marilyn Hoffman (auth), Art, Christian Sci Monitor, 1/3/51; Kay Loring (auth), Pen named director of art school, 7/24/64 & Edith Weigle (auth), Art critic, 11/28/65, Chicago Tribune.
Memberships: Am Watercolor Soc; Arts Club Chicago; hon mem Union League Civic & Arts Found.
Publications: Auth, Whipping boy or cultural spokesman, 54 & auth, The tongue is quicker than the mind, 66, Art League; auth, Artist-teacher blasts tycoons & pretenders, Chicago Sun Times, 71.
Dealer: Joseph Welna, 105 E Ontario, Chicago, IL 60611.
Mailing Address: 55 W Schiller St, Chicago, IL 60610.

PENCZNER, PAUL JOSEPH
Painter
Preferred Media: Oils, Acrylics, Ink.
b Hungary, Sept 17, 16; U S citizen.
Study & Training: In Hungary & Austria.
Work in Public Collections: Vatican, Rome; Capitol Bldg, Jefferson City; Univ Tenn, Memphis; Univ Mo, Cape Girardeau; Fla State Univ, Talahassee.

Commissions: Works comn by Mayor Walter Chandler, City of Memphis, Sen McKinney, Capitol Bldg, Jefferson City, Univ Tenn, Univ Mo, & family of Virginia Churchill.
Exhibitions: Pa Acad Fine Arts, Philadelphia; Brooks Mem Art Gallery, Memphis; Jersey City Mus; Smithsonian Inst, Washington, D C; El Delgado Mus, New Orleans.
Teaching: Owner & dir, Penczner Fine Art Sch, Memphis.
Memberships: Nat Soc Painters Casein.
Dealer: Penczner's Round Corner Gallery, 1684 Poplar Ave, Memphis, TN 38104.
Mailing Address: 1436 Poplar Ave, Memphis, TN 38104.

PENKOFF, RONALD PETER
Educator, Printmaker
Preferred Media: Intaglio.
b Toledo, Ohio, May 18, 32.
Study & Training: Bowling Green State Univ, BFA, 54; Ohio State Univ, MA, 56; Stanley William Hayter's Atelier 17, Paris, France, 65-66.
Work in Public Collections: Libr of Cong, Washington, D C; Columbus Gallery Art, Ohio; Munson-Williams-Proctor Inst, Utica, N Y; Montclair Mus, N J; Ball State Art Gallery, Muncie, Ind.
Exhibitions: Pennell Int Exhib Prints, Libr of Cong, Washington, D C, 55-57; Indiana Artists, John Herron Art Mus, Indianapolis, 60-64; Conn Acad Fine Arts Ann, Hartford, 61-62; Soc Washington Printmakers, Smithsonian Inst, Washington, D C, 62; Nouvelles Realities, Paris, 66.
Teaching: Asst prof art, State Univ N Y Col Oneonta, 56-59; asst prof art, Ball State Univ, 59-67; prof art, Univ Wis-Waukesha, 67-
Positions: Vis prof, Bath Acad Art, Corsham, Eng, summer 66.
Awards: First award in painting, N Y State Fair, 57; Munson-Williams-Proctor Inst award, Cent N Y Artists, 58-59; first award in painting, Eastern Ind Artists, 64.
Bibliography: W Fabricki (auth), Prints & drawings of Ronald Penkoff, Quartet, 63; Donald Key (auth), Color printing is an elusive endeavor, Milwaukee J, 71.
Publications: Auth, The eye & the object, Forum, 62; auth, Roots of the Ukiyo-E, 65; auth, Sign, signal, symbol, 70.
Dealer: Gallery 2111, 2111 N Prospect, Milwaukee, WI 53202.
Mailing Address: S55 W29261 Saylesville Rd, Waukesha, WI 53186.

PENNEY, BRUCE BARTON
Painter
Preferred Media: Oils.
b Laconia, N H, Aug 9, 29.
Study & Training: Worcester Mus Sch; Cleveland Woodward, illusr; with Eldon Rowland, Well Fleet, Mass; New York Phoenix Sch Design.
Work in Public Collections: Worcester Polytech Inst, Mass; Stockholm Mus, Sweden; Dartmouth Col, Hanover, N H.
Exhibitions: Hanover Gallery, N H; Southern Vt Art Asn, Manchester, 67; one-man shows, Wiener Gallery, New York, N Y, 68, Center St Gallery, Winter Park, Fla, 69 & Gallery 2, Woodstock, Vt, 69-71.
Dealer: Wiener Gallery, 963 Madison Ave, New York, NY 10021.
Mailing Address: Box 254, Kennebunkport, ME 04046.

PENNEY, CHARLES RAND
Collector, Patron
b Buffalo, N Y, July 26, 23
Study & Training: Yale Univ, BA; Univ Va, LLB & JD.
Collections Arranged: Selected Works by Emil Ganso, Kenan Ctr, 69; Prints from The Charles Rand Penney Foundation, Niagara Co Community Col Mus, 71; Staffordshire Pottery Portrait Figures, Niagara Co Hist Soc, 72.
Positions: Dir & trustee, The Charles Rand Penney Found, 64-
Memberships: Am Fedn Arts (trustee); Gallery Asn N Y (dir); hon life mem Patteran Soc; Buffalo Soc Artists (trustee); Mem Art Gallery Art Comt.
Collections: International contemporary art; works of Charles E Burchfield & Emil Ganso; Western New York artists; Spanish-American Santos & Retablos; Victorian Staffordshire pottery portrait figures; American antique historic glass; American antique pressed glass.
Mailing Address: Olcott, NY 14126.

PENNEY, JAMES
Painter, Educator
Preferred Media: Oils.
b St Joseph, Mo, Sept 6, 10.
Study & Training: Univ Kans, BFA, 31, with Albert Bloch & Karl Mattern; Art Stud League New York, 31-34, with George Grosz, Von Schlegell, John Sloan & Thomas Benton.
Work in Public Collections: Fort Worth Mus, Tex; Columbus Gallery Fine Arts, Ohio; Springfield Art Mus, Mass; Wichita Art Mus, Kans; New Britain Mus Am Art, Conn; plus others.

Commissions: Mural, comn by Works Progress Admin, Flushing High Sch Lobby, N Y, 38; murals, Fed Art Proj, Post Off Bldgs, Union & Palmyra, Mo, 40-43; Hamilton: Four Seasons (mural), Dunham Hall, Hamilton Col, Clinton, N Y, 59; Nebraska Settlers (three murals), Main Vestibule, Nebr State Capitol, Lincoln, 63; Fields in Spring (painting), comn by Omaha Nat Bank for Joslyn Mus, Nebr, 66.
Exhibitions: Artists for Victory, Metrop Mus Art, New York, N Y, 41; Pa Acad Fine Arts Ann, Philadelphia, 51-68; Am Inst Arts & Lett Ann, New York, 53, 59 & 71; Nature in Abstraction, Whitney Mus Am Art Ann, New York, 57, 59 & 63; Nat Acad Design Ann, New York, 72; plus others.
Teaching: Instr painting, drawing & graphics, Bennington Col, 46-47; instr painting, drawing & graphics, Munson-Williams-Proctor Inst, 48-55; prof painting & drawing, Hamilton Col, 48-; asst prof painting & drawing, Vassar Col, 55-56; Yaddo fel, 56 & 61; vis artist, Calif Col Arts & Crafts, 60.
Positions: Bd control & v pres, Art Stud League New York, 41-46; trustee, Am Fine Arts Soc, 44-48.
Awards: Medal, Midwestern Artists Ann, Kansas City Art Inst, 31; medal & award, Paintings of the Year, Pepsi-Cola, 48; prize, Audubon Artists Ann, 67.
Bibliography: James Penney paints an interior, In: Oil Painting, Watson-Guptill, 53; John I H Bauer (auth), Nature in Abstraction, Whitney Mus Am Art, 58; Nebraskaland masterpiece, Nebr Land Mag, 64; plus others.
Memberships: Nat Acad Design; Audubon Artists; Nat Soc Mural Painters; life mem Munson-Williams-Proctor Inst; Am Fedn Arts; plus others.
Publications: Auth, Cross section New York '72, Hamilton Col, 72; ed, Charles Saxon exhibition, Hamilton Col, 72; ed, Mural designs—James Penney, Utica Col, 72; plus other catalogues & forewords.
Dealer: Kraushaar Galleries, 1055 Madison Ave, New York, NY 10028.
Mailing Address: 101 Campus Rd, Clinton, NY 13323.

PENNY, AUBREY JOHN ROBERT
Painter
Preferred Media: Acrylics.
b London, Eng, July 30, 17; U S citizen.
Study & Training: Univ Calif, Los Angeles, BA(art & art hist), 53, MA(art), 55; also with Dr Danes.
Work in Public Collections: Contemp Art Soc, London, Eng; Edward Dean Mus, Cherry Valley, Calif.
Exhibitions: Los Angeles Co Mus Art, Calif, 54-57; Corcoran Gallery Art, Washington, D C, 57; Am Watercolor Soc, New York, N Y, 57-58; Pa Acad Fine Arts, Philadelphia, 59; two-man shows, Madison Gallery, New York, 63 & Int De Deauville, France, 72.
Positions: Owner, No-os Gallery, Los Angeles, 55-; mem art coun, Univ Calif, Los Angeles, 55-
Awards: Prize for drawing, Emanual Sch, London, 31; award of merit, Calif Nat Watercolor Soc, 55; hon mention, Los Angeles City Art Festival, 58.
Memberships: Contemp Art Soc, London, Eng; Victoria Inst, London; Am Soc Aesthetics & Art Criticism.
Research: Originator of style No-osism or mind-line based on primacy of mind in the continuum, that chemical-electrical relationships leads to neural energy to feeling to act.
Mailing Address: No-os Gallery, 1551 A Cahuenga Blvd, Los Angeles, CA 90028.

PEPPER, BEVERLY
Sculptor, Painter
Preferred Media: Steel, Acrylics.
b Brooklyn, N Y, Dec 20, 24.
Study & Training: Pratt Inst; Art Stud League New York; also with Fernand Léger & Andre L'Hôte, Paris, France.
Work in Public Collections: Albright-Knox Art Gallery, Buffalo, N Y; Mass Inst Technol, Boston; Fogg Art Mus, Cambridge, Mass; Walker Art Ctr, Minneapolis, Minn; Galleria Civica Arte Mod, Turin, Italy; plus others.
Commissions: Contrappunto (stainless steel), comn by William Kaufman Co, U S Plywood Bldg, New York, N Y, 63; Kennedy Mem (stainless steel), Weizmann Inst, Israel, 65; Torre (stainless steel), Flags Over Ga, Atlanta, 69; Sudden Presence (Cor-ten), City of Boston, New Chardon St, 71; Land Canal & Hillside Automobile-oriented (Cor-ten, earth & sod), R D Nasher Co, North Park, Dallas, Tex, 71.
Exhibitions: Sculpture in the City, Festival dei due Mondi, Spoleto, Italy, 62; Plus by Minus, Today's Half Century, Albright-Knox Art Gallery, 68; Outdoor Sculpture, Jewish Mus, New York, 68; Sculpture, Mus Contemp Art, Chicago, Ill, 69; Biennale, Venice, Italy, 72.
Awards: Gold medal & purchase award for sculpture, XVII Mostra Int Fiorino, 66; first prize & purchase award, Jacksonville Art Mus, 70; Best Art in Steel, Iron & Steel Inst, 70.

Bibliography: Jan Van der Marck (auth), Beverly Pepper (catalog), Marlborough Gallery, 69; Wayne Andersen (auth), Sculpture today, Mass Inst Technol Press, 70; Vittorio Armentano (auth), B P making sculpture (film), G Ungaretti, narrator, 70.
Dealer: Marlborough Gallery, 41 E 57th St, New York, NY 10022.
Mailing Address: Vicolo del Cinque, 30, 00153 Rome, Italy.

PERHAM, ROY GATES
Painter
Preferred Media: Oils.
b Paterson, N J, Apr 18, 16.
Study & Training: Grand Cent Art Sch; also with Frank V Dumond & Frank J Reilly.
Work in Public Collections: Americana Mus, Univ S C; Plimoth Plantation, Plymouth, Mass; Salisbury Pub Libr, Md; Maywood Pub Libr, N J.
Commissions: Portrait of Dr O Howard, D D, by friends at Diocesan Col, McGill Univ, 56; Jordan River (mural), Rutherford Baptist Church, N J, 57; portrait of Dr Arthur Armitage, South Jersey Col, Rutgers Univ, Camden, 61; portrait of Dr Milton Hoffman, D D, Cent Col, Pella, Iowa, 66; portrait of H Bruce Palmer, Conf Bd, New York, N Y, 71.
Exhibitions: Allied Artists Am, New York, 66; Fairleigh Dickinson Univ, Rutherford, N J, 67; Fair Lawn Art Asn, N J, 68; Bergen Mall Exhib, Paramus, N J, 70.
Awards: Purchase prize, Bergen Mall, 64.
Memberships: Hackensack Art Club (pres, 48); Bergen Co Artists Guild.
Dealer: Portraits, Inc, 41 E 57th St, New York, NY 10022.
Mailing Address: 268 Raymond St, Hasbrouck Heights, NJ 07604.

PERKINS, ANN
Art Historian
b Chicago, Ill, Apr 18, 15.
Study & Training: Univ Chicago, AB, 35, AM, 36, PhD, 40.
Teaching: Res assoc ancient art, Yale Univ, 55-65; assoc prof ancient art, Univ Ill, Urbana, 65-69, prof ancient art, 69-
Awards: Guggenheim fel, 54-55.
Memberships: Archaeol Inst Am; Col Art Asn Am.
Research: Chiefly art of the Eastern Roman Empire.
Publications: Auth, The art of Dura-Europos (in press).
Mailing Address: 1009 W Clark St, Champaign, IL 61820.

PERKINS, G HOLMES
Architect, Educator
b Cambridge, Mass, Oct 10, 04.
Study & Training: Harvard Univ, AB, 26, MArch, 29, LLD, 72.
Teaching: Chmn dept archit & dean grad sch fine arts, Univ Pa, 51-71, prof archit & urbanism, 71-
Positions: Ed, J Am Inst Planners, 50-52; chancellor col of fels, Am Inst Architects, 64-66.
Memberships: Fel Am Inst Architects; hon corres mem Royal Inst Architects Can.
Publications: Auth, Comparative outline of architectural history, 37; contribr, articles in prof jour.
Mailing Address: Dept of Architecture, University of Pennsylvania, Philadelphia, PA 19104.

PERKINS, MABEL H
Collector
b Grand Rapids, Mich, July 26, 80.
Study & Training: Vassar Col, BA.
Positions: Bd mem, secy, v pres & pres, Grand Rapids Art Mus; established print gallery in Grand Rapids Art Mus.
Collection: Fine prints of all categories, specializing in Durer and Rembrandt.
Mailing Address: 327 Washington St S E, Grand Rapids, MI 49503.

PERKINS, ROBERT EUGENE
Art Administrator
b Pittsfield, Mass, Oct 20, 31.
Study & Training: Sioux Falls Col, BA, 56; Columbia Univ, MA, 57; Univ S Dak.
Positions: Asst prin, Canton High Sch, S Dak, 59-61; dir admis, Sioux Falls Col, 61-63, dean stud, 63-70; pres, Ringling Sch Art, Sarasota, Fla, 71-
Publications: Co-auth, Profile of the South Dakota high school graduate of 1968, 69; auth, The maestro, 70.
Mailing Address: 3424 S Lockwood Ridge Rd, Sarasota, FL 33580.

PERLESS, ROBERT
Sculptor
Preferred Media: Bronze, Stainless Steel.
b New York, N Y, Apr 23, 38.
Study & Training: Univ Miami.
Work in Public Collections: Whitney Mus Am Art, New York.

Commissions: Polished bronze kinetic sculptures, Eastern Airlines, Boston, Mass, Guggenheim Int, New York, Avon Corp, New York & Boone Co Nat Bank, Columbia, Mo; polished bronze hanging kinetic sculpture, Haskins & Sells, New York.
Exhibitions: One-man shows, Bodley Gallery, New York, 68 & Bernard Danenberg Galleries, New York, 72; New Acquisitions Exhibit, Whitney Mus Am Art, New York, 70; Kinetic Show, Hudson River Mus, 70.
Dealer: Bernard Danenberg Galleries, 1020 Madison Ave, New York, NY 10021.
Mailing Address: 43 Greenwich Ave, New York, NY 10014.

PERLIN, BERNARD
Painter, Illustrator
b Richmond, Va, Nov 21, 18.
Study & Training: Nat Acad Design, with Leon Kroll, 36-37; Art Stud League New York, with Isabel Bishop, William Palmer & Harry Sternberg, 36-37; also in Poland.
Work in Public Collections: Mus Mod Art; Tate Gallery, London; Springfield Mus Art, Mass; Calif Palace of Legion of Honor; Va Mus Fine Arts; plus others.
Commissions: U S Post Off Dept, 40; U S Treasury Dept.
Exhibitions: Cincinnati Mus Asn, 58; Brussels World's Fair, 58; Detroit Inst Art, 60; Pa Acad Fine Arts, 60; retrospective, Univ Bridgeport, 69; plus many other group & one-man shows.
Teaching: Instr, Wooster Community Art Ctr, Danbury, Conn, 67-69.
Awards: Fulbright fel, 50; Guggenheim fels, 54-55 & 59; Nat Inst Arts & Lett Award, 64; plus others.
Bibliography: Lloyd Goodrich & John I H Baur (auth), American art of our century, Whitney Mus Am Art, 61; Daniel M Mendelowitz (auth), A history of American art, Holt, Rinehart & Winston, 61; Selden Rodman (auth), Conversations with artists, Capricorn Press, 61; plus others.
Publications: Contribr, illus, In: Life & Fortune Mags.
Mailing Address: Shadow Lake Rd, Ridgefield, CT 06877.

PERLIN, RAE
Painter, Collector
Preferred Media: Oils
b Saint John's, Newf.
Study & Training: With Samuel Brecher, 41, 42 & 46 & Hans Hofmann, 47 & 48, New York, N Y; Acad Grande Chaumière, Paris, France; Acad Ranson, Paris.
Work in Public Collections: Mem Univ Newf Permanent Collection, Can.
Exhibitions: Mem Univ Newf Art Gallery, 71; plus others from 62-72.
Positions: Art critic, Saint John's Daily News, 60-71; art critic, Saint John's Eve Tel, 64-67.
Awards: Arts & lett, Newf Govt, 56 & 62-67; Can Coun grant, 70.
Collection: Contemp works of Can artists; prints, drawings, constructions & paintings.
Publications: Contribr, A history of art in Newfoundland, In: Book of Newfoundland, Vol 4, 67; illusr, Spindrift & morning light, 68.
Mailing Address: 11A Monkstown Rd, Saint John's, Newfoundland, Can.

PERLMAN, RAYMOND
Educator, Illustrator
Preferred Media: Watercolors, Collage.
b Sheboygan, Wis, May 17, 23.
Study & Training: Univ Ill, Champaign, BFA, 48, MFA, 53; Art Ctr Col Design, Los Angeles, MPA, 52.
Work in Public Collections: Watercolors, Univ Ill, Champaign.
Exhibitions: Creativity on Paper, Mead Paper Co, New York, N Y, 65; Chicago 3, Ill, 70; Art Dir Club New York 49th Ann, 70; Printing Job of the Year, 3M Co, 70; TDC 17, Type Dir Club New York, 71.
Teaching: Prof art & in charge graphic design, Univ Ill, Champaign, 49-
Awards: U N Int Poster Competition, 49; Eighth Ann Watercolor & Drawing Exhib, Artists Guild Chicago, 66; various cert merit, design exhibs, 65-
Memberships: Soc Typographic Arts, Chicago.
Art Interests: Photography & all printing processes.
Publications: Illusr, Our wonderful world, Grolier, 53-59; illusr, Rocks & minerals, 57, illusr, Fossils, 62, Golden Nature Guide & illusr, Geology, Golden Sci Guide, 72, Western Publ; illusr, World Book & Childcraft, Field Enterprises, 58-
Mailing Address: 40 Oakwood Dr, Park Hills, Mahomet, IL 61853.

PERLMUTTER, JACK
Painter, Printmaker
b New York, N Y, Jan 20, 20.
Work in Public Collections: Nat Gallery Art, Phillips Collection & Corcoran Gallery Art, Washington, D C; Metrop Mus Art, New York; Nat Mus Mod Art, Tokyo, Japan.

Commissions: First Saturn Moon Rocket Launching (painting), 67 & Saturn V, Apollo 6 (painting), 68, NASA, Kennedy Space Ctr, Fla; Woodcuts for Apollo 16, Mission Control Ctr, Houston, Tex, 72.
Exhibitions: Four Corcoran Gallery Art Am Art Biennials, 49-61; American Prints Today, Print Coun Am, exhibited in ten cities, 59-60; Third & Fourth Expos Gravure, Ljubljana, Yugoslavia, 59 & 61; Third Nat Invitational Exhib Printmaking, Univ Wis, 71; Second Nat Invitational Print Show, Fine Arts Gallery, San Diego, Calif, 71.
Teaching: Chmn dept graphics, Corcoran Sch Art, 61-
Positions: Dir, Dickey Gallery Art, D C Teachers Col, 56-68.
Awards: Fulbright grant in art & printmaking to Tokyo, Japan, 59-60; print prize, First Int Exhib Fine Arts Saigon, 62; also numerous purchase awards.
Bibliography: A Perlmutter original, Washington Star Sun Mag, 11/62; reproduction, In: Art Today, Holt, Rinehart & Winston, 4th ed; Eyewitness to space, Abrams, 72.
Memberships: Soc Am Graphic Artists; Cosmos Club (art comt, 63-).
Publications: Contribr, Transactions of 5th International Conference of Orientalists (Toho Gakkai), In: Japanese Prints Today, 7/60; auth, Western art influences in Japan, In: Today's Japan Orient/West, 8/60; auth, Painting in a land of transition (with reproductions), Inst Int Educ Mag, 1/61.
Mailing Address: 2511 Cliffbourne Pl N W, Washington, DC 20009.

PERLS, FRANK (RICHARD)
    Art Dealer, Collector
b Zehlendorf, Ger, Oct 23, 10.
Study & Training: Univ Vienna; Univ Munich; Univ Berlin.
Positions: Dir, Frank Perls Gallery, Beverly Hills, Calif.
Memberships: Art Dealers Asn Am.
Research: Fifteenth century Cologne School.
Collection: Picasso, Braque, Matisse & Lautrec.
Publications: Auth, var articles on art.
Mailing Address: 9777 Wilshire Blvd, Beverly Hills, CA 90212.

PERLS, KLAUS G
    Art Dealer
b Berlin, Ger, Jan 15, 12; U S citizen.
Study & Training: Univ Basel, Switz, PhD, 33.
Positions: Partner, Perls Galleries, 37-
Memberships: Art Dealers Asn Am (dir & past pres, 66-68).
Specialty of Gallery: Modern masters.
Publications: Auth, Complete works of Jean Fouquet, 40; auth, Maurice de Vlaminck, 41.
Mailing Address: 1016 Madison Ave, New York, NY 10021.

PERRET, GEORGE ALBERT
    Writer, Lecturer
b New York, N Y.
Study & Training: Munson-Williams-Proctor Inst, Utica, N Y; Utica Col, Syracuse Univ; Art Stud League New York, N Y; Nat Acad Design Sch Art, New York.
Collections Arranged: Artists of the South Fork, 65, The Wyeth Family, 66 & Mary Cassat, 67, Parrish Mus, Southampton, N Y.
Teaching: Instr art hist, Southampton Col, Long Island Univ, 63-68.
Positions: Dir, Parrish Art Mus, 63-68; cur, Am Contemp Artists Gallery, 68-72; dir publ, Assoc Am Artists, 72-
Memberships: Westbeth Graphic Artists Group (prog dir).
Research: American painting, 1860-1950.
Publications: Contribr, Art news and reviews (weekly column), Suffolk Sun, 65-68; auth, Levon West, 66; auth, George Elmer Browne, 66; co-auth, Tully Filmus Drawings, 71; auth, Moses Soyer Drawings, 71.
Mailing Address: Indian Wells Hwy, Amagansett, NY 11930.

PERRET, NELL FOSTER
    Painter
Preferred Media: Graphics.
b Brooklyn, N Y.
Study & Training: Pratt Inst; Art Stud League New York, N Y; Design Lab.
Work in Public Collections: Southampton Col, Long Island Univ; East Hampton Guild Hall; St Mary's Univ; Wichita State Univ.
Exhibitions: St Mary's Univ, Md, 71; Audubon Artists, Nat Acad Design Gallery, 71; Westbeth Graphics Workshop, Palacio Bellas Artes, Mex, 71-72; East Hampton Guild Hall Ann; Southampton Col Ann.
Teaching: Instr graphics, Parrish Art Mus, Southampton, 60-68; adj prof graphics, Southampton Col, 68-70.
Awards: Two awards, East Hampton Guild Hall, 61 & 62; three awards for graphics, Parrish Art Mus, 63, 64 & 67.
Bibliography: Esther Greenwood (auth), Long Island Art, Long Island Press, 62; Jean Paris (auth), Review of my work, Newsday, 63; Gordon Brown (auth), Review, Arts Mag, summer 71.
Memberships: East Hampton Guild Hall; Westbeth Graphic Artists Workshop (publ dir, 70-72); Audubon Artists.
Mailing Address: 463 West St, 628A, Westbeth, New York, NY 10014.

PERRIN, C ROBERT
    Painter, Illustrator
Preferred Media: Watercolors.
b Medford, Mass, July 13, 15.
Study & Training: Sch Practical Art, scholar, also with John Whart & Lester Stevens, four yrs.
Work in Public Collections: Ford Motor Co Collection Am Watercolors; Lyman Allyn Mus, New London, Conn.
Exhibitions: Am Watercolor Soc, 58-; U S Info Agency World Tour, 59; Boston Watercolor Soc, 60-; Nat Acad Design; Boston Arts Festival.
Teaching: Artist, lectr & demonstr, Boston & Nantucket Island, Mass, 50.
Positions: Free lance illusr, Boston, Mass, 39-42 & 46-68.
Awards: Purchase prize, Boston Soc Independent Artists, 52; Richard Mitlou Mem Award, 32nd Ann Exhib Painting by Contemp New Eng Artists, 61; first award, Copley Soc, 65.
Bibliography: James S Geggis (auth), Art studio on wheels, United Press, 47; Patricia Boyd Wilson (auth), The home forum, Christian Sci Monitor, 66; Norman Kent (auth), 100 watercolor techniques, Watson-Guptill, 68.
Memberships: Am Watercolor Soc; Boston Watercolor Soc; Artist Asn Nantucket; Rockport Art Asn; Guild Boston Artists.
Publications: Co-auth, Watercolor page, 59, co-auth, Making a rug mural, 66, Am Artist Mag; contribr, The folk arts & crafts of New England, 65; contribr, Creating art from anything, 68.
Dealer: Grand Central Art Galleries, 40 Vanderbilt Ave, New York, NY 10017.
Mailing Address: 50 Washington St, Nantucket Island, MA 02554.

PERROT, PAUL N
    Art Administrator, Lecturer
b Paris, France, July 28, 26; U S citizen.
Study & Training: Inst Fine Arts, New York Univ, 46-52.
Collections Arranged: Three Great Centuries of Venetian Glass, 58; most exhibs shown at The Corning Mus Glass, 60-72.
Teaching: Instr glass hist, Corning Community Col & Alfred Univ.
Positions: Asst, The Cloisters, Metrop Mus Art, 48-52; asst to dir, Corning Mus Glass, 52-55, asst dir, 55-60, dir, 60-72; ed, J of Glass Studies, 59-72; asst secy mus progs, Smithsonian Inst, 72-
Memberships: Am Asn Mus (coun mem, exec comt, v pres); U S Int Coun Mus (chmn); Col Art Asn Am; Am Archaeol Inst; Spec Libr Asn.
Publications: Auth, Three great centuries of Venetian glass, 58; auth, articles, In: Antiques, Apollo, Arts in Va, Col Art J & others.
Mailing Address: Smithsonian Institution, Washington, DC 20560.

PERROTT, JAMES STANFORD
    Art Administrator, Educator
Preferred Media: Watercolors.
b Nov 3, 17; Can citizen.
Study & Training: Alta Col Art, Calgary; Banff Sch Fine Arts, Alta; Hans Hofmann Sch Art, Provincetown, Mass; Art Stud League New York; Pa Acad Fine Arts.
Work in Public Collections: Univ Calgary; Glenbow-Alta Inst, Calgary.
Exhibitions: Alta Soc Artists, Edmonton, 55-70; Western Ont Ann, London, Ont, 62; Art Inst Ont Touring Exhib, 65.
Teaching: Instr hist, drawing, design & anat, Alta Col Art, 46-67, head dept, 67-
Awards: Scholarship ann award.
Memberships: Alta Soc Artists (pres, 65).
Collection: Paintings, prints, sculpture, antiques, glass, ceramics & pottery.
Mailing Address: Alberta College of Art, 1301 16th Ave N W, Calgary, Alta. T2M 0L4, Can.

PERRY, CHARLES OWEN
    Sculptor
Preferred Media: Metals, Plastics.
b Helena, Mont, Oct 18, 29.
Study & Training: Columbia Univ, 54; Yale Univ, with J Albers, 54-58, BArch, 58.
Work in Public Collections: Mus Mod Art, New York, N Y; Art Inst Chicago, Ill; Mus Contemp Art, London, Eng; San Francisco Mus Art, Calif; Joseph Hirshhorn Collection.
Commissions: Aluminum sculpture, Torrington Mfg, 69; bronze sculpture, Harvard Bus Sch, 71; chrome sculpture, Equitable Assurance, St Louis, Mo, 71; painted steel sculpture, Fed Reserve Bank, Minneapolis, Minn, 72; aluminum sculpture, Embarcadero Ctr, San Francisco, 72-73.
Exhibitions: Whitney Mus Am Art Sculpture Biennial, New York, 64-66; Science Age Totems, San Francisco Mus Art, Calif, 65; Directions 1: Options 1968, Milwaukee Art Ctr, Wis & Mus Contemp Art, Chicago, 68; Superlimited, Books, Boxes & Things, Jewish Mus, 69; Venice Biennial, Italy, 72.

Positions: Sculptor-in-residence, Am Acad Rome, 70-71.
Awards: Prix de Rome, Am Acad Rome, 64 & 66; design in steel
   award, Am Iron & Steel Inst, 70 & 71; premio for Emelia, Cir-
   colo della Stampa, Bologna, 71.
Bibliography: L B Jackson (auth), Return to a Rome prize winner,
   Am Inst Architects J, 4/68; Charles Perry & solid geometry,
   Archit Forum, 4/72.
Dealer: Waddell Gallery, 50 W 57th St, New York, NY 10022.
Mailing Address: Via Ippolito Pindemonte, 14, 00152 Rome, Italy.

PERRY, REGENIA ALFREDA
   Art Historian
b Virgilina, Va, Mar 30, 41.
Study & Training: Va State Col, BS, 61; Case Western Reserve Univ,
   Va Mus Fine Arts Out of State fel, 61-62, MA, 62; Yale Univ, 63-
   64; Univ Pa, PhD (art hist), 66.
Teaching: Asst prof art hist, Howard Univ, 65-66; asst prof art
   hist, Ind State Univ, Terre Haute, 66-67; assoc prof art hist, Va
   Commonwealth Univ, 67-
Positions: Spec res asst, Cleveland Mus Art, Ohio, 64-65; vis
   scholar, Piedmont Univ Ctr, Winston-Salem, N C, 71-72.
Awards: Danforth Found post-doctoral fel, 70-71.
Memberships: Col Art Asn Am; Am Asn Mus; Soc Archit Historians;
   Am Asn Univ Prof.
Publications: Auth, A history of Afro-American art 1619-1972, Holt,
   Rinehart & Winston, 73; auth, James Van Derzee—photographer,
   73.
Mailing Address: 2800 Monument Ave, No 3, Richmond, VA 23221.

PERSHING, LOUISE
   Painter, Sculptor
Preferred Media: Oils, Stainless Steel, Brass, Aluminum, Cor-ten
   Steel.
b Pittsburgh, Pa.
Study & Training: Pa Acad Fine Arts; Carnegie-Mellon Univ; Univ
   Pittsburgh, with Philip Elliot; also with Hans Hoffman.
Work in Public Collections: Earle Ludwig Collection, Chicago, Ill;
   Gulf Oil Corp, Pittsburgh; Pittsburgh Pub Sch Collection; Univ
   W Va; also in private collections in U S & S Am.
Exhibitions: Carnegie Int, 37 & 50; Painting in the U S, Carnegie Inst,
   43-49; one-man shows, Westinghouse Corp, Pittsburgh, 65, Gulf
   Oil Corp, Pittsburgh, 66, Univ W Va, Art Alliance, Philadelphia
   & Artist of the Year, Pittsburgh Arts & Crafts Ctr, 72; plus many
   others.
Awards: Twelve awards, Assoc Artists Pittsburgh, 30-72; Artist of
   the Year, Pittsburgh Chamber Commerce, 66; Nat Soc Arts &
   Letters Award of Merit, 69.
Dealer: King Gallery, 1251 N Negley Ave, Pittsburgh, PA 15206.
Mailing Address: 916 College Ave, Pittsburgh, PA 15232.

PETERDI, GABOR F
   Painter, Printmaker
Preferred Media: Oils, Intaglio.
b Pestujhely, Hungary, Sept 17, 15; U S citizen.
Study & Training: Hungarian Acad, Budapest; Acad Julien, Paris,
   France; Atelier 17, Paris, with Hayter.
Work in Public Collections: Whitney Mus Am Art, Mus Mod Art &
   Metrop Mus Art, New York, N Y; Art Inst Chicago, Ill; Boston
   Mus Fine Arts, Mass; & over 150 mus in the U S & abroad.
Exhibitions: Retrospectives, Brooklyn Mus, 59, Cleveland Mus, 62,
   Corcoran Gallery Art & Yale Univ Art Gallery, 64 & Honolulu
   Acad Arts, 68; over 100 one-man shows & 22 retrospectives.
Teaching: Instr, Brooklyn Mus Art Sch, 48-52; assoc prof, Hunter
   Col, 52-59; prof art, Yale Univ, 60-
Awards: Prix du Rome, 30; Mus Western Art, Tokyo, 64; Guggen-
   heim fel, 64-65.
Bibliography: V Johnson (auth), Graphic work 1934-69, Touchstone,
   69.
Memberships: Silvermine Guild Artists (v pres, 65-); Florentine
   Acad Design; Nat Drawing Soc.
Publications: Auth, Printmaking, Macmillan, 59; auth, Great prints
   of the world, 69, Macmillan; auth, Printmaking, Encyclopaedia
   Britannica.
Dealer: Grace Borgenicht Gallery, 1018 Madison Ave, New York, NY
   10021.
Mailing Address: 108 Highland Ave, Rowayton, CT 06853.

PETERS, CARL W
   Painter
Preferred Media: Oils, Watercolors.
b Rochester, N Y, Nov 14, 97.
Study & Training: Rochester Inst Technol; Nat Acad Summer Sch,
   Woodstock, N Y; also with John F Carlson.
Work in Public Collections: Many in pub collections.
Commissions: Evolution of Contemporary Commerce in Rochester
   (mural), Genessee Valley Trust, Rochester, 30; From Painting
   Man to Modern Lines (mural), Madison High Sch, Rochester,

U S Govt, 37; Settling of Genessee Valley (mural), West High Sch,
   Rochester, U S Govt, 38; mural at Charlotte High Sch, U S Govt,
   40; Tribute to Devotion (mural), Rochester Acad Med, 41.
Exhibitions: Nat Acad Design, New York, N Y; Pa Acad Fine Arts,
   Philadelphia; Corcoran Gallery Art, Washington, D C; Art Inst
   Chicago, Ill; Am Watercolor Soc, New York.
Teaching: Prof life class, Univ Rochester; instr pvt sch.
Awards: Fairchild gift, Univ Rochester, 24; first, second & third
   Hallgarten Prizes, Nat Acad Design, 26, 28 & 32; gold medal,
   Rockport Art Asn, 71; plus many others.
Bibliography: Many bibliographies.
Memberships: Am Watercolor Soc; Rockport Art Asn; Rochester
   Art Club; Acad Artists; Genessee Group.
Mailing Address: 208 Jefferson Ave, Fairport, NY 14450.

PETERSEN, ROLAND CONRAD
   Painter, Printmaker
b Endelave, Denmark, Mar 31, 26; U S citizen.
Study & Training: Univ Calif, Berkeley, AB, 49, MA, 50; San Fran-
   cisco Art Inst, 51; Calif Col Arts & Crafts, summer 54; Atelier
   17, Paris, France, 50, 63 & 70, with Stanley W Hayter.
Work in Public Collections: Mus Mod Art & Whitney Mus Am Art,
   New York, N Y; Philadelphia Mus Art, Pa; Nat Collection Fine
   Arts, Washington, D C; M H De Young Mem Mus, San Francisco,
   Calif.
Commissions: Dams of the West (portfolio of 25 color prints), U S
   Dept Interior, Bur Reclamation, Washington, D C, 70.
Exhibitions: Illinois Biennial, Urbana, 61-69; Carnegie Int, Pitts-
   burgh, Pa, 64; 25th Ann Exhib Contemp Art, Art Inst Chicago, 65;
   American Painting, Va Mus Fine Arts, Richmond, 66-70; Trois
   Graveurs et Un Sculpteur, Ctr Cult Am, Paris, France, 71; plus
   many one-man exhibs.
Teaching: Instr painting, Washington State Univ, 52-56; assoc prof
   painting & printmaking, Univ Calif, Davis, 56-; instr printmak-
   ing, Univ Calif, Berkeley, summer 65.
Positions: Mem educ process, Col Lett & Sci, Univ Calif, Davis,
   65, mem exec comt, 65-66.
Awards: Guggenheim fel, 63; appointee, Inst Creative Arts, Univ
   Calif, 67 & 70; Fulbright travel award, 70.
Bibliography: Philip Leider (auth), rev, In: Art in Am, 63; Michael
   Benedikt (auth), rev, In: Art News, 67; James Mellow (auth), rev,
   In: Art Int, 67; plus others.
Memberships: Intercontinental Biog Asn; Calif Soc Etchers; San
   Francisco Art Mus.
Dealers: Staempfli Gallery, 47 E 77th St, New York, NY 10021; Bed-
   narz Galleries, 902 N La Cienega Blvd, Los Angeles, CA 90069.
Mailing Address: Art Dept, University of California, Davis, CA
   95616.

PETERSHAM, MAUD FELLER
   Illustrator, Writer
b Kingston, N Y, Aug 5, 89.
Study & Training: Vassar Col; N Y Sch Fine & Appl Art.
Awards: Caldecott Medal, 46.
Publications: Auth & illusr, Bird in hand, 67, David, 67, co-auth,
   American ABC, 67 & co-auth, Rooster crows, 71, Macmillan;
   auth & illusr, Let's learn about sugar, Harvey, 69; plus many
   others.
Mailing Address: Woodstock, NY 12498.

PETERSON, A E S
   Painter
Preferred Media: Watercolors, Casein, Graphics.
b Northampton, Mass, June 30, 08.
Study & Training: Herman Itchkawich, Providence, R I; C Gordon
   Harris, Lincoln, R I.
Work in Public Collections: Nat Shawmut Bank Boston, Mass;
   Grant Capitol Mgt Corp, Providence; Tillinghast Stiles, Inc,
   East Providence, R I.
Exhibitions: Am Watercolor Soc, Nat Acad Design Gallery, New
   York, N Y, 68-72; Audubon Artists, 69, 70 & 72; Painters &
   Sculptors Soc N J, Jersey City Mus, 69-72; Butler Inst Am
   Art, Youngstown, Ohio, 70; Knickerbocker Artists, Nat Arts
   Club, New York, 71-72.
Positions: Treas, Providence Watercolor Club, 62-70, rec secy,
   71-
Awards: Naomi Lorne Mem Medal for Old Barn, Nat Soc Painters
   Casein, 68; Sadie & Max Tesser Award for Old Barn, Audubon
   Artists, 69; gold medal for Cabanas, Catharine Lorillard Wolfe
   Art Club, 71.
Bibliography: R Stevens (auth), Nobody home, La Rev Mod, 11/1/65;
   Ralph Fabri (auth), Old barn, Syndicate Mag, 6/69 & Cabanas,
   Today's Art Mag, 5/72.

Memberships: Am Watercolor Soc; Nat Soc Painters Casein &
Acrylic (dir, 70-); Allied Artists Am; Catharine Lorillard Wolfe
Art Club; Providence Art Club.
Mailing Address: 27 Holbrook Ave, Rumford, East Providence, RI
02916.

PETERSON, JOHN DOUGLAS
Art Administrator, Designer
b Peshtigo, Wis, July 9, 39.
Study & Training: Layton Sch Art, cert indust design, BFA; Cran-
brook Acad Art, MFA.
Exhibitions: Made of Plastic, Bloomfield Art Asn, 70; Detroit Art-
ists, Mkt, 71.
Collections Arranged: Dr & Mrs Hilbert De Lawter-African Collec-
tion, 67; Miava Grottel Retrospective-Ceramics, 67; Wallace
Mitchell Retrospective-Painting, 71.
Teaching: Instr exhib design, Cranbrook Acad Art, 70-72.
Positions: Pres, Romaine Gallery, 64-65; asst dir, Cranbrook Acad
Art/Galleries, 68-70, assoc dir, 70-71, dir & dean stud, Acad,
71-
Memberships: Arts Coun Triangle (chmn, 71-); Cranbrook Acad Art
Alumni Asn (bd mem, 69-70, v pres, 71-72); Am Asn Mus; Mich
Mus Asn.
Mailing Address: 29 Academy Way, Bloomfield Hills, MI 48013.

PETERSON, LARRY D
Painter, Educator.
Preferred Media: Watercolors, Acrylics.
b Holdrege, Nebr, Jan 1, 35.
Study & Training: Kearney State Col, BA, 58; Northern Colo Univ,
MA, 62; Univ Kans, 72-
Work in Public Collections: Univ Minn; The Gallery, Kearney, Nebr;
250 works in pvt collections.
Commissions: Oil paintings, Trenton High Sch, 59; watercolor ATO
Fraternity, Kearney State Col, 67; acrylic & oil paintings, First
Methodist Church, Kearney, 72.
Exhibitions: Five State Exhib, Washburn Univ, Topeka, Kans, 65;
26th Nat Watercolor Exhib, Jackson, Miss, 67; 5th Nat Art Exhib,
New Orleans, La, 69; Kans Univ Ann, Lawrence, 71; Nat Art Ex-
hib, Rock Springs, Wyo, 71.
Teaching: Instr art, North Platte Pub Schs, 58-65; instr art, North
Platte Col, 66-67; asst prof art, Kearney State Col, 67-; grad
asst, Univ Kans, Lawrence, 70-71.
Awards: Chadron State Col First Award, 63; Nebr Art Teachers Asn
Distinguished Serv Award, 69; award of excellence, Nat Art Ex-
hib, Rock Springs, 71.
Bibliography: Nancy Kalis (auth), one-man rev, Art Rev, Des Moines,
Iowa, 68; Rêva Remy (auth), one-man rev, In: Rev Mod Art, Paris,
France, 68.
Memberships: Nat Art Educ Asn; Nebr Art Teachers Asn (past
pres); Asn Nebr Art Clubs (past pres); Nebr State Educ Asn;
Kappa Pi (past pres, Beta Beta Chap).
Publications: Contribr, Art in action, Nat Art Publ, 62-64; co-auth,
Nebraska art guide K-6, Elem Art Curric, State Nebr, 66.
Dealer: Ware House Gallery, 123 W Fourth St, Grand Island, NE
68801.
Mailing Address: 3507 Linden Dr, Kearney, NE 68847.

PETERSON, ROBERT BAARD
Painter, Draughtsman
Preferred Media: Oils.
b Elmhurst, Ill, July 5, 43.
Study & Training: Gallaudet Col, 60-62; Univ N Mex, 62-65, with
Lez Haas, Ralph Lewis, Sam Smith, Walther Kuhlmann, Norman
Zammitt & John Kacere.
Work in Public Collections: Sim Hunter, New York, N Y; Northern
Trust, Chicago; First City Bank Chicago, Brussels, Belg; Mus
N Mex, Santa Fe; Wurlitzer Found, Taos, N Mex.
Exhibitions: Second Nat Painting Show, Washington & Jefferson Col,
Pa, 69; Southwest Fine Arts Biennial, Santa Fe, 70; Fuller
Lodge Competition, Los Alamos, N Mex, 70; one-man shows,
Unitarian Church, Albuquerque, N Mex, 70 & Willard Gallery,
New York, 72.
Awards: Hon mention & purchase award, Southwest Fine Arts Bi-
ennial, 70; purchase prize, Fuller Lodge Competition, 70;
Wurlitzer Found grant, 70.
Bibliography: Eye on New York, Art Gallery Mag, 1/72; David L
Shirley (auth), Review, New York Times, 1/8/72; Bruce Wolmer
(auth), Reviews & previews, Art News, 2/72.
Dealer: Willard Gallery, 29 E 72nd St, New York, NY 10021.
Mailing Address: 1014 Washington S E, Albuquerque, NM 87108.

PETHEO, BELA FRANCIS
Painter, Educator
Preferred Media: Oils, Acrylics, Graphics.
b Budapest, Hungary, May 14, 34; U S citizen.
Study & Training: Univ Budapest, MA, 56; Acad Fine Arts, Vienna,

57-59, with A P Guetersloh; Univ Vienna, 58-69; Univ Chicago,
MFA, 63.
Work in Public Collections: Hungarian State Mus Fine Arts, Buda-
pest; Kunstmus, Basel, Switz; Univ Minn Permanent Collection,
Minneapolis; Carleton Col Permanent Collection, Northfield,
Minn; plus others.
Commissions: Kindliche Untugenden (mural), Asn Austrian Boy-
scouts, Vienna, 58; The History of Handwriting (exhib panel),
Noble & Noble Publ for Hall of Educ, World's Fair, New York,
N Y, 64; plus others.
Exhibitions: Hamline Univ, 66; Coffman Gallery, Univ Minn, 68;
Moorhead State Col, 69; Biennale Wis Printmakers, 71; Rochester
Art Ctr, 72; plus others.
Teaching: Instr art, Univ Northern Iowa, 64-66; assoc prof art &
artist-in-residence, St John's Univ, 66-
Awards: Belobende Anerkennung, Acad Fine Arts, Vienna, 58;
graphic prize, Univ Chicago, 62.
Bibliography: Arturo Carlo Quintavalle (auth), Bela Petheo, Univ
Parma & St John's Univ Res Coun Publ, 67; plus others.
Memberships: Col Art Asn Am; Int Platform Asn.
Publications: Auth, Rembrandt's pupils in the Museum of Fine Arts
in Budapest, Szabad Muveszet, 6/56; auth, Creativity versus convention: an illustrator's challenge, Rec, winter 67; auth, Poly-
mer-coated lithographic transfer paper, In: Five artists—their
printmaking methods, Artists Proof, 68; auth, The college art
gallery, Art J, summer 71; plus others.
Mailing Address: St John's University, Collegeville, MN 56321.

PETRIE, FERDINAND RALPH
Painter, Designer
Preferred Media: Watercolors.
b Hackensack, N J, Sept 17, 25.
Study & Training: Parsons Sch Design, New York, N Y, cert advert,
49; Art Stud League New York, with Frank Reilly; Famous Art-
ists Course Illus, cert, 59.
Work in Public Collections: Nat Collection Fine Art, Smithsonian
Inst, Washington, D C; Audubon Naturalists Soc, Chevy Chase,
Md; Hammond Mus, North Salem, N Y; U S Navy Combat Art
Gallery, Washington, D C.
Exhibitions: One-man exhib, Audubon Naturalists Soc, 70; Allied
Artists Am, Nat Acad Design Gallery, New York, 71; N J Wa-
tercolor Soc, Mus Arts & Sci, Morristown, 71-72; Am Artists
Prof League Grand Nat, New York, 71 & 72; San Clemente White
House Loan Exhib from Smithsonian Inst, 70-72.
Teaching: Instr painting & drawing, Fairleigh Dickinson Univ,
Rutherford, 69-70; instr watercolor, Annex Gallery, Montclair,
N J, 70-72; pvt instr watercolor, 72-
Positions: Illusr, J Gans Assoc Studio, New York, 50-69.
Awards: First prize for watercolor, Atlantic City Boardwalk Show,
69; Salmagundi Club Purchase Prize, 70; Grand Nat Award, Am
Artists Prof League, 71.
Memberships: N J Watercolor Soc (exhib chmn); Salmagundi Club
(art comt); Rockport Art Asn; Hudson Valley Art Asn; Am Art-
ists Prof League.
Publications: Illusr, New York Life Ins Calendar, 70 & 72; illusr,
Provident Mutual Life Ins Co Calendar, 71; illusr, educ poster,
Educ Syst & Publ, 72; illusr, Becton-Dickinson Co Publ, 72.
Dealers: Callahan-Petrie Gallery, 13 Main St, Rockport, MA 01966;
Grand Central Galleries, 40 Vanderbilt Ave, New York, NY
10017.
Mailing Address: 51 Vreeland Ave, Rutherford, NJ 07070.

PETRO, JOSEPH (VICTOR), JR
Painter, Illustrator
b Lexington, Ky, Nov 4, 32.
Study & Training: Transylvania Col, with Victor Hammer; grad sch,
Cincinnati Med Sch, art as appl to med.
Work in Public Collections: Paintings in pvt collections throughout
U S.
Commissions: Covers, Family Weekly Mag, N Y; Brown & Bigelow
calendars; Brown-Forman Distillers, Louisville, Ky; 32 horse
paintings, Keeneland Collection, Keeneland Racing Asn, Lexing-
ton, Ky; 27 portraits of pres of Transylvania Col, 1794-, pres
rm, Transylvania Col; plus others.
Exhibitions: One-man shows, Transylvania Col, 63, Univ Ky, 65,
Abercrombie-Fitch, N Y, 68, Bass Galleries, Louisville, 68 &
Clossons, Cincinnati, Ohio, 69; plus others.
Positions: Publ, series ltd number collector prints horses, 54-69;
consult, Spindletop Res, Inc, Lexington, 65-68.
Memberships: Am Fedn Arts.
Publications: Illusr, Cincinnati Pictorial Enquirer, Thoroughbred
Rec, Nat Geog, Holiday, Better Homes & Gardens & others.
Mailing Address: 305 Henry Clay Blvd, Lexington, KY 40502.

PETROFF, GILMER
Painter, Designer
Preferred Media: Watercolors, Acrylics.
b Saranac Lake, N Y, Mar 20, 13.
Study & Training: Yale Univ; Univ Wis Summer Sch; Cape Cod Sch Art; also with Richard E Miller.
Work in Public Collections: O'Hara Collection; High Mus, Atlanta, Ga; Columbia Mus, S C; Florence Mus, S C; Staten Island Hist Soc, N Y; plus one other.
Commissions: Murals, Clemson House, Clemson Univ, 51, Tapps Dept Store, Columbia, 54 & S C Hwy Dept, Columbia, 56 & Yachtsman Motel, Myrtle Beach, S C, 71.
Exhibitions: Saint Paul Mus, 39; Columbia Mus Art, S C, 51; Florence Mus Art, S C, 69; Staten Island Mus Art, N Y.
Teaching: Assoc prof archit, Clemson Univ, 46-50; instr, Richland Art Sch, Columbia, 50-60.
Positions: Designer, Lyles, Bissett, Carlisle & Wolfe, Architects, Columbia, 50-60; chief designer, Stanley Smith & Sons, Builders, 60-
Awards: Purchase awards, High Mus Art, Atlanta, Ga, 47 & Columbia Mus Art, 65.
Memberships: S C Art Asn (pres, 55); Columbia Artists Guild (pres, 57).
Publications: Illusr, Textile leaders of the South, 64.
Mailing Address: 5318 Pinestraw Rd, Columbia, SC 29206.

PEZZATI, PIETRO
Painter
b Boston, Mass, Sept 18, 02.
Study & Training: Child-Walker Sch Art; also with Charles Hopkinson; in Europe.
Work in Public Collections: Med Sch & Bus Sch, Harvard Univ; Sch Med & Sch Educ, Univ Pa; Mass Gen Hosp; Yale Sch Med; Mass Hist Soc; plus many others.
Exhibitions: Exhibited regionally & nat in group & one-man shows.
Teaching: Instr, schs & pvt classes; demonstr technique & slide lect hist of portraiture, pvt groups.
Mailing Address: Fenway Studios, 30 Ipswich St, Boston, MA 02215.

PFAHL, CHARLES ALTON, III
Painter
Preferred Media: Pastels, Oils.
b Akron, Ohio, May 15, 46.
Study & Training: With Robert Brackman, Madison, Conn, John Koch, New York, N Y & Jack Richard, Cuyahoga Falls, Ohio.
Exhibitions: Allied Artists Ann, 69-71, Am Watercolor Ann, 70 & 71 & Audubon Artists Ann, 70-72, Nat Acad Design, New York, N Y; one-man show, Harbor Gallery, Long Island, N Y, 71; Butler Inst Am Art Ann, Youngstown, Ohio, 72.
Awards: Green Shields grant, Can, 71; John F & Anna Lee Stacy grant, 72; Hudson Valley Gold Medal of Hon, 72.
Memberships: Salmagundi Club; Nat Arts Club; Hudson Valley Artists.
Dealer: Harbor Gallery, Main St, Cold Springs Harbor, NY 11724.
Mailing Address: 481 Eastern Pkwy, Brooklyn, NY 11216.

PFEIFER, BODO
Painter, Sculptor
b Dusseldorf, Ger, July 17, 36; Can citizen.
Study & Training: Ecole Beaux Artes, Montreal; Acad Fine Arts, Hamburg, Ger; Vancouver Sch Art, B C, dipl.
Work in Public Collections: Vancouver Art Gallery; Nat Gallery, Ottawa, Ont; Art Gallery Ont, Toronto; Montreal Mus Fine Art, P Q; Can Coun, Ottawa, Ont.
Commissions: Mural, Dept Transport, Ottawa, Vancouver Int Airport, 68; mural, McCarter Nairne & Partners, Architects for Moore's Off Bldg, Vancouver, 68.
Exhibitions: Canada 101, Edinburgh Int Festival, 68; Survey 68, Montreal Mus Fine Art, 68; Can Artist, Art Gallery Ont, 68; The New Art of Vancouver, Newport Harbour Art Mus, Seventh Biennial Exhib, Nat Gallery Can, Ottawa, 68; The New Art of Vancouver, Newport Harbour Art Mus, 69.
Teaching: Sessional instr painting & drawing, Univ Calgary, 71-
Awards: Can Coun grants, 66-71; Can Group Painters Award in Painting, 67; award in painting, Survey 68, Montreal Mus Fine Art, 68.
Bibliography: Thomas H Garver (auth), The new art of Vancouver, Newport Harbour Art Mus, 69; W Townsend (auth), Canadian art today, Studio Int, 70; Artists of pacific Canada, Nat Film Bd Can, 71.
Mailing Address: 2197 W Second Ave, Vancouver, B C, Can.

PFRIEM, BERNARD
Painter
b Cleveland, Ohio, Sept 7, 16.
Study & Training: John Huntington Polytech Inst, 34-36; Cleveland Inst Art, 36-40; Europ study, 50-52.

Work in Public Collections: Mus Mod Art; Chase Manhattan Bank, N Y; Dorado Beach Hotel, P R; Columbia Banking, Savings & Loan Asn, Rochester, N Y; Metrop Mus, New York; plus others.
Commissions: Murals, Guerrero & Mexico City, Mex; plus many portraits.
Exhibitions: Six shows, Iolas Gallery, N Y, 49-63; Whitney Mus Am Art, 52 & 65; retrospective, Cleveland Inst Art, 63; Richard Feigen Gallery, Chicago, Ill, 67; Carnegie Inst; also in France, Ger & Italy; plus others.
Teaching: Instr drawing & painting, Peoples Art Ctr, Mus Mod Art, 46-51; instr drawing, Cooper Union Sch Art & Archit; instr, Silvermine Col Art, New Canaan, Conn; instr, Sarah Lawrence Col, 69-70.
Positions: Dir, studio arts sessions in southern France for Sarah Lawrence Col.
Awards: Mary Ranney traveling scholar, Western Reserve Univ; Copley Award painting, 59; prize drawing, Norfolk Mus Arts & Sci; plus many others.
Bibliography: Patrick Waldberg (auth), Bernard Pfriem (monogr), William & Noma Copley Found, 61 & Main et marvielles, Mercure, France, 61; Patricia Allen Dreyfus (auth), The inward journey (monogr), Am Artist, 9/72.
Mailing Address: 115 Spring St, New York, NY 10012.

PHARR, MR & MRS WALTER NELSON
Collectors
Mr Pharr, b Greenwood, Miss, Nov 9, 06; Mrs Pharr, b Detroit, Mich, Apr 1, 23.
Study & Training: Mr Pharr, Washington & Lee Univ; Mrs Pharr, Garland Jr Col, Boston, Mass.
Collection: International modern art; marine paintings including 18 by J E Butterworth, others by R Salmon & T Birch; plus others.
Mailing Address: 154 E 66th St, New York, NY 10021.

PHELAN, LINN LOVEJOY
Designer, Educator
Preferred Media: Ceramics.
b Rochester, N Y, Aug 25, 06.
Study & Training: Rochester Inst Technol, dipl, 28; Ohio State Univ, BFA (ceramic art), 32; Alfred Univ, MS (educ), 55.
Exhibitions: Rochester Mem Art Gallery, 28-58; Everson Mus, Syracuse, N Y, 32-50; Albright-Knox Mus, Buffalo, N Y, 51; York State Craftsman, Ithaca Col, N Y, 54-71; N Y State Fair, Syracuse, 60-70.
Teaching: Instr pottery, Sch Am Craftsman, 44-50; instr art, Alfred-Almond Cent Sch, 50-67; lectr art, State Univ N Y Col Ceramics, Alfred Univ, 67-
Positions: Mgr fair, York State Craftsmen, Inc, 57-59; exec comt, N Y State Art Teachers, Albany, 58-61, pres, 60-61.
Mailing Address: 114 S Main St, Almond, NY 14804.

PHELPS, NAN DEE
Painter, Photographer
Preferred Media: Oils.
b London, Ky.
Study & Training: Self-taught; scholar to Cincinnati Art Mus, Ohio.
Work in Public Collections: The Henry Ford Collection, Dearborn, Mich; Chamber of Commerce, Pulaski, Va; also in pvt collections.
Commissions: Water Along Autumn Path, Emanuel Baptist Church, Hamilton, Ohio, 48; The Coming of the Lord, First Church of God, Middletown, Ohio, 49; Sunset on Water, First Church of God, New Miami, Ohio, 52; Country Scenery, Mr & Mrs Steve Derdourski, Gary, Ind, 52; The Shepherd & Sheep, Orphanage, Trinidad Island, 65.
Exhibitions: All-American Fine Art Show, Cincinnati, Ohio; Cincinnati Art Mus, 42-56.
Awards: First place, Ford Motor Co, 60; first place mag cover, Kiwanis Club, Cincinnati, Ohio, 60; award from Greater Hamilton Art Club.
Bibliography: Della Hicks (auth), Never, never land.
Publications: Auth, Self-taught artist, Ford Times News, 58; auth, Christmas shopping through the windshield, 72-73.
Mailing Address: 1721 Green Wood Ave, Hamilton, OH 45011.

PHILBRICK, MARGARET ELDER
Printmaker, Painter
Preferred Media: Intaglio, Mixed Media.
b Northampton, Mass, July 4, 14.
Study & Training: Mass Col Art, grad; De Cordova Mus Workshop, with Donald Stoltenberg.
Work in Public Collections: Libr of Cong, Washington, D C; Wiggin Collection, Boston Pub Libr, Mass; Nat Bezalel Mus, Jerusalem; First Nat Bank, Boston; New Britain Mus, Conn.
Exhibitions: U S Info Agency Serv Exhib to Far East, 58-59; Second Int Miniature Print Exhib, Pratt Graphic Art Ctr, New York, N Y, 66; Boston Printmakers 23rd Nat Exhib, De Cordova Mus, Lincoln, Mass, 71; Soc Am Graphic Artists 51st Nat, Kennedy Gal-

leries, New York, 71; Margaret Philbrick— A Retrospective Exhib, Ainsworth Gallery, Boston, 72.
Awards: Carl Zigrosser Multum in Parvo Award, Pratt Graphic Art Ctr, 66; Alice Standish Buel Mem purchase award, Soc Am Graphic Artists, 71; John Taylor Arms Mem Prize, Nat Acad Design, 72.
Memberships: Boston Printmakers (exec bd, 72); Boston Watercolor Soc; Soc Am Graphic Artists; Nat Acad Design; Am Color Print Soc.
Publications: Illusr, On gardening, 64 & illusr, In praise of vegetables, 66, Scribners; illusr, Natural flower arrangements, Doubleday, 72; illusr, West Dedham & Westwood 300 years, 72.
Dealer: Westwood Gallery, 36 Hartford St, Westwood, MA 02090.
Mailing Address: 323 Dover Rd, Westwood, MA 02090.

PHILBRICK, OTIS
Painter, Printmaker
b Mattapan, Mass, Oct 21, 88.
Study & Training: Mass Sch Art, Boston.
Work in Public Collections: Boston Pub Libr; Libr Cong; Bezalel Mus, Jerusalem; Amherst Col; Fogg Mus Art; plus others.
Exhibitions: Carnegie Inst; Boston Watercolor Soc Ann; Boston Art Festival, 53-55, 58 & 61; Am Exhibs in France, Israel, Italy & Eng; U S State Dept Traveling Exhib, Far East; plus others.
Teaching: Emer prof painting, Mass Col Art.
Positions: Pres, Boston Printmakers.
Awards: Prizes, Cambridge Art Asn, 54 & 59 & Jordan Marsh Co, 63; Mohawk Paper Co purchase award, 63; plus others.
Memberships: Boston Soc Watercolor Painters; Soc Am Graphic Artists; Boston Printmakers; Copley Soc; Boston Watercolor Soc.
Mailing Address: 323 Dover Rd, Westwood, MA 02090.

PHILIPP, ROBERT
Painter
b New York, N Y, Feb 2, 95.
Study & Training: Art Stud League, with DuMond & Bridgman, 10-14; Nat Acad Design, with Volk & Maynard, 14-17.
Work in Public Collections: Whitney Mus Am Art; Brooklyn Mus; Mus Fine Arts Houston; Corcoran Gallery Art; Norton Gallery Art; plus many others.
Exhibitions: Exhibited nationally.
Teaching: Vis prof, Univ Ill, 40; instr, High Mus Art, 46; instr, Art Stud League New York; instr, Nat Acad Design.
Awards: Prizes, Nat Acad Design, 22, 47 & 51; bronze medal, Allied Artists Am, 58; W C Osborne Award, Am Watercolor Soc, 67; plus others.
Memberships: Academician Nat Acad Design; Lotos Club; Benjamin Franklin fel Royal Soc Art London.
Mailing Address: 881 Seventh Ave, New York, NY 10019.

PHILLIPS, DOROTHY W
Art Administrator, Writer
b Camden, N Y, Mar 6, 06.
Study & Training: Wellesley Col, BA; New York Univ Grad Inst Fine Arts; Inst Art & Archéol, Sorbonne, Paris.
Positions: Asst curator, Egyptian dept, Metrop Mus Art, New York, NY, 30-48; curator collections & res & ed & compiler, miscellaneous catalogues for loan exhibs of Am art, Corcoran Gallery of Art, Washington, DC, 59-
Publications: Contribr, ancient Egyptian art articles, In: Metrop Mus Art Bull, 41-48 & auth, Ancient Egyptian animals, Metrop Mus Art picture book with text, 48; contribr, Am art articles, In: Corcoran Gallery Bull & Nat Retired Teachers Asn J, 63-72; co-auth & ed, A catalogue of the collection of American paintings in the Corcoran Gallery of Art, Vol I, 66, Vol II (in press).
Mailing Address: Corcoran Gallery of Art, 17th & E Sts, N W, Washington, DC 20006.

PHILLIPS, GIFFORD
Collector, Writer
b Washington, D C, June 30, 18.
Study & Training: Stanford Univ, 36-38; Yale Univ, BA, 42.
Memberships: Mus Mod Art, New York (trustee, 66-); Phillips Collection (trustee); Pasadena Art Mus (trustee, 67-); Mus Mod Art Int Coun (bd dirs); Los Angeles Co Mus Art Contemp Art Coun.
Collection: Contemporary American painting and sculpture.
Publications: Auth, Arts in a democratic society, 66; auth, articles, In: Art News, Artforum & Art in Am.
Mailing Address: 825 S Barrington Ave, Suite 302, Los Angeles, CA 90049.

PHILLIPS, IRVING W
Cartoonist, Illustrator
b Wilton, Wis, Nov 29, 05.
Study & Training: Chicago Acad Fine Arts.

Commissions: Stage play adaptations, One foot in heaven, Gown of glory, Mother was a bachelor & Rumple, Alvin Theatre, New York, N Y, 55; plus others.
Positions: Cartoon humor ed, Esquire Mag, 37-39; cartoon staff, Chicago Sun-Times Syndicate, 40-52; motion picture assignments with Warner Bros, RKO, Charles Rodgers Prod & United Artists; auth & illusr, syndicated strip appearing int in 180 papers in 22 countries, The strange world of Mr Mum.
Awards: Int first prize & cup, Salone dell'Umorismo of Bordighera, Italy, 69.
Memberships: Writers Guild Am; Dramatists Guild; Nat Cartoonists Soc; Mag Cartoonists Guild; Newspaper Cartoon Coun; plus others.
Publications: Auth & illusr, The strange world of Mr Mum, 65; auth, The twin witches of fingle fu, 69; auth, No comment by Mr Mum, Popular Libr, 71; auth & co-auth, 260 TV scripts; contribr, scripts & animation to ABC-TV children's prog, Curiosity Shop; contribr, Sat Eve Post; plus many others.
Mailing Address: 2807 E Sylvia St, Phoenix, AZ 85032.

PHILLIPS, JOHN GOLDSMITH
Museum Curator
b Glens Falls, N Y, Jan 22, 07.
Study & Training: Harvard Univ, AB.
Teaching: Lectr var aspects Europ art & new installations, Metrop Mus Art, New York, N Y.
Positions: Former chmn western Europ arts, Metrop Mus Art, chmn emer western Europ arts, 71-
Awards: Guggenheim fel, 57.
Publications: Auth, Early Florentine designers and engravers, Metrop Mus Art, 55; auth, China-trade porcelain, 56.
Mailing Address: 170 E 77th St, New York, NY 10021.

PHILLIPS, MARGARET McDONALD
Painter, Educator
Preferred Media: Oils.
b New York, N Y.
Study & Training: Hunter Col, BA; Grand Cent Sch Art, MA; with Eric Pape, Frank Schwartz & Edmund Greacen; Wayman Adams Sch Portraiture; Univ Paris, scholar, 42; St Andrews Col, PhD.
Work in Public Collections: Indira Ghandi (portrait), Indira Ghandi Collection, New Delhi, India; Portrait of a Mountaineer, Fla Southern Col; Muskingum Col, Ohio; St Luke's Hosp, New York.
Commissions: Portrait of Mme V Pandil commissioned by UN, hanging in New Delhi, 54; portrait of Mme Paul Manfort, Berlitz Sch Language, Paris, France, 65; portrait of John S Bennell, Fifth Ave Presby Church, New York, 67; portrait of Walter H Aldridge, Columbia Univ, New York, 69; portrait of Pres Richard M Nixon, commissioned by Pres Heritage Club, Republican Club Hdq, 72; plus others.
Exhibitions: Galerie Int, New York, 60; 50 Am Artists, Schoeneman Art Gallery, New York, 65; Nat Art Club 23rd Ann, New York, 69; Ogunquit Art Ctr, Maine, 69; Academic Artists, W Springfield, Mass, 70.
Teaching: Mem admin staff, New York Phoenix Sch Design, 54-, head portrait painting dept, 68-; instr pvt classes.
Awards: Nancy Ashton Prize, 42; citation, Fla Southern Col, 69.
Bibliography: Su San (auth), Artist captures the essence, Sun, 69; Wagsan (auth), She paints the greats, J Am; Lesley Kuhn (auth), Psychosomatic paintings, Int Press Asn, 69.
Memberships: The 50 Am Artists (pres, 54-); Royal Soc Arts, London; Acad Artists, W Springfield, Mass; Palm Beach Art League; Rockport Art Asn.
Publications: Illusr, King of Siam & Queen of Persia, N Y Graphic Soc, 47; auth, You & your portrait, 55; auth, Judging an art exhibition, 60; auth, Aesthetic enjoyment, 68.
Dealer: Rembrandt Art Gallery, 80th & Madison Ave, New York, NY 10016.
Mailing Address: 19 E 37th St, New York, NY 10016.

PHILLIPS, MARJORIE
Museum Director, Painter
Preferred Media: Oils.
b Bourbon, Ind, Oct 25, 94.
Study & Training: Art Stud League New York; also with Kenneth Hayes Miller & Boardman Robinson.
Work in Public Collections: Whitney Mus Am Art, New York, N Y; Corcoran Gallery Art, Washington, D C; Yale Univ Art Gallery, New Haven, Conn; Phillips Collection, Washington, D C; Mus Fine Arts, Boston, Mass.
Exhibitions: Exhibition of American Painting, Tate Gallery, London, Eng, 46; Carnegie Int, Pittsburgh, Pa, several yrs; one-man shows, Calif Palace of Legion of Honor, San Francisco, 59 & Edward Root Art Ctr, Munson-Williams-Proctor Inst, Utica, N Y, 65.

Collections Arranged: Seymour Lipton's Sculpture, 64; Giacomotti Sculpture and Painting, 65; Alexander Calder Sculpture, 67; Contemporary Sculpture, 68; Cezanne Exhib (with Art Inst Chicago & Boston Mus Fine Arts), to celebrate 50th Anniversary of Phillips Collection opening, 71; Forty Paintings by Washington, D C, Artists, 71-72.
Positions: Assoc dir Phillips Collection, 25-66, dir, 66-72.
Awards: Award of Merit, Pa Mus Sch Art, 59.
Memberships: Am Fedn Arts
Publications: Auth, Duncan Phillips and his collection, Atlantic Mo Press, Little, 71.
Mailing Address: 2101 Foxhall Rd N W, Washington, DC 20007.

PHILLIPS, MATT
Painter
Preferred Media: Watercolors, Oils
b New York, N Y.
Study & Training: Univ Chicago, MA; Stanford Univ; Barnes Found.
Work in Public Collections: Metrop Mus Art; Nat Gallery Art; Philadelphia Mus Art; New Brit Mus Am Art.
Exhibitions: Galerie Marcel Bernheim, New York, 62-65; Peter Deistsch, New York, 62 & 65; Princeton Gallery Fine Art, 71; Smithsonian Inst Traveling Exhib, 72; William Zierler Gallery, New York, 72; plus others.
Teaching: Head dept art, Bard Col, 64-
Publications: Auth, Maurice Prendergast: the monotypes (catalog), 67 & Milton Avery: works on paper (catalog), 71, Bard Col; auth, The monotype today, Artist's Proof, 69; The monotype: an edition of one, Smithsonian Inst Traveling Exhib, 72.
Dealer: William Zierler Gallery, 956 Madison Ave, New York, NY 10021.
Mailing Address: Bard College, Annandale-on-Hudson, NY 12004.

PHIPPS, CYNTHIA
Collector
Mailing Address: 3 E 77th St, New York, NY 10021.

PHIPPS, MR & MRS OGDEN
Collectors
Memberships: Art Collectors Club.
Mailing Address: 635 Park Ave, New York, NY 10021.

PIATEK, FRANCIS JOHN
Painter
Preferred Media: Oils, Acrylics.
b Chicago, Ill, Dec 9, 44.
Study & Training: Sch Art Inst Chicago, BFA & MFA.
Work in Public Collections: Art Inst Chicago.
Commissions: Mural, Main State Bank Chicago, 72.
Exhibitions: Chicago & Vicinity Shows, 67-69 & 71 & Soc Contemp Art Exhib, 70 & 71, Art Inst Chicago; Whitney Mus Am Art Ann Exhib Contemp Am Painting, 68; one-man shows, Hyde Park Art Ctr, 69 & Phyllis Kind Gallery, 72.
Teaching: Instr painting, Art Inst Chicago, 70-71.
Awards: Art Inst traveling fel, Francis Ryerson, 67; Pauline Potter Palms award, 68 & John G Curtis Prize, 69, Chicago & Vicinity Shows.
Dealer: Phyllis Kind Gallery, 226 E Ontario St, Chicago, IL 60611.
Mailing Address: 3925 N Troy St, Chicago, IL 60618.

PICARD, LIL
Painter, Sculptor
b Landau, Ger; U S citizen.
Study & Training: Col Strassbourg, Alsace-Loraine; study in Vienna, Austria & Berlin, Ger; Art Stud League New York, with Jevza Modell.
Work in Public Collections: Schniewind Collection, Nevege, Ger; Hahn Collection, Cologne, Ger.
Exhibitions: Parnass Gallery, Wuppethal, Ger, 62; Insel Gallery, Hamburg, Ger, 63; Smolin Gallery, New York, N Y, 65; Kunsthalle, Baden-Baden, Ger; Stedelijk Mus, Holland; plus others.
Positions: Art critic, Kunstwerk, Baden-Baden & Die Welt, Hamburg.
Art Interests: Self performances in personal realism style.
Publications: Contrib ed, Inter/View.
Mailing Address: 40 E Ninth St, New York, NY 10003.

PICK, JOHN
Educator, Art Administrator
b West Bend, Wis, Sept 18, 11.
Study & Training: Univ Notre Dame, BA, 29; Univ Wis, MA, 34, PhD, 38; Grad study at Harvard & Oxford.
Work in Public Collections: Milwaukee Art Ctr; Marquette Univ Art Collection.
Collections Arranged: Marquette University Art Collection including editing two catalogues, Marquette University Art Collection & the supplement.

Teaching: Fulbright lectr, Royal Univ Malta, 55-56.
Positions: Chmn, Univ Comt Fine Arts, Marquette University, 51-; cultural attaché, Embassy of Malta, Washington, D C, 68-
Memberships: Am Asn Univ Prof; Mod Lang Asn Am; Eng-Speaking Union; fel Royal Soc Arts, London.
Research: Brochures on icons, Spanish colonial art and others.
Publications: Auth, Gerard Manley Hopkins: priest and poet, Oxford Univ Press, 42; A Hopkins reader, Oxford Univ Press, 52; Hopkins—the windhover, Merrill, 68.
Mailing Address: Marquette University, Milwaukee, WI 53233.

PICKEN, GEORGE
Painter, Printmaker
b New York, N Y, Oct 26, 98.
Study & Training: Art Stud League New York, 24; & in Europe.
Work in Public Collections: Corcoran Gallery Art; Lowe Art Ctr, Syracuse Univ; Lowe Art Gallery, Miami Univ; Hudson River Mus; Whitney Mus Am Art; plus many others.
Commissions: Murals, U S Post Off, Edward & Hudson Falls, N Y & Chardon, Ohio.
Exhibitions: Corcoran Gallery Art, 41, 43, 45 & 61; Whitney Mus Am Art, 42-46 & 60; Va Mus Fine Arts, 42, 44 & 46; Pa Acad Fine Arts, 44-46; Carnegie Inst, 44-46; plus many other group & one-man shows.
Teaching: Instr art, Cooper Union Art Sch, 43-64; asst prof painting & dept rep, sch painting & sculpture, Columbia Univ, 43-64; spec asst prof fine arts, Hofstra Univ, 65-66; vis prof painting, Kansas City Art Inst, 65-66; vis prof painting, Univ Hartford, 67-68; instr painting, Lenox Sch Boys, Mass, 67-68.
Awards: Prize, Corcoran Gallery Art, 43.
Memberships: Fedn Mod Painters & Sculptors; Soc Am Graphic Artists; Am Asn Univ Prof.
Mailing Address: Church St, Tyringham, MA 01264.

PICKENS, ALTON
Painter, Educator
b Seattle, Wash, Jan 19, 17.
Study & Training: Reed Col.
Work in Public Collections: Mus Mod Art.
Teaching: Prof art, Vassar Col, 56-
Mailing Address: Dept of Art, Vassar College, Poughkeepsie, NY 12601.

PICKENS, VINTON LIDDELL
Painter
b Charlotte, N C.
Study & Training: Corcoran Art Sch, with Eugene Weisz, Washington, D C; Am Univ, with Ben L Summerford.
Work in Public Collections: Butler Inst Am Art, Youngstown, Ohio; Watkins Gallery, Washington, D C; Miami Mus Mod Art, Fla; Univ Maine; Art-in-the-Embassies Prog, State Dept.
Exhibitions: Corcoran Biennial; Soc Washington Artists; Irene Leach Mem Exhibs, Norfolk, Va; Va Artists Biennial, Richmond; N C Artists Biennial, Raleigh.
Memberships: Artists Equity Asn (Washington, D C Chap).
Publications: Auth & illusr, Paint an elephant, Atlantic, 58; auth, article, In: Serendipity.
Mailing Address: Janelia Farm, Ashburn, VA 22011.

PICKFORD, ROLLIN, JR
Painter
Preferred Media: Watercolors, Oils, Acrylics.
b Fresno, Calif.
Study & Training: Fresno State Col; Stanford Univ, BA; also with Alexander Nepote, Ralph DuCasse, James Weeks & Joseph Mugnaini.
Work in Public Collections: Springfield Art Mus, Mo; State of Calif Collection, Sacramento; Ford Motor Co, Dearborn, Mich; Fresno Arts Ctr; City of Santa Paula, Calif.
Exhibitions: All-California Invitational, Laguna Beach, Calif, 60; Watercolor U S A, Springfield, Mo, 62, 65 & 66; Mainstreams '68, Marietta, Ohio, 68; Calif Nat Watercolor Soc Traveling Show, Riverside Mus, New York & Va Mus, Richmond; Austrian-Am Exchange Exhib, Linz, Salzburg & Vienna, Austria, 72.
Teaching: Instr art, Fresno State Col, 48-62.
Positions: Pres, Fresno Art League, 46-47.
Awards: Best of show, All-California Invitational, 60; first prize & purchase award, Watercolor U S A, 62; first prize & purchase award, Calif State Fair, 63.
Memberships: West Coast Watercolor Soc; Carmel Art Asn; Fresno Arts Ctr; Old Bergen Art Guild.
Publications: Illusr, stories by William Saroyan, Lincoln-Mercury Times & Ford Times, 50's; auth, A philosophical approach to watercolor, Am Artist, 69.
Mailing Address: 1839 Van Ness, Fresno, CA 93721.

PICKHARDT, CARL
Painter
b Westwood, Mass, May 28, 08.
Study & Training: Harvard Univ, AB, 31; study with Harold Zimmerman, 30-35.
Work in Public Collections: Mus Mod Art, New York, N Y; Mus Fine Arts, Boston, Mass; Newark Art Mus, N J; Libr Cong, Washington, D C; Brooklyn Art Mus, N Y.
Exhibitions: Int Biennial of Color Lithography, 51; Carnegie Int, 52; Int Exhib, Japan, 52; Am Drawing Biennial, Norfolk, Va, 66; Pa Acad Fine Arts, Philadelphia, 68.
Teaching: Instr printmaking, Worcester Mus Art Sch, 49-50; instr printmaking, Art Stud League New York, 51; instr painting, Fitchburg Art Mus, 51-62.
Awards: Schope Prize, Nat Acad Design, 42.
Bibliography: Parker Tyler (auth), Carl Pickhardt, Horizon, 72.
Dealer: Doris Meltzer, 783 Madison Ave, New York, NY 10021.
Mailing Address: 66 Forest St, Sherborn, MA 01770.

PIERCE, DELILAH W
Painter, Educator
Preferred Media: Oils, Acrylics.
b Washington, D C, Mar 3, 04.
Study & Training: D C Teachers Col, dipl; Howard Univ, BS; Columbia Univ, MA; also with Lois Jones, Céline Tabary, Ralph Pearson, James Lesene Wells & Jack Perlmutter.
Work in Public Collections: Howard Univ Gallery Art, Washington, D C; D C Teachers Col, Washington; Anacostra Mus, Smithsonian Affil.
Commissions: Portrait of Dr Eugene A Clark comn by family for Eugene A Clarke Pub Sch, Washington, D C, 69.
Exhibitions: Atlanta Univ Art Show, 52 & 53; Area Show, 57-59 & Travel Exhib, 60-61, Corcoran Gallery Art; Baltimore Gallery Art Area Show, 59; Smith-Mason Gallery Nat Exhib, 71; Trenton Mus, 72.
Teaching: Instr art, secondary pub schs, Washington, D C, 25-52; instr art & art educ, D C Teachers Col, 52-56, prof art & art educ, 56-69, vis prof art educ, 70-71; vis prof art educ, Howard Univ Sch Educ, 64-67.
Awards: Agnes Meyer summer fel, 62; award for achievement in field of art & art educ, Phi Delta Kappa, 63; mus donor prog purchase award, Am Fedn Art, 64; plus one other.
Bibliography: Cedric Dover (auth), American Negro art, N Y Graphic Soc, 60; J E Atkinson (auth), Black dimensions in contemporary American art, Carnation Co, 71.
Memberships: Soc Washington Artists (treas, 69-); Artist Equity Asn; Washington Watercolor Asn (mem chmn, 72); Nat Conf Artists (regional chmn, 70-72); D C Art Asn (chmn exhib comt, 70-72).
Publications: Auth, Can art serve as a balance wheel in education?, Educ Arts Asn J, 49; auth, The significance of art experiences in the education of the Negro, J Negro Life & Hist.
Dealer: Artists Mart, 1361 Wisconsin Ave, Washington, DC 20012.
Mailing Address: 1753 Verbena St N W, Washington, DC 20012.

PIERCE, ELIZABETH R
Painter
Preferred Media: Oils.
b Brooklyn, N Y.
Study & Training: Art Stud League New York, with John Groth, John Stewart Curry & Anne Goldthwaite; Art League Long Island, New York, with Edgar A Whitney; Columbia Univ Exten; Hunter Col.
Work in Public Collections: Children's room, Jamaica Pub Libr, N Y.
Exhibitions: Nat Asn Women Artists Ann, Nat Acad Design Galleries; Nova Scotia Soc Artists, Halifax; Nat Mus, Washington, D C; Crowell's Downeaster Gallery, Yarmouth, N S.
Teaching: Instr adult educ oil painting, Nova Scotia Dept Educ, Yarmouth, 59-67.
Memberships: Nat Asn Women Artists; life mem Art Stud League New York.
Mailing Address: R R 1, Yarmouth, N S, Can.

PIEROTTI, JOHN
Cartoonist
b New York, N Y.
Study & Training: Art Stud League New York; Cooper Union; Mechanics Inst.
Work in Public Collections: Collection of All Works, Syracuse Univ; Wayne State Univ; Univ Wis.
Commissions: Numerous commissions.
Exhibitions: Man & this World, Montreal, Can; Yugoslavia; Metrop Mus Art, New York.
Awards: Five Silurian Awards for best ed cartoon, 65-71; Page One Award for best sports cartoon, 65-68; Page One Award for best ed cartoon, 68 & 70-72.
Memberships: Nat Cartoonists Soc (pres, 57-59); Artists & Writers.

Publications: Illusr, sports & ed cartoonist, New York Post, at present.
Mailing Address: New York Post, 75 West St, New York, NY 11214.

PIERRE-NOEL, LOIS JONES
Painter, Designer
Preferred Media: Oils, Acrylics.
b Boston, Mass, 05.
Study & Training: Boston Mus Sch Fine Arts, scholar, 4 yrs; Boston Normal Art Sch; Designers Art Sch; Harvard Univ; Columbia Univ; Howard Univ, AB; Acad Julien, Paris, France, with Berges, Montezin, Maury & Adler; Acad Grande Chaumiere, Paris.
Work in Public Collections: Brooklyn Mus, N Y; Phillips Collection, Washington, D C; Palais Nat, Haiti; Corcoran Gallery Art, Washington, D C; Am Embassy, Luxembourg; plus others.
Exhibitions: Nat Acad Design, New York, N Y; Rhodes Nat Gallery, S Rhodesia; Trenton Mus, N J; San Francisco Mus Art, Calif; Salon Artistes Francais, Grand Palais Champs-Elysees, Paris; plus many others.
Teaching: Prof design & watercolor painting, Howard Univ, 30-
Awards: Gen Educ Bd foreign fel for study in France & Italy, 37-38; oil painting award, 8th Ann Area Exhib, Corcoran Gallery Art, 53; Chevalier, Nat Order Merit of Honor, Govt Haiti for achievement in art; plus others.
Bibliography: Cedric Dover (auth), American negro art, N Y Graphic Soc, 60; Dr Samella S Lewis & Ruth G Waddy (auth), Black artists on art, Contemp Crafts Publ, Vol I, 69; Elsa H Fine (auth), The Afro-American artist: a search for identity, Holt, Rinehart & Winston, 72.
Memberships: Fel Royal Soc Arts; Artists Equity Asn; Soc Washington Artists; Art Dirs Club Metrop Washington; Nat Conf Artists (1st v pres).
Research: The Black visual arts, encompassing the contemporary art of African, Haitien and Afro-American artists.
Publications: Auth, Lois Mailou Jones peintures—1937-1951, Georges Frere, Tourcoing, France, 52.
Mailing Address: 1220 Quincy St NE, Washington, DC 20017.

PIKE, JOHN
Illustrator, Painter
b Boston, Mass, June 30, 11.
Study & Training: Hawthorne Sch Art, 28-31; also with Richard Miller.
Commissions: Paintings, USAF Hist Found, France, Ger, Greenland, Ecuador, Columbia, Panama & others; advert for, Lederle Labs, Alcoa, Standard Oil & Falstaff; plus others.
Exhibitions: Grand Cent Art Gallery; Saint Petersburg Art Club, Fla, Oklahoma City Mus Conserv Art, Great Plains Mus, Lawton, Okla & San Diego Fine Arts Festival, 60-61; also over 50 one-man shows plus others.
Teaching: Instr, John Pike Watercolor Sch, Woodstock, N Y, summers.
Awards: Salmagundi Black & White Prizes, 41; Am Watercolor Soc Award, 42; Halgarten Prize, Nat Acad Design, 45; plus others.
Memberships: Academician Nat Acad Design; Am Watercolor Soc; Soc Illusr; Salmagundi Club; Woodstock Art Asn; plus others.
Publications: Contribr, illus & covers, In: Colliers, Reader's Digest, Life, Fortune & True Mags.
Mailing Address: P O Box 428, Woodstock, NY 12498.

PINARDI, ENRICO VITTORIO
Sculptor, Painter
Preferred Media: Wood.
b Cambridge, Mass, Feb 11, 34.
Study & Training: Apprentice with Pelligrini & Cascieri, five yrs; Boston Archit Ctr; Sch Mus Fine Arts, Boston; Mass Col Art, BS(educ); R I Sch Design, MFA.
Work in Public Collections: Worcester Art Mus, Mass; De Cordova Mus, Lincoln, Mass; Inst Contemp Art, Boston, Mass; Chase Manhattan Bank, New York, N Y; Kanegis Gallery, Boston.
Exhibitions: New England Art Part IV Sculpture, 64 & Surrealism, 70, De Cordova Mus; 21 Sculptors & Painters, Boston Univ, 64; New England Art Today, Northeastern Univ, 65; 10 Sculptors, Nashua, N H, 68.
Teaching: Instr sculpture, Worcester Art Mus Sch, 63-67; asst prof sculpture, R I Col, 67-
Dealer: Sidney Kanegis Gallery, 244 Newbury, Boston, MA 02116.
Mailing Address: 87 Child, Hyde Park, MA 02136.

PINCUS-WITTEN, ROBERT A
Art Historian, Writer
b New York, N Y, Apr 5, 35.
Study & Training: Cooper Union, Emil Schweinburg grant, 56; Univ Chicago, dept fel, 61-63, MA & PhD; Univ Paris exchange fel, Sorbonne, 63-64.
Teaching: Asst prof art hist, Queens Col, 66-
Positions: Assoc ed, Artforum.

Research: Symbolism; the history of contemporary art.
Publications: Auth, Les Salons de la Rose & Croix, Picadilly Gallery (London), 68; auth, The konography of symbolist art, Artforum, 1/70; auth, Against order: poetical sources of chance art, In: Against order, chance and art, Inst Contemp Art, Univ Pa, 70; auth, The disintegration of minimalism: five pictorial sculptors, In: Materials and methods, a new view, Katonah Gallery, 71; auth, White on white: from tonalism to monochromism, In: White on white, Mus Contemp Art, Chicago, 72.
Mailing Address: Dept of Art, Queens College, Flushing, NY 11367.

PINDELL, HOWARDENA DOREEN
Painter, Art Administrator
b Philadelphia, Pa, Apr 14, 43.
Study & Training: Boston Univ, BFA, 65; Yale Univ, MFA, 67.
Work in Public Collections: Whitney Mus Am Art, New York; plus private collections.
Exhibitions: Twenty-six Contemporary Women Artists, Larry Aldrich Mus, Ridgefield, Conn, 71; Contemporary Black Artists in America, 71 & Whitney Ann, 72, Whitney Mus Am Art; Oversize Drawings, N Y Univ, 72; American Women Artists, Kunsthaus Hamburg, Ger, 72.
Collections Arranged: Pop Art Prints, Drawings & Multiples, 70, California Prints, 72, Chuck Close, Lilliana Porter, 73 & California Printstour of mus in U S A until 74, Mus Mod Art, New York.
Teaching: Guest lectr mus & the printmaker, Pratt Inst, New York, 72-; guest lectr women artists, Hunter Col, New York, 72-
Positions: Asst cur prints & illustrated bks, Mus Mod Art, New York, 71-
Awards: Nat Endowment Arts Found Award, 72.
Bibliography: Hans Bhalla (auth), Exhibition at Spelman Col, 11/71; Carter Ratcliff (auth), Whitney annual, Artforum Mag, 4/72; Lucille Naimer (auth), The Whitney annual, Arts Mag, 3/72.
Research: Contemporary American art.
Publications: Auth, Mary Quinn Sullivan, Notable American women, Harvard Univ Press, 71; auth, California prints, Arts Mag, 5/72; auth, Jan Groth: the constructed line, Craft Horizons, 8/72; auth, Ed Ruscha: interview, Print Collectors News Letter, fall 72.
Mailing Address: Westbeth Artists' Housing, 463 West St, New York, NY 10014.

PINEDA, MARIANNA (MARIANNA PINEDA TOVISH)
Sculptor
Preferred Media: Bronze, Wood, Stone, Ivory, Wax.
b Evanston, Ill, May 10, 25.
Study & Training: Cranbrook Acad Art, 42, with Carl Milles; Bennington Col, 42-43, with Moselsio; Univ Calif, Berkeley, 43-45, with R Puccinelli; Columbia Univ, 45-46, with Maldarelli; also with Ossip Zadkene, Paris, France, 49-50.
Work in Public Collections: Walker Art Ctr, Minneapolis, Minn; Mus Fine Arts, Boston, Mass; Munson-Williams-Proctor Inst, Utica, N Y; Addison Gallery Am Art, Andover, Mass; Dartmouth Col, N H.
Commissions: Medallion for Jan Veen Mem Libr, Boston Conserv Music.
Exhibitions: Metrop Mus Art, New York, N Y, 51; four Whitney Mus Am Art Ann, New York, 54-59; Art Inst Chicago, Ill, 57 & 61; Carnegie Int, Pittsburgh, Pa, 60; Mus Mod Art, New York, 60.
Teaching: Instr sculpture, Newton Col, Mass, 72-
Awards: Mather Prize for Sculpture, Art Inst Chicago, 57; grand prize, Boston Arts Festival, 60; Radcliffe Inst Independent Study scholar, 62-64.
Memberships: Artists Equity Asn (secy, Boston Chap, 57-59); Sculptors Guild; academician Nat Acad Design; Boston Visual Artists Union.
Publications: Contribr & illusr, Art in Am, 2/55 & Audience Mag, winter 60.
Dealer: Alpha Gallery, 121 Newbury St, Boston, MA 02116.
Mailing Address: 164 Rawson Rd, Brookline, MA 02146.

PINES, NED L
Collector
b Malden, Mass, Dec 10, 05.
Collection: Modern art.
Mailing Address: 355 Lexington Ave, New York, NY 10017.

PINKERTON, CLAYTON (DAVID)
Painter
b San Francisco, Calif, Mar 6, 31.
Study & Training: Calif Col Arts & Crafts, BAEd, MFA; Harwood Found, Univ N Mex.
Work in Public Collections: De Young Mus, San Francisco; Calif Palace Legion of Honor, San Francisco; Ill Bell Tel, Chicago.

Exhibitions: Recent Painting U S A: The Figure, Mus Mod Art, New York, N Y, 63; Contemp Am Painting & Sculpture, Univ Ill, 67 & 69; Violence in Recent American Art, Mus Contemp Art, Chicago, 69; Human Concern, Whitney Mus Am Art, New York; Three Centuries of Am Painting, Calif Palace Legion of Honor, 71.
Teaching: Prof fine arts, Calif Col Arts & Crafts, 60-; dir grad div.
Awards: Fulbright scholar, 57-58; James Phelan Award, 57 & 61; San Francisco Art Asn.
Bibliography: Joan Mondale (auth), Politics in art.
Memberships: San Francisco Art Inst.
Mailing Address: 35 Washington St, Richmond, CA 94801.

PINKNEY, HELEN LOUISE
Art Administrator, Art Historian
b Decatur, Ill.
Study & Training: Dayton Art Inst Sch, grad.
Collections Arranged: The Camera the Paper & I, collection of photographs by Jane Reece, 52; The Wonderful World of Photography: Jane Reece Memorial Exhibition, 63; Oriental & European Textiles Exhib, 72.
Positions: Registrar of collections, Dayton Art Inst, 36-45, cur, 45-59, librarian, 45-, assoc cur textiles, 59-
Memberships: Am Asn Mus; Spec Libr Asn, Mus Div.
Research: Extensive research on Jane Reece Photographic Collection; general research as curator on collections, including textiles; bibliographic research as librarian for museum & school.
Publications: Auth, Articles & catalogues on Jane Reece Collection, In: Dayton Art Inst Bull, 52 & 63.
Mailing Address: 37 Stoddard Ave, Dayton, OH 45405.

PINKOWSKI, EMILY JOAN
Painter, Instructor
Preferred Media: Acrylics.
b Chicago, Ill.
Study & Training: Mundelein Col, scholar; Univ Chicago, PhB; Am Acad Art, com art cert.
Exhibitions: Butler Inst Am Art, Youngstown, Ohio, 69-72; New Horizons in Art, Ill Competition, Chicago, 70-72; A Styka Mem Exhib Nat Show, Am Artists Polish Descent, Am Coun Polish Cult Clubs, Doylestown, Pa, 71; Women '71, Northern Ill Univ, DeKalb, 71; Mainstreams '72, Marietta Col Int Exhib, Ohio, 72.
Teaching: Instr painting, Northbrook Art League, Ill, 68-; instr painting, North Shore Art League, Winnetka, Ill, 70-; instr painting, Deerpath Art League, Lake Forest, Ill, 71-
Awards: Second prize, New Horizons in Art, Ill Competition, North Shore Art League, 71; second prize, Styka Show, Am Coun Polish Cult Clubs, 71; Borg-Warner purchase award, 72.
Bibliography: Ann Feuer (auth), Artist in the news, Hollister Papers, 69; Robert Glauber (auth), The mechanical image (monograph for one-man show), 71.
Memberships: North Shore Art League; Deerpath Art League; Northbrook Art League; Soc Polish Arts & Lett; Polish Arts Club.
Mailing Address: 3085 Blackthorn Rd, Riverwoods, IL 60015.

PINSKY, ALFRED
Painter, Educator
b Montreal, P Q, Mar 31, 21.
Study & Training: Montreal Mus Fine Arts; also with Anne Savage.
Exhibitions: Can Soc Graphic Art; Can Group Painters; Montreal Mus Fine Arts.
Teaching: Prof fine arts, Sir George Williams Univ, presently.
Positions: Former chmn dept fine arts, Sir George Williams Univ; auth critical rev of exhibs, CBC, Montreal.
Awards: Scholar, Montreal Mus Fine Arts, 38-39.
Mailing Address: Dept of Fine Arts, Sir George Williams University, Montreal 107, P Q, Can.

PINTO, JAMES
Painter, Sculptor
Preferred Media: Acrylics, Bronze.
b Bijelina, Yugoslavia, Apr 24, 07; U S citizen.
Study & Training: Univ Zagreb, Yugoslavia; Chouinard Art Inst, Angeles, Calif; mural painting with David Alfaro Siqueiros; also with Jean Charlot.
Work in Public Collections: Witte Mem Mus, San Antonio, Tex; Mus Contemp Art, Belgrad, Yugoslavia; Berg Art Ctr, Concordia Col, Moorehead, Minn; Mala Umetnicka Galeria, Sarajevo, Yugoslavia; Univ Art Gallery, Univ N Mex, Albuquerque; plus many others.
Commissions: Regional fiesta mural, Inst Allende, San miguel, 51 & 54; co-worker with Rico Lebrun on Genesis Mural, Pomona Col, Calif, 60; outdoor sculpture mural, Nell Fernandez Harris, San Miguel, 68; indoor mural, Hotel Inst Allende, 70.
Exhibitions: American Painting Today, Metrop Mus Art, New York, N Y, 52; 15th Ann Contemp Art, Art Inst Chicago, Ill, 55; Instituto Nacional Bellas Artes, Mexico City, Mex, 58; 62nd Ann Western Artists, Denver Art Mus, Colo, 62; 1st Anual de Escultura, Museo Arte Moderno, 71-72.

Teaching: Instr painting, Escuela Univ Bellas Artes, San Miguel, 48-50; dean faculty, Inst Allende, 50-
Awards: First prize, First Nat Vet Exhib, Santa Monica, Calif, 47; first prize, Nat Univ Mex & U S Embassy, Mexico City, 49; purchase prize, Life-Day Exhib Contemp Art, Fargo, N Dak, 57.
Bibliography: Felipe Cossio del Pomar (auth), Critica de arte de baudelaire a malraux, Fondo de Cultura Economica, 56; Brooks (auth), Painting & understanding of abstract art, 64 & Baldwin (auth), Contemporary sculpture techniques, 67, Reinhold.
Dealer: Galeria de Arte Misrachi, Genova 20, Mexico, DF.
Mailing Address: Apdo Postal 12, San Miguel de Allende, Gto, Mexico.

PITZ, HENRY CLARENCE
Painter, Writer
Preferred Media: Watercolors, Oils, Acrylics.
b Philadelphia, Pa, June 16, 95.
Study & Training: Pa Mus Sch Art, grad; Spring Garden Inst, grad.
Work in Public Collections: Pa Acad Fine Arts, Philadelphia; Nat Gallery Art, Washington, D C; Philadelphia Mus Art, Pa; Nat Acad Design, New York, N Y; Libr of Cong Collection, Washington, D C; plus many others.
Commissions: Three mural panels commissioned by Smithsonian Inst for Chicago World's Fair; illusr for five classics, Limited Ed Club, 52-67; off NASA artist, Apollo 10 Flight, 69; off artist, U S Environ Protection Agency, 72.
Exhibitions: Pa Acad Fine Arts, Philadelphia, 30-69; Am Watercolor Soc, New York, 46-68; Nat Acad Design, New York, 50-72; Exhibition of Space Artists, Nat Gallery Art, Washington, D C, 70; Exhib Western Artists, Phoenix Art Mus, Ariz, 72; plus many others.
Teaching: Prof decoration & illus & dir dept, Philadelphia Col Art, 34-60; instr drawing & watercolor, Pa Acad Fine Arts, summers 37-42; vis lectr art, Univ Pa, 42.
Positions: Pres, Philadelphia Sketch Club, 36-39; assoc ed, Am Artist, 42-; bd ed, Am Artist Bk Club, 68-
Awards: Dana Gold Medal, 34; bronze medal, Paris Int Exhib, 38; literary award medal, Philadelphia Athenaeum, 70.
Bibliography: Ernest W Watson (auth), Forty illustrators, Watson-Guptill, 46; Richard Ellis (auth), Book illustration, history & development, Kingsport, 52; Walter Reed (auth), The illustrator in America, Reinhold, 66.
Memberships: Philadelphia Art Alliance (v pres in charge art, 33-59, bd dirs, 42-); Nat Acad Design; hon mem Soc Illustrators; Woodmere Art Gallery (bd trustees, 68-); Philobiblon Club.
Research: Artists of Brandywine Valley, Pa; art techniques.
Publications: Auth, Treasury of American book illustrations, 41; auth, Ink drawing techniques, 57; co-auth, Early American dress, 62; auth, The Brandywine tradition, 69; auth, Charcoal drawing, 71.
Mailing Address: 3 Cornelia Pl, Philadelphia, PA 19118.

PITZ, MOLLY WOOD
Painter
b Ambler, Pa, May 12, 13.
Study & Training: Philadelphia Mus Sch Indust Art.
Work in Public Collections: Pa State Univ; also in pvt collections.
Exhibitions: Philadelphia Watercolor Club, 39-45 & 63; Woodmere Art Gallery, 43-46 & 48-52; William Jeanes Mem Libr, 48-55 & 59-69; Philadelphia Mus Col Art, 59; Philadelphia Art Alliance, 65; plus others.
Awards: Hartford Found fel, 64.
Memberships: Philadelphia Art Alliance; Philadelphia Watercolor Club; Bryn Mawr Art Ctr, Art Teachers Workshop; Allen Lane Art Ctr; Philadelphia Mus Sch Art Alumni Asn.
Mailing Address: 3 Cornelia Pl, Philadelphia, PA 19118.

PLAGENS, PETER
Painter, Instructor
b Dayton, Ohio, Mar 1, 41.
Study & Training: Univ Southern Calif, BFA, 62; Syracuse Univ, MFA, 64.
Exhibitions: Wide White Space, Antwerp, Belg, 68; Contemp Am Drawings, Oakland Art Mus, Calif, 69; First Ann Drawing Exhib, St John's Univ, N Y, 70; Nat Drawing Invitational, Southern Ill Univ, Carbondale, 71; Twenty-Four Los Angeles Artists, Los Angeles Co Mus Art, Calif, 71; plus many other group & one-man shows.
Teaching: Instr art, Calif State Univ, Northridge.
Positions: Cur, Long Beach Mus, Calif, 65-66; contribr ed, Artforum.
Publications: Auth, A meditation on painting, 3/71 & West coast blues, 2/71, Artforum; auth, Zip: Barnett Newman, Art in Am, 11/71; auth, Some problems in recent paintings, Art J, winter 71.
Mailing Address: c/o Reese Palley, 93 Prince St, New York, NY 10012.

PLAMONDON, MARIUS GERALD
Sculptor, Craftsman
b Quebec, P Q, July 21, 19.
Study & Training: Ecoles Beaux-Arts, Quebec; also in France & Italy.
Commissions: Stone carvings, stained glass, numerous churches, univ bldgs, hotels & hosps.
Exhibitions: Exhibited nationally & int.
Positions: Pres, Ecoles Beaux Arts, Quebec; pres, Soc Sculptors Can, 59-61; v pres, Int Asn Plastic Arts, UNESCO.
Awards: Scholar to Europe, 38-40; Royal Soc fel, 55-56.
Memberships: Sculptors Soc Can; Stained Glass Asn Am; Royal Can Acad.
Mailing Address: 1871 Sheppard Ave, Quebec 6, P Q, Can.

PLATE, WALTER
Painter, Educator
b Woodhaven, N Y, June 9, 25.
Study & Training: Grand Cent Sch Art, N Y, 42-43; Ecole Beaux-Arts & Grande Chaumiere, Paris, France, 47-50.
Work in Public Collections: Corcoran Gallery Art; Whitney Mus Am Art; Johnson Found Collection; also in pvt collections.
Exhibitions: Art Inst Chicago, 59 & 61; Corcoran Gallery Art, 59 & 61; Pa Acad Fine Arts, 60; Walker Art Ctr, Minneapolis, Minn, 60; Albany Inst Hist & Art, 61; plus others.
Teaching: Instr, Art Stud League New York, summers, 59-65; adj assoc prof archit, Rensselaer Polytech Inst, 64-
Awards: Prizes, Corcoran Gallery Art, 59 & Albany Inst Hist & Art, 51; Woodstock Klienert Award, 61; plus others.
Mailing Address: Box 292, Woodstock, NY 12498.

PLATH, IONA
Designer, Writer
b Dodge Center, Minn, May 24, 07.
Study & Training: Westmoreland Col; Art Stud League New York; Art Inst Chicago.
Teaching: Instr art & design, 30-
Positions: Free lance designer, 47-
Publications: Auth & illusr, Decorative arts of Sweden, Scribner's, 48 & Dover, 65; auth & illusr, Hand weaving, Scribner's, 64 & 72.
Mailing Address: 17 Mountain View Ave, Woodstock, NY 12498.

PLATT, ELEANOR
Sculptor
b Woodbridge, N J, May 6, 10.
Study & Training: Art Stud League New York.
Work in Public Collections: Boston Mus Fine Arts; Metrop Mus Art; Truman Libr; Hebrew Univ, Jerusalem; Harvard Univ Law Sch Libr; plus many others.
Commissions: Bas-reliefs, Louis Brandeis Wehle, Samuel J Tilden & Arthur T Vanderbilt; plaques, Orison Marden & Charles S Whitman, N Y Sch Law; busts, Arnold Grant, Syracuse Univ Law Sch; plus many others.
Positions: Mem, New York City Art Comn, 64-67.
Awards: Chaloner scholar, 39-41; Am Acad Arts & Lett grant, 44; Guggenheim fel, 45.
Memberships: Nat Acad Design; Nat Sculpture Soc.
Mailing Address: Hotel Park Plaza, 50 W 77th St, New York, NY 10024.

PLAUT, JAMES S
Art Administrator, Writer
b Cincinnati, Ohio, Feb 1, 12.
Study & Training: Harvard Univ, AB, 33, AM, 35.
Collections Arranged: Int exhibs for Inst Contemp Art, Boston, 39-56; in charge of all exhib planning, U S Pavilion, Brussels World's Fair, 58, New York World's Fair, 64, Montreal, 67 & Osaka, 70.
Teaching: Lectr hist art, Harvard Univ, 34-35, 37-38; lectr hist art, New Eng Conserv Music, 38-39.
Positions: Asst cur paintings, Mus Fine Arts, Boston, 35-39; dir, Inst Contemp Art, Boston, 39-56; v pres, Old Sturbridge Village, 59-62; secy gen, World Crafts Coun, 67-; adv, N J State Mus & Pac Northwest Arts Ctr.
Awards: Chevalier, Legion of Honor, Fr Govt, 46; Off, Royal Order St Olav, Norway, 50; Comdr, Royal Order of Leopold, Belg Govt, 58.
Memberships: Art Vis Comt of Wheaton Col (chmn); MacDowell Colony; Coun Arts, Mass Inst Technol.
Publications: Auth, Oskar Kokoschka, 48; auth, Steuben glass, 48, 51 & 72; auth, Assignment in Israel, 60.
Mailing Address: 64 Fairgreen Pl, Chestnut Hill, MA 02167.

PLEASANTS, FREDERICK R
Collector, Patron
b Upper Montclair, N J, Nov 30, 06.
Study & Training: Princeton Univ, BS; Harvard Univ, MA.

Teaching: Lectr, Ariz State Mus, 60-64.
Positions: Cur, Brooklyn Mus, 50-58; cur, Ariz State Mus, 58-64.
Research: Primitive art, problems of anthropology in relation to museums in America.
Collection: Primitive art of Africa, Oceania and pre-Columbian America.
Mailing Address: 5 Sierra Vista Dr, Tucson, AZ 85719.

PLEISSNER, OGDEN MINTON
Painter
Preferred Media: Oils, Watercolors.
b Brooklyn, N Y, Apr 29, 05.
Study & Training: Brooklyn Friends Sch; Art Stud League New York.
Work in Public Collections: Metrop Mus Art, New York, N Y; Nat Collection Fine Arts, Washington, D C; Philadelphia Mus, Pa; Brooklyn Mus; Toledo Mus Art, Ohio.
Exhibitions: Carnegie Int, Pittsburgh, Pa; Art Inst Chicago, Ill; Nat Acad Design, New York; Am Watercolor Soc, New York; American Art, Metrop Mus Art.
Positions: Mem Fine Arts Comn, Nat Collection Fine Arts; dir & trustee, Louis C Tiffany Found; trustee, Shelburne Mus.
Awards: Joseph Pennell Medal, Philadelphia Watercolor Club, 54; gold medal, Am Watercolor Soc, 56; Altman Prize, Nat Acad Design, 59.
Bibliography: Alexander Eliot (auth), American painting; Norman Kent (auth), articles, In: Am Artist.
Memberships: Nat Acad Design (v pres); Am Watercolor Soc; Century Asn; Philadelphia Watercolor Club; Royal Soc Arts.
Dealer: Hirschl & Adler, 21 E 67th St, New York, NY 10021.
Mailing Address: 35 E Ninth St, New York, NY 10003.

PLETCHER, GERRY
Painter, Printmaker
Preferred Media: Etchings, Woodcuts, Acrylics, Oils.
b State College, Pa.
Study & Training: Edinboro State Col, BSArt Educ; Pa State Univ, MA; also with Montenegro, Carol Summers, Harold Altman, Nelson Sandgren & Shobaken.
Work in Public Collections: Evansville Mus Arts & Sci, Ind; Fisk Univ, Nashville, Tenn; Jacksonville State Univ, Ala; Watkins Art Inst, Nashville; Tenn Arts Comn, Nashville.
Exhibitions: 31st Southeastern Competition & Exhib, Gallery Contemp Art, Winston-Salem, N C, 69; Cent South Art Exhib, Nashville, 69, 70 & 71; Graphics U S A 1970, Nat Art Exhib, Dubuque, Iowa, 70; Ark Nat Art Exhib, Ark State Univ, 70; Nat Acad Design 145th Ann, New York, N Y, 70; plus others.
Teaching: Instr printmaking, Univ Tenn, Nashville, 68-
Awards: First prize purchase award in graphics, 9th Ann Tenn All-State Artists Exhib, Nashville, 69; graphics purchase award, 22nd Ann Mid-States Art Exhib, Evansville Mus Arts & Sci, 69; 7 purchase prizes, Tenn Arts Comn, 72; plus one other.
Bibliography: Gerry Pletcher, La Rev Mod, 2/71; Sweimal drei, Aufbau, 3/19/71.
Memberships: Tenn Art League.
Dealers: The Gallery Upstairs, Inc, 200 23rd Ave N, Nashville, TN 37205; Galerie Artist-Centre, 8330 Pfaffikon-Zurich, Switz.
Mailing Address: 605 Brook Hollow Rd, Nashville, TN 37205.

PLIMPTON, RUSSELL A
Art Administrator
b Hollis, N Y, Aug 26, 91.
Study & Training: Princeton Univ, AB, 14; Univ Minn, hon MA, 56; pvt study art hist, Europe.
Collections Arranged: Increased collections & arranged many exhibs, Minneapolis Art Inst.
Teaching: Lectr painting & decorative arts, radio & TV, Minneapolis, Minn.
Positions: Asst cur decorative arts dept, Metrop Mus Art, New York, N Y, 16-21; dir, Minneapolis Art Inst, 21-56; dir, Soc Four Arts, Palm Beach, Fla, 56-69; dir emer 69-
Memberships: Asn Art Mus Dirs (pres, 56); Am Asn Mus; Am Fedn Arts; plus others.
Publications: Contribr, Minneapolis Art Inst Bull.
Mailing Address: 10 Four Arts Plaza, Palm Beach, FL 33480.

PLOCHMANN, CAROLYN GASSAN
Painter
Preferred Media: Oils, Acrylics, Graphics.
b Toledo, Ohio, May 4, 26.
Study & Training: Toledo Mus Art Sch Design, 43-47; Univ Toledo, BA, 47; State Univ Iowa, MFA, 49; with Alfeo Faggi, 50; South Ill Univ, 51-52.
Work in Public Collections: Selden Rodman Collection, Oakland, N J; Evansville Mus Arts & Sci, Ind; Fleishmann Found Collection, Cincinnati, Ohio; Butler Inst Am Art, Youngstown, Ohio; plus others.
Commissions: Mural, North Side Old Nat Bank, Evansville, 53.

Exhibitions: One-man shows, Witte Mus, San Antonio, Tex, 68 & Toledo Mus Art, 68; 164th Prints & Drawings Ann, Pa Acad Fine Arts, Philadelphia, 69; 52nd Ann Mem Exhib, Philadelphia Watercolor Club, 69; Woodstock Artists Asn 50th Ann, N Y, 69.
Teaching: Supvr art, Allyn Training Sch, South Ill Univ, Carbondale, 49-50.
Awards: George W Stevens fel, Toledo Mus Art, 47-49; Tupperware Art Fund First Award, 53; Emily Lowe Found Competition Award, 58.
Bibliography: Louise Bruner (auth), Art notes, Toledo Blade, 10/10/65; Donald Key (auth), rev, In: Milwaukee J, 6/18/69.
Memberships: Silvermine Guild Artists; Woodstock Art Asn; Philadelphia Watercolor Club; Toledo Fedn Art Socs.
Publications: Auth, University portrait: nine paintings by Carolyn Gassan Plochmann, South Ill Univ Press, 59; auth, bk rev, In: The Egyptian; auth, cover article, In: Prize-winning graphics, 66.
Dealer: Kennedy Galleries, Inc, 20 E 56th St, New York, NY 10022.
Mailing Address: Rte 1, Carbondale, IL 62901.

PLUMMER, JOHN II
Art Administrator, Educator
b Rochester, Minn, Dec 15, 19.
Study & Training: Carleton Col, AB; Columbia Univ, PhD.
Teaching: Instr & lectr, Columbia Univ, instr, Barnard Col, 52-56; vis prof, univ, 61; vis lectr, Harvard Univ, 63; adj prof, Columbia Univ, 64-
Positions: Res assoc, Pierpont Morgan Libr, New York, N Y, 55-56, cur mediaeval & renaissance mss, 56-66, res fel for art, 66-
Research: Mediaeval and modern art.
Publications: Auth, Liturgical manuscripts, 64 & The Glazier collection of illuminated manuscripts, 68, Pierpont Morgan; auth, The hours of Catherine of Cleves, Pierpont Morgan, Boston Bk & Braziller, 66.
Mailing Address: 453 N Western Hwy, Blauvelt, NY 10913.

PNEUMAN, MILDRED Y
Painter
Preferred Media: Oils.
b Oskaloosa, Iowa, Sept 15, 99.
Study & Training: Univ Colo, BA & BEd, 21, MFA, 47.
Work in Public Collections: Univ Colo Mus; Univ Colo Faculty Club; PEO Mem Libr, Des Moines, Iowa.
Exhibitions: Hoosier Salon Asn, Marshall Fields, Chicago, Ill, 28-40; Am Color Print Soc; Colo State Fairs, 65-68; Denver Metrop, 69; Northern Colo Exhibs, Boulder Art Asn, 70.
Teaching: Instr art, Los Angeles Pub Schs, 21-23; instr art, Gary Pub Schs, 23-25.
Positions: Mem bd, Boulder Pub Libr Art Gallery, 67-70.
Awards: Colo State Fair Awards, 44; Tri Kappa Prizes, 65-66.
Memberships: Boulder Artists Guild (pres, 69-70); Boulder Art Asn.
Collection: 130 prints, woodcuts, lithographs, etchings, serigraphs and others, from the United States, Europe and Asia.
Publications: Auth, A study of the mountain form in painting, Univ Colo, 47.
Mailing Address: 1380 Running Springs Rd, Apt 4, Walnut Creek, CA 94595.

POHL, LOUIS G
Painter, Printmaker
b Cincinnati, Ohio, Sept 14, 15.
Study & Training: Cincinnati Art Acad.
Work in Public Collections: Cincinnati Mus Asn; Honolulu Acad Art.
Exhibitions: Butler Inst Am Art, 39 & 44; Art of Cincinnati, 40-42; one-man shows, Cincinnati Mus Asn, Contemp Art Ctr, 61 & Honolulu Acad Art; plus others.
Teaching: Instr, Univ Hawaii, 53-56; instr, Honolulu Sch Art; instr drawing, painting & illus, Honolulu Acad Art.
Positions: Cartoonist, daily cartoon School Daze, Honolulu Advertizer.
Awards: Four prizes, Honolulu Acad Art, 47-57; McInerny Found grant, 54-55; Printmaker of the Year, 65; plus others.
Memberships: Hawaii Painters & Sculptors League; Honolulu Printmakers.
Mailing Address: 3507 Nuuanu Pali Dr, Honolulu, HI 96187.

POINDEXTER, ELINOR FULLER
Art Dealer
b Montreal, Can; U S citizen.
Positions: Dir, Poindexter Gallery.
Memberships: Art Dealers Asn Am.
Specialty of Gallery: Contemporary painting & sculpture, especially American.
Collection: Contemporary works.
Mailing Address: 24 E 84th St, New York, NY 10028.

POLAN, LINCOLN M
Collector
b Wheeling, W Va, Feb 12, 09.
Study & Training: New York Univ; Univ Va; Ohio State Univ.
Positions: Mem bd dirs, Huntington Galleries, W Va.
Memberships: Metrop Mus Art.
Collection: Line and wash drawings by Rodin; drawings by French
    impressionists; American paintings, predominantly of the ash
    can school; Renaissance portraits of men; Renaissance prints
    and engravings. Collections exhibited at Huntington Galleries
    Art Museum, University of West Virginia Art Museum, Museum
    of Fine Arts, Houston, Texas & Phoenix Art Museum, Arizona.
Mailing Address: 2 Prospect Dr, Huntington, WV 25701.

POLAN, NANCY MOORE
Painter
Preferred Media: Watercolors.
b Newark, Ohio.
Study & Training: Marshall Univ, AB; Huntington Galleries; also
    with Fletcher Martin, Hilton Leech, Paul Puzinas & Al Schmidt.
Work in Public Collections: Huntington Galleries, W Va; Admiral
    House, Naval Observ, Washington, D C.
Exhibitions: Am Watercolor Soc, 61, 66 & 72 & traveling exhib, 72-
    73; Nat Arts Club, New York, 62-72; Joan Miro Graphics, Bar-
    celona, 70 & traveling exhib, Spain & U S A, 70-71; 21st Contemp
    Art La Scala, Florence, Italy, 71; one-man show, New York
    World's Fair, 65; plus many other group & one-man shows.
Positions: Hon rep, Centro Studi e Scambi Internazionali, Rome,
    Italy, 68-72.
Awards: Ralph & Elizabeth C Norton Mem Award, Third Nat Jury
    Show Am Art, Chautauqua, N Y, 60; Nat Arts Club Watercolor
    Award, New York, 69; bronze medal, Centro Studi e Scambi
    Internazionali, Rome, 71.
Bibliography: Pierre Mornand (auth), Portrait, La Rev Mod, 66.
Memberships: Nat Arts Club; assoc Allied Artists Am; Acad Inter-
    nazionale Leonardo de Vinci Roma (corresp, 72); Int Platform
    Asn (art comt, 67-72); Am Fedn Arts.
Publications: Contribr, La Rev Mod, 61 & 66.
Mailing Address: 2 Prospect Dr, Huntington, WV 25701.

POLESKIE, STEPHEN FRANCIS
Painter, Printmaker
b Pringle, Pa, June 3, 38.
Study & Training: Wilkes Col, BA(econ), 59; New Sch Social Res, 61.
Work in Public Collections: Whitney Mus Art, Metrop Mus Art &
    Mus Mod Art, New York, N Y; Walker Art Ctr, Minneapolis,
    Minn; Fort Worth Art Ctr, Tex.
Commissions: Seven ed silk-screen prints, Assoc Am Artists, 65-
    72; Seagansett-Patchogue (ed silk-screen prints), Int Graphic
    Arts Soc, 72.
Exhibitions: Contemporary American Printmakers, S London Mus,
    London, Eng, 67; Word & Image- Posters and Typography (1879-
    1967), Mus Mod Art, New York, 68; Recent Acquisitions: Prints
    and Drawings, Metrop Mus Art, 69; Oversize Prints, Whitney Mus
    Am Art, 71; Primera Bienal Americana de Artes Graficas, Mus
    Tertulia, Carton Colombia, S Am, 71.
Teaching: Asst prof silk-screen & drawing, Cornell Univ, 68-
Dealers: Associated American Artists, 663 Fifth Ave at 52nd St,
    New York, NY 10022; Fendrick Gallery, 3059 M St N W, Washing-
    ton, DC 20007.
Mailing Address: 306 Stone Quarry Rd, Ithaca, NY 14850.

POLITINSKY, F AUGUSTA (FLORA)
Painter, Sculptor
Preferred Media: Wax, Watercolors, Casein, Oils, Papier Maché,
    Copper, Aluminum Wire.
b Paterson, N J.
Study & Training: Am Art Sch, New York; Nat Acad Design; Newark
    Mus; Art Stud League New York.
Work in Public Collections: Many pvt collections.
Exhibitions: Nat Acad Sch, Gotham Painters, New York, 60; Pater-
    son Mus, 63; Ahda Artzt Gallery, New York, 67-69; Burr Artists,
    Jersey City Mus, 69; Empire Savings, Hannover Trust, New
    York, 71.
Awards: Best in show, Gotham Painters, 65; hon mention, Compos-
    ers, Auth, Artists Am, 72.
Memberships: Paterson Art Asn; Burr Artists; Fair Lawn Asn;
    Gotham Painters, New York (treas, 63); Composers, Authors &
    Artists Am.
Mailing Address: 490 Park Ave, Paterson, NJ 07504.

POLLACK, PETER
Photographer, Writer
b Wing, N Dak, Mar 21, 11.
Study & Training: Art Inst Chicago; Inst Design, Chicago, Ill.
Work in Public Collections: (Photographs) Art Inst Chicago; Worces-
    ter Art Mus; Whitney Mus Am Art.

Positions: Cur photog, Art Inst Chicago, 45-57; dir, Am Fedn Arts,
    62-64; hon cur photog, Worcester Art Mus, 64-; dir art, W J
    Sloane, New York, 65-70; dir photog, Harry N Abrams, Inc, 70-;
    ed, series of facsimile editions publ by Amphoto Press, 71-
Publications: Auth, Understanding primitive art (Sula's Zoo), 68;
    auth, The picture history of photography, rev ed, 70.
Mailing Address: 6 W 77th St, New York, NY 10024.

POLLACK, REGINALD MURRAY
Painter, Writer
Preferred Media: Oils.
b Middle Village, N Y, July 29, 24.
Study & Training: Apprentice to Moses Soyer, 41; study with Wallace
    Harrison, 46-47; Acad Grande Chaumiere, Paris, France, 48-52.
Work in Public Collections: Whitney Mus Am Art & Mus Mod Art,
    New York, N Y; Brooklyn Mus, N Y; Collection de l'Etat, France;
    Tel Aviv Mus, Jerusalem Mus & Haifa Mus, Israel; plus many
    other pub & pvt collections.
Commissions: Ed of color lithography, Int Coun, Mus Mod Art, New
    York, 59; Peace (greeting card), Jewish Mus, New York, 61;
    painting for Great Thoughts of Western Man series, Container
    Corp Am, 64; cover for State of N Y Dir, Bell Tel Co, 68-69;
    Chinese animal destiny calendar, Colgate-Palmolive Co, 72; plus
    others.
Exhibitions: 12 one-man shows, Peridot Gallery, New York, 49-69;
    Mixed Emotions, Long Beach Mus, Calif, 69; The Artist Collects,
    Lytton Art Ctr, Los Angeles, 69; Collectors Choice, Hall Gal-
    lery, Miami Beach, Fla, 72; 15 one-man shows plus many other
    group shows.
Teaching: Vis critic art, Yale Univ, 62-63; instr art, Cooper Union,
    63-64; staff mem, Human Relations Training Ctr, Univ Calif, Los
    Angeles, at Lake Arrowhead, 66; instr, Quaker Half-Way House,
    Los Angeles, 68.
Awards: Prix Othon Friesz - V, Paris, 56; Prix des Peintres
    Etrangers - Laureate, Paris, 58; Ingram-Merrill Found grants
    in painting, 64, 70-71.
Art Interests: Developed a technique for producing original litho-
    graphs from high speed offset presses.
Publications: Illusr, O is for overkill, Viking Press, 68; auth &
    illusr, The magician and the child, Atheneum, 71; illusr, The
    willow tree, Holt, Rinehart & Winston, 72; illusr, Ctr for Dem
    Insts Mag, 3/72; auth, To artists with love & Brancusi's sculp-
    ture versus his home, Art News; plus one other.
Mailing Address: 205 River Bend Rd, Great Falls, VA 22066.

POLLAK, THERESA
Painter, Educator
Preferred Media: Oils, Ink.
b Richmond, Va, Aug 13, 99.
Study & Training: Richmond Art Club; Westhampton Col, Univ
    Richmond, BS; Art Stud League New York; Fogg Mus, Harvard
    Univ, Carnegie fel; Steiger Paint Group, Edgertown, Mass; with
    Hans Hofmann, Provincetown, Mass.
Work in Public Collections: Va Commonwealth Univ, Richmond; Va
    Mus Fine Arts, Richmond; Chrysler Mus Norfolk, Va; Univ Va,
    Charlottesville; Washington & Lee Univ, Lexington, Va.
Exhibitions: 12th Biennial Exhib Contemp Am Painting, Corcoran
    Gallery Art, Washington, D C, 30; 1st Biennial Contemp Am
    Painting, Whitney Mus Am Art, New York, N Y, 32; New Eng Soc
    Contemp Art, Boston Mus Fine Arts, Mass, 33; 19th Irene
    Leache Mem Regional Painting Exhib, Chrysler Mus Norfolk, 68;
    Virginia Artists 1971, Va Mus Fine Arts, Richmond, 71.
Teaching: Instr drawing & painting, Va Commonwealth Univ, 28-35,
    prof drawing & painting, 35-69, faculty chmn, 42-50; instr draw-
    ing & painting, Westhampton Col, Univ Richmond, 30-35.
Awards: Distinguished alumna award, Westhampton Col, 64; cert
    distinction, Va Mus Fine Arts, 71; Theresa Pollak Bldg of Fine
    Arts, Va Commonwealth Univ, 71.
Memberships: Richmond Artists Asn (v pres, 58-59); Art Stud
    League New York; Marquis Biographical Libr Soc; Va Mus Fine
    Arts; Valentine Mus, Richmond.
Publications: Contribr, art criticisms, In: Richmond Newsleader &
    Richmond Times Dispatch, 31-49.
Mailing Address: 3912 Stuart Ave, Richmond, VA 23221.

POLLARD, DONALD PENCE
Designer, Painter
Preferred Media: Crystal, Oils.
b Bronxville, N Y, Sept 13, 24.
Study & Training: Pvt study with Harriet Lumis; R I Sch Design,
    BFA; Brown Univ.
Work in Public Collections: Eisenhower Mus; Kennedy Collection;
    Govt of Can, Ottawa, Ont; also in pvt collections in the U S,
    Europe, Asia & the Far East.
Commissions: Design of the Great Ring of Canada (with Alexander
    Seidel); other comns as assigned by Steuben Glass.

Exhibitions: Conn Nat Acad, 42; all major Steuben Exhibs, 53-; Phillips Mall Ann, 72.
Positions: Sr designer, Steuben Glass, 50-
Mailing Address: Steuben Glass, 715 Fifth Ave, New York, NY 10022.

POLLARO, PAUL
Painter
Preferred Media: Acrylics, Oils, Collage
b Brooklyn, N Y.
Study & Training: Flatiron Sch Art, New York, N Y; Art Stud League New York.
Work in Public Collections: Finch Col Mus, New York; Notre Dame Univ, Ind; Manhattanville Col, Purchase, N Y; Wagner Col, Staten Island, N Y; MacDowell Colony Collection, Peterborough, N H.
Exhibitions: 159th Ann, Pa Acad Fine Arts, Philadelphia, 64; Am Acad Arts & Lett, New York, 66 & 72; Nat Inst Arts & Lett, New York, 69 & 72; Artists of the 20th Century, Gallery Mod Art, New York, 70; Artists at Work, Finch Col Mus, 71.
Teaching: Instr painting, New Sch Soc Res, 64-69; asst prof painting, Wagner Col, 69-; vis artist, Notre Dame Univ, summers 65 & 67.
Awards: Second prize, Jersey City Mus, 62; fel, MacDowell Colony, 66, 68 & 71; Tiffany Found grant, 67.
Dealer: Babcock Galleries, 805 Madison Ave, New York, NY 10021.
Mailing Address: 7005 Shore Rd, Brooklyn, NY 11209.

POLLOCK, MERLIN F
Painter, Educator
Preferred Media: Acrylics, Watercolors.
b Manitowoc, Wis, Jan 3, 05.
Study & Training: Ecole Beaux Arts, Paris, France; Fountainbleau, Paris; Art Inst Chicago, BFA, MFA.
Work in Public Collections: Syracuse Univ, N Y; Munson-Williams-Proctor Inst, Utica, N Y; Everson Mus, Syracuse; State Univ N Y Col Forestry, Syracuse.
Commissions: Steel (fresco), Tildon Tech High Sch, Chicago, Ill; First Post Office (mural), O'Fallon Post Off, Ill, comn by U S Treas Dept.
Exhibitions: Michigan Invitational, Flint Inst Art, Mich, 57; Dr Vance Inaugural Invitational, Wesleyan Univ, Lincoln, Nebr, 58; Rocky Mountain Nat Invitational Art Exhib, Utah State Univ, Logan, 58; One Hundred Twenty-Five Years of New York State Painting & Sculpture Invitational, N Y State Fair, 66; one-man shows, Mich State Univ, East Lansing, 59 & Everson Mus, Syracuse, 66.
Teaching: Instr mural painting, fresco & drawing, Sch Art, Art Inst Chicago, 35-43; prof painting, Syracuse Univ, 46-71.
Positions: Supvr mural painting, Ill Art Proj, Works Proj Admin, 40-43; chmn grad prog, Syracuse Univ Sch Art, 47-71; acting dean sch art, Syracuse Univ, 60-61, 67-68 & 69-70.
Awards: James Nelson Raymond fel, Art Inst Chicago, 30; Syracuse Ann, Everson Mus, 50, 60, 64 & 66; Finger Lakes Ann, Rochester Mem Mus, 56-58 & 60.
Mailing Address: 120 Wellwood Dr, Fayetteville, NY 13066.

POLONSKY, ARTHUR
Painter, Educator
Preferred Media: Oils, Tempera.
b Lynn, Mass, June 6, 25.
Study & Training: Boston Mus Sch, with Karl Zerbe, 43-48, dipl (with honors), 48, European traveling fel, 48-50.
Work in Public Collections: Fogg Mus, Harvard Univ, Cambridge, Mass; Mus Fine Arts, Boston; Addison Gallery Am Art; Brandeis Univ, Waltham, Mass; Stedelijk Mus, Amsterdam, Holland.
Commissions: Portrait of Dr William Dameshek, Tufts-New England Med Ctr, Boston, 66; Stone with the Angel (portfolio of ten original lithographs), Impressions Workshop, Inc, Boston, 69; portrait of Dr Sidney Farber, Harvard Med Sch for Boston Children's Hosp, 71.
Exhibitions: Salon des Jeunes Peintres, Paris, France, 49; Art Today-1950, Metrop Mus Art, New York, N Y, 50; Exhib Am Art, Stedelijk Mus, Amsterdam, Holland, 50; Carnegie Int Expos, Pittsburgh, Pa, 51; View, Inst Contemp Art, Boston, 60.
Teaching: Instr painting & head dept, Boston Mus Sch, 50-60; from instr to asst prof painting & drawing, Brandeis Univ, 54-65; assoc prof painting, drawing & design, Boston Univ Sch Fine & Applied Arts, 65-
Positions: Mem & dir, Artists Equity Asn, 48-67.
Awards: Tiffany Found grant for painting, 51-52; first prize, Boston Arts Festival, 54.
Bibliography: Article on young artists, In: Life Mag, 12/48; reviews of exhibs, In: Art News, 48 & 65; microfilm records of papers, documents, letters, reviews & tape recorded interviews, In: Archives Am Art, Smithsonian Inst, 72.
Dealer: Boris Mirski Gallery, 166 Newbury St, Boston, MA 02115.
Mailing Address: 364 Cabot St, Newtonville, MA 02160.

POLSKY, CYNTHIA
Painter
Preferred Media: Acrylics, Watercolors.
b New York, N Y, Feb 16, 39.
Study & Training: Art Stud League New York, with Will Barnet; New Sch Social Res, with Julian Levy; Columbia Univ.
Work in Public Collections: Palm Springs Desert Mus, Calif; Joseph E Hirshhorn Collection; Rand Corp Off, Los Angeles, Calif.
Commissions: Wooden painted murals, Manhattanville Col Music Festival, 66; rec jacket, UNICEF, 66.
Exhibitions: One-man shows, Benson Gallery, Bridgehampton, L I, N Y, 68, Comara Gallery, Los Angeles, 69, Artisan Gallery, Houston, Tex, 70 & Palm Springs Desert Mus, 72-73; Laguna Beach Art Asn Exhib 10, 71; Watercolor Exhib, Comara Gallery, 72.
Bibliography: Henry Seldio (auth), catalogue preface for exhib, Palm Springs Desert Mus, 72-73.
Dealers: Comara Gallery, 617 N La Cienega Blvd, Los Angeles, CA 90069; Benson Gallery, Bridgehampton, NY 11932.
Mailing Address: 50 E 79th St, New York, NY 10021.

POMERANCE, LEON
Collector, Patron
b New York, N Y, Aug 2, 07.
Study & Training: New York Univ, BS, Law Sch, LLB & LLM.
Positions: Trustee, Archaeol Inst Am, 65-, pres, N Y chap, 68-70; co-sponsor excavations, Kato Zakro, Crete, Greece.
Collection: Ancient pre-Greek, Greek and Near Eastern art.
Mailing Address: 7 Amherst Rd, Great Neck, NY 11021.

PONCE DE LEON, MICHAEL
Printmaker, Painter
b Miami, Fla, July 4, 22.
Study & Training: Univ Mex, BA; Art Stud League New York; Nat Acad Design; Brooklyn Mus Art Sch; also in Europe.
Work in Public Collections: Mus Mod Art, New York, N Y; Nat Gallery Art, Washington, D C; Smithsonian Inst, Washington, D C; Metrop Mus Art, New York; Brooklyn Mus, N Y; plus others.
Commissions: Many print editions, 60-; 10 prints, U S State Dept, 66; glass sculpture Steuben Glass, 71.
Exhibitions: Mus Arte Mod, Paris, France; Victoria & Albert Mus, London, Eng; Venice Bienale, 70; Mus Mod Art, New York; Metrop Mus, New York; plus others.
Teaching: Instr printmaking, Hunter Col, 59-66; instr printmaking, Art Stud League New York, 66-; prof printmaking Columbia Univ, 72.
Positions: Int Cult Exchange, U S State Dept, lect & travel Yugoslavia, 65, India & Pakistan, 67-68 & Spain, 71.
Awards: Tiffany Found grant, 55; Fulbright grant, 56; Guggenheim Found grant, 67.
Bibliography: J Ross & C Romano (auth), The complete printmaker, Macmillan, 72; J Heller (auth), Prints, Holt, Rinehart & Winston, 72; G Peterdi (auth), Printmaking, Macmillan, 72.
Memberships: Soc Am Graphic Artists (treas, 68); Asn Am Univ Prof.
Publications: Contribr, Experiments in three dimensions, Art in Am, 68; auth, Artist proof, 71; auth, The collage intaglio, 72.
Dealer: Jane Haslem Gallery, 2121 P St N W, Washington, DC 20036.
Mailing Address: 463 West St, New York, NY 10014.

POND, CLAYTON
Painter, Printmaker
b Long Island, N Y, June 10, 41.
Study & Training: Carnegie Inst Technol, BFA, 64; Pratt Inst, MFA, 66.
Work in Public Collections: Nat Collection Fine Arts, Washington, D C; Mus Mod Art, New York, N Y; Boston Mus Fine Arts, Mass; Philadelphia Mus Art, Pa; Art Inst Chicago, Ill.
Exhibitions: Whitney Mus Am Art Ann, New York, N Y, 67; one-man exhibs, paintings, Martha Jackson Gallery, New York, 68 & 72 & paintings & prints, De Cordova Mus, Lincoln, Mass, 72; Int Exhib Colored Graphics, Mus Mod Art, Paris, France, 70; U S Pavilion, World's Fair, Osaka, Japan, 70.
Teaching: Instr photog & printmaking, C W Post Col, Long Island Univ, 66-68; adj instr serigraphy, Sch Visual Arts, New York, 68-70; guest lectr, Univ Wis-Madison, spring 72.
Awards: State Dept grant, Smithsonian Inst Int Art Prog & Abby Gray Found, 67; Boston Mus Purchase Award, Boston Printmakers 20th Ann, 68; Color Print U S A Purchase Award, W Tex Mus, 69; plus others.
Bibliography: Richard S Field (auth), Silkscreen, the media medium, Art News Mag, 1/72; Jules Heller (auth), Printmaking today, Holt, Rinehart & Winston, 72; Marshall B Davidson (auth), Artists' America, Am Heritage, 73.
Memberships: Am Color Print Soc; Print Coun Am; Boston Printmakers; Philadelphia Print Club.
Dealer: Martha Jackson Gallery, 32 E 69th St, New York, NY 10021.
Mailing Address: 130 Greene St, New York, NY 10012.

POONS, LARRY
Painter
b Tokyo, Japan, Oct 1, 37.
Study & Training: Boston Mus Fine Arts Sch, 58.
Work in Public Collections: Mus Mod Art; Albright-Knox Art Gallery; Stedelijk Mus, Holland; Woodward Found, Washington, D C.
Exhibitions: Art Inst Chicago, 66; Corcoran Gallery Art, 67; Carnegie Inst, 67; Documenta IV, Kassel, Ger, 68; Whitney Mus Am Art Ann, 68 & 72; plus many others.
Teaching: Vis faculty, N Y Studio Sch, 67.
Bibliography: Lawrence Alloway (auth), Systemic painting, Guggenheim Mus, 66; Gregory Battcock (ed), Minimal art: a critical anthology, Dutton, 68; E C Goosen (auth), The art of the real U S A 1948-1968, Mus Mod Art, 68; plus others.
Dealer: Lawrence Rubin Gallery, 49 W 57th St, New York, NY 10019.
Mailing Address: 295 Church St, New York, NY 10005.

POOR, ANNE
Painter
Preferred Media: Oils, Watercolors.
b New York, N Y, Jan 2, 18.
Study & Training: Bennington Col; Art Stud League New York, N Y, with Alexander Brook, William Zorach & Yasuo Kuniyoshi; Acad Julian, Paris, painting with Jean Lureat & Abraham Rattner; also asst for murals in fresco to Henry Varnum Poor.
Work in Public Collections: Whitney Mus Am Art; Brooklyn Mus; Art Inst Chicago; Wichita Mus; Des Moines Art Ctr.
Commissions: Murals, Pub Works Admin, 37; Murals in true fresco, comn by Nathaniel Saltonstall, Wellfleet, Mass, 51-52, Skowhegan Sch Painting & Sculpture, 54, South Solon Free Meeting House, Maine, 57 & mr & Mrs Robert Graham, Stamford, Conn, 58.
Exhibitions: Artists For Victory, Metrop Mus Art, 42; Am Brit Art Ctr, New York, 44, 45 & 48; Maynard Walker Gallery, New York, 50; five shows, Graham Gallery, New York, 57-71; plus others.
Teaching: Mem fac painting & dir, Skowhegan Sch Painting & Sculpture, 47-61, gov & trustee, 63-
Awards: Edwin Austin Abbey Mem fel for mural painting, 48 & first prize for landscape painting, 70, Nat Acad Design; Nat Inst Arts & Lett grant in art, 57.
Bibliography: Alan Gussow (auth), A sense of place, Friends of Earth, Sat Rev Press, 72.
Memberships: Artists Equity Asn.
Publications: Illusr, Greece, Viking Press, 64.
Dealer: Graham Gallery, 1014 Madison Ave, New York, NY 10021.
Mailing Address: 92 S Mountain Rd, New City, NY 10956.

POOR, ROBERT JOHN
Art Historian
b Rockport, Ill, July 10, 31.
Study & Training: Boston Univ, BA (art hist), 53, MA (art hist), 57; Univ Chicago, with Ludwig Bachhofer, PhD (art hist), 61.
Collections Arranged: Art of India (exhibition catalogue), 69 & Far Eastern Art in Minnesota Collections (exhibition catalogue), 70, Univ Minn Gallery; Hanga, The Modern Japanese Print (exhibition catalogue), Minn Mus Art, Saint Paul, 72.
Teaching: Asst prof Asian art, Dartmouth Col, 61-65; assoc prof Asian art, Univ Minn, Minneapolis, 65-
Positions: Consult Asian art, Minneapolis Inst Art; cur Asian art, Minn Mus Art, Saint Paul.
Research: Chinese bronzes.
Publications: Auth, Notes on the Sung archaeological catalogs, 65 & auth, Some remarkable examples of I-Hsing ware, 66-67, Archives of Chinese Art Soc Am; Auth, Ancient Chinese bronzes, Inter-Cult Arts Press, 68; auth, Evolution of a secular vessel-type, 68 & auth, On the Mo-tzu-Yu, 70, Oriental Art.
Mailing Address: Dept of Art History, University of Minnesota, Minneapolis, MN 55455.

POPE, ANNEMARIE HENLE
Art Administrator
b Dortmund, Ger; U S citizen.
Study & Training: Heidelberg Univ, PhD, 32; Radcliffe Col, Harvard Univ, exchange fel, 33-34.
Positions: Asst dir, Portland Art Mus, Ore, 41-42; dir in charge exhibs, Am Fedn Arts, 47-51; chief traveling exhibs, Smithsonian Inst, 51-64; pres, Int Exhibs Found, 65-
Awards: Royal Swedish Order of Polar Star, 57; Order of Merit, First Class, Ger, 64.
Memberships: Am Asn Mus; Washington Friends of Am Mus Bath, Eng (chmn); Am Fedn Arts; Master Drawings Asn; Corcoran Gallery Art; plus others.
Publications: Auth, acknowledgments for catalogues publ by Int Exhibs Found in connection with traveling exhibs.
Mailing Address: International Exhibitions Foundation, 1729 H St, N W, Washington, DC 20006.

POPE, JOHN ALEXANDER
Museum Director
b Detroit, Mich, Aug 4, 06.
Study & Training: Yale Col, BA, 30; Harvard Univ, MA, 40, PhD, 55.
Teaching: Lectr Chinese art, Columbia Univ, 41-43; res prof oriental art, Univ Mich, 62-71; lectr, U S, Europe & Far East, 66-69.
Positions: Assoc in res, Freer Gallery Art, Washington, D C, 43-46, asst dir, 46-62, dir, 62-71; co-chmn, Manila Trade Pottery Sem, Manila, 68.
Memberships: Am Oriental Soc; Oriental Ceramic Soc, London; Asn Asian Studies; Asia Soc; Japan Soc.
Publications: Compiler, A descriptive and illustrative catalogue of Chinese bronzes, 46; auth, Fourteenth century blue and white: a group of Chinese porcelains in the Topkapu Sarayi Müzesi, Istanbul, Freer Gallery Art Occasional Papers, Vol 2, No 1; auth, Chinese porcelains from the Ardebil Shrine, Freer Gallery Art, 56; sr co-auth, Freer Chinese bronzes, Freer Gallery Art Oriental Studies, Vol 1, No 7; contribr, Harvard J Asiatic Studies; plus others.
Mailing Address: c/o Freer Gallery of Art, Washington, DC 20560.

POPE, MARY ANN IRWIN
Painter
Preferred Media: Acrylics.
b Louisville, Ky, Mar 8, 32.
Study & Training: Art Ctr, Louisville; Univ Louisville; Cooper Union.
Work in Public Collections: Nat Collection Fine Art, Washington, D C; Mint Mus, Charlotte, N C; Quarter Print Collector, New Orleans, La.
Exhibitions: Soc 4 Arts, Palm Beach, Fla, 69; Frontal Images, Jackson, Miss, 70; Mid-South, Brooks Art Gallery, Memphis, Tenn, 71 & 72; 38th Ann Nat Exhib Miniature Artists, Washington, D C, 71; Piedmont Painting & Sculpture Exhib, Mint Mus, Charlotte, N C, 72.
Teaching: Instr painting, Art Ctr, 59; instr painting, Huntsville Art League, Ala, 66-, dir, adult classes, 67-
Awards: Shaw Warehouse Award, 32nd Nat Watercolor Exhib, 72; Mint Mus Purchase Award, Piedmont Painting & Sculpture Exhib, 72.
Memberships: Huntsville Art League & Mus Asn; Ala Watercolor Soc.
Mailing Address: 1705 Greenwyche Rd S E, Huntsville, AL 35801.

POPE, RICHARD CORAINE
Painter, Designer
Preferred Media: Opaque Watercolor.
b Spokane, Wash, Aug 5, 28.
Study & Training: Univ Louisville, BA & MA; Cincinnati Art Acad, with Noel Martin.
Exhibitions: Work has been widely exhibited in regional shows.
Teaching: Instr graphic design, Univ Louisville, 65-66; assoc prof graphic design, Univ Ala, Huntsville, 66-
Positions: Art dir, Staples Advert, Louisville, 57-64.
Memberships: Huntsville Art League & Mus Asn (dir, 70-72); Huntsville Mus Bd.
Mailing Address: 1705 Greenwyche Rd S E, Huntsville, AL 35801.

PORTANOVA, JOSEPH DOMENICO
Sculptor, Designer
Preferred Media: Bronze.
b Boston, Mass, May 16, 09.
Study & Training: With Cyrus E Dallin.
Work in Public Collections: Dr Lee de Forest (sculpture), Smithsonian Inst, Washington, D C; Dr Robert A Millikan (sculpture), Calif Inst Technol, Pasadena; Dr Fabien Sevitzky (sculpture), Dade Co Auditorium, Miami, Fla; Richard Bard (sculpture), Lake Bard, Ventura Co, Calif; J B (Cap) Haralson (sculpture), Amateur Athletic Union, Indianapolis, Ind.
Commissions: Dr Charles LeRoy Lowman (sculpture), Orthopaedic Hosp, Los Angeles, Calif, 62; Leo M Harvey (sculpture), Harvey Aluminum Co, Torrance, Calif, 62; ten bas-relief tablets, Los Angeles Mem Coliseum, 63-; John E Longden (bust), 66, Santa Anita Park, 66 & William Shoemaker (bust), Arcadia, Calif, 71, Los Angeles Turf Club.
Exhibitions: Los Angeles Co Mus Art, 58; Laguna Beach Art Asn, Calif, 60; Calif Art Club, Los Angeles, 62; Calif State Fair, Sacramento, 63; Nat Acad Design, New York, N Y, 64.
Positions: V pres design, Hoffman Electronics Corp, 44-65; dir design, Teledyne-Packard Bell, 65-
Awards: First prize, Laguna Beach Art Asn, 60; first prize, Calif Art Club, 62; gold medal, Calif State Fair, 63.
Bibliography: Clay & bronze, Saturday Night, 1/39; Janice Lovoos (auth), The portrait sculpture of Joseph Portanova, Am Artist, 1/65.

Memberships: Calif Art Club (second v pres & bd dirs, 63); fel Am Inst Fine Arts (v pres, 64).
Mailing Address: 13741 Romany Dr, Pacific Palisades, CA 90272.

PORTER, (EDWIN) DAVID
Painter, Sculptor
b Chicago, Ill, May 18, 12.
Work in Public Collections: Whitney Mus Am Art; Miami Mus Mod Art; Chrysler Art Mus; Norfolk Mus Arts & Sci; Parish Art Mus, Southampton; plus many others.
Exhibitions: Editions in Plastic, Jewish Mus, New York, N Y, 69; Outdoor Sculpture, Artists of the Region, Guild Hall, N Y, 70; Artists at Dartmouth Retrospective, City Hall, Boston, Mass, 71; Hemisphere Club, Time-Life Bldg, New York, 71; Artists of Suffolk County, Part V, New Directions, Heckscher Mus, Huntington, N Y, 71; plus many other group & one man shows.
Teaching: Artist-in-residence, Dartmouth Col, fall 64 & spring 65; artist-in-residence, Cooper Union, 67-68; lectr art, Corcoran Gallery Art, Washington, D C, 68 & 69.
Awards: Gold medal of Pres Gronchi of Italy, Sassoferrato, Italy, 61; Beaux Arts Award in painting, Beaux Arts Club, 69; grant, Nat Inst Arts & Lett, 70; plus many others.
Bibliography: Today's living, New York Herald Tribune, 56; The making of a construction (tv film interview), Voice Am, 57; maj articles on work publ in newspapers in Norway & Sweden, 60.
Publications: Auth, Why I ran away, Am Weekly, 7/10/60.
Mailing Address: Wainscott, NY 11975.

PORTER, ELMER JOHNSON
Painter, Educator
Preferred Media: Watercolors.
b Richmond, Ind, May 5, 07.
Study & Training: Art Inst Chicago, BAE; Ohio State Univ, MA; Earlham Col; Univ Cincinnati; Univ Colo; Butler Univ; San Carlos Univ, Guatemala.
Exhibitions: Hoosier Salon, Chicago, Ill; Art League, Columbus, Ohio; Cincinnati; New York, N Y; Art Asn Richmond, Ind.
Teaching: Instr art, McKinley High Sch, Cedar Rapids, Iowa, 30-37; instr art, Hughes High Sch, Cincinnati, 38-46; prof art, Ind State Univ, Terre Haute, 46-
Awards: Applied arts prize, Indianapolis Art Asn, 29; watercolor award, Art League, Columbus, 38; Bonsib purchase prize, Hoosier Salon, 39.
Memberships: Art Educ Asn Ind (pres, 52-53, secy-treas, 54-67); Kappa Pi (int secy, 70-); Nat Art Educ Asn; Am Soc Bookplate Collectors & Designers; Pen & Brush Club.
Publications: Auth, Bookplates of Ernest Haskel, Bookplate Ann, 51.
Mailing Address: 3115 Margaret Ave, Terre Haute, IN 47802.

PORTER, FAIRFIELD
Painter, Lecturer
b Winnetka, Ill, June 10, 07.
Study & Training: Harvard Col, BS, 28; Art Stud League, with Boardman Robinson & Thomas Hart Benton, 28-30.
Work in Public Collections: Mus Mod Art; Wadsworth Atheneum; Univ Nebr; Purdue Univ; Univ N Mex; plus others.
Commissions: Numerous portraits comns.
Exhibitions: Six shows, Whitney Mus Am Art, 59-68; Univ Ala, 64; Univ Southern Ill, 64; retrospective, Cleveland Mus Art, 67; Colby Col, 69; plus others.
Teaching: Lectr aesthet, univs & cols; adj prof art, Southampton Col, Long Island Univ; instr, Queens Col, N Y, 69; prof & artist-in-residence, Amherst Col, 69-70.
Positions: Ed assoc, Art News, 51-58; art critic, Nation Mag, 59.
Awards: Longview Found Award for criticism in The Nation, 59; purchase prize, Purdue Univ, 66.
Bibliography: John W McCoubrey (auth), American tradition in painting, Braziller, 63.
Memberships: Int Asn Art Critics.
Publications: Auth, Thomas Eakins (monogr), Braziller, 59; contribr, Art News, The Nation, Art in Am & Art & Lit; plus others.
Dealer: M Knoedler & Co, 21 E 70th St, New York, NY 10021.
Mailing Address: 49 S Main St, Southampton, Long Island, NY 11968.

PORTER, J ERWIN
Painter
b Medina, N Y, Jan 13, 03.
Study & Training, Rochester Inst Technol.
Work in Public Collections: Marine Midland Bank; Monroe Co Savings Bank; Rochester Savings Bank; New Paltz Savings Bank; Charles Rand Penny Found; plus others.
Exhibitions: Four shows, Am Watercolor Soc, 61-68; Nat Acad Design, 63 & 65; six shows, Allied Artists Am, 63-71; one-man shows, Smithsonian Inst, 67; Nat Arts Club Ann, 67-70; plus others.
Awards: Rochester Art Club Awards, 64, 65, 68 & 69; Widmer Wine Co Award, Mem Art Gallery Finger Lakes Exhib, 68.

Bibliography: Article, In: Am Artist, 6/66.
Memberships: Fel Rochester Mus & Sci Ctr; Am Watercolor Soc; Allied Artists Am; Rochester Art Club; Genesee Group.
Mailing Address: 1501 N Miracle Mile, Tucson, AZ 85705.

PORTER, PRISCILLA MANNING
Craftsman, Educator
b Baltimore, Md, Feb 1, 17.
Study & Training: Bennington Col, BA, 40.
Work in Public Collections: Bowl in collection of Pottery Sch, Faenza, Italy; fused & epoxied glass panel, New Britain Mus, Conn; fused glass animal in permanent collection of Corning Mus Glass, N Y.
Commissions: Fused glass cross, St John's Episcopal Church, Washington, Conn, 62; fused weed-ash cross, Emmanuel Episcopal Church, Baltimore, Md, 63; Noah's Ark (fused glass epoxied to plate glass panels), North Shore Unitarian Soc, Plandome, Long Island, 71.
Exhibitions: San Jose State Col Glass Exhib, 64; Craftsmen of the Eastern States, sponsored by Smithsonian Inst, 66.
Teaching: Instr ceramics, dept educ, Mus Mod Art, New York, N Y, 52-61.
Awards: Cert of merit, Artist-Craftsmen New York, 68.
Memberships: Soc Conn Craftsmen; Artist-Craftsmen New York.
Mailing Address: Plumb Hill Rd, Washington, CT 06793.

PORTMANN, FRIEDA BERTHA ANNE
Painter, Sculptor
b Tacoma, Wash.
Study & Training: With Fernand Leger, Glenn Lukens, Clifford Still, Norman Lewis Rice, Peter Camfferman, Edward Du Penn, Julius Heller, Hayter, Lasansky & H Matsumoto.
Work in Public Collections: Univ Southern Calif, Los Angeles; Art Inst Chicago, Ill; Calif Col Fine Arts, Oakland; plus many in pvt collections.
Commissions: Sacajewea (wooden garden sculpture), Seattle, Wash; Beer & Skittles (mural), pvt home, Seattle; Pioneer Teacher (oils), Pioneer Asn, Seattle; Lily Madonna (ceramics), in garden, Catholic Sch, Seattle; numerous portraits in oils, Seattle.
Exhibitions: Prints, Boston Mus Arts; paintings, prints, sculpture & crafts, Seattle Art Mus; sculpture, Denver Mus Art; painting & print, Oakland Mus Art; paintings, Argent Gallery, New York.
Teaching: Art dir, Walla Walla Pub Schs, Wash; instr art & orchestra, Aberdeen Pub Schs, Wash; instr jr & high sch art, Seattle Pub Schs.
Memberships: Northwest Printmakers (pres); Women Painters Wash(secy).
Mailing Address: 1330 Boren Ave, Apt 301, Seattle, WA 98101.

POSEN, STEPHEN
Painter
b St Louis, Mo, Sept 27, 39.
Study & Training: Washington Univ, BFA, Milliken traveling scholar, 64-65; Fulbright grant, Italy, 64-66; Yale Univ, MFA.
Work in Public Collections: Va Mus Fine Arts; Chase Manhattan Collection.
Exhibitions: Highlight of the 1971 Season, Aldrich Mus Contemp Art, Ridgefield, Conn, 71; The New Realists, Chicago Mus Contemp Art, 71; Relativating Realism, Stedelijk Van Abbe Mus, Eindhoven, Holland, 72; Whitney Mus Am Art Ann, New York, N Y, 72; Documenta 5, Kassel, W Ger, 72.
Teaching: Instr drawing, Cooper Union.
Bibliography: David Shirey (auth), Downtown art scene, N Y Times, 4/3/71; Ivan Karp (auth), Rent is the only reality, Arts Mag, 1/72; John Canaday (auth), Whitney annual, N Y Times, 2/6/72.
Mailing Address: c/o O K Harris Gallery, 465 W Broadway, New York, NY 10012.

POSES, MR & MRS JACK I
Collectors
Mr Poses, b Russia, Dec 28, 99; U S citizen.
Study & Training: Mr Poses, New York Univ, BCS, 23, MBA, 24; Brandeis Univ, LLD, 68.
Positions: Mr Poses, v chmn, New York City Bd Higher Educ, 63-; mem bd trustees, mem educ & budget comts, founder Poses Inst Fine Arts & chmn coun fine arts, Brandeis Univ; founder, Einstein Med Sch.
Awards: Mr Poses, Chevalier, Legion Hon, 58; citation distinguished & exceptional serv to City New York, Mayor Lindsay, 67; plus others.
Art Interests: Established numerous scholarships at many leading universities, as well as devoting active support to major art museums.
Collection: French and American.
Mailing Address: 1107 Fifth Ave, New York, NY 10028.

POSEY, LESLIE THOMAS
Sculptor, Educator
Preferred Media: Stone.
b Harshaw, Wis, Jan 20, 00.
Study & Training: Wis Sch Fine & Appl Arts, with Ferd Koenig, 19-23; Pa Acad Fine Art, scholar, 23, also with Albert Laessle; Art Inst Chicago, 24 & with Albin Polasek, 29-30.
Work in Public Collections: Manatee Art League, Bradenton, Fla; Contemp Arts Gallery, Pinellas Park, Fla; Longboat Key Art Ctr, Fla.
Commissions: Beethoven (limestone), Dr O Seivert, Wildwood Park, Wis, 33; decorative cast stone, Church of the Redeemer, Sarasota, Fla, 52; garden figure in cast stone, Nat Coun Garden Clubs, Athens, Ga, 54; Kellogg portrait (stone), Dept Fire Control, Oneco, Fla, 58; Terry portrait (bronze), Longboat Key Art Ctr, 70.
Exhibitions: Wisconsin Sculptors & Painters, 23 & Lincoln Int, 30, Milwaukee Art Inst; Am Artists Exhib, Art Inst Chicago, 30; Hoosier Salon, Marshall Fields Gallery, Chicago, Ill, 30; Fla Int, Lake Land, 50.
Teaching: Dir sculpture, Posey Sch Sculpture, 37-; instr sculpture, Manatee Art League, Bradenton, Fla, 52-61; instr sculpture, Longboat Key Art Ctr, 61-71.
Positions: Sculptor, Am Terra-Cotta Co, Chicago, 25-26; head sculpture & design, Indianapolis Terra-Cotta Co, Ind, 26-29.
Awards: Medal & award, Milwaukee Art Inst, 23; first prize, Hoosier Salon, Katherine Barker Hickox, 30; first prize, Sarasota Art Asn, Fla Fed Art, 40.
Memberships: Longboat Key Art Ctr; Sarasota Art Asn (dir, 71-73).
Mailing Address: 401 N Tuttle Ave, Sarasota, FL 33580.

POSNER, DONALD
Art Historian
b New York, N Y, Aug 30, 31.
Study & Training: Queens Col, AB, 56; Harvard Univ, AM, 57; N Y Univ, PhD, 62.
Teaching: Instr art hist, Queens Col, 57; asst prof art hist, Columbia Univ, 61-62; prof art hist, N Y Univ Inst Fine Arts, 62-
Positions: Art historian-in-residence, Am Acad Rome, 68-69; ed-in-chief, Art Bull, 68-71.
Awards: Phi Beta Kappa award, 56; Rome prize fel, Am Acad Rome, 59-61; ACLS grant, 65.
Memberships: Col Art Asn Am (dir, 70-74); Renaissance Soc Am; Am Soc Eighteenth Century Studies.
Research: Italian painting of sixteenth through eighteenth century; French painting of eighteenth century.
Publications: Auth, Annibale Carracci, 71; auth, Caravaggio's homo-erotic early works, Art Quart, 71; co-auth, 17th & 18th century art, 72; auth, The true path of Fragonard's Progress of Love, Burlington Mag, 72; auth, Watteau's Lady at her Toilet, 73.
Mailing Address: Institute of Fine Arts, New York University, 1 E 78th St, New York, NY 10021.

POST, GEORGE (BOOTH)
Painter, Educator
b Oakland, Calif, Sept 29, 06.
Study & Training: Calif Sch Fine Arts.
Work in Public Collections: San Francisco Mus Art; Seattle Art Mus; Calif Palace of Legion of Honor; San Diego Fine Arts Soc; Metrop Mus Art; plus many others.
Exhibitions: Metrop Mus Art; San Francisco Mus Art; DeYoung Mem Mus; Seattle Art Mus; San Diego Fine Arts Gallery; plus many others.
Teaching: Instr, Stanford Univ, 40; prof fine arts, Calif Col Arts & Crafts, 47-; instr, San Jose Col, 51-52.
Awards: Prizes, Mother Lode Exhib, 55, 58 & 60; purchase awards, Watercolor U S A, Springfield Mus Art, Mo, 66 & Jack London Square Art Festival, 68; plus many others.
Memberships: Am Watercolor Soc; San Francisco Art Asn; Calif Watercolor Soc; Int Inst Arts & Lett; W Coast Watercolor Soc.
Publications: Contribr, illus, In: Fortune, Calif Arts & Archit, Art Digest, Am Artist & Ford Times Mags.
Mailing Address: 327 Cumberland St, San Francisco, CA 94114.

POTAMKIN, MEYER P
Collector
b Philadelphia, Pa, Nov 11, 09.
Study & Training: Dickinson Col, PhB, 32; Temple Univ, MEd, 41.
Collection: American art, heavy 1880 to 1915 from Hicks to Levine.
Mailing Address: 1808 Delancey Pl, Philadelphia, PA 19103.

POTTER, (GEORGE) KENNETH
Painter, Designer
Preferred Media: Watercolors, Oils, Acrylics.
b Bakersfield, Calif, Feb 26, 26.
Study & Training: Acad Art, San Francisco, 47 & 48; Acad Frochot, Paris, France, with Jean Metzinger (theoritician of cubism), 50-

52; Inst Statale dei Belli Arte, Florence, Italy, summer 51; study in Sicily, 53; Col Marin, AA, 72.
Work in Public Collections: City San Francisco Art Comn, Calif, 58; Univ San Francisco Collection, 65; Fed Housing & Urban Development, regional off, San Francisco, 69; Col Marin, Kentfield, Calif, 72.
Commissions: Golf Match (egg tempera), Olympic Club Lakeside Lobby, San Francisco, 60; mural (acrylic on wallboard), Macy's —Sacramento, 63; mural (acrylic on canvas), Macy's—Stockton, 65; hist mural (ink & acrylic on canvas), Corte Madera Town Council-Town Hall, 68; two murals (ink & acrylic on canvas), Regional Off Moore Bus Forms, 69.
Exhibitions: Phelan Awards Competition, San Francisco Mus Art, 49; 94th Ann Am Watercolor Soc, Nat Acad Design Gallery, New York & Nat Travel Show, 61; A City Buys Art, Calif Palace Legion of Hon, San Francisco, 63; Fukuoka, Japan Exchange Show, Oakland, Calif, 64; one-man show, Brazilian-Am Inst, Rio de Janeiro, 55.
Teaching: Instr watercolor, Civic Art Ctr, Walnut Creek, Calif, 68-70; instr watercolor, Acad Art, San Francisco, 70.
Positions: Art dir, McCann-Erikson Advert, Rio de Janeiro, 54-55; art dir, Johnson & Lewis Advert, San Francisco, 57; art dir, Michelson Advert, Palo Alto, Calif, 59-60.
Awards: Purchase award for watercolor, San Francisco Art Comn, 58; non-purchase award for watercolor, Calif State Fair & Expos, 58 & 72; first award for watercolor, Delta Ann, Antioch, Calif, 69.
Bibliography: Harold Rogers (auth), Color out of the West, Christian Sci Monitor, 2/26/49; Mabel Greene (auth), I began to draw, then to talk, San Francisco News-Editorial, 11/13/52; Milton Goldring (auth), O pintor Americano Kenneth Potter, Correio da Manha, Rio de Janeiro, 6/2/55.
Memberships: West Coast Watercolor Soc (pres, 68-70); Artists Equity Asn (bd dirs, Northern Calif chap, 72-73); East Bay Artists Asn (v pres, 70); San Francisco Soc Communicating Arts.
Publications: Contribr, Golden Gate Bridge, 5/27/62, A walk in Chinatown, 6/10/62 & A walk in the art world, 9/29/63, Bonanza, San Francisco Chronicle; contribr, Mission San Antonio, Calif Automobile Asn, 9/67; contribr, Marin portfolio, Image Mag, 10/67.
Dealer: Maxwell Galleries, Ltd, 551 Sutter St, San Francisco, CA 94102.
Mailing Address: 105 Sonora Way, Corte Madera, CA 94925.

POTTER, TED
Painter, Art Administrator
b Springhill, Kans, Dec 6, 33.
Study & Training: Univ Kans; Univ Calif Grad Sch, Berkeley; Calif Col Arts & Crafts, MFA, 62.
Work in Public Collections: Salem Col, Winston-Salem, N C; N C Nat Bank, Charlotte; Arts Coun Winston-Salem; Glide Found, San Francisco, Calif; Calif Col Arts & Crafts.
Positions: Dir art, Glide Found, 65-67; dir, Gallery Contemp Art, Winston-Salem, 68-72; dir, Tampa Bay Art Ctr, Fla, 72-
Memberships: N C State Arts Soc (adv coun, 69-72); Nat Endowment for the Arts (individual artist fel panel, visual arts div, 71-72); N C State Arts Coun (bd mem).
Specialty of Gallery: Contemporary American art.
Mailing Address: Gallery of Contemporary Art, 500 S Main St, Winston-Salem, NC 27101.

POTTS, DON
Painter, Educator
b San Francisco, Calif, Oct 5, 36.
Study & Training: San Jose State Col, BA, 36, MA, 65; Univ Iowa, 63.
Work in Public Collections: Univ Iowa, Iowa City; Joslyn Art Mus, Omaha, Nebr; La Jolla Mus Art, Calif; Pasadena Art Mus, Calif; San Francisco Mus Art; plus others.
Exhibitions: Los Angeles Munic Art Gallery, Calif, 68; Excellence, Univ Calif Art Mus, Berkeley, 70; Recent Acquisitions, San Francisco Mus Art, 71; What is Technological Art?, Calif State Univ, Hayward, 71; one-man shows, Hansen Fuller Gallery, San Francisco, 64, 66 & 70; plus many other group & one-man shows.
Teaching: Asst prof art, Univ Calif, Berkeley, at present.
Awards: First prize, Print Sculpture Ann, Richmond Art Ctr, Calif, 66; Nat Coun Arts fel, Nat Endowment Arts, 70; Adeline Kent Award, San Francisco Art Inst, 70; plus others.
Mailing Address: c/o Hansen Fuller Gallery, 228 Grant Ave, San Francisco, CA 94108.

POUCHER, ELIZABETH MORRIS
Sculptor
Preferred Media: Graphics.
b Yonkers, N Y.
Study & Training: Vassar Col, AB; N Y Univ; Columbia Univ; Art Stud League New York; Alexander Archipenko; Acad Grande Chaumière, Paris, France; Ecole Animalier, Paris; also with Andre L'Hote.

Work in Public Collections: Nat Portrait Gallery, Smithsonian Inst, Washington, D C; Taylor Art Gallery, Vassar Col, Poughkeepsie, N Y; Mus City New York; plus many pvt collections.
Commissions: Many portraits for pvt commissions, 70-72.
Exhibitions: Bronxville, N Y Ann, 68-71; Hudson Valley Art Asn, White Plains, N Y, 68-71; Pen & Brush, New York, 68-72; Allied Artists Am, New York, 68-72; Nat Sculpture Soc Exhibs, 68-72.
Awards: Silver medal for sculpture, Pen & Brush, 70; hon mention, Hudson Valley Art Asn, 70; first prize for sculpture, Bronxville, N Y Ann, 71.
Memberships: Nat Sculpture Soc; Allied Artists Am; Pen & Brush (bd dirs, 69-72); Hudson Valley Art Asn.
Mailing Address: 9 Brooklands, Bronxville, NY 10708.

POUSETTE-DART, RICHARD
Painter
b Saint Paul, Minn, June 8, 16.
Study & Training: Bard Col, hon DHL, 65.
Work in Public Collections: Mus Mod Art; Whitney Mus Am Art; Addison Gallery Am Art, Andover, Mass; Albright-Knox Art Gallery; Johnson Wax Collection; plus many others.
Exhibitions: Abstract Painting & Sculpture in America, 44 & Traveling Exhibs, 69 & 71, Mus Mod Art, New York, N Y; The New Decade, 55 & Retrospective Exhib, 63, Whitney Mus Am Art, New York; New York School Exhibition, Los Angeles Mus Fine Arts, Calif; Documenta 2, Mus Mod Art, 59 & Corcoran Gallery Art, Washington, D C, 64; American Abstract Expressionists & Imagists, Solomon Guggenheim Mus, 61; plus many other group & one-man shows.
Teaching: Lectr, Boston Mus Sch Fine Arts, 59; instr painting, New Sch Social Res, 59-61; instr advan paintings, Sch Visual Arts, New York, 65; lectr, Minneapolis Inst Fine Arts, 65; guest critic, Columbia Univ, 68; instr painting, Sarah Lawrence Col, 71, 73.
Awards: Second prize, Corcoran Gallery Biennale, 64; Comstock Prize, Art Inst Chicago, 65; Nat Arts Coun Award, 66; plus many others.
Bibliography: Richard Pousette-Dart: transcendental expressionist, 61, Lawrence Campbell (auth), Pousette-Dart: circles and cycles 63 & Charlotte Willard (auth), Yankee Vedanta, 67, Art News; plus many others.
Mailing Address: 286 Haverstraw Rd, Suffern, NY 10901.

POWELL, LESLIE (JOSEPH)
Painter, Designer
Preferred Media: Oils, Watercolors, Pastels.
b Minneapolis, Kans, Mar 16, 06.
Study & Training: Okla Univ, 22-23; Chicago Acad Fine Arts, 24-25; Art Stud League New York, fall 27; Columbia Univ, 49-51, BFA, 52, MFA, 54.
Work in Public Collections: Brooklyn Mus Art; Newark Mus Art, N J; Univ Ga Mus Art; Mus N Mex Gallery Art, Santa Fe; Okla Art Ctr; plus others.
Commissions: Power (with Boyd Cruise), Industry, Communication & others, Samuel L Peters H S Commerce, New Orleans, La, 30 & 31; Town & Country (painting), Security Bank & Trust Co, Lawton, Okla, 48.
Exhibitions: Okla Art Ctr, Oklahoma City; Philbrook Mus Art, Tulsa, Okla; one-man shows, Charles Morgan Gallery, New York, N Y, 38 & 39; Norlyst Gallery, New York, 57; Bodley Gallery, New York, 60; plus many other group & one-man shows.
Teaching: Instr art, Fort Sill I & E Ctr, Okla, 26; instr design & painting, Arts & Crafts Club, New Orleans, 26; instr merchandising, Tulane Univ La Sch Archit, 29-30.
Positions: Designer, Richard Hudnut Co, 27-47; free lance designer, various firms, 27-
Awards: Blanche Benjamin Award for best La Landscape, 31.
Memberships: Artists Equity Asn New York; Audubon Soc.
Research: Chinese art.
Art Interests: Modern art-abstract interpretations of classical & modern music; ballet paintings.
Publications: Auth, reviews, In: Villager, 67-69.
Dealer: Art for Industry, 663 Fifth Ave, New York, NY 10022.
Mailing Address: 39½ Washington Square S, New York, NY 10012.

POWERS, MARILYN
Painter
Preferred Media: Oils.
b Brookline, Mass, May 23, 25.
Study & Training: Mass Col Art, 42-45; Boston Mus Sch, 45-49, with Karl Zerbe.
Work in Public Collections: Fleming Mus, Univ Vt.
Commissions: Portraits, of Mrs Jane Stahl, comn by Frederick T Stahl, 65, Mrs John Deknatel, comn by John Deknatel, Boston, 69 & family portraits, comn by Warren Bennis, pres, Univ Cincinnati, 70; plus other portraits, Boston.

Exhibitions: Boston Art Festival, 52-58; View, Inst Contemp Arts, Boston, 62; Boston Mus Fine Arts, 69; Providence Art Festival, R I, 70; Direct Vision, Boston City Hall, 72.
Teaching: Instr painting, Harriet Tubman Settlement House, 53-54; instr painting, Boston & Brookline Adult Educ, 63; instr painting, Direct Vision Art Sch, 69-, pres, Direct Vision Inc, 72-
Awards: Awards, Fleming Mus, Univ Vt, 52 & Silvermine, Conn, 53.
Bibliography: Neil Hansen (auth), This mighty space, New Renaissance, 68; P Boyd Wilson (auth), Marilyn Powers, Christian Sci Monitor, 69; Edgar Driscoll (auth), Review, Boston Globe, 69.
Publications: Contribr, painting reproduced, Art News, 52, drawings reproduced, Audience Mag, 58 & 59, Christian Sci Monitor, 65 & New Boston Renaissance, 69.
Dealer: Joan Peterson Gallery, 561 Boylston St, Boston, MA 02116.
Mailing Address: 40 University Rd, Brookline, MA 02146.

POZZATTI, RUDY O
Printmaker, Painter
b Telluride, Colo, Jan 14, 25.
Study & Training: Univ Colo, BFA & MFA; also with Wendell H Black, Max Beckmann & Ben Shahn.
Work in Public Collections: Mus Mod Art, New York, N Y; Libr Cong, Washington, D C; Art Inst Chicago, Ill; Sheldon Mem Art Gallery, Lincoln, Nebr; Cleveland Mus Art, Ohio.
Commissions: (Spec Print Editions) Cleveland Print Club, Cleveland Mus Art, 54; Int Graphic Arts Soc, New York, 58-61 & 63; Conrad Hilton Hotel, New York, 61; Clairol, Inc, for New York World's Fair, 63; Ferdinand Roten Galleries, Baltimore, Md, 67 & 68.
Exhibitions: Work of Rudy Pozzatti, Cleveland Mus Art, 55; Young Americans, Whitney Mus Am Art, New York, 61; Stampe di Due Mondi: Prints of Two Worlds, Tyler Sch Art, Rome, Italy, 67; 20 Year Retrospective, Sheldon Mem Art Gallery, Univ Nebr, 69; Artists Abroad, Inst Int Educ, Am Fedn Arts, New York, 69.
Teaching: Asst prof printmaking & painting, Univ Nebr, 50-56; prof printmaking, Indiana Univ, 56-72, distinguished prof, 72-
Awards: Assoc Am Artists Prize, 100 Prints of the Year Exhib, 62; Guggenehim fel, 63-64; George Norlin Silver Medal, Assoc Alumni of Univ Colo, 72; plus others.
Bibliography: Norman Geske (auth), Rudy Pozzatti: American printmaker, Univ Kans Press, 71; Richard Taylor (auth), Pozzatti (film), Artists in America, NETV, 71; Nancy Carroll (auth), A visit with Rudy Pozzatti, North Shore Art League, 72.
Memberships: Soc Am Graphic Artists; Boston Printmakers; Print Coun Am (adv bd).
Dealers: Jane Haslem Gallery, 2121 P St N W, Washington, DC 20007; Weyhe Gallery, 794 Lexington Ave, New York, NY 10021.
Mailing Address: 117 S Meadowbrook Ave, Bloomington, IN 47401.

PRAEGER, FREDERICK A
Collector, Publisher
b Vienna, Austria, Sept 16, 15; U S citizen.
Study & Training: Univ Vienna.
Positions: Pres, Frederick A Praeger, Publ, New York, 50-68; chmn, Phaidon Publ, Ltd, London, 67-68; gen mgr, Ed Praeger, Munich, 69-
Collection: Contemporary art.
Mailing Address: 7 Schmidschneider Strasse, D 8036 Herrsching bei München, West Germany.

PRAGER, DAVID A
Collector
b Long Branch, N J, July 25, 13.
Study & Training: Columbia Univ, BA & LLD; also with Jack Tworkov.
Positions: Asst secy, Friends of Whitney Mus Am Art, New York, N Y, 59-63, secy, 63-67; mem acquisitions comt, Whitney Mus Am Art, 60-61, 67-68 & 70-71; bd trustees, Am Fedn Arts, 67-, treas, 69-; treas, Munic Art Soc, 67-69, bd dirs, 69-, pres, 72-
Memberships: Century Asn.
Collection: Contemporary American painting.
Mailing Address: 14 E 90th St, New York, NY 10028.

PRATT, DALLAS
Patron, Collector
b New York, N Y, Aug 21, 14.
Study & Training: Yale Univ, BA; Columbia Univ, MD.
Positions: Ed, Columbia Libr Columns, 51-; co-founder & trustee, Am Mus Britain, 59-; ed, Am in Britain, 63-64; founder, John Judkyn Mem, Bath, Eng, 64-
Collection: Renaissance maps & manuscripts.
Publications: Auth, Discovery of a world-early maps of America, Antiques Mag, 12/69 & 1/70; auth, Angel-motors, Columbia Libr Columns, 5/72.
Mailing Address: 228 E 49th St, New York, NY 10017.

PRATT, DUDLEY
Sculptor
b Paris, France, June 14, 97; U S citizen.
Study & Training: Yale Univ; Boston Mus Art Sch, with Charles
Grafly; Acad Grande Chaumière, with Emile Antoine Bourdelle;
Univ Wash, with Archipenko.
Work in Public Collections: Three works in Seattle Art Mus; Park
Ave Gallery, Mount Kisco, N Y; Galeria San Miguel, San Miguel
Allende, Mex.
Commissions: 12 over life-size groups, Univ Wash Med Sch, 48;
Gold Star Mother, war Mem on Pub Safety Bldg, City of Seattle,
Wash, 49; The Student (limestone), Holland Libr, Wash State
Univ, Pullman, 50; plus many others.
Exhibitions: Pennsylvania-Detroit, 1958, 58; Art U S A, 1958, Madi-
son Square Garden, New York, N Y, 58; Mount Kisco Ann, Mount
Kisco, N Y, 60, Northern Westchester, 64; Audubon Artists 18th
Ann, 60; one-man show, Sculpture Ann, New York, 59; plus
many others.
Mailing Address: Calle del Recreo 39, San Miguel de Allende,
Guanajuato, Mexico.

PRATT, FRANCES (FRANCES ELIZABETH USUI)
Painter, Art Dealer
b Glen Ridge, N J, May 25, 13.
Study & Training: New York Sch Applied Design for Women; Art
Stud League New York, with Richard Lahey; Hans Hofmann Sch
Art.
Work in Public Collections: Brooklyn Mus, N Y; Va Mus Fine Arts,
Richmond.
Exhibitions: Denver Art Mus Ann, 42; Addison Gallery, 45; Cleve-
land Mus Art, 47; Brooklyn Mus Watercolor Int, 47, 49 & 51;
Corcoran Gallery Art Biennial, 49.
Collections Arranged: Ancient Mexico in Miniature, Am Fedn Arts,
64-66; Guerrero, Stone Sculpture from the State of Guerrero,
Mex, Finch Col Mus Art, 65.
Teaching: Instr painting, Ballard Sch New York, 42-59; instr paint-
ing, Parsons Sch Design, 48-51.
Positions: Owner-dir, Frances Pratt, Inc, Gallery.
Awards: Anne Payne Robertson Prize, Nat Asn Women Artists Ann,
46; prize for oil, Nat Asn Women Artists Ann, 50; Audubon Prize
for crayon mixed media, Audubon Artists Ann, 52.
Research: Pre-classic cultures of Mexico (1500 B C - A D 200).
Specialty of Gallery: Antiquities; Oriental pottery; modern paintings,
Collection: Paintings, prints, Japanese tea bowls.
Publications: Co-auth, Encaustic, methods and materials, 49; illusr,
Mezcala stone sculpture: the human figure, Mus Primitive Art,
67; illusr, Chalcacingo: Akademische Druck—U Verlagsanstalt,
Graz, Austria, 71; illusr, Paleolithic and Megalithic traits in the
Olmec tradition of Mexico, Institutum Canarium, Graz, Austria,
72.
Mailing Address: 33 W 12th St, New York, NY 10011.

PRENTICE, DAVID RAMAGE
Painter, Designer
Preferred Media: Acrylics.
b Hartford, Conn, Dec 22, 43.
Study & Training: Hartford Art Sch.
Work in Public Collections: Wadsworth Atheneum, Hartford; Yale
Univ, New Haven, Conn; Mus Mod Art, New York, N Y.
Exhibitions: One-man shows, Teuscher Gallery, 66 & Sonnabend
Gallery, 70, New York; Other Ideas, Detroit Inst Fine Arts,
Mich, 69; Prospect, Dusseldorf, Ger, 69; Whitney Mus Am Art
Ann, New York, 70.
Teaching: Guest instr painting, Hartford Art Sch, Univ Hartford,
fall 70.
Dealer: Sonnabend Gallery, 924 Madison Ave, New York, NY 10021.
Mailing Address: 654 Broadway, New York, NY 10012.

PRESTINI, JAMES LIBERO
Sculptor, Designer
Preferred Media: Steel, Aluminum, Wood.
b Waterford, Conn, Jan 13, 08.
Study & Training: Yale Univ, BS, 30, Sch Educ, 32; Univ Stockholm,
38, with Carl Malmsten; Inst Design, Chicago, 39, with L Moholy-
Nagy; also study in Italy, 53-56.
Work in Public Collections: Mus Mod Art & Metrop Mus Art, New
York, N Y; Art Inst Chicago, Ill; Nat Collection Fine Arts, Smith-
sonian Inst, Washington, D C; San Francisco Mus Art, Calif.
Commissions: Aluminum sculpture, R S Reynolds Mem Sculpture
Award, Richmond, Va, 72.
Exhibitions: James Prestini, Sculpture from Structural Steel Ele-
ments, San Francisco Mus Art, 69; James Prestini, Art Inst Chi-
cago, 69; Contemporary American Painting & Sculpture, Univ Ill,
Champaign, 69; Excellence: Art from the University, Univ Calif,
Berkeley, 70; International Collection of 20th Century Design,
Mus Mod Art, New York, 72.

Teaching: Instr design, Lake Forest Acad, 33-42; instr design, Inst
Design, Chicago, 39-46; assoc prof design, N Tex State Univ, 42-
43; instr design, Inst Design, Chicago, 52-53; prof design, Univ
Calif, Berkeley, 56-, res prof, Creative Arts Inst, 67-68.
Awards: Best res report prize, Int Competition for Low-Cost
Furniture Design, Mus Mod Art, New York, 49; Guggenheim fel
for sculpture, 72-73; award for excellence in fine art in steel,
Am Iron & Steel Inst, New York, 71.
Bibliography: Edgar Kaufmann (auth), Prestini's art in wood, Pan-
theon, 50; Gerald Nordland (auth), James Prestini, sculpture
from structural steel elements, San Francisco Mus Art, 69;
George Staempfli (auth), James Prestini, recent sculpture,
Staempfli Gallery, 71.
Memberships: Life fel Metrop Mus Art.
Publications: Co-auth, The place of scientific research in design,
48; co-auth, Research in low-cost seating for homes, 48; co-auth,
Survey on construction materials demonstration & training cen-
ter, 51; auth, Survey of Italian furniture industry (Milan), 54;
auth, Proposed policy statement on architectural research for
the College of Architecture of the University of California,
Berkeley, 58.
Dealers: Triangle Gallery, 251 Post St, San Francisco, CA 94108;
Staempfli Gallery, 47 E 77th St, New York, NY 10021.
Mailing Address: 2324 Blake St, Berkeley, CA 94704.

PRESTON, MALCOLM H
Art Critic, Painter
Preferred Media: Oils.
b West New York, N J, May 25, 19.
Study & Training: Univ Wis, BA; Columbia Univ, MA & PhD.
Work in Public Collections: Hofstra Univ Collection; Dayton Art
Inst; Portland Mus.
Exhibitions: Wis Salon; Pa Acad Fine Arts; Audubon Artists; Art
U S A; Provincetown Art Asn.
Teaching: Asst instr fine arts, New Sch Social Res, 40-41; instr fine
arts, Adelphi Univ, 47-48; prof fine arts, Hofstra Univ, 49-
Positions: Dir, Inst of the Arts, Hofstra Univ, 60-64; art critic,
Newsday, 68-; art critic, Boston Herald Traveler, 70-
Awards: Joe & Emily Lowe Found educ res grant, 50; Ford Found
grant, 56 & 57; Shell Oil res grant, 64.
Mailing Address: Box 182, Truro, MA 02666.

PRESTOPINO, GREGORIO
Painter
Preferred Media: Oils, Watercolors.
b New York, N Y, June 29, 07.
Study & Training: Nat Acad Design.
Work in Public Collections: Whitney Mus Am Art, New York; Walker
Art Ctr, Minneapolis, Minn; Joseph H Hirshhorn Collection,
Washington, D C; Art Inst Chicago, Ill; N J State Mus, Trenton.
Commissions: Mosaic, comn by Dr Rebecca Notterman, Prof Bldg,
Princeton.
Exhibitions: Whitney Mus Am Art Am Painting Ann, 45; Mus Mod
Art, New York; Pa Acad Fine Arts, Philadelphia; Corcoran
Gallery Art, Washington, D C; Phillips Acad, Andover, Mass.
Teaching: Artist (painting), Brooklyn Mus Sch, 46-51; artist (paint-
ing), New Sch Social Res, 50-67; artist-in-residence, Mich
State Univ, 60.
Awards: Temple God Medal, Pa Acad Fine Arts, 46; Nat Inst Arts
& Lett grant, 61; B Altman Figure Painting Award, Nat Acad De-
sign, 72.
Bibliography: J Hubley (auth), Harlem Wednesday (film), Story-
board, Inc, 56; J G Smith (auth), Watercolors of Gregorio Pres-
topino, Am Artist, 10/57.
Memberships: MacDowell Colony (dir, 71).
Dealer: Lerner-Heller Gallery, 789 Madison Ave, New York, NY
10021.
Mailing Address: Roosevelt, NJ 08555.

PRETSCH, JOHN EDWARD
Cartoonist, Illustrator
b Philadelphia, Pa, Apr 14, 25.
Positions: Formerly, Sun supplement artist, news artist & promo-
tional layout artist, Philadelphia Eve Bull, news artist, 66-;
former advert layout artist, Sears Roebuck & Co.
Publications: Illusr, Five years, five countries, five campaigns
with the 141st infantry regiment, 45; constribr, cartoons, In:
Colliers, Sat Eve Post & Philadelphia Eve Bull.
Mailing Address: 4337 H St, Philadelphia, PA 19124.

PREUSS, ROGER
Painter, Writer
Preferred Media: Oils, Watercolors.
b Waterville, Minn.
Study & Training: Minneapolis Col Art & Design.
Work in Public Collections: Mont Hist Mus, Helena; Brigham Young
Univ, Harris Fine Arts Ctr, Provo, Utah; Smithsonian Hall

Philately, Washington, D C; Mont State Univ Inabnit Collection, Missoula; U S Fed Bldg & Minn State Capitol, Saint Paul; also in European pub collections.
Commissions: 1949-50 Fed Duck Stamp Design, U S Dept Interior, Washington, D C, 48; 16 painting wildlife series, Shedd-Brown Collection, Minneapolis, Minn, 50; 150 paintings of wildlife, Thos D Murphy Co, Red Oak, Iowa, 54; 20 paintings, Michael's Restaurant Preuss Collection, Golden Valley, Minn, 55; Minnesota Wildlife (12 painting panel), Greater Minneapolis C of C, 68.
Exhibitions: Contemp Bird Painting Biennial, Joslyn Art Mus, Omaha, Nebr, 48; Kerr's Gallery, Beverly Hills, Calif, 48; Nat Wildlife Art Exhib, Milwaukee, Wis, 54; Gallery Western Art, Mont Hist Soc, Helena, 64; 13th Int Exhib, Galerie Int, New York, N Y, 71.
Teaching: Sem lectr wildlife painting, Minneapolis Col Art; consult, Art & Educ Asn.
Awards: Fed duck stamp design award, U S Fish & Wildlife Serv, 49; Audubon Soc art award, 59; art-print-of-the-year award, Nat Wildlife Fedn, 64.
Bibliography: Black ducks along the border (film), produced by Lane Film Studios, Inc, 62; Marion McKinley (auth), Roger Preuss—artist, S Dak Conserv Digest, 1/70; Dean Durken (auth), Preuss master of wildlife painting, Saint Paul Pioneer Press, 11/29/70.
Memberships: Soc Animal Artists; fel Int Inst Arts; Minn Artists Asn (dir & past v pres, 53-56); Am Artists Prof League; Minneapolis Soc Fine Arts.
Publications: Auth & illusr, The official wildlife of America calendar, 55-; auth & illusr, Outdoor horizons, 57; contribr, National wildlife, 63; co-auth & illusr, Minnesota today, 68; illusr, Twilight over the wilderness, 71.
Dealers: Gokey Gallery, 21 W Fifth St, Saint Paul, MN 55102; Merrill's Gallery, Taos, NM 87571.
Mailing Address: 2224 Grand Ave, Minneapolis, MN 55405.

PREUSSER, ROBERT ORMEROD
Painter, Educator
Preferred Media: Mixed Media.
b Houston, Tex, Nov 13, 19.
Study & Training: Pvt study with McNeill Davidson, Houston, 30-39; Inst Design, Chicago, 39-40; Newcomb Sch Art, Tulane Univ, 40-41; Inst Design, Chicago, 41-42; Art Ctr Sch, Los Angeles, 46-47.
Work in Public Collections: Mus Fine Arts Houston; Contemp Arts Mus, Houston; Witte Mem Mus, San Antonio, Tex; Tex Christian Univ, Fort Worth; Addison Gallery Am Art, Andover, Mass.
Exhibitions: Directions in American Painting, Carnegie Inst, Pittsburgh, Pa, 41; Abstract and Surrealist American Exhibition, Art Inst Chicago, Ill, 47; Art Inst Chicago Am Artists Ann, 51; Survey of American Painting, Am Fedn Arts Circulating Exhib, 57-58; Texas Painting & Sculpture—The 20th Century, Owens Arts Ctr Circulating Exhib, Dallas, 71-72.
Teaching: Instr painting, Houston Mus Fine Arts Sch, 47-54; instr painting, Univ Houston, 51-54; assoc prof visual design, Mass Inst Technol, 54-; instr drawing, Harvard Univ Grad Sch Design, 55-56.
Positions: Art ed, Tex Cancer Bull, 48-50; co-dir, Contemp Arts Mus, Houston, 49-51; stage set designer, Tex Stage, Houston, 50-51; assoc cur educ, Mus Fine Arts Houston, 52-54.
Awards: Purchase prize, 16th Ann Houston Artists Exhib, Mus Fine Arts Houston, 40; Contemp Arts Mus Purchase Prize, 27th Ann Houston Artists Exhib, 52; nominated Promising New Talent in U S A, Art in Am Rev, 56.
Bibliography: Ralph M Pearson (auth), chap 3, In: The modern renaissance in American art, Harper & Row, 54; Vision in engineering (interview), Int Sci & Technol, 10/65.
Publications: Auth, Visual education for science and engineering students, In: Education of vision, George Braziller, 65, Fr & Ger ed, 67; auth, Art and the engineer, Mech Eng, 12/67.
Dealer: Joan Peterson Gallery, 561 Boylston St, Boston, MA 02116.
Mailing Address: 2 Willard Street Ct, Cambridge, MA 02138.

PREZAMENT, JOSEPH
Painter
Preferred Media: Oils.
b Winnipeg, Man, Jan 3, 23.
Study & Training: Winnipeg Sch Art; Montreal Mus Fine Arts; Ecole des Beaux Arts.
Exhibitions: Royal Can Acad, Montreal Mus Fine Arts, 67; Burnaby Art Soc, B C, 67; Can Painters & Engravers, Toronto, 68; Can Soc Graphic Artists, Toronto, 68; Canadian Printmakers Showcase, Toronto, 69.
Memberships: Can Soc Graphic Artists.
Dealer: Waddington Galleries, 1456 Sherbrooke St W, Montreal, PQ, Can.
Mailing Address: 4832 Wilson Ave, Montreal 253, PQ, Can.

PRIBBLE, EASTON
Painter, Educator
Preferred Media: Oils, Acrylics, Pastels.
b Falmouth, Ky, July 31, 17.
Study & Training: Univ Cincinnati.
Work in Public Collections: Whitney Mus Am Art, New York, N Y; Munson-Williams-Proctor Inst, Utica, N Y; Joseph Hirshhorn Collection, Washington, D C; Parrish Mus, Southampton, N Y; Utica Col, N Y.
Commissions: Painted wood relief mural, Munson-Williams-Proctor Inst Sch Art, 61; painted wood relief mural, Oneida Co Off Bldg, N Y, 69.
Exhibitions: Whitney Ann Am Painting, Whitney Mus Am Art, 50, 54 & 55; Univ Nebr Ann, Lincoln, 56; Everson Mus, Syracuse, N Y, 63.
Teaching: Instr painting, Munson-Williams-Proctor Inst Sch Art, 57-; instr hist art, Utica Col, 60-
Awards: Painting award, Everson Mus, 60 & 64; painting award, Munson-Williams-Proctor Inst, 63.
Publications: Contribr, Contemporary American culture, Chicago Rev, 54; contribr, New talent in America, Art in Am, 56.
Mailing Address: 1407 Sunset Ave, Utica, NY 13502.

PRICE, GEORGE
Cartoonist
b Coytesville, N J, June 9, 01.
Positions: Cartoonist & bk illusr.
Publications: Contribr, cartoons, In: New Yorker Mag, 26-; auth & illusr, We buy old gold, 52 & George Price's characters, 55; auth & illusr, My dear five hundred friends, S&S, 63; auth & illusr, People zoo, 71.
Mailing Address: 81 Westervelt Ave, Tenafly, NJ 07670.

PRICE, KENNETH
Printmaker, Sculptor
b Los Angeles, Calif, 1935.
Study & Training: Univ Calif; Otis Art Inst; Chouinard Art Inst; Univ Southern Calif, BFA, 56; State Univ N Y Albany, MFA, 58.
Work in Public Collections: Los Angeles Co Mus Art.
Exhibitions: Fifty California Artists, San Francisco Mus Art, 62; New American Sculpture, Pasadena Art Mus, 64; two-man show, 66 & American Sculpture of the Sixties, 67, Los Angeles Co Mus Art; Ten from Los Angeles, Seattle Art Mus, 66; one-man show, 69 & ann group show, 72, Whitney Mus Am Art; plus many other group & one-man shows.
Awards: Tamarind fel, 68-69.
Bibliography: Peter Selz (auth), Funk, Univ Calif Press, 67.
Mailing Address: 2360 S Robertson Blvd, Los Angeles, CA 90034.

PRICE, ROSALIE PETTUS
Painter
Preferred Media: Acrylics, Oils, Ink.
b Birmingham, Ala.
Study & Training: Birmingham-Southern Col, AB; Univ Ala, MA.
Work in Public Collections: Birmingham Mus Art; Springfield Art Mus, Mo; Spain Ctr Collection, Univ Ala, Birmingham; Samford Univ, Birmingham; Birmingham Trust Nat Bank.
Exhibitions: Watercolor U S A, Springfield, 68, 71-72; 35th Ann Midyear Show, Butler Inst Am Art, Youngstown, Ohio, 70; 50th Ann Exhib, Calif Nat Watercolor Soc, Laguna Beach, Calif, 70; Watercolor Invitational, Chico State Col, Calif, 72; 18th Ann Drawing & Small Sculpture Show, Ball State Univ, Muncie, Ind, 72.
Teaching: Instr drawing & watercolor, Birmingham Mus Art, 67-70; instr art appreciation, color & design, Samford Univ, 69-70.
Awards: Little House on Linden purchase award, Birmingham Art Asn, 68; W Alden Brown Mem Prize, Nat Soc Painters Casein, 70; purchase award, Watercolor U S A, 72.
Bibliography: Martin Hames (interviewer), The implacable abstraction of objects, Ala Educ TV, 1/13/72.
Memberships: Calif Nat Watercolor Soc; Watercolor Soc Ala (secy, 48-49); La Watercolor Soc; Birmingham Art Asn (pres, 47-49); Nat Soc Painters Casein & Acrylic.
Mailing Address: 300 Windsor Dr, Birmingham, AL 35209.

PRICE, VINCENT
Collector, Art Dealer
b St Louis, Mo, May 27, 11.
Study & Training: Yale Univ, BA, 33; Univ London, 34-35; Ohio Wesleyan, hon LLD; Calif Col Arts & Crafts, hon DFA; Columbia Col, hon DFA.
Positions: Founder, Mod Inst Art, 45; pres, Univ Calif, Los Angeles Art Coun; dir, Vincent Price Art Gallery; art consult, Sears Roebuck & Co.
Memberships: Indian Arts & Crafts Bd, Dept Interior (chmn, 68-72).

Publications: Auth, Vincent Price on art, syndicated column, Chicago Tribune, 3 yrs; auth, many articles on art in nat magazines & newspapers; auth, I like what I know, The book of Joe & Treasury of American art; plus others.
Mailing Address: 9371 Beverlycrest, Beverly Hills, CA 90210.

PRIDE, JOY
Painter, Writer
Preferred Media: Oils, Graphics.
b Lexington, Ky.
Study & Training: Univ Ky, BA, MA; Barnes Found, Merion, Pa; Art Stud League New York; New Sch Soc Res; Scand Acad; Julian Acad; Acad Andre L'Hote, Paris, France; also with Stuart Davis.
Work in Public Collections: Home of Henry Clay-Ashland, Senate Off Bldg, Washington, D C; Lexington Pub Schs.
Commissions: Hist Ky Landmarks, Ky Schs.
Exhibitions: Speed Mus Regional, Louisville, Ky, 30; Nat Asn Women Artists Ann, 45-60; Pen & Brush, 45-66; one-man shows, Lexington, Ky, 35, Los Angeles, Calif, 45 & Newburyport, Mass, 72.
Teaching: Head dept art, Barmore Sch, New York, N Y; head dept art, Murray State Teachers Col; instr art, Univ Ky.
Positions: Art dir gen publ, Christian Sci Publ Soc; art dir-prod ed, McCormack Mathers Publ Co; sr art ed, Macmillan Co.
Awards: Hon mention, Nat Asn Women Artists, 52; Am Inst Graphic Arts Fifty Bks of Yr Award.
Memberships: Nat Asn Women Artists; Pen & Brush; Newburyport Art Asn (pres).
Research: Influences on modern schools of painting other than painting traditions.
Publications: Auth, Sing of America, Crowell; auth, America sings, Hansen; designer, Psychology; designer, Story of American freedom & designer, World history, Macmillan.
Mailing Address: Christian Science Publishing Society, One Norway St, Boston, MA 02115.

PRIEST, HARTWELL WYSE
Painter, Printmaker
Preferred Media: Graphics.
b Brantford, Ont, Jan 1, 01; U S citizen.
Study & Training: Smith Col, 24; Paris-Atelier, with Andre L'Hote; also with Hans Hofmann, New York, N Y.
Work in Public Collections: Etching, Libr of Cong, Washington, D C; etching, Newark Pub Libr, N J; lithograph, Norton Gallery, West Palm Beach, Fla; lithograph, Longwood Col, Farmville, Va; Univ Maine; plus others.
Commissions: Murals in children's ward, Univ Va Hosp, Charlottesville, 55; flowers & woodland scene for ann report, Hunt Bot Libr, Pittsburgh, Pa, 71.
Exhibitions: Nat Asn Women Artists Ann, 44-; Soc Am Graphic Artists Ann, 56-; Artistes Feminins, Exhib Les Services Americans d'information, Ostende & Brussels, Berne, 56; Audubon Artists, New York, 68; Nat Asn Women Artists Foreign Exhib, Palazzo Vechio, Florence, Italy, 72.
Teaching: Instr graphics, Va Art Inst, 67-
Positions: Pres, Summit, N J Art Asn, 45-46.
Awards: Medal of honor, 53, Alice S Buell Mem Award for graphics, 70 & John Carl Georgi Mem Award, 72, Nat Asn Women Artists; award, Pen & Brush, 72.
Memberships: Nat Asn Women Artists (mem jury, 55, exten comt, 70-72); Soc Am Graphic Artists; Washington Watercolor Club.
Dealer: Current Scene Gallery, High St, Charlottesville, VA 22901.
Mailing Address: 41 Old Farm Rd, Charlottesville, VA 22901.

PRIMERANO, JOAN WALTON
Painter
Preferred Media: Oils.
b Buffalo, N Y, Oct 9, 26.
Study & Training: Albright Art Sch, Buffalo; Art Inst Buffalo.
Exhibitions: Benedictine Art Awards, New York, 70; Audubon Artists Exhib, New York, 71 & 72; Mainstreams '72, Marietta Col, Ohio, 72; Allied Artists Exhib, New York, 72.
Awards: Harold J Cleveland Mem Award, 14th Nat Juried Show, Chautauqua, N Y, 71.
Mailing Address: 72 University Ave, Buffalo, NY 14214.

PRINGLE, BURT EVINS
Graphic Artist, Designer
Preferred Media: Tempera, Acrylics, Gouaches.
b Savannah, Ga, Feb 11, 29.
Work in Public Collections: Hall of Fame Portraits, Gator Bowl, Jacksonville, Fla.
Commissions: Murals, USA, Stuttgart, Ger, 54; Migratory Bird Treaty Commemorative Postage Stamp, 66 & V I Commemorative Postage Stamp, 67, U S Post Off.
Exhibitions: Jacksonville Arts Festival, 61-64; one-man show, Norton Gallery & Sch Art, West Palm Beach, Fla, 68.

Positions: Display dir, Retail stores, 46-
Awards: Soc L'Exploition Burssels World's Fair, Pan Am Airways, 58; 1 bronze & 2 gold medals, Display World Mag, 58-59; 16 honorariums, UN Postal Admin, 66-72.
Bibliography: Lily Freed (auth), article, In: Scotts Monthly J, 66-67; Belmont Faries (auth), Stamp design, S P A Jour, 67; A Beltramo (auth), La personale filatelico, Collezionista, Italy, 68.
Memberships: Am Fedn Arts.
Mailing Address: 7028 Altama Rd, Jacksonville, FL 32216.

PRINS, (J) WARNER
Painter, Illustrator
b Amsterdam, Holland, July 24, 01.
Work in Public Collections: Metrop Mus Art; Jewish Mus, N Y; Munson-Williams-Proctor Inst, Utica, N Y.
Commissions: Ceramic murals, pub bldg, N Y & Int Hotel, Airport, New York, N Y.
Exhibitions: One-man shows, Carlebach Gallery, N Y, 50, Archit League, N Y, 52, The Contemporaries, N Y, 53 & Juster Gallery, N Y, 59.
Memberships: Artists Equity Asn.
Publications: Illusr, An old faith in the new world; illusr, Phedre, 68; illusr, Haggadah, A S Barnes, 69.
Mailing Address: 888 Park Ave, New York, NY 10021.

PRIOR, HARRIS KING
Art Administrator, Educator
b Hazardville, Conn, Mar 10, 11.
Study & Training: Trinity Col, BS, 32, MA, 35; Harvard Univ; Yale Univ; Univ Paris; Univ Brussels; Inst Fine Arts, New York Univ; Calif Col Arts & Crafts, hon DFA, 59.
Collections Arranged: Paintings by Arthur B Davies, Whitney Mus Am Art, Munson-Williams-Proctor Inst, Rochester Mem Art Gallery & others, 62-63.
Teaching: Asst instr Eng & fine arts, Trinity Col, 32-36; head sch fine arts, Olivet Col, 37-39; prof fine arts, Univ Rochester, 62-
Positions: Dir community arts prog, Munson-Williams-Proctor Inst, 47-56; dir, Am Fedn Arts, 56-62; dir Mem Art Gallery, Univ Rochester, 62-
Memberships: Asn Art Mus Dirs (v pres, 68, secy, 71, treas, 72); Am Asn Mus; Col Art Asn Am; Century Asn; Rotary Club.
Publications: Auth, Ten painters of the Pacific Northwest (exhib catalog), 48; auth, Paintings of Arthur B Davies (exhib catalog), 62; auth, articles, In: Italian Encycl, Mus News, Ore Hist Quart, Art in Am & Art Stud League Quart.
Mailing Address: 2813 Elmwood Ave, Rochester, NY 14618.

PRITZLAFF, MR & MRS JOHN, JR
Collectors
Mr Pritzlaff, b Milwaukee, Wis, May 10, 25.
Study & Training: Princeton Univ, BA, 49.
Positions: U S Ambassador to Malta, 69-; bd dirs, Heard Mus.
Mailing Address: 4954 E Rockridge Rd, Phoenix, AZ 85018.

PROBST, JOACHIM
Painter
Preferred Media: Oils.
b New York, N Y, Sept 1, 13.
Work in Public Collections: St Petersburg Mus, Fla; Chrysler Mus, Norfolk, Va; Delgado Mus, La; Grace Cathedral, San Francisco, Calif; Fairleigh Dickinson Univ, Madison, N J; plus many others.
Exhibitions: Grace Cathedral, San Francisco, 62; St Louis Univ, Mo, 66; Chrysler Mus, Norfolk, 70; St Petersburg Mus, Fla, 71; Probus Rex Gallery, New York, 71-72; plus many others.
Awards: Sullivan Co Art Show, 61-62 & New York State Exhib, 63, Greer Gallery.
Bibliography: Bennett Schiff (auth), In the art galleries, New York Post 11/10/57; Roger Ortmayer (auth), Frontiers of faith presents the art of Joachim Probst, produced on NBC-TV, 7/15/62; The Horizon history of christianity, Am Heritage Publ Co, 64; plus many others mags & newspapers.
Mailing Address: c/o Probus Rex Gallery, 943 Madison Ave, New York, NY 10021.

PROCTOR, GIFFORD MacGREGOR
Sculptor, Designer
Preferred Media: Bronze.
b New York, N Y, Feb 5, 12.
Study & Training: Yale Univ, BFA; Am Acad in Rome, Prix de Rome fel, 35; apprentice to A Phimister Proctor (father); study & travel abroad, 5 yrs.
Commissions: Four heroic granite eagles, U S Govt, Fed Off Bldg, New Orleans, La, 40; first spec serv force mem, Helena, Mont, 48; two portrait statues, comn by State of Ore, Nat Capitol Bldg, Wash, D C, 53; relief globe of moon, Washington Plaza Hotel, Seattle, Wash, 69; many medals, portrait busts, garden & decorative sculpture.

Teaching: Artist-in-residence, Beloit Col, 40-42.
Positions: Asst to pres, Chandler Cudlipp Assts N Y, N Y Interior Planning & Design, 58-65; coordr planning & design, Stud Union, San Fernando Valley State Col, Northridge, Calif, 69-
Bibliography: Clement Morro (auth), The Valley Forge Washington, La Rev Mod, 38; sci ed (auth), Want to buy a moon?, Life Mag, 11/30/62.
Memberships: Nat. Sculpture Soc.
Mailing Address: 341 Camino Al Lago, Menlo Park, CA 94025.

PROHASKA, RAY
    Painter, Illustrator
b Muo, Yugoslavia, Feb 5, 01; U S citizen.
Study & Training: Calif Sch Fine Art, San Francisco.
Work in Public Collections: Butler Inst Am Art, Youngstown, Ohio; Krannert Art Gallery, Univ Ill, Champaign; Guild Hall, East Hampton, N Y; Int Tel & Tel Co, New York; New Britain Mus, Conn.
Commissions: Communications (mural), Washington & Lee Univ, Lexington, Va, 67.
Exhibitions: Va Mus Biennial, Richmond, 65-69; N C Mus Art, 71; Benson Gallery, Bridgehampton, N Y; Southampton Col, N Y; Guild Hall, East Hampton, N Y.
Teaching: Instr illus, Art Stud League New York, 61-62; artist-in-residence, Washington & Lee Univ, 64-69; artist-in-residence, Wake Forest Univ, 69-73.
Awards: John Marin Mem Award, Springfield Art Mus, 62; gold medal for painting, 63, Hall of Fame & Soc Medal of Hon, 72, one-man show award, Guild Hall, 63; plus one other.
Memberships: Soc Illustrators (pres, 59-60).
Publications: Illusr, Eddie-no-name, 63; illusr, Who's afraid, 63; auth, A basic course in design—introduction to drawing & painting, 71.
Mailing Address: Box 726, Bridgehampton, NY 11932.

PROOM, AL
    Painter, Designer
b Nevada City, Calif, June 11, 33.
Exhibitions: Calif Palace of Legion of Honor, 62-64; Oakland Art Mus, 62 & 64; Butler Inst Am Art, 64; Rochester Mem Art Gallery, 64; McNay Art Inst, San Antonio, 65; plus many other group & one-man shows.
Awards: Purchase prize for City Beautification, San Francisco, 67; purchase prize, Butler Inst Am Art, 69.
Mailing Address: 1780 Eighth Ave, San Francisco, CA 94118.

PROSS, LESTER FRED
    Educator, Painter
Preferred Media: Oils, Watercolors, Acrylics.
b Bristol, Conn, Aug 14, 24.
Study & Training: Oberlin Col, BA, 45, MA, 46; Ohio Univ, with Ben Shahn, summer 52; Skowhegan Sch Painting & Sculpture, summer 53; also with Simon, Zorach, Levine, Hebald & Bocour.
Exhibitions: Louisville Art Ctr Ann, 61-64; Midstates Ann, Evansville, 64; Face of Kentucky I & II Traveling Exhib, 68-70; Appalachian Corridors II Traveling Exhib, 70-71; Preview '71, 71.
Teaching: Prof art, Berea Col, 46-, chmn dept, 50-; Fulbright lectr painting & art hist, Univ Panjab, 57-58; vis assoc prof art educ & hist, Union Col, summer 61; vis prof art, Am Univ Cairo, 67-68.
Positions: Pres, Ky Art Educ Asn, 55; chmn adv bd, Appalachian Mus, Berea Col, 69-
Awards: Haskell traveling fel, Oberlin Col, 57-58.
Memberships: Col Art Asn Am; Mid-Am Col Art Asn; Ky Guild Artists & Craftsmen (pres, 61-63); Asn Asian Studies; Asia Soc.
Publications: Illusr, Mountain life & work.
Mailing Address: 1287 CPO, Berea, KY 40403.

PROSSER, M, see ALLEN, MARGARET PROSSER.

PRUITT, A KELLY
    Painter, Sculptor
Preferred Media: Oils, Bronze.
b Waxahachie, Tex, Feb 9, 24.
Work in Public Collections: Mus N Mex, Santa Fe; Diamond M Mus, Snyder, Tex.
Commissions: The Plainsman (bronze), Frank Phillips Col, Borger, Tex, 67.
Exhibitions: Guest artist, Tex State Fair, Dallas, 69; 19th Ann Tucson Festival Exhib, Tucson Art Ctr, Ariz, 69; one-man exhib, Okla Mus Art at Red Ridge, Oklahoma City, 72.
Bibliography: A lamp out of the west, Chyka Carey Prod, 64; Jane Pattie (auth), A Kelly Pruitt: cowboy with a paint brush, Cattleman Mag, 66; Ed Ainsworth (auth), The cowboy in art, World, 68.

Publications: Illusr, The Cattleman, 66 & 68; illusr, The Paint Horse J, 67; illusr & auth, article, In: The Paint Horse J, 67.
Dealers: Cross Galleries, 3629 W Seventh St, Fort Worth, TX 76107; Spanish Steps Gallery, Taos Plaza, Taos, NM 87571.
Mailing Address: Ranchos de Taos, NM 87557.

PUCCINELLI, RAIMONDO
    Sculptor
b San Francisco, Calif, May 5, 04.
Study & Training: Calif Sch Fine Arts, San Francisco; Rudolph Schaeffer Sch Design, San Francisco; apprentice to woodcarvers, stone cutters & masters of plaster; Univ Calif, Berkeley.
Work in Public Collections: Maria (terra-cotta), San Francisco Mus Art; Seated Figure (bronze), Museo d'Arte Moderna, Florence, Italy; Edgard Varese (granite portrait), Columbia Univ Music Libr, New York, N Y; Mother & Child (porphyry), Fresno Mall, Calif; Hans Rothe (bronze portrait), Stadt Theatre Mus, Schleswig, Ger.
Commissions: Panther (polished diorite), Salinas Col, Calif, 40; Polar Bear (polished marble), Mills Col, Oakland, Calif, 41; Bear (diorite), Univ Calif, Berkeley, 44; San Franciscan Saints, 57-58, bronze doors, 58 & St Bernadette & Virgin (terra-cotta), 58, House of Theology, Franciscan Monastery, Centerville, Ohio; Cross (bronze), St Andrew's Church, Mayo, Md, 60.
Exhibitions: Twenty Contemporary Sculptors, Grand Cent Galleries, New York, 46; Contemporary American Sculpture, Whitney Mus Am Art, New York, 48 & 49; Sculpture Exhib, Nat Inst Arts & Lett, New York, 53, 55 & 57; Biennale Int del Bronzetto, Padova, Italy, 67; Modern Sculpture, Corcoran Gallery Art, Washington, D C, 62; plus numerous one-man exhibs in the U S A, Latin America & Europe.
Teaching: Instr sculpture & drawing, Mills Col, 38-47; prof sculpture & drawing, Univ Calif, Berkeley, 42-47; asst prof sculpture & drawing, Univ N C, Chapel Hill, 47-48; instr design & art hist, Queens Col, New York, 48-51; dean sculpture & drawing, Rinehart Sch Sculpture, Peabody Inst & Md Inst Col Art, 58-60; prof sculpture, Int Univ Arts, Florence, presently.
Positions: Cult envoy for Latin Am, U S Dept State, 56.
Awards: Sculpture prize, San Francisco Mus Art, 37 & 38; sculpture award, Los Angeles Co Mus Art, 39; medaglio d'oro for Il Fiorino, Palazzo Strozzi, Florence, Italy, 66.
Bibliography: Wanda Svevo (auth), Puccinelli & his sculpture, Habitat Mag, 58; Carra & Cavallo (auth), Puccinelli, Il Castello, 71; Italo Sesti (auth), Raimondo Puccinelli—scultore del visibile, Scena Illustrata, 71.
Memberships: Hon mem Florentine Acad.
Publications: Auth, Bronze sculpture, Arts & Archit, 39; auth, Sculpture, a visual language, Architects' Report, winter 61.
Mailing Address: Piazza Donatello 18, Florence, Italy 50132.

PUCKER, BERNARD H
    Art Dealer
b Kansas City, Mo, Oct 19, 37.
Study & Training: Columbia Univ, BA, 59; Hebrew Univ Jerusalem, 60; Brandeis Univ, MA, 66.
Positions: Dir, Pucker Safrai Gallery, Boston, Mass.
Specialty of Gallery: Contemporary artists; Chagall graphics; Israeli artists; New England artists.
Mailing Address: 171 Newbury St, Boston, MA 02116.

PULITZER, JOSEPH, JR
    Collector
b Saint Louis, Mo, May 13, 13.
Study & Training: Harvard Univ, AB, 36.
Collection: Contemporary art, paintings.
Mailing Address: 9501 Clayton Rd, Saint Louis, MO 63108.

PURDY, DONALD R
    Painter, Art Dealer
Preferred Media: Oils.
b Conn, Apr 10, 24.
Study & Training: Univ Conn, BA; Boston Univ, MA.
Work in Public Collections: New Britain Mus; Colby Col; Chase Manhattan Bank Collection: Kansas Univ; Chrysler Mus.
Exhibitions: U S A Int Show; Silvermine Guild Artists; Audubon Artists; Allied Artists Am.
Awards: Gold medal, Allied Artists Am; first prize, Silvermine Guild Artists; Jane Peterson Award, Audubon Artists.
Bibliography: F Whitaker (auth), article, In: Am Artist.
Memberships: Am Fedn Arts; Allied Artists Am; Silvermine Guild Artists.
Collection: American & Barbizon.
Dealer: Schoneberg Galleries, 823 Madison Ave, New York, NY 10021.
Mailing Address: 163 Westport Rd, Wilton, CT 06897.

PURVES, AUSTIN
Painter, Sculptor
Preferred Media: Tempera, Aluminum Casting.
b Philadelphia, Pa, Dec 31, 00.
Study & Training: Pa Acad Fine Arts, with Daniel Garber; Acad Julien, Paris, France; Am Conserv, Fontainebleau, France, with Paul Baudoin.
Work in Public Collections: Litchfield Hist Soc; Waterbury Mus.
Commissions: Altar painting, comn by William Olcott, St Paul's Church, Duluth, Minn, 27; altar painting, comn by Byron Miller, Grace Church, Honesdale, Pa, 48; mosaic chapel, Am Battle Monument, Draguignan, 48; aluminum bas reliefs, U S Lines, SS United States, 50; east apse mosaics, Nat Shrine Immaculate Conception, Washington, D C, 60.
Teaching: Instr painting, Yale Univ, 27-28; dir Cooper Union Art Sch, 31-38; instr painting, Bennington Col, 46-47.
Positions: Dir, Design Studio, R H Macy, New York, 27-29.
Memberships: Nat Soc Mural Painters (pres, 55); Archit League New York (v pres, 30).
Mailing Address: Litchfield, CT 06759.

PUTNAM, MRS JOHN B
Collector
b Cleveland, Ohio, June 19, 03.
Memberships: Art Collectors Club.
Collection: Paintings and modern art.
Mailing Address: 12817 Lake Shore Blvd, Cleveland, OH 44108.

PUTNAM, WALLACE (BRADSTREET)
Painter, Writer
Preferred Media: Oils.
b West Newton, Mass, Apr 16, 99.
Study & Training: Art schs in Boston, Mass.
Work in Public Collections: Mus Mod Art, New York, N Y; Yale Univ Societe Anonyme Collection; Univ Southern Ill; Roy Nenberger Collection.
Exhibitions: Int Exhib Mod Art, Societe Anonyme, Brooklyn Mus, 26; Fantastic Art, Dada, Surrealism, Mus Mod Art, New York, 36.
Publications: Auth & illusr, Manhattan manners, 35; auth & illusr, Miracle enough, 68.
Mailing Address: Rte 1, Box 270, Yorktown Heights, NY 10598.

PUTTERMAN, FLORENCE GRACE
Painter, Collector.
b Brooklyn, N Y, Apr 14, 27.
Study & Training: N Y Univ, BS; Bucknell Univ; Pa State Univ.
Work in Public Collections: Bucknell Univ, Lewisburg, Pa; Lycoming Col, Williamsport, Pa.
Exhibitions: Butler Inst Am Art, 65; Northwest Printmakers Ann, Seattle, Wash; Images 70, Miss State Art Festival, Jackson, 70; 3rd Nat Print Ann, Ga State Univ, Atlanta, 72; Colorprint U S A, Tex Tech Univ, Lubbock, 72.
Teaching: Artist in residence, Federal title III program, 67-68, 69-70.
Positions: Founder & pres, Arts Unlimited, Selinsgrove, Pa, 65-; cur, Milton Shoe Co Print Collection, Pa, 70-.
Awards: 1st prize, graphics, Berwick Art Ctr, 66-67; Best-in-show award, Everhart Mus, Scranton, Pa, 68.
Memberships: Am Fedn Arts; Hunterdon Co Art Ctr; Art Alliance Cent Pa; Mid-State Artists (treas, 70-).
Collection: African & Indian art.
Mailing Address: 101 Charles Ave, Selinsgrove, PA 17870.

Q

QUANCHI, LEO
Painter
b New York, N Y, Sept 23, 92.
Study & Training: City Col New York; Nat Acad Design; Art Stud League New York; Parsons Sch Design.
Work in Public Collections: Whitney Mus Am Art, New York; Newark Art Mus, N J; Pa Acad Fine Arts, Philadelphia; Bloomfield Col Collection, N J; plus many in pvt collections.
Exhibitions: Whitney Mus Am Art, New York; Des Moines Art Ctr, Iowa; Metrop Mus Art, New York; Monmouth Col, N J, 61; New Jersey Art Today, Fairleigh Dickinson Univ, 65; plus many other group exhibs & sixteen one-man shows.
Awards: Salmagundi Club prize, 68; first prize, Nat Asn Univ Women, 70; ann exhib, State N J; plus many others.
Mailing Address: Maple Extension, Kent, CT 06567.

QUAT, HELEN S
Printmaker, Painter
b Brooklyn, N Y, Oct 2, 18.
Study & Training: Skidmore Col; Columbia Univ; Art Stud League New York, N Y; also with Raphael Soyer, Joseph Solman & Leo Manso.
Work in Public Collections: Univ Mass, Amherst; N J State Mus, Trenton.
Exhibitions: Pratt Graphics Ctr 3rd Int Miniature Print Exhib, 68; Pa Acad Fine Arts 164th Ann, 69; Int Exhib Women Artists, Ont & France, 69; State Univ N Y Potsdam 10th Print Ann, 69-70; Nat Exhib Prints & Drawings, Okla Art Ctr, 69-72.
Awards: Vadley Art Co Award for Graphics, Catharine Lorillard Wolfe Art Club, 67; purchase prize, Hunterdon Art Ctr, N J, 70; Mr & Mrs Benjamin Ganeles Prize, Nat Asn Women Artists, 71.
Memberships: Nat Asn Women Artists; Long Island Artists Alliance; Print Club, Philadelphia; fel MacDowell Colony.
Dealer: Alonzo Gallery, 26 E 63rd St, New York, NY 10021.
Mailing Address: 16 Elliot Rd, Great Neck, NY 11021.

QUAYTMAN, HARVEY
Painter
b Far Rockaway, N Y, Apr 20, 37.
Study & Training: Syracuse Univ; Tufts Univ; Boston Mus Fine Arts Sch, BFA.
Work in Public Collections: Pasadena Art Mus; Whitney Mus Am Art; Dartmouth Col; Houston Mus Fine Arts; Mus Mod & Experimental Arts, Santiago de Chile; plus others.
Exhibitions: Inst Contemp Art, Houston, Tex, 67; Whitney Mus Am Art Ann, 69 & 72; L'art Vivant aux Etats Unis, Fondation Maeght, St Paul de Vence, France, 70; Structure of Color, Whitney Mus Am Art, 70; Chicago Art Inst Biannual, 72; plus others.
Teaching: Former instr, Boston Mus Fine Arts Sch, Middlebury Col, Essex Col Art, Colchester, Eng & Sch Visual Arts, New York; instr, Cooper Union, at present.
Awards: J W Paige traveling fel, Boston Mus Fine Arts, 60-61.
Dealer: Paula Cooper Gallery, 96 Prince St, New York, NY 10012.

QUEST, CHARLES FRANCIS
Painter, Educator
Preferred Media: Oils.
b Troy, N Y, June 6, 04.
Study & Training: Wash Univ Sch Fine Arts, 24-29; advan study in Paris, France, 29; summer study, Spain, France & England, 60.
Work in Public Collections: Brit Mus, London, Eng; Victoria & Albert Mus, London; Bibliotheque Nat, Paris; Mus Mod Art, New York, N Y; Metrop Mus Art, New York; plus many others in mus & pvt collections throughout world.
Commissions: Altar painting, St Mary's Church, Helena, Ark, 34; baptistry murals, St Michael & St George Episcopal Church, St Louis, Mo, 34; altar painting, Trinity Episcopal Church, St Louis, 35; altar painting, Old Cathedral, St Louis, 59-60.
Exhibitions: Les peintres Graveurs Actuels Aux Etats-Uni, Bibliotheque Nat, Paris, 51; Am Watercolor, Drawings & Prints Exhib, Metrop Mus Art, New York, 52; Art in the Embassies Program, Dept of State, Washington, D C, 67; 51st Exhib, Soc Am Graphic Artists, New York, 71; plus many group & one-man exhibs in mus & galleries throughout world.
Teaching: Instr art, St Louis Pub Schs, Mo, 29-44; prof art, Wash Univ Sch Fine Arts, 44-71, emer prof, 71-
Awards: Purchase prize, 3rd Ann Nat Print Exhib, Brooklyn Mus, 49; purchase prize, Nat Print Exhib, Libr of Cong, 52; purchase prize, 51st Ann Print Exhib, Soc Am Graphic Artists, 71; plus many others.
Bibliography: Article, In: St Louis Post Dispatch, 60; demonstr printmaking, 68 & demonstr figure drawing, 68, Art in St Louis, prog produced on KMOX-TV, St Louis.
Memberships: St Louis Artists Guild; Soc Am Graphic Artists.
Mailing Address: 200 Hillswick Rd, Tryon, NC 28782.

QUEST, DOROTHY (JOHNSON)
Painter, Instructor
Preferred Media: Oils.
b Saint Louis, Mo, Feb 28, 09.
Study & Training: Wash Univ Sch Fine Arts, 28-33; study in Europe, 29; Columbia Univ, summer 37.
Work in Public Collections: Wash Univ Olin Libr, Saint Louis, Mo; Saint Louis Univ Med Sch; Univ Eastern Ill, Charleston; Eden Seminary, Saint Louis; Washington & Lee Univ, Va.
Commissions: Sixteen murals for sanctuary, Church of Epiphany, Saint Louis, 48; twelve Mem portraits, Dodge Mem Hall, Boston, Mass, 57; Mrs Clay Jordan, Philanthropist, Mem home, Saint Louis, 63; John Lilly, Pres, Saint Louis Co Nat Bank, 63; portrait of Pierre Laclede, Pierre Laclede Bldg, Saint Louis, 64; plus over 600 portraits, 31-72.
Exhibitions: Saint Louis City Art Mus Ann; Saint Louis Artists Guild Ann; one-man show, Tryon Fine Arts Ctr, N C, 72.

Teaching: Instr art, Community Sch, Saint Louis, 36-38; head art dept, Acad Sacred Heart, Saint Louis, 39-41; head art dept, Maryville Col, Saint Louis, 44-45; instr art, Tryon Fine Arts Ctr, 71-
Bibliography: Eloise Lang (auth), article, In: Saint Louis Post Dispatch, 65; Walter Orthwein (auth), article, 67 & Lynn Hawkins (auth), article, 69, In: Saint Louis Globe Democrat.
Memberships: Tyron Painters & Sculptors, Inc (chmn exhibs out-of-town artists, 70-); Spartanburg Art Asn.
Art Interests: Lectr painting, Saint Louis City Art Mus, radio stations KMOX & KSD, pvt clubs, churches & schs.
Dealer: Tryon Painters & Sculptors, Inc, Melrose Ave, Tryon, NC 28782.
Mailing Address: 200 Hillswick Rd, Tryon, NC 28782.

QUICK, BIRNEY MacNABB
Painter, Educator
Preferred Media: Oils, Watercolors.
b Proctor, Minn, Nov 9, 12.
Study & Training: Vesper L George Sch, Boston, Mass; Minneapolis Col Art Design; Louis Comfort Tiffany fel & Chaloner fel, 38.
Work in Public Collections: Minneapolis Inst Art; Univ Minn Art Gallery; Gen Mills Collection; Int Multifood Corp Collection; Northwestern Nat Life Collection.
Commissions: Oil on canvas, Med Arts Bldg, Duluth, Minn, 46; oil on canvas, Minn Mutual Life Ins Co, Saint Paul, 58; oil on canvas, Minn Fed Savings Loan, Saint Paul, 60; oil on canvas, Grand Marais St Bank, Minn, 68; oil on canvas, St John's Catholic Church, Grand Marais, 72.
Exhibitions: Am Painters & Sculptors Show, Art Inst Chicago; Minn Biennial, Minneapolis Art Inst; Independent Artist's Show, Boston, Mass; one-man shows, Walker Art Ctr & Minneapolis Art Inst; Tweed Gallery, Univ Minn, Duluth.
Teaching: Prof painting, Minneapolis Sch Art, 46-
Positions: Dir studies abroad, Am Cols Art, 70-71.
Awards: Biennial award in drawing, Minneapolis Art Inst, 60.
Dealer: Martin Gallery, 2115 Second Ave S, Minneapolis, MN 55404.
Mailing Address: 4537 Dupont Ave S, Minneapolis, MN 55409.

QUINN, HENRIETTA REIST
Collector
b Lancaster, Pa, Dec 11, 18.
Study & Training: Edgewood Park Jr Col.
Collection: American primitive paintings; eighteenth century porcelain; eighteenth century miniature memoribilia; eighteenth century American & English furniture.
Mailing Address: Rolling Meadows, Cornwall, PA 17016.

QUINN, NOEL JOSEPH
Painter, Educator
Preferred Media: Watercolors.
b Pawtucket, R I, Dec 25, 15.
Study & Training: R I Sch Design, grad, 36, fel, Paris, France; Parsons Sch Fine & Appl Arts, Paris & Italy, cert dipl; Ecole Beaux Arts; also with Andre L'hote & Andre Cassandre; Nat Gallery & Kaiser Frederick Mus, Berlin, Ger.
Work in Public Collections: Butler Art Inst, Youngstown, Ohio; Air Force Acad, Denver, Colo; Pentagon, Libr of Cong & House of Rep, Washington, D C; Calif State Agr Collection, Sacramento; Los Angeles Turf Club, Santa Anita Park, Arcadia, Calif.
Commissions: Thoroughbred Racing (portfolio of paintings), Los Angeles Turf Club, 60.
Exhibitions: American Paintings & Prints, Metrop Mus Art, New York, N Y, 52; Hallmark Int Show, Wildenstein Galleries, New York, 53; Southwest Watercolor Soc Show, Southern Methodist Univ, Dallas, 69; one-man show, Yoseido Gallery, Tokyo, Japan, 55; plus many others.
Teaching: Instr watercolor, Otis Art Inst, 53-; instr, Los Angeles City Col, 72.
Awards: First prize award, State Agr Comt, Calif State Fair, 49; Hallmark Int Award, 52; Watercolor U S A, show award, Springfield Art Mus, 64.
Memberships: Calif Nat Watercolor Soc (pres, 62-63); Soc Motion Picture Illustrators (pres, 63-65).
Art Interests: Part of each year devoted to educating the blind in terms of their sight by their study and active participation in art work; creator of new language of symbols for color and value in bas-relief; paintings reproduced in the language overlay provide the pertinent clues which enable them to complete the picture.
Publications: Auth, article, In: Am Artist Mag, 5/03; auth, Scene, Southwestern Watercolor Soc Mag.
Mailing Address: 3946 San Rafael Ave, Los Angeles, CA 90065.

QUIRK, FRANCIS JOSEPH
Painter, Museum Director
Preferred Media: Oils, Acrylics, Watercolors, Charcoal, Pastel, Ink.
b Pawtucket, R I, June 3, 07.

Study & Training: R I Sch Design, grad, 29; Univ Pa, 42; Provincetown Sch Art; also study in Woodstock, N Y, Italy, France, Ger & Czech.
Work in Public Collections: Nat Portrait Gallery & Smithsonian Inst, Washington, D C; Canton Art Inst, Ohio; Ga Mus Art, Athens; Univ Notre Dame, Inc.
Commissions: Portrait of Pres Strider, Colby Col Alumni, Maine; portrait of Dr John Leitner, bd dirs, Monroe Co Med Ctr; portrait of pres, Lehigh Univ; portrait of Carl Sandberg, comn by Pres Abby Sutherland Brown, Ogontz Col, Pa; portrait of Edgar Lee Masters, comn by Writers Guild Pa.
Exhibitions: Pa Acad Fine Arts, Philadelphia; Philadelphia Mus Art; Nat Acad Design, New York, N Y; also in Buffalo & Syracuse, N Y & Newport, R I.
Teaching: Prof drawing & painting & chmn fine arts dept, Ogontz Col, 35-50; prof painting & perspective, Hussian Sch Arts, Philadelphia, 43-50; chmn fine arts, Lehigh Univ, 50-69.
Positions: Dir exhibs, Lehigh Univ, 50-, cur permanent collections, 59-
Awards: Tiffany Found fel, 40; Lineback Award, 65; Ossabaw Island Proj, 68 & 72.
Memberships: Univ Club; Am Artists Prof League; Art Alliance Philadelphia; Am Asn Mus; Am Fedn Arts; plus others.
Art Interests: Library and art collection of the Ossabaw Island Project.
Collection: Oriental prints; contemporary American prints; primative American paintings.
Publications: These our own (TV prog), WFIG TV, 59-61; Art & us (TV & radio prog), Lehigh Valley & Easton, 61; auth, Prendergast (Maurice P—paints), Ariz State Univ, 65.
Dealers: Phoenix Gallery, 939 Madison Ave at 74th St, New York, NY 10021; Ogunquit Gallery, Ogunquit, ME 03907.
Mailing Address: Peterspen, 219 Magada Rd E, Bethlehem, PA 18017.

QUIRK, THOMAS CHARLES, JR
Painter, Educator
Preferred Media: Watercolors, Oils.
b Pittsburgh, Pa, Dec 31, 22.
Study & Training: Edinboro State Col, BS, 48; Univ Pittsburgh, MEd, 64.
Work in Public Collections: Butler Inst Am Art, Youngstown, Ohio; Chatham Col, Pittsburgh; Pittsburgh Pub Schs.
Exhibitions: Pa Acad Fine Arts Ann, Philadelphia, 69; Nat Acad Design Ann, New York, N Y, 71; Am Drawing Biennial XXIV, Norfolk, Va, 71; Drawing & Small Sculpture Ann, Ball State Univ, 71; Philadelphia Watercolor Club Ann, 72.
Teaching: Asst prof painting & drawing, Kutztown State Col, 66-
Positions: Artist-in-residence, Everhart Mus, Scranton, Pa, 72-
Awards: Hon mention, Philadelphia Watercolor Club Ann, 70; prize, Drawing Ann, Ball State Univ, 71.
Memberships: Philadelphia Watercolor Club.
Dealer: Larcada Gallery, 23 E 67th St, New York, NY 10021.
Mailing Address: 310 E Main St, Kutztown, PA 19530.

QUISGARD, LIZ WHITNEY
Painter, Sculptor
b Philadelphia, Pa, Oct 23, 29.
Study & Training: Md Inst Col Art, dipl, 49, BFA (summa cum laude), 66; also with Morris Louis, 57-60; Rinehart Sch Sculpture, MFA, 66.
Work in Public Collections: Univ Ariz Ghallager Mem Collection, Tucson; Lever House, New York, N Y; Univ Baltimore, Md; Hampton Sch, Towson, Md; plus many pvt collections.
Commissions: Two murals, Belfort, Baltimore, 54.
Exhibitions: Corcoran Biennial Am Painting, Corcoran Gallery Art, Washington, D C, 63; Univ Colo Invitational Show, 63; Am Painting & Sculpture Ann, Pa Acad Fine Arts, Philadelphia, 64; Art Inst Chicago Ann, Ill, 65; one-man show, Univ Md, 69; plus other group & many one-man shows.
Teaching: Instr painting & design, Baltimore Hebrew Congregation, 62-; instr painting & color theory, Md Inst, Baltimore, 65-; lectr design, Goucher Col, 66-69; lectr art hist, Univ Md, Catonsville, 69-70.
Positions: Theatre designer, Goucher Col, Theatre Hopkins & Ctr Stage, Baltimore, 66-; art critic, Baltimore Sun, 69 & 70; area reviewer, Craft Horizons Mag, 69-
Awards: Artists prize, Baltimore Mus Regional Exhib, 58; Rinehart fel, Md Inst, 64-66; best in show, Loyola Col Invitational, 66.
Bibliography: B Rose (auth), review, In: Art Int, 11/62; review, In: Arts Mag, 11/62; review, In: Art News, 11/62.
Publications: Auth, Baltimore's top twelve, Baltimore Mag, 5/69; auth & illusr, An artist's travel log (series of 3 articles), Baltimore News Am, 71.
Mailing Address: 321 Rossiter Ave, Baltimore, MD 21212.

R

RABB, MR & MRS IRVING W
Collectors
Study & Training: Mr Rabb, Harvard Univ, AB, Harvard Bus Sch; Mrs Rabb, Smith Col, AB; Radcliffe Col, AM.
Collection: Twentieth century sculpture, including Henry Moore, Giacometti, Maillot, Arp, Lipshitz, Calder, Neuelson & Laurens; twentieth century drawings and collages, with emphasis on Cubism and sculpture drawings.
Mailing Address: 1010 Memorial Dr, Cambridge, MA 02138.

RABIN, BERNARD
Art Restorer
b New York, N Y, Nov 1, 16.
Study & Training: Newark Art Sch; New Sch Social Res; Brooklyn Mus, with Sheldon & Caroline Keck; also restoration at the Uffizi, Florence, Italy.
Work in Public Collections: (Restoration Works) Montclair Art Mus, Princeton Univ Art Mus, Carnegie-Mellon Mus, N J Hist Soc, & in pvt collections.
Commissions: Restoration of Monet's Water Lilies, Mus Mod Art, New York, 59.
Teaching: Lectr, Int Conf Conservators, Lisbon, 10/72.
Positions: Official restorer, Newark Mus, Montclair Art Mus, Princeton Univ Art Mus, Carnegie-Mellon Mus & N J Hist Soc; head Am restorers, Comt Rescue Ital art, 67.
Memberships: Am Asn Mus; fel Int Inst Conserv.
Publications: Auth, articles, In: J Int Inst Conserv, 59-70.
Mailing Address: Rear 38 Halsey St, Newark, NJ 07102.

RABINOVICH, RAQUEL
Painter, Sculptor
Preferred Media: Oils, Glass.
b Buenos Aires, Arg, Mar 30, 29.
Study & Training: Univ. Córdoba, Arg; Univ Edinburgh; Atelier André Lothe, Paris, France.
Work in Public Collections: Mus Mod Art, Buenos Aires; Genaro Perez Mus, Córdoba; Fondo Nac Art, Buenos Aires.
Exhibitions: Soc Scottish Artists, Edinburgh, 57; Salón Art Visuales Contemp, Arg, 61; Salón Premio Honor Ver y Estimar, Buenos Aires, 63; Primer Salón Artistas Jóvenes Latin Am, Mus Art Mod, Arg, 65; New Directions (Artists of Suffolk Co), Hecksher Mus, Huntington, N Y, 71; plus others.
Awards: Salón munic prize, Arg, 54; Salon Parques Nac Prize, 63; Fondo Nac Art fel, 64.
Bibliography: E Rodriguez (auth), Raquel Rabinovich, Exposiciones, 62; J Barnitz (auth), Raquel Rabinovich, Arts Mag, New York, 70; M Preston (auth), Raquel Rabinovich, Newsday, New York, 72.
Dealer: Lerner-Heller Galleries, 789 Madison Ave, New York, NY 10021.
Mailing Address: 14 Donna Ct, Huntington, NY 11743.

RABINOVITCH, WILLIAM AVRUM
Painter
Preferred Media: Oils, Acrylics, Watercolors.
b New London, Conn, Sept 16, 36.
Study & Training: Worcester Polytech Inst, BSME; Boston Mus Sch Fine Arts; San Francisco Art Inst, MFA; also with Tom Holland.
Work in Public Collections: Monterey Peninsula Col, Calif.
Exhibitions: One-man shows, Monterey Peninsula Mus Art, 65 & Am Embassy & Asn Cult Hisp Norteamericano, 68; Silvermine Competitive, Conn, 69; New York City Ann, Avanti Gallery, 70; one-man show, Large Paintings, Monterey Jazz Festival, 71.
Awards: First prize, Monterey Peninsula Mus Art & Monterey Jazz Festival, 65 & first prize, Monterey Co Fair, 70.
Dealer: Maxwell Gallery, 551 Sutter St, San Francisco, CA 94102.
Mailing Address: 638 Lottie St, Monterey, CA 93940.

RABKIN, LEO
Sculptor, Painter
Preferred Media: Sculptural Constructions.
b Cincinnati, Ohio, July 21, 19.
Study & Training: Univ Cincinnati; N Y Univ; also with Iglehart, Tony Smith & Baziotes.
Work in Public Collections: Mus Mod Art, New York, N Y; Whitney Mus Am Art, New York; Solomon R Guggenheim Mus, New York; N C Mus Art, Raleigh; Brooklyn Art Mus, N Y.
Exhibitions: Seven Painting & Sculpture Biennials, Whitney Mus Am Art, 59-69; three-man show, New Talents, Mus Mod Art, 60; Light/Motion/Space, Walker Art Ctr, Minneapolis, Minn, 67; A Plastic Presence, San Francisco Mus Art, Milwaukee Art Ctr & Jewish Mus, 70; Retrospective, Storm King Art Ctr, Mountainville, N Y, 70; plus others.

Awards: Ford Found Award for Watercolor, 61; first prize for watercolor, Silvermine Guild Artists, 61; popular award for sculpture, First Ann Westchester, 67.
Memberships: Am Abstr Artists (pres, 64-); U S Comn Int Asn Art (secy, 68-70); Fine Arts Fedn New York (mem bd dirs, 70-); Sculptors Guild; Fedn Mod Painters & Sculptors.
Collection: Whirligigs; Shaker furniture and tools; American primitive toys and dolls.
Publications: Ed, American Abstract artists, 1936-1966, 66.
Mailing Address: 218 W 20th St, New York, NY 10011.

RABUT, PAUL
Illustrator, Painter
b New York, N Y, Apr 6, 14.
Study & Training: City Col New York; Nat Acad Design; Art Stud League New York; also with Jules Gottlieb, Harvey Dunn & Lewis Daniel.
Work in Public Collections: USA Med Mus, Washington, D C; U S Postal Serv Collection; Gen Elec Collection.
Commissions: Designed 6 cent Natural Hist Commemorative U S Postage Stamp, Haida Ceremonial Canoe, 5/6/70 & 11 cent Airmail Commemorative U S Postage Stamp, City of Refuge, Nat Park Ser, 4/3/72.
Exhibitions: Soc Illusr, 41-72; Art Dirs Club, 42-53; Art Inst Chicago, 43; Nat Acad Design, 50; State Dept Traveling Exhib Advert Art, Europe & S Am, 52-53; plus others.
Teaching: Lectr illus, photog, primitive arts of Africa & northwest coast & South Seas.
Positions: Consult primitive art, galleries & collectors; art dir & stylist animated films, Fed Aeronaut Admin, U S Army, U S Navy & Fr Govt.
Awards: Medal, Nat Acad Design, 32; prizes, Art Dirs Club, 42, 43, 46 & 51.
Memberships: Soc Illusr; Westport Artists.
Collection: Primitive art, especially Africa, oceanic, pre-Colombian America & American Indian.
Publications: Auth & illusr, Paul Rabut visits the tall timber, True Mag, 49; auth & illusr, My life as a head hunter, Argosy Mag, 53; illusr, leading nat mags.
Mailing Address: 104 Easton Rd, Westport, CT 06880.

RACHELSKI, FLORIAN W
Painter, Sculptor
Preferred Media: Wood, Stone, Bronze, Marble.
b Poland; U S citizen.
Study & Training: Ecole Nat Beaux Arts, Paris, France.
Commissions: Monument of Christ, St Mary's Church, Paris, 53; monument of the Madonna, St Trinity Church, Osining, N Y, 59.
Exhibitions: Salon Nat Beaux Arts, Paris; Salon des Artistes Francais, Paris; Salon d'Hiver, Paris; Nat Acad Design, New York, N Y; Nat Sculpture Soc, New York.
Awards: Bronze medal, 55 & silver medal, 56, Salon des Artistes Francais; Prix Bingguely le Jeune, Winter Salon, Paris, 58.
Memberships: Syndicat Nat des Artistes Createur Prof, 53; fel Nat Sculpture Soc.
Publications: Auth articles in, J l'Amateur d'Art, La Rev Mod, Masgue et Visages, Nat Sculpture Rev & Le Livre D'Or Sculpture.
Mailing Address: 18 St Marks Pl, New York, NY 10003.

RACZ, ANDRE
Painter, Educator
b Cluj, Romania, Nov 21, 16; U S citizen.
Study & Training: Univ Bucharest, BA, 35.
Work in Public Collections: Mus Mod Art, New York, N Y; Whitney Mus Am Art; New York Pub Libr; Libr Cong, Washington, D C; Bibliot Nat, Paris.
Exhibitions: 50 Yrs Am Art, Mus Mod Art, Paris, London, Belgrade & Barcelona, 55; First Int Biennial, Mex, 58; First Biennial Relig Art, Salzburg, Austria, 58; Int Watercolor Biennial, Brooklyn Mus, 61; Nat Inst Arts & Lett, New York, 68.
Teaching: Prof painting & chmn div painting & sculpture, Columbia Univ, 51-
Awards: Guggenheim fel printmaking, 56; Fulbright res scholar, Chile, 57; Ford Found fel, 62.
Bibliography: Carmen Valle (auth), Poets on painters and sculptors, Tiger's Eye, 49; Rosamel del Valle (auth), Una tarde con el pintor Andre Racz, Nacion, 49; Antonio Romera (auth), Andre Racz pintor y grabador, Ed Pacifico, 50.
Memberships: Soc Am Graphic Artists; Am Asn Univ Prof.
Publications: Auth, The reign of claws, 45, XII prophets of Aleijadinho, 47, Via crucis, 48, Mother and child, 49 & Canciones negras, 53.
Mailing Address: P O Box 43, Demarest, NJ 07627.

RADIN, DAN
Painter
Preferred Media: Oils, Acrylics.
b New York, N Y, May 12, 29.
Study & Training: High Sch Music & Art; Queens Col; Cranbrook Acad Art, BFA & MFA.
Work in Public Collections: Cranbrook Mus, Bloomfield Hills, Mich; Detroit Inst Arts, Mich; Butler Inst Am Art, Youngstown, Ohio; Lowe Gallery, Univ Miami, Coral Gables, Fla.
Exhibitions: Butler Inst Am Art 26th Ann, 61; Painting Part II, 63 & Landscape II, 71, De Cordova Mus; Am Acad Ann, Rome, 64; Contemp Surv, J B Speed Mus, Louisville, Ky, 66.
Teaching: Instr painting, Swain Sch Design, New Bedford, Mass, 64-71; instr painting & drawing, Univ Conn, 72; instr drawing, R I Sch Design, 72.
Awards: Louis Comfort Tiffany Found awards in painting, 62 & 64; second purchase award, Lowe Gallery, 63.
Mailing Address: Rte 1, Norwich, CT 06360.

RADOCZY, ALBERT
Painter
Preferred Media: Oils.
b Stamford, Conn, Oct 24, 14.
Study & Training: Parsons Sch Design; Cooper Union, grad.
Work in Public Collections: Brooklyn Mus, N Y; Ball State Teachers Col, Ind; Lyman Allyn Mus, Conn.
Commissions: Tapestry murals, Allegheny Col, Meadville, Pa, 66.
Exhibitions: N J State Mus Ann, Trenton, 61; Whitney Mus Am Art Ann, New York, N Y, 62; Brooklyn Mus Nat Print Exhib, N Y, 62; Mus Mod Art Lending Collection, 65.
Teaching: Lectr drawing, Cooper Union, 50-55; prof design, City Col New York, 55-
Awards: Purchase award, Ball State Teachers Col, 59.
Mailing Address: 61 Cedar St, Cresskill, NJ 07626.

RADULOVIC, SAVO
Painter, Craftsman
b Montenegro, Yugoslavia, Jan 27, 11; U S citizen.
Study & Training: Saint Louis Sch Fine Arts, Wash Univ, 30-32; Fogg Mus Art, Harvard Univ, Carnegie fel, 37; Acad Belle Arte, Rome, Italy, Fulbright fel, 49-50.
Work in Public Collections: City Art Mus Saint Louis; Univ Ariz; Hist Sect, War Dept, Pentagon, Washington, D C; Col William & Mary, Williamsburg, Va; Mus Mod Art, Miami Beach, Fla; also in pvt collections U S & abroad.
Exhibitions: Nat Acad Design; Pa Acad Fine Arts; Whitney Mus Am Art; City Art Mus Saint Louis; Philadelphia Mus Art; plus many others.
Positions: Owner & dir, Artists Little Gallery, New York, N Y, 46-
Awards: Purchase prize, City Art Mus Saint Louis, 41.
Memberships: Artists Equity Asn.
Mailing Address: 750 Lexington Ave, New York, NY 10022.

RAE, EDWIN C
Art Historian, Educator
b New Canaan, Conn, Aug 31, 11.
Study & Training: Harvard Col, BA, 33, Harvard Univ, MA, 34, PhD, 43.
Teaching: Instr hist art, Brown Univ, 38-39; instr hist art, Univ Ill, Urbana, 39-42, prof hist art, 47-
Awards: Legion Honneur scholars & res grants.
Memberships: Soc Archit Historians (asst ed jour, 41); Col Art Asn Am; Archaeol Inst Am; Royal Soc Antiquaries Ireland.
Research: Gothic architecture and sculpture, particularly in Ireland.
Publications: Auth, The education of the artist, Art J, 61; auth, The sculpture of the cloister of Jerpoint Abbey, 66 & Irish sepulchral monuments of the later middle ages, 70-71, J Royal Soc Antiquaries Ireland; auth, The rice monument in Waterford Cathedral, Royal Irish Acad Proceedings, 70.
Mailing Address: Fine Arts Bldg, University of Illinois, Champaign, IL 61820.

RAFFAEL, JOSEPH
Painter
Preferred Media: Oils.
b Brooklyn, N Y, Feb 22, 33.
Study & Training: Cooper Union Art Sch, cert; Yale Univ, BFA.
Work in Public Collections: Metrop Mus Art, New York, N Y; San Francisco Mus Art, Calif; Art Inst Chicago, Ill; Los Angeles Co Art Mus, Calif; Univ Art Mus, Univ Calif, Berkeley.
Exhibitions: Ninth Sao Paulo Bienial, Brazil, 68; Human Concern, Personal Torment, Whitney Mus Am Art, 70; American Painting (organized by Paul Selz), Richmond Art Mus, Va, 70; Darmstadt Biennial, Ger, 70; 70th Am Exhib, Art Inst Chicago, 72.
Teaching: Instr art, Sch Visual Arts, 66-69; assoc prof art, Univ Calif, Berkeley, 69; prof art, Sacramento State Univ, 69-

Awards: Fulbright award, 58-60; L C Tiffany Found fel, 60.
Bibliography: Pincus-Witten (auth), A Conversation with Joe Raffael, Artforum, 12/66; Grace Glueck (auth), O to be born under pisces, New York Times, 1/69; Gloria Smith (auth), The eyes have it: Joseph Raffael (film), NBC TV, 72.
Dealer: Nancy Hoffman Gallery, 429 W Broadway, New York, NY 10012.
Mailing Address: P O Box 77, San Geronimo, CA 94963.

RAFFEL, ALVIN ROBERT
Painter, Educator
Preferred Media: Oils, Watercolors.
b Dayton, Ohio, Dec 25, 05.
Study & Training: Chicago Acad Fine Arts; Art Inst Chicago, with F DeForest Schook.
Work in Public Collections: Dayton Art Inst; Canton Art Mus, Ohio.
Commissions: Seascape (oil), George E Morris, Chicago, Ill, 33; portrait of A H Allen, comn by Mrs A H Allen, Chicago, 34; portrait of Karl Koeker, comn by Karl Koeker, Dayton, 35; portrait of S H McCoy, Springfield H S, Ohio, 56; landscape (oil), Widow's Home, Dayton, 58.
Exhibitions: Ohio Ann, Dayton Art Inst, 45; Cincinnati Ann, Cincinnati Art Mus, Ohio, 45; Portrait of America, New York, N Y, 46; Carnegie Ann, Pittsburgh, Pa, 46-48; Provincetown Arts Festival, Mass, 58.
Teaching: Prof painting & life drawing, Sch of Dayton Art Inst, 46-
Awards: First purchase prize for Fellaheen, Dayton Art Inst, 45; award for Holiday on the Ice, Mrs G S Weng, 48; award for The Lesser Light to Rule the Night, Jefferson Patterson, 51.
Memberships: Am Asn Univ Prof; Dayton Soc Painters & Sculptors.
Publications: Auth, Art, Exponent, 61.
Mailing Address: 6720 Mad River Rd, Dayton, OH 45459.

RAFSKY, JESSICA C
Collector
b New York, N Y, Sept 18, 24.
Study & Training: George Washington Univ; New York Univ.
Memberships: Assoc Guggenheim Mus; sustaining mem Mus Mod Art; assoc Metrop Mus Art; Friend of Whitney Mus; Mus Primitive Art; plus others.
Collection: Contemporary art.
Mailing Address: 200 E 62nd St, New York, NY 10021.

RAGLAND, JACK WHITNEY
Painter, Printmaker
Preferred Media: Acrylics, Serigraphy.
b El Monte, Calif, Feb 25, 38.
Study & Training: Ariz State Univ, BA & MA, with Dr Harry Wood, Arthur Jacobson & Ben Goo; Univ Calif, Los Angeles, with Dr Lester Longman, Sam Amato & William Brice; Akad Angewandte Kunst; Akad Bildenden Künste; Graphische Bundes-Lehr- und Versuchsanstalt, Vienna.
Work in Public Collections: Albertina Mus, Vienna, Austria; Phoenix Art Mus, Ariz; Graphische Bundes-Lehr-und Versuchsanstalt, Vienna; Kunsthaus, Basel, Switz.
Exhibitions: Ariz Ann Exhib, Phoenix, Ariz, 61; Tucson Southwest Exhib, Ariz, 61; Exhib Nat Recognized Artists, Seattle, Wash, 63 & Fort Lauderdale, Fla, 64 & 65; Iowa Ann Exhib, Des Moines, 70 & 72.
Teaching: Grad asst drawing & painting, Univ Calif, Los Angeles, 61-64; instr drawing & painting, Ariz State Univ, summer, 63; assoc prof drawing, printmaking & art history, Simpson Col, 64-
Awards: Grand purchase prize, Ariz Ann, Phoenix Art Mus, 61; painting selected as one of top representational painting in USA, Allied Publ, 62.
Bibliography: Applause, N Y Mag Arts, 11/3/71.
Memberships: Col Art Asn; Mid-Am Col Art Asn.
Publications: Contrib, statement, In: Prize-winning paintings book II, Allied, 62; auth, Works of Wilhelm Jarushka, Graphische Bundes-Lehr-und-Versuchsanstalt Mag, 71.
Mailing Address: 1005 Ann Parkway, Indianola, IA 50125.

RAHJA, VIRGINIA HELGA
Painter, Educator
b Aurora, Minn, Apr 21, 21.
Study & Training: Hamline Univ, BA, 44; Sch Assoc Arts, DFA, 66.
Exhibitions: Many exhibs & ann, Walker Art Ctr, Minn Art Inst, St Paul Gallery, Minn State Fair & Hamline Galleries.
Teaching: Assoc prof painting, Hamline Univ, 43-48 & dir, Hamline Galleries, 45-48; prof painting, Sch Assoc Arts, St Paul, 48-65, dean, 48-
Positions: Asst supt fine arts, Minn State Fair, 44-48.
Memberships: Minn Art Educators Asn; Nat Asn Interior Designers; Am Asn Univ Women; Midwest Col Art Conf.
Mailing Address: 360 S Lexington Pkwy, St Paul, MN 55105.

RAHR, FREDERIC H
Collector, Patron
b Malden, Mass, Apr 23, 04.
Study & Training: Harvard Col; Famous Artists Sch; Nat Acad Sch Fine Arts; also with Francis Scott Bradford.
Collection: Paintings, prints, engravings.
Mailing Address: 9 E 56th St, New York, NY 10022.

RAIN, CHARLES (WHEDON)
Painter
b Knoxville, Tenn, Dec 27, 11.
Study & Training: Art Inst Chicago, 31-33; pvt study in Berlin, Vienna & Paris, 33-34.
Work in Public Collections: Springfield Mus Fine Arts; Univ Ill; Ariz State Univ, Tempe; DeBeers Mus, Johannesburg, S Africa; Va Mus Fine Arts.
Exhibitions: Springfield Mus Fine Arts, 47 & 63; five shows, Univ Ill, 49-57; Los Angeles Mus Art, 51 & 56; Denver Art Mus, 57; Albright-Knox Art Gallery, Buffalo, 61; plus many others.
Awards: Purchase prizes, Springfield Mus Fine Arts, Mass, 47 & Univ Ill, 50.
Dealer: FAR Gallery, 746 Madison Ave, New York, NY 10021.
Mailing Address: 10 Mitchell Pl, New York, NY 10017.

RAINEY, FROELICH GLADSTONE
Art Administrator, Writer
b Black River Falls, Wis, June 18, 07.
Study & Training: Univ Chicago, PhB, 29; Am Sch in France, 30; Yale Univ, PhD, 35.
Teaching: Asst prof anthrop, Univ Puerto Rico, 35; prof anthrop, Univ Alaska, 35-42; prof anthrop, Univ Pa, 47-
Positions: Asst in anthrop, Peabody Mus, Yale Univ, 31-35; anthrop res in West Indies, 33-35; dir, Univ Mus, Univ Pa, 47-, dir, Applied Sci Ctr for Archaeol, 60-, archaeol res in Italy, 61-, supvr archaeol res, Univ Mus expeds all over the world.
Awards: Grants for res, Am Mus Natural Hist, 34-42; Comdr, Order of Merit, Italian Repub.
Memberships: Am Asn Mus (pres, 61-63, exec comt, 63-); Int Coun Mus; Mus Coun Philadelphia; Soc Am Archaeol; Soc Pa Archaeol; plus others.
Publications: Auth, Archaeology, 70, Dating the past, 71 & Archaeology, 72, Encycl Britannica Yearbk Sci & the future; auth, The Ipiutak culture. Excavations at Point Hope, Alaska, Addison-Wesley, 71; auth, Looting of archaeological sites, Sci Yr (in press).
Mailing Address: The University Museum, University of Pennsylvania, 33rd & Spruce Sts, Philadelphia, PA 19104.

RAKOCY, WILLIAM (JOSEPH)
Painter, Educator
Preferred Media: Oils, Watercolors, Acrylics.
b Youngstown, Ohio, Apr 14, 24.
Study & Training: Butler Inst Am Art, with Clyde Singer, 39-41; Am Acad Art, 44; Kansas City Art Inst, with Ross Braught, Ed Lanning & Bruce Mitchell, MFA, 51.
Work in Public Collections: Mural, U S N T S, Gt Lakes, Ill; mural, YMCA, Youngstown; watercolor, Butler Inst Am Art, Youngstown; drawings & prints, El Paso Mus Art, Tex.
Commissions: Mural, Woodrow Wilson High Sch, Youngstown, 46; four murals (with Robert Sonoga & Chet Kwiecinski), McSorleys Colonial Rest, Pittsburgh, Pa, 55; three murals, YMCA, Youngstown.
Exhibitions: Butler Inst Am Art Ann, 55.
Teaching: Instr painting & drawing, Mohn Sch Art, 54-56; asst prof painting & drawing, Col Artesia, 66-67, assoc prof painting & drawing, 67-71.
Awards: Art travel grant to study in Italy, Italian Businessmen, Kansas City, Mo, 53; first award in watercolor, Butler Inst Am Art, 56.
Memberships: Kansas City Area Artists Asn; El Paso Art Asn; Mogollon Artists Asn (pres); Western Asn Art Schs & Univ Mus; El Paso Hist Soc.
Art Interests: Promoter of art auctions to assist artists via sales and scholarships.
Publications: Auth, Sketches on Mogollon, 64; auth, A western portfolio, 65; auth, Art reporter, El Paso, Texas, Painting Place Art News, 72; auth, Sketches & observations, 72; auth, Art look, South West Gallery Mag; plus others.
Dealer: Nancy Crook International Gallery, 1220 Wyoming St, El Paso, TX 79912.
Mailing Address: 4210 Emory Way, El Paso, TX 79902.

RALSTON, J(AMES) K(ENNETH)
Painter, Illustrator
Preferred Media: Oils, Ink, Watercolors.
b Choteau, Mont, Mar 31, 96.
Study & Training: Art Inst Chicago; hon DFA, Rocky Mt Col, 71.
Work in Public Collections: Jefferson Nat Expansion Mem, Saint Louis, Mo; Custer Battlefield Nat Monument, Mont; Mont Hist Soc Mus & Galleries, Helena; Buffalo Bill Hist Ctr, Whitney Gallery Western Art, Cody, Wyo; Western Heritage Mus Treasures of West Collection, Billings, Mont.
Commissions: Murals, The Crossing, Jordan Hotel, Glendive, Mont, 52 & Billings Munic Airport, Logan Field, 58; paintings, After The Battle, Treasures of West Collection, 55, Into The Unknown, Jefferson Nat Expansion Monument, 64 & The Return, First Westdie Nat Bank, Great Falls, Mont, 71.
Exhibitions: Gainsborough Gallery, Calgary, Alta, 59; Charles M Russell Gallery, Great Falls, 62 & 71; Mont Hist Soc, 64; Galeries Lafayette, Paris, France, 66; Yellowstone Art Ctr, Billings, 67 & 71.
Bibliography: Michael Kennedy (auth), Man who avoids footprints of CMR, Mont Mag Western Hist, 61; R W Fenwick (auth), J K Ralston and his art, Empire Mag, 67; Ed Ainsworth (auth), The cowboy in art, Bk World Publ, 68.
Memberships: Mont Inst Arts; Billings Arts Asn; Yellowstone Art Ctr (chmn ann art auction).
Publications: Auth & illusr, Rhymes of a cowboy, Rimrock Publ, 69.
Mailing Address: 2103 Alserson Ave, Billings, MT 59102.

RAMBERG, CHRISTINA (CHRISTINA RAMBERG HANSON)
Painter
Preferred Media: Acrylics.
b Camp Campbell, Ky, Aug 21, 46.
Study & Training: Sch Art Inst Chicago, BFA, 68.
Exhibitions: Famous Artists, 69 & Chicago Imagist Art, 72, Mus Contemp Art, Chicago, Ill; Spirit of the Comic in the 50's & 60's, Univ Pa, Philadelphia, 69; False Image II, Hyde Park Art Ctr, Chicago, 69; Whitney Ann, Whitney Mus Am Art, New York, N Y, 72.
Teaching: Vis artist-instr painting, Univ Colo, Boulder, 72.
Dealer: Phyllis Kind Gallery, 226 E Ontario St, Chicago, IL 60611.
Mailing Address: 709 W Buena, Chicago, IL 60613.

RAMBO, JAMES I
Museum Curator
b San Jose, Calif, June 28, 23.
Study & Training: San Jose State Col, BA, 48; Calif Sch Fine Arts; Tex A&M Univ.
Positions: Mem staff, Cooper Union Mus, New York, N Y, keeper decorative arts, 50-52; mem staff, Calif Palace of Legion of Honor, San Francisco, Calif, 53-, cur collections, 55-66, chief cur, 66-
Publications: Contribr, articles in prof publ & catalogues.
Mailing Address: California Palace of Legion of Honor, Lincoln Park, San Francisco, CA 94121.

RAMIREZ, EDUARDO VILLAMIZAR
Sculptor
Preferred Media: Metal Constructions, Concrete Constructions.
b Pamplona, Colombia, Aug 27, 23.
Study & Training: Nat Univ Colombia Archit Sch; Nat Univ Colombia Art Sch.
Work in Public Collections: Mus Mod Art, New York, N Y; Chase Manhattan Bank, New York; Mass Inst Technol Art Collection, Cambridge, Mass; Mus Mod Art, Bogota, Colombia; Notre Dame Univ Art Collection, Ind.
Commissions: Wood relief & gold leaf, Banco Bogota, Colombia; precast concrete walk, Gaseosas Lux, Cali, Colombia; sculpture & wood panels, American Bank, New York; sculpture in concrete, Fort Tryon, New York.
Exhibitions: The Classic Spirit, Sidney Janis Gallery, New York, 64; White on White Show, De Cordova Mus, Lincoln, Mass, 65; Art of Latin America Since Independence, Yale Univ, New Haven, Conn, 66; Tenth São Paulo Biennial, Brazil, 68; Am Acad Arts & Letters, 72.
Awards: Guggenheim Int Award, 58; first award, Salon Artistas Colombianos, Bogota, 64; second int prize, Tenth São Paulo Biennial, 68.
Mailing Address: 463 West St, New York, NY 10014.

RAMOS, MELVIN JOHN
Painter, Educator
Preferred Media: Oils.
b Sacramento, Calif, July 24, 35.
Study & Training: Sacramento Jr Col, 54, with Wayne Thiebaud; San Jose State Col, 55; Sacramento State Col, 55-58 & MA.
Work in Public Collections: Mus Mod Art, New York, N Y; Neue Galerie, Aachen, Ger; Oakland Art Mus, Calif; San Francisco Art Mus, Calif; Univ Mus, Potsdam, N Y.
Commissions: Paintings, Time Inc, New York, 68 & Syracuse Univ, N Y, 70.

Exhibitions: Pop Art U S A, Oakland Mus & Six More, Los Angeles
Co Mus, Calif, 63; Human Concern, Personal Torment, Whitney
Mus-Am Art, New York & Pop Art Revisited, Hayward Gallery,
London, Eng, 69; Looking West, Joslyn Art Mus, Omaha, Nebr, 70.
Teaching: Assoc prof painting, Calif State Univ, Hayward, 66-
Bibliography: R Skelton (auth), The art of Mel Ramos, Art Int, Switz,
68; S Suzuki (auth), Mel Ramos-1935-, Mizue, Tokyo, 70; Pops
girls (pictorial), Playboy, 72.
Publications: Contribr, History of modern art, 69, Erotic art 2, 70,
Art now/new age, 71, The high art of cooking & Art as image and
idea, 72.
Dealer: French & Co, 980 Madison Ave, New York, NY 10021.
Mailing Address: 5941 Ocean View Dr, Oakland, CA 94618.

RAND, PAUL
Painter, Designer
b New York, N Y, Aug 15, 14.
Study & Training: Pratt Inst; Art Stud League New York, with George
Grosz; Parsons Sch Design.
Work in Public Collections: Mus Mod Art; Smithsonian Inst, Washington, D C.
Exhibitions: One-man shows, Composing Room, 47, Am Inst Graphic
Arts Gallery, 58 & IBM Gallery, 71; Brooklyn Mus, 72; many
shows, Art Dirs Club New York.
Teaching: Instr design, Cooper Union, 42; instr graphic design,
Pratt Inst, 46-47; prof graphic design, Yale Univ, 56-69.
Positions: Art dir, Esquire Apparel Arts, 37-41; art dir, Weintraub
Advert Agency, 41-54; design consult, IBM Corp & Westinghouse
Elec Corp, 56-
Awards: Citation, Philadelphia Col Art, 62; gold medal, Am Inst
Graphic Arts, 66; Art Dirs Hall of Fame, 72.
Bibliography: Georgine Oeri (auth), Paul Rand, Graphis Mag, 47;
Y Kamekura (auth), The work of Paul Rand, Zokeisha, Tokyo, 58;
article, In: Am Artist, 70.
Memberships: Art Dirs Club New York; Am Inst Graphic Arts; Alliance Graphique Int, Paris; Benjamin Franklin fel, Royal Soc
Arts & Sci, London.
Publications: Auth, Thoughts on design, Wittenborn, 47 & Van
Nostrand Reinhold, 70; auth, Black in the visual arts, Harvard
Univ Press, 49; illusr, I know a lot of things, 56, Sparkle & spin,
57, Little 1, 62 & Listen, listen, 70, Harcourt; auth, The trademarks of Paul Rand, Wittenbron, 60.
Mailing Address: 87 Goodhill Rd, Weston, CT 06880.

RANDALL, (LILLIAN) PAULA
Sculptor, Designer
Preferred Media: Wood, Stone, Plastics, Welded Metals.
b Plato, Minn, Dec 21, 95.
Study & Training: Minneapolis Inst Arts; Univ Southern Calif; Otis
Art Inst, Los Angeles.
Work in Public Collections: Western Div Nat Audubon Soc, Sacramento, Calif; Off Tournament Roses, Pasadena, Calif.
Exhibitions: All Calif Exhib, Laguna Beach Art Mus, Calif, 64; Univ
Taiwan, Formosa, 64; Calif Inst Technol, Dabney Hall, Pasadena,
65; Brandeis Univ Exhib, Granada Hills, Calif, 67; Form and the
Inner Eye Tactile Show, Calif State Univ, Los Angeles & Pierce
Col, San Fernando, Calif, 72.
Teaching: Instr sculpture, pvt studio, 69-; instr sculpture, Pasadena
Sch Fine Arts, 70.
Awards: Laguna Beach Art Mus Award, All Calif Show, 64; spec
achievement award, All Calif Exhib, Indio, 66; Pasadena Soc Artists Spec Award, 71.
Bibliography: Russ Leadabrand (auth), Meet artist Paula Randall,
Pasadena Star-News, 69; Don Ham (dir), The art of age (film),
privately produced, 71; Jim Norris (auth), An artist who perseveres with a blowtorch, Pasadena Union, 71; plus others.
Memberships: Pasadena Soc Artists (secy-treas publicity, 62-72);
Pasadena Artist Assocs; Laguna Beach Art Mus; Los Angeles Co
Art Gallery.
Mailing Address: 441 Ramona Ave, Sierra Madre, CA 91024.

RANDALL, RUTH HUNIE
Designer, Educator
Preferred Media: Ceramics.
b Dayton, Ohio, Sept 30, 96.
Study & Training: Cleveland Art Inst, design & art educ; Syracuse Univ, BFA, MFA; State Univ N Y Col Ceramics, Alfred Univ;
Kunstgewerbe Schule, Vienna; also with Ruth Reeves & Ivan
Mestrovic.
Work in Public Collections: Everson Mus, Syracuse, N Y; Walker
Art Mus, Youngstown, Ohio; San Antonio Mus, Tex; Syracuse
Univ.
Commissions: Ceramic sculpture relief, exterior br libr, Syracuse
Bd Educ Bldg Comt, 60.
Exhibitions: World's Fairs; San Francisco; New York, N Y; Paris
Decorative Arts; Nat Ceramic Exhibs, 30-62.
Teaching: Prof design & crafts, Syracuse Univ Sch Art, 30-62.

Awards: Second prize awards, Nat Ceramic Shows, 30, 36 & 56;
first prize for ceramic sculpture, Rochester Mus, N Y, 62.
Bibliography: Article on personal ceramic collection, Syracuse Mus
Bull, 60.
Memberships: Southwest Fla Craft Guild; N Y State Craftsmen (bd
dirs, 58-60); Syracuse Ceramic Guild (pres, 56).
Collection: Japanese Mingei ceramics & Peruvian ceramics for
Syracuse Univ Art Sch Collection.
Publications: Illusr, ceramics page, Craft Horizons, 39; auth, Ceramic sculpture, Watson Guptill, 46.
Dealer: Artizan Shop, Sanibel, FL 33957.
Mailing Address: 334 N E La Salle Ave, Port Charlotte, FL 33950.

RANDALL, THEODORE A
Sculptor, Educator
b Indianapolis, Ind, Oct 18, 14.
Study & Training: Yale Univ, BFA, 38; State Univ N Y Col Ceramics,
Alfred Univ, MFA, 49.
Commissions: Pottery, Syracuse Mus Fine Arts & St Stephens
Church, Albany, N Y.
Teaching: Lectr motives & meaning in art & ceramics today; instr
State Univ N Y Col Ceramics, Alfred Univ, 52-53, asst prof, 53-
56, head div art, 56-, prof ceramics, 60-
Awards: Prizes, Albright Art Gallery, Smithsonian Inst & York
State Craftsmen; plus others.
Memberships: Fel Am Ceramic Soc; fel Acad Int Ceramics; fel Nat
Coun Educ for Ceramic Arts (past pres); fel Nat Asn Schs Art
(pres); SUNY Coun Art Dept Chmn.
Publications: Auth, Notions about the usefulness of pottery, Pottery
Quart, 61; contribr, articles, In: Am Ceramic Soc J & Bull, Ceramic Age, Ceramic Indust & Ceramics Monthly.
Mailing Address: Jericho Hill Rd, Alfred, NY 14802.

RANDELL, RICHARD K
Sculptor
b Minneapolis, Minn, 1929.
Work in Public Collections: Minneapolis Art Inst; Univ Minn; Saint
Paul Gallery; Walker Art Ctr, Minneapolis.
Exhibitions: Walker Art Ctr Biennial, 56, 58, 62 & 66; Ohio State
Univ, 66; Univ Ill, 67; American Sculpture of the Sixties, Los
Angeles Co Mus Art, 67; Southern Ill Univ, 67; plus many others.
Teaching: Instr, Hamline Univ, 54-61; instr, Macalester Col, 61;
instr, Univ Minn, 61-65; instr, Sacramento State Col, 66.
Awards: Purchase prizes, Walker Art Ctr Biennial, 56, 62 & 66;
first prize & purchase prize, 57 & hon mention, 59, Minneapolis
Art Inst; purchase prize, Saint Paul Art Gallery, 61.
Bibliography: Maurice Tuchman (auth), American sculpture of the
sixties, Los Angeles Co Mus Art, 67.
Mailing Address: c/o Royal Marks Gallery, 19 E 71st St, New York,
NY 10021.

RANDOLPH, GLADYS CONRAD
Painter, Writer
b Whitestone, N Y.
Study & Training: N Y Sch Fine & Appl Art; Terry Art Inst; Portland Art Mus, Ore; Univ Pa; New York Univ; also with Hobson
Pittman & Revington Arthur.
Work in Public Collections: Lowe Gallery Art; Columbus Mus Art,
Ga.
Exhibitions: League Am Pen Women, 50; Fla Southern Col, 52; Ringling Mus Art, Fla; Miami Art League; Am Artists Prof League;
plus many others.
Awards: Prizes, Miami Art League, Blue Dome & Fla Fedn Artists;
plus others.
Memberships: Fla Fedn Artists; Miami Watercolor Soc; Artists Equity Asn; Arts Coun, Inc, Miami (art chmn); Fla Art Group; plus
many others.
Publications: Contribr, articles, In: Mineralogist, Portland Oregonian, Ore J, Am Boy & other publ & newspapers.
Mailing Address: Sailboat Bay Apts, 2951 S Bayshore Dr, Apt B4,
Miami, FL 33133.

RANKIN, DON
Painter
b Dec 9, 42.
Study & Training: Famous Artists' Sch; also with Bill Yeager; Samford Univ, BA(fine art & psychol).
Work in Public Collections: Numerous collections in southeast &
New England states.
Commissions: Birmingham Centennial Seal, 69; Birmingham Centennial commemorative coins, Arlington Shrine, 70, Univ Ala Med
Complex, 71 & Birmingham Jefferson, 71.
Exhibitions: Ala Watercolor Soc, 67-71; Birmingham Art Asn Ann,
68 & Ala Centennial Show, 71, Birmingham Mus Art; plus other
group & one-man shows.

Memberships: Ala Watercolor Soc (past v pres, bd dirs); charter mem La Watercolor Soc (reporter-at-large); assoc Am Watercolor Soc.
Mailing Address: 614 Hambaugh Ave, Homewood, AL 35209.

RANKINE, V V
Sculptor, Painter
Preferred Media: Plexiglas
b Boston, Mass.
Study & Training: Amedée Ozenfant Sch, New York, N Y; Black Mt Col, with Alberts & De Kooning.
Work in Public Collections: Nat Collection Fine Arts, Washington, D C; Corcoran Gallery Art, Washington, D C; Oklahoma City Mus; Indianapolis Mus Art; Woodward Found, Washington, D C.
Commissions: Altar painting, Robert Owen Shrine, New Harmony, Ind, 65.
Exhibitions: Six shows, Jefferson Pl Gallery, Washington, D C, 63-72; Betty Parsons Gallery, New York, N Y, 66, 69 & 70; 30th Corcoran Biennial, Washington, D C, 67-68; Four Americans, Axiom Gallery, London, Eng, 68; Painting & Sculpture Today, Indianapolis Mus, 69.
Teaching: Dir art dept, Madeira Sch, Greenway, Va, 67-70; artist-in-residence, Inst Man & Sci, Rensselaer, N Y, summer 68; humanities art instr, Hunter Col High Sch, New York, 70-71.
Awards: Painting prize, Corcoran Gallery Ann Exhib, 55.
Bibliography: Leslie Judd Ahlander (auth), article, In: Art Int, 11/64; Lawrence Campbell (auth), article, In: Art News, 3/69; Legrace Benson (auth), article, In: Art Int, 12/69.
Dealer: Jefferson Place Gallery, 2144 P St NW, Washington, DC 20037.
Mailing Address: c/o Betty Parsons Gallery, 24 W 57th St, New York, NY 10019.

RANNIT, ALEKSIS
Art Historian, Educator
b Kallaste, Estonia, Oct 14, 14.
Study & Training: Tartu State Univ, dipl art hist; Columbia Univ, MS.
Teaching: Prof art hist, Ecole Superieure Arts et Metiers, Freiburg, Ger, 46-50; prof art hist, res assoc & cur Slavic & E Europ collections, Yale Univ, presently.
Positions: Chief cur prints & rare bks, Lithuanian Nat Libr, Kaunas, 41-44; sci secy, div fine arts, Fr High Comn, Ger, 50-53; art ref librn & cataloger prints, art & archit div, New York Pub Libr, 53 & 61.
Awards: Olsen Found fel res & writing on Coptic art & symbolism, 55.
Memberships: Int Asn Art Critics; Int Pen Clubs, London (exec comt); Asn Ger Art Historians; Estonian Lit Soc (pres); academician Acad Int Sci & Lett, Paris; plus others.
Publications: Auth, Eduard Wiiralt (monogr), 43 & 46 & V K Jonynas (monogr), 47; auth, M K Ciurlionis (monogr), UNESCO, 49; auth, Honegger, Swiss purist artist (monogr), 71; contribr, Brockhaus Encycl & Schweizer Lexicon; plus others.
Mailing Address: Yale University, Box 1603A, New Haven, CT 06520.

RANSON, NANCY SUSSMAN
Painter, Serigrapher
Preferred Media: Oils, Acrylics, Silkscreen.
b New York, N Y.
Study & Training: Pratt Inst Art Sch, cert; Art Stud League New York; Brooklyn Mus Art Sch; also with Alexander Brook; Robert Laurent & Jean Charlot.
Work in Public Collections: Fogg Mus Art, Harvard Univ, Cambridge, Mass; Mus City of New York; Philadelphia Free Libr, Pa; Nat Art Gallery New South Wales, Sydney, Australia; Nat Mus Mod Art, New Delhi, India.
Exhibitions: Critics Choice Show, Grand Cent Galleries, New York, 46; Whitney Mus Am Art, New York, 51; Nat Exhib Contemp Artists U S, Pomona, Calif, 56; Pa Acad Fine Arts, 57; Color Prints of Americas, N J State Mus, 70.
Awards: Medal of Honor in Graphics, Nat Asn Women Artists, 56; MacDowell Found fel, 64; first prize in graphics, Am Soc Contemp Artists, 70.
Memberships: New York Soc Women Artists (v pres, 68-69); Am Soc Contemp Artists (pres, 69-71); Nat Asn Women Artists (chmn, for exhibs, 63-67, chmn admis, 69-71); Audubon Artists (dir, graphics, 70-73); Am Color Print Soc.
Mailing Address: 1299 Ocean Ave, Brooklyn, NY 11230.

RAPP, LOIS
Painter, Educator
Preferred Media: Watercolors, Oils, Pastels.
Study & Training: Philadelphia Col Art, dipl teacher's training & cert illus, 25-29; also with Earl Horter.

Work in Public Collections: Woodmere Art Gallery, Philadelphia, Pa; Valley Forge Mem Chapel, Pa; Gwynedd-Mercy Col, Gwynedd Valley, Pa; Norristown Pub Libr, Pa; Montgomery Hosp, Norristown.
Exhibitions: Am Drawing Ann XV, Norfolk, Va, 57; Am Watercolor Soc 91st Ann, New York, N Y, 58; Regional Exhib, Philadelphia Mus Art, Pa, 59; Philadelphia Watercolor Club, Pa, 71; Woodmere Art Gallery, Philadelphia, 72.
Teaching: Instr art, Mater Misericordiae Acad, Merion, Pa, 33-45; instr art, Collegeville Trappe Pub Schs, Pa, 35-48; instr art, Conshocken Art League, Pa, 35-57.
Awards: Gold medal for Along the Schuylkill River, Lansdale Art League, 52; awards for Meeting House Interior, 60 & Falls of the Potomac, 63, Woodmere Art Gallery.
Memberships: Am Watercolor Soc; Woodmere Art Gallery (exhib comt, 65-69); Philadelphia Watercolor Club (bd dirs, 68-70).
Mailing Address: 116 Haws Ave, Norristown, PA 19401.

RAPPIN, ADRIAN
Painter
Preferred Media: Oils.
b New York, N Y, Jan 20, 34.
Study & Training: Acad Fine Arts, Rome, Italy; Brandeis Univ, BA; Art Acad Cincinnati; Art Stud League New York.
Work in Public Collections: Staten Island Mus, New York; Gibbes Gallery, Charleston Mus, S C; Lincoln Univ, Oxford, Pa; Randolph Macon Col, Lynchburg, Va; Kellogg Found, Battle Creek, Mich.
Exhibitions: Allied Artists Am, Nat Acad Design Galleries, 61-72; one-man exhibs, Barzansky Gallery, 64, 66 & 69; 50 Am Artists, New York, 65-69; UNICEF Int, Monaco, 65-67; Kalamazoo, Mich, 70; plus others.
Memberships: Allied Artists Am; 50 Am Artists; Intercontinental Artists; Am Artists Prof League.
Publications: Reproductions painting, Christmas Fund, New York Times, 67-70, Songs of our times, Hansen, 73 & The bookshelf for boys & girls, Univ Soc Press, 73-74.
Mailing Address: 14 W 68th St, New York, NY 10023.

RASCOE, STEPHEN THOMAS
Painter, Educator
Preferred Media: Oils.
b Uvalde, Tex, May 8, 24.
Study & Training: Univ Tex, Austin; Art Inst Chicago, BFA, MFA.
Work in Public Collections: Houston Mus Fine Arts, Tex; Dallas Mus Fine Arts, Tex; Southern Methodist Univ, Dallas; Ford Motor Co, Dearborn, Mich; Ling-Temco-Vought Res Ctr, Grand Prairie, Tex.
Commissions: Rancho Seco Land & Cattle Co, Corpus Christi, Tex, 67; Tex Instruments Corp, Dallas, 67; Arlington Bank & Trust Co, Tex, 69; First Nat Bank Dallas, 69; Lakewood Bank, Dallas, 71.
Exhibitions: Longview Invitational Ann, Tex, 57-72; Artists West of the Mississippi, Denver, Colo, 67; San Antonio Hemisphere, Tex, 68.
Teaching: Asst prof art, Univ Tex, Arlington, 64-
Positions: Pres, S Tex Art League, 60-61; pres, Arlington Art Asn, Tex, 67-68.
Awards: Houston Mus Fine Arts purchase award, Tex Show, 56; first prize, Tex Painting & Sculpture Show, Dallas Mus, 57; D D Feldman award, 58.
Memberships: Dallas Art Asn; Fort Worth Art Asn; Mus S Tex, Corpus Christi.
Dealer: Mary Nye Contemporary Art, 5906 Norway Rd, Dallas, TX 75230.
Mailing Address: 2002 Westview Terrace, Arlington, TX 76013.

RATH, HILDEGARD
Painter, Lecturer
Preferred Media: Oils, Pastels, Watercolors, Charcoal.
b Freudenstadt, Württemberg, Ger, Mar 22, 09; U S citizen.
Study & Training: Atelier House, Stuttgart, Ger, with Adolf Senglaub; Kunstgewerbe Sch, Stuttgart; Akad Bildenden Kunste, Berlin, Ger; also with Otto Manigk, Berlin.
Work in Public Collections: Wurttembergische Kultministerium, Stuttgart; Metrop Mus Art, New York, N Y; New York Pub Libr; Brooklyn Mus, N Y; Libr Cong, Washington, D C; over 800 works in mus & pvt collections.
Commissions: Oil paintings, portraits & landscapes, comn by Willi Eiselen, Ulm, Donau, Ger, 32; portraits, landscapes & still lifes, comn by Walter Freudenberg, Baden, Ger, 46; Triplets, comn by Mrs Sig Buchmeyer, Paris, France, 48; Mrs Siegtraut Gauss-Glock, Wurttemberg, Ger, 54; Madonna, comn by Klaus Heuck, Frankfurth, Ger, 59.
Exhibitions: Weissenhof Ausstellung Stuttgart Int, 27; Allied Artists Am, Nat Acad Design Galleries, New York, 51; Artists Equity Bldg Fund Exhib, Whitney Mus Am Art, 51; Artists Equity Asn, 52; 15th Nat Print Exhib, Libr Cong, 57.

Teaching: Dir painting, Europ Sch Fine Art, 49-54; lectr hist art, Great Neck Pub Schs, 61-62; lectr serigraphy, N Shore Art Ctr, 61-62.

Awards: Dr Blaicher Award, 27; Grumbacher Award, 52; Prix de Paris, 63.

Bibliography: Hennemann-Bayer (auth), Zur Ausstellung, Schwarzwalder Bote Stuttgart, 59; Dannecker (auth), Von werken, Stuttgarter Nachrichten, 59; P H Buhner (auth), Hildegard Rath im Kunsthaus Schaller, Stuttgarter Zeitung, 59.

Memberships: Int Platform Asn; Wurttembergischer Kunstverein, Stuttgart; Southern Vt Art Asn; Knickerbocker Artists; Artists Equity Asn N Y.

Publications: Auth, articles, In: Art Digest, 52, Schwarzwald Zeitung, 59 & Am Artist, 63; contribr, Enciclopedia int degli artisti, 70-71.

Dealer: Galerie Internationale, 1095 Madison Ave, New York, NY 10028; Weintraub Gallery, 992 Madison Ave, New York, NY 10021.

Mailing Address: 3 Cypress Ave, Kings Point, NY 11024.

RATHBONE, PERRY TOWNSEND
Museum Director

b Germantown, Pa, July 3, 11.

Study & Training: Harvard Col, AB, 33, Harvard Univ, 33-34; Wash Univ, hon DFA, 58; Northeastern Univ, hon DHL, 60; Bates Col, hon DFA, 64; Suffolk Univ, hon DHL, 69; Williams Col, 70; Boston Col, hon DFA, 70.

Positions: Cur, Detroit Inst Art, 36-40; secy & dir masterpieces of art, N Y World's Fair, 39; dir, City Art Mus Saint Louis, 40-55; dir, Boston Mus Fine Arts, Mass, 55-72; mem, Mayor of Boston's Art Adv Comt, 69-; chmn bd, Metrop Boston Art Ctr; trustee, New Eng Conserv Music; Inst Contemp Art, Boston; Boston Art Festival; v chmn comt to visit fine arts dept, Harvard Univ; trustee, R I Sch Design; Int Exhibs Found, Washington, D C; mem fine arts vis comt, R I Sch Design; mem vis comt art & archeol, dept fine arts, Wash Univ; mem art adv comt, Chase Manhattan Bank, New York; trustee, Am Fedn Arts.

Awards: Chevalier, Legion of Hon.

Memberships: Am Asn Mus (v pres, 60-, mem coun); Asn Art Mus Dirs (pres, 59-60, 69-70); Benjamin Franklin fel Royal Soc Arts, London.

Publications: Auth, Max Beckmann, 48, Mississippi panorama, 49, Westward the way, 54, Lee Gatch, 60 & Handbook for the Forsyth Wickes collection, 68; contribr, art mags & mus bull.

Mailing Address: 151 Coolidge Hill, Cambridge MA 02138.

RATKAI, GEORGE
Painter, Sculptor

b Budapest, Hungary, Dec 24, 07.

Work in Public Collections: Tel-Aviv Mus, Israel; Abbott Labs Collection; Univ Ill; Butler Inst Am Art; Univ Nebr; plus many others.

Exhibitions: Audubon Artists, 55-65; Provincetown Art Asn, 56-64; Relig Art Exhib, Univ Nebr, 65; Mansfield State Col, Pa, 65; Bass Mus Art, Miami, 65; plus many others.

Awards: Prize, Art of Dem Living, 51; gold medals, 53 & 65 & mem medal, 56, Audubon Artists; Childe Hassam Award, 59.

Memberships: Artists Equity Asn; Audubon Artists; fel Int Inst Arts & Lett; Am Fedn Arts; Nat Soc Painters in Casein; plus others.

Mailing Address: 350 W 57th St, New York, NY 10019.

RATTNER, ABRAHAM
Painter

b Poughkeepsie, N Y, July 8, 95.

Study & Training: Corcoran Sch Art, 13-15; George Washington Univ, 13-14; Pa Acad Fine Arts, 15-17; Ecoles Beaux Arts, Paris, 21-23; Acad Ransom, Paris, 23-24; Acad Grande Chaumiere, 24-25; Sorbonne, 25-26.

Work in Public Collections: Mus Mod Art; Whitney Mus Am Art; Pa Acad Fine Arts; Albright-Knox Art Gallery, Buffalo; Art Inst Chicago; plus many others.

Commissions: Mosaic mural, St Francis Monastery, Chicago, 56; mosaic columns & tapestry murals, Fairmount Temple, Cleveland, Ohio, 57; stained glass facade, Loop Synagogue, Chicago, Ill, 58; De Waters Art Ctr, Flint, Mich, 58; facade, St Leonard's Friary & Col; plus others.

Exhibitions: Pa Acad Fine Arts; Corcoran Gallery Art; Art Inst Chicago; Univ Ill; Carnegie Inst; plus many other group & one-man shows U S & abroad.

Teaching: Instr, Skowhegan Sch Art, summers 49-50; artist-in-residence, Am Acad in Rome, 51; vis prof, Pa Acad Fine Arts, 55; vis prof, Columbia Univ, 55-56; instr & artist-in-residence, many leading schs & univs.

Awards: Prize, Univ Ill, 48; citation & gold medal, one-man show, Temple Univ, Philadelphia, Pa, 55; gold medal, Art Dirs Club, Philadelphia, 56; plus many others.

Bibliography: Lloyd Goodrich & John I H Baur (auth), Four American expressionists, Whitney Mus Am Art, 49; Daniel M Mendelowitz (auth), A history of American art, Holt, Rinehart & Winston, 61; S W Hayter (auth), About prints, Oxford Univ Press, 62; plus many others.

Memberships: Fr Soc Arts Decoratif; Nat Inst Arts & Lett.

Dealer: Kennedy Galleries, Inc, 20 E 56th St, New York, NY 10022.

Mailing Address: 830 Greenwich St, New York, NY 10014.

RAUCH, JOHN G
Collector, Patron

b Indianapolis, Ind, July 16, 90.

Study & Training: Harvard Col, AB, 11, Harvard Law Sch, 11-12; Butler Univ, hon LLD, 68.

Positions: Trustee, Art Asn Indianapolis, 40-62, pres bd trustees, 62-; chmn bd trustees, Ind Hist Soc, 50-

Mailing Address: 3050 N Meridian St, Indianapolis, IN 46208.

RAUH, FRITZ
Painter

b Wuppertal, Ger, Nov 25, 20.

Study & Training: Art Sch, Braunschweig, Ger.

Exhibitions: One-man shows, De Young Mus, San Francisco, Calif, 56, San Francisco Mus Art, Calif, 67, William Sawyer Gallery, San Francisco, 71 & Oakland Art Mus, Calif, 71; Int Show, Expo '70, Osaka, Japan, 70.

Dealer: William Sawyer Gallery, 3045 Clay St, San Francisco, CA 94115.

Mailing Address: 235 Scenic Ave, San Anselmo, CA 94960.

RAUSCHENBERG, ROBERT
Painter

b Port Arthur, Tex, Oct 22, 25.

Study & Training: Kansas City Art Inst & Sch Design, 46-47; Acad Julian, Paris, 47; Black Mt Col, with Josef Albers, 48-49; Art Stud League New York, with Vaclav Vytlacil & Morris Kantor, 49-50.

Work in Public Collections: Albright-Knox Art Gallery; Whitney Mus Am Art; White Mus, Cornell Univ; Tate Gallery, London, Eng; Goucher Col; also in many pvt collections.

Exhibitions: Dada, Surrealism and Their Heritage, Mus Mod Art, 68; Directions I: Options, Milwaukee Art Ctr, 68; Arts Coun Gt Brit, 68; Whitney Mus Am Art Ann, 69 & 70; Guggenheim Mus, 72; plus many other group & one-man shows U S & abroad.

Awards: Winner, Venice Biennale, 64; awards, Corcoran Biennial Contemp Am Painters, 65 & Art Inst Chicago, 66; plus others.

Bibliography: Dore Ashton (auth), The unknown shore, Little, 62; Tracy Atkinson (auth), Directions I: options 1968, Milwaukee Art Ctr, 68; Gregory Battcock (ed), Minimal art: a critical anthology, Dutton, 68; plus many others.

Mailing Address: 381 Lafayette St, New York, NY 10003.

RAVESON, SHERMAN HAROLD
Painter, Writer

Preferred Media: Oils.

b New Haven, Conn.

Study & Training: Cumberland Univ, AB, 27 & LLB, 29; Art Stud League New York.

Work in Public Collections: Nat Mus Racing, Saratoga, N Y; Hall of Fame of Trotter, Goshen, N Y; Sporting Gallery, N Y; Hialeah Race Course Clubhouse, Fla; Saratoga Raceway, N Y.

Exhibitions: Am Watercolor Soc, New York, N Y, 34-58; Eleven paintings of N Y Racetracks, New York World's Fair, 64-65; Carnegie Inst, Pittsburgh, Pa, 65; Grand Cent Art Gallery, New York, 65-67; Assoc Am Artists, New York, 65-67.

Positions: V pres & art dir, Sterling Advert, New York, 51-58; publ, Classified Boating Dir, 67-68; pres, Mountain Living Mag, 70-

Awards: Hans Obst purchase prize, Am Watercolor Soc, 56; Nat Arts Club Medal of Hon, 61; first recipient of John Hervey Citation for distinguished contribution in harness racing art, Harness Tracks Am, 64.

Memberships: Am Watercolor Soc; Philadelphia Watercolor Club; Grand Central Art Gallery.

Publications: Art dir, Life Mag, 35-37; auth, Literary America, 50; art dir, 70- & illusr, 72-, Mountain Living Mag.

Dealer: Grand Central Art Galleries, 40 Vanderbilt Ave, New York, NY 10017.

Mailing Address: Wayah Valley Rd, Franklin, NC 28734.

RAWSKI, CONRAD HENRY
Educator, Lecturer

b Vienna, Austria, May 25, 14.

Study & Training: Univ Vienna, PhD; Western Reserve Univ, MS in LS; Harvard Univ; Cornell Univ.

Teaching: Prof, Ithaca Col, 40-56; lectr, Schenectady Mus, 46-48; lectr hist of the bk, lit of humanities & fine arts librarianship; assoc prof libr sci, sch libr sci, Case Western Reserve Univ, 62-65; prof libr sci & coordr PhD prog, 65-

Positions: Head fine arts dept, Cleveland Pub Libr, 57-62.
Awards: Ford Found fel, 52-53.
Memberships: Am Soc Aesthet; Mediaeval Acad Am; Am Libr Asn; Ohio Libr Asn; Am Musicol Soc.
Publications: Auth, Petrarch: four dialogues for scholars, Case Western Reserve Univ Press, 67; contribr, criticisms, articles & rev in publ on art, music & medieval aesthet.
Mailing Address: School of Library Science, Case Western Reserve University, Cleveland, OH 44106.

RAY, ROBERT (DONALD)
Painter, Sculptor
b Denver, Colo, Oct 2, 24.
Study & Training: Univ Southern Calif, BFA(cum laude); Centro Estudios Universitarios, Mexico City, Mex, MA(magna cum laude).
Work in Public Collections: Baltimore Mus Art, Md; Brooklyn Mus Art, N Y; Denver Art Mus, Colo; Mus N Mex, Santa Fe; Columbia Mus Art, S C.
Exhibitions: The West—80 Contemporaries, Univ Ariz Art Gallery, Tucson, 67; one-man show, Colo Springs Fine Arts Ctr, Colo, 68; Three Cultures—Three Dimensions, 69 & Southwestern Artists Biennial, 70, Mus N Mex; 73rd Ann Exhib Western Art, Denver Art Mus, 71.
Awards: Purchase award, Ball State Teachers Col, 59; first prize for sculpture, Mus N Mex, 69; graphics award, Taos Art Asn, N Mex, 72.
Bibliography: Fels (auth), Compression and expansion in the works of Blackburn and Ray, 72; Harmsen (auth), Harmsen's Western Americana, Northland, 72.
Memberships: Taos Art Asn.
Dealer: Mission Gallery, Taos, NM 87571.
Mailing Address: 115 Los Cordovas Rte, Taos, NM 87571.

RAY, RUTH (MRS JOHN REGINALD GRAHAM)
Painter
Preferred Media: Oils, Gouache, Pencil.
b New York, N Y, Nov 8, 19.
Study & Training: Swarthmore Col; Art Stud League New York, with Bridgeman, Corbino & Kantor.
Work in Public Collections: Nat Acad Design, New York; Columbus Art Mus, Ga; Springfield Mus Fine Arts, Mass; Norfolk Mus Art, Va; Nat Art Mus Sport, New York.
Commissions: Many commissions.
Exhibitions: Nat Acad Design, New York; Carnegie Inst, Pittsburgh, Pa; Whitney Mus Am Art, New York; Pa Acad Fine Arts, Philadelphia; Allied Artists Am, New York.
Positions: V pres, Nat Asn Women Artists.
Awards: Purchase prize, Springfield Mus, 46; medal of hon, Am Artists Mag, 53; bronze medal, Allied Artists Am, 57.
Memberships: Nat Acad Design (coun, 69-72); Silvermine Guild Artists; Allied Artists Am; Grand Cent Art Gallery, New York.
Dealer: Grand Central Art Gallery, 42 Vanderbilt Ave, New York, NY 10017.
Mailing Address: 291 Mansfield Ave, Darien, CT 06820.

RAYDON, ALEXANDER R
Art Dealer, Collector
Study & Training: Tech Univ Munich, grad engr.
Positions: Dir, Raydon Gallery.
Research: American art of the nineteenth and early twentieth centuries.
Specialty of Gallery: Paintings, sculpture, prints and drawings from the Renaissance to the present, with emphasis on the nineteenth and early twentieth centuries.
Publications: Ed, America's vanishing resource, 70, America the beautiful, 71, Americans abroad, 72 & Charles Burchfield—master doodler, 72.
Mailing Address: 1091 Madison Ave, New York, NY 10028.

RAYEN, JAMES WILSON
Painter, Instructor
Preferred Media: Acrylics.
b Youngstown, Ohio, Apr 9, 35.
Study & Training: Yale Univ, BA, BFA & MFA; also with Josef Albers, Sewell Sillman & Rico Lebrun.
Work in Public Collections: Addison Gallery Am Art, Andover, Mass; Yale Univ, New Haven, Conn; Wellesley Col, Mass; First Nat Bank, Boston, Mass.
Exhibitions: One-man show, Durlacher Brothers Gallery, New York, N Y, 66; Young New England Painters, Ringling Mus, Sarasota, Fla, 69; one-man show, Eleanor Rigelhaupt Gallery, Boston, Mass, 68; Landscape II, De Cordova Mus, Lincoln, Mass, 71; one-man show, 10 Year Retrospective, Brockton Art Ctr, Mass, 73.
Teaching: Assoc prof, Wellesley Col, 61-

Awards: Ital Govt grant in painting, 59-60; Ford Found grant in the humanities, 69-70.
Mailing Address: Box 219, Wellesley, MA 02181.

READ, HELEN APPLETON
Art Historian, Art Critic
b Brooklyn, N Y, Aug 25, 87.
Study & Training: Smith Col, AB, 08, with Alfred Vance Churchill, Robert Henri, Frank Vincent Dumond, William Chase, Charles Frieseke & Richard Miller.
Positions: Art critic, Brooklyn Daily Eagle, 22-38; assoc art ed, Vogue Mag, 23-31; dir, Art Alliance Am, 24-30; dir, Portraits, Inc, 43-57, pres, 57-
Awards: Salmagundi Club Medal, 67; Smith Col Medal, 68.
Memberships: Arch Am Art; Am Fedn Art; Brooklyn Mus; Whitney Mus Am Art; Cosmopolitan Club.
Research: American art; German art; Romantic art.
Specialty of Gallery: Contemporary portraiture.
Publications: Auth, Robert Henri, 29, 500 years of German art, 36 & Caspar David Friedrich, apostle of Romanticism, 39.
Mailing Address: Portraits, Inc, 41 E 57th St, New York, NY 10022.

REARDON, MARY A
Painter
Preferred Media: Oils, Watercolors, Acrylics, Charcoal.
b Quincy, Mass.
Study & Training: Radcliffe Col, AB; Yale Univ Sch Fine Arts, BFA; also with Eugene Savage, Jean Charlot & David Siqueiros.
Work in Public Collections: Mural drawings, De Cordova Mus, Lincoln, Mass; Radcliffe Col, Cambridge, Mass.
Commissions: Mosaic chapel, Our Lady of Guadalupe, 65 & mosaic ceilings, Last Judgment & Creation, Nat Shrine Immaculate Conception, Washington, D C, 72; fresco, Formation of a Priest, St Johns Sem, Brighton, Mass; altarpiece & figures, Baltimore Cathedral, Md, 67.
Exhibitions: First & Second Int Exhibs Relig Art, Trieste, Italy, 61 & 66; Seventh Centennial Exhib, Basilica St Anthony, Padua, Italy, 63; one-man exhib, Trieste, 71.
Teaching: Instr adult educ, Boston Mus Fine arts; assoc prof studio courses, Emmanuel Col, Boston, 51-70.
Positions: Mem ladies comt, Boston Mus Fine Arts.
Awards: President's Medal, Second Int Exhib Relig Art, 66.
Memberships: Nat Soc Mural Painters; Cambridge Art Asn; N Shore Arts Asn, Copley Soc.
Publications: Co-auth, Pope Pius XII—rock of peace; illusr, Snow treasure, They came from Scotland, Bird in hand & Grenfell.
Mailing Address: 30 Ipswich St, Boston, MA 02215.

REAVES, ANGELA WESTWATER
Art Editor, Writer
b Columbus, Ohio, July 6, 42.
Study & Training: Smith Col, BA; New York Univ, MA.
Positions: Asst dir, Ctr Int Studies, New York Univ, 67-69; res assoc, Inst Govt, Univ Ga; ed, Ga Govt Rev, 69-71; managing ed, Artforum, 72-
Mailing Address: Artforum, 667 Madison Ave, New York, NY 10021.

REBECK, STEVEN AUGUSTUS
Sculptor
b Cleveland, Ohio, May 25, 91.
Study & Training: With Carl Bitter; Cleveland Sch Art, with Carl Heber.
Commissions: Shakespeare (bust in stone), for garden, Cleveland; Soldiers Mem, Alliance, Ohio; Spanish War Veteran (bronze); Lincoln (bronze); sphinx statue, Masonic Temple, Saint Louis, Mo.
Awards: Awards & medals for portraits & busts, Cleveland Mus Art, 23.
Art Interests: Portraits & memorial tablets.
Mailing Address: 1028 Roanoke Rd, Cleveland Heights, OH 44118.

REBERT, JO LIEFELD
Painter, Lecturer
b Detroit, Mich, Sept 30, 15.
Study & Training: Detroit Soc Arts & Crafts, grad; Detroit Inst Musical Art, artists dipl; also with Joseph Canzanni.
Work in Public Collections: Eastland Bank, Anaheim; Lytton Savings & Loan, Los Angeles; Mus Belles Artes, Mexico City; Calif State Fair Collection; Brentwood Savings & Loan, Hollywood, Calif; plus others.
Exhibitions: Watercolor U S A; Calif Nat Watercolor Soc; Calif State Fair; one-man matted traveling show, U S univs, 70-71; plus many one-man shows, Brand Art Ctr, Glendale, 71 & Palos Verdes Mus, 72; plus others.
Teaching: Instr painting, Downey Mus Art Sch, Calif, 60-69; instr painting, Chouinard Art Inst, Los Angeles, 66-67; demonstrated lects for art groups in the West; instr painting, Univ Southern Calif at Idyllwild, 72.

Positions: Juror, Calif Nat Watercolor Soc, Calif State Fair & other shows.
Awards: Seven awards, Calif Nat Watercolor Soc, 58-70; awards, Calif State Fair, 66-71; Arches Paper Award, Watercolor U S A, 71 (total of 94 awards).
Bibliography: Margaret Harold (auth), Prize-winning watercolor, Bks II & VII, 65 & 68; Edward Reep (auth), Content of watercolor, Van Nostrand Reinhold, 70; Gerald Brommer (auth), Watercolor, 73.
Memberships: Calif Nat Watercolor Soc (treas & historian, 64-67); Pasadena Soc Artists; Los Angeles Women's Art Coun.
Publications: Auth, Handbook on copper enameling, Ceramics Monthly Mag, 55; auth, The challenge of painting, 70; plus others.
Dealer: Jacqueline Anhalt Gallery, 750 N La Cienega Blvd, Los Angeles, CA 90069.
Mailing Address: 2960 Glenmanor Pl, Los Angeles, CA 90039.

REBOLI, JOSEPH JOHN
Painter, Illustrator
Preferred Media: Oils.
b Port Jefferson, N Y, Sept 25, 45.
Study & Training: Paier Sch Art, New Haven, Conn.
Work in Public Collections: New Haven Paint & Clay Club; Awixa Pond Art Asn, Bay Shore, N Y.
Exhibitions: Conn Classic Art Exhib, Trumbull, Conn, 64; Nat Benedictine Art Awards, New York, N Y, 65; 23rd New Eng Exhib of Painting & Sculpture, Silvermine, Conn, 72.
Awards: Best in show, Conn Classic Art Exhib, 64; purchase award, New Haven Paint & Clay Club, 65; first prize, White Plains Art Festival, 72.
Memberships: Salmagundi Club.
Publications: Illusr, Guideposts Mag, 11/71; illusr, Ralston's ring, Ballentine, 71; illusr, Good Housekeeping Mag, 7/72 & 9/72; illusr, Clothes Mag, 5/72.
Dealer: Barney Kane Inc, 137 E 47th St, New York, NY 10017.
Mailing Address: 87 Cedar St, Stony Brook, NY 11790.

RECCHIA, RICHARD (HENRY)
Sculptor
Preferred Media: Bronze, Marble.
b Quincy, Mass.
Study & Training: Boston Art Mus Sch Art; also study in France & Italy.
Work in Public Collections: Bas reliefs on bldg, Boston Art Mus & replica, J B Speed Mus, Louisville, Ky; Brookgreen Gardens Mus, S C.
Commissions: Bas reliefs, Gov Curtis Guild, Boston Common, 16; Sam Walter Foss, Brown Univ, 16 & Phi Beta Kappa, Harvard Univ, 17; Gov Oliver Ames Mem, Northeaston, Mass, 21; Gov John Stark equestrian statue, State of N H, Manchester, 48.
Exhibitions: Int Expos, Bologna, Italy, 31; many ann, Nat Acad Design, New York, N Y; Corcoran Gallery Art, Washington, D C; many ann, Nat Sculpture Soc, New York; New York World's Fair, 42.
Positions: Founder, Boston Soc Sculptors.
Awards: Gold Cross & Medal of Honro, Int Expos, Bologna, 31; Watrous Gold Medal, Nat Acad Design, 42; Lindsay Morris Mem Prize for Bas Relief, Nat Sculpture Soc, 49.
Bibliography: Richard Recchia creates heroic size equestrian, Am Art, 6/50; Meara (auth), A garden where statues grow, N Shore Mag, 68; Stickler (auth), Stark holds symbol of freedom high, N H Sun News, 9/27/70.
Memberships: Nat Acad Design; Nat Sculpture Soc.
Publications: Illusr, Down to earth, 64.
Mailing Address: 6 Summer, Rockport, MA 01966.

REDDEN, ALVIE EDWARD
Painter, Instructor
b Hamilton, Tex, July 22, 15.
Study & Training: W Tex State Col, BS, 40; Univ Colo, MFA, 51; Ohio State Univ; Columbia Univ; Mexico City Col; Latin-Am Cult Workshop; also with Grant Reynard.
Teaching: Prin, Samnorwood Elem Schs, 40-42 & 45; instr art, W Tex State Univ, 46; art dir, Mesa Col, 47-, chmn div fine arts, 64-; non resident art instr, Univ Colo, 49-
Memberships: Mesa Co Fine Arts Ctr (trustee, 53-63); Nat Art Educ Asn; Colo Art Educ Asn; Pac Art Asn.
Mailing Address: Dept of Art, Mesa College, Grand Junction, CO 81501.

REED, DOEL
Painter, Educator
Preferred Media: Graphics.
b Logansport, Ind, May 21, 94.
Study & Training: Art Acad Cincinnati, with L H Meaken, James R Hopkins & H H Wessel.

Work in Public Collections: Bibliot Nat, Paris; Victoria & Albert Mus, London; Metrop Mus Art, New York, N Y; Rosenwald Collection, Philadelphia; Pa Acad Fine Arts, Philadelphia.
Commissions: Six murals, Okla State Off Bldg, Oklahoma City, 41.
Exhibitions: Many ann, Nat Acad Design, Audubon Artists, Allied Artists Am, Soc Am Graphic Artists & Nat Soc Painters Casein.
Teaching: Prof art & chmn dept, Okla State Univ, 24-59.
Awards: Gold Medal of Honor, 51 & John Taylor Arms Mem Medal, 54, Audubon Artists; Samuel Morse Medal, Nat Acad Design, 65.
Bibliography: Doel Reed makes an aquatint, Mus N Mex Press, 65.
Memberships: Nat Acad Design; Allied Artists Am; Audubon Artists; Soc Am Graphic Artists; Nat Soc Painters Casein.
Dealers: Mission Gallery, Taos, NM 87571; Blair Galleries, Ltd, Canyon Rd, Santa Fe, NM 87501.
Mailing Address: Box 1244, Taos, NM 87571.

REED, HAL
Painter, Sculptor
Preferred Media: Oils, Acrylics, Bronze.
b Frederick, Okla, Feb 22, 21.
Study & Training: Trade Tech Col Los Angeles; Art Ctr Sch Design; Art League San Francisco; also with Nicolai Fechin.
Work in Public Collections: State of Calif Gov Off, Sacramento; Los Angeles City Hall Permanent Collection; plus other public & private collections.
Commissions: Robert Fulton Medal, Nat Commemorative Soc, 71; Eleanor Roosevelt Medal, Soc Commemorative Femmes Celebres 71; Atomic Age Medal, Soc Medalists, 71.
Exhibitions: Nat Open, Miniature Painters, Sculptors & Gravers Soc, Washington, D C, 72; Nat Open, Miniature Art Soc N J, 72; Am Artists Prof League, New York, 72; Calif State Fair, Sacramento, 72; Olive Hyde Art Ctr Second Ann, Fremont, Calif, 72; plus many others.
Teaching: Instr color, compos, anat, perspective & advan painting, Art League Los Angeles, 65-
Positions: Founder, Art League Los Angeles, 65-
Awards: First award in sculpture, portrait, seascape & graphics, San Fernando Art Guild, 69; first in sculpture & McLeod Award, Miniature Painters, Sculpture Soc, Washington, 72; first in sculpture & purchase award, Miniature Art Soc N J, 72.
Memberships: Coun Traditional Artists Socs (pres, 71-72); fel Am Artists Prof League; fel Am Inst Fine Arts; Valley Artists Guild, Los Angeles (past pres, 58-72); Calif Art Club.
Publications: Auth, How to compose pictures & achieve color harmony, Walter Foster Publ, 69-72.
Mailing Address: 18237 Jovan St, Reseda, CA 91335.

REED, HAROLD
Art Dealer
b Newark, N J, Jan 11, 37.
Study & Training: Stanford Univ, BA; Art Stud League New York.
Positions: Dir, Harold Reed Gallery, New York, N Y.
Mailing Address: Harold Reed Gallery, 118 E 78th St, New York, NY 10021.

REED, PAUL ALLEN
Painter, Educator
Preferred Media: Acrylics.
b Washington, D C, Mar 28, 19.
Study & Training: San Diego State Col; Corcoran Sch Art.
Work in Public Collections: Corcoran Gallery Art, Washington, D C; Nat Collection Fine Arts, Washington, D C; Detroit Inst Art, Mich; Walker Art Ctr, Minneapolis, Minn; Albright-Knox Art Gallery, Buffalo, N Y.
Exhibitions: 25th Ann Soc Am Art, Art Inst Chicago, 65; Washington Color Painters, Washington, D C, Tex, Calif, Mass & Minn, 65-66; 250 Yrs Am Art, Corcoran Gallery Art, 66; Jackson Pollock to the Present, Steinberg Gallery, Wash Univ, St Louis, Mo, 69; Washington 20 Yrs, Baltimore Mus Art, 70.
Teaching: Instr painting, Art League Northern Va, 71-; instr, Corcoran Sch Art, 71-
Bibliography: Barbara Rose (auth), The primacy of color, 5/64 & Legrace Benson (auth), The Washington scene, 69, Art Int; Walter Hopps (auth), The Vincent Melzac collection, Corcoran Gallery Art, 71.
Dealer: Bertha Schaefer Gallery, 41 E 57th St, New York, NY 10022.
Mailing Address: 3541 N Utah St, Arlington, VA 22207.

REEP, EDWARD ARNOLD
Painter, Educator
Preferred Media: Oils.
b Brooklyn, N Y, May 10, 18.
Study & Training: Art Ctr Col Design, cert, 41; also with E J Bisttram, Stanley Reckless & Willard Nash.
Work in Public Collections: Los Angeles Co Mus, Los Angeles, Calif; 66 works, U S War Dept, Pentagon; Grunwald Graphic Arts Collection, Univ Calif, Los Angeles; Lytton Collection, Los Angeles; State of Calif Collection, Sacramento.

Commissions: Three panels of early conquests in Calif, S Am & U S (with Gordon Mellor), USA Private's Club, Fort Ord, Calif, 41; Painter's Impression of International Airports (10 pages in full color), Life Mag, 6/56.
Exhibitions: Whitney Mus Am Art Ann, New York, N Y, 46-48; Los Angeles Co Mus Ann, 46-60; Corcoran Gallery Art Biennial, Washington, D C, 49; Nat Acad Design, New York; Nat Gallery Art, Washington, D C.
Teaching: Instr painting & drawing, Art Ctr Col Design, Los Angeles, 46-50; instr painting & drawing, Chouinard Art Inst, Los Angeles, 50-69; prof painting, chmn dept & artist-in-residence, E Carolina Univ, 70-
Positions: Coord art chmn, Los Angeles City Art Festival Exhibs, 51.
Awards: Guggenheim Found fel, 46; first purchase prize for watercolor, Los Angeles Co Mus, 51; first prize in oil painting, Los Angeles All City Ann, 63.
Bibliography: Niece (auth), Art, an approach, William C Brown, 59; Schaad (auth), Realm of contemporary still-life, 62 & Mugnaini (auth), Drawing, a search for form, 65, Van Nostrand Reinhold.
Memberships: Calif Nat Watercolor Soc (pres, 51-52); hon life mem Calif Parent-Teachers Asn.
Publications: Auth, The content of watercolor, Van Nostrand Reinhold, 69.
Dealer: Garden Gallery, Rte 8, Box 172A, Raleigh, NC 27612.
Mailing Address: 201 Poplar Dr, Greenville, NC 27834.

REEVE, JOHN SEBASTIAN
Sculptor
Preferred Media: Mixed Media.
b Oakland, Calif, Jan 5, 43.
Study & Training: Ariz State Univ, BFA, 67, MFA, 71.
Exhibitions: Pac Northwest Arts & Crafts Fair, Bellevue, Wash, 67 & 68; First Four Corners Biennial, 71 & Invitational Show, 72, Phoenix Art Mus; North-West Ann, Seattle Art Mus, 71; Ariz State Univ, 71.
Awards: Hon mention, Phoenix Art Mus, 71.
Mailing Address: 780 Mission Canyon Rd, Santa Barbara, CA 93105.

REEVES, MR & MRS BENJAMIN
Collectors
Mailing Address: 150 Central Park S, New York, NY 10019.

REEVES, J MASON, JR
Painter
b Washington, D C, Nov 29, 98.
Study & Training: Pa Acad Fine Arts; Acad Julian, Paris, France; also with Edmund Tarbell & others.
Work in Public Collections: USN Dept; Univ Calif; State of Calif; Los Angeles Co; St Francis Hosp; plus others; also in pvt collections.
Exhibitions: Bohemian Club; Calif Art Club; Painters & Sculptors Club; Artists of the Southwest; Santa Cruz, Calif; plus others.
Awards: Prizes, Painters & Sculptors Club & Calif Art Club; award of merit, Los Angeles Art Asn; plus others.
Memberships: Artists of the Southwest (pres, 60-61); Painters & Sculptors Club; Calif Art Club; Laguna Beach Art Asn; Am Inst Fine Arts; plus others.
Mailing Address: 749 N Kenmore Ave, Los Angeles, CA 90029.

REFREGIER, ANTON
Painter
b Moscow, Russia, Mar 20, 05; U S citizen.
Study & Training: R I Sch Design, 20-25; also with Hans Hoffman, Munich, Ger, 27.
Work in Public Collections: Mus Art, Univ Wyo; Corcoran Gallery, Washington, D C; Smithsonian Inst, Washington, D C; St Laurence Univ, Canton, N Y.
Commissions: Glass constructs, Burlington Mills, New York, N Y; mural, lobby, Gracie Square Hosp, New York; mural, lobby, psychiat addition, Metrop Hosp, New York, 70; mosaic mural, 1199 Hosp Workers Union, 70; paintings Grand Coulee Dam, U S Dept Interior, 71.
Exhibitions: Philadelphia Art Alliance, 62; Moscow Mus Fine Arts, Leningrad, 66; plus many others nat & int.
Teaching: Vis instr, Univ Ark, 52; vis instr, Cleveland Sch Fine Arts; assoc prof, Bard Col, 62-64.
Positions: Artist-correspondent, Fortune Mag, UN Original Conf, San Francisco, Calif.
Awards: Hallmark Competition, 53.
Memberships: Artists Equity Asn; Nat Soc Mural Painters.
Publications: Auth, Natural figure drawing, 49, An artist's journey, 65 & We make our tomorrow, 65; contribr, Fortune, What's New & other mags.
Mailing Address: Glasco Turnpike, Rte 1, Box 345, Woodstock, NY 12498.

REGAT, MARY E
Sculptor
Preferred Media: Stone.
b Duluth, Minn, Nov 12, 43.
Study & Training: Univ Alaska.
Work in Public Collections: Anchorage Fine Arts Mus, Alaska; Pfeils Prof Travel Agency, Anchorage; Post Oak Towers Bldg, Alaska Interstate Corp, Houston, Tex; Anchorage Natural Gas.
Exhibitions: All Alaska Juried Art Show, Anchorage; Design I, Anchorage; one-man show, Color Ctr Gallery, 70 & 71; one-man show, Artique Gallery, 72.
Awards: Sculpture award, Design I, 71; purchase award, Anchorage Fine Arts Mus, 71.
Bibliography: Voula Crouch (auth), Carving a canoe, Alaska Sportsman, 71 & Sam—Sculpture in soapstone, Alaska J, winter 72.
Memberships: Alaska Artist Guild; Anchorage Fine Arts Mus Asn.
Dealer: Artique, Ltd, 314 G St, Anchorage, AK 99504.
Mailing Address: 3530 Purdue Dr, Anchorage, AK 99504.

REGENSBURG, SOPHY P
Painter, Collector
Preferred Media: Acrylics.
b New York, N Y, July 28, 85.
Study & Training: New York Sch Art, with William Merrit Chase & Robert Henri.
Work in Public Collections: Guild Hall East Hampton, N Y; Smith Col Mus Art, Northampton, Mass.
Exhibitions: Parrish Art Mus, Southampton, N Y, 56 & 72; Nat Soc Painters Casein, New York, 56 & 58; Guild Hall East Hampton, 60-71; Saint Louis Art Mus, Mo, 67; Butler Inst Am Art Mid-Year Ann, 72; plus many one-man shows.
Awards: First prize gold medal & third prize bronze medal, 52 & silver medal, 53, Nat Amateur Painters Competition.
Collection: Contemporary American paintings & drawings.
Dealer: Babcock Galleries, 805 Madison Ave, New York, NY 10021.
Mailing Address: 200 E 71st St, New York, NY 10021.

REGENSTEINER, ELSE F(RIEDSAM)
Educator, Designer
b Munich, Ger, Apr 21, 06; U S citizen.
Study & Training: Univ Munich; Inst Design, Chicago; Black Mountain Col, with Moholy-Nagy, Marli Ehrman & Anni & Josef Albers.
Work in Public Collections: Cooper Union Mus, New York, N Y; Art Inst Chicago, Ill; Ill State Univ.
Exhibitions: Designer-Craftsmen U S A, circulated by Smithsonian Inst, 53; Designer-Craftsmen Ill, Ill State Mus, Springfield, 66; Decorative Arts Nat, Wichita, Kans, 70; Textiles for Collectors, Art Inst Chicago, 71; Fabrications, Cranbrook Acad Art, 72.
Teaching: Instr weaving, Hull House, Chicago, 41-45; instr weaving, Inst Design, Chicago, 42-46; prof weaving, Sch Art Inst Chicago, 45-71.
Awards: First prize for drapery & upholstery, Int Textile Exhib, Univ N C, 46; five citations of merit, Am Inst Interior Design, 47, 48 & 51; hon mention, State Mus Art, Springfield, 66.
Memberships: Am Crafts Coun; Handweavers Guild Am (bd dirs, 71-72).
Publications: Contribr, Craftsmen in Illinois, Directions 1965, 65 & Weaving in Illinois, Directions 1970, 70, Ill Art Educ Asn & articles, In: Handweaver & Craftsman, 65 & 69; auth, The art of weaving, Van Nostrand Reinhold, 70; contribr, articles, In: Shuttle, Spindle & Dyepot, 71 & 72.
Mailing Address: 1416 E 55th St, Chicago, IL 60615.

REGINATO, PETER
Sculptor
Preferred Media: Steel.
b Dallas, Tex, Aug 19, 45.
Study & Training: San Francisco Art Inst, 63-66.
Exhibitions: Park Place Invitational, 67; Whitney Mus Am Art Sculpture Ann, 70; Highlights of the Season, Aldrich Mus, 70-71; two one-man shows, Tibor de Nagy Gallery, New York, N Y, 71.
Teaching: Adj lectr sculpture, Hunter Col, 71-
Bibliography: Pincus-Witten (auth), Peter Reginato, Artforum, 71; Shireley (auth), Joe Lo Guidio Gallery, N Y Times, 72.
Dealer: Tibor de Nagy Gallery, 29 W 57th St, New York, NY 10019.
Mailing Address: 60 Greene St, New York, NY 10012.

REHBERGER, GUSTAV
Painter, Educator
b Riedlingsdorf, Austria, Oct 20, 10; U S citizen.
Study & Training: Art Inst Chicago, Ill, scholar; Art Instr Schs, Minneapolis, Minn, scholar.
Teaching: Instr, Am Art Sch, New York, N Y, 69-; instr, Art Stud League New York, 72-
Mailing Address: Studio 1206, Carnegie Hall, New York, NY 10019.

REIBACK, EARL M
Sculptor, Painter
b New York, N Y, May 30, 38.
Study & Training: Lehigh Univ, BA & BS (eng physics); Mass Inst Technol, MS nuclear eng).
Work in Public Collections: Whitney Mus Am Art, New York; Philadelphia Mus Art, Pa; Milwaukee Art Ctr; New Orleans Mus Art, La; Wichita Art Mus, Kans.
Commissions: Three light sculptures & projs, Coty Show, Metrop Mus Art, 66; lumia light wall, Int Hotel, Las Vegas, Nev, 69; lumia light sculpture, Mus N C, Raleigh, 70.
Exhibitions: Light and Motion Show, Worcester Art Mus, Mass, 67; Milwaukee Art Ctr, Wis, 67; Experiments in Light and Technology, Brooklyn Mus, N Y, 68; Bienal de Arte, Coltejer Medellin, Colombia, S Am, 71; U S Info Serv Exhib, 15 Europ & Middle Eastern countries, 71-73.
Teaching: Lectr, New York Univ, Columbia Univ, City Col New York, Univ Denver & Northwood Col.
Bibliography: Articles, In: Time, Fortune & House & Garden; color plates, In: Encycl Britannica Ann, 71.
Art Interests: Lumia, kinetic light, light projections.
Publications: Auth, articles, In: House and Garden, 1/69 & Electronics Age, spring 70.
Mailing Address: 20 E Ninth St, New York, NY 10003.

REIBEL, BERTRAM
Sculptor, Graphic Artist
Preferred Media: Wood, Bronze, Stone.
b New York, N Y, June 14, 01.
Study & Training: Art Inst Chicago; also with Alexander Archipenko.
Exhibitions: Metrop Mus Art, New York; Nat Acad Design, New York; Pa Acad Fine Arts, Philadelphia; Northwest Printmakers; Libr of Cong, Washington, D C; plus others.
Memberships: Artists Equity Asn; Asn Int Arts Plastiques.
Mailing Address: 1127 Hardscrabble Rd, Chappaqua, NY 10514.

REICH, NATHANIEL E
Painter
Preferred Media: Oils.
b Brooklyn, N Y.
Study & Training: Art Stud League New York, N Y; Pratt Inst; Brooklyn Inst Arts & Sci.
Work in Public Collections: Huntington Hartford Collection, Gallery Mod Art, New York; Joe & Emily Lowe Mus, Univ Miami, Fla; Washington Co Mus Fine Arts, Hagerstown, Md; Evansville Mus Arts & Sci, Ind; New York Heart Asn; plus others.
Exhibitions: Eighth Serv Command Competition USA, 44; Fourth Har Zion Temple Art Show, Philadelphia, 66; Prospect Park Centennial Invitational, 66; Mus Mod Art, Paris, 70; Boston Inst Fine Arts, 71.
Awards: St Gaudens Medal, 23; first prize, Eighth Serv Command Competition, USA, 44.
Memberships: Artists Equity Asn.
Mailing Address: 1620 Ave I, Brooklyn, NY 11230.

REICHEK, JESSE
Printmaker, Painter
b Brooklyn, N Y, Aug 16, 16.
Study & Training: Inst Design, Chicago, 41-42; Acad Julian, Paris, 47-51.
Work in Public Collections: Amon Carter Mus Western Art, Fort Worth, Tex; Art Inst Chicago; Bibliot Nat, Paris, France; Grunwald Graphic Arts Found, Univ Calif, Los Angeles; La Jolla Art Mus; plus many others.
Exhibitions: Mus Mod Art, 62, 65 & 69; one-man shows, Am Cult Ctr, Florence, Italy, 64 & Univ N Mex Mus, 66; retrospective, Univ Southern Calif Art Mus, 67; San Francisco Mus Art, 69; plus many other group & one-man shows.
Teaching: Assoc prof design, Univ Calif, Berkeley, 58-60, prof, 60-; artist-in-residence, Tamarind Lithography Workshop, Los Angeles, 66; res prof, Creative Arts Inst, Univ Calif, 66-67.
Awards: Co-partic, Graham Found grant, 62; res travel grant, Creative Arts Inst, Univ Calif, summer 63.
Publications: Auth, Jesse Reichek-Dessins, Ed Cahiers Art, Paris, 60; auth, La montee de la nuit, 61 & Fontis, 61, P A Benoit, Alex; auth, Etcetera, New Directions, 65; auth, The architect and the city, Mass Inst Technol Press, 66; plus many others.
Dealer: Betty Parsons Gallery, 24 W 57th St, New York, NY 10019.
Mailing Address: 2801 Ashby Ave, Berkeley, CA 94705.

REICHERT, DONALD KARL
Painter, Educator
Preferred Media: Acrylics, Oils, Ink.
b Libau, Man, Jan 11, 32.
Study & Training: Univ Man Sch Art, with Robert A Nelson & George Swinton & BFA, 56; Inst Allende, Mex, with James Pinto;

Emma Lake Artist's Workshops, with Jules Olitzki, Stepan Wolpe, Lawrence Alloway, John Cage & Frank Stella.
Work in Public Collections: Nat Gallery Can; Art Gallery Ont; Winnipeg Art Gallery; Mt Allison Univ; Montreal Mus Fine Arts.
Exhibitions: Winnipeg Show Nat Biennial; Montreal Spring Show Nat; Nat Gallery Biennial; Visua '67, Nat Exhib; Midwest Painters Invitational.
Teaching: Artist-in-residence, Univ N B, 61-62; asst prof painting, Univ Man Sch Art, 64-
Awards: Bursary, 62 & sr nat award, 67, Can Coun.
Mailing Address: 228 Glenwood Crescent, Winnipeg R2L 1J9, Man, Can.

REICHERT, DONALD O
Painter, Art Administrator
Preferred Media: Watercolors, Collage
b Chicago, Ill, Nov 10, 12.
Study & Training: Am Int Col; with Emmy Zweybruck, Paval Tchelitchew & Owne Smith; Attingham, Nat Trust, England.
Work in Public Collections: Mus Fine Arts, Springfield, Mass; Pittsfield Mus Art, Mass; Fitchburg Mus Art, Mass; Olsen Found, Leete's Island, Conn.
Collections Arranged: Maxfield Parrish Retrospect, 66; David Bumbeck, 66; Michael Skop-George Harrington, 68; Otto & Gertrud Natzler, 70.
Positions: Asst dir, Yale Univ, 51-54; asst dir, Olsen Found, Leetes Island, 54-55; cur, George Walter Vincent Smith Art Mus, Springfield, Mass, 55-70, dir, 70-
Awards: Barstow Award; Springfield Art League Award; Fitchburg Award.
Memberships: Am Asn Mus.
Publications: Co-auth, Maxfield Parrish Retrospect, 66; co-auth, The George Walter Vincent & Belle Townsley Smith Collection of islamic rugs, 71; author of catalogues current with most museum exhibits.
Mailing Address: George Walter Vincent Smith Art Museum, 222 State St, Springfield, MA 01103.

REICHMAN, FRED(RICK) (THOMAS)
Painter
Preferred Media: Oils, Acrylics.
b Bellingham, Wash, Jan 28, 25.
Study & Training: Univ Calif, Berkeley, BA (cum laude) & MA; San Francisco Art Inst.
Work in Public Collections: San Francisco Mus Art, Calif; Oakland Mus, Art Div, Calif; Okla Art Ctr, Oklahoma City; City & Co San Francisco; Bank Am World Hq, San Francisco; plus others.
Commissions: Murals, Stanford Univ Med Sch, Palo Alto, Calif, 61 & San Francisco Art Festival, Civic Ctr, 68.
Exhibitions: Art Inst Chicago 64th Ann, 61; 50 Calif Artists, Whitney Mus Am Art, New York, N Y, 62; one-man exhib, San Francisco Mus Art, 69; Expo 70, Osaka, Japan, 70; 7 Bay Area Artists, Oakland Mus, 71.
Teaching: Instr art, Univ Calif Exten, San Francisco, 66-
Awards: Artist's Coun Prize, San Francisco Art Asn Ann, 54; purchase award, San Francisco Art Festival, 64; award of merit, Art Festival City & Co San Francisco, 68.
Bibliography: Gerald Nordland (auth), Catalogue, San Francisco Mus Art, 4/69.
Dealers: Silvan Simone Gallery, 11579 Olympic, Los Angeles, CA 90035; Rose Rabow Galleries, 2130 Leavenworth, San Francisco, CA 94133.
Mailing Address: 1235 Stanyan St, San Francisco, CA 94117.

REICHMAN, GERSON
Collector
Mailing Address: 64 Lincoln Ave, Portchester, NY 10573.

REID, (WILLIAM) RICHARD
Painter
b Regina, Sask, Apr 3, 30.
Study & Training: Univ Man Sch Art, BFA; Inst Allende, Mex; also with Oskar Kokoschka.
Exhibitions: London, Eng, 60-63; Paris, France, 63; one-man shows, Griffiths Gallery, Vancouver, 68, Albert White Gallery, Toronto, 68 & Pandora's Box Gallery, Victoria, 68; plus many others.
Teaching: Instr painting, Univ B C.
Awards: Can Coun Awards, 63-64 & 67.
Mailing Address: 268 River Rd, Richmond, B C, Can.

REID, ROBERT DENNIS
Painter, Instructor
Preferred Media: Oils.
b Atlanta, Ga, 24.
Study & Training: Clark Col, 41-43; Art Inst Chicago, 43-46; Parson Sch Design, New York, N Y, 48-50.

Work in Public Collections: Myers Col, Birmingham, Ala; Mus African Art, Washington, D C; Laura Musser Mus, Muscatine, Iowa; Univ Notre Dame, South Bend, Ind; Cornell Univ, Ithaca, N Y; plus many others.
Exhibitions: U S Info Serv Tour, Paris, Brest, Vannes & Tours, 71; Black Artists: Two Generations, 71 & Recent Acquisitions, 71, Newark Mus; Black Artists Am, Whitney Mus Am Art, 71; one-man shows, Alonzo Gallery, 72 & N C Cent Univ, Durham, 72; plus many other group & one-man shows.
Teaching: Instr painting, Summit Art Ctr, N J, 70-71; asst prof drawing, R I Sch Design, 70-
Awards: Childe Hassam Purchase Award, Am Acad Arts & Lett, 69.
Bibliography: Many articles & reviews.
Dealer: Alonzo Gallery, 26 E 63rd St, New York, NY 10021.
Mailing Address: 233 Lafayette St, New York, NY 10012.

REIDER, DAVID H
Designer, Photographer
b Portsmouth, Ohio, Apr 6, 16.
Study & Training: Univ Buffalo; Cleveland Sch Art.
Work in Public Collections: Milwaukee Art Inst, Wis; Mus Saarbrucken, Ger.
Exhibitions: Milwaukee Art Inst; Albion Col; Univ Mich; Saarbrucken, Ger; Am Fedn Arts Exhib, 59-61.
Teaching: Lectr design, Buffalo State Teachers Col, 42; instr design, Univ Buffalo, 42-46; head dept design, Albright Art Sch, 42-47; asst prof design, Univ Mich, Ann Arbor, 47-54, assoc prof, 55-59, prof, 59-
Memberships: Am Asn Univ Prof; Mus Mod Art (comt art educ); Soc Photog Educ.
Publications: Contribr, numerous archit & indust publ.
Mailing Address: Dept of Art, University of Michigan, Ann Arbor, MI 48104.

REIF, RUBIN
Painter, Educator
b Warsaw, Poland, Aug 10, 10.
Study & Training: Cooper Union Art Sch; Art Stud League New York; Hans Hofmann Sch Fine Arts; Acad Fine Arts, Florence, Italy.
Work in Public Collections: Ohio Univ; Art Stud League New York; Cooper Union Collection; Ark Indust Develop Comn; also in many pvt collections.
Exhibitions: Am Fedn Arts Traveling Exhib, 48-49 & 67-69; Cincinnati Mus Asn; Ark Art Ctr, Little Rock, 60, 61 & 67-69; Springfield Art Mus, Mo, 67-69; Oklahoma Art Ctr, 67-69; plus many other group & one-man shows.
Teaching: Assoc prof art, Univ Ark, Fayetteville, presently.
Awards: Prizes, Ohio State Fair, 52, Ark Festival Arts, 62 & 63 & Okla Ann, 64; plus many others.
Mailing Address: Dept of Art, University of Arkansas, Fayetteville, AR 72701.

REIFF, ROBERT FRANK
Art Historian, Painter
Preferred Media: Oils, Acrylics.
b Rochester, N Y, Jan. 23, 18.
Study & Training: Univ Rochester, AB, 41; Colo Springs Fine Arts Ctr, 42, with Boardman Robinson & Adolf Dehn; Columbia Univ, MA, 50, PhD, 60; also with Hans Hofmann, 51.
Work in Public Collections: Rochester Mem Art Gallery; Pasadena Art Inst; Middlebury Col; Allen Mem Art Gallery, Oberlin, Ohio.
Exhibitions: Rochester Mem Art Gallery, 36-69; Albright-Knox Art Gallery, Buffalo, 52; Walker Art Ctr, 57; Berkshire Art Asn, 58; Stratton Mountain Summer Exhib, Vt, 71.
Teaching: Instr sculpture, Muhlenberg Col, 47-49; instr sculpture & design, Oberlin Col, 50-55; asst prof humanities, Univ Chicago, 55-56; asst prof art hist, Saint Cloud State Col, Minn, 56-57; prof art hist, Middlebury Col, 58-
Positions: Trustee, Sheldon Mus, Middlebury, Vt, 60-
Awards: Awards, Rochester Mem Art Gallery, 41, 45, 58 & 62, Walker Art Ctr, 52 & for Before Processing, Albright-Knox Art Gallery, 56.
Memberships: Col Art Asn Am; Am Asn Univ Prof (pres local chap, 71-72).
Research: Late painting of Arshile Gorky; modern art; nineteenth century European and Far Eastern art.
Publications: Auth, Indian miniatures: the Rajput painters, Tuttle, 59 & Renoir, McGraw, 68; contribr, McGraw-Hill dict art, 69 & Encycl world art, Vol 14, 70; auth, articles, In: Col Art J, winter 70-71 & winter 71-72.
Mailing Address: 20 Gorham Lane, Middlebury, VT 05753.

REIMANN, WILLIAM P(AGE)
Sculptor, Educator
Preferred Media: Plexiglass, Stainless Steel, Pencil.
b Minneapolis, Minn, Nov 29, 35.
Study & Training: Yale Univ, BA, 57, BFA, 59, MFA, 61; with Josef

Albers, Rico Lebrun, Robert M Engman, James Rosati, Gilbert Franklin, Seymour Lipton, Gabor Peterdi, Neil Welliver & Bernard Chaet.
Work in Public Collections: Mus Mod Art, New York, N Y; Boston Mus Fine Arts, Mass; Whitney Mus Am Art, New York; Rockefeller Univ, New York.
Commissions: Sculpture, Yale Univ Dept Art & Archit, 64; suspended sculptures, Endo Labs, Garden City, N Y, 65 & Rockefeller Univ, 70-71; courtyard sculpture, Harvard Col Observ, Cambridge, Mass, 72; sculpture, Transformation of a Rectangle, Revere Copper & Brass Corp, New York.
Exhibitions: Structured Sculpture, Galerie Chalette, New York, 61-68; Sculpture Ann, 64-65 & Young Americans, 65, Whitney Mus Am Art; Int Exhib Contemp Painting & Sculpture, Carnegie Inst, Pittsburgh, 67-68; Transformations, Carpenter Ctr Visual Arts, Harvard Univ, 72.
Teaching: Asst prof art, Old Dom Col, 61-64; lectr visual & environ studies, Harvard Univ, 64-, acting coord studies, Carpenter Ctr Visual Arts, spring 71.
Dealer: Galerie Chalette, 9 E 88th St, New York, NY 10028.
Mailing Address: Gerry's Landing, Cambridge, MA 02138.

REINDORF, SAMUEL
Painter
Preferred Media: Oils, Pastels, Watercolors.
b Warsaw, Poland, Sept 1, 14; U S citizen.
Study & Training: Cent Tech Sch, Toronto; Am Artists Sch, New York, N Y, scholar, with Saul Wilson & Nahum Tscacbasov.
Work in Public Collections: Fairfield Mus, Conn; Toronto Art Gallery, Ont; Riverside Mus, New York; Hall of Art, New York; Tygeson Gallery, Toronto.
Exhibitions: Toronto Art Gallery, 34-38; Riverside Mus, 39-40; New York World's Fair, 63-65; Butler Inst Am Art, 63-65; 26th Ann Exhib Contemp Am Painting, Palm Beach, 64; plus others.
Awards: First prize, 26th Exhib Contemp Am Painting, 64; hon mention for Clown, Conn Acad Fine Art, 68.
Bibliography: Emily Genauer (auth), article, In: Herald Tribune, 63; Lotta Dempsey (auth), article, In: Toronto Daily Star, 66; Richard Ray (auth), article, In: Bridgeport Post, 70.
Memberships: Artists Equity Asn New York.
Publications: Auth, articles, In: Art News, 64, Toronto Star, 65, Toronto Globe & Mail, 66, Excelsior, Mexico City, 67 & Dallas Morning News, 67.
Dealer: Washington Irving Galleries, 126 E 16th St, New York, NY 10003; Agra Gallery, 1721 De Sales N W, Washington, DC 20036.
Mailing Address: 92 Bayberry Lane, Westport, CT 06880.

REINER, MR & MRS JULES
Collectors, Patrons
Mr Reiner, b New York, N Y, Mar 3, 18.
Study & Training: Mr Reiner, St Johns Univ, LLB; Mrs Reiner, N Y Univ, BA.
Memberships: Friends Whitney Mus Am Art; Assoc Solomon R Guggenheim Mus; Contribr Mus Mod Art; Metrop Mus Art; Friends Hofstra Univ Mus.
Collection: Late nineteenth century art; twentieth century art.
Mailing Address: 295 Madison Ave, New York, NY 10017.

REINHARDT, SIEGFRIED GERHARD
Painter, Designer
b Eydkuhnen, Ger, July 31, 25; U S citizen.
Study & Training: Wash Univ, AB.
Work in Public Collections: Am Acad Arts & Lett; City Art Mus Saint Louis; Concordia Teachers Col; Southern Ill Univ; Whitney Mus Am Art; plus many others.
Commissions: Murals, Rand McNally, Skokie, Ill, Edison Bros Shoe Co, Saint Louis, Teamsters Local 88 Med Bldg & Nooter Corp, Saint Louis.
Exhibitions: 14 shows, City Art Mus Saint Louis, 43-61; Whitney Mus Am Art, 51-55 & 60; Cincinnati Art Ctr, 55, 58 & 61; Pa Acad Fine Arts, 60-61; plus many other group & one-man shows.
Teaching: Lectr, pvt groups, TV & radio; instr painting & drawing, Wash Univ, 55-70.
Positions: Designer & executor stained glass windows, Emil Frei, Inc, 48-; painted Man of Sorrows, weekly TV show, 55, 57 & 58.
Awards: Six awards, Saint Louis Art Guild, 51-58; awards, Cincinnati Contemp Art Ctr, 58 & Int Exhib Sacred Art, Trieste, Italy, 61; plus many others.
Bibliography: Nathaniel Pousette-Dart (ed), American painting today, Hastings, 56; Lee Nordness (ed), Art: U S A: Now, C J Bucher, 62.
Memberships: Saint Louis Art Guild.
Dealers: Midtown Galleries, 11 E 57th St, New York, NY 10022; Albrecht Gallery of Art, 2818 Frederick Blvd, Saint Joseph, MO 64506.
Mailing Address: 635 Craig Woods Dr, Kirkwood, MO 63122.

REININGHAUS, RUTH (RUTH REININGHAUS SMITH)
Painter, Instructor
Preferred Media: Oils.
b New York, N. Y.
Study & Training: Hunter Col, 44-46 & 50-52; Nat Acad Design,
Nell Boardman scholar, with Morton Roberts, 62; Frank Reilly
Sch, Robert Lehman scholar, with Frank Reilly, 63; Art Stud
League New York, with Robert Phillips & Robert Beverly Hale,
66; New York Univ, scholar, 68.
Exhibitions: Catharine Lorillard Wolfe Art Asn Ann, Nat Arts Club,
N Y, 66; Hudson Valley Art Asn Ann, Westchester Community
Ctr, N Y, 69-72; Am Artists Prof League Ann, Lever House, N Y,
69-72; Allied Artists Am Ann, Nat Acad Design, N Y, 71; Berk-
shire Art Asn, Pittsfield Mus, Mass, 72.
Teaching: Instr oil painting, Kittredge Club Women, New York, 64-;
instr oil painting, Bankers Trust Co, New York, 71-
Positions: Free lance artist & fine arts comns; tech illusr, Sound
Publ Co, 66-
Awards: Nell Boardman Award, Nat Acad Design, 62; Robert Leh-
man Award, Frank Reilly Sch, 63; New York Univ scholar, 68.
Bibliography: Lucien Mandosse (auth), 58th ann exhibition of Allied
Artists of America, La Rev Mod, 72.
Memberships: Allied Artists Am; Am Artists Prof League; Hudson
Valley Art Asn; Berkshire Art Asn.
Publications: Tech illusr, Telephony for the sound contractor, 72.
Dealer: Hammer Galleries Inc, 51 E 57th St, New York, NY 10022.
Mailing Address: 418 E 88th St, New York, NY 10028.

REINSEL, WALTER NEWTON
Painter
Preferred Media: Watercolors, Oils, Acrylics.
b Reading, Pa, Aug 11, 05.
Study & Training: Pa Acad Fine Arts, with Arthur Carles; also with
Andre L'Hote, Paris & Mirmande, France.
Work in Public Collections: Philadelphia Mus Art; Reading Pub Mus,
Pa; Woodmere Art Gallery, Philadelphia; Container Corp, Chi-
cago, Ill; Oil, Capehart Farnsworth.
Exhibitions: Many ann, Pa Acad Fine Arts, 38-60 & one-man show,
48; Philadelphia Watercolor Club Ann, 50-72; Am Watercolor Soc,
58-62; Audubon Artists; also 12 one-man shows.
Positions: Art dir & supvr, N W Ayer & Son, 30-65.
Awards: Harrison Morris Prize, Pa Acad Fine Arts Fel, 53-57;
Philadelphia Watercolor Club Medal & Award, 67 & T Oakley
Mem Prize, 68.
Memberships: Artists Equity Asn, Philadelphia Chap; Philadelphia
Watercolor Club; Pa Acad Fine Arts; Philadelphia Art Alliance
(mem oil comt).
Mailing Address: 721 Walnut St, Philadelphia, PA 19103.

REIS, MRS BERNARD J
Collector, Patron
b New York, N Y, Sept 15, 00.
Study & Training: Univ Mich.
Positions: Trustee, Jewish Mus, New York; mem arts comt, Bran-
deis Univ, Waltham, Mass.
Mailing Address: 252 E 68th St, New York, NY 10021.

REISMAN, PHILIP
Painter, Illustrator
Preferred Media: Oils, Watercolors.
b Warsaw, Poland, July 18, 04; U S citizen.
Study & Training: Art Stud League New York, N Y, illus & compos
with Wallace Morgan, life drawing with George Bridgeman; also
etching & compos with Harry Wickey.
Work in Public Collections: Bibliot Nat, Paris; Syracuse Univ Col-
lection, N Y; Bates Col, Maine; Wadsworth Atheneum, Hartford,
Conn; Norfolk Mus, Va.
Commissions: Mural, Bellevue Psychiat Hosp, New York, 38.
Exhibitions: Mural Show, Mus Mod Art, New York, 32; Whitney Mus
Am Art, New York; Nat Acad Design, 56; Art U S A, 59; Pa Acad
Fine Arts, Philadelphia.
Teaching: Instr art, Workshop Sch, New York, 54-56; instr art, Five
Towns Arts Found, 68-70; instr art, Educ Alliance, New York,
71-72.
Awards: Mickiewitz Centennial Comt Prize, 55; Joseph Isidor Gold
Medal, Nat Acad Design, 56; Childe Hassam Purchase Prize, 68.
Bibliography: Lincoln Kirstein (auth), Philip Reisman, Hound &
Horn, 33; Henry Goodman (auth), Philip Reisman, A D, 41;
illustrations reproduced by Life, 41.
Memberships: Artists Equity Asn New York (v pres, pres).
Publications: Illusr, Anna Karenina, Vols I & II, 40 & Crime and
punishment, 44, Random.
Dealer: ACA Gallery, 25 E 73rd St, New York, NY 10022.
Mailing Address: 4 W 18th St, New York, NY 10011.

REISS, LEE
Painter
Preferred Media: Oils.
b New York, N. Y.
Study & Training: Art Alliance Sch; Art Stud League New York; Am
Art Sch; Queens Col; Cornell Univ.
Work in Public Collections: Washington Co Mus, Hagerstown, Md;
Norfolk Mus; also in pvt collections.
Exhibitions: Am Artists Prof League; Long Island Art League; Nat
Acad Design; Nat Arts Club; Norfolk Mus Arts & Sci; plus many
others.
Teaching: Instr painting, Nat Art League, Long Island.
Positions: Chmn traveling oil shows, Nat Asn Women Artists.
Memberships: Allied Artists Am; Nat Art League, Long Island; Nat
Asn Women Artists.
Mailing Address: 75-30 Vleigh Pl, Flushing, NY 11367.

RELIS, ROCHELLE R
Painter
Preferred Media: Oils, Ink, Watercolors.
b Lwow, Poland; U S citizen.
Study & Training: Theatre Acad, Lwow; Art Sch, Lwow; also with
Herman Frenkiel, Paris, France.
Work in Public Collections: Synagogue Mus, Graz, Austria; over 50
pvt collections in U S, Europe & Israel.
Commissions: Jewish Folklore Albume Series, Fidler on the roof,
72.
Exhibitions: Int Arts Exhibs, New York; Spring Arts Festivals, New
York; Atlantic City Arts Shows, N J; Galerie Int, New York; also
numerous selected nat & regional juried shows.
Teaching: Instr painting, summer resorts, 70-71.
Awards: Hon master fine arts, Univ Eastern Fla, 71.
Memberships: Berkshire Art Asn; Tex Fine Arts Asn; Nat Acad TV
Arts & Sci; Am Guild Variety Artists; Am Fedn TV & Radio Art-
ists.
Dealer: Galerie Internationale, 1095 Madison Ave, New York, NY
10028.
Mailing Address: 45-35 44th St, Long Island City, NY 11104.

REMBSKI, STANISLAV
Painter, Writer
Preferred Media: Oils, Crayons, Pencils.
b Sochaczew, Poland.
Study & Training: Technol Inst, Warsaw, Poland; Ecole Beaux Arts,
Paris, France; Royal Acad Fine Arts, Berlin, Ger.
Work in Public Collections: Pres Woodrow Wilson, Woodrow Wilson
House, Washington, D C; Pres Franklin D Roosevelt, F D R Mem
Libr, Hyde Park, N Y; Lawrence Cardinal Shehan, Archbishop's
House, Baltimore, Md; Fleet Admiral William D Leahy, Hist Soc,
Madison, Wis; Leon Dabo, Nat Acad Design, New York, N Y.
Commissions: Conversion of William Duke of Acquitaine, Trustees
of St Bernard's Sch, Gladstone, N J, 31; I Am the Life, Mem
Episcopal Church, 62.
Exhibitions: One-man shows, Dudensing Galleries, New York, 27,
Carnegie Hall Gallery, New York, 34, Arthur U Newton Galler-
ies, New York, 35, Baltimore Mus Art, Md, 47; Baltimore Inst
Art, Md, 50.
Positions: Vis critic, Md Inst Art, 52-55.
Memberships: Salmagundi Club; Allied Artists Am; Nat Soc Mural
Painters; Am Artists Prof League; Charcoal Club, Baltimore.
Publications: Auth, Mysticism in art, Leonardo da Vinci Forum, 36;
auth, Freedom, New Age, 72.
Mailing Address: 1404 Park Ave, Baltimore, MD 21217.

REMENICK, SEYMOUR
Painter
Preferred Media: Oils.
b Detroit, Mich, Apr 3, 23.
Study & Training: Tyler Sch Fine Arts, 40-42; Hans Hofmann Sch,
46-48.
Work in Public Collections: Philadelphia Mus; Pa Acad Fine Arts;
R I Sch Design; Phoenix Art Mus; Dallas Mus Contemp Art.
Exhibitions: Am painting, Rome, Italy, 55; 4 Young Americans, R I
Sch Design, 56; 11 Contemp Am Painters, Paris, France, 56; Art
Inst Chicago Ann, 61; Drawing Show, Philadelphia Mus, 65.
Awards: Louis Comfort Tiffany Found grant, 55; Benjamin Altman
Landscape Prize, Nat Acad Design, 60; Hallmark Purchase
Award, 60.
Dealer: Pearl Fox Gallery, 103 Windsor Ave, Melrose Park, PA
19126.
Mailing Address: 1836 Pine St, Philadelphia, PA 19103.

REMINGTON, DEBORAH WILLIAMS
Painter
Preferred Media: Oils.
b Haddonfield, N J, June 25, 30.
Study & Training: Calif Sch Fine Arts, San Francisco, cert, 52; San
Francisco Art Inst, BFA, 55; also study in Asia, 55-58.

Work in Public Collections: Whitney Mus Am Art, New York, N Y; Mus XXème Siècle, Paris, France; Addison Gallery Am Art, Andover, Mass; Van Boymans Mus, Rotterdam, Holland.
Exhibitions: Whitney Mus Am Art Painting Ann, 65, 67 & 72; Art Vivant Am, Fond Maeght, Saint Paul de Vence, France, 70.
Bibliography: Knute Stiles (auth), The mysterious machine, Artforum, 2/66; Simon Watson-Taylor (auth), Space machines, Art & Artists, 8/67; Sabine Marchand (auth), Deborah Remington, Cimaise, 2/72.
Dealers: Bykert Gallery, 24 E 81st St, New York, NY 10028; Pyramid Galleries, Ltd, 2121 P St, N W, Washington, DC 20037.
Mailing Address: 309 W Broadway, New York, NY 10013.

REMSING, (JOSEPH) GARY
Painter, Sculptor
b Spokane, Wash, Sept 18, 46.
Study & Training: San Jose State Univ, BA & MA.
Work in Public Collections: De Saisset Mus, Univ Santa Clara, Calif.
Exhibitions: One-man exhibs, de Saisset Mus, 69, Atherton Gallery, Menlo Park, Calif, 70 & 72, William Sawyer Gallery, San Francisco, 71 & 73 & Gerard John Hayes Gallery, Los Angeles, Calif, 72; Selection of Young Contemp Calif Artists, 69 & 70; Looking West 1970, Joslyn Art Mus, Omaha, Nebr, 70; plus other group & one-man exhibs.
Teaching: Instr, Modesto Jr Col, 71-
Awards: Walnut Creek Civic Arts Ctr Gallery, 69, Maryville Col, Tenn, 70 & Calif Arts Comn, 70.
Publications: Auth, articles, In: San Francisco Chronicle, 9/8/69 & 5/7/71; auth, article, In: West Art, 9/69; auth, articles, In: Artforum, 11/69; auth, articles, In: Art Wk, 5/71 & 4/72.
Dealers: Gerard John Hayes Gallery, 722 N La Cienega Blvd, Los Angeles, CA 90069; William Sawyer Gallery, 3043 Clay St, San Francisco, CA 94115.
Mailing Address: 1418 Oakwood Dr, Modesto, CA 95350.

RENK, MERRY (MERRY CURTIS)
Designer, Sculptor
b Trenton, N J, July 8, 21.
Study & Training: Sch Indust Arts, Trenton, N J; Inst Design, Chicago, Ill.
Work in Public Collections: San Francisco State Col Libr, Calif; San Francisco Art Comn; Univ Wis; Johnson's Wax Collection, Objects U S A; Oakland Mus Art, Calif.
Commissions: Wedding crown, Johnson's Wax Collection, Objects U S A, 70.
Exhibitions: One-woman show, Nordness Galleries, New York, N Y, 70; Objects U S A Traveling Exhib, U S A & Europe, 70-72; one-woman shows, De Young Mem Mus, San Francisco, 71 & Mus Hist & Technol, Smithsonian Inst, 71-72.
Awards: San Francisco Art Comn Awards, 54 & 59; San Francisco Women Artists Award, 65.
Bibliography: Uchida (auth), Jewelry by Merry Renk, Crafts Horizons, 11 & 12/61; C McCann (auth), Three fine craftsmen, Artweek, 2/71; A Fried (auth), article, In: San Francisco Examr, 3/71.
Memberships: Metal Arts Guild (pres, 53).
Dealer: Nordness Galleries, 237 E 75th St, New York, NY 10021.
Mailing Address: 17 Saturn St, San Francisco, CA 94114.

RENNELS, F M
Sculptor
Preferred Media: Steel, Aluminum.
b Sioux City, Iowa, June 4, 42.
Study & Training: Eastern Ill Univ, BS; Stanford Univ, summer grad study sculpture; Cranbrook Acad Art, Bloomfield Hills, Mich, MFA.
Work in Public Collections: Elgin Civic Plaza, Ill; Judson Col, Elgin.
Exhibitions: Kent State Blossom Summer Outdoor Sculpture Show, Ohio, 71; Mich Artist Show, Detroit Art Inst, 71; Multiples U S A, Kalamazoo, Mich, 71; group & one-man show, Spectrum Gallery, New York, N Y, 72.
Awards: Cranbrook Acad Art Ann Founders Award, 70; Multiples U S A Award, Kalamazoo, 70; Troy Sculpture Competition Award, Mich, 71.
Mailing Address: 1023 N Spring, Elgin, IL 60120.

RENNIE, HELEN (SEWELL)
Painter, Designer
Preferred Media: Oils, Acrylics.
b Cambridge, Md.
Study & Training: Corcoran Sch Art, hon student; Nat Acad Design; also with Charles W Hawthorne.
Work in Public Collections: Phillips Gallery Collection, Washington, D C; Am Univ C Law Watkins Collection, Washington, D C; U S Dept Commerce, Washington, D C; U S Dept State, Washington, D C; Clarendon Trust Co, Arlington, Va.
Commissions: Mural design, Roosevelt High Sch, Washington, D C, Pub Works Art Proj, 33-34.
Exhibitions: Mus Mod Art, New York, N Y, 46 & Recent Drawings U S A, 56; Corcoran Gallery Art Biennial, Washington, D C, 59; Baltimore Mus Regional, Md, 64; Washington Artists, Phillips Gallery, Washington, D C, 71-72.
Teaching: Instr drawing & painting, Phillips Gallery Sch; instr drawing & painting, Art League Washington.
Positions: Artist-designer, War Food Admin, Washington, D C, 40-45; art dir, U S Navy Dept, Washington, D C, 48-51; visual info off, U S Off Price Stabilization, Washington, D C, 51-53.
Awards: Five awards from various donors, Soc Washington Artists, 48-71; Baltimore Mus Regional, 59 & 60.
Memberships: Soc Washington Artists (v pres); Artists Equity Asn; Women in the Visual Arts.
Dealer: Franz Bader Gallery, 2124 Pennsylvania Ave N W, Washington, DC 20037.
Mailing Address: 1306 30th St N W, Washington, DC 20007.

RENOUF, EDWARD PECHMANN
Painter, Sculptor
Preferred Media: Acrylics, Steel.
b Hsiku, China, Nov 23, 06; U S citizen.
Study & Training: Phillips Andover Acad, 24; Harvard Univ, 28; Columbia Univ, 36-40; also drawing & painting with Carlos Merida, Mex, 41.
Commissions: Steel sculpture, 65 & mural painting, 67, Horace Mann Sch, Riverdale, N Y.
Exhibitions: Whitney Mus Am Art Sculpture Ann, 60 & 64; three-man show, Zabriskie Gallery, New York, 60; Conn Acad Show, Wadsworth Atheneum, Hartford, 61; Pa Acad Fine Arts 161st Ann, Philadelphia, 66.
Teaching: Vis artist painting, Akad Bildenden Kunste, Munich, Ger, fall 70.
Awards: Hon mention, Conn Acad, 61; second prize for sculpture, Sharon Creative Arts Found, 64.
Bibliography: John Canaday (auth), Art: an image is created, New York Times, 1/5/60; Brian O'Doherty (auth), article, In: New York Times, 3/31/62; Stuart Preston (auth), article, In: New York Times, 2/27/65.
Memberships: Sculptors Guild; Fedn Mod Painters & Sculptors.
Publications: Contribr, Dyn, Mex, 42.
Dealer: Spectrum Gallery, 464 W Broadway, New York, NY 10012.
Mailing Address: East St, Washington, CT 06793.

REOPEL, JOYCE
Sculptor
b Worcester, Mass, Jan 21, 33.
Study & Training: Ruskin Sch Drawing & Fine Arts, Oxford Univ, Eng; Yale-Norfolk Art Sch, fel; Worcester Mus Art Sch, grad.
Work in Public Collections: Ohio State Univ, Columbus; Fogg Art Mus, Cambridge, Mass; Pa Acad Fine Arts, Philadelphia; Addison Gallery Am Art, Andover, Mass; Univ Mass, Amherst; plus others.
Exhibitions: Boston Arts Festival; Nat Inst Arts & Lett; Worcester Mus Art; De Cordova & Dana Mus, Lincoln, Mass; Victoria & Albert Mus, London, Eng; plus others.
Awards: Nat Inst Arts & Lett; Wheaton Col for res; Ford Found grant; plus others.
Mailing Address: c/o Forum Gallery, 1018 Madison Ave, New York, NY 10021.

RESIKA, PAUL
Painter
b New York, N Y, Aug 15, 28.
Study & Training: With S Wilson, 40-44 & Hans Hofmann, 45-47, New York; also in Venice & Rome, 50-54.
Work in Public Collections: Indianapolis Mus Art; Sheldon Mem Gallery, Univ Nebr, Lincoln; Joseph H Hirshhorn Collection, Washington, D C; Sara Roby Found; Mus Contemp Art, Bordighera, Italy.
Exhibitions: One-man exhibs, George Dix Gallery, New York, 48 & Peridot-Washburn Gallery, New York, 64, 65 & 67-71; Nat Acad Design, New York, 61 & 72; Am Landscape, Smithsonian Inst, Washington, D C, 68; Hassam Exhib, Am Acad Arts & Lett, 69-71.
Teaching: Adj prof painting & drawing, Cooper Union, 66-; instr painting, Art Stud League New York, 68-69.
Positions: Artist-in-residence, Dartmouth Col, spring 72.
Awards: Louis Comfort Tiffany Found grant, 59; Ingram Merrill Prize, 69; Hassam Purchase Prize, Am Acad Arts & Lett, 71.
Bibliography: Claire Nicholas White (auth), Resika's ... mountains, Art News, 4/67; Mimi Shorr (auth), Passions in balance, Am Artist, 12/72; also numerous reviews & articles, In: New York Times, Time, Arts, Art News, Art Int, Am Artist.
Dealer: Washburn Gallery, 820 Madison Ave, New York, NY 10021.
Mailing Address: 114 E 84th St, New York, NY 10028.

RESNICK, MILTON
Painter
b Bratslav, Russia, Jan 8, 17; U S citizen.
Study & Training: Paris, France & New York, N Y.
Work in Public Collections: Calif Mus Fine Arts, Berkeley, Calif; Mus Mod Art; Whitney Mus Am Art; Wadsworth Atheneum; Wake Forest Col, Winston-Salem, N C; also many others including pvt collections.
Exhibitions: One-man show, DeYoung Mem Mus, San Francisco, 55; four shows, Whitney Mus Am Art, 57-67; San Francisco Mus Art, 63; Univ Tex Art Mus, 64 & 68; Jewish Mus, N Y, 67; plus many other group & one-man shows.
Teaching: Instr, Pratt Inst, Brooklyn; vis lectr & critic, var schs, R I, Yale Summer Sch, Wagner Col & Silvermine; vis prof, Univ Calif, Berkeley, 55-56; instr, New York Univ, 64-; vis lectr & critic, N Y Studio Sch, 65-; vis prof, Univ Wis-Madison, 66-67.
Dealer: Howard Wise Gallery, 2 W 13th St, New York, NY 10019.
Mailing Address: 80 Forsyth St, New York, NY 10002.

REVINGTON, GEORGE D, III
Collector
Collection: Modern American painting and sculpture, exhibited at the American Federation of Arts, Museum of Modern Art and at various galleries and art shows.
Mailing Address: 1211 Ravinia Rd, West Lafayette, IN 47906.

REVOR, REMY, SSND
Designer, Educator
b Chippewa Falls, Wis, Sept 17, 14.
Study & Training: Mt Mary Col, BA; Sch Art Inst Chicago, BFA & MFA.
Work in Public Collections: Milwaukee Art Ctr; Saint Paul Art Ctr, Minn; Mus Tex Tech Univ; Objects U S A, Johnson Collection Contemp Crafts.
Exhibitions: Wis Designer Craftsmen Ann, 53-72; Mus Contemp Crafts, New York, 62, 63 & 66-68; Wichita Art Asn, 64; Chicago Pub Libr, 64.
Teaching: Assoc prof textile design, Mt Mary Col, 52-70, prof, 70-; instr textile design, Arrowmont Sch Arts & Crafts, Gatlinburg, Tenn, summers 69-72.
Awards: Louis Comfort Tiffany Found Award For Textiles, 62; Am Inst Architects Gold Medal Award For Craftsmanship, 67; Fulbright Award res textile design, Finland, 69-70.
Memberships: Wis Designer Craftsmen (publ chmn, 66-68); Col Art Asn Am.
Mailing Address: Mt Mary College, Milwaukee, WI 53222.

REWALD, JOHN
Art Historian, Educator
b Berlin, Ger, May 12, 12; U S citizen.
Study & Training: Univ Hamburg, 31; Univ Frankfort-on-Main, 31-32; Sorbonne, PhD, 36.
Teaching: Lectr visits with artists in Europe & forgeries of modern art; vis prof, Princeton Univ, 61; prof art hist, Univ Chicago, 64-71; prof art hist, grad ctr, City Univ New York, 71-
Positions: Cur pvt collection, John Hay Whitney; assoc, Mus Mod Art, 43-
Awards: Prix Charles Blanc, Acad Française, 41; Knight, Legion of Hon, 54.
Publications: Auth, The history of impressionism, 46, 62 & 69 & Post-impressionism—from Van Gogh to Gauguin, 56 & 62, Mus Mod Art; auth, Paul Cezanne: a biography, Schocken, 68; auth, bks on Bonnard, Pissarro, Seurat, Manzù, Degas & Maillol; plus many others.
Mailing Address: 1075 Park Ave, New York, NY 10028.

REY, H A
Illustrator, Writer
Preferred Media: Gouache, India Ink, Crayon.
b Hamburg, Ger, Sept 16, 98; U S citizen.
Study & Training: Univ Munich; Univ Hamburg.
Work in Public Collections: Kerlan Collection; Univ Southern Miss; Univ Ore.
Memberships: Am Craftsmans Coun.
Publications: Numerous illustrated childrens books, Harper, 41-62 & including Curious George series & others, Houghton, 41-66.
Mailing Address: 14 Hilliard St, Cambridge, MA 02138.

REYNAL, JEANNE
Mosaic Artist
b White Plains, N Y, Apr 1, 03.
Study & Training: Atelier, Paris, France, apprentice with Boris Anrep, 30-38.
Work in Public Collections: Ford Found, White Plains; Mus Mod Art, New York, N Y; Walker Art Ctr, Minneapolis, Minn; Whitney Mus Am Art, New York; Rockefeller Univ; plus many others.

Commissions: Ford Found Prog Adult Educ, White Plains, 59; Our Lady of Florida, Palm Beach, 62; Cliff House, Avon, Conn, 62; Nebr State Capital, Lincoln, 65 & 66; SS Joachim & Ann Church, Queens Village, N Y, 67; plus many others.
Exhibitions: Loeb Stud Ctr, N Y Univ, 61; PVI Gallery, New York, 64; San Francisco Mus Art traveling exhib, Boston, Mass, Montreal, Can, Lincoln, Nebr & Amarillo, Tex, 64; Betty Parsons Gallery, 71 & Newport Art Asn, R I, 71; plus many others.
Awards: Emmanuel Walter fund purchase prize for Yuba (mosaic), San Francisco Art Asn, 45.
Bibliography: Hans Unger (auth), Practical mosaic, 65; Barbara Poses Kafka (auth), Art & architecture, Craft Horizons, 1-2/68; Paul Falkenberg (producer & ed), Mosaics: the work of Jeanne Reynal (film), 68.
Mailing Address: 240 W 11th St, New York, NY 10014.

REYNARD, CAROLYN COLE
Painter, Instructor
Preferred Media: Acrylics.
b Wichita, Kans, Aug 6, 34.
Study & Training: Wichita State Univ, BFA; Ohio Univ, MFA.
Work in Public Collections: Wichita State Univ.
Exhibitions: Air Capitol Annual, Wichita Art Mus, Kans, 56; Exhibition 80, Huntington Galleries, W Va, 57-59; Santa Barbara Art Mus, Calif, 60; Artists of Santa Barbara, Faulkner Gallery, Santa Barbara, 60-62; Artists of Central New York, Munson-Williams-Proctor Inst Mus Art, Utica, N Y, 64-65 & 67.
Teaching: Instr art, Ohio Univ, 58-59; asst prof art, State Univ N Y Col Oswego, 63-69; instr art, Wappingers Cent Sch Dist, N Y, 69-
Memberships: N Y State Art Teachers Asn; Dutchess Co Art Asn.
Publications: Auth, I can't draw, School Arts, 71.
Mailing Address: 104 College Ave, Poughkeepsie, NY 12603.

REYNOLDS, HARRY REUBEN
Art Historian, Photographer
b Centerburg, Ohio, Jan 29, 98.
Study & Training: Art Inst Chicago; State Univ Iowa, 39-40; Brooks Inst Photog, 61.
Work in Public Collections: Photo murals, Utah State Univ, Logan.
Commissions: Photo murals, College Hill & Logan LDS Temple, Cache Co, Utah, 47 & Cache Co scenes, Bluebird Candy Co, Logan, 47.
Collections Arranged: Faculty Show Multimedia, 67, Concrete & Abstr, 68, Ansel Adams Photog Exhib, 68 & Forms Upon The Frontier, Folk Life and Folk Arts, 68.
Teaching: From instr art to emer prof, Utah State Univ, 23-, cur galleries, 67-
Mailing Address: 519 N Sixth St E, Logan, UT 84321.

REYNOLDS, JOSEPH GARDINER
Designer
Preferred Media: Stained Glass.
b Wickford, R I, Apr 9, 86.
Study & Training: R I Sch Design.
Work in Public Collections: Stained glass windows, Washington Cathedral; Mem Chapel & Am Church, Paris, France; Wellesley Mem Chapel, Mass; St George's Sch Chapel, Newport, R I.
Exhibitions: U S Pavilion, Paris, France; Mus Fine Arts, New York, N Y; Providence Art Club.
Memberships: Medieval Acad.
Research: Medieval cathedrals; medieval stained glass.
Mailing Address: 296 Payson Rd, Belmont, MA 02178.

REYNOLDS, NANCY DU PONT
Sculptor
Preferred Media: Bronze, Lucite.
b Greenville, Del, Dec 28, 19.
Commissions: Lucite carving on copper bases, Stevenson Ctr Natural Sci, Vanderbilt Univ, Nashville, Tenn; lucite carving for meditation chapel, Lutheran Towers Bldg, Wilmington, Del; lucite carving, Goldsborough Off Bldg, Wilmington; lucite carvings, Wilmington Trust Co; bronze statue of a child (in memory of Dr Warren), Childrens Bur, Wilmington.
Exhibitions: Corcoran Gallery Art, Washington, D C; Nat Acad Design, New York, N Y; Del Art Mus, Wilmington; one-man shows, Rehoboth Art League, Del & Caldwell's, Wilmington.
Memberships: Nat League Am Pen Women (Diamond State Br); Burr Artists; Del Art Mus; Rehoboth Art League; Catharine Lorillard Wolfe Art Club.
Mailing Address: Foxwood, Old Kennett Rd, Greenville, DE 19807.

REYNOLDS, RALPH WILLIAM
Educator, Painter
Preferred Media: Watercolors.
b Albany, Wis, Nov 10, 05.
Study & Training: Art Inst Chicago, 25-27 & 31; Beloit Col, BA, 38; State Univ Iowa, MA, 39; also with Grant Wood, Jean Charlot,

Eliot O'Hara, Charles Burchfield, William Thon, Clarence Carter & Millard Sheets.
Work in Public Collections: Indiana Univ Pa; Westminster Col, New Wilmington, Pa; One Hundred Friends Pittsburgh Art, Pa; Univ Club, Pittsburgh; also many pub schs, banks & indust concerns in western Pa.
Commissions: Many portraits, Pa, 42-72.
Exhibitions: Over 100 exhibs incl Pittsburgh Watercolor Soc, Arts & Crafts Ctr, 51-72, Am Watercolor Soc, Nat Acad Design Galleries, 59 & Am Artists Prof League's Grand Nat, Lever House, New York, 72; over 20 one-man shows incl Univ Club Pittsburgh & Westminster Col, 68.
Teaching: Stud instr art, Beloit Col, 33-38; head dept art, S Dak State Univ, 40-41; prof art, Indiana Univ Pa, 41-71, emer prof, 72.
Positions: Commercial artist, var studios, Chicago, Ill & Cleveland, Ohio, 27-33.
Awards: 20 awards, Ann Allied Artists Johnstown, Pa, 51-72; 5 Ida Smith Mem Awards & First Prize, Pittsburgh Watercolor Soc, 51-63; 7 purchase awards, Penelec & U S Bank Shows, 60-69; plus others.
Memberships: Indiana Art Asn, Pa (pres, 42); Allied Artists Johnstown, Pa; Pittsburgh Watercolor Soc (v pres, 52); Assoc Artists Pittsburgh; fel Am Artists Prof League.
Dealer: Arts & Crafts Center, Fifth & Shady Ave, Pittsburgh, PA 15232.
Mailing Address: 363 S Third St, Indiana, PA 15701.

REYNOLDS, RICHARD (HENRY)
Sculptor, Painter
Preferred Media: Stone, Wood, Metal, Acrylics, Polymers.
b New York, N Y, May 16, 13.
Study & Training: San Bernardino Valley Col, AA, 33; Univ Calif, Berkeley, BA, 36; cert, 39; Univ Calif, Los Angeles, SS, 39; Mills Col, SS, 40, with Moholy-Nagy; Univ of the Pac, MA, 42; Rudolph Schaefer Sch; Ore State Univ, Shell grant.
Commissions: Wall sculpture, steel tiger, Women's Dorm, Univ of the Pac, 64; steel Viking symbol, Edison High Sch, Stockton, Calif, 64; metal Bengal tiger, Class of 1950, Univ of the Pac, 65; cast stone building, Manteca Union High Sch, Calif, 65; bronze relief, New Wing Stockton Rec Bldg, Stockton, 66.
Exhibitions: West Coast, Sculptors, Eric Locke Gallery, San Francisco, 60; Painting in May 66, Purdue Univ, 66; Northern Calif Arts Painting Open, Sacramento, Calif, 70; Da Vinci Int, New York Coliseum, 70; Post-Sabbatical Exhib, Stockton Fine Arts Gallery, 72.
Teaching: Instr art & asst chmn div arts & lett, Stockton Col, 38-48; prof art & chmn dept art, Univ of the Pac, 48-; guest prof art educ, summer 54; guest lectr, Alaska Methodist Univ, spring 62.
Awards: Second prize for sculpture, Sexology Mag, 57; Transparent Painting Award, Northern Calif Spring Art Festival, 68; purchase award for painting, Lodi-Acampo Open, 70.
Memberships: Life fel Int Inst Arts & Lett; Col Art Asn Am; Pac Arts Asn (ed, Journalette & pres, Northern Calif Sect, 51-52, chmn nat mem comt, 52-53); San Francisco Art Inst; hon mem Stockton Art League (pres, 52-53).
Research: Art education; sculpture.
Publications: Auth & contribr, Arts & Archit, 1/48; auth, The shell and the kernel, Pac Rev, 10/51; auth, A plea for wider distribution of art values, Col Art J, winter 51-52; auth, Aspects of creativity, Univ of the Pac Press, 60; auth, A buffalo sculpture for a California high school, 1/66.
Dealer: Stockton Fine Arts Gallery, 7153 Pacific Ave, Stockton, CA 95207.
Mailing Address: 1656 W Longview Ave, Stockton, CA 95207.

RHOADS, EUGENIA ECKFORD
Painter
Preferred Media: Watercolors, Oils.
b Dyesburg, Tenn, Jan 9, 01.
Study & Training: Miss State Col Women, AB, 23; Columbia Univ, MA, 24; Am Beaux Art Sch, Fontainbleau, summer 32; also with Robert Brackman, Francis Speight, Walter Stuemig, Helen Sawyer & Henry Pitz.
Work in Public Collections: Del Art Mus, Wilmington; Miss State Col Art Collection, Columbus; Univ Del Art Collection, Newark; Du Pont Co Collection, Wilmington & Atlanta; Wilmington Trust Co.
Exhibitions: Brooks Mem Art Gallery, Memphis, Tenn, 55; Nat Collection, Smithsonian Inst, Washington, D C, 56-58; Birmingham Art Mus, Ala, 62; Allied Art, Nat Acad, 66; Am Watercolor Soc, 67.
Teaching: Instr art & design, N C Col Women, 24-26; instr art educ, Univ N C, summers 29 & 30; dir Tower Hill Sch, Wilmington, 27-35.

Positions: Mem adv comn, Rohoboth Art League, Del, 36-; chmn educ coun, Wilmington Art Mus, 40-48; mem visual arts coun, Del State Arts Coun, 69-.
Awards: Fresh Flowers Today Award, Wilmington Soc Fine Arts, 46; The Trio Award, Birmingham Mus Art, 62; Breath of Spring Award, Nat League Am Pen Women, 63.
Memberships: Nat League Am Pen Women (pres, Diamond State Br, 54); Wilmington Soc Fine Arts (secy bd, 69-); Philadelphia Art Alliance; Allied Artists Am; Am Watercolor Soc.
Publications: Auth, Wonder windows, Dutton, 31.
Dealer: Warehouse Gallery, Arden, DE 19803.
Mailing Address: 108 School Rd, Wilmington, DE 19803.

RHODEN, JOHN W
Sculptor
b Birmingham, Ala, 18.
Study & Training: With Richmond Barthe, 38; Columbia Univ Sch Painting & Sculpture, with Oronzio Maldarelli, Hugo Robus & William Zorach.
Work in Public Collections: Stockholm Mus; Carl Milles Collection; Heinz Collection, Pittsburgh, Pa; Steinberg Collection, Saint Louis, Mo; Delaware Mus; plus many others.
Commissions: Zodiacal structure and curved wall (metals & jewel glass), Sheraton Hotel, Philadelphia, Pa, 57; Monumental Bronze, Harlem Hosp, 66; Monumental Abstraction, Metrop Hosp, 68; Clifton Sr High Sch, Baltimore, Md, 71.
Exhibitions: Metrop Mus Art; Audubon Ann; Pa Acad Fine Arts; Nat Acad Design; Am Acad Arts; plus many others.
Positions: Specialist, U S Dept State Tour Iceland, Europe & Northern Africa, 55-56; mem artist deleg, U S Dept State Tour, U S S R, Poland & Yugoslavia, 59 & Asia, 60; consult, Seni-Rupa Inst Teknol, Bandung, Indonesia, 62.
Awards: Rockefeller grant, 59; Medal Pro Sculptura Egregia, Howard Univ, 61; Guggenheim fel, 61.
Memberships: Life mem Munic Art Soc; Am Soc Contemp Artists.
Mailing Address: 23 Cranberry St, Brooklyn, NY 11201.

RHODES, REILLY PATRICK
Art Museum Director
b Bloomington, Ill, Mar 28, 41.
Study & Training: Kansas City Art Inst, BFA, 66; Wichita State Univ, MFA, 68; Sterling Inst, Boston, Mass, art gallery mgt, 69; Syracuse Univ, mus mgt, 70; Univ Mo-Columbia, pub rels, 70.
Work in Public Collections: Gen Mills, Inc, Minneapolis, Minn; Macy's Inc, Kansas City, Mo; Wichita State Univ; Albrecht Gallery Mus Art, St Joseph, Mo.
Exhibitions: Raydon Gallery, New York, N Y.
Collections Arranged: 12 collections for Mus Art, Albrecht Gallery, 68-71; William Grooper: Fifty Years of Drawing 1921-1971 (200 works); Moses Soyer: A Human Approach; Jack Zajac Sculpture; Viviane Woodard Corporation Collection (French Impressionists); Charles Burchfield: Master Doodler; Alexander Archipenko: The American Years; Joseph Gotto: Drawings & Sculpture; Gaston Lachaise: Drawings & Sculpture; Lamar Dodd: Retrospective; Bruno Lucchesi: Sculpture; Paintings by Greg Rossi; Ohio University Alumni Invitational Exhibition; Robert Wick: Sculpture; all for the Canton Art Inst, 71-
Teaching: Instr drawing, Mo Western Col, 69-70.
Positions: Med illusr (film making), Kansas City Gen Hosp & Med Ctr, 66; mem staff, Longstreet Art Gallery, Wichita, Kans, 67-68; dir, Albrecht Gallery, Saint Joseph, Mo, 68-71; dir, Canton Art Inst, Ohio, 71-
Awards: Macy's Ann Exhib Award, 65.
Memberships: Col Art Asn Am; Am Asn Mus; Assoc Coun of the Arts.
Publications: Auth, Public relations catalogue, Albrecht Gallery; auth, introductions to var catalogues incl L E Shafer bronzes, An exhibition of sculpture and drawings by O V Shaffer, Moses Soyer: a selection of paintings 1960-1970 & Moses Soyer: a human approach, The art of Irving Ramsey Wiles (1861-1948) & All Ohio (Canton Art Inst Ann).
Mailing Address: Canton Art Institute, 1001 Market Ave N, Canton, OH 44702.

RIBA, PAUL F
Painter, Illustrator
Preferred Media: Oils.
b Cleveland, Ohio, Jan 25, 12.
Study & Training: Pa Acad Fine Arts, Philadelphia; Cleveland Inst Art, grad, 36.
Work in Public Collections: White House, Washington, D C; Smithsonian Inst, Washington; Cleveland Mus Art, Ohio; Rochester Mus Art, N Y; Ohio State Capitol, Columbus.
Commissions: Elements of Aviation (mural), Cleveland Airport, Ohio, 37; Travel (mural), Cleveland Auto Club, 47; Industrial Products (mural), Warner & Swasey Co, Cleveland, 53; illustration of Jack London's Call of the Wild, Harris-Intertype Corp,

Cleveland, 62; African Scene (mural), bd rm for Apcoa Corp, 67.
Exhibitions: Cleveland Mus Art, 37-55; Carnegie Int, Pittsburgh, Pa, 47-49 & 52; Nat Acad Design, New York, N Y, 53; Flint Invitational, Mich, 66; Art in U S A, New York.
Teaching: Instr drawing & illus, Cleveland Inst Art, 49-62.
Awards: Spec awards & first prizes, Cleveland Mus Art, 37-55; Best Wallcovering Yr Int Award, Am Inst Interior Designers, 62; best of show award, Ziuta & J J Akston Found, 72.
Bibliography: Ernest W Watson (auth), The paintings of Paul Riba, Am Artist Mag, 11/53 & (auth), Composition in landscape & still life, Watson-Guptill, 59; Kenneth Bates (auth), Principles of basic design, World.
Memberships: Artists Guild of Palm Beach Art Inst (mem bd, 72-).
Dealer: Brian Riba, 308 Peruvian Ave, Palm Beach, FL 33480.
Mailing Address: 112 Worth Ct S, West Palm Beach, FL 33405.

RICCI, JERRI
Painter
b Perth Amboy, N J.
Study & Training: N Y Sch Appl Design for Women, 35; Art Stud League New York, with Scott Williams, George Bridgman, Mahonri Young & others, 35-38.
Work in Public Collections: Fairleigh Dickinson Col; Parrish Mus, Southampton, N Y; Am Acad Arts & Lett; Clark Univ, Butler Art Inst; Addison Gallery Am Art, Andover, Mass; plus others.
Exhibitions: Toledo Mus Art; Pa Acad Fine Arts; Art Inst Chicago; Dayton Art Inst; Addison Gallery Am Art; plus others.
Awards: Silver medal, Catharine Lorrillard Wolfe Art Club, 54; Clara Obrig Award, Nat Acad Design; gold medal, Audubon Artists, 55; plus many others.
Memberships: Am Watercolor Soc; Allied Artists Am; assoc Nat Acad Design; Philadelphia Watercolor Club; Audubon Artists; plus others.
Mailing Address: 1 Atlantic Ave, Rockport, MA 01966.

RICE, DAN
Painter, Instructor
Preferred Media: Oils.
b Long Beach, Calif, June 17, 26.
Study & Training: Univ Calif, Los Angeles; Black Mountain Col, BA; Univ Calif, Berkeley; Mass Inst Technol, MA(arch); also with De-Kooning, Kline, Shahn, Motherwell, Stamos, Tworkov, Guston, Albers, Bolotowski & Rothko.
Work in Public Collections: Wadsworth Atheneum, Hartford, Conn; Albright-Knox Art Gallery, Buffalo, N Y; Mus Mod Art, New York, N Y; Princeton Univ Mus, N J; Dillard Univ Mus, New Orleans, La.
Teaching: Instr painting & drawing, Black Mountain Col, N C, 56-57; instr painting, Art Stud League New York, 68-69; vis prof painting, State Univ N Y Buffalo, summer 70; instr life drawing, Univ Conn, 71-72.
Positions: Consult, Franz Kline Estate, New York, 63-; cataloguer works of Mark Rothko, New York, 69-70.
Awards: Longview Found grant, 62.
Bibliography: Jonathan Williams (auth), Dan Rice, painter, Art Int Mag, 60.
Publications: Illusr, The disolving fabric, 55; illusr, All that is lovely in men, 56; illusr, The dutiful son, 60; illusr, Corrosive sublimate, 71; illusr, The plum poems, 72.
Dealer: Catherine Viviano Gallery, 250 E 65th St, New York, NY 10022.
Mailing Address: Rock Landing Rd, Haddam Neck, East Hampton, CT 06424.

RICE, HAROLD RANDOLPH
Educator, Writer
b Salineville, Ohio, May 22, 12.
Study & Training: Univ Cincinnati, BSAA & BS(art educ), 34, MEd, 42; Columbia Univ, Arthur Wesley Dow scholar, 43-44, EdD, 44; Moore Col Art, hon LHD, 63.
Teaching: Art supvr, Wyoming Pub Schs, Ohio, 34-42; adj instr, Univ Cincinnati, 40-42; teaching fel, Columbia Univ, 42-44; head dept art, Univ Ala, 44-46; dean, Moore Inst Art, 46-62; first pres, 51-62; pres & dean, Moore Col Art, 62-63; dean, Col Design, Archit & Art, Univ Cincinnati, 63-
Positions: Chmn comt on art, Ohio Elem Educ Policies Comt, 40-42; chmn arts & skills corps, Am Red Cross, Ala, 44-46; dir, Philadelphia Art Alliance, 47-63; nat scholar juror, Scholastic Arts Awards, seven yrs, 49-71; adv art ed, Bk Knowledge, 50-63; mem bd dirs, Contemp Arts Ctr, 64-69; mem adv bd, 69-
Memberships: Fel & life mem Nat Asn Schs Art (secy, 50-55, pres, 55-57); life mem Eastern Arts Asn (v pres, 56-58, pres, 58-60); Nat Art Educ Asn (coun mem, 60-63); hon mem Cincinnati Art Club; Int Coun Fine Arts Deans; plus others.
Publications: Auth, numerous articles for prof mag & jour, 29-; contrib art ed, Jr Arts & Activities, 37-46; plus others.
Mailing Address: 640 Evening Star Lane, Cincinnati, OH 45220.

RICE, NORMAN LEWIS
Painter, Educator
b Aurora, Ill, July 22, 05.
Study & Training: Univ Ill, BA, 26; Sch Art Inst Chicago, 26-30.
Teaching: Instr drawing & design, Sch Art Inst Chicago, 28-43; prof painting, Syracuse Univ, 46-54; prof painting & hist art, Carnegie-Mellon Univ, 54-
Positions: From asst dean to dean, Sch Art Inst Chicago, 30-43; dir, Sch Art, Syracuse Univ, 46-54; dean, Col Fine Arts, Carnegie-Mellon Univ, 54-72, dean emer, 72-
Memberships: Fel Nat Asn Schs Art; fel Am Coun Arts in Educ; plus others.
Mailing Address: 222 Carnegie Pl, Pittsburgh, PA 15208.

RICE, PHILIP SOMERSET
Painter, Art Administrator
Preferred Media: Acrylics.
b Mobile, Ala, July 3, 44.
Study & Training: Mid Tenn State Univ, BS(art), 67; Pratt Contemp Printmaking Ctr, with Jurgen Fischer, 67; Southern Ill Univ, Carbondale, MFA, 71.
Work in Public Collections: Rose Hulman Inst Technol, Terre Haute, Ind; univ galleries, Southern Ill Univ, Carbondale; Mid Tenn State Univ Galleries, Murfreesboro.
Commissions: Historical oil painting, Murfreesboro C of C, 66.
Exhibitions: The Print in America, Peabody Mus, Nashville, Tenn, 66; Wabash Valley Ann, Terre Haute, 71; Chapel Hill Nat Printmakers, N C, 71; Brooks Goldsmith's Ann, Memphis, Tenn, 72; Quincy Art Ann, Ill, 72.
Teaching: Dir art, Isaac Litton Jr High, Nashville, 67-70; asst instr art, Pratt Contemp Printmaking Ctr, 67; instr drawing & painting, Southern Ill Univ, Carbondale, 70-71; instr, Springfield Art Asn, 71-72.
Positions: Exec dir, Springfield Art Asn, 71-72.
Bibliography: Parisian Arts Int.
Memberships: Col Art Asn; Am Fedn Arts.
Mailing Address: 817 N Fifth St, Springfield, IL 62702.

RICH, DANIEL CATTON
Art Administrator, Lecturer
b South Bend, Ind, Apr 16, 04.
Study & Training: Univ Chicago, PhB; Harvard Univ.
Collections Arranged: The Two Tiepolos; Toulouse-Lautrec, 31; Rembrandt and His Circle, 35; The Art of Fr Goya, 41; Hogarth, Constable & Turner, 46; Henri Rousseau, 46; Chauncey McCormick Memorial Exhibition, 55; Georges Seurat, 58; plus many others.
Teaching: Lectr Degas, the two Tiepolos, all phases of painting & sculptures, especially in 17th, 18th & 19th century painting; vis lectr, Harvard Col, 60.
Positions: Ed, Bull, Art Inst Chicago, 27-32, asst cur painting & sculpture, 29-31, assoc cur, 31-38, dir fine arts, 38-43, cur, 38-70, dir fine arts, 43-58, trustee, 55-58, hon gov life mem; dir, Worcester Art Mus, Mass, 58-70; trustee, Guggenheim Mus, New York, N Y, 61-; v chmn, Mass Bd Higher Educ, 69-70.
Awards: Officer, Legion Hon; Off, Order of Orange Nassau; Knight of Merit, Italy.
Memberships: Int Coun Mus; Am Inst Design; hon mem Am Inst Architects (Chicago Chap); Asn Art Mus Dirs; Am Asn Mus; plus others.
Publications: Auth, Seurat and the evolution of La Grande Jatte, 35, Charles H and Mary F S Worcester Collection Catalogue, 38 & Degas, 51; contribr, Atlantic Monthly & art jours; plus others.
Mailing Address: 10 W 66th St, New York, NY 10023.

RICH, FRANCES L
Sculptor, Photographer
Preferred Media: Bronze.
b Spokane, Wash, Jan 8, 10.
Study & Training: Smith Col, BA, 31; sculpture with Malvina Hoffman & frescoes with Angel Zarraga, Paris, France, 33-35; Beaux Art Acad; Boston Mus Sch, 35-36, with Alexander Iacovleff; Cranbrook Acad Art, 37-40, sculpture with Carl Mills; Claremont Col, 46, with Millard Sheets.
Work in Public Collections: Marble portrait bust of Alice Stone Blackwell, Boston Pub Libr; Nude Bronze, Palm Springs Desert Mus, Calif; St Catherine of Sienna, libr entrance, Santa Catalina Sch, Monterey, Calif; Christ Crucified, Collection Father Edward Doyle, Holy Trinity Church, Bremerton, Wash.
Commissions: Army Navy Nurse, Arlington Nat Cemetery, Va, 38; bronze bas relief Nunc Dimittis, comn by Mr & Mrs James Coonan, St Peters Episcopal Church, Redwood City, Calif, 55; bronze Our Lady of Combermere, Madonna House, Ont, 56; bronze bust of Katherine Hepburn, Am Shakespeare Festival Theatre, Stratford, Conn, 60; bronze St Francis of Assisi, St Margarets Episcopal Church, Palm Desert, 70 & Pierce Col, Athens, Greece, 71; plus others.

Exhibitions: One-man shows, Santa Barbara Mus Art, 52, Calif Palace Legion of Honor, 55 & retrospective, Palm Springs Desert Mus, 69; Calif Relig Artists, De Young Mem, 52; Lenten Exhib Liturgical Arts, Denver Art Mus, 55.
Bibliography: Articles, In: Liturgical Arts Quart; also in newspapers.
Memberships: Archit League New York; Alumna Cranbrook Acad Art.
Mailing Address: P O Box 213, Palm Desert, CA 92260.

RICH, GARRY LORENCE
Painter
b Newton Co, Mo, Nov 11, 43.
Study & Training: Kansas City Art Inst, BFA; N Y Univ, MA.
Work in Public Collections: Whitney Mus Am Art, New York, N Y; Aldrich Mus Contemp Art, Ridgefield, Conn; Phoenix Art Mus, Ariz; Nelson Gallery Art, Kansas City, Mo; Miami Art Ctr, Fla.
Exhibitions: Whitney Mus Am Art Ann, 71; Highlights of the Season, Aldrich Mus Contemp Art, Ridgefield, 71; one-man shows, Max Hutchinson Gallery, New York, 71-72; Henri Gallery, Washington, D C, 72 & Gallery A, Sydney, Australia, 72.
Teaching: Asst prof painting, N Y Univ, 65-71; asst prof painting, Hofstra Univ, 71-72; asst prof painting, Bard Col, 72-
Awards: Max Beckman fel, Brooklyn Mus, 66; Nat Coun Arts Nat Endowment, 67; Anderson fel, N Y Univ, 68.
Bibliography: Domingo (auth), Color abstractionism, 12/70 & Bowling (auth), Color and recent painting, 72, Arts Mag; Ratcliff (auth), Young New York painters, Art News, 70.
Dealer: Max Hutchinson Gallery, 127 Green St, New York, NY 10013.
Mailing Address: 492 Broome St, New York, NY 10013.

RICHARD, BETTI
Sculptor
Preferred Media: Bronze.
b New York, N Y, Mar 16, 16.
Study & Training: Art Stud League New York; also with Paul Manship.
Work in Public Collections: Phoenix Art Mus, Ariz; San Joachin Pioneer Mus & Haggin Art Galleries, Stockton, Calif; Melick Libr, Eureka Col, Ill; Hackley Sch, Tarrytown, N Y; Rosary Hill Col, Buffalo, N Y.
Commissions: St Francis Statue, St Francis of Assisi Church, New York, 57; marble statue of Our Lady, House Theol, Centerville, Ohio, 58; St John Baptiste de la Salle, St John Vianney Sem, E Aurora, N Y, 63; busts of Mozart & Wagner, Metrop Opera, New York, 63 & 70; Cardinal Gibbons Mem, Baltimore, Md, 67.
Exhibitions: Allied Artists Ann, 42-71; Nat Acad Design Ann, 44-71; Nat Sculpture Soc Ann, 47-72; Third Int Exhib, Philadelphia Mus, Pa, 49; Fall Exhib Kuenstlerhaus, Vienna, Austria, 54.
Awards: Barnett Prize, Nat Acad Design, 47; gold medal for sculpture, Allied Artists Am, 56; John Gregory Award, Nat Sculpture Soc, 60.
Bibliography: Jacques Schnier (auth), Sculpture in modern America, Univ Calif Press, 49; Norman Kent (auth), The sculpture of Betti Richard, Am Artist Mag.
Memberships: Fel Nat Sculpture Soc (secy, 71-); Archit League New York (v pres sculpture, 61-63); Allied Artists Am; Nat Arts Club; Audubon Artists.
Mailing Address: 15 Gramercy Park S, New York, NY 10003.

RICHARD, PAUL
Art Critic
b Chicago, Ill, Nov 22, 39.
Study & Training: Harvard Col, BA, 61; Univ Pa Grad Sch Fine Arts.
Positions: Art critic, Washington Post, Washington, D C, 68-
Mailing Address: 1150 15th St N W, Washington, DC 20005.

RICHARDS, JEANNE HERRON
Etcher, Painter
b Aurora, Ill.
Study & Training: Univ Iowa, BFA, 52, MFA, 54, with Mauricio Lasansky; Fulbright grant, Paris, 54-55, Atelier 17, Paris, 54, with Stanley William Hayter.
Work in Public Collections: Lessing J Rosenwald Collection, Nat Gallery Art; Prints & Photographs, Libr Cong, Washington, D C; Nat Collection Fine Arts, Washington, D C; Nelson-Atkins Gallery Art, Kansas City, Mo; Sheldon Mem Art Galleries, Univ Nebr, Lincoln.
Exhibitions: Five Libr Cong Pennell Exhibs Prints, 47-61; Prints From Brooklyn Mus Nat, Am Fedn Arts U S Tour, 56; Intaglio Prints U S A, U S Info Agency Tour S Am, 59; one-man exhib prints, Univ Ill, Champaign, 69; Olga N Sheldon Collection, Univ Nebr Galleries, Lincoln, 70.
Teaching: Asst instr drawing, Univ Iowa, 55-56; asst prof prints & drawing, Univ Nebr, Lincoln, 57-63.

Awards: Purchase award & mem, Corcoran Gallery Art, 57; purchase award, Print Club Albany 13th Nat, 69.
Memberships: Col Art Asn Am; Soc Washington D C Printmakers; Print Club Albany; Northern Va Fine Arts Asn.
Dealer: Mickelson Gallery, 707 G St N W, Washington, DC 20001.
Mailing Address: 3506 Cameron Mills Rd, Alexandria, VA 22305.

RICHARDS, KARL FREDERICK
Educator, Painter
Preferred Media: Oils.
b Youngstown, Ohio, June 14, 20.
Study & Training: Cleveland Inst Art, dipl, 44; Western Reserve Univ, BSEd, 44; State Univ Iowa, MA, 47; Ohio State Univ, PhD, 56.
Teaching: Asst prof art, Bowling Green State Univ, 47-56; prof art & chmn dept, Tex Christian Univ, 56-71; prof art & chmn div, Ark State Univ, 71-
Mailing Address: P O Box RR, State University, AR 72467.

RICHARDSON, CONSTANCE (COLEMAN)
Painter
Preferred Media: Oils.
b Indianapolis, Ind, Jan 18, 05.
Study & Training: Pa Acad Fine Arts.
Work in Public Collections: Indianapolis Mus Art, Ind; Detroit Inst Arts, Mich; Santa Barbara Mus Art, Calif; Columbus Gallery Fine Arts, Ohio; Pa Acad Fine Arts, Philadelphia.
Commissions: This Land is Ours (painting), Omaha Nat Bank, Nebr, 66.
Exhibitions: Am Painting Today, Metrop Mus Art, New York, N Y, 50; Am Landscape, A Changing Frontier, Nat Collection Fine Arts, Washington, D C, 66; Fifty Artists from Fifty States Circulating Exhib, Am Fedn Arts, 67-68; Am Paintings of Ports & Harbors, 1774-1968, Jacksonville-Norfolk, 69; Remnants of Things Past, Jacksonville-Saint Petersburg, 71.
Bibliography: Louise Bruner (auth), Constance Richardson, Am Artist, 1/61; Alan Gussow (auth), A sense of place: the artist & the American land, Sat Rev, 71.
Dealer: Kennedy Galleries, 20 E 56th St, New York, NY 10022.
Mailing Address: 285 Locust St, Philadelphia, PA 19106.

RICHARDSON, EDGAR PRESTON
Art Administrator
b Glens Falls, N Y, Dec 2, 02.
Study & Training: Univ Pa; Williams Col; Pa Acad Fine Arts.
Positions: Ed, Art Quart, 38-64; dir, Detroit Inst Arts, 45-62; dir, H F du Pont Winterthur Mus, 62-66; chmn, Smithsonian Art Comn, 63-66; pres, Pa Acad Fine Arts, 68-70.
Memberships: Arch Am Art (dir); Am Philos Soc; Hist Soc Pa (coun); Nat Portrait Gallery Comn.
Publications: Auth, The way of Western art, 39 & 67, Am Romantic painting, 44, Washington Allston, 48 & 67, Painting in America—the story of 450 years, 56 & 65 & A short history of painting in America, 63.
Mailing Address: 285 Locust St, Philadelphia, PA 19106.

RICHARDSON, GERARD
Painter, Designer
b New York, N Y, 1910.
Study & Training: In Europe.
Work in Public Collections: Fr Naval Club, Paris; Nat Naval Mem Mus, Washington, D C; Adm Jerauld Wright Bldg, Norfolk Naval Base; Lyndon B Johnson Ranch; Sam Rayburn Libr, Tex; plus others.
Commissions: Large oil painting, The (PT) 109, Kennedy Libr.
Art Interests: Portrayal of nautical, sportscar, and air activities, historical combat scenes and all-subject murals.
Mailing Address: 1534 N 22nd St, Arlington, VA 22209.

RICHARDSON, GRETCHEN (GRETCHEN ROSE FREELANDER)
Sculptor
Preferred Media: Stone, Marble, Alabaster.
b Detroit, Mich.
Study & Training: Wellesley Col, BA; Acad Julian, Paris, France; Art Stud League New York, with William Zorach & Jose de Creeft.
Work in Public Collections: Work in pvt collections only.
Exhibitions: Int Arts Club, London, Eng; Pa Acad Fine Arts, Philadelphia; Audubon Artists; Knickerbocker Artists; Nat Acad Design; plus several one-man shows.
Awards: I A R Wylie prize 52, Amelia Peabody prize, 55 & Mary Kellner Mem prize, 59, Nat Asn Women Artists; plus many others.
Memberships: Audubon Artists (sculpture jury, 71); Nat Asn Women Artists (exec comt, 52-55, sculpture jury, 69-71); New York Soc Women Artists; Artists Equity Asn New York.
Dealer: Bodley Gallery, 1063 Madison Ave, New York, NY 10028.
Mailing Address: 530 Park Ave, New York, NY 10021.

RICHARDSON, JUDITH HEIDLER
Art Administrator, Art Dealer
b Newport, R I, Feb 4, 42.
Study & Training: Swarthmore Col; Bennington Col, BA; Sorbonne Univ Paris, Ecole des Lettres.
Positions: Asst dir, Pace Gallery, New York, N Y, 66-69; dir, Sonnabend Gallery, New York, 69-
Specialty of Gallery: Contemporary painting & sculpture; art deco & art moderne.
Mailing Address: Sonnabend Gallery, 924 Madison Ave, New York, NY 10021.

RICHARDSON, SAM
Painter, Educator
b Oakland, Calif, July 19, 34.
Study & Training: Calif Col Arts & Crafts, BA, 56 & MFA, 60.
Exhibitions: Paints Behind the Painters, Palace Legion of Hon Mus, San Francisco, Calif, 67; Illinois Biennial, Univ Ill, 67; Plactic as Plastic, Mus Contemp Crafts, New York, N Y, 69; New Methods & Materials, Mus Mod Art, New York, N Y, 69; Reed Col Invitational, Ore, 69; plus many other group & one-man shows.
Teaching: Instr art, Oakland City Col, 60-61; art dir, Mus Contemp Crafts, New York, 61-63; asst prof art, San Jose State Col, 63-66, assoc prof art, 67-
Mailing Address: c/o Hansen Fuller Gallery, 228 Grant Ave, San Francisco, CA 94108.

RICHENBURG, ROBERT BARTLETT
Painter, Sculptor
b Boston, Mass, July 17, 17.
Study & Training: George Washington Univ; Boston Univ; Corcoran Sch Art; Art Stud League New York; Ozenfant Sch Art; Hans Hofmann Sch Fine Art.
Work in Public Collections: Chrysler Mus Art; Univ Tex Art Mus, Austin; Berkeley Mus Art, Univ Calif; Whitney Mus Am Art; Mus Mod Art, New York; plus many others.
Exhibitions: One-man shows, Tibor de Nagy Gallery, 59-64; Am Fedn Arts Traveling Exhibs, 60-61, 64-65 & 68-69; Whitney Mus Am Art Painting Ann, 61 & 64, Sculpture Ann, 68; one-man shows, Dana Arts Ctr, Colgate Univ, 70 & Ithaca Col Mus Art, 71; plus many other one-man & group shows.
Teaching: Instr art, City Col New York; instr art Pratt Inst; instr art, Cooper Union; instr art New York Univ; assoc prof art, Cornell Univ, 64-67; assoc prof art, grad adv art dept, fac coun mem & chmn self-study comt, Hunter Col, 67-70; Aruba Res Ctr, City Univ Prog, 70; prof art, Ithaca Col, 70-
Awards: Am Fedn Arts Award, 64.
Memberships: Art Educ Asn (comt Int Cult Relations); Am Asn Univ Prof; Col Art Asn Am; life mem Art Stud League New York.
Mailing Address: 121 E Remington Rd, Cayuga Heights, Ithaca, NY 14850.

RICHMAN, ROBERT M
Art Administrator, Writer
b Connersville, Ind, Dec 22, 14.
Study & Training: Western Mich Univ, AB(Eng) & AB(hist); Univ Mich, AM.
Collections Arranged: Arranged over 90 exhibits of recent work by contemporary artists from Europe, Asia and the Americas.
Teaching: Instr, Univ Mich, 38-45; prof, Adelphi Col, 45-47; lectr philos art, Nat Gallery Art, Phillips Gallery & Libr Cong.
Positions: Founder & pres, Inst Contemp Arts, Washington, D C, 47, trustee, mem exec comt & bd trustees, 47-; lit & art ed, New Repub Mag, 51-54; mem, President's Fine Arts Comt, 56-, chmn, 60-; mem, Washington Festival, 57-, dir, 58; mem, Am Nat Theatre & Acad, 58-; trustee, Nat Cult Ctr, 59-; trustee, Opera Soc Washington, 59-; trustee, Meridian House Found, 60-; trustee, Arena Stage, Washington Drama Soc, 60-; consult arts, Dept State, 61; trustee, Ctr Arts of Indian Am, 65-
Awards: Hopwood Awards, 42-44; Comdr Brit Empire, 59.
Memberships: Am Asn Mus Dirs; Am Asn Mus; fel Int Inst Arts & Lett; Col Art Asn Am; Artists Equity Asn; plus others.
Publications: Publ, The potter's portfolio, 50; ed, The arts at mid-century, 54; auth, Nature in the modern arts; contribr, New Repub & Kenyon Rev; plus others.
Mailing Address: 3102 R St N W, Washington, DC 20007.

RICHMOND, FREDERICK W
Collector, Patron
b Boston, Mass, Nov 15, 23.
Study & Training: Harvard Univ, 42-43; Boston Univ, AB, 45; Pratt Inst, LLD.
Positions: Chmn bd, Carnegie Hall Corp, 61; mem, N Y State Coun Arts; chmn, New York Comt Young Audiences; co-chmn, Mayor's Comt Scholastic Achievement; bd mem, New York Studio Sch.
Collection: Modern art.
Mailing Address: 43 Pierrepont St, Brooklyn, NY 11201.

RICHMOND, LAWRENCE
Collector
b Hollis, N Y, Oct 30, 09.
Study & Training: Dartmouth Col, AB.
Positions: Trustee, Provincetown Art Asn, 62, 71 & 72; pres, Provincetown Symphony Soc, 68-69.
Collection: Primarily modern American painting and sculpture; African sculpture.
Mailing Address: 7 Woodcrest Rd, Great Neck, NY 11024.

RICKEY, GEORGE W
Sculptor
Preferred Media: Stainless Steel.
b South Bend, Ind, June 6, 07.
Study & Training: Trinity Col, Scotland; Balliol Col, Oxford Univ, BA, MA, 41; Ruskin Sch Drawing, Oxford Univ; Acad Andre Lhote & Acad Mod, Paris, France; Knox Col, hon DFA, 70.
Work in Public Collections: Albright-Knox Art Gallery, Buffalo, N Y; Corcoran Gallery Art, Washington, D C; Mus Boymans-van Beuningen, Rotterdam, Neth; Mus Mod Art, New York, N Y; Neue Nationalgalerie, Berlin, Ger.
Commissions: Kinetic sculpture, Joseph H Hirshhorn Collection, 62, Kunsthalle, Hamburg, Ger, 63, Rijksmuseum Kroller-Muller, Otterlo, Neth, 65, Nordpark, Dusseldorf, Ger, 65 & Nat Collection Fine Arts, Washington, D C, 67.
Exhibitions: Directions in Kinetic Sculpture, Univ Art Mus, Univ Calif, Berkeley, 66; Sculpture from Twenty Nations, Solomon R Guggenheim Mus, New York, 67; Plus by Minus, Albright-Knox Art Gallery, 68; Int Sculptors' Symp, Osaka, Japan, 69; Kinetic Art, Arts Coun Gr Brit, Hayward Gallery, London, 70.
Awards: Nat Fine Arts Honor Award, Am Inst Architects, 72.
Bibliography: Robert Coates (auth), The art galleries/innovations, New Yorker, 10/21/61; Engineer of movement, Time Mag, 11/4/66; Peter Riedl (auth), George Rickey: kinetische objekte, Philipp Reclam J, Stuttgart, 70.
Publications: Auth, Constructivism: origins and evolution, Braziller, 67.
Dealer: Staempfli Gallery, 47 E 77th St, New York, NY 10021.
Mailing Address: East Chatham, NY 12060.

RIDABOCK, RAY (BUDD)
Painter, Instructor
b Stamford, Conn, Feb 16, 04.
Study & Training: Williams Col, 22-24; Columbia Univ Exten, 28-29; also with Amy Jones, Anthony di Bona, Peppino Mangravite & Xavier Gonzalez.
Work in Public Collections: New Brit Art Mus; Munson-Williams-Proctor Inst; State Teachers Col, Indiana, Pa; U S Embassy, Lima, Peru; Norfolk Mus Arts & Sci; plus many others.
Exhibitions: Am Watercolor Soc Traveling Exhibs, 62-64; Audubon Artists; Boston Arts Festival, Baltimore Mus; Butler Inst Am Art; Pa Acad Fine Arts; plus many other group & one-man shows.
Teaching: Instr, Silvermine Guild Artists, 58-; instr, Greenwich Art Soc, 62-
Awards: Conn Watercolor Soc Awards, 63, 67 & 68; Painters in Casein Medal of Merit, 65; award, Greenwich Art Soc, 67; plus many others.
Memberships: Am Watercolor Soc; Artists Equity Asn; Audubon Artists; Conn Acad Fine Arts; fel Silvermine Guild Artists (bd dirs, 58-65, 67-).
Mailing Address: South Lane, Redding Ridge, CT 06876.

RIDLON, JAMES A
Sculptor, Educator
b Nyack, N Y, July 11, 34.
Study & Training: Syracuse Univ, BA, 57; San Francisco State Col, 58-59; Syracuse Univ, MFA, 65.
Work in Public Collections: Munson-Williams-Proctor Mus, Utica, N Y; State Univ N Y Agr & Tech Col Morrisville; Rochester Mem Gallery, N Y; Everson Mus, Syracuse, N Y.
Commissions: Sculptured mural, C & U Broadcasting, 58; Bert Bell Mem Trophy, Long Island Athletic Club, 68; assemblage, Merchants Nat Bank Bldg, Rochester, 71.
Exhibitions: One-man exhibs, Wells Col, Aurora, N Y & Schuman Gallery, Rochester, 71; Mirrors, Motors, Motion, Albert-Knox Art Gallery, Buffalo, N Y, 70; Graphics 71, Nat Print & Drawing Exhib, Western N Mex Univ, 71; three-man exhib, Lubin House Gallery, New York, N Y, 71.
Teaching: Asst sculpture, San Francisco State Col, 58; lectr art educ, Syracuse Univ, 65-67, assoc prof sculpture & synaesthetic educ, 68-
Awards: Purchase prize, 32nd Ann Exhib, Munson-Williams-Proctor Mus, 68; Graphics 1969 Award, N Y State Fair, 69; first prize in sculpture, 10th Ann Westchester Art Soc Exhib, 70.
Memberships: Nat Art Educ Asn; N Y State Art Teachers Asn; Assoc Artists Syracuse; Cooperstown Art Asn.
Publications: Contribr, Synaesthetic education, Syracuse Univ Press, 71.

Dealer: Schuman Gallery, 267 Oxford, Rochester, NY 14607; Adam Gallery, 21 E 73rd St, New York, NY 10021.
Mailing Address: 128 Lincklaen St, Cazenovia, NY 13035.

RIES, MARTIN
Painter, Art Historian
b Washington, D C, Dec 26, 26.
Study & Training: Corcoran Gallery Art, 40-44; Am Univ, BA, 50, with Jack Tworkov & Leo Steppat; Hunter Col, MA, 68, with Leo Steinberg, William Rubin & Ad Reinhardt.
Work in Public Collections: Pace Col Mus, Pleasantville, N Y; Riverside Mus Collection, Rose Art Mus, Brandeis Univ; Inst Cult Hisp, Madrid, Spain.
Exhibitions: Corcoran Gallery Art, 52; Inst Cult Hisp, Univ Madrid, 55; Mus Mod Art, 56; Toledo Mus, Ohio, 57; Paul Gallery, Tokyo, Japan, 68.
Teaching: Instr medieval art hist, Marymount Col, 59; instr mod art hist, Hunter Col, 63-67; asst prof hist art, drawing & painting, L I Univ, 68.
Positions: Asst dir pub rels, Nat Cong Comt, 51; asst dir, Hudson River Mus, Yonkers, N Y, 57-67; adv, Westchester Cult Ctr, 65-67.
Awards: Hon mention, 52nd Nat Soc Arts & Lett Award, 57, Corcoran Gallery Art; Critics Choice, Whyte Gallery, 57.
Research: Minotaur in Western art, from ancient Greek myth to contemporary art.
Publications: Auth, Elusive Goya, New Repub, 57 & monthly articles, In: Hudson River Mus Bull, 57-67; auth, Hudson River art—past & present, 59, Endowments for great society, Art Voices Mag, 65 & New Art, 66.
Dealer: Mann Gallery, 1226 Third Ave, New York, NY 10021.
Mailing Address: 36 Livingston Rd, Scarsdale, NY 10583.

RIESS, LORE
Painter, Printmaker
Preferred Media: Oils.
b Berlin, Ger; U S citizen.
Study & Training: Art Acad, Contempora (Bauhaus Sch), Berlin; Sumi Drawing & Calligraphy, Tokyo, Japan; Art Stud League New York.
Work in Public Collections: Corcoran Gallery Art, Washington, D C; Israel Mus, Jerusalem; Tel-Aviv Mus, Israel; U S Embassy, Tokyo; Rutgers Univ, N J.
Commissions: Ed of etchings, Mickelson Gallery, Washington, D C, 71.
Exhibitions: One-man shows, Nihon Bashi Gallery, Tokyo, 65, Nat Asn Women Artists, 69, Painters & Sculptors Soc Nat, Old Jaffa Nora Gallery, Israel, 70, Painters & Sculptors Soc Nat, 71 & Int Miniature Print Exhib, 71.
Awards: William McNulty Merit Award, Art Stud League New York, 64; M J Kaplan Prize, Nat Asn Women Artists, 69; Gallery of Graphic Art Award, Int Miniature Print Exhib, 71.
Bibliography: T Ichinose (auth), Colorful abstract oils by Lore Riess, Mainichi Daily News, 65; articles, In: Art News, 5/66, Washington Post, 1/67 & Jerusalem Post, 7/70 & 3/71.
Dealer: Phoenix Gallery, 939 Madison Ave, New York, NY 10021.
Mailing Address: Apt 37F, 15 W 72nd St, New York, NY 10023.

RIFKIN, DR & MRS HAROLD
Collectors
Collection: American art of the early twentieth century.
Mailing Address: 35 E 75th St, New York, NY 10021.

RIGSBY, JOHN DAVID
Painter
Preferred Media: Oils, Acrylics.
b Tallassee, Ala, Oct 10, 34.
Study & Training: Univ Ala, BFA & MS(urban studies); Southern Conn State Col; Columbia Univ, with Leon Goldin.
Work in Public Collections: Telfair Acad Arts & Sci, Savannah, Ga; Univ Ala Gallery Collection; Beaufort Mus, S C; U S Embassy, Tunis, Tunisia; Brit Coun, Tunis.
Commissions: Sculpture, Mobile Art Ctr, Ala, 63.
Exhibitions: Ala Artists Ann, Birmingham, 62; Artists of Southeast & Tex, New Orleans, La, 63; one-man shows, Delgado Mus, New Orleans, 64, Galerie Munic, Tunis, 67, Telfair Acad, 69 & Columbia Mus, S C, 71; Am Artists Tunisia, U S Info Serv, 66; Guild S C Artists Ann, 71.
Teaching: Nat Endowment Arts artist-in-residence, Beaufort Pub Sch Syst, S C, 70-73.
Positions: Consult art, Ctr Urban Educ, New York, N Y, 68-69; dir Vol Community Serv Prog, Action Bridgeport Community Develop, Conn, 68-69.
Awards: Merit award, Artists of Southeast & Tex, Delgado Mus, 63; merit award, Guild S C Artists Exhib, 71; Springs Mills Traveling Exhibit Award, 72.
Bibliography: Al Wardi (auth), Dans le tournoi de l'art avec John David Rigsby, L'Action, 3/29/67; Gaynor Pearson (auth), The one

room school now has wheels, Conn Educ, 2/68; Oliver & Sisk (auth), Artist-in-residence—a first for South Carolina, S C Educ J, winter 71.
Memberships: Guild S C Artists; Nat Art Educ Asn; Col Art Asn Am.
Research: The design of cultural enrichment programs as a basis for community participation.
Dealer: Neikrug Gallery, 224 E 68th St, New York, NY 10021.
Mailing Address: 2805 Azalea Dr, Beaufort, SC 29902.

RILEY, ART (ARTHUR IRWIN)
Painter, Photographer.
Preferred Media: Watercolors, Oils.
b Boston, Mass, Sept 14, 11.
Study & Training: Art Ctr Sch Los Angeles.
Exhibitions: Am Watercolor Soc, New York, N Y; Calif Watercolor Soc, Los Angeles Co Mus Art; Springfield Art Mus, Mo; Youngstown Art Mus, Ohio; one-man show, Pacific Grove, Calif Art Mus.
Positions: Artist, MGM Studios, five yrs; artist, Walt Disney Studios, 37-65.
Awards: Am Watercolor Soc award; Laguna Beach Art Asn award; Butler Inst Am Art award; plus others.
Memberships: Acad Motion Picture Arts & Sci; Am Watercolor Soc.
Art Interests: Direct painting on location.
Publications: Auth & illusr, article, In: Am Artist Mag; contribr, Sat Eve Post, Ariz Highways, Ford Times, Life Mag & others.
Dealers: Pebble Beach California Gallery, Pebble Beach, CA 93953; The Palette, Carmel, CA 93921.
Mailing Address: 615 N First St, Burbank, CA 91502.

RILEY, CHAPIN
Collector
Memberships: Art Collectors Club.
Collection: Modern painting and sculpture.
Mailing Address: 9 Old Colony Rd, Worcester, MA 01609.

RILEY, GERALD PATRICK
Designer, Instructor
Preferred Media: Constructed Objects, Leather, Metal, Assorted Fibers.
b Oklahoma City, Okla, Sept 6, 41.
Study & Training: Univ Okla, BFA, 64, MA(art educ), 71.
Work in Public Collections: Ark Arts Ctr, Little Rock; Contemp Arts Found, Oklahoma City.
Exhibitions: 11th & 12th Ann Eight State Exhib Painting & Sculpture, 69 & 70 & Okla Biennial Exhib, 71, Okla Art Ctr, Oklahoma City; 4th Ann Okla Designer Craftsman Exhib, Philbrook Art Ctr, Tulsa, 71; 4th Ann Prints, Drawings & Crafts Exhib, Ark Arts Ctr, Little Rock, 71.
Teaching: Instr gen art, Okla Art Ctr, Oklahoma City, 66-71; instr art & chmn dept, John Marshall High Sch, Oklahoma City, 68-
Positions: Educ dir, Okla Art Ctr, Oklahoma City, 67-69; dir creative educ lab, Oklahoma City Arts Coun, 71-72.
Awards: Jewelry award, Okla Designer Craftsman, 70 & 71; purchase award, Ark Arts Ctr, Little Rock, 71.
Bibliography: Exhibitions, 3-4/69, 1-2/70 & 11-12/71, Craft-Horizons.
Memberships: Nat Art Educ Asn (states assembly, 67-71); Okla Art Educ Asn (pres, 69-71); Okla City Art Educ Asn (pres, 67-68); Am Crafts Coun; Okla Designer Craftsman Asn (v pres, 69-71).
Mailing Address: 3508 S W 21st St, Oklahoma City, OK 73108.

RILEY, ROY JOHN
Painter, Designer
Preferred Media: Oils.
b Independence, Kans, Apr 19, 03.
Study & Training: Calif Arts & Crafts; Detroit Art Sch; Huettles Art Sch, Chicago; Univ Tulsa, with Franz Vanderlachen; also with Merlin Enabnet.
Commissions: Mural, Travel & Transport Bldg, Chicago World's Fair, Ill, 33.
Exhibitions: Assoc Artists Philbrook, Tulsa, Okla; Ruskin Club, Tulsa; Verdigris Valley Art Exhib, Independence, Kans; Scottsdale Artist League, Ariz; two one-man shows, Philbrook Art Gallery, Tulsa.
Positions: Demonstr Artist in Action shows, Philbrook Art Gallery, Tulsa, Art Asns in Bartlesville, Okla, Fort Smith, Ark, civic groups in Scottsdale, Ariz & univs.
Awards: Awards for South of the Border (painting), Philbrook Art Gallery, 45 & Ruskin Club, 45; award for The Boulders (painting), Scottsdale Artist League, 69.
Art Interests: Sculpture compositions in primitive art; light plastics representative of stone.
Dealer: La Galeria, Sedona, AZ 86336.
Mailing Address: 140 W Granada Rd, Phoenix, AZ 85003.

RIMMEL, E P GREBE, see GREBE

RING, EDWARD ALFRED
Collector, Art Dealer
b New York, N Y.
Collections Arranged: Focus On Light, sponsored, N J State Mus, Trenton, 67.
Teaching: Mem N J State Coun Arts, 67-, chmn, 71-
Positions: Owner Carter Gallery.
Memberships: Am Fedn Arts; Metrop Mus Art; Mus Mod Art; Los Angeles Mus Art.
Mailing Address: R R 1, Box 303, Titusville, NJ 08560.

RIPPEY, CLAYTON
Painter, Educator
Preferred Media: Acrylics.
b La Grande, Ore, Apr 24, 23.
Study & Training: Northwestern Univ; Stanford Univ, BA & MA, with Daniel Mendelowitz, Ray Faulkner & Anton Refrigier; San Jose State Col, with George Post; Inst Allende, Mex, with James Pinto & Fred Samuelson.
Work in Public Collections: Cunningham Mus, Bakersfield, Calif; Wakayama Castle, Japan.
Commissions: Pylon design & mural, Bakersfield Col, Calif, 58; two murals, Porterville Col, Calif, 66; two murals, Valley Plaza Mall, Bakersfield, 67; mural, Monache High Sch, Porterville, 68; three dimensional mural, Tenneco Corp Hq, Bakersfield, 69; plus others.
Exhibitions: Lucian Labaudt Gallery, San Francisco, Calif, 55; Cunningham Mem Mus, Bakersfield, 58, 61 & 66; Circulo de Belles Artes, Palma, Spain, 60; Pioneer & Haggen Mus, Stockton, Calif, 64; Port Townsend Art Ctr (festival guest exhibitor), Wash, 65; plus 32 one-man shows.
Teaching: Prof painting, Bakersfield Col, 49-, chmn dept, 68-72; prof painting, Maui Community Col, Univ Hawaii, 67-68.
Positions: Dir Exhibs, Cunningham Mus, Bakersfield, 54-55; dir exhibs, Bakersfield Col Gallery, 61-62.
Awards: 13 awards (single painting), traveling show, Kern Co, 60; best of show, Kern Co Fair Asn, 63, 65 & 67; best of show, Taft Art Asn, 72.
Memberships: Taft Art Asn (hon life mem); Bakersfield Art Asn (v pres, 54); Calif Art Educ Asn.
Dealer: Gallery Yves Jaubert, 75 Farbour St Honore, Paris 8, France.
Mailing Address: Cézanne Gallery, P O Box 2354, Bakersfield, CA 93303.

RISING, DOROTHY MILNE
Painter, Instructor
Preferred Media: Oils, Watercolors.
b Tacoma, Wash, Sept 13, 95.
Study & Training: Pratt Inst, dipl, 16; Cleveland Sch Art, with Henry Keller, 20; Univ Wash, BA, 32, MFA, 33.
Work in Public Collections: Seattle Art Mus, Wash; Frye Art Mus, Seattle; Pac Nat Bank Washington, Tacoma; Three Grumbacher Collections; Lakeside Sch.
Exhibitions: Northwest Ann, 69 & Northwest Watercolor Soc, 69, Art Mus Pavilion; West Coast Oil Exhib, 69 & Puget Sound Area Exhib, 71, Frye Art Mus; Pac Northwest Art Ann, Erb Mem Art Gallery, Eugene, Ore, 72; plus others.
Teaching: Instr, Univ Puget Sound, 16-17; instr & supvr art, Western Wash Col, 17-19; instr art, Seattle High Schs, 33-66.
Awards: Purchase prize, Spokane Womens Club, 49; Music & Art Found First Prize, Henry Gallery, 50; Best watercolor in show, Nat League Am Pen Women, Smithsonian, 55.
Bibliography: Around the world through an artist's eyes, Pen Woman, 67; Edna Daw (auth), A word about Dorothy Rising, Age of Achievement, 71.
Memberships: Fel Royal Soc Art, London; Nat League Am Pen Women (pres Seattle br, 70-72); Women Painters Wash (pres, 49); Northwest Watercolor Soc; Artists Equity Asn.
Publications: Auth & illusr Contemporary versus academic art, Town Crier, 34; auth, The silver Bible, Christian Sci Monitor, 64; auth & illusr, Vanished landmarks, 71, Preserving our open spaces, 71 & Great snow mountain, 72, Age of Achievement.
Mailing Address: 5033 17th Ave N E, Seattle, WA 98105.

RISLEY, JOHN HOLLISTER
Sculptor, Educator
b Brookline, Mass, Sept 20, 19.
Study & Training: Amherst Col, BA(cum laude); R I Sch Design, BFA; Cranbrook Acad Art, MFA.
Work in Public Collections: Wesleyan Univ, Conn; Henry E Huntington Art Gallery, Calif; Fred Olsen Found, Conn; Hartford Jewish Community Ctr, Conn; Rose Art Gallery, Brandeis Univ.
Commissions: Reliefs, wood & metal, IBM Hq, New York, 65; wrought iron, Cleveland Garden Ctr, Ohio, 66 & copper, Nat Bank, Quarryville, Pa, 71; sculptures, wood & metal, Brookside Elementary Sch, Waterville, Maine & bronze, Univ Maine, Portland, 70.

Teaching: Prof sculpture, Wesleyan Univ, 54-, chmn dept art, 68-
Awards: First prize for furniture, U S Designer Craftsman, 53; Drakenfield Prize, 18th Ceramic Ann, 54; New Haven Arts Festival Sculpture Prize, 66.
Mailing Address: 30 Maple Shade Rd, Middletown, CT 06457.

RITCHIE, ANDREW C
Art Administrator, Art Historian
b Bellshill, Scotland, Sept 18, 07; U S citizen.
Study & Training: Univ Pittsburgh, BA, MA; Yale Univ, hon MA; Univ London, PhD.
Teaching: Lectr art & res asst, Frick Collection, New York, N Y, 35-42; vis lectr art, New York Univ, 36-40; lectr Brit art, Fr & Spanish Post-Renaissance painting & mod art.
Positions: Dir, Albright-Knox Art Gallery, Buffalo, N Y, 42-49; dir dept painting & sculpture, Mus Mod Art, New York, 49-57; dir, Yale Univ Art Gallery, New Haven, Conn, 57-70, emer dir, 70-
Awards: Decorated Cross Legion of Hon, France, 46; Order of Orange Nassau, Netherlands, 48; Off Cross of Order of Merit, Fed Repub Ger, 57.
Memberships: Col Art Asn Am; Asn Am Mus Dir.
Publications: Auth, English painters, Hogarth to Constable, 42; auth, Abstract painting & sculpture in America, 51 & Arno, 70; auth, Edouard Vuillard, 54 & Arno, 70; auth, Three American precisionist painters, Arno (in prep); co-auth, Selected paintings & sculpture from the Yale University Art Gallery, Yale Univ Press, 72; plus many others.
Mailing Address: R F D, New Canaan, CT 06018.

RIU, VICTOR
Sculptor
Preferred Media: Granite.
b Italy, July 18, 87.
Study & Training: In Italy.
Work in Public Collections: Pa Acad Fine Arts, Philadelphia; Lehigh Univ; Woodmere Art Gallery, Philadelphia, Pa; Fed Reserve Saving & Loan Pub Art Collection, Philadelphia; Mus Civico, Trieste, Italy.
Exhibitions: One-man shows, Leigh Univ, Woodmere Art Gallery & Allentown Art Mus; Philadelphia Artists Alliance; Pa Acad Fine Arts, 58, 64 & 71; plus others.
Awards: Charles K Smith Award, 66; Phillip Mills Award, New Hope, Pa, 71-72; Lehigh Art Alliance Gold Medal Award, 72; plus others.
Memberships: Lehigh Artists Alliance; Woodmere Art Gallery; Allentown Art Mus; Pa Acad Fine Arts.
Mailing Address: 201 E State St, Coopersburg, PA 18036.

RIVERS, LARRY
Painter
b New York, N Y, 1923.
Study & Training: Hans Hofmann Sch Fine Arts, 47-48; New York Univ.
Work in Public Collections: Brooklyn Mus; Corcoran Gallery Art; Kansas City Art Inst; Metrop Mus Art; Minneapolis Inst Art; plus many others including pvt collections.
Commissions: Outdoor billboard, First New York Film Festival, 63.
Exhibitions: Nine shows, Whitney Mus Am Art, 54-64; Pa Acad Fine Arts, 63; retrospective exhib, Jewish Mus, N Y, 65; Marlborough Gallery, 68; Gotham Gallery, 68; plus many other group & one-man shows.
Teaching: Artist-in-residence, Slade Sch Fine Arts, London, 64.
Awards: Corcoran Gallery Art Award, 54.
Bibliography: William Gaunt (auth), The observer's book of modern art from impressionism to the present day, Frederick Warne & Co Ltd, London, 64; Lucy R Lippard (auth), Pop art, Praeger, 66; Sam Hunter (auth), Larry Rivers (monogr), Abrams, 70; plus many others.
Publications: Illusr, When the sun tries to go on.
Dealer: Marlborough Gallery Inc, 41 E 57th St, New York, NY 10022.
Mailing Address: 92 Little Plains Rd, Southampton, NY 11968.

RIZK, ROMANOS
Painter, Instructor
Preferred Media: Acrylics, Polymer, Collage.
b Providence, R I, Aug 12, 27.
Study & Training: Vesper George Sch Art, Boston, Mass; Butera Sch Art, Boston; Cape Sch Art, Provincetown, Mass, with Henry Hensche.
Work in Public Collections: Mus Fine Arts, Mobile, Ala; State St Bank Bldg Gallery, Boston.
Exhibitions: Cape Cod Art Asn & Provincetown Art Asn Juried Shows, 53-72; Cape Cod Art Asn Invitational, Hyannis, Mass, 63, 65 & 72; one-man show, Bristol Art Mus, R I, 70; Provincetown Art Asn Invitational, 71 & 72; one-man show, Arwin Galleries, Detroit, Mich, 72.

Teaching: Instr painting & dir, Romanos Rizk Sch Painting, Provincetown, 62-
Positions: Mem gov bd, Fine Arts Work Ctr, Provincetown, 68-70, mem adv comt, 70-
Awards: First prize, Falmouth Artists' Guild, 65, Cape Cod Art Asn, 65, 68 & 71 & Artists' Asn Nantucket, 66.
Memberships: Provincetown Art Asn (trustee, 67-).
Publications: Print ed painting, Int Art Publ Co, 70.
Dealer: The Arwin Galleries, 222 Grand River W, Detroit, MI 48226.
Mailing Address: 8 Kiley Ct, Provincetown, MA 02657.

ROBB, DAVID M
Educator, Art Historian
b Tak Hing Chau, China, Sept 19, 03; U S citizen.
Study & Training: Oberlin Col, AB, 26, AM, 27; Carnegie Found fel fine arts, 27-30; Princeton Univ, AM, 31, MFA, 35, Inst Advan Study fel, 38-39, PhD, 41.
Teaching: Assoc prof hist art, Colgate Univ, 30-35; assoc prof hist art, Univ Minn, 35-39; prof hist art, Univ Pa, 39-
Awards: Fulbright & Guggenheim fel.
Memberships: Col Art Asn Am (pres, 60-62); Soc Archit Historians; Philadelphia Art Alliance.
Research: Medieval art.
Publications: Co-auth, Art in the Western world, 35 & 62; auth, Harper history of painting, 52; auth, Art of the illuminated manuscript, 73.
Mailing Address: 506 Narberth Ave, Merion Station, PA 19066.

ROBB, MR & MRS SIDNEY R
Collectors
Mr Robb, b Boston, Mass, Oct 20, 00.
Study & Training: Mr Robb, Harvard Univ; Tufts Univ, hon LLD, 61; Harvard Univ, hon MA, 62; Boston Col, hon LHD, 64; Suffolk Univ, hon DCS, 66.
Positions: Mr Robb, trustee, Boston Mus Fine Arts.
Awards: Mr Robb, hon alumni, Hebrew Univ Jerusalem, 65.
Collection: Impressionists, primarily Degas, Pissarro, Vuillard, Mary Cassatt, Bonnard and Moore; sculptures—Degas, Maillol, Lehmbruck & Moore.
Mailing Address: 65 Commonwealth Ave, Boston, MA 02116.

ROBBIN, ANTHONY STUART
Painter
Preferred Media: Acrylics.
b Washington, D C, Nov 24, 43.
Study & Training: Columbia Col, BA; Yale Univ Sch Art, BFA & MFA.
Work in Public Collections: Addison Gallery Am Art, Andover, Mass.
Exhibitions: Group shows, Bykert Gallery, New York, N Y, 71 & Paley & Lowe Inc, New York, 72; guest exhib, Tyler Sch Art, Temple Univ, 72; Whitney Mus Am Art Ann, 72.
Publications: Auth, Smithson sites & non sites, Art News, 69; auth, Two ocean projects, 69 & auth, A protein sensibility, 71, Arts Mag; auth, Hutchison ecological art, Art Int, 70.
Mailing Address: 71 Franklin St, New York, NY 10013.

ROBBINS, DANIEL J
Educator, Art Historian
b New York, Jan 15, 33.
Study & Training: Univ Chicago, BA; Yale Univ, MA; N Y Univ Inst Fine Arts; Univ Paris.
Collections Arranged: Cezanne & Structure, 63 & Albert Gleizes Retrospective, 64-65, Guggenheim Mus Art; Contemp Wall Sculpture, 63-64 & Decade of New Talent, 64-65, Am Fedn Arts.
Teaching: Instr, Ind Univ, 55; prof, Brown Univ, 65-71; lectr, Harvard Univ.
Positions: Cur, Nat Gallery Art, Washington, D C, 59-60; cur, Guggenheim Mus Art, 61-64; dir, Mus Art, R I Sch Design, 64-71; dir, Fogg Art Mus, Harvard Univ, 71-
Awards: French Govt fel, Paris, 58; Fulbright grant, 58-59.
Publications: Auth, Painting between the wars, 65; auth, Joaquin Torres Garcia, Guggenheim Mus, 71; contribr, Art J, Art France, Art Int, Art News, Apollo, Studio Int & Bull Baltimore Mus Art.
Mailing Address: Fogg Art Museum, Harvard University, Cambridge, MA 02138.

ROBBINS, FRANK
Cartoonist, Illustrator
b Boston, Mass, Sept 9, 17.
Study & Training: Boston Mus Fine Arts Sch; Nat Acad Design.
Commissions: Portrait, Polyclinic Hosp, N Y.
Exhibitions: Whitney Mus Am Art, 56; Corcoran Gallery Art, 57 & 58; Toledo Mus Art, 57 & 58; Nat Acad Design, 57 & 58; Audubon Artists, 57 & 58; plus others.
Positions: Auth & illusr comic strip, Scorchy Smith, 39-44; auth & illusr comic strip, Johnny Hazard, Kings Features Syndicate, presently.

Awards: Prize, Nat Acad Design, 36.
Memberships: Nat Cartoonists Soc.
Publications: Contribr, Life, Look, Cosmopolitan & other nat mags.
Mailing Address: 285 Central Park West, New York, NY 10024.

ROBBINS, HULDA D
Painter, Printmaker
Preferred Media: Oils.
b Atlanta, Ga, Oct 19, 10.
Study & Training: Pa Mus Sch Indust Art, Philadelphia; Prussian Acad, Berlin, with Ludwig Bartning; Barnes Found, Merion, Pa.
Work in Public Collections: Metrop Mus Art, New York, N Y; Victoria & Albert Mus, London, Eng; Bibliot Nat, Paris; Art Mus Ont; Smithsonian Inst, Washington, D C.
Exhibitions: Portrait of America, New York & Tour, 45-46, Current Am Prints, Carnegie Inst, Pittsburgh, Pa, 48; Nat Print Ann, Brooklyn Mus & Tour, 48-49; Nat Exhib Prints, Libr Cong, Washington, D C, 56; U S Info Agency Print Exhib Europ Tour, 72-
Teaching: Instr, basic & advan serigraphy, Nat Serigraph Soc Sch, 54-60; instr creative painting, Atlantic Co Jewish Community Ctr, Margate, N J, 60-67.
Awards: Purchase award, Prints For Children, Mus Mod Art, 41; Paintings By Printmakers Award, 47 & Babette S Kornblith Purchase Prize, 49, Nat Serigraph Soc.
Memberships: Am Color Print Soc.
Mailing Address: 16 S Buffalo Ave, Ventnor, NJ 08406.

ROBBINS, WARREN M
Art Administrator, Educator
b Worcester, Mass, Sept 4, 23.
Study & Training: Univ N H, BA(eng), 45; Univ Mich, MA(hist), 49.
Collections Arranged: Traditional African Art from the Peabody Museum, 66; The Heritage of African Art, 67; Edward Mitchell Bannister, 67; Ben Shahn on Human Rights, 68; The Art of Henry O Tanner, 69; The Language of African Art, 70; African Art— The De Havenon Collection, 71; African Art in Washington Collections, 72.
Teaching: Lectr African art, Mus African Art, Washington, D C, 64-; lectr influence of African sculpture on mod western art, mus & univs in U S A, 68-
Positions: Founder/dir, Mus African Art, 64-
Research: Influence of African sculpture on modern western art.
Publications: Auth, African art in American collections, Praeger, 66; contribr, article, In: Art in Society, Vol 5, No 3; ed, The art of Henry O Tanner (exhib catalogue), 69; auth, The language of African Art (exhib catalogue), 70; auth, The impact of African sculpture on modern western art, Praeger, (in prep).
Mailing Address: Museum of African Art, 318 A St N E, Washington, DC 20002.

ROBERDS, GENE ALLEN
Printmaker
b Cole Camp, Mo, May 4, 35.
Study & Training: Eastern Ill State Col, BS, 57; Univ Ill, MFA, 61.
Work in Public Collections: Jacksonville Art Mus, Fla; Jacksonville Jr Col Gallery; Carver Orgn, Evansville, Ind.
Commissions: Vignette for stock cert, Dayton Corp, Minneapolis, Minn, 67.
Exhibitions: Minnesota Artists, Walker Art Ctr, 66; Art of Two Cities, New York, N Y, 66; Nat Invitational Print Show, San Diego, Calif, 71.
Teaching: Instr printmaking, Murray State Col, 61-64; asst prof printmaking, Minneapolis Sch Art, 64-68; asst prof printmaking, Jacksonville Univ, 68-71.
Positions: Owner-artist, St Augustine Prints, 70-
Memberships: Intercontinental Biog Asn.
Publications: Illusr, Minn Rev, 66; illusr, The metaphysical giraffe, 67.
Mailing Address: 15 1/2 St George St, St Augustine, FL 32084.

ROBERTS, CLYDE HARRY
Painter, Educator
Preferred Media: Watercolors.
b Sandusky, Ohio, June 12, 23.
Study & Training: Cleveland Inst Art, dipl, 46; Columbia Univ, MA, 49; also with John Pike & Robert Brackman.
Work in Public Collections: Washington Co Mus Fine Arts, Hagerstown, Md; Ford Times Gallery, Dearborn, Mich; Hill Top House, Harpers Ferry, W Va; Artists Unlimited, Washington, D C.
Exhibitions: Many exhibs, Baltimore Watercolor Open, Cumberland Valley Exhib, Miss Art Asn Open & Cleveland Mus May Show.
Teaching: Instr painting, Wash Co Mus Art, Hagerstown, 49-70; dir Sch, 68-70; instr painting, Hagerstown Jr Col, 57-; supvr art, Wash Co Bd Educ, 68-
Awards: First award, Miss Art Asn, 50; popular prize, Cumberland Valley Artists, 71; Artists Members Award, Baltimore Watercolor Club, 71.

Bibliography: Jerome Palms (auth), article, In: Ford Times Mag, 58; G Horn (auth), article, In: Art Today, 68.
Memberships: Baltimore Watercolor Club; Md Art Asn (secy, 62-64); Nat Art Educ Asn; Wash Co Arts Coun.
Publications: Illusr, Ford Times Mag, 58; contribr, Sch Arts, 68 & Artists News Unlimited, 71.
Dealer: Artists Unlimited, 11702 Mentone Rd, Silver Spring, MD 20906.
Mailing Address: 219 N Colonial Dr, Hagerstown, MD 21740.

ROBERTS, COLETTE (JACQUELINE)
Art Critic, Art Administrator
b Paris, France, Sept 16, 10; U S citizen.
Study & Training: Sorbonne, MA; Acad Ranson, with Roger Bissiere, 25-31; Ecole Louvre, 28-37; Inst Art & Archeol, with Henri Focillon.
Exhibitions: Exhibited extensively throughout France.
Collections Arranged: Organized exchange cult exhibs, sponsored by Am & Fr Embassies.
Teaching: The road to mod art summer lect series, Coun Int Educ Exchange, 51-; instr, Queens Col, N Y, 60; instr, New York Univ, 60, adj asst prof art hist, 68-
Positions: Directed & organized meet the artist prog, New York Univ; gallery dir, Nat Asn Women Artists, New York, 47-49; secy to cur Far Eastern art, Metrop Mus Art, 50-51; dir, Grand Cent Mod Gallery, N Y, 52-68; assoc dir, Sachs Gallery, New York, 68-
Awards: Palmes Academiques, 60; McDowell Colony fel, 60.
Specialty of Gallery: Modern American art.
Publications: Auth, Mark Tobey, 60, Louise Nevelson, sculptor, 64 & Pocket museum, 64; contribr, art ed, In: Fr-Am, 53-
Mailing Address: 510 E 85th St, New York, NY 10028.

ROBERTS, GILROY
Sculptor
b Mar 11, 05; U S citizen.
Study & Training: Frankford High Sch Eve Art Class, Philadelphia, Pa; Corcoran Gallery Art Sch; also with John R Sinnock & Heinz Warnsks.
Work in Public Collections: U S Mint, Philadelphia; Smithsonian Inst, Washington, D C; Franklin Mint, Franklin Ctr, Pa.
Commissions: Portrait of Anthony Drexel, Drexel Inst, Philadelphia, 38; Kennedy half dollar, U S Mint, Philadelphia, 63; portrait of Albert Einstein, Inst Advan Study, Princeton, N J; portrait of David Sarnoff, RCA Corp; portrait of Ernie Pyle, Scripps Howard News Alliance.
Exhibitions: Pa Acad Fine Arts, Philadelphia, 36-37; Corcoran Gallery Art, Washington, D C, 42; Nat Sculpture Soc, New York, N Y; Madrid, Spain, 51; Rome, Italy, 61.
Positions: Picture engraver, Bur Engraving & Painting, Washington, D C, 38-44; chief sculptor & engraver, U S Mint, Philadelphia, 48-64; chmn & chief sculptor, Franklin Mint, 64-
Awards: Hon mention, Nat Sculptors Soc, 51; gold medal & citation, Int Exhib Coins & Medals, Madrid, Spain, 51; gold medal, Numismatic Asn, 51.
Bibliography: Willard Garvin (auth), The suburb that has its own mint, Sunday Bull Mag, 1/51; Thomas Baker (auth), The creation of the Kennedy half dollar, Coin Asn Mag, 6/72.
Memberships: Fel Nat Sculpture Soc; Franklin Inst; Rittenhouse Astron Soc; Philadelphia Sketch Club.
Art Interests: Coins, medals & plaques.
Publications: Auth, Birth of a dime design, 10/67 & auth, Creating designs in circles, 5/68, Coins Mag.
Mailing Address: 7 Llangollen Lane, Newtown Square, PA 19073.

ROBERTS, (WILLIAM) GOODRIDGE
Painter
b Barbados, B W I, Sept 24, 04.
Study & Training: Beaux-Arts, Montreal, 24-26; Art Stud League New York, 27-29; Univ N B, LLD, 60.
Work in Public Collections: Nat Gallery Can; Montreal Mus Fine Arts; Vancouver Art Gallery; Winnipeg Art Gallery; Bezalel Mus, Israel; plus many others.
Commissions: Painting of Quebec landscape presented to Queen Elizabeth by Royal Can Air Force Asn, 54.
Exhibitions: Carnegie Inst, 52 & 55; Valencia Int, 55; Mexico City, Mex, 58; Brussels, Belg, 58; Tate Gallery, London, Eng, 64; plus many other group & one-man shows.
Teaching: Vis fel, Univ N B, 59-60.
Positions: Off war artist, RCAF, 43-45.
Awards: Prizes, Montreal Mus Fine Arts, 48 & 56 & Winnipeg Art Gallery, 57; Glazebrook Award, 59; plus many others.
Memberships: Can Group Painters; Can Soc Graphic Art; Can Soc Painters in Water Colour; Contemp Arts Soc, Montreal; Royal Can Acad; plus others.
Mailing Address: 355 Lansdowne Ave, Montreal, P Q, Can.

ROBERTS, LUCILLE D (MALKIA)
Painter, Educator
Preferred Media: Oils, Acrylics.
b Washington, D C.
Study & Training: Howard Univ; Univ Mich, AM; N Y Univ; Acad Grande Chaumière, Paris, France; Univ Ghana; also with Jose Gutierriez, Mexico City, Mex.
Work in Public Collections: Atlanta Univ Collection; W Va State Col Collection; Jefferson Community Col, Water Town, N Y.
Exhibitions: Nat Exhib Black Artists, Smith-Mason Gallery, Washington, D C, 71; Black Artists Exhib, Afro-Am Cult Ctr, Cleveland State Univ, 72; one-man shows, Porter Gallery, Howard Univ, 71 & Col Mus, Hampton Inst, 72.
Teaching: Asst prof art, D C Teachers Col, Washington, 65-; vis assoc prof African & Afro-Am art, State Univ N Y Col Oswego, 70-71.
Awards: First prize, mem show, 65 & Evening Star Award, 66, Soc Wash Artists; James A Porter Award, Cleveland State Univ, 72.
Bibliography: Lewis (auth) & Wadday (auth), Black artists on art, 69; J Edwin Atkinson (auth), Black dimensions in contemporary art, Carnation Co, 70.
Memberships: Nat Conf Artists; Black Acad Arts & Lett; Soc Washington Artists; D C Art Asn.
Mailing Address: 7333 New Hampshire Ave, Hyattsville, MD 20783.

ROBERTS, PRISCILLA WARREN
Painter
Preferred Media: Oils.
b Glen Ridge, N J, June 13, 16.
Study & Training: Art Stud League New York; Nat Acad Design.
Work in Public Collections: Metrop Mus Art, New York, N Y; Dallas Mus Fine Arts, Tex; Walker Art Ctr, Minneapolis, Minn; Butler Inst Am Art, Youngstown, Ohio; IBM Collection, New York.
Exhibitions: Carnegie Int, Pittsburgh, 50; Nat Acad Design, New York, 69; Corcoran Gallery Art, Washington, D C; Univ Ill, Urbana; Allied Artists, New York.
Awards: Hallgarten prizes & Proctor Portrait Prize, Nat Acad Design, 47; third prize, Carnegie Int, 50.
Memberships: Nat Acad Design; hon mem Catharine Lorillard Wolfe Asn.
Publications: Contribr, Pictures, painters, and you-Ray Bethers.
Dealer: Grand Central Galleries, 40 Vanderbilt Ave, New York, NY 10017.
Mailing Address: Box 281, Wilton, CT 06897.

ROBERTS, THOMAS (KIETH)
Painter
Preferred Media: Oils, Watercolors, Acrylics.
b Toronto, Ont, Dec 22, 09.
Study & Training: Cent Tech Sch, Toronto; Ont Col Art, Toronto.
Work in Public Collections: Ford Motor Co; Rio-Algom; Seagrams; plus collections of many other Can co & insts.
Exhibitions: Many Ann, Royal Acad Arts, Montreal & Toronto, Montreal Mus Fine Arts & Ont Soc Artists, Toronto, 29-
Awards: Ralph Clarke Stone Award, 49.
Memberships: Royal Can Acad; Ont Soc Artists.
Dealer: Eaton's Fine Art Galleries, Yonge & College Sts, Toronto, Ont, Can.
Mailing Address: 1312 Stavebank Rd, Port Credit, Ont, Can.

ROBERTSON, BRYAN
Writer
Positions: Staff mem, Arts Mag.
Publications: Ed, Jackson Pollock, In: Library of modern master ser, Abrams, 60.
Mailing Address: 70 E 96th St, New York, NY 10028.

ROBERTSON, D HALL
Painter
Preferred Media: Oils.
b Washington, D C, Aug 12, 18.
Study & Training: Corcoran Sch Art, Washington; Art Stud League New York.
Commissions: Mural, U S Govt Post Off, Miss, 40.
Exhibitions: Two Corcoran biennials, 39-45 & one-man show, 47, Corcoran Gallery Art, Washington; Carnegie Inst Print Exhib, 52; Best American Art During Last Five Years, Metrop Mus Art, New York, 54.
Teaching: Instr oil painting, U S Army, Pentagon, Washington, 69-
Position: Art dir, U S Army Hq Mil Dist, Washington, 54-
Awards: First prize in oils, 59 & first prize in watercolors, 69, Northern Va Fair.
Memberships: Am Fedn Arts.
Mailing Address: 140 E North St, Leesburg, VA 22075.

ROBINSON, FREDERICK B
Art Administrator
b Boston, Mass, Dec 23, 07.
Study & Training: Harvard Univ, Fogg Art Mus fel Study in Europe, BS; Western New Eng Col, hon LHD, 62.
Teaching: Prof art hist, Springfield Tech Community Col, 69-
Positions: Former dir, Mus Fine Arts, Springfield, Mass.
Awards: Outstanding Servant Pub, WWLP TV, 64; Benjamin Franklin fel, Royal Soc Encouragement Arts, London, Eng, 68.
Publications: Contribr, mus bull, art mags & newspapers.
Mailing Address: 135 Forest Glen Rd, Longmeadow, MA 01106.

ROBINSON, JAY THURSTON
Painter
b Detroit, Mich, Aug 1, 15.
Study & Training: Yale Col, BA; Cranbrook Acad Art, MFA.
Work in Public Collections: Cranbrook Mus, Bloomfield Hills, Mich; Detroit Inst Art, Mich; Houston Mus Fine Arts, Tex; J B Speed Mus, Louisville, Ky; Philbrook Art Ctr, Tulsa, Okla.
Exhibitions: Audubon Artists, New York, N Y; Carnegie Int, Pittsburgh, Pa; Corcoran Gallery Art Biennial, Washington, D C; Nat Acad Design, New York; Pa Acad Fine Arts, Philadelphia.
Awards: Louis Comfort Tiffany Found fel, 49; seven purchase awards, Childe Hassam Fund, Am Acad Arts & Lett.
Memberships: Artists Equity Asn New York.
Art Interests: Non-objective; semi-abstract on human themes; portraits.
Mailing Address: 60 Church St, Pleasantville, NY 10570.

ROBINSON, MARY TURLAY
Painter, Lecturer
Preferred Media: Oils.
b South Attleboro, Mass, Sept 7, 87.
Study & Training: Vassar Col, AB, 10; Art Stud League New York, N Y; Fontainebleau, France.
Commissions: Fresco (with La Montagne St Hubert), Expos Arts Decoratifs, 25.
Exhibitions: Salon Automne, Paris, France, 25; Kraushaar Gallery Shows; Fontainebleau Alumni Asn, Archit League; Am Woman's Asn; Cooper Union League; plus others.
Teaching: Lectr Background In Art, mem Metrop Mus Art & other mus & galleries, New York; lectr, Forming Collections, Jr League New York.
Awards: Best in Show, Am Woman's Asn; Jurors Choice, Art Asn Nantucket, 71.
Memberships: Art Asn Nantucket (jury comt, 70); nat mem Smithsonian Assocs; Artists Equity Asn New York (bd dirs); life mem Art Stud League New York (woman's v pres, 22 & 23); Fontainebleau Alumni Asn (liaison officer, 28).
Collection: American and French artists' paintings of the nineteenth and twentieth centuries.
Publications: Auth, articles in art mags & col publ, 71.
Mailing Address: 171 W 12th St, New York, NY 10011.

ROBINSON, ROBERT DOKE
Painter, Educator
b Kansas City, Kans, Nov 11, 22.
Study & Training: Minneapolis Sch Art; Walker Art Ctr Sch; Univ Minn, with S Chatwood Burton, BA, BS & MA; Okla State Univ, with Ivan Doseff & Schaefer-Simmern, cert.
Work in Public Collections: Chaffee Art Mus, Rutland, Vt; Lawrence Recreation Ct, Rutland.
Exhibitions: S Vt Art Ctr, Manchester, 61.
Teaching: Lectr art & the community & art educ, art clubs, gallery groups, high schs & cols; asst prof art & chmn dept, Castleton State Col, 60-
Positions: Owner & pres, R D Robinson Advert Co, 51-58; art dir, Grubb-Clealand Advert Agency; pres, Mid-Vt Artists, 63-65.
Memberships: Delta Phi Delta; Nat Art Educ Asn; Eastern Art Asn.
Publications: Contribr illus, nat & int mod med publ & others.
Mailing Address: Dept of Art, Castleton State College, Castleton, VT 05735.

ROBINSON, THOMAS
Art Dealer, Collector
b Fort Worth, Tex, Feb 9, 38.
Study & Training: Tex Christian Univ; Tex Wesleyan Col.
Positions: Dir, Robinson Galleries, Inc, 69-
Bibliography: Brochure, 1/71; article, In: S W Art Gallery Mag, 6/71.
Specialty of Gallery: Art of the nineteenth & twentieth centurys in America; American sculpture, paintings & graphics.
Mailing Address: Robinson Galleries, Inc, 3220 Louisiana St, Houston, TX 77006.

ROBINSON, WAHNETA THERESA
Curator, Art Historian
b Adrian, Mich.
Study & Training: Long Beach City Col, AA; Long Beach State Univ, BA & MA; Univ Calif, Los Angeles, with Dr E Maurice Bloch.
Collections Arranged: Nineteenth Century American Landscape Painting, 66; Seven Decades of Design, 67; African Art, 68; Alexander Calder's Gouaches, 70; American Portraits—Old & New, 71; Masuo Ikeda—Prints, 71; Hans Burkhardt—Retrospect, 72; William Gropper—Paintings & Graphics, 72.
Positions: Cur, Long Beach Mus Art, Calif, 66-
Memberships: Col Art Asn; Art Historians Southern Calif; Am Asn Univ Women.
Research: Essential historical data gathered about artists and art works for exhibition, publication and lectures.
Publications: Auth catalogues, Nineteenth century American landscape painting, 66, Seven decades of design, 67, Alexander Calder's gouaches, 70, American portraits—old & new, 71 & Masuo Ikeda—prints, 71.
Mailing Address: 2300 E Ocean Blvd, Long Beach, CA 90803.

ROBLES, ESTHER WAGGONER
Art Dealer, Collector
b Sacramento, Calif.
Study & Training: Cumnock Sch Girls & Sch Expression, Los Angeles; Univ Calif, Los Angeles; Univ Paris; toured art monuments in Europe.
Collections Arranged: Co-organizer & catalog, Karel Appel West Coast Exhib, La Jolla Art Mus, Pasadena Mus, Phoenix Art Mus, San Francisco Art Mus & Santa Barbara Art Mus, 61-62; Robert Cremean Sculpture Exhib with catalog, Sheldon Mem Art Gallery, Univ Nebr, Univ Tex, Univ Colo, Fort Worth Art Ctr, State Univ Iowa, Krannert Art Mus of Univ Ill & Munic Art Dept, Barnsdalle Galleries, Los Angeles, 64-66; Robert Cremean Sculpture Tour with catalog, Calif Arts Comn, 66-67.
Teaching: Lectr, Development of La Cienega and Los Angeles as a Major Art Center & Current Materials of Art: Light/Sound/Movement/Plastics.
Positions: Adv, Fed Arts Proj, Calif Arts Comn; art corresp, Los Angeles newspapers, Venice Biennale & Documenta 4, Kassel, Ger; v pres, Southern Calif Art Dealers Asn, 70-72; hon mem art adv panel, Comn Internal Revenue, 70-72; organizer & pres, Art Sponsors, Inc; ed, The Lively Arts; dir exhibs, Esther Robles Gallery.
Memberships: Los Angeles Co Mus Art (graphic arts coun & contemp art coun); Western Asn Mus; Pasadena Mus; Univ Calif, Los Angeles, Alumni Asn.
Specialty of Gallery: Twentieth century and vanguard painting and sculpture.
Collection: American & European artists, toured by Western Association of Art Museums; works by Appel, Bissier, Capograossi, Davie, Ehrenhalt, Frost, Hartung, Hofmann, Matta, Jenkins, Robles, Scott, Magritte, Seuphor, Falkenstein, Hayter, Tapies, Feininger, Giacometti, Battenberg, Cremean and Hajdu.
Mailing Address: 12947 San Vicente Blvd, Los Angeles, CA 90049.

ROBLES, GLENN (WAGGONER)
Printmaker, Painter
b Los Angeles, Calif.
Study & Training: Seong Moy Graphic Sch; Los Angeles City Col; Univ Calif, Los Angeles.
Work in Public Collections: Many pvt collections.
Exhibitions: West Side Jewish Community Ctr, Los Angeles, 63; La Jolla Mus Art, Calif, 64; Long Beach Mus Art, Calif, 64; Los Angeles Co Mus Art, 64; N Y/L A Drawings of the 60's, 66; plus many other group & one-man shows.
Mailing Address: c/o Esther-Robles Gallery, 665 N La Cienega Blvd, Los Angeles, CA 90069.

ROBLES, JULIAN
Painter, Sculptor
b Bronx, N Y, June 24, 33.
Study & Training: Nat Acad Art & Design, with Robert Phillip; Art Stud League New York, with Sidney Dickinson.
Work in Public Collections: N Mex State Fair Gallery, Albuquerque; Diamond M Mus, Snyder, Tex.
Commissions: Portraits, Haruke Fujita, wife of Consul Gen Japan, 67, Adm Edward O McDonnell, Lincoln Family, Oyster Bay, L I, 68, Ernestine Evans, Secy State N Mex, 69, Margaret Jamison, Santa Fe, N Mex, 70 & Jean & Merle Rosenbaum, Santa Fe, 71.
Exhibitions: N Mex State Fair Art Exhib, Albuquerque, 71.
Awards: First award-purchase prize, N Mex State Fair, 71; second prize (pastels), N Mex Fine Art Award, 72.
Research: Researching and recording authentic western Indian life and ceremonials.
Mailing Address: P O Box 1845, Taos, NM 87571.

ROCHE, JIM
Sculptor, Painter
Preferred Media: Ceramic, Wire, Plastic, Ink.
b Jackson Co, Fla, Nov 21, 43.
Study & Training: Fla State Univ, BA; Univ Dallas, MA & MFA.
Exhibitions: Whitney Sculpture Ann, Whitney Mus Am Art, New York, N Y, 70; Project: South/Southwest, Fort Worth Art Ctr Mus, Tex, 70; Six Major Pieces by Six Young Sculptors, A Clean Well Lighted Place, Austin, Tex, 71; Drawings 71-72, Janie C Lee Gallery, Dallas, Tex, 71-72; Interchange, Dallas Mus Fine arts & Walker Art Ctr, Minn, 72-73.
Awards: Exhib awards, Fort Worth Art Ctr Mus, 70 & 71.
Bibliography: Martha Utterback (auth), Texas, Artforum, 1/71; Janet Kutner (auth), Texas/a new environment, Art Gallery Mag, 7/72; Kent Biffle (auth), Art/Big D, Newsweek, 8/72.
Dealer: Dave Hickey, 306 E 50th St, New York, NY 10022.
Mailing Address: P O Box 1252, Irving, TX 75060.

ROCKBURNE, DOROTHEA
Sculptor
b Verdun, P Q, Can.
Study & Training: Black Mountain Col, BA.
Work in Public Collections: Mus Mod Art, New York, N Y; Walker Art Ctr, Minneapolis, Minn.
Exhibitions: One-man show, Sannabend Gallery, Paris, 71; Mus Mod Art, New York, 71; one-man show, Bykert Gallery, New York, 70, 72 & 73; Documenta 5, Kassel, W Ger, 72.
Teaching: Instr art theory, Sch Visual Arts, New York, 70-
Awards: Guggenheim fel, 72-73.
Bibliography: Robert Pincus-Witten (auth), article, In: Artforum, 2/71; Gregoire Muller (auth), Materialith Painterlines, Arts Mag, 10/71; cover photo & three articles, Artforum, 4/72.
Mailing Address: c/o Bykert Gallery, 24 E 81st St, New York, NY 10028.

ROCKEFELLER, MR & MRS DAVID
Collectors
Mr Rockefeller, b New York, N Y, June 12, 15.
Study & Training: Mr Rockefeller, Harvard Univ, BS, 36; Univ Chicago, PhD, 40; Columbia Univ, LLD, 54, Bowdoin Col, 58, Jewish Theol Sem, 58, Williams Col, 66, Wagner Col, 67, Harvard Univ, 69, Pace Col, 70.
Positions: Trustee & chmn bd trustees, Mus Mod Art, New York.
Collections: Paintings, modern art.
Mailing Address: 146 E 65th St, New York, NY 10021.

ROCKEFELLER, JOHN DAVISON, III
Collector, Patron
b New York, N Y, Mar 21, 06.
Study & Training: Princeton Univ, BS, 29.
Positions: Bd mem, Am Mus Natural Hist, 33-55; dir, Lincoln Ctr Performing Arts, Inc, chmn, 61-70, hon chmn, 70-; emer trustee, Princeton Univ.
Memberships: Asia Soc (pres & trustee, 56-64, chmn, 65-); Am Asn Mus; life mem Brooklyn Mus & Metrop Mus Art; corp mem Mus Mod Art; Mus Primitive Art; plus others.
Collection: Emphasis on Asian art.
Mailing Address: 30 Rockefeller Plaza, New York, NY 10022.

ROCKEFELLER, MRS LAURANCE S
Collector
Mailing Address: 834 Fifth Ave, New York, NY 10021.

ROCKEFELLER, NELSON ALDRICH
Collector, Patron
b Bar Harbor, Maine, July 8, 08.
Study & Training: Dartmouth Col, AB, 30.
Positions: Trustee, Mus Mod Art, 32-, pres, 39-41 & 46-53, chmn, 57-58; founder, trustee & pres, Mus Primitive Art, 54-; hon trustee, Metrop Mus Art.
Memberships: Am Asn Mus; Asia Soc; Assocs Guggenheim Mus; life mem Col Art Asn Am; Coun Nat Mus France.
Collection: Emphasis on modern art.
Mailing Address: The Executive Mansion, Albany, NY 12202.

ROCKEFELLER, MR & MRS WINTHROP
Collectors
Mr Rockefeller, b New York, N Y, May 1, 12.
Study & Training: Mr Rockefeller, Yale Univ, 31-34; Univ Ark, hon LLD, Hendrix Col, Col William & Mary, Col Ozarks; New York Univ, LHD; Univ San Francis Xavier, Suere, Bolivia, HHD; Southwestern at Memphis, DCL.
Positions: Chmn bd, Colonial Williamsburg & Williamsburg Restoration.
Collection: Paintings and furniture.
Mailing Address: 1 East End Ave, New York, NY 10021.

ROCKLIN, RAYMOND
Sculptor, Lecturer
Preferred Media: Bronze, Steel, Wood.
b Moodus, Conn, Aug 18, 22.
Study & Training: Educ Alliance, New York, N Y, with Abbo Ostrovsky; Cooper Union Art Sch, with Milton Hebald & John Hovannes.
Work in Public Collections: Whitney Mus Am Art, New York; Provincetown Mus Art, Mass; Temple Israel, Saint Louis; Skowhegan Sch Painting & Sculpture.
Commissions: Wall brass, comn by Mrs Beskind, New York, 62 & Mrs Nina Waller, Baltimore, 63.
Exhibitions: Young Am, Whitney Mus Am Art, 56; Oakland Art Mus, 59; Gallerina Tiberina, Rome, 59; Univ Calif, Berkeley, 60; Claude Bernard Gallery, Paris, 60.
Teaching: Guest artist, Am Univ, 56; asst prof art, Univ Calif, Berkeley, 59-60; guest artist, Ball State Teachers Col, summer 64.
Awards: Cooper Union Art Sch scholar to Skowhegan Sch Painting & Sculpture, 51; Fulbright grant, Italy, 52-53; Yaddo Found fel, 56.
Bibliography: M Seuphor (auth), Raymond Rocklin, The sculpture of this century, 61; F Hazan (auth), article, In: Dictionary of modern sculpture.
Memberships: Sculptors Guild; Am Abstr Artists; Fedn Mod Painters & Sculptors.
Dealer: Sculptors Guild, 122 E 42nd St, New York, NY 10017.
Mailing Address: 232B Watch Hill Rd, Peekskill, NY 10566.

ROCKMORE, NOEL
Painter
b New York, N Y, Dec 28.
Exhibitions: Cleveland Mus Art, Ohio; Isaac Delgado Mus Art, New Orleans, La; Butler Inst Am Art, Youngstown, Ohio; Whitney Mus Am Art, Mus Mod Art & Metrop Mus Art, New York, N Y; Pa Acad Fine Arts, Philadelphia; plus one-man shows.
Awards: Hallgarten prize, 56 & 57 & Wallace Truman prize, 59, Nat Acad Design; Tiffany Found fels, 56 & 63; Ford Found & Am Fedn Arts grant, 64; plus others.
Publications: Auth, Preservation Hall portraits, 68.
Mailing Address: 638 Royal St, New Orleans, LA 70130.

ROCKWELL, NORMAN
Illustrator
b New York, N Y, Feb 3, 94.
Study & Training: Art Stud League New York; Univ Vt, DFA, 49; Middlebury Col, HHD, 54; Univ Mass, DFA, 61; also with George Bridgeman & Thomas Fogarty.
Work in Public Collections: Metrop Mus Art, New York.
Memberships: Soc Illusr.
Publications: Auth, Norman Rockwell, illustrator, 46, Norman Rockwell: my adventures as an illustrator, 59 & The Norman Rockwell Album, 61; contribr, Sat Eve Post & Look Mag; plus others.
Mailing Address: Stockbridge, MA 01262.

RODMAN, SELDEN
Writer, Collector
b New York, N Y, Feb 19, 09.
Study & Training: Yale Univ, 31.
Positions: Art comnr, State N J, 64-65.
Art Interests: Initiated and directed tempera murals by eight self-taught artists in Cathedral St-Trinité, Port-au-Prince, Haiti, 49-51; comn three murals by Seymour Leichman and sculpture by James Kearns, 60-68.
Collection: Contemporary figurative painting and sculpture; collection has been widely shown in the United States and Mexico, and has been catalogued by Vanderbilt University and by San Carlos Academy, Mexico.
Publications: Auth, The eye of man, 56, Conversations with artists, 57 & The insiders, 59.
Mailing Address: 659 Valley Rd, Oakland, NJ 07436.

RODRIGUEZ LUNA, ANTONIO
Painter
Preferred Media: Oils.
b Montoro, Spain, June 22, 10; Mex citizen.
Study & Training: Sch Fine Arts, Seville, 23-27; Royal Acad San Fernando, Madrid, 27-29.
Work in Public Collections: Nat Mus Mod Art, Madrid, Spain; Fine Arts Gallery San Diego, Calif; Nat Mus Mod Art, Mexico City, Mex.
Exhibitions: One-man shows, Venice Biennial (representing Spain), 34, Nat Mus, Washington, D C, 41, Retrospective, Nat Palace Fine Arts, Mexico D F, 59, Fine Arts Gallery San Diego, 67 & Wenger Gallery, San Francisco, Calif, 70.
Teaching: Prof painting, San Carlos Acad, Nat Univ Mex, 49-69.

Awards: First prize for painting, Nat Contest Painting & Design, Barcelona, 38; Guggenheim fel, 41-43; first prize for painting, Nat Inst Fine Arts Ann, Mex, 63.
Bibliography: M Nelkin (auth), El expresionismo Mexicano, Inst Nac Bellas Artes, 64; Image of Mexico, Tex Quart, 69; Juan Rejano (auth), Antonio Rodriguez Luna, Nat Univ Mex, 71.
Mailing Address: c/o Wenger Gallery, 855 Montgomery St, San Francisco, CA 94133.

ROEBLING, MARY G
Collector, Patron
b Collingswood, N J, July 29, 05.
Awards: Am Art Asn; Arch Am Art; Philadelphia Print Club; N J Cult Ctr Adv Coun (first chmn); Metrop Mus Art.
Collection: Paintings, sculpture, fine porcelain and glass.
Mailing Address: Lafayette House, 777 W State St, Trenton, NJ 08618.

ROELOFS, MRS RICHARD, JR
Collector
Mailing Address: 115 E 67th St, New York, NY 10021.

ROESCH, KURT (FERDINAND)
Painter
b Berlin, Ger, Sept 12, 05; U S citizen.
Study & Training: Acad Art, Berlin.
Work in Public Collections: Mus Mod Art, New York, N Y; Albright-Knox Art Gallery, Buffalo, N Y; Metrop Mus Art, New York; Currier Gallery, Manchester, N H; Univ Nebr.
Exhibitions: Four exhibs at Carnegie Inst, 41-58; Documenta, Kassel, Ger, 55; one-man shows, Curt Valentin Gallery, 49-53; Currier Gallery, 55.
Positions: Emer mem faculty, Sarah Lawrence Col.
Memberships: N H Art Asn.
Mailing Address: Richards Lane, New Canaan, CT 06840.

ROESLER, NORBERT LEONHARD HUGO
Collector
b Plankenberg, Austria, Aug 8, 01; U S citizen.
Memberships: Drawing Soc; fel Pierpont Morgan Libr.
Collection: Drawings by Dutch, French, Italian, English and others.
Mailing Address: 785 Park Ave, New York, NY 10021.

ROGALSKI, WALTER
Printmaker, Lecturer
b Glen Cove, N Y, Apr 10, 23.
Study & Training: Brooklyn Mus Sch, with Xavier Gonzalez, Arthur Osver, C Seide & Gabor Peterdi, 47-51.
Work in Public Collections: Mus Mod Art; Brooklyn Mus; Cleveland Mus Art; Fogg Mus Art; Seattle Art Mus; plus many others.
Exhibitions: Six shows, Brooklyn Mus, 51-68; Soc Am Graphic Artists, 66 & 69; Cincinnati Mus Asn, 68; Am Fedn Arts Traveling Exhib, 69; Nat Print Exhib, Potsdam, N Y, 69; plus many others.
Teaching: Lectr etching, engraving, lithography & photo silk-screening; assoc prof graphic art, grad sch art & design, Pratt Inst.
Awards: Prizes, DeCordova & Dana Mus, 61 & Yale Gallery Fine Arts, 61; purchase prize, Assoc Am Artists, 66; plus others.
Memberships: Soc Am Graphic Artists.
Publications: Auth, Prints and drawings by Walter R Rogalski (catalogue), Print Club Cleveland & Cleveland Mus Art, 54; contribr, Artists Proof Mag.
Mailing Address: 15 Cross St, Locust Valley, NY 11560.

ROGERS, CHARLES B
Painter, Museum Director
b Great Bend, Kans, Jan 27, 11.
Study & Training: Nat Acad Design; Tiffany Found; Bethany Col, BFA; Calif Col Arts & Crafts, MFA; with Dong Kingman; Jay Connaway Sch Art.
Work in Public Collections: Libr of Cong Pennell Collection, Washington, D C; Metrop Mus Art Arms Collection, New York, N Y; Inst Mex Notreamericanos, Mexico City; Philadelphia Mus Art; Boston Pub Libr.
Commissions: Mural, U S Govt Post Off, Council Grove, Kans, 40; Smoky Valley Landscape, Citizens Bank Mem, Ells, Kans, 69; Splitter Farm, Dr Stan Splitter, Oakland, Calif, 71; Autumn in Kansas, C L Clark Law Off, Salina, Kans, 72.
Exhibitions: One-man exhibs, U S Nat Mus, Smithsonian Inst, Washington, D C, Inst Mex Norteamericano, Mexico City, Munic Tower Galleries, Los Angeles, Calif, Galleries de Arte, Monterrey, Mex & Inst Technol, Rochester, N Y; plus many other group & one-man shows.
Collections Arranged: The Great West-Paintings & Prints by Charles B Rogers; Paintings of the Southwest by Peter Hurd, Bethany College.

Teaching: Head sch art, Bethany Col, 47-53; head sch art, Kans Wesleyan Univ, 66-67.
Positions: Mgr & asst dir, Huntington Hartford Found, 54-66; dir, Rogers House Mus-Gallery, 67-
Awards: Over 130 art awards including, Am Inst Fine Arts & Mikami Award.
Bibliography: Ed Smith (auth), Charles B Rogers—artist, Kans State Publ, 68; art professor Charles B Rogers, Kans State Univ, 69.
Memberships: Soc Am Graphic Artists; Carmel Art Asn, Calif; Prairie Watercolor Painters; Kans Fedn Art (v pres, bd mem, 71-).
Specialty of Gallery: Paintings & prints of the great west.
Publications: Auth, Painting the American west, Artists Mag, London; auth, Charles B Rogers pleads for the spirit in art, Am Artist Mag, 8/63; auth, Heart of art, Art & Artists, 65; auth, Quill of the Kansan, privately publ, 70.
Mailing Address: Rogers House Museum-Gallery, Snake Row, Ellsworth, KS 67439.

ROGERS, JAMES B
Painter
Preferred Media: Acrylics.
b Detroit, Mich.
Study & Training: Univ Ill; Univ Miami; Md Inst Art, BFA.
Work in Public Collections: Long Beach Mus Art, Calif; Douglas Col, New Brunswick, N J; Founder's Collection, Calif State Col Syst; New Brunswick Pub Libr, N J; U S NATO Hq, Brussels, Belgium.
Commissions: Series of industrial paintings, Chem Bank World Hq, New York, N Y; series of paintings, Kidder-Peabody Corp World Hq, New York, 70.
Exhibitions: All Maryland, Baltimore Mus Art, 56; Conn Biennial, Wadsworth Atheneum, Hartford, 65; Newport Ann, R I, 66; Jersey City Ann, Jersey City Mus Art, 67; Hortt Mem, Fort Lauderdale Mus Art, Fla, 71.
Awards: Contemp Am Art-World Tour, U S State Dept, 64; travel exhib award, Salmagundi Club, 68.
Memberships: Provincetown Art Asn.
Dealer: McKenzie Gallery, 861 N La Cienega Blvd, Los Angeles, CA 90069.
Mailing Address: 9275 Flicker Pl, Los Angeles, CA 90069.

ROGERS, JOHN
Painter, Lecturer
Preferred Media: Watercolors.
b Brooklyn, N Y, Dec 9, 06.
Study & Training: Art Stud League New York, N Y.
Exhibitions: Am Watercolor Soc, 41-72; Brooklyn Mus Int, 46; Watercolor U S A, Springfield, Mo, 62; Watercolor Soc, London, 65; Nat Acad Design, 70.
Teaching: Instr watercolors, Garden City Adult Sch, 55-70; instr watercolors, Elmont Adult Prog, 57-70.
Positions: Artist, New York Times, 28-30; artist & illusr, New York Post, 50-55.
Awards: Am Watercolor Soc Silver Medal, 42; first prize in watercolor, Salmagundi Club, 70; gold medal, Am Artists Prof League.
Bibliography: Norman Kent (auth), John Rogers, watercolorist, Am Artist, 48.
Memberships: Am Watercolor Soc (exhib chmn, 68); Am Artists Prof League; Salmagundi Club; Art League Nassau Co (pres, 66); Art Stud League New York.
Publications: Auth, articles, In: Am Artist, 48, Design Mag, 51, Artist's Mag, London, 52 & Watercolor Simplified, 65.
Dealer: Garden City Gallery, 923 Franklin Ave, Garden City, NY 11530.
Mailing Address: 2107 Renfrew Ave, Elmont, NY 11003.

ROGERS, JOHN H
Sculptor, Educator
Preferred Media: Bronze, Wood.
b Walton, Ky, Dec 20, 21.
Study & Training: Eastern Ky Univ; Tyler Sch Art, Temple Univ, BFA & MFA.
Work in Public Collections: Ala Archives, Montgomery; Marine Corps Combat Art Collection, Marine Corps Mus, Washington, D C; Auburn Univ, Ala.
Commissions: Bust of Gen H M Smith USMC, Ala Archives, Montgomery, 69.
Exhibitions: Minneapolis Womens Club Ann Print Show, Minn, 66; Armed Forces of U S as Seen by the Contemporary Artist, Smithsonian Inst, Washington, 68; Artists in Vietnam, Smithsonian Traveling Exhib Serv, 68-70; Atlanta Sch Art Faculty Exhib, High Mus Art, Ga, 72.
Teaching: Sr seminar humanities, Atlanta Sch Art, 70-71.
Positions: Acad dean, Minneapolis Col Art & Design, 64-68; asst

head, Marine Corps Combat Art Prog, Washington, 68-69, head, 69-70; dean, Atlanta Sch Art, Ga, 70-
Awards: Mem award, Minneapolis Womens Club, 66.
Memberships: Nat Asn Schs Art (del, 71-72); Southeastern Col Art Conf (del, 72); Col Art Asn (del, 71-72).
Publications: Auth, Minn Educ Asn J, 67.
Mailing Address: 1153 Cumberland Rd N E, Atlanta, GA 30306.

ROGERS, LEO M
Collector
b Boston, Mass, Dec 24, 02.
Study & Training: Columbia Col, BA, 23; Columbia Univ, ChE, 25.
Collection: Cezanne, Manet, Degas, Soutine, Modigliani, Sisley, Signac, Rouault, Vuillard, Picasso, Pascin, Lautrec, Cassat, Renoir, Pisarro, Van Gogh, Morisot, Daumier, Brach, Homer & Ryder.
Mailing Address: 601 Longboat Club Rd, Sarasota, FL 33577.

ROGERS, MILLARD FOSTER, JR
Art Administrator, Art Historian
b Texarkana, Tex, Aug 27, 32.
Study & Training: Mich State Univ, BA(hon), 54; Univ Mich, MA, 58; Victoria & Albert Mus, London, 59, with John Pope-Hennessy.
Collections Arranged: New Eng Glass Co, 1818-1880, Toledo Mus Art, 63; Indian Miniature Painting, 71 & Canadian Landscapes, 73, Univ Wis.
Teaching: Assoc prof mus training & connoisseurship, Univ Wis-Madison, 67-
Positions: Asst to dir, Toledo Mus Art, Ohio, 59-63, cur Am art, 64-67; dir, Elvehjem Art Ctr, Univ Wis-Madison, 67-
Awards: Gosline fel, Toledo Mus Art, 58-59.
Memberships: Asn Art Mus Dirs; Am Asn Mus.
Research: Junius Brutus Stearns, 1815-1885.
Publications: Auth, La pintura Española en el Museo de Arte de Toledo, Goya, 8/62, The salutation of Beatrice by Dante Gabriel Rossetti, Connoisseur, 7/63, Benjamin West and the caliph: two paintings for Fonthill Abbey, Apollo, 6/66; Ivydia, popular Victorian image, Antiques, 3/70 & Randolph Rogers, American sculptor in Rome, Univ Mass Press, 71.
Mailing Address: Elvehjem Art Center, University of Wisconsin-Madison, 800 University Ave, Madison, WI 53706.

ROGERS, OTTO DONALD
Painter, Educator
Preferred Media: Acrylics.
b Kerrobert, Sask, Nov 19, 35.
Study & Training: Sask Teacher's Col, teacher cert, 53; Univ Wis, BSc(Art educ), 58, MA(fine art), 59.
Work in Public Collections: Nat Gallery Can, Ottawa; Montreal Mus Fine Arts; Nat Mus Iceland, Reykjavik; Fredericton Art Gallery, N B; Windsor Art Gallery, Ont.
Commissions: Sculpture in steel (with George Kerr, architect), Prince Albert Regional Libr, 65.
Exhibitions: Biennial, 66 & Royal Can Acad Art Exhib, 70, Nat Gallery Can; Directors Choice Exhib, sponsored by Can Coun, Confedn Art Gallery & Mus, Charlottetown, Prince Edward Island, 68; Art in Saskatchewan, Waddington Fine Arts Gallery, Montreal, 69; Art Bank Can Exhib, Mendel Gallery, Saskatoon, 72.
Teaching: Assoc prof painting, Univ Sask, 59-, head art dept, 73-
Positions: Mem acquisitions comt, Mendel Gallery, 72-73.
Awards: Sr award for study in Europe, Can Coun, 67-68.
Bibliography: R Harper (auth), History of Canadian painting, 66; W Townshend (auth), Canadian art today, Studio Int, 70; C McConnell (auth), Otto Rogers, Arts Can, 71.
Memberships: Assoc Royal Can Acad Art.
Mailing Address: Dept of Art, University of Saskatchewan, Saskatoon, Sask, Can.

ROGERS, P J
Printmaker, Painter
Preferred Media: Graphics.
b Rochester, N Y, June 13, 25.
Study & Training: Wells Col, Aurora, N Y, BA; Univ Buffalo Grad Sch; Acad Fine Arts, Vienna; Art Stud League New York; also with Victor Hammer, Lazlo Szabo & Robert Brackman.
Commissions: Portrait comns, Buffalo, N Y, Akron, Ohio, Los Angeles, Calif & Hudson, Ohio, 52-72; murals for Hall of Man, Buffalo Mus Sci, 53-55; portrait of founder, Novatny Elec Co, Akron, 67; poster for opening of new theater, Akron Weathervane Theater, 70.
Exhibitions: Big Bend Nat, Tallahassee, Fla, 68; Akron Art Inst May Show, 69; 34th Ohio Artists & Craftsmen Show, Massillon Mus, Ohio, 70; Canton Art Inst Ann All Ohio Fall show, 70 & 71; plus others.
Teaching: Instr painting, Buffalo Mus Sci, 55; instr arts-crafts, Univ Akron Spec Progs, 58.
Positions: Art preparator, Buffalo Mus Sci, 52-55.
Awards: Second prize, Univ Akron, 69; hon award, Ohio Print Show, Cuyahoga Valley Art Inst, 69.

Memberships: Women's Art League Akron (corres secy, 68-70).
Dealers: Summerfeld Gallery, Dobbs Ferry, NY 10522; Drawing Room Gallery, Rte 303, Main St, Peninsula, OH 44264.
Mailing Address: 954 Hereford Dr, Akron, OH 44303.

ROGERS, PETER WILFRID
Painter
Preferred Media: Oils, Acrylics, Ink.
b London, Eng, Aug 24, 33.
Study & Training: St Martins Sch Art, London, Eng.
Work in Public Collections: Bristol Art Gallery, Eng; Roswell Mus, N Mex; Macnider Mus, Mason City, Iowa; Mus of Southwest, Midland, Tex.
Commissions: Mural, Tex State Archives & Libr, Austin, 64; 48 paintings & drawings of Alaska, Atlantic Richfield Co, New York, N Y, 70-71.
Exhibitions: Royal Soc Brit Artists, 57-59; Religious Paintings, Birmingham Mus Art, Ala, 67; Biennial, Santa Fe, N Mex, 70.
Publications: Auth & illusr, The quest.
Dealer: Artium Orbis Gallery, 558 Canyon Rd, Santa Fe, NM 87501.
Mailing Address: San Patricio, NM 88348.

ROGOVIN, HOWARD SAND
Painter
b Ashville, N C, Feb 22, 27.
Study & Training: Northwestern Univ, BS; Art Stud League New York, with Kantor & Grosz; Univ Colo, MFA.
Teaching: Vis artist, Kansas City Art Inst, Mo, 68-69; assoc prof drawing, Univ Iowa, 69-72.
Awards: Yaddo, 60; Nat Coun Arts, 69; Old Gold Medal, Univ Iowa, 70.
Dealer: Babcock Gallery, 805 Madison Ave, New York, NY 10021.
Mailing Address: 1428 Lexington Ave, New York, NY 10028.

ROHLFING, CHRISTIAN
Art Administrator, Curator
b Philadelphia, Pa, Nov 11, 16.
Study & Training: Univ Chicago.
Positions: Bd dirs & adv bd, Four Winds Mus Theatre; adminr & cur exhibs, Cooper-Hewitt Mus Design, New York, N Y, presently.
Mailing Address: 343 E 30th St, New York, NY 10016.

ROHM, ROBERT
Sculptor
b Cincinnati, Ohio, Feb 6, 34.
Study & Training: Pratt Inst, BID, 56; Cranbrook Acad Art, Bloomfield Hills, Mich, MFA, 60.
Work in Public Collections: Mus Mod Art, New York, N Y; Kunsthalle, Zurich, Switz; Finch Col Mus, New York; Columbus Gallery Fine Art, Ohio; Allen Art Mus, Oberlin Col, Ohio.
Exhibitions: Anti-illusion: Procedures/Materials, 69 & Sculpture Ann, 70, Whitney Mus Am Art; 955,000, Vancouver Art Mus, B C, 70; one-man exhib, O K Harris, Works of Art, New York, 70 & 71; U S Sect, Triennial, New Delhi, India, 71.
Teaching: Instr sculpture, Columbus Col Art & Design, 56-59; instr sculpture, Pratt Inst, 60-65; assoc prof sculpture, Univ R I, 65-, res grant-in-aid, 65, 66 & 69.
Awards: Guggenheim Found fel, 64; Cassandra Found Award, 67.
Bibliography: Ralph Pomeroy (auth), An interview with Robert Rohm, Artforum, 4/70 & Robert Rohm, Arts Can, 4/70; Kenneth Baker (auth), The way works of art behave, Christian Sci Monitor, 12/14/70.
Dealer: O K Harris, Works of Art, 469 W Broadway, New York, NY 10012.
Mailing Address: 26 Lake St, Wakefield, RI 02879.

ROJO, VICENTE
Painter
Preferred Media: Oils.
b Barcelona, Spain, Nov 15, 32.
Work in Public Collections: Mus Mod Art, Mex; Banco Cedulas Hipotecarias S A, Mex; Casa de las Americas, Havana, Cuba; Biblioteca Luis Arango, Bogota, Colombia.
Commissions: Portfolio of five lithographs, Lublin Inc, New York, N Y, 69.
Exhibitions: Sixth Biennial São Paulo, Brazil, 61; Second Biennial De Jovenes, Paris, France, 61; Mexico: The New Generation, traveled throughout the U S A, 66; Expo '67, Montreal, P Q, 67; First Triennial India, New Delhi, 68.
Bibliography: J J Gurrola (producer), Rojo (film), Nat Univ Mex, 66; Octavio Paz (auth), Discos visuales, Ediciones Era, 68; J Garcia Ponce (auth), Vicente Rojo, Nat Univ Mex, 71.
Dealer: Galeria Juan Martin, Amberes 17, Mexico D F 6, Mex.
Mailing Address: Dulce Olivia 57, Mexico D F 21, Mex.

ROJTMAN, MRS MARC B
Collector
Positions: Bd gov, New York Cult Ctr; fel, Morgan Libr; pres Rojtman Found Inc.

Memberships: Art Collectors Club; Drawing Soc; fel in perpetuity Metrop Mus Art; Inst Fine Arts, New York Univ (mem bd adv); Cooper Hewitt Mus, Smithsonian Inst (mem adv coun).
Mailing Address: 22 E 64th St, New York, NY 10021.

ROLLER, MARION BENDER
Sculptor, Painter
Preferred Media: Terra-Cotta, Bronze, Watercolors.
b Boston, Mass.
Study & Training: Vesper George Sch Art, dipl; Art Stud League New York, with John Hovannes; Greenwich House, with Lu Duble; also watercolors with Edgar Whitney.
Commissions: Head of child, Nassau Ctr for Emotionally Disturbed Children, Woodbury, N Y, 68; plus many other pvt commissions.
Exhibitions: Allied Artists Am, 59-72; Nat Acad Design, New York, N Y, 62-69; Am Artists Prof League, 65, 66 & 68; Audubon Artists, 66; Nat Sculpture Soc, New York, 69-72; plus two one-man shows.
Teaching: Instr art, Fashion Inst Technol, 67.
Awards: Anonymous prize, 59 & hon mention, 65, Allied Artists Am; Mrs John Newington Award, 65 & Archer Milton Huntington Award, 68, Am Artists Prof League; gold medal, Pen & Brush, 71.
Bibliography: G Kramer (auth), Profile, Hudson Register Star, 65.
Memberships: Nat Sculpture Soc; Allied Artists Am (asst corresp secy, 66-71); Pen & Brush (co-chmn, 67-); Catharine Lorillard Wolfe Art Club; Hudson Valley Art Asn.
Mailing Address: 1 W 67th St, New York, NY 10023.

ROMANO, CLARE CAMILLE
Printmaker, Painter
b Palisade, N J.
Study & Training: Cooper Union Sch Art, 39-43; Ecole Beaux-Arts, Fontainebleau, France, 49; Inst Statale Arte, Florence, Italy, Fulbright grant, 58-59.
Work in Public Collections: Mus Mod Art, Whitney Mus Am Art & Metrop Mus Art, New York, N Y; Libr Cong & Nat Collection Fine Arts, Washington, D C.
Commissions: Tapestry, Mfrs Hanover Bank, New York, 69.
Exhibitions: Invitational of American Prints, South London Art Gallery, Eng, 67; Cincinnati Mus Art Print Invitational, 68; First Biennial Am Graphic Art, Columbia, S Am, 71; Second Triennial Int Exhib Woodcuts, Ugo Carpi Mus, Italy, 72; American Prints, U S Info Agency Invitational, Australian Nat Mus, Canberra, 72.
Teaching: Instr printmaking, New Sch Social Res, 60-; adj asst prof printmaking, Pratt Graphic Arts Ctr, 63-; adj asst prof printmaking, Pratt Inst, 64-
Awards: Louis Comfort Tiffany grant, 52; Fulbright grant, 58; citation for prof achievement, Cooper Union Sch Art, 66.
Bibliography: Patricia Boyd Wilson (auth), article, In: Christian Sci Monitor, 67; Faulkner & Ziegfeld (auth), Art today, Holt, Rinehart & Winston, 69; Pat Gilmour (auth), Modern prints, Studio Vista (London), 70.
Memberships: Soc Am Graphic Artists (pres, 70-72); Print Club Philadelphia; Boston Printmakers; Mod Painters & Sculptors; assoc Nat Acad Design.
Publications: Co-illusr, Spoon River anthology, 63; co-illusr, Leaves of grass, 64; auth, Artist's proof, 64 & 66; auth, American encyclopedia, 71; co-auth, The complete printmaker, 72.
Dealer: Associated American Artists, 663 Fifth Ave, New York, NY 10022.
Mailing Address: 110 Davison Pl, Englewood, NJ 07631.

ROMANO, EMANUEL GLICEN
Painter, Illustrator
b Rome, Italy, Sept 23, 97.
Study & Training: In Switz; also with Enrico Glicenstein.
Work in Public Collections: Univ Art Mus, Univ Tex, Austin; Fogg Mus Art; Metrop Mus Art, New York, N Y; Detroit Inst Art; Mus Ville Paris; plus others.
Commissions: Mural, Klondike Bldg, Welfare Island, N Y; portraits in many pvt collections.
Exhibitions: Whitney Mus Am Art; City Col New York; Fort Worth Art Asn; one-man shows, Greenville Mus Art, S C, 62 & Haifa Mus & Tel-Aviv Mus, Israel; plus many others.
Teaching: Lectr mural painting in ancient & mod times.
Memberships: Artists League Am.
Publications: Contribr, drawings, In: The waste land, The hollow men, Waiting for Godot, Beckett, Rhinoceros & Ionesco; plus many others.
Mailing Address: 163 E 74th St, New York, NY 10021.

ROMANO, JAIME (LUIS)
Painter
Preferred Media: Acrylics.
b Santurce, P R, May 10, 42.
Study & Training: Univ P R, BA(humanities), 66; Am Univ, MA, 69.

Work in Public Collections: Mus Bellas Artes, Ponce, P R; Ateneo Puertorriqueño, San Juan, P R; Inst Cult Puertorriqueña, San Juan; Mus Antropologia y Arte, Univ P R, Rio Piedras; C Law Watkins Mem Collection, Am Univ, Washington, D C.
Exhibitions: Certamen Navidad Ateneo Puertorriqueño, San Juan, 66-68 & 71; David Lloyd Kreeger Award Exhib, Washington, 69; Expos Panamericana Artes Gráficas, Cali, Colombia, 70; Primera & Segunda Bienal Grabado Latinoamericano, San Juan, 70 & 72.
Teaching: Instr advan drawing & painting, Univ P R, Rio Piedras, 69-71; acad adv, 70-71.
Positions: V pres, Fondo Becas Artes Plásticas, Inc, San Juan, 70-
Awards: First prize in painting, Soc Amigos de Cristobal Ruiz, 67; first prize in painting, David Lloyd Kreeger Award Exhib, 68; first prize in painting, Certamen Ateneo Puertorriqueño, 68.
Bibliography: Ernesto Alvarez (auth), Jaime Romano, Artes Graficas, 66; Antonio Molina (auth), Lo ultimo de Romano, El Mundo, 68; The seven minutes, San Juan Star, 10/15/72; plus one other.
Publications: Auth, Ernesto Alvarez, 66; auth, Art in Puerto Rico-boom or bust?, 71; auth, On criticism, critics & criteria, 72.
Dealer: Galeria Santiago, 207 Calle del Cristo, San Juan, PR 00901.
Mailing Address: 472 Soldado H L Alvarado (Altos), Hato Rey, PR 00918.

ROMANO, SALVATORE MICHAEL
Painter, Sculptor
Preferred Media: Acrylics, Plaster, Plastics, Wood, Metals, Water.
b Cliffside Park, N J, Sept 12, 25.
Study & Training: Art Stud League New York, with Jon Corbino; Acad Grande Chaumière, Paris, France, with Edouard Georges & Ehrl Kerkam.
Exhibitions: Primary Structures, Jewish Mus, New York, N Y, 66; Cool Art Show, 67 & Highlights of the Season, 68-69, 69, Aldrich Mus Contemp Art, Ridgefield, Conn; one-man shows, A M Sachs Gallery, New York, 68 & Max Hutchinson Gallery, New York, 71.
Teaching: Adj instr sculpture, Cooper Union Sch Arts & Archit, 68-70; lectr painting, sculpture & drawing, Herbert H Lehman Col, City Univ New York, 69-
Bibliography: Corinne Robins (auth), Floating sculpture, 65 & Grace Glueck (auth), New York Gallery notes, 9/10/71, Art in Am; Carl Baldwin (auth), It floats, Art News, 11/71.
Publications: Auth, article, In: Lehman Col Art News Letter, 71.
Dealer: Max Hutchinson Gallery, 127 Greene St, New York, NY 10012.
Mailing Address: 679 Broadway, New York, NY 10012.

ROMANO, UMBERTO ROBERTO
Painter, Sculptor
Preferred Media: Oils, Acrylics, Bronze, Marble.
b Naples, Italy, Feb 26, 06; U S citizen.
Study & Training: Nat Acad Design, New York, N Y, 21-26; Tiffany Found, summer 25; Am Acad Rome, 26-27.
Work in Public Collections: Nat Collection Fine Arts, Washington, D C; Whitney Mus Am Art; Roosevelt Libr, Hyde Park, N Y; Corcoran Gallery, Washington, D C; Smith Mus, Springfield, Mass.
Commissions: Mural, Three Centuries of New England History, Springfield Post Off, 38; Portrait of Sara Delano Roosevelt, March-of-Dimes, Hyde Park Libr, 42; mosaic mural, After Chaos Came Order, Munic Ct House, New York, 61; Pupil Learns from Past & Looks Toward The Future, P S 234, Brooklyn, 64; Mother and Child (stained glass window), Allen Stevenson Sch, New York, 67.
Exhibitions: Carnegie Int, Pittsburgh, Pa, 33-49; one-man shows, Worcester Art Mus, Mass, 35 & Galerie Andre Weil, Paris, 49; Oriental Fragment, U S Govt Traveling Show, Orient, 50-52; Fragment—Man Weeps, U S Govt Traveling Relig Show, Italy, France, Spain & Ger, 58-61.
Teaching: Instr painting & sculpture & dir, Worcester Art Mus Sch, 33-40; instr painting & sculpture & dir, Romano Sch Art, Gloucester, Mass, 33-60; instr painting & sculpture & dir, Romano Sch Art, New York, 50-72.
Positions: First v pres, Int Asn Plastic Arts, 65-; first v pres, Nat Acad Design, 65-; dir, Abbey Found, 66-; pres, Audubon Artists, 71-72.
Awards: Pulitzer Prize, Columbia Univ, 26; Carnegie Award, Nat Acad Design, 54; gold medal of honor, Century Asn, 69.
Bibliography: Edward Alden Jewell (auth), Romano portrays horrors of war, New York Times, 44; Harry Salpeter (auth), Renaissance of Umberto Romano, Esquire, 45; Richard Merrifield (auth), Umberto Romano, Yankee Mag, 52.
Memberships: Century Asn (exhib comt, 70-); Rockport Art Asn; Nat Mural Soc (dir, 62-); Provincetown Art Asn; Castle Hill Found (dir, 50-58).
Publications: Contribr, American art today, Nat Art Soc, 39; illusr, Dante's the divine comedy, 46 & contribr, Best of art, 48, Double-

day; contribr, Contemporary American painting, Univ Ill Press, 49; contribr, Expressionism in art, Liveright, 58.
Dealers: Wellfleet Art Gallery, Cape Cod, MA 02650; Galerie Moos, 1430 Sherbrooke St W, Montreal 25, P Q, Can.
Mailing Address: 162 E 83rd St, New York, NY 10028.

ROMANS, CHARLES JOHN
Painter
Preferred Media: Oils.
b New York, N Y, Mar 4, 91.
Study & Training: Buffalo State Teachers Col, cert; N Y Univ; Nat Acad Design, with Leon Kroll & Siguard Skou; also with George E Browne, Provincetown, Mass.
Work in Public Collections: Jersey City Pub Mus, N J; Union Mus, Albany, Ga; La Salle Col Union Permanent Collection, Philadelphia, Pa; Kosciuszko Found, New York.
Exhibitions: Montclair Mus N J Exhib, 37 & 50; Allied Artists Am Ann, 37-71; Am Watercolor Soc Ann, 39 & Nat Acad Design Ann, 41, Nat Acad Design Galleries; Riverside Mus Spec Exhib, 52-54.
Teaching: Instr fine arts, Dickinson High Sch, Jersey City, 45-55; pvt instr art workshop, 55-71; instr art workshop, Seven Mile Beach Art League, Avalon, N J, 57-60.
Awards: Jersey City Mus Award, Art Coun N J, 50-51; Dr M Woodrow Award, Hudson Valley Art Asn, 54; Anonymous Award, Allied Artists Am, 71.
Bibliography: Philbrook Smith (auth), The Romans' concentrate careers, N J Music & Arts, 3/69.
Memberships: N J Painters & Sculptors Soc (treas & v pres, 44-54); Allied Artists Am (secy, 52-54); Nat Asn Painters Casein; Prof Artists S Jersey (pres, 57-71); Atlantic City Art Ctr Gallery (adv, 64).
Dealer: Old Bergen Art Guild, 43 W 33rd St, Bayonne, NJ 07002.
Mailing Address: 1033 New York Ave, Cape May, NJ 08204.

ROMANSKY, ALVIN S
Collector, Patron
b Houston, Tex, Mar 15, 07.
Study & Training: Univ Penn; Univ Tex; Univ Houston; Univ Calif, Davis, LLB.
Exhibitions: Dallas Mus Fine Arts; Witte Mem Mus; Tex Gen Exhib & Nat Photo Exhib, 35-40, Houston Mus Fine Art.
Collections Arranged: Rufino Tamayo Exhib & Contemp In Cotton, Contemp Arts Mus; Ashanti Goldwrights, Univ Tex, 71; plus many others.
Positions: V pres, Contemp Arts Mus, 47-52.
Awards: Three prizes, Houston Mus Fine Arts.
Bibliography: Tamayo catalogue, Contemporary in cotton; plus others.
Memberships: Chambre Syndicate Estampe Dessin Tableaux, France.
Research: Ashanti art; gold weights.
Art Interests: Donated collection of graphics to the University of Texas; donated Alvin Romansky Print Room to the University of Houston Museum of Fine Arts.
Collection: French graphics; contemporary French art; Ashanti objects.
Mailing Address: Apt 2214, Lamar Towers, 2929 Buffalo Speedway, Houston, TX 77006.

ROME, HAROLD
Collector, Painter
b Hartford, Conn, May 27, 08.
Study & Training: Yale Univ, BA, 29, Yale Law Sch, 28-30, Yale Sch Archit, BFA, 34.
Exhibitions: One-man show paintings & songs, Marble Arch Gallery, New York, N Y, 64; one-man show paintings, Bodley Gallery, New York, 70.
Positions: Composer & writer.
Memberships: Dramatists Guild.
Collection: African sculpture; large collection of West African heddle-pulleys.
Publications: Composer, Fanny, 54, Destry rides again, 59, I can get it for you wholesale, 62, Zulu and the Zayda, 65, Scarlett (mus adaptation Gone with the wind), Imperial Theatre, Tokyo, 70; plus many others.
Mailing Address: c/o Chappell & Co, 609 Fifth Ave, New York, NY 10017.

ROMELING, W B
Painter
Preferred Media: Watercolors.
b Schenectady, N Y, Feb 26, 09.
Study & Training: Pratt Inst, Brooklyn, N Y; Syracuse Univ; Sch Fine Arts; also with Ogden Pleissner.
Work in Public Collections: Schenectady Mus; Cooperstown Art Asn.
Exhibitions: Central New York, Munson-Williams-Proctor Inst, Utica, N Y, 62; Invitational Watercolor Show, Sharon, Conn, 67-

68; one-man show, Bennington Gallery, Vt, 70-71; Cooperstown Ann, N Y, 70-71; one-man show, Muggleton Gallery, Auburn, N Y, 70-71.
Teaching: Instr art, Owen D Young Sch, Van Hornesville, N Y, 43-69.
Awards: Purchase prize, Schenectady Mus, 63; first prize, still life, 66 & Godley Watercolor Award, 70, Cooperstown Art Asn.
Memberships: Cooperstown Art Asn (pres, 70-72); Southern Vt Artists.
Dealer: Richard Comins, 125 North St, Bennington, VT 05201.
Mailing Address: Box 53, Van Hornesville, NY 13475.

ROMOSER, RUTH AMELIA
Painter, Sculptor
Preferred Media: Oils, Acrylics.
b Baltimore, Md, Apr 26, 16.
Study & Training: Baltimore Art Inst, grad; sculpting courses with Xavier Corbera, Barcelona, Spain; Robert Motherwell Workshop; graphics with Joseph Ruffo.
Work in Public Collections: Miami Mus Mod Art, Fla; Lowe Mus, Univ Miami, Fla; Miami Herald; Nat Cardiac Hosp, Miami; Int Gallery, Baltimore, Md.
Commissions: Two paintings for 12 productions, Actors Studio M, Coral Gables, Fla, 63-64.
Exhibitions: Ringling Southeast Nat Art Show, Sarasota, Fla, 61-63; Nat Drawing Exhib, Cheltenham, Pa, 64; Four Arts Plaza Nat, Palm Beach, 66; Hortt Mem Regional, Fort Lauderdale Mus Arts, 66; one-man show, Nat Design Ctr, New York, N Y, 67.
Awards: Eighth Ann Hortt Mem Award, Fort Lauderdale Mus Arts, 67; Design Derby Award, Designers-Decorators Guild, 69; Artspo 70, Coral Gables, 70.
Bibliography: Nellie Bower (auth), Arriving at a style, Miami Daily News, 65; Bernard Davis (auth), Romoser foreward (catalogue), Miami Mus Mod Art, 68; Doris Reno (auth), Lively arts, Miami Herald, 69.
Memberships: Blue Dome Art Fel; Fla Artists Group; Lowe Mus; Miami Art Ctr.
Publications: Ed, All Florida Artist in the House Mag, 63; contribr, rev, In: Art News Mag, 67.
Dealer: Bernard Davis, Miami Museum of Modern Art, Bayshore at 20th St, Miami, FL 33137.
Mailing Address: 8025 S W 64th St, Miami, FL 33143.

RONALD, WILLIAM
Painter
b Stratford, Ont, Aug 13, 26; U S citizen.
Study & Training: Ont Col Art, hon grad, 51.
Work in Public Collections: Mus Mod Art, New York, N Y; Guggenheim Mus, New York; Whitney Mus Am Art, New York; Nat Gallery Can, Ottawa, Ont; Carnegie Inst, Pittsburgh, Pa.
Commissions: Acrylic mural, Nat Art Ctr, Ottawa, 70.
Exhibitions: Carnegie Int, 58; Brussels World's Fair & traveling exhib, 58; Sao Paulo Biennale, Mus Arte Mod, 59; Whitney Mus Am Art Ann, 59; Can Biennial, Nat Gallery Can, 68.
Positions: Host of TV show on arts, Can Broadcasting Corp, Toronto, Ont, 66-67.
Awards: Hallmark Corp Art Award for watercolor, 52; nat award, Can sect, Int Guggenheim Awards, 56; award, Second Biennial Exhib Can Painting, Nat Gallery Can, 57.
Bibliography: David Ralston & Hugo McPherson (auth), The Ronald Chapel in Toronto Harbour, Can Art, 4/66; William Cameron (auth), Portrait of the artist as a violently honest man, Macleans Mag, 2/71.
Mailing Address: 392 Brunswick Ave, Toronto 179, Ont, Can.

RONAY, STEPHEN ROBERT
Painter
Preferred Media: Oils, Graphics.
b Arad, Roumania, Nov 27, 00; U S citizen.
Exhibitions: Art Inst Chicago, 37; Cincinnati Mus Art, 38; Mus Mod Art, New York, N Y, 40; Parrish Art Mus, Southampton, N Y, 60-72; Va Mus Fine Arts, 68; plus one-man shows, New York.
Awards: The Poet's Garden Award, 69 & Garden & Beach Award, 70, Parrish Art Mus.
Mailing Address: 10 E Ridge Dr, Flower Hill, Roslyn, NY 11576.

RONEY, HAROLD ARTHUR
Painter, Lecturer
Preferred Media: Oils.
b Sullivan, Ill, Nov 7, 99.
Study & Training: Chicago Acad Art; Art Inst Chicago; also with Harry Leith-Ross, John Folinsbee & George A Aldrich.
Work in Public Collections: Sullivan Pub Libr, Ill; Witte Mem Mus; Austin Pub Libr, Tex; South Bend Pub Sch, Ind; Southwest Tex State Univ; plus others.
Exhibitions: River Square Gallery, San Antonio, Tex, 71; Coppini Acad Fine Arts, San Antonio, 71; plus many other group & one-man shows.

Teaching: Instr oil landscape, Froman Sch Art, 58-
Mailing Address: R R No 8, Box 294B, San Antonio, TX 78228.

ROOT, MRS EDWARD W
Collector
Mailing Address: College Hill, Clinton, NY 13323.

ROSATI, JAMES
Sculptor, Educator
b Washington, Pa, June 9, 12.
Work in Public Collections: Yale Gallery Fine Arts; New York
Univ; Whitney Mus Am Art; Geigy Chem Corp, Ardsley, N Y;
Hopkins Art Ctr, Dartmouth Col; also in many pvt collections.
Commissions: Sculpture, St John's Abbey, Collegeville, Md.
Exhibitions: Six shows, Whitney Mus Am Art Ann, 52-66; Int Coun
Mus Mod Art Exhib, France, Ger & Scandinavia, 65-66; Flint
Inst, 66; Colby Col, 67; Mus Contemp Crafts Traveling Exhib,
67-68; plus many other group & one-man shows.
Teaching: Instr, Pratt Inst & Cooper Union, N Y; vis critic sculp-
ture, Hopkins Art Ctr, Dartmouth Col, spring 63; adj assoc prof
sculpture, Yale Univ, 64-
Awards: Logan Medal & Prize, Art Inst Chicago, 62; Carborundum
Major Abrasive Mkt Award, 63; Guggenheim fel, 64; plus others.
Bibliography: Michel Seuphor (auth), The sculpture of this century,
dictionary of modern sculpture, A Zwemmer Ltd, London, 59;
Jean Selz (auth), Modern sculpture, Braziller, 63; Herbert Read
(auth), A concise history of modern sculpture, Praeger, 64.
Dealer: Marlborough Gallery, 41 E 57th St, New York, NY 10028.
Mailing Address: 252 W 14th St, New York, NY 10011.

ROSE, ARTHUR
Painter, Sculptor
Preferred Media: Oils, Steel.
b Charleston, S C, May 26, 21.
Study & Training: Claflin Col, BA; N Y Univ, MA; also with William
Baziotes, Peter Busa, Hale Woodruff & James Podzez; plus
many others.
Work in Public Collections: S C State Art Collection; Columbia
Mus Art; Citizens & Southern Nat Bank, Columbia, S C; Ind
Univ, Bloomington, Ind; Johnson Publ Co, Inc, Chicago, Ill.
Exhibitions: Cafe Tortilla, Bloomington, 67; Stillman Col, Tusca-
loosa, Ala, 69; Columbia Mus Art First Invitational, S C, 69;
Sandlapper Gallery, Columbia, 71; The Gallery, Spartanburg,
S C, 72.
Teaching: Instr sculpture & oil painting & head dept art, Claflin
Col, 52-
Awards: Hon mention, Springs Cotton Mills, Lancaster, S C, 61;
best in show award, J O Endris & Son Jewelers, New Albany,
Ind, 67; second award, Nat Conf Artists, 70.
Bibliography: Paul Lin (auth), Buried sand treasures, Literary
Star, 60; Jack A Morris (auth), Contemporary artists of S C,
privately pub, 71; J Edward Atkinson (auth), Black dimensions
in contemporary American art, Carnation, 71.
Memberships: Nat Conf Artists (regional dir, 58-62); S C Asn Sch
Art; Smithsonian Assocs, Guild S C Artists.
Dealer: Sandlapper Gallery, Hwy 378, Columbia, SC 29202.
Mailing Address: Claflin College, Orangeburg, SC 29115.

ROSE, DOROTHY
Painter
Preferred Media: Oils, Watercolors.
b Brooklyn, N Y.
Study & Training: Beaux Arts Inst Design, 33-35; New Sch Soc Res,
49-50; Art Stud League New York, N Y, 51-55; with Robert Hale,
John Carroll, Reginald Marsh & Morris Kantor.
Work in Public Collections: Staten Island Mus Arts & Sci, N Y.
Exhibitions: Five one-man shows, Panoras Gallery, 55-65; Silver-
mine Guild Ann, 56; exhibs, New York City Ctr, 56-58; Ringling
Mus 10th Ann, Sarasota, Fla, 60; 15 Brooklyn Artists, Brooklyn
Mus, 63; plus others.
Positions: Juror, Janaf Art Exhib, fall 68.
Awards: Prize winner, 59 & Four Man Show Award, 59, Village Art
Ctr.
Memberships: Artists Equity Asn New York; Village Art Ctr (mem
coun, 59); life mem Art Stud League New York.
Mailing Address: 312 E 21st St, Apt 3G, Brooklyn, NY 11226.

ROSE, HANNA TOBY
Art Administrator
b New York, N Y.
Study & Training: Wellesley Col, BA, with Alfred Barr, Jr & grad
study with Meyer Shapiro.
Positions: Cur educ, Brooklyn Mus, 47-71, asst dir for educ, 71-
Memberships: Int Coun Mus (pres, Int Educ Comt, 53-62); Am Asn
Mus; Mus Asn Gt Brit; Nat Comt Art Educ (coun mem); Int Soc
Educ Art.
Research: Art and disadvantaged children.
Publications: Co-auth, Exploring New York, 56; ed, Museums and

teachers, 56; ed, Role of the arts in meeting social and educa-
tional needs of disadvantaged, 67; auth, articles, In: UNESCO
Occasional Papers, Sch Arts & Mus.
Mailing Address: 55 E Ninth St, New York, NY 10003.

ROSE, HERMAN
Painter, Printmaker
Preferred Media: Graphics.
b Brooklyn, N Y, Nov 6, 09.
Study & Training: Nat Acad Design, 27-29.
Work in Public Collections: Mus Mod Art; Whitney Mus Am Art;
Univ Tex; Univ Calif; Smithsonian Inst Print Collection; also in
many pvt collections.
Exhibitions: Mus Mod Art, 48 & 52; six shows, Whitney Mus Am
Art, 48-58; Pa Acad Fine Arts, 52; ACA Gallery, 55 & 56; one-
man show, Forum Gallery, N Y, 62.
Teaching: Instr, Brooklyn Col, 49-51; instr, New Sch Social Res,
54-55; instr, Brooklyn Col, 58-61; instr, Hofstra Col, 59-60;
instr, New Sch Social Res, 63-; artist-in-residence, Univ Va, 66.
Awards: Yaddo Found fel, 55; Longview Award, 60 & 61.
Dealer: Zabriskie Gallery, 699 Madison Ave, New York, NY 10021.
Mailing Address: 130 W 186th St, New York, NY 10033.

ROSE, PETER HENRY
Art Dealer
b New York, N Y, Feb 25, 35.
Study & Training: Hamilton Col, BA; Univ Pa, MA; Columbia Univ;
Ecole Superieuré, Univ Paris.
Positions: Owner-dir, Peter Rose Gallery.
Specialty of Gallery: Twentieth century contemporary American art.
Mailing Address: Peter Rose Gallery, 340 E 52nd St, New York, NY
10022.

ROSE, THOMAS ALBERT
Sculptor
Preferred Media: Plastics, Polyester, Fiber Glass.
b Washington, D C, Oct 15, 42.
Study & Training: Univ Wis-Madison, 60-62; Univ Ill, Urbana, with
Frank Gallo & Roger Majarowitz, 62-65, BFA, 65; Univ Calif,
Berkeley, with Peter Voulkos, Harold Paris, William King &
George Miyasaki, 65-67, MA, 67, study grant to Univ Lund, 67-
68.
Work in Public Collections: Univ N Mex Mus, Albuquerque; Libr
Cong, Washington, D C; Metromedia Collection Los Angeles,
Calif, John Bolles, San Francisco, Calif; San Francisco Art
Comn; plus others.
Exhibitions: Sculpture, Plastics West Coast, Hanson Gallery, San
Francisco, 67; First Int Exhib Erotic Art, Lund, Sweden, 68;
Realities Exhib, Contemp Gallery, Dallas, Tex, 72; Graphic
Form, Leger Galerie, Malmo, Sweden, 72; Midwest Biennial,
Joslyn Mus, Omaha, Nebr, 72; plus others.
Teaching: Asst to Richard O'Hanlon, sculpture class, Univ Calif,
Berkeley, 66-67; asst to Bertil Lundberg, lithography, A B F
Sch, Malmo, Sweden, 67-68; instr sculpture, Univ Calif, Berke-
ley, 68-69; instr sculpture & graphics, N Mex State Univ, 69-72;
instr sculpture, Univ Minn, Minneapolis, 72-
Awards: Nat Endowment Arts vis artist grant & State Arts Comn
grant, N Mex State Univ, 72-73; Kresge Found grant, 72-73;
plus others.
Dealer: Bolles Gallery, 10 Gold, San Francisco, CA 94133.
Mailing Address: 4210 Harriet Ave S, Minneapolis, MN 55409.

ROSEBERG, CARL ANDERSSON
Sculptor, Art Historian
b Vinton, Iowa, Sept 26, 16.
Study & Training: Univ Iowa, BFA, 39, MFA, 47; Cranbrook Acad
Arts, summers 47 & 48; Univ Va, summer 64; Univ Mysore, sum-
mer 65; Tyler Sch Art, summer 67.
Work in Public Collections: Springfield Art Mus, Mo; Chrysler Mus,
Norfolk, Va; Va Mus Fine Arts, Richmond; Longwood Col, Va;
Univ Iowa.
Commissions: Bronze Hwy Markers, Rockingham Co Citizens Comt,
Va, 55; William & Mary Medallion, Marshall-Wythe Sch Law, 67,
Col William & Mary Medallion, 68 & Donald W Davis Commemo-
rative Plaque, Life Sci Bldg, Col William & Mary, 70.
Exhibitions: One-man show, 63 & 12 Va Sculptors, 70, Norfolk Mus
Arts & Sci; Am Art Today, New York World's Fair, 64; Va Sculp-
tors Traveling Exhib, 70-72; Tidewater Col Faculty Exhib, Chry-
sler Mus, 72.
Teaching: Instr, Col William & Mary, 47-52, asst prof fine arts, 52-
57, assoc prof, 57-66, prof & Heritage fel, 66-
Awards: Fulbright fel, India; award of honor, Va Chap Am Inst Ar-
chitects, 68; Thomas Jefferson Award, Robert McConnell Found,
71; plus many others.
Memberships: Asian Soc; Am Asn Mus; Audubon Artists; Twentieth
Century Gallery (mem bd); Tidewater Artists.
Research: Art of India.

Publications: Illusr, Little Red Riding Hood & big bad wolf, 53 & roll titles for The colonial naturalist (film), 64.
Mailing Address: P O Box 1166, Williamsburg, VA 23185.

ROSEN, HY(MAN) (JOSEPH)
Cartoonist
Preferred Media: Inks.
b Albany, N Y, Feb 10, 23.
Study & Training: Art Inst Chicago; Art Stud League New York, N Y; State Univ N Y Albany; Stanford Univ, fel jour.
Positions: Ed cartoonist, Albany Times-Union, 45; ed cartoonist, Hearst Newspapers.
Awards: Top award, Freedom Found, Valley Forge, Pa, 50, 55 & 60; top award, Nat Conf Christians & Jews, 62.
Memberships: Asn Am Ed Cartoonists (pres, 72).
Mailing Address: Times-Union, Sheridan Ave, Albany, NY 12201.

ROSEN, ISRAEL
Collector
b Baltimore, Md, Dec 28, 11.
Study & Training: Johns Hopkins Univ, AB, 31; Univ Md Sch Med, MD, 35.
Memberships: Baltimore Mus Art (accessions comt contemp art, 61-67, comt spec funds & develop, 70-, bd trustees, 72-); Univ Calif Art Mus, Berkeley (nat comt, 70-).
Collection: Modern art, with special emphasis on abstract expressionism, including works by Pollock, de Kooning, Still, Kline, Rothko, Baziotes, Tobey, Rauschenberg, as well as works by twentieth century European artists such as Picasso, Mondrian, Kindinsky, Klee, Leger & Gris.
Publications: Auth, Toward a definition of abstract expressionism, Baltimore Mus News, 59; auth, Edward Joseph Gallagher III mem collection, Baltimore Mus Art, 64 & Metrop Mus Art, 65.
Mailing Address: 1 E University Pkwy, Baltimore, MD 21218.

ROSENBERG, HAROLD
Writer, Educator
b New York, N Y, Feb 2, 06.
Study & Training: City Col New York, 23-24; Brooklyn Law Sch, LLB; St Lawrence Univ, 27; Lake Forest Col, LittD, 68; Md Inst, Col Art, DFA, 70.
Teaching: Regents lectr, Univ Calif, 62; lectr, Christian Gauss Sem, Princeton Univ, 63; lectr, Baldwin Sem, Oberlin Col; vis prof, Univ Southern Ill, 66; prof art & mem comt social thought, Univ Chicago, 67-
Positions: Art ed, Am Guide Series, 38-40; art critic, New Yorker, 67-
Awards: Frank Jewett Mather Award, Col Art Asn, 64; citation, Univ Calif, Berkeley, 70.
Memberships: Int Asn Art Critics.
Publications: Auth, The tradition of the new, McGraw, 59 & 65; auth, The anxious object, New Am Libr, 64 & 69; auth, Artworks and packages, Horizon, 69; auth, Act and the actor, World, 71; auth, The De-definition of art, Horizon, 72; contribr, Art News & Art News Ann; plus many others.
Mailing Address: New Yorker Magazine, 25 W 43rd St, New York, NY 10036.

ROSENBERG, JAKOB
Writer, Educator
b Berlin, Ger, Sept 5, 93.
Study & Training: Univ Bern; Univ Zurich; Univ Frankfurt-am-Main; Univ Munich, PhD, 22; Harvard Univ, hon MA, 42, hon DA, 61.
Teaching: Resident fel & lectr, Harvard Univ, 37-39, assoc prof, 40-47, prof fine arts, 48-64, emer prof, 64-; Robert Sterling Clark prof, Williams Col, 64-65; sr fel, Nat Gallery, Washington, D C, 66-67.
Positions: Cur prints, Fogg Mus Art, Harvard Univ, 39.
Memberships: Col Art Asn Am; fel Am Acad Arts & Sci; hon fel Pierpont Morgan Libr.
Publications: Auth, Great Draughtsmen from Pisanello to Picasso, Harvard Univ Press, 59; auth, Zeichnungen Cranachs, 60; auth, Rembrandt, life and work, Phaidon, 64; auth, On quality in art, Princeton Univ Press, 67; co-auth, Dutch art and architecture, Penguin, 72; plus many others.
Mailing Address: 19 Bellevue Rd, Arlington, MA 02174.

ROSENBERG, LOUIS CONRAD
Printmaker, Illustrator
b Portland, Ore, May 6, 90.
Study & Training: Mass Inst Technol, 12-14, traveling fel, 20-22; Royal Col Art, London, Eng, 25-26.
Work in Public Collections: Smithsonian Inst; Libr Cong; New York Pub Libr; Boston Pub Libr; Boston Mus Fine Arts; plus many others.
Exhibitions: Nat Acad Design; Art Inst Chicago; Albany Inst Hist & Art; Albany Print Club; Wichita Art Asn; plus others.

Awards: Prizes, Art Inst Chicago, 32 & Albany Print Club, 40; fine arts gold medal, Am Inst Architects, 48; plus others.
Memberships: Academician Nat Acad Design; fel Royal Soc Painters, Etchers & Engravers, London; Am Inst Architects.
Publications: Auth, Davanzati palace, 22; illusr, Bridges of France, 24 & Middle East war projects of Johnson-Drake & Piper, 43; contribr, print mags; plus others.
Mailing Address: 555 Country Club Rd, Lake Oswego, OR 97034.

ROSENBLATT, ADOLPH
Painter, Lithographer
b New Haven, Conn, Feb 23, 33.
Study & Training: Sch Design, Yale Univ, with Albers, Brooks & Marca-Relli.
Work in Public Collections: Libr Cong, Washington, D C.
Exhibitions: Am Fedn Traveling Exhib, 58; Boston Arts Festival, 61; Riverside Mus, New York, N Y, 62; Provincetown, Mass, 63; Dorsky Gallery, 63, 64 & 72.
Mailing Address: c/o Dorsky Galleries, 111 Fourth Ave, New York, NY 10003.

ROSENBLOOM, CHARLES J
Collector
Mailing Address: 1036 Beechwood Blvd, Pittsburgh, PA 15206.

ROSENBLUM, JAY
Painter
Preferred Media: Acrylics.
b New York, N Y, Oct 12, 33.
Study & Training: Pratt Inst, with Richard Lindner; Bard Col, BA, 55, with Louis Schanker; Cranbrook Acad Art, MFA, 56, with Fred Mitchell.
Work in Public Collections: Larry Aldrich Mus Contemp Art, Ridgefield, Conn; Mus Mod Art Lending Serv, New York; Albright-Knox Mus Lending Serv, Buffalo, N Y; 180 Beacon St Collection, Cambridge, Mass.
Commissions: Painting, comn by Larry Aldrich, Phoenix, Ariz, 71.
Exhibitions: Festival of Two Worlds, Spoleto, Italy, 56; Detroit Inst Art, 56; Highlights of 1970 Season, Aldrich Mus, 70; one-man shows, A M Sachs Gallery, 70 & Blue Parrot Gallery, New York, 72; Recent Prints U S A, New York Cult Ctr, 72.
Teaching: Instr painting, Dalton Sch, N Y, 63-; instr painting, 92nd St YMHA, New York, 65-; adj lectr painting, Queensboro Community Col, 69-; adj lectr painting, Lehman Col, 71-
Awards: Carlos Lopez Mem Prize in Painting, Detroit Inst Art, 56; Painter of Yr, 1970, Larry Aldrich, 70; City Walls Inc grant, 72.
Bibliography: Cindy Nemser (auth), rev, In: Arts Mag, 10/70; Carter Ratcliff (auth), rev, In: Art Int, 2/71; Ward Jackson (auth), Art now: New York, 5/71.
Dealers: A M Sachs Gallery, 29 W 57th St, New York, NY 10019; Blue Parrot Print Gallery, 1057 Madison Ave, New York, NY 10028.
Mailing Address: 502 E 11th St, New York, NY 10009.

ROSENBLUM, ROBERT
Art Historian
b New York, N Y, July 24, 27.
Study & Training: Queens Col, BA; Yale Univ, MA; N Y Univ, PhD.
Teaching: Instr hist art, Univ Mich, 55-56; assoc prof hist art, Princeton Univ, 56-66; prof hist art, N Y Univ, 67-
Research: Modern art, 1760 to the present.
Publications: Auth, Cubism and twentieth century art, 60, Transformations in late eighteenth century art, 67, Ingres, 67 & Frank Stella, 70.
Mailing Address: 1 E 78th St, New York, NY 10021.

ROSENBLUM, SADIE SKOLETSKY
Painter, Sculptor
Preferred Media: Oils.
b Odessa, Russia, Feb 12, 99; U S citizen.
Study & Training: Art Stud League New York; New Sch Soc Res; also with Raphael Soyer, Kunioshr, Ben-Zion & Samuel Adler.
Work in Public Collections: Philadelphia Mus Art, Pa; Ohio Univ, Athens; El Paso Mus Art, Tex; Brandeis Univ Mus, Waltham, Mass; Lowe Art Mus, Univ Miami, Coral Gables; plus many others.
Exhibitions: Mus Mod Art, New York, N Y; Corcoran Gallery Art, Washington, D C; one-man shows, Mus Arts, Fort Lauderdale, Fla, 62 & 65, Lowe Art Mus, Univ Miami, 64 & Columbia Mus, S C, 72; plus many other group & one-man shows.
Positions: Assoc mem adv bd, Peabody Col.
Mailing Address: 5750 Collins Ave, Apt 12 F, Miami Beach, FL 33140.

ROSENBORG, RALPH M
Painter
b Brooklyn, N Y, June 9, 13.
Study & Training: Sch Art League, N Y; Am Mus Nat Hist.

Work in Public Collections: Mus Mod Art; Guggenheim Mus; Phillips Collection, Washington, D C; Metrop Mus Art; Cleveland Art Mus; plus many others.
Exhibitions: More than 300 group exhibs, 34-; 53 one-man shows, New York & other prin cities in U S, 35-
Teaching: Instr art, Brooklyn Mus, 36-38; instr, Ox-Bow Summer Sch, Saugatuck, Mich, 49.
Awards: Purchase Award, Am Acad Arts & Lett, 60.
Memberships: Fedn Mod Painters & Sculptors.
Mailing Address: 165 Lexington Ave, New York, NY 10016.

ROSENDALE, HARRIET
　Painter
Preferred Media: Oils.
b Buffalo, N Y.
Study & Training: New York Sch Fine & Appl Art; Art Stud League New York, N Y, with Frank Vincent DuMond & Jon Corbino.
Exhibitions: Nat Asn Women Artists; New Eng Regional New Canaan, Conn; Springfield Art League, Mass; Conn Acad Fine Art, Hartford; Sarasota Art Asn, Fla.
Awards: Awards, New Eng Regional, 57 & Nat Asn Women Artists, 59 & 61.
Memberships: Nat Asn Women Artists; Conn Acad Fine Arts; Sarasota Art Asn; Springfield Art League.
Publications: Works reproduced by Am Artists Group, Bk of Month Club, Cameo & E E Fairchild.
Dealer: Munson Gallery, 275 Orange St, New Haven, CT 06511.
Mailing Address: 1700 Ben Franklin Dr, Sarasota, FL 33577.

ROSENHOUSE, IRWIN JACOB
　Printmaker, Illustrator
Preferred Media: Graphics.
b Chicago, Ill, Mar 1, 24.
Study & Training: Cooper Union, cert, 50.
Work in Public Collections: Metrop Mus Art; Cooper Union Mus; New York Pub Libr Graphics Collection, N Y; Everhart Mus, Pa; Brooklyn Col, N Y.
Exhibitions: Am Fedn Arts; Libr of Cong; Mus Mod Art, New York; Pa Acad Fine Arts; Boston Printmakers.
Teaching: Instr drawing, painting & graphics, Mus Mod Art Educ Ctr, 68-70; instr graphics, Brooklyn Col, 72.
Positions: Owner & operator, Rosenhouse Gallery New York, 63-71; free lance designer & illusr, 72.
Awards: Award for graphics, Louis Comfort Tiffany Found; resident artist, Huntington Hartford Found, 59 & 61.
Publications: Illusr, What kind of feet does a bear have?, Bobbs, 63; illusr, Have you seen trees?, Young-Scott, 67.
Dealer: Rosenhouse Gallery, 33 Greenwich Ave, New York, NY 10014.
Mailing Address: 722 Broadway, New York, NY 10003.

ROSENQUIT, BERNARD
　Painter, Printmaker
Preferred Media: Oils, Gouache, Wood.
b Hotin, Roumania, Dec 26, 23; U S citizen.
Study & Training: Inst Art & Archeol, Paris; Fontainebleau Sch Fine Arts, France; Brooklyn Mus Sch Fine Art, N Y; Atelier 17, New York; Art Stud League New York, N Y.
Work in Public Collections: Metrop Mus Art, New York; Brooklyn Mus Fine Art; Victoria & Albert Mus, London, Eng; Smithsonian Inst, Washington, D C; New York Pub Libr Print Collection; plus others.
Exhibitions: Honolulu Acad Fine Arts, Hawaii; Boston Mus Fine Arts, Mass; Mus Mod Art, New York; Newark Mus Art, N J; seven one-man shows, Roko Gallery, New York, 51-71; plus others.
Awards: Fulbright grant painting, Paris, 58; Louis Comfort Tiffany Found grant printmaking, 59.
Memberships: Artists Equity Asn New York; life mem Art Stud League New York.
Dealer: Roko Gallery, 90 E 10th St, New York, NY 10003.
Mailing Address: 1437 First Ave, New York, NY 10021.

ROSENTHAL, MRS ALAN H
　Collector
Collection: Ethnographica.
Mailing Address: 169 E 69th St, New York, NY 10021.

ROSENTHAL, BERNARD J
　Sculptor
Preferred Media: Metal.
b Highland Park, Ill, Aug 9, 14.
Study & Training: Univ Mich, BFA, 36; Cranbrook Acad Art.
Work in Public Collections: Mus Mod Art, New York, N Y; Whitney Mus Am Art; Middleheim Mus, Antwerp, Belg; Israel Mus, Jerusalem; Albright-Knox Art Gallery, Buffalo.

Commissions: Cube, Alamo, New York, 66; Large Cube, Univ Mich, Ann Arbor, 68; Bronze disk, Rondo, New York Pub Libr, 69; Sun Disk, Financial Ctr Pac, Honolulu, Hawaii, 71; Pedestrian Plaza Sculpture, New York, 72.
Exhibitions: Nine Whitney Mus Am Art Ann, 53-69; Third Bienal, Sao Paulo, Brazil, 55; Recent Sculpture U S A, Mos Mod Art, 59; Biennale, Middleheim Mus, Antwerp, Belg, 71.
Awards: Honor award, Am Inst Architects, 59; Ford Found Purchase Prize, Krannert Art Mus, 63; outstanding achievement award, Univ Mich, 67.
Bibliography: Bernard Rosenthal, Life, 52; Gibson Danes (auth), Bernard Rosenthal, Art Int, 68; Sam Hunter (auth), Rosenthal: sculptures, 68.
Dealer: M Knoedler, 21 E 70th St, New York, NY 10021.
Mailing Address: 358 E 57th St, New York, NY 10022.

ROSENTHAL, GERTRUDE
　Art Historian, Art Administrator
b Mayen, Ger, May 19, 03; U S citizen.
Study & Training: Univ Paris, 25-26; Univ Cologne & Univ Bonn, PhD(magna cum laude), 32, with A E Brinckmann; hon LHD, Goucher Col, 68; hon DFA, Md Inst Baltimore Col Art, 68.
Collections Arranged: Bacchiacca & His Friends, 60, Four Paris Painters—Manet, Degas, Morisot & Mary Cassatt, 62, Baltimore Mus Art; Nineteen Hundred Fourteen, 64, From El Greco To Pollock, Early & Late Works by Am & Europ Artists, 68; Cone Collection, Mary Frick Jacobs Collection, Daingerfield Collection, & Wurtzburger Primitive Art Collection.
Teaching: Vis prof, Johns Hopkins Univ, 48-50, vis lectr, 52-53.
Positions: Res asst, Courtauld Inst, Univ London, 39-40; art librn, Goucher Col, Baltimore, 40-45; from cur to chief cur, Baltimore Mus Art, 45-69, emer chief cur, 69-; ed, Baltimore Mus News, 59-63; consult, Western Col Honolulu Acad Arts, 72-
Awards: Nat Found Arts res grant Am & Ger Romantic nineteenth century painting, 68; studies in hon of G Rosenthal, 68 & 72.
Memberships: Am Asn Mus; Col Art Asn Am; Mus Mod Art; Walters Art Gallery; Baltimore Mus Art.
Research: European and American art from the sixteenth century to 1965.
Publications: Auth, articles on Gauguin, 52, Matisse, 56 & German Expressionism, 57, Baltimore Mus News; ed, Biennale Venezia 1960, Stati Uniti d'America, 60; auth & ed, Four Paris painters, 62, Nineteen Fourteen, 64 & From El Greco to Pollock, early and late works by European and American artists, 68; auth & ed, Annual II, studies on Thomas Cole, Baltimore Mus Art, 68.
Mailing Address: 3925 Beech Ave, Baltimore, MD 21211.

ROSENTHAL, SEYMOUR JOSEPH
　Painter
Preferred Media: Watercolors, Oils, Tempera, Lithography.
b New York, N Y, Aug 14, 21.
Work in Public Collections: 39 lithographs, Metrop Mus Art Permanent Collection, New York; Herron Mus Art, Indianapolis, Ind; Suffolk Mus, Stony Brook, N Y; Technion Bldg, Haifa, Israel; Harry S Truman Libr, Independence, Mo.
Commissions: Drawings of children, New York Bd Educ, 57; painting of Moses, Borough Pres, Queens, N Y, 62.
Exhibitions: Civil Rights Art Show, Brooklyn Mus, 62; one-man shows, Herzl Inst, 64, Suffolk Mus, 68 & ACA Gallery, New York, 69; Major Drawings of 19th & 20th Century Exhib, 64-65 & Art Dealers Choice Exhib, 67, Gallery Mod Art, New York; Indianapolis Mus Art, 72.
Awards: St Gauden's Medal, Benjamin Franklin High Sch, 39.
Bibliography: Jeanne Paris (auth), Artist has a great future, Long Island Press, 66; Edwin Newman (auth), Today Show, NBC TV, 70; Theo Metzger (auth), Directions, ABC TV, 71.
Memberships: Artists Equity Asn; Comt Arts & Lit In Jewish Life, Jewish Fedn Philanthropies.
Publications: Illusr, Parke Davis Med J, 56 & Scope, 56; contribr, Commonweal, Vol 90, No 15.
Dealers: Associated American Artists, 663 Fifth Ave, New York, NY 10022; ACA Gallery, 25 E 73rd St, New York, NY 10021.
Mailing Address: 161-08 Jewel Ave, Flushing, NY 11365.

ROSENTHAL, STEPHEN
　Painter
Preferred Media: Tempera.
b Richmond, Va, May 28, 35.
Study & Training: Art Stud League New York, N Y, with Edwin Dickinson; Tyler Sch Fine Arts, Philadelphia, Pa, with Boris Blai & BFA, 60.
Work in Public Collections: Arts Club Chicago, Ill; Yale Univ Art Gallery, New Haven, Conn; Art Fund, New York.
Exhibitions: Am Acad Arts & Lett, New York, 63; Amon Carter Mus, Fort Worth, Tex, 64; Int Watercolor Biennial, Brooklyn Mus, N Y, 65; Herron Inst, Indianapolis, Ind, 67; Pa Acad Fine Arts Biennial Exhib, Philadelphia, 67.

Teaching: Instr design, Cooper Union, New York, 66-67; lectr painting, Univ N C, Greensboro, 71-72.
Positions: Bk reviewer, Arts Mag, New York, 71-72.
Awards: Mason Lord prize, Baltimore Mus Art, 67.
Bibliography: Raymond Charmet (auth), Un jeune Americain, Arts, 66; Leach Levy (auth), The drawn line in painting, Parker St 470, 71.
Dealer: 55 Mercer, 55 Mercer St, New York, NY 10013.
Mailing Address: 42 Grand St, New York, NY 10013.

ROSENWALD, BARBARA K
Collector
b Norfolk, Va, July 30, 24.
Study & Training: Boston Mus Sch Fine Arts; Fogg Mus, Harvard Univ; Stella Elkins Tyler Sch Fine Arts; also in Paris, France & Florence, Italy.
Collection: Modern Italian art, including works by Afro, Campigli, Moscha; French modern art, including works by Pignon and others.
Mailing Address: Box 496, Rushland, Bucks County, PA 18956.

ROSENWALD, LESSING JULIUS
Collector, Patron
b Chicago, Ill, Feb 10, 91.
Study & Training: Cornell Univ; Univ Pa, hon DHL; Lincoln Univ, hon DHL; Jefferson Med Col, hon LLD.
Positions: Hon mem bd gov, Philadelphia Mus Art; former trustee, Free Libr Philadelphia; trustee, Rosenbach Found, Philadelphia; assoc, Blake Trust, London; trustee & benefactor, Nat Gallery Art; benefactor, Libr Cong, Washington, D C; hon mem, Inst Advan Study, Philadelphia Mus Art.
Awards: Philadelphia Award, Artists Equity Asn, 61; distinguished achievement award, Philadelphia Art Alliance, 63.
Memberships: Grolier Club, N Y; Benjamin Franklin fel Royal Soc Arts, Eng; Print Coun Am.
Collection: Prints, drawings, miniatures & rare illustrated books, including, Fior di Virtu 1491 and The nineteenth book.
Mailing Address: 1146 Fox Chase Rd, Jenkintown, PA 19046.

ROSIN, HARRY
Sculptor, Educator
Preferred Media: Bronze.
b Philadelphia, Pa.
Study & Training: Pa Acad Fine Arts; also study in Paris.
Work in Public Collections: Pa Acad Fine Arts; Philadelphia Mus.
Commissions: Connie Mack, Philadelphia Stadium; J B Kelly & Quaker & Puritan, Schuykill River, Philadelphia; Deerfield Boy, Mass; four large stone reliefs, Westchester, Pa Ct House.
Exhibitions: One-man show, Pa Acad Fine Arts; World's Fairs, San Francisco, Chicago, New York & Dallas.
Teaching: Sr instr sculpture, Pa Acad Fine Arts, 39-
Awards: Widener Gold Medal; Am Acad Arts & Lett grant; Bouregy Prize, Audubon Artists.
Memberships: Assoc Nat Acad Design.
Mailing Address: New Hope, PA 18938.

ROSKILL, MARK WENTWORTH
Art Historian, Art Critic
b London, Eng, Nov 10, 33.
Study & Training: Trinity Col, Cambridge, Eng, BA, 56; Harvard Univ, MA, 57; Courtald Inst, Univ London, 57; Trinity Col, Cambridge, MA, 61; Princeton Univ, MFA & PhD, 61.
Teaching: Instr & asst, Princeton Univ, 59-61; from instr to asst prof, Harvard Univ, 61-68; assoc prof, Univ Mass, Amherst, 68-
Awards: Am Coun Learned Socs fel, 65-66.
Memberships: Col Art Asn Am.
Research: Nineteenth and twentieth century art; criticism; methodology of art history.
Publications: Auth, English painting from 1500 to 1865; ed, The letters of Vincent Van Gogh, 63; auth, Dolce's Aretino and Venetian art theory of the cinquecento, 68; auth, Van Gogh, Gauguin and the Impressionist circle, 70; contribr, Atlantic brief lives, 71.
Mailing Address: Dept of Art, University of Massachusetts, Amherst, MA 01002.

ROSOFSKY, SEYMOUR
Painter
Preferred Media: Oils, Watercolors, Pastels.
b Chicago, Ill, Aug 4, 24.
Study & Training: Art Inst Chicago, BFA, 49, MFA, 50.
Work in Public Collections: Mus Mod Art, New York, N Y; Art Inst Chicago; Los Angeles Co Mus; Brooklyn Mus; Pasadena Mus.
Exhibitions: Mythology in our Time, Bologna, Italy, 66; Fantasy & Figure, Am Fedn Arts Touring Exhib, 68-69; Human Concern & Personal Torment, Whitney Mus Am Art, 69; Chemin de la Creation, France, 70; Tamarind Touring Exhib, U S & S Am, 70; plus many one-man shows in U S & Europe.
Teaching: Prof art, City Cols Chicago, 53-

Awards: Fulbright award, 58-59; Guggenheim fel, 62-63, 63-64; Tamarind fel, 68.
Memberships: Alumni Asn Art Inst Chicago.
Dealers: Galerie du Dragon, Rue du Dragon 19, Paris, France; Graphics Gallery, 1 Embarcadero Ctr, San Francisco, CA 94111.
Mailing Address: 859 Fullerton, Chicago, IL 60614.

ROSS, ALEXANDER
Painter
Preferred Media: Watercolors, Acrylics, Oils.
b Dunfermline, Scotland, Oct 28, 08; U S citizen.
Study & Training: Carnegie Inst Technol, with Robert Lepper; Boston Col, hon MA.
Work in Public Collections: New Britain Mus, Conn; Waterbury Mus, Conn; U S Air Force Collection, Denver, Colo; Am Acad Design, New York, N Y; Mormon Church.
Commissions: Many portrait comns, by pvt individuals & major Am publ.
Exhibitions: Am Watercolor Soc, Royal Soc Painters, London, 66; 200 Yrs Watercolor, Metrop Mus Art, New York, 67; 18th Ann New Eng Exhib, Silvermine Guild, Conn, 68; Landscape One, De Cordova Mus, Lincoln, Mass, 70; Spring Rebirth, S New Eng Invitational, Fairfield Univ, Conn, 70.
Teaching: Lectr creative painting, Cath Univ Am, summer 54.
Positions: Mem Art Comt, Fairfield Univ, 69-
Awards: First prize Popular Opinion Award, Los Angeles Co Fair, 60; Thomas Saxe Found Award, New Canaan Ann, 67; Adolf & Cedar Obrig Award, Nat Acad Design, 72.
Bibliography: Robert Ulrich Godsoe (auth), Alex Ross: reluctant prophet, Esquire, 48.
Memberships: Nat Acad Design; Conn Acad Fine Arts; Am Watercolor Soc; Silvermine Guild Artists; Conn Watercolor Soc.
Publications: Illusr, covers, Good Housekeeping, 42-54, Sat Eve Post, 43-50, Cosmopolitan, 44-60, Ladies Home J, 45-60 & McCalls, 45-60; auth, How I use watercolor, Am Artist, 62 & New directions in watercolor (film), Electrographic Corp, 71.
Dealers: Collectors Gallery, Nashville, TN 37205; Joe Demers, 5 Harbour House, Harbourtown, Hilton Head Island, SC 29928.
Mailing Address: Hawthorn Trail, Ridgefield, CT 06877.

ROSS, ALVIN
Painter, Educator
Preferred Media: Oils.
b Vineland, N J, Jan 12, 20.
Study & Training: Tyler Sch Fine Arts, Temple Univ, BFA & BSEd, 44; Barnes Found; Acad Belle Arti, Florence; also with Louis Bouche, Franklin Watkins, Earl Horter, Peggy Bacon & Furman J Finck.
Work in Public Collections: Minneapolis Inst Arts; La Jolla Art Ctr; New York Hilton Collection; Univ Nebr.
Exhibitions: Art Inst Chicago Ann, 61; Am Acad Arts & Lett, 62; Butler Inst Am Art, 70; Nat Acad Design, 72; Nat Inst Arts & Lett, 72.
Teaching: Prof hist art & chmn dept, Pratt Inst, 52-
Awards: Bronze medal of honor in painting, Nat Arts Club, 70.
Mailing Address: 127 W 20th St, New York, NY 10011.

ROSS, CHARLES
Sculptor
b Philadelphia, Pa, Dec 17, 37.
Study & Training: Univ Calif, AB, 60, MA, 62.
Work in Public Collections: William Rockhill Nelson Gallery Art, Kansas City, Mo; Whitney Mus Am Art.
Exhibitions: Directions I: Options 1968, Milwaukee Art Ctr, 68; Prospect '68, Dusseldorf, 68; Made of Plastic, Flint Inst, 68; Univ Pa, 69; Whitney Mus Am Art Sculpture Ann, 69; plus many others.
Teaching: Instr, Univ Calif, 62; instr, Cornell Univ, 64; instr, Univ Calif, 65; artist-in-residence, Univ Ky, 65; instr, Sch Visual Arts, New York, 67; instr, Herbert Lehman Col, 68.
Positions: Co-dir & collabr, Dancers Workshop Co, San Francisco, 64-66.
Awards: James D Phelan traveling scholar, Univ Calif, 62.
Bibliography: Tracy Atkinson (auth), Directions I: Options 1968, Milwaukee Art Ctr, 68.
Mailing Address: 80 Wooster St, New York, NY 10012.

ROSS, CONRAD HAROLD
Printmaker, Educator
Preferred Media: Collage Intaglio.
b Chicago, Ill, Apr 26, 31.
Study & Training: Univ Ill, BFA, 53; Univ Chicago, 54; Univ Iowa, MFA, 59.
Work in Public Collections: Libr Cong, Washington, D C; Springfield Art Mus, Mo; Norfolk Mus Arts & Sci, Va; Dallas Mus Fine Arts, Tex; Okla Printmakers Soc, Oklahoma City.

Exhibitions: The Artist Chooses Contemporary Art, Ackland Art Mus, Univ N C, Chapel Hill, 68; Drawing Nat, San Francisco Mus Art, Calif, 70; Second Ann Exp in Art & Technol Exhib, High Mus, Atlanta, Ga, 70; The Henderson Series—Prints, Drawings Constructions, Birmingham-Southern Art Gallery, Ala, 71; Seventh Dulin Nat Print & Drawing Competition, Knoxville, Tenn, 71; plus others.

Teaching: Instr drawing, design, lettering & art appreciation, La Polytech Inst, 61-63; asst prof drawing & printmaking, Auburn Univ, 63-; vis lectr drawing & printmaking, Kans Univ, 68.

Awards: Louis Comfort Tiffany Found grant printmaking, 60; Auburn Univ res grant-in-aid, 65-67; purchase award, Prints & Drawings, Jacksonville, Fla, 66.

Memberships: Print Coun Am; Southern Graphic Arts Circle; Col Art Asn Am; Philadelphia Print Club; Nat Art Workers Community; plus others.

Publications: Contribr, Artists' proof the annual of prints and printmaking, 70.

Mailing Address: 447 Wrights Mill Rd, Auburn, AL 36830.

ROSS, JAMES MATTHEW
Painter, Educator
b Ann Arbor, Mich, Sept 8, 31.
Study & Training: Univ Mich, AB; Cranbrook Acad Art, MFA; Rockham Sch Grad Studies, Ann Arbor; Accad Belle Arti, Rome.
Work in Public Collections: Butler Inst Am Art; Cranbrook Mus Art; Detroit Inst Art.
Exhibitions: Michigan Artists, 51-60 & 63; Detroit Inst Art & Pa Acad Fine Arts, 59-60; Walker Art Ctr, 59-60; Wis Painters & Sculptors Ann, Milwaukee Art Ctr, 63-65; Univ Wis-Whitewater, 65; plus others.
Teaching: Asst prof art, Univ Wis-Platteville, 62-
Awards: Fulbright grant painting to Italy, 60 & 61; prizes, Wis Painters & Sculptors, 63 & Mich Fine Arts Exhib, 64; plus others.
Memberships: Col Art Asn Am; Wis Painters & Sculptors Soc; Am Asn Univ Prof.
Mailing Address: Dept of Art, University of Wisconsin-Platteville, Platteville, WI 53818.

ROSS, JEAN G
Painter, Instructor
Preferred Media: Oils.
b Ridgewood, N J, May 16, 25.
Study & Training: Paterson State Teachers Col; Park Col, Mo.
Exhibitions: Am Artists Prof League Grand Nat, New York, N Y, 69-72; Governor's Reception, Garden State Art Ctr, 71 & 72; Franklin Arts Coun, Millstone, N J, 71 & 72; Am Asn Univ Women, Bernardsville, N J, 71 & 72; Suburban Artists Guild, Highland Park, N J.
Teaching: Instr oil painting, Ridgewood Art Asn, N J, 61-66; instr oil painting, Somerset Art Asn, Bernardsville, 66-
Positions: V pres activities, Somerset Art Asn.
Awards: First prize for oils, 71 & gold medal for oils, 72, Am Artists Prof League; first prize prof, Suburban Arts Coun, 71.
Memberships: Am Artists Prof League.
Dealer: The Carriage House, Hilltop Rd, Mendham, NJ 07945.
Mailing Address: 102 Liberty Corner Rd, Warren, NJ 07060.

ROSS, JOHN T
Printmaker, Educator
b New York, N Y, Sept 25, 21.
Study & Training: Cooper Union Art Sch, grad, 48, with Morris Kantor & Will Barnet; New Sch Social Res, with Antonio Frasconi & Louis Schanker; Columbia Univ, 53.
Work in Public Collections: Nat Collection Fine Arts, Washington, D C; Hirshhorn Collection; Metrop Mus Art, New York; Libr Cong, Washington, D C; Cincinnati Art Mus.
Commissions: Ed prints, Hilton Hotel, 63, Assoc Am Artists, 64, 66 & 72, Philadelphia Print Club, 67, N Y State Coun Arts, 67 & Int Poetry Forum, 68.
Exhibitions: Second Int Color Print Exhib, Grenchen, Switz, 61; Int Biennale Gravure, Cracow, Poland, 68; Prize-winning Am Prints, Pratt Graphic Art Ctr, New York, 68; Nat Acad Fine Arts, Amsterdam, Netherlands, 68; Biennial Print Exhib, Calif State Col, Long Beach, 69; plus many group & one-man shows.
Teaching: Instr printmaking, New Sch Soc Res, 57-; instr printmaking, Pratt Graphic Ctr, 63-; assoc prof art, Manhattanville Col, 64-; demonstr & lectr, U S Info Agency Exhib, Romania & Yugoslavia, 64-66.
Positions: Dir, Art Ctr Northern N J, 66-67; pres, U S Comt-Int Asn Art, 67-69; chmn adv panel, Cooper Union Art Sch, 67-69.
Awards: Louis Comfort Tiffany Found grant printmaking, 54; Purchase Prize for 100 Prints of the Year, AAA Gallery, 63; citation for prof achievement, Cooper Union Art Sch, 66.

Bibliography: Articles, In: Am Artist, 52; Artists Proof, 64 & Art in Am, 65.
Memberships: Soc Am Graphic Artists (pres, 61-65, exec coun, 65-); assoc Nat Acad Design; Boston Printmakers; Philadelphia Print Club; Am Color Print Soc.
Publications: Illusr, many bks; co-auth, The complete printmaker, Macmillan, 72.
Dealer: Associated American Artists, 663 Fifth Ave, New York, NY 10022.
Mailing Address: 110 Davison Pl, Englewood, NJ 07631.

ROSS, (ROBERT) KENNETH
Art Administrator
b El Paso, Tex, Aug 1, 10.
Study & Training: Pasadena Jr Col; Chouinard Art Inst; Art Ctr Sch Los Angeles; Nat Acad, Florence, Italy; Acad Grande Chaumiere, Paris; Euston Rd Sch Drawing & Painting, London.
Teaching: Lectr hist art & art appreciation, Univ Southern Calif.
Positions: Dir, Pasadena Art Inst, Calif; dir, Mod Inst Art, Beverly Hills, Calif; art critic, Pasadena Star News; art critic, Los Angeles Daily News, Calif; dir, Los Angeles Munic Arts Dept, 50-
Memberships: Jr Arts Ctr Los Angeles (bd trustees); Munic Art Patrons, Los Angeles.
Mailing Address: Municipal Arts Dept, Rm 1500, City Hall, Los Angeles, CA 90012.

ROSS, MARVIN CHAUNCEY
Museum Curator, Art Historian
b Moriches, N Y, Nov 21, 04.
Study & Training: Harvard Univ, AB, AM; N Y Univ; Univ Berlin; Centro de Estudios Historicos, Madrid, Spain.
Collections Arranged: Early Christian & Byzantine Art, Walters Art Gallery, Baltimore, Md, 47; Raoul Dufy, Los Angeles Co Mus Art, Calif, 53.
Positions: Cur medieval art, Walters Art Gallery, Baltimore, 34-52; chief cur art, Los Angeles Co Mus Art, 52-55; cur, Hillwood (art collection of Mrs Merriweather Post), Washington, D C, 59-
Memberships: Am Asn Mus; Archaeol Inst Am; Am Ceramic Circle; English Ceramic Circle.
Publications: Ed, The west of Alfred Jacob Miller, 51 & 67; ed, George Catlin, last rambles with the Indians, 59; auth, catalogue of the Byzantine antiquities in Dumbarton Oaks collection, 62 & 65; auth, The art of Karl Fabergé & his contemporaries, 65; auth, Russian porcelains: Merriweather Post collection, 68.
Mailing Address: 2230 California St N W, Washington, DC 20008.

ROSSE, MARYVONNE
Sculptor
Preferred Media: Clay, Plaster, Wood, Bronze.
b Palo Alto, Calif, Mar 4, 17.
Study & Training: Acad Fine Arts, The Hague, Netherlands, dipl.
Work in Public Collections: Mus Holland, Mich.
Commissions: Plaques, J Bos, Netherlands, 38; medals, Koninklyk Begeer, Netherlands, 38; portraits, D Tutein Noltenius, Netherlands, 42; garden ornaments, Nederlandshe Olie Fabriek, Delft, Netherlands, 46; commercial prototypes, D G Williams Inc, Brooklyn, 48-66.
Exhibitions: Pulchri Studios, The Hague, 36-47; New York World's Fair, 39; Pen & Brush Club, 67-72; Catharine Lorillard Wolfe Art Club, 67-72; Nat Sculpture Soc, 71-72.
Collections Arranged: Catharine Lorillard Wolfe Art Club, Nat Acad Gallery; Nat Arts Club.
Teaching: Instr sculpture, Rockland Found, Nyack, N Y, 47; instr art, King Coit Theatre Sch Children, New York, N Y, 47-48.
Positions: Sculpture, D G Williams, Brooklyn, N Y, 48-66; ed news lett, Catharine Lorillard Wolfe Art Club, 68-72.
Awards: Hon mention, Catharine Lorillard Wolfe Art Club, Nat Acad, 70; Pen & Brush Solo Exhib Award, 71; gold medal, Catharine Lorillard Wolfe Art Club Ann, 72.
Memberships: Nat Sculpture Soc; Pen & Brush Club (sculpture chmn, 69-); Burr Artists (historian, 68-); Catharine Lorillard Wolfe Art Club (bd mem & sculpture chmn, 69-).
Mailing Address: 431 Buena Vista Rd, New City, NY 10956.

ROSSI, BARBARA
Painter, Printmaker
b Chicago, Ill.
Study & Training: Art Inst Chicago Sch, MFA.
Work in Public Collection: Art Inst Chicago.
Exhibitions: Spirit of the Comics, Inst Contemp Art, Univ Pa, Philadelphia, 69, also circulating exhib under auspices of Am Fedn Arts, 70; Prints by Seven, Whitney Mus Am Art, New York, N Y, 70; Chicago & Vicinity, Art Inst Chicago, 71; Chicago Imagist Art, Mus Contemp Art, Chicago, 72; Chicago Painters, Nat Gallery Can, Ottawa, 72.
Teaching: Instr intaglio processes, Art Inst Chicago Sch, 71-

Awards: Anna Louise Raymond traveling fel, Art Inst Chicago Sch, 70.
Bibliography: Franz Schulze (auth), Fantastic images, Chicago art since 1945, Follett, 72.
Mailing Address: c/o Phyllis Kind Gallery, 226 E Ontario, Chicago, IL 60611.

ROSSI, JOSEPH O
Painter, Instructor
b Paterson, N J.
Study & Training: Newark Sch Fine & Indust Art; Columbia Univ; also with John Grabach & Harvey Dunn.
Work in Public Collections: Salmagundi Club Collection; Norfolk Mus, Va; Bergen Mall Collection; Newark Hosp Collection; also in pvt collections.
Exhibitions: Am Watercolor Soc Ann, New York; Allied Artists Am Ann, New York; Audubon Artists Ann, New York; Nat Acad Design Ann, New York; Watercolor U S A, Mo.
Teaching: Instr watercolor, oil & life drawing, Newark Sch Fine & Indust Art; also pvt instr & instr for var art groups.
Awards: Salmagundi Oil Award, Herman Wick Mem, 70; N J Watercolor Award, hon Peter H B Frelinghuysen, 71; N J Artist of Yr Award, Am Artist Prof League.
Memberships: Am Watercolor Soc (chmn social affairs); N J Watercolor Soc (past v pres & del-at-lg); Allied Artist Am (past current work chmn); Salmagundi Club (past art chmn); Audubon Artist Am.
Publications: Auth, Watercolor page, Am Artist, 8/72.
Mailing Address: 45 Lockwood Dr, Clifton, NJ 07013.

ROSTER, FRED HOWARD
Sculptor, Educator
b Palo Alto, Calif, June 27, 44.
Study & Training: Gavilan Col, AA; San Jose State Col, BA & MA; Univ Hawaii, MFA & with Herbert H Sanders.
Work in Public Collections: Honolulu Acad Art, Hawaii; State Found Cult & Arts, Honolulu; Contemp Arts Ctr Hawaii; Hawaii State Dept Educ; Hawaii Loa Col, Kailua.
Commissions: Ceramic sculptural pots, Flora Pacifica, Honolulu, 70; stained glass mural, Vladimir Ossipoff Corp for Hilo, Hawaii, 71.
Exhibitions: San Francisco Potters Asn Ann, DeYoung Mus, 68; Design Ten, Calif, 68; Artists of Hawaii Ann, Honolulu Acad Art, 69-72; Hawaii Craftsmen's Ann, Honolulu, 69-72; one-man show, Contemp Arts Ctr Hawaii, 72.
Teaching: Instr ceramics, San Jose State Col, 68-69; asst prof sculpture, Univ Hawaii, 69-
Awards: Elizabeth Moses Award, San Francisco Potter's Asn, 68; sculptural grand award, Windward Artists Guild, 71; res grant, Univ Hawaii, 71.
Memberships: Honolulu Acad Art.
Dealer: Downtown Gallery Ltd, 125 Merchant St, Honolulu, HI 96813.
Mailing Address: 3891 Manoa Rd, Honolulu, HI 96822.

ROSTON, ARNOLD
Painter, Patron
b Racine, Wis, June 29, 18.
Study & Training: City Col New York, 35-37; Nat Acad Design, 37-39; New Sch Social Res, 39-40, with Alexey Brodovitch.
Work in Public Collections: Metrop Mus Art, New York, N Y; Mus Mod Art, New York; New York Pub Libr Print Collection; Vatican Collection, Rome, Italy; Larry Aldrich Old Hundred Mus, Ridgefield, Conn.
Commissions: Copper mural wall, Great Publ Works, Great Neck Pub Libr, N Y, 71.
Exhibitions: New York World's Fair, N Y; Pa Acad Fine Arts, Philadelphia; Brooklyn Mus Art Ann Instructors Show; Cooper Union Art Sch 90th Yr Instructors Show, Cooper-Hewitt Mus, N Y; Nat Ann Exhibs Advert & Ed Art, New York.
Teaching: Instr graphic design, Cooper Union, 46-53; instr graphic design, Brooklyn Mus Art Sch, 54-55; instr graphic design, Pratt Inst, 54-55.
Positions: Visual info specialist, U S Off Emergency Mgt, 41-43; creative dir, RKO-MBS, 44-58; art group head, Grey Advert Agency, 56-58; pres, Roston & Co, Great Neck, N Y, 59-; mem art adv bd, New York Community Col, 72-
Awards: Yaddo Found resident fel, 38; Hemispherical Poster Awards, Mus Mod Art, 40-41; Art Dirs Gold Medal, Nat Exhib Advert & Ed Art, 54.
Bibliography: Many articles in trade press, mags & ann catalogues.
Memberships: Art Dirs Club (secy, 71-73); Art Dirs Scholar Fund (pres, 62-); Assoc Coun Arts; Sch Art League of New York Bd Educ (trustee, 69-).

Art Interests: Works of master artists donated to Whitney Museum of American Art, Hofstra University, Joseph and Emily Lowe Museum, National Portrait Gallery of the Smithsonian and others.
Collection: Master drawings, from Penni, Turner and Zuccaro to Ben Shahn, Warhol and Kuniyoshi; prints, from Pissarro, Matisse and Picasso to Castellon, Teichman and Roston.
Mailing Address: 102 Station Rd, Great Neck, NY 11023.

ROSZAK, THEODORE
Painter, Sculptor
b Poland, May 1, 07; U S citizen.
Study & Training: Art Inst Chicago, 22-29; Univ Chicago; Univ Ill; Columbia Univ.
Work in Public Collections: Mus Mod Art, New York, N Y; Whitney Mus Am Art; Yale Gallery Art, New Haven, Conn; Pa Acad Fine Arts; plus others.
Commissions: Spire & Bell Tower, Mass Inst Technol, Cambridge, 56; U S Embassy Eagle, London, Eng, 60; Invocation V, Maremont Bldg, Chicago, Ill, 62; Flight, New York World's Fair, 64; Sentinel, Pub Health Lab, New York, 68.
Exhibitions: Whitney Mus Am Art Retrospective, 56; Tate Gallery, London, 59; U S Nat Exhib, Moscow, U S S R, 59; Venice Biennale, 60; Guggenheim Int, New York, 64; plus others.
Teaching: Prof sculpture, Sarah Lawrence Col, 40-56; vis critic, Columbia Univ, 70-72.
Awards: Frank G Logan Medal For Sculpture, 47 & 51 & Campagna Award, 62, Art Inst Chicago; George G Widener Gold Medal, Pa Acad Fine Art, 56.
Bibliography: Peter Selz (auth), Theodore Roszak, Mus Mod Art, 59; Michel Conil Lacolste (auth), Theodore Roszak, Dict Mod Sculpture, 60; H H Arnason (auth), Theodore Roszak, Sculptor, Art Am, 61.
Memberships: Drawing Soc (adv coun, 72); Louis Comfort Tiffany Found (trustee, 64-); Skowhegan Sch Painting & Sculpture (mem bd gov, 60-); Nat Inst Arts & Lett (v pres, 70).
Publications: Auth & illusr, In pursuit of an image, 55.
Dealer: Pierre Matisse Art Gallery, 41 E 57th St, New York, NY 10021.
Mailing Address: One St Lukes Pl, New York, NY 10014.

ROTAN, WALTER
Sculptor
b Baltimore, Md, Mar 29, 12.
Study & Training: Md Inst; Pa Acad Fine Arts; also with Albert Laessie.
Work in Public Collections: Pa Acad Fine Arts; Brookgreen Gardens, S C.
Exhibitions: Nat Acad Design; Pa Acad Fine Arts; Art Inst Chicago; Philadelphia Mus Art; Carnegie Inst; plus many others
Teaching: Head art dept, Taft Sch, Watertown, Conn, 38-53.
Awards: Cresson traveling scholar, 33 & prize, 46, Pa Acad Fine Arts; four prizes, Nat Acad Design, 36-45; prize, Allied Artists Am, 56; plus others.
Memberships: Fel Nat Sculpture Soc; Audubon Artists; fel Pa Acad Fine Arts.
Mailing Address: 45 Christopher St, New York, NY 10014.

ROTENBERG, HAROLD
Painter
Preferred Media: Oils.
b Attleboro, Mass, July 12, 05.
Study & Training: Mus Fine Arts, Boston; Harvard Summer Sch; Acad Grande Chaumière, Paris, France; Bezalel Art Sch, Jerusalem; also with Charles Hawthorne, Provincetown, Mass.
Exhibitions: Rockport Art Asn, Mass, 40-72; Safad, Israel, 42-72; Vose Art Gallery, Boston, Mass, 52-62; Babcock Gallery, New York, N Y, 55-60; Soc des Artistes Independants, Paris, 62-72.
Teaching: Instr drawing, Sch Practical Art, Boston, 29-37; instr drawing, Boston Mus Fine Arts, 29-40.
Positions: Dir art, Hecht House, Boston, 30-52.
Memberships: Artists Equity Asn New York; Rockport Art Asn; Soc Artistes Independants, Paris; Israel Artists Asn.
Mailing Address: 200 E 62nd St, New York, NY 10021.

ROTH, FRANK
Painter
b Boston, Mass, Feb 22, 36.
Study & Training: Cooper Union Art Sch, 54; Hans Hofmann Sch Fine Arts, 55.
Work in Public Collections: Albright-Knox Art Gallery, Buffalo, N Y; Whitney Mus Am Art; Santa Barbara Mus Art, Calif; Baltimore Mus Art, Md; Walker Art Ctr, Minneapolis, Minn; plus many others.
Exhibitions: Midland Group, Nottingham, Eng, 66; Ulster Mus, Belfast, Ireland; Art in Embassies, 69; Philadelphia Art Alliance, 69; Toledo Mus Art, 69; plus many other group & one-man shows.

Teaching: Instr painting, State Univ Iowa, summer 64; instr painting & drawing, Sch Visual Arts, N Y, 63-; Ford Found artist-in-residence, Univ R I, 66; instr, Univ Calif, Berkeley, 68; instr, Univ Calif, Irvine, 71.

Awards: Ford Found purchase award, 62; Guggenheim fel, 64; Minister For Affairs Award, Int Exhib Young Artists, Tokyo, Japan, 67; plus others.

Bibliography: William H Gerdts, Jr (auth), Painting and sculpture in New Jersey, Van Nostrand-Reinhold, 64.

Mailing Address: c/o Martha Jackson Gallery, 32 E 69th St, New York, NY 10021.

ROTH, JAMES BUFORD
Art Restorer, Painter

b Moniteau Co, Mo, May 11, 10.

Study & Training: Kansas City Art Inst, with Ernest Lawson & Ross Braught; Fogg Mus, Harvard Univ, Carnegie grantee.

Commissions: Rearidos, Grace & Holy Trinity Church, Kansas City, Mo, 39 & Rockhurst Col Chapel, Kansas City, 40.

Teaching: Lectr painting tech, Kansas City Art Inst, 40-49; lectr painting tech, Univ Kans, 50-; lectr painting tech, Univ Mo, 50-; lectr painting tech, Am Asn Mus Workshops, 70 & 72.

Positions: Art conservator & restorer, William Rockhill Nelson Gallery Art, 33-; art conservator & restorer, Atkins Mus Fine Arts, 38-; also pvt restorer.

Awards: Bronze medal for painting, Midwestern Exhib Kansas City Art Inst, 32; first prize, Sweepstakes, Kansas City Art Inst.

Bibliography: Many.

Memberships: Fel Int Inst Conserv Artistic Hist Works; Int Inst Conserv, Am Group (mem coun).

Research: Transfer techniques for paintings; in-painting restorations using plastics as media.

Publications: Co-auth, Separation of two layers of Chinese wall painting, 52; auth, Wax relining, Am Asn Mus Bull, Notes on transfer technique, Expos Painting Conserv, 62, Conservation of paintings, Mus Roundup & Unique painting technique of George Caleb Bingham, Int Inst Conserv, 71.

Mailing Address: 4525 Oak St, Kansas City, MO 64111.

ROTH, RICHARD LEE
Painter

b Brooklyn, N Y, June 22, 46.

Study & Training: R I Sch Design; Cooper Union, BFA.

Work in Public Collections: Akron Art Inst, Ohio; Chase Manhattan Bank Collection, New York, N Y.

Exhibitions: Four Painters for Spring, Castelli Warehouse, New York, 69; group show, Parker St 470, Boston, Mass, 69; 1969 Ann Exhib Contemp Am Painting, Whitney Mus Am Art, New York, 70; one-man shows, O K Harris Gallery, New York, 70 & 72.

Teaching: Adj asst prof, N Y Univ, 71-

Dealer: O K Harris Gallery, 469 W Broadway, New York, NY 10012.

Mailing Address: 25 E Fourth St, New York, NY 10003.

ROTH, RUBI
Painter, Instructor

Preferred Media: Watercolors, Oils, Collage.

b New York, N Y, Dec 1, 05.

Study & Training: N Y Univ; Cooper Union; Columbia Univ.

Work in Public Collections: Norfolk Mus, Va; Seton Hall, N J; Forbes Mus, New York; Long Beach Libr, New York; Beth El Day Sch, New York.

Commissions: Murals commissioned by Dr George Novis, Manhasset, N Y, 70 & Louis Kerber, Belle Harbor, N Y, 71.

Exhibitions: Am Artists Prof League, Lever House, New York, 71; Am Watercolor Soc, Nat Acad Design, New York, 71; Nat Asn Women Artists, Nat Acad Design, New York & Lever House, New York, 72; Nat Art League, Douglaston, N Y, 72.

Teaching: Instr art, Nat Art League, 57-, demonstrator, 72.

Positions: Art judge, Police Athletic League, New York, 71.

Awards: First prize, Am Artists Prof League, 67; second prize, Flushing Merchants Asn, 71; third prize, Nat Art League, 72.

Memberships: Am Watercolor Soc; Nat Asn Women Artists; Am Artists Prof League; Artists Equity Asn; Nat Art League (bd dirs, 72).

Publications: Illusr, Little calypsos, 70; contribr, Arts & crafts activities desk book, Parker.

Mailing Address: 211 Beach 134th St, Belle Harbor, NY 11694.

ROTHMAN, SIDNEY
Art Dealer, Art Critic

b U S A, May 7, 18.

Study & Training: Brooklyn Col; Columbia Univ, BA (lang & art hist); New York Sch Archit Design.

Collections Arranged: New Jersey Artists Show, 68; South American Collection, 69; Yugoslavian Printmakers, 72; Collection of European Prints, Fordham Univ, 72.

Teaching: Lectr art, Women's Club Island, Beach Haven, N J, 67-

68; lectr art, Deborah Hosp, Browns Mills, N J, 69; lectr art, Long Beach Found, Loveladies, N J, 71.

Positions: Art dealer, Philadelphia area, 46-66, Barnegat Light, 58-; assessor of paintings, Long Beach Found Arts & Sci, 71 & 72 season.

Bibliography: Dorothy Grafly (auth), articles, In: Art in Am, 53 & Art Focus, 11/72; Alda Stewart (auth), Observer-Courier Sun, Toms River, 6/16/72.

Memberships: Long Beach Found Arts & Scis; Artists Equity Asn.

Research: Spanish art of time of Velasquez thru Ribera.

Specialty of Gallery: Showing only living artists of all mediums, & sponsoring foreign contemporary artists.

Publications: Auth, articles, In: Beach Haven Times, 67-71; contribr, Arts of Asia, Hong Kong, 71.

Mailing Address: 21st on Central Ave, Barnegat Light, NJ 08006.

ROTHOLZ, RINA
Printmaker

b Israel; U S citizen.

Study & Training: Pratt Graphic Arts Ctr, New York, N Y; Brooklyn Mus Art Sch, N Y.

Work in Public Collections: Boston Mus Fine Arts; Rose Art Mus, Brandeis Univ; Mus Mod Art, New York; Israel Mus, Jerusalem; Albright-Knox Mus, Buffalo, NY; plus many other public & private collections.

Commissions: Edition of 50 prints, 69 & edition of 200 prints, Commentary Libr Collection of Art Treasure; Blue Disc (greeting card design), UNICEF, 72.

Exhibitions: One-man show, Pucker/Safari Gallery, Boston, Mass, 72; group exhibs, De Cordova Mus, Lincoln, Mass, 71; five exhibs, Audubon Artists, 62-71; Boston Printmakers Ann & Traveling Shows, 67-72; New Direction in American Printmaking, 68 & 69; plus many other group & one-man shows.

Teaching: Lectr & demonstrations, Bd Coop Educ Serv, Scholars in Residence Prog, Nassau Co, N Y.

Awards: First prize for graphics, Port Washington Sixth Ann; purchase prize, Nassau Community Second Graphic Exhib; prize in graphics, Nat Asn Women Artists, 72.

Memberships: Boston Printmakers; Nat Asn Women Artists; Prof Artists Guild.

Research: Discovered process of Tuilegraphy, which is the carving of vinyl asbestos tiles while they are still warm, then printing the tiles as intaglio plates to achieve a variety of textures, shapes, and high reliefs.

Publications: Auth, Tuilegraphy, Artist's Proof, Vol 7.

Mailing Address: 42 Shepherd Lane, Roslyn Heights, NY 11577.

ROTHSCHILD, LINCOLN
Sculptor, Writer

Preferred Media: Wood.

b New York, N Y, Aug 9, 02.

Study & Training: Columbia Univ, AB, 23, AM, 33; N Y Univ Inst Fine Arts; Art Stud League New York, N Y, with Kenneth Hayes Miller, Boardman Robinson & Allen Tucker.

Work in Public Collections: Wood carving, Mother & Child, Whitney Mus Am Art.

Teaching: Instr art hist, Columbia Univ, 25-35; asst prof art hist & chmn dept art, Adelphi Col, 46-50; lectr art hist, City Col New York, 64-68.

Positions: Dir, New York Unit Index Am Design, 37-40; nat exec dir, Artists Equity Asn, 51-57; ed, Pragmatist In Art, 64-

Awards: First prize for sculpture, Village Art Ctr, 49.

Memberships: Col Art Asn Am; Am Soc Aesthetics; life mem Art Stud League New York (mem bd control, 31); Am Artists Cong (treas, 36-41).

Research: Interpretation of style; American art.

Publications: Auth, Sculpture through the ages, 42, Style in art, 60 & Hugo Robus, 60.

Mailing Address: 63 Livingston Ave, Dobbs Ferry, NY 10522.

ROUSE, MARY JANE DICKARD
Educator

b Monroe, La, Oct 17, 24.

Study & Training: La Polytech Inst, BA; Inst Design, Chicago; La State Univ, MA; Stanford Univ, PhD.

Teaching: Instr, art dept, La Polytech Inst, 56-60; from asst prof to assoc prof art educ, Ind Univ, Bloomington, 63-

Awards: Danforth col teacher fel, 60-61; Stanford fel, 61-62.

Research: Experimental aesthetics; evaluation; curriculum.

Publications: Auth, articles on res & curric & res monogr.

Mailing Address: Dept of Art Education, Indiana University, Bloomington, IN 47401.

ROUSSEAU, THEODORE, JR
Museum Curator

b Freeport, N Y, Oct 8, 12.

Study & Training: Eton Col, Windsor, 24-29; Sorbonne, 33; Harvard Univ, BA, 34, MA, 37.

Collections Arranged: Van Gogh Exhibition, Metrop Mus Art & Art Inst Chicago, 49-50; Cezanne Exhibition, 52, Metrop Mus Art & Art Inst Chicago; Vienna Art Treasures, 50; Dutch Painting: The Golden Age, Metrop Mus Art, Toledo Mus Art & Art Gallery Toronto, 54-55.
Teaching: Lectr painting, univs & mus.
Positions: Asst cur paintings, Nat Gallery Art, Washington, D C, 40-41; assoc cur paintings, Metrop Mus Art, 47, cur Europ paintings, 48-67, chmn dept paintings, 67-68, v-dir & cur in chief, 68-
Awards: Legion of Hon, France; Order of Orange-Nassau; Comdr, Order of Alfonso X el Sabio, Spain, 62; plus others.
Memberships: Century Asn; Grolier Club.
Publications: Auth, Paul Cezanne, 53; auth, Titian, Abrams, 55 & 70; Auth, The Metropolitan Museum, 57; contribr, Art News, Rev Paris, Metrop Mus Art & other mus bull.
Mailing Address: Metropolitan Museum of Art, Fifth Ave at 82nd St, New York, NY 10028.

ROUSSEAU-VERMETTE, MARIETTE
Craftsman
Preferred Media: Tapestry.
b Trois Pistoles, P Q, Aug 29, 26.
Study & Training: Ecole Beaux Arts, Quebec, 48; Liebes Studio; Oakland Col Arts & Crafts, Calif.
Work in Public Collections: Galerie Nat Can, Ottawa; Mus Quebec; many Can embassies; Univ Vancouver Arts Faculty Hall; Vancouver Art Gallery.
Commissions: Theater stage curtains, Govt Nat Art Ctr Performing Art, 65 & J F Kennedy Ctr, Washington, D C, 71; tapestries, Macmillan Bloedel Hall, Vancouver, 68, Hall of Justice Perce, 68 & Hall of the Toronto Star, 71-72.
Exhibitions: 4 Biennales, Lausanne, Switz, 62, 65, 69 & 71; Quebec & Ont Contemp Painters Centennial Exhib, 65; 300 Yrs Art, Nat Gallery Can, 67; Mus Mod Art, New York, N Y, 69; Mus Beaux Arts, Montreal, 71.
Teaching: Prof tapestry, Ctr Art Ste-Adele, P Q, 52-56; prof tapestry, Ctr Art Laval, P Q, 70-
Positions: Dir, Can Conf Arts, 58-
Awards: First prize, P Q Art Contest, 57; Can Art Coun traveling bursary, 67; Cult Inst Rome, Italy bursary, 72-73.
Bibliography: Le grande livre de la tapisserie, Time, 63; Guy Robert (auth), Symphonies en laines et couleurs, Vie Arts, 64; Eugene Cloutier (auth), Retrospective (catalogue), 72.
Memberships: Conf Arts; assoc Can Royal Acad; Asn Artistes Prof; World Craft Coun; Montreal Mus Fine Art.
Collection: Canadian paintings, sculptures and tapestries; graphic art; Polish tapestries, icons and paintings.
Dealer: Marlborough-Godard Galleries, 1490 Sherbrooke St W, Montreal, P Q, Can; Marlborough-Godard Galleries, 22 Hatelton, Toronto, Ont, Can.
Mailing Address: Ste-Adele en haut, P Q, Can.

ROUSSEL, CLAUDE PATRICE
Sculptor, Instructor
Preferred Media: Wood, Stone, Steel, Plastics.
b Edmundston, N B, July 6, 30.
Study & Training: Ecole Beaux-Arts, Montreal, P Q, 50-56; Can Coun sr traveling fel, Europe, 61.
Work in Public Collections: Smithsonian Inst, Washington, D C; N B Mus, St John; Confedn Art Gallery, Charlottetown, P E I; Univ Moncton, N B; Mt Allison Univ, Sackville, N B.
Commissions: Mural, Frederickton Airport, N B, 64; mural, N B Centennial Bldg, 66; monument, fishermen, Escuminac, N B, 69; exterior sculpture & interior mural, Univ Moncton Nursing Pavillion, 71; archit sculpture for City Hall, City of St John, 72; plus 20 other archit projs.
Exhibitions: Survey 69, Montreal Mus Fine Arts, 69; N B Mus, 70; Confedn Art Gallery, 70; Air & Space Mus, Smithsonian Inst, 71; Man & His World, Montreal, 71.
Teaching: Art instr, Edmundston Pub Schs, 56-59; art instr, Univ Moncton, 63-
Positions: Asst curator, Beaverbrook Art Gallery, Frederickton, 59-61.
Awards: Allied Arts Medal, Royal Archit Soc Can, 64; St John City Hall Sculpture Competition, City of St John, 72.
Bibliography: Painting a province, Nat Film Bd, 60; J Villon (auth), L'art en acadie, Rev Liberté, 70; E Michel (auth), Reseau soleil, C B C, 71; plus one other.
Memberships: Can Artist Representation (Moncton rep, 72); Can Sculptor Soc.
Mailing Address: 905 Amirault, St Anselme, N B, Can.

ROVELSTAD, TRYGVE A
Sculptor, Designer
b Elgin, Ill.
Study & Training: Art Inst Chicago; Univ Wash; also with Lorado Taft.

Work in Public Collections: Designed & ed, Am Roll Honor World War II, Am Chapel St Paul's Cathedral, London, Eng; portrait of Sen William Barr, Capitol Bldg, Springfield, Ill; dedication plaque of Gov Stratton, Ill State Off Bldg; plus others.
Commissions: Screaming Eagle Medal, 101st Airborne Div Asn, 69; Captive Nations Proclamation Medal, 69; Chicago Coin Club 50th Anniversary Medal, 69; Chicago Fire Centennial Medal, Chicago Hist Soc, 71; Martin Delaney Commemorative Medal, Am Negro Commemorative Soc, 72; plus others.
Exhibitions: A Thousand Yrs Calligraphy & Illum, Peabody Inst City of Baltimore, Md, 59-60; Hudson Valley Art Asn Ann, 70 & 72; Am Artists Prof League Grand Nat, 71 & 72.
Positions: Sculptor, U S War Dept, Shrivenham, Eng, 45-46; designer-sculptor, var firms & studios; heraldic artist & medalist, Off Qm, Washington, D C, auth & lithographer, Coast & Geodetic Surv, Map Div, Washington, D C; pres, Pioneer Mem Found Ill; gov, Assoc Soc Chicago; pres & dir, Pathfinder Inc, Elgin, Ill.
Awards: Sculpture Award for Pioneer Father, Am Artists Prof League Grand Nat, 71.
Memberships: Fel Am Artists Prof League; Alumni Asn Sch Art Inst Chicago.
Mailing Address: 535 Ryerson Ave, Elgin, IL 60120.

ROWAN, DENNIS MICHAEL
Printmaker, Educator
Preferred Media: Intaglio.
b Milwaukee, Wis, Jan 6, 38.
Study & Training: Univ Wis, BS, 62; Univ Ill, MFA, 64.
Work in Public Collections: Art Inst Chicago, Ill; Boston Mus Fine Arts, Mass; Seattle Art Mus, Wash; Okla Art Ctr, Oklahoma City; Honolulu Acad Arts, Hawaii.
Exhibitions: Eight shows, Boston Printmakers Exhib, 61-72; six shows, Northwest Printmakers Int Exhib, Seattle, 63-71; Nat Acad Design 140th Ann, 65; 22nd Int Printmaking Biennale, Buenos Aires, Arg, 70; 22nd Prints Nat, Libr Cong, Washington, D C, 71.
Teaching: Prof art, Univ Ill, Urbana-Champaign, 64-, assoc, Ctr Advan Study, 71-
Awards: Purchase award, Second Biennale Int Gravure, Cracow, Poland, 68; Yorkshire Arts Asn Purchase Prize, Brit Int Print Biennale, 70; Juror's prize, Graphikbiennale Wien, Europahaus, Vienna, Austria, 72.
Memberships: Boston Printmakers; Calif Soc Printmakers.
Publications: Contribr, Prize-winning graphics, Vol 3, 65 & Vol 4, 66.
Mailing Address: 143 Fine Arts Bldg, University of Illinois, Champaign, IL 61820.

ROWAN, FRANCES PHYSIOC
Painter, Printmaker
Preferred Media: Graphics.
b Ossining, N Y.
Study & Training: Randolph-Macon Woman's Col, 29-30; Cooper Union, cert, 36; also graphics with Harry Sternberg & woodcuts with Carol Summers.
Work in Public Collections: Randolph-Macon Woman's Col, Lynchburg, Va; Freeport High Sch, N Y.
Exhibitions: Brooklyn Mus 11th Nat Print Show, 58; Audubon Artists, 58 & 59; Am Fedn Arts Traveling Show, 58-59; Knickerbocker Artists, 61; Silvermine Guild Artists 6th Nat Print Show, 66.
Teaching: Instr drawing & painting, Country Art Gallery, Westbury, N Y, 55-66; instr drawing & painting, Five Towns Music & Art Found, 70-
Awards: First prizes, Malverne Artists, 52 & Hofstra Univ, 57; Sam Flax Award, Knickerbocker Artists, 61.
Memberships: Prof Artists Guild; Silvermine Guild Artists.
Mailing Address: 210 Pine St, Freeport, NY 11520.

ROWAN, HERMAN
Painter, Educator
Preferred Media: Oils.
b New York, N Y, July 20, 23.
Study & Training: Cooper Union; San Francisco State Col; Kans State Univ, BS; State Univ Iowa, MA & MFA.
Work in Public Collections: Walker Art Ctr, Minneapolis; Brooklyn Mus, N Y; Univ Notre Dame, South Bend, Ind; Columbus Mus, Ohio; San Diego Gallery Fine Arts, Calif.
Exhibitions: Art U S A, New York, 60; San Francisco Mus Nat Ann, 63; Southwest Ann, Houston Mus, 63; Walker Art Ctr Invitational, 65; Box-Top Art, Tour N Z Galleries, 71-72.
Teaching: Prof painting, Univ Minn, Minneapolis, 64-
Awards: Lyman Award, Albright Gallery, 59; purchase prize, San Diego Gallery Fine Arts, 63; hon mention, Calif Western Univ, 63.
Dealer: Martin Gallery, 2116 Second Ave S, Minneapolis, MN 55404.
Mailing Address: 1778 Emerson Ave S, Minneapolis, MN 55403.

ROWE, REGINALD M
Painter, Sculptor
b New York, N Y, Dec 8, 20.
Study & Training: Princeton Univ, BA, 44; Art Stud League New York, with Louis Bosa, 46-47; Inst Allende, Univ Guanajuato, 58-59, MFA, 59.
Work in Public Collections: Marion Koogler McNay Mus, San Antonio, Tex.
Commissions: Mural & outdoor sculpture, Hemisfair 1968, San Antonio, Tex, 68.
Exhibitions: San Miguel Allende, Mex, 60; 18th Exhib Southwest Prints & Drawings, Dallas Mus, 69; Artists of the Southeast & Texas, Isaac Delgado Mus Art, New Orleans, La, 71; two-man show, Witte Mus, San Antonio, 68; one-man New York shows, Wellons Gallery, 52, 53 & 56, Bianchini Gallery, 60 & Ruth White Gallery, 64 & 70.
Teaching: Chmn faculty painting, drawing & design, San Antonio Art Inst, 64-
Positions: Chmn exhibs, Witte Mus, 65-67.
Awards: San Miguel Allende, 60.
Bibliography: Ernest Hemingway (auth), catalogue statement for first New York show, 52; reviews, In: Arts, Art News, Pictures on Exhib, Times, Tribune & Art Int, 52-70.
Dealer: Ruth White Gallery, 401 E 74th St, New York, NY 10021.
Mailing Address: 219 W Gramercy, San Antonio, TX 78212.

ROWLAND, ELDEN HART
Painter
b Cincinnati, Ohio, May 31, 15.
Study & Training: Cincinnati Art Acad; Cent Acad Commercial Art, Cincinnati; San Antonio Art Inst, Tex; also Jerry Farnsworth, Cape Cod & Robert Brackman, Conn.
Work in Public Collections: Joe & Emily Lowe Gallery, Coral Gables, Fla; New Col, Sarasota, Fla; Stetson Univ, Deland, Fla; Spring Hill Col, Mobile, Ala; Berkshire Art Asn, Pittsfield, Mass.
Commission: Mural paintings, Monsanto Chem, Springfield, 55.
Exhibitions: Soc Four Arts, Palm Beach, Fla, 60; Lowe Gallery Mem Ann, 62; Cooperstown Ann, 71; Greater Schenectady Ann, N Y, 71; Berkshire Art Asn Ann, 71.
Teaching: Instr painting, Hilton Leech Art Sch, Sarasota.
Awards: First purchase awards, Joe & Emily Lowe Art Gallery, 62, Spring Hill Col, 63 & Berkshire Art Asn, 71.
Memberships: Am Fedn Arts; Sarasota Art Asn; Schenectady Art Mus; Ringling Mus Art.
Publications: Auth, Painters' sutra, 72.
Dealer: Gail Hinchen Gallery, 56 Jean Rd, Manchester, CT 06040.
Mailing Address: 5453 Avenida del Mare, Sarasota, FL 33581.

ROWLANDS, TOM
Painter, Designer
b Pleasant City, Ohio, Mar 8, 26.
Study & Training: Parsons Sch Design; Art Stud League New York; Cooper Union; New Sch Social Res; Belle Arte, Florence, Italy.
Work in Public Collections: Carnegie Mus, Pittsburgh, Pa; Westmoreland Co Mus Art, Greensburg, Pa; Pa Acad Fine Arts, Philadelphia.
Exhibitions: Carnegie Int, Pittsburgh, Pa.
Teaching: Artist-in-residence, Westmoreland Co Mus Art.
Dealer: Ward Nasse Gallery, 178 Prince St, New York, NY 10012.
Mailing Address: 56 Main St, Yarmouth Port, MA 02675.

ROYSHER, HUDSON (BRISBINE)
Designer, Art Administrator
Preferred Media: Silver, Gold, Bronze.
b Cleveland, Ohio, Nov 21, 11.
Study & Training: Cleveland Art Inst, grad dipl, 34; Western Reserve Univ, MS, 34; Univ Southern Calif, MFA, 48.
Work in Public Collections: Mace, Univ Buffalo, N Y; Mace, Univ Southern Calif, Los Angeles; Mace, Syracuse Univ, N Y; Mace, Calif State Univ, Los Angeles; Mace, Bethune-Cookman Col, Daytona Beach, Fla.
Exhibitions: U S State Dept Traveling Exhib, 50-52; Eleven Southern Californians, De Young Mem Mus, San Francisco, Calif, 52; Smithsonian Inst Traveling Exhib, 53-55; Designer Craftsmen of the West Traveling Exhib, 57; Masters of Contemporary American Crafts Exhib, Brooklyn Mus, 61.
Teaching: Asst prof indust design, Univ Southern Calif, 39-42; head div indust design, Chouinard Art Inst, 45-50; prof art, Calif State Univ, Los Angeles, 50-70, chmn dept art, 72.
Awards: Spec award for continued excellence, Cleveland Mus Art, 40 & 46; outstanding prof award, 66 & outstanding educator award, 72, trustees of Calif State Univ & Cols.
Bibliography: A welded steel education, Design Mag, London, 1/51; H E Winter (auth), Three American silversmiths, Amerika, 5/53; Churches & temples, Progressive Archit, 10/56.

Memberships: Indust Designers Soc Am (chmn west coast chap, 46); Am Asn Univ Prof (chap pres); Southern Calif Designer Craftsmen (chap pres, 58-59); Am Craftsman's Coun; Asn Calif State Univ Prof (chap pres, 63-65 & 71-72).
Mailing Address: 1784 S Santa Anita Ave, Arcadia, CA 91006.

RUBEN, RICHARDS
Painter, Educator
b Los Angeles, Calif, Nov 29, 25.
Study & Training: Chouinard Art Inst.
Work in Public Collections: Wooster Mus, Mass; Brooklyn Mus, N Y; Los Angeles Co Mus Art; Corcoran Gallery Art, Washington, D C; Pasadena Art Mus, Calif.
Exhibitions: Pittsburgh Int, 55; São Paulo 111rd Biennial, Brazil, 55; 1st Paris Biennial, France, 59; Arte de America y Espana, Madrid, Spain, 63; San Francisco Mus Art, Calif, 71.
Teaching: Asst prof drawing & painting, Pomona Col, 58-62; asst prof drawing & painting, N Y Univ, 63-; instr drawing & painting, Pratt Inst, 67-71.
Awards: First prize for oil, San Francisco Mus Art, 53; Tiffany grant, 54; Tamarine fel, 61.
Mailing Address: c/o Poindexter Gallery, 24 E 84th St, New York, NY 10028.

RUBENSTEIN, LEWIS W
Painter, Educator
b Buffalo, N Y, Dec 15, 08.
Study & Training: Harvard Univ, AB, traveling fel, Europe; also with Leger & Ozenfant, Paris, frescoes with Rico Lebrun & lithography with Emil Ganso, Rome, plastic painting media with Jose Guttierez & sumi with Keigetsu, Tokyo.
Work in Public Collections: Ford Found, New York, N Y; Am Univ, Washington, D C; Vassar Col Art Gallery, Poughkeepsie, N Y; U S Info Agency; Addison Gallery Am Art.
Commissions: Frescoes, Busch-Reisinger Mus, Cambridge, Mass, 37 & asst to Orozco, Mus Mod Art, New York, 40; murals, Post Off, U S Sect Fine Arts, Wareham, Mass, 40 & entrance, Jewish Ctr, Buffalo, 50; four paintings, Marine Midland Nat Bank, Poughkeepsie, 65.
Exhibitions: Whitney Mus Am Art, New York, 38; Nat Acad Design, New York, 46, 52, 56 & 63; Libr Cong, Washington, D C, 52-60; Soc Am Graphic Artists, New York, 52-72; Am Watercolor Soc, New York, 55 & 64.
Teaching: Instr fresco painting, Boston Mus Sch Art, 37-38; prof painting, Vassar Col, 39-; instr fresco painting, Univ Buffalo, summer 41.
Awards: Am Artists Group & Knobloch Prizes, Soc Am Graphic Artists, 52 & 54; Fulbright grant, Japan, 57-58; Fairfield Award, Silvermine Guild Artists, 59.
Bibliography: Guillermo Rivas (auth), Lewis Rubenstein, Mex Life, 8/51; Erica Beckh Rubenstein (auth), Lewis Rubenstein's time painting, Vassar Alumnae Mag, 5/57; Masao Ishizawa (auth), Rubenstein and his sumi painting, Hoshun, Japan, 2/25/59.
Memberships: Soc Am Graphic Artists.
Publications: Auth, Fresco painting today, Am Scholar, 35; Time painting by Lewis Rubenstein (film), 56-57 & Ceremony for a new planet (film), 72, Vassar Col; illusr, For Serv J, 58-66; co-auth, Psalm 104 (film), Weston Woods Studios, 70.
Dealer: Three Arts, 56 Raymond Ave, Poughkeepsie, NY 12603.
Mailing Address: Dept of Art, Vassar College, Poughkeepsie, NY 12601.

RUBIN, MR & MRS HARRY
Collectors
Mailing Address: 700 Park Ave, New York, NY 10021.

RUBIN, IRWIN
Painter, Designer
b Brooklyn, N Y, July 26, 30.
Study & Training: Brooklyn Mus Sch Art; Cooper Union Art Sch; Yale Univ, BFA & MFA.
Exhibitions: Fla State Univ, 60; Baltimore Mus Art, 60; Bertha Schaefer Gallery, N Y, 60-63; Stable Gallery, N Y, 64; Byron Gallery, 65; plus others.
Teaching: Instr drawing & color design, Univ Tex, 55; asst prof, Fla State Univ, 56-58; instr, Pratt Inst, Brooklyn, 64-; asst prof archit, Cooper Union Art Sch, 67-
Positions: Art dir, McGraw-Hill Bk Co, New York, N Y, 58-63; art dir, Harcourt Brace Jovanovich, Inc, New York, 71-
Publications: Auth, Permanency in collage, Arts Mag, 57.
Mailing Address: 126 Lincoln Pl, Brooklyn, NY 11217.

RUBIN, LAWRENCE
Art Dealer, Collector
b New York, N Y, Feb 22, 33.
Study & Training: Brown Univ; Columbia Univ, BA; Univ Paris.
Positions: Owner & dir, Lawrence Rubin Gallery.

Specialty of Gallery: Painters Stella, Motherwell, Poons, Louis, Bannard, Olitski, Holland, Sander and Dzubas; sculptors Caro, Arman and Scott.
Collection: Contemporary painting and sculpture.
Mailing Address: 49 W 57th St, New York, NY 10019.

RUBIN, WILLIAM
Art Curator, Art Historian
b New York, N Y, Aug 11, 27.
Study & Training: Columbia Univ, AB, MA & PhD; Univ Paris.
Collections Arranged: Dada, Surrealism & Their Heritage, 68, New Am Painting & Sculpture, 69, Stella, 70 & Picasso in the Collection of Mus Mod Art, 72.
Teaching: Prof art hist, Sarah Lawrence Col, 52-67; prof art hist, City Univ New York Grad Div, 60-67; prof art hist, N Y Univ, Grad Div, 60-68; adj prof art hist, N Y Univ Inst Fine Arts, 68-
Positions: Am art ed, Art Int Mag, 59-64; chief cur painting & sculpture, Mus Mod Art, New York, 68-
Publications: Auth, Modern sacred art and the Church of Assy, 61, Dada, surrealism and their heritage, 68, Dada and surrealist art, 69, Stella, 70 & Picasso in the collection of the Museum of Modern Art, 72; plus others.
Mailing Address: Museum of Modern Art, 11 W 53rd St, New York, 10019.

RUBINS, DAVID KRESZ
Sculptor
b Minneapolis, Minn, Sept 5, 02.
Study & Training: Beaux Arts Inst Design, New York, N Y; Ecole Beaux Arts, Paris; Acad Julian, Paris, asst to James E Fraser.
Work in Public Collections: Minneapolis Inst Art, Minn; Ind Univ, Bloomington; Indianapolis Mus Art, Ind.
Commissions: Figure on Steps, Arch Bldg, Washington, D C, 33; work in Riley Hosp, Indianapolis, 36-72; Lilly Monument, Crown Hill Cemetery, Indianapolis, 61; Lincoln Monument, State Off Bldg Plaza, Indianapolis, 64.
Exhibitions: Archit League New York, 33; Nat Acad Design, New York, 33; Ind Artists Ann, Indianapolis, 36-70; Am Sculpture Today, Metrop Mus Art, 51.
Teaching: From instr to prof sculpture & anat, Herron Sch Art, Indianapolis, 35-
Awards: Fel Am Acad Rome, 28; Nat Inst Arts & Lett grant sculpture, 54.
Publications: Auth, The human figure—an anatomy for artists, Viking Press, 53.
Mailing Address: 3923 La Salle Ct, Indianapolis, IN 46205.

RUDA, EDWIN
Painter
Preferred Media: Mixed Media.
b New York, N Y, May 15, 22.
Study & Training: Columbia Univ, MA, 49; Sch Painting & Sculpture, Mexico City, 49-51; Univ Ill, MFA, 56.
Work in Public Collections: State of N Y Collection, Albany Mall; Indianapolis Mus Art, Ind; Dallas Mus Fine Art, Tex; Allentown Art Mus, Pa.
Exhibitions: Smithsonian Traveling Exhib, Latin Am, 66; Systemic Painting, Guggenheim Mus, New York, 66; Whitney Mus Am Art Painting Ann, New York, 69; Two Generations of Color Painting, Inst Contemp Art, Philadelphia, 70; Gallery A, Sydney, Australia, 71.
Teaching: Instr painting, Univ Tex, Austin, 56-59; instr painting, Sch Visual Arts, New York, 67-71.
Positions: Co-founder, Park Pl Gallery Art Res.
Bibliography: David Bourdon (auth), E=MC² a go go, 1/66 & Carter Ratcliff (auth), Striped for action, 2/72, Artnews; Dore Ashton (auth), New York Commentary, Studio Int, 2/70.
Publications: Auth, Park Place 1963-67: some informal notes in retrospect, Art Mag, 67; auth, Jack Krueger: frontiers of zero, Artforum, 4/68.
Mailing Address: c/o Paula Cooper Gallery, 96 Prince St, New York, NY 10012.

RUDDLEY, JOHN
Art Administrator, Painter
Preferred Media: Acrylics, Oils, Watercolors.
b New York, N Y, Oct 29, 12.
Study & Training: Cooper Union Sch Art & Archit, with Tully Filmus, Ernest Fiene & Paul Feeley; DaVinci Sch Art; Columbia Univ, BS(hist art); Columbia Univ, MA(art educ).
Work in Public Collections: Corcoran Sch Art, Washington, D C; Arts Club Washington.
Exhibitions: Corcoran Gallery Art, Washington, 63; Arts Club Washington, 63; Corcoran Sch Art, 63-64; Avant Gallery, Alexandria, Va, 64; Columbia Univ Gallery, New York, N Y, 65.

Teaching: Prof design & painting, Corcoran Sch Art, 62-64; prof hist art, Lab Inst Design, New York, 64-69; prof painting, Pace Col, Pleasantville, N Y, 70-71.
Positions: Dean & head, Corcoran Sch Art, 62-65; supvr art, Westchester Co, White Plains, N Y, 65-; dir, Westchester Art Workshop, 65-; trustee, Hammond Mus, North Salem, N Y, 69-; bd govs, Cooper Union, New York, 69-
Memberships: Am Soc Aesthetics; Arts Club Washington; Inst Study Art; Int Soc Educ Art; Nat Art Educ Asn.
Publications: Auth, Series of book reviews, Nat Art Educ Asn J, 64-72.
Mailing Address: Westchester Art Workshop, County Center, White Plains, NY 10606.

RUDOLPH, MR & MRS C FREDERICK
Collectors
Mailing Address: Ide Rd, Williamstown, MA 01267.

RUDQUIST, JERRY JACOB
Painter, Educator
Preferred Media: Oils.
b Fargo, N Dak, June 13, 34.
Study & Training: Minneapolis Col Art & Design, BFA, 56; Cranbrook Acad Art, MFA, 58.
Work in Public Collections: Walker Art Ctr, Minneapolis, Minn; Minneapolis Inst Arts; Univ Gallery, Univ Minn, Minneapolis; Saint Cloud State Col, Minn; Anoka Ramsey State Jr Col, Minn.
Exhibitions: Art Across America, Mead Nat Painting Exhib, Columbus, Ohio, 65; New Art From the Twin Cities, Chicago, 70; Drei Amerikaner aus dem Mittleren Western, Mannheimer Symposion der Kunste, W Ger, 72; one-man exhibs, Walker Art Ctr, Minneapolis, 63 & Minneapolis Inst Arts, 64 & 71.
Teaching: Prof art, Macalester Col, 58-; vis lectr & critic art, Boston Univ, summer 69.
Awards: Spec donor & purchase award, Walker Art Ctr, 62; purchase award, Minneapolis Inst Arts, 65; Mead Award for poster design, 71.
Bibliography: Dan Paris (auth), Rudquist (film), produced by Minneapolis Inst Arts, Macalester Col & Minn State Arts Coun, 71; Samuel Sachs II (auth), Jerry Rudquist: recent works, Minneapolis Inst Arts, 71.
Art Interests: Lithography.
Dealer: Suzanne Kohn Gallery, 1690 Grand Ave, Saint Paul, MN 55105.
Mailing Address: 2322 Seabury Ave S, Minneapolis, MN 55406.

RUDY, CHARLES
Sculptor
Preferred Media: Stone, Bronze, Wood, Terra Cotta.
b York, Pa, Nov 14, 04.
Study & Training: Pa Acad Fine Arts, Philadelphia.
Work in Public Collections: Pa Mus Fine Arts; Brookgreen Gardens, Georgetown, S C; Philadelphia Mus, Pa; Metrop Mus Art, New York; Carnegie Inst, Pittsburgh, Pa.
Commissions: U S Post Off, Bronx, N Y, 39; U S Govt Bldg, 39; five stone figures (with Roy Larson), Va Polytech Inst, Blacksburg, 54; sculpture (with Willard Hahn), Lehigh Co Ct House, 64; bronze gates (with Edward Green), William Penn Hist Mus, Harrisburg, Pa, 64.
Exhibitions: Pa Acad Fine Arts, Philadelphia, 28-68; Whitney Mus Am Art, New York, 36-53; Art Inst Chicago, Ill, 39-52; Metrop Mus Art, New York, 50; Nat Acad Design, New York, 50-71.
Teaching: Head dept sculpture, Cooper Union, 31-41; instr sculpture, Pa Acad Fine Arts, 50-52.
Positions: Mem Art Comn Pa, 49-72.
Awards: Guggenheim Found fel, 42; Am Acad Arts & Lett Award, 44; John Howe Sculpture Award, Pa Acad Fine Arts, 47.
Bibliography: Scrap sculpture welding, Life, 12/20/43.
Memberships: Nat Acad Design; Nat Sculpture Soc; Pa Acad Fine Arts.
Publications: Auth, Challenge to form, Mag Art, 40.
Mailing Address: P O Box 106, Ottsville, PA 18942.

RUELLAN, ANDRÉE
Painter
Preferred Media: Oils, Gouache, Graphics
b New York, N Y, Apr 6, 05.
Study & Training: Art Stud League New York, scholar, 20-22; Maurice Sterne Sch, Rome, Italy, scholar, 22-23; Acad Suédoise, Paris, France, with Per Krogh & Charles Dufresne.
Work in Public Collections: Oils, Fogg Mus, Harvard; Metrop Mus Art, New York; Phillips Mem Gallery, Washington, D C & Columbia Mus Art, S C; drawings, Whitney Mus Am Art, New York.
Commissions: Murals, Post Off, Emporia, Va, 40 & Lawrenceville, Ga, 41.

Exhibitions: Many Carnegie Int, 30-50; 10 ann, Whitney Mus Am Art; Grantees Exhib, Am Acad Arts & Lett, 45; Am Painting Today, Metrop Mus Art, 50; Storm King Art Ctr Retrospective, 66.
Teaching: Vis artist, Pa State Univ, summer 57.
Awards: Am Acad Arts & Lett grant arts, 45; Pennell Mem Medal, Philadelphia Watercolor Club, 45; Guggenheim Found fel, 50-51.
Bibliography: Harry Salpeter (auth), About Andrée Ruellan, Coronet, 12/38; Ernest Watson (auth), Andrée Ruellan, Am Artist, 10/43; Arthur Zaidenburg (auth), The art of the artist, Crown, 51.
Memberships: Woodstock Artists Asn; Art Stud League New York; Philadelphia Watercolor Club.
Dealer: Kraushaar Galleries, 1055 Madison Ave, New York, NY 10028.
Mailing Address: Shady, NY 12479.

RUEPPEL, MERRILL C
Art Administrator
b Haddonfield, N J, May 7, 25.
Study & Training: Beloit Col, BA, 49; Univ Wis-Madison, MA, 51, PhD, 55.
Positions: Res asst, Minneapolis Inst Arts, 56-57, asst to dir, 57-59, asst dir, 59-61; asst dir, City Art Mus, Saint Louis, 61-64; dir, Dallas Mus Fine Arts, 64-.
Memberships: Asn Art Mus Dirs; Am Asn Mus; Archaeol Inst Am.
Mailing Address: Dallas Museum of Fine Arts, Fair Park, Dallas, TX 75226.

RUFFO, JOSEPH MARTIN
Printmaker, Designer
b Norwich, Conn, Dec 6, 41.
Study & Training: Pratt Inst; Cranbrook Acad Art.
Work in Public Collections: Brooks Mem Art Gallery, Memphis, Tenn; Ark Art Ctr, Little Rock; Mus Mod Art, Salvador, Brazil; Memphis Acad Arts, Tenn; Miss Art Asn, Jackson.
Exhibitions: 48th Ann Print Exhib, Soc Am Graphic Artists, New York, N Y, 67; 12th Ann Mid South Exhib, Memphis, 67; 10th Dixie Ann, Montgomery Mus Art, 69; Nat Print & Drawing Exhib, Miss Art Asn, 69; Miami Art Ctr Mem Exhib, 71.
Teaching: Instr art, Memphis Acad Arts, 64-68; instr art, Fla Mem Col, 69-; asst prof art & chmn dept, Barry Col, 69-.
Awards: Fulbright grant, Brazil, 63; best in show, 12th Ann Mid South Exhib, 67; purchase prize, 10th Dixie Ann Prints & Drawings, 68.
Art Interests: Silkscreen & etching.
Mailing Address: 7230 S W 64th Ct, South Miami, FL 33143.

RUMSEY, DAVID MacIVER
Sculptor, Designer
b New York, N Y, Apr 29, 44.
Study & Training: Yale Univ, BA, 66, BFA & MFA, 69.
Exhibitions: Boston Pub Gardens, outdoor environments sponsored by Housing & Urban Develop, 68; Spaces, Mus Mod Art, New York, 70; Work for New Spaces, Walker Art Mus, Minneapolis, Minn, 71; Pulsa & Television Sensoriums, Automation House, 71; Pulsa, Philadelphia Mus Fine Arts, 71.
Teaching: Lectr art, Yale Univ, 68-72; vis artist, Calif Inst Arts, 70-73.
Positions: Mem Pulsa Group.
Art Interests: Environmental art, using television, film, electronics, light and sound.
Mailing Address: 155 Bowers Hill Rd, Oxford, CT 06483.

RUSCHA, EDWARD JOSEPH
Painter, Photographer
b Omaha, Nebr, Dec 16, 37.
Study & Training: Chouinard Art Inst.
Work in Public Collections: Mus Mod Art, New York, N Y; Los Angeles Co Mus Art, Los Angeles; Whitney Mus Am Art, New York; Joseph Hirshhorn Collection, Washington, D C; Oakland Mus Art, Calif.
Exhibitions: Drawings U S A, Minn Mus Art, Saint Paul, 71; Continuing Surrealism, La Jolla Mus Art, Calif, 71; Top Boxed Art, Ill State Univ, Normal, 71; 11 Los Angeles Artists, Hayward Gallery, London, 71; Art Systems, Centro Arte Y Comunication, Buenos Aires, Arg, 71; plus many other group & one-man shows.
Teaching: Lectr painting, Univ Calif, Los Angeles, 69-70.
Bibliography: Joyce Haber (auth), article, In: Los Angeles Times, 5/19/71; Rosalind Kraus (auth), rev, In: Artforum, 5/71; Reyner Banham (auth), A London-Los Angeles love affair, West, 6/6/71; plus many others.
Publications: Auth, On the sunset strip, 66, Thirty-four parking lots, 67, Royal road test, 67, Business cards, 68 & Nine swimming pools, 68, Heavy Indust Publ; plus many others.

RUSH, ANDREW
Printmaker, Painter
b Mich, Sept 24, 31.
Study & Training: Univ Ill, BFA(hons), 53; Univ Iowa, MFA, 58; Fulbright fel, Florence, Italy, 58-59.
Work in Public Collections: Uffizi Mus, Florence, Italy; Brooklyn Mus, N Y; Libr of Cong, Washington, D C; Dallas Mus, Tex; Seattle Mus, Wash.
Commissions: Law Prints (portfolio of three offset lithographs), Lawyers Publ Co, 68; mem bd ed etching, Asn Am Artists, New York, 68; ed etchings, Tucson Art Ctr, 71.
Exhibitions: USIS Traveling Exhib to Europe & Latin Am, 60-65; Graphic Art U S A, Am prints to Soviet Union, 63; Brooklyn Mus Biennial, 64; 50 American Printmakers, Am Pavilion, New York Worlds Fair, 64-65; Intag 71, 30 Printmakers, San Fernando State Univ, 71.
Teaching: Assoc prof art, Univ Ariz, 59-69; vis artist-in-residence, Ohio State Univ, 70.
Awards: Seattle Mus Int Printmakers, 63 & purchase award, Brooklyn Mus Biennial, 64.
Bibliography: Andrew Rush, Southwest Art Gallery Mag, 3/72.
Dealers: Graphics Gallery, 4656 Oracle Rd, Tucson, AZ 85704; Associated American Artists, 663 Fifth Ave, New York, NY 10022.
Mailing Address: P O Box E, Oracle, AZ 85623.

RUSKIN, LEWIS J
Collector, Patron
b London, Eng, July 30, 05.
Study & Training: Ariz State Univ, hon LLD, 68.
Positions: Chmn, Ariz Comn Arts & Humanities, 67-.
Awards: Hon fel, Phoenix Art Mus.
Art Interests: Donated Renaissance and Baroque paintings to the Phoenix Art Museum and Renaissance, Baroque and Barbizon paintings and sculpture to Arizona State University Gallery.
Collection: Sixteenth, seventeenth and eighteenth century paintings.
Mailing Address: 5800 E Foothill Dr N, Paradise Valley, AZ 85253.

RUSKIN, MICKEY
Collector
Mailing Address: Max's Kansas City, 213 Park Ave S, New York, NY 10003.

RUSSELL, (GEORGE) GORDON
Painter
Preferred Media: Oils.
b Altoona, Pa, July 15, 32.
Study & Training: Pa State Univ, with Hobson Pittman; Pa Acad Fine Arts, with Walter Stuempfig; Barnes Found.
Work in Public Collections: Pa Acad Fine Arts, Philadelphia; Fogg Art Mus, Harvard Univ, Cambridge, Mass; Mus Fine Arts, Bowdoin Col, Brunswick, Maine; Krannert Art Mus, Univ Ill, Urbana; New York Hosp Collection, N Y.
Exhibitions: Pa Acad Fine Arts Ann & Fel Ann; Contemporary Paintings, Yale Univ Art Gallery, 62; one-man shows, six at Durlacher Bros, New York, 57-67, Fort Worth Art Ctr, Tex, 62 & Larcada Gallery, New York, 69 & 71.
Awards: Lewis S Ware Mem, 53, J Henry Schiedt Mem, 54 & Toppan prize, 54, Pa Acad Fine Arts.
Memberships: Fel Pa Acad Fine Arts.
Dealer: Larcada Gallery, 23 E 67th St, New York, NY 10021.
Mailing Address: 117 E Caroline Ave, Altoona, PA 16602.

RUSSELL, HELEN DIANE
Art Historian
b Kansas City, Mo, Apr 8, 36.
Study & Training: Vassar Col, AB; Radcliffe Grad Sch; Johns Hopkins Univ, PhD.
Collections Arranged: Protest & Social Comment in Prints, 70; Kathe Kollwitz, 71; Rare Etchings by G B & G D Tiepolo, 72.
Teaching: Prof lectr 15th-17th cent European painting & graphic arts, Am Univ, Washington, D C, 66-72.
Positions: Asst to chief, Smithsonian Inst Traveling Exhib Serv, Washington, 60-61; mus cur, Nat Gallery Art, Washington, 64-70, asst cur graphic arts, 70-.
Awards: Woodrow Wilson Nat fel, 58-59.
Memberships: Col Art Asn Am.
Research: Prints & drawings of the sixteenth through eighteenth centuries.
Publications: Auth, rev of Louise Lucas, Art books a basic bibliography, 68 & Andre Mellerio, Odilon Redon, 69, Mus News; auth, A museum worker speaks, Washington Print Club Newsletter, 72; auth, rev Aldo Rizzi, The etchings of the Tiepolos, Print Collectors Newsletter 72; auth, Rare etchings Giovanni Battista & Giovanni Domenico Tiepolo, 72.
Mailing Address: National Gallery Art, Washington, DC 20565.

RUSSELL, JAMES SPENCER
Painter
b Monticello, Ind, Apr 7, 15.
Study & Training: Univ N Mex, BFA, with Raymond Jonson; Yale Univ, MFA, with Donald Oenslager.
Work in Public Collections: Contemp Am Art, Am Embassy, Beirut, Lebanon.
Exhibitions: Contemp Wall Sculpture, Am Fedn Arts, 64 & R I Sch Design, Providence, 65; Small Environments, Southern Ill Univ, Carbondale, 72.
Mailing Address: 250 E 77th St, New York, NY 10021.

RUSSELL, SHIRLEY (XIMENA)
Painter
Preferred Media: Oils.
b Del Rey, Calif.
Study & Training: Stanford Univ, AB, 07; Univ Hawaii; also with Andre L'Hote, Hans Hofmann, Rico Le Brun, Serisawa & Norman Ives.
Work in Public Collections: Honolulu Acad Arts; State Found Cult & Arts, Capitol Bldg, Honolulu; Tennant Art Found Gallery; Castel & Cooke Art Collection; Tokyo Nat Mus Art.
Commissions: Portraits, Leslie B Hicks, Hawaiian Elec Co, Honolulu & Chief Justices Perry & Kemp, Bar Asn Honolulu; also pvt comns.
Exhibitions: Mus Fine Arts, Los Angeles, 37; Palace Legion of Honor, San Francisco, 46; Honolulu Acad Arts Show & Matsonia Tour, 63-65; Mex-Hawaiian Exchange Exhib, 68; Honolulu Acad Arts Ann.
Teaching: Instr Calif schs, 08-18; instr, Univ Hawaii, summers 30-39; instr art, McKinley High Sch, Honolulu, 46; instr, Honolulu Acad Arts, 54-55.
Positions: Secy, Asn Honolulu Artists, 39-41, pres, 41-42.
Awards: Grand Prize for Paukahana, 33 & first prize for still life, 46, Honolulu Acad Arts; Grand Prize for U S Mail, Territorial Fair, Honolulu, 53; plus many others.
Biography: Meg Torbet & Kenneth Kimgrey (auth), Art in Hawaii, Design Quart, Walker Art Ctr, 60; plus others.
Memberships: Painters & Sculptors League Honolulu; Honolulu Acad Arts.
Dealer: Downtown Gallery, 125 Richards St, Honolulu, HI 96813.
Mailing Address: 4220 Puu Panini Ave, Honolulu, HI 96816.

RUSSIN, ROBERT I
Sculptor, Educator
Preferred Media: Marble, Bronze.
b New York, N Y, Aug 26, 14.
Study & Training: City Univ New York, BA & MA; Beaux Arts Inst Design.
Work in Public Collections: Colo Springs Fine Arts Ctr, Colo; Palm Springs Desert Mus, Calif; Pomona Col, Claremont, Calif; Gettysburg Mus, Pa; Brookhaven Nat Labs, N Y.
Commissions: Two aluminum figures, Evanston Post Off, Ill, 39; Lincoln Monument, State of Wyo, Lincoln Hwy, 59; bronze group, Fed Bldg, Cheyenne, Wyo, 66; fountain sculpture, City of Hope Nat Med Ctr, Calif, 67; carved wood reliefs, Fed Bldg, Denver, Colo, 68; plus many others.
Exhibitions: Pa Acad Fine Arts Sculpture Biennial, Philadelphia, 66; one-man shows, Tucson Art Ctr, Ariz, 66, Colo Springs Fine Arts Ctr, 67, Palm Springs Desert Mus, 70 & Magnes Mus, Berkeley, Calif, 70.
Teaching: Instr sculpture, Cooper Union Art Inst, 44-47; prof sculpture, Univ Wyo, 47-
Awards: Ford Found fel, 53-54; Lincoln Sesquicentennial Medal, U S Cong, 59; Charles G B Steele Sculpture Award, Pa Acad Fine Arts, 66.
Bibliography: Rebecca Northen (auth), Robert Russin, sculptor to Wyoming, Western Farm Life, 9/50; O A Sealy (auth), Russin's metal magic, 2/56 & F K Frame (auth), Russin's Lincoln, 2/65, Empire Mag; Tom Francis (auth), Robert Russin, Wyoming sculptor, Am Artist, 1/60.
Memberships: Nat Sculpture Soc; Sculptors Guild (exec secy, 46).
Publications: Contribr, A new sculptural medium, Col Art J, 56, The Lincoln monument on the Lincoln highway, Lincoln Herald, 61 & A university bronze foundry, Am Artist, 63.
Dealer: Heritage Gallery, 718 N La Cienega Blvd, Los Angeles, CA 90069.
Mailing Address: 716 Ivinson Ave, Laramie, WY 82070.

RUSSO, ALEXANDER PETER
Painter, Educator
Preferred Media: Acrylics, Oils, Plastics, Metals.
b Atlantic City, N J, June 11, 22.
Study & Training: Pratt Inst, 40-42; Swarthmore Col, 47; Bard Col, summer, 47; Guggenheim fel, 48-50; Breevort-Eickenmeyer fel, Columbia Univ, 50-52, BFA, 52; Fulbright grant, Acad Fine Arts, Rome, Italy, 52-54; Univ Buffalo, 55.
Work in Public Collections: Albright-Knox Gallery, Buffalo, N Y; Corcoran Gallery Art, Washington, D C; Nat Collection Fine Arts, Washington, D C; Fed Ins Deposit Corp, Washington; Acad Arts & Letters, New York.
Commissions: Encaustic mural, Telesio Interlandi, Capo San Andrea, Sicily, 53; silk screen murals, Birge Co, Buffalo, 56; various design commissions, Doubleday Publ Co, Dutton Publ, Cohn Hall Marx, plus many others, 58-60; acrylic painting series, U S Navy Dept, Washington, 64; acrylic mural, Dr Martin Cherkasky, N Y, 70.
Exhibitions: Carnegie Nat, Pittsburgh, Pa, 46; Int Exhib, Bordighera, Italy, 53 & 54; Four Am Artists Exhib, Biblioteca, Rome, Italy, 54; Albright-Knox Gallery Regional, Buffalo, N Y, 56; Corcoran Biennials, Washington; plus many one-man shows.
Teaching: Assoc prof painting & drawing, Corcoran Sch Art, 61-70, chmn faculty & painting dept, 66-69; prof art & chmn dept, Hood Col, 71-
Positions: U S Navy combat artist, U S Navy Dept, Washington, 42-46; acting art dir, Sewell, Thompson, Caire Advertising, New Orleans, La, 48-49; free lance artist & designer, various agencies & orgns, New York, 58-60; guest lectr art, Roanoke & Hollins Cols, Univ South Ill, Miss Art Asn, plus others.
Bibliography: Carl Fortes (auth), Tape on aesthetics & teaching methods of Alexander Russo, Boston Univ, 68; Anne M Jonas (auth), Focus on: Alexander Russo, The Art Scene, 70/71.
Memberships: Col Art Asn; Arts Club Washington (chmn exhibs, 70-71); Artists Equity; Soc Washington Artists; Edward McDowell Colony.
Research: Contemporary & Medieval Italian art.
Publications: Illusr, To all hands, an amphibious adventure, 44 & illusr, Many a watchful night, 45, McGraw; auth, The Italian experience, Inst Int Educ, 53.
Dealer: Frank Rehn Galleries, 60th & Madison Ave, New York, NY 10010.
Mailing Address: Hood College, Frederick, MD 21701.

RUST, DAVID E
Art Historian, Collector
b Bloomington, Ill.
Study & Training: N Y Univ Inst Fine Arts, MA, 63.
Collections Arranged: English Drawings & Watercolors, 62; Old Master Drawings from Chatsworth, 69; Nathan Cummings Collection, 70.
Positions: Mus cur, Nat Gallery Art, Washington, D C, 61-
Collection: Paintings & drawings, mostly European Sixteenth-Eighteenth Century, some nineteenth century; American Nineteenth Century & some contemporary.
Publications: Auth, Twentieth century paintings & sculpture of the French School in the Chester Dale Collection, 65; auth, Eighteenth and nineteenth century paintings & sculpture of the French School in the Chester Dale Collection, 65; auth, The drawings of Vincenzo Tamagni da San Gimignano, Report & Studies Hist Art, 68.
Mailing Address: National Gallery Art, Washington, DC 20565.

RUST, EDWIN C
Sculptor, Art Administrator
b Hammonton, Calif, Dec 5, 10.
Study & Training: Cornell Univ; Yale Univ, BFA; also with Archipenko & Milles.
Work in Public Collections: U S Ct House, Washington, D C; Univ Tenn, Knoxville; Univ Miss; LeMoyne-Owen Col, Memphis, Tenn; Memphis Acad Arts, Tenn.
Exhibitions: Whitney Mus Am Art, New York, N Y, 40; Carnegie Inst, Pittsburgh, Pa, 40; Philadelphia Mus Art, Pa, 40 & 49; Mus Mod Art, New York, 42; Brooks Mem Mus, 50 & 52.
Teaching: Assoc prof sculpture, Col William & Mary, 36-43, head fine arts dept, 39-43.
Positions: Dir, Memphis Acad Arts, 49-
Mailing Address: 3725 Waynoka Ave, Memphis, TN 38111.

RUTA, PETER PAUL
Painter, Editor
Preferred Media: Oils.
b Dresden, Ger, Feb 7, 18; U S citizen.
Study & Training: Art Stud League New York, with Morris Kantor & Jean Charlot, 38-42 & 45-46; Acad Fine Arts Venice, 47-49, degree; Acad Venice, with Guido Cadorin, 48.
Work in Public Collections: Uffizi Gallery, Florence, Italy; Univ Southern Ill.
Exhibitions: One-man shows, Stonington Gallery, Conn, 60, Angeleski Gallery, New York, N Y, 62, Hacker Gallery, New York, 62, Surebaja Gallery, New York, 67 & Graham Gallery, New York, 72.
Awards: First prize, Westchester Art Soc, 65.
Publications: Ed, Arts Mag, 68-71; ed, Int Art Exhibs, 69.

Dealer: Graham Gallery, 1014 Madison Gallery, New York, NY 10021.
Mailing Address: 463 West St, New York, NY 10014.

RUTHLING, FORD
Painter, Designer
Preferred Media: Oils.
b Santa Fe, N Mex, Apr 23, 33.
Study & Training: With Randall Davey.
Work in Public Collections: Mus N Mex; Wichita Falls Fine Art Mus; Univ Utah Collection.
Commissions: Various commissions.
Exhibitions: Nelson Atkins Mus; Mus N Mex; Oklahoma City Mus Fine Art; Dallas Mus Fine Art; Wichita Falls Mus Fine Art.
Mailing Address: 313 E Berger St, Santa Fe, NM 87501.

RUTLAND, EMILY EDITH
Painter
Preferred Media: Oils, Acrylics.
b Lee Co, Tex.
Work in Public Collections: Centennial Mus, Corpus Christi, Tex; Corpus Christi Mus; Dallas Mus, Tex; Tex Tech Univ.
Exhibitions: Corpus Christi Nat, 47; Tex Fine Arts Invitational, Austin, 65; Corpus Christi Art Found, 68; Tex Fine Arts Regional, Tex A&I Univ, 71 & 72; plus many others.
Awards: Many.
Memberships: Tex Fine Arts Asn; Tex Watercolor Soc; S Tex Art League; Art Found Corpus Christi.
Mailing Address: 615 W Nettie, Kingsville, TX 78363.

RUTSCH, ALEXANDER
Painter, Sculptor
b Austria.
Study & Training: Acad Fine Art, Belgrade, Yugoslavia; Vienna, Austria; govt study grant, Paris, France.
Work in Public Collections: Albertina Graphic Art Collection, Austria; Austrian Gallery, Belvedere, Vienna; Munic Mus, Vienna; Munic Mus, Vienna; Mus Mod Art, Paris; Mus Liege, Belgium.
Exhibitions: Foreign Artists in France (represented Austria), Petit Palais, Paris, 62; International Sculptors, Mus Rodin, Paris, 62-63; one-man show, Galerie Vendome, Brussels, Belgium, 65; Int Exhib, Grand Palais de Champs Elyses, Paris, 66; Galerie St Louis, Morges, Switz, 71.
Awards: Silver medal of arts, sci & letters & bronze medal for art, City of Paris, 58; first prize (three portraits of Picasso), Salon Artistique Int de Sceaux, 54.
Bibliography: Jean Desville (producer), The world of Rutsch (film), 64; Carlton Lake (auth), In quest of Dali, Putnams, 69; Roger Seiler (auth), Inner eye of Alexander Rutsch (film), produced by IBM, 72.
Mailing Address: 222 Highbrook Ave, Pelham, NY 10803.

RUVOLO, FELIX EMMANUELE
Painter, Educator
b New York, N Y, Apr 28, 12.
Study & Training: In Catania, Sicily.
Work in Public Collections: Krannert Art Mus, Univ Ill, Urbana; Art Inst Chicago, Ill; Walker Art Ctr, Minneapolis, Minn; Oakland Mus, Calif; Univ Calif Mus Fine Arts, Berkeley.
Commissions: Colored lithograph, Collectors Press, 67.
Exhibitions: Abstr & Surrealist Art Am, Mus Mod Art, New York, N Y, 51; 60 Americans—1960, Walker Art Ctr, 60; Invitational Am Drawing, Moore Col Art Gallery, Philadelphia, Pa, 68; Drawings 1969, Ithaca Col Art Gallery, N Y, 69; Am Drawing & Sculpture, 1948-1969, Krannert Art Mus, 71.
Teaching: Prof art, Art Inst Chicago, 44-48; prof art, Univ Calif, Berkeley, 50-; prof art, Univ Southern Calif, summer 63.
Awards: Award, San Francisco Mus Art, 64; Hall of Justice Competition Award, San Francisco Art Comn, 67; grants, Univ Calif Inst Creative Arts, 64 & 71.
Bibliography: K Kuli (auth), Felix Ruvolo, Mag Art, 47 & Painters who teach, Pictorial Living, 59; N Pousette Dart (auth), American painting today, Hastings, 57.
Mailing Address: 78 Strathmoor Dr, Berkeley, CA 94705.

RYERSON, MARGERY AUSTEN
Painter, Etcher
Preferred Media: Watercolors, Oils.
b Morristown, N J.
Study & Training: Vassar Col, AB; Art Stud League New York, N Y, with Robert Henri; also with Charles Hawthorne, Provincetown, Mass.
Work in Public Collections: Oil portrait, Vassar Col Gallery, Poughkeepsie; Fr Mus, Seattle, Wash; etchings, Metrop Mus Art, New York; oil portrait, Philbrook Art Ctr, Tulsa, Okla; etching, Bibliot Nat, Paris, France.
Commissions: Many portraits.

Exhibitions: Allied Artists Am, 71, New York; N J Watercolor Soc, Morristown, 71; Am Watercolor Soc, 72; Nat Acad Design, New York; Audubon Artists, New York, 72.
Positions: Corresp secy, Audubon Artists, 58-59; rec secy, Soc Am Graphic Artists; v pres, Allied Artists Am, 52-53.
Awards: Maynard Prize, Nat Acad Design, 59; Hook Prize, Am Watercolor Soc, 62; silver medal, Nat Arts Club, 71.
Bibliography: E Hobson (auth), An artist and a child, Foster's Daily Democrat, Dover, N H, 8/15/70; Doris di Savino (auth), Yesterday and today, Trends, 3/26/72.
Memberships: Nat Acad Design; life mem Am Watercolor Soc; life mem Allied Artists Am; N J Watercolor Soc; Nat Arts Club.
Publications: Ed, The art spirit, 23 & Hawthorne on painting, 36; illusr, Winkie boo, 48; contribr, The artist, 60; contribr, Am Artist.
Dealer: Grand Central Art Galleries, 43rd St & Madison Ave, New York, NY 10017.
Mailing Address: 15 Gramercy Park S, New York, NY 10003.

RYMAN, ROBERT
Painter
b Nashville, Tenn, May 30, 30.
Study & Training: Tenn Polytech Inst, 48-49; George Peabody Col, 49-50.
Work in Public Collections: Mus Mod Art, New York, N Y; Whitney Mus Am Art, New York; Milwaukee Art Ctr, Wis; Wadsworth Atheneum, Hartford, Conn; Stedelijk Mus, Amsterdam, Netherlands.
Exhibitions: Systemic Painting, 66, Sixth Guggenheim Int, 71 & one-man show, Robert Ryman, 72, Guggenheim Mus; Anti-Illusion—Procedures, Materials, Whitney Mus Am Art, New York, 69; Documenta, Kassel, W Ger, 72.
Bibliography: Lucy R Lippard (auth), The silent in art, Art Am, 1-2/67; Carter Ratcliff (auth), New York letter, Art Int, 2/20/71 & 5/20/71; D Waldman (auth), Robert Ryman (catalogue), Guggenheim Mus, 72.
Dealers: John Weber Gallery, 420 W Broadway, New York, NY 10012; Konrad Fischer, Dusseldorf, Ger.
Mailing Address: 637 Greenwich St, New York, NY 10014.

S

SAAR, BETYE
Painter, Designer
Preferred Media: Mixed Media.
b Los Angeles, Calif, July 30, 26.
Study & Training: Univ Calif, Los Angeles, BA; Univ Southern Calif; Long Beach State Col; San Fernando Valley State Col.
Work in Public Collections: Univ Mass, Amherst; Wellington Evest Collection, Boston, Mass; Golden State Mutual Life Ins Collection, Los Angeles, Calif; Los Angeles Co Mus Art; Home Savings & Loan Art Collection, Los Angeles.
Exhibitions: 25 Calif Women of Art, Lytton Ctr Visual Art, Los Angeles, 68; Dimensions of Black, La Jolla Fine Arts Mus, Calif, 70; Sculpture Ann, 70 & Contemporary Black Artists in America, 71, Whitney Mus Am Art, New York, N Y; Black Artist Invitational, Los Angeles Co Mus Art, 72.
Teaching: Vis artist, Calif State Univ, Hayward, fall 71.
Positions: Costume designer, Inner City Cult Ctr, Los Angeles, 68-71.
Awards: Purchase award for graphics, Pasadena Watercolor Soc, 70; purchase award for Small Images, Calif State Col, Los Angeles, 72; purchase award, Downy Mus Art, 72.
Bibliography: Black talent speaks, Los Angeles Fine Arts/FM Mag, 1/67; Scatterly talents, Arts Mag, 68; Lewis (auth) & Waddy (auth), Black artist on art, Contemp Crafts, 69.
Publications: Auth, Handbook, 67.
Mailing Address: 8074 Willow Glen Rd, Los Angeles, CA 90046.

SABATINI, RAPHAEL
Painter, Educator
b Philadelphia, Pa, Nov 26, 98.
Study & Training: Pa Acad Fine Arts, Cresson traveling scholarships; also with Arthur B Carles, Fernand Leger, Antoine Bourdelle & Constantin Brancusi.
Work in Public Collections: Philadelphia Mus Art; Pa Acad Fine Arts, Philadelphia; Sturgis R Ingersoll Collection, Pennlyn, Pa.
Commissions: Frieze for Fine Art Bldg, Sesquecentennial, Philadelphia, Pa, 26; Mother Mary Drexel Chapel, Langhorn, Pa, 29; N W Ayer Bldg, Philadelphia, 28.

Exhibitions: Sesquecentennial, Philadelphia, 26; Golden Gate Expos, San Francisco; Pa Acad Fine Art Ann.
Teaching: Prof painting & sculpture, Tyler Sch Art, Temple Univ, 36-66, emer prof, 66-
Positions: Comnr, Philadelphia Art Comn, 65-68; comnr, Fine Art Comn Philadelphia Redevelop Auth, 71-72.
Awards: Limback Found Award for distinguished teaching, 62; Percy Owens Mem Award for distinguished Pa artist, 63; 400th Anniversary of Michelangelo Award, Am Inst Ital Cult, 64.
Memberships: Artists Equity Asn; Philadelphia Art Alliance (v pres, 57-); Philadelphia Art Mus; fel Pa Acad Fine Arts.
Publications: Auth, Sculpture processes, Prothman Baldwin, 57.
Mailing Address: 7318 Oak Lane Rd, Melrose Park, PA 19126.

SABINE, JULIA
Art Librarian
b Chicago, Ill, Feb 4, 05.
Study & Training: Cornell Univ, BA; Yale Univ; Inst Art & Archaeol, Paris; Univ Chicago, PhD.
Teaching: Former vis instr, Univ Ky & Rutgers Univ.
Positions: Former supv art & music librn, Newark Pub Libr.
Mailing Address: 1416 Genesee St, Utica, NY 13502.

SACHS, A M
Art Dealer, Collector
b New York, N Y.
Study & Training: Univ Mich, Ann Arbor, BA.
Positions: Dir, A M Sachs Gallery.
Memberships: Art Dealers Asn Am.
Specialty of Gallery: Contemporary American painters.
Collection: Altalio, Salemme, John Ferren Howard Mehring, Giorgio Cavollon, Warren Brandt, Peter Hutchinson and other contemporary American painters.
Mailing Address: 29 W 57th St, New York, NY 10019.

SACHS, SAMUEL, II
Art Administrator, Art Historian
b New York, N Y, Nov 30, 35.
Study & Training: Harvard Univ, AB (cum laude); N Y Univ Inst Fine Arts, AM.
Collections Arranged: Chinese Art from the Collection of His Majesty, The King of Sweden, 67; The Past Rediscovered, XIX Century French Painting 1800-1900, 69.
Teaching: Lectr art hist, Univ Mich, Ann Arbor, 62-63; lectr art hist, Minneapolis Inst Arts, 64-
Positions: Asst prints & drawings, Minneapolis Inst Arts, 58-60, chief cur, 64-; asst dir, Univ Mich Mus Art, 62-64.
Memberships: Am Asn Mus; Am Fedn Arts (exhib comt), Col Art Asn Am.
Research: Fakes and forgeries; American nineteenth and twentieth century painting.
Publications: Auth, Reconstructing the whirlwind of 26th st, Art News, 2/63; auth, Drawings and watercolors of Thomas Moran, In: Thomas Moran (catalogue), Univ Calif, Riverside, 63; coauth, The past rediscovered: French painting 1800-1900 (catalogue), 69; auth, American paintings at the Minneapolis Institute of Arts, 71; auth, Art forges ahead, Auction Mag, 1/72.
Mailing Address: 201 E 24th St, Minneapolis, MN 55404.

SACHSE, JANICE R
Painter, Printmaker
Preferred Media: Oils, Watercolors, Graphics.
b New Orleans, La, May 6, 08.
Study & Training: La State Univ, with Albrizio; Newcomb Col, Tulane Univ, with William Woodward.
Work in Public Collections: Anglo Am Mus, La State Univ; La State Univ, Alexandria Libr Collection; two prints, La State Art Comn; Arts & Sci Mus, Baton Rouge; Pine Bluff Art Ctr, Ark; plus others.
Exhibitions: Volkfest Exhib New Orleans Galleries, Int House, Berlin, Ger, 68; Art On Paper, Witherspoon Gallery, Univ N C, 68; 11th Midwest Biennial, Joslyn Art Mus, Omaha, Nebr, 70; Sally Jackson Gallery, Hong Kong, 70; La State Univ Union Art Gallery, 72; plus others.
Awards: First Prize, La State Art Comn, 54; First Bd Dirs Prize, Beaumont Art Mus, 65; Sears Judges Prize, Vincent Price Gallery, 66 & 67.
Memberships: La Coun Performing Arts; Am Fedn Art; La Craft Coun; La Watercolor Soc.
Collection: German Expressionists Nolde, Heckle, Davis, H Moore, Burliuk, Rioux, Luks, Bellows & Tomayo.
Publications: Auth, Janice R Sachse 1960-1970, Marco Polo Publ, Hong Kong, 70 & Meet the artist series, La State Univ, Alexandria, 72.
Dealers: Downtown Gallery, 532 Chartre St, New Orleans, LA 70130; Baton Rouge Art Gallery, 205 N Fourth, Baton Rouge, LA 70801.
Mailing Address: 370 S Lakeshore Dr, Baton Rouge, LA 70808.

SADEK, GEORGE
Educator, Art Administrator
b Czech, Oct 12, 28; U S citizen.
Study & Training: Hunter Col; City Univ New York, BA; Ind Univ, MFA.
Work in Public Collections: Mus Mod Art, New York, N Y; Libr of Cong, Washington, D C; Morgan Libr.
Exhibitions: Type Dir Club New York, 69; Am Inst Graphic Arts, 70; Typomondus, Frankfurt, Ger, 71.
Teaching: From instr to asst prof graphic design, Ind Univ, 60-66; prof graphic design, Cooper Union, 66-, chmn dept art, 66-68.
Positions: Dean Sch Art & Archit, Cooper Union, 68-
Bibliography: Article, In: Am Inst Graphic Arts J, 68; article, In: Print, 70.
Memberships: Nat Asn Schs Art (bd mem, 68-71); Am Inst Graphic Arts (bd mem, 69-72); Col Art Asn (bd mem, 71-).
Mailing Address: Cooper Union School of Art & Architecture, Cooper Square, New York, NY 10003.

SAFER, JOHN
Sculptor
Preferred Media: Acrylics, Brass.
b Washington, D C, Sept 6, 22.
Work in Public Collections: Baltimore Mus Art, Md; Corcoran Gallery Art, Washington, D C; New York Cult Ctr, N Y; Philadelphia Mus Art, Pa; San Francisco Mus Art, Calif.
Exhibitions: One-man shows, Pyramid Gallery, Washington, D C, 70, Westmoreland Co Mus, Greensburg, Pa, 71, New York Cult Ctr, 71, U S Embassy, London, Eng & Montclair Mus Art, N J, 72.
Bibliography: Gerald Nordland (auth), John Safer and the light fantastic, Art Gallery Mag, 2/72.
Dealer: Gimpel Weitzenhoffer Ltd, 1040 Madison Ave, New York, NY 10021.
Mailing Address: 7420 Hampden Lane, Bethesda, MD 20014.

SAFFORD, RUTH PERKINS
Painter
Preferred Media: Watercolors.
b Boston, Mass.
Study & Training: Mass Col Art, BS; also with Henry B Snell.
Work in Public Collections: Farnsworth Mus, Rockland, Maine; Va Mus Fine Arts, Richmond; Mint Mus, Charlotte, N C; Navy Hist Mus, Washington, D C; Ball Mus, Muncie, Ind.
Commissions: Portraits of interiors, Nat Cathedral, Mt Vernon, Lee Mansion, Hyde Park & Gunstor Hall; plus many others.
Exhibitions: Critics Choice, Cincinnati; New Eng Contemp Art; Am Watercolor Soc; Corcoran Gallery Art; Mellon Found Traveling Exhib, three yrs.
Teaching: Instr art, Harvard Educ Sch.
Awards: Many.
Bibliography: Var articles in newspapers.
Memberships: Am Watercolor Soc; N Art Asn; Washington Watercolor Soc; Northern Art Asn; assoc Smithsonian Inst.
Publications: Auth, article, In: Am Artist.
Dealers: Guild Boston Artists, 162 Newbury, Boston, MA 02116; Grand Central Galleries, 40 Vanderbilt Ave, New York, NY 10017.
Mailing Address: 2821 Dumbarton Ave N W, Washington, DC 20007.

SAHRBECK, EVERETT WILLIAM
Painter
Preferred Media: Watercolors.
b East Orange, N J, Nov 4, 10.
Study & Training: Univ N Y.
Work in Public Collections: Montclair Art Mus; Newark Art Mus; Overlook Hosp, Summit, N J; First Nat Bank Boston.
Exhibitions: Am Watercolor Soc Ann, 54-72; Montclair Art Mus Statewide Ann, 55-67; Royal Soc Painters Watercolors, London, 63; Landscape I, De Cordova Mus, 70.
Positions: Art dir, Reach, McClinton & Co, 34-68.
Awards: Am Watercolor Soc Ann Prize, 61; silver medal of honor, N J Watercolor Soc, 70; Cape Cod Art Asn Watercolor Prize, 71 & 72.
Memberships: Am Watercolor Soc; N J Watercolor Soc (pres); Cape Cod Art Asn (pres, 71-72).
Dealer: Munson Gallery, Chatham, MA 02633 & Osterville, MA 02655.
Mailing Address: Box 401, South Harwich, MA 02661.

SAIDENBERG, DANIEL
Art Dealer
b Winnipeg, Man, Oct 12, 06.
Study & Training: Julliard Sch Music.
Positions: Pres, Saidenberg Gallery.
Specialty of Gallery: Twentieth century European and American masters.
Mailing Address: 16 E 79th St, New York, NY 10021.

ST AMAND, JOSEPH
Painter
Preferred Media: Oils.
b New York, N Y, Nov 10, 25.
Study & Training: Univ Calif, Berkeley; Calif Sch Fine Art, San
Francisco.
Work in Public Collections: Cathedral Sch, Kristiansand, Norway.
Exhibitions: San Francisco Mus Art 75th Ann, 57; Palace Legion of
Honor Winter Invitational, Calif, 60-64; Carnegie Inst, Pittsburgh, Pa, 64; Univ Calif, Santa Cruz, 69.
Mailing Address: 953 Kansas St, San Francisco, CA 94107.

ST CLAIR, MICHAEL
Art Dealer
b Bradford, Pa, May 28, 12.
Study & Training: Kansas City Art Inst, Vanderslice scholar, with
Thomas Hart Benton; Art Stud League New York, N Y, with
George Grosz; Colo Springs Fine Arts Ctr, scholar, with Boardman Robinson.
Exhibitions: One-man exhib, Okla Art Ctr, Oklahoma City.
Teaching: Instr drawing & painting, Okla Art Ctr Sch.
Positions: Dir, Babcock Galleries, New York, 59-
Memberships: Art Dealers Asn Am.
Specialty of Gallery: Nineteenth and twentieth century American
paintings.
Mailing Address: 865 First Ave, New York, NY 10017.

ST JOHN, BRUCE
Art Administrator, Art Historian
b Brooklyn, N Y, Jan 10, 16.
Study & Training: Middlebury Col, AB, 38; Columbia Univ, 40; New
York Univ, 46; Neth Inst Art Hist Sem, 64.
Collections Arranged: The Independents of 1910, 60; The Life and
Times of John Sloan, 61; The Calder Family, 61; Jerome Myers,
66.
Positions: Dir, Mint Mus Art, 50-55; cur, Delaware Art Mus, 55-57,
dir, 57-
Research: John Sloan and the Eight.
Publications: Ed, John Sloan's New York scene 1906-1913, Harper
& Row, 65; auth, Jerome Myers (catalogue), Del Art Mus, 66;
auth, John Sloan, Praeger, 71; auth, John Sloan in Philadelphia
1888-1904, Am Art J, 71.
Mailing Address: Rushmore Rd, Stormville, NY 12582.

SAINZ, FRANCISCO
Painter, Designer
b Santander, Spain, May 8, 23.
Study & Training: Acad Fine Arts, Madrid; also with F Sainz de la
Maza, Barcelona.
Exhibitions: Knickerbocker Artists; FAR Gallery; Assoc Am Artists;
Downtown Community Sch.
Teaching: Lect, Wrought Iron & Spanish Art.
Publications: Design illusr, Antique French paperweights, 55.
Mailing Address: 178 Second Ave, New York, NY 10003.

SAITO, SEIJI
Sculptor
Preferred Media: Stone, Bronze, Wood.
b Japan, 1933.
Study & Training: Tokyo Univ Art, BFA & MFA; Brooklyn Mus Art
Sch; also stone carving with Kametaro Akashi & Odilio Beggi.
Work in Public Collections: Isaac Delgado Mus Art, New Orleans;
Methodist Hosp Brooklyn, N Y.
Exhibitions: Ann Art Festival, Tochigi-Kaikan, Japan, 58; one-man
shows, Samanthé Gallery, New York, 68 & 70; Nat Sculpture Soc
Ann, Lever House, New York, N Y, 70 & 72.
Memberships: Nat Sculpture Soc.
Mailing Address: 925 Union St, Apt 1G, Brooklyn, NY 11215.

SAKAOKA, YASUE
Sculptor, Instructor
Preferred Media: Bronze, Marble, Steel.
b Himaji-City, Japan, Nov 12, 33.
Study & Training: Reed Col; Portland Mus Art Sch, BA; Univ Ore,
MFA; Rinehart Inst Sculpture, 63-65; also with Fredrick Litman,
Michel Russo, Manuel Izquierdo & Jan Zach.
Work in Public Collections: Parkside Gardens, Baltimore, Md; Jasper Park, Ore; Verlane, Lutherville, Md.
Commissions: Four concrete panels, Lake Co Recreation Comn, Eugene, Ore, 63; two totem sculptures, Welsh Construct Co, Baltimore, 65; play sculptures, Hollygrove Camp Broadnax, Va, 70-
71; play sculptures in concrete, South Hill City Coun, Va, 71.
Exhibitions: Northwest Inst Sculpture Ann, 62 & 63; Rinehart Inst
Ann, Baltimore, 64 & 65; Int Gallery Int Exhib, Baltimore, 65;
Southern Asn Sculptors, Inc Ann Traveling Exhib, 70-71; Galerie
Int Exhib, N Y, 71.

Teaching: Instr sculpture, Md Inst Eve Sch, Baltimore, 63-65; asst
prof art, St Paul's Col, Lawrenceville, Va, 65-
Positions: Dir arts & crafts prog, YW-YMHA Summer Camp, East
Orange, N J, 72.
Awards: Comn awards, Jr C of C, Albany, Ore, 60, Welsh Construct
Co, 63 & South Hill City Coun, 70.
Memberships: Col Art Asn Am; Nat Art Educ Asn; Va Art Educ Asn.
Dealer: Eric Shindler Gallery, 2305 E Broad St, Richmond, VA
23220.
Mailing Address: St Paul's College, Lawrenceville, VA 23868.

SALAMONE, GLADYS L
Painter
Preferred Media: Oils.
b New York, N Y.
Work in Public Collections: Albuquerque Nat Bank Eastdale Off;
Sandia Officers' Club, Kirtland AFB; New Mex Art League Old
Town Gallery, Albuquerque.
Exhibitions: Sierra Art Soc, Truth Or Consequences, N Mex, 72;
Fifth Ann Nat, Fine Arts League Southern Colo, La Junta, 72;
N Mex 100 Invitational Nor Este Art Asn Show, Albuquerque, 72;
N Mex Art League, 72; Uncompahgre Art Guild Ann Art Festival,
Montrose, Colo, 72.
Awards: First prize for oils, Sierra Art Soc, 72; second pl & purchase prize in oils, Uncompahgre Art Guild Ann Art Festival, 72;
second prize in oils, Hotchkiss Fine Arts Show, 72; plus others.
Memberships: Am Artists Prof League; N Mex Art League; Nor
Este Art Asn, Albuquerque.
Mailing Address: 8301 Pickard Ave N E, Albuquerque, NM 87110.

SALAZAR, JUAN
Painter, Designer
Preferred Media: Oils.
b Mexico City, Mex, Apr 11, 34.
Study & Training: Inst Politecnico Nac; Escuela Pintura y
Escultura Inst Nac Bellas Artes, with Carlos Orozco Romero.
Commissions: Engravings, Carton y Papel, S A, Mexico City, 71.
Exhibitions: One-man shows, Galeria Arte Mex, Mexico City, 69,
Agra Gallery, Washington, D C & Mus Nac Arte Mod, Mexico
City, 72.
Bibliography: Enrique Gual (auth), Intereses varios, Excelsior, 69
& article, In: Catalogo Expos, 72; Ines Amor (auth), article, In:
Catalogo Expos, 72.
Dealer: Galeria de Arte Mexicano, Milan 18, Mexico City, Mex.
Mailing Address: Madrid 209/3, Mexico City, Mex 21.

SALDIVAR, JAIME
Painter
b Mex, Dec 26, 23.
Work in Public Collections: Mus Mod Art, Mexico City, Mex; Pres
House los Finos Mex.
Commissions: Zocalo, Count Mariguy Hourlon; Villa, Pres Diaz
Ordaz; Suave Patria, Pres Echeverria; Cathedral, Manuel Marron Collection.
Exhibitions: Mizrachi Gallery, 65 & 69; Arte Naif Hispanamericano,
Madrid, 67; Naif Triennial, Bratislava, Czech, 68; Retahlos de
poetos, Castle of Chapultepec, 71.
Research: Art naif.
Publications: Auth, Naif painters, 70; auth, 400 years of plastic arts
in Mexico, 71.
Dealer: Mizrachi Gallery, Genova 20, Mexico D F, Mex.
Mailing Address: Covarrubias At 97 Z 18, Mexico D F, Mex.

SALEMME, LUCIA (AUTORINO)
Painter, Educator
Preferred Media: Oils, Watercolors, Ink.
b New York, N Y, Sept 23, 19.
Study & Training: Nat Acad Design, 36; Art Stud League New York,
38.
Work in Public Collections: Whitney Mus Am Art; Nat Gallery Art,
Washington, D C; Italian Embassy; New York Pub Libr Print
Collection.
Commissions: Mosaic mural, Mayer & Whittlesey, New York, 58;
many portraits, 59-72; art restoration, Art Stud League Painting
Collection, New York, 72.
Exhibitions: Watercolors Selected By Sect Fine Arts, Nat Gallery
Art, 41; Trends Watercolors Today, Brooklyn Mus, 43, 45, 57 &
59; Am Watercolor, Art Inst Chicago, Ill, 44 & 45; Sculpture &
Watercolor Ann, 49-51 & 58 & Ann Exhib Contemp Am Painting,
56-59, Whitney Mus Am Art.
Teaching: Instr, People's Art Ctr, Mus Mod Art, 57-61; asst prof
painting & drawing, N Y Univ, 59-; instr painting & drawing, Art
Stud League New York, 70-
Awards: Solomon R Guggenheim Found scholar, 42; MacDowell
Colony fel, 62.
Memberships: Artists Equity Asn.

Publications: Auth, Color exercises for the painter, 70 & Compositional projects for the painter, 73, Watson-Guptill.
Dealer: William Zierler Gallery, 956 Madison Ave, New York, NY 10021.
Mailing Address: 112 W 21st St, New York, NY 10011.

SALEMME, MARTHA
Painter
b Geneva, Ill, Aug 30, 12.
Study & Training: With Antonio Salemme.
Work in Public Collections: New York Hospital.
Exhibitions: Guild Hall, East Hampton, N Y; Hudson River Mus; Jersey City Mus; Int Platform Asn Exhib, Washington, D C, 69-71; Pietrantonio Gallery, N Y; plus others.
Memberships: Int Platform Asn.
Mailing Address: R D 4, Easton, PA 18042.

SALERNO, CHARLES
Sculptor, Educator
Preferred Media: Stone.
b Brooklyn, N Y, Aug 21, 16.
Study & Training: Art Stud League New York, N Y; Acad Grande Chaumiére, Paris; Escuela Pintura Y Escultura, Mexico City; State Univ N Y, teaching cert.
Work in Public Collections: Mus Art R I Sch Design; Ariz State Univ Collection Am Art; Atlanta Art Asn, Ga; Wadsworth Atheneum, Hartford, Conn; Grand Rapids Art Mus, Mich.
Exhibitions: Fairmont Park Int, Philadelphia, 49; Carvers, Modelers, Welders, Mus Mod Art, 50; Am Pavilion, Brussels Fair, Belg, 58; World's Fair, New York, 64; Nat Acad Design, New York, 72; plus several one-man shows, Weyhe Gallery.
Teaching: Asst prof sculpture, City Col New York, 64-
Awards: Louis Comfort Tiffany Found fel sculpture, 48; purchase prize, Staten Island Mus, 59; Margaret Hirsch-Levine Prize in Sculpture, Audubon Artists Ann, 71.
Bibliography: Frances Christoph (auth), Salerno sculpture, Weyhe Gallery, 65.
Memberships: Audubon Artists (dir sculpture); Nat Acad Design; Sculptors Guild (v pres, 65); Nat Sculpture Soc.
Dealer: Weyhe Gallery, 794 Lexington Ave, New York, NY 10021.
Mailing Address: 269 Little Clove Rd, Staten Island, NY 10301.

SALINAS, BARUJ
Painter
Preferred Media: Acrylics.
b Havana, Cuba, July 6, 35; U S citizen.
Study & Training: Kent State Univ, BArch.
Work in Public Collections: Inst Nac Bellas Artes, Mexico City, Mex; Beit Uri Mus, Kineret, Israel; Inst Int Educ, New York, N Y; Miami Mus Mod Art, Fla; Fort Lauderdale Mus Arts, Fla; plus others.
Exhibitions: Exposicion 68 Año Olimpico, Mer Kup Gallery, Mexico City, 68; Watercolor U S A, Springfield Mus, Mo, 68 & 70; Seventh Grand Prix Int Peinture, Cannes, France, 71; one-man shows, Fort Lauderdale Mus, 69 & Palacio Bellas Artes, Mex, 71; plus others.
Awards: Best transparent watercolor, Tex Watercolor Soc, 64; best watercolor, Tenth Hortt Mem Ann, 68; Cintas Found competition grant, 70 & 71.
Bibliography: Rêva Rémy (auth), Grand prix Cote d'Azur: Baruj Salinas, La Rev Mod, 71; Wifredo Fernandez (auth), Baruj Salinas su mundo pictórico, Ed Punto Cardinal, 71; Merle De Kuper (auth), Twenty-eight artists in Mexico, Ed Montauriol, 72.
Publications: Illusr, Calendario del hombre Descalzo, 70 & Resumen A I P, 71.
Dealer: Harmon Gallery, 1258 Third St S, Naples, FL 33940.
Mailing Address: 2740 S W 92nd Ave, Miami, FL 33165.

SALMOIRAGHI, FRANK
Photographer, Instructor
b Herrin, Ill, Apr 27, 42.
Study & Training: South Ill Univ, BS, 65; Ohio Univ, MFA, 68.
Work in Public Collections: Int Mus Photog, George Eastman House; Nat Mus Can.
Exhibitions: Young Photographers, Univ N Mex, 68; Vision and Expression, George Eastman House, 68-69; Serial and Modular Imagery, Purdue Univ, 69; one-man shows, South Ill Univ, 64 & A Presence Beyond Reality, Honolulu Art Acad, 71.
Teaching: Teaching asst photog, Ohio Univ, 66-68; instr photog, Univ Hawaii, 68-71.
Positions: Free-lance photographer.
Awards: Intramural res grant, 68-70 & honorarium to document vis artists Tony Smith & Harold Tovish, 69-70, Univ Hawaii.
Publications: Illusr, Popular Photog Ann; illusr, Young photographers (cat), Univ N Mex, 68; illusr, Contemporary photographers: vision and expression (cat), George Eastman House, 68; illusr, nude in the window, In: Camera Mag, 71.

Dealer: The Foundry, Waimanu & Kamani Sts, Honolulu, HI 96813.
Mailing Address: P O Box 11237, Moiliili Station, Honolulu, HI 96814.

SALMON, LARRY
Curator
b Winfield, Kans, May 5, 45.
Study & Training: Univ Kans, BA, 67; Harvard Univ, AM, 68.
Positions: Curatorial asst, City Art Mus St Louis, Mo, summer 68; asst cur textiles, Mus Fine Arts, Boston, Mass, 68-69, actg cur textiles, 69-71, cur textiles, 71-
Memberships: Am Asn Mus; Ctr Int Etude Textiles Anciens.
Mailing Address: Museum of Fine Arts, Boston, MA 02115.

SALTER, JOHN RANDALL
Painter, Sculptor
Preferred Media: Oils, Watercolors, Acrylics, Wood.
b Boston, Mass, Apr 16, 98.
Study & Training: Art Inst Chicago, BFA; Univ Iowa, MA & MFA.
Work in Public Collections: Northern Ariz Univ, Flagstaff; Menninger Clin, Topeka, Kans; var Roman Cath Churches; Univ Iowa, Iowa City.
Commissions: Chapel (paintings, archit design, sculpture, tiles & stained glass), Church of the Epiphany, Flagstaff, 63; woodblock wall mural, St Pius Church, Flagstaff, 69.
Exhibitions: Wichita Nat Exhib, Kans, 63; Allied Artists Painting Nat, Nat Acad Design Galleries, 66; Watercolor Biennial, Phoenix Art Mus, 69; Collectors Choice, Northern Ariz Univ, 70; Exhib Prints, Fedn Rocky Mountain States, 71; plus others.
Teaching: Assoc prof art, Northern Ariz Univ, 46-66.
Bibliography: Bugatti (auth), entry, In: Encyclopaedia internazionale degli artisti, 71.
Publications: Auth, A comparison of three fertility figures, Univ Iowa Press, 54.
Dealers: The Gallery, 105 E State St, Rockford, IL 61104; Gallery 3, 3819 N Third St, Phoenix, AZ 85012.
Mailing Address: 811 N Humphrey St, Flagstaff, AZ 86001.

SALTMARCHE, KENNETH CHARLES
Painter, Art Administrator
b Cardiff, Wales, Sept 29, 20; Can citizen.
Study & Training: Ont Col Art, Toronto, assoc, 46; Art Stud League New York, N Y, with Julian Levi.
Work in Public Collections: Art Gallery Hamilton, Ont; London Art Mus, Ont; Govt Ont, Toronto.
Collections Arranged: Some Canadians in Spain, 65; William G R Hind: Confederation Painter in Can, 67; Things: Still Life Painting 17th to 20th Century, 70.
Positions: Dir, Art Gallery Windsor, 46-; art critic, Windsor Star, 47-
Memberships: Ont Asn Art Galleries (pres, 68-69); Can Art Mus Dirs Orgn (secy, 62-64); Can Mus Asn.
Mailing Address: 995 Chilver Rd, Windsor 15, Ont, Can.

SALTONSTALL, ELIZABETH
Painter
Preferred Media: Oils.
b Chestnut Hill, Mass, July 26, 00.
Study & Training: Sch Mus Fine Arts, Boston, dipl; also painting with Andre L'Hote, Paris & lithography with Stow Wengenroth.
Work in Public Collections: Libr Cong, Boston Mus Fine Arts; Boston Pub Libr; Yale Univ Art Gallery; Bixler Mus, Colby Col, Maine.
Exhibitions: Libr Cong, Washington, D C, 42, 44, 45 & 49; Carnegie Inst Graphics Invitationals, 46, 47 & 50; Boston Printmakers, 58, 67 & 69; Audubon Artists Ann, 60, 67 & 69; Print Club Albany, 71.
Teaching: Instr painting, Winsor Sch, Boston, 23-28; instr painting, Milton Acad, Mass, 28-65.
Memberships: Artists Equity Asn; Audubon Artists; Nat Asn Women Artists; Pen & Brush Club; Boston Printmakers.
Mailing Address: 231 Chestnut Hill Rd, Chestnut Hill, MA 02167.

SALTZMAN, WILLIAM
Painter, Designer
Preferred Media: Oil, Wood, Copper, Stained Glass.
b Minneapolis, Minn, July 9, 16.
Study & Training: Univ Minn, BS, 40.
Work in Public Collections: Mayo Clin, Rochester, Minn; Minneapolis Inst Art; Walker Art Ctr, Minneapolis; Joslyn Mus, Omaha, Nebr.
Commissions: Exterior mural, glazed brick, YMCA-YWCA Bldg, Rochester, Minn, 64; Welded sculpture, Ten Commandments, Eternal Light & candelabra, B'nai Abraham Synagogue, St Louis Park, Minneapolis, 65; stained glass windows & meditation chapel, Univ Minn Hosps, Minneapolis, 65; plus many others.
Exhibitions: Abstract and Surrealist American Art, 58th Ann Exhib Am Paintings & Sculpture, Art Inst Chicago, Ill, 48; 13th Ann

Watercolor Exhib, San Francisco Art Asn, San Francisco Mus Art, Calif, 49; Ann Exhib Contemp Am Painting, Whitney Mus Am Art, New York, N Y, 52; 1952 Pittsburgh Int Exhib Contemp Painting, Carnegie Inst, Pa, 52; 5th Midwest Biennial Exhib, Joslyn Art Mus, 58; plus many other group & one-man shows.
Teaching: Instr painting & drawing, Exten Div, Univ Minn & asst & acting dir, Univ Minn Gallery, Minneapolis, 46-48; guest instr, St Olaf Col, 51-54; vis prof, Univ Nebr, Lincoln, spring 64; assoc prof art, Macalester Col, 66-
Positions: Supvr art, Fairmont Pub Schs, Minn; camouflage adv, USA Engrs, 42-46; mem Gov Comt, Minn State Art Soc, 46-50; resident artist & dir, Rochester Art Ctr, 48-64; juror, many exhibs, Iowa, Wis & Minn, 48-
Awards: Popular Award, 48th Ann Minn State Fair, Saint Paul, 59; Popular Award & President's Medal for Illuminated Skyline (oil), Second Ann Exhib Minn Artists, Golden Rule, Minn, 59; award, Ball State 10th Ann Show, 64; plus many others.
Memberships: Col Art Asn Am; Nat Soc Mural Painters & Sculptors.
Dealer: Suzanne Kohn Gallery, 1690 Grand Ave, Saint Paul, MN 55105.
Mailing Address: 5140 Lyndale Ave S, Minneapolis, MN 55419.

SAMARAS, LUCAS
Sculptor
b Kastoria, Greece, Sept 14, 36; U S citizen.
Study & Training: Rutgers Univ, BA, 59, with Alan Kaprow; Columbia Univ, 59-62, with Meyer Schapiro.
Work in Public Collections: Mus Mod Art, New York, N Y; Albright-Knox Art Gallery, Buffalo, N Y; Los Angeles Co Mus Art, Calif; Walker Art Ctr, Minneapolis, Minn; City Art Mus, Saint Louis, Mo.
Exhibitions: Chicago Art Inst, Ill, 67; The Obsessive Image, Inst Comtemp Art, London, 68; Dada, Surrealism and Their Heritage, Mus Mod Art, New York, 68; Documenta IV, Kassel, Ger, 68; Whitney Mus Am Art Ann, 72; plus others.
Bibliography: Lawrence Alloway (auth), Samaras: selected works 1960-1966, Pace Gallery, 66; Christopher Finch (auth), Pop art: object and image, Dutton, 68; Max Kozloff (auth), Renderings, Simon & Schuster, 68; plus others.
Mailing Address: 52 W 71st St, New York, NY 10023.

SAMERJAN, GEORGE E
Designer, Painter
b Boston, Mass, May 12, 15.
Study & Training: Art Ctr Col, grad, 38; Chouinard Art Inst, 33; Otis Art Inst, 40-41; also with Alexander Brook & Willard Nash.
Work in Public Collections: San Diego Fine Arts Soc; Fla Southern Col; Abbott Labs; Ford Motor Co Collection; Cole of California, Los Angeles; plus others.
Commissions: Murals, U S Post Off, Maywood, Calexico & Culver City, Calif; murals, Lexington Hospital, Ky, Am Red Cross & New York Hospital; designed Arctic Commemorative Stamp, 59, Adlai Stevenson Mem Stamp, 65 & Erie Canal Sesquicentennial Stamp, 67, U S Post Off Dept; S C Tricentennial, 70.
Exhibitions: Nat Acad Design; Pa Acad Fine Arts, Philadelphia; Denver Art Mus, Colo; Corcoran Gallery Art, Washington, D C; Riverside Mus, New York; Liege Belg & Paris, France; plus many others.
Teaching: Lect, Introduction to the Graphic Arts, New York Univ, adj asst prof, New York Univ.
Positions: Doc artist, USAF in the Arctic & elsewhere; chmn, Soc Illustrators Sem, 62-63.
Awards: Am Inst Graphic Arts, Art Dirs Club Philadelphia & Calif Watercolor Soc; plus others.
Memberships: Am Watercolor Soc; Audubon Artists.
Mailing Address: Cantitoe St, Katonah, NY 10536.

SAMPLE, PAUL
Painter
Preferred Media: Oils, Watercolors, Acrylics.
b Louisville, Ky, Sept 14, 96.
Study & Training: With Jonas Lie, F Tolles Chamberlain & Stanton MacDonald Wright.
Work in Public Collections: Boston Mus Fine Arts; Pa Acad Fine Arts; Metrop Mus Art; Art Inst Chicago; Brooklyn Mus.
Commissions: Murals, Nat Life Ins Co, Montpelier, Vt, Brevoort Hotel, New York, N Y, Appanaug Post Off, R I, Redondo Beach Post Off, Calif & Mass Mutual Ins Co, Springfield.
Exhibitions: Carnegie Int, Pittsburgh; Nat Acad Design, New York; Pa Acad Fine Arts, Philadelphia; Corcoran Gallery Art Biennial, Washington, D C; Paul Sample Retrospective, Currier Gallery Art, Manchester, N H, 48.
Teaching: Artist-in-residence, Dartmouth Col, 38-62.
Awards: Temple Medal, Pa Acad Fine Arts, 36; hon mention, Carnegie Int, 36; First Benjamin Altman Prize, Nat Acad Design, 62.
Memberships: Nat Acad Design; Am Watercolor Soc.

Dealers: Capricorn Galleries, 8003 Woodmont Ave, Bethesda, MD 20014; Eric Galleries, 61 E 57th St, New York, NY 10022.
Mailing Address: Norwich, VT 05055.

SAMPLINER, MR & MRS PAUL H
Collectors
Collection: French impressionist paintings.
Mailing Address: 150 Central Park S, New York, NY 10019.

SAMSTAG, GORDON
Painter, Sculptor
b New York, N Y, June 21, 06.
Study & Training: Nat Acad Design Sch; Art Stud League New York; also schs in Paris, France.
Work in Public Collections: Toledo Mus, Ohio; Santa Barbara Mus; Aldridge Collection, Australia.
Commissions: Paintings, Reidsville, N C Post Off & Scarsdale, N Y Post Off; 23D Collage, Diamond Christensen, Adelaide.
Exhibitions: Pa Acad Fine Arts; Corcoran Gallery Art, 58; Carnegie Int, 59; Contemp Art Soc Interstate, Hobart Tas, Melbourne & Sydney, 67-70.
Teaching: Dir, Am Art Sch, New York, 51-61; sr lectr fine art, painting & sculpture, South Australian Sch Art, 61-71.
Awards: Clarke Prize, Nat Acad Design, 49; Lippincott Prize, Pa Acad Fine Arts, 50; Woodville Critics Prize, 68.
Memberships: Nat Acad Design; Contemp Art Soc (pres, 68); Royal South Australian Soc Art; Burnside Painting Group (pres, 64).
Publications: Ed, Bull Australian Soc Educ Through Art, 68, Contemp Art Soc Quart, 69 & Collection, Elliot Aldridge, 70.
Mailing Address: P O Box 641, Cairns, North Queensland, Australia 4870.

SAMUELSON, FRED BINDER
Painter, Educator
Preferred Media: Acrylics.
b Harvey, Ill, Nov 29, 25.
Study & Training: Sch Art Inst Chicago, BFA, 51, MFA, 53; Univ Chicago, 46-53.
Work in Public Collections: Oil, Denver Art Mus, Colo; watercolor, Witte Mus, San Antonio, Tex; acrylics, Ohio Univ, Athens & Tex Fine Arts Asn, Laguna Gloria Mus, Austin.
Commissions: Acrylic mural, Hemisfair 68, San Antonio, 68.
Exhibitions: 60th Ann Exhib Western Art, Denver Art Mus, 54; 20th Ann Tex Painting & Sculpture Exhib, Dallas Mus Fine Art, 58; Southwest Am Art Ann, Okla Art Ctr, 60; Segundo Festival Pictorico Acapulco, 64; 53rd Tex Fine Arts Asn Ann, 64.
Teaching: Instr painting & drawing, Inst Allende, San Miguel de Allende, Mex, 55-63; chmn faculty, San Antonio Art Inst, 63-64; head grad studies & painting, Inst Allende, 65-
Bibliography: Leonard Brooks (auth), Oil painting traditional and new, 59 & Wash drawings, 61, Van Nostrand Reinhold; interview, Time-Life, 65.
Dealer: Four Winds Gallery, Kalamazoo, MI 49001.
Mailing Address: Apartado Postal 70, San Miguel de Allende, Mex.

SANBORN, HERBERT J
Lithographer, Painter
b Worcester, Mass, Oct 28, 07.
Study & Training: Nat Acad Design, Pulitzer traveling fel, 29; teachers col, Columbia Univ; Univ Chicago.
Work in Public Collections: Libr Cong; Nat Collection Fine Arts, Smithsonian Inst; Hunterdon Co Art Ctr.
Exhibitions: 10th Biennial Nat Print Exhib, Print Club Albany, 63; Jacksonville Coun Arts Festival, 64; Print Club Philadelphia Mem Exhib, 64; Va Artists, Va Mus Art, 65; Corcoran Gallery Art Area Ann, 65.
Positions: Dir, Davenport Munic Art Gallery, 33-35; dir mus, Oglebay Inst, Wheeling W Va, 36-42; exhibs officer, Libr Cong, Washington, D C, 46-
Awards: Third prize, Third Ann Va Printmakers, Univ Va, 62; purchase prize, Hunterdon Co Art Ctr, 64.
Bibliography: Eugene Ettenberg (auth), Modern influences on printing design, Am Artist, 9/56.
Memberships: Washington Chap Am Inst Graphic Arts (pres, 71); Print Club Philadelphia; Watercolor Soc Washington; Inter-Soc Color Coun.
Publications: Auth, Hill towns of Spain (lithographs), 30; auth, Modern art influences on printing design, 56.
Mailing Address: 3541 Forest Dr, Alexandria, VA 22302.

SANCHEZ, EMILIO
Painter
b Nuevitas, Cuba, June 10, 21; U S citizen.
Study & Training: Art Stud League New York.
Work in Public Collections: Metrop Mus Art, New York, N Y; Mus Mod Art, New York; Brooklyn Mus, N Y; Philadelphia Mus Art, Pa; Albright-Knox Mus, Buffalo, N Y.

Exhibitions: Colteser Bienal, Medellin, Colombia; Bienal 1 & 2, San Juan, P R; Pa Acad Fine Arts; Am Color Print Ann.
Awards: Eyre Medal, Pa Acad Fine Arts, 69; David Kapan Purchase Award, Am Color Print Soc, 70.
Mailing Address: c/o Coe Kerr Gallery, Inc, 49 E 82nd St, New York, NY 10028.

SANDECKI, ALBERT EDWARD
Painter, Instructor
Preferred Media: Watercolors, Oils.
b Camden, N J, Oct 10, 35.
Study & Training: Pa Acad Fine Arts, 53-59.
Work in Public Collections: McNay Art Inst, Tex; Lubbock Mus, Tex; Corcoran Gallery Art, Washington, D C; Albright-Knox Mus, Buffalo, N Y; plus many others in pvt collections.
Exhibitions: Audubon Artists, 57; Pa Acad Fine Arts Ann, 57-60; Nat Acad Design Ann, 58; Wadsworth Atheneum Ann, 60; Philadelphia Watercolor Soc, 60-67; plus many other group & one-man shows.
Teaching: Instr portraiture & still life, Sanski Art Ctr, 59-
Bibliography: Edith De Shazo (auth), article, In: Courier-Post; John Cannady (auth), article, In: New York Times.
Memberships: Fel Pa Acad Fine Arts.
Art Interests: Conservator of paintings.
Dealer: James Graham & Sons, Inc, 1014 Madison Ave, New York, NY 10021.
Mailing Address: 50 Tanner St, Haddonfield, NJ 08033.

SANDER, LUDWIG
Painter
Preferred Media: Oils, Graphics.
b New York, N Y, July 18, 06.
Work in Public Collections: Whitney Mus Am Art, New York; Solomon R Guggenheim Mus, New York; Corcoran Gallery Art, Washington, D C; Art Inst Chicago; San Francisco Mus Art.
Exhibitions: Salon Realités Nouvelles, Paris, 68; Neue Kunst U S A, Mod Art Mus, Munich, 68; Form of Color, Toledo Mus Art, Ohio, 70; Plus By Minus—Today's Half Century, Albright-Knox Art Gallery, Buffalo; From Synchronism Forward, Am Fedn Arts Traveling Show.
Awards: Nat Coun Arts Award, 67; J S Guggenheim Mem Found fel, 68; Nat Inst Arts & Lett Award Art, 71.
Bibliography: Andrew Hudson (auth), Washington—an American salon, 4/67 & Carter Ratcliff (auth), New York letter, 4/72, Art Int; Hilton Kramer (auth), article, In: New York Times, 1/22/72.
Dealer: Lawrence Rubin Gallery, 49 W 57th St, New York, NY 10019.
Mailing Address: 68 E 12th St, New York, NY 10003.

SANDERS, ANDREW DOMINICK
Painter, Instructor
Preferred Media: Oils.
b Erie, Pa, Dec 22, 18.
Study & Training: Philadelphia Mus Sch Art, dipl, 42.
Exhibitions: Int Gulf-Carribbean, Mus Fine Arts, Houston, Tex, 56; Nat Acad Design 146th Ann, New York, N Y, 71; Audubon Artists 30th Ann, Nat Acad Design Galleries, 72; Mainstreams '72 5th Ann, Marietta Col, Ohio, 72; Butler Inst Am Art 38th Midyear Ann, Youngstown, Ohio, 72.
Teaching: Instr drawing, painting & art hist, Ringling Sch Art, Sarasota, Fla, 49-59; instr drawing & painting, Columbus Col Art & Design, 60-63; dir drawing & painting, Art Sch, Erie, 64-
Awards: First prize, All Fla Ann, 53 & first prize paintings of circus, 54, Ringling Mus Art, Sarasota; hon mention, Mainstreams '72, Marietta Col, 72.
Mailing Address: The Art School, 18 N Park Row, Erie, PA 16501.

SANDERS, JOOP A
Painter
Preferred Media: Oils, Acrylics, Watercolors.
b Amsterdam, Holland, Oct 6, 22; U S citizen.
Study & Training: Art Stud League New York, N Y, with George Grosz; also with De Kooning.
Work in Public Collections: Stedelijke Mus, Amsterdam; Munic Mus, The Hague; Belzalel Mus, Jerusalem; Dillard Univ.
Exhibitions: Ninth St Show, 51; Stable Shows, 52-55; one-man retrospective, Stedelijke Mus, 60; Carnegie Int, 60; Options, Mus Contemp Art, Chicago, 68.
Teaching: Vis lectr, Carnegie Inst Technol, spring 65; prof painting, State Univ N Y Col New Paltz, 66-, Res Found awards, 71-72; vis lectr, Univ Calif, Berkeley, spring 68.
Awards: Longview Found fel, 60-61.
Bibliography: Tom Hess (auth), Forward to catalogue, Stedelijke Mus, 60.
Dealer: New Bertha Schaefer Galleries, 51 E 57th St, New York, NY 10022.
Mailing Address: 35 Bond St, New York, NY 10012.

SANDGREN, ERNEST NELSON
Painter, Educator
b Dauphin, Man, Dec 17, 17.
Study & Training: Univ Ore, BA & MFA; Univ Michoacan, Mex; Chicago Inst Design.
Work in Public Collections: Portland Art Mus, Ore; Am Embassy Collection; Victoria & Albert Mus, London.
Commissions: Murals in Eugene, Ore, State Univ Libr, Corvallis & Portland, Ore.
Exhibitions: Denver Art Mus; Santa Barbara Mus Art; Brooklyn Mus, N Y; also nat tours; Am Cult Ctr, Paris, France; Turin & Bordighera, Italy & Johannesburg, S Africa; 46 U S A Printmakers, New Forms Gallery, Athens, Greece, 64.
Teaching: Instr art, Univ Oregon, 47; prof art, Oregon State Univ, 48-; guest printmaker instr, Pa State Univ, summer 66; guest printmaker instr, Cent Ore Col, summers 70-72.
Positions: Exped artist, Am Quintana Roo Mex Exped, 65 & 66; exped artist, CEDAM Exped to Durango, Mex, 70.
Awards: Northwest Painting Exhib, Spokane, Wash, 57; M H de Young Mem Mus, 58; Yaddo fel, 61; plus others.
Memberships: Ore Artists Alliance; Portland Art Mus.
Publications: Co-auth, A search for visual relationships & Northwest four and two (color art films).
Mailing Address: Art Dept, Oregon State University, Corvallis, OR 97331.

SANDGROUND, MARK BERNARD, SR
Collector, Patron
b Boston, Mass, June 6, 32.
Study & Training: Univ Mich, BA, 52; Univ Va, LLB, 55, JD, 71.
Teaching: Prof humanities & cooking, Free Col Belgravia, Lower Sch, 65-66.
Positions: Pres, La Nicoise.
Awards: La Chaine des Les Robsier Chevalier, 71; Klip & Klop Gold Medal, 72.
Bibliography: D Kane (auth), Killer Kock and the white princess, McGraw, 72; The Gypsie princess (film), 72.
Memberships: Friends of Corcoran Gallery Art (bd dir, 67-, pres, 68-70); Pyramid Gallery (bd dir, 71-).
Research: Graphic works of Jose Louis Cuevas.
Collection: Cuevas, Rico Lebrun, Lowell Nesbitt & Anne Truitt.
Publications: Auth, Collected letters from unknown artists, 1846-1871, privately pub, 52; auth, Erotica from the Falls Church Collection, 72.
Mailing Address: 700 Colorado Bldg, Washington, DC 20005.

SANDLER, IRVING HARRY
Art Critic, Art Historian
b New York, N Y, July 22, 25.
Study & Training: Temple Univ, BA, 48; Univ Pa, MA, 50.
Teaching: Instr art hist, New York Univ, 60-71; instr art hist, State Univ N Y Col Purchase, 71-
Positions: Art critic, Art News, 56-62; art critic, New York Post, 60-65; vis critic, State Univ N Y, 69-70; contrib ed, Art Am, 72.
Awards: Tona Shepherd Fund grant travel in Ger & Austria; Guggenheim Found fel, 65.
Bibliography: Jay Jacobs (auth), Of myths and men, Art Am, 3-4/70; Rosalind Constable (auth), The myth of the myth-makers, Washington Post Bk World, 11/29/70; Gesture-makers and colour-fieldsmen, Times Lit Suppl, 6/8/71.
Memberships: Int Asn Art Critics (pres, 70-); Col Art Asn Am; Inst Study Art Educ.
Research: American art since 1930.
Publications: Contribr, The New York school, some younger artists, 59; contribr, Minimal art: a critical anthology, 68; auth, The triumph of American painting, a history of abstract expressionism, 70; ed, Alex Katz, 71; ed, Art criticism and art education, 72.
Mailing Address: 100 Bleecker St, New York, NY 10012.

SANDOL, MAYNARD
Painter
b Newark, N J, 30.
Study & Training: Newark State Col, 52; also with Robert Motherwell.
Work in Public Collections: Newark Mus Art; Wadsworth Atheneum, Hartford, Conn; Princeton Univ, N J; Finch Col Mus, New York, N Y; Joseph Hirshhorn Collection, Washington, D C; also pvt collections.
Exhibitions: Corcoran Gallery of Art, Washington, D C; Mus Mod Art, New York, N Y; N J Pavilion, New York World's Fair; Am Greetings Gallery, New York; N J State Mus, Trenton; plus others.
Bibliography: William H Gerdts, Jr (auth), Paintings and sculpture in New Jersey, Van Nostrand, 64.
Mailing Address: Box 985, Rte 2, Parker Rd, Chester, NJ 07830.

SANGUINETTI, EUGENE F
Art Administrator, Lecturer
b Yuma, Ariz, May 12, 17.
Study & Training: Univ Santa Clara, BA, 39; Univ Ariz, 60-62.
Collections Arranged: Selected Drawings from the Collection of Edward Jacobson, 70; Drawings by Living Americans, Objects from Buddhist Cultures & Etching Renaissance in France: 1850-1880, 71; Drawings by New York Artists, Prehistoric Utah Petroglyphs & Pictographs & Ron Resch and the Computer, 72; plus 9 retrospective & 11 one-man exhibs, 67-72.
Teaching: Lectr art hist, Univ Ariz, 62-64; adj assoc prof art, Univ Utah, 67-
Positions: Dir, Tucson Mus & Art Ctr, Ariz, 64-67; dir, Utah Mus Fine Arts, Univ Utah, Salt Lake City, 67-; judge, five art shows, Colo, Utah & Idaho, 68-72.
Memberships: Asn Am Mus; Western Asn Art Mus; Col Art Asn Am; Asn Archit Historians; Am Fedn Arts.
Research: American art of the first half of the twentieth century.
Specialty of Gallery: Paintings, tapestries and furniture from American and European periods, Oriental material, Egyptian and Cyprist antiquities; French and English objects and decoration.
Publications: Contribr, Alexander H Wyant Retrospective, 68, John Marin Drawings Retrospective, 69, Etching Renaissance in France: 1850-1880, 71, Alex Katz Retrospective, 71 & Drawings by New York Artists, 72.
Mailing Address: 104 Arts & Architecture Center, University of Utah, Salt Lake City, UT 84112.

SANTIAGO, HELENE
Art Dealer, Collector
b Paris, France, Aug 28, 10; U S citizen.
Study & Training: Univ Vienna, 2 yrs; Sorbonne, 1 yr.
Positions: Dir, Galeria Santiago.
Specialty of Gallery: Mainly abstract and avant-garde paintings and graphics of contemporary Puerto Rican artists.
Collection: Paintings and graphics of local contemporary artists.
Mailing Address: c/o Galeria Santiago, Calle del Cristo 207, San Juan, PR 00901.

SARFF, WALTER
Painter, Designer
b Pekin, Ill, Oct 29, 05.
Study & Training: Sch Mod Photog, New York, N Y, grad, 49; Sch Portrait & Commercial Photog, New York; also with Alexey Brodovitch & Adolph Fassbender; Nat Acad Art, Chicago, traveling scholar, 31, grad; Grand Cent Sch Art, New York; Art Stud League New York; Woodstock Sch Painting, N Y; also with Hubert Ropp, Chicago & Yasuo Kuniyoshi, New York.
Work in Public Collections: Collections of George Hillenbrand, M Owen Page & Anna Carolan.
Exhibitions: Springfield Art Mus, Mass; Worcester Art Mus, Mass; Denver Art Mus, Colo; San Francisco Art Mus, Calif; Seattle Art Mus, Wash; plus many others.
Teaching: Instr & asst registr, Nat Acad Art, Chicago, 29-31; pvt instr, 31-42.
Positions: Dir, Sawkill Gallery, Woodstock; chmn exec bd, Woodstock Artists Asn, 39 & juror; exec secy, Ulster Co Artists Union Union; pres, Sarff-Zumpano, Inc.
Memberships: Am Soc Mag Photogr; Artists Equity Asn; Art Stud League New York; hon mem Hypo Club; Mus Mod Art; plus others.
Publications: Contribr, Am Ann Photog, cover, Am Photog, Art Photog, Cath Digest & Charm; plus others.
Mailing Address: 15 W 36th St, New York, NY 10018.

SARGENT, MARGARET HOLLAND
Painter
Study & Training: Univ Calif, Los Angeles, 45-47; watercolor classes, Tokyo, Japan, 56; oil painting with Herbert Abrams, New York, 59-61 & Marcos Blahove, Fairfax, Va, 69.
Commissions: Portrait, Arg Embassy, Ankara, Turkey.
Exhibitions: One-man shows, Turkish Am Asn, Ankara, 63, Art Research Northern Va, 68 & Frye Art Mus, 71; Coupeville Days, Wash, 71; Bellevue Art Festival, Wash, 72; Gordon Woodside Galleries, Seattle, 72; Frye Art Mus, Seattle, 72; plus others.
Awards: Blue ribbon for portrait of Lt Gen William F Cassidy, Washington, D C; gold seal award, Montgomery Co Ann, Md.
Mailing Address: 800 First Ave N, Apt 42, Seattle, WA 98109.

SARKIS (SARKIS SARKISIAN)
Painter
Preferred Media: Oils, Mixed Media.
b Smyrna, Turkey, May 15, 09; U S citizen.
Study & Training: John P Wicker Art Sch; Art Sch Soc Arts & Crafts, with John Carroll.
Work in Public Collections: Detroit Inst Arts; Butler Inst Am Art, Youngstown, Ohio.
Commissions: Mosaic tile, Map of the World, Ford Admin Bldg, Dearborn, Mich; Reredos & 16 other relig paintings, Church of Incarnation, Detroit, 41; portrait of Gen Calladay, Flint Armory, Mich.
Exhibitions: Mus Mod Art, New York, N Y; Carnegie Inst Art, Pittsburgh; Wayne State Univ; Henry Ford Community Col; Women's City Club, Detroit.
Teaching: Painting instr & dir, Art Sch Soc Arts & Crafts, Detroit, 33-66.
Awards: Awards, Univ Mich, Ann Arbor & Butler Inst Am Art; three Art Founder's Prizes, Detroit Inst Arts; plus many others.
Bibliography: Morley Driver (auth), Sarkis, the grand old man of Detroit's art world, Detroit Mag, 12/26/65; Joy Hakanson (auth), His eyesight is limited but not his vision, Sun Mag, Detroit News, 3/26/72.
Memberships: Art Founder's Soc & Friends Mod Art, Detroit Inst Arts; Scarab Club.
Dealers: Detroit Artists Market, 1452 Randolph St, Detroit, MI 48226; Arwin Galleries, 222 W Grand River, Detroit, MI 48226.
Mailing Address: 1352 Joliet Pl, Detroit, MI 48207.

SARNOFF, ARTHUR SARON
Painter
Preferred Media: Oils, Acrylics.
b Brooklyn, N Y, Dec 30, 12.
Study & Training: Indust Sch Art; Grand Cent Sch Art; also with Harvey Dunne.
Work in Public Collections: Bass Mus; Springfield Mus; Parrish Mus; Hartford Mus; Grand Cent Galleries & Nat Art Mus Sport, New York, N Y.
Commissions: Fine art prints, Arthur Kaplan Co, Donald Art Co & Cataldi Fine Prints.
Exhibitions: Int Art Galleries; Continental Art Galleries; Sports in Action, Grand Cent Art Galleries; Nat Acad Art; Allied Art Show; plus others.
Awards: Outdoor advert award, Art Dirs Club.
Memberships: Soc Illusrs; Allied Artists Am.
Publications: Contribr, all leading mags.
Dealer: Grand Central Galleries, 40 Vanderbilt Ave, New York, NY 10017.
Mailing Address: 2 Beechwood Dr, Glen Head, NY 11545.

SARNOFF, LOLO
Sculptor, Collector
Preferred Media: Fibers, Acrylics.
b Frankfurt am Main, Ger, Jan 9, 16; U S citizen.
Study & Training: Reimann Art Sch, Berlin, Ger, grad, 36.
Work in Public Collections: Nat Acad Sci, Washington, D C; Kennedy Ctr, Washington, D C; Corning Glass Ctr, Corning, N Y.
Commissions: Light sculptures, U S Embassy, New Delhi, 70 & flame, Kennedy Ctr, 71.
Exhibitions: One-man shows, Agra Gallery, Washington, D C, 68 & Corning Mus Glass, 70; two-man shows, Gallery Two, Woodstock, Vt, 69 & Gallery Marc, Washington, D C, 71; Art 72, Int Artmart, Basel, Switz, 72.
Memberships: Artists Equity Asn.
Collection: Twentieth century drawings, paintings and sculptures; eighteenth century Fayence; eighteenth century porcelain.
Dealers: Gallery Marc, 2121 P St N W, Washington, DC 20037; Gallery Liatowitsch, 51 Steinenbachgaesslein, Basel, Switz.
Mailing Address: 7507 Hampden Lane, Bethesda, MD 20014.

SARNOFF, ROBERT W
Collector
b New York, N Y, July 2, 18.
Positions: Trustee, John F Kennedy Libr Corp; bd dirs, Bus Comt for Arts.
Collection: Contemporary art.
Mailing Address: 30 Rockefeller Plaza, New York, NY 10020.

SARSONY, ROBERT
Painter, Printmaker
Preferred Media: Oils, Watercolors, Graphics.
b Easton, Pa, Jan 1, 38.
Work in Public Collections: Butler Inst Am Art, Youngstown, Ohio; Ga Mus Art, Athens; Joslyn Art Mus, Omaha, Nebr; Sara Roby Found, New York, N Y; Univ Kans Mus Art, Lawrence; plus others.
Exhibitions: Allied Artist Show, New York, 63-65; one-man shows, Capricorn Galleries, Bethesda, Md, 67-71; Mainstream 71, Marietta Col, Ohio, 71; Three Young Realists, ACA Galleries, New York, 71; New Jersey Contemporary Masters, Heritage Arts, South Orange, 71-72; plus others.
Bibliography: John S Le Maire (auth), Robert Sarsony, N J Bus Mag, 69; George Albert Perret (auth), Robert Sarsony—painter, Heritage Arts, 71.

Dealer: Capricorn Galleries, 8003 Woodmont Ave, Bethesda, MD 20014.
Mailing Address: Gristmill Rd, R D 3, Dover, NJ 07801.

SATO, TADASHI
Painter, Sculptor
Preferred Media: Oils.
b Maui, Hawaii, Feb 6, 23.
Study & Training: Honolulu Sch Art; Brooklyn Mus Art Sch; New Sch Social Res, New York, with Davis; aslo with Ralston Crawford, Stuart Davis, John Ferren & Wilson Stamper.
Work in Public Collections: Guggenheim Mus, New York, N Y; Whitney Mus Am Art, New York; Honolulu Acad Arts, Hawaii; Univ Art Gallery, Tucson, Ariz.
Commissions: Oil mural, Maui War Mem Gym, Wailuka, Hawaii, 62; concrete relief wall, State Libr, Kahului, Maui, 63; two oil murals, State Libr, Aina Haina, Oahu, Hawaii, 65; mosaic floor design, Hawaii State Capitol Bldg, Honolulu, 69; mosaic mural, West Maui Mem Gym, Maui, 72.
Exhibitions: 52 Young Painters of America, Guggenheim Mus, 54; Pacific Heritage Exhibit, Los Angeles, Calif, 63; Four Contemporary Painters, McRoberts & Tunnard Ltd, London, 64; White House Festival of Arts, White House, Washington, D C, 65; American Paintings in Berlin Art Festival, Ger, 67.
Awards: John Hay Whitney Found Opportunity fel, 53; McInerny Found Honolulu Community fel, 55; best painting in show, Honolulu Acad Arts, 57.
Memberships: Hui No Eau, Kahului, Maui (bd dirs, 72); Lahaina Art Soc, Maui; Hawaii Painters & Sculptors League.
Dealer: Willard Gallery, 29 E 72nd St, New York, NY 10021.
Mailing Address: P O Box 476, Lahaina, Maui, HI 96761.

SATORSKY, CYRIL
Printmaker, Illustrator
b London, Eng.
Study & Training: Leeds Col Art, nat dipl design; Royal Col Art, Royal scholar, traveling scholar, res scholar, ARCA & first class hon degree.
Work in Public Collections: Cincinnati Art Mus; Wooster Col; Essex Community Col.
Exhibitions: Philadelphia Print Club Ann; Rental Gallery, Baltimore Mus, 70; Sixth Dulin Nat Print Show, Knoxville, Tenn, 70.
Teaching: Prof illus & printmaking, Md Inst Col Art, 65-
Positions: Adv to univ publ, Univ Tex, Austin, 62-65.
Memberships: Philadelphia Print Club.
Publications: Auth & illusr, A pride of Rabbis, Aquarius, 70; illusr, The Frenchman & the seven deadly sins, Scribners, 71; illusr, Sir Gawain & the green knight, Limited Ed Club, 72.
Dealer: Ferdinand Roten, 123 W Mulberry St, Baltimore, MD 21201.
Mailing Address: 2906 N Calvert St, Baltimore, MD 21218.

SATURENSKY, RUTH
Painter
b Denver, Colo, Jan 18, 20.
Study & Training: Colo Woman's Col; Otis Art Inst; Jepson Art Inst; Chouinard Art Inst.
Commissions: Auth & dir, three theatre pieces (with Alex Haye's Los Angeles Summer Theatre Piece Lab), 67.
Exhibitions: Pa Acad Fine Arts; Fine Arts Gallery San Diego; Long Beach Art Mus; Jewish Community Ctr; Santa Barbara Mus Art; plus others.
Positions: Founder, Changes (theatre co), 67; dir, The Ensemble Group (exp art theatre), Los Angeles, presently.
Awards: Prizes, Los Angeles Mus Art, 60; Westside Jewish Community Ctr, Los Angeles, 63 & First Methodist Church, Santa Monica, 63.
Mailing Address: 2124 N Beachwood Dr, Apt 17, Los Angeles, CA 90028.

SAUCY, CLAUDE GERALD
Painter, Educator
Preferred Media: Graphics.
b Thayngen, Switz, Nov 24, 29.
Study & Training: Kunstgewerbe Schule, Zurich; Univ Zurich.
Work in Public Collections: Mus Mod Art, New York, N Y; Wadsworth Atheneum, Hartford, Conn.
Exhibitions: Invitational Artist, New Haven Art Festival, Conn, 69; Invitational Artists, Sharon Creative Arts Found, Conn, 70.
Teaching: Chmn dept art & art hist, Kent Sch, 66-
Awards: Hon mention, New Haven Festival Art, 67; art prize, Sharon Creative Arts Found, 69.
Bibliography: H Steiner (auth), Claude Saucy, Schaffhauser-Nachrichten, 10/65.
Dealer: Far Gallery, 746 Madison Ave, New York, NY 10021.
Mailing Address: Skiff Mountain, Kent, CT 06757.

SAUL, PETER
Painter
b San Francisco, Calif, Aug 16, 34.
Study & Training: Stanford Univ; Calif Sch Fine Arts, 50-52; Wash Univ, BFA, 56, with Fred Conway.
Work in Public Collections: Art Inst Chicago; Oberlin Col; Mus Mod Art, New York, N Y; Univ Mass.
Exhibitions: One-man exhibs, San Francisco Art Inst, Reed Col & Calif Col Arts & Crafts, 68; Mus Mod Art, New York, 68; Univ Okla, 68; Univ Ill, 69; one-man exhib, Mus St Etinne, France, 71; plus others.
Awards: New Talent Award, Art in Am Mag, 62; William & Noma Copley Found grant, 62.
Dealer: Allan Frumkin Gallery, 620 N Michigan Ave, Chicago, IL 60611.
Mailing Address: 383 Lovell St, Mill Valley, CA 94941.

SAUNDERS, AULUS WARD
Painter, Educator
Preferred Media: Watercolors, Acrylics, Oils.
b Perry, Mo, Sept 22, 04.
Study & Training: Westminster Col (Mo), BA; Saint Louis Sch Fine Arts; Wash Univ, MA; Univ Iowa, PhD; Also with Charles Cagle.
Work in Public Collections: State Univ N Y Col Oswego.
Exhibitions: Midwestern Ann Art Exhib, Kansas City Art Inst, 35; 30th & 31st Ann Exhib Paintings Am Artists, Saint Louis City Art Mus, 36 & 37; 18th Ann Exhib Artists Cent N Y, Munson-Williams-Proctor Inst, Utica, N Y, 55; one-man show watercolors, State Univ N Y Col, Morrisville, 67.
Teaching: Prof art, State Univ N Y Col Oswego, 37-70; vis prof, Southern Ill Univ, Carbondale, summer 49; vis prof, Pa State Univ, University Park, summers 50-52.
Research: Psychology of art, especially genesis and stability of art talent in children.
Publications: Auth, The stability of artistic attitude, Psychol Monogr, 36; auth, Feeling and form, Sch Arts, 10/70.
Mailing Address: 165 E Third St, Oswego, NY 13126.

SAUNDERS, J BOYD
Printmaker, Educator
Preferred Media: Graphics.
b Memphis, Tenn, June 12, 37.
Study & Training: Memphis State Univ, BS; Univ Miss, MFA; Bottega Arte Grafica, Florence, Italy.
Work in Public Collections: Denison Univ Print Collection, Ohio; Columbia Mus Art Print Collection, S C; S C State Collection, Columbia; Bottega Arte Grafica Collection; Univ Ariz Print Collection, Tucson.
Commissions: Mixed media altar panel, Guess Chapel, Univ Church, Oxford, Miss, 62; mem portrait comn, Tipoff Club, Columbia, S C, 69; oil mural, Univ House, Univ S C, 72.
Exhibitions: Soc Washington Printmakers 24th Nat, Smithsonian Inst, Washington, D C, 62; 1st Int Printmaker's Exhib, Gallerie Bottega & Arte Grafica, Florence, 67; 34th Graphic Arts & Drawing Nat, Wichita, Kans, 69; 5th Dulin Print & Drawing Competition Nat, Knoxville, Tenn, 70; 15th N Dak Print & Drawing Ann, Grand Forks, 72.
Teaching: Instr art, Univ Miss, 61-62; instr art, Southwest Tex State Col, 62-65; asst prof art, Univ S C, 65-
Positions: Staff artist, Dan Kilgo & Assocs, Tuscaloosa, Ala, 59-60; designer-illusr, Chaparral Press, Kyle, Tex, 63-65; art purchasing comt, S C Collection, Columbia, 69-70; steering comt mem, Fiesta '72, Columbia, 72.
Awards: Third prize, 6th Ann Mid-South Exhib Paintings, Prints & Drawings, Memphis, Tenn, 61; grand prize, Guild Columbia Artists, 71; purchase prize, 15th N Dak Ann Print & Drawing Competition, 72.
Bibliography: Jack Morris (auth), Boyd Saunders, printmaker, Contemp Artists S C, 69; Harriet Door (auth), 2 forceful exhibitions, Charlotte Observer, N C, 72; Adger Brown (auth), Boyd Saunders/vital forces, State-Rec, Columbia, 72.
Memberships: Print Coun Am; Guild S C Artists (adv bd, 56); Columbia Art Asn; Southeastern Graphics Soc (pres); Am Asn Univ Prof.
Publications: Illusr, Bosque territory; a history of an agrarian community, 64; illusr, Lyndon Baines Johnson; the formative years, 65; auth, A summer's printmaking in Florence, Art Educ J, 68.
Dealer: Hubris Press, Columbia, SC 29210.
Mailing Address: 2103 Marley Dr, Columbia, SC 29210.

SAUNDERS, RAYMOND JENNINGS
Painter, Educator
b Pittsburgh, Pa, Oct 28, 34.
Study & Training: Pa Acad Fine Arts, nat scholastic scholar; Univ Pa, nat scholastic scholar; Carnegie Inst Technol, BFA; Calif Col Arts & Crafts, MFA.

Work in Public Collections: Mus Mod Art, New York, N Y; Whitney
Mus Am Art, Andover Collection Am Art; Pa Acad Fine Arts; Nat
Inst Arts & Lett.
Exhibitions: Mus Mod Art, 71; one-man shows, San Francisco Mus
Art, 71 & Providence Mus Art, 72; Whitney Mus Am Art Ann, 72;
Pa Acad Fine Arts, 72.
Teaching: Prof painting, Calif State Univ, Hayward, 68-; vis critic,
R I Sch Design, 68, vis artist, 72; vis artist, Yale Univ, 72.
Positions: Nat consult urban affairs, Volt Tech Serv, New York, 68-;
art consult, Dept Black Studies, Univ Calif, Berkeley, 69-; mem
Afro-Am Acquisitions Comt, Univ Art Mus, Berkeley, 71-
Awards: Thomas Eakins Prize, Pa Acad Fine Arts, 55; Nat Acad
Arts & Lett Award, Nat Inst Arts & Lett, 63; Prix de Rome, Am
Acad Rome, 64-66.
Bibliography: Bearden & McHolty (auth), The painter's mind, Crown,
69.
Memberships: Fel Am Acad Rome.
Publications: Auth, Black is a color, privately publ, 68.
Dealer: Terry Dintenfass Gallery, 18 E 67th St, New York, NY
10021.
Mailing Address: 6007 Rock Ridge Blvd, Oakland, CA 94618.

SAVAS, JO-ANN
Painter, Illustrator
Preferred Media: Watercolors.
b Opelika, Ala, Jan 30, 34.
Study & Training: Auburn Univ, Alpha Delta Pi scholar, BS(art educ).
Exhibitions: Nat Acad Galleries, New York, N Y; New York World's
Fair; Chateau de la Napole, Cannes, France; Southern Contem-
poraries Collection of Sears-Roebuck & Juried Int Women's
Show, 66; Nat Women's Watercolor Exhib, 67 & 68; plus 27 major
one-man shows & other group shows.
Teaching: Pvt art instr, Huntsville.
Positions: Tech illusr, Army Ballistic Missile Agency, Redstone
Arsenal, Ala, 57-58.
Memberships: Huntsville Art League & Mus Asn (first pres); Nat
Asn Women Artists.
Mailing Address: 3506 Mae Dr S E, Huntsville, AL 35801.

SAVOY, CHYRL LENORE
Sculptor, Educator
Preferred Media: Woods, Metals.
b New Orleans, La, May 23, 44.
Study & Training: La State Univ, BA(art); Acad Fine Arts, Florence,
with Gallo & Berti; Wayne State Univ, MFA(sculpture).
Work in Public Collections: Our Lady Bayous Convent, Abbeville,
La; Herrod Jr H S Libr, Abbeville; Mamou H S Libr, La.
Commissions: Renovation & redesigning of chapel, Dominican Rural
Missionaries, Abbeville, 72; sculpture, Our Lady Queen of All
Saints, Ville Platte, La, 72.
Exhibitions: 58th Exhib Mich Artists, Detroit Inst Arts Mus, 71;
1971 Artist's Biennial Exhib of Artists of Southwest & Tex, New
Orleans Mus Art, 71; 27th Ann State Art Exhib Prof Artists, La
Art Comn Galleries, Baton Rouge, 71; 14th Ann Delta Art Exhib,
Ark Art Ctr, Little Rock, 71; one-man show, New Orleans Mus
Art, La, 72.
Teaching: Asst sculpture, Wayne State Univ, summer 70.
Awards: Purchase award, New Orleans Mus Art, 71.
Mailing Address: 1009 Poinciana Ave, Mamou, LA 70554.

SAWYER, ALAN R
Art Consultant
b Wakefield, Mass, June 18, 19.
Study & Training: Bates Col, BS, 41; Boston Mus Fine Arts Sch;
Boston Univ, 47-48; Harvard Univ, MA(art hist), 49; Bates Col,
hon DFA, 69.
Collections Arranged: Designer-Craftsmen U S A, 54, Design in
Scandinavia, 56, coordr of Midwest Designer-Craftsmen Exhib,
57 & installation of all primitive art exhibs, 52-59, Art Inst Chicago; installation of rug & textile exhibs, Textile Mus, 59-71;
cur, Master Craftsmen of Ancient Peru Exhib, Solomon R Guggenheim Mus, 65-69.
Teaching: Instr art dept, Tex Woman's Univ, 49-52; group discussion leader, Looking at Modern Art, Ford Found, Art Inst Chicago, 55-57; lectr, pub lect prog, Univ Chicago-Art Inst Chicago,
59; adj prof art & archaeol, Columbia Univ, 68-69; lectr, Smithsonian Assocs, 71-
Positions: Cur primitive art, Tex Woman's Univ, 49-52; asst to cur
decorative arts, Art Inst Chicago, 52-54, asst cur decorative
arts in charge Early Americana & pre-Columbian art, 54-56,
assoc cur in charge primitive art, 56-58, cur primitive art, 58-
59; dir, Textile Mus, 59-71; dir, Park Forest Art Ctr; mem, Univ
Pa Archeol Exped to Bolivia, 55; leader of Textile Mus Archaeol
Exped to Peru, 60; leader, Brooklyn Mus Study Tour to Peru, 65;
independent art consult, 71-

Memberships: Archaeol Inst Am; Soc Am Archaeol; Inst Andean
Studies.
Publications: Auth, Handbook of the Nathan Cummings Collection of
ancient Peruvian art, 54 & Animal sculpture in pre-Columbian
art, 57, Art Inst Chicago; auth, A group of early Nasca sculptures
in the Whyte Collection, Archaeol Mag, 62; auth, Ancient Peruvian
ceramics, Metrop Mus Art, 66; auth, Ancient Peruvian art, 68;
plus numerous other articles & catalogs on Peruvian art.
Mailing Address: 5504 33rd St N W, Washington, DC 20015.

SAWYER, CHARLES HENRY
Museum Director
b Andover, Mass, Oct 20, 06.
Study & Training: Yale Univ, AB; Harvard Law Sch & Harvard Grad
Sch; Amherst Col, hon LHD; Univ N H, hon DFA; Clark Univ, hon
LHD.
Teaching: Prof hist art, Sch Archit & Design, Yale Univ, 47-56; prof
mus practice & hist art, Univ Mich, Ann Arbor, 57-
Positions: Dir, Addison Gallery Am Art, Andover, Mass, 30-40,
mem art comt, 40-; dir, Worcester Mus Art, Mass, 40-47; mem
Mass Art Comn, 43-45; trustee, Corning Mus Glass, 50-; mem
Smithsonian Art Comn, 54-; dir, Univ Mich Mus Art, 57-72.
Memberships: Am Asn Mus; Asn Art Mus Dirs; Col Art Asn Am;
Am Antiquarian Soc; Am Acad Arts & Lett.
Publications: Auth, Art education in English public schools, 37; auth,
Report of committee on visual arts at Harvard, 54-55; auth, In-
tegration in the arts, 57 & The college art department and the
work of art, 65, Col Art J; contribr, var art mags.
Mailing Address: Museum of Art, Alumni Memorial Hall, Ann Ar-
bor, MI 48104.

SAWYER, HELEN (HELEN SAWYER FARNSWORTH)
Painter, Writer
Preferred Media: Oils, Watercolors.
b Washington, D C.
Study & Training: Masters Sch, Dobbs Ferry; Nat Acad Design Sch,
with Charles Hawthorne.
Work in Public Collections: Whitney Mus Am Art; Pa Acad Fine
Arts; Toledo Mus; Atlanta Mus; Indianapolis Mus.
Commissions: Paintings, Blue Ridge Spring, Chesapeake & Ohio R R,
New York, First Nat City Bank & Circus Parade, G Lister Car-
lyle.
Exhibitions: Carnegie Nat & Int, Pittsburgh; Am Painting Today,
Metrop Mus Art; Century of Prog, Chicago; San Francisco
World's Fair; New York World's Fair; plus one-man shows,
throughout U S & abroad.
Awards: Award for The Bareback Rider, Ringling Mus; first hon
mention for Trees by the Turn, Art Inst Chicago; first prize for
landscape & still life, Atlanta Mus.
Bibliography: Ernest Watson (auth), Helen Sawyer, Am Artist.
Memberships: Nat Acad Design; Fla Artists Group (pres, 53-55);
Audubon Artists; Nat Asn Women Painters & Sculptors.
Research: Material on life and work in Syracuse University Ar-
chives and Archives of American Art.
Publications: Auth, Peter Sawyer master mariner, Cape Cod Com-
pass; auth, Paintings in oils on paper, Am Artists; auth, Living
among the modern primitives, Scribner.
Dealer: Frank Oehlschlaeger Gallery, 28 Blvd of the Presidents,
St Armands Key, Sarasota, FL 33578.
Mailing Address: 3842 Flamingo, Sarasota, FL 33581.

SAWYER, WILLIAM
Art Dealer, Collector
b Lindsay, Okla, Feb 16, 20.
Positions: Dir, William Sawyer Gallery, San Francisco, Calif.
Specialty of Gallery: Contemporary American painting, sculpture
and graphics.
Collection: Contemporary American and Mexican paintings, sculp-
ture and graphics.
Mailing Address: 3045 Clay St, San Francisco, CA 94109.

SAXON, CHARLES DAVID
Cartoonist, Illustrator
Preferred Media: Pencil, Ink.
b New York, N Y, Nov 13, 20.
Study & Training: Columbia Univ, BA; Hamilton Col, LHD.
Work in Public Collections: Brooklyn Mus, N Y; Libr Cong; Colum-
bia Univ.
Awards: Gold medal, Art Dirs Club New York, 62; spec award for
TV cartoon, Venice Film Festival, 65.
Bibliography: Jack Dillon (auth), article, In: Graphis, 71.
Publications: Auth & illusr, Oh, happy, happy, happy!, 59-60; con-
tribr, New Yorker anthologies; contribr, Great cartoons of the
world, 69-71.
Mailing Address: 228 Weed St, New Canaan, CT 06840.

SAYPOL, MR & MRS RONALD D
Collectors
Mr Saypol, b New York, N Y, Nov 12, 29.
Study & Training: Dickinson Col, BA, 51; Brooklyn Law Sch, LLB, 55.
Mailing Address: 1160 Park Ave, New York, NY 10028.

SAYRE, ELEANOR AXSON
Curator
b Philadelphia, Pa, Mar 26, 16.
Study & Training: Bryn Mawr Col, AB, 38; Harvard Univ, 38-40.
Collections Arranged: Rembrandt: Experimental Etcher, in collaboration with Morgan Library; Albrecht Duerer: Master Printmaker.
Teaching: Intermittent seminars in prints through Harvard Univ & Radcliffe Col for students of five cols.
Positions: Asst in exhibs, Yale Univ Art Gallery, 40-41; gallery asst, Lyman Allyn Mus, New London, Conn, 42; asst dept educ, R I Sch Design Mus, 42-45; from asst cur to cur prints & drawings, Mus Fine Arts, Boston, Mass, 45-
Publications: Auth, A Christmas book, 66; co-auth, Rembrandt: experimental etcher, 69; auth, Late caprichos of Goya, 71; co-auth, Duerer: master printmaker, 72.
Mailing Address: Dept of Prints & Drawings, Museum of Fine Arts, Boston, MA 02115.

SAZEGAR, MORTEZA
Painter
Preferred Media: Acrylics.
b Teheran, Iran, Nov 11, 33; U S citizen.
Study & Training: Univ Tex, El Paso, BA, 55, BS, 56; Baylor Univ Col Med, 56-57; Cornell Univ, 58-59.
Work in Public Collections: Whitney Mus Am Art, New York, N Y; San Francisco Mus Art, Calif; Riverside Mus, New York; Univ Mass, Amherst; Int Minerals & Chem Corp, Chicago, Ill.
Exhibitions: Four one-man shows, Poindexter Gallery, New York, 64-71; Art Inst Chicago, 65; Detroit Inst Arts, Mich, 65; Whitney Mus Am Art Ann, 69-70; Univ Tex Art Mus, Austin, 72.
Dealer: Poindexter Gallery, 24 E 84th St, New York, NY 10028.
Mailing Address: R R 1, Cochranville, PA 19330.

SCANGA, ITALO
Sculptor, Educator
b Lago, Italy, June 6, 32; U S citizen.
Study & Training: Mich State Univ, BA & MA.
Work in Public Collections: Metrop Mus Art, New York, N Y; Milwaukee Art Ctr, Wis; Univ Wis-Madison; Mus Art, R I Sch Design, Providence; Pa Acad Fine Arts, Philadelphia.
Exhibitions: Whitney Mus Am Art Sculpture Ann, New York, 70; Mus Mod Art, New York, 71; Mus Contemp Art, Chicago, Ill, 71; Corcoran Gallery Art, Washington, D C, 71; Pa Acad Fine Arts, 72.
Teaching: Asst prof sculpture, R I Sch Design, 64-66; assoc prof sculpture, Tyler Sch Art, Philadelphia, 67-
Awards: Best in show, 48th Ann Wis Painters & Sculptors Show, 62; Howard Found grant, Brown Univ, 70; Cassandra Found grant, 72.
Bibliography: Article, In: Arts Yearbook Contemp Sculpture, 65; Meilach & Seiden (auth), Direct metal sculpture, Crown, 66; Willoughby Sharp (auth), Pythagoras & Christ, Avalanche Mag, 71.
Dealer: Henri Gallery, 1500 21st St N W, Washington, D C 20036.
Mailing Address: 2225 Menlo Ave, Glenside, PA 19038.

SCARAVAGLIONE, CONCETTA MARIA
Sculptor
Preferred Media: Wood, Stone, Bronze, Copper, Terra-cotta.
Study & Training: Nat Acad Design; Art Stud League New York, N Y, with Boardman Robinson; Master Inst, with Robert Laurent.
Work in Public Collections: Whitney Mus Am Art; Mus Mod Art, New York; Roerich Mus; Pa Acad Fine Arts; Glasgow Mus.
Commissions: Railroad Express Postman 1862, Main Post Off, Washington, D C, 36; wood relief, Aborigines, Post Off, Drexel Hill, Pa, 39; agricultural relief, Fed Trade Comn Bldg, 40; Girl With Mountain Sheep, U S Govt Bldg, New York World's Fair; Girl With Gazelle, several high schs, New York.
Exhibitions: Whitney Mus Am Art, 55; Mus Mod Art, New York, 59; Brooklyn Mus; Art Inst Chicago; Pa Acad Fine Arts.
Awards: Widner Gold Medal, Pa Acad Fine Arts, 36; Am Arts & Lett grant, 46; Prix de Rome, Am Acad Rome, 47-50.
Dealer: Kraushaar Galleries, 1055 Madison Ave, New York, NY 10028.
Mailing Address: 441 W 21st St, New York, NY 10011.

SCARBROUGH, CLEVE KNOX, JR
Art Administrator, Art Historian
b Florence, Ala, July 17, 39.
Study & Training: Florence State Univ, BS, 62; Univ Iowa, MA, 67.
Collections Arranged: Graphics by Four Modern Swiss Sculptors, Mint Mus Art, circulated by Smithsonian Traveling Serv, 72-

Teaching: Grad asst, Univ Iowa, 64-67; asst prof art hist, Univ Tenn, Knoxville, 67-69.
Positions: Dir, Mint Mus Art, 69-
Memberships: Col Art Asn; Am Asn Mus; N C Mus Coun (bd mem, 70-72).
Publications: Ed, North Carolinians collect, 71 & Graphics by four modern Swiss sculptors, 72.
Mailing Address: 501 Hempstead Pl, Charlotte, NC 28207.

SCARPITTA, SALVATORE
Sculptor
b New York, N Y, 19.
Study & Training: Study in Italy, 36-59.
Work in Public Collections: Stedelijk Mus, Amsterdam, Holland; Albright-Knox Art Gallery, Buffalo, N Y; Los Angeles Co Mus Art, Calif; Mus Mod Art, New York, N Y; Tel-Aviv Mus, Israel.
Exhibitions: Corcoran Gallery Art, Washington, D C, 63; First Salon Int Galeries Pilotes, Mus Cantonal Beaux-Arts, Lausanne, Switz, 63; one-man exhib, Royaux Mus, Brussels, Belg, 64; Md Inst, 64; Art Inst Chicago, Ill, 64; Univ Ill, 65; plus others.
Teaching: Vis critic, Md Inst, Col Art, 66-
Bibliography: Harriet Janis & Rudi Blesh (auth), Collage, personalities—concepts—techniques, Chilton, 62; Allen S Weller (auth), The joys and sorrows of recent American art, Univ Ill, 68; B H Friedman (auth), The ivory tower, Art News, 4/69.
Dealer: Leo Castelli Gallery, 4 E 77th St, New York, NY 10021.
Mailing Address: 240 E 94th St, New York, NY 10028.

SCHABACKER, BETTY B
Painter, Lecturer
Preferred Media: Watercolors, Collage.
b Baltimore, Md, Aug 14, 25.
Study & Training: Conn Col Women; Marian Carey Art Asn Newport, R I; Coronado Sch Art, Calif, with Monty Lewis; also with Gerd & Irene Koch, Ojai, Calif.
Work in Public Collections: B K Smith Gallery, Lake Erie Col, Painesville, Ohio; First Nat Bank Pa, Erie; Western Union, New York, N Y; Erie Art Ctr.
Exhibitions: Mus Art Mod, Paris, France, 61-63; four shows, Butler Inst Am Art Ann, 64-69; Chautauqua Exhib Am Art, 66 & 67 & one-man show, Lake Erie Col, 71.
Awards: Grumbacher Award, Providence Art Club, R I, 59; Nancy Hubbard Lance Award, Lake Erie Col, 71.
Memberships: Calif Nat Watercolor Soc; Albright-Knox Mus Rental Gallery; Los Angeles Art Asn.
Dealers: Galerie 8, Colony Plaza, Erie, PA 16505; Galerie des Beaux Arts, Scranton, PA 18503.
Mailing Address: 315 Monoca Dr, Erie, PA 16505.

SCHACHTER, JUSTINE RANSON
Painter, Designer
Preferred Media: Stone, Graphics.
b Brooklyn, N Y, Dec 18, 27.
Study & Training: Tyler Sch Fine Arts, Temple Univ, scholar; Brooklyn Mus Art Sch, with John Bindrum, Milton Hebald & John Ferren; Art Stud League New York, N Y, with Will Barnett.
Work in Public Collections: Bellmore Pub Libr, N Y; Island Trees Pub Libr, Levittown, N Y; Wantagh High Sch, N Y.
Commissions: N Y State Poster, N Y State Parent-Teacher Asn, all N Y pub schs, 70-71.
Exhibitions: One-man show, Ruth White Gallery, 61; Nat Asn Women Artists Traveling Graphics Show, U S & Europe, 69-70; Am Soc Contemp Artists, New York, 69-71.
Teaching: Artist-in-residence, Community Arts Prog, Wantagh High Sch, 72.
Positions: Dir graphic arts, Audio-Visual Educ TV, Mineola Pub Sch, 64-65.
Awards: Award for graphics, Brooklyn Soc Artists Ann, 49; awards for mixed media, Nassau Co Off Cult Develop, 70 & Am Soc Contemp Artists, 71.
Bibliography: Elyse Frommer (auth), Rock and stone craft, Crown, 72.
Memberships: Am Soc Contemp Artists (chmn admis, 68-71); Nat Asn Women Artists; Artists Equity Asn; Int Asn Arts; Art Forms Creative Ctr (exec dir, 71-).
Publications: Illusr, Long Island Free Press, 70-71.
Mailing Address: 14 Trumpet Lane, Levittown, NY 11756.

SCHAEFER, CARL FELLMAN
Painter
Preferred Media: Watercolors, Egg Tempera.
b Hanover, Ont, Apr 30, 03.
Study & Training: Ont Col Art, Toronto, with J E H MacDonald & Arthur Lismer; Cent Sch Arts & Crafts, London, Eng.
Work in Public Collections: Nat Gallery Can; Art Gallery Ont; Art Gallery Hamilton; Art Gallery London; Va Mus Fine Arts, Richmond.

Commissions: Ser of paintings on prod, Can Packers, Ltd, Toronto, 42.

Exhibitions: Coronation Exhib George VI, London, Eng, 37; Century of Can Art, Tate Gallery, London, 38; 18th Int Art Inst Chicago, Ill, 39; 11th Int, Brooklyn Mus, 41: First Biennial, São Paulo Mus Arte Mod, 51.

Teaching: Instr painting, Cent Tech Sch, Toronto, 30-40; dir art, Hart House, Univ Toronto, 34-40; instr & dir painting, Ont Col Art, 48-55, emer chmn dept drawing & painting, 68-

Positions: Off war artist, Europ Theatre Opers & Iceland, RCAF, 43-46.

Awards: J S Guggenheim Mem Found fel, 40; Queen's Coronation Medal, Elizabeth II, 53; Can Centennial Medal, Dom Can, 67.

Bibliography: Robert H Hubbard (auth), An anthology of Canadian art, Oxford Univ Press, Toronto, 40; Donald W Buchanan (auth), The growth of Canadian painting, Collins, London, 50; J Russell Harper (auth), Painting in Canada, a history, Univ Toronto Press, 66.

Memberships: Can Soc Graphic Art; Can Soc Painters Watercolour (pres, 38-40); Can Group Painters; Royal Can Acad Arts; life fel Int Inst Arts & Lett.

Publications: Auth, Iceland, Atlantis on the Arctic Circle, Can Art Mag, 46.

Dealer: Roberts Gallery, 641 Yonge St, Toronto, Ont, Can.

Mailing Address: 157 St Clements Ave, Toronto 12, Ont, Can.

SCHAEFER, HENRI BELLA
Painter

b New York, N Y.

Study & Training: Columbia Univ Exten; Art Alliance Française, Acad L'Hote & Acad Grande Chaumiere, Paris, France; with William A MacKay, 35-38; Fashion Inst Technol, cert, 61.

Work in Public Collections: Fla Southern Col; Butler Inst Am Art, Youngstown, Ohio; Norfolk Mus Arts & Sci, Va; Va Mus Fine Art Arts, Richmond; Le Moyne Col; also in pvt collections.

Exhibitions: Five shows, Nat Asn Women Artists, Nat Acad Galleries, New York, 60-69; Chateau de Napoule, Cannes, 65; Cognac Mus, 65 & 66; Int Women's Salon, Cannes, 66; Spring Arts Festival Educ & Cult Trust Fund of Elec Indust, 70 & 71; plus many other group & one-man shows.

Positions: Chmn, Helen West Heller Mem Comt, 56; trustee, Dorothy Yepez Art Gallery, Saranac, N Y.

Awards: Marcia Brady Tucker Prize & Medal of Honor, Nat Asn Women Artists, 62.

Memberships: Nat Asn Women Artists (oil jury, 63-65); Artists Equity Asn (exec bd, N Y Chap, 54-, dir, N Y Chap, 56-57, nat sec & nat exec comt, nat dir, 60-, chmn grants & fels fine arts, 63-); Nat Hist Shrines Found.

Mailing Address: 111 Bank St, New York, NY 10014.

SCHAEFFER, RUDOLPH FREDERICK
Designer, Educator

b Clare, Mich, June 26, 86.

Study & Training: Thomas Normal Training Sch, Detroit, grad; study with Ernest Batchelder, Ralph Johonnot & Douglas Donaldson; study in Paris, Munich, Vienna & the Orient; res indust design & color for U S Dept Educ, Munich, Ger, 14.

Teaching: Prof color & design, Univ Calif, Berkeley & Stanford Univ, 16-24.

Positions: Art dir, Greek Theatre, Univ Calif, Berkeley, 23-24; founder & dir, Rudolph Schaeffer Sch Design, San Francisco, 26-

Bibliography: Arts in American life, McGraw-Hill, 33.

Memberships: Am Inst Interior Designers; Nat Soc Interior Designers; Soc Asian Art.

Collection: Oriental art—Sung Dynasty ceramics and paintings.

Publications: Auth, Flower Arrangement Folio, 35.

Mailing Address: 2255 Mariposa St, San Francisco, CA 94110.

SCHAEFFLER, LIZBETH
Sculptor, Ceramist

Preferred Media: Terra-cotta.

b Somerville, Mass, Oct 27, 07.

Study & Training: Pratt Inst; Nat Acad Design; Art Stud League New York, with Charles Keck, Mahonri Young & Adolph Weinman.

Commissions: Portrait relief Mem comn by Mrs Fred B Smith for Church of Highlands, White Plains, N Y, 40; bronze medal, Dahlia Asn Am, 60; bronze portrait relief, Mem comt for William Gardner, Nantucket, Mass, 70.

Exhibitions: Silvermine Guild Artists Exhib, Conn; Nat Sculpture Soc, New York; Westchester Co Fair, White Plains; New Rochelle Art Asn, N Y; Kenneth Taylor Galleries, Nantucket.

Positions: Exec secy, Kenneth Taylor Galleries, 57-65.

Awards: First prize, Westchester Co Fair.

Memberships: Artists Asn Nantucket.

Mailing Address: 6 Lily St, Nantucket, MA 02554.

SCHAFER, ALICE PAULINE
Printmaker

Preferred Media: Wood, Linoleum.

b Albany, N Y, Feb 11, 99.

Study & Training: Albany Sch Fine Arts, grad (cum laude).

Work in Public Collections: Metrop Mus Art; Southern Vt Art Ctr, Manchester, Vt; New York Pub Libr; Carnegie-Mellon Univ, Pittsburgh, Pa; Butler Inst Am Art, Youngstown, Ohio.

Commissions: Etchings, facade, Nat Commercial Bank & Trust, Albany, 50 & Doll Lady, Print Club Albany, 61.

Exhibitions: 3rd Nat Buffalo Printmakers, N Y, 40; 123rd Ann, Nat Acad Design, New York, 49; Royal Soc, Exchange, London, 54; Soc Am Graphic Artists 51st Ann, New York, 71; Nat Asn Women Artists 83rd Ann, 72.

Positions: Registr, Albany Inst Hist & Art, 52-64.

Awards: Alice Standist Buell Mem Award for The Music Shell, Pen & Brush Club, 65; gold medal for Going to St Ives, Am Artists Prof League, 66; John Taylor Mem Prize for Some Journeys Begin, Print Club Albany, 68.

Memberships: Print Club Albany (pres, 50); Southern Vt Artists; Soc Am Graphic Artists; Nat Asn Women Artists; Miniature Painters, Sculptors & Gravers Soc Washington, D C.

Collection: Contemporary printmakers.

Mailing Address: 33 Hawthorne Ave, Albany, NY 12203.

SCHAFFER, ROSE
Painter, Lecturer

Preferred Media: Oils, Casein, Acrylics, Wood.

b Newark, N J.

Study & Training: Art Stud League New York, N Y, 35-40, with George Bridgeman & Ivan Oninsky; also with Bernard Karfiol, Sol Wilson, Seong Moy & Antonio Frasconi.

Work in Public Collections: Smithsonian Inst, Washington, D C; Norfolk Mus Arts & Sci, Va; Springfield Mus Art, Mass; Montclair Mus, N J; State N J Cult Ctr.

Exhibitions: Nat Acad Design; New York; Boston Mus Art, Mass; Delgado Mus, New Orleans; Brooklyn Mus, N Y; Philadelphia Print Club, Pa.

Teaching: Lectr mod art, Parent-Teacher Asn & other orgn.

Awards: Awards, Terry Nat, Miami Beach, Fla, 55 & Seton Hall Univ, 56; two purchase prizes, Art For Overlook, 55-60; plus others.

Memberships: Nat Asn Women Artists (graphic jury); Nat Fedn Arts; Summit Art Asn; Artists Equity Asn; Artists Equity Asn N J.

Mailing Address: 320 S Harrison St, East Orange, NJ 07018.

SCHANG, FREDERICK, JR
Collector

b New York, N Y, Dec 15, 93.

Study & Training: Columbia Univ, BLit, 15.

Positions: Pres, Columbia Artists Mgt, 49-60.

Awards: Ritter of Danneborg, Govt Denmark; Order of Vasa, Govt Sweden.

Collection: Works of Paul Klee; collection shown at Minn Mus Art, Soc Four Arts, Palm Beach & var cols & mus.

Publications: Auth, Visiting cards of celebrities, F Hazen, Paris, 71.

Mailing Address: 200 Mac Farlane Dr, Delray Beach, FL 33444.

SCHANKER, LOUIS
Printmaker, Painter

b New York, N Y, July 20, 03.

Study & Training: Art Stud League New York; Cooper Union Art Sch; Educ Alliance; also abroad.

Work in Public Collections: Brooklyn Mus, N Y; Metrop Mus Art, Whitney Mus Am Art & Mus Mod Art, New York; Philadelphia Mus Art, Pa; Art Inst Chicago, Ill; plus others.

Exhibitions: Solomon R Guggenheim Mus, New York; San Francisco Mus Art, Calif; Soc Am Graphic Artists; Libr Cong, Washington, D C; Victoria & Albert Mus, London, Eng; plus many other group & one-man shows.

Teaching: Instr art, New Sch Social Res, 40-60; assoc prof art, Bard Col, 49-64, prof emer, 64-; Univ Colo, 53; Univ Minn, 59.

Awards: Prizes, Brooklyn Mus, 47; Yaddo fel, 58; Univ Ill, 58; plus others.

Bibliography: S W Hayter (auth), About prints, Oxford Univ Press, 62.

Memberships: Fedn Mod Painters & Sculptors; Sculptors Guild.

Publications: Auth, Line-form-color, 44.

Mailing Address: Box 359, Stamford, CT 06904.

SCHAPIRO, MEYER
Educator, Art Historian

b Shavly, Russia, Sept 23, 04; U S citizen.

Study & Training: Columbia Univ, AB, MA & PhD.

Teaching: Prof hist art, Columbia Univ, 28-

Research: Early Christian, medieval and modern art.

Mailing Address: Columbia University, New York, NY 10014.

SCHAPIRO, MIRIAM
Painter
b Toronto, Ont, Nov 15, 23; U S citizen.
Study & Training: Univ Iowa, BA, 45, MA, 46, MFA, 49.
Work in Public Collections: Whitney Mus Am Art, New York, N Y; Mus Mod Art, New York; New York Univ Permanent Collection; Stanford Univ, Palo Alto, Calif; Saint Louis City Art Mus.
Exhibitions: Carnegie Int, 58; seven one-woman shows, Andre Emmerich Gallery, New York, 58-71; Toward A New Abstraction, Jewish Mus, 63; Paul Brach & Miriam Schapiro—Double Retrospective, Newport Harbor Art Mus, 69; Women In Collection, Whitney Mus Am Art, 71; Am Women 20th Century, Lakeview Ctr Arts & Sci, Ill, 72.
Teaching: Co-originator Feminist Art Prog, Calif Inst Arts, 72-
Awards: Ford Found Tamarind fel, 64.
Bibliography: L Campbell (auth), M Schapiro paints a painting, Art News, 5/67; B Rose (auth), Abstract illusionism, Artforum, 10/68; Hermine Freed (auth), M Schapiro in her studio in Easthampton (video tape), 8/72.
Publications: Auth, The education of women as artists, project womanhouse, Col Art J, summer 72; co-auth, Womanhouse (catalogue), 72; contribr, On womanhouse (taped interview), KCET Los Angeles, 72.
Dealer: Andre Emmerich Gallery, 41 E 57th St, New York, NY 10021.
Mailing Address: 642 Moreno Ave, Los Angeles, CA 90049.

SCHARFF, CONSTANCE KRAMER
Printmaker, Painter
b New York, N Y.
Study & Training: Brooklyn Mus Art Sch, grad; also with Adja Jounkers & Abraham Rattner.
Work in Public Collections: Brooklyn Mus, N Y; Philadelphia Mus Art, Pa; Norfolk Mus, Va; Furman Univ, Greenville, S C; Israel Mus, Jerusalem.
Commissions: Ed prints, Contemp Arts Asn, N Y, 56 & 60 & Am Asn Contemp Arts, 68.
Exhibitions: Libr Cong, Washington, D C, 54, 55 & 63; Long Island Artists Biennials, 55 & Nat Print Biennial, 66, Brooklyn Mus; Silvermine Guild, 65; Soc Am Graphic Artists, 65-71; Potsdam Nat Print Show, 66.
Positions: Chmn traveling shows, Am Soc Contemp Arts, 55-57, mem bd, 62-; juror, All N J State Show, 71.
Awards: Medals of honor, Audubon Artists, 55 & Nat Asn Women Artists, 68; first prize for printmaking, Original Graphics & Brit Printmakers, 62.
Memberships: Soc Am Graphic Artists; Nat Soc Painters Casein & Acrylic (rec secy, 67-); Audubon Artists; Nat Asn Women Artists (watercolor & print juries, 60-); Washington Printmakers.
Dealers: Discovery Art Galleries, 1191 Valley Rd, Clifton, NJ 07013; Etchings International, 200 E 58th St, New York, NY 10022.
Mailing Address: 115 Jaffrey St, Brooklyn, NY 11235.

SCHARY, SUSAN
Painter
Preferred Media: Oils.
b Philadelphia, Pa, Aug 7, 36.
Study & Training: Tylor Sch, Temple Univ, BFA (hons); also with Vladamir Shatolov.
Work in Public Collections: City Hall, Philadelphia; Temple Univ, Philadelphia; Thomas Paine Ctr, Philadelphia; Villanova Univ, Philadelphia.
Exhibitions: Florence Art Gallery, Italy, 65; 100 Distinguished Philadelphia Artists, 67; Fleisher Art Mem Faculty Show, 67; Munic Arts Festival, Los Angeles, 70 & 71; one-woman shows, Philadelphia, 64 & 67 & Los Angeles, 71 & 72.
Teaching: Instr, Harcum Jr Col, Bryn Mawr, Pa, 60-62; instr painting & drawing, Fleisher Art Mem, 66-68.
Awards: Gimble Awards, 47-50; hon mention, Fidelity Bank Ann, 58; Dean's Prize, Tyler Sch, 58.
Memberships: Artists Equity Asn.
Mailing Address: 672 S Bronson Ave, Los Angeles, CA 90005.

SCHEIBE, FRED KARL
Painter, Writer
Preferred Media: Enamels.
b Kiel, W Ger, Dec 2, 11; U S citizen.
Study & Training: Clark Univ, BA, 38; Univ Pa, MA, 41; Univ Cincinnati, PhD, 54.
Work in Public Collections: First Man on the Moon, Eisenhower Mus, Abilene, Kans; Galaxy, Nelson D Rockefeller Collection, New York, N Y; Mexico, A Poem, Langenheim Mem Libr, Greenville, Pa; Starry Night, Hartwick Col Art Collection, Oneonta, N Y.
Commissions: Industry is King (mural), C of C, Abingdon, Va, 63.

Exhibitions: Va Intermont Art Ctr, Bristol, 62; Idioplasmic Precipitates, Die Galerie, Munich, W Ger, 71; one-man shows, Stuttgart, W Ger, 63; Yager Mus, Hartwick Col, 70 & Exhib of Idioplasmic Precipitates, Two Rivers Gallery, Robinson Ctr, N Y, 71.
Bibliography: Frank Perretta (auth), Idioplasmic precipitates, Oneonta Star, 3/25/67.
Memberships: Cooperstown Art Asn.
Art Interests: Idioplasmic precipitates; developed secret enamel formula which produces vividly colored paintings.
Dealer: Golden Matador, 209 N Atlantic Ave, Cocoa Beach, FL 32931.
Mailing Address: 379 Harbor Dr, Cape Canaveral, FL 32920.

SCHEIN, EUGENIE
Painter, Instructor
Preferred Media: Oils, Acrylics, Watercolors.
U S citizen.
Study & Training: Hunter Col, BA; Columbia Univ, MA; Martha Graham Sch Dance; Nat Univ Mex.
Work in Public Collections: Carvell Mus, La; Ga Mus Art, Athens; Lowe Art Mus, Coral Gables, Fla; Miami Mus Mod Art, Fla.
Exhibitions: Int Watercolors, Brooklyn Mus; Cincinnati Mus; Riverside Mus, New York, N Y; Soc Four Arts, Palm Beach; Fla Artists Asn.
Teaching: Instr mod dance, Hunter Col, 26-52; instr mod dance, Univ Miami, 56-
Memberships: Lowe Art Mus; Miami Mus Mod Art; Artists Equity Asn (v pres, 72-).
Mailing Address: 1070 Stillwater Dr, Miami Beach, FL 33141.

SCHELLIN, ROBERT WILLIAM
Painter, Educator
Preferred Media: Acrylics, Clay.
b Akron, Ohio, July 28, 10.
Study & Training: Univ Wis Milwaukee, BA, 33; with Hans Hofmann, New York, 39-40; Univ Wis-Madison, MA, 48.
Work in Public Collections: Milwaukee Art Ctr, Wis; Madison Art Asn; Univ Wis-Milwaukee; Kenosha Pub Mus, Wis.
Exhibitions: U S Info Agency Am Crafts Exhib, Europe, 61-62; Wis Craftsmen, Smithsonian Inst, Washington, D C, 62; Four Ceramists, Tweed Gallery, Duluth, Minn, 63; Wis Art, 1850 To Today, 63 & Commemorative Exhib Wis Art, 64, Milwaukee Art Ctr.
Teaching: Instr painting, Milwaukee State Col, 45-51; prof ceramics, Univ Wis-Milwaukee, 51-
Positions: Mem Milwaukee Art Comn, 62-70, chmn, 68-70.
Awards: Silver Medal, Milwaukee Art Inst, 33; Design Excellence Award, 57 & first award for ceramics, 62, Milwaukee Art Ctr.
Memberships: Wis Painters & Sculptors; Wis Designer Craftsmen; Am Craftsmen Coun.
Mailing Address: 3335 N Bartlett Ave, Milwaukee, WI 53211.

SCHEU, LEONARD
Painter, Lecturer
Preferred Media: Watercolors, Oils.
b San Francisco, Calif, Feb 19, 04.
Study & Training: Calif Sch Fine Arts, San Francisco; Art Stud League New York, N Y, drawing with George Bridgeman.
Work in Public Collections: Ford Motor Co Collection, Dearborn Mus, Mich.
Commissions: Calif Motherlode & Jacksonville, Ore, Ford Motor Co.
Exhibitions: U S Naval Acad, Annapolis, Md, 65; Butler Inst Am Art, Youngstown, Ohio, 68; Holyoke Mus, Mass, 69; Erie Pub Mus, Pa, 70; Anchorage Fine Arts Mus, Alaska, 71.
Teaching: Instr painting & drawing, Whittier Sch Syst, Calif, 61-70; prof art, Banff Sch Fine Arts, Univ Alta, 62-65; instr painting, drawing & art hist, Orange Coast Col, 62-67.
Positions: Juror, local & nat exhibs, 53-
Awards: Hon mention, Laguna Beach Art Asn.
Bibliography: M Jackson (auth), article, In: Laguna Beach Post, 55; Margaret Paige (auth), article, In: S Coast News, 64; article, In: St Vincent, Latrobe, Pa, 66.
Memberships: Laguna Beach Art Asn (mem bd, 56-, pres, 56-57, exhib chmn, 56-58); Calif Nat Watercolor Soc; Nat Soc Painters Casein (bd mem, 56-59); Soc Western Artists; Painters & Sculptors Soc N J.
Publications: Illusr, Good ghost towns never die, Lincoln Mercury Times, 54; illusr, Saga of Cinnabar, New Almaden, 54 & Gold rush town that took its time, 61, Ford Times.
Dealer: William D Gorman, 43 W 33rd St, Bayonne, NJ 07002.
Mailing Address: 309 Agate St, Laguna Beach, CA 92651.

SCHIFF, LONNY
Painter, Printmaker
Preferred Media: Oils, Watercolors, Graphics.
Study & Training: Univ Ill, BA(hons), 53; Worcester Art Mus Sch, fine arts cert, 64; etching study, Impressions Workshop, 65.

Commissions: Complete restoration of 18 portraits for Framingham Hist Soc, 67; suite of 11 paintings, Radler Assoc, Wellesley, Mass, 68.

Exhibitions: Cape Cod Art Asn, 70-; Spectrum Gallery, 72; Providence Art Club, 71; one-woman shows, Cambridge Art Asn, 72, Copley Soc, Boston, 73 & Brandeis Univ, 73; plus others.

Teaching: Instr, adult oil painting classes, Worcester Art Mus, 63-67; instr art appreciation & techniques class, Sudbury Art Asn, 68-69; printmaking workshop, Charles River Art Ctr, 68.

Awards: First prize in graphics, & Larry Newman prize in oils, Cape Cod Art Asn, 71; Minna Pinter Prize in Graphics, Cambridge Art Asn, 71; plus others.

Memberships: Nat Asn Women Artists; Cambridge Art Asn (former dir); Copley Soc; Sudbury Art Asn; Int Inst for Conserv, London; plus others.

Research: Lost old masters, conservation.

Dealer: Spectrum Gallery, Rte 6A, Brewster, MA 02631.

Mailing Address: Box 2156, Framingham Centre, MA 01701.

SCHILLER, BEATRICE
Painter, Graphic Artist

Preferred Media: Watercolors, Graphics, Acrylics.

b Chicago, Ill.

Study & Training: Inst Design; Ill Inst Technol; Art Inst Chicago; also with Richard Florsheim, Jack Kearney, Herbert Davidson; Kwak Wai Lau & Stanley Mitruk.

Exhibitions: Nat Exhib Small Paintings, Purdue Univ, Lafayette, 64; 17th Ann Nat Exhib Realistic Art, Mus Fine Arts, Springfield, Mass, 66; Art Inst Chicago Art Rental & Sales Gallery, Ill, 66-; Butler Inst Am Art, Youngstown, Ohio, 67; New Horizons in Sculpture & Painting, Chicago, 70; plus others.

Awards: Reinhardt H Jahn Purchase Prize, Sixth Union League Art Show, 65; Herbert C Brook Purchase Prize, Seventh Union League Art Show, 67; hon mention, Munic Art League Chicago, 71; plus others.

Memberships: Chicago Soc Artists; Ill Inst Technol (alumni); Munic Art League Chicago; Art Inst Chicago Art Rental & Sales Gallery; N Shore Art League; plus others.

Dealer: Art Rental & Sales Gallery, Art Institute of Chicago, Michigan Ave & Adams St, Chicago, IL 60603.

Mailing Address: 3150 N Lake Shore Dr, Chicago, IL 60657.

SCHIMMEL, NORBERT
Collector

b Sept 2, 04; U S citizen.

Positions: Trustee, Am Archaeol Inst; mem vis comt, Fine Arts Dept, Harvard Univ & Fogg Art Mus, mem vis comt, Egyptian, Near Eastern & Greek & Roman Art, Metrop Mus Art, New York.

Collection: Ancient art, especially Etruscan, Egyptian, Greek, Near Eastern and Iranian; works exhibited Metrop Mus Art, 59 & Fogg Art Mus, 64.

Publications: Auth, Herbert Hoffmann.

Mailing Address: 20 Cooper Sq, New York, NY 10003.

SCHIMMEL, WILLIAM BERRY
Painter, Lecturer

Preferred Media: Watercolors, Oils.

b Olean, N Y, July 21, 06.

Study & Training: Rutgers Univ, BLitt; Nat Acad Design; also with Gerry Pierce & Roy Mason.

Work in Public Collections: Phoenix Fine Art Mus, Ariz; Cincinnati Mus Fine Art, Ohio; Univ Mus, Univ N C; Phoenix Pub Libr; Nat Casualty Life Ins Bldg, Phoenix.

Exhibitions: Nat Acad Ann Watercolor Exhib, three yrs; Am Watercolor Soc Exhibs, eight yrs; Butler Inst Am Art, Youngstown, Ohio.

Teaching: Instr watercolor & oil, Seattle Art Asn, Wash, Fort Worth Pub Sch Syst, Texas, Sch Mines, Brainerd, Minn, Flagstaff Art Asn, Ariz, Tucson Watercolor Guild & Phoenix Art Mus, Ariz, also pvt classes in Denver & Estes Park, Colo, Jackson, Wyo, Prescott & Phoenix, Ariz.

Positions: Art dir, Benton & Bowles, New York, N Y, 35-38.

Awards: Am Watercolor Soc Emily Goldsmith Award, 70; Eight Valley Nat Bank Purchase Awards, Ariz State Fair.

Memberships: Am Watercolor Soc; Am Artists Prof League; Nat Arts Club New York; Int Inst Arts of Lett.

Publications: Auth, Watercolor, the happy medium, Macmillan, 58.

Dealer: Buck Saunders, N Brown Ave, Scottsdale, AZ 85251.

Mailing Address: 6539 E Cheney Rd, Scottsdale, AZ 85253.

SCHLAGETER, ROBERT WILLIAM
Art Administrator

b Streator, Ill, May 10, 25.

Study & Training: Univ Ill, BA, MFA; Univ Heidelberg, cert; Univ Chicago, Harvard Univ.

Collections Arranged: Fifty Years of American Art (1900-1950), 68; Age of Dunlap; Art of the Early Republic Exhibition.

Teaching: Asst prof art hist, Univ Tenn, Knoxville, 52-58.

Positions: Dir, Mint Mus Art, Charlotte, N C, 58-66; assoc dir, Downtown Gallery, New York, N Y, 67; assoc dir, Ackland Art Ctr, Univ N C, Chapel Hill, 67-

Mailing Address: Ackland Art Center, University of North Carolina, Chapel Hill, NC 27514.

SCHLAIKJER, JES WILHELM
Painter, Illustrator

Preferred Media: Oils.

b New York, N Y, Sept 22, 97.

Study & Training: Ecole Beaux-Arts, France; Art Inst Chicago; also with Forsberg, Cornwell & Dunn.

Work in Public Collections: Nat Acad Design; U S War Dept; U S Naval Acad; Dept State; Georgetown Univ; plus others.

Exhibitions: Many nat exhibs.

Positions: Off artist, U S War Dept, Washington, D C, 42-44, art consult, 45-

Awards: Prizes, Nat Acad Design, 26, 28 & 32.

Memberships: Nat Acad Design.

Mailing Address: 4526 Verplanck Pl N W, Washington, DC 20016.

SCHLECHT, RICHARD
Painter, Illustrator

Preferred Media: Oils, Acrylics, Ink.

b Dallas, Tex, Nov 9, 36.

Study & Training: Univ Denver, BA.

Exhibitions: 30th Ann Midyear Show, Butler Inst Am Art, Youngstown, Ohio, 65; Nat Acad Design, New York, N Y, 67; New York Art Dirs Ann, 68; Audubon Artists Ann, New York, 68; Mainstreams '70, Marietta Col, Ohio, 70.

Awards: Third prize for oils, Am Artists League of Washington, D C 26th Ann, 63; Henry Ward Ranger Purchase Award, 67.

Dealers: Mickelson Gallery, 708 G St N W, Washington, DC 20001; Green Street Gallery, 196 Green St, Annapolis, MD 21401.

Mailing Address: 426 Severn Ave, Annapolis, MD 21403.

SCHLEMM, BETTY LOU
Painter

Preferred Media: Watercolors.

b Jersey City, N J, Jan 13, 34.

Study & Training: New York Phoenix Sch Design, scholar; Nat Acad Design, New York, scholar.

Work in Public Collections: USN; Grand Cent Art Galleries, New York; also in many pvt collections.

Exhibitions: Am Watercolor Soc; Butler Inst Am Art; Nat Acad Design; Allied Artists Am; Audubon Artists.

Awards: Silver medal, Am Watercolor Soc, 64; gold medal, Hudson Valley Art Asn, 65; Robert Lehman travel grant, Washington Sq Outdoor Art Exhib, 67.

Bibliography: Article, In: Christian Sci Monitor, 67; 100 watercolor techniques, Watson-Guptill, 69.

Memberships: Am Watercolor Soc; Allied Artists Am (secy, 64-65); Rockport Art Asn (mem bd, 70-); Boston Artists Guild; N J Watercolor Soc.

Publications: Auth, Watercolor page, Am Artist, 64; Margaret Harold (auth), Prize winning art, 66 & Prize winning watercolors, 67.

Dealer: Grand Central Art Galleries, 40 Vanderbilt Ave, New York, NY 10017.

Mailing Address: Caleb's Lane, Rockport, MA 01966.

SCHLEMOWITZ, ABRAM
Sculptor

b New York, N Y, July 19, 11.

Study & Training: Beaux-Arts Inst Design, 28-33; Art Stud League New York, 34; Nat Acad Design, 35-39.

Work in Public Collections: Chrysler Mus, Provincetown, Mass; Univ Calif, Berkeley.

Exhibitions: One-man shows, Howard Wise Gallery, 61-67; Collaboration: Artist and Architect, Mus Contemp Crafts, 62; 12 New York Sculptors, Riverside Mus, 62; Humanists of the 60's, New Sch Social Res, 63; Art In Embassies Traveling Exhib, Mus Mod Art, circulated int, 63-64; plus others.

Teaching: Instr, Contemp Art Ctr, YMHA, New York, 36-39; instr, Pratt Inst, 62-63; instr, Univ Calif, Berkeley, 63-64; instr, Univ Ky, 65; instr, Univ Wis, 65-67; instr, Kingsborough Col, City Univ New York, 70-

Positions: Organizing chmn, New Sculpture Group, 57-58.

Awards: Guggenheim fel, 63.

Research: Bronze casting.

Mailing Address: 139 W 22nd St, New York, NY 10011.

SCHLEY, EVANDER DUER (VAN)
Conceptual Artist, Photographer

Preferred Media: Videotape, Film.

b Montreal, P Q, Apr 21, 41; U S citizen.

Work in Public Collections: Place and Process (film), in collections of Fort Worth Art Ctr, Miami-Dade Col & Boston Mus Fine Arts.

Exhibitions: Place & Process, Edmonton, Alta, 69; Architecture of Joy, Archit League New York, N Y, 70; Software, Jewish Mus, New York, 70; Information, Mus Mod Art, New York, 70; Encuentros de Espana, Pamplona, Spain, 72.
Teaching: Lectr art & archit, Univ Calif, Santa Barbara, spring 72.
Awards: Avalanche Mag art award, 72.
Bibliography: Billy Adler (auth), In the midnight hour (videotape), 69 & Run (videotape), GBF, Inc, 72.
Publications: Auth, Signs, 72.
Mailing Address: 20705 Cheney Dr, Topanga, CA 90290.

SCHLICHER, KARL THEODORE
Painter, Educator
b Terre Haute, Ind, May 14, 05.
Study & Training: Univ Wis, BS & MS; Colt Sch Art; Art Inst Chicago; Univ Chicago; Ohio State Univ, PhD; also with Reynolds, Giesbert, Coats, Hopkins, Grimes & others.
Work in Public Collections: Portraits in pvt collections.
Exhibitions: Contemp Art of the Southwest, 56; Lufkin Art League; Nacogdoches Fair; Stephen F Austin State Col Fac Exhibs.
Teaching: Prof art, Stephen F Austin State Univ, 48-, head dept art, 48-65.
Positions: Ed & publ, Tex Trends in Art Educ, 51-56.
Memberships: Col Art Asn Am; Tex Fine Arts Asn; Tex Art Educ Asn (pres, 56-58); Royal Soc Arts; Nat Art Educ Asn; plus others.
Publications: Contribr to Tex Outlook, Western Arts Asn Res Bull & Tex Trends in Art Educ.
Mailing Address: Art Dept, Stephen F Austin State Univ, Nacogdoches, TX 75961.

SCHLOSS, EDITH
Painter, Art Critic
Preferred Media: Oils, Watercolors.
U S citizen.
Study & Training: Art Stud League New York.
Exhibitions: Assemblage, Mus Mod Art, New York, N Y, 61; Women in Art, Stamford Mus, Conn, 72; one-woman shows, Il Segno, Rome, 68, Am Acad Rome, 71 & Green Mountain Gallery, 72.
Positions: Ed assoc, Art News, 55-61; art critic for Italy, Int Herald Tribune, Paris, France, 69-
Bibliography: Claudia Terenzi (auth), Poetic imagination (paintings by Edith Schloss), Paese Sera, Rome, 3/71; James Mellon (auth), The private sensibility of Edith Schloss, New York Times, 3/25/72; Lawrence Campbell (auth), Oils & watercolors by Edith Schloss, Art News, 4/72.
Art Interests: Assemblage.
Publications: Auth, The unfinished cathedral of Antonio Gaudi, Art News, 58; auth, Braibanti, Village Voice, New York, 70; auth, Art & politics, one of Rome's most daring exhibitions, 2/71, auth, Tiepolo al a Doge's palace, 10/71 & auth, How to catch the moon, 1/72, Int Herald Tribune.
Dealers: Green Mountain Gallery, 135 Greene St, New York, NY 10012; Galleria Il Segno, Via Capole le Case, Rome, Italy.
Mailing Address: Via Della Vetrina 18, Rome, Italy 00186.

SCHMALZ, CARL (NELSON, JR)
Painter, Educator
Preferred Media: Watercolors.
b Ann Arbor, Mich, Dec 26, 26.
Study & Training: Eliot O'Hara Watercolor Sch, summers 43 & 44; Harvard Col, AB, 48; Harvard Univ, MA, 49, PhD, 58.
Work in Public Collections: Walker Art Mus, Brunswick, Maine; Jones & Laughlin Steel Corp, Cleveland, Ohio; Diners Club Am; Blue Cross-Blue Shield; Hampshire Col; plus others.
Exhibitions: Colby Col Invitational, Maine, 58; Portland Summer Art Festival, 58 & 59; Am Watercolor Soc, 66, 68 & 70; Watercolor U S A, Springfield, Mo, 70; Wichita Centennial Nat Art Exhib, Kans, 70; plus others.
Teaching: Asst prof art hist & assoc dir, Bowdoin Col, 53-62; prof art hist, Amherst Col, 62-
Positions: V pres & mem bd dirs, Portland Mus Art, Maine, 57-62; art consult, O'Hara Picture Trust, 69-
Awards: First prize (watercolor), Cambridge Art Asn Ann, 47; first prize (traditional watercolor), Virginia Beach Boardwalk Show, 65; Southern Mo Trust Purchase Award, Watercolor U S A, 70.
Memberships: Col Art Asn; Am Archaeol Inst; Acad Artists Asn.
Publications: Contribr, A staining and transparent palette, In: Watercolor portraiture, Putnam, 49; auth, The watercolor page, 2/72 & Eliot O'Hara, great teacher of watercolor, 3/72, Am Artist Mag; plus others.
Dealer: Anne Gray, Eric Schindler Gallery, 2305 E Broad St, Richmond, VA 23223.
Mailing Address: 40 Arnold Rd, Amherst, MA 01002.

SCHMECKEBIER, LAURENCE E
Sculptor, Educator
b Chicago Heights, Mar 1, 06.
Study & Training: Univ Wis, BA, 27; Univ Marburg, 27-28; Sorbonne, 28; Univ Munich, PhD, 30.
Work in Public Collections: Syracuse Univ Collection, N Y.
Exhibitions: Cleveland Mus Ann May Show, 49-54; Rochester Mem Mus Finger Lakes Exhib, 55-57; Regional Artists Exhib, Everson Mus, Syracuse, 56, 57, 59 & 60; Cent N Y Artists, 56, 58 & 59; Munson-Williams-Proctor Inst, Utica, N Y, Corning Glass Ctr Ann May Show, N Y, 70.
Teaching: Asst prof art hist, Univ Wis-Madison, 31-38; prof fine arts & chmn dept, Univ Minn, Minneapolis, 38-46; prof art hist & dir, Cleveland Inst Art, Ohio, 46-54; prof fine arts & dean, Syracuse Univ, 54-71, emer prof, 71-
Awards: Cert of merit, May Show, Cleveland Mus Art, 49-51; George L Herdle Award, Rochester Mem Mus, 55; first prize for sculpture, Chautauqua Art Asn Exhib, 56.
Memberships: Col Art Asn Am.
Research: Italian Renaissance painting; modern Mexican art; contemporary American art.
Publications: Auth, Italian Renaissance painting, 38 & 71; Modern Mexican art, 39, John Steuart Curry's pageant of America, 43, Art in red wing, 46 & Ivan Mestrovic, sculptor and patriot, 59.
Mailing Address: R D 1, Lyme, NH 03768.

SCHMEIDLER, BLANCHE J
Painter
b New York, N Y, Nov 1, 15.
Study & Training: Hunter Col; Columbia Univ, BA; Samuel Brecher Art Sch; Art Stud League New York, with Vytlacil; Seong Moy Graphics Workshop.
Work in Public Collections: St Vincent's Col, Latrobe, Pa; Seton Hall Univ, Newark, N J; John Herron Art Mus, Indianapolis, Ind; also in pvt collections.
Exhibitions: Nat Acad Design; Audubon Artists; Nat Arts Club; Whitney Mus Am Art; Silvermine Guild; plus many other group & one-man shows.
Teaching: Lect, History & Application of Woodcut, Nat Acad Design.
Awards: Prizes, Nat Asn Women Artists, 59 & Grumbacher prize, 60; Painters & Sculptors Soc N J, 61.
Memberships: New York Soc Women Artists (chmn mem comt, 62-65, bd dirs, 63-66); Am Soc Contemp Artists (chmn traveling exhibs, 63-66); Nat Asn Women Artists; Silvermine Guild Artists; Painters & Sculptors Soc N J; plus others.
Mailing Address: 35-35 75th St, Jackson Heights, NY 11372.

SCHMID, RICHARD ALAN
Painter
Preferred Media: Oils, Watercolors, Conté, Crayon, Stone, Wood.
b Chicago, Ill, Oct 5, 34.
Study & Training: Am Acad Art, Chicago, 52-55, with William Mosby.
Exhibitions: Invitational Drawing Exhib, Otis Art Inst, Los Angeles, Calif, 66; 33rd Ann, Butler Inst Am Art, Youngstown, Ohio, 68; 23rd Am Drawing Biennial, Norfolk Mus Arts & Sci, 69; 164th Ann, Pa Acad Fine Arts, Philadelphia, 69; Am Watercolor Soc Ann, Nat Acad Design Galleries, New York, 70-71; plus many one-man shows throughout U S A, 58-72.
Awards: Jane Peterson Prize, Allied Artists Am, 67; gold medal of honor, Am Watercolor Soc, 71; Am Watercolor Soc Gold Medal of Honor for Marianne, Am Artist, 72; plus others.
Dealers: Talisman Gallery, Bartlesville, OK 74003; Welna Gallery, 105 E Ontario, Chicago, IL 60611.
Mailing Address: Spring Lake Rd, Sherman, CT 06784.

SCHMIDT, ARNOLD ALFRED
Painter, Sculptor
Preferred Media: Acrylics.
b Plainfield, N J, Jan 9, 30.
Study & Training: Art Stud League New York, 49-50; Cooper Union, cert, 56; Hunter Col, BA & MA, 65; also with Hannes Beckmann, Neil Welliver & Tony Smith.
Work in Public Collections: Mus Mod Art; Rose Art Inst, Brandeis Univ; Newark Mus; Fairleigh Dickinson Univ; Stedelijk Mus, Schiedam, Netherlands.
Exhibitions: The Responsive Eye, 65, Optical Art, 66 & Recent Acquisitions, 66, Mus Mod Art; Op Art and Others, Newark Mus, 67; Form and Color, Stedelijk Mus, 67; American Paintings of the Nineteen Sixties, Currier Mus Art, 70; plus others.
Bibliography: Alfred Barr (auth), What is modern art, Mus Mod Art, 67; Ray Faulkner & Edwin Ilegfeld, Art Today, Holt-Reinhart & Winston, 69.
Mailing Address: 505 La Guardia Pl, New York, NY 10012.

SCHMIDT, FREDERICK LEE
Painter, Educator
Preferred Media: Acrylics, Oils.
b Hays, Kans, Dec 11, 37.
Study & Training: Univ Northern Colo, BA; Univ Iowa, with Stuart
Edie, MFA; also with Joe Patrick, Howard Rogovin & James
Lechay.
Work in Public Collections: Northwestern Col, Orange City, Iowa;
Sioux City Art Ctr, Iowa; Western Carolina Univ, Cullowhee, N C;
Univ Iowa, Iowa City.
Exhibitions: Sioux City 32nd Ann, 69; Des Moines State Capitol, Iowa,
69; Benedicta Arts Ctr 2nd Invitational Drawing Exhib, Saint
Joseph, Mo, 71; 34th Semi-Ann Southeastern Exhib, Winston-
Salem, N C, 72; group show, Asheville Art Gallery, N C, 72.
Teaching: Asst prof art, Northwestern Col, 68-70; asst prof art,
Western Carolina Univ, 70-72; asst prof art, Va Polytech Inst &
State Univ, 72-
Awards: Northwestern Col summer grant, 69; hon mention, Assoc
Artists N C, 71; Helene Wurlitzer Found grant, 72.
Memberships: Nat Col Art Asn.
Dealer: Oliva Associates, New York, NY 10001.
Mailing Address: Apt H2, 800 Broce Dr, Blacksburg, VA 24060.

SCHMIDT, JULIUS
Sculptor
Preferred Media: Bronze, Iron.
b Stamford, Conn, June 2, 23.
Study & Training: Okla Agr & Mech Col; Cranbrook Acad Art, BFA,
MFA; with Ossip Zadkine, Paris, France, 53; Acad Belle Arti,
Florence, Italy.
Work in Public Collections: Mus Mod Art, New York, N Y; Art Inst
Chicago, Ill; Albright-Knox Art Gallery, Buffalo, N Y; Princeton
Mus Art, N J; Whitney Mus Am Art, N Y.
Exhibitions: Sixteen Americans, Mus Mod Art, New York, 59; The
Hirshhorn Collection, Guggenheim Mus, New York, 62; Seventh
Biennial, Sao Paulo, Brazil, 63; Sculpture in the Open Air, Bat-
tersea Park, London, Eng, 63; Biennial, Middleham, Belg, 71.
Teaching: Chmn sculpture dept, Kansas City Art Inst, 54-59;
sculpture dept, R I Sch Design, 59-60; vis artist, sculpture dept,
Univ Calif, Berkeley, 61-62; chmn sculpture dept, Cranbrook
Acad Art, 62-72; head sculpture dept, Univ Iowa, 72-
Awards: Guggenheim fel, 64.
Bibliography: Sixteen Americans, Mus Mod Art, New York, 59; H
Read (auth), Concise history of modern sculpture, Praeger, 64;
Redstone (auth), Art in architecture, McGraw, 68.
Dealer: Marlborough Galleries, 41 E 57th St, New York, NY 10022.
Mailing Address: Dept of Art, University of Iowa, Iowa City, IA
52240.

SCHMIDT, KATHERINE (KATHERINE SCHMIDT SHUBERT)
Painter
Preferred Media: Oils, Pencils, Conté.
b Yenia, Ohio, Aug 15, 98.
Study & Training: Art Stud League New York; study mus in Europe,
25-28.
Work in Public Collections: Whitney Mus Am Art; Metrop Mus Art;
Mus Mod Art; Newark Mus; Santa Barbara Mus Art.
Exhibitions: Daniel Gallery; Downtown Gallery; Issacson Gallery;
Durlacher Gallery; Zabriskie Gallery.
Bibliography: E Halpert (auth), Director Downtown Gallery; B Bur-
roughs (auth), article, In: Aris Mag.
Dealer: Zabriskie Gallery, 29 W 57th St, New York, NY 10019.
Mailing Address: Taylors Lane, Little Compton, RI 02837.

SCHMIDT, RANDALL BERNARD
Sculptor, Educator
Preferred Media: Ceramics, Vinyls.
b Fort Dodge, Iowa, Oct 2, 42.
Study & Training: Hamline Univ, BA; Univ N Mex, MA.
Work in Public Collections: Univ N Mex Art Mus, Albuquerque; Univ
Art Collections, Ariz State Univ, Tempe; Col Art Collection, Ariz
West Col, Yuma; Univ Art Collections, Pac Lutheran Univ,
Tacoma, Wash; Yuma Fine Arts Asn.
Exhibitions: Nat Crafts Invitational, Univ N Mex Art Mus, 68; 25th
Ceramics Nat, Everson Mus Art, Syracuse, N Y, 68-70; Media
68 & Media 72, Civic Arts Gallery, Walnut Creek, Calif, 68-72;
Southwest Crafts '70, Am Crafts Coun, Los Angeles, Calif, 70;
Crafts 72, Richmond Art Ctr, Calif, 72.
Teaching: Asst prof ceramics, Ariz State Univ, 68-; guest artist,
Pac Lutheran Univ, summer 71.
Awards: Best of show, First Ann Invitational Art Exhib, Phoenix
Jewish Community Ctr, 68; award, Media 68, Civic Arts Gallery,
68; award, Four Corner Painting & Sculpture Biennial, Phoenix
Art Mus, Ariz, 71; plus others.
Memberships: Ariz Designer-Craftsmen; Nat Coun Educ for Ce-
ramic Arts.

Research: Exploration of expanded vinyl as a sculptural material.
Publications: Contribr, Teaching secondary school art, W Brown
Co, 71.
Mailing Address: 834 W 12th St, Tempe, AZ 85281.

SCHMIDT, STEPHEN
Museum Director
b New York, N Y, Dec 11, 25.
Study & Training: Mohawk Col, N Y; Univ N Mex, BA.
Positions: Dir, Fort Concho Preservation & Mus.
Memberships: Am Asn Mus; Mountain-Plains Mus Conf; Am Asn
State & Local Hist; Nat Trust Hist Preserv; Tex Hist Found; plus
others.
Mailing Address: Ft Concho Preservation & Museum, 716 Burges
St, San Angelo, TX 76901.

SCHMUTZHART, BERTHOLD JOSEF
Sculptor, Educator
Preferred Media: Wood, Steel, Bronze.
b Salzburg, Austria, Aug 17, 28; U S citizen.
Study & Training: Acad Appl Art, Vienna, Austria; masterclass for
ceramics & sculpture, with Robert Obsieger.
Work in Public Collections: Fredericksburg Gallery Mod Art, Va.
Commissions: Christ (wood), 62 & (bronze), 64, St James Church,
Washington, D C; bacchus fountain, Fredericksburg Gallery, 67;
Christ (steel), 68 & processional cross (bronze), 71, St Clements
Church, Inkster, Mich.
Exhibitions: Southern Sculpture, Little Rock, Ark, 66 & Louisville,
Ky, 68; Washington Artists, Massilon Mus, Ohio, 69; Twenty
Washington Artists, Nat Collection Fine Arts, Washington, D C,
70; Art Barn, U S Dept Interior, Washington, D C, 71.
Teaching: Assoc prof sculpture & drawing, Corcoran Sch Art, Wash-
ington, D C, 63-; assoc prof sculpture, Montgomery Col, Takoma
Park, Md, 71-
Awards: First prize, Washington Religious Arts Soc, 60 & Southern
Sculpture, 66; first prize silver medal, Audubon Soc, 71.
Bibliography: Off Econ Opportunity (auth), A face for the future
(film), Booker Assocs, Reston, Va, 65; Tools for learning (film),
Kingsbury Ctr, Washington, D C, 71.
Memberships: Am Asn Univ Prof; Guild Religious Archit; Artist's
Equity Asn (first v pres, Washington, D C Chap, 71-).
Dealer: Franz Bader Gallery, 2124 Pennsylvania Ave, Washington,
DC 20037.
Mailing Address: 1011 E Capitol St, Washington, DC 20003.

SCHNACKENBERG, ROY
Painter, Sculptor
b Chicago, Ill, Jan 14, 34.
Work in Public Collections: Whitney Mus Am Art, New York, N Y;
Art Inst Chicago.
Exhibitions: Whitney Recent Acquisitions Show, 67 & Whitney Ann,
67-69; New American Realists, Göteberg, Sweden, 70; Beyond
Illustration, The Art of Playboy (world tour), 71-; Recent Ac-
quisitions Show, Art Inst Chicago, 71.
Awards: Copley Found Award, 67.
Mailing Address: 50 E Scott Rd, Barrington, IL 60010.

SCHNEEBAUM, TOBIAS
Painter
Preferred Media: Oils.
b New York, N Y, Apr 25, 21.
Study & Training: Work Prog Admin, 35-36; City Col New York, BA,
42; Brooklyn Mus Art Sch, with R Tamayo, 46 & A Osver, 47.
Work in Public Collections: Mus Estado, Guadalajara, Mex; Mus
Nat, Cuzco, Peru.
Exhibitions: Smithsonian Inst, Washington, D C, 55; Univ Nebr, 63;
Art Inst Chicago, 64; Univ Colo, 65.
Teaching: Instr painting, Ajijic Sch Art, Mex, 47-49.
Awards: Yaddo fel, 53 & 55; Fulbright fel, 55 & 56.
Publications: Illusr, The girl in the abstract bed, 54 & Jungle
journey, 59.
Dealer: Peridot-Washburn Gallery, 820 Madison Ave, New York,
NY 10021.
Mailing Address: 463 West St, New York, NY 10014.

SCHNEIDER, JO ANNE
Painter
Preferred Media: Oils.
b Lima, Ohio, Dec 4, 19.
Study & Training: Sch Fine Arts, Syracuse Univ.
Work in Public Collections: Butler Inst Am Art, Youngstown, Ohio;
Syracuse Univ, N Y; Allentown Mus, Pa; St Lawrence Univ, Can-
ton, N Y; Colby Col, Maine.
Exhibitions: Corcoran Gallery Art; Whitney Mus Am Art Ann; 50
Yrs Am Art, Am Fedn Art, 64; Childe Hassam Fund Exhib, Am
Acad Arts & Lett, 71; plus nine one-man exhibs, 54-72.

Awards: First prize, Guild Hall, 67; Marion K Haldenstein Mem Prize, Nat Asn Women Artists, 70; Stanley Grumbacher Mem Award, Audubon Artists, 72.
Dealer: Frank Rehn Gallery, 655 Madison Ave, New York, NY 10021.
Mailing Address: 35 E 75th St, New York, NY 10021.

SCHNEIDER, NOEL
Sculptor
Preferred Media: Wood, Stone, Steel.
b New York, N Y, July 31, 20.
Study & Training: Art Stud League New York, with William Zorach; City Univ New York.
Work in Public Collections: Bergen Co YMHA, N J.
Commissions: Willner Mem Bas Relief, Bergen Co YMHA, 64.
Exhibitions: One-man show, Bosshart Art Mus, N J State Col, 62; Stamford Mus Nat, Conn, 68; one-man slide show, City Univ New York, 69; two-man show, Meet Sculptor Ser, Sculpture Ctr, New York, 69; 28th Ann Nat Exhib Painters & Sculptors, Jersey City Mus, 69.
Awards: Ann purchase prizes, Collectors Am Art, 62-64; first prize for sculpture, Am Vet Soc Artists, 68 & gold medal, 70.
Memberships: Am Vet Soc Artists.
Dealer: Sculpture Center, 167 E 69th St, New York, NY 10021.
Mailing Address: 124 Oxford St, Manhattan Beach, Brooklyn, NY 11235.

SCHNEIDERMAN, DOROTHY
Art Dealer
b New York, N Y, Apr 11, 19.
Positions: Dir, Harbor Gallery, 65-
Specialty of Gallery: Contemporary American realists.
Mailing Address: 43 Main St, Cold Spring Harbor, NY 11724.

SCHNIER, JACQUES
Sculptor
Preferred Media: Bronze.
b Dec 25, 98; U S citizen.
Study & Training: Stanford Univ, AB(civil eng); Univ Calif, MA; Calif Sch Fine Arts, San Francisco.
Work in Public Collections: Oakland Art Mus, Calif; Legion of Honor Mus, San Francisco; Stanford Univ Mus; Santa Barbara Mus Art, Honolulu Acad Art.
Commissions: U S Half Dollar, commemorating San Francisco-Oakland Bay Bridge, 36; archit relief, Berkeley High Sch, Calif, 39; wood relief sculpture, State of Hawaii, Cong Club, Washington, D C, 48; bronze wall sculpture, Col Archit Alumni, Univ Calif, Berkeley, 60; carved acrylic sculpture, Calif Col Arts & Crafts Founders Centennial Award for Neil Armstrong, 72.
Exhibitions: Third Sculpture Int, Philadelphia Mus, 49; one-man shows, Sculpture, Stanford Univ Mus, 62, Sculpture, Santa Barbara Mus Art, 63, Bronze Sculpture, Ryder Gallery, Univ Calif, Berkeley, 65 & Transparency and Reflection, Judah Magnes Mus, Berkeley, 71.
Teaching: Instr sculpture, Calif Col Arts & Crafts, Oakland, 35-36; from lectr sculpture to prof, Univ Calif, Berkeley, 36-66.
Positions: Chmn adv bd, Nat Sculpture Ctr, Univ Kans, 71-; mem adv bd, Int Sculpture Symp, Eugene, Ore, 71-74; mem adv bd, Sect L, AAAS, 72.
Awards: First sculpture award, San Francisco Art Asn, 28; first sculpture prize & gold medal, Oakland Art Mus, 48; Inst Creative Arts fel, Univ Calif, 63.
Bibliography: Yvonne Greer Thiel (auth), Artists and people, Philos Libr, 59; Irving Stone (ed), There was light, Doubleday, 70; Harry Hollander (auth), Plastics for artists, Watson-Guptill, 72.
Publications: Auth, The Tibetan Lamaist ritual: Chöd, Int J Psychoanal, Vol 37, No 6; auth, Reinforced polyester plastic and acrylic color for sculpture, Proceedings of Fifth Nat Sculpture Conf, 68 & Reflection and transparency in carved acrylic sculpture, Proc Sixth Nat Sculpture Conf, 70; auth, The cubic element in my sculpture, 69 & Transparency and reflection as entities in sculpture of carved acrylic resin, 72, Leonardo.
Mailing Address: 4081 Happy Valley Rd, Lafayette, CA 94549.

SCHNITTMANN, SASCHA S
Sculptor, Museum Director
Preferred Media: Marble, Bronze.
b New York, N Y, Sept 1, 13.
Study & Training: Cooper Union Art Sch; Nat Acad Design; Beaux Arts Inst Design; Ecole Beaux Artes, Paris, France; also study with Olympio Brindisi, George Grey Barnard, Attilio Piccirilli, Charles Keck, Robert Aitken, Alexandre Sambougnac, Ceasare Stea, Gaetano Cecere & others.
Work in Public Collections: Pan-Am Soc; Am Mus Natural Hist; Dayton Art Inst; Kansas City Art Inst; Moscow State Univ, Russia; plus many others.

Commissions: Am Legion Monument, Saint Louis, Mo; aluminum figures for War Mem Stadium, Little Rock, Ark; Morgan Horse (life-size bronze), State Vt, 67; Martin Luther King, Jr (heroic Mem portrait bust four times life size), 68; fountain figures, Henry Ford Centennial Libr, Dearborn, Mich & Darsa Fountain, Saint Louis, Mo; also many busts, Mem & monuments including busts & portraits of notable persons throughout the world.
Exhibitions: Saint Louis Art Guild, 42; City Art Mus Saint Louis, 42; Seattle Art Mus, Wash, 42; Whitney Mus Am Art, New York, 43; Chicago Art Club, Ill, 43; plus others.
Positions: Dir & cur, Triton Mus Art.
Awards: Soc Independent Artists, 42; City Art Mus Saint Louis, 42; Art Inst Chicago, 43; plus many others.
Bibliography: Sculptor Schnittmann gives church valuable bronzes, San Jose Mercury, 12/16/71; Leonard Neft (auth), St Joseph's celebration, The Mercury, 3/19/71; Bust of Martin Luther King unveiled at Grace Cathedral, Voice of the People, 2/26/72.
Memberships: Life fel Russian Sculpture Soc; Am Acad Sculptors; hon life mem Ecole Beaux Arts, Paris; Soc Independent Artists; Am Inst Archit Sculptors; plus many others.
Publications: Auth & illusr, Anatomy & dissection for artists, 39; auth & illusr, Plastic histology, 40; contribr to archit mags.
Mailing Address: 915 Commercial St, San Jose, CA 95112.

SCHNURR-COLFLESH E
Painter
b Sandusky, Ohio, July 21, 32.
Study & Training: Cleveland Inst Art, BFA.
Exhibitions: Recent Paintings U S A: The Figure, Mus Mod Art, New York, N Y, 62; Butler Inst Am Art, Youngstown, Ohio, 63; Pa Acad Fine Arts, Philadelphia, 66; one-man shows, Caravan House Gallery, New York, 72 & Earl Hall, Columbia Univ, New York, 72.
Mailing Address: 507 W 111th St, New York, NY 10025.

SCHOELKOPF, ROBERT J, JR
Art Dealer
b New York, N Y, Nov 9, 27.
Study & Training: Yale Col, BA.
Positions: Dir & owner, Robert Schoelkopf Gallery.
Memberships: Art Dealers Asn Am.
Specialty of Gallery: Nineteenth and twentieth century American painting, sculpture and photography.
Mailing Address: 825 Madison Ave, New York, NY 10021.

SCHOEN, MR & MRS ARTHUR BOYER
Collectors
Mr Schoen, b Pittsburgh, Pa, Apr 17, 23; Mrs Schoen, b New York, N Y, Sept 27, 15.
Study & Training: Mr Schoen, Princeton Univ, BA; Mrs Schoen, Columbia Univ; Grand Cent Sch Art, New York.
Awards: Mrs Schoen, six United Hosp Fund Awards, 60-72.
Memberships: Parrish Art Mus (Mrs Schoen, pres, 70-); Metrop Mus Art; Mus City of New York; Mrs Schoen, York Club (pres).
Collection: Paintings: eighteenth century Lowestoft (Chinese export); tenth and twelfth century Persian pottery; eighteenth century English and American furniture.
Mailing Address: 17 E 89th St, New York, NY 10028.

SCHOENER, ALLON
Art Consultant
b Cleveland, Ohio, Jan 1, 26.
Study & Training: Yale Univ, BA, 46; Courtauld Inst Art, Univ London, 47-48; Yale Univ, MA, 49.
Collections Arranged: Lower East Side: Portal To American Life, 66 & Word From Jerusalem, 72, Jewish Mus; Erie Canal; 1817-1967, N Y State Coun Arts, 67; Harlem On My Mind, Metrop Mus Art, 69.
Positions: Asst dir, Jewish Mus, 66-67; visual arts prog dir, N Y State Coun Arts, 67-
Publications: Ed, Portal to America, Holt, Rinehart & Winston, 67; ed, Harlem on my mind, Random, 69.
Mailing Address: Grafton, VT 05146.

SCHOENER, JASON
Painter, Educator
Preferred Media: Oils, Watercolors, Gouache.
b Cleveland, Ohio, May 17, 19.
Study & Training: Cleveland Inst Art, dipl; Western Reserve Univ, BS; Art Stud League New York, N Y; Columbia Univ, MA.
Work in Public Collections: Cleveland Mus Art; Whitney Mus Am Art, New York; Calif Palace Legion of Honor, San Francisco; Columbus Gallery Fine Art, Ohio; Munson-Williams-Proctor Inst, Utica, N Y.
Exhibitions: San Francisco Mus Art Painting Ann, 53-65; Brooklyn Mus Int Watercolor Exhibs, 59 & 61; Pa Acad Fine Arts Water-

color Ann, 59-69; Calif Palace Legion of Honor Winter Invitationals, 68 & 70; Landscape I & II, De Cordova Mus, 70 & 71.
Teaching: Instr, Munson-Williams-Proctor Inst, 49-53; assoc prof, Calif Col Arts & Crafts, Oakland, 53-61, dir, pub rels & spec serv, 53-55, chmn dept fine arts, 55-70, dir, eve col, 55-69, prof, 61-, dir, fine arts div, 70-; vis lectr, Mills Col, 62-63; vis prof, Athens Technol Inst, Greece, 64-65.
Awards: Awards, Richmond Art Ctr, Calif, 57, Calif State Fair, 58 & Maine Art Gallery, 61.
Memberships: San Francisco Art Inst; Col Art Asn Am; Art Stud League New York; Am Asn Univ Prof.
Publications: Contribr, Art patronage in Greece, Art J, winter 66-67.
Dealers: Midtown Galleries, 11 E 57th St, New York, NY 10022; Gumps Gallery, 250 Post St, San Francisco, CA 94118.
Mailing Address: 74 Ross Circle, Oakland, CA 94618.

SCHOLDER, FRITZ
Painter, Printmaker
b Breckenridge, Minn, Oct 6, 37.
Study & Training: Univ Kans; Wis State Univ; Sacramento City Col, with Wayne Thiebaud; Sacramento State Univ, BA; Univ Ariz, MFA.
Work in Public Collections: Brooklyn Mus; Houston Mus Fine Arts; Phoenix Art Mus; San Diego Gallery Fine Art; Dallas Mus Fine Art.
Exhibitions: Winter Invitational, Palace Legion of Honor, San Francisco, 61; Am Indian Art, Edinburgh Art Festival & Berlin Festival, 66; Indian Painting, Mus Bellas Artes, Buenos Aires & Bibliot Nac, Chile, 67; Two Am Painters, Nat Collection Fine Art, Smithsonian Inst, 72; Two Am Painters, Madrid, Berlin, Bucharest, Belgrade, Ankara, Athens & London, 72-73.
Awards: Southwest Indian Art Proj scholar, Rockefeller Found, 61-62; purchase award, Ford Found, 62; Opportunity fel, John Hay Whitney Found, 62-63.
Bibliography: J J Brody (auth), Indian painters and white patrons, Univ N Mex Press, 71; Breeskin & Turk (auth), Scholder/Indians, Northland Press, 72; J Mondale (auth), Art and politics, Lerner Publ, 72.
Dealer: Cordiér & Ekstrom, 980 Madison Ave, New York, NY 10021.
Mailing Address: Galisteo, NM 87540.

SCHOLDER, LAURENCE
Printmaker, Educator
Preferred Media: Intaglio.
b Brooklyn, N Y, Nov 23, 42.
Study & Training: Carnegie Inst Technol, BFA; Univ Iowa, MA.
Work in Public Collections: Fort Worth Art Ctr, Tex; Houston Mus Fine Arts, Tex; Okla Art Ctr, Oklahoma City; Ark Art Ctr, Little Rock; McNay Art Inst, San Antonio, Tex.
Exhibitions: American Graphic Workshops '68, Cincinnati Art Mus, Ohio, 68; Multiples U S A, West Mich Univ, Kalamazoo, 70; Midwest Biennial, Joslyn Art Mus, Omaha, Nebr, 70 & 72; Seattle Print Int, Seattle Art Mus, Wash, 71; Libr Cong 22nd Print Nat, Washington, D C, 71.
Teaching: Asst prof printmaking, South Methodist Univ, 68-
Positions: Artist's rep, bd trustees, Dallas Mus Fine Art, 71-72.
Awards: Purchase award, Young Printmakers, Herron Art Inst, 67; purchase award, Print & Drawing Nat, Okla Art Ctr, 68; merit award, Southwest Graphics Invitational, San Antonio, 72.
Dealer: Cranfill Gallery, 2710 Routh St, Dallas, TX 75201.
Mailing Address: 3109 Drexel Dr, Dallas, TX 75205.

SCHOLZ, JANOS
Collector, Writer
b Sopron, Hungary, Dec 20, 03.
Study & Training: Royal Hungarian Col Agr, Dipl Ing; Royal Hungarian Conserv Music, dipl.
Teaching: Adj prof art hist, Columbia Univ, 65; sr fel, New York Univ.
Research: Italian drawings.
Collection: Drawings by the Old Italian Masters; porcelain; fayences; carpets.
Publications: Auth, articles & bks on Italian drawings.
Mailing Address: 863 Park Ave, New York, NY 10021.

SCHONBERGER, FRED
Painter, Sculptor
Preferred Media: Oils, Fiberglass, Steel.
b Arnhem, Holland, Dec 16, 30; Can citizen.
Study & Training: Kunst Nyverheid, Arnhem, with Jacob Van Arnhem & Hoff; Uffizi, Florence, Italy, with Kroller Muller.
Work in Public Collections: Queens Univ, Kingston, Ont; Reyerson Inst, Toronto, Ont; Wallack Galleries, Ottawa, Ont; County Court House, Kingston; plus others.

Commissions: Mural, Holy Name Parish, Kirkland Lake, Ont, 59; Cement Fondu Sculpture, County Court House, Kingston, 68; mural, Rene Turgeon, Ottawa, 72; fiberglass group sculpture, Marquette Stage, Queens Univ, in prep.
Exhibitions: Lady Dunn Int Exhib, Beaver Brook Gallery, Fredericton, 61; Kingston Art Asn Ann Spring Exhib, 63-68; Expos Provinciale Quebec, 64; Nine Kingston Artists, Can Art Coun, 67-68; two-man invitational, Agnes Etherington Art Ctr, Queens Univ, Kingston, 68.
Teaching: Instr drawing, painting & sculpting, Ont Dept Educ, Community Prog Br, Ont, 62-71; instr drawing, painting & sculpting, Queens Univ, 63-70.
Positions: Pres, Kingston Artists Workshop, 63-65; chmn & exec mem, Gallery Asn & Comt for Children's Art, 66-69.
Awards: Grand Prix for Mars-1964 & fourth prize for Love, Concours Nat Art Quebec, 64.
Memberships: Soc Can Artists; Can Artists Representatives (rep, Kingston Chap, 72-).
Dealer: Gilhooly Galleries, Billings Bridge, Ottawa, Ont, Can.
Mailing Address: 557 Union St, Kingston, Ont, Can.

SCHONWALTER, JEAN FRANCES
Painter, Instructor
Preferred Media: Oils, Bronze.
b Philadelphia, Pa.
Study & Training: Moore Col Art, scholar, BFA; Pa Acad Fine Arts, grad fel.
Work in Public Collections: Philadelphia Mus Art, Pa; N J State Mus, Trenton; Brooklyn Mus, N Y; Slater Mus, Norwich, Conn; New York Pub Libr, N Y.
Commissions: Two paintings of Temple B'Nai Jeshurun, N J, 59.
Exhibitions: Libr Cong, Washington, D C; N J State Mus Exhibs; Boston Mus Exhibs; Butler Inst Am Art, Youngstown, Ohio; Nat Acad Design, New York.
Teaching: Instr life painting, Newark Sch Fine & Indust Art, N J, 69-
Awards: Pennypacker Prize for graphics, Soc Am Graphic Artists, 66; purchase prize, N J State Mus, 67; first prize & medal of honor for graphics, Nat Asn Women Artists, 71.
Bibliography: Dona Meilach (auth), Direct metal sculpture, Crown, 58; E F Singer (auth), Meet the artist—Jean Schonwalter, Suburban Life, 70.
Memberships: Artists Equity Asn N J; Soc Am Graphic Artists; Assoc Artists N J; Nat Asn Women Artists.
Dealer: Schoneman Galleries, 823 Madison Ave, New York, NY 10021.
Mailing Address: 67 Fielding Ct, South Orange, NJ 07079.

SCHOOLER, LEE
Collector
b Chicago, Ill, June 15, 23.
Study & Training: Roosevelt Univ, BA, 46.
Memberships: Am Fedn Arts; Mus Mod Art, New York; Art Inst Chicago.
Collection: Contemporary painting & sculpture; pre-Columbian sculpture.
Mailing Address: 43 E Elm St, Chicago, IL 60611.

SCHOOLEY, ELMER WAYNE
Painter, Educator
Preferred Media: Oils, Wood.
b Lawrence, Kans, Feb 20, 16.
Study & Training: Univ Colo, BFA, 38; State Univ Iowa, MA, 41.
Work in Public Collections: Paintings, Mus Mod Art, New York, N Y, Hallmark Collection, Kansas City, Mus N Mex, Santa Fe & Roswell Mus, N Mex; lithograph, Metrop Mus Art, New York.
Commissions: Fresco (with Gussie Du Jardin), Las Vegas, N Mex Hosp, 50.
Exhibitions: Houston Southwestern Exhib, Tex, 62; Kansas City Mid-Am Exhib, 64; Tucson Festival Art Exhib, Ariz, 64; Eight State Exhib, Oklahoma City, 68; Biennial Southwestern Exhib, Santa Fe, 72.
Teaching: Asst prof, N Mex Western Univ, 46-47; prof arts & crafts & head dept, N Mex Highlands Univ, 47-
Awards: Purchase prizes, Ford Found, 62 & Southwest Biennial, 70 & 72; hon mention, Kansas City Hallmark Purchase, 64.
Mailing Address: P O Box 5, Montezuma, NM 87731.

SCHORR, JUSTIN
Painter, Educator
Preferred Media: Oils.
b New York, N Y, June 10, 28.
Study & Training: City Col New York, BSS, 50; Columbia Univ Teachers Col, EdD, 62.
Work in Public Collections: Butler Inst Am Art, Youngstown, Ohio; Waldemar Res Found; Lock Haven State Col, Pa.

Exhibitions: Brooklyn Mus, N Y, 58; Nat Acad Design, New York, 59; Pa Acad Fine Arts, Philadelphia, 63; Butler Inst Am Art, Youngstown, Ohio, 64.
Teaching: Assoc prof painting, Columbia Univ Teachers Col, 62-
Publications: Auth, Aspects of art, A S Barnes, 67.
Dealer: West Broadway Gallery, 431 W Broadway, New York, NY 10012.
Mailing Address: 788 Riverside Dr, New York, NY 10032.

SCHOTT, JOSEPH JOHN
Painter
Preferred Media: Oils.
b Newark, N J, Feb 19, 22.
Work in Public Collections: Fanwood Mem Libr, N J.
Exhibitions: Contemp N J Art Exhib, Bambergers, Newark, 67; Contemp Am Realism Exhib, Hammond Mus, North Salem, N Y, 68; Representational Works of Art Nat, Springfield Mus, Mass, 68 & 69; Nat Acad Design 144th Ann, Nat Acad Galleries, New York, 69; Am Artists Prof League Grand Nat, Lever House, New York, 69, 70 & 72.
Awards: Award for realistic painting, Painters & Sculptors Soc Nat, Jersey City, N J, 67; award for traditional painting, Art Ctr of Oranges Statewide Exhib, East Orange, N J, 67; best in show, Summit Art Ctr Statewide Exhib, N J, 72.
Bibliography: Article, In: Plainfield Courier News, N J, 3/15/67; Michael Lenson (auth), article, In: Newark Sun News, 12/20/70; Verdi Johnson (auth), article, In: Sun Star Ledger, Newark, 5/21/72.
Memberships: Am Artists Prof League; Acad Artists Asn; charter mem Federated Art Asns N J; Hudson Valley Art Asn; Art Exhibs Coun N J.
Mailing Address: 185 Watson Rd, Fanwood, NJ 07023.

SCHRACK, JOSEPH EARL
Painter
Study & Training: Art Inst Chicago; Art Stud League New York, with Frank Vincent Dumond, John Sloan & Robert Henri; John Herron Art Inst; also with Hans Hofmann & George Inness, Jr.
Commissions: Murals, First Fed Savings Bank, San Diego & First Nat Bank, El Cajon, Calif; Adm Robert E Coontz, U S N (portrait), Pentagon, Washington, D C; Ike & Mamie Eisenhower (portrait), House Off Bldg, Washington, D C; plus many other pvt commissions.
Exhibitions: Allied Artists Am; Audubon Artists; La Jolla Art Ctr; San Diego Fine Arts Soc; Carlsbad Art Asn; plus many others.
Teaching: Instr art, San Diego Fine Arts Gallery; instr fine arts, Balboa Univ; instr art, pvt classes.
Awards: Prizes, Art Inst Chicago, 13; Carlsbad Art Asn, 54.
Memberships: Men's Art Inst, San Diego; La Jolla Art Ctr; San Diego Fine Arts Soc; Alumni Asn Art Inst Chicago.
Art Interests: History & theory of classical & modern art.
Mailing Address: 2965 Front St, San Diego, CA 92103.

SCHRAG, KARL
Painter
Preferred Media: Oils, Gouache, Graphics.
b Karlsruhe, Ger, Dec 7, 12; U S citizen.
Study & Training: Ecole Beaux Arts, Geneva & Paris; Acad Ranson, Paris; Art Stud League New York, N Y, with Lucien Simon, Roger Bissiere, Harry Sternberg & S W Hayter.
Work in Public Collections: Nat Gallery Art; Metrop Mus Art; Mus Mod Art; Whitney Mus Am Art; Art Inst Chicago; plus many others.
Exhibitions: Several one-man exhibs painting, Kraushaar Galleries, New York, 47-70; Mod Art In U S, Tate Gallery, London & other Europe mus, 56; Am Fedn Arts one-man exhib paintings & prints, Brooklyn Mus & tour, 62; Whitney Mus Am Art Painting Ann, 65; Retrospective Exhib Prints, Nat Collection Fine Arts, Washington, D C, 72.
Teaching: Dir etching, Atelier 17, New York, 50-51; instr printmaking, Brooklyn Col, 53-54; instr drawing & printmaking, Cooper Union, 54-68.
Awards: Purchase awards, Brooklyn Mus Print Ann, 47 & 50; cert of merit for best exhib U S, Fourth Int Exhib Contemp Art, New Delhi, India, 62; Am Acad Arts & Lett grant, 66.
Bibliography: John Gordon (auth), Karl Schrag, Am Fedn Arts, 60; U S Info Agency staff (auth), Printmakers U S A (film), Sidney Stiber Prod, 61; Una E Johnson (auth), Karl Schrag, a catalogue raisonné of the graphic works, 1939-1970, Sch Art, Syracuse Univ, 71.
Memberships: Soc Am Graphic Artists; Artists Equity Asn; Art Stud League New York.
Publications: Auth, Some thoughts on art, Cable, 58; auth, Happiness and torment of printmaking, Artist's Proof, 66; auth, The artist alone versus the artist in the workshop, New Univ Thought, autumn 67.

Dealer: Kraushaar Galleries, 1055 Madison Ave, New York, NY 10028.
Mailing Address: 127 E 95th St, New York, NY 10028.

SCHRAMM, JAMES SIEGMUND
Collector, Patron
b Burlington, Iowa, Feb 4, 04.
Study & Training: Coe Col, hon LLD, 54; Amherst Col, hon LHD, 61; Grinnell Col, hon DFA, 72.
Positions: Pres & trustee, Des Moines Art Ctr, 42-; trustee, Chicago Mus Contemp Art, 69-70; hon chmn, Amherst Col Asn Art, 71-
Awards: Distinguished Serv Award, Univ Iowa, 71.
Memberships: Am Fedn Art (exec comt, 42-, pres, 56-58); Whitney Mus Am Art (Friends, 68-); Guggenheim Mus (Friends, 69-).
Art Interests: Supporting art departments in colleges and universities; encouraging American contemporary artists.
Collection: American painting and sculpture from the 30's; some European, Japanese and American prints; African sculpture.
Mailing Address: 2700 S Main St, Burlington, IA 52601.

SCHRECK, MICHAEL HENRY
Painter, Sculptor
Preferred Media: Oils, Bronze.
b Austria; U S citizen.
Study & Training: Art Stud League New York; also with Tom Von Dreger, Vienna & Colin Collahan, London.
Work in Public Collections: Heckscher Mus, N Y; Miami Mus Mod Art, Fla; N Y Univ; N Y Univ Med Ctr; State Univ N Y Buffalo.
Commissions: Mexican Mural, Thomaston, N Y, 69; Sculpture Garden, R Gimbel, New York.
Exhibitions: Mus Fine Arts, Montreal, 53-56; Dom Gallery, Montreal, 54-56; Jersey City Mus, N J, 59; one-man show, Selected Artists Gallery, New York, 61; Mus Art Mod, Paris, 64.
Awards: Grand Prix Int, Deauville, France, 64; Prix Int de Vichy, Mention Grand Finale, 64; Prix Rencontre Int, Chateau de Senou, France, 65.
Bibliography: P Mornand (auth), Au Musee d'Art Moderne, La Rev Mod, 64; J J Leveque (auth), Le tour de galeries, Galerie Arts, 3/65; J Paris (auth), article, In: Long Island Art Rev, 66.
Memberships: Life fel Royal Soc Arts, London; Am Fedn Arts; Smithsonian Inst.
Dealers: Gloria Luria Gallery, 14700 Biscayne Blvd N, Miami, FL 33161; Dominion Gallery, 1438 Sherbrooke St W, Montreal, PQ, Can.
Mailing Address: 3111 N Ocean Dr, Hollywood, FL 33020.

SCHREIBER, EILEEN SHER
Painter, Lecturer
Preferred Media: Collage, Acrylics, Watercolors.
b Denver, Colo.
Study & Training: Univ Utah, 42-45; New York Univ Exten, 66-68; also with Tom Vincent & Alan Goldstein.
Work in Public Collections: Morris Mus Arts & Sci, Morristown, N J; Seton Hall Univ, South Orange, N J; Bloomfield Col, N J; Morris Co State Col, Dover, N J; also in collection of Sen Harrison Williams, N J.
Commissions: Painting on N J beach area, Broad Nat Bank, Newark, 70; Wolfgang Rapp Architects, Elkins Park, Pa, 72.
Exhibitions: Morristown Mus Arts & Sci, 65-72; N J Mus in Trenton, 69; Am Watercolor Soc Nat, Nat Acad Galleries, New York, N Y, 70; Audubon Artists, New York, 70; Pallazzo Vecchio, Florence, Italy, 72; plus one other.
Teaching: Lectr.
Awards: N J Watercolor Soc Award, 69; second watercolor, Nat Asn Women Artists, 70; first in watercolor, collage, Hunerdon Mus Art Gallery, 71.
Bibliography: D Bainbridge (auth), Commentaries on artists, N J Music & Arts Mag, 4/68; M Lenson (auth), rev, In: Newark Eve News, 4/70.
Memberships: Nat Asn Women Artists (watercolor jury, 70-72); Artists Equity Asn; Nat Painters & Sculptors Soc; Hunterdon Art Asn; Summit Art Asn.
Dealers: Betty Kardo, Highgate Gallery, 182 Cooper, Upper Montclair, NJ 07043; Sidney Rothman, Barnegat Light, NJ 08006.
Mailing Address: 236 S Valley Rd, West Orange, NJ 07052.

SCHREIBER, GEORGES
Painter
Preferred Media: Oils, Watercolors, Graphics.
b Brussels, Belg, Apr 25, 04; U S citizen.
Study & Training: Art Crafts Sch Elberfeld, W Ger; Acad Fine Arts Duesseldorf & Berlin, Ger; also in London, Florence & Paris.
Work in Public Collections: Metrop Mus Art, New York; Whitney Mus Am Art, New York; Toledo Mus, Ohio; Bibliot Nat, Paris; Libr Cong, Washington, D C; plus many others.

Exhibitions: Int Watercolor Exhib, Art Inst Chicago; Carnegie Exhib, Pittsburgh, Pa; New York World's Fair, 39; Artists For Victory, Metrop Mus Art; Pa Acad Fine Arts, Philadelphia.
Teaching: Instr watercolor & painting, New Sch Social Res, 59-
Awards: William Tuthill Prize, Int Watercolor Show, Art Inst Chicago; first prize, Mus Mod Art; first prize & gold medal, New York Art Dirs Club.
Publications: Auth & illusr, Portraits and self-portraits, Houghton Mifflin, 36 & Bks Libr, 69; auth & illusr, Bambino the clown, Viking Press, 57.
Dealer: Kennedy Galleries, 20 E 56th St, New York, NY 10022.
Mailing Address: 8 W 13th St, New York, NY 10011.

SCHREIBER, MARTIN
Sculptor, Painter
Preferred Media: Acrylics, Steel.
b Berlin, Ger, Nov 8, 23; U S citizen.
Study & Training: Art Stud League New York; Brooklyn Mus Art Sch; also with Ruben Tam.
Work in Public Collections: Nassau Community Col; Contemp Arts Ctr, Cincinnati, Ohio; Mary Washington Col, Va; Corcoran Mus, Washington, D C.
Exhibitions: 3rd Ann Op Art Festival, E Hampton Gallery, New York, N Y, 66; Op Art and It's Antecedents, Am Fedn Arts Traveling Exhib, 67; five shows, Silvermine Ann; Gallery MacKay, Montreal, 68; one-man show, Spectrum Gallery, New York, 71.
Awards: First prize in acrylic, Silvermine, Conn, 65.
Memberships: Art Dirs Club N Y.
Dealer: Spectrum Gallery, 464 W Broadway, New York, NY 10029.
Mailing Address: 1578 Pea Pond Rd, North Bellmore, NY 11710.

SCHREYER, GRETA L
Painter, Lecturer
Preferred Media: Oils, Watercolors, Lithography.
b Vienna, Austria, July 28, 23; U S citizen.
Study & Training: Acad Arts, Vienna; Columbia Univ, with Seong Moy; Art Stud League New York; Pratt Inst; also with Moses Soyer & Fred Taubes.
Work in Public Collections: Mus Ha'aretz, Tel-Aviv, Israel; Jersey City State Col, N J; New Sch Social Res, Art Ctr, New York, N Y; Pasadena Mus, Calif; Mus Art & Sci, Norfolk, VA; plus others.
Exhibitions: Four shows, New Sch Art Ctr, New York, 60-68; Knickerbocker Artists, New York; one-man shows, St Olaf Col, Northfield, Minn, 66 & Panama Art Asn, Fla, 67; Roko Gallery, New York, 72; plus other one-man shows.
Teaching: Guest lectr, Brandeis Univ, 67-68; guest lectr, Women Comt, Westbury Chap, 68-69; guest lectr, Mus Mod Art, Metrop Mus Art, Whitney Mus Am Art & Guggenheim Mus, New York, 69-
Awards: Grumbacher Awards, 56 & 69.
Memberships: Am Fedn Arts; Artist's Equity Asn New York.
Dealer: Roko Gallery, 90 E Tenth St, New York, NY 10003.
Mailing Address: 54 W 74th St, New York, NY 10023.

SCHROEDER, ERIC
Museum Curator, Writer
b Sale, Eng, Nov 20, 04.
Study & Training: Corpus Christi Col; Oxford Univ, BA; Harvard Univ.
Positions: Keeper Islamic art, Fogg Art Mus, Harvard Univ, 38-70.
Publications: Auth, Iranian book painting, 40; co-auth, Iranian & Islamic art, 51; auth, Persian miniatures in the Fogg Museum, 42; auth, Muhammad's people, 55; auth, Visions of element, 63; also contribr to Collier's Encycl, Bk of Knowledge, Survey Persian Art, Ars Islamica & other art publ.
Mailing Address: 9 Follen St, Cambridge, MA 02138.

SCHROYER, ROBERT McCLELLAND
Designer, Illustrator
b Oakland, Calif, Aug 13, 07.
Study & Training: Carnegie Inst; Parsons Sch Design, scholar, 29; Acad Grande Chaumiére, Paris, France.
Exhibitions: Lowe Gallery, Miami, Fla.
Teaching: Asst instr stage design, Parsons Sch Design, New York, 29; instr interior design, Paris, 30-31.
Positions: Designer, Delineator Mag, 31-35; free lance designer & illusr, all major mags & advert agencies, 35-
Awards: House & Garden scholar, 30; Upholstery Leather Group Asn Award; Advert A Award, Burdine Advert Coun, Fla, 59.
Memberships: Parsons Sch Design Alumni; Am Inst Interior Designers.
Mailing Address: 6250 S W 49th St, Miami, FL 33155.

SCHRUP, JOHN EDMUND
Painter, Instructor
Preferred Media: Oils.
b Madison, Wis, Apr 25, 37.
Study & Training: Univ Wis-Madison, BS, MS & MFA, with Robert

Grilley, Alfred Sessler, Leo Steppat & Dean Meeker.
Work in Public Collections: Wichita Art Mus, Kans; Univ Wis-Madison; Univ Wis-La Crosse.
Exhibitions: Wis Painters & Sculptors, Milwaukee, 64; Kans Ann, Wichita, 65 & 66; one-man show, Wichita Art Mus, 66; Tex Ann, Dallas, 67; Contemp Gallery, Dallas, 69.
Teaching: Grad teaching asst drawing, Univ Wis-Madison, 62-64; instr painting & drawing, Wichita State Univ, 65-66; instr painting & drawing, El Centro Community Col, Dallas, 70-
Positions: Artists' Equity alternate rep to Dallas Mus Fine Arts Bd, 71.
Memberships: Artists' Equity Asn (pres, Dallas Chap, 71-72).
Mailing Address: 10211 Lake Gardens, Dallas, TX 75218.

SCHUCKER, CHARLES
Painter
b Gap, Pa, Jan 19, 08.
Study & Training: Md Inst Fine & Mech Arts, grad, 34; traveling scholar, Europe, 35.
Work in Public Collections: Whitney Mus Am Art; Brooklyn Mus; Newark Mus Asn; New Brit Mus Am Art; Howard Wise Collection; plus others.
Exhibitions: Amherst Col; Carnegie Inst, Pittsburgh; Walker Art Ctr, Minneapolis; Art Inst Chicago; Pa Acad Fine Arts; plus many one-man exhibs.
Teaching: Instr art, City Col New York; instr art, N Y Univ; prof art, Pratt Inst, 56-
Positions: Mem Fed Art Proj, Works Prog Admin, 38-42; mem bd dirs, Yaddo Found Creative Arts.
Awards: Guggenheim Found fel.
Dealer: Max Hutchinson Gallery, 127 Greene St, New York, NY 10012.
Mailing Address: Studio 33, Middagh St, Brooklyn Heights, NY 11201.

SCHUELER, JON R
Painter, Lecturer
b Milwaukee, Wis, Sept 12, 16.
Study & Training: Univ Wis, BA (econs), 38, MA (Eng lit), 40; Calif Sch Fine Arts, 48-51, with David Park, Elmer Bischoff, Richard Diebenkorn, Hassel Smith, Clyfford Still & Clay Spohn.
Work in Public Collections: Whitney Mus Am Art, New York, N Y; Union Carbide Corp Collection.
Commissions: Lithographs, New York Hilton Hotel, 62.
Exhibitions: Whitney Mus Am Art; Corcoran Gallery Art, Washington, D C; Walker Art Ctr, Minneapolis, Minn; Md Inst; Cornell Univ; plus others.
Teaching: Lect, Painting, Yale Univ Summer Sch Art & Md Inst, Col Art Asn Am & others.
Bibliography: John I H Baur (auth), Nature in abstraction, Macmillan, 58; B H Friedman (ed), School of New York, Grove Press, 59; Lloyd Goodrich & John I H Baur (auth), American art of our century, Whitney Mus Am Art, 61.
Publications: Contribr, Letter on the sky, It Is Mag.
Mailing Address: 80 Wig Hill Rd, Chester, CT 06412.

SCHULHOF, MR & MRS RUDOLPH B
Collectors
Collection: Modern art since 1945.
Mailing Address: Dock Lane, Kings Point, NY 11024.

SCHULLER, GRETE
Sculptor
Preferred Media: Stone, Wood.
b Vienna, Austria; U S citizen.
Study & Training: Vienna Lyzeum; Vienna Kunstakademie; Art Stud League New York, N Y, sculpture with W Zorach; Sculpture Ctr, New York.
Work in Public Collections: Norfolk Mus Arts & Sci, Va; Mus Natural Hist, New York; Mus Sci, Boston, Mass.
Exhibitions: Des Moines Art Ctr, Iowa, 52; Acad Arts & Lett, 55; Univ Notre Dame, South Bend, Ind, 59; Detroit Inst Arts & Pa Acad Fine Arts, Philadelphia, 59-60; 150 Yrs Am Art, New Westbury Garden, N Y, 60.
Awards: Hon mention Archit League New York, 54; Ellen P Speyer Prize, Nat Acad Design, 71; Pauline Law Prize, Allied Artists Am, 72.
Memberships: Fel Nat Sculpture Soc; Allied Artists Am; Audubon Artists.
Publications: Contribr, The form is in the fieldstone, Nat Sculpture Rev, fall 71.
Dealer: Gallery Madison/90, 1248 Madison Ave, New York, NY 10028.
Mailing Address: 116 E 83rd St, New York, NY 10028.

SCHULMAN, JACOB
Collector
b New York, N Y, July 2, 15.
Study & Training: Sch Educ, New York Univ, BS.
Collection: Contemporary painters and sculptors with emphasis on Jewish or Biblical themes, including works by Baskin, Bloom, Levine, Rattner, Shahn, Weber and Zorach.
Mailing Address: 117 First Ave, Gloversville, NY 12078.

SCHULTE, MR & MRS ARTHUR D
Collectors
Mr Schulte,b New York, N Y, 06.
Study & Training: Mr Schulte, Yale Univ; Mrs Schulte, Hunter Col; Columbia Univ; New York Univ.
Collection: French, American, Italian and Greek paintings and sculpture.
Mailing Address: 810 Fifth Ave, New York, NY 10021.

SCHULTZ, HAROLD A
Painter, Educator
b Grafton, Wis, Jan 6, 07.
Study & Training: Layton Sch Art; Northwestern Univ, BS & MA.
Exhibitions: Art Inst Chicago; Chicago Soc Artists; Brooklyn Mus; Ferargil Gallery.
Teaching: Lect, American Art Today; head art dept, Francis W Parker Sch, Chicago, 32-40; prof art educ, Univ Ill, 40-
Memberships: Ill Art Educ Asn; Nat Art Educ Asn; Western Art Asn; Int Soc for Educ through Art, UNESCO.
Publications: Co-auth, Art in the elementary school, 48.
Mailing Address: Fine Arts Bldg, University of Illinois, Urbana, IL 61801.

SCHULTZ, ROGER d
Painter, Sculptor
Preferred Media: Acrylics, Copper, Bronze.
b Troy, Ohio, Nov 17, 40.
Study & Training: Univ Cincinnati, BS.
Work in Public Collections: Fine Arts Mus N Mex, Santa Fe; Fine Arts Collection, Univ Cincinnati, Ohio; First Nat Bank Ariz, Phoenix; Westinghouse Corp, Norman, Okla; Ansul Co, Marinette, Wis.
Commissions: Sphere sculpture, Bank N Mex, Albuquerque, 69; sculpture, First Northern Savings & Loan Asn, Santa Fe, 70; adobe residence, Dr & Mrs Robert M Zone, Santa Fe, 71; sculpture, Horizon Country Club, Belen, N Mex, 72.
Exhibitions: N Mex Biennial, 67, 69 & 71 & Southwest Biennial, 68 & 72, Fine Arts Mus N Mex; Sesquicentennial Fine Arts Exhib, Univ Cincinnati, 68; 11th & 12th Midwest Biennials, Joslyn Art Mus, Omaha, Nebr, 70 & 72; Mainstreams '72, Marietta Col, Ohio, 72.
Awards: Alfred Morang Competition First Pl Award, 67; Univ Cincinnati Purchase Award, 68; major award & purchase award, Fine Arts Mus N Mex, 71.
Dealer: Janus Gallery, 116½ E Palace Ave, Santa Fe, NM 87501.
Mailing Address: Arroyo Hondo Rd, Rte 3, Box 72A, Santa Fe, NM 87501.

SCHULZ, CHARLES MONROE
Cartoonist
b Minneapolis, Minn, Nov 25, 22.
Study & Training: Anderson Col, hon LHD, 63.
Positions: Cartoonist, Saint Paul Pioneer Press & Sat Eve Post, 48-49; created syndicated comic strip Peanuts, 50-
Awards: Outstanding Cartoonists of the Year, Nat Cartoonists Soc, 55; Outstanding Humorist of the Year, Yale Univ, 57; Emmy Award for CBS cartoon spec, 66; plus others.
Publications: Auth & illusr, Love is walking hand in hand, 65, A Charlie Brown Christmas, 65, You need help, Charlie Brown, 66, Charlie Brown's all-stars, 66 & You've had it, Charlie Brown, 69; plus more than 100 others.
Mailing Address: 2162 Coffee Lane, Sebastopol, CA 95472.

SCHULZE, FRANZ
Educator, Art Critic
b Uniontown, Pa, Jan 30, 27.
Study & Training: Northwestern Univ, 43; Univ Chicago, PhB, 45; Sch Art Inst Chicago, BFA, 49, MFA, 50; Acad Fine Arts, Munich.
Teaching: Instr, Purdue Univ, 50-52; prof, Lake Forest Col, 52-
Positions: Art critic, Chicago Daily News, 62-
Awards: Ford Found critic's fel, 64; Harbison Award, Danforth Found, 71; Graham Found Advan Fine Arts fel, 71.
Memberships: Col Art Asn Am; Arch Am Art; Am Asn Univ Prof; Louis Corinth Mem Found.
Research: Art and architecture in the Midwest, especially Chicago.

Publications: Auth, Art, architecture and civilization, 68; auth, Fantastic images: Chicago art since 1945, 72.
Mailing Address: Dept of Art, Lake Forest College, Highland Park, IL 60035.

SCHULZE, JOHN H
Photographer, Educator
b Scottsbluff, Nebr, June 7, 15.
Study & Training: Kans State Teachers Col, BS; Univ Iowa, MFA.
Work in Public Collections: Nihon Univ, Tokyo; Haydon Gallery, Mass Inst Technol; Univ Ala; Waterloo Munic Gallery; Oakland Mus.
Commissions: Photog mural, Sci Bldg, Univ Northern Iowa, 71.
Exhibitions: American Photography: The Sixties, Sheldon Mem Art Gallery, Nebr, 66; Photography in Fine Arts V, Metrop Mus Art, 67; Photography U S A, DeCordova Mus, 68; Light Seven, Haydon Gallery, Mass Inst Technol, 68; Focus Gallery, San Francisco, 68.
Teaching: Prof photog, sch art, Univ Iowa, 48-; res prof, 68-69; artist-in-residence, Washburn Univ, 72; artist-in-residence, Northwest Mo State Col, 72.
Bibliography: Kay Finch (auth), Elusive shadow (film), Univ Iowa Camera, 65.
Memberships: Soc Photog Educ (chmn, 70); Col Art Asn Am; Mid Am Col Art Asn.
Publications: Auth, London Times (educ suppl), 64, Camera International, 65 & Contemporary photographer, 67; contribr, Aperture & Photog Ann, 69.
Mailing Address: 5 Forest Glen, Iowa City, IA 52240.

SCHULZE, PAUL
Designer, Instructor
Preferred Media: Glass, Mixed Media.
b New York, N Y, Feb 7, 34.
Study & Training: Parsons Sch Design, cert; New York Univ, BS (indust design), 60.
Commissions: Crystal cross, Steuben Glass, St Clement's Episcopal Church, New York.
Exhibitions: Studies in Crystal 1966, Steuben Glass, New York, 65; Islands in Crystal, Steuben Glass, New York, 66.
Teaching: Instr eng drawing & three dimensional design, Parsons Sch Design, 62-70.
Positions: Off interior design, Bus Equip Sales Co, New York, 60-61; designer, Steuben Glass, 61-69, asst dir design, 69-70, dir design, 70-
Awards: Stud Competition Award, Am Soc Indust Designers, 59.
Memberships: Guild for Organic Environment; Nat Alumni Coun Parsons Sch Design.
Publications: Illusr, Organics, Steendrukkerij & Co, Holland, 61; illusr, articles, In: Indust Design & Progressive Archit.
Mailing Address: 102 N Washington Ave, Hartsdale, NY 10530.

SCHUMAN, ROBERT CONRAD
Painter, Instructor
b Baldwin, N Y, July 12, 23.
Study & Training: New York Univ, 48; Columbia Univ, 48; Pratt Inst Art Sch, BFA, 50; Univ Hawaii, MEd, 59; pvt study with Robert Brackman & Jean Charlot.
Exhibitions: Easter Art Exhib, Honolulu, 63 & 65; Libr Hawaii, Honolulu, 65; Hui Noeau, Maui, 65 & 68; Waldorf Astoria Art Gallery, N Y, 66; Balik Art Show, Lahaina Art Gallery, 70; plus others.
Teaching: Instr art, Baldwin, N Y, 48-50; instr, Nanakuli, Oahu, 51, Eleele Kauai, 51-57; art supvr, Univ Hawaii, 58-64; instr art, Honolohua, Maui, 65; art instr & dept chmn, Baldwin High Sch, Maui, 66-67; instr art, Lahainaluna High Sch, 68-
Positions: Judge, Children's Art Show, Honolulu Acad Arts, 57; dir, State Art Week, 59.
Awards: Prizes, Hui Noeau, 64; Maui Co Fair, 64.
Memberships: Nat Art Educ Asn; Hawaii Educ Asn; Hawaii Arts Coun; Hui Noeau (bd dirs); Pacific Art Asn; plus others.
Publications: Contribr, articles to prof art journals.
Mailing Address: Box 470-C, R R 1, Honokeana St, Lahaina, HI 96761.

SCHUSTER, EUGENE IVAN
Art Dealer, Art Historian
b St Louis, Mo, Dec 8, 36.
Study & Training: Wayne State Univ, BA & MA; Univ Mich, Ann Arbor, 59-62; Warburg Inst, Univ London, Fulbright scholar with E H Gombrich, 62-65; Courtauld Inst, Univ London & London Sch Econ, 62-65.
Teaching: Lectr art hist, Wayne State Univ, 59-62; lectr art hist, Eastern Mich Univ, 60; lectr art hist, Rackham Exten, Univ Mich, 61; lectr art hist, Nat Gallery, London, 62-65.
Positions: Dir, London Arts Gallery.

Awards: Louis La Med Prize for outstanding masters thesis on topic of Jewish cultural concern.
Memberships: Founders Soc, Detroit Inst Arts; Detroit Art Dealers Asn; Appraisers Asn Am.
Research: Quattrocento in Florence, especially formative changes caused by humanistic studies and leading to the Renaissance.
Specialty of Gallery: Old and modern master graphics; western painting and sculpture from the fifteenth to twentieth centuries.
Publications: Auth, Les peintres maudits: a study of the cultural relationship of the Jewish artists of Paris, 60; auth, Sir Charles Locke Eastlake, Plymouth Art Mus, Eng, (in prep).
Mailing Address: 321 Fisher Bldg, Detroit, MI 48202.

SCHUTZ, ANTON
Etcher, Writer
b Berndorf, Ger, Apr 19, 94; U S citizen.
Study & Training: Univ Munich, ME, 20; Munich Acad Fine Arts, 19-23; Art Stud League New York, 24-25, with Joseph Pennell.
Work in Public Collections: Libr Cong, Washington, D C; Brit Mus, London; Bibliot Nat, Paris, France; Uffizi, Florence, Italy; Cleveland Mus Art, Ohio; plus others.
Exhibitions: In the U S & abroad.
Positions: Founder & pres, New York Graphic Soc, 25-66, dir & consult, 66-; past pres, Inter-Am Graphics, Ltd; publ & co-ed, UNESCO World Art Series, 54-60.
Memberships: Soc Am Graphic Artists; Chicago Soc Etchers.
Publications: Auth, New York in etchings, 39; auth, Fine art reproduction of old and modern masters, 41, 61 & 65; auth, Hand book of fine art color reproductions, 45; auth, Blue book color reproductions, 51; auth, Reproductions of American paintings, 61; plus others.
Mailing Address: 4 Heathcote Rd, Scarsdale, NY 10583.

SCHWAB, ELOISA (MRS A H RODRIGUEZ)
Painter
Preferred Media: Oils.
b Habana, Cuba, July 4, 94; U S citizen.
Study & Training: Acad Julien, Paris, France; Art Stud League New York, with Bridgman & Miller.
Work in Public Collections: Kate Duncan Smith DAR Sch Grant, Ala; Hickory N C Mus; N J Mus, Paterson; Arnot Art Mus, Elmira, N Y; Art Stud League New York, N Y; plus one other.
Exhibitions: Pa Acad Fine Arts; Paterson Art League; Fair Lawn Art Asn; Composers, Authors, Artists of Am; Burr Artists; plus many one-man shows.
Positions: State pres N J Chap, Composers, Authors, Artists Am.
Awards: State show, Paterson, N J; award, Gotham Painters, first prize, Fair Lawn Art Asn Outdoor Show.
Memberships: Burr Artists (corresp secy, 70-); Gotham Painters (corresp secy, 65-); Am Fedn Art; Fair Lawn Art Asn; life mem Art Stud League New York.
Mailing Address: 15-26B Plaza Rd, Fair Lawn, NJ 07410.

SCHWABACHER, ALFRED
Collector
b Felheim, Ger, Dec 1, 79.
Collection: French impressionists.
Mailing Address: 91 Central Park W, New York, NY 10023.

SCHWABACHER, ETHEL K
Painter, Art Critic
Preferred Media: Acrylics.
b New York, N Y, May 20, 03.
Study & Training: With Max Weber, 28; in Europe, 28-33; with Arshile Gorky, 35-36.
Work in Public Collections: Whitney Mus Am Art, New York; Albright-Knox Gallery, Buffalo; Rockefeller Univ, New York; Syracuse Univ, N Y; Wichita State Univ, Kans.
Exhibitions: Whitney Mus Am Art Ann, 52-65; Mexico City Biennale, 60; Walker Art Ctr, 60; Carnegie Int, 61; Brooklyn Mus Watercolor Int, 61-62; plus several one-man shows, N Y.
Publications: Auth, Arshile Gorky, Whitney Mus Am Art & Macmillan, 57 & Arte Visivi, Rome, 62.
Mailing Address: 1192 Park Ave, New York, NY 10028.

SCHWACHA, GEORGE
Painter
b Newark, N J, Oct 2, 08.
Study & Training: With Arthur W Woelfle & John Grabach.
Work in Public Collections: Albany Inst Hist & Art; Mint Mus Art; Elisabet Ney Mus; Am Watercolor Soc; New Haven Paint & Clay Club; plus many others.
Exhibitions: Corcoran Gallery Art; Currier Gallery Art; Denver Art Mus; Elgin Acad Art; Delgado Mus Art; plus many others.
Awards: Awards, Meriden Arts & Crafts, 52 & Fla Southern Col, 52; gold medal, Audubon Artists, 61; plus others.

Publications: Margaret Harold (auth), Prize-winning paintings, Bk IV.
Mailing Address: 273 Glenwood Ave, Bloomfield, NJ 07003.

SCHWALBACH, MARY JO
Painter, Sculptor
Preferred Media: Mixed Media.
b Milwaukee, Wis, July 8, 39.
Study & Training: Pine Manor Jr Col, AA; Univ Wis, BS; New York Univ Inst Fine Arts; Sch Visual Arts; also in Paris & Rome.
Work in Public Collections: Univ Calif Mus, Berkeley; Jazz Mus, New York, N Y; Kellogg State Bank, Green Bay, Wis; Am City Bank, Menomonee Falls, Wis; Kimberly State Bank, Wis.
Commissions: Sculpture, 1st Fed Savings & Loan, Menomonee Falls, 69; three hockey sculptures, Philadelphia Flyers, The Spectrum, Philadelphia, Pa, 70; sculpture of Mario Andretti, Clipper Mag, New York, 72; sculpture, Computer TV Gulf & Western Bldg, New York, 72; Am Baseball Asn, 72.
Exhibitions: One-man shows, Rhoda Sande Gallery, New York, 69; West Bend Mus Fine Arts, Wis, 69 & Dannenberg, New York, 72; retrospective, Bergstrom Mus, Neenah, Wis, 70; Beyond Realism, Upstairs Gallery, East Hampton, N Y, 72.
Teaching: Asst instr printmaking, Mus Mod Art Sch, New York, 65.
Positions: Mem staff, Mus Mod Art, 62-67.
Bibliography: S Walton (auth), Mary Jo Schwalbach-sports artist, Sporting News, 71; article, In: Clipper Mag, 8/72; S Fischler (auth), Mary Jo Schwalbach-sports action, Sports Hockey, 72.
Publications: Illusr, Down Beat, 65-72 & Prestige Record Jackets, 66-69; illusr, art reproduced, In: New Yorker, 70.
Dealer: Bernard Dannenberg, 1020 Madison Ave, New York, NY 10021.
Mailing Address: 14 E 80th St, New York, NY 10021.

SCHWARCZ, JUNE THERESE
Craftsman
Preferred Media: Enamels.
b Denver, Colo, June 10, 18.
Study & Training: Univ Colo, 36-38; Univ Chicago, 38-39; Pratt Inst, 39-41; Inst Design, Chicago, Ill, with Moholy Nagy.
Work in Public Collections: Kunstgewerbermuseum, Zurich, Switz; Johnson Wax Collection; Minn Mus Art, St Paul, Oakland Art Mus, Calif.
Commissions: Enameled bowl with technique deomonstration bowls, Mus Contemp Crafts, 58; three piece panel, Cent Nat Bank, Enid, Okla, 62.
Exhibitions: New Talent U S A, Art in Am, 60; one-man show, Mus Contemp Crafts, 65; Objects U S A, Johnson Wax Collection & Exhib, 69; one-man shows, Mus Bellerive (Kunstgewerbermuseum), Zurich, Switz, 71 & Schmuckmuseum, Pforzheim, Ger, 72.
Awards: Purchase award, Ceramic Nat, Everson Mus, Syracuse, 60; First Calif Craftsmen's Biennial, Oakland Mus, 61; Goldsmith 70, ex-Minn Mus Art, 70.
Bibliography: Uchida (auth), June Schwarcz, 9/59 & Ventura (auth), June Schwarcz: electroforming, 11/65, Crafts Horizons; Nordress (auth), Objects: U S A, Viking Press, 70.
Memberships: Am Crafts Coun; Soc North Am Goldsmiths.
Publications: Contribr, Craftmen's world, 59 & Research in crafts, 61, Am Crafts Coun Publ; auth, The arts turn to plating, J Electroplaters Soc, 11/67.
Mailing Address: 18 Wray Ave, Sausalito, CA 94965.

SCHWARTZ, AUBREY E
Printmaker, Sculptor
b New York, N Y, Jan 13, 28.
Study & Training: Art Stud League New York; Brooklyn Mus Art Sch.
Work in Public Collections: Nat Gallery Art, Washington, D C; Brooklyn Mus Art; Philadelphia Mus Art; Libr Cong, Washington, D C; Art Inst Chicago.
Commissions: Ed lithographs, Predatory Birds, Gehenna Press, 58; Midget & Dwarf, Tamarind Workshop, 60 & Bestiary, Kanthos Press, 61; ed etchings, Mothers & Children, New York, 59 & Wildflowers, New York, 66.
Exhibitions: Young Am Whitney Mus Am Art, 57; Print Coun Am Show, 57; one-man show prints & drawings, Grippi Gallery, New York, 58; Art U S A, New York Coliseum, 59; Contemp Graphic Art, U S State Dept, 59.
Awards: Guggenheim Found fel creative printmaking, 58-60; Tamarind fel creative lithography, 60; first prize for graphic art, Boston Arts Festival, 60.
Bibliography: Carl Zigrosser (auth), catalogue, Print Coun Am, 59; Allan Fern (auth), catalogue, U S State Dept, 61; Harold Joachim (auth), A bestiary, Kanthos Press, 61.
Mailing Address: Harpur College, State University of New York at Binghamton, Binghamton, NY 13901.

SCHWARTZ, BARBARA J
Art Administrator
b Detroit, Mich, Dec 15, 47.
Study & Training: Univ Wis-Madison, BS.
Positions: Dir, Contemp Arts Gallery, New York Univ, N Y, 71-
Mailing Address: 77 Seventh Ave, New York, NY 10011.

SCHWARTZ, CARL E
Painter, Instructor
Preferred Media: Acrylics.
b Detroit, Mich, Sept 21, 35.
Study & Training: Art Inst Chicago, BFA; Univ Chicago, BFA.
Work in Public Collections: Art Inst Chicago; Libr Cong, Washington, D C; Ball State Univ, Muncie, Ind; Univ Minn; Va Beach Art Asn, Va.
Exhibitions: Ann Exhib Mich Artists, Detroit Art Inst, 55, 65 & 69; Butler Inst Am Art Nat, 63-65; Art Across Am, Columbus Gallery Fine Arts & 28 mus, 65-67; Am Painting Exhib, Smithsonian Inst, Washington D C & Tour, 72; 18th Nat Print Exhib, Brooklyn Mus, 72-73.
Teaching: Instr figure painting & drawing, N Shore Art League, 58-; instr figure painting & drawing, Suburban Fine Arts Ctr, 60-71.
Awards: Logan Medal & Award, Art Inst Chicago, 58; Commonwealth Prize, Detroit Art Inst, 65; best of show award, Va Beach Art Asn, 69.
Bibliography: Allan Davidson (auth), article, In: Art League News, 67; Thomas Carbol (auth), The printmaker in Illinois, Ill Art Educ Asn, 72.
Memberships: Arts Club Am; Artists Guild Chicago; Contemp Art Mus Chicago; N Shore Art League; Art Inst Chicago.
Publications: Illusr, Playboy, 65 & 67; auth, article, In: N Shore Art League News, 69.
Mailing Address: 4228 N Hazel, Chicago, IL 60613.

SCHWARTZ, EUGENE M
Collector, Patron
b Butte, Mont, Mar 18, 27.
Study & Training: New Sch Social Res; New York Univ; Columbia Univ; Univ Wash.
Positions: Acquisitions Comt, Whitney Mus Am Art, 67-68, 68-69.
Collection: Contemporary American art since World War II, chiefly of the sixties: parts of the collection shown as a group at Jewish Museum, Everson Museum of Art and the Albany Institute of History and Art.
Mailing Address: 1160 Park Ave, New York, NY 10028

SCHWARTZ, HENRY
Painter, Instructor
Preferred Media: Oils.
b Winthrop, Mass, Oct 27, 27.
Study & Training: Sch Mus Fine Arts, Boston, Mass, traveling fel & dipl, 53; Akad Bildendekunst, Salzburg, Austria, dipl, with Oskar Kokoschka.
Work in Public Collections: Mus Fine Arts, Boston; Wheaton Col, Mass.
Exhibitions: Boston Arts Festivals, 54-58; five one-man shows, Boris Mirski Gallery, 56-68; Carnegie Int, 61.
Teaching: Instr painting, Sch Mus Fine Arts, 56-
Publications: Illusr, filmstrip, United Churches of Christ, 61; illusr, Boston Mag, 64-65.
Dealer: Boris Mirski Gallery, 166 Newbury St, Boston, MA 02116.
Mailing Address: 8 Garrison St, Boston, MA 02116.

SCHWARTZ, MARVIN D
Art Historian
b New York, N Y, Feb 15, 26.
Study & Training: City Col New York, BS, 46; Inst Fine Arts, New York Univ, 47-51; Univ Del, MA, 54.
Teaching: Lectr, City Col New York, 48-51, 56-64; State Univ N Y Col Purchase, 69-
Positions: Jr cur, Detroit Inst Arts, 51-52; cur decorative arts & indust design lab, Brooklyn Mus, 54-68, ed publ, 59-60; ed, New York News & Views, Apollo Mag, 57-60; adv to Fine Arts Comt of the White House & dept design, Sears, Roebuck & Co, 64-; lectr & consult, Metrop Mus Art, 68-; trustee, Jerome Levy Found.
Awards: Recipient stipend, Belg-Am Educ Found.
Memberships: Soc Archit Historians; Col Art Asn Am; fel H F DuPont Winterthur Mus.
Publications: Auth, weekly antiques column, New York Times, 66-; auth, Collectors guide to antique American ceramics; auth, Collectors guide to antique American glass; co-auth, New York Times book of antiques, 72; auth, articles on Am furniture, Am ceramics, calligraphy & enamels.
Mailing Address: Office of Public Information, Metropolitan Museum of Art, Fifth Ave at 82nd St, New York, NY 10028.

SCHWARTZ, THERESE
Painter, Writer
b New York, N Y.
Study & Training: Corcoran Sch Art, Washington, D C; Am Univ; Brooklyn Mus Art Sch, N Y.
Work in Public Collections: Corcoran Gallery Art; Howard Univ; Fred C Olsen Found; Monroe Geller Found; Barnet Aden Collection.
Commissions: Traveling Watercolor Show, Howard Univ under Cong grant, Southern univs & mus, 53-54.
Exhibitions: Phillips Mem Gallery, 54; Mus Art Mod, Paris, 56; Univ N C, 69; Stanford Mus, Conn, 72; Suffolk Co Mus, 72; plus others.
Teaching: Instr painting, plastic & sculpture, Great Neck Adult Prog, 67-70.
Positions: Ed, New York Element, 68-
Awards: Second prize for oils, Corcoran Gallery Art Regional Show, 52; New Talent U S A Award, Art Am, 62.
Bibliography: S Zimmerman (auth), The unencumbered icon, 9/66 & G Brown (auth), Reviews, 9/69, Arts Mag; P Scheldjahl, New York, Art Int, 10/69.
Memberships: Women In Arts.
Publications: Auth, var articles, New York Element, 68-72; auth, Plastic sculpture and collage, Hearthside, 69; auth, The political scene, column in Arts Mag, 70-71; auth, The politicalization of the avant-garde (ser), Art in Am, 11/71, 3/72 & 3/73.
Dealer: A M Sachs Gallery, 29 W 57th St, New York, NY 10019.
Mailing Address: 161 W 75th St, Apt 9A, New York, NY 10023.

SCHWARTZ, WILLIAM SAMUEL
Painter
b Smorgon, Russia, Feb 23, 96; U S citizen.
Study & Training: Vilna Art Sch, Russia, scholar, 08-12; Art Inst Chicago; Auditorium Conserv Music, Chicago, with Karl Stein, 15-18; also with Francesco Daddi, 18-19.
Work in Public Collections: Art Inst Chicago; Detroit Inst Arts; Libr Cong; Dept Labor, Washington, D C; Dallas Mus Fine Arts; plus many others.
Exhibitions: Many nat & int exhibs, 18-
Awards: Corpus Christi Art Found Award, 45; Mr & Mrs Jules F Brower Prize, 45 & Munic Art League Prize, 52, Art Inst Chicago; plus many others.
Mailing Address: 880 N Lake Shore Dr, Apt 18B, Chicago, IL 60611.

SCHWARZ, FELIX CONRAD
Painter, Educator
Preferred Media: Oils.
b New York, N Y, Apr 13, 06.
Study & Training: Corcoran Sch Art; George Washington Univ; Columbia Univ; also study in Eng, France, Belg, Italy, Holland & Switz.
Work in Public Collections: George Washington Univ.
Commissions: Many portraits for pvt comns.
Exhibitions: One-man shows, Wis State Univ, 65, Birmingham Mus Art, 68, Montgomery Mus Fine Arts, 68, Spring Hill Col, Mobile, 69 & Thor Gallery, Louisville, Ky, 69; plus many others.
Teaching: Prof fine arts at the State Univs of Va, N C, Minn & Wis over a period of 40 yrs.
Positions: Former ed, Advanced Sch Digest.
Bibliography: Rev articles, In: La Rev Mod, Art News, New York Times, New York Herald Tribune & others.
Mailing Address: 1500 North Dakota Ave N E, Saint Petersburg, FL 33703.

SCHWARZ, HEINRICH
Museum Curator, Educator
b Prague, Czech, Nov 9, 94.
Study & Training: Univ Vienna, PhD; Wesleyan Univ, MA.
Teaching: Vis lectr, Wellesley Col, 52; vis lectr, Mt Holyoke Col, 54; vis prof, Wesleyan Univ, 54-56, prof hist art, 56-62; vis lectr, Yale Univ, 58; vis prof, Columbia Univ, 66-67, 67-68.
Positions: Asst, Albertina Mus, Vienna, 21-23; cur, Austrian State Gallery, Vienna, 23-38; res asst, Albright-Knox Art Gallery, 41-42; cur paintings, drawings & prints, Mus Art, R I Sch Design, 43-53; cur collections, Davison Art Ctr, Wesleyan Univ, 54-72.
Awards: Austrian Cross of Honor for Sci & Art, First Class, 64.
Memberships: Col Art Asn Am; Am Fedn Arts; Drawing Soc (nat comt); Print Coun Am (bd dirs); Master Drawings (ed adv bd).
Publications: Auth, Amicis (yearbk of Austrian State Gallery), 27; co-auth, D O Hill, Master of photography, 31; auth, Carl Schindler (monogr), 31; auth, Salzburg und das Salzkammergut, 36 & 58; plus others; contribr, scientific articles to Europ & Am mag.
Mailing Address: Davison Art Center, Wesleyan University, Middletown, CT 06457.

SCHWARZ, MYRTLE COOPER
Painter, Educator
Preferred Media: Stained Glass, Ceramics.
b Breckenridge Co, Ky, Dec 10, 00.
Study & Training: Western Ky State Univ, AB; Col William & Mary, MA; Columbia Univ, MA & EdD.
Teaching: Exten Serv, Univ Ky; prof educ, Col William & Mary; prin high sch & supt schs, Va & Ky; prof art educ & dir, Community Ctr, Phillips Univ; prof educ & dir art educ, Okla State Univ; vis prof, Monticello Col; prof English, Wis State Univ; prof art, Livingston Univ.
Positions: Chmn math & pres art sect, Va Educ Asn; mem comt, Seven Coop Univs Teacher Training; chmn Lang Arts Develop, Va State Curriculum; mem comt, Prof Standards & Develop, Nat Educ Asn; dir, Community Art Ctr, Enid, Okla.
Memberships: Enid Artists League; Univ Women's Serv Club; Nat Art Educ Asn (chmn Div Higher Educ & Teacher Training).
Publications: Auth, articles, In: Va J Educ, In Ky & Okla J Educ.
Mailing Address: 1500 N Dakota Ave N E, St Petersburg, FL 33703.

SCHWEITZER, GERTRUDE
Painter, Sculptor
b New York, N Y.
Study & Training: Pratt Inst; Nat Acad Design, New York; Acad Julian, Paris.
Work in Public Collections: Metrop Mus Art, New York; Art Inst Chicago; Toledo Mus Art, Ohio; Brooklyn Mus, N Y; Whitney Mus Am Art, New York, N Y; plus many others.
Exhibitions: One-man exhibs, Norton Gallery Art, West Palm Beach, Fla, 47 & 66, Galerie Charpentier, Paris, 48, 54 & 61, Hanover Gallery, London, 53, Philadelphia Art Alliance, Pa, 69 & Hokin Gallery, Palm Beach, Fla, 71; plus many others.
Positions: Chmn arts & skill corps, Am Red Cross, 42-45.
Awards: Am Watercolor Soc Medal, 34; Soc Four Arts Awards, watercolor, 48 & 59 & oils, 50 & 51; first prize as best woman painter N J State Exhib, Montclair Art Mus, 52; plus many others.
Bibliography: René Barotte (auth), G Schweitzer, peintures et dessins, Ed Chene, Paris, 65.
Memberships: Nat Acad Design; Audubon Artists; Am Artists Prof League; Am Watercolor Soc.
Mailing Address: Box 287, Palm Beach, FL 33480.

SCHWEITZER, M R
Art Dealer, Collector
b Sept 7, 11.
Positions: Owner, M R Schweitzer Galleries.
Memberships: Charter mem, Am Soc Appraisers.
Research: American painting by little-known masters, 1830-1930.
Specialty of Gallery: American painting, 1830-1930; European painting, sixteenth to nineteenth centuries.
Collection: American and English nineteenth century; Spanish and Italian seventeenth century.
Mailing Address: 958 Madison Ave, New York, NY 10021.

SCHWIEGER, CHRISTOPHER ROBERT
Printmaker, Educator
Preferred Media: Graphics.
b Scottsbluff, Nebr, Dec 5, 36.
Study & Training: Nebr West Col, AA; Chadron State Col, BFA; Univ North Colo, MA; Univ Denver.
Work in Public Collections: Ohio State Univ, Columbus; Univ North Colo; West N Mex Univ, Silver City; S Dak Mem Art Ctr, Brookings; Miss Art Asn Galleries, Jackson.
Commissions: Gilded gold & mixed media on glass mural, Univ North Colo Stud Ctr, Greeley, 66.
Exhibitions: Manisphere 99 and 100 Int Exhibs, Winnipeg, Can, 70 & 71; 12th & 14th Print & Drawing Nat, Okla Art Ctr, 70 & 72; 42nd Int Northwest Printmakers Exhib, Seattle Art Mus, Wash, 71; 12th Midwest Biennial, Joslyn Art Mus, Omaha, Nebr, 72; one-man show, Ohio State Univ, 72.
Teaching: Chmn div fine & appl arts, Minot State Col, 67-
Awards: Miss Art Asn Purchase Awards, 69-71; West N Mex Univ Purchase Awards, 71; jury commendation, Northwest Printmakers, Seattle Art Mus, 71.
Memberships: Nat Art Educ Asn; Manisphere Group Artists.
Publications: Contribr, Col Educ Rec, 6/69.
Mailing Address: 401 Hillcrest Dr, Minot, ND 58701.

SCOTT, DAVID WINFIELD
Art Administrator
b Fall River, Mass, July 10, 16.
Study & Training: Art Stud League New York; Harvard Col, AB; Claremont Grad Sch, MA & MFA; Univ Calif, Berkeley, PhD.
Positions: From lectr art to prof, Scripps Col, 46-63; dir, Nat Collection Fine Arts, Washington, D C, 64-69; consult, Nat Gallery Art, Washington, D C, 69-
Mailing Address: 3016 Cortland Pl N W, Washington, DC 20008.

SCOTT, HENRY (EDWARDS), JR
Painter, Educator
Preferred Media: Watercolors, Oils.
b Cambridge, Mass, Aug 22, 00.
Study & Training: Harvard Univ, Sachs fel, 25, Bacon art scholar, 26-28, BA & MA; Art Stud League New York; also with Edward Forbes in Italy & George Bridgman in New York.
Work in Public Collections: Fogg Art Mus, Cambridge; Univ Kans Med Ctr; Univ Kans Law Sch; Amherst Col; Regency House, Kansas City.
Commissions: Originated & directed stage production of Giotto's Frescoes of the Nativity, Pittsburgh, Pa, 32-33, Amherst Col, periodically since 35; stage designs for Amherst Masquers, 35-36 & Univ Kans City Playhouse, 49-50.
Exhibitions: Amherst Col, 41; Springfield, Mass, 42; Boston & Cambridge, Mass, 47; four shows, Martha's Vineyard, 47-63; Kansas City, Mo, 50-69; plus others.
Collections Arranged: Eight exhibs yearly, Univ Kans, Kansas City, 48-65.
Teaching: Lectr & asst head tutor, Div Fine Arts, Harvard Univ & Radcliffe Col, 23-26; Instr art, Univ Rochester, 28-29; asst prof art, Univ Pittsburgh, 29-34; assoc prof art, Amherst Col, 35-43; assoc prof art, Univ Mo-Kansas City, 47-59, chmn art dept, 47-64, prof, 59-70, prof emer, 70-
Positions: Asst to dir, Mem Art Gallery, Univ Rochester, 28-29; cur art, Amherst Col, 38-43; mem, Munic Art Comn, Kansas City, Mo, 54-69.
Awards: Prize, Rochester Art Asn, 28.
Memberships: Col Art Asn Am; Am Asn Univ Prof.
Publications: Auth, Historical outline of the fine arts, 36.
Mailing Address: South Rd, Chilmark Post Office, West Tisbury, MA 02575.

SCOTT, JONATHAN
Painter
Preferred Media: Oils, Watercolors.
b Bath, Eng, Oct 30, 14.
Study & Training: Heatherly Sch, London; Mauritz Heymann Sch, Munich; The Accad, Florence.
Work in Public Collections: Pasadena Art Mus, Calif; Santa Fe, N Mex; Lindsay Art Asn, Calif; San Marino High Sch, Calif; G G de Silva Collection, Los Angeles.
Commissions: Paintings, USN Art Prog, 63-64; also portrait comns.
Exhibitions: New English Art Club, London, 38; Butler Mus, Youngstown, Ohio, 54; Los Angeles Mus; Frye Mus, Seattle; McNay Mus, San Antonio, Tex, 62.
Teaching: Instr drawing & painting, Univ Southern Calif, 46; instr drawing & painting, Pasadena Art Mus, 47-48; instr drawing & painting, Riverside Art Asn, 62-63.
Awards: Awards, Pasadena Soc Artists, 42-61, Calif Watercolor Soc, 55 & Laguna Beach Art Asn, 61.
Memberships: Calif Nat Watercolor Soc (pres, 60); Taos Art Asn (art comt & mem bd, 72).
Dealer: Gallery A, Taos, NM 87571.
Mailing Address: P O Box 1154, Taos, NM 87571.

SCOTT, MARIAN (DALE)
Painter
Preferred Media: Acrylics.
b Montreal, P Q, June 26, 06.
Study & Training: Montreal Art Asn, 17-20, scholar; Monument Nat, 18-20, with Dionnet; Ecole Beaux Arts, Montreal, 23-25; Slade Sch, London, Eng.
Work in Public Collections: Nat Gallery Can, Ottawa; Montreal Mus Fine Arts; Mus Quebec; Dept External Affairs, Ottawa; Mus Art Contemporain, Montreal.
Commissions: Oils, Endocrinology, Dr Hans Selye, McGill Univ, 43 & Tree of Life, Mrs Paul Sise, Montreal Gen Hosp Chapel, 58.
Exhibitions: New York World's Fair, 39; Panorama, Peinture du Quebec, Mus Art Contemporain, 40-66; Biennale, Sao Paulo, Brazil, 51-53; 50 Yrs Can Painting, Nat Gallery Can; Expos Createurs Quebec, 71.
Teaching: Instr painting, St George's Sch, Montreal, 37-39; instr painting, Montreal Mus Fine Arts, 42-45.
Awards: First prize for painting, Can Group Painters, 66; purchase award, Thomas More Inst, Montreal, 67; Baxter Purchase Award, Ont Soc Artists.
Memberships: Soc Artistes Prof Quebec; Can Artists Representation, assoc Royal Can Acad Arts.
Mailing Address: 451 Clarke Ave, Montreal 217, P Q, Can.

SCRIVER, ROBERT MACFIE (BOB)
Sculptor
Preferred Media: Clay, Bronze.
b Browning, Mont, Aug 15, 14.
Work in Public Collections: Glenbow Found, Calgary, Alta; Whitney Gallery Western Art, Cody, Wyo; Mont Hist Soc, Helena; Cowboy

Hall Fame, Oklahoma City, Okla; Panhandle Plains Mus, Canyon, Tex.

Commissions: Over life size statue of bison, Great Falls H S, Mont, 67; Bill Linderman (heroic statue), Rodeo Cowboy Asn for Cowboy Hall of Fame, Oklahoma City, 68; Rustler (statue), C M Russel H S, Great Falls, 68.

Exhibitions: Soc Animal Artists, New York, N Y, 61; Audubon Artists, New York, 64; Nat Acad Design, New York, 64; Acad Artists, Springfield, Mass, 64; Int Art Guild, D'Palais de la Scala, Monte Carlo, Monaco, 67; plus many one-man shows.

Awards: Gold medals, 69, 70 & 71 & silver medal, 72, Cowboy Hall of Fame.

Bibliography: Article, In: Am Artist Mag, 63; article, In: La Rev Mod, 64; article, In: Mont Hist Soc.

Memberships: Salmagundi Club; Nat Sculpture Soc; Cowboy Artists Am.

Mailing Address: Box 172, Browning, MT 59417.

SCRUGGS-SPENCER, MARY, see SPENCER

SCULL, ROBERT C
Collector
U S citizen.
Mailing Address: 1010 Fifth Ave, New York, NY 10028.

SCULLY, VINCENT
Art Historian, Educator
b New Haven, Conn, Aug 21, 20.
Study & Training: Yale Univ, BA, 40, MA, 47, PhD, 49.
Teaching: Asst, Yale Univ, 47-48, instr, 49-52, Morse fel, 51, asst prof, 52-56, assoc prof, 56-61, prof, 61-66, Col John Trumbull prof hist art, 66-
Awards: Fulbright grant to Italy, 51-52; Billings Mem fel, Greece, 55; Howard Found fel, Sicily, 56 & Bollingen fel to Greece & Turkey, 57-58.
Memberships: Col Art Asn Am; Soc Archit Historians; Am Inst Archeol; Conn Acad Arts & Sci.
Publications: Auth, Modern architecture, In: Great ages of world architecture series, Braziller, 61; auth, The earth, the temple and the gods, Yale Univ Press 62 & Praeger, 69; Louis I Kahn, In: Makers of contemporary architecture series, Braziller, 62; auth, American architecture and urbanism, Praeger, 69; auth, Pueblo architecture of the Southwest: a photographic essay, In: Amon Carter Museum of Western Art series, Univ Tex Press, 71; plus others.
Mailing Address: 389 St Ronan St, New Haven, CT 06511.

SCURIS, STEPHANIE
Sculptor, Educator
b Lacedaemonos, Greece, Jan 20, 31.
Study & Training: Sch Art & Archit, Yale Univ, BFA & MFA, with Josef Albers.
Work in Public Collections: Jewish Community Ctr, Baltimore, Md, West View Ctr, Baltimore.
Commissions: Sculpture, Bankers Trust Co, New York, N Y; lobby sculpture, Cinema I & II, New York.
Exhibitions: New Haven Art Festival, 58-59; Art: U S A, traveling exhib, 58 & 60; Mus Mod Art, New York, 62; Whitney Mus Am Art, New York, 64; plus others.
Teaching: Instr sculpture, Md Inst Art, 61-
Awards: Winterwitz Award, prize for outstanding work & alumni award, Yale Univ; Peabody Award, 61-62; Rinehart fel, 61-64.
Mailing Address: Maryland Institute of Art, 116 W Lanvale St, Baltimore, MD 21217.

SEABOURN, BERT DAIL
Painter, Illustrator
Preferred Media: Oils, Watercolors.
b Iraan, Tex, July 9, 31.
Study & Training: Oklahoma City Univ, cert in art; Famous Artists Schs, Westport, Conn, cert in art; Okla Cent State Univ.
Work in Public Collections: Okla Art Ctr, Oklahoma City; Five Civilized Tribes Mus, Muskogee, Okla; Heard Mus, Phoenix, Ariz; Indian Arts & Crafts Bd, Washington, D C; Pac Northwest Indian Ctr, Gonzaga Univ, Spokane, Wash.
Exhibitions: Kans Printmakers Nat, Wichita, 61; Contemp Am Art Ann, Oklahoma City, 64; Int Petrol Art Exhib, Tulsa, Okla, 66; Ctr Arts of Indian Am, Washington, D C, 68; Eight State Painting & Sculpture Ann, Oklahoma City, 71.
Positions: Artist & Journalist, USN, 51-55; art dir & artist, Okla Gas & Elec Co, Oklahoma City, 55-
Awards: Purchase award, Okla Art Ctr, 69; first pl, Heard Mus, 69; second pl, Five Civilized Tribes Mus, 71.
Memberships: Artists of Okla, Inc (pres, 69); Art Dirs Club Oklahoma City (pres, 70); Okla Art Guild (pres, 70); Okla Mus Art; Okla City Advert Club.
Publications: Auth & illusr, Indian Gallery, 72.
Mailing Address: 3123 S W 63rd St, Oklahoma City, OK 73159.

SEAMAN, DRAKE F
Painter
Preferred Media: Oils.
b U S citizen.
Study & Training: Kachina Art Sch, 59-63, with Jay Datus; also murals with Ray Strong, 70.
Commissions: Landscape mural, Seventh Day Adventist Church, Santa Barbara, Calif.
Exhibitions: Palace Arts & Sci, San Francisco, Calif, 70; Santa Barbara Mus Art, 70; O'Brien's Art Emporium, Scottsdale, Ariz, 70-71; Troys Cowboy Art Gallery, Scottsdale, 71-72; Jamison Gallery, Tucson, Ariz, 72; plus others.
Teaching: Instr landscape, Brooks Fine Arts Ctr, Santa Barbara, 69-70.
Bibliography: Bob Austin (auth), Reflections on oil, Austin Gallery, 70.
Dealer: Dan May, P O Box 874, Tempe, AZ 85281.
Mailing Address: Williams, AZ 86046.

SEARLES, CHARLES ROBERT
Painter
Preferred Media: Acrylics, Watercolors.
b Philadelphia, Pa, July 11, 37.
Study & Training: Fleisher Art Mem, Philadelphia; Pa Acad Fine Arts, Philadelphia.
Commissions: Mural, Ile, Ife Afro-Am Mus, Philadelphia, 73.
Exhibitions: Afro American Artist 1900-1969, Philadelphia Civic Ctr, 69; New Black Artist, Brooklyn Mus, New York, N Y, 69; Contemporary Black Artist in America, Whitney Mus Am Art, New York, 71; All Phases Due II, Studio Mus, New York, 71; one-man show, Bryn Mawr Col, Philadelphia, 72; plus many others.
Teaching: Lectr drawing, Philadelphia Mus Art, summer 70; art instr, Model Cities Cult Arts, 70-
Positions: Bd mem, Philadelphia Northern Arts Coun, 71-; mem exhib comt, Peale Galleries, Pa Acad Fine Arts, 72.
Awards: Drake Press Award, 70, Cresson traveling scholar, 71 & Ware traveling awards, 73, Pa Acad Fine Arts; Quaker Storage Co Prize, 73.
Mailing Address: 4834 Cedar Ave, Philadelphia, PA 19143.

SEARLES, STEPHEN
Sculptor, Instructor
Preferred Media: Bronze, Stone.
b Leonia, N J.
Study & Training: Art Stud League New York, with George Bridgman, Frank V DuMond & Reginald Marsh; Grand Cent Sch Art, New York, N Y, with Georg Lober; also with Gelin, Fontainebleau, France.
Commissions: Our Lady of Good Voyage statue, Church of Our Lady of Good Voyage, Gloucester, Mass; Thar She Blows whaler & other sculptures made of Gloucester fishermen; sculpture for African Hall, Am Mus Natural Hist, New York; plus many portrait busts in bronze of well-known people.
Exhibitions: Sculpture Exhibs, Grassy Gallery, Biarritz, France, 46; Palace of Fontainebleau, France, 49; Guild of Boston Artists, Mass, 72 & E Rockport Art Asn, Mass, 72.
Teaching: Instr drawing & sculpture, Biarritz Am Univ, 45-46; instr life drawing & sculpture, Newark Sch Fine & Indust Art, 50-53; instr life drawing, Vesper George Sch Art, Boston, 62
Awards: Best sculpture awards, Salmagundi Club, New York, 52, Soc Acad Artists, Springfield Mus Art, Mass, 65 & 69 & Rockport Art Asn, 68.
Memberships: Nat Sculpture Soc; Am Artists Prof League; Rockport Art Asn; Am Vet Soc Artists.
Dealer: Guild of Boston Artists, 162 Newbury St, Boston, MA 02116.
Mailing Address: 30 Ipswich St, Boston, MA 02215.

SECKEL, PAUL BERNHARD
Painter, Graphic Artist
Preferred Media: Acrylics, Oils.
b Osnabrueck, Ger, July 18, 18; U S citizen.
Study & Training: London Cent Sch Arts & Crafts; Univ Buffalo, BFA & Yale Univ, MFA.
Exhibitions: Recent Drawings, U S A, Mus Mod Art, New York, N Y, 56; Drawings by Invitation, Flint Inst Art, 57; Exhib of Paintings Eligible for Purchase, Am Acad Arts & Lett, 63; plus various Audubon Artists Ann.
Awards: Emily Lowe Award, 63.
Memberships: Westchester Art Asn.
Publications: Auth, How to make original color lithographs—a manual for professional artists, 70.
Dealer: Alessandro Oliva, 818 Madison Ave, New York, NY 10021.
Mailing Address: 12 Van Etten Blvd, New Rochelle, NY 10804.

SECKLER, DOROTHY GEES
Art Critic, Lecturer
b Baltimore, Md, July 9, 10.
Study & Training: Teachers Col, Columbia Univ, BS(art educ); Md

Inst Art, traveling scholar, 31; New York Univ; also in Europe.
Work in Public Collections: Mus Mod Art, New York, N Y.
Teaching: Lect, Modern Art; lectr, Mus Mod Art, 45-49; part-time instr, New York Univ, 47-52; lectr & instr, City Col New York, 57-60; lectr & instr, Pratt Inst, 60-61.
Positions: Assoc ed, Art News & Art News Ann, 50-55; gallery ed, Art in Am, 55-61; spec contribr fine arts, MD (Med News Mag), 57-61.
Awards: Am Fedn Arts Award for art criticism, 54.
Publications: Co-auth, The questioning public, Mus Mod Art Bull, 49; co-auth, Mod art sect, In: Famous artist's course, 53; co-auth, figure drawing comes to life, 57; contribr, Encycl world art, 59; contribr, numerous articles, Art News; also reviews on exhibs & monographs.
Mailing Address: 64 Sagamore Rd, Bronxville, NY 10708.

SECUNDA, (HOLLAND) ARTHUR
Painter, Sculptor
b Jersey City, N J, Nov 12, 27.
Study & Training: New York Univ; Art Stud League New York; Acad Grande Chaumiere; Acad Julian; with Zadkine & L'hote, Paris, France, 48-50; Inst Meschini, Rome; also study in Mex.
Work in Public Collections: Smithsonian Inst, Washington, D C; Nat Collection Fine Arts, Washington, D C; Mus Mod Art, New York, N Y; Art Inst Chicago, Ill; Brooklyn Mus, N Y; plus many others in U S A, Sweden, Belg & Switz.
Exhibitions: One-man shows, La Jolla Art Mus, Calif, 66, Galerie Richard Foncke, Gent, Belg, 68, Fleischer-Anhalt Gallery, Los Angeles, Calif, 68, Konstsalongen Kavaletten, Uppsala, Sweden, 71, Galerie Leger, Malmo, Sweden plus many others.
Awards: Tamarind fel, Calif, 70 & N Mex, 72.
Dealer: Malvina Miller Gallery, 3489 Sacramento St, San Francisco, CA 94118.
Mailing Address: 463 West St, New York, NY 10014.

SEDERS, FRANCINE LAVINAL
Art Dealer
b Paris, France, Dec 12, 32; U S citizen.
Study & Training: Univ Paris Law Sch, MLaws; Univ Wash, MCS.
Positions: Mgr, Otto Seligman Gallery, Seattle, Wash, 65-66, mgr-owner, 66-70; mgr-owner, Francine Seders Gallery, Seattle, 70-
Specialty of Gallery: Contemporary paintings, sculpture and graphics.
Mailing Address: 6701 Greenwood Ave N, Seattle, WA 98103.

SEERY, JOHN
Painter
Work in Public Collections: Art Inst Chicago, Ill; Whitney Mus Am Art, New York, N Y; Boston Mus Fine Arts, Mass; Cincinnati Mus Contemp Art, Ohio; R I Sch Design Mus.
Exhibitions: Andre Emmerich Gallery, 70 & 72; Spoleto Art Festival, Italy; 2 Generations of Lola Field Painting, Univ Pa; 10 Americans, Australia; one-man shows, New York & Chicago.
Bibliography: Sdzeleahl (auth), From creative plumbing to lyrical abstraction, New York Times, 70; Marandel (auth), La nouvelle peinture abstraction Americaine, Opus (Fr), 71; Ratcliff (auth), Painterly vs painted, Art News J, 72.
Mailing Address: c/o Andre Emmerich Gallery, 41 E 57th St, New York, NY 10022.

SEFF, MR & MRS MANUEL
Collectors
Mailing Address: 120 East End Ave, New York, NY 10028.

SEGAL, GEORGE
Sculptor
b New York, N Y, Nov 26, 24.
Study & Training: New York Univ, BS (art educ), 50, Rutgers Univ, MFA, 63.
Work in Public Collections: Mus Mod Art, New York; Mus Mod Art, Stockholm, Sweden; Art Gallery Ont, Toronto; Nat Gallery Can, Ottawa, Ont; Art Inst Chicago, Ill; plus others.
Exhibitions: Mus Contemp Art, Chicago, 68; Vancouver Art Gallery, B C, 69; Haywood Gallery, London, 69; Galerie Speyer, Paris, France, 69; Whitney Mus Am Art, New York, 72; plus many other group & one-man shows.
Teaching: N J High Schs, 57-63.
Awards: Walter K Gutman Found Award, 62; first prize, Art Inst Chicago, 66.
Bibliography: Gregory Battcock (ed), Minimal art: a critical anthology, Dutton, 68; Wayne Craven (auth), Sculpture in America, Thomas Y Crowell, 68; Christopher Finch (auth), Pop art: object and image, Dutton, 68; plus others.
Dealer: Sidney Janis Gallery, 6 W 57th St, New York, NY 10019.
Mailing Address: R F D 4, Box 323, North Brunswick, NJ 08902.

SEGY, LADISLAS
Art Dealer, Collector
b Budapest, Hungary, Feb 10, 04; U S citizen.
Study & Training: Cent State Univ, hon DLitt, 53.
Collections Arranged: Circulating Exhib African Sculpture, throughout U S, 49-
Teaching: Lectr, African Sculpture & Its Background & African Sculpture & Mod Art, throughout U S.
Positions: Dir & owner, Segy Gallery.
Research: African art.
Specialty of Gallery: African sculpture.
Collection: African art; French and American modern painting and sculpture; Peruvian textiles; Mexican Mascala sculptures; prehistoric axes.
Publications: Auth, Geometric art and aspects of reality, fall 57 & The phenomenological approach to the perception of artworks, summer 65, Cent Rev Arts & Sci; auth, The Ashanti Akua'Ba statues as archetype, and the Egyptian Ankh, Anthropos, 63; auth, The Yoruba Ibeji statue, Acta Tropica, Vol 27, No 2; auth, The Mossi doll, an archetypal fertility figure, Tribus, 73; plus many others.
Mailing Address: 50 W 57th St, New York, NY 10019.

SEIBERLING, DOROTHY BUCKLER LETHBRIDGE
Writer
b Akron, Ohio, Mar 7, 22.
Study & Training: Vassar Col, AB, 43.
Positions: Mem staff, Life Mag, 43-49, co-ed art dept, 50-54, art ed, 54-, sr ed, 65-
Awards: Penney-Missouri Mag Award for Life Mag ser on The woman problem, 72.
Mailing Address: Life Magazine, Rockefeller Center, New York, NY 10020.

SEIDE, CHARLES
Painter, Educator
Preferred Media: Oils, Acrylics.
b Brooklyn, N Y, May 14, 15.
Study & Training: Nat Acad Design, 32-37, with Leon Kroll.
Work in Public Collections: Fogg Mus Art, Cambridge, Mass.
Exhibitions: Paintings of Yr, Pepsi-Cola Co, 46 & 48; Nat Acad Design, 51 & 57; Pa Acad Fine Arts, 52; Art U S A, 58.
Teaching: Instr painting & mat tech, Brooklyn Mus Art Sch, 46-62; assoc prof art, Cooper Union, 50-, dir, Eve Sch, 66-68, head dept art, 68-70, head dept painting, 70-71; instr painting, Silvermine Col Art, 66-67.
Positions: Nat dir, Artists Equity Asn, 53-54; v pres, Brooklyn Soc Artists, 53-55.
Awards: Prize for painting, 46 & Regional fel, 48, Pepsi-Cola Co; graphics prize, Brooklyn Soc Artists, 57.
Bibliography: Dorothy Seckler (auth), Changing means to new ends, Art News, 52; Vincent Longo (auth), Studio talk, Arts Mag, 5/56.
Memberships: Am Asn Univ Prof.
Publications: Contribr, Encaustic, materials and methods, 49; contribr, Diameter, 51; illusr, Brooklyn Heights Press, 53.
Mailing Address: 1 Washington Sq Village, New York, NY 10012.

SEIDENBERG, (JACOB) JEAN
Sculptor, Educator
Preferred Media: Bronze, Lead, Mixed Media, Wood.
b New York, N Y, Feb 14, 30.
Study & Training: Brooklyn Mus Sch; Mus Mod Art Sch; Syracuse Univ.
Work in Public Collections: Ark Art Ctr, Little Rock; Ball State Univ Art Gallery, Muncie, Ind.
Commissions: Welded steel figure, Oil & Gas Bldg, New Orleans, La, 60; bronzes, Children on Glide, Simon-Diaz Pediat Clin, New Orleans, 62, five life-size figures, Corpus, St Joseph, Mary, St Rita & Sacred Heart, Stations, St Rita Cascia Church, Harahan, La, 64 & St Richard, St Richard's Cath Church, Jackson, Miss, 66; La-Gettysburg design, La Gettysburg Monument Comn, 68.
Exhibitions: Exhib of Nine, La State Univ Centennial Yr, Baton Rouge, 59; Photogr Choice, Univ Ind, Bloomington, 59; Recent Painting U S A, The Figure, Mus Mod Art, New York, 62; Art in Embassies Prog, U S Dept State, 66; Volkfest 68, West Berlin, Ger, 68; plus one-man exhibs, La, Ark, Vt & New York.
Teaching: Instr photog, Tulane Univ La, 57-65; asst prof sculpture, Fla State Univ, 72-
Awards: Awards, New Orleans Art Asn Ann, Delgado Mus, 51, 53 & 58 & La State Art Comn Ann, 51 & 54; Louis Comfort Tiffany Found fel painting, 60.
Memberships: Col Art Asn Am.
Dealer: Bienville Gallery, 539 Bienville St, New Orleans, LA 70130.
Mailing Address: Dept of Art, Florida State University, Tallahassee, FL 32306.

SEIDLER, DORIS
Painter, Printmaker
b London, Eng.
Study & Training: Atelier 17, New York, N Y, with Stanley William Hayter.
Work in Public Collections: Libr Cong, Washington, D C; Smithsonian Inst, Washington, D C; Philadelphia Mus Art; Brooklyn Mus; Seattle Mus Art.
Exhibitions: Brooklyn Mus Bi-Ann; Vancouver Int Print Exhib; First Hawaii Nat Print Exhib, Honolulu Acad Arts; Pa Acad Fine Arts, Philadelphia; Soc Am Graphic Artists, Kennedy Gallery, 71.
Awards: Awards, Print Club Philadelphia, 67; purchase award, Brooklyn Mus, 68; medal for creative graphics, Audubon Artists, 72.
Memberships: Soc Am Graphic Artists (rec secy, 64-71); Soc Can Painter-Printmakers; Print Club Philadelphia.
Publications: Auth, articles, In: Artist Proof.
Dealer: Roko Gallery, 90 E Tenth St, New York, NY 10003.
Mailing Address: 14 Stoner Ave, Great Neck, NY 11021.

SEITZ, WILLIAM CHAPIN
Educator, Art Historian
b Buffalo, N Y, June 19, 14.
Study & Training: Albright Art Sch, Buffalo, 32-33; Art Inst Buffalo, 33-35; Univ Buffalo, BFA, 46; study in Europe, 49; Princeton Univ, jr fel, 50-51; Procter fel, 51-52, MFA, 52, Am Coun Learned Socs fel, 52-53, PhD, 55; Fulbright grant to France, 56-57.
Exhibitions: One-man shows, Arista Gallery, New York, N Y, 38, Princeton Univ Art Mus, 49 & 50 & Willard Gallery, New York, 49, 50 & 53.
Collections Arranged: Claude Monet: Seasons and Moments, 60, The Art of Assemblage, 61, Arshile Gorky & Mark Tobey, 62, Hans Hofmann, 63, Art Israel, 64 & The Responsive Eye, 64, Mus Mod Art, New York; Louise Nevelson, Adolph Gottlieb, James Rosati & others, Rose Art Mus, 65-71; U S Exhib at 9th Ann Biennial, São Paulo, Brazil, 67; 7th Biennial of Canadian Painting, Nat Gallery Can, Ottawa, 68.
Teaching: Instr painting & drawing, Art Inst Buffalo, 41; instr, Univ Buffalo, 46-48, asst prof, 48-49; instr Albright Art Sch & N Y State Col for Teachers, Buffalo, 48-49; critic-in-residence, Princeton Univ, 52, lectr & critic, 53-55, asst prof, 55-56; prof fine arts, Brandeis Univ, 65; vis prof, Harvard Univ, 70-71; William R Kenan, Jr prof hist art, Univ Va, 71-; Kress prof, Nat Gallery Art, 71-72.
Positions: New York City Fed Art Proj, 35-38; chief draftsman, Hewitt Rubber Co, Buffalo, 41-43, proj engr, 43-45; bicentennial preceptorship, Princeton Univ, 57-60; assoc cur, Dept Painting & Sculpture Exhibs, Mus Mod Art, New York, 60-64, cur, 65; dir, Rose Art Mus & Poses Inst Fine Arts, Brandeis Univ, 65.
Memberships: Col Art Asn Am (bd mem, 72); Am Asn Mus Dirs; Am Asn Univ Prof; Eng Speaking Union; Nat Found on Arts (bd mem, 72).
Publications: Auth, Assemblage & Collage, Encycl Americana, 68; auth, Kinetic Art, The Peter Stuyvesant Collection, Abrams, Amsterdam, 69; auth, Sculpture, Quality: Its Image in the Arts, Atheneum, 69; auth, Manet & Turner, Atlantic Brief Lives, Atlantic Mo Press, 71; auth, George Segal, Abrams, 72; plus many exhib catalogs & articles in nat art mag.
Mailing Address: Fayerweather Hall, University of Virginia, Charlottesville, VA 22903.

SELDIS, HENRY J
Art Critic, Educator
b Berlin, Ger, Feb 23, 25.
Study & Training: New York Univ, BA; Columbia Univ; New Sch Social Res; also criticism with Donald Bear, Santa Barbara.
Collections Arranged: The Image Retained, 62 & Pac Heritage, 64, Munic Art Galleries, Los Angeles, Rico Lebrun Retrospective, Los Angeles Co Mus Art, 68; Henry Moore Exhib, 73.
Teaching: Lectr art, Univ Calif, Santa Barbara, 55-58; lectr art, Exten, Univ Calif, Los Angeles, 58-59; lectr art, Univ Southern Calif, 59-60; lectr art, Calif State Univ, Los Angeles, 67-69; also, pub lectr.
Positions: Art critic, Santa Barbara News-Press, 50-58; art ed & sr art critic, Los Angeles Times, 58-; art consult, Century City, 67-68; dir traveling exhibs, Munic Art Galleries, Los Angeles.
Awards: Frank Jewett Mather Award, Col Art Asn Am, 53; Taft & Rita Schreiber Found res grant, 70.
Memberships: Col Art Asn Am; Am Fedn Arts; Am Soc Aesthet & Criticism; Venice Comt (exec v chmn Los Angeles Chap, 70-); Comt Rescue Ital Art (exec chmn Southern Calif Chap, 66-67); plus others.
Publications: Co-auth, Sculpture of Jack Zajac, 61; auth, Rico Lebrun (monogr) & Henry Moore in America; contribr, Art Int & Art Am.
Mailing Address: Los Angeles Times, Times-Mirror Sq, Los Angeles, CA 90053.

SELEY, JASON
Sculptor
b Newark, N J, May 20, 19.
Study & Training: Cornell Univ, AB, 40; Art Stud League New York, with Ossip Zadkine; Ecole Nat Superieur des Beaux Arts, Atelier Gaumond.
Work in Public Collections: Mus Mod Art, New York, N Y; Whitney Mus Am Art, New York; Nat Gallery, Ottawa, Can; N J State Mus, Trenton; Univ Mus, Univ Calif, Berkeley.
Commissions: Taliesmen (bronze abstract), Casper Col, Wyo, 69-70.
Exhibitions: The Art of Assemblage, 61 & Americans 1963, 63, Mus Mod Art, New York; Festival of Two Worlds, Spoleto, Italy, 62; Sculpture in the Open Air, Battersea Park, London, Eng, 63; Documenta III, Kassel, Ger, 64.
Teaching: Assoc prof sculpture, Hofstra Univ, 53-65; assoc prof sculpture, N Y Univ, 65-67; prof sculpture & chmn art dept, Cornell Univ, 68-
Awards: Maintenance & travel grant for Haiti, U S State Dept & U S Off Educ, 47-49; Fulbright scholar for France, Inst Int Educ, 49-50; artist-in-residence for Berlin, Deutscher Akademischen Austauschienst, 70-71.
Bibliography: William Seitz (auth), The art of assemblage, 61 & Dorothy Miller (auth), Americans 1963, 63, Mus Mod Art, New York; Herbert Read (auth), A concise history of modern sculpture, Praeger, 65.
Memberships: Col Art Asn Am.
Art Interests: Sculpture with automobile bumpers.
Mailing Address: 209 Hudson St, Ithaca, NY 14850.

SELIG, MR & MRS MANFRED
Collectors, Patrons
Collection: Old and modern paintings; graphic art.
Mailing Address: Empire Children's Wear Co, 2609 First Ave, Seattle, WA 98121.

SELIG, MARTIN
Collector
Mailing Address: 408 39th E, Seattle, WA 98112.

SELIGER, CHARLES
Painter, Designer
Preferred Media: Oils, Acrylics.
b New York, N Y, June 3, 26.
Work in Public Collections: Mus Mod Art, New York; Whitney Mus Am Art, New York; Seattle Mus Art, Wash; Addison Mus Art, Andover, Mass; Munson-Williams-Proctor Inst, Utica, N Y.
Exhibitions: Abstract & Surrealist American Art, 47 & 65th Am Exhib, 62, Art Inst Chicago, Ill; Abstract Art in America, Mus Mod Art, New York, 51; Art of Organic Forms, Smithsonian Inst, Washington, D C, 68; Miniaturen '70 Int, Galerie 66 h g Krupp, Hofheim, Ger, 70.
Teaching: Instr painting, Mount Vernon Art Ctr, N Y, 50-53.
Positions: V pres design, Pictorial Prod Inc, Mount Vernon, 60-
Dealer: Willard Gallery, 29 E 72nd St, New York, NY 10021.
Mailing Address: 616 E Lincoln Ave, Mount Vernon, NY 10552.

SELLA, ALVIN CONRAD
Painter, Educator
b Union City, N J, Aug 30, 19.
Study & Training: Yale Univ Sch Art; Art Stud League New York, with Brackman & Bridgman; Columbia Univ, with Machau; Col Fine Arts, Syracuse Univ; Univ N Mex; also in Mex.
Work in Public Collections: Bristol Iron & Steel Co; Collectors of Am Art; Sullins Col.
Exhibitions: Am Fedn Arts Traveling Exhib, 61-62; one-man exhibs, Centenary Col, Lauren Rogers Mus Art, Laurel, Miss, Munic Art Gallery, Jackson, Miss & Birmingham Mus Art, Ala, 69; plus many others.
Teaching: Head dept art, Sullins Col, 48-61; prof art, Univ Ala, 61-; vis prof, Miss Art Colony, spring workshops, 62-64; vis prof, Shreveport Art Colony, 64-68; artist-in-residence, Summer Sch Arts, Univ S C, 68.
Awards: First award, 54th Ann Miss Juried Exhib; third prize, 7th Juried Mobile Art Exhib, 72; first & second prize, 32nd Ann Watercolor Exhib, Birmingham Mus Art, 72.
Memberships: Art Stud League New York; Am Asn Univ Prof; Col Art Asn Am; fel Int Inst Arts & Lett.
Mailing Address: Dept of Art, University of Alabama, University, AL 35486.

SELLERS, CHARLES COLEMAN
Art Historian
b Overbrook, Pa, Mar 16, 03.
Study & Training: Haverford Col, BA, 25; Harvard Univ, 26.
Teaching: Inst Am art, Dickinson Col, 50-56; librn, Waldron Phoenix Belknap Jr, Res Libr Am Painting, 56-59.
Awards: Bancroft Prize, Columbia Univ, 70.

Publications: Auth, Charles Willson Peale, 47 & rev ed, 69; auth, Portraits and miniatures by C W Peale, 52; ed, American colonial painting, 59; auth, Benjamin Franklin in portraiture, 62; auth, Charles Willson Peale with patron and populace, 69.
Mailing Address: 161 W Louther St, Carlisle, PA 17013.

SELLERS, WILLIAM FREEMAN
Sculptor, Lecturer
Preferred Media: Metals, Wood, Plastics.
b Bay City, Mich, June 1, 29.
Study & Training: Univ Mich, BArch, 54, MFA, 62.
Work in Public Collections: Suspension, Six Cubes & Converging Cubes, Mem Art Gallery, Rochester, N Y.
Commissions: Four Squares (painted steel), Stud Asn, N Y State Univ Col Cortland, 69.
Exhibitions: Sculpture & Prints Ann, 66 & Contemp Am Sculpture Ann, 68, Whitney Mus Am Art, New York, N Y; Plus by Minus: Today's Half-Century, Albright-Knox Art Gallery, Buffalo, N Y, 68; American Sculpture of the Sixties, Grand Rapids Art Mus, Mich, 69; Painting and Sculpture Today, Indianapolis Mus Art, Ind, 70; plus other one-man shows.
Teaching: Instr design, Rochester Inst Technol, 62-65; asst prof sculpture, Univ Rochester, 66-70; lectr sculpture, ceramics, drawing & design, Lehman Col, 70-
Awards: Jurors' show award, Mem Art Gallery, 66.
Dealer: Max Hutchinson Gallery, 127 Greene St, New York, NY 10012.
Mailing Address: Salt Point Turnpike, Salt Point, NY 12578.

SELONKE, IRENE A
Painter
Preferred Media: Watercolors, Oils.
b Chicago, Ill, Sept 4, 10.
Study & Training: Art Inst Chicago; Kansas City Art Inst; also with Joseph Fleck, Taos, N M & Olga Dormandi, Paris, France.
Work in Public Collections: Ralph Foster Mus, Point Lookout, Mo; Gill Studios, Olatha, Kans; Johnson Co Nat Bank, Prairie Village, Kans; Three-Thirty-Three Myer Bldg, Kansas City, Mo; Golden Ox, Washington, D C.
Commissions: Tron furs, Sylvan Tron, Kansas City, 60; hist mural & many portraits, Mr & Mrs Dave Lorenz, Platt Woods, Mo, 66.
Exhibitions: Coun Am Artists, Lever House, New York, N Y, 64; Nat League Am Pen Women Biennial State Show, Saint Louis, Mo, 65; Nat League Am Pen Women Regional State Show, Kansas City, 65; Greater Kansas City Art Asn Exhibs, 66; Nat League Am Pen Women Nat Exhib, Salt Palace, Salt Lake City, Utah, 69.
Positions: Illusr, Mod Handcraft Mag, Kansas City, 59-61.
Awards: Four awards, Nat League Am Pen Women, 62-69; five awards, Greater Kansas City Art Asn, 62-68; Pikes Peak Nat Award, 72.
Memberships: Nat League Am Pen Women (state art chmn, 71-72).
Publications: Contribr, Workbasket Mag & Workbench Mag, 59-61.
Dealer: Ken Gilbert 83rd & Summerset, Prairie Village, KS 66208.
Mailing Address: 3318 W 95th St, Leawood, KS 66206.

SELVIG, FORREST HALL
Art Historian, Writer
b Tacoma, Wash, Jan 3, 24.
Study & Training: Harvard Col, AB, 49; Univ Calif, Berkeley, 53-56.
Collections Arranged: Selections From Richard Brown Baker Collection, 60; The Nabis, 61; Pavel Tchelitchew, 64; Jean Hélion, 65; Charles Demuth, 68; plus others.
Positions: Asst dir, Minneapolis Art Inst, Minn, 61-63; asst dir, Gallery Mod Art, New York, N Y, 63-65; dir, Akron Art Inst, Ohio, 66-68; ed, New York Graphic Soc, Greenwich, Conn, 68-71.
Memberships: Am Asn Mus.
Research: Late nineteenth century French painting, especially the Nabis and the Symbolists.
Publications: Auth, The Nabis and their circle, 62; auth, American collections, 63; auth, Charles Demuth, 68; auth, Review of the Whitney Sculpture Annual, 69; ed, 19th century landscape painting, 71.
Mailing Address: Botsford Hill, Roxbury, CT 06783.

SELZ, PETER H
Art Historian, Art Museum Director
b Munich, Ger, Mar 27, 19.
Study & Training: Univ Chicago, fel, 46-49, MA & PhD; Univ Paris, Fulbright award, 49-50, Calif Col Arts & Crafts, hon DFA, 67.
Collections Arranged: Directions In Kinetic Sculpture, 65; Funk, 67; Richard Lindner, 69; Pol Bury, 70; Excellence, 70; Harold Paris, 72; Ferdinand Hodler, 72; plus many earlier exhibs arranged at Pomona Col, Mus Mod Art, New York & Univ Art Mus, Berkeley.
Teaching: Asst prof art hist, Inst Design, Univ Chicago, 53-54; prof art hist, Univ Calif, Berkeley, 65-

Positions: Head Art Educ Prog, Inst Design, Ill Inst Technol, 53-55; chmn dept art & dir art gallery, Pomona Col, 55-58; cur painting & sculpture exhibs, Mus Mod Art, 58-65; dir Univ Art Mus, Univ Calif, Berkeley, 65-; ed, Art Am; mem consult comt, Art Quart.
Awards: Belg-Am Educ Found fel, 53; Order of Merit, Fed Ger Repub, 63; sr fel, Nat Endowment Humanities, 72; plus others.
Memberships: Col Art Asn Am (dir, 59-68); Soc Archit Historians.
Publications: Auth, Alberto Giacomatti, 65; auth, Directions in kinetic sculpture, 66; auth, Funk, 67; auth, Harold Paris; the California years, Univ Calif Art Mus, 72; auth, Ferdinand Hodler, 72; contribr, Art Bull, Art News, Art J, Arts, Arts & Archit, Sch Arts, Penrose Ann & Encycl Britanica; plus many others.
Mailing Address: University Art Museum, University of California, Berkeley, CA 94720.

SEMANS, JAMES HUSTEAD
Patron
b Uniontown, Pa, May 30, 10.
Study & Training: Princeton Univ, AB; Johns Hopkins Univ, MD.
Positions: Chmn, bd trustees, N C Sch Arts, 64-; bd mem, Mary Duke Biddle Found.
Mailing Address: 1415 Bivins St, Durham, NC 27707.

SENIOR, DOROTHY ELIZABETH
Painter
Preferred Media: Oils & Pastels.
b Willimantic, Conn.
Study & Training: Converse Art Sch of Norwich Free Acad, Conn; Chestnut Hill Art Sch; with Walter Olin Green; also with Herman Itchkawich, R I & Helen Van Wyk, Mass; plus others.
Work in Public Collections: Admiral Inn, Cumberland, R I.
Exhibitions: Rockport Art Asn, Mass, 69; Acad Artists Asn, Mus Fine Arts, Springfield, Mass, 69; Nat Arts Club, New York, N Y, 71; Nat Soc Painters in Casein & Acrylic, New York, 71; Pen & Brush, New York, 72; plus one other.
Awards: Award for Kim and Kris (oil portrait), Slater Mus, Pawtucket, R I, 65; award for Woodland (oil), S Co Art Asn, R I, 66; award for Gloucester Sea (oil), Nat Arts Club, New York, 67.
Memberships: Nat Arts Club; Nat Soc Painters in Casein & Acrylic; Pen & Brush; Am Artists Prof League; Acad Artists Asn.
Mailing Address: 20 Garden Dr, Lincoln, RI 02865.

SENNHAUSER, JOHN
Painter, Designer
Preferred Media: Oils, Collage.
b Rorschach, Switz; U S citizen.
Study & Training: Royal Acad, Venice, Italy; Cooper Union Art Sch; Florence Acad Fine Art, Italy.
Work in Public Collections: Whitney Mus Am Art, New York, N Y; S R Guggenheim Mus, New York; Philbrook Art Ctr, Tulsa, Okla; Munson-Williams-Proctor Inst, Utica, N Y; Birla Acad Art & Cult, Calcutta, India; plus one other.
Commissions: Murals, Salomon Bros, New York, 70; Price-Waterhouse, Washington, D C, 71 & Boston Harbor, Clark, Dodge & Co, Boston, 72.
Exhibitions: Pa Acad Fine Arts, 36 & 52; Brooklyn Mus Watercolor Int, 43, 49 & 51-53; Art Inst Chicago, 47; Whitney Mus Am Art, 48-51, 53, 55 & 56; Walker Art Ctr, Minneapolis, Minn, 53; plus many one-man shows, N Y, R I & Mass.
Teaching: Instr life drawing & painting, Leonardo Da Vinci Art Sch, 36-39; dir, Contemp Art Sch, 39-42.
Positions: Asst to cur, Mus Non-Objective Painting, New York, 43-45; designer, R Guertler Studio, New York, 45-57; art dir, C R Gracie & Sons, New York, 57-72.
Awards: Purchase awards, Whitney Mus Am Art, 51 & Philbrook Art Ctr, 51; Mark Rothko Found grant, 71 & 72.
Bibliography: Saul Dworkin (auth), Collage film, 70.
Memberships: Am Abstr Artists (secy-treas, 50-52); Fedn Mod Painters & Sculptors (pres, 66-68); Int Inst Arts & Lett, Zurich, Switz.
Mailing Address: 255 W 84th St, New York, NY 10024.

SEPESHY, ZOLTAN L
Painter, Educator
Preferred Media: Tempera, Graphics.
b Kassa, Hungary, Feb 24, 98; U S citizen.
Study & Training: Acad Fine Art & Art Teachers, Budapest, Hungary, MFA; also studies in Vienna, Paris, Ger & Italy.
Work in Public Collections: Metrop Mus Art, New York, N Y; Art Inst Chicago, Ill; Detroit Inst Art, Mich; Toledo Mus Art, Ohio; City Art Mus, St Louis, Mo; plus others.
Commissions: Secco murals, City of Dearborn, Mich, 28, U S Govt, Nashville, Ill, 40, Mich Eng Soc, Rackham Bldg, Detroit, 45 & Fed Bank & Loan Co, Kalamazoo, Mich, 50.
Exhibitions: Carnegie Int, Pittsburgh, Pa, Brooklyn Int, N Y, Chicago Int & Corcoran Biennial Nat, Washington, D C, several yrs;

New York World's Fair, 39; retrospective exhib, Cranbrook Acad Art & Syracuse Univ, N Y (catalogued Libr Cong), 65.
Teaching: Instr painting & drawing, Sch Social Arts & Crafts, Detroit, 26-28; resident artist, Cranbrook Acad Art, Bloomfield Hills, Mich, 31-67.
Positions: From dir to pres, Cranbrook Acad Art, 47-66.
Awards: Nat Acad Arts & Lett & Nat Inst Arts & Lett grant, 46; first prize, Carnegie Inst, Pittsburgh, 47; Morse Medal, Nat Acad Design, New York, 64.
Bibliography: H Salpeter (auth), At home in two worlds, Esquire Mag, New York, 42; Sepeshy tempera painting, Am Artist, 44; L Schmeckebier (auth), Complete catalog, Syracuse Univ, 65.
Memberships: Nat Inst Arts & Lett; Nat Acad Design; Nat Soc Mural Painters.
Publications: Auth, Manual on tempera painting, Crowell Collier; auth, articles, In: Fine Arts Mag, Art Digest & Col Art J.
Dealer: Midtown Galleries, 11 E 57th St, New York, NY 10022.
Mailing Address: 787 Harmon, Birmingham, MI 48009.

SEREDY, KATE
Illustrator
Preferred Media: Pencil, Crayon.
b Budapest, Hungary; U S citizen.
Study & Training: Budapest Acad Arts, grad, 20.
Work in Public Collections: May Massee Mem, William White Libr, Emporia State Col.
Awards: John Newberry Medal, Am Libr Asn, 37.
Bibliography: Articles, In: Horn Bk, Publ Weekly & Elementary English.
Publications: Auth & illusr, The good master, 35, The white stag, 37, The singing tree, 38, Tree for Peter, 40 & The chestry oak, 48, Viking Press.
Mailing Address: Weaver St, Montgomery, NY 12549.

SERGER, HELEN
Art Dealer
b Skoczow, Poland, Feb 1, 01; U S citizen.
Memberships: Art Dealers Asn Am.
Specialty of Gallery: Paintings, drawings and graphics by German and Austrian expressionists; twentieth century masters.
Mailing Address: 9 E 82nd St, New York, NY 10028.

SERISAWA, IKUO
Art Dealer
U S citizen.
Study & Training: Art Inst Chicago, 43-47.
Positions: Owner & dir, I Serisawa Gallery.
Specialty of Gallery: Contemporary paintings and graphics; also antique Oriental prints and modern Oriental graphics.
Mailing Address: 8320 Melrose Ave, Los Angeles, CA 90069.

SERISAWA, SUEO
Painter
Preferred Media: Oils.
b Yokohama, Japan, Apr 10, 10; U S citizen.
Study & Training: Study with Yoichi Serisawa (father) & George Barker; Otis Art Inst.
Work in Public Collections: Metrop Mus Art, New York, N Y; Los Angeles Co Mus Art, Calif; Santa Barbara Mus Art, Calif; Pasadena Art Mus, Calif; San Diego Fine Arts Gallery, Calif.
Exhibitions: Carnegie Int, Pittsburgh, Pa, 52; Tokyo Int, Japan, 52; São Paulo Biennale, Brazil, 55; Whitney Mus Am Art, New York, N Y, 60; Pacific Heritage, U S State Dept, Berlin, Ger, 65; plus others.
Teaching: Instr painting, Kann Inst Art, 48-51; instr painting, Scripps Col, 49-50.
Awards: Carol H Beck Gold Medal, Pa Acad Fine Arts, 47; purchase award, Metrop Mus Art, 50; purchase award, Los Angeles Co Mus, 50, 56 & 57.
Bibliography: Arthur Millier (auth), Inner development of artist, Am Artist, 50; Ed Biberman (auth), 20 artists (film), Los Angeles Mus & Univ Calif, Los Angeles, 70; Joe Mugnaini (auth), Oil painting techniques and materials, 69 & Logics of drawing, 73, Reinholt; plus others.
Dealer: I Serisawa Gallery, 8320 Melrose Ave, Los Angeles, CA 90069.
Mailing Address: 10552 Santa Monica Blvd, Los Angeles, CA 90025.

SERRA, RICHARD
Sculptor
b San Francisco, Calif, 39.
Study & Training: Univ Calif, Berkeley; Univ Calif, Santa Barbara, BA; Yale Univ, BA & MFA.

Exhibitions: Stedelijk Mus, Amsterdam, Holland, 69; Kunsthalle, Bern, Switz, 69; Solomon R Guggenheim Mus, New York, N Y, 69; Larry Aldrich Mus Contemp Art, Ridgefield, Conn, 69; Whitney Mus Am Art, New York, 72; plus many others.
Mailing Address: 319 Greenwich Ave, New York, NY 10013.

SERRA-BADUE, DANIEL
Painter, Educator
b Santiago de Cuba, Sept 8, 14.
Study & Training: Escuela Munic Bellas Artes, Santiago de Cuba, 24-26; Studio of Jose Simont & Art Stud League New York, 27-28; with Monturiol, Barcelona, 29, Hernandez Giro, Santiago de Cuba, 30-31, Borrell-Nicolau & Luis Muntane, Escuela Bellas Artes, Barcelona, 32-36; Art Stud League New York, Nat Acad Design & Columbia Univ, 38-40; Escuela Nac Bellas Artes, Havana, 43; Pratt Inst Graphic Art Ctr, New York, 64; Art Critics Workshop, Am Fedn Arts, 67.
Exhibitions: Int Exhib Graphics, Univ Conn Mus Art, Storrs, 71; Am Soc Contemp Artists Ann, New York, 71 & 72; Pintura Cubana, Miami Art Ctr, Fla, 72; one-man shows, John Wanamaker's Fine Arts Gallery, Philadelphia, Saint Peter's Col, Jersey City, Columbia Mus Art, S C & Cisneros Gallery, New York, 72; plus many other group & one-man shows.
Teaching: Prof drawing, Prov Sch Plastic Arts, Santiago de Cuba, 43-45; prof artistic anatomy & perspective, Sch Plastic Arts, Santiago de Cuba, 45-60; insr art, Univ Oriente, Cuba, summers, 48 & 50; prof design, Sch Journalism, Santiago de Cuba, 54-59; prof still life painting, Nat Sch Fine Arts, Havana, 60-62; lectr painting, Columbia Univ, 62-63; instr drawing & painting, Brooklyn Mus Art Sch, 62-; instr art, Saint Joseph's Col Women, New York, summers 64-65; asst prof art hist, Saint Peter's Col, 67-70, chmn dept, 67-, assoc prof, 70-
Positions: Asst dir cult, Ministry Educ, Havana, 59-60.
Awards: John Simon Guggenheim Mem Found fel, 38 & 39; Oscar B Cintas Found fel, 63 & 64; winner print contest, Potentials Gallery, Calif, 64; plus many others.
Bibliography: Rene Buch (auth), Simbolos silenciosos: la pintura de Serra Badue, Vision, New York, 11/17/61; Florencio Garcia Cisneros (auth), 40 Latin American painters in New York, Rema Press, Miami, 64; Cindy Hughes (auth), Geometry, people mixed in palette, New York World-Telegram, 2/28/64; plus many others.
Publications: Auth, weekly articles, In: Diario de la Marina, Havana, 3/3/46 to 6/22/47 & Diario de Cuba, Santiago de Cuba, 12/8/57 to 12/28/58; auth, The plastics arts in Santiago de Cuba (XVI to XIX centuries), (in press); plus others.
Mailing Address: Department of Art History, Saint Peter's College, Kennedy Blvd, Jersey City, NJ 07306.

SESSLER, STANLEY SASCHA
Painter, Etcher
Preferred Media: Oils.
b St Petersburg, Russia, Mar 28, 03; U S citizen.
Study & Training: Mass Col Art, dipl fine arts, 27 & dipl art educ, 28, with Major, Hamilton & Andrews; Courtauld Inst Art, London; in Europe, 55.
Work in Public Collections: Univ Notre Dame, Ind; Philbrook Art Ctr, Tulsa, Okla; Columbus Mus Arts & Crafts, Ga; Univ of the South, Sewanee, Tenn; Beverly Art Gallery, Chicago, Ill.
Commissions: Hist map & landscapes, Buchanan Pub Libr, Mich; altar piece, Ascencion, St Mary's Church, Floyd's Knobs, Ind; Early Hist South Bend, Robertson's Dept Store.
Exhibitions: Hoosier Show, Chicago, Ill & Indianapolis, Ind; Springfield Mus Art, Mass; Ill State Fair Exhib, Springfield; Nat Exhib Realistic Art, Springfield, Mass; Ogunquit Art Ctr, Maine.
Teaching: Instr drawing, Vesper George Sch Art, Boston, Mass, 27-28; from instr art to emer prof, Univ Notre Dame, 28-70, head dept, 37-60.
Awards: P C Reilly first prize for painting, Hoosier Salon, Chicago, 38; first prize for painting, 55 & outstanding work in show, 66, Northern Ind Art Show, Hammond, Ind.
Memberships: Fel Royal Soc Arts, London, Eng; fel Int Inst Arts & Lett; Midwestern Col Art Conf; Acad Art Asn, Springfield, Mass.
Dealer: Heritage Art Galleries, 1973 W 111th St, Chicago, IL 60643.
Mailing Address: Box 117, Dawn Hill Rd, Rte 1, Siloam Springs, AR 72761.

SETTERBERG, CARL GEORG
Painter, Illustrator
Preferred Media: Oils, Watercolors.
b Las Animas, Colo.
Study & Training: Art Inst Chicago; Am Acad Fine Arts.
Work in Public Collections: McChord AFB, Washington, D C; Air Force Acad, Colorado Springs, Colo; Columbus Mus, Ga; De Beers Collection; Soc Illusr.
Commissions: 14 doc paintings, USAF; portraits, Air Force Acad.

Exhibitions: Am Watercolor Soc, 42-72; Allied Artists Am, 48-71; Nat Acad Design, 48-71; Royal Acad, 60; Western Art Asn, Phoenix Art Mus, 71.
Positions: Illusr, McCalls, Colliers, Womans Home Companion, Am, Rd Bk & others.
Awards: Ranger Fund Award, Nat Acad Design, 58; Watercolor U S A Award, 67 & William Church Osborne Award, 69, Am Watercolor Soc.
Bibliography: Norman Kent (auth), Watercolor techniques, Watson-Guptill, 68; Ralph Fabri (auth), American Watercolor Society, 69.
Memberships: Nat Acad Design; Am Watercolor Soc; Audubon Artists; Salmagundi Club; Soc Illusr (v pres).
Publications: Auth, Treatise, Am Artist, 61.
Mailing Address: 45 Tudor City Pl, New York, NY 10017.

SEVERINO, D(OMINICK) ALEXANDER
Educator, Art Administrator
b Boston, Mass, Sept 14, 14.
Study & Training: Mass Sch Art, BS; Boston Univ, EdM; Harvard Univ, EdD.
Teaching: Instr art, R I Col Educ, 39-43; prof art, Univ Wis, 52-55.
Positions: Asst dean art & design, R I Sch Design, 47-48; chmn dept art, Bradford Durfee Tech Inst, 48-52; dir fine & appl art, Ohio State Univ, 55-57, assoc dean Col Educ, 57-
Memberships: Col Art Asn Am; Nat Art Educ Asn; Am Fedn Art; Asn Sch Adminr; Nat Educ Asn.
Mailing Address: 6215 Olentangy River Rd, Worthington, OH 43085.

SEWELL, JACK VINCENT
Museum Curator
b Dearborn, Mo, June 11, 23.
Study & Training: Saint Joseph Jr Col, Mo, 41-43; City Col New York, 43-44; Univ Chicago, MFA, 50; Harvard Univ, 51-53.
Collections Arranged: Complete reinstallation of Oriental Collections, Art Inst Chicago, 58.
Teaching: Lect, Indian and Far Eastern Art, The Arts of China, Strength in Delicacy—A Study of Archaic Chinese Bronzes & Sculpture of Gandhara.
Positions: Mem staff, Oriental dept, Art Inst Chicago, 50-56, assoc cur Oriental art, 56-58, cur, 58-
Memberships: Far Eastern Ceramic Group; Japan-Am Soc Chicago (dir, v pres); The Cliff Dwellers; Arts Club Chicago.
Publications: Contribr, Archaeol & Chicago Art Inst Quart.
Mailing Address: 1350 N Lake Shore Dr, Chicago, IL 60610.

SEXAUER, DONALD RICHARD
Printmaker, Educator
Preferred Media: Intaglio.
b Erie, Pa.
Study & Training: Col William & Mary; Edinboro State Col, BS; Kent State Univ, MA.
Work in Public Collections: Butler Inst Am Art, Youngstown, Ohio; New York Pub Libr; Boston Pub Libr; Mint Mus Art, Charlotte, N C; Montgomery Mus Fine Arts, Ala.
Commissions: Print eds, Woman, Assoc Am Artists, 66 & To Fly, To Fly, Int Graphic Arts Soc, 66; Vietnam Fragments (folio), Off, Chief Mil Hist, Washington, D C, 71.
Exhibitions: Soc Am Graphic Artists, 64-72; New Talent In Printmaking, New York, 66; 140th Ann, Nat Acad Design, 66; San Diego Print Invitational, Calif, 71; 16th Hunterdon Nat, Clinton, N J, 72.
Teaching: Prof printmaking, Sch Art, E Carolina Univ, 60-
Awards: Print prize, 140th Ann, Nat Acad Design, 66; purchase award, Piedmont Print Ann, Mint Mus, 71; purchase award, Bradley Print Show, Peoria.
Memberships: Soc Am Graphic Artists; Acad Artists Asn.
Publications: Illusr, Red clay reader number 5, Southern Lit Rev, 68.
Dealer: Garden Gallery, Hwy 70 W, Raleigh, NC 27611.
Mailing Address: 109 Greenbriar Dr, Greenville, NC 27834.

SEXTON, LEO LLOYD, JR
Painter
Preferred Media: Oils.
b Hilo, Hawaii, Mar 24, 12.
Study & Training: Sch Mus Fine Arts, Boston, Mass, Cummings travel scholar; Slade Sch, Univ London.
Work in Public Collections: Honolulu Acad Arts, Hawaii.
Exhibitions: Boston Art Club, Mass, 33; Bournemouth Mus, Eng, 36; Royal Acad, London, 36 & 39; Oakland Mus, Calif, 40; Artists of Hawaii, Honolulu Acad Arts, 55-56.
Awards: First prize for life drawing, Univ London.
Memberships: Hawaii Painters & Sculptors League (pres, 60).
Mailing Address: 4575 Aukai Ave, Honolulu, HI 96816.

SEYFRIED, JOHN LOUIS
Sculptor
b St Louis, Mo, Sept 26, 30.
Study & Training: Wash Univ, BFA, 58; Syracuse Univ; Cranbrook Acad Art, MFA, 62.

Work in Public Collections: Albreit Mus; Charleston Art Gallery; Tenn Arts Comn.
Commissions: Heroic fountain group, Chase Park Plaza, St Louis, Mo, 63-64; divider screen, I E Milestone, St Louis, 64; wall mural, Fred Seidel, New York, N Y, 66; five welded reliefs, Self Mem Hosp, Greenville, S C, 67; heroic mem & wall relief, Prof Photo Am, Des Plaines, Ill, 68-69.
Exhibitions: Mich Show, Detroit, 61-62; Mo Show, St Louis, 62-64; Drawings Int, Detroit, 64; Mid-South Show, Memphis, Tenn, 66, 68, 70 & 72; New Media Sculpture Show, Atlanta, Ga, 69; plus one other.
Teaching: Instr sculpture & ceramics, Webster Col, St Louis, 62-63; asst prof art, Merimec Community Col, Kirkwood, Mo, 63-64; assoc prof sculpture, Memphis Acad Arts, Tenn, 65-
Positions: Exec dir, People's Art Ctr, 62-63.
Dealer: New Bertha Schaefer Gallery, 57th St, New York, NY 10022.
Mailing Address: 2375 Circle, Memphis, TN 38112.

SEYLER, DAVID W
Sculptor, Educator
Preferred Media: Stone, Ceramics, Bronze.
Study & Training: Art Acad Cincinnati, dipl; Art Inst Chicago; Univ Chicago, BFA; Univ Wis, MFA.
Work in Public Collections: Syracuse Univ, N Y; Univ Chicago, Ill; Cincinnati Art Mus, Ohio; Sheldon Art Gallery, Lincoln, Nebr.
Commissions: Mural, U S Navy Gt Lakes Training Sta, 43; stained glass & altar, Holy Trinity Episcopal Church, Lincoln, 62-72; mural, KOLN-TV, Lincoln, 68-69.
Teaching: Prof sculpture, drawing & design, Univ Nebr, Lincoln, 48-
Awards: Drakenfeld first prize, Nat Ceramic Exhib; Woods Found travel grant, Italy, 59-60; Univ Nebr Found grant, Eng, 71-72.
Bibliography: Warren E Cox (auth), Pottery & porcelain & Herbert Peck (auth), The book of Rookwood pottery, Crown.
Memberships: Nebr Art Asn; Col Art Asn; fel Int Soc Arts & Lett.
Art Interests: Prints-paintings as gifts to local museum.
Collection: Prints & paintings.
Dealer: Sheldon Gallery & Lakewood Arts Studio, Lincoln, NE 68501.
Mailing Address: 3434 S 28th St, Lincoln, NE 68502.

SEYMOUR, CATRYNA TEN EYCK, see TEN EYCK, CATRYNA

SEYMOUR, CHARLES, JR
Art Historian, Curator
b New Haven, Conn, Feb 26, 12.
Study & Training: Yale Univ, Sterling fel, 35-37, BA & PhD; Univ Paris; Cambridge Univ.
Teaching: Prof art hist, Yale Univ, 49-; vis Mellon Prof art hist, Univ Pittsburgh, 65.
Positions: Cur sculpture & asst chief cur, Nat Gallery Art, 39-49; cur Renaissance art, Yale Univ Art Gallery, 49-
Awards: Guggenheim Found fel, 54-55.
Memberships: Renaissance Soc Am; Col Art Asn Am.
Research: Medieval and Renaissance art, especially architecture, sculpture and painting.
Publications: Auth, Notre Dame of Noyon, 39 & 70; auth, Masterpieces of sculpture in The National Gallery of Art, 49; auth, Tradition and experiment in modern sculpture, 49; auth, Sculpture in Italy 1400-1500, In: Pelican history of art, 66; auth, Sculpture of Verrocchio, 71.
Mailing Address: 145 Cliff St, New Haven, CT 06511.

SHACKELFORD, SHELBY
Painter
Preferred Media: Casein.
b Halifax, Va, Sept. 27, 99.
Study & Training: Md Inst Art, Baltimore, grad, with Marguerite & William Zorach, Othon Friesz & Fernand Leger.
Work in Public Collections: Baltimore Mus Art; New York Pub Libr; Morgan State Col; Western Md Col, Westminster; plus others.
Exhibitions: Eastern Show Regional, 68; Notre Dame Col, 72; Jewish Community Ctr, Baltimore, 72; many Md Regional Shows.
Teaching: Head dept art, St Timothy's Sch, Stevenson, Md, 44-62; instr painting, Baltimore Mus Art, 50-65.
Awards: First prize for painting, 59 & two purchase prizes, Baltimore Mus Art; prize for drawing, Eastern Art Asn.
Publications: Auth & illusr, Now for creatures, 34 & Electric eel calling, 40.
Mailing Address: 300 Northfield Pl, Baltimore, MD 21210.

SHACKNOVE, RETA
Painter, Sculptor
Preferred Media: Mixed Media, Collage.
b Hamilton, Ont; U S citizen.
Study & Training: Hunter Col, BA; New York Univ, MA; with Leo Manso, Hans Hofmann, Genichiro Inokuma & Gregorio Prestopino.

Work in Public Collections: Chrysler Mus, Norfolk, Va; Newark Art Mus, N J; Syracuse Univ, N Y; N C Mus Art, Raleigh; St Lawrence Univ.

Commissions: Interior fixtures for store (with Ferris Shacknove), Raymond Loewy, New York, N Y, 48; interior props design collection of lamps & bowls (with Ferris Shacknove), Gottschalk Sales Co, New York, 50-60; sculptures in wire, papier mache & plaster (with Ferris Shacknove), Bergdorf Goodman, Bonwit Teller, Lord & Taylor, Tiffany & Kislav, New York, 50; theatrical props (with Ferris Shacknove) for The King & I, New York; Posters (collages), Filium, Inc, Buenos Aires, Arg, 72.

Exhibitions: Thirteenth Ann New Eng Exhib, Silvermine Guild Artists, Conn, 62; New Finds, Joan Avnet Gallery, Great Neck, Long Island, 65; St Scholastica Educ Ctr, Fort Smith, Ark, 72; Rangely Col, Colo, 72; one-man show, Univ Mo-Columbia, 72.

Teaching: Instr design & art hist, Samuel J Tilden H S, New York, 38-43; chmn art seminars, Fairleigh Dickinson Univ, 69-71; lectr art, Am Soc Appraisers, 70.

Positions: Secy New York chap, Indust Designers Inst, 55; co-founder, secy & treas, Communicating Arts Found, New York, 70; bd overseers & co-chmn comn fine arts, Fairleigh Dickinson Univ, 72; trustee, Inst Advan Study Theatre Arts, 72.

Awards: Golden Jubilee Award for best designed windows, Fifth Ave Asn, New York, 50.

Bibliography: Structural modern, Design Mag, 52.

Publications: Co-auth, No art: an American psycho-social phenomenon, Leonardo, 71.

Mailing Address: 12 E 87th St, New York, NY 10028.

SHADDOLT, JACK LEONARD
Painter
b Shoeburyness, Eng, Feb 4, 09.
Study & Training: Euston Rd Group, London, Eng; Andre Lhote, Paris, France; Art Stud League New York.
Work in Public Collections: Art Gallery Toronto, Ont; Nat Gallery Can; Montreal Mus Fine Arts; Seattle Art Mus, Wash; Vancouver Art Gallery; plus others.
Commissions: Murals, Hart House, Toronto, Edmonton Int Airport & Charlottetown Mem Ctr; other comn in pvt collections.
Exhibitions: Can Traveling Exhibs; São Paulo, Brazil; Caracas, Venezuela; Carnegie Inst; Seattle World's Fair, 62; plus others.
Teaching: Head drawing & painting sect, Vancouver Sch Art.
Publications: Auth, articles on contemp art problems in Can.
Mailing Address: 461 N Glynde St, Vancouver, B C, Can.

SHADRACH, JEAN H
Painter, Art Dealer
Preferred Media: Acrylics.
b La Junta, Colo.
Study & Training: Univ N Mex; Sumié, Okinawa; Constatine & Roman Chatov Studio, Atlanta, Ga; Alaska Methodist Univ & Anchorage Community Col.
Work in Public Collections: Anchorage Fine Arts Mus; Pfeils Prof Travel Serv, Anchorage; also in collection of Sen Ted Stevens, Washington, D C.
Exhibitions: Cent Ga Juried Exhib, 67; All Alaska Juried Art Exhib, Anchorage, 68-72; Northwestern Watercolor Soc Ann, Seattle, Wash, 70; Design I, Anchorage, 71; Artists of Alaska, traveling show in U S, 71-73; plus one-woman show.
Positions: Co-owner, Artique, Ltd, Fine Art Gallery, Anchorage, 71-
Awards: Best of show, Elmendorf AFB, 69; drawing award, All Alaska Juried Art Exhib, 70; Governor's Award, Alaska, 70.
Memberships: Alaska Artist Guild (pres, 70-71).
Specialty of Gallery: Alaskan artists work.
Publications: Auth, Okinawa Sketchbook, 62.
Dealer: Artique, Ltd, 314 G St, Anchorage, AK 99501.
Mailing Address: 3530 Purdue Dr, Anchorage, AK 99504.

SHANE, FREDERICK E
Painter, Educator
Preferred Media: Oils, Casein.
b Feb 2, 06; U S citizen.
Study & Training: Kansas City Art Inst, 23-24; also with Randall Davey, Santa Fe, N Mex, 24; Broadmoor Art Acad, summers 25 & 26.
Work in Public Collections: City Art Mus, Saint Louis, Mo; Denver Mus Art, Colo; Springfield Mus Art, Mo; Nat Collection, Mus Art, Tel-Aviv, Israel; IBM Corp Collection; plus many others.
Commissions: Paintings of Army Medicine, War Dept, Abbott Collection, Washington, D C; Portrait of James M Wood, Stephens Col; mural, U S Post Off, Eldon, Mo; Scruggs-Vandervoort-Barney Collection, Univ Mo; Jefferson City Jr Col.
Exhibitions: Art Inst Chicago; Corcoran Gallery Art, Washington, D C; Pa Acad Fine Arts, Philadelphia; Carnegie Inst, Pittsburgh, Pa; New York World's Fair, 39-40 & 64-65; plus many other group & one-man shows.

Teaching: Prof art, Univ Mo, 38-71, chmn dept, 58-67, emer prof fine arts, 71-
Positions: Artist corresp, Army Med Corps, 44.
Awards: Second painting prize, Davenport Mus Art, Iowa, 50; popular painting prize, Columbia Art League, 60; Byler Award for achievement in art & teaching, 71; plus many others.
Publications: Auth, Fred Shane drawings, Univ Mo Press.
Mailing Address: 633 N Foothill Rd, Beverly Hills, CA 90210.

SHANKS, BRUCE McKINLEY
Editorial Cartoonist
b Buffalo, N Y, Jan 29, 08.
Work in Public Collections: Dept Justice, Washington, D C; Supreme Ct Off, Washington, D C.
Exhibitions: Var schs, banks, cols.
Positions: Ed cartoonist, Buffalo Eve News, at present.
Awards: Pulitzer Prize, 58; Grand Award, Nat Safety Coun, 61; Cartoon Citation, All-Am Conf Combat Communism, Washington, D C, 64; plus others.
Publications: Auth, cartoons, In: New York Times, Newsweek, U S News & World Report, Time & others.
Mailing Address: 675 Delaware Ave, Buffalo, NY 14202.

SHANNON, JOSEPH
Painter
Preferred Media: Acrylics, Crayon.
b Lares, P R.
Study & Training: Corcoran Sch Art, Washington, D C, 54; Temple Sch Art, Tucson, Ariz, 55; Smithsonian Inst, with Peter Paul DeAnna, 68.
Exhibitions: One-man shows, Studio Gallery, Tucson, 56 & 57; Tucson Fine Arts Ctr, 62; one-man shows, Corcoran Gallery, 69, Poindexter Gallery & Henri Gallery, Washington, D C, 71.
Awards: Prize, Southwestern Artists Exhib, Tucson Fine Arts, Ctr, 56.
Dealer: Poindexter Gallery, 24 E 84th St, New York, NY 10028.
Mailing Address: 8005 Mimosa Dr, Vienna, VA 22180.

SHANNON, (DAVID) PATRIC
Art Administrator
b Durant, Okla, May 6, 20.
Study & Training: Stanford Univ, hons prog, AB; Univ Calif, MA; study with Hans Hofmann; Univ Calif, 63-64.
Work in Public Collections: Pvt collections only.
Exhibitions: Los Angeles Co Art Mus, 48; Whitney Mus Am Art, New York, N Y, 50; Oakland Mus Art Ann, 50; San Francisco Mus Art, 50; Tex Ann, Dallas Mus Fine Arts, 57.
Collections Arranged: Washington Gallery Modern Art Collection; Winston and Ada Eason Monuments of American Master Prints; Trebor Collection of Mexican Artists' Works; Dorothy Doughty Porcelain Bird Collection; Jerome Westheimer Collection of Contemporary Paintings.
Teaching: Lectr design, San Jose State Col, 64; dir theatre arts, El Camino Col, 56-57; chmn art dept, Austin Col, 57-61.
Positions: Ed asst to dir, Oakland Art Mus, 50-51; color consult, W & J Sloane's, San Francisco, 51-53; staff designer, Cleveland Playhouse, 53-54; drama instr, C K McClatchey High Sch, Sacramento, Calif, 55-56; dir, Oklahoma Art Ctr, 65-72; dir, Contemp Art Gallery, Inc, Santa Fe, 72-
Awards: Humanities award for art, Stanford Univ, 49; visual arts adv, Okla Arts & Humanities Coun, 65-72.
Memberships: Col Art Asn Am; Am Asn Mus; Western Asn Art Mus; Am Fedn Arts (Okla State Adv, 70).
Specialty of Gallery: Non-provincial contemporary paintings and architectural sculpture by nationally known, Santa Fe area-related American painters and sculptors; monumental work for public buildings, corporations, architects, decorators and collectors.
Publications: Ed, Weiner sculpture collection, Times-Journal Publ, 65; ed, Les Fauves, Norman Transcript Press, 67; ed, Invitational, past jurors, Norman Transcript Press, 69; auth, The role of the trustee in the 70's (bk rev), Mus News, 6/72.
Mailing Address: The Contemporary Art Gallery, Inc, Number One, 1st Northern Plaza E, Santa Fe, NM 87501.

SHAPIRO, BABE
Painter
Preferred Media: Acrylics.
b Irvington, N J, May 4, 37.
Study & Training: State Teachers Col, Newark, N J, BS; Hunter Col, MA, with Robert Motherwell.
Work in Public Collections: Kresge Art Ctr, Mich State Univ, East Lansing; Newark Mus; Andrew Dickson White Mus, Cornell Univ, Ithaca, N Y; Albright-Knox Art Gallery, Buffalo, N Y; Cooper-Hewitt Mus, Smithsonian Inst, New York, N Y.
Exhibitions: Am Fedn Arts, 60; Biennial Exhib Contemp Am Painting, Univ Ill, 63; New York World's Fair, 65; Cincinnati Art Mus, 66; Indianapolis Mus Art, 70.

Teaching: Instr painting, Md Inst Col Art, Baltimore, 64-
Awards: Newark Mus Triennial Purchase Prize Award, 58 & 61;
first prize in painting, Monmouth Col, N J, 63; Ford Found
Artist-in-Residence, Quincy Art Club, Ill, 66.
Dealers: A M Sachs Gallery, 29 W 57th St, New York, NY 10019;
Gertrude Kasle Gallery, 310 Fisher Bldg, Detroit, MI 48202.
Mailing Address: 31 Walker St, New York, NY 10013.

SHAPIRO, DAISY VIERTEL
Collector, Patron
b New York, N Y, July 8, 92.
Study & Training: Painting with Louise Pollet & Alex Redein.
Memberships: Art Collectors Club Am; Friends of Whitney Mus Am
Art, Mus Mod Art, New York; Solomon R Guggehneim Mus; Arch
Am Art.
Art Interests: Donations of many works of art to museums and
colleges including Dartmouth College.
Collection: Contemporary American painting and sculpture.
Mailing Address: 200 East End Ave, New York, NY 10028.

SHAPIRO, DAVID
Painter
b New York, N Y, June 26, 44.
Study & Training: Skowhegan Sch, Maine, 65; Pratt Inst, BFA, 66;
Ind Univ, Bloomington, MFA, 68.
Work in Public Collections: Ind Univ Art Mus, Bloomington; Westinghouse Corp, Pittsburgh, Pa.
Exhibitions: Two-man show, Gertrude Kasle Gallery, Detroit, Mich,
70; Beaux Arts, Columbus Gallery Fine Art, Ohio, 71; one-man
shows, Pointdexter Gallery, New York, 71 & Owen Gallery, Den-
ver, Colo, 72; Color Forum, Univ Tex Art Mus, Austin, 72.
Teaching: Instr art hist, John Herron Art Sch, Indianapolis, Ind, 66-
67; instr drawing, Pratt Inst, 69-71; guest artist, Drake Univ, 70;
instr painting, Univ Bridgeport, fall 71.
Awards: Milton Avery Mem scholar, Mr & Mrs Roy Nueberger, 65.
Dealer: Poindexter Gallery, 24 E 84th St, New York, NY 10028.
Mailing Address: 315 Riverside Dr, New York, NY 10025.

SHAPIRO, IRVING
Painter, Instructor
Preferred Media: Watercolors.
b Chicago, Ill, Mar 28, 27.
Study & Training: Art Inst Chicago; Chicago Acad Fine Art; Am
Acad Art, Chicago.
Work in Public Collections: Univ Vt; Columbus Mus Art, Ga; Lake-
view Mus Art, Peoria, Ill; Ill State Mus, Springfield; Macon Mus
Art, Ga.
Exhibitions: Am Watercolor Soc Ann, Nat Acad Design Gallery, 58-
72; Union League Club Chicago, 55, 57 & 59; Butler Inst Am Art,
Youngstown, Ohio, 62; Art Inst Chicago Sales & Rental Galleries,
66-68.
Teaching: Instr watercolors, Am Acad Art, 45-, dir, 71-
Awards: First watercolor awards, Union League Club Chicago, 55 &
57; Ranger Award, Am Watercolor Soc, 58; Ill State Mus Pur-
chase Award, 66-67.
Memberships: Am Watercolor Soc; Artists Guild Chicago.
Publications: Auth & illusr, article, In: Am Artist Mag, 59; contribr,
100 watercolor techniques, 70, Acrylic watercolor, 71 & Palette
talks, 72.
Dealer: Blair Galleries, Santa Fe, NM 87501.
Mailing Address: 3330 Maple Leaf Dr, Glenview, IL 60025.

SHAPIRO, JOEL (ELIAS)
Sculptor
Preferred Media: Mixed Media.
b New York, N Y, Sept 27, 41.
Study & Training: New York Univ, BA & MA.
Work in Public Collections: Fogg Art Mus; Univ Mass; Whitney
Mus Am Art, New York; Lannan Found, Fla; Weatherspoon Art
Gallery, Univ N C.
Exhibitions: Anti-Illusion: Procedure/Material, 69 & Sculpture
Ann, 70, Whitney Mus Am Art; Hanging/Leaning, Emily Lowe
Gallery, Hofstra Univ, L I, N Y, 70; one-man show, Paula Cooper
Gallery, New York, 70 & 72; Works on Paper, Soc Contemp Art
31st Ann, Art Inst Chicago, Ill, 71; Kid's Stuff?, Albright-Knox
Gallery, Buffalo, N Y, 71.
Bibliography: Marcia Tucker & James Monte (auth), Anti-illusion:
procedure/material, Whitney Mus Am Art, 69; Robert Pincus-
Witten (auth), New York, Artforum, 5/70; Denise Wolmer (auth),
In the galleries, Arts Mag, 3/72.
Dealer: Paula Cooper Gallery, 100 Prince St, New York, NY 10012.
Mailing Address: 54 Leonard St, New York, NY 10013.

SHAPLEY, FERN RUSK
Museum Curator, Writer
b Mahomet, Ill, Sept 20, 90.
Study & Training: Univ Mo, AB, AM, PhD, AED; Bryn Mawr Col.

Positions: Asst art & archaeol, Univ Mo, 16-17, asst prof art, 25;
res asst, Nat Gallery Art, 43-47, cur paintings, 47-56, asst chief
cur, 56-60, cur res, Samuel H Kress Found, 60-
Awards: Fel, Bryn Mawr Col; European fel, 15; fel, Univ Mo, 15-16.
Publications: Auth, George Caleb Bingham, the Missouri artist, 17;
auth, European paintings from the Gulbenkian collection, 50;
auth, Paintings from the Samuel H Kress collection: Italian
schools, XIII-XV century, 66; auth, Paintings from the Samuel H Kress collection: Italian schools, XV-XVI century, 68; co-
auth, Comparisons in art, 57; contribr, articles, In: Gazette
Beaux Arts, Art Quart, Art in Am, Am J Archaeol, plus others.
Mailing Address: National Gallery Art, Constitution Ave at Sixth
St N W, Washington, DC 20025.

SHAPLEY, JOHN
Art Historian
b Mo.
Study & Training: Univ Mo, AB; Princeton Univ, MA; Univ Vienna,
PhD.
Teaching: Prof art, N Y Univ, 24-29; prof art, Univ Chicago, 29-39;
prof art, Cath Univ Am, 52-60; prof art, Univ Baghdad, 60-63;
prof art, Howard Univ, 63-70.
Awards: Carnegie Corp Medal; Decoration, Shah of Iran, 60.
Publications: Illusr, Editorial board: survey of Persian art, 33-;
co-auth, Comparisons in art, Praeger, 57; auth, many articles &
reviews; contribr, var serials, In: Art Bull, Archeol & others.
Mailing Address: 326 A St S E, Washington, DC 20003.

SHAPSHAK, RENE
Sculptor
b Paris, France; U S citizen.
Study & Training: Ecole Beaux Arts, Paris; Ecole Beaux Arts,
Bruxelles; Art Sch, London, Eng.
Work in Public Collections: Philathea Col Mus Mod Art, London,
Ont; Butler Inst Am Art, Youngstown, Ohio; Munic Mus, Paris;
Cecil Rhodes Mus, Bishop-Stortford, Eng; Pinakotheki, Athens,
Greece; plus many others.
Commissions: Marble bas-relief, 42 & granite bas-relief, 42, New
Gen Post Off, Capetown, S Africa; metal sculptures, S African
Broadcasting Corp, 50 & munition factory, Pretoria, 54; fountain,
City of New York, 72; plus many others.
Exhibitions: One-man exhib, UN, 55; Palais Beaux Arts, Paris, 55;
Whitney Mus Am Art, New York, N Y, 56; Mus Art Mod, Paris,
71-72; plus others.
Positions: Dir, Rene Shapshak Mus Mod Art, London, Ont.
Memberships: Archit League; Am Fedn Arts; Fr Art Theatre; Am
Int Inst; Syndicate African Artists.
Mailing Address: Hotel Chelsea, 222 W 23rd St, New York, NY
10011.

SHARP, HAROLD
Illustrator
Preferred Media: Watercolors, Ink.
b New York, N Y, Mar 2, 19.
Study & Training: Nat Acad Design, 37-41; Columbia Univ, BA; Hun-
ter Col, MA.
Awards: Ashton Award, Hunter Col.
Publications: Illusr, L W Frolich Agency, New York Times, Gray
Agency, J Am Med Asn & Physician Publ.
Mailing Address: 3973 Saxon Ave, New York, NY 10463.

SHARP, MARION LEALE
Painter
b New York, N Y.
Study & Training: Art Stud League New York, 09; also with Lucia
Fairchild Fuller.
Exhibitions: Paris Salon; Am Soc Miniature Painters, New York; Pa
Acad Fine Arts, Philadelphia; Baltimore Mus Art, Md; Los Ange-
les Mus Art, Calif; plus others.
Awards: First prize for oil portrait, Nat League Am Pen Women,
38; first prize for portrait miniatures, Nat League Am Pen
Women Exhib, Smithsonian Inst, 46; first prize, Nat Collection
Fine Arts, 52; plus others.
Memberships: Nat League Am Pen Women; Baltimore Watercolor
Club; Metrop Mus Art.
Mailing Address: 66 Harmon Ave, Pelham, NY 10803.

SHATALOW, VLADIMIR MIHAILOVICH
Painter
Preferred Media: Oils, Tempera, Acrylics.
b Belgorod, Russia, July 20, 17; U S citizen.
Study & Training: Inst Art, Kharkov, 34-36 & Inst Art, Kiev,
U S S R, 38-41.
Exhibitions: Butler Inst Am Art, Youngstown, Ohio, 68; Watercolor
Show, Pa Acad Fine Arts, Philadelphia, 69; Am Watercolor Soc
Ann, New York, N Y, 70; Wichita Centennial Watercolor Compe-
tition, Kans, 71; Watercolor U S A Nat, Springfield, Mo, 72.

Awards: Gold medal hon for oil painting, Allied Am Artists, New
York, 65; gold medal for watercolor, Nat Arts Club, New York,
68; grand award plaque for watercolor, Wichita Centennial, 71.
Memberships: Allied Am Artists; Artists Equity Asn; Audubon
Artists; Philadelphia Watercolor Club; Pa Acad Fine Arts.
Mailing Address: 2104 Poplar St, Philadelphia, PA 19130.

SHAW, CHARLES GREEN
Painter, Writer
b New York, N Y, May 1, 92.
Study & Training: Yale Univ, PhB, 14; Columbia Univ, 15; Art Stud
League New York; also with Thomas Hart Benton & George Luks.
Work in Public Collections: Philadelphia Mus Art, Pa; Boston Mus
Art, Mass; Detroit Inst Art, Mich; Mus Mod Art, Metrop Mus Art,
Solomon R Guggenheim Mus & Whitney Mus Am Art, New York;
plus many others.
Commissions: Covers for Vanity Fair Mag; poster for Shell-Mex
Ltd.
Exhibitions: Art Inst Chicago, Ill; Walker Art Ctr, Minneapolis,
Minn; Inst Mod Art, Boston; Hemisfair, San Antonio, Tex; Am
Fedn Arts traveling exhib to Europe & Japan; plus many other
group & one-man shows.
Awards: First prize for painting, Century Asn; prize, 58 & first
prize, 60, Nantucket Art Asn.
Memberships: Fel Int Inst Arts & Lett; Nantucket Art Asn (exec
comt); Mus Mod Art, New York (adv bd, 37-41); Am Abstract
Artists; Fedn Mod Painters & Sculptors; plus others.
Publications: Auth, New York oddly enough, 38, The giant of Central
Park, 40 & Moment of the now, 69; illusr, The milk that Jack
drank, 44, Black and white, 44 & It looked like spilt milk, 45,
plus many others.
Dealer: Bertha Schaefer Galleries, 41 E 57th St, New York, NY
10022.
Mailing Address: 340 E 57th St, New York, NY 10022.

SHAW, DONALD EDWARD
Painter, Sculptor
Preferred Media: Mixed Media.
b Boston, Mass, Aug 24, 34.
Study & Training: Boston Mus Sch Fine Arts.
Exhibitions: One-man shows, Nova Gallery, Boston, 56, 57 & 58;
Inst Aragon, Guadalahara, Mex & Univ Guadalahara, 68; David
Gallery, Houston, 72; Gallery Mod Art, Taos, N Mex, 71.
Bibliography: Ann Holmes (auth), Fantastic artists, Southwest Art
Gallery Mag, 2/72.
Publications: Contribr, logo, Agencia Noticias Mex, 69 & cover illus,
Southwest Art Gallery Mag, 72.
Mailing Address: c/o Dianne David Gallery, 2243 San Felipe,
Houston, TX 77019.

SHAW, HARRY HUTCHISON
Painter
Preferred Media: Oils, Acrylics, Watercolors.
b Savannah, Ohio, Oct 4, 97.
Study & Training: Univ Mich; Cleveland Sch Art; Pa Acad Fine Arts;
Russ Moffet Sch, Provincetown; Ohio State Univ, BFA & MA; Nat
Univ Mex; Stanford Univ.
Work in Public Collections: Smithsonian Inst, Washington, D C; Mod
Mus Art, Mexico City; Lord Neuffield Found, London, Eng; U S
Embassy, Mexico City; Ford Motor Co, Dearborn, Mich.
Commissions: Akron YWCA, 29; Women's League Chapel, Univ Mich,
Ann Arbor, 30; Pub Libr, Lafayette, La.
Exhibitions: Inst Mex-Am Cult Rels, Mexico City, 64-68; Inst Cult
Rels, Guadalajara, Mex, 68; Mus Art, Columbia, S C, 70; Butler
Inst Am Art, Youngstown, Ohio; Pa Acad Fine Arts, Philadelphia;
plus many others.
Teaching: Instr, Miami Univ, 25-26; instr painting, Art Mus Sch,
Clearwater, Fla, 41-42; assoc prof art, Univ Southwestern La,
42-59.
Positions: Head dept art, Marietta Col, 36; dir Summer Sch, Ohio
Sch Painting, 36-38.
Bibliography: Conroy Maddox (auth), article, In: Arts Rev, London,
62.
Memberships: Cent Stud E Scambi Int, Rome; Longboat Key Art Asn.
Mailing Address: 501 Sloop Lane, Sarasota, FL 33577.

SHAW, (GEORGE) KENDALL
Painter, Educator
Preferred Media: Acrylics.
b New Orleans, La, Mar 30, 24.
Study & Training: Ga Inst Technol, 44-46; Tulane Univ, BS, 49; La
State Univ, 50; New Sch Social Res, 50-52; Brooklyn Mus Art
Sch, 53; Tulane Univ, MFA, 59; also with Edward Corbett, Ral-
ston Crawford, Stuart Davis, O Louis Guglielmi, George Rickey
& Mark Rothko.
Work in Public Collections: Albright-Knox Art Gallery, Buffalo,
N Y; Mus Contemp Art, Nagaoka, Japan; New York Univ, N Y;
Tulane Univ, New Orleans.

Exhibitions: Four one-man exhibs, Tibor de Nagy Gallery, New
York, 64-68; Contemporary Painting, Mus Contemp Art, Nagaoka,
65; Modular Painting, Albright-Knox Art Gallery, 70; Sets for
The First Reader by Gertrude Stein, Mus Mod Art & Metrop Mus
Art, New York, 70-71; one-man exhib, John Bernard Myers Gal-
lery, New York, 72.
Teaching: Instr painting, Parsons Sch Design, 66-; instr painting,
Brooklyn Mus Art Sch, 69-, chmn painting dept, 72-
Memberships: Col Art Asn Am.
Dealer: John Bernard Myers Gallery, 50 W 57th St, New York, NY
10019.
Mailing Address: 916 President, Brooklyn, NY 11215.

SHAW, RICHARD BLAKE
Sculptor
Preferred Media: Ceramics, Wood, Mixed Media.
b Hollywood, Calif, Sept 12, 41.
Study & Training: Orange Coast Col, 61-63; San Francisco Art Inst,
BFA, 65; Alfred Univ, 65; Univ Calif, Davis, MA, 68.
Work in Public Collections: Oakland Mus, Calif; Objects U S A,
Johnson's Wax Collection; U S Info Agency, traveling exhibs.
Exhibitions: One-man show, Dilexi Gallery, San Francisco, Calif,
68; Objects U S A, Johnson's Wax Collection, 69; Whitney Mus Am
Art Sculpture Ann, New York, N Y, 70; Contemporary American
Ceramic, Mus Mod Art, Kyoto & Tokyo, Japan, 71-72; Interna-
tional Ceramics, 1972, Victoria & Albert Mus, London, Eng, 72.
Teaching: Chmn ceramics dept, San Francisco Art Inst, 65-; mem
faculty, Univ Wis-Madison, summer 71.
Awards: Agnus Brandenstein fel, 64-65; Nat Endowment Arts, 70-71.
Bibliography: Articles, In: Arts Int, 5&6/66, Objects U S A, Viking
Press, 69 & Arts Can, summer 71.
Memberships: Order Golden Brush.
Dealer: Ruth Braunstein, c/o Quay Gallery, 2 Jerome Alley, San
Francisco, CA 94133.
Mailing Address: Box 274, Stinson Beach, CA 94970.

SHAYN, JOHN
Painter, Designer
b Ukraine, Jan 15, 01; U S citizen.
Study & Training: Mass Normal Art Sch, 17-18; Boston Univ, 19-21;
Mus Fine Arts Sch, Boston, 22-23; Art Stud League New York, 24.
Work in Public Collections: Union of Am Hebrew Congregations;
Berg Found; Frank Llloyd Wright Found, Wis.
Exhibitions: Miami, Fla, Chicago, Ill, Boston, Mass, Great Neck,
N Y; one-man shows, New York, N Y.
Teaching: Radio & TV lects on Bible art & symbolism.
Awards: First prize, New York Bldg Cong, 27; second prize, East-
ern Fine Paper Grand Nat Award, 66.
Memberships: Artists Equity Asn; Inst Graphic Arts; Art Stud
League New York.
Art Interests: Inventor, wax color tempera medium.
Publications: Auth, True craftsmanship as applied to design; illusr,
Art and the Bible.
Mailing Address: 20 E 67th St, New York, NY 10021.

SHEA, BEVERLY
Art Dealer
b Albany, Calif, Dec 29, 38.
Positions: Owner, Beverly Shea Gallery.
Specialty of Gallery: Contemporary oils.
Mailing Address: P O Box 112, Canyon, CA 94516.

SHEAD, S RAY
Painter, Sculptor
Preferred Media: Acrylics, Epoxy.
b Cartersville, Ga, Nov 27, 38.
Study & Training: Atlanta Art Inst, BFA, 60; Art Ctr Col Design,
BPA, 63; also with John Rodgers & Loser Fiedelson, Los Ange-
les, Calif.
Work in Public Collections: Columbus Mus, Ga; Montgomery Mus,
Ala; Opelika Art League, Ala; Atlanta High Mus, Ga; Southwest
Ga Art Mus, Albany.
Commissions: Painting, Chrysler Corp, Atlanta, 60; sculpture,
Dibco-Wayne Corp, Atlanta, 68; painting, Callaway Gardens, Ga,
70.
Exhibitions: Southeastern Ann, Atlanta, 60; Dixie Ann, Montgomery,
Ala, 60; 6th Ann Callaway Gardens Exhib, Ga, 69; 49th Shreve-
port Art Exhib, La, 70; Ga Artists Exhib I & II, Atlanta, 71-72.
Teaching: Assoc prof art & head dept, LaGrange Col, 68-
Positions: Art dir, Compton Advert, New York, N Y, 63-67.
Awards: Second Dixie Ann Award, 60; Southern Contemp Award, 69;
Sixth Ann Columbus Exhib Award, 70.
Memberships: Col Art Asn Am.
Dealer: Beverly Singlee, Youngsmill Rd, LaGrange, GA 30240.
Mailing Address: P O Box 907, LaGrange, GA 30240.

SHEAKS, BARCLAY
Painter, Educator
Preferred Media: Acrylics, Polymers.
b East Chicago, Ind.
Study & Training: Va Commonwealth Univ, BFA; Col William & Mary, teaching cert.
Work in Public Collections: Va Mus Fine Arts, Richmond; Butler Inst Am Art, Youngstown, Ohio; Columbia Mus Fine Arts, S C; Mobile Mus, Ala; Mariners Mus, Newport News, Va.
Commissions: Relief sculpture, Riverside Hosp, Newport News, 63; portrait of USS Am, USN, 64; portrait of USS Enterprise, comn by off of ship, 65; portrait of USS John F Kennedy, City of Newport News, 69; painting series, exec suite, Tenneco Corp, Newport News Shipyard, 72.
Exhibitions: Nat Drawing Biennial (drawing selected for Smithsonian Inst Nat Traveling Exhib), Norfolk Mus, Va, 65; Butler Inst Am Art Mid-Year Show Am Painting, 65, 66 & 67; 99 Exhibition, Am Watercolor Soc, Nat Acad Design, New York, N Y, 66; Juried Art Exhib, Corcoran Gallery Art, Washington, D C, 67; Ten Top Realists S E, Gallery Contemp Art, Winston-Salem, N C, 69-70.
Teaching: Head art dept, Newport News Pub Schs, 49-69; assoc prof art, Va Wesleyan Col, 69-
Positions: Art consult, Hunt Mfg Co, Philadelphia, Pa, 65; lectr, Va Mus, Richmond, 70; artist-in-residence, Richmond Humanities Ctr, 71.
Bibliography: Russel Woody (auth), chap, In: Painting in synthetic media & Complete guide to polymer painting, Van Nostrand-Reinhold; chap, In: Prize winning paintings, 66.
Memberships: Tidewater Artists Asn; Salmagundi Club.
Publications: Auth, Painting with acrylics from start to finish, Davis Mass, 72.
Dealer: Chester Smith, Seaside Art Gallery, Nags Head, NC 27959.
Mailing Address: 51 Hopkins St, Newport News, VA 23601.

SHECTER, PEARL S
Painter, Instructor
Preferred Media: Acrylics, Gold Leaf, Collage.
b New York, N Y, Dec 17, 10.
Study & Training: Hunter Col, BFA; Columbia Univ, MFA; Hans Hofmann Sch Painting; Archipenko Sch Art, New York; New Bauhaus Sch Design, with Moholy-Nagy; Acad Grande Chaumiere, Paris.
Work in Public Collections: N Y Univ; John F Kennedy Libr; Miami Univ, Ohio; Int Rels Found, New York.
Exhibitions: Walker Art Ctr, Minn, 63; Carnegie Endowment Ctr, New York, 63; Lehigh Univ, Allentown, Pa, 67; Mfr Hanover Trust Bank, 70 & 71; Union Carbide Gallery, New York, 72.
Teaching: Lectr studio courses, N Y Univ, 58-69; instr studio courses, Newton-Harvard Creative Art Ctr, 63.
Positions: Art dir, Elisabeth Irwin High Sch, 72.
Awards: Carnegie Found grant, 50; gold medal Patronato Scholastico Arti, Italy, 63; cert of merit, Int Biog, Eng, 70.
Bibliography: Entry, In: Encyclopedia internationale degli artisti, 71; Artists New York (tape), Voice of Am, 72.
Memberships: Exp Art & Technol; Int Asn Art Bull UNESCO; Group 8 Artists New York (pres, 72).
Publications: Contribr, articles, In: Art News, Art Digest & Art Now, 63-70.
Dealer: Surgil Associates, 663 Fifth Ave, New York, NY 10022.
Mailing Address: 60 E Ninth St, New York, NY 10003.

SHEEHE, LILLIAN CAROLYN
Painter, Instructor
Preferred Media: Fired Glass, Oils, Copper Enameling.
b Conemaugh, Pa, Oct 16, 15.
Study & Training: Indiana Univ Pa, BS(art); ceramics & sculpturing with Sheldone Grumbling, majolica with Hugh Geise & painting & sculpturing with George Ream.
Work in Public Collections: U S Bank Gallery; Art Assocs Gallery; Court of Gabrielle (serigraph), David Glosser Libr; Trees at Christmastime in California (serigraph), Flood Mus; 130 glass-fired paintings & sagged bottle collection, C of C, Johnstown, Pa.
Commissions: Golf mural, J Cover, Johnstown, Pa, 44; designed & printed Christmas cards, Pa Rehab Ctr & Bur Voc Rehab, 59-71; emblem design, Lee Hosp Rehab Med Dept, 66; landscape mosaic, Mrs Lyn Hoffman, 70; art calendar, Allied Artists Am, 71.
Exhibitions: All Allied Artists Juried Shows, 36-; Pittsylvania Ceramic Guild all-Pa competition, 64-71; Three Rivers Arts Festival, 65 & 66; Allied Artists Graphic Arts Show, 70; one-man show, Johnstown C of C, 72.
Teaching: Art supvr, East Conemaugh Schs, 36-42; instr art & world hist, Westmont High Sch, 44-45 & 53-54; instr art & art supvr, Ferndale-Dale Grade & High Schs, 55-59; instr arts & crafts, Pa Voc Rehab Ctr, 59-72.
Positions: Designer & coordr, Around About Now in Johnstown, 71-72.

Awards: Purchase award, U S Bank Show, 61; Allied Artists Best of Show, U S Bank Show, 70; Phoebe Jerema Award, Pittsylvania Ceramic Guild, 71.
Bibliography: Art Exhibit (two TV shows on glass work), George Mengelson, Producer, 69.
Memberships: Allied Artists (mem bd, many yrs, pres, 70-72); Pittsylvania Ceramic Guild; Area Arts Coun; Arts Assocs; Cult Affairs Comt (coordr, spec events publ).
Research: Experimented twenty years on uses of fired glass and its combinations for pictorial work.
Collection: Eighty photogravures on satin, circa 1885.
Publications: Auth & illusr, Allied Artists Fall Show Catalog (plus cover design), 58; auth, Useless to useful, Leather Craftsman Mag, 61; auth & illusr, Antiquity in a day, Ceramics Arts & Crafts, 64; auth & illusr, Textbook on photo—tinting—color—oils, Bur Voc Rehab, 65; plus others.
Mailing Address: 1333 Christopher St, Johnstown, PA 15905.

SHEETS, MILLARD OWEN
Designer, Painter
b Pomona, Calif, June 24, 07.
Study & Training: Chouinard Art Inst, 28; Otis Art Inst, MFA, 63; Univ Notre Dame, hon LLD, 64.
Work in Public Collections: Metrop Mus Art, New York, N Y; Art Inst Chicago, Ill; Los Angeles Mus Art, Calif; The White House, Washington, D C; San Francisco Mus Art, Calif; plus many others.
Commissions: Libr tower granite mosaic, Univ Notre Dame, South Bend, Ind; mosaic dome & chapel, Nat Shrine, Washington, D C; mosaic facade, Detroit Pub Libr; mural, Rainbow Tower, Hilton Hotel, Honolulu, Hawaii; two large murals, Los Angeles City Hall, East Los Angeles, Calif; numerous banks & savings & loan bldgs & murals in Calif & Tex.
Exhibitions: Univ Nebr; Albright-Knox Art Gallery, Buffalo, N Y; Art Inst Chicago, Ill; Va Mus Fine Arts, Richmond; Sao Paulo, Brazil; plus many others.
Teaching: Chouinard Art Inst, 28-35; prof art, Scripps Col, 31-, head dept art, 32-55; dir, Otis Art Inst, 55-62.
Positions: Artist, Life Mag, Burma-India front, 43-44; U S State Dept Specialist Prog to Turkey & Russia, 60-61; trustee, Scripps Col, 66-70; trustee, Calif Inst Arts, 68-
Awards: Prizes from Chicago Art Inst, Arizona State Fair & Calif Watercolor Soc; plus many others.
Memberships: Nat Acad Design; Calif Watercolor Soc; Am Watercolor Soc; Soc Motion Picture Art Dirs; Bohemian Club.
Mailing Address: Box 150, Barking Rocks, Gualala, CA 95445.

SHEETS, NAN JANE
Art Administrator, Painter
Preferred Media: Oils.
b Albany, Ill.
Study & Training: Valparaiso Univ; Univ Utah; Broadmoor Art Acad; also with John F Carlson, Robert Reid, Everett L Warner, Birger Sandzen & Hugh H Breckenridge.
Work in Public Collections: Springfield Art Asn, Mo; Okla Art Ctr, Oklahoma City; Univ Okla Art Mus, Norman; Philbrook Art Ctr & Mus, Tulsa, Okla; Cowboy Hall of Fame & Western Heritage Ctr, Oklahoma City; plus one other.
Exhibitions: Midwestern Artists Traveling Show, Am Fedn Arts, 23; Artists U S, Brooklyn Mus, 28; Woman's Int Exhib, Detroit, Mich, 29; Off Exhib New York World's Fair, 39 & 40; Coronado Cuarto Centennial Expos, Albuquerque, N Mex, 40.
Collections Arranged: Many exhibs, Okla Art Ctr, 35-65.
Positions: Auth, Nan Sheets By-line, weekly column in Sun Oklahoman, 34-62; dir, Okla-Work Proj Admin Fed Art Prog & supvr, State of Okla Art Proj, 35-42; dir, Okla Art Ctr, 35-65.
Awards: Birger Sandzen Prize for best landscape, Broadmoor Art Acad, 23; purchase prize, Midwestern Art Exhib, 24; Mrs Adolph Wagner Prize, Witte Mem Mus, 29.
Bibliography: Leila Macklun (auth), article, In: Am Mag Art, 8/27; Victor Harlow (auth), article, In: Harlows Weekly, 3/2/31; Marilyn Hoffman (auth), article, In: Christian Sci Monitor, 2/3/48.
Mailing Address: 401 N W 18th St, Oklahoma City, OK 73103.

SHELDON, OLGA N
Patron, Collector
b Lexington, Nebr, Aug 25, 97.
Awards: Distinguished Nebraskan Award, Nebr Soc Washington, D C, 71.
Collection: Works of Robert Henri; American art; works on loan or donated to Sheldon Memorial Art Gallery, University of Nebraska, Lincoln; Philip Johnson Building donated by family.
Mailing Address: 611 N Madison, Lexington, NE 68850.

SHELL, MR & MRS IRVING W
Collectors
Collection: Includes works by Emilio Greco, Reg Butler, Julio Le Parc, Yuichi Inoue, Zubel Kachadoorian, Siqueiros and Morio Hoshi.
Mailing Address: 442 Wellington Ave, Chicago, IL 60657.

SHENG, SHAO FANG
Painter, Instructor
Preferred Media: Acrylics, Watercolors, Silver, Copper.
b Tientsin, China, Sept 13, 18; U S citizen.
Study & Training: Painting with Old Master of Peking; Taliesin East & West, archit with Frank Lloyd Wright; Fla Southern Col; Marietta Col.
Work in Public Collections: Norfolk Mus Arts & Sci; Zanesville Art Inst, Ohio.
Commissions: Paintings & frescoes, Chinese Govt, 45; paintings, Frank Lloyd Wright, 48-49; mural & five paintings, Herbert Randall, 59; paintings, Noah Ganz, 68 & Charleston Nat Bank, 71; plus others.
Exhibitions: Taliesen East & West, 48-49; Fla Southern Col, Lakeland, 50; one-man show, Art Inst Chicago, 50; Am Fedn Arts Traveling Exhib, mus & galleries U S, 51; Contemp Art Gallery, Palm Beach, 68-69.
Teaching: Instr painting, Fla Southern Col, 48-49; instr painting & Chinese lang, Chatauqua Inst, 55-; instr painting & Chinese lang, 71-72.
Positions: Res painter, Acad Sinic, Manking, China, 42-44.
Awards: First prizes, for Yin-Yang, The Creative & Receptive, Appalachian Corridors, 60, Dream of Rockhound (oil), Chatauqua Art Gallery, 69 & Facet 3D (sculpture), Allied Artists W Va, 71; plus others.
Memberships: Int Platform Asn; Nat Soc Arts & Lett; Ohio Arts & Crafts Guild; W Va Artists & Craftsmen Guild; Allied Artists W Va.
Mailing Address: Rte 1, Williamstown, WV, 26187.

SHEPHERD, DOROTHY G (MRS ERNST PAYER)
Museum Curator
b Wellend, Ont, Aug 15, 16.
Study & Training: Univ Mich, AB & MA; Inst Fine Arts, New York Univ.
Teaching: Lect, Islamic Art & Architecture, Art & Architecture of Spain, Islamic & Medieval Textiles & Art of the Ancient Near East; adj prof hist art, Case-Western Reserve Univ, at present.
Positions: Monuments off, Monuments & Fine Arts Sect, SHAEF, Berlin, 45-47; cur Textiles & Near Eastern Art, Cleveland Mus Art, 54-
Memberships: Col Art Asn Am; Archaeol Soc Am; Am Res Ctr in Egypt; Centre Int Etudes Textiles Anciens, Middle East Inst; Am Soc Aesthet.
Publications: Contribr to Arts Orientalis & Cleveland Mus Art Bull.
Mailing Address: Cleveland Museum of Art, 11150 East Blvd, Cleveland, OH 44106.

SHEPLER, DWIGHT (CLARK)
Painter, Writer
Preferred Media: Watercolors, Oils.
b Everett, Mass, Aug 11, 05.
Study & Training: Boston Mus Fine Arts Sch, 28-29; Williams Col, BA, 28; also with Leslie P Thompson, Philip Hale & Harry Sutton, Jr.
Work in Public Collections: Boston Mus Fine Arts, Mass; Williams Col; Borough Mus, Dartmouth, Eng; portraits, Harvard Univ Grad Schs & Libr; U S Navy Collection.
Commissions: Habitat group, Boston Mus Science; mural decorations, Sclussverein Ski Club, Glen, N H, 39-40; mural decorations, U S Naval Acad, Annapolis, Md, 45-47; mural decorations, Williams Col, 46-52; Hubbard Mem (sculpture), Artic Inst N Am, Ellesmore Island, Arctic, 52.
Exhibitions: Watercolor Ann, Pa Acad Fine Arts, 36; American Watercolors, Nat Acad Design, 43 & 45; Boston Watercolor Soc, Boston Mus Fine Arts, 51-68; Navy Paintings Invitational, Nat Gallery Art, Washington, D C, 56; one-man show, Guild Boston Artists, 70.
Positions: Off U S Navy combat artist, 42-46.
Memberships: St Botolph Club (v pres, 64-); Boston Watercolor Soc (chmn exhibs); Guild Boston Artists (pres, 69-); Weston Art Asn; Concord Art Asn.
Publications: Contribr, The navy at war, 43; contribr, History of U S Naval operations in World War II, 48; contribr, Life's picture history of World War II, 48; contribr, American Heritage, to 70; auth, Dwight Shepler: an artist's horizons, Barre Publ, (in prep).
Dealer: Guild of Boston Artists, 162 Newbury St, Boston, MA 02116.
Mailing Address: 27 School St, Weston, MA 02193.

SHEPPARD, CARL DUNKLE
Art Historian
b Washington, D C, Jan 11, 16.
Study & Training: Amherst Col, BA; Harvard Univ, MA, 42, PhD, 47.
Teaching: Instr, Univ Mich, Ann Arbor, 46-49; from asst prof to prof, Univ Calif, Los Angeles, 50-64; prof art hist & chmn dept, Univ Minn, Minneapolis, 64-
Awards: Del Amo Found grant, Spain, 57; Fulbright lectureship, Istanbul, 62-63; McMillan travel grant, Italy, 68.
Memberships: Col Art Asn Am (mem bd dirs, 70-); Soc Archit Historians; Int Ctr Medieval Art (adv bd); Medieval Acad; Int Cong Art Historians.
Publications: Auth, introd & chapters 7, 8 & 11, Looking at modern painting, Norton, 62; auth, Subtleties of Lombard marble sculpture of the VIIth and VIIIth centuries, Gazette Beaux Arts, 64; auth, Carbon 14 dating and Santa Sophia, Dumbarton Oaks Papers, Istanbul, 65; auth, Byzantine carved marble slabs, Art Bull, 3/69; auth, The bronze doors of Augsburg Cathedral, Festschrift, 72.
Mailing Address: Dept of Art History, 108 Jones Hall, University of Minnesota, Minneapolis, MN 55455.

SHEPPARD, JOHN CRAIG
Painter, Educator
Preferred Media: Watercolors, Oils.
b Lawton, Okla, July 22, 14.
Study & Training: Univ Okla, BFA(painting), 37, BFA(sculpture), 38; also in Norway, France & Mex.
Work in Public Collections: Mus Art Mod, Paris; Brooklyn Mus, N Y; El Paso Mus Art; Gilcrease Mus Art, Tulsa, Okla; Mus Great Plains, Lawton.
Commissions: Murals, Bus Admin Bldg, Univ Okla, Norman, 41, Stud Union Bldg, Mont State Univ, Bozeman, 42, Will Rogers Theater, Tulsa, 46 & in pvt homes, Okla, Nev, Kans & Tex; Arthur Orvis Portrait, Univ Nev, Reno, 68.
Exhibitions: Mus Art, Bergen, Norway, 56; De Young Mus Art, San Francisco, 58; Salon Art Libre & Mus Beaux Arts, Paris, 62; Brooklyn Mus, 63; Watercolor U S A, Springfield Art Mus, 68.
Teaching: Instr sculpture & painting, Mont State Univ, 40-42; Chmn dept art, Univ Nev, Reno, 47-71; guest lectr Indian art, Univ Oslo, 55-56.
Positions: Dir prod illus, Douglas Aircraft Co, Tulsa, 42-46.
Awards: Bronze medal, Denver Art Mus, 41; silver medal, Kansas City Midwest Ann, 44; purchase prize, Mus Art Mod, Paris, 62.
Bibliography: Green Peyton (auth), America's heartland: the southwest, Univ Okla Press, 48; Per Rom (auth), Kunsten Idag, W Nygaard, Oslo, 59; Robert Laxalt (auth), Nevada, Coward, 70.
Memberships: Am Asn Univ Prof; Pac Art Asn (regional rep, 50-); Western Asn Mus Dirs (regional dir, 48-65); Nev State Arts Coun (chmn, 62); Nev Art Gallery (bd dirs, 50-62).
Publications: Illusr, Horses of the conquest 49 & Life and death of an oilman, 51, Univ Okla Press; co-auth & illusr, Landmarks on the emigrant trail, University of Nevada Press, 71.
Mailing Address: 1000 Primrose St, Reno, NV 89502.

SHEPPARD, JOSEPH SHERLY
Painter, Sculptor
Preferred Media: Oils.
b Owings Mills, Md, Dec 20, 30.
Study & Training: Md Inst Art, cert fine art; also with Jacques Maroger.
Work in Public Collections: Baltimore Mus Art, Md; Butler Inst Am Art, Youngstown, Ohio; Davenport Munic Art Gallery, Iowa; Univ Ariz Mus; Norfolk Mus Arts & Sci, Va.
Commissions: Portrait of Pres Hawkins, Towson State Col, Md, 67; Discovery of Scurvy, Pub Health Hosp, Baltimore, 68; Battle of Ft McHenry, Equitable Trust Co, Baltimore, 69; Christ Crowned With Thorns, Lutheran High Sch, Baltimore Co, Md, 70; seven hist murals, Baltimore Police Dept, 70-71.
Exhibitions: Allied Artists Nat, 56 & 59; Realists, Laguna Beach, 64; Regional, Butler Inst Am Art Nat, 67 & one-man show, 72; Baltimore Mus Art Regional, 71; Westmoreland Co Mus, Greenburg, Pa, 72.
Teaching: Instr oil painting, Dickinson Col, 55-57; instr oil painting, Md Inst Art, 63-
Awards: Emily Lowe Prize, Allied Artists, 56; Guggenheim Found fel, 57-58; purchase prize, Butler Inst Am Art, 67.
Memberships: Allied Artists Am.
Dealers: Grand Central Galleries, 40 Vanderbilt Ave, New York, NY 10017; IFA Gallery, 2023 Connecticut Ave NW, Washington, DC 20008.
Mailing Address: 222 Wendover Rd, Baltimore, MD 21218.

SHERBELL, RHODA
Sculptor, Collector
Preferred Media: Bronze.
b Brooklyn, N Y.
Study & Training: Art Stud League New York, N Y, with William

Zorach; Brooklyn Mus Art Sch, with Hugo Robies; also study in Italy & France.

Work in Public Collections: The Dancers, Okla Mus Art, Oklahoma City; The Flying Acrobats, Colby Col Art Mus, Waterville, Maine.

Commissions: Marguerite & William Zorach Bronze, Nat Arts Collection, Smithsonian Inst, Washington, D C, 64; Casey Stengel, Country Art Gallery Long Island, Baseball Hall of Fame, Cooperstown, N Y; Yogi Berra, comn by Percy Uris.

Exhibitions: Pa Acad Fine Arts & Detroit Inst Art, 60; Am Acad Arts & Lett, 60; Brooklyn Mus Art Award Winners, 65; Nat Acad Design & Heckscher Mus Show, 67; Retrospective Sculpture & Drawing Show, Huntington Hartford Gallery, New York, 70.

Awards: Am Acad Arts & Lett & Nat Inst Arts & Lett grant, 60; Ford Found Purchase Award, 65; Louis Comfort Tiffany Found grant, 66.

Bibliography: The artist and the sportsman, Nat Art Mus Sport, 68; Alfredo Valente (auth), Rhoda Sherbell sculpture, New York Cult Ctr & Fairleigh Dickinson, 70.

Memberships: Allied Artists Am; Audubon Artists; New York Soc Women Artists; Catharine Lorillard Wolfe Art Club.

Collection: Contemporary American realistic work, including M Soyer, W Zorach, Marguerite Zorach, Mervin Honig, Harry Sternberg, John Koch Agostine H Jackson and others.

Dealer: Frank Rehn, Inc, 655 Madison Ave, New York, NY 10021.

Mailing Address: 64 Jane Ct, Westbury, NY 11590.

SHERMAN, LENORE (WALTON)
Painter, Lecturer
Preferred Media: Oils, Watercolors, Acrylics.
b New York, N Y, May 11, 20.
Study & Training: With Leon Franks, Hayward Veal, Orrin A White & Sergei Bongart, watercolor with James Couper Wright, portrait with Eignar Hansen.
Work in Public Collections: San Diego Law Libr; Chateaubriand Restaurant, San Diego; var banks.
Commissions: Comns from pvt collectors.
Exhibitions: San Diego Art Inst 18th Ann, 71; Mission Valley Expos Art, Calif, 67; Rancho Calif Invitational, 70-71; Southern Calif Expos, Del Mar, Calif, 70-72; Calif Federated Women's Clubs Fine Arts Festival, 71.
Teaching: Instr oil painting, Del Gardens Art Asn, San Diego, spring 72; instr oil painting, Foothills Art Asn, La Mesa, Calif, summer 72; also pvt sem.
Awards: First award for oils, San Diego Landmarks Theme, Southern Calif Expos, 70; first award for Calif landmarks & second award for still life, Calif Fedn Clubs Fine Arts Festival, 71; purchase award, San Diego Art Inst 18th Ann, 71.
Bibliography: Ed Ainsworth (auth), The cowboy in art, World Publ, 68; articles, In: San Diego Union, 60-72.
Memberships: San Diego Art Inst.
Dealer: Challis Galleries, 1390 S Coast Hwy, Laguna Beach, CA 92652.
Mailing Address: 6217 Winona Ave, San Diego, CA 92120.

SHERMAN, SARAI
Painter, Designer
Preferred Media: Oils, Graphics.
b Philadelphia, Pa.
Study & Training: Temple Univ Tyler Sch Art, BFA, BS (educ); Barnes Found; Univ Iowa, MFA.
Work in Public Collections: Whitney Mus Am Art, New York, N Y; Mus Mod Art, New York; Hirshhorn Collection, Smithsonian Inst, Washington, D C; Uffizi Gallery Print Collection, Florence, Italy; Tel Aviv Mus, Israel.
Exhibitions: Whitney Mus Am Art Painting Ann, 52-64; Recent Painting U S A: The Figure, Mus Mod Art, New York, int tour, 62-63; Premio Marzotto, Milan, Paris, Hamburg, London & Belgrade, 67-68; Childe Hassam Acquisition Fund, 70; Venice Biennial, Int Graphics: U S A, Italy, 72.
Awards: Fulbright scholar, 52-54; award for painting, Nat Inst Arts & Lett, 64; European Community Prize, Premio Marzotto, 67.
Bibliography: Bryant (auth) & Venturoli (auth), Painting of Sarai Sherman (monogr), Galleria Penelope, Rome, 63; Pastorino (auth), Pittura come vita, Documenta Film, Rome, 68; Bernari (auth), Folk rock, blues, flower children, Ed Grafica Romero, 69.
Dealer: Forum Gallery, 1018 Madison Ave, New York, NY 10028.
Mailing Address: 17 W Ninth St, New York, NY 10011.

SHERMAN, WINNIE BORNE
Painter, Lecturer
Preferred Media: Watercolors.
b New York, N Y, Nov 10, 02.
Study & Training: Teachers Col, Columbia Univ, with Haney & Grace Cornell; Cooper Union Art Sch, with Perard & Traphagen, BFA, 23; Nat Acad Design, with Ivan Olinsky & Hawthorn; Art Stud

League New York, with Bridgman, Dumond, Lever & Pennell; also with Dean Cornwell.

Work in Public Collections: Seton Hall Univ Libr, N J; Thomas Watson Pvt Collection, IBM, New York; Houston Mus, Tex; Okla Art Inst, Tulsa; Grumbacher Artists' Palette Collection, New York; plus many others including pvt collections.

Exhibitions: One-man shows, Westchester Co Ctr, White Plains, N Y, New Rochelle Pub Libr, N Y, Burr Gallery, New York, Archit League, New York & New Sch, New York; plus many other group shows.

Teaching: Instr fine arts, New York City high schs, 25-35; instr pvt classes, 35-; art dir, Beaupré Sch Mus & Art, 46-48; instr fine arts, Hunter Col H S Art & Design, 57-65; instr art, City Col New York, 60-64; instr art, Inst Ret Prof, New Sch Social Res, 66-69.

Positions: Hospitality chmn & exhib comt, Westchester Arts & Crafts Guild, 53-57; chmn art sect, Women's Club, New Rochelle, 55-58; social chmn & exhib comt, Nat Arts Club, 58-62; juror for various exhibs.

Awards: Award for watercolor, Am Artist Mag, 53; first prize for graphics, Westchester Arts & Crafts Guild, 54; award for watercolor, Nat Arts Club, 61; plus others.

Memberships: Catharine Lorillard Wolfe Art Club (pres, 68-71); Nat Soc Arts & Lett (corresp secy, 62-64, N Y art chmn, 62-66, first v pres & pres, 68-70, Empire State Chap; nat art chmn, 66-68); Nat League Am Pen Women (art chmn, 66-68, first v pres, 68-72; hon fel Royal Soc Arts, London; Am Artists Prof League.

Mailing Address: 500 E 77th St, Apt 934, New York, NY 10021.

SHERRY, WILLIAM GRANT
Painter, Sculptor
Preferred Media: Oils, Wax.
b Amagansett, N Y, Dec 7, 14.
Study & Training: Acad Julian, Paris, France, cert, with Pierre Jerome; Heatherly Sch Art, London, Eng, with Ian McNab.
Work in Public Collections: Farnsworth Mus, Rockland, Maine; Mod Mus Art, Fort Lauderdale, Fla; Am Embassy, Pakistan; Parliament Bldg, Can; Springfield Mus Fine Art, Mass.
Exhibitions: De Young Mus, San Francisco, Calif; Colby Col, Maine; Ringling Mus, Sarasota, Fla, 49; Boston Arts Festival, Mass, 56; Art U S A, Madison Sq Garden, New York, 58.
Teaching: Chief instr painting & art dir, Fla Gulf Coast Art Ctr, Beleair, Fla, 57-64; art instr, Hamilton AFB, Ignacio, Calif, 65-67.
Awards: Laguna Beach Festival Arts, Nat Painting Contest, 51; purchase prize, Springfield Mus, Mass, Mr & Mrs Chauncey A Steiger, 57.
Dealers: Center Street Gallery, 136 Park Ave S, Winter Park, FL 32789; ADI Gallery, 530 McAllister St, San Francisco, CA 94102.
Mailing Address: 51 Park Terr, Mill Valley, CA 94941.

SHERWOOD, A
Sculptor, Printmaker
b Birmingham, Ala, Sept 12, 32.
Study & Training: Univ Fla; Hampton Inst; Wesley Col; Del State Col; Univ Philippines.
Work in Public Collections: Lilliputian Found, Washington, D C; Acad Art, Easton, Md; U S Navy; U S Air Force.
Commissions: Oil paintings for Phillips Elem Sch, Hampton, Va, 66.
Exhibitions: Norfolk Mus, Va, 66 & 67; Va Mus Fine Arts, Richmond, 67; Audubon Soc, Washington, D C, 69; Rehoboth Art League, Del, 70; Royal Art Gallery, Manila, Phillippines, 72.
Teaching: Instr art, Pope AFB, N C, 61-63; instr art, Alexander Graham Bell Jr H S, Fayetteville, N C, 62-63.
Positions: TV art illusr, Univ Fla Agr Ed Dept, 58-60; art illusr, spec serv, Pope AFB, 61-63; art illusr, Mag O'Club, Langley AFB, 63-65.
Awards: Award for Owl Fury (sculpture), Atlantic City Nat Art Show, 69; award for Roadrunner (sculpture), Acad Arts, 69; award for Vulture (sculpture), Rehoboth Art League, 70.
Bibliography: Joe Aaron (auth), Air Force wife successfully combines, Daily Press, Va, 67; Murray Bond (auth), Artist finds found objects, Airlifter, 68; S Stern Berger (auth), Art is where she finds it, Eve J, Del, 70.
Collection: Pre-Columbia pottery; Central America stone ware; celadon; Sung, Ming & Ching porcelain; brass from Asia.
Publications: Illusr, Elavet News, Gainesville, Fla, 58-60; illusr, various bulls, Gainesville, Fla, 58-60; illusr, Agr News & Univ Fla, 59.
Mailing Address: 6665 W Sixth Ave, Hialeah, FL 33012.

SHERWOOD, BETTE (WILSON)
Painter, Sculptor
Preferred Media: Oils.
b Sheffield, Ala.
Study & Training: Chicago Art Inst; Corcoran Sch Art; Miss State Col Women; Inst Allende, San Miguel Allende; also with Henri Gadbois.

Work in Public Collections: Lions Camp, Kerrville, Tex; Tenn Valley Art Mus; River Oaks Bank & Trust Co; also in collection of Mr & Mrs Herbert Douglas.

Commissions: Portrait of daughter, Mrs Eugenie Feffer, Haifa, Israel, 70; children's portraits, James T Fox, Bellaire, Tex, 71; portrait of Mrs E E Hunter, Morristown, N J, 71; portraits, comn by Jimmy Lyon, Houston, Tex, 71.

Exhibitions: Nat League of Am Pen Women, Houston, 68 & 69; Southwestern Watercolor Soc, 69; Art League of Houston, 69; Galerie Int, New York, N Y, 71; Med Soc Art Show, Houston Oaks Hotel, 71.

Awards: Best of show & hon mention, Nat League Am Pen Women, 68.

Memberships: Int Platform Asn; Nat League Am Pen Women (pres, Houston Br, 68-70, founder Mem Br, 70); Int Poetry Soc; Southwestern Watercolor Soc; River Oaks Ladies Reading Club.

Mailing Address: 9215 Bronco, Houston, TX 77055.

SHESTACK, ALAN
Museum Director, Art Historian
b New York, N Y, June 23, 38.
Study & Training: Wesleyan Univ, BA; Harvard Univ, MA.
Collections Arranged: Fifteenth Century Engravings of Northern Europe, catalog & exhib, Nat Gallery Art, Washington, D C, 67; Master E S (catalog & exhib), Philadelphia Mus Art, 67; The Danube School (catalog & exhib), Yale Univ Art Gallery, 68.
Positions: Cur, Lessing J Rosenwald Collection, Nat Gallery Art, 65-67; curator prints & drawings, Yale Univ Art Gallery, 67-71, dir, 71-
Memberships: College Art Asn; Print Coun Am; Asn Art Mus Dirs; Am Asn Mus.
Research: Specialist in fifteenth century German art and history of printmaking.
Publications: Auth, Master E S, 67, Fifteenth century engravings of northern Europe, 67, The complete engravings of Martin Schongauer, 69, Master L Cz and Master W B, 72 & auth, articles, In: Art News, Burlington Mag, Master Drawings & Art Quart.
Mailing Address: Box 2006, Yale Station, New Haven, CT 06520.

SHIBLEY, GERTRUDE
Painter
Preferred Media: Oils.
b Brooklyn, N Y.
Study & Training: Brooklyn Col, BA; with Francis Criss, 42; Hans Hofmann Sch Fine Arts, 52-53.
Work in Public Collections: Wichita State Univ Mus Collection, Kans; Philadelphia Mus Fine Arts Rental Collection, Pa.
Exhibitions: World's Fair, New York, N Y, 40; Nat Asn Women Painters, Nat Acad Design Gallery, 51-52; Prizewinners Village Art Ctr, Whitney Mus Am Art, New York, 54; Art U S A, New York, 58; Southampton Col Invitational, 71; plus others.
Teaching: Instr painting, Halloran Hosp, Staten Island, 42-44; instr painting, Ruth Ettinger Sch, New York, 55-56.
Positions: Ceramist, Design Technics, 44-48.
Awards: Prize for one-man show, Village Art Ctr, 49; hon mention, Terry Art Award, Miami, Fla, 52.
Memberships: Guild Hall.
Dealer: Phoenix Gallery, 939 Madison Ave, New York, NY 10021.
Mailing Address: 351 W 24th St, New York, NY 10011.

SHIELDS, ALAN J
Designer, Painter
b Lost Springs, Kans, Feb 4, 44.
Study & Training: Kans State Univ.
Work in Public Collections: Mus Mod Art, New York, N Y; Whitney Mus Am Art, New York; Solomon R Guggenheim Mus, New York; Akron Art Inst, Ohio; Fort Worth Art Ctr, Tex.
Dealer: Paula Cooper, 96-100 Prince St, New York, NY 10012.
Mailing Address: P O Box 1554, Shelter Island, NY 11964.

SHIKLER, AARON
Painter
b Brooklyn, N Y, Mar 18, 22.
Study & Training: Tyler Sch Fine Arts, Temple Univ, BFA, BS Educ & MFA; Barnes Found; Hans Hofmann Sch.
Work in Public Collections: Metrop Mus Art, New York, N Y; Mint Mus Art, Charlotte, N C; Parrish Mus Art, Southampton, N Y; Nat Acad Design; Montclair Art Mus, N J.
Commissions: Portraits of Pres & Mrs John F Kennedy for White House.
Exhibitions: New Britain Mus Art, Conn, 64; Gallery Mod Art, New York, 65; Nat Acad Design, 65; Brooklyn Mus, 71; Calif Palace of Legion of Honor, San Francisco, 71; plus others.
Awards: Ranger Award, 59; Proctor Prize, Nat Acad Design, 59 & 60; Thomas B Clarke Prize, 61; plus others.
Bibliography: Shikler & Levine, Brooklyn Mus, 4/71; articles, In: Am Artist, 9/71 & Current Biog, 12/71.

Memberships: Nat Acad Design; Century Asn.
Publications: Contribr, two chaps, In: Pastel painting, 68.
Dealer: Davis Galleries, 231 E 60th St, New York, NY 10022.
Mailing Address: 44 W 77th St, New York, NY 10024.

SHIMODA, OSAMU
Sculptor, Painter
Preferred Media: Iron.
b Manchuria, June 4, 24.
Study & Training: St Paul Univ, Tokyo; Acad Grande Chaumiere, Paris.
Work in Public Collections: St Paul Univ, Tokyo; Syracuse Mus; Nat Mus Mod Art, Tokyo.
Commissions: Murals, Hawaii Chamber of Commerce & Indust, 59.
Exhibitions: Granite Gallery, New York, 66; Nat Mus Mod Art Ann, Tokyo, 67; Suzanne Kohen Gallery, Minneapolis, 70; Bertha Schaefer Gallery, 70; Sculptors Guild, 71 & 72.
Memberships: Sculptors Guild.
Mailing Address: c/o New Bertha Schaefer Gallery, 41 E 57th St, New York, NY 10022.

SHIMON, PAUL
Painter, Illustrator
Preferred Media: Gouache, Tempera, Oils.
b New York, N Y.
Study & Training: Art Stud League New York; also with Jean Liberté.
Work in Public Collections: Butler Inst Am Art, Youngstown, Ohio; four U S Info Agency Embassy bldgs, Africa.
Exhibitions: Audubon Artists, 54; Macdowell Alumni Show, 71.
Awards: Emily Lowe Watercolor Award, 53; Macdowell Colony fel, 60.
Memberships: Artists Equity Asn.
Publications: Illusr, The alluring avocado, 66.
Dealer: Skylight Gallery, 1 Union Sq W, New York, NY 10003.
Mailing Address: 457 Franklin Delano Roosevelt Dr, New York, NY 10002.

SHINER, NATE
Painter, Educator
Preferred Media: Acrylics.
b Vallejo, Calif, Mar 13, 44.
Study & Training: Napa Col, AA; Sacramento State Col, BA & MA.
Exhibitions: San Francisco Art Inst Centennial, San Francisco Mus Art, Calif, 71; Contemporary Painting in America, Whitney Mus Am Art, New York, N Y, 72; Sacramento Sampler, Oakland Art Mus, Calif, 72; Invitational (traveling exhib), São Paulo, Buenos Aires, Brazilia Porto Alegre, E B Crocker Art Gallery, Calif, 72.
Teaching: Instr drawing, Sacramento State Col, 70-71; instr drawing & painting, Sacramento City Col, 71-
Dealer: Candy Store Art Gallery, 605 Sutter, Folsom, CA 95630.
Mailing Address: 2131 51st St, Sacramento, CA 95817.

SHIPLEY, JAMES R
Educator, Designer
b Marion, Ohio, Dec 26, 10.
Study & Training: Cleveland Inst Art, dipl, 35, with Viktor Schreckengost; Western Reserve Univ, BS, 36; Univ Southern Calif; Inst Design, Chicago; Univ Ill, AM, 48.
Exhibitions: May Show, Cleveland Mus Art, 35; Mich Artists Ann, Detroit Inst Art, 37.
Teaching: Prof art & head dept art & design, Univ Ill, Champaign, 39-; instr prod design, Inst Design, Chicago, summer 48; acad dir design, Advan Studies for Designers, Inst Contemp Art, Boston, Mass, summer 58.
Positions: Commercial artist, J H Maish Advert Agency, Marion, Ohio, 29-31; designer, Gen Motors Corp, Detroit, 36-38; free lance designer & art dir, var Midwestern firms, 44-
Awards: Univ Ill Res Bd grant, visual pollution, 70-72.
Memberships: Nat Asn Schs Art (v pres, 60-61, pres, 61-63); Midwest Col Art Asn (v pres, 60-61, pres, 61-62, chmn accreditation comt, 63-70); Indust Designers Soc Am (educ comt, 65-70); Adv Panel Visual Arts, Ill Arts Coun.
Publications: Auth, Programs in art in the state universities, Print, 1-2/60; auth, Interior design, Small Homes Coun, rev ed, 69; co-auth, The new artist, In: Contemporary American painting and sculpture 1969, Univ Ill Press, 69; contribr, Graduate education in the humanities and the arts, State Ill Bd Higher Educ, 70.
Mailing Address: Dept of Art & Design, University of Illinois at Champaign, Champaign, IL 61820.

SHOEMAKER, PETER
Painter, Educator
b Newport, R I, Jan 9, 20.
Study & Training: Calif Sch Fine Arts, San Francisco, cert, with Clyfford Still, Clay Spohn & Elmer Bischoff, 47-50; Univ Calif, Berkeley, BA, 51.

Work in Public Collections: Calif Palace of Legion of Honor, San Francisco; Richmond Art Ctr, Calif; Oakland Mus, Calif.
Exhibitions: III Biennial, São Paulo, Brazil, 55; Corcoran Biennial, Washington, D C, 57; Pacemakers, Contemp Arts Mus, Houston Tex, 57; Carnegie Int, Pittsburgh, Pa, 58; Painters Behind Painters, Calif Palace of Legion of Honor, 67.
Teaching: Assoc prof painting, Calif Col Arts & Crafts, Oakland, 60-
Bibliography: Mary Fuller (auth), Was there a San Francisco school?, Artforum, 1/71.
Memberships: San Francisco Art Inst.
Dealer: John Bolles Gallery, 10 Gold St, San Francisco, CA 94133.
Mailing Address: 622 Panoramic Way, Berkeley, CA 94704.

SHOEMAKER, VAUGHN
Editorial Cartoonist, Painter
b Chicago, Ill, Aug 11, 02.
Study & Training: Chicago Acad Fine Arts, Ill.
Work in Public Collections: Huntington Libr, San Marino, Calif; Syracuse Univ, N Y; Del Mesa Carmel, Calif.
Exhibitions: Obrien Galleries, Chicago, 35 & 36; Marshall Field Galleries, Chicago, 38.
Teaching: Instr ed cartooning, Chicago Acad Fine Arts, 27-42; instr ed cartooning, Studio Sch Art, Chicago, 43-45.
Positions: Cartoonist, Chicago Daily News, 22-25; chief ed cartoonist, 25-52; ed cartoonist, New York Herald Tribune, 56-61; chief ed cartoonist, Chicago Am-Chicago Today, 61-
Awards: Pulitzer Prizes, Columbia Univ, 38 & 47; Headliners Award, Atlantic City, 43.
Bibliography: Gerald W Johnson (auth), The lines are drawn, Lippincott, 58.
Memberships: Hon mem Palette & Chisel Acad Fine Arts, Chicago; hon mem Ridge Art Asn, Chicago.
Publications: Auth, '38 A D, '39 A D, '40 A D, '41-42 A D & '43-44 A D.
Mailing Address: Drawer V, Carmel, CA 93921.

SHOKLER, HARRY
Painter, Serigrapher
Preferred Media: Oils.
b Cincinnati, Ohio, Apr 25, 96.
Study & Training: Cincinnati Art Acad; Pa Sch Fine Arts, summer; New York Sch Fine & Appl Arts; Colorossi, Paris.
Work in Public Collections: Metrop Mus Art, New York, N Y; Philadelphia Mus, Pa; Carnegie Inst, Pa; Libr of Cong, Washington, D C; Syracuse Mus, N Y.
Exhibitions: Paris Salon, 28; Nat Acad Design, New York; Pa Acad Fine Arts, Philadelphia; Southern Vt Artists; Dayton Art Inst; plus one other.
Teaching: Lectr serigraphy, Princeton Univ, Columbia Univ & others, 41-45; instr oil painting, Southern Vt Artists.
Awards: Award for Pigeon Cove, Chaffee Art Mus, 69; award for Tunisian Coffee House, Albany Print Biennial; award for West River in March, Miller Art Ctr.
Memberships: Southern Vt Artists (art comt & trustee, 71); Miller Art Ctr; Chaffee Art Mus; Chester Art Guild; West River Artists.
Publications: Auth, Artists manual for silk screen printmaking.
Dealer: Grand Central Art Galleries, 40 Vanderbilt Ave, New York, NY 10017.
Mailing Address: Londonderry, VT 05148.

SHONNARD, EUGENIE F
Painter, Sculptor
b Yonkers, N Y, 86.
Study & Training: New York Sch Appl Design for Women, with Alphonse Mucha; Art Stud League New York, with James Earl Fraiser; also with Auguste Rodin & Emile Bourdelle, Paris, France.
Work in Public Collections: Brittany Peasant (bronze head), Metrop Mus Art, New York, N Y; Mus Guethary, France; Jardin des Plantes, Paris; Cleveland Mus, Ohio; Colorado Springs Fine Arts Ctr, Colo; plus many others including pvt collections.
Commissions: Decorative wooden panels for Waco, Tex Post Off, U S Treas Dept; decoration in terra-cotta for Ruth Hanna Mem Wing, Presby Hosp, Albuquerque, N Mex; chapel in wood, Mrs Frederick M P Taylor, Black Forest, Colo; Miguel Chavez (portrait bust in bronze), St Michael's Col, Santa Fe, N Mex; Chief Justice Charles Rufus Brice (portrait plaque in bronze), Supreme Ct Bldg, Santa Fe; plus many others.
Exhibitions: Art Inst Chicago; Pa Acad Fine Arts; Mus Mod Art, New York; Whitney Mus Am Art; Brooklyn, Mus; plus many others.
Awards: Grand prize, 40 & first prize, 41, N Mex State Fair; hon fel fine arts, Sch Am Res & Mus N Mex, 54.
Memberships: Fel Nat Sculpture Soc.
Mailing Address: 226 Hickox, Santa Fe, NM 87501.

SHOOK, GEORG E
Painter
Preferred Media: Watercolors.
b Charleston, Miss, May 24, 32.
Study & Training: Orange Voc Col, Orlando, Fla; Univ Fla; Ringling Inst Art, Sarasota, Fla.
Work in Public Collections: Ellen J Martin Collection, Springfield, Mo; City of Springfield Collection & Watercolor U S A Collection, Springfield Art Mus; Artist's Registry, Brooks Mem Art Gallery, Memphis, Tenn.
Exhibitions: 9th-11th Tenn All-State Artists Ann, Nashville, 69-71; 14th-16th Mid-south Ann, Brooks Art Gallery, Memphis, Tenn, 69-71; Watercolor U S A, Springfield Art Mus, 71 & 72; 7th Cent South Ann, Parthenon Galleries, Nashville, 72; 105th Am Watercolor Soc Ann, New York, N Y, 72; plus others.
Positions: Art dir, Memphis Publ Co, 61-
Awards: Ellen J Martin Purchase Award, 71 & purchase award, 72, Watercolor U S A, Springfield; Southern Postcard Co Watercolor Award, Cent South Exhib, Nashville, 72; Little Art Shop Award, Tenn Watercolor Soc First Ann, 72.
Memberships: Art Dirs Club Memphis (pres, 70-72); Memphis Watercolor Soc (co-founder & dir, 69-); Tenn Watercolor Soc (pres, 71-72); Artist's Registry, Brooks Mem Art Gallery.
Mailing Address: 1239 Cherrydale Cove, Memphis, TN 38111.

SHORE, CLOVER VIRGINIA
Painter, Educator
Preferred Media: Oils, Watercolors, Graphics.
b Durango, Texas, Aug 1, 06.
Study & Training: Abilene Christian Col, BA; George Peabody Col, MA; Tex Woman's Univ; Univ Colo, Boulder; also with Clyfford Still, Mark Rothko, Jacob G Smith & Frederic Taubes.
Work in Public Collections: Science Bldg, Tex Christian Univ; Cent Mus, Utrecht, Neth; Fort Worth Osteop Hosp, Tex; Abilene Christian Col, Fort Worth Campus.
Exhibitions: Butler Art Inst Ann, Youngstown, Ohio, 56; Tex Fine Arts, Austin; Birmingham Mus Fine Arts, Ala, 60-62; Nat Watercolor Show, Jackson Mus Art, Miss, 61; Local Artists, Fort Worth Art Ctr, 64.
Teaching: Asst prof art, Tex Christian Univ, 46-48; lectr, Univ Tex, Arlington, 57-58 & 60-63; chmn art dept, Abilene Christian Col, Fort Worth Campus, 68-
Awards: First pl in graphics, West Tex Mus, Abilene, 51; Tex Fine Arts citation awards, 56 & 64; Blanche McVeigh Print Award, 64.
Memberships: Life mem Tex State Teachers Asn; Fort Worth Art Ctr; Tex Fine Arts Asn.
Dealer: Cross Galleries, 3629-A W Seventh St, Fort Worth, TX 76107.
Mailing Address: 2200 Glenco Terr, Fort Worth, TX 76110.

SHORE, MARY
Painter
b Philadelphia, Pa, Mar 19, 12.
Study & Training: Cooper Union Art Sch, scholar; Art Inst Chicago.
Work in Public Collections: Permanent Collections of Addison Gallery Am Art, Andover, Mass, Fitchburg Art Mus, Mass & Baltimore Art Mus, Md.
Exhibitions: One-man shows, oils, Boris Mirski Gallery, Boston, 64, constructions, masks, assemblage & collage, Philadelphia Art Alliance, 65; oils & watercolors, Hilliard Gallery, Martha's Vineyard, Mass, 71; two solo exhibs, Fitchburg Art Mus, 65; Pingree Sch Gallery, Hamilton, Mass, 72; plus many others.
Awards: Blanche E Colman Art Found Award, 66.
Memberships: Artists Equity Asn (past pres Northeast Chap).
Mailing Address: Page St, Gloucester, MA 01930.

SHORE, RICHARD PAUL
Sculptor
b Jersey City, N J, Aug 27, 43.
Study & Training: Marietta Col, BA, 66; New Sch Soc Res, New York, N Y, 66-67.
Work in Public Collections: Storm King Art Ctr Mus Art (on loan), Mountainville, N Y; Aldrich Mus Contemp Art (on loan), Ridgefield, Conn.
Exhibitions: Sculpture in the Park, Van Saun Park, Paramus, N J, 71; Audubon Artists Nat, Nat Acad Galleries, New York, 71; Bergen Community Mus Art, Paramus, 72; Jersey City Mus, 72; invited exhib, Greenwich, Conn, 72; plus others.
Teaching: Guest lectr aesthet, Caldwell Col, 70-71; mem faculty, Art Ctr Northern N J, 72-
Awards: Saks Award, Westchester Art Soc, 71; Ellen A Ross Mem Prize, 71 & Painters & Sculptors Soc Prize, 72, Jersey City Mus Nat Exhib.
Memberships: Mod Arts Guild; Painters & Sculptors Soc N J.
Dealers: Alonzo Gallery, 26 E 63rd St, New York, NY 10021; Kornbluth Gallery, 7-21 Fair Lawn Ave, Fair Lawn, NJ 07410.
Mailing Address: 250 Engle St, Tenafly, NJ 07670.

SHORES, (JAMES) FRANKLIN
Painter
Preferred Media: Watercolors, Oils.
b Hampton, Va, Nov 9, 42.
Study & Training: Pa Acad Fine Arts.
Work in Public Collections: Pa Acad Fine Arts, Philadelphia.
Exhibitions: Pa Acad Fine Arts Ann, 67 & 69; Phila Watercolor
Club Exhibs, 68-72.
Awards: Cresson Europ traveling scholar & Eakins Figure Painting
Prize, 64, Pa Acad Fine Arts.
Mailing Address: 1834 Callowhill St, Philadelphia, PA 19130.

SHORTER, EDWARD SWIFT
Painter, Collector
Preferred Media: Oils.
b Columbus, Ga, July 2, 02.
Study & Training: Mercer Univ, AB & LLD; Corcoran Sch Art; Fon-
tainbleu, Paris, with Andre L'Hote, Wayman Adams & Hugh
Breckenridge; Boston Mus Sch Art.
Work in Public Collections: Corcoran Gallery Art; Atlanta Art Asn;
Ft Hays, Kans; Wesleyan Col, Macon, Ga; Mercer Univ, Macon,
Ga.
Commissions: Portrait, Mercer Univ; paintings, Housing Auth Co-
lumbus, Tift Col & St Francis Hosp.
Exhibitions: Pa Acad Fine Arts; Corcoran Gallery Art; Southern
States Art League; Soc Washington Artists; Southeastern Art Ann.
Collections Arranged: Am Traditionalists of Twentieth Century; Spec
Exhib Old Master Drawings & Graphics; Contemp Exhib Ga Art-
ists.
Positions: Acting dir, Columbus Mus Arts & Crafts, 53-55, dir, 55-
68, emer dir, 68-; pres, Asn Ga Artists, 55-57.
Awards: Gari Melcher Award, Artists Fel; Algenon Sydney Sullivan
Award, Mercer Univ.
Memberships: Am Asn Mus; Artists Equity Asn; Am Artists Prof
League; Salmagundi Club; Soc Washington Artists.
Collection: American paintings; European porcelains; Oriental
ivories and rugs.
Mailing Address: P O Box 1374, Columbus, GA 31906.

SHOSTAK, EDWIN BENNETT
Sculptor
Preferred Media: Wood.
b New York, N Y, Aug 23, 41.
Study & Training: Ohio Univ; Cooper Union.
Work in Public Collections: Phillip Johnson Collection, New Canaan,
Conn.
Exhibitions: Walter Chrysler Art Mus, Provincetown, Mass, 63;
group show, Bykert Gallery, New York, 68; Whitney Mus Sculp-
ture Ann, New York, 69; one-man show, Fischbach Gallery, New
York, 71; Critic's Choice, Sculpture Ctr, New York, 72.
Bibliography: Bob Hughes (auth), In search of the new, pursuit of the
old, Time Mag, 1/71; Garrit Hery (auth), New York letter, Art
Int, 10/71; Denise Green (auth), New York reviews, Arts Mag,
11/71.
Dealer: Fischbach Gallery, 29 W 57th St, New York, NY 10019.
Mailing Address: 76 Jefferson St, New York, NY 10002.

SHOTWELL, HELEN HARVEY
Painter, Photographer
b New York, N Y, Apr 21, 08.
Study & Training: Painting with Henry Lee McFee, Edwin Scott &
Paul Pusinas; photog with Flora Pitt Conrey.
Work in Public Collections: IBM Collection; Fitchburg Art Mus;
Columbia Univ; Albert Schweitzer Found; China Inst New York.
Exhibitions: Dayton Art Inst; High Mus Art; Carnegie Inst; Pa Acad
Fine Arts; Corcoran Gallery Art; plus others; photographs
shown in int salons in New Zealand, Iceland, India, Spain, S Am
& U S.
Memberships: Nat Acad Women Artists; Woodstock Art Asn; fel Int
Inst Arts & Lett; Jackson Heights Art Club; Fitchburg Art Mus.
Mailing Address: 257 W 86th St, New York, NY 10024.

SHOULBERG, HARRY
Painter
Preferred Media: Oils.
b Philadelphia, Pa, Oct 25, 03.
Study & Training: Am Artists Sch; also with Carl Holty & Sol Wil-
son.
Work in Public Collections: Metrop Mus Art, New York, N Y; Car-
negie Inst, Pittsburgh, Pa; Norfolk Mus Arts & Sci, Va; Denver
Mus, Colo.
Exhibitions: Am Oil Painting, Corcoran Gallery Art, Washington,
D C, 41; Print & Watercolor Exhib, Pa Acad Fine Arts, Phila-
delphia, 46; Libr Cong Print Exhib, Washington, D C, 47; Audu-
bon Artists 28th Ann, New York, 70; Nat Acad Design 146th Ann,
New York, 71.

Awards: Emily Lowe Award, 56; Kapp Award, Silvermine Guild, 57;
M J Kaplan Mem Award, Am Soc Contemp Artists, 66.
Bibliography: H Shokler (auth), Artists manual for silk screen
printmaking, 46 & A Reese (auth), American prize prints of the
20th century, 49; Am Artists Group; Margaret Harold (auth),
Prize winning art, bk 7, 66.
Memberships: Audubon Artists; Am Soc Contemp Artists; N J Soc
Painters & Sculptors; Artists Equity Asn New York.
Dealer: Harbor Gallery, 43 Main St, Cold Spring Harbor, NY 11724.
Mailing Address: 112-114 W 14th St, New York, NY 10011.

SHOWELL, KENNETH L
Painter
Preferred Media: Acrylics.
b Huron, S Dak, Oct 22, 39.
Study & Training: Kansas City Art Inst, BFA, 63; Ind Univ, MFA,
65.
Work in Public Collections: Art Inst Chicago, Ill; Whitney Mus Am
Art, New York, N Y; Michener Collection, Univ Tex, Austin;
Akron Mus, Ohio.
Exhibitions: Whitney Mus Am Art Ann, 67-69; Highlights of the
1969-1970 Art Season, Aldrich Mus, Ridgefield, Conn; Lyrical
Abstraction, Whitney Mus Am Art, New York, 71; Spray, Santa
Barbara Mus Art, 71; Painting and Sculpture Today 1972,
Indianapolis Mus Art, Ind, 72.
Bibliography: R Pincus-Witten (auth), New York (rev), Artforum,
1/70; C Ratcliff (auth), The new informalists, Art News, 2/70.
Mailing Address: 11 Lispenard St, New York, NY 10013.

SHUCK, KENNETH MENAUGH
Art Administrator, Painter
Preferred Media: Watercolors, Acrylics.
b Harrodsburg, Ky, May 21, 21.
Study & Training: Ohio State Univ, BS(art educ) & MA(art hist); Univ
Chile, Inst Int Educ scholar, 50.
Exhibitions: Denver Art Mus Ann; Watercolor U S A & 10 State Re-
gional, Springfield, Mo.
Collections Arranged: 10 State Regional Exhib, 51-72; Watercolor
U S A, 61-72.
Positions: Dir, Springfield Art Mus, Mo, 51.
Memberships: Midwest Mus Conf (pres, 63); Mo State Coun Arts
(chmn visual arts, 66-68); Am Asn Mus; Am Fedn Arts.
Mailing Address: 1111 E Brookside Dr, Springfield, MO 65804.

SHUFF, LILY (LILLIAN SHIR)
Painter, Engraver
Preferred Media: Oils, Watercolors.
b New York, N Y.
Study & Training: Hunter Col, BA; Columbia Univ; Brooklyn Acad
Fine Art; Art Stud League New York, with Morris Kantor; also
with Adja Junkers & Jerry Farnsworth.
Work in Public Collections: Metrop Mus Art, New York; Libr of
Cong, Washington, D C; Yale Univ Art Gallery, New Haven, Conn;
Butler Inst Am Art, Youngstown, Ohio; Bezalel Nat Mus, Jerusa-
lem, Israel; plus 32 other mus collections.
Exhibitions: Ten Years of American Prints 1947-1956, Brooklyn
Mus, N Y, 56; Munic Mus Art, Uneo Park, Tokyo, Japan, 60;
Mus Nac Bellas Artes, Buenos Aires, Arg, 63; Royal Scottish
Acad, Edinburgh, Scotland, 63; Int Cult Ctr, New Delhi, India, 66.
Awards: Gold medal of hon for watercolor, N J Mus, 56 & 62; Win-
sor & Newton Prize for oil, Am Soc Contemp Artists, 66, 68 &
70; Elizabeth Rungius Fulda Prize for oil, Nat Asn Women Art-
ists, 69 & 70; plus many others.
Bibliography: Article, In: Think, 59; Alfred Khouri Collection, Norfolk Mus, 63.
Memberships: Nat Asn Women Artists (chmn mem jury, 56-58 & 64-
66; bd dirs, 58-67); Nat Soc Painters Casein (rec secy, 57-64);
New York Soc Women Artists (bd govs, 56-71); Audubon Artists
(graphics dir, 70-72); N J Painters & Sculptors (admission jury,
71).
Art Interests: Slides of paintings circulated in univs & cols in U S A
by Ga Mus Fine Art, Athens.
Publications: Contribr, Art collector's almanac, 65; contribr, Prize
winning paintings, 67; contribr, Prize winning art, 67; contribr,
Today's art, 70; contribr, How to paint a prize winner, 70.
Dealer: East Side Gallery, 307 E 37th St, New York, NY 10016.
Mailing Address: 465 West End Ave, New York, NY 10024.

SHULMAN, JOSEPH L
Collector
Collection: Includes works by Modigliani, Picasso, Gris, Valaden,
Marini, Metzinger, Laurencin, Pascin, Renior, Guttuso, Le
Corbusier, Bauchant, Matisse, Lipchitz, Fresnay, Hofmann,
Gates, Du Fresne, Liberte, Kermelouk, Mirko, Marino, Botkin,
Vespianna and Epstein.
Mailing Address: 162 Mountain Ave, Bloomfield, CT 06002.

SHULMAN, LEON
Art Curator, Instructor
b Worcester, Mass, Dec 18, 36.
Study & Training: Worcester Art Mus Sch, cert; San Francisco Art Inst, MFA.
Collections Arranged: Light and Motion; The Direct Image in Contemporary Painting; Marisol.
Teaching: Instr art hist & painting, Sch of Worcester Art Mus.
Positions: Assoc curator contemp art, Worcester Art Mus.
Publications: Auth, Light and motion (cat), 67, The direct image (cat), 69 & Marisol (cat), 71.
Mailing Address: 22 Lancaster St, Worcester, MA 01608.

SHUNNEY, ANDREW
Painter
Preferred Media: Oils, Acrylics, Gouache.
b Attleboro, Mass, Mar 12, 21.
Study & Training: R I Sch Design; Art Stud League New York, N Y; also with Diego Rivera, Mex.
Work in Public Collections: Art in Embassies Prog, State Dept, Washington, D C; Kenneth Taylor Gallery, Nantucket, Mass; Buehrle Collection, Zurich, Switz; Salon Automne, Paris, France; Countess Guy de Toulouse-Lautrec Collection.
Dealer: Hammer Galleries, 51 E 52nd St, New York, NY 10021.
Mailing Address: 154 Main St, Nantucket, MA 02554.

SHUTE, BEN E
Painter, Instructor
b Altoona, Wis, July 13, 05.
Study & Training: Art Inst Chicago; Chicago Acad Fine Arts.
Work in Public Collections: High Mus Art, Atlanta, Ga; Columbus Mus Arts & Crafts, Ga; Ga Inst Technol, Atlanta; Emory Univ, Atlanta; Mus Art, Columbia, S C; plus others.
Exhibitions: Calif Palace of Legion of Honor, San Francisco, Calif; Pasadena Art Inst; Butler Inst Am Art, Youngstown, Ohio; Telfair Acad Art; Brooklyn Mus, N Y; plus others.
Teaching: Lect, Contemporary American Painting; instr art, Atlanta Art Inst, 28-43, head fine arts dept, 43-70.
Positions: Chmn, Southeastern Ann Exhib, 16 yrs; mem bd, Ga Art Asn.
Awards: Atlanta Watercolor Club, 60; Mead Paper Co Award, 61; Southeastern Ann, 61; plus others.
Memberships: Asn Ga Artists; Nat Soc Painters in Casein.
Mailing Address: 1002 Cardova Dr N E, Atlanta, GA 30324.

SIBLEY, CHARLES KENNETH
Painter, Educator
Preferred Media: Oils, Acrylics, Watercolors.
b Huntington, W Va, Dec 20, 21.
Study & Training: Ohio State Univ, BS; Art Inst Chicago; Columbia Univ, MA; State Univ Iowa, MFA.
Work in Public Collections: Metrop Mus Art, New York, N Y; N C Mus, Raleigh; Va Mus, Richmond; Rochester Mem Mus, N Y; Harvard Univ, Cambridge, Mass.
Commissions: Panels, USS Kennedy, 71 & Seventeen Mag, 72; Virginia landscape (oil), Gov Mansion, Richmond, 72.
Exhibitions: Carnegie Int, Pittsburgh, 57; Whitney Mus Am Art Bi-Ann, New York, 57-59; Nat Soc Arts & Lett, 59; Nat Acad Design, 61; 50 Artists—50 States, Am Fedn Arts, 68.
Teaching: Instr painting & design, Duke Univ, 50-51; prof painting & design, Old Dom Univ, 55-, chmn dept, 55-70.
Awards: Louis Comfort Tiffany grant, 55; Stern Medal, Nat Acad Design, 61; Irene Leache Mem First Prize, Norfolk Mus, 71.
Mailing Address: Rte 1, Box 147F, Cape Charles, VA 22310.

SICARD, LOUIS GABRIEL
Painter, Lecturer
Preferred Media: Oils.
b New Orleans, La.
Study & Training: Tulane Univ La, with Elswoodward; also with Luis Granier, understudy of Sorola & Chas Wellington Boyle.
Commissions: Negroes Gathering Cotton, Chamber of Commerce, New Orleans, 28; Prometheus Depicting Power-Humanity, Southwestern Elec Power Co, Shreveport, La, 56; plantation scenes, B & B Syst Adv Co, Shreveport, 58; old fashioned tailor at work, Selber Bros, 60; two portraits depicting La hist, La State Exhib Mus, Shreveport, 67.
Exhibitions: Coun Am Artist Socs Nat, 64 & 65 & Am Artists Prof League Grand Nat, 72, Lever House, New York, N Y; Witte Mus, San Antonio, Tex, 65; Coppini Acad Fine Arts, 72-
Teaching: Instr landscape, portrait & still life, Louis G Sicard F R S A Sch Art, 45-
Positions: Organized, La Artists Inc, Shreveport, 55; emer dir, Shreveport Art Club, 60; organized, Men's Art Guild, 68 & Men's Prof Art League, 72.

Memberships: Am Artists Prof League; Coppini Acad Fine Arts; Men's Prof Art League; Artists & Craftsmen Asn; fel Royal Soc Art.
Mailing Address: c/o Gallery Ten-Ten, 1010 W Tenth Ave, Amarillo, TX 79101.

SICKMAN, JESSALEE BANE
Painter, Instructor
Preferred Media: Oils.
b Denver, Colo, Aug 17, 05.
Study & Training: Univ Colo; Goucher Col; Corcoran Sch Art, Washington, D C; also with Richard Lahey & Eugen Weisz.
Work in Public Collections: Corcoran Gallery Art.
Commissions: Portrait, comn by Mr Pach, Cleveland, Ohio, 51; Pigeons, comn by Mrs Bruton, Alexandria, Va, 55; figure study, comn by Mrs Woods, San Diego, Calif, 71.
Exhibitions: One-man watercolor show, Pub Libr, Washington, D C, 42; Corcoran Gallery Art Biennial Exhibs, 42-50; Colony Club, Washington, D C, 58 & 62; Soc Washington Artists, Smithsonian Inst, 68 & Arts Club.
Teaching: Instr still life, Warrentown Country Sch, Va, 40; instr life portrait, Corcoran Sch Art, 40-63; instr portrait & still life, Sickman Studios, Washington, D C, 64-
Awards: Landscape Award, Corcoran Sch Art, 37; Alice Barney Mem Portrait Award, 38.
Memberships: Artists Equity Asn; Soc Washington Artists.
Mailing Address: 1215 Eye St N W, Washington, DC 20015.

SICKMAN, LAURENCE CHALFONT STEVENS
Art Administrator, Art Historian
b Denver, Colo, Aug 27, 06.
Study & Training: Harvard Univ, AB(cum laude), 30, Harvard-Yenching fel China Peking, 30-35, resident fel, Fogg Art Mus, 37-39; hon DFA, Rockhurst Col, 72.
Teaching: Lectr hist art, Univ Kans, 70-; lectr hist art, Univ Mo-Kansas City, 70-
Positions: Cur Oriental art, Nelson Gallery Art, Kansas City, Mo, 35-45, v dir, 46-53, dir, 53-; ed, Arch Asian Art, 66-
Awards: Knight Order of the Pole Star, H M King of Sweden, 68.
Memberships: Asn Art Mus Dirs (pres, 64); Am Asn Mus (coun mem, 63-69); Col Art Asn Am (bd dirs, 63-68); Chinese Art Soc Am (bd gov, 48-, ed, Arch, 48-66); Am Coun Learned Socs (comt Far Eastern Studies, 48-53).
Research: Far Eastern art, especially Chinese paintings and sculpture.
Publications: Ed, The university prints, Oriental art, series O, early Chinese art, 38; co-auth, The art and architecture of China, Pelican history of art, 56; ed & contribr, Chinese calligraphy and painting in the collection of John M Crawford, Jr, 62.
Mailing Address: Nelson Gallery—Atkins Museum, 4525 Oak St, Kansas City, MO 64111.

SIDER, DENO
Painter, Sculptor
Preferred Media: Oils, Clay, Ink, Charcoal.
b Norwich, Conn, Mar 2, 26.
Study & Training: Norwich Acad, dipl; also with Leon Franks.
Work in Public Collections: Mattatuck Mus, Conn.
Commissions: Map of U S & decor, Aldo, Hollywood, 56; side panels & fish murals (mixed media), Aquarium, Tarzana, 66.
Exhibitions: Int Madonna Festival, Los Angeles, 58-61 & 63-64; Calif State Show, Sacramento, 62 & 66; Los Angeles Co Art Show, Los Angeles, 66; Hollywood Bowl Art Festival, Los Angeles, 68-69; Gallery Tour, distrib by Ira Roberts.
Teaching: Instr art & oils & owner, Sider Art Sch, Hollywood, 54-64; instr art & oils, Leedes Art Sch, Encino, Calif, 64-
Positions: Partner, Leedes Art Gallery, 64-71, owner, 71-
Awards: Mattatuck Mus Purchase Award, 64; Madonna Festival Award, Methodist Church, Los Angeles, 64; Hollywood Bowl Best of Show, 68 & 69.
Memberships: Life mem San Fernando Valley Art Club; Calif Art Club; Valley Artist Guild; Burbank Art Asn.
Specialty of Gallery: French academic Impressionist sculpture and paintings.
Collections: Leon Franks; Egyptian 18th Dynasty art; G McGregor; T'sung Dynasty scrolls.
Publications: Illusr, Epicurean Mag, 69-70; illusr & ed, Prospector News, 71-
Mailing Address: 17620 Ventura Blvd, Encino, CA 01316.

SIDERIS, ALEXANDER
Painter
b Skopelos, Greece, Feb 21, 98.
Study & Training: Art Stud League New York, N Y; Acad Julian, Paris, France; also with George Bridgman & Pierre Laurence.
Work in Public Collections: Amarillo Mus, Tex; Wesleyan Col, Macon, Ga; Greek Church, Philadelphia, Pa; murals, Church of

the Annunciation, Pensacola, Fla; Byzantine mural, Greek
Cathedral, New York; plus others.
Exhibitions: Allied Artists Am, 40-44 & 57; Barbizon Gallery, 54;
Nat Arts Club, 55; Knickerbocker Artists, 59-61; one-man
show, Hellenic Am Union Gallery, Athens, Greece, 68; plus
other group & one-man shows.
Awards: Prize, Am Artists Prof League, 53; award, Nat Arts Club,
61; gold medal prize, 64 & hon mention for oil, 70, Knicker-
bocker Artists.
Memberships: Am Artists Prof League (v pres N Y Chap, 56-58).
Mailing Address: 116 Pinehurst Ave, New York, NY 10033.

SIEBER, ROY
Educator, Museum Curator
b Shawano, Wis, Apr 28, 23.
Study & Training: New Sch Social Res, BA, 49; Univ Iowa, MA, 51,
PhD, 57.
Teaching: Lect, African Art to cols, Peace Corps & others; from
instr to asst prof art hist, Univ Iowa, 50-62; mem fac, Ind Univ,
62-64; prof art hist, 64-, chmn fine arts dept, 67-70; vis prof
Univ Ghana, 64, 67; vis prof, Univ Ife, Nigeria, 71.
Positions: Mem for area fel prog, Africa Screening Comt, 59-63;
cur primitive art, Ind Univ Fine Arts Mus, 62-; mem primitive
art adv comt, Metrop Mus Art; mem joint comt Africa, Am Coun
Learned Socs-Social Sci Res Coun, 62-70; trustee, Mus African
Art.
Awards: African-Am Univ grant, 64; Ind Univ Int Studies grant, 64,
67; Nat Endowment for Humanities sr fel, 70-71; plus others.
Memberships: Royal Anthrop Inst; African Studies Asn (chmn arts
& humanities comt, 63); Col Art Asn Am; Am Asn Univ Prof; Mid-
west Art Asn (secy, 63).
Research: African art.
Publications: Auth, Sculpture of northern Nigeria, Mus Primitive
Art, N Y, 61; co-auth, Sculpture of Black Africa, Los Angeles Co
Mus Art, 68; auth, African textiles and decorative arts, Mus Mod
Art, N Y, 72; plus numerous articles & symp.
Mailing Address: 114 Glenwood Ave E, Bloomington, IN 47401.

SIEGEL, ADRIAN
Photographer, Painter
b New York, N Y, July 17, 98.
Work in Public Collections: Philadelphia Mus Art; Mus Mod Art,
New York.
Commissions: Circulating exhibs, Musicians at Work & People &
Art, Philadelphia Mus Art.
Exhibitions: Three Photographers, Philadelphia Mus Art; Six Pho-
tographers, Mus Mod Art, 49; Pa Acad Fine Arts Ann, Philadel-
phia; Pepsi Cola Show, Metrop Mus Art, New York; Artists Eq-
uity Exhib, Civic Ctr, Philadelphia, 72.
Positions: Official Photogr, Philadelphia Orch, 37.
Awards: Gold medal, Art Dirs Club, New York, 49.
Bibliography: Orchestra man looks at the world's great musicians,
Life, 43; Charles D Sigsbee (auth), Idol moments in the orches-
tra, Sun Mag, 52; A lens among the strings, High Fidelity Mag,
55.
Memberships: Philadelphia Art Alliance; Artists Equity Asn; fel
Royal Soc Art, Eng; Philadelphia Print Club; Pa Acad Fine Arts.
Publications: Auth, Concerto for camera, Philadelphia Orchestra
Asn.
Mailing Address: 1907 Pine St, Philadelphia, PA 19103.

SIEGEL, (LEO) DINK
Illustrator
Preferred Media: Watercolors, Inks, Oils, Gouache.
b Birmingham, Ala.
Study & Training: Nat Acad Design; Art Stud League New York; Am
Sch Art; also with Robert Brackman.
Memberships: Soc Illustrators.
Publications: Illusr, Redbook, Cosmopolitan, Sat Eve Post, Good
Housekeeping, New Yorker & Playboy.
Mailing Address: 100 W 57th St, New York, NY 10019.

SIEGEL, IRENE
Painter
b Chicago, Ill.
Study & Training: Northwestern Univ, BS; Univ Chicago; Ill Inst
Technol Inst Design, Moholy-Nagy scholar, 54, MS.
Work in Public Collections: Art Inst Chicago; Mus Mod Art, New
York, N Y; Los Angeles Co Mus; World Bank, Washington, D C;
Pasadena Mus, Calif.
Exhibitions: Drawing Soc Show, Mus Fine Arts, Houston, Tex, 65;
Form & Fantasy, Am Fedn Art, 69; Tamarind Prints, Mus Mod
Art, 69; Soc Contemp Art, Art Inst Chicago, 71; Relativerend
Realisme, Van Abbemuseum, Eindhoven, Holland, 72.
Awards: Mr & Mrs Frank Logan Prize, 66; Tamarind fel, Ford
Found, 67.

Bibliography: William S Lieberman (auth), Homage to lithography,
Mus Mod Art, 69; Garo Antreasian (auth), The Tamarind book of
lithography, Abrams, 71; Franz Schulze (auth), Fantastic images,
Follett, 72.
Publications: Illusr, Barnyard epithets and other obscenities, 70.
Dealer: LoGiudice Gallery, 59 Wooster, New York, NY 10013.
Mailing Address: 421 Roslyn Pl, Chicago, IL 60614.

SIEGRIEST, LUNDY
Painter, Instructor
Preferred Media: Oils, Mixed Media.
b Oakland, Calif, Apr 4, 25.
Study & Training: Calif Col Arts & Crafts, Oakland, cert.
Work in Public Collections: Whitney Mus Am Art, New York, N Y;
Denver Art Mus, Colo; Libr Cong, Washington, D C; Santa Bar-
bara Mus, Calif; Oakland Mus.
Exhibitions: 3rd Biennale Sao Paulo, Brazil, 55; Carnegie Inst Int,
Pittsburgh, 55; Young Am Under 35, 58 & Contemp Am Painting,
60, Whitney Mus Am Art; 17 Am Painters, Brussels World's
Fair, 58.
Teaching: Instr painting, Acad Art, San Francisco, Calif, 51-64;
instr painting, Jr Ctr Art, Oakland, 53-71; instr painting, Civic
Arts, Walnut Creek, Calif, 64.
Awards: Albert M Bender grant, 52; purchase awards, Calif Palace
Legion of Honor, 52 & Santa Barbara Mus, 55.
Bibliography: New talent, art U S A, Art Am, 57; Contemporary
American painting, Univ Ill Press, 63.
Dealer: Bolles Gallery, 10 Gold St, San Francisco, CA 94133.
Mailing Address: 479 Cavour St, Oakland, CA 94618.

SIEVAN, MAURICE
Painter
Preferred Media: Oils, Watercolors, Pastels.
b Ukraine, Russia, Dec 7, 98; U S citizen.
Study & Training: Nat Acad Design, New York, N Y, with Leon Kroll
& Charles Hawthorne; Art Stud League New York; also with
Andre L'Hote, Paris, France.
Work in Public Collections: Mus Mod Art, New York; Brooklyn Mus,
N Y; Baltimore Mus, Md; Butler Inst Am Art, Youngstown, Ohio;
Walter Chrysler Mus, Provincetown, Mass.
Exhibitions: Salon Automne, Paris, France, 31; Brooklyn Mus Int
Watercolor Exhibs, 41 & 53; Artists For Victory, Metrop Mus
Art, New York, 42; Painting U S A, Carnegie Inst Fine Arts,
Pittsburgh, Pa, 43, 44 & 45; Romantic Painting Am, 43, Recent
Drawings, 56 & New Acquisitions 64-65, Mus Mod Art.
Teaching: Instr art, Summit Art Asn, 40-50; instr art, Queens Col,
Flushing, N Y, 46-68.
Awards: Newhouse Mem Award, Audubon Artists, 46; first prize,
Queens Bot Gardens, 49; Invitation Award Res Studios, Maitland,
Fla, 53.
Bibliography: Elizabeth McCausland (auth), Work for artists, Am
Artists Group, 47; Lawrence Campbell (auth), Maurice Sievan,
Art News, 5/55; Ivan Karp (auth), Seven paintings by Sievan,
Barone Gallery, 1/60.
Memberships: Woodstock Art Asn; Fedn Mod Painters & Sculptors
(all comts); Col Art Asn Am; Artists Equity Asn.
Mailing Address: 924 West End Ave, New York, NY 10025.

SIGEL, BARRY CHAIM
Painter
Preferred Media: Oils, Watercolors, Feathers.
b Baltimore, Md, Sept 22, 43.
Study & Training: Md Inst Art; Acad Art, New Haven; with Mrs
Rosenfield, N Truro, Mass; also with A G Giovanni, Giorzinko,
Sicily.
Work in Public Collections: Union Plumbers Am Hall, Pasadena;
Harvey House Rest, Baltimore; Grand Canyon Hist Mus, Ariz;
Royal Mus, Bombay, India.
Commissions: Portraiture & bust, Richard Lyttle, New Haven, Conn,
68; mural, Pierre's Beauty Salon, New York, N Y, 69; watercolor,
Mr & Mrs Dilly McKenzie, Cape Cod, Mass, 69; outdoor sign,
Right-on Church of Good Vibes, Mesa, Wyo, 70; collage (with Ann
Kutti), Layed Back'n Mello Rest Home, San Francisco, Calif, 72.
Exhibitions: Baltimore Mus Art, 65 & 66; Datza Mabot Gallery,
Pecarino, Sicily, 67; Grand Prix de Still Life, Ostend, Belg, 68;
Greenwich Village Outdoor Show, 69; Green Mountain Art Gallery,
New York, 71.
Teaching: Critic painting, Scungia Acad, Sicily, 69.
Awards: Louis Waitsman prize, Baltimore Arts Asn, 66; Chalk
Championship New York, 71.
Bibliography: N P Clark (auth), article, In: Baltimore News Post, 66;
Tworkov (auth), You call these paintings?, N H Hist Mag, 68.
Memberships: Charcoal Club Baltimore.
Dealer: Green Mountain Art Gallery, 135 Greene St, New York, NY
10012.
Mailing Address: 28 E Broadway, New York, NY 10002.

SIGISMUND, VIOLET M
Painter, Printmaker
Preferred Media: Oils, Watercolors, Woodblock.
b New York, N Y.
Study & Training: Art Stud League New York; also with Sidney Laufman & George Grosz.
Exhibitions: Pa Acad Fine Arts, Philadelphia, 47; Audubon Artists, New York, 47, 48 & 61; Butler Inst Am Art, Youngstown, Ohio, 62; Nat Acad Design, New York, 62 & 64; Nat Asn Women Artists, Int Festival Cannes, France, 65; group print shows, Albany Inst Arts, 71, Cayuga Mus, 73 & Washington Co Mus, Md, 71-73.
Awards: Silver medal, Knickerbocker Artists, 52; Friend's Award, Silvermine Guild, 60; Sargent Prize, Nat Asn Women Artists, 63.
Memberships: Knickerbocker Artists; National Asn Women Artists; Provincetown Art Asn; Artists Equity Asn New York (exec bd, 60-73, chmn mem, 60-73).
Dealers: Clinton Seeley, Rye Beach, NH 03871; Paul Kessler, Provincetown, MA 02657.
Mailing Address: 1 Sheridan Sq, New York, NY 10014.

SIHVONEN, OLI
Painter
Preferred Media: Acrylics, Oils.
b Brooklyn, N Y, Jan 31, 21.
Study & Training: Art Stud League New York; Black Mt Col, N C, with Josef Albers & Buckminster Fuller.
Work in Public Collections: Mus Mod Art, New York, N Y; Whitney Mus Am Art, New York; Corcoran Gallery Art, Washington, D C; Dallas Mus Fine Arts, Tex; Art Inst Chicago, Ill.
Commissions: Lobby wall painting, State Agency Bldg, S Mall, Albany, N Y, 68; painting, Northwestern Univ, Evanston, Ill, 69.
Exhibitions: Geometric Abstraction in America, 62 & Whitney Ann, 63, 65 & 67, Whitney Mus Am Art; The Responsive Eye, Mus Mod Art, New York, 65; 30th Biennial Am Painting, Corcoran Gallery Art, 67; Plus X Minus Todays Half Century, Albright-Knox, Buffalo, N Y, 68.
Awards: Nat Coun Arts Award, 67; purchase award, Corcoran Biennial, 67.
Mailing Address: 245 Grand St, New York, NY 10002.

SILBERSTEIN, MURIEL ROSOFF
Instructor, Painter
Preferred Media: Assemblage, Collage.
b Brooklyn, N Y.
Study & Training: Carnegie Inst Technol, BFA; Philadelphia Mus Art, with Hobson Pitman; Inst Mod Art, with Victor D'Amico, Donald Stacy & Jane Bland.
Commissions: Prog drawings, Philadelphia Symphony Orch Children's Concerts, 49; murals & other projs, Mt Sinai Hosp & Philadelphia Psychiat Hosp.
Exhibitions: Jewish Community Ctr Group Show, 71-72; one-woman show, Panoras Gallery, New York, N Y, 72.
Teaching: Instr art, Inst Mod Art, Mus Mod Art, New York, N Y, 63; guest lectr art educ, var cols & community groups, New York, 67-; instr, Int Playgroups Art Workshops, New York, 70-; instr, Staten Island Community Col, 70-; instr, parent-child classes, Metrop Mus Art.
Positions: Assoc dir & scene designer, Pittsburgh Playhouse, 44-46; interior display designer, var Pittsburgh dept stores, 46-47; art educ consult, Staten Island Ment Health Schs, Head Start, Staten Island Community Col & others.
Awards: Woman of Achievement, Staten Island Advan, 67; achievement award, Lambda Kappa Mu Sorority.
Memberships: New York Art Comn (comnr, 70-); Metrop Mus Art (trustee, 71-); Staten Island Coun Arts; New York Cult Coun (visual arts comt, 72); Heritage House (dir).
Research: Art education; community arts projects.
Publications: Contribr, Art Caravan.
Mailing Address: 144 Clinton Ave, Staten Island, NY 10301.

SILINS, JANIS
Painter, Educator
Preferred Media: Oils, Watercolors.
b Riga, Latvia, June 1, 96; U S citizen.
Study & Training: Univ Moscow; Riga Univ, MA & PhD; Univ Stockholm; Univ Marburg; Art Sch Ilya Mashkov, Moscow; Art Sch Kazan.
Work in Public Collections: Univ Art Collection, Riga; Art Mus Jelgava, Latvia.
Exhibitions: Nat Art Exhib, Riga, 28; Exhib Artists In Exile, Stuttgart, Ger, 48; Ringling Mus Art, Sarasota, 63; Latvian Exhib Arts & Crafts, Boston, 64; Latvian Artist Group New York, N Y, 67.
Collections Arranged: Hugh Gowan Miller Collection Paintings, Norfolk Mus, Va, 55; Arts of Norway, Morse Art Gallery, Winter Park, Fla & Tour, 58; plus many others.

Teaching: Instr art hist, Riga Univ & Latvian Acad Art, 31-44; instr art hist, Univ Würzburg, 46-51; instr art hist, Rollins Col, 56-63.
Positions: Dir art mus, Riga Univ, 41-44; art consult, Norfolk Mus, 55-; exec dir, Morse Gallery Art, 56-60.
Awards: Order of Three Stars, Govt Latvia, 36; Kriskian Baron Award, Riga Univ, 37.
Bibliography: J Kadilis (auth), Janis Silins, Cels, 46; L Liberts (auth), Janis Silins, 46 & A Annus (auth), Seeking for beauty and truth, 66, Laiks; plus others.
Memberships: Latvian Artist Group New York; Sarasota Art Asn; Orlando Art Asn (mem bd, 62); Asn Artists, Sadarbs, Riga (secy, 24-38); Am Asn Univ Prof.
Research: Basic problems of art philosophy, especially ontology of art; principles of modern art; Latvian art.
Publications: Auth, Rudolph Perle, 28; auth, Michelangelo, 31; auth, Karlis Zale, his monumental sculpture, 38 & 43; auth, Laudolf Liberts, painter and stage designer, 42; auth, Janis Gailis, a Latvian landscape painter, 48; plus one other.
Mailing Address: 1258 Chestnut St, Roselle, NJ 07203.

SILKOTCH, MARY ELLEN
Painter
b New York, N Y, Sept 12, 11.
Study & Training: Van Emburgh Sch Art; also with Jonas Lie, Sigismund Ivanowski & Dudley Gloyne, summers.
Work in Public Collections: Work in pvt collections.
Exhibitions: Nat Acad Women Artists; Montclair Art Mus, N J; Am Artists Prof League; Atlantic City Art Ctr; Irvington Mus & Art Asn; plus others.
Teaching: Instr art, Van Emburgh Sch, Plainfield, 44-64; instr art, Adult Educ, Dunellen, N J, 48-57; instr art, Bound Brook Adult Educ, 50-57; instr art, North Plainfield, 51-54.
Positions: V pres, Academic Artists, 67-; v pres, Trailside Mus Arts Ctr N J.
Awards: Prizes, Am Artists Prof League, Plainfield Art Asn & East Orange, N J; plus others.
Memberships: Nat Asn Women Artists; Plainfield Art Asn (pres, 52-60); Am Artists Prof League (pres, N J Chap, 69-); N J Adult Educ Asn; Westfield Art Asn.
Mailing Address: 341 Hazelwood Pl, Piscataway, NJ 08854.

SILLS, THOMAS ALBERT
Painter
b Castalia, N C, Aug 20, 14.
Work in Public Collections: Whitney Mus Am Art, New York, N Y; Metrop Mus Art, New York; Mus Mod Art, New York; Chase Manhattan Collection, New York; Sheldon Mem Gallery, Lincoln, Nebr; plus many others.
Exhibitions: Wilson Col, Chambersberg, Pa, 68; Stud Ctr Art Gallery, Brooklyn Col, N Y, 69; New Am Painting & Sculpture, The First Generation, Mus Mod Art, New York, 69; Afro-Am Artists Exhib, Mus Philadelphia Civic Ctr, Pa, 69; Mt Holyoke Col, South Hadley, Mass, 69; plus other group & one-man exhibs.
Awards: William & Norma Copley Found Award, 57.
Mailing Address: 240 W 11th St, New York, NY 10014.

SILVERCRUYS, SUZANNE (MRS EDWARD FORD STEVENSON)
Sculptor, Lecturer
b Maeseyck, Belg; U S citizen.
Study & Training: Les Filles de la Croix, Liege; Newham Col, Cambridge Univ; Georgetown Visitation Convent, Washington, D C; Yale Univ Sch Fine Arts, BFA, 28; study in Paris & Belg; Temple Univ, hon LHD, 42; Mt Allison Univ, LLD.
Work in Public Collections: Busts, plaques & Mem, Louvain Libr; McGill Univ, Can; Yale Univ Sch Med; Reconstruct Hospital, N Y; Mus Mod Art, New York, N Y; plus many others.
Commissions: Amelia Earhart Trophy, Zonta Club; bust of Cardinal Cushing, Stonehill Col, Northeaston, Mass; statue of Padre Kino of Ariz for Statuary Hall, Rotunda, U S Capitol, Washington, D C; Hon Joseph W Martin, Rotunda of old House of Rep, Washington, D C; war Mem, Shawinigan Falls, Can; plus many others including portrait busts of prominent people.
Exhibitions: Corcoran Gallery Art, Washington, D C; Nat Inst Archit Educ; Salon de Printemps, 31.
Teaching: Lectr process of sculpture making.
Positions: Radio artist, NBC-TV.
Awards: First prize, Rome Alumni Competition, 27; Chevalier de L'Ordre de Leopold; Officer de l'ordre de la Couronne, Belg; plus many others.
Publications: Auth, Suzanne of Belgium; auth, A primer of sculpture, 42.
Mailing Address: 3001 E Camino de Bravo, Tucson, AZ 85718.

SILVERMAN, BURTON PHILIP
Painter, Illustrator
Preferred Media: Oils, Watercolors, Pastels.
b Brooklyn, N Y, June 11, 28.
Study & Training: Pratt Inst; Art Stud League New York, 46-49;

Columbia Univ, BA, 49.
Work in Public Collections: Brooklyn Mus; Philadelphia Mus Art, Pa; Anchorage Mus Art, Alaska; New Britain Mus Am Art, Conn; Parrish Mus Art, Southampton, N Y.
Exhibitions: Pa Acad Art Ann, Philadelphia, 49; Seven Shows, Butler Inst Am Art Ann, Ohio, 54-70; Nat Acad Design, New York, 64-71; San Diego Arts Festival, Calif, 66; Childe Hassam Exhib, Nat Inst Arts & Lett, New York, 67.
Teaching: Instr drawing & painting, Sch Visual Arts, New York, 64-67.
Awards: Henry W Ranger Purchase Prize, 65 & Benjamin Altman Figure Prize, 69, Nat Acad Design; Dillard Collection Purchase Prize, Art on Paper, Univ N C, 66.
Bibliography: Fredrick Whitaker (auth), Four realists, 10/64 & Elizabeth Case (auth), Burton Silverman captures the moment, 6/71, Am Artist Mag; Joseph Singer (auth), Pastel portraits, Watson-Guptill (in prep).
Memberships: Academician, Nat Acad Design.
Publications: Co-auth, A new look at the eight, Art News, 2/58; auth, Homage to Thomas Eakins, 67 & Art for Pablo Picasso's sake, 68, Book World.
Dealers: FAR Gallery, 746 Madison Ave, New York, NY 10021; Kenmore Galleries, 122 S 18th St, Philadelphia, PA 19103.
Mailing Address: 324 W 71st St, New York, NY 10023.

SILVERMAN, RONALD H
Educator
Study & Training: Univ Calif, Los Angeles, BA, 52; Los Angeles State Col, MA, 55; Stanford Univ, EdD, 62.
Teaching: Prof art, Los Angeles State Univ, 55-
Mailing Address: Art Dept, Calif State Univ, Los Angeles, 5151 State University Dr, Los Angeles, CA 90032.

SIME, JOHN
Art Administrator
b Milford Haven, Wales, Nov 5, 25.
Study & Training: Trinity Col, Cambridge Univ, MA.
Positions: Dir, Artist's Workshop, Holkley Valley Sch, New Sch Art, 62-70; exec dir, Three Schs Art, Toronto, Ont, 70-; dir, Mus Contemp Art, Toronto.
Awards: Can Coun travel grants, 68 & 72.
Bibliography: Vera Frenkel (auth), The new school of art: insight-explosions, Arts Can, 10/68.
Mailing Address: 296 Brunswick Ave, Toronto 179, Ont, Can.

SIMON, BERNARD
Sculptor, Instructor
b Russia, Jan 6, 96.
Study & Training: Educ Alliance & Art Workshop, New York.
Work in Public Collections: Slater Mem Mus, Norwich, Conn; Norfolk Mus Arts & Sci, Va; also in pvt collections.
Exhibitions: Audubon Artists; Silvermine Guild Art; Boston Arts Festival; Provincetown Group; Hyannis Art Asn; plus others.
Teaching: Instr, Mus Mod Art, New York; instr, New Sch Social Res; instr, Bayonne Art Ctr.
Awards: Prizes, Knickerbocker Artists, Audubon Artists & N J Soc Painters & Sculptors; plus others.
Memberships: Silvermine Guild Arts; Brooklyn Soc Artists; Knickerbocker Artists; Provincetown Art Asn; Cape Cod Art Asn.
Mailing Address: 490 West End Ave, New York, NY 10024.

SIMON, ELLEN R
Designer, Painter
b Toronto, Ont, Apr 15, 16.
Study & Training: Ont Col Art; Art Stud League New York; New Sch Social Res; also with Joep Nicolas & Yvonne Williams.
Work in Public Collections: Albertina Collection, Vienna; New York Pub Libr; Brooklyn Mus, N Y; Nat Gallery Can; Art Gallery Ont.
Commissions: Stained glass windows in many churches & synagogues in Can; Sidney Hillman Mem Window, Hastings-on-Hudson, N Y; Church of St Michael & All Angels, Toronto, 60-67; windows for Holy Family Narthex, Princeton Univ Chapel, 66; Adlai Stevenson Mem Window; plus others.
Exhibitions: Nat Gallery Can; Philadelphia Mus Art, Pa; Smithsonian Inst; Carnegie Libr, Pittsburgh, Pa; Mus Contemp Crafts, New York; plus others.
Teaching: Instr in stained glass, Riverside Church Arts & Crafts Prog, N Y, 65-
Publications: Auth & illusr, The critter book, 40; illusr, Inga of Porcupine Mine, 42, Americans all, 44 & Music in early childhood, 52.
Mailing Address: 419 W 119th St, New York, NY 10027.

SIMON, HOWARD
Illustrator, Painter
Preferred Media: Watercolors, Oils, Wood.
b New York, N Y, July 22, 03.
Study & Training: Nat Acad Design, New York; Acad Julian, Paris.
Work in Public Collections: Metrop Mus Art; New York Pub Libr Print Collection; Mills Col Print Collection, Calif; Brooks Mem, Memphis; Univ Ore Libr; plus others.
Exhibitions: 50 Prints of Yr; 50 Bks of Yr; Victoria & Albert Mus, London; one-man show, Smithsonian Inst; Art Ctr, New York; plus others.
Teaching: Adj asst prof painting & drawing, New York Univ Sch Visual Arts, 45-65.
Publications: Illusr, many bks, 26-; auth, Cabin on a ridge, Follett, 69.
Mailing Address: Stanfordville, NY 12581.

SIMON, NORTON
Collector
b Portland, Ore, Feb 5, 07.
Positions: Mem bd mus assocs, Los Angeles Co Mus Art; pres & trustee, Hunt Foods & Industries Mus Art.
Collection: Paintings.
Mailing Address: 1645 W Valencia Dr, Fullerton, CA 92633.

SIMON, SIDNEY
Sculptor, Painter
b Pittsburgh, Pa, May 21, 17.
Study & Training: Carnegie Inst Technol; Pa Acad Fine Arts, Emlen Cresson fel, 40 & Edwin Austin Abbey fel, 40-41, BFA, with George Harding; Univ Pa, BA; Barnes Found.
Work in Public Collections: Metrop Mus Art, New York, N Y; Arch-Hist Div, U S War Dept, Washington, D C; Am Embassy, Paris, France; Cornell Univ Med Ctr, Kramer Col, Ithaca, N Y.
Commissions: Crucifix & St John, Our Lady of Angels, Glenmont, N Y; bronze grill, State Univ N Y Downstate Med Ctr, entrance hall; wall design, Walt Whitman High Sch, Yonkers, N Y; The Circus (mobile), Woodland House, Hartford, Conn; entrance sculpture, 747 Bldg, New York, 72.
Exhibitions: Pa Acad Fine Arts Ann, 48-52 & 62-72; Am Painting, Metrop Mus Art, 50; Nine Whitney Mus Am Art Ann, 50-62; Mus Mod Art Assemblage Exhib, 62; L'Aquarelle Contemporaine aux Etats Units, State Dept, 63.
Teaching: Instr drawing, New Sch Social Res; instr & founding dir, Skowhegan Sch Painting & Sculpture, Maine, 45-58; instr painting, Brooklyn Mus Sch; vis prof, Salzburg Sem Am Studies, 71.
Positions: Artist-in-residence, Am Acad Rome, Italy, 69-70; vis sculptor, Sarah Lawrence Col, 71-72.
Bibliography: Robert Rice (auth), Sidney Simon, Motel on Mountain, 60; Richard McLanathan (auth), Sidney Simon, Grippi Gallery, 64; Barbara Kafka (auth), Craft Horizon, 67.
Memberships: Artists Equity Asn New York; Century Asn; Archit League; Skowhegan Sch Painting & Sculpture; Provincetown Art Asn.
Dealer: Graham Gallery, 1014 Madison Ave, New York, NY 10021.
Mailing Address: 95 Bedford St, New York, NY 10014.

SIMON, SIDNEY
Educator, Art Historian
b Pittsburgh, Pa, June 13, 22.
Study & Training: Carnegie Inst, BFA; Harvard Univ, PhD.
Collections Arranged: Collaborated on Gerhard Marcks, Sculptor, 53, Reality and Fantasy 1900-1954, Expressionism 1900-1955, Sculpture of Theodore Roszak, 56, Paintings by Stuart Davis, 57, The 18th Century: One Hundred Drawings by One Hundred Artists, 61, The 19th Century: 125 Master Drawings, 62 & 20th Century Master Drawings, 63.
Teaching: Assoc prof art, Univ Minn, 59-67, prof art hist, 68-
Positions: Sr cur, Walker Art Ctr, 53-59; dir Univ Minn Art Gallery, 59-67.
Awards: Fulbright res fel, 59.
Memberships: Col Art Asn Am.
Mailing Address: 2668 Inglewood Ave S, Minneapolis, MN 55416.

SIMONI, JOHN PETER
Painter, Educator
b Denver, Colo, Apr 12, 11.
Study & Training: Colo State Col Educ, BA & MA; Nat Univ Mex; Kansas City Art Inst, with Thomas Hart Benton; Colo Univ, with Max Beckmann; Ohio State Univ, PhD; Mass Inst Technol; also in Trentino, Italy.
Work in Public Collections: Colo Friends of Art Collection.
Commissions: Reliefs, sculpture, murals, Southwest-Citizens Fed Savings & Loan Asn, Wichita, Kansas State Bank, Newton, Fine Arts Ctr Theatre, Univ Wichita, East Heights Methodist Church & Citizens Nat Bank, Emporia, Kans; plus others.

Exhibitions: Mulvane Mus Art; Wichita Art Mus; Colo State Univ; Birger Sandzen Mem Gallery, Lindsborg, Kans; Univ Wichita.
Collections Arranged: Organized Elsie Allen Art Gallery & assembled the Allen Collection of paintings, Baker Univ; arranged & catalogued the Bloomfield Collection of paintings, Univ Wichita, 56.
Teaching: Lect, Art Education Today, Italian Renaissance, Art in Religion & others; head dept art, Baker Univ, 37-55; prof art, Univ Wichita, 55-57, chmn dept art, 57-63; prof art, Wichita State Univ, 64-
Positions: Gallery dir, Baker Univ, 37-55; dir Univ Galleries, Univ Wichita, 57-63; color consult, Western Lithograph Co, Wichita, Kans & Houston, Tex, 61-63; co-dir, Univ Gallery, Wichita State Univ, 64-67; designer, John Coultis Interiors, 64-
Awards: Trentino Prize, Italy, 28; Carter Prize, Denver, 31; Knight Off, Order of Merit, Rep Italy, 66.
Memberships: Am Soc Aesthet; Col Art Asn Am; Kansas Fedn Art; Southwestern Col Art Conf (pres, 62-64); fel Int Inst Arts & Lett; plus others.
Publications: Contribr, book reviews, In: Col Art J, Art Critic: weekly art column for Wichita Eagle; monthly art column, The Baldwin Ledger, 65-
Mailing Address: 1816 Harvard St, Wichita, KS 67208.

SIMONT, MARC
Illustrator
b Paris, France, Nov 23, 15; U S citizen.
Study & Training: Acad Ranson; Nat Acad Design; also with Andre L'Hote.
Awards: Caldecott Medal, Am Libr Asn, 57.
Bibliography: Elizabeth Lansing (auth), biog paper, in: Caldecott Medal books, Horn bk, 57.
Memberships: Auth League.
Publications: Illusr, The happy day, 49, The thirteen clocks, 51 & A tree is nice, 57; auth & illusr, The lovely summer, 52 & A child's eye view of the world, 72.
Mailing Address: Town St, West Cornwall, CT 06796.

SIMPER, FREDERICK
Painter
Preferred Media: Watercolors.
b Mishawaka, Ind, July 31, 14.
Work in Public Collections: Detroit Inst Arts, Mich; South Bend Art Mus, Ind; U S Embassies Collection.
Exhibitions: Detroit Inst Arts, 38-68; Chicago Inst Art, Ill, 48; Watercolor U S A, Springfield, Mo, 65; Butler Inst Art, Youngstown, Ohio; Pa Acad Fine Arts, Philadelphia.
Teaching: Instr watercolor, Soc Arts & Crafts, Detroit, 48-51; instr watercolor, Bloomfield Art Asn, Birmingham, Mich, 68-70.
Positions: Art dir, D'Arcy, MacManus Int, 49-
Awards: Detroit Inst Arts Founders Soc Award, 42; Baltimore Sun Award for black & white drawing, 45; Mich Watercolor Soc Award, 72.
Memberships: Mich Watercolor Soc.
Dealer: Arwin Galleries, 222 Grand River W, Detroit, MI 48226.
Mailing Address: 3075 Spring Ct, West Bloomfield, MI 48033.

SIMPKINS, HENRY JOHN
Painter, Illustrator
Preferred Media: Watercolors.
b Winnipeg, Man, Jan 16, 06.
Study & Training: Winnipeg Sch Art, with Frans Johnson; also with Lemoine Fitzgerald & Jessie Dow.
Commissions: Mural (oil), Trans Can Tel Co, Expos 67.
Exhibitions: Can Nat Gallery Travelling Exhib, 37; Royal Can Acad Art, 58; one-man shows, Klinkhoff Gallery, Montreal, 69 & Wallack Gallery, Ottawa, 70 & 72.
Positions: Illusr, Brigden's Ltd, Winnipeg, 25-28; illusr, Rice Studio, New York, N Y, 28-29; illusr, Rapid Grip & Battens, Montreal, 30-58.
Awards: First prize for watercolor, Jessie Dow, 32 & 34.
Memberships: Assoc mem Royal Can Acad Arts; Montreal Arts Club.
Dealers: Klinkhoff Galleries, 1200 Sherbrooke St W, Montreal, P Q, Can; Wallack Galleries, 202 Bank St, Ottawa, Ont, Can.
Mailing Address: 313 Pine Beach Blvd, Dorval, P Q, Can.

SIMPSON, DAVID
Painter, Educator
Preferred Media: Acrylics.
b Pasadena, Calif, Jan 20, 28.
Study & Training: Calif Sch Fine Arts, with Clifford Still & others, BFA, 56; San Francisco State Col, MA, 58.
Work in Public Collections: San Francisco Mus Art, Calif; Oakland Art Mus, Calif; Mus Mod Art, New York, N Y; Philadelphia Mus Art, Pa; Baltimore Mus Art, Md.

Exhibitions: Carnegie Int, Pittsburgh, Pa, 61 & 64; Americans 1963, Mus Mod Art, New York, 63; Post Painterly Abstraction, Los Angeles, Calif, 66; plus others.
Teaching: Prof art, Univ Calif, Berkeley, 65-
Dealer: Hank Baum Gallery, 1 Embarcadero Center, San Francisco, CA 94111.
Mailing Address: P O Box 248, Richmond, CA 94807.

SIMPSON, LEE
Painter
Preferred Media: Oils.
b Cisco, Tex, Oct 9, 23.
Study & Training: Columbia Univ, with Arnold Leondar; also with Louise Nevelson & Elaine DeKooning, New York, N Y.
Work in Public Collections: Couse Mus, Taos, N Mex; Johnson-Everheart Collection, Miami Beach, Fla; State Nat Bank, El Paso, Tex; Whirlpool Corp, Benton Harbor, Mich; UN Plaza, New York.
Commissions: Mural, Perryton Nat Bank, Tex, 69.
Exhibitions: Spec Group Show, Panhandle-Plains Hist Mus, Canyon, Tex, 69; Ninth & Tenth Ann Awards Show, Taos Art Asn, 71 & 72; Southwest Fine Arts Biennial, Mus N Mex, Santa Fe, 72; one-man show, W Tex State Univ, Canyon, 68.
Teaching: Guest lectr oil painting, W Tex State Univ, 69; guest instr oil painting, Amarillo Jr Col, 69-70.
Positions: Owner & instr oil painting, Simpson Gallery & Studio, Amarillo, 62-70.
Awards: Juror's citation award, State Citation Show, Tex Fine Arts Asn, 68 & 69; first award, Ninth Ann Awards Show, Taos Art Asn, 72.
Memberships: Taos Art Asn.
Dealer: Gallery A, P O Box 1221, E Kit Carson St, Taos, NM 87571.
Mailing Address: P O Box 1209, Taos, NM 87571.

SIMPSON, MARILYN JEAN
Painter, Instructor
Preferred Media: Pastels, Oils.
b Birmingham, Ala, Aug 24, 29.
Study & Training: Univ Ala; Art Stud League New York; Inst Allende, San Miguel Allende, Mex; Madison Art Sch, Conn; also with Robert Brackman; Am Univ Avignon, France.
Work in Public Collections: Gov Bldg, Tallahassee, Fla; VZTop Gallery, Pensacola, Fla; Shelby Studio, Goeppingen, Ger.
Exhibitions: Smithsonian Inst, Washington, D C; Paula Insel Gallery, New York, N Y; Birmingham Mus, Ala; Mobile Art Gallery, Ala; Fla Fedn Art, De Bary, Fla; plus one-man shows.
Teaching: Instr art, pvt sch, Fort Walton Beach, Fla, 69-
Awards: Best in show (oil), Beaux Arts, 62; first in portraits (pastels), Arts & Design Show, Fla, 63; first in portraits (pastels), Fla Second Ann Art Exhib, 70.
Memberships: Pensacola Art Ctr; Prof Artist Guild N W Fla (secy, 70); Arts & Design Soc (v pres, 63).
Dealer: VZTop Gallery, Serville Square, Pensacola, FL 32507.
Mailing Address: 4 Williams, P O Box 1107, Fort Walton Beach, FL 32548.

SIMPSON, MAXWELL STEWART
Painter, Sculptor
Preferred Media: Oils, Watercolors.
b Elizabeth, N J, Sept 11, 96.
Study & Training: Schs Nat Acad Design, 14 & 18; Art Stud League New York, N Y, summer 16; in Eng, France & Italy, 23, 24 & 29.
Work in Public Collections: Etching, Nat Gallery Art, Washington, D C; oils, N J; oils, drawings & watercolor, Newark Mus, N J; oil, etching & drawings, Shelburne Art Mus, Vt.
Commissions: Murals, Stage House Inn, comn by Mrs William G Mennen, Jr, Scotch Plains, N J, 60 & Savings Bank Cent N J, 71; portraits, Mrs William Casford, Chatham, N J, 69, Mr Charles Hoffman, Elizabeth, N J, 71 & Mrs Ian Prior, West Caldwell, N J, 72.
Exhibitions: Soc Nat Beaux Arts, Paris Salon, 24; 10th Int Water-Exhib, Art Inst Chicago, 30; Surv Am Art, Baltimore Mus Art, 34; New York World's Fair, 39; Homage To Isadora Duncan, San Francisco World's Fair, 39; plus one-man shows, New York.
Teaching: Instr figure drawing & painting, Elizabeth Art Club Studio, 25-28; instr figure drawing, Newark Sch Fine & Indust Arts, 36-46; instr portrait painting, Simpson Studio, Elizabeth, 36-46.
Awards: Hon mention for Old Woman, Terry Nat Art Exhib, Miami, Fla, 52; Emily Lowe Competition Award for Spring Landscape, 58; N J Artist of Yr Award, 59.
Bibliography: Frederic Whitaker (auth), The paintings of Maxwell Stewart Simpson, Am Artist, 5/63.
Memberships: Assoc Artists N J.
Publications: Auth, The relationship of modern art to modern industry, Dun's Rev, 4/38.
Dealer: Grand Central Galleries, 40 Vanderbilt Ave, New York, NY 10017.
Mailing Address: Old Raritan Rd, Scotch Plains, NJ 07076.

SIMPSON, MERTON D
Painter, Art Dealer
b Charleston, S C, Sept 20, 28.
Study & Training: N Y Univ; Cooper Union Art Sch, with Robert Motherwell & Baziotes; also with William Halsey.
Work in Public Collections: James J Sweeney Collection, Guggenheim Mus; Howard Univ, Washington, D C; Scott Field Mus, Chicago; Atlanta Univ; Gibbs Art Gallery.
Exhibitions: Guggenheim Mus, New York; Metrop Mus Art, New York; Brooklyn Mus, N Y; Nat Gallery, Paris; Nat Mus Japan.
Awards: Awards, Red Cross Exchange Exhib, Tokyo & Paris, 50; Atlanta Univ, 50, 51 & 56 & Oakland Art Mus, 52.
Specialty of Gallery: Primitive art, especially African.
Mailing Address: 1063 Madison Ave, New York, NY 10028.

SIMPSON, WILLIAM KELLY
Art Historian, Educator
b New York, N Y, Jan 3, 28.
Study & Training: Yale Univ, BA, 47, MA, 48, PhD, 54; Ecole Practique Hautes Études, Paris, France.
Collections Arranged: The Pennsylvania-Yale Expedition to Nubia, Peabody Mus, Yale Univ, New Haven, Conn, 63; Recent Accessions in Egyptian and Ancient Near Eastern Art & The Horace L Mayer Collection, 72, Mus Fine Arts, Boston, Mass; also Metrop Mus, New York & Univ Pa Mus, Philadelphia.
Teaching: Prof Egyptol, Yale Univ, 56-; vis prof Egyptol, Univ Pa.
Positions: Cur Egyptian Art, Mus Fine Arts, Boston, 70-
Awards: Guggenheim Found fel, 65.
Memberships: Archaeol Inst Am; Am Oriental Soc; Am Res Ctr in Egypt; Egypt Explor Soc; Soc Française Egyptologie.
Research: Art, History, and literature of ancient Egypt.
Publications: Auth, Papyrus Reisner I-records of a building project, 63; auth, Papyrus Reisner II-accounts of the dockyard workshop, 65; auth, Papyrus Reisner III-records of a building project in the early twelfth dynasty, 69; co-auth, The ancient Near East: a history, 71; co-auth, The literature of ancient Egypt, 72.
Mailing Address: Katonah's Wood Rd, Katonah, NY 10536.

SIMS, AGNES
Painter, Sculptor
b Rosemont, Pa, Oct 14, 10.
Study & Training: Philadelphia Sch Design for Women; Pa Acad Fine Arts.
Work in Public Collections: Mus N Mex; Colorado Springs Fine Arts Ctr; Denver Art Mus.
Commissions: Mural, N Mex Petroglyphs, Mutual Bldg & Loan, 70.
Exhibitions: One-man show, Mus N Mex; Colorado Springs Fine Arts Ctr; Santa Barbara Mus Art, Calif; Walker Art Center, Minneapolis, Minn; exhib of wall hangings based on Southwest Indian Petroglyphs for U S Info Serv at U S Embassy, London, Eng, 64; plus others.
Collections Arranged: Exhib of reproductions of Southwest Indian petroglyphs, Brooklyn Mus, 53 & Mus L'Homme, Paris, 54.
Awards: Am Philos Soc grant for res & recording Southwest Indian Petroglyphs, 49; Neosho grant, 52; Ingram Merrill Found grant, 60.
Memberships: Hon assoc Archaeol, Sch Am Res; Artists Equity Asn.
Publications: Auth & illusr, San Cristobal Petroglyphs, 50.
Mailing Address: 600 Canyon Rd, Santa Fe, NM 87501.

SIMSON, BEVLYN A
Painter, Printmaker
b Columbus, Ohio, Sept 9, 17.
Study & Training: Ohio State Univ, BA & MFA; also with David Black, Sidney Chafetz, Charles Czuri, Robert Gatrell, E H Hebner, Robert King, Hoyt Sherman, Rose Lazar & Stanley Twardowcicz.
Work in Public Collections: Pres Richard M Nixon Collection, Washington, D C; Columbus Gallery Fine Arts, Ohio; Kresge Collection, Detroit, Mich; Ohio State Univ Libr, Rare Books & Mss Collection, Columbus; plus others.
Commissions: Three panel acrylic paintings, First Investment Co, Columbus, & Raymond Lappin, former pres, Fed Nat Mortgage Asn, Washington, D C, 70; paintings, Ohio State Nisonger Ctr Ment Retardation.
Exhibitions: Salon 1969 Soc l'Ecole Francais Salles d'Exposition La Ville Paris, 69; one-man shows, J B Speed Mus, Louisville, Ky, 70 & 72; Huntington Gallery, Columbus, 70 & Bodley Gallery, New York, N Y, 71; Print & Drawing Nat, Western Ill Univ, Macomb, 72; Palais Beaux-Arts, Rome, Italy, 72; plus others.
Awards: Columbus Gallery Fine Arts Painting Award, 69 & 71; awards, Eighth Grand Prix Int, La Cote d'Azur, Cannes, France, 72; six awards, 23rd Grand Prix Int, Deauville, France, 72.
Bibliography: Salles d'exposition de la ville de Paris, La Rev Mod, Paris, 1/70; L Soretsky (auth), Hard-edge geometrics, City-East-

ern Cepcor, Inc, New York, 2/71; Artirnomis (auth) revs, In: Arts Mag & Art Digest, Inc, New York, 2/71, plus others.
Memberships: Int Platform Asn; Am Fedn Arts; Bexley Area Art Guild; Columbus Art League (secy-treas).
Publications: Auth, Prints and poetry, 69.
Dealers: Bodley Gallery, 1063 Madison Ave, New York, NY 10021; Gilman Galleries, 103 E Oak St, Chicago, IL 60611.
Mailing Address: 289 S Roosevelt Ave, Columbus, OH 43209.

SINAIKO, (AVROM) ARLIE
Sculptor, Collector
Preferred Media: Wood, Bronze.
b Kapule, Russia, Oct 1, 02; U S Citizen.
Study & Training: Univ Wis, BS; Northwestern Univ, MD; Art Inst Chicago; Sculpture Ctr, New York; Art Stud League New York; Atelier, with Archipenko, Lassaw & Harkavy.
Work in Public Collections: Lincoln Ctr Performing Arts, New York, N Y; Pa Acad Fine Arts, Philadelphia; Walker Art Ctr, Minneapolis, Minn; Isaac Delgado Mus, New Orlans, La; Santa Barbara Art Mus, Calif; plus many others.
Exhibitions: Pa Acad Fine Arts; Detroit Inst Art; Riverside Mus, N Y; Art U S A 1959; Provincetown Art Asn, Mass.
Positions: Chmn art comn, Int Synagogue, N Y.
Awards: Purchase prize, Pa Acad Fine Arts, 61; hon mention for sculpture, Audubon Artists, 68; Kellner Award for sculpture, Am Soc Contemp Artists, 71.
Memberships: Am Soc Contemp Artists (exec comt, 67); Artists Equity Asn; Audubon Artists (exec comt, 72); Provincetown Art Asn.
Collection: Renoir sculpture; Klee drawing; also works of Derain, Dufy, Fujita & many contemporary artists & many lithographs & etchings of Picasso, Braque, Matisse, Roualt & Miro; early American primitive painters.
Dealer: Bodley Gallery, 787 Madison Ave, New York, NY 10021.
Mailing Address: 115 Central Park W, New York, NY 10023.

SINE, DAVID WILLIAM
Sculptor, Painter
b Verde Valley, Ariz, Aug 13, 21.
Commissions: Murals, Last Supper, Rev Camillas, Pisinimo, Papago Reservation, Ariz, 68 & Station of the Cross, Rev Joseph Bauer, Topawa, Papago Reservation, Ariz, 69.
Exhibitions: Scottsdale Nat Indian Arts Coun Inc, Ariz, 65-71.
Awards: Hon mention for Skywalkers of Apache Pass, Scottsdale Nat Indian Arts, 72.
Mailing Address: P O Box 324, Sells, AZ 85634.

SING HOO (SING HOO YUEN)
Sculptor, Painter
Preferred Media: Bronze, Marble, Wood, Clay, Wax.
b Canton, China, May 15, 08; Can citizen.
Study & Training: Toronto Col Art; Ont Col Art, assoc, with A Barnes & Emannual Hahn; Slade Sch, Univ London, with Turner.
Work in Public Collections: London Mus, Eng; Nat Gallery Ottawa, Ont; Royal Ont Mus, Toronto.
Commissions: Sun Dial & bronze figures of daughter & gardener, parks, Toronto.
Exhibitions: Ont Soc Artists, 32-68; Can Nat Exhib, 32-68; Royal Can Acad Art, 36-72; Sculptor's Soc Can, 40-67.
Teaching: Lectr Oriental & Western art, Chinese Sch, 36-40.
Positions: Asst paleont dept, Royal Ont Mus, 34-40.
Mailing Address: 139 Livingstone Ave, Toronto, Ont, Can.

SINGER, BURR (BURR LEE FRIEDMAN)
Painter
b Saint Louis, Mo.
Study & Training: Saint Louis Sch Fine Arts; Art Inst Chicago; Art Stud League New York; also with Waltar Ufer.
Work in Public Collections: Warren Flynn Sch, Clayton, Mo; Libr Cong, Washington, D C; Beverly-Fairfax Jewish Community Ctr, Los Angeles, Calif; Child Guidance Clinic, Los Angeles.
Exhibitions: Calif Watercolor Soc, 40-45, 53-58, 68, & traveling exhib; Frye Mus Art, Seattle, Wash, 60 & 62; Art of Los Angeles & Vicinity, 61 & 69; Kramer Gallery, Los Angeles, Calif, 63; Watercolor: U S A, Springfield, Mo, 64; plus others.
Awards: Los Angeles Co Fair, 51, 53; prize, Marineland Exhib, 55.
Memberships: Calif Watercolor Soc (v pres, 58); Artists Equity Asn; Los Angeles Art Asn; Coun Allied Artists.
Mailing Address: 2143 Panorama Terr, Los Angeles, CA 90039.

SINGER, CLYDE J
Painter
Preferred Media: Oils.
b Malvern, Ohio, Oct 20, 08.
Study & Training: Columbus Art Sch, Ohio; Art Stud League New York, N Y, with Kenneth Hayes Miller, John Steuart Curry & Thomas Hart Benton.

Work in Public Collections: Pa Acad Fine Arts, Philadelphia; Columbus Gallery Fine Arts, Ohio; Thomas Gilcrease Inst Hist & Art, Tulsa, Okla; Butler Inst Am Art, Youngstown, Ohio; Canton Art Inst, Ohio.
Commissions: Mural, Skaters, Post Off, New Concord, Ohio, 40.
Exhibitions: Carnegie Mus Int, Pittsburgh, Pa, 36-39; Corcoran Gallery Art Biennial, Washington, D C, 37; Golden Gate Int Expos, San Francisco, Calif, 39; Whitney Mus Am Art Painting & Sculpture Biennial, 41; Artists For Victory, Rockefeller Ctr, New York, 45.
Positions: Art critic, Vindicator, Youngstown, 40-; asst dir, Butler Inst Am Art, 40-
Awards: Norman Wait Harris Silver Medal, Art Inst Chicago, 35; First Hallgarten Prize, Nat Acad Design, 38; first prize, Ohio State Fair Fine Arts Exhib, 68.
Bibliography: Roger Bonham (auth), Clyde Singer; Ohio painter, Am Artist, 2/69; Paul Chew (auth), Singer retrospective 1932-1972, Westmoreland Co Mus Art, 3/72.
Mailing Address: 210 Forest Park Dr, Youngstown, OH 44512.

SINGER, ESTHER FORMAN
   Painter, Art Critic
Preferred Media: Oils, Mixed Media.
b New York, N Y, Oct 14.
Study & Training: Art Stud League New York, 40-41; Temple Univ, 41-44; New York Univ, 47-49; New York Sch Social Res, 68-70.
Work in Public Collections: Newark Mus, N J; N J State Mus, Trenton; Finch Mus Contemp Art, New York; Hudson River Mus, Yonkers, N Y; Seton Hall Univ Collection, South Orange, N J.
Exhibitions: New York World's Fair, 65; Kenosha Pub Mus, Wis, 70; one-man shows, Centenary Col, Hackettstown, 70 & Bloomfield Col, N J, 71; Ohio Univ, St Clairsville, Ohio, 72.
Teaching: Instr childrens' exp art, South Orange Community Ctr, 68-69; lectr contemp art, Deborah Hosp, 68-
Positions: Guest panelist, Art Forms, WOR TV, 67-68; ed, Jewish Standard Newspaper, 70-71; Jersey J Newspaper, 70-72 & Suburban Life Mag N J, 70-; judge, Menlo Park Outdoor-Indoor Art Show, 71; adv, Art Exhibs Coun, N J, 71-72; judge, Art Exhibs Coun Art Show, 72; art ed, Newark News Newspaper, 72-
Awards: Nat Design Ctr Award for Contemp Art, 66; first prize for oils, Roseland Festival Art, 66, 67 & 68; first prize for oils, Summit Art Ctr-Collage, 68.
Bibliography: Smith (auth), feature story & cover photo, In: N J Music & Art Mag, 10/65; Nancye Kallis (auth), rev, In: Art Rev Mag, 4/66; Carlette Winslow (auth), article, In: N J Suburban Life Mag, 3/70.
Memberships: Artist's Equity Asn New York; Artist's Equity Asn; N J Art Exhibs Coun; Painters & Sculptors Soc N J; Miniature Artists Asn N J.
Publications: Contribr, Am Artist Mag, 4/72.
Dealers: Gallery 9, Chatham, NJ 07928; Gallery 52, 52 S Orange Ave, South Orange, NJ 07079.
Mailing Address: 70 Glenview Rd, South Orange, NJ 07079.

SINGER, WILLIAM EARL
   Painter, Sculptor
b Chicago, Ill, July 10, 10.
Study & Training: Univ Chicago; Art Inst Chicago; Andre L'Hote, Paris, France; also with Charles Wilimovsky & John Norton.
Work in Public Collections: Grand Rapids Art Gallery; Ill State Mus; Scopus Col, Melbourne, Australia; Presidential Palace, Colombia; Israeli Govt; Am Embassy, Paris, France; plus many others.
Commissions: Thomas Mann Mem, Zurich, Switz; Gertrude Lawrence Mem, London, Eng; Am Embassy, London; Oscar Hammerstein Mem, New York; bronze monument of Vincent Van Gogh for the City of Arles, France, 68; plus others.
Exhibitions: Art Inst Chicago; New York World's Fair; Denver Art Mus; Toronto Art Mus; Haarlem Mus, Netherlands; plus many others.
Teaching: Lect, Contemporary Painting & the Old Masters.
Positions: Color consult, Chicago World's Fair & Brussels Int.
Awards: Medal of Honor of France, 68; decorated by Andre Malraux, Palais Royale, Paris; Citizen Honoraire, France, 68; Chevalier de l'Ordre des Arts et des Lettres, 69; also honored by Italy & Neth.
Bibliography: Andre Blum (auth), William Earl Singer, Mus Louvre, Paris, 51; Maximilian Gauthier (auth), An American in Paris, 62; Alex Drier (auth), The world of William Earl Singer (documentary), 68; plus others.
Memberships: Fel Int Inst Arts & Lett; Calif Watercolor Soc; Chicago Sculptors Asn; Beaux-Arts Soc Paris, France.
Publications: Auth & illusr, Paintings of Israel; contribr to New horizons in American art, Mus Mod Art & American art today, Nat Art Soc.
Mailing Address: 12897 San Vicente Blvd, Los Angeles, CA 90049.

SINGLETARY, ROBERT EUGENE
   Graphic Artist
Preferred Media: Graphite Lead.
b Bloomington, Ill, Dec 4, 45.
Study & Training: Ill State Univ with Walter Bock & Harold Boyd; Corcoran Gallery Art, Washington, D C.
Work in Public Collections: Phila Mus Art, Pa; State Dept, Washington, D C.
Exhibitions: Fourth Biennial of Drawings U S A, St Paul, Minn, 69; Nat Drawing Exhib, San Francisco Mus, 70; Drawing Soc 70 Nat Exhib, Corcoran Gallery Art, 70; one-man show, Fendrick Gallery, Washington, D C, 72.
Awards: Purchase award, Phila Mus Art, 70.
Bibliography: Am Fedn Art, Drawing society's 1970 national exhibition, 70; Cornelia Noland (auth), The Singletary style, Washingtonian, 8/71; Joanna Eagle (auth), Washington, D C, Art Gallery Mag, 4/72.
Dealer: Fendrick Gallery, 3059 M St, Washington, DC 20007.
Mailing Address: 211 N Fairfax St, Apt 9, Alexandria, VA 22314.

SINGLETON, ROBERT ELLISON
   Painter, Printmaker
b Jacksonville, N C, Dec 13, 37.
Study & Training: Col William & Mary; Richmond Prof Inst; also with Teresa Pollock.
Work in Public Collections: Mint Mus Art, Charlotte, N C; Loch Haven Art Ctr, Orlando, Fla; Fla Gas, Orlando; Twentieth Century Gallery, Williamsburg, Va; Archit Designers Inc, Dallas, Tex.
Commissions: Murals & paintings, Sentinel Star Co, Orlando, 68 & 71; paintings, Loger Properties, San Antonio, Tex, Jacksonville & Orlando, 69 & 71; paintings, George Barley Inc, 70-72; painting, Tupperware Int, Orlando, 72; paintings, Bank E Orange, Orlando, 72.
Exhibitions: One-man shows, Mus Arts & Sci, Daytona Beach, Fla, 68, Coconut Grove Playhouse Gallery, Miami, Fla, 69, Ludwig Katzenstein Gallery, Baltimore, Md, 70 & Loch Haven Art Ctr, Orlando, 70; Piedmont Graphics Competition, Mint Mus Art, Charlotte, 71 & 72.
Teaching: Instr painting, Loch Haven Art Ctr, Orlando, 68-; lect & sem critiques throughout southeastern states, 68-
Positions: Cur exhibits, Jamestown Festival Park, Va, 62-63.
Awards: First pl, Int Winter Park Sidewalk Art Festival, 67-69; MacDowell Colony grant, 70-72.
Bibliography: Articles, In: Orlando Sentinel, 68-72; filmed documentary, WFIA TV, Tampa, 71; series of interviews (video-tape), WMFE TV, Orlando, 72-73.
Dealer: Gallery International, 401-B Park Ave N, Winter Park, FL 32789.
Mailing Address: P O Box 626, 201 Holly St, Altamonte Springs, FL 32701.

SINNARD, ELAINE (JANICE)
   Painter, Sculptor
Preferred Media: Oils.
b Fort Collins, Colo, Feb 14, 26.
Study & Training: Art Stud League New York, 48-49, with Reginald Marsh; New York Univ, 51, with Samuel Adler; also with Robert D Kaufmann, 51; Sculpture Ctr, 55, with Dorothea Denslow; Acad Grande Chaumiere, Paris, France, 56; also with Betty Dodson, 60.
Commissions: Five wall hangings (with Mrs Louise Darlington, Marlin Studios), Scandinavian Airline, New York, 61; three oil paintings, Basker Bldg Corp 5660, Miami Beach, Fla, 70.
Exhibitions: City Ctr Gallery, New York, 54; Riverside Mus Eighth Ann, New York, 55; First Ann Metrop Young Artists, Nat Arts Club, New York, 58; one-woman shows, Ward Eggleston Galleries, New York, 59 & Fairleigh Dickinson Univ, N J, 60.
Bibliography: Article, In: Art News, 54; James E Duffy (auth), article, In: World Telegram, 59; Fran Hepperle (auth), article, In: Times Herald Record, 72.
Dealers: Lord & Taylor Art Gallery, Fifth & 39th St, New York, NY 10016; Zantman Galleries Ltd, Carmel-by-the-Sea, CA 93921.
Mailing Address: R D 1, Box 133, Westtown, NY 10998.

SINSABAUGH, ART
   Photographer, Educator
b Irvington, N J, Oct 31, 24.
Study & Training: Ill Inst Technol Inst Design, BS, with Moholy-Nagy & Harry Callahan, MS, with Aaron Siskind.
Work in Public Collections: Mus Mod Art, New York, N Y; Art Inst Chicago; George Eastman House, Rochester, N Y; Exchange Nat Bank, Chicago; Smithsonian Inst, Washington, D C.
Commissions: The Quality of Life (mural), Chicago City Planning Comn, First City Plan of Chicago, 61-63; midwest landscape photograph mural, Univ Ill Med Ctr, Chicago, 65.

Exhibitions: Abstract Photography, Am Fedn Arts, New York, 55;
The Photographer and the American Landscape, Mus Mod Art,
New York, 63; one-man show, Art Inst Chicago, 63; one-man
show, Gallery 500d, Chicago, 65; Photography U S A, De Cordova
Mus, Lincoln, Mass, 68.
Teaching: Instr photography, Ill Inst Technol Inst Design, 49-58;
prof art & head dept Photography & cinematography, Univ Ill,
Champaign, 58-
Awards: Arts in Am Mag Award, New Talent, U S A Award Show,
62; Guggenheim fel, 69; assoc, Univ Ill Ctr Advan Studies, Cham-
paign, 72.
Bibliography: Gene Thornton (auth), Two tales of one city, New
York Times, 3/22/70; Great print makers of today, Life Libr
of Photography, 70; Allen Porter (auth), Sinsabaugh, Camera,
Switz, 6/72.
Memberships: Founding mem Soc Photog Educ.
Publications: Co-auth, 6 Mid-Am charts/11 midwest photographs,
64; contribr, portfolio of works, Tri Quart, winter 65; contribr,
portfolio of works & cover, New Lett, spring, 72.
Mailing Address: 132 Fine Arts Bldg, University of Illinois, Cham-
paign, IL 61820.

SINTON, NELL (WALTER)
Painter, Instructor
Preferred Media: Acrylics.
b San Francisco, Calif.
Study & Training: San Francisco Art Inst, with Maurice Sterne; Inst
Creative & Artistic Develop.
Work in Public Collections: San Francisco Mus Art; Oakland Mus
Art, Calif; Chase Manhattan Bank, New York, N Y; Lytton Trust
Co, San Jose, Calif.
Exhibitions: San Francisco Mus Art, 57, 63 & 70; Stanford Res Inst,
Palo Alto, Calif, 58; Staempfli Gallery, New York, 60; Am Acad
Arts & Lett, New York, 67; Univ Calif, Berkeley, 72; plus others.
Teaching: Instr drawing, San Francisco Art Inst, 70-71.
Positions: Artist mem, San Francisco Art Comn, City & Co, 58-63.
Awards: San Francisco Art Inst Award, De Young Mus, 56; Oakland
Mus Art Awards, 58 & 61.
Bibliography: M Tapié (auth), Morphologie autre, 60; F Martin
(auth), Review San Francisco, Art Int, 63 & Artforum, 63 & 67.
Memberships: San Francisco Art Inst (trustee, 66-).
Publications: Auth, reviews, In: Clear Creek Mag, 70 & 71.
Dealer: Quay Gallery, 2 Jerome Alley, San Francisco, CA 94133.
Mailing Address: 1020 Francisco St, San Francisco, CA 94109.

SIPIORA, LEONARD PAUL
Museum Director, Writer
b Lawrence, Mass, Sept 1, 34.
Study & Training: Vanderbilt Univ; Univ Mich, Ann Arbor, AB (cum
laude), 55, MA, 56.
Collections Arranged: Ann Nat Sun Carnival Exhib; Biennial, Int
Designer Craftsmen; W S Horton Retrospective, 70; Tom Lea
Retrospective, 71; Walter Griffin Retrospective, 71.
Positions: Co-founder & pres, El Paso Arts Coun, 69-70, dir, 71-;
bd mem, Tex Mus Conf; mem chmn, Mountain-Plains Mus Conf.
Memberships: Kappa Pi; Am Asn Mus; Am Fedn Arts; Am Platform
Asn; Nat Soc Arts & Lett (first v pres, El Paso Chap).
Collection: American paintings and graphics.
Publications: Auth, The universality of Tom Lea (catalog), 71;
auth, A community oriented art museum, Southwest Gallery Art
Mag, 71; contribr, foreword to Biography of John Enneking, 72.
Mailing Address: 1211 Montana St, El Paso, TX 79902.

SIPORIN, MITCHELL
Painter, Educator
Preferred Media: Oils, Watercolors.
b New York, N Y, May 5, 10.
Study & Training: Crane Col, Chicago, Ill; Art Inst Chicago.
Work in Public Collections: Whitney Mus Am Art, New York; Mus
Mod Art, New York; Metrop Mus Art, New York; Fogg Art Mus,
Harvard Univ, Cambridge, Mass; Art Inst Chicago.
Commissions: Frescoes, U S Treas Dept, Post Off, Decatur, Ill, 37
& Saint Louis, Mo, 39.
Exhibitions: Am Painting, Art Inst Chicago, 38-39; Americans 1942,
Mus Mod Art, 42; San Francisco World's Fair; New York
World's Fair; Art U S A Now, 62-67.
Teaching: Prof painting, Brandeis Univ, 51-
Awards: Guggenheim Found fels, 45-46; Prix de Rome for painting,
Am Acad Rome, 50; Sr Fulbright fel, Italy, 66-67.
Bibliography: S Cheney (auth), Expressionism in art, Liveright, 34;
H Cahill (auth), New horizon in American art, Mus Mod Art, 39;
Americans 1942, Mus Mod Art, 42.
Mailing Address: 300 Franklin St, Newton, MA 02158.

SIQUEIROS, DAVID ALFARO
Painter
b Santa Rosalia, Mex, Dec 29, 96.
Study & Training: Acad San Carlos.

Work in Public Collections: Mus Arte Mod, Mexico City; Mus Mod
Art, New York, N Y; Philadelphia Mus Art.
Commissions: La América Tropical, Mural Block Painters, Los An-
geles, Calif, 32; Retrato de la Burguesia, Sindicato Mex Elec-
tricistas, Mexico City, 39; Por Una Seguridad Social Para Todos
los Mexicanos, Inst Mex Seguro Socialm, Mexico City, 51-54;
Del Porfirismo a la Revolucion, Mus Nac Hist, Mexico City, 57-
66; La Marcha de la Humanidad, Manuel Suárex, Mexico City,
66-71.
Exhibitions: 25th Bienal Internacional Arte Venecia, 50; Mus Nat
Art Mod, Paris, 52; Los Angeles Co Mus Art, 63; Siqueiros,
Exposición Retrospectiva: 1907-1967, Nat Univ Mex, 67; Expos
Retrospective Mus Cent Art, Tokyo, Japan, 72.
Teaching: Instr, Chouinard Sch Art, Los Angeles, 32; prof, Escuela
Pintura San Miguel Allende, 48-49; instr murals, Escuela Taller
Siqueiros, Cuernavaca, 66-71.
Awards: Premio Int Venecia, Mus Art Mod, São Paulo, 50; Premio
Nac Art, Gobierno Mex, 67; Premio Lenin de la Paz, U S S R-
Gobierno, 67.
Bibliography: La Pintura Mural de la Revolucion Mexicana, Fondo
Ed Plastica Mexicana, 60; De Micheli (auth), D Alfaro Siqueiros,
Fratelli Fabbri Ed, 68; Muros de Fuego (film), Mentor Films, 67-
70.
Memberships: Nat Acad Arts (past pres); Acad Artes Florencia;
Acad Artes Berlin; Acad Artes Moscow.
Publications: Auth, Como se pinta un mural, 51; auth, El nuevo
realismo Mexicano, Integración Plástica, 66; auth, A un joven
pintor Mexicano, 67; co-auth, Un Mexicano y su obra, 69.
Mailing Address: c/o Sala de Arte Público, Tres Picos 29, Mexico
City 5, Mex.

SIRENA (CONTESSA ANTONIA MASTROCRISTINO FANARA)
Painter, Collector
b White Plains, N Y.
Work in Public Collections: Mus Mod Art, Rome, Italy; Mus Castello
Sforzesco, Milano, Italy; Mus Campidoglio, Rome; Regione
Fruili Venezia Giulia, Regione Siciliana; Regione Sarda.
Commissions: Paintings for Federico Fellini, Frankie Laine, Gina
Lollobrigida, Vittorio de Sica, The Vatican & Pope Paul XI.
Exhibitions: One-woman shows, Van Diemen-Lillienfield Galleries,
New York, 66, Gallerie Andre Weil, Paris, 68, Mike Douglas TV
Show Exhib, 68, Palazzo delle Esposizioni, Comune di Roma,
Rome, 69 & State Gallery in Teatro Massimo, Palermo, Sicily,
70; plus many others.
Teaching: Lectr art, colleges & orgn, internationally, 70-
Positions: Art gallery dir, Sirena Art Galleries, Long Island, N Y,
63-
Awards: Gold Cup (First Int Prize), Quadriennale of Europe, 67;
Dame of Grand Cross Award, Order of St Constantine, 68; Gold
medal of pres of Senate, Mayor of Rome, 72; plus many others.
Bibliography: Aurelio Prete (auth), Sirena, ERS, Rome, 66; Guilio
Bolaffi (auth), Bolaffi on modern art, Torino, Italy, 70 & 72; Gio-
vanni Quattrucci (auth), Sirena, Europe Ed, 72.
Memberships: Accad oli Paestum Accad dei 500; Accad Tiberina;
Int Comt Cult, Rome; Metrop Mus Art.
Art Interests: Art exhibitions and awards for talented artists,
national and international.
Collections: Paintings of new artists, contemporary art and old
masters; antique furniture, clocks, candelabras and other art.
Mailing Address: 1724 Hempstead Turnpike, East Meadow, NY
11554.

SIRUGO, SALVATORE
Painter
Preferred Media: Acrylics, Casein.
b Pozzallo, Italy; U S citizen.
Study & Training: Art Stud League New York, N Y, 48-49; Brooklyn
Mus Art Sch, N Y, 50-51.
Work in Public Collections: Pace Col, New York; Southern Ill Univ,
Carbondale; Dillard Univ, New Orleans, La; Ciba-Geigy Corp,
Harrison, N Y.
Exhibitions: Whitney Mus Am Art Ann, New York, 52; Pa Acad Fine
Arts Ann, Philadelphia, 53; Art U S A: 58, New York, 58; Prov-
incetown Arts Festival, Mass, 58; one-man exhibs, Camino Gal-
lery, 59, Tanager Gallery, 61, K Gallery, 63 & Great Jones Gal-
lery, 66.
Awards: Emily Lowe Award, Joe & Emily Lowe, 51; Woodstock
Found Award, Woodstock Artists Asn, 52; Longview Found
Award, 62.
Bibliography: Natalie Edgar (auth), The private worlds of Sal
Sirugo, Art News, 11/66; F W McDarrah (auth), The artist's
world in pictures, Dutton, 61.
Memberships: Life mem Art Stud League New York (bd control,
61); Artists' Club.
Mailing Address: 321 W 24th St, New York, NY 10011.

SISSONS, LYNN E
Painter
Preferred Media: Watercolors.
b Portage La Prairie, Man.
Study & Training: Winnipeg Sch Art, 20; Univ Man Sch Art.
Work in Public Collections: Winnipeg Art Gallery; Can Dent Soc, Toronto, Ont; Man Hist Soc; Medicine Hat Alta Gallery; Man Schs Libr Art; also in pvt collections.
Commissions: Reprod of old forts of Winnipeg, Hist Mus.
Exhibitions: Winnipeg Sketch Club Ann, 21-; Man Soc Artists in Winnipeg & traveling Shows, 29-; one-man show, 50th Anniversary Winnipeg Art Gallery, 63; One Hundred & Fifty Years of Art in Manitoba, Legis Bldg, 70; Simpson Co-Toronto Art Gallery; plus others.
Awards: George Wilson first prize for best sketch in Man, 27; first prize & hon mention, Man Soc Artists Ann, 67; prize for best painting for sch, Investors Group; plus others.
Memberships: Man Soc Artists (all off, 29-68); Winnipeg Sketch Club (all off, 20-72); Poetry Soc Winnipeg (bd mem & treas, 60-70); Man Theatre Soc (working mem, 23-40).
Publications: Many articles written & publ in Free Press & Winnipeg Tribune.
Mailing Address: 3B-405 Assinniboine Ave, Winnipeg, Man, Can.

SISTER THOMASITA (MARY THOMASITA FESSLER, OSF)
Sculptor, Educator
b Milwaukee, Wis, Feb 23, 12.
Study & Training: St Mary's Acad; Univ Wis-Milwaukee, BE; Art Inst Chicago, BFA & MFA.
Commissions: Two wood mosaic murals, Marquette Univ Mem Libr; mahogany carved sanctuary crucifix, outdoor stone sculpture, rectory crucifix & wood mosaic stations of the cross for the Sisters' Chapel, St Cyprian's Church, River Grove, Ill; stained glass windows, St Xavier's Hosp, Dubuque, Iowa; plus many others for homes, schs, churches & pub bldgs.
Exhibitions: New York, Washington, D C, Dayton, Ohio, Seattle, Wash, Chicago, Ill, plus many others.
Teaching: St Anthony's High Sch, Sterling, Colo; St Mary's Acad, Milwaukee; chmn art dept, Cardinal Stritch Col, 47-; also summer sessions at Cath Univ, Univ Notre Dame, St Martin's Col, Maryhurst Col, Holy Name Col & Marquette Univ; also worldwide lect on liturgical art.
Positions: Mem Am Deleg to First Int Cong Cath Artists, Rome, 50; Milwaukee Art Ctr Exhib Comt, 50-; bd mem, Milwaukee Children's Arts Prog, 52-; U S rep, Fourth Int Assembly Int Soc Educ through Art, Montreal, P Q, 63; Gov Coun on Arts, 63-; adv bd Arts & Activities Mag; adv bd, Wis Montessori Soc, 63-
Awards: Friends of Art Award, 64; Quota Club Women of Achievement Award, 64; Theta Sigma Phi Award to Do'ers of the 70's, 70; plus others.
Bibliography: Articles, In: Liturgical Arts, J Arts & Lett, Cath Art Quart & many others.
Memberships: Liturgical Arts Asn; Col Art Asn Am; Nat Art Educ Asn; Int Soc for Educ through Art; Wis Art Educ Asn.
Publications: Auth, articles, In: New World, Everyday Art, Cath Trends in Art Educ, Salesianum & Sch Arts; plus many others.
Mailing Address: Studio San Damiano, Milwaukee, WI 53217.

SISTI, ANTHONY J
Collector, Painter
b New York, N Y, Apr 21, 01.
Study & Training: Albright Art Sch, Buffalo; Royal Acad, Florence, Italy; Dr degree, with Falice Carena; Acad Julian, Paris, France; Royal Acad, Munich.
Commissions: Portrait, Hon Frank A Sedita, mayor of Buffalo, Fedn Ital Socs of Buffalo, 70.
Exhibitions: One-man & group exhibs, Mus Mod Art, Mus of City of New York & Riverside Mus, New York; Calif Palace of Legion of Honor, San Francisco; Howard Univ, Washington, D C; Albright-Knox Art Gallery; plus others.
Positions: Chmn, First Allentown Exhib, 56; pres, Patteran Soc, 57; chmn, Civic Art Festival, Buffalo, 65.
Awards: Prizes, Patteran Soc, 43, Western New York Exhib, Buffalo, 47 & Buffalo Soc Artists, 47; plus others.
Collection: Old masters, impressionists, modern art.
Mailing Address: 469 Franklin St, Buffalo, NY 14203.

SIVARD, ROBERT PAUL
Painter, Art Administrator
Preferred Media: Casein.
b New York, N Y, Dec 7, 14.
Study & Training: Pratt Inst; Nat Acad Design; Acad Julien, Paris.
Work in Public Collections: N J State Mus Art; Libr Cong.
Commissions: Murals (with Frank Schwartz), Ore State Capitol, 39 & Treasure Island San Francisco, City of San Francisco, 40; commemorative postage stamp, The American Woman, 60.

Exhibitions: Mus Art Mod, Paris, 54; Carnegie Invitational, 57; Galerie Charpentier, 59; Philadelphia Mus, 60; Dallas Mus, 65.
Collections Arranged: U S Nat Exhib Moscow, 59; Off U S Exhibs, São Paulo Bienales, 59, 61, 63 & 65 & Venice Bienales, 62 & 64.
Positions: Dir visual & art serv, U S Embassy Paris, 50-55; chief Exhibs Div, U S Info Agency, 58-65, agency art dir, 66-
Awards: 11th Ann Corcoran Mus Award, 57; Thomas B Clarke Award for painting, Nat Acad Design, 58; gold medal, Art Dirs Club, 58.
Bibliography: Sivard, Time, 55; Un Americain a Paris, Illus, France, 55; Sivard, shopping with, Horizon, 59.
Memberships: Am Inst Graphic Arts.
Dealer: Midtown Gallery, 11 E 57th St, New York, NY 10022.
Mailing Address: 3013 Dumbarton Ave N W, Washington, DC 20007.

SKEGGS, DAVID POTTER
Designer, Painter
b Youngstown, Ohio, Feb 5, 24.
Study & Training: Denison Univ, AB; Iowa State Univ, MA; also with Hans Hofmann.
Work in Public Collections: Akron Art Inst; Butler Inst Am Art, Youngstown, Ohio; Joslyn Mus Art; Sioux City Art Ctr; U S Embassies, abroad; plus other pub & pvt collections.
Exhibitions: Canton Art Inst; Art Inst Chicago; Syracuse Mus Fine Arts; Libr Cong; Wadsworth Atheneum; plus many others.
Teaching: Asst prof art, Youngstown Col, 48-52, head dept art, 52-54.
Positions: Dir, Sioux City Art Ctr, 54-57; designer, Garth Andrew Co, Bath, Ohio, 57-65; designer, Skeggs Design Studio, 60-; designer, Far Corners, Inc, 65-
Memberships: Ohio Designer-Craftsmen; Am Crafts Coun; Artists Equity Asn.
Mailing Address: 1854 Orchard Dr, Bath, OH 44210.

SKELTON, PHILLIS HEPLER
Painter
Preferred Media: Watercolors.
b Pittsburgh, Pa, Dec 31, 98.
Study & Training: Univ Southern Calif, BA(cum laude); Scripps Col, MA, with Eliot O'Hara, Dong Kingman, Phil Dike, Millard Sheets & David Scott.
Work in Public Collections: Pasadena Art Mus, Calif; Bowdoin Col, Brunswick, Maine.
Exhibitions: Calif Nat Watercolor Soc; Pasadena Art Gallery; Scripps Col, Claremont, Calif; Laguna Art Gallery, Calif; Am Watercolor Soc.
Teaching: Instr, Calif, 20-23; pvt instr, 50-; Scripps instr art, Claremont, 59-67; head dept art, Mayfield Sr High Sch, Pasadena, 60-68.
Awards: Awards, Pasadena Art Mus, Laguna Art Gallery & Calif Nat Watercolor Soc.
Memberships: Calif Nat Watercolor Soc; Laguna Art Gallery.
Mailing Address: 543 S College Ave, Claremont, CA 91711.

SKEMP, ROBERT OLIVER
Painter
Preferred Media: Oils.
b Scotdale, Pa, Aug 22, 10.
Study & Training: Art Stud League New York, N Y, with Thomas Hart Benton, George Bridgman, Frank Dumond & Robert Laurent; Grand Cent Sch Art; in France & Spain; also with George Luks.
Work in Public Collections: Rayburn Bldg, Washington, D C; U S Coast Guard, Washington, D C; R J Reynolds Tobacco Co, Winston-Salem, N C; Ackland Gallery, Univ N C, Chapel Hill; Springfield Art Mus, Ill.
Commissions: Man's Search For Happiness, Church of Jesus Christ of Latter Day Saints, World's Fair, New York, 64; portraits, Chief Judge Paul V Rao, Fed Ct, New York, 67, Mr Haakon Romnes, New York, 69, Dean Douglas Brown, Princeton Univ, N J, 69 & Mrs Roger Blough, Pittsburgh, 70; plus others.
Exhibitions: Ann Exhib Advert Art, 49-63; Art: U S A, New York, 64.
Awards: Gold medal, 51, two gold medals, 52 & second & third places, 53, Art Dirs Club Chicago.
Bibliography: Howard Munce (auth), Portrait painting, Northlight Mag, winter 70.
Dealers: Portraits, Inc, 41 E 57th St, New York, NY 10022; Grand Central Art Gallery, 40 Vanderbilt Ave, New York, NY 10017.
Mailing Address: 32 Hyde Lane, Westport, CT 06880.

SKINNER, CLARA (CLARA SKINNER GUY)
Painter, Printmaker
U S citizen.
Study & Training: Univ Southern Calif; Art Stud League New York; also with Hans Hofmann.
Work in Public Collections: Metrop Mus Art Print Collection, New York, N Y; San Francisco Mus Art, Calif; Cleveland Mus Art, Ohio; Detroit Mus Art, Mich; Saint Louis Mus Fine Arts, Mo; plus others.

Exhibitions: 50 Best American Prints Travelling Exhib, Am Fedn Arts, 35; Mod Mus Moscow, Russia, 40; Responsive Eye, Mus Mod Art, New York, 50; one-man show, Castallone Gallery, 58.
Teaching: Assoc prof art, MacMurray Col, 46-56.
Mailing Address: c/o Syme, R F D, Camden, ME 04843.

SKINNER, ELSA KELLS
Painter, Illustrator
Preferred Media: Watercolors.
b Syracuse, N. Y.
Study & Training: Syracuse Univ, BFA; Univ N Mex, with Randall Davey & Kenneth Adams; also with Rex Brant, Milford Zornes, Robert E Wood Jr, Bud Biggs & George Post.
Work in Public Collections: Old Mine at Golden, Albuquerque City Hall, N Mex; Seminole Child, Bernalillo Co Health Bldg, Albuquerque; Out Cerrillos Way, N Mex Bank & Trust Co, Hobbs.
Commissions: Oil portrait of Oñate, N Mex Hist Soc, N Mex State Univ, Las Cruces.
Exhibitions: Nat Asn Am Penwomen Nat, Smithsonian Inst, Washington, D C, 60; Mus N Mex Biennial, Santa Fe, 63; Southwestern Regional, Oklahoma City, Okla, 64; Reno Regional, Nev, 65; El Paso Sun Carnival Nat, Tex, 67.
Positions: Painter & designer, Charles Hall, New York, N Y, 32-33; free lance bookjacket designer, Thomas Nelson & Sons, 34-35; designer, Decorative Utilities Corp, Newark, N J, 34-40; free lance illusr & designer, Berland Printing Co, New York, 35-39.
Awards: The Humming-bird, first prize watercolor, 62 & Gold and Brown, first prize mixed & The Creatures, first prize acrylic, 67, N Mex State Fair; Old Mine at Golden, first purchase award, City of Albuquerque, 68.
Memberships: Southwestern Watercolor Soc (mem chmn, N Mex Chap, 71-72).
Dealer: Wagon Trails Gallery, 108 Romero N W, Old Town, Albuquerque, NM 87104.
Mailing Address: 2245 Inez Dr, Albuquerque, NM 87110.

SKINNER, ORIN ENSIGN
Designer
Preferred Media: Stained Glass.
b Sweden Valley, Pa, Nov 5, 92.
Study & Training: Rochester Atheneum Art Sch, N Y, grad, 15, with Herman J Butler; also res in France & Eng, 23-25.
Commissions: Stained glass windows, Princeton Univ Chapel, 30, St John the Divine Cathedral, New York, N Y, 32, Heinz Mem Chapel, Univ Pittsburgh, 38, St Patrick's Cathedral, New York, 56 & Grace Cathedral, San Francisco, 66.
Positions: Designer, Charles A Baker, Rochester, 12-16; designer, R Toland Wright, Cleveland, Ohio, 17-19; mgr, treas & pres, Charles J Connick Assocs, 20-; ed, Stained Glass, 30-48.
Awards: Master craftsman, Boston Soc Arts & Crafts, 40.
Memberships: Fel Int Inst Arts & Lett; fel Stained Glass Asn Am (pres, 48-49).
Research: Restoration of Great Western Rose Window of Rheims Cathedral.
Publications: Contribr, Am Architect, 27, Liturgical Arts, 37, Am Fabricks, 50 & Holy Cross Mag, 67.
Mailing Address: 37 Walden St, Newtonville, MA 02160.

SKLAR, DOROTHY
Painter
Preferred Media: Watercolors, Acrylics.
b New York, N. Y.
Study & Training: Univ Calif, Los Angeles, BE; Chouinard Art Ctr Sch, Los Angeles; also with S Macdonald Wright & Millard Sheets.
Work in Public Collections: Los Angeles Munic Art Comn, Los Angeles City Hall; Baptist Univ, Shawnee, Okla; Westside Jewish Community Ctr, Los Angeles.
Exhibitions: Pa Acad Fine Arts, 53, 54 & 57; Los Angeles Co Mus Art, 55; Butler Inst Am Art, Youngstown, Ohio, 63-68; Frye Mus, Seattle, Wash, 66; Calif State Fair, Sacramento, 66.
Teaching: Instr art, Santa Monica City Schs, 43.
Awards: Award in oil, Laguna Art Asn, 60; Ida M Holiday Mem Award, Nat Asn Women Artists, 60; Child Hassan Award, Frye Mus, 66.
Memberships: Calif Nat Watercolor Soc (treas, 61, v pres, 62); Southern Calif Chap Artists Equity Asn (treas, 51); Nat Soc Painters Casein; Nat Asn Women Artists; Laguna Beach Art Asn.
Dealer: Kramer Art Gallery, 710 N La Cienega Blvd, Los Angeles, CA 90069.
Mailing Address: 6612 Colgate, Los Angeles, CA 90048.

SKLAR-WEINSTEIN, ARLENE (JOYCE)
Painter, Printmaker
Preferred Media: Acrylics.
b Detroit, Mich, Oct 25, 31.
Study & Training: Parsons Sch Design; Mus Mod Art, New York, scholar & with Bernard Pfreim; Albright Art Sch; New York Univ,
with Hale Woodruff, BA, 52, MS(art educ), 55; Pratt Graphics Ctr, with Andrew Stasik.
Work in Public Collections: Mus Mod Art, New York, N Y; New York Pub Libr Permanent Print Collection; Grace Gallery, New York City Community Col, Brooklyn; Hudson River Mus Permanent Collection, Yonkers, N Y; Mfrs Hanover Trust Co, Mount Vernon, N Y.
Exhibitions: Regional juried graphics, Albright-Knox Gallery, Buffalo, N Y, 52; The Visionaires, East Hampton Galleries, New York, 68; Juried Regional, Yonkers Art Asn, Hudson River Mus, 70 & 71; Juried Nat, Nat Asn Women Artists, Lever House, New York, 72; one-man show, Evolutions, Hudson River Mus, 71 & one-man show, West Broadway Gallery, 72.
Teaching: Chmn dept art for jr high sch, Plainedge Schs, Farmingdale, N Y, 53-56; instr art & dir art sch, YM-YWHA, Inwood-Wa Washington Heights, N Y, 56-58; coord-instr art workshops, H Hastings Creative Arts Coun, N Y, 62-68.
Positions: Visual arts coordr, Coun Arts Westchester, White Plains, N Y, 69-70.
Awards: Geigy award for painting, Ciba-Geigy Corp, 69; first prize, Regional Juried at Hudson River Mus, Yonkers Art Asn, 71; award at print competition, Gestetner Corp, 71.
Bibliography: Masters (auth) & Houston (auth), Psychedelic art, Grove, 68; H H Arnason (auth), History of modern art, Abrams, 69; Barry N Schwartz (auth), introduction to catalogue, Hudson River Mus, 71.
Memberships: Yonkers Art Asn, Hudson River Mus (pres, 70-72); Women in Art (rotating leadership, 72); Nat Asn Women Artists.
Dealer: West Broadway Gallery, 431 W Broadway, New York, NY 10013.
Mailing Address: 18 Harvard Lane, Hastings-on-Hudson, NY 10706.

SKOP, MICHAEL
Sculptor, Educator
Preferred Media: Bronze, Polyester, Wood, Stone.
b Lakewood, Ohio, June 14, 32.
Study & Training: Syracuse Univ, with Ivan Mestrovic, BFA; Univ Notre Dame, MFA; Danish Royal Art Acad, with Mogens Boggild; Univ Perugia, Italy; Am Scandinavian grant to Denmark, 59; Fulbright grant to Florence, Italy, 60.
Work in Public Collections: Danish Royal Art Acad, Copenhagen; Univ Mass, Amherst; Jewish Community Ctr, Cincinnati, Ohio.
Commissions: Crucifix, St Josaph Ukranian Church, Cleveland, Ohio, 59; Walter Draper Mem, Queen City Club, Cincinnati, 63; relig compos, Christ Church, Cincinnati, 65; Mem, Oper Engrs, New Haven, Conn, 72; plus numerous pvt comns.
Exhibitions: Syracuse Art Mus, N Y, 53; Danish Royal Art Acad, 59; Cincinnati Art Mus, Art Acad Faculty, 63-66; Brecksville Art Gallery, Ohio, 63-72; one-man show, Smith Art Mus, Springfield, Mass, 68.
Teaching: Instr sculpture, Cincinnati Art Acad, 63-67; asst prof sculpture, Southern Conn State Col, 67-
Positions: Asst to Ivan Mestrovic, Syracuse Univ, 53-55; grad asst cur, Univ Notre Dame, 58-59; consult, Trait Tex Indust, Cleveland, 70-
Bibliography: Michael Skop sculptor, Arte Armonia, Florence, Italy, 60; Arthur Darrach (auth), Michael Skop, Cincinnati Enquirer, 63; Donald Reichert (auth), Michael Skop, Smith Mus Catalog, Mass, 68.
Memberships: Nat Art Educ Asn.
Dealer: Brecksville Art Gallery, Mill Rd, Brecksville, OH 44141.
Mailing Address: Creamery Rd, Durham, CT 06422.

SLACK, DEE
Painter
Preferred Media: Oils.
b Salisbury, Md, Apr 5, 46.
Study & Training: Md Inst Col Art, BFA.
Commissions: Portrait of Robert Gordon, commissioned by Mr & Mrs Gordon, Scranton, Pa, 72; painting of Bob Keitel, commissioned by Robert S Keitel, New York, N Y, 72; tropical seascape, commissioned by Mr & Mrs A Kaupinis, Houston, Tex.
Exhibitions: Women Artists in Revolution, Soho, New York, 69; Painterly Realism, traveling show, Am Fedn Arts, 70-72; Multi-Media '71 & Drawing Each Other, 71, Brooklyn Mus, N Y; one-woman show, Green Mountain Gallery, New York, 72.
Dealer: Green Mountain Gallery, 135 Greene St, New York, NY 10012.
Mailing Address: 165 W Fourth St, New York, NY 10014.

SLADE, ROY
Painter, Educator
Preferred Media: Acrylics.
b Cardiff, Wales, July 14, 33.
Study & Training: Cardiff Col Art, NDD, 54; Univ Wales, ATD, 54.
Work in Public Collections: Arts Coun Gt Brit; Contemp Art Soc; Nuffield Found; Westinghouse Corp; Brit Overseas Airways Corp.

Exhibitions: Contemp Painting, Nat Mus Wales, 53-60; Art in Alliance, Washington, D C, 68; one-man shows, Jefferson Pl Gallery, Washington, D C, 68, 70 & 72; Washington Art, State Univ N Y Col, Potsdam & State Univ N Y, Albany, 71; Nat Print Club, Nat Col Fine Art, Washington, D C, 72; plus others

Teaching: Sr lectr post-grad studies, Leeds Col Art, Eng, 64-69; prof painting, Corcoran Sch Art, Washington, D C, 67-68, dean, 70-

Positions: Vis, Boston Sch of Mus Fine Art, 70-; mem, D C Comn Arts, 72-; lectr, numerous univs & schs.

Awards: Fulbright-Hays scholar, 67.

Publications: Auth, Up the American Vanishing Point, 11/68 & Report from Washington, 1/72, Studio Int; auth, A new cultural centre, Yorkshire Post, 2/69; auth, Artist in America, Contemp Rev, 5/69.

Dealer: Nesta Dorrance, Jefferson Place Gallery, 2144 P St N W, Washington, D C 20037.

Mailing Address: 2327 Ashmead Pl N W, Washington, DC 20009.

SLATE, JOSEPH FRANK
Painter, Writer
b Holliday's Cove, W Va, Jan 19, 28.
Study & Training: Univ Wash, BA, 51; printmaking, Tokyo, Japan, 57; Yale Univ Sch Art & Archit, Alumni fel & BFA, 60, with Josef Albers, Gabor Peterdi, Neil Welliver, Bernard Chaet & William Bailey; Dante Aligheri Inst, Florence, Italy, 71.
Work in Public Collections: Drawing, Yale Univ.
Exhibitions: 12th Nat Print Show, Brooklyn Mus, 60; Pioneer Gallery, Cooperstown, N Y, 61; Artist-in-Residence Exhib, Milton Col, Univ Wis, 63; one-man show of paintings, Kenyon Col, 71.
Teaching: Prof art & chmn dept, Kenyon Col, 62-, chmn fine arts div, 67-69.
Positions: Consult, Studies on Aesthet & Perception, Yale Univ Dept Psychol, 60-65; mem exec comt, Kress Found Consortium Art Hist, 65-69.
Awards: Hon mention for painting, Ohio Expos, 62.
Memberships: Mid-Ohio Cols Art Asn (pres, 64-65); Col Art Asn Am; Mid-Am Col Art Asn.
Research: Perception.
Publications: Auth, Those old Italians, 62 & Respect, 64, New Yorker; auth, This heavy folk thing, Kenyon Rev, 69; auth, So hard to look at, Contempora, 70; contribr, The art of drawing, 72.
Dealer: Accent House, 405 N Main, Mount Vernon, OH 43050.
Mailing Address: Box 417, Gambier, OH 43022.

SLAUGHTER, LURLINE EDDY
Painter
Preferred Media: Acrylics, Oils.
b Heidelberg, Miss, June 19, 19.
Study & Training: Miss State Col Women, Columbus, grad; Miss Art Colony Workshops, with Alvin Sella, Fred Mitchell, Ida Kohlmeyer, Howard Goodson, Frank Engel, Andrew Bucci, Alex Russo & Bob Gelinas; also with Marie Hull & Malcolm Norwood.
Work in Public Collections: Pine Bluff Arts Ctr, Ark; Miss State Col Women; Univ of the South, Sewanee, Tenn; Miss State Univ, Starkville.
Exhibitions: Six Nat Oil Painting Exhibs, Jackson, Miss, 60-69; Hunter Gallery Ann, Chattanooga, Tenn, 65; Cent S Ann, Parthenon Mus, Nashville, Tenn, 66; Masur Mus Ann, Monroe, La, 66; Fine Arts Registry, Brooks Mem Mus, Memphis, Tenn, 70; plus one-man shows, N Y, Miss, Tenn & Ark.
Awards: Outstanding Artist Award, Fine Arts Registry, 66; best in show awards, Southern Contemp Art Festival, Greenville, Miss, 66 & Holiday Arts Festival, McComb, Miss, 67.
Memberships: Miss Art Colony (bd dirs, 65-); Miss Art Asn (state adv comt, 67-); Tenn Art League; Gulf S Arts Coun, McComb & Greenville, Miss (gallery artist); McCartys Galleries, Merigold, Miss & Monteagle, Tenn (gallery artist); plus one other.
Mailing Address: Seldom Seen Plantation, Silver City, MS 39166.

SLES, STEVEN LAWRENCE
Painter
Preferred Media: Oils, Ink, Glass.
b Jersey City, N J, June 16, 40.
Study & Training: Inst Allende, Mex; Bard Col; Univ Madrid; Swarthmore Col; Art Stud League New York; also with Hans Hoffman & Sol Wilson.
Work in Public Collections: Swarthmore Col, Pa; Vereinigung Mund und Fussmalenden Kunstler Gallery, Florence, Italy; Vereinigung Der Mund und Fussmalenden Kunstlen in Aller Welt Gallery, Munich, Ger & Liechtenstein.
Exhibitions: FAR Gallery, New York, N Y; Provincetown Art Asn, Mass; Jersey City Mus; Petchburi Gallery, Bangkok, Thailand; Galeria Toison, Madrid, Spain; plus others.
Positions: Dir, personal art staff, Valencia, Spain, 66-; dir, Galerie Privée, Valencia, Spain, 70-; mem, Worldwide Asn Mouth & Footpainting Artists, Inc, Vaduz, Lichtenstein.

Awards: Purchase prize, Pearson Gallery, Swarthmore Col, 62; Charles T Bainbridge Award, Jersey City, 70; first & second prizes, Kenny Inst Int Mus Art Show, Minn, 71; plus others.
Bibliography: Articles, In: Elizabeth Daily J, 4-9/64; Agramunt (auth), article, In: Avanzada, Madrid, 9/70; Sheer determination (film), Vereinigung Der Mund und Fussmalenden Kunstler in Aller Welt Gallery, 64-71; plus others.
Memberships: Fel Royal Soc Arts; Int Arts Guild (hon v pres, Span Comt, 70); Free Painters & Sculptors, London; Arte Actual, Valencia; dipl mem Vereinigung Mund und Fussmalenden Kunstler in Aller Welt.
Publications: Auth, Ahora que te has ido, Poesía Española, Madrid, 70; auth, Amor, río que estas dormido, Poesía de Venezuela, Caracas, 70; auth, Mujer en la oscuridad del día, Azor, Barcelona, Spain, 70; auth, Three poetries, Arbol de fuego, Caracas, 70; auth, El guerrero y la guerra de la vida, Mensaje, Lérida, Spain, 70.
Mailing Address: Conde Altea, 49, Valencia, Spain.

SLETTEHAUGH, THOMAS CHESTER
Painter, Educator
Preferred Media: Mixed Media.
b Minneapolis, Minn, May 8, 25.
Study & Training: Univ Minn, BS, 49, MEd, 50, with Walter Quint, Malcolm Myers & John Rood; Pa State Univ, DEd, 56, with Viktor Lowenfeld; spec study at Williams Col, Univ S C, Univ Ga & Syracuse Univ.
Work in Public Collections: Bucharest Univ, Romania; Cult Ctr, Budapest, Hungary; Cortland Gallery, State Univ N Y, Cortland.
Commissions: Symbol of excellence, comn by admin, Miss State Col Women, 70; Miss State Col Women Crest for Apollo 14, comn by Alumni Asn, 71.
Exhibitions: Baltimore Mus Art Regional, Md, 68; Corcoran Gallery Art Regional, Washington, D C, 69; Carnegie Mus Regional, Pittsburgh, Pa, 70; one-man show of prints, Outer Space Concepts, Kunstforom Gallery, Garmisch-park, W Ger, 71; one-man show of prints, Grape Le af—Variations, Bucharest Univ, 72.
Collections Arranged: Max Klager—Printmaker (etchings & silkscreen), Heidelberg Univ, W Ger; Bruce Carter—Woodcuts, Carnegie-Mellon Univ.
Teaching: Prof art, Frostburg State Col, 62-68; prof fine arts, Miss State Col Women, 68-70; assoc prof grad studies art educ, Univ Minn, 70-
Positions: Cur art, Frostburg State Col, 62-68; coun mem, Md Arts Coun, 66-68; gallery dir, Miss State Col Women, 68-70; coun mem, Miss Coun Arts, 68-70; coun mem, Minn Art Educators, 71-72.
Awards: Intercultural Art of Hungary & America Award, Off Int Progs, Univ Minn, 71; psychoaesthetics develop award, Col Educ, Univ Minn, 71.
Bibliography: Hans Stumbauer (auth), Art education in Austria, Art Sch Linz, 71; Marzio Bugatti (auth), article, In: Encycl Int Degli Artist (Italy), 71; Paul Cornel Chitic (auth), articles, In: Tribune & Art Rev, Bucharest, Romania, 72.
Memberships: Int Soc Educ in Art; Int Soc Aesthet; Int Soc Art Hist; Int Soc Empirical Aesthet; Int Coun Educ for Teaching.
Research: Creative intellect of artists and perceptive development of the individual.
Publications: Auth, Psychoaesthetics, the tactile modalities and creative thinking, 70; auth, The creative use of tactile modalities & creative thinking, 70; auth, Art education as a means to international understanding, 72; auth, Non visual motivations for art expressions, 72; auth, Perceptual understanding based on tactile art experience, 72.
Mailing Address: 135 Wulling Hall, University of Minnesota, Minmeapolis, MN 55455.

SLICK, JAMES NELSON
Painter, Sculptor
Preferred Media: Oils.
b Salt Lake City, Utah, Aug 26, 01.
Study & Training: Cornell Univ; also with William McDermot.
Work in Public Collections: Permanent Collections of Los Angeles Turf Club, Arcadia, Calif Bay Meadows Race Track, Golden Gate Fields, Keeneland Race Course & Hialeah Race Track; two in Hall of Fame & others in mus proper, Thoroughbred Nat Mus Racing, Saratoga, N Y; plus others.
Commissions: Adios (life-size bronze), Meadows Race Track, Pittsburgh, Pa, 68; plus over 300 pvt comns.
Teaching: Instr horse portraiture, Studio Club, Lexington, Ky, 65-66.
Awards: First Prize Blue Grass Fair, 64.
Bibliography: Kent Cockran (auth), articles, In: Racing Form; articles, In: Calif Thoroughbred & Thoroughbred Rec.
Mailing Address: 287 Cabrillo St, Costa Mesa, CA 92627.

SLIFKA, MR & MRS JOSEPH
Collectors
Mailing Address: 870 Fifth Ave, New York, NY 10021.

SLIVE, SEYMOUR
Educator, Writer
b Chicago, Ill, Sept 15, 20.
Study & Training: Univ Chicago, AB, 43, PhD, 52; Harvard Univ, hon MA, 58.
Teaching: Instr fine arts, Oberlin Col, 50-51; asst prof & chmn art dept, Pomona Col, 52-54; asst prof fine arts, Harvard Univ, 54-57, assoc prof, 57-61, prof fine arts, 61-, chmn dept fine arts, 67-70; exchange prof, Univ Leningrad, 61; Ryerson lectr, Yale Univ, 62; Slade prof, Oxford Univ, 73.
Positions: Mem ed staff, Art Quart, 63.
Awards: Fulbright fel to the Netherlands, 51-52; Guggenheim fel, 56-57; Fulbright res scholar, Univ Utrecht, 59-60.
Memberships: Fel Am Acad Arts & Sci; hon mem Karel van Mander Soc; Col Art Asn Am (dir, 58-62, 65-69); Renaissance Soc.
Publications: Auth, Catalogue of Frans Hals Exhibition held in Haarlem, 62; auth, Frans Hals, Das Festmahl der St Georgs-Schutzengild 1616, 62; auth, Rembrandt drawings, 65; co-auth, Dutch painting: 1600-1800, 66; auth, Frans Hals, 2 vols, 70; plus others.
Mailing Address: 1 Walker Street Pl, Cambridge, MA 02138.

SLIVKA, DAVID
Sculptor
Preferred Media: Bronze, Wood, Marble.
b Chicago, Ill.
Study & Training: Calif Sch Fine Arts.
Work in Public Collections: Univ Tex Mus, Austin; Walker Art Ctr, Minneapolis; Univ Calif, Berkeley; Brooklyn Mus, N Y; Stuttgart Mus, Ger.
Exhibitions: Hirshhorn Collection Mod Sculpture, 62-63; Univ Tex Mus, 66; Brandeis Univ Creative Arts Award Winners, Aldrich Mus Contemp Art, Conn, 66; one-man show, Southern Ill Univ, Carbondale, 68; Selections From Chase Manhattan Bank Collection, 71.
Teaching: Prof sculpture, Univ Mass, Amherst, 64-67; artist-in-residence, Southern Ill Univ, Carbondale, 67-68; Queens Col, N Y, 71-73.
Awards: Brandeis Univ Creative Arts Award For Am Sculpture, 62.
Bibliography: Harvey Arnason (auth), Modern sculpture from the Joseph Hirshhorn collection, Guggenheim Mus, 62; Georgine Oeri (auth), The sculpture of David Slivka, Quadrum, 63; Harold Rosenberg (auth), The anxious object, Illus, 65.
Dealer: Helen Gee, 263 W 11th St, New York, NY 10014.
Mailing Address: Box 537, New York, NY 10011.

SLIVKA, ROSE
Art Editor
Positions: Ed-in-chief & writer, Craft Horizons.
Mailing Address: Craft Horizons, 16 E 52nd St, New York, NY 10022.

SLOAN, MR & MRS J SEYMOUR
Collectors, Patrons
Collection: Primarily American art, but also includes works by Europeans such as Moore, Jongkind, Gromaire, Fraser and Matisse.
Mailing Address: 30 E 65th St, New York, NY 10021.

SLOAN, ROBERT SMULLYAN
Painter, Art Dealer
Preferred Media: Oils.
b New York, N Y, Dec 5, 15.
Study & Training: City Col New York, AB, 36; Inst Fine Arts, N Y Univ, 37-39.
Work in Public Collections: IBM Collection; Bradford Jr Col, Haverhill, Mass; White Art Mus, Ithaca, N Y.
Commissions: Many covers & spec features, Time, Coronet & Colliers, 41-50; posters, Russian War Relief, 43 & Doing All You Can, Brother, U S Treas, 43.
Exhibitions: Nat Soldier Art Show, Nat Gallery Art, Washington, D C, 45; Carnegie Inst, 48; Corcoran Biennial, 49; Portraits of Yr, Portraits, Inc, 49; Am Watercolor Soc Exhib, Nat Acad Design Gallery, 56.
Positions: Independent art dealer.
Awards: Citation for distinguished serv, U S Treas, 43; watercolor div award, Nat Soldier Art Show, USA, 45.
Bibliography: George Wiswell (auth), Discovery of a Copley portrait, Am Heritage Mag, 60.
Memberships: Appraisers Asn Am; Mamaroneck Artists Guild (pres, 54).
Specialty of Gallery: American and European painting.
Collection: Hudson River school.
Publications: Illusr, Army Educ Prog & other mags.
Mailing Address: 1412 Arlington St, Mamaroneck, NY 10543.

SLOANE, ERIC
Illustrator, Writer
b New York, N Y, Feb 27, 10.
Study & Training: Art Stud League New York; Sch Fine Arts, Yale Univ, 29; New York Sch Fine & Applied Art, 35.
Commissions: Designed & executed Willett's Mem, Am Mus Natural Hist; murals, Int Silver Co, Meriden, Conn, Morton Salt Co, Chicago & Wings Club, New York; plus others.
Collections Arranged: Donor, Eric Sloane Mus Early Am Tools, Kent, Conn.
Awards: Gold Medal, Hudson Valley Art Asn, 64; Freedom Found Award, 65.
Memberships: Nat Acad Design; Salmagundi Club.
Publications: Auth, Skies and the artist, 51, Return to Taos, 60, Museum of early American tools, 64, Reverence for Wood, 65, Remember America, 71 plus many others.
Mailing Address: Weather Hill, Cornwall Bridge, CT 06754.

SLOANE, JOSEPH CURTIS
Art Historian, Educator
b Pottstown, Pa, Aug 8, 09.
Study & Training: Princeton Univ, AB, 31, MFA, 34, Hodder fel, 48, PhD, 49.
Teaching: Instr art hist, Princeton Univ, 35-37; asst prof art hist & chmn dept art, Rutgers Univ, 37-38; from assoc prof art hist to prof & chmn dept art, Bryn Mawr Col, 38-58; prof art hist & chmn dept art, Univ N C, Chapel Hill, 58-, dir, William Hayes Ackland Art Ctr.
Positions: Pres, Nat Coun Arts Educ, 69-71; N C State Art Soc.
Awards: Fulbright sr res grant, 52; alumni distinguished prof, Univ N C, 63-
Memberships: Col Art Asn Am (past pres); N C State Arts Coun; Am Soc Aesthet; Am Coun Arts Educ (past pres).
Research: Nineteenth and twentieth century art, especially painting.
Publications: Auth, French painting between the past and the present, Princeton Univ Press, 51; auth, Paul Marc Joseph Chenavard, Univ N C Press, 62; auth, articles, In: Art Bull, Art Quart, Gazette Beaux-Arts, Art J & others.
Mailing Address: 407 Morgan Creek Rd, Chapel Hill, NC 27514.

SLOANE, MARY (HUMPHREYS)
Painter
b New York, N Y, Aug 18, 12.
Study & Training: Wells Col, AB, 31; Columbia Univ; also with George Picken.
Work in Public Collections: In pub & pvt collections.
Exhibitions: Minot State Teachers Col, N Dak, 62; two-man show, N Mex Highlands Univ, 62; Unitarian Soc, Amherst, Mass, 68; Int Group, Roland Gibson Art Found, 68; St Paul's Sch, Concord, N H, 69; plus others.
Teaching: Lect on art to cols & libr asns.
Positions: Mass State Art Chmn; Am Asn Univ Women Art Leader, Nine-State Northeast Conf, 60.
Awards: Medal of honor, Nat Asn Women Artists, 57; Silvermine Guild Art, 57; silver medal, Springfield Art League, 59; plus others.
Memberships: Artists Equity Asn; Nat Asn Women Artists; Cape Cod Art Asn; Provincetown Art Asn; Springfield Art League, Mass; plus others.
Publications: Auth, Strong cables rising, 42.
Mailing Address: R F D, Bernardston, MA 01337.

SLOANE, PATRICIA HERMINE
Painter
b New York, N Y, Nov 21, 34.
Study & Training: Dayton Art Inst, 47-49, scholar, 49; R I Sch Design, scholar, 53-54, BFA, 55; Ohio Univ Grad Col, scholar, 55-56; Nat Acad Design, 56-58; Hunter Col, MA, 68; also with Hans Hofmann; New York Univ, PhD, 72.
Work in Public Collections: Mus Mod Art Lending Collection, New York; Andrew Dickson White Mus, Cornell Univ; Univ Notre Dame, Ind.
Commissions: Bk jacket design & bk design for New York City publ.
Exhibitions: Riverdale YMHA, 64; Emanu-el Midtown YMHA, 64; Chelsea Exhib, St Peter's Episcopal Church, 64; one-man show, Grand Cent Moderns, 68; Fordham Univ; Univ R I, 68; plus others.
Teaching: Instr, introduction to fine arts, Ohio Univ, 56; instr arts & crafts, Jewish Community Ctr, Providence, R I; instr, Scarsdale Studio Workshop, 65-; instr, Univ R I, Community Col of City Univ New York, Trenton Jr Col & others; gallery lectr, Whitney Mus Am Art; asst prof, City Univ New York.
Memberships: Col Art Asn Am; Am Soc Aesthet.
Publications: Contribr, drawings, In: Village Voice; contribr, critical articles, In: East (newspaper of the arts).
Mailing Address: 79 Mercer St, New York, NY 10012.

SLOBODKIN, LOUIS
Sculptor, Illustrator
b Albany, N Y, Feb 19, 03.
Study & Training: Beaux Arts Inst Design, 18-23.
Commissions: U S Post Off, Washington, D C; statue of Lincoln,
 Symbol of Unity, for Fed Bldg garden; Young Abe Lincoln (bronze
 statue), Interior Bldg, Washington, D C; two panels, Madison Sq
 Post Off, New York; Tropical Postman (aluminum); plus others.
Exhibitions: Whitney Mus Am Art, New York; Pa Acad Fine Arts,
 Philadelphia; Art Inst Chicago, Ill; 50 Best Books Exhib, Am Inst
 Graphic Art; 20 Best Children's Books, Am Fedn Arts Traveling
 Exhib; plus others.
Teaching: Lect, Contemporary Sculpture & Designing & Illustrating
 Children's Books; head sculpture dept, Master Inst, New York,
 34-37; head sculpture div, New York City Art Proj, 41-42.
Awards: Caldecott Medal, 43.
Bibliography: An Am Group (pres, 45-46); Sculptors Guild (bd
 dirs, 40-45); Am Inst Graphic Arts (chmn artists comt); Nat
 Sculpture Soc; Artists Equity Asn (bd nat dirs).
Publications: Auth & illusr, Read about the postman, 66, Read
 about the fireman, 67, Read about the busman, 57, Round trip
 spaceship, 68, Wilbur the warrior, 71 plus many others; contribr
 to Mag of Art & Horn Bk.
Mailing Address: 9341 E Bay Harbor Dr, Bay Harbor Island, FL
 33154.

SLOSHBERG, LEAH PHYFER
Art Administrator
b New Albany, Miss, Feb 21, 37.
Study & Training: Miss State Col Women, BFA; Tulane Univ La, MA.
Collections Arranged: Burgoyne Diller Retrospective, 66; Focus on
 Light, 67; Ben Shahn Retrospective, 69.
Positions: Cur arts, N J State Mus, Trenton, asst dir, 69-71, dir,
 71-
Memberships: Am Asn Mus.
Mailing Address: State Museum, P O Box 1868, 205 W State St, Cul-
 tural Center, Trenton, NJ 08625.

SLOTNICK, MORTIMER H
Painter
b New York, N Y, Nov 7, 20.
Study & Training: City Col New York; Columbia Univ.
Work in Public Collections: In pvt collections only.
Exhibitions: Whitney Mus Am Art, Riverside Mus, Hudson River
 Mus, New York Pub Libr, Nat Acad Design, New York, plus
 others.
Teaching: Prof art & art educ, City Col New York; supvr arts &
 humanities, City Sch Dist, New Rochelle, N Y; lectr art educ,
 Col New Rochelle.
Memberships: Allied Artists Am; Am Artists Prof League; Am Vet
 Soc Artists; Westchester Art Asn; New Rochelle Art Asn.
Mailing Address: 43 Amherst Dr, New Rochelle, NY 10804.

SMALL, AMY GANS
Sculptor, Instructor
Preferred Media: Wood, Stone, Metal.
b New York, N Y.
Study & Training: Hartford Art Sch, 8 yrs; Art Stud League New
 York, with Zorack; New Sch Social Res, with Seymour Lipton;
 Nat Park Col, Forest Glen, Md; Sculpture Ctr, New York; Cent
 Cult, Inst Nat Bellas Artes, Mexico City, Mex, 71-72; also with
 Lothar J Kestenbaum & many others.
Work in Public Collections: Selected Artists Gallery, New York &
 in pvt collections.
Commissions: Head of Ann Buckman (clay & cast stone), Dr Moses
 Buckman, Westchester, N Y, 50; stone figures for sculpture
 garden, Evan Frankel, Easthampton, N Y, 61.
Exhibitions: Woodstock Presentation Show, N Y, 50; Woodstock Art
 Asn, 25 yrs; one-man shows, Krasner Gallery, New York, 58 &
 59; one-man shows, Selected Artists Gallery, New York, 61 & 68;
 Easthampton Guild Shows, 61, 67 & 68; plus many others.
Teaching: Instr sculpture, Lighthouse Sch for the Blind, New York,
 60-61; head sculpture sect, Woodstock Sch Art, 69-71; head pvt
 sch, Easthampton & Woodstock, 69-72; instr sculpture, Univ
 Poughkeepsie, 70-71.
Awards: Best in show, Westchester Arts & Crafts Guild Show;
 Presentation Show Award, Woodstock Artists Asn, 48.
Bibliography: Zaidenberg (auth), Anyone can sculpt, Harper & Row,
 52; Howard DeVree & Stuart Preston (auth), articles, In: New
 York Times, 61; Zaidenberg (auth), New & classic sculpture
 methods, World Publ, 72; plus many others.
Memberships: Woodstock Art Asn (mem bd, three times); Artists
 Equity Asn New York (bd·mem twice).
Dealers: Lewis Gallery, Woodstock, NY 12498; Herbert H Kende,
 655 Madison Ave & 60th St, New York, NY 10021.
Mailing Address: Box 307, Plochmann Lane, Woodstock, NY
 12498.

SMART, MARY-LEIGH
Collector, Patron
b Springfield, Ill, Feb 27, 17.
Study & Training: Oxford Univ, dipl, extra mural delegacy, 35; Wel-
 lesley Col, BA, 37; Columbia Univ, MA, 39; also with Bernard
 Karfiol, 38-39.
Memberships: Barn Gallery Assocs (founding secy & prog dir, 58-
 69, pres, 69-70, hon dir, 70-); Inst Contemp Art, Boston (corpora-
 tor, 65-); DeCordova Mus (acquisitions comt, 66-); Strawberry
 Banke (overseer, 71-); Am Fedn Arts.
Art Interests: Contemporary art and organizations promoting it;
 publisher of two works of conceptual art by Christopher C Cook.
Collection: Twentieth century New England painting and sculpture;
 American, European and Asian contemporary graphics.
Publications: Ed & auth, Hamilton Easter Field Art Foundation Col-
 lection (catalogue), 66; ed, Art: Ogunquit, a national exhibition of
 artists who have worked in Ogunquit (catalogue), 67; auth, Barn
 Gallery Assocs in action, 69 & The Barn Gallery, 70.
Mailing Address: Beachmere Pl, Ogunquit, ME 03907.

SMILEY, RALPH JACK
Painter, Instructor
Preferred Media: Oils.
b New York, N Y, July 24, 16.
Study & Training: Art Stud League New York; Nat Acad Design; also
 with George B Bridgman, Frank Vincent DuMond, Charles S Chap-
 man, Jules Gotlieb & Sidney E Dickenson.
Commissions: Portraits & still lifes, pvt comns throughout world.
Exhibitions: Greek Theatre Los Angeles, 56; Calif Art Club, 57;
 Painters & Sculptors Club Los Angeles, 58; Ebell Club, 59; Fri-
 day Morning Club, 60.
Teaching: Instr anat & drawing & lectr painting, Hollywood Art Ctr
 Sch, 59-
Awards: First prizes for portrait, Calif Art Club, 57, Painters &
 Sculptors Club, 58 & Friday Morning Club, Los Angeles, 60.
Memberships: Art Stud League New York; Calif Art Club; Los Ange-
 les Art Asn; Painters & Sculptors Club Los Angeles; Am Inst
 Fine Arts.
Mailing Address: 1759 Orchid Ave, Hollywood, CA 90028.

SMITH, ALVIN
Painter, Educator
Preferred Media: Mixed Media.
b Gary, Ind, Nov 27, 33.
Study & Training: State Univ Iowa, BA, 55; Kansas City Art Inst, 57;
 Univ Ill, AM, 60; teachers col, Columbia Univ, Heft Scholar, 67-
 69.
Work in Public Collections: Atlanta Univ; Dayton Mus, Ohio; teach-
 ers col, Columbia Univ; Kerlan Collection, Univ Minn; Mt Hol-
 yoke Col.
Exhibitions: Childe Hassam Exhib, Am Acad Arts & Lett, 68; Allu-
 sions, Community Gallery, Brooklyn Mus, 70; Eight Afro-Am
 Artists, Rath Mus, Geneva, Switz, 71; Irish Exhib Living Art,
 Dublin, Ireland, 72; Young American Artists, Gentofte Kunstven-
 ner, Copenhagen, Denmark, 72.
Teaching: Lectr art educ, Queens Col (N Y), 67-
Positions: Art corresp, Art Int, 72.
Awards: Painting purchase awards, Dayton Mus, 62 & 72; Dow
 Painting Award, Columbia Univ; Creative Artists Pub Serv
 grant, Cult Coun Found, N Y State Coun Arts, 72.
Bibliography: Peter Schjeldahl (auth), A triumph rather than a
 threat, New York Times, 4/27/69; Barbara Rose (auth), article,
 In: Art in Am, 9/10/70; Jean-Luc Daval (auth), article, In: Art
 Int, 10/20/71.
Memberships: Brooklyn Mus (adv comt, Community Gallery, 69-);
 Inst Soc Educ Through Art; Nat Art Educ Asn.
Research: Fine art by Afro-Americans: 1945-1970.
Publications: Illusr, Shadow of a bull, 65, illusr, cover, Art Int,
 summer 71.
Mailing Address: 27 E 22nd St, New York, NY 10010.

SMITH, ARTHUR HALL
Painter
Preferred Media: Oils, Acrylics, Ink.
b Norfolk, Va, Mar 23, 29.
Study & Training: Ill Wesleyan Univ, BFA, 51; Ecole Beaux-Arts
 (Atelier Souverbie), Paris, Fulbright fel, 51; Atelier 17, Paris,
 52, with S W Hayter; grad study, Univ Wash, 55; also with Mark
 Tobey, Seattle, Wash, 55-57.
Work in Public Collections: Chrysler Mus, Norfolk; Corcoran Gal-
 lery Art, Washington, D C; Phillips Collection, Washington, D C;
 Baltimore Mus Art, Md; Seattle Art Mus.
Commissions: Centennial murals, Mem Ctr, Ill Wesleyan Univ,
 Bloomington, Ill, 50; Mammals in World Art, Mammal Hall, U S
 Mus Natural Hist, Smithsonian Inst, Washington, D C, 58; Truckee
 Storage Triptych, Bur Water Reclamation, U S Dept Interior,
 Washington, D C, 72.

Exhibitions: Seventh Ann Va-N C Painting, Norfolk Mus Arts, 49; Va Artists Ann, Va Mus Fine Arts, Richmond, 51; one-man show, Washington Artists Series, Corcoran Gallery Art, 61; Huit Americains de Paris, Ctr Cult Am, Paris, France, 64; The American Artist and Water Reclamation, Nat Gallery Art, Washington, D C, 72.
Awards: Merwin Medal for painting, Bloomington Art Asn, 48; painting prize, 15th Area Exhib, Corcoran Gallery Art, 62.
Dealer: Franz Bader Gallery, 2124 Pennsylvania Ave N W, Washington, DC 20037.
Mailing Address: 2131 Florida Ave N W, Apt 23, Washington, DC 20008.

SMITH, MRS BERTRAM
Collector, Patron
b Dallas, Tex.
Study & Training: New York Inst Fine Arts.
Positions: Patron, trustee, mem painting & sculpture acquisitions comt & secy int coun, Mus Mod Art.
Collection: Post-impressionist, School of Paris paintings, drawings and sculpture.
Mailing Address: 907 Fifth Ave, New York, NY 10021.

SMITH, C R
Collector
Mailing Address: 510 Park Ave, New York, N Y 10022.

SMITH, CHARLES (WILLIAM)
Painter, Educator
Preferred Media: Oils, Acrylics.
b Lofton, Va, June 22, 93.
Study & Training: Corcoran Sch Art, Washington, D C; Yale Univ, cert in art.
Work in Public Collections: Mus Mod Art, New York, N Y; Rosenwald Collection, Nat Mus, Washington, D C; Guggenheim Mus, New York; Seattle Art Mus, Wash; Yale Univ, New Haven, Conn.
Commissions: Mosaics for pub schs & banks.
Exhibitions: Over forty one-man shows in mus, galleries, cols & univs throughout U S A.
Teaching: Instr graphic art & painting, Bennington Col, Vt, 38-46; prof painting, Univ Va, 46-63, chmn dept art, 47-63.
Bibliography: Schniewind (auth), Abstractions, Charles Smith, Johnson, 39; O'Neal (auth), Prints & paintings, 58; Charles Smith, Univ Va Press.
Publications: Auth, Linoleum block printing, 25; auth, Old Va in block prints, 29; auth, Old Charleston, 33; auth, Experiments in relief print making, 54; auth, My zoological garden (portfolio block paintings), 56.
Mailing Address: 211 Fourth St, Charlottesville, VA 22901.

SMITH, DAVID LOEFFLER
Painter, Educator
Preferred Media: Oils.
b New York, N Y, May 1, 28.
Study & Training: Bard Col, BA; Cranbrook Acad Art, MFA; also with Hans Hofmann & Raphael Soyer.
Exhibitions: Carnegie Inst, 60 & 61; Seligman Gallery, New York, N Y; one-man show, First St Gallery, 72.
Teaching: Dean & dir, Swain Sch Design, New Bedford, Mass; acting chmn dept art, Chatham Col.
Awards: Henry Posner Prize, Carnegie Inst, 61.
Publications: Auth, articles, In: Am Artist, 59-62, Antiques Mag, 11/67, Arts Mag, 3/68 & Art & Artists, 1/70 & 5/71.
Dealer: First Street Gallery, 305 Bowery, New York, NY 10003.
Mailing Address: 122 Hawthorn St, New Bedford, MA 02740.

SMITH, DOLPH
Painter, Educator
Preferred Media: Watercolors.
b Memphis, Tenn, July 26, 33.
Study & Training: Memphis State Univ; Memphis Acad Arts, BFA, 60.
Work in Public Collections: Ark State Univ, Jonesboro; Brooks Mem Art Gallery, Memphis, Tenn; Southwestern at Memphis; Tenn Arts Comn, State of Tenn, Nashville; N C Nat Bank, Charlotte.
Commissions: Paintings for various locations nationwide, Holiday Inns Am, 65-72; painting for Tenn Exec Mansion Christmas Card, Gov & Mrs Winfield Dunn, 71; painting for Sen Albert Gore, Democratic Party, Shelby Co, Tenn, 71.
Exhibitions: Watercolor U S A, Springfield, Mo, 65; Am Watercolor Soc, New York, N Y, 66; Invitational (one of four mid-south artists chosen to celebrate Memphis sesquicentennial with an exhib), Brooks Mem Art Gallery, 69; one-man shows, Brooks Mem Art Gallery, 65 & Charles Bowers Mem Mus, Santa Ana, Calif, 67.
Teaching: Asst prof painting & drawing, Memphis Acad Arts, 64-; vis instr painting, Southwestern Col, 66-68.

Positions: Art dir, Ward Archer Assoc, Memphis, 64-67.
Awards: First prize for watercolor, Mid-South Exhib, Brooks Mem Art Gallery, 64.
Bibliography: Jo Potter (auth), The real world of Dolph Smith, produced on WKNO-TV, 65; Margaret Harold (compiler), Prize-winning watercolors, 65; William Thomas (auth), Dolph Smith's Mid-South, Mid-South Mag, 2/9/69.
Publications: Illusr, Delta Rev Mag, 10/67, 11-12/69 & fall 70; illusr, Mid-South Mag, 12/71.
Dealer: Memphis Academy of Arts, Overton Park, Memphis, TN 38104.
Mailing Address: 1458 Vinton, Memphis, TN 38104.

SMITH, EMILY GUTHRIE
Painter, Instructor
Preferred Media: Pastels, Oils.
b Fort Worth, Tex, July 8, 09.
Study & Training: Tex Woman's Univ; Art Stud League New York, N Y; Univ Okla; also with Mitchell Jamieson & Frederic Taubes.
Work in Public Collections: Fort Worth Art Ctr Mus; Dallas Mus Fine Arts, Tex; W Tex Mus Fine Arts, Lubbock, Tex; Lone Star Gas Co Collection, State of Tex; Univ Tex, Arlington.
Commissions: Portraits, comn by Mary Martin, 46 & Major Carswell, Carswell AFB, Fort Worth, 57; murals, Western Hills Hotel, Fort Worth, 51, Fort Worth Savings & Loan, 54 & mosaic, All Saints Hosp, Fort Worth, 56.
Exhibitions: Tex Pavilion, Hemisfair, San Antonio, 68; Am Watercolor Soc, New York, N Y; Va Biennial, Richmond Mus Fine Arts; one-man retrospective, Fort Worth Art Ctr Mus.
Teaching: Instr portrait painting, mosaics & drawing, Fort Worth Art Ctr Mus, 55-70; instr, Taos, N Mex & Las Vegas, Tex, summers 60-69.
Awards: Tex Ann Award, Dallas Mus Fine Arts, 63; top award, Tarrant Co Ann, Fort Worth Art Ctr Mus, 65; first award, Longview Invitational, Jr Serv League, 68.
Memberships: Fort Worth Art Ctr Mus; Dallas Mus Fine Arts.
Collection: Contemporary painting.
Dealer: Carlin Galleries, 710 Montgomery, Fort Worth, TX 76107.
Mailing Address: 708 Crestwood Dr, Fort Worth, TX 76107.

SMITH, FRANK ANTHONY
Painter
Preferred Media: Acrylics.
b Salt Lake City, Utah, Aug 4, 39.
Study & Training: Univ Utah, BFA, 62, MFA, 64.
Work in Public Collections: Univ Utah Mus Fine Art; Utah State Univ; Salt Lake Art Ctr; Max Hutchinson Gallery, New York, N Y.
Commissions: Buffalo dance piece 66 & Diamond dance piece (with Linda C Smith), 71, Repertory Dance Theatre; Stimuli sensory environ for children, Salt Lake Art Ctr, 70; mural, Univ Utah Biol Bldg, 72.
Exhibitions: Drawings U S A, 63; three-man show, Mickelson Gallery, Washington, D C, 65; Artists West of the Mississippi, 67; 73rd Western Ann, Denver, Colo, 72; Realist Painting 12 Viewpoints, 72.
Teaching: Asst prof painting & drawing, Univ Utah, 68-
Awards: San Francisco Art Dirs Gold Medal, 64; purchase award, Third Intermt Biennial, 68.
Dealer: Max Hutchinson Gallery, 127 Greene St, New York, NY 10012.
Mailing Address: 953 First Ave, Salt Lake City, UT 84103.

SMITH, GARY M
Art Dealer
b Vinita, Okla, Jan 23, 44.
Study & Training: Kansas City Art Inst, Mo; Cooper Union.
Specialty of Gallery: Contemporary American painting and pre-Columbian artifacts.
Mailing Address: 99 Bowery St, New York, NY 10002.

SMITH, GEORGE W
Sculptor, Educator
Preferred Media: Steel, Bronze.
b Buffalo, N Y, Apr 21, 41.
Study & Training: San Francisco Art Inst, BFA; Hunter Col, City Univ New York, MA, with Tony Smith.
Work in Public Collections: Newark Mus, N J; Everson Mus Art, Syracuse, N Y; collection of Reese Palley, New York, N Y.
Commissions: 22nd ann theme sculpture, City & Co Art Comn, San Francisco, Calif, 68; sculptures, San Jose Br, Nat Asn Advan Colored People, in connection with Olympics in Mex, 68.
Exhibitions: One-man show, Reese Palley Gallery, New York, 70; Contemp Am Black Artists, Hudson River Mus, Yonkers, N Y, 70; Whitney Mus Am Art Sculpture Ann, 70-71; Black Artists-Two Generations, Newark Mus, 71; one-man show, Everson Mus Art, Syracuse, 72.

Teaching: Asst prof sculpture, State Univ N Y Buffalo, 72-
Awards: John Simon Guggenheim Mem Found fel in sculpture, 71-72.
Bibliography: S S Lewis (auth), Black artists on art, Vol II, Contemp Crafts, Inc, Calif, 71.
Dealer: Reese Palley Gallery, 93 Prince St, New York, NY 10012.
Mailing Address: 37 Williamstowne Ct, Apt 12, Cheektawaga, NY 14225.

SMITH, GORD
Sculptor, Painter
b Montreal, P Q, Oct 8, 37.
Study & Training: Sir George Williams Univ.
Work in Public Collections: Nat Gallery Can; Montreal Mus Fine Art; Mus Art Contemporaine Montreal; Sir George Williams Univ; McGill Univ; plus others.
Commissions: Bronze relief, Waterloo Trust Co, Kitchener, 63; steel screen, Can Pavilion, Expo '67; stainless steel relief, Int Nickel Co Can, Toronto, 67; bronze sculpture, Can Embassy, Bonn, Ger, 68; stainless steel split circle, Confedn Ctr, P E I, 72; plus others.
Exhibitions: Six shows, Waddington Galleries, Montreal, 59-69; Three Canadians Exhibition, Art Gallery Toronto, 61-62; Montreal Mus Fine Art, 62; Can Outdoor Sculpture Competition, Nat Gallery Can, 61-64; Isaacs Gallery, Toronto, 63; plus others.
Teaching: Assoc prof sculpture, Univ Victoria, 72-
Awards: First prize, Nat Fedn Can Univs, 57; first prize, Beth Tzedec Art Exhib, Toronto, 68; Nat Design Coun Chmns Award, 70; plus others.
Bibliography: Gordon Burwash (auth), Focus (film), Nat Film Bd Can, 63; Anita Aarons (auth), article, In: Royal Archit Inst Can Allied Arts Catalogue, 66.
Memberships: Assoc Royal Can Acad Art; Que Sculptor's Asn.
Publications: Contribr, The Can Architect, 62; contribr, Can Art Mag, 64; contribr, Ecole Montreal, 64; contribr, Symp Que, 65; co-auth, Gord Smith, sculptor (monogr), Que Sculptor's Asn, 72.
Dealer: Waddington Galleries, 1456 Sherbrooke St W, Montreal, P Q, Can.
Mailing Address: 2611 Richmond Ave, Victoria, B C, Can.

SMITH, GORDON
Painter, Educator
b Brighton, Eng, June 18, 19.
Study & Training: Winnipeg Sch Art; Vancouver Sch Art; Calif Sch Fine Arts; Harvard Univ Summer Sch.
Work in Public Collections: Nat Gallery Can; Art Gallery Toronto; Art Gallery Winnipeg; London Mus Art, Ont; Hart House, Univ Toronto; plus others.
Exhibitions: Saõ Paulo, Brazil, 61; Can Exhib, Warsaw, Poland, 62; Can Biennial, 63; Seattle World's Fair, Wash, 63; New Design Gallery, Vancouver, B C, 64; plus others.
Teaching: Former assoc prof art, Univ B C.
Awards: Can Biennial, 56; Can Coun sr fel for study abroad, 60-61.
Memberships: B C Soc Art; Can Soc Painter-Etchers & Engravers; assoc Royal Can Acad Arts; Can Group Painters.
Mailing Address: 5030 The Byway, West Vancouver, B C, Can.

SMITH, GORDON MACKINTOSH
Museum Director
b Reading, Pa, June 21, 06.
Study & Training: Williams Col, BA, 29; Grad Sch Arts & Sci, Harvard Univ, 29-31; in Europe, 31-32; hon LittD, D'Youville Col, 63.
Positions: Cur, Berks Co Hist Soc, 35-36; asst regional dir, New Eng Fed Art Proj, Works Prog Admin, 36-41; chief, Plans & Intel Unit, Engr Bd, Fort Belvoir, Va, 42-44; proj specialist, Off Strategic Serv, Washington, D C, 44-46; dir, Currier Gallery Art, 46-55; dir, Albright-Knox Art Gallery, Buffalo, N Y, 55-
Memberships: Benjamin Franklin fel, Royal Soc Arts, London; Am Fedn Arts; Asn Art Mus Dirs; Col Art Asn Am; Intermuseum Conserv Asn.
Mailing Address: Albright-Knox Art Gallery, Buffalo, NY 14222.

SMITH, HASSEL W, JR
Painter
b Sturgis, Mich, Apr 24, 15.
Study & Training: Northwestern Univ, BS; Calif Sch Fine Arts, with Maurice Sterne.
Work in Public Collections: Tate Gallery, London, Eng; Albright-Knox Art Gallery, Buffalo, N Y; Corcoran Gallery Art, Washington, D C; Whitney Mus Am Art, New York, N Y; San Francisco Mus Art, Calif; plus others.
Exhibitions: Retrospective, Pasadena Art Mus, 61; Painters of the Southwest Traveling Exhib, 62; John Moore's Ann Invitational, Liverpool, Eng, 63; retrospective, San Francisco State Col, 64; one-man show, Santa Barbara Mus Art, Calif, 69; plus many others.

Teaching: Instr, Calif Sch Fine Arts, 45-48; instr, San Francisco State Col, 46-47; instr, Univ Ore, 48-49; instr, Calif Sch Fine Arts, 49-52; instr, Presidio Hill Elem Sch, San Francisco, 52-55; lectr, Univ Calif, Berkeley, 63-64, 64-65.
Awards: Abraham Rosenberg fel, 41-42.
Mailing Address: c/o David Stuart Gallery, 807 N La Cienega Blvd, Los Angeles, CA 90046.

SMITH, HELEN M
Illustrator, Painter
b Canton, Ohio, Oct 19, 17.
Study & Training: Univ Melbourne, Australia, 42-43; Wash Univ, BFA, 53, MA, 58; Art Instr, Inc, cert; St Louis Univ.
Exhibitions: St Louis Artists Guild; Ann Mo Exhib; Liturgical Art, Seattle; Cath Art Exhib, Calif; Springfield Art Mus, Mo; plus others.
Teaching: Instr art, Villa Duchesne, St Louis, 53-56; instr art & head art dept, Maryville Col, 58-60, asst prof art & archaeol & dir art dept, 60-61, asst prof & dir art & archaeol depts, 61-68; lectr, Harvard Univ & Oriental Inst Archaeol, Yale Univ, 60; asst prof art hist & dir instr graphics, Southern Ill Univ, 68.
Positions: Med Illusr, St Louis Univ Med Ctr, 61-65; dir med illus, dept ophthal, Washington Univ, 64-68; consult, Am Col Radiol, 64-
Awards: Ruth Kelso Renfrow Art Club Award, 55; first, second & third prizes, Soc Tech Writers & Publ Exhib.
Memberships: St Louis Artists Guild; Archaeol Soc Am; Oriental Archaeol Soc; fel Int Inst Arts & Lett; Ill Art Educ Asn.
Publications: Illusr, Aghios Kosmos, 59; illusr, many med journals & bks.
Mailing Address: 11447 Clayton Rd, St Louis, MO 63131.

SMITH, HENRY HOLMES
Photographer, Educator
b Bloomington, Ill, Oct 23, 09.
Study & Training: Ill State Univ; Art Inst Chicago; Ohio State Univ; New Bauhaus (Chicago Sch Design); Ind Univ; also with L Moholy-Nagy, Gyorgy Kepes, Hin Bredendieck, Alexander Archipenko.
Work in Public Collections: Mus Mod Art, New York, N Y; Eastman House, Rochester, N Y; Mus Fine Arts, St Petersburg, Fla; Univ Nebr Mus Art, Lincoln; Art Inst Chicago Mus, Ill.
Exhibitions: Abstract Photography, Mus Mod Art, New York, 51; Photography at Mid-Century, Eastman House, 59; Photographers Choice, Ind Univ Art Gallery, Bloomington, 59; Sense of Abstraction, Mus Mod Art, New York, 60; Twentieth Century Photographers, Eastman House, Rochester, 66; plus others.
Teaching: Instr photog, New Bauhaus, Chicago, 37-38; prof photog, dept art, Ind Univ, Bloomington, 47-
Memberships: Found mem Soc Photog Educ (v chmn, 63-67, mem bd dirs, 63-).
Research: Esthetics of photography.
Publications: Auth, Image, obscurity & interpretation, 57 & Museum taste and the taste of our time, 62, Aperture Quart; auth, Photographs of Van Deren Coke, Photography (London), 63; auth, New figures in a classic tradition, In: Aaron Siskind Photographer, 65 & Photography in our time, In: Photographers on Photography, 66.
Dealer: The Gallery, N Grant St, Bloomington, IN 47401.
Mailing Address: 725 University St, Bloomington, IN 47401.

SMITH, HOWARD ROSS
Museum Curator
b Los Angeles, Calif, Aug 21, 10.
Study & Training: Univ Calif, MA; Calif Col Arts & Crafts; also with Eugen Neuhaus.
Teaching: Head dept art, Univ Maine, 42-49.
Positions: Cur, Calif Palace of Legion of Honor, 51-55, asst dir, 55-70, assoc dir, 70-
Mailing Address: California Palace of the Legion of Honor, Lincoln Park, San Francisco, CA 94121.

SMITH, JEROME IRVING
Museum Curator, Librarian
b New York, N Y, Nov 24, 10.
Study & Training: Columbia Univ, BA, 32.
Positions: Librn, cur fire-fighting collection & manuscripts & dir publicity, Mus of City of New York, 33-50; dir, Mus Hist & Indust, Seattle, 51-52; registr, Henry Ford Mus & Greenfield Village, 53-66, librn, 66-69, chief librn, 69-
Memberships: Am Asn Mus (nat chmn registr sect, 58); Spec Libr Asn (nat chmn mus librns, 38, v chmn mus, humanities & picture librns sect, 72); Am Libr Asn; Detroit Bk Club; Founders Soc, Detroit Inst Arts.
Publications: Contribr, Country Life, Antiques, Art In Am, The Connoisseur, Avocations & other magazines & newspapers.
Mailing Address: 546 Neff Rd, Grosse Point, MI 48236.

SMITH, J(OHN) B(ERTIE)
Educator, Painter
Preferred Media: Watercolors.
b Lamesa, Tex, June 5, 08.
Study & Training: Baylor Univ, AB, 29; Univ Chicago, AM, 31; Columbia Univ, EdD, 46.
Work in Public Collections: Arroyo Hondo (watercolor), Denver Art Mus.
Exhibitions: Denver Art Mus Ann, 38-42; Artists West of Miss, Colo Springs Fine Arts Ctr, Colo, 45; Southeastern Art Ann, Atlanta, Ga, 47; one-man show, Mobile Art Ctr, Ala, 48; Tex Watercolor Soc, San Antonio, 55.
Teaching: Chmn dept art, Adams State Col, 31-39; chmn dept art, Univ Wyo, 39-45; chmn dept art, Univ Ala, 45-49; dean, Kansas City Art Inst, 49-54; chmn dept art, Hardin-Simmons Univ, 54-60; chmn dept art, Baylor Univ, 60-
Positions: Pres, Southeastern Arts Asn, 49-50; pres, Midwestern Col Art Conf, 54-55; pres, Tex Fine Arts Asn, 58-59; pres, Tex Art Educ Asn, 69-71.
Memberships: Am Asn Univ Prof; Col Art Asn Am.
Mailing Address: 2109 Charboneau Dr, Waco, TX 76710.

SMITH, JOSEPH A(NTHONY)
Painter, Illustrator
Preferred Media: Pencil, Wax.
b Bellefonte, Pa, Sept 5, 36.
Study & Training: Pa State Univ, undergrad, 55, 56 & 57, grad, 60, with Hobson Pittman; Pratt Inst, BFA.
Work in Public Collections: Pa Acad Fine Arts, Philadelphia; Bloomsburg State Col, Pa.
Exhibitions: Pa Acad Fine Arts, 61, 67 & 69; Fourth Collectors Choice Exhib, City Mus Saint Louis, Mo, 62; one-man exhib paintings, drawings & sculpture, Staten Island Inst Arts & Sci, 66; Nat Acad Arts & Lett, New York, N Y, 68; Am Drawings: The Last Decade, Katonah Gallery, N Y, 71; plus others.
Teaching: Asst prof fine art, Pratt Inst, 61-; asst prof fine art, Pa State Univ, University Park, summers 69-
Positions: Design consult, Brooks Bros, 70-; exhib designer & consult, Staten Island Inst Arts & Sci, 70-; mem bd dirs, Staten Island Coun Arts, 71-
Awards: Mary S Litt Award for watercolor, 100th Ann Am Watercolor Soc, 67; hon mention, Pa Acad Fine Arts Bi-Ann Exhib Watercolors, Prints & Drawings, 67; first prize juror's choice, Third Ann Arts Festival, Pa State Univ, University Park, 71.
Memberships: Philadelphia Watercolor Club; Am Fedn Arts.
Publications: Contribr & illusr, Pangolin Mag, 69; illusr, Nat Parks Mag, 70-71; illusr, Sierra Club Survival Songbook, 71; illusr, David Johnson passed through here, 71; illusr, Harper's Mag, 72.
Mailing Address: 8 N Saint Austin Pl, Staten Island, NY 10310.

SMITH, JUSTIN V
Art Administrator, Collector
b Minneapolis, Minn, Oct 25, 03.
Study & Training: Princeton Univ, AB, 25.
Positions: Pres, T B Walker Found, Minneapolis; mem bd dirs, Walker Art Ctr, Minneapolis.
Collection: Painting and sculpture of the twentieth century.
Mailing Address: 1221 Hennepin Ave, Minneapolis, MN 55403.

SMITH, LAWRENCE M C
Collector, Patron
b Philadelphia, Pa, Oct 4, 02.
Study & Training: Univ Pa, AB, 23, LLB, 28; Magdalen Col, Oxford Univ, BA, 25, MA, 46.
Positions: Pres, Am Fedn Arts, 48-52, now trustee; trustee, Philadelphia Mus Art; chmn bd, Civic Ctr Mus, 57-60.
Memberships: Benjamin Franklin fel, Royal Soc Arts; Art Collectors Club.
Collection: Paintings and graphic art.
Mailing Address: 3460 School House Lane, Philadelphia, PA 19144.

SMITH, LEON POLK
Painter, Sculptor
b Chickasha, Okla, May 20, 06.
Study & Training: E Cent State Col, BA, 34; Columbia Univ, MA, 38.
Work in Public Collections: Guggenheim Mus; Metrop Mus Art; Mus Mod Art; Mus Bellas Artes, Caracas; Cleveland Mus.
Exhibitions: Construction Geometry In Painting, New York, N Y, 60; one-man shows, Mus Bellas Artes, 62 & Galeria Muller, Stuttgart, Ger, 64; New Shapes of Color, Stedelijk Mus, Amsterdam, Holland, 66; Retrospect, San Francisco Mus & Rose Mus, 68.
Teaching: Lectr, Brandeis Univ, 68; artist-in-residence, Univ Calif, Davis, 72.
Awards: Grants, Longview Found, 56, Nat Coun Arts, 67 & Tamarind, 68; plus others.
Mailing Address: Ashley Lane, Shoreham, NY 11786.

SMITH, MRS LOUIS
Collector
Collection: Ethnographia.
Mailing Address: 907 Fifth Ave, New York, NY 10021.

SMITH, MOISHE
Printmaker
Preferred Media: Intaglio.
b Chicago, Ill, Jan 10, 29.
Study & Training; New Sch Social Res, BA, 50; Univ Iowa, with Lasansky, MFA, 53; Skowhegan Sch Painting & Sculpture; Acad Florence; also with Giorgio Morandi.
Work in Public Collections: Mus Boymans, Beuningen, Rotterdam; Kestner Mus, Hannover; Galleria Degli Uffizi, Florence; Metrop Mus Art, New York, N Y; Nat Gallery Art, Washington, D C.
Exhibitions: São Paulo Int, Brazil, 55; Print Coun Am Traveling Exhib, 59 & 62; Int Prints, Cincinnati Mus, Ohio, 62; Salon de Mai, Paris, 65; Libr Cong, 69 & 71.
Teaching: Vis artist printmaking, Univ Wis, 66-67; vis artist printmaking, Ohio State Univ, spring 71; vis artist, Univ Iowa, autumn 71; vis artist, Univ Wis-Parkside, 72-
Awards: Four Seasons res grant, Southern Ill Univ, 57; Fulbright fel, 59-61; Guggenheim Found fel, 67.
Memberships: Soc Am Graphic Artists.
Mailing Address: University of Wisconsin-Parkside, Racine, WI 53406.

SMITH, OLIVER
Painter
b Lynn, Mass, Oct 1, 96.
Study & Training: R I Sch Design; also with Charles Hawthorn, Provincetown, Mass.
Work in Public Collections: Univ Fla, Gainesville; Remington Rand Corp.
Commissions: Stained glass, Princeton Univ Chapel, Temple Emanu-El, New York, Wittenberg Univ, Springfield, Ohio, Mellon Cathedral, Pittsburgh, Pa & Nazareth Hosp Chapel, Philadelphia.
Exhibitions: Am Watercolor Soc; Audubon Artists; Philadelphia Watercolor Club; Smithsonian Inst, Washington, D C; Rockport Art Asn, Mass.
Awards: Awards, Gulf Coast Art Ctr, Rockport Art Asn & St Petersburg Art Club, Fla.
Memberships: Salmagundi Club; Rockport Art Asn; St Petersburg Art Club; Clearwater Art Asn; Gulf Coast Art Ctr.
Research: Stained glass windows; glass blowing by hand.
Mailing Address: 223 Shore Dr, Ozona, FL 33560.

SMITH, PAUL J
Museum Director
b Sept 8, 31.
Study & Training: Art Inst Buffalo; Sch for Am Craftsmen.
Collections Arranged: Made with Paper; Plastic as Plastic; Object in the Open Air; Fantasy Furniture; Amusements Is; Objects: U S A.
Positions: V pres, Louis Comfort Tiffany Found; former bd mem, N Y State Craftsmen & Artist-Craftsmen of New York; bd mem, Elder Craftsmen Shop New York; bd mem, Haystack Mountain Sch Crafts; dir, Mus Contemp Crafts, New York, at present.
Memberships: Int Coun Mus; Mus Coun New York; N Y State Asn Mus.
Mailing Address: Museum of Contemporary Crafts, 29 W 53rd St, New York, NY 10019.

SMITH, PAUL K
Painter
b Cape Girardeau, Mo, Feb 27, 93.
Study & Training: Saint Louis Sch Fine Arts; Denver Art Acad.
Exhibitions: Denver Art Mus, 23-56, 62-64; 15 Colorado Artists, 49-65; Denver Metrop Exhibs, 50-64; Mulvane Art Ctr, Topeka, 56 & 64; Lever House, New York, N Y, 64; plus many other group & one-man shows.
Awards: Central City, 64; Canon City, Colo, 69; Denver Art Guild, 69; plus many others.
Memberships: Gilpin Co Art Asn; Denver Art Guild; Denver Art Mus.
Mailing Address: 3041½ S Broadway, Denver, CO 80216.

SMITH, PAUL ROLAND
Painter, Educator
Preferred Media: Oils, Ink, Watercolors.
b Colony, Kans, Sept 12, 16.
Study & Training: Pittsburg State Col, BS; Univ Iowa, MFA.
Work in Public Collections: Des Moines Art Ctr, Iowa; Wright Mus, Beloit, Wis; Univ Iowa, Iowa City; Sioux City Art Ctr, Iowa; St Cloud Mus, St Cloud State Col, Minn.

Teaching: Prof painting & drawing, Univ Northern Iowa, 51-65; prof, painting & drawing & chmn dept art, Hamline Univ, 65-
Positions: Dir Int Exhib, Kappa Pi, 65-; mem bd dirs, Minn Mus Art, 71-
Awards: First awards, Des Moines Art Ctr, 57, Minn Centennial State Fair, 58 & Sioux City Art Ctr, 59.
Memberships: Artists Equity Asn (pres, 64-67); Midwest Col Art Asn (prog dir, 69); Col Art Asn Am; Walker Art Ctr; Minn State Arts Coun (chmn visual arts, 71-).
Publications: Auth, Adult nursery rhymes, Waverly Publ Co, 72.
Mailing Address: Dept of Art, Hamline University, Saint Paul, MN 55101.

SMITH, R HARMER
Painter, Etcher
Preferred Media: Watercolors.
b Jersey City, N J, July 27, 06.
Study & Training: Sch Fine & Appl Art, Pratt Inst, cert archit; Sch Fine Arts, Yale Univ, BFA; Art Stud League New York, N Y.
Work in Public Collections: USN Art Collection, Washington, D C; Jersey City Pub Libr; Old Bergen Church, Jersey City.
Exhibitions: Am Watercolor Soc; Archit League; Jersey City Mus Asn; Madison Pub Libr, N J.
Awards: Trustees' Prize for Upstream, Jersey City Mus Asn, 53; Jersey J Medal for Snug Berth, 61; Patrons' Prize for From The Bridge, Hudson Artists, 67.
Bibliography: Fred H Scherff (auth), R Harmer Smith, Pencil Points, 10/37.
Memberships: Jersey City Mus Asn (gov); hon mem Hudson Artists; N J Watercolor Soc; Salmagundi Club.
Publications: Auth & illusr, Pencil sketches by R Harmer Smith, Pencil Points, 7/31; contribr, reproductions, In: Pencil Points & Am Artist, 30-40.
Mailing Address: 44 Hamilton St, Madison, NJ 07940.

SMITH, RALPH ALEXANDER
Writer, Educator
b Ellwood City, Pa, June 12, 29.
Study & Training: Columbia Univ, AB, teachers col, MA & EdD.
Teaching: Instr art hist & art educ, Kent State Univ, 59-61; asst prof art hist & art educ & chmn dept art, Wis State Univ-Oshkosh, 61-63; asst prof art hist & art educ, State Univ N Y Col New Paltz, 63-64; asst prof aesthet educ, Univ Ill, Urbana, 64-67, assoc prof, 67-71, prof, 71-
Memberships: Am Soc Aesthet; Philos Educ Soc; Nat Art Educ Asn; Inst Study Art In Educ; World Future Soc.
Research: Theoretical foundations of aesthetic and humanistic education.
Publications: Ed, Aesthetics and criticism in art education, Rand, 66; auth, Aesthetic education: a role for the humanities program, Teachers Col Rec, 1/68; ed, Aesthetic concepts and education, 70 & Aesthetics and problems of education, 71, Univ Ill Press; auth, Aesthetic foundations, In: The teacher's handbook, Scott F, 70.
Mailing Address: 228B Education, University of Illinois at Urbana-Champaign, Urbana, IL 61801.

SMITH, RAY WINFIELD
Collector, Art Historian
b Marlboro, N H, June 4, 97.
Positions: Ed consult, J Glass Studies; chmn, Int Comt Ancient Glass.
Research: Technological research with Brookhaven National Laboratory on ancient glass.
Collection: Ancient glass; medieval furniture, rugs and paintings.
Publications: Auth, Glass from the ancient world, 57; many radio & TV interviews; TV prog, Nefertiti & the Computer, BBC, 3/20/71.
Mailing Address: P O Box 43, Dublin, NH 03444.

SMITH, ROBERT ALAN
Painter, Instructor
Preferred Media: Oils.
b Pasadena, Calif.
Study & Training: Chouinard Art Inst, Los Angeles, Calif, 46; Inst Allende, San Miguel de Allende, Mex, 48; painting with David Alfaro Siqueiros, Mex; Chouinard Art Inst, 53.
Work in Public Collections: Libr Cong, Washington, D C; Nat Collection, Smithsonian Inst, Washington, D C; Metrop Mus Art, New York, N Y; Philadelphia Mus, Pa; Pasadena Art Mus, Calif.
Exhibitions: Ann Print Exhib, Libr Cong, 59 & 60; 50 Am Printmakers, De Cordova Mus, Mass, 61; Santa Barbara Mus Art, Calif, 64; Am Art Today, New York World's Fair, 65; White House, Washington, D C, 67.
Teaching: Instr painting, Calif Inst Arts, Los Angeles, 65; instr, Ventura Col, 65-
Awards: Purchase awards, Libr Cong, 60 & Pasadena Art Mus, 62; James D Phelan Award for Calif Painters, 61.

Bibliography: Langsner (auth), Art news from Los Angeles, Art News Mag, 2/59 & 2/60 & Los Angeles letter, Art Int, 3/62; Seldis (auth), Art, Los Angeles Times, 10/61.
Memberships: Western Serigraph Inst.
Art Interests: Paintings of the Holy Spirit.
Publications: Contribr, Western Serigraph Inst Bull, 61 & Ventura Fine Arts Mag, 62; illusr, Long ago elf, 68 & Crocodiles have big teeth all day, 70, Follett.
Mailing Address: 1218 Ayers Ave, Ojai, CA 93023.

SMITH, ROBERT C
Educator
b Cranford, N J, Feb 26, 12.
Study & Training: Harvard Univ, AB, 33, AM, 34, Sachs fel, 34-35, PhD, 36.
Teaching: Assoc fine arts, Univ Ill, 37-39; assoc prof hist art, Sweet Briar Col, 45-46; assoc prof hist art, Univ Pa, 48-56, prof, 56-
Positions: Asst dir, Hispanic Found, Libr Cong, 39-45; res assoc, Winterthur Mus, 59-
Awards: Guggenheim fel, 46-47; Gulbenkian fel, 62-
Memberships: Corresp mem Hispanic Soc; corresp mem Acad Am Franciscan Hist; corresp mem Nat Acad Fine Arts, Port.
Research: Luso-Brazillian art; art of the United States.
Publications: Auth, Guide to the art of Latin America, Govt Printing Off, 48 & Arno, 71; auth, Cadeirais de Portugal, Horizonte, Lisbon, 68; auth, The art of Portugal, Weidenfeld & Nicolson, London, 68; auth, S Oporto, 68; auth, Art of Portugal: fifteen hundred to eighteen hundred, Hawthorn, 68; plus others.
Mailing Address: R D 1, Glenmoore, PA 19343.

SMITH, SAM
Painter, Educator
Preferred Media: Watercolors, Oils.
b Thorndale, Tex, Feb 11, 18.
Study & Training: With Randall Davey, Jack Levine, Ben Turner & Carl von Hassler.
Work in Public Collections: War Dept Hist Properties Sect; Santa Fe Mus; Univ N Mex; N Mex State Fair Collection; Panhandle Mus Fine Art.
Commissions: Mural, Camp Barkley, Tex, War Dept, 42; paintings, Infantry Weapons, Camp Barkley, 42.
Exhibitions: One-man show, Corcoran Gallery Art, Washington, D C, 48; Santa Fe Mus Fine Art, N Mex, 49; Botts Mus Art, Albuquerque, N Mex, 64; Panhandle-Plains Hist Mus, Canyon, Tex, 64; Roswell Mus Art, N Mex, 65.
Teaching: Prof art, Univ N Mex, 56-
Awards: Questa, N Mex purchase prize, 62 & first prize for watercolor, 62, N Mex State Fair; first prize for watercolor, Ouray Alpine Show, Colo, 64.
Bibliography: Robert Ruark (auth), Sam Smith, artist, Assoc Press, 48.
Memberships: Life mem N Mex Art League; Artists Equity Asn (pres).
Dealer: M James Hall Gallery, Ruidoso, NM 88345.
Mailing Address: 213 Utah N E, Albuquerque, NM 87108.

SMITH, SHIRLANN
Painter
b Wichita, Kans.
Study & Training: Kans State Univ, BFA; Provincetown Workshop Art Sch, Mass; Art Stud League New York.
Work in Public Collections: Whitney Mus Am Art, New York, N Y; Berkeley Univ Art Mus, Calif; Wichita State Univ Art Mus, Kans; Aldrich Mus Contemp Art, Ridgefield, Conn; Phoenix Art Mus, Ariz.
Exhibitions: Young Provincetown Painters, Chrysler Mus, Provincetown, Mass, 64; New England Exhib, Silvermine, Conn, 67; American Painting 1970, Va Mus, Richmond, 70; Lyrical Abstraction, Aldrich Mus Contemp Art, Ridgefield, Conn, 70; Recent Acquisitions & Lyrical Abstraction, Whitney Mus Am Art, New York, 71.
Awards: Grumbacher Artists Material Co award for mixed media, New England Exhib, Silvermine, 67.
Bibliography: Gordon Brown (auth), review, In: Arts Mag, summer 70; Dorothy Grafley (auth), Lyrical abstraction, Art in Focus, 10/70.
Dealer: 55 Mercer Gallery, 55 Mercer, New York, NY 10013.
Mailing Address: 20 E Broadway, New York, NY 10002.

SMITH, TONY
Sculptor
b South Orange, N J, 12.
Study & Training: Art Stud League New York, 34-35; archit stud, New Bauhaus, Chicago, 37-38; archit apprentice of Frank Lloyd Wright, 38-40.

Exhibitions: Wadsworth Atheneum, Hartford, Conn, 64 & 67; Jewish Mus, New York, N Y, 67; Philadelphia Inst Contemp Art, 67; Whitney Mus Am Art Ann, 70.
Dealer: Knoedler Gallery, 14 E 57th St, New York, NY 10022.
Mailing Address: 647 Berkeley Rd, Orange, NJ 07050.

SMITH, WILLIAM ARTHUR
Painter, Printmaker
Preferred Media: Oils, Watercolors.
b Toledo, Ohio, Apr 19, 18.
Study & Training: Keane's Art Sch, Toledo; Art Stud League New York, N Y; Grand Cent Art Sch, New York; Ecole Beaux Arts, Paris; Acad Grande Chaumiére, Paris; Univ Toledo, MA.
Work in Public Collections: Metrop Mus Art, New York; Los Angeles Co Mus, Calif; Libr Cong, Washington, D C; Nat Acad Design, New York.
Commissions: Mural of hist Md, State of Md, Md House, Aberdeen, 68.
Exhibitions: Contemp Arts U S, Los Angeles, 56; 200 Yrs Watercolor Painting Am, Metrop Mus Art, 66-67; 27 one-man exhibs, major cities Europe, Asia, & U S.
Teaching: Lectr, var univs & art schs, Europe, Asia & U S.
Awards: Two Nat Acad Design Awards, 49 & 51; Nat Acad Design prize for oil painting, Adolf & Clara Obrig, 51; two grand prize & gold medals, Am Watercolor Soc, 56 & 65.
Memberships: Nat Acad Design (mem coun & rec secy, 54-55); Am Watercolor Soc (pres, 56-57; hon pres, 57-); Int Asn Art (exec comt, 63-69, v pres, 66-69, pres U S Comt, 70-); Audubon Artists; Philadelphia Watercolor Club.
Publications: Auth & Illusr, Art behind the iron curtain, 2/60 & The changing art of the Orient, 8/65, Harpers Bazaar; auth, Ben Shahn, In: Ben Shahn, Osaka Shiritsu Bijutsukan-Mainichi Shimbun, Japan, 70.
Mailing Address: Windy Bush Rd, Pineville, PA 18946.

SMITHSON, ROBERT I
Sculptor, Lecturer
b Passaic, N J, Jan 2, 38.
Study & Training: Art Stud League New York.
Work in Public Collections: Whitney Mus Am Art, New York, N Y. Mus Mod Art, New York; Milwaukee Art Ctr, Wis; Neue Galerie, Aachen, Ger.
Commissions: Spiral Jetty (earth works), Great Salt Lake, Utah; Broken Circle & Spiral Hill (earth works), Emmen Holland.
Exhibitions: Albright-Knox Art Gallery, Buffalo, 68; Tate Gallery, London, Eng, 68; Haags Gemeentemuseum, The Hague, 68; Andrew Dickson White Mus Art, Cornell Univ, 69; Stedelijk Mus, Amsterdam, Holland, 69; plus others.
Teaching: Lect, Art in the City, Making Art in Yucatan & Minimal Art at Columbia Univ, Yale Univ & New York Univ.
Positions: Consult, Tibbetts, Abbott, McCarthy and Stratton, Architects & Engineers, 66-67.
Awards: Art Inst Chicago Award, 72.
Bibliography: Douglas MacAgy (auth), Plus by minus: today's half-century, Albright-Knox Art Gallery, 68; Lucy R Lippard, (auth), Minimal art, Haags Gemeentemuseum, 68; E C Goossen (auth), The art of the real U S A 1948-1968, Mus Mod Art, 68; plus others.
Art Interests: A concern for combining earth works with reclamation projects.
Publications: Auth, Incidents of mirror travel in the Yucatan, Artforum, 69; auth, The spiral jetty, art of the environment, 72.
Dealer: John Weber Gallery, 420 W Broadway, New York, NY 10012.
Mailing Address: 799 Greenwich St, New York, NY 10014.

SMUL, ETHEL LUBELL
Painter, Instructor
Preferred Media: Oils, Watercolors, Graphics.
b New York, N Y, Sept 11, 97.
Study & Training: Maxwell Sch Teachers; Hunter Col, BA & MA; Pratt Graphic Art Ctr; also with John Sloan, Boardman Robinson, Brackman, Olinsky, Barnet & Bob Blackburn.
Work in Public Collections: Cincinnati Art Mus; Riverside Mus.
Exhibitions: Carnegie Inst, 49; Cincinnati Art Mus Second Int Biennial Contemp Color Lithography, 53; Riverside Mus, 53, 54, 56 & 58; Traveling Shows, 53, 54 & 58; Nat Acad Design, 56, 57 & 64.
Teaching: Instr fine arts & crafts & Eng, sec schs, New York, 36-59.
Memberships: Am Soc Contemp Artists (treas, 59-, dir); New York Soc Women Artists (dir); Nat Asn Women Artists.
Mailing Address: 165 W 20th St, New York, NY 15011.

SMYTH, CRAIG HUGH
Art Administrator, Art Historian
b New York, N Y, July 28, 15.
Teaching: Lectr, Frick Collection, New York, 46-50; from asst prof to prof, Inst Fine Arts, New York Univ, 50-, acting dir & acting head dept fine arts, 51-53, dir & head grad dept fine arts, 53-

Positions: Res asst & sr mus aide, Nat Gallery Art, Washington, D C, 41-42.
Memberships: Col Art Asn Am (dir, 53-57, secy, 56); Comite Int Hist Art (alt U S mem, 70-); U S Nat Comt Hist Art; Metrop Mus Art (hon trustee, 68-); Vis Comt, Dept Art & Archaeol, Princeton Univ.
Research: Sixteenth century Italian painting and drawing; sixteenth century Italian architecture.
Publications: Auth, The early works of Bronzino, Art Bull, 49; auth, Mannerism and Maniera, 63; auth, The sunken courts of the Villa Giula and the Villa Imperiale, In: Essays in memory of Karl Lehmann, 63; co-auth, Michelangelo and St Peter's—I: the attic as originally built on the south hemicycle, Burlington Mag, 69; auth, Bronzino as draughtsman, 71.
Mailing Address: Institute of Fine Arts, New York University, 1 E 78th St, New York, NY 10021.

SMYTHE, DAVID RICHARD
Sculptor
b Washington, D C, Dec 2, 43.
Study & Training: Corcoran Sch Art, Washington, D C, 62-64; Art Inst Chicago, BFA, 67, MFA, 69.
Work in Public Collections: Whitney Mus Am Art, New York, N Y; also in collections of James Speyers, Art Inst Chicago, Whitney Halsted, Chicago & Ronald Feldman, New York.
Commissions: Relief painting, Blue Cross-Blue Shield, C F Murphy Arch, Chicago, Ill, 69.
Exhibitions: Allan Franklin Gallery, Chicago & New York, 68 & 70; Contemp Am Painting & Sculpture, Univ Ill, Urbana, 69; Inst Contemp Art, Univ Pa, 70; Whitney Mus Am Art, New York, 72; Ronald Feldman Fine Arts, Inc, New York, 72.
Awards: George D Brown traveling fel, Art Inst Chicago, 69 & Richard Rice Jenkins Award, 70; Tamarind Inst fel, Albuquerque, N Mex, 72.
Mailing Address: c/o Ronald Feldman Fine Arts, Inc, 33 E 74th St, New York, NY 10021.

SNEED, PATRICIA M
Art Dealer, Collector
b Spencer, Iowa, Oct 24, 22.
Study & Training: Drake Univ, 40-42; Univ Cincinnati, 45-46.
Collections Arranged: Fifty Artists for Fifty States (nat art exhib), 65-; Art in Other Media, 70.
Positions: Pres & bd trustees, Burpee Art Mus; owner & dir, Sneed Gallery, 35, 58-; mem art adv panel, State of Ill, 66-
Memberships: Am Fedn Arts.
Specialty of Gallery: Contemporary American art.
Collection: Contemporary American art.
Publications: Auth, Show me a picture (children's art appreciation prog).
Mailing Address: 2024 Harlem Blvd, Rockford, IL 61103.

SNELGROVE, WALTER H
Painter
b Seattle, Wash, Mar 22, 24.
Study & Training: Univ Wash; Calif Sch Fine Arts, with Hassel Smith, Antonio Sotamayor and James Weeks; Univ Calif, Berkeley, BA & MA, with James McCray & M O'Hagan.
Work in Public Collections: Whitney Mus Am Art, New York, N Y; Oakland Mus, Calif; Colorado Springs Fine Arts Ctr, Colo; Calif Palace of Legion of Honor; Stanford Univ.
Exhibitions: Carnegie Int, Pittsburgh, Pa; Art Inst Chicago, Ill; Albright-Knox Art Gallery, Buffalo, N Y; Va Mus Fine Arts, Richmond; retrospective, Foothill Col, 67; plus others.
Teaching: Instr, Univ Calif, 51-53.
Awards: Prizes, Oakland Mus, 62; San Francisco Mus Art, 63; Kelham Mem Awards, Calif Palace of Legion of Honor; plus others.
Memberships: San Francisco Art Asn.
Mailing Address: 2966 Adeline St, Berkeley, CA 94703.

SNELSON, KENNETH D
Sculptor
Preferred Media: Steel.
b Pendleton, Ore, June 29, 27.
Work in Public Collections: Whitney Mus Am Art, New York, N Y; Mus Mod Art, New York; Milwaukee Art Ctr, Wis; Kröller Müller Mus, Otterloo, Holland; Staedelijk Mus, Amsterdam, Holland.
Commissions: Tower of Light Pavillion, N Y World's Fair, 64; Japan Iron & Steel Fedn, Expo-70, Osaka, Japan, 70.
Exhibitions: Sculpture of the Sixties, Los Angeles Co Mus, Calif, 67; Five Monumental Sculptures, Kröller Müller Mus, 69; Int Sculpture Symp, Osaka, Japan, 69; Kunsthalle Düsseldorf, Ger, 70; Snelson Sculpture Exhib, Hannover Kunstuerein, Hannover, Ger, 71.

Publications: Auth, A design for the atom, Indust Design, 2/63; auth, Continuous tension, discontinuous compression structures, 65 & A model for atomic forms, 66, U S Patent Off.
Mailing Address: 140 Sullivan St, New York, NY 10012.

SNODGRASS, JEANNE OWENS
Art Administrator, Lecturer
b Muskogee, Okla, Sept 12, 27.
Study & Training: Art Instr, Inc; Northeastern State Col; Okla Univ.
Collections Arranged: 214 exhibs of Indian art & artifacts, Philbrook Art Ctr, 55-68; Am Indian Artists Nat Competition Ann, Philbrook Art Ctr, 55-68.
Teaching: Lect, American Indian Painting: Its History and Its Artists.
Positions: Asst to dir & cur Am Indian Art, Philbrook Art Ctr, 55-68; admin asst to pres, Educ Dimensions, Inc, 69-71; assoc, Am Indian Affairs & mem Arts & Crafts Adv Comt; consult, Gilcrease Mus; juror, many nat & regional Indian Art Exhibs.
Awards: Outstanding contrib to Indian art, U S Dept Interior, 67.
Memberships: Okla Mus Asn (secy); Ethno-Hist Asn; Tulsa Hist Soc.
Publications: Auth, American Indian paintings, 64; ed, American Indian basketry, 64; auth, American Indian painters: a biographical directory, Heye Found, 68.
Mailing Address: 1003 Maple St, Muskogee, OK 74401.

SNOW, JOHN
Printmaker, Painter
b Vancouver, B C, Dec 12, 11.
Work in Public Collections: Victoria & Albert Mus, London, Eng; Nat Gallery Can; Univ Toronto; Can Coun.
Exhibitions: Premiere Expos Bienale Int Gravure, Tokyo & Osaka, Japan, 57; Fifth Int Biennial Color Lithography, Cincinnati, 58; Royal Acad Arts, London, 63; Cardiff Commonwealth Arts Festival, Cardiff & Brit Isles, 65; Salon Beaux Arts, Paris, 69.
Awards: C W Jeffrey's Award, Can Soc Graphic Art, 61; Jessie Dow Award, Montreal Mus Fine Arts, 62.
Memberships: Can Soc Graphic Art; assoc Royal Can Acad Arts.
Dealer: Marlborough Godard Ltd, 1490 Sherbrooke St W, Montreal 7109, P Q, Can.
Mailing Address: 915 18th Ave S W, Calgary, Alta T2T 0H2, Can.

SNOW, MICHAEL
Painter, Film Maker
b Toronto, Ont, Dec 10, 29.
Study & Training: Ont Col Art, Toronto.
Work in Public Collections: Mus Mod Art, New York, N Y; Art Gallery Toronto; Montreal Mus Fine Arts; Nat Gallery Can; Anthol Film Arch, New York; plus others.
Exhibitions: Gallery Mod Art & Whitney Mus Am Art, New York; Carnegie Inst, Pittsburgh, Pa; Mus Mod Art, New York; Isaacs Gallery, New York & Toronto; represented Can, Venice Bienale, Italy, 70; plus many others.
Awards: Grand Prize, Fourth Int Experimental Film Festival, Brussels, Belg, 68; Guggenheim fel, 72.
Dealers: Bykert Gallery, 24 E 81st St, New York, NY 10028; Isaacs Gallery, 832 Yonge St, Toronto, Ont, Can.
Mailing Address: Box 199, Church St Sta, New York, NY 10008.

SNYDER, JAMES WILBERT (WILB)
Painter, Writer
Preferred Media: Watercolors.
b Philadelphia, Pa.
Study & Training: Univ Pa Sch Fine Arts, BFA; New York Univ, MA, PhD; Cambridge Univ; Am Univ Beirut; also with Elliot O'Hara.
Work in Public Collections: Pvt collections throughout U S A.
Exhibitions: One-man & group shows in Philadelphia, Cape Cod, N J & Southwest Fla.
Teaching: Social sci, Univ Pa, New York Univ & Athens Col, Greece.
Awards: Various blue ribbons & hon mentions in shows & exhibs.
Memberships: Sanibel-Captiva Art League (mem bd); Art Coun Southwest Fla; Soc N Am Artists.
Mailing Address: Gulf Dr, Sanibel, FL 33957.

SNYDER, JOAN
Painter
Preferred Media: Oils, Acrylics.
b New Brunswick, N J, Apr 16, 40.
Study & Training: Rutgers Univ, MFA.
Work in Public Collections: Allan Mus, Oberlin Col, Ohio.
Exhibitions: Whitney Mus Am Art Ann, New York, N Y, 72; Grids, Inst Contemp Art, Philadelphia, Pa, 72; Am Woman Artist Show, Kunsthaus, Hamburg, Ger, 72; one-woman shows, Paley & Lowe Inc, New York, 71 & Parker 470, Boston, Mass.
Teaching: Instr child art, State Univ N Y Stony Brook, 68-70.

Bibliography: Marcia Tucker (auth), The anatomy of a stroke: recent paintings by Joan Snyder, 5/19/71 & Lizzie Bordon (auth), New York, 1/72, Artforum; Kenneth Baker (auth), article, In: Christian Sci Monitor, 4/20/72.
Dealer: Paley & Lowe Inc, 59 Wooster St, New York, NY 10012.
Mailing Address: 105 Mulberry St, New York, NY 10013.

SNYDER, SEYMOUR
Illustrator, Instructor
Preferred Media: Oils, Watercolors, Gouache.
b Newark, N J, Aug 11, 97.
Study & Training: Pa Acad Fine Arts; Grand Cent Sch Art; Art Stud League New York, N Y; Newark Sch Art, N J.
Commissions: Advert & promotional work, var nat co.
Exhibitions: Lynn Kottler Gallery, 68; Am Artists Prof League, New York, 69; Nat Arts Club, New York, 70.
Teaching: Instr commercial art & lectr art hist, High Sch Art & Design & New York Adult Educ Prog, 62-69; instr illus & design, Pels Sch Art, New York, 70-
Awards: Watercolor Prize, Salmagundi Club, 69.
Memberships: Life mem Art Stud League New York; Am Artists Prof League; Artists Equity Asn.
Publications: Illusr, McCalls, House & Gardens, Better Homes & Gardens, Successful Farming & Am Home; illusr, var calendars.
Mailing Address: 315 E 68th St, New York, NY 10021.

SOBY, JAMES THRALL
Writer, Critic
b Hartford, Conn, Dec 14, 06.
Study & Training: Williams Col, 24-26, hon LHD, 62.
Positions: Asst dir, Mus Mod Art, 43, dir painting & sculpture, 43-45, trustee, 43-, hon chmn comt on mus collections, mem exec & prog comt, v pres, 61-; art critic, Sat Rev Lit, 46-57; actg ed, Mag of Art, 50-51, chmn ed bd, 51-52.
Awards: Star of Solidarity, Ital Govt.
Publications: Auth, Modern art and the new past, 57, Juan Gris, 58, Joan Miro, 59, Ben Shahn: paintings, 63 & Magritte, 65; plus many earlier publ; contribr, articles & criticism, leading art publ.
Mailing Address: Brushy Ridge Rd, New Canaan, CT 06840.

SOFFER, SASSON
Sculptor
Preferred Media: Glass.
b Baghdad, Iraq, June 1, 25; U S citizen.
Study & Training: Brooklyn Col, 50-54, with Mark Rothko.
Work in Public Collections: Whitney Mus Am Art, New York, N Y; Indianapolis Mus Fine Art, Ind; Albright-Knox Gallery, Buffalo, N Y; Rockefeller Inst, New York; Butler Inst Am Art, Youngstown, Ohio.
Exhibitions: Whitney Mus Am Art, New York; Carnegie Int, Pittsburgh, Pa; Yale Univ Art Gallery; Harvard Univ; Boston Mus Fine Art.
Awards: Ford Found Purchase Award, Whitney Mus Am Art, 62; Ford Found artist-in-residence, Portland Mus, 66.
Mailing Address: 505 La Guardia Pl, New York, NY 10012.

SOGLOW, OTTO
Cartoonist
b New York, N Y, Dec 23, 00.
Study & Training: Art Stud League New York, 19-25, with John Sloan.
Positions: Cartoonist, New York World, 25-26, cartoonist, King Features Syndicate, 33-
Awards: Reuben Award as outstanding cartoonist of the year, Nat Cartoonist Soc, 67.
Memberships: Soc Illustrators; Nat Cartoonists Soc.
Publications: Auth & illusr, Pretty pictures, Everything's rosey & The little king; co-auth & illusr, Wasn't the depression terrible; contribr, New Yorker, Colliers, Life & other mags.
Mailing Address: 330 W 72nd St, New York, NY 10023.

SOKOLE, MIRON
Painter, Educator
Preferred Media: Oils, Acrylics.
b Odessa, Russia; U S citizen.
Study & Training: Cooper Union, cert; Nat Acad Art, with Ivan Olinsky.
Work in Public Collections: Butler Inst Am Art, Youngstown, Ohio; Mus Tel Aviv, Israel; Univ Minn, Minneapolis; IBM Collection; Upjohn Collection.
Exhibitions: Int Expos, Mus Art Mod, Paris, 46; Watercolors Show, Whitney Mus Am Art, New York, N Y, 53 & 54; Corcoran Gallery Art Biennial, Washington, D C, 58; Audubon Artists, New York, 64; 21st Ann, Norfolk Mus, Va, 65.

Teaching: Instr painting & drawing, Am Artists Sch, New York, 38-41; artist-in-residence, Kansas City Art Inst, Mo, 47-51; prof art, Fashion Inst Technol, New York, 62-
Positions: Free lance stage designer, 35-38; stage & indust designer, 42-46.
Bibliography: Salpeter (auth), Miron Sokole, Esquire, 9/45; A Guskin (auth), Painting in U S A, 54; Martha Cheney (auth), Modern art in America, Tudor.
Memberships: Woodstock Artists Asn; Exp Art & Technol; Artists Equity Asn (nat dir, 52).
Dealer: Jarvis Gallery, Woodstock, NY 12498.
Mailing Address: 250 W 22nd St, New York, NY 10011.

SOLERI, PAOLO
Architect-Environmental Planner, Sculptor
b Torino, Italy, 19.
Study & Training: Polytech Torino, Frank Lloyd Wright fel.
Work in Public Collections: Mus Mod Art, New York, N Y.
Commissions: II Donnone (sculpture), Phoenix Civic Ctr, Ariz, 72.
Exhibitions: Corcoran Gallery Art, Washington, D C, 70; Whitney Mus Am Art, New York, 70; Mus Contemp Art, Chicago, Ill, 70; Nat Conf Ctr, Ottawa, Can, 71; Univ Art Mus, Berkeley, Calif, 71; plus others.
Awards: Graham Found, 62; Guggenheim Found, 64 & 67.
Publications: Auth, Arcology: the city in the image of man, 69 & The sketchbooks of Paolo Soleri, 71, Mass Inst Technol Press; auth, The bridge between matter & spirit is matter becoming spirit, Doubleday, 73.
Mailing Address: Cosanti Foundation, 6433 Doubletree Rd, Scottsdale, AZ 85253.

SOLINGER, DAVID M
Collector, Patron
Positions: Mem bd trustees, Am Fedn Arts, 54-; pres bd trustees, Whitney Mus Am Art, 66-
Collection: Twentieth century paintings and sculpture.
Mailing Address: 250 Park Ave, New York, NY 10017.

SOLMAN, JOSEPH
Painter, Instructor
Preferred Media: Oils, Gouache.
b Vitebsk, Russia, Jan 25, 09; U S citizen.
Study & Training: Nat Acad Design, New York, N Y, 26-29; Art Stud League New York, 29-30.
Work in Public Collections: Whitney Mus Am Art, New York; Phillips Gallery, Washington, D C; Fogg Mus, Cambridge, Mass; Butler Inst Am Art, Youngstown, Ohio; Los Angeles Co Mus, Los Angeles, Calif.
Exhibitions: Whitney Mus Am Art Ann, 52, 53 & 55; Int Asn Plastic Arts Europ Traveling Show Am Art, 56; Second Expos Contemp Art, Inst Brasil-Estados Unidos, Rio de Janeiro, 60.
Teaching: Instr oil painting, Mus Mod Art, 52-54; instr oil painting, New Sch Social Res, 64-66; instr oil painting, City Col New York, 67-
Positions: Ed & co-ed, Art Front Mag, 37-39.
Awards: Nat Inst Arts & Lett Award For Painting, 61; Isaac N Maynard Prize For Portrait, 69 & Saltus Gold Medal For Merit, 71, Nat Acad Design.
Bibliography: D Seckler (auth), Solman paints a picture, Art News, summer 51; S Burrey (auth), Joseph Solman: the growth of conviction, Arts, 10/55.
Memberships: Fedn Mod Painters & Sculptors (pres, 65-67, v pres, 67-).
Publications: Auth, Joseph Solman, Crown, 66.
Dealer: ACA Galleries, 25 E 73rd St, New York, NY 10021.
Mailing Address: 156 Second Ave, New York, NY 10003.

SOLOMON, DANIEL
Painter
Preferred Media: Acrylics.
b Topeka, Kans, July 13, 45.
Study & Training: Univ Ore, BSc.
Commissions: Outdoor mural, Benson & Hedges Tobacco Co, 71.
Exhibitions: Can Artists, Art Gallery Ont, 68; Survey 69, Montreal Mus Fine Arts, 69; one-man shows, Isaacs Gallery, 70 & 71.
Teaching: Instr painting, Ont Col Art, Toronto, 70-
Awards: Can Coun Bursary for Painting, 70 & 72.
Bibliography: L Lippard (auth), rev, 2/69 & M Greenwood (auth), rev, 8 & 9/71, Arts Mag; also rev, Arts Mag, 6/70.
Mailing Address: c/o Isaacs Gallery, 832 Yonge St, Toronto, Ont, Can.

SOLOMON, HYDE
Painter
Preferred Media: Oils.
b May 3, 11; U S citizen.
Study & Training: Art Stud League New York, N Y.

Work in Public Collections: Whitney Mus Am Art, New York; Wadsworth Atheneum, Hartford, Conn; Munson-Williams-Proctor Inst, Utica, N Y; Art Mus Princeton Univ, N J; Univ Calif Mus, Berkeley.
Exhibitions: Talent 1950, Kootz Gallery, New York; Carnegie Int, Pittsburgh, Pa, 57-59; 60 Am Painters, Walker Art Ctr, Minneapolis, 60; Nature In Abstraction, Whitney Mus Am Art, New York, 60; 157th Ann, Pa Acad Fine Arts, 62.
Positions: Artist-in-residence, Princeton Univ, 59-62.
Awards: Mus Purchase Award, Gloria Vanderbilt, 57; Childe Hassam Fund Purchase Award, Acad Arts & Lett, 70.
Bibliography: Thomas B Hess (auth), U S painting: some recent directions, Art News Ann, 56; Martica Sawin (auth), Profile of Hyde Solomon, Arts Mag, 11/58.
Dealer: Poindexter Gallery, 24 E 84th St, New York, NY 10028.
Mailing Address: 463 West St, New York, NY 10014.

SOLOMON, MR & MRS SIDNEY L
Collectors
Mr Solomon b Salem, Mass, Feb 21, 02; Mrs Solomon b Boston, Mass, May 15, 09.
Study & Training: Mr Solomon, Harvard Col, Harvard Univ Bus Sch; Mrs Solomon, Radcliffe Col, AB; Simmons Col, BS.
Collection: Sculpture of the twentieth century to contemporary, including Giacometti, Lipchitz, Marini, Nevelson, Dubuffet, Arp, Chadwick, Calder, Schmidt, Doris Cassar & Trova; painting collection includes Sargent, Vuillard, Tomayo, Leger, Giacometti, Monet and Matta; drawings of Maillol, Archipenko, Degas, Lachaise & many others; watercolors of Nolde & Marini; also a collection of pop art.
Mailing Address: 834 Fifth Ave, New York, NY 10021.

SOLOMON, SYD
Painter, Instructor
b Uniontown, Pa, July 12, 17.
Study & Training: Art Inst Chicago, 34; Ecole Beaux-Arts, Paris, France, 45.
Work in Public Collections: Delgado Mus Art, New Orleans, La; Butler Inst Am Art, Youngstown, Ohio; Birmingham Mus Art, Ala; Whitney Mus Am Art & Solomon R Guggenheim Mus, New York, N Y; plus many others.
Exhibitions: Nat & int exhibs incl Univ Ill, New Eng Ann, Silvermine Guild Art, Painting of the Year, Art Inst Chicago, Guild Hall, East Hampton, N Y & many others.
Teaching: Dir painting classes, Ringling Mus Art, 52-; dir fac, Famous Artists Sch, 53-; vis prof art, New Col, Sarasota, 66-68.
Positions: Camouflage designer, Engrs Bd, Washington, D C, 42.
Awards: First prize, Ringling Mus Art, 62; Silvermind Guild, 62; Ford Found Purchase Prize, 65.
Memberships: Artists Equity Asn; Allied Arts Coun.
Dealer: Saidenberg Gallery, 1037 Madison Ave, New York, NY 10021.
Mailing Address: 9210 Blind Pass Rd, Sarasota, FL 33581.

SOLOWAY, RETA
Painter, Lecturer
Preferred Media: Oils.
b Washington, D C, June 10, 11.
Study & Training: Corcoran Sch Art, 22-27; Parsons, 28-30; Phoenix Sch Design, 28-30; Philadelphia Mus Sch Art, 31-35; Philadelphia Graphic Sketch, 35-36; Nat Acad Sch, 69; New Sch, 71; also with Umberto Romano, Thornton Oakley, Henry Pitz, S G Schell, Joseph Stefanelli & Eric Isenburger.
Work in Public Collections: Gregory Mus, Hicksville, L I.
Commissions: Portraits, Maj Gen Arthur Gaines, Denver, Colo, 70 & Dean Emer, Charles Smythe, Pennington Prep Sch, 71.
Exhibitions: Nat Art League, 65-72; Malverne Artists L I, 65-72; Knickerbocker Artists, 69; Allied Artists Am, 69-72; Catharine Lorillard Wolfe Art Club, 72.
Teaching: Instr painting, Re-Art Studio, Elmont, N Y, 66-; demonstr, Nat Arts Club, Malverne Libr, 70-; IPA Nat Convention, Washington, D C, 72.
Awards: Best in show, Gregory Mus Inc, 71; first in oil, Long Beach Open Spring Exhib, 71; first in oil, Malverne Artists 28th Open Exhib, 72.
Memberships: Allied Artists Am (adv, 69-72, asst corresp secy, 71-73); Nat Art League (Bull ed, 70-71); Catharine Lorillard Wolfe Art Club; Am Artists Prof League; Malverne Artists L I (pres, 70-71, adv, 70-).
Publications: Contribr, Portrait in occupational therapy, 46 & Portrait of the world, 65.
Dealer: The Art Mart, 1000 Broadway, Woodmere, NY 11598.
Mailing Address: 1561 Hempstead Turnpike, Elmont, NY 11003.

SOLOWEY, BEN
Painter, Sculptor
b Warsaw, Poland, Aug 29, 00; U S citizen.
Study & Training: Graphic Sketch Club, Philadelphia, Pa; Pa Acad

Fine Arts, Philadelphia.
Work in Public Collections: Portraits in Phila Gen Hosp, Kensington Hosp, Philadelphia, Philadelphia Bd Educ & Pa Sch Soc Works, Univ Pa, Philadelphia; plus others.
Exhibitions: Nat Acad Design, New York, N Y; Pa Acad Fine Arts; Art Inst Chicago, Ill; Wilmington Soc Fine Arts, Del; Woodmere Art Gallery, Philadelphia.
Teaching: Instr drawing, Phila Mus Col Art, 57-59.
Awards: Pa Acad Fine Arts Gold Medal Award, 54; Woodmere Gallery Sculpture Award, Philadelphia, 70; Allentown Art Mus Drawing Award, Pa, 71.
Memberships: Allentown Art Mus; Am Watercolor Soc; fellowship Pa Acad Fine Arts; Philadelphia Watercolor Club; Woodmere Art Gallery.
Mailing Address: Bedminster, Bucks County, PA 18910.

SOLWAY, CARL E
Art Dealer
b Chicago, Ill, Jan 12, 35.
Positions: Dir, Carl Solway Gallery.
Memberships: Art Dealers Asn Am.
Specialty of Gallery: Twentieth century American and European painting, sculpture and graphics; urban environment and wall projects; Eye Editions, publisher of graphic works by John Cage, Richard Hamilton and Nancy Graves.
Mailing Address: 204 W Fourth St, Cincinnati, OH 45202.

SOMMERBURG, MIRIAM
Painter, Sculptor
Preferred Media: Wood, Stone, Stained Glass.
b Hamburg, Ger; U S citizen.
Study & Training: Sculpture with Richard Luksch, Ger & design with Friedrich Adler, Ger.
Work in Public Collections: Metrop Mus Art, New York, N Y; Butler Inst Am Art, Youngstown, Ohio; Springfield Mus, Mo; Norfolk Mus, Va.
Exhibitions: Exhibs, Edinburgh, Scotland, 63, Birmingham, Eng, 64, Mus Cognac, Cannes,France, 65-66; New Delhi, Bombay & Calcutta, India, 65-66 & Palazzo Vecchio, Florence & Pompeiian Pavilo, Naples, Italy, 72; plus many others.
Positions: Life fel, Intercontinental Biog Asn, Eng, 72-
Awards: First, second & third prizes for sculpture & graphics, Village Art Ctr, 46-60; Member's Award For Sculpture, Nat Asn Women Artists, 61; Medal For Creative Sculpture, Audubon Artists, 66.
Bibliography: Joseph L Young (auth), Mosaics, principles & practice, Van Nostrand Reinhold, 63; Carlo E Bugatti (auth), Enciclopedia internazionale degli artisti, 71.
Memberships: Audubon Artists (sculpture jury, 68); Am Asn Contemp Artists; Nat Asn Women Artists (sculpture jury, 62-65, graphics jury, 66-69); Print Coun Am; Fedn Am Arts.
Mailing Address: c/o Westbeth-Artists Housing, 463 West St, Apt G227, New York, NY 10014.

SONENBERG, JACK
Painter
b Toronto, Ont, Dec 28, 25; U S citizen.
Study & Training: Ont Col Art, Toronto; N Y Univ; Wash Univ, BFA.
Work in Public Collections: Guggenheim Mus, New York, N Y; Whitney Mus Am Art, New York; Metrop Mus Art, New York; Nat Gallery Can, Ottawa.
Commissions: Steel wall construction, Ciba-Geigy Corp, Ardsley, N Y, 71.
Exhibitions: Pa Acad Fine Arts 152nd Ann, 57; Contemp Am Painting & Sculpture, Krannert Art Mus, 63; Art in Process, Finch Col Mus, New York, 65; Fourth Int Japan Cult Forum, Tokyo, 67; Whitney Mus Am Art Painting Ann, 67.
Teaching: Instr painting & printmaking, Sch Visual Arts, New York, 64-; instr painting & printmaking, Pratt Inst, 68-
Positions: Ford Found & Am Fedn Arts artist-in-residence grant, Hampton Inst, 66.
Awards: First prize for painting, 13th New Eng Ann, 62; premio, Fourth Am Print Biennial, Chile, 70.
Dealer: Brooke Alexander, 328 E 78th St, New York, NY 10021.
Mailing Address: 217 E 23rd St, New York, NY 10010.

SONFIST, ALAN
Painter
b New York, N Y, June 26, 46.
Study & Training: Western Ill Univ; Pratt Inst; Hunter Col, MA.
Exhibitions: One-man show, Reese Palley, New York, 70; Boston Element Show, Mus Fine Arts, 71; Stedijk Mus, Holland, 71; Harcus Karkow, Boston, 71.
Teaching: Prof, Montclair State Col, 70-71.
Bibliography: Gracie Gliuck (auth), Nature artist, New York Times, 11/70; Cindy Nemser (auth), Sonfist-phenomenist, Art in Am, 3/71; Benthall (auth), Sonfist & Haague, Studio Int, 6/71.

Dealer: Palley & Lowe, 101 Wooster St, New York, NY 10012.
Mailing Address: Box 382, Gracie Station, New York, NY 10028.

SONNENBERG, MR & MRS BENJAMIN
Collectors
Collection: Ancient art, ethnographica.
Mailing Address: 19 Gramercy Park, New York, NY 10003.

SONNENSCHEIN, HUGO, JR
Patron, Art Historian
b Chicago, Ill, Feb 22, 17.
Study & Training: Swarthmore Col; Lake Forest Col, BA; Univ Va, LLB & JD; John Marshall Law Sch, Chicago, LLM.
Positions: Ed, Chicago Bar Rec, 50-66; trustee, Lake Forest Col, 69-
Memberships: Gov life mem Art Inst Chicago; Mus Mod Art; Soc Contemp Art.
Research: Prints and drawings; legal art.
Art Interests: Donor, Sonnenschein Collection to Lake Forest Col & Lake Forest Acad.
Mailing Address: 135 S La Salle St, Chicago, IL 60603.

SORBY, J RICHARD
Painter, Educator
Preferred Media: Acrylics, Watercolors, Mixed Media.
b Duluth, Minn, Dec 21, 11.
Study & Training: Univ Minn; Univ Northern Colo, AB, 37, MA, 51; Art Inst Chicago; Univ of the Americas; Univ Calif, Los Angeles, with John Ferren; Univ Colo, with Jimmy Ernst.
Work in Public Collections: William Rockhill Nelson Gallery, Kansas City, Mo; Denver Art Mus, Colo; Joslyn Mem Mus Art, Omaha, Nebr; Brigham Young Univ; Rural Electrification Admin, Washington, D C.
Commissions: Spaulding Mem, Papantla (pyroxylin), Univ Northern Colo, Greeley, 58.
Exhibitions: Denver Art Mus Ann Western Artists, 40-59; Nat Watercolor Competition, Nat Gallery Art, Washington, D C, 41; First & Second Ann Rocky Mountain Nat Invitational, Utah State Univ, 57 & 58; Northern Calif Artists Ann, Crocker Art Gallery, Sacramento, 61-68; First Nat Exhib Polymer Paintings, Eastern Mich Univ, 67.
Teaching: Instr art, Univ Nebr, Lincoln, 40-42; assoc prof painting, Sch Art, Univ Denver, 47-59; prof painting & design, Calif State Univ, San Jose, 59-72, emer prof, 72-
Awards: First award & purchase for Crown of Light. 4th Biennial 10 State Exhib, Joslyn Mem Mus, 56; first prize for Passing Shadows (acrylic collage), Univ Santa Clara Sullivan-Hickson Fund, 66; first award & purchase for Mountain Stream, 27th Ann, Cedar City, Utah, 67.
Bibliography: Arneil (auth), The work of Richard Sorby, Empire Mag, Denver Post, 11/58; M L Stribling (auth), Painting in found materials, 71.
Memberships: East Bay Artists Asn(v pres, 67-68); Group 21 (v pres, 72).
Publications: Illusr, Lincoln-Mercury Times, 54, Ford Times, 56 & Empire Mag, Denver Post, 58.
Dealer: Copenhagen Galleri, Hamlet Sq, Solvang, CA 93463.
Mailing Address: Morningsun Studio, Glen Haven, CO 80532.

SORIA, PAOLA (PAOLA SORIA SERENI)
Painter
Preferred Media: Oils.
b Rome, Italy, Apr 30, 08; U S citizen.
Study & Training: Acad Belle Arti, with Umberto Coromaldi & Carlo Siviero; also with Antonio Fabres & Giacomo Balla; Art Stud League New York, with Robert Brackman; Nat Acad Design, with Louis Bosa.
Work in Public Collections: Landscape, Norfolk Mus, Va; Brandeis Univ Libr, Boston, Mass.
Commissions: Mr Lee M Freidman (portrait), Jewish Hist Soc.
Exhibitions: Fifty American Artists, 61, 63 & 65; Am Artists Prof League Grand Nat, 63; Nat Arts Club; Salmagundi Club; Burr Artists Asn, 70; plus other group & one-man shows.
Awards: Palais des Beaus Arts, 67th Salon, 51; Prix de Paris, 64 & 67.
Mailing Address: 301 E 66th St, New York, NY 10021.

SOUDEN, JAMES G
Educator, Painter
b Chicago, Ill, Oct 14, 17.
Study & Training: Art Inst Chicago; Univ Ariz, BFA & MA; Inst Design, Ill Inst Technol, MS (art educ).
Teaching: Assoc prof art, Univ Ariz, 49-62, actg head art dept, 62; prof art & dean col, Otis Art Inst, 62-
Mailing Address: Otis Art Inst, 2401 Wilshire Blvd, Los Angeles, CA 90057.

SOWERS, MIRIAM R
Painter, Art Dealer
Preferred Media: Oils.
b Bluffton, Ohio, Oct 4, 22.
Study & Training: Miami Univ; Art Inst Chicago; Univ N Mex.
Work in Public Collections: Tex A&I Univ; Houston Baptist Col;
Lovelace Clin, Albuquerque; Int Arch, London, Eng; New York
World's Fair.
Commissions: Many comn portraits; stained glass mural.
Exhibitions: Dayton Art Inst, Ohio; Butler Inst Am Art; Akron Art
Inst; one-man show, Ann Bible Soc Gallery, New York; Toledo
Mus Art; plus other group & one-man shows.
Positions: Owner, Symbol Gallery Art, 61-
Awards: Prizes, Toledo Mus Art, Ouray Colo Nat & N Mex State
Fair; plus others.
Bibliography: Walter Trimble (auth), Insight, Encanto Mag; articles,
In: Albuquerque Tribune, Albuquerque Clubwoman Mag & Albu-
querque Jour.
Specialty of Gallery: Symbolic portraits and figurative landscapes,
oils on gold leaf.
Mailing Address: 2049 S Plaza N W, Albuquerque, NM 87104.

SOYER, ISAAC
Painter, Instructor
Preferred Media: Oils.
b Russia, Apr 20, 02; U S citizen.
Study & Training: Nat Acad Design; Cooper Union; also in Paris,
France & Madrid, Spain.
Work in Public Collections: Employment Agency, Whitney Mus Am
Art, New York, N Y; Portrait of My Father, Brooklyn Mus; Re-
becca, Albright-Knox Mus, Buffalo, N Y; The Art Beauty Shoppe,
Dallas Mus Fine Arts, Tex; Cafeteria, Brooks Mem Gallery,
Memphis, Tenn.
Exhibitions: Mus Mod Art, New York; Art Inst Chicago, Ill; Pa Acad
Fine Arts Philadelphia; Corcoran Gallery Art, Washington, D C;
New York World's Fair.
Teaching: Instr painting & drawing, Educ Alliance Art Sch, New
York, 50-; instr painting & drawing, New Sch Social Res, 68-;
instr painting & drawing, Art Stud League New York, 69-
Awards: First prize, Western N Y Exhib, 44; first prize for land-
scape, Audubon Artists Exhib, 45.
Bibliography: John H Bauer (auth), Revolution and tradition in
American art, 51; L Goodrich & J Bauer (auth), American art of
our century, 61; Edmund Feldman (auth), Varieties of visual ex-
perience, Abrams, 72.
Mailing Address: 122 E 61st St, New York, NY 10021.

SOYER, MOSES
Painter
b Russia, Dec 25, 1899; U S citizen.
Study & Training: Cooper Union Art Sch; Nat Acad Design; Beaux
Arts Inst Design; Educ Alliance Art Sch; also with Robert Henri
& George Bellows.
Work in Public Collections: Metrop Mus Art, Mus Mod Art & Whit-
ney Mus Am Art, New York, N Y; Brooklyn Mus, N Y; Detroit
Inst Arts, Mich; Everson Mus Art, Syracuse, N Y; plus many
others.
Commissions: Mural, U S Post Off, Philadelphia, Pa.
Exhibitions: Libr Cong & Phillips Collection, Washington, D C;
Toledo Mus Art, Ohio; Newark Mus, N J; Butler Inst Am Art,
Youngstown, Ohio; Nat Acad Design; plus many others.
Teaching: Contemp Sch Art, New York; New Sch Social Res; Educ
Alliance Art Sch.
Bibliography: Bernard Smith (auth), Moses Soyer (monogr), ACA
Gallery, 44; Charlotte Willard (auth), Moses Soyer, World Publ,
62; plus others.
Memberships: An Am Group; Am Soc Painters, Gravers & Sculp-
tors; Nat Inst Arts & Lett.
Publications: Auth, Painting the human figure, Watson-Guptill, 64;
illusr, First book of ballet.
Mailing Address: 222 W 23rd St, New York, NY 10011.

SOYER, RAPHAEL
Painter
Preferred Media: Oils, Graphics.
b Russia, Dec 25, 99; U S citizen.
Study & Training: Cooper Union; Nat Acad Design; Art Stud League
New York, N Y.
Work in Public Collections: Metrop Mus Art, New York; Whitney
Mus Am Art, New York; Mus Mod Art, New York; Addison Mus
Art, Andover, Mass; Philadelphia Mus Art, Pa.
Exhibitions: Carnegie Int, Pittsburgh, Pa; Whitney Mus Am Art;
Calif Palace Legion of Honor, San Francisco; Pa Mus Fine Arts;
Art Inst Chicago.
Teaching: Instr painting, Art Stud League New York; instr painting,
Am Art Sch; instr painting, New Sch Social Res.

Bibliography: Lloyd Goodrich (auth), Raphael Soyer, Praeger, 67;
Sylvan Cole (auth), 50 years of printmaking, Da Capo, 67; Joseph
K Foster (auth), Watercolors and drawings, Crown, 69.
Memberships: Nat Acad Design; Am Acad Arts & Lett.
Publications: Auth & illusr, A painter's pilgrimage, 62, Homage to
Thomas Eakins, 66 & Self revealment, 69.
Dealer: Forum Gallery, 1018 Madison Ave, New York, NY 10021.
Mailing Address: 88 Central Park W, New York, NY 10023.

SPAETH, ELOISE O'MARA
Collector, Writer
b Decatur, Ill, June 19, 04.
Study & Training: Millikin Univ.
Positions: Trustee, Dayton Art Inst, 38-44, dir, Mod Gallery, 40-44;
trustee, Am Fedn Arts, 45-, chmn exten serv, 47-59; trustee,
Guild Hall Mus, 50-, chmn acquisitions comt, 62-; trustee &
v pres, Arch Am Art, 59; chmn, East Div Arch, 59; dir, Friends
of Whitney Mus Am Art; mem, Smithsonian Inst Fine Art Comn.
Memberships: Am Asn Mus; Col Art Asn Am; Art Collectors Club.
Collection: Contemporary religious art; antiquities; contemporary
American and European art.
Publications: Auth, American art museums and galleries, 60, 66 &
69; auth, Collecting art, 68; contribr to art & relig publ.
Mailing Address: 120 E 81st St, New York, NY 10028.

SPAGNOLO, KATHLEEN MARY
Printmaker, Illustrator
Preferred Media: Graphics.
b London, Eng, Sept 12, 19.
Study & Training: Bromley Art Sch; Royal scholar & Princess of
Wales scholar to Royal Col Art, London, 39-42; Sch Design, with
E W Tristram; Am Univ, with Robert Gates & Krishna Reddy.
Work in Public Collections: Dept of Interior, Washington, D C; Univ
Va, Charlottesville; George Washington Univ, Washington, D C;
Libr Cong.
Commissions: Rendering (bench), Index Am Design, Nat Gallery Art,
Washington, D C, 69.
Exhibitions: Corcoran Gallery Art, Washington, D C, 62; Philadel-
phia Print Club, 63; Silvermine Guild Artists, 63; Soc Washing-
ton Printmakers, 69-72.
Memberships: Soc Washington Printmakers; Washington Water-
color Asn; Washington Print Club; Artist's Equity Asn.
Dealer: Hensley Gallery, 113 N Fairfax St, Alexandria, VA 22314.
Mailing Address: 7401 Recard Lane, Alexandria, VA 22307.

SPAMPINATO, CLEMENTE
Sculptor
Preferred Media: Bronze, Marble.
b Italy, Jan 10, 12; U S citizen.
Study & Training: Acad Fine Arts, Rome, Italy; Fr Acad Nude,
Rome; Sch of Governatorate, Rome; Royal Sch of the Medal,
Rome.
Work in Public Collections: Nat Mus Sport, New Madison Square
Garden, New York, N Y; Rockwell Gallery Western Art, Corning,
N Y; Isaac Delgado Mus Art, New Orleans, La; Notre Dame Univ,
Ind; Oklahoma Art Ctr, Oklahoma City.
Commissions: Soccer trophy, int competition, Ital Govt, 40; Navy
Goat (bronze statue), comt class 1915, U S Naval Acad, Annapo-
lis, Md, 57; several archit reliefs, Bd Educ & Dept Pub Works,
New York, 57-72; three different bronze statues of Columbus,
Huntington, N Y, 64, Mineola, N Y, 65 & Bridgeport, Conn, 71;
two lime-stone bas reliefs, Brooklyn Heights Br Libr, N Y, 60;
plus one other.
Exhibitions: Sport Sculpture Nat, Rome, 40-48; Allied Artists Am,
New York, 46-51; Am Artists Prof Art League, New York, 51;
Nat Sculpture Soc, New York, 52-72; Nat Acad Design, New York,
64-72; plus other group & one-man shows.
Awards: First prize, Nat Competition Sport Figure, Rome, 39; first
prize, Nat Competition Ski Trophy Olympic Games, Rome, 40;
gold medal, Grand Award Munic Art League, Chicago, Ill, 70.
Memberships: Fel Nat Sculpture Soc; Circolo Artistico Int; Int Fine
Arts Coun; Int Am Inst.
Dealer: Campanile Galleries, Inc, 200 S Michigan Ave, Chicago, IL
60604.
Mailing Address: 36 Littleworth Lane, Sea Cliff, NY 11579.

SPANDORF, LILY GABRIELLA
Painter
Preferred Media: Gouache, Watercolors, Mixed Media.
Study & Training: Acad Arts, Vienna, grad.
Work in Public Collections: Smithsonian Inst, Washington, D C; Libr
Cong, Washington, D C; Washington Co Mus Fine Arts, Hagers-
town, Md; Munic Mus, Rome, Italy; The White House, Washing-
ton, D C.

Commissions: Paintings, presented as gifts of State to HRH Princess Margaret, Pres of Korea, Chung Hee Park & former pres of Iceland, Asgeir Asgeirsson by President Lyndon B Johnson; designed U S postage stamp for Christmas, 63, Post Off Dept.
Exhibitions: Washington Watercolor Asn Nat, 61-67; Am Drawing Ann & Smithsonian Travel Exhib, Norfolk Mus, Va, 63; Metrop Art Exhib, Smithsonian Inst, 63-66; one-man shows, Agra Gallery, 65-67, 70 & 72 & Bodley Gallery, New York, plus others; exhibited widely, Europe, Eng, Italy & U S.
Awards: Numerous awards, Italy, Eng & U S.
Memberships: Washington Press Club; Artist's Equity Asn; Washington Watercolor Asn.
Dealer: Agra Gallery, 1721 De Sales St N W, Washington, DC 20036.
Mailing Address: 1603 19th St N W, Washington, DC 20009.

SPARK, VICTOR DAVID
Art Dealer
b Brooklyn, N Y, May 16, 98.
Study & Training: N Y Univ, BS, 21.
Positions: Dir, Victor D Spark Art Gallery.
Specialty of Gallery: American and foreign paintings, drawings and other works of art; appraisals of fine art.
Mailing Address: 1000 Park Ave, New York, NY 10028.

SPAULDING, WARREN DAN
Painter, Educator
Preferred Media: Watercolors, Acrylics, Oils, Pencil, Ink.
b Boston, Mass, Oct 7, 16.
Study & Training: Mass Sch Art, cert painting, 37; Sch Fine Art, Yale Univ, Alice K English fel foreign travel & study, 49, BFA & MFA.
Work in Public Collections: Univ Maine, Orono; Joslyn Art Mus, Omaha; U S Sect Fine Arts, Marine Hosp, Carville, La, Branford Col, Yale Univ, New Haven, Conn; St Louis Artists Guild, Mo.
Exhibitions: Cincinnati Art Mus Am Art Ann, 40; Am Watercolors, Nat Gallery Art, Washington, D C, 40; Exhib Current Am Prints, Carnegie Inst, 47; Pa Acad Fine Arts Painting & Sculpture Ann, 51 & 54; Midwest Biennial, Joslyn Art Mus, 56 & 58.
Teaching: Instr painting, Sch Fine Arts, Yale Univ, 49-50; art dir, Taft Sch, Watertown, Conn, 50-51; prof compos, Sch Fine Arts, Wash Univ, 51-61.
Awards: Nat Watercolor Competition Purchase Award, U S Sect Fine Art, 40; first prize for oil & sculpture exhib, St Louis Artists Guild, 51; purchase prize, Midwest Biennial, Joslyn Art Mus, 58.
Memberships: Main Art Gallery.
Dealer: Main Street Gallery, 459 Main St, Rockland, ME 04841.
Mailing Address: South Thomaston, ME 04858.

SPAVENTA, GEORGE
Sculptor
b New York, N Y, Feb 22, 18.
Study & Training: Leonardo da Vinci Art Sch; Beaux Art Inst Design; Acad Grande Chaumiere, Paris, France.
Work in Public Collections: Univ Calif, Berkeley; Mass Inst Technol, Cambridge.
Exhibitions: Carnegie Inst, 49-50; Mus Mod Art, New York, traveling exhib, U S, 64-65, Paris & other Europ cities, 65-66.
Teaching: Sculpture, New York Studio Sch, 64-; sculpture, Skowhegan Sch Painting & Sculpture, 68; sculpture, Md Inst Art, 69.
Dealer: Poindexter Gallery, 24 E 84th St, New York, NY 10028.
Mailing Address: 463 West St, New York, NY 10014.

SPEIGHT, FRANCIS
Painter, Educator
b Windsor, N C, Sept 11, 96.
Study & Training: Wake Forest Col, DHL; Corcoran Gallery Art; Pa Acad Fine Arts; Col of the Holy Cross, DFA, 64.
Work in Public Collections: Mus Mod Art; Toronto Gallery Art; Pa Acad Fine Arts; Rochester Mem Gallery; Butler Inst Am Art; plus many others.
Exhibitions: Retrospective, N C Mus Art, Raleigh, 61.
Teaching: Instr, Pa Acad Fine Arts, 26-61; prof art & artist-in-residence, E Carolina Univ, 61-
Awards: Percy Owens Award, Pa Acad Fine Arts, 61; prize, Pa Nat Exhib, Ligonier Valley, 61; Gold Medal For Achievement In Art, State of N C, 64; plus many others.
Memberships: Nat Acad Design; Nat Inst Arts & Lett; N C Art Soc (adv bd).
Mailing Address: East Carolina University, Greenville, NC 27834.

SPELMAN, JILL SULLIVAN
Painter
Preferred Media: Acrylics.
b Chicago, Ill, Feb 17, 37.
Study & Training: Hilton Leech Art Sch, Sarasota, Fla, 55-57; also with Paul Ninas, New Orleans, 56-58.

Work in Public Collections: Univ Mass, Amherst.
Exhibitions: Three-man show, Sarasota Art Asn, Fla, 58; Watercolor U S A, Springfield Art Mus, Mo, 67; Mainstreams '70, Marietta Col, Ohio, 70; three-man show, The Landscape of the Mind, Phoenix Gallery, New York, N Y, 71; Salon 72, Ward Nasse Gallery, New York, 72.
Teaching: Lectr, Ringling Mus Art, Sarasota, 58-60.
Positions: Pres, Phoenix Coop Gallery, 72-
Awards: Sarasota Art Asn First Prize, Art Stud Exhib, 57; Hamel Prize, Sarasota Art Asn Ann, 58; Grumbacher Oil Prize, Knickerbocker Artists Ann, 70.
Memberships: Nat Soc Painters in Casein & Acrylic (corresp secy, 71).
Dealer: Phoenix Gallery, 939 Madison Ave, New York, NY 10021.
Mailing Address: 22 W 96th St, New York, NY 10025.

SPENCER (MARY SCRUGGS-SPENCER)
Painter, Instructor
Preferred Media: Oils.
b Ancon, Panama, Dec 5, 09; U S citizen.
Study & Training: Univ Ala; Southern Methodist Univ, with DeForrest Judd.
Commissions: Romantic garden scene, Riff's Bridal Salon, Longview, Tex, 57.
Exhibitions: Butler Mus Fine Arts Nat Exhib, Youngstown, Ohio, 64; Artists of the Gulf States, Delgado Mus, New Orleans, La, 64; Sun Carnival Nat Exhib, El Paso Mus Fine Arts, Tex, 65-67; one-woman show, Parthenon, Nashville, Tenn, 65; two-woman show, Beaumont Mus, Tex, 70.
Teaching: Instr hobby art, night dept, Kilgore Jr Col, Tex, 66-72; instr art, St Mary's, Longview, Tex, 72; instr, Longview Mus & Arts Ctr; instr, pvt workshops.
Positions: Dir-at-large, Tex Watercolor Soc, 72-73.
Awards: Hon mention, Tex Fine Arts Asn, 63; Grumbacher Award, Elizabet Ney Mus, 64; Fred Miller Award, Beaumont Mus, 67.
Bibliography: Ashford (auth), Arts, San Antonio Express, 1/13/63; Stevens (auth), Aux Etats Unis, La Rev Mod, 2/65; Hieronymus (auth), Art & theatre, Nashville Tennessean, 3/14/65 & 4/18/65.
Memberships: Tex Fine Arts Asn; E Tex Fine Arts Asn (bd mem, 70-71); Tex Watercolor Asn (mem-at-large, 72); Gregg Art Guild; Tyler Art League.
Collection: Contemporary regional artists.
Dealer: Frederick-Nila, 306 N Fourth, Longview, TX 75601.
Mailing Address: 106 Skyline Dr, Longview, TX 75601.

SPENCER, ELEANOR PATTERSON
Writer, Art Historian
b Northampton, Mass.
Study & Training: Smith Col, BA & MA; Radcliffe Col, PhD; hon LHD, Goucher Col, 67.
Teaching: Prof hist art, Goucher Col, 30-62.
Positions: Trustee, Walters Art Gallery, Baltimore, 62; trustee, Baltimore Mus Art, 62; trustee, Peale Mus, Baltimore, 62.
Awards: Sachs fel, Harvard Univ, 28; Fulbright fel, 62.
Memberships: Col Art Asn Am.
Research: Illuminated manuscripts of the fifteenth century in France.
Publications: Auth, articles, In: Scriptorium, 63, 65 & 69; auth, articles, In: Burlington Mag, 65 & 66.
Mailing Address: 7 rue Fustel de Coulanges, Paris, France, 75005.

SPENCER, HUGH
Illustrator, Photographer
b Saint Cloud, Minn, July 19, 87.
Study & Training: Chicago Sch Appl & Normal Art; Art Stud League New York, N Y; N Y Eve Sch Indust Art; also with Charles Chapman & Arthur Covey.
Exhibitions: Capital Wood Carvers Asn Show, 72.
Positions: Illusr, nature & sci readers & textbooks.
Awards: Hon mention, Weinstock's Photo Exhib & Competition, Sacramento, Calif, 62.
Memberships: Soc Conn Craftsmen; Meriden Arts & Crafts; Conn Bot Soc (pres, 63-64); Sierra Camera Club; Capital Wood Carvers Asn.
Publications: Contribr, Natural Hist; contribr, Nature.
Mailing Address: 3711 El Ricon Way, Sacramento, CA 95825.

SPENCER, JOHN R
Art Historian, Art Administrator
b Moline, Ill, Sept 20, 23.
Study & Training: Grinnell Col, BA, 47, hon DFA, 72; Yale Univ, MA, 51, PhD, 53; also with Charles Seymour, Jr.
Teaching: Instr & asst prof art, Yale Univ, 52-58; assoc prof art & acting chmn dept, Univ Fla, 58-62; prof hist art, Oberlin Col, 62-
Positions: Dir mus, Oberlin Col, 62-72.
Memberships: Col Art Asn Am (secy, 67, v pres, 71); Am Asn Mus; Asn Art Mus Dir; Instituto per la Storia dell'arte lombarda; Am Fedn Arts.

Research: Fifteenth century Italian art, with emphasis on painting & theoretical writings.
Publications: Auth, L B Alberti, on painting, 55 & 67; auth, Filarete's treatise on architecture, 65.
Mailing Address: National Endowment for the Arts, 806 15th St N W, Washington, DC 20506.

SPERAKIS, NICHOLAS GEORGE
Painter, Printmaker
b New York, N Y, June 8, 43.
Study & Training: Pratt Inst, scholar, fall 60; Nat Acad Design Sch Fine Art, New York, scholar, painting with Louis Boucie, 60-61; Art Stud League New York, scholar, 61-63, painting with Joseph Hirsch, Charles Alsom, Edwin Dickenson, Will Barnet & Harry Sternberg & graphics with Harry Sternberg; Pratt Graphic Art Ctr, scholar, printmaking with Sid Hammer, Clair Romano & Ed Casserella.
Work in Public Collections: Brooklyn Mus Print Collection, N Y; Philadelphia Mus Fine Art Print Collection, Pa; Chrysler Mus Permanent Collection, Provincetown, Mass; Norfolk Mus Arts & Sci, Va; 42nd St Pub Libr, New York.
Commissions: Portraits, Johnethan Charnolble, Collection of Carla Rueban, Mari Galleries, Larchmont, N Y, 66, Dr John Courins, Maplewood, N J, 66, Marvin Bolotzky, New York, 67, Chaim Gross, New York, 69 & George Viener, Redding, Pa, 71.
Exhibitions: Three Brooklyn Mus Biennials, 64, 66 & 70; 100 Prints From Pratt Graphic Art Ctr, Jewish Mus, New York, summer 64; New Acquisitions, Chrysler Mus, Provincetown, Mass, 64 & 65, New Acquisitions, Norfolk Mus Arts & Sci, 65.
Teaching: Instr painting & graphics, Art Sch Educ Alliance, 68-69; instr graphics, 92nd St YMHA, New York, 70-71; instr graphics, Brooklyn Mus Art Sch, 71-72.
Awards: Purchase Prize, Mercyhurst Col Paint Ann, 64; Lawrence & Hinda Rosenthal fel, Am Acad Arts & Lett & Nat Inst Arts & Lett, 60; J S Guggenheim Mem Found fel graphics, 70.
Bibliography: Robert Henkes (auth), The crucifixion as depicted by contemporary artists, Nazarine Col, 72; Barry Shwarts (auth), 20th century humanist art, Praeger, 73; Una Johnson (auth), American printmaking, Brooklyn Mus, (in prep).
Memberships: Fedn Am Art; Artists Equity Asn; Rhino Horn Orgn Humanist Art.
Dealer: Paul Kessler Gallery, 108 Commercial St, Provincetown, MA 02657.
Mailing Address: 27 Eldridge St, Second Floor, New York, NY 10002.

SPEYER, A JAMES
Art Administrator
b Pittsburgh, Pa.
Study & Training: Carnegie Inst Technol, BS; Chelsea Polytechnique, London, Eng; Sorbonne; Ill Inst Technol, MA, with Mies van der Rohe.
Collections Arranged: Am Bi-Ann, Twentieth Century Sculpture Exhib, 67 & Mies van der Rohe Retrospective, 68, Art Inst Chicago.
Teaching: Instr advan archit, Ill Inst Technol, 46-61; vis prof archit, Nat Univ Athens, 57-60; instr mod art, Ford Found sem, Art Inst Chicago.
Positions: Pvt architect, 46-57, Chicago corresp, Art News Mag, 55-57; cur contemp art, Art Inst Chicago, 61-
Mailing Address: Art Institute of Chicago, Michigan Ave & Adams St, Chicago, IL 60603.

SPICKETT, RONALD JOHN (SR)
Painter, Instructor
Preferred Media: Oils.
b Regina, Sask, Apr 11, 26.
Study & Training: Alta Col Art, Calgary, Dipl; Ont Col Art, Toronto; Inst Allende Mex, scholar, 55.
Work in Public Collections: Nat Gallery Ottawa; Dept External Affairs, Can Govt; London Art Gallery, Ont; Art Gallery Toronto; Edmonton Art Gallery.
Commissions: Sculpture, Med Arts Bldg, Calgary, 60; sculpture, Bank of Montreal, Edmonton, 62; mural painting, Bowlen Bldg, Govt Alta, Calgary, 68-69.
Exhibitions: Nat Gallery Can Biennial; Mem Univ Gallery, Newfoundland, Can, 70; Banff Festival Arts, Alta, 71; Environment '71, Calgary, 71.
Teaching: Instr painting & drawing, Univ Calgary, 69-
Awards: Can Coun Award, Govt Can, 63 & 69.
Bibliography: Articles, In: Can Art, 59-61.
Memberships: Royal Can Acad Art.
Mailing Address: Dept of Art, University of Calgary, Calgary, Alta T2N 1N4, Can.

SPIDELL, ENID JEAN
Painter, Educator
b Hampton, N B, June 5, 05.
Study & Training: Parsons Sch Design; New York Univ, BS (art educ); Teachers Col, Columbia Univ, MA; pvt study with George Pearse Ennis; Art Stud League New York; Syracuse Univ Exten, Taxco, Mex.
Exhibitions: In mem orgns; one-man shows, New Rochelle Pub Libr, 56 & 64, Bronxville Pub Libr, 64 & New Rochelle, 68.
Teaching: Assoc prof art & chmn fashion arts, Pratt Inst.
Awards: Prize in design competition, 43.
Memberships: Am Watercolor Soc; Int Soc Color Coun; New Rochelle Art Asn (dir, 56-59, pres, 59-63, dir, 63-).
Mailing Address: 50 Jackson St, New Rochelle, NY 10801.

SPIEGEL, SAM
Collector
b Austria, Nov 11, 04.
Study & Training: Univ Vienna.
Memberships: Art Collectors Club.
Collection: Modern impressionist art.
Mailing Address: 475 Park Ave, New York, NY 10022.

SPITZ, BARBARA S
Printmaker
Preferred Media: Intaglio.
b Chicago, Ill, Jan 8, 26.
Study & Training: Art Inst Chicago; R I Sch Design; Brown Univ, AB; also with Leon Golub, Franz Schulze & Letterio Calapai.
Work in Public Collections: Art Inst Chicago; De Cordova Mus, Lincoln, Mass; Okla Art Ctr, Oklahoma City; First Nat Bank Boston, Mass.
Exhibitions: Art Inst Chicago 71st Ann, 68; The Print Club, Philadelphia, Pa, 69 & 72; Soc Am Graphic Artists 51st Ann, Kennedy Galleries, New York, N Y, 71; one-man show, Benjamin Galleries, Chicago, 71; Boston Printmakers 23rd & 24th Ann, De Cordova & Rose Art Mus, 71 & 72.
Awards: Munic Art League Prize, Art Inst 71st Ann, 68; purchase awards, Boston Printmakers 23rd & 24th Ann, De Cordova Mus, 71 & 72; purchase award, Okla Art Ctr 14th Ann, 72.
Bibliography: T & B Carbol (ed), article, In: The printmaker in Illinois, Ill Art Educ Asn, 72.
Memberships: Artist Equity Asn; Chicago Soc Artists; Arts Club Chicago; Boston Printmakers; Renaissance Soc, Univ Chicago.
Dealer: Benjamin Galleries, 900 N Michigan Ave, Chicago, IL 60611.
Mailing Address: 150 Indian Tree Dr, Highland Park, IL 60035.

SPITZER, FRANCES R
Collector
b New York, N Y, Mar 31, 18.
Study & Training: Syracuse Univ, BS.
Collection: French impressionists; contemporary American art.
Mailing Address: 200 E 66th St, New York, NY 10021.

SPONENBURGH, MARK
Art Historian, Sculptor
b Cadillac, Mich, June 15, 16.
Study & Training: Cranbrook Acad Art, scholar, 40; Wayne Univ; Ecole Beaux-Arts, Paris, France; Univ London; Univ Cairo.
Work in Public Collections: Detroit Inst Art; Portland Art Mus; Univ Ore; Mus Mod Art, Egypt; Pakistan Arts.
Exhibitions: Pa Acad Fine Arts; Durand-Ruel & Paris Salon, France; Inst Fine Arts Cairo; Nat Gallery, Pakistan; 25 one-man exhibs, sculpture; plus others.
Collections Arranged: Sculpture Pac Northwest, Univ Ore, 55; 2000 Yrs Horse & Rider In Arts of Pakistan, 59 & Folk Arts of Swat, 61, Nat Col Arts, Pakistan; C R I A, Corvallis Arts Coun, 67-
Teaching: Assoc prof, Univ Ore, 46-56; vis prof, Royal Col Arts, 56-57; prof & prin, Nat Col Arts, Pakistan, 58-61; prof, Ore State Univ, 61-
Awards: Tiffany Found fel, 41; Fulbright Found fel, 51-53; purchase prizes, Detroit Art Inst & Portland Art Mus; plus others.
Memberships: Col Art Asn Am; Northwest Inst Sculpture; Am Asn Mus.
Publications: Contribr, Arts Quart, J Inst Egypte, Rev Caire, Near E Bull & J Near E Studies; plus others.
Mailing Address: Dept of Art, Oregon State University, Corvallis, OR 97331.

SPONGBERG, GRACE
Painter, Photographer
Preferred Media: Watercolors.
b Chicago, Ill, Apr 25, 06.
Study & Training: Art Inst Chicago.
Work in Public Collections: Horace Mann Sch, Chicago; Bennett Sch, Chicago; Byford Sch, Chicago; Mus Vaxco, Sweden.
Exhibitions: Pa Acad Fine Arts; Art Inst Chicago; Joslyn Art Mus; Chicago Soc Art; Riverside Mus; plus others.
Memberships: Chicago Soc Art.
Mailing Address: 909 N Rush St, Chicago, IL 60611.

SPRAGUE, MARK ANDERSON
Painter, Educator
Preferred Media: Oils, Polymers, Collage.
b Champaign, Ill, Jan 5, 20.
Study & Training: Univ Ill, BFA, 46, MFA, 49.
Work in Public Collections: Ill State Univ Mus, Bloomington.
Commissions: Painting for Great Ideas of Western Man, Container
Corp Am, Chicago, Ill.
Exhibitions: Am Fedn Arts Circulating Exhib, Washington, D C, 49;
Art Inst Chicago 60th Am Ann, 51; Western Art Ann, Denver,
Colo, 51-52; Corcoran Gallery Art Biennial, Washington, D C,
51-53; Nat Acad Design Ann, New York, 58-62.
Teaching: Prof art, Univ Ill, Champaign, 46-
Mailing Address: 912 Devonshire Dr, Champaign, IL 61820.

SPRAGUE, NANCY KUNZMAN
Sculptor
b New York, N Y, Sept 27, 40.
Study & Training: R I Sch Design; Univ Pa, BFA; Tyler Sch Art,
Temple Univ; Univ Kans; Univ Iowa, MA & MFA.
Work in Public Collections: Tenn Sculpture '71, Tenn Arts Comn,
Fairleigh Dickinson Univ.
Commissions: Bronze sculpture, Friends of Elvis Presley, 71.
Exhibitions: One-man show, Ruth White Gallery, New York, 69;
Young Sculptors Competition, Sculptors Guild, New York, 69;
16th Ann Drawing & Small Sculpture, Ball State Univ, 70; Mid
S Art Exhib, Brooks Mem Art Gallery, Memphis, 71; 24th Ann
Iowa Artists Exhib, Des Moines Art Ctr, 72.
Memberships: Col Art Asn Am.
Dealer: Ruth White Gallery, 401 E 74th St, New York, NY 10021.
Mailing Address: Windham Way, Rte 1, Iowa City, IA 52240.

SPRAYREGEN, MORRIS
Collector
Collection: Primarily French impressionist and post-impressionist
art.
Mailing Address: 812 Park Ave, New York, NY 10021.

SPRIGGS, EDWARD S
Museum Director
Positions: Dir, Studio Mus Harlem.
Mailing Address: Studio Museum in Harlem, 2033 Fifth Ave, New
York, NY 10035.

SPRUCE, EVERETT FRANKLIN
Painter, Printmaker
b Faulkner Co, Ark, Dec 25, 08.
Study & Training: Dallas Art Inst, 25-29; pvt study with Olin H
Travis & Thomas M Stell.
Work in Public Collections: Mus Fine Arts Houston, Tex; Mus Mod
Art, New York, N Y; Calif Palace of Legion of Honor, San Fran-
cisco; Mus Fine Arts Rio de Janeiro, Brazil; Nelson Gallery,
Kansas City, Mo; plus many others.
Exhibitions: Carnegie Inst, Pittsburgh, Pa; Corcoran Gallery Art,
Washington, D C; Brussels, Belg & Bordighera, Italy; Ford
Found Retrospective, circulated nationally by Am Fedn Arts;
Pan-Am Union, Washington, D C; Dallas Mus Fine Arts, Tex;
plus others.
Teaching: Instr, Dallas Mus Sch, 36-40; instr art, Univ Tex, Aus-
tin, 40-44, asst prof, 44-47, chmn dept art, 48-50, prof art &
mem grad fac, 54-
Positions: Gallery asst, Dallas Mus Fine Arts, 31-34, registrar, 35,
asst dir, 35-40.
Awards: Bordighera, Italy, 54; D D Feldman Award, Tex State Fair,
55; Dallas Mus Fine Arts Prize, 55; plus others.
Bibliography: John I H Baur (auth), Revolution and tradition in mod-
ern American art, Harvard Univ Press, 59; John Leeper (auth),
Everett Spruce, Am Fedn Arts, 59; portfolio of paintings, Vol I,
In: Blaffer Series, Univ Tex Press.
Mailing Address: 15 Peak Rd, Austin, TX 78746.

SPRUYT, E LEE
Painter
Preferred Media: Oil & Gouache, Encaustic
b Lisbon, Port, Feb 10, 31; U S citizen.
Study & Training: Apprentice (at 14) to Pachita Crespi; Pratt Inst
Night Sch; Art Stud League New York; R I Sch Design; Carnegie
Inst Technol, scholar to Atheneum Sch, Finland, 3 yrs; study with
Robert Rabinowitz & Samuel Rosenberg.
Work in Public Collections: In Europe & U S.
Exhibitions: Group show, Lord & Taylor, 64, five one-man shows,
65-73; group show, Artists Equity Asn Gallery, New York; Archit
League New York, 70 & 72; Portrait of the Old Met, Mus Per-
forming Arts, Lincoln Ctr, 72-73; 48 drawings & gouache, New
York City.
Teaching: Instr drawing, Carnegie-Mellon Univ; instr art, Boys
Club R I.

Bibliography: 10 drawings, In: Show Mag, 2/70, 3/70; articles, In:
New York Times, 10/72 & Metropolitan Opera Program, 11/72.
Memberships: Artists Equity Asn New York.
Dealer: Lord and Taylor Gallery, 424 Fifth Ave, New York, NY
10018.
Mailing Address: 419 E 91st St, New York, NY 10028.

SPURGEON, SARAH (EDNA M)
Painter, Educator
b Harlan, Iowa, Oct 30, 03.
Study & Training: Univ Iowa, BA & MA; Harvard Univ; Grand Cent
Sch Art; also with Grant Wood, Paul Sachs & others.
Work in Public Collections: Iowa Mem Union, Iowa City; Seattle
Art Mus, Wash; Ginkgo Mus, Vantage, Wash; Henry Gallery, Univ
Wash, Seattle.
Commissions: Mural, Univ Experimental Sch, Iowa City.
Exhibitions: Kansas City Art Inst; Joslyn Mus; Des Moines Art
Salon; Seattle Art Mus; Gumps, San Francisco, Calif; plus
others.
Teaching: Assoc prof art, Cent Wash State Col, 39-42, 44-71,
emer, 71-
Awards: Carnegie fel, 29-30; prizes, Iowa Art Salon, 30 & 31;
prizes, Univ Iowa, 31.
Memberships: Nat Educ Asn; Am Asn Univ Prof; Wash Educ Asn;
Women Painters Wash.
Publications: Contribr to Design & Childhood Educ Mag.
Mailing Address: 204 E 9th St, Ellensburg, WA 98926.

SQUIER, JACK LESLIE
Sculptor, Educator
Preferred Media: Resin, Fiber Glass, Bronze.
b Feb 27, 27; U S citizen.
Study & Training: Ind Univ, BS, 50; Cornell Univ, MFA, 52.
Work in Public Collections: Mus Mod Art, New York, N Y; Whitney
Mus Am Art, New York; Everson Mus, Syracuse, N Y; Johnson
Mus, Cornell Univ; Stanford Univ Mus.
Commissions: Disc (fiber glass & aluminum leaf sculpture), Ithaca
Col, 68.
Exhibitions: Carnegie Int, Pittsburgh; Brussels World's Fair; Re-
cent Sculpture U S A, Mus Mod Art; 30 Americans Under 35, 57
& many ann, Whitney Mus Am Art.
Teaching: Prof sculpture, Cornell Univ, 58-
Bibliography: William Lipke (auth), Disc, by Jack Squier, Cornell
Univ, 68.
Memberships: Int Asn Art (dep v pres, 72-); Sculptors Guild.
Mailing Address: 221 Berkshire Rd, Ithaca, NY 14850.

SQUIRES, GERALD LEOPOLD
Painter, Educator
Preferred Media: Acrylics, Clay.
b Nfld, Can, Nov 17, 37.
Study & Training: Danforth Tech, Toronto; Ont Col Art, Toronto.
Work in Public Collections: Vincent Price Collection; Montreal Mus
Fine Arts; Mem Univ Nfld; Univ Toronto; Saidye & Samuel Bronf-
man Collection, Montreal.
Exhibitions: Ont Soc Artist, 65; Western Ont Ann, 66; Montreal Mus
Fine Arts, 67; Painters in Nfld, 68-71.
Teaching: Art instr, Mem Univ Nfld, 70-, exten artist-in-residence,
72.
Awards: First & second prize, Great Northern AUK Workshop Con-
ceptual Partic Painting & Sculpture, Nfld Arts & Lett Competi-
tion, 72.
Bibliography: Kat Kritzweiser (auth), From a modern squires an
old monk's dream, Globe & Mail Toronto; Nat C B C Show
(recently shown).
Memberships: Great Northern AUK Workshop; founding mem
Oshawa Art Gallery.
Dealers: Ron Mason, Mt Scio Rd, St John's, Nfld, Can; George
Ruckus, Picture Loan Gallery, Toronto, Ont, Can.
Mailing Address: Ferryland, Nfld, Can.

SQUIRES, NORMA-JEAN
Sculptor, Painter
Preferred Media: Wood, Aluminum, Mirrors, Motors.
b Toronto, Ont; U S citizen.
Study & Training: Art Stud League New York; Cooper Univ, cert, 61;
also spec studies with James Rosati, sculptor.
Work in Public Collections: Sterling Forest Gardens, Long Island,
N Y; Galeria Vandres, Madrid, Spain.
Exhibitions: One-woman shows, Hudson River Mus, Yonkers, N Y,
66 & East Hampton Gallery, New York, 69; Affect-Effect, La Jolla
Mus Art, Calif, 69; Recent Trends in American Art, Westmore-
land Co Mus Art, Greensburg, Pa, 69; Sculptured Light, Suffolk
Co Mus, Long Island, N Y, 70; plus others.
Teaching: Instr sculpture, Lucinda Art Sch, Tenafly, N J, 67-69.
Awards: Sarah Cooper Hewitt Award for the Advan of Sci & Art,
Cooper Union, 61.

Bibliography: Shirley Fischler (auth), newspaper profile, In: Toronto Daily Star, 4/68; Burton Wasserman (auth), Modern painting—the movements, the artists, their work, Davis Publ, 70.
Dealer: Orlando Gallery, 17037 Ventura Blvd, Encino, CA 91316.
Mailing Address: 2764 Woodwardia Dr, Los Angeles, CA 90024.

STACHELBERG, MRS CHARLES G
Collector, Patron
b New York, N Y.
Study & Training: Columbia Univ Exten; New York Univ.
Collection: Late nineteenth and twentieth century art.
Mailing Address: 169 E 69th St, New York, NY 10021.

STACKS, LEON
Painter, Art Restorer
Preferred Media: Oils, Acrylics.
b Charlotte, N C, Apr 25, 28.
Study & Training: With W Lester Stevens, 43-45 & William J Potter, 46.
Work in Public Collections: USN Collection, Mariner's Mus, Norfolk, Va; N C Nat Bank, Charlotte; Greenville Art Ctr, N C; Goldsboro Art Ctr, N C; State Univ N Y, Albany; plus other corporate & pvt collections.
Commissions: Restoration commissions, pvt & corporate collections, govt bldgs & univs incl Davidson Col, Wofford Col, Univ S C, Wake Forest Univ, Univ N C, Clemson Col & Winthrop Col, 45-
Exhibitions: Rockport Art Asn Mem Exhib, Mass, 44-46; Piedmont Exhib, Mint Mus, Charlotte, 50; Assoc Artists N C Ann, 69-72; Nat Soc Painters in Casein & Acrylic Open Exhib, New York, 72; Washington Soc Miniature Painters, 72; plus others; also 50 one-man shows at galleries & mus, 45-72.
Collections Arranged: Asst, Elliott Daingerfield Retrospective, Mint Mus, Charlotte & N C State Mus, Raleigh, 71; also contribr to catalog.
Positions: Dir & charter mem, Rockport Summer Group, 45-; mem bd, N C Arts Coun, 72-75.
Memberships: Am Art Soc; Assoc Artists N C (dir, 70-72); Salmagundi Club; Assoc Artists Winston-Salem; Nat Arts Club.
Dealers: American Art Society, Newport News, VA 23607; Shepherd-Lambeth Co, Winston-Salem, NC 27102.
Mailing Address: P O Box 276, Blowing Rock, NC 28605.

STADLER, ALBERT
Painter
Preferred Media: Acrylics.
b New York, N Y, Aug 12, 23.
Study & Training: Univ Pa; Univ Fla.
Exhibitions: Corcoran Gallery Art, Washington, D C; Dayton Art Inst, Ohio; Los Angeles Co Mus Art, Calif; Walker Art Ctr, Minneapolis, Minn; Art Gallery Toronto, Ont; plus many others.
Art Interests: Color, in all its changing hues, chroma's & lights.
Dealer: Fishbach Gallery, 29 W 57th St, New York, NY 10019.
Mailing Address: 1568 Second Ave, New York, NY 10028.

STAEMPFLI, GEORGE W
Art Dealer, Painter
b Bern, Switz, Dec 6, 10; U S citizen.
Study & Training: Univ Erlangen, PhD, 35.
Exhibitions: One-man shows, M Knoedler & Co, New York, 41 & 47.
Positions: Cur, Mus Fine Arts, Houston, Tex, 55-57; coordr fine arts, Am Pavilion, Brussels Expo, 57-58; pres, Staempfli Gallery, 59-
Specialty of Gallery: Contemporary European and American painting and sculpture.
Mailing Address: 47 E 77th St, New York, NY 10021.

STAHL, BEN (ALBERT)
Painter, Illustrator
b Chicago, Ill, Sept 7, 10.
Work in Public Collections: (Illus) Hall of Fame; New Britain Mus Am Art; Albion Col; Adelphi Col; Duke Univ.
Commissions: 14 stations of cross for Cath Bible & Cath Press, Chicago, 55.
Exhibitions: Art Inst Chicago; Nat Acad Design; Audubon Mus; Bridgeport Univ, 69; Fort Lauderdale, Fla, 70; plus others.
Teaching: Mem founding fac, Famous Artists Schs, Westport, Conn, 49-
Positions: Mem bd adv, Am Art Found; founder & v pres, Mus of the Cross, Sarasota, Fla, 65-
Awards: Saltus Gold Medal, Nat Acad Design, 49; Art Dirs Club, Chicago, 49; Art Dirs Club, New York, 52; plus others.
Memberships: Soc Illustrators; Westport Artists (co-founder); Sarasota Art Asn (v pres, 53); Am Artists Prof League; Int Platform Asn.

Publications: Auth & illus, Blackbeard's Ghost, 65; illus, Gone with the wind, anniversary ed; auth & illus, The secret of Red Skull, 71; illusr, Sat Eve Post & other nat mag.
Mailing Address: Siesta Key, Sarasota, FL 33581.

STALEY, ALLEN
Art Historian
b Saint Louis, Mo, June 4, 35.
Study & Training: Princeton Univ, BA, 57; Yale Univ, MA, 60, PhD, 65.
Teaching: Lectr, Frick Collection, New York, 62-65; assoc prof, Columbia Univ, 69-
Positions: Asst cur, Philadelphia Mus Art, 65-68.
Research: English painting.
Publications: Co-auth, Victorian artists in England (catalogue), 65; co-auth, Romantic art in Britain (catalogue), 68; ed, From realism to symbolism: Whistler and his world (catalogue), 71.
Mailing Address: 1 W 72nd St, New York, NY 10023.

STAMATS, PETER OWEN
Collector, Patron
b Cedar Rapids, Iowa, July 20, 29.
Study & Training: Dartmouth Col, BA, 51.
Positions: Mem, Iowa State Arts Coun, 66-70.
Memberships: Am Fedn Arts; Cedar Rapids Art Asn (dir, 58-, pres, 59-60).
Art Interests: Support of Cedar Rapids Art Ctr.
Collection: Fifteenth century to nineteenth century prints.
Mailing Address: 427 Sixth Ave S E, Cedar Rapids, IA 52406.

STAMATY, STANLEY
Cartoonist, Illustrator
Preferred Media: Ink, Watercolors, Acrylics.
b Dayton, Ohio, May 21, 16.
Study & Training: Cincinnati Art Acad.
Commissions: Poster for Fire Prev Wk, Am Ins Asn.
Exhibitions: De Young Mus Cartoon Exhib, 43; Metrop Mus Art Cartoon Exhib.
Positions: Mem adv bd, Guild Creative Art, 65-
Memberships: Nat Cartoonists Soc; Mag Cartoonists Guild (chmn mem comt); Art Dirs Club N J.
Publications: Auth, Fun can be work, Writer's Digest, 49; illusr, McGraw, Am Bk Co, Am J Nursing & Dynamic Maturity.
Mailing Address: P O Box 75, 1019 Woodgate Ave, Elberon, NJ 07740.

STAMM, JOHN DAVIES
Collector
b Milwaukee, Wis, May 2, 14.
Study & Training: New York Univ, BS.
Collection: Modern American paintings; lithographs by Lautrec, as well as books, catalogues, magazines and papers pertaining to him.
Publications: Auth, exhibition catalogue of Lautrec posters & lithographs, Milwaukee Art Inst, 65; auth, introduction to Philip Evergood Exhibition (catalogue).
Mailing Address: 666 Fifth Ave, New York, NY 10018.

STAMOS, THEODOROS (S)
Painter, Educator
b New York, N Y, Dec 31, 22.
Study & Training: Am Artists Sch.
Work in Public Collections: Mus Mod Art, New York; Metrop Mus Art, New York; Whitney Mus Am Art, New York; Univ Calif Mus, Berkeley; N J State Mus, Trenton.
Commissions: Oil mural, SS Arg, 46 & tapestry, New York, 71, Moore McCormack Lines.
Exhibitions: Documenta, Kassel, Ger; New Am Painting, Paris, Zurich, New York, London, Madrid & others; Abstr Expressionists & Imagists, Guggenheim Mus, New York; Dada, Surrealism & Their Inheritors, Mus Mod Art.
Teaching: Instr art, Art Stud League New York; lectr art, Columbia Univ; prof art, Brandeis Univ.
Awards: Brandeis Univ Creative Arts Award; Tiffany Found fel; Nat Arts grant.
Bibliography: K Sawyer (auth), Stamos, Mus Poche Paris, 60; R Pomeroy (auth), Theodoros Stamos, Abrams, 73.
Memberships: Life fel Metrop Mus Art.
Publications: Illusr, Sorrows of cold stone, Dodd.
Dealer: Marlborough Gallery, 41 E 57th St, New York, NY 10022.
Mailing Address: East Marion, NY 11939.

STAMPER, WILLSON YOUNG
Painter, Educator
Preferred Media: Oils.
b New York, N Y, Jan 5, 12.
Study & Training: Art Stud League New York, with Kimon Nocolaides & Rico Lebrun, 32-36; Cincinnati Art Acad, 38-39; schs, USN.

Work in Public Collections: Mus Mod Art, New York; Cincinnati Art Mus, Ohio; Marion Hendrie Collection, Cincinnati; Honolulu Acad Art, Hawaii; State Found Cult & Art, State Capitol, Honolulu.
Commissions: Murals & ceramic tile, State Hawaii Int Airport Bldg, 72.
Exhibitions: World's Fair, San Francisco, 39; Expressionism, El Greco to Picasso, Cincinnati Art Mus, 41; Invitational, Albright-Knox Art Gallery, Buffalo, N Y, 51; Carnegie Int, Pittsburgh, Pa, 52.
Teaching: Instr drawing & painting & head conservator, Cincinnati Art Acad, 37-43; dir art sch & head conservator, Honolulu Acad Art, 45-62.
Awards: First prize, Artists Greater Cincinnati, Cincinnati Art Mus, 42; Grand Prize, 19th Ann, 48 & purchase award, 66, Honolulu Acad Art.
Bibliography: Madge Tennent (auth), Miracle in art, Paradise Pac, 58; Art in Hawaii, House Beautiful, 58. Willson Stamper, La Rev Mod, Paris, 49.
Memberships: Painters & Sculptors Hawaii.
Publications: Co-auth, Stamper, Abels, Richardson, 39; contribr, The development of Eugene, Am Psychol, 40.
Dealer: Downtown Gallery, 125 Merchant St, Honolulu, HI 96813.
Mailing Address: 224 N Kalaheo Ave, Kailua, HI 96734.

STAMPFLE, FELICE
Art Curator, Writer
b Kansas City, Mo, July 25, 12.
Study & Training: Wash Univ, AB & AM; Radcliffe Col.
Positions: Cur drawings & prints, Pierpont Morgan Libr, 45-; ed, Master Drawings, 63-
Research: Drawings, especially eighteenth century Italian.
Publications: Auth, var articles, reviews & exhib catalogues.
Mailing Address: 450 E 63rd St, New York, NY 10021.

STANCZAK, JULIAN
Painter, Educator
b Borownica, Poland, Nov 5, 28; U S citizen.
Study & Training: Uganda, Africa & London, Eng; Cleveland Inst Art, BFA, 54; Yale Univ, MFA, 56, with Albers & Marca-Relli.
Work in Public Collections: Dayton Art Inst, Ohio; Albright-Knox Art Gallery, Buffalo, N Y; Larry Aldrich Mus, Ridgefield, Conn; Des Moines Art Ctr, Iowa; Libr Cong, Washington, D C; plus others.
Exhibitions: One-man shows, Kent State Univ & Dartmouth Col, 68; Albright-Knox Art Gallery, 68; Univ Ill, 69; Herron Mus Art, Indianapolis, Ind, 69; plus other group & one-man shows.
Teaching: Instr, Art Acad Cincinnati, 57-64, instr painting & drawing, Cleveland Inst Art, 64-; artist-in-residence, Dartmouth Col, 68.
Awards: Cleveland Fine Arts Award, 70; Outstanding Educ Am, 70; Ohio Arts Coun Award, 72.
Bibliography: George Rickey (auth), Constructivism: origins and evolution, Braziller, 67; Udo Kultermann (auth), Neue formen des bildes, Verlag Ernst Wasmuth, Tubingen, 69; Kenneth F Bates, (auth), Basic design, World Publ, 70; plus many others.
Memberships: Am Abstract Artists; Am Int Platform Asn.
Research: Pioneer in optical art.
Dealer: Martha Jackson Gallery, 32 E 69th St, New York, NY 10021.
Mailing Address: 6229 Cabrini Lane, Seven Hills, OH 44131.

STANDEN, EDITH APPLETON
Art Historian
b Halifax, N S, Feb 21, 05; U S citizen.
Study & Training: Oxford Univ, BA.
Positions: Art secy, Joseph Widener Collection, Elkins Park, Pa, 29-42; assoc cur, Metrop Mus Art, New York, N Y, 49-70, cur consult, 70-
Memberships: Col Art Asn Am.
Research: European post-medieval tapestries.
Publications: Auth, var articles, In: Metrop Mus Bull, Metrop Mus J & Art Bull, 51-72; co-auth, Art treasures of the Metropolitan, 52 & Decorative art from the Samuel H Kress Collection, 64.
Mailing Address: Metropolitan Museum of Art, Fifth Ave & 82nd St, New York, NY 10028.

STANKIEWICZ, RICHARD PETER
Sculptor, Educator
Preferred Media: Metals.
b Philadelphia, Pa, Oct 18, 22.
Study & Training: With Hans Hofmann, Fernand Leger & Ossip Zadkine.
Work in Public Collections: Whitney Mus Am Art, New York, N Y; Mus Mod Art, New York; Mus Mod Art, Stockholm; Guggenheim Mus, New York; Albright-Knox Mus, Buffalo.
Exhibitions: Venice Biennale, 58; Pittsburgh Int, Carnegie Inst, 58-61; Bienal, Sao Paulo, 61; Four Americans, Mod Mus, Stockholm, 62; Nat Gallery Victoria, Melbourne.

Teaching: Prof art, State Univ N Y Albany, 67-; vis artist, Amherst Col, 70-71.
Awards: Awards, Brandeis Univ & Nat Coun Arts.
Dealer: Zabriskie Gallery, 29 W 57th St, New York, NY 10019.
Mailing Address: Star Rte, Huntington, MA 01050.

STANLEY, BOB
Painter
Preferred Media: Acrylics.
b Yonkers, N Y, Jan 3, 32.
Study & Training: Ogelthorpe Univ, BA; Columbia Univ; Art Stud League New York; Brooklyn Mus Art Sch, Max Beckman painting scholar, 55 & 56.
Work in Public Collections: Whitney Mus Am Art, New York, N Y; Milwaukee Art Ctr, Wis; Wash Univ Mus, St Louis, Mo; Fogg Art Mus, Cambridge, Mass; Metrop Mus Art, New York.
Exhibitions: Whitney Mus Am Art Painting Ann, 67, 69 & 72; Documenta 4, Kassel, Ger, 68; Obsessive Image, Inst Contemp Arts, London, Eng, 68; 29th Ann, Art Inst Chicago, Ill, 69; Monumental Art, Contemp Arts Ctr, Cincinnati, Ohio, 71.
Awards: Cassandra Found Award, 69.
Bibliography: Christgau (auth), Big paintings, Cheetah Mag, 68; Honnef (auth), Mythen des alltags-transzendiert, Gegenverkehr, Aachen, 69; Gassiot-Talabot (auth), Robert Stanley, Opus Int, 12/71-1/72.
Dealer: Paul Bianchini, 14 E 77th St, New York, NY 10021.
Mailing Address: 3 Crosby St, New York, NY 10013.

STANTON, MARTHA ZELT
Printmaker, Instructor
b Washington, Pa, Nov 16, 30.
Study & Training: Conn Col; Pa Acad Fine Arts; New Sch Social Res, with Antonio Frasconi; Mus Arte Mod, Brazil, with John Friedlaender; Univ N Mex, with Garo Antreasian; Temple Univ, BA.
Work in Public Collections: Philadelphia Free Libr, Pa.
Exhibitions: Salao Arte Mod, Rio de Janeiro, Brazil, 61; Int Bienale, São Paulo, Brazil, 61; Pa Acad Fine Arts Nat Ann, 61-70; Var Print Club Nat Exhibs, Philadelphia, 61-; Cheltenham Art Ctr Print Nat, Pa, 71.
Teaching: Instr silk screen, Pa Acad Fine Arts, 68-; instr printmaking, Philadelphia Mus Art, 68-; instr silk screen, Philadelphia Col Art, 69-
Positions: Dir, graphic workshop prof artists, Pa Acad Fine Arts, 63-65; demonstrating artist-printmaker, Prints-in-Progress, Philadelphia, 63-71; secy, Exp in Art & Technol, Inc, Philadelphia, 68.
Awards: Cresson traveling award, 54 & Scheidt Mem traveling award, Pa Acad Fine Arts; Print Club fel, 65.
Memberships: Print Club; fel Pa Acad Fine Arts.
Mailing Address: 605 N Ithan Ave, Rosemont, PA 19010.

STAPP, RAY VERYL
Educator, Painter
Preferred Media: Oils.
b Norton, Kans, July 10, 13.
Study & Training: Bethany Col, Lindsborg, Kans, BFA, with Birger Sandzen; Kansas City Art Inst, life with Thomas Hart Benton; Art Stud League, New York, N Y, with Dumond, Reilly & Trafton; teachers col, Columbia Univ, BA, with Ziegfield; Pa State Univ, EdD, with Lowenfeld.
Work in Public Collections: Painting, Lowenfeld Mem Collection, Pa State Univ.
Exhibitions: Nat Craft & Ceramics Show, Wichita Art Asn, Kans, 57; Erie Art Asn, Pa, 60; 18th Ann Area Show, Peoria, Ill, 69.
Teaching: Instr & asst prof design & art educ, Bethany Col, 49-56; asst prof & assoc prof art, Edinboro State Col, 57-64; assoc prof & prof design & art educ, Eastern Ill Univ, 64-
Positions: Engraver & lithographer, Hallmark Card Co, 37-39; advert artist, Armstrong Cork Co, 48-49; prod illusr, Boeing Airplane Co, 56-57.
Memberships: Nat Art Educ Asn; Western Arts; Ill Art Educ Asn (coun mem, 69-70).
Research: Relationships of measures of creativity, general intelligence and memory; extension of research used as criteria for evaluating children in grades 4-8.
Publications: Auth, You can mix your own glazes, 58 & Planning an art lesson, 67, Arts & Activities.
Mailing Address: 42 Circle Dr, Charleston, IL 61920.

STAPRANS, RAIMONDS
Painter, Sculptor
Preferred Media: Oils, Plastics.
b Riga, Latvia, Oct 13, 26; U S citizen.
Study & Training: Sch Art, Esslinger, Stuttgart, 46; Univ Wash, BA, 52; Univ Calif, MA, 55; also with Archipenko.

Work in Public Collections: Calif Palace Legion of Honor, San Francisco, Calif; Oakland Mus, Calif; Santa Barbara Mus, Calif; Los Angeles Co Mus; Phoenix Art Mus.
Exhibitions: Portland Art Mus, Ore, 56 & 57; Oakland Art Mus, 57; Palace Legion of Honor Winter Invitational, 57, 59 & 60; Litton Industs, 62; Am Acad Arts & Lett, New York, N Y, 70; plus many one-man shows in U S, Can & Europe.
Bibliography: California canvas (film), KRON, San Francisco, 66; Artists eye (film), Motion Media, 67.
Dealer: Maxwell Galleries, 551 Sutter, San Francisco, CA 94102.
Mailing Address: 2052 20th St, San Francisco, CA 94107.

STARK, GEORGE KING
Educator, Sculptor
Preferred Media: Brass.
b Schenectady, N Y, June 14, 23.
Study & Training: State Univ N Y Col Buffalo, BS(art educ); teachers col, Columbia Univ, MA; State Univ N Y Buffalo, EdD; also with Dorothy Denslow.
Work in Public Collections: IBM Collection; Lowe Art Mus, Univ Miami, Fla; Am Art Clay Co; State Univ N Y Col Buffalo; State Univ N Y Col Oswego; also in pvt collections.
Commissions: Sculptured light fixtures, Savoy Hilton Hotel, New York, 59; Space Modulator, Sheraton-Palace Hotel, San Francisco, Calif, 60; divider screen, Park-Sheraton Hotel, New York, 60; wall relief sculpture, Prudential Steamship Lines, New York, 61; sculptured fountain, comn by Robert E Maytag, Newton, Iowa, 71.
Exhibitions: 17th & 19th Ceramic Nat, 52 & 56 & Ceramic Int Exhib, 58, Syracuse Mus Fine Arts; Western N Y Ann, Albright-Knox Gallery, Buffalo, 57 & 60; one-man show, Lowe Art Mus, 67.
Teaching: Prof art, State Univ N Y Col Oswego, 64-
Awards: Shared first prize for ceramic sculpture, 19th Ceramic Nat, 56; Am Inst Architects Sculpture Award, Albright-Knox Gallery, 57 & 60.
Research: Analysis of artist-teacher's statements on their creativity.
Publications: Auth, Silent images, 11/63 & Mass communication and faculty/student dialogue, 4/69, Art Educ J; auth, On sculpture, Sch Arts, 3/64; auth, A games theory in education, Sch & Soc, fall 67; auth, Think stream, S & W, fall 69-winter 70.
Mailing Address: 229 E Seventh St, Oswego, NY 13126.

STARK, MELVILLE F
Painter, Educator
Preferred Media: Oils, Watercolors, Pastels, Acrylics.
b Honesdale, Pa, Sept 29, 03.
Study & Training: East Stroudsburg State Col; Univ Pa, MS; Mus Col Fine Arts, Philadelphia; Syracuse Univ, with Cullan Yates & W E Baum; also in Eng & France.
Work in Public Collections: Several U S Embassies; Lehigh Co Ct House, Allentown, Pa; Allentown City Hall; Reading Art Mus, Pa; plus many others.
Exhibitions: Am Watercolor Soc; Pa Acad Fine Arts; Nat Soc Painters Casein; Mus Fine Arts, Springfield, Mass; Philadelphia Watercolor Club.
Teaching: Head dept painting, Baum Art Sch Allentown Art Mus, 31-62, dir, Sch, 56-62; head dept painting, Cedar Crest Col, 40-55; head dept art hist, Muhlenberg Col, 55-60.
Positions: Dir, Allentown Art Mus, 54-60.
Awards: First Myers Mem Award, Nat Soc Painters Casein; first prize for landscape, Manatee Art League, Brandenton, Fla; hon mention, Mus Fine Arts, Springfield.
Memberships: Mus Fine Arts, Springfield; Rockport Art Asn; N Shore Art Asn; Sarasota Art Asn; Knickerbocker Art Club.
Mailing Address: R D 1, Zionsville, PA 18092.

STARK, RONALD C
Photographer, Lecturer
b Sidney, N Y, June 27, 44.
Study & Training: Univ Denver; N Y State Univ, BA.
Work in Public Collections: Baltimore Mus Art, Md; Smithsonian Inst, Washington, D C.
Commissions: Walt Disney Movie Stills, comn by M Goldfarb, Denver, Colo, 65; photo exhib, comn by L Hager, Woodland Mus, Cooperstown, N Y, 67 & 68; photo exhib, N Y State Univ, 68.
Exhibitions: Baltimore Mus Art, 70; Mass Inst Technol Gallery, Boston, 71; one-man shows, Studio Gallery, Washington, D C & Graphiks Biennale, Vienna, Austria, 72; Corcoran Gallery Art, 72.
Teaching: Stud lectr commun, Univ Denver, 62-64; stud lectr photog, film & TV, State Univ N Y, 66-68; mem faculty, Smithsonian Inst, 69-
Dealers: Studio Gallery, 1735 Connecticut Ave N W, Washington, DC 20009; Neikrug Gallery, 224 E 68th St, New York, NY 10021.
Mailing Address: 6048½ Ramshorn Pl, McLean, VA 22101.

STARKS, ELLIOTT ROLAND
Art Administrator, Educator
b Madison, Wis, Feb 24, 22.
Study & Training: Univ Wis-Madison, BS, 43, MS, 46.
Collections Arranged: Wis Union Collection Original Art, 51-; Frank Lloyd Wright, 55; Alexander Calder Exhib, 56; Leo Steppat Mem Sculpture Exhib, 67.
Teaching: Instr art, Amphitheater Sch, Tucson, Ariz, 46-47; instr art, Thomas Sch, Tucson, 48-50; asst prof social educ & dir Wis Union, Univ Wis-Madison, 51-
Memberships: Madison Art Asn; Elvehjem Art Ctr; Wis Arts Coun; Int Asn Col Unions.
Publications: Auth, Arts and crafts in the college union, 62.
Mailing Address: Wisconsin Union Galleries, 800 Langdon St, Madison, WI 53706.

STARRS, MILDRED
Painter, Instructor
Preferred Media: Watercolors.
b Brooklyn, N Y.
Study & Training: Maxwell Training Sch Teachers; Pratt Inst; New York Univ, cert, with J Haney.
Work in Public Collections: Meadowbrook Hosp, L I; John F Kennedy Bldg Art Gallery; George Washington Univ Law Sch, Washington, D C; Nat Gallery Sports, New York, N Y.
Commissions: Toni, Lauri, Dr & Mrs Alfred Lapin, N Y; Terri, Mr & Mrs Richard Wheeler, N Y; Jennifer, Mr & Mrs Victor Borod, Miami, Fla; Summer & Winter (two), Mr & Mrs Michael McCormack, N Y; Hollywood, Mrs Frederick Paulsen, N Y.
Exhibitions: One-man shows, Barbizon Gallery, New York, 65-67 & George Washington Univ, 66; Acad Artists Asn, Springfield Mus, Mass, 65-72; Nat Gallery, Catharine Lorillard Wolfe Art Club, 67; Allied Artists Am, Nat Gallery, New York, 71.
Teaching: Instr art, Bd Educ, New York, 27-61; chmn art, 46-61.
Awards: First prize, St Luke Art Guild, 63 & 64; best in show, Catharine Lorillard Wolfe Art Club, 67; spec award, Nat Art League, 70.
Memberships: Am Artists Prof League (treas, 67-); Nat Art League (v pres, 62-); Catharine Lorillard Wolfe Art Club (mem bd dirs, 71-); Hudson Valley Art Asn; Acad Artists Asn.
Mailing Address: 301 Park Lane, Douglaston, NY 11363.

STASACK, EDWARD ARMEN
Painter, Printmaker
b Chicago, Ill, Oct 1, 29.
Study & Training: Univ Ill, BFA & MFA.
Work in Public Collections: Libr Cong, Washington, D C; Honolulu Acad Arts, Hawaii; Philadelphia Mus Art, Pa; Boston Pub Libr, Mass; Achenbach Found Collection, San Francisco, Calif; Palace Legion of Honor.
Commissions: Precast concrete murals, City of Honolulu, Fort St Mall, 68, Chart House Restaurant, Honolulu, 69 & Honolulu Community Col, 72.
Exhibitions: Japan Print Biennial, Tokyo, 62; Carnegie Int, Pittsburgh, Pa, 65; one-man show, Downtown Gallery, New York, N Y, 65; Krakow Print Biennial, Poland, 70; Buenos Aires Print Biennial, Arg, 70.
Teaching: Prof art & chmn dept, Univ Hawaii, 69-
Positions: Mem adv comt, Contemp Arts Ctr Hawaii, 69-; mem bd, Artist-In-Residence Prog, State of Hawaii, 70-; mem adv comt, Hawaii 200th Cong U S & Hawaii Bicentennial Celebrations, 71-
Awards: Tiffany Found fel, 58; Rockefeller Found fel, 59; MacDowall Colony Found fel, 71.
Bibliography: George Tahara (auth), Drawing—painting—Stasack (film), 67.
Memberships: Soc Am Graphic Artists; Honolulu Printmakers (pres, 59-61); Hawaii Painters & Sculptors; Boston Printmakers.
Publications: Auth, Hawaiian petroglyphs, Malamalama Mag, 67; auth, reviews, Honolulu Star-Bull, 68; co-auth, Hawaiian petroglyphs, Bishop Mus, 70.
Mailing Address: 2560 Campus Rd, Honolulu, HI 96822.

STASIK, ANDREW J
Painter, Educator
b New Brunswick, N J, Mar 16, 32.
Study & Training: New York Univ; Columbia Univ, BFA, 54; Univ Iowa; Ohio Univ, MFA, 56.
Work in Public Collections: Mus Fine Arts, Budapest, Hungary; Nat Mus, Krakow, Poland; Metrop Mus Art, New York, N Y; Nat Collection Fine Arts, Washington, D C; Cleveland Mus Fine Art; plus many others.
Exhibitions: Int Biennale Graphics, Krakow, Poland, 66, 68, 70 & 72; Int Expos Original Drawings, Rijeka, Yugoslavia, 68; Prints/Multiples, Univ Wash, 70; Fourth Am Biennale Santiago, Chile, 70; plus many other group & one-man shows in Austria, Norway, Yugoslavia, Porto Alegre, Romania, P R, Poland, Can, Sweden, New York, Japan, Pa & Ohio.

Teaching: Asst prof printmaking, Pratt Inst.
Positions: Vis critic printmaking, Yale Univ; ed, Print/Printmaking Rev; dir, Pratt Graphics Ctr.
Awards: Purchase award, Okla Art Ctr, 12th Ann Nat Exhib Prints & Drawings, 70; purchase prize, Multiples Exhib, Western Mich Univ, 70; President's award in graphics, Audubon Artists Ann, 70; plus many others.
Publications: Auth & illusr, Prints and poems (folio), 63; ed, Printmaking in Eastern Europe, Abrams, 71.
Mailing Address: Pratt Graphics Center, 831 Broadway, New York, NY 10003.

STATMAN, JAN B
Painter
Preferred Media: Oils, Acrylics, Watercolors.
b New York, N Y.
Study & Training: Hunter Col, with William Baziotes, Bernard Klonis & Richard Lippold, AB; also with Saul Berliner
Work in Public Collections: Mus Mod Art Alto Aragón, Huesca, Spain; Civic Mus Contemp Art, Sasso Ferrato, Italy; Longview Bank & Trust Co, Tex; Temple Emanu-El, Longview; plus others.
Exhibitions: Jr Serv League Ann, Longview, 65-72; 1st Ann Small Paintings Exhib, N Mex Art League, Albuquerque, 71; 13th Ann Nat Sun Carnival Art Exhib, El Paso Mus Art, Tex, 71; 32nd Ann Nat Exhib, Cedar City Art Comt, Utah, 72; Ann 9-State Exhib, Barnwell Art Ctr, Shreveport, La, 70.
Teaching: Consult art, Longview Independent Sch Dist, 60-64; instr painting, Red Barn Arts Crafts Ctr, Longview, 69-71; instr painting, Longview Mus & Arts Ctr, 72-
Awards: Circuit merit, Laguna Gloria Mus, Tex Fine Arts Spring Exhib, 63; merit award & jury mention, N Mex Art League W & Southwest Exhib, 70; Longview Bank & Trust Co Award, E Tex Fine Arts Asn, 70.
Memberships: Tex Fine Arts Asn; E Tex Fine Arts Asn.
Publications: Auth, Art notes (weekly column), Longview News, 65-70; auth, Artist's world (weekly column), Women's World Weekly, 70-
Dealer: L & L Gallery, 1107 N Fourth St, Longview, TX 75601.
Mailing Address: 27 Country Pl, Longview, TX 75601.

STEADMAN, WILLIAM EARL
Museum Director
b Pigeon, Mich, Jan 31, 21.
Study & Training: With Josef Albers & Willem De Kooning; Mich State Univ, BS, 42; Univ Ariz, BFA (art hist), 46; Yale Univ, BFA (archit & design), 50, MFA (archit & design), 51.
Collections Arranged: Charles Burchfield, His Golden Year, 65-66; Homage to Seurat, 68-69; East Side, West Side (Reginald Marsh Retrospective), 69; Van Dongen Retrospective (1st in America), 71; Childe Hassam Retrospective, 72.
Positions: Asst dir & head mus art sch, N Mex Mus, Roswell, 51-52; asst dir & head mus art sch, Canton Art Inst, Ohio, 52-53; cur fine arts, U S Mil Acad, West Point, N Y, 53-58; dir, Mus Fine Arts, Little Rock, Ark, 58-59; dir, Univ Ariz Mus Art, 61-
Publications: Ed, Charles Burchfield, his golden year (catalogue), 65; auth & ed, Homage to Seurat (catalogue), 68; ed, East side, west side (catalogue), 69; ed, Cornelius Theodorus Marie Van Dongen (catalogue), 71; auth & ed, Childe Hassam (catalogue), 72.
Mailing Address: University of Arizona Museum of Art, Olive & Speedway, Tucson, AZ 85721.

STEBBINS, THEODORE ELLIS, JR
Art Historian, Art Administrator
b New York, N Y, Aug 11, 38.
Study & Training: Yale Univ, BA, 60; Harvard Univ Law Sch, JD, 64, Harvard Univ, PhD, 71.
Collections Arranged: Luminous Landscape, Fogg Art Mus, 66; Martin Johnson Heade, Whitney Mus Am Art, 69; New Haven Scene, New Haven Colony Hist Soc, 70.
Teaching: Instr hist art, Smith Col, 67; asst prof hist art, Yale Univ, 69-, Morse fel, 72.
Positions: Assoc cur, Garvan Collections, Yale Univ Art Gallery, 68-, cur Am painting & sculpture, 71-
Awards: Chester Dale fel, Nat Gallery Art, Washington, D C, 66.
Memberships: Col Art Asn Am; Am Fedn Arts.
Research: American landscape painting of the nineteenth century; history of American drawings and watercolors.
Collection: Nineteenth and twentieth century American art.
Publications: Auth, Richardson and Trinity Church, J Soc Archit Historians, 68; Thomas Cole at Crawford Notch, Nat Gallery Art, 68, Martin Johnson Heade, Whitney Mus Am Art, 69 & American landscape: some new acquisitions at Yale, Yale Univ Art Gallery Bull, autumn 71; contrib auth, 19th century American painting from Cole to Whistler, In: Britannica Encycl of Am Art, Chanticleer Press, 73.
Mailing Address: Yale University Art Gallery, New Haven, CT 06510.

STECHOW, WOLFGANG
Art Historian
b Kiel, Ger, June 5, 96; U S citizen.
Study & Training: Univ Freiburg, 14; Univ Berlin, 20; Univ Göttingen, PhD, 21; Univ Mich, hon LHD, 66; Oberlin Col, hon DFA, 67.
Teaching: From instr art hist to asst prof, Univ Göttingen, 26-36; from asst prof art hist to assoc prof, Univ Wis, 36-40; prof art hist, Oberlin Col, 40-63; vis prof, Univ Mich, Williams Col, Smith Col, Vassar Col, Yale Univ, Cleveland Mus, Nat Gallery & others, 63-72.
Positions: Consult comt, Art Quart & Calif Studies in the History of Art; ed, Art Bull, 50-52.
Memberships: Col Art Asn Am (v pres, 45-46); Nat Comt Hist Art; Am Soc Aesthet; Archaeol Inst Am.
Research: Fifteenth to seventeenth century northern painting; iconography.
Publications: Auth, Apollo und Daphne, 32 & 65, Salomon van Ruysdael, 38, Dutch landscape painting of the 17th century, 66 & 68, Rubens and the classical tradition, 67 & Bruegel, 69.
Mailing Address: 21 Robin Park, Oberlin, OH 44074.

STECZYNSKI, JOHN MYRON
Sculptor, Educator
b Chicago, Ill, June 22, 36.
Study & Training: Art Inst Chicago; Craft Ctr, Worcester, Mass; Univ Notre Dame, BFA; Yale Univ, Woodrow Wilson fel, 58, MFA; Acad Fine Arts, Polish Govt grant, 60, Warsaw; also with Umberto Romano.
Commissions: Wood relief panels, Ursuline Provincialate, Kirkwood, Mo; wood sculpture, Moreau Sem, Notre Dame, Ind; banners, Little Flower Church, South Bend, Ind; St Mark's Episcopal Church, Worcester, Mass & others.
Exhibitions: One-man shows, Warsaw, Poland & Worcester Art Mus, 61; Craftsmen of the Northeastern States, Worcester, Mass, 63; Craftsmen of the Eastern States, circulated by Smithsonian Inst, 63-64; Christocentric Arts Festival, Univ Ill, 64; Prints for Collectors, Worcester Craft Ctr, 64; plus others.
Teaching: Lect, Modern Liturgical Art, Polish Folk Art & Byzantine Art to clubs & univ groups; prof art, Worcester Art Mus Sch; instr art hist, Boston Mus Fine Arts Sch, 61-63; asst prof & chmn dept art, Newton Col of the Sacred Heart, at present.
Awards: Univ Ill, 53; Polish Arts Club Chicago Prize, 59; Chopin Fine Arts Club Award, Butler Inst Am Art, 61.
Mailing Address: 16 Sunnyside Lane, R F D 2, Lincoln, MA 01773.

STEELE, IVY (NEWMAN)
Sculptor, Educator
Preferred Media: Bronze, Wood, Resins.
b Saint Louis, Mo, Apr 15, 08.
Study & Training: Wash Univ Art Sch; Art Inst Chicago; Wellesley Col, BA; also with Cosmo Campoli, Chicago.
Work in Public Collections: Wellesley Art Mus, Mass.
Commissions: Epoxy exterior relief, Covenant Methodist Church, Evanston, Ill, 68; Flight (bronze sculpture), Highland Park Hosp, Ill, 70; relief sculpture (polyester resin), Ravinia Nursery Sch, Highland Park, 71.
Exhibitions: 4th Ann Watercolors, Drawings & Prints, Oakland Art Gallery, Calif, 36; 1st Nat Exhib Lithography, Okla Art Ctr, Oklahoma City, 39; Sculpture By Chicago Artists, Art Inst Chicago, 40; one-man show, Am Inst Architects, Chicago Chap, 59; Sculpture Show, Ruth White Gallery, 64-65.
Teaching: Instr art, Francis W Parker Sch, Chicago, 41-45; instr art, Hull House Art Sch, 45-54; instr art, Psychom & Psychiat Res Inst Chicago, 60-71.
Bibliography: Ivy Steele, La Rev Mod, 38; article, In: Inland Architect, 59.
Memberships: Arts Club Chicago; Renaissance Soc Univ Chicago; Artists Equity Asn (v pres, secy, dir, mem var comts); Chicago Soc Artists (secy, dir, first v pres); Col Art Asn Am.
Dealer: Berenice Green, 1209 Astor St, Chicago, IL 60657.
Mailing Address: 456 Barry Ave, Chicago, IL 60657.

STEFANELLI, JOSEPH J
Painter
b Philadelphia, Pa, Mar 20, 21.
Study & Training: Philadelphia Mus Col Art, 38-40; Pa Acad Fine Arts, 40-41; New Sch Social Res, New York, N Y, 49-50; Art Stud League New York, 50-51; Hans Hofmann Sch Painting, New York, 51-52.
Work in Public Collections: Whitney Mus Am Art; Walker Art Ctr; Norfolk Art Mus; Baltimore Mus; New York Univ; plus others.
Exhibitions: Many ann, Whitney Mus Am Art, Corcoran Gallery Art, Carnegie Int & Art Inst Chicago; one-man shows, Westbeth Galleries, 71 & New Sch Social Res, 72; plus other group & one-man shows.

Teaching: Instr, Univ Calif, Berkeley, summers 60 & 63; vis critic, Cornell Univ; artist-in-residence, Princeton Univ, 63-66; Spear Res Fund Award, Rome, summer 65; vis critic, Univ Ark; instr, Columbia Univ, 66-; instr, New Sch Social Res, 66-
Awards: Fulbright Award for Rome, 58-59; Am Res Ctr Egypt fel, 66-67; N Y State Coun Arts Award, 71.
Mailing Address: 463 West St, New York, NY 10014.

STEFANOTTY, ROBERT ALAN
Art Dealer
b Arlington, N J, Feb 1, 47.
Study & Training: Bowland Col, Univ Lancaster, Eng, AB (hons), aesthet with Prof Sibley; Bryn Mawr Grad Sch.
Positions: Mgr, Felix Landau Gallery, Los Angeles, 70-71; asst dir, La Boetie, New York, 71-72; dir, Gimpel & Weitzenhoffer, Ltd, 72-
Mailing Address: 1040 Madison Ave, New York, NY 10021.

STEG, J L
Printmaker
b Alexandria, Va.
Study & Training: Rochester Inst Technol, 3 yr cert; State Univ Iowa, BFA & MFA.
Work in Public Collections: Libr Cong, Washington, D C; Smithsonian Nat Collection, Washington, D C; Brooklyn Mus, N Y; Mus Mod Art, New York, N Y; Fogg Mus, Cambridge, Mass.
Commissions: Ed of 50 prints, Assoc Am Artists, 66.
Exhibitions: Eighth Int Print & Drawing Exhib, Lugano, Switz, 64; Eight Am Intaglio Printmakers, Ger, 65; Graphic Arts U S A to Russia, 66; Prints of Two Worlds, Rome & Philadelphia, 66; Big Prints U S A, State Univ N Y Col New Paltz, 68.
Teaching: Instr drawing & painting, Cornell Univ, 49-51; prof drawing & printing, Tulane Univ La, 51-
Awards: Charles Lea Prize, Philadelphia Print Club, 50-64; purchase prize, Eighth Int Print & Drawing Exhib, Lugano, 64; purchase prizes, State Univ N Y Col Potsdam Print Exhib, 64-68.
Memberships: Am Color Print Soc.
Publications: Auth, article, In: Artists proof, 66.
Dealer: Associated American Artists, 663 Fifth Ave, New York, NY 10022.
Mailing Address: Newcomb College Dept of Art, Tulane University, New Orleans, LA 70118.

STEGALL, JAMES PARK
Painter, Instructor
Preferred Media: Oils.
b Wichita Falls, Tex, Feb 8, 42.
Study & Training: Pa Acad Fine Arts, Philadelphia; restoration of painting with Marilyn Roswell Weidner; also with Walter Stuempfif & Ben Kamihira, Spain.
Exhibitions: Nat Acad Design, New York, 56-64; Pa Acad Fine Arts Ann, 63-65, Pa Acad Fine Arts fel, 65; Pittsburgh Nat, 65, Pa; Tarrant Co Ann, Fort Worth, Tex, 68.
Teaching: Instr art, Fort Worth Art Ctr Mus, 68-
Awards: Cresson Mem Award, Pa Acad Fine Arts, 64; first purchase award, Pittsburgh Nat, 65; first prize, Tarrant Co Ann, 69.
Dealer: Carlin Galleries, 710 Montgomery, Fort Worth, TX 76107.
Mailing Address: 5110 Byers, Fort Worth, TX 76107.

STEGEMAN, CHARLES
Painter, Educator
Preferred Media: Oils, Acrylics.
b Ede, Netherlands, June 5, 24; Can citizen.
Study & Training: Acad Beeldende Kunst, The Hague; Acad Royale Beaux Arts, Brussels; Inst Nat Superieur Beaux-Arts, Antwerp.
Work in Public Collections: Nat Gallery Can; Ont Art Gallery; Vancouver Art Gallery; Art Gallery Greater Victoria; Univ B C.
Exhibitions: Western Art Circuit, Western Can, 52-53; Toronto Art Gallery, 61; Winnipeg Biann, 61; Montreal Mus Fine Arts, 62; Chicago Centennial Exhib, Ill, 63.
Teaching: Assoc prof painting, Art Inst Chicago, 62-69; assoc prof painting & chmn dept, Haverford Col, 69-
Dealer: Harold Patton, 17500 Fenway Dr, Detroit, MI 48221.
Mailing Address: 1930 Lafayette Rd, Gladwyne, PA 19035.

STEIDER, DORIS
Painter
Preferred Media: Egg Tempera.
b Decatur, Ill, 24.
Study & Training: Purdue Univ, BS(appl design), 45; Univ N Mex, MA(fine art), 65.
Commissions: Christmas card design for Int Cardiovascular Found, 60; Christmas card for N Mex Crippled Children's Soc, 64; cover brochure for Nat Coun Teachers Math, 69; Christmas card for Delta Gamma Sorority, 70; murals, St Joseph's Hosp, Albuquerque; plus others.

Exhibitions: Smithsonian Inst; Army Traveling Print Shows, 63 & 64; Albuquerque Invitational, 64, Ann Traveling Shows, 66- & Southwest Biennials, Mus N Mex; Witte Mus Western Art Show, San Antonio, Tex; El Paso Sun Carnival, Tex; plus many other group & one-man shows.
Awards: Popular awards, 63-65, first prize prints & drawings, 64, first prize acrylics & second prize oils, 67 & 69, purchase prizes 70 & 71, N Mex State Fair; Spec Award for traditional oils, Nat League Am Pen Women Shows, Tulsa, 65; second prize, 14th Ann Black Canyon Painters Parade, Hotchkiss, Colo, 72; plus others.
Bibliography: Article & illus, In: Trailer Life, 6/69; article & cover, In: Pen Woman Mag, 3/69 & 6/72; plus others.
Memberships: Nat League Am Pen Women (nat art bd); Artists Equity Asn; N Mex Arts & Crafts Fair (bd mem, six yrs); Albuquerque Fine Arts Advisory Bd.
Publications: Illus, Check series for Citizen's Bank, Albuquerque; paintings reproduced for cards, nat distribution, Saga Printers.
Dealers: Brandywine Galleries, 122 Tulane Dr S E, Albuquerque, NM 87106; Baker Collector Gallery, P O Box 1920, Lubbock, TX 79408.
Mailing Address: 1601 Kirby N E, Albuquerque, NM 87112.

STEIG, WILLIAM
Cartoonist, Sculptor
Preferred Media: Wood.
b New York, N Y, Nov 14, 07.
Study & Training: City Col New York, 23-25; Nat Acad Design, 25-29.
Work in Public Collections: Wood sculpture, R I Mus Art & Smith Col; paintings, Brooklyn Mus.
Exhibitions: One-man wood sculpture exhib, Downtown Gallery, New York, 39; drawings & sculpture, Smith Col, 40; plus others.
Awards: Caldecott Medal, 70.
Publications: Auth & illusr, Sylvester and the magic pebble, 69, The bad island, 69, An eye for elephants, 70, Amos & Boris, 71 & Male/female, 71; contribr, New Yorker & other leading mag.
Mailing Address: 82 Washington Pl, New York, NY 10011.

STEIN, HARVE
Painter, Educator
Preferred Media: Watercolors.
b Chicago, Ill, Apr 23, 04.
Study & Training: Art Inst Chicago, 22-26; Julian Acad, Paris, France, 27; Art Stud League New York, 30-33; also with Harvey Dunn.
Work in Public Collections: U S State Dept; Univ Minn; Brown Univ; Pub Arch, Toronto; Montclair Art Mus, N J; plus others.
Exhibitions: Nat Watercolor Exhibs throughout U S.
Teaching: Instr painting, Conn Col, 46, 47 & 51; instr, New London Art Stud League, 48-59; Mitchell Col, summer session, 55-56; emer prof fine art, R I Sch Design.
Positions: Dir, Stone Ledge Studio Art Galleries, Noank, Conn, 63-
Awards: Providence Watercolor Club, 56; New Haven Paint & Clay Club, 57; Providence Art Club, 63; plus others.
Memberships: Hon life mem Soc Illustrators; Am Watercolor Soc; Audubon Artists; Artists Fel; Appraisers Asn Am; plus others.
Publications: Illusr, many bks; contribr, nat mags; auth, The illustrator explains, Am Artist Mag, 58.
Mailing Address: P O Box 237, Noank, CT 06340.

STEIN, MAURICE JAY
Painter, Designer
b New York, N Y, Mar 26, 98.
Study & Training: Cooper Union; Pratt Inst, City Col New York; Acad Venice; Columbia Univ.
Work in Public Collections: Seaman & Int Inst Gallery, New York; Univ Maine, Orono; St Peters Episcopal Church, Rockland, Maine; Yeshiva Univ, New York; Col John Hamilton Gillespie Mus, Sarasota, Fla.
Commissions: Portraits, Dr Jonas E Salk, Virus Res, Univ Pittsburgh, 59, Capt Eddie Rickenbacker, USA, 60 & Lt Gen August Shomburg, USA, 61; Christ, St Peters Episcopal Church, 68; Profet Micah, Temple Judea, Manhasset, N Y, 70.
Exhibitions: United Irish Charities, New York, 62; Nat Soc Arts & Lett, 63; Farnsworth Mus, Rockland, 63 & 64; Palette Scholar Award Show, New York, 67; 20 Selected Professionals, March of Dimes, 68.
Teaching: Instr oil painting, Treasure Art Guild, Paramus, N J, 62-65; instr oil painting, Synagogue Golden Age Group, 64-67.
Positions: Designer of jewelry for var mfrs, 20-50; chmn, Palette Scholar Award Comt, 67.
Awards: Grumbacher award of merit, 61; first prize gold medal, United Irish Co Charities, Hunter Col 30th Art Exhib, 62; gold medal for yr, Cath Fine Arts Soc, 70; plus others.
Memberships: Hon mem Kappi Pi; fel Royal Soc Arts; Nat Soc Arts & Lett (treas, 66); hon mem Cath Fine Arts Soc.

Art Interests: Founded Palette Scholarship Award for honor art high school students in 1967; now has three chapters with plans made for national coverage.
Mailing Address: 969 Park Ave, Studio 6A, New York, NY 10028.

STEIN, RONALD JAY
Sculptor
Preferred Media: Plastic.
b New York, N Y, Sept 15, 30.
Study & Training: Cooper Union, cert fine art, with Will Barnet; Yale Univ, BFA, with Joseph Albers; Rutgers Univ, MFA.
Work in Public Collections: Carnegie Inst, Pittsburgh, Pa; Guggenheim Mus, New York; Tenn Fine Arts Ctr, Nashville; Wadsworth Atheneum, Hartford, Conn; Loch Haven Art Ctr, Fla.
Commissions: Mosaic murals (with Lee Krasner Pollock), Uris Bros, New York, 58.
Exhibitions: Carnegie Int, 57; Inst Contemp Art, Boston, 58; Art Inst Chicago Int, 60; one-man show, Marlborough Gallery, London, Eng, 67; Art in the Mirror, Mus Mod Art, New York, 70.
Dealer: Marlborough Gallery, 41 E 57th St, New York, NY 10022.
Mailing Address: 76 E 79th St, New York, NY 10021.

STEIN, WALTER
Painter, Sculptor
Preferred Media: Oils, Watercolors, Aluminum, Plastic.
b New York, N Y, Nov 30, 24.
Study & Training: Art Stud League New York; Cooper Union; New York Univ; New Sch Social Res; Acad Belle Arti, Florence.
Work in Public Collections: Phillips Collection, Washington, D C; Indianapolis Mus Art; Fogg Art Mus, Cambridge, Mass; Mus Mod Art, New York; Metrop Mus Art, New York.
Teaching: Instr painting, Scarsdale Art Ctr, N Y, 68-69; instr drawing, Cooper Union, 69-70; instr painting, Five Towns Art Ctr, N Y, 70-71.
Publications: Ed & illusr, Common botany, 53; illusr, Histoires naturelles, Harvard Univ Press, 60; ed & illusr, Tichborne's elegy, 68.
Mailing Address: 11 Cooper Sq, New York, NY 10003.

STEINBERG, ISADOR N
Painter, Designer
b Odessa, Russia, June 14, 00.
Study & Training: Sch Design & Lib Arts, scholar; Art Stud League New York; New York Univ; Grand Chaumiere, Paris, France; also with John Sloan & Max Weber.
Commissions: USA courses in Botany, Surveying, Lettering, Mechanical Drawing & others.
Exhibitions: Newark Art Club; Am Inst Graphic Arts Fifth Books of the Year & Textbook Exhib, plus others.
Teaching: Lect, Sch of Design; former instr advert design, Columbia Univ Exten.
Positions: Consult bk prod & illus, Pentagon, 43; owner, York Studios, New York.
Awards: Fifty Bks of the Yr Award, 39.
Publications: Illusr, Evolution of physics, Artist's materials and techniques, Tools of war, Military roentgenology, Exploring science & others.
Mailing Address: 12 E 75th St, New York, NY 10021.

STEINBOMER, DOROTHY H
Sculptor, Art Librarian
b Bayonne, N J, May 27, 12.
Study & Training: Our Lady of the Lake Col, BA & MLS; Univ of the Americas, Mexico City, MFA; also with Harding Black, Etienne Ret, Michael Frary, Dan Lutz & Fletcher Martin.
Commissions: Stained glass windows, Jefferson Methodist Chapel, Redeemer Lutheran Church, Northwood Presbyterian Church & Aldersgate Methodist Church, San Antonio, Tex; fused glass hanging cross, First Presbyterian Church, Midland, Tex; fused glass & metal sculpture, Holiday Inn, Dallas, Tex; screen, McClaugherty Chapel, San Antonio; fused glass sculpture, Med Ctr, Houston, Tex; also in pvt collections.
Exhibitions: Two-man show, Tex Fine Arts Asn, 57; Witte Mem Mus, 57 & 60; Tex A&M Univ, 59; Artisans Gallery, Houston, 60; Craft Guild San Antonio, 62-65; numerous studio shows of stained glass in Southwest.
Collections Arranged: Community Arts Forum, San Antonio; Faith into Form, Church Archit Guild Nat Exhib, Dallas, 64; two int exhibs for Hemisfair, San Antonio, 68.
Teaching: Lect, visual arts series, St Mary's Univ; asst prof & art libr, 67-
Memberships: Stained Glass Asn Am; Am Crafts Coun; Craft Guild San Antonio; San Antonio Art League (pres, 56-58); Mex-Am Cult Exchange Inst (pres, 65); plus others.
Mailing Address: 800 Burr Rd, San Antonio, TX 78209.

STEINER, MICHAEL
Sculptor
Preferred Media: Steel, Aluminum, Brass.
b New York, N Y, 1945.
Work in Public Collections: Storm King Art Ctr; Boston Mus Fine Arts; Mus Mod Art.
Exhibitions: Light Show, Inst Contemp Art, Philadelphia, Pa, 64; Larry Aldrich Mus, Ridgefield, Conn, 68; Minimal Art, Gemeentemuseum, The Hague, Holland, 68; 8 American Sculptors, Pioneer Court, Chicago, Ill, 68; Norman MacKenzie Art Gallery, Univ Sask, Regina, 70; plus one other.
Teaching: Instr, Emma Lake Workshop, Univ Sask, Regina, 69; vis artist, Cranbrook Art Inst, Bloomfield Heights, Mich, 69.
Awards: Guggenheim Award, 71.
Bibliography: Terry Fenton (auth), article, In: Art Int, 70.
Mailing Address: c/o Marlborough Gallery, 41 E 57th St, New York, NY 10022.

STEINFELS, MELVILLE P
Painter, Designer
b Salt Lake City, Utah, Nov 3, 10.
Study & Training: Art Inst Chicago; Chicago Sch Design.
Work in Public Collections: Murals (buon fresco, fresco secco, mosaic, ceramic tile), Church of the Epiphany, Chicago, Loyola Univ, Chicago, St Mary's Capuchin Sem, Crown Point, Ind, Newman Club, Ann Arbor, Mich, St Mary Magdalen Church, Melvindale, Mich & many others.
Commissions: Eight murals, Resurrection Mausoleum, Justice, Ill.
Teaching: Artist-in-residence, Siena Heights Col, 45-50; instr drawing, painting & design.
Mailing Address: 332 Talcott Pl, Park Ridge, IL 60068.

STEINHOUSE, TOBIE (THELMA)
Painter, Printmaker
b Montreal, Que.
Study & Training: Sir George Williams Univ; Art Stud League New York, with Morris Kantor & Harry Sternberg, 46-47; Ecole Beaux-Arts, Paris; Atelier 17, Paris, France, with W S Hayter, 61-62.
Work in Public Collections: Nat Gallery Can, Ottawa; Montreal Mus Fine Arts, Que; Confederation Art Gallery, Charlottetown, P E I; Ministry of External Affairs of Can, Moscow Embassy, U S S R; McMichael Conserv Collection, Kleinburg, Ont.
Commissions: Songes et Lumiére (portfolio of 8 color engravings), Reverberations (portfolio of color engravings), 70, The Edge of Day, 71 & Songes et Lumiére, 72, Graphic Guild Montreal.
Exhibitions: One-man show, Galerie Lara Vincy, France, 57; Montreal Mus Fine Arts, 59 & 63; Second Int Biennial Engraving, Santiago, Chile, 65; First & Third Brit Int Print Biennial, Bradford, Eng, 68 & 72; Ninth Int Biennial Art, Menton, France, 72; plus six one-man shows, 58-72.
Positions: Judge, Can Soc Graphic Art & Soc Can Painter-Etchers & Engravers Exhib, 70.
Awards: Sterling Trust Award, Soc Can Painter-Etchers & Engravers, 63; Jessie Dow First Prize Award, Montreal Mus Fine Arts, 63; Govt Can Centennial Medal Hon, 67; plus others.
Bibliography: Guy Viau (auth), La Peinture moderne au Canada Français, Ministére Affaires Cult, Que, 64; Guy Robert (auth), Ecôle de Montréal, Collection Artistes Can, 65; V Nixon (auth) Tobie Steinhouse-artist, Vie des Arts Mag, summer 72; plus others.
Memberships: Assoc mem Royal Can Acad Arts; Can Group Painters (pres, 66-68); L'Atelier Libre Recherches Graphique; Soc Can Painter-Etchers & Engravers; Can Soc Graphic Art; plus others.
Dealer: L'Atelier Renée Le Sieur, 46, Côte de la Montagne, Quebec, P Q, Can.
Mailing Address: 208 Côte St Antoine Rd, Montreal 217, P Q, Can.

STEINITZ, KATE TRAUMAN
Writer, Art Historian
b Beuthen, Ger, Aug 2, 89; U S citizen.
Study & Training: With Lovis Corinth, Berlin, Ger; Univ Berlin, with Woefflin; Paris Sorbonne; Hanover Tech Hochschule, with Schubring.
Work in Public Collections: Hanover Provincial Mus; Los Angeles Co Mus Art, Calif; plus in some European collections.
Exhibitions: New York Pub Libr, 40; one-woman exhib, Los Angeles Co Mus Art, 68.
Teaching: Substitute instr Renaissance art hist, Pomona Col.
Positions: Res librarian, Elmer Belt Libr of Vinciana, 45-61, hon cur, Elmer Belt Libr, Univ Calif, Los Angeles, 61-
Awards: Grant, U S State Dept, 51; grant to Italy, Kress Found, 69.
Memberships: Am Fedn Art; Verband Deutscher Kunsthistoriker; Mus Mod Art, New York; Los Angeles Co Mus Art; Kestner Gesellschaft, Hanover.
Research: Leonardo da Vinci; modern art.

Art Interests: Art history; art literature.

Collection: Graphic art; prints distributed by Kestner Gesellschaft Hanover, from Kubin to Kokoschka, from Daumier to Duchamps, collages by Kurt Schwitters.

Publications: Auth, Leonardo da Vinci's manuscripts, 48, Leonardo da Vinci's Trattato della pittura (res monography), 56, Kurt Schwitters Erinnerungen & Gespräche, Zurich, Arche, 63, Eng version, 68, Early art bibliographies, who did the first?, Burlington Mag, 72 & Two drawings by Parmigianino in the Woodner Collection, Graphic Arts Coun Newsletter, Vol 7, No 4; plus many other articles, bks & reviews.

Mailing Address: 11842 Goshen Ave, Los Angeles, CA 90049.

STEINKE, BETTINA
Painter
Preferred Media: Oils, Pastels, Charcoal.
b Biddeford, Maine, June 25, 13.
Study & Training: Fawcett Art Inst, Newark, N J; Cooper Union, New York, N Y; Phoenix Art Inst, New York.
Work in Public Collections: Nat Cowboy Hall of Fame & Western Heritage, Oklahoma City, Okla; Fort Worth Mus, Tex; Gilcrease Mus, Tulsa, Okla; Philbrook Mus, Tulsa; also in pvt collections in U S & abroad.
Exhibitions: Watercolor Show, Curacao, Neth, 47; one-man shows, Well Known Personalities, Philbrook Mus, 54, The Eskimo, Winnipeg, 56 & Portraits Around U S, Oklahoma City, 68.
Awards: Fred Whitaker (auth), Painter of people, Am Artist, 1/71; plus many others.
Memberships: Soc Illusr.
Publications: Illusr, N B C Symphony Orch, 37; illusr, articles, In: Lamp, 50-53; also illusr for var mags & bks.
Mailing Address: c/o Blair Galleries, Ltd, P O Box 2342, Santa Fe, NM 87501.

STEINMANN, MR & MRS HERBERT
Collectors
Mailing Address: 9 E 81st St, New York, NY 10028.

STEINMETZ, GRACE ERNST TITUS
Painter, Lecturer
Preferred Media: Oils, Casein, Acrylics.
b Lancaster, Pa.
Study & Training: Pa Acad Fine Arts; Barnes Found; Millersville State Col, BS; Univ Pa, MS.
Work in Public Collections: Univ Southern Fla, Lakeland; Franklin & Marshall Col; Elizabethtown Col, Pa; Millersville State Col, Pa; Lancaster Co Art Asn, Pa.
Exhibitions: Am Watercolor Soc, 68; Painters & Sculptors Soc N J, 69; Knickerbocker Soc, 70; Moore Col Art, 70; Nat Soc Painters Casein & Acrylic, 72.
Teaching: Assoc prof art hist, Elizabethtown Col, 64-65, adj prof oil painting, 69.
Awards: Best of show, Lancaster Co Art Asn, 67; award for nontraditional watercolor, Painters & Sculptors Soc N J, 68; Grumbacher First Prize, Nat Soc Painters Casein & Acrylic, 69.
Memberships: Nat Soc Painters Casein & Acrylic; Echo Valley Art Group; fel Royal Soc Arts.
Mailing Address: Box 270, R D 2, Manheim, PA 17545.

STELL, H KENYON
Educator, Painter
Preferred Media: Acrylics, Oils, Wood.
b Adams, N Y, Jan 22, 10.
Study & Training: Syracuse Univ, BFA(illus) & cert art educ; New York Univ, MA(educ admin); Syracuse Univ.
Work in Public Collections: Marine Midland Bank, Cortland, N Y.
Exhibitions: Nassau-Suffolk Art League, Garden City, N Y, 46; Assoc Artists Syracuse, Mus Fine Art, 48; State Univ Art Faculties Exhib, 54-56.
Teaching: Instr art & supvr, Toaz Jr High Sch & Huntington High Sch, Huntington, N Y, 39-47; prof art & chmn dept, State Univ N Y Col Cortland, 47-66, prof art hist, 66-, vis prof art, Univ Maine, Orono, summer 51.
Positions: Chmn art, State N Y Teachers Col Faculty Asn, 50; dir Art Show, 51 & mem art adv comt, N Y State Fair; pres, Cortland Col Chap, Am Asn Univ Prof, 52 & dir & organizer, Art in Western Europe, study abroad prog, summer 63, State Univ N Y Col Cortland; juror art exhibs, Roberson Mem Show, Buffalo Soc Artists, 62-70; consult, Marine Bank Art Collection, 69.
Awards: 15 yr citation, Nat Art Educ Asn, 60.
Memberships: Nat Art Educ Asn; Col Art Asn Am.
Research: John Trumbull.
Mailing Address: Cosmos Hill Rd, Cortland, NY 13045.

STELLA, FRANK
Painter
b Malden, Mass, May, 1936.
Study & Training: Phillips Acad, with Patrick Morgan; Princeton

Univ, with William Seitz & Stephen Greene.
Work in Public Collections: Mus Mod Art; Whitney Mus Am Art; Pasadena Art Mus; Albright-Knox Art Gallery, Buffalo, N Y; Walker Art Ctr, Minneapolis, Minn; plus many others.
Exhibitions: Int Biennial Exhib Paintings, Tokyo, Japan, 67; Documenta IV, Kassel, Ger, 68; The Art of the Real, 68 & retrospective, 70, Mus Mod Art; Philadelphia Mus Art, 68; Whitney Mus Am Art Ann, 69 & 72; plus many other group & one-man shows.
Awards: First prize, Int Biennial Exhib Paintings, Tokyo, 67.
Bibliography: Lawrence Alloway (auth), Systemic painting, Guggenheim Mus, 66; Oto Bihalji-Merin (auth), Adventures of modern art, Abrams, 66; Gregory Battcock (ed), Minimal art: a critical anthology, Dutton, 68; plus many others.
Dealer: Lawrence Rubin Gallery, 49 W 57th St, New York, NY 10019.
Mailing Address: 17 Jones St, New York, NY 10013.

STELZER, MICHAEL NORMAN
Sculptor
b Brooklyn, N Y, Jan 6, 38.
Study & Training: Pratt Inst, 56; Art Stud League New York, 60-62; Nat Acad Sch Fine Arts, Edward Mooney traveling scholar, 66 & Nat Sculpture Soc Joseph Nicolosi grant, 67; also with Nathaniel Choate, 64, Michael Lantz, 64-67 & Donald DeLue, 68 & 69.
Commissions: Relief painting, Worcester Polytech Inst, 64.
Exhibitions: Am Artists Prof League Grand Nat, 63; Nat Arts Club, 63-64; Nat Acad Design, 64-67 & 70-71; Allied Artists Am, 67 & 71; Nat Sculpture Soc Lever House Exhib, 68-72.
Teaching: Instr pvt classes, Brooklyn Heights, N Y, 68-
Awards: Helen Foster Barnett Prize, Nat Acad Design, 66; Dr H DeBellis First Prize Sculpture, Salmagundi Club, 69; first prize sculpture, New Rochelle Art Asn, 71.
Bibliography: Article, In: Pen & Brush, 66; Opportunities offered the young sculptor, 67 & Interpreting the human figure, 68, Nat Sculpture Rev.
Memberships: Nat Sculpture Soc; Salmagundi Club; Allied Artists Am.
Mailing Address: 8 Everit St, Brooklyn, NY 11201.

STENBERY, ALGOT
Painter
Preferred Media: Gouache, Oils.
b Cambridge, Mass, Apr 24, 02.
Study & Training: Hartford Art Sch, with Albertus Jones; Boston Mus Art Sch, with Frederick Bosley; Art Stud League New York, N Y, with Kimon Nicolaides.
Work in Public Collections: Metrop Mus Art, New York; G R Dick Collection; Edith Wetmore Collection.
Commissions: Murals, Work Proj Admin, Harlem Housing Proj Social Rm, 34 & Post Off, Wayne, Mich, 38, tiles, Chrysler Bldg, New York, 36 & Liner Bremen grand staircase, 68.
Exhibitions: World's Fair, 35; Long Island Art Asn, 61; Am Watercolor Soc, 66; Nat Soc Casein Painters, 70; Salmagundi Club, 70.
Teaching: Instr drawing & painting, Cooper Union, 33-40; instr drawing & painting, Am Artists Sch, 40-42.
Mailing Address: 144 Bleecker St, New York, NY 10012.

STEPHENS, CURTIS
Designer, Educator
Preferred Media: Plastics.
a Athens, Ga, Dec 13, 32.
Study & Training: Univ Ga, MFA.
Work in Public Collections: Objects U S A, Johnson's Wax Collection; Ill State Mus, Springfield.
Exhibitions: Designed for Production, Mus Contemp Crafts, 64; Objects U S A, Johnson's Wax Collection, Smithsonian Inst, 69; 24th & 25th Ill Invitational Exhib, Ill State Mus, 71 & 72.
Teaching: Asst prof art, LaGrange Col, 61-63; asst prof art, Univ Northern Mich, 66-68; assoc prof art & design, Univ Ill, Champaign-Urbana, 68-
Positions: Designer, Callaway Mills, LaGrange, Ga, 63-66.
Bibliography: Lee Nordness (auth), Objects: U S A, Viking Press, 70, Jay Hartley Newman & Lee Scott Newman (auth), Plastics for the craftsman, Crown, 72.
Mailing Address: Dept of Art, University of Illinois, Champaign, IL 61820.

STEPHENS, NANCY ANNE
Sculptor, Film Maker
Preferred Media: Magnets, Ceramics, Plastics, Fluids.
b Santa Barbara, Calif, Nov 18, 39.
Study & Training: Univ Kans Art Dept, 57; Northwestern Univ Theatre, 58-59; Univ Kans Theatre, 59-62; Kans City Art Inst, 63.
Work in Public Collections: Art Res Ctr, Kansas City, Mo; Galeria Grada Zagreba, Zagreb, Yugoslavia.
Commissions: Tapestry, Kansas City Parks & Recreation Dept, Mo, 69; graphics, Harrison St Rev & Westport Trucker, 71-72.

Exhibitions: New Ctr U S Art Series, 63-64; Art Res Ctr Series, 66-72; Sir George Williams Univ, Montreal, P Q, 67; Anonima Studio, New York, N Y, 68; Novo Tendencija 4, Zagreb, Yugoslavia, 69.
Positions: Lithoartist, Hallmark Cards, Kansas City, 62-64; dir II watercolor, ceramics & sculpture, Kansas City Parks & Recreation Dept, Mo, 66-70; ed & contribr, Art Res Ctr Mag, 66-71; pres, Art Res Ctr, Kansas City, 72-
Bibliography: Donald Hoffman (auth), articles, In: Kansas City Star, 66-72; Yves Robillard (auth), article, In: art sect, Montreal La Presse, 9/67; Lawrence Alton et al (auth), articles, In: New York Element, 68, 70 & 71.
Memberships: Kansas City Writers, Artists & Musicians (directing comt, 72-); New Tendencies Int Movement, Europ.
Publications: Contribr, Harrison St Rev, 72 & Westport Trucker, 71-72.
Mailing Address: 820 E 48th St, Kansas City, MO 64110.

STEPHENS, THOMAS MICHAEL
Sculptor, Designer
Preferred Media: Plastics, Steel, Aluminum.
b Elkins, Ark, Feb 21, 41.
Study & Training: Univ Kans, 59-63, four yrs independent study.
Work in Public Collections: Jewish Community Ctr, Kansas City, Mo; Rockhurst Col, Kansas City; Art Res Ctr, Kansas City; Galerija Grada, Zagreba, Zagreb, Yugoslavia.
Commissions: Landscaping, bldgs & sculpture for ten playgrounds, Parks & Recreation Dept, Kansas City, Mo, 66-67; design & art works, Midway Cafe, Kansas City, 71-72; design, Green Bindery, Kansas City, 72.
Exhibitions: Exhib Series, New Ctr U S Art, 63-64 & Art Res Ctr, 66-72; Sir George Williams Univ, Montreal, P Q, Can, 67; Anonima Studio, New York, N Y, 68; Buffalo State Univ, N Y, 68; Novo Tendencija 4, Zagreb, Yugoslavia, 69.
Teaching: Lectr hist & sci in art, Jewish Community Ctr, Kansas City, 70-71; lectr res in art, Art Res Ctr, Kansas City, 70-72; lectr art & technol, Kansas City Art Inst, Mar 71.
Positions: Prod designer, Topeka Civic Theatre, Kans, 61-62; dir, New Ctr U S Art Coop Gallery, Kansas City, 64; art supvr & design consult, Kansas City Parks & Recreation Dept, Mo, 64-67; contribr & ed, Art Res Ctr Mag, 66-72; coordr, Art Res Ctr, Kansas City, 69-72.
Awards: Fine arts guest lectr & exhibitor, Northwest Mo State Col, 65; humanities guest lectr & exhibitor, William Jewell Col, 66; Kansas City Asn Trusts & Found individual faculty develop grant, 70.
Bibliography: Donald Hoffman (auth), articles, In: art sect, Kansas City Star, 66-72; Yves Robillard (auth), article, In: art sect, Montreal La Presse, 9/67; Larry Alton et al & (auth), Testament of ARC, New York Element, 7/70 & 7/71.
Memberships: New Tendencies Movement, Europ; Kansas City Writers, Artists & Musicians (directing comt, 72-).
Publications: Contribr, Novo Tendenciji 4 Catalogue, 69; contribr, Bit Int J Art & Cybernet, 69; contribr, Harrison St Rev, 70 & 72; contribr, The Shelter, 71 & Westport Trucker, 72.
Mailing Address: 820 E 48th St, Kansas City, MO 64110.

STEPHENSON, JOHN H
Sculptor, Educator
Preferred Media: Mixed Media, Ceramics, Metals.
b Waterloo, Iowa, Oct 27, 29.
Study & Training: Univ Northern Iowa, BA; Cranbrook Acad Art, MFA.
Work in Public Collections: Int Mus Ceramics Faenza, Italy; Everson Mus, Syracuse, N Y; Detroit Mus Art, Mich; Parrish Art Mus, South Hampton, N Y; St Paul Art Ctr, Minn.
Commissions: The Wall (ceramic mural), Arbor A, Int Mkt, Ann Arbor, Mich, 71.
Exhibitions: Fiber, Clay and Metal, St Paul Art Ctr, 64; Concorso Int Della Ceramica Arte, Faenza, 65; Objects U S A, Smithsonian Inst, Washington, D C, 70; Crafts 1970, Boston City Hall, Mass, 70; Arts U S A II, Northern Ill Univ Mus, DeKalb, Ill, 71.
Teaching: Instr ceramics, Cleveland Inst Art, 58-59; prof ceramics, Univ Mich, Ann Arbor, 59-
Awards: Rackham res grants, Japan, 62 & mixed media, 69, Univ Mich; Medaglia Oro Della Citta Faenza, 65.
Dealer: Deson-zaks Gallery, Inc, 226 E Ontario St, Chicago, IL 60611.
Mailing Address: 4380 Waters Rd, Ann Arbor, MI 48103.

STERN, MR & MRS ARTHUR LEWIS
Collectors
b Mr Stern, Rochester, N Y, Apr 11, 11; Mrs Stern, New York, N Y, Apr 21, 13.
Study & Training: Mr Stern, Yale Univ, BA; Harvard Law Sch, JD; Mrs Stern, Goucher Col, BA; Rochester Inst Technol.

Positions: Mr Stern, mem bd dirs, Mem Art Gallery, Rochester, N Y, 60-, pres, 67-69; Mrs Stern, chmn art selection comt, Mem Art Gallery, 64-
Memberships: Mem Art Gallery, Rochester; Am Fedn Art; Mus Mod Art.
Collection: Modern painting and sculpture; Greek, Asian and European artifacts.
Mailing Address: 3365 Elmwood Ave, Rochester, NY 14610.

STERN, H PETER
Collector
Study & Training: Harvard Univ, AB(magna cum laude), 50; Columbia Univ, MA, 52; Law Sch, Yale Univ, LLB, 54.
Positions: V pres, Ralph E Ogden Found, Mountainville, N Y; trustee, Vassar Col; trustee, Int Fund Monuments, New York; trustee, Hudson Valley Philharmonic Soc; trustee, Nat Temple Hill Asn, Vail's Gate, N Y, 64-71; trustee, Old Mus Village of Smith's Cove, Monroe, N Y, 67-71; v chmn, Mid-Hudson Pattern for Prog, 68-; pres & mem bd trustees, Storm King Art Ctr.
Collection: Contemporary paintings, graphics and sculpture.
Mailing Address: Taylor Rd, Mountainville, NY 10953.

STERN, HAROLD PHILLIP
Museum Director, Writer
b Detroit, Mich, May 3, 22.
Study & Training: Ctr Japanese Studies, Univ Mich, BA, MA & PhD.
Teaching: Lectr Ukiyoe, Tokugawa painting, life in 14th century Japan, Korean imperial treasures & Japanese art, mus, galleries, univs & Japan Soc; instr Ukiyoe painting, Univ Mich, hon lectr.
Positions: Adv, two Japanese Govt loan exhibs, 53 & 65-66; adv, Korean Govt Loan Exhib, 57-58; asst dir, Freer Gallery Art, Washington, D C, 62-72, dir, 72-
Awards: Freer fel, 50.
Memberships: Japan-Am Soc Washington; Am Oriental Soc.
Publications: Auth, Masterpieces of Korean art, 57 & Hokusai: paintings and drawings in the Freer Gallery of Art, 60; co-ed, Art treasures from Japan, 65; auth, Master prints of Japan, Abrams, 69.
Mailing Address: Freer Gallery of Art, Jefferson Dr at 12th St S W, Washington, DC 20560.

STERN, JAN PETER
Sculptor
Preferred Media: Highly Polished Stainless Steel, Metals.
b Nov 14, 26; U S citizen.
Study & Training: Syracuse Univ Col Fine Arts, BID; New Sch Social Res.
Work in Public Collections: Nat Collection Smithsonian Inst, Capitol Mall, Washington, D C; Pasadena Art Mus; Joseph H Hirshhorn Mus; Univ Mich Inst Sci & Technol; Atlantic Richfield Collection; plus others.
Commissions: Monumental sculptures, Prudential Ctr, Boston, 66, Maritime Plaza, Golden Gateway Ctr, San Francisco, 67, Alcoa Hq, Chicago, 68, Cardinal Spellman Retreat House, New York, N Y, 69 & Los Angeles City Hall Mall, 72.
Exhibitions: Phoenix Art Mus, 67; Mus Contemp Art, 68; Saint Louis Art Mus, 68; San Francisco Mus Art, 70; Marlborough Gallery, New York, 70; plus other group & one-man shows.
Bibliography: Monumental sculpture show, Artforum, 2/68; Louis Redstone (auth), Art in architecture, 68 & Garrett Eckbo (auth), The landscape we see, 69, McGraw, documented by Nat Educ TV; plus others.
Mailing Address: 14640 Hilltree Rd, Santa Monica, CA 90402.

STERNBERG, HARRY
Painter, Educator
Preferred Media: Acrylics.
b New York, N Y, July 9, 04.
Study & Training: Art Stud League New York; also graphics with Harry Wickey.
Work in Public Collections: Mus Mod Art, New York; Metrop Mus Art, New York; Fogg Mus, Boston; Victoria & Albert Mus, London; Bibliot Nat, Paris.
Commissions: Murals, U S Treas Dept, Sellersville, Pa, 36 & Chicago, Ill, 38.
Exhibitions: Whitney Mus Am Art Ann, New York, 48-50; Am Acad Arts & Lett, New York, 72.
Teaching: Instr painting & graphics, Art Stud League New York, 34-68; instr graphics, New Sch Social Res, 42-45; head dept art, Idyllwild Sch Music & Art, Univ Southern Calif, 59-69.
Awards: J S Guggenheim Mem Found fel, 63; purchase award, Am Acad Arts & Lett, 72.
Publications: Auth, Silk screen color printing & Modern methods and materials of etching, McGraw; auth, Composition, Woodcut & Abstract-realist drawing, Pitman.
Dealer: ACA Gallery, 25 E 73rd St, New York, NY 10021.
Mailing Address: 1606 Conway Dr, Escondido, CA 92025.

STERNE, DAHLI
Painter, Sculptor
Preferred Media: Oils.
b Stettin, Ger, Jan 3, 01; U S citizen.
Study & Training: Kaiserin Auguste Victoria Acad, BA; also with
Albert Pels, Ludolf Liberts & Josef Shilhavy, U S.
Work in Public Collections: Oklahoma City Art Ctr; Evanston Mus
Art; Fla Southern Col; Seton Hall Univ; Gracie Mansion, New
York; plus others.
Exhibitions: Nat Arts Club, 53-58; Allied Artists Am, 55; 50 Am Art-
ists, 55-58; Col Mt St Vincent, New York; Allied Artists Am; plus
others.
Positions: Art dir, Nat Coun Jewish Women.
Awards: Citation, Okla Art Asn, 54; award, Am Artists Prof League,
55; gold medal, Ogunquit Art Ctr, 57.
Memberships: Am Artists Prof League; Catharine Lorillard Wolfe
Art Club; Artists Equity Asn; 50 Am Artists; Nat Soc Arts & Lett
(v pres, 71-72).
Mailing Address: 315 W 70th St, New York, NY 10023.

STERNE, HEDDA
Painter
b Bucharest, Roumania, Aug 4, 16; U S citizen.
Study & Training: Pvt study in Paris, Bucharest & Vienna.
Work in Public Collections: Univ Ill; Metrop Mus Art; Mus Mod Art;
Univ Nebr; Art Inst Chicago; plus many others.
Exhibitions: Painting & Sculpture Today, Art Asn Indianapolis, 65-
66; Flint Inst Invitational, 66-67; The Visual Assault, Univ Ga,
67-68 & Barnard Col, 68; Univ Colo, 68; Phillips Collection,
Westmoreland Mus, 69; plus many other group & one-man shows.
Teaching: Instr art hist, Carbondale Col, 64; conducted workshop
for art teachers, N Y State Coun Arts, 68.
Awards: Fulbright fel to Venice, 63; first prize, Art Inst Newport
Ann, 67; Tamarind fel, 67; plus others.
Bibliography: Robert Motherwell & Reinhardt (ed), Modern artists
in America, Wittenborn, 51; Nathaniel Pousette-Dart (ed),
American painting today, Hastings, 56; Herbert Read (auth), The
quest and the quarry, Rome-New York Art Found Inc, 61; plus
others.
Dealer: Betty Parsons Gallery, 24 W 57th St, New York, NY 10019.
Mailing Address: 179 E 71st St, New York, NY 10021.

STEVENS, EDWARD JOHN, JR
Painter, Educator
Preferred Media: Gouache.
b Jersey City, N J, Feb 4, 23.
Study & Training: N J State Teachers Col, Newark, BA, 43; Colum-
bia Univ Teachers Col, MA, 44, Art Exten, 44-47, with Henry
Varnum Poor & George Picken.
Work in Public Collections: Whitney Mus Am Art, New York, N Y;
N J State Mus, Trenton; Art Inst Chicago, Ill; Pa Acad Fine Arts;
Honolulu Acad Arts, Hawaii.
Exhibitions: 22 one-man exhibs, Weyhe Gallery, New York, 44-71;
Whitney Mus Am Art Ann, 54; Brooklyn Mus Int Watercolor Ex-
hib, 55; Pa Acad Fine Arts Ann, 63; Newark Mus N J Triennial,
64.
Teaching: Instr painting, Newark Sch Fine & Indust Art, 47-59, co-
ord dir, 59-
Awards: Artist of Yr, Hudson Artists, 54; bronze medal, N J Ter-
centenary, 64; Henry Ward Ranger Fund Purchase Award, Nat
Acad Design, 68.
Memberships: Philadelphia Watercolor Club; Audubon Artists.
Dealer: E Weyhe, 794 Lexington Ave, New York, NY 10021.
Mailing Address: 621 Palisade Ave, Jersey City, NJ 07307.

STEVENS, ELISABETH GOSS
Writer, Art Critic
b Rome, N Y, Aug 11, 29.
Study & Training: Wellesley Col, BA, 51; Columbia Univ, MA (high
hons), 56.
Positions: Ed assoc, Art News, 64-65; art critic, Washington Post,
65; free lance art critic & writer, 65-
Publications: Auth, The gallery, art column in Wall St J, 70-; auth,
An archeological find named Iris Love, New York Times Mag,
3/7/71; auth, The urban museum crisis (ser), Washington Post,
6-7/72; auth, articles, In: Atlantic, New Repub, Sat Rev, Book-
world, Art Am, Arts & many others.
Mailing Address: 22 Fox Meadow Rd, Scarsdale, NY 10583.

STEVENS, LAWRENCE TENNEY
Sculptor
Preferred Media: Marble, Bronze, Wood.
b Brighton, Mass, July 16, 96.
Study & Training: Mus Sch Fine Arts, Boston; Tufts Med Sch; Prix-
de-Rome, Am Acad, Tiffany Found scholars, 23-25; also with
John Wilson, Bela Pratt, Philip Hale & Charles Grafly.

Work in Public Collections: Brookgreen Gardens; Philbrook Art Ctr,
Tulsa, Okla; Civic Ctr, Scottsdale, Ariz; Phoenix Art Mus, Ariz;
Ball Mus, Muncie, Ind.
Commissions: John Harrison, bronze, Fairmont Park Asn City Art
Comt, Philadelphia, 30; six heroic statues, Tex Centennial, Dal-
las, 36; Protecting Hand, Woodmen Accident & Life Ins Co, Lin-
coln, Nebr, 56; rodeo series (nine bronzes), Valley Nat Bank,
Phoenix, Ariz, 59-70; terra cotta bas-reliefs, hist of Palm
Springs, Calif, Security First Nat Bank, 60.
Exhibitions: Archit League Winter Exhib, New York, N Y, 25; Mus
Fine Arts, Boston, Mass, 25; Boston Art Club, 25; Philbrook Art
Ctr, 45; Invitational Sculpture Exhib, Philadelphia, Pa, 52.
Positions: In charge of sculpture, Tex Centennial, Dallas, 36.
Awards: Nat competition for sculpture, Fine Arts Bldg, Pomona,
Calif, 37.
Memberships: Nat Sculpture Soc; fel Am Acad in Rome.
Mailing Address: 519 W University Dr, Tempe, AZ 85281.

STEVENS, MAY
Painter
Preferred Media: Oils, Acrylics.
b Boston, Mass, June 9, 24.
Study & Training: Mass Col Art, BFA, 46; Art Stud League New
York, N Y, 47; Acad Julian, Paris, 49.
Work in Public Collections: Whitney Mus Am Art; Wash Univ, Saint
Louis, Mo; Jacksonville Mus, Fla; Schenectady Mus, N Y; Brook-
lyn Mus.
Exhibitions: Pa Acad Fine Arts, 64; Nat Inst Arts & Lett, 69; Re-
cent Acquisitions & Women Artists From Permanent Collection,
Whitney Mus Am Art, 70; Am Women Artists Invitational, Ham-
burg, Ger, 72.
Teaching: Instr painting, Sch Visual Arts, 62-; adj lectr art, Queens
Col(N Y), 64-; vis artist, Ball State Univ, 68.
Awards: New Eng Ann Landscape Prize, Silvermine Guild Artists,
Conn, 58; Childe Hassam Purchase Award, Nat Inst Arts & Lett,
68 & 69; MacDowell Colony fel, 71-72.
Bibliography: A L Chanin (auth), preface to catalogue for one-woman
exhib, Galerie Mod, 55; Howard Devree (auth), preface to cata-
logue for one-woman exhib, De Aenlle Gallery, 61; Barry
Schwartz (auth), Humanism in modern art, Praeger, 73.
Memberships: Artists Equity Asn New York.
Mailing Address: 97 Wooster St, New York, NY 10012.

STEVENS, WALTER HOLLIS
Painter, Educator
Preferred Media: Watercolors, Acrylics, Oils.
b Mineola, N Y, Aug 5, 27.
Study & Training: Drake Univ, BFA, 51; Univ Ill, Urbana, MFA, 55.
Work in Public Collections: Birmingham Mus Art, Ala; Ark Art
Ctr, Little Rock; Mint Mus Art, Charlotte, N C; Okla Art Ctr,
Oklahoma City; Tenn Fine Arts Ctr, Nashville.
Exhibitions: One-man shows, Contemp Arts, Inc, New York, N Y,
60 & 64; Contemporary Arts, Traveling Exhib to S Am, 60 & 65;
Mid-South Exhib, Brooks Mem Art Gallery, Memphis, Tenn, 62-
66, 69 & 71; Seven Delta Exhibs, Ark Art Ctr, 61-70; Three Wa-
tercolor U S A Exhibs, Springfield, Mo, 68-72.
Teaching: Prof painting, Univ Tenn, 57-
Awards: First purchase awards, Ala Watercolor Nat, Birmingham
Mus, 57 & 60; first purchase award, Cent South Exhib, Nashville,
66; purchase award, Tenn Watercolorists, Chattanooga, 72.
Bibliography: New talent issue, Art in Am, 57; Robert Schlageter
(auth), Walter H Stevens, Mint Mus, 59.
Memberships: Tenn Watercolor Soc; Knoxville Watercolor Soc.
Dealer: Rothery's, 7301 Kingston Pike N W, Knoxville, TN 37919.
Mailing Address: 2305 Woodson Dr, Knoxville, TN 37920.

STEVENSON, A BROCKIE
Painter
Preferred Media: Acrylics.
b Montgomery Co, Pa, Sept 24, 19.
Study & Training: Pa Acad Fine Arts, Philadelphia; Barnes Found,
Merion, Pa; Skowhegan Sch Painting & Sculpture, Maine.
Work in Public Collections: Corcoran Gallery Art, Washington, D C;
Nat Collection Fine Arts, Washington, D C; Pa Acad Fine Arts;
State Univ, Potsdam, Univ Mass, Amherst.
Exhibitions: American Artists Report the War, Nat Gallery Art,
London, Eng, autumn 44; four shows, Painting & Sculpture Ann,
Pa Acad Fine Arts, 48-51; four shows, Soc Bellas Artes Peru,
Lima, 53-56; Washington Art, State Univ N Y, Potsdam & Albany,
71; Eight Washington Artists, Columbia Mus Art, S C, 71.
Teaching: Instr compos, Sch Fine Arts, Wash Univ, 60-62; assoc
prof design, Corcoran Sch Art, Washington, D C, 65-
Positions: War artist corresp, Europ Theater Opers Southern Base
Sect, USA, Eng, 43-44 & Off Chief Eng, France, 44-45.
Bibliography: Art by armed forces, Life Mag, 7/6/42; Lincoln
Kirstein (auth), Am battle art, 1588-1944, Mag Art, 5/44; Paul
Richards (auth), rev, In: Washington Post, 6/21/70.

Dealer: Pyramid Galleries Ltd, 2121 P St N W, Washington, D C 20037.

Mailing Address: Corcoran School of Art, 17th & New York Ave N W, Washington, DC 20006.

STEVENSON, BRANSON GRAVES
Painter, Designer

Preferred Media: Graphics.

b Franklin Co, Ga, Apr 5, 01.

Study & Training: Inst Nac, Panama; Col Great Falls, Mont; also with Margarite Wildenhain, Bernard Leach & Shoji Hamada.

Work in Public Collections: Mont Inst Arts, Helena; C M Russell Gallery, Great Falls, Mont; Mont Hist Soc, Helena; Univ Ore, Eugene.

Commissions: Fresco mural, Great Falls, 45; Story of Paper (glass mural), Great Falls Pub Libr, 68; doc TV film, Jr League Great Falls, 71; 138 proofs of lithographs, First Nat Bank, Great Falls, 71-72.

Exhibitions: Retrospective exhib, Russell Gallery, 70; one-man show, Yellowstone Art Ctr, Billings, Mont, 72; Mont Hist Soc, 72; Northern Mont Col, 72; Ore Arts Comn, Eugene, 72.

Teaching: Lectr humanities, Col Great Falls, 63-

Positions: Founder, dir, secy & trustee, Archie Bray Found, Helena, 51-

Awards: Purchase prize for Rhubarb (lithograph), Univ Ore; awards for emulsion wax watercolors, etching, drawings & lithographs, Mont State Fair.

Bibliography: Kathleen Cronin (auth), article, In: Mobil World, 71; Ray Steele (auth), Branson G Stevenson, the man and his works, KRTV, 72.

Memberships: C M Russell Mus (dir, 53-); Mont Hist Soc & Art Gallery (mem bd trustees, 64-); life mem & fel Mont Inst Arts.

Collection: Etchings and graphics, including etchings by Rembrandt and Seymore Haden, sculpture by C M Russell and painting by Florencio Molino Campos.

Publications: Contribr, Craft Horizons, Ceramic Indust, Mont Arts & others.

Dealer: Glass Art Shop, 505 First Ave N, Great Falls, MT 59401.

Mailing Address: 715 Fourth Ave N, Great Falls, MT 59401.

STEVENSON, FLORENCE EZZELL
Painter, Lecturer

Preferred Media: Oils, Watercolors.

b Russellville, Ala.

Study & Training: Athens Col (Ala), grad; Conserv Art & Music, Tuscaloosa, Ala, grad; Sch Art Inst Chicago, Ill, grad.

Work in Public Collections: Gage Park Sch, Chicago; Munic Bldg, Russellville, Ala; Morgan Park High Sch, Chicago; Hanover Col; Sutherland Sch, Chicago; plus others.

Commissions: Oil painting, Century of Prog, Rosenwald Mus Sci & Indust, Chicago, 33-34.

Exhibitions: Smithsonian Inst, Washington, D C; many exhibs, Art Inst Chicago; Parthenon, Nashville, Tenn; Brooks Mem Gallery, Memphis, Tenn; Ridge Art Asn, Chicago; plus many other group & one-man shows.

Teaching: Lectr art, var groups; head dept art, Conserv Art & Music, Tuscaloosa.

Positions: Adv mem, Marquis Biog Libr Soc; trustee, Vanderpoel Art Gallery, Chicago.

Awards: Mrs Frank G Logan Prize; All Ill Soc Fine Arts Gold Medal Award; var prizes, Nat League Am Pen Women, 45-57; plus many others.

Bibliography: Article & reproduction, In: Christian Sci Monitor.

Memberships: Arts Club, Chicago, Ill; Nat League Am Pen Women; Am Artists Prof League; Munic Art League, Chicago; Int Platform Asn; plus many others.

Mailing Address: 8020 S Chicago Ave, Chicago, IL 60617.

STEVENSON, ROBERT BRUCE
Sculptor, Lecturer

Preferred Media: Plexiglass.

b San Diego, Calif, May 18, 24.

Study & Training: Univ Calif, Los Angeles, BA, 50; San Fernando Valley State Col, MA, 65.

Work in Public Collections: Downey Mus; Los Angeles Co Mus, Calif; Long Beach Art Mus, Calif; also in collections of Mr & Mrs Braunstein, San Francisco, Calif & Mr & Mrs George Richey, New York, N Y.

Commissions: Large plexiglass struct, Charles Cowles, Los Angeles Co Mus, 65-66; two large plexiglass struct, Joseph Hirschhorn, Nat Gallery, Washington, D C, 66 & Mrs & Mrs J L Wolgin, Philadelphia Art Mus, 68.

Exhibitions: Looking West, Joslyn Art Mus, Omaha, Nebr, 70; Traveling Embassy Show, U S Info Agency, 71; Fine Arts Gallery, San Diego Rental Gallery, 71; Dimensions in Plastics, Jewish Community Ctr Gallery, 71; Long Beach Mus Tenth Ann, 72; plus others.

Teaching: Lectr art, Los Angeles City Schs, 54-

Positions: Vis artist, Proj Advan Creative Art, San Bernardino, Inyo & Mono Co, 68.

Awards: Downey Mus Purchase Prize, New Talent Show, 68; purchase award, Long Beach Mus Tenth Ann, 72.

Bibliography: Susan Ellis (auth), They're taking odd shapes, Los Angeles Herald Examr, 1/8/67; Design for living: Robert Stevenson, Arts Mag, 9-10/67; William Wilson (auth), Juried show in Long Beach, Los Angeles Times, 4/1/68.

Mailing Address: c/o Esther Robles Art Gallery, 665 N La Cienega Blvd, Los Angeles, CA 90069.

STEVENSON, RUTH ROLSTON
Painter

Preferred Media: Watercolors, Oils, Pencil.

b Brooklyn, N Y.

Study & Training: Pratt Inst, dipl, with Walter Beck; Art Stud League New York, with John Sloan.

Work in Public Collections: Watercolor landscape, Norfolk Mus; watercolor portrait, Huntington Mus, W Va; oil mural, Seamans Church Inst, New York, N Y.

Commissions: 20 children's portraits in pvt collections, 28; 5 children's portraits in Rome, Italy, 71; oil landscape of New York, in Chile, S Am, 71.

Exhibitions: Nat Art Club, New York, 57; Am Artists Prof League, 59; Nat Asn Women Artists, 60; Am Watercolor Soc 100th Travel Exhib, 67; Pen & Brush Club, 71 & 73.

Teaching: Art instr, Pratt Inst, 20-24; art instr, Newark Pub Sch Fine Indust Art, 27-36.

Awards: Gold medal for Mountain Garden (watercolor), Nat Arts Club, 57; award for Wood Companions (oil), Am Artists Prof League, 59; Solo Award for Double Bouquet (watercolor), Pen & Brush Club, 72 & 73.

Memberships: Nat Arts Club (art comn, 61); Am Watercolor Soc; Nat Asn Women Artists; Pen & Brush Club (art comt, 50); Am Artists Prof League.

Mailing Address: 26 W Ninth St, New York, NY 10011.

STEWART, ALBERT T
Sculptor

b Kensington, Eng, Apr 9, 00.

Study & Training: Beaux-Arts Inst Design; Art Stud League New York; also with Paul Manship.

Work in Public Collections: Metrop Mus Art; Fogg Mus Art; Reading Mus Art.

Commissions: Tablets, panels, figures, doors & fountains, Seamen's Mem, N Y, Buffalo City Hall, N Y, Saint Paul City Hall & Court House, St Bartholomew's Church, N Y & Am Battle Monument, Thiacourt, France; plus many others.

Awards: Prize, 31 & citation, 55, Nat Acad Design; prizes, Pasadena Art Inst, 48 & Chaffey Art Asn, 51; plus others.

Memberships: Nat Sculpture Soc; Am Mus Natural Hist; academician Nat Acad Design.

Mailing Address: 4215 Via Padova, Claremont, CA 91711.

STEWART, ARTHUR
Painter

Preferred Media: Watercolors, Oils, Acrylics.

b Marion, Ala, July 29, 15.

Study & Training: Auburn Univ; Art Inst Chicago; also with Kelly Fitzpatrick.

Work in Public Collections: Birmingham Mus Art, Ala; Montgomery Mus Art, Ala; Norfolk Mus Arts & Sci, Va; Atlanta Art Asn, Ga; also in collection of Queen Elizabeth II, Eng.

Commissions: Four murals (with Kelly Fitzpatrick), Bank of Tallassee, Ala.

Exhibitions: Art In War Traveling Exhib, Life Mag, 41-42; four Southeastern Ann, 49-59; Norfolk Mus Arts & Sci Traveling Exhib, 64; Ala Watercolor Soc, 69-70; Am Watercolor Soc.

Teaching: Instr drawing, Birmingham Mus Art; pvt instr.

Positions: Chmn Beaux Arts Ball, Birmingham Mus Art, 59, mem bd, 65-66.

Awards: Purchase award for Spanish Bouquet, Norfolk Mus Arts & Sci, 64; award for Early Light, Meade Co, 64; Harriete Murray Award for Rosalie, Birmingham Centennial Exhib, 72; plus others.

Bibliography: Alfred Frankfurter (auth), Parisian scenes, San Francisco Chronicle, 49; Richard Howard (auth), Arthur Stewart florals, Crescenzi Gallery, 67.

Memberships: Birmingham Art Asn (v pres, 65-66); Ala Watercolor Soc (pres, 65-67); Ala Art League; Ala Art Asn.

Dealer: Elizabeth Agee, 1915 11th Ave S, Birmingham, AL 35205.

Mailing Address: 2969 Pump House Rd, Birmingham, AL 35243.

STEWART, DOROTHY S
Painter
Preferred Media: Oils, Watercolors.
b Brooklyn, N Y.
Study & Training: Art Stud League New York; Nat Acad Sch Fine Art, New York; also with Edgar Whitney, Paul Puzinas & Anthony Toney.
Work in Public Collections: Gregory Mus, Hicksville, N Y; Mercy Hosp, Rockville Centre, N Y.
Exhibitions: Nat Arts Club 71st Ann Watercolor Exhib, New York, 69; Allied Artists Am 56th & 58th Ann, 69 & 71, Catharine Lorillard Wolfe Art Club 73rd-75th Ann, 69-71 & Am Watercolor Soc 105th Ann, 72, Nat Acad Galleries; Am Artists Prof League Grand Nat, Lever House, New York, 72.
Teaching: Instr art, Malverne Sr High Sch, N Y, 65-66.
Awards: M Grumbacher Award, Nat Art League 41st Ann, 71; first prize oil painting, Gregory Mus, 72; Washington Sq Bus & Prof Women's Club Award, Washington Sq Outdoor Art Exhib, 72; plus others.
Memberships: Catharine Lorillard Wolfe Art Club (dir, 70, 2nd v pres, 71-74); Allied Artists Am (chmn, pub rels comt, 72-); Nat Art League; Art League Nassau Co (treas, 59-61); Am Artists Prof League.
Publications: Contribr, Prize-winning art-book 7, Allied Publ, Inc, Fort Lauderdale, Fla, 67.
Dealer: Garden City Galleries Ltd, 933 Franklin Ave, Garden City, NY 11530.
Mailing Address: 1296 Forest Ave, Baldwin, NY 11510.

STEWART, JACK
Painter, Educator
Preferred Media: Acrylics.
b Atlanta, Ga, Jan 27, 26.
Study & Training: With Steffen Thomas, Atlanta; Yale Univ Sch Fine Arts, BFA; Columbia Univ Sch Archit.
Commissions: Mural on facade of Versailles Hotel, Miami Beach, Fla, 55; six mosaic murals on S S Santa Paula, Grace Lines, 57; mural on facade of Hotel Aruba Caribbean, Netherlands Antilles, 58; two mosaic murals in pub sch 28, Manhattan, N Y, 58; stained glass for off of Cinerama, Inc, New York, N Y, 60.
Exhibitions: Pa Acad Fine Arts, Philadelphia, 53; New York City Ctr Show, 56; Inform & Interpret, Nat Fedn Arts Nat Traveling Show, 65-66; Art East Shows, New York, 65-68; Grippi & Wadell Gallery, 63-64.
Teaching: Lectr art & archit, New Sch Social Res, 53-58; instr design, Pratt Inst, 55-61; lectr drawing & painting, Columbia Univ, 67-; assoc prof drawing & painting, Cooper Union Sch Art & Archit, 60-, chmn dept, 71-
Publications: Contribr, Mosaic art today, 59; ed, Modern mosaic techniques, Watson Guptill, 67; auth, short articles on drawing & mosaic, In: Jefferson Encycl, World, 69; contribr, The art of mosaic, 69.
Mailing Address: 31 E 7th St, New York, NY 10003.

STEWART, JARVIS ANTHONY
Educator, Painter
Preferred Media: Acrylics, Oils.
b Marville, Mo, Dec 28, 14.
Study & Training: St Joseph Jr Col, 32-33; Phillips Univ, BFA, 42, with E J McFarland; Ohio State Univ, MA, 47; also with Ernest Thurn, Pablo O'Higgins Felipe Cossio & Hoyt Sherman.
Work in Public Collections: Columbus Gallery Fine Arts, Ohio; Otterbein Col, Westerville, Ohio; Phillips Univ, Enid, Okla.
Teaching: Instr design, Phillips Univ, 42-43; prof design & art hist, Ohio Wesleyan Univ, 43-
Positions: Asst for murals, Am Hotels Corp, Robidoux Hotel, Saint Louis, Mo, 39-40.
Research: Craftsmen of the Mexican Bajio; sociology of art.
Mailing Address: 61 Westgate Dr, Delaware, OH 43015.

STEWART, JOHN LINCOLN
Educator, Writer
b Alton, Ill, Jan 24, 17.
Study & Training: Denison Univ, AB, 38; Ohio State Univ, MA, 39, PhD, 47; Denison Univ, hon DA, 64.
Teaching: From asst prof to prof, Dartmouth Col, 49-64; prof Am lit & provost, John Muir Col, Univ Calif, San Diego, 64-
Positions: Provost & adv to chancellor arts, Univ Calif, 47-49; assoc dir, Hopkins Art Ctr, Dartmouth Col, 62-64.
Awards: Dartmouth faculty fel, 62-63.
Research: Contemporary American and British literatures.
Publications: Auth, John Crowe Ransom, Univ Minn Press, 62; auth, The burden of time, the fugitives and agrarians, Princeton Univ Press, 65; plus others.
Mailing Address: Office of the Provost, John Muir College, University of California, San Diego, La Jolla, CA 92037.

STEWART, JOHN P
Printmaker, Sculptor
b Fort Leavenworth, Kans, Mar 11, 45.
Study & Training: Univ Colo, BFA, 67, with Roland Reiss & Wendel Black; Univ Calif, Santa Barbara, MFA, 69.
Work in Public Collections: Corcoran Gallery Art, Washington, D C; Whitney Mus Am Art, New York, N Y; Kalamazoo Art Inst, Mich; Santa Barbara Mus Art; Peabody Mus, Nashville, Tenn.
Exhibitions: Northwest Printmakers 40th Int, Seattle Art Mus, 69; Art on Paper, Greensboro, N C, 71; Whitney Mus Recent Acquisitions, New York, 72; Objective Drawings, 100 Acres, New York, 72; one-man show, Pyramid Gallery, Washington, D C, 72.
Teaching: Instr printmaking, Univ N C, Greensboro, 69-
Dealer: Pyramid Gallery, 2121 P St N W, Washington, DC 20037.
Mailing Address: Art Dept, University of North Carolina at Greensboro, Greensboro, NC 27412.

STEWART, PATRICIA KAYE
Art Administrator
b El Paso, Tex, Oct 26, 47.
Study & Training: Univ Pa, BA; Columbia Univ.
Collections Arranged: Comix, Mus Contemp Art, Chicago, Ill, 72 & arrangements, selections & cataloging all exhibs, 72-
Positions: Curator, Mus Contemp Art, 72-
Publications: Auth, Comix, 72.
Mailing Address: Museum of Contemporary Art, 237 E Ontario St, Chicago, IL 60611.

STILL, CLYFFORD
Painter
b Grandin, N Dak, Nov 30, 04.
Study & Training: Spokane Univ, BA, 33; Wash State Col, MA.
Work in Public Collections: Baltimore Mus Art; Albright-Knox Art Gallery, Buffalo, N Y; Mus Mod Art; Phillips Collection, Washington, D C; Whitney Mus Am Art; plus others.
Exhibitions: One-man show, San Francisco Mus Art, 43; Fifteen Americans Traveling Exhib, 52, The New American Painting, circulating Europe, 58-59 & The New American Painting and Sculpture, 69, Mus Mod Art; retrospective, Albright-Knox Art Gallery, 59; Documenta II, Kassel, Ger, 59; one-man show, Univ Pa, 64; plus others.
Teaching: Mem fac, Yaddo, 34, 35, Wash State Col, 33-41, Richmond Prof Inst, Col William & Mary, 43-45, Calif Sch Fine Arts, 46-50; originated Subject of the Artist, New York, N Y, 47-48, Brooklyn Col, 52, Univ Pa, 63 & Hunter Col, 52.
Mailing Address: Box 337, New Windsor, MD 21776.

STILLMAN, E CLARK
Collector
b Eureka, Utah, Oct 24, 07.
Study & Training: Univ Mich, AB & AM.
Research: African sculpture; medieval and modern book illumination and illustration.
Collection: Traditional Congolese sculpture; manuscript and printed Books of Hours.
Mailing Address: 24 Gramercy Park, New York, NY 10003.

STILWELL, WILBER MOORE
Educator, Writer
Preferred Media: Oils.
b Covington, Ind, Feb 2, 08.
Study & Training: Kans State Teachers Col, BSEduc; Univ Iowa, MA; Kansas City Art Inst, Mo.
Exhibitions: Midwestern Artists Exhib, Kansas City, 33, 36 & 39; Nat Watercolor Show, Pa Acad Fine Arts, 34; Mo Artists Exhib, 38.
Teaching: Prof art, Univ S Dak, Vermillion, 41-
Positions: Nat co-dir, Am Art Wk, 65-66.
Awards: First award in lithography, Kansas Artists Exhib, Topeka, 41; medals, for distinguished serv Am art, Am Artists Prof League, New York, 66 & distinguished serv educ in art, Nat Gallery Art, 66.
Research: Picture design and composition.
Publications: Co-auth, New—blottergraph printing, 3/56, Transwax—a new art process, 2/58, Mobile printing, 3/61, Scraper paper, 9/61 & Waxbrush printing, 2/62, Sch Arts Mag.
Mailing Address: 711 E Lewis St, Vermillion, SD 57069.

STINSKI, GERALD PAUL
Painter, Collector
Preferred Media: Oils.
b Menasha, Wis, June 15, 29.
Work in Public Collections: Pvt & corporate collections.
Commissions: Del Monte Foods, Gallo Wineries, Consolidated Foods (Nathan Cummings Collection), plus others.
Exhibitions: Southeastern Regional, Atlanta, Ga; Tidewater Art Asn, Norfolk, Va.
Bibliography: Haddad's fine art reproductions, 72.

Collection: Sixteenth century drawings including Raphael; pre-Columbian sculpture, Etruscan and early Christian santos.
Dealers: Zantman Galleries, P O Box 5818, Carmel-by-the-sea, CA 93921; Conacher Galleries, 134 Maiden Lane, San Francisco, CA 94108.
Mailing Address: 65 Manzanita Rd, Fairfax, CA 94930.

STIPE, WILLIAM S
Painter
b 16.
Study & Training: Univ Iowa, BA & MA, 36; Mus Sch, Boston, with Karl Zerbe, 40; Inst Design, Chicago, 47.
Work in Public Collections: Springfield Art Mus, Mo; Ohio Univ, Athens; Northern Trust Co, Chicago; Int Minerals & Chem Corp, Skokie, Ill; Kans State Univ, Manhattan.
Commissions: Wall painting, Evanston Chamber Commerce, Davis L Bus Stop, 71.
Exhibitions: Denver Art Mus, Colo; Mus Fine Arts, Boston, Mass; Butler Inst Am Art, Youngstown, Ohio; Columbia Mus Art, S C; one-man shows, Culver-Stockton Col, Canton, Mo & Ill Arts Coun Gallery, Chicago, 72; plus many other group & one-man shows.
Teaching: Mem faculty, Northwestern Univ, 48.
Awards: Second prize, Washington, D C Watercolor Club, 49; Pauline Palmer Second Prize, 59th Ann Chicago Show, Art Inst, 56; first prize for painting, Old Orchard Art Fair, Skokie, Ill, 70.
Mailing Address: 1216 W Jarvis, Chicago, IL 60626.

STITES, RAYMOND SOMERS
Art Historian, Writer
b Passaic, N J, June 19, 99.
Study & Training: Brown Univ, MA & PhB; R I Sch Design; Univ Vienna, PhD.
Exhibitions: Metrop Mus Art; Denver Archaeol Mus; Dayton Art Inst; Am Mus Natural Hist.
Teaching: Lectr Leonardo da Vinci; chmn dept art & aesthet, Antioch Col, 30-48.
Positions: Cur in charge educ, Nat Gallery Art, Washington, D C, 48-70, asst to dir educ servs, 68-70; dir, Cult Films, Inc.
Memberships: Col Art Asn Am; Am Archaeol Soc; Ohio Valley Art Asn.
Publications: Auth, The sculptures of Leonardo da Vinci, 30, The arts and man, 40 & The self psychoanalysis of Leonardo da Vinci, 69; co-auth, Sublimations of Leonardo da Vinci, Smithsonian, 70; contribr, art mags.
Mailing Address: 11212 Kenilworth Ave, Garrett Park, MD 20766.

STODDARD, DONNA MELISSA
Art Administrator, Educator
b Saint Petersburg, Fla, July 1, 16.
Study & Training: Fla Southern Col, BS, 37; Pittsburgh Art Inst; Pa State Col, MEd, 42; N Y Sch Interior Design, 53; Univ Tampa, 59; Univ Fla, 60; Philathea Col, hon LHD, 68.
Collections Arranged: Directed Fla Int Art Exhib, 52; organized & installed permanent contemp art collection, Fla Southern Col.
Positions: Exec dept off art, Fla Southern Col, 40-; WEDU-TV Co Art Chmn Art Auction, 68-69.
Awards: Am Cult Award, 52; Grumbacher Award, 53; Miami Women's Club Gold Medal, 53; plus others.
Memberships: Am Asn Univ Women; Col Art Asn Am; Southeastern Col Art Asn; fel Royal Soc Art, London; Am Asn Univ Prof; plus others.
Publications: Contribr, Design Mag.
Mailing Address: Dept of Art, Florida Southern College, Lakeland, FL 33802.

STODDARD, HERBERT C
Painter, Educator
b Brooklyn, N Y, Aug 31, 10.
Study & Training: Col Archit, Univ Va; Col Archit, New York; Ringling Sch Art, Sarasota, Fla.
Exhibitions: Sarasota Art Asn, Ringling Mus, 55-59; Tampa Art Inst; Soc Four Arts, Palm Beach, Fla; Sarasota Art Asn Ann; Fla Art Group.
Teaching: Asst prof art, New Col, Fla.
Positions: Dir, Sarasota Sch Art, 57-
Awards: Prizes, Sarasota Art Asn, Manatee Art Ctr & Clearwater Art Inst.
Memberships: Artists Equity Asn; Fla Artists Group.
Mailing Address: 1543 Palmetto Lane, Sarasota, FL 33580.

STODDARD, WHITNEY SNOW
Art Historian
b Greenfield, Mass, Mar 25, 13.
Study & Training: Williams Col, BA, 35; Harvard Univ, MA, 38 & PhD, 41, with Koehler, Post & Sachs.

Teaching: Instr art, Williams Col, 38-43, asst prof, 43-49, assoc prof, 49-54, prof, 54-, chmn dept, 69-
Awards: Fulbright advan res grant, 54.
Memberships: Col Art Asn Am; Soc Archit Historians; Medieval Acad Am; Int Ctr Medieval Art (v pres, 72).
Research: Provencal Romanesque sculpture.
Publications: Auth, The west portals of Saint-Denis and Chartres, Harvard Univ Press, 52; auth, Adventure in architecture, building the new St Johns, 58; auth, Monastery and cathedral in France, 68 & The facade of Saint-Gilles-du-Gard, 72, Wesleyan Univ Press.
Mailing Address: Williams College, Williamstown, MA 01267.

STOFFA, MICHAEL
Painter, Lecturer
Preferred Media: Oils.
b Hlinne, Czech; U S citizen.
Study & Training: Newark Sch Fine & Indust Arts, scholar, 42; Pa Acad Fine Arts; Art Stud League New York.
Commissions: Portrait of J F Kennedy, Munic Bldg, Clark Court House, N J, 64; portrait of Dr Lozo, Edison, N J, 65; many other portrait comns in Westfield, N J area.
Exhibitions: Foreign Friends of Acapulco, Hilton Hotel, Acapulco, Mex, 69 & 70; Greenwich Village Art Exhib, New York, N Y, 69 & 70; Sullivan Parque, Mexico City, Mex, 69-72; North Shore Art Asn, Gloucester, Mass, 72; North Atlantic Exhib, East Gloucester, Mass, 72.
Teaching: Instr painting & still life portraits, Rahway Art Ctr & New Brunswick Art Ctr, N J, 59-67; also pvt classes in own studio, 59-69.
Awards: Popular award, Westfield Art Asn, 68; Bruce Stevens Award, Greenwich Village Show, 68.
Memberships: North Shore Art Asn; Jardin de Arte, Mexico City.
Mailing Address: 4 Dock Sq, Rockport, MA 01966.

STOIANOVICH, MARCELLE
Painter
Study & Training: Col d'Art Appliqué à'Industrie, Paris, France.
Work in Public Collections: Work in pvt collections.
Commissions: Posters for Am Christmas Fund, Paris; book jacket designs for Doubleday & Co; hand-made jewelry.
Exhibitions: Salon des Artistes Français, Paris, France; Maison Française, Columbia Univ, New York, N Y; Assoc Am Artists, New York; American Club, Athens & Macedonian Ctr, Salonika, Greece; Venable Gallery, Washington, D C; plus many others.
Awards: Hon mention for watercolor, Beaux-Arts, Paris, 50; hon mention, Soc Artistique de Clichy, Paris, 52.
Mailing Address: 60 Rector St, Metuchen, NJ 08840.

STOKES, THOMAS PHELPS
Painter
Preferred Media: Oils.
b New York, N Y, Mar 15, 34.
Exhibitions: Collectors Exhib, Cleveland Mus, Ohio, 64; Members Gallery-Albright-Knox Art Gallery, Buffalo, N Y, 66; Phillips Collection, Washington, D C, 69; Gift of Time, Mus N Mex, Santa Fe, 70; Univ Art Gallery, Va Polytech Inst & State Univ, Blacksburg, Va, 71; plus others.
Bibliography: John Canaday (auth), rev, In: New York Times, 5/4/68 & 9/27/69; Anita Feldman (auth), Thomas Stokes, summer 68 & rev, fall 69, Arts Mag; C Ratcliff (auth), article, In: Art Int, 11/69.
Dealer: Betty Parsons Gallery, 24 W 57th St, New York, NY 10019.
Mailing Address: 11 Carlyle Mansions, Cheyne Walk, London SW 3525, England.

STOKSTAD, MARILYN JANE
Art Historian, Educator
b Lansing, Mich, Feb 16, 29.
Study & Training: Carleton Col, BA, 50; Mich State Univ, MA, 53; Univ Mich, PhD, 57.
Teaching: Prof hist art, Univ Kans, 58-, chmn dept, 61-72, dir, Mus Art, 61-67, assoc dean, Col Arts & Sci, 72.
Positions: Res cur medieval art, Nelson Gallery, Kansas City, 69-
Awards: Fulbright fel, 51-52.
Memberships: Col Art Asn Am (bd dirs, 71); Medieval Soc Kans (pres, 68-70); Midwest Col Art Conf (pres, 64-65); Soc Archit Historians (bd dirs, 71); Am Asn Univ Prof (nat coun, 72-).
Research: Medieval art, especially sculpture; Irish art.
Publications: Auth, Handbook of the Museum of Art, University of Kansas, 62; auth, Notes on a Barcelon silver reliquary, Regist, Vol 2, No 9-10; auth, Renaissance art outside Italy, Art Horizons, 68; auth, Three apostles from Vich, Nelson Gallery Bull, Vol 4, No 11.
Mailing Address: 2020 W Ninth St, Lawrence, KS 66044.

STOLL, MRS BERRY VINCENT
Collector
b Louisville, Ky, Feb 2, 06.
Study & Training: Bryn Mawr Col; Louisville Art Sch.
Positions: V pres, J B Speed Art Mus, Louisville.
Collection: Paintings and antiques.
Mailing Address: 3905 Lime Kiln Lane, Louisville, KY 40222.

STOLL, TONI
Painter
Preferred Media: Oils, Watercolors.
b New York, N Y, Nov 5, 20.
Study & Training: Syracuse Univ, BFA; Grad Sch, Rutgers Univ.
Work in Public Collections: New Brunswick Pub Libr, N J; Long
Beach Island Jewish Community Ctr, N J.
Exhibitions: Am Artists Prof League, Nat Arts Club, 61-62; Smith-
sonian Inst, Washington, D C, 61-63; Painters & Sculptors Soc,
Jersey City Mus, 61-66; Fairleigh Dickenson Univ, Madison, 63;
Douglass Col, Rutgers Univ N J Centennial, New Brunswick, 64.
Teaching: Instr art, Lafayette Sch, Highland Park, N J, 53-58; pvt
instr, 53-
Positions: Art liaison chmn, Anshe Emett Mem Temple Art Show,
59 & 60; judge, Roebling-Boehm Art Scholar Competition, 62,
Spring Conf Exhib Gen Fedn Women's Clubs N J, 64 & Cinema
Theater Children's Exhib, Menlo Park, 68.
Awards: Grumbacher first prize for best in oils, 60 & 62, Drew Univ
second prize, 63 & hon mention, 64, Am Artists Prof League
Shows.
Bibliography: Toni Stoll exhibition, N J Music & Arts, 63; Paula
Hasslocher (auth), Women artists of New Jersey, Fairleigh Dick-
enson Univ Press, 64; Waylande Gregory (auth), Highland Park
artist chosen, Daily Home News, New Brunswick, 65.
Memberships: Am Artists Prof League; Hunterdon Art Asn; Guild
Creative Art; Cent N J Art Asn; Am Fedn Arts.
Dealer: Guild of Creative Art, 620 Broad St, Rte 35, Shrewsbury,
NJ 07701.
Mailing Address: 64 Johnson St, Highland Park, NJ 08904.

STOLOFF, CAROLYN
Painter
b New York, N Y.
Study & Training: Univ Ill; Columbia Univ, BA; Art Stud League New
York; Atelier 17; with Xavier Gonzalez, Eric Isenburger & Hans
Hofmann; also poetry with Stanley Kunitz.
Exhibitions: Whitney Mus Am Art; Pa Acad Fine Arts; Audubon Art-
ists; Nat Asn Women Artists; N J Soc Painters & Sculptors; plus
many other group & one-man shows.
Teaching: Former instr painting & drawing, Manhattanville Col,
chmn dept art, 58-63, now lectr art & Eng.
Awards: Silver anniversary medal, 67 & hon mention, 72, Audubon
Artists; Nat Coun Arts grant for poetry, 68; Helene Wurlitzer
Found residence grant for poetry, 72 & 73.
Mailing Address: 24 W 8th St, New York, NY 10011.

STOLOFF, IRMA
Sculptor
b New York, N Y.
Study & Training: Art Stud League New York, N Y, with Alexander
Stirling Calder, Boardman Robinson, Howard Giles, Yasuo
Kuniyoshi & Alexander Archipenko.
Work in Public Collections: Sculptures, Butler Inst Am Art, Youngs-
town, Ohio & Rose Art Mus, Brandeis Univ, Waltham, Mass;
sculpture & watercolor, Norfolk Mus, Va & Sheldon Swope Art
Gallery, Terre Haute, Ind; watercolor, Gibbs Art Gallery,
Charleston, S C.
Commissions: Portraits, bas-reliefs & figure compositions, pub &
pvt comns.
Exhibitions: Allied Artists Am, 66, New York Soc Women Artists,
70, Audubon Artists, 72 & Nat Asn Women Artists, 72, Nat Acad
Design Galleries; Nat Arts Club Ann, 69; plus others.
Teaching: Pvt instr.
Awards: Barstow Prize for sculpture, Nat Asn Women Artists, 53;
Excalibur Award for sculpture, Catharine Lorillard Wolfe Art
Club, 69; Mr & Mrs Michael J Solomone Prize for sculpture,
Audubon Artists, 71.
Bibliography: Datos biograficos de Irma Stoloff, Espacios, Mexico
City, 11/53; Irma Stoloff y la escultura abstracta, La Prensa,
11/53; Cornelia Justice (auth), The artists outpouring, Ledger
Star, 68; plus others.
Memberships: Audubon Artists (exec bd, 65-70); Nat Asn Women
Artists (sculpture jury, 52-54, 55-57, 68-70 & 72-74, finance
comt, 65-66, prog comt, 70); Silvermine Guild Artists; New York
Soc Women Artists (exhib comt, 66); Artists Equity Asn.
Mailing Address: 46 E 91st St, New York, NY 10028.

STOLTENBERG, DONALD HUGO
Painter, Printmaker
b Milwaukee, Wis, Oct 15, 27.
Study & Training: Inst Design, Ill Inst Technol, BS (visual design).
Work in Public Collections: Boston Mus Fine Art, Mass; Addison
Gallery Am Art, Andover, Mass; De Cordova Mus, Lincoln, Mass;
Portland Mus Art, Maine; Springfield Art Mus, Mass.
Exhibitions: Venice Observed, Fogg Mus, Cambridge, Mass, 56; Bos-
ton Arts Festival, 56-61; Corcoran Gallery Art Exhib, Washing-
ton, D C, 63; Landscape, De Cordova Mus, 71; Am Art Exhib, Art
Inst Chicago.
Teaching: Instr painting & printmaking, De Cordova Mus Sch; vis
critic, R I Sch Design.
Awards: Grand prize, 57 & first prize in painting, 59, Boston Arts
Festival; first purchase prize, Portland Mus Arts Festival.
Memberships: Boston Printmakers (mem bd, 71-).
Dealer: Kanegis Gallery, 249 Newbury St, Boston, MA 02116.
Mailing Address: Setucket Rd, Brewster, MA 02631.

STOMPS, WALTER E, JR
Painter, Educator
Preferred Media: Acrylics.
b Hamilton, Ohio, July 13, 29.
Study & Training: Miami Univ, BFA; Art Inst Chicago, with Boris
Anisfeld, Paul Weighardt, Isabelle MacKinnon & Edgar Pillet &
MFA; Syracuse Univ.
Work in Public Collections: Cleveland Mus Art, Ohio; Dayton Art
Inst, Ohio; Miami Univ, Oxford, Ohio.
Commissions: Ctr City Murals Proj, Dayton, Ohio, Nat Endowment
Arts, 72; Gen Motors (Frigidaire), Dayton, Ohio.
Exhibitions: Everson Mus Painting Exhib, Syracuse, N Y, 63; Ohio
Painting & Sculpture Exhib, Dayton, 66; Nat Drawing & Sculpture
Exhib, Muncie, Ind, 67; Ohio Print & Drawing Exhib, Dayton, 68;
Cincinnati Invitational, 72.
Teaching: Instr painting & drawing, Dayton Art Inst Sch, 63-, chmn
fine arts dept, 69-
Awards: James Nelson Raymond Award, Art Inst Chicago, 59; pur-
chase award, Ohio Painting & Sculpture Exhib, Dayton Art Inst,
66; purchase award, Ohio Print & Drawing Exhib, Dayton Art
Inst, 68.
Publications: Illusr, Dayton U S A, 72.
Dealer: Dayton Art Institute, Dayton, OH 45405.
Mailing Address: 335 Sherman Ave, Hamilton, OH 45013.

STONE, ALEX BENJAMIN
Art Dealer, Collector
b Sczuczyn, Poland, Mar 14, 22.
Study & Training: St John's Univ; Kans State Univ, DVM; Stanford
Univ Med Sch.
Positions: Mem bd dir, Friends Art, Davenport, Iowa, 71-
Memberships: Am Fedn Art; Mus Mod Art; Davenport Art Mus
(acquisitions comt).
Specialty of Gallery: Nineteenth century American landscapists;
contemporary American and European prints.
Collection: Eclectic—fifteenth century Venetians to twentieth cen-
tury surrealists.
Mailing Address: 4520 Fourth Ave, Moline, IL 61265.

STONE, JOHN LEWIS, JR
Painter, Instructor
Preferred Media: Watercolors, Oils, Tempera.
b Presidio, Tex, Nov 24, 37.
Study & Training: Fort Worth Mus Fine Arts; Tex Christian Univ;
Univ Tex, Arlington; Pa Acad Fine Arts.
Work in Public Collections: Pvt collections of individuals & corpora-
tions.
Exhibitions: 34th & 35th Ann, Miniature Painters, Sculptors &
Gravers Soc, Washington, D C; Heritage Hall Mus, Ft Worth, Tex,
71; one-man show, Cross Gallery, 71 & 72; Snyder Mus Fine
Art, 71; Longview Invitationals, 71 & 72.
Teaching: Instr watercolor workshop, Tex Christian Univ.
Awards: Borjorne' Egli Award, 34th Ann & Elizabeth Curtis Award,
35th Ann, Miniature Painters, Sculptors & Gravers Soc; first
prize in drawing, Heritage Hall Mus, 70; Beggs Award for water-
color, Snyder Mus Fine Art, 71.
Dealer: Gross Galleries, 3629 W Seventh St, Fort Worth, TX 76107.
Mailing Address: 2548 Cockrell St, Fort Worth, TX 76109.

STONE, SYLVIA
Sculptor
Preferred Media: Plexiglas.
b Toronto, Ont; U S citizen.
Study & Training: Pvt study in Can; Art Stud League New York.
Work in Public Collections: Whitney Mus Am Art, New York, N Y;
Hartford Antheneum, Conn; Xerox Corp, New York; Larry Al-
drich Mus, Ridgefield, Conn.

Commissions: Sunrise Mall, New York, comn by Tankoos-Muss Corp, 73.
Exhibitions: One-woman shows, Tibor de Nagy Gallery, 67-69 & Andre Emmerich Gallery, 72; 14 Sculptors—Industrial Edge, Walker Art Ctr, Minneapolis, Minn, 69; Whitney Mus Am Art Sculpture Ann, New York, 69, 71 & 73; Plastic Presence, Jewish Mus, Milwaukee Art Ctr & San Francisco, 70.
Awards: CAPS Award, New York State, 71.
Bibliography: M Friedman (auth), Sylvia Stone: industrial edge, Art Int, 70; Irv Sandler (auth), Sylvia Stone at Emmerich, Art in Am, 72.
Dealer: Andre Emmerich Gallery, 420 W Broadway, New York, NY 10012.
Mailing Address: 138 Prince St, New York, NY 10012.

STONEBARGER, VIRGINIA
Painter
b Ann Arbor, Mich, Mar 9, 26.
Study & Training: Antioch Col, BA, 50; Colorado Springs Fine Arts Ctr, 50-51; Art Stud League New York, 51-52; Hans Hofmann Sch, 54; New York Univ, 54 & 56; Univ Wis-Milwaukee, MS, 72.
Exhibitions: Univ Minn, 54; Art: U S A, 58; Univ Wis, 59; Milwaukee Art Ctr, 59-61; one-man shows, Lakeland Col, 69 & Univ Wis, 71; plus many other group & one-man shows.
Teaching: Instr art, Univ Lake Sch, Hartland, Wis, 59-62; instr painting, Watertown Adult Voc Sch, Wis, 67-68; instr art, Waukesha Co Tech Inst, 70-72.
Awards: Prizes, Watertown, Wis, 58 & Milwaukee Art Ctr, 60; Danforth Found fel, 69; plus others.
Memberships: Wis Painters & Sculptors Asn.
Mailing Address: 4850 Easy St, Hartland, WI 53029.

STOOPS, JACK DONALD
Film Maker, Educator
b Los Angeles, Calif, July 29, 14.
Study & Training: Univ Calif, Los Angeles, BA; Univ Southern Calif, MA; Columbia Univ, EdD; Leicester Col Arts, Eng.
Work in Public Collections: Art films in pub schs, U S.
Teaching: Asst prof art, Univ Calif, Los Angeles, 50-65; prof art, Univ Tenn, Knoxville, 65-66; prof art, Univ Wash, 68-
Positions: Pres, Pac Arts Asn, 63-65.
Awards: Awards for films, Discovering Color, Biennale Venezia, Italy, 61 & Discovering Creative Pattern, Edinburgh Film Festival, Scotland, 65; Golden Eagle Award, Coun Int Nontheatrical Events, 71.
Memberships: Nat Art Educ Asn (mem bd, 64-67).
Publications: Auth, articles, In: Art Educ J, 56-70; auth, Sch Arts, 58; auth, Craft Horizons, 65.
Mailing Address: 2415 42nd Ave E, Seattle, WA 98102.

STORM, HOWARD
Painter
Preferred Media: Acrylics.
b Newton, Mass, Oct 26, 46.
Study & Training: Denison Univ; apprenticeship, J Ferguson Stained Glass Studio, Weston, Mass; San Francisco Art Inst, BFA, 69; Univ Calif, Berkeley, MA, 70, MFA, 72.
Work in Public Collections: Roswell Mus, N Mex; Denison Univ, Granville, Ohio; Mount St Joseph Col, Cincinnati, Ohio; Ky Arts Comn, Frankfort.
Exhibitions: San Francisco Art Inst Centennial, San Francisco Mus Art, 71; 73rd Western Ann, Denver Mus, 71; one-man shows, San Francisco Art Inst, 69, Roswell Mus, 71 & Berkeley Mus, 72.
Teaching: Instr painting, Northern Ky State Col, 72-
Positions: Artist-in-residence grant, Roswell Mus, 71-72.
Awards: Eisner Prize, Univ Calif, Berkeley, 72; purchase award, Preview '73; purchase award, Huntington Galleries.
Memberships: Col Art Asn Am.
Dealer: Artium Orbis Gallery, 558 Canyon Rd, Santa Fe, NM 87501.
Mailing Address: 247 Licking Pike, Alexandria, KY 41001.

STORM, LARUE
Painter, Sculptor
Preferred Media: Graphics.
b Pittsburgh, Pa.
Study & Training: Univ Miami, AB & MA; Art Stud League, Woodstock, N Y; also printmaking with Calvaert Brun, Paris, & study in Los Angeles & Mich.
Work in Public Collections: Lowe Mus, Coral Gables, Fla; Columbia Mus Art, Ga; Norton Gallery Art, West Palm Beach, Fla.
Exhibitions: 50 Fla Painters, Ringling Mus, Sarasota, Fla, 55; Corcoran Gallery Art Biennial, Washington, D C, 57; Butler Inst Am Art, Youngstown, Ohio, 58-60; Miami Six, El Paso Mus, Tex, 65; Fla Creates, var mus Fla, 71-
Teaching: Instr drawing & design, Univ Miami, 67-
Publications: Auth, Jose Guadalupe Posada: guerrilla fighter of the throwaways, Carrell, 70.

Mailing Address: 3737 Justison Rd, Coconut Grove, Miami, FL 33133.

STORY, WILLIAM EASTON
Painter, Museum Director
b Valley City, N Dak, Feb 13, 25.
Study & Training: Art Inst Chicago, BFA; Ball State Teachers Col, MA; also with Stanley William Hayter.
Work in Public Collections: Butler Inst Am Art, Youngstown, Ohio; Ball State Univ Art Gallery, Muncie, Ind.
Exhibitions: Whitney Mus Am Art Ann, 57; Corcoran Gallery 25th Biennial, Washington, D C, 57; Cincinnati Art Mus Second Interior Valley Competition, 58; Artistas Brasileiros E Am, Mus Art Mod, São Paulo, Brazil, 60; Collages by American Artists, Ball State Univ Art Gallery, 72.
Collections Arranged: Metals in Muncie, Ball State Univ Art Gallery, 59; American Trompe L'Oeil & John Ferren—Paintings, Parrish Art Mus, Southampton, N Y, 69.
Teaching: Asst prof art & supvr, art gallery, Ball State Univ, Muncie, 56-66.
Positions: Asst dir, Am Mus in Brit, Bath, Eng, 66-68; dir, Parrish Art Mus, Southampton, 68-69; dir, Ella Sharp Mus, Jackson, Mich, 69-72; dir, Ball State Univ Art Gallery, 72-
Memberships: Am Asn Mus; Midwest Mus Asn.
Publications: Contribr, America in Britain, 67 & 68.
Mailing Address: 418½ N Calvert St, Muncie, IN 47306.

STOUT, GEORGE LESLIE
Art Consultant
b Winterset, Iowa, Oct 5, 97.
Study & Training: Univ Iowa, BA, 21; Harvard Univ, AM, 29; hon LittD, Clark Univ, 55.
Positions: Head conserv, Fogg Art Mus, Harvard Univ, 29-47; dir, Worcester Art Mus, 47-54; dir, Isabella Stewart Gardner Mus, Boston, 55-70.
Publications: Co-auth, Painting materials, Van Nostrand Reinhold, 42; auth, The care of pictures, Columbia Univ Press, 48; auth, Treasures of the Isabella Stewart Gardner Museum, Crown, 69.
Mailing Address: 350 Sharon Park Dr, C 23, Menlo Park, CA 94025.

STOUT, MYRON STEDMAN
Painter
b Denton, Tex, Dec 5, 08.
Work in Public Collections: Brooklyn Mus, N Y; Carnegie Mus, Pittsburgh, Pa; Guggenheim Mus, New York, N Y; Mus Mod Art, New York.
Exhibitions: Whitney Mus Am Art, 58; Mus Mod Art, 59; Jewish Mus, 63; Guggenheim Mus, 64-65; Corcoran Biennial, 69.
Dealer: Richard Bellamy, 1078 Madison Ave, New York, NY 10028.
Mailing Address: 4 Brewster St, Provincetown, MA 02657.

STOUT, RICHARD GORDON
Painter
Preferred Media: Acrylics.
b Beaumont, Tex, Aug 21, 34.
Study & Training: Cincinnati Art Acad, 52-53; Sch Art Inst Chicago, BFA, 57; Univ Tex, MFA, 69.
Work in Public Collections: Mus Fine Arts, Houston, Tex; Dallas Mus Fine Arts, Tex; Marion Koogler McNay Art Inst, San Antonio, Tex; Rice Univ; Univ Houston, Tex.
Commissions: Mural, Tex Fine Arts Asn for Hemisfair, now in libr lobby, Univ Houston, 68.
Exhibitions: Momentum Mid Continental Exhib, Chicago, Ill, 56-57; Second Int Triennial Oriental Coloured Graphic, Basel, Switz, 61; Hallmark Int, 62; One Hundred Contemporary American Draftsmen, Univ Mich, 63; Marion Koogler McNay Art Inst, 64 & 71.
Teaching: Instr painting, Mus Fine Arts, Houston, 58-67; asst prof drawing & painting, Univ Houston, 67-
Awards: First painting award, Dallas Mus Fine Arts, 64; Longview Purchase Prize, Jr Serv League, 65 & 72; Tex Fine Arts Asn Awards, 66 & 71.
Dealer: Houston Galleries, 2323 San Felipe, Houston, TX 77019.
Mailing Address: 1213 Bonnie Brae, Houston, TX 77006.

STOVALL, LUTHER McKINLEY (LOU)
Printmaker
b Athens, Ga, Jan 1, 37.
Study & Training: R I Sch Design; Howard Univ, BFA.
Work in Public Collections: Nat Collection Fine Arts, Smithsonian Inst, Washington, D C; Ringling Mus; Corcoran Gallery Art; Washington Post Co.
Commissions: Poster, VISTA, Washington, D C, 69; poster, Peace Corps, Washington, D C, 70; poster, Houston Mus Fine Arts, Tex, 70; posters, Corcoran Gallery Art, Washington, D C, 70 & 71; Bikes Have Equal Rights (poster), D C Dept Motor Vehicles, Washington Ecol Ctr, 70-72.

Exhibitions: Prints & Posters, Corcoran Gallery Art, Du Pont Ctr, Washington, D C, 69-71; Johns Hopkins Ctr Advan Int Study, Washington, D C, 70-71; Atlantic Christian Col, N C, 72; Frostburg Col, Md, 72; Traveling Exhib Prints & Posters, Baltimore Mus Art, Md, 72-73; plus others.
Teaching: Master printmaking & silkscreen, workshop, Corcoran Gallery Art, 69-72.
Positions: Dir, Workshop, Inc, 68.
Awards: Sterm grant, 68-72; individual artist grant, 72 & workshop grant, 72, Nat Endowment Arts.
Bibliography: Silkscreen printmaking (film), produced on WTOP-TV, 69; Jay Jacobs (auth), We have to like the way you look, Art Gallery, 3/70.
Mailing Address: Workshop, Inc, 2301 S St N W, Washington, DC 20008.

STOWMAN, ANNETTE BURR
Painter
Preferred Media: Oils.
b Paris, France, Jan 21, 09; U S citizen.
Study & Training: Vassar Col, AB, 29; Art Stud League New York, 56-58.
Work in Public Collections: Hickory Art Mus, N C; Greenville Mus Art, S C; Tamahassee D A R Sch, S C; Riveredge Found Collection, Can.
Exhibitions: Yorktown Heights Regional Show, N Y, 57; New York City Ctr Gallery, N Y, 61; Nat Artists Club Exhib, 62; Colorama Gallery, N Y World's Fair, 65; Volusia Co, Fla Regional Show, 68.
Teaching: Instr art, Dayton Community Col Div Continuing Educ, 70-
Awards: Second prize, Yorktown Heights Art Show, 57; hon mention, Nat Artists Club, 62; equal award, Volusia Co Art Show, 68.
Memberships: Burr Artists (parliamentarian, 66-); life mem Art Stud League New York; New Smyrna Beach Artists Workshop (prog chmn, 69-70); Daytona Beach Art Ctr; Fla Fedn Art.
Dealer: Burr Artists, 15 Gramercy Park S, New York, NY 10003.
Mailing Address: P O Box 278, Edgewater, FL 32032.

STRAIGHT, MICHAEL
Collector
b Southampton, N Y, Sept 1, 16.
Study & Training: Cambridge Univ, MA.
Collection: Fifteenth, sixteenth and seventeenth century French and Italian paintings.
Mailing Address: 3017 N St N W, Washington, DC 20007.

STRALEM, DONALD S
Collector, Patron
b Port Washington, N. Y.
Study & Training: Harvard Univ, 24; Cambridge Univ, 25.
Positions: Pres, Palm Springs Desert Mus, Calif.
Memberships: Fogg Art Mus (overseers comt).
Collection: Impressionists, naifs.
Mailing Address: 40 Wall St, New York, NY 10005.

STRATER, HENRY
Painter
Preferred Media: Oils.
b Louisville, Ky, Jan 21, 96.
Study & Training: Acad Julien, Paris; Art Stud League New York, N Y; Pa Acad Fine Arts, with Arthur Carles & Charles Grafly; Acad San Fernando, with Sorolla; Acad Grande Chaumiére, Paris; Ecole M Denis, with Edouard Vuillard; also with Ignacio Zuloaga, Spain.
Work in Public Collections: Oils, Philadelphia Mus Art, Art Mus Princeton Univ, N J, Detroit Inst Arts, City Art Mus St Louis & Butler Inst Am Art, Youngstown, Ohio.
Exhibitions: Salon Automne, Paris, France, 22; Whitney Studio Club Portrait Exhib, 26; Brooklyn Mus Watercolor Ann, 26; Corcoran Gallery Art Biennial, Washington, D C, 32; IBM Gallery Sci & Art, Golden Gate Expos, San Francisco, Calif, 39-40.
Positions: Trustee, Mus Art Ogunquit, Maine, 52-
Awards: Second prize, Golden Gate Expos, IBM Fine Arts Collection, 39; third prize for oil, Soc Four Arts, 47; first prize for drawing, Norton Gallery Art, 60.
Bibliography: Edward F Fry (auth), foreward, In: H S, 62; Sarah Lansdell (auth), An adventure in color, Courier-J Sun Illus Mag, 65; Betty Chamberlain (auth), Henry Strater: form and adventure through color, Am Artist, 5/72.
Memberships: Ogunquit Art Asn (pres, 46-48); The Players, New York; Arts Club, Louisville; Soc Four Arts; Palm Beach Art Inst.
Publications: Illusr, 14 cantos, Ezra Pound, Three Mts Press, Paris, France, 23; contribr, Living American art, 35-37; auth, 24 drawings by Henry Strater, Anthoenson Press, 58; ed, Henry Strater, 62; ed, Henry Strater, new paintings, Frank Rehn Gallery, 67.
Dealer: Frank Rehn Gallery, 655 Madison Ave, New York, NY 10021.
Mailing Address: Shore Rd, Ogunquit, ME 03907.

STRATTON, DOROTHY (DOROTHY STRATTON KING)
Painter, Printmaker
b Worcester, Mass.
Study & Training: Pratt Inst, cert, 42; Brooklyn Mus Sch, N Y, 42-43; Univ Calif, Los Angeles Summer Sch, 56 & 57, with Rico Lebrun; Univ Calif, Los Angeles, 61; Univ Calif, San Diego, 66-67.
Work in Public Collections: Long Beach Mus Art, Calif; Tunisian Ministry Cult Affairs, Tunis; Los Angeles Munic Art Collection, City Hall; Art In Embassies Permanent Collection, Dept of State, Washington, D C; Southwestern Col, Chula Vista, Calif.
Exhibitions: One-man shows, Pasadena Art Mus, Calif, 59, La Jolla Mus Art, Calif, 62 & Tunisian Comt Cult Coop U S Info Serv, Tunis, 65; Art In Embassies Prog, 10 countries, 65-72; Calif Soc Printmakers Nat, Richmond Art Ctr, 72.
Positions: Miniature set decorator, George Pal Prod, 45-46; gallery receptionist & ed publicity, Munic Art Dept, Los Angeles, 52-61.
Awards: First prize West Competition, Motorola, Inc, 62; first purchase prizes, Regional Exhib, Southwestern Col, 63; Kogo Time-Life Awards & first purchase prizes, Art Guild Exhib, Fine Arts Gallery San Diego, 63.
Memberships: Artists Equity Asn (publicity comt, 46-50); life mem Westwood Art Asn (pres, 56-57); Arts Coun, Univ Calif, Los Angeles (fine arts comt rep, 57-62); La Jolla Mus Art (registr & mem secy, 64-65, chmn art ref libr, 66-70); Fine Arts Soc & Art Guild Comt, Fine Arts Gallery San Diego (chmn art guild comt, 63-66, v chmn, 72-).
Mailing Address: 1465 Torrey Pines Rd, P O Box 2151, La Jolla, CA 92037.

STRAWBRIDGE, EDWARD RICHIE
Painter
Preferred Media: Oils, Watercolors.
b Nov 22, 03; U S citizen.
Memberships: Am Watercolor Soc; Soc Western Artists; Philadelphia Sketch Club; Philadelphia Watercolor Club.
Mailing Address: 8210 Crittenden St, Philadelphia, PA 19118.

STRAWN, MELVIN NICHOLAS
Painter, Sculptor
Preferred Media: Oils.
b Boise, Idaho, Aug 5, 29.
Study & Training: Chounaird Art Inst; Los Angeles Co Art Inst; Jepson Art Inst; Calif Col Arts & Crafts, BFA & MFA.
Work in Public Collections: Oakland Art Mus; Antioch Col; Colo State Univ.
Commissions: Environ design (sculpture), Ottawa Col, Kans, 72.
Exhibitions: Colo State Univ Centennial Exhib, 70; Cedar City Nat, Utah, 72; I-25 Artists Alliance, Colorado Springs Fine Arts Ctr, 72; plus others, 55-72.
Teaching: Instr art, Midwestern Univ, Mich State Univ, Antioch Col & Univ Denver, 56-72; chmn art dept, Antioch Col, 66-69; dir, sch art, Univ Denver, 69-
Awards: First purchase award, Colo State Univ Centennial, 70.
Memberships: I-25 Artists Alliance; Col Art Asn Am.
Mailing Address: 7 S Lane, Cherry Hills Village, CO 80110.

STREETER, TAL
Sculptor
Preferred Media: Steel.
b Oklahoma City, Okla, Aug 1, 34.
Study & Training: Univ Kans, BFA, MFA; Colorado Springs Fine Arts Ctr, with Robert Motherwell; Colo Col; with Seymour Lipton, three yrs.
Work in Public Collections: Mus Mod Art, New York, N Y; San Francisco Mus Art, Calif; Wadsworth Atheneum, Hartford, Conn; Nat Collection Fine Arts, Smithsonian Inst, Washington, D C; Smith Col Mus Art.
Commissions: Sculpture, Ark Art Ctr, Little Rock; two sculptures, Gt Southwest Park, Atlanta, Ga; sculpture, Sheldon Mem Art Gallery, Lincoln, Nebr; Sculpture in Environment, New York City Parks Dept; sculpture, Hong-Ik Univ, Seoul, Korea.
Exhibitions: American Sculpture, Sheldon Mem Art Gallery, Lincoln, 70; Painting & Sculpture Today, Indianapolis Mus Art, Ind, 70; Cool Art & Highlights of the Season, Larry Aldrich Mus, Ridgefield, Conn, 70; Red Line in the Sky: Tal Streeter's Kites, Univ Kans Mus Art, Lawrence, 72; Outdoor Sculptors Indoors, Storm King Art Ctr, Mountainville, N Y, 72.
Teaching: Vis artist, Fairleigh Dickinson Univ, Madison Campus, 62; vis artist-in-residence, Dartmouth Col, 63; vis artist, Univ N C, Greensboro, 70; Fulbright prof, Seoul, Korea, 71; vis lectr, U S Info Serv, Japan, 72; vis artist, Univ N C, Greensboro, 72-73.
Awards: State Univ N Y Int Studies grant, Japan, 69; Fulbright professorship, Korea, 71.
Bibliography: Mark Sadan (auth), Sculpture song (film biog), Film-Makers Coop, 66; E Amel (auth), New York City's Endless Column, Space Design, 70; Joseph Love (auth), Dolmens in the vast field of a domed sky, Minami Gallery, 71.

Publications: Co-auth, Seymour Lipton, the sculptor's way, 61 & auth, Kite: red line in the sky, 72, Univ Kans Mus Art; auth, Red line to the sky: notebook for a contemporary monument, Space Design, 71; auth, Japan's flying art: kites, Weatherhill/Lippincott, 72.
Dealers: A M Sachs Gallery, 29 W 57th, New York, NY 10019; Lippincott Large-Scale Sculpture, 400 Sackett Point Rd, North Haven, CT 06473.
Mailing Address: Old Verbank School, Millbrook, NY 12545.

STREETT, TYLDEN WESTCOTT
Sculptor, Educator
b Baltimore, Md, Nov 28, 22.
Study & Training: Johns Hopkins Univ; St John's Col; Md Inst Col Art, BFA & MFA, with Sidney Waugh & Cecil Howard; also asst to Lee Lawrie.
Commissions: Archit sculpture, Kirk-in-the-Hills, Bloomfield Hills, Mich, 57; archit sculpture (with Lee Lawrie) West Point, N Y, 58; archit sculpture, Washington D C Cathedral, 59, Roland Park Presby Church, 59 & Kuwait Embassy, Washington, D C, 65.
Exhibitions: Corcoran Gallery Art, Washington, D C, 60; Baltimore Mus Art, 69.
Teaching: Instr sculpture, Md Inst Col Art, Baltimore, 59-; dir Grad Studies, 66-; instr sculpture, Jewish Community Ctr, Baltimore, 63-65.
Awards: Rinehart traveling fel, 53; Louis Comfort Tiffany Found Award, 56; John Gregory Award, 62.
Memberships: Nat Sculpture Soc; Artists Equity Asn.
Publications: Auth, Plaster casting using a waste mold (film), 70.
Dealer: Phoenix Galleries, 5 W Chase St, Baltimore, MD 21201.
Mailing Address: 4622 Keswick Rd, Baltimore, MD 21210.

STRICKLAND, THOMAS J
Painter
Study & Training: Newark Sch Fine & Indust Arts, N J; Am Art Sch & Nat Acad Fine Arts, New York, N Y, with Robert Philipp.
Exhibitions: Metrop Young Artists First Ann, 58 & Am Artists Prof League, 58 & 61, Nat Arts Club; Butler Inst Am Art Fine Arts Festival, Youngstown, Ohio, 63; Seventh Grand Prix Int Peinture Cote d'Azur, Cannes, France, 71; Art Show Temple Beth Am, Miami, 72; plus others.
Awards: Digby Chandler Prize, Knickerbocker Artists Exhib, 65; first prize, Hollywood Arts & Crafts Guild Ann Mems Art Exhib, 72; first prize, Seven Lively Arts Festival Circle Art Show, Hollywood, 72.
Memberships: Grove House, Miami; Hollywood Arts & Crafts Guild, Fla; Miami Art Ctr; Miami Palette Club.
Mailing Address: 2598 Taluga Dr, Miami, FL 33133.

STRIDER, MARJORIE VIRGINIA
Sculptor
Preferred Media: Plastics.
b Guthrie, Okla.
Study & Training: Kansas City Art Inst, Mo; Okla Univ, BFA.
Work in Public Collections: Albright Knox Mus, Buffalo, N Y; Larry Aldrich Mus, N Y; plus others.
Exhibitions: Am Fedn Art Traveling New York Show, 66; one-man show, Park Col, Kansas City, 68; Whitney Sculpture Ann, Whitney Mus Am Art, New York, 70; Collage of Indignation II, New York Cult Ctr, 71; one-man show, Hoffman Gallery, New York, 73; plus others.
Teaching: Instr sculpture, Sch Visual Arts, New York, 68-; instr sculpture, Univ Iowa, summer 70; instr sculpture, Univ Ga, summer 72.
Bibliography: M Kirby (auth), chap, In: The art of time, 69 & L Lippard (auth), chap, In: Conceptual art, 72, Dutton; M Compton (auth), chap, In: Movements of modern art, Hamlyn, 70.
Publications: Auth, Moving out-moving up, Art News, 1/71; auth, Radical scale, Art & Artists, 1/72; illusr & contribr, Modern American painting & sculpture, Abrams, 72.
Dealer: Nancy Hoffman, 429 W Broadway, New York, NY 10012.
Mailing Address: 113 Greene St, New York, NY 10012.

STRINGER, MARY EVELYN
Educator, Art Historian
b Huntsville, Mo, July 31, 21.
Study & Training: Univ Mo, AB; Univ N C, AM; Harvard Univ, univ traveling fel, 66-67, with Ernst Kitzinger.
Teaching: Assoc prof art, Miss State Col Women, 47-
Awards: Fulbright scholar, 55-56; Danforth Found teacher study grant, 59-60 & 64-65.
Memberships: Col Art Asn Am; Medieval Acad; Int Ctr Medieval Art; Southeastern Col Art Conf.
Publications: Auth, Review of Andrew Martindale, Gothic Art, 69; auth, Composite nativity-adoration of English medieval alabasters, N C Mus Art Bull, 70.
Mailing Address: Box 1109, College Station, Columbus, MS 39701.

STRISIK, PAUL
Painter
Preferred Media: Oils, Watercolors, Acrylics.
b Brooklyn, N Y, Apr 21, 18.
Study & Training: Art Stud League New York, N Y, with Frank Vincent Dumond.
Work in Public Collections: Parrish Mus Art, Southampton, N Y; Percy H Whitney Mus, Fairhope, Ala; Mattatuck Mus, Conn; Utah State Univ; Union Carbide & Chem Collection.
Exhibitions: Each ann, Am Watercolor Soc, Nat Acad Design, Allied Artists Am & other nat shows.
Awards: Bronze medal of honor, Nat Arts Club, 70; best in show, Am Artists Prof League Grand Nat, 72; Obrig Prize, Nat Acad Design, 72; plus many others.
Memberships: Rockport Art Asn (pres, 68-72); assoc Nat Acad Design; Am Watercolor Soc; Allied Artists Am; Knickerbocker Artists.
Publications: Auth, Watercolor page, Am Artist, 4/70.
Mailing Address: 10 Main St, Rockport, MA 01966.

STROBEL, THOMAS C
Painter, Graphic Artist
b Bellemeade, Tenn, Sept 6, 31.
Study & Training: Art Inst Chicago, BFA; Univ Chicago; pvt study in Ger.
Work in Public Collections: State Art Acad, Ger; Krannert Mus, Univ Ill; Art Inst Chicago; Int Minerals & Chem Corp; IBM Collection; plus others, including pvt collections.
Exhibitions: Albright-Knox Art Gallery, Buffalo, N Y, Worcester Mus Art, Mass, Cleveland Mus Art, Walker Art Ctr, Minneapolis, Minn & Art Inst Chicago, 65; plus many other group & one-man shows.
Teaching: Former instr painting & drawing, Northwestern Univ, Chicago.
Awards: Gold medal, Chicago Sun Times, 60; Fulbright Award painting, Dusseldorf, Ger, 60-61; Graham Found grant, 68-69; plus many others.
Memberships: Chicago Art Club; N Shore Art Ctr; Evanston Art Ctr.
Mailing Address: 204 Otis Rd, Barrington Hills, IL 60010.

STROMBOTNE, JAMES
Painter
b Watertown, S Dak, 1934.
Study & Training: Pomona Col, BA; Claremont Grad Sch, MFA.
Work in Public Collections: Whitney Mus Am Art; Pasadena Art Mus; Cleveland Art Mus; Amon Carter Mus Western Art; Santa Barbara Mus; plus many others.
Exhibitions: Whitney Mus Am Art, 60-63; Carnegie Int, 64; Am Fedn Arts, 64; New Sch Social Res, N Y, 64 & 68; Corcoran Gallery Art, 67; plus many other group & one-man shows.
Teaching: Mem, Inst Creative Arts, Univ Calif, 65-66.
Awards: Honnold traveling fel, Pomona Col, 56; Guggenheim fel, 62-63; Tamarind Lithography Workshop fel, 68; plus others.
Mailing Address: 666 Griffith Way, Laguna Beach, CA 92651.

STRONG, CHARLES RALPH
Painter, Educator
Preferred Media: Acrylics.
b Greeley, Colo, Dec 25, 38.
Study & Training: Coronado Sch Fine Art, 57; San Francisco Art Inst, BFA, 62, MFA, 63; also with Elmer Bischoff, Jack Jefferson, Frank Lobdell & James Weeks.
Work in Public Collections: de Saisset Art Gallery, Univ Santa Clara, Calif; Oakland Mus, Calif; San Francisco Art Inst.
Exhibitions: California Works of Paper 1950-1971, Univ Art Mus, Berkeley, Calif, 72; one-man shows, Richmond Art Ctr, Calif, 69, Galerie Smith-Anderson, Palo Alto, Calif & Chief Joseph Series, Crown Col, Univ Calif, Santa Cruz, 72; three-man show, Painted Images, Oakland Mus, 71.
Teaching: Instr painting & drawing, San Francisco State Col, 65-68; lectr painting & drawing, Stanford Univ, summers 70 & 71; asst prof painting & drawing, Col Notre Dame, Calif, 70-
Awards: Fulbright fel to Eng, 64.
Dealer: Galerie Smith-Anderson, 200 Homer Ave, Palo Alto, CA 94301.
Mailing Address: Star Rte, Box 79, Redwood City, CA 94062.

STROTHER, JOSEPH WILLIS
Painter, Instructor
Preferred Media: Acrylics.
b New Orleans, La, Dec 14, 33.
Study & Training: La Col, BA; Univ Ga, MA & EdD.
Work in Public Collections: Chattahoochee Art Asn Collection; N C Nat Bank Collection; Wachovia Bank State Collection; Ga Mus; Dillard Collection, Weatherspoon Gallery, Univ N C, Greensboro.

Exhibitions: Mead Painting of Year, Atlanta, 61; four shows, Nat Art on Paper, Greensboro, N C, 64-69; N C Artist Ann, 71; Ga Artist Ann, 72.
Teaching: Art supvr, Marietta City Schs, Ga, 57-61; instr art, Montgomery Co, Md, 61-64; instr art, Univ N C, Greensboro, 64-66; instr art, Univ Ga, 66-
Awards: Purchase award, Chattahooche Art Asn, 69; award, Ocala Jr Col, 69; purchase award, N C Sch Ment Health Exten, Chapel Hill, 71.
Memberships: Nat Art Educ Asn; Col Art Asn Am.
Mailing Address: Dept of Art, University of Georgia, Athens, GA 30601.

STROUD, PETER ANTHONY
Painter, Educator
Preferred Media: Acrylics.
b London, Eng, May 23, 21.
Study & Training: Teacher Training Col, London Univ, Centralo Hammersmith Schs Art, 48-53.
Work in Public Collections: Tate Gallery, London; Guggenheim Mus, New York, N Y; Los Angeles Co Mus, Calif; Detroit Inst Fine Arts, Mich; Pasadena Art Mus, Calif.
Commissions: Murals, Int Union Archit Congress Bldg, London, 61; State Sch Leverkusen, Ger, 63 & Mfrs Hanover Trust Co, New York, 69.
Exhibitions: Carnegie Int, Pittsburgh, Pa, 61 & 64; Guggenheim Mus Int, 64; The Responsive Eye, Mus Mod Art, New York, 65; European Painters Today, Jewish Mus, New York, 68.
Teaching: Prof visual studies, Bennington Col, 63-68; prof painting, Rutgers Univ Grad Sch, New Brunswick, 68-
Awards: Pasadena Mus fel, 64.
Bibliography: Lawrence Allowey (auth), Catalog Introduction, Int Contemp Art, London, 61; Dore Ashton (auth), Peter Stroud's relief-paintings, Studio Int, 66; John Coplans (auth), Interview with Peter Stroud, Artforum, 66.
Dealer: Max Hutchinson Gallery, 127 Greene St, New York, NY 10012.
Mailing Address: 311 Church St, New York, NY 10013.

STRUPPECK, JULES
Sculptor, Educator
b Grangeville, La, May 29, 15.
Study & Training: Univ Okla, BFA; La State Univ, MA.
Exhibitions: Am Fedn Arts Traveling Exhib, 41; Bertha Schaefer Gallery, 53; Whitney Mus Am Art, 54; Archit League, 54; San Francisco Mus Art, 66.
Teaching: Prof sculpture, Newcomb Col, Tulane Univ La, presently.
Awards: Prizes, Gallery Art, Miami, Bertha Schaefer Gallery & Marine Hosp, New Orleans, La; plus others.
Publications: Auth, The creation of sculpture, Holt, Rinehart & Winston, 52; contribr, Design Mag.
Mailing Address: Dept of Art, Newcomb College, Tulane University of Louisiana, New Orleans, LA 70118.

STUART, DAVID
Art Dealer, Lecturer
b Scotland, S Dak.
Study & Training: Otis Art Inst, Los Angeles.
Positions: Dir, David Stuart Galleries.
Memberships: Art Dealers Asn Am.
Specialty of Gallery: Contemporary painting and sculpture; pre-Columbian and African arts.
Mailing Address: 807 N La Cienega Blvd, Los Angeles, CA 90069.

STUART, JOSEPH MARTIN
Painter, Museum Director
Preferred Media: Acrylics.
b Seminole, Okla, Nov 9, 32.
Study & Training: Univ N Mex, BFA, 59, MA, 62.
Work in Public Collections: Art Mus, Univ N Mex, Albuquerque; Jewett Gallery, Col Idaho, Caldwell; Melick Libr Collection, Eureka Col, Ill; Salt Lake Art Ctr, Salt Lake City, Utah.
Commissions: Mural, Donald B Anderson, Roswell, N Mex, 61.
Exhibitions: 10th & 11th Mid-Am Exhibs, Nelson Mus, Kansas City, Mo, 60 & 61; Western Artists 68th Ann, Denver Art Mus, Colo, 62; two-man show, Mus Art, Univ Ore, Eugene, 63; Northwest Artists 50th & 52nd Ann, Seattle Art Mus, Wash, 64 & 66; two-man show, Jonson Gallery, Univ N Mex, Albuquerque, 69.
Collections Arranged: Jannis Spyropoulos: Paintings, Roswell Mus & Art Ctr, N Mex, 62; Edward Kienholz: Sculpture, Boise Gallery Art, Idaho, 67; Lure of the West, Salt Lake Art Ctr, 71.
Teaching: Lectr introd to art, Univ Utah, 69; asst prof art hist, S Dak State Univ, 71-
Positions: Cur, Mus Art, Univ Ore, 62-63; dir, Boise Gallery Art, 64-68; dir, Salt Lake Art Ctr, 68-71; dir, S Dak Mem Art Ctr, Brookings, 71-; dir, res proj, Surv Art in S Dak, State & Nat Endowment on the Art grant, 72-74.

Awards: First prize in painting, Cheney Cowles Mem Mus, Spokane, Wash, 65; Salt Lake Art Ctr Purchase Award, 67.
Memberships: Am Soc Archit Historians; S Dak Mem Art Ctr; Brookings Area Arts Coun (dir); Brookings Fine Arts Club.
Publications: Auth, Nature in abstract-expressionism, Roswell Mus Bull, 60; auth, The need for art education in the public schools, Pac Art Asn Rev, 62; auth, An interview with Billy Apple, Boise Art Asn Bull, 66; auth, Stimuli, Utah Archit, fall 69.
Mailing Address: 719 Eighth St, Brookings, SD 57006.

STUART, KENNETH JAMES
Art Director
b Milwaukee, Wis.
Study & Training: Pa Acad Fine Arts, with Arthur B Carles; also in Paris, France.
Work in Public Collections: Hitler, Libr Cong, Washington, D C.
Teaching: Head, dept illus & advert, Moore Col Art, Philadelphia, Pa, 39-44, bd managers, 44-56.
Positions: Mag & bk illusr & painter, 44; art ed, Sat Eve Post, Philadelphia, 44-62; art dir, Reader's Digest, New York, 62-
Awards: Award for distinctive merit, N J Art Dirs Club, 62; three citations for merit, Soc Illusr, 63; New York Type Dirs Club Award, 63; plus others.
Memberships: Salmagundi Club.
Mailing Address: 295 Ridgefield Rd, Wilton, CT 06897.

STULER, JACK
Photographer, Educator
b Homestead, Pa, Aug 30, 32.
Study & Training: Phoenix Col, 57; Ariz State Univ, BA, 60, with Van Deren Coke, 61, MFA, 63; workshop with Ansel Adams, 66.
Work in Public Collections: George Eastman House, Rochester, N Y; Gen Aniline Films, New York, N Y; Univ Collections, Ariz State Univ, Tempe; Yuma Art Ctr, Ariz; Phoenix Col.
Exhibitions: Three Photogr, George Eastman House, 63; Photog 63/Int Exhib, 63, George Eastman House; Photog In Twentieth Century, Nat Gallery Can, 67; Am Photog: The Sixties, Sheldon Mem Art Gallery, Univ Nebr, Lincoln, 66; Photog U S A, De Cordova Mus, Lincoln, Mass, 68.
Teaching: Asst prof photog art, Ariz State Univ, 66-, summer fel, 68.
Awards: First Award Biennial Photog, Phoenix Art Mus, 67; Best of Show, Third Southwestern Art Invitational, Yuma Fine Arts Asn, 68.
Bibliography: Nathan Lyons (auth), The younger generation, Art Am, 12/63.
Memberships: Soc Photog Educ; Inst Cult Exchange Through Photog (mem adv bd, 66-).
Publications: Contribr, Photography in the twentieth century, Horizon, 67, Photog Ann, 69, Being without clothes, Aperture 15:3, 70 & Camera, Lucerne, Switz, 11/71.
Mailing Address: 1134 E Broadmor Dr, Tempe, AZ 85282.

STURTEVANT, HARRIET H
Painter, Designer
b Manchester, N H, May 2, 06.
Study & Training: Albright Art Sch; Parsons Sch Design, New York & Paris, 28-30.
Exhibitions: Nat Arts Club, 54-64; Catharine Lorillard Wolfe Art Club, 54-65 & 67; Knickerbocker Artists, 58-64; Watercolor: U S A, 62 & 63; one-man show, Pen & Brush Club, 69; plus others.
Positions: Free-lance designer, 64-
Awards: Prizes, Long Island Art League, 53 & 64, prizes, 57, 60 & 63 & gold medal, 67, Catharine Lorillard Wolfe Art Club; prizes, Knickerbocker Artists, 62 & 64; plus others.
Memberships: Am Watercolor Soc; Pen & Brush Club; Allied Artists Am; Catharine Lorillard Wolfe Art Club; Knickerbocker Artists.
Mailing Address: 35-50 77th St, Jackson Heights, NY 11372.

SUBA, SUSANNE
Painter, Illustrator
b Budapest, Hungary.
Study & Training: Pratt Inst, grad.
Work in Public Collections: Metrop Mus Art, New York, N Y; Brooklyn Mus, N Y; Art Inst Chicago, Ill; Mus City of New York; Kalamazoo Inst Art, Mich.
Exhibitions: Ansdell Gallery, London, Eng; Hammer Gallery, New York; Kalamazoo Inst Art; Art Inst Chicago; Mus Mod Art, New York.
Awards: Awards, Am Inst Graphic Art, Art Dirs Club New York & Art Dirs Club Chicago.
Mailing Address: 1019 Third Ave, New York, NY 10021.

SUBLETT, CARL C
Painter, Educator
Preferred Media: Watercolors, Oils, Acrylics.
b Johnson Co, Ky, Feb 4, 19.
Study & Training: Western Ky Univ; Univ Study Ctr, Florence, Italy; Univ Tenn.
Work in Public Collections: Dulin Gallery Art, Knoxville, Tenn; Hunter Gallery Art, Chattanooga, Tenn; Mint Mus, Charlotte, N C; Stephens Col, Springfield, Mo; Tenn Arts Comn, Nashville, Tenn.
Exhibitions: Several exhibs, Southeastern Art Ann, Atlanta, Ga, Paintings of Yr, Atlanta & New Painters of South, Birmingham, Ala; Watercolor U S A, Springfield, Mo, 64-72; Am Watercolor Soc, New York, N Y, 72.
Teaching: Assoc prof art, Univ Tenn, 66-
Awards: Rudolph Lesch Award, Am Watercolor Soc, 72; purchase awards, Am Collection, Hunter Gallery Art, 72 & Collection Tenn Art League & Parthenon, Nashville, 72.
Bibliography: Margaret Harold (auth), Prize winning watercolors, Allied, 64.
Memberships: Dulin Gallery Art, (adv bd, 71-); Knoxville Watercolor Soc; Tenn Watercolorists; Mus Mod Art; Port Clyde Arts & Crafts Soc, Maine.
Publications: Contribr, Artist and advocates, Mead Corp; contribr, Nat Drawing Soc.
Dealer: Collectors Gallery, 6019 W Gate Ctr, Nashville, TN 37205.
Mailing Address: 2104 Lake Ave, Knoxville, TN 37916.

SUDLOW, ROBERT N
Painter, Educator
Preferred Media: Oils.
b Holton, Kans, Feb 25, 20.
Study & Training: Univ Kans, BFA; Univ Calif, Berkeley; Calif Col Arts & Crafts, Oakland, MFA; Acad Grande Chaumiere, Paris, France; Acad Andre L'Hote, Paris.
Work in Public Collections: City Art Mus, Saint Louis, Mo; Mulvane Art Ctr, Washburn Univ, Topeka, Kans; Joslyn Art Mus, Omaha, Nebr; Stephens Col, Columbia, Mo.
Exhibitions: Contemp Painting Invitational, Ashland Col, Ohio, 71; Wichita Art Mus, Kans, 71; U S Senate, Washington, D C, 71; one-man show, Spiva Art Ctr, 71; Nelson Art Mus Summer Invitational, 72.
Teaching: Prof painting & sculpture, Univ Kans, 47-; Watkins faculty fel, 58; instr drawing & painting, Spiva Art Ctr, 71.
Awards: Huntington Hartford fel, 57-59; Villa Montalvo fel, 60.
Dealer: Nelson-Atkins Art Galleries, Sales & Rental Gallery, 45th & Oak, Kansas City, MO 64111.
Mailing Address: 1416 W Seventh, Lawrence, KS 66044.

SUFI, AHMAD ANTUNG
Sculptor
Preferred Media: Bronze, Concrete, Polyester, Resin.
b Palembang, Indonesia, Sept 7, 30.
Study & Training: Craft Stud League, New York; New Sch Social Res, scholar, 66; Educ Alliance; Haystack Mountain Sch Arts & Crafts.
Work in Public Collections: Pvt collections of Dr Edna S Levine, Ivan Spane, Dr Walter Drauss, George L Sherry & Mrs Gloria Furman.
Commissions: Loft bed & interior design, Buck Clark, New York, N Y, 68; mural-window (plexiglas), Mrs Teannie Clark, New York, 71; resin sculpture, Mrs Ruth Ann Pippenger, Brooklyn, N Y, 72.
Exhibitions: Art exhib for benefit of UNICEF, UN Art Gallery, 67; Int Art Exhib, Minneapolis/Saint Paul, Minn, 72; Artist-Craftsmen New York Summer Show, 72; Gallery 91, Brooklyn, 72; Sculptors Guild, Inc, 72.
Teaching: Instr glass craft, pvt studio, 70-
Awards: Second prize, Brooklyn Heights Promenade Art Show, 71; best in sculpture, Artist-Craftsmen New York Ann Show, 72.
Bibliography: Article, 67 & Dinky Di (auth), article, 72, In: UN Secretarial News; Corine Coleman (auth), article, In: Phoenix Newspaper, 72.
Memberships: Heights-Hills Artists Coop; Artist-Craftsmen New York; UN Art Club; Sculptors Guild.
Art Interests: Works are non-representational in the traditional sense, concerned with manifestation of being and the expression of total whole by the most economical means of plastic language, both in form and content, elementally archetypal, yet externalized somewhat in the order of constructivism principle.
Mailing Address: 429 Hicks St, Brooklyn, NY 11201.

SUGARMAN, GEORGE
Sculptor, Painter
Preferred Media: Metal, Acrylics.
b New York, N Y, May 11, 12.
Study & Training: City Col New York, BA; Atelier Zadkine, Paris, 51.

Work in Public Collections: Sculptures, Walker Art Ctr, Minneapolis, Minn, Kunstmuseum, Zurich, Switz, Albert List Family Collection, New York & Kaiser Wilhelm Mus, Krefeld, W Ger; lithographs, Mus Mod Art, New York.
Commissions: Wood wall sculpture, Ciba-Geigy Chem Co, 60; metal sculptures, Xerox Data Systs, El Segundo, Calif, 69, South Mall Proj, Albany, 70, First Nat Bank, Saint Paul, Minn, 71 & Greenfield Sch, Philadelphia, Pa, 72.
Exhibitions: Whitney Mus Am Art Sculpture Ann, 60-70; Pittsburgh Int, Carnegie Inst, 61; Sao Paulo Biennal, Brazil, 63; Sculpture of the Sixties, Los Angeles Co Mus Art, 67; Int Pavilion, Venice Biennal, 69.
Teaching: Assoc prof sculpture, Hunter Col, 60-70; vis prof sculpture, Grad Sch Art & Archit, Yale Univ, 67-68.
Awards: Second prize for sculpture, Pittsburgh Int, 61-62; Longview Found grants, 61-63; Nat Art Coun Award, 66.
Bibliography: A Goldin (auth), introd to catalogue, Kunsthalle, Basel, Switz, 69; I Sandler (auth), Sugarman-sculptural complex, First Nat Bank Saint Paul, 71; H Freed (auth), Audio-visual tape, 72.
Mailing Address: 21 Bond St, New York, NY 10012.

SUGIMOTO, HENRY Y
Painter, Instructor
Preferred Media: Oils, Watercolors, Wood.
U S citizen.
Study & Training: Calif Col Arts & Crafts, BFA; Calif Sch Fine Arts; Acad Colarossi, Paris.
Work in Public Collections: Mus Crecy, France; Calif Palace Legion of Honor, San Francisco; Hendrix Col Fine Art Mus, Ark; Wakayama Mod Art Mus, Japan; Univ Ark Art Mus.
Exhibitions: Salon Automne, Paris, 31; Fine Art Exhib, San Francisco World Expos, 39; U S Exhib, Mod World Exhib, Tokyo, Japan, 50; Salon Artistes Français, Paris, 63; Months of Waiting, Doc Painting Traveling Exhib, 72.
Teaching: Instr art, Denson High Sch, Ark, 43-44.
Positions: Art consult, War Relocation Authority, 43-45.
Awards: Art Concour Award, Found Western Art, 37; recognition medal, San Francisco World's Fair, 39; recognition plaque for Months of Waiting, Los Angeles Co Bd Supervisors, 72.
Bibliography: New America, Life & War Relocation Authority, 46.
Memberships: Washington Printmaker Soc; Nika-Kai Art Asn, Tokyo.
Research: Documentary painting of the War Relocation Centers of Japanese during World War II.
Publications: Illusr, Songs for the land of dawn, 49, Toshio and Tama, 49 & New friends for Susan, 51; contribr, Beauty behind barbed wire, 52 & Nisei, 69.
Dealer: Wiener Gallery, 963 Madison Ave, New York, NY 10021.
Mailing Address: 600 W 146th St, New York, NY 10031.

SULLINS, ROBERT M
Painter, Educator
Preferred Media: Acrylics, Polyester Resins.
b Los Angeles, Calif, Aug 31, 26.
Study & Training: Univ Wyo, 46-47; Univ Ill, 47-48; Univ Wyo, BA (art), 50, MA(art), 58; Fulbright fel, 59-60; Inst Allende, San Miguel Allende, Mex, MFA, 66.
Work in Public Collections: Norfolk Mus Arts & Sci, Va; Northern Ill Univ, DeKalb; Cicic Ctr, Scottsdale, Ariz; Inst Int Educ, New York, N Y.
Commissions: Crucifixion (mural), St Joseph's Cath Church, Rawlins, Wyo, 61; Upstatescape (painting), State Univ N Y, Col Oswego, 66; mural, The Flame Room, Rawlins, 67; kenetic machine, Mirrors, Motors & Motion Show, Rochester Mus, N Y, 70.
Exhibitions: One-man shows, Jason Gallery, New York, 66 & Aspect/Aegis Gallery, New York, 68; Childe Hassam Exhib, Am Acad Arts & Lett, 69; Kinetic Art Show, Albright-Knox Art Gallery, Buffalo, 70; Am Drawing Biennial, XXIV, Norfolk Mus Arts & Sci, 71; plus others.
Teaching: Prof art, State Univ N Y Col Oswego, 60-
Positions: Supvr art, Pub Schs Rawlins, Wyo, 55-59.
Awards: Robert Ahl Mem grant, 60; State of N Y res fel, 71.
Memberships: Col Art Asn Am.
Dealer: Abe Rothstein-Horizon Galleries, 10345 W Olympic Blvd, Los Angeles, CA 90064 & 43 Glendale Rd, Newton Center, MA 02159.
Mailing Address: 167 W Fifth St, Oswego, NY 13126.

SULLIVAN, GENE
Painter, Illustrator
Preferred Media: Watercolors.
b Sauquoit, N Y.
Study & Training: Parsons Sch Design; Art Stud League New York, N Y; also with Everet Shinn, New York.
Work in Public Collections: In pvt collections of William Thetford, Elizabeth Sandberg & Mrs Vernon La Chance, New York.

Exhibitions: Nat Acad Design, 49; Am Watercolor Soc Exhibs, 49-70; Allied Artists Am; Audubon Artists, 50-53; one-man shows, Ferargil Art Gallery; one-man show, Grand Cent Art Gallery, 56; plus others.
Teaching: Instr interior delineation, Pratt Inst, 45-49; pvt instr oils & watercolors.
Positions: Dir, Gene Sullivan Art Gallery, New York, 56-57; free lance designer & illusr, var mags & co.
Awards: Gold medal for watercolor, Catharine Lorillard Wolfe Art Club; Albers Mem Award, 54.
Memberships: Am Watercolor Soc; Pa Acad Fine Arts.
Mailing Address: 69 W 55th St, New York, NY 10019.

SULLIVAN, JIM
Painter
Preferred Media: Acrylics.
b Providence, R I, Apr 1, 39.
Study & Training: R I Sch Design, Providence, Fulbright scholar & BFA, 61; grad work, Stanford Univ, 62-63.
Work in Public Collections: Whitney Mus Am Art, New York, N Y; Worcester Art Mus, Mass; Albany State Mus, N Y.
Exhibitions: Whitney Mus Am Art Ann, 67, 69 & 72; Lyrical Abstraction, Larry Aldrich Mus, Conn & Whitney Mus Am Art, 70-71; Beautiful Painting, Columbus Gallery Fine Arts, Ohio, 71; group show—small works, Mus Mod Art, New York, 71; group show, Ind Mus Art, Indianapolis, 72.
Teaching: Asst prof painting, Bard Col, 65-
Awards: Guggenheim Found grant, 72.
Bibliography: David Shirey (auth), art rev, In: New York Times, 10/23/71; Peter Schsedahl (auth), Rev with reprod, In: Art in Am, 2/72; Carter Ratcliff (auth), Whitney annual part I, Artforum, 4/72.
Dealer: Paley & Lowe Gallery, Inc, 59 Wooster St, New York, NY 10012.
Mailing Address: 484 Broome St, New York, NY 10013.

SULLIVAN, MAX WILLIAM
Art Administrator
b Fremont, Mich, Sept 27, 09.
Study & Training: Western Mich Univ, AB, 32; Harvard Univ, AM, 41; Providence Col, hon LLD, 50.
Teaching: Instr, Cranbrook Sch, 33-35; instr arts & crafts, Middlesex Sch, Concord, Mass, 35-38; head art dept, Groton Sch, Mass, 38-42; consult art educ, Harvard Sch Educ, 40-42; dir educ, R I Sch Design, 44-45.
Positions: Dir, exhib New Eng handicrafts, Worcester Mus Art, 42-43; consult, Metrop Mus Art, 43-44; dean sch, R I Sch Design, 45-47, pres corp, 47-55; dir, Portland Art Mus, Portland Art Asn & Mus Art Sch, 56-61, secy, bd trustees, 57-60; dir, Everson Mus Art, Syracuse, N Y, 61-71; prog dir, Kimbell Art Mus, Fort Worth, Tex, 71-
Memberships: Am Inst Architects; Fort Worth Club; Am Asn Mus; Harvard Club.
Research: Contemporary architecture and contemporary sculpture; classical studies, especially Magna Graecia.
Publications: Auth & ed, Contemporary New England handicrafts, Worcester Art Mus, Mass, 43; contribr & ed, Calligraphy: the golden age & its modern revival, Portland Art Mus, 58; contribr, Everson dedication portfolio, 69 & American ship portraits & marine painting, 70, Everson Mus, Syracuse, N Y; contribr, Catalogue of the collection, Kimbell Art Mus, Fort Worth, Tex, 72.
Mailing Address: Kimbell Art Museum, Will Rogers Rd W, Fort Worth, TX 76107.

SUMM, HELMUT
Painter, Educator
Preferred Media: Oils, Watercolors, Graphics.
b Hamburg, Ger, Mar 10, 08; U S citizen.
Study & Training: Univ Wis, grad, 30; Marquette Univ, MED, 46; also with Umberto Romano, Carl Peters & Robert Von Neumann.
Work in Public Collections: Milwaukee Art Ctr Collection; Milwaukee J Gallery Wis Art; Univ Wis-Green Bay Contemp Art Collection; Lakeland Col Collection Wis Art; Gimbel's Airscapes, Milwaukee.
Commissions: Murals, St John's Lutheran Sch, Glendale, Wis, 56 & Home for Aged Lutherans, Milwaukee, 57; oil painting, Cudahy YMCA, Wis.
Exhibitions: Midwest Mem Exhib, Milwaukee, 46; Soc Am Etchers, Nat Acad Design Galleries, 48; Univ Okla Nat, 50; Am Watercolor Soc Traveling Exhib, 60; Milwaukee Art Ctr Friends of Art, 64-72.
Teaching: Instr art, Milwaukee Pub Schs, 31-48; dir dept art, Univ Wis-Milwaukee Exten, 48-56, prof art & art educ, Univ Wis-Milwaukee & Exten, 56-
Awards: Award for oil painting, Am Inst Architects, 63; purchase award for oil, Beloit & Vicinity Exhib, 64; watercolor award, Wis Salon, 65.

Bibliography: Don Key (auth), Review of Theodore's Gallery, 65 & Violet Dewey (auth), What's new in art, 67, Milwaukee J; reproduction, In: Wis Beautiful, 67.
Memberships: Wis Watercolor Soc; Wis Painters & Sculptors (pres, 63); Delta Phi Delta.
Publications: Auth, University of Wisconsin Extension art programs, WTMJ.
Dealer: Friends of Art, Milwaukee Art Center, 750 N Lincoln Memorial Dr, Milwaukee, WI 53202.
Mailing Address: 6183 N Lake Dr, Milwaukee, WI 53217.

SUMMER, (EMILY) EUGENIA
Painter, Sculptor
Preferred Media: Acrylics, Polyesters, Wood, Metal.
b Newton, Miss, June 13, 23.
Study & Training: Miss State Col Women, BS; Columbia Univ, MA; Sch Art Inst Chicago; Calif Col Arts & Crafts; Penland Sch Crafts, N C; Seattle Univ.
Work in Public Collections: Miss Art Asn, Munic Art Gallery, Jackson; First Nat Bank Collection, Jackson; Nat Bank Commerce Collection, Columbus, Miss; First Nat Bank, Laurel, Miss; Sears Roebuck Collection, Laurel.
Exhibitions: Contemp Am Paintings, Soc Four Arts, Palm Beach, Fla, 60; Am Fedn Arts Circulating Exhib, many U S mus, 61-62; Art In Embassies Prog, U S State Dept, Rio de Janeiro, Brazil, 66-67; many Mid-South Exhibs Brooks Mem Art Gallery, Memphis, Tenn; Eighth Decade: Painters Choice, Ga Col Milledgeville, 71.
Teaching: Assoc prof art, Miss State Col Women, 50-
Awards: Dumas Milner Purchase Award, 62 & jurors award, 68, Nat Watercolor Exhib, Jackson; first prize in watercolor painting, Mid-South Exhib, Brooks Gallery, 65; also recipient Miss State Col Women grants for studying & producing works in plastics.
Memberships: Col Art Asn Am; Miss Art Asn; Am Crafts Coun; Southern Asn Sculptors; Kappa Pi.
Mailing Address: 915 Fifth Ave S, Columbus, MS 39701.

SUMMERFORD, BEN LONG
Painter, Educator
Preferred Media: Oils.
b Montgomery, Ala, Feb 3, 24.
Study & Training: Am Univ, BA & MA; Ecole Beaux-Arts, Paris; also with Karl Knaths & Jack Tworkov.
Work in Public Collections: Corcoran Gallery Art, Washington, D C; Phillips Gallery, Washington, D C; Fort Wayne Mus Art, Ind.
Exhibitions: Fulbright Painters, Whitney Mus Am Art, 59; one-man show, Jefferson Pl Gallery, Washington, D C, 64 & 67.
Teaching: Prof painting, Am Univ, 50-, chmn dept art, 57-
Awards: Fulbright fel, France, 49-50.
Mailing Address: 10216 Brown's Mill Rd, Vienna, VA 22180.

SUMMERS, CAROL
Printmaker
Preferred Media: Wood.
b Kingston, N Y, Dec 26, 25.
Study & Training: Bard Col, BA, 51.
Work in Public Collections: New York Pub Libr; Metrop Mus Art, New York; Mus Mod Art, New York; Victoria & Albert Mus, London; Bibliot Nat, Paris.
Awards: Ital Govt grant, Italy, 55; Louis Comfort Tiffany Found fels, 55 & 61; Guggenheim Found fel, 59.
Memberships: Print Coun Am (artist adv bd); Print Club Philadelphia.
Mailing Address: 523 W 45th St, New York, NY 10036.

SUMMERS, DUDLEY GLOYNE
Painter, Illustrator
Preferred Media: Oils, Casein.
b Birmingham, Eng, Oct 12, 92; U S citizen.
Study & Training: New Sch Art, Boston, Mass; Art Stud League New York, N Y.
Work in Public Collections: Four Chaplains, Nat Conf Christians & Jews, New York; Sojourner Truth, State Univ N Y Col New Paltz.
Teaching: Instr illus, New York Sch Design; instr painting, Plainfield, N J.
Memberships: Salmagundi Club; Soc Illusr.
Publications: Illusr, Sat Eve Post, Am Boy, Red Bk, Cosmopolitan & Boy's Life.
Mailing Address: 77 Glasco Turnpike, Woodstock, NY 12498.

SUMMY, ANNE TUNIS
Painter
Preferred Media: Acrylics.
b Baltimore, Md.
Study & Training: Philadelphia Acad Fine Arts; Inst Allende, Mex.

Work in Public Collections: William Penn Mem Mus Contemp Collection, Harrisburg, Pa; Court Art Trust, Washington, D C; Bloomsburg Col, Pa; Rehoboth Art League, Del.

Commissions: Portrait, Armstrong Cork Co, Lancaster, Pa, 69.

Exhibitions: Butler Inst Am Art Midyear Show, Youngstown, Ohio, 68; Women in Fine Arts, Moore Col Art, Philadelphia, Pa, 68-69; Baltimore Mus Art Md Invitational, 69; Pa Acad Fine Arts Fel Shows, Philadelphia, 69-70; one-man show, William Penn Mem Mus, 71.

Awards: Newman Medal, 68 & Lorne Medal, 69, Nat Soc Painters in Casein & Acrylics; Landscape Painters Pa Purchase Award, Bloomsburg Col, 70.

Bibliography: Article, In: La Rev Mod, 1/70.

Memberships: Nat Soc Painters in Casein & Acrylic; Philadelphia Art Alliance; Peale Club.

Dealer: Camp Hill Gallery, 2208 Market St, Harrisburg, PA 17011.

Mailing Address: 2885 Gulf Shore Blvd N, Naples, FL 33940.

SUNDBERG, CARL GUSTAVE
Painter, Designer
Preferred Media: Porcelain, Enamels, Graphics.
b Erie, Pa, June 23, 28.
Study & Training: Albright Art Sch, Univ Buffalo, grad; study with Joseph Plaucan, Virginia Cuthbert, Albert Blaustien, Letterio Calipia & Robert Bruce.
Work in Public Collections: Butler Inst Am Art, Youngstown, Ohio; Tyler Mus Art, Tex; Erie Pub Mus, Pa; Erie Pub Libr, Pa; Union Bank Erie, Pa; Albright-Knox Rental Art Gallery.
Commissions: Porcelain coat of arms, Episcopal Diocese of Erie, 68; six porcelain panels (mod motif with coins), Union Bank, Erie, 69.
Exhibitions: Chautauqua Nat Jury Shows, N Y, 67-72; Midyear Shows, Butler Inst Am Art, Youngstown, 68, 70 & 72; Washington & Jefferson Nat Exhib, Washington, Pa, 69 & 72; Miss Nat Arts Festival, 70; Audubon Artists, New York, N Y, 71.
Teaching: Instr painting, Erie Art Ctr, 64-
Positions: Artist-designer, Erie Ceramic Arts Co, 53-; dir, Galerie 8, Erie, 67-
Awards: Purchase prize, Mid Year Show, Butler Inst Am Art, 70; purchase prize, Juried Arts Seventh Nat Exhib, Tyler Mus Art, 70; prize for non-traditional, Chautauqua Exhib, 72.
Bibliography: Clyde Singer (auth), article, In: Youngstown Vindicator, 6/28/70; Ada C Tanner (auth), article, In: Chautauqua Daily, 8/17/70; Peggy Krider (auth), art demonstration film produced by Villa Maria Col, 70.
Memberships: Erie Art Ctr (pres, 67-69); Erie Arts Coun (v pres, 70-71); Albright-Knox Art Gallery; Chautauqua Art Asn.
Specialty of Gallery: Paintings & graphics of well known area & national artists.
Dealer: Galerie 8, 2594 W Eighth, Erie, PA 16505.
Mailing Address: 5518 Bondy Dr, Erie, PA 16509.

SUNDBERG, WILDA (REGELMAN)
Painter
Preferred Media: Watercolors.
b Erie, Pa, Oct 5, 30.
Study & Training: Albright Art Sch, Univ Buffalo, 49-51; Gannon Col, Erie, 64-66; also with Joseph Plaucan, Al Blaustein & Virginia Cuthbert.
Work in Public Collections: Erie Pub Libr.
Commissions: Illustrate pvt homes, M O Smith, 70, Warren Omark, 70, John Colwell, 70 & Wm H Piper, Erie, 72.
Exhibitions: Nat Chautauqua Jury Show, N Y, 69-71; Catharine Lorillard Wolfe Art Club, Nat Acad Design, New York, N Y, 70; Erie Summer Festival Arts, Tri State, Great Lakes Juried, 70; Muse Art Gallery, Springfield Art Mus, Mo, 71; Albright Knox Mem Gallery, Buffalo, N Y, 71.
Teaching: Pvt instr, Erie, 64-66; instr art, Erie Art Ctr, 64-72.
Positions: Fashion illusr, Erie Dry Goods, 51-55.
Awards: Chautauqua Nat Watercolor Award, Chautauqua Art Asn, 70; third award watercolor, Edinboro, Pa Summer Gallery, 70.
Bibliography: Peggy Krider (producer), Watercolor demonstration (film), Villa Maria Col, Erie, 70; Ada Tanner (auth), article, In: Chautauqua N Y News, 70; Meg Loncharic (auth), Women in the arts, Erie Times, 70.
Memberships: Erie Art Ctr (bd dirs, 71-72); Albright Knox Art Gallery; Chautauqua Art Asn; Erie Arts Coun.
Dealer: Galerie 8, West Eighth St, Erie, PA 16505.
Mailing Address: 5518 Bondy Dr, Erie, PA 16509.

SUNDERLAND, ELIZABETH READ
Art Historian
b Ann Arbor, Mich, June 12, 10.
Study & Training: Univ Mich, AB; Univ Munich, Ger; Radcliffe Col, AM & PhD.

Teaching: Instr fine art, Duke Univ, 39-42; asst prof fine art, Wheaton Col (Mass), 42-43; asst prof fine art, Duke Univ, 43-51, assoc prof, 51-71, prof hist art, 71-, Endowment res grant, Italy, 65-66.
Positions: Dir, Soc Archit Historians.
Memberships: Am Asn Archit Historians; Mediaeval Acad Am (counr); Col Art Asn Am; hon mem Soc Amis Arts Charlieu; hon mem La Diana; plus others.
Research: Medieval architecture of the eighth through eleventh centuries.
Publications: Auth, Charlieu a l'epoque medievale, Lyon, 71; contribr to Col Art J, J Soc Archit Historians, Art Bull, Speculum, J Archit Inst Japan & others.
Mailing Address: Dept of Art, College Station, Duke University, Durham, NC 27706.

SUNKEL, ROBERT CLEVELAND
Art Historian, Sculptor
Preferred Media: Wood.
b Clarksville, Tex, Jan 19, 33.
Study & Training: Kilgore Col, Tex, AA; Tex Christian Univ, BFA & MFA; Herron Sch Art, Ind Univ; Temple Univ; Northern Ill Univ.
Teaching: Instr art, Henderson State Col, 58-60; instr art, Northwest Mo State Univ, 60-63, acting chmn dept, 63-71, asst prof, 71-
Positions: Cur, Percival De Luce Mem Collection, Northwest Mo State Univ, 71-
Memberships: Soc Archit Historians; Am Asn Univ Prof; Col Art Asn Am; Mid-Am Col Art Conf; Am Fedn Arts.
Research: English Baroque and Palladian architecture, particularly the work of Wren, Gibbs and Hawksmoor.
Mailing Address: P O Box 75, Maryville, MO 64468.

SUROVEK, JOHN HUBERT
Painter, Museum Director
Preferred Media: Acrylics, Watercolors.
b East Chicago, Ind, Apr 29, 46.
Study & Training: Ball State Univ, BS; also with Fred Messersmith & Alice Welty Nichols.
Collections Arranged: Cuban Paintings—Finest Collection in the World, Gift of Gen & Mrs Fulgenco Batista; Fla Invitational: First Annual (limited to 12 southeastern artists), 72.
Teaching: Instr humanities & art, Deland Sr High Sch, Fla, 69-71, admin asst, 70-
Positions: Chmn art dept, Hagerstown Sch Corp, 68-69; dir, Mus Arts & Sci, Daytona Beach, Fla, 72-
Memberships: Southeastern Mus Conf; Am Asn Mus; Fla Fedn Arts; Nat Art Educ Asn; Fla Art Educ Asn.
Publications: Co-auth, Motivational Handbook for Schs, ESEA Title III, 9/69.
Mailing Address: 1040 Museum Blvd, Daytona Beach, FL 32014.

SURREY, MILT
Painter
Preferred Media: Oils.
b New York, N Y, Mar 18, 22.
Work in Public Collections: Cincinnati Art Mus, Ohio; Columbia Mus Art, S C; Detroit Inst Arts, Mich; Evansville Mus Art, Ind; Miami Mus Mod Art, Fla.
Exhibitions: Soc Four Arts, Palm Beach, Fla, 69; Nat Arts Club, New York, 69; Cape Coral Nat Art Show, Fla, 70; George Walter Vincent Smith Art Mus, Springfield, Mass, 70; Parrish Art Mus, Southampton, N Y, 70.
Awards: John Knecht Mem Award, Berwick Arts Festival, 69; third pl award, Garden Valley Nat Art Show, 69; second pl award, Roslyn Art Show, 70.
Mailing Address: 201 Montrose Rd, Westbury, N Y 11590.

SURREY, PHILIP HENRY
Painter
Preferred Media: Acrylics, Oils, Watercolors, Pastels.
b Calgary, Alta, Oct 8, 10.
Study & Training: Winnipeg Sch Art, with Lemoine Fitzgerald; Vancouver Sch Art, with Frederick Varley & Jock Macdonald; Art Stud League New York, N Y, with Alexander Abels.
Work in Public Collections: Nat Gallery Can, Ottawa; Art Gallery Ont, Toronto; Montreal Mus Fine Arts; Mus Quebec, Quebec City; Art Gallery Hamilton, Ont.
Exhibitions: Hamilton Art Gallery Winter Exhibs, 58-71; 25 Quebec Painters, Montreal Mus Fine Arts, 61; Master Can Painters & Sculptors, London, 63; one-man retrospective, Peintre Dans La Ville, Mus Art Contemporain, Montreal 71 & Ctr Cult Can, Paris, 72.
Teaching: Instr drawing, Sir George Williams Univ.
Awards: First prize, Montreal Spring Show, 53; second prize, Winnipeg Show, 60.

Bibliography: J De Roussan (auth), Le peintre des reflets de la ville, Vie Arts, 63 & Philip Surrey, Ed Lidec, Montreal, 68; Robert Ayre (auth), The city and the dream, Can Art, 64.
Dealer: Galerie Gilles Corbeil, 2175 Crescent St, Montreal, P Q, Can.
Mailing Address: 478 Grosvenor Ave, Montreal 217, P Q, Can.

SUSSMAN, ARTHUR
Painter
b Brooklyn, N Y, Mar 30, 27.
Study & Training: Syracuse Univ, BFA; Brooklyn Mus Sch Art.
Work in Public Collections: N Mex Mus Fine Art, Santa Fe; Okla Art Ctr.
Exhibitions: One-man shows, Inst Cult Rels, Mexico City, Mex, 61, Malaga, Spain, 63, Miami Mus Mod Art, 64, Artists House, Haifa, Israel, 64 & Bernard Black Gallery, N Y, 65; plus many others.
Teaching: Artist-in-residence, Univ Albuquerque.
Awards: Oriental Studies Found grant, 62.
Dealers: Brandywine Galleries Ltd, 120 Morningside Dr S E, Albuquerque, NM 87108; New West, 5908 Lomas Blvd N E, Albuquerque, NM 87110.
Mailing Address: 10309 Santa Paula Ave N E, Albuqueruqe, NM 87111.

SUTHERLAND, SANDY
Painter, Writer
Preferred Media: Oils, Watercolors.
b Cincinnati, Ohio, Apr 10, 02.
Study & Training: Art Stud League New York, N Y; Mech Inst, N Y.
Work in Public Collections: Kenneth Taylor Gallery; Nat Arts Club.
Exhibitions: Metrop Mus Art Exhib Am Watercolors, 52; Am Watercolor Soc, 70; Allied Artists Am, 71; Grand Cent Art Galleries, 72; Nat Arts Club, 72.
Awards: Am Watercolor Soc Prize for Non-mem, 51; Hoe Medal for free hand drawing, Mech Inst, 55; first award of merit for painting, Kenneth Taylor Gallery, 58.
Memberships: Allied Artists Am (dir); Am Watercolor Soc (rec secy, treas); Grand Cent Art Gallery; life mem Art Stud League New York; Nat Arts Club.
Publications: Auth, Figure sketching in watercolor, 63 & Painting in oil on paper, 68, Am Artist.
Mailing Address: 15 Gramercy Park S, New York, NY 10003.

SUTTMAN, PAUL
Sculptor
Preferred Media: Bronze, Marble.
b N Mex, July 16, 33.
Study & Training: Univ N Mex, BFA, 55; Cranbrook Acad Art, MFA, 57.
Work in Public Collections: Joseph H Hirshhorn Mus, Washington, D C; Mus Mod Art, New York, N Y; Art Mus, Macomb Col, Mich; Kalamazoo Art Ctr; Roswell Art Ctr.
Commissions: Two figures, Eastland Shopping Ctr, Detroit, Mich, 65; figure, Martha Cooke Bldg, Univ Mich, 68.
Exhibitions: Sculpture From Hirshhorn Collection, Guggenheim Mus, 62; Sculptors From Midwest, John Herron Inst, 63; Biennale Sculpture Contemporaine, Rodin Mus, Paris, 68 & 70; U S Info Serv Traveling Exhib, Istanbul & Ankara, Turkey, 72; After Surrealism, Metaphors & Sinides, Ringling Art Mus, Sarasota, Fla, 72.
Teaching: Instr sculpture, Univ Mich, Ann Arbor, 58-62; artist-in-residence, Dartmouth Col, spring 73.
Awards: Rackham Found res grant, Italy, 60; Fulbright fel Paris, Inst Int Educ, 63; Prix de Rome fel, Am Acad Rome, 65-68.
Bibliography: The bronze man, Nat Educ TV, 60.
Dealers: Donald Morris Gallery, 20082 Livernois, Detroit, MI 48221; Terry Dintenfass, Inc, 18 E 67th St, New York, NY 10021.
Mailing Address: c/o 18 E 67th St, New York, NY 10021.

SUTTON, GEORGE MIKSCH
Painter, Illustrator
b Lincoln, Nebr, May 16, 98.
Study & Training: Bethany Col, BS, 19; Univ Pittsburgh, 23-25; Cornell Univ, PhD, 32; Bethany Col, ScD, 52.
Teaching: George Lynn Cross emer res prof zool, Univ Okla, presently.
Positions: Emer cur birds, Stovall Mus, 68-; ornithologist, Okla Biol Surv.
Awards: John Burroughs Award, 62; Knight Cross Order of the Falcon, Iceland, 72.
Memberships: Wilson Ornithol Soc (past pres); Arctic Inst N Am; Cooper Ornithol Soc; Am Geog Soc; Am Ornithologists' Union (past councilman); plus others.

Publications: Auth & illusr, Mexican birds, 51 & Iceland summer, 61; auth & illusr, Oklahoma birds, Univ Okla Press, 67; auth & illusr, High arctic, 71 & At a bend in a Mexican river, 72, Eriksson; plus many others.
Mailing Address: Dept of Zoology, University of Oklahoma, Norman, OK 73069.

SUZUKI, KATSKO (KATSKO SUZUKI KANNEGIETER)
Art Dealer
b Nagoya, Japan.
Study & Training: Kinjyo Female Col, Nagoya; Bunka Fukuso Gakuin, Tokyo, Japan.
Positions: Dir & pres, Suzuki Graphics, Inc, New York, N Y, 70-; juried Sumi-E Soc Am Exhib, 5/72.
Bibliography: Article, In: Graphics: New York, 9/70; MaCnow (auth), article, In: High Fashion, 12/70; Kawabata (auth), article, In: Bungei Syunju Weekly, 1/71.
Specialty of Gallery: Mainly specialized in graphics. Many gallery artists are international.
Mailing Address: 797 Madison Ave, New York, NY 10021.

SUZUKI, SAKARI
Painter
Preferred Media: Oils.
b Iwateken, Japan; U S citizen.
Study & Training: Calif Sch Fine Arts, San Francisco; Art Stud League New York, N Y, Metrop scholar, 34.
Work in Public Collections: High Mus Art, Atlanta, Ga; Dept Labor, Washington, D C.
Commissions: Mural, Willard Parker Hosp, New York, N Y, 37.
Exhibitions: Corcoran Gallery Art, Washington, D C, 34; one-man shows, ACA Gallery, New York, 36, Artists Gallery, New York, 48 & 51 & Mandel Bros Art Gallery, Chicago, Ill, 55; Pa Acad Fine Arts, Philadelphia, 52.
Teaching: Instr painting, Am Artists Sch, New York, 38-40.
Positions: Scenic artist, Munic Opera, St Louis, Mo, 53-55; scenic artist, Starlight Theatre, Kansas City, Mo, 56-69; scenic artist, Gen Motors Futurama, 62-64; scenic artist, Lyric Opera, Chicago, 65-70.
Awards: Am Artists Cong Prize, 36; hon mention, Terry Nat Art Exhib, Miami, Fla, 52.
Memberships: United Scenic Artists Am.
Mailing Address: 5040 Marine Dr, Chicago, IL 60640.

SVENSON, JOHN EDWARD
Sculptor, Collector
Preferred Media: Wood, Bronze.
b Los Angeles, Calif, May 10, 23.
Study & Training: Claremont Grad Sch, Calif; sculpture with Albert Stewart.
Work in Public Collections: Los Angeles Co Fair Collection, Pomona, Calif; Ahmanson Ctr, Los Angeles; Nat Orange Show Permanent Collection, San Bernardino, Calif.
Commissions: Bronze, wood and fibreglass sculpture for five Santa Fe Fed Savings & Loan bldgs; two hist panels, San Gabriel Mission Chapel, Calif, 58; bldg facade & cast stone free form, Purex Corp, Lakewood, Calif, 60; over life size bronze groups, Home Savings & Loan, Calif, 63-72; bronze Alaska Tlingit medal, Soc Medalists Ann Issue, 72.
Exhibitions: Otis Art Inst Galleries, Los Angeles, 60; Lang Galleries, Scripps Col, Claremont, 61; Los Angeles Co Mus Art, 62; Newman Galleries, Philadelphia, Pa, 71; Kennedy Galleries, New York, N Y, 72.
Positions: Art dir, Los Angeles Co Fair, 57-; trustee, Alaska Indian Arts, Inc, Port Chilkoot, 67-
Awards: First prize, Greek Theater, Los Angeles, 51 & 54; award for excellence in sculpture, Am Inst Archit, 57 & 61; first prize, Laguna Art Festival, 61.
Memberships: Fel Nat Sculpture Soc; Soc Medalists, New York.
Collection: Northwest Coast Indian; Pre-Columbian Inca, Mexican & others; sculptures by Antoine Barye & Paul Manship; paintings by Ramos Martinez & Henry Lee McFee.
Mailing Address: 593 Bolsa Chica, Green Valley Lake, CA 92341.

SVET, M (MRS DORE SCHARY)
Painter
b Newark, N J, Apr 15, 12.
Study & Training: Faucett Art Sch; Nat Acad Design; Art Stud League New York, with George Bridgman & Frank V Dumond; also with Carl Von Schleusing, Newark.
Work in Public Collections: Los Angeles City Hall; Brandeis Univ; Fairleigh Dickinson Col, Teaneck, N J.
Commissions: Portraits in many pvt collections.
Exhibitions: One-man shows, Assoc Am Artists, 51 & 56, Vigeveno Gallery, Westwood, Calif, 54, Los Angeles Art Asn Biann, Nessler Gallery, N Y, 62-64 & Corcoran Rental Gallery, Washington, D C, 64.

Memberships: Am Fedn Arts; Los Angeles Art Asn.
Mailing Address: 50 Sutton Pl S, New York, NY 10022.

SWAN, BARBARA
Painter
Preferred Media: Graphics.
b Newton, Mass, June 23, 22.
Study & Training: Wellesley Col, BA; Boston Mus Sch.
Work in Public Collections: Philadelphia Mus Art; Boston Mus Art; Worcester Mus; Fogg Art Mus; Boston Pub Libr.
Exhibitions: Carnegie Ann, 49; Contemporary American Painting, Univ Ill, 50; View 1960, Inst Contemp Arts, Boston, Mass, 60; Brooklyn Mus Biennial Print Exhib, 65; New England Landscape Painting, De Cordova Mus, 71.
Teaching: Instr painting, Wellesley Col, 46-49; instr art, Milton Acad, 51-54; instr painting & drawing, Boston Univ, 60-65.
Awards: Albert Whitin travelling fel, Boston Mus Art, 48; assoc scholar, Inst Independent Study, Radcliffe Col, 61-63; George Roth Prize, Philadelphia Print Club, 65.
Dealer: Alpha Gallery, 122 Newbury St, Boston, MA 02116.
Mailing Address: 808 Washington St, Brookline, MA 02146.

SWANN, ERWIN
Collector, Patron
b New York, N Y, Dec 9, 06.
Study & Training: Univ Va, 19; Univ Wis, 20; New York Univ, 21.
Positions: Ed, Countrybrook, 40-46; mem adv coun, dept art hist & archaeol, Columbia Univ, New York, presently.
Art Interests: Founder, Swann Collection caricature and cartoon; producer films on art and cultural subjects.
Collection: French impressionist art; modern European and American art; Indian and Far Eastern; original drawings of caricature and cartoon artists of the eighteenth, nineteenth and twentieth centuries.
Publications: Auth, Red squares, 68.
Mailing Address: 24 W 55th St, New York, NY 10019.

SWANSON, DEAN
Museum Curator
b Saint Paul, Minn, Sept 7, 34.
Study & Training: Univ Minn, BA & MA.
Collections Arranged: Robert Rauschenberg, 65; Nicholas Kurshenick, 68; Richard Lindner, 69; Joan Miró Sculptures, 71.
Teaching: Teaching asst, Univ Minn, 57-60.
Positions: Asst cur, Walker Art Ctr, Minneapolis, Minn, 62, assoc cur, 64, chief cur, 67-
Mailing Address: Walker Art Center, 807 Hennepin Ave, Minneapolis, MN 55403.

SWARZ, SAHL
Sculptor
Preferred Media: Bronze, Steel.
b New York, N Y, May 4, 12.
Study & Training: Clay Club New York; Art Stud League New York.
Work in Public Collections: Whitney Mus Am Art, New York; Minneapolis Inst Fine Arts; N J State Mus, Trenton; Richmond Mus Fine Arts, Va; Rose Art Mus, Brandeis Univ, Waltham, Mass.
Commissions: Guardian (bronze), Brookgreen Gardens Mus, S C, 39; Equestrian Mem to Gen Bidwell, Buffalo, N Y, 49; symbolic wood figures, U S Courthouse, Statesville, N C, 45; mall sculpture, Pittsfield, Mass, 71; fountain sculpture, State of N J, Spruce Run Recreational Park, 72.
Exhibitions: Whitney Mus Am Art Ann, 48-62; Pa Acad Fine Arts, 49-58; Ill Biennial, 57 & 59; Dept State Traveling Exhib, 58; Bronzetto Int Padua, Italy, 59 & 61.
Teaching: Instr sculpture, Brandeis Univ, 64-65; instr sculpture, Univ Wis-Madison, 66; asst prof sculpture, Columbia Univ, 66-; instr sculpture, New Sch Soc Res, 67-70.
Awards: Am Acad Arts & Lett grant, 55; J S Guggenheim Mem Found grants, 55 & 58; Gov Purchase Prize, N J State Mus, 65.
Memberships: Sculpture Ctr (assoc dir, 34-53).
Publications: Auth & illusr, Blueprint for the future of American sculpture, 44; auth, Monograph on Ilse Erythropel.
Dealer: Sculpture Center, 167 E 69th St, New York, NY 10021.
Mailing Address: 245 Palisade Ave, Cliffside Park, NJ 07010.

SWARZENSKI, HANNS PETER
Art Historian, Writer
b Berlin, Ger, Aug 30, 03; U S citizen.
Study & Training: Univ Bonn, PhD, 27; Fogg Art Mus, Harvard Univ, 27-28.
Work in Public Collections: Berlin State Mus; Nat Gallery Art, Washington; Boston Mus Fine Arts.
Collections Arranged: Rathbone Yrs, Boston Mus Fine Arts, 72.
Teaching: Spec lectr medieval art, Warburg Inst, Univ London, 46-54.

Positions: Res fel, Inst Advan Study, Princeton, N J, 36-48; acting cur sculpture, Nat Gallery Art, Washington, D C, 44-46.
Memberships: Am Acad Arts & Sci.
Research: Medieval manuscripts, metalwork and sculpture.
Publications: Auth, Deutsche buchmalerei des 13 jahrhunderts, 36; auth, The Berthold missal, 43; co-auth, English sculptures of the 12th century, 52; auth, Monuments of Romanesque art, 53.
Mailing Address: Boston Museum of Fine Arts, Boston, MA 02115.

SWAY, ALBERT
Painter, Illustrator
b Cincinnati, Ohio, Aug 6, 13.
Study & Training: Cincinnati Art Acad; Art Stud League New York.
Work in Public Collections: Metrop Mus Art, New York, N Y; New York Pub Libr; Carnegie Inst; Pa State Univ; Soc New York Hosp.
Exhibitions: Libr Cong, 43-45; Albright-Knox Art Gallery, 51; Soc Am Graphic Artists, 51-; Royal Soc Painters, Etchers & Engravers, London, Eng, 54; Am-Japan Contemp Print Exhib, Tokyo, 67; plus many other group & one-man shows.
Teaching: Instr drawing & painting, New York Hosp League, 63-64.
Awards: First prize in graphics, Cincinnati Mus Asn, 39.
Memberships: Soc Am Graphic Artists.
Publications: Illusr, Lamb's sectional histories of New York State, Frank E Richards; illusr filmstrips on New York State history, produced by Our York State, N Y, 50-; med illusr, A syllabus for health visitors, Navajo Tribal Coun, Ariz, 60; med illusr, Respiratory diseases, Nat Tuberculosis Asn, 61; med illusr, Hepatic excretory function (ser filmstrips), Am Gastroenterol Asn, 72; also med illus in sci jours.
Mailing Address: 445 E 68th St, New York, NY 10021.

SWAZO (PATRICK SWAZO HINDS)
Painter, Lecturer
Preferred Media: Oils.
b Tesuque Pueblo, N Mex, Mar 25, 29.
Study & Training: Calif Col Arts & Crafts, BA; Mexico City Col; Art Inst Chicago.
Work in Public Collections: Oakland Art Mus, Calif; Am Indian Hist Soc, San Francisco, Calif; Bur Indian Affairs, Washington, D C; Heard Mus, Phoenix, Ariz; Mus Northern Ariz, Flagstaff.
Exhibitions: Calif Palace Legion of Hon, San Francisco, 63; San Francisco Mus Art, 66; Heard Mus, Phoenix, 68; Philbrook Art Ctr, Tulsa, Okla, 69; Mus N Mex Southwest Biennial, Santa Fe, 70.
Teaching: Instr oil painting & sketch class, Arts & Crafts Coop, Inc, Berkeley, Calif, 68-69; lectr Indian art, Navajo Col, Ariz, 72; lectr Indian art, Colo Col, Colorado Springs, 72.
Awards: First award, Scottsdale Nat Indian Art Exhib, 66, 67, 70 & 71; first award, Ctr Indian Art, Washington, D C, 68; first award, Heard Mus, Phoenix, 70.
Bibliography: Clara Lee Tanner (auth), The Bialse Collection of Southwest Indian painting; Dorothy Dunn (auth), American Indian painting; J O Snodgrass (auth), American Indian painters.
Publications: Illusr, The Indian historian, 12/67.
Mailing Address: 224 Sena St, Santa Fe, NM 87501.

SWEENEY, JAMES JOHNSON
Art Administrator, Lecturer
b Brooklyn, N Y, May 30, 00.
Study & Training: Georgetown Univ, AB, 22 & hon LHD, 63; Jesus Col, Cambridge Univ, 22-24; Sorbonne, Paris, 25; Univ Siena, 26; Grinnell Col, hon DFA, 57, Univ Mich, 60, Univ Notre Dame, 61 & Univ Buffalo, 62; hon LHD, Rollins Col, 60, Col of the Holy Cross, 60 & Univ Miami, 68; Ripon Col, hon ArtsD, 60.
Collections Arranged: Many exhibs, Univ Chicago, Mus Mod Art, New York, N Y, Art Gallery Toronto, Va Mus Fine Arts, Mass Inst Technol, Mus Art Mod, Paris, Tate Gallery, London & Honolulu Acad Arts.
Teaching: Lectr, many univs & mus, U S, 35-
Positions: Dir painting & sculpture, Mus Mod Art, New York, 45-46; dir, Solomon R Guggenheim Mus, New York, 52-60; dir, Mus Fine Arts, Houston, Tex, 61-68, consult dir, 68-; gallery consult, Nat Capital Develop Comn, Canberra, Australia, 68-; mem vis comt Visual & Performing Arts, Harvard Univ, & Fine Arts, Fogg Art Mus, 69-; adv purchase, Arts Coun Northern Ireland, Belfast, 70-72; art adv, Israel Mus, 72-; also mem bd dirs, trustee, adv, fel or hon mem many art orgns, socs, comts, acad, workshops, asn, clubs, insts, coun & found, U S & Europe.
Awards: Chevalier, Legion d'Honneur, France, 55; Officier, Ordre des Arts et des Lettres, Paris, 59; Art Am Award, 63.
Memberships: Asn Int Art les Moyens Audio-Visuels (v pres, 72-); hon mem Arts Club Chicago; hon mem Buffalo Fine Arts Acad; hon mem Int Coun Mus Mod Art; hon mem Am Inst Interior Designers; plus many others.

Publications: Auth, Vision and image, 68, African sculpture, 70, Joan Miro, 70, Alexander Calder, 71 & Pierre Soulages, 72; plus many other bks, articles & films.
Mailing Address: 120 East End Ave, New York, NY 10028.

SWEENY, BARBARA ELEANOR
Museum Curator
b Philadelphia, Pa.
Study & Training: Wellesley Col, BA, 26.
Teaching: Instr hist art, Rosemont Col, 28-29, hist painting, 39-42.
Positions: Asst, John G Johnson Collection, Philadelphia, 31-56, assoc cur, 56-69, cur, 69-
Publications: Auth, Catalogue Italian paintings, J G Johnson Collection, 66 & Catalogue Flemish-Dutch paintings, J G Johnson Collection, 72.
Mailing Address: John G Johnson Collection, P O Box 7646, Philadelphia, PA 19101.

SWENEY, FRED
Illustrator, Writer
Preferred Media: Oils.
b Holidaysburg, Pa, June 5, 12.
Study & Training: Cleveland Sch Art, Ohio.
Work in Public Collections: In pvt collections.
Teaching: Instr, Ringling Sch Art, 49-
Positions: Supvr, Leece-Neville Co; artist-illusr, Brown & Bigelow, 49-
Awards: Nat Offset Lithographic Award, 60, Lithographic Award, 61 & Graphic Arts Award, 62, Brown & Bigelow.
Bibliography: J M Ethridge (auth), Contemporary authors, Gale, 62.
Publications: Auth & illusr, Techniques of drawing and painting wildlife, 59, Drawing and painting birds, 61 & Painting the American scene in watercolor, 64; illusr, Nat Geog; auth, illusr & contribr, Sports Afield Mag.
Mailing Address: 4576 Cooper Rd, Sarasota, FL 33580.

SWENSEN, MARY JEANETTE HAMILTON (JEAN)
Painter, Lithographer
Preferred Media: Watercolors, Graphics.
b Laurens, S C, June 25, 10.
Study & Training: Columbia Univ, with Hans Mueller, BS, 56, with Arthur Young, MA (graphic arts), 60; Fine Arts Sch for Am, Fountainbleau, France, with Lucien Fontanerosa; Ariz State Univ, with Prof Arthur Hahn, five summers.
Work in Public Collections: Two lithographs, Metrop Mus Art, New York, N Y; one lithograph, Nat Graphic Arts Collection, Smithsonian Inst, Washington, D C; one lithograph, Graphic Arts Collection, New York Pub Libr Main Br; one lithograph, Laurens Pub Libr, S C.
Exhibitions: Soc Western Artists, M H de Young Mus, San Francisco, Calif, 64; Nat Art Roundup, Las Vegas, Nev, 65; Fine Arts Bldg, Colo State Fair, Pueblo, 65.
Awards: Hon mention for drawing, Soc Western Artists, 64.
Memberships: Soc Western Artists; Delta Phi Delta.
Mailing Address: 684 W 99th Ave, Denver, CO 80221.

SWENSON, ANNE
Painter, Instructor
Preferred Media: Oils, Watercolors.
b Stafford Springs, Conn.
Study & Training: Art Stud League New York; also with William Fisher, Vincent Drennan, Paul Giambertone & Tetsuya Kochi.
Work in Public Collections: St Peter's Rectory, Staten Island, N Y.
Exhibitions: Staten Island Mus, New York, N Y, 55-61; Art & Sci Mus, Statesville, N C, 67; Civic Art Ctr, Rapid City, S Dak, 68; Nat Arts Club, New York, 69; Wash Mus Fine Arts, Hagerstown, Md, 71; plus others.
Teaching: Lectr & demonstr mosaics, Staten Island Mus, 59-; instr art & head dept, St Peter's Elem Sch, Staten Island, 60-62.
Awards: Anna D Morse Gold Medal, Gotham Painters, 66; second pl award for watercolor, Composers, Auth & Artists Am, New York City Chap, 69; hon mention for oil, Composers, Auth & Artists of Am, Nat Exhib, 71.
Bibliography: Bibliography with photos of works, Staten Island Advan, 59, 60 & 69; Anne Swenson, Composers, Authors & Artists of Am, Vol 26, No 1 & Vol 26, No 4.
Memberships: Burr Artists (dir, 67-72); Gotham Painters; Composers, Auth & Artists Am, Inc (treas, New York City Chap, 70-72).
Publications: Illusr, Indian Asn Am; auth, Rugs through the ages, New Bull Staten Island Mus, Vol 9, No 3.
Mailing Address: 10 Phelps Pl, Staten Island, NY 10301.

SWIFT, DICK
Printmaker, Educator
Preferred Media: Graphics.
b Long Beach, Calif, Nov 29, 18.
Study & Training: Los Angeles State Col, BA; Claremont Grad Sch,

MFA; Chouinard Art Inst; Art Stud League New York.
Work in Public Collections: San Jose Col; Univ Ill; Cincinnati Mus Asn; Drake Univ; Zanesville Art Inst; plus many others.
Exhibitions: One-man show, Santa Barbara Mus; Otis Art Inst, Calif Palace of Legion of Honor, Los Angeles Mus Art, Pasadena Mus Art & Pa Acad Fine Arts, 65-69; plus many other group & one-man shows.
Teaching: Prof art, Calif State Univ, Long Beach, 58-
Awards: Prizes, Am Color Print Soc, 65, Philadelphia Mus Art, 68 & Otis Art Inst, 69; plus many others.
Memberships: Am Color Print Soc; Los Angeles Print Soc (pres, 68-69).
Mailing Address: Dept of Art, California State University, 6101 E Seventh St, Long Beach, CA 90840.

SWIGGETT, JEAN DONALD
Educator, Painter
Preferred Media: Oils.
b Franklin, Ind, Jan 6, 10.
Study & Training: Chouinard Inst Fine Art, Los Angeles, 30-31; San Diego State Col, AB, 34; Univ Southern Calif, MFA, 39; Claremont Grad Sch, 50-52.
Work in Public Collections: Long Beach Mus Art, Calif; Fine Arts Gallery, San Diego, Calif.
Commissions: Murals, Post Off, Franklin, Ind, 39 & S S President Jackson & S S President Adams, 40-41.
Exhibitions: Southwest Exhib, Tucson Art Ctr, 68; Long Beach Mus Art Ann, 68; Calif-Hawaii Regionals, San Diego Fine Arts Gallery, 71 & 72; Reality-Illusion, Downey Mus Art, 72; Calif State Expos Art Exhib, 72.
Teaching: Teaching asst drawing, Univ Southern Calif, 40-41; instr painting, Wash State Col, 41-42; prof painting & drawing, Calif State Univ, San Diego, 46-
Awards: San Diego Art Inst Ann, 71; Calif-Hawaii Regional Award, San Diego Fine Arts Gallery, 72; Riverside Art Ctr Ann, Calif, 72.
Memberships: Art Guild Fine Art Soc, San Diego (pres, 51-52).
Research: Romanesque architecture and sculpture.
Mailing Address: 9275 Briarcrest Dr, La Mesa, CA 92041.

SWINTON, GEORGE
Painter, Writer
Preferred Media: Oils, Watercolors.
b Vienna, Austria, Apr 17, 17; Can citizen.
Study & Training: McGill Univ, BA, 46; Montreal Sch Art & Design, 47; Art Stud League New York, N Y.
Work in Public Collections: Nat Gallery Can; Vancouver Art Gallery; Winnipeg Art Gallery; Hamilton Art Gallery; Confederation Art Ctr, Charlottetown.
Exhibitions: 2 retrospectives, Winnipeg Art Gallery; 4 Can Biennials; 3 Montreal Spring Exhibs; 11 Winnipeg Shows; 31 one-man shows.
Teaching: Lectr art, Smith Col, 50-53; prof art, Univ Man, 54-, adj prof anthrop, 70-
Awards: Three Can Coun grants.
Research: Prehistoric and contemporary Eskimo art.
Publications: Auth, Eskimo sculpture/sculpture Esquimaude, 65; illusr, Red River of the north, 67; co-auth, Sculpture/inuit, 71; auth, Sculpture of the Eskimo, 72.
Dealer: Upstairs Gallery, Edmonton St, Winnipeg 1, Man, Can.
Mailing Address: 730 Waverly St, Winnipeg, Man. R3M 3L7, Can.

SWIRNOFF, LOIS (LOIS SWIRNOFF CHARNEY)
Painter, Lecturer
Preferred Media: Acrylics, Gouache, Oils.
b Brooklyn, N Y, May 9, 31.
Study & Training: Cooper Union, cert of grad, 51; Yale Univ, with Josef Albers, BFA, 53, MFA, 56.
Work in Public Collections: Addison Gallery Am Art, Andover; Radcliffe Inst, Harvard Univ; Jewett Art Ctr, Wellesley Col.
Exhibitions: Americans in Italy, Munson-Williams-Proctor Inst, Utica, N Y; American Fulbright Painters, Duveen-Graham Gallery, New York, 57; Boston Arts Festivals, 63-64; Affect/Effect, La Jolla Mus, Calif, 68.
Teaching: Instr art, Wellesley Col, 56-60; asst prof art, Univ Calif, Los Angeles, 63-68; lectr visual & environ studies, Harvard Univ, 68-
Awards: Fulbright fel to Italy, 51-52; fel of Radcliffe Inst Independent Study, 61, 62 & 63; Univ Calif fel for jr faculty, 67.
Mailing Address: Carpenter Center for Visual Art, Harvard University, 19 Prescott St, Cambridge, MA 02138.

SYKES, (WILLIAM) MALTBY
Painter, Printmaker
b Aberdeen, Miss, Dec 13, 11.
Study & Training: With Wayman Adams, John Sloan, Diego Rivera, Andre Lhote, Fernand Leger & Stanley William Hayter.

Work in Public Collections: Mus Mod Art, New York, N Y; Stedelijk Mus, Amsterdam; Metrop Mus Art, New York; Boston Mus Fine Arts; Philadelphia Mus Art.
Commissions: Color engravings, ed 210 prints, Trellis, 55, Cathedral Interior 58 & Floating Still Life, 62, Int Graphic Arts Soc.
Exhibitions: Salon d'Automne, Paris, 51; Int Biennial Contemp Color Lithography, Cincinnati Art Mus, 52; Am Watercolors, Drawings & Prints, Metrop Mus Art, New York, 52; Curator's Choice Exhib, Philadelphia Print Club, 56; Contemp Am Graphic Art, U S Info Agency & Tour Abroad, 61.
Teaching: Prof art, Auburn Univ, 42-, artist-in-residence, 68-
Awards: Albany Inst Hist & Art Purchase Award, Print Club Albany, 63; Philip & Esther Klein Award, Am Color Print Soc, 65; sabbatical award, Nat Endowment Arts, 67-68.
Memberships: Soc Am Graphic Artists.
Publications: Contribr, American prize prints of the 20th century, 49; auth, The multimetal lithography process, Artists Proof, 68; contribr, Printmaking today, Holt, Rinehart & Winston, rev ed, 72; contribr, Art of the print, Abrams, 73.
Mailing Address: 712 Brenda Ave, Auburn, AL 36830.

SYLVESTER, LUCILLE
Painter, Writer
Preferred Media: Oils.
b Russia; U S citizen.
Study & Training: Acad Julian, Paris, France, with Pierre Montézin; Art Stud League New York, N Y, with Robert Brackman & Robert Phillips.
Exhibitions: One-man show, Hammer Gallery, New York, 39; First Ann Contemp Drawings, Nat Acad Design, New York, 44-45; Allied Artists Am Ann, Nat Acad Design Galleries, 55; Nat Arts Club, New York, 57; Mus Art, Springville, Utah, 68.
Teaching: Instr art, jr high schs, New York; lectr art, var schs, clubs & groups, 59.
Positions: Juror, Queensboro Outdoor Art Ann, 52; chmn jury of awards, Third Ann Art Exhib Jewish Teachers Asn New York, 63.
Awards: First prize, Knickerbocker Artists Ann, 52; Lewis & Lewis Award, 57 & Grumbacher Mat Award, 59, Catharine Lorillard Wolfe Art Club Ann.
Bibliography: Article & reproduction, In: New York Times, 3/27/38; Andrew Danzak (auth), article, In: Chelsea-Clinton News, 4/52; Gordon Sinclair (auth), Let's be personal (broadcast), CFRB, 2/9/65.
Memberships: Knickerbocker Artists (first v pres, 62-65, bd dirs, 69-71); fel Am Artists Prof League; Audubon Artists; Catharine Lorillard Wolfe Art Club; life mem Art Stud League New York.
Publications: Auth, The meaning of art (play), Plays Mag, 11/47; auth, This changing world: the story of the flag, 48; auth, Loyal Queen Esther, 56; auth & illusr, Portrait in prose and paint, 12/64; auth & illusr, six hist articles on New York, 68-69.
Mailing Address: 200 W 20th St, New York, NY 10011.

SYLVESTRE, GUY
Art Critic, Writer
b Sorel, P Q, May 17, 18.
Study & Training: Col Ste Marie, Montreal; Univ Ottawa, MA.
Positions: Ed, Gants du ciel, 43-46; nat librn, Nat Libr, Ottawa, presently.
Memberships: Fedn Can Artists; Soc Ecrivains Can; Can Libr Asn; Royal Soc Can Acad Can Française.
Publications: Auth, Anthologie de la poesie Canadienne-Française, Beauchemin, 64; auth, Panorama des lettres Canadiennes Françaises, 64 & Literature in French Canada, 67, EOQ; auth, Ecrivains Canadiens, HMH, 64 & McGraw, 67; auth, Structures sociales du Canada Français, Laval, 66; plus many others.
Mailing Address: 1870 Rideau Garden, Ottawa, Ont, Can.

SYLVIA, LOUIS
Painter
b New Bedford, Mass, May 17, 11.
Study & Training: Swain Sch Design; Nat Acad Design; Art Stud League New York, N Y; also with Harry Neyland & Aldro Hibbard.
Work in Public Collections: Sandjford Mus, Norway; Sharon Mus, Mass; Lisbon Mus, Port.
Commissions: First Nat Bank, New Bedford, 66-72; Bank of Italia, New York, 67; Pocasset Country Club, R I, 68; West Hartford Bank, Conn, 69-70; South Eastern Bank, New Bedford, 70.
Exhibitions: Jordan Marsh Co, Boston, 59-63; Mystic Art Festival, Conn, 63-72; Int Platform, Washington, D C, 66-72; Post Off, New Bedford, 70; Wamsutta Club, New Bedford, 72.
Teaching: Instr art, Roosevelt Jr High Sch, New Bedford, 57-65.
Awards: Awards for watercolor & oil, Dartmouth Art Festival, 59; first awards for watercolor, Mystic Art Festival, 63 & 64; first purchase award, Fla Seaside Art Festival, 72.
Bibliography: Articles, In: New York World's Fair, 38, Yachting Mag, 41 & New Mar Marine Co, 72.
Mailing Address: 38 Howland St, Dartmouth, MA 02714.

SZARAMA, JUDITH LAYNE
Printmaker, Instructor
Preferred Media: Pencil, Graphics.
b Stamford, Conn, Aug 12, 40.
Study & Training: Swain Sch Design, New Bedford, Mass, dipl.
Work in Public Collections: Mint Mus, Charlotte, N C; Miami Art Ctr, Fla; Miami Pub Libr Lending Print Collection.
Commissions: Flight-tourist attractions on schedule of airline, Eastern Air Lines, Hartley Training Ctr, Miami, 69.
Exhibitions: One-man show, Prints & Drawings, Baker Gallery, Coconut Grove, Fla, 67; Soc Am Graphic Artists 51st Print Ann, Kennedy Gallery, New York, N Y, 71; 33 Miami Artists, Miami Art Ctr, 71; 9th Nat Biennial Print Exhib, Silvermine Guild Artists, New Canaan, Conn, 72; Drawings, Fort Lauderdale Mus Arts, Fla, 72.
Teaching: Instr anat & figure drawing, etching & painting, Miami Art Ctr, 70-
Positions: Tech illustrator, Eastern Air Lines, Miami, 67-70.
Awards: Mint Mus Purchase Award, 70; best in show (graphics), YMHA-YWHA, Miami & Temple Beth Am, Miami, 71-72.
Bibliography: Frank Laurent (auth), Art, 68 & Bob Watters (auth), Where to let your art hang out, 71, Village Post, Coconut Grove.
Memberships: Mangrove . . . (rec secy, 70).
Mailing Address: 6867 S W 52nd St, Miami, FL 33155.

T

TABUENA, ROMEO VILLALVA
Painter
Preferred Media: Acrylics, Oils, Watercolors.
b Iloilo City, Panay Island, Philippines, Aug 22, 21.
Study & Training: Univ Philippines, with Diosdado Lorenzo; Art Stud League New York, Thekla M Barneys grant, 52-53, with Will Barnet; Acad Grande Chaumiére, Paris, with Goertz.
Work in Public Collections: New York Pub Libr Print Div; Philippine Nat Mus, Manila; Palace Fine Arts, Mexico City; Mus Mod Arte, Mexico City; Mus Mod Art, São Paulo, Brazil.
Commissions: Filipiniana (mural), Govt Philippines, for Washington Embassy, 57.
Exhibitions: One-man shows, Assoc Am Artists Galleries, New York, 53 & Palace Fine Arts, Mexico City, 62 & 69; Prize Winners Show, Whitney Mus Am Art, New York, 53; Tabuena Ten Yrs Retrospective, Philippine Art Gallery, Manila, 59; Eighth Biennal São Paulo, Mus Mod Art, Brazil, 65.
Teaching: Lectr, Art of today, Far Eastern Univ, 51.
Positions: Art dir, Eve News, Manila, 49-52.
Awards: Gold medal in painting, Sch Fine Arts, Univ Philippines, 41; second prize, Art Asn Philippines Ann, 49.
Bibliography: Emily Genauer (auth), Romeo V Tabuena, What's New, Abbot Labs, 55; Lyd Arguilla (auth), Ten years of Tabuena's art, Philippine Art Gallery, 59; Arias de la Canal (auth), Tabuena—sensibilidad, disciplinada & poetica, El Norte, Mex, 69.
Memberships: Art Asn Philippines.
Publications: Auth, Tabuena (Watercolor page), Am Artist Mag, 56; auth, Painting a still life, In: Painting in acrylics, Watson-Guptill, 65.
Dealers: Galleria de Arte Misrachi, Genova 20, Mexico City, Mex; Tasende Gallery, Costera Y Yanez Pinzon, Acapulco, Mex.
Mailing Address: Santo Domingo 12, San Miguel de Allende, Guanajuato, Mex.

TAHIR, ABE M, JR
Art Dealer
b Greenwood, Miss, Feb 18, 31.
Study & Training: Univ Miss, BBA; George Washington Univ, MBA.
Positions: Dir, Tahir Gallery.
Specialty of Gallery: Original prints.
Mailing Address: 823 Chartres St, New Orleans, LA 70116.

TAIT, CORNELIA DAMIAN
Painter, Sculptor
Preferred Media: Oils.
b Philadelphia, Pa.
Study & Training: Graphic Sketch Club; Fleisher Art Mem; Temple Univ, with Alexander Abels & Boris Blai, BS (educ); Tyler Sch Fine Arts, with Raphael Sabatini, BFA (honors), MFA.
Work in Public Collections: Temple Univ Permanent Collection, Philadelphia; Tyler Art Sch, Elkins Park, Pa; Nara Philos Study Ctr, Duncannon, Pa; Christian Endeavor Bldg, World Hq, Columbus, Ohio; St Mary's Romanian Orthodox Church Mus, Cleveland, Ohio.

Commissions: Three murals on musical themes, Morris Rotenberg, Philadelphia, 46; portraits of church donors, Romanian-Orthodox Cathedral, Detroit, Mich, 49; 21 altar screen paintings, Holy Trinity Romanian-Orthodox Cathedral, Detroit, 49-50; portrait of founder of Christian Endeavor, comn by Joseph Holton Jones, Columbus, 55.
Exhibitions: Nat Exhib, Pittsburgh, Pa, 61 & Ecclesiastical Crafts Exhib, Cleveland, 62, Church Archit Guild Am; Art with Architecture & Regional Paintings Exhibs, 50th Anniversary of Philadelphia Art Alliance, 65; Pa Acad Fine Arts Regional, Philadelphia, 66; Signs in Cloth, nat traveling exhibs in 36 major U S A cities, 68-71; Int Graphics Collectors' Exhib, E Stroudsburg State Teachers Col, 66.
Teaching: Instr art, Settlement Music Sch, 42-44; instr sculpture, Philadelphia Mus Art, 44-45; instr art & supvr, Buckingham Friends Sch, 50-53; supvr art, Albington Township Cult Ctr, 63.
Awards: Purchase awards, Temple Univ, 57-60; Mania Blai Painting Award, Tyler Sch Fine Arts, 58; painting award, Phillips Mill Art Asn, 65; plus others.
Bibliography: Look up & live, 67 & 68 & Lamp unto my feet, 68 & 69, produced on CBS-TV.
Memberships: Artists Equity Asn; Woodmere Art Gallery; Philadelphia Art Alliance; Nat Forum Prof Artists; Violet Oakley Mem Found.
Research: Byzantine architecture & monuments; folk art in Romania; folk arts of the Southwest Indians.
Publications: Contribr, Process of underpainting (film), 52; contribr, Friends J, 52; contribr, New Leaves, 65 & 66; contribr articles for newspapers, 60's.
Mailing Address: 10 Armour Rd, Hatboro, PA 19040.

TAIT, KATHARINE LAMB
Painter, Designer
Preferred Media: Stained Glass.
b Alpine, N J, June 3, 95.
Study & Training: Friends Sem, N Y; Nat Acad Design; Art Stud League New York; Cooper Union Art Sch.
Work in Public Collections: Education (Hugo B Froehlich Mem window), Newark Mus, N J.
Commissions: All nave & rose windows in both Protestant & Roman Cath chapels, U S Marine Corps, Camp Lejeune, N C; all windows, Old Mariners Church, Detroit, Mich; all windows, All Saints Episcopal Church, Detroit; all windows, Calvary Methodist Church, Dumont, N J.
Exhibitions: Guild Relig Archit, Detroit; Nat Arts Club, New York, N Y; Tenafly Pub Libr, N J; Stained Glass Asn Am.
Teaching: Instr design, Cooper Union Women's Art Sch, 22-26.
Positions: Artist & designer, J & R Lamb Studios, 21-
Memberships: Nat Soc Mural Painters; Stained Glass Asn Am; Bergen Co Artists Guild.
Publications: Auth & illusr, Children of Paris, New York Times Bk Rev; auth & illusr, A child's day in court, New York Times Mag.
Mailing Address: Lambs Lane, Box 102, Cresskill, NJ 07626.

TAJIRI, SHINKICHI
Sculptor, Educator
b Los Angeles, Calif, Dec 7, 23.
Study & Training: Art Inst Chicago, with Ossip Zadkine; with F Leger, Paris, France; Acad Grande Chaumière, Paris.
Work in Public Collections: Stedelijk Mus, Amsterdam; Mus Mod Art, New York; Louisiana, Copenhagen; Roysman Mus, Rotterdam; CNAC, Paris.
Commissions: AKU fountain, 60.
Exhibitions: Stedelijk Mus, Amsterdam, 60-67; Venice Biennial, 62; Andre Emmerich Gallery, New York, 65; Kunsthalle, Basel, Switz, 69; Kunsthalle Lund, Sweden, 71.
Teaching: Guest prof sculpture, Minneapolis Col Art & Design, 64-65; prof sculpture, Stadtliche Höchschule für Bildende Kunste, West Berlin, Ger, 69-
Awards: Golden Lion, Eighth Int Festival Amateur Films, Cannes, France, 55; Mainichi Shibum prize for sculpture, Mainchi Newspapers, Tokyo, 63; Grand Prix, The Wet Dream Film Festival, Amsterdam, 70.
Bibliography: L Freed (auth), Seltsame spiele, Barmieyer & Nikel, 69.
Publications: Ed, Ferdi, 69; auth, Shake well before using, 69; auth, The wall, 70; auth, Mayday, 70; auth, Land mine, 70.
Dealer: Court Gallery, Ostergade 24, Copenhagen, Denmark.
Mailing Address: Castle Scheres, Baarlo (Limburg), Netherlands.

TAKAI, TEIJI
Painter
Preferred Media: Oils.
b Osaka, Japan, Feb 5, 11.
Study & Training: Shinano Bashi Art Inst, Osaka.

Work in Public Collections: Corcoran Gallery, Washington, D C; Mod Art Mus, Tokyo, Japan; Columbia Mus, S C; Uniontown Art Club, Pa; Wakayama Mod Art Mus, Japan.
Exhibitions: Several one-man shows, Poindexter Gallery, 59-72; Whitney Mus Am Art Ann, New York, N Y, 59 & 61; Corcoran Biennial, 61-62; Carnegie Int, Pittsburgh, 61-62; Retrospective, Takashimaya Tokyo, 67.
Teaching: Vis prof art, Winthrop Col, fall 70 & 72.
Awards: Okada Prize, 40; Fukushima Prize, 64.
Memberships: Niki Art Asn; Int Artist Asn.
Dealer: Poindexter Gallery, 24 E 84th St, New York, NY 10028.
Mailing Address: 253 W 103rd St, New York, NY 10025.

TAKAL, PETER
Painter
b Bucharest, Romania, Dec 8, 05; U S citizen.
Study & Training: Paris, France.
Work in Public Collections: Mus Mod Art, New York, N Y; Metrop Mus Art, New York; Whitney Mus Am Art, New York; Cleveland Mus Art, Ohio; Los Angeles Co Mus Art, Calif; plus in over 100 mus collections in U S A & abroad.
Commissions: City Roofs (print), 56 & Trees & Fields (print), 57, Print Club Cleveland; four prints, Int Graphic Arts Soc, New York, 56-65; Meditation (print), Assoc Am Artists, New York, 58; suite of 20 lithographs, Tamarind Lithography Workshop, Los Angeles, 64; two prints, Hollander Workshop, New York, 69; plus others.
Exhibitions: Pa Acad Fine Arts Biennial, Philadelphia, 53-67; Whitney Mus Am Art Ann, 55-63 & 69; Recent Drawings U S A, Mus Mod Art, New York, 56; American Prints Today, traveling exhib, Print Coun Am, 59, 62 & 63; White House, Washington, D C, 66 & 70; plus more than 50 one-man shows in U S A & abroad, 32-72.
Teaching: Lectr art, Cleveland Mus Art, 58; lectr art, Beloit Col, 65; lectr art, Cent Col, 68.
Awards: Fel, Yaddo Found, 61; purchase award, Third Nat Print Exhib, Pasadena Art Mus, 62; Ford fel, Tamarind Lithography Workshop, 63-64; plus others.
Bibliography: Pierre Mornand (auth), Takal portraitiste lineaire evocateur de l'insaisissable, Le Courrier Graphique, 37; Norman Kent (auth), What is good drawing?, Am Artist Mag, 45; Leonia E Prasse (auth) & Louise Richards (auth), Recent works of Peter Takal, Cleveland Mus Art, 58; plus others.
Memberships: Print Club Philadelphia (juror, 58); Artists Equity Asn New York; Print Coun Am; Soc Am Graphic Artists; Am Color Print Soc (juror, 59).
Publications: Auth, Selected works of Peter Takal, drawings & poems, Int Univ Press, 45; co-auth, Peter Takal at the Strozzina, Palazzo Strozzi (catalogue), 60; auth, Between the lines, Artists Proof, Vol I, No 2; illusr, Mother & child in modern art, Duell, 64; auth, About the invisible in art, Lyman Wright Art Ctr, 65.
Dealer: Weyhe Gallery, 794 Lexington Ave, New York, NY 10021.
Mailing Address: 116 E 68th St, New York, NY 10021.

TAKEMOTO, HENRY TADAAKI
Craftsman, Sculptor
Preferred Media: Ceramics.
b Honolulu, Hawaii, July 23, 30.
Study & Training: Univ Hawaii, BFA; Los Angeles Co Art Inst, MFA.
Work in Public Collections: Smithsonian Inst.
Exhibitions: Second Int Exhib Contemp Ceramics, Ostend, Belg, 59; Third Int Exhib Contemp Ceramics, Prague, Czech, 62; Studio Potter Exhib, Victoria & Albert Mus, London, Eng, 66-70; Objects: U S A Johnson Wax Collection Contemp Crafts, Smithsonian Inst, Washington, D C, 70-73; Contemp Ceramic Art, U S, Can, Mex, Japan, Kyoto & Tokyo, 71-72.
Teaching: Instr ceramics, Calif Sch Fine Arts, San Francisco; instr ceramics, Scripps Col, 65-69.
Positions: Designer & glaze chemist, Interpace Corp, 69-
Awards: Double purchase prize, Wichita Art Asn, 59; silver medal for sculpture, Ostend, Belg, 59; bronze medal, Mus Contemp Crafts, N Y, 60; plus others.
Mailing Address: 1951 Redesdale Ave, Los Angeles, CA 90039.

TALBOT, WILLIAM (H M)
Sculptor
Preferred Media: Concrete, Stained Glass.
b Boston, Mass, Jan 10, 18.
Study & Training: Pa Acad Fine Arts, 36 & 41; with George Demetrios, Gloucester, Mass, 37-40; Acad Beaux Arts, Paris, France, 45-46.
Work in Public Collections: Whitney Mus Am Art, New York, N Y; St Lawrence Univ, Canton, N Y; Earlham Col, Richmond, Ind; Bryn Mawr Col, Pa; St John's Church, Washington, Conn.

Commissions: Fountain (with Carl Koch & G Kepes), Fitchburg Youth Libr, Mass, 50; fountain, Nat Coun State Garden Clubs Am Nat Hq, St Louis, Mo, 59; Mem (sculpture & stairwell at rehab ctr), Mrs Charles Belknap for Barnes Hosp, St Louis, Mo, 64.
Exhibitions: Pa Acad Fine Arts Ann, 42, 49 & 66; Philadelphia Mus Third Int, 49; De Cordova & Dana Mus Sculpture Exhib, 49; Whitney Mus Am Art Sculpture Ann, 50, 51 & 63; Arts Club Chicago, 72.
Teaching: Vis prof sculpture, dept archit & design, Univ Mich, spring 49.
Awards: Prix de Rome, Am Acad Rome, 41; Cresson traveling fel, 41 & Steele Sculpture Prize, 49, Pa Acad Fine Arts.
Bibliography: Peter Blake (auth), article, In: Archit Forum, 51; Edward Renouf (auth), The sculpture of William Talbot, Harvard Art Rev, spring-summer, 67; D Meilach (auth), Contemporary art with stone, Crown, 69.
Memberships: Sculptors Guild (pres, 65-68, v pres publ, 68-72).
Dealer: Frank Rehn Gallery, 655 Madison Ave, New York, NY 10021.
Mailing Address: Bell Hill, Washington, CT 06793.

TALLEUR, JOHN J
Printmaker
Preferred Media: Intaglio.
b Chicago, Ill, May 29, 25.
Study & Training: Art Inst Chicago Sch; Univ Chicago, BFA, 47; Iowa State Univ, MFA, 51.
Work in Public Collections: Mus Mod Art, New York, N Y; Carnegie Inst, Pittsburgh, Pa; Metrop Mus, New York; Whitney Mus Am Art, New York; Art Inst Chicago, Ill.
Commissions: Print, Lakeside Studios, 72; print, Jewish Community Ctr, Kansas City, Mo, 72.
Teaching: Instr printmaking, Carleton Col, 47-49; instr printmaking, Saint Paul Gallery & Sch Art, 49; prof printmaking, Univ Kans, 53-
Bibliography: Bret Waller (auth), John Talleur, Univ Kans Mus Art, 66.
Memberships: Artists Equity Asn; Delta Phi Delta; Print Coun Am.
Mailing Address: 242 Concord, Lawrence, KS 66073.

TALVACCHIO, HELEN STEINER
Painter
Preferred Media: Oils, Watercolors.
b Akron, Ohio, May 5, 21.
Study & Training: Cleveland Inst Art, four yr cert, Ohio; Univ Akron.
Exhibitions: Butler Nat, Youngstown, Ohio, 63; Am Vet Show, New York, N Y, 66; Cooperstown Art Asn, N Y, 66 & 68; Catharine Lorillard Wolfe Art Club, New York, 68; Knickerbocker Artists, Nat Arts Club, New York, 71.
Awards: First in prints, Cleveland Mus May Show, 49; second in oils, Nat League Am Pen Women, Washington, 68 & Salt Lake City, 70.
Memberships: Nat League Am Pen Women (Western Reserve Br, v pres & treas, 66-).
Dealer: Malvina Freedson Gallery, Winton Pl, Lakewood, OH 44107.
Mailing Address: 24217 Emery Rd, Cleveland, OH 44128.

TAM, REUBEN
Painter, Educator
Preferred Media: Oils, Acrylics, Inks.
b Kapaa, Hawaii, Jan 17, 16.
Study & Training: Univ Hawaii, BA, 37, fifth yr cert, 38; Calif Sch Fine Arts; Columbia Univ, with Meyer Schapiro; New Sch Soc Res.
Work in Public Collections: Mus Mod Art, New York, N Y; Metrop Mus Art, New York; Whitney Mus Am Art, New York; Brooklyn Mus, N Y; Nat Collection Fine Arts, Smithsonian Inst, Washington, D C.
Exhibitions: Contemp Am Painting, Whitney Mus Am Art, New York, 41-65; Contemp Am Painting, Krannert Art Mus, Univ Ill, Urbana-Champaign, 49-69; Am Painting, Metrop Mus Art, New York, 53; Pittsburgh Int Exhib, Carnegie Inst Mus Art, 64 & 67; Landscape in Maine (1820-1970), Colby Col Art Mus, Maine, 70.
Teaching: Instr advan painting, Brooklyn Mus Art Sch, 46-; prof painting, Ore State Univ, summer 66; vis artist, Ore State Syst Higher Educ, summer 71.
Awards: First nat prize, Golden Gate Expos, San Francisco, Calif, 39; Guggenheim fel, 48; first prize, Brooklyn Mus Biennial, 52 & 56.
Bibliography: Burrey (auth), Reuben Tam: painter of the intimate landscape, Arts Mag, 2/58; Nordness (auth) & Weller (auth), Art U S A now, Viking, 62; Gussow (auth), A sense of place: the artist & the American land, Sat Rev, 72.
Dealer: Coe Kerr Gallery, Inc, 49 E 82nd St, New York, NY 10028.
Mailing Address: 549 W 123rd St, New York, NY 10027.

TAMAYO, RUFINO
Painter
b Oaxaca, Mex, 99.
Work in Public Collections: Mus Mod Art, New York, N Y; Mus Art Mod, Paris, France; Mus Arte Mod, Rome, Italy; Mus Royale, Brussels, Belg; Phillips Mem Gallery, Washington, D C.
Commissions: Murals, Govt Mex, Palace Fine Arts, Mexico City, 52, Mus Nac Antropologia, Mexico City, 64 & UN, New York, 72; murals, Dallas Mus Fine Arts, 53 & UNESCO Bldg, Paris, 58.
Exhibitions: One-man shows, San Francisco Mus Art, 53, Kunsternes Hus Oslo, Norway, 59, Phoenix Art Mus, Ariz, 68 & Biennal Venice.
Awards: Oficiel Legion d'Honeur, France; Comendator Repub Italiana; Premio Nac Mex.
Bibliography: Many.
Memberships: Inst & Acad Arts & Lett; Acad Arte, Buenos Aires, Arg; Acad Diseno, Florence, Italy.
Dealer: Perl's Gallery, 1016 Madison Ave, New York, NY 10021.
Mailing Address: Callejon del Santisimo 12, San Angel, Mexico City, Mex.

TAMBELLINI, ALDO
Painter, Sculptor
Preferred Media: Mixed Media.
b Syracuse, N Y, Apr 29, 30.
Study & Training: Syracuse Univ, BFA, 54; Univ Notre Dame, teaching fel, MFA, 58, with Ivan Mestrovic; Grad Sch Archit & Allied Arts, Univ Ore, teaching fel.
Work in Public Collections: Black Film Ser, Mus Mod Art Film Arch.
Commissions: Relief, Le Moyne Col, Syracuse, 65; Black Gate Cologne, WDR TV, Cologne, Ger, 68; 0 + 0, Intermedia Inst, New York, 71.
Exhibitions: TV As Creative Medium, Howard Wise Gallery, New York, 67; Vision & TV, Rose Art Mus, Brandeis Univ, Waltham, Mass, 70; Cineprobe, Mus Mod Art, New York, 70; Black Film Ser, Jewish Mus, New York, 70; Black Video No 3, Whitney Mus Am Art, New York, 70.
Teaching: Instr painting & sculpture, Syracuse Mus Fine Arts, 51-53; instr sculpture, Pratt Inst, 64; instr creative electrography, Dist 5, New York, 69-
Awards: Syracuse Mus Prize, 52; Int Grand Prix, Oberhausen Film Festival, Ger, 69.
Bibliography: J Margoles (auth), TV the next medium, Art Am, 69; G Youngblood (auth), Expanded cinema, Dutton, 70; Kultermann (auth), Art & life, Praeger, 71.
Publications: Illusr & contribr, Black Issue, Arts Can, 67; auth, Impermanence, Arts Can, 68; auth, Radican software, First Video Newsletter, 70.
Mailing Address: c/o Howard Wise Gallery, 2 W 13th St, New York, NY 10019.

TANIA (SCHREIBER)
Sculptor, Painter
b Warsaw, Poland, Jan 11, 24.
Study & Training: McGill Univ, MA, 42; Columbia Univ, 42-44; Art Stud League, with Yasuo Kuniyoshi, Morris Kantor, Vaclav Vytlacil & Harry Sternberg, 48-51.
Work in Public Collections: Rose Art Mus, Brandeis Univ; New York Univ; Morgan State Col; New York Civic Ctr Synagogue.
Commissions: Two walls, comn by New York City, Vest Pocket Parks, Brooklyn & Bronx, 67-68.
Exhibitions: Two-man show, New York Univ Loeb Ctr, 64 & 67; Univ Va, 64 & 68; Milwaukee Art Inst, 65; Univ Del, 65; four-man show show, Mus Mod Art, 69; plus many others.
Teaching: Instr fundamentals of design & drawing, New York Univ, 63-69.
Dealer: Bertha Schaefer Galleries, 41 E 57th St, New York, NY 10022.
Mailing Address: 345 Fireplace Rd, East Hampton, NY 11937.

TANKSLEY, ANN
Painter
Preferred Media: Oils.
b Pittsburgh, Pa, Jan 25, 34.
Study & Training: Carnegie Inst Technol, BFA.
Work in Public Collections: Johnson Publ Co, Chicago, Ill.
Exhibitions: 15 Women, N C A&T State Univ, Greensboro, 69; Freedomways Exhib, Hudson River Mus, Yonkers, N Y, 71; U S A 1971, Carnegie Inst, Pittsburgh, 71; Acts of Art, New York, 72; Black Women Artist, Mount Holyoke Col, South Hadley, Mass, 72; plus others.
Teaching: Instr art, Queens Youth Ctrs Arts, N Y, 59-62; instr art, Art Ctr Northern N J, 63; substitute instr art, Malvern Pub Schs, 71-
Dealer: Acts of Art, 15 Charles St, New York, NY 10014.
Mailing Address: 18 Carlton Rd, Great Neck, NY 11021.

TANNER, JAMES L
Craftsman
Preferred Media: Wood, Glass, Ceramics.
b Jacksonville, Fla, July 22, 41.
Study & Training: Fla A&M Univ, BA, 64; Aspen Sch Contemp Art, summer 64; Univ Wis-Madison, MS, 66, MFA, 67.
Work in Public Collections: Johnson Wax Collection, Smithsonian Inst, Washington, D C; N Hennepin State Jr Col, Minneapolis, Minn; Mankato State Col, Minn.
Exhibitions: Young America 1969, Mus Contemp Crafts, 69; Objects U S A, circulated by Smithsonian Inst, 69-70; Glass 2000 BC-1971 AD, John Michael Kohler Art Ctr, Sheboygan, Wis, 71; Reflections on Glass, Long Beach Mus Art, Calif, 71-72; Toledo Glass Nat, 72.
Bibliography: Daniel Wilson (auth) & David Wayne (auth), With these hands, 70; Lee Nordness (auth), Objects U S A, 70.
Memberships: Nat Coun Educ Ceramic Arts; Am Craftsman Coun; Minn Craftsman Coun (bd dirs, 72-73).
Mailing Address: Rte 1, Good Thunder, MN 56037.

TARNOPOL, GREGOIRE
Painter, Collector
Preferred Media: Gouache.
b Odessa, Russia, Feb 24, 91; U S citizen.
Study & Training: Acad Art, Munich; Acad Art, Saint Petersburg; Acad Art, Copenhagen.
Exhibitions: Barzansky Gallery, New York, N Y, 41.
Collection: French modern: from Delacroix to Picasso.
Mailing Address: 47 E 88th St, New York, NY 10028.

TARR, WILLIAM
Sculptor
Preferred Media: Steel.
b New York, N Y, May 31, 25.
Work in Public Collections: Whitney Mus Am Art, New York; Art Inst Chicago, Ill.
Commissions: Morningside Heights (welded steel), 68 & Martin Luther King, Jr Mem (welded steel), 72, Bd Educ, New York; concrete sculpture, Buchanan Sch, Washington, D C, 69.
Exhibitions: Sculpture Ann, Whitney Mus Am Art, New York, four from 62-68; Am Sculpture Show, Flint Inst Fine Arts, 65.
Awards: Purchase award, Ford Found, 62; cert merit, Munic Art Soc, 68.
Mailing Address: 102 Greene St, New York, NY 10012.

TASCONA, ANTONIO TONY
Painter, Sculptor
b St Boniface, Man, Mar 16, 26.
Study & Training: Winnipeg Sch Art, dipl; Univ Man Sch Fine Arts.
Work in Public Collections: Winnipeg Art Gallery, Man; Confederation Art Gallery & Mus Charlottetown, P E I; Art Gallery Ont, Toronto; Nat Gallery Can, Ottawa; Can Coun Collection, Ottawa.
Commissions: Aluminum bas relief, Man Centennial Art Ctr, 67-68; lacquer painting on aluminum, Winnipeg YWCA, 68; sculpture, Fletcher Argue Bldg, Univ Man, 69; epoxy resin disks, in steel rings, Fed Dept Pub Works for Freshwater Inst, Univ Man, 72.
Exhibitions: Walker Art Ctr Biennial, Minneapolis, 58; Expos Concours Artistiques, Montreal Beaux Arts, 63 & Quebec Mus, 64; Can Prints & Drawings, Cardiff Commonwealth Arts Festival, Wales, 65; Nat Gallery Can Traveling Exhib Australia, 67; Nat Gallery Can Biennial, Ottawa, 68.
Awards: Purchase awards, Western Ont Ann, 65 & 66; Arts Medal Award, Royal Archit Inst Can, Ottawa, 70; Can Coun Arts Award fel, 72.
Bibliography: Rene Ostiguey (auth), Western Canadian art, Vie Arts Montreal, 66; Anita Aarons (auth), Royal Inst Can, 70; P Fry (auth), Tony Tascona, Arts Can Mag, 72; plus others.
Memberships: Winnipeg Art Gallery; Can Artist Representation; assoc Royal Can Acad Arts.
Mailing Address: 151 Tache Ave, Winnipeg, Man R2H 1Z4, Can.

TATMAN, VIRGINIA DOWNING
Craftsman, Painter
b Kenosha, Wis, July 5, 17.
Study & Training: Univ Wis-Milwaukee.
Exhibitions: Wis State Fair; Wis Designer-Craftsmen Ann; Milwaukee Art Ctr Ann Summer Fair; one-man show, Kenosha Pub Mus; plus others.
Teaching: Instr art, Kenosha Tech Inst; instr, State Wis D V R.
Positions: Former cur, Kenosha Pub Mus.
Awards: Prizes, Winter Art Fair, Kenosha, 69, Kenosha Art Asn, 69 & Kenosha Art Fair, 72.
Memberships: Wis Designer-Craftsmen; Greater Kenosha Art Coun (v pres).
Mailing Address: 2703 73rd St, Kenosha, WI 53140.

TATSCHL, JOHN
Craftsman, Sculptor
Preferred Media: Wood, Glass, Bronze.
b Vienna, Austria, June 30, 06.
Study & Training: Teachers Col, Vienna; Acad Appl Art & Acad Fine Arts, Master Sch Sculpture, Vienna.
Work in Public Collections: Mus N Mex, Santa Fe.
Commissions: Mural, U S Post Off, Vivian, La; ten stained glass windows, St Michael Church, Albuquerque; stained glass windows, Am Bank Commerce, Albuquerque; stained glass for churches, Las Cruces, Los Alamos & Albuquerque, N Mex; fountain, Roswell Mus; plus others.
Exhibitions: Southwest Exhibits regularly, 46-56.
Teaching: Asst prof, Park Col, 43-46; prof art, Univ N Mex, 46-
Awards: Purchase awards, Roswell Mus & Mus N Mex; Univ N Mex res grants, 50 & 53; Am Inst Architects Award for art in archit, 63.
Mailing Address: Dept of Art, University of New Mexico, Albuquerque, NM 87106.

TATTI, BENEDICT MICHAEL
Sculptor, Painter
b New York, N Y, May 1, 17.
Study & Training: Masters Inst Roerich Mus, with L Slobodkin; Da Vinci Art Sch, with A Piccirilli; State Univ N Y; Art Stud League New York, with William Zorach & O Zadkine; Hans Hofmann Sch Art, with Hans Hofmann.
Work in Public Collections: Harper's Row, Mr & Mrs Cass Canfield, New York; Mr & Mrs Zero Mostel, New York; Dr Maurice Hexter, Fedn Jewish Philanthropies, New York; Boccour Paints, Mr & Mrs Sam Golden, N J; Lasdon Found, Mr & Mrs Lloyd Lasdon, New York.
Commissions: Sundial, R W Bliss for Dumbarton Oaks, Washington, D C, 52; Bison, E Taylor for Tokyo Park, Japan, 60; D'Aragon Mem, A D'Aragon, Hartsdale, N Y, 69; medallions of D Sarnoff, D Eisenhower & Mark Twain, Newell & Lennon, New York.
Exhibitions: Artists for Victory, Metrop Mus Art, New York, 42; Pa Acad Fine Arts, Philadelphia, 50-54; Mus Mod Art, New York, 60; Claude Bernard Gallery, Paris, France, 60; Roko Gallery, New York, 67.
Teaching: Instr sculpture & head dept, H S Art & Design, 65-; instr sculpture, Craft Stud League, 66-67.
Positions: Consult restoration, Alexanders Sculpture Studio, 46-72; sculptor-designer, Loewy-Smith Assocs, 52-65.
Awards: Artist-in-residence, Nat Ctr Experiments TV, San Francisco, Calif, 69; grant, creative arts prog, N Y State Coun Arts, 72; medal of hon for sculpture, Painters & Sculptors Soc N J, 72.
Memberships: Am Soc Contemp Artists; Sculptors League, New York; Painters & Sculptors Soc N J (v pres, at present).
Dealer: Alexander Gallery, 117 E 39th St, New York, NY 10016.
Mailing Address: 214 E 39th St, New York, NY 10016.

TAUBES, FREDERIC
Painter, Writer
b Lwow, Poland, Apr 15, 00; U S citizen.
Study & Training: Munich Art Acad, with F von Stuck & M Doerner; Bauhaus, Weimar, with J Itten.
Work in Public Collections: Metrop Mus Art, New York, N Y; San Francisco Mus Art, Calif; De Young Mem Mus, San Francisco; Mills Col Collection, Oakland; William Rockhill Nelson Gallery, Kansas City; plus many others.
Exhibitions: Over one hundred one-man exhibs in mus & galleries in U S A.
Teaching: Carnegie vis prof art, Univ Ill; vis prof art, Univ Wis, Univ Okla, Univ Hawaii, Colo State Col, State Teachers Col, Lansing, Mich, New York Univ, Cooper Union, Art Stud League New York, plus many others; lectr art, Royal Col Art, Royal Soc Art, Slade Sch, London Univ, John Ruskin Sch Art, Oxford Univ, Edinborough Col Art, Camberwell Sch Art & Crafts, plus many others.
Positions: Contrib ed, Taubes Page, Am Artist Mag, 43-59; Am ed, The Artist Mag with the Taubes Page as ed feature, at present.
Awards: Col in State N Mex; hon citizen of San Antonio, Tex; hon citation, New Iberia; plus others.
Memberships: Fel Royal Soc Arts; fel Int Soc Arts & Lett.
Research: Formulator of Taubes Varnishes & Copal Painting Media.
Publications: Auth forty bks on paint techniques & esthetics; contribr, Encycl Britannica; Yearbooks, Grolier Encycl & others.
Mailing Address: Haverstraw, NY 10927.

TAUCH, WALDINE AMANDA
Sculptor, Collector
b Schulenburg, Tex.
Study & Training: With Pompeo Coppini.
Work in Public Collections: Witte Mem Mus, San Antonio, Tex; Pan Handle Plains Hist Mus, Campos, Tex; Wesleyan Mus, Ga.
Commissions: Heroic monument to Bedford, Ind, State Ind, 22; The Doughboy Statue, Am Legion, Austin, Tex, 31; Moses Austin

Monument, State Tex, 41; Higher Education, comn by Mr & Mrs Andrew Casoles for Trinity Univ (Tex), 68; Gen Douglas MacArthur, Howard Payne Col, Brownwood, Tex, 69.
Exhibitions: Nat Sculpture Soc Traveling Show, 31; Women Painters & Sculptors, New York, N Y, 32; Coppini Acad Fine Arts, 54-; Witte Mem Mus; Nat Acad Design, New York; plus others.
Bibliography: Shaffer (auth), Making the Texas Ranger of to-day, San Antonio Express, 61; John Field (auth), Unveiling of Gen Douglas MacArthur.
Memberships: Coppini Acad Fine Arts (sponsor, 57-, pres emer, 60-); fel Nat Sculpture Soc; Am Acad Arts & Lett; Panhandle Plains Hist Soc & Mus (dir arts, 72-73); fel Am Artists Prof League.
Collections: Paintings by Van Driest, Rolla Taylor, Harold Roney & Frank Garvari.
Mailing Address: 115 Melrose Pl, San Antonio, TX 78212.

TAULBEE, DAN J
Painter, Art Dealer
Preferred Media: Oils, Watercolors.
b Charlo, Mont, Apr 7, 24.
Study & Training: With pvt instructors.
Work in Public Collections: Farnsworth Mus, Maine; Peabody Mus, Cambridge, Mass; Plains Indian Mus, Browning, Mont; C M Russell Mus, Helena, Mont; Southern Plains Mus, Anadarko, Okla.
Exhibitions: Farnsworth Mus Show; Peabody Mus Show; Nat Acad Design, New York, N Y; Burr's Int Show.
Positions: Owner, Heritage Am Art Gallery, Butte, Mont.
Awards: Gold medal, Burr Gallery.
Memberships: Grand Cent Watercolorists Soc.
Specialty of Gallery: Historical plains Indian art & Western Americana.
Art Interests: Pictorial history of the Plains Indian.
Dealers: Grand Central Galleries, 40 Vanderbilt Ave, New York, NY 10017; La Galleria, 2161 Ave de la Playa, La Jolla, CA 92037.
Mailing Address: 2706 Nettie St, Butte, MT 59701.

TAWNEY, LENORE
Weaver
Preferred Media: Cloth, Collages.
b Lorain, Ohio.
Study & Training: Univ Ill, 43-45; Inst Design, Ill, with Archipenko, 46-47; also with Martha Taipale, Finland, 54.
Work in Public Collections: Mus Contemp Crafts, New York, N Y; Mus Mod Art, New York; Kunstgewerbe Mus, Zurich; Brooklyn Mus, N Y; Cooper-Hewitt Mus.
Exhibitions: Brussels World's Fair, 59; Kunstgewerbe Mus, Zurich, 64; one-man shows, Art Inst Chicago, Contemp Crafts Mus, Seattle World's Fair & Staten Island Mus, New York, 61.
Dealer: Willard Gallery, 29 E 72nd St, New York, NY 10021.
Mailing Address: 37 E Fourth St, New York, NY 10003.

TAYLOR, CHARLES
Painter
Preferred Media: Oils, Watercolors.
b Philadelphia, Pa, Dec 15, 10.
Study & Training: Fleisher Mem Sch; also with Maurice Molarsky.
Work in Public Collections: N Y Univ Col Eng; Philadelphia Art Mus, Pa; Montclair Mus; Woodmere Art Gallery; Harcum Jr Col.
Exhibitions: Nat Acad Design Ann; Am Watercolor Soc; Philadelphia Watercolor Club; Pa Acad Fine Arts Ann; Carnegie Inst.
Awards: Second Altman figure prize, Nat Acad Design, 55; Am Artist Mag medal, 60; Seley purchase prize, Salmagundi Club, 61.
Bibliography: Article, In: The Studio, 9/55; article, In: Am Artist Mag, 5/60; article, In: Charette, 5/63.
Memberships: Salmagundi Club; Am Watercolor Soc; Philadelphia Watercolor Club (pres); Audubon Artists; Philadelphia Art Alliance.
Mailing Address: 2021 Waverly St, Philadelphia, PA 19146.

TAYLOR, (BERTHA) FANNING
Painter, Lecturer
Preferred Media: Oils, Watercolors, Graphics.
b New York, N Y, July 30, 83.
Study & Training: Hunter Col Woman's Art Sch; Cooper Union, with Bryson Burroughs; Univ Montpellior, France; Sorbonne; Ecole Louvre; Atelier d'Art Sacre, with Maurice Denis.
Work in Public Collections: Sacred Maternity (oil), Norfolk Mus; Sermon on the Mount (oil), St Peter's Church Sun Sch, Spotswood, N J; portraits of Bishop Brown & Rev Payton Williams, Christ & St Luke's Church, Norfolk, Va; Guild House.
Commissions: Virgin & St Hubert (murals), Mrs Morgan Richards, Paris, France, 37; small portable reredos, commissioned by chaplain for Navy chapel, Norfolk, 48.
Exhibitions: Sect Artistes Français, Salon Beaux Arts, Paris, 30-39; Salon Artistes Independants, Paris, 30-39; Salon d'Automne,

Paris, 30-39; Salon Tuileries, Paris, 30-39; one-man show, Norfolk Mus, 66.
Teaching: Lectr art theory, classes, clubs & libraries, 39-; lectr art hist, Hermitage Found, 45-49; lectr art appreciation, Norfolk Div, Col William & Mary, 49-52; oil painting, Norfolk Mus Art Class, 52-60.
Positions: Lectr, Louvre Mus, Paris, 29-39; cur collections, Hermitage Found, 45-49.
Awards: Medaille da Bronze, Ministere l'Educ, France; award, City of Norfolk, 70; award, Fedn Woman's Clubs, 72.
Memberships: Col Art Asn Am; Am Artists Prof League; Pen & Brush Club; Tidewater Artists (pres); Artistes Moderne, Americain et Anglais, Paris (founder & dir).
Research: Medieval & eleventh century of the French School; Renaissance period of the Italian School.
Publications: Auth, Form & feeling in painting, 59; auth, My fifteen years in France, 68.
Mailing Address: 434 Pembroke Ave, Norfolk, VA 23507.

TAYLOR, FREDERICK BOURCHIER
Painter, Sculptor
Preferred Media: Oils.
b Ottawa, Ont, July 27, 06.
Study & Training: McGill Univ, BArch, 30; Univ London Goldsmiths Col Art, with Stanley Anderson; London Co Coun Sch Arts & Crafts; Byam Shaw Sch Painting, with Ernest Jackson.
Work in Public Collections: Nat Gallery Can, Ottawa; Pub Archives Can, Ottawa; Art Gallery Ont, Toronto; Montreal Mus Fine Arts; Mus Que, P Q; plus many others.
Commissions: Etching, Govt Can, Ottawa, 32; etchings & paintings for corps in Can & U S A, 32-72; portrait paintings, McGill Univ, 41-66; series of paintings, Algoma Steel Corp, Saulte Ste Marie, Ont, 46-47; plus many other pvt commissions.
Exhibitions: Ont Soc Artists, Toronto, 31-; Royal Can Acad Arts, Toronto, 31-72; many group & int travelling exhibs in Can, U S A & Mex, 31-72; Royal Inst Painters, London, 36.
Teaching: Instr & lectr drawing & modeling, McGill Univ Sch Archit, 40-43.
Positions: Chmn Que region, Fedn Can Artists, 44-45, nat v pres, 45-46.
Memberships: Royal Can Acad Arts (coun & comts, 48-); Can Soc Graphic Art; Soc Can Painter-Etchers & Engravers.
Dealer: Galeria San Miguel, Portal Allende 8, San Miguel de Allende, Gto, Mex.
Mailing Address: Apartado Postal 101, San Miguel de Allende, Gto, Mex.

TAYLOR, GRACE MARTIN
Painter, Educator
Preferred Media: Oils, Casein, Acrylics, Graphics.
b Morgantown, W Va.
Study & Training: Pa Acad Fine Arts; W Va Univ, AB, MA; Ohio Univ; Art Inst Chicago; Art Stud League New York; Bisttram Sch Art; Hans Hofmann Sch Fine Arts.
Work in Public Collections: Am Color Print Soc; Laskin Galleries, Charleston, W Va; Hallmark Co; Charleston Art Gallery, W Va; plus many pvt collections.
Exhibitions: Nat Acad Design, New York, N Y, 44 & 48; Am Watercolor Soc, New York, 58 & 59; Am Drawing Biennial, Norfolk Mus, 65; Contemp Gallery, Palm Beach, Fla, 67; one-man show, Artist of the Yr, W Va Univ, 58.
Teaching: Assoc prof art & head dept, Mason Col Music & Fine Arts, 34-56; assoc prof art, Morris Harvey Col, 56-68; lectr, W Va Univ Div Exten Credit, 67-71.
Positions: Dean, Mason Col Music & Fine Arts, 50-55, pres, 55-56.
Awards: First prize for prints, Seven State Exhib, Va Intermont Col, 48; first prize & jurors award, Three State Ann, Huntington Galleries, 54; Citizen of the Yr in Art in W Va, W Va Rhododendron Arts Festival, 71.
Bibliography: Haas (auth) & Packer (auth), Instruction in audio-visual aids, 50 & Morris Davidson (auth), Painting with purpose, 64, Prentice-Hall.
Memberships: Provincetown Art Asn; Allied Artists W Va (pres, 35 & 36); Am Asn Univ Prof; Int Platform Asn.
Research: Art education in colleges & universities of the East.
Art Interests: Creative production & teaching.
Collection: Portfolios of drawings & watercolors; paintings in all media.
Mailing Address: 1604 Virginia St E, Charleston, WV 25311.

TAYLOR, DR & MRS J E
Collectors
Mailing Address: 142 Lodges Lane, Bala-Cynwyd, PA 19004.

TAYLOR, JOHN (WILLIAMS)
Painter
Preferred Media: Oils, Gouache, Watercolors, Graphics.
b Baltimore, Md, Oct 12, 97.
Study & Training: J Francis Smith Art Sch, 20-22; Art Stud League Los Angeles, with S McDonald Wright, 23; Art Stud League New York, with Boardman Robinson, 26-27; study in Paris, France, 29.
Work in Public Collections: Oil, Va Mus, Richmond; oil, Mus New Britain Inst, Conn; gouache, John Herron Mus, Indianapolis, Ind; oil, Nat Acad Design Ranger Fund Collection, New York, N Y; oil, Morse Gallery Art, Rollins Col, Fla.
Commissions: Mural painting for Richfield Springs Post Off, N Y, comn by Dept Interior Sect Fine Arts, 42.
Exhibitions: Va Mus Art Biennial, Richmond, 48; Carnegie Inst Int, Pittsburgh, Pa, 50; Pa Acad Fine Arts Ann, Philadelphia, 54; Whitney Mus Am Art Ann, New York, 59; Nat Acad Design Ann, New York, 61.
Teaching: Instr painting, Art Stud League New York Woodstock Summer Sch, 48-54; assoc prof painting & vis artist, Tulane Univ La, 56, 58 & 59; prof painting & vis artist, Univ Fla, 60-62.
Awards: John Barton Payne Medal & purchase award, Va Mus, Richmond, 46; citation & grant, Am Acad Arts & Lett, 48; Guggenheim fel, 54.
Bibliography: Lawrence Campbell (auth), Poet of the levee & the level sands, Art Stud League New York News, 9/1/50 & John Taylor, Art News, 3/63; Ray Bethers (auth), How paintings happen, Norton, 51.
Memberships: Academician Nat Acad Design; life mem Woodstock Artists Asn (trustee, 65-70).
Publications: Contribr, The art of the artist, Crown, 51.
Mailing Address: Shady, Ulster County, NY 12479.

TAYLOR, JOHN C E
Painter, Educator
Preferred Media: Oils, Pencil.
b New Haven, Conn, Oct 22, 02.
Study & Training: Acad Julian, Paris, France, 26-28; also with Walter Griffin, France, 26-28; Yale Univ, MA, 40.
Work in Public Collections: Mus Am Art, New Britain, Conn.
Commissions: Designs for wood carvings, 57-62 & crypt chapel doors, 72, Trinity Col Chapel, Hartford, Conn; Westover award tablet, Westover Sch, Middlebury, Conn, 58; design for wood carvings, St James Church, Glastonbury, Conn, 62.
Exhibitions: Spring Salon, Paris, 28; Corcoran Gallery Art Biennial, Washington, D C, 35 & 39; Artists for Victory Traveling Exhib, 45-46; John C E Taylor Retrospective, Trinity Col, Hartford, 70.
Teaching: Mem faculty art, Trinity Col, 41-56, prof art hist, 56-70, head fine arts dept, 45-64; instr art hist, Loomis Sch, 55-72;
Positions: Scholar-in-residence, Loomis Sch, 70-72.
Awards: Cooper prize, Conn Acad Fine Arts, 35; second prize, New Orleans Art Asn, 46; black & white prize, Rockport Art Asn, 55.
Bibliography: E A Jewell (auth), Exploring realism & abstraction, New York Times, 31; F Berkman (auth), Much avant-garde art profonation of nature, Hartford Times, 70; J Goldenthal (auth), Taylor work in retrospect, Hartford Courant, 70.
Memberships: Conn Acad Fine Arts; Rockport Art Asn; North Shore Arts Asn; Washington Arts Asn, Conn.
Mailing Address: 30 Four Mile Rd, West Hartford, CT 06107.

TAYLOR, JOSHUA CHARLES
Educator, Art Historian
b Hillsboro, Ore, Aug 22, 17.
Study & Training: Mus Art Sch, Portland, Ore, 35-39; Reed Col, BA, 39, MA, 46; Princeton Univ, MFA, 49, PhD, 56.
Teaching: Instr theatre, Reed Col, 39-41; instr hist art, Princeton Univ, 48-49; prof humanities & hist art, Univ Chicago, 49-63, William Rainey Harper prof humanities & prof art, 63-
Positions: Dir, Nat Collection Fine Arts, 70-
Awards: Quantrell Award, Univ Chicago, 56.
Memberships: Asn Art Mus Dir; Col Art Asn Am (bd mem); Int Inst Conserv of Hist & Artistic Works; Benjamin Franklin fel Royal Soc Arts.
Research: Nineteenth & twentieth century painting & artistic theory in Italy & United States.
Publications: Auth, William Page, the American Titian, 57; auth, Learning to look, 57; auth, Futurism, 61; auth, Graphic works of Umberto Boccioni, 61; auth, Vedere prima di Credere, 70.
Mailing Address: 1250 31st St N W, Washington, DC 20007.

TAYLOR, MARIE
Sculptor
b Saint Louis, Mo, Feb 22, 04.
Study & Training: Art Stud League New York; Wash Univ Sch Art, 23-24.
Work in Public Collections: Cleveland Art Mus; also in many pvt collections.

Commissions: Main altar, St Paul's Church, Peoria, Ill, 60; Jefferson Mem Nat Expansion, Saint Louis Riverfront, for Mansion House, Saint Louis, 67.
Exhibitions: Joslyn Mus Art; Kansas City Art Inst; Southern Ill Univ, Carbondale, 52; Brooks Mem Art Gallery, Memphis, Tenn, 55; Sculpture 1969, Span Int Pavillion, 69; plus others.
Awards: Prizes, Cleveland Art Mus, Saint Louis Art Guild & Nat Asn Women Artists; plus others.
Bibliography: M King (auth), Christmas exhibits at Saint Louis galleries, Saint Louis Post Dispatch, 12/14/69; Dona Z Meilach (auth), Creative carving, Turtle, 69 & Contemporary stone sculpture, Oracle, 70; plus many others.
Memberships: Sculptors Guild, N Y; Nat Soc Arts & Lett.
Mailing Address: c/o Betty Parsons Gallery, 24 W 57th St, New York, NY 10019.

TAYLOR, PRENTISS (HOTTEL)
Lithographer, Instructor
Preferred Media: Watercolors, Graphics.
b Washington, D C, Dec 13, 07.
Study & Training: Art Stud League New York, with Charles W Hawthorne, Charles Locke, Eugene Fitsch, Anne Goldthwaite & others.
Work in Public Collections: Boston Mus Fine Arts, Mass; Mus Mod Art, New York, N Y; Libr of Cong, Washington, D C; Phillips Collection, Washington, D C; Smithsonian Inst, Washington, D C; plus many others.
Commissions: Mural in tempera for bath, commissioned by Mr & Mrs R F Flint, New Haven, Conn, 40; mural in oil, Christian Sci Hq, Washington, D C, 49.
Exhibitions: Chicago Int Watercolors & Prints, Art Inst Chicago, 30's; Nat Print Exhib, Libr of Cong, Washington, D C, 43-; Painting & Watercolor Graphics Ann, Whitney Mus Am Art, New York, 45; Painting in the U S, 1946-1949, Carnegie Inst, Pittsburgh, Pa; Am Drawing Biennials, Norfolk Mus, Va, 60's; plus many others.
Teaching: Lectr painting, Am Univ, Washington, D C, 55-
Positions: Pres, Artists Guild Washington; pres, Washington Watercolor Club; art therapist, St Elizabeth Hosp, Washington, D C, 43-54; art therapist, Chestnut Lodge, Rockville, Md, 58-
Awards: Purchase awards in several ann, Nat Print Exhib, Libr of Cong, Washington, D C, 43-; purchase awards in watercolors, Va Artists, Va Mus Fine Arts, 43; Cannon prize in graphic arts, Nat Acad Design, 54.
Bibliography: L Ward (auth), Printmakers of tomorrow, Parnassus, 3/39; H Salpeter (auth), Prentiss Taylor, Coronet, 4/39; A Cohen (auth), Prentiss Taylor, D C Gazette, 70.
Memberships: Assoc Nat Acad Design (graphics class); Soc Am Graphic Artists; Philadelphia Watercolor Club; Artists Equity Asn (bd mem, 71); Soc Washington Printmakers (pres, 43-).
Research: Art as psychotherapy; How art may reintegrate the disordered mind; Talent/status vs expectancy achievement.
Publications: Illusr, Negro mother, 31; illusr, Scottsboro limited, 32; illusr, Why birds sing, 33; illusr, American herb calendar, 37.
Dealer: Franz Bader, 2124 Pennsylvania Ave N W, Washington, DC 20037.
Mailing Address: J 718 Arlington Towers, Arlington, VA 22209.

TAYLOR, RALPH
Painter, Printmaker
Preferred Media: Oils.
b Russia, Jan 18, 97; U S citizen.
Study & Training: Pa Acad Fine Arts; also study in Italy, France & Eng.
Work in Public Collections: Fleisher Art Mem; La France Art Inst; Pa Acad Fine Arts.
Exhibitions: Corcoran Gallery Art, 26; Rochester Mem Gallery, 26; Nat Acad Design, 30; Philadelphia Art Alliance, 63; Pa Acad Fine Arts; plus many other group & one-man shows.
Teaching: Instr painting, Graphic Sketch Club, Philadelphia, 20-23; instr painting, Com Illus Studios, New York, 28-30.
Awards: Mary Butler Mem Prize for Concert, Fel Pa Acad Fine Arts, 54; Da Vinci Gold Medal for City at Night, Da Vinci Alliance, 59; award for Animated Conversation, Philadelphia Art Alliance, 63.
Bibliography: Benezit (auth), article, In: Dictionnaire critique et documentaire des peintres.
Memberships: Fel Acad Fine Arts; Philadelphia Art Alliance; Philadelphia Print Club.
Mailing Address: 135 S 18th St, Philadelphia, PA 19103.

TAYLOR, ROBERT
Art Critic, Writer
b Newton, Mass, Jan 19, 25.
Study & Training: Colgate Univ, AB, 47; Brown Univ Grad Sch, 48.
Teaching: Vis lectr, Wheaton Col, 60-

Positions: Art critic, Boston Herald, 52-67; Boston corresp, Pictures on Exhibit, 54-59; mem staff, Boston Globe Mag, 68-
Publications: Auth, In red weather, 61; ed, publs, Inst Contemp Art, Boston, 67.
Mailing Address: 1 Thomas Circle, Marblehead, MA 01945.

TAYLOR, ROSEMARY
Craftsman
Preferred Media: Stoneware.
b Joseph, Ore.
Study & Training: Cleveland Inst Art; New York Univ; Greenwich House.
Exhibitions: One-man shows, Only Originals, N J, 70, West Chester Col, Pa, 71, Artisan Gallery, Princeton, N J, 72, Warren Libr, 72 & Georg Jensen, 72.
Memberships: N J Designer-Craftsman; Artist-Craftsmen N Y; Am Craft Coun.
Publications: Contribr, McCall's Needlework & Craft Mag.
Mailing Address: Box 46, River Rd, Lumberville, PA 18933.

TAYLOR, SANDRA J
Painter
Preferred Media: Oils, Acrylics, Inks.
b Los Angeles, Calif, Apr 27, 36.
Study & Training: Univ Calif, with William Brice & Sam Amato & BA; Iowa State Univ, with Byron Burford, MA.
Work in Public Collections: Univ Iowa, Iowa City; Macy's Corp, New York, N Y; John S Bolles Collection, San Francisco, Calif; Univ Calif Res Libr, Los Angeles.
Exhibitions: 13th Ann Drawing & Small Sculpture Show, Ball State Univ, Muncie, Ind, 67; 4th Ann Nat Drawing Exhib, Bucknell Univ, Lewisburg, Pa, 68; Invited Artist Civic Ctr Art Show, San Francisco & Hayward Area Festival Show, 69-71; Rental Gallery Exhib, San Francisco Mus Art, 71; Northern Calif 18th Ann Open Art Exhib, Pauls Gallery, Sacramento, Calif, 72.
Positions: Gallery asst, John Bolles Gallery, 70-71.
Bibliography: Thomas Albright (auth), reviews, In: San Francisco Chronicle, 68 & 71; Cecil McCan (auth), reviews, In: West Art, 68 & Art Week, 71; E M Polley (auth), review, In, Sunday Times-Herald, 71.
Memberships: Col Art Asn Am.
Dealer: John Bolles Gallery, 10 Gold St, San Francisco, CA 94133.
Mailing Address: 845 Diamond St, San Francisco, CA 94114.

TAYSOM, WAYNE PENDLETON
Sculptor, Educator
b Afton, Wyo, Oct 10, 25.
Study & Training: Univ Wyo; Columbia Univ; Univ Utah, BFA; Ecole Beaux-Arts, Paris; Teachers Col, Columbia Univ, MA; Cranbrook Acad Art.
Work in Public Collections: Portland Art Mus; Ore State Univ Mem Union; Corvallis Clin, Ore; Univ Ore Erb Mem Union, Eugene; U S Nat Bank Ore, Portland.
Commissions: Archit sculpture, Lane Co Courthouse, Eugene; Masonic Temple; Corvallis Br, U S Nat Bank Ore; fountain & doors, Ore State Univ Libr; coun chamber doors, Salem Civic Ctr, Salem, Ore; many portrait & pvt comns.
Exhibitions: One-man show, 54 & Paper Works, 72, Portland Art Mus; Seattle World's Fair, 62; Am Crafts Coun, Western Craftsmen, 64; Hunnicutt Art Gallery, Hawaii, 67; plus many others.
Teaching: Prof sculpture, Univ Ore, 51-52; prof art, Ore State Univ, 53-
Awards: Purchase prize, Portland Art Mus, 56.
Memberships: Am Asn Univ Prof; Portland Art Asn.
Mailing Address: Dept of Art, Oregon State University, Corvallis, OR 97331.

TCHENG, JOHN T L
Painter
Preferred Media: Inks, Oils.
b Shanghai, China, Sept 21, 18; U S citizen.
Study & Training: With S C Chao, Shanghai; with C C Wang, New York, N Y.
Exhibitions: 11 one-man shows from coast to coast, 56-
Memberships: Cincinnati Art Club.
Research: Chinese calligraphy; modern painting.
Mailing Address: Pine Studios, P O Box 252, Fort Thomas, KY 41075.

TEAGUE, DONALD
Painter
Preferred Media: Watercolors.
b Brooklyn, N Y, Nov 27, 97.
Study & Training: Art Stud League New York; also with Norman Wilkinson, London.

Work in Public Collections: Va Mus Fine Arts, Richmond; Frye Mus, Seattle, Wash; Air Force Acad, Colorado Springs, Colo; Mills Col Art Gallery, Oakland, Calif; State of Calif Collection, Sacramento.
Exhibitions: Am Watercolor Soc, New York, N Y; Mus Watercolor, Mexico City, Mex; Art Inst Chicago, Ill; Royal Watercolor Soc, London, Eng; Kyoto Mus, Japan.
Awards: Gold medal of hon, 53 & 64, Am Watercolor Soc; Morse Gold Medal, Nat Acad Design, 62.
Bibliography: Ernest Watson (auth), Donald Teague, illustrator, Am Artist, 44.
Memberships: Am Watercolor Soc; Nat Acad Design; Salmagundi Club.
Mailing Address: P O Box 745, Carmel, CA 93921.

TEDESCHI, PAUL VALENTINE
Painter, Educator
b Worcester, Mass, Nov 1, 17.
Study & Training: Vesper George Sch Art, Boston; Art Inst Chicago; Yale Univ, BFA & MFA; Columbia Univ.
Exhibitions: Boston Festival Art; Providence Festival Art; Silvermine Guild Artists; Conn Watercolor Soc; Conn Acad Fine Arts; plus other group & one-man shows.
Teaching: Asst prof art, Southern Conn State Col, 54-69, chmn dept fine arts, 54-55, assoc prof art, 69-
Awards: New Haven Paint & Clay Club Purchase Prize, 49; Silvermine Guild Artists, 58.
Mailing Address: Dept of Fine Arts, Southern Connecticut State College, New Haven, CT 06515.

TEE-VAN, HELEN DAMROSCH
Painter, Illustrator
Preferred Media: Oils, Watercolors.
b New York, N Y, May 26, 93.
Study & Training: New York Sch Display; also with George De Forest Brush & Jonas Lie.
Work in Public Collections: Berkshire Mus, Pittsfield, Mass; Bronx Zoo, New York.
Commissions: Murals & display, Berkshire Mus, Pittsfield, 38-39; murals & exhibs, New York Zool Soc, 41-62.
Exhibitions: Am Mus Natural Hist, New York, 25; Warren Cox Gallery, New York, 31; Buffalo Mus Sci, N Y, 35; Gibbs Mem Gallery, Charleston, S C, 35; Berkshire Mus, Pittsfield, 36.
Positions: Scientific artist, scientific artist tropical res & artist on N Y expeds, tropical dept, 22-62, New York Zool Soc.
Memberships: Soc Woman Geographers; Soc Animal Artists; life mem New York Zool Soc.
Art Interests: Undersea landscape; black & white illustrations.
Publications: Auth & illusr, Red howling monkey, Macmillan, 26; illusr, Story of the platypus, 59, auth & illusr, Insects are where you find them, 63, auth & illusr, Small mammals are where you find them, 66 & illusr, Story of Alaskan grizzly, 69, Knopf; plus many natural hist bk illus for various scientific & juvenile bks.
Mailing Address: Rte 1, Box 275, Sherman, CT 06784.

TEICHMAN, SABINA
Painter, Sculptor
Preferred Media: Oils, Watercolors, Clay.
b New York, N Y.
Study & Training: Columbia Univ, BA & MA; also with Charles J Martin & Arthur J Young.
Work in Public Collections: Whitney Mus Am Art; Butler Inst Am Art; Smithsonian Inst; Fogg Mus Art, Harvard Univ; San Francisco Mus Art.
Exhibitions: Whitney Mus Am Art Ann; Art U S A, 58; Provincetown Art Asn; Butler Inst Am Art Ann; Audubon Artists Ann.
Awards: Prize for painting, Womens Westchester Ctr, 50.
Bibliography: Baur & Goodrich (auth), Art of the 20th century; Baron (auth), 31 contemporary artists; Frank Crotty (auth), Provincetown profiles.
Memberships: Audubon Artists (corresp secy); Provincetown Art Asn.
Dealer: ACA Galleries, 25 E 73rd St, New York, NY 10021.
Mailing Address: 27 E 22nd St, New York, NY 10010.

TEILMAN, HERDIS BULL
Art Administrator, Curator
b Paris, France; U S citizen.
Study & Training: Barnard Col, BA; N Y Univ Inst Fine Arts, 61; Univ Paris Inst Art & Archeol, 61-62; N Y Univ Inst Fine Arts, 63-64, with Lopez-Rey & Horst Gerson.
Collections Arranged: Forerunners of Am Abstraction, Mus Art, Carnegie Inst, winter 71.
Positions: Secy-registr, Nat Serigraph Soc, 61; asst, Kunst Arbeidsplassen, Oslo, Norway, 62-63; cur painting & sculpture, Newark Mus, N J, 68-70; asst dir, Mus Art, Carnegie Inst, 70-
Memberships: Am Asn Mus.

Publications: Auth, Frank Wilbert Stokes (1858-1955), Meltzer Gallery, New York, N Y, 60; contribr, The museum, Vol 21, Nos 3 & 4, Newark Mus, N J; auth, Forerunners of American abstraction, Carnegie Inst, 71; contribr, Carnegie Mag, Carnegie Inst & Libr, Pittsburgh, 71-72.
Mailing Address: 3955 Bigelow Blvd, Pittsburgh, PA 15213.

TEITZ, RICHARD STUART
Art Administrator, Art Historian
b Fall River, Mass, July 18, 42.
Study & Training: Yale Univ, AB; Harvard Univ, MA.
Collections Arranged: Etruscan Art, 67, Victorian Art, 69, Am Contemp Art, 69, Toulouse-Lautrec, 71, Marisol, 71 & Escher, 71.
Teaching: Instr archit hist, Boston Archit Ctr, Mass, 63-66; instr art hist, Clark Univ, 66-67.
Positions: Dir, Wichita Art Mus, Kans, 67-69; assoc dir, Worcester Art Mus, Mass, 69-70, dir, 70-
Memberships: Col Art Asn Am; Asn Art Mus Dirs; Int Coun Mus; Am Asn Mus.
Research: Classical and Renaissance art.
Collection: Old master drawings.
Publications: Auth, Masterpieces of Etruscan art, 67; auth, Masterpieces of religious art, 67; auth, American Victoriana, 69.
Mailing Address: 55 Salisbury St, Worcester, MA 01608.

TELLER, JANE (SIMON)
Sculptor
Preferred Media: Wood, Graphics.
b Rochester, N Y.
Study & Training: Rochester Inst Technol; Barnard Col, BA; also with Ibram Lassaw.
Work in Public Collections: Olsen Found, Stamford, Conn; Geigy Collection, Ardsley, N Y; N J State Mus, Trenton.
Commissions: Menorah (iron & plexiglass) & Eternal Light (iron & plexiglass), Temple Judea, Doykstown, Pa, 69; Magic Muse (wood sculpure), N J State Mus, 72.
Exhibitions: N J State Mus, Trenton, 65-72; Newark Mus, N J, 68; Sculptors Guild Ann, Lever House, New York, N Y, 70; Hudson River Mus, Yonkers, N Y, 71; Mus Mod Art, New York.
Awards: Purchase award, N J State Mus, 71; Nat Asn Women Artists; 50th Anniversary Exhib prize, Philadelphia Art Alliance.
Bibliography: David R Campbell (auth), Art & architecture, Craft Horizons, 6/62; Art & architecture, Aujourd 'Hui, 63; David Van Dommellen (auth), Walls—enrichment & ornamentation, Funk & Wagnalls, 65.
Memberships: Sculptors Guild; Artists Equity Asn.
Mailing Address: 200 Prospect Ave, Princeton, NJ 08540.

TEMES, MORTIMER (ROBERT)
Cartoonist, Designer
b Jersey City, N J, Apr 15, 28.
Study & Training: Art Stud League New York, with William McNulty, Jon Corbino, Frank Reilly & Robert B Hale, 47-49; N Y Univ, 49-53, BA, 53.
Positions: Prof free lance cartoonist, 50-; dir spec serv, Newark Col Eng, 58-
Memberships: Nat Cartoonists Soc; Mag Cartoonists Guild; Am Col Pub Relations Asn.
Publications: Illusr, Engineers & engineering—some definitions, 68; illusr, Making tomorrow happen, 70; cartoons have appeared in many nat mags & in many cartoon anthologies.
Mailing Address: 10 Sycamore Dr, Hazlet, NJ 07730.

TEMPLE, MR & MRS ALAN H
Collectors
Collection: Contemporary art.
Mailing Address: 11 Paddington Rd, Scarsdale, NY 10583

TEN EYCK, CATRYNA (CATRYNA TEN EYCK SEYMOUR)
Painter
Preferred Media: Graphics, Acrylics.
b New York, N Y, June 30, 31.
Study & Training: Smith Col; Art Stud League New York.
Work in Public Collections: Calif Palace Legion of Hon, San Francisco; Denver Art Mus, Colo; Honolulu Acad Arts, Hawaii; Albany Inst Hist & Art, N Y; Munson-Williams-Proctor Inst, Utica, N Y.
Exhibitions: Seventh Ann Nat Print Exhib, Springfield Col, Mass, 71; Thirty-Sixth Ann Exhib, Cooperstown Art Asn, N Y, 71; Sixtieth Am Ann Exhib, Art Asn Newport, R I, 71; Fifty-First Ann Nat Exhib Paintings, Ogunquit Art Ctr, Maine, 71; Ann Juried Exhib, Sharon Creative Arts Found, Conn, 71.
Awards: First prize for graphics, Springfield Art League, 71.
Memberships: Southern Vt Artists, Inc; Cooperstown Art Asn.
Dealer: Tunnel Gallery, 232 E 59th St, New York, NY 10022.
Mailing Address: 290 W Fourth St, New York, NY 10014.

TENNYSON, MERLE BERRY
Painter, Instructor
Preferred Media: Acrylics, Oils.
b Brandon, Miss, Mar 17, 20.
Study & Training: Miss State Col Women, BS; Univ Miss, MA; also with Ida Kohlmeyer, New Orleans, Andrew Bucci, Washington, Alvin Sella, Alex Russo, Frederick, Md & Tom Chimes, Philadelphia.
Work in Public Collections: R W Norton Art Gallery, Shreveport, La; Bankers' Trust Co, First Nat Bank, First Fed Savings & Loan & Miss Art Asn, Jackson, Miss.
Commissions: Paintings, comn by Mr & Mrs Francis Stevens, Washington, D C, 70 & William D Rowell, Jackson, Miss.
Exhibitions: Nat Arts & Crafts, Miss Arts Festival, Jackson, 65, 69, 70 & 71; Frontal Images, Miss Art Asn, Jackson, 67-69; Mid-South Exhib, Brooks Mem Art Gallery, Memphis, Tenn, 68 & 69; 47th Regional, Shreveport, 69; Delta Ann, Ark Art Ctr, Little Rock, Ark, 69 & 71.
Teaching: Instr drawing & painting, Univ Miss Continuation Study Prog, Millsaps Col, 58-66.
Awards: Purchase awards, Regional, 69 & Lafont Art Colony, S Cent Bell Tel, 70; Best in Show Award, Edgewater Ann, 71.
Memberships: Miss Art Asn (pres, 66-67, exec comt & bd dirs, 67-); Miss Arts Ctr (bd gov, 67-); Millsaps Col Arts & Lect Ser (bd dirs); Miss Art Colony (bd dirs, 69-).
Publications: Auth, Painting and ceramics used as occupational therapy in working with the mentally ill, 58.
Mailing Address: 1437 Rebel Dr, Jackson, MS 39211.

TERENZIO, ANTHONY
Painter, Educator
Preferred Media: Oils.
b Settefrati, Italy, Feb 10, 23; U S citizen.
Study & Training: Pratt Inst, BFA; Columbia Univ, MA; Am Art Sch, with Raphael Soyer & Jack Levine.
Work in Public Collections: Lowe Ctr, Syracuse Univ.
Exhibitions: Brooklyn Artists Biennial, Brooklyn Mus, N Y, 49; Butler Inst Am Art Biennial, Ohio, 57; Boston Arts Festival, 58; Eight From Connecticut, Wadsworth Atheneum, Hartford, 60; New England Drawing Exhib, Smith Col, Northampton, Mass, 64.
Teaching: Prof painting & drawing, Univ Conn, 55-
Awards: Emily Lowe Award, 50; first award, Ann Conn Artists, Norwich Art Asn, 57 & 60.
Bibliography: Baker (auth), Prize winning paintings-1960, Allied, 61.
Mailing Address: R F D No 2, Box 197, Storrs, CT 06268.

TERESI, JOSEPH ANTHONY
Painter, Instructor
Preferred Media: Oils.
b New York, N Y, Apr 29, 21.
Study & Training: Harrison Art Sch, Chicago, Ill, scholar; Art Inst Chicago, with Max Kahn & John Fabion; Columbia Col (Ill); also with David Olere, Paris, France & Karl Eberle, Frankfurt, Ger.
Work in Public Collections: Evanston Sch Syst Collection, Ill; Edward G Robinson Collection, Calif; Vincent Price Collection, Calif; Manfred Kuhnard Gallery, Glendale, Calif; Americana Galleries, Northfield, Ill.
Exhibitions: Kerrigan-Hendrick Gallery, Chicago, 62; Manfred Kuhnard Gallery, 63; one-man shows, Raymond Burr Galleries, Beverly Hills, Calif, 63 & Vincent Price Gallery, Beverly Hills, 64; Fair is our Land, Americana Galleries, 65.
Teaching: Instr oil painting & drawing, Americana Art Sch, 65-
Mailing Address: c/o 271 Waukegan Rd, Northfield, IL 60093.

TERKEN, JOHN
Sculptor
Preferred Media: Bronze.
b Rochester, N Y, Jan 11, 12.
Study & Training: Beaux Arts Inst Design, with Chester Beach, Lee Lawrie & Paul Manship; N Y Sch Fine & Indust Arts; Columbia Sch Fine Arts; also Europ art ctrs.
Work in Public Collections: Roswell Mus, N Mex; Grand Cent Galleries, New York, N Y; Gregory Mus, Hicksville, N Y.
Commissions: Monument, Am Soc Prev Cruelty Animals Hq, New York, 55; Benjamin Franklin Mem, Franklin Nat Bank, Garden City, N Y, 61; Eagle Fountain, Salisbury Park, East Meadow, N Y, 61; New Horizons, Hempstead Town Plaza, 69; Richard Henry Dana Monument, San Juan Capistrano Hist Soc, Calif, 72.
Exhibitions: Nat Acad Design, New York, 68; Nat Arts Club, New York, 70; Hudson Valley Art Asn, Westchester, N Y, 71; Acad Artists Asn, Springfield, Mass, 71; Nat Sculpture Soc, New York, 72.
Teaching: Lectr sculpture, East Meadow High Sch, 51-
Positions: Advert mgr, Nat Sculpture Rev, 49-65, mem ed bd, 70-, mem Bd Coop Educ Serv, Long Island Dist, 69-, deleg to Fine Arts Fedn New York, 70-

Awards: Louis Comfort Tiffany Found Award, 49; Lindsey Morris
Mem Prize, Nat Sculpture Soc, 65; Coun Am Artists Award, Am
Artists Prof League, 72.
Memberships: Fel Nat Sculpture Soc (mem coun, 62-, secy, 68-
70); fel Hudson Valley Art Asn; assoc Int Inst Conservators;
Acad Artists Asn; Art League Nassau Co.
Mailing Address: 386 Chambers Ave, East Meadow, NY 11554.

TERRELL, ALLEN TOWNSEND
Sculptor
b Riverhead, N Y, Nov 2, 97.
Study & Training: Columbia Univ Sch Archit, cert proficiency, 21;
Art Stud League New York, with Edward McCartan; Pa Acad Fine
Arts, with Albert Laessle; Ecoles Am Fontainebleau, France;
Acad Julien, Paris, France; also with Charles Despiau.
Work in Public Collections: Suffolk Co Hist Soc, Riverhead; Metrop
Mus Art, New York, N Y; Mus City New York; Brooklyn Mus,
N Y.
Commissions: Vermil ye Medal, Franklin Inst, Philadelphia, Pa,
35; childrens playrm, 39 & cabin in class lounge (with John Mars-
man), 46, S S America, U S Lines.
Exhibitions: Salon D'Automne, 30; Nat Arts Club, 59; Allied Artists
Am, 65; Nat Acad Design, 72.
Teaching: Instr watercolor & still life, Parsons Sch Design, 34-35.
Awards: Bronze medal of hon for sculpture, Nat Arts Club, 59;
Awards Comt prize for sculpture, Allied Artists Am, 65; Dessie
Greer Prize for sculpture, Nat Acad Design, 72.
Memberships: Nat Sculpture Soc; Allied Artists Am; Am Watercolor
Soc; Nat Arts Club; Fontainebleau Asn (trustee, 40).
Art Interests: Drawings & watercolors collections.
Mailing Address: 42 Stuyvesant St, New York, NY 10003.

TERRY, DUNCAN NILES
Designer, Craftsman
Preferred Media: Glass.
b Bath, Maine, Nov 6, 09.
Study & Training: Sch Mus Fine Arts, Boston; Cent Sch Arts &
Crafts, London; also with Ferdnand Leger, Paris.
Commissions: Carved glass windows, Riverside Church, New York,
N Y, 50 & St James Episcopal Church, Long Branch, N J, 62-67;
windows & wood & stone Mem, Trinity Cathedral, Trenton, N J,
60-72; windows, doors & Mem, All St's Church, Torresdale, Pa,
60-72; stained glass, Bnai Emunah Synagogue, Tulsa, Okla, 62;
windows, doors, facade & mosaic mural, St Mary's Church,
Kittanning, Pa, 67.
Art Interests: Developing new techniques in glass decoration and
using them alone and in combination with established techniques.
Mailing Address: 1213 Lancaster Ave, Rosemont, PA 19010.

TERRY, EMALITA NEWTON
Painter, Instructor
Preferred Media: Watercolors, Acrylics, Oils, Graphics.
b San Angelo, Tex, Jan 15.
Study & Training: Howard Payne Col, dipl; also with Xavier Gon-
zalez, New York, N Y, Jose Arpa, Seville, Spain, Adele Brunet,
Dallas, Tex & New York & Will Stevens, New Orleans, La.
Work in Public Collections: M Grumbacher, New York; Art League
Las Vegas, Nev; Laguna Gloria Gallery, Austin, Tex; Mus Fine
Arts, San Antonio, Tex; Tex A&M Univ, College Station.
Exhibitions: Tex Fine Arts Asn, Laguna Gloria Gallery, 52-58; D D
Feldman Contemp Exhib, Dallas, 55-57; Art League Houston,
Houston Fine Arts Mus, Tex, 57; Nat Asn Women Artists 66th
Exhib, Nat Acad Galleries, New York, 58; Art League Las Vegas,
Art League Galleries, 67; plus others.
Teaching: Instr painting & drawing, Tex A&M Univ, 49-59; instr
painting & drawing, Terry's Art Studio, Las Vegas, 59-
Positions: Dir gallery, Tex A&M Univ, 51-59; bd dirs, Tex Fine
Arts Asn, 54-57, chmn & v pres bd dirs, 57-59; instr art theory
& appreciation & adv, Jr League Las Vegas, 71-72.
Awards: Distinguished art serv award, Tex A&M Col, 52-53; two
awards of merit, M Grumbacher, 55-57; Emily Goldman Mem
Award, Nat Asn Women Artists, 58; plus others.
Memberships: Tex Watercolor Soc; Allied Arts Coun; Art League
Las Vegas; plus others.
Dealer: Nevada Frames Galleries, 1815 Industrial Rd, Las Vegas,
NV 89102.
Mailing Address: 3215 Medicine Man Way, Las Vegas, NV 89109.

TERRY, HILDA (HILDA TERRY D'ALESSIO)
Cartoonist, Writer
b Newburyport, Mass, June 25, 14.
Study & Training: Art Stud League New York; Nat Acad Design;
N Y Univ.
Commissions: Fulton Fish Market (acrylics), Sam Marg, New
York, N Y, 71.
Teaching: Instr cartooning, New Sch Social Res, 68; instr cartoon-
ing, New York Phoenix Sch Art & Design, 69-71.

Positions: Animation designer, Am Info, at present; pres, Hilda
Terry Prod, at present; directress, Hilda Terry Gallery, New
York; artist, animation prog for Kansas City Royals Baseball
Club, 72.
Awards: Wohelo award, Camp Fire Girls; best Waste-Not cartoon,
New York Times, 42.
Memberships: Nat Cartoonists Soc (talent pool ed, 71-72).
Specialty of Gallery: Fine art humor.
Art Interests: Animated cartoons for computerized boards (sports
stadium scoreboards).
Publications: Auth, Teena (comic strip), 41-; auth, Teena (comic
bks), 46-49; auth, Originality in art, 54; assoc ed, Art collectors
almanac, 65.
Mailing Address: 8 Henderson Pl, New York, NY 10028.

TERRY, MARION (E)
Painter, Art Critic
Preferred Media: Oils, Acrylics.
b Evansville, Ind, June 4, 11.
Study & Training: Albright Art Sch; Univ Buffalo; also with Xavier
Gonzalez.
Work in Public Collections: New York Hosp Soc, N Y; Univ Bank,
Coral Gables, Fla; Abbott Labs, Chicago, Ill; Ford Motor Co,
Dearborn, Mich; Honeywell Mfg Co, Philadelphia, Pa.
Commissions: Living War Mem (476 portraits of every Dade Co
serviceman who lost his life in World War II); seven paintings,
Com Bank, Winter Park, Fla; four paintings, First Nat Bank,
Winter Park; City Nat Bank, Clearwater, Fla.
Exhibitions: Southeastern Ann; Ford Motor Co traveling exhibs, 55,
57-58; Fort Worth, Tex, 58; Fla Gulf Coast Art, Clearwater, 71;
Saint Petersburg Art Club; plus many other group & one-man
shows.
Teaching: Instr painting, Craft Village, Saint Petersburg, 44-69;
instr painting, C of C, Madeira Beach, Fla, 69-72; instr pvt
classes.
Positions: Pres & head fine arts dept, Terry Art Inst, 44-54.
Awards: Award for Horses in the Surf, Gulf Coast, 71; award for
Pennsylvania Town, 71 & award for Reflections, 72, Art Guild,
Treasure Island, Fla.
Memberships: Fla Art Group; Fla Fedn Arts; Pen & Brush Club;
Village Art Ctr, New York.
Publications: Illusr, cover for 50th anniversary & auth, articles, In:
Saint Petersburg Times; art critic, Gulf Beach J.
Dealers: Laura's Art Center, Largo, FL 33540; Mirell Gallery,
3421 Main Highway, Miami, FL 33133.
Mailing Address: 14080 N Bayshore Dr, Madeira Beach, FL 33708.

TETTLETON, ROBERT LYNN
Painter, Educator
Preferred Media: Oils.
b Ruston, La, Dec 23, 29.
Study & Training: La Polytech Inst, BA, 50; La State Univ, Baton
Rouge, MA, 53.
Exhibitions: La Art Comn, Baton Rouge, 52; Delgado Mus, New Or-
leans, La, 53; Gainesville Fine Arts Asn, Fla, 61; Mid-South Art
Show, Brooks Mem Art Gallery, Memphis, Tenn, 69; one-man
shows, Little Theater, Monroe, La, 54 & Mary Buie Mus, Oxford,
Miss, 70.
Teaching: Instr art, Northeast La State Col, 55-56; asst prof art,
Univ Fla, 61-65; prof art & chmn dept, Univ Miss, 65-
Memberships: Fla Art Educ Asn; Southeastern Col Art Asn (pres,
69-70); Gainesville Fine Arts Asn (pres, 65); Am Asn Univ Prof.
Mailing Address: 137 Leighton Rd, Oxford, MS 38677.

TEWI, THEA
Sculptor
Preferred Media: Stone.
U S citizen.
Study & Training: Art Stud League New York; Greenwich House,
with Lou Duble; Clay Club, with D Denslow; New Sch Social
Res, with Seymour Lipton.
Work in Public Collections: Nat Collection Fine Arts, Smithsonian
Inst, Washington, D C; Cincinnati Art Mus, Ohio; Norfolk Mus
Arts & Scis, Va; Notre Dame Univ, Ind; Am Ins Co Corp Collec-
tion, Galveston, Tex; plus many others.
Exhibitions: 18th-20th Ann New Eng Exhib, Silvermine Guild Art-
ists, 65 & 67-69; Nat Arts Club Exhib Relig Art, 66; Erie Sum-
mer Festival Arts, Pa State Univ, 68; Sixth Biennial of Sculpture,
Carrara, Italy, 69; plus many other group & 10 one-man shows.
Awards: Spec award for outstanding merit in craftsmanship, Art-
ists-Craftsmen New York, 67; medal of hon & first prize for
sculpture, Nat Asn Women Artists, 69; first prize for sculpture,
Am Soc Contemp Artists, 71; plus many others.
Bibliography: D Meilach (auth), Contemporary stone sculpture,
Crown, 70; Margaret Harold (auth), Prize winning sculpture &
Prize winning art, Allied; Int Encycl Art, Ancona, Italy.

Memberships: Sculptors League (pres, 71-); League Present Day Artists (hon pres); Nat Asn Women Artists (chmn sculpture jury, 69-72); Am Soc Contemp Artists; Artists-Craftsmen New York.
Mailing Address: 100-30 67th Dr, Forest Hills, NY 11375.

TEXOON, JASMINE
Painter, Instructor
Preferred Media: Oils.
b New York, N Y, Sept 19, 24.
Study & Training: Nat Acad Design, with Gilford Beal, H Hildebrandt & Charles Hinton, four yrs with honors; Brooklyn Mus Art Sch, with Bocour; Art Stud League New York, with Byron Browne.
Work in Public Collections: Christ the King (mural), Marian Col Art Gallery Permanent Collection, Fond du Lac, Wis; relig mural, Monastery St Lazarro Mus, Venice, Italy; painting, Col Armeno Permanent Collection, Venice; relig paintings, St Mary's Convent, Yonkers & Church Holy Cross Sch, New York.
Commissions: Painting of home, Mr & Mrs Zambetti, Sr, New York, 50; painting of boy & his dog, Mr & Mrs Russell, New York, 54; three landscapes, Mr & Mrs Alexander Walker, Yonkers, 67; portrait of a little girl, Donata Pellegrini, Yonkers, 68.
Exhibitions: Raymond Duncan Gallery, Paris, France, 62, 65, 68 & 69; Lynn Kotler Gallery, New York, 63; Int Exhib Drawings, Florence, Italy, 71; one-man shows, Manhattan Col, New York, 55 & Burr Gallery, New York, 59.
Teaching: Instr pvt classes, 49-61 & 71-; instr art, New York City Bd Educ, 57-
Positions: Occup therapist for prof patients, Bronx, N Y, 55-62; occup therapist, Rockland State Hosp, 64-
Awards: Scholar, High Sch Music & Art, 44; hon for art work, Nat Acad Design Sch, 47; Prix de Paris, Ligoa Duncan Gallery, 62, 65, 68 & 69.
Bibliography: Article, In: J Am, 59; Leonardo da Vinci, Cahiers d'Art, 70; Enciclopedia Internazionale Degli Artisti, Bugatti, 70.
Memberships: Life mem Art Stud League New York; Burr Artists; Centro Studi E Scambi Internazionale Rome, Italy.
Mailing Address: 3523 Riverdale Ave, New York, NY 10463.

TEYRAL, JOHN
Painter, Instructor
b Yaroslav, Russia, June 10, 12.
Study & Training: Cleveland Inst Art; Boston Mus Fine Arts Sch; Grande Chaumiere, Paris; Accad Belli Arti, Florence, Italy.
Work in Public Collections: Cleveland Mus Art; City of Cleveland, Ohio; Butler Inst Am Art; Pepsi Cola Collection; Montclair Mus Art, N J.
Commissions: Mural, President Garfield Mem, Cleveland; many portraits of prominent persons.
Exhibitions: Carnegie Inst; Metrop Mus Art; Va Mus Fine Arts; Corcoran Gallery Art; Univ Nebr; plus many others.
Collections Arranged: 32 Realists, Cleveland Inst Art, 72.
Teaching: Instr painting & drawing, Cleveland Inst Art, 39-
Awards: Prizes, Cleveland Mus Art, 41-61 & Butler Inst Am Art, 44; Fulbright grant to Italy, 49-50; plus others.
Mailing Address: Cleveland Institute of Art, 11141 East Blvd, Cleveland, OH 44106.

THACHER, JOHN SEYMOUR
Museum Director
b New York, N Y, Sept 5, 04.
Study & Training: Yale Univ, BA, 27; Univ London, PhD, 36.
Positions: Asst to dir, Fogg Mus Art, Cambridge, Mass, 36-40, asst dir, 40-46, exec off, Dumbarton Oaks Res Libr & Collection, 40-45, actg dir, 45-46, dir & treas, 46-69; trustee, Harvard Univ; trustee & assoc in fine arts, Yale Univ, 53-; former treas, Byzantine Inst, Inc, Washington, D C.
Memberships: Century Asn; Cosmos Club; assoc Int Inst Conserv Mus Objects; fel Pierpont Morgan Libr; Grolier Club; plus others.
Publications: Auth, Paintings of Francisco de Herrara, the elder, Art Bull, 37.
Mailing Address: 1692 31st St N W, Washington, DC 20007.

THEK, PAUL
Sculptor
b Brooklyn, N Y, Nov 2, 33.
Study & Training: Cooper Union; Art Stud League New York; Pratt Inst, 51-54; also study in Europe.
Commissions: Sets & costumes for Area (ballet), Nederlands Dans Theater, 69.
Exhibitions: One-man shows, The Stable Gallery, 64, 67 & 69; Documenta IV, Kassel, 68 & Cologne, 69; Stedelijk Mus, Amsterdam, 69; Nat Mus, Stockholm, 69; two-man show, Galerie 20, Amsterdam, 69; plus others.
Awards: Fulbright fel, 67.
Mailing Address: c/o M E Thelen Gallery, Lindenstrasse 20, Cologne, Germany.

THELIN, VALFRED P
Painter, Lecturer
Preferred Media: Watercolors, Acrylics.
b Waterbury, Conn, Jan 8, 34.
Study & Training: Layton Sch Art; Art Inst Chicago; Int Design Conf Ctr, Insel Mainau, W Ger; plus art seminars in six European countries & Mex.
Work in Public Collections: Reading Mus, Pa; Springfield Mus, Mass; Fort Wayne Mus, Ind; Butler Inst Am Art, Youngstown, Ohio; Corcoran Gallery Art.
Exhibitions: Watercolor U S A, Springfield Mus, Mo, 63-72; Am Watercolor Soc, Nat Acad Galleries, New York, N Y, 63-72; Art in the Embassies, sponsored by Smithsonian Inst, Washington, D C, 68-73; Landscape 1 & Art Expo '72, De Cordova Mus, Lincoln, Mass, 70 & 72; Six by Eight (eight watercolorists invited from the U S A), Philbrook Art Mus, Tulsa, Okla, 71.
Awards: Jurors Award of Distinction, Hermann Fine Arts Mus, 68; John Singer Sargeant Award, Watercolor U S A, Springfield Mus, 68; Henry Ward Ranger Award, Audubon Artists, Nat Acad Design, 69.
Bibliography: Joshua Kind (auth), Chicago, Art News, 2/66; Safer (auth), New York reviews, Arts Mag, 4/68; B Sheaks (auth), Painting with acrylics, Davis, 6/72.
Memberships: Ogunquit Art Asn (pres, 71-72); life mem Rockport Art Asn (juror); Pa Acad Fine Arts; Sarasota Art Asn (juror demonstrations, 72-73).
Publications: Contribr, Art in Am, 3/67, 68 & 72 & The Art Gallery, 71 & 72.
Mailing Address: 190 Shore Rd, Ogunquit, ME 03907.

THEPOT, ROGER FRANÇOIS
Painter
Preferred Media: Acrylics, Gouache.
b Landeleau, France, 25.
Work in Public Collections: Mus Mod Art, New York, N Y; Mus d'Art Mod, Paris, France; Nat Gallery, Ottawa, Can; Art Gallery Ont, Toronto; Mendel Art Gallery, Saskatoon, Can.
Exhibitions: Construction & Geometry in Painting, Galerie Chalette, New York, 60; Ecole de Paris, Galerie Charpentier, Paris, 61; Prix Europe de Peinture, Ostende, Belg, 62; Thirteen French Artists, Nippon Gallery, Tokyo, Japan, 67; Canada 67, Mus Mod Art, New York, 67.
Teaching: Instr colour, Ont Col Art, 67-
Awards: Baxter Award, 67.
Bibliography: M Seuphor (auth), La peinture abstraite, Flammarion, 62; G Rickey (auth), Constructivism—origins & evolution, Braziller, 67; Roger Francois Thepot, Ed Prisme, 72.
Memberships: Realites Nouvelles; Royal Can Acad.
Dealer: Gallery Moos Ltd, 138 Yorkville, Toronto, Ont, Can.
Mailing Address: 80 Alcina Ave, Toronto, Ont, Can.

THIEBAUD, (MORTON) WAYNE
Painter, Educator
b Mesa, Ariz, Nov 15, 20.
Study & Training: Sacramento State Col, BA, 51, MA, 52.
Work in Public Collections: Mus Mod Art; Whitney Mus Am Art; Libr Cong; Albright-Knox Art Gallery; Washington Gallery Mod Art, plus many others.
Commissions: Fountain mobile structure, Calif State Fair, 52; mosaic mural, Munic Utility Dist Bldg, Sacramento, 59; producer 11 educ motion picture, Bailey Films, Hollywood, Calif.
Exhibitions: One-man show, DeYoung Mem Mus, 62; Dayton Art Inst; Int Contemp Art, Houston, Tex; San Francisco Mus Art, São Paulo Biennale, Brazil, 68; plus many other group & one-man shows.
Teaching: Chmn art dept, Sacramento City Col, 51; guest instr, San Francisco Art Inst, 58; prof art, Univ Calif, Davis, 60-; prof art & artist-in-residence, Cornell Univ, 66; artist-in-residence, Viterbo Col, 69.
Awards: Golden Reel Film Festival Award, 56; Scholastic Art Awards for films Space & Design, 61; Creative Res Found grant, 61; plus others.
Bibliography: Sam Hunter (ed), New art around the world: painting and sculpture, Abrams, 66; Lucy R Lippard (auth), Pop art, Praeger, 66; Allen S Weller (auth), The joys and sorrows of recent American art, Univ Ill Press, 68.
Publications: Auth, American rediscovered, 63 & Delights, 65.
Mailing Address: Dept of Art, University of California, Davis, CA 95616.

THIESSEN, (CHARLES) LEONARD
Art Administrator, Writer
b Omaha, Nebr, May 3, 02.
Study & Training: Univ Nebr, Lincoln; Royal Acad Art Sch, Stockholm, Sweden; Acad Grande Chaumiere, Paris, France; Heatherley Sch Art, London, Eng; Creighton Univ, hon DFA, 72.

Work in Public Collections: Joslyn Art Mus, Omaha, Nebr; Sheldon Art Gallery, Lincoln, Nebr; Univ Nebr, Omaha; Kans Wesleyan Univ, Salina; Herbert Inst Art, Augusta, Ga.
Commissions: Mural in cocktail rm, Paxton Hotel, Omaha, 38; baptistry triptych, St Paul's P E Church, Omaha, 41; hist dioramas (with Bill J Hammon), Nebr Hist Soc, Lincoln, 52-53; mural decorations for power house, Lewis & Clark Reservoir, Corps of Eng, Yankton, S D, 55; exterior mosaic (with Bill J Hammon), Pershing Mem Auditorium, City of Lincoln, 55-56.
Exhibitions: Young Contemporaries, London, 49; Royal Soc Brit Artists, London, 49; Nat Soc, London, 49; Midwest Biennial, Joslyn, 52; Mid-America, Kansas City, 53.
Positions: State dir, fed arts prog, Works Proj Admin, Des Moines, 40-42; exec secy, Nebr Arts Coun, 66-
Publications: Art ed, Omaha World-Herald, 39-71.
Mailing Address: c/o Nebraska Arts Council, 1112½ Farnam St, Omaha, NE 68102.

THOM, ROBERT ALAN
Illustrator, Painter
b Grand Rapids, Mich, Mar 4, 15.
Study & Training: Columbus Inst Fine Arts, Ohio; also with Robert Brackman.
Work in Public Collections: Parke, Davis Co; Bohn Aluminum & Brass Co; Univ Md; Cranbrook Acad Arts; Nat Asn Retail Druggists Hq, Chicago; plus others.
Exhibitions: Vancouver Art Gallery, B C; Smithsonian Inst; Sheldon Swope Gallery Art; Oregon Mus Nat Hist; Pioneer Mus, Stockton, Calif; plus many others.
Memberships: Soc Illustrators; Bloomfield Art Asn; Birmingham, Mich (founding pres).
Publications: Auth & illusr, article on Wine Festival, Burgundy, France, In: Gourmet Mag, 61.
Mailing Address: 6160 W Surrey Rd, Birmingham, MI 48010.

THOMAS, ALMA WOODSEY
Painter
Preferred Media: Oils, Acrylics.
b Columbus, Ga, Sept 22, 96.
Study & Training: Howard Univ, BS, 24; Columbia Univ, MFA, 34; Am Univ, 50-60; also in Europe, 58, under auspices Temple Univ.
Work in Public Collections: Corcoran Gallery Art, Washington, D C; Smithsonian Inst Collection Fine Arts, Washington, D C; George Washington Univ Gallery Art, Washington, D C; Fisk Univ Gallery Art, Nashville, Tenn; Whitney Mus Am Art, New York, N Y.
Exhibitions: Retrospective, Howard Univ Gallery Art, 66; Franz Bader Gallery, Washington, D C, 68 & 70-72; Fisk Univ Gallery Art, Nashville, Tenn, 71; Whitney Mus Am Art, 72; Retrospective, Corcoran Gallery Art, 72.
Teaching: Instr art, jr high sch, 24-60.
Awards: Purchase prize, Howard Univ, 63; Soc Washington Artists, 63, 68 & 71; Am-Austrian Soc Art Exhib Award, 68.
Bibliography: Cedric Dover (auth), American Negro art, Studio, 60; The art gallery, Hollycroft, 4/70.
Memberships: Am Fedn Arts; Corcoran Gallery Art; Soc Washington Artists; Washington Watercolor Asn; Smithsonian Inst.
Dealer: Franz Bader Gallery, 2124 Pennsylvania Ave N W, Washington, DC
Mailing Address: 1530 15th St N W, Washington, DC 20005.

THOMAS, ED B
Educator, Lecturer
b Cosmopolis, Wash, Nov 30, 20.
Study & Training: Columbia Univ; New York Univ; Univ Wash, BA & MFA.
Commissions: Recorded TV series for sch use—Man's story, Treasure trips, Our neighbors, The Japanese, Electronic tour of Masterpieces of Korean Art, 58, Van Gogh, 59 & Treasures of Japan, 60, Seattle Art Mus.
Exhibitions: Nat Serigraphy Soc; San Francisco Mus Art; Seattle Art Mus; regional exhibs, 50-
Teaching: Lect, weekly TV art prog, Seattle, 51-; instr art hist, Cornish Sch, Seattle, 52-58; from vis prof & lect to assoc prof art, Western Wash State Col, 67-
Positions: Cur educ, Seattle Art Mus & Seattle Ctr Art Pavilion, 51-54, educ dir, 54-61, asst dir, 61-63, assoc, dir, 63-67; arts adv bd, Seattle World's Fair, 58-62; bd trustees, Allied Artists Seattle, 59-62; secy, Fine Arts, Inc, 62; v pres, Western Asn Art Mus, 63-64.
Awards: Prize for sch telecasts, Am Exhib of Educ Radio-TV Prog, Ohio Univ, 56; plus other TV awards.
Memberships: Pacific Art Asn (first v pres, 60-62); Wash Art Asn; Nat Comt on Art Educ; Am Asn Mus; Northwest Printmakers; plus others.
Publications: Auth, Guide to Life's illuminations exhibit, Time, Inc, 58; auth, Mark Tobey, 59; ed & narrator, Chinese ink & watercolor (film), 61.
Mailing Address: 1500 42nd St, Seattle, WA 98102.

THOMAS, ELAINE FREEMAN
Educator, Art Administrator
b Cleveland, Ohio, July 21, 23.
Study & Training: Northwestern Univ, Evanston, 44; Tuskegee Inst, BS(magna cum laude), 45; Black Mountain Col, 45, with Josef Albers & Robert Motherwell; N Y Univ, Bodden fel, MA, 49, with Hale Woodruff; Mexico City Col, 56; Berea Col, 61; N Y Univ, 62; Univ Paris, 66; Southern Univ Workshop, 68; Columbia Univ, 70.
Collections Arranged: One-man exhib, Winston-Salem State Univ, 70; Discovery 70, Univ Cincinnati; George Washington Carver Exhib, White House, 71; Ala Black Artists Exhib, Birmingham Festival Art, 72; plus others.
Teaching: Asst prof art & chmn dept, Tuskegee Inst, 45-, mus dir & cur, George W Carver Mus, 61-
Awards: Distinguished participation, Am Artists Prof League, 68; Beaux Arts Festival Award.
Memberships: Am Asn Mus; Col Art Asn Am; Nat Art Educ Asn; Nat Conf Artists; Ala Art League.
Mailing Address: Tuskegee Institute, AL 36088.

THOMAS, GEORGE R
Educator, Designer
b Portsmouth, Va, Dec 8, 06.
Study & Training: Univ N C, 24-25; Carnegie Inst Technol, BArch, 30; Columbia Univ, 38; study in Europe.
Teaching: Instr art, Mary Washington Col, 35; from instr to prof archit & arts, Univ N H, 31-, dir art gallery, 37-, chmn dept arts, 40-
Memberships: Am Inst Architects; Am Asn Univ Prof; N H Art Asn; Coun League N H Arts & Crafts; N H Soc Architects.
Publications: Contribr, articles on archit design & educ to various publ.
Mailing Address: Dept of the Arts, University of New Hampshire, Durham, NH 03824.

THOMAS, LIONEL ARTHUR JOHN
Painter, Sculptor
Preferred Media: Enamel, Oils.
b Toronto, Ont, Can, Apr 3, 15.
Study & Training: John Russell Acad; Toronto; Ont Col Art, Toronto; Calif Sch Fine Art, San Francisco; also with Hans Hofmann, Provincetown, Mass.
Work in Public Collections: Fla State Col, Lakeland; Nat Gallery, Ottawa; Art Gallery Toronto; Vancouver Art Gallery; Univ Victoria, B C.
Commissions: Bronze fountain, Edmonton City Hall, Alta, 58; Vancouver Pub Libr, 61; enamel doors, St Thomas More Col, Saskatoon, Sask, 62; B C Prov Govt Mus, Victoria, 68; oil on panels, (with L & P Thomas), Stud Union Bldg, Univ B C, 69.
Teaching: Assoc prof design, Sch Archit, 50-64; assoc prof design, Univ B C, 64.
Positions: Chmn, Comt Appl Design B C Govt, Victoria, 65-68.
Awards: Allied Arts Medal, Royal Archit Inst Can, 56.
Bibliography: Rene Boux (auth), New star, Can Art; Stephen Franklin (auth), Artist and a briefcase, Weekend Mag, 58; article, In: B C Beautiful, spring 70; plus articles in other mags.
Memberships: Assoc Royal Can Acad; Am Craftsmen Coun; Am Soc Archeologists; Can Fedn Artists; Ont Crafts Found; plus others.
Mailing Address: 3351 Craigond Rd, West Vancouver, B C, Can.

THOMAS, REYNOLDS
Painter, Sculptor
b Wilmington, Del, Jan 21, 27.
Study & Training: Pa Acad Fine Arts; Univ Fine Arts, Mex.
Work in Public Collections: Del Art Ctr, Wilmington; Northern Trust Co, Chicago, Ill; Hempstead Bank, Long Island, N Y; Farnsworth Mus, Rockland, Maine; Northern Ind Art Asn Permanent Collection, Hammond; plus many others.
Commissions: Twelve oil paintings of Alpine scenes, Garcia Ski Corp, Teaneck, N J, 69; HSH Princess Grace de Monaco (portrait), Palace, Monaco, 71; plus many other pvt commissions.
Exhibitions: Int Grand Prix Contemp Art, Monte Carlo, Monaco, 72; one-man shows, Hotel de Paris, Monte Carlo, Am Wk Celebration, 66, Country Art Gallery, Long Island, N Y, 62, 67, 68 & 71, Int Art Ctr, Milan, Italy, Galleria al Porto, Arenzano, Italy, 71, Kennedy Galleries, 64 & 65 & Galerie Michel-Ange, Chateau Perigord, Monte Carlo, 72; plus many other group & one-man shows.
Awards: Thouron prize, 52 & scholar, 54, Pa Acad Fine Arts; prizes, Del Art Ctr, 56; int grand prize & trophy (painting), La Stanza Letteraria, Rome, Italy, 72.
Memberships: Am Fedn Arts; Int Art Guild, Monte Carlo, France.
Dealers: Country Art Gallery, Locust Valley, Long Island, NY 11560; Galleria al Porto, No 4, Arenzano, Genoa, Italy.
Mailing Address: Casa Sul Porto, No 4, Arenzano, Genoa, Italy 16010.

THOMAS, ROBERT CHESTER
Sculptor
Preferred Media: Stone, Wood, Bronze.
b Wichita, Kans, Apr 19, 24.
Study & Training: With David Green, Pasadena, Calif, 46-47 & Ossip Zadkine, Paris, France, 48-49; Univ Calif, Santa Barbara, BA, 51; Calif Col Arts & Crafts, MFA, 52.
Work in Public Collections: Santa Barbara Mus Art, Calif; Univ Calif, Santa Barbara; Joseph H Hirshhorn Collection, Washington, D C.
Commissions: Painted wood sculpture, J Magnin, Century City, Calif, 66; bronze figure, Class of 1967, Univ Calif, Santa Barbara, 67; ceramic fountain, comn by Phyllis Plous, Santa Barbara, 68.
Exhibitions: Int Salon de Mai, Paris, France, 49; San Francisco Mus Art, 52, 53, 56 & 57; one-man shows, Santa Barbara Mus Art, 55, La Jolla Art Ctr, Calif, 60 & Adele Bednarz Galleries, Los Angeles, Calif, 70-72; Retrospective, Univ Calif, Santa Barbara, 66.
Teaching: Prof sculpture, Univ Calif, Santa Barbara, 54-
Awards: Bronze medal for sculpture, City of Los Angeles, 49; silver medal for sculpture, Calif State Fair, 54; purchase prize for sculpture, Santa Barbara Mus Art, 59.
Dealer: Adele Bednarz Galleries, 902 N La Cienega Blvd, Los Angeles, CA 90069.
Mailing Address: 38 San Mateo Ave, Goleta, CA 93017.

THOMAS, STEFFEN WOLFGANG
Sculptor, Painter
Preferred Media: Bronze.
b Fürth, Ger, Jan 7, 06; U S citizen.
Study & Training: Sch Appl Arts, Nürnberg, Ger; Acad Fine Arts, Munich, Ger, with Herman Hahn, Bernhart Bleeker & Josef Wakerle.
Work in Public Collections: High Mus, Atlanta, Ga; Agnes Scott Col, Decatur, Ga; State Capitol, Atlanta; Am Col Surg, Chicago, Ill; Univ Edinborough, Scotland.
Commissions: Marble portrait bust, comn by Martha Berry, Berry Sch Libr, Rome, Ga, 36; bronze portrait bust of George Washington Carver, Tuskegee Inst, Ala, 45; bronze monument to Gov Eugene Talmadge, Talmadge Mem Comt, State Capitol Grounds, Atlanta, 49; Bronze Ala Confederate monument, State of Ala, Vicksburg Nat Mil Park, Miss, 51; aluminum bas relief murals, Fulton Nat Bank, Atlanta, 54.
Exhibitions: Glas Palast, Munich, 27; one-man show, High Mus, 36; Nat Sculpture Soc, New York, N Y, 48; Southeastern Art Show, Atlanta Art Asn, 49-51; Nat Soc Miniature Arts, Smithsonian Inst, Washington, D C, 52.
Positions: Art dir Ga, Nat Youth Admin, 39-42.
Awards: First & purchase prize for Head of Youth, City of Fürth, 25; hon mention, Fine Arts Acad, Munich, 28.
Bibliography: Katerine Barnwell (auth), Artist's studio or lion's den, Atlanta J-Constitution Mag, 3/4/62; Ann Carter (auth), Reaching higher, Sun Atlanta J-Constitution, 2/2/69, Ethel Kerlin & staff (auth), Mr Steffen Thomas, WETV, 69.
Mailing Address: 848 Mentelle Dr N E, Atlanta, GA 30308.

THOMASITA see SISTER THOMASITA.

THOMPSON, (JAMES) BRADBURY
Designer, Art Director
b Topeka, Kans, Mar 25, 11.
Study & Training: Washburn Univ, AB, 34, DFA, 65.
Commissions: Book design for Annual of advertising art, 43 & 54, Graphic arts production yearbook, 48 & 50, Westvaco Inspirations & American Classics, 39-72, Homage to the book, 68 & The quality of life, 68; plus many others.
Exhibitions: Int Exhib Graphic Art, Paris, France, 55, London, Eng, 56, Milan, Italy, 61, Amsterdam, 62 & Hamburg, Ger, 64; traveling one-man exhib, Am Inst Graphic Art, 58.
Teaching: Vis critic, Sch Art & Archit, Yale Univ, 56-; bd gov, Philadelphia Col Art, 56-59.
Positions: Art dir, Capper Publ, 34-38; art dir, Rogers, Kellogg, Stillson, Inc, 38-41; art dir, Off War Info, 42-45; art dir, Mademoiselle, 45-59; publ art dir, Street & Smith Publ, 45-59; consult, Westvaco Corp, 45-; des dir, Art News & Art News Ann, 45-72; art dir, Living for Young Homemakers, 47-49; consult, Famous Artists Schs, 59-; consult, McGraw Hill Publ, 60-; consult, Time-Life Bks, 64-70; consult, Harvard Bus Rev, 64-67; consult, Field Enterprises Educ Corp, 64-; consult, Cornell Univ, 65-
Awards: Wash Univ Distinguished Serv Award; Gold T-Square Award, Nat Soc Art Dirs, 50; multiple awards, Art Dirs Club.
Memberships: Art Dirs Club (first v pres, exec comt); Soc Illustrators; Am Inst Graphic Arts (bd dirs); Alliance Graphique Int; Nat Soc Art Dirs (rep, 58-64); plus others.
Publications: Auth, The Monalphabet, 45 & Alphabet 26, 50.
Mailing Address: Jones Park, Riverside, CT 06878.

THOMPSON, DOROTHY BURR
Art Historian, Lecturer
b Delhi, N Y, Aug 19, 00.
Study & Training: Bryn Mawr Col, AB, 23, European fel, 23, AM, PhD, 31; Wooster Col, hon DFA, 72.
Collections Arranged: Comment in Clay (spec exhib), Royal Ont Mus, 47.
Teaching: Lectr archaeol for circuit, Archaeol Inst Am, 40-; lectr classical archaeol, Univ Toronto, 43-47; prof classical archaeol, Univ Pa, 52 & 68; vis lectr archaeol, Oberlin Col, 68; prof classical archaeol, Princeton Univ, 69-70; vis lectr, Univ Sydney, 72.
Positions: Acting dir, Royal Ont Mus, 46-47.
Memberships: Archaeol Inst Am (exec comt, 48-); corresp mem Deutsches Archäologisches Inst.
Research: Classical greek subjects such as figurines, garden art & pvt life.
Publications: Auth, Terracottas from Myrina in Museum of Fine Arts, Boston, privately publ, 34; auth, Swans & Amber (translations of Greek lyrics), Univ Toronto Press, 49; auth, Troy, the terracotta figurines of the Hellenistic period, Princeton Univ Press, 63; auth, Ptolemaic Oinochoai and portraits in Faince, Oxford Press, 73; contribr various journals.
Mailing Address: Institute for Advanced Study, Princeton, NJ 08540.

THOMPSON, F RAYMOND (RAY)
Illustrator, Writer
Preferred Media: Watercolors.
b Philadelphia, Pa, Aug 9, 05.
Study & Training: Temple Univ, 26-27 & 50-52; Mus Sch Art, Philadelphia; Spring Garden Inst, Philadelphia; Charles Morris. Price Sch Journalism & Advert, Philadelphia.
Publications: Auth & illusr, You can draw a straight line!, 63; auth & illusr, Washington along the Delaware, 70; auth & illusr, Washington at Germantown, 71; auth & illusr, Betsy Ross, last of Philadelphia's free Quakers, 72.
Mailing Address: 1107 Montgomery Ave, Fort Washington, PA 19034.

THOMPSON, GEORGE LOUIS
Designer
Preferred Media: Glass.
b Winnetoon, Nebr, Oct 14, 13.
Study & Training: Univ Minn, BSA; Mass Inst Technol, MS.
Work in Public Collections: Metrop Mus Art, New York, N Y; Palais Louvre, Paris, The Hermitage, Leningrad, U S S R; William Rockhill Nelson Gallery Art, Kansas City, Mo; Nat Gallery Mod Art, New Delhi, India.
Commissions: Eisenhower Cup, comn by his cabinet, Washington, D C, 53; Papal Cup, Cardinal Spellman, New York, 56; Lafayette Medallion, Collection Pres René Coty, France, 57; Angel Stele, Kennedy Found, 62; Eleanor Roosevelt Memorial, Eleanor Roosevelt Libr, 71.
Exhibitions: 5 Steuben Traveling Exhibs, 36-53; New York World's Fair, 39-40; Designs in Glass by 27 Contemporary Artists, New York, 40; Brit Artists in Crystal, New York, 54; Poetry in Crystal, New York, 66.
Positions: Sr designer, Steuben Glass, New York, 36-
Awards: Boston Soc Archit Prize & class medal, Mass Inst Technol, 36.
Bibliography: Poetry in crystal, 63 & Five masterworks, 72, Steuben Glass.
Mailing Address: 210 E 63rd St, New York, NY 10021.

THOMPSON, JOANNE
Painter, Sculptor
Preferred Media: Oils, Bronze, Conté.
b Chicago, Ill.
Study & Training: Univ Colo; also with Gilkerson, Los Angeles.
Work in Public Collections: Americana Galleries, Northfield, Ill.
Exhibitions: Nat Arts Club Gallery, New York, N Y, 65-69; Mus Fine Arts, Springfield, Mass, 65-70; Am Artists Prof League Grand Nat, New York, 66-70; Hammond Mus, Westchester, N Y, 68; one-man shows, Americana Galleries, 68 & 70.
Teaching: Instr oil painting, Americana Galleries, 67-68.
Awards: Best of Show/Jury's Choice, Orange Co Fair, Calif, 64; hon mention for still life, Acad Artists, 67; first prize for sculpture, Mt Prospect, Ill, 68.
Bibliography: Catharine Lorillard Wolfe prof women's show (catalogues), Nat Art Club Gallery, 65-69; Grand nat show (catalogue), Am Artists Prof League, 70; The art of technique and color, Grumbacher, 73.
Memberships: Am Artists Prof League; Artists Guild Chicago; Acad Artists; Catharine Lorillard Wolfe Prof Women's Club.
Dealer: Showcase Gallery, 1420 South Coast Hwy, Laguna Beach, CA 92651.
Mailing Address: 310 Avenida Granada, San Clemente, CA 92672.

THOMPSON, KENNETH WEBSTER
Illustrator, Painter
Preferred Media: Gouache, Watercolors.
b New York, N Y, Apr 26, 07.
Study & Training: Grand Cent Sch Art; also with George Pierce Ennis.
Work in Public Collections: Wartime illustrations, Libr of Cong, Washington, D C.
Exhibitions: Am Watercolor Soc Ann; Soc Illusrs; Nantucket Artists Asn.
Awards: Eight awards, New York Art Dir Club; thirteen awards, Chicago Art Dir Club; three awards, N J Art Dir Club.
Memberships: Life mem Soc Illusr (past dir); Am Watercolor Soc; Nantucket Artists Asn (past dir); Artists Guild (past dir).
Publications: Illusr, The continent we live on (series), 62-68; illusr, The sea, 66.
Mailing Address: 20 W 11th St, New York, NY 10011.

THOMPSON, LOCKWOOD
Collector
b Cleveland, Ohio, 01.
Study & Training: Williams Col, AB, 23; Harvard Law Sch, LLB, 26.
Positions: Mem adv Coun, Cleveland Mus Art, 49; mem Int Coun, Mus Mod Art, New York, N Y, 62.
Collection: Contemporary art.
Mailing Address: 11901 Carlton Rd, Cleveland, OH 44106.

THOMPSON, MALCOLM BARTON
Painter, Sculptor
Preferred Media: Acrylics, Watercolors.
b Coraopolis, Pa, Dec 25, 16.
Study & Training: Pratt Inst, grad; Art Stud League New York, N Y; also illus with Nicholas Riley.
Commissions: U S Army in Action Ser, Pentagon, 49.
Exhibitions: Soc Casein Artists, New York, 70; Slater Mem Mus, Norwich, Conn, 71; Conn Watercolor Soc, Hartford, Conn, 71; Mainstreams 71, Marietta, Ohio, 71; Am Watercolor Soc, New York, 72.
Teaching: Instr watercolor & anat, McLane Art Inst, New York, 38-40.
Awards: Marjorie Salembier Award, Conn Classic Arts, 68; first prize, New Canaan Art Show, 70; Grumbacher Acrylic Award, Am Artists Prof League, 71.
Dealer: Lord & Taylor Galleries, 39th St & Fifth Ave, New York, NY 10016.
Mailing Address: R F D 3, Georgetown, CT 06829.

THOMPSON, PAUL LELAND
Painter
Preferred Media: Oils, Acrylics, Watercolors.
b Buffalo, Iowa, May 20, 11.
Study & Training: Calif Sch Fine Arts; Corcoran Sch Art; with Heinrich Pfieffer, Provincetown, Mass.
Work in Public Collections: Marine Ins Co, Pittsburgh, Pa; Fairleigh Dickinson Univ, Rutherford, N J.
Commissions: Two murals, Shiloh Baptist Church, Plainfield, N J, 57.
Exhibitions, Corcoran Gallery Art Biennial, 45; Calif Palace Legion of Hon Nat Exhib, San Francisco, Calif, 49; Nat Watercolor Exhib, Nat Acad Design, 56; Statewide Exhibs, Hunterdon Co Art Ctr, 64-67 & 72.
Awards: First prize for watercolor, Art Ctr Oranges, 57; first prize for oil painting, 64 & second prize for oil painting, 67, Hunterdon Co Art Ctr.
Memberships: Artists Equity New York; Artists Equity N J; N J Watercolor Soc; Hunterdon Co Art Ctr; Plainfield Art Asn, N J.
Dealer: Barton Barry, 475 Park Ave, Scotch Plains, NJ 07060.
Mailing Address: 224 E Front St, Plainfield, NJ 07060.

THOMPSON, RALSTON CARLTON
Painter, Educator
Preferred Media: Oils, Watercolors.
b Ironton, Ohio, Mar 28, 04.
Study & Training: Wittenberg Univ, AB, 25; Dayton Art Inst, 25-26; Chicago Acad Fine Arts, 32-33; Ohio State Univ, MFA, 38.
Work in Public Collections: Cincinnati Art Mus, Ohio; Butler Inst Am Art, Youngstown, Ohio; Dayton Art Inst, Ohio; Columbus Gallery Fine Arts, Ohio; Chubb Gallery, Ohio Univ, Athens; plus many others.
Exhibitions: 22nd Int Exhib Watercolors, 43 & 57th Ann Exhib Am Watercolors & Drawings, 46, Art Inst Chicago; Pittsburgh Int Exhib Contemp Paintings, Carnegie Inst, Pa, 55; Drawings U S A, St Paul Gallery Art, Minn, 61; Art Across America, Mead Corp, 65; plus many other group & one-man shows.
Teaching: Instr drawing & painting, Ohio State Univ, 35-41; chmn fine arts dept, Wittenberg Univ, 41-65, prof fine arts, 47-69, emer prof, 69-

Positions: Guest artist, Cincinnati Art Acad, 49-50; mem visual arts working artists adv panel, Ohio Arts Coun, 67-69.
Awards: Fifty seven awards since 41.
Mailing Address: 254 Circle Dr, Springfield, OH 45503.

THOMPSON, SUSIE WASS
Painter
Preferred Media: Watercolors.
b Addison, Maine, July 15, 92.
Work in Public Collections: Univ Maine, Orono.
Commissions: Many in U S A, Can, Eng, France, Italy & Scotland.
Exhibitions: One-woman shows, Colby Col, 59, Northeast Harbor, Maine, 62, 63 & 65, Pietrantonio Gallery, New York, N Y, 63, Blue Hills, Maine, 66 & Rochester, N Y; plus many others.
Memberships: Kennebec Valley Art Asn; Am Fedn Arts.
Mailing Address: Cape Split, Addison, ME 04606.

THOMSON, CARL L
Art Dealer, Designer
Preferred Media: Watercolors.
b Brooklyn, N Y, Mar 6, 13.
Study & Training: Pratt Inst, with Arthur Schweider.
Work in Public Collections: Salmagundi Club; Burr Artists Group.
Exhibitions: Salmagundi Club Ann Watercolor & Oil Shows, 59-72.
Teaching: Instr drawing, Salmagundi Club, 61-63.
Positions: Advert designer, C Thomson Assoc, 47-59; art dir, Am Home Prod Corp, 59-70; owner, Thomson Gallery, New York, 70-
Awards: Graphic arts award, Printing Industs Am, 69; cert spec merit, Printing Industs Metrop New York, 70.
Memberships: Salmagundi Club (v pres & mem bd dirs).
Specialty of Gallery: Contemporary and representational fine art.
Mailing Address: 19 E 75th St, New York, NY 10021.

THON, WILLIAM
Painter
b New York, N Y, Aug 8, 06.
Study & Training: Art Stud League, 24-25; Bates Col, hon DFA, 57.
Work in Public Collections: Swope Art Gallery; Metrop Mus Art; Butler Inst Am Art; Munson-Williams-Proctor Inst, Utica, N Y; Calif Palace of Legion of Honor, San Francisco; plus over 45 maj U S mus.
Exhibitions: Corcoran Gallery Art, Washington, D C; Pa Acad Fine Arts, Philadelphia; Va Mus Fine Arts, Richmond; Art Inst Chicago, Ill; Whitney Mus Am Art, New York, N Y; plus many others.
Positions: Trustee, Am Acad in Rome.
Awards: Dawson Medal, Philadelphia Watercolor Club, 68; Altman Prize, Nat Acad Design, 69; Gold Medal of Honor, Am Watercolor Soc, 70; plus many others.
Memberships: Assoc Nat Acad Design; Salmagundi Club; Brooklyn Soc Art; Nat Inst Arts & Lett; Am Acad Arts & Lett.
Dealer: Midtown Galleries, 11 E 57th St, New York, NY 10022.
Mailing Address: Port Clyde, ME 04855.

THORNDIKE, CHARLES JESSE (CHUCK)
Cartoonist, Writer
b Seattle, Wash, Jan 20, 97.
Study & Training: Univ Wash; Seattle Art Sch; Calif Sch Fine Arts; also with Lee F Randolph, Rudolph Schaefer, Harold Von Schmidt & Johonnot.
Work in Public Collections: Smithsonian Inst, Washington, D C; Mus Natural Hist, New York, N Y; Mus Arts & Sci, Miami, Fla; Cartoonists Exchange, Pleasant Hill, Ohio; Washington Sch Art, D C.
Exhibitions: Cartoon Mus, Orlando, Fla Travelling Exhib U S Army, Europe.
Teaching: Instr cartooning & com art, Com Art Sch, 34-35; instr cartooning & com art, New York Sch Design, 35-36; instr cartooning & com art, Terry Art Sch, Miami, Fla, 49-51; instr cartooning & com art, Univ Miami, 51-
Positions: Art dir, Gen Motors Acceptance Corp, New York, 28-31; art dir, U S Navy, 41-46.
Memberships: Jockey Club, Miami.
Publications: Auth & illusr, The secrets of cartooning, House Little Bks, 35; Auth & illusr, The art of cartooning, 36; auth & illusr, The art & use of the poster, 37; auth & illusr, Arts & crafts for children, 38; auth & illusr, Oddities of nature (syndicated newspaper feature), 48.
Mailing Address: 11660 Canal Dr, North Miami, FL 33161.

THORNE, GORDON (KIT)
Painter, Designer
Preferred Media: Acrylics, Watercolors.
b Stanway, Eng, Aug 21, 96; Can citizen.
Study & Training: Vancouver Sch Art, with Scott, Varley & McDonald; Goldsmiths Col, with Speed, Gardner & Stanley Anderson.

Work in Public Collections: Centennial Mus, Vancouver, B C; Leningrad Arts, Russia; Vancouver Pub Libr; Lipsett Mus, Vancouver; Libr of Cong, Washington, D C.
Commissions: Blackstone Hotel, Vancouver, 68; Railway Mens Club, Vancouver, 72.
Exhibitions: Western Art Circle, Vancouver, 52-71; Can Painters & Etchers, Toronto, 60-70.
Teaching: Instr art, Fedn Can Artists, 52-56.
Memberships: Life mem Vancouver Mus Asn; life mem Western Art Circle; Can Painters & Etchers.
Publications: Auth, Occasional notes, of Vancouver & Victoria, 68; auth, Strolling & sketching, McNeil.
Dealer: Art Emporium, 2956 Granville St, Vancouver, B C, Can.
Mailing Address: 1460 Nelson St, Vancouver 5, B C, Can.

THORNE, M ART
Painter
b Devon, N B, Nov 15, 09.
Study & Training: Ont Col Art, AOCA, with John Alfsen, George Pepper, Gustav Hahn & Emanuel Hahn; Art Stud League New York, with Vythacil, Marsh & Kantor.
Commissions: Murals, Brit Am Oil Co, Toronto & Casa Loma, Toronto.
Exhibitions: Can Soc Graphic Art; Can Younger Artists; Royal Ont Mus; Art Gallery Toronto; Rochester Mus Arts & Sci; plus others.
Positions: Art dir, Forest Hill Art Club, Toronto.
Mailing Address: 40 Delisle Ave, Toronto, Ont, Can.

THORNE, THOMAS ELSTON
Painter, Art Historian
Preferred Media: Oils, Acrylics.
b Lewiston, Maine, Oct 5, 09.
Study & Training: Portland Sch Fine & Appl Art, cert, 32; Yale Sch Fine & Arts, BFA, 40; Art Stud League New York, with Reginald Marsh.
Work in Public Collections: Old Williamsburg (painting), Col William & Mary, Williamsburg, Va; Jamestown Creek (painting) & Deep Creek (painting), Colonial Williamsburg Found, Va.
Commissions: The Circus (mural), donated by Alexander Bower to children's ward, Maine Gen Hosp, Portland, 32; James Blair (mural), PTA of James Blair H S, Williamsburg, 61.
Exhibitions: Pa Acad Fine Arts Watercolor Show, Philadelphia, 30; New York Watercolor Club, N Y, 40; Int Watercolor Show, Baltimore, Md, 46; Am Drawing Ann, Norfolk, Va, 61; Irene Leehe Mem Exhib, Norfolk, 62.
Teaching: From instr to prof painting, Col William & Mary, 40-, head fine arts dept, 43-69.
Memberships: Col Art Asn Am; Va Hist Soc; Va Mus Fine Arts; 20th Century Gallery; Asn Preservation Va Antiquities.
Research: Early painting in Virginia.
Publications: Contribr, The earliest American nude, William & Mary Quart, 50; contribr, Southern American painting, 54 & contribr, William Byrd & the duchess, 63, Mag Antiques; contribr, Charles Bridges, Limner, Art in Va, 69.
Mailing Address: 209 Burns Lane, Williamsburg, VA 23185.

THORPE, EVERETT CLARK
Painter, Educator
Preferred Media: Oils, Collages, Acrylics, Metalics.
b Providence, Utah, Aug 22, 07.
Study & Training: Utah State Univ, BS, MFA; Syracuse Univ; Hans Hofmann Sch Art.
Work in Public Collections: Springville Nat Gallery; Maxwell Galleries; Utah Inst Fine Arts; Utah State Capitol Bldg; Sigman Phi Epsilon Nat Hq, Richmond, Va; plus many pvt collections.
Commissions: Six murals, Sigman Phi Epsilon, Utah State Univ; Provo Fed Bldg, Fed Govt, 12 Fonders; mural at state capitol, Utah State Univ & Cache Co; Tabernacle, Logan Stake; History of Communication, Utah State Univ Libr, Sr Class 69.
Exhibitions: Utah Art at New York Madison Square, Hawthorn & Provincetown; Springville Nat; Utah Biennial; Tucson Invitational; Maxwell Galleries; plus many others.
Teaching: Prof art, Utah State Univ, 34-
Awards: Terry Int, 55; Springville Int, 65-67; Utah purchase award, Utah Inst, 72.
Bibliography: Looking back on Everett Thorpe, Merrill Gallery Art; Lendhart (auth), An American artist, Univ Wyo Press, 71.
Memberships: Nat Soc Mural Painters; Utah State Inst Fine Arts; Fedn Painters; Alliance of Artists.
Art Interests: Portrait painting; mural design; sprots & portrait illustration.
Publications: Sports illusr, Salt Lake Tribune, 38-40; sports illusr, Deseret News, 41-; illusr, New art education, 55; illusr, Sayings of a saint, 60; illusr, History of biology, 60.
Mailing Address: Merrill Gallery, Utah Art Center, Utah State University, Logan, UT 84321.

THRALL, ARTHUR
Printmaker, Educator
Preferred Media: Intaglio, Acrylics.
b Milwaukee, Wis, Mar 18, 26.
Study & Training: Wis State Col, Milwaukee, BS & MS; Univ Wis-Madison; Univ Ill, Urbana; Ohio State Univ.
Work in Public Collections: Butler Inst Am Art, Youngstown, Ohio; Libr Cong, Washington, D C; Art Inst Chicago, Ill; Brooklyn Mus, N Y; Smithsonian Inst, Washington, D C.
Commissions: 100 print ed, New York Hilton Hotel, 62.
Exhibitions: Carnegie Int Print Exhib, Pittsburgh, Pa, 51; Young American Printmakers, Mus Mod Art, New York, N Y, 53; one-man show, Smithsonian Inst, 60; 160th Ann, Pa Acad Art, Philadelphia, 64; 143rd Ann, Nat Acad Design, New York, 67.
Teaching: Assoc prof art, Milwaukee-Downer Col, 56-64; prof art, Lawrence Univ, 64-; vis prof art, Univ Wis-Madison, 66-67.
Awards: Louis Comfort Tiffany Found fel graphics, 63; purchase award, 14th Ann, Brooklyn Mus, 63; Cannon Prize, 143rd Ann, Nat Acad Design, 67.
Bibliography: M Fish (auth), Arthur Thrall, Wis Architect, 65; M Harold (auth), Prize-winning graphics, Margaret Harold Publ, 65 & 66; D Anderson (auth), The art of written forms, Holt Rinehart & Winston, 69.
Memberships: Soc Am Graphic Artists; Boston Printmakers; Calif Soc Printmakers.
Dealer: Associated American Artists, 663 Fifth Ave, New York, NY 10022.
Mailing Address: 59 Bellaire Ct, Appleton, WI 54911.

THWAITES, CHARLES WINSTANLEY
Painter
b Milwaukee, Wis, Mar 12, 04.
Study & Training: Univ Wis; Layton Sch Art.
Work in Public Collections: Univ Wis; Univ Mex; Marquette Univ; Milwaukee Fed Court; Milwaukee Co Court; Milwaukee Art Ctr.
Commissions: Murals, U S Post Off, Greenville, Mich, Plymouth, Chilton, Wis & Windom, Minn; portraits, pres of St John's Col, Annapolis, Md & Santa Fe, N Mex; mural designs for fed bldgs, Pub Bldgs Admin.
Exhibitions: Eight shows, Mus N Mex, Santa Fe, 55-68; one-man show, St John's Col, 65; Southwest Biennials & Fiesta Ann, 66-68; traveling exhibs, 66-68; Fedn Rocky Mountain States Eight States Exhib, 68; plus many other nat & regional exhibs.
Awards: Prizes, Milwaukee Art Inst, 33-44; 48 State Competition Prize, 39; prizes & medal, Calif Palace of Legion of Honor, 46.
Bibliography: Article, In: The Studio, London, Eng, Vol 131, No 634; Dr Francis V O'Connor (auth), Federal art patronage, Univ Md, 66; Forbes Watson (auth), American painting today, Am Fedn Arts.
Mailing Address: Sunmount, Box 4454, Santa Fe, NM 87501.

TIBBS, THOMAS S
Museum Director, Lecturer
b Indianapolis, Ind, Aug 30, 17.
Study & Training: Univ Rochester, AB, MFA; Columbia Univ.
Exhibitions: Craftsmanship in a Changing World, 56; Louis Comfort Tiffany Retrospective, 58; Six Decades of American Painting, 61; Affect & Effect, 68; Jose de Rivera Forty Year Retrospective, 72.
Teaching: Lectr art hist, Calif State Univ, San Diego, 69-
Positions: Assoc dir educ, Rochester Mem Art Gallery, 47-52; dir, Huntington Galleries, W Va, 52-56; dir, Mus Contemp Crafts, New York, 56-60; dir, Des Moines Art Ctr, Iowa, 60-68; dir, La Jolla Mus Contemp Art, 68-
Memberships: Am Asn Mus; Asn Art Mus Dir; fel Royal Soc Art, London.
Mailing Address: 700 Prospect St, La Jolla, CA 92037.

TIFFANY, MARGUERITE BRISTOL
Painter, Weaver
Preferred Media: Oil.
b Syracuse, N Y.
Study & Training: Syracuse Univ, BS; Columbia Univ, MA; Newark Sch Fine & Appl Arts, cert; Parsons Sch, New York, N Y, cert; N Y Univ; and with Emile Walters, Iceland & William Zoroch, New York.
Exhibitions: N J State Ann, Montclair Mus, 33, 34, 35, 37; Am Womans Asn, New York, 41-42; Panhellenic House Asn, New York, 42-43; Ogunquit Art Ctr Ann, Maine, 41-70; Am Artistic Prof League Ann, Spring Lake, N J, 41-71; plus five one-man shows, N J.
Teaching: Prof art, Rutgers Univ, 25-40; William Paterson Col, 29-56; Fairleigh Dickinson Univ, 56-65.
Positions: Art Comt, N J chmn, Metrop Opera Guild, 52-58; state pres, Nat League Am Penwomen, 66-68; N J state pres, Assoc Handweavers, 68-70.
Awards: Cert, contrib art educ, Eastern Arts Asn, 60; hon mention ribbon, State Fedn Womens Clubs N J, 72.

Memberships: Am Artists Prof League, N J chap (corresp secy, 61-68); Paterson Art League (pres, 58-60); Fair Lawn Art Asn; Ridgewood Art Asn; Eastern Arts Asn (chmn speaker's conv, 40; exec bd, 44-48); plus others.
Publications: Auth, Art and picture study (monogr), N J Dept Educ, 30; Educ Mag (art issue), 2/46; contribr, Art education in principle and practice, 33; Art room planning guide, Dept Educ, Trenton, N J, 60-63; illusr, two articles, Newark Sunday News, 4/12 & 4/14/70.
Mailing Address: 330 E 33rd St, Paterson, NJ 07504.

TIFT, MARY LOUISE
Printmaker
Preferred Media: Graphics.
b Seattle, Wash, Jan 2, 13.
Study & Training: Univ Wash, BFA; Art Ctr Col Design; San Francisco State Col.
Work in Public Collections: Philadelphia Mus Art, Pa; Seattle Art Mus, Wash; Achenbach Print Collection, San Francisco Palace Legion of Honor; Bell Tel Co Ill Print & Drawing Collection, Chicago; Standard Oil Co Calif, San Francisco.
Exhibitions: First & second Nat Print Invitational, Fine Arts Gallery, San Diego, Calif, 69 & 71; Second Brit Biennale Prints, Yorkshire, Eng, 70; Fifth Int Triennal Colored Graphics, Grencehn, Switz, 70; Graphics 71, circulated by Smithsonian Inst; Fifth Int Print Biennale, Cracow, Poland, 72.
Teaching: Asst prof design, Calif Col Arts & Crafts, Oakland, 49-57.
Positions: Coordr design, San Francisco Art Inst, 57-60.
Awards: Purchase awards, Pratt Graphic Int Miniature Print Show, 68, Northwest Printmakers Int, 69 & Print Club Philadelphia, 69.
Memberships: Calif Soc Printmakers (coun mem, 70-72); Los Angeles Printmakers Soc; Print Club Philadelphia.
Mailing Address: 607 Chapman Dr, Corte Madera, CA 94925.

TIGERMAN, STANLEY
Painter, Architect
Preferred Media: Acrylics.
b Chicago, Ill, Sept 20, 30.
Study & Training: Mass Inst Technol, 48-49; Inst Design, 49-50; Yale Univ, BArch, 60 & MArch, 61.
Commissions: Modular structure, Metrop Structures, Chicago, 71.
Exhibitions: Soc Contemp Artists Show, Art Inst Chicago, Ill, 65; Eight Chicago Artists, Walker Art Ctr, Minneapolis, Minn, 65; one-man shows, Evanston Art Ctr, Ill, 69, Art Res Ctr, Kansas City, Mo, 69 & Springfield Arts Asn, Ill, 70.
Teaching: Prof archit & art, Univ Ill, Chicago Circle, 65-71.
Positions: Prin, Stanley Tigerman & Assocs, Chicago, 62-
Awards: Graham Found fel advan study fine arts, 65; honor awards, Nat Am Inst Architects & Housing & Urban Develop, 70 & Chicago Chap Am Inst Architects, 71.
Bibliography: R A M Stern (auth), New directions in American architecture, Braziller, 69; Faulkner & Ziegfield (auth), Art today, Holt, Rinehart & Winston, 69; Dahinden (auth), Urban structures of the future, Praeger, 72.
Memberships: Am Inst Architects; Yale Art Asn (past pres); Ill Arts Coun (archit adv comt, 68-69).
Publications: Contribr, Young architects in America, Zodiac Int, 64; contribr, Instant city, Archit Jour Hui, 66; contribr, City shape 21, Toshi Jutaku, Tokyo, 68; auth, Formal generators of structure, Leonardo, 68.
Mailing Address: 233 N Michigan Ave, Chicago, IL 60601.

TILLEY, LEWIS LEE
Painter
Preferred Media: Oils, Acrylics.
b Parrott, Ga, May 17, 21.
Study & Training: High Mus Sch Art, 37-39; Emory Univ, 37-39; Univ Ga, BFA, 42; Colorado Springs Fine Arts Ctr, with Boardman Robinson, Adolph Dehn & John Held, 42-45; Inst Allende, Mex, MFA, 68.
Work in Public Collections: Post Card No 2, Colorado Springs Fine Arts Ctr, Colo; Cañon City Art Ctr, Colo; State Fair Colo Collection; Ga Art Asn; Southern States Art League.
Commissions: Mural in bird house, Broadmoor Cheyenne Mountain Zoo, Colorado Springs, 58; dragon wall mural, Victor Hornbein House, Denver, Colo, 59; mural in bd dirs rm, First Nat Bank, Colorado Springs, 59; four polyester resin sculptures, Colorado Springs Eye Clin, 60; exterior wall mural, Horace Mann Jr H S, Colorado Springs, 62.
Exhibitions: Am Fedn Arts; Graphic Arts Chicago; Denver Ann & Biennial; Artists West of the Mississippi; Washington Cathedral Religious Exhib.
Teaching: Instr painting, life drawing & design, Colorado Springs Fine Arts Ctr, 45-51; assoc prof art, painting, graphic design & drawing, Southern Colo State Col, 65-

Positions: Producer & dir, Alexander Film Co, 58-62; communications media adv, U S Agency Int Develop, Ind Univ, 62-64.
Awards: First purchase award for oil, Cañon City Blossom Festival, 69; first purchase award for oil, Colo State Fair, 70.
Bibliography: Discovery No 49, Mod Photog, 58.
Art Interests: Film making.
Publications: Auth, History of writing & painting, 63; illusr, English with the twins, 63; illusr, History of medicine, 63; ed, The story of Nok culture, 63.
Mailing Address: 30 Mesa Rd, Colorado Springs, CO 80903.

TILLIM, SIDNEY
Painter
Preferred Media: Oils.
b Brooklyn, N Y, June 16, 25.
Study & Training: Syracuse Univ, BFA, 50.
Work in Public Collections: Michener Collection, Univ Tex, Austin; Ludwig Collection, Neue Galerie, Aachen, Ger; Weatherspoon Art Gallery, Univ N C, Greensboro; Mus Art, Ogunquit, Maine; Joseph H Hirshhorn Mus & Sculpture Garden.
Exhibitions: Contemp Realism In Figure & Landscape, Wadsworth Atheneum, Hartford, Conn, 64; Realism Now, Vassar Col Art Gallery, Poughkeepsie, N Y, 68; Aspects of New Realism, Milwaukee Art Ctr, 69; 22 Realists, 70 & Ann, 72, Whitney Mus Am Art.
Teaching: Instr art hist & drawing, Pratt Inst, 64-68; instr art hist & painting, Bennington Col, 66-
Positions: Contrib ed, Arts, 59-65; contrib ed, Artforum, 65-69.
Dealer: Richard Bellamy, c/o Noah Goldowsky Gallery, 1078 Madison Ave, New York, NY 10028.
Mailing Address: 166 E 96th St, New York, NY 10028.

TIMMAS, OSVALD
Painter
Preferred Media: Watercolors, Acrylics, Oils.
b Estonia, Sept 17, 19; Can citizen.
Study & Training: Tartu State Univ; Atelier Schs Tartu & Tallinn, Estonia, with Nicholas Kummits & Gunther Reindorff.
Work in Public Collections: London Art Mus, Ont; Art Gallery Hamilton; Art Gallery Windsor; Canton Art Inst, Ohio; Rodman Hall Art Ctr, St Catharines, Ont.
Exhibitions: Can Watercolors, Drawings & Prints, Nat Gallery Can, Ottawa, 66; Audubon Artists, New York, N Y, 66-69; Am Watercolor Soc, New York, 66, 67 & 69; Nat Acad Design, New York, 67, 68 & 71; Royal Can Acad Arts, Nat Gallery Can, 70; plus one-man shows.
Awards: Medal & award for creative aquarelle, Audubon Artists, 67 & 68; Major Award for Watercolor Painting, Coutts-Hallmark Co Can, 69 & 70; John Labatt Ltd Award, 71.
Bibliography: Anthony Ferry (auth), A floating world, 2/20/65 & It's now time for Timmas, 11/11/65, Toronto Star; Stevens (auth), Osvald Timmas, La Rev Mod, 11/66.
Memberships: Assoc Royal Can Acad Arts; Am Watercolor Soc; Can Soc Painters Watercolor (dir, 67-69); Ont Soc Artists (v pres, 71-).
Dealer: Merton Gallery, 68 Merton St, Toronto 7, Ont, Can; Gallerie Fore 405 Selkirk Ave, Winnipeg 4, Can.
Mailing Address: 776 Marlee Ave, Toronto 19, Ont, Can.

TIMMINS, WILLIAM FREDERICK
Painter, Illustrator
Preferred Media: Oils.
b Chicago, Ill.
Study & Training: Am Acad Art, Chicago; Art Stud League New York, with George Bridgman; Grand Cent Art Sch, New York, with Harvey Dunn & Mario Cooper.
Work in Public Collections: House of Four Winds, Calif Hist Bldg, Monterey.
Commissions: Mural, Independent Savings & Loan Asn, Salinas, Calif, 72; also many comns for pvt protraits & paintings.
Exhibitions: One-man show, Perry House Gallery, 69.
Memberships: Carmel Art Asn; Soc Western Artists.
Publications: Illusr, Boy Scout Handbook, 68 & Winnie the pooh, Western Publ, 68.
Dealers: Perry House Gallery, 201 Van Buren, Monterey, CA 93940; Carmel Valley Gallery, Carmel Valley, CA 93924.
Mailing Address: P O Box 5685, Carmel, CA 93921.

TING, WALASSE
Painter
b Shanghai, China, Oct 13, 29.
Work in Public Collections: Mus Mod Art, New York, N Y; Guggenheim Mus, New York; Carnegie Inst, Pittsburgh, Pa; Stedelijk Mus, Amsterdam, Holland; Israel Nat Mus, Jerusalem.
Exhibitions: Paul Facchetti, Paris, France, 54; Martha Jackson Gallery, 60; Galerie Birch, 63; Galerie ed France, 68; Lefebre Gallery, 71.

Awards: Guggenheim fel, 70.
Publications: Auth, My shit & my love, 61; auth, One cent life, 64; auth, Chinese moonlight, 67; auth, Hot & sour soup, 69; auth, Green banana, 71.
Dealer: Lefebre Gallery, 47 E 77th St, New York, NY 10028.
Mailing Address: 100 W 25th St, New York, NY 10001.

TINNING, GEORGE CAMPBELL
Painter
Preferred Media: Watercolors, Acrylics.
b Saskatoon, Sask, Feb 25, 10.
Study & Training: Elliot O'Hara Sch, Maine; Art Stud League New York.
Work in Public Collections: Nat Gallery Art, Ottawa, Ont, Can; Montreal Mus Fine Arts, P Q; Ford Motor Co, Dearborn, Mich; Charlottetown Art Mus, Prince Edward Island; Montreal Star, P Q.
Commissions: Mural on stair wall, Jenkins Valve Co, Lachine, Que, 60; mural, pres lounge, Bank Montreal, 61; murals, Ritz Carlton Hotel, Montreal, 67.
Teaching: Pvt classes.
Positions: War artist, hist sect, Can Army, 43-46.
Awards: Dow awards for watercolor, 42 & 48, Montreal Mus Fine Arts.
Memberships: Assoc Royal Can Acad Art; Can Soc Painters Watercolour.
Publications: Auth, Can Art, spring 49; auth & illusr, Lincoln Mercury times, 50-59.
Dealer: Waddington Galleries Inc, 1456 Sherbrooke St W, Montreal 109, P Q, Can.
Mailing Address: Apt 53, 1509 Sherbrooke St W, Montreal 109, P Q, Can.

TIRANA, ROSAMOND (MRS EDWARD CORBETT)
Painter
b New York, N Y, Jan 29, 10.
Study & Training: Swarthmore Col, BA, 31; London Sch Econs, 31-32; Univ Geneva, 31 & 32; painting with Bernice Cross, E R Rankine & Hans Hofmann.
Exhibitions: Corcoran Gallery Art, Washington, D C, 56-59 & 66; Provincetown Art Asn, Mass, 57-65; Art for Embassies, Nat Collection Fine Arts, 68, U S Embassy, Turkey, 69; Franz Bader Gallery, Washington, D C, 69; plus others.
Positions: For corresp, Chicago Daily News, London Clarion & Milwaukee Leader, 32-34.
Awards: Prizes, Lycee Mooiere, Paris, France, 24; Va Regional Exhib, 59; Washington Post Area Competition, 59.
Memberships: Am Fedn Arts.
Mailing Address: 3500 35th St N W, Washington, DC 20016.

TITTLE, GRANT HILLMAN
Printmaker, Designer
b Haleyville, Ala, Nov 21, 32.
Study & Training: Auburn Univ, BFA, with Maltby Sykes; Pratt Inst, MFA, with Walter Rogalski; also with Max Kahn, Chicago, Dolf Reiser, London & Henry Cliff, Bath, Eng.
Work in Public Collections: Univ Chicago, Ill; Alcoa Aluminum, Pan-Am Bldg, New York; Mint Mus, Charlotte, N C; Pratt Inst, Brooklyn, N Y.
Exhibitions: One-man shows, Metal Multiples & Medallions, Pratt Inst, 70 & E G Gallery, New York, 70; Sixth Ann Piedmont Graphics Exhib, Mint Mus, 70; Colorprint U S A Exhib, Tex Christian Univ, Lubbock, 71; Ga Artists, High Mus, Atlanta, 72.
Teaching: Tutor/lectr, lithography & design, Bath Acad Art, Corsham, Eng, 66-68; asst prof printmaking & design, Univ Ga, 70-
Positions: Designer, Sears Nat Display Dept, 56-58; art prod mgr, Sci Res Assoc, 58-60; assoc designer, Bud Donahue & Assocs, 62-65.
Awards: First purchase award in Sixth Graphics Ann, Mint Mus, 70.
Bibliography: A Stasik (ed), Artist proof, Pratt/New York Graphics Soc, 72; C Romano & J Ross (ed), Printmaking: techniques and innovations, McMillan, 72; Colorprint U S A 1971, Tex Christian Univ, 72.
Memberships: Col Art Asn Am; Exp Art & Technol.
Mailing Address: 140 Parkway Dr, Athens, GA 30601.

TOBEY, ALTON S
Painter, Lecturer
Preferred Media: Oils, Acrylics.
b Middletown, Conn, Nov 5, 14.
Study & Training: Yale Univ Sch Fine Arts, BFA, 37, MFA, 47.
Work in Public Collections: Two murals, Smithsonian Inst, Washington, D C; Jewish Mus, New York, N Y; Nat Acad Design Edwin Abbey Collection, N Y; Proj 400, Chadds Ford, Pa.
Commissions: Mural for Campfield Ave Libr, comn by Charles Goodwin, 37; mural for East Hartford Post Off, 38; Life of Gen MacArthur (six murals), Edwin Abbey Mural Fund for MacArthur

Mem, 65; two murals on anthrop, Smithsonian Mus Natural Hist, 67; fourteen murals on Am hist, comn by dir of Proj 14, Chadds Ford, Pa, 70.
Exhibitions: Conn Acad Fine Arts, 34-37; City Ctr Galleries, 50-53; Riverside Mus, 52-54; Norfolk Mus Arts & Sci, 66; Loeb Ctr, N Y Univ, 69-71.
Teaching: Instr & lectr styles, techniques & hist art, Yale Sch Fine Arts, 45-49; lectr hist art, City Col New York, 50-51.
Positions: Pres, Mamaroneck Art Guild; dir, Artists Equity New York, 70-; v pres, Nat Soc Mural Painters, 72-
Mailing Address: 296 Murray Ave, Larchmont, NY 10538.

TOBEY, MARK
Painter
Preferred Media: Oils, Tempera.
b Centerville, Wis, Dec 11, 90.
Study & Training: Art Inst Chicago; also with Teng Kwei, Shanghai.
Work in Public Collections: Seattle Art Mus, Wash; Metrop Mus Art, New York, N Y; Mus Mod Art, New York; Whitney Mus Am Art, New York; Boston Mus Fine Arts, Mass.
Commissions: Mural for libr at Olympia, Wash, 58; mural for libr, Wash State Univ, 62; mural for opera house, Seattle, Wash, 64.
Exhibitions: One-man shows, Seattle Art Mus, 35, 42 & 71, San Francisco Mus Art, 45, Whitney Mus Am Art, 51, Art Inst Chicago, 55 & Mus Arts Decoratifs, 61.
Teaching: Resident artist, Darlington Hall, Eng, 31-39.
Awards: Grand nat prize for painting, Venice Biennial, 58; award, Art in Am, 58; first prize for painting, Carnegie Int, 61.
Bibliography: Colette Roberts (auth), Mark Tobey, Grove, 60; Tobey, the world of a market, Univ Wash Press, 64; Wieland Schmied (auth), Tobey, Ed Pierre Tisne, Paris, 66.
Memberships: Am Acad Arts & Lett.
Mailing Address: c/o Willard Gallery, 29 E 72nd St, New York, NY 10021.

TOBIAS, ABRAHAM JOEL
Painter, Sculptor
Preferred Media: Plastics, Metals, Stones.
b Rochester, N Y, Nov 21, 13.
Study & Training: Cooper Union Art Sch, 30-31; Art Stud League New York, 31-33; Fed Art Proj, New York, 38-40.
Work in Public Collections: Brooklyn Mus, N Y; Los Angeles Co Mus Art, Calif; New York Pub Libr, N Y; Howard Univ, Washington, D C; Rochester Pub Libr, N Y.
Commissions: The Student (fresco mural), Howard Univ, Washington, D C, 45; two war Mem fresco panels, James Madison H S, Brooklyn, 52; acrylic mural, Domestic Rels Ct, Dept Pub Works, New York, 56; two plexiglass panels for entrance, Polytech Inst Brooklyn, 58; mosaic & terrazzo mural, Henrietta Szold Sch, New York Bd Educ, 60.
Exhibitions: Mus Mod Art, New York; San Francisco Mus, Calif; Brooklyn Mus, N Y; Adelphi Col; Archit League New York; plus many others including one-man shows.
Teaching: Lectr mural painting, Howard Univ, 45; artist-in-residence, Adelphi Univ, 47-57; lectr mural painting, Asn Am Cols Prog, 52 & 55.
Positions: Art dir, intelligence div, U S Air Forces, Washington, D C, 43-44; graphic designer, Off Strategic Serv, Washington, D C, 44-45; instr artist, Polytech Inst Brooklyn, 70-
Awards: Post off mural comn, Nat Fine Arts Comn, 40; award for mural painting, Archit League New York, 52.
Bibliography: Joseph L Young (auth), Mosaics: principles & practice, Reinhold, 64; Lawrence N Jensen (auth), Synthetic painting media, Prentice Hall, 64; Louis Botto (auth), In the know, Look Mag, 69.
Publications: Auth, Mural painting, 2/57 & auth, A mural painting for science & technology, 3/69, Am Artist Mag.
Mailing Address: 98-51 65th Ave, Rego Park, Queens, NY 11374.

TOBIAS, JULIUS
Sculptor, Instructor
Preferred Media: Concrete.
b New York, N Y, Aug 27, 15.
Study & Training: Atelier Fernand Leger, Paris, 49-52.
Work in Public Collections: Pasadena Mus Art, Calif.
Exhibitions: Pa Acad Fine Arts, Philadelphia, 58; Mus Mod Art Traveling Exhib, Tokyo, 59; New Eng Exhib, Silvermine, Conn, 60; Whitney Mus Am Art Sculpture Ann, 68; Indianapolis Mus Art, Ind, 70.
Teaching: Instr painting, New York Inst Technol, 66-71; instr sculpture, Queens Col(N Y), 71-
Awards: N Y Cult Coun Found Creative Artists Pub Serv Prog grant, 71; Guggenheim fel, 72-73.
Bibliography: Corrine Robbins (auth), Six artists and the new extended vision, Arts Mag, 9-10/65; Barbara Rose (auth), A gallery without walls, Art Am, 3-4/68; James R Mellow (auth), Two sculptors worlds apart, New York Times, 1/31/71.

Dealer: Max Hutchinson Gallery, 127 Greene St, New York, NY 10012.
Mailing Address: 9 Great Jones St, New York, NY 10012.

TODD, MICHAEL CULLEN
Sculptor, Painter
Preferred Media: Steel, Aluminum.
b Omaha, Nebr, June 20, 35.
Study & Training: Univ Notre Dame, BFA, 57; Univ Calif, Los Angeles, MA, 59.
Work in Public Collections: Whitney Mus Am Art, New York, N Y; Los Angeles Co Mus Art, Los Angeles, Calif; Southwestern Col, Chula Vista, Calif.
Exhibitions: Four Whitney Mus Am Art Sculpture Ann, 64-70; Sculpture of 60's, Los Angeles Co Mus Art, 65 & Philadelphia Mus, 66; Living Am Art, Maeght Found, France, 71; var exhibs large scale sculpture, Lippincott Corp.
Teaching: Instr sculpture, Bennington Col, 66-68; asst prof sculpture, Univ Calif, San Diego, 68-
Awards: Woodrow Wilson fel, 59; Fulbright fel, France, 61.
Bibliography: T Garver (auth), Recent sculpture 1968-70, Univ Calif, Los Angeles & Salk Inst, 69; L Goldberg (auth), Sculpture, Circle series, 1970-72, Art Gallery, Calif State Univ, Fullerton, 72.
Memberships: Mus Mod Art; Whitney Mus Am Art; Fine Art Gallery, San Diego.
Mailing Address: 172 Neptune St, Encinitas, CA 92024.

TOIGO, DANIEL JOSEPH
Painter, Educator
Preferred Media: Oils, Watercolors.
b Albia, Iowa, May 20, 12.
Study & Training: Apprenticeship with Herb Olsen, Dale Nichols & Ben Stahl; Chouinard Art Inst, with William Moore.
Work in Public Collections: Paintings, State Capitol Bldg, Sacramento, Calif, San Diego Art Inst, Calif, Santa Paula Chamber of Commerce, Calif & Ahmanson Collection, Los Angeles, Calif.
Exhibitions: Los Angeles All City Art Festival, 67-71; Frye Mus, Seattle, Wash, 68; Santa Paula Ann Art Exhib, 68-71; Am Artists Prof League Grand Nat, 68-72; Calif State Fair, Sacramento, 70-71.
Teaching: Private instr landscape, 45-
Awards: Los Angeles All City Purchase Award, Howard Ahmanson, 68 & 69; San Diego Art Inst Award, Walter Scott, 68; Am Artists Prof League Award, 71.
Bibliography: Artist—Dan Toigo (film), Chico State Col, 70.
Memberships: Fel Am Artists Prof League; Am Inst Fine Arts; Calif Art Club; San Gabriel Fine Arts Asn (dir, 67-); Valley Artists Guild.
Mailing Address: 5278 Ellenwood Dr, Los Angeles, CA 90041.

TOLGESY, VICTOR
Sculptor
Preferred Media: Steel.
b Miskolc, Hungary, Aug 22, 28; Can citizen.
Work in Public Collections: Nat Gallery Can, Ottawa; Etherington Art Ctr, Queen's Univ, Kingston, Ont; Charlottetown Confedn Art Gallery, Prince Edward Island, Can; Waterloo Univ, Ont; Willistead Art Gallery, Windsor, Ont.
Commissions: Hungarian freedom monument, Can-Hungarian Fedn, Toronto, 66; sculpture for Expo '67, 67; sculpture, Jeffery Hall, Queen's Univ, 71; sculptures, Ottawa Pub Libr, 72.
Exhibitions: Sculpture 67, Toronto, 67; Royal Can Acad Show, 67 & Montreal & Charlottetown, 71; 11th Winnipeg Show, 68; Ont Soc Artists 100th Ann Exhib, Toronto, 72.
Awards: Can Coun sr fel, 65; sculpture prize, Royal Can Acad, Waterloo Univ, 67; sculpture prize, Soc Can Artists, 71.
Memberships: Assoc Royal Can Acad Art.
Mailing Address: 90 Kirby Rd, Ottawa, Ont, Can.

TOLPO, CARL (AXEL EDWARD)
Sculptor, Painter
Preferred Media: Plaster, Oils.
b Ludington, Mich, Dec 22, 01.
Study & Training: Augustana Col; Univ Chicago; Art Inst Chicago.
Work in Public Collections: Heroic Lincoln Head Bronze, Lincoln Mus, Washington, D C; Grand Canyon of the Yellowstone, Washington, D C; plus many others.
Commissions: 14 oil portraits of gov, lt gov, senate pres & speakers, State of Ill, 55-72; plus many pvt commissions, 29-
Exhibitions: Nat Sculpture Soc, New York, N Y, 67; plus many others.
Teaching: Lectr Fine Use of the Creative Order, 69.
Mailing Address: Sky Ridge Rd, Rte 2, Box 180A, Stockton, IL 61085.

TOLPO, LILY
Sculptor, Painter
Preferred Media: Plaster, Oils, Acrylics.
b Chicago, Ill, Sept 13, 17.
Study & Training: Chicago Acad Fine Arts.
Commissions: Comns from educators in pub schs, 64-70; gigantic chandelier sculpture in Rotunda of New Lake Co Court House Complex, Waukegan, Ill, 70; plus many pvt comns.
Exhibitions: One-woman shows, Former All-Ill Soc Fine Arts, 41 & Freeport Country Club, Ill, 72.
Art Interests: Noted for original technique of biographical portrait painting.
Mailing Address: Sky Ridge Rd, Rte 2, Box 180A, Stockton, IL 61085.

TOMLINSON, FLORENCE KIDDER
Painter, Instructor
Preferred Media: Oils, Watercolors.
b Austin, Ill.
Study & Training: Colt Sch Art, dipl; Stillwater Art Colony; Univ Minn Summer Sch; Univ Wis, teachers cert; also with Ralph Pearson, Frederick Taubes & Myra Werten.
Work in Public Collections: Milwaukee Art Inst, Wis; lithograph, Nat League Am Pen Women, Washington, D C; two oil paintings, Oshkosh Paper Co, Wis; oil painting, Madison Pub Libr, Wis; plus pvt collections.
Commissions: History of Cooperation (mural in oil), Midland Coop, Inc, Minneapolis, Minn, 48; Trade & Industry (mural in oil), Madison Tech Col, Madison, 55; plus many pvt commissions.
Exhibitions: Nat Exhib Prints, Libr of Cong, Washington, D C, six from 45-54; Northwest Printmakers 18th Int, Seattle, Wash, 46; Walker Art Gallery Regional Exhib, Minneapolis, 46; Soc Am Graphic Artists, Kennedy Galleries, New York, N Y, 53; Wisconsin Painters & Sculptors, Milwaukee Art Inst, Wis, 61.
Teaching: Instr figure & portrait painting & design, Madison Adult Vocational Sch, days & eve, 30-62; instr art, Shorewood Sch, 40-41; instr drawing, Univ Wis Summer Art Tour Europe, 61.
Awards: Purchase award for Eve (wood engraving), Milwaukee Art Inst, 44; award for Sharkies (oil painting), Wis Salon Art, 56; first award for Dreams (lithograph), Nat League Am Pen Women, 64.
Bibliography: Al Sessler (auth), The Tomlinson exhibition, 52 & Elizabeth Gould (auth), A thing about clowns, 68, Wis State J; Frank Custer (auth), Mrs Tomlinson's record, Capitol Times, 11/18/61; Dorish Goodhue (auth), About our cover, Pen Woman, 1/69.
Memberships: Artists Equity Asn; Wis Painters & Sculptors; Madison Art Asn (bd mem & chmn tours, 58-61); hon mem Madison Art Guild (pres, 45-47); Nat League Am Pen Women (pres Madison br, 52-54, state art chmn, 55, state pres, 66-68).
Publications: Illusr & contribr, Design in nature's silhouettes, Country Life in Am, 39; illusr & contribr, Wood engravings, Wis Hort, 44; illusr, Am Bee J, 48 & 49; illusr & contribr, Block prints are fun, Nature Mag, 56; contribr, House & Garden.
Mailing Address: 703 Glenway St, Madison, WI 53711.

TOMPKINS, ALAN
Painter, Educator
Preferred Media: Oils.
b New Rochelle, N Y, Oct 29, 07.
Study & Training: Columbia Univ, BA; Yale Univ, BFA.
Commissions: Mural paintings comn by U S Treas Dept for post off at Indianapolis, Ind, 36, Martinsville, Ind, 37 & Boone, N C, 40; mural painting, Gen Elec Co, Bridgeport, Conn, 44; mural painting, Cent Baptist Church, Hartford, Conn, 58.
Exhibitions: Ind Artists Ann, 37-38; Art Inst Chicago Ann, 38; Conn Acad Ann, 52-71.
Teaching: Instr painting, Cooper Union Art Sch, 38-43; lectr painting, Columbia Univ, 46-51; prof painting & art hist, Univ Hartford, 51-
Positions: Dir, Hartford Art Sch, Univ Hartford, 57-69; comnr, Fine Arts Comn, 59-69; v chancellor, Univ Hartford, 60-
Awards: First prize for painting, 68-70, Conn Acad.
Memberships: Conn Acad (v pres, 70-72); Conn Watercolor Soc.
Research: Twentieth century art.
Mailing Address: 11 Milburn Dr, Bloomfield, CT 06002.

TONER, PAUL
Art Dealer
b New York, N Y, July 22, 48.
Study & Training: State Univ N Y Stony Brook Inst Fine Arts.
Positions: Dir, John Weber Gallery, 71-
Specialty of Gallery: Minimal sculpture; conceptual art.
Mailing Address: 420 W Broadway, New York, NY 10013.

TONEY, ANTHONY
Painter, Educator
Preferred Media: Oils.
b Gloversville, N Y, June 28, 13.
Study & Training: Syracuse Univ, BFA; teachers col, Columbia Univ, MA & EdD.
Work in Public Collections: Whitney Mus Am Art, New York; Nat Acad Design, New York; Syracuse Univ, N Y; Univ Ill, Urbana; St Lawrence Univ, Canton, N Y.
Commissions: Murals, Bowne Hall, 68 & 6 panels, Brockway Cafeteria, St Mary's Dorm, Roslyn, N Y, 71; Mrs Mollie Bergman, 72 & Diana Lucas, New York, N Y, 72.
Exhibitions: Carnegie Inst, 49; Whitney Mus Am Art Ann, 50-60; Pa Acad Fine Arts Ann, 50-68; Audubon Artists Ann, 55-72; Nat Acad Design Ann, 60-72; plus others.
Teaching: Instr creative art, Hofstra Univ, 52-55; instr creative painting, New Sch Social Res, 52-; instr creative painting, Five Towns Music & Art Found, 52-
Awards: Ranger Fund Purchase Award, Nat Acad Design, 66; Childe Hassam Purchase Award, Nat Inst Arts & Lett, 68; medal of honor, Audubon Artists, 68.
Memberships: Nat Acad Design; Audubon Artists (mem bd, 65-); Nat Soc Mural Painters; Artists Equity Asn (mem bd dirs, 71-); Int Inst Arts & Lett.
Publications: Contribr, article, In: Reality, 55; contribr, Tune of the calliope, 57; ed, 150 masterpieces of drawing, 65; auth, Creative painting and drawing, 66.
Dealer: ACA Gallery, 25 E 73rd St, New York, NY 10021.
Mailing Address: 16 Hampton Pl, Katonah, NY 10536.

TOOKER, GEORGE
Painter
b Brooklyn, N Y, Aug 5, 20.
Study & Training: Phillips Acad, grad, 38; Harvard Univ, AB, 42; Art Stud League New York, 43-44, with Reginald Marsh, Kenneth Hayes Miller & Harry Sternberg.
Work in Public Collections: Whitney Mus Am Art, Metrop Mus Art & Mus Mod Art, New York, N Y; Walker Art Ctr, Minneapolis, Minn; Johnson Collection, Smithsonian Inst, Washington, D C.
Teaching: Instr, Art Stud League New York, 65-68.
Awards: Nat Inst Arts & Lett grant, 60.
Memberships: Nat Acad Design, New York.
Mailing Address: c/o Frank K M Rehn, Inc, 655 Madison Ave, New York, NY 10021.

TOPOL, ROBERT MARTIN
Collector
b New York, N Y, Mar 9, 25.
Collection: Frescos, oils & sculptures.
Dealer: Greer Gallery, E 53rd St, New York, NY.
Mailing Address: 825 Orienta Ave, Mamaroneck, NY 10543.

TORAL, MARIA TERESA
Engraver, Designer
Preferred Media: Inks, Oils, Collage.
b Madrid, Spain.
Study & Training: Escuela Artes y Oficios, Madrid; Taller Ciudadela, Inst Nac Bellas Artes, Mex; also with Guillermo Silva Santamaría & Yukio Fukasawa.
Work in Public Collections: Mus Arte Mod, Mex; Mus Arte Contemporáneo, Chile; Univ Mus, Tex; Living Arts Found, New York, N Y; Joods Historisch Mus, Amsterdam.
Exhibitions: Bienal de Chile, 63; Salón del OPIC, Mex, 66; Exposición Solar, Inst Bellas Artes, Mex, 68; Salón de Grabado, Salon Plastica Mexicana, 69, 70 & 72; Int Miniature Prints Exhib, Pratt Graphics Ctr, New York, 69 & 71.
Bibliography: Margarita Nelken (auth), Siete anos de grabado de María Teresa Toral, Acta Politecnica, 68.
Memberships: Salón Plástica Mexicana; Pratt Ctr Contemp Printmaking.
Dealer: Galería Misrachi, Génova 20, México D F, Mex.
Mailing Address: Avenida México 167-F, México 11 DF, Mex.

TORBERT, MARGUERITE BIRCH
Designer, Writer
b Faribault, Minn, Sept 30, 12.
Study & Training: Univ Minn, BA; Univ Iowa, MA.
Positions: Cur of design & ed, Design Quart, Walker Art Ctr, 50-63; film dir, Minnimath, Nat Sci Found, 65-70; interior designer, Int Design Ctr, 72-
Mailing Address: 2116 Irving Ave S, Minneapolis, MN 55405.

TORMEY, JAMES
Painter, Designer
Preferred Media: Oils.
b New York, N Y.
Study & Training: Pratt Inst; Art Stud League New York, with William Zorach, five yrs.

Exhibitions: Nat Acad Design, New York, 69-72; Allied Artists Am, New York, 71; Audubon Artists, New York, 71-72; Gallery Madison 90, New York.
Mailing Address: c/o Gallery Madison 90, 1248 Madison Ave, New York, NY 10028.

TORREANO, JOHN FRANCIS
Painter, Lecturer
Preferred Media: Acrylics.
b Flint, Mich, Aug 17, 41.
Study & Training: Cranbrook Acad Art, BFA, 63; Ohio State Univ, MFA, 67; also with Robert King & Hoyt L Sherman.
Work in Public Collections: Whitney Mus Am Art, New York, N Y; Larry Aldrich Mus Contemp Art, Ridgefield, Conn; Michener Collection, Univ Tex.
Exhibitions: Am Fedn Arts Traveling Exhib; Erasable Structures, Visual Arts Gallery, New York; Ann Exhib Contemp Am Painting, 69 & Lyrical Abstraction, 71, Whitney Mus Am Art; Butler Inst Am Art, Youngstown, Ohio, 72.
Teaching: Asst prof painting, Univ S Dak, 67-68; instr painting, Sch Visual Arts, 69-70; vis artist, Art Inst Chicago, 72.
Bibliography: C Ratcliff (auth), New York Lett, Art Int, 70 & Painterly vs painted, Art News Ann, 71; B Richardson (auth), California review, Arts Mag, 71.
Mailing Address: 103 Franklin St, New York, NY 10013.

TORRES, JOHN, JR
Sculptor, Art Administrator
Preferred Media: Stone.
b Bronx, N Y, Mar 7, 39.
Study & Training: Md State Col, 56-57; Mich State Univ, 58-59; New Sch Soc Res, 59-62; Art Stud League New York, 59-68; Brooklyn Mus Sch, 63-64; R I Sch Design, BFA, 72; also with Arnold Prince, Seymour Lipton & William Zorach.
Exhibitions: Whitney Mus Am Art, New York, N Y, 71; Nat Collection Fine Art, Smithsonian Inst, Washington, D C, 71; one-man shows, R I Sch Design, 70 & Guest of Govt Mex, 70.
Teaching: Lectr Afro art hist, Brown Univ; assoc sculpture, R I Sch Design.
Positions: Dir Vt Proj, Art Stud League New York; admin asst to dean, R I Sch Design.
Awards: Ford Found grant for Vt summer; Edward MacDowell Colony fel; Nat Endowment grant.
Bibliography: Patterson (auth), Encyclopedia of black cultural contributions; Fax (auth), Seventeen black artists, Dodd; article, In: Sepia Mag, 7/68.
Memberships: Art Stud League New York (bd mem); Afro Art Ctr (bd mem); Salmagundi Club.
Mailing Address: 2 College St, Providence, RI 02903.

TOULIS, VASILIOS (APOSTOLOS)
Printmaker, Painter
b Clewiston, Fla, Mar 24, 31.
Study & Training: Univ Fla, BDes, with Fletcher Martin & Carl Holty; Pratt Inst, BFA, with Richard Lindner, Fritz Eichenberg, Jacob Landau & Walter Rogalski.
Work in Public Collections: U S State Dept, Washington, D C; Mus Arte Mod, Mexico City, Mex; Caravan House, New York, N Y.
Commissions: Portfolio of prints, Ctr for Contemp Printmaking, 68.
Exhibitions: Brooklyn Mus, N Y, 66; Fleischcer Mem, Philadelphia, Pa, 66; Mus Arte Mod, Mexico City, 67; Int Miniature Print Exhib, 68; New Paltz Nat Print Exhib, 68; plus others.
Teaching: Lect, Serigraphic Printmaking, Univ R I, 67 & Pratt Inst seminar, 69; head graphic workshops, Pratt Inst, 66-, instr printmaking, 69-71, asst prof & head undergrad printmaking, 71-
Positions: Printmaking adv to dir, Hudson River Mus, New York.
Awards: Tiffany Found grant in printmaking, 67.
Memberships: Am Asn Univ Prof.
Mailing Address: 235 E 31st St, New York, NY 10010.

TOUSIGNANT, CLAUDE
Painter, Instructor
b Montreal, P Q, Dec 23, 32.
Study & Training: Sch Art & Design, Montreal; Acad Ranson, Paris, France.
Work in Public Collections: Nat Gallery Can; Phoenix Art Mus, Ariz; Larry Aldrich Mus, Ridgefield, Conn; York Univ; Mus Contemp Art, Montreal & Quebec; plus others.
Exhibitions: Solomon R Guggenheim Mus, New York, N Y, 65; Can Art, Paris, Rome & Brussels; Lausanne, Switz, 68; Mass Inst Technol, Cambridge; Washington Gallery Mod Art; plus many other group exhibs & 13 one-man shows.
Teaching: Instr design, Sch Art & Design, Montreal.
Positions: Pres, Calude Tousignant, Inc.
Awards: Prize, Salon de la Jeune Peinture, 62 & Centennial Exhib, 67.
Memberships: Artistes Prof de Montreal; Royal Can Acad Arts.
Mailing Address: 3684 St Laurent, Montreal, P Q, Can.

TOVISH, HAROLD
Sculptor
Preferred Media: Bronze.
b New York, N Y, July 31, 21.
Study & Training: Columbia Univ, 40-43; Ossip Zadkine Sch Sculpture, Paris, France, 49-50; Acad Grande Chaumière, Paris, 50-51.
Work in Public Collections: Whitney Mus Am Art, New York; Boston Mus Fine Art, Mass; Philadelphia Mus Art, Pa; Art Inst Chicago, Ill; Mus Mod Art, New York.
Commissions: Epitaph (sculpture), State of Hawaii, 70.
Exhibitions: 28th Venice Biennial, Italy, 56; Carnegie Int, 58; Recent Sculpture: U S A, Mus Mod Art, New York, 59; Whitney Mus Am Art Ann, 66; Guggenheim Int Award Exhib, Solomon R Guggenheim Mus, 68; plus others including one-man shows.
Teaching: Asst prof sculpture & drawing, Univ Minn, 51-54; vis prof sculpture, Univ Hawaii, 64-70; prof sculpture & drawing, Boston Univ, 71-
Awards: Grant, Am Inst Arts & Lett, 60 & 71; sculptor-in-residence, Am Acad, Rome, 66; Guggenheim fel, 67.
Bibliography: H Harvard Arneson (auth), New talent, Art in Am, 54 & Harold Tovish (catalogue), Watson Gallery, 67.
Memberships: Boston Visual Artists Union.
Dealer: Terry Dintenfass, Inc, 18 E 67th St, New York, NY 10021.
Mailing Address: 164 Rawson Rd, Brookline, MA 02146.

TOWN, HAROLD BARLING
Painter, Writer
b Toronto, Ont, June 13, 24.
Study & Training: Ont Col Art, grad, 44; hon LHD, York Univ, 66.
Work in Public Collections: Tate Gallery, London, Eng; Mus Mod Art, New York, N Y; Stedelijk Mus, Amsterdam, Holland; Solomon R Guggenheim Mus, New York; Nat Gallery Can.
Commissions: Mural on canvas, Ont Hydro Comn, St Lawrence Seaway Power Proj, 57; decorative exterior enamel frieze, North York Pub Libr, Toronto, 59; two part mural & sculptural screen, Toronto Int Airport, Malton, Can Govt, 62; mural & collage, Tel Bldg, Toronto, 64; mural on canvas, Queens Park Proj, Ont Govt, 69.
Exhibitions: Sixth São Paulo Biennial, 61; Cezanne & Structure in Modern Painting, Guggenheim Mus, 63; Documenta, Kassel, Ger, 64; Can Govt Pavilion, Expo '67, Can, 67 & Expo '70, Osaka, Japan, 70; one-man shows, Venice Biennial, Italy, 56, 64 & 72.
Positions: Mem bd gov, Ont Art Col, 71.
Awards: Fel, Inst Cult Hispanica, Arte de Am y Espana, Madrid, 63; medal serv, Order Can, 68.
Bibliography: Herbert Read (auth), A concise history of modern painting, Praeger, 59; J Russel Harper (auth), Painting in Canada, Univ Toronto Press, 66; R Fulford (auth), The multiplicity of Harold Town, Arts Can, 4/71.
Memberships: Royal Can Acad.
Publications: Illusr, Love where the nights are long, 62; auth, Enigmas, 64; co-auth, Drawings of Harold Town, 69; auth, Silent stars, sound stars, film stars, 71.
Dealer: Mazelow Gallery, 3463 Yonge St, Toronto 319, Ont, Can.
Mailing Address: 9 Castel Frank Crescent, Toronto 5, Ont, Can.

TOWNLEY, HUGH
Sculptor, Printmaker
Preferred Media: Wood, Concrete.
b Lafayette, Ind, Feb 6, 23.
Study & Training: Univ Wis, 46-48; also with Ossip Zadkine, Paris, 48-49; London Co Coun Arts & Crafts, 49-50.
Work in Public Collections: Mus Mod Art; Whitney Mus Am Art; Boston Mus Fine Arts; Fogg Mus Art, Harvard Univ; Los Angelles Co Mus Art.
Commissions: Cast concrete reliefs & archit walls, Old Stone Bank, Bristol, R I, 65; wood relief, Bristol Hosp, Conn, 69; three concrete pieces, Class of 65, Brown Univ, Providence, R I, 70; three hanging wood sculptures, Retail Planning Corp, Nashville, Tenn, 71; three concrete pieces, State of Ky Comprehensive Training Ctr, Somerset, Ky, 72.
Exhibitions: New Talent Show, Mus Mod Art, 55; Carnegie Inst Biennial, 58; Am Painting & Sculpture, Univ Ill, 61 & 63; Ann Drawings & Sculpture, Whitney Mus Am Art, 62 & 63; 65th Am Painting & Sculpture Exhib, Art Inst Chicago, 64.
Teaching: Instr sculpture & drawing, Layton Sch Art, Milwaukee, Wis, 51-56; asst prof sculpture, Beloit Col, 56-57; asst prof sculpture & drawing, Boston Univ, 57-61; prof art, Brown Univ, 61-; vis prof, Univ Calif, Berkeley, 61; vis lectr, Harvard Univ, 67; vis prof, Univ Calif, Santa Barbara, 68; vis lectr, Ft Wright Col, 71.
Awards: Grant for creative work in art, Nat Inst Arts & Lett, 67; artist fel, Tamarind Lithography Workshop, 69; Gov Award, State of R I Coun Arts, 72.
Bibliography: Frank Getlein (auth), article, In: Art Am, 12/56.

Dealer: Graphics Gallery, 1 Embarcadero Ctr, San Francisco, CA 94111.
Mailing Address: 1 Resolute Lane, Bristol, RI 02809.

TOWNSEND, MARVIN J
Cartoonist
Preferred Media: Inks.
b Kansas City, Mo, July 2, 15.
Study & Training: Kansas City Art Inst; Col Com Art Sch.
Work in Public Collections: Syracuse Univ Permanent Collection, N Y.
Awards: Cert of merit, Dict Int Biog.
Publications: Strips, gag cartoons & illus for trade, business & prof mags, 41-; auth, Bert (cartoon strip), Nat Safety News, 58-; auth, Moontoons jokes & riddles, 70; auth, Ghostly ghastly cartoons, 71.
Mailing Address: 631 W 88th St, Kansas City, MO 64114.

TRACY, (LOIS) BARTLETT
Painter, Writer
Preferred Media: Acrylics, Oils.
b Jackson, Mich.
Study & Training: Rollins Col, 29; with Hans Hofmann, 45-46; Mich State Univ, MA, 58; New Col Workshop, 65, with Balcomb Greene, Afro, James Brooks, Marca-Relli & Sid Solomon.
Work in Public Collections: Air & Space Mus, Smithsonian Inst, Washington, D C; Norton Gallery Art, Palm Beach, Fla; Univ Va, Charlottesville; Univ N C, Chapel Hill; Southeastern Col, Univ Ky.
Exhibitions: Many exhibs, Nat Asn Women Artists, New York, 40-60; many Fla Artists Group Traveling Shows, 40-72; Assoc Artists N C Traveling Shows, 60-63; Audubon Artists, New York; Southeastern Shows, Atlanta, Ga; plus others.
Teaching: Instr, Exten, Univ Va, 52-59 & 64-65; head dept art, Clinch Valley Col, 53-58; head dept art, Southeastern Col, Univ Ky, 64-66; head dept art, Edison Jr Col, Ft Myers, Fla, 68-
Positions: Pres, N H Art Asn; mem bd, Nat Asn Women Artists, Pen & Brush & Assoc Artists N C.
Awards: First award, Fla Artists Group, 68; Watercolor award, Southeastern Ann, High Mus Art; gold medal, New York World's Fair, State of Fla; plus others.
Bibliography: Cosmic artist, Yankee, 7/49; Bartlett Tracy, N H Profiles, 4/52.
Memberships: Am Asn Univ Prof; Fla Artists Group; Sarasota Art Asn; Galerie Int New York; Int Fine Arts Gallery, Fort Meyers.
Publications: Auth, Painting principles and practices, 65, 67, 69 & 71; auth, The art of art.
Dealers: Center Street Gallery, Winter Park, FL 32789; Fine Arts Gallery, Fort Meyers, FL 33302.
Mailing Address: 580 Artist Ave, Englewood, FL 33533.

TRAHER, WILLIAM HENRY
Painter, Lecturer
Preferred Media: Acrylics.
b Rock Springs, Colo, Apr 6, 08.
Study & Training: Nat Acad Design, 30-33; Yale Univ Sch Fine Art, 38-39.
Work in Public Collections: Diorama backgrounds, Denver Mus Natural Hist.
Commissions: Cole Jr High, Denver, Colo, 35 & De Witt Ark Post Off, 41, U S Treas Dept; cloud recognition mural, Williams Air Force Field, Ariz, 43; wilderness murals, Columbia Savings & Loan, Pueblo, Colo, 68; four landscape murals, Saint Louis Arch, Nat Park Serv, 70; plus twenty-two dioramas.
Exhibitions: Fifth Int Exhib Lithography & Wood Engraving, Art Inst Chicago, 36; New Horizons in American Art, Mus Mod Art, New York, N Y, 36; Second Nat Exhib Am Art, Munic Art Comt, New York, 37; Fine Art in Advertising, Art Dir Club, New York, 50; Surrealism, exhib from Mus Mod Art, Denver Art Mus, 62.
Positions: Art dir, Philip H Gray Advert Agency, 45-47; artist & researcher, Jeppesen Map Co, Denver, 52-53; tech illusr, Lowry Air Force Base, Denver, 53-54; chief artist, Denver Mus Natural Hist, 54-
Awards: Purchase prize, Penny Art Fund, Colo Fedn Woman's Clubs, 36; second nat exhib, Beaux Arts Inst Design, 38; medal for originality, Sixth Southwest Int Exhib, 55.
Bibliography: D Bear (auth), Some younger artists of Colorado, Parnassus, 4/37; J Devran (auth), Studio in a cigarette case, Rocky Mountain Life, 1/48; D Evans (auth), A maker of visions, Denver Mag, 6/65.
Memberships: Denver Art Mus (bd trustees, 50-53); hon life mem Denver Artists' Guild (pres, 50-52); Int Platform Asn.
Publications: Illusr, Stars & men, Bobbs, New York & Arnolds, London, 39; illusr, Wyoming design, state series, Container Corp, 49; illusr, Index of American design, Christensen, 54; illusr, U S Golf Asn Ann, 60; auth, The artist cornered, Photog Soc Am J, 65.
Mailing Address: 2331 Niagara St, Denver, CO 80207.

TRAUERMAN, MARGY ANN
Painter, Instructor
Preferred Media: Watercolors.
b Sioux Falls, S Dak.
Study & Training: Iowa State Univ, BFA; Am Acad Art; Art Stud League New York, with Jacob Getlar Smith.
Exhibitions: Am Watercolor Soc Ann, 53-68; Pa Acad Fine Arts Ann, 53 & 61; N Y Figurative Painting, New York & traveling exhib, 71; one-man shows, Chatham Col, Pittsburgh, Pa, 61, Patrons of Art, McAllen, Tex, 71 & 1st Gallery, 72.
Teaching: Instr art, Art & Design H S, New York, 52-
Awards: Hon mention, Knickerbocker Artists Ann, 57; award, 67 & medal, 68, Painters & Sculptors Soc N J.
Bibliography: David Loeffler Smith (auth), Celebrated women artists, 1/62 & Heritage of the thirties, 10/62, Am Artist.
Memberships: Soc Painters & Sculptors N J; Am Watercolor Soc.
Dealer: 1st St Gallery, 118 Prince St, New York, NY 10012.
Mailing Address: 2 W 67th St, New York, NY 10023.

TRAVERS, GWYNETH MABEL
Graphic Artist
b Kingston, Ont, Apr 6, 11.
Study & Training: Queen's Univ, BA, 33; Queen's Summer Sch; also with Andre Bider, Ralph Allen & George Swinton.
Work in Public Collections: Acadia Univ, Wolfsville, N S; Nat Gallery Can, Ottawa; Queen's Univ, Kingston; Montreal Mus Fine Arts, P Q; Winnipeg Art Gallery, Man.
Exhibitions: Can Painter-Etchers & Engravers, Toronto, Ont, 57-70; Winnipeg Show, Man, 58-60; Nat Gallery Can Biennial, Ottawa, 58 & 71; Agnes Etherington Art Centre, Queen's Univ, Kingston, 60-69 & one-man show woodblock prints, 72; Brockville I O D E Invitational, 69 & 71.
Awards: Reid award, Can Painter-Etchers & Engravers, 58; Dept Educ, P Q, 63 & first prize in graphics, 65, Expos Provincial.
Mailing Address: 234 Albert St, Kingston, Ont, Can.

TRAVIS, OLIN (HERMAN)
Painter, Lecturer
Preferred Media: Oils.
b Dallas, Tex, Nov 15, 88.
Study & Training: Art Inst Chicago, five yrs.
Work in Public Collections: Tex Fine Arts Mus, Austin; Highland Park Art Mus; Dallas Mus Fine Arts; also many portraits & landscapes in pvt collections.
Commissions: Eutra, East Texas Rm, Hall of State, Dallas; Love Field Airport, Tex; habitat backgrounds for Dallas Mus Natural Hist & Corpus Christi Mus, Tex.
Exhibitions: San Francisco Nat, Calif; plus many other group & one-man shows including New York, N Y, Saint Louis, Mo, Milwaukee, Wis, Houston, Dallas & Abilene, Tex & Okla Univ.
Teaching: Instr art, San Antonio Art Inst, Tex; instr art, Austin Col, Sherman, Tex.
Positions: Founder & dir, Dallas Art Inst, 24-44; dir, Dallas Art Asn, eight yrs.
Awards: Gold medal for portraiture, Art Inst Chicago Sch; first landscape award, Southern States Art League, Memphis, Tenn; plus many others.
Mailing Address: 8343 Santa Clara Dr, Dallas, TX 75218.

TREADWELL, GRACE (ANSLEY)
Painter, Lecturer
Preferred Media: Oils, Watercolors.
b Martha's Vineyard Island, Mass, July 13, 93.
Study & Training: Boston Mus Sch, four yrs; Art Stud League New York, one yr; Acad Grande Chaumiére, Paris, France, one yr.
Work in Public Collections: Albright-Knox Gallery, Buffalo, N Y; Gov Off, Hartford, Conn; St Mark's Church, New York, N Y; Father Flannigan's Boys Home, Nebr; Grace Church, Trumbull, Conn.
Commissions: Last Supper, Episcopal Minister, Smethport, Pa; Madonna for St George's Church, Mrs Henry Hill Pierce, New York; Nativity, dedicated to Mr Bird S Coler, Bird S Coler Hosp, New York; St Joseph's Manor, Mother Bernadette de Lourdes (Carmelite Order), Trumbull.
Exhibitions: Nat Asn Woman Artists, 20 yrs; Mus & Galleries U S A Traveling Exhib; Brooklyn Mus; Allied Artists, New York; Miss Art Asn, Nat Arts Club, New York.
Teaching: Lectr watercolor for young children, St George's Church, 49; lectr watercolor for young children, Bird S Coler Hosp, 62-66; lectr oil for adults, St Joseph's Manor, 66-72.
Awards: Miss Art Asn; many awards, Pen & Brush Club; United Hosp, New York.
Bibliography: Article, In: Miss Porter's Sch Bull; article, In: Bridgeport Post; article, In: Trumbull Times; plus others.
Memberships: Nat Asn Women Artists (pres, 46-49, chmn watercolor jury, 51, mem bd, 10 yrs); Pen & Brush Club (chmn watercolor jury, 53).

Art Interests: Teaching art to young children with special attention to retarded & cerebral palsy children.
Mailing Address: 6448 Main St, Trumbull, CT 06611.

TREADWELL, HELEN
Painter, Designer
b Chihuahua, Mex.
Study & Training: Vassar Col; Sorbonne, Paris, France.
Commissions: Many murals in hotels & clubs in U S, also Hotel Bermudiana, Hamilton, Bermuda, Hotel O'Higgins, Chile, Chase Manhattan Bank, San Juan P R, Marine Midland, N Y & others; five mosaic murals, New York Pub Sch Syst; many others in ships, trains & pvt homes; mosaic panels, Church of the WORD Luthern, Rochester, N Y.
Exhibitions: One-man shows, Arthur Newton Gallery, Rockefeller Ctr, Archit League, Crespi Gallery & Contemp Gallery, 34-65.
Awards: Spec award for mural paintings in Munic Bldgs, Chile; pres medal for extraordinary serv in promotion of relationship between archit & fine arts of mural painting & sculpture, Archit League, 69.
Memberships: Nat Soc Mural Painters (pres, 63-68); Archit League (first v pres, 52-54, 64-66, mem exec comt); U S Comn Int Asn Art (treas); Fine Arts Fedn New York (v pres); Artists Equity Asn; plus others.
Mailing Address: 33 W 67th St, New York, NY 10023.

TREASTER, RICHARD A
Painter, Instructor
Preferred Media: Watercolor, Tempera.
b Lorain, Ohio, July 14, 32.
Study & Training: Cleveland Inst Art, BFA.
Work in Public Collections: Butler Inst Am Art, Youngstown, Ohio; Canton Art Inst, Ohio; Miami Univ, Oxford, Ohio; Lehigh Univ, Bethlehem, Pa; Nat Acad Design, New York, N Y.
Exhibitions: 200 Yrs Am Watercolor, Metrop Mus Art, 66; View of Contemp Am Watercolor, Cleveland Inst Art, 68; Mainstream Int, 68-72; Watercolor U S A, 72; Cleveland May Show, 72.
Teaching: Instr painting, Cooper Sch Art, Cleveland, 66-67; instr painting, Cleveland Inst Art, 66-
Awards: Mainstreams Award of Excellence, Marietta Col, 69; Emily Goldsmith Award, Am Watercolor Soc, 69; Ohio Fine Arts Coun honorarium, 71.
Bibliography: Ralph Fabri (auth), Medal of merit, Today's art, 8/66; Norman Kent (auth), Richard Treaster—American artist, Am Artist, 1/72.
Memberships: Am Watercolor Soc.
Dealer: A B Closson Jr Co, 400 Race St, Cincinnati, OH 45202.
Mailing Address: 1228 Virginia Ave, Lakewood, OH 44107.

TREBILCOCK, PAUL
Painter
Preferred Media: Oils.
b Chicago, Ill, Feb 13, 02.
Study & Training: Univ Ill; Art Inst Chicago; & also study in Europe.
Work in Public Collections: Art Inst Chicago; Cranbrook Mus; Cincinnati Mus; U S Embassy, London, Eng; plus many univs & cols.
Commissions: Many portraits of prominent persons.
Awards: William Randolph Hearst prize, 26 & Frank G Logan Medal & first prize, 28, Art Inst Chicago; first Hallgarten prize, Nat Acad Design, 31.
Bibliography: Ernest Watson (auth), Paul Trebilcock, Am Artist Mag, 12/44 & Paul Trebilcock, portrait painter, In: Twenty painters and how they work, Watson-Guptill, 50.
Memberships: Nat Acad Design; Century Asn; Chelsea Arts Club, London, Eng.
Dealer: Portraits, Inc, 41 E 57th St, New York, NY 10022.
Mailing Address: 44 W 77th St, New York, NY 10024.

TREIMAN, JOYCE WAHL
Painter
Preferred Media: Oils.
b Evanston, Ill, May 29, 22.
Study & Training: Univ Iowa, BFA.
Work in Public Collections: Whitney Mus Am Art, New York, N Y; Art Inst Chicago, Ill; Denver Art Mus, Colo; Oberlin Allen Art Mus; Grunwald Found, Univ Calif, Los Angeles.
Exhibitions: American Painting, Art Inst Chicago, Ill, 46-60; American Painting & Sculpture, Univ Ill, 50-63; Whitney Mus Am Art, New York, 51-53, 57 & 58; Carnegie Int, Pittsburgh, Pa, 55 & 57; Recent Painting: The Figure, Mus Mod Art, New York, 62.
Teaching: Vis prof painting, Art Ctr Col Design, summer 68; vis prof painting, San Fernando Valley State Col, 68-69; vis lectr painting, Univ Calif, Los Angeles, 69-70.
Awards: Tiffany fel, 47; Logan prize, Art Inst Chicago, 51; Tamarind Lithography fel, Ford Found, 62.

Dealers: Forum Gallery, 1018 Madison Ave, New York, NY 10021;
Adele Bednarz Gallery, 902 N La Cienega Blvd, Los Angeles, CA
90069.
Mailing Address: 712 Amalfi Dr, Pacific Palisades, CA 90272.

TRIANO, ANTHONY THOMAS
Painter, Art Administrator
Preferred Media: Oils.
b Newark, N J, Aug 25, 28.
Study & Training: Newark Sch Fine & Indust Art, 46-50; with Reuben
Nakian, 47-52; also with Samuel Brecher.
Work in Public Collections: Newark Mus, N J; Lowe Mus, Coral
Gables, Fla; Paterson State Col, Wayne, N J; Hartford Art Found,
Conn; Seton Hall Univ, South Orange, N J; plus others.
Exhibitions: Five Newark Artists, Newark Mus, 58; East Hampton
Collectors, Guild Hall, Long Island, N Y, 62; Gallery Selections,
J L Hudson Gallery, Detroit, Mich, 64; New Jersey & the Artist,
N J State Mus, Trenton, 65; Boochever Art Collection, Paterson
State Col, 68; plus others including over twelve one-man shows.
Teaching: Artist-in-residence & prof art, Seton Hall Univ, 70-
Positions: U S Govt art surveyor & consult, 72.
Awards: 25th Ann N J State art award, Montclair Mus, 57; purchase
award, Newark Mus, 59.
Bibliography: Mike Berg (auth), The life & world of Triano, Seton
Hall Univ, 68; William Sheppard (auth), Inside the arts, produced
on WNYC-TV by Brooklyn Col, 70; D Simon (auth), Profiles, TV
prog produced by Seton Hall Univ, 71.
Publications: Illusr, Exploring nature's rythms, 60 & illusr, Duck
fever, 61, Abbott Labs; contribr, H & G colors for your personal
bed & bath, 56 & contribr, House of color, 67, House & Garden.
Mailing Address: 586 Devon St, Kearny, NJ 07032.

TRIESTER, KENNETH
Painter, Sculptor
b New York, N Y, Mar 5, 30.
Study & Training: Univ Miami; Univ Fla, BArch, 53.
Work in Public Collections: Norton Gallery, Palm Beach, Fla; Mi-
ami Mus Mod Art, Fla; Fla Supreme Ct, Tallahassee.
Commissions: Family of God (limited ed of bronze menoras), 69 &
series of six bronze plaques depicting hist of Jews, United Jewish
Appeal; series of ten paintings depicting 4,000 yr hist of Jews,
Temple Israel, Miami.
Exhibitions: Greenwich Gallery, New York; Mus Fine Arts, Colum-
bus, Ga; Lowe Art Gallery, Coral Gables, Fla; Contemp Art Mus,
Houston, Tex; High Mus, Atlanta, Ga; plus several one-man
shows.
Awards: First prize for Four Conversations (sculpture), Nat Ce-
ramic Exhib, Lowe Art Gallery, 53.
Memberships: Blue Dome Soc, Miami; Fla Sculptural Soc; Southern
Asn Sculptors.
Art Interests: Photopainting, a new technique of combining photo-
graphs & paintings.
Publications: Contribr articles to many archit, sch & bldg publs.
Mailing Address: 1460 Brickell Ave, Miami, FL 33131.

TRIFON, HARRIETTE
Painter, Sculptor
b Philadelphia, Pa.
Study & Training: Pratt Inst, grad; Adelphi Univ; Art Stud League
New York.
Work in Public Collections: Birmingham Mus Art, Ala; Jewish Mus,
New York, N Y; Staten Island Mus, N Y; Woodward Found, Wash-
ington, D C; Abilities Inc Bldg, Hempstead, N Y.
Commissions: The Road (surrealistic & semi-abstract acrylic) &
sculpture mural of large surrealistic & semi-abstract flowers,
69, Samuel Lichtenstein Archit, Lawrence, Long Island.
Exhibitions: Birmingham Mus Art, 55; Hofstra Univ Nat Show, 58;
Pa Acad Fine Art, Philadelphia, 59; Corcoran Gallery Art,
Washington, D C, 60; Brooklyn Mus Print Show, N Y, 61.
Teaching: Owner & instr art, Harriette Trifon Creative Workshop,
59-
Positions: Dir art gallery, Woodmere-Hewlett Libr, 70-; dir art,
St Albans Naval Hosp, for '52 Orgn, 70-71.
Awards: Birmingham Mus Art, 55; Hofstra Univ, 58; Long Island
Artists Nat Show, 62.
Dealer: Loring's Art Gallery, Central Ave, Cedarhurst, NY 11516.
Mailing Address: 84 Laurel Hill Dr, Valley Stream, NY 11581.

TRIMM, H WAYNE
Illustrator
b Albany, N Y, Aug 16, 22.
Study & Training: Cornell Univ, 40; Augustana Col, BS, 48; Kans
State Univ, 49; Col Forestry, Syracuse Univ, MS, 53.
Commissions: Dioramas, Springfield Mus Art; three murals, Jug
End Barn, South Egremont, Mass, 61; three ecol dioramas, Au-
gustana Col, 67; movie for Audubon Screen Tour, 68-69; Cleve-
land Mus Art.

Exhibitions: Am Bird Artists Traveling Exhib, sponsored by Audubon Artists; Joslyn Mus Art; Buffalo Mus Sci; San Jose State
Univ; New York Coliseum Sportsman's Show; plus others.
Teaching: Lect, Conservation, Wildlife Painting & Alaskan Bow-
hunting.
Positions: Staff artist, N Y State Conserv Dept & Conserv Educ Div,
53-
Memberships: Columbia Co Arts & Crafts; Soc Animal Artists; hon
mem Tuscarora Indian Tribe; Am Ornithologists Union.
Publications: Illusr, Manual of museum techniques, 48 & The mam-
mals of California and its coastal waters, 54; illusr, Collier's
Encycl, 60-61; field paintings for The birds of Tikal, 63-64 & The
birds of Colorado, 66; contribr, illus to Audubon Mag & N Y State
Conservationist.
Mailing Address: Sketch Book Farm, Chatham, NY 12037.

TRIPLETT, MARGARET L
Educator, Painter
b Vermillion, S Dak, Dec 30, 05.
Study & Training: Univ Iowa, BA; Boston Mus Fine Arts Sch; Yale
Univ, MA; also with Grant Wood.
Work in Public Collections: Munson-Williams-Proctor Inst, Utica,
N Y; Slater Mem Mus, Norwich, Conn.
Exhibitions: Am Watercolor Soc; Conn Watercolor Soc; De Cordova
& Dana Mus; Slater Mus Art; Lyman Allyn Mus; plus others.
Teaching: Instr art, Norwich Art Sch, 29-43, dir, 43-70, retired.
Positions: Trustee, Hartford Art Sch, Univ Hartford, 62-70.
Awards: Jesse Smith Noyes Found grant, 69.
Memberships: Conn Art Asn (pres, 54-56); Conn Watercolor Soc;
Mystic Art Asn (bd dirs, 72); life mem Nat Educ Asn; plus others.
Research: Study of students of the Norwich Art School.
Publications: Co-auth, The Norwich Art School, a study of the direc-
tors, in combination with an on-going study of former students,
71.
Mailing Address: 1 Prunier Court, Norwich, CT 06360.

TRISSEL, JAMES NEVIN
Painter, Educator
Preferred Media: Oils.
b Davenport, Iowa, Nov 7, 30.
Study & Training: State Univ Iowa, BA; Colo State Col, MA; State
Univ Iowa, MFA.
Work in Public Collections: Univ Wis; Beloit Col; Colo Col; Colo-
rado Springs Fine Arts Ctr.
Exhibitions: One-man show, Beloit Col, 57; Wis Salon, 58; El Paso
Biennial, 64 & 66; one-man show, Colorado Springs Fine Arts
Ctr, 66 & 72.
Teaching: Instr art, Beloit Col, 58-60; asst prof art & art theory,
Univ Calif, Los Angeles, 60-64; assoc prof art & art hist, Colo
Col, 64-, chmn dept art, 71-
Positions: Actg dir, Wright Art Ctr, Beloit Col, 58-59; dir, Univ
Exten Prog in Art, Univ Calif, Los Angeles, 62-64.
Mailing Address: 1724 N Tejon St, Colorado Springs, CO 80907.

TRIVIGNO, PAT
Painter, Educator
Preferred Media: Acrylics, Oils.
b New York, N Y, Mar 13, 22.
Study & Training: Tyler Sch Art; New York Univ; Columbia Univ,
BA, MA.
Work in Public Collections: Solomon R Guggenheim Mus, New York;
Brooklyn Mus, N Y; Everson Mus, Syracuse, N Y; New York
Times, N Y; Delgado Mus, New Orleans, La.
Commissions: Murals, Lykes Steamship Lines.
Exhibitions: Whitney Mus Am Art Ann; Art Inst Chicago; Pa Acad
Fine Arts; Am Acad Arts & Lett; Univ Ill Biennial; plus 12 one-
man shows.
Teaching: Prof art, Tulane Univ La, 50-
Positions: Bd trustees, Delgado Mus, New Orleans, La.
Bibliography: Articles, In: New York Times, 10/8/50 & 1/10/60;
R Pearson (auth), Modern renaissance in American art, Harper;
John Alford (auth), exhibition catalogue, Seligman Gallery.
Dealer: Saidenberg Gallery, 1035 Madison Ave, New York, NY 10021.
Mailing Address: 1831 Marengo St, New Orleans, LA 70115.

TROSKY, HELENE ROTH
Printmaker, Writer
b Monticello, N Y.
Study & Training: New Sch Soc Res, with Kuniyoshi Egas; Manhattanville Col, BA, with Al Blaustein & John Ross.
Exhibitions: Nat Asn Women Artists, Nat Acad Design Galleries,
67-69; Conn Acad Fine Arts, 67 & 68; Charles Z Mann Gallery,
67 & 69; Silvermine Guild, 68-70; one-man show, Hudson River
Mus, Yonkers, N Y, 69.
Teaching: Art dir, Westchester Co Music & Art Camp, 65, 66, 71
& 72; lectr art hist, Brandeis Univ Women, 66-; instr printmaking, Manhattanville Col, 71-

Positions: Columnist, Muse roundup, Harrison Independent Green-burgh Rec & Yonkers Rec, 60-; art consult, Westchester Libr Syst, 65-70; dir, second Regional Plan, New York, N Y, 65-
Awards: Westchester Art Soc Award, 67; Northern Westchester Award, 68; Nat Asn Women Artists Award, 69.
Memberships: Silvermine Guild; Conn Acad Fine Arts; Westchester Art Soc (exec dir & chmn bd, 60-); Artists Equity New York; Nat Asn Women Artists; plus others.
Dealer: Raydon Gallery, 1091 Madison Ave, New York, NY 10028; Charles Z Mann Gallery, 1226 Third at 71st St, New York, NY 10021.
Mailing Address: Yarmouth Rd, Purchase, NY 10577.

TROVA, ERNEST TINO
Sculptor, Painter
b Saint Louis, Mo, Feb 19, 27.
Work in Public Collections: Paintings, Mus Mod Art, New York, Tate Gallery, London & Am Container Corp; sculpture, Mus Mod Art, Whitney Mus Am Art & Solomon Guggenheim Mus, New York; City Art Mus, Saint Louis.
Exhibitions: Documenta IV, Kassel, Ger; Los Angeles Co Mus Art, Calif; Solomon R Guggenheim Mus; Jewish Mus, New York; Nat Mus Mod Art, Tokyo, Japan.
Dealer: Pace Gallery, 32 E 57th St, New York, NY 10022.
Mailing Address: 6 Layton Terr, Saint Louis, MO 63124.

TROVATO, JOSEPH S
Painter
b Guardavalle, Italy, Feb 6, 12.
Study & Training: Art Stud League New York; Nat Acad Design; Sch Related Arts & Sci, Utica, N Y; Munson-Williams-Proctor Inst Sch Art; Hamilton Col, hon DFA, 63.
Work in Public Collections: Munson-Williams-Proctor Inst; Utica Col; Libr Cong, Washington, D C.
Exhibitions: Munson-Williams-Proctor Inst; Utica Col; Albany Inst Hist & Art; E W Root Art Ctr, Hamilton Col; Everson Mus Art.
Collections Arranged: Charles Burchfield, 62; 50th Anniversary Exhib of the Armory Show, 63; Edward Hopper, 64; Learning About Pictures from Mr Root, 65; 125 Years of New York Painting and Sculpture for N Y State Coun on the Arts; The Nature of Charles Burchfield (Mem Exhib incl catalogue), Munson-Williams-Proctor Inst, 70.
Teaching: Vis asst prof art, Hamilton Col, 65-66.
Positions: Asst to dir, Munson-Williams-Proctor Inst, 39-; in charge exhib prog, Edward W Root Art Ctr, Hamilton Col, 58-; field researcher for N Y State, Arch Am Art for The New Deal and the Arts, 64-65; consult, N Y State Coun on the Arts.
Publications: Contribr, Art in Am.
Mailing Address: 12 Hamilton Pl, Clinton, NY 13323.

TRUBNER, HENRY
Art Historian
b Munich, Ger, June 10, 20; U S citizen.
Study & Training: Fogg Art Mus, Harvard Univ, BA & MA.
Collections Arranged: Chinese Ceramics; Arts of T'ang Dynasty, Los Angeles Co Mus Art, 52 & 57; Arts of Han Dynasty, Chinese Art Soc, Asia House, 61; Ceramic Art Japan: 100 masterpieces From Japanese Collections, Seattle Art Mus, Nelson Art Gallery, Asia House & Los Angeles Co Mus Art, 72-73.
Teaching: Assoc prof Asian art, Univ Toronto, 58-68.
Positions: Cur Oriental art, Los Angeles Co Mus Art, 47-58; cur Far Eastern Dept, Royal Ont Mus, Toronto, 58-68; cur Dept Asiatic Art, Seattle Art Mus, Wash, 68-
Memberships: Asia Soc (mem adv comt); Japan Soc; Oriental Ceramic Soc, London; Col Art Asn Am; Am Oriental Soc.
Research: Japanese ceramics.
Publications: Auth, Chinese ceramics, Los Angeles Co Mus Art, 52; auth, Arts of the T'ang dynasty, 57; auth, Arts of Han dynasty, Viennese Art Soc, 61; co-auth, Art treasures from Japan, 65-66; auth, Ceramic art of Japan: 100 masterpieces from Japanese collections, Kodansha Int, Tokyo, 72.
Mailing Address: Seattle Art Museum, Volunteer Park, Seattle, WA 98102.

TRUDEAU, YVES
Sculptor
Preferred Media: Bronze, Plexiglass, Steel.
b Montreal, P Q, Dec 3, 30.
Study & Training: Ecole Beaux Arts Montreal, sr matriculant with Marie Mediatrice.
Work in Public Collections: Mus Quebec; Galerie Nat Can; Mus Art Contemporain Montreal; Mus Art Prague, Czech; Mus Plein Air D'Ostrava, Czech.
Commissions: Vivace, J M C Camp Musical, Mont-Orford, P Q, 60; Vie Interieur, comn by N D De L'Enfant, Sherbrooke, P Q, 66; Phare Du Cosmos, Expo 67, Universe Plaza, 67; concrete relief,

Univ Sherbrooke; bronze relief, Ecole Arts & Metiers De Riviere-Du-Loup, P Q, 68.
Exhibitions: Third Int Contemp Sculpture Biennial, 66 & Panorama Sculpture Quebec, 70, Mus Rodin, France; Int Symp Sculpture, Ostrava, 69; one-man show, Mus Quebec, 70; Biennale Middle-heim, Anvers, Belg, 71; Premiere Biennale Petite Sculpture, Budapest, Hungary, 71.
Teaching: Prof sculpture, Ecole Beaux-Arts Montreal, 67-69; prof sculpture concept & metal, Univ Que, Montreal, 69-
Awards: Can Coun Awards, 63 & 69; Ministere Educ Quebec Award, 70-71.
Bibliography: Robert Guy (auth), Yves Trudeau, sculptor, Asn Sculpteurs Quebec, 71.
Memberships: Can Conf Arts (councellor, 67-68); Asn Sculpteurs Quebec (pres, 60-66); Int Conf Mus; Int Asn Plastic Art.
Publications: Auth, article, In: Metiers D'Arts Quebec, 63; co-auth, Catalogue, Galerie Nat Can, 66; auth, Confrontation 67 (catalogue), 67.
Mailing Address: c/o Galerie de Montreal, 2060 Rue MacKay, Montreal, P Q, Can.

TRUE, VIRGINIA
Painter, Educator
Preferred Media: Acrylics, Pastels, Ink, Oils.
b Saint Louis, Mo, Feb 7, 00.
Study & Training: John Herron Art Inst, dipl painting, 24 with William Forsyth; Pa Acad Fine Arts, scholar, with Merriman, 25; John Herron Art Inst, BAE, 31; Cornell Univ, MFA, 37, with Christian Midjo; Columbia Univ, summer; Univ Colo, summer; also in Rome, Italy, 55.
Work in Public Collections: Painting, Colo State Univ, Fort Collins, portraits, Univ Colo, Boulder; portrait, Purdue Univ Lafayette, Ind; carved wood panel, Cornell Univ, Ithaca, N Y.
Commissions: Mural, hist of home econ, Col Home Econ, Cornell Univ, 37.
Exhibitions: Rochester Mem Art Gallery Ann Regional, N Y, 39; Trends Am Art, Carnegie Inst, Pittsburgh, Pa, 41; Retrospective Exhib, Andrew Dickson White Mus Art, Cornell Univ, 65.
Teaching: Art instr, John Herron Art Inst, 26-28; art instr, Univ Colo, Boulder, 29-36; from instr art to prof, Cornell Univ, 36-65; prof & head dept housing & design, 45-65, emer prof, 65-; art instr, Cape Cod Art Asn, summers 68-69.
Positions: Bk designer & art consult, Barnes & Noble, 48.
Awards: First prizes, Colo Artists Exhib, Denver Art Mus, 32 & 33; first prize, Midwest Artists Exhib, Kansas City Art Inst, 34; Nelson Eddy Purchase Prize, Rochester Mem Art Gallery, 39.
Memberships: Am Fedn Arts; Cornell Andrew Dickson White Mus Art Assoc; Mus Fine Arts, Boston; Provincetown Art Asn.
Dealer: Cobb House Gallery, Main St, Barnstable, MA 02630.
Mailing Address: 20 Tee Way, South Yarmouth, MA 02664.

TRUETTLER, WILLIAM
Art Administrator
Positions: Assoc cur 18th & 19th century painting & sculpture, Nat Collection Fine Arts.
Mailing Address: Smithsonian Institution, Washington, DC 20560.

TRUEX, VAN DAY
Painter, Designer
b Delphos, Kans, Mar 5, 04.
Study & Training: Parsons Sch Design, New York, N Y; Kans Wesleyan, MA.
Work in Public Collections: Calif Palace Legion of Honor, San Francisco; Mus Univ Kans, Manhattan; Nelson Rockhill Mus, Kansas City, Mo; Philadelphia Mus Art, Pa; Metrop Mus Art, New York.
Teaching: Pres, Parsons Sch Design, 41-51.
Positions: Designer, Yale & Towne Mfg Co, 51-53; designer, Tiffany & Co, 51-
Awards: Chevalier, Legion d'honneur, France, 51.
Dealer: Graham Gallery, 1014 Madison Ave, New York, NY 10021.
Mailing Address: 84560 Ménerbes, France.

TRUITT, ANNE (DEAN)
Sculptor
Preferred Media: Woods, Acrylics.
b Baltimore, Md, Mar 16, 21.
Study & Training: Bryn Mawr Col, BA, 43; Inst Contemp Art, Washington, D C, 48-49; Dallas Mus Fine Arts, 50.
Work in Public Collections: Corcoran Gallery Art, Washington, D C; Saint Louis Mus Art, Mo; Univ Ariz Mus Art, Tucson; Nat Collection Fine Arts, Washington, D C.
Exhibitions: Seven Sculptors, Inst Contemp Art, Philadelphia, Pa, 65; American Sculpture of the 60's, Los Angeles Co Mus Art, Calif, 67; The Pure & Clear: American Innovations, Philadelphia Mus Art, Pa, 68; Whitney Mus Am Art Ann, New York, N Y, 68 & 70; Washington, Twenty Years, Baltimore Mus Art, Md, 70.
Awards: Guggenheim fel, 71; Nat Endowment Arts, 72.

Bibliography: Gregory Battcock (auth), Minimal art, a critical anthology, Dutton, 68; Clement Greenberg (auth), Anne Truitt: American artist, Vogue, 68 & article, In: Art Int, Vol 11, No 4.
Dealers: Andre Emmerich, 41 E 57th St, New York, NY 10021; Pyramid Gallery, 2121 P St N W, Washington, DC 20037.
Mailing Address: 3506 35th St N W, Washington, DC 20016.

TSAI, WEN-YING
Sculptor, Painter
Preferred Media: Stainless Steel.
b Amoy, China, Oct 13, 28; U S citizen.
Study & Training: Univ Mich, ME, 53; Art Stud League New York, 53-57; Grad Faculty Polit & Social Sci, New Sch Social Res, 56-58.
Work in Public Collections: Tate Gallery, London, Eng; Centre Nat D'Art Contemporain, Paris, France; Kaiser Wilhelm Mus, Krefeld, Ger; Albright-Knox Art Gallery, Buffalo, N Y; Whitney Mus Am Art, New York, N Y.
Exhibitions: The Responsive Eye, 65 & The Machine Show, 68, Mus Mod Art, New York; Cybernetic Serendipity, Inst Contemp Arts, London, 68; Third Salon Int Galeries Pilotes, Mus Cantonal Beaux Arts, 70; Pittsburgh Int, Carnegie Inst Mus Art, 70.
Positions: Proj engr, Guy B Panero, Engineers, New York, 56-60; proj mgr, Cosentini Assocs, Engineers, New York, 62-63.
Awards: Whitney fel, 63; fel of Ctr Advan Visual Studies, Mass Inst Technol, 69-71; design in steel award, Am Iron & Steel Inst, 71.
Bibliography: Art for tomorrow-the 21st century, produced on CBS-TV, 69; Jonathan Benthall (auth), Cybernetic sculpture of Tsai, Studio Int, 3/69; Fred Barzyk (auth), Video variations (with Boston Symphony Orchestra), produced on WGBH-TV, 71.
Art Interests: The use of electronic controls & scientific instruments in kinetic art.
Dealer: Galerie Denise René, 124 Rue La Boetie, Paris 8, France.
Mailing Address: 1 Avenue Niel, Paris 17, France.

TSCHACBASOV, NAHUM
Painter, Printmaker
b Baku, Russia, Aug 30, 99; U S citizen.
Study & Training: Lewis Inst, Chicago; Armour Inst Technol; Columbia Univ; also in Paris, France.
Work in Public Collections: Metrop Mus Art & Whitney Mus Am Art, New York, N Y; State Dept, Washington, D C; Dallas Mus Fine Arts, Tex; Tel-Aviv Mus, Israel; Philadelphia Mus Art, Pa; Butler Inst Am Art, Youngstown, Ohio; plus many others.
Exhibitions: Carnegie Inst, Pittsburgh, Pa; Art Inst Chicago, Ill; Corcoran Gallery Art, Washington, D C; Va Mus Fine Arts, Richmond; Univ Texas, Austin; plus many other group & one-man shows in the U S & Europe.
Teaching: Former instr, Am Artists Sch & Art Stud League New York.
Positions: Owner, Tschacbasov Sch Fine Arts; pres, Am Arch World Art, Inc.
Awards: Pepsi-Cola Award, 47.
Memberships: An Am Group.
Publications: Publ, two portfolios of etchings, 47; auth & publ, The American library compendium and index of world art, 61 & An illustrated survey of western art; contribr, articles to Art Stud League New York Quart & Numero.
Mailing Address: 222 W 23rd St, New York, NY 10011.

TSELOS, DIMITRI THEODORE
Art Historian, Writer
b Kerasea, Greece, Oct 21, 01; U S citizen.
Study & Training: Univ Chicago, PhD, 26, MA, 28; Princeton Univ, Carnegie Found scholarships, 28-32; MA, 29, MFA, 31, PhD, 33; Inst Fine Arts, New York Univ, 29-30, with Richard Offner & Walter Cook; also with Charles R Morey.
Teaching: From instr medieval & mod art to assoc prof, Inst Fine Arts, New York Univ, 31-49; lectr mod art, Swarthmore Col, 37-41; lectr mod art, Univ Southern Calif, summers, 37-41; vis prof, Vassar Col, 44-46; prof art, Univ Minn, 49-71, emer prof & consult, 71-
Awards: Fulbright res grants, Greece, 55-56 & 63-64.
Memberships: Col Art Asn Am (dir, 55-60); Archaeol Inst Am; Soc Archit Historians; Am Asn Univ Prof; Minn Hist Soc.
Research: Medieval painting; modern architecture; modern Greek art.
Publications: Auth, Exotic influences in the architecture of F L Wright, Mag Art, 53; auth, The sources of the Utrecht psalter miniatures, 55; auth, Modern illustrated books, 59; auth, Defensive addenda on the origins of the Utrecht psalter, Art Bull, 67; auth, F L Wright and world architecture, J Archit Historians, 69.
Mailing Address: 1494 Branston St, St Paul, MN 55108.

TSUCHIDANA, HARRY SUYEMI
Painter
Preferred Media: Oils.
b Waipahu, Hawaii, May 28, 32.
Study & Training: Honolulu Acad Arts, Hawaii; Corcoran Sch Art,

Washington, D C.
Work in Public Collections: Honolulu Acad Arts; State Found Cult & Arts, Honolulu; Free Libr Philadelphia, Pa.
Exhibitions: Young Talent, Corcoran Gallery Art, Washington, D C, 56; Ankrum Gallery, Los Angeles, Calif, 67; one-man shows, Libr of Hawaii, Honolulu, 61, Gima's Gallery, Honolulu, 63 & Contemp Arts Ctr Hawaii, Honolulu, 66.
Awards: John Hay Whitney fel, 59.
Mailing Address: 1269 S Beretania St, Honolulu, HI 96814.

TSUTAKAWA, GEORGE
Sculptor, Painter
Preferred Media: Bronze, Watercolors.
b Seattle, Wash, Feb 2, 10.
Study & Training: With Alexander Archipenko, 36; Univ Wash Sch Art, BFA, 37, MFA, 50.
Work in Public Collections: Seattle Art Mus, Wash; Denver Art Mus, Colo; Santa Barbara Mus Art, Calif; Henry Art Gallery, Univ Wash, Seattle.
Commissions: Fountain of Wisdom (bronze), Seattle Pub Libr, 60; Waiola (fountain sculpture in bronze), Ala Moana Ctr, Honolulu, Hawaii, 66; Garth Fountain (bronze), Nat Cathedral, Washington, D C, 68; bronze fountain sculpture, Franklin Murphy Sculpture Garden, Univ Calif, Los Angeles, 69; fountain sculpture in bronze, Jefferson Plaza, Indianapolis, Ind, 71.
Exhibitions: 3rd Biennial, São Paulo, Brazil, 55; San Francisco Painting & Sculpture Ann, San Francisco Mus Art, Calif, 55, 58 & 60; 3rd Pac Coast Biennial, Santa Barbara Mus Art, Calif, 59; 66th Ann Exhib Western Art, Denver Art Mus, Colo, 60; Int Art Festival, Amerika Haus, Berlin, E Ger, 66.
Teaching: Prof art, Univ Wash, 46-
Awards: Award for Obos No 5 (wood), Santa Barbara Mus Art, 59; awards for Obos No 9 (wood), San Francisco Mus Art & Denver Art Mus, 60.
Bibliography: Henry Seldis (auth), Pacific heritage: exhibition review, Art in Am, 2/65; Gervais Reed (auth), The fountains of George Tsutakawa, Am Inst Archit J, 7/69; Marcell R Heinley (auth), George Tsutakawa fountain sculptor, Designers West, 2/70.
Mailing Address: 3116 S Irving St, Seattle, WA 98144.

TUBIS, SEYMOUR
Painter, Sculptor
Preferred Media: Oils, Intaglio, Bronze, Wood, Bone.
b Philadelphia, Pa, Sept 20, 19.
Study & Training: Temple Univ; Philadelphia Mus Sch; Art Stud League New York; with Georges Braque; Acad Grande Chaumière, Paris, France; Inst d'Arte, Florence, Italy; also with Hans Hofmann.
Work in Public Collections: Metrop Mus Art, New York, N Y; Libr of Cong, Washington, D C; Soc Am Graphic Artists, New York; Pa State Col; Univ Calgary, Alta, Can.
Exhibitions: Carnegie Int, Pittsburgh, Pa, 48; Nat Exhib Prints, Drawings & Watercolors, Metrop Mus Art, 52; Traveling Exhib Am Prints, Royal Soc London, Eng, 54; Int Exhib Graphics, Seattle Art Mus, 68; one-man show, Retrospective of Paintings & Sculpture, Mus N Mex, Santa Fe, 64.
Teaching: Instr painting, design & graphic arts, Inst Am Indian Arts, 62-, chmn dept fine arts, 65-
Positions: Artist-designer, New York Times, 59-62.
Awards: Noyes Mem prize for intaglio, Soc Am Graphic Artists, 48; fourth purchase award in painting, Joe & Emily Lowe Found, 50; first prize in painting, Am Newspaper Guild, 52.
Bibliography: Michelle Seuiere (auth), Les exposition Seymour Tubis, Opera, 7/26/50; John MacGregor (auth), Seymour Tubis experiments with printmaking, Pasatiempo, 8/27/67; Martha Buddeke (auth), Seymour Tubis takes two directions, J Arts, Albuquerque J, 11/21/71.
Memberships: Life mem Art Stud League New York; Soc Am Graphic Artists; Col Art Asn Am; Santa Fe Designer/Craftsmen.
Publications: Contribr, 72nd annual, Royal Soc Painters, Etchers & Engravers, 54; contribr, Western review, Western N Mex Univ, 66; illusr, Pembroke Mag; illusr, Yerma, Santa Fe N Mex, 71; contribr, Indian painters & white patrons, El Palacio, 71.
Dealers: The New West, 5908 Lomas N E, Albuquerque, NM 87110; Daniel Frishman Gallery of Art, Main St, Osterville, MA 02655.
Mailing Address: 414 Canyon Rd, Santa Fe, NM 87501.

TUCHMAN, MAURICE
Museum Curator
b Jacksonville, Fla, Nov 30, 36.
Study & Training: Nat Univ Mex; City Col New York, BA, 57; Columbia Univ, MA, 59.
Collections Arranged: Five Younger Calif Artists, 65; Edward Kienholz, 66; Irwin-Price, 66; John Mason, 66; Am Sculpture of 60's, 67; Soutine, 68; Art & Technol, 71; 11 Los Angeles Artists, Arts Coun Gt Brit, 71.

Positions: Art ed mod art sect, Columbia Encycl, 62; mem curatorial & lect staff, Guggenheim Mus, 62-64, organizer, summer 64; sr cur, Los Angeles Co Mus Art, 64-
Awards: Fulbright scholar, 60-61.
Publications: Auth, (catalogues), New York School, 65, American sculpture of the 60's, 67, Soutine, 68, Art and technology, 1971, 71 & 11 Los Angeles artists, 71.
Mailing Address: Los Angeles County Museum of Art, 5905 Wilshire Blvd, Los Angeles, CA 90036.

TUCKER, CHARLES CLEMENT
Painter
Preferred Media: Oils.
b S C, Sept 13, 13.
Study & Training: Art Stud League New York, scholar & with Frank Vincent DuMond, Ivan G Olinsky & George B Bridgman.
Work in Public Collections: Comt Rm For Affairs, Washington, D C; Mass Inst Technol, Cambridge, Mass; Mint Mus Charlotte, N C; Fourth Circuit Ct Appeals, Richmond Fed Bldg, Va; Univ N C, Charlotte; plus numerous other univs & mus throughout the U S A.
Exhibitions: Metrop Mus Art, New York, N Y, 42; Nat Acad Design, New York, 50; Coun Am Artist Socs, New York, 66; Hudson Valley Art Asn, New York, 68-72; Allied Artist Am, New York, 71-72.
Awards: First award, N C Nat Exhib, 58 & 59; dirs award, Coun Am Artist Soc, 66; Artist of the Year, Charlotte-Mecklenburg Bi-Centennial, 68.
Bibliography: Harold H Martin (auth), & Harper Gault (auth), Gay banker, Sat Eve Post, 11/23/46; Legette Blythe (auth), Miracle in the hills, McGraw, 53 & Call down the storm, Holt, 58.
Memberships: Allied Artist Am; Hudson Valley Art Asn; life mem Art Stud League New York; Am Artist Prof League; Int Platform Asn.
Art Interests: Portraits.
Mailing Address: 3621 Arborway Dr, Charlotte, NC 28211.

TUCKER, JAMES EWING
Museum Curator, Painter
Preferred Media: Oils, Watercolors, Graphics.
b Rule, Tex, Aug 13, 30.
Study & Training: Midwestern Univ; Univ Tex, Austin, BFA; Univ Iowa, MFA.
Work in Public Collections: Miss Art Asn, Jackson; N C State Univ, Raleigh; Pine Bluff Art Ctr, Ark; Witte Mus, San Antonio.
Exhibitions: Many.
Collections Arranged: Art on Paper, 65-72, Cone Collection & Dillard Collection, Weatherspoon Art Gallery.
Positions: Cur, Weatherspoon Art Gallery, 59-, ed Bull, 65-
Awards: Purchase awards, Miss Art Asn, 59 & 60, Winston-Salem Gallery Contemp Art, 61 & N C Mus Art, 63.
Dealer: Garden Gallery, Rte 8, Box 169, Raleigh, NC 27607.
Mailing Address: 632 Scott Ave, Greensboro, NC 27403.

TUCKER, MARCIA
Art Historian, Educator
b New York, N Y, Apr 11, 40.
Study & Training: Ecole du Louvre & Acad Grande Chaumière, Paris, France, 59-60; Conn Col, BA(fine arts), 61; New York Univ Inst Fine Arts, MA, 69.
Collections Arranged: Anti-Illusion: Procedures/Materials, 69, Robert Morris, 70, The Structure of Color, 71 & James Rosenquist: Retrospective Exhibition, 72, plus many others, Whitney Museum American Art, New York.
Teaching: Instr art, Univ R I, summer 66 & 68 & fall 67; instr art, City Univ New York, fall 67 & spring 68; instr art, Sch Visual Arts, 69-
Positions: Cur, William N Copley Collection, 63-66; ed assoc, Art-News, 65-69; assoc cur, Whitney Mus Am Art, 69-
Publications: Auth, Robert Morris (catalogue), Praeger; auth, Robert Natkin, ArtNews, 68; auth, Ferdinand Howald Collection of American paintings (catalogue), 69; auth, Phenaumanology, 12/70 & auth, The anatomy of a brush stroke: recent paintings by Joan Snyder, 5/71, Artforum; plus others.
Mailing Address: 36 W 26th St, New York, NY 10010.

TUCKER, MRS NION
Collector
Mailing Address: 80 New Place Rd, Hillsborough, CA 94010.

TUCKER, PERI
Writer, Illustrator
Preferred Media: Watercolors, Inks.
b Kashau, Austria-Hungary, July 25, 11; U S citizen.
Study & Training: Columbus Sch Fine Arts; also with E C Van Swearingen.

Exhibitions: Regional Ann, Akron Art Inst, Ohio, 40-46; Touring Show, Ohio Watercolor Soc, 43; Regional Invitational, Sci Ctr, Saint Petersburg, Fla, 68-69; one-man show, Fla Gulf Coast Art Ctr, Belleair, Fla, 67.
Positions: Free lance writer & artist, 67-
Publications: Children's bk illusr, Saalfield Publ Co, 38-51; art writer & news artist, Akron Beacon J, 42-51; art writer & news artist, Saint Petersburg Times, 52-66.
Mailing Address: 201 Driftwood Lane, Harbor Bluffs, Largo, FL 33540.

TUDOR, TASHA
Illustrator, Writer
b Boston, Mass, Aug 28, 15.
Study & Training: Boston Mus Fine Arts Sch.
Commissions: Creator of the Tasha Tudor Christmas Cards.
Exhibitions: Currier Gallery Art.
Publications: Auth & illusr, A is for Annabelle, Walck, 54, Rand, 71, One is one, Hale, 56, Rand, 71 & Corgiville Fair, T Y Crowell, 71, plus many others; illusr, Doll's house, Viking Press, 62 & 70 & The secret garden, Lippincott, 62 & Dell, 71; plus many others.
Mailing Address: R F D 1, Contoocook, NH 03229.

TULK, ALFRED JAMES
Painter
Preferred Media: Oils, Watercolors.
b London, Eng, Oct 3, 99; U S citizen.
Study & Training: Oberlin Col; Nat Acad Design, cert; Art Stud League New York, cert; Yale Univ Sch Art, BFA, 23; Inst Bellas Artes, Guanajuato, Mex, MFA, 63.
Work in Public Collections: Painting, Birmingham Mus Art, Ala; portrait painting, Orlando Pub Libr, Fla.
Commissions: Stained glass window, Col W Africa, Monrovia, Liberia, 40; murals for lobby, Salvation Army Hosp, Flushing, N Y, 48; Iconastasis, Franciscan Monastery, New Canaan, Conn, 52; mural for reception rm, D A Long Co Bldg, Hamden, Conn, 59; three murals, Picuris Indian Pueblo, Penasco, N Mex, 63.
Exhibitions: One-man shows, Recent Paintings, Art Mus, Stamford, Conn, 60 & 62, Recent Paintings, Stiles Col, Yale Univ, New Haven, 65, Exhib of Paintings, Mus Art, Birmingham, 68, Instructors Show, Art League, Bradenton, Fla, 68 & Expressionistic Paintings, United Gt Hall, New Haven, Conn, 71.
Teaching: Instr drawing & painting, Dept Adult Educ, City of Stamford, 54-58; instr drawing & painting, Dept Adult Educ, City New Haven, 63-67; instr drawing & painting, Art Guild North Haven, 65-70.
Positions: Dir dept mural painting, Rambusch Decorating Co, New York, N Y, 26-46; gen designer, Karl Hackert Studios, Chicago, Ill, 46-72; assoc designer, Studios of George Payne, Paterson, N J, 48-52.
Awards: Drawing prize, Yale Art Sch, 21; bronze medal, Beaux Arts Inst Design, 22; first prize for oil painting, Greenwich Art Sch, 58.
Memberships: Nat Soc Mural Painters; New Haven Arts Coun; North Haven Art Guild (adv).
Mailing Address: 210 Upper State St, North Haven, CT 06473.

TUNIS, EDWIN
Writer, Illustrator
b Cold Spring Harbor, N Y, Dec 8, 97.
Study & Training: Md Inst; also with C Y Turner, Joseph Lauber & Hugh Breckenridge.
Commissions: Murals, McCormick & Co, Baltimore, Title Guarantee Co & City Hosp, Baltimore, Md.
Awards: Gold medal for Wheels, Boys' Club Am, 56; Edison Fund Award for Colonial Living, 57.
Memberships: Pen Club; Author's Guild.
Publications: Auth & illusr, Frontier living, 61, Colonial craftsmen, 65; Shaw's fortune, 66 & Young United States, 69, World Publ; auth & illusr, Chipmunks on the doorstep, T Y Crowell, 71; plus others.
Mailing Address: R F D 1, Box 78, Reisterstown, MD 21136.

TURANO, DON
Sculptor, Medalist
Preferred Media: Bronze, Wood.
b New York, N Y, Mar 9, 30.
Study & Training: Sch Indust Art, with Albino Cavalido; Corcoran Sch Art, with Heinz Warneke; Skowhegan Sch Painting & Sculpture, with H Tovish; Rinehart Sch Sculpture, with R Puccinelli.
Commissions: Silver & wood mace, Am Col Physicians, Philadelphia, Pa, 64; carved oak panels, First Presby Church, Royal Oak, Mich, 65; limestone figures, Cathedral of St Peter & St Paul, Washington, D C, 69; four arks (locust wood), Temple Micah, Washington, D C, 71; silver Medallion, Univ Notre Dame, Ind, 72.

Exhibitions: Pa Acad Fine Arts, Philadelphia, 63; St Louis Mus, Mo, 64; Univ Colo, Boulder, 65; Audubon Ann, Nat Acad Design Galleries, 66; Xerox Corp, Rochester, N Y, 71.
Teaching: Instr sculpture, George Washington Univ, 61-65; instr sculpture, Corcoran Sch Art, 61-65.
Awards: First prizes, Corcoran Gallery Art, 66, Festival Relig Art, 67 & George Washington Univ, 68.
Memberships: Nat Sculpture Soc; assoc Washington Relig Art Comn.
Dealer: Downeast Gallery, 2140 Cathedral Ave N W, Washington, DC 20008.
Mailing Address: 2625 Connecticut Ave N W, Washington, DC 20008.

TURK, RUDY H
Museum Director, Art Historian
b Sheboygan, Wis, June 24, 27.
Study & Training: Univ Wis; Univ Tenn; Ind Univ; Univ Paris, Fulbright scholar, 56-57.
Collections Arranged: The Works of John Roeder, Richmond Art Ctr, Calif, 61-62; Contemporary Glass, Fine Arts Gallery San Diego, 67; Paintings by Tom Holland, 68, The World of David Gilhooly, 69 & Enamels by June Schwarcz, 70, Ariz State Univ.
Teaching: Assoc prof art, Ariz State Univ, 67-
Positions: Art historian & dir art gallery, Univ Mont, 57-60; dir, Richmond Art Ctr, 60-65; asst dir, Fine Arts Gallery San Diego, 65-67; dir Univ Art Collections, Ariz State Univ, 67-
Awards: Award of merit, Calif Col Fine Arts, 65.
Memberships: Western Asn Art Mus; Asn Am Mus; Western Asn Art Depts & Univ Mus; Col Art Asn Am.
Research: Contemporary art; eighteenth century French art; humanities; American ceramics.
Collection: Eighteenth century French prints; contemporary American art.
Publications: Auth, I L Udell, Univ Art Collections, Tempe, 71; co-auth, Scholder/Indians, Northland, 72; co-auth, The search for personal freedom, William C Brown, Vols I & II, 72; plus various art reviews.
Mailing Address: University Art Collections, Arizona State University, Tempe, AZ 85281.

TURNBULL, GRACE HILL
Sculptor, Painter
Preferred Media: Marble, Wood, Oils, Pastels.
b Baltimore, Md, Dec 31, 80.
Study & Training: Md Inst Art, Baltimore; Art Stud League New York, with Joseph De Camp; Pa Acad Fine Arts, Philadelphia, with William Chase & Cecilia Beaux; outdoor painting with Willard Metcalf.
Work in Public Collections: Painting & sculptures, Baltimore Art Mus; sculpture in Corcoran Art Gallery, Washington, D C, Worcester Art Mus, Mass & Metrop Mus Art, New York, N Y.
Exhibitions: Art Inst Chicago 25th Ann, 12; Salon Beaux Arts, Paris, France, 14; Artists for Victory Exhib, Metrop Mus Art, 42-43; many ann, Nat Sculpture Soc, Nat Asn Women Artists & Pa Acad Fine Arts.
Awards: Anna Hyatt Huntington Prizes, Nat Asn Women Artists, 32 & 44; Metrop Mus Art Purchase Prize, 42; Baltimore Mus Art Awards, 45 & 47.
Memberships: Fel Nat Sculpture Soc; Nat Asn Women Artists; Baltimore Mus Art.
Art Interests: Presented the Reese Memorial Monument to Baltimore City; also given scholarships to art students.
Publications: Auth, Tongues of fire, 28; ed, The essence of Plotinus, 34; ed, Fruit of the vine, 50; auth, Chips from my chisel, 51; auth, The uncovered well, 52.
Mailing Address: 223 Chancery Rd, Baltimore, MD 21218.

TURNER, (CHARLES) ARTHUR
Painter, Instructor
Preferred Media: Oils, Acrylics, Charcoal.
b Houston, Tex, Nov 17, 40.
Study & Training: N Tex State Univ, BA, 62; Cranbrook Acad Art, Bloomfield Hills, Mich, MFA, 66, with Zoltan Shepeshy.
Work in Public Collections: Mus Fine Arts, Houston, Carrol Reese Mus, E Tenn State Univ, Johnson City; Alcoa Aluminum Co, Detroit, Mich; The Galleries, Cranbrook Acad Art; Del Mar Col, Corpus Christi, Tex.
Exhibitions: Artist of Southeast & Tex, Isaac Delgado Mus, New Orleans, 61; Prints 1966, State Univ N Y Potsdam, 66; Drawing Soc Nat, Am Fedn Art, New York, N Y, 70; 24th Am Drawing Biennial, Norfolk Mus Art, Va, 71; The Other Coast, Calif State Col, Long Beach, 71.
Teaching: Asst prof painting, Madison Col(Va), 66-68; instr painting, Sch Art, Mus Fine Arts, Houston, 69-
Awards: Award in 34th Ann Painting & Sculpture Exhib, Dallas Mus Fine Arts, 63; second award, Southwestern Watercolor Soc 7th Ann, 71; first purchase award, Beaumont Art Mus 20th Ann, 71.

Bibliography: Richard Hutchens (auth), Arthur Turner—painter, Forum, summer 68 & Arthur Turner, Facets, 6/69.
Memberships: Southwestern Watercolor Soc; Tex Fine Arts Asn; Tex Watercolor Soc; Col Art Asn Am.
Dealer: Smither Gallery, 2817 Allen St, Dallas, TX 75204.
Mailing Address: 915 Hawthorne, Studio 2, Houston, TX 77006.

TURNER, BRUCE BACKMAN
Painter
Preferred Media: Oils.
b Worcester, Mass, Oct 28, 41.
Work in Public Collections: In pvt collections throughout the U S.
Exhibitions: Ogunquit Art Ctr Ann Exhibs, Maine, 71 & 72; Am Artists Prof League Grand Nat, New York, N Y, 71 & 72; Hudson Valley Art Asn Ann, White Plains, N Y, 72; Chautauqua Art Asn Nat Exhib, 72; North Shore Arts Asn Ann, East Gloucester, Mass, 72.
Teaching: Pvt classes in oil painting, Rockport, Mass, 71-72.
Positions: Owner, Bruce Turner Gallery, Rockport, Mass.
Awards: Mrs Helen Logan Award for Ogunquit Spume, Chatauqua Nat, 72; hon mention for Open Sea, Ogunquit Nat, 72; plus thirteen awards in regional shows in past two years.
Memberships: Am Artists Prof League; Copley Soc Boston; North Shore Arts Asn; Chautauqua Art Asn; Salmagundi Club.
Art Interests: Oil paintings, done in a traditional style, landscapes and seascapes.
Mailing Address: 4 Story St, Rockport, MA 01966.

TURNER, DICK
Cartoonist
Preferred Media: Inks.
b Indianapolis, Ind, Aug 11, 09.
Study & Training: John Heron Art Inst; De Pauw Univ, AB; Chicago Acad Fine Arts; Cleveland Art Sch.
Memberships: Nat Cartoonist Soc.
Publications: Auth & illusr, Carnival (cartoon panel), 40-
Mailing Address: 555 Flamevine Lane, Vero Beach, FL 32960.

TURNER, EVAN HOPKINS
Museum Director
b Orono, Maine, Nov 8, 27.
Study & Training: Harvard Univ, AB, MA, PhD; Sir George Williams Univ, hon LHD, 65; Swarthmore Col, hon LHD, 67.
Teaching: Adj prof art hist, Univ Pa, 70-
Positions: Lectr & res asst, Frick Collection, New York, N Y, 53-56; gen cur & asst dir, Wadsworth Atheneum, Hartford, Conn, 55-59; dir, Mont Mus Fine Arts, 59-64; dir, Philadelphia Mus Art, 64-
Memberships: Nat Endowment Arts (chmn mus panel); Am Asn Mus (mem coun); Asn Art Mus Dirs (chmn prof practices comt); Benjamin Franklin fel Royal Soc Arts; Am Fedn Arts (bd mem).
Research: Thomas Eakins; eighteenth century American sculpture.
Mailing Address: P O Box 7646, Philadelphia, PA 19101.

TURNER, JANET E
Printmaker, Educator
Preferred Media: Graphics, Mixed Media.
b Kansas City, Mo, Apr 7, 14.
Study & Training: Stanford Univ, AB, 36; Kansas City Art Inst, with Thomas H Burton, dipl, 41; Claremont Col, with Millard Sheets & Henry McFee, MFA, 47; Columbia Univ, EdD, 60.
Work in Public Collections: Metrop Mus Art, New York, N Y; Philadelphia Mus Art, Pa; Victoria & Albert Mus, London; Bibliotheque Nat, Paris, France; Libr of Cong, Washington, D C.
Exhibitions: American Painting Today, 50 & Watercolors & Prints, 52, Metrop Mus Art, New York; Ninth Nat Exhib, Libr of Cong, Washington, D C, 51; Nat Acad Design, New York, 61; Fourth Int Bordighera Biennale, Italy.
Teaching: Instr art, Girl's Collegiate Sch, 42-47; asst prof art, Stephan F Austin State Col, 47-56; from asst prof to prof art, Chico State Col, 59-
Positions: Pres, Nat Serigraph Soc, 57-59, v pres, 59-62.
Awards: Guggenheim fel, 53; Tupperware Art Found fel, 56; Cannon prize, Nat Acad Design, 61.
Memberships: Assoc Nat Acad Design; Soc Am Graphic Artists; Nat Asn Women Artists; Am Color Print Soc; Los Angeles Printmaking Soc.
Publications: Illusr, The yazoo, Rinehart, 52.
Dealers: Galerie Internationale, 1095 Madison Ave, New York, NY 10028; Bay Window, Mendocino, CA 95460.
Mailing Address: 567 E Lassen, Sp 701, Chico, CA 95926.

TURNER, JOSEPH
Patron
b New York, N Y, Feb 6, 92.
Study & Training: Jefferson Med Col, BS, MD.

Art Interests: Kodachrome photography (non-profit) of works of art & donating the transparencies to museums & universities.
Mailing Address: 1150 Park Ave, New York, NY 10028.

TURNER, RAYMOND
Sculptor
Preferred Media: Wood, Bronze.
b Milwaukee, Wis, May 25, 03.
Study & Training: Milwaukee Art Inst; Layton Sch Art; Wis State Univ; Beaux Arts Inst, New York, N Y.
Work in Public Collections: Fort Wadsworth, Staten Island, N Y; Smithsonian Inst, Washington, D C; Baseball Hall of Fame, Cooperstown, N Y.
Commissions: Commemorative coins of Robert E Lee, Nat Commemorative Soc, 68, Fats Waller, Am Negro Commemorative Soc, 70, Theodore Roosevelt, Int Fraternal Commemorative Soc, 70 & Emily Dickinson, Soc Commémorative Femmes Célebres, 70.
Exhibitions: Detroit Art Inst, Mich, 27; Salon Aulomne, Paris, 28; Pa Acad Fine Arts, Philadelphia, 40; Nat Acad Design, New York, 67; Nat Sculpture Soc, New York, 72.
Awards: August Helbig Prize for Man, Detroit Art Inst, 27; Guggenheim found fel, 28; Pauline Law Prize, for Girl, Allied Artists Am, 66.
Memberships: Fel Nat Sculpture Soc.
Mailing Address: 51 Seventh Ave S, New York, NY 10014.

TURNER, ROBERT CHAPMAN
Educator, Ceramist
Preferred Media: Clay.
b Port Washington, N Y, July 22, 13.
Study & Training: Swarthmore Col, BA; Pa Acad Fine Arts; State Univ N Y Col Ceramics, Alfred Univ, MFA.
Work in Public Collections: Walker Art Ctr, Minneapolis; Univ Ill, Urbana; Smithsonian Inst, Washington, D C; Los Angeles Co Fair Asn; State Univ N Y Albany.
Exhibitions: Int Ceramic Exhib, Palais Miramar, Brussels, Belg, 58; Nat Mus Art, Buenos Aires, Arg, 63 & Victoria & Albert Mus, London, Eng, 72; Objects U S A, traveling exhib sponsored by Johnson Wax Co, 70; one-man show, Bonniers, New York, N Y, 57.
Teaching: Instr ceramics, Black Mountain Col, 49-51; prof ceramic art, State Univ N Y Col Ceramics, Alfred Univ, 58-; instr ceramic art, Penland Sch Crafts, summers, 69-71.
Awards: Prize, Ceramic Nat Exhib, Everson Mus, Syracuse, 51, 54 & 66; silver medal, Cannes, France, 54 & silver medal, Prague, 62, Int Exhib Ceramics.
Bibliography: Daniel Rhodes (auth), Robert Turner, 57 & Howard Yana Shapiro (auth), Bob Turner, 72, Craft Horizons.
Memberships: Nat Coun Educ Ceramic Arts (pres, 68-69); N Y State Craftsmen (bd mem, 55-68); Am Crafts Coun (trustee, 58-60); Int Acad Ceramics, Geneva, Switz.
Mailing Address: Cook Rd, Alfred Station, NY 14803.

TURNER, THEODORE ROY
Painter, Educator
Preferred Media: Watercolors, Oils.
b Frederick Hall, Va, Jan 10, 22.
Study & Training: Richmond Prof Inst, Col William & Mary, BFA, 43; New Sch Soc Res, New York, N Y, 46-50, painting with Abraham Rattner & printmaking with Louis Shanker; N Y Univ Inst Fine Arts, MA, 50.
Work in Public Collections: New York Pub Libr Print Collection; Va Mus Fine Arts, Richmond; Miss Art Asn, Jackson; Dartmouth Col, Hanover, N H; Univ Va, Charlottesville.
Exhibitions: Brooklyn Mus Print Ann, 51 & 55; Am Fedn Arts Traveling Exhib Prints, 55; Va Mus Biennials, 59, 67 & 71; Watercolor U S A, Springfield, Mo, 64; one-man shows, Babcock Galleries, New York, 68 & 69.
Teaching: Instr medieval archit, Dartmouth Col, 50-52; assoc prof painting, Univ Va, 52-, acting chmn McIntire Dept Fine Arts, 62-67; vis artist, Roanoke Fine Arts Ctr, Va, 71.
Awards: Cert distinction & purchase award, Va Mus Fine Arts, 59; purchase award, 20th Watercolor Nat, Miss Art Asn, 61; painting award, 18th Irene Leache Mem, Norfolk Mus, 66.
Bibliography: Sue Dickinson (auth), Theodore Turner, Richmond Times-Dispatch, 6/23/68; Theodore Turner, New York Mag, 6/24/68; Larry Campbell (auth), Theodore Turner's watercolors, Art News, 12/69.
Memberships: Va Ctr Creative Arts (adv bd, 71-72).
Dealer: Babcock Galleries, 805 Madison Ave, New York, NY 10021.
Mailing Address: 916 Old Farm Rd, Charlottesville, VA 22903.

TUROFF, MURIEL PARGH
Sculptor, Painter
Preferred Media: Metals, Enamels.
b Odessa, Russia, Mar 1, 04; U S citizen.
Study & Training: Art Stud League New York; Pratt Inst; Univ Colo.

Work in Public Collections: Smithsonian Inst Portrait Gallery, Washington, D C; Jewish Mus, New York, N Y.
Exhibitions: Syracuse Mus Art, N Y, 45; Mus Natural Hist, New York, 58; Cooper Union Mus, New York, 60; Lowe Mus Beaux Arts, Miami, Fla, 68; YM-YWHA, Miami, Fla, 71.
Teaching: Instr art & ceramics, Riverdale Neighborhood House, New York, 43-47; instr ceramics in occup ther, Vet Hosp, Bronx, 45-46; instr basic design, Westchester Co Ctr, 59-61; instr enamelling, Miami Art Ctr, 70-72.
Awards: Blue ribbon for best in show, Blue Dome Art Fel, 66; second prize, YM-YWHA, 71.
Memberships: Artists Equity Asn; Fla Sculptors; Blue Dome Art Fel (treas, 64-68); Am Craftsmen's Coun; Fla Craftsmen.
Publications: Auth, How to make pottery, Crown, 49.
Mailing Address: 517 Gerona Ave, Coral Gables, FL 33146.

TUTTLE, RICHARD
Painter
b Rahway, N J.
Study & Training: Trinity Col(Conn); Cooper Union.
Work in Public Collections: Drawings, Betty Parsons Collection; James A Michener Found; Nat Gallery, Can; Corcoran Gallery Art, Washington, D C; Kaiser-Wilhelm Mus, Ger; plus other pub & pvt collections.
Exhibitions: One-man shows, Betty Parsons Gallery, 65-67, 68 & 70; Galeria Schmela, Dusseldorf, 68 & Nicholas Wilder Gallery, Los Angeles, 69; Anti Illusion: Procedures/Materials, Whitney Mus Am Art, 69; Corcoran Gallery Art 31st Biennial, 69; Soft Art, N J State Mus, 69; Am Paintings Of 60's, Am Fedn Arts, 69; plus others.
Bibliography: The avant garde: subtle, cerebral, elusive, Time, 11/22/68; This is the loose paint generation, Nat Observer, 8/4/69; Robert Pincus-Witten (auth), The art of Richard Tuttle, Artforum, 2/70; plus many others.
Publications: Contribr, Art Int.
Mailing Address: c/o Betty Parsons Gallery, 24 W 57th St, New York, NY 10019.

TWARDOWICZ, STANLEY JAN
Painter, Photographer
b Detroit, Mich, July 8, 17.
Study & Training: Meinzinger Art Sch, Detroit, 40-44; Skowhegan Sch Painting & Sculpture, Maine, summers 46 & 47.
Work in Public Collections: Mus Mod Art, New York, N Y; Los Angeles Co Mus Art; Milwaukee Art Ctr; Am Fedn Arts; New York Univ, N Y.
Exhibitions: Guggenheim Mus, 54; Art Inst Chicago, 54, 55 & 61; Carnegie Int, 55; five exhibs, Mus Mod Art, 57-69; Mus Fine Arts, Boston, 66.
Teaching: Instr art, Ohio State Univ, 46-51; asst prof art, Hofstra Univ, 65-
Awards: Guggenheim Found fel, 56-57.
Dealer: Peridot-Washburn Gallery, 820 Madison Ave, New York, NY 10021.
Mailing Address: 57 Main St, Northport, NY 11768.

TWIGGS, LEO FRANKLIN
Painter, Educator
Preferred Media: Batik.
b St Stephen, S C, Feb 13, 34.
Study & Training: Claflin Col, Orangeburg, S C; Art Inst Chicago; N Y Univ, With Jason Seley & Hale Woodruff; Univ Ga, with Sam Adler.
Work in Public Collections: Johnson Publ Co, Chicago; Spring Mills, New York; Wachovia Bank & Trust Co, N C; Atlanta Univ, Ga; Citizens & Southern Bank, S C.
Exhibitions: Sch Pub Health Art Exhib, Univ N C, 71; Nat Exhib Black Artists, Washington, D C, 71; Artists U S A, Carnegie Inst, Pittsburgh, Pa, 71-72; Salute to Black Artists, N J State Mus, Trenton, 72; Scholastic Mag Nat Art Competition, 72.
Teaching: Assoc prof art, S C State Col, 64-
Positions: Comnr, S C Arts Comn, 70-
Awards: Best in show, Nat Conf Artists, 69; merit prize, Guild S C Artists, 70; award of distinction, Smith Mason Gallery, 71.
Bibliography: J Edward Atkinson (auth), Black dimensions in contemporary American art, 70; Ruth Waddy & Samella Lewis (auth), Black artists on art, Vol II, 71; Mary Mebane (auth), article, In: Instr Mag, 72.
Memberships: Col Art Asn Am; Nat Art Educ Asn; Nat Conf Artists (chmn, educ div, 72); Guild S C Artists; S C Arts Comn (comnr, 70-72).
Research: Using a method of art criticism with Black underprivileged children.
Publications: Auth, articles, In: Explor Educ, 70, Design Mag, 72, Negro Educ Rev, 72, Sch Arts, 72 & Mus News, 72.
Mailing Address: P O Box 1691, South Carolina State College, Orangeburg, SC 29115.

TWIGGS, RUSSELL GOULD
Painter
Preferred Media: Acrylics.
b Sandusky, Ohio, Apr 29, 98.
Study & Training: Carnegie-Mellon Univ.
Work in Public Collections: Whitney Mus Am Art, New York, N Y; Wadsworth Atheneum, Hartford, Conn; Mus Art, Carnegie Inst, Pittsburgh, Pa; Brooklyn Mus, N Y; Westmoreland Co Mus Art, Greensburg, Pa.
Exhibitions: Abstr & Surrealist Painting, Art Inst Chicago, Ill, 47; Whitney Mus Am Art Ann, 55; five Carnegie Int, 55-67; Mus Mod Art Drawing Show, 56; Corcoran Gallery Art, Washington, D C, 57.
Positions: Massier, Carnegie-Mellon Univ, 24-
Awards: Carnegie Inst Group Prize, Assoc Artists Pittsburgh, 49; second prize for painting, Cincinnati Art Mus, 55; Mrs Henry J Heinz, II Award, 62.
Bibliography: Paul Lancaster (auth), The artist, Wall St J, 57; Paul Chen (auth), Russell Twiggs retrospective, Westmoreland Co Mus Art, 64; Connie Kienzle (auth), Russell Twiggs, Roto-Pittsburgh Press, 71.
Memberships: Pittsburgh Plan Art.
Dealer: Pittsburgh Plan For Art, 1251 N Negley Ave, Pittsburgh, PA 15206.
Mailing Address: 652 Maryland Ave, Pittsburgh, PA 15232.

TWITTY, JAMES (WATSON)
Painter, Educator
Preferred Media: Acrylics, Oils.
b Mt Vernon, N Y, Apr 13, 16.
Study & Training: Art Stud League New York, N Y, with Edwin Dickenson, Stephen Greene & Morris Kantor; Univ Miami, with Xavier Gonzalez & Eliot O'Hara.
Work in Public Collections: Nat Collection Fine Arts, Washington, D C; Baltimore Mus Art, Md; Corcoran Gallery Art, Washington, D C; High Mus Art, Atlanta, Ga; Mus Fine Arts, Dallas, Tex.
Exhibitions: One-man shows, Corcoran Gallery Art, 66, Lehigh Univ, Bethlehem, Pa, 67, Valley House Gallery, Dallas, 69, Findlay Gallery, New York, 71 & McNay Art Inst, San Antonio, Tex, 72.
Teaching: Assoc prof painting, Corcoran Sch Art, 64-; lectr fine arts, George Washington Univ, 64-
Awards: Award of merit, Allied Artists Am, 61; second prize, Soc Washington Artists, 65; hon mention, First Ann Exhib, Miami, Fla, 66.
Memberships: Life mem Art Stud League New York.
Dealers: Findlay Galleries, 990 Madison Ave, New York, NY 10021; Pyramid Galleries, 2121 P St N W, Washington, DC 20037.
Mailing Address: 1600 S Joyce St, Arlington, VA 22202.

TWOMBLY, CY
Painter
b Lexington, Va, Apr 25, 28.
Study & Training: Boston Mus Sch Fine Arts, 48-49; Washington & Lee Univ, 50; Art Stud League New York, 51; Black Mountain Col, 52, with Frank Kline & Robert Motherwell.
Work in Public Collections: Represented in pvt collections in New York, Chicago, Washington, D C & Europe.
Exhibitions: New York Univ, N Y, 67; Whitney Mus Am Art Ann, New York, 67; one-man shows, Milwaukee, Wis, 68 & Nicholas Wilder Gallery, 69; Herron Inst Art, Indianapolis, Ind, 69; plus others.
Teaching: Head art dept, Southern Sem & Jr Col, Buena Vista, Va, 55-56.
Awards: Va Mus Fine Arts fel for travel in Europe & Africa, 52-53.
Bibliography: Pierre Restany (auth), Lyrisme et abstraction, Edizioni Apollinairi, Milan, 60.
Dealer: Leo Castelli Gallery, 4 E 77th St, New York, NY 10021.
Mailing Address: 149 via Monsevato, Rome, Italy.

TWORKOV, JACK
Painter
b Biala, Poland, Aug 15, 00; U S citizen.
Study & Training: Columbia Univ, 20-23, hon LHD, 72; Nat Acad Design, 23-25; Art Stud League New York, 25-26.
Work in Public Collections: Albright-Knox Art Gallery, Buffalo, N Y; Cleveland Mus Fine Art, Ohio; Mus Mod Art, New York, N Y; Nat Collection Fine Art, Smithsonian Inst, Washington, D C; Whitney Mus Am Art, New York; plus others.
Exhibitions: New American Painting, Int Traveling Show, Nionia, 58; Osaka Festival, Gutai 9, 58; Documenta II, Kassel, Ger, 59; American Abstract Expressionists, Guggenheim Mus, 61; Whitney Mus Am Art Ann, 69-71.
Teaching: Leffingwell prof art & chmn dept, Yale Univ, 63-69; vis prof painting, Cooper Union, 70-72; vis prof painting, Columbia Univ, spring 73.
Awards: William A Clark Prize & Corcoran Gold Medal, Corcoran Gallery Art, 63; Guggenheim fel, 71.

Bibliography: D Ashton (auth), The unknown shore, Little, 62; L Slate (auth), Jack Tworkov, film produced by Nat Educ TV, 63; Ed Bryant (auth), Jack Tworkov, Whitney Mus, 64; plus others.
Publications: Auth, The wandering soutine, 11/50 & auth, Flowers & realism, 5/54, Art News; auth, articles, In: It Is, spring 58, autumn 58 & 59.
Mailing Address: 161 W 22nd St, New York, NY 10011.

TYLER, VALTON
Printmaker
Preferred Media: Aquatint.
b Texas City, Tex, Mar 30, 44.
Study & Training: Dallas Art Inst, Tex, 67.
Work in Public Collections: Tyler Mus Art, Tex.
Exhibitions: First Fifty Prints, Valton Tyler, Pollock Galleries, Southern Methodist Univ, Dallas, Tex, 72; Eighth Ann New Talent in Printmaking, Assoc Am Artists, New York, N Y, 72; First Fifty Prints, Valton Tyler, Tyler Mus Art, 72.
Bibliography: Reynolds (auth), The fifty prints— Valton Tyler, Southern Methodist Univ Press, 72.
Dealer: Valley House Gallery, 6616 Spring Valley Rd, Dallas, TX 75240.
Mailing Address: 5601 Goodwin, Dallas, TX 75206.

TYSON, MRS CHARLES R
Collector
Mailing Address: 6910 Wissahickon Ave, Philadelphia, PA 19119.

TYSON, MARY (MRS KENNETH THOMPSON)
Painter
Preferred Media: Watercolors.
b Sewanee, Tenn, Nov 2, 09.
Study & Training: Grand Cent Art Sch, with George P Ennis, Howard Hildebrandt & Wayman Adams; New Sch Social Res, with Julian Levi.
Work in Public Collections: Artists Asn Nantucket Permanent Collection; Amherst Collection; Guild Hall Collection.
Exhibitions: Watercolors by Contemporary Americans, Addison Gallery, 35; Int Exhib, Brooklyn Mus, 35 & 37; Nat Arts Club Watercolor Exhib, 68; Allied Artists, 70; one-man show, Bruce Mus, Greenwich, Conn, 71.
Awards: Solo award, 68, Elizabeth Morse Genius Mem award, 70 & second brush award, 71, Pen & Brush Club.
Memberships: Am Watercolor Soc; Pen & Brush Club; Easthampton Guild Hall; Nantucket Artists Asn.
Mailing Address: 20 W 11th St, New York, NY 10011.

TYTELL, LOUIS
Painter
Preferred Media: Oils.
b New York, N Y, Jan 8, 13.
Study & Training: City Col New York, BS, 34; Columbia Univ, MA, 35; Skowhegan Sch Painting & Sculpture; New Sch Social Res.
Work in Public Collections: Newark Mus.
Exhibitions: 200 American Watercolors, Whitney Mus Am Art, Nat Gallery Art & Carnegie Inst, 41; 110 American Painters, Walker Art Ctr, 44; Pa Acad Fine Arts Ann, 49 & 66; Nat Acad Design Ann, 62, 66 & 68; Nat Inst Arts & Lett, 67.
Teaching: Chmn art dept, H S Music & Art, 61-67; assoc prof art, City Col New York, 67-69; chmn art dept, H S Mus & Art, 69-
Awards: Purchase for permanent print collection, Libr of Cong, 54; Tiffany fel, 62; grant, Am Inst Arts & Lett, 67.
Dealer: Roko Gallery, 90 E 10th St, New York, NY 10003.
Mailing Address: 14 Washington Pl, New York, NY 10003.

U

UCHIMA, ANSEI
Printmaker, Painter
Preferred Media: Wood.
b Stockton, Calif, May 1, 21.
Work in Public Collections: Art Inst Chicago, Ill; Rijks Mus, Amsterdam; Libr of Cong, Washington, D C; Philadelphia Mus, Pa; Metrop Mus Art, New York, N Y.
Exhibitions: Tokyo Int Print Biennials, 57 & 60; Grenchen Int Print Triennials, 58, 61 & 70; Fifth Sao Paulo Int Biennial, 59; Vancouver Int Print Exhib, 67; 35th Venice Int Biennial, 70.
Teaching: Mem faculty printmaking, Sarah Lawrence Col, 62-; lectr printmaking, Columbia Univ, 68-

Awards: Guggenheim fel, 62-63 & 70-71.
Memberships: Soc Am Graphic Artists; Japan Print Asn.
Mailing Address: 664 W 163rd St, New York, NY 10032.

UDINOTTI, AGNESE
Sculptor, Painter
Preferred Media: Steel, Oils.
b Athens, Greece, Jan 9, 40; U S citizen.
Study & Training: Ariz State Univ, BA & MA.
Work in Public Collections: Phoenix Art Mus, Ariz; Ariz Western
Col, Yuma; Yuma Fine Arts Asn; Glendale Community Col,
Ariz; Ministry of Educ, Athens; Scottsdale Civic Ctr, Ariz.
Commissions: Sculpture, comn by Mrs Eugene T Savage, Yuma, 62;
steel doors, Wilson Jones & Assocs, Scottsdale, Ariz, 70 &
Imagineering, Tucson, Ariz, 72; relief, comn by Mrs M Ehrlich,
Phoenix, 70; steel diptych, comn by Har Oude Jans, Amsterdam,
Holland, 72.
Exhibitions: One-man shows, Vorpal Galleries, San Francisco,
Calif, 68 & 71, Art Forms Gallery, Athens, 69 & 71 & Ariz Chap
Arts & Humanities Traveling Exhib, 71-72; Southwestern Bi-
ennial, Phoenix Art Mus, 71; 6th Ann, Yuma Fine Arts Asn, 72.
Teaching: Workshop leader welded sculpture, Orme Sch Fine Arts
Prog, Mayer, Ariz, Feb 71 & Feb 72; Univ Southern Calif, sum-
mer 72.
Awards: Hellenic Am Union Sculpture Award, 68; Sculpture Prize,
Phoenix Art Mus First Biennial, 71; Solomos Prize for Sculp-
ture, Panos Nikoli Tselepi, Athens, 71.
Bibliography: Seiden Meilach (auth), Direct metal sculpture, Crown,
66 & Creating art from anything, Reilly & Lee, 68.
Mailing Address: c/o 4215 N Marshall Way, Scottsdale, AZ 85251.

UDVARDY, JOHN WARREN
Sculptor, Painter
Preferred Media: Wood, Canvas, Metals, Plastic.
b Elyria, Ohio, May 27, 36.
Study & Training: Skowhegan Sch Painting & Sculpture, scholar, sum-
mer 57; Cleveland Inst Art, scholar, 55-58, BFA, 63; Yale Univ,
scholar, 64-65, MFA, 65.
Work in Public Collections: Cleveland Inst Art, Ohio; Columbia
Broadcasting Syst, New York; N Y; Fogg Mus, Cambridge, Mass;
Princeton Univ, N J.
Commissions: Design of symbol & emblem for Ecol Action R I, 70.
Exhibitions: One-man shows, Michael Walls Gallery, San Francisco,
Calif, 67, Bristol Art Mus, R I, 69, Cleveland Inst Art, 70 &
Annmary Brown Mem, Providence, R I, 71; Young New Eng
Painters, Sarasota, Fla, Portland, Maine & Manchester, N H, 69.
Teaching: Instr drawing, Cleveland Inst Art, 62-63; asst printmaking,
Yale Univ, 64-65; asst prof painting & design, Brown Univ, 72.
Positions: Regional judge, Nat Scholastic Competition, 67; critic &
guest lectr, Atlanta Sch Art, Ga, Mar, 70; vis critic, R I Sch De-
sign, May 70 & May 71.
Awards: Mary C Page Europ Traveling scholar, Cleveland Inst Art,
60-61.
Publications: Illusr, Los, fall 68 & spring 70.
Dealer: Lenore Gray Gallery, 15 Meeting St, Providence, RI 02912.
Mailing Address: 900 Hope St, Bristol, RI 02809.

UELSMANN, JERRY
Photographer
b Detroit, Mich, June 11, 34.
Study & Training: Rochester Inst Technol, BFA, 57; Ind Univ, MS,
58, MFA, 60.
Work in Public Collections: Mus Mod Art, New York, N Y; Phila-
delphia Mus Art, Pa; Art Inst Chicago, Ill; Nat Gallery Can,
Ottawa; Int Mus Photog, George Eastman House, Rochester, N Y.
Exhibitions: Photography in America 1850-1965, Yale Univ Art
Gallery, 65; Photography in the Twentieth Century, George East-
man House in collab with Nat Gallery Can, 67; one-man shows,
Mus Mod Art, New York, 67, Philadelphia Mus Art, 70 & Art Inst
Chicago, 72.
Teaching: Prof photog, Univ Fla, 60-
Awards: Guggenheim fel, 67; grant, Univ Fla, 70; photog fel, Nat
Endowment Arts, 73.
Bibliography: Jerry N Uelsmann (monograph), Aperture Inc, 70;
W E Parker (auth), Eight photographs: Jerry Uelsmann, Double-
day, 70; John Ward (auth), The criticism of photography as art:
the photographs of Jerry Uelsmann, Univ Fla Press, 70.
Memberships: Founding mem Soc Photog Educ; fel Royal Photog
Soc Gt Brit.
Publications: Contribr, Contemporary Photographer, 64, Camera,
67, Aperture, 67, 68 & 70, Life, 69 & Infinity.
Dealer: Witkin Gallery, 243 E 60th St, New York, NY 10022.
Mailing Address: 5701 S W 17th Dr, Gainesville, FL 32601.

UHL, EMMY
Sculptor
b Bremen, Ger, Mar 10, 19; U S citizen.
Work in Public Collections: Hudson River Mus, Yonkers, N Y.

Exhibitions: Yonkers Art Asn Ann, N Y, 67-70; Westchester Art
Soc Ann, N Y, 69-71; N Shore Community Arts Ctr, L I, N Y, 70;
Knickerbocker Artists Ann, New York, N Y, 70-72; Audubon Art-
ists, New York, 71; plus others.
Awards: Armbruster Award, Yonkers Art Asn, 67; Knickerbocker
Artists Award Merit, 72.
Bibliography: Jerry G Bowles (auth), rev, In: Art News, 6/70; Car-
ter Ratcliff (auth), rev, In: Art Int, 6/70; Beatrice Dain (auth),
Gallery previews in New York, Pictures on Exhib, 6/70.
Memberships: Yonkers Art Asn.
Dealer: Sindin Harris, Hartsdale Ave, Hartsdale, NY 10530.
Mailing Address: 71 Burkewood Rd, Mount Vernon, NY 10552.

ULIN, DENE
Collector, Art Consultant
b Detroit, Mich, Sept 6, 30.
Study & Training: Conn Col; Art Inst Chicago.
Collections Arranged: Personal collection & representative artists
shown, J Walter Thompson Co, New York, Neiman-Marcus, Dal-
las, Salcowitz, Houston, Hall's, Kansas City, Cooper Union Mus,
New York, Tiffany's windows, New York & Joan Rivers Show,
NBC-TV, 69.
Positions: Adv to purchasers of fine arts, in relationship with 40
New York galleries & dealers, for paintings, sculpture & draw-
ings; exclusive agent in the U S for William Accorsi, toy sculp-
ture & Luba Krejci, lace constructions.
Collection: Contemporary art.
Publications: Auth, articles in art mag.
Mailing Address: 27 E 65th St, New York, NY 10021.

ULLMAN, MRS GEORGE W
Collector
Collection: French furniture and paintings, Louis XV and Louis XVI
periods; Haitian paintings; contemporary paintings of Philip
Curtis.
Mailing Address: 4642 N 56th St, Phoenix, AZ 85018.

ULLMAN, HAROLD P
Collector
b Chicago, Ill, Jan 30, 99.
Study & Training: Univ Mich Sch Engr.
Positions: Bd mem, Los Angeles Co Mus Art, 59-64; bd mem, Pasa-
dena Art Mus, 65-; bd mem, Grunwald Ctr Graphic Arts, Univ
Calif, Los Angeles.
Collection: Rouault graphics; sculpture from India and Nepal;
primitive art.
Mailing Address: 12001 San Vicente Blvd, Los Angeles, CA 90049.

ULLRICH-ZUCKERMAN, B
Painter, Photographer
b Evanston, Ill.
Study & Training: Northwestern Univ, BA(with honors in Eng), 30;
Art Inst Chicago, BFA, 34; with Boris Anisfeld & Francis Chapin;
also with Edward Weston, 42; Univ Chicago, MA, 48.
Work in Public Collections: Remembrance of Things Past, Univ Ariz
Collection Am Painting, Tucson; photog in Hall of Justice, San
Francisco, Calif; Midwest Color Slide Art Collection, Chicago
Main Pub Libr, Ill; plus in many pvt collections throughout U S A.
Exhibitions: Cent Am Traveling Exhib, 41; Painting in the United
States, Carnegie Inst, Pittsburgh, Pa, 43 & 44; Photography at
Mid Century, Eastman House, Rochester, N Y, 60; Western Asn
Art Mus Traveling Exhibs, 66-69; one-man show paintings, 40 &
photog, 70, San Francisco Mus Art.
Teaching: Instr pvt classes, 46-
Awards: Kistler Print Prize, Laguna Beach Mus, Calif; 38; hon men-
tion, San Francisco Mus Art, 39; hon award, Newspaper Photog
Awards, Nat Salon, Washington, D C, 59.
Memberships: Artists Equity Asn (secy Chicago chap, 55-56, nomi-
nating comt); San Francisco Women Artists; Friends of Photog;
Bay Area Photog (secy, 71-).
Publications: Contribr, Am Heritage, 2/65; reproduced painting,
Mardi Gras.
Mailing Address: 2206 44th Ave, San Francisco, CA 94116.

UMLAUF, CHARLES
Sculptor
Preferred Media: Bronze, Marble.
b Mich, July 17, 11.
Study & Training: Art Inst Chicago, with Albin Polasek; Chicago Sch
Sculpture, with Viola Norman.
Work in Public Collections: Krannert Art Mus, Univ Ill, Urbana; Des
Moines Art Ctr, Iowa; Metrop Mus Art, New York, N Y; Okla Art
Ctr; Mus Fine Arts, Houston, Tex; plus nine other Tex mus.
Commissions: Marble reredos relief, St Michael & All Angels
Church, Dallas, Tex, 61; Spirit of Flight (bronze fountain sculp-
ture), at entrance of Lovefield Airport, Dallas, 61; Torch Bear-
ers (bronze), acad ctr entrance, Univ Tex, Austin, 63; Icarus

(bronze), in lobby of Phillips Petrol Bldg, Bartlesville, Okla, 64; Family Group (three figural bronze), at entrance of Houston Mus Natural Sci, Tex, 72.
Exhibitions: Third Int Sculpture Exhib, Philadelphia Mus Art, Pa, 49; American Sculpture, 1951, Metrop Mus Art, New York, N Y, 51; Int Relig Biennial, Salzburg, Austria, Ger, Spain & Eng, 58-59; 20th Ceramic Int, Everson Mus, Syracuse, N Y & tour, 59-60; 161st Ann, Pa Acad Fine Arts, Philadelphia, 66; plus various other exhibs & presentations of artistic endeavors in mus, galleries & univs.
Teaching: Prof sculpture, Univ Tex, Austin, 52-
Awards: Guggenheim grant, 49-50; purchase award, Ford Found, 60; grant, Univ Tex, 66.
Bibliography: Gibson A Danes (auth), The sculpture of Charles Umlauf, sculptor, Univ Tex Press, 67; Earl Miller (dir), Bronze sculpture- (in the making), produced by Univ Tex, 69.
Dealers: Dalzell Hatfield Galleries, Box K Ambassador Hotel, Los Angeles, CA 90070; Valley House Gallery, 6616 Spring Valley Rd, Dallas, TX 75240.
Mailing Address: 506 Barton Blvd, Austin, TX 78704.

UNDERWOOD, EVELYN NOTMAN
Painter
Preferred Media: Watercolors.
b St Catharines, Ont; U S citizen.
Study & Training: Pratt Inst, grad; Berkshire Summer Sch Art, grad; State Univ N Y Col Buffalo; State Univ N Y Buffalo; Millard Fillmore Col; also with Charles Burchfield, Millard Sheets, Ernest Watson & Rex Brandt.
Work in Public Collections: Roswell Park Inst, Buffalo, N Y; Vet Hosp, Buffalo.
Exhibitions: Butler Inst Am Art 19th Ann, Youngstown, Ohio, 54; Indust Niagara Art Exhib, 65; Int Platform Asn Art Shows, Sheraton Hotel, Washington, D C, 70 & 71; Burchfield Ctr, State Univ N Y Col Buffalo, 70 & 72; Nat League Am Pen Women Regionals, New York, N Y; plus others.
Teaching: Instr art, Buffalo Pub Schs; instr, Buffalo Mus Sci, 50-51; instr art, Arcade Cent Sch, N Y, 63-64.
Awards: Purchase award & first prize, Ten Yellow Steps Gallery, 53; first prize, Nat League Am Pen Women; Regional Shows.
Memberships: Int Platform Asn (secy, 58-59, mem coun); Nat League Am Pen Women (art chmn, 66-68, deleg, for Assoc Art Orgn Western N Y, 68-72).
Collection: Landscape and travel paintings.
Publications: Illusr, Bull Millard Fillmore Hosp, 56; illusr, cover, Pen Woman, Vol 47, No 4.
Mailing Address: 362 Linden Ave, East Aurora, NY 14052.

UNTERMYER, JUDGE & MRS IRVING
Collectors
Collection: Porcelains.
Mailing Address: 960 Fifth Ave, New York, NY 10021.

UNTERSEHER, CHRIS CHRISTIAN
Sculptor
Preferred Media: Ceramics.
b Portland, Ore, May 14, 43.
Study & Training: San Francisco State Col, BA, 65; Univ Calif, Davis, MA, 67.
Work in Public Collections: Objects U S A, Johnson Wax Collection, Racine, Wis; Allan Stone Galleries Collection, New York, N Y; Jim Newman Found, San Francisco, Calif; Mem Union Art Gallery Collection, Univ Calif, Davis.
Exhibitions: Objects U S A, Johnson Wax Collection, int traveling show, 69-73; 20 Americans, Mus Contemp Crafts, New York, 71; one-man shows, Hansen-Fuller Gallery, San Francisco, 67-70, Trains, De Young Mus, San Francisco, 68 & Allan Stone Galleries, New York, 69.
Teaching: Instr ceramics, Univ Calif, Davis, 68-69; instr ceramics, Univ Cincinnati, 69-70; asst prof ceramics, Univ Nev, Reno, 70-
Awards: Purchase award, Mem Union Art Gallery, Univ Calif, Davis, 68; purchase award, Ann Graphics Competition, Nev Art Gallery, Reno, 71.
Bibliography: David Zack (auth), Art news: nut art in quake time, Newsweek, 70; Nordness (auth), Objects: U S A, Viking, 70; Lowell Darling (auth), Clay without tears, Art Ctr World, 71.
Memberships: Am Crafts Coun.
Dealer: Wenger Gallery, 855 Montgomery St, San Francisco, CA 94133.
Mailing Address: 948 Washington, Reno, NV 89503.

UNWIN, NORA SPICER
Painter, Printmaker
Preferred Media: Watercolor, Collage, Graphics.
b Surbiton, Eng.
Study & Training: Leon Underwood Studio; Kingston Sch Art; Royal Col Art, ARCA; also with George Demetrios, Boston & Donald Stoltenberg, De Cordova Mus, Lincoln.
Work in Public Collections: Brit Mus & Victoria & Albert Mus, London, Eng; Metrop Mus Art, New York, N Y; Libr Cong, Washington, D C; Wiggin Collection, Boston Pub Libr, Mass.
Exhibitions: Royal Acad, London, Eng; Bibliot Nat, Paris, France; Worcester Art Mus, Mass; Springfield Mus Art, Mass; Metrop Mus Art, New York.
Awards: Prize for graphics, Nat Acad Design, 58; prize for watercolor, Boston Watercolor Soc, 65; prize for graphics, Cambridge Art Asn, 68.
Memberships: Nat Acad Design; Soc Am Graphic Artists; Boston Printmakers (exec bd); Boston Watercolor Soc; N H Art Asn.
Publications: Auth & illusr, Proud pumpkin, Joyful the morning, 63, Two too many, 63 & The midsummer witch, 66, McKay; auth & illusr, Sinbad the cygnet, John Day Co, 70.
Mailing Address: Pine-Apple Cottage, Old Street Rd, Peterborough, NH 03458.

UPJOHN, EVERARD MILLER
Art Historian
b Scranton, Pa, Nov 7, 03.
Study & Training: Harvard Univ, AB, 25, MArch, 27.
Teaching: Asst prof hist art, Univ Minn, Minneapolis, 25-35; from asst prof to prof hist art, Columbia Univ, 35-70, emer prof art hist, 70-
Research: History of American architecture.
Publications: Auth, Richard Upjohn, architect & churchman, 39; co-auth, History of world art, 49, rev ed, 58; contribr, Encycl American, 50; co-auth, Highlights, an illustrated history of art, 63.
Mailing Address: 47-06 U Meadow Lakes, Hightstown, NJ 08520.

URBAN, MYCHAJLO RAPHAEL
Sculptor, Painter
Preferred Media: Plywood, Acrylics, Welded Steel.
b Luka, Ukrainian SSR, Sept 27, 28; U S citizen.
Study & Training: Univ Chicago, 56-59; Sch Art Inst Chicago, BFA, 59; Ill Inst Technol, with Misch Kohn, 64-65.
Work in Public Collections: Concordia Teachers Col, River Forest, Ill.
Exhibitions: Ravinia Festival Art Exhib, Highland Park, Ill, 59; 64th Ann Artists Chicago & Vicinity, 61; 161st Ann, Pa Acad Fine Art, Philadelphia, 66; 13th Ball State Univ Ann, Muncie, Ind, 67; 150 Years Ill Traveling Show, 69-71.
Teaching: Instr sculpture, Evanston Art Ctr, 70-
Awards: Edward L Ryerson For Traveling fel, 59; prizes, Art Inst Chicago & Univ Wis-La Crosse, 65.
Bibliography: D Z Meilach (auth), Contemporary art with wood, Crown, 68 & Creative carving, Reilly & Lee, 69.
Dealer: Michael Wyman Gallery, 233 E Ontario St, Chicago, IL 60611.
Mailing Address: 2006 W Chicago Ave, Chicago, IL 60622.

URBAN, REVA
Painter, Sculptor
Preferred Media: Oils, Aluminum.
b Brooklyn, N Y, Oct 15, 25.
Study & Training: Art Stud League New York, Carnegie scholar, 43-45.
Work in Public Collections: Mus Mod Art, New York, N Y; Art Inst Chicago, Ill; Univ Mus, Berkeley, Calif; Finch Col Mus, New York; Averthorp Gallery, Jenkintown, Pa.
Exhibitions: Pittsburgh Int, 58-; First Biennale Chrislicher Kunst der Gegenwart, Salzburg, Austria, 58; Continuity & Change, Wadsworth Atheneum, Hartford, Conn, 62; Documenta III, Kassel, Ger, 64; Seven Decades-Crosscurrents in Modern Art 1895-1965, exhib at ten New York galleries, 65.
Bibliography: Sam Wagstaff, Jr (auth), Reva, Am Abstract Painters & Sculptors, 62; Peter Selz (auth), Reva Urban, Catalogue, 65 & Univ Art Collections, 66.
Mailing Address: 845 Eighth Ave, New York, NY 10019.

URQUHART, TONY
Sculptor, Painter
Preferred Media: Plywood.
b Niagara Falls, Ont, Apr 9, 34.
Study & Training: Albright Art Sch, dipl, 56; Univ Buffalo, BFA, 58; Yale Univ Summer Sch, fel, 55.
Work in Public Collections: Nat Gallery Can, Ottawa; Art Gallery Ont, Toronto; Winnipeg Art Gallery; Walker Art Ctr, Minneapolis, Minn; Mus Mod Art.
Commissions: 12 murals, Niagara Falls, Skylon Tower, CPR Restaurants, 65; mural, Prov Ont Govt Bldg, 67.
Exhibitions: Carnegie Int, Pittsburgh, Pa, 58; Guggenheim Int, New York, N Y, 58; Paris Biennial, France, 63; Art Am & Spain, Madrid, Barcelona, Rome & Paris, 64; Sculpture '67, Toronto, 67.

Teaching: Lectr lettering, Univ Buffalo, 57-58; lectr basic design, McMaster Univ, 66-67; asst & assoc prof basic design & fine art, Univ Western Ont, 67-72; prof fine art, Univ Waterloo, 72-
Positions: Artist-in-residence, Univ Western Ont, 60-63 & 64-65.
Awards: Baxter Award, Ont Soc Artists Exhib, 61; Can Coun fel, 63 & 67.
Bibliography: J Russell Harper (auth), Painting in Canada, Univ Toronto Press, 66; John Chandler (auth), Drawing reconsidered, 10/11/70 & Dorothy Cameron (auth), A reunion with Tony Urquhart, 4/5/71, Arts Can.
Memberships: Can Artists Representation (nat secy, 68-72); Can Conf Arts (bd gov, 70-73, second v pres, 71).
Publications: Illusr, A sketchbook of Canadian & European drawings, 63 & The broken ark—a book of beasts, 71.
Dealers: Nancy Poole Studio, Waterloo St, London & Toronto; Bau-Xi Gallery, 3003 Granville St, Vancouver, B C, Can.
Mailing Address: 102-271 West Court Pl, Waterloo, Ont, Can.

URRUTIA, LAWRENCE
Art Administrator
b Los Angeles, Calif, July 5, 35.
Collections Arranged: Projections: Anti Materialism, 70, Continuing Surrealism, 71 & Helen Lundeberg, 72.
Positions: Asst dir, La Jolla Mus Contemp Art, Calif.
Mailing Address: La Jolla Museum of Contemporary Art, La Jolla, CA 92037.

URRY, STEVEN
Sculptor
Preferred Media: Aluminum.
b Chicago, Ill, Sept 5, 39.
Study & Training: Chicago Art Inst, 57-59; Univ Chicago, BA, 59.
Work in Public Collections: Chicago Art Inst.
Commissions: Monumental sculpture, Libr Bldg, Loyola Univ, Ill, 69.
Exhibitions: Hemisphere, Am Pavillion, Tex, 68; Univ Nebr Ann, 70; Whitney Mus Am Art, New York, N Y, 70; Art Inst Chicago, 70; Chicago 8 Sculptors, Pioneer Plaza Ctr.
Mailing Address: c/o Zabriskie Gallery, 29 W 57th St, New York, NY 10019.

USHENKO, AUDREY ANDREYEVNA
Painter, Instructor
Preferred Media: Oils.
b Princeton, N J, July 28, 45.
Study & Training: Ind Univ, BA, 65; Sch Art Inst Chicago; Northwestern Univ, MFA, 67, with George M Cohen.
Exhibitions: Ind Artists Salon, Indianapolis Mus, 66-68; two-man show, Evanston, Ill, 67; Phalanx Four & Phalanx Five, Chicago, 67 & 68; one-man shows, Sloan Galleries, Valparaiso, Ind, 68 & 70; five-man faculty show, South Bend, 72.
Teaching: Instr art, Valparaiso Univ, 68-
Memberships: New Art Asn; Col Art Asn Am.
Research: Late eighteenth century English topographical watercolors.
Mailing Address: Dept of Art, Valparaiso University, Valparaiso, IN 46383.

UZIELLI, GIORGIO
Collector
b Florence, Italy, June 5, 03.
Study & Training: Univ Florence, LLD.
Memberships: Am-Italy Soc (pres).
Collection: Aldine editions; first editions of Dante; paintings and bronzes.
Mailing Address: 1107 Fifth Ave, New York, NY 10028.

V

VACCARO, NICK DANTE
Painter, Educator
Preferred Media: Mixed Media.
b Youngstown, Ohio, Apr 09, 31.
Study & Training: Univ Wash, BA, 58; Univ Calif, Berkeley, MA, 60; also with David Park.
Work in Public Collections: San Francisco Art Asn, Calif; Dallas Mus Fine Art, Tex; Montgomery Mus Fine Art, Ala; Univ Calif Berkeley; Youngstown Univ, Ohio.
Commissions: Mosaic, Pac Coast Paper Mills, Seattle, Wash, 57.

Exhibitions: Butler Inst Ann, Youngstown, 56 & 59; San Francisco Art Mus Ann, 58; Riverside Mus Print Int, New York, 59; Calif Palace Legion of Hon, San Francisco, 61; Mid-Am, Nelson Gallery, Kansas City, 64-66 & 70.
Teaching: Instr drawing & painting, dept art, Univ Tex, 60-61, asst prof drawing color, sch archit, 61-63; prof drawing & painting, Univ Kans, 63-, chmn dept art, 63-67; vis artist, Pa State Univ, 70.
Awards: Purchase awards, San Francisco Mus Art, 58, Dallas Mus Fine Arts, 61 & Montgomery Mus Fine Art, 62.
Publications: Illusr, Tex Quart, Vol 5, No 1; illusr, Image, Univ Tex, Austin, 63; auth, Gorky's debt, Art J, 63.
Mailing Address: 535 Kansas St, Lawrence, KS 66044.

VACCARO, PATRICK FRANK (PATT VACCARO)
Printmaker, Painter
Preferred Media: Oils.
b New Rochelle, N Y.
Study & Training: Ohio State Univ; Youngstown State Univ, BS (art educ).
Work in Public Collections: U S Govt for foreign embassies; Butler Inst Am Art, Youngstown, Ohio; St Peters Col, Jersey City, N J; Farnsworth Mus, Wellesley Col, Mass; Canton Art Inst, Ohio.
Commissions: Preservation print, Friends Am Art, Youngstown, 69.
Exhibitions: Boston Libr Tour Italy, 55-59; Boston Printmakers Ann, Boston Mus Fine Arts, 55-; Am Colorprint Soc Ann, Philadelphia, Pa, 59-; Butler Inst Am Art Midyrs, Youngstown, 62-67; Cleveland Mus Art Nat U S Tour, 67.
Teaching: Instr art, Youngstown Pub Schs, 52-; instr art, Youngstown State Univ, 59-70.
Positions: Trustee, Soc N Am Artists, 71-72.
Awards: Medal of hon in graphics, Painters & Sculptors Soc N J, 63; Quaker Storage Award, Am Colorprint Soc, 69; first in ceramics, Butler Inst Am Art, 70.
Memberships: Hunterdon Art Ctr; Boston Printmakers; Am Colorprint Soc; Painters & Sculptors Soc N J; Springfield Art League.
Publications: Illusr, Christian Herald; illusr, Together, Methodist Monthly, 69; illusr, Strategy, Presby-Westminster Press, 71-72.
Dealer: American Art Society, Newport News, VA 23607.
Mailing Address: 3 Oak Dr, Poland, OH 44514.

VALENTINE, DeWAIN
Sculptor
Preferred Media: Polyester Resin.
b Fort Collins, Colo, Aug 27, 36.
Study & Training: Univ Colo, BFA, 58; Yale-Norfolk Art Sch, Yale Univ fel, 58; Univ Colo, MFA, 60.
Work in Public Collections: Whitney Mus Am Art, New York, N Y; Los Angeles Co Mus Art; Pasadena Art Mus; Milwaukee Art Ctr; Stanford Univ Art Mus.
Exhibitions: Whitney Mus Am Art Ann, 66, 68 & 70; Sculpture of the Sixties, Los Angeles Co Mus Art, 66; Plastic Presence, Jewish Mus, New York, Milwaukee Art Ctr & San Francisco Art Mus, 69; 14 Sculptors: The Industrial Edge, Walker Art Ctr, 69; Art Inst Chicago Am Ann, 70; plus others.
Teaching: Instr design & drawing, Univ Colo, 58-61; instr plastics, Univ Calif, Los Angeles, 65-67.
Bibliography: Kurt Von Mier (auth), An interview with DeWain Valentine, 5/68 & Plagens (auth), Five artists—Ace Gallery, 10/71, Artforum; E A Danielli (auth), DeWain Valentine, Art Int, 11/69.
Mailing Address: 69 Market St, Venice, CA 90291.

VALIER, BIRON (FRANK)
Painter, Printmaker
Preferred Media: Collages.
b West Palm Beach, Fla, Mar 13, 43.
Study & Training: Yale Univ, MFA; Cranbrook Acad Art, BFA; Univ Ark; Woodstock Artist's Asn Graphic Workshop; Art Stud League New York; Norton Gallery & Sch Art; Palm Beach Jr Col; Fla State Univ; Mexico City Col.
Work in Public Collections: Butler Inst Am Art, Youngstown, Ohio; DeCordova Mus, Lincoln, Mass; Mus Fine Arts, Boston, Mass; Norton Gallery Contemp Collection, West Palm Beach; Print Collection, Boston Pub Libr.
Exhibitions: Nat Acad Design Ann, New York, N Y, 65; Young Printmakers 1967 Traveling Exhib, 67; New Talent Show, Alpha Gallery, Boston, 69; Landscape II, DeCordova Mus, Lincoln, 71; Food Show, Inst Contemp Art, Boston, 72.
Teaching: Instr art, Wheelock Col, 69-72; part-time instr, R I Col, fall 72.
Awards: Purchase prize, Butler Inst Am Art, 66; award of merit, Fla State Fair Fine Arts Exhib, 66 & 68; purchase prize, DeCordova Mus, Boston Printmakers Exhib, 71.
Bibliography: Peter Fierz (auth), New talent: James Piskoti, Biron Valier, Kunstnachrichten, 11/69; Robert Taylor (auth), Biron

Valier's work tough, bold, Boston Globe, 11/10/72; Katherine Nahum (auth), Biron Valier: trains of thought, Newton Times, 11/8/72.
Memberships: Boston Visual Artist's Union; Am Fedn Arts.
Art Interests: Acrylic & aluminum collages.
Publications: Contribr, Paula's dream world of trains, 72.
Dealer: Athena Gallery, 278 Orange St, New Haven, CT 06510.
Mailing Address: 2 Park Rd, Belmont, MA 02178.

VALIUS, TELESFORAS
Graphic Artist, Educator
b Riga, Latvia, July 10, 14; Can citizen.
Study & Training: Kaunas Sch Fine Arts, 37; Ont Col Educ, 66.
Work in Public Collections: Vytautas Mus, Kaunas, Lithuania; Art Mus Fine Arts, Vilnius, Lithuania; Art Mus, London, Ont; Mus Fine Arts, Montreal, Can; Art Inst Ont, Toronto.
Exhibitions: Canadian Religious Art Today, Regis Col, Jesuit Seminary, Scarboro, Ont, 63; 30th Ann Exhib Am Color Print Soc, Asn Am Artists, New York, N Y, 69; Color Prints of the Americas, New Jersey State Mus, Cult Ctr, Trenton, 70; Exhib Prints sponsored by Can Soc Graphic Arts & Can Embassy, Washington, D C, 71; Canadian Prints & Drawings, sponsored by Can Soc Graphic Arts, Inst Studies Educ Tour, 71.
Teaching: Prof graphic arts, Vilnius Acad Art, 42-44; head graphic arts, Ecole des Arts et Metiers, Freiburg, 46-49; instr art, Winston Churchill Col, 67-
Positions: Pres, Lithuanian Art Inst, 49-57; pres, Soc Can Painters, Etchers & Engravers, 62-65; pres, Can Soc Graphic Art, 65-66.
Awards: C W Jeffery's Award, Can Soc Graphic Art, 58; sterling trust award, Soc Can Painters, Etchers & Engravers, 61; centennial silver medal, Can Govt, 67.
Bibliography: Albert Bechtold (auth), Telesforas Valius, Ourer's L'Imprimerie de Lustenau, 45; Algimantas Mackus (auth), Telesforas Valius, Lithuanian Mag, 64; Algimantas Banelis (auth), Su telesforu valiumi, Lithuanian Cult Mag, 70.
Memberships: Am Colo Print Soc; life fel Int Inst Arts & Lett; Int Platform Asn; mem honoris causa Int Acad Literature, Arts & Sci.
Dealer: Picture Loan Gallery, 3 Charles St W, Toronto, Ont, Can.
Mailing Address: 84 Pine Crest Rd, Toronto 9, Ont, Can.

VALLEE, JACK (LAND)
Painter
Preferred Media: Watercolor.
b Wichita Falls, Tex, Aug 23, 21.
Study & Training: Midwestern Univ; Art Stud League New York, with Reginald Marsh, Howard Trafton & Frank DuMond.
Work in Public Collections: Springfield Mus Art; Univ Okla; Okla Art Ctr; Berkshire Mus, Pittsfield, Mass; Holyoke Mus Art.
Exhibitions: Five shows, Am Watercolor Soc, 58-65; Conn Acad Fine Arts, 59-65; Holyoke Mus, 64 & 68; Fisher Gallery, Washington, D C, 65 & 68; plus others.
Awards: Okla Art Festival, 62-64; McDowell Colony fel, 63; Watercolor: U S A, 64.
Memberships: Allied Artists Am; Washington Watercolor Club; Am Watercolor Soc; Nat Arts Club; Asn Okla Artists.
Mailing Address: 1216 N E 50th St, Oklahoma City, OK 73111.

VALLEE, WILLIAM OSCAR
Painter
Preferred Media: Watercolors.
b South Paris, Maine, June 18, 34.
Study & Training: Univ Alaska.
Work in Public Collections: Many in pvt collections.
Exhibitions: Anchorage Fur Rendezvous, 63; Easter Arts Festival, 63; Alaska Festival Music & Art, 63 & 64; one-man shows, Anchorage Petrol Club, 63 & Anchor Galleries, 63.
Positions: Instituted (in coop with Am Artists Prof League), Am Art Wk, 63; treas, Soc Alaskan Arts, 63; co-founder, Alaska-Int Cult Arts Ctr, secy, 64-; bd dirs & co-founder, Anchorage Community Art Ctr; pres & chmn bd, Alaska Map Serv, Inc.
Awards: Anchorage Fur Rendezvous, 63; Easter Art Festival, 63; Artist of the Month, Alaska Art Guild, 63.
Memberships: Alaska Art Guild (pres & chmn, 64); Alaska Watercolor Soc (pres, 63-); Am Soc Photogrammetry; Am Artist Prof League.
Mailing Address: 4118 Irene Dr, Anchorage, AK 99504.

VALTMAN, EDMUND
Cartoonist
Preferred Media: India Ink.
b Tallinn, Estonia, May 31, 14; U S citizen.
Study & Training: Pvt studios, 36-39; Tallinn Art & Appl Art Sch, 42-44.
Work in Public Collections: Lyndon Johnson Libr, Austin, Tex; Univ Southern Miss Libr; Univ Cincinnati Libr, Ohio; State Hist Soc Mo, Columbia; Wichita State Univ Libr, Kans.

Exhibitions: The Great Challenge, Ed Cartoon Exhib, Washington, Tokyo & London, 58-59; Politics 1960, Columbia Univ, New York, N Y, 60; Int Salon Cartoons, Montreal, Can, 68-71; World Cartoon Festival, Knokke-Heist, Belg, 71; one-man cartoon exhib, Trinity Col, Hartford, Conn, 65.
Awards: Pulitzer Prize for Cartooning, Columbia Univ, 62; Frank Tripp Award, Gannett Newspapers, 63; Pub interest award, Nat Safety Coun, 58.
Memberships: Asn Am Ed Cartoonists; Nat Cartoonists Soc; Conn Acad Fine Arts.
Collection: Editorial cartoons.
Mailing Address: Hartford Times, 10 Prospect St, Hartford, CT 06101.

VAN AALTEN, JACQUES
Painter
b Antwerp, Belg, Apr 12, 07.
Study & Training: Nat Acad Design, 26-30, grad; Art Stud League New York, 32-34; Acad Grande Chaumière, Paris, France, 55; Tulane Univ La, 70-71.
Work in Public Collections: Portrait of Pope Pius XII, Vatican Mus Permanent Collection, Rome, Italy; Relig Ministry Bldg, Jerusalem; Truman Libr, Independence, Mo; La State Art Collection, New Capitol Bldg, Baton Rouge; Rockport Art Asn, Mass; plus many others in pvt collections in U S A & abroad.
Exhibitions: Munic Artists, New York, N Y, 41; Detroit Inst Art Mus, Mich, 46; Isaac Delgado Mus Art, New Orleans, La, 58-59; Rockport Art Asn, Mass, 62-71; La Artists Group, La Art Comn Gallery, Old Capitol Bldg, Baton Rouge; plus many other group & one-man shows.
Teaching: Instr art, Nassau Conservatory Art, Long Island, N Y, 40; instr art, van Aalten Studio Sch, Detroit, 44-47.
Awards: Sydam Medal, 30; Tiffany scholar, 30.
Memberships: Life mem Rockport Art Asn; life mem Art Stud League New York; Nat Soc Mural Painters; Isaac Delgado Mus Art Asn.
Mailing Address: 30 W 60th St, New York, NY 10023.

VAN ARSDALE, DOROTHY THAYER
Art Administrator
b Malden, Mass, Jan 14, 17.
Study & Training: Simmons Col, BS(bus admin).
Collections Arranged: Art Treasure of Turkey, 66, Tunisian Mosaics, 67, Colonial Art from Ecuador, 68 & Swiss Drawings, 69, Washington, D C & nat tour; Selection of New Belgian Painting, Fla & nat tour, 71.
Positions: Chief traveling exhib serv, Smithsonian Inst, Washington, D C, 64-70; dir, Dorothy T Van Arsdale Assocs, Traveling Exhib Serv & Gallery, Fla.
Awards: Knight, Order Dannebrog, King of Denmark, 71.
Memberships: Am Asn Mus.
Publications: Contribr, Paintings & drawings, 66, Sculptures & drawings, 66, Islamic art from the collection of Edwin Binney 3rd, 66 & Carl-Henning Pedersen, 69; contribr & ed, 140 years of Danish glass, 68.
Mailing Address: 830 Montrose St, Clermont, FL 32711.

VAN ATTA, HELEN ULMER
Collector
b Midland, Tex, Mar 3, 14.
Memberships: Art Collectors Club.
Collection: Contemporary American art.
Mailing Address: 4850 Preston Rd, Dallas, TX 75205.

VAN BUREN, RAEBURN
Illustrator, Cartoonist
b Pueblo, Colo, Jan 12, 91.
Study & Training: Art Stud League New York, 13.
Work in Public Collections: Boston Univ Libr; Syracuse Univ.
Teaching: Lect, Comic Strip Art.
Positions: Creator of comic strip Abbie & Slats, syndicated by United Feature Syndicate, over 200 daily newspapers.
Awards: Cartoonist of the Year, B'nai B'rith, Philadelphia, Pa, 58.
Memberships: Nat Cartoonists Soc; life mem Soc Illustrators; Artists & Writers Soc.
Publications: Contribr, illus for Sat Eve Post, Collier's, Redbook, New Yorker, McClure Syndicate & King Features Syndicate, plus others.
Mailing Address: 21 Clover Dr, Great Neck, NY 11021.

VAN BUREN, RICHARD
Sculptor
b Syracuse, NY, 37.
Study & Training: Mexico City Col; Univ Mex; San Francisco State Col.
Work in Public Collections: Mus Mod Art, New York, N Y; Walker Art Ctr, Minneapolis, Minn.

Commissions: 3-unit wall sculpture, Walker Art Ctr, 71.
Exhibitions: Primary Structures, Jewish Mus, New York, 66; Whitney Sculpture Ann, Whitney Mus Am Art, New York, 68 & 70.
Bibliography: Phyllis Tuchman (auth), An interview with Richard Van Buren, Artforum, 12/69; Carter Ratcliff (auth), Solid color, Art News, 5/72.
Mailing Address: c/o Paula Cooper Gallery, 96 Prince St, New York, NY 10012.

VANCE, GEORGE WAYNE
Ceramist, Sculptor
Preferred Media: Clay.
b Macomb, Ill, Oct 29, 40.
Study & Training: Knox Col, BA, 62; Univ Iowa, MA, 68; Univ Colo, MFA, 72.
Work in Public Collections: Wis State Univ-Platteville.
Commissions: Casserole, Sheldon Mem Gallery, Lincoln, Nebr, 69.
Exhibitions: All Iowa Artist, Des Moines Art Ctr, 67; Tenth Ann Rochester Festival Relig Art, N Y, 68; Iscals, Tex Technol Col Mus, 69; Kitchen Keramik Exhib, Sheldon Mem Gallery, 69; Midwest Biennial, Joslyn Mus, Omaha, Nebr, 70-72.
Teaching: Instr ceramics, Dak State Col, 68-70.
Awards: First prize sculpture, Rochester Festival Relig Art, 68; first prize sculpture 70 & jurors award, 71, Own Your Own, Southern Colo State Col.
Bibliography: Paul Arnold (auth), article, In: Craft Horizons, 68; Ray Schemore (auth), article, In: Craft Horizons, 70.
Memberships: Am Crafts Coun.
Mailing Address: Jamestown Star Rte, Boulder, CO 80302.

VANCO, JOHN LEROY
Art Administrator, Photographer
b Erie, Pa, Aug 21, 45.
Study & Training: Allegheny Col, BA(art hist & hist); Whitney Mus Am Art.
Positions: Exec dir, Erie Art Ctr, 68-
Awards: Best prof, ESFA Photog Exhib, 72.
Publications: Auth, What ever happened to Louis Eilshemius?, 67; contribr, American art & western wildlife, 72; illusr, Roger Misiewicz: wolfman of the blues, 72.
Mailing Address: 1317 Parade St, Erie, PA 16503.

VAN DE BOGART, WILLARD GEORGE
Sculptor, Designer
Preferred Media: Media Hardware.
b New York, N Y, Dec 29, 39.
Study & Training: Ohio Univ, BBA, 65; McGill Univ, with Dr Donald Theall, 69; Nat Film Bd Can, with Mark Slade, 69; Calif Inst Arts, with Nam June Paik & Morton Subotnick, 70-71, MFA, 71.
Commissions: Third Eye (oil mural, with Leon Arkus), PPG Indust & Carnegie Mus Art, Market Sq, Pittsburgh, Pa, 71.
Exhibitions: Three Rivers Art Festival, Bell Tel Theatre, Pittsburgh, 70; Propositions for Unrealized Projects, Howard Wise Gallery, New York, N Y, 70; Los Angeles Philharmonic Orchestra Symphonies for Youth, Dorothy Chandler Pavilion, Los Angeles, Calif, 71; Int Glass & China Exhib, Atlantic City Convention Hall, N J, 71; Ninth Ann New York Avant Garde Festival, Sea Port Mus, New York, 72.
Teaching: Instr film arts, Ivy Sch Prof Art, Pittsburgh, 69-70; instr media environ, Calif Inst Arts, 70-71; instr media prod, Univ Pittsburgh, 71-72.
Awards: A W Mellon Award, 69; Robert Flaherty Scholarship Award, Int Film Seminars, 70; Calif Inst Arts Scholarship award, 70.
Bibliography: Jean Lipman (auth), Period rooms—the sixties & seventies, Art in Am, 70; Jim Burns (auth), Arthropods—New design futures, Praeger, 72; Doug Davis (auth), Art into the future, Praeger, 73.
Memberships: Pittsburgh Independent Filmmakers (founder, 69); Experiments in Art & Technology; Am Film Inst.
Research: Performing and experimentation with sound and light generating systems within specifically designed environments incorporating bio-feedback systems.
Art Interests: Video, electronic music, bio-feedback, film, lasers.
Publications: Auth, Filmmakers Newsletter, 69, 70 & 71; auth, Radical software, 70 & 72; auth, article, In: Arts Mag, 72; contribr, Industrial art methods, 72.
Mailing Address: 24 Donati Rd, Pittsburgh, PA 15241.

VAN DER MARCK, JAN
Art Historian, Museum Curator
b Roermond, Netherlands, Aug 19, 29.
Study & Training: Univ Nijmegen, BA, MFA, PhD (hist art), 56; Univ Utrecht; Columbia Univ.
Collections Arranged: Charles Biederman, 65 & Lucio Fontana, 66, Walker Art Ctr, Minneapolis, Minn; Pictures to be Read/Poetry to be Seen, 67, Christo: Wrap In Wrap Out, 69 & Art by Telephone, 69, Mus Contemp Art, Chicago, Ill.

Teaching: Assoc prof art hist, Univ Wash, 72-
Positions: Cur, Gemeentemuseum, Arnhem, Netherlands, 59-61; dep dir fine arts, Seattle World's Fair, Wash, 61-62; cur, Walker Art Ctr, Minneapolis, 63-67; dir, Mus Contemp Art, Chicago, 67-70; dir, Valley Curtain Corp, 71-72; cur contemp art, Henry Gallery, Univ Wash, 72-; contrib ed, Art in Am.
Awards: Fel, Netherlands Org Pure Res, 54-55; fel, Rockefeller Found, 57-59.
Memberships: Am Asn Mus; Col Art Asn Am; Am Fedn Arts (nat exhib comt, 68-).
Research: Art of the twentieth century with emphasis on the last fifteen years.
Publications: Auth, Romantische boekillustratie in Belgie, Romen, 56; auth, The sculpture of George Segal, Abrams, 73; plus many articles in periodicals including, Art in Am, Arts Can & Art Int.
Mailing Address: 8048 Crest Dr N E, Seattle, WA 98115.

VAN DER POEL, PRISCILLA PAINE
Educator, Painter
b Brooklyn, N Y, Apr 9, 07.
Study & Training: Smith Col, AB & AM; Art Stud League New York; Brit Acad in Rome; also with Frank DuMond, George Bridgman, Sherrill Whiton & others.
Exhibitions: Studio Club, Tryon Mus, Northampton, Mass, 36-45.
Teaching: Lect on mod art; instr art, Smith Col, 35-39, asst prof art, 39-45, assoc prof art, 45-60, chmn dept art, 54-58, actg chmn, summers 59 & 61, prof art, 60-72, emer prof, 72-
Memberships: Col Art Asn Am; Am Asn Univ Prof; Northampton Hist Asn; Cosmopolitan Club, N Y.
Mailing Address: 222 Elm St, Northampton, MA 01060.

VAN DERPOOL, JAMES GROTE
Educator, Art Historian
b New York, N Y, July 21, 03.
Study & Training: Mass Inst Technol, BArch; Harvard Univ, MFA; Am Acad Rome, Italy; Atelier Gromort; Ecole Beaux Arts, Paris, France.
Teaching: Prof hist archit, Univ Ill, 32-39, head dept art, 39-46; prof archit & head Avery Libr, Columbia Univ, 46-, acting dean & assoc dean, 59-61.
Positions: Consult various hist preserv projs, 50-; archit ed, Columbia Encycl, 52-54; chmn design construct, Hist St. Luke's Church, Smithfield, Va, 52-56; co-ed, Complete Libr World Art, 57-62; exec dir, Landmarks Preserv Comn New York, 62-65; chmn design ballroom wing, Grace Mansion, New York, 64.
Awards: George McAneny Medal, Am Scenic & Hist Preserv Soc, 64; Benjamin Franklin fel, Royal Soc Arts, London, 65; fel, Am Inst Archit, 68.
Memberships: Int Fund for Monuments (v chmn, 68, trustee, 69-); Save Venice, Nat Comt (co-chmn U S A); Soc Archit Historians (nat pres, 55-57); Col Art Asn Am; Am Scenic & Hist Preserv Soc (trustee, 36-).
Art Interests: Historic preservation; Renaissance painting & eighteenth century American arts.
Collection: Italian, Dutch & American paintings.
Publications: Contribr, Encycl Britannica & others.
Mailing Address: 570 Park Ave, New York, NY 10021.

VANDER SLUIS, GEORGE J
Painter, Educator
Preferred Media: Acrylics.
b Cleveland, Ohio, Dec 18, 15.
Study & Training: Cleveland Inst Art; Colorado Springs Fine Arts Ctr; Fulbright scholar, Italy, 51-52.
Work in Public Collections: Rochester Mem Art Gallery, N Y; Everson Mus Art, Syracuse, N Y; Munson-Williams-Proctor Inst, Utica, N Y; State Univ N Y Albany, N Y; Hamline Univ, St Paul, Minn; plus many others.
Commissions: Mural for post off, Rifle, Colo, 40 & Riverton, Wyo, 41, U S Govt Sect Fine Arts; wall painting for Hotel Syracuse, City Walls New York & N Y State Coun Arts, 71; Barn Door decorations in N Y State, N Y State Coun on the Arts grant, 66.
Exhibitions: American Paintings 1945-1957, Minneapolis Inst Arts, 57; Contemp Painting & Sculpture, Univ Ill, 61; 125 Years of New York Painting & Sculpture, N Y State Expos, Syracuse, 66; American Art, White House, Washington, D C, 66; The Door, Mus Contemp Crafts, New York, 68; plus many other group & one-man shows.
Teaching: Instr painting & drawing, Colorado Fine Arts Ctr, 40-42 & 45-47; prof painting & drawing, Syracuse Univ, 47-
Awards: Jurors award, Rochester Mem Art Gallery, 58 & 69.
Bibliography: J Albino (auth), Barn door painting, Dodge News, 11/67.
Dealer: Krasner Gallery, 1043 Madison Ave, New York, NY 10028.
Mailing Address: School of Art, Syracuse University, Syracuse, NY 13210.

VAN DER STRAETEN, VINCENT ROGER
　Art Dealer
b New York, N Y, June 9, 29.
Positions: Dir, Van Der Straeten Gallery, New York.
Memberships: Art & Antique Dealers League Am (v pres).
Specialty of Gallery: Contemporary American, English and French
　paintings, master graphics and sculpture.
Mailing Address: 981 Madison Ave, New York, NY 10021.

VAN DER VOORT, AMANDA VENELIA
　Painter
Preferred Media: Oils, Watercolors, Graphics.
b Alliance, Ohio.
Study & Training: Pratt Inst, grad. Grand Cent Sch Art; Metrop Sch
　Art; Nat Acad Sch Fine Arts; Columbia Univ; N Y Univ; also with
　Helen Lorenz, Ogden Pleisner, Romanovsky, Robert Philipp, Dong
　Kingman & Howard Hildebrandt.
Commissions: Painting of El Jardin, comn by W Alton Jones, La
　Gorce Island, Fla, 61; portrait of Mrs Rosen, Dr Theodore Rosen,
　New York, N Y, 63; flower painting, E H Blanchard, Warwick,
　N Y, 67; high St, Rockport, Mass, Dr J Wolfe, Houston, Tex, 68;
　Gloxinias, comn by George E Martin, Greenwich, Conn, 71.
Exhibitions: Allied Artists Am, New York, 56-57; Am Artists Prof
　League, New York, 56-72; Nat Acad Design, New York, 57; Hud-
　son Valley Art Asn, White Plains, N Y, 59-72; Acad Artists Asn,
　Springfield, Mass, 65-71.
Positions: Dir & rec secy, Hudson Valley Art Asn, 66-; dir & first
　v pres, Pen & Brush, 67-; dir nat bd, Am Artists Prof League,
　70-
Awards: Awards for figure painting, Catharine Lorillard Wolfe Art
　Club, 70 & Art Soc Old Greenwich, 71; best in show for oil
　portrait, Conn State Fedn Women's Clubs, 72.
Memberships: Catharine Lorillard Wolfe Art Club (dir & chmn nat
　Exhib, 60-); Contemp Art Club Greenwich (art chmn, 72-); Nat
　League Am Pen Women (art chmn, 72-); fel Nat Acad Design; fel
　Royal Soc Arts, Eng.
Mailing Address: 17 Stonehedge Dr S, Greenwich, CT 06830.

VAN DE WIELE, GERALD
　Painter
b Detroit, Mich, 32.
Study & Training: Art Inst Chicago; Black Mountain Col.
Work in Public Collections: Baltimore Mus Art, Md; Borg Warner
　Corp, Chicago; Singer Mfg Co; Owens Corning Fiberglass Corp;
　Coca-Cola Co; also in pvt collections.
Exhibitions: Albright-Knox Art Gallery, Buffalo, N Y, 63; Riverside
　Mus, New York, 64 & 66; Smithsonian Inst Traveling Exhib, 68;
　Ill Wesleyan Univ, Bloomington, 68; Peridot Gallery, New York,
　69; plus others.
Awards: Nat Coun on the Arts grant, 68.
Mailing Address: Apt 3A, 57 W 86th St, New York, NY 10024.

VAN HOESEN, BETH (MRS MARK ADAMS)
　Printmaker
Preferred Media: Intaglio.
b Boise, Idaho, June 27, 26.
Study & Training: Stanford Univ, BA; San Francisco Art Inst; San
　Francisco State Col; Escuela Esmeralda, Mex; Acad Fontain-
　bleau; Acad Grande Chaumière; Acad Julian.
Work in Public Collections: San Francisco Mus, Calif; Brooklyn
　Mus, N Y; Mus Mod Art, New York, N Y; Smithsonian Inst,
　Washington, D C; Victoria-Albert Mus, London, Eng.
Exhibitions: Two Decades of American Prints, 16th Nat Print Ex-
　hib, Brooklyn Mus, 47-68; 116th Ann Exhib, Pa Acad Fine Arts,
　65; Amerikanische Radierugen, touring exhib ten print makers,
　U S Info Bur; Contemp Prints from Northern Calif, Art in Em-
　bassies Prog, U S State Dept, 66; Graphics '71, West Coast
　U S A, Univ Ky, 71.
Awards: San Francisco Mus Art 25th Ann, 61; Pasadena Mus pur-
　chase award, Fourth Biennial Print Exhib, 64; Hawaii Nat Bi-
　ennial, 71.
Bibliography: One woman renaissance in prints, Esquire, 55; A port-
　folio by Beth Van Hoesen, Ramparts, summer 64; Mendelowitz
　(auth), A history of American art, Holt, 70.
Memberships: San Francisco Women Artists; Bay Area Print-
　makers.
Publications: Illusr, A collection of wonderful things, Scrimshaw,
　72.
Dealers: Gump's Gallery, 250 Post St, San Francisco, CA 94108;
　Hanson-Fuller Gallery, 228 Grant Ave, San Francisco, CA 94108.
Mailing Address: 3816 22nd St, San Francisco, CA 94114.

VAN HOOK, DAVID H
　Painter, Art Administrator
b Danville, Va, Dec 25, 23.
Study & Training: Univ S C, with Edmund Yaghijian.

Work in Public Collections: Jacksonville Mus Art, Fla; Greenville Co
　Mus, S C; C & S Nat Bank, Columbia, S C; murals, Caughman Rd
　Sch, Columbia; Columbia Mus Art.
Exhibitions: Mint Mus, Charlotte, N C, 66; Columbia Mus Art, 67;
　C & S Nat Bank Exhib, 68; Pfeiffer Col, Misenheimer, N C, 69;
　Contemp Artist of S C Tricentennial Exhib, Columbia, Greenville
　& Charleston, S C, 70; plus many other group & one-man shows.
Collections Arranged: Jasper Johns Print Travelling Exhibit, 71;
　Eight Washington Artists, 71.
Positions: Registrar, Columbia Mus Art, 51-58, asst to dir, 58-60,
　cur exhibs, 61-
Awards: Rose Talbert Award, 54; hon award, Columbia Mus Art, 59;
　purchase prize, Guild S C Artists, 61.
Memberships: Guild S C Artists; Am Asn Mus; Southeastern Mus
　Conf.
Dealer: Jefferson Place Gallery, 2144 P St N W, Washington, DC
　20036.
Mailing Address: Columbia Museum of Art, Bull & Senate Sts, Co-
　lumbia, SC 29201.

VAN HOOK, NELL
　Painter, Sculptor
Preferred Media: Oils, Clays, Stone, Bronze.
b Richmond, Va.
Study & Training: Hamilton Col; Columbia Univ; Nat Acad Design.
Work in Public Collections: Syracuse Mus; Columbia Univ; Col
　Physicians & Surg, New York, N Y; Gibney Found, Calif; Univ
　Ky; plus others.
Commissions: Two murals, churches in Atlanta, Ga; two paintings,
　World's Fair, New York; portrait, William Bender Collection.
Exhibitions: Catharine Lorillard Wolfe Art Club; Nat Pen Women
　Am, Washington, D C; Gloucester Soc Arts; plus many others.
Awards: First in oils & first in sculpture, Gloucester Soc Arts;
　two first prizes in oils, Catharine Lorillard Wolfe Art Club;
　sculpture prize, Nat Pen Women Am.
Memberships: Burr Artists; Catherine Lorillard Wolfe Art Club;
　Col Art Asn Am, N Y Cahp.
Mailing Address: 501 Theodore Fremd Ave, Rye, NY 10580.

VAN LEER, MRS W LEICESTER
　Collector
b Warwick, N Y, Jan 29, 05.
Study & Training: Smith Col; also with Mary Turlay Robinson.
Collection: Includes works by Delacroix, Matisse, Boudin, Dufy,
　Burchfield, Wyeth, Prendergast, Davies, Bishop, Homer,
　Segonzac, Marin, Cropsey, Utrillo, Beal, Andrew Wyeth and
　others.
Mailing Address: 12 E 73rd St, New York, NY 10017.

VAN LOEN, ALFRED
　Sculptor, Educator
Preferred Media: Stone, Acrylic.
b Oberhausen-Osterfeld, Ger, Sept 11, 24; U S citizen.
Study & Training: Royal Acad Art, Amsterdam, Holland, 41-46.
Work in Public Collections: Metrop Mus Art, New York, N Y; Mus
　Mod Art, New York; Brooklyn Mus, N Y; Nat Mus, Jerusalem,
　Israel.
Commissions: Brass fountain, James White Community Ctr, Salt
　Lake City, Utah, 58; Peace Window, Community Church, New
　York, 63; Crescendo, State Univ N Y Agr & Tech Col Farming-
　dale, 69; Jacob's Dream (brass), Little Neck Jewish Ctr, N Y,
　70; bronze & acrylic portrait of Guy Lombardo, Hall of Fame,
　Stony Brook, N Y, 72.
Exhibitions: Nat Acad Art, New York, 64; Whitney Mus Am Art Ann,
　New York, 67; Emil Walters Gallery, New York, 68; Stony Brook
　Mus, 68; Heckshere Mus, Huntington, N Y, 71.
Teaching: Instr, Hunter Col, 53-54; instr, N Shore Community Art
　Ctr, N Y, 55-61; asst prof sculpture, C W Post Col, L I Univ, 62-
Awards: First prize, Village Art Ctr, 49; Louissa Robbins Award,
　Silvermine Guild Artists, 56; first prize sculpture, Am Soc Con-
　temp Artists, 64.
Bibliography: Paul Moscanyi (auth), Alfred Van Loen, Channel Press,
　60; Mark Smith (auth), Alfred Van Loen, portrait, Long Island
　Mag, 64; Sculptured emotion of A V L, Mod Castings, 65.
Memberships: Artists Equity Asn, New York; Am Soc Contemp
　Artists; Am Crafts Coun; Long Island Univ Pioneer Club; Hunting-
　ton Artists Group.
Publications: Auth, Simple methods of sculpture, Channel Press, 58;
　auth, Instructions to sculpture, C W Post Col, 66; auth, Origin of
　structure and design, Hamilton Press, 67; auth, Drawings by
　Alfred Van Loen, Harbor Gallery Press, 69.
Dealer: Harbor Gallery, 43 Main St, Cold Spring Harbor, NY 11724.
Mailing Address: 221 Beverly Rd, Huntington Sta, NY 11746.

VAN METER, MARY
Painter, Educator
Preferred Media: Acrylics.
b Knox County, Ind, Feb 5, 19.
Study & Training: Vincennes Univ Jr Col, AA, 40; Ind State Univ, BS, 50; Ind Univ, MA, 56; also with Alma Eikerman, Alton Pickens & Jack Tworkov.
Work in Public Collections: Vincennes Univ Art Dept Gallery, Inc; Old Bank Gallery, Vincennes.
Exhibitions: Art for Religion, Lutheran Church, Indianapolis, Ind, 61; one-man show, Old Bank Gallery, 67; Northwest Territory Art Guild Exhib, 67 & Wabash Valley Exhib, 68, Swope Art Gallery, Terre Haute, Ind.
Teaching: Instr art, Washington High Sch, Ind, 52-54; instr art & critic, Ind Univ Sch Educ, Bloomington, 54-56; elem art supvr, Vincennes Pub Schs, Ind, 56-57; instr art, Washington High Sch, 57-65; assoc prof art, Vincennes Univ Jr Col, 66-71, prof art & art coordr, 71-
Awards: Ind Univ Cert scholastic achievement, 56; first prize, oil painting, Little Gallery, Bloomfield, Ind, 60; first hon mention, print, Art for Relig, Lutheran Church, 61.
Bibliography: Theodore Bowie (auth), A critical guide (film), Ind Univ AV Ctr, 57.
Memberships: Northwest Territory Art Guild (pres, 69, corres secy, 71); Indianapolis Mus Art; Ind State Arts Comn; Hoosier Art Salon.
Publications: Contribr, Hoosier college verse, Evansville Univ Press, 39-40; auth, article on collecting dolls, Hobbies Mag, 56; auth, High school art, Sch Arts Mag, 57; auth, Art notes for today's collector, Valley Advan, 67-70; co-auth, Appreciation of the visual arts (in prep).
Dealer: Old Bank Gallery, 1212 Burnett Lane, Vincennes, IN 47591.
Mailing Address: 1002 N First, Vincennes, IN 47591.

VANN, LOLI (MRS LILIAN VAN YOUNG)
Painter
Preferred Media: Oils, Watercolors, Pastels.
b Chicago, Ill, Jan 7, 13.
Study & Training: Art Inst Chicago Sch; also with Sam Ostrowsky.
Work in Public Collections: Chaffey Col, Ontario, Calif; Hollenbeck H S, Los Angeles, Calif.
Exhibitions: Exhib Am Paintings, Carnegie Inst, Pittsburgh, Pa; Am Painting, Metrop Mus Art, New York, N Y; Corcoran Gallery Art Biennial, Washington, D C; Am Paintings & Int Watercolor Exhibs, Art Inst Chicago.
Awards: Purchase prize, Chaffey Community Art Asn; hon mention, Calif Watercolor Soc; second prize, Los Angeles Co Mus Art.
Mailing Address: 2293 Panorama Terrace, Los Angeles, CA 90039.

VAN ROIJEN, HILDEGARDE GRAHAM
Painter, Sculptor
Preferred Media: Metal, Graphics.
b Washington, D C, Nov 1, 15.
Study & Training: Rollins Col; Am Univ; Corcoran Gallery Sch Art, Washington, D C.
Work in Public Collections: Drawings of Egypt, Brooklyn Mus, N Y.
Commissions: Watercolor, Jr League Hq, Washington, D C.
Exhibitions: Int Printmakers Show & Int Watercolor Show, Smithsonian Inst; Phillips Gallery; Am House, Vienna, Austria; Va Mus, Richmond; Corcoran Gallery Art, Washington, D C.
Positions: Art therapist, St Elizabeth's Hosp, Washington, D C.
Awards: First for Pride's Sin, Univ Va, Charlottesville, 71.
Memberships: Artists Equity Asn; Studio Gallery Washington, D C; Northern Va Artists.
Mailing Address: 2911 M St (rear), Washington, DC 20007.

VAN VEEN, STUYVESANT
Painter, Educator
Preferred Media: Oils, Watercolors, Gouache.
b New York, N Y, Sept 12, 10.
Study & Training: City Col New York; Pa Acad Fine Arts; Nat Acad Design; Art Stud League New York; New York Sch Indust Art; also with Daniel Garber, Thomas Benton & David Karfunkel.
Work in Public Collections: Norfolk Mus Arts & Sci, Va; Newark Mus, N J; Fairleigh Dickinson Univ, N J; Smithsonian Inst, Washington, D C; New York Hist Soc.
Commissions: Pittsburgh Panorama (mural), Pittsburgh Post Off, Courthouse, commissioned by U S Treas Dept, 37; The Story of Pharmacy (mural), New York World's Fair, World's Fair Corp, 38; Synthesis (mural) & Security (mural), for courtrooms in Philadelphia Munic Ct Bldg, Philadelphia Art Comn; Bridge of Wings (mural), Wright-Paterson Air Force Base, Ohio Hq Bldg, U S Air Force, 45; Dodgers Victories, murals for seven lobbies at Ebbets Field Apts, Brooklyn, N Y, HFH Corp, 63.
Exhibitions: Carnegie Inst Int, Pittsburgh, 29 & 43; Am Ann, Art Inst Chicago Century Progress, six from 33-46; Cincinnati Mus

Ann, five from 36-49; Whitney Mus Am Art Am Ann, 39-40; Nat Acad Design Ann, 65-69.
Teaching: Instr art, pvt classes, 30-41; instr & supvr painting & drawing, Cincinnati Art Acad, 46-49; assoc prof art, City Col New York, 49-
Positions: Res assoc, dept anthrop, Columbia Univ, 35-38; art dir, Cincinnati Ord Dist, War Dept, 42-43; co-founder & set designer, Stage Inc, Cincinnati Civic Theater, 48-49; art & mural consult, Int Fair Consult, 62-63.
Awards: Childe Hassam purchase award, Am Acad Arts & Lett, 61; Nelson Whitehead Prize, Am Soc Contemp Artists, 66; prize, New Eng Ann, Silvermine Guild Artists, 68.
Memberships: Am Watercolor Soc; Nat Soc Painters Casein (bd dirs, 53); Nat Soc Mural Painters (treas, 60); Artists Equity Asn New York (pres, 58-59); Nat Inst Arts & Lett.
Publications: Illusr, Fortune Mag, 35; illusr, Gesture & environment, Kings Crown, 35-38, Mouton, 72; illusr, The rebel mail runner, Holiday, 54; illusr, Garibaldi, Random, 57; illusr, The art of making the dance, Rinehart, 60; illusr & comment, Gesture, lace and culture, rev ed.
Dealer: ACA Gallery, 25 E 73rd St, New York, NY 10021.
Mailing Address: 320 Central Park W, New York, NY 10025.

VAN WOLF, HENRY
Sculptor, Painter
b Regensburg, Bavaria, Apr 14, 98; U S citizen.
Study & Training: Munich Art Sch, 12-16; sculpture & bronze technique with Ferdinand von Miller, 19-22, 23-26.
Commissions: Bronze statue of an Indian (Fernando), Van Nuys Mall, Calif; bronze mem bust of Einstein, erected at Albert Einstein Med Ctr, Philadelphia, Pa; sculpture group, Garden Grove, Calif; sculptured bronze doors, St Nicholas Episcopal Church, Encino, Calif; bronze monument of Martin Luther King, Jr, Martin Luther King Elem Sch, Compton, Calif; plus many others.
Exhibitions: Brooklyn Mus, N Y; Springfield Mus Art; Int Comtemp Relig Sculptured Medals, Rome, Italy, 63; Int Exhib Contemp Sculptured Medals, Athens, Greece, 66 & Paris, France, 67; plus many others.
Awards: Los Angeles City Art Exhib, 49, 66 & 70; Nat Award, Nat Sculpture Soc, 62; seven awards, Valley Art Guild, 48-72.
Bibliography: Article, In: Enciclopedia Int Degli Artisti, 70-71; article, In: Margaret Harold publications of prize-winning sculpture book 7; plus others.
Memberships: Nat Sculpture Soc; fel Am Inst Fine Arts; Valley Artist's Guild (founder, past pres); Fedn Int Medaille; Traditional Artists Soc (dir coun).
Mailing Address: 5417 Hazeltine Ave, Van Nuys, CA 91401.

VAN YOUNG, OSCAR
Painter, Instructor
Preferred Media: Oils.
b Vienna, Austria; U S citizen.
Study & Training: Art Acad, Odessa, Russia; with Sam Ostrowsky, Paris, France & Chicago, Ill; Calif State Univ, Los Angeles, BA, MA.
Work in Public Collections: Los Angeles Co Mus Art, Calif; Chaffey Col, Ontario, Calif; Frye Mus, Seattle, Wash; Int Lithography & Engraving, City of Chicago; Mother & Child (drawing), Santa Barbara Mus, Calif.
Exhibitions: Am Paintings & Int Watercolor Shows, Art Inst Chicago; 10 Painters of the West, Encycl Britannica Collection; Golden Gate World's Fair Expos, San Francisco, Calif; Va Mus Biennial; Corcoran Gallery Art Biennial, Washington, D C.
Teaching: Instr advan painting, Otis Art Inst, 54-56; instr design, painting & drawing, Pasadena City Col, 59-; asst prof advan painting, Los Angeles State Univ, 61-63.
Awards: Bartels prize, Art Inst Chicago; purchase prize, Chaffey Col; purchase award, Frye Mus.
Bibliography: Arthur Millier (auth), article, In: Los Angeles Times; Jules Langsner (auth), article, In: Art News; Ronald D Scofield (auth), California Painter turns against early realism, Santa Barbara.
Dealer: Maxwell Galleries, 551 Sutter St, San Francisco, CA 94102.
Mailing Address: 2293 Panorama Terrace, Los Angeles, CA 90039.

VARGA, FERENC
Sculptor
Preferred Media: Bronze, Marble, Wood.
b Szekesfehervar, Hungary; U S citizen.
Study & Training: Acad Fine Arts, Budapest, Hungary, with Prof Eugene Broy & Prof Francis Sidlo; govt scholar, Italy, 38 & France, 42.
Work in Public Collections: Nat Art Gallery, Budapest; Mus Fine Arts, Budapest; Vatican Mus, Rome, Italy; Mus Zurich, Switz.

Commissions: Portrait, Vice-regent of Hungary, Budapest, 42; monument, City of Windsor, Ont, Can, 50; group of statues, Ft Lincoln Mem, Washington, D C, 55; monument, City of Detroit, Mich, 66; bust, Ford Auditorium, Detroit, 72.
Exhibitions: Nat Art Gallery, Budapest, 42; Exhib Ecclesiastical Arts Guild, Detroit, 52; Nat Sculpture Soc, New York, 59; one-man show, Masters' Gallery, Toronto, Ont, 64; Eszterhazy Gallery, Palm Beach, Fla, 71.
Teaching: Assoc prof sculpturing, Acad Fine Arts, Budapest, 28-40.
Awards: Lord Rothermere Award, 28 & Ball Ede scholar, Govt Hungary, 42; Medal of Bethlehem Distinction, Fine Arts & Sci Soc of Church of Hungary, 47.
Bibliography: Dr E Schwartz (auth), Ferenc Varga, Ons Volk (Brussels), 49 & Last uns nach Bethlehem eilen, Am-Ung Verlag (Cologne), 59; J P Danglade (auth), Magnificent statue of the Christ by sculptor Varga, The Cemeterian (Columbus), 62.
Memberships: Fine Arts & Sci Soc of Church of Hungary, Budapest; Acad Cath Hungarica Sci Atrib Prov, Vatican City; Nat Sculpture Soc.
Mailing Address: 296 N E Sixth Ave, Delray Beach, FL 33444.

VARGA, MARGIT
Painter, Writer
Preferred Media: Oils.
b New York, N Y, May 5, 08.
Study & Training: Art Stud League New York, with Boardman Robinson & Robert Laurent.
Work in Public Collections: Metrop Mus Art; Springfield Mus Fine Arts, Mass; Univ Ariz, Tucson; IBM Collection; Pa Acad Fine Arts.
Commissions: Mural for lobby, Kidder, Meade & Co, Paramus, N J.
Exhibitions: Whitney Mus Am Art, 51; Univ Ill, 51; Art Inst Chicago; Carnegie Inst; Corcoran Gallery Art.
Positions: Art ed, Life Mag, 36-56, asst art dir, 56-60; art consult, Time, Inc, 60-70.
Publications: Co-auth, Modern American painting, 39; auth, Waldo Peirce, 41; auth, Carol Brant, 45; ed, America's arts & skills, 57; contribr, Mag Art, Studio Publ & Life Mag.
Dealer: Midtown Galleries, 11 E 57th St, New York, NY 10022.
Mailing Address: Box 784 Hildreth Lane, Bridgehampton, NY 11932.

VARGAS, RUDOLPH
Sculptor
b Uruapan, Mex, Apr 20, 04; U S citizen.
Study & Training: San Carlos Acad Fine Arts, Mexico City, Mex.
Work in Public Collections: Hand woodcarved madonna, Vatican Mus, Rome, Italy; 30 works of hand woodcarved statues & panels, Santa Teresita Hosp, Duarte, Calif; Life of Father Junipero Serra (five scenes), San Juan Capistrano Mission, Calif; scenes of life of Christ, San Fernando Mission, Calif.
Commissions: Large figures, Reno, Nev; Albert Pyke (bronze bust), Scottish Rite Cathedral, Pasadena, Calif.
Exhibitions: One-man show, Santa Teresita Hosp, Duarte, 72.
Positions: Sculptor, Warner Bros Studios, 67; sculptor, Walt Disney Studios, 68-70.
Bibliography: Phil Gilkerson (auth), Southland artist, 65; Garcia Mendez (auth), Ideas: eventos latinos, 69; article, In: Enciclopedia Internazionale Degli Artisti, Bugatti Editore, 70-71.
Mailing Address: 3661 Whittier Blvd, Los Angeles, CA 90023.

VARGO, JOHN
Educator, Painter
Preferred Media: Tempera, Watercolors.
b Cleveland, Ohio, Aug 9, 29.
Study & Training: Cleveland Inst Art, with Louis Bosa.
Work in Public Collections: Cleveland Mus Art; Syracuse Univ, N Y; Munson-Williams-Proctor Inst, Utica, N Y; LeMoyne Col, Syracuse.
Commissions: The Erie Canal (mural), First Fed Savings Syracuse, 60.
Exhibitions: Cooperstown 35th Ann Exhib, N Y, 70; Rochester Finger Lakes Exhib, N Y, 71; one-man shows, Pa State Univ, New Kensington, 69, May Mem, Syracuse, 70 & LeMoyne Col, 71.
Teaching: Prof illus & serigraph, Syracuse Univ, 58-
Positions: Illusr, Advance Art, Cleveland, 51-58.
Awards: Eagan Pres Plaza Award, 64 & popular prize, 64, N Y State Fair; first prize for portrait painting, Cooperstown Art Asn, 70; award for painting, Mem Art Gallery, Univ Rochester, 71.
Bibliography: Anna W Olmsted (auth), rev, 4/19/70 & Ann Hartranft (auth), rev, 12/12/71, In: Syracuse Herald-Am; Gordon Muck (auth), Syracuse Post Standard, 12/6/71.
Mailing Address: 6319 Danbury Dr, Jamesville, NY 13078.

VARIAN, ELAYNE H
Art Administrator, Art Historian
b San Francisco, Calif.
Study & Training: Art Inst Chicago; Univ Chicago, MA.

Collections Arranged: Art in Process, I, II, III & IV, 65-69; Art Nouveau, 69; Art Deco, 70; N Dimensional Space, 70; Artists' Videotape Performances, 71; Prints from Hollanders Workshop, 72; Women in the Arts Festival, 72; Mr & Mrs George Rickey's Private Collection: Constrictivist Art, 72.
Teaching: Instr museology, Finch Col, 65-72.
Positions: Asst to pres, Duveen Bros, Inc, 53-62; dir & cur, Contemp Wing, Finch Col Mus Art, 64-; adv, N Y State Coun Arts, 67-; McDowell Colony fel; dir, Heathcote Art Found; past pres, Attingham Summer Sch, Eng; mem, Mayor's Citizens Comt & Gov's Citizens Comt; mem, Artists' Cert Comt, New York Dept Cult Affairs.
Memberships: Am Asn Mus; Int Coun Mus; Col Art Asn Am; Gallery Asn N Y State (co-dir exhib comt, 72).
Publications: Contribr, Art in Am, Arts Mag & Art Int.
Mailing Address: 62 E 78th St, New York, NY 10021.

VASA (VASA VELIZAR MIHICH)
Sculptor, Educator
Preferred Media: Plastics.
b Yugoslavia, Apr 25, 33; U S citizen.
Study & Training: Sch Appl Art, Beograd, Yugoslavia, 47-51; dipl; Acad Appl Art, Beograd, 52-54, dipl.
Work in Public Collections: Mus Mod Art, Beograd; Denver Art Mus, Colo; Univ N Mex Art Mus, Albuquerque; Larry Aldrich Mus, Ridgefield, Conn; plus many others including pvt collections.
Commissions: Wood inlay mural, Hotel Metropol, Beograd, 57; plastic sculpture, Frederick Weisman, Toyota Auto Industs, Japan, 71; plastic sculpture, Max Palevsky, Palm Springs, Calif, 71; plastic sculpture, Winmar Co, Inc, Severence Ctr, Cleveland, Ohio, 72.
Exhibitions: New Modes in California Painting & Sculpture, La Jolla Mus Art, Calif, 66; Univ Ill Biennial Exhib Contemp Painting & Sculpture, Champaign, 67; American Sculpture of the Sixties, Los Angeles Co Mus Art, Calif, 67; 73rd Western Ann, Inaugural Exhib, Denver Art Mus, Colo, 71; Vasa Sculptures, Mus Mod Art, Beograd, 72; plus many others including one-man shows.
Teaching: Assoc prof art, Univ Calif, Los Angeles, 67-; assoc prof visual fundamentals, Univ Southern Calif, 70-71.
Awards: Grant, Univ Calif, Los Angeles, 70; Judith Thomas Found grant, 71; Creative Arts Inst appointment, Univ Calif, 72-73; plus others.
Bibliography: Joseph H Krause (auth), The nature of art, Prentice Hall, 69; William Wilson (auth), Sculpture by Vasa in USC show, Los Angeles Times, 70; Donald Brewer (auth), Vasa sculptures (catalogue), Mus Mod Art, Beograd, 72; plus others.
Mailing Address: 360 Sunset Ave, Venice, CA 90291.

VASS, GENE
Painter, Sculptor
Preferred Media: Oils, Inks, Woods.
b Buffalo, N Y, July 28, 22.
Work in Public Collections: Mus Mod Art, New York, N Y; Whitney Mus Am Art, New York; Guggenheim Mus, New York; Albright-Knox Art Gallery, Buffalo; Baltimore Mus, Md; plus others including many in pvt collections.
Exhibitions: Carnegie Int, 65; Whitney Ann, 65 & New Acquisitions, 69, Whitney Mus Am Art; New Acquisitions, Guggenheim Mus, 66; Select Artists, Des Moines Art Ctr, Iowa, 67; plus many others.
Mailing Address: 159 Mercer St, New York, NY 10012.

VASSOS, JOHN
Painter, Designer
b Greece, Oct 23, 98; U S citizen.
Study & Training: Robert Col, Constantinople; Fenway Art Sch, Boston; Boston Mus Fine Arts Sch; Art Stud League New York, 21-22; New York Sch Design.
Work in Public Collections: Athens Mus, Greece; Athens Pub Libr; Syracuse Univ.
Commissions: Design, U S Trade Fair pavilions at Karachi, Pakistan & New Delhi, India; mosaic mural, entrance of Military Electronic Ctr, Van Nuys, Calif; mural, radio-TV station, Philadelphia, Pa, Conadado Beach Hotel, Puerto Rico, RCA Electronic Ctr, Palm Beach; developed hist complex for city of Norwalk, Conn; plus many others.
Exhibitions: New York Pub Libr; Toledo Pub Libr; New Sch Social Res; Riverside Mus; Silvermine Guild Art; plus others.
Positions: Indust designer, RCA Corp, 38-; also designs for Remington, Du Pont, Savage Arms & others.
Awards: Silver medal, Indust Design Inst, 61; medal, Am Packaging; the Paidea Award, Hellenic Univ Club New York, 63; plus many others.
Memberships: Silvermine Guild Art (pres); Philadelphia Art Alliance; Indust Designers Soc Am (chmn bd); plus others.
Publications: Contribr, art & design mag.
Mailing Address: Comstock Hill, Norwalk, CT 06850.

VAUX, RICHARD
Painter
Preferred Media: Acrylics, Oils, Graphics.
b Greensburg, Pa, Sept 15, 40.
Study & Training: Miami Univ, DFA, 63; Northern Ill Univ, MFA, 69.
Work in Public Collections: Hofstra Univ, Hempstead, N Y; Northern Ill Univ, Nassau Community Col, Garden City, N Y; C W Post Col, Greenvale, N Y; Adelphi Univ, Garden City.
Exhibitions: N Y State Pavilion, New York World's Fair, Dayton Art Inst, Ohio, 63; Butler Inst Am Art, Youngstown, Ohio, 68; Stamford Mus, Conn, 70; Minn Mus Art, Saint Paul, 71.
Teaching: Asst prof art, Adelphi Univ, 64-
Awards: Awards for painting, Hofstra Univ Ann, 63 & Westchester Art Ann, 70; award for drawing, Northern Ill Univ Ann, 68.
Dealers: Bertha Schaefer Gallery, 41 E 57th St, New York, NY 10022; Artium Gallery, 402 Main St, Port Washington, NY 11050.
Mailing Address: 36 Ave A, Holbrook, NY 11741.

VAZQUEZ, PAUL
Painter
Preferred Media: Oils.
b Brooklyn, N Y, Sept 19, 33.
Study & Training: Ohio Wesleyan Univ, BFA, 56; Univ Ill, Kate Neal Kinley fel & MFA, 57.
Work in Public Collections: Butler Inst Am Art, Youngstown, Ohio; Univ Ill, Urbana; Ball State Teachers Col, Muncie, Ind.
Exhibitions: Pa Acad Fine Arts 152nd Ann, 57; Allen Stone Gallery, New York, 70; Galerie Biesj, Amsterdam, Holland, 70; one-man show, Paley & Lowe, 71 & 72; Am Painting, Chicago Inst Am Art, 72.
Teaching: Instr art hist, Bennett Col, 63-66; asst prof humanities, Western Conn State Col, 66-69; asst prof drawing & design, Univ Bridgeport, 69-
Awards: Purchase award, Butler Inst Am Art, 58.
Dealer: Paley & Lowe, 59 Wooster St, New York, NY 10012.
Mailing Address: 134 Duane St, New York, NY 10013.

VELA, ALBERTO
Painter
Preferred Media: Oils.
b Mexico City, Mex, 20.
Study & Training: Acad Fine Arts, Mexico City; also with José Clemente Orozco & Carlos Ruano Llopis, Mex.
Commissions: Posters, Plaza de Toros, Mexico City, 48-49.
Exhibitions: Gallery Otto, Vienna, 67; Colline Gallerie, Paris, 68; Northwest Galleries, Seattle, Wash, 69; Cabinet Comt Opportunity for Span Speaking People, Washington, D C, 70; Americana Galleries, Chicago, Ill, 71.
Mailing Address: c/o Americana Galleries, 271 Waukegan Rd, Northfield, IL 60093.

VELARDE, PABLITA
Painter, Illustrator
b Santa Clara Pueblo, N Mex, Sept 19, 18.
Study & Training: U S Indian Sch, Santa Fe, with Dorothy Dunn.
Commissions: Murals, Maisel Bldg, Albuquerque, N Mex, 40; Bandelier Nat Monument Mus, N Mex, 46; Foote Cafeteria, Houston, 57; Western Skies Hotel, Albuquerque, 58.
Exhibitions: Denver Art Mus, Colo; M H de Young Mem Mus, San Francisco, Calif; Mus N Mex; Calif Palace of Legion of Honor, San Francisco; Philbrook Art Ctr; plus others.
Teaching: Painting demonstrations, KOB-TV, Albuquerque.
Awards: Palmes Academique, Fr Govt, 55; grand prizes, Gallup Ceremonial, N Mex, 55-59; New Mexico State Fair, 59; plus others.
Memberships: Art League New Mex; Nat League Am Pen Women; Inter-Triban Indian Ceremonial Asn.
Publications: Illusr, cover of Indians of Arizona; auth & illusr, Old father, the story teller, 60.
Mailing Address: 805 Adams St N E, Albuquerque, NM 87100.

VERMES, MADELAINE
Craftsman
b Hungary, Sept 15, 15.
Study & Training: Alfred Univ; Craft Stud League; Greenwich House Potters.
Work in Public Collections: Cooper Union Mus; Mus Int delle Ceramiche, Faenza, Italy.
Exhibitions: Coliseum, New York, N Y, 57; Art League Long Island, N Y, 58; Int Ceramic Arts, Smithsonian Inst, Washington, D C; Philadelphia Art Alliance, Pa; one-man show, Brentano's Gallery, New York, 57; plus many other group & one-man shows.
Memberships: Artist-Craftsmen New York; Nat League Am Pen Women; York State Craftsmen.
Mailing Address: 315 E 65th St, Apt 10F, New York, NY 10021.

VERMEULE, CORNELIUS CLARKSON, III
Art Historian, Writer
Preferred Media: Bronze, Marble.
b Queenstown, Ireland, Aug 10, 25; U S citizen.
Study & Training: Harvard Univ, AB, 47, MA, 51; Univ Col, Univ London, PhD, 53.
Work in Public Collections: Mus Fine Arts, Boston; Nat Mus, Pylos, Hellas.
Collections Arranged: Many exhibs, Fogg Mus Art, 50-72; Sir John Soane's Mus, London; Mus Fine Arts, Boston.
Teaching: Asst prof fine arts, Univ Mich, Ann Arbor, 53-55; asst prof archaeol, Bryn Mawr Col, 55-57; prof classics, Yale Univ, 72-73.
Positions: Asst, Sir John Soane's Mus, 51-53; cur classical art, Mus Fine Arts, Boston, 57-; acting dir, 72-; cur coins, Mass Hist Soc, Boston, 69-
Memberships: Life mem Col Art Asn Am; fel Royal Numismatic Soc; life fel Am Numismatic Soc (mem coun, 60-); life mem Archaeol Inst Am; life mem Hellenic & Roman Soc.
Research: European painting, Greek and Roman art; numismatics.
Collection: Greek and Roman art; drawings; all on loan to Museum of Fine Arts, Boston.
Publications: Auth, European art and the classical past, 64; auth, Roman imperial art in Greece and Asia Minor, 68; auth, Polykleitos, 69; auth, Numismatic art in America, 71; co-auth, Greek, Etruscan and Roman art, 72.
Mailing Address: Museum of Fine Arts, Boston, MA 02115.

VERNON, ALEXANDRA
Painter
b Reading, Pa, Sept 6, 44.
Study & Training: Study in Rome, London & New York.
Work in Public Collections: Los Angeles Art Asn Galleries, Calif; Las Vegas Art Club Mus, Nev; Newport Harbor Art Mus, Balboa, Calif; plus others.
Exhibitions: Las Vegas Art League Round-Up, 69; one-woman show, I Magnin & Co, Los Angeles, Calif, 69; Exhib Relig Art, First Fed Savings & Loan Asn, Los Angeles, 71; Ankrum Gallery Exhib for Nat Comt on U S-China Relations, Los Angeles, 72.
Bibliography: D Simmons (auth), Collage by Alex Vernon, Designers West, 7/72.
Memberships: Los Angeles Art Asn.
Dealer: Los Angeles Art Association Galleries, 825 La Cienega Blvd, Los Angeles, CA 90069.
Mailing Address: 1429 N Alta Vista Blvd, Los Angeles, CA 90046.

VERSHBOW, MR & MRS ARTHUR
Collectors
Mr Vershbow b Boston, Mass, Mar 22, 22; Mrs Vershbow b Boston, Mass, June 12, 24.
Study & Training: Mr Vershbow, Mass Inst Technol, BS & MS; Mrs Vershbow, Radcliffe Col, AB.
Collection: Prints, particularly works by Redon, Piranesi and Callot; illustrated books, especially fifteenth to seventeenth centuries.
Mailing Address: 54 Bishopsgate Rd, Newton, MA 02159.

VERZYL, JUNE CAROL
Art Dealer, Collector
b Huntington, N Y, Feb 5, 28.
Study & Training: Parsons Sch Design.
Positions: Gallery dir, Verzyl Gallery, Northport, N Y, 66-
Specialty of Gallery: Contemporary American paintings, sculpture and graphics.
Collection: Contemporary American, including Filmus, Refregier, Benda, Twardowicz, Clawson & Christopher; nineteenth century engravings.
Mailing Address: 377 Rte 25A, Northport, NY 11768.

VEVERS, ANTHONY MARR
Painter, Educator
Preferred Media: Oils, Mixed Media.
b London, Eng, May 20, 26; U S citizen.
Study & Training: Yale Univ, BA, 50; Accad Belle Arte, Florence, Italy, 50; Hans Hofmann Sch, New York, N Y, 52-53.
Work in Public Collections: Isaac Delgado Mus, New Orleans, La; Univ Mass, Amherst; Purdue Univ, Lafayette, Ind; Fairleigh Dickinson Univ, N J; J H Hirshhorn Collection.
Exhibitions: Am Acad Arts & Lett, New York, 64; Younger Painters, Yale Univ, 65; Pa Acad Fine Arts Ann, 66; Evansville Mus Show, Ind, 67; 350th Anniversary Exhib New Eng Art, Mass, 71.
Teaching: Lectr painting, Univ N C, Greensboro, 63-64; prof painting & art hist, Purdue Univ, Lafayette, 64-; vis staff, Fine Arts Work Ctr, Provincetown, Mass, 70-71, consult, 71-72.
Positions: Consult, Ind State Arts Comn, 70-; v pres, Art Asn Provincetown, 71-72.

Awards: Grants, Nat Coun Arts, 67 & Purdue Univ, 70; New Eng
Painting & Sculpture Prize, 71.
Dealer: Babcock Galleries, 805 Madison Ave, New York, NY 10021.
Mailing Address: Dept of Creative Arts, Purdue University,
Lafayette, IN 47907.

VICENTE, ESTEBAN
Painter
Preferred Media: Oils, Collage.
b Turegeno, Spain, Jan 20, 04; U S citizen.
Study & Training: Acad Belles Artes, Madrid, Spain.
Work in Public Collections: Whitney Mus Am Art, New York; Art
Inst Chicago, Ill; Honolulu Acad Arts, Hawaii; Mus Mod Art, New
York; Nat Collection Fine Arts, Smithsonian Inst, Washington,
D C.
Exhibitions: Eighth St Art Show, 49; Carnegie Int, Carnegie Inst,
Pittsburgh, Pa; Whitney Mus Am Art Ann; plus many others.
Teaching: Instr art, Black Mountain Col, 48; instr art, Univ Calif,
Berkeley, 54 & 58; instr art, New York Univ, 59-69; instr art,
Yale Univ, 60-61; instr art, Univ Calif, Los Angeles, 62; artist-
in-residence, Des Moines Art Ctr, 65; artist-in-residence,
Princeton Univ, 65-66 & 69-72; artist-in-residence, Honolulu
Acad Fine Arts, 69.
Awards: Purchase awards, 60 & 61 & Tamarind fel, 62, Ford Found;
Childe Hassam purchase award, Am Acad Arts & Lett, 71.
Bibliography: Elaine De Kooning (auth), Vicente paints a collage,
Art News, 52; David Shirey (auth), article, In: New York Times,
4/22/72; John Ashberry (auth), article, In: Art News, 5/72.
Dealer: Andre Emmerich, 41 E 57th St, New York, NY 10022.
Mailing Address: Main St, Bridgehampton, NY 11932.

VICKERS, GEORGE STEPHEN
Educator
b St Catharines, Ont, Dec 19, 13.
Study & Training: McMaster Univ, BA; Harvard Univ, AM.
Teaching: Prof & chmn dept fine art, Univ Toronto, at present; also
coun mem.
Awards: Harvard Univ jr fel, 39-42.
Publications: Co-auth, Art and man, 3 vols, 64; contribr, Art Bull
& Burlington Mag.
Mailing Address: 31 Rosedale Rd, Toronto, Ont, Can.

VICKERY, CHARLES BRIDGEMAN
Painter
Preferred Media: Oils, Acrylics.
b Hinsdale, Ill, July 16, 13.
Study & Training: Art Inst Chicago; Am Acad Fine Art, Chicago;
also with Ben Stahl.
Work in Public Collections: Univ Club, Chicago, Ill; Union League
Club, Chicago, Ill; prints, Royal Acad, London, Eng.
Exhibitions: Rockport Art Asn, Mass; Union League Club; Ackerman
Gallery, London, Eng; Springfield Mus, Ill; Pallette & Chisel
Acad, Chicago.
Awards: Diamond Medal Award, Pallette & Chisel Acad, 68; Waters
of the World Prize, N Shore Art Asn, Gloucester, 70; Union
League Club Prize, 72.
Bibliography: Eleanor Jewett (auth), article, In: Chicago Tribune, 45;
C. J Bulliet (auth), article, In: Chicago Daily News, 8/51.
Memberships: Pallette & Chisel Acad (dir, 67-69); Rockport Art
Asn; N Shore Art Asn.
Dealer: W Russell Button Gallery, 955 Center St, Douglas, MI
49406.
Mailing Address: 4533 Wolf Rd, Western Springs, IL 60558.

VICKREY, ROBERT REMSEN
Painter
Preferred Media: Tempera.
b New York, N Y, Aug 20, 26.
Study & Training: Yale Univ, BA; Art Stud League New York; Yale
Sch Fine Arts, BFA; also with Kenneth Hayes Miller & Reginald
Marsh.
Work in Public Collections: Syracuse Univ; Metrop Mus Art, New
York; Whitney Mus Am Art; Butler Inst Am Art; Mus Arte Mod,
Rio de Janeiro.
Commissions: Covers for Time Mag; also portraits & bk jackets.
Exhibitions: Whitney Mus Am Art; Mus Mod Art, New York; Santa
Barbara Mus, Calif; Mus Fine Arts, Houston, Tex; Univ Nebr.
Awards: Edwin Austin Abbey mural fel, 49; Am Watercolor Soc, 56;
Nat Acad Design, 58.
Memberships: Am Watercolor Soc; Audubon Artists; Nat Acad De-
sign.
Dealer: Midtown Galleries, 11 E 57th St, New York, NY 10022.
Mailing Address: 390 Harbor Rd, Southport, CT 06490.

VIDAL, (MARGARITA) HAHN
Painter
Preferred Media: Oils.
b Hamburg, Ger, Mar 11, 19; U S citizen.
Study & Training: With Eduardo Couce Vidal.
Work in Public Collections: Eduardo Sivori, Mus Artes Plasticas,
Buenos Aires, Arg; Juan B Castagnino, Museo Cuidad Rosario,
Arg; Mus Seattle, Wash; Mus Mobile, Ala; Hist Mus Taiwan,
China.
Commissions: Hahn Vidal Rm, Arvida Corp, Boca Raton Hotel &
Club, Fla, 69.
Exhibitions: Mus Bellas Artes, Rio de Janeiro, Brazil, 52; Galeria
Arg, Buenos Aires, 55, 57, 60 & 68; Flowers from Argentina,
Kennedy Gallery, New York, N Y, 61; Doll & Richards, Boston,
Mass, 63 & 70; Flower Painters of the World, Tryon Gallery,
London, Eng, 68; plus others.
Memberships: Grand Cent Art Galleries; Hudson Valley Art Asn;
Am Artist Prof League.
Dealer: Grand Central Art Gallery, Inc, 40 Vanderbilt Ave, New
York, NY 10019.
Mailing Address: 345 W 58th St, New York, NY 10019.

VIERTHALER, ARTHUR A
Craftsman, Educator
b Milwaukee, Wis, Sept 15, 16.
Study & Training: Milwaukee State Teachers Col, BS; Univ Wis, MS.
Commissions: Many comns for jewelry, relig articles & others.
Exhibitions: Milwaukee Designers; Midwestern Designers; Smith-
sonian Traveling Exhib; Designer-Craftsmen Traveling Exhibs;
Wis State Fair; plus others.
Teaching: Lect, Pre-Historic Design, Contemporary Design, Natu-
ral Phenomena of Design Elements in Minerals, Gemstones,
Mining for Gemstones & others; art instr, Madison Pub Schs;
prof art, Sch Educ, Univ Wis, at present.
Awards: Wis Designer-Craftsmen; Madison Art Asn; Miss River
Exhib, 61; plus others.
Mailing Address: Dept of Art, University of Wisconsin, Madison, WI
53706.

VIESULAS, ROMAS
Printmaker, Educator
Preferred Media: Graphics.
b Lithuania, Sept 11, 18; U S citizen.
Study & Training: Ecole des Arts et Metiers, Ger, grad; Ecole des
Beaux Arts, Paris, France.
Work in Public Collections: Mus Mod Art, New York, N Y; Mus
Mod Art, Kamakura, Japan; Biblioteque Nat, Paris; Art Gallery
N S W, Sydney, Australia; Nat Gallery Art, Washington, D C.
Commissions: Spring (ed), Print Club, Philadelphia, Pa, 65; Up-on
(100 prints), Int Graphic Arts Soc, New York, 68; Ascent (ed),
Acquarius Press, 70.
Exhibitions: Int Exhibs Graphic Arts, Ljubljana, Yugoslavia, 59, 61
& 65; Whitney Mus Am Art Ann, 66; Biennial Graphic Arts, Kra-
kow, Poland, 66, 68 & 70; Two Decades of American Prints 1947-
1968, Brooklyn Mus, 69; 35th Biennial of Venice & one-man show,
Italy, 70.
Teaching: Prof printmaking, Tyler Sch Art, Temple Univ, 60-
Awards: Guggenheim fels, 58, 64 & 69; Tamarind fel, 60; medal,
Biennial Graphic Arts, Krakow, 70.
Memberships: Print Club Philadelphia; Soc Am Graphic Artists.
Dealer: Weyhe Gallery, 794 Lexington Ave, New York, NY 10021.
Mailing Address: Dept of Printmaking, Tyler School of Arts, Temple
University, Beech & Penrose Aves, Philadelphia, PA 19126.

VIGTEL, GUDMUND
Art Administrator
b July 9, 25; U S citizen.
Study & Training: Isaac Grunewald's Sch Art, Stockholm, 43-44; Univ
Ga, BFA, 52, MFA, 53.
Collections Arranged: The New Tradition, 63; An Anthology of Mod-
ern American Art, 64; The Beckoning Land, 71; The Modern
Image, 72; plus numerous others.
Positions: Admin asst, Corcoran Gallery Art, 54-57, asst to dir, 57-
61, asst dir, 61-63; dir, High Mus Art, 63-
Memberships: Am Asn Mus; Asn Art Mus Dirs.
Publications: Numerous exhib catalogues.
Mailing Address: High Museum of Art, 1280 Peachtree St N E, At-
lanta, GA 30309.

VILDER, ROGER
Sculptor
Preferred Media: Kinetics.
b Beyrouth, Lebanon, Nov 29, 38; Can citizen.
Study & Training: Sir George Williams Art Sch, dipl; Sir George
Williams Univ, BFA; McGill Univ.
Work in Public Collections: Mus Contemp Art, Montreal.

Commissions: Kinetic works, World's Fair, Montreal, 70-71 & Can Govt, Osaka, Japan, 70; kinetic wall, Ministry External Affairs, Ottawa, 71-72.
Exhibitions: Artists 68, Art Gallery Ont, Toronto, 68; Concours Quebec Prov, Mus Contemp Art, Montreal, 68, 69 & 71; Some More Beginning, Brooklyn Mus, 69; 11th & 12th Winnipeg Biennial, Man, 69-71; Kinetics, Hayward Gallery, London, Eng, 70.
Teaching: Prof painting & sculpture, Mus Art Sch, Montreal, 67-69; prof advan design, Sir George Williams Univ, 69-70; prof painting & sculpture, Col Old Montreal, 69-
Positions: Counr, Quebec Sculptors Asn, 69-71; adv & mem exec comt, Soc Prof Artists Quebec, 70-71.
Awards: Concours Artistique P Q, Mus Contemp Art, 68; Can Arts Coun grants, 69-70 & 71-72.
Bibliography: Frank Popper (auth), Kinetics art, Studio Vista, Holland, 68; William Townsend (auth), Canadian art today, Studio Int, London, 70; Jasia Reichardt (auth), Kinetics, Archit Design, London, 71.
Memberships: Quebec Sculptor Asn (mem exec comt, 69-); Asn Artistes Prof Quebec; Can Artist Rels.
Publications: Auth, Sculpture and lights, Arts Can, Dec 68; auth, Lumiere dans l'art, Forces, spring 69; ed, London exhibitions, Arts Mag, 11/70; auth, Technology and art, Studio Int, 11/70; auth, Le paradoxe magique de Roger Vilder, Vie Arts, fall 71.
Mailing Address: c/o The Electric Gallery, 272 Avenue Rd, Toronto, Ont, Can.

VILLA, CARLOS
Painter
b Dec 11, 36.
Study & Training: San Francisco Art Inst, BFA, 61; Mills Col, MFA, 63.
Exhibitions: Park Pl Group, Daniel's Gallery, New York, N Y, 65; Park Pl Invitational, Park Pl Gallery, New York, 65; Second Ann Arp To Artschwager Exhib, Goldowsky Gallery, New York, 67; two-man exhibs, Wyndham Col, Vt, 68 & San Francisco Art Inst, Calif, 69; plus other group & one-man exhibs.
Teaching: Asst, Mills Col, 61-63; asst, Studio 1, Oakland, Calif, 61-63; instr, Tel Hill Neighborhood Ctr, Urban Arts, San Francisco, 69-70; chm interdepartmental studies, San Francisco Art Inst, at present; asst prof art, Calif State Univ, Sacramento, at present.
Awards: Hon mention, Richmond Art Ctr Ann, 58.
Bibliography: Rev, 12/70 & Emily Wasserman (auth), article, 1/71, In: Artforum.
Mailing Address: c/o Hansen Fuller Gallery, 228 Grant Ave, San Francisco, CA 94108.

VILLENEUVE, JOSEPH ARTHUR
Painter
b Chicoutimi, P Q, Jan 4, 10.
Work in Public Collections: Mus Beaux Arts Montreal; Musee du Québec; Nat Gallery Can, Ottawa.
Exhibitions: Mus Quebec; Vancouver Art Gallery; Galerie Art Can Chicoutimi; Galerie Morency, Montreal; Galerie Waddington, Montreal.
Bibliography: Marcel Carriere (auth), Off Nat Film, 7/5/65; Henri-Pierre Fortier (auth), Off Radio-TV Française, 4/26/72. Arthur Villeneuve's Quebec Chronicles (exhib catalogue), Montreal Mus Fine Arts.
Dealer: Galerie Morency, 1564 St Denis, Montreal, P Q, Can.
Mailing Address: 669 Rue Tache, Chicoutimi, P Q, Can.

VINCENT, TOM
Painter
Preferred Media: Polymer, Liquitex, Oils.
b Kansas City, Mo, 30.
Study & Training: Kansas City Art Inst, BFA & MFA.
Work in Public Collections: Kansas City Art Inst; Springfield Mus Fine Arts, Mo; Atlanta Mus, Ga; Montclair Art Mus, N J; Milwaukee Art Ctr, Wis.
Commissions: Painting, Charles S Gehrie Presto Int, 40; Jazz (painting), Venice Film Festival, 62; mural, Schering Corp, 68; mural, Montclair Travel Bollinger, 71.
Exhibitions: Mus Mod Art, New York, N Y; Corcoran Gallery Art, Washington, D C; Pa Acad Fine Arts, Philadelphia; Caravan de France Galleries, New York; Galerie Cernuschi, Paris, France.
Teaching: Instr drawing, Montclair Art Mus, 70-
Awards: Speiser Mem Award for Procession, 62; Silvermine Guild Award for Composition, 69; Montclair Mus Award for Triptic, 70.
Bibliography: Russel O Hoddy (auth), Polymer painting, Van Nostrand Reinhold, 71.
Memberships: Pa Acad Fine Arts; Am Watercolor Soc; United Scenic Artists.
Dealer: Galerie Cernuschi, Paris 8, France.
Mailing Address: c/o Caravan de France Galleries, 121 E 57th St, New York, NY 10022.

VINER, FRANK LINCOLN
Sculptor, Designer
Preferred Media: Vinyl, Cheesecloth, Dyes.
b Worcester, Mass, Aug 9, 37.
Study & Training: Sch Worcester Art Mus; Yale Univ, BFA, 61, MFA, 63.
Work in Public Collections: Rose Art Mus, Brandeis Univ; Milwaukee Art Ctr, Wis; Riverside Mus, New York, N Y.
Commissions: Five wearable sculptures, Berkshire Int, 68; yellow environ room, Wadsworth Atheneum, Hartford, Conn, 69.
Exhibitions: Eccentric Abstraction, Fischbach Gallery, New York, 66; Options, Directions, Milwaukee Art Ctr & Mus Contemp Art, Chicago, 68; Whitney Mus Am Art Sculpture Ann, New York, 68; Op Losse Schroeven/Square Tags in Round Holes, Stedelijk Mus, Amsterdam, 69; A Plastic Presence, Jewish Mus, New York, Milwaukee Art Ctr & San Francisco Mus Art, 70.
Teaching: Instr fine art, Sch Visual Arts, New York, 63-, vis artist, Univ Colo, Boulder Grad Sch Art, 72; Rhinehart critic sculpture, Md Inst Art, 72.
Bibliography: D Judd (auth), Hard edge painting, Arts Mag, 2/63; H Kramer (auth), And now eccentric abstraction, New York Times, 11/66; L R Lippard (auth), Collected essays in art criticism, 71.
Publications: Contribr, Art by telephone (recording), Mus Contemp Art Chicago, 69; contribr, If I had a mind . . . concept-art project-art, 71.
Dealer: 55 Mercer Gallery, 55 Mercer St, New York, NY 10013.
Mailing Address: 163 Bowery, New York, NY 10002.

VIRET, MARGARET MARY (MRS FRANK IVO)
Painter, Lecturer
Preferred Media: Watercolors, Oils, Acrylics.
b New York, N Y, Apr 18, 13.
Study & Training: Terry Art Sch; Miami Art Sch; Miami Art Ctr; Univ Miami; also with Dong Kingman, Eliot O'Hara, Xavier Gonzalez, Eugene Massin, Georges Sellier & Jack Amoroso plus many other prominent instructors.
Work in Public Collections: Fla Fedn Art, De Bary; Mirell Gallery; Norton Gallery; Lowe Art Gallery; Bacardi Art Gallery, Fla.
Commissions: Cuba Home Scene, Miami Woman's Club, 63; ballet scenes, Pauline Hill Co, Miami, 65; Spring Flowers (watercolors), Fla C of C, 69; Fla Everglades Scene for wall, Capt Gene, 70; Fla Flowers for wall, Laura, Pompano Beach, Fla.
Exhibitions: Tampa Art Mus, 55; Fla Fedn Art, 55-56; Bass Art Mus, Miami Beach, 55-57, 62 & 63; Lowe Art Gallery, 60, 62 & 70; American Contemporary, Four Arts Soc, 65; plus others.
Teaching: Instr art, Miami Art League, 55-56; instr art, adult classes, YWCA & YMCA, Miami, 63-68; instr art adult classes, Dade Co Schs, 68-73.
Positions: Chmn, Dade Co Art Chmn, 56-58; art dir, Fla Fedn Women's Clubs, 56-63; pres, Laramore Rader Poetry Group, Miami, 70-72; art dir, Miami Women's Club, 67-73.
Awards: Best watercolor for Flowers, Fla Fedn Women's Clubs, 61; best watercolor for Marine, Bass Art Mus, 62; best watercolor for Flowers, Burdines Coral Gables Art Club, 63.
Bibliography: Violet Barker (auth), Dade County, Community Press, 63; Irene Gramling (auth), Sphinx, Franklin Press, 65 & 66; Edna Chauser (auth), Cultural Alliance, Chase, 71.
Memberships: Miami Art League (pres, 55-56); Fla Fedn Art (v pres, 56-58); hon mem Hibiscus Fine Arts Guild; Coral Gables Art Club; hon mem Allied Arts N Miami.
Mailing Address: 294 N E 55th Terrace, Miami, FL 33137.

VODICKA, RUTH KESSLER
Sculptor, Instructor
Preferred Media: Bronze, Brass, Wood.
b New York, N Y.
Study & Training: City Col New York; with O'Connor Barrett, 46-49; Sculpture Ctr, New York, 48-52; Art Stud League New York, 56-57 & 69; New Sch Soc Res, 65; New York Univ, 69.
Work in Public Collections: Norfolk Mus, Va; Montclair State Col, N J; Grayson Co State Bank, Sherman, Tex.
Commissions: Eternal Light (bronze sculpture), Temple of Jewish Community Ctr, Harrison, N J, 65.
Exhibitions: Whitney Mus Ann, New York, 52-57; Am Fedn Arts Travelling Exhib, 57-58; Galerie Claude Bernard, Paris, France, 60; Walk-Through-Dance-Through Sculpture, New York Cult Arts Festival, Bryant Park, 67; plus nine one-man shows, 56-71.
Teaching: Instr sculpture, Queens Youth Ctr, Bayside, 53-56; instr sculpture, Emanuel Midtown YM & WHA, New York, 66-69; instr sculpture, Great Neck Arrandale Sch, 69-70.
Awards: Joseph W Beatman Award (top prize for best work in any medium & first prize), Silvermine Guild Artists, 57; medal of hon, Painters & Sculptors Soc N J, 62; Julia Ford Pew Prize, Nat Asn Woman Artists, 66; plus others.
Bibliography: Vivian Campbell (auth), Sculptor's torch pays off, Life Mag, 56; Fred W McDarrah (auth), The artist's world, Dutton, 61;

Louis Calta (auth), Multi-purpose sculpture on view in Bryant Park, New York Times, 10/67.
Memberships: Am Soc Contemp Artists; Audubon Artists; Nat Asn Women Artists; Sculptors Guild (exec bd, 72); Women in Arts.
Art Interests: Total art-music, theatre, dance, literature, film, poetry, architecture & painting.
Publications: Contribr, Feminist Art J, 72; contribr, Women & Art, 72.
Mailing Address: 97 Wooster St, New York, NY 10012.

VOGEL, DONALD
Printmaker, Instructor
b Poland, Dec 24, 02; U S citizen.
Study & Training: Parson Sch Design; Columbia Univ, BS, MA.
Work in Public Collections: Seattle Art Mus; Pa State Univ; Metrop Mus Art, New York, N Y; Munson-Williams-Proctor Inst; Soc Am Graphic Artists; plus others.
Exhibitions: Brooklyn Mus, 50; Am Fedn Arts Traveling Exhib, 50; Royal Soc Painters, Etchers & Engravers, 54; Cal Western Univ, San Diego, 60; Pratt Graphic Art Ctr, 64; plus many others.
Teaching: Instr art, H S Art & Design, New York.
Awards: Munson-Williams-Proctor Inst, 43; Northwest Printmakers, 43 & 46; Libr of Cong, 50.
Memberships: Soc Am Graphic Artists.
Publications: Contribr to Print Collector's Quart, La Rev Mod, Am Prize Prints 20th Century & others.
Mailing Address: 415 E 52nd St, New York, NY 10022.

VOGEL, DONALD S
Painter, Art Dealer
Preferred Media: Oils.
b Milwaukee, Wis, Oct 21, 17.
Study & Training: Corcoran Gallery Art, Washington, D C; Art Inst Chicago; Work Prog Admin Easel Proj, Chicago.
Work in Public Collections: Fort Worth Art Ctr, Tex; Dallas Mus Fine Arts, Tex; Beaumont Mus Art, Tex; Mobile Art Ctr, Ala; Philbrook Art Ctr, Tulsa, Okla.
Exhibitions: 47th Ann Am Art, Cincinnati Art Mus, Ohio, 40; Artists of Chicago & Vicinity Ann, 40 & 42; 61st Ann Paintings, San Francisco Art Asn, San Francisco Mus Art, 41; Artists for Victory Exhib, Metrop Mus Art, New York, N Y, 42; Univ Ill Exhib Contemp Paintings & Sculpture, 53.
Collections Arranged; Clara McDonald Williamson, Nov, 66 & Velox Ward, May, 72, Amon Carter Mus Art, Fort Worth; Valton Tyler, Southern Methodist Univ, Feb, 72.
Positions: Dir, Valley House Gallery.
Awards: Bronze medal, Am Acad Rome, 42; Dallas Allied Arts Ann Awards, Dallas Mus Fine Arts, 44-46; Eighth Tex Gen Exhib Award, Houston Mus Fine Arts, 46.
Memberships: Art Dealers Asn Am; Am Fedn Arts; Dallas Mus Fine Arts.
Specialty of Gallery: Paintings and sculpture of the nineteenth and twentieth centuries.
Publications: Co-auth & ed, Passion: Georges Rouault (catalogue), 62; co-auth, Aunt Clara, 66; ed, The paintings of Hugh H Breckenridge (catalogue), 67; ed, Valton Tyler, 71; ed, Velox Ward (catalogue), 72.
Mailing Address: c/o Valley House Gallery, 6616 Spring Valley Rd, Dallas, TX 75240.

VOGEL, EDWIN CHESTER
Collector
Positions: Chmn, Coun Fine Arts & Archaeol, Columbia Univ, 57-67, hon chmn, 67-
Collection: French Impressionists of the nineteenth & twentieth century; Chinese porcelain; English eighteenth century furniture.
Mailing Address: 654 Madison Ave, New York, NY 10021.

VOIGT, ROBEN
Sculptor, Educator
Preferred Media: Steel.
b Philadelphia, Pa, June 6, 40.
Study & Training: Tyler Sch Art, MFA, with Boris Blai, Aldo Casanova, Raphael Sabatini & Adolf Dioda; San Francisco Art Inst, with Roger Jacobsen; Haystack Sch Crafts, Deer Isle, Maine.
Work in Public Collections: Wilmington Soc Fine Arts Mus; also in numerous pvt collections.
Exhibitions: Sculpture, High Mus Art, Atlanta, Ga, 68; Piedmont Arts Festival Ann, Atlanta, 69; Agnes Scott Col Invited Sculpture Show, Atlanta, 70; Callaway Gardens Art Ann, La Grange, Ga, 71; Sculptors Guild Ann, Lever House, New York, N Y, 71.
Teaching: Instr sculpture, Wilmington Art Ctr, Del, 64-67; asst prof art, Berry Col, 67-72; art consult, Griffin-Spalding Co Schs, Ga, 72-
Awards: Frist prize in sculpture, Rittenhouse Sq Clothesline Exhib, 63; purchase prize, Wilmington Soc Fine Arts Mus, 65; first prize in sculpture, Coosa Valley Fair Art Show, Rome, Ga, 67.

Bibliography: Clyde Burnett (auth), article, In: Atlanta J, 11/27/70.
Memberships: Col Art Asn Am; Sculptors Guild; Ga Art Educ Asn.
Mailing Address: 316 Hammond Dr, Griffin, GA 30223.

VOLLMER, RUTH
Sculptor
Preferred Media: Plastics.
b Munich, Ger; U S citizen.
Work in Public Collections: Nat Collection Fine Arts, Smithsonian Inst, Washington, D C; Mus Mod Art, New York, N Y; Whitney Mus Am Art, New York; New York Univ Art Collection; Rose Art Mus, Brandeis Univ; plus many others including pvt collections.
Commissions: Mus Mod Art Exhibs, Art in Progress, 15th Anniversary Exhib, 44, Elements of Stage Design, toured U S A, 47-50 & several children's art dept including Brussels World's Fair, 58; relief mural for lobby, New York; sculpture to each of 15 founders on 25th anniversary, Comt Econ Develop, 67.
Exhibitions: Univ Colo, 61; Mus Mod Art Lending Serv, New York, 63-; For Eyes & Ears, Cordier Ekstrom Gallery, New York, 64; Whitney Mus Am Art Ann, 64-70; Second Salon Int Galeries Pilotes, Lausanne, Switz, 66; plus many other group & one-man shows.
Bibliography: B H Friedman (auth), The quiet world of Ruth Vollmer, Art Int, Vol 9, No 12; Robert Smithson (auth), Quasi-infinities & the waning of space, Arts Mag, Vol 41, No 1; Sol LeWitt (auth), Paragraphs on conceptual art, Art Forum, summer 67; plus many others.
Memberships: Am Abstract Artist; Sculptors Guild.
Art Interests: Plastics, predominantly transparent metals fabricated & cast.
Dealer: Betty Parsons Gallery, 24 W 57th St, New York, NY 10019.
Mailing Address: 25 Central Park W, New York, NY 10023.

VON ADLMANN, JAN ERNST
Museum Director, Art Historian
b Rockland, Maine, Sept 18, 36.
Study & Training: Univ Calif, Berkeley, with Peter Selz; Free Univ W Berlin; Univ Vienna, with Fritz Novotny; New York Univ Inst Fine Arts, with Robert Goldwater, MA (hist art).
Collections Arranged: Kitsch: The Grotesque Around Us, 70; Max Klinger: A Glove, and other Images of Reverie & Apprehension, 71; Civilization Revisited, 71 & 72.
Teaching: Instr art hist, State Univ N Y Buffalo, 65; vis asst prof art hist, Univ Colo, 66-67.
Positions: Cur asst, Albright-Knox Art Gallery, N Y, 64-65; dir, Tampa Bay Art Ctr, Fla, 67-69; dir, Wichita Art Mus, Kans, 69-72; dir, Long Beach Mus Art, Calif, 72-
Awards: Fel, Salzburg Austro-Am Soc, 60; fel, Austrian Govt, 61; fel, Fed Repub W Ger, 63.
Memberships: Am Asn Mus; Col Art Asn Am; Int Coun Mus; Mountain-Plains Mus Conf; Western Asn Art Mus.
Research: First U S exhib & documentation of graphic works of Max Klinger.
Publications: Auth, Kitsch: the grotesque around us (catalogue), 70; auth, Max Klinger: a glove, & other images of reverie & apprehension (catalogue), 71; contribr, Art News Mag, 72; contribr, Art Gallery Mag, 72.
Mailing Address: Long Beach Museum of Art, 2300 E Ocean Blvd, Long Beach, CA 90803.

VON GROSCHWITZ, GUSTAVE
Museum Director
b New York, N Y, Apr 16, 06.
Study & Training: Columbia Univ, BA, 27; New York Univ, Col Art Asn fel, 45-46, MA, 49.
Teaching: Instr art, Wesleyan Univ, 38-45, actg chmn art dept, 42-45; adj prof art, Univ Cincinnati, 53-63.
Positions: Cur prints, Wesleyan Univ Art Mus, 38-45; sr cur & cur prints, Cincinnati Art Mus, 47-63; dir, Mus Art, Carnegie Inst, 63-68; assoc dir, Mus Art, Univ Iowa, 68-; trustee, Tamarind Lithography Workshop.
Awards: Am Asn Mus grant, summer 39.
Memberships: Print Coun Am.
Publications: Ed, Lehman Collection Catalogue; contribr, Collier's Encycl, 50.
Mailing Address: Museum of Art, University of Iowa, Iowa City, IA 52240.

VON GUNTEN, ROGER
Painter
Preferred Media: Oils, Acrylics.
b Zurich, Switz, Mar 29, 33.
Study & Training: Kunstgewerbeschule Zurich, 48-53; Iberoamerican Univ, Mex, 59-60.
Work in Public Collections: Mus Arte Mod, Mexico City; Univ Oaxaca, Mex; Mus Univ Veracruzana, Xalapa, Mex; Centro Arte Mod, Guadalajara, Mex.

Commissions: Paintings, Mex Pavilions Expo 67, Montreal, 67 & Hemisfair 68, San Antonio, Tex, 68; murals, Mex Pavilion, Expo 67, Osaka, Japan, 69 & Centro Arte Mod, Guadalajara, Mex, 70.

Exhibitions: 20th Biennial Watercolors, Brooklyn Mus, N Y, 58; Confrontacion 66, Mus Bellas Artes, Mexico City, 66; 2nd Bienal Coltejer, Medellin, Colombia, 70; 11th Premi Int Dibuix, Barcelona, Spain, 72.

Awards: Soc Amigos Acapulco First Prize, 2nd Festival Pictorico Acapulco, Mex, 64.

Bibliography: J Garcia Ponce (auth), Nueve pintores Mexicanos, Ed Era, Mex, 68 & Aparicion de lo invisible, Ed Siglo XXI, Mex, 68.

Mailing Address: c/o Galeria Juan Martin, Amberes 17, Mexico City 6, Mex.

von MEYER, MICHAEL
Sculptor

b Russia, June 10, 94; U S citizen.

Study & Training: Calif Sch Fine Arts, San Francisco.

Work in Public Collections: Daily Californian Newspaper Bldg, Salinas; House Off Bldg, Washington, D C; U S Post Off, Santa Clara, Calif; Church of Transfiguration, Denver, Colo; Marina Heights, Vallejo, Calif.

Commissions: St Innocent Eastern Orthodox Church, Encino, Calif; St Therese's Shrine, Fresno, Calif; Russian Orthodox Holy Trinity Cathedral, San Francisco; Russian Cath Ctr; Beach Chalet, San Francisco.

Exhibitions: San Francisco Mus Art; Corcoran Gallery Arts, Washington, D C; Oakland Art Gallery, 36; Pomeroy Galleries, San Francisco, 66; Monterey Peninsula Mus Art, 69.

Awards: Winner, Woman's Art Asn San Francisco, 26; bronze medal, Oakland Art Gallery Fourth Ann Sculpture, 34.

Bibliography: E M Polley (auth), Art and artists, Sun Times Herald, Vallejo, Calif; Robert Hagan (auth), The walls they left behind, San Francisco Mag, 64.

Mailing Address: c/o Hoover Gallery, 710 Sansome St, San Francisco, CA 94111.

VON NEUMANN, ROBERT A
Sculptor, Educator

Preferred Media: Clay, Wood, Metals.

b Berlin, Ger, Nov 15, 23; U S citizen.

Study & Training: Sch Art Inst Chicago, BFA; Univ Wis, MS.

Work in Public Collections: Des Moines Art Ctr, Iowa; Detroit Mus Art, Mich; Newark Mus Art, N J; Ill State Univ, Normal; Ind State Col, Indianapolis.

Commissions: Sculpture to illus article in Playboy Mag, 69 & 72.

Exhibitions: Aspects of Christian Art, Newark Mus Art, 56; Craftsmen in a Changing World, Mus Contemp Crafts, New York, 57; American Crafts, Am Pavilion, World's Fair, Brussels, Belg, 58; American Decorative Arts, Europe, U S & Near East, U S State Dept, 59-61; Int Sterling Silver Flatware Design Competition, Europe & U S, 60-61.

Teaching: From instr to asst prof art, Iowa State Teachers Col, 50-55; prof art, Univ Ill, Urbana, 55-

Awards: Chosen by competition to study with Baron Frik Fleming, Court Silversmith to King of Sweden, 50; one of 21 awards, First Int Design Competition for Sterling Silver Flatware, 60; chosen by Int Coop Comn to study Japanese handicraft industries, 60.

Bibliography: Elizabeth Drews (auth), The Creative Personality (series of films), Dept Educ, Mich State Univ, 58.

Memberships: Am Craftsmens Coun.

Publications: Auth, The decorative arts: an aesthetic stepchild?, 60 & bd rev of The arts of the Japanese Sword, 63, Col Arts J; auth, The design and creation of jewelry, Chilton, 60 & rev ed, 72.

Dealer: Gilman Gallery, 103 E Oak St, Chicago, IL 60611.

Mailing Address: R R 1, Saint Joseph, IL 61873.

VON SCHLEGELL, DAVID
Sculptor

Preferred Media: Stainless Steel, Aluminum.

b St Louis, Mo, May 25, 20.

Study & Training: Univ Mich, 40-42; Art Stud League New York, 46-48.

Work in Public Collections: Whitney Mus Am Art, New York, N Y; Carnegie Inst, Pittsburgh, Pa; Storm King Art Ctr, Mountainville, N Y; Mass Inst Technol, Cambridge, Mass; N Y State Albany Man Proj.

Commissions: Sculpture, Lannon Found, Palm Beach, Fla, 69; sculpture, Storm King Art Ctr, Mountainville, 70; sculpture, Harbor Towers, Boston, Mass, 72.

Exhibitions: Whitney Ann, 68 & Lipman Found, 69, Whitney Mus Am Art, New York; Carnegie Int, Pittsburgh, Pa, 70; Sculpture for New Spaces, Walker Art Ctr, Minneapolis, Minn, 71; Middleheim Biennial, Belg, 71; plus many other group & one-man shows.

Teaching: Vis lectr sculpture, Univ Calif, Santa Barbara, 68; instr painting, Sch Visual Arts, 68-69; vis instr sculpture, Cornell Univ, 69-70; dir studies sculpture, Yale Univ, 71-

Awards: Purchase prize, Carnegie Int, 67; St Buttolph Award, 69; Nat Found Arts, 69.

Bibliography: Jacobs (auth), The artist speaks: D V S, Art in Am, 5-6/68.

Dealer: Reese Palley, 93 Prince St, New York, NY 10012.

Mailing Address: 173 Christopher St, New York, NY 10014.

VON SCHNEIDAU, CHRISTIAN
Painter, Sculptor

b Smaland, Sweden, Mar 24, 93.

Study & Training: Acad Fine Arts, Sweden; Art Inst Chicago; also with J Wellington Reynolds, Charles Hawthorne, Richard Miller & others.

Commissions: Portraits & murals in numerous theatres, churches, hotels & clubs throughout the U S & abroad.

Exhibitions: Nationally.

Teaching: Dir, Von Schneidau Sch Art, Los Angeles & Palm Springs, Calif; prof art, Bus Men's Art Inst, Los Angeles; instr portrait painting, Bakersfield Art Asn & Cunningham Mem Mus.

Awards: Prizes, Swedish-Am Exhib, Chicago; Scandinavian-Am Art Soc; Grumbacher Award, 68; plus many others.

Memberships: Calif Watercolor Soc; Fairbanks Art Guild; Swedish Club Los Angeles; Scandinavian-Am Art Soc; Kern River Valley Art Asns; plus others.

Mailing Address: 1023 Emerald Bay, Laguna Beach, CA 92651.

VON WIEGAND, CHARMION
Painter, Writer

Preferred Media: Oils.

b Chicago, Ill.

Study & Training: Barnard Col, Columbia Univ; also jour & playwriting with Minor Latham & Hatcher Hughes, Byzantine art hist with Wittemore, Florentine & Siena painting with Richard Offner & Oriental art with Riefstahl.

Work in Public Collections: Mus Mod Art, New York, N Y; Whitney Mus Am Art, New York; Cincinnati Art Mus, Ohio; Seattle Art Mus, Wash; Joseph Hirshhorn Mus, Washington, D C.

Commissions: Painting, Container Corp Am.

Exhibitions: Women, Peggy Guggenheim's Art of This Century, 45; Classic Tradition In Contemp Art, Walker Art Inst, 53; Konkrete Kunst: 50 Yrs Develop, Zurich, Switz, 60; Art & Writing, Stedelijk Mus, Amsterdam & Baden Baden, Ger, 63; Mondrian, DeStijl & Their Impact, Marlboro-Gerson Gallery, 64.

Positions: Pres, Am Abstr Artists, 51-53.

Awards: Award, Soc Typographic Arts, Chicago, 68; first prize in painting on Tibetan theme, Sixth Relig Biennale, Cranbrook Acad Art, Mich, 69.

Collection: Tibetan art; constructivists.

Publications: Auth, The meaning of Mondrian, J Aesthet, 43; auth, The Russian arts, In: Encycl Arts, 46; auth, The Oriental tradition and abstract art; auth, The world of abstract art; auth, Memoir on Mondrian, Arts Ann, 61.

Mailing Address: 333 E 34th St, New York, NY 10016.

VOORHEES, DONALD EDWARD
Painter

Preferred Media: Watercolors.

b Neptune, N J, May 6, 26.

Study & Training: Acad Arts, Newark, N J, with Stanley Turnbull, Avery Johnson & Edmund Fitzgerald; Art Stud League New York, with Mario Cooper; also with John Pike & Edgar Whitney.

Exhibitions: N J Watercolor Soc State Ann, Morris Mus, 54-72; Knickerbocker Artists Ann, Nat Arts Club, 71-72; Art Ctr Oranges State Ann, N J, 72; Am Watercolor Soc 105th Ann, 72 & Nat Traveling Exhib, 72-73.

Teaching: Instr watercolor, Guild Creative Art, Shrewsbury, N J, 64-; also private instr.

Positions: Mem Art Adv Comn, Monmouth Co Bd Freeholders, 69-

Awards: Mary Lawrence Mem Award, N J Watercolor Soc State Ann, 71; hon mention, Ringwood Manor Mus State Ann, 71 & Garden State Arts Ctr Ann, 71.

Memberships: N J Watercolor Soc (secy, 71-72, exhib chmn, 72-73); Guild Creative Art.

Dealer: Guild of Creative Art, 620 Broad St, Shrewsbury, NJ 07701.

Mailing Address: 125 Manor Pkwy, Lincroft, NJ 07738.

VORIS, ANNA MAYBELLE
Art Administrator

b Mount Rainier, Md, Aug 5, 20.

Study & Training: George Washington Univ, BA; Cath Univ Am, MA; Johns Hopkins Univ.

Positions: Mus cur, Nat Gallery Art, Washington, D C.

Mailing Address: 4801 Kenmore Ave, Alexandria, VA 22304.

VORIS, MARK
Educator, Painter
b Franklin, Ind, Sept 20, 07.
Study & Training: Franklin Col; Art Inst Chicago; Inst Allende, Mex; Univ Ariz; also with Paul Dougherty.
Exhibitions: Stanford Univ; M H de Young Mem Mus; Cochise Col; Univ Ariz; Tucson Art Ctr.
Teaching: Prof art, Col Fine Arts, Univ Ariz, 46-, actg head dept art, 62-63.
Mailing Address: 2626 E Lee St, Tucson, AZ 85716.

VOULKOS, PETER
Sculptor, Educator
b Bozeman, Mont, Jan 29, 24.
Study & Training: Montana State Univ, BS; Calif Col Arts & Crafts, MFA; Montana State Univ, hon LHD, 68.
Work in Public Collections: Baltimore Mus Art, Md; Denver Art Mus, Colo; Smithsonian Inst, Washington, D C; Japanese Craft Mus; San Francisco Mus Art, Calif; plus many others.
Exhibitions: Brussels World's Fair, 58; Seattle World's Fair, 62; Int Sculpture Exhib, Battersea Park, London, 63; Los Angeles State Col, 64; Univ Calif, Irvine, 66; plus many other group & one-man shows.
Teaching: Instr, Archie Bray Found, Black Mountain Col, Los Angeles Co Art Inst, Montana State Univ, Greenwich House Pottery & Teachers Col, Columbia Univ; prof art & design, Univ Calif, Berkeley, 59-
Awards: Silver medal, Int Ceramic Exhib, Ostend, Belg, 54; gold medal, Int Ceramic Exhib, Cannes, France; Rodin Mus Prize in Sculpture, I Paris Biennial, 59; plus many others.
Mailing Address: 1306 Third St, Berkeley, CA 94710.

VOYER, SYLVAIN JACQUES
Painter
Preferred Media: Acrylics.
b Edmonton, Alta, Jan 22, 39.
Study & Training: Alta Col Art, Calgary, with Deli Sacilotto.
Work in Public Collections: Nat Gallery Can, Ottawa; Edmonton Art Gallery; Willistead Art Gallery, Windsor, Ont; Univ Calgary.
Exhibitions: Sixth Biennial Can Painting, 65 & Can Watercolors, Prints & Drawings, 66, Nat Gallery Can; Edmonton Art Gallery, 71.
Positions: Mem bd, Edmonton Art Gallery, 72-
Memberships: Can Artist Representation (rep, 71 & 72).
Mailing Address: 10024-102nd St, Edmonton, Alta, Can.

VRANA, ALBERT S
Sculptor
Preferred Media: Bronze, Concrete.
b Cliffside Park, N J, Jan 25, 21.
Study & Training: Univ Miami.
Work in Public Collections: Captive (cast bronze), Atlanta Mem Art Ctr, Ga; War Flower (bronze), Lowe Art Gallery, Univ Miami, Fla; Fuego (wood), Univ Miami.
Commissions: Sand cast stone relief for Miami Beach Pub Libr Rotunda, City Miami Beach, Fla, 62; cast stone relief from styrofoam molds, U S Govt for Fed Off Bldg, Jacksonville, Fla, 66; cast stone relief from styrofoam molds, Morris Burk, Prof Arts Ctr, Miami, 66; free-standing monument (ferro cement & bronze), Arlen House, Miami Beach, 69; monumental mural (ferro cement & hammered bronze), State of Fla for Fla Int Univ, Miami, 72.
Exhibitions: Penland Show, Gallery Contemp Art, Winston-Salem, N C, 68; one-man shows, Lowe Art Gallery, Univ Miami, 60 & 63, Fairleigh Dickinson Univ Art Gallery, Madison, N J, 64, ACA Galleries, New York, N Y, 66 & Berenson Gallery, Miami, 68, 69 & 72.
Teaching: Instr sculpture, Miami-Dade Jr Col, 66-67; instr sculpture, Penland Sch, summers 68-
Awards: Tiffany grant, 63.
Bibliography: Art Mandler (auth), Artist in concrete (film), produced by Portland Cement Asn, 66; Le beton sculpte par moulage, Batir Mag, Paris, 67; Harry Forgeron(auth), Sculptured structures molded in plastic foam, New York Times, 67.
Memberships: Sculptors of Fla (v pres, 65).
Publications: Contribr, Sculpture from plastics, 67; contribr, Spiel mit form und struktur, 68; contribr, Contemporary art with wood, 68; contribr, Plastics as an art form, 69; contribr, Contemporary stone sculpture, 70.
Dealer: Berenson Gallery, 1128 Kane Concourse, Bay Harbor Islands, FL 33154.
Mailing Address: 6824 S W 81st St, Miami, FL 33143.

VYTLACIL, VACLAV
Painter, Educator
Preferred Media: Oils, Acrylics, Tempera.
b New York, N Y, Nov 1, 92.
Study & Training: Art Inst Chicago; Art Stud League New York;
Bavarian Royal Acad Art, Munich, Ger; Hans Hofmann Sch Art, Munich.
Work in Public Collections: Whitney Mus Am Art, New York; Metrop Mus Art, New York; Pa Acad Fine Arts, Philadelphia; Duncan Philips Mus Art, Washington, D C; Rochester Mus Art, N Y.
Exhibitions: Whitney Mus Am Art, New York, 40-62; Carnegie Int, Carnegie Inst, Pittsburgh, Pa, 42, 44 & 45; Artists for Victory, Metrop Mus Art, New York, 44; Pa Acad Fine Arts, Philadelphia, 52; Duncan Philips Mus Art, Washington, D C, 55; plus many other group & one-man shows.
Teaching: Instr art, Minneapolis Sch Art, 17-21; lectr mod art & artist-in-residence, Univ Calif, Berkeley, 28-29; instr art, Calif Col Arts & Crafts, summers 36 & 37; lectr hist art & chmn dept art, Queen's Col, 42-45; instr art, Colorado Springs Fine Art Ctr, 51-53; instr art, Univ Ga, 68; instr painting & lectr hist mod art, Art Stud League New York, 35-
Positions: Jury mem, Pepsi-Cola Nat Art Competition, 48; regional jury mem, Nat Exhib Art, Metrop Mus Art, New York, 50.
Awards: Hon mention, 14 & William M R French Gold Medal, 36, Soc Am Artists, Art Inst Chicago.
Memberships: Fedn Mod Painters & Sculptors; Am Abstract Artists; Art Stud League New York.
Mailing Address: Sparkill, NY 10976.

W

WAAGE, FREDERICK O
Art Historian, Educator
b Philadelphia, Pa, Oct 7, 06.
Study & Training: Univ Pa, AB, 28; Princeton Univ, MA, 29, MFA, 35, PhD, 43.
Teaching: Instr archaeol, Cornell Univ, 35-38, asst prof hist art & archaeol, 38-41, assoc prof, 41-45, chmn dept fine arts, 42-60, prof hist art & archaeol, 45-72, emer prof, 72-; vis lectr art, Elmira Col, 52-58; lectr art, Ithaca Col, 58-72.
Memberships: Col Art Asn Am; Archaeol Inst Am.
Publications: Auth, Numismatic notes and monographs, No 70, N Y; auth, Antioch on the Orontes, Part 1, Vol IV, Princeton, 48; auth, Prehistoric Art, Dubuque, 67; contribr, Am J Archaeol & Antiq; plus others.
Mailing Address: 103 Comstock Rd, Ithaca, NY 14850.

WAANO-GANO, JOE
Painter, Lecturer
Preferred Media: Oils, Watercolors, Acrylics, Charcoals.
b Salt Lake City, Utah, Mar 3, 06.
Study & Training: T N Lukits Acad Art; Hanson Puthuff Art Sch; Univ Southern Calif; also with Dean Cornwell.
Work in Public Collections: Southwest Mus, Los Angeles, Calif; Gardena H S, Calif; Hist & Art Mus, Los Angeles; Cedar City H S, Utah; Bur Indian Affairs, Washington, D C.
Commissions: Sioux Ghost Dance Chant (mural), ticket off, Rapid City, S Dak, 30 & Sacred Deerskin Dance (mural), ticket off, San Francisco, 44, Western Air Lines; mural for children's ward, Los Angeles Gen Hosp, 30; Theme (mural) & Education (mural), Sherman Indian Inst, Arlington, Calif, 34.
Exhibitions: Am Artists Prof League, New York, N Y, 40-; Nat Ann Indian Art Exhib, Indian Ctr, Los Angeles, 55-69; Am Indian Artists Nat Exhib, Philbrook Mus, Tulsa, Okla, 57-; Nat Am Indian Exhib, Scottsdale, Ariz, 60-; Ctr Arts Indian Am, Washington, D C, 64-68.
Positions: Bd dirs, Painters & Sculptors, Los Angeles, 50-64, pres, 62-63.
Awards: Award for Moonlight Madonna, Int Madonna Festival, 52; award for Flight of the Great Head, Tulsa Indian Womens Club, 63; award for Chief Strong Bear, Greek Theatre, 65.
Bibliography: Ada Wallis (auth), Cherokee Indian, gifted artist, Widening Horizons, 60; Jeanne Snodgrass (auth), Joe Waano Gano, Am Indian Painters, 68; Marion Gridley (auth), Joe Waano Gano, Indians of Today, 71.
Memberships: Valley Artists Guild (pres, 51-52); Artists of the Southwest (bd dirs, 51-); fel Am Artists Prof League; fel Am Inst Fine Art; life mem Traditional Art Guild of Paramount.
Publications: Auth & illusr, Art of the American Indian, Western Art Rev, 51.
Mailing Address: 8926 Holly Pl, Los Angeles, CA 90046.

WACHSTETER, GEORGE
Illustrator
Preferred Media: Inks, Watercolors.
b Hartford, Conn, Mar 12, 11.
Work in Public Collections: New York Pub Libr Theatre Collection;

U S Steel Collection; NBC Collection; plus works in pvt collections.
Exhibitions: One-man traveling exhib for NBC Book of Stars, 58.
Positions: Illusr for major advert agencies, theatrical & motion picture productions, 36-; illusr for CBS, ABC, NBC radio & TV networks, 37-; weekly contribr illus & caricature to drama pages, New York Herald Tribune, 41-50; contribr illus & caricature drama & political pages, New York Times, 42-50, TV artist, 50-51; caricaturist for Theatre Guild on the Air, produced by U S Steel, 45-63; drama artist, New York J-Am, 56-63, TV mag cover artist, 58-63; drama artist, New York World Tel, 64-66; syndicated feature illusr for Hallmark TV Drama series, 64-69.
Publications: Illusr, NBC book of stars, Simon & Schuster, 57.
Mailing Address: 85-05 Elmhurst Ave, Elmhurst, NY 11373.

WADDELL, JOHN HENRY
Sculptor
Preferred Media: Bronze.
b Des Moines, Iowa, Feb 14, 21.
Study & Training: Art Inst Chicago, BFA, MFA, BAE & MAE.
Work in Public Collections: Phoenix Art Mus, Ariz; Univ Ariz, Tucson; Ariz State Univ, Tempe; Coe Col; Eureka Col.
Commissions: Dance Mother, Phoenix Art Mus, 59-62; That Which Might Have Been, Unitarian Church, Phoenix, 63-64; The Family, Maricopa Co Complex, 65-67; Dance, Phoenix Civic Ctr, 70-73.
Exhibitions: One-man shows, La Jolla Mus, 62; Phoenix Art Mus, 60, 63 & 64 & Hellenic Am Union, Athens, Greece, 66; touring one-man show, Ariz, 69.
Teaching: Asst prof art, Inst Design, Chicago, 55-57; prof art, Ariz State Univ, 57-61.
Awards: Valley Beautiful grant, 65-67; Ariz Comn on Art & Humanities grant, 70-72; Nat Found Art & Humanities grant, 71-72.
Mailing Address: Kerr Ranch, Box 482, Cottonwood, AZ 86326.

WADDELL, RICHARD H
Art Dealer
b New York, N Y.
Study & Training: Amherst Col, BA; Columbia Univ, MS.
Positions: Dir, Waddell Gallery, New York.
Specialty of Gallery: Generally avant-garde, with emphasis on European artists, mainly sculptors.
Mailing Address: Waddell Gallery, 50 W 57th St, New York, NY 10019.

WADE, JANE
Art Dealer
b Dallas, Tex, June 30, 25.
Study & Training: Univ Ariz; in Europe; Curt Valentin Gallery, New York, N Y; Otto Gerson Gallery, New York.
Collections Arranged: Drawings By Sculptors, Smithsonian Inst & U S Tour.
Positions: Secy & asst, Curt Valentin Gallery, 48-56; secy & assoc, Otto Gerson Gallery, 56-63; v pres, Marlborough-Gerson Gallery, 63-64; juror, Mid-West Ann, William Rockhill Nelson Gallery Art, Kansas City, Mo; owner & dir, Jane Wade Ltd.
Bibliography: Jay Jacobs (auth), By appointment only, Art Am, 7-8/67; By appointment only, Newsweek, 9/4/67; By appointment only, Time, 8/3/70.
Memberships: Art Dealers Asn Am.
Specialty of Gallery: Twentieth century painting and sculpture.
Mailing Address: 45 E 66th St, New York, NY 10021.

WADE, ROBERT SCHROPE
Painter, Photographer
b Austin, Tex, Jan 6, 43.
Study & Training: Univ Tex, Austin, BFA, 65; Univ Calif, Berkeley, MA, 66.
Work in Public Collections: Okla Art Ctr, Oklahoma City; Witte Mus, San Antonio, Tex; McLennan Col, Waco, Tex; Mountainview Col, Dallas, Tex; Northwood Inst, Cedar Hill, Tex.
Exhibitions: Whitney Contemp Am Painting Ann, Whitney Mus Am Art, New York, N Y, 69; Project South-Southwest, Fort Worth Art Ctr Mus, Tex, 70; one-man shows, Kornblee Gallery, New York, 71 & Chapman Kelley Gallery, Dallas, Tex, 71; Painting and Sculpture Today—1972, Indianapolis, Mus Art, 72.
Teaching: Instr, McLennan Col, 66-70; artist-in-residence, Northwood Inst, 70-72, dir, Northwood Exp Art Inst, Dallas, 72-
Awards: Purchase prize, Okla Art Ctr Ann, 68; 34th Ann Exhib Award, Fort Worth Art Ctr Mus, 71.
Bibliography: Robert Pincus-Witten (auth), New York, Artforum, 12/71; Big D, Newsweek, 8/7/72; Janet Kutner (auth), The Houston-Dallas axis, Art in Am, 9-10/72.
Memberships: Tex Fine Arts Soc (bd dirs, 70-72); Col Art Asn Am; Artists Equity Asn.
Dealers: Kornblee Gallery, 58 E 79th St, New York, NY 10021; Smither Gallery, 2817 Allen, Dallas, TX 75201.
Mailing Address: 302½ S Beckley, Dallas, TX 75203.

WADSWORTH, FRANCES LAUGHLIN
Sculptor, Painter
b Buffalo, N Y.
Study & Training: Albright Art Sch, with Antoinette Hollister, Gutzon Borglum, Charles Teft & John Effl.
Commissions: Safe Arrival (sculpture), Travelers Ins Co, Hartford, Conn; Founder's Monument, Am Sch Deaf, West Hartford; Thomas Hooker, Soc Decendents Founders of Hartford; Gallaudet Monument; portraits & garden sculpture.
Exhibitions: Conn Acad Fine Arts, 30-58; Hartford Soc Women Painters, 30-58; Acad Artists, Springfield, 35-60; Nat League Am Pen Women, 56 & 58; Nat Sculpture Soc, New York, N Y, 70.
Teaching: Lectr sculpture, Inst Living, Hartford, 30-58.
Awards: Nat League Am Pen Women, 56-58.
Bibliography: Ursula Toomey (auth), The charm of her sculpture, Hartford, 62.
Memberships: Nat League Am Pen Women (pres, Hartford Br, 68-70); Acad Artists, Springfield; Conn Acad Arts; Hartford Soc Women Painters; Hartford Art Club (pres, 30-40).
Mailing Address: 129 Day St, Granby, CT 06035.

WAGNER, G NOBLE
Painter, Sculptor
Preferred Media: Stainless Steel.
b Pa, Nov 20, 07.
Study & Training: Temple Univ Tyler Sch Art, BFA, MFA, 59.
Work in Public Collections: Albright-Knox Art Gallery, Buffalo, N Y; Blank, Rome, Klaus & Comisky, Attorneys, Philadelphia, Pa.
Exhibitions: Philadelphia Print Club, 69; Nat Print & Watercolor Exhib, Pa Acad Fine Arts, 69; New York State Fair, Syracuse, 69; Philadelphia Art Mus, 70; Cheltenham Art Centre Tenth Ann Regional Sculpture Exhib, Philadelphia Civic Ctr, 71.
Teaching: Instr art & philos, 51-56; instr art, Oak Lane Co Day Sch, Temple Univ, 59-60, instr art educ, univ, 60-65; instr art educ, elem educ teachers for state cert, 62-63; instr philos art educ, Cheltenham Township Art Centre, 61-, instr painting & sculpture, 62-
Positions: Co-founder & dir educ, Cheltenham Sch Fine Arts, Cheltenham Township Art Centre, 40-, pres, 41-42, chmn bd gov, 42-43, established Aegean Sch Fine Arts, Greece; mem coun, Exp Art & Technol, 67; mem coun, Pa Art Educ Asn, 69; dir art tours abroad, 63 & 66.
Awards: Tyler alumni award, 68 & 70, Temple Univ; first Addie Rubin Mem Award, 22nd ann award exhib, 69 & print exhib award, 71, Cheltenham Art Centre.
Memberships: Pa Acad Fine Arts; Philadelphia Print Club; Mus Mod Art, New York; Philadelphia Mus Art; Peale Club, Philadelphia.
Research: The nature of a meaningful art education course for elementary education student teachers.
Mailing Address: 7955 Waltham Rd, Cheltenham, PA 19012.

WAGNER, JOHN PHILIP
Painter
b Philadelphia, Pa, July 29, 43.
Study & Training: Philadelphia Col Art, BFA; Md Inst Col Art, MFA; spec study with David Hare & Dennis Leon.
Commissions: Poly-chrome sculpture, Baltimore Parks Comn, Md, 65.
Exhibitions: Baltimore Mus Art Regional Show, 65; Soc Illusrs Show, New York, N Y, 69; Southwest Fine Arts Biennial, Santa Fe, N Mex, 70.
Teaching: Instr drawing, Md Inst Col Art, summer 68.
Positions: Artist-in-residence, State Arts Comn, 70-71.
Awards: Rinehart Sch Sculpture fel, 65; Nat Endowment Arts N Mex State Artist-in-Residence grant, 70-71.
Publications: Illusr, Grove Press & Evergreen Rev, 68-69; illusr, Avante Garde Mag, 69; illusr, N Mex Mag, 69; illusr, children's bks for Macmillan & Crowell Collier, 69-70; contribr, Western rev, 72.
Dealer: Jamisons Galleries, 111 E San Francisco St, Santa Fe, NM 87501.
Mailing Address: Rte 1, Box 295-A, El Rancho, NM 87501.

WAGNER, RICHARD ELLIS
Painter
Preferred Media: Acrylics, Oils.
b Trotwood, Ohio, June 18, 23.
Study & Training: Antioch Col; Dayton Art Inst, Ohio; Univ Colo, BFA & MFA.
Work in Public Collections: Denver Art Mus, Colo; Libr Cong, Washington, D C; Dartmouth Col, Hanover, N H; De Cordova Mus, Lincoln, Mass; Rochester Mus, N Y.
Commissions: Murals, Horizon House, Naples, Fla, 71.
Exhibitions: Recent Drawings, U S A, Mus Mod Art, New York, N Y, 56; Art U S A, Madison Sq Gardens, 58; Boston Arts Festival, Mass, 58, 60 & 62; Jefferson Arts Festival, New Orleans, La, 69; Youngstown Art Festival, Butler Inst Am Art, 70.

Teaching: Assoc prof art, Dartmouth Col, 53-66.
Awards: Purchase prizes, Denver Art Mus, 50 & Libr Cong, 52;
City of Manchester Award, Currier Gallery, Manchester, N H, 56.
Publications: Illusr, Ford Times, 58-70.
Dealer: Grand Central Art Galleries, 40 Vanderbilt Ave, New York,
NY 10017.
Mailing Address: P O Box 456, Telluride, CO 81435.

WALD, SYLVIA
Painter
b Philadelphia, Pa.
Study & Training: Moore Inst Art, Philadelphia.
Work in Public Collections: Mus Mod Art, New York, N Y; Metrop
Mus Art, New York; Whitney Mus Am Art; Nat Gallery Art,
Washington, D C; Brooklyn Mus, N Y; plus others.
Exhibitions: Second Biennial, Sao Paulo, 53; Curator's Choice,
Smithsonian Inst & Tour U S, 54; 50 Yrs Am Art, Mus Mod Art
& Tour Europe, 55; Am Prints Today, 62; U S Info Serv Show,
Palacio Bellas Artes, Mex, 64.
Bibliography: Seiberling (auth), Looking into art, Henry Holt, 59;
The art of printmaking, In: Master prints from nineteenth and
twentieth centuries, Libr Cong & Univ Nebr Art Gallery, 66.
Memberships: Am Fedn Arts.
Dealer: Tunnel Gallery, 232 E 59th St, New York, NY 10022.
Mailing Address: 37 E Fourth St, New York, NY 10003.

WALDMAN, PAUL
Painter
b Erie, Pa, 36.
Study & Training: Brooklyn Mus Art Sch; Pratt Inst.
Work in Public Collections: Paintings, New York Univ, Newark Mus
& White Mus, Cornell Univ; drawing & lithographs, Mus Mod Art;
sculpture collage, Rose Art Mus, Brandeis Univ; plus many oth-
ers.
Exhibitions: Group Paintings & Prints, Sch Visual Arts, 68; Second
Kent Invitational, Ohio, 68; Group Show From Collection, Newark
Mus, 68; Dominant Female, Finch Col Mus Art, 68; three shows,
Knoedler Gallery, 71; plus many others.
Teaching: Instr, Greenwich Art Ctr, spring 63; instr New York Com-
munity Col, 63-64; instr, Brooklyn Mus Art Sch, 63-67; vis art-
ist, Ohio State Univ, Jan 66; vis prof, Univ Calif, Davis, spring
66; instr, Sch Visual Arts, 66-
Positions: Ford Found artist-in-residence, 65.
Mailing Address: c/o M Knoedler & Co, 21 E 70th St, New York, NY
10021.

WALDRON, JAMES MacKELLAR
Curator, Painter
b Hazleton, Pa, Sept 3, 09.
Study & Training: Kutztown State Col, BS; Tyler Sch Fine Arts, Tem-
ple Univ, MFA; Univ Calif, Los Angeles, summer 37.
Work in Public Collections: Kutztown State Col, Pa; Reading Pub
Mus & Art Gallery, Pa; Reading Mus, Eng; Wilson Pub Sch, West
Lawn, Pa; Gov Mifflin Schs, Shillington, Pa.
Commissions: Mural, First Baptist Church, Reading, 52.
Exhibitions: Regional Exhibs, Reading Pub Mus & Art Gallery, 36-
69; one-man exhibs, Kutztown State Col, 49 & Berks Art Alliance,
Reading, Pa, 58.
Collections Arranged: Over 100 exhibs, Reading Pub Mus & Art Gal-
lery, 58-68.
Teaching: Instr & supvr art, West Reading Sch Dist, Pa, 36-58; adj
instr art, Kutztown State Col, 50-58; cur art, Reading Mus & Art
Gallery, 58-71.
Positions: Pres, Co Art Supvr, 39-40; pres, Berks Art Alliance, 50-
71.
Awards: Gen Alumni Asn Citation, Kutztown State Col, 61.
Memberships: Int Inst Conserv.
Research: Pennsylvania German art.
Collection: Drawings, paintings, lithographs & etchings by contempo-
rary and local artists, including Marin, Kuhns, Cadmus, Dehn,
Kenneth Hayes Miller, Boardman Robinson, Conrad Roland &
Earl Poole.
Publications: Illusr, I like you because, Parent-Teachers Asn West
Reading, 47; illusr, Berks County stamp and story, 48; illusr,
Art Bull, 55; illusr, Berks Co Hist Rev Mag.
Mailing Address: 23 S Seventh Ave, West Reading, PA 19602.

WALKER, HERBERT BROOKS
Sculptor, Museum Director
Preferred Media: Sheet Metals, Bronze.
b Brooklyn, N Y, Nov 30, 27.
Study & Training: Art Stud League New York, with Harry Sternberg
& Robert B Hale, 43; Yale Sch Fine Arts, BFA, with R Eberhardt,
R Zallinger, Graziani, R Albers and De Konning.
Work in Public Collections: Photographs of Antionio Gaudis Work,
Mus Mod Art, New York, N Y; Barbados Mus, B W I; Walker Mus.

Commissions: Paintings, movie, photographs, Gahagan Dredging,
Orinoco River, Venezuela, 53-54; paintings & photographs, U S
Steel, Cerro Bolivar, Venezuela; earth sculpture, Walker Mus,
60.
Exhibitions: One-man shows, Stony Brook Mus, Long Island, N Y,
52, Barbados Mus, 54 & IORC, Abadan, Iran, 58; Walker Mus,
60-; group show, Rodin Mus, 70.
Collections Arranged: Spec exhibs for pub schs, 60-72 & Walker
Mus, Fairlee, Vt, 60-; Oil Exhibs, IORC, Abadan, Iran, 58 & 59.
Teaching: Instr art, Thetford Acad, 64-66.
Positions: Materials prod head, IROC, Abadan, Iran, 58-59; dir,
Walker Mus, 59-
Bibliography: H Brooks Walker, 1951, EYE Mag, Yale Univ, 67.
Memberships: Life mem Art Stud League New York; Yale Arts
Alumni Asn.
Publications: Illus, Gaudi, Mus Mod Art, 57.
Mailing Address: Fairlee, VT 05045.

WALKER, HERSCHEL CAREY
Collector
Memberships: Art Collectors Club.
Mailing Address: 510 Park Ave, New York, NY 10022.

WALKER, HUDSON D
Collector, Art Administrator
b Minneapolis, Minn, June 17, 07.
Study & Training: Fogg Mus Art, Harvard Univ, with Paul Sachs,
Edward Forbes & Arthur Pope, 28-30.
Collections Arranged: Marsden Hartley Retrospective, Mus Mod
Art, New York, N Y, 44.
Positions: First cur, Univ Gallery, Univ Minn, Minneapolis, 34.
Memberships: Fine Arts Work Ctr, Provincetown (pres, 71-); T B
Walker Found (v pres & trustee); Am Fedn Arts (trustee, 44-71,
pres, 45-47); hon mem Artists Equity Asn (exec dir, 47-53).
Art Interests: Pvt collections given or loaned to Univ Gallery, Univ
Minn, Minneapolis.
Collection: Marsden Hartley & Alfred H Maurer; graphics by Harry
Sternberg, Joseph Hirsch & Albert Christ-Janer.
Publications: Auth, Marsden Hartley, Kenyon Rev, 47.
Mailing Address: 40 Deepdene Rd, Forest Hills, NY 11375.

WALKER, JAMES ADAMS
Painter, Printmaker
b Connersville, Ind, Jan 24, 21.
Study & Training: Western Mich Univ, BS, 46; Univ Mich, 47-48;
teachers col, Columbia Univ, MA, 49; East Carolina Univ, 49-56;
teachers col, Columbia Univ, prof dipl, 58; Claremont Grad Sch,
59; Mich State Univ, MFA, 61.
Work in Public Collections: Dulin Gallery Art, Knoxville, Tenn;
Flint Inst Arts, Mich; Mercyhurst Col, Erie, Pa; Western Mich
Univ, Kalamazoo, Mich; Butler Inst Am Art, Youngstown, Ohio.
Exhibitions: 19th Nat Competition Prints, Libr Cong, Washington,
D C, 63; 14th & 15th Nat Brooklyn Mus Print Exhib, 64 & 66; 32nd
Nat Graphic Arts Drawing Exhib, Wichita Art Asn, Kans, 65; 11th
Nat Biennial Print Exhib, Print Club Albany, N Y, 66.
Teaching: Art supvr & critic instr, E Carolina Univ, 49-56; art instr,
Northern Community High Sch, Flint, 56-66; art instr, Nat Music
Camp, Interlochen, Mich, summer 63; asst prof art, Kent State
Univ, Warren, Ohio, 66-
Awards: Purchase award, 25th Ann Mich Acad Sci, Arts & Lett, 66;
Hugh J Baker Mem Prize for prints, 43rd Ann Hoosier Salon,
Indianapolis, Ind, 67; first print purchase award, Butler Inst Am
Art, 68.
Bibliography: Arne W Randall (auth), Murals for schools, Davis
Mass, 56; Charles E Meyer (auth), Papers of the Michigan Acad-
emy of Science, Arts and Letters, Univ Mich Press, 62; Eleanor
Nelson (auth), Faculty focus, Kent State Univ Press, 71.
Memberships: Mich Acad Sci, Arts & Lett (chmn, fine arts sect, 65-
67); Trumbull Art Guild (bd dirs & bd trustees, 69-); Kalamazoo
Inst Arts; Canton Art Inst; Steel Valley Art Teachers Asn.
Publications: Auth, Newsprint, paste and chicken wire, 50, Let's
scribble a mural, 53 & Buttermilk and chalk drawing, 54, Sch
Arts Mag; auth, Cypress knees, Indust Arts Mag, 59.
Mailing Address: 8778 Gull Rd, Richland, MI 49083.

WALKER, JEROME
Painter, Educator
Preferred Media: Mixed Media, Graphics.
b Peoria, Ill, 1937.
Study & Training: Art Inst Chicago, scholar; Chicago Acad Fine
Arts.
Work in Public Collections: Bernard Horwich Ctr, Chicago, Ill; Ill
Inst Technol, Chicago; Inst Contemp Arts.
Exhibitions: Art Inst Chicago Vicinity Show, 66; Univ Chicago Mo-
mentum II, 67; Festival of the Arts & Spectrum, McCormick Pl,
Chicago; Participating Artists of Chicago & Eye on Chicago, Ill
Inst Technol, 67.

Teaching: Head printmaking dept, Chicago Acad Fine Art, 71-
Memberships: Artists Int Asn, London; Inst Contemp Arts, London; Partic Artists Chicago.
Mailing Address: c/o Americana Galleries & Art Center, Inc, 271 Waukegan Rd, Northfield, IL 60093.

WALKER, MORT
Cartoonist
Preferred Media: Ink.
b El Dorado, Kans, Sept 3, 23.
Study & Training: Univ Mo, BA.
Work in Public Collections: Bird Libr, Syracuse Univ; Boston Univ Libr; Kans State Univ; Montreal Humor Pavilion; Smithsonian Inst.
Exhibitions: Metrop Mus Art, New York, N Y, 52; Brussels World's Fair, 64; Mus Louvre, Paris, 65; New York World's Fair, 67; Expo, Montreal, 69.
Positions: Creator of Beetle Bailey, King Features Syndicate, 50-, Hi & Lois, 54-, Sam's Strip, 61-63 & Boner's Ark, 68-
Awards: Reuben Award, 54 & two Best Humor Strip Plaques, 66 & 69, Nat Cartoonists Soc; Silver Lady, Banshees Soc, 55.
Bibliography: Many articles, bks & TV specials.
Memberships: Nat Cartoonists Soc (pres, 60); Newspaper Comics Coun; Artists & Writers Asn.
Publications: Ed, Nat Cartoonists Soc Album, 61, 65 & 72; auth, Most, 71 & Land of lost things, 72; auth, Hi and Lois, 2 vols; auth & illusr, Beetle Bailey, 6 vols.
Dealer: Graham Gallery, 1014 Madison Ave, New York, NY 10021.

WALKER, MRS PHILIP
Collector
Collection: Paintings.
Mailing Address: 115 Sargent Rd, Brookline, MA 02146.

WALKER, MR & MRS RALPH
Collectors
Collection: Antiques and contemporary art.
Mailing Address: 3784 Tenth Ave, New York, NY 10034.

WALKER, ROBERT MILLER
Educator
b Flushing, N Y, Dec 10, 08.
Study & Training: Princeton Univ, BA, 32, MFA, 36; Harvard Univ, PhD, 41.
Teaching: Instr, Williams Col, 36-38; asst prof art hist, Swarthmore Col, 41-47, chmn dept, 41-71, assoc prof, 47-52, prof, 52-
Memberships: Col Art Asn Am; Soc Archit Historians; Philadelphia Print Club; Am Archaeol Soc; Print Coun Am; plus others.
Mailing Address: 212 Elm Ave, Swarthmore, PA 19081.

WALKEY, FREDERICK P
Museum Director
b Belmont, Mass, May 29, 22.
Study & Training: Duke Univ; Boston Mus Fine Arts Sch; Tufts Col, BSEd.
Positions: Exec dir, De Cordova Mus, Lincoln, Mass, presently.
Memberships: Am Asn Mus; Am Fedn Arts.
Mailing Address: De Cordova Museum, Sandy Pond Rd, Lincoln, MA 01773.

WALLACE, DAVID HAROLD
Art Historian, Art Administrator
b Baltimore, Md, Dec 24, 26.
Study & Training: Lebanon Valley Col, BA; Columbia Univ, MA, PhD.
Collections Arranged: Peale-Sharples Collection of Early American Portraits, Independence Nat Historical Park, Philadelphia, Pa.
Positions: Asst ed, N Y Hist Soc, New York, 52-56; mus cur, Independence Nat Hist Park, Philadelphia, 58-68; asst chief, Br Mus Opers, Nat Park Serv, 68-71, chief, 71-
Research: American artist biographies.
Publications: Co-auth, Dictionary of artists in America, 1564-1860, N Y Hist Soc, 57; auth, John Rogers, the people's sculptor, 67.
Mailing Address: 9 W Third St, Frederick, MD 21701.

WALLACE, SONI
Painter
Preferred Media: Watercolors, Acrylics.
b London, Eng, Apr 18, 31; U S citizen.
Study & Training: Silvermine Art Guild, New Canaan, Conn; Mus Mod Art, with Zolten Hecht; Pratt Graphics, New York, N Y.
Work in Public Collections: Gibbes Art Mus, Charleston, S C.
Commissions: Three covers for mag, Distinguished Resorts, 68, 70 & 71.
Exhibitions: Conn Watercolor Soc 31st Ann, Fairfield Univ, 69; Love/Peace, Am Greetings Gallery, New York, 69; Northwest Printmakers 41st Int Exhib, Seattle Art Mus, Wash, 70; one-man shows, Pacem in Terris Gallery, New York, 70 & Danbury Libr Gallery, Conn, 71.
Awards: Award for watercolor show, Pen & Brush, New York, 69; Max Granick Award, Am Soc Contemp Artists, N Y, 71; award, Washington Art Asn, Conn, 72.
Memberships: Nat Asn Women Artists (prog chmn, 72); Am Soc Contemp Artists; Silvermine Guild Artists; Washington Art Asn.
Dealer: Silvermine Guild of Artists, Silvermine Rd, New Canaan, CT 06840.
Mailing Address: 975 Park Ave, New York, NY 10028.

WALSH, JOHN STANLEY
Painter, Writer
Preferred Media: Watercolors.
b Brighton, Eng, Aug 16, 07.
Study & Training: London Cent Sch Art, Eng.
Work in Public Collections: Montreal Mus Fine Arts; Toronto Art Mus.
Exhibitions: Am Watercolor Soc, 61; Can Soc Painter in Water Colour; Can Soc Graphic Art; Royal Can Acad Art; numerous one-man shows, Montreal, New York & Toronto.
Teaching: Lectr watercolor painting.
Memberships: Can Watercolor Soc; Can Soc Graphic Art.
Publications: Contribr, articles & illus, In: Am Artists, New York Times, Esquire, Harper's Bazaar & Field & Stream; plus others.
Mailing Address: 142 52nd Ave, Lachine, P Q, Can.

WALTER, MAY E
Collector, Patron
Positions: Mem art adv coun, Univ Notre Dame; secy, trustee & mem exec comt, Am Craftsman's Coun.
Art Interests: Patron, New York Univ Art Collection, Notre Dame Univ.
Collection: Twentieth century masters, includes cubism & futurism.
Mailing Address: 923 Fifth Ave, New York, NY 10021.

WALTER, VALERIE HARRISSE
Sculptor
Preferred Media: Marble, Teak, Mahogany, Bronze.
b Baltimore, Md.
Study & Training: Md Inst, Baltimore; Art Stud League New York, N Y; apprentice to Augustus Lukeman; Hunter Col; Col Notre Dame, Md; McCoy Col, Johns Hopkins Univ.
Work in Public Collections: Gen Umberto Nohle, Aeronaut Ministry, Rome, Italy; John Daniel II & Bamboo, Baltimore Zoo.
Commissions: Marble bust, Geheimnat Carl van Noorden, Frankfurt, Ger & Vienna, 34; bronze head, Charlotte, comn by Mason Faulkner Lord, Baltimore, 57; bronze bas-relief, Dr & Mrs W Waldemar Argow, Unitarian Church, Baltimore, 62; bronze, Toni, comn by Mrs Richard O'Brien; bronze bust, Nathalie, comn by Mr J Sawyer Wilson.
Exhibitions: Corcoran Gallery Art, Washington, D C; Pa Acad Fine Arts, Philadelphia; Paris Salon; San Francisco Mus Art; Hispanic Mus, New York.
Awards: First prize for sculpture, Soc Washington Artists Ann.
Mailing Address: 202 E 31st St, Baltimore, MD 21218.

WALTNER, BEVERLY RULAND
Painter
Preferred Media: Acrylics.
b Kansas City, Mo.
Study & Training: Yale Univ, with Joseph Albers; Univ Miami, BA; Northern Ill Univ, MFA; Kent State Univ, Blossom-Kent Art Prog, with Richard Anuszkiewicz.
Work in Public Collections: Northern Ill Univ, De Kalb.
Exhibitions: 10th Midwest Biennial, Joslyn Art Mus, Omaha, Nebr, 68; Mid-Am I, Nelson Gallery Art, Kansas City & City Art Mus, Saint Louis, Mo, 68; 35th Ann Midyear Show, Butler Inst Am Art, Youngstown, Ohio, 70; 33rd Ann Exhib Contemp Am Painting, Soc Four Arts, Palm Beach, Fla, 71; Ann Exhib Nat Soc Painters in Casein, Inc, Nat Arts Club, New York, N Y, 72.
Teaching: Instr art, Barry Col, Miami Shores, Fla, 70-71.
Awards: Top award, New Horizons in painting, N Shore Art League, Chicago, Ill, 66; first pl, Chautauqua Exhib Am Art, 68 & Louis E Seiden Mem Award, 70, Chautauqua Art Asn.
Bibliography: Margaret Harold (auth), Top award in new horizons exhibit, Prize-Winning Art Bk 7, Allied Fla, 67; Donald L Hoffmann (auth), The color image, Kansas City Star, 1/19/69; Bill von Mauer (auth), Colors get her vivid messages across, Miami News, 2/8/72.
Memberships: Chatauqua Art Asn; Miami Art Ctr.
Mailing Address: 604 Tibidabo Ave, Coral Gables, FL 33143.

WALTON, FLORENCE GOODSTEIN (GOODSTEIN-SHAPIRO)
Painter, Art Historian
Preferred Media: Oils, Charcoals, Acrylics, Pastels.
b New York, N Y, July 22, 31.
Study & Training: Cooper Union, 50-51; City Col New York, BS (art

educ), 52; Hans Hofmann Sch Fine Arts, 56-57; Univ Minn, MA (art hist), 73.
Work in Public Collections: Bonython Gallery, Sydney, Australia; Martin Luther King Collection, Atlanta, Ga; Augsburg Col Collection, Minneapolis, Minn; Juana Mordo Gallery, Madrid, Spain; Merton Simpson Gallery, New York.
Exhibitions: Am Watercolor Soc, Smithsonian Inst, Washington, D C, 63; Cooper Union Gallery, New York, 67; Los Angeles Co Mus Art, Calif, 69; Boynthon Art Gallery, Sydney, 69; Tweed Gallery, Univ Minn, Duluth, 71.
Teaching: Instr art hist, Lakewood State Jr Col, 71-
Positions: Art prog dir, Emanuel-Midtown Y Community Ctr, 63-65; secy & pub rels dir, Aspects Gallery, New York, 64-66; dir, Artists Against War Exhib, New York, 67-68.
Awards: STA award for excellence, Art Inst Chicago, 54.
Bibliography: New voices, Village Voice, 3/64; Artist paints death, Australian, 9/30/69; Shades of Whispering Glades, Sydney Morning-Herald, 9/30/69.
Memberships: Col Art Asn Am; Am Inst Archaeol; Exp Art & Technol.
Research: Pre-Hellenic Greek ware; Goya's black paintings; Indian Gupta architecture.
Publications: Auth, Lumen room, Technol & the Environ, 70.
Mailing Address: 8066 Ruth St N E, Minneapolis, MN 55432.

WALTON, HARRY A, JR
Collector
b Covington, Va, Sept 24, 18.
Study & Training: Univ Va, 37; Columbia Univ, 39; Lynchburg Col, AB, 39.
Memberships: Fel Pierpont-Morgan Libr, N Y; Univ Va Bibliog Soc.
Collection: Early books and manuscripts, Bibles, fine binding, Aldinae and first editions; works have been exhibited in libraries at: Trinity College, Washington, D C, College of William and Mary, Norfolk Museum of Arts and Sciences, University of Virginia and Lynchburg College.
Mailing Address: White Oak Dairy, Covington, VA 24426.

WALTON, MARION (MARION WALTON PUTNAM)
Sculptor
Preferred Media: Marble, Bronze, Wood.
b New Rochelle, N Y, Nov 19, 99.
Study & Training: Bryn Mawr Col; Art Stud League New York; Acad Grande Chaumière, Paris, with Antoine Bourdelle.
Work in Public Collections: Lincoln Mus, Nebr; plus many pvt collections in U S A, France & Sweden.
Commissions: World's Fair, U S Govt, 39; post off mural, U S Govt; plus many pvt commissions for portraits, gardens & interiors.
Exhibitions: Mus Mod Art, New York, N Y; Whitney Mus Am Art, New York; Metrop Mus Art, New York; Art Inst Chicago, Ill; La Jeune Sculpture, Rodin Mus, Paris, France; plus many others.
Teaching: Prof sculpture, Sarah Lawrence Col, 50-51.
Memberships: Sculptors Guild; Artists Equity Asn.
Dealer: New Bertha Schaefer Gallery, 41 E 57th St, New York, NY 10022.
Mailing Address: 49 Irving Pl, New York, NY 10003.

WANG, YINPAO
Painter, Writer
Preferred Media: Watercolors.
b Suchow, China, Mar 11, 18; U S citizen.
Study & Training: Chao Tung Univ, BA; Univ Pa, MBA.
Work in Public Collections: Henry Ford Mus, Detroit, Mich; Detroit Art Mus; China Inst in Am, New York, N Y; Gracie Mansion, New York; James Cash Penney Collections, New York.
Exhibitions: One-man shows, Art Stud League New York, 38, Detroit Art Mus, 58, Columbia Univ, New York, 68, Nat Mus, Taipei, Taiwan, 70 & Jefferson Univ, Philadelphia, Pa, 71.
Teaching: Instr painting, Art Stud League New York, 37-38; prof art, Kwang Si Univ, 46-47.
Positions: Founder, Peking Art Asn, China, 28-32; publ, Peking Pictorial, 29-32; v pres, Chinese Art League in New York, 37-41.
Awards: Merit award, Grumbacher, 54; int awards, Am Inst Interior Designers, 61 & 63; spec award, Int Platform Asn, 65; plus others.
Memberships: Fel Royal Soc Arts; hon mem Kappa Pi; life mem Harrisburg Art Asn; art mem Philadelphia Art Alliance; Nat Soc Arts & Lett.
Publications: Contribr, The mysterious fifth dimension, 58; auth, Techniques of Chinese painting, 70, We live in art, 70 & Thoughts in Chinese art, 72.
Mailing Address: 52 Breece Dr, Yardley, PA 19067.

WARBURG, EDWARD M M
Collector
b White Plains, N Y, June 5, 08.
Study & Training: Harvard Col, BS, 30; Brandeis Univ, hon DHL,

Jewish Inst Religion, Hebrew Union Col.
Teaching: Art instr, Bryn Mawr Col, 31-33.
Positions: Mem archaeol exped to photograph Islamic archit, Iran, 33; staff mem, Mus Mod Art, 34-35; trustee, Am-Israel Cult Found; chmn, Am Patrons of Israel Mus; founder, former mem exec comt, now hon trustee, Mus Mod Art, New York; hon trustee, Inst Int Educ.
Collection: Contemporary art.
Mailing Address: 730 Park Ave, New York, NY 10021.

WARD, LYLE EDWARD
Painter, Educator
Preferred Media: Oils.
b Topeka, Kans, Feb 4, 22.
Study & Training: Stevens Point State Teachers Wis, 43; Univ Kansas City, 50; Kansas City Art Inst, BFA, 51, MFA, 52; also with Miron Sokole, New York, N Y.
Work in Public Collections: Brooklyn Mus, N Y; Mus Art, Univ Okla, Norman; Mulvane Art Mus, Topeka.
Exhibitions: One-man shows, Superior St Gallery, Chicago, Ill, 60 & Univ Miss, Oxford, 72; Contemp Americans, Ark Arts Ctr, Little Rock, 66; Ark State Pavilion, Hemisfair, San Antonio, Tex, 68; Inaugural Exhib Artists U S A, State Univ N Y Col Oswego, 68.
Teaching: Assoc prof art & chmn dept, Col of the Ozarks, Clarksville, Ark, 56-
Awards: Arts Festival Award, Worthen Bank, Little Rock, 60 & 62; first prize, Delta Exhib, Ark Arts Ctr, 63, 65 & 67; 18th Arts Festival Award, Fort Smith Festival Bd, Ark, 68.
Bibliography: Ed Albin (auth), article, In: Ark Gazette, Little Rock, 59; Margaret Harold (auth), Prize winning paintings, bk 6, Allied Publ, 66.
Memberships: Col Art Asn Am; Mid-Am Art Asn; Southeast Art Conf.
Dealer: Reflections Gallery, 3445 Peachtree Rd, N E, Atlanta, GA 30304.
Mailing Address: 610 Johnson St, Clarksville, AR 72830.

WARD, LYND (KENDALL)
Illustrator, Writer
b Chicago, Ill, June 26, 05.
Study & Training: Teachers Col, Columbia Univ, BS, 26; Staatliche Akad Graphische Kunst, Leipzig, Ger, 26-27.
Work in Public Collections: Libr Cong; New York World's Fair, 39; Nat Acad Design; Newark Mus; Metrop Mus Art; Montclair Art Mus, N J.
Exhibitions: Am Art Cong; New York World's Fair, 39; Nat Acad Design; John Herron Art Inst.
Awards: Prize, 49 & John Taylor Arms Mem Prize, 62, Nat Acad Design; Samuel F B Morse Gold Medal, 66; Rutgers Medal, 69; plus others.
Memberships: Academician Nat Acad Design; Soc Am Graphic Artists (pres, 53-59); Soc Illusr.
Publications: Auth & illusr, God's man, 29, Madman's drum, 30, Song without words, 36 & Vertigo (novels in woodcuts), 37; auth & illusr, Nic of the woods, 65; plus others.
Mailing Address: Lambs Lane, Cresskill, NJ 07626.

WARD, VELOX BENJAMIN
Painter
b Mount Vernon, Tex, Dec 21, 01.
Work in Public Collections: Smithsonian Inst, Washington, D C; Am Nat Collection; Am Nat Ins Co, Galveston, Tex; Amon Carter Mus, Fort Worth, Tex.
Commissions: Paintings of old homesteads for Johnnie Hartman, Dallas, Tex, 61, Mrs Jean Roberts, Longview, Tex, 62, Mrs Henry Foster, Longview, 67, Mrs Nila Boatner, Longview, 69 & Mrs Joan Cotton, Longview, 69.
Exhibitions: Heirloom House, Inc, Dallas, 65; Texas Painting & Sculpture Exhib, Dallas Mus Fine Arts, 66; The Sphere of Art, Hemisfair 68, San Antonio, Tex, 68; Amon Carter Mus, 72.
Dealer: Donald S Vogel, 6616 Spring Valley Rd, Dallas, TX 75240.
Mailing Address: 2303 Stardust, Longview, TX 75601.

WARDLAW, GEORGE MELVIN
Painter
Preferred Media: Acrylics.
b Baldwyn, Miss, Apr 9, 27.
Study & Training: Memphis Acad Arts, BFA, 51; Univ Miss, with David Smith & Jack Tworkov, MFA, 65.
Exhibitions: American Crafts, Smithsonian Inst, Washington, D C, 52; Recent Still Life, R I Sch Design, Providence, 66; Inside-Outside, Smith Col Mus Art, Northampton, Mass, 66; Contemporary Art at Yale, Yale Univ Art Gallery, New Haven, Conn, 66; Abstract Paintings, DeCordova Mus, Lincoln, Mass, 71.
Teaching: Asst prof design, State Univ N Y Col New Paltz, 56-63; assoc prof painting & exec off, Yale Univ, 64-68; prof painting & chmn dept, Univ Mass, Amherst, 68-
Mailing Address: 47 Morgan Circle, Amherst, MA 01002.

WARDLE, ALFRED H
Silversmith, Jeweler
Preferred Media: Sterling Silver, Gold.
b Englewood, N J, May 29, 33.
Study & Training: Art Inst Pittsburgh; Sch Am Craftsmen, Rochester Inst Technol, AAS & BS; Syracuse Univ Sch Art.
Commissions: Mem punch bowl, Rochester Inst Technol, 56; silver chalice with gold cross, Grace Episcopal Church, Utica, N Y, 60; silver chalice, Westminster Presby Church, Utica, 62; large tree of life, Temple Addas Israel, Rome, N Y, 66; presidential mace, Mohawk Valley Community Col, Utica, 69.
Exhibitions: Smithsonian Inst Traveling Exhib, 58; Crafts Exhib, Mus Mod Art, Caracas, Venezuela, 61; R I Arts Festival Show, Providence, 63; one-man show, Three Rivers Arts Festival, Pittsburgh, Pa, 66; two-man show, Munson Williams Proctor Inst, Utica, 68.
Teaching: Instr metal arts, Norwich Free Acad, Conn, 59-60; instr silversmithing, Munson Williams Proctor Inst, 60-
Positions: Color coordr, restoration comt, Unitarian Church Barneveld, N Y, 70-72.
Awards: Young Americans second prize, Mus Contemp Crafts, 54; hollow-ware first prize, R I Arts Festival, 63; crafts first prize, Syracuse Regional Art Show, 63-65.
Bibliography: Nicolas Haney, Trilling & Lee (auth), Art for young America, Bennett Co, 60.
Memberships: N Y State Craftsmen.
Mailing Address: R D 1, Hinman Rd, Barneveld, NY 13304.

WARHOL, ANDY
Painter, Craftsman
b Cleveland, Ohio, Aug 8, 31.
Study & Training: Carnegie Inst Technol.
Work in Public Collections: Albright-Knox Art Gallery, Buffalo, N Y; Los Angeles Co Mus Art; Mus Mod Art; Whitney Mus Am Art; Walker Art Ctr, Minneapolis, Minn; plus others.
Exhibitions: The 1960's, Mus Mod Art, 67; Jewish Mus, 68; Documenta IV, Kassel, Ger, 68; Directions I: Options, Milwaukee Art Ctr, 68; Whitney Mus Am Art Ann, 68 & 69; plus many others.
Awards: Sixth Film Cult Award, 64; Los Angeles Film Festival Award, 64.
Bibliography: Samuel Adams Green (auth), Andy Warhol (catalogue), Inst Contemp Art, Philadelphia, 65; Tracy Atkinson (auth), Directions I: Options 1968, Milwaukee Art Ctr, 68; Gregory Battcock (ed), Minimal art: a critical anthology, Dutton, 68; plus many others.
Memberships: Film Co-op.
Mailing Address: c/o Leo Castelli Gallery, 4 E 77th St, New York, NY 10021.

WARK, ROBERT RODGER
Art Administrator, Art Historian
b Edmonton, Alta, Oct 7, 24; U S citizen.
Study & Training: Univ Alta, BA & MA; Harvard Univ, MA & PhD.
Teaching: Instr art, Harvard Univ, 52-54; instr art, Yale Univ, 54-56; lectr art, Calif Inst Technol, 60-; lectr art, Univ Calif, Los Angeles, 65-
Positions: Cur art, Huntington Libr & Art Gallery, 56-
Memberships: Col Art Asn Am; Asn Art Mus Dirs.
Research: English art of the Georgian period.
Publications: Ed, Sir Joshua Reynolds, discourses on art, 59; auth, Rowlandson's drawings for a tour in a post-chaise, 63; auth, Early British drawings in the Huntington Collection 1700-1750, 69; auth, Drawings by John Flaxman in the Huntington Collection, 70; auth, Ten British pictures 1740-1840; plus others.
Mailing Address: Henry E Huntington Library & Art Gallery, San Marino, CA 91108.

WARNEKE, HEINZ
Sculptor
Preferred Media: Granite.
b Bremen, Ger, June 30, 95; U S citizen.
Study & Training: Kunstschule, Bremen; Staatliche Kunstgewerbe Schule & Acad, masters degree; with Blossfeld, Haberkamp, Wakele & others
Work in Public Collections: Art Inst Chicago, Ill; Corcoran Gallery Art, Washington, D C; Brookgreen Gardens, Georgetown, S C; Santa Fe Mus, N Mex; The Immigrant, P Samuel Mem, Fairmount Park, Philadelphia, Pa; Nat Collection Am Art, Smithsonian Inst.
Commissions: Prodigal Son (granite), 38, Last Supper, tympanium at s portal, 55 & entire decoration of clerestory at s transcept, 56-60, Washington Cathedral, Washington, D C; granite elephant group, commissioned by pvt group for Philadelphia Zool Gardens, 63; portrait plaque of Allen C Dulles, pvt commission for C I A Bldg, Langley, Va, 69.
Exhibitions: Salon des Tuileries, Paris, France, 29; Art Inst Chicago Ann, 30; Pa Acad Fine Arts Ann, Philadelphia, 34-42; Mus Mod Art Ann, New York, 36-46; Whitney Mus Am Art Ann, New York, 36-46.
Teaching: Head sculpture, Warneke Sch Art, 40-42; head sculpture, Corcoran Sch Art, 43-68; prof sculpture, George Washington Univ, 43-68.
Positions: Mem, Ger Monuments Comn, World War I, Bucharest, Romania, 14-18.
Awards: Logan prize for best in show, 30; Widener Gold Medal, Pa Acad Fine Arts, 35; first prize, Washington D C Artists Ann, Corcoran Gallery Art, 43-44; plus others.
Bibliography: Olin Dows (auth), Art for housing tenants, Mag Art, 11/38; Walter Nathan (auth), Living forms: the sculptor Heinz Warneke, Parnassus Mag, 2/41; New Last Supper, Life Mag, 9/19/55.
Memberships: Nat Acad Design; fel Nat Sculpture Soc; assoc Salon des Tuileries; New England Sculptors Soc; life fel Int Inst Arts & Lett.
Publications: Auth, First & last & sculptor, Mag Art, 2/39.
Mailing Address: The Mowings, East Haddam, CT 06423.

WARNER, BOYD, JR
Painter
Preferred Media: Sand, Watercolors, Oils, Acrylics.
b Kaibeto, Ariz, May 26, 37.
Work in Public Collections: Buck Saunders, Scottsdale, Ariz; James T Bialec, Phoenix, Ariz; Dick Van Dyke, Cave Creek, Ariz & Gen Motors Corp, Detroit, Mich.
Exhibitions: Scottsdale Nat Indian Art & Crafts Show, 68-71; Inter Tribal Ceremonial, Gallup, N Mex, 68-72; Heard Mus Indian Art Show, Phoenix, 69-71; Ariz State Fair, Phoenix, 69-71; 27th Indian Art Show, Philbrook Art Ctr, Tulsa, Okla, 72.
Awards: Elkus Mem Award, 71 & first & second award in mixed media, 72, Inter Tribal Ceremonial; hon mention, Heard Mus Indian Arts & Crafts, 71.
Mailing Address: 606 N Fourth St, Apt 1, Phoenix, AZ 85004.

WARNER, HARRY BACKER, JR
Writer
b Chambersburg, Pa, Dec 19, 22.
Positions: Art critic & writer on art, Hagerstown Herald-Mail, Md, 43-
Mailing Address: 423 Summit Ave, Hagerstown, MD 21740.

WARNER, JO
Painter
Preferred Media: Oils.
b Clayton, N Mex, Apr 30, 31.
Study & Training: Univ Colo, Boulder, BFA; Skowhegan Sch Painting & Sculpture, Maine, with Jack Levine & Henry V Poor; Art Stud League New York, with Morris Kantor & Byron Brown.
Exhibitions: Tenth Street, Mus Contemp Art, Houston, Tex, 59; Recent American Painting & Sculpture, Mus Mod Art Circulating Exhib, 61-63; West Side Artists-New York City, Riverside Mus, 64.
Dealer: Phoenix Gallery, 939 Madison Ave at 74th St, New York, NY 10021.
Mailing Address: 142 West End Ave, New York, NY 10023.

WARREN, BETTY
Painter
Preferred Media: Oils, Pastels.
b New York, N Y.
Study & Training: Nat Acad Design; Cape Sch Art, with Henry Hensche.
Work in Public Collections: Albany Inst Hist & Art, N Y; State Univ N Y, Albany; Hartwick Col, Oneonta, N Y; N Y State Supreme Court, Albany; Grand Lodge Masons N Y State, New York.
Exhibitions: Artists of the Mohawk, Hudson Region, Schenectady, N Y, 60-71; Allied Artists Am, New York, 65 & 67; Am Watercolor Soc, New York, 66; Nat Arts Club Nat, New York, 69-71; Knickerbocker Artists, New York; over 25 one-man shows in mus & galleries.
Teaching: Instr painting & drawing, Albany Inst Hist & Art, 59-; co-owner & dir, Malden Bridge Sch Art, N Y, 65-
Awards: Purchase prize, Albany Inst Hist & Art, 64; gold medal, Catharine Lorillard Wolfe; grand prize, Cooperstown 29th Ann Exhib.
Bibliography: Cover article, In: Prize Winning Paintings, 64 & 65; Norman Kent (auth), The paintings of Betty Warren, Am Artist, 67; rev, In: Grand Cent Galleries Yearbook, 67, 69 & 70.
Memberships: Grand Cent Art Club; Nat Arts Club; Am Artists Prof League; Nat League Am Pen Women; Pen & Brush.
Dealer: Grand Central Art Galleries, Hotel Biltmore, New York, NY 10017.
Mailing Address: 76 Western Ave, Albany, NY 12203.

WARREN, FERDINAND EARL
Painter, Art Administrator
Preferred Media: Oils.
b Independence, Mo, Aug 1, 99.
Study & Training: Kansas City Art Inst.
Work in Public Collections: Metrop Mus Art, New York, N Y; Brooklyn Mus Art, N Y; Rochester Mem Gallery, Youngstown, Ohio; Currier Gallery Art, Springfield, N H; NASA Permanent Collection, Nat Gallery Art, Washington, D C.
Commissions: Two war bond posters, U S Treas Dept, 43; History of the Printed Word (mural), Foote & Davies, Atlanta, Ga, 57; Robert Frost (portrait from life), Agnes Scott Col, Decatur, Ga, 58; copper enamel cross, Saint Agnes Episcopal Church, Atlanta, 63; Apollo 14 (painting), NASA, Washington, D C, 71.
Exhibitions: Richmond Va Ann, 48-49; Corcoran Gallery Art, Washington, D C, 49; Art in the Embassies, U S Dept State, 66-70; Nat Acad Design Ann, New York; Carnegie Inst Int, Pittsburgh, Pa.
Positions: Artist-in-residence, Univ Ga, 50-51; chmn dept art, Agnes Scott Col, 52-69.
Awards: Silver medal, Am Watercolor Soc, 50; purchase prize, Butler Inst Am Art, 54; Edwin Palmer prize, Nat Acad Design, 61.
Bibliography: Forbes Watson (auth), Painting today; Ernest Watson (auth), Composition in landscape.
Mailing Address: 227 E Hancock St, Decatur, GA 30030.

WARREN, MRS GEORGE HENRY
Collector
b Oakland, Calif, Jan 29, 97.
Awards: Legion of Hon, France.
Collection: Cubist and abstract art.
Mailing Address: 118 Mill St, Newport, RI 02840.

WARREN, JEFFERSON TROWBRIDGE
Museum Director
b Louisville, Ky, Oct 4, 12.
Study & Training: Univ Minn, George T Slade scholar, 47, BA(magna cum laude) & MA; in Europe; Minneapolis Sch Art.
Positions: Cur, Minneapolis Pub Mus, 46-57; del, UNESCO, 50; dir, John Woodman Higgins Armory, Worcester, Mass, 57-62; dir, Vizcaya-Dade Co Art Mus, Miami, Fla, 62-; supt, mus div, Dade Co Park & Recreation Dept, Miami, 62-
Memberships: Am Assn Mus; Southeastern Mus Conf; Mus Dirs Coun Greater Miami (treas); Dade Co Cult Facilities Study Comt.
Publications: Auth, Exhibit methods, 9/72; contribr, var encycl, prof jour & popular mag.
Mailing Address: Vizcaya, 3251 S Miami Ave, Miami, FL 33129.

WARREN, L D
Editorial Cartoonist
b Wilmington, Del, Dec 27, 06.
Positions: Ed cartoonist, Cincinnati Enquirer, 47-
Mailing Address: 1815 William H Taft Rd, Cincinnati, OH 45206.

WARREN, PETER WHITSON, see WHITSON

WARSHAW, HOWARD
Painter
Preferred Media: Acrylics, Offset Lithography.
b New York, N Y, Aug 14, 20.
Study & Training: Pratt Inst; Nat Acad Design Sch; Art Stud League New York.
Work in Public Collections: Carnegie Inst, Pittsburgh; Pa Acad Fine Arts; Philadelphia; Santa Barbara Mus Art, Calif; Los Angeles Co Mus Art, Calif; Univ Southern Calif Collection.
Commissions: Murals, Wyle Res, El Segundo, Calif, 53, Ortega Commons, Univ Calif, Santa Barbara, 60, Revelle Commons, Univ Calif, San Diego, 67, Bowdoin Col Libr, Brunswick, Maine, 69 & Univ Calif, Los Angeles, Reed Neurol Res Ctr, 71.
Exhibitions: Corcoran Gallery Art, Washington, D C; Guggenheim Mus, New York; Whitney Mus Am Art, New York; Carnegie Int; Mus Art Mod, Paris.
Teaching: Prof art, Univ Calif, Santa Barbara, 55-
Awards: First prize for oil painting & first prize for watercolor, Los Angeles Co Mus Art Centennial, 50.
Bibliography: Russel Lynes (auth), foreward to catalogue, Bowdoin Col Mus Art, 11/72.
Art Interests: Originated a graduate program in which offset lithography and video tape are used as media for drawing.
Publications: Auth, The return of naturalism as the avant-garde, Nation, 60; auth, The wild goose chase for reality, Ctr Mag, 69.
Dealers: Silvan Simone Gallery, 11579 Olympic, West Los Angeles, CA 90064; Jacques Seligman Gallery, 5 E 57th St, New York, NY 10022.
Mailing Address: 250 Toro Canyon Rd, Carpinteria, CA 93013.

WARSINSKE, NORMAN GEORGE, JR
Sculptor, Painter
Preferred Media: Metal, Bronze, Steel.
b Wichita, Kans, Mar 4, 29.
Study & Training: Univ Mont, BA; Kunstwerkschule, Darmstadt, Ger; Univ Wash, BA.
Commissions: Steel screen, Univ Unitarian Church, Seattle, Wash, 59; bronze fountains, King Co Med Bldg, Seattle, 65 & Theodora Retirement Home, Seattle, 66; brass & steel screen, Yellowstone Boy's Ranch, Billings, Mont, 69; gold leaf steel stabile, IBM bldg lobby, Seattle, 71.
Exhibitions: Northwest Ann, Seattle Art Mus, 59-65; Northwest Sculpture Inst Show, Portland Art Mus, 61; Santa Barbara Invitational, Calif, 63; Sculpture Invitational, Los Angeles Co Mus Art, 64; one-man show, Northwest Craft Ctr, Seattle, 69-70.
Teaching: Asst instr drawing, Univ Wash, 58-59.
Awards: First prize for sculpture, Bellevue Art Festival, 60; best of all categories, Henry Art Gallery, 66.
Bibliography: Louis Redstone (auth), Art in architecture, McGraw, 68; M R Heinley (auth), Norman Warsinske—metal artistry, Designers W, 6/70.
Memberships: Seattle Munic Art Comn (v pres, 65-69); Northwest Craft Ctr (pres, 65-).
Publications: Illusr, cover, Am Inst Architects J, 8/71.
Dealer: Miller-Pollard, Inc, 4538 University Way N E, Seattle, WA 98105.
Mailing Address: 3823 94th N E, Bellevue, WA 98004.

WASEY, JANE
Sculptor
Preferred Media: Stone, Wood.
b Chicago, Ill, June 28, 12.
Study & Training: With Paul Landowski, Paris; Simon Moselsio, New York; also with John Flanagan & Heinz Warneke.
Work in Public Collections: Ariz State Univ, Tempe; Univ Colo; Dartmouth Col; Univ Nebr; Pa Acad Fine Arts; plus others.
Exhibitions: Art Inst Chicago; Brooklyn Mus; Univ Chicago; Detroit Inst Arts; one-man shows, Montross Gallery, 34, Delphic Studio, 35, Philbrook Art Ctr, 49, Weathervanes Contemp, New York, 54 & Kraushaar Galleries, 56 & 71; plus others.
Teaching: Instr sculpture, Bennington Col, 48-49, pvt instr, 50-60.
Awards: First prizes for sculpture, Parrish Art Mus & Guild Hall, N Y; Mrs John Henry Hammond Award, Nat Asn Women Artists, 51; Phillips Mem Prize, Archit League, 55; plus others.
Bibliography: Brumme (auth), Contemporary American sculpture; Anton Henze (auth), Contemporary church art; Design for learning, Town & Country, 10/49; plus others.
Memberships: Sculptor's Guild; Nat Asn Women Artists; Nat Sculpture Soc; Audubon Artists.
Dealer: Kraushaar Galleries, 1055 Madison Ave, New York, NY 10028.
Mailing Address: Sneden's Landing, Palisades, NY 10964.

WASHBURN, GORDON BAILEY
Gallery Director
b Wellesley Hills, Mass, Nov 7, 04.
Study & Training: Deerfield Acad; Williams Col, AB, 28; Fogg Mus Art, Harvard Univ; Williams Col, hon MFA, 38; Allegheny Col, hon DFA, 59; Univ Buffalo, hon DFA, 62; Washington & Jefferson Col, hon DFA, 68.
Collections Arranged: Pittsburgh International (triennially); French Painting 1100-1900 & Pictures of Everyday Life-Genre Painting in Europe, 1500-1900, Carnegie Inst; American Painting in the 1950's, Am Fedn Arts, 68; three exhibitions per yr, Asia House Gallery, 62-69.
Teaching: Lect art hist.
Positions: Dir, Albright Art Gallery, Buffalo, N Y, 31-42; dir, Mus Art, R I Sch Design, 42-49; dir dept fine arts, Carnegie Inst, Pittsburgh, Pa, 50-62; dir, Asia House Gallery, New York, N Y, 62-
Awards: Guggenheim fel, 49-50; Chevalier, Legion of Hon, 52.
Memberships: Col Art Asn Am; Asn Art Mus Dirs; Am Assn Mus.
Publications: Auth, Pictures of everyday life-Genre painting in Europe, 1500-1900, 54, American classics of the nineteenth century, 57, The 1958 Pittsburgh international exhibition of contemporary painting & sculpture, 58 & Retrospective exhibition of paintings from previous internationals, 58, Carnegie Inst; auth, Structure and continuity in exhibition design, Nature & Art of Motion, 65; plus many others.
Mailing Address: Asia House Gallery 112 E 64th St, New York, NY 10021.

WASHBURN, JOAN T
Art Dealer
b New York, N Y, Dec 26, 29.
Study & Training: Middlebury Col, BA.
Collections Arranged: Jean Xceron (1890-1967)—Paintings from

1930-1940, 71; Joshua Johnston (1796-1824), 71; Tinsel Paintings (folk art) from the E Leight Collection, 71; Martin Johnson Heade (1819-1904)—Paintings after 1880, 72; William Trost Richards (1833-1905).
Positions: Dir, Washburn Gallery, New York.
Specialty of Gallery: Nineteenth and twentieth century American and European painting and sculpture.
Mailing Address: Washburn Gallery, 820 Madison Ave, New York, NY 10021.

WASHINGTON, JAMES, JR
Painter, Sculptor
Preferred Media: Oils, Tempera, Pastels, Granite, Marble.
b Gloster, Miss.
Study & Training: Nat Landscape Inst; also with Mark Tobey.
Work in Public Collections: Seattle Art Mus, Wash; San Francisco Art Mus, Calif.
Commissions: The Creation (series 4), YWCA, Seattle, 66; The Creation (series 6), Seattle Pub Libr, 67; The Creation (series 7-10), Seattle First Nat Bank Main Br, 68; busts of hist men, Progress Plaza, Philadelphia, Pa, 69; The Creation (series 5), Meany Jr H S, Seattle, 70.
Exhibitions: Third Pacific Coast Biennial, Santa Barbara Mus Art, Calif, 59; Willard Gallery, New York, N Y, 60-64; Northwest Today, Seattle World's Fair, 62; Grosvenor Gallery Int Exhib, London, Eng, 64; Expo '70, Osaka, Japan, 70.
Positions: Secy, Seattle Chap, Artists Equity Asn, 49-53, pres, 60-62; mem gov coun art, State of Wash, 59-60, state art comnr, 61-66.
Awards: Award for Bird Hatching, Oakland Munic Art Mus, 57; award for Wounded Bird, Seattle World's Fair, 62; gov sculpture award, 70.
Bibliography: Ann Faber (auth), James Washington's stone sculpture excellence, Seattle Post Intelligence, 56; Pauline Johnson (auth), James Washington speaks, Art Educ J, 68.
Memberships: Int Platform Asn.
Mailing Address: 1816 26th Ave, Seattle, WA 98122.

WASILE, ELYSE
Painter, Designer
Preferred Media: Acrylics, Gouache, Oils.
b New York, N Y, May 27, 20.
Study & Training: Univ Calif, Los Angeles.
Work in Public Collections: Nassau Art Gallery, Bahamas; Commonwealth of Bahamas Post Off, Nassau.
Commissions: Murals, Widner Estate, Palm Beach, Fla, 51, Palm Beach Int Airport, 60 & Nassau Beach Hotel, 61; definitive stamp issue (15), Post Off Dept, Bahamas, 71.
Exhibitions: S Fla Fair & Expos, 60; Bahamas Art Soc, Nassau, 67; Nassau Art Gallery Ann.
Awards: Blue ribbon, S Fla Fair & Expos, 60.
Bibliography: Jody Allan (auth), Women in unusual jobs, 67, Nancy Savage (auth), Paintings & restoration, 69 & Stamp designing, 71, Nassau Tribune.
Memberships: IIC Nat Gallery, London; Bahamas Hist Soc.
Dealer: Nassau Art Gallery, Bay St, Nassau, Bahamas.
Mailing Address: P O Box N 1334, Nassau, Bahamas.

WASSER, PAULA KLOSTER
Painter, Educator
b Hatton, N Dak.
Study & Training: Univ Minn; Minneapolis Sch Art; Univ N Dak, BS; Stanford Univ, MA; Chouinard Art Inst; Art Stud League New York; Univ Southern Calif; also with Dan Lutz, Carlos Merida, Jean Charlot & Frank McIntosh.
Exhibitions: Phoenix Fine Arts Asn; Tucson Fine Arts Festival; Ariz Art Guild; Ariz State Fair; Univ Nev, Reno; one-man shows, Phoenix, Ariz; plus others.
Teaching: Instr art, jr high sch, Grand Forks, N Dak, 23-25; supvr stud art, State Teachers Col, Valley City, N Dak, 26-27; actg head dept art, Ariz State Univ, head dept 33-54, prof art, 49-64, cur Am collection, 50-64, emer prof art, 65-
Awards: Prizes, Ariz State Fair, 30 & 31.
Memberships: Fel Int Inst Arts & Lett; Sierra Club; Calif Roadside Coun; plus other conserv groups & civic clubs.
Publications: Compiled brochures of College Collection, 50-52, 55-56, 59-63; auth, The Arizona State College collection of American art, 54; co-auth, A guide for the improvement of the teaching of art in the schools of Arizona; contribr, Am Homes Mag & Design; plus others.
Mailing Address: 181 Lassen Circle, Vacaville, CA 95688.

WASSERMAN, ALBERT
Painter, Designer
Preferred Media: Oils.
b New York, N Y, Aug 22, 20.
Study & Training: Art Stud League New York, 37-39, with Charles

Chapman; Nat Acad Design, 38-40; with Sidney Dickinson; U S Army Univ, France.
Work in Public Collections: Traphagen Collection, Ariz.
Commissions: Portraits, pvt comns.
Exhibitions: Nat Acad Design, New York, 41; Allied Artists Am, New York, 41-72; N J Painters & Sculptors Soc, 41-72; Am Watercolor Soc, New York, 53-69; Audubon Artists, New York, 60.
Teaching: Instr & lectr, Jackson Heights Art Asn, 55-; instr & lectr, Nat Art League, 67-69.
Positions: Graphic design consult, var agencies, 48-
Awards: Pulitzer Prize scholar, 40 & Nat Acad Design, 41, E H & E C Friedrichs Prize, Allied Artists Am, 41.
Bibliography: Ethel Traphagen (auth), article, In: Fashion Digest, 54.
Memberships: Allied Artists Am; N J Painters & Sculptors Soc; Assoc Am Watercolor Soc; Nat Art League; Artists Equity Asn.
Mailing Address: 34-24 82nd St, New York, NY 11372.

WASSERMAN, BURTON
Painter, Printmaker
Preferred Media: Oils, Silkscreen, Spray Enamels.
b Brooklyn, N Y, Mar 10, 29.
Study & Training: Brooklyn Col, BA, with Burgoyne Diller & Ad Reinhardt; Columbia Univ, MA & EdD.
Work in Public Collections: Philadelphia Mus Art, Pa; Montreal Mus Fine Arts; Norfolk Mus Arts & Sci, Va; Philadelphia Civic Ctr Mus; N J State Mus, Trenton; plus others.
Commissions: Relief triptych, Mr & Mrs Herbert Kurtz, Melrose Park, Pa, 71.
Exhibitions: 21st Am Drawing Biennial, Norfolk Mus Arts & Sci, 65; U S A Pavilion, Int Expos, Osaka, Japan, 70; Color Prints of the Americas, N J State Mus, 70; Int Graphics Exhib, Montreal Mus Art, 71; Silkscreen: History of a Medium, Philadelphia Mus Art, 71-72; plus others.
Teaching: Prof art, Glassboro State Col, 60-
Awards: Brickhouse Drawing Prize, 21st Am Drawing Biennial, Norfolk Mus Arts & Sci, 65; Ryan Purchase Prize, Art from N J Ann Exhib, N J State Mus, 67; Esther-Philip Klein Award, Am Color Print Soc Ann, 70; plus others.
Memberships: Artists Equity Asn (nat pres, 71-73); Am Color Print Soc (mem exec coun, 65-73); Philadelphia Watercolor Club (v pres, 70-73).
Publications: Auth, articles, In: Am Artist, Art Int, Art Educ, Sch Arts, Arts & Activities & many more, 59-72; auth, Modern painting: the movements, the artists, their work, 70 & co-auth, Basic silkscreen printmaking, 71, Davis, Mass; auth, Bridges of vision: the art of prints and the craft of printmaking, N J State Mus, 70.
Dealer: McCleaf Gallery, 1713 Walnut St, Philadelphia, PA 19103.
Mailing Address: 204 Dubois Rd, Glassboro, NJ 08028.

WASSERMAN, JACK
Art Historian, Art Administrator
b New York, N Y, Apr 27, 21.
Study & Training: Washington Square Col, New York Univ, BA; New York Univ Inst Fine Arts, with Karl Lehmann & Richard Krautheimer, MA, PhD.
Teaching: Instr art, Univ Conn, 53-60; asst prof art, Ind Univ, Bloomington, 60-62; prof Renaissance art, Univ Wis-Milwaukee, 62-
Awards: Fulbright grant, 52; Am Coun Learned Soc grant, 70; Am Philos Soc grant, 71.
Memberships: Col Art Asn Am; Soc Archit Historians (bd dirs, 70-); Royal Soc Arts; Amici di Brera.
Publications: Auth, Quirinal Palace in Rome, 63 & The dating & patronage of Leonardo's Burlington House cartoon, 71, Art Bull; auth, Ottaviano Mascarino, Accad di San Luca, Rome, 66; auth, Michelangelo's Virgin & Child with St Anne at Oxford, Burlington Mag, 69.
Mailing Address: 2715 N Lake Dr, Milwaukee, WI 53211.

WATERHOUSE, RUSSELL RUTLEDGE
Painter
Preferred Media: Watercolors.
b El Paso, Tex, Aug 11, 28.
Study & Training: Tex A&M Univ, BS, 50; Art Ctr Col Design, Los Angeles, 54-56.
Work in Public Collections: Tex Tech Univ Mus Art, Lubbock; El Paso Mus Art; Univ Tex, El Paso.
Exhibitions: Baker Collectors Gallery, Lubbock, 65; one-man show, El Paso Mus Art, 72; one-man show, Wichita Falls Tex Cult Ctr & Mus Art, 72.
Positions: Mem, Tex Comn Arts & Humanities, 70-75.
Publications: Illusr, Goodbye to a river, Knopf, 60; illusr, The legal heritage of El Paso, 63 & Pass of the North, 68, Tex Western Press.
Mailing Address: 5500 Westside Dr, El Paso, TX 79932.

WATFORD, FRANCES MIZELLE
Painter, Instructor
Preferred Media: Watercolors, Acrylics, Oils.
b Thomasville, Ga, Sept 6, 15.
Study & Training: Hilton Leech Art Sch, summers 52-59; Sarasota Sch Art, Portas Studio & Ringling Sch Art, Fla, summers 59-64; spec workshop with Dong Kingman, Columbus, Ga, 66; Famous Artists Sch, grad, 69.
Work in Public Collections: Montgomery Mus Fine Arts, Ala; Birmingham Mus Art, Ala; Houston Mem Libr, Dothan, Ala; Dothan High Sch Gallery, Ala.
Commissions: Portraits, pvt collections, Dothan, 58 & 62, Elba, Ala, 60 & 64 & Graceville, Fla, 60; murals, pvt collections, Dothan, 64-66.
Exhibitions: Dothan-Wiregrass Art League, 61-68; Bienniale Int Vichy, France, 64; Honored Exhibitor, Birmingham, Ala, 66; Arts & Crafts Festival Dothan, 71-72; one-man shows, Montgomery Mus Fine Arts, 61, Dothan, 61, 64 & 70 & Columbus Mus Arts & Crafts, Ga, 66; plus others.
Teaching: Instr art fundamentals & creative art, Frances Watford Studio, Dothan, 49-
Positions: Dir, Attic Gallery, Dothan, 58-
Awards: Purchase awards, 58-61 & 59 & Cline Award, 66, Ala Art League; dipl d'honneur, Bienniale Vichy, 64; plus others.
Bibliography: L'art a l'etranger, 10/63 & En province, 1/65, La Rev Mod; Grace Burgess (auth), Student showcase, Famous Artists Mag, 11/71.
Memberships: Ala Art League (regional v pres, 63-67); Watercolor Soc Ala (regional v pres, 56); Arts & Crafts Festival Dothan (receiving comt, 71-72).
Specialty of Gallery: Paintings in all media.
Mailing Address: 106 Montezuma Ave, Dothan, AL 36301.

WATKINS, FRANKLIN CHENAULT
Painter
Preferred Media: Oils.
b New York, N Y, Dec 30, 94.
Study & Training: Univ Va; Univ Pa; Pa Acad Fine Arts, Philadelphia.
Work in Public Collections: Metrop Mus Art, New York; Mus Mod Art, New York; Whitney Mus Am Art, New York; Philadelphia Mus Art; Corcoran Gallery Art, Washington, D C.
Exhibitions: Retrospectives, Mus Mod Art, 50 & Philadelphia Mus Art, 64; one-man exhib, Second Inter-Am Biennial Mex, Salon Honor, Palacio Bellas Artes, 60.
Teaching: Mem fac, Pa Acad Fine Arts, 25 yrs, retired, mem bd dirs, 70-
Awards: First prize & Lehman Prize, Carnegie Int, 31; gold medal, Corcoran Gallery Bi-Ann, 39; gold medal of honor, Pa Acad Fine Arts, 49.
Bibliography: Ben Wolf (auth), Watkins, portrait of a painter, Univ Pa Press; Watkins (film), Philadelphia Mus Art; catalogue of retrospective exhib, Mus Mod Art; plus others.
Memberships: Assoc Am Acad Design; Nat Inst Arts & Lett; Am Philos Soc.
Dealer: Kennedy Galleries, 20 E 56th St, New York, NY 10022.
Mailing Address: 682 17th Ave S, Naples, FL 33940.

WATKINS, LOUISE LOCHRIDGE
Museum Director, Lecturer
b Springfield, Mass, July 6, 05.
Study & Training: Skidmore Col, BS.
Collections Arranged: Springfield Color Slide International Exhibition.
Teaching: Lectr decorative arts, hist of Cloisonne, hist of enameling & Chinese jades; instr, George Walter Vincent Smith Art Mus, Springfield, Mass, 36-38.
Positions: Asst, George Walter Vincent Smith Art Mus, 36-38, asst to dir, 38-50, dir, 51-71; secy-treas, New Eng Mus Asn, 50-60; mem, State Comn Art Curric for Mass Schs, 68-70.
Memberships: Am Asn Mus; Springfield Art League; hon mem Springfield Photog Soc.
Publications: Contribr, George Walter Vincent Smith Art Mus Bull.
Mailing Address: 56 Wenonah Rd, Longmeadow, MA 01106.

WATROUS, JAMES SCALES
Painter, Art Historian
Preferred Media: Mosaics.
b Winfield, Kans, Aug 3, 08.
Study & Training: Univ Wis, BS, MA & PhD.
Work in Public Collections: Lawrence Univ; Kans State Univ; Milwaukee Art Ctr.
Commissions: Symbols of Printing (mural), Webcrafters Press, Madison, Wis, 52; Justice (aluminum), Wis Bar Ctr, Madison, 58; The Conjurer (mosaic mural), Wash Univ, St Louis, Mo, 59; mosaics, Man: Creator of Order & Disorder, 64 & Symbols of Communication, 72, Univ Wis.
Teaching: Prof art hist & art, Univ Wis-Madison, 36-, Hagen Prof art hist, 64-, chmn dept art hist, 52-61.
Awards: Inst Advan Educ faculty fel, Italy, 54; award of merit, Wis Chap Am Inst Architects, 62; Wis Gov Award in Arts, 69.
Memberships: Mid-Am Col Art Asn (pres, 59); Col Art Asn Am (pres, 62-64); Nat Soc Mural Painters.
Research: Technical studies in the fine arts.
Publications: Auth, The craft of old-master drawings, Univ Wis Press, 57.
Mailing Address: 2809 Sylvan Ave, Madison, WI 53705.

WATSON, ALDREN AULD
Illustrator, Designer
b Brooklyn, N Y, May 10, 17.
Study & Training: Yale Univ, 35; Art Stud League New York, with George Bridgman, Charles Chapman, Robert Brackman, William Auerbach-Levy & others.
Work in Public Collections: Illus bks in libr, U S, Can & Europe & in pvt collections.
Commissions: Mural, S S Pres Hayes, Thomas Crowell Co Off, 64.
Exhibitions: Fifty Bks Shows, Soc Illusr Ann.
Positions: Textbk designer, D C Health & Co, Boston, 65-66; chief ed curric oriented mat, Silver Burdett Co, Morristown, N J, 66-; off NASA artist, Apollo 8, 68.
Awards: Prize, Domesday Bk Illus Competition, 45.
Bibliography: Chap, In: Forty illustrators and how they work.
Memberships: Auth Guild.
Publications: Auth & illusr, My garden grows, 62 & Maple tree begins, 70, Viking Pres; auth & illusr, Hand bookbinding, 63 & 68; auth & illusr, Very first words for writing and spelling, Holt, Rinehart & Winston, 66; auth & illusr, Village blacksmith, Crowell, 68; plus many others.
Mailing Address: River Rd, Putney, VT 05346.

WATSON, CLARISSA H
Art Dealer
b Ashland, Wis.
Study & Training: Layton Art Sch, Milwaukee, Wis; Univ Wis-Milwaukee; Milwaukee-Downer Col, BA; Country Art Sch, with Harry Sternberg.
Collections Arranged: Long Island Artists, Washington, D C, 67; The Collectors' Collections, Adelphi Univ, Garden City, Long Island, 68; Gabriel Spat (1890-1967) Retrospective, Fine Arts Asn Willoughby, Cleveland, Ohio, 70; Nobility of the Horse in Art—to save America's Wild Horses, Washington, D C, 71.
Positions: Dir-founder, Country Art Sch, Westbury, Long Island, 53-68; dir & co-founder, Country Art Galleries, Locust Valley & Southampton, Long Island, 53-; art consult, Adelphi Univ, 67-69; dir film festivals, 7 Village Arts Coun, Locust Valley, 69-71; dir-producer, Mediaeval Christmas Festival, Locust Valley, 70 & 71-
Specialty of Gallery: Nineteenth and twentieth century American realism and American and European naifs.
Publications: Auth, The art virus, This Wk Mag, 64; auth, Ateliers of Paris, 65 & The art balloon, 67, Locust Valley Leader; auth, Art as an investment, Oyster Bay Guardian, Long Island, L I, 66; ed, The artists' cookbook, Stevenson, 71.
Mailing Address: The Country Art Gallery, The Plaza, Locust Valley, Long Island, NY 11560.

WATSON, ROBERT
Painter
Preferred Media: Oils on Canvas.
b Martinez, Calif, Feb 28, 23.
Study & Training: Univ Calif; Univ Ill; Univ Wis.
Work in Public Collections: Toledo Mus, Ohio; Calif Palace of Legion of Honor, San Francisco; Rochester Univ, N Y; St Mary's Col, Moraga, Calif.
Exhibitions: Fifth Ann Exhib Contemp Am Art, Calif Palace of Legion of Honor, 52; Calif State Fair, Sacramento, 53; Exhib Contemp Am Art, Univ Ill, 54; Nat Acad Design, New York, N Y, 54.
Awards: First prize, Calif State Fair, 54.
Bibliography: Arthur Watson (quth), article, In: Am Artist, 9/53.
Memberships: Soc Western Artists.
Mailing Address: c/o Martin Gallery, Pima Plaza E, Scottsdale, AZ 85251.

WATSON, SYDNEY HOLLINGER
Art Administrator, Designer
b Toronto, Ont, Apr 6, 11.
Work in Public Collections: Nat Gallery Can, Ottawa; Queen's Univ, Kingston, Ont; McLaughlin Gallery, Oshawa, Ont; Hart House, Univ Toronto; McMichael Conserv Collection Art, Toronto.
Commissions: Mural (oil on canvas), Bd Rm, Imp Oil Head Off, Toronto, 55; acrylic wall paintings, Chapel, Trinity Col Sch, Port Hope, Ont, 65; mosaic mural, Head Off, Can Imperial Bank Commerce, Montreal, P Q, 66; sand blasted slate mural, Excelsior

Life Ins Head Off, Toronto, 67; exterior wall panels (porcelain on steel), Chem Bldg, Univ Toronto, 68.
Exhibitions: Many ann, Ont Soc Artists, Royal Can Acad Arts, Can Soc Painters Watercolor & Can Group Painters.
Teaching: Instr design, Ont Col Art, 46-49, v prin, 49-54, prin, 54-70.
Awards: Art Dirs Club Medal, Toronto, 64; Can Centennial Medal, Govt Can, 67; Royal Can Acad Arts Medal, 68.
Memberships: Royal Can Acad Arts (mem coun); Ont Soc Artists (pres, 54-57); Can Group Painters (dir, 68-).
Publications: Auth & illusr, lettering text, W W Gage, Toronto, 55; auth & illusr, A history of printing, Gaylord Printing Co, Toronto, 58.
Dealer: Roberts Gallery, 641 Yonge St, Toronto 5, Ont, Can.
Mailing Address: 2 Nesbitt Dr, Toronto 5, Ont, Can.

WATTS, ROBERT M
Designer
Preferred Media: Mixed Media.
b U S, June 14, 23.
Study & Training: Univ Louisville, BME, 44; Art Stud League New York, N Y, 46-48; Columbia Univ, AM, 51.
Work in Public Collections: Mod Museet, Stockholm; Houston Art Mus; Albright-Knox Art Mus, Buffalo; Art Inst Chicago.
Exhibitions: New Media, New Forms II, Martha Jackson Gallery, New York, 60; Assemblage, 61 & The Machine, 68, Mus Mod Art; Whitney Mus Am Art Ann Contemp Am Sculpture, 65; Happening & Flexus, Koelnischer Kunstverein, Koln, Ger, 71.
Teaching: Prof film & mixed media, Rutgers Univ, New Brunswick, 52-, univ res coun grant for film & mixed media, 64-71; Carnegie Corp vis artist & consult, Univ Calif Santa Cruz, 68.
Awards: Exp Workshop Award, Carnegie Corp, 64.
Bibliography: Max Kosloff (auth), Pop culture and the new vulgarians, Art Int, 62; Brian O'Dougherty (auth), Art: machines in revolt, 62 & Grace Glueck (auth), If its art you want...67, New York Times.
Memberships: Life mem Art Stud League New York.
Publications: Co-auth, Newspaper, 63; auth, Flexus, assorted events and objects, 64-72; auth, Postage stamps, fluxpost, 65; contribr, The arts on campus: the necessity for change, 70; co-auth, Proposals for art education, 70.
Mailing Address: R D 3, Bangor, PA 18013.

WAUGH, COULTON
Painter, Writer
Preferred Media: Oils.
b St Ives, Eng, Mar 10, 96; U S citizen.
Study & Training: With Frederick J Waugh; Art Stud League New York, with George Bridgeman & Frank Vincent Dumond.
Work in Public Collections: Paintings, Syracuse Univ, N Y; paintings, Univ Wichita, Kans; Cooperstown Art Asn Permanent Collection, N Y; Toledo Mus Art, Ohio; Mus Art, Davenport, Iowa.
Commissions: Set of eight murals (with Frederick J Waugh) in lobby, First Nat Bank, Provincetown, Mass, 31.
Exhibitions: One-man shows, Lotte Jacobi Gallery, New York, N Y, 55, Grand Cent Art Galleries, New York, 62, 68 & 71 & Cooperstown Art Asn, N Y, 64.
Teaching: Instr art, eve div, Orange Co Community Col, 58-63.
Positions: Cur, Storm King Art Ctr, Mountainville, N Y, 59.
Awards: Purchase prize, 64 & hon mention, 66, Cooperstown Art Asn.
Memberships: Grand Cent Art Galleries; Pioneer Gallery.
Publications: Auth, The comics, Macmillan, 47; auth, Painting with fire, 11/62, auth Technique of old masters, 4/64 & auth, Keep out of the mud, summer 69, Am Artist Mag; auth, How to paint with a knife, Watson-Guptill, 71.
Dealer: Grand Central Art Galleries, 40 Vanderbilt Ave, New York, NY 10017.
Mailing Address: R R 2, Box 133, Newburgh, NY 12550.

WAYNE, JUNE
Painter
b Chicago, Ill.
Work in Public Collections: Bibliot Nat France; Bibliot Royale Beuxelles; Mus Mod Art, New York, N Y; Nat Collection Fine Art, Smithsonian Inst, Washington, D C; Rosenwald Collection, Alverthorpe Gallery, Jenkintown, Pa.
Exhibitions: Oversize Prints, Whitney Mus Am Art, New York, 71; Bienal Am Artes Graficas, Colombia, 71; Biennale Epinal Int Estampes, France, 71; Concert of Tapestry, Gallery Demeure, Paris, 72.
Positions: Dir, Tamarind Lithography Workshop & adv, Tamarind Inst, Univ N Mex, 60-; mem bd dirs, Grunwald Graphic Arts Found, Univ Calif, Los Angeles, 65-, mem exec comt & adv to Chancellor, Arts Mgt Prog, Grad Sch Admin, 69-; mem overseers comt, Sch Visual & Environ Arts, Harvard Univ, 71-
Awards: Prix du Biennale, Int Estampes Epinal, 71; plus many others.

Bibliography: Baskett (auth), The art of June Wayne, Abrams, 68.
Dealers: Gallery La Demeure, Pl St Sulpice, Paris 6, France; Peter Plone Associates, 1108 N Tamarind Ave, Los Angeles, CA 90038.
Mailing Address: 1108 N Tamarind Ave, Los Angeles, CA 90038.

WEAVER, HOWARD SAYRE
Educator
U S citizen.
Teaching: Dean, Yale Univ Sch Art, 68-
Mailing Address: 1605 Yale Station, New Haven, CT 06520.

WEAVER, JOHN BARNEY
Sculptor
Preferred Media: Bronze.
b Anaconda, Mont, Mar 28, 20.
Study & Training: Art Inst Chicago, Albert Kuppenhiemer scholar, 41; dipl; also monumental sculpture with Albin Polasek.
Work in Public Collections: Bronzes, Charles Russell, Statuary Hall, Washington, D C, Adm Nimitz, Annapolis Naval Acad Mus & Trophies For The Brave, Canton Art Inst; Miss Indian America, Mont State Hist Soc, Helena; heads & figures, Anthrop Hall, Smithsonian Inst.
Commissions: Cast stone, War Memorial, Butte, Mont, 44; three Indians, Nat Geog Soc, Washington, D C, 63; bronzes, The Stake, Prov Mus & Arch, Alta, 67 & Chief Red Crow, Blood Tribal Coun, Cardston, Alta, 69; Archaic Indian, Grandfather Mountain Mus, N C, 65.
Exhibitions: Chicago & Vicinity, Art Inst Chicago, 47; 1st Exhib Old Northwest Territory, Springfield, Ill, 47; Denver Art Mus 54th Ann, 48; Wis Painters & Sculptors, Milwaukee Art Inst, 51; 68th Exhib Soc Washington Artists, Natural Hist Bldg, Washington, D C, 61.
Teaching: Instr life drawing, Layton Sch Art, Milwaukee, 46-51.
Positions: Sculptor, Mont Hist Soc, 55-60; sculptor, Smithsonian Inst, 61-66.
Bibliography: R T Taylor (auth), Jack Weaver—sculptor, Mont Inst Arts, 55; Ruth Bowen (auth), Alberta art in bronze, My Golden West, 70; B Schwartz (auth), Talented hands, CBC TV, Edmonton, Alta, 70.
Memberships: Nat Sculpture Soc.
Dealer: Montana Gallery & Book Shop, Box 181, 11th & California, Helena, MT 59601.
Mailing Address: 10904-126th St, Edmonton, Alta T5M 0P3, Can.

WEBB, AILEEN OSBORN
Patron, Collector
b Garrison, N Y, June 25, 92.
Study & Training: Calif Col Arts & Crafts, hon DFA, 60.
Positions: Chmn bd, Am Craftsmen's Coun; pres, World Crafts Coun; pres, Am House, New York, N Y.
Awards: Sustaining mem award, Jr League of City of New York, 63; Trail Blazer Award, New York Chap, Nat Home Fashions League, 64.
Collection: Modern art.
Mailing Address: 340 E 72nd St, New York, NY 10021.

WEBER, ALBERT JACOB
Painter, Educator
b Chicago, Ill, July 10, 19.
Study & Training: Art Inst Chicago, BFA; Mexico City Col, MAA.
Exhibitions: Five shows, Univ Mich, 56-69; Soc Washington Printmakers, 57 & 60; Detroit Inst Art, 57, 60 & 66; Bloomfield Art Asn, 57 & 67; Am Fedn Arts Traveling Exhibs, 58-60; plus many other group & one-man shows.
Teaching: Instr, Mexico City Col; prof art, Univ Mich, Ann Arbor, 55-69.
Awards: Prize, Grand Rapids Art Gallery, 58; purchase prizes, Butler Inst Am Art, 59-61; purchase prize, Graphic Art & Drawing Exhib, Olivet Col, Mich, 62; plus others.
Memberships: Ann Arbor Art Asn.
Mailing Address: 1106 Lincoln St, Ann Arbor, MI 48104.

WEBER, IDELLE LOIS
Painter, Sculptor
Preferred Media: Oils, Plexiglass.
b Chicago, Ill.
Study & Training: Scripps Col; Univ Calif, Los Angeles, AA, BA & MA.
Work in Public Collections: Albright-Knox Gallery, Buffalo; also pvt collections.
Exhibitions: Mus Mod Art, 56; Bertha Schaefer Gallery, New York, 62-64; Solomon R Guggenheim Mus, 64; Providence Mus Fine Arts, R I, 65; Albright-Knox Gallery, 63.
Awards: Nat Scholastic Art Awards, Scripps Col, 50.
Bibliography: Notiziario: arte, Domus, 64; Douglas MacAgy (auth), The city idyll, Lugano Rev, 65; Lucy R Lippard (auth), Pop art, Praeger, 66.
Mailing Address: 35 Sidney Pl, Brooklyn, NY 11201.

WEBER, JEAN M
Art Administrator, Educator
b Boston, Mass, Apr 2, 33.
Study & Training: Brown Univ; R I Sch Design, BA; Edinburgh Univ; State Univ Iowa.
Collections Arranged: The Summer Place, 70; American Impressions, 70; Commedia dell'Arte, 71; Objects and Images, 71; Tantric Art of Tibet, 72.
Teaching: Adj prof, Southampton Col, 70-
Positions: Dir, Jr Art Gallery, Louisville, Ky, 66-69; asst & actg dir, Parrish Art Mus, Southampton, N Y, 69-70, dir, 70-
Awards: Danforth Found fel, 54-55; Int Mus Sem award, N Y State Coun Art, Metrop Mus, 72.
Memberships: Am Asn Mus; Am Fedn Arts; Nat Art Educ Asn; Int Coun Mus; N Y State Asn Mus.
Mailing Address: Henry St, Sag Harbor, NY 19963.

WEBER, JOHN
Art dealer
Positions: Pres, John Weber Gallery.
Specialty of Gallery: Contemporary art.
Mailing Address: 420 W Broadway, New York, NY 10012.

WEBSTER, DAVID S
Art Administrator
Positions: Asst dir, Shelburne Mus.
Mailing Address: Shelburne Museum, Shelburne, VT 05482.

WEBSTER, LARRY RUSSELL
Designer, Painter
Preferred Media: Watercolors.
b Arlington, Mass, Mar 18, 30.
Study & Training: Mass Col Art, BFA; Boston Univ, MS.
Work in Public Collections: De Cordova Mus, Lincoln, Mass; Grand Rapids Art Mus, Mich; Munic Gallery, Davenport, Iowa; Springfield Art Mus, Mo.
Exhibitions: Nat Acad Design, New York, 70; Allied Artists Am, 71; Am Watercolor Soc, New York, 72; Watercolor U S A.
Teaching: Asst prof typographic design, hist type & watercolor painting, Mass Col Art, 64-65.
Positions: Package designer, Union Bay & Paper Corp, 53-54; illusr, USA, 54-56; graphic designer, v pres & dir, Thomas Todd Co, Boston, 56-
Awards: Obrig Prize for watercolor, Nat Acad Design, 68 & 70; silver medal of honor, Am Watercolor Soc, 68 & 72; gold medal of honor, Allied Artists Am, 71.
Memberships: Am Watercolor Soc; Allied Artists Am; Soc Printers, Boston; Boston Watercolor Soc.
Mailing Address: 116 Perkins Row, Topsfield, MA 01983.

WECHSLER, HERMAN J
Art Consultant, Writer
b New York, N Y, Aug 21, 04.
Study & Training: New York Univ, BS; Harvard Univ, MA; Ecole Louvre, Paris; also with Paul S Sachs, John Shapley, Adolf Goldschmidt, Meyer Shapiro & others.
Positions: Founder, pres & dir, FAR Gallery, New York, 34-
Specialty of Gallery: Graphic art of nineteenth and twentieth centuries.
Publications: Auth, Pocket books of—Old masters & Gods and goddesses in art and legend; auth, Lives of famous French painters, Wash Square Press; auth, Introduction to prints and printmaking; auth, Great prints and printmakers, 68.
Mailing Address: 333 Central Park W, New York, NY 10025.

WECHTER, VIVIENNE THAUL
Educator, Painter
b New York, N Y.
Study & Training: Jamaica Teachers Col, with Hunter, BP; Columbia Univ; New York Univ; Pratt Inst; Sculpture Ctr, New York; Art Stud League New York; with Robert Beverly Hale & de Creeft; Morris Davidson Sch Mod Art.
Work in Public Collections: Corcoran Gallery Art, Washington, D C; Berkeley, Calif; Rose Mus, Brandeis, Mass; Jewish Mus, New York; Mus Fine Art, Houston & Fort Worth, Tex.
Exhibitions: Art: U S A; Provincetown Art Asn; Mus Mod Art, New York; Riverside Mus, New York; Fedn Mod Painters & Sculptors; plus many one-man shows.
Teaching: Artist-in-residence, Fordham Univ, 64-, chmn acquisitions & exhibs, 64- & prof fine arts, 67-
Positions: Dir, Urban Arts Corps, 68-; chmn univ coalition, Bronx Coun Arts, 70-; dir, Bronx Mus Arts, 71-
Awards: Riverside Mus; Am Soc Artists; Jersey City Mus.
Bibliography: G Brown (auth), article, 68 & R Gurin (auth), article, 68, In: Arts Mag.
Memberships: Soc Esthetics; Col Art Asn; Fedn Mod Painters & Sculptors (exec comt, 71-); Am Soc Artists; Am Asn Univ Prof.

Publications: Illusr, The park of Jonas, 67; ed, Five museums come to Fordham, 68; ed, Visual Fordham, 69 & 70; auth, A view from the ark, Barlenmir House, 72; contribr, Reconsidering the nonfigurative in painting.
Mailing Address: Dept of Fine Arts, Fordham University, Bronx, NY 10458.

WEDDIGE, EMIL
Lithographer, Educator
b Sandwich, Ont, Dec 23, 07; U S citizen.
Study & Training: Eastern Mich Univ, BS; Univ Mich, MDes; also with Emil Ganse, Morris Kantor & E Desjobert, France.
Work in Public Collections: Metrop Mus Art, New York, N Y; Cape Kennedy, Fla; Libr of Cong, Washington, D C; Philadelphia Mus Art, Pa; Detroit Art Inst, Mich.
Commissions: Lithography in color, Chrysler Motor Car Co, 55; suite of lithographs in color, Parke, Davis & Co, 56; History of Paper (suite), Dow Chem Co, 57; portrait of a city, Detroit Edison Co, 58; Sesquicentennial Suite, Univ Mich, 66.
Exhibitions: Joseph Pennel Exhib, 34-68; Am Color Print Soc, 48-71; Print Club, 48-71; Biennial Color Print Exhib, 52 & 54; Van Gogh Mem Exhib, Pontoise, France, 60.
Teaching: Instr art, Eastern Mich Univ, 36-37; prof art, Univ Mich, Ann Arbor, 37-
Awards: Founders prize, Detroit Inst Arts, 42; best print award, Am Color Print Soc, 56; James Cleating Print Prize, Michigan Exhib, 64.
Bibliography: Article, In: Statesman, India, 60; Joy Hakanson (auth), Art, Detroit News, 69; William Tall (auth), Art, Detroit Freepress, 69.
Memberships: Am Fedn Arts; Am Color Print Soc; Print Club; Print Coun Am; Int Platform Asn (spec adv to art chmn, 68-).
Art Interests: Stone lithography.
Publications: Auth, Lithography, 66.
Dealer: Birmingham Gallery, 1028 Haynes St, Birmingham, MI 48011.
Mailing Address: 870 Stein Rd, Ann Arbor, MI 48103.

WEDIN, ELOF
Painter
Preferred Media: Oils.
b Sweden, June 28, 01; U S citizen.
Study & Training: Minneapolis Sch Art; Art Inst Chicago.
Work in Public Collections: Minneapolis Inst Arts; Univ Minn, Minneapolis; Smith Col.
Commissions: U S Post Off, U S Govt Art Proj.
Exhibitions: Art Inst Chicago, Ill; San Francisco World's Fair, Calif; Minneapolis Inst Arts, Minn; Walker Art Ctr, Minneapolis; Minn State Fair.
Awards: Minneapolis Inst Arts; Walker Art Ctr; Minn State Fair.
Mailing Address: 3512 James Ave, Minneapolis, MN 55412.

WEEBER, GRETCHEN
Painter
Preferred Media: Watercolors.
b Albany, N Y.
Study & Training: Albany Inst Hist & Art; Inst Allende, San Miguel Allende, Mex; also with Betty Warren.
Work in Public Collections: Rensselaer Co Hist Soc, Troy, N Y; Home Savings Bank, Albany; New York State Conf Mayors, Albany; First Lutheran Church, Albany; Robert Appleton Collection, Albany; plus others in pvt collections.
Exhibitions: New York State Expos, Syracuse, 64; Eastern States Expos, Springfield, Mass, 65; Berkshire Ann, Pittsfield, Mass, 68; Artists of the Upper Hudson, Albany Inst Hist & Art, 70; Artists Asn Nantucket, Kenneth Taylor Galleries, Mass, 72; plus many other group shows, including one one-man show.
Awards: Raymond Scofield Prize for best watercolor, Albany Artists Group, 64; first prize, Rennselaer Co Hist Soc, 68; first prize for Nantucket Subjects, Artists Asn Nantucket, 69.
Memberships: Artists Asn Nantucket (bd mem, 72).
Dealer: Main Street Gallery, Main St, Nantucket, MA 02554.
Mailing Address: 7 Mulberry St, Nantucket, MA 02554.

WEEGE, WILLIAM
Printmaker, Educator
b Milwaukee, Wis.
Study & Training: Univ Wis-Milwaukee; Univ Wis-Madison, MA, 67, MFA, 68.
Work in Public Collections: Akron Art Inst; Brooklyn Mus; Art Inst Chicago; Frankfurt Libr, Ger; Mus Mod Art, New York; plus many others.
Exhibitions: U S Pavillion, World's Fair, Japan, 70; Seventh Int Biennial Exhib Prints, Tokyo, 70; Beyond Realism, Assoc Am Artists, New York, N Y, 70; Mechanics in Printmaking, 70 & Artist as Adversary, 70, Mus Mod Art, New York; Large Print Show, Whitney Mus Am Art, 71; plus many other group & one-man shows.

Teaching: From instr lettering to asst prof art, Univ Wis-Madison, 67-
Positions: Dir photo-offset area proj, Univ Wis-Madison, 67-68, graphics area specialist, 68; dir exp workshop for Smithsonian Inst, 35th Venice Biennale, summer 70; dir, Shenanigan Press, Ltd, Venice, Italy.
Mailing Address: Box 259, Rt 1, Barneveld, WI 53507.

WEEKS, JAMES (DARRELL) (NORTHRUP)
Painter
b Oakland, Calif, Dec 1, 22.
Study & Training: Calif Sch Fine Arts, 40-42 & 46-48; Hartwell Sch Design, 47; Escuela Pintura, Mexico City.
Work in Public Collections: Corcoran Gallery Art, Washington, D C; San Francisco Mus Art; Am Fedn Art, New York, N Y; Howard Univ, Washington, D C; Oakland Mus.
Exhibitions: Corcoran Gallery Invitational, 63; Carnegie Int, Pittsburgh, 64; one-man shows, San Francisco Mus Art, 65 & Boston Univ Art Gallery, 71; Expo 70, Osaka, Japan, 70.
Teaching: Instr painting, San Francisco Art Inst, 58-67; instr painting, Univ Calif, Los Angeles, 67-70; instr grad painting & chmn dept, Boston Univ, 70-
Bibliography: A Ventura (auth), James Weeks: the plain path, Arts Mag, 2/64; James Weeks, paintings, Felix Landau Gallery, 64.
Dealer: Poindexter Gallery, 24 E 84th St, New York, NY 10028.
Mailing Address: 118 Page Rd, Bedford, MA 01730.

WEEKS, LEO ROSCO
Painter, Illustrator
Preferred Media: Oils, Watercolors.
b La Crosse, Ind, June 23, 03.
Study & Training: Am Acad Art; also with Glen Sheffer.
Work in Public Collections: Pub schs in Cairo, Herrin, Downers Grove & Rock Island, Ill.
Exhibitions: Hoosier Salon, Indianapolis, Ind, 40's; Palette & Chisel Acad Fine Arts, Chicago, Ill, 42-62; All Ill Soc Fine Arts, Chicago, 42-62; Garden State Watercolor Soc, Princeton, N J, 70; Scotch Plains-Fanwood Art Asn, 71 & 72 & Westfield Art Asn, Union Col, Cranford, 65-67 & 72, N J State Shows.
Positions: Asst art dir, Popular Mech Mag, Chicago, 43-62, New York, 62-68; retired.
Awards: Gold medal for oils, Palette & Chisel Acad Fine Arts, 44; first prize for watercolor, All-Ill Soc Fine Arts, 46 & 52; Honeywell prize for Still Life in oil painting, Hoosier Salon, 48.
Memberships: Palette & Chisel Acad Fine Arts (secy, 44-47, pres, 48); Westfield Art Asn, N J.
Publications: Illusr, miscellaneous western bks for children, 30-43; illusr, Penny wise, 42; illusr, Popular Mech Mag, 43-68.
Mailing Address: 7 Glenwood Rd, Fanwood, NJ 07023.

WEEMS, KATHARINE LANE
Sculptor
Preferred Media: Bronze.
b Boston, Mass, Feb 22, 99.
Study & Training: May Sch, Boston; Sch Mus Fine Arts, Boston; also with Anna Hyatt Huntington, Brenda Putnam, Charles Grafly & George Demetrios.
Work in Public Collections: Mus Fine Arts, Boston; Mus Sci, Boston; Reading Mus, Pa; Calgary Mus, Alta; Brookgreen Gardens, S C.
Commissions: Brick carvings of geog distribution of animals of world & entrance doors, Biol Labs, Harvard Univ; Lotta Fountain, Esplanade, Boston; U S Legion of Merit & Medal For Merit, U S Govt; Goodwin Medal, Mass Inst Technol, Cambridge, Mass.
Exhibitions: Paris Salon, France; Nat Acad Design, New York, N Y.
Awards: Widener Gold Medal, Philadelphia Acad Fine Arts, 27; Saltus Gold Medal for Merit, 60 & Speyer Prize, 72, Nat Acad Design.
Bibliography: From Clay to bronze (film), Harvard Univ & Mus Fine Arts, Boston; Patricia Barnard (auth), The contemporary mouse, Coward, 54; Tatiana Browne (auth), A bevy of bears, Heredities Inc, 72.
Memberships: Nat Acad Design; Nat Sculpture Soc (mem coun, 49); Nat Inst Arts & Lett; Guild Boston Artists; Archit League New York.
Dealer: Guild of Boston Artists, 162 Newbury St, Boston, MA 02116.
Mailing Address: P O Box 126, Manchester, MA 01944.

WEESE, MYRTLE A
Painter
b Roslyn, Wash, Oct 30, 03.
Study & Training: Los Angeles Co Art Inst; also with George Flower & Ejnar Hansen.
Work in Public Collections: Paintings & portraits in pvt collections.
Exhibitions: One-man shows, Bowers Mem Mus, Santa Anna, Sierra Madre City Hall, Los Angeles City Hall, Descanso Gardens, 61 & Sierra Madre, 67; plus others.

Awards: Prizes, Brea Women's Club, 61 & Las Artistas, 61, gold medal, Greek Theatre, Los Angeles, 61.
Memberships: Scand-Am Soc; Am Inst Fine Arts; Las Artistas Art Club; Prof Artists Los Angeles.
Mailing Address: 4766 E 25th St, Tucson, AZ 85711.

WEHR, PAUL ADAM
Illustrator, Designer
b Mount Vernon, Ind, May 16, 14.
Study & Training: John Herron Art Inst, BFA.
Work in Public Collections: Herron Art Inst.
Exhibitions: Indiana Artists, 37, 42 & 43; Pa Acad Fine Arts, 40 & 43; Ind Art Club, 44; Advert Art Exhib, N Y, 45; Art Dirs Club, Chicago, 45 & 54; plus others.
Positions: Head commercial art dept, John Herron Art Inst, Indianapolis, Ind, 37-45; illusr, Stevens, Gross Studios, Inc, Chicago, Ill.
Awards: Prizes, Ind Artists, 42, 44, 51 & 56 & Hoosier Salon, 43, 44 & 69; first award, Ind Sesquicentennial Design Competition, Seal & Commemorative Stamp, 65; plus others.
Memberships: Ind Art Club.
Publications: Illusr, covers for, Popular Mech, Sports Afield, Coronet & Country Gentleman Mags; illusr, Collier's Mag; plus others.
Mailing Address: 6038 Allisonville Rd, Indianapolis, IN 46220.

WEHR, WESLEY CONRAD
Painter
Preferred Media: Mixed Media.
b Everett, Wash, Apr 17, 29.
Study & Training: Univ Wash, BA & MA; also with Mark Tobey.
Work in Public Collections: Munic Gallery Mod Art, Dublin, Ireland; Art Gallery Greater Victoria, B C; Lyman Allyn Mus, Conn Col, New London, Conn; Carpenter Art Galleries, Dartmouth Col, Hanover, N H; Henry Art Gallery, Univ Wash, Seattle.
Exhibitions: Wash State Art Mobile, State Capitol Mus, Olympia, 69-70; Expo 70, Wash State Pavilion, Osaka, Japan, 70; Gov Invitational, State Capitol Mus, Olympia, 70; Retrospective, Whatcom Mus Hist & Art, Bellingham, Wash, 70; Northwest Drawings, Henry Art Gallery, Univ Wash, Seattle, 72.
Awards: Painting award, Arts & Crafts Festival, Bellevue, Wash, 66; painting award, Arts Festival, Anacortes, Wash, 67; first pl & hon mention, Tacoma Art League, 69.
Bibliography: Mary Randlett (auth), Portraits by Mary Randlett, Seattle Times, 71; Elizabeth Bishop (auth), The artist and his environment (monogr), Univ Press, Seattle, 73.
Publications: Illusr, Poetry Northwest, Seattle, 66; contribr, People/the arts/the city, Munic Art Comn Report, Seattle, 66; contribr, The artist and his environment, Univ Press, Seattle, 73.
Dealers: Francine Seders Gallery, 6701 Greenwood Ave N, Seattle, WA 98103; Humboldt Galleries, 575 Sutter St, San Francisco, CA 94115.
Mailing Address: Henry Art Gallery, University of Washington, Seattle, WA 98105.

WEIDENAAR, REYNOLD HENRY
Etcher, Painter
Preferred Media: Watercolors, Casein.
b Grand Rapids, Mich, Nov 17, 15.
Study & Training: Kendall Sch Design, 35-36; Kansas City Art Inst, scholar, 38, 38-40.
Work in Public Collections: Libr Cong, Washington, D C; Detroit Inst Arts, Mich; Nat Gallery South Wales, Liverpool, Eng; Honolulu Acad Fine Arts, Hawaii; Hackley Art Gallery, Muskegon, Mich.
Commissions: Murals, church hist, La Grave Ave Christian Reformed Church, 65 & Urban Renewal, Mich Consolidated Gas Co, Grand Rapids.
Exhibitions: Regular exhibitor, Nat Acad Design, Detroit Inst Arts & Libr Cong.
Teaching: Instr life drawing & painting, Kendall Sch Design, 56-; pvt instr.
Awards: Guggenheim Found award, 44; Tiffany Found scholar, 48.
Memberships: Nat Acad Design; Soc Am Graphic Artists; Am Watercolor Soc.
Publications: Auth, Our changing landscape, Wake-Brook House, 70.
Dealer: Hefner Galleries, 52 Market Ave S W, Grand Rapids, MI 49502.
Mailing Address: Oakwood Manor, 547 Cherry St S E, Grand Rapids, MI 49503.

WEIDNER, ROSWELL THEODORE
Painter, Instructor
Preferred Media: Oils, Charcoal, Pastels.
b Reading, Pa, Sept 18, 11.
Study & Training: Pa Acad Fine Arts, Philadelphia, Cresson For traveling scholar, 35; Barnes Found, Merion, Pa.

Work in Public Collections: Pa Acad Fine Arts; Philadelphia Mus Art; Pa State Univ; Metrop Mus Art, New York, N Y; Libr Cong, Washington, D C.
Commissions: Portraits, of Herman Beerman, Univ Pa, Philadelphia, 68, Robert C Sale, Conn State Libr, Hartford, 69 & Clair R McCollough, Nat Asn Broadcasters, Washington, D C, 70.
Exhibitions: Pa Acad Fine Arts Ann, Philadelphia, 36-70; World's Fair, New York, 39; Directions Am Painting, Carnegie Inst, Pittsburgh, Pa, 43; Drawing Soc 2nd Eastern Cent Exhib, Philadelphia Mus Art, 70; 24th Am Drawing Biennial, Norfolk Mus Arts & Sci, Va & Smithsonian Traveling Exhib, 71.
Teaching: Sr instr painting, Pa Acad Fine Arts, 38-; instr painting, Philadelphia Col Art, 49-51.
Positions: Mem exhib comt, Philadelphia Art Alliance, 65-70.
Awards: Fel prize, Pa Acad Fine Arts Ann, 43; Dawson Mem Medal, Philadelphia Watercolor Club, 64-72.
Memberships: Fel Pa Acad Fine Arts (pres, 54-67, v pres, 67-); Philadelphia Watercolor Club (bd dirs, 65-); Artists Equity Asn; Print Club Philadelphia; Int Inst Conserv Hist & Artistic Works.
Dealers: Investment Art, Fort Worth, TX 76101; Langman Gallery, Jenkintown, PA 19046.
Mailing Address: 612 Spruce St, Philadelphia, PA 19106.

WEIL, MR & MRS RICHARD K
Collectors
Mailing Address: 6372 Forsyth Blvd, St Louis, MO 63101.

WEILL, ERNA
Sculptor, Instructor
Preferred Media: Stone, Metal, Concrete.
b Frankfurt am Main, Ger; U S citizen.
Study & Training: Univ Frankfurt, with Helene von Beckerath; also with John Hovannes, New York, N Y.
Work in Public Collections: Ga Mus Art, Athens; Birmingham Mus, Ala; Jewish Mus, New York; Hyde Park Libr, New York; Israel Mus, Hebrew Univ, Jerusalem; plus many others.
Commissions: Bronze archit sculptures, Teaneck Jewish Ctr, N J, 55, White Plains Jewish Ctr, N Y, 58 & Temple Har El, Jerusalem, Israel, 63; bronze portrait sculptures, Linus Pauling, Portula Valley, Calif, Martin Buber, Hebrew Univ & Leonard Bernstein; plus many more.
Exhibitions: New York World's Fair; N J State Mus, Trenton; Brooklyn Mus; Montclair Mus; Newark Mus; plus one-man shows, N Y & N J, 51-72.
Teaching: Instr sculpture, Brooklyn Mus, Forest Hills Pub Schs, Forest Hills Jewish Ctr & Teaneck Jewish Ctr; instr sculpture, Adult Educ Prog, Ft Lee, N J; pvt instr, sculpture; lectr, Fairleigh Dickinson Univ; lectr, var clubs & temples, N J.
Awards: Mem Found Jewish Cult grant for relig sculpture.
Bibliography: Bernard Buranelli (auth), World of Erna Weill, Rec Mag, 64; Avram Kampf (auth), Contemporary synagogue art, Union Am Hebrew Congregations, 65.
Memberships: Artists Equity Asn New York; New York Soc Artists Craftsmen; Mod Artists Guild, N J.
Publications: Auth, Any child can model in clay, Design; co-auth, article, In: Crisis, 10/65; contribr, Libr J & N J Educ Rev.
Mailing Address: 886 Alpine Dr, Teaneck, NJ 07666.

WEILL, MR & MRS MILTON
Collectors
Mr Weill, b New York, N Y, Oct 21, 91.
Study & Training: Mr Weill, Columbia Univ, AB, 13.
Memberships: Art Collectors Club.
Mailing Address: 769 John Ringling Blvd, Sarasota, FL 33577.

WEILLER, LEE GREEN
Painter
Preferred Media: Oils.
b London, Eng, Aug 27, 02; U S citizen.
Study & Training: Philadelphia Sch Design for Women; Pa Acad Fine Arts, fel; Acad Grande Chaumiere, Paris, France.
Work in Public Collections: In pvt collections only.
Exhibitions: Corcoran Biennial, Corcoran Gallery Art, Washington, D C; Am Fedn Arts Traveling Exhib; Moore Inst Art, Philadelphia, Pa; Woodmere Art Gallery, Philadelphia.
Teaching: Instr art, Wharton Ctr & Janette Whitehill Rosenbaum Art Ctr, Philadelphia, 58-64.
Awards: John Frederick Louis Medal; Pearl Aiman Van Sciver Prize.
Memberships: Philadelphia Mus Art; Fellowship Pa Acad Fine Arts; Moore Inst Col Art; Woodmere Art Gallery.
Mailing Address: 8210 Manor Rd, Elkins Park, PA 19117.

WEIN, ALBERT W
Sculptor, Painter
Preferred Media: Bronze, Marble.
b New York, N Y, July 27, 15.
Study & Training: Md Inst, 27-29; Nat Acad Design; Grand Cent Sch

Art; Beaux Arts Inst, with Hans Hofmann.
Work in Public Collections: Vatican Mus Numismatic Collection, Vatican City; New York Univ Hall of Fame; Jewish Mus, New York; Brookgreen Gardens, S C; Palm Springs Desert Mus, Calif.
Commissions: Exterior sculptures, Hillside Mem Park, Los Angeles, 60-68; exterior, St Michael's Episcopal Church, Anaheim, Calif, 67; bas-relief panels, Univ Wyo Phys Sci Ctr, 68; 25th Anniversary Medal, UN, 70; exterior sculpture, Canton Jewish Community Ctr, Ohio, 70.
Exhibitions: Whitney Mus Am Art Ann, New York, 50; Am Sculpture, Metrop Mus Art, New York, 51; San Francisco Mus Art Ann, 57; one-man exhib, Jewish Mus, 58; 30 Yr Retrospective, Palm Springs Desert Mus, 69.
Teaching: Vis prof sculpture, Univ Wyo, 65-67.
Awards: Prix de Rome, Am Acad Rome, 47 & 48; Tiffany Found fel, 49; Huntington Hartford Found fel, 55.
Bibliography: J Lovoos (auth), The art of Albert Wein, Am Artist, 1/63 & Art review, Christian Sci Monitor, 4/67; F Sleight (auth), Retrospective review, Palm Springs Desert Mus, 12/69.
Memberships: Fel Am Acad Rome; fel Int Inst Arts & Lett; fel Huntington Hartford Found; fel Nat Sculpture Soc.
Dealers: The Gallery, 168 N Palm Canyon, Palm Springs, CA 92262; Dalzell Hatfield Galleries, Ambassador Hotel, Los Angeles, CA 90070.
Mailing Address: 5450 Encino Ave, Encino, CA 91316.

WEINBAUM, JEAN
Painter, Sculptor
Preferred Media: Watercolors, Oils, Stained Glass.
b Zurich, Switz, 26.
Study & Training: Zurich Sch Fine Arts, 42-46; Acad Grande Chaumière; Ecole Paul Colin; Acad Andre L'Hote, 47-48.
Work in Public Collections: Musee d'Art Moderne, Paris, France; Nat Collection Fine Arts, Washington, D C; Univ Art Mus, Berkeley, Calif; Stanford Univ Mus, Calif; Calif Palace of Legion of Honor, San Francisco.
Commissions: Eleven stained glass windows, Chapelle de Mosloy, 51; rosette stained glass, Berne sur Oise, 55; twenty-two stained glass windows, St Pierre du Regard, 57; Wall of Light (monumental stained glass window), Escherange, 62; eight windows, Lycee de Jeunes Filles, Bayonne, France, 66.
Exhibitions: Musee d'Art Moderne, Paris, 62, 63 & 65; one-man shows, Galerie Smith-Andersen, Palo Alto, Calif, 70, 71 & 73, Calif Palace of Legion of Honor, 71, Musee Arts Decoratifs, Lausanne, Switz, 72 & Bildungszentrum, Gelsenkirchen, Ger, 72; plus many other group & one-man shows.
Bibliography: Francois Mathey & others (auth), Le vitrail Français, chap, In: Tendances Modernes, Ed Deux Mondes, Paris, 58; Robert Sowers (auth), Stained glass: an architectural art, Universe Bks, New York, 65; Shuji Takashina (auth), Stained glass works by Jean Weinbaum, Space Design, Tokyo, 9/67.
Dealer: Galerie Smith-Andersen, 200 Homer St, Palo Alto, CA 94301.
Mailing Address: P O Box 40291, San Francisco, CA 94140.

WEINBERG, ELBERT
Sculptor, Educator
Preferred Media: Wood, Bronze, Marble.
b Hartford, Conn, May 27, 28.
Study & Training: Hartford Art Sch, with Henry Kreis; R I Sch Design, with Waldemar Raemisch; Yale Univ Sch Fine Arts.
Work in Public Collections: Mus Mod Art, New York, N Y; Whitney Mus Am Art, New York; Jewish Mus, New York; Boston Mus Fine Arts, Mass; Wadsworth Atheneum, Hartford.
Commissions: Bronze procession (sculpture), Mr & Mrs Albert List, Jewish Mus, 59; Jacob Wrestling with Angel (sculpture), Brandeis Univ, Waltham, Mass, 64; Revelation (bronze relief), chapel house, Colgate Univ, Hamilton, N Y, 64; Eagle (bronze), Fed Res Bank, Atlanta, Ga, 64; Shofar (bronze), Rockdale Temple, Cincinnati, Ohio, 69.
Exhibitions: Whitney Mus Am Art, New York, 57, 58, 60 & 64; Carnegie Int, Pittsburgh, Pa, 58 & 61; Sculpture U S A, Mus Mod Art, New York, 59; 64 Americans Exhib, Art Inst Chicago, Ill, 61; Hirschhorn Collection, Guggenheim Mus, New York, 62.
Teaching: Instr sculpture, Cooper Union, 56-59; vis prof sculpture, Boston Univ, 70-
Awards: Prix de Rome, Am Acad Rome, 51-53; Guggenheim fel, 59; sculpture award, Am Inst Arts & Lett, 69.
Bibliography: Articles & photographs in several bks.
Memberships: Sculptors Guild, New York.
Dealers: Grace Borgenicht Gallery, 1018 Madison Ave, New York, NY 10021; Alpha Gallery, 121 Newbury St, Boston, MA 02116.
Mailing Address: Via Appia Antica 20, Rome, Italy.

WEINER, ABE
Painter, Instructor
Preferred Media: Acrylics, Egg Tempera.
b Pittsburgh, Pa, Nov 5, 17.
Study & Training: Carnegie Inst Technol, cert painting & design, 41, with Robert Gwathmey & Samuel Rosenberg.
Work in Public Collections: Hillman Libr, Univ Pittsburgh.
Commissions: Painting & mosaic on aluminum, Alcoa Co Pittsburgh; painting, PPG Industs.
Exhibitions: Assoc Artists Pittsburgh, 40-72 & Shows, 46-49, Carnegie Inst; Carnegie Int, Carnegie Libr Pittsburgh, 50; Contemp Soc Exhib, Art Inst Chicago, 52; 50 Most Promising Artists U S, Metrop Mus Art, 53.
Teaching: Instr painting, Arts & Crafts Ctr, 57-60; instr painting & drawing & asst dir, Ivy Sch Prof Art, 61-; instr painting, Irene Kaufman Ctr, 65-
Awards: First prize & second prize, 41 & 45 & Judge's Prize, 59, Assoc Artists Pittsburgh; Three Rivers Festival Purchase Award, 68.
Memberships: Assoc Artists Pittsburgh.
Mailing Address: 1636 Denniston Ave, Pittsburgh, PA 15217.

WEINER, ANITA, see KUSHNER-WEINER, ANITA MAY

WEINER, EGON
Sculptor, Educator
Preferred Media: Bronze.
b Vienna, Austria, July 24, 06; U S citizen.
Study & Training: Sch Arts & Crafts, Acad Fine Arts, Vienna.
Work in Public Collections: Syracuse Mus Fine Arts; Augsburg Col, Minneapolis; Augustana Col, Rock Island, Ill; plus others.
Commissions: Mem portrait busts of architects Sullivan & Adler for Lobby of Auditorium Theater of Chicago, 69; Polyphone #2 (bronze monument), St Joseph Hospital, Chicago, 69-70; Flame (bronze monument), Oslo, Norway, 71; portrait bust of Sen Beuton (bronze) for Encycl Britannica, Chicago, 70; portrait bust of Dr Eric Oldberg (bronze) for Med Ctr, Chicago, 72; plus others.
Exhibitions: Art Inst Chicago (art rental—juried), 60-70; Art Inst Oslo Juried Ann Exhib, 71; U S Info Serv Libr, Am Embassy, Oslo, 72-73; plus many earlier exhibs.
Teaching: Lectr, U S & abroad; prof sculpture & life drawing, Art Inst Chicago, 45-71, now prof emer; vis prof art, Augustana Col, 56.
Positions: Educ consult, film of Del Prado Mus, Madrid, Spain, 69; educ consult, Int Film Bur, Chicago.
Awards: Prize, 48 & gold medal, 69, Munic Art League, Chicago; medal, 59 & prize, 59, Art Inst Chicago; prize, 55 & citation, 62, Am Inst Architects; Gold Medal, Soc Arts & Lett, 70; plus others.
Memberships: Life fel Int Inst Arts & Lett; Munic Art League, Chicago (dir, 61-64); Cliff Dwellers of Chicago; hon life mem Alumni Asn Sch of Art Inst Chicago; Nat Inst Arts & Lett (adv coun, 68-70); plus others.
Mailing Address: 835 Michigan Ave, Evanston, IL 60202.

WEINER, MRS SAMUEL
Collector
Mailing Address: 737 Park Ave, New York, NY 10021.

WEINER, TED
Collector, Patron
b Fort Worth, Tex, Mar 9, 11.
Positions: Dir, Palm Springs Desert Mus, Calif, 67-; mem Nat Comt, Univ Art Mus, Univ Calif, Berkeley, 69-; mem, President's Adv Comt Arts, John F Kennedy Ctr Performing Arts, 70-
Awards: Cult Award, W Tex Chamber Commerce, 67.
Art Interests: Experimental Art Class for gifted children, Fort Worth.
Collection: Contemporary paintings and sculpture, including works by Henry Moore, Maillol, Marino Marini, Modigliani, Lipchitz, Picasso, Callery, Voulkos, Chadwick, Noguchi, Calder, Laurens, Marchs, de la Fresneye, de Stael, Tamayo, Parker & Kline; selection exhibited at University of Texas at Austin, 66 & Palm Springs Desert Museum, 69.
Mailing Address: P O Box 12405, Fort Worth, TX 76116.

WEINGARTEN, HILDE (MRS ARTHUR KEVESS)
Painter, Printmaker
b Berlin, Ger; U S citizen.
Study & Training: Art Stud League New York, with Morris Kantor; Cooper Union Art Sch, with Morris Kantor, Robert Gwathmey & Will Barnet, 47; Pratt Graphics Ctr.
Work in Public Collections: Bezalel Nat Mus, Jerusalem, Israel; Summit Med Group, N J; Arwood Corp, New York, N Y; Western Electric, N J; Gen Reinsurance Corp.
Exhibitions: Jewish Tercentenary Exhib, 55; Brooklyn & Long Island Artists, Brooklyn Mus, 58; Graphics '71 Print Exhib,

Western N Mex Univ, Silver City, 71; Audubon Artists, Nat Acad Design, New York, 71; plus many other group & six one-man shows.
Awards: Hon mention, Silver Jubilee, Caravan Gallery, 54; Patrons of Art prize for oil painting, Painters & Sculptors Soc N J, 70; Winsor & Newton Award for oil painting, Am Soc Contemp Artists, 71.
Memberships: Artists Equity Asn New York (bd dirs, 64-72); Nat Asn Women Artists (asst chmn foreign exhibs, 71-72); League Present Day Artists (bd dirs, 70-); Am Soc Contemp Artists; Painters & Sculptors Soc N J.
Publications: Illusr, The tune of the calliope, 58 & German folksongs, 68.
Mailing Address: 140 Cadman Plaza W, Brooklyn, NY 11201.

WEINHARDT, CARL JOSEPH, JR
Museum Director
b Indianapolis, Ind, Sept 22, 27.
Study & Training: Harvard Univ, AB(magna cum laude), 48, MA, 49, MFA, 55; Christian Theol Sem, Indianapolis, HHD, 67.
Collections Arranged: 5 Centuries Ger Prints, 56 & 18th Century Design, 60, Metrop Mus Art; 4 Centuries Am Art, Minneapolis Inst Arts, 63; Pavel Tchelitchew, 64 & Lovis Corinth, 65, Gallery Mod Art; Treasures From Metrop, Indianapolis Mus Art, 70.
Teaching: Lectr archit, Boston Archit Ctr, 54-55; lectr fine art, Columbia Univ, 58-60.
Positions: Staff mem, Metrop Mus Art, 55-58, assoc cur prints & drawings, 58-60; dir, Minneapolis Inst Arts, 60-62; dir, Gallery Mod Art, New York, 62-65; dir, Indianapolis Mus Art, 65-
Bibliography: Caroline Geib (auth), A Challenge accepted, Time-Life Broadcasts, 71.
Memberships: Asn Art Mus Dirs; Nat Soc Arts & Lett (nat adv); Drawing Soc (nat comt); Olana Preserv (trustee); Clowes Hall Adv Comt.
Publications: Auth, The etchings of Canaletto, Metrop Mus Art, 56; auth, Beacon Hill, Bostonian Soc, 58; auth, The James Ford Bell American Wing, Minneapolis Inst Art, 63; auth, Newport preserved, Art Am, 65; auth, A catalogue of European paintings in the Indianapolis Museum of Art, 71.
Mailing Address: Newfields, 1100 W 38th St, Indianapolis, IN 46208

WEINMAN, ROBERT ALEXANDER
Sculptor
Preferred Media: Bronze, Stone, Wood, Metals.
b New York, N Y, Mar 19, 15.
Study & Training: Nat Acad Design; Art Stud League New York; Hobart Sculptor's Welding Course; also sculpture with A A Weinman, Lee Lawrie, Paul Manship, E McCartan, C Jennewein & J E Fraser.
Work in Public Collections: Bessie The Belligerent (bronze) & Great Blue Heron (watercolor), Brookgreen Gardens, S C.
Commissions: Limestone tympana, Our Lady Queen of Martyrs Church, Forest Hills, N Y, 39; bronze elk, Benevolent & Protective Order Elks, Walla Walla, Wash, 48; bronze doors, Armstrong Libr, Baylor Univ, Waco, Tex, 51; athletic medals, Nat Collegiate Athletic Asn, 52; Morning Mission (bronze), Tulsa, Okla, 52.
Exhibitions: Nat Acad Design Ann, 37, 38, 49 & 53; Pa Acad Fine Art Ann, 38 & 39; Allied Artists Am, 46; Sculpture Int, Philadelphia, 49; Nat Sculpture Soc, 52, 60, 65, 69 & 70.
Awards: Hon mention for sculpture, Allied Artists Am, 46; Mrs Louis Bennett Prize, Nat Sculpture Soc, 52.
Memberships: Assoc Nat Acad Design; fel Nat Sculpture Soc (secy, 62-65, first v pres, 65-68 & 70-); Soc Animal Artists; Collectors Art Medals (charter dir, 71).
Publications: Contribr, articles, In: Nat Sculpture Rev, 62-71.
Mailing Address: Cross River Rd, R D 1, Bedford, NY 10506.

WEINSTEIN, MR & MRS JOSEPH
Collectors, Patrons
Mr Weinstein, b New York, N Y, Nov 13, 99.
Study & Training: Mr Weinstein, Harvard Univ; Mrs Weinstein, Simmons Col.
Collection: Picasso, Cezanne, Renoir, Rouault, Soutine, Max Weber, Balcomb Greene, Rodin, Zogbaum, Zorach and others; also African sculpture.
Mailing Address: 211 Central Park W, New York, NY 10024.

WEISGARD, LEONARD JOSEPH
Illustrator, Writer
b New Haven, Conn, Dec 13, 16.
Study & Training: Pratt Inst; New Sch Soc Res; also with Alexei Brodovich.
Exhibitions: Metrop Mus Art; Mus Mod Art, New York, N Y; Worcester Mus; Waterbury Mus; plus throughout the Soviet Union.
Teaching: Instr art, Booth Free Sch.

Positions: Dir exhibs, Mattatuck Hist Soc; mem greeting card art
selection, UNICEF; scenic & costume designer.
Awards: Caldecott Award, Am Libr Asn; awards, Am Inst Graphic
Arts.
Bibliography: Articles, In: Horn Bk Mag.
Publications: Auth over thirteen bks; illusr over 250 bks for
children.
Mailing Address: Snoldelevgård, Snoldelev, 4621 per Gadstrup,
Denmark.

WEISGLASS, MR & MRS I WARNER
Collectors
Mailing Address: 475 Park Ave, New York, NY 10022.

WEISMAN, WINSTON ROBERT
Educator, Writer
b New York, N Y, Feb 3, 09.
Study & Training: Ohio Univ, BA (jour & art hist cum laude), 32;
Univ Paris, cert art hist, summer 34; New York Univ Inst Fine
Arts, MA (art hist), 36; Mills Col, fel, 39; Ohio State Univ, PhD
(art hist & studio art), 42.
Teaching: Instr art hist & photog, Mills Col, 37-39; instr art hist,
Univ Ky, 39-40; instr art hist, Ind Univ, 47-50; instr art, Univ
Tex, 50-52; res prof art hist, Pa State Univ, 53-, chmn dept art
& archit hist, 57-64, head dept art hist, 64-71.
Positions: Vis prof, New York Univ Inst Fine Arts, 57; vis prof,
Univ Pa, 59; dir & lectr, Pa State Study Abroad Prog, Univ
Cologne, summer 63; Concora vis lectr, Northwestern Univ,
spring 69; dir, Ctr Study Renaissance & Baroque Art, Pa State
Univ.
Awards: Ind Univ grant, 40-42; Am Coun Learned Soc scholar, 52-
53; Am Philos Soc award, 54-55; plus many others.
Memberships: Col Art Asn Am; Soc Archit Historians; Victorian
Soc Am; Friends of Cast Iron Archit.
Art Interests: Commercial architecture in the U S A & Europe.
Publications: Auth, The emergence of the American mode in architecture, Am Rev, 5/62, Skyscraper, Encycl Britannica, 64, The
origins of the skyscraper, Soc Ingegneri Bull, 4/70, The early
commercial architecture of George B Post, J Soc Archit Hist,
10/72 & Cast iron building technology: the laing stores, Monu-
mentum, 72; plus many others.
Mailing Address: Dept of Art History, Pennsylvania State University, University Park, PA 16802.

WEISMANN, DONALD LEROY
Educator, Painter
Preferred Media: Collage, Film.
b Milwaukee, Wis, Oct 12, 14.
Study & Training: Univ Wis-Milwaukee, BS; Univ Minn; Univ Wis-
Madison, PhM; St Louis Univ; Harvard Univ, Carnegie Corp
scholar, 41; Ohio State Univ, PhD.
Work in Public Collections: Butler Inst Am Art, Youngstown, Ohio;
Chrysler Mus, Provincetown, Mass; Columbia Mus Art, S C; D D
Feldman Collection, Humanities Res Ctr, Univ Tex, Austin; Witte
Mus, San Antonio, Tex.
Commissions: Mural, Ill Centennial Bldg, Springfield, 41; TV video-
tape ser, Mirror of Western Art, Nat Educ TV, 60 & The Visual
Arts, Ford Found & U S Off Educ, 61; films, Terlingua, 71 & Sta-
tion X, 72, Pub Broadcast Corp.
Exhibitions: Ann Exhib Am Art, 40-41 & Int Watercolor Exhib, 42,
Art Inst Chicago, Ill; Ann Exhib Art U S & Territories, Butler
Inst Am Art, 57-58; Gulf-Caribbean Exhib, Houston Mus Fine
Arts, Tex, 58; World's Fair, New York, N Y, 64-65.
Collections Arranged: Ulfert Wilke Retrospective, 53 & Victor Ham-
mer Retrospective, 54, Univ Ky, Lexington.
Teaching: Assoc prof, N Tex State Univ, summer 40; asst prof art &
art hist, Ill State Normal Univ, 40-42 & 46-48; asst prof art hist,
Wayne State Univ, 49-51; prof art & head dept, Univ Ky, 51-54;
prof art, Univ Tex, Austin, 54-, chmn dept, 54-58, grad prof art
hist, 58-, univ prof in arts, 64-, chmn comp studies, 67-
Awards: Purchase award for painting, Butler Inst Am Art, 57;
Bromberg Award for Excellence in Teaching, Univ Tex, Austin,
65; lett of commendation for enhancement of arts in Am, President of U S, 72.
Memberships: Nat Coun Arts; Nat Humanities Fac; Am Asn Univ
Prof; Am Studies Asn; Tex Fine Arts Asn.
Research: Creative process in art and science; language and visual
form.
Publications: Auth & illusr, Some folks went west, 60; auth, Jelly
was the word, 65; auth & illusr, Language and visual form, 68;
contribr, The collage as model, Psychol Issues, Vol 6, No 2;
auth, The visual arts as human experience, 70.
Dealer: Carlin Galleries, 710 Montgomery St, Fort Worth, TX 76107.
Mailing Address: Academic Center 18, University of Texas at Austin, Austin, TX 78712.

WEISS, HARVEY
Sculptor
Preferred Media: Bronze, Welded Brass.
b New York, N Y, Apr 10, 22.
Study & Training: Nat Acad Design; Art Stud League New York; also
with Ossipe Zadkine, Paris.
Work in Public Collections: Albright-Knox Art Gallery; Krannert
Mus; Silvermine Guild Collection; Nelson Rockefeller Collection;
Joseph H Hirshhorn Collection; plus others.
Commissions: Menorah, Temple B'nai Zion, Shreveport, La, 67;
relief, Mt Vernon Synagogue, N Y, 69; relief, Conn Off Bldg,
Westport, 71.
Exhibitions: Five-one-man shows, Paul Rosenberg & Co, 59-70; one-
man show, Silvermine Guild, 68; retrospective, Fairfield Univ,
70; Am Inst Arts & Lett, 70; Sculptor's Guild Ann Shows.
Awards: Three Ford Found purchase awards; Olivetti Award, New
Eng Ann Exhib, 69; Nat Inst Arts & Lett grant, 70.
Memberships: Sculptors Guild (pres, 70-71); Silvermine Guild Art-
ists (bd trustees, 68-70); Auth Guild.
Publications: Auth & illusr, Ceramics, 64, Paint brush & palette, 66,
Collage and construction, 70, The gadget book, 71 & Lens and
shutter, 71; plus others.
Dealer: Paul Rosenberg & Co, 20 E 79th St, New York, NY 10021.
Mailing Address: 42 Maple Lane, Greens Farms, CT 06436.

WEISS, JEAN BIJUR
Painter, Collector
Preferred Media: Acrylics, Watercolors, Ink.
b New York, N Y, Mar 18, 12.
Study & Training: New York Sch Design, cert; Columbia Univ; New
York Univ; Metrop Mus; N Y Sch Social Res; Kunstgewerbe Sch,
Vienna; Silvermine, Mus Mod Art; Art Stud League New York;
Pratt Graphic Arts Ctr, New York; also with Arshile Gorky,
George Grosz & Joseph Binder.
Work in Public Collections: Nat Collection Fine Arts, Washington,
D C; New York Hosp Collection, N Y; Inst Rehab, N Y.
Commissions: Three paintings, pvt collectors, 66-72.
Exhibitions: New Eng Ann, Silvermine, Conn, 56; Am Watercolor
Soc, New York; Northern Westchester Ann; Westchester Ann;
one-man show, Katonah Gallery, 71.
Teaching: Adult educ instr drawing & painting, Chappaqua Pub Schs,
N Y, 63-66.
Awards: Antiques award, New Eng Ann, Silvermine, 56; Lobster
Buoy's award, Westchester Co Arts Festival; Croton Gothic
award, Katonah Gallery, N Y.
Memberships: Silvermine Guild Art; Westchester Art Soc; Yonkers
Art Asn; Katonah Gallery Lending Gallery.
Collection: Arshile Gorky painting and drawings.
Dealers: Silvermine Guild of Art, 1037 Silvermine Rd, New Canaan,
CT 06840; Katonah Gallery, 28 Bedford Rd, Katonah, NY 10536.
Mailing Address: 760 King St, Chappaqua, NY 10514.

WEISS, LEE (ELYSE C WEISS)
Painter
Preferred Media: Watercolors.
b Inglewood, Calif, May 22, 28.
Study & Training: Calif Col Arts & Crafts, 46-47; also with N Eric
Oback, 57 & Alexander Nepote, 58.
Work in Public Collections: Nat Collection Fine Arts, Smithsonian
Inst, Washington, D C; Nat Acad Design, New York, N Y; Exec
Residence, State Wis; Springfield Mus Art, Mo; Dimock Gallery,
George Washington Univ, Washington, D C; plus many others
Commissions: The American Artist & Water Resources, one of 40
Am artists chosen for Bur Reclamation Art Proj, U S Dept Inte-
rior, 71.
Exhibitions: Am Watercolor Soc, New York, 65-; Pa Acad Fine Arts,
Philadelphia, 65 & 68; The Landscape as Interpreted by Twenty-
two Artists, Minneapolis Inst Fine Arts, Minn, 66; The American
Artist & Water Reclamation, Nat Gallery Art, Washington, D C,
72; plus many other group & one-man shows.
Awards: Medal of hon for watercolor, Knickerbocker Artists, 64;
five awards, 65-71 & purchase award, 67, Watercolor U S A,
Springfield Mus; Emily Lowe Award, 66 & Henry Ward Ranger
Fund purchase award, 67, Am Watercolor Soc; plus many others.
Memberships: Am Watercolor Soc; Calif Nat Watercolor Soc; Phila-
delphia Watercolor Club; Wis Painters & Sculptors; Wis Water-
color Soc.
Publications: Co-auth, Lee Weiss watercolors, Col Printing & Publ,
71; auth, article, In: The watercolor page, Am Artist Mag, 9/72.
Dealers: Franz Bader Gallery, 2124 Pennsylvania Ave N W, Wash-
ington, DC 20037; Oehlschaeger Galleries, 107 E Oak, Chicago,
IL 60611.
Mailing Address: 106 Vaughn Ct, Madison, WI 53705.

WEITZENHOFFER, A MAX
Art Dealer
b Oklahoma City, Okla, Oct 30, 39.
Study & Training: Univ Okla, BFA.
Positions: Dir, Gimpel & Weitzenhoffer Ltd.
Memberships: Art Dealers Asn Am.
Specialty of Gallery: Twentieth century American and European
  paintings and sculpture.
Mailing Address: 1040 Madison Ave, New York, NY 10021.

WEITZMANN, KURT
Educator, Art Historian
b Almerode, Ger, Mar 7, 04; U S citizen.
Study & Training: Univ Munster; Univ Wurzburg; Univ Vienna; Univ
  Berlin, PhD, 29; Dr honoris causa, Univ Heidelberg, 67; Dr hon-
  oris causa, Univ Chicago, 68.
Teaching: Assoc prof art & archaeol, Princeton Univ, 45-50, prof
  art & archaeol, 50-72, emer prof, 72-; vis lectr art & archaeol,
  Yale Univ, 54-55; vis prof art & archaeol, Univ Alexandria, 60;
  guest prof art & archaeol, Univ Bonn, 62; vis scholar, Dumbarton
  Oaks, Washington, D C.
Positions: Stipend, Ger Archaeol Inst, Greece, 32 & Berlin, 32-34;
  permanent mem, Inst Advan Study, 35-72; consult cur, Metrop
  Mus Art.
Awards: Prix Gustave Schlumberger, Acad Inscriptions & Belles
  Lett, Paris, France, 69.
Memberships: Fel Medieval Acad Am; Ger Archaeol Inst; Am Philos
  Soc; Col Art Asn Am; Archaeol Inst Am.
Research: Late classical, Byzantine & Medieval art; expeditions to
  Mount Athos & Mount Sinai.
Publications: Co-auth, Die Byzantinischen elfenbeinskulpturen des
  X-XIII jahrhunderts, Vols I & II, 30 & 34; auth, Illustrations in
  roll & codex, 47, rev ed, 70; auth, Greek mythology in Byzantine
  art, 51; co-auth, A treasury of icons, 67; auth, Studies in late
  classical & Byzantine manuscript illumination, 71.
Mailing Address: 30 Nassau St, Princeton, NJ 08540.

WELCH, JAMES HENRY
Collector
b Cleveland, Ohio, June 21, 31.
Study & Training: Western Pa Horological Inst, Pittsburgh, certified
  watchmaker; Col Wooster, BA.
Memberships: Nat Asn Watch & Clock Collectors (pres, Ohio Valley
  Chap, 64-65).
Collection: Seventeenth, eighteenth and early nineteenth century
  decorative watches including enamel automaton repousse and
  complicated watches; eighteenth century English musical clocks;
  American paintings, Hudson River, nineteenth century portraits
  and still lifes; British nineteenth century landscapes and portraits; French Barbizon School landscapes.
Mailing Address: 114 48th St N W, Canton, OH 44709.

WELCH, LIVINGSTON
Sculptor, Painter
Preferred Media: Lead, Brass.
b New Rochelle, N Y, Aug 8, 01.
Study & Training: Hunter Col.
Work in Public Collections: Notre Dame Univ Mus; Casanova Col;
  Hunter Col.
Exhibitions: One-man shows, Wellons Gallery, New York, N Y, 48,
  Caravan Gallery, N Y, 56, World House Gallery, New York, 62-
  65 & Shuster Gallery, New York, 65-69 & Galeria Int, New York.
Mailing Address: c/o Shuster Gallery, 536 Third Ave, New York,
  NY 10016.

WELCH, MR & MRS ROBERT G
Collectors
Mr Welch b Kewanee, Ill, July 9, 15.
Study & Training: Stanford Univ, AB, 37.
Memberships: Cleveland Mus Art; Mus Mod Art, New York (Cleve-
  land growth bd); Cleveland Soc Contemp Art.
Mailing Address: 16800 S Woodland Rd, Cleveland, OH 44120.

WELCH, STUART CARY
Museum Curator
Teaching: Lectr fine arts, Harvard Univ.
Positions: Hon cur Indian & Islamic mss in Harvard Col Libr.
Mailing Address: Fogg Art Museum, Quincy St & Broadway, Cam-
  bridge, MA 02138.

WELLER, ALLEN STUART
Educator, Art Historian
b Chicago, Ill, Feb 1, 07.
Study & Training: Univ Chicago, PhB, 27, PhD, 42; Princeton Univ,
  MA, 29; Ind Cent Col, hon LLD, 65.
Collections Arranged: Contemporary American Painting & Sculp-
  ture, Krannert Art Mus, 48-53, biennially, 55-69.

Teaching: Prof hist art, Univ Mo-Columbia, 29-47; prof hist art,
  head dept, dean col fine & appl arts & dir mus, Univ Ill, 47-71;
  vis prof, Univ Minn; vis prof, Univ Colo; vis prof, Univ Calif;
  vis prof, Univ R I; vis prof, Ore State Univ.
Awards: Legion of Merit, USAF, 46; fel Royal Soc Arts; fel Nat
  Asn Schs Art.
Memberships: Col Art Asn Am (bd dirs); Soc Archit Historians; Nat
  Asn Schs Art (bd dirs); Asn Fine Arts Deans.
Research: Italian Renaissance; contemporary American painting and
  sculpture.
Publications: Auth, Francesco de Giorgio, 1439-1501, 42; auth,
  Abraham Rattner, 56; co-auth, Art U S A now, 62; auth, The joys
  and sorrows of recent American art, 68.
Mailing Address: 412 W Iowa St, Urbana, IL 61801.

WELLINGTON, DUKE
Painter
Preferred Media: Oils.
b Kans, Aug 9, 96.
Study & Training: Kans State Col; Los Angeles Art Ctr; Art Stud
  League New York; also with Eliot O'Hara, Edgar A Whitney, Hay-
  ward Veal, Doel Reed, Alice Harold Murphy, Reed Schmickle &
  Joseph Fleck.
Work in Public Collections: Graphica, Sage Brush Inn, Taos, N Mex;
  in many pvt collection, including Maurice Chevalier, Paris, Irv-
  ing Berlin, N Y & Gustav S Eyssell, N Y.
Commissions: Christ in Kansas mural & 30 religious paintings, Dio-
  cese of Wichita, Kans, 58.
Exhibitions: Kansas City Mo Art Asn, Kansas City Mus, 57; Kans
  Painters Show, Kans State Col Pittsburg, 58; Ozark Artist Guild,
  Joplin, Mo, 58; Spiva Art Ctr, Joplin, 59; Wichita Art Mus, 68.
Positions: Art dir, Tex Theatre, San Antonio, 24-26; art dir, Para-
  mount Theatres, 27-36; art dir, Nat Screen Serv, Los Angeles,
  Calif, 40-56; demonstr art, NBC/KOAM Educ TV, Pittsburg, 66-
  67.
Awards: Award for Clown Lou Jacobs, Ozark Artists Guild, 58;
  award for The Hens, Spiva Art Ctr, 59; award for Finitude, Kans
  Painters Show, 59.
Bibliography: Robert Kelly (auth), San Antonio boy promoted, San
  Antonio Eve News, 5/25/28; George Britt (auth), Lure movie
  fans, New York World Telegram, 10/7/32; R E Breniver (auth),
  Duke, artist deluxe, Signs of the Times, Cincinnati, Ohio, 2/32.
Memberships: Spiva Art Ctr; life mem Scene & Pictorial Painters
  Int; Wichita Art Mus.
Publications: Auth, Theatre poster service, Publix Theatres Publ,
  29-36; auth, Theory and practice of poster art, Signs of Times
  Publ Co, 34.
Dealer: Reynolds Gallery, Taos, NM 87571.
Mailing Address: Ranchos de Taos, NM 87557.

WELLIVER, NEIL G
Painter
b Millville, Pa, July 22, 29.
Study & Training: Philadelphia Mus Col Art; Yale Univ, with Albers,
  Diller, Brooks & Relli.
Work in Public Collections: Whitney Mus Am Art; Vassar Col Mus
  Art.
Exhibitions: Nat Arts Club, 59; Am Fedn Arts Traveling Exhib, 60 &
  68; Realism Now, Vassar Col, 68; Four Views, N J State Mus, 70;
  The New Landscape, Boston Univ, 72; plus many other group &
  one-man shows.
Positions: Critic painting, Cooper Union Art Sch, 54-57; critic
  painting, Yale Univ & Univ Pa.
Awards: Morse fel, 60-61.
Bibliography: Welliver's travels, Art News, 68; Rudolph Burckhardt
  (prod & dir), Green wind (film), 70.
Publications: Contribr, Art News, Craft Horizons & Perspecta.
Dealer: John Bernard Myers Gallery, 50 W 57th St, New York, NY
  10019.
Mailing Address: R D 2, Lincolnville, ME 04849.

WELLS, CHARLES ARTHUR, JR
Sculptor
b New York, N Y, Dec 24, 35.
Study & Training: With Leonard Baskin.
Work in Public Collections: Whitney Mus Am Art, New York; Nat
  Portrait Gallery, Washington, D C; Pa State Univ Mus; Smith
  Col Mus Art, Northampton, Mass; Princeton Univ Art Mus,
  N J; plus others.
Awards: John Taylor Arms Award, 63; Nat Inst Arts & Lett, 64;
  Am Acad Rome, 64-66.
Bibliography: C Chetham (auth), article, In: Mass Rev, 64.
Art Interests: Stone carving, etching.
Mailing Address: Vallecchia-Castello, Lucca 55040, Italy.

WELLS, FRED N
Executive Director
b Lincoln, Nebr, Aug 12, 94.
Study & Training: Univ Calif, Berkeley; Univ Nebr, AB.
Positions: Chmn, Nebr State Capitol Murals Comn, 51-65; pres, Nebr Art Asn, 63-64, exec secy, at present; mem, Nebr Hall of Fame Comn, at present; dir, Lincoln Community Arts Coun, at present; treas & dir, Nebr Arts Coun, at present.
Memberships: Sigma Delta Chi.
Mailing Address: Nebraska Art Association, Sheldon Memorial Art Gallery, Lincoln, NE 68508.

WELLS, JAMES LESESNE
Painter, Lithographer
b Atlanta, Ga, Nov 2, 02.
Study & Training: Lincoln Univ; Teachers Col, Columbia Univ, BS, MA; Nat Acad Design, with Frank Nankivell.
Work in Public Collections: IBM Collection; Hampton Inst; Univ Kans; Thayer Mus Art; Valentine Mus Art; plus others.
Exhibitions: Nat & Int Group Show, Soc Washington Printmakers, Prints of Two Worlds, Stampe di Due Mondi, Philadelphia Mus Art & Temple Univ, Rome, Italy, & Exhib & Symposium on Black Arts, Cleveland Mus Art, 67; two-man show, Carl Van Vechtan Gallery Art, Fisk Univ, 67; one-man show, Smith-Mason Gallery, Washington, D C, 69; group show, Afro-American Images, State Armory, Wilmington, Del, 69; one-man show, Paintings & Prints, Van Vechtan Gallery Art, 72; plus many other group & one-man shows.
Teaching: Prof art, Howard Univ, retired, 68.
Awards: Washington Watercolor Club, 59; Smithsonian Inst, 61; purchase award for Talladega Col, Am Fedn Arts, 64.
Memberships: Am Fedn Arts; Washington Watercolor Club.
Mailing Address: 1333 R St N W, Washington, DC 20009.

WELLS, MAC
Painter
Preferred Media: Acrylics, Watercolors, Oils.
b Cleveland, Ohio, Feb 3, 25.
Study & Training: Oberlin Col, BA, 48; Cooper Union, 48-49; also with Nahum Tschacbasov & Yasuo Kuniyoshi.
Work in Public Collections: Michener Collection, Univ Tex, Austin; Aldrich Mus, Ridgefield, Conn; Herron Mus Art, Indianapolis, Ind; Purdue Univ, West Lafayette, Ind; Univ Mass, Amherst.
Commissions: Three-dimensional card, Mus Mod Art, New York, N Y, 65.
Exhibitions: One-man shows, Aegis Gallery, New York, 63, A M Sachs Gallery, New York, 65 & 67 & Max Hitchinson Gallery, New York, 70 & 72.
Teaching: Instr gen studio, Hunter Col, 66-; instr painting & design, Moore Col Art, Philadelphia, 66-72; instr painting, Skowhegan Sch Painting & Sculpture, Maine, 69.
Bibliography: Article, In: New Talent, Art in Am, 7 & 8/65; Lucy Lippard (auth), New York letter, Art Int, 11/20/65.
Memberships: Am Abstr Artists.
Dealer: Max Hutchinson Gallery, 127 Greene St, New York, NY 10012.
Mailing Address: 64 Grand St, New York, NY 10013.

WENGENROTH, STOW
Printmaker
b Brooklyn, N Y, July 25, 06.
Study & Training: Art Stud League New York, N Y; Grand Cent Sch Art.
Work in Public Collections: Metrop Mus Art, New York; Libr Cong, Washington, D C; Boston Pub Libr, Mass; Mus Mod Art, New York; Baltimore Mus, Md.
Exhibitions: Nat Acad Design, New York; Soc Am Graphic Artists, New York; Audubon Artists, New York; Philadelphia Watercolor Club, Pa; Conn Acad, Hartford.
Awards: Pennel Mem Medal, Philadelphia Watercolor Club, 43; medal of honor, Audubon Artists, 49; S F B Morse Medal, Nat Acad Design, 68.
Memberships: Nat Acad Design; Nat Inst Arts & Lett; Soc Am Graphic Artists; Philadelphia Watercolor Club; Albany Print Club.
Publications: Auth, Making a lithograph, 36; co-auth, Stow Wengenroth's New England, 69.
Dealer: Kennedy Galleries, 20 E 56th St, New York, NY 10022.
Mailing Address: 717 Main St, Greenport, NY 11944.

WENGER, LESLEY
Art Dealer
b New York, N Y, Oct 6, 41.
Study & Training: New York Univ, BA, 63.
Collections Arranged: (Exhibitions) Glass Sculpture/John Anderson, Bruce George, Kim Newcomb, Wenger Gallery, San Francisco, 71; Judith Foosaner—Painting, Wenger Gallery, 71; Laya Bros-toff—Woven Canvases, Wenger Gallery, 72; Ceramic Sculpture/ Dan Snyder, Butterfield, Shannonhouse, Buck, Billick, 72; Ceramic Sculpture/Unterseher, McNamara, Greenley, Cooper, Arrizabalaga, Williamson, Dewey, 72; Sculpture/Mary Gould Quinn and Charlotte Wax, 72.
Positions: Dir, Wenger Gallery, 69-
Mailing Address: 855 Montgomery St, San Francisco, CA 94133.

WENGER, SIGMUND
Art Dealer, Lecturer
b Brooklyn, N Y, Nov 20, 10.
Study & Training: New York Univ, 29-31.
Teaching: Consult & lectr, La Jolla Mus Contemp Art, Calif, 65-69; consult & lectr, Fine Arts Gallery San Diego, Calif, 65-; consult & lectr, Nat Inst Fine Arts, Mexico City, Mex, 66-70.
Positions: Dir, Galerias Carlota, Tijuana, Baja California, Mex; co-dir, Wenger Gallery, San Francisco & La Jolla, Calif.
Specialty of Gallery: Mexican and contemporary art.
Mailing Address: P O Box 3-B, San Ysidro, CA 92073.

WENTWORTH, MURRAY JACKSON
Painter, Instructor
Preferred Media: Watercolors.
b Boston, Mass, Jan 18, 27.
Study & Training: Art Inst Boston.
Work in Public Collections: Farnsworth Mus Art, Rockland, Maine; Springfield Mus Art, Mo; First Nat Bank, Boston; Mech Nat Bank, Worcester, Mass; Utah State Univ, Logan.
Exhibitions: Metrop Mus Art, New York, N Y, 66; Mex Art Inst & Watercolor Mus, Mexico City, 68; Butler Inst Am Art, Youngstown, Ohio, 69; Brockton Fuller Mem Mus, Mass, 70; one-man show, Farnsworth Mus, 72.
Teaching: Instr watercolor, Art Inst Boston, 57-
Awards: Ranger Fund Purchase Prize, Nat Acad Design, 65; Nat Arts Club Bronze Medal Hon, 68; Am Watercolor Soc Bronze Medal Hon, 69.
Memberships: Am Watercolor Soc; Allied Artists Am; Boston Watercolor Soc (v pres, 71-); Salmagundi Club; assoc Nat Acad Design.
Publications: Contribr, watercolor page, Am Artist Mag, 70.
Mailing Address: 132 Central St, Norwell, MA 02061.

WERNER, ALFRED
Critic, Writer
Study & Training: Univ Vienna; New York Univ Inst Fine Arts.
Teaching: Lectr hist mod art, Guggenheim Mus, Mus Mod Art, Nat Gallery Art & Jewish Mus; instr art hist, Wagner Col & City Col New York.
Positions: U S corresp, Pantheon, Munich, Ger; bk rev ed, Am Artist, New York.
Awards: Prof Honoris Causa, Austrian Govt, 67; officer's cross, Ger Order Merit.
Memberships: Int Asn Art Critics.
Publications: Twenty bks published including works on Modigliani, Pascin, Chagall & Barlach; contribr to Arts Mag, Art J, Am Artist, Kenyon Rev & Antioch Rev.
Mailing Address: 230 W 54 th St, New York, NY 10019.

WERNER, DONALD (LEWIS)
Painter, Designer
Preferred Media: Watercolors, Collage.
b Fresno, Calif, Feb 2, 29.
Study & Training: Fresno State Col, BA, with Adolf & Ella Odorfer & Jane Gale; Chouinard Art Inst, Los Angeles; also costuming with Marjorie Best.
Work in Public Collections: Murals, Dan River Mills, New York, N Y; Wellington Sears, New York; Martex, New York; Fresno Art Ctr, Calif; Hudson River Mus, Yonkers, N Y.
Commissions: Collage murals, New York World's Fair.
Exhibitions: Many one-man shows, Gallery 84, New York, 59-72, Painting & Photog, Fresno Art Gallery, 67, Photog, Focus Gallery, San Francisco, 68, Painting & Photog, Hudson River Mus, 69 & 72 & Photog, St Paul Civic Ctr, Minn, 70.
Collections Arranged: Art in Westchester, 69, African Art, 71, Light, Motion, Sound, 71, Sky, Sand & Spirits, 72, 20th Century Sculpture, 72 & James Renwick Brevoort, 72, Hudson River Mus.
Positions: Display designer, Seventeen Mag, 11 yrs; store designer & displayer, Gimbels, 68-69; mus artist & designer, Hudson River Mus, 68-69.
Awards: First prize for watercolor, Fresno Art Ctr, 60.
Bibliography: Beeching (auth), Theatrical displays and display techniques (film), Scope Prod, 69.
Memberships: Gallery 84; Yonkers Art Asn.
Dealer: Gallery 84, 1046 Madison Ave, New York, NY 10016.
Mailing Address: 65 W 92nd St, New York, NY 10025.

WERNER, NAT
Sculptor
b New York, N Y, Dec 8, 08.
Study & Training: City Col New York, BA; Columbia Univ, MA; Art Stud League New York, with Robert Lourent.
Work in Public Collections: Whitney Mus Am Art, New York; Lyman Allen Mus, Lew London, Conn; Mt Sinai Hosp, Detroit; Tel Aviv Mus, Israel; Howard Univ Gallery, Washington, D C.
Commissions: Bas-relief, Fowler Post Off, Ind; sculptures, New York World's Fair, 39 & Artus Res, New York, bronze, New York Eng Soc & wood, James Madison High Sch, New York.
Exhibitions: Whitney Mus Am Art Ann, 36-63; Pa Acad Fine Arts, 39-56; Brussels Int, 46; Fairmount Int, Philadelphia, 50; Art U S A, New York, 58-59.
Teaching: Instr sculpture, Stuyvesant Adult Ctr, 60-
Awards: First hon mentions, New York World's Fair, 39 & New Orleans Sculpture, 42; first prize, Guildhall Easthampton, 53-54.
Memberships: Sculptors Guild (pres, 63-65).
Dealer: ACA Galleries, 25 E 73rd St, New York, NY 10021.
Mailing Address: 225 E 21st St, New York, NY 10010.

WERTH, KURT
Illustrator
Preferred Media: Wood, Inks.
b Leipzig, Ger; U S citizen.
Study & Training: State Acad Graphic Arts, Leipzig, with Walter Tiemann, grad.
Work in Public Collections: Mus Fine Arts, Leipzig.
Commissions: Murals for canteens in many factories in Ger, 30-34.
Publications: Illusr, Shakespeare: Trollus & Cressipa, 25, The merry miller, 52 & One mitten Lewis, 55; auth & illusr, The monkey, the lion, & the snake, 67 & Lazy Jack, 70.
Mailing Address: 645 W 239th St, Bronx, NY 10463.

WERTHEIM, MRS MAURICE
Collector
Memberships: Art Collectors Club.
Mailing Address: 43 E 70th St, New York, NY 10021.

WESCHLER, ANITA
Sculptor, Painter
Preferred Media: Stone, Aluminum, Plastic, Wood, Terra-cotta, Bronze.
b New York, N Y.
Study & Training: Parsons Sch Design, grad; Nat Acad Design; Pa Acad Fine Arts, with Albert Laessle; Art Stud League New York, with William Zorach; Columbia Univ; Barnes Found.
Work in Public Collections: Whitney Mus Am Art; Norfolk Mus Arts & Sci; Mus Amherst; Alliance Repub Turkey; Mus Tel-Aviv; plus other pub & pvt collections.
Commissions: Sculpture, U S Treas Dept.
Exhibitions: (Group) Whitney Mus Am Art; Metrop Mus Art; Philadelphia Mus Art; Mus Mod Art; plus others; also 25 one-man shows nationwide since 64.
Positions: Del to U S Comt Int Asn Art; del to Fine Arts Fedn New York; del to Conf Am Artists.
Awards: Prizes, Corcoran Gallery Art & San Francisco Mus Art; Audubon Artists Medal of Honor.
Memberships: Archit League; Fedn Mod Painters & Sculptors; Nat Asn Women Artists (juror); Sculptor's Guild (mem exec bd); Artist-Craftsmen New York (juror).
Publications: Auth, Nightshade, Colony Press; auth, A sculptor's summary.
Mailing Address: 136 Waverly Pl, New York, NY 10014.

WESSELMANN, TOM
Painter
Preferred Media: Oils.
b Cincinnati, Ohio, Feb 23, 31.
Study & Training: Hiram Col; Univ Cincinnati, BA; Art Acad Cincinnati; Cooper Union Art Sch, cert.
Work in Public Collections: Albright-Knox Art Gallery, Buffalo, N Y; Mus Mod Art & Whitney Mus Am Art, New York, N Y; Suermondt Mus, Aachen, Ger; Atkins Mus Fine Arts, Kansas City, Mo; plus others.
Exhibitions: One-man shows, Tanager Gallery, 61, Green Gallery, 62, 64 & 65 & Sidney Janis Gallery, New York, 66, 68, 70 & 72; Mus Contemp Art, Chicago, Ill, 69; De Cordova Mus, Lincoln, Mass, 69; plus many other group & one-man shows.
Dealer: Sidney Janis Gallery, 6 W 57th St, New York, NY 10019.
Mailing Address: 60 E 12th St, New York, NY 10003.

WESSELS, GLENN ANTHONY
Painter, Educator
Preferred Media: Oils, Acrylics.
b Capetown, S Africa, Dec 15, 95.
Study & Training: Univ Calif, AB(psychol), 19; Calif Col Arts & Crafts, BFA, 26; Hofman Schule Bildende Kunst, Munich, 28-30; Univ Calif, Berkeley, MA(art), 32; also with Andre Lhote & Karl Hofer.
Work in Public Collections: San Francisco Mus Art, Calif; Oakland Art Mus, Calif; Univ Calif Art Mus; Seattle Mus Art, Wash; Vancouver Mus Art, B C.
Exhibitions: Santa Barbara Mus, Calif, 46; San Francisco Art Asn Exhibs, 50-68; Oakland Art Mus Exhibs, 50-68; Chrysler Mus, Provincetown; Univ Ill.
Teaching: Prof compos materials art, Calif Col Arts & Crafts, 31-42; prof drawing, painting & art philos, Univ Calif, Berkeley, 46-63, emer prof, 63-67.
Positions: Art critic, San Francisco Fortnightly, 31-33; art ed, San Francisco Argonaut, 34-40; supvr, Works Proj Admin, 35-39; regional gen chmn, Nat Art Wk, 41.
Awards: Grant, 65 & citation, 71, Univ Calif, Berkeley; first award for painting, San Francisco Mus Ann, San Francisco Art Asn, 55.
Memberships: San Francisco Art Inst (bd trustees, 63-72); Friends of Photography, Carmel (bd trustees, 68-72); Oakland Mus (bd trustees).
Mailing Address: 2873 Hilltop Dr, Placerville, CA 95667.

WEST, CLIFFORD BATEMAN
Painter, Film Maker
Preferred Media: Oils.
b Cleveland, Ohio, July 4, 16.
Study & Training: Cleveland Sch Art; Adams State Teachers Col, BA; Colorado Springs Fine Arts Ctr; Cranbrook Acad Art, MA; also with Boardman Robinson, Arnold Blanch & others.
Work in Public Collections: Massillon Mus Art; Iowa State Teacher's Col; Cranbrook Mus Art.
Commissions: Murals, Rackham Mem Bldg, Detroit, Mich, Casa Contenta Hotel, Guatemala, Vet Mem Bldg, Detroit, Colorado State Hist Soc, Denver, Alamosa Nat Bank, Colo & City Bank, Detroit.
Exhibitions: Int Watercolor Exhib, Chicago, Ill, 40; Pa Acad Fine Arts, Philadelphia, 47; Nat Acad Design, New York, N Y, 48; Premier of Eduard Munch Films, Guggenheim Mus, New York, 68; Premier of Nesch Films, Detroit Mus Art, 72.
Teaching: Head dept art, Kingswood Sch, 40-54; instr drawing anat, Cranbrook Acad Art, 40-54.
Positions: Co-founder & pres, Ossabow Island Proj, 61-
Awards: Prix de Rome, Alumni prize, 39; cine golden eagle award for film Harry Bertoia's Sculpture, 69; gold medal, Mich Acad Arts, Sci & Lit, 69.
Mailing Address: 225 Lone Pine Rd, Bloomfield Hills, MI 48013.

WEST, LOWREN
Painter, Illustrator
b New York, N Y, Feb 28, 23.
Study & Training: Pratt Inst Art Sch; Hans Hofmann Sch Fine Arts; Columbia Univ.
Commissions: Graphic designs for Gen Elec, Westinghouse & Life Mag.
Exhibitions: Nat Arts Club, 60 & 62; Mus Mod Art, New York, 60; Riverside Mus, 64; Art in America Exhibition, 67-69; Monogram Art Gallery, New York, 67; plus others.
Awards: Nat Arts Club, 62.
Publications: Contribr illus for New Yorker Mag, Fortune Mag & Graphis.
Dealer: Stable Gallery, 7610 E McDonald Dr, Scottsdale, AZ 85253.
Mailing Address: 300 Riverside Dr, New York, NY 10025.

WEST, W RICHARD (DICK)
Educator, Painter
b Darlington, Okla, Sept 8, 12.
Study & Training: Haskell Inst; Bacone Col; Univ Okla, BFA, MFA; Univ Redlands; also with Olaf Nordmark.
Work in Public Collections: Smithsonian Inst, Washington, D C; Joslyn Mem Art Mus, Omaha, Nebr; Philbrook Art Ctr, Tulsa, Okla; Gilcrease Mus, Tulsa; Bacone Col, Okla.
Commissions: Post off mural, Okemah, Okla, 41; bas-relief panels, Univ Redlands, Calif, 60's; Crucifixion (sculpture), N Am Indian Ctr, Chicago, Ill, 60's.
Exhibitions: Esquire Theater Art Gallery, Chicago, 56; Philbrook Art Ctr, Tulsa, 58; Bacone Col, Okla, 67; Civic Ctr, Muskogee, Okla, 69; Kansas City Mus Hist & Sci, 71.
Teaching: Dir oil painting & perspective, Bacone Col, 47-70; dir Indian art & sculpture, Haskell Indian Jr Col, 70-
Awards: Citation of Indian arts & crafts, 60; first place for sculpture, Philbrook Art Ctr Nat Show, 60; Waite Phillips Award, 64.
Bibliography: Ed Shaw (auth), Another face of Jesus (filmstrip of life & works), produced by Am Baptist Films, 69; Charles Waugaman (auth), Cheyenne artist, Friendship Press, 70; Dorothy Elliot (auth), Dick West artist, Kansas, 71.
Research: Indian art.
Art Interests: Religious paintings & woodcarvings.
Mailing Address: 2543 Cedarwood, Lawrence, KS 66044.

WESTERMANN, HORACE CLIFFORD
Sculptor
Preferred Media: Woods, Metals.
b Los Angeles, Calif, Dec 11, 22.
Study & Training: Art Inst Chicago; also with Paul Weighardt.
Work in Public Collections: Whitney Mus Am Art, New York, N Y; Art Inst Chicago, Ill; Los Angeles Co Mus Art.
Exhibitions: Surrealist Art, Mus Mod Art, New York, 60; Retrospective, Los Angeles Co Mus Art, 68 & Mus Contemp Art, Chicago, 69; Documenta, Ger, 70 & 72.
Awards: Nat Arts Coun, 67.
Mailing Address: Box 28, Brookfield Center, CT 06805.

WESTERMEIR, CLIFFORD PETER
Painter, Educator
b Buffalo, N Y, Mar 4, 10.
Study & Training: Buffalo Sch Fine Arts; Pratt Inst Art Sch; New York Sch Fine & Appl Arts; Univ Buffalo, BS; Univ Colo, PhD.
Work in Public Collections: Albright-Knox Art Gallery; Nat Cowboy Hall of Fame & Western Heritage, Oklahoma City, Okla.
Commissions: Many pvt portrait commissions.
Exhibitions: Albright-Knox Art Gallery; Am Watercolor Soc; Syracuse Mus Fine Art; Boulder, Colo; one-man show, Tucson, Ariz; plus other group & one-man shows.
Teaching: Instr art, Buffalo Sch Fine Art, 35-44; instr art, Univ Buffalo, 35-44; instr hist, Univ Colo, 44-46; asst prof hist, Saint Louis Univ & Maryville Col, 46-52; prof hist, Univ Ark, Fayetteville, 52-64; guest lectr, Univ Tex, 54; guest lectr, Univ Colo, Boulder, 57 & 59, prof hist, 64-
Awards: The Patteran, 39 & 40.
Publications: Auth, Man, beast & dust: the story of rodeo, 47; auth & illusr, Trailing the cowboy, 55 & Who rush to glory, 58; auth, Colorado's first portrait, Univ N Mex Press, 70; contribr, Britannica Jr & Encycl Britannica.
Mailing Address: 1703 Columbine Ave, Boulder, CO 80302.

WETHEY, HAROLD EDWIN
Art Historian
b Port Byron, N Y, Apr 10, 02.
Study & Training: Cornell Univ, AB; Harvard Univ, MA, PhD.
Teaching: From instr to asst prof art hist, Bryn Mawr Col, 34-38; asst prof art hist, Wash Univ, 38-40; assoc prof art hist, Univ Mich, Ann Arbor, 40-46; prof art hist, 46-; vis prof art, Univ Tucaman, Arg, 43; U S State Dept vis prof art, Univ Mex, summer 60.
Positions: Contribr ed, Handbk of Latin-Am Studies, 46-59; mem ed staff, Art Bull, 65-71.
Awards: Fel, Am Coun Learned Soc, 36 & 63-64; Russel lectureship, 64-65 & Guggenheim fel, 71-72, Univ Mich, Ann Arbor; plus others.
Memberships: Col Art Asn Am; Hispanic Soc Am; Soc Archit Historians; Acad de S Fernando; Soc Peruana Historia; plus others.
Art Interests: Spanish & Latin American art; Italian Renaissance & Baroque art.
Publications: Auth, Alonso Cano, painter, sculptor and architect, 55, El Greco and his school, 62, Titian, the religious paintings, 69 & Titian, Vol II, The Portraits, 71; plus many others including contribr to leading encyclopedias & mags.
Mailing Address: 1510 Cambridge Rd, Ann Arbor, MI 48104.

WEXLER, GEORGE
Painter, Educator
Preferred Media: Oils.
b Brooklyn, N Y, Jan 18, 25.
Study & Training: Cooper Union Sch Art; New York Univ, BA; Mich State Univ, MA.
Work in Public Collections: Norfolk Mus Art, Va; Walter P Chrysler Collection, New York, N Y; State Univ N Y Albany; Schenectady Mus Art, N Y; New York Univ Collection.
Commissions: Murals, Detroit, Mich, 55 & Milwaukee, Wis, 56, Victor Gruen Assocs.
Exhibitions: Landscape in America, New Sch Soc Res, 63; one-man shows, Angeleski Gallery, New York, N Y, 61, Albany Inst Art, N Y, 66, First St Gallery, New York, 70 & Schenectady Mus Art, N Y, 72.
Teaching: Asst prof design, Mich State Univ, 50-57; prof painting, State Univ N Y Col New Paltz, 57-
Awards: Hon mention, Michiana, South Bend, Ind, 54; hon mention, Ball State Ann Drawing Exhib, Ind, 62; painting prize, Mid-Hudson Ann, Albany Inst Art, 63-65.
Bibliography: Gussow (auth), A sense of place, Sat Rev, 72.
Publications: Auth, bk rev, In: J Aesthetic Educ, 70.
Dealer: First Street Gallery, 118 Prince St, New York, NY 10012.
Mailing Address: 359 Springtown Rd, New Paltz, NY 12561.

WEYHE, MRS ERHARD
Art Dealer
Specialty of Gallery: Art books and art.
Mailing Address: 794 Lexington Ave, New York, NY 10021.

WHEELER, CLEORA CLARK
Designer, Collector
b Austin, Minn.
Study & Training: Univ Minn, BA & cert eng drafting & advan eng drafting, 43; New York Sch Fine & Appl Art.
Work in Public Collections: Brass wall plaque, libr Kappa Kappa Gamma House, Univ Minn, Minneapolis; complete collection of bookplates in libr at Brown Univ, Columbia Univ, Harvard Univ & New York Pub Libr; plus other univ & pub libr.
Exhibitions: Am Bookplate Soc Ann, 16-25; Bookplate Asn Int, 26-36; New York Times Bk Fair, 37; Nat Collection Fine Arts, Smithsonian Inst, Washington, D C, 46-66; Bookplates, 14th Ann Int Cong of Int Ex Libris Soc, Elsinore, Denmark, 72.
Awards: First award in design, Minn State Soc, 13 & Nat League Am Pen Women, 50; Silver chalice achievement award, Kappa Kappa Gamma, 52.
Memberships: Nat League Am Pen Women (pres Minn Br, 40-42, state pres, 42-44, nat chmn design, 44-46, nat chmn heraldic art, 54-56 & nat chmn illum & inscriptions, 64-66).
Collection: Bookplates.
Publications: Auth, On behalf of accuracy, American Society of Bookplate Collectors and Designers yearbook, 33; auth, ser of six articles on bookplates, In: Minn Med, 7-12/57, reprinted in Univ Minn Bull, 7/72.
Mailing Address: 1376 Summit Ave, Saint Paul, MN 55105.

WHEELER, MONROE
Art Administrator
b Evanston, Ill, Feb 13, 00.
Study & Training: France, Eng & Ger.
Collections Arranged: Dir of following Mus Mod Art Exhibs: Modern Bookbinding by Professor Ignatz Wiemeler, 35, Modern Painters & Sculptors as Illustrators, 36, Prints of Georges Rouault, 38, Britain at War, 41, 20th Century Portraits, 42, Airways to Peace, 43, Modern Drawings, 44, Chaim Soutine, 50, Georges Rouault Retrospective, 53, Textiles & Ornaments of India, 56, The Last Works of Henri Matisse, 61 & Bonnard & His Environment, 64.
Positions: Dir Am sect, Salon Int de Livre, Paris, France, 32; chmn libr comt, Mus Mod Art, New York, N Y, 35, mem adv comt, 37, mem dir, 38, dir publs, 39-, dir exhibs, 40-, trustee, 45-66, hon trustee for life, 66-, chmn comn drawings & prints, 67-, trustee, Ben Sahn Found, 69-
Awards: Chevalier, Fr Legion of Hon, 51.
Memberships: Grolier Club (trustee); New York Genealogical & Biog Soc (v pres & trustee); Int Graphic Arts Soc (pres & trustee); life mem Fr Inst U S; Am Inst Graphic Arts (former trustee).
Publications: Auth or co-auth various publs for Mus Mod Art.
Mailing Address: Hay-meadows, Rosemont, NJ 08556.

WHEELER, ORSON SHOREY
Sculptor, Lecturer
b Barnston, P Q, Sept 17, 02.
Study & Training: Bishop's Univ, BA; RCA classes (honors), Montreal; Cooper Union; Nat Inst Archit Educ; Nat Acad Design; also study in Europe.
Commissions: Bust, Can Pac Railways; bust, Court House, Montreal, P Q; Supreme Court, Ottawa; Robinson Residence for Retired Teachers, Cowansville, P Q; sculpture, Dow Chem Can, Ltd; plus many others including many in pvt collections in U S A & Can.
Exhibitions: Nat Acad Design, New York, N Y, 40; Smith Col, 45; Ottawa, 50; Quebec City, P Q, 51 & 60; Montreal Mus Fine Arts, 52-57; plus many others.
Teaching: Lectr fine arts, Sir George William Univ, 31-; seasonal lectr archit, McGill Univ, 49-
Positions: Chmn permanent collection, Can Handicrafts Guild, 44-64, co-chmn, 64-
Awards: Dominican Govt Centennial Medal, 67.
Bibliography: Quebec Arts '58, film produced by CBC, Madones et abstractions (fr version), shown at Brussels World's Fair, 58.
Memberships: Sculpture Soc Can (treas, 52-67).
Art Interests: Made over 150 scale models of world famous buildings to illustrate the history of architecture, models exhibited at Montreal Mus Fine Arts, 55.
Mailing Address: 1435 Drummond St, Montreal, P Q, Can.

WHEELER, ROBERT G
Art Administrator
b Kinderhook, N Y, Sept 20, 17.
Study & Training: Syracuse Univ; Columbia Univ; N Y State Col Teachers.
Teaching: Instr Am art hist & art appreciation, Russell Sage Col, Albany Div, 50-56.

Positions: Asst dir, Albany Inst Hist & Art, 47-49, dir, 49-56; dir res & publ, Sleepy Hollow Restorations, 56-68; dir crafts, Henry Ford Mus, 68-69, v pres, 69-71, dir mus & dir res & interpretation, 71-
Memberships: Am Asn Mus (pres northeastern conf, 53-54 & 67-68); Am Fedn Arts.
Art Interests: Lectr on seventeenth, eighteenth & nineteenth century arts & crafts of the Hudson Valley.
Publications: Contribr, Antiques Mag, Am Collector, New York Hist Soc Bull, New York Hist, New York Sun & New York World-Tel & Sun.
Mailing Address: 14157 Dolphin, Detroit, MI 48223.

WHINSTON, CHARLOTTE
Painter, Sculptor
b New York, N Y.
Study & Training: New York Sch Fine & Appl Arts, scholar; Nat Acad Design, with George Maynard & sculpture with Fredrick Roth; Art Stud League New York, with George Luks.
Work in Public Collections: Smith Col, Northampton, Mass; Univ Wis-La Crosse; Riverside Mus Collection, Rose Art Mus, Brandeis Univ; Seton Hall Univ, N J; Norfolk Mus, Va.
Commissions: Urban Bldg (exterior mural, porcelain enamel on steel), comn by Henry Goelet, 56.
Exhibitions: New York Soc Women Artists, Riverside Mus Ann, 56, 58 & 62; Asn Greek Women Artists & U S Info Serv, Am Gallery, Athens, Greece, 57; Munic Mus Uneo Park Tokyo, 60; Audubon Artists Ann & Allied Artists Am Ann, Nat Acad Design Galleries, 60-72; Arg Exhib, Mus Nac Artes, Buenos Aires & Rio de Janeiro, 64.
Positions: Dir & chmn nominations, New York Soc Women Artists, 69-71.
Awards: First prize for watercolor, Indiana Univ Pa, 49; first grand prize for watercolor & silver medal, Seton Hall Univ, 58; bronze medal for oil, Nat Asn Women Artists, 69; plus others.
Bibliography: Margaret Harold(auth), Prize winning art, Allied Publ, 68 & 69.
Memberships: Audubon Artists (treas, 63-64 & 71-73); Allied Artists Am Nat Asn Women Artists (v pres, pres & adv); Am Soc Contemp Artists; Nat Soc Painters Casein & Acrylic (chmn traveling exhibs, 60-61 & dir & chmn awards, 71-72).
Publications: Contribr, Today's Art, summer 60; co-auth, article, In: Art Am, 61.
Mailing Address: 2 Tudor City Pl, New York, NY 10017.

WHIPPLE, BARBARA (MRS GRANT HEILMAN)
Printmaker, Writer
b San Francisco, Calif.
Study & Training: Swarthmore Col, BA, 43; Rochester Inst Technol, BS, 56; Tyler Sch, Temple Univ, MFA, 61.
Work in Public Collections: Newark Pub Libr, N J; Elizabethtown Col, Pa; Lancaster Country Day Sch, Pa.
Commissions: Woodcut prints, Jr League Lancaster, Pa.
Exhibitions: One-man show, Swarthmore Col, Pa, 64; two & three-man shows, Oak Ridge Art Ctr, Tenn, 66 & Asheville Art Mus, 67; one-man shows, Elizabethtown Col, Pa, 71 & Lebanon Valley Col, Annville, Pa, 73.
Teaching: Instr art, Mem Art Gallery, Univ Rochester, 55-58; instr art, Rochester Sch Deaf, 56-58; assoc prof art, Geneseo State Teachers Col, 58-59.
Awards: Best of show & purchase prize, Lib Relig Art Exhib, Denver, Colo, 67; first prize, Lancaster Open Award, Pa, 68; juror's award, Reading Regional, Pa, 69.
Bibliography: Barbara Whipple, printmaker, La Rev Mod, 1/66.
Memberships: Philadelphia Watercolor Club; Philadelphia Art Alliance; Philadelphia Print Club; Artists Equity Asn; Swarthmore Col Bd Mgrs.
Publications: Auth, Art for the child from 6 to 9, Instr, 56; auth, Another key: art, Volta Rev, 58; auth, Luigi Rist: printmaker, 71, William E Sharer, painter, 73 & Ford Ruthling, master of the ball point pen, 73, Am Artist.
Mailing Address: Box 328, Lititz, PA 17543.

WHIPPLE, ENEZ MARY
Art Administrator
b Syracuse, N Y.
Study & Training: Syracuse Univ, BS(jour).
Teaching: Adj prof humanities, Southampton Col, L I Univ, 71.
Positions: Exec dir, Guild Hall E Hampton, 48-
Memberships: Am Fedn Arts; Am Asn Mus; N Y State Asn Mus.
Mailing Address: Guild Hall of East Hampton, Box GGGG, 158 Main St, East Hampton, NY 11937

WHITAKER, FREDERIC
Painter, Writer
Preferred Media: Watercolors.
b Providence, R I, Jan 9, 91.
Study & Training: R I Sch Design, 07-11.

Work in Public Collections: Metrop Mus Art, New York, N Y; Boston Mus Fine Arts, Mass; Hispanic Mus, New York; Frye Mus, Seattle, Wash; Salt Lake City Art Mus, Utah.
Exhibitions: Am Watercolor Soc, New York, 38-72; Nat Acad Design, New York, 45-72; Royal Watercolor Soc, London, 62; Watercolor U S A Ann, Springfield, Mo, 62-72; Metrop Mus Art Centennial Am Watercolor Soc, 66.
Teaching: Pvt instr watercolors, 58-64.
Positions: Designer, Gorham Co, Providence, 16-21; designer, Tiffany Co, New York, 22.
Awards: Silver medal, Am Watercolor Soc, 49; best in show, Am Artists Prof League Grand Nat, 69; best in show for all media, Springville Art Asn, Utah, 70.
Bibliography: Norman Kent (auth), Watercolor methods, 55 & Susan Meyer (auth), Twenty-four watercolorists, 72, Watson-Guptill; Janice Lovoos (auth), Frederic Whitaker, Northland, 72.
Memberships: Am Watercolor Soc (pres, 49-56); Nat Acad Design (v pres, 56-57); fel Royal Soc Arts, London; Audubon Artists (pres, 43-46); Int Asn Plastic Arts (v pres, 54-61).
Publications: Auth, 85 monographs, In: Am Artist, 56-72; auth, Whitaker on watercolor, 63 & Guide to painting better pictures, 65, Van Nostrand Reinhold.
Dealer: Grand Central Art Galleries, 40 Vanderbilt Ave, New York, NY 10017.
Mailing Address: 6453 El Camino Del Teatro, La Jolla, CA 92037.

WHITAKER, IRWIN A
Educator, Craftsman
Preferred Media: Ceramics, Enamels, Plastics.
b Wirt, Okla, Oct 19, 19.
Study & Training: San Jose State Col, BA; Claremont Col, MFA, with Richard Pettersen.
Work in Public Collections: Detroit Art Inst.
Exhibitions: Many nat & regional exhibs.
Teaching: Instr ceramics, Southern Ore Col, 49-50; prof ceramics, Mich State Univ, 50-
Awards: First award for ceramics, Calif State Fair, 49; purchase award for ceramics, Univ Nebr, 59; purchase award for enamel, Detroit Inst Art, 62.
Memberships: Midwest Designer-Craftsmen Coun (mem bd, 58-60).
Research: Contemporary Mexican pottery.
Publications: Auth, Crafts and craftsmen, 67.
Mailing Address: 4721 Ottawa Dr, Okemos, MI 48864.

WHITCOMB, JON
Painter, Illustrator
b Weatherford, Okla, June 9, 06.
Study & Training: Ohio Wesleyan Univ, 23-27; Ohio State Univ, AB, 28.
Teaching: Mem faculty portrait painting, Famous Artists Sch, at present.
Positions: Poster artist, RKO Theatres, Chicago, Ill, 28-29; art advert, Cleveland, Ohio, 30-34; v pres, Charles E Cooper, Inc, Advert Art, New York, N Y, 35-64.
Art Interests: Portrait painting.
Publications: Illusr & auth, articles, In: Cosmopolitan; illusr, Ladies Home J, McCall's & Redbook.
Mailing Address: 8 Circle Rd, Darien, CT 06820.

WHITE, BRUCE HILDING
Sculptor
Preferred Media: Aluminum, Steel.
b Bay Shore, N Y, July 11, 33.
Study & Training: Univ Md, BA; Columbia Univ, MA & PhD.
Work in Public Collections: Ind Mus Arts & Sci, Evansville; Western Ill Univ; Columbia Univ; Northern Ill Univ.
Commissions: Stainless steel sculpture, Rogers Libr & Mus Art, Laurel, Miss.
Exhibitions: Chicago & Vicinity Artists 72nd & 73rd Ann, Art Inst Chicago, 69 & 71; Sculpture Nat, Purdue Univ, Ind, 70; Large Sculpture 4th Ann, Blossom Kent Festival, Ohio, 71; 12th Midwest Biennial, Joslyn Art Mus, Omaha, Nebr, 72.
Teaching: Prof sculpture & area chmn sculpture & crafts, art dept, Northern Ill Univ, 68-
Mailing Address: c/o Fairweather Hardin Gallery, 101 E Ontario St, Chicago, IL 60611.

WHITE, CHARLES WILBERT
Painter, Educator
Preferred Media: Inks, Charcoals, Oils.
b Chicago, Ill, Apr 2, 18.
Study & Training: Art Inst Chicago; Art Stud League New York; Taller Grafica Mex; hon DFA, Columbia Col (Ill).
Work in Public Collections: Metrop Mus Art, New York, N Y; Whitney Mus Am Art, New York; Los Angeles Co Mus Art, Calif; Dresden Mus Art, Ger; Govt of Ghana.

Commissions: Mural, Assoc Negro Press, 40; mural, Chicago Pub Libr, Ill, 43; mural, Hampton Inst, Va, 43.
Exhibitions: Howard Univ, Washington, D C, 67; Am Drawings of the Sixties, New Sch Art Ctr, New York, 69; Five Famous Black Artists, Mus Fine Arts, Boston, Mass, 70; Krannert Art Mus, Champaign, Ill, 71; Three Graphic Artists, Los Angeles Co Mus Art, 71.
Teaching: Instr art, Southside Art Ctr, Chicago, 39-40; artist-in-residence, Howard Univ, 45; instr art, Workshop Sch Art, 50-53; prof drawing, Otis Art Inst, 65-.
Awards: Julius Rosenwald fel, 42 & 43; Childe Hassam Award, Am Acad Art, 65.
Bibliography: A Locke (auth), The Negro in art, 40; B Horowitz (auth), Images of dignity, drawings of Charles White, Ward Ritchie, 67; Louis Robinson (auth), Charles White, Ebony Mag, 7/67.
Memberships: Black Acad Arts & Lett (exec bd mem, 69-); assoc Nat Acad Design; Nat Conf Artists; Otis Art Assocs.
Publications: Illusr, Four took freedom, 67 & illusr, Black history, 68, Doubleday.
Mailing Address: c/o Heritage Gallery, 718 N La Cienega Blvd, Los Angeles, CA 90069.

WHITE, DORIS A
    Painter
b Eau Claire, Wis.
Study & Training: Art Inst Chicago.
Exhibitions: Butler Inst Am Art, Youngstown, Ohio; Am Watercolor Soc, New York, N Y; Art Alliance, Philadelphia, Pa; Inst Arte Mex; Ill Mus, Springfield; plus many others.
Awards: Grand Award, Am Watercolor Soc; Ranger Fund Purchase Award, Nat Acad Design & RCA Victor Purchase Award, Lowe Gallery; Assoc Mem Award, Allied Artists Am; plus others.
Memberships: Nat Acad Design; Calif Watercolor Soc; Am Watercolor Soc; Philadelphia Watercolor Club; Wis Watercolor Soc.
Mailing Address: Rte 1, Jackson, WI 53037.

WHITE, IAN McKIBBIN
    Art Administrator, Designer
b Honolulu, Hawaii, May 10, 29.
Study & Training: Cate Sch; Harvard Col, BA(archit), 51; Harvard Univ Grad Sch Design, 51-52; Univ Calif, Los Angeles, 57-58.
Commissions: Designed, Frieda Shiff Warburg Sculpture Garden, Brooklyn Mus, New York, N Y, 66; designed, Peary-McMillan Arctic Mus, Bowdoin Col, Brunswick, Maine, 67.
Positions: Asst dir, Brooklyn Mus, New York, 64-67; dir, Calif Palace Legion of Hon, San Francisco, Calif, 68; dir museums, Calif Palace Legion of Hon & M H de Young Mem Mus, San Francisco, 70-
Awards: Silver medal for oil painting, Cate Sch, 47.
Memberships: U S Nat Comt Int Coun Mus; Am Asn Mus (adv coun, 64-); Am Asn Mus Dir (comt chmn, 69-); Am Fedn Arts (trustee, 71-).
Publications: Auth, articles, In: Curator, Vol 10, No 1 & San Francisco Examiner, 67.
Mailing Address: M H de Young Memorial Museum, California Palace of the Legion of Honor, Lincoln Park, San Francisco, CA 94131.

WHITE, LAWRENCE EUGENE
    Educator
b Abilene, Tex, Dec 2, 08.
Study & Training: Abilene Christian Col, BA; Univ South Calif, MA.
Teaching: Instr art, Abilene Christian Col, 32-36; instr art, Pepperdine Col, 39-44, prof art & chmn dept, Pepperdine Univ, 44-
Positions: Owner, Eugene White Ceramics Studios, 41-48.
Publications: Auth, Art for the child, 50.
Mailing Address: Dept of Art, Pepperdine University, 24255 Pacific Coast Hwy, Malibu, CA 90265.

WHITE, LEO
    Cartoonist
b Holliston, Mass, Apr 8, 18.
Study & Training: Sch Practical Art, Boston; Evans Sch Cartooning, Cleveland.
Positions: Sports & ed cartoonist, Patriot-Ledger, Quincy, Mass.
Publications: Auth & illusr, Hockey stars, Toronto Tel News Serv, TV starscramble, Columbia Features, New York, Little people's puzzle, United Features & Crosswords for kids, Fawcett.
Mailing Address: Patriot-Ledger, 13 Temple Pl, Quincy, MA 02169.

WHITE, NORMAN TRIPLETT
    Sculptor
Preferred Media: Electronics, Plastics.
b San Antonio, Tex, Jan 7, 38.
Study & Training: Harvard Col, with T Lux Feininger, 55-59, BA, 59.

Work in Public Collections: Nat Gallery Can, Ottawa.
Exhibitions: Some More Beginnings, Exp in Art & Technol Show, Brooklyn Mus, New York, N Y, 68; Exp in Art & Technol Show, High Mus Art, Atlanta, Ga, 69; The Canadian Electric Company, Carmen Lamanna Gallery, Toronto, Ont, 69; Norm White at the Electric Gallery, Electric Gallery, Toronto, 71; New Media Art, Can Nat Exhib, Art Gallery Ont, 71.
Awards: Can Coun bursaries, 69-71.
Art Interests: To mimic in as unarbitrary a way as possible the efficiency, flexibility and diversity of biological systems.
Dealer: The Electric Gallery, 272 Avenue Rd, Toronto, Ont, Can.
Mailing Address: 30 St Andrew's St, Toronto, Ont, Can.

WHITE, ROBERT (WINTHROP)
    Sculptor, Educator
Preferred Media: Bronze, Terra-Cotta, Stone, Wood, Tempera, Watercolors.
b New York, N Y, Sept 19, 21.
Study & Training: With Joseph Weisz & Hans Grad, Munich, 32-34; also with John Howard Benson, R I, 34-38; R I Sch Design, 38-42 & 46.
Work in Public Collections: Brooklyn Mus, N Y; R I Sch Design Mus, Providence; Springfield Mus, Mass.
Commissions: Life size bronze fountain, Mr & Mrs Amyas Ames, Martha's Vinyard, Mass, 57; bronze of St Anthony on Padua, St Anthony of Padua Sch, Northport, N Y, 59; A E Verrill Silver Medal, Peabody Mus Natural Hist, Yale Univ, 60; three wooden & metal figures, Mrs Hester Pickman, St Michael's Roman Cath Church, Bedford, Mass, 60-66; bronze relief portrait of Joseph Wilson, Xerox Corp, Stamford, Conn, 72.
Exhibitions: Pa Acad Ann, Philadelphia, 50; Int Exhib Religious Art, Stazione Marittima, Trieste, Italy, 58; The Continuing Tradition of Realism in American Art, Hirschl & Adler Galleries, New York, 62; Eight Americans, Amsterdam, Breda, Nymegen, Holland, 69; The Representational Spirit, Univ Art Gallery, Albany, N Y, 70.
Teaching: Instr life drawing, Parsons Sch Design, New York, 49-52; assoc prof life drawing, State Univ N Y, Stony Brook, 62-
Positions: Sculptor-in-residence, Am Acad in Rome, Italy, 69-70.
Awards: Am Acad in Rome fel, 52-55; Nat Acad Design Proctor Mem Prize, 62; Farfield Found grant, 69.
Publications: Illusr, The enchanted, Pantheon, 51 & The confessions of Nat Turner, Harper's Mag, 67.
Dealer: James Graham & Sons, 1014 Madison Ave, New York, NY 10021.
Mailing Address: Moriches Rd, Saint James, NY 11780.

WHITE, ROGER LEE
    Painter, Educator
Preferred Media: Oils, Watercolors.
b Shelby, Ohio, Nov 27, 25.
Study & Training: Miami Univ, BFA; Univ Denver, MA; Univ Colo; Univ Okla; also study with Mark Rothke, Jimmie Ernst, Wendell H Black, Carl Morris & Richard Diebenkorn.
Work in Public Collections: Okla Art Ctr, Oklahoma City; Oklahoma City Univ; Miami Univ Sch Art, Oxford, Ohio; Univ Okla Mus Art, Norman; Oklahoma Printmakers Soc, Oklahoma City.
Exhibitions: Philbrook Art Ctr, Tulsa, Okla, 56-72; Okla Art Ctr, 56-72; Southwest Painters & Sculptors, Houston, Tex, 63; Nelson Gallery Art, Kansas City, Mo, 64; Okla Univ Mus Art, Norman, 70.
Teaching: Asst prof & chmn art dept, Col of the Ozarks, 57-58; spec instr studio courses, Okla Sci & Arts Found, 58-69; assoc prof studio courses & chmn art dept, Oklahoma City Univ, 58-69.
Positions: Dir, Silver Mountain Summer Art Sch, Empire, 59-72; dir, C & W Art Gallery, 65-68; dir, Silver Mountain Art Gallery, Georgetown, Colo, 69-72; producer, cinematographer & artist, Focal Point Assocs, Oklahoma City, 71-
Awards: Philbrook Mus Art, 59-60; 20th Ann Exhib Okla Artists, 60; Okla Printmakers 5th Nat Exhib Contemp Art, 63.
Bibliography: Betty Neukom (auth), Silver mountain, Silver Mountain Art Studios.
Memberships: Asn Okla Artists; Okla Printmakers Soc (exec bd).
Dealer: Silver Mountain Art Studio, Empire, CO 80438.
Mailing Address: 1424 Northwest 105, Oklahoma City, OK 73114.

WHITE, RUTH
    Art Dealer, Collector
b New York, N Y.
Study & Training: With Kurt Seligmann.
Positions: Owner, Ruth White Gallery.
Specialty of Gallery: Contemporary paintings, sculpture & graphics.
Collection: Kurt Seligmann; Ozenfant; paintings & sculpture by various young American artists.
Mailing Address: 401 E 74th St, New York, NY 10021.

WHITEHEAD, ALFRED
Painter, Educator
b Peterborough, Eng, July 10, 87.
Exhibitions: Montreal Spring Exhibs, 42-47; N S Soc Art, 48, 49 & 52-58; Royal Soc Brit Artists, London, Eng; one-man shows, Dalhousie Univ, 61 & Univ N B, 62; plus many other group & one-man shows.
Teaching: Dean music, Mount Allison Univ, 47-53, emer, 53-
Awards: DrMusic, McGill Univ; hon LLD, Mount Allison Univ; hon LLD, Queen's Univ.
Memberships: Fel Royal Col Organists; N S Soc Art; N S Artists.
Mailing Address: 52 Havelock St, Amherst, N S, Can.

WHITEHEAD, JAMES LOUIS
Art Administrator, Designer
b Demopolis, Ala, Feb 21, 13.
Study & Training: Birmingham-Southern Col, BA, 33; Vanderbilt Univ, MA, 34; Univ Pa, PhD, 42.
Positions: Dir, Staten Island Inst Arts & Sci, 51-61; asst to pres, Pratt Inst, 61-63; dir, Monmouth Mus, 63-67; cur, Franklin D Roosevelt Libr & Mus, 67-
Memberships: Am Asn Mus; Int Coun Mus.
Mailing Address: 50 Spackenkill Rd, Poughkeepsie, NY 12603.

WHITEHILL, FLORENCE (FITCH)
Painter
Preferred Media: Watercolors.
b Hillsdale, N Y.
Study & Training: Mass Col Art, Boston; Grand Cent Sch Art, New York, N Y.
Work in Public Collections: New York Hist Soc; East Hampton Soc, N Y; Tamassee Daughters Am Revolution Sch, S C.
Exhibitions: Allied Artists Am, Nat Acad Design Galleries, New York, 44-52; nine exhibs, Am Artists Prof League Grand Nat, New York, 47-72; Catharine Lorillard Wolfe Art Club Ann, 49-72; Acad Artists Asn, Fine Arts Mus, Springfield, Mass, 56-58, 64 & 67; Nat League Am Pen Women Biennial, Smithsonian Inst, Washington, D C, 58.
Awards: Best in show, 53 & best watercolor, 68, Catharine Lorillard Wolfe Art Club; award of honor for watercolor, Nat League Am Pen Women, 58.
Bibliography: Mary Barbara Reinmuth (auth), The pen woman, New York Br, Nat League Am Pen Women, winter 57-58.
Memberships: Catharine Lorillard Wolfe Art Club (pres, 53-56, corresp secy, 59-71); Am Artists Prof League; Acad Artists Asn; Nat League Am Pen Women (state art chmn, 64-66, N Y br treas, 72-73); life fel Royal Soc Arts, London.
Mailing Address: 7 Peter Cooper Rd, New York, NY 10010.

WHITEHILL, WALTER MUIR
Writer, Art Historian
b Cambridge, Mass, Sept 28, 05.
Study & Training: Harvard Univ, AB, 26, AM, 29, with A Kingsley Porter; Courtald Inst, Univ London, PhD, 34, with W G Constable & Alfred Clapham.
Teaching: Tutor fine arts, Harvard Univ, 26-28, Allston Burr Sr Tutor, Lowell House, 52-56, lectr hist, 56-57.
Positions: Asst dir, Peabody Mus Salem, 36-46; dir & librn, Boston Atheneum, 46-72, emer, 72-; trustee, Mus Fine Arts, Boston, 53-
Bibliography: L H Butterfield (ed), Walter Muir Whitehill, a record, Antheonsen Press, 58; complete bibliog, In: Bull Bibliog, F W Faxon Co, 73.
Memberships: Col Art Asn Am; hon mem Boston Soc Architects; hon mem Am Inst Architects.
Research: Spanish Romanesque architecture and manuscripts; architecture and topography of Boston; histories of various museums, libraries and institutions.
Publications: Auth, Spanish Romanesque architecture of the eleventh century, 41 & 68; auth, Salem East India Society and Peabody Museum of Salem, a sesquicentennial history, 49; auth, Boston Public Library, a centennial history, 56; auth, Boston, a topographical history, 59 & 68; auth, Museum of Fine Arts, Boston, a centennial history, 70.
Mailing Address: 44 Andover St, North Andover, MA 01845.

WHITESIDE, FORBES J
Educator
Study & Training: Univ Minn, BA, 41; Minn Sch Art, cert, 48; Univ Minn, MFA, 51.
Teaching: Asst prof art, Oberlin Col, 51-53, assoc prof, 54-55, prof, 56-
Mailing Address: Art Dept, Oberlin College, Oberlin, OH 44074.

WHITLEY, PHILIP WAFF
Sculptor
Preferred Media: Steel, Bronze.
b Rocky Mount, N C, Nov 24, 43.
Study & Training: Univ N C, Chapel Hill, BA & MFA.
Work in Public Collections: Mint Mus Art, Charlotte, N C; Greenville Co Mus Art, S C; Vardell Gallery, St Andrews Presby Col, Laurinburg, N C; Springs Mills, Lancaster, S C.
Exhibitions: Southern Sculpture: 68, Southern Asn Sculptors, Columbia, S C, 68; Ann Springs Mills Art Show, 69; Ann Piedmont Painting & Sculpture Exhib, Charlotte, N C, 70; two-man show, Greenville Co Mus Art, 71.
Teaching: Instr art, St Andrews Presby Col, 69-70; artist-in-residence, Greenville Co Mus Art Sch, 71-
Memberships: Guild S C Artists; Greenville Art Guild.
Mailing Address: 106 DuPont Dr, Greenville, SC 29607.

WHITLOCK, JOHN JOSEPH
Art Administrator, Educator
b South Bend, Ind, Jan 7, 35.
Study & Training: Ball State Univ, BS, 57, MA, 63; Ind Univ, EdD.
Work in Public Collections: Ball State Univ, Muncie, Ind; Hanover Col, Ind.
Exhibitions: Drawings & Small Sculpture Show, Ball State Univ, 57; one-man shows, Hanover Col, 63 & 67-69, Guild Gallery, Louisville, Ky, 64, Ind Univ Matrix Gallery, Bloomington, Ind, 69 & Franklin Col, Ind, 69.
Collections Arranged: The Senufo Door/A Study of its Iconography, 70; The Ghana Door/A Study of its Origin, 70; A Return to Humanism, 71.
Teaching: Instr educ, Hanover Col, 64-66, asst prof art, 66-69; teaching assoc art educ, Ind Univ, Bloomington, 69-70.
Positions: Dir & cur, Burpee Art Mus, Rockford, Ill, 70-72; dir, Brooks Mem Art Gallery, Memphis, Tenn.
Awards: Ball State Univ Fine Arts Purchase Award, 57.
Memberships: Am Asn Mus; Am Asn Univ Prof; Am Craftsmen's Coun; Nat Art Educ Asn.
Publications: Auth, Art in the small college, Midwest Art Educ Conf, Houston, Tex, 65; auth, The reproduction was better than the painting, Art Educ, 71.
Mailing Address: c/o Brooks Art Gallery, Overton Park, Memphis, TN 38112.

WHITLOW, TYREL EUGENE
Painter, Instructor
Preferred Media: Oils.
b Lynn, Ark, Aug 31, 40.
Study & Training: Ark State Univ, with Dan F Howard, BA; Inst Allende, San Miguel Allende, Mex, with James Pinto, MFA.
Work in Public Collections: Pulaski Savings & Loan Asn Relig Collection, Little Rock, Ark.
Exhibitions: 13th Ann Mid-South Exhib, Brooks Mem Art Gallery, Memphis, Tenn, 68; 5th Monroe Ann, Masur Mus Art, Monroe, La, 68; Contemp Southern Art Exhib, Memphis, 68; 10th Ann Delta Art Exhib, Ark Arts Ctr, Little Rock, 68; Print & Drawing Nat, Northern Ill Univ, 70; Ill State Fair, Springfield, Ill, 72.
Teaching: Inst art, Ill Valley Community Col, 68-
Awards: Top award, Contemp Southern Art Exhib, 68; purchase award, Ark Arts Festival, Pulaski Fed Loan & Savings, Little Rock, 68; watercolor award, Ark State Watercolor Exhib, 68.
Memberships: Am Fedn Arts; Rockford Art Asn; Lakeview Art Ctr; Nat Art Asn; Soc Art Historians.
Dealers: Burpee Museum of Art, 737 N Main St, Rockford, IL 61103; The Collection Gallery, Princeton, IL 61356.
Mailing Address: Illinois Valley Community College, R R 1, Oglesby, IL 61348.

WHITMORE, COBY
Painter, Illustrator
b Dayton, Ohio, June 11, 13.
Study & Training: Art Inst Chicago.
Work in Public Collections: The Pentagon, Washington, D C; U S Air Force Acad; New Britain Mus Am Art, Conn; Syracuse Univ, N Y.
Exhibitions: One-man show, Am Soc Illustrators, New York, N Y, 48.
Positions: Apprentice, Haddon Sundblom, Chicago, 32-35; artist with Carl Jensen, Cincinnati, 38-39; artist, Grauman Studios, Chicago, 39-43; artist, Charles E Cooper, Inc, New York, 42-
Awards: Cert distinctive merit, Art Dirs Club, Philadelphia, 54; award for merit, 33rd Ann Nat Exhib Advert & Ed Art & Design, 54; ann award for outdoor advert, Art Dirs Club, Chicago.
Memberships: Am Soc Illustrators; Mus Mod Art, New York.
Publications: Illusr cover page, Sat Eve Post, Good Housekeeping, Ladies Home J, McCalls & Cosmopolitan.
Mailing Address: 6 N Calibogue Cay Sea Pines, Hilton Head Island, SC 29928.

WHITMORE, LENORE K
Painter
Preferred Media: Mixed Media.
b Lemont, Pa, Aug 9, 20.
Study & Training: Pa State Univ, BS; Herron Sch Art; Provincetown
    Workshop; also with Garo Antresian, Will Barnet, Edward Ma-
    netta, Victor Candell & Leo Manso.
Work in Public Collections: John Calvert Collection; G D Sickert
    Collection; Indianapolis Found; DePauw Univ, Jerone Picker Col-
    lection.
Exhibitions: Hoosier Salon, 62, 63 & 67; Eastern Mich Nat Polymer
    Exhib, 68; Audubon Artists Exhibs; Int de Femme, 69; Painters
    & Sculptors Soc N J.
Teaching: Instr lit & painting, Ridgewood Sch Art, 69 & 70.
Positions: Pres, Indianapolis Art League Found, 59-64.
Awards: Motorola Nat Art Exhib Awards, 61 & 62; Mark A Brown
    Award in Composition, Hoosier Salon, 63; permanent pigments
    award, Painters & Sculptors Soc N J, 68.
Memberships: Nat Asn Women Artists; Pen and Brush Club; Mod
    Artists Guild; Indianapolis Art League; Ind Artists Club.
Mailing Address: Box 802, 203 Oak St, Ridgewood, NJ 07450.

WHITNEY, EDGAR ALBERT
Painter, Instructor
Preferred Media: Watercolors.
b New York, N Y, Apr 16, 91.
Study & Training: Cooper Union; Art Stud League New York; Nat
    Acad Design; Columbia Univ; Grand Cent Sch Art; also with Jay
    Comaway, Eliot O'Hara & Charles W Hawthorne.
Work in Public Collections: Farnsworth Mus, Rockland, Maine; Nat
    Acad Design, N Y; Art Club Saint Petersburg; Lake Worth Art
    Asn, Fla; Lawrence Rockefeller Collection.
Exhibitions: All Am Watercolor Soc Exhibs; All Nat Art League
    Shows; Nat Acad Design, 71 & 72.
Teaching: Instr watercolor & compos, Pratt Inst, 38-52; instr, N Y
    Bot Gardens; creator-instr, Whitney Watercolor Tours, 48-
Positions: Art dir, McCann Erickson, New York, N Y; contrib ed,
    Am Artist Mag.
Awards: Audubon Artists Award, 58; Nat Art League Awards, 52-58;
    Nat Acad Ranger Fund Purchase Prize, 69.
Bibliography: David Clark (auth), Watercolor holiday, Universal
    Films, Hollywood, Calif.
Memberships: Am Watercolor Soc (treas, 54-60); Philadelphia Wa-
    tercolor Club; life mem Art Stud League New York; hon life mem
    Southwestern Watercolor Socs; hon life mem La Watercolor Socs.
Publications: Auth, Watercolor: the hows and whys, 58 & Complete
    guide to watercolor, 65, Watson-Guptill; auth, Watercolor &
    casein articles, In: Grolier Encycl; plus others.
Dealers: Downtown Gallery, 532 Chartres, New Orleans, LA 70130;
    Schram Galleries, Fort Lauderdale, FL 33310.
Mailing Address: 1970 81st St, Jackson Heights, NY 11370.

WHITNEY, JOHN HAY
Art Administrator, Collector
b Ellsworth, Maine, Aug 17, 04.
Study & Training: Yale Univ, 22-26, hon MA; Oxford Univ, 26-27;
    Kenyon Col, hon LHD; Colgate Univ, hon LLD, 58; Brown Univ,
    hon LLD, 58; Exeter Univ, hon LLD, 59; Colby Col, hon LLD, 59;
    Columbia Univ, hon LLD, 59.
Positions: Bd dirs & v pres, Saratoga Performing Arts Ctr; trustee,
    Mus Mod Art, New York; trustee & v pres, Nat Gallery Art.
Awards: Benjamin Franklin Medal, Royal Col Art, Eng; Legion
    Merit; Chevalier, Fr Legion Honneur; plus others.
Mailing Address: 110 W 51st St, New York, NY 10020.

WHITSON (PETER WHITSON WARREN)
Drawer, Educator
b Concord, Mass, Sept 7, 42.
Study & Training: Univ N H, with Christopher Cook, BA, 63; Univ
    Iowa, with James Lechay & Hans Breder, MA & MFA, 67.
Work in Public Collections: Univ Iowa.
Exhibitions: All Iowa Show, Des Moines, 67; 13th Ann N Dak Art
    Show, Univ N Dak, 69, Hopper Show, Art Inst Chicago, 69; West-
    ern Dakota Junk Co Show, Eastern Mont Col, 69; plus many other
    free art shows in U S A & Can, 69-
Teaching: Asst drawing, Univ Iowa, 65-67; instr drawing, Eastern
    Mont Col, 67-69; asst prof drawing, 69-
Positions: Co-pres, Western Dakota Junk Co, Billings, Mont, 69-;
    pres, Lost Lady Mining Co, Billings, 70-; pres, Al's Ham-'N'-
    Egger & Body Shop, Billings, 71-
Publications: Auth, The Western Dakota Junk Co Junker Flyer, 70-
    72; auth, The Lost Lady Newsletter, 70-72; auth & contribr to
    many other free art publs, 69-72.
Mailing Address: The Western Dakota Junk Co, 315 S 34th St,
    Billings, MT 59101.

WHYTE, RAYMOND A
Painter
Preferred Media: Oils.
b Canmore, Alta, Aug 3, 23.
Study & Training: Art Stud League New York, with Edwin Dickinson;
    Venice, Paris & Madrid; Univ Toronto.
Work in Public Collections: Crocker Art Mus, Sacramento, Calif; De
    Beers Mus S Africa.
Commissions: Triptych, Richard Hamilton, 61; mural, Austral Oil
    Co, Houston, Tex, 65; triptych, Gerald B Kara, New York, N Y,
    68; memorabalia, oil, Bernard G Cantor, Beverly Hills, Calif,
    70; plus many other portrait & painting comns.
Exhibitions: Nat Acad, 49-; one-man shows, Galerie DeTours, San
    Francisco, 62-72, De Saisset Art Mus, Santa Clara, Calif, 67,
    Crocker Art Mus, Sacramento, Calif, 67 & E Kuhlik Gallery, New
    York, 72.
Bibliography: Jane Allison (auth), Painter in New York, Indianapolis
    Star, 3/9/61; Doug Scott (auth), Profiles in progress, San Fran-
    cisco Examr, 8/2/64; Kevin Sanders (auth), Contemporary sur-
    realists, ABC TV Art Rev, 2/3/72.
Dealer: Galerie DeTours, 559 Sutter St, San Francisco, CA 94102.
Mailing Address: 30 Fayson Lakes Rd, Kinnelon, NJ 07405.

WICK, PETER ARMS
Curator
b Cleveland, Ohio, May 17, 20.
Study & Training: Yale Univ, BA, BArch; New York Univ Inst Fine
    Arts; Fogg Art Mus, Harvard Univ, MA.
Positions: Asst cur, dept prints & drawings, Boston Mus Fine Arts,
    62-64; dir, Print Coun Am, 65; governor, Gore Place, Waltham-
    Watertown, Mass, 65; asst dir Fogg Art Mus, Harvard Univ, 66-
    67, asst cur Houghton Libr, 67-70, cur printing & graphic arts,
    70-
Art Interests: Prints & drawings.
Publications: Ed, Maurice Prendergast, watercolor sketchbook,
    1899, New York Graphic Soc, 60; auth, Jacques Villion: master of
    graphic art (exhib catalogue) & Honoré Daumier anniversary
    exhibition catalogue, 58, Boston Mus Fine Arts; auth, A summer
    sketchbook by David Levine, 63; co-auth, Arts of the French
    book, 1900-1965: illustrated books of the School of Paris, South-
    ern Methodist Univ Press, 67; auth, Toulouse-Lautrec, book
    covers and brochures, Harvard Univ Libr, 72.
Mailing Address: 35 W Cedar St, Boston, MA 02114.

WICKISER, RALPH LEWANDA
Art Administrator, Painter
Preferred Media: Oils.
b Greenup, Ill, Mar 20, 10.
Study & Training: Art Inst Chicago, 28-31; Eastern Ill Univ, BA, 34,
    hon PhD, 56; Vanderbilt & Peabody, Tiffany fel, 34-35, MA, 35,
    PhD, 38.
Work in Public Collections: Delgado Mus, New Orleans, La; Lehigh
    Univ, Bethlehem, Pa; La Art Comn, Baton Rouge; Mint Mus,
    Charlotte, N C; High Mus, Atlanta, Ga.
Exhibitions: Libr of Cong Ann Print Exhib, 48; George Vinet Trav-
    eling Exhib Relig Prints, 52-58; Whitney Mus Am Art Ann, 53;
    State Dept Exhib Color Lithographs travel through Europe, 54-
    56; New Realism, Suffolk Mus, Stony Brook, N Y, 71.
Teaching: From instr to prof painting & chmn dept, La State Univ,
    37-56; prof painting & dir div art educ, State Univ N Y Col New
    Paltz, 56-59; prof painting, Pratt Inst, 59-, chmn art educ dept,
    59-65.
Awards: Grant for one yr painting & study, 52.
Bibliography: The artist as a teacher, Col Art J, winter 51-52;
    Retrospective, East Ill State Univ, 68; New realism, Suffolk
    Mus, 71.
Memberships: Col Art Asn Am.
Research: Art theory & art education.
Art Interests: Figure & landscape painting.
Publications: Auth, An introduction to art activities, 47; contribr,
    The education of the artist, 51; contribr, A contemporary paint-
    er's attitude toward tradition, 55; auth, An introduction to art
    education, 57; co-auth, Higher education & the arts.
Mailing Address: Pratt Institute, Brooklyn, NY 11205.

WICKS, EUGENE CLAUDE
Painter, Instructor
Preferred Media: Oils.
b Coleharbor, N Dak, Oct 7, 31.
Study & Training: Univ Colo, BFA, MFA, 59.
Work in Public Collections: Art Inst Chicago, Ill; Philadelphia
    Print Club, Pa; Lakeview Art Ctr, Peoria, Ill; Decatur Art Ctr,
    Ill; Am Fedn Arts Overseas Collection.
Exhibitions: Libr of Cong, Washington, D C, 59; Brooklyn Mus
    Print Exhib, 60, 62 & 64; Northwest Printmakers Ann Exhib,
    60-68; Philadelphia Acad 185th Ann, 63; one-man shows, 61-70.

Teaching: Prof painting, Univ Ill, Urbana, 59-, assoc head dept art, 68-, asst head dept art, 61-67.
Positions: Vis artist, dept art, Univ Colo, summer 63.
Memberships: Nat Asn Schs Art.
Mailing Address: 2121 Gunn Dr, Champaign, IL 61820.

WIDSTROM, EDWARD FREDERICK
Sculptor
Preferred Media: Bronze, Metals.
b Wallingford, Conn, Nov 1, 03.
Study & Training: Detroit Sch Art; Art Stud League New York, N Y.
Work in Public Collections: New Haven Paint & Clay, Inc, Conn; Meriden Art & Crafts Asn, Conn; also in pvt collections.
Commissions: 33 Presidents of U S, Int Silver Co, Meriden, 39-70; portrait reliefs, St Stevens Sch, Bridgeport, Conn, 50, Munic Bldg, Meriden, 66 & Marionist Sch, Thompson, Conn, 68.
Exhibitions: Nat Acad Design, New York, 40-72; Nat Sculpture Soc, New York, 60-72; Hudson Valley Art Asn, White Plains, N Y, 60-72; Am Artists Prof League, New York, 69-71; Coun Am Artists, New York.
Awards: Dir Award, Coun Am Artists Soc, 64; Pres Award, Am Artists Prof League, 70; silver medal, Nat Sculpture Soc, 72.
Memberships: Nat Sculpture Soc; Am Artists Prof League; Hudson Valley Art Asn; Conn Acad Fine Arts; Meriden Arts & Crafts Asn.
Mailing Address: 21 Lydale Pl, Meriden, CT 06450.

WIEGAND, ROBERT
Painter
b Mineola, N Y, May 15, 34.
Study & Training: Albright Art Sch, Buffalo, N Y; State Univ N Y Buffalo, BS(art educ); New York Univ.
Work in Public Collections: Murals, New York Dept Parks, Astor Pl, N Y, Lever Bros Co, 53rd & Park Ave, Noble Found, Church & Reade Sts & Reliance Savings Bank, Jamaica Ave & Union Hall St.
Exhibitions: 10 Downtown, New York, 68; Brooklyn Mus, 68; Mus Mod Art, 69; Jewish Mus, 70; Newark Mus, 72; plus other group & one-man shows.
Teaching: Instr painting, Staten Island Acad; adj lectr, Lehman Col.
Positions: V pres, City Walls, Inc.
Awards: New York Bd Trade, 70.
Mailing Address: 16 Greene St, New York, NY 10013.

WIEGHARDT, PAUL
Painter, Educator
b Ger, Aug 26, 97.
Study & Training: Sch Fine Arts, Cologne, Ger; Bauhaus, Weimar, with Klee; Acad Fine Arts, Dresden, Ger.
Work in Public Collections: Albright-Knox Art Gallery, Buffalo, N Y; Barnes Found, Merion, Pa; Berkshire Mus, Pittsfield, Mass; Rosenwald Collection; Smith Col Mus Art, Northampton, Mass; plus others including many in pvt collections.
Exhibitions: French Group, Expos Nat, Paris, France; Art Inst Chicago, Ill; Pa Acad Fine Arts, Philadelphia; Libr of Cong, Washington, D C; Soc Contemp Art, Chicago; plus many other group & one-man shows.
Teaching: Prof art, Art Inst Chicago, 46-63; instr art, Evanston Art Ctr, 48-; instr archit, Ill Inst Technol, 50-
Mailing Address: 1281 Laurel Ave, Wilmette, IL 60091.

WIELAND, JOYCE
Painter, Film Maker
b Toronto, Ont, 31.
Study & Training: Cent Tech Sch, grad.
Work in Public Collections: Nat Gallery Can; Montreal Mus Fine Arts, Can; Philadelphia Mus Art, Pa; Mus Mod Art Film Archives, New York, N Y; Royal Belg Film Archives; plus many other painting & film works in collections of univs, galleries & film archives.
Commissions: Bill's Hat (mixed media), Art Gallery Ont, 67.
Exhibitions: The Wall-Art for Architecture, travelling exhib, Art Gallery Ont, 69 & Rothmans Art Gallery, Stratford, Ont, 70; Oberhausen Film Festival, Austria, 69; Survey '70-Realism(e)s, Montreal Mus Fine Arts & Art Gallery Ont, 70; Eight Artists from Canada, Tel-Aviv Mus, Israel, 70; Directors' Fortnight, Cannes Film Festival, France, 70; plus many other group & one-man exhibs of paintings & films.
Awards: Can Coun grant, 66 & 68; two prizes for Rat Life & Diet in North America, Third Independent Filmmakers' Festival, New York, 68.
Dealer: Isaacs Gallery, 832 Yonge St, Toronto 285, Can.
Mailing Address: 137 Summerhill Ave, Toronto, Ont, Can.

WIENER, GEORGE
Art Dealer
b New York, N Y.
Positions: Owner, Wiener Gallery.
Specialty of Gallery: Late nineteenth and twentieth century French and American.
Mailing Address: 963 Madison Ave, New York, NY 10021.

WIENER, SAMUEL G
Painter
b Dec 26, 96; U S citizen.
Study & Training: Univ Mich, BS; Atelier Corbett-Gugler, N Y; Atelier Gromort-Expert, Paris; also with Eliel Saarinen.
Exhibitions: One-man show, La State Exhib Bldg; 14 States Regional Exhib, Monroe, La; 13 States Regional Exhib, City Mus, Shreveport, La; one-man show, City Mus, Monroe; Women's Dept Club, Shreveport.
Memberships: Fel Am Inst Archit; Shreveport Art Asn; Men's Art Guild.
Publications: Auth & illusr, Venetian houses and details, Architectural, 25.
Mailing Address: 615 Longleaf Rd, Shreveport, LA 71106.

WIER, GORDON D (DON)
Designer, Painter
b Orchard Lake, Mich, June 14, 03.
Study & Training: Univ Mich, AB; Chicago Acad Fine Arts; Grand Cent Sch Art; also with J Scott Williams.
Work in Public Collections: Detroit Inst Art; Mus Rouaux Art et Hist, Brussels, Belg; J D Speed Mem Mus, Louisville, Ky; also in pvt collections of King H M Baudouin I, Belg, King Frederick IX & Queen Ingrid, Denmark, Crown Prince Akihito, Japan & others.
Exhibitions: Baltimore Watercolor Club; Del River Art Asn; Soc Decorators; two-one-man shows, Bridgeport, Conn.
Teaching: Instr, Grand Cent Sch Art, 28-35.
Positions: Designer, Steuben Glass, 45-51, art designer, 52-69; designer, Corning Glass Works, 49-50.
Awards: Cert of Excellence, Inst Graphic Arts, 50 & 51.
Mailing Address: 3601 Husted Dr, Chevy Chase, MD 20015.

WIESE, LUCIE
Art Critic, Writer
U S citizen.
Study & Training: Simmons Col; New Eng Law Sch; Harvard Univ; Sorbonne; Staley Col, hon Dr Art Oratory.
Awards: Bellingen Recognition & William Lyon Phelps Recognition.
Research: American art and artists; twentieth century innovators.
Publications: Ed, The emergency of an American art; ed, Paul Rosenfeld: voyager in the arts; auth, Mr Butterfly (play, in prep); auth, exhib catalogs.
Mailing Address: 130 W 57th St, New York, NY 10019.

WIGGINS, BILL
Painter
Preferred Media: Oils.
b Roswell, N Mex, Sept 24, 17.
Study & Training: N Mex Mil Inst, Roswell; Abilene Christian Col; Am Shrivenham Univ, Eng, with Francis Speight; Fed Art Proj, Work Proj Admin, Roswell.
Work in Public Collections: Roswell Mus & Art Ctr.
Exhibitions: Newport 43rd Ann, R I, 54; Low Ruins Nat, Tubac, Ariz, 65; 5th Juried Arts Nat, Tyler, Tex, 68; Mainstreams 68, Marietta Col, Ohio, 68; Ark State Univ Nat, Jonesboro, 70.
Teaching: Instr art, Roswell Mus & Art Ctr, 55-63.
Bibliography: Elena Montes (auth), Bill Wiggins of Roswell, N Mex Mag, 10/65; United States art, La Rev Mod, Paris, France, 12/65.
Memberships: Artists Equity Asn.
Mailing Address: 711 W Eighth St, Roswell, NM 88201.

WIGHT, FREDERICK S
Painter, Art Administrator
b New York, N Y, June 1, 02.
Study & Training: Univ Va, BA; Harvard Univ, MA.
Exhibitions: One-man shows, M H de Young Mem Mus, San Francisco, Calif, 56, Pasadena Art Mus, Calif, 56, Fine Arts Gallery San Diego, Calif, 60, Esther Robles Gallery, Los Angeles, Calif, 60, Long Beach Mus Art, Calif, 61 & Palm Springs Desert Mus, Calif, 69.
Collections Arranged: Jacques Lipchitz Retrospective, 63, Kurt Schwitters, 65, Henri Matisse Retrospective, 66, Negro in American Art, 66, Jean Arp Memorial, 68 & Gerhard Marcks Retrospective, 69.
Teaching: Instr art hist, Univ Mich, 50; instr art hist, Harvard Univ, 51; instr art hist, Univ Calif, Los Angeles, 53-70, chmn dept art, 63-66.

Positions: Asst dir, Inst Contemp Art, Boston, Mass; dir, Frederick
S Wight Galleries, Univ Calif, Los Angeles, 53-
Memberships: Int Asn Art Critics; UCLA Art Coun.
Publications: Auth, Morris Graves, 56, Hans Hofmann, 57, Arthur
G Dove, 58, Richard Neutra, 58 & Modigliani, 61; plus many
others.
Mailing Address: 405 Hilgard Ave, Los Angeles, CA 90024.

WILBERT, ROBERT JOHN
Painter, Educator
Preferred Media: Oils, Watercolors.
b Chicago, Ill, Oct 9, 29.
Study & Training: Univ Ill, BFA, 51, MFA, 54.
Work in Public Collections: Saginaw Mus, Mich; South Bend Art Ctr,
Ind; Kalamazoo Art Ctr, Mich; Macomb Co Community Col, War-
ren, Mich; Wayne State Univ, Detroit, Mich.
Exhibitions: American Watercolors, Drawings & Prints, Metrop Mus
Art, 52; Butler Inst Am Art 25th Midyear Ann, 60; Pa Acad Fine
Arts 156th Ann, 61; four one-man shows, Donald Morris Gallery,
Detroit, 62-72; A Survey of Contemporary Art, J B Speed Art
Mus, Louisville, Ky, 65.
Teaching: Instr painting, Flint Inst Arts, Mich, 54-56; prof painting,
Wayne State Univ, 56-
Awards: 4th Biennial Michiana Regional Award, South Bend Art Ctr,
66; gallery award, Mich State Fair, 67; Werbe Award, 57th Exhib
Mich Artists, Detroit Inst Arts, 69.
Dealer: Donald Morris Gallery, 20082 Livernois, Detroit, MI 48221.
Mailing Address: 18033 Birchcrest, Detroit, MI 48221.

WILDE, JOHN
Painter, Educator
Preferred Media: Oils, Pencil, Silverpoint.
b Milwaukee, Wis, Dec 12, 19.
Study & Training: Univ Wis, BS & MS.
Work in Public Collections: Whitney Mus Am Art, New York, N Y;
Pa Acad Fine Arts, Philadelphia; Art Inst Chicago; Detroit Inst
Art; Wadsworth Atheneum, Hartford, Conn.
Exhibitions: Contemp Am Art, Univ Ill Biennial, 48-65; several ex-
hibs, Contemp Am Painting & Drawing, Whitney Mus Am Art, 52-
68; Contemp Drawing U S A, Mus Mod Art, 58; Art U S A Now,
U S, Europ & Eastern mus, 62-66; Retrospective, Milwaukee Art
Ctr, 67.
Teaching: Alfred Sessler Distinguished Prof Art, Univ Wis-Madison.
Awards: Lambert Purchase Award, Pa Acad Fine Art, 63; Childe
Hassam Purchase Award, Nat Acad Design, 65; purchase award,
Butler Inst Am Art, 68.
Bibliography: Ed Nordness (auth), Art U S A now, Viking Press, 63;
Great modern drawings, 67; The Wildeworld (film), Milwaukee
Art Ctr, Univ Wis Press & Channel 10, Milwaukee, 68.
Dealer: Lee Nordness Gallery, 236 E 75th St, New York, NY 10021.
Mailing Address: R F D 1, Evansville, WI 53536.

WILDENHAIN, FRANS
Potter, Educator
b Leipzig, Ger, June 5, 05; U S citizen.
Study & Training: Weimar Bauhaus; Acad Amsterdam, Holland.
Work in Public Collections: Smithsonian Inst, Washington, D C;
Rochester Mem Art Gallery, N Y; Everson Mus, Syracuse, N Y;
Stedeljik Mus, Amsterdam; Boymans Mus, Rotterdam; plus
many others.
Commissions: Mural, Strasenburgh Lab, Rochester, N Y; Nat Libr
Med, Bethesda, Md; Summit Hosp, Overlook, N Y; Rochester Inst
Technol, Rochester Stud League.
Exhibitions: Mus Contemp Crafts, 56 & 62-64; Miami Nat, 57 & 58;
Brussels World's Fair, 58; Syracuse Invitational, 71; Am Crafts
Coun Gallery, New York, N Y; plus many others.
Teaching: From prof ceramics to emer prof, Sch Am Craftsman,
Rochester Inst Technol.
Awards: Fairchild award, twice, Rochester; Brussels World's
Fair; plus many others.
Bibliography: Article, In: Crafts Horizons.
Memberships: Am Crafts Coun; World Crafts Coun.
Publications: Contribr, Am Artist Mag & Crafts Horizons.
Mailing Address: 6 Laird Lane, Pittsford, NY 14534.

WILDER, MITCHELL ARMITAGE
Art Administrator
b Colorado Springs, Colo, Aug 19, 13.
Study & Training: McGill Univ, AB, 35; Univ Calif, Berkeley.
Positions: Dir, Colo Springs Fine Arts Ctr, 45-53; dir, Abby Aldrich
Rockefeller Collection, Williamsburg, Va, 54-58; dir, Chouinard
Art Inst, Los Angeles, 58-61; dir, Amon Carter Mus, Fort Worth,
61-
Memberships: Asn Art Mus Dirs.
Mailing Address: Box 2365, Fort Worth, TX 76101.

WILEY, WILLIAM T
Painter
b Bedford, Ind, Oct 21, 37.
Study & Training: San Francisco Art Inst, BFA, 60, MFA, 62.
Work in Public Collections: San Francisco Mus Art; Whitney Mus
Am Art, New York, N Y; Univ Calif Mus, Berkeley; Los Angeles
Co Mus Art, Calif; Oakland Mus, Calif.
Exhibitions: Univ Nev Ann Art Festival, Reno, 69; Looking West,
Joslyn Art Mus, Omaha, Nebr, 70; Kompas IV Exhib, Stedelijk
van Abbemuseum, Eindhoven & Dortmund, Netherlands, 70 &
Kunsthalle, Berne, Switz, 70; Studio Marconi, Milan, Italy, 71;
one-man exhibs, Art Inst Chicago, 72 & Corcoran Gallery Art,
Washington, D C, 72; plus other group & one-man shows.
Teaching: Assoc prof art, Univ Calif, Davis, 62-
Awards: Sculpture purchase award, Los Angeles Co Mus Art, 67;
purchase prize, Whitney Mus Am Art, 68; Nealie Sullivan Award,
San Francisco Art Inst, 68; plus others.
Bibliography: James R Mellow (auth), Realist William Wiley, New
York Times, 10/11/70; John Perrault (auth), Toward a new meta-
physics, Village Voice, 10/15/70; Cecile Mc Cann (auth), Probing
the western ethic, Artweek, 5/15/71; plus others.
Publications: Co-auth, The great blondino (film), shown Belg Film
Festival, 67; contribr, Over evident falls (theater event), Sacra-
mento State Col, 68; auth, Man's nature (film), shown Hansen
Fuller Gallery, 71.
Dealer: Hansen Fuller Gallery, 228 Grant Ave, San Francisco, CA
94108.
Mailing Address: Box 654, Woodacre, CA 94973.

WILKE, ULFERT S
Painter, Art Administrator
Preferred Media: Oils, Acrylics.
b Bad Tölz, Ger, July 14, 07; U S citizen.
Study & Training: With Willy Jaeckel, 23; Arts & Crafts Sch, Bruns-
wick, 24-25; Acad Grande Chaumiere, 27-28; Acad Ranson, Paris,
27-28; Harvard Univ, 40-41; State Univ Iowa, MA, 47.
Work in Public Collections: Philadelphia Mus, Pa; Solomon R Gug-
genheim Mus, New York, N Y; Cleveland Mus Art, Ohio; Whitney
Mus Am Art, New York; Mus Tel Aviv, Israel.
Exhibitions: Younger Am Artists, Solomon R Guggenheim Mus, 54;
Italy Rediscovered, Smithsonian Traveling Exhib, 55-56; Letter-
ing By Mod Artists, Mus Mod Art, New York, 64; Tokyo Biennial,
tour Japan, 67; Ulfert Wilke, Recent Works, Des Moines Art Ctr,
Columbus Gallery Fine Arts, Joslyn Art Mus & San Francisco
Mus Art, 70-71.
Collections Arranged: Oscar Kokoschka, Kalamazoo Inst Arts, 40;
As Found, Inst Contemp Art, Boston, 66; Very Small Paintings,
Objects & Works On Paper, Univ Iowa Mus Art, 72.
Teaching: Asst prof art, Univ Louisville, 48-55; vis grad prof paint-
ing, Univ Ga, 55-56; assoc prof art, Rutgers Univ, New Bruns-
wick, 62-67.
Positions: Head dept art & dir, Kalamazoo Col & Inst Arts, Mich,
40-42; art & educ dir, Springfield Art Asn, Ill, 46-47; dir, Univ
Iowa Mus Art, 68-
Awards: Albrecht Durer Prize, Ger, 27; Guggenheim Found fels
study in Europe, 59-60 & 60-61.
Bibliography: J Langsner (auth), Art, 11/61 & G Nordland (auth),
Calligraphy and the art of Ulfert Wilke, 4/71, Art Int.
Memberships: Asn Am Mus Dirs.
Publications: Illusr, portfolios, Music to be seen, 56, Fragments
from nowhere, 58 & One, two and more, 60.
Mailing Address: University of Iowa Museum of Art, Iowa City, IA
52240.

WILKINS, RUTH LOIS
Art Administrator, Art Historian
b Boston, Mass, Nov 20, 26.
Study & Training: Wellesley Col, AB.
Collections Arranged: Chinese Export Porcelain, 65; American
Painting from 1830, 65; Some Recent Images in American Paint-
ing, 68; Chinese Art from the Cloud Wampler Collection, 68;
American Ship Portraits & Marine Painting, 70.
Positions: Registrar, Everson Mus Art, 60-62, ed of publ, 63-70,
cur collections, 66-70; consult, Mus Am China Trade, 71; cur
educ, Kimbell Art Mus, 71-
Awards: Woman of Achievement in Arts, Post Standard, 68.
Memberships: Col Art Asn Am; Am Asn Mus.
Research: Chinese gold & silver from the T'ang Dynasty; Chinese
export silver for the Anglo-American market; classical studies,
particularly Western Greek foundations of Sicily and Magna
Graecia.
Collection: American silver of the Colonial period.
Publications: Ed, American painting from 1830, 65; ed, Chinese art
from the Cloud Wampler & other collections, 68; auth, What is an
art museum?, 68; ed, American ship portraits & marine paint-
ing, 70; co-auth, China trade silver, 1790-1870, 72; plus others.
Mailing Address: 308 Ridglea Village, 6035 Westridge Lane, Fort
Worth, TX 76116.

WILKINSON, CHARLES K
Museum Curator
b London, Eng, Oct 13, 97.
Study & Training: Slade Sch & Univ Col, Univ London, 15-17 & 19-20.
Teaching: Adj prof Columbia Univ, 64-69; adj prof, New York Univ, 66-67.
Positions: Mem Egyptian expedition, Metrop Mus Art, 20-32, Iranian expedition, 32-40, sr res fel, 42-47, assoc cur Near Eastern archaeol, 47-53, cur, 53-63, cur emer, 63-; Hagop Kevorkian cur Middle East art & archaeol, Brooklyn Mus, 69-; trustee, Am Schs Oriental Res; dir, Colt Archaeol Inst; mem Coun Brit Sch Archaeol in Iraq.
Memberships: Am Oriental Soc; Brit Inst Persian Studies; Archaeol Inst Am; Century Asn.
Mailing Address: Sharon, CT 06069.

WILKINSON, KIRK COOK
Art Dealer, Painter
Preferred Media: Watercolor, Casein, Acrylic.
b New York, N Y, Nov 23, 09.
Study & Training: Parson's Sch Design; watercolor painting with Felice Waldo Howell.
Work in Public Collections: Scarborough Art Gallery, N Y; Pocker Art Gallery, New York; Kendall Art Gallery, Wellfleet, Mass.
Exhibitions: Art Dir Club New York, 34-; Art Dir Club Philadelphia, 54 & 56; Jr League Westchester Ann, 66-69; Westchester Art Asn Ann, 69; Cape Cod Art Asn Ann, 70-72; plus others.
Teaching: Instr graphics & ann lectr, Parson's Sch Design, 31-52.
Positions: Art dir, Country Life, Am Home Mag, N Y, 35-36; art dir, House Beautiful Mag, New York, 36-37; art dir, Conde Nast, New York, 37-39; art dir, Women's Day Mag, New York, 38-70; pres & organizer, Parson's Sch Design Alumni Coun, 44; owner, Kendall Art Gallery.
Awards: Gold medal, New York Art Dir Club, 54; gold medal, Philadelphia Art Dir Club; second prize watercolor, Jr League Westchester Show, 69; plus others.
Bibliography: Charles Coiner (auth), Commentary on the art and layout of Women's Day, Art Direction Mag, 4/54.
Memberships: Am Fedn Arts; Soc Illusr; Century Asn; Dutch Treat Club; Provincetown Art Asn; plus others.
Specialty of Gallery: Contemporary art, sculpture and ceramics.
Publications: Auth, Let's talk about your pictures, Popular Photog, 4/54; auth, Lighting is the news, 10/59 & The new thinking man, 2/62, Art Direction.
Dealer: Scarborough Art Gallery, Scarborough, NY 10510.
Mailing Address: c/o Kendall Art Gallery, Box 742, Wellfleet, MA 02667.

WILL, JOHN A
Printmaker, Painter
Preferred Media: Graphics.
b Waterloo, Iowa, June 30, 39.
Study & Training: Univ Iowa, MFA, 64; Rijsacadamie von Beeldende Kunston, Amsterdam, 64-65; Tamarind, Albuquerque, N Mex, Ford Found grant, 70-71.
Work in Public Collections: New York Pub Libr, N Y; Art Inst Chicago, Ill; Univ Calgary, Alta; Hamline Univ, Minneapolis, Minn; Mus N Mex, Santa Fe.
Exhibitions: Libr Cong Nat Print Exhib, 66; Drawings '70 Nat Drawing Exhib, Saint Paul, Minn, 68; Drawings U S A Fourth Biennial Nat Drawing Exhib, San Francisco Mus Art, 70; Colorprint U S A Nat Print Exhib, Lubbock, Tex, 71; West 71, Edmonton Art Gallery, Alta, 71.
Teaching: Asst prof drawing, Univ Wis-Stout, 65-70; artist-in-residence, Yale Univ, summer 66; artist-in-residence, Peninsula Sch Art, Fish Creek, Wis, summer 68; asst prof lithography, Univ Calgary, 71-
Awards: Fulbright fel to Holland, 64-65.
Mailing Address: Dept of Art, University of Calgary, Calgary, Alta. T2N 1N4, Can.

WILLARD, CHARLOTTE
Writer, Art Critic
Study & Training: New York Univ; Columbia Univ, BA; New Sch Social Res, with Jose de Creeft.
Positions: Art ed, Look, 50-55; contrib ed, Art Am, 58-68; art critic, New York Post, 64-68.
Awards: MacDowell Colony fel, 71-72.
Research: Renaissance painting.
Publications: Contribr, Story behind painting, 60, Moses Soyer, 61, What is a masterpiece, 64, Cezanne to op art, 71 & Frank Lloyd Wright, 72.
Mailing Address: 340 E 63rd St, New York, NY 10021.

WILLE, O LOUIS
Sculptor
Preferred Media: Wood, Stone, Bronze.
b Apr 27, 17; U S citizen.
Study & Training: Univ Minn, MA.
Work in Public Collections: Univ Minn Gallery; Sculpture Ctr, New York, N Y.
Exhibitions: Minneapolis Art Inst; Walker Art Ctr; Denver Art Mus; San Francisco Mus Art; Everson Mus, Syracuse.
Mailing Address: The Tyrol, Box 1145, Aspen, CO 81611.

WILLENBECHER, JOHN
Sculptor
b Macungie, Pa, May 5, 36.
Study & Training: Brown Univ, BA, 58; New York Univ Inst Fine Arts, 58-61.
Work in Public Collections: Whitney Mus Am Art, New York, N Y; Albright-Knox Art Gallery, Buffalo, N Y; James A Michener Found Collection, Univ Tex, Austin; Aldrich Mus Contemp Art, Ridgefield, Conn; Solomon R Guggenheim Mus, New York.
Exhibitions: Mixed Media & Pop Art, Albright-Knox Art Gallery, Buffalo, 63; Paintings & Constructions of the 1960's, R I Sch Design, Providence, 64; Young Americans, Whitney Mus Am Art, New York, 65; Kunst-Lucht-Kunst, Stedelijk Mus, Eindhoven, Holland, 66; Painting & Sculpture Today, Indianapolis Mus Art, Ind, 70.
Teaching: Lectr painting, Philadelphia Col Art, 72-73.
Bibliography: David Bourdon (auth), Out there with Willenbecher, Art Int, 9/20/68.
Mailing Address: 145 W Broadway, New York, NY 10013.

WILLER, JIM
Sculptor, Painter
b Fulham, Eng, Feb 25, 21; Can citizen.
Study & Training: Hornsey Sch Art, London, Eng; Royal Acad, Amsterdam; Winnipeg Sch Art & Univ Man, BA, 52.
Work in Public Collections: Nat Gallery Can, Ottawa; Winnipeg Art Gallery, Man; Univ Winnipeg; Univ Man, Winnipeg.
Commissions: Sun dial & two hanging screens, Polo Park Shopping Ctr, Winnipeg, 59; sculpture, Charleswood Hotel, Winnipeg, 61; marble portrait, Mrs William Morton, Sackville, N B, 63; red square, Greenwin Award for Arts, Toronto, 69; five murals for Image I, Vancouver, 70-71.
Exhibitions: Can Scholar Winner's Abroad Exhib, Nat Gallery Ottawa, 56; Can Biennial, 56-57; Univ Man Exhib Winnipeg Artists, 61; Sculpture '67, Toronto City Hall, 67; 3D into the 70's, East Can on Tour, 70; plus others.
Teaching: Instr design, Vancouver Sch Art, 64-65.
Awards: Can Govt overseas grant, 54; Can award to Netherlands, Imp Tobacco, 67-68; Greenwin Award Arts, Al Latner, Toronto, 69.
Bibliography: Interview, On: CBC-TV, 59; Polo Park sculpture, Can Art, 59; 3 part sculpture, Art Int, 68.
Memberships: Can Artists (rep).
Publications: Auth, Paramind, McClelland, 72.
Dealer: Bau-xi Gallery, 555 Hamilton St, Vancouver, B C, Can.
Mailing Address: Sunset Beach, West Vancouver, B C, Can.

WILLET, HENRY LEE
Craftsman
Preferred Media: Glass, Gold.
b Pittsburgh, Pa, Dec 7, 99.
Study & Training: Princeton Univ; Univ Pa; with father, William Willet; Europ study & travel; Lafayette Col, hon ArtD, 51; Geneva Col, hon LHD, 66; Ursinus Col, hon LHD, 67; St Lawrence Univ, hon DFA, 72.
Work in Public Collections: Children's Gallery, Metrop Mus Art, New York, N Y.
Commissions: Stained glass, Cadet Chapel, W Point Mil Acad, 10-72, Am Lutheran Church, Oslo, Norway, 66, Hall of Sci, New York World's Fair, 67 & Nat Presby Church Ctr, Washington, D C, 68; stained glass & tower window, San Francisco Grace Cathedral, 66.
Exhibitions: One-man shows, Columbia Mus Art, S C, 61, Atlanta Art Asn, Ga, 61, Taft Mus, Cincinnati, Ohio, 69 & Mus Am Art, New Britain, Conn, 71; Archit Glass, Mus Contemp Crafts, New York, 68.
Teaching: Instr hist stained glass, Philadelphia Sch Apprentices Stained Glass, 03-; instr sem symbolism & color, Nantucket Sch Ecclesiastical Needlery, summer 71.
Positions: Pres, Willet Stained Glass Studios, 30-65, chmn bd, 65-
Awards: Medal of achievement, Philadelphia Art Alliance, 52; Conover Award, Guild Relig Archit, 63; Frank P Brown Medal, Franklin Inst, 71.
Bibliography: Article, In: Time, 10/11/37; A new luster in churches, Life, 4/11/55; Anne Hoene (auth), Stained glass—what future?, Art Gallery, 12/68.

Memberships: Hon mem Am Inst Architects; fel Stained Glass Asn Am (pres, 42-44); fel Royal Soc Arts, London; Guild Relig Archit; fel Am Soc Church Archit.
Publications: Co-auth, Stained glass, In: Encycl Americana, 48.
Mailing Address: 10 E Moreland Ave, Philadelphia, PA 19118.

WILLIAMS, BENJAMIN FORREST
Museum Curator, Art Historian
b Lumberton, N C, Dec 24, 25.
Study & Training: Corcoran Sch Art, with Eugene Weisz; George Washington Univ, AA; Univ N C, AB; Columbia Univ, Paris Exten, Ecole du Louvre; Netherlands Inst Art Hist; Art Stud League New York.
Work in Public Collections: Atlanta Art Asn; N C Mus Art; Duke Univ; Greenville Civic Art Gallery, N C; Knoll Assoc, New York, N Y.
Exhibitions: Va Intermont, Bristol; Weatherspoon Gallery, Greensboro; Person Hall Gallery, Chapel Hill, N C; Asheville Art Mus; Am Fedn Arts traveling exhibs; plus many others.
Collections Arranged: Francis Speight—Retrospective; Sculptures of Tilmann Riemenschneider; Carolina Charter Tercentenary Exhibition; Young British Art; North Carolina Collects; The Retrospectives for Josef Albers, Hobson Pittman, Jacob Marling, Victor Hammer, Fedor Zakharov, Henry Pearson, & the collections of the N C Mus Art; assisted with, Rembrandt & His Pupils & E L Kirchner.
Positions: In charge of Ann N C Artists' Exhib; prin investr, Black Mountain Col Res Proj; gen cur, N C Mus Art, at present.
Awards: Ronsheim Mem award, Corcoran Sch Art, 46; Washington Soc Arts, 47; prizes, Southeastern Ann, 47.
Memberships: Am Asn Mus; Southeastern Mus Conf; Col Art Asn Am.
Publications: Contribr articles on nineteenth century American painting & sculpture to N C Mus Art Bull & N C Hist Rev.
Mailing Address: North Carolina Museum of Art, Raleigh, NC 27611.

WILLIAMS, FRANKLIN
Painter
Preferred Media: Acrylics.
b Ogden, Utah, Feb 5, 40.
Study & Training: Calif Col Arts & Crafts, BFA & MFA.
Work in Public Collections: Oakland Art Mus; Univ Calif Mus; Lytton Ctr Visual Arts.
Exhibitions: Some New Art in the Bay Area, San Francisco Art Inst, 63; Lithographs by Bay Area Artists, San Francisco Mus Art, 64; Funk Art Show, Univ Calif, Berkeley, 67; Whitney Mus Painting Ann, 67 & Whitney Mus Sculpture Ann, 68, Whitney Mus Am Art, New York, N Y.
Teaching: Instr painting, San Francisco Art Inst, 66-; instr painting, Calif Col Arts & Crafts, 71-
Awards: Spencer Macky Mem scholar, 65-66; Ford Found grant, 66; Nat Endowment Arts Award, 68.
Publications: Auth, articles, In: Art Int, 63, Artforum, 63, 67 & 69, Art Mag, 68 & Art News, 72.
Dealer: Marc Moyens, 2121 P St NW, Washington, DC 20037.
Mailing Address: 713 Elm Dr, Petaluma, CA 94952.

WILLIAMS, GARTH MONTGOMERY
Illustrator, Designer
b New York, N Y, Apr 12, 12.
Study & Training: Westminster Sch Art, London, Eng; Royal Col Art, London, spec talent scholar painting & exten scholar, ARCA.
Exhibitions: Royal Acad Arts Ann, London, 33-35 & 41; Exhib Original Textile Designs, Cotton Bd, Cent Gallery, Manchester, Eng, 41.
Awards: Prix de Rome for sculpture, Soc Rome Scholars, London, 36.
Publications: Illusr, Stuart Little, 45, Charlotte's web, 52 & The little house books, 53, Harper & Row; auth & illusr, The adventures of Benjamin Pink, 51 & The rabbit's wedding, 58, Harper & Row.
Mailing Address: Apartado Postal 123, Guanajuato, Guanajuato, Mex.

WILLIAMS, GERALD
Sculptor, Potter
Preferred Media: Clays.
b Asansol, India, Jan 5, 26; U S citizen.
Study & Training: Cornell Col; Notre Dame Col (N H), hon DFA, 71.
Work in Public Collections: Currier Gallery Art, Manchester, N H; Fitchburg Art Mus, Mass; Syracuse Univ, N Y; Objects U S A, Johnson Collection.
Commissions: Ceramic mural, Sunapee & resin mural, Laconia, State of N H; resin mural, Int Paper Box Machine Co, Nashua, N H; ceramic mural, Sheen, Finney, Bass & Green Law Off, Manchester.

Exhibitions: Am Studio Pottery, 67 & Ceramic Int, 72, Victoria & Albert Mus, London, Eng; Syracuse Ceramic Nat, 70; one-man shows, Contemp Crafts Mus, New York, 69 & Currier Gallery Art, Manchester, 70.
Teaching: Instr sculpture, Currier Gallery Sch Art, 52-72; instr ceramics, Dartmouth Col, 64-65; instr ceramics, Haystack Sch Crafts, 66 & 69-
Positions: Trustee, Soc Arts & Crafts, Boston, Mass, 67-72; mem adv bd, N H Comn Arts.
Bibliography: Nordness (auth), Objects: U S A, 70.
Memberships: N H Art Asn; League N H Craftsmen.
Research: Wet-firing process; photo-resist process.
Publications: Auth, Textiles of Oaxaca, 64; contribr, Craft Horizons, 69; ed, The Studio Potter, 72.
Mailing Address: R F D 1, Goffstown, NH 03045.

WILLIAMS, GLUYAS
Illustrator, Cartoonist
b San Francisco, Calif, July 23, 88.
Study & Training: Harvard Univ, AB, 11.
Work in Public Collections: Libr Cong.
Exhibitions: Boston Mus Fine Arts, 46.
Publications: Auth, The Gluyas Williams book, 29, Fellow citizens, 40 & The Gluyas Williams gallery, 57; illusr, Daily except Sunday, 38, People of note, 40 & Father of the bride, 49 (bks by Robert Benchley); contribr, cartoons, In: New Yorker & other mags.
Mailing Address: 14 Sylvan Ave, West Newton, MA 02165.

WILLIAMS, GUY
Painter
b San Diego, Calif, June 21, 32.
Study & Training: Chouinard Art Sch, Los Angeles, Calif.
Work in Public Collections: Long Beach Mus Art, Calif; La Jolla Mus Art, Calif.
Exhibitions: New Modes in Calif Painting & Sculpture, La Jolla Mus, 66; Tokyo Int Exhib, Japan, 67; Am Fedn Arts Traveling Exhib, 68; Long Beach Mus Art, 69; Whitney Ann, Whitney Mus Am Art, New York, N Y, 72; plus others.
Teaching: Instr painting, Chouinard Art Sch, Calif Inst Arts, 65-67; asst prof painting, Pomona Col, 67-; asst prof painting, Claremont Grad Sch, 67-
Awards: James Phelan awards, 61-63; Am Fedn Arts Award, 68; purchase award, Long Beach Mus, 69.
Bibliography: Barbara Rose (auth), California art, Art in Am, 1/66; Carter Ratcliff (auth), Whitney annual, Artforum, 6/72.
Publications: Auth, Art & technology, Artforum, 2/69; auth, Random notes on painting, Pomona Col Publ, 71.
Mailing Address: 470 N Indian Hill Blvd, Claremont, CA 91711.

WILLIAMS, HERMANN WARNER, JR
Art Administrator, Writer
b Boston, Mass, Nov 2, 08.
Study & Training: Harvard Univ, Prince Greenleaf & Burr scholar, AB(cum laude), 31, Univ scholar, 31, MA, 33; Courtald Inst, Univ London, stud asst, PhD, 35; Inst Fine Arts, New York Univ, Carnegie Tuition fels, 35-41.
Collections Arranged: Biennial Exhib Contemp Am Painting, 47-68, Visionaries & Dreamers, 56, Am Stage, 57, Civil War: The Artists' Rec, 61 & Past & Present: 250 Yrs Am Art, Corcoran Gallery Art; plus many others.
Teaching: Lectr, Metrop Mus Art, Mus Fine Arts, Boston, Col Art Asn Am, Nat Gallery Art, Norton Gallery Art, Dayton Art Mus, Brooks Mem Mus, Toledo Mus Art, Fla Art League, Norfolk Mus, Washington Co Mus Art & Montgomery Mus Fine Arts.
Positions: Docent, Fogg Mus & Mus Fine Arts, Boston; stud asst Oriental Study Rm, Fogg Mus; asst to George Stout, restoration work, Royal Ont Mus Art & Archaeol, Toronto; asst Dept Arms & Armor, Metrop Mus Art; Rockefeller Found intern, Brooklyn Mus, 35, asst cur Renaissance & mod art, 36; from asst to asst cur paintings, Metrop Mus Art, 37-46; asst dir, Corcoran Gallery Art, 45, dir & secy, 47-68, emer dir, 68-; juror, Baltimore Mus Art, Va Mus Art & many others.
Memberships: Am Asn Mus; fel Co Mil Historians (past gov); Asn Art Mus Dirs; Am Fedn Art; Am Soc Arms Collectors; plus many others.
Collection: Nineteenth and twentieth century American art; pre-Civil War American military items.
Publications: Co-auth, William Sidney Mount, 44; auth, The civil war: the artists' record, 61; auth, Mirror to the American past; a survey of American nineteenth century genre painting, 72.
Mailing Address: Corcoran Gallery of Art, 17th St & New York Ave, Washington, DC 20006.

WILLIAMS, HIRAM DRAPER
Painter, Educator
Preferred Media: Oils.
b Indianapolis, Ind, Feb 11, 17.
Study & Training: Williamsport Sketch Club, with George Eddinger;

Pa State Univ, BS, with Victor Lowenfeld & MEd, with Hobson Pittman & Lowenfeld.
Work in Public Collections: Mus Mod Art, New York, N Y; Whitney Mus Am Art, New York; Milwaukee Art Ctr; Nat Art Collection, Washington, D C; Corcoran Gallery Art, Washington, D. C.
Exhibitions: Art U S A: Painting, Mus Mod Art, 61; Art U S A II; Carnegie Int, Pittsburgh, 64; Art Across Am, 65; Art: U S A: Now, 66.
Teaching: Asst prof art educ, Univ Southern Calif, 53-54; asst prof art educ, Univ Tex, Austin, 54-60, res grant, 58; prof painting, Univ Fla, 60-
Awards: D D Feldman Award, 58; Guggenheim Found fel, 63.
Bibliography: Donald Weisman (auth), Recent painting of Hiram Williams, Univ Tex Quart, 59; William B Stephens (auth), On creating and teaching, Col Art J, summer 71.
Publications: Auth, Notes for a young painter, Prentice-Hall, 63; co-auth, Forms, Univ Tex Press, 69.
Dealer: Nordness Galleries, 236 E 75th St, New York, NY 10021.
Mailing Address: 2804 N W 30th Terr, Gainesville, FL 32601.

WILLIAMS, LEWIS W, II
Art Historian
b Champaign, Ill, Apr 24, 18.
Study & Training: Univ Ill, BFA, 46, MFA, 58; Univ Chicago, PhD, 58.
Teaching: Instr art hist, Univ Mo-Columbia, 48-50; asst art hist, Northwestern Univ, Evanston, 53-55; prof art hist, Beloit Col, 55-
Positions: Dir, Assoc Cols Midwest Arts London & Florence, Florence, Italy, 71-72.
Awards: Teacher of Yr, Beloit Col, 66.
Memberships: Col Art Asn Am; Am Asn Univ Prof (pres local chap, 67).
Research: American sculpture.
Mailing Address: Dept of Art, Beloit College, Beloit, WI 53511.

WILLIAMS, MARY FRANCES
Art Historian, Lecturer
b Providence, R I, Apr 26, 05.
Study & Training: Radcliffe Col, BA, MA, PhD.
Collections Arranged: 41st-61st Ann Loan Exhibitions of American Art, Randolph-Macon Woman's Col.
Teaching: Asst prof art, Hollins Col, 36-39; asst prof art, Mt Holyoke Col, 39-42; prof art hist & cur, Randolph-Macon Woman's Col, 52-
Positions: Mem, Va State Art Comn, 56-70.
Awards: Jonathan Fay Prize, 27 & Caroline Wilby Prize, 31, Radcliffe Col; Gillie A Larew distinguished teaching award, Randolph-Macon Woman's Col, 72.
Memberships: Nat League Am Penwomen; Col Art Asn Am; Mus Mod Art, New York; Lynchburg Fine Arts Ctr; Lynchburg Art Club.
Publications: Auth, Catalogue of the collection of American painting at Randolph-Macon Woman's College, 65; auth, Time makes ancient good uncouth, Randolph-Macon Alumnae bull, 72.
Mailing Address: 239 Westmoreland St, Lynchburg, VA 24503.

WILLIAMS, NEIL
Painter, Film Maker
b Bluff, Utah, Aug 19, 34.
Study & Training: Calif Sch Fine Arts, BFA, 59.
Work in Public Collections: Whitney Mus Am Art, New York, N Y; Richmond Mus, Calif; Mass Inst Technol, Cambridge.
Exhibitions: One-man exhibs, Green Gallery, 64, Dwan Gallery, 66, Andre Emmerich Gallery, New York, 66 & 68 & Logiudice Gallery, 72.
Bibliography: Richard Hirsch (auth), Private affinities & public users, Arts Mag, Vol 40, No 7; John Perreault (auth), Systematic painting, Art Forum, 11/66; Lucy Lippard (auth), Peverse perspectives, Art Int, 3/67.
Dealer: Walter Kelly Inc, 10 E Elm St, Chicago, IL 60601.
Mailing Address: c/o Wyoming, 333 Park Ave S, New York, NY 10010.

WILLIAMS, SHIRLEY C
Sculptor
Preferred Media: Wood.
b Hackensack, N J, Aug 22, 30.
Study & Training: Art Stud League New York, with Sidney Dickenson, Gene Scarpantoni & William Dobbin; Frank Reilly Sch Art, New York, with Jack Faragasso; Craft Stud League, New York, with Domenico Facci; John C Campbell Folk Art Sch, N C.
Work in Public Collections: Northeastern Loggers Exhib Hall, Old Forge, N Y.
Commissions: William of Orange coat of arms, Dutch Reformed Church, Spring Valley, N Y, 67; symbol, Smokey Bear, in the round, State of Vt, 69; Arabian show horse portrait, John R

Zehner, Nyack, N Y, 70; audubon owl accoutrements, Tippy Arnold, Ho-Ho-Kus, N J, 71; regional estate carving, Lakewood Sch, Congers, N Y, 71.
Exhibitions: Catharine Lorillard Wolfe Art Club 70th Ann, Gramercy Park, New York, 67; Vermont Lumberjack Roundup, State of Vt, Lake Dunmore-Killington, 68-71; Int Wood Collectors Exhib, U S Nat Arboretum, Washington, D C, 71; Am Artists Prof League Grand Nat, New York, 72; Northeastern Loggers Exhib Hall, 72.
Awards: Am Artists Prof League Hon Mention, 72.
Bibliography: Sybil C Harp (auth), The lady woodcarver, Creative Crafts Mag, fall 67; Ed Gallenstein (auth), Profile of Shirley C Williams, Chip Chats Nat Wood Carvers Mag, winter 68; George Fowler (auth), Woodcarving with the feminine touch, Northern Logger Mag, 12/71.
Memberships: Fel Am Artists Prof League; Int Wood Collectors Soc; Nat Wood Carvers Asn; Am Forestry Asn; Northeastern Loggers Asn.
Publications: Auth, Introduction to wood sculpture, Int Wood Collectors Soc Bull, 70.
Mailing Address: Box 43, Lake Rd, Rockland Lake, NY 10989.

WILLIAMS, TOMMY CARROLL
Art Historian, Painter
Preferred Media: Acrylics.
b Childress, Tex, July 6, 40.
Study & Training: Lubbock Christian Col, AA; W Tex State Univ, BS; Univ Okla, MEd.
Work in Public Collections: Okla Christian Col, Oklahoma City; Cent Art Galleries, New York, N Y; Southwest Tex State Univ, San Marcos.
Exhibitions: The Cutting Edge, Oklahoma City, 67; Statewide Faculty Show, Cent State Univ, Edmond, 68.
Teaching: Instr art, Okla Christian Col, 62-67, asst prof art, 67-69; asst prof art hist & gallery dir, Southwest Tex State Univ, 70-
Awards: First pl in painting, St Luke's Methodist Church Cutting Edge, Statewide Painting & Sculpture, Oklahoma City, 67.
Bibliography: Articles, In: local newspapers, Tex & Okla, 62-
Memberships: Col Art Asn Am; Kappa Pi.
Research: Specializing in nineteenth-twentieth century European and American art.
Publications: Auth, Notebook for art appreciation courses, 65 & 67; illusr, Oklahoma oil journal, 68.
Mailing Address: 414-B Sarah Dr, San Marcos, TX 78666.

WILLIAMS, WALTER (HENRY)
Painter, Printmaker
b Brooklyn, N Y, Aug 11, 20.
Study & Training: Brooklyn Mus Art Sch, 51-55; Skowhegan Sch Painting & Sculpture, summer 53; also with Ben Shahn, spring 52.
Work in Public Collections: Whitney Mus Am Art, New York, N Y; Brooklyn Mus; Nat Gallery Arts, Washington, D C; Riverside Mus, New York; Metrop Mus Art, New York.
Exhibitions: Five shows, Whitney Mus Ann, 53-63; Int Watercolor Biennial, Brooklyn Mus, 63; Corner, Charlottenborg, Copenhagen, Denmark, 63; Pa Acad Ann, 66; Nat Acad Design, 147th Ann, 72.
Teaching: Artist-in-residence, Fisk Univ, 68-69.
Awards: John Hay Whitney Found fel, 55; Nat Inst Arts & Lett grant, 60; Adolph & Clara Obrig Prize, Nat Acad Design, 72.
Bibliography: Cedric Dover (auth), American negro art, Studio, London, 58; Janet Erickson & Adelaide Sproul (auth), Printmaking without a press, Reinhold, 67.
Memberships: Billed Kunstnernes Forbund, Denmark.
Dealer: Terry Dintenfass Inc, 18 E 67th St, New York, NY 10021.
Mailing Address: Hospitalsvej 4, Copenhagen, Denmark F 2000.

WILLIAMS, WARNER
Sculptor, Designer
b Henderson, Ky, Apr 23, 03.
Study & Training: Berea Col; Herron Art Inst; Art Inst Chicago, BFA.
Work in Public Collections: Martin Luther King bas-relief portrait, King Mem, Atlanta, Ga; Albert Schweitzer medallion, Schweitzer Mem Mus, Switz; Queen Marie medal, Vienna Diplomatic Acad & Theresianische Acad; Thomas Edison Commemorative Medal, Smithsonian Inst & Edison Mus, East Orange, N J; Helen Keller medallion, 35 schs for blind, U S; plus many other mem, medals, medallions, bas-reliefs & busts.
Positions: Artist-in-reidence, Culver Mil Acad, Ind, 40-68.
Awards: Six awards, Hoosier Salon, 28-42; award, City of Chicago, 38; prize, Art Inst Chicago, 41; plus others.
Memberships: Chicago Art Club; Chicago Art Asn; Hoosier Salon; Nat Sculpture Soc.
Mailing Address: Geodesic Dome Studio, Culver, IN 46511.

WILLIAMSON, CLARA McDONALD
Painter
Preferred Media: Oils.
b Iredell, Tex, Nov 20, 75.
Work in Public Collections: Dallas Mus Fine Arts, Inc, Amon Carter Mus, Fort Worth, Tex; Valley House Gallery, Dallas; Mus Mod Art, New York, N Y; Wichita Art Mus, Kans.
Exhibitions: One-man show, Dallas Mus Fine Arts, 48; American Painting of Today, 1950, Metrop Mus, New York, 50; Am Contemp Natural Painters, 53-54 & Am Primitive Painting Exhib, 58-59, Smithsonian Inst, Washington, D C; Int Exhib Primitive Art, Bratislava, Czech, 66; plus others.
Awards: Raiberto Comini Purchase Award, 45 & 47, Dealey Purchase Award, 46 & Summerfield G Roberts Award, 54, Dallas Mus Fine Arts.
Bibliography: Vogel (auth), The paintings of Aunt Clara, Univ Tex Press, 66.
Mailing Address: c/o Valley House Gallery, 6616 Spring Valley Rd, Dallas, TX 75240.

WILLIS, ELIZABETH BAYLEY
Art Historian, Collector
b Somerville, Mass, May 9, 02.
Study & Training: Univ Wash, AB, with Lyonel Feininger, Mark Tobey & Morris Graves.
Positions: Assoc, Willard Gallery, New York, 43-46; cur, Henry Gallery, Univ Wash, 46-48; cur, San Francisco Mus Art, 48-50; acting asst dir, Calif Palace Legion of Honor, 50-51; consult decorative arts, prod & mkt, Mingei Kan, Tokyo, 51-52; mem UN Tech Asst Bd for Taiwan, Vietnam, India & Morocco, 52-59; consult textile export, India, 55-57.
Research: Tribes of India's northeast frontier, especially their arts and textiles; textile arts of India; folk arts of Japan.
Collection: Artifacts, pottery and textiles from Tibet, Bhutan, Japan & Morocco, now in the Permanent Collection of the Smithsonian Institution; costumes and textiles from the same countries now in Permanent Collections of the University of Washington and the Washington State Museum; Ming and Ch'ing paintings in a private collection.
Mailing Address: Rte 8, Box 8835, Bainbridge Island, WA 98110.

WILLSON, ROBERT
Sculptor, Educator
Preferred Media: Glass, Enamel, Ceramics.
b Mertzon, Tex, May 28, 12.
Study & Training: Univ Tex, BA; Univ Bellas Artes, Guanajuato, Mex, MFA; also with Jose Clemente Orozco.
Work in Public Collections: Mus Correr, Venice, Italy; Nat Glass Mus, Murano, Italy; Nat Mus, Auckland, N Z; Witte Art Mus, San Antonio, Tex; Lowe Art Mus, Coral Gables, Fla.
Commissions: Glass sculptures, comn by Harmon Gallery, Naples, Fla, 69; ceramic sculptures, comn by Mrs Robert Hoffman, Naples, 70; glass sculpture doorway, comn by Herbert Martin, Miami, Fla, 72; enamel sculpture, Exec Plaza, Miami, 72.
Exhibitions: Painting & Sculpture Nat, San Francisco Mus Art, 57; Int Glass Sculpture, 64, 66 & 68, Venice, 68; one-man shows, Robert Willson Glass Sculpture, Mus Correr, 68, Ringling Art Mus, Sarasota, Fla, 70 & Corning Mus Glass, N Y, 71; Biennale Exhib, Venice, Italy, 72.
Collections Arranged: 3500 Yrs Colombian Art, Lowe Art Mus, 60; Fragments of Egypt, Peoria Art Mus, 69.
Teaching: Chmn dept art, Tex Wesleyan Col, 40-48; assoc prof art, Univ Miami, 52-
Positions: Dir, Coun Ozark Artists, 50-52; pres & dir, Fla Craftsmen, 52-58.
Awards: Nat hon mention for sculpture, San Francisco Mus Art, 57; Shell Co Found grant for glass sculpture, 71; grand medal award winner for sculpture, Garden Mod Art, Miami, 72.
Bibliography: Roland Fleischer (auth), Some recent experiments in glass, 65 & Paul Perrot (auth), Robert Willson—sculptor in glass 69, Col Art J; Frank Wills (auth), Robert Willson glass sculpture, Mnemosyne, 68.
Memberships: Col Art Asn Am; Am Asn Mus.
Research: History of glass as sculpture.
Publications: Ed, Kress Collection, 61 & auth, Art concept in clay, 67, Univ Miami Press; auth, College-level art curriculum in glass, Dept Health, Educ & Welfare, 68.
Dealers: Galerie 99, 1135 Kane Concourse, Bay Harbor Island, Miami, FL 33154; Harmon Art Gallery, 1258 Third St S, Naples, FL 33940.
Mailing Address: 7955 S W 126 Terr, Miami, FL 33156.

WILMARTH, CHRISTOPHER MALLORY
Sculptor, Instructor
Preferred Media: Glass, Steel, Wood.
b Sonoma, Calif, June 11, 43.
Study & Training: Cooper Union, BFA, 65.
Work in Public Collections: Mus Mod Art, New York, N Y; Philadelphia Mus; Art Inst Chicago; Woodward Found, Washington, D C; Lannan Found, Palm Beach, Fla.
Exhibitions: Whitney Ann, Whitney Mus Am Art, New York, 66, 68 & 70; one-man show, Graham Gallery, New York, 68; Art Vivant Estats Unis, Dore Ashton Found, Maeght, France, 70; one-man shows, Paula Cooper Gallery, New York, 71 & 72; Am Ann, Art Inst Chicago, 72.
Teaching: Adj prof sculpture, Cooper Union, 69-; vis critic sculpture, Yale Univ, 71-72.
Awards: Nat Coun Arts grant, 69; John Simon Guggenheim Mem fel, 70-71; Howard Found fel, 72.
Bibliography: Dore Ashton (auth), Radiance & reserve, Arts Mag, 3/71; Robert Pincus Witten (auth), C Wilmarth a note on pictorial sculpture, 5/71 & Joseph Masheck (auth), rev, 6/72, Artforum.
Dealer: Paula Cooper Gallery, 96 Prince St, New York, NY 10012.
Mailing Address: P O Box 85, Prince St Station, New York, NY 10012.

WILMETH, HAL TURNER
Art Historian, Painter
b Lincoln, Nebr, July 9, 17.
Study & Training: Kansas City Art Inst, with Thomas Hart Benton, BFA; Univ Chicago, with W Middeldorf & O Von Simson, MA; Univ degli Studii, Florence, Italy, with Longhi & Salmi.
Work in Public Collections: Univ Okla.
Teaching: Instr art hist, Univ Nebr, 48-54; dean stud, art hist & humanities, Calif Col Arts & Crafts, 55-60; chmn dept art hist, Dominican Col, 61-
Positions: Dir, Gumps Art Gallery, San Francisco, Calif, 54-60.
Awards: Fulbright grant, Italy, 49-51.
Memberships: Am Asn Univ Prof; Col Art Asn Am.
Mailing Address: 96 Half Moon Rd, Novato, CA 94947.

WILNER, MARIE SPRING
Painter
Preferred Media: Oils, Watercolors, Collage, Plastic.
b Paris, France; U S citizen.
Study & Training: Hunter Col, BA; Art Stud League New York, N Y; New Sch Social Res, with Camillo Egas & Samuel Adler.
Work in Public Collections: Tweed Mus, Univ Minn; Norfolk Mus, Va; Mus Ga; Bridgeport Mus, Conn; Birmingham Mus, Ala.
Exhibitions: Pa Acad Fine Arts, 61; Butler Inst Am Art, 63; Sheldon Swope Mus, 68; Tweed Mus, Univ Minn, 69; Salon Autumn, Paris, 72.
Awards: Gold medal, Ann Exhib Am Artists Prof League; Grumbacher Purchase Prize, Nat Asn Women Artists Ann; bronze medal, Third Biennale Int, Ancona, Italy.
Bibliography: Vallobra (auth), De l'honneur et du deshonneur des hommes; article & cover, In: Design, 62.
Memberships: Life fel Royal Soc Art, London; Int Arts Guild, Monaco; Nat Assoc Arts & Lett; Nat Asn Women Artists (gallery chmn, 62, jury mem, 65 & chmn jury awards, 67); Soc Encouragement Progres, Paris (chevalier, 68, officer, 71).
Dealers: Dickson Gallery, 3237 P St N W, Washington, DC 20007; Sue Fischman, Fort Lauderdale, FL 33310.
Mailing Address: 1248 White Plains Rd, Bronx, NY 10473.

WILSON, ALBERT LEON
Sculptor, Illustrator
b Jamaica, N Y, June 23, 20.
Work in Public Collections: Men & Minotaurs (sculpture & print), Roberson Art Ctr, Binghampton, N Y; Our Man on the Moon (sculpture), Strassenburg Planetarium, Rochester, N Y; Busted Bike, Roy Neuberger Collection to N Y State Mus, Albany; also in collection of Gov Nelson A Rockefeller.
Commissions: Phoenix, Allendale Sch, Rochester, 68; baptismal font, Faith Lutheran Church, Webster, N Y, 69; main altar, Faith Lutheran Church, Webster, 69; Eagle, Munic Bldg Courtroom, Fulton, N Y, 70; Comet (busted bike), Kaufman Bldg, New York, N Y, 72; plus others.
Exhibitions: York State Craft Fair, Ithaca Col, N Y; Northeast Craft Fair, Am Craftmen's Coun, Mount Snow, Vt, 67; two-man show, 71 & Finger Lakes Exhib, 71, Univ Rochester Mem Art Gallery; New American Sculpture, U S Info Agency touring exhib to Europe, Asia & Africa, 71-72; plus others.
Positions: Layout artist & designer, J C Penney Co, New York, 46-54; art dir, Sibley, Lindsay & Curr, Rochester, 56-58; art dir, illusr & free lance photog, 58-59; art group supvr, Rumrill-Hoyt, Inc, 58-67.
Awards: Over twenty graphic art awards, Rochester Soc Communicating Artists, 57-67.
Bibliography: Iron man, Upstate, 68; David Spengler (auth), He unleashes his art on the steel girder, N J Papers, 71; article, In: U S Info Serv Photo Bull, 9/72; plus others.

Memberships: Am Craftsmen's Coun; York State Craftsmen; Lake Country Craftsmen; Sculpt-your-own-bronze Club; Nantucket Artist's Asn.
Art Interests: Originator of box-beam sculpture and sculpture printing.
Mailing Address: c/o Wilson Gallery, 695 Park Ave, Rochester, NY 14607.

WILSON, BEN
Painter, Lecturer
Preferred Media: Oils.
b Philadelphia, Pa, June 23, 13.
Study & Training: Nat Acad Design, 31-33; City Col New York, with Eggers, BSS, 35; Acad Julien, Paris, France, 53-54.
Work in Public Collections: Everhart Mus, Scranton, Pa; Fairleigh Dickinson Collection Self Portraits; Norfolk Mus, Va; Faberge Collection, Ridgefield, N J; Almeras Collection, Paris.
Exhibitions: Riverside Mus, 55; Newark Mus, 56, triennial, 61; Montclair Mus nine from 56-72; Everhart Mus, 65 & 66; N J Pavilion, New York World's Fair, 65-66.
Teaching: Instr painting & drawing, City Col New York, 46-48; instr life drawing, Jamesine Franklin Sch Art, 50; lectr mod art, New York Univ, 62-68.
Awards: Agnes B Noyes Award for watercolor, 59 & Skinner award for abstract oils, 63, Montclair Mus; Ford Found artist-in-residence, Everhart Mus, 65.
Bibliography: Bugatti (auth), International encyclopedia of artists, Univ Europa, 70-71.
Memberships: Mod Artists Guild (v pres, 63); Assoc Artists N J.
Publications: Auth, Cobra, Artists Proof, 66.
Dealer: Galerie A G, rue de l'universite, Paris, France.
Mailing Address: 596 Broad Ave, Ridgefield, NJ 07657.

WILSON, CHARLES BANKS
Painter, Lithographer
Preferred Media: Egg Tempera.
b Springdale, Ark, Aug 6, 18.
Study & Training: Art Inst Chicago, lithography with Francis Chapin, painting with Louis Riman & Boris Anisfeld & watercolor with Hubert Ropp.
Work in Public Collections: Metrop Mus Art, New York, N Y; Corcoran Gallery Art, Washington, D C; Gilcrease Inst Am Hist & Art, Tulsa, Okla; Joslyn Art Mus, Omaha, Nebr; Smithsonian Inst, Washington, D C.
Commissions: 50 Watercolors, Ford Motor Co, 51-69; oil mural, comn by J D Rockefeller, Jr, Jackson Lake Lodge, Wyo, 55; portraits, of Thomas Gilcrease, Gilcrease Inst Am Hist & Art, 57 & Will Rogers, Okla Press Asn, Oklahoma City, 61; rotunda murals, Okla State Legis, 70; plus others.
Exhibitions: Int Watercolor Exhib, Art Inst Chicago, 39; Am Watercolor Exhib, Springfield, Mo, 70; some 200 nat & regional exhibs.
Teaching: Head art, Northeastern Okla Agr & Mech Col, 47-60.
Awards: Chicago Soc Lithographers & Etchers Award, 39; first prize for prints, Brooklyn Mus, 43; Libr Cong Purchases, Nat Print Exhibs, 44-54.
Bibliography: An Indian party, Collier's Mag, 7/25/42; Hold before the young, Okla Today, 69; Painting mural portraits, Am Artists, 11/69.
Publications: Illusr, Treasure island, 48, Company of adventures, 49, The mustangs, 52 & Geronimo, 58; auth, Indians of eastern Oklahoma, 57.
Mailing Address: 100 N Main St, Miami, OK 74354.

WILSON, EDWARD N
Sculptor, Educator
Preferred Media: Metals, Concrete.
b Baltimore, Md, Mar 28, 25.
Study & Training: Univ Iowa, BA, MA; Univ N C.
Work in Public Collections: Howard Univ; plus numerous pvt collections.
Commissions: Mem in bronze, Duke Univ, Durham, N C, 65; JFK (park design & sculpture), City of Binghamton & Sun Bull Fund, N Y, 66-69; Second Genesis (aluminum sculpture), City of Baltimore for Lake Clifton Sch, Md, 70-71; Mem in bronze, Harlem Commonwealth Coun, 72; Middle Passage (concrete & bronze), City of New York, Brooklyn, N Y, 72-73.
Exhibitions: N C Mus Art, Raleigh, N C, 55, 61 & 62; 155th Ann Exhib Am Painting & Sculpture, Pa Acad Fine Arts & Detroit Inst Arts, 60; Am Negro Art, Univ Calif, Los Angeles, 66, Univ Calif, Davis, 66, San Diego & Oakland, Calif, 67; Artists of Central New York, Munson-Williams-Proctor Mus, 66-68; 30 Contemporary Black Artists, nat circulated, 68-70.
Teaching: Prof sculpture, State Univ N Y Binghamton, 64-, chmn dept art & art hist, 68-72.
Positions: Artist-in-residence, humanities div, Western Mich Univ, 69.

Awards: Award for sculpture, Md Artists 24th Ann, Baltimore Mus Art, 56; purchase prize for sculpture, New Vistas in Am Art, Howard Univ, 61; fel, State Univ N Y, 66-68.
Bibliography: Cedric Dover (auth), American Negro art, N Y Graphic Soc, 60; Art & rebuttal, Christian Sci Monitor, 4/21/71; H Hope (auth), article, In: Art J, spring Vol 31, No 3.
Memberships: Col Art Asn Am (bd dirs, 70, secy & chmn artists comt, 71-); State Univ N Y-Wide Comt Arts.
Publications: Auth, Contemporary sculpture: some trends & problems, 63; auth, Statement, Arts in Soc, fall-winter 68-69; auth, CAA & Negro colleges, Art J, winter 68-69.
Mailing Address: Dept of Art & Art History, State University of New York at Binghamton, Binghamton, NY 13901.

WILSON, JANE
Painter
b Seymour, Iowa, Apr 29, 24.
Study & Training: Univ Iowa, BA, MA.
Work in Public Collections: Mus Mod Art, New York, N Y; Whitney Mus Am Art, New York; Wadsworth Atheneum, Hartford, Conn; New York Univ; Rockefeller Inst, New York; plus many others.
Exhibitions: Whitney Mus Am Art, New York, 63 & 68; Smithsonian Traveling Exhib, 68; Newport Festival Art, 68; Univ Iowa, 69; Finch Col, N Y, 69; plus many other group & one-man shows.
Teaching: Instr art hist, Pratt Inst, 67-69.
Awards: Tiffany grant, 67.
Dealer: Graham Galleries, 1014 Madison Ave, New York, NY 10021.
Mailing Address: 177 E 87th St, New York, NY 10028.

WILSON, MAY
Sculptor
b Baltimore, Md, Sept 28, 05.
Work in Public Collections: Whitney Mus Am Art, New York, N Y; Baltimore Mus; Goucher Col, Baltimore; Corcoran Gallery Art, Washington, D C; Dela Banque de Pariset, Brussels, Belg.
Exhibitions: New Idea, New Media Show, Martha Jackson Gallery, New York, 60; Mus Mod Art Traveling Assemblage, New York, 62; Am Fedn Arts Patriotic Traveling Show, New York, 68; Human Concern Show, 69 & Whitney Sculpture Ann, 70, Whitney Mus Am Art.
Awards: Awards, Baltimore Mus Art Shows, 52 & 59.
Bibliography: Bill Wilson (auth), Grandma Moses of the underground, Art & Artists, 5/68; Woo who? May Wilson (film), Amalie Rothschild, 70; May Wilson (videotape), Lee Ferguson, 7/14/71.
Dealer: Gimpel & Weitzenhoffer, 1040 Madison Ave, New York, NY 10021.
Mailing Address: 208 W 23rd St, New York, NY 10011.

WILSON, SOL
Painter
Preferred Media: Oils, Casein, Watercolors.
b Poland, Aug 23, 96; U S citizen.
Study & Training: Cooper Union, 18; Nat Acad Design, 20-22; Beaux Arts, New York; also with George Bellows & Robert Henri.
Work in Public Collections: Whitney Mus Am Art, New York, N Y; Brooklyn Mus, N Y; Youngstown Mus Art, Ohio; Metrop Mus Art, New York; Libr of Cong, Washington, D C.
Commissions: Delmar Post Off, N Y, 44, Westhampton Beach Post Off, 46, Fed Art Proj, U S Treas Dept.
Exhibitions: Carnegie Inst Int Exhib, 47; Corcoran Gallery Art Nat Exhib, Washington, D C, 47; Inst Arts & Lett Ann, 50; Butler Inst Am Art, Youngstown, Ohio, 65; Nat Acad Design Ann, New York, 68.
Teaching: Instr painting, Am Artists Sch, 38; instr painting, Sch Art Studies, 46-49; instr painting, Art Stud League New York, 68-69.
Awards: Corcoran Biennial, 47; Carnegie Inst Ann, 47; grant, Am Acad Arts & Lett.
Bibliography: Earnest Watson (auth), American drawing, 57 & Landscape painting, 62; Sol Wilson, Horizon Mag, 61.
Memberships: Nat Acad Design; Audubon Artists; Artists Equity Asn; Provincetown Art Asn.
Dealer: Babcock Galleries, 805 Madison Ave, New York, NY 10021.
Mailing Address: 200 W 72nd St, New York, NY 10023.

WILSON, SYBIL
Painter, Designer
Preferred Media: Acrylics.
b Tulsa, Okla, Mar 20, 23.
Study & Training: Art Stud League New York, with Ernest Fiene; Yale Univ Sch Art & Archit, with Josef Albers, BFA & MFA; also with Anni Albers.
Work in Public Collections: New York Univ Collection; Univ Ky Collection; Univ Mass Collection; Univ Bridgeport Collection; Chase Manhattan Bank Collection; plus others.

Exhibitions: One-man shows, Grand Cent Mod Gallery, New York, N Y, 62 & 65; Retinal Art in U S Traveling Exhib, 66; one-man shows, East Hampton Gallery, New York, 70 & Woods, Gerry Gallery, R I Sch Design, 72.
Teaching: Prof art, Univ Bridgeport, 54-; adj prof art, R I Sch Design, 70-72.
Awards: Am Inst Graphic Arts 50 Best Bks Award, 60.
Publications: Ed, Anni Albers: on designing, Pellango Press, New Haven, 60.
Dealer: East Hampton Gallery, 450 W 27th St, New York, NY 10025.
Mailing Address: 66 Rennell St, Bridgeport, CT 06602.

WILSON, TOM MUIR
Designer
Preferred Media: Graphics.
b Bellaire, Ohio, Dec 6, 30.
Study & Training: W Va Inst Technol; Cranbrook Acad Art, BFA; Rochester Inst Technol, MFA.
Exhibitions: One-man shows, Rochester, N Y & Wheeling, W Va, 57, 59 & 61; Boston Art Festival, 61; Photog Exhib, George Eastman House, Rochester, N Y, 63; Western N Y Ann, Buffalo, 63 & 64; Art of Two Cities, Minneapolis, 65; plus others.
Teaching: Prof art & instr photog & graphic design, Minneapolis Sch Art; instr photog, Rochester Inst Technol; instr sculpture & design, Nazareth Col Rochester.
Positions: Designer exhib galleries, George Eastman House Mus Photog, 61-62; free lance photogr & graphic designer, New York, Rochester & Minneapolis, 61-
Awards: Award for sculpture, Art Inst Am Inst Architects, 56; prize, Philadelphia Print Club, 61.
Mailing Address: 13720 Vincent Ave S, Burnsville, MN 55378.

WILSON, (RONALD) YORK
Painter
b Toronto, Ont, Dec 6, 07.
Study & Training: Cent Tech Sch, Toronto; Ont Col Art.
Work in Public Collections: Nat Gallery Can; Nat Mus Art Mod, Paris; Mus Mod Art, Mex; Birla Acad Mus, Calcutta, India; Art Gallery Ont.
Commissions: Murals, McGill Univ, Montreal, 54, Imp Oil, Toronto, 57, O'Keefe Ctr, Toronto, 59 & Gen Hosp, Port Arthur, 65; mosaic, Carleton Univ, Ottawa, 70.
Exhibitions: New York World's Fair, 39; Carnegie Int, Pittsburgh, Pa, 52; Bienial São Paulo, Brazil, 63; Main Gallery, Mus Galliera, 63; one-man show, Bellas Artes, Mex, 69.
Awards: Winnipeg Show Award, 56; Baxter Award, Toronto, 60; Can Centennial Medal, 67.
Bibliography: Mural (film), Crawley Films, 57; Michael Foytenay (auth), York Wilson (film), Nat Film Bd, 62; Michel Seuphor (auth), York Wilson (catalog), 64.
Memberships: Royal Can Acad; Ont Soc Artists (pres, 46-49); Can Group Painters (pres, 68).
Publications: Illusr, Face at the bottom of the world, Hagiwara Sukitaro Publ, Tokyo.
Dealer: Roberts Gallery, 641 Yonge St, Toronto, Ont, Can.
Mailing Address: 41 Alcina Ave, Toronto 176, Ont, Can.

WIMBERLEY, FRANK WALDEN
Painter, Sculptor
Preferred Media: Collage.
b Pleasantville, N J, Aug 31, 26.
Study & Training: Howard Univ, with Lois M Jones, James Wells & James Porter.
Work in Public Collections: Mus Mod Art, New York, N Y; Storefront Mus, New York.
Exhibitions: C W Post Col, N Y, 69; Whitney Rebuttal, Acts of Art Gallery, New York, 71; Hudson River Mus, Yonkers, N Y, 71; Seton Hall Univ, N J, 71; Dutchess Co Col, N Y, 72.
Memberships: Guild Hall, East Hampton, Long Island.
Dealer: Acts of Art Gallery, 15 Charles St, New York, NY 10003.
Mailing Address: 99-11 35th Ave, Corona, NY 11368.

WINCHESTER, ALICE
Art Editor
b Chicago, Ill, July 26, 07.
Study & Training: Smith Col, BA, 29.
Positions: Ed, Mag Antiques, 38-72; temporary cur, Whitney Mus Am Art, 72-74.
Memberships: Am Asn Mus; Soc Archit Historians; Furniture Hist Soc; Asn Preserv Technol; Am Ceramic Circle.
Research: American decorative arts; American folk art.
Publications: Co-ed, Primitive painters in America 1750-1950, 50; auth, How to know American antiques, 51; ed, The antiques treasury of furniture and other decorative arts, 59, Collectors and collections, 61 & Living with antiques, 63.
Mailing Address: 4 Currituck Rd, Newtown, CT 06470.

WINDFOHR, ROBERT F
Collector
Positions: Chmn bd, Fort Worth Art Ctr, Tex.
Mailing Address: 1900 Spanish Trail, Fort Worth, TX 76107.

WINER, ARTHUR HOWARD
Sculptor, Educator
Preferred Media: Steel.
b Lowell, Mass, Dec 11, 40.
Study & Training: Univ Mass, BA, 62; Univ Chicago, MFA, 63; Hobart Sch Welding, Troy, Ohio, 70; also with Hiroaki Morino & Katherin Nash.
Work in Public Collections: Univ Mass, Amherst; Rock Valley Col, Rockford, Ill; Art Inst Zanesville, Ohio; Cherryvale Shopping Ctr, Rockford, Ill; Hobart Sch Welding.
Commissions: Concrete relief, Mr Addison, Marietta, Ohio, 70; relief, James Mills, Marietta, 70; welded steel relief, Franklin Lee, Marietta, 71; free standing welded steel, Dr & Mrs G Krivchenia, Marietta, 71; welded steel relief & free standing, First Bank Marietta, 71 & 72.
Exhibitions: 27th & 29th Int Concorso Ceramica Arte, Faenza, Italy, 69 & 71; Butler Inst Am Art, Youngstown, Ohio, 69-71; U S A Nat, Mobile, Ala, 70; Metal Show, Am Soc Metals, Cleveland, Ohio, 70; Appalachain Corridors 3, Charleston, W Va, 72.
Teaching: Instr art, Rock Valley Col, 65-66; asst prof sculpture & ceramics, Marietta Col, 66-
Positions: Juror, Mainstreams Int Exhib, Marietta, 68-72; dir, Marietta Col Crafts Regional, 72.
Awards: Shell Oil-Marietta Col grants, 68-71.
Memberships: Col Art Asn Am; Am Asn Univ Prof; Nat Coun Educ Ceramic Arts; Am Crafts Coun; World Crafts Coun.
Publications: Contribr, Contemporary American ceramics (catalogue), 69.
Dealer: Park Avenue Gallery, Mount Kisco, NY 10549.
Mailing Address: 214 Rathbone Rd, Marietta, OH 45750.

WINER, DONALD ARTHUR
Museum Curator, Instructor
Preferred Media: Ceramics.
b St Louis, Mo, Oct 26, 27.
Study & Training: Univ Mo, BS, MA.
Collections Arranged: William Singer, Jr Retrospective, 67; Edwin W Zoller Retrospective, 68; Pennsylvania '71; George Hetzel Retrospective, 72; Pennsylvania Heritage, 72.
Teaching: Instr painting, drawing & art hist, Elizabethtown Col, 69-
Positions: Cur, Springfield Art Mus, Mo, 54-57; asst dir, Brooks Art Gallery, Memphis, Tenn, 57-59; dir, Montgomery Mus Fine Arts, Ala, 59-62; dir, Everhart Mus Art & Sci, 62-66; cur, Pa Collection Fine Arts, Pa Hist & Mus Comn, 66-
Memberships: Am Asn Mus; Northeastern Mus Conf; Pa Guild Craftsmen; Mid-State Artists.
Research: Pennsylvania painters; pottery of Pennsylvania.
Collection: American earthenware, especially slip decorated red ware.
Mailing Address: 3112 Schoolhouse Lane, Harrisburg, PA 17109.

WINES, JAMES N
Sculptor
b Oak Park, Ill, June 27, 32.
Study & Training: Syracuse Univ Sch Art, BA, 55.
Work in Public Collections: Albright-Knox Art Gallery, Buffalo, N Y; Stedelijk Mus, Amsterdam, Holland; Whitney Mus Am Art, New York, N Y; Tate Gallery, London, Eng; Walker Art Ctr, Minneapolis, Minn.
Commissions: Plaza sculpture, Hoffmann-La Roche Res Ctr, Nutley, N J, 64; plaza sculpture for libr, Univ Wis-Milwaukee, 65; lobby sculpture, Dana Arts Ctr, Colgate Univ, Hamilton, N Y, 67; sculpture for mall, State Capital Bldg, Albany, N Y, 68; sculpture for lobby, Treadwell Corp, New York, 68.
Exhibitions: Whitney Mus Am Art Sculpture Biennial, New York, 61-67; American Sculpture, São Paulo Biennial, Brazil, 63; Pittsburgh Int, Pa, 64; American Sculpture, Walker Art Ctr, Minneapolis, 64; International Sculpture, Tate Gallery, London, 65.
Teaching: Instr environ art, Sch Visual Art, 65-; instr environ workshop, New York Univ, 65-71.
Positions: Dir, Site, Inc, New York, 69-; mem, Arts & Bus Coop Coun, New York, 71-; mem, Fed Design Assembly, Washington, D C, 72; mem arts adv coun, Bicentennial Celebration, Washington, D C, 72.
Awards: Design in Steel, Iron & Steel Inst, 71.
Bibliography: David Sellin (auth), James Wines—sculpture, Colgate Univ Press, 66.
Publications: Auth, The case for site-oriented art, Landscape Archit, 7/71; auth, Site, Art & Artists, London, 10/71; co-auth, Street art, TA/BK, Holland, 1/72; co-auth, Peekskill melt, Art Gallery, 3/72; auth, The case for the big duck, Archit Forum, 4/72.

Dealer: Marlborough Gallery, 41 E 57th St, New York, NY 10022.
Mailing Address: 60 Greene St, New York, NY 10022.

WINGATE, ARLINE (HOLLANDER)
Sculptor
b New York, N Y.
Work in Public Collections: Syracuse Univ Mus, N Y; Nat Mus Stockholm, Sweden; Ghent Mus Belg; Farnsworth Mus, Rockland, Maine; Parrish Mus, Southampton, N Y; plus many others including pvt collections.
Exhibitions: Metrop Mus Art, New York; Whitney Mus Am Art, New York; Wadsworth Atheneum Mus; San Francisco Mus Art; Baltimore Mus, Md; plus many others in Paris, France, Belg, Buenos Aires, Arg, London, Eng & U S A including five one-man shows.
Dealer: Frank Rehn Gallery, 655 Madison Ave, New York, NY 10021.
Mailing Address: Baiting Hollow Rd, East Hampton, NY 11937.

WINGERT, PAUL STOVER
Educator, Writer
b Waynesboro, Pa, Nov 13, 00.
Study & Training: Columbia Col, AB; Columbia Univ, MA & PhD; Univ London; Sorbonne, Paris.
Collections Arranged: Arts of S Seas, Mus Mod Art, 46; African Negro Sculpture, De Young Mem Mus, 48; Prehistoric Stone Sculpture of Pac Northwest, Portland Art Mus, Ore, 51; Melanesian Art, War Mem Mus, Auckland, N Z, 52; S Pac Art, 53; African Sculpture, Baltimore Mus Art, 55-56; plus others.
Teaching: Cur fine arts & archaeol, 34-42, Columbia Univ, instr, 42-49, asst prof fine arts & archaeol, 49-54, assoc prof, 54-58, prof, 58-66, prof emer, 66-
Awards: Wenner-Gren grant S Seas, 52; Guggenheim Found fel, 55.
Memberships: Col Art Asn Am; Am Ethnol Soc; Polynesian Soc; Am Anthropol Asn; fel AAAS; plus others.
Publications: Auth, The sculpture of Negro Africa, 50, Art of the South Pacific Islands, 53 & Primitive Art, 62 & 65; co-auth, The Tsimshian: their arts and music, 51; contribr, articles & rev, In: Art Bull, Am Anthropologist, Transactions of New York Acad Sci, Col Art J, Art Digest, Sat Rev & others.
Mailing Address: 117 Highland Ave, Montclair, NJ 07042.

WINKEL, NINA
Sculptor
Preferred Media: Copper, Terra-cotta.
b Westfalen, Ger, May 21, 05; U S citizen.
Study & Training: Staedel Mus Sch, Frankfurt, Ger.
Work in Public Collections: Wall panel, Keene Valley Libr, N Y.
Commissions: Lassiter Mem, Lassiter Family, Charlotte, N C; Early Moravians (wall panels), Hanes Corp, Winston-Salem, N C; War Mem, Seward Park High Sch, New York, N Y; Group of Children, City of Wiesbaden, Albert Schweitzer Sch.
Exhibitions: Int Fairmount Park Exhib; Am Acad Arts & Lett; one-man show, Univ Notre Dame, 54; many shows, Nat Acad Design; Retrospective, Sculpture Ctr, 72.
Teaching: Instr sculpture, Clay Club Servicemen Canteen, 42-46.
Awards: E Watrous Gold Medal, 45 & Samuel F B Morse Gold Medal, 64, Nat Acad Design; bronze medal, Nat Sculpture Soc, 67-71.
Bibliography: Nancy Dryfoos (auth), Nina Winkel, Nat Sculpture Rev, 71.
Memberships: Fel Nat Sculpture Soc (secy, 65-68); assoc Nat Acad Design; Sculptors Guild; Sculpture Ctr (pres, 70-).
Research: Antiques; Byzantine mosaics.
Publications: Auth, var articles on sculpture & mosaics in periodicals.
Mailing Address: Keene Valley, NY 12943.

WINOKUR, JAMES L
Collector, Patron
b Philadelphia, Pa, Sept 12, 22.
Study & Training: Univ Pa, BS(econ), 43.
Positions: Trustee & mem mus art comt, Carnegie Inst, 67-; v pres & gov, Pittsburgh Plan for Art, 67-; fel Mus Art, Carnegie Inst, 68-; bd dirs, Arts & Crafts Ctr, Pittsburgh, 69-; trustee, Sara Mellon Scaife Found, 72-
Art Interests: Joseph Goto, American sculptor in welded steel.
Collection: Cobra paintings, drawings and sculpture including Carl-Henning Pedersen, Jorn, Corneille, Alichinsky, Ubac, Reinhoud and others; twentieth century American paintings, drawings and sculpture including John Kane, Dove, Avery, Joan Mitchell, Feininger, Wines, Sam Francis, Joseph Goto and others; prints from Old Masters to the twentieth century.
Mailing Address: 5625 Darlington Rd, Pittsburgh, PA 15217.

WINSHIP, FLORENCE SARAH
Illustrator
b Elkhart, Ind.
Study & Training: Chicago Acad Fine Arts; Art Inst Chicago.
Publications: Illusr, Woofus & Miss Sniff, Santa's surprise, The night before Christmas & The bird book; plus many other bks for children.
Mailing Address: 1111 Oxford Rd, Deerfield, IL 60015.

WINSOR, V JACQUELINE
Sculptor
b Nfld, Can, Oct 20, 41; U S citizen.
Study & Training: Yale Summer Sch Art & Music, 64; Mass Col Art, BFA, 65; Rutgers Univ, MFA, 67.
Exhibitions: American Women Artists, Hamburg Kunsthaus, Ger, 72; one-woman show, Nova Scotia Col Art & Design, Halifax, 72; group show, Va Commonwealth Univ, Richmond, 72; group show, Paula Cooper Gallery, New York, N Y, 72; Whitney Mus Am Art Ann of Painting & Sculpture, 73; plus other earlier shows.
Teaching: Instr art introd & ceramics, Douglass Col, 67; instr art introd, Middlesex Co Col & Newark State Teachers' Col, 68 & 69; instr ceramics, Mills Col Educ, 68 & 71; instr graphics, Loyola Univ, New Orleans, summer 69; instr ceramics, Greenwich House Pottery Sch, New York, 69-72; instr sculpture, Sch Visual Arts, New York, spring 71; instr art introd, Hunter Col, 72-73.
Bibliography: Grace Glueck (auth), Art notes, New York Times, 5/30/71; Elizabeth Bear (auth), Rumbles, 9/71 & Interview with Jackie Winsor, spring 72, Avalanche; plus others.
Mailing Address: 141 Canal Street, New York, NY 10002.

WINTER, CLARK
Sculptor
b Cambridge, Mass, Apr 4, 07.
Study & Training: Harvard Univ, AB; Ind Univ, MFA; Fontainebleau Acad Art; Art Stud League New York, N Y.
Work in Public Collections: Mus Art, Carnegie Inst; Aldrich Mus Contemp Art; Carnegie-Mellon Univ; Pittsburgh Hilton Hotel.
Exhibitions: Am Sculpture Exhib, Metrop Mus Art, 51; Sculpture Ann, Whitney Mus Am Art, 54; San Francisco Mus Art, 54; Third Int, Philadelphia Mus Art; Soc Sculptors.
Teaching: Instr, Ind Univ, 47-49; head dept sculpture, Kansas City Art Inst, 49-53; vis assoc prof, Univ Calif, Berkeley, 53 & 55; assoc prof sculpture, Carnegie-Mellon Univ, 55-70, emer prof, 72-
Mailing Address: 110 Birch Ave, Corte Madera, CA 94925.

WINTER, LUMEN MARTIN
Sculptor, Painter
Preferred Media: Watercolors, Oils.
b Ellery, Ill, Dec 12, 08.
Study & Training: Grand Rapids Jr Col; Cleveland Sch Art; Nat Acad Design; also study in France & Italy.
Work in Public Collections: Washington Co Mus, Hagerstown, Md; Libr of Cong, Washington, D C; Mus Contemp Art, Dallas, Tex; Columbus Mus Arts & Crafts, Ga; Vatican, Rome, Italy; plus many others.
Commissions: Lady of the Thruways (bronze figure), Knights of Columbus for Lady of Good Counsel Col, White Plains, N Y, 59; mosaic & bas-relief sculpture for chapels, U S Air Force Acad, Colorado Springs, Colo, 60-61; Apollo 13 official medallion for Capt James A Lovell, Jr, Houston, Tex, 70; Titans mural (oil on linen), United Nations, New York, N Y, 72; space age mosaic, AFL-CIO Hq Bldg, Washington, D C, 72.
Exhibitions: Nat Acad Design, New York; Int Color Lithography, Cincinnati Art Mus, Ohio, 44; Am Watercolor Soc Ann & traveling shows, 50-; Int Watercolor, Pa Acad Fine Arts, Philadelphia, 51; Geneva, Switz, 55; plus others.
Positions: V pres, Archit League New York, 55-57; art juror, various art shows.
Awards: Purchase award, Nat Acad Design, 65; Peterson Award, Salmagundi Club, 69; medallion, New York Bicentennial, Am Numismatic Soc, 72.
Bibliography: Norman Kent (auth) & Ernest Watson (auth), Lumen Martin Winter, Am Artist Mag, 50, 52, 59 & 66; Ralph Fabri (auth), Lumen Martin Winter, Today's Art, 66.
Memberships: Salmagundi Club (comts & juries, 50-); Am Watercolor Soc; Nat Soc Mural Painters (v pres, 53-55); New Rochelle Art Asn (pres, 52-54).
Research: Art works of Leonardo da Vinci.
Art Interests: Reconstruction of full size Last Supper.
Publications: Co-auth, The Last Supper of Leonardo da Vinci, Coward McCann, 53.
Mailing Address: 144 Overlook Circle, New Rochelle, NY 10804.

WINTER, ROGER
Painter, Educator
Preferred Media: Oils, Pencils.
b Denison, Tex, Aug 17, 34.
Study & Training: Univ Tex, BFA, 56; Univ Iowa, MFA, 60; Brooklyn Mus Sch, Beckmann scholar, 60.
Work in Public Collections: Mus Art, Univ Okla, Norman; Dallas Mus Fine Arts, Tex; Pollock Gallery, Southern Methodist Univ, Dallas; Nicholson Mem Libr & Mus, Longview, Tex; Oak Cliff Savings & Loan, Dallas.
Exhibitions: Texas Painting & Sculpture, 20th Century, Dallas, 71-72; two-man show, Whitte Mus, San Antonio, Tex, 67; one-man shows, Pollock Gallery, 68 & One i at a Time, 71, Southern Methodist Univ, Dallas & Delgado Mus Art, New Orleans, La, 68.
Teaching: Instr painting, Fort Worth Art Ctr, 61; instr painting, Dallas Mus Fine Arts, 62-68; assoc prof painting, Southern Methodist Univ, 65-
Positions: Installation asst, Dallas Mus Contemp Arts, 62-63; gallery tours & lectr, Dallas Mus Fine Arts, 63-
Awards: Purchase award, Univ Okla Art Mus, 62; top award, Dallas Ann, Dallas Mus Fine Arts, 64.
Bibliography: Douglas McAgy (auth), One i at a time (exhib catalogue), Southern Methodist Univ Press, 71; film on work produced on KERA-TV, Dallas, 71.
Dealer: Cranfill Gallery, 2710 Routh, Dallas, TX 75201.
Mailing Address: 3228 Rankin, Dallas, TX 75205.

WINTER, RUTH
Painter
Preferred Media: Oils.
b New York, N Y, Jan 17, 13.
Study & Training: New York Univ, BS, 31, MA, 32; Art Stud League New York, with Corbino, Bosa & Morris Kantor, 57-61.
Work in Public Collections: In collections of Reginald Cabral, Provincetown, Mass, Marlo Lewis, Scarsdale, N Y, Mr Frantz, Great Neck, N Y, Lawrence Koenisberg, South Lawrence, N Y & Seymour S Alter, West Hempstead, N Y.
Exhibitions: Am Art at Mid-century, Orange, N J, 57; Nat Asn Women Artists, 57-68; Art U S A, Provincetown, Mass, 58; Brooklyn Mus, 60; Nat Acad Design, 60.
Awards: Marcia Brady Tucker Prize, Nat Asn Women Artists, 57; Max Low Award, 59; Mr & Mrs Gomes Award, Mahopac Art League, 59.
Bibliography: Robert M Coates (auth), The art galleries, New Yorker, 5/57; Stuart Preston (auth), Art: a game of styles, New York Times, 5/57; Painting televised, Boston, 7/58.
Memberships: Nat Asn Women Artists; life mem Art Stud League New York; Mahopac Art League.
Mailing Address: 98-50 67th Ave, Rego Park, NY 11374.

WINTERNITZ, EMANUEL
Museum Curator, Writer
b Vienna, Austria, Aug 4, 98.
Study & Training: Univ Vienna, LLD.
Teaching: Lectr music, Fogg Mus & many U S univs & mus, 38-41; lectr music, Columbia Univ, 47-48; vis prof music, Yale Univ Sch Music, 49-60; vis prof music, Rutgers Univ, 61-68; prof music, City Univ New York, 68-
Positions: Mem staff, Metrop Mus Art, 42-49, cur musical instruments & musical collection, 49-, reorganized, Crosby Brown Collection Musical Instruments.
Awards: Guggenheim fel, 46; Am Coun Learned Soc fel, 62; Am Philos Soc grant, 69.
Memberships: Am Musicol Soc (coun mem, 56-58, chmn, N Y Chap, 60-62); Col Art Asn Am; Int Phenomenol Soc; Music Libr Asn; Soc Ethnomusicol.
Publications: Auth, Musical autographs from Monteverdi to Hindemith, Princeton Univ Press, 55; auth, Keyboard instruments in the Metropolitan Museum of Art, 61; auth, Musical instruments of the western world, McGraw, 67; auth, Musical instruments & their symbolism in western art, 67; plus contribr to many articles in prof publs, journals & mus bulletins.
Mailing Address: Metropolitan Museum of Art, Fifth Ave at 82nd St, New York, NY 10028.

WINTERS, DENNY
Painter
b Grand Rapids, Mich, Mar 17, 07.
Study & Training: Art Inst Chicago; Chicago Acad Fine Arts.
Work in Public Collections: Philadelphia Mus Art, Pa; San Francisco Mus Art, Calif.
Exhibitions: Mus Mod Art, New York; Art Inst Chicago, Ill; Pa Acad Fine Arts, Philadelphia; San Francisco Mus Art; Carnegie Inst, Pittsburgh, Pa; plus many other group & one-man shows.
Awards: Guggenheim fel, 48; Butler Inst Am Art Purchase Prize; Denver Mus First Prize Ann Art Show.

Publications: Illusr, Full fathom five & Savage summer; jacket design, Wilderness river.
Mailing Address: Rockport, ME 04856.

WINTERS, JOHN L
Painter, Printmaker
Preferred Media: Oils, Intaglio.
b Zalite, Latvia, Dec 10, 35; U S citizen.
Study & Training: R I Sch Design, BFA; Tulane Univ, MFA; Inst Allende, San Miguel Allende, Mex.
Work in Public Collections: Miss State Col Women Art Gallery, Columbus.
Exhibitions: Artist's Ann, 67 & Artists of the Southeast & Texas, 69, Delgado Mus, New Orleans, La; 57th Nat, Jackson, Miss, 67; Memphis Sesquicentennial, Brooks Art Gallery, Memphis, Tenn, 69; The Arts: The 8th Decade, Ga Col, Milledgeville, 71.
Teaching: Instr drawing, painting & printmaking, Miss State Col Women, 65-70; asst prof drawing, painting & printmaking, Univ Miss, 70-
Memberships: Col Art Asn Am.
Dealer: Dos Patos Gallery, 915 S Tancahua, Corpus Christi, TX 78403.
Mailing Address: P O Box 144, University, MS 38677.

WINTERSTEEN, BERNICE McILHENNY
Art Administrator, Collector
b Philadelphia, Pa, June 16, 03.
Study & Training: Smith Col, BA; Ursinius Col, hon LHD, 65; Villanova Univ, hon DFA, 67; Wilson Col, DFA, 68; Moore Col Art, DFA, 68.
Positions: Bd gov & trustee, womens comt, Philadelphia Mus Art, 47-64, pres, 64-68; organizer & first chmn vis comt, Smith Col Art Mus, 51; bd gov, Philadelphia Mus Col Art, 55-64; adv coun mem, Princeton Univ Mus Art, 58-; mem vis comt, design & visual arts dept, Harvard Univ, 64-; hon chmn, Nat Trust Preserv Conf, Philadelphia, 66; chmn, Philadelphia Art Festival, 67; hon chmn, Philadelphia Friends Am Mus Britain; mem mayor's comt for 1976 Bicentennial Observ & 1976 World's Fair Comt; plus many civic, art & state positions.
Awards: Distinguished Daughter of Pennsylvania, 64.
Memberships: Philadelphia Art Comn; charter mem Philadelphia Ctr Performing Arts.
Collection: Nineteenth & twentieth century French painting & sculpture; French Impressionist & Post-Impressionist paintings, including fifteen paintings by Picasso & Matisse's Lady in Blue.
Mailing Address: 1425 Mt Pleasant Rd, Villanova, PA 19085.

WIPER, THOMAS WILLIAM
Art Administrator, Painter
Preferred Media: Mixed Media, Watercolors, Acrylics, Film.
b San Francisco, Calif, June 1, 38.
Study & Training: Univ Ariz, with Charles Littler, BFA & MFA; Univ Calif, Berkeley, with Carl Kasten.
Exhibitions: Regional exhibs, 64-
Teaching: Instr, Foothill Col, 65-66; instr, Univ Ariz, 66-68.
Positions: Dir educ, Tucson Art Ctr, Ariz, 68-
Memberships: Am Fedn Arts; Tucson Coun Arts.
Mailing Address: Tucson Art Center School, 179 N Main Ave, Tucson, AZ 85705.

WISE, HOWARD
Art Dealer
b Cleveland, Ohio, Nov 6, 03.
Study & Training: Clare Col, Cambridge Univ, BA(honors); Western Reserve Univ; Cleveland Inst Art.
Positions: Estab Howard Wise Gallery of Present Day Painting & Sculpture, Cleveland, 57; dir, Howard Wise Gallery, New York, N Y, 60-
Specialty of Gallery: Kinetic & light art.
Mailing Address: 2 W 13th St, New York, NY 10011.

WISNOSKY, JOHN G
Painter, Educator
Preferred Media: Acrylics, Intaglio, Mixed Media.
b Springfield, Ill, Mar 21, 40.
Study & Training: Yale Univ Summer Sch Art, 61; Univ Ill, Urbana, BFA, 62, MFA, 64.
Work in Public Collections: Honolulu Acad Arts, Hawaii; Southern Ill Univ, Carbondale; Contemp Arts Ctr Hawaii, Honolulu; State Hawaii Found Cult & Arts; Mint Mus, Charlotte, N C.
Commissions: Pan Pac hall design, Hawaii Pavilion, Expo 70, Osaka, Japan, 70; sculpture, Ewa Beach Publ Libr, Oahu, Hawaii, 71; flora pacifica design, Ethnobotanical Expos, 71.
Exhibitions: Northwest Printmakers Int, Seattle, Wash, 65; Soc Am Graphic Artists, New York, N Y, 65; Presentation Artist Show in

conjunction with Boston Printmakers, Boston Mus Fine Art, 66; Drawings-U S A, Saint Paul Art Ctr, Minn, 67; Am Printmakers Exhib, Otis Art Inst, 68.
Teaching: Instr painting & design, Va Polytech Inst & State Univ, 64-66; asst prof painting, design, printmaking & advan drawing, Univ Hawaii, 66-
Positions: Owner, J Wisnosky Design Serv, 70-
Awards: Henry B Shope Prize, Soc Am Graphic Artists, 65; purchase Award, Honolulu Acad Arts, 70.
Bibliography: Jean Charlot (auth), rev, In: Honolulu Star-Bull, 9/13/67, 1/12/71 & 7/1/71; Webster Anderson (auth), rev, In: Honolulu Advertiser, 3/9/69 & 6/30/71.
Memberships: Honolulu Printmakers (pres, 69-70); Hawaii Painters & Sculptors League (pres, 69-70).
Dealer, Downtown Gallery, 125 Merchant St, Honolulu, HI 96822.
Mailing Address: 2110 Brown Way, Honolulu, HI 96822.

WITHAM, VERNON CLINT
Painter, Collector
Preferred Media: Mixed Media.
b Eugene, Ore, Dec 6, 25.
Study & Training: Univ Ore; Calif Sch Fine Arts, San Francisco.
Work in Public Collections: Univ Ore Mus Art, Eugene; Univ Wyo Mus Art, Laramie.
Exhibitions: Under 25, Seligmann Gallery, New York, N Y, 49; Artists of Oregon, Portland Art Mus, 53; one-man show, Calif Palace of Legion of Honor, San Francisco, 60; Maxwell Gallery, San Francisco, 61; The American Landscape, Peridot Gallery, New York, 68.
Teaching: Artist in residence, Univ Wyo, 71
Awards: Purchase award, Northwest Painting Ann, 72.
Collection: Antique primitive art from around the world.
Publications: Co-auth, 12 new painters (serigraph folio), 53; contribr, insert 4, The written palette, 62.
Dealer: Grandtour Gallery, 19 W Eighth, Eugene, OR 97401.
Mailing Address: 2100 Greiner, Eugene, OR 97405.

WITHROW, WILLIAM J
Art Administrator
b Toronto, Ont, Sept 30, 26.
Study & Training: Univ Toronto, BA, 50, BEd, 55 & MEd, 58, MA, 60.
Teaching: Head art dept, Earl Haig Col, 51-59.
Positions: Dir, Art Gallery Ont, Toronto, 60-
Awards: Can Centennial Medal, 67.
Memberships: Can Mus Asn; Am Asn Mus; Am Asn Art Mus Dirs; Can Art Mus Dirs Orgn; Can Nat Comt for Int Coun Mus.
Publications: Auth, Sorel Etrog sculpture, 67 & Contemporary Canadian painting, 72.
Mailing Address: c/o Art Gallery of Ontario, Grange Park, Toronto 133, Ont, Can.

WITKIN, JEROME PAUL
Painter, Educator
Preferred Media: Oils.
b Brooklyn, N Y, Sept 13, 39.
Study & Training: Cooper Union Art Sch, 57-60; Skowhegan Sch Painting & Sculpture; Berlin Acad, W Ger, Pulitzer traveling fel, 60; Univ Pa, MFA, 70.
Work in Public Collections: Minn Mus Art, Saint Paul; Univ N H, Durham; B K Smith Gallery, Lake Erie Col, Painesville, Ohio.
Exhibitions: One-man shows, Morris Gallery, New York, N Y, 62-64; A History of Collage, Grosvenor Gallery, London, 66; The Transatlantic, U S Artists in Eng, U S Embassy, London, 66; Drawings U S A, Minn Mus Art, 71; Drawings, Kraushaar Gallery, New York, 71.
Teaching: Instr drawing, Md Inst Art, Baltimore, 63-65; lectr painting, Manchester Col Art, Eng, 65-67; vis prof design, drawing & painting, Moore Col, 68-71; assoc prof art, Syracuse Univ, 71-
Awards: Guggenheim Found fel painting, 63-64.
Dealer: Kraushaar Galleries, 80th St & Madison Ave, New York, NY 10021.
Mailing Address: Lowe Art Center, 309 University Pl, College of Visual & Performing Arts, Syracuse University, Syracuse, NY 13210.

WITMEYER, STANLEY HERBERT
Art Administrator, Designer
Preferred Media: Watercolors, Mixed Media.
b Palmyra, Pa, Feb 14, 13.
Study & Training: Sch Art & Design, Rochester Inst Technol, dipl; State Univ N Y Col Buffalo, BS; Syracuse Univ, MFA; Univ Hawaii, with Ben Norris.
Work in Public Collections: Pvt collections.
Exhibitions: Rochester Mem Art Gallery; Albright-Knox Gallery, Buffalo; Honolulu Acad Fine Arts; Everson Mus, Syracuse.

Teaching: Instr art Cuba Pub Schs, N Y, 39-44; prof painting & design, Sch Art & Design, Rochester Inst Technol, 46-52.
Positions: Dir, Sch Art & Design, Rochester Inst Technol, 52-68, assoc dean Col Fine & Appl Arts, 68-
Awards: Distinguished Alumni Awards, State Univ N Y Col Buffalo, 68 & Rochester Inst Technol, 71; Athletic Hall of Fame Award, Rochester Inst Technol, 71.
Memberships: Rochester Torch Club (pres, 52); Nat Art Educ Asn; Rochester Art Club (pres, 56); Rochester Inst Technol Alumni Asn (pres, 52); N Y State Art Teachers Asn.
Collection: American printmakers and painters.
Publications: Auth, articles, In: Everyday Art, Design Mag, Sch Arts, Nat Art Educ J & N Y Art Teachers Bull.
Mailing Address: 51 Kron St, Rochester, NY 14619.

WITT, NANCY CAMDEN
Sculptor, Painter
b Richmond, Va, Oct 24, 30.
Study & Training: Randolph-Macon Woman's Col; Old Dom Univ, BA; Va Commonwealth Univ, MFA.
Work in Public Collections: Valentine Mus, Richmond; Chrysler Mus, Norfolk, Va; Mint Mus, Charlotte, N C; Univ Va, Charlottesville; Va Mil Inst, Lexington.
Commissions: Portrait, Ferrum Col, Va, 69; mobile construct, Philip Morris Tobacco Co, Richmond, 69-70; mural, Security Fed Savings & Loan Co, Richmond, 71.
Exhibitions: Five shows, Va Mus Biennial, Richmond, 61-69; Ringling Mus, Fla, 63; Miami Nat Painting Exhib, Coral Gables, Fla, 64; Southeastern Exhib, Atlanta, Ga, 64; Southeastern Exhib Prints & Drawings, Jacksonville, Fla, 65.
Teaching: Actg chmn art dept, Richard Bland Col, Col William & Mary, 61-63 & 64-65.
Dealer: Eric Schindler Gallery, 2305 E Broad St, Richmond, VA 23223.
Mailing Address: Rte 3, Box 643, Ashland, VA 23005.

WITTENBORN, GEORGE
Collector, Art Dealer
b Ger, May 13, 05; U S citizen.
Positions: Pres, art import & export co; publ & distribr bks & periodicals on fine & appl arts.
Memberships: Mus Mod Art; Metrop Mus Art.
Specialty of Gallery: Ultra modern art and statements.
Collection: Contemporary and experimental art.
Publications: Ed, Nelson Howe: body image & Paul Klee: nature of nature.
Mailing Address: 109 Edgemont Rd, Scarsdale, NY 10583.

WITTMANN, OTTO
Museum Director, Art Administrator
b Kansas City, Mo, Sept 1, 11.
Study & Training: Harvard Univ.
Collections Arranged: The Splendid Century, Masterpieces from France; Painting in Italy in 18th Century; The Age of Rembrandt; The Art of Van Gogh.
Teaching: Inst art hist, Skidmore Col, 38-41.
Positions: Cur, Hyde Collection, Glens Falls, N Y, 38-41; asst dir, Portland Mus Art, Ore, 41; assoc dir, Toledo Mus Art, 53-59, dir, 59-, ed, Mus News, 14 yrs; mem, Nat Endowment Arts Mus Adv Panel.
Awards: Chevalier, Legion d'Honneur, France; Commander, Order of Merit, Italy; Off, Order of Orange-Nassau, Netherlands.
Memberships: Asn Art Mus Dir (pres, 71-72); Am Asn Mus (coun); Nat Collection Fine Arts Comn; Col Art Asn Am (former dir); Int Coun Mus (comt glass; secy gen).
Publications: Co-auth, Travellers in Arcadia; auth numerous articles in art mags.
Mailing Address: Toledo Museum of Art, Box 1013, Toledo, OH 43697.

WOELFFER, EMERSON
Painter
Preferred Media: Oils, Acrylics.
b Chicago, Ill, July 27, 14.
Study & Training: Art Inst Chicago; Inst Design, Chicago, BA & hon DFA.
Work in Public Collections: Art Inst Chicago; Whitney Mus Am Art, New York, N Y; Mus Mod Art, New York; Univ Ill; plus others.
Exhibitions: Gallery 16, Graz, Austria, 65; one-man shows, Santa Barbara Mus, Calif, 64; David Stuart Gallery, Los Angeles, Calif, 65 & 69; Quay Gallery, San Francisco, Calif, 68 & Jodi Scully Gallery, Los Angeles, 72; Calif Inst Arts Invitational, 72; plus many other group & one-man shows.
Teaching: Instr, Sch Design, Chicago, 42; vis prof, Black Mountain Col, 49; instr, Colo Springs Fine Arts Ctr, 50; instr, Chouinard Art Inst, 59; vis prof painting, Univ Southern Calif, summer 62.

Positions: Topog draftsman, USAAF, 39-40; artist-in-residence, Honolulu Acad Arts, Hawaii, 70.
Awards: Guggenheim Found fel, France, Italy, Spain & Eng, 67-68; purchase award, All City Art Festival, 68; Raymond A Speiser Mem Prize, Pa Acad Fine Arts, 68; plus others.
Collection: African, New Guinea & pre-Columbian works; surrealist paintings.
Mailing Address: 475 Dustin Dr, Los Angeles, CA 90065.

WOFFORD, PHILIP
Painter, Writer
b Van Buren, Ark, Aug 14, 35.
Study & Training: Univ Ark, BA, 57; Univ Calif, Berkeley, 57-58.
Work in Public Collections: Whitney Mus Am Art, New York, N Y; Michener Found Collection, Austin, Tex; R I Sch Design, Providence.
Exhibitions: San Francisco Mus Ann, 58; Whitney Mus Ann Exhib Am Painting, 69 & 72; Corcoran Gallery Art, Washington, D C.
Teaching: Instr art, New York Univ Exten, 64-68; instr art, Bennington Col, 69-
Bibliography: Carter Ratcliff (auth), The new informalists, Art News, 2/70; Peter Scheldajl (auth), Return to the sublime, New York Times, 4/18/71.
Publications: Auth, article, In: Art Now: New York, 70; auth, Grand Canyon search ceremony, Barlenmir House, 72.
Dealer: Andre Emmerich Gallery, 41 E 57th St, New York, NY 10022.
Mailing Address: R D 2, Hoosick Falls, NY 12090.

WOJCIK, GARY THOMAS
Sculptor
Preferred Media: Welded Metal.
b Chicago, Ill, Feb 26, 45.
Study & Training: Sch Art Inst Chicago, BFA; Univ Ky, MA.
Work in Public Collections: High Mus Art, Atlanta, Ga; New York Port Auth, N Y; Chicago Park Dist, Hyde Park, Chicago.
Exhibitions: Whitney Sculpture Ann, Whitney Mus Am Art, 68; Univ Ill Biennial Painting & Sculpture Exhib, 69; Soc Contemp Art 29th Ann, Art Inst Chicago, 69; Viewpoints Painting & Sculpture Invitational, Colgate Univ, 70; Painting & Sculpture 1972, Storm King Art Ctr, Mountainville, N Y, 72.
Teaching: Part-time asst prof sculpture, Ithaca Col, 69-
Awards: Art Inst Chicago traveling fel.
Bibliography: Rev, In: New York Times, 11/29/70, Art News Mag, 1/29/71 & Art Int, 2/20/71.
Dealer: Kornblee Art Gallery, 58 E 79th St, New York, NY 10021.
Mailing Address: 273 Bundy Rd, Ithaca, NY 14850.

WOJINSKI, FRANCIS ANN, O P
Printmaker, Educator
Preferred Media: Intaglio.
b Detroit, Mich, June 30, 10.
Study & Training: Siena Heights Col, BA; De Paul Univ, MA; Univ Southern Calif, with Jules Heller & Carlton Ball, MFA.
Work in Public Collections: Colgate Rochester Divinity Sch, Rochester, N Y; St John Fisher Col, Rochester; Siena Heights Col, Adrian, Mich; Univ Tex Mus, Austin.
Exhibitions: Rochester Festival Relig Arts, 65; Bay Artist-Educator Asn, Oakland Art Mus, Calif, 66; Incarnate Word Col Fine Arts Gallery, San Antonio, Tex, 69; 40th San Antonio Artists Exhib, 70; Retrospective Exhib, Tex Univ Med Sch, San Antonio, 71.
Teaching: Instr all subj & art, St Edmund Sch, Oak Park, Ill, 30-40; instr social sci & art, St Scholastica Sch, Detroit, Mich, 40-50; instr Latin & art, Holy Cross High Sch, Santa Cruz, Calif, 50-60; instr Latin & art, Bishop O'Dowd High Sch, Oakland, 60-65; instr graphics, Siena Heights Col, 65-68; instr graphics, Incarnate Word Col, 69-71.
Awards: Award, Rochester Festival Relig Arts, 65; award, 40th Ann Artists Exhib San Antonio, 70.
Memberships: Int Graphic Art Soc; Print Coun Am; Pratt Art Ctr Contemp Prints; Nat Cath Art Asn.
Publications: Auth & illusr, Reading readiness book for first grade, 40, Art course of study for primary grades, 42, Art course of study for elementary grades, 44 & Art course of study for high school, 60.
Mailing Address: 421 N Decatur Blvd, Las Vegas, NV 89107.

WOLFE, ANN (ANN WOLFE GRAUBARD)
Sculptor, Instructor
Preferred Media: Bronze.
b Mlawa, Poland; U S citizen.
Study & Training: Hunter Col, BA; studies sculpture in Manchester, Eng & Paris, France; Acad Grande Chaumière, with Despiau & Vlerick.

Work in Public Collections: Morris Raphael Cohen Libr, City Univ New York, N Y; Jerusalem Mus Art, Israel; Nat Mus Korea, Seoul; Mus Western Art, Moscow, Russia; Wangensteen-Phillips Med Ctr, Univ Minn.
Commissions: Dr Morris R Cohen (bronze head), alumni of City Univ New York, 43; Pres Syngman Rhea (bronze head), Dr R Oliver, Washington, D C, 47; Dr W R Ramsey (bronze head), Children's Hosp, St Paul, Minn, 57; welded relief in steel & bronze, Mt Zion Temple, St Paul, 65; Dr O H Wangensteen (bronze head), alumni of dept surgery, Univ Minn, 65.
Exhibitions: Third Sculpture Int, Philadelphia Mus Art, Pa, 49; Pa Acad Fine Arts, Philadelphia, 51; Fifth Six-State Sculpture Show, 51 & Biennial From the Upper Midwest, 56 & 58, Walker Art Ctr, Minneapolis, Minn; Sculpture '54, Sculpture Ctr, New York, 54.
Teaching: Instr pvt studio, 62-70; instr sculpture, Minnetonka Ctr Arts & Educ, 71-
Awards: Allied Artists Am, 36; Soc Washington Artists, 44 & 45; Minneapolis Inst Arts, 51.
Publications: Contribr, Worcester Tel-Gazette, 40-60.
Dealer: Adele Bednarz Galleries, 902 N La Cienega Blvd, Los Angeles, CA 90069.
Mailing Address: 2928 Dean Blvd, Minneapolis, MN 55416.

WOLFE, TOWNSEND DURANT
Painter, Art Administrator
Preferred Media: Oils, Bronze.
b Hartsville, S C, Aug 15, 35.
Study & Training: Ga Inst Technol; Atlanta Art Inst, BFA; Cranbrook Acad Art, MFA; Inst Art Admin, Harvard Univ, cert.
Work in Public Collections: Ark Arts Ctr, Little Rock; Mint Mus Art, Charlotte, N C; Okla Arts Ctr, Oklahoma City; Miss Art Asn, Jackson; Carroll Reece Mem Mus, E Tenn State Univ, Johnson City.
Exhibitions: Four shows, Ball State Teacher's Col Drawing Nat, Muncie, Ind, 59-67; Mead Painting of Yr Exhib, Atlanta, Ga, 62; Watercolors U S A, Springfield, Mo, 63-64; Bucknell Ann Drawing Nat, Lewisberg, Pa, 65; Audubon Artist Nat, New York, N Y, 68.
Teaching: Instr painting & drawing, Memphis Acad Art, Tenn, 59-64; instr painting & drawing, Scarsdale Studio Workshop, N Y, 64-65.
Positions: Dir, Wooster Community Art Ctr, Danbury, Conn, 65-68; art dir, Upward Bound Proj, Danbury, summers 66-68; exec dir, Ark Arts Ctr, 68-
Awards: M J Kaplan Painting Award, Nat Soc Casein Painters, 65; Silvermine Guild Award Painting, 18th Ann New Eng Exhib, 67; award merit & purchase prize, 57th Nat Painting Exhib, Miss Art Asn, 67.
Memberships: Am Asn Mus; Am Fedn Arts; Southeastern Asn Mus.
Mailing Address: MacArthur Park, Little Rock, AR 72203.

WOLFF, ROBERT JAY
Painter, Writer
Preferred Media: Oils.
b Chicago, Ill, July 27, 05.
Study & Training: Yale Univ, 27; Ecole Beaux Arts, Paris, France.
Work in Public Collections: Tate Gallery, London, Eng; Guggenheim Mus, New York, N Y; R I Mus, Providence; Brooklyn Mus, N Y; Brooklyn Col, City Univ New York.
Exhibitions: Realities Nouvelles, Paris & other European cities, 48-51; traveling exhib to France, Italy, Ger & Switz, 56; Pa Acad Fine Arts Ann, Philadelphia; Corcoran Gallery Art, Washington, D C, 58; Whitney Mus Am Art Ann, New York, 58; plus nine one-man shows, New York, 39-58.
Teaching: Dean, Sch Design, Chicago, 38-42; prof art, Brooklyn Col, City Univ New York, 46-71; vis prof design, Mass Inst Technol, 61.
Bibliography: Sidney Janis (auth), Abstract art in America, Reynal & Hitchcock, 44; L Moholy-Nagy (auth), Vision in motion, Theobold-Chicago, 48; M Seuphor (auth), Dictionary of abstract art, Tudor, 57.
Publications: Auth, Elements of design-educational portfolio, Mus Mod Art, 46; contribr, Education of vision, Braziller, 65; auth, Seeing red, Feeling blue & Hello yellow, Scribners, 68; auth, On art & learning, Grossman, 71; contribr, prof jours.
Mailing Address: Garland Rd, New Preston, CT 06777.

WOLFSON, SIDNEY
Painter, Sculptor
Preferred Media: Oils.
b New York, N Y.
Study & Training: Art Stud League New York, N Y; Pratt Inst; Cooper Union.
Work in Public Collections: Whitney Mus Am Art; Wadsworth Atheneum; Herbert F Johnson Mus, Cornell Univ; Vassar Col; Columbia Univ.

Exhibitions: Six Am Abstr Painters, Arthur Tooth Gallery, London, 61; Carnegie Int, Pittsburgh, 62; Geometric Abstraction, Whitney Mus Am Art, 62; one-man show, Bennington Col, Vt, 63; New Acquisitions, 71 & Retrospective, 72, Vassar Col; plus others.
Teaching: Artist-in-residence, Creative Arts Acad, New York, summer 68; asst prof art, Dutchess Community Col, Poughkeepsie, N Y, 69-70.
Mailing Address: Salt Point, NY 12578.

WOLINS, JOSEPH
Painter
Preferred Media: Oils.
b Atlantic City, N J, Mar 26, 15.
Study & Training: Nat Acad Design, 31-35.
Work in Public Collections: Metrop Mus Art, New York, N Y; Norfolk Mus Arts & Sci, Va; Albrecht Mus, St Joseph, Mo; Fiske Univ Art Gallery, Ala; Ein Harod Mus, Israel.
Exhibitions: Corcoran Gallery Art Biennial, Washington, D C, 47; Pa Acad Fine Arts Ann, Philadelphia, 48; Whitney Mus Am Art Ann, 49-53; Mus Mod Art Ann, São Paulo, Brazil, 62; Butler Inst Am Art Ann, Youngstown, Ohio, 65.
Awards: Mark Rothko Found award for painting, 71.
Memberships: Artists Equity Asn.
Mailing Address: 463 West St, New York, NY 10014.

WOLLE, MURIEL SIBELL
Painter, Writer
Preferred Media: Lithographic Crayon, Watercolors.
b Brooklyn, N Y, Apr 3, 98.
Study & Training: New York Sch Fine & Appl Art, two diplomas; New York Univ, BS, 28; Univ Colo, MA, 30.
Work in Public Collections: Springfield Mus, Mo; Univ Colo Mem Ctr, Boulder; Mont State Mus, Helena.
Exhibitions: Denver Art Mus Ann Show, 28-47; Nat Asn Women Artists, 30-48; Artists West of the Mississippi, 39; one-man shows, Denver Art Mus, 56 & Iowa State Univ Gallery, Mem Union, 67.
Teaching: Instr art, Col Indust Art, 20-23; instr art, New York Sch Fine & Applied Art, 23-26; from instr to prof art & head dept, Univ Colo, Boulder, 26-66, emer prof, 66-
Awards: Norlin Medal, 57 & Stearns Award, 66, Univ Colo; Laureate Key, Delta Phi Delta, 58.
Bibliography: Jessie Palmer (auth), Colorado woman, art professor, ghost town authority, writes guide to Montana mining camps, Great Falls Tribune, 3/22/64; Barbara Gigone (auth), Artist-writer recalls career, Denver Post, 3/23/66.
Memberships: Nat Asn Women Artists; Delta Phi Delta (second v pres, first v pres & nat alumni pres); Boulder Artists Guild; Colo Auth League, Denver; Woman's Press Club.
Art Interests: Visiting, sketching & collecting historic ghost mining town data of the twelve western states.
Publications: Auth & illusr, Ghost cities of Colorado, 33, Cloud cities of Colorado, 34, Stampede to Timberline, 49, The bonanza trail, 53 & Montana pay dirt, 63.
Mailing Address: 500 Mohawk Dr, No 204, Boulder, CO 80303.

WOLPERT, ELIZABETH DAVIS
Painter, Instructor
Preferred Media: Oils.
b Fort Washington, Pa, Sept 12, 15.
Study & Training: Moore Col Art, BFA; Pa State Univ, MAEd; also with Hobson Pittman.
Work in Public Collections: Woodmere Art Gallery, Philadelphia, Pa; Pa State Univ, University Park; Temple Univ, Philadelphia; Bob Jones Univ, Greenville, S C; Univ Miami, Coral Gables, Fla.
Exhibitions: Pa Acad Fine Arts, Philadelphia, 48; Philadelphia Mus Art, 62; Butler Inst Art, Youngstown, Ohio, 65; many shows, Woodmere Art Gallery; Cheltenham Art Ctr, 66; plus many one-man shows.
Teaching: Instr art, pub & pvt schs, 38-
Awards: Charles K Smith First Prize & First Mem Prize, Woodmere Art Gallery, 53; first purchase prizes, Junto, Philadelphia, 58-59.
Memberships: Artists Equity Asn; Philadelphia Art Alliance; Philadelphia Mus Art; Woodmere Art Gallery; Nat Art Educ Asn.
Mailing Address: 100 Bethlehem Pike, Ambler, PA 19002.

WOLSKY, MILTON LABAN
Illustrator, Painter
Preferred Media: Oils.
b Omaha, Nebr, Jan 23, 16.
Study & Training: Univ Nebr, Omaha; Art Inst Chicago; also with Julian Levi & Hans Hofmann, New York.
Work in Public Collections: Gov Mansion, State of Nebr; U S Embassy, Lebanon; Air Force Hist Soc; U S Nat Bank, Omaha.
Exhibitions: Am Watercolor Soc, New York, 53; one-man exhib, Joslyn Art Mus, Omaha, 60; Nebr Centennial, Sheldon Art Gallery, Lincoln, 67.

Teaching: Instr painting, Joslyn Art Mus, 58-62.
Positions: Art dir, Bozell & Jacobs, Inc.
Awards: First award & purchase prize, Gov Art Show, 64.
Memberships: Soc Illusr.
Collection: Wolsky Collection of contemporary paintings; donation to Joslyn Art Mus, 67.
Publications: Auth, Basic elements of painting, 59; auth & illusr, Rock people, 70.
Mailing Address: 5804 Leavenworth St, Omaha, NE 68106.

WONG, FREDERICK
Painter, Instructor
Preferred Media: Watercolors.
b Buffalo, N Y, May 31, 29.
Study & Training: Univ N Mex, BFA, MA.
Work in Public Collections: Butler Inst Am Art, Youngstown, Ohio; Atlanta Art Asn, Ga; Reading Mus Art, Pa; Philbrook Art Ctr, Tulsa, Okla; Neuberger Collection, Purchase, N Y.
Exhibitions: Los Angeles Co Mus Art, Calif, 59; Butler Inst Am Art, Youngstown, 60; Am Watercolor Soc, New York, N Y, 60-69; Watercolor U S A, Springfield, Mo, 63; Mainstreams '69, Marietta, Ohio, 69.
Teaching: Instr form & structure, Pratt Inst, 66-69; instr painting, drawing & design, Hofstra Univ, 70-
Awards: Bronze medal, Butler Midyr Ann, Butler Inst Am Art, 60; gold medal, Nat Arts Club, 61; award of excellence, Mainstreams '69, Marietta Col, 69.
Memberships: Am Watercolor Soc; Allied Artists Am.
Dealer: Kenmore Galleries, Inc, 122 S 18th St, Philadelphia, PA 19103.
Mailing Address: 315 Riverside Dr, New York, NY 10025.

WONG, JASON
Executive Director
b Long Beach, Calif, May 12, 34.
Study & Training: Long Beach City Col, AA, 54; Univ Calif, Los Angeles, BA, 63.
Collections Arranged: 7 Decades of Design, organized through Calif Arts Comn grant for state tour, 67-68; The Art of Alexander Calder - Gouaches, western states tour, 70; Max Beckmann Graphics, Nat Tour, 73.
Positions: Asst cur, Long Beach Mus Art, 59-64; art dir, Audiorama Corp, Am-Quest Int, 64-65; cur, Long Beach Mus Art, 65, dir, 65-72; dir, Tucson Art Ctr, 72-
Awards: Nat Ed Asn grant for res in museological studies, 72.
Memberships: Am Asn Mus, Western Asn Art Mus (v pres); Am Fedn Arts.
Mailing Address: Tucson Art Center, 325 W Franklin St, Tucson, AZ 85705.

WONNER, PAUL (JOHN)
Painter
b Tucson, Ariz, Apr 24, 20.
Study & Training: Calif Col Arts & Crafts; Univ Calif, Berkeley, MA, MLS.
Work in Public Collections: Guggenheim Mus, New York, N Y; San Francisco Mus Art, Calif; Nat Collection Fine Arts, Smithsonian Inst, Washington, D C; Oakland Mus, Calif; Joseph H Hirshhorn Found; plus others.
Exhibitions: Carnegie Inst, Pittsburgh, Pa, 58 & 64; Whitney Mus Am Art, New York, 59; Art Inst Chicago, Ill, 61 & 64; Univ Ill, 61, 63 & 65; Mus Mod Art, New York, 62; plus many other group & one-man shows.
Teaching: Instr painting, Univ Calif, Los Angeles, 63-64; instr painting, Otis Art Inst, 66-68.
Mailing Address: 131 Hermosillo Rd, Montecito, CA 93103.

WOOD, HARRY EMSLEY, JR
Educator, Painter
b Indianapolis, Ind, Dec 10, 10.
Study & Training: Univ Wis, BA, MA; Ohio State Univ, MA, PhD; Acad Belli Arti, Florence, Italy, with Ottono Rosai; also with John Frazier, Provincetown, Mass & Emil Bisttam, Taos, N Mex.
Work in Public Collections: Mem Union, Ariz State Univ, Tempe; Phoenix Art Mus, Ariz.
Commissions: Murals, Gt Cent Ins Co, Peoria, Ill; plus many portraits of prominent people.
Exhibitions: Florence, Italy, 50; Phoenix Art Mus, 61; Phoenix & Tucson Ann, 61; Ariz State Univ, Tempe; Northern Ariz Univ, Flagstaff; plus many other group & one-man shows.
Teaching: Prof art, Ill Wesleyan Univ, 42-44; dean, col fine arts, Bradley Univ, 44-50; prof art, Ariz State Univ, 54-, chmn dept art, 54-66.
Positions: V pres, Mind³ Commun Group, 71-
Awards: Purchase prize, Artist Guild, 59.

Memberships: Col Art Asn Am; Nat Art Educ Asn (nat coun, 58-62); Pac Art Asn (pres, 58-60); Am Soc Aesthetics; Ariz Art Educ Asn (pres, 54-55).
Publications: Auth, Lew Davis, 25 years of painting in Arizona, 61, Soul, an interpretation of That which might have been, Birmingham, 63, A sculpture by John Waddell & The faces of Abraham Lincoln, 70.
Mailing Address: 104 Vista del Cerro, Tempe, AZ 85281.

WOOD, JAMES ARTHUR (ART)
Cartoonist, Lecturer
b Miami, Fla, June 6, 27.
Study & Training: Washington & Lee Univ, BA; Mich State Univ.
Work in Public Collections: Libr of Cong, Washington, D C; Alderman Libr Permanent Collection, Univ Va, Charlottesville; Univ Akron Collection, Ohio; William Allen White Collection, Univ Kans; Truman Libr Collection.
Exhibitions: Brussels World's Fair, 58; one-man show, Pittsburgh Press, 59; The Great Challenge, Int Cartoon Exhib, 59-60; Cartoon Show, Nat Portrait Gallery, 72.
Positions: Ed cartoonist, Richmond Newsleader, 50-56; chief political cartoonist, Pittsburgh Press Club, 56-63; cartoonist & dir info, U S Independent Tel Asn, 63-
Awards: Freedoms Found awards, 53, 54 & 58-60; Christopher Award, 54; Golden Quill Awards, 60 & 62.
Memberships: Asn Am Ed Cartoonist (bd mem, 59-63); Nat Cartoonists Soc; Nat Press Club.
Mailing Address: 7008 Tilden Lane, Rockville, MD 20852.

WOOD, JAMES NOWELL
Art Historian, Art Administrator
b Boston, Mass, Mar 20, 41.
Study & Training: Williams Col, BA; Inst Fine Arts, New York Univ, MA.
Positions: Asst to dir, Metrop Mus Art, New York, N Y, 67-68, asst cur, dept 20th century art, 68-70; cur, Albright-Knox Art Gallery, Buffalo, N Y, 70-
Research: Nineteenth and twentieth century American and European painting, sculpture and decorative arts.
Publications: Auth, Rockne Krebs, 71 & Six painters, 71.
Mailing Address: Albright-Knox Art Gallery, Buffalo, NY 14222.

WOODEN, HOWARD EDMUND
Museum Director, Art Critic
b Baltimore, Md, Oct 10, 19.
Study & Training: Johns Hopkins Univ, BS & MA.
Collections Arranged: The Rose Hulman Institute Collection of British Watercolors, 67-72; Sculptures by Ernst Eisenmayer, 67-68; B M Jackson: oils, 70; John Silk Deckard: 1960-1970, 70-71.
Teaching: Fulbright instr, Athens Col, 51-52; lectr art hist, Univ Evansville, 55-63; assoc prof, Univ Fla, 63-66; assoc prof art hist, Ind State Univ, Terre Haute, 67-
Positions: Dir, Sheldon Swope Art Gallery, Terre Haute, 66-
Awards: Fulbright grant, U S Dept State, 51-52.
Memberships: Col Art Asn Am; Am Asn Mus; Soc Archit Historians; Archaeol Inst Am.
Research: British watercolor painting of the eighteenth and nineteenth centuries; American architecture of the nineteenth century; meaning in contemporary art.
Publications: Auth, Architectural heritage of Evansville, 62; auth, The Rose Hulman Institute collection of British watercolors, 69; auth, Fifty paintings and sculptures from the collection of the Sheldon Swope Art Gallery, 72; plus numerous articles & brochures.
Mailing Address: Sheldon Swope Art Gallery, 25 S Seventh St, Terre Haute, IN 47807.

WOODHAM, DERRICK JAMES
Sculptor
Preferred Media: Mixed Media.
b Blackburn, Eng, Nov 5, 40.
Study & Training: S E Essex Tech Col Sch Art, intermediate dipl design; Hornsey Col Arts & Crafts, nat dipl design; Royal Col Art, dipl.
Work in Public Collections: Tate Gallery, London, Eng; Mus Contemp Art, Nagaoka, Japan.
Commissions: Sculpture J Meeker, Fort Worth, Tex, 69; sculpture, S P Steinberg, Newlett, N Y, 71.
Exhibitions: New Generation, 1965, Whitechapel Gallery, London, 65; Paris Bienalle, Mus Art Mod, 65; Primary Structures, Jewish Mus, New York, N Y, 66; British Sculpture of the 60's, Nash House Gallery, London, 70; Der Geist Surrealismus, Baukunst Galerie, Koln, Ger, 71.
Teaching: Instr sculpture, Philadelphia Col Art, 68-70; asst prof art forms found, Univ Iowa Sch Art, 70-
Awards: Stuyvesant Found bursary, 65; Prix de la Ville, Sculpture, Paris Bienalle, 65.

Bibliography: Grace Gluek (auth), British sculptures, Art in Am, 66; Robert Kudielka, Abscheid vom object, Kunstwerke, 10/68; Otto Kulturman (auth), The new sculpture, Praeger, 69.
Dealer: Richard Feigen & Co, 27 E 79th St, New York, NY 10021.
Mailing Address: 905 N Dodge St, Iowa City, IA 52240.

WOODHAM, JEAN
Sculptor, Lecturer
Preferred Media: Metals.
b Midland City, Ala, Aug 16, 25.
Study & Training: Auburn Univ, BA; Sculpture Ctr, New York, N Y; Univ Ill, Kate Neal Kinley Mem fel.
Work in Public Collections: Massillon Mus Permanent Collection, Ohio; Nuclear Ship Savannah, Telfair Acad Arts & Sci, Savannah, Ga; Alfred Khouri Mem Collection, Norfolk Mus Arts & Sci, Va; Westport Permanent Collection, Conn.
Commissions: The River (welded steel wall piece), Int Bank Reconstruction & Develop, New York, N Y, 64; Menorah (welded bronze), Jewish Community Ctr, Harrison, N Y, 66; Wings (welded bronze), Ala State Univ, Montgomery, 67; fountain sculptures, Flintkote Corp Hq, White Plains, N Y, 68-69; fountain pieces, Gen Elec Credit Corp, Stamford, Conn, 71-72.
Exhibitions: Pa Acad Fine Arts Ann, Philadelphia, 50-54; Womens Int Art Club, New Burlington Gallery, London, Eng, 55; New Eng Ann, Silvermine Guild, Conn, 55-60; U S Info Agency Exhibs, Arg, Brazil, Chile & Mex, 63; Selected Sculptors Guild, Albright-Knox Gallery, Buffalo, N Y, 71; plus others.
Teaching: Head dept sculpture, Silvermine Guild Artists, 55-56; instr sculpture, Stamford Mus, Conn, 67-69; vis asst prof sculpture, Auburn Univ, 70.
Positions: Chmn sculpture, New York Fedn Women's Clubs, 50-51; mem bd mgrs, Silvermine Guild Artists, 58-60; mem exec bd, Rowayton Art Ctr, Conn, 66-67.
Awards: Jacobs Award for best sculpture & Beatman Award for best of show, New Eng Ann, 60; Audubon Artists Medal for creative sculpture, 62; medal of honor for sculpture, Nat Asn Women Artists, 66.
Bibliography: Jacques Schnier (auth), Sculpture in modern America, Univ Calif Press, 48; Jean Woodham—sculptress, Veritas Corp, 66; Margaret Harold (auth), Prize winning sculpture, bk 7, Allied Publ, 67.
Memberships: Sculptors Guild (treas, 60-65, exec bd, 66-68, secy, 72-); Archit League New York; Audubon Artists (juror, 64); Artists Equity Asn New York; Nat Asn Women Artists (juror, 60, 61, & 63-66, chmn sculpture, 65-66).
Mailing Address: 26 Pin Oak Lane, Westport, CT 06880.

WOODLOCK, ETHELYN HURD
Painter
Preferred Media: Oils.
b Hallowell, Maine, June 9, 07.
Study & Training: Copley Sch Commercial Art, Boston, Mass.
Work in Public Collections: Valley Hosp, Ridgewood, N J; The Carlson Collection, Ramsey, N J; Bd Trades Bldg, Nassau, Bahamas; Hickory Art Mus, S C; Fort Lauderdale Pub Libr, Fla.
Exhibitions: 64th Am Show, Art Inst Chicago, Ill, 61; Contemporary Portraits, Fitchburg Art Mus, Mass, 62; Awards Artists Exhib, Montclair Art Mus, 66; Contemporary American Realism, Hammond Mus, Salem, N Y, 68; two-man show, Bergen Community Mus, 71.
Awards: Purchase award, Ringwood Manor State Exhib, 68; purchase award, Bergen Mall, Paramus, N J, 71; judge's choice, Am Artists Prof League, 71.
Bibliography: Rodger (auth), Non-verbal communication, Am Soc Clin Hypnosis, 72.
Memberships: Nat Asn Women Artists; Catharine Lorillard Wolfe Art Club; Am Artists Prof League; Allied Artists Am.
Mailing Address: 15 Franklin Ave, Midland Park, NJ 07432.

WOODNER, IAN
Collector
Memberships: Art Collectors Club.
Mailing Address: 39 W 67th St, New York, NY 10023.

WOODRUFF, HALE A
Painter, Educator
Preferred Media: Oils, Watercolors.
b Cairo, Ill, Aug 26, 00.
Study & Training: John Herron Art Inst, Indianapolis, Ind; Fogg Art Mus, Harvard Univ; Acad Scandinave & Acad Mod, Paris; Morgan State Col, hon DFA; also fresco painting with Diego Rivera, Mex.
Work in Public Collections: Newark Mus, N J; Libr Cong, Washington, D C; IBM Collection; Howard Univ, Washington, D C; Lincoln Univ, Jefferson City, Mo; plus other pub & pvt collections.
Exhibitions: Galerie Jeune Peinture, Paris; First Nat Exhib Am Art, New York, N Y; Whitney Mus Am Art; one-man shows, Int Print Soc, State Mus N C, Kansas City Art Inst, Univ Mich, Ann

Arbor, Hampton Inst & Univ N C, Chapel Hill & Greensboro; plus other group & one-man shows at mus, cols, schs & galleries throughout U S.
Teaching: Lectr, Drew Univ, Denver Mus, Univ Mass, Amherst, Queensboro Jewish Ctr, Vassar Col, Univ Colo, Boulder & many other clubs, schs & art groups throughout U S; prof art educ, New York Univ, emer prof, 68-
Positions: Art dir, Atlanta Univ.
Awards: Julius Rosenwald fel continued creativity art, 43-45; bronze award & hon mention, Harmon Found; first award, High Mus Art, Atlanta; plus others.
Bibliography: Alain Locke (auth), Negro art past and present & article, In: Am Mag Art; Ralph M Pearson (auth), Experiencing pictures, Simon & Schuster, New art education, Harpers & article, In: Forum Mag; Ralph McGill (auth), article, In: Atlanta Constitution; plus others.
Dealer: Bertha Schaefer Gallery, 41 E 57th St, New York, NY 10022.
Mailing Address: 22 E Eighth St, New York, NY 10003.

WOODS, GURDON GRANT
Sculptor, Educator
Preferred Media: Concrete.
b Savannah, Ga, Apr 15, 15.
Study & Training: Art Stud League New York, N Y; Brooklyn Mus Sch; San Francisco Art Inst, hon DArts, 66.
Work in Public Collections: City of San Francisco.
Commissions: Steel fountain & concrete relief panels, IBM Corp, San Jose, Calif; aluminum fountain, Paul Masson Winery, Saratoga, Calif; concrete panels, McGraw-Hill, Novato, Calif; plus others.
Exhibitions: San Francisco Art Inst Ann; San Francisco Art Festivals; Denver Mus Ann; São Paulo Biennial; Southern Sculpture Ann; plus others.
Teaching: Instr sculpture, San Francisco Art Inst, 55-65; assoc prof art, Univ Calif, Santa Cruz, 66-, chmn dept, 66-70.
Positions: Dir, Col San Francisco Art Inst, 55-65; sculptor mem, San Francisco Art Comn, 54-56; sculptor mem, Santa Cruz Art Comn, 70-
Awards: Four purchase awards, San Francisco Ann & Festivals; also found grants & citations.
Memberships: San Francisco Art Inst (exec dir, 55-64); Col Art Asn Am; San Francisco Mus Coun.
Dealer: Bolles Gallery, 10 Gold St, San Francisco, CA 94133.
Mailing Address: 1238 Escalona Dr, Santa Cruz, CA 95060.

WOODS, RIP
Painter, Educator
Preferred Media: Mixed Media.
b Idabel, Okla, Aug 15, 33.
Study & Training: Ariz State Univ, MAE, 58.
Work in Public Collections: Phoenix Art Mus, Ariz; Ariz State Univ, Tempe; Ark State Univ, Jonesboro; Yuma Fine Arts Ctr, Ariz; Ariz Western Col, Yuma.
Commissions: Relief-assemblage mural (with Ray Fink), Nat Housing Industs, Phoenix, 70; mosaic & bas relief painting (with Ray Fink), Greyhound-Armour, Phoenix, 71.
Exhibitions: Drawing U S A, Calif Palace of Legion of Honor, San Francisco, Calif, 60; one-man show, Phoenix Art Mus, 68; Art on Paper, Weatherspoon Gallery, N C, 69; Ill Bell Traveling Exhib, Chicago, 70-71; 73rd Western Ann, Denver, Colo, 71.
Teaching: Assoc prof painting, drawing & printmaking, Ariz State Univ, 65-; assoc prof painting, Colorado Springs Fine Art Ctr, Colo, summer 67.
Mailing Address: 7817 S 13th Pl, Phoenix, AZ 85040.

WOODS, SARAH LADD
Collector, Patron
b Lincoln, Nebr, May 8, 95.
Study & Training: Wellesley Col, BA; Univ Nebr, LHD.
Positions: Patron, past pres & life trustee, Nebr Art Asn.
Art Interests: Thomas C Woods Collection, Sheldon Gallery, University of Nebraska.
Collection: Contemporary American.
Mailing Address: 2475 Lake St, Lincoln, NE 68502.

WOODS, THEODORE NATHANIEL, III
Sculptor
Preferred Media: Plastics, Wood.
b Akron, Ohio, Jan 1, 48.
Study & Training: Ariz State Univ, with Ben Goo, BFA & MFA.
Work in Public Collections: Ariz State Univ; also numerous pvt collections.
Exhibitions: Southwest Fine Arts Biennial, Santa Fe, N Mex, 70; First Four Corners Biennial, Phoenix, Ariz, 71; Yuma Fine Arts Invitational, Ariz, 72; Dimensions '72, Phoenix, 72; Phoenix Art Mus Exhib, 72.

Teaching: Nat Endowment Arts artist-in-residence, Mesa, Ariz, 72-73.
Awards: Third pl crafts, Fine Arts, 70; first pl sculpture, First Four Corners Biennial, 71; merit award sculpture, Dimensions '72.
Memberships: L'Assemblage; Tempe Five.
Mailing Address: c/o Robert L Dickson, 3338 W Belmont, Phoenix, AZ 85021.

WOODS, WILLIS FRANKLIN
Museum Director
b Washington, D C, July 25, 20.
Study & Training: Brown Univ, AB; Am Univ; Univ Ore.
Teaching: Instr art, Palm Beach Jr Col, 58-62.
Positions: Asst dir, Corcoran Gallery Art, Washington, D C, 47-49; dir, Norton Gallery & Sch Art, West Palm Beach, Fla, 49-62; dir, Detroit Inst Arts, 62-
Memberships: Soc Arts & Crafts (trustee, 62-); Arch Am Art (trustee, 62-); Art Quart (ed bd, 62-); Am Asn Mus; Am Asn Mus Dirs.
Mailing Address: Detroit Institute of Arts, 5200 Woodward Ave, Detroit, MI 48202.

WOODSIDE, GORDON WILLIAM
Art Dealer, Collector
b Seattle, Wash.
Study & Training: Univ Wash.
Positions: Dir, Gordon Woodside Galleries, Seattle.
Specialty of Gallery: Artists of the Pacific Northwest.
Collection: Representative works by prominent artists of the Northwest.
Mailing Address: 803 E Union St, Seattle, WA 98122.

WOODWARD, CLEVELAND LANDON
Painter, Illustrator
Preferred Media: Oils, Watercolors.
b Glendale, Ohio, June 25, 00.
Study & Training: Cincinnati Art Acad, scholar, 23-26; Charles Hawthorne's Cape Cod Sch Art, summer 24; Brit Art Acad, Rome Italy, 28-29.
Work in Public Collections: Mobile Art Gallery, Langan Park, Ala; Arctic Mus, Brunswick, Maine; Boardman Press, Nashville, Tenn; United Lutheran Publ House, Philadelphia, Pa; Christian Bd Publ, Saint Louis, Mo.
Commissions: Samuel and Eli (mural), Seventh Presbyterian Church, Cincinnati, Ohio, 49; painting for Donald B MacMillan of Arctic Mus, Brunswick, Maine, 52; sixteen watercolor illus for World Bible, World Publ Co, 62; Peter and John (mural), West End Baptist Church, Mobile, Ala, 72; plus others.
Exhibitions: Cincinnati Art Mus Spring Exhib, 25; one-man shows, Traxel Art Gallery, Cincinnati, 29, Mobile Art Mus, 68, Percy Whiting Mus, Fairhope, Ala, 69, Mobile Art Gallery, 71 & Percy Whiting Mus, Fairhope, Ala, 71.
Teaching: Lectr Biblical art, schs, cols & mus, many yrs; instr oil painting, Eastern Shore Acad Fine Arts, 72-
Positions: Co-founder & mem first bd dirs, Cape Cod Art Asn.
Memberships: Eastern Shore Art Asn (bd dirs, 71-74); Adv Comt, Eastern Shore Acad Fine Arts.
Publications: Illusr, By an unknown disciple, Harper Bros, The other wise man, Harper Bros, Painting Christ head, Abingdon Press & Kudla and his polar bear, Dodd Mead & Co.
Dealer: Orleans Art Gallery, Main St, Orleans, Cape Cod, MA 02653.
Mailing Address: 354 Boone Lane, Fairhope, AL 36532.

WOODY, (THOMAS) HOWARD
Sculptor, Educator
Preferred Media: Bronze, Assemblage.
b Salisbury, Md, Sept 26, 35.
Study & Training: Richmond Prof Inst, BFA; E Carolina Univ, MA; Univ Iowa; Art Inst Chicago; Kalamazoo Art Ctr; Univ Ky.
Work in Public Collections: Miami Mus Mod Art, Fla; Mint Mus Art, Charlotte, N C; Birmingham Mus Art, Ala; Columbus Mus Arts & Crafts, Ga; Royal Ont Mus, Toronto.
Exhibitions: Smithsonian Touring Sculpture Exhib, 69; Art in Embassies Int Prog, U S Dept State, 69; Ball State Nat Small Sculpture Exhib, Muncie, Ind, 71; Atmospheric One-man Presentations, De Waters Art Ctr, Flint, Mich, 72 & Akron Art Inst, Ohio, 72.
Teaching: Instr sculpture, Roanoke Fine Art Ctr, Va, 59-61; assoc prof sculpture, Pembroke State Univ, 62-67; prof sculpture, Univ S C, 67-, Russell Creative Res Award, 72.
Awards: Spec Citation Award, Atlanta Festival Sculpture, 68; S C State Art Collection Award, S C Arts Comn, 71.
Bibliography: J A Morris (auth), Contemporary artists of South Carolina, Greenville Co Mus Art, 70.

Memberships: Southern Asn Sculptors (pres, 65-70); Nat Sculpture Ctr (adv, 66-); Guild S C Artists (mem bd, 69); S C Craftsmen (mem bd, 68); Southeastern Col Art Conf.
Mailing Address: 433 Arrowwood Rd, Columbia, SC 29210.

WOOF, MAIJA (MAIJA GEGERIS ZACK PEEPLES)
Painter
Preferred Media: Oils, Acrylics, Clay, Watercolors, Dye.
b Riga, Latvia, Nov 21, 42.
Study & Training: Univ Calif, Davis, BA, 64, MA, 65; also with William T Wiley, Robert Arneson & Wayne Thiebaud.
Work in Public Collections: Crocker Art Gallery, Sacramento, Calif; La Jolla Mus Art, Calif; Matthews Art Ctr, Tempe, Ariz; San Francisco Mus Art, Calif; Norman MacKenzie Art Gallery, Regina, Sask.
Commissions: Beast rainbow painting, City of San Francisco, Civic Ctr, 67; rainbow house, pvt party, San Francisco, 67-68; ceiling murals, Rainbow House, San Francisco, 67-68; crocheted, woven & sewn beast curtains, Univ Calif Art Bldg, Davis, 71.
Exhibitions: One-man shows, Candy Store Gallery, Folsom, Calif, 65-72; Grotesque Show, San Francisco, Boston, Mass & Philadelphia, Pa, 69; Sacramento Sampler 1, Crocker Art Gallery, Oakland Mus & Brazil, 71-72; The World of Woof, throughout Ariz, 71-72; Beast Retrospective, Univ Calif Gallery, Davis, 72.
Collections Arranged: The Nut Show, for Kaiser-Aetna, Tahoe Verdes, Calif, 72.
Teaching: Instr art, Laney Col, Oakland, Calif, 68-69; instr art, Univ Calif, Davis, 71-72; instr art, Sierra Col, Rocklin, Calif, 71-
Bibliography: Andrew Gale (auth), An art original, Sacramento Bee, 71.
Dealer: Candy Store Gallery, 605 Sutter St, Folsom, CA 95630.
Mailing Address: 2012 D St, Sacramento, CA 95814.

WOOLFENDEN, WILLIAM EDWARD
Art Administrator, Art Historian
b Detroit, Mich, June 27, 18.
Study & Training: Wayne State Univ, BA, MA.
Positions: Asst cur Am art, Detroit Inst Arts, 45-49, dir educ, 49-60; asst dir, Archives Am Art, Detroit, Mich, 60-62, exec dir, 62-64, dir, 64-70, dir, Archives Am Art, Smithsonian Inst, New York, N Y, 70-; mem vis comt, dept Am paintings & sculpture, Metrop Mus Art, New York; adv drawings, Minn Mus Art, Saint Paul.
Memberships: Am Asn Mus; Col Art Asn; Soc Archit Historians; Nat Trust Hist Preservation.
Research: American art; American drawings.
Mailing Address: 219 E 69th St, New York, NY 10021.

WORTH, PETER JOHN
Sculptor, Art Historian
b Ipswich, Eng, Mar 16, 17; U S citizen.
Study & Training: Ipswich Sch Art, 34-37; Royal Col Art, London, 37-39, ARCA, 46, with E W Tristram, Paul Nash, Edward Bawden, Douglas Cockerell, Roger Powell & others.
Work in Public Collections: Denver Art Mus; Joslyn Art Mus; Permanent Collection, Sheldon Gallery Art, Univ Nebr.
Exhibitions: San Francisco Mus Art, 50; Nelson Gallery Art, 50, 53, 54 & 57; Art Inst Chicago, 51; Walker Art Ctr, 51, 52 & 56; Denver Art Mus, 52, 53, 55-57 & 60-63.
Teaching: Prof art hist, Univ Nebr, Lincoln, 59-
Memberships: Egypt Explor Soc, London; Col Art Asn Am.
Research: Stylistic transformations in late antique and early medieval art, especially in iconography.
Publications: Photogr, Life library of photography, 70 & Bilder, Stuttgart, 70.
Mailing Address: Dept of Art, Woods Hall, University of Nebraska, Lincoln, NE 68508.

WORTHAM, HAROLD
Painter, Art Consultant
Preferred Media: Oils.
b Shawnee, Okla, Jan 24, 09.
Study & Training: Yard Sch Fine Arts, Washington, D C; Art Stud League New York, N Y, with K H Miller, Brackman & Dickinson; San Fernando Acad Fine Arts, Madrid, Spain, with Gregorio Toledo & Francisco Nuñez Losada.
Work in Public Collections: Rosenberg Libr, Galveston, Tex.
Commissions: Restoration work in Mus Santa Cruz, Toledo, Spain; Mus Pontevedra, Spain; Monasterio Nuestra Señora de Guadalupe, Spain; Cathedral, Murcia, Spain; Iglesia, Zumaya & Parrochial Church, Arenillas, Zamora, Spain.
Exhibitions: Metrop Arts, Washington, D C, 36; Rosenberg Libr, Galveston, 42 & 53; Casa Am, Madrid, 52; Prado Sala, Madrid, 59; Galeria Fortuny, Madrid, 64.

Positions: Consult restoration & conservation paintings, Span Govt, Cent Inst Restoration, Govt Spain, Madrid, 64-
Awards: Purchase prize award, Independent Artists, Metrop Exhib, 36; Famous Amateurs Award first prize for oils, UNICEF Exhib, 51; hon awards for restoration, San Fernando Acad, 53-54.
Memberships: Art Stud League New York; Int Inst Arts & Lett, Switz; Int Coun Mus (Conserv), Rome.
Dealer: Jasper Galleries, 5433 Westheimer Rd, Houston, TX 77027.
Mailing Address: Serrano 63, Madrid 6, Spain.

WORTHEN, WILLIAM MARSHALL
Sculptor
Preferred Media: Steel, Bronze.
b Wellsberg, W Va, Mar 1, 43.
Study & Training: Univ N Mex, BS.
Exhibitions: New Mexico Professional Invitational, Albuquerque, 68 & 72; Mainstreams, Marietta, Ohio, 71 & 72; The West Artists & Illustrators, Tucson Art Ctr, Ariz, 72.
Awards: Award for Falcon, 67, Falcon on Gauntlet & Buffalo, 71, N Mex State Fair.
Dealer: Gallery A, E Kit Carson Rd, Taos, NM 87571.
Mailing Address: 441 Loma Hermosa Dr N W, Albuquerque, NM 87105.

WRAY, DICK
Painter
b Houston, Tex, Dec 5, 33.
Study & Training: Univ Houston.
Work in Public Collections: Albright-Knox Art Gallery, Buffalo, N Y; Mus Fine Arts, Houston.
Exhibitions: Mus Contemp Art, Houston, 61; Southwest Painting & Sculpture, Houston, 62; Hemisfair, Houston, 68; Homage to Lithography, Mus Mod Art, New York, 69.
Awards: Purchase prizes, Ford Found, 62 & Mus Fine Arts, Houston, 63.
Mailing Address: 4012 Amherst St, Houston, TX 77005.

WRIGHT, BARTON ALLEN
Painter, Illustrator
Preferred Media: Scratchboard, Acrylics.
b Bisbee, Ariz, Dec 21, 20.
Commissions: Display, Wupatki Nat Monument, Flagstaff, 62.
Exhibitions: First Regional Art Exhib, Phoenix, Ariz, 67; Calif Centennial Exhib, San Diego, Calif, 69; La Jolla Art Asn, Calif, 69; Festival of Arts, Lake Oswego, 71.
Collections Arranged: M R F Colton, 58; G E Burr, 59; Indian Artists, 60; Western Artists, 62; Paul Dyck, 64; Am Art, 65; Flagstaff Art 66; Southwest Art, 68; Widforss, 69; Santa Fe Indian Art, 70; Nat Park Illusr, 71; N Fechin, 72.
Positions: Cur arts & exhib, Mus Northern Ariz, 55-58, cur mus, 58-
Publications: Illusr, San Caetano del Tumacacori, 55, Throw stone, 61 & Little cloud, 62; auth, This is a Hopi kachina, 64 & illusr, Dinosaurs of northern Arizona, 68, Mus Northern Ariz.
Mailing Address: Museum of Northern Arizona, Box 1389, Flagstaff, AZ 86001.

WRIGHT, CATHARINE MORRIS
Painter, Writer
Preferred Media: Oils, Watercolors.
b Philadelphia, Pa, Jan 26, 99.
Study & Training: Philadelphia Sch Design Women, 17-18; also with Henry B Snell & Leopold Seyffert.
Work in Public Collections: Pa Acad Fine Arts, Philadelphia; Philadelphia Mus Art; Woodmere Art Gallery; Univ Pa; Nat Acad Design.
Commissions: Many pvt portrait commissions.
Exhibitions: Pa Acad Fine Arts, 18-52; Corcoran Gallery Art, 21-41; Nat Acad Design, 30-52; Am Watercolor Soc; Carnegie Inst.
Teaching: Founder, Fox Hill Sch Art, 50-
Awards: Second Hallgarten prize, Nat Acad Design, 33; prize, Allied Artists Am, 41; prize, Silvermine Guild Artists, 55.
Memberships: Am Watercolor Soc; Audubon Artists; Allied Artists Am; Philadelphia Watercolor Club (v pres, 49-57); Newport Art Asn; Nat Acad Design.
Publications: Auth, The simple nun, 29, Seaweed their pasture, 46, The color of life, 57, plus prose & verse in nat mags including Atlantic Monthly, Sat Eve Post & many others.
Dealer: Vose Galleries of Boston, Inc, 238 Newbury St, Boston, MA 02116.
Mailing Address: Fox Hill, Jamestown, RI 02835.

WRIGHT, FRANK
Painter, Printmaker
Preferred Media: Oils, Graphics.
b Washington, D C, Oct 10, 32.
Study & Training: Am Univ, BA, 54; Univ Ill, Urbana, MA, 57; fel,

Fogg Mus, Harvard Univ, 60-61.
Work in Public Collections: Bibliot Nat, Paris, France; Nat Collection Fine Arts, Washington, D C; Univ Seattle Law Sch, Wash.
Commissions: Deepbite etching demonstration plate & ed, Lessing J Rosenwald, Jenkintown, Pa, 68.
Exhibitions: One-man shows, Watkins Gallery, Washington, D C, 59 & Mickelson Gallery, Washington, D C, 65; two-man show, Galeria Nice, Buenos Aires, Arg, 65; Atelier 17 et Son Maitre S W Hayter, Bibliot Nat, 66; one-man show, Gallery Marc, Washington, D C, 71; plus others.
Teaching: Instr master drawing, Corcoran Sch Art, Washington, D C, 66-70; asst prof design & graphics, George Washington Univ, 70-
Awards: Nat Soc Arts & Lett scholar, 50-54; Leopold Schepp Found fel Europ studies, 56-58; Paul J Sachs fel graphic arts, Print Coun Am, 59-62; plus others.
Bibliography: Rafael Squirru (auth), Washington mannerists or the foresight to look backward, Americas, 1/57.
Dealer: Gallery Marc, 2121 P St N W, Washington, DC 20037.
Mailing Address: 3520 Bradley Lane, Chevy Chase, MD 20015.

WRIGHT, FRANK COOKMAN
Painter, Instructor
Preferred Media: Oils, Acrylics.
b Cincinnati, Ohio, June 6, 04.
Study & Training: Yale Univ, AB, with Sydney Dickenson & Eugene Soragu; Grand Cent Sch Art, with Edmund Graecen; Nat Acad Design Sch, with Dean Cornwell; also with Dimitry Romanovsky.
Work in Public Collections: Hammond Mus, North Salem, N Y; Tarrytown Pub Libr, N Y; also in pvt collections, 42 states & 10 countries.
Commissions: Gateway Arch—Saint Louis, Nat Marine Serv, 66; plus others.
Exhibitions: Macbeth Galleries, 35; one-man shows, Copley Soc Boston; Newport Art Asn, R I; Am Artists Prof League Grand Nat; Hudson Valley Art Asn; plus others.
Teaching: Pvt instr; lectr & demonstr radio & TV progs.
Positions: Ed, News Bull, 59-
Awards: First prize for portraits, Hudson Valley Art Asn, 35; hon mention for oil landscapes, Am Artists Prof League, 62.
Memberships: Am Artists Prof League (pres, 67-); Coun Am Artist Socs (pres, 68-); Hudson Valley Art Asn (pres, 31-37, dir); fel Am Inst Fine Arts; Copley Soc Boston.
Publications: Contribr, many editorials, articles & reviews.
Mailing Address: 222 E 71st St, New York, NY 10021.

WRIGHT, G ALAN
Sculptor
Preferred Media: Bronze, Stone.
b Seattle, Wash, Mar 31, 27.
Study & Training: Honolulu Sch Art; also with Willson Stamper & Ralston Crawford.
Work in Public Collections: Johnson Wax Collection; Seattle Art Mus; Denver Art Mus.
Commissions: The Great Gull in bronze, D E Skinner, Seattle Sci Pavillion, World's Fair, 62; bronze lion cub, First Nat Bank, Spokane, Wash, 63; bronze owl, City Hall, Renton, Wash, 68; bronze crane, Seattle First Nat Bank, 69; crane, First Nat Bank, Tacoma, Wash, 69.
Exhibitions: Northwest Ann Show, Seattle Art Mus, 62-65; Gov Invitational Exhib, Wash, 67; Sara Roby Gallery, Racine, Wis, 68; Whitney Mus Am Art, New York, N Y, 68; Lee Nordness Gallery, New York, 68 & 69.
Positions: Serigraph artist, Honolulu Acad Arts, Hawaii; bd dirs & founding mem, Allied Art, Renton, 62-64; pres, Renton Art Festival, 62-64; comnr, Mayor's Art Comn, Renton, 62-65.
Awards: First prizes, Renton Art Festival, 62 & 64; first prize, New Arts & Crafts Fair, Bellevue, Wash, 63; Ford Found Purchase Award, 64.
Bibliography: Article, In: Christian Sci Monitor, 62 & 64; J Canaday (auth), article, In: New York Times, 68; M Randlett (auth), Living artists of the Pacific Northwest, 72.
Dealers: Gordon Woodside Gallery, 803 E Union St, Seattle, WA 98122; Lee Nordness Galleries, 236-238 E 75th St, New York, NY 10021.
Mailing Address: 1234 S Third St, Renton, WA 98055.

WRIGHT, NINA KAIDEN
Art Consultant
b New York, N Y, May 18, 31.
Study & Training: Emerson Col, BA.
Positions: Mem nat adv coun, Mus Graphic Art, New York; mem art adv coun, New York Bd Trade; consult to Philip Morris for Two Hundred Years of North American Indian Art & When Attitudes Become Form; consult to Mead Corp for European Painters Today; consult to Am Motors Co, Gulf & Western Industries,

Bristol-Myers, Coca-Cola, J C Penney, Capital Res & others; pres, Ruder & Finn Fine Arts, at present.
Mailing Address: Ruder & Finn Fine Arts, 110 E 59th St, New York, NY 10022.

WRIGHT, RUSSEL
Designer, Sculptor
b Lebanon, Ohio, Apr 3, 04.
Study & Training: Cincinnati Acad Art, with Frank Duveneck; Art Stud League New York, with Kenneth Hayes Miller & Lentelli; Princeton Univ, 22-24; Sch Archit, Columbia Univ, 23; Sch Archit, New York Univ, 38-39.
Commissions: Styling elec appliances, merchandising wood & basket prod, Japan, 57-58; design, Dragon Rock (experimental home & arboretum), Garrison-on-Hudson, N Y, 60; designed dinnerware & glassware, Japan, 64; design, Shun Lee Dynasty (Chinese restaurant), 66.
Exhibitions: Home furnishings designs exhibited Metrop Mus Art, Mus Mod Art, Good Design Show & others in U S & Europe.
Positions: Stage mgr & designer stage prod, with Norman Bel Geddes, The Theatre Guild Neighborhood Playhouse & Group Theatre; owner, Russel Wright Assocs, 54-; consult in master planning & programming of parks, Nat Park Serv, 67-; dir, Summer in Parks Prog, Washington, D C, 68; consult on developing handicrafts, Govt Barbados, 70.
Awards: Tiffany Award for sculpture; two Trail Blazer Awards, 51; Good Design Awards, Mus Mod Art, 50 & 53; plus others.
Memberships: Am Soc Indust Designers (founder, pres, 52-53); Harlem Sch Arts (founding mem, bd dirs).
Art Interests: Design of modern home furnishings for easier living, including furniture, lamps, floor coverings, fabrics, tableware and others.
Publications: Co-auth, Easier living, 51.
Mailing Address: 221 E 48th St, New York, NY 10017.

WRIGHT, STANLEY MARC
Painter, Instructor
Preferred Media: Oils, Watercolors, Acrylics.
b Irvington, N J, May 24, 11.
Study & Training: Sch Fine Art, Pratt Inst, grad (highest hon), 33; Jerry Farnsworth Sch Art, Tiffany Found fel, 35.
Work in Public Collections: Portraits, of Gov Deane C Davis & Sen George D Aiken, State House, Montpelier, Vt, Joe Kirkwood, Golf Hall of Fame, Foxberg, Pa, George A Wolf, Med Ctr, Univ Kans & A G Mackay, Med Ctr, Burlington, Vt.
Commissions: Portrait & landscape paintings, U S & Europe.
Exhibitions: Metrop Mus Art; Brooklyn Mus; Newark Mus; Montclair Mus; Washington Cong Galleries.
Teaching: Head portrait & landscape, Newark Sch Fine Arts, 44-50; instr portrait & landscape & dir, Wright Sch Art, Stowe, Vt, 50-; lectr, demonstr & instr painting, many orgn.
Awards: Many prizes for nat exhibs & one-man shows.
Bibliography: Articles, In: Cue Mag, Vt Life Mag, Times, Newark News, Free Press & others.
Memberships: Salmagundi Club; Audubon Artists; Fel Int Inst Arts & Lett; hon mem Vt Artists; Vt Coun Arts.
Mailing Address: R F D 2, Stowe, VT 05672.

WRIGHT, MR & MRS WILLIAM H
Collectors
Collection: Modern paintings & watercolors; Pre-Columbian sculpture, mostly from Colima, Mexico.
Mailing Address: 12921 Evanston St, Los Angeles, CA 90049.

WRIGHTSMAN, CHARLES BIERER
Collector
b Pawnee, Okla, June 13, 95.
Study & Training: Stanford Univ, 14-15; Columbia Univ, 15-17.
Positions: Trustee, Metrop Mus Art, New York, N Y, chmn bd trustees, Inst Fine Arts.
Mailing Address: First City National Bank Bldg, 1021 Main St, Houston, TX 77002.

WRISTON, BARBARA
Educator, Art Historian
b Middletown, Conn, June 29, 17.
Study & Training: Oberlin Col, AB; Brown Univ, AM.
Positions: Dir mus educ, Art Inst Chicago, 61-
Memberships: Soc Archit Historians (pres, 60-61); Furniture Hist Soc; Victorian Soc; Victorian Soc Am; U S Nat Comt Int Coun Monuments & Sites; Am Nat Comt Educ & Cult Action, Int Coun Mus (chmn, 66-70).
Research: Seventeenth and eighteenth century English and American architecture and furniture.
Publications: Auth, When does architecture become history, Inland Architect, 62; auth, Who was the architect of the Indiana Cotton

Mill, 1849-1850?, J Soc Archit Historians, 5/65; auth, Joiner's tools in The Art Institute of Chicago, 67 & The Howard Van Doren Shaw Memorial Collection in The Art Institute of Chicago, 69, Mus Studies; auth, Visual arts in Illinois, 68.
Mailing Address: Art Institute of Chicago, Michigan at Adams St, Chicago, IL 60603.

WUERMER, CARL
Painter, Fine Art Appraiser
Preferred Media: Oils.
b Munich, Ger, Aug 3, 00; U S citizen.
Study & Training: Art Inst Chicago, 20-24; Art Stud League New York, N Y.
Work in Public Collections: High Mus Art, Atlanta, Ga; IBM Corp Art Collection, Endicott, N Y; Encycl Britannica Collection Am Art; Royal Globe Ins Co, London, Eng; Syracuse Univ Art Collection, N Y.
Exhibitions: Var ann, Am Painting & Sculpture, Art Inst Chicago & Nat Acad Design; Corcoran Gallery Art Bi-Ann, 32; Painting In U S, Carnegie Inst, 46-49; Fifth Ann Painting & Sculpture, Grover M Hermann Fine Arts Ctr, Marietta, Ohio, 72.
Awards: J Francis Murphy Mem prize, Nat Acad Design, 28; Popular Vote Prize, Carnegie Inst, 49; hon mention, Allied Artists Am 58th Ann, 71.
Bibliography: G Pagano (auth), The Encyclopedia Britannica Collection of American painting, 46.
Memberships: Grand Cent Art Galleries; Allied Artists Am; Artists Fel (pres, 57-59); Hudson Valley Art Asn.
Research: Research for the appraisal of the Frick Collection, New York, High Museum of Art Collection, Eleutherian Mills-Hagley Foundation Collection, Wilmington, Delaware and others.
Mailing Address: R F D 253 B, Woodstock, NY 12498.

WUJCIK, THEO
Printmaker, Educator
Preferred Media: Graphics.
b Detroit, Mich, Jan 29, 36.
Study & Training: Soc Arts & Crafts Art Sch, Detroit, Mich, dipl; Creative Graphic Workshop, New York, N Y; Tamarind Lithography Workshop, Calif, Ford Found grant, 67-68.
Work in Public Collections: Mus Mod Art, New York; Los Angeles Co Mus Art, Calif; Amon Carter Mus Western Art, Fort Worth; Pasadena Art Mus, Calif; Libr Cong, Washington, D C.
Exhibitions: Int Original Prints, Calif Palace of Legion of Honor, San Francisco, Calif, 64; Boston Printmakers 19th Ann, Mus Fine Arts, Boston, Mass, 67; 17th Print Nat, Brooklyn Mus, N Y, 70; Prints by Seven, Whitney Mus Am Art, New York, 70; Int Miniature Print Exhib, Pratt Graphic Art Ctr, New York, 71.
Teaching: Instr graphics, Soc Arts & Crafts Art Sch, 64-70; asst prof lithography, Univ S Fla, 72-
Positions: Co-founder, Detroit Lithography Workshop, 68-70; shop dir, graphicstudio, Univ S Fla, 70-
Awards: Louis Comfort Tiffany Found Award Graphics, 64.
Dealer: Brooke Alexander Inc, 26 E 78th St, New York, NY 10021.
Mailing Address: 411 Berwick Ave, Tampa, FL 33617.

WUNDER, RICHARD PAUL
Art Historian, Art Administrator
b Ardmore, Pa, May 31, 23.
Study & Training: Harvard Univ, AB, 49, MA, 50, PhD, 55.
Collections Arranged: The Architect's Eye, Cooper Union Mus, 62; Theater Drawings from the Donald Oenslager Collection, Minneapolis Inst Arts & Yale Univ Art Gallery, 63-64; Frederic Edwin Church, Nat Collection Fine Arts, Smithsonian Inst, 66.
Positions: Asst to dir, Fogg Art Mus, Harvard Univ, 53-54; cur drawings & prints, Cooper Union Mus, 55-64; cur & asst dir, Nat Collection Fine Arts, Smithsonian Inst, 64-69; dir, Cooper-Hewitt Mus Design, 69-70.
Awards: John Thornton Kirkland fel, Harvard Univ, 54.
Memberships: Col Art Asn Am; Drawing Soc (dir, 64-72); Soc l'Histoire l'Art Francais; Archives Am Art (adv bd, 68-); Art Quart (adv bd, 67-).
Research: Italian & French drawings of the seventeenth & eighteenth centuries; American painting, sculpture & drawings of the nineteenth century.
Publications: Auth, Extravagent drawings of the 18th century, Lambert-Spector, 62; auth, Architectural & ornament drawings, Univ Mich Mus, 65; auth, Hiram Powers, Smithsonian Inst, 73.
Mailing Address: Brookside, Orwell, VT 05760.

WUNDERLICH, RUDOLF G
Art Dealer
b Tarrytown, N Y, Nov 13, 20.
Study & Training: New York Univ.
Positions: Dir, Kennedy Galleries, Inc.
Specialty of Gallery: Early American eighteenth, nineteenth & twentieth century paintings, drawings & watercolors; also Western

Americana & old & modern master prints; works of modern masters; modern sculpture & graphics.
Mailing Address: Kennedy Galleries, Inc, 20 E 56th St, New York, NY 10022.

WURTZBURGER, JANET E C
Collector, Patron
b Cleveland, Ohio, Jan 29, 08.
Memberships: Walters Art Gallery (v pres, at present); Baltimore Mus (trustee); Md Inst Col Art (trustee); Mus Mod Art (int coun); Am Acad at Rome (trustee).
Art Interests: Contemporary sculpture.
Collection: Modern sculpture from Rodin to Calder; primitive art collection is now being exhibited at Baltimore Mus.
Mailing Address: Timberlane, Stevenson, MD 21153.

WYATT, STANLEY
Painter, Educator
Preferred Media: Oils, Tempera, Graphite.
b Denver, Colo, Sept 20, 21.
Study & Training: Columbia Col, with Frank Mechau, BA, 43; Art Inst Chicago, 46; Columbia Univ, with Meyer Shapiro, MA, 47; Brooklyn Mus, with Rufino Tamayo, 48.
Work in Public Collections: N Am-Mexican Cult Inst, Mexico City; Packaging Inst, Toronto, Can; Nyack Pub Libr, N Y.
Commissions: Illus, Nat Educ Asn J, 52-65, Columbia Univ Alumni News, 53-57, New York Times Mag, 57-61, Col Entrance Bd Rev, 59-72 & Rockefeller Univ Rev, 68.
Exhibitions: Barnard Col, New York, N Y, 59; Regis Col, Denver, 61; La Galeria Collectionistas, Mexico City, 62; N Am-Mexican Cult Inst, Mexico City, 63; Casa Italiana, Columbia Univ, New York, 71.
Teaching: Assoc prof art & chmn dept, Waynesburg Col, 49-51; instr art, Columbia Univ, 52-60; assoc prof art, City Col New York, 60-; assoc prof art & chmn dept, Rockland Community Col, 61-63.
Positions: Dir dept art, Del Piombo Art Ctr, 59-61; art dept rep, Baruch Sch, 61-69; supvr art dept, eve div, City Col New York, 69-72.
Awards: Brainard Sr prize, Columbia Col, 43; distinction in illustration, Am Asn Alumni Mags, 57; gold ribbon for prints, Fifth Ann Bergen Mall Exhibs, 66.
Bibliography: Graphic art of Stanley Wyatt, Anon, Univ Mich, 70.
Memberships: Fel Royal Soc Arts, London; Salmagundi Club; Newcomen Soc N Am; United Fedn Col Teachers.
Publications: Ed, Jester, Columbia Univ, 43; auth, Thanks to Shanks, 58; illusr, Poetry of the damned, Peter Pauper, 60; illusr, 20th century views & 20th century interpretations, 60-72 & The great American forest, 65, Prentice Hall.
Mailing Address: 75 River Rd, Grand View-on-Hudson, NY 10960.

WYCKOFF, SYLVIA SPENCER
Painter, Educator
Preferred Media: Watercolors.
b Pittsburgh, Pa, Nov 14, 15.
Study & Training: Col Fine Arts, Syracuse Univ, BFA, 37, MFA, 44.
Work in Public Collections: Radio Station WSYR, Syracuse, N Y; R E Dietz Co, Syracuse; also incl in pvt collections.
Exhibitions: Munson-Williams-Proctor Inst, Utica, N Y; Mem Art Gallery, Rochester, N Y; Everson Mus Art, Syracuse; Cooperstown Art Asn, Cooperstown, N Y; Nat Asn Women Artists, New York, N Y.
Teaching: Prof watercolor & drawing, Syracuse Univ, 42-
Awards: First prize for watercolor, Syracuse Regional, 45; League Prize for watercolor, Nat League Am Pen Women Nat Show, 48; Gordon Steele Award, Assoc Artists Syracuse, 68.
Memberships: Nat Asn Women Artists; Nat League Am Pen Women; Assoc Artists Syracuse; Daubers Club Syracuse.
Mailing Address: 705 E Molloy Rd, Syracuse, NY 13211.

WYETH, ANDREW NEWELL
Painter
Preferred Media: Tempera, Watercolors.
b Chadds Ford, Pa, July 12, 17.
Study & Training: With N C Wyeth; Harvard Univ, hon DFA, 55; Colby Col, hon DFA, 55; Dickinson Col, hon DFA, 58; Swarthmore Col, hon DFA, 58.
Work in Public Collections: Metrop Mus Art, New York, N Y; Mus Fine Arts, Boston, Mass; Los Angeles Co Mus Art, Calif; Art Inst Chicago, Ill; Farnsworth Mus, Rockland, Maine; plus many others.
Exhibitions: Currier Gallery Art, Manchester, N H; Pa Acad Fine Arts, Philadelphia; Fogg Art Mus, Mass; Univ Ariz, Tucson; Mus Fine Arts, Boston; plus many other group & one-man shows.
Awards: Pa Acad Fine Arts; Carnegie Inst; Am Watercolor Soc; plus many others.

Bibliography: Richard Merryman (auth), Andrew Wyeth, Houghton.
Memberships: Nat Acad Design, Audubon Artists; Am Watercolor
   Soc; Nat Acad Arts & Lett; Am Acad Arts & Lett.
Mailing Address: c/o Coe Kerr Gallery, 49 E 82nd St, New York,
   NY 10028.

WYETH, HENRIETTE (MRS PETER HURD)
   Painter
b Wilmington, Del, Oct 22, 07.
Study & Training: Normal Art Sch, Boston; Pa Acad Fine Arts; also
   with N C Wyeth.
Work in Public Collections: Wilmington Soc Fine Arts; Roswell Mus
   Art; New Britain Mus Art, Conn; Lubbock Mus Art, Tex; Tex
   Tech Univ; portraits in pvt collections.
Exhibitions: Carnegie Inst, Pittsburgh, Pa; Art Inst Chicago, Ill;
   Metrop Mus Art, New York; Roswell Mus Art, N Mex; New York
   City & others.
Awards: Four first prizes, Wilmington Soc Fine Arts; Pa Acad Fine
   Arts.
Mailing Address: Sentinel Ranch, San Patricio, NM 88348.

WYETH, JAMES BROWNING
   Painter
Preferred Media: Oils, Watercolors.
b Wilmington, Del, July 6, 46.
Work in Public Collections: William Farnsworth Mus, Rockland,
   Maine; Brandywine River Mus, Chadds Ford, Pa; Del Art Mus,
   Wilmington.
Bibliography: Joseph Roody (auth), Another Wyeth, Look Mag,
   4/2/68; Wyeth phenomenon (film), CBS TV, 69; Richard Meryman
   (auth), Wyeth Christmas, Life Mag, 12/17/71.
Memberships: Nat Acad Design; Am Watercolor Soc; Nat Endow-
   ment Arts.
Dealer: Coe Kerr Gallery, 49 E 82nd St, New York, NY 10028.
Mailing Address: Chadds Ford, PA 19317.

WYMAN, WILLIAM
   Craftsman
Preferred Media: Ceramics.
b Boston, Mass, June 13, 22.
Study & Training: Mass Col Art, BS; Columbia Univ, MA; Alfred
   Univ.
Work in Public Collections: Des Moines Art Ctr; Saint Paul Gallery
   Art; Mus Contemp Crafts; Everson Mus Art; Smithsonian Inst;
   plus others.
Commissions: Ceramic monument, Weymouth High Sch, 65.
Exhibitions: Work exhibited in every major ceramic exhib nat & int
   incl Metrop Mus Art, Inst Contemp Arts, Boston, Victoria & Al-
   bert Mus, London, World Ceramic Exhib, New York, Brussels
   World's Fair; plus many others.
Teaching: Workshops & lect, many univs, cols & art orgn, nat & in
   Can; instr ceramics & sculpture, Boston Mus Fine Arts Sch, at
   present.
Positions: Operator, Herring Run Pottery, East Weymouth.
Awards: R I Festival Arts; Smithsonian Inst; Am Crafts Coun; plus
   others.
Memberships: Am Crafts Coun; Am Asn Univ Prof.
Mailing Address: 9 Iron Hill St, East Weymouth, MA 02189.

WYNN, DONALD JAMES
   Painter, Lecturer
b Brooklyn, N Y, Sept 26, 42.
Study & Training: Pratt Inst, BFA, 67; Ind Univ, MFA, 69.
Work in Public Collections: Pratt Inst; Ind Univ; Greenshields Fedn,
   Montreal.
Exhibitions: Hofstra Ann, Hofstra Univ, Hempstead, N Y, 67; Indiana
   Artists, Herron Mus, Indianapolis, Ind, 68; Poetic American Real-
   ism, Gallerie R P Hartmann, Munich, Ger, 69; 22 Realists, Whit-
   ney Mus Am Art, New York, N Y, 70; The Realist Revival, Am
   Fedn Arts Traveling Exhib, New York Cult Ctr, 72.
Teaching: Teaching asst painting & drawing, Ind Univ, Bloomington,
   67-69; instr drawing, Eastern Mich Univ, 72.
Positions: Guest artist, Yale Univ, New Haven, Conn, 70; guest art-
   ist, Skidmore Col, Saratoga Springs, N Y, 71; vis artist, Art Inst
   Chicago, Ill, 72-73; vis artist, Ohio Univ, 72.
Awards: Herron Mus Art Award, 68; Elizabeth T Greenshields Found
   Mem grant, 70; Fine Arts Work Ctr residence grant, Provinces-
   town, Mass, 71.
Bibliography: Muller-Mellis (auth), Poetic American Realism, Gallerie R P Hartmann, 69; James Monte (auth), 22 Realists, Whit-
   ney Mus Am Art, 70; Carter Ratcliff (auth), New York, Art Int,
   4/70.
Mailing Address: 255 77th St, Brooklyn, NY 11209.

WYNNE, ALBERT GIVENS
   Painter, Instructor
b Colorado Springs, Colo, Jan 3, 22.
Study & Training: Univ Denver; Iowa Wesleyan Col, BA; Univ Iowa,
   MA; also with S Carl Fracassini, Boardman Robinson, James
   Lechay & others.
Exhibitions: Joslyn Art Mus; Butler Inst Am Art; Anchorage, Alaska;
   Am Fedn Arts traveling exhib; Roswell, N Mex; plus many other
   group & one-man shows.
Teaching: Honoraria instr, Univ Colo, Colorado Springs Fine Arts
   Ctr.
Awards: Prizes, Art Exhib, Anchorage Alaska & Des Moines Art
   Ctr.
Mailing Address: 7420 Swan Rd, Colorado Springs, CO 80908.

WYNSHAW, FRANCES
   Art Dealer
b New York, NY.
Positions: Dir, Avanti Galleries, New York.
Specialty of Gallery: Contemporary American and European art.
Mailing Address: 145 E 72nd St, New York, NY 10021.

WYRICK, PETE (CHARLES LLOYD WYRICK, JR)
   Art Critic, Writer
b Greensboro, N C, May 5, 39.
Study & Training: Davidson Col, BA; Univ N C, MFA; Univ Mo.
Exhibitions: Corcoran Biennial Exhib Am Painting, 67; Assoc Art-
   ists N C Ann, 68; Univ Va Print Exhib, 68.
Collections Arranged: Art from the Ancient World, The Human Fig-
   ure in Art, A Wyeth Portrait & Light as a Creative Medium, Va
   Mus Fine Arts, 66-68.
Teaching: Instr lit, Stephens Col, 64-66.
Positions: Artmobile coordr & asst head progs div, Va Mus Fine
   Arts, Richmond, 66-68; exec dir, Asn Preservation Va Antiq,
   68-70; pres, Fine Arts Consults, Richmond, 71-; art critic,
   Richmond News Leader, 71-
Memberships: Am Asn Mus; Col Art Asn Am; Soc Archit Historians;
   Am Acad Consults.
Research: Contemporary American painting; eighteenth-twentieth
   century American architecture.
Publications: Auth, Art and urban aesthetics (weekly column), Rich-
   mond News Leader; auth, A Wyeth portrait, 67 & Contemporary
   art at the Virginia Museum, 72, Arts in Va; co-auth, Richmond's
   17th Street market (in prep); auth, A Richmond guide (in prep).
Mailing Address: 9 E Franklin St, Richmond, VA 23219.

WYSE, ALEXANDER JOHN
   Painter, Sculptor
Preferred Media: Oils, Wood, Glass, Ink, Tin, Pencil.
b Gloucestershire, Eng, Sept 8, 38; Can citizen.
Study & Training: Cheltenham Col Art, Gloucestershire; Royal Col
   Art, London, Eng.
Work in Public Collections: Mt Allison Univ, NB; Can Coun Collec-
   tion.
Exhibitions: Nat Children's Art Exhib, Eng; Brit Young Contempo-
   raries; first Can one-man show, Pa Acad Fine Arts Peace Gal-
   lery; Arwin Galleries, Detroit, Mich; Pollock Gallery, Toronto,
   Ont.
Teaching: Instr, Northwest Territories, Can, 62-63; instr engraving,
   W Baffin Eskimo Coop, Baffin Island; lectr, Ont Elem Schs, 71.
Awards: Am Soc Graphic Arts Award, Alphabet book, 68; Can Coun
   grants, 68 & 70.
Publications: Co-auth, Alphabet book, Univ Toronto Press, 68-69.
Dealers: Arwin Galleries, 222 Grand River W, Detroit, MI 48226;
   Pollock Gallery, Toronto, Ont, Can.
Mailing Address: 125 Noel St, Ottawa, Ont, Can.

Y

YAGHJIAN, EDMUND
   Painter, Educator
Preferred Media: Acrylics.
b Harpoot, Armenia; U S citizen.
Study & Training: R I Sch Design, BFA; Art Stud League New York,
   with Stuart Davis.
Work in Public Collections: New York Pub Libr, N Y; New York
   Univ; High Mus Art, Atlanta, Ga; Gibbes Art Mus, Charleston,
   S C; West Point Mus, N Y; plus many others including over 450
   in pvt collections.
Exhibitions: New York World's Fair; San Francisco World's Fair,
   Calif; Carnegie Int, Pittsburgh, Pa, 36; Whitney Mus Am Art,

New York, 40; Metrop Mus Art, New York, 41; 40 Year Retrospective, Univ S C, 72; plus many other group & one-man shows.
Teaching: Instr art, Art Stud League New York, 38-42; guest instr painting, Univ Mo, 44-45; head dept art, Univ S C, 45-66, artist-in-residence, 66-72; instr painting, Columbia Mus Art, 72-
Awards: Numerous prizes & awards in local & regional shows.
Bibliography: Articles in art mags & bks.
Memberships: Am Fedn Arts; Col Art Asn Am; Southeastern Col Art Asn (pres); life mem Art Stud League New York; S C Artists Guild (pres & founder).
Mailing Address: 1510 Adger Rd, Columbia, SC 29205.

YATER, GEORGE DAVID
Painter, Art Administrator
Preferred Media: Oils, Watercolors.
b Madison, Ind, Nov 30, 10.
Study & Training: John Herron Art Sch, 28-32, dipl; Cape Sch Art, Provincetown, with Henry Hensche, summers 31-34; also with Edwin Dickinson & Richard Miller.
Work in Public Collections: Chrysler Collection, Norfolk Art Gallery, Va; Ford Motor Co, Dearborn, Mich; Paper Mill Playhouse, Millburn, N J; Ind Univ, Bloomington; De Pauw Univ, Greencastle, Ind.
Exhibitions: Nat Acad Design, New York, N Y; Pa Acad Fine Arts, Philadelphia; Am Watercolor Soc, New York; Indianapolis Mus Art, Ind; Chrysler Art Mus, Provincetown, Mass.
Positions: Dir, Provincetown Art Asn, 47-61; dir, Sarasota Art Asn, 55-56; dir & instr, Middletown Fine Arts Ctr, 70-71.
Awards: Alumni prize, Ind Artists Ann, John Herron Art Mus, 53; outstanding oil, Hoosier Salon, Indianapolis, 54; first prize for oil, 61 & 69, Falmouth Artists Guild.
Bibliography: Ernie Pyle (auth), article, In: Scripps-Howard Feature, 36; Jack Stinnet (auth), In New York, AP Feature, 36; Robert Hatch (auth), At the tip of Cape Cod, Horizon Mag, 61.
Publications: More than 75 watercolors have been used as illus in Ford Times, Lincoln-Mercury Times & New Eng Journeys, 52-60.
Mailing Address: Castle Rd, Truro, MA 02666.

YATES, SHARON DEBORAH
Painter
Preferred Media: Oils.
b Rochester, N Y, Apr 3, 42.
Study & Training: Syracuse Univ, scholar to Florence, Italy, 63, BFA, 64; Tulane Univ La, MFA, 66.
Work in Public Collections: Okla Art Ctr, Oklahoma City.
Exhibitions: Am Fedn Arts Traveling Exhib, New York, 67-; Okla Art Ctr Tenth Ann, 68; Mainstreams '70, Marietta Col Fine Arts Ctr, Ohio, 70; Exhib Contemp Realists, Cleveland Inst, Ohio, 72; one-man show, Univ Louisville, Ky, 67; plus many other group & one-man shows.
Teaching: Instr printmaking, painting & drawing, Univ Louisville, 66-68; instr painting & drawing, Md Inst Col Art, 68-
Awards: Seed grant as artist-in-residence, Am Beautiful Fund of Natural Area Coun, 70; grand prize, Mainstreams, 70; Prix de Rome, 72.
Bibliography: Barbara Gold (auth), Art! ?, film produced on Channel 2, Baltimore, Md, 3/72.
Publications: Contribr, A sense of place, The artist & The American land, 72.
Mailing Address: American Academy in Rome, Via Angelo Masina 5, Rome, Italy 00153.

YEKTAI, MANOUCHER
Painter
Preferred Media: Oils.
b Tehran, Iran, Dec 22, 22; U S citizen.
Study & Training: Univ Tehran; Ecole Superior Beaux Arts, Paris, France, with Auzenfant, 45-47; Art Stud League New York, 47-48.
Work in Public Collections: Many collections.
Exhibitions: Poindexter Gallery, New York, N Y, five from 57-64; Gumps Gallery, San Francisco, Calif, 59, 64 & 65; Piccadilly Gallery, London, Eng, 61 & 70; Anderson-Meyer Gallery, Paris, 62; Gestrude Kasle Gallery, Detroit, Mich, 65-70; plus many others.
Mailing Address: 1235 Park Ave, New York, NY 10028.

YEPEZ, DOROTHY
Art Administrator, Painter
Preferred Media: Pastels.
b Philadelphia, Pa, Feb 22, 18.
Study & Training: Univ Pa; Temple Univ; New York Univ; Cooper Union; New Sch Soc Res; also privately.
Work in Public Collections: Amistad Res Ctr, New Orleans, La; Saranac Lake Free Libr, N Y.
Exhibitions: Dorothy Yepez Galleries, Saranac Lake, 59, 62, 67 & 72; pen & Pallette Ann Exhib, Saranac Lake, 65 & 66.

Collections Arranged: Leon Slwinski, Warsaw, Poland, 61; The Gay 90's, 61; Military Lore (Civil War), 62; Arts & Crafts from the Clinton Prison Hobby Shop, Dannemora, N Y, 62; Dolls of all Nations & Original Christmas Cards, 63; Stamp Show: Vatican Series from the collection of His Eminence Cardinal Spellman, 63; Meet the Artists: Naomi Lorne, Lilly Shiff, May Heiloms, Montifore Hosp Libr, N Y.
Positions: Dir-adminstr, Dorothy Yepez Galleries, 52-
Awards: Grumbacher award, 57.
Bibliography: Enciclopedia Int Degli Artisti, Bugatti Editore, 70-71.
Memberships: Charter mem New York State Coun Arts; Smithsonian Assocs; Am Fedn Arts; Am Asn Mus; Mus Mod Art, New York.
Specialty of Gallery: American antiques.
Art Interests: Fine arts from all over the world.
Collection: 150 yr old sch house; furniture, glassware, crockery, tinware & other antiques.
Mailing Address: Bloomingdale Rd, Saranac Lake, NY 12983.

YOAKUM, DELMER J
Painter, Designer
Preferred Media: Oils, Watercolors.
b Saint Joseph, Mo, Dec 6, 15.
Study & Training: Chouinard Art Inst & Jepson Art Inst, Los Angeles, Calif; Kansas City Art Inst; Univ Southern Calif.
Work in Public Collections: Butler Inst Am Art, Youngstown, Ohio; San Diego Art Mus, Calif; Calif Nat Watercolor Soc; Las Vegas Art League; Glendale Savings & Loan, Calif.
Exhibitions: Los Angeles Mus, Calif, 47-58; Butler Inst Am Art, 53-71; Calif Nat Watercolor Soc, Los Angeles, 54-72; Watercolor U S A, Springfield, Mo, 66-72; Nat Acad Design, New York, N Y, 70.
Teaching: Instr art, Sedona, Ariz.
Positions: Scenic artist, Motion Picture Studios, Hollywood, Calif, 52-72.
Awards: Edouvard Manet Award, Frye Art Mus, 58 & 63; best of show, City of Avalon, Calif, 67; John Marin Mem Award, Watercolor U S A, 71.
Memberships: Calif Nat Watercolor Soc (past pres); Inglewood Art League (hon life mem); Sedona Arts Ctr.
Dealer: The Martin Gallery, Brown Ave at Pima Plaza, Scottsdale, AZ 85251.
Mailing Address: 57 Chapel Hills Rd, Sedona, AZ 86336.

YOCHIM, LOUISE DUNN
Educator, Painter
Preferred Media: Oils, Watercolors.
b Jitomir, Ukraine, July 18, 09; U S citizen.
Study & Training: Art Inst Chicago, cert, 32, BAE, 42, MAE, 52; Univ Chicago, 56.
Work in Public Collections: Bir-Bejan, Russia; Eilat Mus, Israel; Bernard Horwich Ctr, Chicago, Ill; Northeastern Ill Univ, Chicago; A Werbe Gallery, Detroit, Mich.
Exhibitions: Chicago & Vicinity Exhib, Art Inst Chicago, 35-44; Chicago Soc Artists Exhib, Riverside Mus, New York, N Y, 51; Nat Exhib, Terry Mus Art, Fla, 52; Assoc Artists Gallery, Washington, D C, 62; one-woman show, Northeastern Ill Univ, 72; plus many others.
Teaching: Instr art, Chicago Pub H S, Ill, 34-50; instr art, Chicago Acad Fine Arts, 51-52; instr art, Chicago Teachers Col, 60-61.
Positions: Art supvr, Chicago Pub Schs, 50-71; consult, elem & high schs, 71-; consult art, Rand McNally Publ, 67-; consult art, Encycl Britannica, 68-
Awards: Todros Geller Award for painting, Am Jewish Arts Club, 48 & 61; award, Chicago Soc Artists, 53.
Bibliography: Frank Holland (auth), Renaissance unit's show to cap season, Chicago Sun Times, 57; Doris Lane Butler (auth), Winnetka to open art fair season, Chicago Daily News, 57; Frank Getlein (auth), Associated artists, Sunday Star, Washington, D C, 62.
Memberships: Chicago Soc Artists (pres, 72); Renaissance Soc Art; Nat Art Educ Asn; Nat Comt Art Educ.
Publications: Auth, Building human relationships through art, 54, Perceptual growth in creativity, 67 & Art in action, 69.
Dealer: Four Arts Gallery, 1629 Oak Ave, Evanston, IL 60203.
Mailing Address: 9545 Drake Ave, Evanston, IL 60203.

YOSHIDA, RAY KAKUO
Painter, Educator
Preferred Media: Oils, Acrylics.
b Kapaa, Kauai, Hawaii, Oct 3, 30.
Study & Training: Sch Art Inst Chicago, BA; Syracuse Univ, MFA; Univ Chicago; Univ Hawaii; also with A D Reinhardt.
Work in Public Collections: Everson Mus, Syracuse, N Y; Art Inst Chicago, Ill; Delgado Mus, New Orleans, La.
Exhibitions: Spirit of the Comics, Inst Contemp Art, Univ Pa, 69; Chicago & Vicinity Exhibs, Art Inst Chicago, 69 & 71; Am Paint-

ing 1972, Indianapolis Mus Art, 72; Mus Contemp Art, Chicago; Brooklyn Mus; plus others.
Teaching: Prof painting, Sch Art Inst Chicago, 60-
Awards: Thomas C Thompson Purchase Prize, Everson Mus, 53; Walter M Campana Prize, 60 & Frank G Logan Medal & Prize, 71, Art Inst Chicago.
Bibliography: Franz Schulze (auth), Chicago art, Follett, 72; article, In: Art Int; article, In: Art News.
Memberships: Art Inst Chicago.
Dealer: Phyllis Kind Gallery, 226 E Ontario, Chicago, IL 60611.
Mailing Address: 915 Lakeside Pl, Chicago, IL 60640.

YOUNG, CLIFF
Painter, Instructor
Preferred Media: Oils, Acrylics.
b New Waterford, Ohio, Dec 27, 05.
Study & Training: Art Inst Pittsburgh; Art Inst Chicago; Nat Acad Design; also with George Oberteuffer, Charles Schroeder, John Norton, J Wellington Reynolds & Harvey Dunn.
Work in Public Collections: U S Navy Art Gallery & U S Marine Corps Collection, Washington, D C; Fed Hall, New York, N Y.
Commissions: Murals, St Francis Monastery, Utuado, P R, 58, Berkshire Life Ins Co, Pittsfield, Mass, 61, Church of Our Lady of Victory, New York, 62, Norweg Children's Home, Brooklyn, N Y, 63 & Pub Sch 232, Queens, N Y, 65.
Teaching: Chmn found courses, Phoenix Sch Design, New York, 67-; instr painting Salmagundi Club, New York, 70-
Memberships: Archit League New York; Salmagundi Club (chmn art comt, 70-71); Nat Soc Mural Painters (treas, 71-72); Soc Illusr; Artists Guild (pres, 72).
Publications: Auth, Figure drawing without a model, 46; auth, Drawing drapery, 47; auth, Figure construction, 66.
Mailing Address: 24 W 45th St, New York, NY 10036.

YOUNG, JOHN CHIN
Painter, Collector
Preferred Media: Oils.
b Honolulu, Hawaii, Mar 26, 09.
Work in Public Collections: Hawaii State Found Cult & Arts, Honolulu; Honolulu Acad Arts; Smithsonian Inst Art in Embassy Prog, Washington, D C; Dept Educ Hawaii State Artmobile Prog, Honolulu.
Commissions: Oil mural painting, Hana Ranch, Maui, Hawaii.
Exhibitions: Am Art Today, Metrop Mus Art & Va Art Mus, 50 & 58; one-man exhibs, Los Angeles Co Mus Art, Calif, Place Legion of Honor, Calif & Honolulu Acad Art; Pac Heritage Traveling Exhib to Berlin.
Teaching: Instr painting, Honolulu Acad Art, 60-61.
Positions: Art critic, Honolulu Star Bull, 65-66; chmn cult activities comt, East West Ctr, Honolulu, 71-72; dir, John Young Gallery.
Awards: First prize in watercolors, 50, first prize in oil painting, 54 & best in show, 55, Honolulu Acad Art.
Memberships: Hawaii Painters & Sculptors League (pres); Tennent Art Found (trustee, 72).
Collection: Oriental, pre-Columbian, African and Oceanic art works.
Mailing Address: Kahala Hilton, Honolulu, HI 96816.

YOUNG, JOSEPH LOUIS
Sculptor, Art Administrator
Preferred Media: Multi-Media.
b Pittsburgh, Pa, Nov 27, 19.
Study & Training: Westminister Col, AB, 41, hon LLD, 60; Boston Mus Sch Fine Art, hon grad, 51; Carnegie Inst Technol; Mass Inst Technol; Cranbrook Acad Art; Art Stud League New York; also with Karl Zerbe, David Aronson, Mitchell Siporin, Oskar Kockoshka & Gyorgy Kepes.
Commissions: Granite bas-relief, Los Angeles Co Hall Record, Los Angeles Civic Ctr, Calif, 64; sixteen stained glass windows, Congregation Beth Sholom, San Francisco, Calif, 65; west apse, Nat Shrine Immaculate Conception, Washington, D C, 67; History of Math (mosaic mural), math sci bldg, Univ Calif, Los Angeles, 70; The Triforium (multi-media tower), Los Angeles Mall, 73; plus over forty major archit commissions throughout the U S A.
Exhibitions: Ten Year Retrospective, Art in Architecture, Palm Springs Desert Mus, 63; Int Exhib Muralists, Brussels, Belg, 65; one-man shows, Archit League New York, 51 & Falk Raboff Gallery, Los Angeles, 53.
Teaching: Dir, Mosaic Workshop, 55-; artist-in-residence, Brandeis Inst, 62-; chmn dept archit arts, Santa Barbara Art Inst, 70-; lectr, Art in Architecture, at various institutions of higher learning.
Positions: Designer 400th Anniversary of Michelangelo, Italian Trade Comn; nat v pres, Artists Equity Asn, 61-62; nat v pres, Nat Soc Mural Painters, 71-72; owner, Art in Archit.

Awards: Edwin Austin Abbey scholar, 50; Am Acad Rome, Italy, 51; Huntington Hartford Found fel, 52.
Memberships: Fel Int Inst Arts & Lett; Nat Sculpture Ctr, Lawrence, Kans; Nat Soc Mural Painters.
Art Interests: Sound-light in architectural environments.
Publications: Auth, Bibliography of mural painting in U S A, 46, A plan for mural painting in Israel, 52, The world of mosaic (film), produced by Univ Calif, Los Angeles, 57; Arts & crafts in architecture, Creative Crafts, Vol 2, No 1 & Mosaics: principles & practice, Reinhold, 63; Dialogues in art, KNBC-TV Series, 67.
Mailing Address: Art in Architecture, 8422 Melrose Ave, Los Angeles, CA 90069.

YOUNG, KENNETH VICTOR
Painter, Designer
b Louisville, Ky, Dec 12, 33.
Study & Training: Ind Univ; Univ Louisville, BS.
Work in Public Collections: Corcoran Gallery Art, Washington, D C; Va Nat Bank, Alexandria; Johnson Publ Co, Chicago, Ill.
Exhibitions: J B Speed Mus, Louisville, 63; Inst Contemp Arts, Washington, D C, 67; Baltimore Mus, Md, 69; Ill Bel Co, Chicago, 71; Indianapolis Mus, Ind, 72.
Collections Arranged: Music Machines, Hall of Graphic Arts, Women and Politics, Gandhi Centennial Exhib, Explorers N Z.
Teaching: Instr painting, Louisville Pub Sch, 62-63; instr design & painting, Corcoran Sch Art, 70-
Positions: Designer, Smithsonian Inst, 64-
Bibliography: B Rose (auth), Black artist in America, Art Am, 70.
Dealer: Studio Gallery, 1735 Connecticut Ave, Washington, DC 20009.
Mailing Address: 1827 Riggs Pl N W, Washington, DC 20009.

YOUNG, MAHONRI S
Art Administrator
b New York, N Y, July 23, 11.
Study & Training: Dartmouth Col, AB; New York Univ, MA.
Collections Arranged: Howald, Wildenstein & British collections.
Teaching: Instr hist art, Sarah Lawrence Col, 41-50.
Positions: Acting dir, Munson-Williams-Proctor Inst, 51-53; dir, Columbus Gallery Fine Arts, 53-
Memberships: Asn Art Mus Dir.
Publications: Am corresp, Apollo Mag.
Mailing Address: 480 E Broad St, Columbus, OH 43215.

YOUNG, MARJORIE WARD
Painter, Instructor
Preferred Media: Watercolors, Pen & Pencil.
b Chicago, Ill, June 25, 10.
Study & Training: With Florence Reed, Chicago, 24; Art Inst Chicago Sat Sch, 25-27, Day Sch, 28-32; with William B Schimmel, 55-56, Jossey Bilan, 58-62, Edgar A Whitney, 69 & 71, Richmond Yip, 70 & J Douglas Greenbowe & Milford Zornes, 72.
Work in Public Collections: Ariz Bank, Phoenix; First Nat Bank Ariz, Phoenix; Walter Bimson Collection, Phoenix; Phoenix Country Club.
Exhibitions: Low Ruins Spring Nat, Tubac, Ariz, 65; 16th Ann Tucson Festival Art, Ariz, 66; Fine Arts Festival S Dak State Univ, 69; 2nd Ariz Watercolor Biennial, Phoenix Art Mus, 70; Nat Diamond Biennial, Nat League Am Pen Women, Washington, D C, 72.
Teaching: Instr drawing & watercolor, Phoenix Art Mus, 70-72; instr watercolor, Creative Living Found, 72.
Positions: Background artist, Fleischer, Famous & Paramount Studios, Miami, Fl, 38-42; gallery dir, Phoenix YWCA, 70-72.
Awards: Second in watercolor for Filibusters, Low Ruins Spring Nat, 65; best of show for watercolor, 71 & hon mention for A Study in Brief, Nat Diamond Biennial, 72, Nat League Am Pen Women.
Memberships: Ariz Artists Guild (pres, 61-62); Ariz Watercolor Asn (pres, 68); Nat League Am Pen Women (br art chmn, 72); Phoenix Art Mus Fine Arts Asn; Contemp Watercolorists Ariz.
Publications: Illusr, Many lives of the lynx, 64; illusr, Functional Spanish, 68.
Dealer: Camelback Galleries, 4521 N Scottsdale Rd, Scottsdale, AZ.
Mailing Address: 320 W Montecito, Phoenix, AZ 85013.

YOUNG, WEBB
Painter
Preferred Media: Watercolors, Oils.
b Covington, Ky, Sept 2, 13.
Study & Training: Art Inst Chicago; Famous Artists Sch; with Gerald Cassidy, 25-27; Inst San Miguel Allende, Mex.
Work in Public Collections: N Mex State Fair Permanent Art Collection; plus many works in pvt collections.
Art Interests: Painting the Southwest.
Publications: Auth, Student steps to watercolor painting, Mexico sketches & A sketchbook of Southwestern life.
Mailing Address: Nambre Rt 1, Box 175, Santa Fe, NM 87501.

YOUNGERMAN, JACK
Painter
b Louisville, Ky, 26.
Study & Training: Univ N C, Chapel Hill; Univ Mo-Columbia; Ecole des Beaux Arts, Paris, France.
Work in Public Collections: Albright-Knox Art Gallery, Buffalo, N Y; Art Inst Chicago, Ill; Corcoran Gallery Art, Washington, D C; Whitney Mus Am Art, New York, N Y; Nat Collection Fine Arts; Phillips Collection, Washington, D C; plus many others in mus, galleries & univs.
Exhibitions: Corcoran Biennial Traveling Exhib, 67; American Prints Today, Mus Art, Munson-Williams-Proctor Inst, Utica, N Y, 68; Whitney Ann, 69; L'Art Vivant aux Etats-Unis, Fondation Maeght, Paris, 70; Carnegie Int, 71; plus many other group & one-man shows in the U S & abroad.
Positions: Designer stage sets & costumes, Histoire de Vasco, Paris, 56 & Death Watch, New York, 58.
Awards: Nat Coun Arts & Sci Award, 66.
Bibliography: Portrait—Jack Youngerman, Art in Am, 9-10/68; Drawings by Jack Youngerman, Harpers, 10/68; Barbara Rose (auth), Getting it physical, Vogue, 2/71; plus many other articles & catalogues.
Dealer: Pace Gallery, 32 E 57th St, New York, NY 10022.
Mailing Address: 70 Fulton St, New York, NY 10038.

YOUNGLOVE, RUTH ANN (MRS BENJAMIN RHEES LOXLEY)
Painter
Preferred Media: Watercolors.
b Chicago, Ill, Feb 14, 09.
Study & Training: Univ Calif, Los Angeles, BE; also with Orrin A White & Marion K Wachtel.
Work in Public Collections: Bank of Am, Pasadena, Calif; El Tovar Hotel, Grand Canyon, Ariz.
Exhibitions: Laguna Beach Art Asn Gallery; Calif Nat Watercolor Soc, Los Angeles, 67 & Laguna Beach, 71; one-woman shows, Flintridge Prep Sch, La Can, 72 & Community Serv Ctr, Pasadena, 72.
Teaching: Instr pvt classes, 55-65.
Awards: Second prize for landscape, Artists League Seal Beach, 68.
Memberships: Pasadena Soc Artists (patron chmn, 58-68); Pasadena Artist Assocs (secy, 61-64); life mem Laguna Beach Art Asn; Calif Nat Watercolor Soc; assoc Am Watercolor Soc.
Art Interests: Landscape painting.
Mailing Address: 1180 Yocum St, Pasadena, CA 91103.

YOUNGQUIST, JOHN
Draftsman
b Crookston, Minn, Sept 19, 18.
Study & Training: Univ Minn, BA; Minn Sch Art; Univ Iowa, MFA; Art Stud League New York; Slade Sch, Univ London; Inst Allende, San Miguel, Mex; N Y Univ.
Work in Public Collections: Minn Inst Art, Minneapolis; Minn Mus Art, St Paul; N Dak State Univ, Fargo; Moorhead State Col, Minn; Univ Iowa, Iowa City.
Exhibitions: Drawing U S A, St Paul, 71; Manisphere Int, Winnipeg, 71; Red River Ann, Moorhead, 72; Ball State Drawing Exhib, Muncie, Ind; Minneapolis Art Inst Biennial.
Teaching: Instr calligraphy, Minn Sch Art, 54-59; instr, Univ Minn Exten, 57-58; assoc prof drawing, Moorhead State Col, 61-
Positions: Bd dirs, Red River Art Ctr, Moorhead, 66-68.
Awards: Seagram Award for Drawing, Manisphere Exhib, 71; purchase award, Drawings U S A, St Paul, 71.
Memberships: Col Art Asn Am.
Dealer: Rourke Art Gallery, 523 S Fourth St, Moorhead, MN 56560.
Mailing Address: 908 Eighth St, Moorhead, MN 56560.

YRISARRY, MARIO
Painter
Preferred Media: Acrylics.
b Manila, Philippines, Mar 29, 33; U S citizen.
Study & Training: Queens Col (N Y), BA; Cooper Union.
Work in Public Collections: Whitney Mus Am Art, New York, N Y; Baltimore Mus Art, Md; Indianapolis Mus Art, Ind; Rose Art Mus, Brandeis Univ, Mass; Mass Inst Technol Mus Art.
Commissions: Poster, Albert A List Found, Lincoln Ctr, New York, 72.
Exhibitions: American Painting & Sculpture, Indianapolis Mus Art, 70; Using Walls (indoors), Jewish Mus, New York, 70; Structure of Color, Whitney Mus Am Art, New York, 71; Grids, Inst Contemp Art, Univ Pa, 72; Painting & Sculpture 1972, Storm King Art Ctr, 72.
Bibliography: Donald Judd (auth), rev, In: Arts Mag, 10/64; Carter Ratcliff (auth), rev, In: Art News, 12/69; Robert Pincus-Witten (auth), New York, Artforum, 2/70.
Publications: Auth, The new work, first person singular-2, Art Gallery, Conn, 5/71.
Dealer: O K Harris Gallery, 469 W Broadway, New York, NY 10012.
Mailing Address: 297 Third Ave, New York, NY 10010.

YRIZARRY, MARCOS
Painter, Graphic Artist
b Mayaguez, P R, Oct 7, 36.
Study & Training: Acad Cent San Fernandeo, Madrid, Spain.
Work in Public Collections: Mus Mod Art, New York, N Y; Bibliot Nat, Paris, France; Ponce Mus, P R; Univ P R, Rio Piedras.
Exhibitions: Int Graphic Biennial, Yugoslavia, 67 & Poland, 68; Galeria Colibri, San Juan, P R; Casa de las Americas, Havana, Cuba.
Awards: Medalla de oro del XV Salon, Madrid, Spain; premio Javier Baez, Casa de las Americas.
Mailing Address: Box 1734, San Juan, PR 00903.

YUDIN, CAROL
Printmaker, Painter
b Brooklyn, N Y.
Study & Training: Pratt Graphic Ctr, with Sid Hammer, Michael Ponce de Leon, Roberto di Lamonica, Andrew Stasik & painting with Michael Lenson.
Work in Public Collections: N J State Mus, Trenton; Jersey City Mus, N J; St Peters Col, Jersey City; Miniature Art Soc N J, Paramus; Belleville Pub Libr, N J.
Commissions: Tree of Life, Congregation Ahavath Achim, Belleville, 65.
Exhibitions: Art From N J, N J State Mus, 69; Fourth Int Miniature Print Exhib, 71; Seventh Triennial N J Artists, Newark Mus, N J, 71; 31st Ann Painters & Sculptors Soc N J, 71; Nat Asn Women Artists, Jersey City & New York, 71.
Teaching: Instr oil painting, Nutley Adult Sch, N J, 66-; instr oil painting, Temple Emanuel, Paterson, N J, 66-69.
Awards: Purchase awards, N J State Mus, 69, Painters & Sculptors Soc N J, 69 & Nat Miniature Art Soc Exhib, 70.
Memberships: Nat Asn Women Artists (graphic juror, 72-75); Painters & Sculptors Soc N J (secy, 62-70, pres, 71-73); Artists Equity N J; Art Exhibs Coun; Hunterdon Art Ctr.
Dealers: Pratt Graphic Ctr Gallery, 831 Broadway, New York, NY 10003; Korby Gallery, 479 Pompton Ave, Cedar Grove, NJ 07009.
Mailing Address: 490 Joralemon St, Belleville, NJ 07109.

YUNKERS, ADJA
Painter, Educator
Preferred Media: Graphics, Pastels, Oils, Acrylics.
b Riga, Latvia, July 15, 00; U S citizen.
Study & Training: Leningrad, Paris, Berlin & Rome.
Work in Public Collections: Represented in over fifty institutions including Mus Mod Art, New York, N Y, Solomon R Guggenheim Mus, New York, Whitney Mus Am Art, New York, Metrop Mus Art, New York & Albright-Knox Art Gallery, Buffalo, N Y.
Commissions: A Human Condition (mural), Syracuse Univ, 66; tapestry for stud union, State Univ N Y Stony Brook, 67.
Exhibitions: Numerous group shows including, Abstract Expressionists & Imagists, Guggenheim Mus, New York, 61, The New American Painting & Sculpture: The First Generation, Mus Mod Art, New York, 69 & Etats Unis, Fondation Maeght, Saint Paul de Venice, France; plus many others including over forty one-man shows.
Teaching: Instr art, New Sch Social Res, 47-56; instr art, Cooper Union, 56-67; instr art, Barnard Col, 69-; instr summer sessions at several western univs.
Positions: Ed, Creation, Ars & Ars-Portfolio, Stockholm, 42-45; vis critic, Columbia Univ, 67-69.
Awards: Guggenheim fel, 49-50, 54-55; Ford Found grant, 60; plus numerous other awards.
Publications: Ed, Prints in the desert, 50.
Mailing Address: 217 E 11th St, New York, NY 10003.

YUST, DAVID E
Painter, Educator
Preferred Media: Acrylics.
b Wichita, Kans, Apr 3, 39.
Study & Training: Birger Sandzen; Wichita State Univ; Kans State Univ; Univ Kans, BFA, 63; Univ Ore, MFA, 69.
Work in Public Collections: Denver Art Mus, Colo; Mulvane Art Ctr, Topeka, Kans; Colo State Univ, Fort Collins; Kans State Univ, Manhattan; Univ Ore, Eugene.
Exhibitions: Artists Choice, Nelson Gallery Art, Kansas City, Mo, 65, 66; Am Embassy Arts Prog, State Dept Traveling Exhib, 66-68; Artists Choice, Friends of Contemp Art, Denver, 70; Selected Artists, Mulvane Art Ctr, 70 & 71; 73rd Western Ann, Denver Art Mus, 71.
Teaching: Asst prof painting & drawing, Colo State Univ, 65-
Awards: Purchase awards, Selected Artists, Mulvane Art Ctr, 70, 11th Biennial, Kans State Univ, 70 & Colo State Univ Centennial, 70.
Dealer: Fountain Gallery Art, 115 S W Fourth Ave, Portland, OR 97220.
Mailing Address: 1301 Patton, Fort Collins, CO 80521.

Z

ZABARSKY, MELVIN JOEL
Painter, Educator
Preferred Media: Oils.
b Worcester, Mass, Aug 21, 32.
Study & Training: Sch Worcester Art Mus, Ruskin Sch Drawing & Fine Arts, Univ Oxford; Sch Fine & Appl Arts, Boston Univ, BFA; Univ Cincinnati, MFA.
Work in Public Collections: Mus Mod Art, New York: N Y; De Cordova Mus, Lincoln, Mass; Addison Gallery Am Art, Andover, Mass; Wiggins Collection, Boston Pub Libr, Mass; Currier Gallery Art, Manchester, N H.
Exhibitions: One-man exhibs, Boris Mirski Gallery, Boston, 62, Tragos Gallery, Boston, 66 & De Cordova Mus, 70; Surreal Images, De Cordova Mus, 68; New Eng Painters Traveling Exhib, Ringling Mus, Sarasota, Fla, 69.
Teaching: Instr painting, Swain Sch Design, New Bedford, Mass, 60-64; asst prof painting, Wheaton Col, 64-69; assoc prof painting, Univ N H, 69-
Awards: Painting prize, Boston Arts Festival, 62; Ford Found grant in humanities, 68.
Bibliography: C Goldstein (auth), Zabarsky (catalogue), De Cordova Mus, 70; B Schwartz (auth), Humanism in twentieth century art, Praeger, 73.
Mailing Address: Dept of Art, University of New Hampshire, Durham, NH 03824.

ZABRISKIE, VIRGINIA M
Art Dealer
b New York, N Y.
Study & Training: Washington Square Col, New York Univ, BA; New York Univ Inst Fine Arts, MA.
Positions: Dir, Zabriskie Gallery, 54-
Memberships: Art Dealers Asn.
Specialty of Gallery: Twentieth century American art.
Mailing Address: 29 W 57th St, New York, NY 10019.

ZACHARIAS, ATHOS
Painter
Preferred Media: Acrylics.
b Marlborough, Mass, June 17, 27.
Study & Training: Art Stud League New York, summer, 52; R I Sch Design, BFA, 52; Cranbrook Acad Art, MFA, 53.
Work in Public Collections: Mus Art, Providence, R I; Inst Contemp Art, Boston, Mass; Kalamazoo Inst Art, Mich; Phoenix Art Mus, Ariz; Westinghouse Corp, Pittsburgh, Pa.
Commissions: Decor for Manhattan Festival Dancers, commissioned by Robert Ossorio, New York, N Y, 63.
Exhibitions: Art U S A, New York, 59; N C Mus Art, Raleigh, 59; Pan-Pacific Show, Kyoto, Japan, 61; one-man shows, Gallery Mayer, New York, 61 & Louis Alexander Gallery, New York, 63.
Teaching: Instr painting, Brown Univ, 53-55; instr painting, Parsons Sch Design, 63-65; instr painting, Wagner Col, 69-
Awards: Best in show award, Guild Hall, 61; grant, Longview Found, 62; festival arts purchase award, Southampton Col, 68.
Publications: Illusr, cover, In: Sci & Technol, 63.
Mailing Address: 463 West St, Apt B-946, New York, NY 10014.

ZADOK, MR & MRS CHARLES
Collectors
Mailing Address: 40 Central Park S, New York, NY 10019.

ZAHN, CARL FREDERICK
Designer, Art Administrator
b Louisville, Ky, Mar 9, 28.
Study & Training: Harvard Univ, AB, 48.
Exhibitions: Fifty Books Exhibition, Am Inst Graphic Arts, 60-72; one-man show, Dreitzer Gallery, Brandeis Univ, 69.
Positions: Graphics designer, Mus Fine Arts, Boston, 56-, ed-in-chief, 71-
Bibliography: William Seitz (auth), Carl Zahn (catalogue of exhib at Brandeis Univ), 69.
Memberships: Am Inst Graphic Arts (bd dirs, 68-71).
Mailing Address: 479 Huntington Ave, Boston, MA 02115.

ZAJAC, JACK
Sculptor, Painter
b Youngstown, Ohio, Dec 13, 29.
Study & Training: Scripps Col, 49-53; also with Millard Sheets, Henry McFee & Sueo Serisawa; Am Acad in Rome.
Work in Public Collections: Mus Mod Art, New York, N Y; Los Angeles Mus Art, Calif; Pa Acad Fine Arts, Philadelphia; Milwaukee Art Inst, Wis; Nelson Gallery Art, Kansas City, Mo; plus others.

Commissions: Reynolds Metals Co, 68.
Exhibitions: Drawings by Sculptors, Smithsonian Inst, circulated in the U S, 61-63; American Painting, Va Mus Fine Arts, Richmond, 62; Fifty California Artists, Whitney Mus Mod Art, New York, 62-63; retrospectives, Newport Harbor Art Mus, Balboa, Calif, 65 & Temple Univ, Rome, 69; plus many other group & one-man shows.
Teaching: Instr, Pomona Col, 59.
Awards: Prix de Rome, 54, 56 & 57; Am Acad Arts & Lett grant, 58; Guggenheim fel, 59.
Bibliography: Henry J Seldis & Ulfert Wilke (auth), The sculpture of Jack Zajac, Gallard Press, 60; Allen S Weller (auth), The joys and sorrows of recent American art, Univ Ill, 68.
Dealer: Fairweather Hardin Gallery, 101 E Ontario Ave, Chicago, IL 60611.
Mailing Address: Pizza del Biscione 95, Rome, Italy.

ZAKANYCH, ROBERT
Painter
b Elizabeth, N J, May 24, 35.
Work in Public Collections: Whitney Mus Am Art, New York, N Y; Blue Cross, Blue Shield, Chicago, Ill; Solomon, Cordwell, Buenz, Assoc, Chicago; Munich Mus Mod Art, W Ger; collection of Peggy Cass, New York; plus others.
Exhibitions: Int Drawing Show, Iarmstadt, Ger, 71; Structure of Color, 71 & Recent Acquisitions, 71, Whitney Mus Am Art; New York Painting, J L Hudson Gallery, Detroit, Mich, 71; Intimate Selection Of Am Spirit I, Miriam Willard Gallery, New York, 71; Group Show, 71 & one-man show, 71, Reese Palley, New York; plus others.
Mailing Address: c/o Reese Palley, 93 Prince St, New York, NY 10012.

ZALSTEM-ZALESSKY, MRS ALEXIS
Collector
Collection: Contemporary art.
Mailing Address: Cloud Wald Farm, New Milford, CT 06776.

ZAMMITT, NORMAN
Sculptor
b Toronto, Ont, Feb 3, 31; U S citizen.
Study & Training: Pasadena City Col, scholar, AA, 57; Otis Art Inst, scholar, MFA, 61.
Work in Public Collections: Mus Mod Art, New York, N Y; Hirschhorn Mus, New York; Libr of Cong, Washington, D C; Otis Art Gallery, Los Angeles, Calif; Larry Aldrich Mus, Conn.
Exhibitions: Young West Coast Artists, 65 & Show of New Acquisitions, 67, Mus Mod Art, New York; American Sculpture of the Sixties, Los Angeles Co Mus Art & Philadelphia Mus Art, Pa, 67; Felix Landau at Studio Marconi, Milan, Italy, 70; one-man shows, Beverly Hills & Los Angeles, Calif & New York, 62-72.
Teaching: Instr drawing & painting, Calif Inst Arts, 67; vis prof design, sch archit, Univ Southern Calif, 68-69; lectr design, Univ Calif, Los Angeles, 71-72.
Awards: Tamarind fel, 67; purchase prize, 50th Anniversary Sculpture Exhib, Otis Art Inst, 68; Guggenheim fel, 68.
Bibliography: Various articles in Art Int, Artforum, Art in Am & Los Angeles Times.
Art Interests: Three dimensional art.
Mailing Address: 3574 Tacoma Ave, Los Angeles, CA 90065.

ZAMPARELLI, MARIO ARMOND
Designer, Collector
b New York, N Y.
Study & Training: Pratt Inst; Univ Paris.
Commissions: Murals in Acrylics, Trans World Airlines; graphic works & environ designs for Kimberly-Clark, Union Bank, Hughes Airwest & Summa Corp.
Positions: Owner, Mario Armond Zamparelli & Co; pres, Art Index, Inc.
Awards: J W Alexander Medal, City of New York; Haskel traveling fel, Pratt Inst; Paul Hoffman Gold Medal.
Bibliography: Articles, In: Esquire Mag, Sundancer Mag & Los Angeles Times.
Specialty of Gallery: International art curatorial and exhibition service.
Collection: Renaissance art, contemporary and ethnic art.
Mailing Address: Art Index, Inc, 3111 Los Feliz Blvd, Los Angeles, CA 90039.

ZANTMAN, HANS
Art Dealer
b Sumbawa, Dutch East Indies, Dec 27, 19; U S citizen.
Study & Training: Private instr, Netherlands.
Positions: Dir, Zantman Art Galleries, Ltd, Carmel, Calif.

Specialty of Gallery: Living artists from U S A & Europe, especially France.
Mailing Address: P O Box 5818, Carmel, CA 93921.

ZAPKUS, KESTUTIS EDWARD
Painter
Preferred Media: Acrylics, Oils.
b Dabikine, Lithuania, Apr 22, 38; U S citizen.
Study & Training: Art Inst Chicago, BFA, 60; Syracuse Univ, Ryerson fel, 60, MFA, 62.
Work in Public Collections: Art Inst Chicago, Ill; plus pvt collections in U S A & Paris, France.
Exhibitions: Six Americans Signal, Paris, 64; Whitney Mus Am Art Ann, 69; one-man shows, Gres Gallery, Chicago, 62, Stable Gallery, 68 & Paula Cooper Gallery, New York, N Y, 71.
Awards: Invitational first prize, Chicago Arts Festival, 63.
Dealer: Paula Cooper Gallery, 100 Prince, New York, NY 10012.
Mailing Address: 35 Bond St, New York, NY 10012.

ZAVEL (ZAVEL SILBER)
Sculptor, Painter
b Latvia, Mar 29, 10; U S citizen.
Study & Training: Vicar Art Sch, Detroit, Mich; Art Inst Chicago, Ill; Univ Southern Calif; also with Charles Despiau, Paris, Vira Mockina & William Sherwood, France.
Commissions: Abstr sculpture, comn by Mr & Mrs Albert Miller, Detroit, 54; metal sculpture & fireplace, comn by Mr & Mrs George Hall, Pittsburgh, Pa, 65; metal centerpiece, comn by Mr & Mrs Leonard Epstein, Paramus, N J, 67; bronze centerpieces, comn by Mr & Mrs Phil Brant, Detroit, 69 & Dr & Mrs Leonard Brant, Port Richmond, Calif, 70.
Exhibitions: Salon Carnot, Paris, 36; Detroit Inst Fine Arts, 55; Am Ceramic Soc, Los Angeles, Calif, 58; Am Art, Orange, N J, 62; Old Print Ctr, New York, N Y, 70.
Mailing Address: 463 West St, Apt 648, New York, NY 10014.

ZECKENDORF, MRS GURI LIE
Collector
Memberships: Art Collectors Club.
Mailing Address: 1100 Park Ave, New York, NY 10028.

ZEISLER, RICHARD SPIRO
Collector, Patron
b Chicago, Ill, Nov 28, 16.
Study & Training: Amherst Col, BA; Harvard Univ.
Memberships: Mus Mod Art, New York (comt painting & sculpture); Brandeis Univ (fine arts awards adv comt); Mount Holyoke Col (art adv comt); Assocs Fine Arts, Amherst Col (exec comt); fel Pierpont Morgan Libr.
Collection: European painting of the twentieth century.
Mailing Address: 767 Fifth Ave, New York, NY 10022.

ZELANSKI, PAUL JOHN
Painter
Preferred Media: Acrylics, Plexiglass.
b Hartford, Conn, Apr 13, 31.
Study & Training: Cooper Union, cert, 55; Yale Univ, BFA, 57; Bowling Green State Univ, MA, 58.
Work in Public Collections: Univ Mass, Amherst; Slater Mus, Norwich, Conn; Manchester Community Col, Conn; Hampshire Col, Northampton, Mass.
Exhibitions: Turn Toward Peace, Boston, Mass; New England in Five Parts, De Cordova Mus, Lincoln, Mass; CREIA, Hartford Univ Carpenter Ctr, Boston; New Directions in Painting, Univ Mass, Amherst; Hard Eye, Amel Gallery, New York, N Y.
Teaching: Instr painting, drawing & design, N Tex State Univ, 58-61; instr painting, Fort Worth, Tex, 61-62; assoc prof art, Univ Conn, 62-
Awards: Award for painting, 69 & best in show, 71, Slater Mus; plaza seven, New Eng Framing Corp, 69.
Bibliography: Alan Graham Collier (auth), Form, space & vision, Prentice-Hall; Barnard Chaet (auth), Artists at work, Webb.
Memberships: Mystic Art Asn (bd dirs, 62-); Conn Acad Fine Arts; Springfield Art League; New England Art Today (bd dirs, 64, 66 & 68); Tex Men Art.
Mailing Address: Dept of Art, U-99, University of Connecticut, Storrs, CT 06268.

ZEMER, YIGAL
Sculptor, Printmaker
b Israel, Aug 26, 38.
Study & Training: Am Inst, Tel Aviv, Israel, 58; study in Bezalel, Jerusalem, 63-64; study in London, Eng, 69; Art Stud League New York, 70-71; Pratt Graphics Ctr, 72.
Work in Public Collections: Art Inst Chicago; Los Angeles Co Mus Art, Calif; Univ Minn, Minneapolis; San Francisco Mus Art, Calif; Libr of Cong, Washington, D C.

Commissions: Open Garden (sculpture monument), Messilot, Israel, 67; Mem area sculpture, Nir-oz, Israel, 67; print ed, Int Graphic Art Soc, New York, N Y, 72; ed, Pratt Inst, New York, 72; ed, Nabis Fin Art, New York, 72.
Exhibitions: Young Artists From Around the World, Union Carbide Bldg, New York, N Y, 71; one-man shows, Gallery Zzo, 66 & Old Gaffa Gallery, 69, Tel Aviv.
Mailing Address: 205 W 15th St, New York, NY 10011.

ZEVON, IRENE
Painter
Preferred Media: Oils.
b New York, N Y, Nov 24, 18.
Study & Training: With Nahum Tschacbasov.
Work in Public Collections: Butler Inst Am Art, Youngstown, Ohio; La Jolla Art Ctr, Calif; Kenosha Pub Mus, Wis; Mary Buie Mus, Oxford, Miss; Univ Ga Mus, Athens; plus many others including pvt collections.
Exhibitions: Kenosha Pub Mus, Wis; Saint Louis Pub Libr, Mo; Long Island Univ, N Y; Nat Acad Design, New York; Nat Asn Women Artists Ann, New York, 72; plus many other group & one-woman shows in univs, mus & galleries.
Awards: Marion K Haldenstein Mem Prize, Nat Asn Women Artists, 72.
Memberships: Nat Asn Women Artists.
Mailing Address: 222 W 23rd St, New York, NY 10011.

ZIB, TOM (THOMAS A ZIBELLI)
Cartoonist
b Mount Vernon, N Y.
Study & Training: Grand Cent Sch Art; Com Illus Studios.
Publications: Contribr, King Features Syndicate, 50-; contribr, Look, 50-60's; contribr, Parade, 70-; contribr, Med Econ, 70-; contribr, Wall St J, 70-
Mailing Address: 167 E Devonia Ave, Mount Vernon, NY 10552.

ZIEGFELD, EDWIN
Educator, Writer
b Columbus, Ohio, Aug 15, 05.
Study & Training: Ohio State Univ, BS & BS(educ); Harvard Univ, MLA; Univ Minn, PhD.
Teaching: Chmn & prof emer, Art Educ Dept, Teachers Col, Columbia Univ.
Positions: Pres, Nat Art Educ Asn, 47-51; coun mem, Nat Comt on Art Educ, Mus Mod Art, New York, 48-51 & 53-56; pres, Int Soc for Educ Through Art, 54-60.
Awards: Outstanding achievement award, Univ Minn, 56; award for distinguished serv to art & educ, Nat Gallery Art, Washington, D C, 66.
Publications: Co-auth, Art today, 41, rev ed, 49, 5th ed, 69; co-auth, Art for daily living, 44; ed, Art and education (a symposium), 53; auth, Art for the academically talented student, 62.
Mailing Address: 62 Morton St, New York, NY 10014.

ZIEMANN, RICHARD CLAUDE
Printmaker, Educator
b Buffalo, N Y, July 3, 32.
Study & Training: Albright Art Sch; Yale Univ, BFA & MFA; painting with Albers & Brooks; printmaking with Peterdi; drawings with Chaet.
Work in Public Collections: Brooklyn Mus, N Y; Silvermine Guild Art; Seattle Art Mus, Wash; De Cordova & Dana Mus; Libr Cong & Nat Gallery Art, Washington, D C; plus many others.
Commissions: Print Editions for Int Graphic Arts Soc, 58 & 60, Yale Univ Alumni Asn, 60 & Pan-Am Airlines, 62.
Exhibitions: American Prints Today, touring exhib to most maj print exhibs, 58-65, 24 mus, 62-63 & Paris Biennale, 63; one-man shows, Springfield Col, 66, Allen R Hite Art Inst, Univ Louisville, 67, Alpha Gallery, Boston, 67 & Univ Conn Art Gallery, 68; Oversize prints, Whitney Mus Am Art.
Teaching: Asst prof art, Hunter Col, 66; instr printmaking, Yale Univ Summer Sch, 66-67; assoc prof art, Lehman Col, at present.
Positions: Supvr, Graphic Workshop in Graphic Arts U S A, exhib touring the Soviet Union, 63-64; Artist-in-residence, Dartmouth Col, summer 71.
Awards: Fulbright grant to the Netherlands, 58-59; Nat Inst Arts & Lett grant, 66; Tiffany Found grant, 60-61; plus many other awards & prizes.
Memberships: Soc Am Graphic Artists.
Dealers: Jane Haslem Gallery, 1669 Wisconsin Ave N W, Washington, DC 20007; Alpha Galleries, 121 Newbury St, Boston, MA 02116.
Mailing Address: Maple St, Chester, CT 06412.

ZIERLER, WILLIAM
Art Dealer
b New York, N Y, Oct 5, 28.
Study & Training: Washington & Jefferson Col.

Positions: Pres & dir, William Zierler Gallery, 68-
Specialty of Gallery: Twentieth century paintings and sculpture,
representing Malcolm Bailey, Paul Camacho, Ken Danby,
Stephen Greene, Budd Hopkins, Alvin Loving and Matt Phillips.
Publications: Contribr, Arts Mag, 4/71.
Mailing Address: c/o 956 Madison Ave, New York, NY 10021.

ZIGROSSER, CARL
Writer
b Indianapolis, Ind, Sept 28, 91.
Study & Training: Columbia Univ, AB; Temple Univ, hon LittD, 61.
Exhibitions: Curatorial Retrospective, Philadelphia Mus Art, 64.
Collections Arranged: Between Two Wars, Prints by American Artists 1914-1941, Whitney Mus Am Art, New York, N Y, 42; Alfred Stieglitz: 291 & After, selections from the Stieglitz Collection, 44 & Masterpieces of Drawing in America, 50, Philadelphia Mus Art.
Positions: Dir, Weyhe Gallery, New York, 19-40; cur prints & drawings, Philadelphia Mus Art, 41-63, v dir, 55-63, hon trustee, 72-; trustee, Guggenheim Mus, New York, 51.
Awards: Guggenheim fel, 39-40; achievement medal, Philadelphia Art Alliance, 59.
Memberships: Print Coun Am (v pres, 56-70).
Publications: Auth, The expressionists, a survey of their graphic art, 57, The complete etchings of John Marin, a catalogue raisonne, 69, Prints & drawings of Kaethe Kollwitz, 69; The appeal of prints, 70 & My own shall come to me, 71.
Mailing Address: Villarasio, Montagnola, 6926, Switzerland.

ZILZER, GYULA
Printmaker, Painter
Preferred Media: Graphics.
b Budapest, Hungary, Feb 3, 98.
Study & Training: Royal Acad Art, Budapest; Hans Hofmann Sch Art, Munich; Royal Polytech Univ, Budapest; Acad Colorossi, Paris, France.
Work in Public Collections: Graphische Cabinet, Munich; Mus Mod Art, Budapest; Mus Mod Art, Metrop Mus Art & New York Pub Libr, New York, N Y; Los Angeles Mus Art, Calif; Luxembourg Mus, Paris; plus others.
Commissions: Portraits of U S Dist Court for Southern Dist New York.
Exhibitions: In Europe, 25-35; Art Inst Chicago, Ill; Bloomsbury Gallery, London, Eng; Mellon Gallery, Philadelphia, Pa; New Sch Social Res; M H de Young Mem Mus; plus others.
Positions: Prod designer & art dir, major films, Hollywood, Calif, 38-48, Cinerama, 58.
Awards: Purchase prize, Int Exhib, Moscow, 27; Int Exhib, Bordeaux, France, 27; Fr Govt Scholar, 28.
Publications: Illusr, The mechanical man, 61, Kaleidoscope (lithography album) & Edgar Allen Poe (Paris).
Mailing Address: 27 W 96th St, New York, NY 10025.

ZIMILES, MURRAY
Painter, Educator
b New York, N Y, Nov 30, 41.
Study & Training: Univ Ill, BFA; Cornell Univ, MFA; Ecole Nat Superieure Beaux-Arts, Paris, France.
Work in Public Collections: Brooklyn Mus, N Y; New York Pub Libr; Rosenwald Collection; Nat Collection Fine Arts; U S Embassy, Bogata, Colombia.
Exhibitions: Prints from Portfolios & Invitational, Brooklyn Mus, 70; Fourth Bienal Am Grabado, Santiago, Chile, 70; one-man shows, Zingale Gallery, New York, 71 & Kunstnerforbundet Gallery, Oslo, Norway, 72.
Teaching: Instr printmaking, Pratt Graphics Ctr, New York, 68-71; asst prof drawing & printmaking, Silvermine Col Art, New Canaan, Conn, 68-71; asst prof drawing & printmaking, State Univ N Y, New Paltz, 72-
Awards: Found Etats-Unis fel, Paris, France, 65-66; Royal Norweg Govt fel, 71.
Bibliography: New talent, Artist Proof Ann, 71.
Publications: Co-auth, The technique of fine art lithography, 70, Early American mills & The lithographic workshop, 73.
Dealer: Associated American Artists Gallery, 663 Fifth Ave, New York, NY 10022.
Mailing Address: 1 W 67th St, New York, NY 10023.

ZIMMERMAN, PAUL WARREN
Painter, Educator
Preferred Media: Oils.
b Toledo, Ohio, Apr 29, 21.
Study & Training: John Herron Art Sch, BFA.
Work in Public Collections: Pa Acad Fine Arts, Philadelphia; Houston Mus Fine Art, Tex; Butler Inst Am Art, Youngstown, Ohio; Springfield Mus Fine Art, Mass; Wadsworth Atheneum, Hartford, Conn.

Commissions: Mural, First New Haven Nat Bank, Conn, 65.
Exhibitions: Indiana Artists Exhibition, John Herron Art Mus, Indianapolis, 57; American Painting & Sculpture, Univ Ill, 61; Pa Acad Fine Arts, Philadelphia, 62; 144th Ann Exhib, Nat Acad Design, New York, N Y, 69; Midyear Show, Butler Inst Am Art, Youngstown, 70.
Teaching: Prof painting & design, Univ Hartford Art Sch, 47-
Awards: First prize, Conn Watercolor Soc, 64; Altman Landscape Prize for second place, 67 & first place, 69, Nat Acad Design.
Bibliography: Henry Pitz (auth), Paintings of Paul Zimmerman, Am Artist Mag, 1/60.
Memberships: Nat Acad Design; Conn Acad Fine Arts; Conn Watercolor Soc (pres, 52-53).
Dealer: J Seligmann & Co, 5 E 57th St, New York, NY 10022.
Mailing Address: 257 Victoria Rd, Hartford, CT 06114.

ZIMMERMAN, WILLIAM HAROLD
Painter, Illustrator
b Dillsboro, Ind, Oct 1, 37.
Study & Training: Cincinnati Art Acad.
Work in Public Collections: Cincinnati Mus Natural Hist, Ohio; Pomona Col, Calif.
Commissions: Private comns.
Exhibitions: Cincinnati Animal Art Show, 66; Soc Animal Artists Ann, New York, N Y, 67; one-man shows in New York, San Francisco, Chicago & Cincinnati.
Awards: Award for Magpie, Cincinnati Animal Art Show, 66.
Bibliography: Oscar Godbout (auth), Wood, field and stream, New York Times, 10/18/64; Bill Thomas (auth), Dillsboro's Audubon, Nat Observer, 11/12/65; Jay Shuler (auth), A real artist has to work for himself, Carolina Outdoors, 9/71.
Memberships: Soc Animal Artists.
Publications: Co-auth & illusr, Topflight, speed index to waterfowl, 66; auth, North American waterfowl, (in press).
Dealer: Frame House Gallery, 110 E Market St, Louisville, KY 40202.
Mailing Address: P.O Box 272, Dillsboro, IN 47018.

ZIOLKOWSKI, KORCZAK
Sculptor
b Boston, Mass, Sept 6, 08.
Work in Public Collections: San Francisco Art Mus; Judge Baker Guidance Ctr, Boston; Symphony Hall, Boston; Vassar Col; marble portraits of Paderewski, Georges Enesco, Artur Schnable, Wilbur L Cross, John F Kennedy & Crazy Horse at Crazy Horse Mem.
Commissions: Noah Webster Statue (marble), Town Hall Lawn, W Hartford, Conn; granite portrait of Wild Bill Hickok, Deadwood, S Dak; Chief Sitting Bull (granite portrait), Mobridge, S Dak; Robert Driscoll, Sr (marble), First Nat Bank Black Hills, Rapid City, S Dak; carving mountain into equestrian figure of Sioux Chief Crazy Horse at request of Indians as mem to Indians of N Am, Custer, S Dak, 48-
Positions: Chmn bd, Crazy Horse Found; asst to Cutzon Borglum, Mount Rushmore Nat Mem, S Dak.
Awards: First sculptural prize for marble portrait of Paderewski, New York World's Fair, 39.
Memberships: Nat Sculpture Soc.
Mailing Address: Crazy Horse, Custer, SD 57730.

ZIPKIN, JEROME R
Collector
b New York, N Y.
Study & Training: Princeton Univ.
Memberships: Art Collectors Club.
Collection: Contemporary paintings and sculpture.
Mailing Address: 1175 Park Ave, New York, NY 10028.

ZIRKER, JOSEPH
Graphic Artist, Lecturer
b Los Angeles, Calif, Aug 13, 24.
Study & Training: Univ Calif, Los Angeles, 43-44, 46-47; Univ Denver, BFA, 49; with Jules Heller & Francis de Erdely, Univ South Calif, MFA, 51.
Work in Public Collections: Brooklyn Art Mus, N Y; Tamarind Archives, Tamarind Lithography Workshop (printer fel, 62-63, res fel, 64); Stanley Freenean Collection, Los Angeles Co Mus; Martin Gluck Collection, San Diego Mus, La Jolla Art Ctr; Achenbach Found, Palace of Legion of Hon, San Francisco, Calif.
Exhibitions: Artists of Los Angeles & Vicinity, Los Angeles Co Mus, 52; 7th Nat Print Ann, Brooklyn Mus, 53; Young Am Printmakers, Mus Mod Art, New York, N Y, 53-54; New Dimensions of Lithography, Tamarind Lithographs, Univ South Calif, 64; Calif Printmakers, Achenbach Found, Palace of Legion of Hon, 71.
Teaching: Lect graphic arts, Univ South Calif, 63; instr, Chouinard Art Inst, Los Angeles, Calif, 63; instr drawing, San Jose City Col, 66-

Positions: Dir, Joseph Press, Venice, Calif, 63-64.
Awards: 3rd Nat Print Exhib, Bradley Univ, Ill, 52; 2nd Nat Exhib of Prints, Univ South Calif, 52; 7th Ann Print Exhib, Brooklyn Mus, 53.
Memberships: Col Art Asn Am.
Publications: Cover designs for Baja California 1533-1950, 51; Embryo, a literary quarterly, 54-55; Art Is One exhibition, catalogue, 61.
Dealer: Gallerie Smith-Andersen, Homer Ave & Emerson St, Palo Alto, CA 94301.
Mailing Address: 330 Palo Alto Ave, Palo Alto, CA 94301.

ZIROLI, NICOLA
Painter, Educator
b Montenero, Italy, May 8, 08; U S citizen.
Study & Training: Art Inst Chicago, grad, 30.
Work in Public Collections: Metrop Mus Art & Whitney Mus Am Art, New York, N Y; Chicago Pub Libr; Butler Inst Am Art, Youngstown, Ohio; New Orleans Mus Art, La; plus many others.
Exhibitions: Albright-Knox Art Gallery, Buffalo, N Y; Va Mus Fine Arts, Richmond; Corcoran Gallery Art, Washington, D C; Los Angeles Mus Art; Pa Acad Fine Arts, Philadelphia; plus many others.
Teaching: Prof art, Univ Ill, at present.
Awards: El Paso Mus Art; First prize for oil painting, 7th Ann Nat Exhib, Mead Competition Watercolor Prize; first prize oils for still life, Evansville Mus Fine Arts; plus many others.
Memberships: Audubon Artists; Am Watercolor Soc; Int Platform Asn; Nat Soc Painters in Casein; Philadelphia Watercolor Club; plus others.
Mailing Address: 1111 McHenry St, Urbana, IL 61801.

ZISLA, HAROLD
Painter, Educator
b Cleveland, Ohio, June 28, 25.
Study & Training: Cleveland Inst Art; Western Reserve Univ, BS Educ & AM.
Exhibitions: Cleveland Mus Art; South Bend Michiana; John Herron Art Mus; Fort Wayne Art Mus; Kalamazoo Art Inst; plus others.
Teaching: Instr, South Bend Art Ctr, 53-; instr, Indiana Univ Exten, South Bend, 55; assoc prof & asst chmn dept art, Ind Univ, South Bend, 66-
Positions: Dir & bd mem, South Bend Art Ctr, 57-; bd mem, Asn Prof Artists of Ind.
Mailing Address: Indiana University at South Bend, Northside at Greenlawn, South Bend, IN 46615.

ZOELLNER, RICHARD C
Printmaker, Painter
Preferred Media: Intaglio.
b Portsmouth, Ohio, June 30, 08.
Study & Training: Cincinnati Art Acad.
Work in Public Collections: Mus Mod Art, New York, N Y; Philadelphia Mus Art, Pa; Brooklyn Mus Art, N Y; Pa Acad Fine Art, Philadelphia; Andover Mus Am Art, Mass.
Exhibitions: First & Fifth Nat Print Ann, Brooklyn Mus, 48 & 53; Ann Painting Exhib, Pa Acad Fine Arts, 55; Birmingham Festival Arts, Birmingham Mus Art, Ala, 63; Am Color Print Soc, Philadelphia, 63; 18th Ann Piedmont Graphic Exhib, Mint Mus, Charlotte, N C, 71.
Teaching: Instr art, Cincinnati Art Mus, 45-48; prof art, Univ Ala, 48-
Positions: Vis artist, May Washington Col, 51, Univ Miss, 52-53 & Univ Fla, 53-54.
Awards: Award, Ann Ala Arts Club Print Exhib, Auburn Univ, 66; award for Images on Paper, Miss Art Asn, 71; award, 13th Dixie Ann, Montgomery Mus Fine Art, 72.
Memberships: Soc Am Graphic Artists; Am Color Print Soc.
Dealer: Franz Bader Inc, 2124 Pennsylvania Ave N W, Washington, DC 20037.
Mailing Address: 14 Guilds Wood, Tuscaloosa, AL 35401.

ZONA, RINALDO A
Painter, Sculptor
Preferred Media: Oils, Acrylics.
b New York, N Y, Feb 24, 19.
Work in Public Collections: Rose Art Mus & Riverside Mus Collection, Brandeis Univ, Waltham, Mass; Finch Col Mus, New York.
Exhibitions: Childe Hassam Fund Exhib, Am Acad Arts & Lett, New York, 67; one-man show, East Hampton Gallery, New York, 66-68 & 70.
Mailing Address: 40 Turtle Cove Lane, Huntington, NY 11743.

ZORNES, JAMES MILFORD
Painter, Designer
Preferred Media: Watercolors.
b Camargo, Okla, Jan 25, 08.
Study & Training: With F Toles Chamberlin & Millard Sheets, 35-

38; Otis Art Inst, 38; Pomona Col, 46-50.
Work in Public Collections: Metrop Mus Art, New York, N Y; Los Angeles Co Mus Art, Calif; Butler Inst Am Art, Youngstown, Ohio; Nat Acad Design, New York; White House Collection, Washington, D C; plus many others including pvt collections.
Commissions: Murals for post off at Campo, Tex, 37 & Claremont, Calif, 38, U S Govt.
Exhibitions: Chicago Int Watercolor Exhib, Art Inst Chicago, 38; San Francisco World's Fair, Calif, 38-40; Metrop Mus Art, New York, 41; 96th Ann Am Watercolor Soc, 63; Watercolor U S A, 72; plus many others.
Teaching: Instr painting, Otis Art Inst, 38-46; instr painting, Pomona Col, 46-50; instr painting, Univ Calif, Santa Barbara, 48-49.
Positions: Off Army artist, U S Govt, 43-45.
Awards: Award for In the Cove, Nat Acad Design; William Tuthill Prize for Well at Guadalupe, 38; Am Artist Medal for Beach Party, 63; plus many others.
Bibliography: Article, In: Am Artist Mag, 11/63; Edgar A Whitney (auth), Complete guide to watercolor painting, 65; One hundred watercolor techniques, Watson-Guptill, 68; plus others.
Memberships: Assoc Nat Acad Design; Am Watercolor Soc; Calif Watercolor Soc (past pres); West Coast Watercolor Soc (former v pres); Riverside Art Asn (bd dirs, 66-67).
Mailing Address: P O Box 24, Mt Carmel, UT 84755.

ZOX, LARRY
Painter
b Des Moines, Iowa, May 31, 36.
Study & Training: Univ Okla; Drake Univ; Des Moines Art Ctr, with George Grosz.
Work in Public Collections: Whitney Mus Am Art, New York, N Y; Oberlin Col, Ohio; Joseph H Hirshhorn Collection; Des Moines Art Ctr; Mus Mod Art, New York; plus many others.
Exhibitions: Riverside Mus, Calif, 68; First Indian Triennale, 68; The Direct Image, Worcester Art Mus, Mass, 69; Whitney Mus Am Art Ann, New York, 69-70 & 72; Indianapolis Mus Art, Ind, 72; plus many other group & one-man shows.
Teaching: Artist-in-residence, Juniata Col, 64; guest critic, Cornell Univ, 67; artist-in-residence, Univ N C, Greensboro, 67; instr art, Sch Visual Arts, 67-; instr art, Dartmouth Col, winter 69.
Awards: Guggenheim fel, 67; Nat Coun Arts Award, 69.
Dealer: Kornblee Gallery, 58 E 79th St, New York, NY 10021.
Mailing Address: 238 Park Ave S, New York, NY 10003.

ZUCCARELLI, FRANK EDWARD
Painter, Illustrator
Preferred Media: Oils.
b Pa, Oct 23, 21.
Study & Training: Newark Sch Fine & Indust Art, with William J Aylward & John Grabach; Art Stud League New York, with Robert Philip; Newark State Teachers Col, BA.
Work in Public Collections: U S Navy & Marine Mus, Washington, D C; Marine Corps Base, Barstow, Calif; Abraham Sharpe Found, New York; Malcolm Forbes Collection, New York.
Commissions: Paintings for U S Navy, Newport R I, 71; Dahlgren Weapons Lab, Va, 71 & Mediterranean Sixth Fleet, 72.
Exhibitions: Newark Sch Indust & Fine Arts Alumni Show, Newark Mus, N J; Westfield Art Asn State Show, 68; Am Vet Soc Artists, Salmagundi Club, New York, 70; Am Artists Prof League Grand Nat, 70; USN Combat Art Collection, Salmagundi Club, New York, 72.
Teaching: Private instr oils, 58-; instr oils & pictorial illus, Spectrum Inst, Somerville, N J, 72-
Positions: Illusr, Ruffa Advert Agency & Street & Smith Publ.
Awards: Purchase award, Westfield Art Asn, 69; Salmagundi Prize, 69 & hon mention, 71, Salmagundi Club.
Bibliography: Doris Brown (auth), New England—artist's forte, New Brunswick Home News, 68 & Artist's assignment pays off, Sun Home News, New Brunswick, 71; Colleen Zirnite (auth), Artist speaks of many things, Spectator, 72.
Memberships: Naval Art Coop & Liaison Comt (combat artist); Salmagundi Club (resident artist, juror); fel Am Artists Prof League; Am Vet Soc Artists; Burr Artists.
Publications: Illusr, Cath Home Messenger.
Mailing Address: 61 Appleman Rd, Somerset, NJ 08873.

ZUCKER, JACQUES
Painter
Preferred Media: Oils, Pastels, Gouache, Sanguine.
b Radom, Poland, June 15, 00; U S citizen.
Study & Training: Bezalel Art Sch, Jerusalem; Acad Grande Chaumière; Colarossi Acad, Paris.
Work in Public Collections: Bezalel Art Mus, Jerusalem; Mus Mod Art, Tel-Aviv, Israel; Helena Rubenstein Mus, Tel-Aviv; Mus Mod Art, Paris, France; plus many others including pvt collections in France, Israel, Eng, Sweden, Japan, U S A & world over.

Exhibitions: Mus Mod Art, New York, N Y; Carnegie Inst, Pittsburgh, Pa; Pa Acad Fine Arts, Philadelphia; Art Inst Chicago, Ill; Whitney Mus Am Art, New York; plus many other group shows including twenty-eight one-man shows.
Bibliography: Harry Salpeter (auth), article, In: Esquire Mag, 38; articles, In: Menorah Mag; Claude Roger (auth), Marx: Jacques Zucker, Paul Petrides Ed, 12/69.
Memberships: Artists Equity Asn; Fedn Artists & Sculptors.
Art Interests: Art qualities & expression.
Collection: Paintings in oils, watercolors, gouache & pastels; drawings in charcoal, sepia & sanguine.
Publications: Illusr many stories.
Dealer: Schoeneman Galleries, 823 Madison Ave, New York, NY 10021.
Mailing Address: 44 W 77th St, New York, NY 10024.

ZUCKER, MURRAY HARVEY
Painter, Sculptor
Preferred Media: Acrylics, Collage.
b New York, N Y, Dec 14, 20.
Work in Public Collections: AFL-CIO Hq, Washington, D C; Community Blood Coun, New York; Omaha Nat Bank, Nebr.
Commissions: Painting, Atlantic Richfield Co, New York, 68; painting, Technicon Corp, Ardsley, N Y, 69; painting, Police Benevolent Asn, New York, 70.
Exhibitions: 10th Ann, Ball State Teachers Col, Muncie, Ind, 64; 16th Ann, Silvermine Guild Artists, Conn, 65; 161st Ann, Pa Acad Fine Arts, Philadelphia, 66; 25th Ann, Audubon Artists, New York, 67; Artists New York '72, New York, 72.
Awards: Hon mention, Pa Acad Fine Arts, 66; hon mention, Am Soc Contemp Artists, 71.
Bibliography: C Crane (auth), Contemporary collages, Interiors, 5/70.
Memberships: Artists Equity Asn New York; Am Soc Contemp Artists; Am Vet Soc Artists.
Mailing Address: 253 E 62nd St, New York, NY 10021.

ZUGOR, SANDOR
Painter
Preferred Media: Graphics, Polymers, Acrylics, Oils.
b Brod, Yugoslavia, Feb 7, 23; U S citizen.
Study & Training: Acad Fine Art, Budapest, 41-45, with Istvan Szonyi; Hungarian Acad Rome, fel, 46-48, graphics with Varga Nandor Lajos.
Work in Public Collections: Mus Fine Art Budapest; Munic Mus Budapest; Ministry Cult Affairs, Vienna.
Exhibitions: Exhib Hist Siena, Munic Mus, Italy, 48; Budapest Nat Exhibs, Nat Gallery Art, 54 & 55; Young Americans, Mus Contemp Crafts, New York, 62; Brooklyn Heights Artists, Brooklyn Mus, 69; Palacio Bellas Artes, Mexico City, 72.
Teaching: Lectr drawing, Brooklyn Col Adult Educ, 66-71.
Positions: Dir, Westbeth Graphics Workshop, 71-
Awards: First prize for Peace & War, Fedn Hungarian Artists, 54.
Mailing Address: 463 West St, New York, NY 10014.

ZUNIGA, FRANCISCO
Sculptor
Preferred Media: Bronze, Marble.
b San Jose, Costa Rica, Dec 31, 11.
Work in Public Collections: Middelhiem Mus, Antwerpen, Belg; Fogg Art Mus, Cambridge, Mass; Fine Arts Galleries San Diego, Calif; Mus Arte Mod, Mexico City, Mex; Phoenix Art Mus, Ariz.
Commissions: Monument, Nuevo Laredo, Mex, 58; Monumento a Cuauhtemoc, Quito, Ecuador, 61; Fuentes Monumentales, Chapultepec, Mexico City, 62; reliefs, Edigicio Secretaria de Communicaciones; Estatua a Benito Juarez, Gobierno de Michoacan, Morelia, Mich.
Exhibitions: Third Sculpture Int, Philadelphia Mus Art, Pa, 49; Expos F Zuniga, Mus Nac, San Jose, Costa Rica, 54; Kunst Mexikaner, Köln, Ger, 59; Expos Zuniga, Fine Arts Gallery San Diego & Phoenix Art Mus, 71.

Awards: Primer Piemio Escultura, Costa Rica, Expos Art Centro Americano, 35; premio for Diego Rivera, Second Biennial Inter-Am Art, 60; premio adquisicion Inst Nac Bellas Artes.
Bibliography: Rosa Gonzalez (auth), Dictionnaire de la sculpture moderne, Paris, 60; Ali Chumxcero (auth), Zuniga, Misrachi, Mexico, 69; Toby Joysmith (auth), Zuniga, Fine Arts Gallery San Diego, 71.
Dealer: Galeria Tasende, Ave M Aleman, Acapulco, Guerrero, Mex.
Mailing Address: Privada de Xontepec 9, Tlalpan, Mexico City, Mex.

ZWEERTS, ARNOLD
Painter, Educator
Preferred Media: Oils, Woodcuts, Mosaic.
b Bussum, Neth, 18; U S citizen.
Study & Training: Sch for Arts & Crafts, Amsterdam; Sch for Art Teacher Training, Royal Acad Art, Amsterdam; Royal Acad Art, Copenhagen, Denmark; Acad Belli Arti, Ravenna, Italy; Inst Allende, Univ Guanajuato, Mex, MFA; also study with Jos Rovers, Riseby, Orselli, Signoriny & Kortlang.
Work in Public Collections: Stedelijk Mus, Amsterdam; Collection of the State, The Hague, Neth; also pvt collections in Denmark, Eng, Norway, Holland, U S & Mex.
Commissions: Mosaics, Hengelo, Neth, 54, Lockhorst, Koldewyn, Van Eyck, Rotterdam Architects, 55-56, Chicago Process Gear Co, 61, Boulder Med Arts Bldg, Colo, 63-64 & Dr Snider, Chicago, 69-70; plus many others.
Exhibitions: First one-man show, Amsterdam, Neth, 48; group show in London, Eng, 53; first one-man show in U S, Chicago Merchandise Mart, 60; group show, Saint Paul Gallery Art, Minn, 62; three-man show, Art Inst Chicago, Ill, 66; plus many others.
Teaching: Instr mosaic & color, Kingston Upon Thames, Surrey, Eng, 51-53; instr appreciation of art, Stedelijk Mus, Rijkmus, Amsterdam, 54-57; asst prof drawing & painting, Art Inst Chicago, 57-; lectr, dept fine arts, Loyola Univ Chicago, 68-
Bibliography: Pieter Scheen (auth), Lexicon Nederlandse Beeldende Kunstenaars 1750-1950, Part II, Kunsthandel P Scheen N V, The Hague, 70.
Memberships: Midwest Designer Craftsmen.
Publications: Auth, articles about art, In: Bussumsche Courant, 50; auth, A renaissance in architectural art?, Delphian Quart, Vol 43, No 4.
Mailing Address: 4805 Forest Ave, Downers Grove, IL 60515.

ZWICK, ROSEMARY G
Sculptor, Printmaker
Preferred Media: Ceramics.
b Chicago, Ill, July 13, 25.
Study & Training: Univ Iowa, with Phillip Guston & Abrizio, BFA, 45; Art Inst Chicago, with Max Kahn, 45-47; De Paul Univ, 46.
Work in Public Collections: Oak Park Libr Collection, Ill; Albion Col Print Collection, Mich; Rearis Sch Collection, Chicago; Phoenix Pub Schs Collection, Ariz; Crow Island Sch, Winnetka, Ill; plus others.
Commissions: Two sculpture animal forms, Wonderland Shopping Ctr, Livonia, Mich, 60; wall relief, Motorola Co, Chicago, 62; sculpture, Temple B'Nai Jenoshua, Morton Grove, Ill, 68; large seated figure, Blue Island Libr, Ill, 71.
Exhibitions: Ceramic Nat, Everson Mus Art, Syracuse, N Y, 60, 62 & 64; Soc Washington Printmakers, Nat Mus, Washington, D C, 64; Mundelein Col, Chicago, 64-71; Art Inst Chicago, 64-72; Twentieth Wichita, Wichita Art Asn, Kans, 68.
Positions: Staff artist, Jr Arts & Activities Mag, 45-47; assoc, 4 Arts Gallery, Evanston, Ill, 62-
Bibliography: John B Kenny (auth), Ceramic design, Chilton, 63; Wesley Buchwald (auth), Craftsmen in Illinois, Ill Art Educ Asn, 65.
Memberships: Renaissance Soc, Univ Chicago; Am Craftsmen Soc.
Specialty of Gallery: Japanese prints midwestern artists & craftsmen.
Dealers: Truro Art Gallery, Truro, MA 02666; Naples Art Gallery, 1305 Third St S, Naples on Gulf, FL 33940.
Mailing Address: 1720 Washington St, Evanston, IL 60202.

NECROLOGY

ABBELL, SAMUEL. Art Patron (1925-1969).

ADAMS, (MOULTON) LEE. Painter, Illustrator (1922-1971).

ALFSEN, JOHN MARTIN. Painter (-1972).

BARBER, MURIEL V. Painter (-1971).

BARNETT, HERBERT P. Educator, Painter (1910-1972).

BARRETT, H STANFORD. Painter, Educator (1909-1970).

BASS, JOHANNA (MRS JOHN). Collector, Patron (-1970).

BENSON, EMANUEL M. Art Administrator, Art Dealer (1904-1971).

BERMAN, EUGENE. Painter, Designer (1899-1972).

BLACK, WENDELL H. Educator (1919-1972).

BORGHI, GUIDO RINALDO. Painter (1903-1971).

BREGER, DAVE (DAVID). Cartoonist (1908-1970).

BROUILLETTE, GILBERT T. Art Dealer, Consultant-Research.

CAMPBELL, ORLAND. Portrait Painter (1890-1972).

CASTLE, MRS ALFRED L. Art Patron (1886-1970).

CAVALLITO, ALBINO. Sculptor (1905-1966).

CONNAWAY, JAY HALL. Painter (1893-1970).

CORBETT, EDWARD M. Educator, Painter (1919-1971).

CORNELL, JOSEPH. Sculptor (1903-1972).

COSTIGAN, JOHN EDWARD. Painter (1888-1972).

CRAMPTON, ROLLIN. Painter (-1970).

CRESPI, PACHITA. Painter (1900-1971).

DENSLOW, DOROTHEA HENRIETTA. Sculptor (1900-1971).

DUBLE, LU. Sculptor (1896-1970).

ECKE, GUSTAV. Museum Curator (-1971).

ENGEL, HARRY. Painter (1901-1970).

ESHERICK, WHARTON. Sculptor, Designer (1887-1970).

FERREN, JOHN. Painter (1905-1970).

FILTZER, HYMAN. Sculptor, Restorer (1901-1967).

FLORY, ARTHUR L. Graphic Artist, Painter (1914-1972).

FOX, MILTON S. Painter (1904-1971).

GARTH, JOHN. Painter (1894-1971).

GAYNE, CLIFTON ALEXANDER, JR. Educator (1912-1971).

GEESEY, TITUS CORNELIUS. Collector, Patron (1893-1969).

GIBBERD, ERIC WATERS. Painter (1897-1972).

GLARNER, FRITZ. Painter (1899-1972).

GREENWOOD, MARION. Painter, Lithographer (1909-1970).

GREGORY, WAYLANDE. Sculptor, Designer (1905-1971).

GRIER, HARRY DODSON MILLER. Museum Director (1914-1972).

GUGGENHEIM, HARRY FRANK. Collector, Publisher, Writer (1890-1971).

HASWELL, ERNEST BRUCE. Sculptor (1889-1965).

HEERAMANECK, NASILI M. Collector, Patron, Art Dealer (1902-1971).

HELM, JOHN F, JR. Educator, Painter (1900-1972).

HERRINGTON, ARTHUR W. Collector, Patron.

HERRINGTON, NELL RAY. Collector, Patron.

HIBBARD, ALDRO THOMPSON. Painter (1886-1972).

HORNYANSKY, NICHOLAS. Etcher (1896-1965).

HUNTLEY, VICTORIA HUTSON. Lithographer (1900-1971).

HUTCHINSON, MARY ELIZABETH. Painter (1906-1970).

ISAACS, BETTY LEWIS. Sculptor (1894-1971).

JAFFE, WILLIAM B. Collector (-1972).

JANSSEN, HANS. Educator, Museum Curator.

JOHN, GRACE SPAULDING. Painter, Writer (1890-1972).

KENT, NORMAN. Engraver, Book Designer (1903-1972).

KENT, ROCKWELL. Painter (1882-1971).

KILGORE, RUPERT. Educator (1910-1971).

KIMAK, GEORGE. Painter (1921-1972).

KNATHS, (OTTO) KARL. Painter (1891-1971).

KOHLHEPP, DOROTHY IRENE. Painter (-1964).

LARKIN, OLIVER. Educator (1896-1970).

LAURENT, ROBERT. Sculptor, Collector (1890-1970).

LAYTON, GLORIA (MRS HARRY GEWISS). Painter.

LENSON, MICHAEL. Painter (1903-1971).

LIEBES, DOROTHY (MRS RELMAN MORIN). Textile Designer (1899-1972).

LONG, STANLEY M. Painter (1892-1972).

LUKE, ALEXANDRA. Painter.

MACDONALD, HERBERT. Painter (1898-1972).

MARANTZ, IRVING. Painter (1912-1972).

MARKUS, HENRY A. Collector.

MASON, ALICE TRUMBULL. Painter (1904-1971).

MASON, ROY MARTELL. Painter (1886-1972).

MAST, GERALD. Painter (1908-1971).

MATTSON, HENRY (ELIS). Painter (1887-1971).

MENCONI, RALPH JOSEPH. Sculptor (1915-1972).

MILLER, BARSE. Painter, Educator (1924-1973).

MITCHELL, GLEN. Painter (1894-1972).

MOFFETT, ROSS E. Painter.

MORISSET, GERARD. Educator (1898-1970).

NASON, THOMAS W. Engraver (1889-1971).

NATZLER, GERTRUD. Ceramic Craftsman.

NEUMEYER, ALFRED. Art Historian (1901-1973).

NEWBERRY, CLARE TURLAY. Illustrator (1903-1970).

NEWMAN, BARNETT. Painter (1905-1970).

OCHTMAN, DOROTHY (MRS W A DEL MAR). Painter (1892-1971).

OGG, OSCAR. Designer, Writer (1908-1971).

O'HARA, ELIOT. Painter (1890-1969).

PATRICK, RANSOM R. Educator (1906-1971).

PAUL, BORIS DuPONT. Painter.

PECK, EDWARD. Director University Galleries (-1970).

PEIRCE, WALDO. Painter.

PEREIRA, I RICE. Painter (1901-1971).

PITTMAN, HOBSON. Painter (1900-1972).

POLKES, ALAN H. Collector, Patron.

POLLACK, LOUIS. Art Dealer (1921-1970).

POOLE, EARL LINCOLN. Illustrator, Art Administrator (1891-1972).

POOR, HENRY VARNUM. Painter (1888-1970).

QUANDT, RUSSELL JEROME. Museum Art Restorer (1919-1970).

RICHTER, GISELA MARIE AUGUSTA. Museum Curator, Writer (1882-1972).

RIGGS, ROBERT. Lithographer (1896-1970).

ROGERS, MEYRIC REYNOLD. Museum Curator (1893-1972).

ROJANKOVSKY, FEODOR STEPANOVICH. Illustrator (1891-1970).

ROSE, IVER. Painter (1899-1972).

ROSENBERG, SAEMY. Art Dealer.

ROSENBERG, SAMUEL. Painter (1896-1972).

ROSENTHAL, DORIS. Painter, Lithographer.

ROTHKO, MARK. Painter (-1970).

ROWLAND, BENJAMIN, JR. Educator (1904-1972).

SACHS, JAMES H. Collector, Patron (1907-1971).

SCHNAKENBERG, HENRY. Painter (1892-1970).

SCHUSTER, CARL. Art Historian, Writer.

SCHWARTZ, MANFRED. Painter (1909-1970).

SHERMAN, JOHN K(URTZ). Critic.

SHRYOCK, BURNETT HENRY, SR. Painter (1904-1971).

SMITH, WALT ALLEN. Sculptor, Designer (1910-1971).

SOPHER, AARON. Painter, Illustrator (1905-1972).

SPRINGWEILER, ERWIN FREDERICK. Sculptor (1896-1968).

STEINBERG, MRS MILTON (EDITH). Art Director (1910-1970).

SUSSMAN, RICHARD N. Painter, Graphic Artist (1908-1971).

TENGGREN, GUSTAV ADOLF. Painter (1896-1970).

TOBIAS, THOMAS J. Collector, Museum Trustee (1906-1970).

TRAVIS, KATHRYNE HAIL. Painter (1894-1972).

TROCHE, E GUNTER. Museum Director (1909-1971).

VON WICHT, JOHN. Painter, Graphic Designer (1888-1970).

WEBER, HUGO. Painter (1918-1971).

WEINGAERTNER, HANS. Painter (1896-1970).

WESCOTT, PAUL. Painter (1904-1970).

WESTON, HAROLD. Painter (1894-1972).

WILFORD, LORAN. Painter, Educator (1892-1972).

WILLIAMS, WHEELER. Sculptor (1897-1972).

WOODWARD, STANLEY. Painter (1890-1970).

WORCESTER, EVA. Painter (1892-1970).

ZACKS, SAMUEL JACOB. Collector, Patron (1904-1970).

ZERBE, KARL. Painter, Educator (1903-1972).

GEOGRAPHICAL INDEX

ALABAMA

Auburn

Hatfield, Donald Gene. Painter, Educator
Ross, Conrad Harold. Printmaker, Educator
Sykes, (William) Maltby. Painter, Print-
maker

Birmingham

Howard, Richard Foster. Art Administrator
Hulsey, William Hansell. Collector
Kennedy, Doris Wainwright. Painter
Price, Rosalie Pettus. Painter
Stewart, Arthur. Painter

Brundidge

Godwin, Robert Lawrence. Painter, Sculptor

Dothan

Watford, Frances Mizelle. Painter, Instructor

Fairhope

Woodward, Cleveland Landon. Painter, Illustrator

Hartselle

Howell, Elizabeth Ann. Painter, Illustrator

Homewood

Rankin, Don. Painter

Huntsville

Hudson, Ralph Magee. Art Historian, Edu-
cator
Parrish, David Buchanan. Painter
Pope, Mary Ann Irwin. Painter
Pope, Richard Coraine. Painter, Designer
Savas, Jo-Ann. Painter, Illustrator

Mentone

Graham, John Meredith, II. Museum Director

Mobile

Altmayer, Jay P. Collector
Blackburn, Lenora Whitmire. Collector
Lassiter, Vernice (Vernice Lassiter Brown).
Painter

Montgomery

Brooks, Louise Cherry. Collector, Ceramist

Ozark

Deloney, Jack Clouse. Painter, Illustrator

Tuscaloosa

Zoellner, Richard C. Printmaker, Painter

Tuskegee Institute

Jarkowski, Stefania Agnes. Painter, Edu-
cator
Thomas, Elaine Freeman. Educator, Art
Administrator

University

Brough, Richard Burrell. Educator, Designer
Sella, Alvin Conrad. Painter, Educator

ALASKA

Anchorage

Appel, Keith Kenneth. Painter, Printmaker
Kimura, William Yusaburo. Painter,
Instructor
Regat, Mary E. Sculptor
Shadrach, Jean H. Painter, Art Dealer
Vallee, William Oscar. Painter

Palmer

Machetanz, Fred. Painter

ARIZONA

Carefree

Harris, Robert George. Painter, Illustrator

Cave Creek

Hack, Phillip S & Patricia Y. Collectors

Cottonwood

McGrew, Ralph Brownell. Painter
Waddell, John Henry. Sculptor

Flagstaff

Danson, Edward B. Museum Director,
Writer
Salter, John Randall. Painter, Sculptor
Wright, Barton Allen. Painter, Illustrator

Mesa

Gillingwater, Denis Claude. Painter

Nogales

Cabot, Hugh. Painter, Sculptor

Oracle

Rush, Andrew. Printmaker, Painter

Paradise Valley

Keane, Bil. Cartoonist
Ruskin, Lewis J. Collector, Patron

Phoenix

Airola, Paavo. Painter, Writer
Bales, (Leeoma) Jewel. Painter
Bergamo, Dorothy Johnson. Painter, In-
structor
Bermudez, Jose Ygnacio. Sculptor, Painter
Blair, Helen (Helen Blair Crosbie). Sculp-
tor, Illustrator
Broadley, Hugh T. Art Historian, Art Ad-
ministrator
Colburn, Carol (Harriet). Painter, Photog-
rapher
Cole, Frances. Painter
Coze-Dabija, Paul. Painter, Writer
Darius, Denyll. Painter
Datus, Jay. Painter, Art Administrator
Dewey, Kenneth Francis. Painter, Illus-
trator
Dignac, Geny (Eugenia M Bermudez). Sculp-
tor, Painter
Dorr, Goldthwaite Higginson, III. Art Ad-
ministrator
Frerichs, Ruth Colcord. Painter
Golubic, Theodore Roy. Sculptor

Phoenix (cont)

Jacobson, Arthur Robert. Painter, Printmaker
Lewis, William R. Instructor, Painter
Mahaffey, Merrill Dean. Painter, Instructor
Marshall, Alice Lord. Painter
Moore, Ina May. Instructor, Painter
Parker, James Varner. Art Administrator, Designer
Phillips, Irving W. Cartoonist, Illustrator
Pritzlaff, Mr & Mrs John, Jr. Collectors
Riley, Roy John. Painter, Designer
Schmidt, Randall Bernard. Sculptor, Educator
Ullman, Mrs George W. Collector
Warner, Boyd, Jr. Painter
Woods, Rip. Painter, Educator
Woods, Theodore Nathaniel, III. Sculptor
Young, Marjorie Ward. Painter, Instructor

Prescott

Chethlahe (David Chethlahe Paladin). Painter, Designer

Rimrock

Dyck, Paul. Painter, Lecturer

San Carlos

Naha, Raymond. Painter

Scottsdale

Curtis, Philip Campbell. Painter
Davis, Lew E. Painter
Gentry, Warren Miller. Educator, Painter
Goo, Benjamin. Sculptor, Painter
Greenbowe, F Douglas. Painter
Lang, Margo Terzian. Painter
Manning, Reg (West). Cartoonist, Writer
Schimmel, William Berry. Painter, Lecturer
Soleri, Paolo. Architect-Environmental Planner, Sculptor
Udinotti, Agnese. Sculptor, Painter
Watson, Robert. Painter

Sedona

Lunge, Jeffrey (Roy). Painter
Yoakum, Delmer J. Painter, Designer

Sells

Sine, David William. Sculptor, Painter

Tempe

Harter, Tom John. Educator, Painter
Stevens, Lawrence Tenney. Sculptor
Stuler, Jack. Photographer, Educator
Turk, Rudy H. Museum Director, Art Historian
Wood, Harry Emsley, Jr. Educator, Painter

Tucson

Bolster, Ella S. Designer-Weaver, Lecturer
De Grazia, Ettore Ted. Painter
Edgerly, Beatrice (Beatrice Edgerly MacPherson). Painter, Writer
Haas, Lez. Painter, Educator

Hanna, Boyd Everett. Illustrator, Painter
Hay, Dorothy B. Painter, Etcher
Heric, John F. Sculptor
Hupp, Frederick Duis. Painter, Educator
Hyslop, Alfred John. Sculptor, Educator
Johnson, Patricia Paul. Painter
Knight, Frederic Charles. Painter, Educator
Loney, Doris Howard. Painter
McMillan, Robert W. Painter, Educator
Martin, Lucille Caiar (Lucille Martin Hampton). Painter
Pleasants, Frederick R. Collector, Patron
Porter, J Erwin. Painter
Silvercruys, Suzanne (Mrs Edward Ford Stevenson). Sculptor, Lecturer
Steadman, William Earl. Museum Director
Voris, Mark. Educator, Painter
Weese, Myrtle A. Painter
Wiper, Thomas William. Art Administrator, Painter
Wong, Jason. Executive Director

Williams

Seaman, Drake F. Painter

Window Rock

Gorman, Carl Nelson (Kin-Ya-Onny Beyeh). Painter, Lecturer

ARKANSAS

Clarksville

Ward, Lyle Edward. Painter, Educator

Eureka Springs

Freund, Harry Louis. Painter, Illustrator

Fayetteville

Reif, Rubin. Painter, Educator

Little Rock

Graham, Bill (William Karr). Cartoonist
Josus (Josephine Hutson Graham). Painter, Educator
Mapes, Doris Williamson. Painter
Wolfe, Townsend Durant. Painter, Art Administrator

Scott

Altvater, Catherine Tharp. Painter

Siloam Springs

Sessler, Stanley Sascha. Painter, Etcher

State University

Richards, Karl Frederick. Educator, Painter

CALIFORNIA

Albany

Kerr, Leslie. Painter

Altadena

Baker, George. Sculptor
Green, David Oliver. Sculptor, Educator

Anaheim

Macaray, Lawrence Richard. Painter, Educator

Arcadia

Huseby, Arleen. Painter, Instructor
Roysher, Hudson (Brisbine). Designer, Art Administrator

Arcata

Berry, Glenn. Painter, Educator

Bakersfield

Rippey, Clayton. Painter, Educator

Belvedere

De Christopher, Eugene Louis. Sculptor, Designer
Ludekens, Fred. Painter, Illustrator

Berkeley

Bechtle, Robert Alan. Painter
Bischoff, Elmer Nelson. Painter, Educator
Blos, May (Elizabeth). Illustrator, Painter
Blos, Peter W. Painter, Instructor
Cahill, James Francis. Art Historian, Educator
Chipp, Herschel Browning. Educator, Museum Curator
Davis, Jerrold. Painter
Elliott, Lillian. Weaver, Designer
Harris, Lucille. Painter
Hartman, Robert Leroy. Painter, Educator
Hoare, Tyler James. Sculptor, Printmaker
Kasten, Karl Albert. Painter, Printmaker
Leon, Dennis. Sculptor
Lipofsky, Marvin B. Sculptor, Glass Blower
Loran, Erle. Painter, Writer
Nelson, Lucretia. Painter, Educator
Prestini, James Libero. Sculptor, Designer
Reichek, Jesse. Printmaker, Painter
Ruvolo, Felix Emmanuele. Painter, Educator
Selz, Peter H. Art Historian, Art Museum Director
Shoemaker, Peter. Painter, Educator
Snelgrove, Walter H. Painter
Voulkos, Peter. Sculptor, Educator

Beverly Hills

Bensinger, B Edward, III. Collector
Brown Greene, Lucille. Painter, Lecturer
Halff, Robert H. Collector
Lewin, Bernard. Art Dealer, Collector
Longstreet, Stephen. Painter, Art Historian
Mesches, Arnold. Painter, Educator
Perls, Frank (Richard). Art Dealer, Collector
Shane, Frederick E. Painter, Educator

Big Sur

Ligare, David H. Painter

Bolinas

Harris, Paul. Sculptor
Okamura, Arthur. Painter

Burbank

Riley, Art (Arthur Irwin). Painter, Photographer

Burlingame

Lilienthal, Mr & Mrs Philip N, Jr. Collectors

Cambria

Clark, Robert Charles. Painter, Lecturer
Paradise, Phil (Herschel). Painter, Sculptor

Canyon

Corson, Gordon Melvin. Painter
Shea, Beverly. Art Dealer

Carlsbad

Hagen, Ethel Hall. Painter

Carmel

Ashley, Frank Nelson. Painter
Beson, Roberta (Roberta Beson Hill). Painter, Art Administrator
Disgard, James Dewey. Collector, Patron
Dooley, Helen Bertha. Painter, Art Dealer
Hill, Dale Logan. Painter, Instructor
Huth, Hans. Art Historian, Art Administrator
Huth, Marta. Painter, Photographer
Lagorio, Irene R. Sculptor, Painter
Laycox, (William) Jack. Painter, Designer
Norman, Emile. Painter, Sculptor
Oehler, Helen Gapen. Painter, Lecturer
Shoemaker, Vaughn. Editorial Cartoonist, Painter
Teague, Donald. Painter
Timmins, William Frederick. Painter, Illustrator
Zantman, Hans. Art Dealer

Carmel Valley

Baker, Eugene Ames. Painter
Parker, Alfred. Illustrator

Carpinteria

Warshaw, Howard. Painter

Chico

Turner, Janet E. Printmaker, Educator

Claremont

Ackerman, Gerald Martin. Art Historian, Educator
Ames, Arthur Forbes. Painter, Educator
Ames, Jean Goodwin. Designer, Painter
Benjamin, Karl Stanley. Painter, Instructor
Blizzard, Alan. Painter, Educator
Dike, Philip Latimer. Painter Designer
Hueter, James Warren. Sculptor, Painter

Clovis

Laury, Jean Ray (Jean Ray Bitters). Designer, Writer

Corona Del Mar

Brandt, Rexford Elson. Painter, Writer
DeLap, Tony. Sculptor
Partch, Virgil Franklin, II. Cartoonist, Illustrator

Corte Madera

Tift, Mary Louise. Printmaker
Winter, Clark. Sculptor

Costa Mesa

Kushner, Dorothy Browdy. Painter, Instructor
Slick, James Nelson. Painter, Sculptor

Dana Point

McLaughlin, John D. Painter

Davis

Arneson, Robert Carston. Sculptor, Educator
Nelson, Richard L. Painter, Educator
Petersen, Roland Conrad. Painter, Printmaker
Thiebaud, (Morton) Wayne. Painter, Educator

Del Mar

Fredman, Faiya R. Sculptor, Painter
Herman, Vic. Painter, Writer
Hutchison, Milburn Robert. Painter, Illustrator

Encino

Hoowij, Jan. Painter
Hutchison, Elizabeth S. Painter
Sider, Deno. Painter, Sculptor
Wein, Albert W. Sculptor, Painter

Escondido

Sternberg, Harry. Painter, Educator

Fairfax

Frances, Harriette (Anton). Painter, Printmaker
Fried, Robert Samuel. Printmaker, Painter
Kreitzer, David Martin. Painter
Stinski, Gerald Paul. Painter, Collector

Fresno

Musselman, Darwin B. Painter, Educator
Odorfer, Adolf. Sculptor, Educator
Pickford, Rollin, Jr. Painter

Skelton / Stewart / Williams

Skelton, Phillis Hepler. Painter
Stewart, Albert T. Sculptor
Williams, Guy. Painter

Fullerton

Arnold, Florence M. Painter
Cannon, Margaret Erickson. Painter, Instructor
Frankel, Dextra. Sculptor, Craftsman
Ivy, Gregory Dowler. Educator, Painter
Partin, Robert (E). Painter, Educator
Simon, Norton. Collector

Goleta

Thomas, Robert Chester. Sculptor

Green Valley Lake

Svenson, John Edward. Sculptor, Collector

Gualala

Sheets, Millard Owen. Designer, Painter

Hillsborough

Tucker, Mrs Nion. Collector

Hollywood

Asmar, Alice. Painter, Designer
Band, Max. Painter, Sculptor
Houser, Vic Carl. Sculptor, Painter
Ruscha, Edward Joseph. Painter, Photographer
Smiley, Ralph Jack. Painter, Instructor

Kentfield

Moquin, Richard Attilio. Sculptor, Instructor

Lafayette

Schnier, Jacques. Sculptor

Laguna Beach

Blacketer, James Richard. Painter, Art Dealer
Darrow, Paul Gardner. Painter, Educator
De Mille, Leslie Benjamin. Painter
Kauffman, Robert Craig. Painter, Sculptor
Kinghan, Charles Ross. Painter
Kuntz, Roger Edward. Painter, Sculptor
Moreton, Russell. Painter
Peche, Dale C. Painter
Scheu, Leonard. Painter, Lecturer
Strombotne, James. Painter
Von Schneidau, Christian. Painter, Sculptor

Laguna Niguel

Armstrong, Roger Joseph. Painter, Cartoonist
Enman, Tom Kenneth. Painter, Art Administrator

Lagunitas

Holman, Arthur (Stearns). Painter

La Jolla

Ellison J Milford. Painter, Graphic Artist
Geisel, Theodor Seuss (Dr Seuss). Illustrator, Writer
Harrison, Newton A. Sculptor, Educator

La Jolla (cont)

Jones, Douglas McKee (Doug). Painter, Art
    Dealer
Key-Oberg, Ellen Burke. Sculptor
Levy, Beatrice S. Painter
Mark, Bendor. Painter
Monaghan, Eileen (Mrs Frederic Whitaker).
    Painter
O'Hara, (James) Frederick. Printmaker,
    Educator
Olten, Carol (Carol Mirabile). Writer
Stewart, John Lincoln. Educator, Writer
Urrutia, Lawrence. Art Administrator
Whitaker, Frederic. Painter, Writer

La Mesa

Swiggett, Jean Donald. Educator, Painter

Lemon Grove

Clark, John Dewitt. Sculptor

Loleta

Graves, Morris. Painter

Long Beach

Hay-Messick, Velma. Painter
Messick, Ben (Newton). Painter, Instruc-
    tor
Robinson, Wahneta Theresa. Curator, Art
    Historian
Swift, Dick. Printmaker, Educator
Von Adlmann, Jan Ernst. Museum Director,
    Art Historian

Los Altos Hills

Hobbs, (Carl) Fredric. Sculptor, Film
    Maker

Los Angeles

Adler, Billy (Telethon). Sculptor, Photog-
    rapher
Anaya, Stephen Raul. Printmaker
Andersen, Andreas Storrs. Educator,
    Painter
Anhalt, Jacqueline Richards. Art Dealer
Aron, Kalman. Painter
Asher, Betty M. Collector
Bailey, Walter Alexander. Painter, Art
    Administrator
Bales, George Carson (Bob). Painter, Illus-
    trator
Berg, Phil. Collector, Patron
Berman, Nancy Mallin. Art Administrator,
    Art Historian
Biberman, Edward. Painter, Lecturer
Blankfort, Dorothy. Collector
Blankfort, Michael. Collector
Bloch, E Maurice. Art Historian, Educa-
    tor
Blower, David Harrison. Painter
Blumberg, Ron. Painter, Instructor
Brach, Paul H. Painter, Educator
Brendel, Bettina. Painter, Lecturer
Brewer, Donald J. Museum Director, Art
    Historian
Brice, William. Painter, Educator
Broderson, Morris. Painter
Brody, Mr & Mrs Sidney F. Collectors
Bueno, Jose. Sculptor, Painter
Burkhardt, Hans Gustav. Painter, Collector
Chicago, Judy. Painter
Cho, David. Sculptor
Chuey, Robert Arnold. Painter, Lecturer
Cremean, Robert. Sculptor

Crown, Keith Allen. Painter, Educator
Crutchfield, William Richard. Painter,
    Printmaker
Darricarrere, Roger Dominique. Sculptor,
    Craftsman
Daves, Delmer. Collector
Davidson, J LeRoy. Art Historian
Dentzel, Carl Schaefer. Museum Director,
    Writer
Dill, Guy Girard. Sculptor
Dimondstein, Morton. Sculptor, Painter
Donahue, Kenneth. Art Administrator, Art
    Historian
Dreiband, Laurence. Painter
Ellis, George Richard. Museum Director
Elsky, Herb. Sculptor
Ewing, Edgar Louis. Painter
Falzone, Michael Joseph. Painter, Sculptor
Feitelson, Lorser. Painter
Fenci, Renzo. Sculptor
Finch, Keith Bruce. Painter
Finkelstein, Max. Sculptor, Instructor
Forst, Miles. Painter, Educator
Foulkes, Llyn. Painter
Francis, Sam. Painter
Freed, Ernest Bradfield. Printmaker,
    Painter
Gibson, George. Painter, Art Administra-
    tor
Gill, Gene. Painter, Printmaker
Goedike, Shirl. Painter
Goodman, Calvin Jerome. Art Consultant,
    Lecturer
Hansen, Robert William. Painter
Herschler, David. Sculptor
Hoopes, Donelson Farquhar. Museum
    Curator, Art Historian
Hough, Richard. Photographer, Designer
Howard, Robert A. Sculptor, Educator
Hubenthal, Karl Samuel. Cartoonist
Johnston, Ynez. Painter, Printmaker
Kanemitsu, Matsumi. Painter, Lecturer
Kayser, Stephen S. Educator, Writer
Kent, Corita, I H M. Serigrapher, Educator
Kester, Lenard. Painter
Kisch, Gloria. Painter
Kubly, Donald R. Designer, Art Adminis-
    trator
Landau, Felix. Art Dealer
Lark, Raymond. Painter, Draftsman
Lauritz, Paul. Painter
Lecoque. Painter, Writer
Leeper, John P. Painter
Lem, Richard Douglas. Painter
Lewis, Samella Sanders. Painter, Art
    Historian
Love, Rosalie Bowen. Painter, Instructor
Lubner, Martin Paul. Painter
Lundeberg, Helen (Helen Lundeberg Feitel-
    son). Painter
Mason, John. Sculptor
Moser, Julon. Painter
Mugnaini, Joseph Anthony. Painter, Writer
Natzler, Otto. Ceramist, Sculptor
Nordland, Gerald John. Museum Director,
    Art Critic
Palmer, Herbert Bearl. Art Dealer, Art
    Critic
Peake, Channing. Painter
Penny, Aubrey John Robert. Painter
Phillips, Gifford. Collector, Writer
Portanova, Joseph Domenico. Sculptor,
    Designer
Price, Kenneth, Printmaker, Sculptor
Price, Vincent. Collector, Art Dealer
Quinn, Noel Joseph. Painter, Educator
Rebert, Jo Liefeld. Painter, Lecturer
Reed, Hal. Painter. Sculptor
Reeves, J Mason, Jr. Painter
Robles, Esther Waggoner. Art Dealer,
    Collector
Robles, Glenn (Waggoner). Printmaker,
    Painter
Rogers, James B. Painter
Ross, (Robert) Kenneth. Art Administrator
Saar, Betye. Painter, Designer
Saturensky, Ruth. Painter

Schapiro, Miriam. Painter
Schary, Susan. Painter
Seldis, Henry J. Art Critic, Educator
Serisawa, Ikuo. Art Dealer
Serisawa, Sueo. Painter
Silverman, Ronald H. Educator
Singer, Burr (Burr Lee Friedman). Painter
Singer, William Earl. Painter, Sculptor
Sklar, Dorothy. Painter
Smith, Hassel W, Jr. Painter
Souden, James G. Educator, Painter
Squires, Norma-Jean. Sculptor, Painter
Steinitz, Kate Trauman. Writer, Art
    Historian
Stern, Jan Peter. Sculptor
Stevenson, Robert Bruce. Sculptor, Lec-
    turer
Stuart, David. Art Dealer, Lecturer
Takemoto, Henry Tadaaki. Craftsman,
    Sculptor
Toigo, Daniel Joseph. Painter, Educator
Treiman, Joyce Wahl. Painter
Tuchman, Maurice. Museum Curator
Ullman, Harold P. Collector
Vann, Loli (Mrs Lilian Van Young). Painter
Van Young, Oscar. Painter, Instructor
Vargas, Rudolph. Sculptor
Vernon, Alexandra. Painter
Waano-Gano, Joe. Painter, Lecturer
Wayne, June. Painter
White, Charles Wilbert. Painter, Educator
Wight, Frederick S. Painter, Art Admin-
    istrator
Woelffer, Emerson. Painter
Wright, Mr & Mrs William H. Collectors
Young, Joseph Louis. Sculptor, Art Ad-
    ministrator
Zammitt, Norman. Sculptor
Zamparelli, Mario Armond. Designer,
    Collector

Los Gatos

Kruskamp, Janet Elaine. Painter

Malibu

Davis, Ronald Wendel. Painter, Collector
Getty, J Paul. Collector, Writer
White, Lawrence Eugene. Educator

March Air Force Base

Amelio, Gilbert Neil. Sculptor, Painter

Mendocino

Bothwell, Dorr. Painter, Printmaker

Menlo Park

Defenbacher, Daniel S. Designer, Lec-
    turer
Proctor, Gifford MacGregor. Sculptor,
    Designer
Stout, George Leslie. Art Consultant

Mill Valley

Allan, William George. Painter
Anderson, Jeremy Radcliffe. Sculptor, Edu-
    cator
O'Hanlon, Richard E. Sculptor, Educator
Saul, Peter. Painter
Sherry, William Grant. Painter, Sculptor

Millbrae

Nepote, Alexander. Painter, Educator

Modesto

Remsing, (Joseph) Gary. Painter, Sculptor

Montecito

Backus, Standish, Jr. Painter, Illustrator
Ludington, Wright S. Collector, Patron
Wonner, Paul (John). Painter

Monterey

Bowman, Dorothy (Louise). Painter,
    Printmaker
Bradford, Howard. Serigrapher, Painter
Dedini, Eldon Lawrence. Cartoonist
Rabinovitch, William Avrum. Painter

Monterey Park

Medearis, Roger. Painter

North Hollywood

D'Agostino, Vincent. Painter

Northridge

Hammons, Verily. Painter

Novato

Wilmeth, Hal Turner. Art Historian,
    Painter

Oakdale

Ayling, Mildred Shoob. Painter, Photog-
    rapher

Oakland

Albright, Thomas. Art Critic, Writer
Baird, Roger Lee. Sculptor, Instructor
Batchelor, Jonathan David. Painter,
    Sculptor
Beasley, Bruce. Sculptor
Breschi, Karen Lee. Sculptor
Foosaner, Judith Ann. Painter
Johnson, Doris Miller (Mrs Gardiner John-
    son). Painter
Lederer, Wolfgang. Designer, Educator
Logan, Maurice. Painter, Illustrator
McLean, Richard Thorpe. Painter, Edu-
    cator
Melchert, James Frederick. Sculptor,
    Educator
Neubert, George Walter. Sculptor, Art
    Administrator
Paris, Harold Persico. Sculptor
Ramos, Melvin John. Painter, Educator
Saunders, Raymond Jennings. Painter,
    Educator
Schoener, Jason. Painter, Educator
Siegriest, Lundy. Painter, Instructor

Ojai

Dominique, John August. Painter
Johnson, Wesley E. Painter, Instructor
Smith, Robert Alan. Painter, Instructor

Orange

Boaz, William G. Sculptor, Educator

Oro Grande

Bender, Bill. Painter

Pacific Palisades

Brokaw, Lucile. Painter
Campbell, Richard Horton. Painter, Print-
    maker
Longman, Lester Duncan. Art Historian
Macdonald-Wright, Stanton. Painter

Palm Desert

Rich, Frances L. Sculptor, Photographer

Palm Springs

Caniff, Milton Arthur. Cartoonist, Writer
Olsen, Frederick L. Potter, Sculptor

Palo Alto

Boyle, Keith. Painter, Educator
Kirkby, Paula Zolloto. Art Dealer
Lobdell, Frank. Painter
Zirker, Joseph. Graphic Artist, Lecturer

Pasadena

Carmichael, Jae. Painter, Art Adminis-
    trator
Edmondson, Leonard. Etcher
Grieger, (Walter) Scott. Sculptor
Kaprow, Allan. Painter, Educator
Levy, Hilda. Painter
Younglove, Ruth Ann (Mrs Benjamin Rhees
    Loxley). Painter

Paso Robles

Sorby, J Richard. Painter, Educator

Pebble Beach

Kaller, Robert Jameson. Art Dealer
Lewis, Jeannette Maxfield. Painter,
    Etcher

Petaluma

McChesney, Robert Pearson. Painter
Williams, Franklin. Painter

Placerville

Wessels, Glenn Anthony. Painter, Educa-
    tor

Port Costa

De Forest, Roy Dean. Painter, Sculptor

Redwood City

Bowman, Richard. Painter
Strong, Charles Ralph. Painter, Educator

Richmond

Haley, John Charles. Painter, Sculptor
Kim, Ernie. Ceramist, Art Administra-
    tor
Pinkerton, Clayton (David). Painter
Simpson, David. Painter, Educator

Riverside

Blum, Shirley Neilsen. Art Historian, Edu-
    cator

Sacramento

Kaltenbach, Stephen James. Painter, Sculp-
    tor
Marcus, Irving E. Painter, Graphic Artist
Shiner, Nate. Painter, Educator
Spencer, Hugh. Illustrator, Photographer
Woof, Maija (Maija Gegeris Zack-Peeples).
    Painter

Salinas

Butterbaugh, Robert Clyde. Sculptor, Edu-
    cator

San Anselmo

Rauh, Fritz. Painter

San Bernardino

Harrison, Robert Rice. Educator

San Clemente

Thompson, Joanne. Painter, Sculptor

San Diego

Anderson, Brad J. Cartoonist
Beach, Warren. Painter
Fisch, Arline Marie. Goldsmith, Educator
Friedman, Kenneth Scott. Sculptor, In-
    structor
Gardiner, Henry Gilbert. Art Administra-
    tor, Art Historian
Jackson, Everett Gee. Painter, Illustrator
Kerr, Kenneth A. Painter, Designer
Kilian, Austin Farland. Painter, Educator
Lopez, Rhoda Le Blanc. Sculptor, Instruc-
    tor
Schrack, Joseph Earl. Painter
Sherman, Lenore (Walton). Painter, Lec-
    turer
Stratton, Dorothy (Dorothy Stratton King).
    Painter, Printmaker
Tibbs, Thomas S. Museum Director, Lec-
    turer
Todd, Michael Cullen. Sculptor, Painter

San Francisco

Acton, Arlo C. Sculptor
Adams, Mark. Designer, Painter
Anargyros, Spero. Sculptor
Asawa, Ruth (Ruth Asawa Lanier). Sculptor,
    Graphic Artist
Beetz, Carl Hugo. Painter, Instructor
Benton, Fletcher. Sculptor
Berggruen, John Henry. Art Dealer
Bolles, John S. Art Dealer, Collector
Bouquet, Gus. Painter, Sculptor
Brandon, Warren Eugene. Painter, Writer
Brooks, (John) Alan. Painter, Educator
Brown, William Henry. Painter
Clark, G Fletcher. Sculptor
Close, Marjorie (Perry). Painter, Lecturer
Conner, Bruce. Painter, Film Maker
Cox, E Morris. Collector
Davis, Stephen A. Painter
Dickinson, Eleanor Creekmore. Painter,
    Sculptor
Elder, Muldoon. Painter, Sculptor
Evans, Henry. Printmaker
Fitch, George Hopper. Collector, Patron

San Francisco (cont)

Fox, Terry Alan. Sculptor
Frankenstein, Alfred Victor. Art Critic,
  Art Historian
Fried, Alexander. Art Critic
Fried, Howard Lee. Sculptor
Fuller, Diana. Art Dealer
Garver, Thomas H. Art Administrator,
  Writer
Gecse, Helene. Painter, Etcher
Giambruni, Tio. Sculptor
Goddard, Vivian. Painter
Gooch, Gerald. Artist, Painter
Graham, F Lanier. Art Historian, Art
  Administrator
Gutkin, Peter. Painter
Gutmann, John. Painter, Educator
Hack, Howard Edwin. Painter
Hansen, Wanda. Art Dealer
Harvey, Robert Martin. Painter
Henry, Jean. Painter, Instructor
Hershman, Lynn Lester. Painter
Hinkhouse, Forest Melick. Art Consultant
Holland, Tom. Painter
Hoover, F Herbert. Art Dealer, Writer
Howard, Robert Boardman. Sculptor
Howe, Thomas Carr. Museum Director
Howell, Raymond. Painter,
  Photographer
Jackson, Suzanne (Fitzallen). Painter,
  Writer
Jolley, Jerry (Geraldine Hazel Jolly).
  Painter, Sculptor
Jonniaux, Alfred. Painter
Keith, David Graeme. Museum Curator
King, Hayward Ellis. Art Dealer,
  Instructor
Kingsbury, Robert David. Sculptor, Crafts-
  man
Koblick, Freda. Sculptor
Kussoy, Bernice (Helen). Sculptor
Leighton, Thomas Charles. Painter, In-
  structor
Lew, Weyman Michael. Painter
Loberg, Robert Warren. Painter, Instruc-
  tor
Lomahaftewa, Linda (Linda Joyce Slock).
  Painter, Educator
Lupper, Edward. Painter
Majdrakoff, Ivan. Painter, Educator
Martin, Fred Thomas. Painter
Martin, William Henry (Bill). Painter,
  Sculptor
Miller, Mrs Robert Watt. Patron
Mundt, Ernest Karl. Sculptor,
  Educator
Nadalini, (Louis) (Ernest). Painter
Pearson, Louis O. Sculptor
Post, George (Booth). Painter, Educator
Potter, (George) Kenneth. Painter, De-
  signer
Potts, Don. Painter, Educator
Proom, Al. Painter, Designer
Rambo, James I. Museum Curator
Reichman, Fred(rick) (Thomas). Painter
Renk, Merry. Designer, Sculptor
Richardson, Sam. Painter, Educator
St Amand, Joseph. Painter
Sawyer, William. Art Dealer,
  Collector
Schaeffer, Rudolph Frederick. Designer,
  Educator
Sinton, Nell (Walter). Painter, Instructor
Smith, Howard Ross. Museum Curator
Staprans, Raimonds. Painter, Sculptor
Taylor, Sandra J. Painter
Ullrich-Zuckerman, B. Painter, Photog-
  rapher
Van Hoesen, Beth (Mrs Mark Adams). Print
  Printmaker
Villa, Carlos. Painter
von Meyer, Michael. Sculptor
Weinbaum, Jean. Painter, Sculptor
Wenger, Lesley. Art Dealer
White, Ian McKibbin. Art Administrator,
  Designer

San Geronimo

Raffael, Joseph. Painter

San Jose

Freimark, Robert (Matthew). Printmaker,
  Painter
French, James C. Museum Curator, Lec-
  turer
Hunter, John H. Painter, Educator
Schnittmann, Sascha S. Sculptor, Museum
  Director

San Juan Capistrano

Honeyman, Robert B, Jr. Collector

San Marino

Wark, Robert Rodger. Art Administrator,
  Art Historian

San Ysidro

Wenger, Sigmund. Art Dealer, Lecturer

Santa Barbara

Cavat, Irma. Painter, Educator
Dole, William. Painter, Educator
Dorra, Henri. Art Historian, Educator
Fenton, Howard Carter. Painter
Frame, Robert (Aaron). Painter
Gebhard, David. Art Administrator, Art
  Historian
Jarvaise, James J. Painter
Lutz, Dan S. Painter
Mallory, Margaret. Collector
Mills, Paul Chadbourne. Museum Curator
Moir, Alfred. Art Historian
Parshall, Douglass Ewell. Painter
Reeve, John Sebastian. Sculptor

Santa Cruz

Auvil, Kenneth William. Educator, Printmaker
Woods, Gurdon Grant. Sculptor, Educator

Santa Monica

Andrews, Oliver. Sculptor
Bongart, Sergei R. Painter, Educator
Diebenkorn, Richard. Painter
Haines, Richard. Painter, Educator
Margolies, John Samuel. Photographer,
  Educator
Mullican, Lee. Painter, Educator
Owyang, Judith Francine. Art Critic

Santa Rosa

Barr, Roger Terry. Sculptor, Painter

Saratoga

Caswell, Helen Rayburn. Painter, Writer

Sausalito

Schwarcz, June Therese. Craftsman

Sebastopol

Schulz, Charles Monroe. Cartoonist

Sierra Madre

Randall, (Lillian) Paula. Sculptor, Designer

Sonoma

Anderson, Gunnar Donald. Painter, Illustrator
Jacobsen, Ray (Eugene). Painter

South Laguna

Jones, John Paul. Painter, Printmaker

South Pasadena

Matson, Victor (Stanley). Painter

Spring Valley

Greene, Ethel Maud. Painter

Stanford

Eisner, Elliot Wayne. Educator
Eitner, Lorenz E A. Art Historian, Educa-
  tor
Elsen, Albert Edward. Art Historian
Faulkner, Ray N. Educator, Writer
Mendelowitz, Daniel Marcus. Painter,
  Writer

Stinson Beach

Hudson, Robert H. Sculptor
Shaw, Richard Blake. Sculptor

Stockton

Dennison, Keith Elkins. Art Administrator,
  Art Historian
Gyermek, Stephen A. Educator
Reynolds, Richard (Henry). Sculptor,
  Painter

Studio City

Block, Irving Alexander. Painter, Educator
Jensen, Eve. Painter
Nelson, Donald Richard. Painter

Sylmar

Gebhardt, Harold. Sculptor, Educator
Gebhardt, Peter Martin. Sculptor

Tarzana

Kendall, Viona Ann. Painter, Printmaker

Thousand Oaks

Janss, Edwin, Jr. Collector
Martino, Antonio P. Painter

Tiburon

Baird, Joseph Armstrong, Jr. Writer, Educator

Topanga

Schley, Evander Duer (Van). Conceptual
  Artist, Photographer

Trinidad

Groth, Bruno. Sculptor

Vacaville

Wasser, Paula Kloster. Painter, Educator

Van Nuys

Van Wolf, Henry. Sculptor, Painter

Venice

Bengston, Billy Al. Painter
Boyce, Richard. Sculptor, Lecturer
Eversley, Frederick John. Sculptor
Falkenstein, Claire. Sculptor
Irwin, Robert. Painter
Valentine, DeWain. Sculptor
Vasa (Vasa Velizar Mihich). Sculptor,
Educator

Ventura

Herron, Jason. Sculptor
Koch, Gerd (Herman). Painter, Educator
Koch, Irene Mabel. Painter, Lecturer

Walnut Creek

Dennis, Charles Houston. Cartoonist
Eaton, Myrwyn Lake. Educator, Painter
Pneuman, Mildred Y. Painter

West Covina

Cross, Watson, Jr. Painter, Instructor

Whitethorn

Gill, James (Francis). Painter, Sculptor

Woodacre

Wiley, William T. Painter

COLORADO

Aspen

Bayer, Herbert. Painter, Designer
Wille, O Louis. Sculptor

Boulder

Drewelowe, Eve. Painter, Sculptor
Eades, Luis Eric. Painter, Educator
Geck, Francis Joseph. Painter, Educator
Matthews, Gene (Eugene Edward). Painter,
Educator
Megrew, Alden Frick. Art Historian, Educator
Neher, Fred. Cartoonist
Vance, George Wayne. Ceramist, Sculptor
Westermeir, Clifford Peter. Painter, Educator
Wolle, Muriel Sibell. Painter, Writer

Breckenridge

Howell, Frank. Painter, Art Dealer

Cherry Hills Village

Strawn, Melvin Nicholas. Painter, Sculptor

Colorado Springs

Abbot, Hazel Newnham. Painter
Arnest, Bernard. Painter
Bessemer, Auriel. Painter, Illustrator
Naeve, Milo M. Art Administrator, Art
Historian
Tilley, Lewis Lee. Painter
Trissel, James Nevin. Painter, Educator
Wynne, Albert Givens. Painter, Instructor

Denver

Bach, Otto Karl. Museum Director, Writer
Billmyer, John Edward. Craftsman, Educator
Bunn, Kenneth Rodney. Painter
DeAndrea, John Louis. Sculptor
DeMaree, Elizabeth Ann (Betty). Painter,
Collector
Hansen, Frances Frakes. Educator, Painter
Jagman, Edward. Painter
Johnston, Richard M. Sculptor, Educator
Kelley, Ramon. Painter
Kirkland, Vance Hall. Painter, Collector
Smith, Paul K. Painter
Swensen, Mary Jeanette Hamilton (Jean).
Painter, Lithographer
Traher, William Henry. Painter, Lecturer

Englewood

Jellico, John Anthony. Art Administrator,
Writer

Evergreen

Kaplinski, Buffalo. Painter

Fort Collins

De Waal, Ronald Burt. Collector
Forsyth, Robert Joseph. Art Historian,
Collector
Yust, David E. Painter, Educator

Golden

Deaton, Charles. Sculptor, Architect

Grand Junction

Redden, Alvie Edward. Painter, Instructor

Gunnison

Julio, Pat T. Educator, Craftsman

Littleton

Bartlett, Fred Stewart. Art Administrator
Britton, Edgar. Sculptor

Longmont

Fulton, W Joseph. Museum Director,
Educator

Telluride

Wagner, Richard Ellis. Painter

CONNECTICUT

Bethany

Herbert, Robert L. Art Historian

Bethel

Farris, Joseph G. Cartoonist, Painter

Bloomfield

Shulman, Joseph L. Collector
Tompkins, Alan. Painter, Educator

Bridgeport

Lam, Jennett (Brinsmade). Painter, Educator
Wilson, Sybil. Painter, Designer

Brookfield Center

Beall, Lester Thomas. Painter, Designer
Westermann, Horace Clifford. Sculptor

Byram

List, Vera G. Patron, Collector

Chester

Killam, Walt. Painter, Art Dealer
Schueler, Jon R. Painter, Lecturer
Ziemann, Richard Claude. Printmaker,
Educator

Cornwall Bridge

Gray, Cleve. Painter, Sculptor
Sloane, Eric. Illustrator, Writer

Cos Cob

Kane, Margaret Brassler. Sculptor

Coventry

Hayes, David Vincent. Sculptor

Darien

Black, Lisa. Painter
Neilson, Katharine B. Educator, Lecturer
Newman, Ralph Albert. Cartoonist, Illustrator
Ray, Ruth (Mrs John Reginald Graham).
Painter
Whitcomb, Jon. Painter, Illustrator

Durham

Skop, Michael. Sculptor, Educator

East Haddam

Warneke, Heinz. Sculptor

East Hampton

Rice, Dan. Painter, Instructor

East Norwalk

Broudy, Miriam Levine. Painter

Easton

Eliscu, Frank. Sculptor

Enfield

Fitzsimmons, James Joseph. Painter, Architect

Falls Village

Blagden, (Frederic) Allen. Painter
Fransioli, Thomas Adrian. Painter
Lathrop, Dorothy. Illustrator, Writer
Lathrop, Gertrude K. Sculptor

Georgetown

Thompson, Malcolm Barton. Painter, Sculptor

Granby

Wadsworth, Frances Laughlin. Sculptor, Painter

Greens Farms

Weiss, Harvey. Sculptor

Greenwich

Aakre, Richard B. Painter, Photographer
Baruch, Mr & Mrs Joseph M. Collectors
Brown, William Ferdinand, II. Illustrator, Writer
Carr, J Gordon. Architect, Painter
Cherepov, George. Painter, Instructor
Gimbel, Mrs Bernard F. Collector, Patron
Hirshhorn, Joseph H. Collector
Kaep, Louis Joseph. Painter
Motherwell, Robert. Painter, Printmaker
Van Der Voort, Amanda Venelia. Painter
Walker, Mort. Cartoonist

Groton

Mac Gillis, Robert Donald. Painter, Illustrator
Nelson, Harry William. Painter, Printmaker

Hamden

Keller, Deane. Educator, Painter

Hartford

Ballinger, Harry Russell. Painter, Writer
Barton, Eleanor Dodge. Educator
Behl, Wolfgang. Sculptor, Educator
Elliott, James Heyer. Art Administrator
Huntington, John W. Collector, Patron
Mitchell, Clifford. Painter, Architect
Neill, T Joseph. Sculptor, Educator
Valtman, Edmund. Cartoonist
Zimmerman, Paul Warren. Painter, Educator

Ivoryton

Bendig, William Charles. Painter, Instructor
Jensen, Leo (Vernon). Sculptor, Painter
Jensen, Pat. Painter

Kent

Howard, Len R. Craftsman, Designer
Nelson, George Laurence. Painter, Art Restorer
Quanchi, Leo. Painter
Saucy, Claude Gerald. Painter, Educator

Lakeville

Blagden, Thomas P. Painter
Hubbard, Earl Wade. Painter

Litchfield

Cain, Michael Peter. Painter, Sculptor
Landeck, Armin. Painter, Engraver
Purves, Austin. Painter, Sculptor

Lyme

Hardin, Adlai S. Sculptor

Madison

Bauermeister, Mary Hilde Ruth. Sculptor
Davies, Kenneth Southworth. Painter, Educator

Mansfield Center

Forman, Kenneth Warner. Painter, Educator
Knobler, Lois Jean. Painter

Meriden

Widstrom, Edward Frederick. Sculptor

Middletown

Frazer, John Thatcher. Film Maker, Painter
Gourevitch, Jacqueline. Painter
Green, Samuel Magee. Art Historian, Painter
Risley, John Hollister. Sculptor, Educator
Schwarz, Heinrich. Museum Curator, Educator

Milford

Johnson, Lester F. Painter, Educator

Monroe

Bogart, Richard Jerome. Painter

Moodus

Guy, James M. Painter, Educator

Mystic

Bates, Gladys Edgerly. Sculptor
Bates, Kenneth. Painter
Fuller, Harvey Kenneth. Painter, Illustrator

New Britain

Ferguson, Charles. Painter, Art Historian

New Canaan

Barton, August Charles. Designer, Painter
Cavalli, Dick. Cartoonist
Eberman, Edwin. Art Administrator, Educator
Ernst, Jimmy. Painter, Educator
Johnson, Philip Cortelyou. Collector, Architect
Margolies, Ethel Polacheck. Painter, Art Administrator
Noyes, Eliot. Architect, Designer
Ritchie, Andrew C. Art Administrator, Art Historian
Roesch, Kurt (Ferdinand). Painter
Saxon, Charles David. Cartoonist, Illustrator
Soby, James Thrall. Writer, Critic

New Fairfield

Austin, Darrel. Painter
Nevelson, Mike. Sculptor

New Haven

Bailey, William H. Painter
Chaet, Bernard. Painter, Educator
Crosby, Sumner McKnight. Art Historian
Fussiner, Howard. Painter
Gardner, Joan A. Painter, Film Maker
Garston, Gerald Drexler. Painter
Gruppe, Charles. Painter
Gute, Herbert Jacob. Painter, Educator
Jensen, Lawrence N. Painter
Kubler, George Alexander. Art Historian, Writer
Lee, George J. Art Administrator, Photographer
Mermin, Mildred (Shire). Painter
Montgomery, Charles Franklin. Art Administrator, Educator
Rannit, Aleksis. Art Historian, Educator
Scully, Vincent. Art Historian, Educator
Seymour, Charles, Jr. Art Historian, Curator
Shestack, Alan. Museum Director, Art Historian
Stebbins, Theodore Ellis, Jr. Art Historian, Art Administrator
Tedeschi, Paul Valentine. Painter, Educator
Weaver, Howard Sayre. Educator

New London

Bonamarte, Lou. Painter, Designer
Lukosius, Richard Benedict. Painter, Educator
Mayhew, Edgar De Noailles. Educator, Museum Director

New Milford

Zalstem-Zalessky, Mrs Alexis. Collector

New Preston

Wolff, Robert Jay. Painter, Writer

Newington

Chapps, John. Sculptor
Martin, G W. Painter, Educator

Newtown

Caparn, Rhys (Rhys Caparn Steel). Sculptor
Getz, Ilse. Painter
Inman, Pauline Winchester. Printmaker, Illustrator
Winchester, Alice. Art Editor

Niantic

Dennis, Roger Wilson. Painter

Noank

Brackman, Robert. Painter, Educator
Stein, Harve. Painter, Educator

Norfolk

Kelemen, Pal. Art Historian

North Haven

Tulk, Alfred James. Painter

Norwalk

Chappell, Warren. Illustrator, Designer
Frasconi, Antonio. Illustrator, Painter
Koch, Robert. Art Historian, Writer
Lasker, Joseph (L). Painter, Illustrator
Lovell, Tom. Painter, Illustrator
Pellew, John Clifford. Painter
Vassos, John. Painter, Designer

Norwich

Radin, Dan. Painter
Triplett, Margaret L. Educator, Painter

Old Greenwich

Giles, Newell Walton, Jr. Painter

Old Lyme

Chandler, Elisabeth Gordon. Sculptor
Hilles, Susan Morse. Collector, Patron
Ingle, Tom. Painter, Lecturer
Olinsky, Tosca (Mrs Charles F Barteau). Painter

Orange

Albers, Josef. Painter, Printmaker

Oxford

Chaplin, George Edwin. Painter, Educator
Fuge, Paul H. Sculptor
Rumsey, David MacIver. Sculptor, Designer

Plainville

Brzozowski, Richard Joseph. Painter

Putnam

Davis, Wayne Lambert. Painter, Illustrator

Redding Ridge

Ridabock, Ray (Budd). Painter, Instructor

Ridgefield

Drummond, Sally Hazelet. Painter
Perlin, Bernard. Painter, Illustrator
Ross, Alexander. Painter

Riverside

Thompson, (James) Bradbury. Designer, Art Director

Rowayton

Peterdi, Gabor F. Painter, Printmaker

Roxbury

Arnason, H Harvard. Art Historian, Writer
Calder, Alexander. Sculptor
Ericson, Dick. Cartoonist, Illustrator
Selvig, Forrest Hall. Art Historian, Writer

Salisbury

Osborn, Elodie C. Art Administrator
Osborn, Robert. Painter, Drawer

Sharon

Broemel, Carl William. Painter, Illustrator
Wilkinson, Charles K. Museum Curator

Sherman

Blume, Peter. Painter
Schmid, Richard Alan. Painter
Tee-Van, Helen Damrosch. Painter, Illustrator

Simsbury

Cowing, William R. Painter, Instructor

South Kent

Aymar, Gordon Christian. Painter, Art Historian

Southbury

Ettenberg, Eugene M. Designer, Educator
Frishmuth, Harriet Whitney. Sculptor

Southport

Vickrey, Robert Remsen. Painter

Stamford

Bechtle, C Ronald. Painter
Burt, David Sill. Sculptor, Writer
Bushmiller, Ernie Paul. Cartoonist
Connolly, Jerome Patrick. Painter, Illustrator
Hausman, Fred S. Painter, Sculptor
Krushenick, Nicholas. Painter, Lecturer
MacLean, Arthur. Painter, Lithographer
Schanker, Louis. Printmaker, Painter

Sterling

Holden, Raymond James. Painter, Illustrator

Stonington

Cale, Robert Allan. Printmaker

Stony Creek

London, Jeff. Sculptor, Lecturer

Storrs

Crossgrove, Roger Lynn. Painter, Educator
Gregoropoulos, John. Painter
Knobler, Nathan. Sculptor, Educator
Terenzio, Anthony. Painter, Educator
Zelanski, Paul John. Painter

Torrington

Abbate, Paul S. Sculptor

Trumbull

Treadwell, Grace (Ansley). Painter, Lecturer

Uncasville

Cuming, Beatrice. Painter
McCloy, William Ashby. Painter, Sculptor

Voluntown

Caddell, Foster. Painter, Instructor

Wallingford

Neff, John A. Painter, Designer

Warren

Abrams, Herbert E. Painter, Lecturer

Washington

Grausman, Philip. Sculptor
Porter, Priscilla Manning. Craftsman, Educator
Renouf, Edward Pechmann. Painter, Sculptor
Talbot, William (H M). Sculptor

Washington Depot

Beineke, Dr & Mrs J Frederick. Collectors
Frazier, Paul D. Sculptor

Watertown

Cajori, Charles F. Painter

West Cornwall

Mangravite, Peppino Gino. Painter, Lecturer
Simont, Marc. Illustrator

West Hartford

Fairchild, Isabel Shelton. Designer, Painter
Taylor, John C E. Painter, Educator

West Redding

Dieringer, Ernest A. Painter
Giusti, George. Designer, Sculptor

Weston

Bleifeld, Stanley. Sculptor, Instructor
Camacho, Paul. Painter
Cowan, Woodson Messick. Cartoonist, Painter
Fogel, Seymour. Painter, Sculptor
Nonay, Paul. Painter, Instructor
Rand, Paul. Painter, Designer

Westport

Boulton, Joseph L. Sculptor, Designer
Cherner, Norman. Designer
Chernow, Ann. Painter, Educator
Chernow, Burt. Educator, Museum Director
Darrow, Whitney, Jr. Cartoonist
Daugherty, James Henry. Painter, Writer
Dohanos, Stevan. Illustrator, Painter
Fisher, Leonard Everett. Painter, Illustrator
Gramatky, Hardie. Painter, Writer
Hurd, Justin G (Jud). Cartoonist
Johnson, Crockett. Painter, Writer
Johnson, Edvard Arthur. Painter, Educator
Olsen, Herb. Painter, Writer
Rabut, Paul. Illustrator, Painter
Reindorf, Samuel. Painter
Woodham, Jean. Sculptor, Lecturer

Wilton

D'Aulaire, Edgar Parin. Illustrator, Lithographer
d'Aulaire, Ingri (Mortenson) Parin. Writer, Illustrator
Lipman, Jean. Art Editor, Writer
Purdy, Donald R. Painter, Art Dealer
Roberts, Priscilla Warren. Painter
Stuart, Kenneth James. Art Director

Woodbridge

Lytle, Richard. Painter, Educator

Woodbury

Leighton, Clare. Engraver, Writer

DELAWARE

Greenville

Reynolds, Nancy Du Pont. Sculptor

Hockessin

Parks, Charles Cropper. Sculptor
Parks, Christopher Cropper. Sculptor, Painter

Newark

Allen, Magaret Prosser. Painter, Educator
Homer, William Innes. Art Historian, Educator
Moss, Joe (Francis). Sculptor, Painter

Wilmington

Blankenship, Roy. Painter, Conservator
Blish, Carolyn Bullis. Painter
Haskell, Harry Garner, Jr. Collector
Hayes, Tua. Painter
Layton, Richard. Painter
Rhoads, Eugenia Eckford. Painter

DISTRICT OF COLUMBIA

Adams, William Howard. Art Administrator, Collector
Atkyns, (Willie) Lee, Jr. Painter, Art Administrator
Bader, Franz. Art Dealer, Collector
Berkowitz, Leon. Painter
Biddle, James. Art Administrator, Collector
Bingham, Lois A. Art Administrator, Lecurer
Bookatz, Samuel. Painter, Sculptor
Breeskin, Adelyn Dohme. Art Administrator
Breitenbach, Edgar. Art Historian
Brown, John Carter. Museum Director
Bullard, Edgar John, III. Museum Curator, Art Historian
Cain, James Frederick, Jr. Printmaker, Museum Curator
Calfee, William Howard. Sculptor
Campbell, Dorothy Bostwick. Painter, Sculptor
Campbell, William Patrick. Art Historian
Carter, Albert Joseph. Museum Curator
Chieffo, Clifford Toby. Painter, Printmaker
Cogswell, Margaret Price. Art Administrator
Conlon, George. Sculptor
Cooke, Hereward Lester. Art Historian, Painter
Cusick, Nancy Taylor. Painter, Educator
D'Arista, Robert. Painter, Educator
Davis, Gene. Painter
Davis, Robert Tyler. Art Administrator, Art Historian
Dorrance, Nesta. Art Dealer
Dulcan, Caril E. Art Dealer, Writer
Eisenstein, Mr & Mrs Julian. Collectors
Ellinger, Ilona E. Painter, Educator
Faul, Roberta Heller. Writer
Fendrick, Barbara Cooper. Art Dealer
Fern, Alan Maxwell. Art Historian, Art Administrator
Ferriter, Clare. Painter, Instructor
Finley, David Edward. Art Administrator
Flint, Janet Altic. Curator, Art Historian
Fontanini, Clare. Educator, Sculptor
Gast, Michael Carl. Painter
Gilliam, Sam. Painter
Glick, Paula Florence. Art Dealer, Collector
Gomez-Sicre, Jose. Art Administrator, Art Critic
Gramberg, Liliana. Painter, Printmaker
Grossman, Sheldon. Museum Curator, Art Historian
Grove, Richard. Art Administrator, Writer
Gumpert, Gunther. Painter
Hadin, Eunice (Barnard). Painter, Illustrator
Haslem, John Arthur & Jane N. Art Dealers, Collectors
Heller, Lawrence J. Collector
Herman, Lloyd Eldred. Art Administrator
Hoffman, Helen Bacon. Painter
Holvey, Samuel Boyer. Sculptor, Designer
Hopps, Walter. Art Administrator
Howland, Richard Hubbard. Art Historian, Writer

Irwin, John N, II. Collector
Isham, Sheila Eaton. Painter
Jackson, Virgil V. Cartoonist, Illustrator
Kerr, John Hoare. Art Administrator, Art Historian
Klavans, Minnie. Painter, Sculptor
Knox, Katharine McCook. Art Historian, Collector
Koch, Virginia Greenleaf. Painter
Krebs, Rockne. Sculptor
Kreeger, David Lloyd. Patron, Collector
Lastra, Luis. Art Dealer, Art Critic
Lazzari, Pietro. Sculptor, Painter
Lewis, Douglas. Art Historian, Art Curator
Lowe, Harry. Art Administrator, Designer
MacAgy, Douglas Guernsey. Art Administrator
MacDonald, William Allan. Art Historian, Educator
McGowin, William Ed. Sculptor, Painter
McGrath, Kyran Murray. Art Administrator
McWhinnie, Harold James. Printmaker, Educator
Marlin, Hilda Van Stockum. Painter
Mehring, Howard William. Painter
Mellon, Paul. Collector, Art Administrator
Millsaps, Daniel. Painter, Writer
Mitchell, Eleanor. Fine Arts Specialist, Librarian
Moore, E Bruce. Sculptor
Neslage, Oliver John, Jr. Art Dealer
Niese, Henry Ernst. Painter, Film Maker
Oberhuber, Konrad J. Art Historian
Parkhurst, Charles. Art Administrator, Writer
Peiperl, Adam. Sculptor
Perlmutter, Jack. Painter, Printmaker
Perrot, Paul N. Art Administrator, Lecturer
Phillips, Dorothy W. Art Administrator, Writer
Phillips, Marjorie. Museum Director, Painter
Pierce, Delilah W. Painter, Educator
Pierre-Noel, Lois Jones. Painter, Designer
Pollack, Reginald Murray. Painter, Writer
Pope, Annemarie Henle. Art Administrator
Pope, John Alexander. Museum Director
Rennie, Helen (Sewell). Painter, Designer
Richard, Paul. Art Critic
Richman, Robert M. Art Administrator, Writer
Robbins, Warren M. Art Administrator, Educator
Roberts, Lucille D (Malkia). Painter, Educator
Ross, Marvin Chauncey. Museum Curator, Art Historian
Russell, Helen Diane. Art Historian
Rust, David E. Art Historian, Collector
Safford, Ruth Perkins. Painter
Sandground, Mark Bernard, Sr. Collector, Patron
Sarnoff, Lolo. Sculptor, Collector
Sawyer, Alan R. Art Consultant
Schlaikjer, Jes Wilhelm. Painter, Illustrator
Schmutzhart, Berthold Josef. Sculptor, Educator
Scott, David Winfield. Art Administrator
Shapley, Fern Rusk. Museum Curator, Writer
Shapley, John. Art Historian
Sickman, Jessalee Bane. Painter, Instructor
Singletary, Robert Eugene. Graphic Artist
Sivard, Robert Paul. Painter, Art Administrator
Slade, Roy. Painter, Educator
Smith, Arthur Hall. Painter
Spandorf, Lily Gabriella. Painter
Spencer, John R. Art Historian, Art Administrator

Stern, Harold Phillip. Museum Director,
  Writer
Stevenson, A Brockie. Painter
Stovall, Luther McKinley (Lou). Printmaker
Straight, Michael. Collector
Taylor, Joshua Charles. Educator, Art
  Historian
Thacher, John Seymour. Museum Director
Thomas, Alma Woodsey. Painter
Tirana, Rosamond (Mrs Edward Corbett)
  Painter
Truettler, William. Art Administrator
Truitt, Anne (Dean). Sculptor
Turano, Don. Sculptor, Medalist
Van Roijen, Hildegarde Graham. Painter,
  Sculptor
Voris, Anna Maybelle. Art Administrator
Wells, James Lesesne. Painter, Lithogra-
  pher
Williams, Hermann Warner, Jr. Art Ad-
  ministrator, Writer
Wright, Frank. Painter, Printmaker
Young, Kenneth Victor. Painter, Designer

FLORIDA

Altamonte Springs

Singleton, Robert Ellison. Painter, Printmaker

Bay Harbor Island

Slobodkin, Louis. Sculptor, Illustrator

Boca Raton

Adams, Robert David. Designer, Painter
Dorst, Claire V. Painter, Educator

Cape Canaveral

Scheibe, Fred Karl. Painter, Writer

Cape Coral

Harsanyi, Charles. Painter
Korjus, Veronica Maria Elisabeth. Painter,
  Lecturer

Clearwater

Arnholt, Waldon Sylvester. Painter, Instructor
Kennedy, J William. Painter, Educator

Clermont

Amateis, Edmond Romulus. Sculptor
Van Arsdale, Dorothy Thayer. Art Administrator

Coconut Grove

Bailey, James Arlington, Jr. Painter,
  Restorer
Massin, Eugene Max. Painter, Educator

Coral Gables

Bergling, Virginia Catherine (Mrs Stephen
  J Kozazcki). Art Book Dealer
Charles, Clayton (Henry). Sculptor, Edu-
  cator
Grodensky, Samuel. Painter

May, E M (Elizabeth M Messiter). Painter,
  Illustrator
Turoff, Muriel Pargh. Sculptor, Painter
Waltner, Beverly Ruland. Painter

Crystal River

Doolittle, Warren Ford, Jr. Art Administrator, Painter

Daytona Beach

Surovek, John Hubert. Painter, Museum
  Director

De Land

Johnson, Robert Lewis. Painter, Photog-
  rapher
Messersmith, Fred Lawrence. Painter,
  Educator

Delray Beach

Schang, Frederick, Jr. Collector
Varga, Ferenc. Sculptor

Edgewater

Stowman, Annette Burr. Painter

El Dora

Leeper, Doris Marie. Painter, Sculptor

Englewood

Tracy, (Lois) Bartlett. Painter, Writer

Fort Lauderdale

Carone, Matthew David. Painter, Art
  Dealer
Chase, Jeanne Norman. Painter
Hope, Henry Radford. Art Historian

Fort Walton Beach

Simpson, Marilyn Jean. Painter, Instructor

Gainesville

Craven, Roy Curtis, Jr. Painter, Educa-
  tor
Hodges, Stephen Lofton. Painter, Art
  Administrator
Holbrook, Hollis Howard. Educator, Painter
Holbrook, Vivian Nicholas. Painter, Art
  Administrator
Kerslake, Kenneth Alvin. Printmaker,
  Educator
Naylor, John Geoffrey. Sculptor, Educator
Uelsmann, Jerry. Photographer
Williams, Hiram Draper. Painter, Educa-
  tor

Hawthorne

Burnham, Lee. Sculptor, Painter

Hialeah

Sherwood, A. Sculptor, Printmaker

Hollywood

Schreck, Michael Henry. Painter, Sculptor

Jacksonville

Brownett, Thelma Denyer. Painter
Dodge, Joseph Jeffers. Painter, Art Ad-
  ministrator
Hicken, Russell Bradford. Art Adminis-
  trator, Lecturer
Koscielny-Parker, Margaret. Painter,
  Sculptor
Mahey, John A. Art Administrator
Pringle, Burt Evins. Graphic Artist, De-
  signer

Jupiter

Connery, Ruth M. Painter, Instructor

Lakeland

Stoddard, Donna Melissa. Art Administrator, Educator

Largo

Tucker, Peri. Writer, Illustrator

Leesburg

Humes, Ralph H. Sculptor

Lynn Haven

Ferguson, Edward Robert. Painter, Printmaker

Madeira Beach

Terry, Marion (E). Painter, Art Critic

Mandarin

Brown, Charles Moses (Charlie). Potter

Marathon

Leake, Gerald. Painter

Miami

Amoroso, Jack Louis. Painter, Collector
Carulla, Ramon A. Painter
Couper, James M. Painter, Instructor
Draper, Robert Sargent. Painter, Art
  Dealer
Evans, Edward Arthur. Painter
Jennings, Frank Harding. Painter, Instruc-
  tor
Luria, Gloria. Art Dealer
McAllister-Kelly, (Rosana). Painter
Martinez-Maresma, Sara (Sara Sofia
  Martinez). Painter, Instructor
Musgrave, Shirley H. Educator, Photogra-
  pher
Pappas, Marilyn. Craftsman, Educator
Randolph, Gladys Conrad. Painter, Writer
Romoser, Ruth Amelia. Painter, Sculptor
Ruffo, Joseph Martin. Printmaker, De-
  signer
Salinas, Baruj. Painter
Schroyer, Robert McClelland. Designer,
  Illustrator
Storm, Larue. Painter, Sculptor
Strickland, Thomas J. Painter

Miami (cont)

Szarama, Judith Layne. Printmaker, Instructor
Triester, Kenneth. Painter, Sculptor
Viret, Margaret Mary (Mrs Frank Ivo). Painter, Lecturer
Vrana, Albert S. Sculptor
Warren, Jefferson Trowbridge. Museum Director
Willson, Robert. Sculptor, Educator

Miami Beach

Bass, John. Collector, Patron
Bernay, Betti. Painter
Fernandez-Yanez, Alvaro. Painter
Gains, Jacob. Painter
Gaston, Marianne Brody. Painter, Illustrator
Hoff, (Syd). Cartoonist, Writer
Leiferman, Silvia W. Painter, Sculptor
Rosenblum, Sadie Skoletsky. Painter, Sculptor
Schein, Eugenie. Painter, Instructor

Miami Shores

Hollinger, (Helen Wetherbee). Painter, Lecturer

Naples

Cord, Orlando. Painter
Geiger, Edith Rogers. Painter
Harmon, (Loren) Foster. Art Dealer
Oppenheim, Samuel Edmund. Painter
Summy, Anne Tunis. Painter
Watkins, Franklin Chenault. Painter

North Miami

Thorndike, Charles Jesse (Chuck). Cartoonist, Writer

North Miami Beach

Aljaman (Alton James Chapman). Painter, Educator
Kessler, Edna Leventhal. Painter, Instructor

Orange Park

Hunt, Julian Courtenay. Painter, Instructor

Orlando

Crane, Roy(ston) (Campbell). Cartoonist, Writer
Criquette (Ruth DuBarry Montague). Painter, Writer
Ivey, James Burnett. Cartoonist, Collector

Osprey

Buzzelli, Joseph Anthony. Painter, Sculptor

Ozona

Banta, E Cabriskie (Mrs Oliver Smith). Painter, Craftsman
Smith, Oliver. Painter

Palm Beach

Brams, Joan. Painter, Sculptor
Cochran, Gifford Alexander. Painter
Gordon, John. Art Administrator, Art Historian
Hare, Channing. Painter
Hare, Stephen Hopkins. Painter
Hokin, Grace E. Art Dealer, Collector
Levin, Jeanne. Painter, Collector
Lukin, Philip. Collector
Plimpton, Russell A. Art Administrator

Pensacola

Carey, John Thomas. Educator, Art Historian
Newton, Earle Williams. Art Administrator, Collector

Perrine

Kleinholz, Frank. Painter, Writer

Ponte Vedra Beach

Greacen, Nan (Nan Greacen Faure). Painter, Instructor

Port Charlotte

Randall, Ruth Hunie. Designer, Educator

Riviera Beach

Hibel, Edna. Painter, Lithographer

St Augustine

Calkin, Carleton Ivers. Painter, Lecturer
Roberds, Gene Allen. Printmaker

St Petersburg

Anderson, David Phillip. Painter, Lecturer
Crane, James. Painter, Cartoonist
Dickey, Helen Pauline. Painter, Instructor
Diman, Homer. Painter
Failing, Frances Elizabeth. Painter, Educator
Goldberg, Norman Lewis. Writer, Art Historian
Hill, Polly Knipp. Etcher, Painter
Hodgell, Robert Overman. Printmaker, Painter
McVeigh, Miriam Temperance. Painter
Malone, Lee H B. Art Administrator
Schwarz, Felix Conrad. Painter, Educator
Schwarz, Myrtle Cooper. Painter, Educator

Sanibel

Snyder, James Wilbert (Wilb). Painter, Writer

Sarasota

Allen, Margo. Sculptor, Painter
Behl, Marjorie. Painter
Bendell, Marilyn. Painter, Instructor
De Diego, Julio. Painter, Illustrator
Farnsworth, Jerry. Painter, Writer
Floethe, Richard. Illustrator, Designer
Held, Philip. Painter, Instructor
Hoppes, Lowell E. Cartoonist
Kelsey, Muriel Chamberlin. Sculptor

Kimbrough, Verman. Educator
Lane, Bent. Painter
Leech, Hilton. Painter, Instructor
Oehlschlaeger, Frank J. Art Dealer
Osborne, Robert Lee. Painter, Instructor
Parton, Nike. Painter, Sculptor
Perkins, Robert Eugene. Art Administrator
Posey, Leslie Thomas. Sculptor, Educator
Rogers, Leo M. Collector
Rosendale, Harriet. Painter
Rowland, Elden Hart. Painter
Sawyer, Helen (Helen Sawyer Farnsworth). Painter, Writer
Shaw, Harry Hutchison. Painter
Solomon, Syd. Painter, Instructor
Stahl, Ben (Albert). Painter, Illustrator
Stoddard, Herbert C. Painter, Educator
Sweney, Fred. Illustrator, Writer
Weill, Mr & Mrs Milton. Collectors

Stuart

Hutchinson, Janet L. Museum Director, Collector
Mosley, Zack T. Illustrator, Cartoonist

Tallahassee

Bosch, Gulnar Kheirallah. Art Historian, Educator
Burggraf, Ray Lowell. Painter, Educator
Deshaies, Arthur. Printmaker
Hurst, Ralph N. Sculptor, Educator
Johnson, Ivan Earl. Educator, Designer
Kuhn, Marylou. Educator, Painter
Seidenberg, (Jacob) Jean. Sculptor, Educator

Tampa

Cardoso, Anthony. Painter, Instructor
Covington, Harrison Wall. Painter, Educator
Gelinas, Robert William. Painter, Educator
Holder, Charles Albert. Painter
Nazarenko, Bonnie Coe. Painter
Wujcik, Theo. Printmaker, Educator

Tarpon Springs

Lenski, Lois. Writer, Illustrator

Vero Beach

Brightwell, Walter. Painter
Turner, Dick. Cartoonist

West Palm Beach

Grove, Edward Ryneal. Sculptor, Painter
Grove, Jean Donner (Mrs Edward R). Sculptor
Houser, James Cowing, Jr. Painter, Educator
Hunter, Edmund Robert. Art Administrator
Leff, Rita. Printmaker, Painter
Norton, Ann. Sculptor
Riba, Paul F. Painter, Illustrator

Winter Park

Genius, Jeannette (Jeannette M McKean). Painter, Designer
McKean, Hugh Ferguson. Painter, Educator
Ortmayer, Constance. Sculptor, Educator

GEORGIA

Athens

Christ-Janer, Albert William. Painter, Printmaker
Dodd, Lamar. Painter, Educator
Feldman, Edmund Burke. Art Historian, Art Critic
Paul, William D, Jr. Museum Director, Painter
Strother, Joseph Willis. Painter, Instructor
Tittle, Grant Hillman. Printmaker, Designer

Atlanta

Beattie, George. Educator, Painter
Bhalla, Hans. Painter, Art Historian
Borochoff, (Ida) Sloan. Painter, Art Dealer
Bruno, Santo Michael. Painter, Instructor
Bryan, Wilhelmus B. Art Administrator, Educator
Chase, Allan Seamans. Sculptor, Designer
Clover, James B. Sculptor, Educator
Daniel, Roxanne. Painter, Photographer
De Noronha, Maria M (Mrs Harold Shafron). Painter, Lecturer
Edwards, Kate Flournoy. Painter
Greco, Anthony Joseph. Painter, Sculptor
Harris, Julian Hoke. Sculptor, Architect
Howett, John. Art Historian
Rogers, John H. Sculptor, Educator
Shute, Ben E. Painter, Instructor
Thomas, Steffen Wolfgang. Sculptor, Painter
Vigtel, Gudmund. Art Administrator

Columbus

Shorter, Edward Swift. Painter, Collector

Decatur

Warren, Ferdinand Earl. Painter, Art Administrator

Griffin

Voigt, Roben. Sculptor, Educator

LaGrange

Shead, S Ray. Painter, Sculptor

Savannah

McNab, Allan. Painter, Printmaker

Suwanee

Creecy, Herbert Lee. Painter, Sculptor

HAWAII

Hilo

Ochikubo, Tetsuo. Painter, Designer

Honolulu

Belshe, Mirella Monti. Sculptor, Art Historian
Charlot, Jean. Painter, Art Historian
Chee, May. Potter
Chesney, Lee R, Jr. Printmaker, Painter
Cox, J Halley. Painter, Educator
DeVis-Norton, Mary M. Museum Educator
Ecke, Betty Tseng Yu-Ho. Painter, Art Historian
Engle, Barbara Jean. Painter, Printmaker
Feher, Joseph. Designer, Painter
Foster, James W, Jr. Art Administrator
Griessler, Franz Anton. Painter
Haar, Francis. Photographer, Lecturer
Hart, Marvell Allison. Museum Curator
Hayward, Peter. Painter, Sculptor
Higa, Charles Eisho. Painter, Instructor
Hudson, Winnifred. Painter
Izacyro (Isaac Jiro Matsuoka). Painter, Instructor
Jameikis, Brone Aleksandra. Designer, Instructor
Karawina, Erica (Mrs Sidney C Hsiao). Designer, Painter
Kenda, Juanita Echeverria. Painter, Educator
Kimura, Sueko M. Painter, Educator
Kingrey, Kenneth. Designer, Educator
Kjargaard, John Ingvard. Painter, Printmaker
Kobayashi, Katsumi Peter. Painter, Lecturer
Kowalke, Ronald Leroy. Painter, Printmaker
Litaker, Thomas (Franklin). Painter
Loring, Clarice. Painter, Muralist
Lux, Gwen (Gwen Lux Creighton). Sculptor
Maehara, Hiromu. Painter, Designer
Marozzi, Eli Raphael. Sculptor, Instructor
Morrison, Boone M. Photographer, Designer
Norris, (Robert) Ben. Painter, Educator
Pohl, Louis G. Painter, Printmaker
Roster, Fred Howard. Sculptor, Educator
Russell, Shirley (Ximena). Painter
Salmoiraghi, Frank. Photographer, Instructor
Sexton, Leo Lloyd, Jr. Painter
Stasack, Edward Armen. Painter, Printmaker
Tsuchidana, Harry Suyemi. Painter
Wisnosky, John G. Painter, Educator
Young, John Chin. Painter, Collector

Kahului

Miller, Barbara Darlene. Painter, Instructor

Kailua

Cooper, Lucille B. Painter, Sculptor
Harvey, Donald Gilbert. Sculptor, Instructor
Stamper, Willson Young. Painter, Educator

Kaneohe

Ingraham, Esther Price. Painter

Lahaina

Hilton, John William. Painter, Illustrator
Sato, Tadashi. Painter, Sculptor
Schuman, Robert Conrad. Painter, Instructor

Lihue

Lai, Waihang. Painter, Instructor

IDAHO

Boise

Auth, Robert R. Painter, Sculptor
Dodworth, Allen Stevens. Art Administrator, Printmaker
Killmaster, John H. Painter, Educator

Moscow

Kirkwood, Mary Burnette. Painter

ILLINOIS

Alton

Freund, Will Frederick. Painter, Educator

Aurora

Ford, Ruth Vansickle. Painter, Educator

Barrington

Schnackenberg, Roy. Painter, Sculptor

Barrington Hills

Strobel, Thomas C. Painter, Graphic Artist

Belleville

Hesse, Don. Cartoonist

Carbondale

Fink, Herbert Lewis. Painter, Educator
Johnson, Evert Alfred. Art Administrator, Painter
Kington, Louis Brent. Sculptor, Educator
Plochmann, Carolyn Gassan. Painter

Champaign

Betts, Edward Howard. Painter, Educator
Britsky, Nicholas. Painter, Educator
Christison, Muriel B. Art Administrator, Instructor
Fehl, Philipp P. Painter, Art Historian
Gammon, Juanita-La Verne. Painter, Educator
Perkins, Ann. Art Historian
Rae, Edwin C. Art Historian, Educator
Rowan, Dennis Michael. Printmaker, Educator
Shipley, James R. Educator, Designer
Sinsabaugh, Art. Photographer, Educator
Sprague, Mark Anderson. Painter, Educator
Stephens, Curtis. Designer, Educator
Wicks, Eugene Claude. Painter, Instructor

Charleston

Moldroski, Al R. Painter, Educator
Stapp, Ray Veryl. Educator, Painter

Chicago

Albright, Malvin Marr. Painter, Sculptor
Ames, (Polly) Scribner. Painter, Sculptor
Anderson, Howard Benjamin. Graphic Artist, Painter

Chicago (cont)

Argeropolos, (Basil) Theodore. Painter, Printmaker
Arnold, Ralph Moffett. Painter, Educator
Aubin, Barbara. Painter, Educator
Bedno, Edward. Designer, Educator
Benda, Richard R. Painter
Bentley, Claude. Painter, Graphic Artist
Berdich, Vera. Printmaker
Bittner, Hans Oskar. Painter, Illustrator
Blair, William McCormick. Patron
Block, Mr & Mrs Leigh B. Collectors
Booth, Laurence Ogden. Sculptor, Architect
Bouras, Harry D. Sculptor
Boz, Alex (Alex Bozickovic). Painter, Lecturer
Brcin, John David. Sculptor
Broadd, Harry Andrew. Painter, Art Historian
Brown, Roger. Painter
Brundage, Avery. Collector
Campoli, Cosmo. Sculptor, Educator
Chapman, Dave. Designer
Colker, Edward. Painter, Designer
Cruz, Emilio. Painter, Educator
Danhausen, Eldon. Sculptor
Davidson, Herbert Laurence. Painter
Davidson, Suzette Morton. Designer, Collector
De Lama, Alberto. Painter, Instructor
Dunn, Cal. Painter
Edwards, Stanley Dean. Painter, Illustrator
Fairweather, Sally H. Art Dealer
Findlay, Helen T. Art Dealer
Florsheim, Richard A. Painter, Printmaker
Garrison, Eve. Painter
Gehr, Mary (Mary Ray). Printmaker, Painter
Gerard, Paula (Mrs Herbert Renison). Graphic Artist, Painter
Ginzel, Roland. Painter, Printmaker
Gray, Richard. Art Dealer
Greene-Mercier, Marie Zoe. Sculptor, Draftsman
Guthman, Leo S. Collector
Hanson, Philip Holton. Painter
Hardin, Shirley G. Art Dealer
Haydon, Harold (Emerson). Painter, Educator
Henry, John Raymond. Sculptor
Horn, Milton. Sculptor, Writer
Hunt, Richard Howard. Sculptor
Hurtig, Martin Russell. Painter, Sculptor
Iervolino, Joseph Anthony. Art Dealer, Collector
Iervolino, Paula. Art Dealer, Collector
Joachim, Harold. Museum Curator
Kapsalis, Thomas Harry. Painter, Sculptor
Kearney, John (W). Sculptor, Educator
Kelly, Walter W. Art Dealer
Kestnbaum, Gertrude Dana. Collector
Kind, Phyllis. Art Dealer
Klein, Medard. Painter
Kohn, Misch. Painter, Printmaker
Kokinas, George. Painter
Koppe, Richard. Painter, Educator
Lanyon, Ellen. Painter, Printmaker
Laslo, Patricia Louise. Sculptor, Instructor
Lewis, Phillip Harold. Museum Curator
Lust, Virginia. Art Dealer
McNear, Everett C. Painter, Designer
Maremont, Arnold H. Collector
Markus, Mrs Henry A. Collector
Maser, Edward Andrew. Art Historian, Educator
Mauldin, Bill. Cartoonist, Writer
Maurice, Alfred Paul. Printmaker, Educator
Maxon, John. Associate Museum Director
Mintz, Harry. Painter
Morrison, Keith Anthony. Painter, Educato
Myers, C Stowe. Designer
Nickle, Robert W. Painter, Educator
Parke, Walter Simpson. Painter, Illustrator
Pen, Rudolph. Painter

Piatek, Francis John. Painter
Ramberg, Christina (Christina Ramberg Hanson). Painter
Regensteiner, Else F(riedsam). Educator, Designer
Rosofsky, Seymour. Painter
Rossi, Barbara. Painter, Printmaker
Schiller, Beatrice. Painter, Graphic Artist
Schooler, Lee. Collector
Schwartz, Carl E. Painter, Instructor
Schwartz, William Samuel. Painter
Sewell, Jack Vincent. Museum Curator
Shell, Mr & Mrs Irving W. Collectors
Siegel, Irene. Painter
Sonnenschein, Hugo, Jr. Patron, Art Historian
Speyer, A James. Art Administrator
Spongberg, Grace. Painter, Photographer
Steele, Ivy (Newman). Sculptor, Educator
Stevenson, Florence Ezzell. Painter, Lecturer
Stewart, Patricia Kate. Art Administrator
Stipe, William S. Painter
Suzuki, Sakari. Painter
Teresi, Joseph Anthony. Painter, Instructor
Tigerman, Stanley. Painter, Architect
Urban, Mychajlo Raphael. Sculptor, Painter
Walker, Jerome. Painter, Educator
White, Bruce Hilding. Sculptor
Wriston, Barbara. Educator, Art Historian
Yoshida, Ray Kakuo. Painter, Educator

Deerfield

Winship, Florence Sarah. Illustrator

De Kalb

Bealmer, William. Craftsman, Educator
Driesbach, David Fraiser. Printmaker, Educator
Kabak, Robert. Painter, Educator

Des Plaines

Grubert, Carl Alfred. Cartoonist

Downers Grove

Zweerts, Arnold. Painter, Educator

Edwardsville

Hampton, Phillip Jewel. Painter, Educator
Huntley, David C. Painter, Educator
Malone, Robert R. Painter, Printmaker

Elgin

Rennels, F M. Sculptor
Rovelstad, Trygve A. Sculptor, Designer

Elizabeth

Locker, Thomas. Painter

Elmhurst

Kauffman, (Camille) Andrene. Painter, Sculptor

Evanston

Becker, Bettie (Bettie Geraldine Wathall). Painter

Breckenridge, James D. Art Historian
Halkin, Theodore. Sculptor, Painter
Lust, Herbert. Art Historian, Collector
Weiner, Egon. Sculptor, Educator
Yochim, Louise Dunn. Educator, Painter
Zwick, Rosemary G. Sculptor, Printmaker

Genoa

Mahmoud, Ben. Painter

Glencoe

Calapai, Letterio. Printmaker, Instructor

Glenview

Barnett, Earl D. Designer, Painter
Shapiro, Irving. Painter, Instructor

Highland Park

Arenberg, Albert L. Collector
Esserman, Ruth. Painter
Flax, Serene. Painter
Lazard, Alice Abraham. Painter
Schulze, Franz. Educator, Art Critic
Spitz, Barbara S. Printmaker

Hinsdale

Larsen, Ole. Painter, Illustrator

Hubbard Woods

Ludgin, Earle. Collector

Lake Bluff

MacAlister, Paul Ritter. Designer, Collector

Lake Forest

Judson, Sylvia Shaw. Sculptor
Lockhart, James Leland. Illustrator, Painter
Mills, George Thompson. Educator, Writer

Libertyville

Holland, Daniel E. Cartoonist

Lombard

Ahlstrom, Ronald Gustin. Painter

Macomb

Bobick, Bruce. Painter, Educator
Loomer, Gifford C. Educator, Painter

Mahomet

Perlman, Raymond. Educator, Illustrator

Metamora

Hedden-Sellman, Zelda. Painter, Instructor

Moline

Stone, Alex Benjamin. Art Dealer, Collector

Normal

Freyberger, Ruth Matilda. Painter, Educator
Hoover, Francis Louis. Collector, Educator
Mills, Frederick Van Fleet. Art Administrator, Educator

Northbrook

Eitel, Cliffe Dean. Painter, Designer
Gross, Earl. Painter, Lecturer

Northfield

Glass, Henry P. Designer, Educator
Vela, Alberto. Painter

Oglesby

Whitlow, Tyrel Eugene. Painter, Instructor

Park Ridge

Steinfels, Melville P. Painter, Designer

Peoria

Altorfer, Gloria Finch. Painter, Designer
Benz, Lee R. Printmaker, Sculptor

Quincy

Irwin, George M. Patron, Collector
Landwehr, William Charles. Art Administrator, Sculptor
Mejer, Robert Lee. Painter, Instructor

Ringwood

Pearson, James Eugene. Instructor, Painter

River Forest

Holt, Charlotte Sinclair. Medical Illustrator, Sculptor

Riverside

Howlett, Carolyn Svrluga. Educator, Designer

Riverwoods

Pinkowski, Emily Joan. Painter, Instructor

Rockford

Argraves, Hugh Oliver. Painter
Heflin, Tom Pat. Painter, Designer
Sneed, Patricia M. Art Dealer, Collector

Roscoe

Bond, Oriel Edmund. Illustrator, Painter

Roselle

Lotton, Iwan Leroy. Painter, Illustrator

St Joseph

Von Neumann, Robert A. Sculptor, Educator

Schaumburg

Martyl (Martyl Schweig Langsdorf). Painter

Springfield

Evans, Robert James. Painter, Museum Curator
Guy, Osmond Sublett. Painter, Educator
Hodge, Roy Garey. Painter, Instructor
Madden, Betty I. Art Historian, Lecturer
Rice, Philip Somerset. Painter, Art Administrator

Stockton

Tolpo, Carl (Axel Edward). Sculptor, Painter
Tolpo, Lily. Sculptor, Painter

Urbana

Bradshaw, Glenn Raymond. Painter, Educator
Creese, Walter Littlefield. Educator
Gallo, Frank. Sculptor, Educator
Jackson, Billy Morrow. Painter
Lecky, Susan. Painter
Schultz, Harold A. Painter, Educator
Smith, Ralph Alexander. Writer, Educator
Weller, Allen Stuart. Educator, Art Historian
Ziroli, Nicola. Painter, Educator

Waterloo

Alling, Clarence (Edgar). Museum Director, Craftsman

Western Springs

Gilmore, Roger. Art Administrator, Educator
Vickery, Charles Bridgeman. Painter

Wilmette

Wieghardt, Paul. Painter, Educator

Winnetka

Alsdorf, James W. Patron, Collector
Mayer, Robert Bloom. Collector
Pattison, Abbott. Sculptor, Painter

INDIANA

Bloomington

Lowe, Marvin. Printmaker, Painter
McGarrell, James. Painter, Educator
Pozzatti, Rudy O. Printmaker, Painter
Rouse, Mary Jane Dickard. Educator

Sieber, Roy. Educator, Museum Curator
Smith, Henry Holmes. Photographer, Educator

Borden

Marsh, (Edwin) Thomas. Potter, Educator

Brazil

Hay, Dick. Sculptor, Educator

Culver

Williams, Warner. Sculptor, Designer

Dillsboro

Zimmerman, William Harold. Painter, Illustrator

Elkhart

Gilbert, Clyde Lingle. Painter, Commercial Artist

Evansville

Eilers, Fred (Anton Frederick). Painter, Designer
Gumberts, William A. Collector, Patron
Ives, Glen Palmer. Museum Director
Knecht, Karl Kae. Editorial Cartoonist
McIver, John Kolb. Painter

Fort Wayne

Bonsib, Louis William. Painter
Fried, Raymond John. Art Administrator, Painter
McBride, James Joseph. Painter, Illustrator

Greencastle

Meehan, William Dale. Painter, Designer

Indianapolis

Block, Amanda Roth. Painter, Printmaker
Brucker, Edmund. Painter, Educator
Clowes, Allen Whitehill. Collector, Patron
Daily, Evelynne B. Painter, Printmaker
Davis, Harry Allen. Painter, Educator
Eagerton, Robert Pierce. Printmaker, Painter
Eiteljorg, Harrison. Collector, Patron
Mattison, Donald Magnus. Painter
Rauch, John G. Collector, Patron
Rubins, David Kresz. Sculptor
Wehr, Paul Adam. Illustrator, Designer
Weinhardt, Carl Joseph, Jr. Museum Director

Lafayette

Dorn, Charles Meeker. Educator, Art Administrator
Vevers, Anthony Marr. Painter, Educator

Michigan City

Harbart, Gertrude Felton. Painter, Instructor

Morgantown

Boyce, Gerald G. Educator, Painter

Muncie

Griner, Ned H. Educator, Craftsman
Keene, Maxine M. Sculptor, Educator
Nichols, Alice W. Painter, Educator
Story, William Easton. Painter, Museum Director

Munster

Meeker, Barbara Miller. Educator, Painter

Nashville

Goth, Marie. Painter, Designer

Notre Dame

Lauck, Anthony Joseph, CSC. Sculptor, Art Administrator

Reelsville

Peeler, Richard. Potter, Sculptor

St Mary-of-the-Woods

Newport, Esther, S P. Painter, Art Administrator

South Bend

Holmes, Paul James & Mary E. Collectors
Hoover, (Sidney) Todd. Printmaker, Instructor
Zisla, Harold. Painter, Educator

Terre Haute

Lamis, Leroy. Sculptor, Educator
Porter, Elmer Johnson. Painter, Educator
Wooden, Howard Edmund. Museum Director, Art Critic

Valparaiso

Ushenko, Audrey Andreyevna. Painter, Instructor

Vincennes

Beard, Marion L Patterson. Educator, Painter
Van Meter, Mary. Painter, Educator

Warsaw

Gerard, Allee Whittenberger. Painter

West Lafayette

Beelke, Ralph G. Educator
Revington, George D, III. Collector

IOWA

Ames

Davis, Alice. Painter

Burlington

Schramm, James Siegmund. Collector, Patron

Cedar Falls

Campbell, Marjorie Dunn. Painter, Educator
Herrold, Clifford H. Educator, Craftsman
Page, John Henry, Jr. Printmaker, Painter

Cedar Rapids

Kocher, Robert Lee. Painter, Art Administrator
Stamats, Peter Owen. Collector, Patron

Davenport

Hoffman, Larry Gene. Art Administrator

Des Moines

Demetrion, James Thomas. Art Administrator
Good, Leonard. Painter, Educator
Kawa, Florence Kathryn. Painter
Kirschenbaum, Jules. Painter, Educator

Fort Dodge

Halm, Robert John. Painter, Instructor

Indianola

Ragland, Jack Whitney. Painter, Printmaker

Iowa City

Burford, Byron Leslie. Painter, Educator
Cuttler, Charles David. Art Historian
Fracassini, Silvio Carl. Painter, Educator
Gorder, Clayton J. Painter, Educator
Lasansky, Mauricio. Printmaker
Lechay, James. Painter
Patrick, Genie H. Painter
Patrick, Joseph Alexander. Painter, Educator
Schmidt, Julius. Sculptor
Schulze, John H. Photographer, Educator
Sprague, Nancy Kunzman. Sculptor
Von Groschwitz, Gustave. Museum Director
Wilke, Ulfert S. Painter, Art Administrator
Woodham, Derrick James. Sculptor

Mason City

Leet, Richard Eugene. Art Administrator, Painter

Waterloo

Held, Alma M. Painter

KANSAS

Ellsworth

Rogers, Charles B. Painter, Museum Director

Emporia

Eppink, Helen Brenan. Educator, Painter
Eppink, Norman R. Printmaker, Painter
Hall, Rex Earl. Painter, Educator

Hays

Moss, Joel C. Painter, Educator

Lawrence

Berger, Klaus. Educator, Writer
Carey, James Sheldon. Educator, Potter
Enggass, Robert. Art Historian
Larsen, Erik. Art Historian, Educator
McKay, John Sangster. Art Administrator, Educator
Stokstad, Marilyn Jane. Art Historian, Educator
Sudlow, Robert N. Painter, Educator
Talleur, John J. Printmaker
Vaccaro, Nick Dante. Painter, Educator
West, W Richard (Dick). Educator, Painter

Manhattan

Howard, Dan F. Painter, Art Administrator

Pittsburg

Krug, Harry Elno. Printmaker, Educator

Topeka

Hunt, Robert James. Painter, Educator

Wichita

Bernard, David Edwin. Printmaker, Educator
Blameuser, Mary Fleurette, B V M. Painter, Instructor
Bosin, Blackbear. Painter, Designer
Connett, (Delores) Dee M. Educator, Painter
Dickerson, William Judson. Painter
Fincher, John H. Painter, Educator
Kiskadden, Robert Morgan. Painter, Educator
Kurdian, Haroutiun Harry. Writer, Collector
Simoni, John Peter. Painter, Educator

KENTUCKY

Alexandria

Storm, Howard. Painter

Berea

Pross, Lester Fred. Educator, Painter

Florence

Goodridge, Lawrence Wayne. Painter, Sculptor

Fort Thomas

Tcheng, John T L. Painter

Lexington

Freeman, Richard Borden. Art Historian, Educator
Petro, Joseph (Victor), Jr. Painter, Illustrator

Louisville

Bright, Barney. Sculptor
Byrum, Mary. Painter
Donson, Jerome Allan. Educator, Sculptor
Kaulitz, Garry Charles. Painter, Printmaker
Kohlhepp, Norman. Painter, Printmaker
Nay, Mary Spencer. Painter, Educator
Page, Addison Franklin. Art Administrator
Stoll, Mrs Berry Vincent. Collector

Murray

Eagle, Clara M. Craftsman, Educator
Head, Robert William. Painter, Educator

Princeton

Granstaff, William Boyd. Painter, Illustrator

Shepherdsville

Lesch, Alma Wallace. Textile Craftsman, Educator

LOUISIANA

Baton Rouge

Boyer, Mrs Richard C. Collector, Patron
Broussard, Jay Remy. Museum Director, Painter
Cavanaugh, Tom Richard. Painter, Educator
Dufour, Paul Arthur. Painter, Designer
Durieux, Caroline Wogan. Printmaker
May, William L. Collector
Sachse, Janice R. Painter, Printmaker

Lake Charles

Holcombe, R Gordon, Jr. Collector, Patron

Mamou

Savoy, Chyrl Lenore. Sculptor, Educator

Metairie

Kohlmeyer, Ida (R). Painter

New Orleans

Brice, Bruce Raymond. Painter
Byrnes, James Bernard. Museum Director, Art Historian
Cook, Richard Lee. Sculptor, Educator
Davis, Mr & Mrs Walter. Collectors, Patrons

Emery, Lin (Lin Emery Braselman). Sculptor
Gordy, Robert P. Painter
Gregory, Angela. Sculptor, Educator
Horton, Jan E. Painter, Writer
Kern, Arthur (Edward). Educator, Sculptor
Lamantia, James. Painter, Collector
Mason, Bette. Painter
Rockmore, Noel. Painter
Steg, J L. Printmaker
Struppeck, Jules. Sculptor, Educator
Tahir, Abe M, Jr. Art Dealer
Trivigno, Pat. Painter, Educator

Shreveport

Cadle, Ray Kenneth. Painter, Craftsman
Francis, Al (Alfred Kade). Painter, Lecturer
Middleton, David V. Painter, Ceramist
Morgan, Arthur C. Sculptor
Morgan, Gladys B. Painter, Instructor
Wiener, Samuel G. Painter

Slidell

Dunbar, George Bauer. Painter

MAINE

Addison

Thompson, Susie Wass. Painter

Bangor

D'Amico, Augustine A. Collector, Patron

Boothbay Harbor

Eames, John Heagan. Etcher, Painter

Bristol

Klebe, Gene (Charles Eugene). Painter, Writer

Brunswick

Beam, Philip Conway. Art Administrator, Educator
Hammond, Ruth MacKrille. Painter

Camden

Iselin, Lewis. Sculptor
Skinner, Clara (Clara Skinner Guy). Painter, Printmaker

Cape Elizabeth

Meissner, Berniece Cram-Gill. Collector
Meissner, Leo J. Painter, Engraver

Cape Neddick

Kuhn, Brenda. Art Administrator

Cape Porpoise

Bacon, Peggy. Painter, Writer

Castine

Ortman, George Earl. Painter, Sculptor

Cushing

Langlais, Bernard. Sculptor, Painter

Damariscotta

Melville, Grevis Whitaker. Painter, Printmaker

Deer Isle

Merritt, Francis Sumner. Painter, Designer

Hancock

Holmbom, James William. Painter

Harborside

McCloskey, Robert. Painter, Illustrator

Hiram

Merrill, David Kenneth. Painter, Instructor

Kennebunkport

Deering, Roger. Painter, Lecturer
Penney, Bruce Darton. Painter

Lincolnville

Welliver, Neil G. Painter

Newcastle

Coggeshall, Calvert. Painter

North Berwick

Hardy, (Clarion) Dewitt. Painter, Art Administrator

Ogunquit

Bartok, John Anthony. Painter
Hallam, Beverly (Linney). Painter, Lecturer
Smart, Mary-Leigh. Collector, Patron
Strater, Henry. Painter
Thelin, Valfred P. Painter, Lecturer

Orono

Hartgen, Vincent Andrew. Painter, Educator
Lewis, Michael H. Painter, Educator

Pleasant Point

Collins, John Ireland. Painter

Port Clyde

Thon, William. Painter

Portland

Dole, George. Cartoonist, Painter

Rockland

Hadlock, Wendell Stanwood. Art Administrator

Rockport

Winters, Denny. Painter

Round Pond

Jackovich, Anthony. Painter

South Harpswell

Burchess, Arnold. Painter, Sculptor
Etnier, Stephen Morgan. Painter

South Thomaston

Spaulding, Warren Dan. Painter, Educator

Stonington

Muir, Emily Lansingh. Painter, Designer

Vinalhaven

McClellan, Robert John. Painter, Illustrator

Waterville

Carpenter, James Morton. Educator, Art Historian

West Boothbay Harbor

Hemenway, Nancy (Mrs Robert D Barton). Painter, Designer

Winter Harbor

Browne, Syd J. Painter

Wiscasset

Laurine (Virginia Laurine Grover). Painter

York

Laurent, John Louis. Painter, Educator

MARYLAND

Annapolis

Schlecht, Richard. Painter, Illustrator

Baltimore

Allwell, Stephen S. Sculptor
Berge, (Edward) Henry. Sculptor
Bilcher, A Earle. Painter
Coplan, Kate M. Designer, Writer

Crosby, Ranice. Medical Illustrator, Educator
Embry, Norris. Painter
Erbe, Joan (Mrs Joan Erbe Udel). Painter
Fendell, Jonas J. Educator, Painter
Ford, John Gilmore. Collector
Freudenheim, Tom Lippman N. Art Administrator
Friedman, Stanley. Painter, Instructor
Gallagher, Edward J, Jr. Collector
Gorski, Daniel Alexander. Sculptor, Painter
Hartigan, Grace. Painter
Hill, Dorothy Kent. Museum Curator
Hoffman, Harry Zee. Painter
Ireland, Richard Wilson (Dick). Painter, Instructor
King, Edward S. Art Administrator
Klitzke, Theodore Elmer. Educator, Art Historian
Kramer, Reuben. Sculptor
Leake, Eugene W. Painter, Art Administrator
Maril, Herman. Painter, Educator
Martin, Keith Morrow. Painter
Miner, Dorothy Eugenia. Museum Curator, Art Historian
Mitchell, John Blair. Painter, Educator
Montenegro, Enrique E. Painter
Moscatt, Paul N. Painter, Instructor
Oppenheimer, Selma L. Painter
Quisgard, Liz Whitney. Painter, Sculptor
Rembski, Stanislav. Painter, Writer
Rosen, Israel. Collector
Rosenthal, Gertrude. Art Historian, Art Administrator
Satorsky, Cyril. Printmaker, Illustrator
Scuris, Stephanie. Sculptor, Educator
Shackelford, Shelby. Painter
Sheppard, Joseph Sherly. Painter, Sculptor
Streett, Tylden Westcott. Sculptor, Educator
Turnbull, Grace Hill. Sculptor, Painter
Walter, Valerie Harrisse. Sculptor
Yates, Sharon Deborah. Painter

Bethesda

Allin, B Warren, Jr. Painter
Apostolides, Zoe. Painter
Ayoroa, Rodolfo (Rudy) E. Painter
Desind, Philip. Art Dealer, Collector
Hauser, Richard. Painter
Safer, John. Sculptor

Bozman

Ernst, James Arnold. Painter, Instructor

Cambridge

Garbisch, Edgar William & Bernice Chrysler. Collectors

Chevy Chase

Asher, Lila Oliver. Printmaker, Educator
Fruhauf, Aline. Painter, Printmaker
Kainen, Jacob. Painter, Printmaker
Wier, Gordon D (Don). Designer, Painter

College Park

Levitine, George. Educator, Art Historian

Emmitsburg

Jungwirth, Irene Gayas. Painter, Designer

Frederick

Gates, Harry Irving. Sculptor, Painter
Russo, Alexander Peter. Painter, Educator
Wallace, David Harold. Art Historian, Art Administrator

Gaithersburg

Bolton, Mimi Du Bois. Painter, Lecturer

Garrett Park

Stites, Raymond Somers. Art Historian, Writer

Hagerstown

Roberts, Clyde Harry. Painter, Educator
Warner, Harry Backer, Jr. Writer

Hampstead

Doster, Rose Wilhelm. Painter, Sculptor

Lanham

Christensen, Erwin Ottomar. Art Historian, Writer

Linthicum Heights

Paul, Bernard H. Craftsman

New Windsor

Mose, Carl C. Sculptor, Lecturer
Still, Clyfford. Painter

Owings Mills

Kissel, William Thorn, Jr. Sculptor

Oxon Hill

Bucci, Andrew A. Painter

Potomac

De Weldon, Felix George Weihs. Sculptor, Architect

Reisterstown

Tunis, Edwin. Writer, Illustrator

Rockville

Edwards, Ellender Morgan. Printmaker, Photographer
Wood, James Arthur (Art). Cartoonist, Lecturer

Silver Spring

Cohen, Harold Larry. Designer, Lecturer
Isen, Harold Bernard. Sculptor, Printmaker
Karaberi, Marianthe. Sculptor, Painter
Lynch, James Burr, Jr. Art Historian

Stevenson

Wurtzburger, Janet E C. Collector, Patron

MASSACHUSETTS

Amherst

Grillo, John. Painter
Matheson, Donald Roy. Printmaker, Educator
Morgan, Charles H. Writer, Educator
Norton, Paul Foote. Art Historian, Educator
Roskill, Mark Wentworth. Art Historian, Art Critic
Schmalz, Carl (Nelson), (Jr). Painter, Educator
Wardlaw, George Melvin. Painter

Andover

Dalton, Frances Louisa. Painter, Instructor
Hayes, Bartlett Harding, Jr. Art Administrator, Writer

Arlington

Dahill, Thomas Henry, Jr. Painter, Educator
Rosenberg, Jakob. Writer, Educator

Bedford

Weeks, James (Darrell) (Northrup). Painter

Belmont

Reynolds, Joseph Gardiner. Designer
Valier, Biron (Frank). Painter, Printmaker

Bernardston

Sloane, Mary (Humphreys). Painter

Beverly

Broudo, Joseph David. Educator, Ceramist

Boston

Aronson, David. Painter, Sculptor
Capp, Al. Cartoonist
Carmack, Paul R. Cartoonist
Cataldo, John William. Educator, Film Maker
Coletti, Joseph Arthur. Sculptor, Writer
Cormier, Robert John. Painter, Instructor
Cox, Gardner. Painter
Crite, Allan Rohan. Painter, Illustrator
Danikian, Caron Le Brun. Writer, Art Critic
Driscoll, Edgar Joseph, Jr. Art Critic
Fairbanks, Jonathan Leo. Art Administrator
Fillman, Jesse R. Collector
Fink, Alan. Art Dealer
Fortess, Karl Eugene. Painter, Printmaker
Gaither, Edmund B. Art Administrator, Art Historian
Ghikas, Panos George. Painter, Educator
Gibran, Kahlil George. Sculptor
Hunter, Robert Douglas. Painter, Instructor
Kanegis, Sidney S. Art Dealer
Kramer, Jack N. Painter, Educator
Lent, Blair. Illustrator, Writer
Lewis, Elma Ina. Art Administrator
McAndrew, John. Art Historian, Educator
Moeller, Robert Charles, III. Art Historian, Art Administrator

Nick, George. Painter, Educator
Peabody, Amelia. Sculptor
Pezzatti, Pietro. Painter
Pucker, Bernard H. Art Dealer
Reardon, Mary A. Painter
Robb, Mr & Mrs Sidney R. Collectors
Salmon, Larry. Curator
Sayre, Eleanor Axson. Curator
Schwartz, Henry. Painter, Instructor
Searles, Stephen. Sculptor, Instructor
Swarzenski, Hanns Peter. Art Historian, Writer
Swirnoff, Lois (Lois Swirnoff Charney). Painter, Lecturer
Vermeule, Cornelius Clarkson, III. Art Historian, Writer
Wick, Peter Arms. Curator
Zahn, Carl Frederick. Designer, Art Administrator

Bradford

Burgy, (Donald) (Thomas). Conceptual Artist

Brewster

Stoltenberg, Donald Hugo. Painter, Printmaker

Brookline

Ablow, Joseph. Painter, Educator
Alcalay, Albert S. Painter
Barron, Harris. Sculptor
Barron, Ros. Painter
Cox, Jan. Painter
Little, Nina Fletcher. Collector, Art Historian
McKibben, Teal. Painter
Nagano, Paul Tatsumi. Painter, Designer
Pineda, Marianna (Marianna Pineda Tovish). Sculptor
Powers, Marilyn. Painter
Swan, Barbara. Painter
Tovish, Harold. Sculptor
Walker, Mrs Philip. Collector

Cambridge

Agoos, Herbert M. Collector
Andersen, Wayne Vesti. Art Historian, Educator
Arnheim, Rudolf. Educator, Writer
Burgess, David Lowry. Painter
Constable, William George. Art Historian, Writer
Coolidge, John. Art Historian, Educator
Deknatel, Frederick Brockway. Art Historian, Educator
Feininger, T Lux. Painter, Writer
Freedberg, Sydney Joseph. Art Historian, Educator
Garvey, Eleanor. Art Administrator
Hanfmann, George M A. Museum Curator, Educator
Hyde, Andrew Cornwall. Art Administrator, Art Consultant
Kepes, Gyorgy. Painter, Educator
Kitzinger, Ernst. Art Historian
Loehr, Max. Museum Curator, Educator
Mazur, Michael B. Painter, Printmaker
Mongan, Agnes. Art Administrator, Art Historian
Neuman, Robert S. Painter, Lecturer
Paeff, Bashka (Bashka Paeff Waxman). Sculptor
Preusser, Robert Ormerod. Painter, Educator
Rabb, Mr & Mrs Irving W. Collectors.
Rathbone, Perry Townsend. Museum Director

Reimann, William P(age). Sculptor, Educator
Rey, H A. Illustrator, Writer
Robbins, Daniel J. Art Historian, Educator
Schroeder, Eric. Museum Curator, Writer
Slive, Seymour. Educator, Writer
Welch, Stuart Cary. Museum Curator

Charlestown

MacLean-Smith, Elizabeth. Sculptor, Lecturer

Charlottesville

Barbee, Robert Thomas. Painter, Graphic Artist

Chatham

Hovey, Walter Read. Art Historian, Lecturer
Orr, Elliot. Painter

Cheshire

Blake, Leo B. Illustrator, Instructor

Chestnut Hill

Plaut, James S. Art Administrator, Writer
Saltonstall, Elizabeth. Painter

Cohasset

Kowal, Dennis J. Sculptor

Conway

Mallary, Robert. Sculptor, Educator

Dartmouth

Sylvia, Louis. Painter

Deerfield

Maniatty, Stephen George. Painter

Dennis

Geissbuhler, Arnold. Sculptor

Duxbury

Bengtz, Ture. Museum Director, Painter

East Weymouth

Wyman, William. Craftsman

Fitchburg

Harris, Mrs Mason Dix. Museum Director

Framingham Center

Schiff, Lonny. Painter, Printmaker

Gloucester

Aarons, George. Sculptor

Gloucester (cont)

Duca, Alfred Milton. Sculptor, Painter
Gage, Harry (Lawrence). Painter, Educator
Grasso, Doris (Ten-Eyck). Painter, Sculptor
Hancock, Walker (Kirtland). Sculptor
Jeswald, Joseph. Painter
Liszt, Maria Veronica. Painter, Designer
Shore, Mary. Painter

Harvard

Chaudhuri, Patricia M. Sculptor, Painter

Harwich

Gilbertson, (Bernice) Charlotte. Painter
Sahrbeck, Everett William. Painter

Haydenville

Gillespie, Gregory Joseph. Painter

Huntington

Stankiewicz, Richard Peter. Sculptor, Educator

Hyde Park

Pinardi, Enrico Vittorio. Sculptor, Painter

Ipswich

Ericson, Susan Kunce. Designer, Painter

Lenox

Hatch, John Davis. Art Consultant, Art Historian

Lexington

Bakanowsky, Louis J. Sculptor, Designer
Cascieri, Arcangelo. Sculptor, Educator
Filipowski, Richard E. Sculptor, Educator

Lincoln

Steczynski, John Myron. Sculptor, Educator
Walkey, Frederick P. Museum Director

Longmeadow

Catok, Lottie Meyer. Painter
Robinson, Frederick B. Art Administrator
Watkins, Louise Lochridge. Museum Director, Lecturer

Manchester

Lothrop, Kristin Curtis. Sculptor
Weems, Katharine Lane. Sculptor

Marblehead

Chamberlain, Samuel. Printmaker, Writer
Taylor, Robert. Art Critic, Writer

Marion

Mellor, George Edward. Educator, Sculptor

Marshfield

Greenamyer, George Mossman. Sculptor, Educator

Montague

Coughlin, Jack. Graphic Artist, Printmaker
Kamys, Walter. Painter, Educator

Nantucket

Schaeffler, Lizbeth. Sculptor, Ceramist
Shunney, Andrew. Painter
Weeber, Gretchen. Painter

Nantucket Island

Maguire, Charles. Art Dealer
Perrin, C Robert. Painter, Illustrator

Natick

Abany, Albert Charles. Painter, Educator
Geller, Esther (Esther Geller Shapero). Painter, Printmaker

New Bedford

Frauwirth, Sidney. Collector
Smith, David Loeffler. Painter, Educator

Newburyport

Pride, Joy. Painter, Writer

Newton

Bahm, Henry. Painter
Grippe, Florence (Berg). Painter, Potter
Grippe, Peter J. Sculptor, Printmaker
Laliberte, Norman. Painter
Siporin, Mitchell. Painter, Educator
Vershbow, Mr & Mrs Arthur. Collectors

Newton Center

Glaser, Samuel. Collector

Newton Centre

Cobb, Ruth. Painter
Kupferman, Lawrence. Painter

Newtonville

Dahl, Francis W. Cartoonist
Polonsky, Arthur. Painter, Educator
Skinner, Orin Ensign. Designer

North Andover

Whitehill, Walter Muir. Writer, Art Historian

North Brookfield

Neal, (Minor) Avon. Writer, Printmaker
Parker, Ann (Ann Parker Neal). Photographer, Printmaker

North Tewksbury

Kaufman, Mico. Sculptor, Writer

North Truro

Allen, Courtney. Illustrator, Sculptor
Bassford, Wallace. Painter, Instructor

Northampton

Baskin, Leonard. Sculptor, Graphic Artist
Chetham, Charles. Museum Director
Cohen, H George. Painter, Educator
Offner, Elliot. Sculptor, Calligrapher
Van Der Poel, Priscilla Paine. Educator, Painter

Norton

Bush, Lucile Elizabeth. Painter, Educator

Norwell

Wentworth, Murray Jackson. Painter, Instructor

Onset

Halberstadt, Ernst. Painter, Sculptor

Pepperell

Cooney, Barbara (Mrs. Charles Talbot Porter). Illustrator, Writer

Pittsfield

Henry, Stuart (Compton). Museum Director, Painter

Provincetown

Davidson, Morris. Painter, Art Administrator
De Nagy, Eva. Painter
Forsberg, James Alfred. Painter, Printmaker
Hensche, Henry. Painter, Instructor
Jensen, Marit. Painter, Serigrapher
Kaplan, Joseph. Painter
Malicoat, Philip Cecil. Painter
Rizk, Romanos. Painter, Instructor
Stout, Myron Stedman. Painter

Quincy

White, Leo. Cartoonist

Reading

Nordstrand, Nathalie Johnson. Painter

Rockport

Andrus, Vera Eugenia. Painter, Lithographer
Callahan, Jack. Painter, Instructor
Davidson, Allan Albert. Painter, Sculptor
Gabin, George Joseph. Painter, Educator
Gellman, Beah (Mrs William C McNulty). Painter, Sculptor
LaFreniere, Isabel Marcotte. Painter
Martin, Roger. Painter, Graphic Artist
Morrell, Wayne (Beam). Painter

Murphy, Gladys Wilkins. Painter, Craftsman
Murphy, Herbert A. Architect, Painter
Nicholas, Thomas Andrew. Painter
Parsons, Kitty (Kitty Parsons Recchia). Painter, Writer
Pearson, Marguerite Stuber. Painter
Recchia, Richard (Henry). Sculptor
Ricci, Jerri. Painter
Schlemm, Betty Lou. Painter
Stoffa, Michael. Painter, Lecturer
Strisik, Paul. Painter
Turner, Bruce Backman. Painter

Roxbury

Avedisian, Edward. Painter
Cox, J W S. Painter, Instructor

Salem

Dodge, Ernest Stanley. Museum Director

Sharon

Avakian, John. Painter, Educator
Brewington, Marion Vernon. Art Historian, Writer
Edmonds, Nicholas Biddle (Nick). Sculptor

Sherborn

Pickhardt, Carl. Painter

Shrewsbury

Jewell, Kester Donald. Museum Curator

Somerville

Brown, Paul Louis. Painter
Corish, Joseph Ryan. Painter

South Easton

Brenner, Mabel. Painter

South Hadley

Cogswell, Dorothy McIntosh. Educator, Painter
DeLonga, Leonard Anthony. Sculptor, Educator
Hayes, Marian. Educator, Art Historian

South Hamilton

Croft, Lewis Scott. Painter

South Yarmouth

True, Virginia. Painter, Educator

Springfield

Reichert, Donald O. Painter, Art Administrator

Stockbridge

Cresson, Margaret French. Sculptor, Writer
Kepets, Hugh Michael. Painter
Rockwell, Norman. Illustrator

Swansea

Doyle, Edward A. Illustrator, Painter

Topsfield

Webster, Larry Russell. Designer, Painter

Truro

Craig, Nancy Ellen. Painter
Preston, Malcolm H. Art Critic, Painter
Yater, George David. Painter, Art Administrator

Tyringham

Davis, Donald Robert. Painter, Art Dealer
Picken, George. Painter, Printmaker

Vineyard Haven

Berresford, Virginia. Painter, Art Dealer
Graves, Maitland. Writer, Painter

Waltham

Keyes, Bernard M. Painter

Ware

Chase, Alice Elizabeth. Educator, Writer

Watertown

Hicken, Philip Burnham. Painter, Educator

Wayland

Bentov, Mirtala. Sculptor
Dergalis, George. Painter

Wellesley

Rayen, James Wilson. Painter, Instructor

Wellfleet

Dickinson, Edwin. Painter
Wilkinson, Kirk Cook. Art Dealer, Painter

West Newton

Burnett, Calvin. Painter, Educator
Williams, Gluyas. Illustrator, Cartoonist

West Tisbury

Scott, Henry (Edwards), Jr. Painter, Educator

Westborough

Bissell, (Charles) Phil. Cartoonist, Illustrator

Weston

Shepler, Dwight (Clark). Painter, Writer

Westwood

Philbrick, Margaret Elder. Printmaker, Painter
Philbrick, Otis. Painter, Printmaker

Williamstown

Bloedel, Lawrence Hotchkiss. Collector
Cunningham, Charles Crehore. Curator, Collector
Faison, Samson Lane, Jr. Museum Director, Educator
Hamilton, George Heard. Museum Director, Art Historian
Rudolph, Mr & Mrs C Frederick. Collectors
Stoddard, Whitney Snow. Art Historian

Worcester

Cronin, Robert (Lawrence). Sculptor
Dresser, Louisa. Art Administrator, Art Historian
Elliott, Bruce Roger. Printmaker, Educator
Farber, George W. Collector
Graziani, Sante. Painter, Designer
Hovsepian, Leon. Painter, Designer
Nigrosh, Leon Isaac. Designer, Instructor
Riley, Chapin. Collector
Shulman, Leon. Art Curator
Teitz, Richard Stuart. Art Administrator, Art Historian

Yarmouth Port

Rowlands, Tom. Painter, Designer

MICHIGAN

Ada

Collins, Kreigh. Illustrator

Albion

Bobbitt, Vernon L. Painter, Educator

Ann Arbor

Cassara, Frank. Painter, Printmaker
Eisenberg, Marvin. Art Historian, Educator
Gooch, Donald Burnette. Educator, Painter
Iglehart, Robert L. Educator
Kamrowski, Gerome. Painter, Educator
La More, Chet Harmon. Painter, Sculptor
Lewis, William Arthur. Painter, Art Administrator
McClure, Thomas F. Sculptor, Educator
McMillan, Constance. Painter
Reider, David H. Designer, Photographer
Sawyer, Charles Henry. Museum Director
Stephenson, John H. Sculptor, Educator
Weber, Albert Jacob. Painter, Educator
Weddige, Emil. Lithographer, Educator
Wethey, Harold Edwin. Art Historian

Birmingham

Fredericks, Marshall Maynard. Sculptor
Kozlow, Richard. Painter, Lecturer
Malbin, Lydia Winston. Collector
Michaels, Glen. Sculptor, Painter
Sepeshy, Zoltan L. Painter, Educator
Thom, Robert Alan. Illustrator, Painter

Bloomfield Hills

De Lawter, Dr & Mrs Hilbert H. Collectors
Grotell, Maija. Ceramist, Educator
Mitchell, Wallace (MacMahon). Museum
    Director, Painter
Peterson, John Douglas. Art Administra-
    tor, Designer
West, Clifford Bateman. Painter, Film
    Maker

Coloma

Martmer, William P. Painter, Photographer

Detroit

Arwin, Lester B. Art Dealer
Barron, Mrs S Brooks. Collector
Binai, Paul Freye. Painter, Art Curator
Bostick, William Allison. Painter, Art
    Administrator
Broner, Robert. Printmaker, Painter
Cartmell, Helen. Painter
Cummings, Frederick James. Art Admin-
    istrator, Art Historian
Driver, Morley (Brooke Lister). Art Critic,
    Collector
Elam, Charles Henry. Art Administrator
Golden, Libby. Printmaker, Painter
Hall, Michael David. Sculptor, Educator
Johnson, Lester L. Painter, Instructor
Kachadoorian, Zubel. Painter, Educator
Kasle, Gertrude. Art Dealer, Collector
Krentzin, Earl. Sculptor, Silversmith
Mandzuik, Michael Dennis. Painter, Print-
    maker
Midener, Walter. Sculptor, Instructor
Miles, Cyril. Painter, Instructor
Morris, Donald Fischer. Art Dealer
Sarkis (Sarkis Sarkisian). Painter
Schuster, Eugene Ivan. Art Dealer, Art
    Historian
Wheeler, Robert G. Art Administrator
Wilbert, Robert John. Painter, Educator
Woods, Willis Franklin. Museum Director

Dexter

Mason, Alice Frances. Lithographer,
    Painter

East Lansing

Alexander, Robert Seymour. Educator,
    Designer
Brainard, Owen. Painter, Educator
Church, C Howard. Painter, Educator
Henricksen, Ralf Christian. Educator,
    Painter

Flint

Davidek, William Stefan. Painter
Hodge, G Stuart. Museum Director

Grand Rapids

Forslund, Carl Victor, Jr. Painter
Inslee, Marguerite T. Painter, Collector
Koster, Marjory Jean. Printmaker
McBride, Walter Henry. Art Administra-
    tor
Myers, Fred A. Art Administrator
Perkins, Mabel H. Collector
Weidenaar, Reynold Henry. Etcher, Painter

Grosse Pointe

Smith, Jerome Irving. Museum Curator,
    Librarian

Highland Park

Brose, Morris. Sculptor

Kalamazoo

Greaver, Hanne. Printmaker
Greaver, Harry. Art Administrator,
    Painter
Kemper, John Garner. Educator, Designer

Mackinac Island

Harsh, Richard. Painter, Educator

Mason

Leepa, Allen. Painter, Educator

Midland

Breed, Charles Ayars. Sculptor, Educator

Oak Park

Barr, David John. Sculptor, Painter
Iden, Sheldon. Painter, Educator

Okemos

Brauner, Erling Bernhardt. Painter,
    Educator
Love, Paul Van Derveer. Gallery Direc-
    tor, Art Historian
Whitaker, Irwin A. Educator, Craftsman

Rochester

Brun, Thomas. Sculptor, Instructor

West Bloomfield

Simper, Frederick. Painter

Whitmore Lake

Davis, Philip Charles. Photographer,
    Educator

MINNESOTA

Burnsville

Wilson, Tom Muir. Designer

Collegeville

Petheo, Bela Francis. Painter, Educator

Duluth

Boyce, William G. Art Administrator, Edu-
    cator
Munoz, Freddy Marcel. Painter

Ely

Gawboy, Carl. Painter

Good Thunder

Tanner, James L. Craftsman

Hastings

Koestner, Don. Painter

Mankato

Artis, William Ellisworth. Educator, Cera-
    mist

Minneapolis

Arnold, Richard R. Designer, Painter
Asher, Frederick M. Art Historian
Bates, Charles T, Jr. Painter
Booth, Cameron. Painter
Bowron, Edgar Peters. Art Administrator,
    Art Historian
Busa, Peter. Painter, Sculptor
Caglioti, Victor. Painter, Sculptor
Clark, Anthony Morris. Museum Director,
    Collector
Dayton, Bruce B. Collector
Fossum, Sydney (Glenn). Painter, Illustra-
    tor
Friedman, Martin. Museum Director
Granlund, Paul Theodore. Sculptor, Instruc-
    tor
Hendler, Raymond. Painter, Sculptor
Herstand, Arnold. Painter, Art Administra-
    tor
Justus, Roy Braxton. Cartoonist
Larkin, Eugene. Printmaker, Educator
McCannel, Mrs Malcolm A. Collector
Mandle, Earl Roger. Art Administrator,
    Art Historian
Maurer, Evan Maclyn. Art Historian, Art
    Administrator
Morris, Edward A. Painter, Illustrator
Munzer, Aribert. Painter, Educator
Myers, Malcolm Haynie. Printmaker,
    Painter
Nash, Katherine E. Sculptor, Educator
Poor, Robert John. Art Historian
Preuss, Roger. Painter, Writer
Quick, Birney MacNabb. Painter, Educa-
    tor
Rose, Thomas Albert. Sculptor
Rowan, Herman. Painter, Educator
Rudquist, Jerry Jacob. Painter, Educator
Sachs, Samuel, II. Art Administrator, Art
    Historian
Saltzman, William. Painter, Designer
Sheppard, Carl Dunkle. Art Historian
Simon, Sidney. Educator, Art Historian
Slettehaugh, Thomas Chester. Painter,
    Educator
Smith, Justin V. Art Administrator, Col-
    lector
Swanson, Dean. Museum Curator
Torbert, Marguerite Birch. Designer,
    Writer
Walton, Florence Goodstein (Goodstein-
    Shapiro). Painter, Art Historian
Wedin, Elof. Painter
Wolfe Ann (Ann Wolfe Graubard). Sculptor,
    Instructor

Minnetonka

Lack, Richard Frederick. Painter, In-
    structor

Moorhead

Boe, Roy Asbjörn. Art Historian, Educator
Youngquist, John. Draftsman

Red Wing

Biederman, Charles (Karel Joseph). Sculptor, Painted Aluminum

St. Paul

Bobleter, Lowell Stanley. Educator, Painter
Boese, Alvin William. Researcher, Collector
Caponi, Anthony. Sculptor, Educator
Celender, Donald Dennis. Art Historian, Painter
Grey, Mrs Benjamin Edwards. Collector, Patron
Kielkopf, James Robert. Painter
Leach, Frederick Darwin. Painter, Art Historian
Lein, Malcolm Emil. Art Administrator, Designer
Myhr, Dean Andrew. Art Administrator
Niemeyer, Arnold Matthew. Collector, Patron
Rahja, Virginia Helga. Painter, Educator
Smith, Paul Roland. Painter, Educator
Tselos, Dimitri Theodore. Art Historian, Writer
Wheeler, Cleora Clark. Designer, Collector

St. Peter

Buranabunpot, Pornpilai. Designer

Winona

Korpela, Edward S. Painter, Educator
Murray, Floretta May. Painter, Educator

MISSISSIPPI

Bay St Louis

Kimbrough, (Sara) Dodge. Painter

Cleveland

Norwood, Malcolm Mark. Painter, Educator

Columbus

Ambrose, Charles Edward. Painter
Dice, Elizabeth Jane. Craftsman, Educator
Stringer, Mary Evelyn. Educator, Art Historian
Summer, (Emily) Eugenia. Painter, Sculptor

Jackson

Hull, Marie (Atkinson). Painter
Tennyson, Merle Berry. Painter, Instructor

McComb

Holmes, Ruth Atkinson. Painter, Sculptor

Oxford

Hamblett, Theora. Painter, Illustrator
Tettleton, Robert Lynn. Painter, Educator

Silver City

Slaughter, Lurline Eddy. Painter

Steens

Frank, David. Potter, Educator

Summit

Barnes, Halcyone D. Painter
Dawson, Bess Phipps. Painter, Art Dealer

University

Winters, John L. Painter, Printmaker

MISSOURI

Cape Girardeau

Bedford, Helen De Wilton. Educator

Columbia

Fernie, John Chipman. Sculptor, Instructor
Larson, Sidney. Painter, Sculptor
McKinin, Lawrence. Educator, Painter

Gower

Nichols, Jeannettie Doornhein. Painter, Instructor

Kansas City

Benton, Thomas Hart. Painter, Writer
Carstenson, Cecil C. Sculptor, Lecturer
Clare, Stewart. Research Artist, Lecturer
Dowling, Daniel Blair. Editorial Cartoonist
Hall, Joyce C. Collector
James, Frederic. Painter
McKim, William Wind. Printmaker, Painter
Roth, James Buford. Art Restorer, Painter
Selonke, Irene A. Painter
Sickman, Laurence Chalfont Stevens. Art Administrator, Art Historian
Stephens, Nancy Anne. Sculptor, Film Maker
Stephens, Thomas Michael. Sculptor, Designer
Townsend, Marvin J. Cartoonist

Kirkwood

Reinhardt, Siegfried Gerhard. Painter, Designer

Maryville

Sunkel, Robert Cleveland. Art Historian, Sculptor

St. Charles

Eckert, William Dean. Painter, Art Historian

St. Louis

Bauer, William. Painter, Illustrator
Betsberg, Ernestine (Mrs Arthur Osver). Painter

Buckley, Charles Edward. Art Administrator, Art Historian
Conway, Fred. Painter, Educator
Duhme, H Richard, Jr. Sculptor, Educator
Hudson, Kenneth Eugene. Painter, Educator
Jones, Howard William. Painter, Sculptor
Krukowski, Lucian. Painter, Educator
May, Morton David. Collector, Patron
Osver, Arthur. Painter
Palmer, Lucie Mackay. Painter, Lecturer
Pulitzer, Joseph, Jr. Collector
Smith, Helen M. Illustrator, Painter
Trova, Ernest Tino. Sculptor, Painter
Weil, Mr & Mrs Richard K. Collectors

Springfield

Albin, Edgar A. Educator, Art Critic
Shuck, Kenneth Menaugh. Art Administrator, Painter

Warrensburg

Ellis, Edwin Charles. Educator

Webster Groves

Boccia, Edward Eugene. Painter, Craftsman

MONTANA

Bigfork

Morgan, Darlene. Painter

Billings

Morrison, Robert Clifton. Printmaker, Painter
Ralston, J(ames) K(enneth). Painter, Illustrator
Whitson (Peter Whitson Warren). Drawer, Educator

Bozeman

Bashor, John W. Educator, Painter

Browning

Scriver, Robert Macfie (Bob). Sculptor

Butte

Lochrie, Elizabeth. Painter, Sculptor
Taulbee, Dan J. Painter, Art Dealer

Great Falls

Cordingley, Mary Bowles. Painter
Gay, Eric Lynn. Painter, Photographer
Stevenson, Branson Graves. Painter, Designer

Missoula

Boussard, Dana. Sculptor
Dew, James Edward. Educator, Painter
Eder, Earl. Painter
Hook, Walter. Painter, Educator

Rollins

Lebkicher, Anne Ross. Painter, Art Administrator

NEBRASKA

Fremont

Hopkins, Ruth Joy. Painter

Kearney

Peterson, Larry D. Painter, Educator

Lexington

Sheldon, Olga N. Patron, Collector

Lincoln

Geske, Norman Albert. Art Administrator
Laging, Duard Walter. Educator
Lux, Gladys Marie. Painter
Seyler, David W. Sculptor, Educator
Wells, Fred N. Executive Director
Woods, Sarah Ladd. Collector, Patron
Worth, Peter John. Sculptor, Art Historian

Omaha

Blackwell, John Victor. Art Historian, Educator
Hammon, Bill J. Painter, Sculptor
Hill, Peter. Painter, Educator
Lubbers, Leland Eugene. Sculptor, Educator
McGonagle, William Albert. Art Administrator
Merriam, John F. Trustee
Thiessen, (Charles) Leonard. Art Administrator, Writer
Wolsky, Milton Laban. Illustrator, Painter

Shelby

Duren, Terence Romaine. Painter, Illustrator

Wayne

Lesh, Richard D. Painter, Instructor

NEVADA

Las Vegas

Lesnick, Stephen William. Painter, Instructor
Terry, Emalita Newton. Painter, Instructor
Wojinski, Francis Ann, O P. Printmaker, Educator

Reno

Cooper, Phillis. Sculptor
Jacobson, Yolande (Mrs J Craig Sheppard). Sculptor
Sheppard, John Craig. Painter, Educator
Unterseher, Chris Christian. Sculptor

NEW HAMPSHIRE

Concord

Barrett, Thomas R. Painter, Instructor
Chandler, John William. Painter, Educator
Hoffmann, Lilly Elisabeth. Weaver, Instructor
Mancuso, Leni (Leni Mancuso Barrett). Painter, Instructor

Dublin

Smith, Ray Winfield. Collector, Art Historian

Dunbarton

Williams, Gerald. Sculptor, Potter

Durham

Hatch, John W. Painter, Educator
Thomas, George R. Educator, Designer
Zabarsky, Melvin Joel. Painter, Educator

Exeter

Lyford, Cabot. Sculptor, Educator

Francestown

Milton, Peter Winslow. Printmaker

Hancock

Dombek, Blanche M. Sculptor

Hanover

Beckmann, Hannes. Painter, Educator
Boghosian, Varujan. Sculptor, Educator
Brackett, Truman H, Jr. Art Administrator, Educator
Coffey, Karita Joyce. Ceramist
Lathrop, Churchill Pierce. Educator, Gallery Director
Nash, Ray. Art Historian

Harrisville

Harris, Paul Stewart. Art Administrator, Art Historian

Keene

Lourie, Herbert S. Painter, Educator

Lyme

Schmeckebier, Laurence E. Sculptor, Educator

Manchester

Brooke, David Stopford. Museum Director
Eshoo, Robert. Painter

Mason

Jones, Elizabeth Orton. Illustrator, Writer

Meredith

Montana, Bob. Cartoonist

Nashua

Hillman, Arthur Staneey. Printmaker, Educator

Northwood

Abeles, Sigmund. Printmaker, Sculptor

Peterborough

Greenleaf, Esther (Hargrave). Painter, Serigrapher
Unwin, Nora Spicer. Painter, Printmaker

Portsmouth

Labrie, Rose. Painter, Writer

Sunapee

Livingstone, Biganess. Painter

Tamworth

Breasted, James Henry, Jr. Art Historian, Lecturer
Olds, Elizabeth. Painter, Printmaker

Warner

Nemec, Nancy. Printmaker

Webster

Tudor, Tasha. Illustrator, Writer

NEW JERSEY

Asbury

Anderson, John S. Sculptor
Konrad, Adolf Ferdinand. Painter

Asbury Park

Cleary, Fritz. Sculptor, Art Critic

Avalon

Gill, Frederick James. Painter, Educator

Barnegat Light

Rothman, Sidney. Art Dealer, Art Critic

Bayonne

Gary, Jan (Mrs William D Gorman). Painter, Printmaker
Gorman, William D. Painter

Belleville

Yudin, Carol. Printmaker, Painter

Berkeley Heights

Hofer, Ingrid (Ingeborg). Painter, Instructor
Lorentz, Pauline. Painter, Instructor

Blairstown

Lenney, Annie. Painter

Bloomfield

Schwacha, George. Painter

Butler

Angelini, John Michael. Painter, Art Director
Law, Pauline Elizabeth. Painter

Caldwell

Lewis, Nat Brush. Painter, Instructor
Mueller, M Gerardine, O P. Sculpture, Educator

Cape May

Gilmore, Ethel (Mrs Charles J Romans). Painter, Instructor
Romans, Charles John. Painter

Chatham

Ellis, Ray G. Painter

Cherry Hill

Conrad, George. Educator, Painter

Chester

Sandol, Maynard. Painter

Cliffside Park

LaMarca, Howard J. Designer, Museum Director
Swarz, Sahl. Sculptor

Clifton

Rossi, Joseph O. Painter, Instructor

Colts Neck

Schweitzer, Gertrude. Painter, Sculptor

Convent

Moore, Fanny Hanna. Collector, Patron

Cranbury

Gould, Stephen. Sculptor, Art Administrator

Cranford

Dawley, Joseph William. Painter, Writer

Cresskill

Mayen, Paul. Designer
Radoczy, Albert. Painter
Tait, Katharine Lamb. Painter, Designer
Ward, Lynd (Kendall). Illustrator, Writer

Demarest

Racz, Andre. Painter, Educator

Denville

Agopoff, Agop Minass. Sculptor

Dover

Johnson, Avery Fischer. Painter, Instructor
Kearns, James Joseph. Sculptor, Painter
Sarsony, Robert. Painter, Printmaker

East Brunswick

Bloom, Donald Stanley. Painter
Bradshaw, Robert George. Painter, Educator
Cantor, Robert Lloyd. Educator, Designer
Maris, Valdi S. Painter, Instructor

East Orange

Schaffer, Rose. Painter, Lecturer

Englewood

Anuszkiewicz, Richard J. Painter
Bell, Enid. Sculptor, Educator
Casarella, Edmond. Graphic Artist, Painter
Grushkin, Philip. Designer, Instructor
Romano, Clare Camille. Printmaker, Painter
Ross, John T. Printmaker, Educator

Fair Lawn

Schwab, Eloisa (Mrs A H Rodriguez). Painter

Fanwood

Schott, Joseph John. Painter
Weeks, Leo Rosco. Painter, Illustrator

Finesville

Kozlow, Sigmund. Painter, Instructor

Fort Lee

Ortlip, Paul Daniel. Painter

Franklin Lakes

Bengert, Elwood George. Painter

Frenchtown

Beline, George. Painter, Sculptor

Gladstone

Duvoisin, Roger. Writer, Illustrator

Glassboro

Wasserman, Burton. Painter, Printmaker

Glen Gardner

Hunt, Kari. Sculptor, Writer

Glen Ridge

Jensen, Alfred. Painter
Kato, Kay. Cartoonist, Illustrator
Konopka, Joseph. Painter

Hackensack

Copeland, Lawrence Gill. Educator, Designer

Haddonfield

Sandecki, Albert Edward. Painter, Instructor

Hampton

Mordvinoff, Nicolas. Painter, Illustrator

Hasbrouck Heights

Perham, Roy Gates. Painter

Hawthorne

Calcia, Lillian Acton. Educator
Falconieri, Virginia. Painter, Instructor

Hazlet

Temes, Mortimer (Robert). Cartoonist, Designer

High Bridge

Burnett, Louis Anthony. Painter
Moore, Martha E (Mrs Louis A Burnett). Painter

Highland Park

Buros, Luella. Painter, Designer
Stoll, Toni. Painter

Hightstown

Upjohn, Everard Miller. Art Historian

Irvington

Grabach, John R. Painter, Educator

Jamesburg

Minnick, Esther Tress. Painter

Jersey City

Craft, Douglas D. Painter, Educator
Mazzone, Domenico. Sculptor, Painter
Mount, (Pauline) Ward. Painter, Sculptor
Murphy, Catherine E. Painter
Serra-Badue, Daniel. Painter, Educator
Stevens, Edward John, Jr. Painter, Educator

Kearney

Triano, Anthony Thomas. Painter, Art Administrator

Kinnelon

Whyte, Raymond A. Painter

Lakewood

du Cret, Dudley Vaughan. Art Administrator, Art Historian

Leonardo

De Lue, Donald. Sculptor

Leonia

Bogert, Grace Warren. Painter, Educator
Dickerson, Daniel Jay. Painter, Educator
Gehner, Marjorie Nielsen. Painter
Johnson, Selina (Tetzlaff). Museologist, Photographer

Lincroft

Voorhees, Donald Edward. Painter

Long Branch

Stamaty, Stanley. Cartoonist, Illustrator

Loveladies

Kelly, Leon. Painter

Madison

Fangor, Voy. Painter
Smith, R Harmer. Painter, Etcher

Manasquan

Markow, Jack. Cartoonist, Painter

Maplewood

Dee, Leo Joseph. Painter
Feldman, Hilda (Mrs Neville S Dickinson). Painter, Educator
Joffe, Bertha. Designer

Margate City

Myers, Legh. Sculptor

Mendham

Hobbie, Lucille. Painter, Illustrator
Notaro, Anthony. Sculptor

Metuchen

Stoianovich, Marcelle. Painter

Midland Park

Woodlock, Ethelyn Hurd. Painter

Milford

Carter, Clarence Holbrook. Painter, Designer

Millington

Keskulla, Carolyn Windeler. Painter, Printmaker

Montclair

Day, Wörden. Sculptor, Printmaker
De Leeuw, Leon. Painter, Sculptor
Gamble, Kathryn Elizabeth. Museum Director
Ordorica, Hilda Trull. Painter
Wingert, Paul Stover. Educator, Writer

Moorestown

Eisenstat, Benjamin. Painter, Illustrator

Morris Plains

Ferris, (Carlisle) Keith. Illustrator, Painter

Mountainside

Domareki, Joseph Theodore. Painter, Sculptor

New Brunswick

Neal, Reginald H. Painter, Educator

New Vernon

Bross, Albert L, Jr. Painter

Newark

Ayaso, Manuel. Painter, Sculptor
Baker, Mildred. Art Administrator
Baretski, Charles Allan. Art Librarian, Art Historian
Dane, William Jerald. Art Librarian
Jones, Benjamin Franklin. Painter, Sculptor
Miller, Samuel Clifford. Museum Director
Nugent, Arthur William. Cartoonist, Illustrator
Rabin, Bernard. Art Restorer

Newton

Kulicke, Robert M. Painter, Craftsman

North Bergen

Makarenko, Zachary Philipp. Painter, Sculptor

North Brunswick

Segal, George. Sculptor

North Haledon

Heusser, Eleanore Elizabeth. Painter

Nutley

Carlin, James. Painter

Oakland

Campanelli, Daniel. Painter, Illustrator
Campanelli, Pauline Eblé. Painter, Instructor
Rodman, Selden. Writer, Collector

Orange

Damron, John Clarence. Painter, Illustrator
Smith, Tony. Sculptor

Park Ridge

De Pol, John. Engraver, Designer

Passaic

Cowdrey, Mary Bartlett. Art Historian, Art Critic

Paterson

Politinsky, F Augusta (Flora). Painter, Sculptor
Tiffany, Marguerite Bristol. Painter, Weaver

Perth Amboy

Hari, Kenneth. Painter, Printmaker

Piscataway

Silkotch, Mary Ellen. Painter

Pitman

Ottiano, John William. Educator, Sculptor

Pittstown

Marsh, Anne Steele. Painter, Printmaker

Plainfield

De Leeuw, Cateau Wilhelmina. Painter, Writer
Graziano, Florence V Mercolino. Painter, Sculptor
Thompson, Paul Leland. Painter

Pluckemin

Hart, Morgan Drake. Painter, Instructor

Princeton

Bannard, Walter Darby. Painter, Art Critic
Brodsky, Judith Kapstein. Printmaker, Painter
Brown, Joseph. Sculptor, Educator
Forsyth, William H. Museum Curator, Writer
George, Thomas. Painter
Greenbaum, Dorothea Schwarcz. Sculptor
Harlow, Robert E. Painter, Instructor
Jones, Frances Follin. Museum Curator

Kelleher, Patrick Joseph. Art Administrator, Art Historian
Kuehn, Frances. Painter
Lee, Rensselaer Wright. Art Historian
McAlpin, David H. Collector
Meiss, Millard. Art Historian, Writer
Teller, Jane (Simon). Sculptor
Thompson, Dorothy Burr. Art Historian, Lecturer
Weitzmann, Kurt. Educator, Art Historian

Ramsey

Hertzberg, Rose. Painter, Printmaker

Ridgefield

Wilson, Ben. Painter, Lecturer

Ridgefield Park

Botto, Richard Alfred. Painter, Educator

Ridgewood

Whitmore, Lenore K. Painter

Ringwood

Backstrom, Florence (Florence Jennie Englert). Painter, Designer
Barbour, Arthur J. Painter, Illustrator

River Edge

Fish, George A. Painter

Roosevelt

Landau, Jacob. Painter, Printmaker
Prestopino, Gregorio. Painter

Roselle

Silins, Janis. Painter, Educator

Rosemont

Wheeler, Monroe. Art Administrator

Rumson

Cocker, Barbara J. Painter, Designer
Langston, Mr & Mrs Loyd H (Mildred J). Art Dealers, Collectors

Rutherford

Barnwell, John L. Painter
Laurer, Robert A. Educator
Petrie, Ferdinand Ralph. Painter, Designer

Scotch Plains

Simpson, Maxwell Stewart. Painter, Sculptor

Somerset

Zuccarelli, Frank Edward. Painter, Illustrator

South Orange

De Foix-Crenascol, Louis. Art Historian, Art Administrator
Gasser, Henry Martin. Painter, Writer
Lozowick, Louis. Painter, Printmaker
Schonwalter, Jean Frances. Painter, Instructor
Singer, Esther Forman. Painter, Art Critic

Springfield

Kaplan, Rhoda B. Painter, Instructor

Stockholm

Jauss, Anne Marie. Painter, Illustrator

Stockton

Farnham, Alexander. Painter, Writer

Summit

Palmer, Fred Loren. Collector, Patron

Teaneck

Borzemsky, Bohdan. Painter, Graphic Artist
Feigl, Doris Louise. Painter
Manhold, John Henry. Sculptor
Weill, Erna. Sculptor, Instructor

Tenafly

Krauser, Joel. Instructor, Printmaker
Price, George. Cartoonist
Shore, Richard Paul. Sculptor

Titusville

Ring, Edward Alfred. Collector, Art Dealer

Trenton

Brooks, Wendell T. Printmaker, Educator
Roebling, Mary G. Collector, Patron
Sloshberg, Leah Phyfer. Art Administrator

Union

Bailin, Hella. Painter
Sles, Steven Lawrence. Painter

Union City

Korn, Elizabeth P. Painter, Educator

Upper Montclair

Coes, Kent Day. Painter, Designer
McQuillan, Frances C. Painter, Instructor

Ventnor

Chester, Charlotte Wanetta. Painter, Sculptor
Harris, Marian D. Painter, Art Critic
Robbins, Hulda D. Painter, Printmaker

Warren

Ross, Jean G. Painter, Instructor

Watchung

Bolley, Irma S. Painter, Designer

Wayne

De Nike, Michael Nicholas. Sculptor
Paris, Lucille M (Lucille M Bichler). Painter

Weehawken

Groshans, Werner (Emil). Painter

West Orange

Hunter, Graham. Cartoonist
Schreiber, Eileen Sher. Painter, Lecturer

Westfield

Hanan, Harry. Cartoonist

Westwood

Jensen, John Edward. Painter, Designer

Woodbine

Durand, Lucille Murphy. Illustrator

Wood-Ridge

Lynds, Clyde Williams. Sculptor

Wyckoff

Carpenter, E. Painter

NEW MEXICO

Abiquiu

O'Keeffe, Georgia. Painter

Albuquerque

Abdalla, Nick. Painter, Educator
Adams, Clinton. Art Administrator, Lithographer
Antreasian, Garo Zareh. Painter, Lithographer
Black, Frederick (Edward). Painter, Art Administrator
Brody, Jacob Jerome. Art Administrator, Educator
Chapian, Grieg Hovsep. Painter, Lecturer
Coke, F Van Deren. Educator, Photographer
Goff, Lloyd Lozes. Painter, Illustrator
Hammersley, Frederick. Painter, Educator
Ingram, Jerry Cleman. Painter, Designer
Jonson, Raymond. Painter, Art Administrator
Kerr, James Wilfrid. Painter, Lecturer
Lehrer, Leonard. Painter, Educator
Newhall, Beaumont. Art Historian, Writer
Peterson, Robert Baard. Painter, Draughtsman

Albuquerque (cont)

Salamone, Gladys L. Painter
Skinner, Elsa Kells. Painter, Illustrator
Smith, Sam. Painter, Educator
Sowers, Miriam R. Painter, Art Dealer
Steider, Doris. Painter
Sussman, Arthur. Painter
Tatschl, John. Craftsman, Sculptor
Velarde, Pablita. Painter, Illustrator
Worthen, William Marshall. Sculptor

El Rancho

Wagner, John Philip. Painter

Galisteo

Scholder, Fritz. Painter, Printmaker

Gallup

Long, C Chee. Sculptor, Painter
Morez, Mary. Painter, Illustrator

Glenwood

Howard, Cecil Ray. Painter, Sculptor

Hobbs

Easley, Loyce Rogers. Painter, Potter

Las Cruces

Guzevich, Kreszenz (Cynthia). Painter, Instructor
Mannen, Paul William. Painter, Educator

Montezuma

Du Jardin, Gussie. Painter, Printmaker
Schooley, Elmer Wayne. Painter, Educator

Penablanca

Lovato, Charles Fredric. Painter

Placitas

Lowney, Bruce Stark. Printmaker

Portales

Gikas, Christopher. Educator, Painter

Ranchos de Taos

Cook, Howard Norton. Painter, Lecturer

Roswell

Ebie, William Dennis. Art Administrator, Painter
Jensen, Hank. Sculptor
Wiggins, Bill. Painter

San Patricio

Hurd, Peter. Painter, Writer
Meigs, John Liggett. Painter, Art Historian
Rogers, Peter Wilfrid. Painter
Wyeth, Henriette (Mrs Peter Hurd). Painter

Santa Fe

Bacigalupa, Andrea. Designer, Painter
Boyd, E. Art Administrator, Writer
Constable, Rosalind. Collector, Writer
Dailey, Charles Andrew (Chuck). Museum Director, Painter
Dutton, Bertha P. Museum Director, Writer
Ellis, Fremont F. Painter
Ettenberg, Franklin Joseph. Draughtsman, Painter
Gallenkamp, Charles & Patricia. Art Dealers
Gobin, Henry (Delano). Painter
Hanbury, Una. Sculptor
Harrill, James. Painter
Henrickson, Paul Robert. Educator, Writer
Hill, Jim. Sculptor, Art Dealer
Hill, Megan Lloyd. Sculptor, Art Dealer
Hotvedt, Kristine J. Printmaker, Instructor
Katz, Theodore (Harry). Educator, Painter
Keener, Anna Elizabeth. Painter, Educator
Lippincott, Janet. Painter
Longley, Bernique. Painter
McGrath, James Arthur. Art Administrator, Painter
Montoya, Geronima Cruz (Po-Tsu-Nu). Painter, Instructor
Moses, Forrest (Lee), (Jr). Painter
Naumer, Helmuth. Painter
New, Lloyd H (Lloyd Kiva). Art Administrator, Designer
Ruthling, Ford. Painter, Designer
Schultz, Roger D. Painter, Sculptor
Shannon, (David) Patric. Art Administrator
Shonnard, Eugenie F. Painter, Sculptor
Sims, Agnes. Painter, Sculptor
Steinke, Bettina. Painter
Swazo (Patrick Swazo Hinds). Painter, Lecturer
Thwaites, Charles Winstanley. Painter
Tubis, Seymour. Painter, Sculptor
Young, Webb. Painter

Shiprock

Cohoe, Grey. Printmaker, Writer

Silver City

McCray, Dorothy M. Printmaker, Educator

Taos

Boyer, Jack K. Museum Director, Curator
Dasburg, Andrew Michael. Painter
Egri, Ted. Sculptor
Gibberd, Eric Waters. Painter
Gorman, R C. Painter, Art Dealer
Harmon, Cliff Franklin. Painter
Kloss, Gene (Alice Geneva Glasier). Etcher, Painter
Larrinaga, Mario. Painter, Designer
Latham, Barbara. Painter, Illustrator
Pruitt, A Kelly. Painter, Sculptor
Ray, Robert (Donald). Painter, Sculptor
Reed, Doel. Painter, Educator
Robles, Julian. Painter, Sculptor
Scott, Jonathan. Painter
Simpson, Lee. Painter
Wellington, Duke. Painter

Velarde

Johnson, (Leonard) Lucas. Painter, Illustrator

NEW YORK

Albany

Frinta, Mojmir Svatopluk. Art Historian, Writer
Mochon, Donald. Painter, Educator
Rockefeller, Nelson Aldrich. Collector, Patron
Rosen, Hy(man) (Joseph). Cartoonist
Schafer, Alice Pauline. Printmaker
Warren, Betty. Painter

Albertson

Madsen, Viggo Holm. Printmaker, Instructor

Alfred

Randall, Theodore A. Sculptor, Educator

Alfred Station

Turner, Robert Chapman. Educator, Ceramist

Almond

Phelan, Linn Lovejoy. Designer, Educator

Altamont

Cowley, Edward P. Educator, Painter

Amagansett

Gwathmey, Robert. Educator, Painter
Perret, George Albert. Writer, Lecturer

Amenia

Hale, Nathan Cabot. Sculptor, Writer

Ancram

Padovano, Anthony John. Sculptor, Lecturer

Angola

Haug, Donald Raymond. Painter, Instructor

Annandale-on-Hudson

Phillips, Matt. Painter

Ardsley

Lysun, Gregory. Painter, Restorer

Ardsley-on-Hudson

Griggs, Maitland Lee. Collector

Armonk

Gressel, Michael L. Sculptor

Astoria

Drummond, (I G). Painter, Sculptor
Halbers, Fred. Painter
Higgins, Thomas J, Jr. Cartoonist

Auburn

Long, Walter Kinscella. Museum Director, Painter

Baldwin

Carter, Granville W. Sculptor
Stewart, Dorothy S. Painter

Barneveld

Wardle, Alfred H. Silversmith

Bay Shore

Berkowitz, Henry. Painter, Designer

Bayside

Feldman, Lilian. Painter
Goldstein, Milton. Printmaker, Educator
Niemann, Edmund E. Painter

Bearsville

Klitgaard, Georgina. Painter, Writer

Bedford

McDonnell, Joseph Anthony. Sculptor
Weinman, Robert Alexander. Sculptor

Bedford Hills

Carter, Bernard Shirley. Painter, Instructor

Bedford Village

Canfield, Jane (White). Sculptor

Beth Page

Paddock, Denis Emil. Collector

Binghamton

De Vito, Ferdinand A. Painter, Educator
Ippolito, Angelo. Painter, Educator
Lindsay, Kenneth C. Art Historian, Writer
Martin, Keith. Museum Director, Painter
Schwartz, Aubrey E. Printmaker, Sculptor
Wilson, Edward N. Sculptor, Educator

Blauvelt

Leber, Roberta (Roberta Leber McVeigh). Ceramist, Instructor
Plummer, John H. Art Administrator, Educator

Brainard

Johnsen, May Anne. Painter, Etcher

Bridgehampton

Benson, Elaine K G. Art Dealer, Writer
Newbill, Al James. Painter, Instructor
Prohaska, Ray. Painter, Illustrator
Varga, Margit. Painter, Writer
Vicente, Esteban. Painter

Bronx

Allen, Patricia (Patricia Allen Bott). Painter, Art Critic
Berg, Siri. Painter
Fastove, Aaron (Aaron Fastovsky). Painter
Ferrara, Frank Vincent. Sculptor, Painter
Florio, Sal Erseny. Sculptor
Jaffe, Irma B. Art Historian
Jennewein, C Paul. Sculptor
Kassoy, Bernard. Painter, Printmaker
Katz, Leo. Painter, Writer
Kaye, George. Educator, Painter
Wechter, Vivienne Thaul. Educator, Painter
Werth, Kurt. Illustrator
Wilner, Marie Spring. Painter

Bronxville

Mawicke, Tran. Painter, Illustrator
Poucher, Elizabeth Morris. Sculptor
Seckler, Dorothy Gees. Art Critic, Lecturer

Brookhaven

Delihas, Neva C. Sculptor

Brooklyn

Albert, Calvin. Sculptor, Educator
Anderson, Lennart. Printmaker, Instructor
Arp, Hilda Dora. Painter, Sculptor
Baumbach, Harold. Painter, Printmaker
Beerman, Herbert. Painter, Educator
Beerman, Miriam H. Painter
Benedict, Nan M. Artist, Educator
Bidner, Robert D H. Painter, Designer
Bothmer, Bernard V. Museum Curator, Art Historian
Cadmus, Paul. Painter, Printmaker
Cameron, Duncan F. Art Administrator, Writer
Carrel, Claudia. Painter, Sculptor
Cramer, Abraham. Painter, Cartoonist
d'Andrea, Albert Philip. Educator, Sculptor
Dechar, Peter. Painter
Duncalfe, Walter John Douglas. Painter, Designer
Ernst, Jimmy. Painter, Educator
Faunce, Sarah Cushing. Museum Curator
Federe, Marion. Painter, Graphic Artist
Fein, Stanley. Painter, Illustrator
Fife, Mary. Painter
Furman, Gloria Violet. Painter, Art Dealer
Gardner, Andrew Bradford. Printmaker, Painter
Grado, Angelo John. Painter, Illustrator
Grebenak, Dorothy. Craftsman
Gurr, Lena. Painter, Graphic Artist
Johnson, J Stewart. Museum Curator
Jones, Nell Choate. Painter
Jones, Tom Douglas. Designer, Educator
Kan, Michael. Art Historian, Art Administrator
Kish, Maurice. Painter
Kozloff, Alexander Ivan. Painter, Printmaker
Kupferman, Murray. Painter, Sculptor
Lerner, Sandy R. Painter, Lithographer
Le Roy, Harold M. Painter, Lecturer
Leventhal, Ethel S. Painter
McNeil, George J. Painter, Educator
Mainardi, Patricia M. Painter, Writer

Mandelbaum, Dr & Mrs Robert A. Collectors
Manilla, Tess (Tess Manilla Weiner). Painter
Marans, Moissaye. Sculptor, Instructor
Marks, Mrs Laurence M. Trustee
Morse, Jennie Greene. Designer, Educator
Moss, Irene.
Nemser, Cindy. Art Critic, Lecturer
Odate, Toshio. Conceptual Artist, Instructor
Pfahl, Charles Alton, III. Painter
Pollaro, Paul. Painter
Ranson, Nancy Sussman. Painter, Seriographer
Rhoden, John W. Sculptor
Richmond, Frederick W. Collector, Patron
Rose, Dorothy. Painter
Rubin, Irwin. Painter, Designer
Saito, Seiji. Sculptor
Scharff, Constance Kramer. Printmaker, Painter
Shaw, (George) Kendall. Painter, Educator
Stelzer, Michael Norman. Sculptor
Sufi, Ahmad Antung. Sculptor
Weber, Idelle Lois. Painter, Sculptor
Weingarten, Hilde (Mrs Arthur Kevess). Painter, Printmaker
Wickiser, Ralph Lewanda. Art Administrator, Painter
Wynn, Donald James. Painter, Lecturer

Brooklyn Heights

Schucker, Charles. Painter

Buffalo

Blair, Robert Noel. Painter, Sculptor
Bowen, Wayne. Painter
Breverman, Harvey. Painter, Printmaker
Buck, Robert Treat, Jr. Art Historian, Art Administrator
Colgrove, Ronald B. Illustrator, Painter
Cuthbert, Virginia. Painter, Instructor
Elliott, Philip Clarkson. Painter, Educator
Hatchett, Duayne. Sculptor, Educator
Johnson, Charlotte Buel. Art Historian, Educator
Knox, Seymour H. Patron
Krims, Leslie Robert. Painter, Photographer
Levick, Mr & Mrs Irving. Collectors
McIvor, John Wilfred. Printmaker, Painter
Moore, Ethel. Art Administrator, Writer
Nichols, Donald Edward. Designer, Educator
Primerano, Joan Walton. Painter
Shanks, Bruce McKinley. Editorial Cartoonist
Sisti, Anthony J. Collector, Painter
Smith, Gordon Mackintosh. Museum Director
Wood, James Nowell. Art Historian, Art Administrator

Callicoon

Mangold, Sylvia Plimack. Painter

Callicoon Center

Mangold, Robert Peter. Painter

Canton

Holladay, Harlan H. Painter, Educator
Lowe, J Michael. Sculptor, Educator

Carmel

Lee, Robert J. Painter, Educator
Mitchell, James E. Illustrator, Painter
Parker, Robert Andrew. Painter

Castleton

Crist, Richard. Painter, Writer

Cazenovia

Ridlon, James A. Sculptor, Educator

Cedarhurst

Lichtenberg, Manes. Painter

Centerport

Fasbender, Walter. Museum Director

Chappaqua

Adelman, Dorothy (Lee) McClintock.
   Printmaker, Painter
Fagg, Kenneth Stanley. Art Administrator,
   Illustrator
Laventhol, Hank. Painter, Etcher
Reibel, Bertram. Sculptor, Graphic Artist
Weiss, Jean Bijur. Painter, Collector

Charlotteville

Artschwager, Richard Ernst. Painter,
   Sculptor

Chatham

Johansen, Anders Daniel. Painter
Trimm, H Wayne. Illustrator

Cheektowaga

Bisone, Edward George. Painter, Illustrator

Clinton

Friedensohn, Elias. Painter, Educator
Ostuni, Peter W. Painter
Penney, James. Painter, Educator
Root, Mrs Edward W. Collector
Trovato, Joseph S. Painter

Cold Spring Harbor

Schneiderman, Dorothy. Art Dealer

Cooperstown

Jones, Louis C. Museum Director
Keck, Sheldon Waugh. Educator, Art
   Conservator

Corning

Buechner, Thomas Scharman. Art Administrator, Painter

Corona

Wimberley, Frank Walden. Painter, Sculptor

Cortland

Stell, H Kenyon. Educator, Painter

Craryville

Bate, Stanley. Painter

Croton-on-Hudson

Biddle, George. Painter, Sculptor

Dix Hills

Ames, Lee Judah. Illustrator, Writer

Dobbs Ferry

Borgatta, Isabel Case. Sculptor, Lecturer
Borgatta, Robert Edward. Painter, Edu-
   cator
Butler, Joseph Thomas. Art Historian,
   Writer
Lissim, Simon. Painter, Educator
Rothschild, Lincoln. Sculptor, Writer

Douglaston

Starrs, Mildred. Painter, Instructor

Eagle Bridge

Moses, Forrest King. Painter

East Aurora

Underwood, Evelyn Notman. Painter

East Chatham

Rickey, George W. Sculptor

East Elmhurst

Clem (Clem Albert Gouveia). Painter

East Hampton

Borgzinner, Jon. Writer, Art Critic
Brooks, James. Painter
Carey, Ted. Collector, Designer
De Kooning, Willem. Painter
De Pauw, Victor. Painter
Hoffmann, Arnold, Jr. Painter, Designer
Jackson, Harlan Christopher. Painter
Krasner, Lee. Painter
Lassaw, Ibram. Sculptor
Levi, Julian (E). Painter, Educator
Levitan Israel (Jack). Sculptor, Lecturer
Little, John. Painter, Sculptor
Ossorio, Alfonso A. Painter, Sculptor
Tania (Schreiber). Sculptor, Painter
Whipple, Enez Mary. Art Administrator
Wingate, Arline (Hollander). Sculptor

East Hills

Newmark, Marilyn (Marilyn Newmark
   Meiselman). Sculptor

East Marion

Stamos, Theodoros (S). Painter, Educator

East Meadow

Finke, Leonda Froelich. Sculptor,
   Draughtsman
Sirena (Contessa Antonia Mastrocristino
   Fanara). Painter, Collector
Terken, John. Sculptor

East Williston

Baderian, Ruth. Painter, Educator

Elmhurst

Berkon, Martin. Painter
Wachsteter, George. Illustrator

Elmira

Fox, Roy Charles W. Painter, Etcher

Elmont

Rogers, John. Painter, Lecturer
Soloway, Reta. Painter, Lecturer

Essex

Lowry, Bates. Art Historian, Art
   Critic

Fairport

Peters, Carl W. Painter

Fayetteville

Goodnow, Frank A. Painter, Educator
Pollock, Merlin F. Painter, Educator

Flushing

Bergere, Richard. Illustrator, Painter
Camurati, Albert. Painter
Cohen, David H. Painter
Gilbert, Creighton Eddy. Art Historian
Goldberg, Chaim Leib. Painter,
   Engraver
Kochta, Ruth (Martha). Painter
Koras, George. Sculptor
Ludwig, Eva. Sculptor
Pincus-Witten, Robert A. Art Historian,
   Writer
Reiss, Lee. Painter
Rosenthal, Seymour Joseph. Painter

Forest Hills

Catan-Rose, Richard. Painter, Educator
De Bellis, Hannibal. Sculptor, Medalist
Leeds, Annette. Painter
Linden, Fred. Painter, Instructor
Lombardo, Josef Vincent. Art Historian,
   Educator
Tewi, Thea. Sculptor
Walker, Hudson D. Collector, Art Admin-
   istrator

Franklin Square

Indiviglia, Salvatore Joseph. Painter,
   Instructor
Newer, Thesis. Painter

Freeport

Brown, Marion B. Painter
de Kooning, Elaine Marie Catherine. Painter, Writer
Lariar, Lawrence. Cartoonist, Writer
Rowan, Frances Physioc. Painter, Printmaker

Garden City

Biedermann, Max. Painter

Garrison

Asoma, Tadashi. Painter
Flavin, Dan. Writer
Locke, Charles Wheeler. Painter, Printmaker

Geneva

Bate, Norman Arthur. Educator, Printmaker

Gilbertsville

Eckmair, Frank C. Printmaker

Glen Cove

Paris, Jeanne C. Art Critic, Writer

Glen Head

Sarnoff, Arthur Saron. Painter

Gloversville

Schulman, Jacob. Collector

Grand View-on-Hudson

Hader, Elmer (Stanley). Illustrator, Writer
Wyatt, Stanley. Painter, Educator

Great Neck

Beck, Margit. Painter, Lecturer
Berne, Gustave Morton. Collector
Eckstein, Ruth. Printmaker, Painter
Filmus, Tully. Painter, Lecturer
Fink, Sam. Painter, Illustrator
Housman, Russell F. Painter, Educator
Kipniss, Robert. Painter
Meyer, Seymour W. Sculptor
Moglia, Luigi (John). Painter, Educator
Pomerance, Leon. Collector, Patron
Quat, Helen S. Printmaker, Painter
Richmond, Lawrence. Collector
Roston, Arnold. Painter, Patron
Seidler, Doris. Painter, Printmaker
Tanksley, Ann. Painter
Van Buren, Raeburn. Illustrator, Cartoonist

Great Neck Estates

Gropper, William. Painter, Lithographer

Greenport

Wengenroth, Stow. Printmaker

Groton

Colby, Victor E. Sculptor, Educator

Hamlin

Marx, Robert Ernst. Painter, Printmaker

Harrison

Neustadter, Edward L. Collector, Patron

Hartsdale

Schulze, Paul. Designer, Instructor

Hastings-on-Hudson

Begg, John Alfred. Designer, Sculptor
Bohnert, Rosetta. Painter, Lecturer
Catti (Catherine James). Painter
Freedman, Maurice. Painter
Nardin, Mario. Sculptor

Haverstraw

Taubes, Frederic. Painter, Writer

Hempstead

Feriola, James Philip. Painter, Art Administrator

Hicksville

Landy, Jacob. Art Historian, Educator

Highland Falls

Heberling, Glen Austin. Painter, Illustrator

Holbrook

Vaux, Richard. Painter

Holland Patent

Christiana, Edward. Painter, Instructor

Hollis

Davies, Theodore Peter. Printmaker, Painter

Honeoye Falls

Coffey, Douglas Robert. Painter, Educator

Hoosick Falls

Lipsky, Pat. Painter
Wofford, Philip. Painter, Writer

Huntington

Brodsky, Stan. Painter
Engel, Michael Martin, II. Painter
Gatling, Eva Ingersoll. Museum Director, Art Historian
Hoehn, Harry. Painter, Printmaker
Hopkins, John Fornachon. Painter, Educator

Rabinovich, Raquel. Painter, Sculptor
Van Loen, Alfred. Sculptor, Educator
Zona, Rinaldo A. Painter, Sculptor

Ithaca

Abbe, Elfriede Martha. Sculptor, Engraver
Daly, Norman David. Sculptor, Painter
Dzubas, Friedel. Painter
Evett, Kenneth Warnock. Painter, Writer
Grippi, Salvatore William. Painter, Educator
Hartell, John (Anthony). Painter
Hoyt, Dorothy (Dorothy Hoyt Dillingham). Painter
Kahn, Peter. Painter, Designer
Leavitt, Thomas Whittlesey. Art Administrator, Art Historian
Mahoney, James Owen. Painter, Educator
Poleskie, Stephen Francis. Painter, Printmaker
Richenburg, Robert Bartlett. Painter, Sculptor
Seley, Jason. Sculptor
Squier, Jack Leslie. Sculptor, Educator
Waage, Frederick O. Art Historian, Educator
Wojcik, Gary Thomas. Sculptor

Jackson Heights

de Gerenday, Laci Anthony. Sculptor
Farian, Babette (Sommerich). Painter, Designer
Freund, Tibor. Painter, Architect
Judkins, Sylvia. Painter
Schmeidler, Blanche J. Painter
Sturtevant, Harriet H. Painter, Designer
Whitney, Edgar Albert. Painter, Instructor

Jamaica

Cade, Walter, III. Painter
Eliasoph, Paula. Painter, Writer
Giffuni, Flora Baldini. Painter, Designer
Jonynas, Vytautas K. Painter, Designer
Lloyd, Tom. Sculptor

Jamesville

Burke, E Ainslie. Painter, Educator

Jefferson

Hacklin, Allan Dave. Painter

Jericho

Bogen, Beverly. Painter
Moss, Milton. Painter, Lecturer

Katonah

Askin, Arnold Samuel. Collector
Baur, John I H. Museum Director, Writer
Giobbi, Edward Gioachino. Painter
Lipinsky De Orlov, Lino S. Painter, Illustrator
Samerjan, George E. Designer, Painter
Simpson, William Kelly. Art Historian, Educator
Toney, Anthony. Painter, Educator

Keene

Mitchell, Bruce Kirk. Painter

Keene Valley

Winkel, Nina. Sculptor

Kenmore

Czurles, Stanley A. Painter, Educator

Kenoza Lake

D'Arcangelo, Allan M. Painter

Kew Gardens

Albee, Grace Thurston Arnold. Engraver,
Painter

Kings Point

Grosz, Franz Joseph. Painter, Designer
Rath, Hildegard. Painter, Lecturer
Schulhof, Mr & Mrs Rudolph B. Collectors

Lake Success

Leaf, Ruth. Printmaker, Instructor

Larchmont

Medrich, Libby E. Sculptor
Tobey, Alton S. Painter, Lecturer

Levittown

Schachter, Justine Ranson. Painter, Designer

Locust Valley

Bush-Brown, Albert. Writer, Educator
Howell, Douglass (Morse). Painter, Art
Historian
Rogalski, Walter. Printmaker, Lecturer
Watson, Clarissa H. Art Dealer

Long Beach

Altabé, Joan Berg. Painter, Educator

Long Island City

Davison, Robert. Painter, Designer
Lerner, Abram. Museum Director
Noguchi, Isamu. Sculptor

Madrid

Hildreth, Joseph Alan. Printmaker,
Painter

Mamaroneck

Goldberger, Mr & Mrs Edward. Collectors,
Patrons
Gumpel, Hugh. Painter
Lekberg, Barbara Hult. Sculptor
Sloan, Robert Smullyan. Painter, Art
Dealer
Topol, Robert Martin. Collector

Manhasset

Catchi (Catherine O Childs). Painter,
Sculptor

Harvey, Jacqueline. Painter
Paley, Mr & Mrs William S. Collectors
Payson, Mr & Mrs Charles S. Collectors

Manlius

Groat, Hall Pierce. Painter

Merrick

Barkan, Bebe (Beverly Adrian). Painter,
Illustrator
Cariola, Robert J. Painter, Sculptor
Johanson, Patricia (Maureen). Sculptor,
Painter

Middletown

Ericson, Beatrice. Painter
Parker, Roy Danford. Painter

Mill Neck

Burrows, Selig S. Collector, Patron

Millbrook

Bluhm, Norman. Painter
Della-Volpe, Ralph Eugene. Painter, Edu-
cator
Streeter, Tal. Sculptor

Millerton

Helck, (Clarence) Peter. Illustrator, Writer

Monsey

Mesibov, Hugh. Painter, Educator

Montgomery

Seredy, Kate. Illustrator

Monticello

De Hoyos, Luis. Collector

Morristown

Frelinghuysen, Mr & Mrs Peter H B, Jr.
Collectors

Mount Kisco

Jones, Amy (Amy Jones Frisbie). Painter,
Educator
Laskey, Dr & Mrs Norman F. Collectors

Mount Vernon

Gilchrist, Agnes Addison. Art & Architec-
tural Historian
Seliger, Charles. Painter, Designer
Uhl, Emmy. Sculptor
Zib, Tom (Thomas A Zibelli). Cartoonist

Mountainville

Mayhall, Dorothy A. Art Administrator,
Sculptor
Ogden, Ralph E. Collector, Patron
Stern, H Peter. Collector

Neponsit

Mount, Charles Merrill. Painter

New City

Corcos, Lucille. Painter, Illustrator
Kantor, Morris. Painter
Poor, Anne. Painter
Rosse, Maryvonne. Sculptor

New Paltz

Bohan, Peter John. Art Historian, Painter
Kammerer, Herbert Lewis. Sculptor
Munsterberg, Hugo. Art Historian, Edu-
cator
Wexler, George. Painter, Educator

New Rochelle

Beling, Helen. Sculptor, Instructor
FeBland, Harriet. Painter, Sculptor
Gross, Irene (Irene Gross Berzon).
Painter, Sculptor
Lantz, Michael F. Sculptor
Liljegren, Frank. Painter, Educator
Meizner, Paula. Sculptor
Mochi, Ugo. Sculptor
Montlack, Edith. Painter
Seckel, Paul Bernhard. Painter, Graphic
Artist
Slotnick, Mortimer H. Painter
Spidell, Enid Jean. Painter, Educator
Winter, Lumen Martin. Sculptor, Painter

New York City

Aach, Herb. Painter, Writer
Abbott, Dorothy. Sculptor, Lecturer
Abramovitz, Mr & Mrs Max. Collectors
Abrams, Harry N. Publisher, Collector
Abrams, Ruth. Painter
Acconci, Vito. Sculptor
Adams, Alice. Sculptor
Addams, Charles Samuel. Cartoonist
Adler, A M. Art Dealer
Adler, Lee. Painter, Printmaker
Adler, Robert. Painter
Adler, Samuel (Marcus). Painter, Educa-
tor
Adrian, Barbara. Painter, Collector
Agostinelli, Mario. Painter, Sculptor
Agostini, Peter. Sculptor
Ahlskog, Sirkka. Craftsman, Sculptor
Akston, Joseph James. Collector, Patron
Alajalov, Constantin. Painter, Illustrator
Albertazzi, Mario. Painter, Art Critic
Albright, Ivan Le Lorraine. Painter
Alcopley, L. Painter, Graphic Artist
Aldrich, Larry. Art Administrator, Col-
lector
Alloway, Lawrence. Educator, Art Critic
Alonzo, Jack J. Art Dealer, Collector
Alston, Charles Henry. Painter, Educa-
tor
Altschul, Arthur G. Collector, Patron
Amaya, Mario Anthony. Museum Direc-
tor, Writer
Amen, Irving. Painter, Printmaker
Amino, Leo. Sculptor
Anderson, David K. Art Dealer, Collector
Anderson, Doug. Illustrator
Andre, Carl. Sculptor
Andrejevic, Milet. Painter
Andrews, Benny. Painter, Lecturer
Andrews, Laddie E. Art Dealer
Angel, Rifka. Painter
Anspach, Ernst. Collector
Anthony, William Graham. Painter,
Draftsman
Antonakos, Stephen. Sculptor
Antonovici, Constantin. Sculptor, Lecturer

Aparicio, Gerardo. Painter
Appel, Karel. Painter, Sculptor
Apt, Charles. Painter
Arakawa, (Shusaku). Painter
Arcilesi, Vincent J. Painter, Educator
Arman. Sculptor
Arnhold, Mr & Mrs Hans. Collectors
Aronson, Boris. Designer, Painter
Aronson, Joseph. Designer, Writer
Ascher, Mary G. Painter
Ashton, Dore. Art Critic, Art Historian
Atkins, David. Painter
Ault, Lee Addison. Collector, Art Dealer
Ay-O. Painter, Printmaker
Aylon, Heléne. Painter
Azuma, Norio. Serigrapher, Painter
Baber, Alice. Painter
Bachrach, Gladys Wertheim. Painter
Baer, Alan. Art Administrator
Baer, Jo. Painter, Writer
Bailey, Malcolm C W. Painter, Illustrator
Baker, Charles Edwin. Art Historian,
  Writer
Baker, Richard Brown. Collector
Baker, Walter C. Collector
Balog, Michael. Painter, Sculptor
Banks, Richard. Painter
Baranik, Rudolf. Painter
Bardazzi, Peter. Painter
Bareiss, Walter. Collector
Barile, Xavier J. Painter, Instructor
Baringer, Richard E. Painter, Designer
Barnet, Will. Painter, Printmaker
Barooshian, Martin. Painter, Art Ad-
  ministrator
Barr, Alfred Hamilton, Jr. Art Historian,
  Art Administrator
Barr-Sharrar, Beryl. Painter, Writer
Barrett, Bill. Sculptor, Educator
Barrie, Erwin S. Painter
Bartle, Annette. Painter, Illustrator
Bartlett, Jennifer Losch. Painter, Writer
Barton, John Murray. Painter, Art Dealer
Barzun, Jacques. Writer, Art Critic
Baskerville, Charles. Painter
Battcock, Gregory. Art Critic, Lecturer
Bauman, Lionel R. Collector
Beal, Jack. Painter
Bean, Jacob. Art Administrator
Bearden, Romare Howard. Painter
Beck, Rosemarie (Rosemarie Beck Phelps).
  Painter, Educator
Belkin, Arnold. Painter, Sculptor
Bell, Clara Louise (Mrs Bela Janowsky).
  Painter
Bell, Leland. Painter
Bellamy, Richard. Art Dealer
Ben-Zion. Painter, Sculptor
Benglis, Lynda. Sculptor, Painter
Benn, Ben. Painter
Bennett, Harriet. Painter
Benney, Robert. Painter
Benno, Benjamin G. Painter, Sculptor
Bensing, Frank C. Painter, Illustrator
Benton, William. Collector
Bergen, Sidney L. Art Dealer
Berger, Samuel A. Collector
Berkman, Aaron. Painter, Instructor
Berman, Ariane R. Painter, Printmaker
Bernstein, Sylvia. Painter, Sculptor
Bernstein, Theresa. Painter, Art Historian
Bettmann, Otto Ludwig. Art Historian
Bevilacqua, Francis. Sculptor, Painter
Bhavsar, Natvar Prahladji. Painter
Bianco, Pamela Ruby. Painter
Bileck, Marvin. Printmaker, Illustrator
Bingham, Mrs Harry Payne. Collector
Birmelin, August Robert. Painter, Print-
  maker
Bisaccio, Philip. Painter
Bisgyer, Barbara G (Barbara G Cohn).
  Sculptor
Bishop, Isabel (Mrs Harold G Wolff).
  Painter, Etcher
Black, Shirley. Painter
Blackwell, Thomas Leo. Painter
Bladen, Ronald. Sculptor

Blaine, Nell. Painter
Blake, Peter Jost. Art Critic, Architect
Blanc, Peter (William Peters Blanc).
  Sculptor, Painter
Blanchard, Carol. Painter, Graphic Artist
Blaustein, Alfred H. Painter, Printmaker
Block, Adolph. Sculptor, Instructor
Blumenthal, Margaret M. Designer
Boardman, Seymour. Painter
Bock, Vera. Illustrator, Designer
Bodin, Paul. Painter
Bohnen, Blythe. Painter
Bomar, Bill. Painter
Bonino, Alfredo. Art Dealer
Borgenicht, Grace (Grace Borgenicht
  Brandt). Art Dealer, Collector
Boris, Bessie. Painter
Boros, Billi (Mrs Philip Bisaccio). Painter,
  Writer
Bostwick, Mr & Mrs Dunbar W. Collectors
Boterf, Chester Arthur (Check). Painter,
  Lecturer
Bothmer, Dietrich Felix Von. Art Historian,
  Art Administrator
Botkin, Henry. Painter, Writer
Bourgeois, Louise. Sculptor
Bowen, Helen Eakins. Painter
Bowie, William. Sculptor
Bowman, Ken. Painter
Bowman, Ruth. Educator, Art Administra-
  tor
Boxer, Stanley (Robert). Sculptor, Painter
Bradley, Peter Alexander. Painter, Art
  Dealer
Branner, Robert. Art Historian
Bransom, (John) Paul. Painter, Illustrator
Brecher, Samuel. Painter, Educator
Breiger, Elaine. Painter, Printmaker
Brendel, Otto J. Art Historian
Brennan, Francis Edwin. Collector, Writer
Brigadier, Anne. Painter, Lecturer
Briggs, Ernest. Painter
Briggs, Judson Reynolds. Painter
Brown, Harry Joe, Jr. Collector, Writer
Brown, Judith. Sculptor
Browning, Colleen. Painter
Bruder, Harold Jacob. Painter, Educator
Brumer, Shulamith. Sculptor
Bruno, Phillip A. Art Dealer, Collector
Brusca, Jack. Painter
Buba, Joy Flinsch. Sculptor, Illustrator
Budd, David. Sculptor, Painter
Bultman, Fritz. Sculptor, Painter
Bunshaft, Mr & Mrs Gordon. Collectors
Burch, Claire R. Painter, Writer
Burden, Carter. Collector
Button, John. Painter
Byron, Charles Anthony. Art Dealer
Calas, Nicolas. Writer
Calcagno, Lawrence. Painter
Callery, Mary. Sculptor
Camins, Jacques Joseph. Painter, Print-
  maker
Campbell, David Paul. Painter
Campbell, Gretna. Painter
Campbell, Kenneth. Sculptor, Painter
Campbell, (James) Lawrence. Painter,
  Writer
Campbell, Vivian (Vivian Campbell Stoll).
  Collector, Writer
Canaday, John Edwin. Art Critic
Candell, Victor. Painter, Educator
Canin, Martin. Painter
Canright, Sarah Anne. Painter
Carewe, Sylvia. Painter, Designer
Carlos, (James) Edward. Painter, Art
  Administrator
Carlson, Cynthia J. Painter
Caro, Frank. Art Dealer
Carr, Sally Swan. Sculptor
Carroll, Robert Joseph. Painter, Illustrator
Castelli, Leo. Art Dealer
Castoro, Rosemarie. Painter, Sculptor
Catlin, Stanton L. Museum Director, Art
  Historian
Cavallon, Giorgio. Painter
Cecere, Ada Rasario. Painter

Cecere, Gaetano. Sculptor, Lecturer
Cernuschi, Alberto C. Art Dealer, Art
  Critic
Chalk, Mr & Mrs O Roy. Collectors
Chamberlain, Betty. Art Administrator,
  Writer
Chamberlain, Elwyn. Painter
Chamberlain, John Angus. Sculptor
Chapellier, George. Art Dealer, Collector
Chapellier, Robert. Art Dealer
Chapin, Louis (Le Bourgeois. Writer, Art
  Critic
Chapman, Mrs Gilbert W. Collector,
  Patron
Chase, Saul Alan. Painter
Chatterton, Clarence Kerr. Painter
Chermayeff, Ivan. Designer, Painter
Cherry, Herman. Painter, Educator
Chi, Chen. Painter
Christ-Janer, Arland F. Painter, Print-
  maker
Christo (Javacheff). Sculptor
Chryssa, Varda. Sculptor
Ciarrochi, Ray. Painter
Cicero, Carmen Louis. Painter, Instructor
Cikovsky, Nicolai. Painter, Printmaker
Cipriano, Anthony Galen. Sculptor
Cisneros, Florencio Garcia (Frank Garcia).
  Art Dealer
Citron, Minna Wright. Painter, Printmaker
Civitello, John Patrick. Painter
Clancy, John. Art Dealer
Clarke, John Clem. Painter
Clawson, Rex Martin. Painter
Clendenin, Eve. Painter, Printmaker
Clerk, Pierre. Painter
Close, Chuck. Painter
Clutz, William. Painter
Coheleach, Guy Joseph. Painter, Illustra-
  tor
Cohen, Mr & Mrs Arthur A. Collectors
Cohen, Elaine Lustig. Painter, Designer
Cohen, Hy. Painter
Cohen, Wilfred P. Collector, Patron
Cole, Alphaeus Philemon. Painter
Cole, Donald. Painter
Cole, Sylvan, Jr. Art Dealer, Writer
Cole, Thomas Casilear. Painter
Colin, Georgia T. Collector, Designer
Colin, Ralph Frederick. Collector
Collins, George R. Art Historian
Conant, Howard Somers. Educator, Painter
Condit, (Eleanor) Louise. Art Administra-
  tor
Conlon, William. Painter, Educator
Connaway, Ina Lee Wallace. Painter,
  Sculptor
Conover, Robert Fremont. Printmaker,
  Painter
Constant, George. Painter
Consuegra, Hugo. Painter, Architect
Cook, Gladys Emerson. Illustrator, Painter
Cooke, Kathleen McKeith. Painter, Sculptor
Cooper, Mario. Painter, Sculptor
Copeland, Lila. Painter, Printmaker
Coplans, John (Rivers). Art Editor, Art
  Critic
Corse, Mary Ann. Painter, Sculptor
Corso, Patrick. Painter
Cortlandt, Lyn. Painter
Cosla, Dr & Mrs O K. Collectors
Cote, Alan. Painter
Cotsworth, Staats. Painter, Illustrator
Cowles, Charles. Publisher, Collector
Cowles, Mr & Mrs Gardner. Collectors
Cowles, Russell. Painter
Cox, Allyn. Painter
Cox, Warren Earle. Collector, Art Dealer
Craig, Martin. Sculptor
Crawford, John McAllister, Jr. Collector,
  Patron
Crawford, Ralston. Painter, Illustrator
Crawford, William H. Cartoonist, Sculptor
Creamer, Paul Lyle. Art Dealer
Crimi, Alfred D. Painter, Instructor
Crispo, Andrew John. Art Dealer, Collec-
  tor

New York City (cont)

Culbertson, Janet Lynn (Mrs Douglas Kaften). Painter, Instructor
Cummings, Nathan. Collector
Cunningham, Benjamin Frazier. Painter, Educator
Cunningham, Francis. Painter
Cushing, George. Industrial Designer
Cusumano, Stefano. Painter, Educator
Cutler, Ethel Rose. Painter, Designer
Cyril, (Ruth). Painter, Printmaker
Daingerfield, Marjorie Jay. Sculptor
Damaz, Paul F. Writer, Collector
Danenberg, Bernard. Art Dealer
Daniels, David M. Collector, Patron
Daphne, Annette. Painter
Daphnis, Nassos. Painter, Sculptor
Daphnis-Avlon, Helen. Painter, Sculptor
Dauterman, Carl Christian. Art Historian, Lecturer
David, Don Raymond. Painter, Instructor
Davidson, Marshall Bowman. Art Critic, Writer
Davies, Jordan Alan. Painter
Davila, Carlos. Painter, Printmaker
Davis, Bradley Darius. Painter
Davis, Douglas Matthew. Art Critic, Artist
Davis, Esther M. Sculptor, Painter
Davis, George. Cartoonist, Illustrator
Davis, Leroy. Art Dealer
Dawson, Eve. Painter
Day, Robert James. Cartoonist
Dean, Abner. Illustrator, Writer
Dean, Peter. Painter, Sculptor
De Blasi, Anthony Armando. Painter
De Botton, Jean Philippe. Painter, Sculptor
de Champlain, Vera Chopak. Painter
De Creeft, Jose. Sculptor, Educator
De Donato, Louis John. Painter
De Graaff, Mr & Mrs Jan. Collectors, Patrons
Dehner, Dorothy. Sculptor, Printmaker
De Kanelba, Sita Gomez. Painter
DeKay, John. Painter
De Knight, Avel. Painter
de Kolb, Eric. Collector, Writer
Delaney, Joseph. Painter, Writer
de Lesseps, Tauni. Sculptor, Painter
De Lisio, Michael. Sculptor
Dellis, Arlene B. Art Administrator
De Maria, Walter. Sculptor
De Martini, Joseph. Painter
Denes, Agnes C. Conceptual Artist
De Niro, Robert. Sculptor, Painter
De Rivera, Jose. Sculptor
Derujinsky, Gleb W. Sculptor, Craftsman
De Ruth, Jan. Painter, Writer
Deskey, Donald. Designer
Deverell, Timothy. Painter
De Vitis, Themis. Painter, Designer
Dewey, Mr & Mrs Charles S, Jr. Collectors
Diao, David. Painter
Diller, Mary Black. Painter, Writer
Dillon, C Douglas. Art Administrator, Collector
Di Meo, Dominick Generoso. Painter, Sculptor
Dine, James. Painter, Sculptor
Dintenfass, Terry. Art Dealer
Di Suvero, Mark. Painter
Dix, George Evertson. Art Dealer
Dobbs, John Barnes. Painter
Dobkin, Alexander. Painter
Dockstader, Frederick J. Museum Director, Collector
Dodd, Lois. Painter, Educator
Dogancay, Burhan Cahit. Painter
Donati, Enrico. Painter, Sculptor
Donneson, Seena. Graphic Artist, Painter
Dorfman, Bruce. Painter, Educator
Dorr, William Shepherd. Collector
Doty, Robert McIntyre. Art Administrator, Curator
Doubrava, Jan. Painter

Dowden, Anne Ophelia Todd. Painter, Illustrator
Dowling, Robert W. Patron
Downey, Juan. Sculptor, Instructor
Doyle, Thomas J. Sculptor, Instructor
Drago, Gabrielle D. Painter
Draper, William Franklin. Painter
Dreitzer, Albert J. Collector, Patron
Drexler, Lynne. Painter
Driggs, Elsie. Painter
Dryfoos, Nancy. Sculptor
Dubin, Ralph. Painter, Sculptor
Dugmore, Edward. Painter
Dulac, Margarita Walker. Painter, Educator
Dunn, Alan. (Cantwell). Cartoonist, Writer
Dunnington, Mrs Walter Grey. Collector, Patron
Dunwiddie, Charlotte. Sculptor
Dworzan, George R. Painter, Sculptor
Edwards, Ethel (Mrs Xavier Gonzalez). Painter
Egan, Charles. Art Dealer
Ehrenbeich, Emma. Painter
Ehrman, Frederick L. Collector
Eidlitz, Dorothy Meigs. Patron, Photographer
Eisler, Colin T. Educator
Ekstrom, Arne H. Art Dealer
Elisofon, Eliot. Painter, Photographer
Elkon, Robert. Art Dealer, Collector
Elliott, Ronnie Rose. Painter
Eloul, Kosso. Sculptor
Emil, Allan D. Collector, Patron
Emil, Arthur D. Collector
Emmerich, Andre. Art Dealer, Writer
Engelhard, Mr & Mrs Charles. Collectors
England, Paul Grady. Painter, Educator
Englander, Gertrud. Ceramist
Ericson, Ernest. Illustrator, Instructor
Erlanger, Elizabeth N. Painter, Lecturer
Esman, Betty (Betty Esman Samuels). Painter
Esman, Rosa M. Art Dealer, Collector
Ets, Marie Hall. Illustrator, Writer
Ettinghausen, Richard. Art Historian, Educator
Everett, Len G. Painter
Evergood, Philip. Painter, Graphic Artist
Eyen, Richard J. Art Dealer, Designer
Fabri, Ralph. Painter, Writer
Facci, Domenico (Aurelio). Sculptor, Instructor
Fahlstrom, Oyvind. Painter
Faragasso, Jack. Illustrator, Painter
Farber, Maya M. Painter
Farr, Fred White. Sculptor
Farrell, Patric. Art Administrator, Writer
Farruggio, Remo Michael. Painter
Faulconer, Mary (Fullerton). Painter, Designer
Fausett, (William) Dean. Painter, Etcher
Feder, Ben. Designer, Painter
Feigen, Richard L. Art Dealer, Collector
Feigenbaum, Harriet (Mrs Neil Chamberlain). Sculptor
Feldman, Ronald. Art Dealer
Felt, Mr & Mrs Irving Mitchell. Collectors
Fenton, Alan. Painter, Instructor
Ferber, Herbert. Sculptor, Painter
Ffrench (Phyllis Marjorie Linnell-Ffrench). Painter
Finck, Furman J. Painter, Educator
Findlay, David B. Art Dealer
Fine, Jud. Sculptor
Fine, Perle. Painter, Educator
Fingesten, Peter. Sculptor, Educator
Fiore, Joseph A. Painter, Educator
Fischbach, Marilyn Cole. Art Dealer, Collector
Fischer, John J. Painter, Sculptor
Fishko, Bella. Art Dealer
Fitzgerald, Harriet. Painter, Lecturer
Flack, Audrey L. Painter, Instructor
Fleischman, Lawrence. Art Dealer, Collector

Flexner, James Thomas. Writer, Art Historian
Floch, Joseph. Painter
Fluek, Toby. Painter
Folds, Thomas McKey. Art Consultant, Educator
Fondren, Harold M. Art Dealer
Ford, Charles Henri. Painter, Photographer
Ford, John Charles. Painter
Fosburgh, James Whitney. Painter, Writer
Foster, Hal. Cartoonist, Painter
Fourcade, Xavier. Art Dealer
Frank, Helen Sophia. Painter, Designer
Frank, Mary. Sculptor
Frankenthaler, Helen. Painter
Fraser, Douglas (Ferrar). Art Historian, Educator
Frater, Hal. Painter
Frazier, Le Roy Dyyon. Painter, Sculptor
Freedman, Doris C. Art Administrator
Freedman, Robert J. Collector
Freeman, Margaret B. Museum Curator, Writer
Freeman, Mark. Painter, Printmaker
Freilich, Ann. Painter
Freilich, Michael Leon. Art Dealer, Collector
Freilicher, Jane. Painter
Frick, Helen Clay. Art Library Director
Fried, Michael. Art Critic
Fried, Theodore. Painter, Etcher
Friedman, Bernard Harper. Writer
Fromer, Mrs Leon. Collector
Frumkin, Allan. Art Dealer
Fuhrman, Esther. Sculptor
Fukui, Nobu. Painter
Fuller, Sue. Sculptor, Instructor
Gahman, Floyd. Painter
Gailis, Janis. Painter
Gaines, Natalie Evelyn. Sculptor, Lecturer
Gardiner, Robert David Lion. Collector
Garrett, Stuart Grayson, Jr. Painter, Educator
Gary, Dorothy Hales. Collector, Writer
Gates, John Monteith. Designer, Painter
Geber, Hana. Sculptor, Instructor
Gechtoff, Sonia. Painter
Gee, Helen. Art Dealer
Geist, Sidney. Sculptor, Art Critic
Gekiere, Madeleine. Painter, Educator
Gelb, Jan. Painter, Printmaker
Gelber, Samuel. Painter, Educator
Geldzahler, Henry. Curator
Genauer, Emily. Art Critic, Writer
Gerardia, Helen. Painter
Gerdts, William H. Art Historian, Educator
Gerst, Hilde W. Art Dealer
Ghent, Henri. Art Administrator, Art Consultant
Giambertone, Paul. Sculptor
Gibbons, Margarita. Painter
Gifford, J Nebraska. Painter
Gikow, Ruth (Ruth Gikow Levine). Painter
Gilbert, Lionel. Painter, Instructor
Gill, Robert Wayne. Painter
Gilvarry, James. Collector
Ginsburg, Max. Painter, Illustrator
Giorgi, Vita. Printmaker, Painter
Giraudier, Antonio. Painter, Writer
Glasgall, Mrs Henry W. Collector
Glezer, Nechemia. Art Dealer, Art Historian
Glickman, Maurice. Sculptor, Writer
Glimcher, Arnold B. Art Dealer, Writer
Glinsky, Vincent. Sculptor, Educator
Glorig, Ostor. Painter
Glover, Euphemia W. Sculptor
Gluckman, Morris. Painter
Glueck, Grace (Helen). Writer
Goings, Ralph Ladell. Painter
Gold, Fay. Painter
Gold, Leah. Painter, Printmaker
Goldberg, Michael. Painter
Goldin, Leon. Painter, Educator

Goldowsky, Noah. Art Dealer
Goldschmidt, Lucien. Art Dealer
Goldsmith, Barbara. Writer, Art Critic
Goldsmith, C Gerald. Collector, Patron
Goldstone, Mr & Mrs Herbert. Collectors
Goldwater, Robert. Art Historian
Gollin, Mr & Mrs Joshua A. Collectors, Patrons
Golub, Leon Albert. Painter
Gomez-Quiroz, Juan Manuel. Painter, Printmaker
Gongora, Leonel. Painter, Educator
Gonzalez, Xavier. Painter, Sculptor
Goodman, Estelle. Sculptor
Goodman, James Neil. Art Dealer, Collector
Goodnough, Robert. Painter
Goodrich, Lloyd. Art Administrator, Writer
Goossen, Eugene Coons. Art Critic, Educator
Gorchov, Ron. Painter
Gottlieb, Abe. Collector, Patron
Gottlieb, Adolph. Painter
Goulet, Lorrie (Lorrie H De Creeft). Sculptor, Instructor
Grace, Charles M. Collector
Graham, James. Art Dealer
Graham, Robert Claberhouse. Art Dealer, Collector
Graves, Nancy Stevenson. Painter, Sculptor
Gray, Francine Du Plessix. Writer
Green, Wilder. Art Administrator, Architect
Greenberg, Clement. Writer, Art Critic
Greenberg, Gloria. Painter, Designer
Greene, Balcomb. Painter
Greene, Daniel E. Painter
Greenspan, George. Collector
Greenwald, Charles D. Collector, Patron
Greenwald, Dorothy Kirstein. Collector
Groell, Theophil. Painter, Instructor
Grooms, Red. Painter
Gross, Alice (Alice Gross Fish). Sculptor
Gross, Chaim. Sculptor, Instructor
Grossman, Nancy. Sculptor, Painter
Grosvenor, Robert. Sculptor
Groth, John August. Illustrator, Painter
Grotz, Dorothy Rogers. Painter
Grube, Ernst J. Writer, Lecturer
Gruskin, Mary Josephine. Art Dealer
Guerrero, Jose. Painter
Guggenheimer, Richard Henry. Painter, Writer
Gursoy, Ahmet. Painter
Gussow, Alan. Painter, Writer
Gussow, Roy. Sculptor, Educator
Guston, Theodore J II. Art Administrator
Haas, Richard John. Printmaker, Painter
Haber, Leonard. Collector, Designer
Habergritz, George Joseph. Painter, Sculptor
Hackenbroch, Yvonne Alix. Museum Curator, Writer
Haddad, Samuel. Art Dealer
Haerer, Carol. Painter
Hahn, Stephen. Art Dealer
Hale, Robert Beverly. Art Administrator, Educator
Halpern, Nathan L. Collector
Hammer, Victor J. Art Dealer
Handler, Mr & Mrs Milton. Collectors, Patrons
Hanson, Duane. Sculptor, Instructor
Hare, David. Sculptor
Harkavy, Minna. Sculptor
Harmon, Lily. Painter, Sculptor
Harnett, Mr & Mrs Joel William. Collectors
Harris, Margo Liebes. Sculptor
Harrison, Tony. Painter, Educator
Harriton, Abraham. Painter
Hart, Agnes. Painter, Educator
Hart, Bill. Art Dealer
Hartford, Huntington. Collector, Patron
Hartl, Leon. Painter
Hartwig, Cleo. Sculptor

Hasen, Burt Stanly. Painter
Haskell, Douglas. Writer, Critic
Hatfield, David Underhill. Painter
Haupt, Mrs Enid. Collector
Haupt, Erik Guide. Painter
Hazen, Joseph H. Collector
Heilemann, Charles Otto. Designer, Educator
Heiloms, May. Painter
Heineman, Bernard, Jr. Collector
Heinemann, Peter. Painter, Educator
Held, Al. Painter
Heliker, John Edward. Painter, Educator
Helioff, Anne Graile (Mrs Benjamin Hirschberg). Painter
Heller, Ben. Collector
Heller, Dorothy. Painter
Heller, Goldie (Mrs. Edward W Greenberg). Collector
Helman, Phoebe. Sculptor
Hendricks, Geoffrey. Painter, Educator
Hendricks, James (Powell). Painter, Educator
Henry, Robert. Painter, Educator
Henselmann, Caspar. Sculptor
Herbert, David. Art Dealer, Collector
Herring, Mr & Mrs H Lawrence. Collectors
Hess, Emil John. Painter
Hess, Thomas B. Art Critic, Writer
Heyman, Mr & Mrs David M. Collectors
Higa, (Yoshiharu). Painter, Photographer
Hightower, John B. Art Administrator
Hildebrand, June Mary Ann. Printmaker, Painter
Hill, Clinton J. Painter
Hill, (James) Jerome. Painter
Hillsmith, Fannie. Painter
Hinman, Charles B. Painter, Sculptor
Hios, Theo. Painter, Graphic Artist
Hirsch, David W (Dave). Cartoonist
Hirsch, Hortense M. Patron
Hirsch, Joseph. Painter
Hirschfeld, Albert. Caricaturist
Hirschl, Norman. Art Dealer
Hitchcock, Henry Russell. Art Historian, Art Critic
Hobson, Katherine Thayer. Sculptor
Hoff, Margo. Painter, Printmaker
Hoffman, Martin (Joseph). Painter, Illustrator
Hoie, Claus. Painter, Etcher
Hollerbach, Serge. Painter, Illustrator
Hollingsworth, Alvin Carl. Painter, Educator
Hollister, Paul. Painter
Holmes, Reginald. Painter, Photographer
Holton, Leonard T. Cartoonist
Holty, Carl Robert. Painter, Writer
Hood, Ethel Painter. Sculptor
Hooker, Mrs R Wolcott. Collector, Patron
Hooton, Bruce Duff. Art Administrator, Writer
Hopkins, Budd. Painter
Hopkins, Peter. Painter, Educator
Horowitz, Nadia. Painter, Designer
Horowitz, Mr & Mrs Raymond J. Collectors
Horowitz, Saul. Collector
Horwitt, Will. Sculptor
Houghton, Arthur A, Jr. Art Administrator
Hovell, Joseph. Sculptor
Hoving, Thomas. Museum Director
Howat, John Keith. Art Museum Curator, Art Historian
Howe, Nelson S. Designer, Lecturer
Howell, Hannah Johnson. Art Librarian
Howell, Marie W. Designer, Instructor
Hoyt, Whitney F. Painter, Collector
Hsiao, Chin. Painter, Sculptor
Hultberg, John Phillip. Painter
Hunter, Sam. Art Historian
Huntington, Jim. Sculptor
Hurt, Susanne M. Painter
Husted-Andersen, Adda. Craftsman, Designer
Hutchinson, Max. Art Dealer
Hutchinson, Peter Arthur. Painter
Hutsaliuk, Lubo. Painter

Hutton, Leonard. Art Dealer
Huxtable, Ada Louise. Critic
Indiana, Robert. Painter, Sculptor
Inokuma, Guenichiro. Painter
Insel, Paula. Art Dealer, Art Administrator
Insley, Will. Painter, Instructor
Inukai, Kyohei. Painter, Sculptor
Iolas, Alexandre. Art Dealer
Isenburger, Eric. Painter
Isserstedt, Dorothea Carus. Art Dealer, Art Historian
Itchkawich, David Michael. Printmaker
Ittleson, Henry, Jr. Collector
Jachmann, Kurt M. Collector
Jackson, Beatrice (Beatrice Jackson Humphreys). Painter
Jackson, Nigel Loring. Painter, Art Administrator
Jackson, Ward. Painter, Editor
Jacobs, Ted Seth. Painter
Jacobs, William Ketchum, Jr. Collector
Jacquemon, Pierre. Painter, Illustrator
Jaffe, Mrs William B. Collector
Jagger, Gillian. Painter, Lecturer
Janis, Conrad. Art Dealer, Collector
Janis, Sidney. Art Dealer, Writer
Janowsky, Bela. Sculptor, Instructor
Janson, Horst Woldemar. Art Historian
Janusas, Ceslovas. Painter
Jaramillo, Virginia. Painter
Jaretzki, Mr & Mrs Alfred, Jr. Collectors
Ject-Key, Elsie. Painter
Jelinek, Hans. Graphic Artist, Educator
Jenkins, Paul. Painter
Jennings, Francis. Sculptor, Painter
Johns, Jasper. Painter
Johnson, Buffie. Painter, Lecturer
Johnson, Cecile Ryden. Painter
Johnson, Clifford Leo. Cartoonist
Johnson, Daniel LaRue. Sculptor, Painter
Johnson, Marian Willard. Art Dealer
Johnson, Ray. Painter
Jones, Edward Powis. Painter, Sculptor
Jordan, Barbara Schwinn. Painter, Illustrator
Jorn, Asger. Painter, Writer
Josten, Peter. Collector
Josten, Mrs Werner E. Collector
Judd, Donald Clarence. Sculptor
Judson, Jeannette Alexander. Painter
Jules, Mervin. Painter, Educator
Kacere, John C. Painter
Kahane, Melanie (Melanie Kahane Grauer). Designer
Kahn, Susan B. Painter
Kahn, Wolf. Painter
Kaish, Luise. Sculptor
Kallem, Herbert. Sculptor, Instructor
Kallir, Otto. Art Dealer, Art Historian
Kallweit, Helmut G. Painter, Sculptor
Kan, Diana. Painter
Kane, Bob Paul. Painter
Kaplan, Alice Manheim. Patron, Collector
Kaplan, Jacques. Collector
Karoly, Andrew B. Painter
Karoly, Fredric. Painter, Sculptor
Karp, Ivan C. Art Dealer, Lecturer
Karshan, Donald H. Museum Director, Collector
Kasak, Nikolas. Sculptor, Painter
Kassoy, Hortense. Sculptor, Painter
Kasuba, Aleksandra. Sculptor
Katz, A(lexander) Raymond. Painter, Lecturer
Katz, Alex. Painter
Katz, Ethel. Painter, Instructor
Katz, Hilda. Painter, Graphic Artist
Katzen, Lila (Pell). Sculptor, Educator
Kaufman, Edgar, Jr. Designer, Writer
Kaufman, Irving. Painter, Educator
Kaufman, Jane A. Painter, Instructor
Kaufman, Joe. Illustrator
Kaupelis, Robert John. Painter, Educator
Kaz (Lawrence Katzman). Designer, Cartoonist
Kaz, Nathaniel. Sculptor, Instructor

New York City (cont)

Keen, Helen Boyd. Painter, Collector
Kelly, Ellsworth. Painter, Sculptor
Kelly, James. Painter
Kempton, Greta. Painter
Kepalas (Elena Kepalaite). Sculptor, Painter
Kerns, Ed (Johnson, Jr). Painter
Kerr, Berta Borgenicht. Art Dealer, Collector
Kerr, E Coe. Art Dealer
Kertess, Klaus D. Art Dealer, Art Historian
Kessler, Alan. Painter
Kessler, Shirley. Painter, Instructor
Kienbusch, William Austin. Painter
Kimball, Yeffe. Painter
King, Ethel May. Collector, Patron
King, Warren Thomas. Cartoonist
King, William Dickey. Sculptor
Kingman, Dong M. Painter, Illustrator
Kinigstein, Jonah. Painter, Designer
Kinstler, Everett Raymond. Painter
Kirstein, Mr & Mrs Lincoln. Collectors
Kiselewski, Joseph. Sculptor
Kissner, Franklin H. Collector
Kitaj, Ronald. Painter, Printmaker
Klein, Doris. Painter, Sculptor
Klein, Sandor C. Painter, Sculptor
Kleinman, Sue. Painter
Kline, Alma. Sculptor
Klonis, Stewart. Painter, Educator
Knapp, Sadie Magnet. Painter, Sculptor
Knight, Hilary. Illustrator, Designer
Knigin, Michael Jay. Painter
Koch, John. Painter, Collector
Kocherthaler, Mina. Painter
Kocsis, Ann. Painter
Koerner, Daniel. Painter, Cartoonist
Kohn, Gabriel. Sculptor
Komodore, Bill. Painter, Sculptor
Komor, Mathias, Art Dealer
Koni, Nicolaus. Sculptor, Painter
Kootz, Samuel M. Art Dealer, Writer
Koplin, Norma-Jean. Painter
Koppelman, Chaim. Printmaker, Educator
Koppelman, Dorothy. Painter, Gallery Director
Korman, Harriet R. Painter
Kotin, Albert. Painter, Educator
Kottler, Lynn. Art Dealer
Kozloff, Joyce. Painter
Kozloff, Max. Art Critic
Kramarsky, Mrs Siegfried. Collector
Kramer, Hilton. Art Critic
Kramer, Marjorie Anne. Painter
Kraner, Florian G. Painter, Educator
Krasner, Oscar. Art Dealer
Kratz, Mildred Sands. Painter
Kraushaar, Antoinette M. Art Dealer
Kredel, Fritz. Illustrator
Kreindler, Doris Barsky. Painter, Lithographer
Kress, Mrs Rush H. Collector
Krevolin, Lewis. Designer, Craftsman
Kreznar, Richard J. Painter, Sculptor
Kriensky (Morris) (E). Painter, Sculptor
Krigstein, Bernard. Painter, Illustrator
Kroll, Leon. Painter, Lithographer
Krueger, Jack. Sculptor
Kruger, Louise. Sculptor
Kuh, Katharine. Art Critic, Art Consultant
Kunié. Painter, Photographer
Kup, Karl. Art Historian
Kurhajec, Joseph A. Sculptor
Kuwayama, Tadaaki. Painter
Lachman, Mr & Mrs Charles R. Collectors
Laderman, Gabriel. Painter, Educator
Laessig, Robert. Painter, Illustrator
La Hotan, Robert L. Painter
Laine, Lenore. Painter
Lamb, Adrian. Painter
Lamont, Frances (Kent). Sculptor
Landis, Lily. Sculptor
Landry, Albert. Art Dealer

Landsman, Stanley. Sculptor
Lane, Alvin Seymour. Collector
Lane, Christopher. Painter
Lang, Daniel S. Painter
Laning, Edward. Painter
La Noue, Terence David. Sculptor
Lansner, Fay. Painter
Lapiner, Alan C. Art Dealer
Larcada, Richard Kenneth. Art Dealer
Larkin, William. Painter, Printmaker
Larsen, Jack Lenor. Designer
Lasker, Mrs Albert D. Collector
Lawrence, Jack. Collector
Lawrence, Marion. Art Historian, Educator
Lebedev, Vladimir. Painter
Lee, Eleanor Gay. Painter
Lee-Smith, Hughie. Painter, Lecturer
Lefebre, John. Art Dealer
Lehman, Irving. Painter, Sculptor
Leiber, Gerson August. Painter, Printmaker
Leichman, Seymour. Painter
Leigh, David I. Collector
Leitman, Norman. Art Dealer
Lekakis, Michael Nicholas. Sculptor
Lembeck, John Edgar. Painter, Art Dealer
Leonardi, Hector. Painter, Instructor
Leonid (Leonid Berman). Painter
Lerman, Leo. Writer, Art Historian
Lerner, Abe. Book Designer, Art Director
Lerner, Alexander. Collector
Lerner, Marilyn Ann. Painter
Lerner, Richard J. Art Dealer
Leslie, Alfred. Painter
Letendre, Rita. Painter
Lev-Landau (Samuel David Landau). Painter
Le Va, Barry. Painter
Leval, Mrs Fernand. Collector
Leventhal, Ruth Lee. Painter, Sculptor
Levering, Robert K. Painter, Illustrator
Levi, Josef. Painter
Levin, Kim (Kim Pateman). Painter, Art Critic
Levine, Jack. Painter
Levine, Les. Sculptor, Museum Curator
Levinson, Fred (Floyd). Designer, Cartoonist
Levinson, Mon. Sculptor
Levit, Herschel. Painter, Illustrator
Levitt, Alfred. Painter
Levy, David Corcos. Photographer, Educator
Levy, Tibbie. Painter
Lewicki, James. Illustrator, Educator
Lewis, Golda. Painter, Sculptor
Lewis, Norman Wilfred. Painter, Instructor
Lewison, Florence (Mrs. Maurice Glickman). Writer, Art Dealer
Lewitt, Sol. Sculptor
Liberman, Alexander. Painter, Sculptor
Lichtenstein, Roy. Painter, Sculptor
Lieberman, Harry. Painter
Lieberman, Meyer Frank. Painter, Printmaker
Lieberman, William S. Art Administrator
Liles, Raeford Bailey. Painter, Sculptor
Lindner, Richard. Painter
Linsky, Mr & Mrs Jack. Collectors
Lipman, Howard W. Collector
Lipman-Wulf, Peter. Sculptor, Printmaker
Lippard, Lucy Rowland. Writer
Lippold, Richard. Sculptor
Lipton, Seymour. Sculptor
Littman, Robert R. Art Administrator, Art Historian
Livingston, Charlotte (Mrs Francis Vendeveer Kughler). Painter, Art Administrator
Livingston, Sidnee. Painter
Lock, Charles K. Art Dealer
Loeb, Mr & Mrs John L. Collectors
Loew, Michael. Painter, Educator
Logemann, Jane Marie. Painter

London, Alexander. Collector, Illustrator
Longo, Vincent. Painter, Educator
Lopez-Rey, Jose. Art Historian
Lorber, Stephen Neil. Painter
Love, Joseph. Painter
Lovet-Lorski, Boris. Sculptor
Lowe, Joe Hing. Painter, Instructor
Lowenthal, Milton. Collector
Lowry, W McNeil. Art Administrator
Lucas, Charles C, Jr. Collector
Lucchesi, Bruno. Sculptor
Lucioni, Luigi. Painter, Etcher
Luck, Robert. Art Administrator, Art Critic
Lukin, Sven. Painter
Lund, David. Painter
Lunde, Karl Roy. Art Historian, Writer
Lusker, Ron. Painter, Educator
Lye, Len. Sculptor, Kinetic Artist
Lynch, James O'Connor. Collector
Lynes, Russell. Writer, Critic
McCarthy, Denis. Painter
McCartin, Jan. Painter
McCartin, William Francis. Painter
McCormick, Harry. Painter
McCormick-Sakvrai, Jo Mary. Painter, Art Critic
McCoy, Jason. Art Dealer
McCracken, John Harvey. Sculptor, Painter
McCray, Porter A. Art Administrator
Machlin, Sheldon M. Sculptor, Printmaker
MacIver, Loren. Painter
MacKay, Hugh. Art Dealer
MacKendrick, Lilian. Painter
McKesson, Malcolm Forbes. Painter, Sculptor
McKinney, Donald. Art Dealer
McKnight, Eline. Printmaker
McLanathan, Richard B K. Art Consultant, Writer
McMahon, James Edward. Art Dealer
MacRae, Emma Fordyce (Emma Fordyce Swift). Painter
Magazzini, Gene. Painter
Magriel, Paul. Collector
Mahaffey, Noel A. Painter
Malkasian, Gregor. Sculptor
Mallory, Ronald. Sculptor
Manca, Albino. Sculptor
Mandel, Howard. Painter, Sculptor
Mandel, John. Painter
Mankowski, Bruno. Sculptor
Mann, David. Art Dealer
Mann, Katinka. Painter, Printmaker
Manship, John Paul. Painter, Sculptor
Manso, Leo. Painter, Educator
Manton, Jock (Archimedes Aristides Giacomantonio). Sculptor, Art Administrator
Manville, Elsie. Painter
Marais (Mary Rachel Brown). Painter
Marca-Relli, Conrad. Painter
Marcus, Marcia. Painter
Marden, Brice. Painter, Educator
Marder, Dorie. Painter
Margo, Boris. Painter, Sculptor
Margulies, Joseph. Painter, Etcher
Marisol, Escobar. Sculptor
Mark, Phyllis. Sculptor
Markell, Isabella Banks. Painter, Graphic Artist
Marks, Mr & Mrs Cedric H. Collectors, Patrons
Marks, Royal S. Art Dealer, Collector
Marks, Stanley A. Collector
Marsicano, Nicholas. Painter, Educator
Marsteller, William A. Collector
Martin, Charles E. Designer, Painter
Martin, Knox. Painter, Sculptor
Martinelli, Ezio. Sculptor
Maryan, Maryan S. Painter
Mason, Frank Herbert. Painter, Educator
Matisse, Pierre. Art Dealer
Mattiello, Roberto. Painter, Sculptor
Mavian, Salpi Miriam. Painter
Max, Peter. Designer, Illustrator

Mayer, Bena Frank. Painter
Mayer, Grace M. Museum Curator, Collector
Mayer, Ralph. Painter, Writer
Mayers, John J. Collector
Mayhew, Richard. Painter, Illustrator
Mayorga, Gabriel Humberto. Painter, Sculptor
Meadmore, Clement L. Sculptor
Meigs, Walter. Painter
Melikian, Mary. Painter
Mellon, James. Printmaker, Painter
Meltzer, Anna E. Painter, Instructor
Meltzer, Doris. Art Dealer, Printmaker
Merkin, Richard Marshall. Painter, Printmaker
Messer, Thomas M. Museum Director, Art Historian
Metz, Frank Robert. Painter, Art Director
Meyer, Mr & Mrs Andre. Collectors
Meyer, Ursula. Sculptor, Photographer
Meyerowitz, William. Painter
Meyers, Dale (Mrs Mario Cooper). Painter, Instructor
Michelson, Annette. Art Critic, Writer
Midgette, Willard Franklin. Painter
Mieczkowski, Edwin. Painter
Mielziner, Jo. Designer, Lecturer
Mikus, Eleanore. Painter, Instructor
Milch, Harold Carton. Art Dealer
Miles, Jeanne Patterson. Painter, Sculptor
Miletti, Clemence M. Painter, Instructor
Miller, Donald Richard. Sculptor
Miller, Dorothy Canning. Museum Curator
Miller, Mrs G Macculloch. Collector
Miller, Harold George. Painter, Designer
Miller, Mitchell. Collector
Miller, Ralph Rillman. Painter, Designer
Miller, Richard Kidwell. Painter
Miller, Richard McDermott. Sculptor
Miss, Mary. Sculptor
Mitchell, (Madison) Fred. Painter
Mitchell, Peter Todd. Painter
Mittleman, Ann. Painter
Miyasaki, George Joji. Printmaker, Painter
Miyashita, Tad. Painter
Mock, Gladys (Gladys Mock Wetter). Painter
Mocsanyi, Paul. Art Administrator
Moe, Henry Allen. Art Administrator
Molin, Brita. Painter, Printmaker
Monroe, Gerald. Painter, Educator
Mont, Frederick. Art Dealer
Monte, James K. Associate Curator
Moore, Robert James. Painter, Instructor
Morales, Armando. Painter
Morgan, Maritza Leskovar. Painter, Illustrator
Morgan, Norma Gloria. Painter, Engraver
Morgan, Randall. Painter
Morris, George Lik. Painter, Sculptor
Morris, Kyle Randolph. Painter
Morris, Robert. Sculptor
Morse, John D. Art Editor
Moseley, Ralph Sessions. Painter
Moses, Ed. Painter
Moskowitz, Robert S. Painter
Moy, Seong. Painter, Graphic Artist
Moyer, Roy. Painter, Art Administrator
Muensterberger, Helene Colcr. Art Dealer
Muensterberger, Werner. Collector, Writer
Mullen, Buell. Painter
Murray, Albert (Ketcham). Painter
Murray, John Michael. Painter
Murray, Robert (Gray). Sculptor
Myers, Forrest Warden. Sculptor
Myers, John. Art Dealer, Collector
Myers, John B. Art Dealer
Nagano, Shozo. Painter
Nakian, Reuben. Sculptor
Namuth, Hans. Photographer, Film Maker
Natkin, Robert. Painter
Navas, Elizabeth S. Collector, Patron
Neel, Alice. Painter
Neikrug, Marjorie. Art Dealer
Neiman, LeRoy. Painter, Printmaker
Nesbitt, Lowell (Blair). Painter, Lecturer

Neuberger, Roy R. Collector, Patron
Nevell, Thomas G. Designer
Nevelson, Louise. Sculptor
Newhouse, Bertram Maurice. Art Dealer
Newman, Arnold. Photographer
Newman, Elias. Painter, Writer
Newton, Douglas. Art Administrator
Niizuma, Minoru. Sculptor
Nivola, Constantino. Sculptor
Noble, Joseph Veach. Art Administrator
Nodel, Sol. Illuminator, Designer
Nordhausen, A Henry. Painter
Nordness, Lee. Art Dealer
Norman, Dorothy (S). Writer, Photographer
Notarbartolo, Albert. Painter
Novak, Barbara (Mrs Brian O'Doherty). Art Historian, Educator
Nuala (Elsa De Brun). Painter
O'Brien, Joan. Painter, Designer
O'Doherty, Brian. Sculptor, Writer
Oenslager, Donald Mitchell. Stage Designer
Offin, Charles Z. Collector, Art Critic
Ohashi, Yutaka. Painter, Sculptor
Ohlson, Douglas Dean. Painter
Ohrbach, Jerome K. Collector
Okada, Kenzo. Painter
Okoshi, Eugenia Sumiye. Painter
Oldenburg, Claes Thure. Sculptor
Oldenburg, Richard Erik. Art Administrator
Olitski, Jules. Painter
Oppenheim, Dennis A. Sculptor
Opper, John. Painter
Orkin, Ruth (Mrs Morris Engel). Photographer, Film Maker
Ortiz, Ralph. Sculptor
Oster, Gerald. Painter, Craftsman
Pace, Stephen S. Painter
Paley, Jeffrey. Art Dealer
Palitz, Mrs Clarence Y. Collector
Palley, Reese. Art Dealer
Palmer-Poroner, Margot. Art Dealer
Paone, Peter. Printmaker, Painter
Paris, Dorothy. Painter
Parish, Betty Waldo. Painter, Writer
Parker, Harry S, III. Museum Educator
Parker, James. Painter
Parker, Raymond. Painter
Parkinson, Elizabeth Bliss. Patron, Collector
Parsons, Betty Bierne. Painter, Art Dealer
Pascal, David. Painter, Cartoonist
Pasilis, Felix. Painter
Passuntino, Peter Zaccaria. Painter, Sculptor
Paternosto, Cesar Pedro. Painter
Pearlman, Henry. Collector
Pearlstein, Philip. Painter, Educator
Pearson, Henry C. Painter
Pease, Roland Folsom, Jr. Art Critic, Collector
Pellicone, William. Painter
Pels, Albert. Painter, Art Administrator
Perless, Robert. Sculptor
Perls, Klaus G. Art Dealer
Perret, Nell Foster. Painter
Pfriem, Bernard. Painter
Pharr, Mr & Mrs Walter Nelson. Collectors
Philipp, Robert. Painter
Phillips, John Goldsmith. Museum Curator
Phillips, Margaret McDonald. Painter, Educator
Phipps, Cynthia. Collector
Phipps, Mr & Mrs Ogden. Collectors
Picard, Lil. Painter, Sculptor
Pierotti, John. Cartoonist
Pindell, Howardena Doreen. Painter, Art Administrator
Pines, Ned L. Collector
Plagens, Peter. Painter, Instructor
Platt, Eleanor. Sculptor
Pleissner, Ogden Minton. Painter

Poindexter, Elinor Fuller. Art Dealer
Pollack, Peter. Photographer, Writer
Pollard, Donald Pence. Designer, Painter
Polsky, Cynthia. Painter
Ponce De Leon, Michael. Printmaker, Painter
Pond, Clayton. Painter, Printmaker
Poons, Larry. Painter
Posen, Stephen. Painter
Poses, Mr & Mrs Jack I. Collectors
Posner, Donald. Art Historian
Powell, Leslie (Joseph). Painter, Designer
Prager, David A. Collector
Pratt, Dallas, Patron, Collector
Pratt, Frances (Frances Elizabeth Usui). Painter, Art Dealer
Prentice, David Ramage. Painter, Designer
Prins, (J) Warner. Painter, Illustrator
Probst, Joachim. Painter
Quaytman, Harvey. Painter
Rabkin, Leo. Sculptor, Painter
Rachelski, Florian W. Painter, Sculptor
Radulovic, Savo. Painter, Craftsman
Rafsky, Jessica C. Collector
Rahr, Frederic H. Collector, Patron
Rain, Charles (Whedon). Painter
Ramirez, Eduardo Villamizar. Sculptor
Randell, Richard K. Sculptor
Rankine, V V. Sculptor, Painter
Rappin, Adrian. Painter
Ratkai, George. Painter, Sculptor
Rattner, Abraham. Painter
Rauschenberg, Robert. Painter
Raydon, Alexander R. Art Dealer, Art Historian
Read, Helen Appleton. Art Historian, Art Critic
Reaves, Angela Westwater. Art Editor, Writer
Reed, Harold. Art Dealer
Reeves, Mr & Mrs Benjamin. Collectors
Regensburg, Sophy P. Painter, Collector
Reginato, Peter. Sculptor
Rehberger, Gustav. Painter, Educator
Reiback, Earl M. Sculptor, Painter
Reich, Nathaniel E. Painter
Reid, Robert Dennis. Painter, Instructor
Reiner, Mr & Mrs Jules. Collectors, Patrons
Reininghaus, Ruth (Ruth Reininghaus Smith). Painter, Instructor
Reis, Mrs Bernard J. Collector, Patron
Reisman, Philip. Painter, Illustrator
Relis, Rochelle R. Painter
Remington, Deborah Williams. Painter
Reopel, Joyce. Sculptor
Resika, Paul. Painter
Resnick, Milton. Painter
Rewald, John. Art Historian, Educator
Reynal, Jeanne. Mosaic Artist
Rich, Daniel Catton. Art Administrator, Lecturer
Rich, Garry Lorence. Painter
Richard, Betti. Sculptor
Richardson, Gretchen (Gretchen Rose Freelander). Sculptor
Richardson, Judith Heidler. Art Administrator, Art Dealer
Riess, Lore. Painter, Printmaker
Rifkin, Dr & Mrs Harold. Collectors
Robbin, Anthony Stuart. Painter
Robbins, Frank. Cartoonist, Illustrator
Roberts, Colette (Jacqueline). Art Critic, Art Administrator
Robertson, Bryan. Writer
Robinson, Mary Turlay. Painter, Lecturer
Rockburne, Dorothea. Sculptor
Rockefeller, Mr & Mrs David. Collectors
Rockefeller, John Davison, III. Collector, Patron
Rockefeller, Mrs Laurance S. Collector
Rockefeller, Mr & Mrs Winthrop. Collectors
Roelofs, Mrs Richard, Jr. Collector
Roesler, Norbert Leonhard Hugo. Collector

New York City (cont)

Rogovin, Howard Sand. Painter
Rohlfing, Christian. Art Administrator, Curator
Rojtman, Mrs Marc B. Collector
Roller, Marion Bender. Sculptor, Painter
Romano, Emanuel Glicen. Painter, Illustrator
Romano, Salvatore Michael. Painter, Sculptor
Romano, Umberto Roberto. Painter, Sculptor
Rome, Harold. Collector, Painter
Rosati, James. Sculptor, Educator
Rose, Hanna Toby. Art Administrator
Rose, Herman. Painter, Printmaker
Rose, Peter Henry. Art Dealer
Rosenberg, Harold. Writer, Educator
Rosenblatt, Adolph. Painter, Lithographer
Rosenblum, Jay. Painter
Rosenblum, Robert. Art Historian
Rosenborg, Ralph M. Painter
Rosenhouse, Irwin Jacob. Printmaker, Illustrator
Rosenquit, Bernard. Painter, Printmaker
Rosenthal, Mrs Alan H. Collector
Rosenthal, Bernard J. Sculptor
Rosenthal, Stephen. Painter
Ross, Alvin. Painter, Educator
Ross, Charles. Sculptor
Roszak, Theodore. Painter, Sculptor
Rotan, Walter. Sculptor
Rotenberg, Harold. Painter
Roth, Frank. Painter
Roth, Richard Lee. Painter
Roth, Rubi. Painter, Instructor
Rousseau, Theodore, Jr. Museum Curator
Ruben, Richards. Painter, Educator
Rubin, Mr & Mrs Harry. Collectors
Rubin, Lawrence. Art Dealer, Collector
Rubin, William. Art Curator, Art Historian
Ruda, Edwin. Painter
Ruddley, John. Art Administrator, Painter
Ruskin, Mickey. Collector
Russell, James Spencer. Painter
Ruta, Peter Paul. Painter, Editor
Ryerson, Margery Austen. Painter, Etcher
Ryman, Robert. Painter
Sachs, A M. Art Dealer, Collector
Sadek, George. Educator, Art Administrator
Saidenberg, Daniel. Art Dealer
St Clair, Michael. Art Dealer
Sainz, Francisco. Painter, Designer
Salemme, Lucia (Autorino). Painter, Educator
Samaras, Lucas. Sculptor
Sampliner, Mr & Mrs Paul H. Collectors
Sanchez, Emilio. Painter
Sander, Ludwig. Painter
Sanders, Joop A. Painter
Sandler, Irving Harry. Art Critic, Art Historian
Sarff, Walter. Painter, Designer
Sarnoff, Robert W. Collector
Saypol, Mr & Mrs Ronald D. Collectors
Scaravaglione, Concetta Maria. Sculptor
Scarpitta, Salvatore. Sculptor
Schaefer, Henri Bella. Painter
Schapiro, Meyer. Educator, Art Historian
Schimmel, Norbert. Collector
Schlemowitz, Abram. Sculptor
Schmidt, Arnold Alfred. Painter, Sculptor
Schneebaum, Tobias. Painter
Schneider, Jo Anne. Painter
Schneider, Noel. Sculptor
Schnurr-Colflesh E. Painter
Schoelkopf, Robert J, Jr. Art Dealer
Schoen, Mr & Mrs Arthur Boyer. Collectors
Scholz, Janos. Collector, Writer
Schorr, Justin. Painter, Educator

Schrag, Karl. Painter
Schreiber, Georges. Painter
Schreyer, Greta L. Painter, Lecturer
Schuller, Grete. Sculptor
Schulte, Mr & Mrs Arthur D. Collectors
Schwabacher, Alfred. Collector
Schwabacher, Ethel K. Painter, Art Critic
Schwalbach, Mary Jo. Painter, Sculptor
Schwartz, Barbara J. Art Administrator
Schwartz, Eugene M. Collector, Patron
Schwartz, Marvin D. Art Historian
Schwartz, Therese. Painter, Writer
Schweitzer, M R. Art Dealer, Collector
Scull, Robert C. Collector
Secunda, (Holland) Arthur. Painter, Sculptor
Seery, John. Painter
Seff, Mr & Mrs Manuel. Collectors
Segy, Ladislas. Art Dealer, Collector
Seiberling, Dorothy Buckler Lethbridge. Writer
Seide, Charles. Painter, Educator
Sennhauser, John. Painter, Designer
Serger, Helen. Art Dealer
Serra, Richard. Sculptor
Setterberg, Carl Georg. Painter, Illustrator
Shacknove, Reta. Painter, Sculptor
Shapiro, Babe. Painter
Shapiro, Daisy Viertel. Collector, Patron
Shapiro, David. Painter
Shapiro, Joel (Elias). Sculptor
Shapshak, Rene. Sculptor
Sharp, Harold. Illustrator
Shaw, Charles Green. Painter, Writer
Shayn, John. Painter, Designer
Shecter, Pearl S. Painter, Instructor
Sherman, Sarai. Painter, Designer
Sherman, Winnie Borne. Painter, Lecturer
Shibley, Gertrude. Painter
Shikler, Aaron. Painter
Shimoda, Osamu. Sculptor, Painter
Shimon, Paul. Painter, Illustrator
Shostak, Edwin Bennett. Sculptor
Shotwell, Helen Harvey. Painter, Photographer
Shoulberg, Harry. Painter
Showell, Kenneth L. Painter
Shuff, Lilly (Lillian Shir). Painter, Engraver
Sideris, Alexander. Painter
Siegel, (Leo) Dink. Illustrator
Sievan, Maurice. Painter
Sigel, Barry Chaim. Painter
Sigismund. Violet M. Painter, Printmaker
Sihvonen, Oli. Painter
Sills, Thomas Albert. Painter
Silverman, Burton Philip. Painter, Illustrator
Simon, Bernard. Sculptor, Instructor
Simon, Ellen R. Designer, Painter
Simon, Sidney. Sculptor, Painter
Simpson, Merton D. Painter, Art Dealer
Sinaiko, (Avrom) Arlie. Sculptor, Collector
Sirugo, Salvatore. Painter
Skemp, Robert Oliver. Painter
Sklar-Weinstein, Arlene (Joyce). Painter, Printmaker
Slack, Dee. Painter
Slifka, Mr & Mrs Joseph. Collectors
Slivka, David. Sculptor
Slivka, Rose. Art Editor
Sloan, Mr & Mrs J Seymour. Collectors, Patrons
Sloane, Patricia Hermine. Painter
Smith, Alvin. Painter, Educator
Smith, Mrs Bertam. Collector, Patron
Smith, C R. Collector
Smith, Gary M. Art Dealer
Smith, George W. Sculptor, Educator
Smith, Joseph A(nthony). Painter, Illustrator
Smith, Leon Polk. Painter, Sculptor
Smith, Mrs Louis. Collector
Smith, Paul J. Museum Director

Smith, Shirlann. Painter
Smithson, Robert I. Sculptor, Lecturer
Smul, Ethel Lubell. Painter, Instructor
Smyth, Craig Hugh. Art Administrator, Art Historian
Smyth, David Richard. Sculptor
Snelson, Kenneth D. Sculptor
Snow, Michael. Painter, Film Maker
Snyder, Joan. Painter
Snyder, Seymour. Illustrator, Instructor
Soffer, Sasson. Sculptor
Soglow, Otto. Cartoonist
Sokole, Miron. Painter, Educator
Solinger, David M. Collector, Patron
Solman, Joseph. Painter, Instructor
Solomon, Hyde. Painter
Solomon, Mr & Mrs Sidney L. Collectors
Sommerburg, Miriam. Painter, Sculptor
Sonfist, Alan. Painter
Sonnenberg, Mr & Mrs Benjamin. Collectors
Sonnenberg, Jack. Painter
Soria, Paola (Paola Soria Sereni). Painter
Soyer, Isaac. Painter, Instructor
Soyer, Moses. Painter
Soyer, Raphael. Painter
Spaeth, Eloise O'Mara. Collector, Writer
Spark, Victor David. Art Dealer
Spaventa, George. Sculptor
Spelman, Jill Sullivan. Painter
Sperakis, Nicholas George. Painter, Printmaker
Spiegel, Sam. Collector
Spitzer, Frances R. Collector
Sprayregen, Morris. Collector
Spriggs, Edward S. Museum Director
Spruyt, E Lee. Painter
Stachelberg, Mrs Charles G. Collector, Patron
Stadler, Albert. Painter
Staempfli, George W. Art Dealer, Painter
Staley, Allen. Art Historian
Stamm, John Davies. Collector
Stampfle, Felice. Art Curator, Writer
Standen, Edith Appleton. Art Historian
Stanley, Bob. Painter
Stasik, Andrew J. Painter, Educator
Stefanelli, Joseph J. Painter
Stefanotty, Robert Alan. Art Dealer
Steig, William. Cartoonist, Sculptor
Stein, Maurice Jay. Painter, Designer
Stein, Ronald Jay. Sculptor
Stein, Walter. Painter, Sculptor
Steinberg, Isador N. Painter, Designer
Steiner, Michael. Sculptor
Steinmann, Mr & Mrs Herbert. Collectors
Stella, Frank. Painter
Stenbery, Algot. Painter
Sterne, Dahli. Painter, Sculptor
Sterne, Hedda. Painter
Stevens, May. Painter
Stevenson, Ruth Rolston. Painter
Stewart, Jack. Painter, Educator
Stillman, E Clark. Collector
Stoloff, Carolyn. Painter
Stoloff, Irma. Sculptor
Stone, Alan. Art Dealer
Stone, Sylvia. Sculptor
Stralem, Donald S. Collector, Patron
Strider, Marjorie Virginia. Sculptor
Stroud, Peter Anthony. Painter, Educator
Suba, Susanne. Painter, Illustrator
Sugarman, George. Painter, Sculptor
Sugimoto, Henry Y. Painter, Instructor
Sullivan, Jim. Painter
Summers, Carol. Printmaker
Sutherland, Sandy. Painter, Writer
Suttman, Paul. Sculptor
Suzuki, Katsko (Katsko Suzuki Kannegieter). Art Dealer
Svet, M (Mrs Dore Schary). Painter
Swann, Erwin. Collector, Patron
Sway, Albert. Painter, Illustrator
Sweeney, James Johnson. Art Administrator, Lecturer
Sylvester, Lucille. Painter, Writer

Takai, Teiji. Painter
Takal, Peter. Painter
Tam, Reuben. Painter, Educator
Tambellini, Aldo. Painter, Sculptor
Tarnopol, Gregoire. Painter, Collector
Tarr, William. Sculptor
Tatti, Benedict Michael. Sculptor, Painter
Tawney, Lenore. Weaver
Taylor, Marie. Sculptor
Teichman, Sabina. Painter, Sculptor
Ten Eyck, Catryna (Catryna Ten Eyck Seymour). Painter
Terrell, Allen Townsend. Sculptor
Terry, Hilda (Hilda Terry D'Alessio). Cartoonist, Writer
Texoon, Jasmine. Painter, Instructor
Thompson, George Louis. Designer
Thompson, Kenneth Webster. Illustrator, Painter
Thomson, Carl L. Art Dealer, Designer
Tillim, Sidney. Painter
Ting, Walasse. Painter
Tobias, Julius. Sculptor, Instructor
Toner, Paul. Art Dealer
Tormey, James. Painter, Designer
Torreano, John Francis. Painter, Lecturer
Toulis, Vasilois (Apostolos). Printmaker, Painter
Trauerman, Margy Ann. Painter, Instructor
Treadwell, Helen. Painter, Designer
Trebilcock, Paul. Painter
Tschacbasov, Nahum. Painter, Printmaker
Tucker, Marcia. Art Historian, Educator
Turner, Joseph. Patron
Turner, Raymond. Sculptor
Tuttle, Richard. Painter
Tworkov, Jack. Painter
Tyson, Mary (Mrs Kenneth Thompson). Painter
Tytell, Louis. Painter
Uchima, Ansei. Printmaker, Painter
Ulin, Dene. Collector, Art Consultant
Untermyer, Judge & Mrs Irving. Collectors
Urban, Reva. Painter, Sculptor
Urry, Steven. Sculptor
Uzielli, Giorgio. Collector
van Aalten, Jacques. Painter
Van Buren, Richard. Sculptor
Van Derpool, James Grote. Educator, Art Historian
Van Der Straeten, Vincent Roger. Art Dealer
Van De Wiele, Gerald. Painter
Van Leer, Mrs W Leicester. Collector
Van Veen, Stuyvesant. Painter, Educator
Varian, Elayne H. Art Administrator, Art Historian
Vass, Gene. Painter, Sculptor
Vazquez, Paul. Painter
Vermes, Madelaine. Craftsman
Vidal, (Margarita) Hahn. Painter
Vincent, Tom. Painter
Viner, Frank Lincoln. Sculptor, Designer
Vodicka, Ruth Kessler. Sculptor, Instructor
Vogel, Donald. Printmaker, Instructor
Vogel, Edwin Chester. Collector
Vollmer, Ruth. Sculptor
Von Schlegell, David. Sculptor
Von Wiegand, Charmion. Painter, Writer
Waddell, Richard H. Art Dealer
Wade, Jane. Art Dealer
Wald, Sylvia. Painter
Waldman, Paul. Painter
Walker, Herschel Carey. Collector
Walker, Mr & Mrs Ralph. Collectors
Wallace, Soni. Painter
Walter, May E. Collector, Patron
Walton, Marion (Marion Walton Putnam). Sculptor
Warburg, Edward M M. Collector
Warhol, Andy. Painter, Craftsman
Warner, Jo. Painter
Washburn, Gordon Bailey. Gallery Director
Washburn, Joan T. Art Dealer
Wasserman, Albert. Painter, Designer

Webb, Aileen Osborn. Patron, Collector
Weber, John. Art Dealer
Wechsler, Herman J. Art Consultant, Writer
Weiner, Mrs Samuel. Collector
Weinstein, Mr & Mrs Joseph. Collectors, Patrons
Weisglass, Mr & Mrs I Warner. Collectors
Weitzenhoffer, A Max. Art Dealer
Welch, Livingston. Sculptor, Painter
Wells, Mac. Painter
Werner, Alfred. Critic, Writer
Werner, Donald (Lewis). Painter, Designer
Werner, Nat. Sculptor
Wertheim, Mrs Maurice. Collector
Weschler, Anita. Sculptor, Painter
Wesselmann, Tom. Painter
West, Lowren. Painter, Illustrator
Weyhe, Mrs Erhard. Art Dealer
Whinston, Charlotte. Painter, Sculptor
White, Ruth. Art Dealer, Collector
Whitehill, Florence (Fitch). Painter
Whitney, John Hay. Art Administrator, Collector
Wiegand, Robert. Painter
Wiener, George. Art Dealer
Wiese, Lucie. Art Critic, Writer
Willard, Charlotte. Writer, Art Critic
Willenbecher, John. Sculptor
Williams, Neil. Painter, Film Maker
Wilmarth, Christopher Mallory. Sculptor, Instructor
Wilson, Jane. Painter
Wilson, May. Sculptor
Wilson, Sol. Painter
Wines, James N. Sculptor
Winsor, V Jacqueline. Sculptor
Winter, Ruth. Painter
Winternitz, Emanuel. Museum Curator, Writer
Wise, Howard. Art Dealer
Wolins, Joseph. Painter
Wong, Frederick. Painter, Instructor
Woodner, Ian. Collector
Woodruff, Hale A. Painter, Educator
Woolfenden, William Edward. Art Administrator, Art Historian
Wright, Frank Cookman. Painter, Instructor
Wright, Nina Kaiden. Art Consultant
Wright, Russel. Designer, Sculptor
Wunderlich, Rudolf G. Art Dealer
Wynshaw, Frances. Art Dealer
Yektai, Manoucher. Painter
Young, Cliff. Painter, Instructor
Youngerman, Jack. Painter
Yrisarry, Mario. Painter
Yunkers, Adja. Painter, Educator
Zabriskie, Virginia M. Art Dealer
Zacharias, Athos. Painter
Zadok, Mr & Mrs Charles. Collectors
Zakanych, Robert. Painter
Zapkus, Kestutis Edward. Painter
Zavel (Zavel Silber). Sculptor, Painter
Zeckendorf, Mrs Guri Lie. Collector
Zeisler, Richard Spiro. Collector, Patron
Zemer, Yigal. Sculptor, Printmaker
Zevon, Irene. Painter
Ziegfeld, Edwin. Educator, Writer
Zierler, William. Art Dealer
Zilzer, Gyula. Printmaker, Painter
Zimiles, Murray. Painter, Educator
Zipkin, Jerome R. Collector
Zox, Larry. Painter
Zucker, Jacques. Painter
Zucker, Murray Harvey. Painter, Sculptor
Zugor, Sandor. Painter

Newburgh

Jackson, Hazel Brill. Sculptor
Waugh, Coulton. Painter, Writer

North Bellmore

Schreiber, Martin. Sculptor, Painter

North Salem

Kipp, Lyman. Sculptor

Northport

Baumhofer, Walter Martin. Illustrator, Painter
Twardowicz, Stanley Jan. Painter, Photographer
Verzyl, June Carol. Art Dealer, Collector

Nyack

Borne, Mortimer. Sculptor, Painter
Dahlberg, Edwin Lennart. Painter
Williams, Shirley C. Sculptor

Olcott

Penney, Charles Rand. Collector,

Old Chatham

Coates, Robert M. Writer, Art Critic
Kratina, K George. Sculptor

Oneida

Colway, James R. Painter

Oneonta

Parish, Jean E. Painter, Educator

Orangeburg

Harootian, Khoren Der. Painter, Sculptor

Ossining

Gebhardt, Roland. Sculptor, Painter

Oswego

O'Connell, George D. Printmaker, Educator
Saunders, Aulus Ward. Painter, Educator
Stark, George King. Educator, Sculptor
Sullins, Robert M. Painter, Educator

Palisades

Breer, Robert C. Sculptor, Film Maker
Katzenbach, William E. Designer, Lecturer
Knowlton, Grace Farrar. Sculptor
Wasey, Jane. Sculptor

Peekskill

Levine, Seymour R. Collector
Rocklin, Raymond. Sculptor, Lecturer

Pelham

Boal, Sara Metzner. Painter, Instructor
Rutsch, Alexander. Painter, Sculptor
Sharp, Marion Leale. Painter

Pelham Manor

Callan, Elizabeth Purvis. Painter

Pine Plains

Becker, Charlotte (Mrs Walter Cox). Illustrator, Painter

Pittsford

Wildenhain, Frans. Potter, Educator

Plainview

Liberi, Dante. Painter, Sculptor

Pleasantville

Handville, Robert T. Painter, Illustrator
Robinson, Jay Thurston. Painter

Port Chester

Blattner, Robert Henry. Painter, Illustrator
Reichman, Gerson. Collector

Potsdam

Gibson, Roland. Collector, Educator

Poughkeepsie

Cikovsky, Nicolai, Jr. Art Historian, Educator
Forman, Alice. Painter, Designer
Havelock, Christine Mitchell. Art Historian
Lindmark, Arne. Painter, Lecturer
Nochlin. Linda (Linda Pommer). Art Historian, Educator
Pickens, Alton. Painter, Educator
Reynard, Carolyn Cole. Painter, Instructor
Rubenstein, Lewis W. Painter, Educator
Whitehead, James Louis. Art Administrator, Designer

Pound Ridge

Bender, Beverly Sterl. Sculptor, Designer
Ferro, Walter. Graphic Artist

Purchase

Danes, Gibson Andrew. Educator
Trosky, Helene Roth. Printmaker, Writer

Purdy Station

McGee, William Douglas. Painter, Educator

Queens

Christman, Reid August. Painter
Tobias, Abraham Joel. Painter, Sculptor

Red Hook

Lax, David. Painter

Rego Park

Aronson, Irene Hilde. Designer, Painter

Riverdale

Carmel, Hilda Anne. Painter
Cooper, Joanne Beckman. Painter
Hnizdovsky, Jacques. Painter, Printmaker
Menkes, Sigmund. Painter

Rochester

Avery, Ralph Hillyer. Painter, Illustrator
Barschel, H J. Designer, Photographer
Brown, Bruce Robert. Painter, Sculptor
Christensen, Hans-Jorgen Thorvald. Designer, Craftsman
Doherty, Robert J, Jr. Art Administrator, Educator
Hambleton, Bud. Sculptor
Herdle, Isabel C. Art Administrator
Holm, Milton W. Painter
Mariano, Anne, Painter
Menihan, John Conway. Painter, Designer
Prior, Harris King. Art Administrator, Educator
Stern, Mr & Mrs Arthur Lewis. Collectors
Wilson, Albert Leon. Sculptor, Illustrator
Witmeyer, Stanley Herbert. Art Administrator, Designer

Rockaway Park

Mina-Mora, Dorise Olson. Painter
Mina-Mora, Raul Jose. Painter, Illustrator

Rockville Centre

Goldberg, Raymond Robert. Painter, Instructor
Goldberg, Virginia Eagan. Painter, Illustrator

Roslyn

Kenny, Thomas Henry. Painter
Ronay, Stephen Robert. Painter

Roslyn Estates

Pall, Dr & Mrs David B. Collectors

Roslyn Heights

Gach, George. Painter, Sculptor
Rotholz, Rina. Printmaker

Rye

Drew, Joan. Printmaker, Sculptor
Guion, Molly. Painter
Morgan, Frances Mallory. Sculptor
Van Hook, Nell. Painter, Sculptor

Sag Harbor

Billings, Henry. Painter, Illustrator
Bolotowsky, Ilya. Painter, Educator
Brook, Alexander. Painter
Knee, Gina (Mrs Alexander Brook). Painter, Etcher
Weber, Jean M. Art Administrator, Educator

Sagaponack

Butchkes, Sydney. Painter, Sculptor
Dash, Robert (Warren). Painter
Georges, Paul. Painter

St. James

White, Robert (Winthrop). Sculptor, Educator

Salt Point

Sellers, William Freeman. Sculptor, Lecturer
Wolfson, Sidney. Painter, Sculptor

Sands Point

Barnet, Mr & Mrs Howard J. Collectors

Saranac Lake

Yepez, Dorothy. Art Administrator, Painter

Saratoga Springs

Baruzzi, Peter B. Painter, Educator
Jones, W Louis. Painter, Sculptor
Pardon, Earl B. Craftsman, Educator

Sayville

Eugenie (Eugenie Muelhauser Murphy). Painter

Scarsdale

Arbeit, Arnold A. Painter, Educator
Barton, Georgie Read. Painter, Educator
Breinin, Raymond. Painter, Sculptor
Burgard, Ralph. Art Administrator
Callisen, Sterling. Educator
Goldsmith, Morton Ralph. Collector, Patron
Hausman, Jerome Joseph. Educator
Kearl, Stanley Brandon. Sculptor
Kizer, Charlotte Elizabeth. Designer, Craftsman
Morgan, Barbara Brooks. Painter, Photographer
Ries, Martin. Painter, Art Historian
Schutz, Anton. Etcher, Writer
Stevens, Elisabeth Goss. Writer, Art Critic
Temple, Mr & Mrs Alan H. Collectors
Wittenborn, George. Collector, Art Dealer

Schenectady

Bittleman, Arnold (Irwin). Painter

Scottsville

Castle, Wendell Keith. Designer, Sculptor
Meyer, Fred (Robert). Sculptor, Painter

Sea Cliff

Jacobs, David (Theodore). Sculptor, Educator
Mellow, James R. Art Critic
Spampinato, Clemente. Sculptor

Setauket

Bishop, Marjorie Cutler. Painter

Shady

Ruellan, Andrée. Painter

Shelter Island

Shields, Alan J. Designer, Painter

Sidney

McClelland, Jeanne C. Printmaker

South Butler

Caster, Bernard Harry. Painter, Enamelist

Southampton

Porter, Fairfield. Painter, Lecturer
Rivers, Larry. Painter

Southold

Gruppe, Karl Heinrich. Sculptor

Sparkill

Vytlacil, Vaclav. Painter, Educator

Stanfordville

Simon, Howard. Illustrator, Painter

Staten Island

Bernstein, Gerald. Painter, Restorer
Hitch, Jean Leason. Painter
Hitch, Robert A. Painter
Lorenzani, Arthur Emanuele. Sculptor
Mulcahy, Freda. Painter, Art Administrator
Nelson, Carey Boone. Sculptor
Salerno, Charles. Sculptor, Educator
Silberstein, Muriel Rosoff. Instructor, Painter
Swenson, Anne. Painter, Instructor

Stone Ridge

Millonzi, Victor. Sculptor

Stony Brook

Reboli, Joseph John. Painter, Illustrator

Stony Point

Dienes, Sari. Painter, Sculptor

Stormville

St John, Bruce. Art Administrator, Art Historian

Suffern

Pousette-Dart, Richard. Painter

Summit

Davis, Gerald Vivian. Painter, Educator

Syracuse

Bakke, Larry Hubert. Educator, Painter
De Tore, John E. Painter, Educator
Freundlich, August L. Educator

Kerfoot, Margaret (Mrs M W Jennison). Painter, Educator
Mack, Rodger Allen. Sculptor, Educator
Vander Sluis, George J. Painter, Educator
Vargo, John. Educator, Painter
Witkin, Jerome Paul. Painter, Educator
Wyckoff, Sylvia Spencer. Painter, Educator

Tappan

Lo Medico, Thomas Gaetano. Sculptor, Designer
Nickford, Juan. Sculptor, Educator

Tillson

Bishop, Benjamin. Painter, Educator

Tonawanda

Bolinsky, Joseph Abraham. Sculptor, Educator

Ulster County

Taylor, John (Williams). Painter

Upper Grandview

Dash, Harvey Dwight. Educator, Painter

Utica

Cimbalo, Robert W. Sculptor
Dwight, Edward Harold. Museum Director
Franco, Barbara. Curator
Loy, John Sheridan. Painter
Moshier, Elizabeth Alice. Painter, Educator
Murray, William Colman. Collector, Patron
Palmer, William C. Painter, Educator
Pribble, Easton. Painter, Educator
Sabine, Julia. Art Librarian

Valley Cottage

Greene, Stephen. Painter
Heaton, Maurice. Designer, Craftsman

Valley Stream

Hart, Allen M. Painter, Educator
Trifon, Harriette. Painter, Sculptor

Van Hornesville

Romeling, W B. Painter

Voorheesville

O'Connor, Thom. Printmaker

Wainscott

Porter, (Edwin) David. Painter, Sculptor

Wantagh

Glaser, David. Designer, Painter

Warwick

Franck, Frederick S. Painter, Writer

Water Mill

Brandt, Warren. Painter
Jackson, Lee. Painter

Webster

Brennan, Harold James. Designer, Craftsman

West Hempstead

Greenberg, Shirlee Bernice. Painter
Hornung, Clarence Pearson. Designer, Writer

Westbury

Cronbach, Robert M. Sculptor
Honig, Mervin. Painter, Painting Conservator
Sherbell, Rhoda. Sculptor, Collector
Surrey, Milt. Painter

Westchester

Hammond, Natalie Hays. Painter, Museum Director

Westtown

Sinnard, Elaine (Janice). Painter, Sculptor

White Plains

D'Amico, Victor Edmond. Educator, Writer
Nickerson, Ruth (Ruth Nickerson Greacen). Sculptor

Whitestone

De Cesare, Sam. Sculptor, Painter

Williston Park

Baum, William. Painter

Wingdale

Bolomey, Roger Henry. Sculptor, Art Historian

Wood Haven

Csoka, Stephen. Painter, Etcher

Woodmere

Brodey, Stanley Carl. Painter

Woodside

Fax, Elton Clay. Painter, Writer
Leitman, Samuel. Painter

Woodstock

Angeloch, Robert (Henry). Painter
Calamar, Gloria. Painter, Lecturer
Chavez, Edward Arcenio. Painter, Sculptor
Currie, Bruce. Painter
Fenton, John Nathaniel. Painter, Etcher
Fite, Harvey. Sculptor

Woodstock (cont)

Guston, Philip. Painter
Handell, Albert George. Painter
Laufman, Sidney. Painter
Lee, Doris. Painter, Illustrator
Lenssen, Heidi (Mrs Fridolf Johnson).
   Painter, Lecturer
Magafan, Ethel. Painter
Neustadt, Barbara (Mrs Gunther Meyer).
   Graphic Artist, Lecturer
Pachner, William. Painter
Petersham, Maud Feller. Illustrator,
   Writer
Pike, John. Illustrator, Painter
Plate, Walter. Painter, Educator
Plath, Iona. Designer, Writer
Refregier, Anton. Painter
Small, Amy Gans. Sculptor, Instructor
Summers, Dudley Gloyne. Painter, Illustra-
   tor
Wuermer, Carl. Painter, Fine Art Ap-
   praiser

Yonkers

Clive, Richard R. Painter
Corwin, Sophia M. Sculptor, Painter
Halley, Donald M, Jr. Art Administrator,
   Instructor
Maltzman, Stanley. Printmaker, Painter

Yorktown Heights

Putnam, Wallace (Bradstreet). Painter,
   Writer

NORTH CAROLINA

Asheville

Bunker, Eugene Francis, Jr (Gene). Potter,
   Educator
Gray, Robert Ward. Art Administrator

Belmont

Mintich, Mary Ringelberg. Sculptor,
   Craftsman

Blowing Rock

McNett, Elizabeth Vardell. Painter,
   Illustrator
Moose, Philip Anthony. Painter, Illustrator
Stacks, Leon. Painter, Art Restorer

Chapel Hill

Foushee, Ola Maie (Mrs John M, Sr).
   Painter, Writer
Ness, (Albert) Kenneth. Painter, Educator
Schlageter, Robert William. Art Adminis-
   trator
Sloane, Joseph Curtis. Art Historian,
   Educator

Charlotte

Dalton, Harry L. Collector, Patron
Franklin, Ernest Washington, Jr.
   Collector
Gatewood, Maud Florance. Painter,
   Educator
Gebhardt, Ann Stellhorn. Painter, Educator
Kortheuer, Dayrell. Painter
Scarbrough, Cleve Knox, Jr. Art Adminis-
   trator, Art Historian
Tucker, Charles Clement. Painter

Dallas

Creech, Franklin Underwood. Painter,
   Instructor

Davidson

Jackson, Herb. Painter, Educator

Durham

Covi, Dario A. Art Historian
Hall, Louise. Educator, Art Historian
Mueller, Earl George. Art Historian,
   Educator
Semans, James Hustead. Patron
Sunderland, Elizabeth Read. Art Historian

Franklin

Raveson, Sherman Harold. Painter,
   Writer

Greensboro

Barker, Walter William. Painter, Writer
Carpenter, Gilbert Frederick (Bert).
   Painter, Educator
Clarke, Ruth Abbott. Painter
Gregory, Joan. Educator, Painter
Miller, Eva-Hamlin. Painter, Educator
Stewart, John P. Printmaker, Sculptor
Tucker, James Ewing. Museum Curator,
   Painter

Greenville

Blakeslee, Sarah (Sarah Blakeslee Speight).
   Painter
Crawley, Wesley V. Sculptor, Educator
Gordley, Metz Tranbarger. Painter
Gray, Wellington Burbank. Educator,
   Designer
Sexauer, Donald Richard. Printmaker,
   Educator
Speight, Francis. Painter, Educator

Hendersonville

Blakely, Joyce (Carol). Painter, Instructor
Hagglund, Irvin (Arvid). Cartoonist

North Wilkesboro

Nichols, Ward H. Painter, Printmaker

Pittsboro

Kachergis, George Joseph. Painter,
   Educator

Raleigh

Bier, Justus. Museum Director, Writer
Broderson, Robert. Painter
Cox, Joseph H. Painter, Educator
Domit, Moussa M. Art Administrator,
   Art Historian
Reep, Edward Arnold. Painter, Educator
Williams, Benjamin Forrest. Museum
   Curator, Art Historian

Tryon

Quest, Charles Francis. Painter, Educator
Quest, Dorothy (Johnson). Painter,
   Instructor

Webster

Morgan, Lucy Calista. Craftsman,
   Instructor

Wilmington

Evans, Minnie. Painter
Howell, Claude Flynn. Painter, Educator

Winston-Salem

King, Joseph Wallace (Vinciata). Painter
Mangum, William (Goodson). Sculptor,
   Painter
Potter, Ted. Painter, Art Administrator

NORTH DAKOTA

Minot

Schwieger, Christopher Robert. Printmaker, Educator

OHIO

Akron

Drumm, Don. Sculptor, Craftsman
Kitner, Harold. Educator
Rogers, P J. Printmaker, Painter

Alliance

Cleveland, Helen Barth. Art Administrator,
   Instructor

Athens

Hostetler, David. Sculptor, Instructor
Kortlander, William (Clark). Painter,
   Educator

Bath

Skeggs, David Potter. Designer, Painter

Canton

Hill, Marvin William. Painter
Rhodes, Reilly Patrick. Art Museum
   Director
Welch, James Henry. Collector

Chillicothe

Gough, Robert Alan. Painter

Cincinnati

Adams, Philip Rhys. Art Administrator
Boulton, Jack. Art Administrator
Boyle, Richard J. Art Administrator, Art
   Historian
Collins, William Charles. Painter, Educator
Cornelius, Francis DuPont. Conservator,
   Painter
DeForest, Julie Morrow. Painter, Writer
Douglas, Edwin Perry. Painter, Educator
Driesbach, Walter Clark, Jr. Sculptor,
   Instructor
Fabe, Robert. Painter, Educator

Fenton, Michael Irwin. Painter, Instructor
Fischer, Mildred (Gertrude). Designer, Weaver
Grooms, Reginald Lesie. Educator, Painter
Hanna, Katherine. Art Administrator
Hayes, Robert T. Painter, Designer
Helwig, Arthur Louis. Painter, Instructor
Klarin, Winifred Erlick. Painter
Knipschild, Robert. Painter, Educator
Krody, Barron J. Designer, Instructor
Longacre, Margaret Gruen. Printmaker, Lecturer
Maciel, Mary Oliveira. Illustrator, Educator
Rice, Harold Randolph. Educator, Writer
Solway, Carl E. Art Dealer
Warren, L D. Editorial Cartoonist

Cleveland

Bickford, George Percival. Collector
Cassill, Herbert Carroll. Printmaker, Educator
Chiara, Alan Robert. Painter
Cooney, John Ducey. Art Administrator, Writer
Czuma, Stanislaw J. Art Historian
Davidovich, Jaime. Painter
Davis, David Ensos. Sculptor
Henning, Edward B. Curator, Educator
Hornung, Gertrude Seymour. Educator, Lecturer
Jankowski, Joseph P. Painter, Educator
Jeffery, Charles Bartley. Educator, Art Administrator
Kowalski, Raymond Alois. Painter
Krausz, Laszlo. Painter
Lee, Sherman Emery. Art Museum Director
McCullough, Joseph. Art Administrator, Painter
McVey, Leza. Sculptor, Designer
McVey, William M. Sculptor, Educator
Miller, Leon Gordon. Designer, Sculptor
Morse, A Reynolds. Collector
Putnam, Mrs John B. Collector
Rawski, Conrad Henry. Educator, Lecturer
Shepherd, Dorothy G (Mrs Ernst Payer). Museum Curator
Talvacchio, Helen Steiner. Painter
Teyral, John. Painter, Instructor
Thompson, Lockwood. Collector
Welch, Mr & Mrs Robert G. Collectors

Cleveland Heights

Dubaniewicz, Peter Paul. Painter
Rebeck, Steven Augustus. Sculptor

Columbus

Black, David Evans. Sculptor
Chafetz, Sidney. Printmaker, Educator
Craig, Eugene. Cartoonist, Lecturer
Gatrell, Marion Thompson. Educator, Painter
Gatrell, Robert Morris. Educator, Painter
Jocda (Joseph Charles Dailey). Painter, Art Administrator
Kuehn, Edmund Karl. Curator, Lecturer
Nicodemus, Chester Roland. Sculptor, Designer
Simson, Bevlyn A. Painter, Printmaker
Young, Mahonri S. Art Administrator

Cuyahoga Falls

Boedeker, Arnold E (Boedie). Illustrator, Painter
Flint, Leroy W. Painter, Educator

Dayton

Clark, Mark A. Museum Curator
Colt, Priscilla C. Art Administrator, Lecturer
Colt, Thomas C, Jr. Museum Director
Evans, Bruce Haselton. Art Administrator, Art Historian
Glover, Donald Mitchell. Curator
Haswell, Mr & Mrs Anthony. Collectors
Koepnick, Robert Charles. Sculptor, Educator
Ostendorf, (Arthur) Lloyd, Jr. Painter, Instructor
Pinkney, Helen Louise. Art Administrator, Art Historian
Raffel, Alvin Robert. Painter, Educator

Delaware

Getz, Dorothy. Sculptor, Educator
Kalb, Marty Joel. Painter
Stewart, Jarvis Anthony. Educator, Painter

Dublin

Chadeayne, Robert Osborne. Painter, Educator

Euclid

Bates, Kenneth Francis. Craftsman, Educator

Findlay

Fowler, Mary Blackford. Sculptor, Painter

Gambier

Boyd, Donald Edgar. Sculptor, Educator
Slate, Joseph Frank. Painter, Writer

Gates Mills

Clague, John Rogers. Sculptor

Grand Rapids

Labino, Dominick. Sculptor, Writer

Hamilton

Phelps, Nan Dee. Painter, Photographer
Stomps, Walter E Jr. Painter, Educator

Hiram

Jagow, Ellen T. Painter

Kent

Grossman, Morton. Painter, Educator
Janicki, Hazel (Mrs Wm Schock). Painter, Instructor
Konzal, Joseph. Sculptor
Novotny, Elmer Ladislaw. Painter, Educator
O'Sickey, Joseph Benjamin. Painter, Educator

Lakewood

Treaster, Richard A. Painter, Instructor

Maple Heights

Grubb, Pat Pincombe. Painter

Marietta

Winer, Arthur Howard. Sculptor, Educator

Marion

Beery, Arthur O. Painter

North Lima

Mohn, Cheri (Ann). Painter

Oberlin

Arnold, Paul Beaver. Educator, Printmaker
Artz, Frederick B. Art Historian, Writer
Bongiorno, Laurine Mack. Art Historian
Buck, Richard D. Conservator
Pearson, John. Painter, Instructor
Stechow, Wolfgang. Art Historian
Whiteside, Forbes J. Educator

Oxford

Fulwider, Edwin L. Painter, Educator

Painesville

Kangas, Gene. Sculptor, Collector

Parma

Jergens, Robert Joseph. Painter, Educator

Poland

Dennison, Dorothy (Dorothy Dennison Butler). Painter, Lithographer
Vaccaro, Patrick Frank (Patt Vaccaro). Printmaker, Painter

Rocky River

Kuekes, Edward D. Cartoonist

Sandusky

Brown, Daniel Quilter. Illustrator, Cartoonist

Seven Hills

Stanczak, Julian. Painter, Educator

Shaker Heights

Hammer, Alfred Emil. Painter, Art Administrator
McGee, Winston Eugene. Painter, Art Administrator
Nelson, Robert Allen. Painter, Printmaker

Springfield

Morgan, Helen Bosart. Sculptor
Thompson, Ralston Carlton. Painter, Educator

Stillwater

McVicker, J Jay. Painter, Educator

Toledo

Bruner, Louise Katherine. Art Critic, Writer
Draper, Line Bloom. Painter
Hutton, William. Museum Curator
Wittmann, Otto. Museum Director, Art Administrator

Urbana

Miller, Nancy. Sculptor, Painter

Warren

Walker, James Adams. Painter, Printmaker

Worthington

Severino, D(ominick) Alexander. Educator, Art Administrator

Wyoming

Gross, Mr & Mrs Merrill Jay. Collectors, Patrons

Yellow Springs

Metcalf, James. Sculptor
Metcalf, Robert M. Designer, Instructor

Youngstown

Butler, Joseph (Green). Art Administrator, Painter
McDonough, John Joseph. Collector, Patron
Murray, Richard Deibel. Painter, Sculptor
Singer, Clyde J. Painter

OKLAHOMA

Ada

Lafon, Dee J. Painter, Sculptor

Ardmore

Beaver, Fred. Painter, Lecturer

Chickasha

Bailey, Clark T. Sculptor, Educator

Miami

Wilson, Charles Banks. Painter, Lithographer

Muskogee

Hill, Joan (Chea-Se-Quah). Painter, Illustrator
Snodgrass, Jeanne Owens. Art Administrator, Lecturer

Norman

Bavinger, Eugene Allen. Painter, Educator
Bogart, George A. Painter
Corsaw, Roger D. Educator, Craftsman
Henkle, James Lee. Sculptor, Educator
Olkinetzky, Sam. Painter, Museum Director
Sutton, George Miksch. Painter, Illustrator

Oklahoma City

Alaupović, Alexandra V. Sculptor, Educator
Cannon, T C (Tom Wayne). Painter, Printmaker
Davis, J Ray. Painter, Printmaker
Faris, Brunel De Bost. Painter, Educator
Goetz, Richard Vernon. Painter, Educator
McAninch, Beth. Painter
McChristy, Quentin L. Painter, Designer
Patterson, Patty (Mrs Frank Grass). Painter, Craftsman
Riley, Gerald Patrick. Designer, Instructor
Seabourn, Bert Dail. Painter, Illustrator
Sheets, Nan Jane. Art Administrator, Painter
Vallee, Jack (Land). Painter
White, Roger Lee. Painter, Educator

Okmulgee

Jones, Ruthe Blalock. Painter

Owasso

Hessing, Valjean McCarty. Painter

Tulsa

Allen, Clarence Canning. Painter, Writer
Allen, Loretta B. Painter, Designer
De Vinna, Maurice (Ambrose, Jr). Critic, Educator
Gussman, Herbert. Collector, Patron
Hogue, Alexandre. Painter, Writer
Humphrey, Donald Gray. Art Administrator, Lecturer
O'Meilia, Philip Jay. Painter, Illustrator
Packer, Clair Lange. Painter, Writer

Wagoner

Dennis, Cherre Nixon. Painter, Etcher

Woodward

Kemoha (George W Patrick Patterson). Painter, Art Historian

OREGON

Astoria

Klep, Rolf. Museum Director, Illustrator

Corvallis

Gilkey, Gordon Waverly. Printmaker, Educator
Jameson, Demetrios George. Painter, Printmaker
Levine, Shepard. Painter, Educator
Sandgren, Ernest Nelson. Painter, Educator
Sponenburgh, Mark. Art Historian, Sculptor
Taysom, Wayne Pendleton. Sculptor, Educator

Eugene

De Matties, Nick Frank. Printmaker
Krause, LaVerne Erickson. Painter, Printmaker
Kutka, Anne (Mrs David McCosh). Painter
McCosh, David J. Painter
McFee, June King. Educator, Writer
Paulin, Richard Calkins. Museum Director, Craftsman
Witham, Vernon Clint. Painter, Collector

Lake Oswego

Hoffman, Elaine Janet. Painter
Rosenberg, Louis Conrad. Printmaker, Illustrator

Lincoln City

Banister, Robert Barr. Gallery Director, Painter

Portland

Andrus, Moulton Loyal. Sculptor, Architect
Bunce, Louis DeMott. Painter
Givler, William Hubert. Painter, Instructor
Goodwin, Alfred. Collector
Griffin, Rachael S. Art Administrator, Writer
Halvorsen, Ruth Elise. Painter, Writer
Hardy, Thomas (Austin). Sculptor
Heidel, Frederick (H). Painter, Educator
Johanson, George E. Painter, Instructor
Kelly, Lee. Sculptor
Kennedy, Leta Marietta. Educator, Craftsman
Littman, Frederic F. Sculptor
McLarty, William James (Jack). Painter, Instructor
Morris, Carl. Painter
Morris, Hilda. Sculptor, Painter
Newton, Francis John. Museum Director

Salem

Hall, Carl Alvin. Painter, Instructor

West Linn

Murphy, Chester Glenn. Painter

PENNSYLVANIA

Alburtis

Kyriakos, Aleko. Sculptor

Allentown

Berman, Muriel Mallin. Collector, Patron
Berman, Philip I. Collector, Patron
Caldwell, Henry Bryan. Museum Director
Dal Fabbro, Mario. Sculptor, Writer
Dreisbach, Clarence Ira. Painter, Lecturer
Gregg, Richard Nelson. Museum Director, Writer
Hoffman, Richard Peter. Painter
Moller, Hans. Painter

Altoona

Russell, (George) Gordon. Painter

Ambler

Lee, Manning De Villeneuve. Illustrator, Painter
Wolpert, Elizabeth Davis. Painter, Instructor

Arcola

Mitchell, Henry (Weber). Sculptor

Ardmore

Atlee, Emilie DeS. Painter, Instructor
Ewing, Thomas R. Painter, Instructor

Bala-Cynwyd

Taylor, Dr & Mrs J E. Collectors

Bangor

Watts, Robert M. Designer

Barto

Bertoia, Harry. Sculptor, Craftsman

Bedminster

Solowey, Ben. Painter, Sculptor

Bethlehem

Quirk, Francis Joseph. Painter, Museum Director

Blue Bell

Martino, Eva E. Painter, Sculptor
Martino, Giovanni. Painter

Broomall

Feld, Augusta. Painter, Instructor
Ingram, Judith. Printmaker, Painter

Bryn Athyn

Ewald, Louis. Painter, Designer

Bryn Mawr

Coolidge, David. Painter

Bucks County

Rosenwald, Barbara K. Collector

Camp Hill

Bartlett, Robert Webster. Painter, Designer

Carlisle

Sellers, Charles Coleman. Art Historian

Chadds Ford

McCoy, John W, (II). Painter, Educator
Parks, Eric Vernon. Sculptor
Wyeth, Andrew Newell. Painter
Wyeth, James Browning. Painter

Chambersburg

Harris, Josephine Marie. Educator, Art Historian

Cheltenham

Wagner, G Noble. Painter, Sculptor

Cheyney

Kamihira, Ben. Painter

Christiana

Miller, Daniel Dawson. Painter, Sculptor

Cochranville

Sazegar, Morteza. Painter

Coopersburg

Riu, Victor. Sculptor

Cornwall

Quinn, Henrietta Reist. Collector

Downingtown

Bostelle, Thomas (Theodore). Painter, Sculptor

Doylestown

Bye, Ranulph (DeBayeux). Painter, Educator

Easton

Higgins, (George) Edward. Sculptor
Salemme, Martha. Painter

Edinboro

Ko, Anthony. Printmaker, Educator
Nicholas, Donna Lee. Potter, Educator

Elkins Park

Berenstain, Stanley. Cartoonist, Writer
Davidson, Abraham A. Educator, Writer
Goodman, Sidney. Painter
Weiller, Lee Green. Painter

Erie

Ahlgren, Roy B. Painter, Printmaker
Burke, Daniel V. Painter, Educator
Kaiser, Vitus J. Painter, Instructor
Kelleher, Daniel Joseph. Painter, Instructor
Sanders, Andrew Dominick. Painter, Instructor
Schabacker, Betty B. Painter, Lecturer
Sundberg, Carl Gustave. Painter, Designer
Sundberg, Wilda (Regelman). Painter
Vanco, John Leroy. Art Administrator, Photographer

Fort Washington

Thompson, F Raymond (Ray). Illustrator, Writer

Freeburg

Bucher, George Robert. Educator, Sculptor

Gibsonia

De Coux, Janet. Sculptor

Glen Campbell

Mallory, Larry Richard. Painter, Instructor

Glenmoore

Smith, Robert C. Educator

Glenside

Scanga, Italo. Sculptor, Educator

Greensburg

Chew, Paul Albert. Art Administrator, Lecturer
Filkosky, Josefa. Sculptor, Educator
Irvin, Mary Francis, S C. Painter, Educator

Harrisburg

Winer, Donald Arthur. Museum Curator, Instructor

Hatboro

Tait, Cornelia Damian. Painter, Sculptor

Haverford

Lloyd, Mrs H Gates. Collector, Patron

Huntingdon

Meltzer, Arthur. Painter, Instructor

Indiana

Kipp, Orval. Painter, Educator
Reynolds, Ralph William. Educator, Painter

Jenkintown

Brown, Bo. Cartoonist
Dioda, Adolph T. Sculptor, Educator
Rosenwald, Lessing Julius

Johnstown

Bradley, Ida Florence. Painter, Instructor
Clemenson, Van Clark. Painter
Hay, George Austin. Painter, Writer
Sheehe, Lillian Carolyn. Painter, Instructor

Kempton

Hesketh. Sculptor

Kutztown

Quirk, Thomas Charles, Jr. Painter, Educator

Lancaster

Kermes, Constantine John. Painter, Printmaker

Steinmetz, Grace Ernst Titus. Painter, Lecturer

Landenberg

Elzea, Rowland Procter. Museum Curator, Painter

Lederach

Hallman, (H) Theodore, (Jr). Craftsman

Lemont

Altman, Harold. Etcher, Educator

Ligonier

Cornelius, Marty. Painter, Illustrator

Lititz

Whipple, Barbara (Mrs Grant Heilman). Printmaker, Writer

Lumberville

Taylor, Rosemary. Craftsman

Malvern

Kramrisch, Stella. Curator, Educator

Manor

Gasparro, Frank. Sculptor, Instructor

Meadville

Fugagli, Alfonso. Painter

Mechanicsville

Coiner, Charles Toucey. Painter

Media

Berd, Morris. Painter, Educator
Hildebrandt, William Albert. Painter, Educator
Hotz, Henry, Jr. Art Administrator
House, James Charles, Jr. Sculptor, Educator

Melrose Park

Sabatini, Raphael. Painter, Educator

Merion Station

Robb, David M. Educator, Art Historian

Millersville

Carson, Sol Kent. Painter, Printmaker

Narberth

Donohoe, Victoria. Art Critic, Writer

New Cumberland

Broh, Minerva Leedy. Painter, Sculptor

New Hope

Autorino, Anthony Michael. Painter
Cheney, Sheldon. Writer, Art Historian
Leith-Ross, Harry. Painter
Moore, Beveridge. Painter
Rosin, Harry. Sculptor, Educator

Newtown Square

Roberts, Gilroy. Sculptor

Norristown

Grimley, Oliver Fetterolf. Painter, Sculptor
Rapp, Lois. Painter, Educator

Ortanna

Berlind, Robert. Painter

Ottsville

Rudy, Charles. Sculptor

Philadelphia

Amarotico, Joseph Anthony. Painter, Conservator
Andrade, Edna Wright. Educator, Painter
Andre, Françoise. Painter
Angelo, Emidio. Cartoonist, Painter
Anliker, Roger (William). Painter, Educator
Ballinger, Louise Bowen. Educator, Writer
Benson, Gertrude Acherman. Writer, Art Critic
Bernstein, Benjamin D. Collector
Blackburn, Morris (Atkinson). Painter, Printmaker
Blai, Boris. Educator, Sculptor
Bookbinder, Jack. Painter, Writer
Bunker, George (Raymond). Painter, Educator
Campbell, Malcolm. Art Historian, Educator
Cramer, Richard Charles. Painter, Educator
Culler, George D. Art Administrator, Educator
De Angeli, Marguerite. Writer, Illustrator
De Costa, Arthur (Archangelo). Painter, Lecturer
Dessner, Murray. Painter
Dillon, Mildred (Murphy). Painter, Printmaker
Drabkin, Stella. Painter, Designer
Easby, Dudley T, Jr. Art Administrator, Art Historian
East, N S, Jr. Designer, Sculptor
Emerson, Edith. Painter, Curator
Etting, Emlen. Painter, Illustrator
Falter, John. Illustrator
Fenton, Beatrice. Sculptor
Ferris, Edythe. Painter, Graphic Artist
Fine, Stanley M. Cartoonist
Frudakis, Evangelos William. Sculptor
Gaul, Arrah Lee. Painter
Gold, Albert. Painter, Educator
Grafly, Dorothy (Mrs Charles H Drummond) Art Critic, Writer
Graham, Frank P. Art Administrator

Greenwood, Paul Anthony. Sculptor, Instructor
Groff, June. Designer, Painter
Hanes, James (Albert). Painter
Hathaway, Calvin Sutliff. Curator
Hathaway, John Wallace. Painter, Printmaker
Havard, James Pinkney. Painter
Hendricks, Barkley Leonnard. Painter
Hood, (Thomas) Richard. Printmaker, Designer
Horter, Elizabeth Lentz. Painter
Howard, Humbert L. Painter
Hutton, Dorothy Wackerman. Designer, Printmaker
Hutton, Hugh McMillen. Cartoonist
Inverarity, Robert Bruce. Designer, Museum Director
Jacobs, Harold. Painter, Sculptor
Johnson, Lois Marlene. Printmaker, Educator
Jones, (Charles) Dexter (Weatherbee), III. Sculptor
Kaplan, Jerome Eugene. Printmaker
Kidder, Alfred, II. Art Administrator
Kimmelman, Harold. Sculptor
Klein, Esther M. Patron, Collector
Kotala, Stanislaw Waclaw. Painter, Art Historian
Kushner-Weiner, Anita May. Painter, Art Administrator
Lechtzin, Stanley. Designer Educator
Le Clair, Charles. Painter, Educator
Lee, Richard Allen. Painter, Collector
Lueders, Jimmy C. Painter, Educator
McGarvey, Elsie Siratz. Curator, Lecturer
McGinnis, Christine. Painter
McIlhenny, Henry Plumer. Collector
Maitin, Samuel (Calman). Printmaker, Designer
Makler, Hope Welsh. Art Dealer
Mangione, Patricia Anthony. Painter
Martell, Barbara Bentley. Painter
Martinet, Marjorie D. Painter
Marzano, Albert. Painter, Designer
Merrick, James Kirk. Painter
Moskowitz, Shirley (Mrs Jacob W Gruber). Painter, Sculptor
Nelson, Leonard. Painter, Educator
Newman, (John) Christopher. Sculptor, Educator
Omwake, Leon, Jr. Painter, Sculptor
Pease, David G. Painter, Educator
Perkins, G Holmes. Architect, Educator
Pitz, Henry Clarence. Painter, Writer
Pitz, Molly Wood. Painter
Potamkin, Meyer P. Collector
Pretsch, John Edward. Cartoonist, Illustrator
Rainey, Froelich Gladstone. Art Administrator, Writer
Reinsel, Walter Newton. Painter
Remenick, Seymour. Painter
Richardson, Constance (Coleman). Painter
Richardson, Edgar Preston. Art Administrator
Searles, Charles Robert. Painter
Shatalow, Vladimir Mihailovich. Painter
Shores, (James) Franklin. Painter
Siegel, Adrian. Photographer, Painter
Smith, Lawrence M C. Collector, Patron
Stegeman, Charles. Painter, Educator
Strawbridge, Edward. Painter
Sweeny, Barbara Eleanor. Museum Curator
Taylor, Charles. Painter
Taylor, Ralph. Painter, Printmaker
Turner, Evan Hopkins. Museum Director
Tyson, Mrs Charles R. Collector
Viesulas, Romas. Printmaker, Educator
Weidner, Roswell Theodore. Painter, Instructor
Willet, Henry Lee. Craftsman

Phoenixville

Hopkins, Kendal Coles. Painter

Pineville

Smith, William Arthur. Painter, Printmaker

Pittsburgh

Arkus, Leon Anthony. Museum Director
Beaman, Richard Bancroft. Painter, Educator
Cantini, Virgil D. Painter, Sculptor
Caplan, Jerry L. Sculptor, Educator
Dixon, Sally Foy. Art Administrator, Lecturer
Farrell, Stephanie Krauss. Art Administrator
Gabriel, Robert A. Sculptor
Gardner, Robert Earl. Printmaker, Educator
Gruber, Aaronel De Roy. Sculptor, Painter
Haggart (Winifred Watkins). Educator, Painter
Josimovich, George. Painter, Designer
Kalinowski, Eugene M. Painter, Sculptor
Karn, Gloria Stoll. Painter, Instructor
Katz, Joseph M. Collector, Patron
Koerner, Henry. Painter, Designer
Lepper, Robert Lewis. Educator, Sculptor
Lewis, Virginia Elnora. Art Administrator, Art Historian
Libby, William C. Painter, Writer
Lieb, Leonard. Painter, Educator
Miller, Donald. Art Critic, Writer
Nama, George Allen. Printmaker, Painter
Owsley, David Thomas. Museum Curator
Pershing, Louise. Painter, Sculptor
Rice, Norman Lewis. Painter, Educator
Rosenbloom, Charles J. Collector
Teilman, Herdis Bull. Art Administrator, Curator
Twiggs, Russell Gould. Painter
Van De Bogart, Willard George. Sculptor, Designer
Weiner, Abe. Painter, Instructor
Winokur, James L. Collector, Patron

Quakertown

Keyser, Robert Gifford. Painter, Educator
Papashvily, George. Sculptor, Writer

Reading

Elliott, B Charles, Jr. Art Administrator, Art Historian

Ridgway

McCloskey, Eunice LonCoske. Painter, Writer

Rochester

Marino, Albert Joseph. Collector

Rosemont

Stanton, Martha Zelt. Printmaker, Instructor
Terry, Duncan Niles. Designer, Craftsman

Royersford

Grebe (E P Grebe Rimmel). Painter, Lecturer

Scranton

Ellis, Carl Eugene. Art Administrator, Instructor

Selinsgrove

Putterman, Florence Grace. Painter, Collector

Sewickley

Heinz, Mr & Mrs Henry J, II. Collectors
Oliver, Henry, Jr. Collector

Sharon

Dunn, Natc. Painter, Instructor

Solebury

Jones, Russell. Painter

State College

McCoy, Wirth Vaughan. Painter, Educator

Sunbury

Karniol, Hilda. Painter, Instructor

Swarthmore

Hollister, Valerie (Dutton). Painter
Walker, Robert Miller. Educator

Titusville

Herpst, Martha Jane. Painter

Uniontown

Leff, Jay C. Collector

University Park

Dickson, Harold Edward. Educator, Writer
Ferguson, Thomas Reed. Painter, Educator
Hoffa, Harlan Edward. Educator
Hyslop, Francis Edwin. Art Historian
Weisman, Winston Robert. Educator, Writer

Valencia

Osby, Larissa Geiss. Painter

Villanova

Wintersteen, Bernice McIlhenny. Art Administrator, Collector

Warrington

Keene, Paul. Painter, Sculptor

Washington

Pablo (Paul Burgess Edwards). Painter, Art Administrator

Wayne

Cooke, Donald Ewin. Writer, Designer
Hoffman, Edward Fenno, III. Sculptor
Key, Ted. Cartoonist
Megargee, Lawrence Anthony (Lawrie). Illustrator

West Chester

Freeland, William Lee. Painter, Sculptor
Hawthorne, Jack Gardner. Educator, Painter
Jamison, Philip (Duane, Jr). Painter

West Reading

Waldron, James MacKellar. Curator, Painter

Wilkes-Barre

Colson, Chester E. Painter, Educator

Wynnewood

Gill, Sue May. Painter, Sculptor
Maxwell, John R. Painter
Merriam, Ruth. Conservator, Collector

Yardley

Wang, Yinpao. Painter, Writer

York

Burickson, Zoel. Sculptor, Lecturer
Case, Andrew W. Painter, Educator
Delgado-Guitart, Jose. Painter

Zionsville

Stark, Melville F. Painter, Educator

RHODE ISLAND

Bristol

Knowlton, Daniel Gibson. Bookbinder
Townley, Hugh. Sculptor, Printmaker
Udvardy, John Warren. Sculptor, Painter

Edgewood

Casey, Elizabeth Temple. Museum Curator

East Providence

Peterson, A E S. Painter

Jamestown

Wright, Catharine Morris. Painter, Writer

Kingston

Cain, Joseph (Lambert). Painter, Educator

Little Compton

Hubbard, Robert. Sculptor
Schmidt, Katherine (Katherine Schmidt Shubert). Painter

Lincoln

Loughlin, John Leo. Painter, Lecturer
Senior, Dorothy Elizabeth. Painter

Newport

Nesbitt, Alexander John. Educator,
  Designer
Warren, Mrs George Henry. Collector

Peace Dale

Eichenberg, Fritz. Illustrator, Printmaker

Providence

Bach, Dirk. Painter, Educator
Day, Martha B Willson. Painter, Collector
Downing, George Elliott. Painter, Educator
Feldman, Walter (Sidney). Painter,
  Educator
Goto, Joseph. Sculptor
Morin, Thomas Edward. Sculptor, Educator
Muench, John. Painter, Graphic Artist
Ostrow, Stephen Edward. Art Historian, Art
  Administrator
Peers, Gordon Franklin. Painter, Educator
Torres, John, Jr. Sculptor, Art Adminis-
  trator

Wakefield

Leete, William White. Painter.
Rohm, Robert. Sculptor

Westerly

Day, Chon (Chauncey Addison). Cartoonist

SOUTH CAROLINA

Anderson

Holcombe, Blanche Keaton. Painter,
  Educator

Beaufort

Rigsby, John David. Painter

Chapin

Mills, Robert James. Painter, Designer

Charleston

Buggel, William Lee. Art Administrator,
  Painter
Goodbred, Ray Edw. Painter, Instructor
Halsey, William Melton. Painter, Educator
Herold, Don G. Museum Director
Hirsch, Willard Newman. Sculptor
Karesh, Ann Bamberger. Painter, Sculptor
Livingston, Virginia (Mrs Hudson Warren
  Budd). Painter, Illustrator
MacBeth, Jerome Russell. Art Adminis-
  trator
McCallum, Corrie (Mrs William Halsey).
  Painter, Instructor

Clemson

McGee, Olivia Jackson. Painter, Illustrator

Columbia

Bardin, Jesse Redwin. Painter, Instructor
Craft, John Richard. Art Administrator
Havens, Elizabeth Carroll. Art Historian,
  Art Dealer
Lafaye, Nell Murray. Painter, Educator
Ledyard, Walter William. Sculptor
McWhorter, Elsie Jean. Painter, Sculptor
Marin, Kathryn Garrison. Painter, Print-
  maker
Mitchell, Dana Covington, Jr. Collector
Mullen, Philip Edward. Drawer
Petroff, Gilmer. Painter, Designer
Saunders, J Boyd. Printmaker, Educator
Van Hook, David H. Painter, Art Adminis-
  trator
Woody, (Thomas) Howard. Sculptor,
  Educator
Yaghjian, Edmund. Painter, Educator

Greenville

Blair, Carl Raymond. Painter, Educator
Bopp, Emery. Painter, Educator
Coburn, Bette Lee Dobry. Painter, Designer
Dreskin, Jeanet Steckler. Painter, Educator
Flowers, Thomas Earl. Painter, Educator
Gustafson, Dwight Leonard. Art Adminis-
  trator
Hunter, Robert Howard. Painter, Sculptor
Koons, Darell J. Painter, Instructor
Morris, Jack Austin, Jr. Art Administrator,
  Writer
Whitley, Philip Waff. Sculptor

Hilton Head Island

Greer, Walter Marion. Painter
Whitmore, Coby. Painter, Illustrator

Isle of Palms

Knerr, Sallie Frost. Painter, Printmaker

Lexington

Flinsch, Harold, Jr. Collector, Patron

Mount Pleasant

Clark, Chevis Delwin. Painter, Instructor

Orangeburg

Rose, Arthur. Painter, Sculptor
Twiggs, Leo Franklin. Painter, Educator

Rock Hill

Freeman, David L. Painter, Educator

Spartanburg

Cook, August Charles. Painter, Engraver
Du Pre, Grace Annette. Painter

SOUTH DAKOTA

Aberdeen

Holaday, William H, Jr. Educator, Painter

Black Hills

Ziolkowski, Korczak. Sculptor

Brookings

Nelson, Signe (Signe Nelson Stuart). Painter
Stuart, Joseph Martin. Painter, Museum
  Director

Sioux Falls

Eide, Palmer. Sculptor, Designer

Vermillion

Howe, Oscar. Painter, Educator
Stilwell, Wilber Moore. Educator, Writer

TENNESSEE

Chattanooga

Bishop, Budd Harris. Art Administrator
Collins, Jim (Lee). Educator, Sculptor
Cress, George Ayers. Painter, Educator

Clarksville

Bryant, Olen L. Sculptor, Educator

Gatlinburg

Gray, Jim. Painter, Instructor

Jackson

Carmichael, Donald Ray. Painter,
  Educator

Knoxville

Ewing, Charles Kermit. Painter,
  Educator
Fulton, Ruth (McConnell). Painter
Le Fevre, Richard John. Painter,
  Educator
Leland, Whitney Edward. Painter,
  Educator
McKeeby, Byron Gordon. Printmaker,
  Educator
Stevens, Walter Hollis. Painter, Educator
Sublett, Carl C. Painter, Educator

Memphis

Anthony, Lawrence Kenneth. Sculptor,
  Educator
Califf, Marilyn Iskiwitz. Painter, Designer
Callicott, Burton Harry. Painter, Callig-
  rapher
Cloar, Carroll. Painter
Goodman, Benjamin. Patron
Govan, Francis Hawks. Educator, Painter
Knowles, Richard H. Painter
Lehman, Louise Brasell. Painter
Moss, Morrie Alfred. Collector
Penczner, Paul Joseph. Painter
Rust, Edwin C. Sculptor, Art Adminis-
  trator
Seyfried, John Louis. Sculptor
Shook, Georg E. Painter
Smith, Dolph. Painter, Educator
Whitlock, John Joseph. Art Administrator,
  Educator

Nashville

Bodo, Sandor. Painter, Sculptor

Brumbaugh, Thomas Brendle. Art
    Historian, Writer
Driskell, David Clyde. Painter, Educator
Jarman, Walton Maxey. Collector
Pletcher, Gerry. Painter, Printmaker

TEXAS

Amarillo

Caballero, Emilio. Educator, Painter
Sicard, Louis Gabriel. Painter, Lecturer

Arlington

Grandee, Joe Ruiz. Painter, Art Gallery
    Director
Joyner, Howard Warren. Painter, Art
    Historian
Rascoe, Stephen Thomas. Painter, Educator

Austin

Beitz, Lester U. Painter, Illustrator
Brezik, Hilarion, CSC. Painter, Educator
Davis, Marian B. Art Historian, Curator
Fearing, Kelly. Painter, Educator
Forsyth, Constance. Painter, Printmaker
Goodall, Donald Bannard. Art Administrator
Guerin, John William. Painter, Educator
Hatgil, Paul. Sculptor
Kelpe, Paul. Painter
Milliken, Gibbs. Painter, Educator
Spruce, Everett Franklin. Painter, Print-
    maker
Umlauf, Charles. Sculptor
Weismann, Donald Leroy. Educator, Painter

Bay City

Bess, Forrest Clemenger. Painter,
    Lecturer

Beaumont

Boughton, William Harrison. Painter,
    Educator
Coe, Matchett Herring. Sculptor

Clint

Herring, Jan(et Mantel). Painter, Writer

Commerce

McGough, Charles E. Printmaker, Educator

Corpus Christi

Cain, Joseph Alexander. Painter, Educator

Dallas

Albrecht, Mary Dickson. Sculptor, Painter
Barnes, Anna Marye. Painter
Bond, Roland S. Collector
Bromberg, Mr & Mrs Alfred L. Collectors
Bywaters, Jerry. Painter, Art Historian
Dozier, Otis. Painter, Printmaker
Froman, Ramon Mitchell. Painter
Harris, Leon A, Jr. Collector, Patron
Kahn, Annelies Ruth. Ceramist, Instructor
Kahn, Ralph H. Art Dealer, Lecturer
Kelley, Chapman. Painter, Art Dealer
Koch, Arthur Robert. Painter, Educator

Leeber, Sharon Corgan. Sculptor
Marcus, Edward S. Collector
Marcus, Stanley. Collector
Mauzey, Merritt. Painter, Illustrator
Meadows, Algur H. Patron
Mudge, Edmund Webster, Jr. Collector
Murchison, John D. Collector
Nagler, Edith Kroger. Painter
Nagler, Fred. Painter
Roche, Jim. Sculptor, Painter
Rueppel, Merrill C. Art Administrator
Scholder, Laurence. Printmaker, Educator
Schrup, John Edmund. Painter, Instructor
Travis, Olin (Herman). Painter, Lecturer
Tyler, Valton. Printmaker
Van Atta, Helen Ulmer. Collector
Vogel, Donald S. Painter, Art Dealer
Wade, Robert Schrope. Painter, Photog-
    rapher
Williamson, Clara McDonald. Painter
Winter, Roger. Painter, Educator

Denton

Mattil, Edward L. Educator, Writer

El Paso

Acosta, Manuel Gregorio. Painter,
    Sculptor
Archer, Dorothy Bryant. Painter, Educator
Enriquez, Gaspar. Designer, Instructor
Jiménez, Luis Alfonso, Jr. Sculptor
Kolliker, William Augustin. Painter,
    Graphic Artist
Krupp, Louis. Painter, Designer
Lea, Tom. Painter, Illustrator
Massey, Robert Joseph. Painter,
    Educator
Morton, Richard H. Painter, Art
    Administrator
Rakocy, William (Joseph). Painter,
    Educator
Sipiora, Leonard Paul. Museum Director,
    Writer
Waterhouse, Russell Rutledge. Painter

Fort Worth

Brown, Richard F. Museum Director
Cantey, Sam Benton, III. Collector
Carlin, Electra Marshall. Art Dealer
Cross, Maria Concetta. Painter, Art
    Dealer
Fuller, Adelaide P & William Marshall.
    Collectors
Johnson, Mrs J Lee, III. Collector, Patron
Lincoln, Richard Mather. Potter, Educator
Malone, James William. Art Administrator
Shore, Clover Virginia. Painter, Educator
Smith, Emily Guthrie. Painter, Instructor
Stegall, James Park. Painter, Instructor
Stone, John Lewis, Jr. Painter, Instructor
Sullivan, Max William. Art Administrator
Weiner, Ted. Collector, Patron
Wilder, Mitchell Armitage. Art Adminis-
    trator
Wilkins, Ruth Lois. Art Administrator,
    Art Historian
Windfohr, Robert F. Collector

Georgetown

Callcott, Frank. Painter

Houston

Adler, Sebastian J. Museum Director
Boynton, James W. Painter, Printmaker
Brochstein, I S. Collector
Collins, Lowell Daunt. Painter, Art Dealer
David, Dianne. Art Dealer, Collector

De Menil, John. Collector
De Montebello, Guy-Philippe Lannes.
    Museum Director
Dreyer, Margaret Webb. Painter, Art
    Dealer
Erdman, R H Donnelley. Art Critic, Art
    Dealer
Hood, Dorothy. Painter
Long, Meredith J. Art Dealer
Love, Jim. Sculptor
O'Neil, John. Painter, Educator
Robinson, Thomas. Art Dealer, Collector
Romansky, Alvin S. Collector, Patron
Shaw, Donald Edward. Painter, Sculptor
Sherwood, Bette (Wilson). Painter, Sculptor
Stout, Richard Gordon. Painter
Turner, (Charles) Arthur. Painter,
    Instructor
Wray, Dick. Painter
Wrightsman, Charles Bierer. Collector

Huntsville

Ahysen, Harry Joseph. Painter, Educator
Breitenbach, William John. Sculptor,
    Draughtsman
Geeslin, Lee Gaddis. Painter, Educator

Irving

Novinski, Lyle Frank. Painter, Educator

Kingsville

Rutland, Emily Edith. Painter

Longview

Elias, Harold John. Painter, Lecturer
Spencer (Mary Scruggs-Spencer). Painter,
    Instructor
Statman, Jan B. Painter
Ward, Velox Benjamin. Painter

Lubbock

Gibbons, Hugh (James). Painter, Educator
Hastie, Reid. Educator, Writer
Howze, James Dean. Educator, Painter
Kingman, Eugene. Painter, Art Adminis-
    trator
Kreneck, Lynwood. Printmaker

Medina

Carrington, Joy Harrell. Painter,
    Illuminator

Nacogdoches

Schlicher, Karl Theodore. Painter,
    Educator

Richardson

Brown, John Hall. Painter, Designer
Pederson, Molly Fay. Painter, Sculptor

San Angelo

Schmidt, Stephen. Museum Director

San Antonio

Duncan, Ruth. Painter

Texas (cont)

Fuchs, Mary Tharsilla, CDP. Educator
Lee, Amy Freeman. Painter, Lecturer
Leeper, John Palmer. Museum Director
McGregor, Jack R. Museum Director
Naylor, Alice Stephenson. Painter
Pace, Margaret Bosshardt. Designer, Painter
Roney, Harold Arthur. Painter, Lecturer
Rowe, Reginald M. Painter, Sculptor
Steinbomer, Dorothy H. Sculptor, Art Librarian
Tauch, Waldine Amanda. Sculptor, Collector

San Marcos

Williams, Tommy Carroll. Art Historian, Painter

Texarkana

Caver, William Ralph. Sculptor, Painter

Waco

Kemp, Paul Zane. Printmaker
Smith, J(ohn) B(ertie). Educator, Painter

UTAH

Logan

Elsner, Larry Edward. Sculptor, Educator
Lindstrom, Gaell. Painter, Educator
Reynolds, Harry Reuben. Art Historian, Photographer
Thorpe, Everett Clark. Painter, Educator

Midvale

Olsen, Don. Painter

Mount Carmel

Zornes, James Milford. Painter, Designer

Orem

Denys, George Frederick. Painter

Provo

Andrus, James Roman. Printmaker, Painter
Coleman, Michael. Painter, Etcher
De Jong, Gerrit, Jr. Educator, Writer
Magleby, Francis R (Frank). Painter, Educator
Myer, Peter Livingston. Sculptor, Painter

Salt Lake City

Beck, Stephen R. Painter, Educator
Cutler, Grayce E. Painter, Writer
Dunn, O Coleman. Collector
Fausett, Lynn. Painter
Friberg, Arnold. Illustrator, Painter
Hicks, Harold Jon (Jack). Sculptor
Sanguinetti, Eugene F. Art Administrator, Lecturer
Smith, Frank Anthony. Painter

Springville

Forster, Peggy Lucille. Art Administrator

VERMONT

Barre

Gaylord, Frank Chalfant. Sculptor, Designer

Barton

Baker, Anna P. Painter, Graphic Artist

Bennington

Adams, Pat. Painter, Educator
Held, Julius S. Educator, Writer

Bristol

Love, Iris Cornelia. Art Historian

Burlington

Graves, Arthur Earle. Painter

Castleton

Robinson, Robert Doke. Painter, Educator

Charlotte

Aschenbach, Paul. Sculptor

Dorset

Bley, Elsa W. Painter
Kouwenhoven, John A. Writer, Educator

East Corinth

Hewitt, Francis Ray. Painter, Educator

Fairlee

Walker, Herbert Brooks. Sculptor, Museum Director

Grafton

Schoener, Allon L-Zimiuare. Art Consultant

Hartland

Tooker, George. Painter

Londonderry

Shokler, Harry. Painter, Serigrapher

Manchester Center

Montague, James L. Art Administrator, Painter

Marlboro

Heiskell, Diana. Painter, Designer

Middlebury

Bumbeck, David A. Printmaker, Educator
Healy, Arthur K D. Painter, Lecturer
Reiff, Robert Frank. Art Historian, Painter

Norwich

Sample, Paul. Painter

Orwell

Wunder, Richard Paul. Art Historian, Art Administrator

Putney

Forakis, Peter. Painter, Sculptor
Ginnever, Charles. Sculptor
Watson, Aldren Auld. Illustrator, Designer

Rutland

Johnson, Katherine King. Art Administrator, Painter

Shaftsbury

Noland, Kenneth. Painter

Shelburne

Emerson, Sterling Deal. Museum Director
Webster, David S. Art Administrator

Springfield

Eldredge, Mary Agnes. Sculptor
Eldredge, Stuart Edson. Painter, Instructor

Stowe

Wright, Stanley Marc. Painter, Instructor

Waitsfield

Carpenter, Harlow. Museum Director

West Townshend

Brodie, Gandy. Painter, Designer
Court, Lee Winslow. Painter

Weston

Landon, Edward August. Printmaker, Painter

Woodstock

Gyra, Francis Joseph, Jr. Instructor, Painter

VIRGINIA

Alexandria

Adams, Katherine Langhorne. Painter, Sculptor
Bailey, Worth. Museum Curator, Art Historian
Banks, Anne Johnson. Painter, Lecturer
Brooks, Phyllis Featherstone. Painter, Instructor
Buhrman, Ruth Ewing. Painter
Caples, Barbara Barrett. Printmaker, Painter

Chapman, Howard Eugene. Designer, Cartoonist
Day, Horace Talmage. Painter, Educator
Evans, Grose. Art Administrator, Art Historian
Genders, Richard Atherstone. Painter
Godwin, Robert Kimball. Painter
Hecht, H Hartman. Collector, Patron
Jamieson, Mitchell. Painter
Mallinson, Constance (Constance Mallinson Alter). Painter
Myers, Denys Peter. Art Historian, Lecturer
Richards, Jeanne Herron. Etcher, Painter
Sanborn, Herbert J. Lithographer, Painter
Spagnolo, Kathleen Mary. Printmaker, Illustrator

Arlington

Fenical, Marlin E. Painter, Art Administrator
Harlan, Roma Christine. Painter, Art Administrator
Reed, Paul Allen. Painter, Educator
Richardson, Gerard. Painter, Designer
Taylor, Prentiss (Hottel). Lithographer, Instructor
Twitty, James (Watson). Painter, Educator

Ashburn

Pickens, Vinton Liddell. Painter

Ashland

Witt, Nancy Camden. Sculptor, Painter

Blacksburg

Carter, Dean. Sculptor, Educator
Huggins, (Leonard) Victor, (Jr). Painter, Educator
Long, Sandra Tardo. Printmaker, Lecturer
Schmidt, Frederick Lee. Painter, Educator

Cape Charles

Sibley, Charles Kenneth. Painter, Educator

Charlottesville

Clark, Eliot Candee. Painter
Hartt, Frederick. Art Historian, Educator
Priest, Hartwell Wyse. Painter, Printmaker
Seitz, William Chapin. Educator, Art Historian
Smith, Charles (William). Painter, Educator
Turner, Theodore Roy. Painter, Educator

Chester

Earl, Jack Eugene. Sculptor

Covington

Walton, Harry A, Jr. Collector

Fairfax

Long, Gwen. Painter, Instructor

Fairfax Station

Jackson, Vaughn L. Painter, Illustrator

Falls Church

Land, Ernest Albert. Painter
Owens, Winifred (Whitebergh). Painter, Lecturer

Lawrenceville

Sakaoka, Yasue. Sculptor, Instructor

Leesburg

Robertson, D Hall. Painter

Lexington

Doyon, Gerard Maurice. Art Administrator, Art Historian
Ju, I-Hsiung. Painter, Educator
Junkin, Marion Montague. Painter, Educator

Lynchburg

Williams, Mary Frances. Art Historian, Lecturer

McLean

Beggs, Thomas Montague. Art Administrator, Painter
Lawson, Edward Pitt. Art Administrator
Orsini (Gwendolyn Orsinger Anderson). Enamelist, Art Dealer
Stark, Ronald C. Photographer, Lecturer

Middleburg

Bowman, Jean (Jean Bowman Magruder). Painter, Illustrator

Newport News

Sheaks, Barclay. Painter, Educator

Norfolk

Jackson, Alexander Brooks (A B). Educator, Painter
Knorr, Jeanne Boardman. Craftsman, Educator
Knorr, Lester. Sculptor, Painter
Lesley, Parker. Art Historian, Educator
McLean, Doris Porter. Painter
Matson, Elina. Weaver
Matson, Greta (Greta Matson Khouri). Painter
Taylor, (Bertha) Fanning. Painter, Lecturer

Powhatan

Binford, Julien. Painter, Sculptor

Reston

Drewes, Werner. Painter, Printmaker

Richmond

Apgar, Nicolas Adam. Painter, Educator
Biehl, Arthur Oliver. Painter, Educator
Brandt, Frederick Robert. Painter, Printmaker
Brown, James Monroe, III. Art Administrator

Burgart, Herbert Joseph. Educator
Freed, David. Printmaker, Photographer
Gaines, William Robert. Art Historian, Painter
McKennis, Gail Collins. Printmaker, Painter
MacNelly, Jeffrey Kenneth. Cartoonist
Martin, Bernard Murray. Painter
Perry, Regenia Alfreda. Art Historian
Pollak, Theresa. Painter, Educator
Wyrick, Pete (Charles Lloyd Wyrick, Jr). Art Critic, Writer

Smithfield

Haack, Cynthia Roach. Painter, Printmaker

South Boston

Cage, Robert Fielding. Painter, Sculptor

Staunton

Desportes, Ulysse Gandvier. Painter, Art Historian

Vienna

Gonzales, Carlotta (Mrs Richard Lahey). Painter, Sculptor
Lahey, Richard (Francis). Painter, Lecturer
Shannon, Joseph. Painter
Summerford, Ben Long. Painter, Educator

Warrenton

Hara, Teruo. Educator, Potter

Williamsburg

Baker, Grace. Painter
George, Walter Eugene, Jr. Designer, Educator
Roseberg, Carl Andersson. Sculptor, Art Historian
Thorne, Thomas Elston. Painter, Art Historian

WASHINGTON

Anacortes

McCracken, Philip. Sculptor

Bainbridge Island Winslow

Willis, Elizabeth Bayley. Art Historian, Collector

Bellingham

Loggie, Helen A. Printmaker, Painter

Ellensburg

Spurgeon, Sarah (Edna M). Painter, Educator

La Conner

Anderson, Guy Irving. Painter

Long Beach

Callahan, Kenneth. Painter

Mary Hill

Dolph, Clifford R. Museum Director

Olympia

Haseltine, James Lewis. Art Administrator,
Painter
Haseltine, Maury (Margaret Wilson
Haseltine). Painter

Pullman

Monaghan, Keith. Painter, Educator

Renton

Wright, G Alan. Sculptor

Seattle

Alps, Glen Earl. Educator, Printmaker
Banks, Virginia. Painter
Brazeau, Wendell (Phillips). Painter
Bush, Beverly. Painter, Sculptor
Celentano, Francis Michael. Painter
Chase, Doris (Totten). Sculptor, Film
Maker
Dailey, Michael Dennis. Painter, Educator
Du Pen, Everett George. Sculptor, Educator
Eckstein, Joanna. Collector, Patron
Fuller, Richard Eugene. Museum Director
Goldberg, Joseph Wallace. Painter
Gonzales, Boyer. Painter, Educator
Hauberg, Mr & Mrs John. Collectors
Herard, Marvin T. Sculptor, Educator
Horiuchi, Paul. Painter
Jenkins, Paul Ripley. Sculptor, Painter
Johnson, Pauline B. Educator, Writer
Jones, Robert Cushman. Painter
Kenny, Bettie Ilene (BIK). Painter, Writer
Kirsten, Richard Charles. Painter, Print-
maker
Kohler, Mel (Otto). Art Dealer
Lawrence, Jacob. Painter, Educator
Levine, Reeva (Anna) Miller. Painter,
Instructor
Maki, Robert Richard. Sculptor
Marshall, John Carl. Craftsman
Mason, Alden C. Painter, Educator
Maytham, Thomas Northrup. Art Adminis-
trator, Lecturer
Meitzler, (Herbert) Neil. Painter, Designer
Monsen, Dr & Mrs R Joseph. Collectors
Moseley, Spencer Altemont. Painter,
Educator
Peck, James Edward. Painter, Designer
Portmann, Frieda Bertha Anne. Painter,
Sculptor
Rising, Dorothy Milne. Painter, Instructor
Sargent, Margaret Holland. Painter
Seders, Francine Lavinal. Art Dealer
Selig, Mr & Mrs Manfred. Collectors,
Patrons
Selig, Martin. Collector
Stoops, Jack Donald. Film Maker, Educator
Thomas, Ed B. Educator, Lecturer
Trubner, Henry. Art Historian
Tsutakawa, George. Sculptor, Painter
Van Der Marck, Jan. Art Historian,
Museum Curator
Warsinske, Norman George, Jr. Sculptor,
Painter

Washington, James W, Jr. Painter, Sculptor
Wehr, Wesley Conrad. Painter
Woodside, Gordon William. Art Dealer,
Collector

Sequim

Henry, John R. Illustrator, Painter

Spokane

Adkison, Kathleen (Gemberling). Painter

Steilacoom

Grigor, Margaret Christian. Sculptor

Sumner

Achepohl, Keith Anden. Printmaker,
Painter

Tacoma

Chubb, Frances Fullerton. Painter,
Educator

Vancouver

Hansen, James Lee. Sculptor

WEST VIRGINIA

Charleston

Black, Mary McCune. Art Administrator,
Painter
Chamness, Ruby Hill. Painter
Keane, Lucina Mabel. Painter, Educator
McNamara, Raymond Edmund. Printmaker,
Painter
Taylor, Grace Martin. Painter, Educator

Huntington

Cornfeld, Melissa Marein. Weaver
Cornfeld, Michael I. Craftsman, Educator
Emerson, Roberta Shinn. Art Administrator
Ettling, Ruth (Droitcour). Printmaker,
Painter
Polan, Lincoln M. Collector
Polan, Nancy Moore. Painter

Morgantown

Couch, Urban. Painter, Designer

Parkersburg

Burnside, Katherine Talbott. Painter

St. Albans

Keeling, Henry Cornelious. Painter,
Educator

Williamstown

Gerhold, William Henry. Painter, Educator
Sheng, Shao Fang. Painter, Instructor

WISCONSIN

Appleton

Brooks, Charles M, Jr. Art Historian,
Educator
Thrall, Arthur. Printmaker, Educator

Barneveld

Weege, William. Printmaker, Educator

Beloit

Boggs, Franklin. Painter, Educator
Ishikawa, Joseph. Art Administrator,
Lecturer
Malsch, Ellen L. Painter, Instructor
Williams, Lewis W, II. Art Historian

Ellison Bay

Austin, Phil. Painter, Lecturer

Evansville

Wilde, John. Painter, Educator

Glendale

Gruen, Shirley Schanen. Painter

Green Bay

King, William Alfred. Painter, Educator

Hartland

Stonebarger, Virginia. Painter

Hollandale

Colescott, Warrington W. Printmaker,
Educator
Myers, Frances. Printmaker

Jackson

White, Doris A. Painter

Kenosha

Faulkner, Kady B. Painter, Educator
Tatman, Virginia Downing. Craftsman,
Painter

Madison

Bohrod, Aaron. Painter, Educator
Butts, Porter. Art Historian, Art
Administrator
Byrd, D Gibson. Educator, Painter
Fiero, Emilie Louise. Sculptor
Grilley, Robert L. Painter, Educator
Kimball, Wilford Wayne, Jr. Lithographer
Logan, Frederick Manning. Educator,
Writer
Lotterman, Hal. Painter, Educator
Meeker, Dean Jackson. Printmaker, Painter
Rogers, Millard Foster, Jr. Art Adminis-
trator, Art Historian
Starks, Elliott Roland. Art Administrator,
Educator
Tomlinson, Florence Kidder. Painter,
Instructor

Vierthaler, Arthur A. Craftsman, Educator
Watrous, James Scales. Painter, Art
　Historian
Weiss, Lee (Elyse C Weiss). Painter

Marinette

La Malfa, James Thomas. Sculptor,
　Educator

Milwaukee

Atkinson, Tracy. Museum Director
Bradley, Mrs Harry Lynde. Collector
Brink, Guido Peter. Painter, Sculptor
Brulc, Dennis. Printmaker, Painter
Burkert, Robert Randall. Painter, Graphic
　Artist
Colt, John Nicholson. Painter, Educator
De Borhegyi, Stephan. Museum Director,
　Writer
Flagg, Mr & Mrs Richard B. Collectors
Green, Edward Anthony. Art Administrator,
　Designer
Grotenrath, Ruth. Painter
Kaiser, Charles James. Painter
Key, Donald D. Art Critic, Writer
Krushenick, John. Painter, Educator
Lewandowski, Edmund D. Painter, Educator
Luntz, Irving. Art Dealer, Writer
Meixner, Mary Louise. Painter, Educator
Melamed, Abraham. Collector, Patron
Meredith, Dorothy Laverne. Weaver,
　Educator
Pick, John. Educator, Art Administrator
Revor, Remy, SSND. Designer, Educator
Schellin, Robert William. Painter, Educator
Sister Thomasita (Mary Thomasita Fessler,
　OSF). Sculptor, Educator
Summ, Helmut. Painter, Educator
Wasserman, Jack. Art Historian, Art
　Administrator

Platteville

Ross, James Matthew. Painter, Educator

Racine

Smith, Moishe. Printmaker

Ripon

Breithaupt, Erwin M. Educator, Art
　Historian

Verona

Littleton, Harvey K. Sculptor, Educator

Waukesha

Penkoff, Ronald Peter. Educator, Print-
　maker

Whitewater

Harrison, Lawrence Victor. Painter,
　Educator

WYOMING

Cody

McCracken, Harold. Art Administrator,
　Art Historian
Meyers, Robert William. Illustrator

Jackson Hole

Kerswill, J W Roy. Painter

Laramie

Deaderick, Joseph. Painter, Educator
Evans, Richard. Painter, Educator
Mueller, Henrietta Waters. Painter,
　Sculptor
Russin, Robert I. Sculptor, Educator

Lysite

Jackson, Harry Andrew. Painter, Sculptor

Sheridan

Martinsen, Ivar Richard. Painter, Educator

Teton Village

Clymer, John F. Painter, Illustrator

PUERTO RICO

Hato Rey

Romano, Jaime (Luis). Painter

Miramar

Homar, Lorenzo. Printmaker, Painter

Ponce

Micheli, Julio. Painter, Printmaker

Rio Piedras

Alicea, Jose R. Printmaker
Balossi, John. Sculptor, Educator
Fontanez, Carmelo. Painter, Instructor
Hernandez-Cruz, Luis. Painter, Educator

San Juan

Buscaglia, José. Sculptor
Dirube, Rolando Lopez. Painter, Sculptor
Irizarry, Carlos. Painter, Printmaker
Lopez, Domingo. Painter, Sculptor
Marrozzini, Luigi. Art Dealer, Lecturer
Molina, Antonio J. Painter, Art Critic
Santiago, Helene. Art Dealer, Collector
Yrizarry, Marcos. Painter, Graphic Artist

VIRGIN ISLANDS

Frederiksted

Irvin, Rea. Painter

St. John

Low, Joseph. Designer, Printmaker

CANADA

ALBERTA

Banff

Leighton, David S R. Art Administrator

Calgary

Dodd, Eric M. Art Administrator,
　Educator
Esler, John Kenneth. Printmaker
Perrott, James Stanford. Art Administrator,
　Educator
Snow, John. Printmaker, Painter
Spickett, Ronald John (Sr). Painter,
　Instructor
Will, John A. Printmaker, Painter

Edmonton

Davey, Ronald A. Art Administrator, Art
　Historian
Dmytruk, Ihor. Painter, Lecturer
Haynes, Douglas H. Painter, Educator
Knowlton, Jonathan. Painter
Manarey, Thelma Alberta. Printmaker,
　Painter
Voyer, Sylvain Jacques. Painter
Weaver, John Barney. Sculptor

Lethbridge

Beny, (Wilfred) Roloff. Photographer,
　Writer

BRITISH COLUMBIA

Campbell River

Andrews, Sybil (Sybil Andrews Morgan).
　Graphic Artist

Cobble Hill

Hughes, Edward John. Painter

Oyama

Mann, Vaughan (Vaughan Grayson). Painter,
　Printmaker

Port Washington

Glyde, Henry George. Painter, Educator

Richmond

Reid, (William) Richard. Painter

Vancouver

Balkind, Alvin Louis. Art Administrator,
　Educator
Bell, Alistair Macready. Printmaker,
　Painter
Burrows, Tom. Sculptor, Educator
Emery, Charles Anthony. Art Administra-
　tor, Educator
Falk, Gathie. Sculptor, Painter

Vancouver (cont)

Fish, Robert (Robert James Field).
 Sculptor, Educator
Harman, Jack Kenneth. Sculptor, Educator
Kanee, Ben. Collector
Knox, George. Art Historian
Korner, John (John Michael Anthony
 Koerner). Painter
Longstaffe, John Ronald. Collector, Patron
Melvin, Grace Wilson. Painter, Illustrator
Onley, Toni. Painter
Pfeifer, Bodo. Painter, Sculptor
Shadbolt, Jack Leonard. Painter
Smith, Gordon. Painter, Educator
Thomas, Lionel Arthur John. Painter,
 Sculptor
Thorne, Gordon (Kit). Painter, Designer
Willer, Jim. Sculptor, Painter

Victoria

Bates, Maxwell Bennett. Painter, Writer
Gowans, Alan. Educator, Writer
Smith, Gord. Sculptor, Painter

West Vancouver

Binning, Bertram Charles. Painter
Cope, Dorothy. Painter
Lennie, Beatrice E C. Sculptor, Designer

MANITOBA

Winnipeg

Eckhardt, Ferdinand. Art Historian, Art
 Administrator
Head, George Bruce. Painter, Designer
Lochhead, Kenneth Campbell. Painter,
 Educator
MacAulay, John Alexander. Collector
Mol, Leo. Sculptor
Reichert, Donald Karl. Painter, Educator
Sissons, Lynn E. Painter
Swinton, George. Painter, Writer
Tascona, Antonio Tony. Painter, Sculptor

NEW BRUNSWICK

Fredericton

Forrestall, Thomas De Vany. Sculptor,
 Painter

Sackville

Colville, Alexander. Painter, Graphic Artist
Harris, Lawren Phillips. Painter, Educator

St. Anselme

Roussel, Claude Patrice. Sculptor,
 Instructor

St. John

Campbell, Rosamond Sheila. Painter,
 Designer

NEWFOUNDLAND

Ferryland

Squires, Gerald Leopold. Painter, Educator

St. John's

Bell, Peter Alan. Painter, Art Administrator
Perlin, Rae. Painter, Collector

NOVA SCOTIA

Amherst

Whitehead, Alfred. Painter, Educator

Halifax

Anderson, Ronald Trent. Painter, Print-
 maker
Brownhill, Harold. Painter, Illustrator
Lindgren, Charlotte. Weaver
Mackay, Donald Cameron. Painter, Art
 Historian

Inverness County

Leaf, June. Painter, Sculptor

Kentville

Fox, Charles Harold. Craftsman
Fox, Winifred Grace. Craftsman, Painter

Peggy's Cove

de Garthe, William Edward. Painter,
 Sculptor

Sydney

Mould, Lola Frowde. Painter

Yarmouth

Pierce, Elizabeth R. Painter

ONTARIO

Ancaster

Panabaker, Frank S. Painter

Aurora

Gilhooly, David James, III. Sculptor

Clarkson

Blackwood, David (Lloyd). Painter,
 Printmaker

Don Mills

Bayefsky, Aba. Painter, Printmaker

Downsview

Bloore, Ronald Langley. Painter,
 Educator

Dundas

Holbrook, Elizabeth Bradford. Sculptor

Glenburnie

Bieler, Andre Charles. Painter, Printmaker

Grimsby

Harley, Harry George. Cartoonist

Guelph

Couling, Gordon Robert. Painter, Educator

Hamilton

MacDonald, Thomas Reid. Art Administrator, Painter

Ingersoll

Crawford, Catherine Betty. Painter

Kingston

Allen, Ralph. Painter, Educator
Hodgson, Trevor. Painter, Photographer
Holmes, David Bryan. Painter, Instructor
MacDonald, Grant. Painter, Illustrator
Schonberger, Fred. Painter, Sculptor
Travers, Gwyneth Mabel. Graphic Artist

Kitchener

Goetz, Peter Henry. Painter, Lecturer

Kleinburg

Jackson, Alexander Young. Painter

London

Ariss, Herbert Joshua. Painter, Illustrator
Bice, Clare. Art Administrator, Painter
Chambers, John. Painter, Film Maker
Cryderman, Mackie. Painter, Graphic
 Artist
Dale, William Scott Abell. Art Historian,
 Art Administrator
Francis, Harold Carleton. Painter, Illustra-
 tor
Lorcini, Gino. Sculptor

Mississagua

Broomfield, Adolphus George. Painter,
 Designer
Dingle, Adrian. Painter
La Pierre, Thomas. Painter, Printmaker

Niagara-on-the-Lake

Benton, Margaret Peake. Painter
Jones, Jacobine. Sculptor

Oakville

Hanson, Jean (Mrs Jean Elphick). Painter, Designer

Orono

Drummond, Arthur A. Painter, Illustrator

Oshawa

Hilts, Alvin. Sculptor

Ottawa

Boggs, Jean Sutherland. Museum Director, Art Historian
Boyd, James Henderson. Printmaker, Sculptor
Groves, Naomi Jackson. Writer, Lecturer
Hubbard, Robert Hamilton. Art Historian, Art Administrator
Hyde, Laurence. Painter, Designer
Karsh, Yousuf. Photographer
Masson, Henri. Painter
Sylvestre, Guy. Art Critic, Writer
Tolgesy, Victor. Sculptor
Wyse, Alexander John. Painter, Sculptor

Port Credit

Roberts, Thomas (Kieth). Painter

Rexdale

Kramolc, Theodore Maria. Painter, Designer

St. Catharines

Harris, Alfred Peter. Painter, Art Administrator

Scarborough

McCarthy, Doris Jean. Painter, Instructor

Thornhill

MacDonald, Thoreau. Illustrator, Painter

Toronto

Aldwinckle, Eric. Designer, Painter
Altwerger, Libby. Painter, Graphic Artist
Arbuckle, Franklin. Painter, Illustrator
Bell, R Murray. Collector
Blazeje, Zbigniew. Sculptor, Painter
Bodolai, Joseph Stephen. Film Maker, Sculptor
Brieger, Peter H. Art Historian, Educator
Brooks, Frank Leonard. Painter, Writer
Bush, Jack. Painter
Cattell, Ray. Painter, Art Director
Clark, Paraskeva. Painter
Collier, Alan Caswell. Painter
Coughtry, John Graham. Painter, Sculptor
Courtice, Rody Kenny. Painter
Dagys, Jacob. Sculptor
Daly, Kathleen (Kathleen Daly Pepper). Painter
Danby, Ken. Painter, Printmaker
Del Junco, Emilio. Collector, Patron
De Pedery-Hunt, Dora. Sculptor, Designer
Deutsch, Peter Andrew. Painter
Dimson, Theo Aeneas. Designer
Drutz, June. Painter, Educator

Etrog, Sorel. Sculptor, Painter
Filipovic, Augustin. Sculptor, Painter
Fleming, Allan Robb. Designer, Calligrapher
Fournier, Alexander Paul. Painter, Printmaker
Franck, Albert Jacques. Painter
Freifeld, Eric. Painter, Educator
Gage, Frances M. Sculptor
Garwood, Audrey. Painter, Printmaker
Gauthier, Joachim George. Painter
Goldhamer, Charles. Painter, Instructor
Gregor, Helen Frances. Tapestry Artist, Designer
Hagan, (Robert) Frederick. Printmaker, Painter
Hall, John A. Painter
Heller, Jules. Printmaker, Art Administrator
Hoenigan, Henry. Painter
Horne, (Arthur Edward) Cleeve. Painter, Sculptor
Isaacs, Avrom. Art Dealer, Art Administrator
Joy, Nancy Grahame. Illustrator, Educator
Kopmanis, Augusts A. Sculptor
Kurelek, William. Painter
Latner, Albert J. Collector, Patron
Luz, Virginia. Painter
Mc Elcheran, William Hodd. Designer, Sculptor
McGeoch, Lillian Jean. Painter, Sculptor
MacKenzie, Hugh Seaforth. Painter
Manning, Jo. Printmaker
Martin, Bernice Fenwick. Painter, Printmaker
Martin, Langton. Painter, Printmaker
Meredith, John. Painter
Mirvish, David. Art Dealer
Mochizuki, Betty Ayako. Painter
Moos, Walter A. Art Dealer
Murphy, Rowley Walter. Painter, Designer
Nakamura, Kazuo. Painter
Neddeau, Donald Frederick Price. Painter, Designer
Oesterle, Leonhard Friedrich. Sculptor, Educator
Ogilvie, Will (William Abernethy). Painter
Pehap, Erich K. Painter, Graphic Artist
Ronald, William. Painter
Schaefer, Carl Fellman. Painter
Sime, John. Art Administrator
Sing Hoo (Sing Hoo Yuen). Sculptor, Painter
Solomon, Daniel. Painter
Thepot, Roger François. Painter
Thorne, M Art. Painter
Timmas, Osvald. Painter
Town, Harold Barling. Painter, Writer
Valius, Telesforas. Graphic Artist, Educator
Vickers, George Stephen. Educator
Watson, Sydney Hollinger. Art Administrator, Designer
White, Norman Triplett. Sculptor
Wieland, Joyce. Painter, Film Maker
Wilson, (Ronald) York. Painter
Withrow, William J. Art Administrator

Waterloo

Urquhart, Tony. Sculptor, Painter

Waubaushene

Gould, John Howard. Painter, Film Maker

Willowdale

Chiarandini, Albert. Painter, Instructor
Gilling, Lucille. Printmaker

Windsor

DeLauro, Joseph Nicola. Sculptor, Educator
Saltmarche, Kenneth Charles. Painter, Art Administrator

QUEBEC

Chicoutimi

Villeneuve, Joseph Arthur. Painter

Cté Portneuf

Beauchemin, Micheline. Painter, Weaver

Dorval

Daoust, Sylvia. Sculptor
Simpkins, Henry John. Painter, Illustrator

Hudson

Cosgrove, Stanley. Painter

Lachine

Walsh, John Stanley. Painter, Writer

Laval

Pellan (Alfred). Painter

Mont-St-Hilaire

Bonet, Jordi. Sculptor, Muralist

Montreal

Adams, Glenn Nelson. Painter
Ayre, Robert Hugh. Writer, Critic
Beament, Harold. Painter
Bellefleur, Leon. Painter, Etcher
Bouchard, Lorne Holland. Painter, Illustrator
Briansky, Rita Prezament. Painter, Printmaker
Bruneau, Kittie. Painter
Carter, David Giles. Art Administrator, Art Historian
Chicoine, Rene. Painter, Instructor
Cooke, Edwy Francis. Painter, Educator
Fox, John. Painter
Gersovitz, Sarah Valerie. Printmaker, Painter
Hebert, Julien. Sculptor, Designer
Kahane, Anne. Sculptor
Lacroix, Richard. Painter, Sculptor
Lewis, Stanley. Sculptor, Printmaker
McEwen, Jean. Painter
McLaren, Norman. Painter, Art Administrator
Masse, Georges Severe. Painter, Lecturer
Menses, Jan. Painter
Molinari, Guido. Painter, Sculptor
Morris, Kathleen Moir. Painter
Muhlstock, Louis. Painter
Pinsky, Alfred. Painter, Educator
Prezament, Joseph. Painter
Roberts, (William) Goodridge. Painter
Scott, Marian (Dale). Painter
Steinhouse, Tobie (Thelma). Painter, Printmaker
Surrey, Philip Henry. Painter
Tinning, George Campbell. Painter
Tousignant, Claude. Painter, Instructor

Montreal (cont)

Trudeau, Yves. Sculptor
Wheeler, Orson Shorey. Sculptor, Lecturer

Morin Heights

Holgate, Edwin Headley. Painter

Perce

Guite, Suzanne. Painter, Sculptor

Quebec

Beament, Tib (Thomas Harold). Painter,
  Instructor
Iacurto, Francesco. Painter, Instructor
Plamondon, Marius Gerald. Sculptor,
  Craftsman

St Adele

Rousseau-Vermette, Mariette. Craftsman

Ste Agathe des Monts

Miller, H McRae. Sculptor, Painter

St Hilaire

Braitstein, Marcel. Sculptor, Educator

St Lambert

Archambault, Louis. Sculptor, Educator
De Tonnancour, Jacques G. Painter,
  Instructor

Sillery

Lemieux, Jean Paul. Painter

Terrebonne

Hurtubise, Jacques. Painter

Westmount

Caiserman-Roth, Ghitta. Painter, Printmaker

SASKATCHEWAN

Regina

Chester, Donovan T. Painter
Levine, Marilyn Anne. Sculptor
Nulf, Frank Allen. Painter, Educator

Saskatoon

Bentham, Douglas Wayne. Sculptor
Bornstein, Eli. Educator, Sculptor
Knowles, Dorothy Elsie (Dorothy Elsie
  Perehudoff). Painter
Lindner, Ernest. Painter
Rogers, Otto Donald. Painter, Educator

MEXICO

FEDERAL DISTRICT

Coyocan

Cesar, Gaston Gonzalez. Sculptor

Mexico, D.F.

Aquino, Edmundo. Painter, Engraver
Bejar, Feliciano. Sculptor, Painter
Beraha, Enrique Misrachi. Art Dealer
Carrillo, Lilia. Painter
Castro (Pacheco Fernando). Painter
Cervantes, Pedro. Sculptor
Corzas, Francisco. Painter
Cruz, Hector. Painter
Cuevas, José Luis. Painter, Illustrator
Escobedo, Augusto Ortega. Sculptor,
  Painter
Escobedo, Helen. Sculptor, Art Adminis-
  trator
Felguerez, Manuel. Painter, Sculptor
Friedeberg, Pedro. Painter, Sculptor
Gironella, Alberto. Painter, Illustrator
Gordon, Maxwell. Painter
Icaza (Francisco De Icaza). Painter,
  Sculptor
Lagunes, Maria (Maria Lagunes Hernandez).
  Sculptor, Painter
Merida, Carlos. Painter
Messeguer, Villoro Benito. Painter,
  Sculptor
Nierman, Leonardo M. Painter, Sculptor
Ocejo, (Jose Garcia). Painter
Rodriguez Luna, Antonio. Painter
Rojo, Vicente. Painter
Salazar, Juan. Painter, Designer
Saldivar, Jaime. Painter
Siqueiros, David Alfaro. Painter
Tamayo, Rufino. Painter
Toral, Maria Teresa. Engraver, Designer
Zuniga, Francisco. Sculptor

GUANAJUATO

Guanajuato

Costa, Olga. Painter, Collector
Edie, Stuart. Painter, Educator
Martin, Fletcher. Painter
Morado, Chavez, Jose. Painter, Educator
Williams, Garth Montgomery. Illustrator,
  Designer

San Miguel de Allende

Dickinson, William Stirling. Educator,
  Art Administrator
Pinto, James. Painter, Sculptor
Pratt, Dudley. Sculptor
Samuelson, Fred Binder. Painter, Educator
Tabuena, Romeo Villalva. Painter
Taylor, Frederick Bourchier. Painter,
  Sculptor

JALISCO

Chapala

Kent, Frank Ward. Painter, Art Administrator

Zapopan

Palau, Marta. Painter, Weaver

MORELOS

Cuernavaca

Angulo, Chappie. Painter, Illustrator
Berger, Jason. Painter
Goeritz, Mathias. Sculptor, Designer

Tepoztlan

Von Gunten, Roger. Painter

NUEVO LEÓN

Monterrey

Ordoñez, Efren. Painter, Sculptor

FOREIGN

AUSTRALIA

Cairns

Samstag, Gordon. Painter, Sculptor

BAHAMAS

Nassau

Wasile, Elyse. Painter, Designer

BELGIUM

Brussels

Crovello, William George. Painter, Sculptor

DENMARK

Copenhagen

Williams, Walter (Henry). Painter, Printmaker

Gadstrup

Weisgard, Leonard Joseph. Illustrator,
  Writer

ENGLAND

Herefordshire

Creo, Leonard E. Painter, Sculptor

London

Gablik, Suzi. Writer, Painter
Kanovitz, Howard. Painter
Stokes, Thomas Phelps. Painter

FRANCE

Arles

Kerkovius, Ruth. Painter

Ménerbes

Truex, Van Day. Painter, Designer

Paris

Briggs, Austin. Collector, Illustrator
Chase-Riboud, Barbara Dewayne. Sculptor
Crotto, Paul. Painter, Sculptor
Gorsline, Douglas Warner. Painter,
    Illustrator
Hayter, Stanley William. Painter,
    Instructor
Koenig, John Franklin. Painter
Levee, John H. Painter, Sculptor
Masurovsky, Gregory. Printmaker,
    Illustrator
Mitchell, Joan. Painter
Parker, Bill. Painter
Tsai, Wen-Ying. Sculptor, Painter
Spencer, Eleanor Patterson. Writer,
    Art Historian
Vilder, Roger. Sculptor

GERMANY

Cologne

Thek, Paul. Sculptor

Munich

Praeger, Frederick A. Collector,
    Publisher

INDIA

New Delhi

Morley, Grace L McCann. Museum
    Director, Writer

IRELAND

Dun Laoghaire

Brady, Charles Michael. Painter

ITALY

Assisi

Congdon, William (Grosvenor). Painter

Camaiore

Lipchitz, Jacques. Sculptor

Carrara

Noordhoek, Harry Cecil. Sculptor

Florence

De Tolnay, Charles. Art Historian, Writer
Fonelli, J Vincent. Painter, Sculptor
Puccinelli, Raimondo. Sculptor

Frosinone

De Marco, Jean Antoine. Sculptor
Fasano, Clara. Sculptor

Genoa

Thomas, Reynolds. Painter

Lavagna

Lionni, Leo. Sculptor, Painter

Lucca

Wells, Charles Arthur, Jr. Sculptor

Rome

Chinni, Peter Anthony. Sculptor, Painter
French, Jared. Painter, Sculptor
Gundersheimer, Herman (Samuel). Art
    Administrator, Art Historian
Hadzi, Dimitri. Sculptor, Printmaker
Hebald, Milton Elting. Sculptor, Graphic
    Artist
Jones, Elizabeth. Sculptor, Medalist
Krauthcimer, Richard. Educator
Leong, James Chan. Painter
Montana, Pietro. Sculptor, Painter
Pepper, Beverly. Sculptor, Painter
Perry, Charles Owen. Sculptor
Schloss, Edith. Painter, Art Critic
Twombly, Cy. Painter
Weinberg, Elbert. Sculptor, Educator
Zajac, Jack. Sculptor, Painter

Siena

D'Almeida, George. Painter

Umbertide (Pg)

Barnes, Robert M. Painter, Educator

Venice

Guggenheim, Peggy. Collector, Patron
Melcarth, Edward. Painter, Sculptor

JAPAN

Tokyo

Gunn, Paul James. Painter, Educator

Yokohama

Block, Joyce. Calligrapher, Instructor

MALI

Bamako

Hanes, Ursula Ann. Sculptor

MOROCCO

Marrakesh

Landau, Rom. Sculptor, Writer

NETHERLANDS

Amsterdam

DeWitt, Floyd Tennison. Sculptor, Painter

Baarlo

Tajiri, Shinkichi. Sculptor, Educator

NEW ZEALAND

Auckland

Hirsch, Richard Teller. Museum Curator,
    Writer

NORWAY

Flateby

Lind, Victor. Painter, Educator

PERU

Miraflores, Lima

Davis, John Harold. Art Administrator,
    Illustrator

SPAIN

Barcelona

Narotzky, Norman David. Painter, Printmaker

Madrid

Balart, Waldo. Painter
Wortham, Harold. Painter, Art Consultant

Malaga

Christopher, William R. Painter

SWITZERLAND

Basel

Tobey, Mark. Painter

Geneva

Ghez, Oscar. Collector
Ketcham, Henry King (Hank). Cartoonist

Montagnola

Zigrosser, Carl. Writer

VENEZUELA

Caracas

Neumann, Hans. Collector

WEST INDIES

Jamaica

Dame, Lawrence. Art Critic, Writer

Tobago

Olmsted, Pat. Painter, Photographer

PROFESSIONAL CLASSIFICATIONS INDEX

(When available, artists' preferred media are entered following names.)

ARCHITECT

Andrus, Moulton Loyal
Blake, Peter Jost
Booth, Laurence Ogden
Carr, J Gordon
Consuegra, Hugo
Deaton, Charles
De Weldon, Felix George Weihs
Fitzsimmons, James Joseph
Freund, Tibor
Green, Wilder
Harris, Julian Hoke
Johnson, Philip Cortelyou
Mitchell, Clifford
Murphy, Herbert A
Noyes, Eliot
Perkins, G Holmes
Soleri, Paolo
Tigerman, Stanley

ART ADMINISTRATOR

Adams, Clinton
Adams, Philip Rhys
Adams, William Howard
Aldrich, Larry
Atkyns, (Willie) Lee, Jr
Baer, Alan
Bailey, Walter Alexander
Baker, Mildred
Balkind, Alvin Louis
Barooshian, Martin
Barr, Alfred Hamilton, Jr
Bartlett, Fred Stewart
Beam, Philip Conway
Bean, Jacob
Beggs, Thomas Montague
Bell, Peter Alan
Berman, Nancy Mallin
Beson, Roberta (Roberta Beson Hill)
Bice, Clare
Biddle, James
Bingham, Lois A
Bishop, Budd Harris
Bothmer, Dietrich Felix Von
Bowron, Edgar Peters
Black, Frederick (Edward)
Black, Mary McCune
Bostick, William Allison
Boulton, Jack
Bowman, Ruth
Boyce, William G
Boyd, E
Boyle, Richard J
Brackett, Truman H, Jr
Breeskin, Adelyn Dohme
Broadley, Hugh T
Brody, Jacob Jerome
Brown, James Monroe, III
Bryan, Wilhelmus B
Buck, Robert Treat, Jr
Buckley, Charles Edward
Buechner, Thomas Scharman
Buggel, William Lee

Burgard, Ralph
Butler, Joseph (Green)
Butts, Porter
Cameron, Duncan F
Carlos, (James) Edward
Carmichael, Jae
Carter, David Giles
Chamberlain, Betty
Chew, Paul Albert
Christison, Muriel B
Cleveland, Helen Barth
Cogswell, Margaret Price
Colt, Priscilla C
Condit, (Eleanor) Louise
Cooney, John Ducey
Craft, John Richard
Culler, George D
Cummings, Frederick James
Dale, William Scott Abell
Datus, Jay
Davey, Ronald A
Davidson, Morris
Davis, John Harold
Davis, Robert Tyler
De Foix-Crenascol, Louis
Dellis, Arlene B
Demetrion, James Thomas
Dennison, Keith Elkins
Dickinson, William Stirling
Dillon, C Douglas
Dixon, Sally Foy
Dodd, Eric M
Dodge, Joseph Jeffers
Dodworth, Allen Stevens
Doherty, Robert J, Jr
Domit, Moussa M
Donahue, Kenneth
Doolittle, Warren Ford, Jr
Dorn, Charles Meeker
Dorr, Goldthwaite Higginson, III
Doty, Robert McIntyre
Doyon, Gerard Maurice
Dresser, Louisa
du Cret, Dudley Vaughan
Easby, Dudley T, Jr
Eberman, Edwin
Ebie, William Dennis
Eckhardt, Ferdinand
Elam, Charles Henry
Elliott, B Charles, Jr
Elliott, James Heyer
Ellis, Carl Eugene
Emerson, Roberta Shinn
Emery, Charles Anthony
Enman, Tom Kenneth
Escobedo, Helen
Evans, Bruce Haselton
Evans, Grose
Fagg, Kenneth Stanley
Fairbanks, Jonathan Leo
Farrell, Patric
Farrell, Stephanie Krauss
Fenical, Marlin E
Feriola, James Philip
Fern, Alan Maxwell
Finley, David Edward

Forster, Peggy Lucille
Foster, James W, Jr
Freedman, Doris C
Freudenheim, Tom Lippmann
Fried, Raymond John
Gaither, Edmund B
Gardiner, Henry Gilbert
Garver, Thomas H
Garvey, Eleanor
Gebhard, David
Geske, Norman Albert
Ghent, Henri
Gibson, George
Gilmore, Roger
Gomez-Sicre, Jose
Goodall, Donald Bannard
Goodrich, Lloyd
Gordon, John
Gould, Stephen
Graham, F Lanier
Graham, Frank P
Gray, Robert Ward
Greaver, Harry
Green, Edward Anthony
Green, Wilder
Griffin, Rachael S
Grove, Richard
Gundersheimer, Herman (Samuel)
Gustafson, Dwight Leonard
Gusten, Theodore J H
Hadlock, Wendell Stanwood
Hale, Robert Beverly
Halley, Donald M, Jr
Hammer, Alfred Emil
Hanna, Katherine
Hardy, (Clarion) Dewitt
Harlan, Roma Christine
Harris, Alfred Peter
Harris, Paul Stewart
Haseltine, James Lewis
Hayes, Bartlett Harding, Jr
Heller, Jules
Herdle, Isabel C
Herman, Lloyd Eldred
Herstand, Arnold
Hicken, Russell Bradford
Hightower, John B
Hodges, Stephen Lofton
Hoffman, Larry Gene
Holbrook, Vivian Nicholas
Hooton, Bruce Duff
Hopps, Walter
Hotz, Henry, Jr
Houghton, Arthur A, Jr
Howard, Dan F
Howard, Richard Foster
Howlett, Carolyn Svrluga
Hubbard, Robert Hamilton
Humphrey, Donald Gray
Hunter, Edmund Robert
Huth, Hans
Hyde, Andrew Cornwall
Insel, Paula
Isaacs, Avrom
Ishikawa, Joseph
Jackson, Nigel Loring

Art Administrator (cont)

Jeffery, Charles Bartley
Jellico, John Anthony
Jocda (Joseph Charles Dailey)
Johnson, Evert Alfred
Johnson, Katherine King
Jonson, Raymond
Kan, Michael
Kelleher, Patrick Joseph
Kent, Frank Ward
Kerr, John Hoare
Kidder, Alfred, II
Kim, Ernie
King, Edward S
Kingman, Eugene
Kocher, Robert Lee
Kubly, Donald R
Kuhn, Brenda
Kushner-Weiner, Anita May
Landwehr, William Charles
Lauck, Anthony Joseph, CSC
Lawson, Edward Pitt
Leake, Eugene W
Leavitt, Thomas Whittlesey
Lebkicher, Anne Ross
Lee, George J
Leet, Richard Eugene
Leighton, David S R
Lein, Malcolm Emil
Lewis, Elma Ina
Lewis, Virginia Elnora
Lewis, William Arthur
Lieberman, William S
Littman, Robert R
Livingston, Charlotte (Mrs Francis
    Vendeveer Kughler
Lowe, Harry
Lowry, W McNeil
Luck, Robert
MacAgy, Douglas Guernsey
MacBeth, Jerome Russell
McBride, Walter Henry
McCracken, Harold
McCray, Porter A
McCullough, Joseph
MacDonald, Thomas Reid
McGee, Winston Eugene
McGonagle, William Albert
McGrath, James Arthur
McGrath, Kyran Murray
McKay, John Sangster
McLaren, Norman
Mahey, John A
Malone, James William
Malone, Lee H B
Mandle, Earl Roger
Manton, Jock (Archimedes Aristides
    Giacomantonio)
Margolies, Ethel Polacheck
Marks, Mrs Laurence M
Maurer, Evan Maclyn
Mayhall, Dorothy A
Maytham, Thomas Northrup
Mellon, Paul
Merriam, John F
Mills, Frederick Van Fleet
Mocsanyi, Paul
Moe, Henry Allen
Moeller, Robert Charles, III
Mongan, Agnes
Montague, James L
Montgomery, Charles Franklin
Moore, Ethel
Morris, Jack Austin, Jr
Morton, Richard H
Moyer, Roy
Mulcahy, Freda
Myers, Fred A
Myhr, Dean Andrew
Naeve, Milo M
Neubert, George Walter
New, Lloyd H (Lloyd Kiva)
Newport, Esther, S P
Newton, Douglas
Newton, Earle Williams
Noble, Joseph Veach

Oldenburg, Richard Erik
Osborn, Elodie C
Ostrow, Stephen Edward
Pablo (Paul Burgess Edwards)
Page, Addison Franklin
Parker, James Varner
Parkhurst, Charles
Pels, Albert
Perkins, Robert Eugene
Perrot, Paul N
Perrott, James Stanford
Peterson, John Douglas
Phillips, Dorothy W
Pick, John
Pindell, Howardena Doreen
Pinkney, Helen Louise
Plaut, James S
Plimpton, Russell A
Plummer, John H
Pope, Annemarie Henle
Potter, Ted
Prior, Harris King
Rainey, Froelich Gladstone
Reichert, Donald O
Rice, Philip Somerset
Rich, Daniel Catton
Richardson, Edgar Preston
Richardson, Judith Heidler
Richman, Robert M
Ritchie, Andrew C
Robbins, Warren M
Roberts, Colette (Jacqueline)
Robinson, Frederick B
Rogers, Millard Foster, Jr
Rohlfing, Christian
Rose, Hanna Toby
Rosenthal, Gertrude
Ross, (Robert) Kenneth
Roysher, Hudson (Brisbine)
Ruddley, John
Rueppel, Merrill C
Rust, Edwin C
Sachs, Samuel, II
Sadek, George
St John, Bruce
Saltmarche, Kenneth Charles
Sanguinetti, Eugene F
Scarbrough, Cleve Knox, Jr
Schlageter, Robert William
Schwartz, Barbara J
Scott, David Winfield
Severino, D(ominick) Alexander
Shannon, (David) Patric
Sheets, Nan Jane
Shuck, Kenneth Menaugh
Sickman, Laurence Chalfont Stevens
Sime, John
Sivard, Robert Paul
Sloshberg, Leah Phyfer
Smith, Justin V
Smyth, Craig Hugh
Snodgrass, Jeanne Owens
Spencer, John R
Speyer, A James
Starks, Elliott Roland
Stebbins, Theodore Ellis, Jr
Stewart, Patricia Kaye
Stoddard, Donna Melissa
Sullivan, Max William
Sweeney, James Johnson
Teilman, Herdis Bull
Teitz, Richard Stuart
Thiessen, (Charles) Leonard
Thomas, Elaine Freeman
Torres, John, Jr
Triano, Anthony Thomas
Truettler, William
Urrutia, Lawrence
Van Arsdale, Dorothy Thayer
Vanco, John Leroy
Van Hook, David H
Varian, Elayne H
Vigtel, Gudmund
Voris, Anna Maybelle
Walker, Hudson D
Wallace, David Harold
Wark, Robert Rodger

Warren, Ferdinand Earl
Wasserman, Jack
Watson, Sydney Hollinger
Weber, Jean M
Webster, David S
Wells, Fred N
Wheeler, Monroe
Wheeler, Robert G
Whipple, Enez Mary
White, Ian McKibbin
Whitehead, James Louis
Whitlock, John Joseph
Whitney, John Hay
Wickiser, Ralph Lewanda
Wight, Frederick S
Wilder, Mitchell Armitage
Wilke, Ulfert S
Wilkins, Ruth Lois
Williams, Hermann Warner, Jr
Wintersteen, Bernice McIlhenny
Wiper, Thomas William
Withrow, William J
Witmeyer, Stanley Herbert
Wittmann, Otto
Wolfe, Townsend Durant
Wong, Jason
Wood, James Nowell
Woolfenden, William Edward
Wunder, Richard Paul
Yater, George David
Yepez, Dorothy
Young, Joseph Louis
Young, Mahonri S
Zahn, Carl Frederick

ART BOOK DEALER

Bergling, Virginia Catherine (Mrs
    Stephen J Kozazcki)

ART CONSULTANT

Folds, Thomas McKey
Ghent, Henri
Goodman, Calvin Jerome
Hatch, John Davis
Hinkhouse, Forest Melick
Hyde, Andrew Cornwall
Kuh, Katharine
McLanathan, Richard B K
Sawyer, Alan R
Schoener, Allon
Stout, George Leslie
Ulin, Dene
Wechsler, Herman J
Wortham, Harold
Wright, Nina Kaiden

ART DEALER

Adler, A M
Alonzo, Jack J
Anderson, David K
Andrews, Laddie E
Anhalt, Jacqueline Richards
Arwin, Lester B
Ault, Lee Addison
Bader, Franz
Barton, John Murray
Bellamy, Richard
Benson, Elaine K G
Beraha, Enrique Misrachi
Bergen, Sidney L
Berggruen, John Henry
Berresford, Virginia
Blacketer, James Richard
Bolles, John S
Bonino, Alfredo
Borgenicht, Grace (Grace Borgenicht
    Brandt)
Borochoff, (Ida) Sloan
Bradley, Peter Alexander
Bruno, Phillip A
Byron, Charles Anthony

Carlin, Electra Marshall
Caro, Frank
Carone, Matthew David
Castelli, Leo
Cernuschi, Alberto C
Chapellier, George
Chapellier, Robert
Cisneros, Florencio Garcia (Frank Garcia)
Clancy, John
Cole, Sylvan, Jr
Collins, Lowell Daunt
Cox, Warren Earle
Creamer, Paul Lyle
Crispo, Andrew John
Cross, Maria Concetta
Danenberg, Bernard
David, Dianne
Davis, Donald Robert
Davis, Leroy
Dawson, Bess Phipps
Desind, Philip
Dintenfass, Terry
Dix, George Evertson
Dooley, Helen Bertha
Dorrance, Nesta
Draper, Robert Sargent
Dreyer, Margaret Webb
Dulcan, Caril E
Egan, Charles
Ekstrom, Arne H
Elkon, Robert
Emmerich, Andre
Erdman, R H Donnelley
Esman, Rosa M
Eyen, Richard J
Fairweather, Sally H
Feigen, Richard L
Feldman, Ronald
Fendrick, Barbara Cooper
Findlay, David B
Findlay, Helen T
Fink, Alan
Fischbach, Marilyn Cole
Fishko, Bella
Fleischman, Lawrence
Fondren, Harold M
Fourcade, Xavier
Freilich, Michael Leon
Frumkin, Allan
Fuller, Diana
Furman, Gloria Violet
Gallenkamp, Charles & Patricia
Gee, Helen
Gerst, Hilde W
Glezer, Nechemia
Glick, Paula Florence
Glimcher, Arnold B
Goldowsky, Noah
Goldschmidt, Lucien
Goodman, James Neil
Gorman, R C
Graham, James
Graham, Robert Claberhouse
Gray, Richard
Gruskin, Mary Josephine
Haddad, Samuel
Hahn, Stephen
Hammer, Victor J
Hansen, Wanda
Hardin, Shirley G
Harmon, (Loren) Foster
Hart, Bill
Haslem, John Arthur & Jane N
Havens, Elizabeth Carroll
Herbert, David
Hill, Jim
Hill, Megan Lloyd
Hirschl, Norman
Hokin, Grace E
Hoover, F Herbert
Howell, Frank
Hutchinson, Max
Hutton, Leonard
Iervolino, Joseph Anthony
Iervolino, Paula
Insel, Paula
Iolas, Alexandre

Isaacs, Avrom
Isserstedt, Dorothea Carus
Janis, Conrad
Janis, Sidney
Johnson, Marian Willard
Jones, Douglas McKee (Doug)
Kahn, Ralph H
Kaller, Robert Jameson
Kallir, Otto
Kanegis, Sidney S
Karp, Ivan C
Kasle, Gertrude
Kelley, Chapman
Kelly, Walter W
Kerr, Berta Borgenicht
Kerr, E Coe
Kertess, Klaus D
Killam, Walt
Kind, Phyllis
King, Hayward Ellis
Kirkby, Paula Zolloto
Kohler, Mel (Otto)
Komor, Mathias
Kootz, Samuel M
Kottler, Lynn
Krasner, Oscar
Kraushaar, Antoinette M
Landau, Felix
Landry, Albert
Langston, Mr & Mrs Loyd H (Mildred J)
Lapiner, Alan C
Larcada, Richard Kenneth
Lastra, Luis
Lefebre, John
Leitman, Norman
Lembeck, John Edgar
Lerner, Richard J
Lewin, Bernard
Lewison, Florence (Mrs Maurice Glickman)
Lock, Charles K
Long, Meredith J
Luntz, Irving
Luria, Gloria
Lust, Virginia
McCoy, Jason
MacKay, Hugh
McKinney, Donald
McMahon, James Edward
Maguire, Charles
Makler, Hope Welsh
Mann, David
Marks, Royal S
Marrozzini, Luigi
Matisse, Pierre
Meltzer, Doris
Milch, Harold Carlton
Mirvish, David
Mont, Frederick
Moos, Walter A
Morris, Donald Fischer
Muensterberger, Helene Coler
Myers, John
Myers, John B
Neikrug, Marjorie
Neslage, Oliver John, Jr
Newhouse, Bertram Maurice
Nordness, Lee
Oehlschlaeger, Frank J
Orsini (Gwendolyn Orsinger Anderson)
Paley, Jeffrey
Palley, Reese
Palmer, Herbert Bearl
Palmer-Poroner, Margot
Parsons, Betty Bierne
Perls, Frank (Richard)
Perls, Klaus G
Poindexter, Elinor Fuller
Pratt, Frances (Frances Elizabeth Usui)
Price, Vincent
Pucker, Bernard H
Purdy, Donald R
Raydon, Alexander R
Reed, Harold
Richardson, Judith Heidler
Ring, Edward Alfred
Robinson, Thomas
Robles, Esther Waggoner

Rose, Peter Henry
Rothman, Sidney
Rubin, Lawrence
Sachs, A M
Saidenberg, Daniel
St Clair, Michael
Santiago, Helene
Sawyer, William
Schneiderman, Dorothy
Schoelkopf, Robert J, Jr
Schuster, Eugene Ivan
Schweitzer, M R
Seders, Francine Lavinal
Segy, Ladislas
Serger, Helen
Serisawa, Ikuo
Shadrach, Jean H
Shea, Beverly
Simpson, Merton D
Sloan, Robert Smullyan
Smith, Gary M
Sneed, Patricia M
Solway, Carl E
Sowers, Miriam R
Spark, Victor David
Staempfli, George W
Stefanotty, Robert Alan
Stone, Alex Benjamin
Stone, Allan
Stuart, David
Suzuki, Katsko (Katsko Suzuki Kannegieter)
Tahir, Abe M, Jr
Taulbee, Dan J
Thomson, Carl L
Toner, Paul
Van Der Straeten, Vincent Roger
Verzyl, June Carol
Vogel, Donald S
Waddell, Richard H
Wade, Jane
Washburn, Joan T
Watson, Clarissa H
Weber, John
Weitzenhoffer, A Max
Wenger, Lesley
Wenger, Sigmund
Weyhe, Mrs Erhard
White, Ruth
Wiener, George
Wilkinson, Kirk Cook
Wise, Howard
Wittenborn, George
Woodside, Gordon William
Wunderlich, Rudolf G
Wynshaw, Frances
Zabriskie, Virginia M
Zierler, William
Zantman, Hans

ART DIRECTOR

Angelini, John Michael
Cattell, Ray
Lerner, Abe
Metz, Frank Robert
Stuart, Kenneth James
Thompson, (James) Bradbury

ART EDITOR

Coplans, John (Rivers)
Jackson, Ward
Lipman, Jean
Morse, John D
Reaves, Angela Westwater
Ruta, Peter Paul
Slivka, Rose
Winchester, Alice

ART HISTORIAN

Ackerman, Gerald Martin
Andersen, Wayne Vesti
Arnason, H Harvard

Art Historian (cont)

Artz, Frederick B
Asher, Frederick M
Ashton, Dore
Aymar, Gordon Christian
Bailey, Worth
Baker, Charles Edwin
Baretski, Charles Allan
Barr, Alfred Hamilton, Jr
Belshe, Mirella Monti
Berman, Nancy Mallin
Bernstein, Theresa
Bettmann, Otto Ludwig
Bhalla, Hans
Blackwell, John Victor
Bloch, E Maurice
Blum, Shirley Neilsen
Boe, Roy Asbjörn
Boggs, Jean Sutherland
Bohan, Peter John
Bolomey, Roger Henry
Bongiorno, Laurine Mack
Bosch, Gulnar Kheirallah
Bothmer, Bernard V
Bothmer, Dietrich Felix Von
Bowron, Edgar Peters
Boyle, Richard J
Branner, Robert
Breasted, James Henry, Jr
Breckenridge, James D
Breitenbach, Edgar
Breithaupt, Erwin M
Brendel, Otto J
Brewer, Donald J
Brewington, Marion Vernon
Brieger, Peter H
Broadd, Harry Andrew
Broadley, Hugh T
Brooks, Charles M, Jr
Brumbaugh, Thomas Brendle
Buck, Robert Treat, Jr
Buckley, Charles Edward
Bullard, Edgar John, III
Butler, Joseph Thomas
Butts, Porter
Byrnes, James Bernard
Bywaters, Jerry
Cahill, James Francis
Campbell, Malcolm
Campbell, William Patrick
Carey, John Thomas
Carpenter, James Morton
Carter, David Giles
Catlin, Stanton L
Celender, Donald Dennis
Charlot, Jean
Cheney, Sheldon
Christensen, Erwin Ottomar
Cikovsky, Nicolai, Jr
Collins, George R
Constable, William George
Cooke, Hereward Lester
Coolidge, John
Covi, Dario A
Cowdrey, Mary Bartlett
Crosby, Sumner McKnight
Cummings, Frederick James
Cuttler, Charles David
Czuma, Stanislaw J
Dale, William Scott Abell
Dauterman, Carl Christian
Davey, Ronald A
Davidson, J LeRoy
Davis, Marian B
Davis, Robert Tyler
De Foix-Crenascol, Louis
Deknatel, Frederick Brockway
Dennison, Keith Elkins
Desportes, Ulysse Gandvier
De Tolnay, Charles
Domit, Moussa M
Donahue, Kenneth
Dorra, Henri
Doyon, Gerard Maurice
Dresser, Louisa
du Cret, Dudley Vaughan

Easby, Dudley T, Jr
Ecke, Betty Tseng Yu-Ho
Eckert, William Dean
Eckhardt, Ferdinand
Eisenberg, Marvin
Eitner, Lorenz E A
Elliott, B Charles, Jr
Elsen, Albert Edward
Enggass, Robert
Ettinghausen, Richard
Evans, Bruce Haselton
Evans, Grose
Fehl, Philipp P
Feldman, Edmund Burke
Ferguson, Charles
Fern, Alan Maxwell
Flexner, James Thomas
Flint, Janet Altic
Forsyth, Robert Joseph
Frankenstein, Alfred Victor
Fraser, Douglas (Ferrar)
Freedberg, Sydney Joseph
Freeman, Richard Borden
Frinta, Mojmir Svatopluk
Gaines, William Robert
Gaither, Edmund B
Gardiner, Henry Gilbert
Gatling, Eva Ingersoll
Gebhard, David
Gerdts, William H
Gilbert, Creighton Eddy
Gilchrist, Agnes Addison
Glezer, Nechemia
Goldberg, Norman Lewis
Goldwater, Robert
Gordon, John
Graham, F Lanier
Green, Samuel Magee
Grossman, Sheldon
Gundersheimer, Herman (Samuel)
Hall, Louise
Hamilton, George Heard
Harris, Josephine Marie
Harris, Paul Stewart
Hartt, Frederick
Hatch, John Davis
Havelock, Christine Mitchell
Havens, Elizabeth Carroll
Hayes, Marian
Herbert, Robert L
Hitchcock, Henry Russell
Homer, William Innes
Hoopes, Donelson Farquhar
Hope, Henry Radford
Hovey, Walter Read
Howat, John Keith
Howell, Douglass Morse
Howett, John
Howland, Richard Hubbard
Hubbard, Robert Hamilton
Hudson, Ralph Magee
Hunter, Sam
Huth, Hans
Hyslop, Francis Edwin
Isserstedt, Dorothea Carus
Jaffe, Irma B
Janson, Horst Woldemar
Johnson, Charlotte Buel
Joyner, Howard Warren
Kallir, Otto
Kan, Michael
Kelemen, Pal
Kelleher, Patrick Joseph
Kemoha (George W Patrick Patterson)
Kerr, John Hoare
Kertess, Klaus D
Kitzinger, Ernst
Klitzke, Theodore Elmer
Knox, George
Knox, Katharine McCook
Koch, Robert
Kotala, Stanislaw Waclaw
Kubler, George Alexander
Kup, Karl
Landy, Jacob
Larsen, Erik
Lawrence, Marion

Leach, Frederick Darwin
Leavitt, Thomas Whittlesey
Lee, Rensselaer Wright
Lerman, Leo
Lesley, Parker
Levitine, George
Lewis, Douglas
Lewis, Samella Sanders
Lewis, Virginia Elnora
Lindsay, Kenneth C
Little, Nina Fletcher
Littman, Robert R
Lombardo, Josef Vincent
Longman, Lester Duncan
Longstreet, Stephen
Lopez-Rey, Jose
Love, Iris Cornelia
Love, Paul Van Derveer
Lowry, Bates
Lunde, Karl Roy
Lust, Herbert
Lynch, James Burr, Jr
McAndrew, John
McCracken, Harold
MacDonald, William Allan
Mackay, Donald Cameron
Madden, Betty I
Mandle, Earl Roger
Maser, Edward Andrew
Maurer, Evan Maclyn
Megrew, Alden Frick
Meigs, John Liggett
Meiss, Millard
Messer, Thomas M
Miner, Dorothy Eugenia
Moeller, Robert Charles, III
Moir, Alfred
Mongan, Agnes
Mueller, Earl George
Munsterberg, Hugo
Myers, Denys Peter
Naeve, Milo M
Nash, Ray
Newhall, Beaumont
Nochlin, Linda (Linda Pommer)
Norton, Paul Foote
Novak, Barbara (Mrs Brian O'Doherty)
Oberhuber, Konrad J
Ostrow, Stephen Edward
Perkins, Ann
Perry, Regenia Alfreda
Pincus-Witten, Robert A
Pinkney, Helen Louise
Poor, Robert John
Posner, Donald
Rae, Edwin C
Rannit, Aleksis
Raydon, Alexander R
Read, Helen Appleton
Reiff, Robert Frank
Rewald, John
Reynolds, Harry Reuben
Ries, Martin
Ritchie, Andrew C
Robb, David M
Robbins, Daniel J
Robinson, Wahneta Theresa
Rogers, Millard Foster, Jr
Roseberg, Carl Andersson
Rosenblum, Robert
Rosenthal, Gertrude
Roskill, Mark Wentworth
Ross, Marvin Chauncey
Rubin, William
Russell, Helen Diane
Rust, David E
Sachs, Samuel, II
St John, Bruce
Sandler, Irving Harry
Scarbrough, Cleve Knox, Jr
Schapiro, Meyer
Schuster, Eugene Ivan
Schwartz, Marvin D
Scully, Vincent
Seitz, William Chapin
Sellers, Charles Coleman
Selvig, Forrest Hall

Selz, Peter H
Seymour, Charles, Jr
Shapley, John
Sheppard, Carl Dunkle
Shestack, Alan
Sickman, Laurence Chalfont Stevens
Simon, Sidney
Simpson, William Kelly
Sloane, Joseph Curtis
Smith, Ray Winfield
Smyth, Craig Hugh
Sonnenschein, Hugo, Jr
Spencer, Eleanor Patterson
Spencer, John R
Sponenburgh, Mark
Staley, Allen
Standen, Edith Appleton
Stebbins, Theodore Ellis, Jr
Stechow, Wolfgang
Steinitz, Kate Trauman
Stites, Raymond Somers
Stoddard, Whitney Snow
Stokstad, Marilyn Jane
Stringer, Mary Evelyn
Sunderland, Elizabeth Read
Sunkel, Robert Cleveland
Swarzenski, Hanns Peter
Taylor, Joshua Charles
Teitz, Richard Stuart
Thompson, Dorothy Burr
Thorne, Thomas Elston
Trubner, Henry
Tselos, Dimitri Theodore
Tucker, Marcia
Turk, Rudy H
Upjohn, Everard Miller
Van Der Marck, Jan
Van Derpool, James Grote
Varian, Elayne H
Vermeule, Cornelius Clarkson, III
Von Adlmann, Jan Ernst
Waage, Frederick O
Wallace, David Harold
Walton, Florence Goodstein (Goodstein-
   Shapiro)
Wark, Robert Rodger
Wasserman, Jack
Watrous, James Scales
Weitzmann, Kurt
Weller, Allen Stuart
Wethey, Harold Edwin
Whitehill, Walter Muir
Wilkins, Ruth Lois
Williams, Benjamin Forrest
Williams, Lewis W, II
Williams, Mary Frances
Williams, Tommy Carroll
Willis, Elizabeth Bayley
Wilmeth, Hal Turner
Wood, James Nowell
Woolfenden, William Edward
Worth, Peter John
Wriston, Barbara
Wunder, Richard Paul

ART LIBRARY DIRECTOR

Frick, Helen Clay

BOOK DESIGNER

Lerner, Abe

BOOKBINDER

Knowlton, Daniel Gibson

CALLIGRAPHER

Block, Joyce. Sumi Ink
Callicott, Burton Harry
Fleming, Allan Robb
Offner, Elliot

CARICATURIST

Hirschfeld, Albert. Ink

CARTOONIST

Addams, Charles Samuel
Anderson, Brad J
Angelo, Emidio
Armstrong, Roger Joseph. Ink
Berenstain, Stanley
Bissell, (Charles) Phil. Ink, Tempera
Brown, Bo. Inks
Brown, Daniel Quilter. Ink, Wash,
   Watercolors, Pencil
Bushmiller, Ernie Paul
Caniff, Milton Arthur. Ink, Watercolors,
   Oils
Capp, Al
Carmack, Paul R
Cavalli, Dick
Chapman, Howard Eugene
Cowan, Woodson Messick
Craig, Eugene
Cramer, Abraham
Crane, James
Crane, Roy (Campbell). Ink
Crawford, William H
Dahl, Francis W
Darrow, Whitney, Jr
Davis, George. Ink
Day, Chon (Chauncey Addison)
Day, Robert James
Dedini, Eldon Lawrence
Dennis, Charles Houston
Dole, George
Dowling, Daniel Blair. Ink, Crayon
Dunn, Alan (Cantwell). Lithographic
   Crayon, Ink
Ericson, Dick
Farris, Joseph G
Fine, Stanley M. Inks
Foster, Hal
Graham, Bill (William Karr)
Grubert, Carl Alfred
Hagglund, Irvin (Arvid)
Hanan, Harry
Harley, Harry George
Hesse, Don
Higgins, Thomas J, Jr
Hirsch, David W (Dave)
Hoff, (Syd). Washes, Ink
Holland, Daniel E
Holton, Leonard T
Hoppes, Lowell E
Hubenthal, Karl Samuel
Hunter, Graham
Hurd, Justin G (Jud)
Hutton, Hugh McMillen. Crayon, Ink
Ivey, James Burnett. Ink
Jackson, Virgil V
Johnson, Clifford Leo
Justus, Roy Braxton
Kato, Kay
Kaz (Lawrence Katzman)
Keane, Bil
Ketcham, Henry King (Hank)
Key, Ted
King, Warren Thomas
Knecht, Karl Kae. India Ink
Koerner, Daniel
Kuekes, Edward D
Lariar, Lawrence
Levinson, Fred (Floyd)
MacNelly, Jeffrey Kenneth. India Ink,
   Watercolors
Manning, Reg (West)
Markow, Jack
Mauldin, Bill
Montana, Bob. Ink
Mosley, Zack T
Neher, Fred
Newman, Ralph Albert. Ink
Nugent, Arthur William
Partch, Virgil Franklin, II
Phillips, Irving W

Pierotti, John
Pretsch, John Edward
Price, George
Robbins, Frank
Rosen, Hy(man) (Joseph). Inks
Saxon, Charles David. Pencil, Ink
Schulz, Charles Monroe
Shanks, Bruce McKinley
Shoemaker, Vaughn
Soglow, Otto
Stamaty, Stanley. Ink, Watercolors,
   Acrylics
Steig, William
Temes, Mortimer (Robert)
Terry, Hilda (Hilda Terry D'Alessio)
Thorndike, Charles Jesse (Chuck)
Townsend, Marvin J. Inks
Turner, Dick. Inks
Valtman, Edmund. India Ink
Van Buren, Raeburn
Walker, Mort. Ink
Warren, L D
White, Leo
Williams, Gluyas
Wood, James Arthur (Art)
Zib, Tom (Thomas A Zibelli)

CERAMIST
   See also Craftsman & Potter

Artis, William Ellisworth
Brooks, Louise Cherry
Broudo, Joseph David
Coffey, Karita Joyce
Englander, Gertrud
Grotell, Maija
Kahn, Annelies Ruth. Clay, Metal, Plastics
Kim, Ernie. Stoneware
Leber, Roberta (Roberta Leber McVeigh)
Middleton, David V
Natzler, Otto
Schaeffler, Lizbeth. Terra-cotta
Turner, Robert Chapman. Clay
Vance, George Wayne. Clay

COLLECTOR

Abramovitz, Mr & Mrs Max
Abrams, Harry N
Adams, William Howard
Adrian, Barbara
Agoos, Herbert M
Akston, Joseph James
Aldrich, Larry
Alonzo, Jack J
Alsdorf, James W
Altmayer, Jay P
Altschul, Arthur G
Amoroso, Jack Louis
Anderson, David K
Anspach, Ernst
Arenberg, Albert L
Arnhold, Mr & Mrs Hans
Asher, Betty M
Askin, Arnold Samuel
Ault, Lee Addison
Bader, Franz
Baker, Richard Brown
Baker, Walter C
Bareiss, Walter
Barnet, Mr & Mrs Howard J
Barron, Mrs S Brooks
Baruch, Mr & Mrs Joseph M
Bass, John
Bauman, Lionel R
Beineke, Dr & Mrs J Frederick
Bell, R Murray
Bensinger, B Edward, III
Benton, William
Berg, Phil
Berger, Samuel A
Berman, Muriel Mallin
Berman, Philip I
Berne, Gustave Morton
Bernstein, Benjamin D

Collector (cont)

Bickford, George Percival
Biddle, James
Bingham, Mrs Harry Payne
Bisgard, James Dewey
Blackburn, Lenora Whitmire
Blankfort, Dorothy
Blankfort, Michael
Block, Mr & Mrs Leigh B
Bloedel, Lawrence Hotchkiss
Boese, Alvin William
Bolles, John S
Bond, Roland S
Borgenicht, Grace (Grace Borgenicht Brandt)
Bostwick, Mr & Mrs Dunbar W
Boyer, Mrs Richard C
Bradley, Mrs Harry Lynde
Brennan, Francis Edwin
Briggs, Austin
Brochstein, I S
Brody, Mr & Mrs Sidney F
Bromberg, Mr & Mrs Alfred L
Brooks, Louise Cherry
Brown, Harry Joe, Jr
Browne, Robert M
Brundage, Avery
Bruno, Phillip A
Bunshaft, Mr & Mrs Gordon
Burden, Carter
Burkhardt, Hans Gustav
Burrows, Selig S
Campbell, Vivian (Vivian Campbell Stoll)
Cantey, Sam Benton, III
Carey, Ted
Chalk, Mr & Mrs O Roy
Chapellier, George
Chapman, Mrs Gilbert W
Clark, Anthony Morris
Clowes, Allen Whitehill
Cohen, Mr & Mrs Arthur A
Cohen, Wilfred P
Colin, Georgia T
Colin, Ralph Frederick
Constable, Rosalind
Cosla, Dr & Mrs O K
Costa, Olga
Cowles, Charles
Cowles, Mr & Mrs Gardner
Cox, E Morris
Cox, Warren Earle
Crawford, John McAllister, Jr
Crispo, Andrew John
Cummings, Nathan
Cunningham, Charles Crehore
Dalton, Harry L
Damaz, Paul F
D'Amico, Augustine A
Daniels, David M
Daves, Delmer
David, Dianne
Davidson, Suzette Morton
Davis, Ronald Wendel
Davis, Mr & Mrs Walter
Day, Martha B Willson
Dayton, Bruce B
De Graaff, Mr & Mrs Jan
De Hoyos, Luis
de Kolb, Eric
De Lawter, Dr & Mrs Hilbert H
Del Junco, Emilio
DeMaree, Elizabeth Ann (Betty)
De Menil, John
Desind, Philip
De Waal, Ronald Burt
Dewey, Mr & Mrs Charles S, Jr
Dillon, C Douglas
Dockstader, Frederick J
Dorr, William Shepherd
Dreitzer, Albert J
Driver, Morley (Brooke Lister)
Dunn, O Coleman
Dunnington, Mrs Walter Grey
Eckstein, Joanna
Ehrman, Frederick L
Eisenstein, Mr & Mrs Julian
Eiteljorg, Harrison

Elkon, Robert
Emil, Allan D
Emil, Arthur D
Engelhard, Mr & Mrs Charles
Esman, Rosa M
Farber, George W
Feigen, Richard L
Felt, Mr & Mrs Irving Mitchell
Fillman, Jesse R
Fischbach, Marilyn Cole
Fitch, George Hopper
Flagg, Mr & Mrs Richard B
Fleischman, Lawrence
Flinsch, Harold, Jr
Ford, John Gilmore
Forsyth, Robert Joseph
Franklin, Ernest Washington, Jr
Frauwirth, Sidney
Freedman, Robert J
Freilich, Michael Leon
Frelinghuysen, Mr & Mrs Peter H B, Jr
Fromer, Mrs Leon
Fuller, Adelaide P & William Marshall
Gallagher, Edward J, Jr
Garbisch, Edgar William & Bernice
    Chrysler
Gardiner, Robert David Lion
Gary, Dorothy Hales
Getty, J Paul
Ghez, Oscar
Gibson, Roland
Gilvarry, James
Gimbel, Mrs Bernard F
Glaser, Samuel
Glasgall, Mrs Henry W
Glick, Paula Florence
Goldberger, Mr & Mrs Edward
Goldsmith, C Gerald
Goldsmith, Morton Ralph
Goldstone, Mr & Mrs Herbert
Gollin, Mr & Mrs Joshua A
Goodman, James Neil
Goodwin, Alfred
Gottlieb, Abe
Grace, Charles M
Graham, Robert Claberhouse
Greenspan, George
Greenwald, Charles D
Greenwald, Dorothy Kirstein
Grey, Mrs Benjamin Edwards
Griggs, Maitland Lee
Gross, Mr & Mrs Merrill Jay
Guggenheim, Peggy
Gumberts, William A
Gussman, Herbert
Guthman, Leo S
Haber, Leonard
Hack, Phillip S & Patricia Y
Halff, Robert H
Hall, Joyce C
Halpern, Nathan L
Handler, Mr & Mrs Milton
Harnett, Mr & Mrs Joel William
Harris, Leon A, Jr
Hartford, Huntington
Haskell, Harry Garner, Jr
Haslem, John Arthur & Jane N
Haswell, Mr & Mrs Anthony
Hauberg, Mr & Mrs John
Haupt, Mrs Enid
Hazen, Joseph H
Hecht, H Hartman
Heineman, Bernard, Jr
Heinz, Mr & Mrs Henry J, II
Heller, Ben
Heller, Goldie (Mrs Edward W Greenberg)
Heller, Lawrence J
Herbert, David
Herring, Mr & Mrs H Lawrence
Heyman, Mr & Mrs David M
Hilles, Susan Morse
Hirshhorn, Joseph H
Hokin, Grace E
Holcombe, R Gordon, Jr
Holmes, Paul James & Mary E
Honeyman, Robert B, Jr
Hooker, Mrs R Wolcott

Hoover, Francis Louis
Horowitz, Mr & Mrs Raymond J
Horowitz, Saul
Hoyt, Whitney F
Hulsey, William Hansell
Huntington, John W
Hutchinson, Janet L
Iervolino, Paula
Inslee, Marguerite T
Irwin, George M
Irwin, John N, II
Ittleson, Henry, Jr
Ivey, James Burnett
Jachmann, Kurt M
Jacobs, William Ketchum, Jr
Jaffe, Mrs William B
Janis, Conrad
Janss, Edwin, Jr
Jaretzki, Mr & Mrs Alfred, Jr
Jarman, Walton Maxey
Johnson, Mrs J Lee, III
Johnson, Philip Cortelyou
Josten, Peter
Josten, Mrs Werner E
Kanee, Ben
Kangas, Gene
Kaplan, Alice Manheim
Kaplan, Jacques
Karshan, Donald H
Kasle, Gertrude
Katz, Joseph M
Keen, Helen Boyd
Kerr, Berta Borgenicht
Kestnbaum, Gertrude Dana
King, Ethel May
Kirkland, Vance Hall
Kirstein, Mr & Mrs Lincoln
Kissner, Franklin H
Klein, Esther M
Knox, Katharine McCook
Koch, John
Kramarsky, Mrs Siegfried
Kreeger, David Lloyd
Kress, Mrs Rush H
Kurdian, Haroutiun Harry
Lachman, Mr & Mrs Charles R
Lamantia, James
Lane, Alvin Seymour
Langston, Mr & Mrs Loyd H (Mildred J)
Lasker, Mrs Albert D
Laskey, Dr & Mrs Norman F
Latner, Albert J
Lawrence, Jack
Lee, Richard Allen
Leff, Jay C
Leigh, David I
Lerner, Alexander
Leval, Mrs Fernand
Levick, Mr & Mrs Irving
Levin, Jeanne
Levine, Seymour R
Lewin, Bernard
Lilienthal, Mr & Mrs Philip N, Jr
Linsky, Mr & Mrs Jack
Lipman, Howard W
List, Vera G
Little, Nina Fletcher
Lloyd, Mrs H Gates
Loeb, Mr & Mrs John L
London, Alexander
Longstaffe, John Ronald
Lowenthal, Milton
Lucas, Charles C, Jr
Ludgin, Earle
Ludington, Wright S
Lukin, Philip
Lust, Herbert
Lynch, James O'Connor
MacAlister, Paul Ritter
McAlpin, David H
MacAulay, John Alexander
McCannel, Mrs Malcolm A
McDonough, John Joseph
McIlhenny, Henry Plumer
Magriel, Paul
Malbin, Lydia Winston
Mallory, Margaret

Mandelbaum, Dr & Mrs Robert A
Marcus, Edward S
Marcus, Stanley
Maremont, Arnold H
Marino, Albert Joseph
Marks, Mr & Mrs Cedric H
Marks, Royal S
Marks, Stanley A
Markus, Mrs Henry A
Marsteller, William A
May, Morton David
May, William L
Mayer, Grace M
Mayer, Robert Bloom
Mayers, John J
Meissner, Berniece Cram-Gill
Melamed, Abraham
Mellon, Paul
Merriam, Ruth
Meyer, Mr & Mrs Andre
Miller, Mrs G Macculloch
Miller, Mitchell
Mitchell, Dana Covington, Jr
Monsen, Dr & Mrs R Joseph
Moore, Fanny Hanna
Morse, A Reynolds
Moss, Morrie Alfred
Mudge, Edmund Webster, Jr
Muensterberger, Werner
Murchison, John D
Murray, William Colman
Myers, John
Navas, Elizabeth S
Neuberger, Roy R
Neumann, Hans
Neustadter, Edward L
Newton, Earle Williams
Niemeyer, Arnold Matthew
Offin, Charles Z
Ogden, Ralph E
Ohrbach, Jerome K
Oliver, Henry, Jr
Paddock, Denis Emil
Paley, Mr & Mrs William S
Palitz, Mrs Clarence Y
Pall, Dr & Mrs David B
Palmer, Fred Loren
Parkinson, Elizabeth Bliss
Payson, Mr & Mrs Charles S
Pearlman, Henry
Pease, Roland Folsom, Jr
Penney, Charles Rand
Perkins, Mabel H
Perlin, Rae
Perls, Frank (Richard)
Pharr, Mr & Mrs Walter Nelson
Phillips, Gifford
Phipps, Cynthia
Phipps, Mr & Mrs Ogden
Pines, Ned L
Pleasants, Frederick R
Polan, Lincoln M
Pomerance, Leon
Poses, Mr & Mrs Jack I
Potamkin, Meyer P
Praeger, Frederick A
Prager, David A
Pratt, Dallas
Price, Vincent
Pritzlaff, Mr & Mrs John, Jr
Pulitzer, Joseph, Jr
Putnam, Mrs John B
Putterman, Florence Grace
Quinn, Henrietta Reist
Rabb, Mr & Mrs Irving W
Rafsky, Jessica C
Rahr, Frederic H
Rauch, John G
Reeves, Mr & Mrs Benjamin
Regensburg, Sophy P
Reichman, Gerson
Reiner, Mr & Mrs Jules
Reis, Mrs Bernard J
Revington, George D, III
Richmond, Frederick W
Richmond, Lawrence
Rifkin, Dr & Mrs Harold

Riley, Chapin
Ring, Edward Alfred
Robb, Mr & Mrs Sidney R
Robinson, Thomas
Robles, Esther Waggoner
Rockefeller, Mr & Mrs David
Rockefeller, John Davison, III
Rockefeller, Mrs Laurance
Rockefeller, Nelson Aldrich
Rockefeller, Mr & Mrs Winthrop
Rodman, Selden
Roebling, Mary G
Roelofs, Mrs Richard, Jr
Roesler, Norbert Leonhard Hugo
Rogers, Leo M
Rojtman, Mrs Marc B
Romansky, Alvin S
Rome, Harold
Root, Mrs Edward W
Rosen, Israel
Rosenbloom, Charles J
Rosenthal, Mrs Alan H
Rosenwald, Barbara K
Rosenwald, Lessing Julius
Rubin, Mr & Mrs Harry
Rubin, Lawrence
Rudolph, Mr & Mrs C Frederick
Ruskin, Lewis J
Ruskin, Mickey
Rust, David E
Sachs, A M
Sampliner, Mr & Mrs Paul H
Sandground, Mark Bernard, Sr
Santiago, Helene
Sarnoff, Lolo
Sarnoff, Robert W
Sawyer, William
Saypol, Mr & Mrs Ronald D
Schang, Frederick, Jr
Schimmel, Norbert
Schoen, Mr & Mrs Arthur Boyer
Scholz, Janos
Schooler, Lee
Schramm, James Siegmund
Schulhof, Mr & Mrs Rudolph B
Schulman, Jacob
Schulte, Mr & Mrs Arthur D
Schwabacher, Alfred
Schwartz, Eugene M
Schweitzer, M R
Scull, Robert C
Seff, Mr & Mrs Manuel
Segy, Ladislas
Selig, Mr & Mrs Manfred
Selig, Martin
Shapiro, Daisy Viertel
Sheldon, Olga N
Shell, Mr & Mrs Irving W
Sherbell, Rhoda
Shorter, Edward Swift
Shulman, Joseph L
Simon, Norton
Sinaiko, (Avrom) Arlie
Sirena (Contessa Antonia Mastrocristino Fanara)
Sisti, Anthony J
Slifka, Mr & Mrs Joseph
Sloan, Mr & Mrs J Seymour
Smart, Mary-Leigh
Smith, Mrs Bertram
Smith, C R
Smith, Justin V
Smith, Lawrence M C
Smith, Mrs Louis
Smith, Ray Winfield
Sneed, Patricia M
Solinger, David M
Solomon, Mr & Mrs Sidney L
Sonnenberg, Mr & Mrs Benjamin
Spaeth, Eloise O'Mara
Spiegel, Sam
Spitzer, Frances R
Sprayregen, Morris
Stachelberg, Mrs Charles G
Stamats, Peter Owen
Stamm, John Davies
Steinmann, Mr & Mrs Herbert

Stern, Mr & Mrs Arthur Lewis
Stern, H Peter
Stillman, E Clark
Stinski, Gerald Paul
Stoll, Mrs Berry Vincent
Stone, Alex Benjamin
Straight, Michael
Stralem, Donald S
Svenson, John Edward
Swann, Erwin
Tarnopol, Gregoire
Tauch, Waldine Amanda
Taylor, Dr & Mrs J E
Temple, Mr & Mrs Alan H
Thompson, Lockwood
Topol, Robert Martin
Tucker, Mrs Nion
Tyson, Mrs Charles R
Ulin, Dene
Ullman, Mrs George W
Ullman, Harold P
Untermyer, Judge & Mrs Irving
Uzielli, Giorgio
Van Atta, Helen Ulmer
Van Leer, Mrs W Leicester
Vershbow, Mr & Mrs Arthur
Verzyl, June Carol
Vogel, Edwin Chester
Walker, Herschel Carey
Walker, Hudson D
Walker, Mrs Philip
Walker, Mr & Mrs Ralph
Walter, May E
Walton, Harry A, Jr
Warburg, Edward M M
Warren, Mrs George Henry
Webb, Aileen Osborn
Weil, Mr & Mrs Richard K
Weill, Mr & Mrs Milton
Weiner, Mrs Samuel
Weiner, Ted
Weinstein, Mr & Mrs Joseph
Weisglass, Mr & Mrs I Warner
Weiss, Jean Bijur
Welch, James Henry
Welch, Mr & Mrs Robert G
Wertheim, Mrs Maurice
Wheeler, Cleora Clark
White, Ruth
Whitney, John Hay
Willis, Elizabeth Bayley
Windfohr, Robert F
Winokur, James L
Wintersteen, Bernice McIlhenny
Witham, Vernon Clint
Wittenborn, George
Woodner, Ian
Woods, Sarah Ladd
Woodside, Gordon William
Wright, Mr & Mrs William H
Wrightsman, Charles Bierer
Wurtzburger, Janet E C
Zadok, Mr & Mrs Charles
Zalstem-Zalessky, Mrs Alexis
Zamparelli, Mario Armond
Zeckendorf, Mrs Guri Lie
Zeisler, Richard Spiro
Zipkin, Jerome R

CONCEPTUAL ARTIST

Burgy, (Donald) (Thomas)
Denes, Agnes C. Graphics, Mixed Media
Odate, Toshio
Schley, Evander Duer (Van). Videotape, Film

CONSERVATOR
See also Restorer

Amarotico, Joseph Anthony
Blankenship, Roy
Buck, Richard D
Cornelius, Francis DuPont

Conservator (cont)

Honig, Mervin
Keck, Sheldon Waugh
Merriam, Ruth

CRAFTSMAN

Ahlskog, Sirkka
Alling, Clarence (Edgar)
Artis, William Ellisworth
Banta, E Zabriskie (Mrs Oliver Smith)
Bates, Kenneth Francis
Bealmer, William
Bertoia, Harry. Copper, Bronze
Billmyer, John Edward
Boccia, Edward Eugene
Brennan, Harold James
Cadle, Ray Kenneth
Christensen, Hans-Jorgen Thorvald.
    Sterling Silver, Metals
Cornfeld, Michael I. Graphics
Corsaw, Roger D. Ceramics
Darricarrere, Roger Dominique. Steel,
    Glass
Derujinsky, Gleb W. Wood, Bronze
Dice, Elizabeth Jane
Drumm, Don
Eagle, Clara M
Fox, Charles Harold
Fox, Winifred Grace
Frankel, Dextra
Grebenak, Dorothy
Griner, Ned H. Silver, Bronze, Brass
Grotell, Maija
Hallman, (H) Theodore, (Jr). Weaving
Heaton, Maurice
Herrold, Clifford H. Metal
Howard, Len R
Husted-Andersen, Adda. Metal
Julio, Pat T
Kennedy, Leta Marietta
Kingsbury, Robert David
Kizer, Charlotte Elizabeth. Gold, Silver
Knorr, Jeanne Boardman
Krevolin, Lewis
Kulicke, Robert M
Lesch, Alma Wallace. Textiles
Marshall, John Carl. Gold, Silver
Mintich, Mary Ringelberg. Metals, Plastics,
    Clay
Morgan, Lucy Calista
Murphy, Gladys Wilkins
Oster, Gerald
Pappas, Marilyn. Collage
Pardon, Earl B
Patterson, Patty (Mrs Frank Grass)
Paul, Bernard H
Paulin, Richard Calkins
Plamondon, Marius Gerald
Porter, Priscilla Manning
Radulovic, Savo
Rousseau-Vermette, Mariette. Tapestry
Schwarcz, June Therese. Enamels
Takemoto, Henry Tadaaki. Ceramics
Tanner, James L. Wood, Glass, Ceramics
Tatman, Virginia Downing
Tatschl, John. Wood, Glass, Bronze
Taylor, Rosemary. Stoneware
Terry, Duncan Niles. Glass
Vermes, Madelaine
Vierthaler, Arthur A
Warhol, Andy
Whitaker, Irwin A. Ceramics, Enamels,
    Plastics
Willet, Henry Lee. Glass, Gold
Wyman, William. Ceramics

CRITIC

Albertazzi, Mario
Albin, Edgar A
Albright, Thomas
Allen, Patricia (Patricia Allen Bott)
Alloway, Lawrence

Ashton, Dore
Ayre, Robert Hugh
Bannard, Walter Darby
Barzun, Jacques
Battcock, Gregory
Benson, Gertrude Acherman
Blake, Peter Jost
Borgzinner, Jon
Bruner, Louise Katherine
Canaday, John Edwin
Cernuschi, Alberto C
Chapin, Louis (Le Bourgeois)
Cleary, Fritz
Coates, Robert M
Coplans, John (Rivers)
Cowdrey, Mary Bartlett
Dame, Lawrence
Danikian, Caron Le Brun
Davidson, Marshall Bowman
Davis, Douglas Matthew
De Vinna, Maurice (Ambrose, Jr)
Donohoe, Victoria
Driscoll, Edgar Joseph, Jr
Driver, Morley (Brooke Lister)
Erdman, R H Donnelley
Feldman, Edmund Burke
Frankenstein, Alfred Victor
Fried, Alexander
Fried, Michael
Geist, Sidney
Genauer, Emily
Goldsmith, Barbara
Gomez-Sicre, Jose
Goossen, Eugene Coons
Grafly, Dorothy (Mrs Charles H
    Drummond)
Greenburg, Clement
Harris, Marian D
Haskell Douglas
Hess, Thomas B
Hitchcock, Henry Russell
Huxtable, Ada Louise
Key, Donald D
Kozloff, Max
Kramer, Hilton
Kuh, Katharine
Lastra, Luis
Levin, Kim (Kim Pateman)
Lowry, Bates
Luck, Robert
Lynes, Russell
McCormick-Sakurai, Jo Mary
Mellow, James R
Michelson, Annette
Miller, Donald
Molina, Antonio J
Nemser, Cindy
Nordland, Gerald John
Offin, Charles Z
Owyang, Judith Francine
Palmer, Herbert Bearl
Paris, Jeanne C
Pease, Roland Folsom, Jr
Preston, Malcolm H
Read, Helen Appleton
Richard, Paul
Roberts, Colette (Jacqueline)
Roskill, Mark Wentworth
Rothman, Sidney
Sandler, Irving Harry
Seckler, Dorothy Gees
Seldis, Henry J
Schloss, Edith
Schulze, Franz
Schwabacher, Ethel K
Singer, Esther Forman
Soby, James Thrall
Stevens, Elisabeth Goss
Sylvestre, Guy
Taylor, Robert
Terry, Marion (E)
Werner, Alfred
Wiese, Lucie
Willard, Charlotte
Wooden, Howard Edmund
Wyrick, Pete (Charles Lloyd
    Wyrick, Jr)

CURATOR

Bailey, Worth
Binai, Paul Freye
Bothmer, Bernard V
Boyer, Jack K
Bullard, Edgar John, III
Cain, James Frederick, Jr
Carter, Albert Joseph
Casey, Elizabeth Temple
Chipp, Herschel Browning
Clark, Mark A
Cunningham, Charles Crehore
Davis, Marian B
Doty, Robert McIntyre
Elzea, Rowland Procter
Emerson, Edith
Evans, Robert James
Faunce, Sarah Cushing
Flint, Janet Altic
Forsyth, William H
Franco, Barbara
Freeman, Margaret B
French, James C
Geldzahler, Henry
Glover, Donald Mitchell
Grossman, Sheldon
Hackenbroch, Yvonne Alix
Hanfmann, George M A
Hart, Marvell Allison
Hathaway, Calvin Sutliff
Henning, Edward B
Hill, Dorothy Kent
Hirsch, Richard Teller
Hoopes, Donelson Farquhar
Howat, John Keith
Hutton, William
Jewell, Kester Donald
Joachim, Harold
Johnson, J Stewart
Jones, Frances Follin
Keith, David Graeme
Kramrisch, Stella
Kuehn, Edmund Karl
Levine, Les
Lewis, Douglas
Lewis, Phillip Harold
Loehr, Max
McGarvey, Elsie Siratz
Mayer, Grace M
Miller, Dorothy Canning
Mills, Paul Chadbourne
Miner, Dorothy Eugenia
Monte, James K
Owsley, David Thomas
Phillips, John Goldsmith
Rambo, James I
Robinson, Wahneta Theresa
Rohlfing, Christian
Ross, Marvin Chauncey
Rousseau, Theodore, Jr
Rubin, William
Salmon, Larry
Sayre, Eleanor Axson
Schroeder, Eric
Schwarz, Heinrich
Sewell, Jack Vincent
Seymour, Charles, Jr
Shapley, Fern Rusk
Shepherd, Dorothy G (Mrs Ernst
    Payer)
Shulman, Leon
Sieber, Roy
Smith, Howard Ross
Smith, Jerome Irving
Stampfle, Felice
Swanson, Dean
Sweeny, Barbara Eleanor
Teilman, Herdis Bull
Tuchman, Maurice
Tucker, James Ewing
Van Der Marck, Jan
Waldron, James MacKellar
Welch, Stuart Cary
Wick, Peter Arms
Wilkinson, Charles K

Williams, Benjamin Forrest
Winer, Donald Arthur
Winternitz, Emanuel

DESIGNER
See also Craftsman

Adams, Mark. Tapestry, Stained Glass
Adams, Robert David. Acrylics
Albers, Anni. Textiles
Aldwinckle, Eric
Alexander, Robert Seymour
Allen, Loretta B
Altorfer, Gloria Finch. Acrylics, Oils,
  Watercolors, Collage
Ames, Jean Goodwin. Acrylics
Arnold, Richard R
Aronson, Boris
Aronson, Irene Hilde
Aronson, Joseph
Asmar, Alice. Casein, Indelible India Inks,
  Acrylics, Oils
Bacigalupa, Andrea
Backstrom, Florence (Florence Jennie
  Englert)
Bakanowsky, Louis J. Mixed Media
Baringer, Richard E
Barnett, Earl D. Oils, Acrylics, Water-
  colors
Barschel, H J. Graphics
Bartlett, Robert Webster. Oils
Barton, August Charles. Watercolors,
  Tempera
Bayer, Herbert
Beall, Lester Thomas
Bedno, Edward
Begg, John Alfred. Bronze
Bender, Beverly Sterl. Marble, Alabaster,
  Wood
Berkowitz, Henry. Oils, Watercolors,
  Mixed Media
Bidner, Robert D H
Blumenthal, Margaret M. Textiles
Bock, Vera
Bolley, Irma S. Watercolors
Bolster, Ella S
Bonamarte, Lou. Watercolors
Bosin, Blackbear. Watercolors, Gouache,
  Acrylics, Charcoal, Pencil
Boulton, Joseph L
Brennan, Harold James
Brodie, Gandy
Broomfield, Adolphus George. Oils, Water-
  colors, Crayon
Brough, Richard Burrell. Watercolors
Brown, John Hall. Watercolors
Buranabunpot, Pornpilai. Textiles
Buros, Luella. Watercolors
Califf, Marilyn Iskiwitz. Oils, Collage
Campbell, Rosamond Sheila
Cantor, Robert Lloyd
Carewe, Sylvia
Carey, Ted
Carter, Clarence Holbrook
Castle, Wendell Keith. Wood
Chapman, Dave
Chapman, Howard Eugene
Chappell, Warren
Chase, Allan Seamans. Steel, Other Metals
Chermayeff, Ivan
Cherner, Norman
Chethlahe (David Chethlahe Paladin).
  Acrylics, Sand
Christensen, Hans-Jorgen Thorvald.
  Sterling Silver, Metals
Coburn, Bette Lee Dobry. Oils, Acrylics,
  Graphics
Cocker, Barbara J. Acrylics
Coes, Kent Day. Watercolor
Cohen, Elaine Lustig
Cohen, Harold Larry
Colin, Georgia T
Colker, Edward
Cooke, Donald Ewin. Watercolors
Copeland, Lawrence Gill. Metal
Coplan, Kate M

Couch, Urban
Cushing, George
Cutler, Ethel Rose. Watercolors, Oils
Davidson, Suzette Morton
Davison, Robert
De Christopher, Eugene Louis. Wood, Metal,
  Plexiglas
Defenbacher, Daniel S
De Pedery-Hunt, Dora
De Pol, John. Wood
Deskey, Donald
De Vitis, Themis
Dike, Philip Latimer. Watercolors, Oils
Dimson, Theo Aeneas. Graphics
Drabkin, Stella. Mosaics
Dufour, Paul Arthur. Sumi, Stained Glass
Duncalfe, Walter John Douglas. Oils,
  Watercolors
East, N S, Jr. Metals
Eide, Palmer. Oils, Acrylics, Wood, Stone,
  Mixed Media
Eilers, Fred (Anton Frederick). Oils
Eitel, Cliffe Dean
Elliott, Lillian. Textiles
Enriquez, Gaspar
Ericson, Susan Kunce. Acrylics, Oils
Ettenberg, Eugene M
Ewald, Louis. Oils, Mosaic, Gold Leaf
Eyen, Richard J
Fairchild, Isabel Shelton. Watercolors
Farian, Babette (Sommerich). Acrylics, Ink,
  Graphics
Faulconer, Mary (Fullerton). Gouache
Feder, Ben
Feher, Joseph. Oils
Fischer, Mildred (Gertrude). Fibers
Fleming, Allan Robb
Floethe, Richard
Forman, Alice
Frank, Helen Sophia. Oils
Gates, John Monteith
Gaylord, Frank Chalfant. Granite
Genius, Jeannette (Jeannette M McKean).
  Oils, Pastels
George, Walter Eugene, Jr
Giffuni, Flora Baldini. Pastels
Giusti, George. Metals
Glaser, David. Oils, Mixed Media
Glass, Henry P
Goeritz, Mathias. Concrete, Steel
Goth, Marie. Oils
Gray, Wellington Burbank. Tempera, Water-
  colors
Graziani, Sante
Green, Edward Anthony. Watercolors
Greenberg, Gloria. Acrylics
Gregor, Helen Frances
Groff, June
Grosz, Franz Joseph. Oils, Glass
Grushkin, Philip
Haber, Leonard
Hanson, Jean (Mrs Jean Elphick). Wool
Hayes, Robert T
Head, George Bruce. Acrylics
Heaton, Maurice
Hebert, Julien
Heflin, Tom Pat. Oils, Acrylics
Heilemann, Charles Otto
Heiskell, Diana
Hemenway, Nancy (Mrs Robert D Barton).
  Bayetage
Hoffmann, Arnold, Jr
Holvey, Samuel Boyer. Metal Direct
  Construction, Lumia
Hood, (Thomas) Richard. Graphics
Hornung, Clarence Pearson
Horowitz, Nadia
Hough, Richard
Housser, Yvonne McKague. Oils, Acrylics,
  Mixed Media, Collage, Watercolors
Hovsepian, Leon
Howard, Len R
Howe, Nelson S
Howell, Marie W
Howlett, Carolyn Svrluga
Husted-Andersen, Adda. Metal
Hutton, Dorothy Wackerman. Graphics

Hyde, Laurence
Ingram, Jerry Cleman. Tempera
Inverarity, Robert Bruce
Jameikis, Brone Aleksandra. Stained Glass
Jensen, John Edward. Watercolors
Joffe, Bertha. Watercolors, Tempera
Johnson, Ivan Earl. Fabrics, Wood
Jones, Tom Douglas
Jonynas, Vytautas K
Josimovich, George. Oils
Jungwirth, Irene Gayas. Egg Tempera, Oils
Kahane, Melanie (Melanie Kahane Grauer)
Kahn, Peter. Graphics
Karawina, Erica (Mrs Sidney C Hsiao).
  Stained Glass
Katzenbach, William E
Kaufman, Edgar, Jr
Kaz (Lawrence Katzman)
Kemper, John Garner. Graphics, Oils
Kerr, Kenneth A. Watercolors
Kingrey, Kenneth
Kinigstein, Jonah
Kizer, Charlotte Elizabeth. Gold, Silver
Knight, Hilary
Koerner, Henry. Watercolors, Oils
Kramolc, Theodore Maria. Oils, Pastels
Krevolin, Lewis
Krody, Barron J
Krupp, Louis. Oils, Watercolors, Charcoal
Kubly, Donald R
LaMarca, Howard J. Graphics
Larrinaga, Mario. Oils
Larsen, Jack Lenor
Laury, Jean Ray (Jean Ray Bitters). Fabric
Laycox, (William) Jack. Oils, Watercolors
Lechtzin, Stanley. Metals, Plastics
Lederer, Wolfgang
Lein, Malcolm Emil
Lennie, Beatrice E C
Levinson, Fred (Floyd)
Liszt, Maria Veronica. Oils
Lo Medico, Thomas Gaetano
Low, Joseph. Graphics
Lowe, Harry
MacAlister, Paul Ritter
McChristy, Quentin L. Transparent Water-
  color, Ink, Pastels
Mc Elcheran, William Hodd
McNear, Everett C
McVey, Leza. Clay
Maehara, Hiromu
Maitin, Samuel (Calman). Graphics
Martin, Charles E. Watercolors, Acrylics,
  Oils, Ink
Marzano, Albert. Acrylics, Oils, Water-
  colors
Max, Peter. Mixed Media
Mayen, Paul
Mcchan, William Dale. Oils
Meitzler, (Herbert) Neil. Acrylics,
  Tempera, Watercolors
Menihan, John Conway
Merritt, Francis Sumner
Metcalf, Robert M. Stained Glass
Mielziner, Jo
Miller, Harold George. Oils
Miller, Leon Gordon
Miller, Ralph Rillman. Oils
Mills, Robert James. Watercolors
Morrison, Boone M
Morse, Jennie Greene. Pastels, Water-
  colors, Gouache
Muir, Emily Lansingh. Oils
Murphy, Rowley Walter. Oils, Watercolors,
  Tempera
Myers, C Stowe
Nagano, Paul Tatsumi. Watercolors, Oils
Neddeau, Donald Frederick Price
Neff, John A. Watercolors
Nesbitt, Alexander John
Nevell, Thomas G
New, Lloyd H (Lloyd Kiva)
Nichols, Donald Edward
Nicodemus, Chester Roland. Ceramics,
  Bronze
Nigrosh, Leon Isaac. Ceramics
Nodel, Sol. Stained Glass

Designer (cont)

Noyes, Eliot
O'Brien, Joan
Ochikubo, Tetsuo. Oils
Oenslager, Donald Mitchell
Pace, Margaret Bosshardt
Parker, James Varner. Collage
Peck, James Edward. Watercolors,
  Enamels, Woods
Peterson, John Douglas
Petrie, Ferdinand Ralph. Watercolors
Petroff, Gilmer. Watercolors, Acrylics
Phelan, Linn Lovejoy. Ceramics
Pierre-Noel, Lois Jones. Oils, Acrylics
Plath, Iona
Pollard, Donald Pence. Crystal, Oils
Pope, Richard Coraine. Opaque Watercolor
Portanova, Joseph Domenico. Bronze
Potter, (George) Kenneth. Watercolors,
  Oils, Acrylics
Powell, Leslie (Joseph). Oils, Watercolors,
  Pastels
Prentice, David Ramage. Acrylics
Prestini, James Libero. Steel, Aluminum,
  Wood
Pringle, Burt Evins. Tempera, Acrylics,
  Gouaches
Proctor, Gifford MacGregor. Bronze
Proom, Al
Rand, Paul
Randall, (Lillian) Paula. Wood, Stone,
  Plastics
Randall, Ruth Hunie. Ceramics
Regensteiner, Else F(riedsam)
Reider, David H
Reinhardt, Siegfried Gerhard
Renk, Merry (Merry Curtis)
Rennie, Helen (Sewell). Oils, Acrylics
Revor, Remy, SSND
Reynolds, Joseph Gardiner. Stained Glass
Richardson, Gerard
Riley, Gerald Patrick. Constructed Objects,
  Leather, Metal, Assorted Fibers
Riley, Roy John. Oils
Rovelstad, Trygve A
Rowlands, Tom
Roysher, Hudson (Brisbine). Silver, Gold,
  Bronze
Rubin, Irwin
Ruffo, Joseph Martin
Rumsey, David MacIver. Television, Film,
  Electronics, Light, Sound
Ruthling, Ford. Oils
Saar, Betye. Mixed Media
Sainz, Francisco
Salazar, Juan. Oils
Saltzman, William. Oils, Wood, Copper,
  Stained Glass
Samerjan, George E
Sarff, Walter
Schachter, Justine Ranson. Stone, Graphics
Schaeffer, Rudolph Frederick
Schroyer, Robert McClelland
Schulze, Paul. Glass, Mixed Media
Seliger, Charles. Oils, Acrylics
Sennhauser, John. Oils, Collage
Shayn, John
Sheets, Millard Owen
Sherman, Sarai. Oils, Graphics
Shields, Alan J
Shipley, James R
Simon, Ellen R
Skeggs, David Potter
Skinner, Orin Ensign. Stained Glass
Stein, Maurice Jay
Steinberg, Isador N
Steinfels, Melville P
Stephens, Curtis. Plastics
Stephens, Thomas Michael. Plastics, Steel,
  Aluminum
Stevenson, Branson Graves. Graphics
Sturtevant, Harriet H
Sundberg, Carl Gustave. Procelain,
  Enamels, Graphics
Tait, Katharine Lamb. Stained Glass
Temes, Mortimer (Robert)

Terry, Duncan Niles. Glass
Thomas, George R
Thompson, (James) Bradbury
Thompson, George Louis. Glass
Thomson, Carl L. Watercolors
Thorne, Gordon (Kit). Acrylics, Water-
  colors
Tittle, Grant Hillman
Toral, Maria Teresa. Inks, Oils, Collage
Torbert, Marguerite Birch
Tormey, James. Oils
Treadwell, Helen
Truex, Van Day
Van De Bogart, Willard George. Hardware
Vassos, John
Viner, Frank Lincoln. Vinyl, Cheesecloth,
  Dyes
Wasile, Elyse. Acrylics, Gouache, Oils
Wasserman, Albert. Oils
Watson, Aldren Auld
Watson, Sydney Hollinger
Watts, Robert M. Mixed Media
Webster, Larry Russell. Watercolors
Wehr, Paul Adam
Werner, Donald (Lewis). Watercolors,
  Collage
Wheeler, Cleora Clark
White, Ian McKibbin
Whitehead, James Louis
Wier, Gordon D (Don)
Williams, Garth Montgomery
Williams, Warner
Wilson, Sybil. Acrylics
Wilson, Tom Muir. Graphics
Witmeyer, Stanley Herbert. Watercolors,
  Mixed Media
Wright, Russel
Yoakum, Delmer J. Oils, Watercolors
Young, Kenneth Victor
Zahn, Carl Frederick
Zamparelli, Mario Armond
Zornes, James Milford. Watercolors

DRAFTSMAN

Anthony, William Graham. Pencil
Breitenbach, William John. Cast Aluminum,
  Polyester Resin, India Ink
Ettenberg, Franklin Joseph. Pen & Ink, Oils
Finke, Leonda Froelich. Bronze, Wood,
  Ink, Silverpoint
Greene-Mercier, Marie Zoe. Bronze, Steel
Lark, Raymond. Oil, Pencil
Peterson, Robert Baard. Oils
Youngquist, John

Draughtsman see Draftsman

DRAWER

Mullen, Philip Edward. Pencil, Pastels
Osborn, Robert
Whitson (Peter Whitson Warren)

Editorial Cartoonist see Cartoonist

EDUCATOR
  See also Instructor

Abany, Albert Charles
Abdalla, Nick
Ablow, Joseph
Ackerman, Gerald Martin
Adams, Pat
Adler, Samuel (Marcus)
Ahysen, Harry Joseph
Alaupović, Alexandra V
Albert, Calvin
Albin, Edgar A
Alexander, Robert Seymour
Aljaman (Alton James Chapman)
Allen, Margaret Prosser

Allen, Ralph
Alloway, Lawrence
Alps, Glen Earl
Alston, Charles Henry
Altabé, Joan Berg
Altman, Harold
Ames, Arthur Forbes
Andersen, Andreas Storrs
Andersen, Wayne Vesti
Anderson, Jeremy Radcliffe
Andrade, Edna Wright
Anliker, Roger (William)
Anthony, Lawrence Kenneth
Apgar, Nicolas Adam
Arbeit, Arnold A
Archambault, Louis
Archer, Dorothy Bryant
Arcilesi, Vincent J
Arneson, Robert Carston
Arnheim, Rudolf
Arnold, Paul Beaver
Arnold, Ralph Moffett
Asher, Lila Oliver
Aubin, Barbara
Auvil, Kenneth William
Avakian, John
Bach, Dirk
Baderian, Ruth
Bailey, Clark T
Baird, Joseph Armstrong, Jr
Bakke, Larry Hubert
Balkind, Alvin Louis
Ballinger, Louise Bowen
Balossi, John
Barnes, Robert M
Barrett, Bill
Barton, Eleanor Dodge
Barton, Georgie Read
Baruzzi, Peter B
Bashor, John W
Bate, Norman Arthur
Bates, Kenneth Francis
Bavinger, Eugene Allen
Bealmer, William
Beam, Philip Conway
Beaman, Richard Bancroft
Beard, Marion L Patterson
Beattie, George
Beck, Rosemarie (Rosemarie Beck Phelps)
Beck, Stephen R
Beckmann, Hannes
Bedford, Helen De Wilton
Bedno, Edward
Beelke, Ralph G
Beerman, Herbert
Behl, Wolfgang
Bell, Enid
Benedict, Nan M
Berd, Morris
Berger, Klaus
Bernard, David Edwin
Berry, Glenn
Betts, Edward Howard
Biehl, Arthur Oliver
Billmyer, John Edward
Bischoff, Elmer Nelson
Bishop, Benjamin
Blackwell, John Victor
Blai, Boris
Blair, Carl Raymond
Blizzard, Alan
Bloch, E Maurice
Block, Irving Alexander
Bloore, Ronald Langley
Blum, Shirley Neilsen
Boaz, William G
Bobbitt, Vernon L
Bobick, Bruce
Bobleter, Lowell Stanley
Boe, Roy Asbjörn
Bogert, Grace Warren
Boggs, Franklin
Boghosian, Varujan
Bohrod, Aaron
Bolinsky, Joseph Abraham
Bolotowsky, Ilya
Bongart, Sergei R

Bopp, Emery
Borgatta, Robert Edward
Bornstein, Eli
Bosch, Gulnar Kheirallah
Botto, Richard Alfred
Boughton, William Harrison
Bowman, Ruth
Boyce, Gerald G
Boyce, William G
Boyd, Donald Edgar
Boyle, Keith
Brach, Paul H
Brackett, Truman H, Jr
Brackman, Robert
Bradshaw, Glenn Raymond
Bradshaw, Robert George
Brainard, Owen
Braitstein, Marcel
Brauner, Erling Bernhardt
Brecher, Samuel
Breed, Charles Ayars
Breithaupt, Erwin M
Brezik, Hilarion, CSC
Brice, William
Brieger, Peter H
Britsky, Nicholas
Brody, Jacob Jerome
Brooks, (John) Alan
Brooks, Charles M, Jr
Brooks, Wendell T
Broudo, Joseph David
Brough, Richard Burrell
Brown, Joseph
Brucker, Edmund
Bruder, Harold Jacob
Bryan, Wilhelmus B
Bryant, Olen L
Bucher, George Robert
Bumbeck, David A
Bunker, Eugene Francis, Jr (Gene)
Bunker, George (Raymond)
Burford, Byron Leslie
Burgart, Herbert Joseph
Burggraf, Ray Lowell
Burke, Daniel V
Burke, E Ainslie
Burnett, Calvin
Burrows, Tom
Bush, Lucile Elizabeth
Bush-Brown, Albert
Butterbaugh, Robert Clyde
Bye, Ranulph (DeBayeux)
Byrd, D Gibson
Caballero, Emilio
Cahill, James Francis
Cain, Joseph (Lambert)
Cain, Joseph Alexander
Calcia, Lillian Acton
Callisen, Sterling
Campbell, Malcolm
Campbell, Marjorie Dunn
Campoli, Cosmo
Candell, Victor
Cantor, Robert Lloyd
Caplan, Jerry L
Caponi, Anthony
Carey, James Sheldon
Carey, John Thomas
Carmichael, Donald Ray
Carpenter, Gilbert Frederick (Bert)
Carpenter, James Morton
Carter, Dean
Cascieri, Arcangelo
Case, Andrew W
Cassill, Herbert Carroll
Cataldo, John William
Catan-Rose, Richard
Cavanaugh, Tom Richard
Cavat, Irma
Chadeayne, Robert Osborne
Chaet, Bernard
Chafetz, Sidney
Chandler, John William
Chaplin, George Edwin
Charles, Clayton (Henry)
Chase, Alice Elizabeth
Chernow, Ann

Chernow, Burt
Cherry, Herman
Chipp, Herschel Browning
Chubb, Frances Fullerton
Church, C Howard
Cikovsky, Nicolai, Jr
Clover, James B
Coffey, Douglas Robert
Cogswell, Dorothy McIntosh
Cohen, H George
Coke, F Van Deren
Colby, Victor E
Colescott, Warrington W
Collins, Jim (Lee)
Collins, William Charles
Colson, Chester E
Colt, John Nicholson
Conant, Howard Somers
Conlon, William
Connett, (Delores) Dee M
Conrad, George
Conway, Fred
Cook, Richard Lee
Cooke, Edwy Francis
Coolidge, John
Copeland, Lawrence Gill
Cornfeld, Michael I
Corsaw, Roger D
Couling, Gordon Robert
Covington, Harrison Wall
Cowley, Edward P
Cox, J Halley
Cox, Joseph H
Craft, Douglas D
Cramer, Richard Charles
Craven, Roy Curtis, Jr
Crawley, Wesley V
Creese, Walter Littlefield
Cress, George Ayers
Crosby, Ranice
Crossgrove, Roger Lynn
Crown, Keith Allen
Cruz, Emilio
Culler, George D
Cunningham, Benjamin Frazier
Cusick, Nancy Taylor
Cusumano, Stefano
Czurles, Stanley A
Dahill, Thomas Henry, Jr
Dailey, Michael Dennis
D'Amico, Victor Edmond
d'Andrea, Albert Philip
Danes, Gibson Andrew
D'Arista, Robert
Darrow, Paul Gardner
Dash, Harvey Dwight
Davidson, Abraham A
Davies, Kenneth Southworth
Davis, Gerald Vivian
Davis, Harry Allen
Davis, Philip Charles
Day, Horace Talmage
Deaderick, Joseph
De Creeft, Jose
De Jong, Gerrit, Jr
Deknatel, Frederick Brockway
DeLauro, Joseph Nicola
Della-Volpe, Ralph Eugene
DeLonga, Leonard Anthony
De Tore, John E
De Vinna, Maurice (Ambrose, Jr)
DeVis-Norton, Mary M
De Vito, Ferdinand A
Dew, James Edward
Dice, Elizabeth Jane
Dickerson, Daniel Jay
Dickinson, William Stirling
Dickson, Harold Edward
Dioda, Adolph T
Dodd, Eric M
Dodd, Lamar
Dodd, Lois
Doherty, Robert J, Jr
Dole, William
Donson, Jerome Allan
Dorfman, Bruce
Dorn, Charles Meeker

Dorra, Henri
Dorst, Claire V
Douglas, Edwin Perry
Downing, George Elliott
Dreskin, Jeanet Steckler
Driesbach, David Fraiser
Driskell, David Clyde
Drutz, June
Duhme, H Richard, Jr
Dulac, Margarita Walker
Du Pen, Everett George
Eades, Luis Eric
Eagle, Clara M
Eaton, Myrwyn Lake
Eberman, Edwin
Edie, Stuart
Eisenberg, Marvin
Eisler, Colin T
Eisner, Elliot Wayne
Eitner, Lorenz E A
Ellinger, Ilona E
Elliott, Bruce Roger
Elliott, Philip Clarkson
Ellis, Edwin Charles
Elsner, Larry Edward
Emery, Charles Anthony
England, Paul Grady
Eppink, Helen Brenan
Ernst, Jimmy
Ettenberg, Eugene M
Ettinghausen, Richard
Evans, Richard
Ewing, Charles Kermit
Fabe, Robert
Failing, Frances Elizabeth
Faison, Samson Lane, Jr
Faris, Brunel De Bost
Faulkner, Kady B
Faulkner, Ray N
Fearing, Kelly
Feldman, Hilda (Mrs Neville S Dickinson)
Feldman, Walter (Sidney)
Fendell, Jonas J
Ferguson, Thomas Reed, Jr
Filipowski, Richard E
Filkosky, Josefa
Fincher, John H
Finck, Furman J
Fine, Perle
Fingesten, Peter
Fink, Herbert Lewis
Fiore, Joseph A
Fisch, Arline Marie
Fish, Robert (Robert James Field)
Flint, Leroy W
Flowers, Thomas Earl
Folds, Thomas McKey
Fontanini, Clare
Ford, Ruth Vansickle
Forman, Kenneth Warner
Forst, Miles
Fracassini, Silvio Carl
Frank, David
Fraser, Douglas (Ferrar)
Freedberg, Sydney Joseph
Freeman, David L
Freeman, Richard Borden
Freifeld, Eric
Freund, Will Frederick
Freundlich, August L
Freyberger, Ruth Matilda
Friedensohn, Elias
Fuchs, Mary Tharsilla, CDP
Fulton, W Joseph
Fulwider, Edwin L
Gabin, George Joseph
Gage, Harry (Lawrence)
Gallo, Frank
Gammon, Juanita-La Verne
Gardner, Robert Earl
Garrett, Stuart Grayson, Jr
Gatewood, Maud Florance
Gatrell, Marion Thompson
Gatrell, Robert Morris
Gebhardt, Ann Stellhorn
Gebhardt, Harold
Geck, Francis Joseph

Educator (cont)

Geeslin, Lee Gaddis
Gekiere, Madeleine
Gelber, Samuel
Gelinas, Robert William
Gentry, Warren Miller
George, Walter Eugene, Jr
Gerdts, William H
Gerhold, William Henry
Getz, Dorothy
Ghikas, Panos George
Gibbons, Hugh (James)
Gibson, Roland
Gikas, Christopher
Gilkey, Gordon Waverly
Gill, Frederick James
Gilmore, Roger
Glass, Henry P
Glinsky, Vincent
Glyde, Henry George
Goetz, Richard Vernon
Gold, Albert
Goldin, Leon
Goldstein, Milton
Gongora, Leonel
Gonzales, Boyer
Gooch, Donald Burnette
Good, Leonard
Goodnow, Frank A
Goossen, Eugene Coons
Gorder, Clayton J
Govan, Francis Hawks
Gowans, Alan
Grabach, John R
Gray, Wellington Burbank
Green, David Oliver
Gregory, Angela
Gregory, Joan
Grilley, Robert L
Griner, Ned H
Grippi, Salvatore William
Grooms, Reginald Lesie
Grossman, Morton
Grotell, Maija
Guerin, John William
Gunn, Paul James
Gussow, Roy
Gute, Herbert Jacob
Gutmann, John
Guy, James M
Guy, Osmond Sublett
Gwathmey, Robert
Gyermek, Stephen A
Haas, Lez
Haggart (Winifred Watkins)
Haines, Richard
Hale, Robert Beverly
Hall, Louise
Hall, Michael David
Hall, Rex Earl
Halsey, William Melton
Hammersley, Frederick
Hampton, Phillip Jewel
Hanfmann, George M A
Hansen, Frances Frakes
Hara, Teruo
Harman, Jack Kenneth
Harris, Josephine Marie
Harris, Lawren Phillips
Harrison, Lawrence Victor
Harrison, Newton A
Harrison, Robert Rice
Harrison, Tony
Harsh, Richard
Hart, Agnes
Hart, Allen M
Harter, Tom John
Hartgen, Vincent Andrew
Hartman, Robert Leroy
Hartt, Frederick
Hastie, Reid
Hatch, John W
Hatchett, Duayne
Hatfield, Donald Gene
Hausman, Jerome Joseph
Hawthorne, Jack Gardner

Hay, Dick
Haydon, Harold (Emerson)
Hayes, Marian
Haynes, Douglas H
Head, Robert William
Heidel, Frederick (H)
Heilemann, Charles Otto
Heinemann, Peter
Held, Julius S
Heliker, John Edward
Hendricks, Geoffrey
Hendricks, James (Powell)
Henkle, James Lee
Henning, Edward B
Henricksen, Ralf Christian
Henrickson, Paul Robert
Henry, Robert
Herard, Marvin T
Hernandez-Cruz, Luis
Herrold, Clifford H
Hewitt, Francis Ray
Hicken, Philip Burnham
Hildebrandt, William Albert
Hill, Peter
Hillman, Arthur Stanley
Hoffa, Harlan Edward
Holaday, William H, Jr
Holbrook, Hollis Howard
Holcombe, Blanche Keaton
Holladay, Harlan H
Hollingsworth, Alvin Carl
Homer, William Innes
Hook, Walter
Hoover, Francis Louis
Hopkins, John Fornachon
Hopkins, Peter
Hornung, Gertrude Seymour
House, James Charles, Jr
Houser, James Cowing, Jr
Housman, Russell F
Howard, Robert A
Howe, Oscar
Howell, Claude Flynn
Howlett, Carolyn Svrluga
Howze, James Dean
Hudson, Kenneth Eugene
Hudson, Ralph Magee
Huggins, (Leonard) Victor, (Jr)
Hunt, Robert James
Hunter, John H
Huntley, David C
Hupp, Frederick Duis
Hurst, Ralph N
Hyslop, Alfred John
Iden, Sheldon
Iglehart, Robert L
Ippolito, Angelo
Irvin, Mary Francis, SC
Ivy, Gregory Dowler
Jackson, A B
Jackson, Herb
Jacobs, David (Theodore)
Jankowski, Joseph P
Jarkowski, Stefania Agnes
Jeffery, Charles Bartley
Jelinek, Hans
Jergens, Robert Joseph
Johnson, Charlotte Buel
Johnson, Edvard Arthur
Johnson, Ivan Earl
Johnson, Lester F
Johnson, Lois Marlene
Johnson, Pauline B
Johnston, Richard M
Jones, Amy (Amy Jones Frisbie)
Jones, Tom Douglas
Josus (Josephine Hutson Graham)
Joy, Nancy Grahame
Ju, I-Hsiung
Jules, Mervin
Julio, Pat T
Junkin, Marion Montague
Kabak, Robert
Kachadoorian, Zubel
Kachergis, George Joseph
Kamrowski, Gerome
Kamys, Walter

Kaprow, Allan
Katz, Theodore (Harry)
Katzen, Lila (Pell)
Kaufman, Irving
Kaupelis, Robert John
Kaye, George
Kayser, Stephen S
Keane, Lucina Mabel
Kearney, John (W)
Keck, Sheldon Waugh
Keeler, Deane
Keeling, Henry Cornelious
Keener, Anna Elizabeth
Keene, Maxine M
Kemper, John Garner
Kenda, Juanita Echeverria
Kennedy, J William
Kennedy, Leta Marietta
Kent, Corita, IHM
Kepes, Gyorgy
Kerfoot, Margaret (Mrs M W Jennison)
Kern, Arthur (Edward)
Kerslake, Kenneth Alvin
Keyser, Robert Gifford
Kilian, Austin Farland
Killmaster, John H
Kimbrough, Verman
Kimura, Sueko M
King, William Alfred
Kingrey, Kenneth
Kington, Louis Brent
Kipp, Orval
Kirschenbaum, Jules
Kiskadden, Robert Morgan
Kitner, Harold
Klitzke, Theodore Elmer
Klonis, Stewart
Knight, Frederic Charles
Knipschild, Robert
Knobler, Nathan
Knorr, Jeanne Boardman
Ko, Anthony
Koch, Arthur Robert
Koch, Gerd (Herman)
Koepnick, Robert Charles
Koppe, Richard
Koppelman, Chaim
Korn, Elizabeth P
Korpela, Edward S
Kortlander, William (Clark)
Kotin, Albert
Kouwenhoven, John A
Kramer, Jack
Kramrisch, Stella
Kraner, Florian G
Krautheimer, Richard
Krug, Harry Elno
Krukowski, Lucian
Krushenick, John
Kuhn, Marylou
Laderman, Gabriel
Lafaye, Nell Murray
Laging, Duard Walter
Lam, Jennett (Brinsmade)
La Malfa, James Thomas
Lamis, Leroy
Landy, Jacob
Larkin, Eugene
Larsen, Erik
Lathrop, Churchill Pierce
Laurent, John Louis
Laurer, Robert A
Lawrence, Jacob
Lawrence, Marion
Lechtzin, Stanley
Le Clair, Charles
Lederer, Wolfgang
Lee, Robert J
Leepa, Allen
Le Fevre, Richard John
Lehrer, Leonard
Leland, Whitney Edward
Lepper, Robert Lewis
Lesch, Alma Wallace
Lesley, Parker
Levi, Julian (E)
Levine, Shepard

Levitine, George
Levy, David Corcos
Lewandowski, Edmund D
Lewicki, James
Lewis, Michael H
Lieb, Leonard
Liljegren, Frank
Lincoln, Richard Mather
Lind, Victor
Lindstrom, Gaell
Lissim, Simon
Littleton, Harvey K
Lochhead, Kenneth Campbell
Loehr, Max
Loew, Michael
Logan, Frederick Manning
Lomahaftewa, Linda (Linda Joyce Slock)
Lombardo, Josef Vincent
Longo, Vincent
Loomer, Gifford C
Lotterman, Hal
Lourie, Herbert S
Lowe, J Michael
Lubbers, Leland Eugene
Lukosius, Richard Benedict
Lusker, Ron
Lyford, Cabot
Lytle, Richard
McAndrew, John
Macaray, Lawrence Richard
McClure, Thomas F
McCoy, John W, (II)
McCoy, Wirth Vaughan
McCray, Dorothy M
MacDonald, William Allan
McDowell, Barrie
McFee, June King
McGarrell, James
McGee, William Douglas
McGough, Charles E
Maciel, Mary Oliveira
Mack, Rodger Allen
McKay, John Sangster
McKean, Hugh Ferguson
McKeeby, Byron Gordon
McKinin, Lawrence
McLean, Richard Thorpe
McMillan, Robert W
McNeil, George J
McVey, William M
McVicker, J Jay
McWhinnie, Harold James
Magleby, Francis R (Frank)
Mahoney, James Owen
Majdrakoff, Ivan
Mallary, Robert
Mannen, Paul William
Manso, Leo
Marden, Brice
Margolies, John Samuel
Maril, Herman
Marsh, (Edwin) Thomas
Marsicano, Nicholas
Martin, G W
Martinsen, Ivar Richard
Maser, Edward Andrew
Mason, Alden C
Mason, Frank Herbert
Massey, Robert Joseph
Massin, Eugene Max
Matheson, Donald Roy
Matthews, Gene (Eugene Edward)
Mattil, Edward L
Maurice, Alfred Paul
Mayhew, Edgar De Noailles
Meeker, Barbara Miller
Megrew, Alden Frick
Meixner, Mary Louise
Melchert, James Frederick
Mellor, George Edward
Meredith, Dorothy Laverne
Mesches, Arnold
Mesibov, Hugh
Messersmith, Fred Lawrence
Miller, Eva-Hamlin
Milliken, Gibbs
Mills, Frederick Van Fleet

Mills, George Thompson
Mitchell, John Blair
Mochon, Donald
Moglia, Luigi (John)
Moldroski, Al R
Monaghan, Keith
Monroe, Gerald
Montgomery, Charles Franklin
Morado, Chavez Jose
Morgan, Charles H
Morin, Thomas Edward
Morrison, Keith Anthony
Morse, Jennie Greene
Moseley, Spencer Altemont
Moshier, Elizabeth Alice
Moss, Joel C
Mueller, Earl George
Mueller, M Gerardine, OP
Mullican, Lee
Mundt, Ernest Karl
Munsterberg, Hugo
Murray, Floretta May
Musgrave, Shirley H
Musselman, Darwin B
Munzer, Aribert
Nash, Katherine E
Nay, Mary Spencer
Naylor, John Geoffrey
Neal, Reginald H
Neill, T Joseph
Neilson, Katharine B
Nelson, Leonard
Nelson, Lucretia
Nelson, Richard L
Nepote, Alexander
Nesbitt, Alexander John
Ness, (Albert) Kenneth
Newman, (John) Christopher
Nicholas, Donna Lee
Nichols, Alice W
Nichols, Donald Edward
Nick, George
Nickford, Juan
Nickle, Robert W
Nochlin, Linda (Linda Pommer)
Norris, (Robert) Ben
Norton, Paul Foote
Norwood, Malcolm Mark
Novak, Barbara (Mrs Brian O'Doherty)
Novinski, Lyle Frank
Novotny, Elmer Ladislaw
Nulf, Frank Allen
O'Connell, George D
Odorfer, Adolf
Oesterle, Leonhard Friedrich
O'Hanlon, Richard E
O'Hara, (James) Frederick
O'Neil, John
Ortmayer, Constance
O'Sickey, Joseph Benjamin
Ottiano, John William
Palmer, William C
Pappas, Marilyn
Pardon, Earl B
Parish, Jean E
Parker, Harry S, III
Partin, Robert (E)
Patrick, Joseph Alexander
Pearlstein, Philip
Pease, David G
Peers, Gordon Franklin
Penkoff, Ronald Peter
Penney, James
Perkins, G Holmes
Perlman, Raymond
Perrott, James Stanford
Peterson, Larry D
Petheo, Bela Francis
Phelan, Linn Lovejoy
Phillips, Margaret McDonald
Pick, John
Pickens, Alton
Pierce, Delilah W
Pinsky, Alfred
Plate, Walter
Plummer, John H
Pollak, Theresa

Pollock, Merlin F
Polonsky, Arthur
Porter, Elmer Johnson
Porter, Priscilla Manning
Posey, Leslie Thomas
Post, George (Booth)
Potts, Don
Preusser, Robert Ormerod
Pribble, Easton
Prior, Harris King
Pross, Lester Fred
Quest, Charles Francis
Quick, Birney MacNabb
Quinn, Noel Joseph
Quirk, Thomas Charles, Jr
Racz, Andre
Rae, Edwin C
Raffel, Alvin Robert
Rahja, Virginia Helga
Rakocy, William (Joseph)
Ramos, Melvin John
Randall, Ruth Hunie
Randall, Theodore A
Rannit, Aleksis
Rapp, Lois
Rascoe, Stephen Thomas
Rawski, Conrad Henry
Reed, Doel
Reed, Paul Allen
Reep, Edward Arnold
Regensteiner, Else F(riedsam)
Rehberger, Gustav
Reichert, Donald Karl
Reif, Rubin
Reimann, William P(age)
Revor, Remy, SSND
Rewald, John
Reynolds, Ralph William
Rice, Harold Randolph
Rice, Norman Lewis
Richards, Karl Frederick
Richardson, Sam
Ridlon, James A
Rippey, Clayton
Risley, John Hollister
Robb, David M
Robbins, Daniel J
Robbins, Warren M
Roberts, Clyde Harry
Roberts, Lucille D (Malkia)
Robinson, Robert Doke
Rogers, John H
Rogers, Otto Donald
Rosati, James
Rosenberg, Harold
Rosenberg, Jakob
Rosin, Harry
Ross, Alvin
Ross, Conrad Harold
Ross, James Matthew
Ross, John T
Roster, Fred Howard
Rouse, Mary Jane Dickard
Rowan, Dennis Michael
Rowan, Herman
Ruben, Richards
Rubenstein, Lewis W
Rudquist, Jerry Jacob
Russin, Robert I
Russo, Alexander Peter
Ruvolo, Felix Emmanuele
Sabatini, Raphael
Sadek, George
Salemme, Lucia (Autorino)
Salerno, Charles
Samuelson, Fred Binder
Sandgren, Ernest Nelson
Saucy, Claude Gerald
Saunders, Aulus Ward
Saunders, J Boyd
Saunders, Raymond Jennings
Savoy, Chyrl Lenore
Scanga, Italo
Schaeffer, Rudolph Frederick
Schapiro, Meyer
Schellin, Robert William
Schlicher, Karl Theodore

Educator (cont)

Schmalz, Carl (Nelson), (Jr)
Schmeckebier, Laurence E
Schmidt, Frederick Lee
Schmidt, Randall Bernard
Schmutzhart, Berthold Josef
Schoener, Jason
Scholder, Laurence
Schooley, Elmer Wayne
Schorr, Justin
Schultz, Harold A
Schulze, Franz
Schulze, John H
Schwarz, Felix Conrad
Schwarz, Heinrich
Schwarz, Myrtle Cooper
Schwieger, Christopher Robert
Scott, Henry (Edwards), Jr
Scully, Vincent
Scuris, Stephanie
Seide, Charles
Seidenberg, (Jacob) Jean
Seitz, William Chapin
Seldis, Henry J
Sella, Alvin Conrad
Sepeshy, Zoltan L
Serra-Badue, Daniel
Severino, D(ominick) Alexander
Sexauer, Donald Richard
Seyler, David W
Shane, Frederick E
Shaw, (George) Kendall
Sheaks, Barclay
Sheppard, John Craig
Shiner, Nate
Shipley, James R
Shoemaker, Peter
Shore, Clover Virginia
Sibley, Charles Kenneth
Sieber, Roy
Silins, Janis
Silverman, Ronald H
Simon, Sidney
Simoni, John Peter
Simpson, David
Simpson, William Kelly
Sinsabaugh, Art
Siporin, Mitchell
Sister Thomasita (Mary Thomasita
    Fessler, OSF)
Skop, Michael
Slade, Roy
Slettehaugh, Thomas Chester
Slive, Seymour
Sloane, Joseph Curtis
Smith, Alvin
Smith, Charles (William)
Smith, David Loeffler
Smith, Dolph
Smith, George W
Smith, Gordon
Smith, Henry Holmes
Smith, J(ohn) B(ertie)
Smith, Paul Roland
Smith, Ralph Alexander
Smith, Robert C
Smith, Sam
Sokole, Miron
Sorby, J Richard
Souden, James G
Spaulding, Warren Dan
Speight, Francis
Spidell, Enid Jean
Sprague, Mark Anderson
Spurgeon, Sarah (Edna M)
Squier, Jack Leslie
Squires, Gerald Leopold
Stamos, Theodoros (S)
Stamper, Willson Young
Stanczak, Julian
Stankiewicz, Richard Peter
Stapp, Ray Veryl
Stark, George King
Stark, Melville F
Starks, Elliott Roland
Stasik, Andrew J

Steczynski, John Myron
Steele, Ivy (Newman)
Stegeman, Charles
Stein, Harve
Stell, H Kenyon
Stephens, Curtis
Stephenson, John H
Sternberg, Harry
Stevens, Edward John, Jr
Stevens, Walter Hollis
Stewart, Jack
Stewart, Jarvis Anthony
Stewart, John Lincoln
Stilwell, Wilber Moore
Stoddard, Donna Melissa
Stoddard, Herbert C
Stokstad, Marilyn Jane
Stomps, Walter E, Jr
Stoops, Jack Donald
Streett, Tylden Westcott
Stringer, Mary Evelyn
Strong, Charles Ralph
Stroud, Peter Anthony
Struppeck, Jules
Stuler, Jack
Sublett, Carl C
Sudlow, Robert N
Sullins, Robert M
Summ, Helmut
Summerford, Ben Long
Swift, Dick
Swiggett, Jean Donald
Tajiri, Shinkichi
Tam, Reuben
Taylor, Grace Martin
Taylor, John C E
Taylor, Joshua Charles
Taysom, Wayne Pendleton
Tedeschi, Paul Valentine
Terenzio, Anthony
Tettleton, Robert Lynn
Thiebaud, (Morton) Wayne
Thomas, Ed B
Thomas, Elaine Freeman
Thomas, George R
Thompson, Ralston Carlton
Thorpe, Everett Clark
Thrall, Arthur
Toigo, Daniel Joseph
Tompkins, Alan
Toney, Anthony
Triplett, Margaret L
Trissel, James Nevin
Trivigno, Pat
True, Virginia
Tucker, Marcia
Turner, Janet E
Turner, Robert Chapman
Turner, Theodore Roy
Twiggs, Leo Franklin
Twitty, James (Watson)
Vaccaro, Nick Dante
Valius, Telesforas
Van Der Poel, Priscilla Paine
Van Derpool, James Grote
Vander Sluis, George J
Van Loen, Alfred
Van Meter, Mary
Van Veen, Stuyvesant
Vargo, John
Vasa (Vasa Velizar Mihich)
Vevers, Anthony Marr
Vickers, George Stephen
Vierthaler, Arthur A
Viesulas, Romas
Voigt, Roben
Von Neumann, Robert A
Voris, Mark
Voulkos, Peter
Vytlacil, Vaclav
Waage, Frederick O
Walker, Jerome
Walker, Robert Miller
Wasser, Paula Kloster
Weaver, Howard Sayre
Weber, Albert Jacob
Weber, Jean M

Wechter, Vivienne Thaul
Weddige, Emil
Weege, William
Weinberg, Elbert
Weiner, Egon
Weisman, Winston Robert
Weismann, Donald Leroy
Weitzmann, Kurt
Weller, Allen Stuart
Wessels, Glenn Anthony
West, W Richard (Dick)
Westermeir, Clifford Peter
Wexler, George
Whitaker, Irwin A
White, Charles Wilbert
White, Lawrence Eugene
White, Robert (Winthrop)
White, Roger Lee
Whitehead, Alfred
Whiteside, Forbes J
Whitlock, John Joseph
Whitson (Peter Whitson Warren)
Wieghardt, Paul
Wilbert, Robert John
Wilde, John
Wildenhain, Frans
Williams, Hiram Draper
Willson, Robert
Wilson, Edward N
Winer, Arthur Howard
Wingert, Paul Stover
Winter, Roger
Wisnosky, John G
Witkin, Jerome Paul
Wojinski, Francis Ann, OP
Wood, Harry Emsley, Jr
Woodruff, Hale A
Woods, Gurdon Grant
Woods, Rip
Woody, (Thomas) Howard
Wriston, Barbara
Wujcik, Theo
Wyatt, Stanley
Wyckoff, Sylvia Spencer
Yaghjian, Edmund
Yochim, Louise Dunn
Yoshida, Ray Kakuo
Yunkers, Adja
Yust, David E
Zabarsky, Melvin Joel
Ziegfeld, Edwin
Ziemann, Richard Claude
Zimiles, Murray
Zimmerman, Paul Warren
Ziroli, Nicola
Zisla, Harold
Zweerts, Arnold

ENAMELIST
See also Craftsman & Designer

Caster, Bernard Harry
Orsini (Gwendolyn Orsinger Anderson).
    Enamels, Watercolors

ENGRAVER

Abbe, Elfriede Martha. Wood
Albee, Grace Thurston Arnold. Wood
Aquino, Edmundo
Cook, August Charles
De Pol, John. Wood
Goldberg, Chaim Leib
Landeck, Armin
Leighton, Clare
Meissner, Leo J. Oils, Mixed Media, Wood
Morgan, Norma Gloria. Copper
Shuff, Lily (Lillian Shir)
Toral, Maria Teresa. Inks, Oils, Collage

ETCHER
See also Printmaker

Altman, Harold
Bellefleur, Leon
Bishop, Isabel (Mrs Harold G Wolff)
Coleman, Michael
Csoka, Stephen
Dennis, Cherre Nixon
Eames, John Heagan
Edmondson, Leonard
Fausett, (William) Dean
Fenton, John Nathaniel
Fox, Roy Charles W
Fried, Theodore
Gecse, Helene. Graphics
Hay, Dorothy B
Hill, Polly Knipp
Hoie, Claus. Graphics
Johnsen, May Anne. Silver Point, Oils
Kloss, Gene (Alice Geneva Glasier)
Knee, Gina (Mrs Alexander Brook)
Laventhol, Hank. Bronze
Lewis, Jeannette Maxfield
Lucioni, Luigi
Margulies, Joseph. Graphics
Richards, Jeanne Herron
Ryerson, Margery Austen
Schutz, Anton
Sessler, Stanley Sascha
Smith, R Harmer
Weidenaar, Reynold Henry

FILM MAKER

Bodolai, Joseph Stephen
Breer, Robert C
Cataldo, John William
Chambers, John
Chase, Doris (Totten)
Conner, Bruce
Frazer, John Thatcher
Gardner, Joan A
Gould, John Howard
Hobbs, (Carl) Fredric
Namuth, Hans
Niese, Henry Ernst
Orkin, Ruth (Mrs Morris Engel)
Snow, Michael
Stephens, Nancy Anne
Stoops, Jack Donald
West, Clifford Bateman
Wieland, Joyce
Williams, Neil

FINE ART APPRAISER

Wuermer, Carl

FINE ARTS SPECIALIST

Mitchell, Eleanor

GALLERY DIRECTOR
See also Museum Director

Banister, Robert Barr
Koppelman, Dorothy
Lathrop, Churchill Pierce
Love, Paul Van Derveer
Washburn, Gordon Bailey

GLASS BLOWER
See also Craftsman & Designer

Lipofsky, Marvin B

GOLDSMITH
See also Craftsman & Designer

Fisch, Arline Marie. Precious Metals

GRAPHIC ARTIST
See also Printmaker

Albers, Anni
Alcopley, L. Inks
Altwerger, Libby
Anderson, Howard Benjamin
Andrews, Sybil (Sybil Andrews Morgan)
Asawa, Ruth (Ruth Asawa Lanier)
Baker, Anna P
Barbee, Robert Thomas
Baskin, Leonard
Bentley, Claude
Blanchard, Carol
Borzemsky, Bohdan
Burkert, Robert Randall
Casarella, Edmond
Colville, Alexander
Coughlin, Jack
Cryderman, Mackie
Donneson, Seena
Ellison, J Milford
Evergood, Philip
Federe, Marion. Woodcuts
Ferris, Edythe
Ferro, Walter. Wood
Gerard, Paula (Mrs Herbert Renison).
    Silverpoint, India Ink, Sumi Ink,
    Watercolors, Tempera
Gurr, Lena
Hebald, Milton Elting. Bronze, Wood,
    Lithography
Hios, Theo
Jelinek, Hans
Katz, Hilda
Kolliker, William Augustin
Marcus, Irving E
Markell, Isabella Banks
Martin, Roger
Moy, Seong
Muench, John
Neustadt, Barbara (Mrs Gunther Meyer).
    Intaglio
Pehap, Erich K
Pringle, Burt Evins
Reibel, Bertram. Wood, Bronze, Stone
Schiller, Beatrice
Seckel, Paul Bernhard
Singletary, Robert Eugene. Graphite Lead
Strobel, Thomas C
Travers, Gwyneth Mabel
Valius, Telesforas
Yrizarry, Marcos
Zirker, Joseph

ILLUMINATOR

Carrington, Joy Harrell
Nodel, Sol

ILLUSTRATOR

Alajalov, Constantin
Allen, Courtney
Ames, Lee Judah. Mixed Media
Anderson, Doug
Anderson, Gunnar Donald. Oils
Angulo, Chappie. Acrylics
Arbuckle, Franklin
Ariss, Herbert Joshua
Avery, Ralph Hillyer. Watercolors
Backus, Standish, Jr
Bailey, Malcolm C W. Acrylics,
    Enamels, Ink, Wash
Bales, George Carson (Bob). Oils, Inks
Barbour, Arthur J. Watercolors
Barkan, Bebe (Beverly Adrian). Acrylics,
    Graphics
Bartle, Annette
Bauer, William. Oils
Baumhofer, Walter Martin. Oils, Casein
Becker, Charlotte (Mrs Walter Cox)
Beitz, Lester U
Bensing, Frank C. Oils
Bergere, Richard

Bessemer, Auriel. Oils
Bileck, Marvin. Graphics
Billings, Henry. Oils
Bisone, Edward George. Acrylics, Water-
    colors, Charcoal, Mixed Media
Bissell, (Charles) Phil. Ink, Tempera
Bittner, Hans Oskar
Blair, Helen (Helen Blair Crosbie)
Blake, Leo B
Blattner, Robert Henry. Watercolors
Blos, May (Elizabeth)
Bock, Vera
Boedeker, Arnold E (Boedie). Watercolors,
    Oils, Acrylics
Bond, Oriel Edmund. Polymer
Bouchard, Lorne Holland. Oils
Bowman, Jean (Jean Bowman Magruder).
    Oils
Bransom, (John) Paul
Briggs, Austin
Broemel, Carl William. Watercolors, Oils
Brown, Daniel Quilter. Ink, Wash, Water-
    colors, Pencil
Brown, William Ferdinand, II
Brownhill, Harold. Watercolors
Buba, Joy Flinsch
Campanelli, Daniel. Pencil, Ink
Carroll, Robert Joseph
Chappell, Warren
Clymer, John F
Coheleach, Guy Joseph. Oils, Tempera
Colgrove, Ronald B. Inks, Acrylics
Collins, Kreigh
Connolly, Jerome Patrick. Oils
Cook, Gladys Emerson. Pastels, Oils
Cooney, Barbara (Mrs Charles Talbot
    Porter)
Corcos, Lucille. Tempera, Acrylics,
    Gouache, Watercolors, Ink, Crayon
Cornelius, Marty. Oils
Cotsworth, Staats
Crawford, Ralston
Crite, Allan Rohan
Crosby, Ranice
Cuevas, José Luis
Damron, John Clarence. Oils, Watercolors
D'Aulaire, Edgar Parin. Mixed Media
D'Aulaire, Ingri (Mortenson) Parin. Oils,
    Pastels, Lithographs
Davis, George. Ink
Davis, John Harold
Davis, Wayne Lambert. Tempera, Water-
    colors, Oils
Dean, Abner
De Angeli, Marguerite. Watercolors, Pencil
De Diego, Julio. Oils, Watercolors,
    Tempera
Deloney, Jack Clouse. Watercolors,
    Acrylics
Dewey, Kenneth Francis. Pen & Ink, Water-
    colors, Oils
Dohanos, Stevan
Dowden, Anne Ophelia Todd. Watercolors
Doyle, Edward A
Drummond, Arthur A. Oils, Watercolors
Durand, Lucille Murphy. Watercolors,
    Graphics
Duren, Terence Romaine
Duvoisin, Roger. Gouache, Collage, Ink
Edwards, Stanley Dean. Oils, Acrylics
Eichenberg, Fritz. Graphics
Eisenstat, Benjamin
Erickson, Dick
Ericson, Ernest
Ets, Marie Hall
Etting, Emlen. Oils, Acrylics
Fagg, Kenneth Stanley. Tempera
Falter, John
Faragasso, Jack. Oils
Fein, Stanley. Oils, Inks
Ferris, (Carlisle) Keith
Fink, Sam
Fisher, Leonard Everett
Floethe, Richard
Fossum, Sydney (Glenn). Oils, Water-
    colors, Pastels
Francis, Harold Carleton

Illustrator (cont)

Frasconi, Antonio. Graphics
Freund, Harry Louis. Oils
Friberg, Arnold
Fuller, Harvey Kenneth. Oils
Gaston, Marianne Brody
Geisel, Theodor Seuss (Dr Seuss)
Ginsburg, Max
Gironella, Alberto
Goff, Lloyd Lozes. Mixed Media
Goldberg, Virginia Eagan. Oils
Gorsline, Douglas Warner. Oils, Water-
  colors
Grado, Angelo John. Oils, Pastels
Granstaff, William Boyd. Oils
Groth, John August. Watercolors, Ink
Haden, Eunice (Barnard)
Hader, Elmer (Stanley)
Hamblett, Theora. Oils
Handville, Robert T. Watercolors,
  Acrylics, Ink, Oils
Hanna, Boyd Everett. Wood, Watercolors,
  Oils
Harris, Robert George. Oils
Heberling, Glen Austin. Oils, Watercolors,
  Acrylics, Tempera, Pastels, Synthetic
  Resins
Helck, (Clarence) Peter. Casein, Tempera
Henry, John R
Hill, Joan (Chea-Se-Quah). Oils, Gouache,
  Acrylics, Collage, Tempera
Hilton, John William. Oils, Wax
Hobbie, Lucille. Watercolors
Hoffman, Martin (Joseph)
Holden, Raymond James
Hollerbach, Serge. Casein, Acrylics, Inks
Holt, Charlotte Sinclair
Howell, Elizabeth Ann. Watercolors,
  Acrylics
Hutchison, Milburn Robert
Inman, Pauline Winchester
Jackson, Everett Gee. Oils
Jackson, Vaughn L. Watercolors, Acrylics,
  Inks
Jackson, Virgil V
Jacquemon, Pierre. Oils
Jauss, Anne Marie. Wash, Oils, Water-
  colors, Linoleum, Dry Point
Johnson, (Leonard) Lucas. Oils
Jones, Elizabeth Orton
Jordan, Barbara Schwinn
Joy, Nancy Grahame. Ink
Kato, Kay
Kaufman, Joe
Kingman, Dong M. Watercolors, Lacquer
Klep, Rolf
Knight, Hilary
Kredel, Fritz. Watercolors, Inks
Krigstein, Bernard. Oils, Watercolors,
  Pastels
Laessig, Robert. Watercolors
Larsen, Ole. Oils, Pastels
Lasker, Joseph (L). Oils
Latham, Barbara. Oils
Lathrop, Dorothy
Lea, Tom
Lee, Doris
Lee, Manning De Villeneuve. Oils, Water-
  colors, Inks
Lenski, Lois
Lent, Blair. Acrylics
Levering, Robert K
Levit, Herschel
Lewicki, James
Lipinsky De Orlov, Lino S. Etching, Oils
Livingston, Virginia (Mrs Hudson Warren
  Budd). Watercolors
Lockhart, James Leland
Logan, Maurice. Watercolors, Oils
London, Alexander
Lotton, Iwan Leroy. Oils
Lovell, Tom. Oils
Ludekens, Fred
McBride, James Joseph. Watercolors
McClellan, Robert John. Oils, Watercolors
McCloskey, Robert

MacDonald, Grant
MacDonald, Thoreau
McGee, Olivia Jackson. Watercolors
Mac Gillis, Robert Donald. Watercolors
Maciel, Mary Oliveira
McNett, Elizabeth Vardell. Oils, Tempera
Masurovsky, Gregory. Ink, Graphics
Mauzey, Merritt
Mawicke, Tran. Oils, Watercolors
Max, Peter. Mixed Media
May, E M (Elizabeth M Messiter). Water-
  colors, Mixed Media, Ceramics
Mayhew, Richard
Megargee, Lawrence Anthony (Lawrie).
  Watercolors, Pastels, Inks
Melvin, Grace Wilson. Watercolors, Mixed
  Media, Acrylics, Collage
Meyers, Robert William
Mina-Mora, Raul Jose
Mitchell, James E. Casein, Oils
Moose, Philip Anthony. Oils, Acrylics
Mordvinoff, Nicholas
Morez, Mary
Morgan, Arthur C. Bronze, Marble
Morgan, Maritza Leskovar
Morris, Edward A
Mosley, Zack T
Newman, Ralph Albert. Ink
Nugent, Arthur William
O'Meilia, Philip Jay
Parke, Walter Simpson. Oils
Parker, Alfred
Partch, Virgil Franklin, II
Perlin, Bernard
Perlman, Raymond. Watercolors, Collage
Perrin, C Robert. Watercolors
Petersham, Maud Feller
Petro, Joseph (Victor), Jr
Phillips, Irving W
Pike, John
Poole, Earl Lincoln. Watercolors
Pretsch, John Edward
Prins, (J) Warner
Prohaska, Ray
Rabut, Paul
Ralston, J(ames) K(enneth). Oils, Ink,
  Watercolors
Reboli, Joseph John. Oils
Reisman, Philip. Oils, Watercolors
Rey, H A. Gouache, India Ink, Crayon
Riba, Paul F. Oils
Robbins, Frank
Rockwell, Norman
Romano, Emanuel Glicen
Rosenberg, Louis Conrad
Rosenhouse, Irwin Jacob. Graphics
Satorsky, Cyril
Savas, Jo-Ann
Saxon, Charles David. Pencil, Ink
Schlaikjer, Jes Wilhelm. Oils
Schlecht, Richard. Oils, Acrylics, Ink
Schroyer, Robert McClelland
Seabourn, Bert Dail. Oils, Watercolors
Seredy, Kate. Pencil, Crayon
Setterberg, Carl Georg. Oils, Watercolors
Sharp, Harold. Watercolors, Ink
Shimon, Paul. Gouache, Tempera, Oils
Siegel, (Leo) Dink. Watercolors, Inks, Oils,
  Gouache
Silverman, Burton Philip. Oils, Water-
  colors, Pastels
Simon, Howard. Watercolors, Oils, Wood
Simont, Marc
Simpkins, Henry John. Watercolors
Skinner, Elsa Kells. Watercolors
Sloane, Eric
Slobodkin, Louis
Smith, Helen M
Smith, Joseph A(nthony). Pencil, Wax
Snyder, Seymour. Oils, Watercolors,
  Gouache
Spagnolo, Kathleen Mary. Graphics
Spencer, Hugh
Stahl, Ben (Albert)
Stamaty, Stanley. Ink, Watercolors,
  Acrylics
Suba, Susanne

Sullivan, Gene. Watercolors
Summers, Dudley Gloyne. Oils, Casein
Sutton, George Miksch
Sway, Albert
Sweney, Fred. Oils
Tee-Van, Helen Damrosch. Oils, Water-
  colors
Thom, Robert Alan
Thompson, F Raymond. Watercolors
Thompson, Kenneth Webster. Gouache,
  Watercolors
Timmins, William Frederick
Trimm, H Wayne
Tucker, Peri. Watercolors, Inks
Tudor, Tasha
Tunis, Edwin
Van Buren, Raeburn
Velarde, Pablita
Wachsteter, George. Inks, Watercolors
Ward, Lynd (Kendall)
Watson, Aldren Auld
Weeks, Leo Rosco. Oils, Watercolors
Wehr, Paul Adam
Weisgard, Leonard Joseph
Werth, Kurt. Wood, Inks
West, Lowren
Whitcomb, Jon
Whitmore, Coby
Williams, Garth Montgomery
Williams, Gluyas
Wilson, Albert Leon
Winship, Florence Sarah
Wolsky, Milton Laban
Woodward, Cleveland Landon. Oils, Water-
  colors
Wright, Barton Allen. Scratchboard,
  Acrylics
Zimmerman, William Harold
Zuccarelli, Frank Edward. Oils

INSTRUCTOR
See also Educator

Anderson, Lennart
Arnholt, Waldon Sylvester
Atlee, Emilie DeS
Baird, Roger Lee
Baker, George P
Bardin, Jesse Redwin
Barile, Xavier J
Barrett, Thomas R
Bassford, Wallace
Beament, Tib (Thomas Harold)
Beetz, Carl Hugo
Beling, Helen
Bendell, Marilyn
Bendig, William Charles
Benjamin, Karl Stanley
Bergamo, Dorothy Johnson
Berkman, Aaron
Blake, Leo B
Blakely, Joyce (Carol)
Blameuser, Mary Fleurette, BVM
Bleifeld, Stanley
Block, Adolph
Block, Joyce
Blos, Peter W
Blumberg, Ron
Boal, Sara Metzner
Bradley, Ida Florence
Brooks, Phyllis Featherstone
Brun, Thomas
Bruno, Santo Michael
Caddell, Foster
Calapai, Letterio
Callahan, Jack
Campanelli, Pauline Eblé
Cannon, Margaret Erickson
Cardoso, Anthony
Carter, Bernard Shirley
Cherepov, George
Chiarandini, Albert
Chicoine, Rene
Christiana, Edward
Christison, Muriel B
Cicero, Carmen Louis

Clark, Chevis Delwin
Cleveland, Helen Barth
Connery, Ruth M
Cormier, Robert John
Couper, James M
Cowing, William R
Cox, J W S
Creech, Franklin Underwood
Crimi, Alfred D
Cross, Watson, Jr
Cuthbert, Virginia
Dalton, Frances Louisa
David, Don Raymond
De Lama, Alberto
De Tonnancour, Jacques G
Dickey, Helen Pauline
Downey, Juan
Doyle, Thomas J
Driesbach, Walter Clark, Jr
Eldredge, Stuart Edson
Ellis, Carl Eugene
Enriquez, Gaspar
Ericson, Ernest
Ernst, James Arnold
Ewing, Thomas R
Facci, Domenico (Aurelio)
Falconieri, Virginia
Feld, Augusta
Fenton, Alan
Fenton, Michael Irwin
Fernie, John Chipman
Ferriter, Clare
Finkelstein, Max
Flack, Audrey L
Fontanez, Carmelo
Friedman, Kenneth Scott
Friedman, Stanley
Fuller, Sue
Gasparro, Frank
Geber, Hana
Gilbert, Lionel
Gilmore, Ethel (Mrs Charles J Romans)
Givler, William Hubert
Goldberg, Raymond Robert
Goldhamer, Charles
Goodbred, Ray Edw
Goulet, Lorrie (Lorrie H De Creeft)
Granlund, Paul Theodore
Gray, Jim
Greacen, Nan (Nan Greacen Faure)
Greenwood, Paul Anthony
Groell, Theophil
Gross, Chaim
Grushkin, Philip
Guzevich, Kreszenz (Cynthia)
Gyra, Francis Joseph, Jr
Hall, Carl Alvin
Halley, Donald M, Jr
Halm, Robert John
Hanson, Duane
Harbart, Gertrude Felton
Harlow, Robert E
Hart, Morgan Drake
Harvey, Donald Gilbert
Haug, Donald Raymond
Hayter, Stanley William
Hedden-Sellman, Zelda
Held, Philip
Helwig, Arthur Louis
Henry, Jean
Hensche, Henry
Higa, Charles Eisho
Hill, Dale Logan
Hodge, Roy Garey
Hofer, Ingrid (Ingeborg)
Hoffmann, Lilly Elisabeth
Holmes, David Bryan
Hoover, (Sidney) Todd
Hostetler, David
Hotvedt, Kristine J
Howell, Marie W
Hunt, Julian Courtenay
Hunter, Robert Douglas
Huseby, Arleen
Iacurto, Francesco
Indiviglia, Salvatore Joseph
Insley, Will

Ireland, Richard Wilson (Dick)
Jameikis, Brone Aleksandra
Janicki, Hazel (Mrs Wm Schock)
Janowsky, Bela
Jennings, Frank Harding
Johanson, George E
Johnson, Avery Fischer
Johnson, Lester L
Johnson, Wesley E
Kahn, Annelies Ruth
Kaiser, Vitus J
Kallem, Herbert
Kaplan, Rhoda B
Karn, Gloria Stoll
Karniol, Hilda
Katz, Ethel
Kaufman, Jane A
Kaz, Nathaniel
Kelleher, Daniel Joseph
Kessler, Edna Leventhal
Kessler, Shirley
Kimura, William Yusaburo
King, Hayward Ellis
Koons, Darell J
Kozlow, Sigmund
Krauser, Joel
Krody, Barron J
Kushner, Dorothy Browdy
Lack, Richard Frederick
Lai, Waihang
Laslo, Patricia Louise
Leaf, Ruth
Leber, Roberta (Roberta Leber McVeigh)
Leech, Hilton
Leighton, Thomas Charles
Leonardi, Hector
Lesh, Richard D
Lesnick, Stephen William
Levine, Reeva (Anna) Miller
Lewis, Nat Brush
Lewis, Norman Wilfred
Lewis, William R
Linden, Fred
Loberg, Robert Warren
Long, Gwen
Lopez, Rhoda Le Blanc
Lorentz, Pauline
Love, Rosalie Bowen
Lowe, Joe Hing
Lueders, Jimmy C
McCallum, Corrie (Mrs William Halsey)
McCarthy, Doris Jean
McLarty, William James (Jack)
McQuillan, Frances C
Madsen, Viggo Holm
Mahaffey, Merrill Dean
Mallory, Larry Richard
Malsch, Ellen L
Mancuso, Leni (Leni Mancuso Barrett)
Marans, Moissaye
Maris, Valdi S
Marozzi, Eli Raphael
Martinez-Maresma, Sara (Sara Sofia Martinez)
Mejer, Robert Lee
Meltzer, Anna E
Meltzer, Arthur
Merrill, David Kenneth
Messick, Ben (Newton)
Metcalf, Robert M
Meyers, Dale (Mrs Mario Cooper)
Midener, Walter
Mikus, Eleanore
Miles, Cyril
Miletti, Clemence M
Miller, Barbara Darlene
Montoya, Geronima Cruz (Po-Tsu-Nu)
Moore, Ina May
Moore, Robert James
Moquin, Richard Attilio
Morgan, Gladys B
Morgan, Lucy Calista
Moscatt, Paul N
Newbill, Al James
Nichols, Jeannettie Doornhein
Nigrosh, Leon Isaac
Nonay, Paul

Odate, Toshio
Osborne, Robert Lee
Ostendorf, (Arthur) Lloyd, Jr
Pearson, James Eugene
Pearson, John
Pinkowski, Emily Joan
Plagens, Peter
Quest, Dorothy (Johnson)
Rayen, James Wilson
Redden, Alvie Edward
Reid, Robert Dennis
Reininghaus, Ruth (Ruth Reininghaus Smith)
Reynard, Carolyn Cole
Rice, Dan
Ridabock, Ray (Budd)
Riley, Gerald Patrick
Rising, Dorothy Milne
Rizk, Romanos
Ross, Jean G
Rossi, Joseph O
Roth, Rubi
Roussel, Claude Patrice
Sakaoka, Yasue
Salmoiraghi, Frank
Sandecki, Albert Edward
Sanders, Andrew Dominick
Schein, Eugenie
Schonwalter, Jean Frances
Schrup, John Edmund
Schulze, Paul
Schuman, Robert Conrad
Schwartz, Carl E
Schwartz, Henry
Searles, Stephen
Shapiro, Irving
Shecter, Pearl S
Sheehe, Lillian Carolyn
Sheng, Shao Fang
Shulman, Leon
Shute, Ben E
Sickman, Jessalee Bane
Siegriest, Lundy
Silberstein, Muriel Rosoff
Simon, Bernard
Simpson, Marilyn Jean
Sinton, Nell (Walter)
Small, Amy Gans
Smiley, Ralph Jack
Smith, Emily Guthrie
Smith, Robert Alan
Smul, Ethel Lubell
Snider, Seymour
Solman, Joseph
Solomon, Syd
Soyer, Isaac
Spencer (Mary Scruggs-Spencer)
Spickett, Ronald John, (Sr)
Stanton, Martha Zelt
Starrs, Mildred
Stegall, James Park
Stone, John Lewis, Jr
Strother, Joseph Willis
Sugimoto, Henry Y
Swenson, Anne
Szarama, Judith Layne
Taylor, Prentiss (Hottel)
Tennyson, Merle Berry
Teresi, Joseph Anthony
Terry, Emalita Newton
Texoon, Jasmine
Teyral, John
Tobias, Julius
Tomlinson, Florence Kidder
Tousignant, Claude
Trauerman, Margy Ann
Treaster, Richard A
Turner, (Charles) Arthur
Ushenko, Audrey Andreyevna
Van Young, Oscar
Vodicka, Ruth Kessler
Vogel, Donald
Watford, Frances Mizelle
Weidner, Roswell Theodore
Weill, Erna
Weiner, Abe
Wentworth, Murray Jackson
Whitlow, Tyrel Eugene

Instructor (cont)

Whitney, Edgar Albert
Wicks, Eugene Claude
Wilmarth, Christopher Mallory
Winer, Donald Arthur
Wolfe Ann (Ann Wolfe Graubard)
Wolpert, Elizabeth Davis
Wong, Frederick
Wright, Frank Cookman
Wright, Stanley Marc
Wynne, Albert Givens
Young, Cliff
Young, Marjorie Ward

LECTURER

Abbott, Dorothy
Abrams, Herbert E
Anderson, David Phillip
Andrews, Benny
Antonovici, Constantin
Austin, Phil
Banks, Anne Johnson
Battcock, Gregory
Beaver, Fred
Beck, Margit
Bess, Forrest Clemenger
Biberman, Edward
Bingham, Lois A
Bohnert, Rosetta
Bolster, Ella S
Bolton, Mimi Du Bois
Borgatta, Isabel Case
Boterf, Chester Arthur (Check)
Boyce, Richard
Boz, Alex (Alex Bozickovic)
Breasted, James Henry, Jr
Brendel, Bettina
Brigadier, Anne
Brown Greene, Lucille
Burickson, Zoel
Calamar, Gloria
Calkin, Carleton Ivers
Carstenson, Cecil C
Cecere, Gaetano
Chapian, Grieg Hovsep
Chew, Paul Albert
Chuey, Robert Arnold
Clare, Stewart
Clark, Robert Charles
Close, Marjorie (Perry)
Cohen, Harold Larry
Colt, Priscilla C
Cook, Howard Norton
Craig, Eugene
Dauterman, Carl Christian
De Costa, Arthur (Archangelo)
Deering, Roger
Defenbacher, Daniel S
De Noronha, Maria M (Mrs Harold Shafron)
Dixon, Sally Foy
Dmytruk, Ihor
Dreisbach, Clarence Ira
Dyck, Paul
Elias, Harold John
Erlanger, Elizabeth N
Filmus, Tully
Fitzgerald, Harriet
Francis, Al (Alfred Kade)
French, James C
Gaines, Natalie Evelyn
Goetz, Peter Henry
Goodman, Calvin Jerome
Gorman, Carl Nelson (Kin-Ya-Onny Beyeh)
Grebe (E P Grebe Rimmel)
Gross, Earl
Groves, Naomi Jackson
Grube, Ernst J
Haar, Francis
Hallam, Beverly (Linney)
Healy, Arthur K D
Hicken, Russell Bradford
Hollinger, (Helen Wetherbee)
Hornung, Gertrude Seymour
Hovey, Walter Read

Howe, Nelson S
Humphrey, Donald Gray
Ingle, Tom
Ishikawa, Joseph
Jagger, Gillian
Johnson, Buffie
Kahn, Ralph H
Kanemitsu, Matsumi
Karp, Ivan C
Katz, A(lexander) Raymond
Katzenbach, William E
Kerr, James Wilfrid
Kobayashi, Katsumi Peter
Koch, Irene Mabel
Korjus, Veronica Maria Elisabeth
Kozlow, Richard
Krushenick, Nicholas
Kuehn, Edmund Karl
Lahey, Richard (Francis)
Lee, Amy Freeman
Lee-Smith, Hughie
Lenssen, Heidi (Mrs Fridolf Johnson)
LeRoy, Harold M
Levitan, Israel (Jack)
Lindmark, Arne
London, Jeff
Long, Sandra Tardo
Longacre, Margaret Gruen
Loughlin, John Leo
McGarvey, Elsie Siratz
MacLean-Smith, Elizabeth
Madden, Betty I
Mangravite, Peppino Gino
Marrozzini, Luigi
Masse, Georges Severe
Maytham, Thomas Northrup
Mielziner, Jo
Mose, Carl C
Moss, Milton
Myers, Denys Peter
Neilson, Katharine B
Nemser, Cindy
Nesbitt, Lowell (Blair)
Neuman, Robert S
Neustadt, Barbara (Mrs Gunther Meyer)
Oehler, Helen Gapen
Owens, Winifred (Whitebergh)
Padovano, Anthony John
Palmer, Lucie Mackay
Perret, George Albert
Perrot, Paul N
Porter, Fairfield
Rath, Hildegard
Rawski, Conrad Henry
Rebert, Jo Liefeld
Rich, Daniel Catton
Robinson, Mary Turlay
Rocklin, Raymond
Rogalski, Walter
Rogers, John
Roney, Harold Arthur
Sanguinetti, Eugene F
Schabacker, Betty B
Schaffer, Rose
Scheu, Leonard
Schimmel, William Berry
Schreiber, Eileen Sher
Schreyer, Greta L
Schueler, Jon R
Seckler, Dorothy Gees
Sellers, William Freeman
Sherman, Lenore (Walton)
Sherman, Winnie Borne
Sicard, Louis Gabriel
Silvercruys, Suzanne (Mrs Edward Ford Stevenson)
Smithson, Robert I
Snodgrass, Jeanne Owens
Soloway, Reta
Stark, Ronald C
Steinmetz, Grace Ernst Titus
Stevenson, Florence Ezzell
Stevenson, Robert Bruce
Stoffa, Michael
Stuart, David
Swazo (Patrick Swazo Hinds)
Swirnoff, Lois (Lois Swirnoff Charney)

Taylor, (Bertha) Fanning
Thelin, Valfred P
Thomas, Ed B
Thompson, Dorothy Burr
Tibbs, Thomas S
Tobey, Alton S
Torreano, John Francis
Traher, William Henry
Travis, Olin (Herman)
Treadwell, Grace (Ansley)
Viret, Margaret Mary (Mrs Frank Ivo)
Waano-Gano, Joe
Watkins, Louise Lochridge
Wenger, Sigmund
Wheeler, Orson Shorey
Williams, Mary Frances
Wilson, Ben
Wood, James Arthur (Art)
Woodham, Jean
Wynn, Donald James
Zirker, Joseph

LIBRARIAN

Baretski, Charles Allan
Dane, William Jerald
Howell, Hannah Johnson
Mitchell, Eleanor
Sabine, Julia
Smith, Jerome Irving
Steinbomer, Dorothy H

LITHOGRAPHER
See also Printmaker

Adams, Clinton
Andrus, Vera Eugenia
Antreasian, Garo Zareh
D'Aulaire, Edgar Parin
Dennison, Dorothy (Dorothy Dennison Butler)
Gropper, William
Hibel, Edna
Kimball, Wilford Wayne, Jr
Kreindler, Doris Barsky
Kroll, Leon
Lerner, Sandy R
MacLean, Arthur
Mason, Alice Frances
Rosenblatt, Adolph
Sanborn, Herbert J
Swensen, Mary Jeanette Hamilton (Jean)
Taylor, Prentiss (Hottel)
Weddige, Emil
Wells, James Lesesne
Wilson, Charles Banks

MEDALIST

De Bellis, Hannibal. Bronze
Jones, Elizabeth. Wax, Plaster, Silver, Gold, Bronze
Turano, Don. Bronze, Wood

MOSAIC ARTIST

Reynal, Jeanne

MURALIST

Bonet, Jordi. Cast Aluminum, Fired Clay, Cement, Plastic
Loring, Clarice. Oils, Mixed Media

MUSEOLOGIST

Johnson, Selina (Tetzlaff)

MUSEUM DIRECTOR
See also Gallery Director

Adler, Sebastian J
Alling, Clarence (Edgar)
Amaya, Mario Anthony
Arkus, Leon Anthony
Atkinson, Tracy
Bach, Otto Karl
Baur, John I H
Bengtz, Ture
Bier, Justus
Boggs, Jean Sutherland
Boyer, Jack K
Brewer, Donald J
Brooke, David Stopford
Broussard, Jay Remy
Brown, John Carter
Brown, Richard F
Byrnes, James Bernard
Caldwell, Henry Bryan
Carpenter, Harlow
Catlin, Stanton L
Chernow, Burt
Chetham, Charles
Clark, Anthony Morris
Colt, Thomas C, Jr
Dailey, Charles Andrew (Chuck)
Danson, Edward B
De Borhegyi, Stephan
De Montebello, Guy-Philippe Lannes
Dentzel, Carl Schaefer
Dockstader, Frederick J
Dodge, Ernest Stanley
Dolph, Clifford R
Dutton, Bertha P
Dwight, Edward Harold
Ellis, George Richard
Emerson, Sterling Deal
Faison, Samson Lane, Jr
Fasbender, Walter
Friedman, Martin
Fuller, Richard Eugene
Fulton, W Joseph
Gamble, Kathryn Elizabeth
Gatling, Eva Ingersoll
Graham, John Meredith, II
Grandee, Joe Ruiz
Gregg, Richard Nelson
Gyermek, Stephen A
Hamilton, George Heard
Hammond, Natalie Hays
Harris, Mrs Mason Dix
Henry, Stuart (Compton)
Herold, Don G
Hodge, G Stuart
Hoving, Thomas
Howe, Thomas Carr
Hutchinson, Janet L
Inverarity, Robert Bruce
Ives, Glen Palmer
Jones, Louis C
Karshan, Donald H
Klep, Rolf
LaMarca, Howard J
Lee, Sherman Emery
Leeper, John Palmer
Lerner, Abram
Long, Walter Kinscella
McGregor, Jack R
Martin, Keith
Maxon, John
Mayhew, Edgar De Noailles
Messer, Thomas M
Miller, Samuel Clifford
Mitchell, Wallace (MacMahon)
Morley, Grace L McCann
Newton, Francis John
Nordland, Gerald John
Olkinetzky, Sam
Paul, William D, Jr
Paulin, Richard Calkins
Phillips, Marjorie
Pope, John Alexander
Quirk, Francis Joseph
Rathbone, Perry Townsend
Rhodes, Reilly Patrick

Rogers, Charles B
Sawyer, Charles Henry
Schmidt, Stephen
Schnittmann, Sascha S
Selz, Peter H
Shestack, Alan
Sipiora, Leonard Paul
Smith, Gordon Mackintosh
Smith, Paul J
Spriggs, Edward S
Steadman, William Earl
Stern, Harold Phillip
Story, William Easton
Stuart, Joseph Martin
Surovek, John Hubert
Thacher, John Seymour
Tibbs, Thomas S
Turk, Rudy H
Turner, Evan Hopkins
Von Adlmann, Jan Ernst
Von Groschwitz, Gustave
Walker, Herbert Brooks
Walkey, Frederick P
Warren, Jefferson Trowbridge
Watkins, Louise Lochridge
Weinhardt, Carl Joseph, Jr
Wittmann, Otto
Wooden, Howard Edmund
Woods, Willis Franklin

PAINTER

Aach, Herb
Aakre, Richard B. Ink
Abany, Albert Charles. Oils, Graphics,
    Mixed Media
Abbot, Hazel Newnham. Watercolors
Abdala, Nick. Mixed Media, Pastels,
    Acrylics
Ablow, Joseph. Acrylics, Pastels,
    Watercolors
Abrams, Herbert E. Oils
Abrams, Ruth
Achepohl, Keith Anden
Acosta, Manuel Gregorio. Oils, Clay
Adams, Glenn Nelson
Adams, Katherine Langhorne. Oils
Adams, Mark
Adams, Pat. Oil/Isobutyl Methacrylate,
    Gouache
Adams, Robert David. Acrylics
Adelman, Dorothy (Lee) McClintock
Adkison, Kathleen (Gemberling). Oils
Adler, Lee. Oils
Adler, Robert. Oils, Ink
Adler, Samuel (Marcus). Oils, Collage
Adrian, Barbara. Oils
Agostinelli, Mario. Oils
Ahlgren, Roy B. Acrylics
Ahlstrom, Ronald Gustin. Collage &
    Acrylics (mixed media)
Ahysen, Harry Joseph. Oils
Airola, Paavo. Oils, Watercolors
Alajalov, Constantin
Albee, Grace Thurston Arnold
Albers, Josef
Albertazzi, Mario. Oils
Albrecht, Mary Dickson
Albright, Ivan Le Lorraine
Albright, Malvin Marr
Alcalay, Albert S. Oils, Plexiglas
Alcopley, L. Oils, Acrylics, Watercolors,
    Inks
Aldwinckle, Eric
Aljaman (Alton James Chapman). Oils,
    Acrylics, Foil
Allan, William George. Acrylics, Water-
    colors
Allen, Clarence Canning. Oils
Allen, Loretta B
Allen, Margaret Prosser
Allen, Margo
Allen, Patricia (Patricia Allen Bott). Oils
Allen, Ralph
Allin, B Warren, Jr. Oils
Alston, Charles Henry. Oils

Altabé, Joan Berg. Opaque Watercolors,
    Acrylics
Altorfer, Gloria Finch. Acrylics, Oils,
    Watercolors, Collage
Altvater, Catherine Tharp. Watercolors
Altwerger, Libby. Watercolors
Amarotico, Joseph Anthony. Acrylics on
    Rag Board or Canvas
Ambrose, Charles Edward. Watercolors,
    Oils
Amelio, Gilbert Neil. Oils on Canvas
Amen, Irving. Oils
Ames, Arthur Forbes
Ames, Jean Goodwin. Acrylics
Ames, (Polly) Scribner
Amoroso, Jack Louis. Acrylics, Lacquer,
    Graphics
Andersen, Andreas Storrs. Oils, Acrylics
Anderson, David Phillip. Acrylics
Anderson, Gunnar Donald. Oils
Anderson, Guy Irving. Oils, Watercolors
Anderson, Howard Benjamin
Anderson, Ronald Trent
Andrade, Edna Wright. Acrylics, Silkscreen
Andre, Françoise. Oils, Acrylics
Andrejevic, Milet. Egg Tempera
Andrews, Benny. Oils & Collage, Ink
Andrus, James Roman. Oils
Andrus, Vera Eugenia
Angel, Rifka. Encaustic
Angelini, John Michael. Watercolors
Angelo, Emidio
Angeloch, Robert (Henry)
Angulo, Chappie. Acrylics
Anliker, Roger (William). Encaustic,
    Gouache, Silverpoint, Graphite
Anthony, William Graham
Antreasian, Garo Zareh
Anuszkiewicz, Richard J
Aparicio, Gerardo
Apgar, Nicolas Adam. Oils
Apostolides, Zoe
Appel, Karel. Acrylics
Appel, Keith Kenneth
Apt, Charles. Oils, Pastels, Watercolors
Aquino, Edmundo. Oils, Silkscreen,
    Lithograph
Arakawa, (Shusaku)
Arbeit, Arnold A. Oils, Watercolors
Arbuckle, Franklin
Archer, Dorothy Bryant. Acrylics, Oils
Arcilesi, Vincent J. Oils, Pastels
Argeropolos, (Basil) Theodore. Acrylics
Argraves, Hugh Oliver. Oils
Ariss, Herbert Joshua
Armstrong, Roger Joseph. Watercolors, Ink
Arnest, Bernard. Oils, Acrylics
Arnholt, Waldon Sylvester. Oils, Pastels,
    Watercolors
Arnold, Florence M. Oils on canvas
Arnold, Ralph Moffett
Arnold, Richard R
Aron, Kalman
Aronson, Boris
Aronson, David. Encaustic, Bronze
Aronson, Irene Hilde
Arp, Hilda Dora. Oils, Watercolors, Pastels
Artschwager, Richard Ernst
Ascher, Mary G. Oils, Watercolors
Ashley, Frank Nelson
Asmar, Alice. Casein, Indelible India Inks,
    Acrylics, Oils
Asoma, Tadashi. Oils
Atkins, David. Oils
Atkyns, (Willie) Lee, Jr. Acrylics
Atlee, Emilie DeS. Oils, Pastels
Aubin, Barbara. Watercolors
Austin, Darrel. Oils
Austin, Phil. Watercolors
Auth, Robert R. Acrylics
Autorino, Anthony Michael
Avakian, John
Avedisian, Edward
Avery, Ralph Hillyer. Watercolors
Ay-O
Ayaso, Manuel. Goldpoint, Mixed Media
Ayling, Mildred Shoob. Watercolors

Painter (cont)

Aylon, Heléne. Aluminum, Plexiglas &
    Acrylics
Aymar, Gordon Christian. Watercolors
Ayoroa, Rodolfo (Rudy) E
Azuma, Nório. Oils
Baber, Alice. Oils, Watercolors
Bach, Dirk
Bachrach, Gladys Wertheim. Oils
Bacigalupa, Andrea
Backstrom, Florence (Florence Jennie
    Englert). Watercolors
Backus, Standish, Jr
Bacon, Peggy
Baderian, Ruth. Watercolors
Baer, Jo. Oils
Bahm, Henry
Bailey, James Arlington, Jr. Oils
Bailey, Malcolm C W. Acrylics, Enamels,
    Ink, Wash
Bailey, Walter Alexander. Oils, Acrylics
Bailey, William H. Oils
Bailin, Hella
Baker, Anna P
Baker, Eugene Ames. Oils, Acrylics,
    Watercolors
Baker, Grace. Oils
Bakke, Larry Hubert. Oils, Collage
Balart, Waldo. Constructions, Mixed Media
Bales, George Carson (Bob). Oils, Inks
Bales, (Leeoma) Jewel. Watercolors
Ballinger, Harry Russell. Watercolors, Oils
Balog, Michael. Multimedia
Band, Max
Banister, Robert Barr. Oils, Watercolors
Banks, Anne Johnson. Acrylics
Banks, Richard. Oils
Banks, Virginia. Watercolors
Bannard, Walter Darby
Banta, E Zabriskie (Mrs Oliver Smith).
    Oils, Watercolors
Baranik, Rudolf. Oils
Barbee, Robert Thomas
Barbour, Arthur J. Watercolors
Bardazzi, Peter
Bardin, Jesse Redwin. Oils on Canvas
Barile, Xavier J
Baringer, Richard E
Barkan, Bebe (Beverly Adrian). Acrylics,
    Graphics
Barker, Walter William
Barnes, Anna Marye. Oils, Acrylics
Barnes, Halcyone D. Watercolors
Barnes, Robert M
Barnet, Will. Graphics
Barnett, Earl D. Oils, Acrylics, Water-
    colors
Barnwell, John L. Oils, Graphics
Barooshian, Martin
Barr, David John
Barr, Roger Terry
Barr-Sharrar, Beryl
Barrett, Thomas R. Acrylics, Casein
Barrie, Erwin S
Barron, Ros
Bartle, Annette
Bartlett, Jennifer Losch
Bartlett, Robert Webster. Oils
Bartok, John Anthony. Oils, Watercolors
Barton, August Charles. Watercolors,
    Tempera
Barton, Georgie Read. Oils
Barton, John Murray
Baruzzi, Peter B
Bashor, John W. Acrylics
Baskerville, Charles. Oils, Acrylics,
    Watercolors
Bassford, Wallace. Oils, Acrylics, Graphics
Batchelor, Jonathan David. Oils, Acrylics
Bate, Stanley. Oils
Bates, Charles T, Jr
Bates, Kenneth. Oils
Bates, Maxwell Bennett. Oils, Watercolors,
    Lithography
Bauer, William. Oils
Baum, William

Baumbach, Harold. Oils
Baumhofer, Walter Martin. Oils, Casein
Bavinger, Eugene Allen
Bayefsky, Aba. Graphics
Bayer, Herbert
Beach, Warren
Beal, Jack. Oils
Beall, Lester Thomas
Beaman, Richard Bancroft. Acrylics
Beament, Harold. Oils
Beament, Tib (Thomas Harold)
Beard, Marion L Patterson. Watercolors
Bearden, Romare Howard
Beattie, George. Acrylics
Beauchemin, Micheline. Acrylics
Beaver, Fred. Watercolors
Bechtle, C Ronald. Watercolors, Gouache
Bechtle, Robert Alan
Beck, Margit. Oils
Beck, Rosemarie (Rosemarie Beck Phelps).
    Oils
Beck, Stephen R. Acrylic Lacquer
Becker, Bettie (Bettie Geraldine Wathall).
    Collage, Acrylics
Becker, Charlotte (Mrs Walter Cox). Oils
Beckmann, Hannes. Oils, Acrylics
Beerman, Herbert
Beerman, Miriam H. Oils
Beery, Arthur O. Oils, Watercolors
Beetz, Carl Hugo. Oils, Acrylics, Water-
    colors, Lithography
Beggs, Thomas Montague. Oils, Fresco,
    Tempera
Behl, Marjorie, Watercolors, Oils
Beitz, Lester U
Bejar, Feliciano
Beline, George
Belkin, Arnold. Acrylics
Bell, Alistair Macready. Watercolors
Bell, Clara Louise (Mrs Bela Janowsky)
Bell, Leland
Bell, Peter Alan. Oils, Acrylics
Bellefleur, Leon
Ben-Zion. Oils, Watercolors
Benda, Richard R. Acrylics & Collage
Bendell, Marilyn. Oils
Bender, Bill. Oils
Bendig, William Charles
Benedict, Nan M
Bengert, Elwood George. Watercolors
Benglis, Lynda
Bengston, Billy Al. Mixed Media
Bengtz, Ture. Oils, Watercolors, Graphics
Benjamin, Karl Stanley
Benn, Ben
Bennett, Harriet. Oils
Benney, Robert
Benno, Benjamin G
Bensing, Frank C. Oils
Bentley, Claude. Acrylics
Benton, Margaret Peake
Benton, Thomas Hart
Berd, Morris. Oils, Acrylics
Berg, Siri. Oils, Acrylics
Bergamo, Dorothy Johnson
Berger, Jason
Bergere, Richard
Berkman, Aaron. Oils, Watercolors, Casein
Berkon, Martin. Oils, Gouache, Ink
Berkowitz, Henry. Oils, Watercolors, Mixed
    Media
Berkowitz, Leon. Oils
Berlind, Robert. Oils on Canvas
Berman, Ariane R. Acrylics, Wood
Bermudez, Jose Ygnacio. Metals
Bernay, Betti. Oils
Bernstein, Gerald. Oils, Watercolors
Bernstein, Sylvia. Watercolors
Bernstein, Theresa. Oils, Aquarelle,
    Graphics
Berresford, Virginia. Oils, Watercolors
Berry, Glenn. Acrylics, Oils
Beson, Roberta (Roberta Beson Hill).
    Oils
Bess, Forrest Clemenger
Bessemer, Auriel. Oils
Betsberg, Ernestine (Mrs Arthur Osver)

Betts, Edward Howard. Acrylics, Water-
    colors
Bevilacqua, Francis
Bhalla, Hans. Collages, Prints
Bhavsar, Natvar Prahladji. Dry Pigment,
    Acrylics
Bianco, Pamela Ruby. Oils
Biberman, Edward. Oils
Bice, Clare. Oils
Biddle, George
Bidner, Robert D H
Biedermann, Max. Acrylics
Biehl, Arthur Oliver. Acrylics
Bieler, Andre Charles. Acrylics, Oils
Bilcher, A Earle. Watercolors, Pastels,
    Charcoal
Billings, Henry. Oils
Binai, Paul Freye. Oils
Binford, Julien. Oils, Egg Tempera,
    Acrylics
Binning, Bertram Charles
Birmelin, August Robert
Bisaccio, Philip
Bischoff, Elmer Nelson. Oils
Bishop, Benjamin. Oils
Bishop, Isabel (Mrs Harold G Wolff)
Bishop, Marjorie Cutler. Oils
Bisone, Edward George. Acrylics, Water-
    colors, Charcoal, Mixed Media
Bittleman, Arnold (Irwin)
Bittner, Hans Oskar
Black, Frederick (Edward). Oils, Acrylics
Black, Lisa. Ink, Acrylics
Black, Mary McCune. Watercolors
Black, Shirley. Watercolors
Blackburn, Morris (Atkinson). Oils, Water-
    colors, Gouache, Sumi
Blacketer, James Richard. Oils
Blackwell, Thomas Leo. Oils
Blackwood, David (Lloyd). Watercolors
Blagden, (Frederic) Allen. Watercolors
Blagden, Thomas P. Oils, Watercolors
Blaine, Nell. Oils, Watercolors
Blair, Carl Raymond. Oils
Blair, Robert Noel. Watercolors, Oils,
    Acrylics
Blakely, Joyce (Carol). Oils
Blakeslee, Sarah (Sarah Blakeslee Speight).
    Oils
Blameuser, Mary Fleurette, B V M. Water-
    colors, Oils, Lithography
Blanc, Peter (William Peters Blanc)
Blanchard, Carol
Blankenship, Roy. Oils
Blattner, Robert Henry. Watercolors
Blaustein, Alfred H
Blazeje, Zbigniew
Bley, Elsa W
Blish, Carolyn Bullis. Watercolors, Oils
Blizzard, Alan
Block, Amanda Roth. Acrylics, Oils
Block, Irving Alexander
Bloom, Donald Stanley. Oils, Watercolors,
    Inks, Pastels
Bloore, Ronald Langley. Oils on Panel
Blos, May (Elizabeth)
Blos, Peter W. Oils, Acrylics
Blower, David Harrison. Oils, Watercolors
Bluhm, Norman. Oils
Blumberg, Ron. Oils, Watercolors
Blume, Peter
Boal, Sara Metzner. Oils
Boardman, Seymour
Bobbitt, Vernon L
Bobick, Bruce. Watercolors
Bobleter, Lowell Stanley
Boccia, Edward Eugene
Bodin, Paul. Oils, Watercolors
Bodo, Sandor
Boedeker, Arnold E. Watercolors, Oils,
    Acrylics
Bogart, George A
Bogart, Richard Jerome. Oils
Bogen, Beverly. Acrylics
Bogert, Grace Warren. Oils
Boggs, Franklin
Bohan, Peter John. Acrylic Resins

Bohnen, Blythe. Acrylics
Bohnert, Rosetta
Bohrod, Aaron
Bolley, Irma S. Watercolors
Bolotowsky, Ilya. Oils, Acrylics, Wood,
　Metal, Plastics
Bolton, Mimi du Bois. Oils
Bomar, Bill
Bonamarte, Lou. Watercolors
Bond, Oriel Edmund. Polymer
Bongart, Sergei R. Oils, Acrylics
Bonsib, Louis William. Oils, Watercolors
Bookatz, Samuel
Bookbinder, Jack. Oils
Booth, Cameron. Oils
Bopp, Emery
Borgatta, Robert Edward. Oils, Marble
Boris, Bessie. Acrylics, Ink, Pastels
Borne, Mortimer
Borochoff, (Ida) Sloan. Oils, Graphics
Boros, Billi (Mrs Philip Bisaccio)
Borzemsky, Bohdan
Bosin, Blackbear. Watercolors, Gouache,
　Acrylics, Charcoal, Pencil
Bostelle, Thomas (Theodore). Oils
Bostick, William Allison. Watercolors,
　Acrylics, Oils
Boterf, Chester Arthur (Check). Acrylics
Bothwell, Dorr. Oils, Acrylics
Botkin, Henry. Oils, Collage
Botto, Richard Alfred. Oils
Bouchard, Lorne Holland. Oils
Boughton, William Harrison. Oils
Bouquet, Gus. Oils, Watercolors, Clay,
　Graphics
Bowen, Helen Eakins. Oils, Polymer
Bowen, Wayne. Oils, Graphics
Bowman, Dorothy (Louise)
Bowman, Jean (Jean Bowman Magruder).
　Oils
Bowman, Ken. Acrylic Polymer, Collage
Bowman, Richard
Boxer, Stanley (Robert)
Boyce, Gerald G. Mixed Media
Boyle, Keith
Boynton, James W. Graphics
Boz, Alex (Alex Bozickovic). Casein, Oils
Brach, Paul H. Oils
Brackman, Robert
Bradford, Howard
Bradley, Ida Florence. Watercolors
Bradley, Peter Alexander. Acrylics
Bradshaw, Glenn Raymond. Watercolors,
　Collage
Bradshaw, Robert George
Brady, Charles Michael. Oils
Brainard, Owen. Acrylics
Brams, Joan. Acrylics
Brandon, Warren Eugene. Oils, Acrylics
Brandt, Frederick Robert. Acrylics
Brandt, Rexford Elson. Watercolors
Brandt, Warren. Oils
Bransom, (John) Paul
Brauner, Erling Bernhardt. Oils
Brazeau, Wendell (Phillips)
Brecher, Samuel. Oils
Breiger, Elaine. Acrylics, Oils
Breinin, Raymond
Brendel, Bettina
Brenner, Mabel. Oils, Casein, Tempera,
　Acrylics
Breverman, Harvey
Brezik, Hilarion, CSC. Watercolors
Briansky, Rita Prezament
Brice, Bruce Raymond. Oils, Acrylics,
　Watercolors
Brice, William
Brigadier, Anne. Oils, Acrylics, Collage,
　Encaustics
Briggs, Ernest
Briggs, Judson Reynolds
Brightwell, Walter. Oils, Watercolors
Brink, Guido Peter
Britsky, Nicholas. Oils, Casein, Water-
　colors
Broadd, Harry Andrew. Oils, Acrylics
Broderson, Morris

Broderson, Robert
Brodey, Stanley Carl. Watercolors
Brodie, Gandy
Brodsky, Judith Kapstein
Brodsky, Stan. Oils, Casein, Watercolors
Broemel, Carl William. Watercolors, Oils
Broh, Minerva Leedy
Brokaw, Lucile. Collage
Broner, Robert
Brook, Alexander. Oils
Brooks, (John) Alan. Oils, Watercolors
Brooks, Frank Leonard
Brooks, James
Brooks, Phyllis Featherstone. Oils, Mixed
　Media, Tempera, Graphics
Broomfield, Adolphus George. Oils, Water-
　colors, Crayon
Bross, Albert L, Jr. Oils
Broudy, Miriam Levine. Oils
Broussard, Jay Remy
Brown, Bruce Robert. Oils
Brown, John Hall. Watercolors
Brown, Marion B. Watercolors
Brown, Marvin Prentiss. Industrial Mate-
　rials
Brown, Paul Louis. Acrylics
Brown, Roger. Oils
Brown, William Henry. Oils on Canvas
Brown Green, Lucille. Acrylics, Oils
Browne, Syd J. Oils, Watercolors
Brownett, Thelma Denyer. Oils
Brownhill, Harold. Watercolors
Browning, Colleen. Oils
Brucker, Edmund. Oils
Bruder, Harold Jacob. Oils
Brulc, Dennis
Bruneau, Kittie. Acrylics, Graphics
Bruno, Santo Michael. Acrylics, Plastics,
　Wood
Brusca, Jack, Acrylics
Brzozowski, Richard Joseph. Watercolors,
　Acrylics
Bucci, Andrew A. Oils, Watercolors
Budd, David
Buechner, Thomas Scharman
Bueno, Jose. Oils
Buggel, William Lee. Clay, Polymer
Buhrman, Ruth Ewing. Acrylics
Bultman, Fritz
Bunce, Louis DeMott. Oils, Acrylics
Bunker, George (Raymond). Oils,
　Lithography
Bunn, Kenneth Rodney
Burch, Claire R. Watercolors, Collage
Burchess, Arnold. Watercolors
Burford, Byron Leslie. Oils, Acrylics
Burgess, David Lowry
Burggraf, Ray Lowell. Acrylics
Burke, Daniel V. Acrylics
Burke, E Ainslie
Burkert, Robert Randall
Burkhardt, Hans Gustav. Oils, Pastels
Burnett, Calvin. Oils
Burnett, Louis Anthony. Oils, Acrylics
Burnham, Lee
Burnside, Katherine Talbott. Paint, Plas-
　tics, Metal
Buros, Luella. Watercolors
Busa, Peter. Oils
Bush, Beverly
Bush, Jack
Bush, Lucile Elizabeth
Butchkes, Sydney. Acrylic Paint
Butler, Joseph (Green). Oils, Watercolors
Button, John
Buzzelli, Joseph Anthony. Enamels, Oils
Bye, Ranulph (DeBayeux). Watercolors, Oils
Byrd, D Gibson. Oils
Byrum, Mary. Oils
Bywaters, Jerry
Caballero, Emilio. Watercolors, Enamel
Cabot, Hugh. Oils, Charcoal, Ink
Caddell, Foster. Oils, Pastels
Cade, Walter, III. Acrylics, Collage
Cadle, Ray Kenneth
Cadmus, Paul. Tempera
Cage, Robert Fielding. Oils

Caglioti, Victor. Acrylics, Oils
Cain, Joseph (Lambert)
Cain, Joseph Alexander. Acrylics
Cain, Michael Peter. Acrylics
Caiserman-Roth, Ghitta. Acrylics, Oils,
　Mixed Media, Graphics
Cajori, Charles F. Oils, Pencil
Calamar, Gloria. Watercolors, Inks,
　Acrylics, Oils, Graphics
Calcagno, Lawrence
Califf, Marilyn Iskiwitz. Oils, Collage
Calkin, Carleton Ivers
Callahan, Jack
Callahan, Kenneth
Callan, Elizabeth Purvis. Watercolors
Callcott, Frank. Oils
Callicott, Burton Harry. Oils
Camacho, Paul. Acrylics
Camins, Jacques Joseph. Oils
Campanelli, Daniel. Pencil, Ink
Campanelli, Pauline Eblé. Oils
Campbell, David Paul. Watercolors, Oils,
　Tempera
Campbell, Dorothy Dostwick
Campbell, Gretna. Oils
Campbell, Kenneth
Campbell, (James) Lawrence. Oils, Water-
　colors
Campbell, Marjorie Dunn
Campbell, Richard Horton. Oils
Campbell, Rosamond Sheila
Camurati, Albert. Oils
Candell, Victor
Canin, Martin. Oils on Canvas
Cannon, Margaret Erickson. Oils, Acrylics
Cannon, T C (Tom Wayne). Oils, Acrylics
Canright, Sarah Anne. Oils, Acrylics
Cantini, Virgil D. Enamels
Caples, Barbara Barrett
Cardoso, Anthony. Oils
Carewe, Sylvia
Cariola, Robert J
Carlin, James. Oils, Watercolors
Carlos, (James) Edward. Oils
Carlson, Cynthia J. Oils
Carmel, Hilda Anne
Carmichael, Donald Ray. Watercolors, Oils
Carmichael, Jae
Carone, Matthew David. Oils, Acrylics
Carpenter, E. Watercolors
Carpenter, Gilbert Frederick (Bert)
Carr, J Gordon. Watercolors
Carrillo, Lilia. Oils, Acrylics
Carrington, Joy Harrell. Oils
Carroll, Robert Joseph
Carson, Sol Kent. Oils, Acrylics
Carter, Bernard Shirley. Watercolors
Carter, Clarence Holbrook
Cartmell, Helen. Oils
Carulla, Ramon A. Oils
Casarella, Edmond
Case, Andrew W. Watercolors
Cassara, Frank
Caster, Bernard Harry
Castoro, Rosemarie
Castro (Pacheco Fernando)
Caswell, Helen Rayburn. Oils
Catan-Rose, Richard
Catchi (Catherine O Childs). Oils, Water-
　colors
Catok, Lottie Meyer. Oils, Watercolors
Cattell, Ray. Acrylics, Watercolors, Oils
Catti (Catherine James). Acrylics, Plexi-
　glas, Enamel, Copper
Cavallon, Giorgio. Oils
Cavanaugh, Tom Richard. Oils
Cavat, Irma. Acrylics, Oils, Mixed Media
Caver, William Ralph
Cecere, Ada Rasario. Oils, Watercolors
Celender, Donald Dennis
Celentano, Francis Michael. Acrylics
Chadeayne, Robert Osborne. Oils, Pastels
Chaet, Bernard
Chamberlain, Elwyn
Chambers, John. Oils, Ink, Pencil
Chamness, Ruby Hill
Chandler, John William

Painter (cont)

Chapian, Grieg Hovsep. Oils
Chaplin, George Edwin. Oils
Charlot, Jean
Chase, Jeanne Norman
Chase, Saul Alan. Acrylics
Chatterton, Clarence Kerr. Oils, Water-
colors, Gouache
Chaudhuri, Patricia M
Chavez, Edward Arcenio
Cherepov, George. Oils
Chermayeff, Ivan
Chernow, Ann. Acrylics, Oils, Silkscreen
Cherry, Herman. Oils
Chesney, Lee R, Jr
Chester, Charlotte Wanetta. Oils, Mixed
Media, Pastels, Watercolors, Silkscreen
Chester, Donovan T. Acrylics
Chethlahe (David Chethlahe Paladin).
Acrylics, Sand
Chi, Chen. Watercolors, Oils
Chiara, Alan Robert. Watercolors
Chiarandini, Albert. Oils
Chicago, Judy
Chicoine, Rene
Chieffo, Clifford Toby. Graphics
Chinni, Peter Anthony
Christ-Janer, Albert William. Watercolors
Christ-Janer, Arland F. Graphics
Christiana, Edward
Christman, Reid August. Oils
Christopher, William R. Acrylics, Oils,
Pencil
Chubb, Frances Fullerton
Chuey, Robert Arnold. Oils, Ink
Church, C Howard
Ciarrochi, Ray. Oils
Cicero, Carmen Louis. Acrylics
Cikovsky, Nicolai
Citron, Minna Wright
Civitello, John Patrick. Acrylics
Clark, Chevis Delwin. Watercolors
Clark, Eliot Candee. Oils, Watercolors,
Pastels
Clark, Paraskeva
Clark, Robert Charles. Tempera, Water-
colors, Oils
Clarke, John Clem. Oils
Clarke, Ruth Abbott
Clawson, Rex Martin
Clem (Clem Albert Gouveia). Watercolors,
Oils, Graphics
Clemenson, Van Clark. Oils
Clendenin, Eve. Acrylics, Ink
Clerk, Pierre
Clive, Richard R. Oils, Pastels
Cloar, Carroll. Acrylics
Close, Chuck. Acrylics
Close, Marjorie (Perry). Oils
Clutz, William
Clymer, John F
Cobb, Ruth. Watercolors
Coburn, Bette Lee Dobry. Oils, Acrylics,
Graphics
Cochran, Gifford Alexander. Watercolors
Cocker, Barbara J. Acrylics
Coes, Kent Day. Watercolors
Coffey, Douglas Robert. Polymers, Oils
Coggeshall, Calvert. Oils
Cogswell, Dorothy McIntosh. Watercolors,
Acrylics
Coheleach, Guy Joseph. Oils, Tempera
Cohen, David H. Oils, Graphics
Cohen, Elaine Lustig
Cohen, H George
Cohen, Hy
Coiner, Charles Toucey. Oils
Colburn, Carol (Harriet). Acrylics, Water-
colors
Cole, Alphaeus Philemon. Oils, Water-
colors
Cole, Donald. Acrylics
Cole, Frances. Watercolors
Cole, Thomas Casilear. Oils
Coleman, Michael. Oils
Colgrove, Ronald B. Inks, Acrylics

Colker, Edward
Collier, Alan Caswell. Oils
Collins, John Ireland. Oils, Watercolors
Collins, Lowell Daunt. Oils
Collins, William Charles. Acrylics
Colson, Chester E
Colt, John Nicholson. Oils, Acrylics,
Pastels
Colville, Alexander
Colway, James R. Watercolors, Acrylics
Conant, Howard Somers. Acrylics, Inks
Congdon, William (Grosvenor). Oils
Conlon, William
Connaway, Ina Lee Wallace. Oils
Conner, Bruce
Connery, Ruth M. Oils, Acrylics
Connett, (Delores) Dee M. Acrylics
Connolly, Jerome Patrick. Oils
Conover, Robert Fremont. Graphics, Oils
Conrad, George. Oils
Constant, George
Consuegra, Hugo. Oils
Conway, Fred
Cook, August Charles. Oils
Cook, Gladys Emerson. Pastels, Oils
Cook, Howard Norton. Oils, Watercolors,
Pastels, Graphics
Cooke, Edwy Francis
Cooke, Hereward Lester. Watercolors
Cooke, Kathleen McKeith. Oils, Dry Point
Coolidge, David. Watercolors, Oils
Cooper, Joanne Beckman. Polymer
Cooper, Lucille B. Oils, Watercolors,
Acrylics
Cooper, Mario. Watercolors
Cope, Dorothy
Copeland, Lila. Oils, Crayon, Lithography
Corcos, Lucille. Tempera, Acrylics,
Gouache, Watercolors, Ink, Crayon
Cord, Orlando
Cordingley, Mary Bowles. Oils, Pencils,
Inks, Acrylics, Pastels
Corish, Joseph Ryan. Oils
Cormier, Robert John
Cornelius, Francis DuPont
Cornelius, Marty. Oils
Corse, Mary Ann
Corso, Patrick. Oils
Corson, Gordon Melvin. Oils
Cortlandt, Lyn. Oils
Corwin, Sophia M. Oils, Acrylics
Corzas, Francisco. Oils
Cosgrove, Stanley
Costa, Olga. Oils
Cote, Alan
Cotsworth, Staats
Couch, Urban
Coughtry, John Graham
Couling, Gordon Robert. Oils, Tempera,
Stained Glass
Couper, James M
Court, Lee Winslow. Oils
Courtice, Rody Kenny. Tempera, Oils,
Watercolors
Covington, Harrison Wall
Cowan, Woodson Messick. Watercolors
Cowing, William R
Cowles, Russell
Cowley, Edward P. Oils
Cox, Allyn
Cox, Gardner. Oils, Watercolors,
Tempera, Acrylics
Cox, J Halley. Watercolors
Cox, J W S
Cox, Jan
Cox, Joseph H
Coze-Dabija, Paul. Oils, Acrylics, Water-
colors, Pastels, Plastics
Craft, Douglas D
Craig, Nancy Ellen. Oils
Cramer, Abraham. Oils, Watercolors,
Pastels
Cramer, Richard Charles
Crane, James
Craven, Roy Curtis, Jr
Crawford, Catherine Betty. Watercolors,
Prints

Crawford, Ralston
Creech, Franklin Underwood. Conte, Char-
coal, Aluminum, Bronze, Clay, Acrylics
Creecy, Herbert Lee
Creo, Leonard E. Oils, Graphics
Cress, George Ayers
Crimi, Alfred D. Oils, Watercolors
Criquette (Ruth DuBarry Montague). Oils
Crist, Richard
Crite, Allan Rohan
Croft, Lewis Scott. Oils, Watercolors
Cross, Maria Concetta. Oils, Watercolors
Cross, Watson, Jr. Watercolors, Oils,
Mixed Media
Crossgrove, Roger Lynn. Pastels, Water-
colors
Crotto, Paul. Oils
Crovello, William George. Acrylics
Crown, Keith Allen. Watercolors, Oils
Crutchfield, William Richard. Watercolors
Cruz, Emilio
Cruz, Hector. Oils
Cryderman, Mackie
Csoka, Stephen
Cuevas, José Luis
Culbertson, Janet Lynn (Mrs Douglas
Kaften). Acrylics, Silver Point
Cuming, Beatrice
Cunningham, Benjamin Frazier. Oils,
Acrylics
Cunningham, Francis. Oils
Curtis, Philip Campbell. Oils
Currie, Bruce. Oils
Cusick, Nancy Taylor. Constructions,
Mixed Media, Acrylics, Oils
Cusumano, Stefano. Oils
Cuthbert, Virginia. Oils
Cutler, Ethel Rose. Watercolors, Oils
Cutler, Grayce E. Watercolors, Acrylics,
Oils
Cyril, (Ruth). Graphics
Czurles, Stanley A
D'Agostino, Vincent. Oils, Watercolors
Dahill, Thomas Henry, Jr
Dahlberg, Edwin Lennart. Watercolors
Dailey, Charles Andrew (Chuck)
Dailey, Michael Dennis. Oils, Watercolors
Daily, Evelynne B
D'Almeida, George. Acrylics, Watercolors
Dalton, Frances Louisa. Oils, Mixed Media,
Ink, Watercolors, Pencil
Daly, Kathleen (Kathleen Daly Pepper).
Oils, Crayon
Daly, Norman David
Damron, John Clarence. Oils, Watercolors
Danby, Ken. Tempera
Daniel, Roxanne. Oils
Daphne, Annette. Oils
Daphnis, Nassos. Epoxy, Plexiglas
Daphnis-Avlon, Helen. Acrylics, Ceramics,
Metal, Graphics, Photo-silkscreen
D'Arcangelo, Allan M
D'Arista, Robert. Oils
Darius, Denyll. Acrylics
Darrow, Paul Gardner. Graphics
Dasburg, Andrew Michael
Dash, Harvey Dwight. Oils
Dash, Robert (Warren). Acrylics, Pastels
Datus, Jay
Daugherty, James Henry
David, Don Raymond. Acrylics, Watercolors
Davidek, William Stefan. Oils, Watercolors
Davidovich, Jaime
Davidson, Allan Albert. Watercolors, Oils,
Graphics
Davidson, Herbert Laurence. Oils
Davidson, Morris. Oils, Watercolors,
Acrylics
Davies, Jordan Alan. Acrylics
Davies, Kenneth Southworth. Oils
Davies, Theodore Peter
Davila, Carlos
Davis, Alice
Davis, Bradley Darius. Acrylics
Davis, Donald Robert. Mixed Media, Oils,
Acrylics
Davis, Esther M

PAINTER / 893

Davis, Gene
Davis, Gerald Vivian. Oils, Gouache, Charcoal, Pastels, Inks
Davis, Harry Allen. Acrylics, Ink, Watercolors
Davis, J Ray
Davis, Jerrold
Davis, Lew E. Oils
Davis, Ronald Wendel. Polyester Resin, Fiberglass
Davis, Stephen A
Davis, Wayne Lambert. Tempera, Watercolors, Oils
Davison, Robert
Dawley, Joseph William. Oils
Dawson, Bess Phipps
Dawson, Eve. Oils
Day, Horace Talmage. Oils, Watercolors
Day, Martha B Willson
Deaderick, Joseph. Oils, Acrylics, Watercolors
Dean, Peter. Oils
De Blasi, Anthony Armando. Acrylics
De Botton, Jean Philippe. Oils
De Cesare, Sam
de Champlain, Vera Chopak. Oils, Watercolors
Dechar, Peter. Oils
De Costa, Arthur (Archangelo). Oils
De Diego, Julio. Oils, Watercolors, Tempera
De Donato, Louis John. Oils
Dee, Leo Joseph. Oils
Deering, Roger
DeForest, Julie Morrow. Oils
De Forest, Roy Dean
de Garthe, William Edward. Oils
De Grazia, Ettore Ted
De Kanelba, Sita Gomez. Acrylics
DeKay, John
De Knight, Avel. Gouache, Oils
de Kooning, Elaine Marie Catherine. Oils
De Kooning, Willem
De Lama, Alberto. Oils
Delaney, Joseph. Oils
De Leeuw, Cateau Wilhelmina. Oils, Wood
De Leeuw, Leon
de Lesseps, Tauni. Lacquer
Delgado-Guitart, Jose
Della-Volpe, Ralph Eugene. Oils
Deloney, Jack Clouse. Watercolors, Acrylics
DeMaree, Elizabeth Ann (Betty). Watercolors
De Martini, Joseph
De Mille, Leslie Benjamin. Oils, Pastels
De Nagy, Eva
De Niro, Robert
Dennis, Cherre Nixon. Watercolors
Dennis, Roger Wilson. Oils, Watercolors
Dennison, Dorothy (Dorothy Dennison Butler). Oils
De Noronha, Maria M (Mrs Harold Shafron)
Denys, George Frederick. Oils
De Pauw, Victor
Dergalis, George
De Ruth, Jan. Oils
Desportes, Ulysse Gandvier. Oils
Dessner, Murray
De Tonnancour, Jacques G
De Tore, John E. Watercolors
Deutsch, Peter Andrew. Acrylics
Deverell, Timothy
De Vitis, Themis
De Vito, Ferdinand A
Dew, James Edward. Acrylics, Watercolors, Oils
Dewey, Kenneth Francis. Pen & Ink, Watercolors, Oils
DeWitt, Floyd Tennison. Oils
Diao, David
Dickerson, Daniel Jay. Acrylics, Oils
Dickerson, William Judson. Oils, Watercolors
Dickey, Helen Pauline. Polymers, Oils
Dickinson, Edwin

Dickinson, Eleanor Creekmore. Mixed Media
Diebenkorn, Richard
Dienes, Sari
Dieringer, Ernest A. Acrylics
Dignac, Geny (Eugenia M Bermudez). Plastics
Dike, Philip Latimer. Watercolors, Oils
Diller, Mary Black
Dillon, Mildred (Murphy)
Diman, Homer. Oils, Watercolors
Di Meo, Dominick Generoso. Mixed Media
Dimondstein, Morton
Dine, James
Dingle, Adrian. Acrylics
Dirube, Rolando Lopez
Di Suvero, Mark
Dmytruk, Ihor. Acrylics
Dobbs, John Barnes. Oils
Dobkin, Alexander
Dodd, Lamar
Dodd, Lois
Dodge, Joseph Jeffers. Oils
Dogancay, Burhan Cahit
Dohanos, Stevan
Dole, George. Oils, Ink, Wash
Dole, William
Domareki, Joseph Theodore. Oils, Multi-Media
Dominique, John August. Oils, Watercolors
Donati, Enrico
Donneson, Seena
Dooley, Helen Bertha. Oils, Watercolors
Doolittle, Warren Ford, Jr
Durfman, Bruce
Dorst, Claire V
Doster, Rose Wilhelm. Watercolors, Ceramics
Doubrava, Jan
Douglas, Edwin Perry
Dowden, Anne Ophelia Todd. Watercolors
Downing, George Elliott
Doyle, Edward A
Dozier, Otis. Graphics
Drabkin, Stella. Mosaics
Drago, Gabrielle D. Oils
Draper, Line Bloom
Draper, Robert Sargent
Draper, William Franklin. Oils
Dreiband, Laurence. Oils, Acrylics
Dreisbach, Clarence Ira. Oils, Watercolors
Dreskin, Jeanet Steckler. Polymers
Drewelowe, Eve. Mixed Media
Drewes, Werner. Oils, Watercolors
Drexler, Lynne. Oils
Dreyer, Margaret Webb. Acrylics, Watercolors, Mixed Media
Driggs, Elsie. Oils
Driskell, David Clyde. Oils, Tempera, Watercolors
Drummond, (I G)
Drummond, Arthur A. Oils, Watercolors
Drummond, Sally Hazelet. Oils
Drutz, June. Tempera, Watercolors
Dubaniewicz, Peter Paul
Dubin, Ralph. Oils
Duca, Alfred Milton. Polymers, Metals
Dufour, Paul Arthur. Sumi, Stained Glass
Dugmore, Edward. Oils
Du Jardin, Gussie. Oils
Dulac, Margarita Walker. Oils
Dunbar, George Bauer. Collage
Duncalfe, Walter John Douglas. Oils, Watercolors
Duncan, Ruth. Oils, Watercolors
Dunn, Cal. Oils, Watercolors
Dunn, Nate. Oils, Acrylics
Du Pre, Grace Annette. Oils
Duren, Terence Romaine
Dworzan, George R. Oils on Canvas
Dyck, Paul. Oils
Dzubas, Friedel
Eades, Luis Eric. Oils, Acrylics
Eagerton, Robert Pierce
Eames, John Heagan

Easley, Loyce Rogers. Oils
Eaton, Myrwyn Lake. Oils, Watercolors, Casein, Ink
Ebie, William Dennis. Acrylics
Ecke, Betty Tseng Yu-Ho. Watercolors, Collage, Plexiglas
Eckert, William Dean. Acrylics
Eckstein, Ruth. Acrylics, Collage
Eder, Earl
Edgerly, Beatrice (Beatrice Edgerly Macpherson). Oils
Edie, Stuart. Oils, Acrylics
Edwards, Ethel (Mrs Xavier Gonzalez)
Edwards, Kate Flournoy. Oils
Edwards, Stanley Dean. Oils, Acrylics
Ehrenbeich, Emma. Oils, Acrylics
Eilers, Fred (Anton Frederick). Oils
Eisenstat, Benjamin
Eitel, Cliffe Dean
Elder, Muldoon. Oils
Eldredge, Stuart Edson. Gouache, Watercolors, Tempera, Oils
Elias, Harold John. Oils, Watercolors, Wire
Eliasoph, Paula
Elisofon, Eliot
Ellinger, Ilona E
Elliott, Philip Clarkson
Elliott, Ronnie Rose. Oils, Collage, Charcoal, Assemblage, Gouache
Ellis, Fremont F
Ellis, Ray G
Ellison, J Milford
Elzea, Rowland Procter. Acrylics
Embry, Norris. Mixed Media
Emerson, Edith. Oils, Watercolors
Engel, Michael Martin, II. Watercolors
England, Paul Grady. Oils
Engle, Barbara Jean. Oils
Enman, Tom Kenneth. Oils, Watercolors
Eppink, Helen Brenan. Acrylics, Oils
Eppink, Norman R. Oils, Watercolors
Erbe, Joan (Mrs Joan Erbe Udel)
Ericson, Beatrice. Acrylics
Ericson, Susan Kunce. Acrylics, Oils
Erlanger, Elizabeth N. Casein, Oils
Ernst, James Arnold. Watercolors
Ernst, Jimmy
Escobedo, Augusto Ortega
Eshoo, Robert. Oils, Watercolors
Esman, Betty (Betty Esman Samuels)
Esserman, Ruth
Etnier, Stephen Morgan. Oils
Etrog, Sorel
Ettenberg, Franklin Joseph. Pen & Ink, Oils
Etting, Emlen. Oils, Acrylics
Ettling, Ruth (Droitcour)
Eugenie (Eugenie Muelhauser Murphy). Watercolors, Oils
Evans, Edward Arthur. Watercolors, Pastels
Evans, Minnie. Watercolors
Evans, Richard. Oils, Acrylics, Intaglio
Evans, Robert James
Everett, Len G. Oils, Pastels
Evergood, Philip
Evett, Kenneth Warnock. Watercolors, Oils
Ewald, Louis. Oils, Mosaic, Gold Leaf
Ewing, Charles Kermit
Ewing, Edgar Louis. Oils
Ewing, Thomas R. Acrylics, Oils, Plastics
Fabe, Robert. Tempera, Watercolors
Fabri, Ralph. Acrylics, Oils, Graphics
Fahlstrom, Oyvind
Failing, Frances Elizabeth. Watercolors, Oils
Fairchild, Isabel Shelton. Watercolors
Falconieri, Virginia. Oils
Falk, Gathie
Falzone, Michael Joseph. Acrylics, Mixed Media
Fangor, Voy. Oils
Faragasso, Jack. Oils
Farber, Maya M. Oils, Acrylics, Collage
Farian, Babette (Sommerich). Acrylics, Ink, Graphics
Faris, Brunel De Bost. Collage

Painter (cont)

Farnham, Alexander. Oils
Farnsworth, Jerry. Oils
Farris, Joseph G
Farruggio, Remo Michael
Fastove, Aaron (Aaron Fastovsky). Oils
Faulconer, Mary (Fullerton). Gouache
Faulkner, Kady B. Oils, Watercolors
Fausett, (William) Dean
Fausett, Lynn. Oils, Tempera
Fax, Elton Clay. Oils
Fearing, Kelly. Oils, Acrylics
FeBland, Harriet. Acrylics, Plexiglas
Feder, Ben
Federe, Marion. Oils
Feher, Joseph. Oils
Fehl, Philipp P. Inks, Watercolors
Feigl, Doris Louise. Oils
Fein, Stanley. Oils, Inks
Feininger, T Lux. Oils, Watercolors
Feitelson, Lorser
Feld, Augusta. Mixed Media
Feldman, Hilda (Mrs Neville S Dickinson).
    Watercolors
Feldman, Lilian. Acrylics
Feldman, Walter (Sidney)
Felguerez, Manuel. Oils, Acrylics
Fendell, Jonas J. Plastic Resins
Fenical, Marlin E. Watercolors, Oils, Ink
Fenton, Alan. Oils, Liquitex
Fenton, Howard Carter. Acrylics, Oils
Fenton, John Nathaniel
Fenton, Michael Irwin. Oils
Ferber, Herbert
Ferguson, Charles
Ferguson, Edward Robert. Oils, Acrylics
Ferguson, Thomas Reed, Jr
Feriola, James Philip. Watercolors
Fernandez-Yanez, Alvaro
Ferrara, Frank Vincent. Oils
Ferris, Edythe. Oils
Ferris, (Carlisle) Keith
Ferriter, Clare. Oils
Ffrench (Phyllis Marjorie Linnell-Ffrench).
    Oils, Watercolors, Pencils, Inks, Crayons
Fife, Mary. Oils
Filipovic, Augustin
Filmus, Tully. Oils
Finch, Keith Bruce
Fincher, John H. Oils, Ink
Finck, Furman J. Oils
Fine, Perle. Oils, Acrylics, Collage
Fink, Herbert Lewis
Fink, Sam
Fiore, Joseph A. Oils, Watercolors
Fischer, John J
Fish, George A. Watercolors
Fisher, Leonard Everett
Fitzgerald, Harriet. Oils
Fitzsimmons, James Joseph. Watercolors
Flack, Audrey L. Oils
Flax, Serene. Watercolors
Flint, Leroy W. Tempera, Acrylics,
    Aluminum
Floch, Joseph. Oils
Florsheim, Richard A. Oils, Lithography
Flowers, Thomas Earl. Acrylics, Oils,
    Mixed Media
Fluek, Toby. Oils
Fogel, Seymour
Fonelli, J Vincent
Fontanez, Carmelo. Watercolors
Foosaner, Judith Ann. Acrylics, Oils
Forakis, Peter
Ford, Charles Henri
Ford, John Charles
Ford, Ruth Vansickle. Watercolors, Oils
Forman, Alice
Forman, Kenneth Warner. Oils, Water-
    colors
Forrestall, Thomas De Vany. Tempera
Forsberg, James Alfred. Oils
Forslund, Carl Victor, Jr. Acrylics
Forst, Miles
Forsyth, Constance. Watercolors, Aquatint
Fortess, Karl Eugene. Oils

Fosburgh, James Whitney. Oils, Water-
    colors
Fossum, Sydney (Glenn). Oils, Watercolors,
    Pastels
Foster, Hal
Foulkes, Llyn. Oils, Acrylics
Fournier, Alexander Paul. Acrylics
Foushee, Ola Maie (Mrs John M, Sr)
Fowler, Mary Blackford
Fox, John. Acrylics
Fox, Roy Charles W. Watercolors
Fox, Winifred Grace
Fracassini, Silvio Carl
Frame, Robert (Aaron). Oils
Frances, Harriette (Anton). Acrylics
Francis, Al (Alfred Kade). Watercolors,
    Oils
Francis, Harold Carleton
Francis, Sam
Franck, Albert Jacques
Franck, Frederick S
Frank, Helen Sophia. Oils
Frankenthaler, Helen
Fransioli, Thomas Adrian. Oils, Acrylics,
    Gouache, Pencil, Silkscreen
Frasconi, Antonio. Graphics
Frater, Hal
Frazer, John Thatcher
Frazier, Le Roy Dyyon
Fredman, Faiya R. Poly-foam, Pencil
Freed, Ernest Bradfield
Freedman, Maurice. Oils, Gouache
Freeland, William Lee. Oils, Pastels,
    Charcoal
Freeman, David L. Acrylics
Freeman, Mark. Oils, Acrylics
Freifeld, Eric. Watercolors, Graphics
Freilich, Ann. Oils, Watercolors
Freilicher, Jane. Oils
Freimark, Robert (Matthew)
French, Jared. Tempera
Frerichs, Ruth Colcord. Watercolors
Freund, Harry Louis. Oils
Freund, Tibor. Acrylics
Freund, Will Frederick. Oils, Watercolors,
    Mixed Media
Freyberger, Ruth Matilda
Friberg, Arnold
Fried, Raymond John
Fried, Robert Samuel
Fried, Theodore
Friedeberg, Pedro
Friedensohn, Elias. Oils
Friedman, Stanley. Oils
Froman, Ramon Mitchell. Oils
Fruhauf, Aline. Graphics
Fugagli, Alfonso
Fukui, Nobu. Acrylics
Fuller, Harvey Kenneth. Oils
Fulton, Ruth (McConnell). Oils, Water-
    colors, Pastels
Fulwider, Edwin L
Furman, Gloria Violet. Collage, Oils,
    Acrylics
Fussiner, Howard. Oils
Gabin, George Joseph. Oils
Gablik, Suzi
Gach, George. Wax, Oils, Plastic
Gage, Harry (Lawrence). Watercolors
Gahman, Floyd. Oils, Watercolors
Gailis, Janis. Oils
Gaines, William Robert. Oils, Acrylics
Gains, Jacob. Oils
Gammon, Juanita-La Verne. Acrylics, Oils,
    Watercolors
Gardner, Andrew Bradford
Gardner, Joan A
Garrett, Stuart Grayson, Jr
Garrison, Eve. Oils, Casein
Garston, Gerald Drexler. Oils
Garwood, Audrey. Oils
Gary, Jan (Mrs William D Gorman).
    Acrylics, Casein
Gasser, Henry Martin. Watercolors
Gast, Michael Carl. Polymers, Oils
Gaston, Marianne Brody
Gates, Harry Irving

Gates, John Monteith
Gatewood, Maud Florance. Polymers
Gatrell, Marion Thompson. Graphics,
    Watercolors
Gatrell, Robert Morris
Gaul, Arrah Lee
Gauthier, Joachim George
Gawboy, Carl. Acrylics
Gay, Eric Lynn. Oils
Gebhardt, Ann Stellhorn
Gebhardt, Roland
Gechtoff, Sonia
Geck, Francis Joseph
Gecse, Helene. Graphics
Geeslin, Lee Gaddis
Gehner, Marjorie Nielsen. Oils, Water-
    colors
Gehr, Mary (Mary Ray). Oils, Acrylics
Geiger, Edith Rogers. Mixed Media
Gekiere, Madeleine. Inks, Oils
Gelb, Jan
Gelber, Samuel. Oils, Watercolors
Gelinas, Robert William. Acrylics
Geller, Esther (Esther Geller Shapero).
    Encaustic, Watercolors
Gellman, Beah (Mrs William C McNulty)
Genders, Richard Atherstone. Watercolors,
    Gouache
Genius, Jeannette (Jeannette M McKean).
    Oils, Pastels
Gentry, Warren Miller. Oils
George, Thomas. Oils, Gouache, Ink
Georges, Paul
Gerard, Allee Whittenberger. Oils
Gerard, Paula (Mrs Herbert Renison).
    Silverpoint, India Ink, Sumi Ink, Water-
    colors, Tempera
Gerardia, Helen
Gerhold, William Henry. Oils, Watercolors
Gersovitz, Sarah Valerie
Getz, Ilse
Ghikas, Panos George. Egg Tempera
Gibberd, Eric Waters. Oils, Acrylics
Gibbons, Hugh (James). Oils, Inks
Gibbons, Margarita. Oils
Gibson, George. Watercolors
Gifford, J Nebraska. Acrylics
Giffuni, Flora Baldini. Pastels
Gikas, Christopher. Stained Glass
Gikow, Ruth (Ruth Gikow Levine). Oils
Gilbert, Clyde Lingle. Oils, Watercolors
Gilbert, Lionel. Oils
Gilbertson, (Bernice) Charlotte. Oils,
    Acrylics, Mixed Media
Giles, Newell Walton, Jr. Watercolors, Oils
Gill, Frederick James. Acrylics, Water-
    colors
Gill, Gene
Gill, James (Francis)
Gill, Robert Wayne. Oils
Gill, Sue May
Gillespie, Gregory Joseph. Oils, Acrylics
Gilliam, Sam
Gillingwater, Denis Claude. Acrylics
Gilmore, Ethel (Mrs Charles J Romans).
    Oils
Ginsburg, Max
Ginzel, Roland
Giobbi, Edward Gioachino. Oils, Mixed
    Media
Giorgi, Vita
Giraudier, Antonio. Acrylics, Mixed Media
Gironella, Alberto
Givler, William Hubert
Glaser, David. Oils, Mixed Media
Glorig, Ostor
Gluckman, Morris
Glyde, Henry George
Gobin, Henry (Delano). Watercolors
Goddard, Vivian. Oils
Godwin, Robert Kimball. Oils
Godwin, Robert Lawrence
Goedike, Shirl. Oils
Goetz, Peter Henry. Watercolors
Goetz, Richard Vernon. Oils
Goff, Lloyd Lozes. Mixed Media
Goings, Ralph Ladell. Oils, Watercolors

Gold, Albert. Oils, Watercolors
Gold, Fay. Oils, Watercolors, Ink, Collage
Gold, Leah. Casein, Graphics, Stained
    Glass
Goldberg, Chaim Leib. Oils, Watercolors
Goldberg, Joseph Wallace. Oils
Goldberg, Michael
Goldberg, Raymond Robert. Watercolors
Goldberg, Virginia Eagan. Oils
Golden, Libby
Goldhamer, Charles
Goldin, Leon. Oils, Gouache
Golub, Leon Albert. Acrylics
Gomez-Quiroz, Juan Manuel. Oils,
    Acrylics
Gongora, Leonel
Gonzales, Boyer. Oils
Gonzales, Carlotta (Mrs Richard Lahey).
    Oils
Gonzalez, Xavier
Goo, Benjamin
Gooch, Donald Burnette. Watercolors,
    Tempera, Oils
Gooch, Gerald
Good, Leonard. Oils, Acrylics, Water-
    colors
Goodbred, Ray Edw. Oils, Pastels
Goodman, Sidney
Goodnough, Robert
Goodnow, Frank A. Oils, Acrylics
Goodridge, Lawrence Wayne. Acrylics
Gorchov, Ron. Oils on Canvas
Gorder, Clayton J. Acrylics
Gordley, Metz Trunbarger. Oils
Gordon, Maxwell
Gordy, Robert P. Acrylics, Ink
Gorman, Carl Nelson (Kin-Ya-Onny Beyeh).
    Oils, Watercolors
Gorman, R C. Acrylics, Oils, Pastels
Gorman, William D. Casein, Tempera,
    Graphics
Gorski, Daniel Alexander. Mixed Media
Gorsline, Douglas Warner. Oils, Water-
    colors
Goth, Marie. Oils
Gottlieb, Adolph
Gough, Robert Alan. Oils, Pencil
Gould, John Howard
Gourevitch, Jacqueline. Oils
Govan, Francis Hawks. Oils, Watercolors
Grabach, John R
Grado, Angelo John. Oils, Pastels
Gramatky, Hardie. Watercolors, Acrylics
Gramberg, Liliana. Graphics
Grandee, Joe Ruiz. Oils, Inks
Granstaff, William Boyd. Oils
Grasso, Doris (Ten-Eyck). Oils, Water-
    colors, Inks, Pastels
Graves, Arthur Earle. Oils
Graves, Maitland
Graves, Morris, Tempera, Oils
Graves, Nancy Stevenson
Gray, Cleve
Gray, Jim. Watercolors
Graziani, Sante
Graziano, Florence V Mercolino. Oils,
    Pastels, Charcoals, Watercolors,
    Graphics
Greacen, Nan (Nan Greacen Faure). Oils
Greaver, Harry. Watercolors
Grebe (E P Grebe Rimmel). Oils
Greco, Anthony Joseph
Green, Samuel Magee. Oils
Greenberg, Gloria. Acrylics
Greenberg, Shirlee Bernice. Acrylics
Greenbowe, F Douglas. Watercolors
Greene, Balcomb
Greene, Daniel E
Greene, Ethel Maud. Acrylics
Greene, Stephen. Oil
Greenleaf, Esther (Hargrave). Acrylics,
    Sand
Greer, Walter Marion. Oils
Gregoropoulos, John
Gregory, Joan. Collage
Griessler, Franz Anton. Charcoal, Oils
Grilley, Robert L

Grillo, John
Grimley, Oliver Fetterolf. Pen & Ink,
    Watercolors
Grippe, Florence (Berg)
Grippi, Salvatore William
Groat, Hall Pierce. Acrylics
Grodensky, Samuel. Oils
Groell, Theophil. Oils
Groff, June
Grooms, Red
Grooms, Reginald Lesie
Gropper, William
Groshans, Werner (Emil). Oils, Pastels
Gross, Earl. Watercolors, Oils
Gross, Irene (Irene Gross Berzon). Oils
Grossman, Morton
Grossman, Nancy
Grosz, Franz Joseph. Oils, Glass
Grotenrath, Ruth
Groth, John August. Watercolor, Ink
Grotz, Dorothy Rogers. Oils
Grove, Edward Ryneal. Oils, Watercolors,
    Intaglio
Grubb, Pat Pincombe. Acrylic Polymers,
    Gouache
Gruber, Aaronel De Roy
Gruen, Shirley Schanen. Acrylics, Water-
    colors
Gruppe, Charles. Oils
Guerin, John William
Guerrero, Jose. Oils
Guggenheimer, Richard Henry. Oils
Guion, Molly
Guite, Suzanne
Gumpel, Hugh. Watercolors
Gumpert, Gunther
Gunn, Paul James. Oils
Gurr, Lena. Oils, Casein
Gursoy, Ahmet. Oils
Gussow, Alan. Oils
Guston, Philip. Oils
Gute, Herbert Jacob. Watercolors
Gutkin, Peter
Gutmann, John
Guy, James M. Oils, Acrylics
Guy, Osmond Sublett. Graphics
Guzevich, Kreszenz (Cynthia). Oils
Gwathmey, Robert. Oils
Gyra, Francis Joseph, Jr
Haack, Cynthia Roach. Graphics
Haas, Lez
Haas, Richard John
Habergritz, George Joseph
Hack, Howard Edwin. Oils,
    Tempera
Hacklin, Allan Dave
Haden, Eunice (Barnard)
Haerer, Carol
Hagan, (Robert) Frederick
Hagen, Ethel Hall. Watercolors
Haggart (Winifred Watkins). Oils
Haines, Richard. Oils
Halbers, Fred
Halberstadt, Ernst
Haley, John Charles. Oils, Watercolors
Halkin, Theodore
Hall, Carl Alvin
Hall, John A
Hall, Rex Earl
Hallam, Beverly (Linney). Acrylics
Halm, Robert John. Oils
Halsey, William Melton. Oils, Casein,
    Collage
Halvorsen, Ruth Elise. Watercolors, Oils
Hamblett, Theora. Oils
Hammer, Alfred Emil. Oils
Hammersley, Frederick. Oils
Hammon, Bill J
Hammond, Natalie Hays. Watercolors
Hammond, Ruth MacKrille. Watercolors,
    Oils, Acrylics, Ink
Hammons, Verily. Oils, Acrylics, Pastels
Hampton, Phillip Jewel. Acrylics
Handell, Albert George. Oils, Pastels
Handville, Robert T. Watercolors, Acrylics,
    Ink, Oils
Hanes, James (Albert). Oils

Hanna, Boyd Everett. Wood, Watercolors,
    Oils
Hansen, Frances Frakes. Acrylics, Water-
    colors
Hansen, Robert William. Lacquer
Hanson, Jean (Mrs Jean Elphick). Oils
Hanson, Philip Holton. Acrylics
Harbart, Gertrude Felton
Hardy, (Clarion) Dewitt. Watercolors
Hare, Channing
Hare, Stephen Hopkins
Hari, Kenneth. Oils, Graphite
Harlan, Roma Christine. Oils, Pastels
Harlow, Robert E. Oils
Harmon, Cliff Franklin. Acrylics, Water-
    colors, Oils
Harmon, Lily. Oils, Graphics
Harootian, Khoren Der
Harrill, James. Acrylics
Harris, Alfred Peter. Oils
Harris, Lawren Phillips
Harris, Lucille
Harris, Marian D. Oils, Watercolors,
    Conté, Pastels
Harris, Robert George. Oils
Harrison, Lawrence Victor
Harrison, Tony
Harriton, Abraham. Oils
Harsanyi, Charles. Oils
Harsh, Richard
Hart, Agnes
Hart, Allen M. Oils, Collage, Mixed Media
Hart, Morgan Drake. Oils, Acrylics, Water-
    colors, Pastels, Crayons
Hartell, John (Anthony). Oils
Harter, Tom John. Casein
Hartgen, Vincent Andrew. Watercolors
Hartigan, Grace
Hartl, Leon
Hartman, Robert Leroy
Harvey, Jacqueline. Oils
Harvey, Robert Martin
Haseltine, James Lewis. Oils
Haseltine, Maury (Margaret Wilson
    Haseltine). Oils, Acrylics
Hasen, Burt Stanly. Oils, Acrylics
Hatch, John W. Watercolors
Hatfield, David Underhill. Oils
Hatfield, Donald Gene. Watercolors
Hathaway, John Wallace. Watercolors,
    Graphics, Mixed Media
Haug, Donald Raymond. Oils
Haupt, Erik Guide. Oils, Pastels
Hauser, Richard. Oils
Hausman, Fred S. Acrylics
Havard, James Pinkney
Hawthorne, Jack Gardner. Watercolors
Hay, Dorothy B. Oils, Watercolors
Hay, George Austin. Oils
Hay-Messick, Velma. Oils
Haydon, Harold (Emerson). Oils,
    Mosaics, Stained Glass
Hayes, Robert T
Hayes, Tua. Oils, Watercolors
Haynes, Douglas H. Acrylics, Mixed Media
Hayter, Stanley William
Hayward, Peter. Oils
Head, George Bruce. Acrylics
Head, Robert William. Mixed Media
Healy, Arthur K D. Watercolors
Heberling, Glen Austin. Oils, Watercolors,
    Acrylics, Tempera, Pastels, Synthetic
    Resins
Hedden-Sellman, Zelda. Acrylics, Water-
    colors
Heflin, Tom Pat. Oils, Acrylics
Heidel, Frederick (H)
Heiloms, May. Oils, Watercolors, Ink,
    Casein
Heinemann, Peter. Oils
Heiskell, Diana
Held, Al
Held, Alma M. Oils, Watercolors
Held, Philip. Oils
Heliker, John Edward. Oils, Watercolors
Helioff, Anne Graile (Mrs Benjamin
    Hirschburg). Oils, Acrylics

Painter (cont)

Heller, Dorothy. Acrylics
Helwig, Arthur Louis. Oils
Hemenway, Nancy (Mrs Robert D Barton).
  Bayetage
Hendler, Raymond. Acrylics, Polystyrene
Hendricks, Barkley Leonnard. Oils,
  Acrylics
Hendricks, Geoffrey. Acrylics, Intermedia
Hendricks, James (Powell). Acrylics, Oils
Henricksen, Ralf Christian. Oils, Water-
  colors
Henry, Jean. Oils
Henry, John R
Henry, Robert. Oils
Henry, Stuart (Compton)
Hensche, Henry. Oils
Herman, Vic. Mixed Media
Hernandez-Cruz, Luis. Oils, Silkscreen
Herpst, Martha Jane. Oils, Watercolors
Herring, Jan(et Mantel)
Hershman, Lynn Lester
Herstand, Arnold
Hertzberg, Rose. Oils, Watercolors
Hess, Emil John. Oils
Hessing, Valjean McCarty. Watercolors
Heusser, Eleanore Elizabeth. Ink, Oils
Hewitt, Francis Ray. Acrylics
Hibel, Edna. Oils
Hicken, Philip Burnham. Acrylics
Higa, (Yoshiharu)
Higa, Charles Eisho. Watercolors, Clay
Hildebrand, June Mary Ann
Hildebrandt, William Albert. Oils
Hildreth, Joseph Alan
Hill, Clinton J. Acrylics
Hill, Dale Logan. Oils
Hill, (James) Jerome
Hill, Joan (Chea-Se-Quah). Oils, Gouache,
  Acrylics, Collage, Tempera
Hill, Marvin William, Sumi Ink, Tempera
Hill, Peter. Acrylics, Oils
Hill, Polly Knipp
Hillsmith, Fannie
Hilton, John William. Oils, Wax
Hinman, Charles B. Acrylics
Hios, Theo. Oils, Acrylics
Hirsch, Joseph
Hitch, Jean Leason. Oils
Hitch, Robert A. Oils
Hnizdovsky, Jacques. Oils
Hobbie, Lucille. Watercolors
Hodge, Roy Garey. Acrylics, Watercolors
Hodgell, Robert Overman
Hodges, Stephen Lofton. Acrylics
Hodgson, Trevor. Mixed Media
Hoehn, Harry. Graphics
Hoenigan, Henry. Oils, Gouache, Water-
  colors, Pastels, Acrylics
Hofer, Ingrid (Ingeborg). Watercolors,
  Graphics
Hoff, Margo. Acrylics, Collage
Hoffman, Elaine Janet. Watercolors
Hoffman, Harry Zee. Acrylics
Hoffman, Helen Bacon. Oils
Hoffman, Martin (Joseph)
Hoffman, Richard Peter
Hoffmann, Arnold, Jr
Hogue, Alexandre. Oils, Watercolors,
  Lithography
Hoie, Claus. Watercolors, Graphics
Holbrook, Hollis Howard. Acrylics
Holbrook, Vivian Nicholas. Oils, Inks
Holcombe, Blanche Keaton. Oils
Holden, Raymond James
Holder, Charles Albert
Holgate, Edwin Headley
Holladay, Harlan H. Oils, Acrylics
Holladay, William H, Jr
Holland, Tom
Hollerbach, Serge. Casein, Acrylics, Inks
Hollinger, (Helen Wetherbee). Oils,
  Pastels, Acrylics
Hollingsworth, Alvin Carl. Acrylics,
  Collage
Hollister, Paul

Hollister, Valerie (Dutton). Acrylics
Holm, Milton W. Oils
Holman, Arthur (Stearns). Oils
Holmbom, James William. Acrylics
Holmes, David Bryan. Tempera
Holmes, Reginald. Acrylics
Holmes, Ruth Atkinson
Holty, Carl Robert. Oils
Homar, Lorenzo
Honig, Mervin. Oils
Hood, Dorothy. Oils, Ink
Hook, Walter. Watercolors
Hoowij, Jan. Oils, Acrylics, Tempera
Hopkins, Budd. Oils, Acrylics
Hopkins, John Fornachon
Hopkins, Kendal Coles. Oils
Hopkins, Peter. Oils
Hopkins, Ruth Joy
Horiuchi, Paul
Horne, (Arthur Edward) Cleeve
Horowitz, Nadia
Horter, Elizabeth Lentz
Horton, Jan E. Oils
Houser, James Cowing, Jr. Acrylics
Houser, Vic Carl
Housman, Russell F
Housser, Yvonne McKague. Oils, Acrylics,
  Mixed Media, Collage, Watercolors
Hovsepian, Leon
Howard, Cecil Ray. Collage, Assemblage
Howard, Dan F. Oils
Howard, Humbert L
Howe, Oscar. Casein
Howell, Claude Flynn. Oils, Watercolors
Howell, Douglass (Morse). Watercolors,
  Graphics
Howell, Elizabeth Ann. Watercolors,
  Acrylics
Howell, Frank. Egg Tempera, Oils, Water-
  colors, Acrylics, Ink
Howell, Raymond
Howze, James Dean. Charcoal, Metal,
  Mixed Media
Hoyt, Dorothy (Dorothy Hoyt Dillingham).
  Oils, Watercolors
Hoyt, Whitney F. Oils, Watercolors,
  Acrylics, Pastels
Hsiao, Chin. Acrylics
Hubbard, Earl Wade
Hudson, Kenneth Eugene
Hudson, Winnifred. Oils, Acrylics, Collage
Hueter, James Warren. Oils
Huggins, (Leonard) Victor, (Jr). Acrylics
Hughes, Edward John. Oils
Hull, Marie (Atkinson). Oils, Watercolors,
  Acrylics, Casein
Hultberg, John Phillip. Oils
Hunt, Julian Courtenay. Oils, Pastels
Hunt, Robert James
Hunter, John H. Collage, Mixed Media
Hunter, Robert Douglas. Oils
Hunter, Robert Howard. Mixed Media
Huntley, David C
Hupp, Frederick Duis. Acrylics
Hurd, Peter
Hurt, Susanne M. Oils
Hurtig, Martin Russell
Hurtubise, Jacques. Acrylics
Huseby, Arleen. Oils
Hutchinson, Peter Arthur. Mixed Media
Hutchison, Elizabeth S
Hutchison, Milburn Robert
Huth, Marta
Hutsaliuk, Lubo. Oils, Watercolors
Hyde, Laurence
Iacurto, Francesco. Oils, Pastels, Charcoal,
  Watercolors
Icaza (Francisco De Icaza). Oils, Acrylics
Iden, Sheldon. Oils, Graphics, Charcoal,
  Pastels
Indiana, Robert. Oils
Indiviglia, Salvatore Joseph. Watercolors
Ingle, Tom
Ingraham, Esther Price. Watercolors
Ingram, Jerry Cleman. Tempera
Ingram, Judith. Acrylics
Inokuma, Guenichiro. Oils, Acrylics

Inslee, Marguerite T. Oils
Insley, Will
Inukai, Kyohei. Oils, Acrylics
Ippolito, Angelo. Oils
Ireland, Richard Wilson (Dick)
Irizarry, Carlos. Mixed Media
Irvin, Mary Francis, SC
Irvin, Rea
Irwin, Robert
Isenburger, Eric. Oils
Isham, Sheila Eaton
Ivy, Gregory Dowler
Izacyro (Isaac Jiro Matsuoka)
Jackovich, Anthony. Oils, Watercolors
Jackson, A B
Jackson, Alexander Young
Jackson, Beatrice (Beatrice Jackson
  Humphreys). Oils
Jackson, Billy Morrow
Jackson, Everett Gee. Oils
Jackson, Harlan Christopher. Acrylics
Jackson, Harry Andrew. Oils
Jackson, Herb. Acrylics, Graphics
Jackson, Lee. Oils
Jackson, Nigel Loring. Oils
Jackson, Suzanne (Fitzallen). Acrylics
Jackson, Vaughn L. Watercolors, Acrylics,
  Inks
Jackson, Ward
Jacobs, Harold. Mixed Media, Multi-Media
Jacobs, Ted Seth. Oils
Jacobsen, Ray (Eugene). Oils
Jacobson, Arthur Robert. Oils
Jacquemon, Pierre. Oils
Jagger, Gillian
Jagman, Edward. Watercolors
Jagow, Ellen T. Acrylics
James, Frederic
Jameson, Demetrios George. Oils
Jamieson, Mitchell
Jamison, Philip (Duane, Jr). Watercolors
Janicki, Hazel (Mrs Wm Schock). Tempera
Jankowski, Joseph P
Janusas, Ceslovas. Oils, Watercolors
Jaramillo, Virginia. Acrylics
Jarkowski, Stefania Agnes. Oils, Water-
  colors
Jarvaise, James J
Jauss, Anne Marie. Wash, Oils, Water-
  colors, Linoleum, Dry Point
Ject-Key, Elsie. Oils, Watercolors
Jenkins, Paul
Jenkins, Paul Ripley. Watercolors
Jennings, Francis
Jennings, Frank Harding. Watercolors
Jensen, Alfred
Jensen, John Edward. Watercolors
Jensen, Lawrence N. Watercolors
Jensen, Leo (Vernon)
Jensen, Marit. Oils
Jensen, Pat
Jergens, Robert Joseph
Jeswald, Joseph
Jocda (Joseph Charles Dailey). Oils,
  Acrylics
Johansen, Anders Daniel. Oils, Watercolors
Johanson, George E
Johanson, Patricia (Maureen)
Johns, Jasper
Johnsen, May Anne. Silver Point, Oils
Johnson, Avery Fischer. Watercolors
Johnson, Buffie. Oils on Canvas
Johnson, Cecile Ryden. Watercolors
Johnson, Crockett
Johnson, Daniel LaRue
Johnson, Doris Miller (Mrs Gardiner
  Johnson). Oils, Gouache, Acrylics,
  Watercolors, Inks, Pencils
Johnson, Edvard Arthur
Johnson, Evert Alfred. Oils, Watercolors
Johnson, Katherine King. Oils
Johnson, Lester F
Johnson, Lester L. Acrylics
Johnson, (Leonard) Lucas. Oils
Johnson, Patricia Paul. Oils
Johnson, Ray
Johnson, Robert Lewis. Watercolors

Johnson, Wesley E
Johnston, Ynez
Jolley, Jerry (Geraldine Hazel Jolley). Oils
Jones, Amy (Amy Jones Frisbie). Oils,
   Watercolors
Jones, Benjamin Franklin
Jones, Douglas McKee (Doug). Oils,
   Pastels
Jones, Edward Powis. Oils, Watercolors
Jones, Howard William
Jones, John Paul
Jones, Nell Choate
Jones, Robert Cushman. Oils
Jones, Russell. Acrylics
Jones, Ruthe Blalock. Watercolors,
   Acrylics, Oils
Jones, W Louis. Acrylics
Jonniaux, Alfred. Oils
Jonson, Raymond. Acrylic Polymer, Oil,
   Watercolor, Casein Tempera, Pencil
Jonynas, Vytautas K
Jordan, Barbara Schwinn
Jorn, Asger
Josimovich, George. Oils
Josus (Josephine Hutson Graham). Plastic
   Resin Paints; Watercolors
Joyner, Howard Warren. Oils, Watercolors
Ju, I-Hsiung. Ink, Acrylics, Watercolors
Judkins, Sylvia. Watercolors, Ink, Acrylics
Judson, Jeannette Alexander. Oils, Acrylics
Jules, Mervin
Jungwirth, Irene Gayas. Egg Tempera, Oils
Junkin, Marion Montague
Kabak, Robert. Oils
Kacere, John C
Kachadoorian, Zubel. Oils, Charcoal, Inks,
   Watercolors, Gold, Silver
Kachergis, George Joseph. Oils, Acrylics
Kaep, Louis Joseph. Watercolors
Kahn, Peter. Graphics
Kahn, Susan B. Oils
Kahn, Wolf. Oils, Pastels
Kainen, Jacob. Oils
Kaiser, Charles James. Oils, Acrylics,
   Watercolors
Kaiser, Vitus J. Acrylics, Watercolors
Kalb, Marty Joel. Oils, Acrylics
Kalinowski, Eugene M
Kallweit, Helmut G
Kaltenbach, Stephen James
Kamihira, Ben
Kamrowski, Gerome. Mixed Media
Kamys, Walter
Kan, Diana. Watercolors
Kane, Bob Paul. Oils
Kanemitsu, Matsumi. Oils, Acrylics,
   Duco, Watercolors
Kanovitz, Howard. Acrylics
Kantor, Morris
Kaplan, Joseph. Oils, Gouache
Kaplan, Rhoda B. Oils, Charcoal, Pastels
Kaplinski, Buffalo
Kaprow, Allan
Kapsalis, Thomas Harry. Oils
Karaberi, Marianthe
Karawina, Erica (Mrs Sidney C Hsiao).
   Stained Glass
Karesh, Ann Bamberger. Acrylics
Karn, Gloria Stoll. Oils
Karniol, Hilda. Oils
Karoly, Andrew B
Karoly, Fredric. Oils, Acrylics
Kasak, Nikolas
Kassoy, Bernard. Oils, Watercolors,
   Pastels
Kassoy, Hortense. Watercolors
Kasten, Karl Albert
Katz, Alex. Oils
Katz, A(lexander) Raymond. Casein, Oils
Katz, Ethel
Katz, Hilda
Katz, Leo. Watercolors, Tempera, Fresco,
   Acrylics, Intaglio, Graphics
Katz, Theodore (Harry). Watercolors,
   Pencil, Ink
Kauffman, (Camille) Andrene. Acrylics,
   Ceremic Glaze, Oils, Watercolors

Kauffman, Robert Craig. Acrylics, Plastic
Kaufman, Irving
Kaufman, Jane A. Acrylics
Kaulitz, Garry Charles. Acrylics
Kaupelis, Robert John. Acrylics, Oils
Kawa, Florence Kathryn. Oils
Kaye, George. Watercolors, Pastels, Mixed
   Media
Keane, Lucina Mabel
Kearns, James Joseph.
Keeling, Henry Cornelious. Watercolors,
   Collage
Keen, Helen Boyd. Oils
Keene, Paul
Keener, Anna Elizabeth. Acrylics, Graphics
Kelleher, Daniel Joseph. Acrylics, Collage
Keller, Deane. Oils
Kelley, Chapman. Oils, Pastels
Kelley, Ramon. Oils, Watercolors,
   Pastels
Kelly, Ellsworth
Kelly, James
Kelly, Leon. Oils
Kelpe, Paul. Oils, Watercolors
Kemoha (George W Patrick Patterson). Oils
Kempton, Greta
Kenda, Juanita Echeverria
Kendall, Viona Ann
Kennedy, Doris Wainwright. Watercolors
Kennedy, J William. Oils
Kenny, Bettie Ilene (Bik). Oils on Linen
   Canvas, Lead Glass
Kenny, Thomas Henry
Kent, Frank Ward
Kepalas (Elena Kepalaite)
Kepes, Gyorgy
Kepets, Hugh Michael
Kerfoot, Margaret (Mrs M W Jennison)
Kerkovius, Ruth
Kermes, Constantine John. Oils, Acrylics
Kerns, Ed (Johnson, Jr). Acrylic Polymer
Kerr, James Wilfrid. Oils
Kerr, Kenneth A. Watercolors
Kerr, Leslie
Kerswill, J W Roy. Watercolors, Oils
Keskulla, Carolyn Windeler. Watercolors
Kessler, Alan. Oils
Kessler, Edna Leventhal. Oils, Watercolors,
   Graphics
Kessler, Shirley. Oils, Watercolors
Kester, Lenard. Oils, Watercolors,
   Gouache
Keyes, Bernard M
Keyser, Robert Gifford. Oils, Watercolors
Kielkopf, James Robert. Oils, Graphite
Kienbusch, William Austin. Casein, Oils
Kilian, Austin Farland. Collage
Killam, Walt. Oils, Gouaches
Killmaster, John H. Acrylics, Resins
Kimball, Yeffe
Kimbrough, (Sara) Dodge. Oils, Pastels,
   Contè, Watercolors
Kimura, Sueko M
Kimura, William Yusaburo
King, Joseph Wallace (Vinciata)
King, William Alfred. Oils, Watercolors
Kinghan, Charles Ross. Watercolors
Kingman, Dong M. Watercolors, Lacquer
Kingman, Eugene. Tempera, Acrylics
Kinigstein, Jonah
Kinstler, Everett Raymond
Kipniss, Robert. Oils
Kipp, Orval
Kirkland, Vance Hall. Oils, Watercolors
Kirkwood, Mary Burnette. Oils
Kirschenbaum, Jules. Acrylics
Kirsten, Richard Charles. Watercolors
Kisch, Gloria. Mixed Media
Kish, Maurice. Oils
Kiskadden, Robert Morgan. Oils, Water-
   colors
Kitaj, Ronald
Kjargaard, John Ingvard. Acrylics
Klarin, Winifred Erlick. Acrylics
Klavans, Minnie
Klebe, Gene (Charles Eugene). Watercolors
Klein, Doris. Oils

Klein, Medard. Oils, Casein, Watercolors,
   Gouache, Pastels, Pencil, Ink
Klein, Sandor C. Oils
Kleinholz, Frank. Oils
Kleinman, Sue. Oils
Klitgaard, Georgina. Oils, Watercolors
Klonis, Stewart. Watercolors
Kloss, Gene (Alice Geneva Glasier). Oils,
   Watercolors
Knapp, Sadie Magnet. Enamels
Knee, Gina (Mrs Alexander Brook). Water-
   colors, Oils
Knerr, Sallie Frost. Watercolors
Knight, Frederic Charles. Oils
Knigin, Michael Jay
Knipschild, Robert. Oils
Knobler, Lois Jean
Knorr, Lester
Knowles, Dorothy Elsie (Dorothy Elsie
   Perehudoff). Oils, Acrylics, Watercolors,
   Charcoal
Knowles, Richard H. Oils
Knowlton, Jonathan. Acrylics
Kobayashi, Katsumi Peter. Oils, Water-
   colors, Pastels
Koch, Arthur Robert. Wood, Plastics
Koch, Gerd (Herman). Oils, Acrylics
Koch, Irene Mabel. Oils
Koch, John. Oils
Koch, Virginia Greenleaf. Acrylics
Kocher, Robert Lee. Dye
Kocherthaler, Mina. Acrylics
Kochta, Ruth (Martha). Oils
Kocsis, Ann
Koenig, John Franklin. Oils, Acrylics
Koerner, Daniel
Koerner, Henry. Ink, Watercolors, Oils
Koestner, Don. Oils
Kohlhepp, Norman
Kohlmeyer, Ida (R). Oils
Kohn, Misch
Kokinas, George
Kolliker, William Augustin. Acrylics
Komodore, Bill. Acrylics, Watercolors, Ink
Koni, Nicolaus
Konopka, Joseph
Konrad, Adolf Ferdinand. Oils
Koons, Darell J. Watercolors, Polymers
Koplin, Norma-Jean. Pencil
Koppe, Richard. Oils, Acrylics, Water-
   colors, Ink
Koppelman, Dorothy
Korjus, Veronica Maria Elisabeth. Oils,
   Pastels
Korman, Harriet R
Korn, Elizabeth P. Mixed Media
Korner, John (John Michael Anthony
   Koerner). Oils, Acrylics
Korpela, Edward S. Watercolors, Acrylics
Kortheuer, Dayrell
Kortlander, William (Clark). Acrylics, Oils,
   Watercolors
Koscielny-Parker, Margaret. Ink, Plexiglas
Kotala, Stanislaw Waclaw. Watercolors,
   Oils
Kotin, Albert. Oils, Acrylics
Kowalke, Ronald Leroy
Kowalski, Raymond Alois. Acrylics,
   Collage
Kozloff, Alexander Ivan. Oils, Watercolors,
   Wood
Kozloff, Joyce. Acrylics
Kozlow, Richard. Acrylics
Kozlow, Sigmund. Oils, Pastels
Kramer, Jack. Oils
Kramer, Marjorie Anne. Oils, Watercolors
Kramolc, Theodore Maria. Oils, Pastels
Kraner, Florian G. Watercolors, Acrylics,
   Oils
Krasner, Lee
Kratz, Mildred Sands. Watercolors
Krause, LaVerne Erickson. Acrylics, Oils
Krausz, Laszlo. Ink, Oils
Kreindler, Doris Barsky. Oils, Watercolors
Kreitzer, David Martin. Oils
Kreznar, Richard J
Kriensky, (Morris) (E). Oils

Painter (cont)

Krigstein, Bernard. Oils, Watercolors, Pastels
Krims, Leslie Robert
Kroll, Leon
Krukowski, Lucian
Krupp, Louis. Oils, Watercolors, Charcoal
Krushenick, John
Krushenick, Nicholas
Kruskamp, Janet Elaine. Oils, Egg Tempera
Kuehn, Frances. Acrylics
Kuhn, Marylou. Encaustic
Kulicke, Robert M
Kunie
Kuntz, Roger Edward. Oils
Kupferman, Lawrence. Acrylics, Tempera
Kupferman, Murray. Casein
Kurelek, William
Kushner, Dorothy Browdy
Kushner-Weiner, Anita May. Watercolors
Kutka, Anne (Mrs David McCosh). Oils
Kuwayama, Tadaaki. Acrylic
Labrie, Rose. Oils
Lack, Richard Frederick. Oils
Lacroix, Richard. Acrylics
Laderman, Gabriel
Laessig, Robert. Watercolors
Lafaye, Nell Murray. Oils
Lafon, Dee J. Oils, Mixed Media
LaFreniere, Isabel Marcotte
Lagorio, Irene R
Lagunes, Maria (Maria Lagunes Hernandez)
Lahey, Richard (Francis). Oils, Watercolors
La Hotan, Robert L. Oils, Watercolors
Lai, Waihang. Watercolors
Laine, Lenore. Acrylics, Oils, Watercolors
Laliberte, Norman
Lam, Jennett (Brinsmade). Oils
Lamantia, James. Oils
Lamb, Adrian. Oils
La More, Chet Harmon. Acrylics, Watercolors
Land, Ernest Albert. Oils
Landau, Jacob. Watercolors
Landeck, Armin
Landon, Edward August
Lane, Bent. Oils
Lane, Christopher
Lang, Daniel S. Acrylics, Oils
Lang, Margo Terzian. Watercolors, Oils
Langlais, Bernard
Laning, Edward
Lansner, Fay
Lanyon, Ellen. Acrylics
La Pierre, Thomas. Oils, Watercolors
Lark, Raymond. Oils, Pencil
Larkin, William
Larrinaga, Mario. Oils
Larsen, Ole. Oils, Pastels
Larson, Sidney
Lasker, Joseph (L). Oils
Lassiter, Vernice (Vernice Lassiter Brown). Mixed Media
Latham, Barbara. Oils
Laufman, Sidney. Oils
Laurent, John Louis. Acrylics, Oils
Laurine (Virginia Laurine Grover). Oils
Lauritz, Paul
Laventhol, Hank. Casein, Oils, Aquatint
Law, Pauline Elizabeth. Oils, Watercolors
Lawrence, Jacob. Gouache, Casein, Tempera
Lax, David. Oils, Polymers, Pastels, Ink
Laycox, (William) Jack. Oils, Watercolors
Layton, Richard
Lazard, Alice Abraham. Oils, Watercolors, Acrylics, Casein
Lazzari, Pietro. Mixed Media
Lea, Tom
Leach, Frederick Darwin. Oils, Acrylics
Leaf, June
Leake, Eugene W
Leake, Gerald
Lebedev, Vladimir. Oils

Lebkicher, Anne Ross. Oils, Gouache, Watercolors, Conté
Lechay, James
Lecky, Susan. Acrylics, Watercolors
Le Clair, Charles. Oils, Acrylics, Watercolors
Lecoque. Oils, Tempera
Lee, Amy Freeman. Watercolors
Lee, Doris
Lee, Eleanor Gay. Oils, Pastels
Lee, Manning de Villeneuve. Oils, Watercolors, Inks
Lee, Richard Allen. Acrylics
Lee, Robert J
Lee-Smith, Hughie. Oils, Watercolors, Pencil, Charcoal
Leech, Hilton. Watercolors
Leeds, Annette. Oils
Leepa, Allen. Acrylics on Canvas
Leeper, Doris Marie
Leeper, John P. Acrylics
Leet, Richard Eugene. Watercolors, Oils
Leete, William White. Acrylics
Le Fevre, Richard John. Acrylics, Watercolors, Oils
Leff, Rita
Lehman, Irving
Lehman, Louise Brasell
Lehrer, Leonard. Oils
Leiber, Gerson August. Graphics
Leichman, Seymour. Oils
Leiferman, Silvia W. Oils, Acrylics
Leighton, Thomas Charles. Pastels
Leith-Ross, Harry. Watercolors
Leitman, Samuel. Watercolors
Leland, Whitney Edward. Acrylics, Watercolors
Lem, Richard Douglas. Oils
Lembeck, John Edgar
Lemieux, Jean Paul
Lenney, Annie. Oils, Watercolors
Lenssen, Heidi (Mrs Fridolf Johnson)
Leonardi, Hector
Leong, James Chan. Mixed Media
Leonid (Leonid Berman). Oils
Lerner, Marilyn Ann. Acrylics
Lerner, Sandy R. Oils, Mixed Media
Le Roy, Harold M. Oils, Serigraph
Lesh, Richard D
Leslie, Alfred
Lesnick, Stephen William. Oils
Letendre, Rita. Acrylics
Lev-Landau (Samuel David Landau). Oils, Casein
Le Va, Barry
Levee, John H. Acrylics, Plexiglas
Leventhal, Ethel S. Watercolors, Oils
Leventhal, Ruth Lee
Levering, Robert K
Levi, Josef
Levi, Julian (E). Oils
Levin, Jeanne
Levin, Kim (Kim Pateman)
Levine, Jack
Levine, Reeva (Anna) Miller. Oils, Acrylics, Watercolors
Levine, Shepard
Levit, Herschel
Levitt, Alfred
Levy, Beatrice S
Levy, Hilda
Levy, Tibbie. Oils
Lew, Weyman Michael. Ink, Watercolors, Acrylics
Lewandowski, Edmund D
Lewis, Golda. Compages
Lewis, Jeannette Maxfield. Oils
Lewis, Michael H. Oils, Film
Lewis, Nat Brush. Watercolors
Lewis, Norman Wilfred. Oils
Lewis, Samella Sanders
Lewis, William Arthur. Watercolors
Lewis, William R. Watercolors
Libby, William C. Oils
Liberi, Dante. Oils
Liberman, Alexander
Lichtenberg, Manes. Oils

Lichtenstein, Roy
Lieb, Leonard. Oils
Lieberman, Harry. Oils
Lieberman, Meyer Frank. Watercolors
Ligare, David H. Oils, Watercolors
Liles, Raeford Bailey
Liljegren, Frank. Oils
Lind, Victor. Graphics
Linden, Fred. Oils, Watercolors
Lindmark, Arne. Watercolors
Lindner, Ernest
Lindner, Richard. Oils, Watercolors
Lindstrom, Gaell
Lionni, Leo. Oils
Lipinsky de Orlov, Lino S. Oils
Lippincott, Janet. Oils, Acrylics
Lipsky, Pat. Acrylics, Oils
Lissim, Simon. Gouache
Liszt, Maria. Oils
Litaker, Thomas (Franklin). Watercolors
Little, John. Oils
Livingston, Charlotte (Mrs Francis Vendeveer Kughler). Watercolors
Livingston, Sidnee. Oils, Watercolors
Livingston, Virginia (Mrs Hudson Warren Budd). Watercolors
Livingstone, Biganess. Charcoal, Acrylics
Lobdell, Frank
Loberg, Robert Warren
Lochhead, Kenneth Campbell
Lochrie, Elizabeth
Locke, Charles Wheeler
Locker, Thomas. Oils
Lockhart, James Leland
Loew, Michael. Oils
Logan, Maurice. Watercolors, Oils
Logemann, Jane Marie. Mixed Media
Loggie, Helen A
Lomahaftewa, Linda (Linda Joyce Slock)
Loney, Doris Howard
Long, C Chee. Casein, Oils
Long, Gwen. Oils
Long, Water Kinscella
Longley, Bernique. Oils, Acrylics
Longo, Vincent
Longstreet, Stephen. Oils
Loomer, Gifford C. Acrylics, Oils
Lopez, Domingo. Graphics
Loran, Erle. Acrylics, Oils, Gouache
Lorber, Stephen Neil
Lorentz, Pauline. Oils, Charcoal
Loring, Clarice. Oils, Mixed Media
Lotterman, Hal. Oils, Lacquer
Lotton, Iwan Leroy. Oils
Loughlin, John Leo. Watercolors
Lourie, Herbert S
Lovato, Charles Fredric. Acrylics
Love, Joseph
Love, Rosalie Bowen. Oils
Lovell, Tom. Oils
Lowe, Joe Hing. Oils, Pastels, Watercolors, Charcoal
Lowe, Marvin
Loy, John Sheridan. Oils
Lozowick, Louis
Lubner, Martin Paul
Lucioni, Luigi
Ludekens, Fred
Lueders, Jimmy C. Acrylics
Lukin, Sven
Lukosius, Richard Benedict. Acrylics
Lund, David
Lundeberg, Helen (Helen Lundeberg Feitelson). Acrylics
Lunge, Jeffrey (Roy). Watercolors
Lupper, Edward. Casein, Oils
Lusker, Ron. Acrylics
Lutz, Dan S. Oils, Watercolors, Acrylics
Lux, Gladys Marie. Watercolors, Oils
Luz, Virginia
Lysun, Gregory. Oils
Lytle, Richard. Oils
McAllister-Kelly, (Rosana). Acrylics
McAninch, Beth. Watercolors, Pencil
Macaray, Lawrence Richard. Oils
McBride, James Joseph. Watercolors

McCallum, Corrie (Mrs William Halsey).
Oils
McCarthy, Denis
McCarthy, Doris Jean. Oils, Watercolors
McCartin, Jan. Oils, Casein
McCartin, William Francis. Acrylics
McChesney, Robert Pearson.
McChristy, Quentin L. Transparent Water-
colors, Ink, Pastels
McClellan, Robert John. Oils, Watercolors
McCloskey, Eunice LonCoske. Oils, Water-
colors
McCloskey, Robert
McCloy, William Ashby. Collage
McCormick, Harry. Oils, Graphics, Water-
colors, Pastels
McCormick - Sakura, Jo Mary
McCosh, David J. Oils
McCoy, John W, (II). Mixed Media
McCoy, Wirth Vaughan. Oils
McCracken, John Harvey
McCullough, Joseph. Acrylics
MacDonald, Grant
MacDonald, Thomas Reid. Oils
MacDonald, Thoreau.
Macdonald-Wright, Stanton. Oils
McEwen, Jean
McGarrell, James
McGee, Olivia Jackson. Watercolors
McGee, William Douglas. Acrylics, Oils,
Watercolors
McGee, Winston Eugene. Oils, Acrylics
McGeoch, Lillian Jean. Oils
Mac Gillis, Robert Donald. Watercolors
McGinnis, Christine. Acrylics, Graphics
McGowin, William Ed
McGrath, James Arthur. Oils, Earth Pig-
ments, Mixed Media
McGrew, Ralph Brownell. Oils, Charcoal
Machetanz, Fred. Oils
McIver, John Kolb. Watercolors, Acrylics
MacIver, Loren
McIvor, John Wilfred
Mackay, Donald Cameron. Oils
McKean, Hugh Ferguson
MacKendrick, Lilian. Oils, Pastels, Water-
colors, Charcoal, Ink
McKennis, Gail Collins. Graphics
MacKenzie, Hugh Seaforth. Tempera,
Watercolors
McKesson, Malcolm Forbes. Watercolors,
Oils, Ink
McKibben, Teal. Oils
McKim, William Wind. Tempera, Acrylics
McKinin, Lawrence. Oils, Acrylics
McLaren, Norman
McLarty, William James (Jack)
McLaughlin, John D. Oils, Acrylics
MacLean, Arthur
McLean, Doris Porter. Oils, Watercolors
McLean, Richard Thorpe. Oils
McMillan, Constance. Oils, Acrylics
McMillan, Robert W
McNab, Allan
McNamara, Raymond Edmund. Graphics
McNear, Everett C
McNeil, George J
McNett, Elizabeth Vardell. Oils, Tempera
McQuillan, Frances C. Watercolors, Oils,
Acrylics
MacRae, Emma Fordyce (Emma Fordyce
Swift). Oils
McVeigh, Miriam Temperance. Oils,
Acrylics
McVicker, J Jay. Acrylics
McWhorter, Elsie Jean
Maehara, Hiromu
Magafan, Ethel. Egg Tempera
Magazzini, Gene. Oils
Magleby, Francis R (Frank).
Oils
Mahaffey, Merrill Dean. Acrylics
Mahaffey, Noel A. Acrylics
Mahmoud, Ben. Acrylics
Mahoney, James Owen
Mainardi, Patricia M. Oils
Majdrakoff, Ivan

Makarenko, Zachary Philipp. Tempera,
Oils, Watercolors, Acrylics
Malicoat, Philip Cecil. Oils, Pencil
Mallinson, Constance (Constance Mallinson
Alter). Acrylics
Mallory, Larry Richard. Pencil
Malone, Robert R. Mixed Media
Malsch, Ellen L. Watercolors
Maltzman, Stanley. Charcoal, Graphics
Manarey, Thelma Alberta. Graphics
Mancuso, Leni (Leni Mancuso Barrett).
Watercolors, Casein
Mandel, Howard. Acrylics, Oils, Water-
colors
Mandel, John
Mandzuik, Michael Dennis. Acrylics, Ink
Mangione, Patricia Anthony. Oils, Acrylics
Mangold, Robert Peter
Mangold, Sylvia Plimack. Acrylics
Mangravite, Peppino Gino. Acrylics
Mangum, William (Goodson). Oils
Maniatty, Stephen George. Oils
Manilla, Tess (Tess Manilla Weiner). Oils,
Collages
Mann, Katinka. Polymers
Mann, Vaughan (Vaughan Grayson).
Mannen, Paul William. Oils, Watercolors
Manship, John Paul. Oils, Gouache, Water-
colors, Mosaics
Manso, Leo. Oils, Acrylics, Collage, As-
semblage
Manville, Elsie. Oils, Pastels
Mapes, Doris Williamson. Watercolors,
Acrylics
Marais (Mary Rachel Brown). Oils
Marca-Relli, Conrad
Marcus, Irving E
Marcus, Marcia. Oils, Acrylics on Canvas
Marden, Brice. Oils
Marder, Dorie
Margo, Boris
Margolies, Ethel Polacheck. Oils, Collage
Margulies, Joseph. Oils, Watercolors,
Graphics
Mariano, Anne. Acrylics
Maril, Herman. Oils, Casein, Acrylics
Marin, Kathryn Garrison. Oils, Pencil,
Mixed Media
Maris, Valdi S. Oils, Acrylics, Mixed Media
Mark, Bendor
Markell, Isabella Banks
Markow, Jack. Oils
Marlin, Hilda Van Stockum. Oils
Marsh, Anne Steele
Marshall, Alice Lord. Watercolors
Marsicano, Nicholas
Martell, Barbara Bentley. Oils, Acrylics,
Mixed Media
Martin, Bernard Murray. Oils
Martin, Bernice Fenwick. Oils, Graphics
Martin, Charles E. Watercolors, Acrylics,
Oils, Ink
Martin, Fletcher. Oils, Watercolors, Print
Media
Martin, Fred Thomas
Martin, G W. Oils
Martin, Keith
Martin, Keith Morrow
Martin, Knox
Martin, Langton. Graphics
Martin, Lucille Caiar (Lucille Martin
Hampton)
Martin, Roger
Martin, William Henry (Bill). Oils
Martinet, Marjorie D
Martinez-Maresma, Sara (Sara Sofia
Martinez). Oils
Martino, Antonio P. Oils
Martino, Eva E. Oils
Martino, Giovanni. Oils, Watercolors
Martinsen, Ivar Richard
Martmer, William P. Oils
Martyl (Martyl Schweig Langsdorf)
Marx, Robert Ernst
Maryan, Maryan S. Oils
Marzano, Albert. Acrylics, Oils, Water-
colors

Mason, Alden C. Oils, Watercolors
Mason, Alice Frances
Mason, Bette. Acrylics, Oils
Mason, Frank Herbert. Oils
Masse, Georges Severe. Oils, Water-
colors, Mixed Media
Massey, Robert Joseph. Egg Tempera
Massin, Eugene Max. Acrylic Sheet
Masson, Henri. Oils
Matson, Greta (Greta Matson Khouri). Oils,
Watercolors
Matson, Victor (Stanley)
Matthews, Gene (Eugene Edward). Acrylics
Mattiello, Roberto. Oils, Mixed Media
Mattison, Donald Magnus. Oils
Mauzey, Merritt
Mavian, Salpi Miriam. Oils
Mawicke, Tran. Oils, Watercolors
Maxwell, John R
May, E M (Elizabeth M Messiter). Water-
colors, Mixed Media, Ceramics
Mayer, Bena Frank. Oils, Watercolors
Mayer, Ralph. Oils
Mayhew, Richard
Mayorga, Gabriel Humberto. Oils, Pastels,
Watercolors
Mazur, Michael B
Mazzone, Domenico
Medearis, Roger. Tempera, Acrylics
Meehan, William Dale. Oils
Meeker, Barbara Miller. Watercolors,
Collage, Acrylics
Meeker, Dean Jackson
Mehring, Howard William. Acrylics
Meigs, John Liggett. Egg Tempera, Water-
colors
Meigs, Walter. Plastic Paints
Meissner, Leo J. Oils, Mixed Media, Wood
Meitzler, (Herbert) Neil. Acrylics, Tem-
pera, Watercolors
Meixner, Mary Louise. Oils, Acrylics
Mejer, Robert Lee
Melcarth, Edward
Melikian, Mary. Watercolors, Oils
Mellon, James
Meltzer, Anna E. Oils, Graphics
Meltzer, Arthur. Oils
Melville, Grevis Whitaker. Oils
Melvin, Grace Wilson. Watercolors, Mixed
Media, Acrylics, Collage
Mendelowitz, Daniel Marcus. Watercolors
Menihan, John Conway
Menkes, Sigmund
Menses, Jan. Tempera
Meredith, John
Merida, Carlos
Merkin, Richard Marshall
Mermin, Mildred (Shire). Oils, Watercolors
Merrick, James Kirk. Watercolors
Merrill, David Kenneth. Acrylics
Merritt, Francis Sumner
Mesches, Arnold
Mesibov, Hugh. Acrylics, Watercolors
Messeguer, Villoro Benito
Messersmith, Fred Lawrence. Water-
colors
Messick, Ben (Newton). Oils
Metz, Frank Robert. Oils
Meyer, Fred (Robert). Gouache
Meyerowitz, William. Oils
Meyers, Dale (Mrs Mario Cooper). Water-
colors
Michaels, Glen
Micheli, Julio. Assemblage
Middleton, David V
Midgette, Willard Franklin. Oils, Acrylics
Mieczkowski, Edwin
Mikus, Eleanore
Miles, Cyril. Acrylics, Collage
Miles, Jeanne Patterson
Miletti, Clemence M. Watercolors, Oils,
Woods
Miller, Barbara Darlene. Acrylics, Intaglio
Miller, Daniel Dawson. Watercolors
Miller, Eva-Hamlin. Acrylics, Oils
Miller, H McRae
Miller, Harold George. Oils

Painter (cont)

Miller, Nancy. Plexiglas, Paper
Miller, Ralph Rillman. Oils
Miller, Richard Kidwell. Oils, Acrylics
Milliken, Gibbs
Mills, Robert James. Watercolors
Millsaps, Daniel. Watercolors
Mina-Mora, Dorise Olson. Watercolors,
    Acrylics
Mina-Mora, Raul Jose
Minnick, Esther Tress. Watercolors
Mintz, Harry. Oils
Mitchell, Bruce Kirk, Oils
Mitchell, Clifford. Oils, Watercolors,
    Graphics
Mitchell, (Madison) Fred
Mitchell, James E. Casein, Oils
Mitchell, Joan
Mitchell, John Blair
Mitchell, Peter Todd. Oils
Mitchell, Wallace (MacMahon)
Mittleman, Ann. Oils
Miyasaki, George Joji
Miyashita, Tad
Mochizuki, Betty Ayako. Watercolor
Mochon, Donald
Mock, Gladys (Gladys Mock Wetter).
    Graphics
Moglia, Luigi (John). Watercolors
Mohn, Cheri (Ann)
Moldroski, Al R
Molin, Brita. Oils, Acrylics
Molina, Antonio J
Molinari, Guido
Moller, Hans. Oils, Watercolors
Monaghan, Eileen (Mrs Frederic
    Whitaker). Watercolors
Monaghan, Keith
Monroe, Gerald. Oils
Montague, James L. Oils, Graphics
Montana, Pietro
Montenegro, Enrique E. Oils
Montlack, Edith. Oils
Montoya, Geronima Cruz (Po-Tsu-Nu)
Moore, Beveridge. Oils
Moore, Ina May. Watercolors
Moore, Martha E (Mrs Louis A Burnett).
    Oils, Acrylics
Moore, Robert James. Oils, Graphics
Moose, Philip Anthony. Oils, Acrylics
Morado, Chavez Jose. Fresco, Oils, Tem-
    pera
Morales, Armando. Oils
Mordvinoff, Nicolas
Moreton, Russell. Oils
Morez, Mary
Morgan, Barbara Brooks
Morgan, Darlene, Ink, Oils
Morgan, Gladys B. Watercolors
Morgan, Maritza Leskovar
Morgan, Norma Gloria. Acrylics, Water-
    color
Morgan, Randall
Morrell, Wayne (Beam). Oils
Morris, Carl. Oils
Morris, Edward A
Morris, George Lik. Oils
Morris, Hilda. Sumi
Morris, Kathleen Moir
Morris, Kyle Randolph. Oils, Acrylics
Morrison, Keith Anthony. Oils, Water-
    colors, Acrylics
Morrison, Robert Clifton. Acrylics
Morton, Richard H. Watercolors
Moscatt, Paul N
Moseley, Ralph Sessions. Acrylics
Moseley, Spencer Altemont. Oils
Moser, Julon. Watercolors
Moses, Ed
Moses, Forrest (Lee), (Jr). Oils
Moses, Forrest King
Moshier, Elizabeth Alice
Moskowitz, Robert S
Moskowitz, Shirley (Mrs Jacob W Gruber).
    Acrylics
Moss, Irene. Oils

Moss, Joe (Francis)
Moss, Joel C
Moss, Milton. Oils
Motherwell, Robert. Collage, Ink, Aquatint
Mould, Lola Frowde. Watercolors, Oils,
    Pastels
Mount, Charles Merrill
Mount, (Pauline) Ward
Moy, Seong
Moyer, Roy
Mueller, Henrietta Waters. Oils, Water-
    colors, Acrylics
Muench, John
Mugnaini, Joseph Anthony. Graphics
Muhlstock, Louis
Muir, Emily Lansingh. Oils
Mulcahy, Freda. Acrylics, Pastels
Mullen, Buell. Stainless Steel, Epoxy,
    Stained Glass
Mullican, Lee. Oils
Munoz, Freddy Marcel. Mixed Media
Munzer, Aribert
Murphy, Catherine E. Oils
Murphy, Chester Glenn. Oils
Murphy, Gladys Wilkins
Murphy, Herbert A
Murphy, Rowley Walter. Oils, Watercolors,
    Tempera
Murray, Albert (Ketcham). Oils, Water-
    colors
Murray, Floretta May. Watercolors,
    Acrylics
Murray, John Michael
Murray, Richard Deibel. Ink, Acrylics
Musselman, Darwin B. Oils, Tempera
Myer, Peter Livingston
Myers, Malcolm Haynie
Nadalini, (Louis) (Ernest). Oils, Acrylics,
    Ink
Nagano, Paul Tatsumi. Watercolors, Oils
Nagano, Shozo. Acrylics
Nagler, Edith Kroger. Oils, Watercolors
Nagler, Fred. Oils
Naha, Raymond. Acrylics
Nakamura, Kazuo. Oils, Watercolors
Nama, George Allen
Narotzky, Norman David. Acrylics, Oils
Natkin, Robert
Naumer, Helmuth
Nay, Mary Spencer
Naylor, Alice Stephenson. Acrylics, Water-
    colors
Nazarenko, Bonnie Coe. Oils
Neal, Reginald H
Neddeau, Donald Frederick Price
Neel, Alice. Oils
Neff, John A. Watercolors
Neiman, LeRoy. Oils, Enamel
Nelson, Donald Richard
Nelson, George Laurence. Oils
Nelson, Harry William. Oils
Nelson, Leonard. Oils, Metal
Nelson, Lucretia
Nelson, Richard L
Nelson, Robert Allen. Stone, Oils
Nelson, Signe (Signe Nelson Stuart)
Nepote, Alexander
Nesbitt, Lowell (Blair). Oils
Ness, (Albert) Kenneth. Oils
Neuman, Robert S
Newbill, Al James
Newer, Thesis. Oils
Newman, Elias. Encaustic, Casein,
    Watercolors
Newport, Esther, SP
Nicholas, Thomas Andrew. Oils, Water-
    colors
Nichols, Alice W. Collage
Nichols, Jeannettie Doornhein. Acrylics,
    Oils, Watercolors
Nichols, Ward H. Oils
Nick, George. Oils
Nickle, Robert W
Niemann, Edmund E
Nierman, Leonardo M. Acrylics
Niese, Henry Ernest. Acrylics, Oils
Noland, Kenneth

Nonay, Paul. Oils, Watercolors, Collage
Nordhausen, A Henry. Oils
Nordstrand, Nathalie Johnson. Water-
    colors, Oils
Norman, Emile. Oils, Acrylics
Norris, (Robert) Ben. Watercolors, Oils
Norwood, Malcolm Mark. Watercolors
Notarbartolo, Albert. Acrylics, Mixed
    Media
Novinski, Lyle Frank. Leather, Acrylics
Novotny, Elmer Ladislaw. Oils, Polymers,
    Watercolors
Nuala (Elsa de Brun). Pastels
Nulf, Frank Allen
O'Brien, Joan
Ocejo, (Jose Garcia)
Ochikubo, Tetsuo. Oils
Oehler, Helen Gapen. Oils, Watercolors
Ogilvie, Will (William Abernethy)
Ohashi, Yutaka. Collage
Ohlson, Douglas Dean. Oils
Okada, Kenzo. Oils
Okamura, Arthur
O'Keeffe, Georgia
Okoshi, Eugenia Sumiye. Oils, Acrylics,
    Graphics
Olds, Elizabeth
Olinsky, Tosca (Mrs Charles F Barteau)
Olitski, Jules. Acrylics
Olkinetzky, Sam. Collage
Olmsted, Pat. Watercolors, Mixed Media
Olsen, Don. Oils, Acrylics
Olsen, Herb. Watercolors
O'Meilia, Philip Jay
Omwake, Leon, Jr. Acrylics
O'Neil, John. Acrylics, Pastels
Onley, Toni. Oils, Watercolors
Oppenheim, Samuel Edmund. Oils
Oppenheimer, Selma L. Oils
Opper, John
Ordoñez, Efren. Oils, Acrylics, Water-
    colors
Ordorica, Hilda Trull. Watercolors
Orr, Elliot. Oils
Ortlip, Paul Daniel. Oils, Mixed Media
Ortman, George Earl
Osborn, Robert
Osborne, Robert Lee
Osby, Larissa Geiss
O'Sickey, Joseph Benjamin. Oils
Ossorio, Alfonso A
Ostendorf, (Arthur) Lloyd, Jr. Watercolors,
    Inks, Oils
Oster, Gerald
Ostuni, Peter W. Oils, Vitreous Enamel,
    Glass, Metals
Osver, Arthur
Owens, Winifred (Whitebergh)
Pablo (Paul Burgess Edwards)
Pace, Margaret Bosshardt
Pace, Stephen S. Oils, Watercolors
Pachner, William. Oils, Watercolors,
    Ink
Packer, Clair Lange. Watercolors, Oils,
    Inks, Crayons
Page, John Henry, Jr
Palau, Marta
Palmer, Lucie Mackay
Palmer, William C
Panabaker, Frank S
Paone, Peter
Paradise, Phil (Herschel). Graphics
Paris, Dorothy. Oils
Paris, Lucille M (Lucille M Bichler)
Parish, Betty Waldo
Parish, Jean
Parke, Walter Simpson. Oils
Parker, Bill. Acrylics
Parker, James. Acrylics, Pencil, Pastels
Parker, Raymond. Oils
Parker, Robert Andrew
Parker, Roy Danford. Oils
Parks, Christopher Cropper
Parrish, David Buchanan. Oils
Parshall, Douglass Ewell. Oils, Water-
    colors
Parsons, Betty Bierne. Acrylics

Parsons, Kitty (Kitty Parsons Recchia).
  Watercolors
Partin, Robert (E). Oils, Acrylics
Parton, Nike. Watercolors
Pascal, David. Inks
Pasilis, Felix
Passuntino, Peter Zaccaria
Paternosto, Cesar Pedro. Acrylics
Patrick, Genie H. Oils
Patrick, Joseph Alexander. Oils
Patterson, Patty (Mrs Frank Grass)
Pattison, Abbott
Paul, William D, Jr
Peake, Channing
Pearlstein, Philip
Pearson, Henry C. Acrylics, Oils
Pearson, James Eugene
Pearson, John
Pearson, Marguerite Stuber. Oils
Pease, David G. Acrylics
Peche, Dale C. Gouache
Peck, James Edward. Watercolors,
  Enamels, Woods
Pederson, Molly Fay. Oils, Acrylics
Peers, Gordon Franklin
Pehap, Erich K
Pellan (Alfred). Oils
Pellew, John Clifford. Watercolors, Oils
Pellicone, William. Oils
Pels, Albert. Oils, Watercolors, Graphics
Pen, Rudolph. Oils, Watercolors
Penczner, Paul Joseph. Oils, Acrylics, Ink
Penney, Bruce Barton. Oils
Penney, James. Oils
Penny, Aubrey John Robert. Acrylics
Pepper, Beverly. Acrylics
Perham, Roy Gates. Oils
Perlin, Bernard
Perlin, Rae. Oils
Perlmutter, Jack
Perret, Nell Foster. Graphics
Perrin, C Robert. Watercolors
Pershing, Louise. Oils
Peterdi, Gabor F. Oils, Intaglio
Peters, Carl W. Oils, Watercolors
Petersen, Roland Conrad
Peterson, A E S. Watercolors, Casein,
  Graphics
Peterson, Larry D. Watercolors, Acrylics
Peterson, Robert Baard. Oils
Petheo, Bela Francis. Oils, Acrylics,
  Graphics
Petrie, Ferdinand Ralph. Watercolors
Petro, Joseph (Victor), Jr
Petroff, Gilmer. Watercolors, Acrylics
Pezzati, Pietro
Pfahl, Charles Alton, III. Pastels, Oils
Pfeifer, Bodo
Pfriem, Bernard
Phelps, Nan Dee. Oils
Philbrick, Margaret Elder. Mixed Media
Philbrick, Otis
Philipp, Robert
Phillips, Margaret McDonald. Oils
Phillips, Marjorie. Oils
Phillips, Matt. Watercolors, Oils, Monotype
Piatek, Francis John. Oils, Acrylics
Picard, Lil
Picken, George
Pickens, Alton
Pickens, Vinton Liddell
Pickford, Rollin, Jr. Watercolors, Oils,
  Acrylics
Pickhardt, Carl
Pierce, Delilah W. Oils, Acrylics
Pierce, Elizabeth R. Oils
Pierre-Noel, Lois Jones. Oils, Acrylics
Pike, John
Pinardi, Enrico Vittorio
Pindell, Howardena Doreen
Pinkerton, Clayton (David)
Pinkowski, Emily Joan. Acrylics
Pinsky, Alfred
Pinto, James. Acrylics
Pitz, Henry Clarence. Watercolors, Oils,
  Acrylics
Pitz, Molly Wood

Plagens, Peter
Plate, Walter
Pleissner, Ogden Minton. Oils, Watercolors
Pletcher, Gerry. Acrylics, Oils
Plochmann, Carolyn Gassan. Oils, Acrylics,
  Graphics
Pneuman, Mildred Y. Oils
Pohl, Louis G
Polan, Nancy Moore. Watercolors
Poleskie, Stephen Francis
Politinsky, F Augusta (Flora). Wax, Water-
  colors, Casein, Oils, Papier Maché
Polsky, Cynthia. Acrylics, Watercolors
Pollack, Reginald Murray. Oils
Pollak, Theresa. Oils, Ink
Pollard, Donald Pence. Crystal, Oils
Pollaro, Paul. Acrylics, Oils, Collage
Pollock, Merlin F. Acrylics, Watercolors
Polonsky, Arthur. Oils, Tempera
Ponce de Leon, Michael
Pond, Clayton
Poons, Larry
Poor, Anne. Oils, Watercolors
Pope, Mary Ann Irwin. Acrylics
Pope, Richard Coraine. Opaque Watercolors
Porter, (Edwin) David
Porter, Elmer Johnson. Watercolors
Porter, Fairfield
Porter, J Erwin
Portmann, Frieda Bertha Anne
Posen, Stephen
Post, George (Booth)
Potter, (George) Kenneth. Watercolors,
  Oils, Acrylics
Potter, Ted
Potts, Don
Pousette-Dart, Richard
Powell, Leslie (Joseph). Oils, Watercolors,
  Pastels
Powers, Marilyn. Oils
Pozzatti, Rudy O
Pratt, Frances (Frances Elizabeth Usui)
Prentice, David Ramage. Acrylics
Preston, Malcolm H. Oils
Prestopino, Gregorio. Oils, Watercolors
Preuss, Roger. Oils, Watercolors
Preusser, Robert Ormerod. Mixed Media
Prezament, Joseph. Oils
Pribble, Easton. Oils, Acrylics, Pastels
Price, Rosalie Pettus. Acrylics, Oils, Ink
Pride, Joy. Oils, Graphics
Priest, Hartwell Wyse. Graphics
Primerano, Joan Walton. Oils
Prins, (J) Warner
Probst, Joachim. Oils
Prohaska, Ray
Proom, Al
Pross, Lester Fred. Oils, Watercolors,
  Acrylics
Pruitt, A Kelly. Oils
Purdy, Donald R. Oils
Purves, Austin. Tempera
Putnam, Wallace (Bradstreet). Oils
Putterman, Florence Grace
Quanchi, Leo
Quat, Helen S
Quaytman, Harvey
Quest, Charles Francis. Oils
Quest, Dorothy (Johnson). Oils
Quick, Birney MacNabb. Oils, Watercolors
Quinn, Noel Joseph. Watercolors
Quirk, Francis Joseph. Oils, Acrylics,
  Watercolors, Charcoal, Pastels, Ink
Quirk, Thomas Charles, Jr. Watercolors,
  Oils
Quisgard, Liz Whitney
Rabinovich, Raquel. Oils
Rabinovitch, William Avrum. Oils, Acrylics,
  Watercolors
Rabkin, Leo. Watercolors
Rabut, Paul
Rachelski, Florian W
Racz, Andre
Radin, Dan. Oils, Acrylics
Radoczy, Albert. Oils
Radulovic, Savo
Raffael, Joseph. Oils

Raffel, Alvin Robert. Oils, Watercolors
Ragland, Jack Whitney. Acrylics
Rahja, Virginia Helga
Rain, Charles (Whedon)
Rakocy, William (Joseph). Oils, Water-
  colors, Acrylics
Ralston, J(ames) K(enneth). Oils, Ink,
  Watercolors
Ramberg, Christina (Christina Ramberg
  Hanson). Acrylics
Ramos, Melvin John. Oils
Rand, Paul
Randolph, Gladys Conrad
Rankin, Don
Rankine, V V
Ranson, Nancy Sussman. Oils, Acrylics
Rapp, Lois. Watercolors, Oils, Pastels
Rappin, Adrian. Oils
Rascoe, Stephen Thomas. Oils
Rath, Hildegard. Oils, Pastels, Water-
  colors, Charcoal
Ratkai, George
Rattner, Abraham
Rauh, Fritz
Rauschenberg, Robert
Raveson, Sherman Harold. Oils
Ray, Robert (Donald)
Ray, Ruth (Mrs John Reginald Graham).
  Oils, Gouache, Pencil
Rayen, James Wilson. Acrylics
Reardon, Mary A. Oils, Watercolors,
  Acrylics, Charcoal
Rebert, Jo Liefeld
Reboli, Joseph John. Oils
Redden, Alvie Edward
Reed, Doel. Graphics
Reed, Hal. Oils, Acrylics
Reed, Paul Allen. Acrylics
Reep, Edward Arnold. Oils
Reeves, J Mason, Jr
Refregier, Anton
Regensburg, Sophy P. Acrylics
Rehberger, Gustav
Reiback, Earl M
Reich, Nathaniel E. Oils
Reichek, Jesse
Reichert, Donald Karl. Acrylics, Oils, Ink
Reichert, Donald O. Watercolors, Collage
Reichman, Fred(rick) (Thomas). Oils,
  Acrylics
Reid, (William) Richard
Reid, Robert Dennis. Oils
Reif, Rubin
Reiff, Robert Frank. Oils, Acrylics
Reindorf, Samuel. Oils, Pastels, Water-
  colors
Reinhardt, Siegfried Gerhard
Reininghaus, Ruth (Ruth Reininghaus Smith).
  Oils
Reinsel, Walter Newton. Watercolors, Oils,
  Acrylics
Reisman, Philip. Oils, Watercolors
Reiss, Lee. Oils
Relis, Rochelle R. Oils, Ink, Watercolors
Rembski, Stanislav. Oils, Crayons, Pencils
Remenick, Seymour. Oils
Remington, Deborah Williams. Oils
Remsing, (Joseph) Gary
Rennie, Helen (Sewell). Oils, Acrylics
Renouf, Edward Pechmann. Acrylics
Resika, Paul
Resnick, Milton
Reynard, Carolyn Cole. Acrylics
Reynolds, Ralph William. Watercolors
Reynolds, Richard (Henry). Acrylics, Poly-
  mers
Rhoads, Eugenia Eckford. Watercolors, Oils
Riba, Paul F. Oils
Ricci, Jerri
Rice, Dan. Oils
Rice, Norman Lewis
Rice, Philip Somerset. Acrylics
Rich, Garry Lorence
Richards, Jeanne Herron
Richards, Karl Frederick. Oils
Richardson, Constance (Coleman). Oils
Richardson, Gerard

Painter (cont)

Richardson, Sam
Richenburg, Robert Bartlett
Ridabock, Ray (Budd)
Ries, Martin
Riess, Lore. Oils
Rigsby, John David. Oils, Acrylics
Riley, Art (Arthur Irwin). Watercolors, Oils
Riley, Roy John. Oils
Rippey, Clayton. Acrylics
Rising, Dorothy Milne. Oils, Watercolors
Rivers, Larry
Rizk, Romanos. Acrylics, Polymer, Collage
Robbin, Anthony Stuart. Acrylics
Robbins, Hulda D. Oils
Roberts, Clyde Harry. Watercolors
Roberts, (William) Goodridge
Roberts, Lucille D (Malkia). Oils, Acrylics
Roberts, Priscilla Warren. Oils
Roberts, Thomas (Kieth). Oils, Watercolors, Acrylics
Robertson, D Hall. Oils
Robinson, Jay Thurston
Robinson, Mary Turlay. Oils
Robinson, Robert Doke
Robles, Glenn (Waggoner)
Robles, Julian
Roche, Jim. Ceramic, Wire, Plastic, Ink
Rockmore, Noel
Rodriguez Luna, Antonio. Oils
Roesch, Kurt (Ferdinand)
Rogers, Charles B
Rogers, James B. Acrylics
Rogers, John. Watercolors
Rogers, Otto Donald. Acrylics
Rogers, P J. Graphics
Rogers, Peter Wilfrid. Oils, Acrylics, Ink
Rogovin, Howard Sand
Rojo, Vicente. Oils
Roller, Marion Bender. Watercolors
Romano, Clare Camille
Romano, Emanuel Glicen
Romano, Jaime (Luis). Acrylics
Romano, Salvatore Michael. Acrylics, Plaster, Plastics
Romano, Umberto Roberto. Oils, Acrylics
Romans, Charles John. Oils
Rome, Harold
Romeling, W B. Watercolors
Romoser, Ruth Amelia. Oils, Acrylics
Ronald, William
Ronay, Stephen Robert. Oils, Graphics
Roney, Harold Arthur. Oils
Rose, Arthur. Oils
Rose, Dorothy. Oils, Watercolors
Rose, Herman. Graphics
Rosenblatt, Adolph
Rosenblum, Jay. Acrylics
Rosenblum, Sadie Skoletsky. Oils
Rosenborg, Ralph M
Rosendale, Harriet. Oils
Rosenquit, Bernard. Oils, Gouache
Rosenthal, Seymour Joseph. Watercolors, Oils, Tempera, Lithography
Rosenthal, Stephen. Tempera
Rosofsky, Seymour. Oils, Watercolors, Pastels
Ross, Alexander. Watercolors, Acrylics, Oils
Ross, Alvin. Oils
Ross, James Matthew
Ross, Jean G. Oils
Rossi, Barbara
Rossi, Joseph O
Roston, Arnold
Roszak, Theodore
Rotenberg, Harold. Oils
Roth, Frank
Roth, James Buford
Roth, Richard Lee
Roth, Rubi. Watercolors, Oils, Collage
Rowan, Frances Physioc. Graphics
Rowan, Herman. Oils
Rowe, Reginald M
Rowland, Elden Hart
Rowlands, Tom

Rubon, Richards
Rubenstein, Lewis W
Rubin, Irwin
Ruda, Edwin. Mixed Media
Ruddley, John. Acrylics, Oils, Watercolors
Rudquist, Jerry Jacob. Oils
Ruellan, Andrée. Oils, Gouache, Graphics
Ruscha, Edward Joseph
Rush, Andrew.
Russell, (George) Gordon. Oils
Russell, James Spencer
Russell, Shirley (Ximena). Oils
Russo, Alexander Peter. Acrylics, Oils, Plastics, Metals
Ruta, Peter Paul. Oils
Ruthling, Ford. Oils
Rutland, Emily Edith. Oils, Acrylics
Rutsch, Alexander
Ruvolo, Felix Emmanuele
Ryerson, Margery Austen. Watercolors, Oils
Ryman, Robert
Saar, Betye. Mixed Media
Sabatini, Raphael
Sachse, Janice R. Oils, Watercolors, Graphics
Safford, Ruth Perkins. Watercolors
Sahrbeck, Everett William. Watercolors
St Amand, Joseph. Oils
Sainz, Francisco
Salamone, Gladys L. Oils
Salazar, Juan. Oils
Saldivar, Jaime
Salemme, Lucia (Autorino). Oils, Watercolors, Ink
Salemme, Martha
Salinas, Baruj. Acrylics
Salter, John Randall. Oils, Watercolors, Acrylics
Saltmarche, Kenneth Charles
Saltonstall, Elizabeth. Oils
Saltzman, William. Oils, Wood, Copper, Stained Glass
Samerjan, George E
Sample, Paul. Oils, Watercolors, Acrylics
Samstag, Gordon
Samuelson, Fred Binder. Acrylics
Sanborn, Herbert J
Sanchez, Emilio
Sandecki, Albert Edward. Watercolors, Oils
Sander, Ludwig. Oils, Graphics
Sanders, Andrew Dominick. Oils
Sanders, Joop A. Oils, Acrylics, Watercolors
Sandgren, Ernest Nelson
Sandol, Maynard
Sarff, Walter
Sargent, Margaret Holland
Sarkis (Sarkis Sarkisian). Oils, Mixed Media
Sarnoff, Arthur Saron. Oils, Acrylics
Sarsony, Robert. Oils, Watercolors, Graphics
Sato, Tadashi. Oils
Saturensky, Ruth
Saucy, Claude Gerald. Graphics
Saul, Peter
Saunders, Aulus Ward. Watercolors, Acrylics, Oils
Saunders, Raymond Jennings.
Savas, Jo-Ann. Watercolors
Sawyer, Helen (Helen Sawyer Farnsworth). Oils, Watercolors
Sazegar, Morteza. Acrylics
Schabacker, Betty B. Watercolors, Collage
Schachter, Justine Ranson. Stone, Graphics
Schaefer, Carl Fellman. Watercolors, Egg Tempera
Schaefer, Henri Bella
Schaffer, Rose. Oils, Casein, Acrylics, Wood
Schanker, Louis
Schapiro, Miriam
Scharff, Constance Kramer
Schary, Susan. Oils
Scheibe, Fred Karl. Enamels

Schein, Eugenie. Oils, Acrylics, Watercolors
Schellin, Robert William. Acrylics, Clay
Scheu, Leonard. Watercolors, Oils
Schiff, Lonny. Oils, Watercolors, Graphics
Schiller, Beatrice. Watercolors, Graphics, Acrylics
Schimmel, William Berry. Watercolors, Oils
Schlaikjer, Jes Wilhelm. Oils
Schlecht, Richard. Oils, Acrylics, Ink
Schlemm, Betty Lou. Watercolors
Schlicher, Karl Theodore
Schloss, Edith. Oils, Watercolors
Schmalz, Carl (Nelson), (Jr). Watercolors
Schmeidler, Blanche J
Schmid, Richard Alan. Oils, Watercolors, Conté, Crayon, Stone, Wood
Schmidt, Arnold Alfred. Acrylics
Schmidt, Frederick Lee. Acrylics, Oils
Schmidt, Katherine (Katherine Schmidt Shubert). Oils, Pencils, Conté
Schnackenberg, Roy
Schneebaum, Tobias. Oils
Schneider, Jo Anne. Oils
Schnurr-Colflesh E
Schoener, Jason. Oils, Watercolors, Gouache
Scholder, Fritz
Schonberger, Fred. Oils
Schonwalter, Jean Frances. Oils, Bronze
Schooley, Elmer Wayne. Oils, Wood
Schorr, Justin. Oils
Schott, Joseph John. Oils
Schrack, Joseph Earl
Schrag, Karl. Oils, Gouache, Graphics
Schreck, Michael Henry. Oils
Schreiber, Eileen Sher. Collage, Acrylics, Watercolors
Schreiber, Georges. Oils, Watercolors, Graphics
Schreiber, Martin. Acrylics
Schreyer, Greta L. Oils, Watercolors
Schrup, John Edmund. Oils
Schucker, Charles
Schueler, Jon R
Schultz, Harold A
Schultz, Roger d. Acrylics
Schuman, Robert Conrad
Schwab, Eloisa (Mrs A H Rodriguez). Oils
Schwabacher, Ethel K. Acrylics
Schwacha, George
Schwalbach, Mary Jo. Mixed Media
Schwartz, Carl E. Acrylics
Schwartz, Henry. Oils
Schwartz, Therese
Schwartz, William Samuel
Schwarz, Felix Conrad. Oils
Schwarz, Myrtle Cooper. Stained Glass, Ceramics
Schweitzer, Gertrude
Scott, Henry (Edwards), Jr. Watercolors, Oils
Scott, Jonathan. Oils, Watercolors
Scott, Marian (Dale). Acrylics
Seabourn, Bert Dail. Oils, Watercolors
Seaman, Drake F. Oils
Searles, Charles Robert. Acrylics, Watercolors
Seckel, Paul Bernhard. Acrylics, Oils
Secunda, (Holland) Arthur
Seery, John
Seide, Charles. Oils, Acrylics
Seidler, Doris
Seliger, Charles. Oils, Acrylics
Sella, Alvin Conrad
Selonke, Irene A. Watercolors, Oils
Senior, Dorothy Elizabeth. Oils & Pastels
Sennhauser, John. Oils, Collage
Sepeshy, Zoltan L. Tempera, Graphics
Serisawa, Sueo. Oils
Serra-Badue, Daniel
Sessler, Stanley Sascha. Oils
Setterberg, Carl Georg. Oils, Watercolors
Sexton, Leo Lloyd, Jr. Oils
Shackelford, Shelby. Casein
Shacknove, Reta. Mixed Media, Collage

Shadbolt, Jack Leonard
Shadrach, Jean H. Acrylics
Shane, Frederick E. Oils, Casein
Shannon, Joseph. Acrylics, Crayon
Shapiro, Babe. Acrylics
Shapiro, David
Shapiro, Irving. Watercolors
Sharp, Marion Leale
Shatalow, Vladimir Mihailovich. Oils,
  Tempera, Acrylics
Shaw, Charles Green
Shaw, Donald Edward. Mixed Media
Shaw, Harry Hutchison. Oils, Acrylics,
  Watercolors
Shaw, (George) Kendall. Acrylics
Shayn, John
Shead, S Ray. Acrylics
Sheaks, Barclay. Acrylics, Polymers
Shecter, Pearl S. Acrylics, Gold Leaf,
  Collage
Sheehe, Lillian Carolyn. Fired Glass, Oils,
  Copper Enameling
Sheets, Millard Owen
Sheets, Nan Jane. Oils
Sheng, Shao Fank. Acrylics, Watercolors,
  Silver, Copper
Shepler, Dwight (Clark). Watercolors, Oils
Sheppard, John Craig. Watercolors, Oils
Sheppard, Joseph Sherly. Oils
Sherman, Lenore (Walton). Oils, Water-
  colors, Acrylics
Sherman, Sarai. Oils, Graphics
Sherman, Winnie Borne. Watercolors
Sherry, William Grant. Oils, Wax
Sherwood, Bette (Wilson). Oils
Shibley, Gertrude. Oils
Shields, Alan J
Shikler, Aaron
Shimon, Paul. Gouache, Tempera, Oils
Shiner, Nate. Acrylics
Shoemaker, Peter
Shoemaker, Vaughn
Shokler, Harry. Oils
Shonnard, Eugenie F
Shook, Georg E. Watercolors
Shore, Clover Virginia. Oils, Watercolors,
  Graphics
Shore, Mary
Shores, (James) Franklin. Watercolors,
  Oils
Shorter, Edward Swift. Oils
Shotwell, Helen Harvey
Shoulberg, Harry. Oils
Showell, Kenneth L. Acrylics
Shuck, Kenneth Menaugh. Watercolors,
  Acrylics
Shuff, Lily (Lillian Shir). Oils, Water-
  colors
Shunney, Andrew. Oils, Acrylics, Gouache
Shute, Ben E
Sibley, Charles Kenneth. Oils, Acrylics,
  Watercolors
Sicard, Louis Gabriel. Oils
Sickman, Jessalee Bane. Oils
Sider, Deno. Oils, Clay, Ink, Charcoal
Sideris, Alexander
Siegel, Adrian
Siegel, Irene
Siegriest, Lundy. Oils, Mixed Media
Sievan, Maurice. Oils, Watercolors,
  Pastels
Sigel, Barry Chaim. Oils, Watercolors,
  Feathers
Sigismund, Violet M. Oils, Watercolors
Sihvonen, Oli. Acrylics, Oils
Silberstein, Muriel Rosoff. Assemblage,
  Collage
Silins, Janis. Oils, Watercolors
Silkotch, Mary Ellen
Sills, Thomas Albert
Silverman, Burton Philip. Oils, Water-
  colors, Pastels
Simon, Ellen R
Simon, Howard. Watercolors, Oils, Wood
Simon, Sidney.
Simoni, John Peter
Simper, Frederick. Watercolors

Simpkins, Henry John. Watercolors
Simpson, David. Acrylics
Simpson, Lee. Oils
Simpson, Marilyn Jean. Pastels, Oils
Simpson, Maxwell Stewart. Oils, Water-
  colors
Simpson, Merton D
Sims, Agnes
Simson, Bevlyn A
Sine, David William
Sing Hoo (Sing Hoo Yuen)
Singer, Burr (Burr Lee Friedman)
Singer, Clyde J. Oils
Singer, Esther Forman. Oils, Mixed Media
Singer, William Earl
Singleton, Robert Ellison
Sinnard, Elaine (Janice). Oils
Sinton, Nell (Walter). Acrylics
Siporin, Mitchell. Oils, Watercolors
Siqueiros, David Alfaro
Sirena (Contessa Antonia Mastrocristino
  Fanara)
Sirugo, Salvatore. Acrylics, Casein
Sissons, Lynn E. Watercolors
Sisti, Anthony J
Sivard, Robert Paul. Casein
Skeggs, David Potter
Skelton, Phillis Helper. Watercolors
Skemp, Robert Oliver. Oils
Skinner, Clara (Clara Skinner Guy)
Skinner, Elsa Kells. Watercolors
Sklar, Dorothy. Watercolors, Acrylics
Sklar-Weinstein, Arlene (Joyce). Acrylics
Slack, Dee. Oils
Slade, Roy. Acrylics
Slate, Joseph Frank
Slaughter, Lurline Eddy. Acrylics, Oils
Sles, Steven Lawrence. Oils, Ink, Glass
Slettehaugh, Thomas Chester. Mixed Media
Slick, James Nelson. Oils
Sloan, Robert Smullyan. Oils
Sloane, Mary (Humphreys)
Sloane, Patricia Hermine
Slotnick, Mortimer H
Smiley, Ralph Jack. Oils
Smith, Alvin. Mixed Media
Smith, Arthur Hall. Oils, Acrylics, Ink
Smith, Charles (William). Oils, Acrylics
Smith, David Loeffler. Oils
Smith, Dolph. Watercolors
Smith, Emily Guthrie. Pastels, Oils
Smith, Frank Anthony. Acrylics
Smith, Gord
Smith, Gordon
Smith, Hassel W, Jr
Smith, Helen M
Smith, J(ohn) B(ertie). Watercolors
Smith, Joseph A(nthony). Pencil, Wax
Smith, Leon Polk
Smith, Oliver
Smith, Paul K
Smith, Paul Roland. Oils, Ink, Watercolors
Smith, R Harmer. Watercolors
Smith, Robert Alan. Oils
Smith, Sam. Watercolors, Oils
Smith, Shirlann
Smith, William Arthur. Oils, Watercolors
Smul, Ethel Lubell. Oils, Watercolors,
  Graphics
Snelgrove, Walter H
Snow, John
Snow, Michael
Snyder, James Wilbert (Wilb). Watercolors
Snyder, Joan. Oils, Acrylics
Sokole, Miron. Oils, Acrylics
Solman, Joseph. Oils, Gouache
Solomon, Daniel. Acrylics
Solomon, Hyde. Oils
Solomon, Syd
Soloway, Reta. Oils
Solowey, Ben
Sommerburg, Miriam
Sonenberg, Jack
Sonfist, Alan
Sorby, J Richard. Acrylics, Watercolors,
  Mixed Media
Soria, Paola (Paola Soria Sereni). Oils

Souden, James G
Sowers, Miriam R. Oils
Soyer, Isaac. Oils
Soyer, Moses
Soyer, Raphael. Oils, Graphics
Spandorf, Lily Gabriella. Gouache, Water-
  colors, Mixed Media
Spaulding, Warren Dan. Watercolors,
  Acrylics, Oils, Pencil, Ink
Speight, Francis
Spelman, Jill Sullivan. Acrylics
Spencer (Mary Scruggs-Spencer). Oils
Sperakis, Nicholas George
Spickett, Ronald John (Sr). Oils
Spidell, Enid Jean
Spongberg, Grace. Watercolors
Sprague, Mark Anderson. Oils, Polymers,
  Collage
Spruce, Everett Franklin
Spruyt, E Lee. Oils & Gouache, Encaustic
Spurgeon, Sarah (Edna M)
Squires, Gerald Leopold. Acrylics, Clay
Squires, Norma-Jean
Stacks, Leon. Oils, Acrylics
Stadler, Albert. Acrylics
Staempfli, George W
Stahl, Ben (Albert)
Stamos, Theodoros (S)
Stamper, Willson Young. Oils
Stanczak, Julian
Stanley, Bob. Acrylics
Stapp, Ray Veryl. Oils
Staprans, Raimonds. Oils, Plastics
Stark, Melville F. Oils, Watercolors,
  Pastels, Acrylics
Starrs, Mildred. Watercolors
Stasack, Edward Armen
Stasik, Andrew J
Statman, Jan B. Oils, Acrylics, Water-
  colors
Stefanelli, Joseph J
Stegall, James Park. Oils
Stegeman, Charles. Oils, Acrylics
Steider, Doris. Egg Tempera
Stein, Harve. Watercolors
Stein, Maurice Jay
Stein, Walter. Oils, Watercolors
Steinberg, Isador N
Steinfels, Melville P
Steinhouse, Tobie (Thelma)
Steinke, Bettina. Oils, Pastels, Charcoal
Steinmetz, Grace Ernst Titus. Oils,
  Casein, Acrylics
Stell, H Kenyon. Acrylics, Oils, Wood
Stella, Frank
Stenbery, Algot. Gouache
Sternberg, Harry. Acrylics
Sterne, Dahli. Oils
Sterne, Hedda
Stevens, Edward John, Jr. Gouache
Stevens, May. Oils, Acrylics
Stevens, Walter Hollis. Watercolors,
  Acrylics, Oils
Stevenson, A Brockie. Acrylics
Stevenson, Branson Graves. Graphics
Stevenson, Florence Ezzell. Oils, Water-
  colors
Stevenson, Ruth Rolston. Watercolors, Oils,
  Pencil
Stewart, Arthur. Watercolors, Oils,
  Acrylics
Stewart, Dorothy S. Oils, Watercolors
Stewart, Jack. Acrylics
Stewart, Jarvis Anthony. Acrylics, Oils
Still, Clyfford
Stinski, Gerald Paul. Oils
Stipe, William S
Stoddard, Herbert C
Stoffa, Michael. Oils
Stoianovich, Marcelle
Stokes, Thomas Phelps. Oils
Stoll, Toni. Oils, Watercolors
Stoloff, Carolyn
Stoltenberg, Donald Hugo
Stomps, Walter E, Jr. Acrylics
Stone, John Lewis, Jr. Watercolors, Oils,
  Tempera

Painter (cont)

Stonebarger, Virginia
Storm, Howard. Acrylics
Storm, Larue. Graphics
Story, William Easton
Stout, Myron Stedman
Stout, Richard Gordon. Acrylics
Stowman, Annette Burr. Oils
Strater, Henry. Oils
Stratton, Dorothy (Dorothy Stratton King)
Strawbridge, Edward. Oils
Strawn, Melvin Nicholas. Oils
Strickland, Thomas J
Strisik, Paul. Oils, Watercolors, Acrylics
Strobel, Thomas C
Strombotne, James
Strong, Charles Ralph. Acrylics
Strother, Joseph Willis. Acrylics
Stroud, Peter Anthony. Acrylics
Stuart, Joseph Martin. Acrylics
Sturtevant, Harriet H
Suba, Susanne
Sublett, Carl C. Watercolors, Oils,
    Acrylics
Sudlow, Robert N. Oils
Sugarman, George. Acrylics
Sugimoto, Henry Y. Oils, Watercolors,
    Wood
Sullins, Robert M. Acrylics, Polyester
    Resins
Sullivan, Gene. Watercolors
Sullivan, Jim. Acrylics
Summ, Helmut. Oils, Watercolors,
    Graphics
Summer, (Emily) Eugenia. Acrylics, Poly-
    esters
Summerford, Ben Long. Oils
Summers, Dudley Gloyne. Oils, Casein
Summy, Anne Tunis. Acrylics
Sundberg, Carl Gustave. Porcelain, Enam-
    els, Graphics
Sundberg, Wilda (Regelman). Watercolors
Surovek, John Hubert. Acrylics, Water-
    colors
Surrey, Milt. Oils
Surrey, Philip Henry. Acrylics, Oils,
    Watercolors, Pastels
Sussman, Arthur
Sutherland, Sandy. Oils, Watercolors
Sutton, George Miksch
Suzuki, Sakari. Oils
Svet, M (Mrs Dore Schary)
Swan, Barbara. Graphics
Sway, Albert
Swazo (Patrick Swazo Hinds). Oils
Swensen, Mary Jeanette Hamilton (Jean).
    Watercolors, Graphics
Swenson, Anne. Oils, Watercolors
Swiggett, Jean Donald. Oils
Swinton, George. Oils,
    Watercolors
Swirnoff, Lois (Lois Swirnoff Charney).
    Acrylics, Gouache, Oils
Sykes, (William) Maltby
Sylvester, Lucille. Oils
Sylvia, Louis
Tabuena, Romeo Villalva. Acrylics, Oils,
    Watercolors
Tait, Cornelia Damian. Oils
Tait, Katharine Lamb. Stained Glass
Takai, Teiji. Oils
Takal, Peter
Talvacchio, Helen Steiner. Oils, Water-
    colors
Tam, Reuben. Oils, Acrylics, Inks
Tamayo, Rufino
Tambellini, Aldo. Mixed Media
Tania (Schreiber)
Tanksley, Ann. Oils
Tarnopol, Gregoire. Gouache
Tascona, Antonio Tony
Tatman, Virginia Downing
Tatti, Benedict Michael
Taubes, Frederic
Taulbee, Dan J. Oils, Watercolors
Taylor, Charles. Oils, Watercolors

Taylor, (Bertha) Fanning. Oils, Water-
    colors
Taylor, Frederick Bourchier. Oils
Taylor, Grace Martin. Oils, Casein,
    Acrylics, Graphics
Taylor, John (Williams). Oils, Gouache,
    Watercolors, Graphics
Taylor, John C E. Oils, Pencil
Taylor, Ralph. Oils
Taylor, Sandra J. Oils, Acrylics, Inks
Tcheng, John T L. Inks, Oils
Teague, Donald. Watercolors
Tedeschi, Paul Valentine
Tee-Van, Helen Damrosch. Oils, Water-
    colors
Teichman, Sabina. Oils, Watercolors, Clay
Ten Eyck, Catryna (Catryna Ten Eyck
    Seymour). Graphics, Acrylics
Tennyson, Merle Berry. Acrylics, Oils
Terenzio, Anthony. Oils
Teresi, Joseph Anthony. Oils
Terry, Emalita Newton. Watercolors,
    Acrylics, Oils, Graphics
Terry, Marion (E). Oils, Acrylics
Tettleton, Robert Lynn. Oils
Texoon, Jasmine. Oils
Teyral, John
Thelin, Valfred P. Watercolors, Acrylics
Thépot, Roger François. Acrylics, Gouache
Thiebaud, (Morton) Wayne
Thom, Robert Alan
Thomas, Alma Woodsey. Oils, Acrylics
Thomas, Reynolds
Thomas, Lionel Arthur John. Enamel, Oils
Thomas, Steffen Wolfgang
Thompson, Joanne. Oils, Bronze, Conté
Thompson, Kenneth Webster. Gouache,
    Watercolors
Thompson, Malcolm Barton. Acrylics,
    Watercolors
Thompson, Paul Leland, Oils, Acrylics,
    Watercolors
Thompson, Ralston Carlton. Oils, Water-
    colors
Thompson, Susie Wass. Watercolors
Thon, William
Thorne, Gordon (Kit). Acrylics, Watercolors
Thorne, M Art
Thorne, Thomas Elston. Oils, Acrylics
Thorpe, Everett Clark. Oils, Collages,
    Acrylics, Metallics
Thwaites, Charles Winstanley
Tiffany, Marguerite Bristol. Oils
Tigerman, Stanley. Acrylics
Tilley, Lewis Lee. Oils, Acrylics
Tillim, Sidney. Oils
Timmas, Osvald. Watercolors, Acrylics,
    Oils
Timmins, William Frederick. Oils
Ting, Walasse
Tinning, George Campbell. Watercolors,
    Acrylics
Tirana, Rosamond (Mrs Edward Corbett)
Tobey, Alton S. Oils, Acrylics
Tobey, Mark. Oils, Tempera
Tobias, Abraham Joel
Todd, Michael Cullen
Toigo, Daniel Joseph. Oils, Watercolors
Tolpo, Carl (Axel Edward). Plaster, Oils
Tolpo, Lily. Plaster, Oils
Tomlinson, Florence Kidder. Oils, Water-
    colors
Tompkins, Alan. Oils
Toney, Anthony. Oils
Tooker, George
Tormey, James. Oils
Torreano, John Francis. Acrylics
Toulis, Vasilios (Apostolos)
Tousignant, Claude
Town, Harold Barling
Tracy, (Lois) Bartlett. Acrylics, Oils
Traher, William Henry. Acrylics
Trauerman, Margy Ann. Watercolors
Travis, Olin (Herman). Oils
Treadwell, Grace (Ansley). Oils, Water-
    colors
Treadwell, Helen

Treaster, Richard A. Watercolor, Tempera
Trebilcock, Paul. Oils
Treiman, Joyce Wahl. Oils
Triano, Anthony Thomas. Oils
Triester, Kenneth
Trifon, Harriette
Triplett, Margaret L
Trissel, James Nevin. Oils
Trivigno, Pat. Acrylics, Oils
Trova, Ernest Tind
Trovato, Joseph S
True, Virginia. Acrylics, Pastels, Ink, Oils
Truex, Van Day
Tsai, Wen-Ying
Tschacbasov, Nahum
Tschidana, Harry Suyemi. Oils
Tsutakawa, George. Watercolors
Tubis, Seymour. Oils, Intaglio
Tucker, Charles Clement. Oils
Tucker, James Ewing. Oils, Watercolors,
    Graphics
Tulk, Alfred James. Oils, Watercolors
Turnbull, Grace Hill. Oils, Pastels
Turner, (Charles) Arthur. Oils, Acrylics,
    Charcoal
Turner, Bruce Backman. Oils
Turner, Theodore Roy. Watercolors, Oils
Turoff, Muriel Pargh. Metals, Enamels
Tuttle, Richard
Twardowicz, Stanley Jan
Twiggs, Leo Franklin. Batik
Twiggs, Russell Gould. Acrylics
Twitty, James (Watson). Acrylics, Oils
Twombly, Cy
Tworkov, Jack
Tyson, Mary (Mrs Kenneth Thompson).
    Watercolors
Tytell, Louis. Oils
Uchima, Ansei
Udinotti, Agnese. Oils
Udvardy, John Warren
Ullrich-Zuckerman, B
Underwood, Evelyn Notman. Watercolors
Unwin, Nora Spicer. Watercolors, Collage,
    Graphics
Urban, Mychajlo Raphael. Acrylics
Urban, Reva. Oils
Urquhart, Tony
Ushenko, Audrey Andreyevna. Oils
Vaccaro, Nick Dante. Mixed Media
Vaccaro, Patrick Frank (Patt Vaccaro).
    Oils
Valier, Biron (Frank). Collages
Vallee, Jack (Land). Watercolors
Vallee, William Oscar. Watercolors
Van Aalten, Jacques
Van der Poel, Priscilla Paine
Vander Sluis, George J. Acrylics
Van Der Voort, Amanda Venelia. Oils,
    Watercolors, Graphics
Van De Wiele, Gerald
Van Hook, David H
Van Hook, Nell. Oils
Van Meter, Mary. Acrylics
Vann, Loli (Mrs Lilian Van Young). Oils,
    Watercolors, Pastels
Van Roijen, Hildegarde Graham. Graphics
Van Veen, Stuyvesant. Oils, Watercolors,
    Gouache
Van Wolf, Henry
Van Young, Oscar. Oils
Varga, Margit. Oils
Vargo, John. Tempera, Watercolors
Vass, Gene. Oils, Inks
Vassos, John
Vaux, Richard. Oils, Graphics
Vazquez, Paul. Oils
Vela, Alberto. Oils
Velarde, Pablita
Vernon, Alexandra
Vevers, Anthony Marr. Mixed Media, Oils
Vicente, Esteban. Oils, Collage
Vickery, Charles Bridgeman. Oils,
    Acrylics
Vickrey, Robert Remsen. Tempera
Vidal, (Margarita) Hahn. Oils
Villa, Carlos

Villeneuve, Joseph Arthur
Vincent, Tom. Polymer, Liquitex, Oils
Viret, Margaret Mary (Mrs Frank Ivo).
  Watercolors, Oils, Acrylics
Vogel, Donald S. Oils
Von Gunten, Roger. Oils, Acrylics
Von Schneidau, Christian
Von Wiegand, Charmion. Oils
Voorhees, Donald Edward. Watercolors
Voris, Mark
Voyer, Sylvain Jacques. Acrylics
Vytlacil, Vaclav. Oils, Acrylics, Tempera
Waano-Gano, Joe. Oils, Watercolors,
  Acrylics, Charcoals
Wade, Robert Schrope
Wadsworth, Frances Laughlin
Wagner, G Noble
Wagner, John Philip
Wagner, Richard Ellis. Acrylics, Oils
Wald, Sylvia
Waldman, Paul
Waldron, James MacKellar
Walker, James Adams
Walker, Jerome. Mixed Media, Graphics
Wallace, Soni. Watercolors, Acrylics
Walsh, John Stanley. Watercolors
Waltner, Beverly Ruland. Acrylics
Walton, Florence Goodstein (Goodstein-
  Shapiro). Oils, Charcoals, Acrylics,
  Pastels
Wang, Yinpao. Watercolors
Ward, Lyle Edward. Oils
Ward, Velox Benjamin
Wardlaw, George Melvin. Acrylics
Warhol, Andy
Warner, Boyd, Jr. Sand, Watercolors, Oils,
  Acrylics
Warner, Jo. Oils
Warren, Betty. Oils, Pastels
Warren, Ferdinand Earl. Oils
Warshaw, Howard. Acrylics
Warsinske, Norman George, Jr
Washington, James W, Jr. Oils, Tempera,
  Pastels
Wasile, Elyse. Acrylics, Gouache, Oils
Wasser, Paula Kloster
Wasserman, Albert. Oils
Wasserman, Burton. Oils, Silkscreen,
  Spray enamels
Waterhouse, Russell Rutledge. Watercolors
Watford, Frances Mizelle. Watercolors,
  Acrylics, Oils
Watkins, Franklin Chenault. Oils
Watrous, James Scales. Mosaics
Watson, Robert. Oils on Canvas
Waugh, Coulton. Oils
Wayne, June
Weber, Albert Jacob
Weber, Idelle Lois. Oils
Webster, Larry Russell. Watercolors
Wechter, Vivienne Thaul
Wedin, Elof. Oils
Weeber, Gretchen. Watercolors
Weeks, James (Darrell) (Northrup)
Weeks, Leo Rosco. Oils, Watercolors
Weese, Myrtle A
Wehr, Wesley Conrad. Mixed Media
Weidenaar, Reynold Henry. Watercolors,
  Casein
Weidner, Roswell Theodore. Oils, Char-
  coal, Pastels
Weiller, Lee Green. Oils
Wein, Albert W
Weinbaum, Jean. Watercolors, Oils, Stained
  Glass
Weiner, Abe. Acrylics, Egg Tempera
Weingarten, Hilde (Mrs Arthur Kevess)
Weismann, Donald Leroy. Collage, Film
Weiss, Jean Bijur. Acrylics, Watercolors,
  Ink
Weiss, Lee (Elyse C Weiss). Watercolors
Welch, Livingston
Wellington, Duke. Oils
Welliver, Neil G
Wells, James Lesesne
Wells, Mac. Acrylics, Watercolors, Oils
Wentworth, Murray Jackson. Watercolors

Werner, Donald (Lewis). Watercolors,
  Collage
Weschler, Anita
Wesselmann, Tom. Oils
Wessels, Glenn Anthony. Oils, Acrylics
West, Clifford Bateman. Oils
West, Lowren
West, W Richard (Dick)
Westermeir, Clifford Peter
Wexler, George. Oils
Whinston, Charlotte
Whitaker, Frederic. Watercolors
Whitcomb, Jon
White, Charles Wilbert. Inks, Charcoals,
  Oils
White, Doris A
White, Roger Lee. Oils, Watercolors
Whitehead, Alfred
Whitehill, Florence (Fitch). Watercolors
Whitlow, Tyrel Eugene. Oils
Whitmore, Coby
Whitmore, Lenore K. Mixed Media
Whitney, Edgar Albert. Watercolors
Whyte, Raymond A. Oils
Wickiser, Ralph Lewanda. Oils
Wicks, Eugene Claude. Oils
Wiegand, Robert
Wieghardt, Paul
Wieland, Joyce
Wiener, Samuel G
Wier, Gordon D (Don)
Wiggins, Bill. Oils
Wight, Frederick S
Wilbert, Robert John. Oils, Watercolors
Wilde, John. Oils, Pencil, Silverpoint
Wiley, William T
Wilke, Ulfert S. Oils, Acrylics
Wilkinson, Kirk Cook. Watercolors,
  Casein, Acrylics
Will, John A. Graphics
Willer, Jim
Williams, Franklin. Acrylics
Williams, Guy
Williams, Hiram Draper. Oils
Williams, Neil
Williams, Tommy Carrol. Acrylics
Williams, Walter (Henry)
Williamson, Clara McDonald. Oils
Wilmeth, Hal Turner
Wilner, Marie Spring. Oils, Watercolors,
  Collage, Plastic
Wilson, Ben. Oils
Wilson, Charles Banks. Egg Tempera
Wilson, Jane
Wilson, Sol. Oils, Casein, Watercolors
Wilson, Sybil. Acrylics
Wilson, (Ronald) York
Wimberley, Frank Walden. Collage
Winter, Lumen Martin. Watercolors,
  Oils
Winter, Roger. Oils, Pencils
Winter, Ruth. Oils
Winters, Denny
Winters, John L. Oils
Wiper, Thomas William. Mixed Media,
  Watercolors, Acrylics, Film
Wisnosky, John G. Acrylics, Intaglio, Mixed
  Media
Witham, Vernon Clint. Mixed Media
Witkin, Jerome Paul. Oils
Witt, Nancy Camden.
Woelffer, Emerson. Oils, Acrylics
Wofford, Philip
Wolfe, Townsend Durant. Oils, Bronze
Wolff, Robert Jay. Oils
Wolfson, Sidney. Oils
Wolins, Joseph. Oils
Wolle, Muriel Sibell. Lithographic Crayon,
  Watercolors
Wolpert, Elizabeth Davis. Oils
Wolsky, Milton Laban. Oils
Wong, Frederick. Watercolors
Wonner, Paul (John)
Wood, Harry Emsley, Jr
Woodlock, Ethelyn Hurd. Oils
Woodruff, Hale A. Oils, Watercolors
Woods, Rip. Mixed Media

Woodward, Cleveland Landon. Oils,
  Watercolors
Woof, Maija (Maija Gegeris Zack Peeples).
  Oils, Acrylics, Clay, Watercolors, Dye
Wortham, Harold. Oils
Wray, Dick
Wright, Barton Allen. Scratchboard,
  Acrylics
Wright, Catharine Morris. Oils, Water-
  colors
Wright, Frank. Oils, Graphics
Wright, Frank Cookman. Oils, Acrylics
Wright, Stanley Marc. Oils, Watercolors,
  Acrylics
Wuermer, Carl. Oils
Wyatt, Stanley. Oils, Tempera, Graphite
Wyckoff, Sylvia Spencer. Watercolors
Wyeth, Andrew Newell. Tempera, Water-
  colors
Wyeth, Henriette (Mrs Peter Hurd)
Wyeth, James Browning. Oils, Watercolors
Wynn, Donald James
Wynne, Albert Givens
Wyse, Alexander John. Oils, Ink, Pencil
Yaghjian, Edmund. Acrylics
Yater, George David. Oils, Watercolors
Yates, Sharon Deborah. Oils
Yektai, Manoucher. Oils
Yepez, Dorothy. Pastels
Yoakum, Delmer J. Oils, Watercolors
Yochim, Louise Dunn. Oils, Watercolors
Yoshida, Ray Kakuo. Oils, Acrylics
Young, Cliff. Oils, Acrylics
Young, John Chin. Oils
Young, Kenneth Victor
Young, Marjorie Ward. Watercolors, Pen &
  Pencil
Young, Webb. Watercolors, Oils
Youngerman, Jack
Younglove, Ruth Ann (Mrs Benjamin Rhees
  Loxley). Watercolors
Yrisarry, Mario. Acrylics
Yrizarry, Marcos
Yudin, Carol
Yunkers, Adja. Graphics, Pastels. Oils,
  Acrylics
Yust, David E. Acrylics
Zabarsky, Melvin Joel. Oils
Zacharias, Athos. Acrylics
Zajac, Jack
Zakanych, Robert
Zapkus, Kestutis Edward. Acrylics, Oils
Zavel, (Zavel Silber).
Zelanski, Paul John. Acrylics, Plexiglas
Zevon, Irene. Oils
Zilzer, Gyula. Graphics
Zimiles, Murray
Zimmerman, Paul Warren. Oils
Zimmerman, William Harold
Ziroli, Nicola
Zisla, Harold
Zoellner, Richard C
Zona, Rinaldo A. Oils, Acrylics
Zornes, James Milford. Watercolors
Zox, Larry
Zuccarelli, Frank Edward. Oils
Zucker, Jacques. Oils, Pastels, Gouache,
  Sanguine
Zucker, Murray Harvey. Acrylics, Collage
Zugor, Sandor. Graphics, Polymers,
  Acrylics, Oils
Zweerts, Arnold. Oils, Woodcuts, Mosaic

PATRON

Akston, Joseph James
Alsdorf, James W
Altschul, Arthur G
Bass, John
Berg, Phil
Berman, Muriel Mallin
Berman, Philip I
Bisgard, James Dewey
Blair, William McCormick
Boyer, Mrs Richard C
Browne, Robert M

Patron (cont)

Burrows, Selig S
Chapman, Mrs Gilbert W
Clowes, Allen Whitehill
Cohen, Wilfred P
Crawford, John McAllister, Jr
Dalton, Harry L
D'Amico, Augustine A
Daniels, David M
Davis, Mr & Mrs Walter
De Graaff, Mr & Mrs Jan
Del Junco, Emilio
Dowling, Robert W
Dreitzer, Albert J
Dunnington, Mrs Walter Grey
Eckstein, Joanna
Eidlitz, Dorothy Meigs
Eiteljorg, Harrison
Emil, Allan D
Fitch, George Hopper
Flinsch, Harold, Jr
Gimbel, Mrs Bernard F
Goldberger, Mr & Mrs Edward
Goldsmith, C Gerald
Goldsmith, Morton Ralph
Gollin, Mr & Mrs Joshua A
Goodman, Benjamin
Gottlieb, Abe
Greenwald, Charles D
Grey, Mrs Benjamin Edwards
Gross, Mr & Mrs Merrill Jay
Guggenheim, Peggy
Gumberts, William A
Gussman, Herbert
Handler, Mr & Mrs Milton
Harris, Leon A, Jr
Hartford, Huntington
Hecht, H Hartman
Hilles, Susan Morse
Hirsch, Hortense M
Holcombe, R Gordon, Jr
Hooker, Mrs R Wolcott
Huntington, John W
Irwin, George M
Johnson, Mrs J Lee, III
Kaplan, Alice Manheim
Katz, Joseph M
King, Ethel May
Klein, Esther M
Knox, Seymour H
Kreeger, David Lloyd
Latner, Albert J
List, Vera G
Lloyd, Mrs H Gates
Longstaffe, John Ronald
Ludington, Wright S
McDonough, John Joseph
Marks, Mr & Mrs Cedric H
May, Morton David
Meadows, Algur H
Melamed, Abraham
Miller, Mrs Robert Watt
Moore, Fanny Hanna
Murray, William Colman
Navas, Elizabeth S
Neuberger, Roy R
Neustadter, Edward L
Niemeyer, Arnold Matthew
Ogden, Ralph E
Palmer, Fred Loren
Parkinson, Elizabeth Bliss
Penney, Charles Rand
Pleasants, Frederick R
Pomerance, Leon
Pratt, Dallas
Rahr, Frederic H
Rauch, John G
Reiner, Mr & Mrs Jules
Reis, Mrs Bernard J
Richmond, Frederick W
Rockefeller, John Davison, III
Rockefeller, Nelson Aldrich
Roebling, Mary G
Romansky, Alvin S
Rosenwald, Lessing Julius
Roston, Arnold

Rothschild, Herbert M
Ruskin, Lewis J
Sandground, Mark Bernard, Sr
Schramm, James Siegmund
Schwartz, Eugene M
Selig, Mr & Mrs Manfred
Semans, James Hustead
Shapiro, Daisy Viertel
Sheldon, Olga N
Sloan, Mr & Mrs J Seymour
Smart, Mary-Leigh
Smith, Mrs Bertram
Smith, Lawrence M C
Solinger, David M
Sonnenschein, Hugo, Jr
Stachelberg, Mrs Charles G
Stemats, Peter Owen
Stralem, Donald S
Swann, Erwin
Turner, Joseph
Walter, May E
Webb, Aileen Osborn
Weiner, Ted
Weinstein, Mr & Mrs Joseph
Winokur, James L
Woods, Sarah Ladd
Wurtzburger, Janet E C
Zeisler, Richard Spiro

PHOTOGRAPHER

Aakre, Richard B
Adler, Billy (Telethon)
Ayling, Mildred Shoob
Barschel, H J
Beny, (Wilfred) Roloff
Coke, F Van Deren
Colburn, Carol (Harriet)
Daniel, Roxanne
Davis, Philip Charles
Edwards, Ellender Morgan
Eidlitz, Dorothy Meigs
Elisofon, Eliot
Ford, Charles Henri
Freed, David
Gay, Eric Lynn
Haar, Francis
Higa, (Yoshiharu)
Hodgson, Trevor
Holmes, Reginald
Hough, Richard
Howell, Raymond
Huth, Marta
Johnson, Robert Lewis
Johnson, Selina (Tetzlaff)
Karsh, Yousuf
Krims, Leslie Robert
Kunie
Lee, George J
Levy, David Corcos
Margolies, John Samuel
Martmer, William P
Meyer, Ursula
Morgan, Barbara Brooks
Morrison, Boone M
Musgrave, Shirley H
Namuth, Hans
Newman, Arnold
Norman, Dorothy (S)
Olmsted, Pat
Orkin, Ruth (Mrs Morris Engel)
Parker, Ann (Ann Parker Neal)
Phelps, Nan Dee
Pollack, Peter
Reider, David H
Reynolds, Harry Reuben
Rich, Frances L
Riley, Art (Arthur Irwin)
Ruscha, Edward Joseph
Salmoiraghi, Frank
Schley, Evander Duer (Van)
Schulze, John H
Shotwell, Helen Harvey
Siegel, Adrian
Sinsabaugh, Art
Smith, Henry Holmes

Spencer, Hugh
Spongberg, Grace
Stark, Ronald C
Stuler, Jack
Twardowicz, Stanley Jan
Uelsmann, Jerry
Ullrich-Zuckerman, B
Vanco, John Leroy
Wade, Robert Schrope

POTTER
See also Ceramist & Craftsman

Brown, Charles Moses (Charlie). Clays
Bunker, Eugene Francis, Jr (Gene). Stoneware, Porcelain
Carey, James Sheldon. Ceramics, Glass
Chee, May
Easley, Loyce Rogers
Frank, David. Clay
Grippe, Florence (Berg)
Hara, Teruo. Ceramics, Steel
Lincoln, Richard Mather. Ceramics
Marsh, (Edwin) Thomas. Ceramics
Nicholas, Donna Lee. Clay
Olsen, Frederick L. Ceramics
Peeler, Richard. Ceramics
Wildenhain, Frans
Williams, Gerald. Clays

PRINTMAKER
See also Graphic Artist, Lithographer & Serigrapher

Abeles, Sigmund
Achepohl, Keith Anden
Adelman, Dorothy (Lee) McClintock
Adler, Lee. Oils, Silkscreen Printing
Ahlgren, Roy B. Acrylics
Albers, Josef
Alicea, Jose R
Alps, Glen Earl
Amen, Irving. Oils
Anaya, Stephen Raul
Anderson, Lennart
Anderson, Ronald Trent
Andrus, James Roman. Oils
Appel, Keith Kenneth
Argeropolos, (Basil) Theodore. Acrylics
Arnold, Paul Beaver. Woodcut, Intaglio
Asher, Lila Oliver. Wood & Linoleum Block
Auvil, Kenneth William
Ay-O
Barnet, Will. Graphics
Bate, Norman Arthur
Baumbach, Harold. Oils
Bayefsky, Aba. Graphics
Bell, Alistair Macready. Woodcut, Intaglio, Watercolors
Benz, Lee R. Woodcut, Cast Stone (Metal), Wood, Alabaster, Marble
Berdich, Vera. Intaglio
Berman, Ariane R. Acrylics, Wood
Bernard, David Edwin. Intaglio
Bieler, Andre Charles. Acrylics, Oils
Bileck, Marvin. Graphics
Birmelin, August Robert
Blackburn, Morris (Atkinson). Oils, Watercolors, Gouache, Sumi
Blackwood, David (Lloyd). Watercolors
Blaustein, Alfred H
Block, Amanda Roth. Acrylics, Oils
Bothwell, Dorr. Oils, Acrylics
Bowman, Dorothy (Louise)
Boyd, James Henderson
Boynton, James W. Graphics
Brandt, Frederick Robert. Acrylics
Breiger, Elaine. Acrylics, Oils
Breverman, Harvey
Briansky, Rita Prezament
Brodsky, Judith Kapstein. Intaglio
Broner, Robert
Brooks, Wendell T
Brulc, Dennis
Bumbeck, David A. Intaglio

Cadmus, Paul. Tempera
Cain, James Frederick, Jr
Caiserman-Roth, Ghitta. Acrylics, Oils,
    Mixed Media, Graphics
Cale, Robert Allan. Graphics
Camins, Jacques Joseph. Oils
Campbell, Richard Horton. Oils
Cannon, T C (Tom Wayne). Oils, Acrylics
Calapai, Letterio
Caples, Barbara Barrett
Carson, Sol Kent. Oils, Acrylics
Cassara, Frank. Intaglio
Cassill, Herbert Carroll. Intaglio, Wood
Chafetz, Sidney
Chamberlain, Samuel. Graphics
Chesney, Lee R, Jr. Intaglio
Chieffo, Clifford Toby. Graphics
Christ-Janer, Albert William. Watercolors,
    Lithography
Christ-Janer, Arland F. Graphics
Cikovsky, Nicolai
Citron, Minna Wright
Clendenin, Eve. Acrylics, Ink
Cohoe, Grey. Intaglio, Oils
Colescott, Warrington W
Conover, Robert Fremont. Graphics, Oils
Copeland, Lila. Oils, Crayon, Lithography
Coughlin, Jack
Crutchfield, William Richard
Cyril, (Ruth). Graphics
Daily, Evelynne B
Danby, Ken. Tempera
Davies, Theodore Peter. Wood
Davila, Carlos
Davis, J Ray
Day, Wörden
Dehner, Dorothy. Bronze
De Matties, Nick Frank
Deshaies, Arthur. Graphics
Dillon, Mildred (Murphy). Wood
Dodworth, Allen Stevens
Dozier, Otis. Graphics
Drew, Joan. Graphics
Drewes, Werner. Watercolors, Woodcut
Driesbach, David Fraiser. Intaglio
Du Jardin, Gussie. Oils
Durieux, Caroline Wogan
Eagerton, Robert Pierce
Eckmair, Frank C
Eckstein, Ruth. Acrylics, Collage
Edwards, Ellender Morgan
Eichenberg, Fritz. Graphics
Elliott, Bruce Roger
Engle, Barbara Jean. Oils
Eppink, Norman R. Oils, Watercolors
Esler, John Kenneth
Ettling, Ruth (Droitcour)
Evans, Henry
Ferguson, Edward Robert. Oils, Acrylics
Florsheim, Richard A. Oils, Lithography
Forsberg, James Alfred. Oils
Forsyth, Constance. Watercolors,
    Aquatint
Fortess, Karl Eugene. Oils
Fournier, Alexander Paul. Acrylics
Frances, Harriette (Anton). Acrylics
Freed, David. Graphics
Freed, Ernest Bradfield
Freeman, Mark. Oils, Acrylics
Freimark, Robert (Matthew)
Fried, Robert Samuel
Fruhauf, Aline. Graphics
Gardner, Andrew Bradford
Gardner, Robert Earl. Intaglio, Lithography
Garwood, Audrey. Oils, Wood
Gary, Jan (Mrs William D Gorman)
Gehr, Mary (Mary Ray). Intaglio, Oils,
    Acrylics
Gelb, Jan
Geller, Esther (Esther Geller Shapero).
    Encaustic, Watercolors
Gersovitz, Sarah Valerie. Silkscreen
Gilkey, Gordon Waverly
Gill, Gene
Gilling, Lucille
Ginzel, Roland
Giorgi, Vita

Gold, Leah. Casein, Graphics, Stained
    Glass
Golden, Libby
Goldstein, Milton
Gomez-Quiroz, Juan Manuel
Gramberg, Liliana. Graphics
Greaver, Hanne
Grippe, Peter J
Haack, Cynthia Roach. Graphics
Haas, Richard John. Intaglio
Hadzi, Dimitri. Bronze
Hagan, (Robert) Frederick
Hari, Kenneth. Oils, Graphite
Hathaway, John Wallace. Watercolors,
    Graphics, Mixed Media
Heller, Jules. Graphics
Hertzberg, Rose. Oils, Watercolors
Hildebrand, June Mary Ann
Hildreth, Joseph Alan. Intaglio
Hillman, Arthur Stanley. Photo Silkscreen
Hnizdovsky, Jacques. Oils, Woodcuts
Hoare, Tyler James. Wood, Metals
Hodgell, Robert Overman
Hoehn, Harry. Graphics
Hoff, Margo. Acrylics, Collage
Homar, Lorenzo. Silkscreen
Hood, (Thomas) Richard. Graphics
Hoover, (Sidney) Todd. Graphics
Hotvedt, Kristine J
Hutton, Dorothy Wackerman. Graphics
Ingram, Judith. Acrylics, Wood Block
    Printing
Inman, Pauline Winchester
Irizarry, Carlos. Mixed Media
Isen, Harold Bernard. Bronze, Polyester
    Resins, Fiber Glass, Clay
Itchkawich, David Michael
Jacobson, Arthur Robert. Oils
Jameson, Demetrios George. Oils
Johnson, Lois Marlene. Intaglio, Silkscreen
Johnston, Ynez
Jones, John Paul
Kainen, Jacob. Oils
Kaplan, Jerome Eugene. Intaglio,
    Lithography
Kassoy, Bernard. Oils, Watercolors,
    Pastels
Kasten, Karl Albert
Kaulitz, Garry Charles. Acrylics,
    Serigraphy
Kemp, Paul Zane. Intaglio, Metal
Kendall, Viona Ann
Kermes, Constantine John. Oils, Acrylics
Kerslake, Kenneth Alvin
Keskulla, Carolyn Windeler. Watercolors
Kirsten, Richard Charles. Watercolors
Kitaj, Ronald
Kjargaard, John Ingvard. Acrylics
Knerr, Sallie Frost. Watercolors, Seri-
    graph, Lithograph
Ko, Anthony. Lithography
Kohlhepp, Norman
Kohn, Misch
Koppelman, Chaim
Koster, Marjory Jean. Wood
Kowalke, Ronald Leroy
Kozloff, Alexander Ivan. Oils, Watercolors,
    Wood
Krause, LaVerne Erickson. Acrylics, Oils,
    Woodcut
Krauser, Joel. Intaglio, Oils
Kreneck, Lynwood
Krug, Harry Elno
Landau, Jacob. Watercolors, Wood
Landon, Edward August
Lanyon, Ellen. Acrylics, Lithography
La Pierre, Thomas. Oils, Watercolors
Larkin, Eugene
Larkin, William
Lasansky, Mauricio
Leaf, Ruth. Graphics
Leff, Rita
Leiber, Gerson August. Graphics
Lewis, Stanley
Lieberman, Meyer Frank. Watercolors
Lipman-Wulf, Peter
Locke, Charles Wheeler

Loggie, Helen A
Long, Sandra Tardo
Longacre, Margaret Gruen. Aquatint, Dry-
    point
Low, Joseph. Graphics
Lowe, Marvin
Lowney, Bruce Stark. Lithography
Lozowick, Louis
McClelland, Jeanne C
McCray, Dorothy M. Intaglio
McGough, Charles E. Graphics
Machlin, Sheldon M
McIvor, John Wilfred
McKeeby, Byron Gordon. Lithography,
    Intaglio
McKennis, Gail Collins. Graphics
McKim, William Wind. Tempera, Acrylics
McKnight, Eline. Graphics
McNab, Allan
McNamara, Raymond Edmund. Graphics
McWhinnie, Harold James. Intaglio
Madsen, Viggo Holm
Maitin, Samuel (Calman). Graphics
Malone, Robert R. Mixed Media
Maltzman, Stanley. Charcoal, Graphics
Manarey, Thelma Alberta. Graphics
Mandzuik, Michael Dennis. Acrylics, Ink
Mann, Katinka. Polymers
Mann, Vaughan (Vaughan Grayson)
Manning, Jo
Marin, Kathryn Garrison. Oils, Pencil,
    Mixed Media
Marsh, Anne Steele
Martin, Bernice Fenwick. Oils, Graphics
Martin, Langton. Graphics
Marx, Robert Ernst. Intaglio
Masurovsky, Gregory. Ink, Graphics
Matheson, Donald Roy
Maurice, Alfred Paul
Mazur, Michael B
Meeker, Dean Jackson
Mellon, James
Meltzer, Doris
Melville, Grevis Whitaker. Oils
Merkin, Richard Marshall
Micheli, Julio. Assemblage
Milton, Peter Winslow
Miyasaki, George Joji
Molin, Brita. Acrylics
Morrison, Robert Clifton. Wood,
    Acrylics
Motherwell, Robert. Collage, Ink, Aquatint
Myers, Frances
Myers, Malcolm Haynie
Nama, George Allen. Intaglio
Narotzky, Norman David. Acrylics, Oils
Neal, (Minor) Avon
Neiman, LeRoy. Oils, Enamel
Nelson, Harry William. Oils
Nelson, Robert Allen. Stone, Oils
Nemec, Nancy
Nichols, Ward H. Oils
O'Connell, George D. Drypoint
O'Connor, Thom
O'Hara, (James) Frederick
Olds, Elizabeth
Page, John Henry, Jr
Paone, Peter
Parker, Ann (Ann Parker Neal)
Penkoff, Ronald Peter. Intaglio
Perlmutter, Jack
Peterdi, Gabor F. Oils, Intaglio
Petersen, Roland Conrad
Philbrick, Margaret Elder. Intaglio, Mixed
    Media
Philbrick, Otis
Picken, George
Pletcher, Gerry. Etchings, Woodcuts,
    Acrylics, Oils
Pohl, Louis G
Poleskie, Stephen Francis
Ponce De Leon, Michael
Pond, Clayton
Pozzatti, Rudy O
Price, Kenneth
Priest, Hartwell Wyse. Graphics
Quat, Helen S

Printmaker (cont)

Ragland, Jack Whitney. Acrylics, Serigraphy
Reichek, Jesse
Riess, Lore. Oils
Robbins, Hulda D. Oils
Roberds, Gene Allen
Robles, Glenn (Waggoner)
Rogalski, Walter
Rogers, P J. Graphics
Romano, Clare Camille
Rose, Herman. Graphics
Rosenberg, Louis Conrad
Rosenhouse, Irwin Jacob. Graphics
Rosenquit, Bernard. Oils, Gouache, Wood
Ross, Conrad Harold. Collage Intaglio
Ross, John T
Rossi, Barbara
Rotholz, Rina
Rowan, Dennis Michael. Intaglio
Rowan, Frances Physioc. Graphics
Ruffo, Joseph Martin
Rush, Andrew
Sachse, Janice R. Oils, Watercolors, Graphics
Sarsony, Robert. Oils, Watercolors, Graphics
Satorsky, Cyril
Saunders, J Boyd. Graphics
Schafer, Alice Pauline. Wood, Linoleum
Schanker, Louis
Scharff, Constance Kramer
Schiff, Lonny. Oils, Watercolors, Graphics
Scholder, Fritz, Printmaker
Scholder, Laurence. Intaglio
Schwartz, Aubrey E
Schwieger, Christopher Robert. Graphics
Seidler, Doris
Sexauer, Donald Richard. Intaglio
Sherwood, A
Sigismund, Violet M. Oils, Watercolors, Woodblock
Simson, Bevlyn A
Singleton, Robert Ellison
Skinner, Clara (Clara Skinner Guy)
Sklar-Weinstein, Arlene (Joyce). Acrylics
Smith, Moishe. Intaglio
Smith, William Arthur. Oils, Watercolors
Snow, John
Spagnolo, Kathleen Mary. Graphics
Sperakis, Nicholas George
Spitz, Barbara S. Intaglio
Spruce, Everett Franklin
Stanton, Martha Zelt
Stasack, Edward Armen
Steg, J L
Steinhouse, Tobie (Thelma)
Stewart, John P
Stoltenberg, Donald Hugo
Stovall, Luther McKinley (Lou)
Stratton, Dorothy (Dorothy Stratton King)
Summers, Carol. Wood
Swift, Dick. Graphics
Sykes, (William) Maltby
Szarama, Judith Layne. Pencil, Graphics
Talleur, John J. Intaglio
Taylor, Ralph. Oils
Thrall, Arthur. Intaglio, Acrylics
Tift, Mary Louise. Graphics
Tittle, Grant Hillman
Toulis, Vasilios (Apostolos)
Townley, Hugh. Wood, Concrete
Trosky, Helene Roth
Tschacbasov, Nahum
Turner, Janet E. Graphics, Mixed Media
Tyler, Valton. Aquatint
Uchima, Ansei. Wood
Unwin, Nora Spicer. Watercolors, Collage, Graphics
Vaccaro, Patrick Frank (Patt Vaccaro). Oils
Valier, Biron (Frank). Collages
Van Hoesen, Beth (Mrs Mark Adams). Intaglio
Viesulas, Romas. Graphics
Vogel, Donald

Walker, James Adams
Wasserman, Burton. Silkscreen, Spray Enamels
Weege, William
Weingarten, Hilde (Mrs Arthur Kevess)
Wengenroth, Stow
Whipple, Barbara (Mrs Grant Heilman)
Will, John A. Graphics
Williams, Walter (Henry)
Winters, John L. Oils, Intaglio
Wojinski, Frances Ann, OP. Intaglio
Wright, Frank. Oils, Graphics
Wujcik, Theo. Graphics
Yudin, Carol
Zemer, Yigal
Ziemann, Richard Claude
Zilzer, Gyula. Graphics
Zoellner, Richard C. Intaglio
Zwick, Rosemary G. Ceramics

PUBLISHER

Abrams, Harry N
Cowles, Charles
Praeger, Frederick A

RESEARCH ARTIST

Clare, Stewart

RESEARCHER

Boese, Alvin William

RESTORER
See also Conservator

Bailey, James Arlington, Jr
Bernstein, Gerald
Lysun, Gregory
Nelson, George Laurence
Rabin, Bernard
Roth, James Buford
Stacks, Leon
Wortham, Harold

SCULPTOR

Aarons, George. Wood, Stone, Bronze & Welded Metals
Abbate, Paul S. Marble, Bronze
Abbe, Elfriede Martha. Wood
Abbott, Dorothy. Marble
Abeles, Sigmund
Acconci, Vito
Acosta, Manuel Gregorio. Clay
Acton, Arlo C
Adams, Alice. Wood, Metal, Rubber
Adams, Katherine Langhorne
Adler, Billy (Telethon)
Agopoff, Agop Minass. Clay, Granite, Marble, Bronze, Wood
Agostinelli, Mario
Agostini, Peter
Ahlskog, Sirkka
Alaupović, Alexandra V. Bronze, Wood, Marble, Welded Steel
Albert, Calvin. Plaster, Metal
Albrecht, Mary Dickson. Steel, Bronze, Metals, Plastics
Albright, Malvin Marr
Allen, Courtney
Allen, Margo. Bronze, Terra-cotta
Allwell, Stephen S. Bronze
Amateis, Edmond Romulus. Stone, Bronze, Acrylics, Wood
Amelio, Gilbert Neil. Terra-cotta
Ames, (Polly) Scribner
Amino, Leo. Plastics
Anargyros, Spero. Bronze, Marble, Stone, Wood
Anderson, Jeremy Radcliffe. Wood

Anderson, John S. Wood
Andre, Carl
Andrews, Oliver
Andrus, Moulton Loyal. Epoxy, Aluminum
Anthony, Lawrence Kenneth. Metal, Wood
Antonakos, Stephen. Neon
Antonovici, Constantin. Marble, Bronze, Wood
Appel, Karel. Acrylics, Aluminum, Wood
Archambault, Louis. Metals
Arman. Plastic
Arneson, Robert Carston. Clay, Ceramics
Aronson, David. Encaustic, Bronze
Arp, Hilda Dora
Artschwager, Richard Ernst
Asawa, Ruth (Ruth Asawa Lanier)
Aschenbach, Paul. Steel, Marble
Auth, Robert R. Acrylics
Ayaso, Manuel. Goldpoint, Mixed Media
Bailey, Clark T. Welded Steel
Baird, Roger Lee. Wood, Metal, Plastics, Mixed Media
Bakanowsky, Louis J. Mixed Media
Baker, George. Bronze, Aluminum
Balog, Michael. Multimedia
Balossi, John. Aluminum
Band, Max
Barr, David John. Masonite
Barr, Roger Terry
Barrett, Bill
Barron, Harris. Bronze, Wood, Granite
Baskin, Leonard
Batchelor, Jonathan David. Acrylics, Bronze, Stone, Wood
Bates, Gladys Edgerly. Wood, Stone, Cast Stone
Bauermeister, Mary Hilde Ruth. Wood, Glass, Light
Beasley, Bruce. Acrylic Plastic, Metal
Begg, John Alfred. Bronze
Behl, Wolfgang. Wood, Bronze, Stone
Bejar, Feliciano. Crystal, Plastic
Beline, George
Beling, Helen. Reinforced Fiber Glass, Bronze
Belkin, Arnold. Acrylics
Bell, Enid. Wood, Terra-cotta, Stone, Marble, Alabaster
Belshe, Mirella Monti. Bronze, Plexiglas, Aluminum
Ben-Zion. Ironwork
Bender, Beverly Sterl. Marble, Alabaster, Wood
Benglis, Lynda
Benno, Benjamin G
Bentham, Douglas Wayne. Steel
Benton, Fletcher
Bentov, Mirtala. Bronze
Benz, Lee R. Stone (Metal), Wood, Alabaster, Marble
Berge, (Edward) Henry
Bermudez, Jose Ygnacio. Metals
Bernstein, Sylvia
Bertoia, Harry. Copper, Bronze
Bevilacqua, Francis. Chisel on Marble & Granite
Biddle, George
Biederman, Charles (Karel Joseph). Painted Aluminum
Binford, Julien. Acrylics, Marbles, Limestones, Beeswax
Bisgyer, Barbara G (Barbara G Cohn)
Black, David Evans. Plastics, Metals
Bladen, Ronald
Blai, Boris. Bronze, Wood, Stone
Blair, Helen (Helen Blair Crosbie). Bronze
Blair, Robert Noel. Acrylics
Blanc, Peter (William Peters Blanc). Wood
Blazeje, Zbigniew
Bleifeld, Stanley. Bronze
Block, Adolph. Bronze
Boaz, William G
Bodo, Sandor
Bodolai, Joseph Stephen. Film, Tape, Contemporary Materials
Boghosian, Varujan. Constructions

Bolinsky, Joseph Abraham. Bronze, Stone, Wood
Bolomey, Roger Henry. Steel, Aluminum
Bonet, Jordi. Cast Aluminum, Fired Clay, Cement, Plastic
Bookatz, Samuel
Booth, Laurence Ogden. Plexiglas, Felt, Steel
Borgatta, Isabel Case. Stone, Wood
Borne, Mortimer
Bornstein, Eli
Bostelle, Thomas (Theodore). Wood
Boulton, Joseph L
Bouquet, Gus. Clay, Graphics
Bouras, Harry D. Steel, Concrete, Bronze
Bourgeois, Louise. Wood, Latex, Plastic & Marble
Boussard, Dana. Fabric
Bowie, William. Metal
Boxer, Stanley (Robert)
Boyce, Richard. Stone, Bronze
Boyd, Donald Edgar. Fiber Glass, Fabrics, Bronze, Wood
Boyd, James Henderson
Braitstein, Marcel. Welded Steel, Bronze, Stainless Steel
Brams, Joan. Acrylics
Brcin, John David
Breed, Charles Ayars. Plastics
Breer, Robert C
Breinin, Raymond
Breitenbach, William John. Cast Aluminum, Polyester Resin
Breschi, Karen Lee. Clay, Mixed Media
Bright, Barney. Bronze, Other Medals
Brink, Guido Peter
Britton, Edgar. Bronze
Broh, Minerva Leedy
Brose, Morris
Brown, Bruce Robert
Brown, Joseph. Bronze
Brown, Judith
Brown, Marvin Prentiss. Industrial Materials
Brumer, Shulamith. Stone
Brun, Thomas
Bryant, Olen L. Wood, Clay
Buba, Joy Flinsch
Bucher, George Robert. Fibers, Polyester
Budd, David
Bueno, Jose. Woods, Oils
Bultman, Fritz
Burchess, Arnold
Burickson, Zoel. Stone, Bronze, Steel, Wood
Burnham, Lee. Bronze, Stone, Ceramics, Wood, Synthetics, Glass
Burrows, Tom. Fiber Glass
Burt, David Sill. Sheet Metal, Electrified Plastics
Busa, Peter. Woods, Plaster
Buscaglia, José. Bronze
Bush, Beverly
Butchkes, Sydney. Acrylic Sheet
Butterbaugh, Robert Clyde. Plastics, Metals, Woods
Buzzelli, Joseph Anthony. Metals, Woods, Plastics
Cabot, Hugh
Cage, Robert Fielding. Brass, Copper, Wood
Caglioti, Victor. Constructions
Cain, Michael Peter. Acrylics
Calder, Alexander
Calfee, William Howard
Callery, Mary
Campbell, Dorothy Bostwick
Campbell, Kenneth
Campoli, Cosmo
Canfield, Jane (White). Marble, Stone, Bronze, Terra-cotta
Cantini, Virgil D. Enamels
Caparn, Rhys (Rhys Caparn Steel). Bronze, Stone
Caplan, Jerry L. Terra-cotta
Caponi, Anthony. Stone
Cariola, Robert J
Carr, Sally Swan. Stone

Carrel, Claudia
Carstenson, Cecil C. Wood
Carter, Dean. Bronze, Wood
Carter, Granville W. Wood, Stone, Metals
Cascieri, Arcangelo
Castle, Wendell Keith. Wood
Castoro, Rosemarie
Catchi (Catherine O Childs). Bronzes
Caver, William Ralph. Metal
Cecere, Gaetano
Cervantes, Pedro. Welded Steel
Cesar, Gaston Gonzalez
Chamberlain, John Angus
Chandler, Elisabeth Gordon. Bronze, Marble
Chapps, John
Charles, Clayton (Henry)
Chase, Allan Seamans. Steel, Other Metals
Chase, Doris (Totten)
Chase-Riboud, Barbara Dewayne. Cast Bronze, Cast Aluminum
Chaudhuri, Patricia M
Chavez, Edward Arcenio
Chester, Charlotte Wanetta
Chinni, Peter Anthony. Bronze, Stainless Steel
Cho, David
Christo (Javacheff)
Chryssa, Varda
Cimbalo, Robert W. Graphics, Wood
Cipriano, Anthony Galen
Clague, John Rogers. Steel, Bronze, Fiber Glass
Clark, G Fletcher. Wood
Clark, John Dewitt. Black Granite, Bronze, Wood
Cleary, Fritz. Bronze
Clover, James B
Coe, Matchett Herring. Bronze, Stone, Wood, Marble
Colby, Victor E. Wood
Coletti, Joseph Arthur. Bronze, Marble, Granite, Limestone, Wood
Collins, Jim (Lee). Wood, Metals
Conlon, George. Marble, Bronze
Connaway, Ina Lee Wallace. Stone, Wood, Bronze
Cook, Richard Lee. Light, Sound, Movement, Neon, Plastic, Electronics
Cooke, Kathleen McKeith. Clay
Cooper, Lucille B. Clays, Acrylics
Cooper, Mario
Cooper, Phillis. Ceramics
Corse, Mary Ann
Corwin, Sophia M. Steel, Marble
Coughtry, John Graham
Craig, Martin. Metal
Crawford, William H
Crawley, Wesley V
Creecy, Herbert Lee
Cremean, Robert
Creo, Leonard E
Cresson, Margaret French. Bronze
Cronbach, Robert M. Direct Metal, Bronze, Concrete, Terra-cotta
Cronin, Robert (Lawrence). Welded Steel
Crotto, Paul
Crovello, William George. Marble, Steel, Acrylics
Dagys, Jacob. Wood, Bronze, Marble & Artificial Materials
Daingerfield, Marjorie Jay. Bronze, Marble
Dal Fabbro, Mario. Wood
Daly, Norman David
d'Andrea, Albert Philip. Bronze, Terra-cotta
Danhausen, Eldon
Daoust, Sylvia
Daphnis, Nassos. Epoxy, Plexiglas
Daphnis-Avlon, Helen. Acrylics, Ceramics, Metal, Graphics, Photo-silkscreen
Darricarrere, Roger Dominique. Steel, Glass
Davidson, Allan Albert. Marble, Bronze
Davis, David Ensos. Steel, Aluminum, Bronze, Wood
Davis, Esther M

Day, Worden
Dean, Peter
DeAndrea, John Louis. Fiber Glass
Deaton, Charles. Concrete, Mixed Media
De Bellis, Hannibal. Bronze
De Botton, Jean Philippe
De Cesare, Sam
De Christopher, Eugene Louis. Wood, Metal, Plexiglas
De Coux, Janet. Stone, Wood
De Creeft, Jose. Stone, Marble
De Forest, Roy Dean
de Garthe, William Edward
de Gerenday, Laci Anthony. Wood, Bronze
Dehner, Dorothy. Bronze
DeLap, Tony
DeLauro, Joseph Nicola. Bronze, Marble, Wood, Plastics
De Leeuw, Leon
de Lesseps, Tauni. Bronze, Lacquer
Delihas, Neva C. Plastics
De Lisio, Michael. Terra-cotta, Bronze
DeLonga, Leonard Anthony. Steel, Stone, Wood
De Lue, Donald. Bronze
De Marco, Jean Antoine
De Maria, Walter. Earth
De Nike, Michael Nicholas. Wood
De Niro, Robert
De Pedery-Hunt, Dora
De Rivera, Jose. Stainless Steel, Bronze
Derujinsky, Gleb W. Wood, Bronze
De Weldon, Felix George Weihs
DeWitt, Floyd Tennison. Bronze, Iron
Dickinson, Eleanor Creekmore. Mixed Media
Dienes, Sari
Dignac, Geny (Eugenia M Bermudez). Plastics
Dill, Guy Girard. Mixed Media
Di Meo, Dominick Generoso. Mixed Media
Dimondstein, Morton. Wood, Bronze
Dine, James
Dioda, Adolph T. Wood
Dirube, Rolando Lopez
Domareki, Joseph Theodore. Multi Media, Steel, Bronze
Dombek, Blanche M. Bronze, Wood, Metal, Clay
Donati, Enrico
Donson, Jerome Allan. Wood
Doster, Rose Wilhelm. Ceramics
Downey, Juan. Electronics
Doyle, Thomas J
Drew, Joan
Drewelowe, Eve. Mixed Media
Driesbach, Walter Clark, Jr. Stone, Wood
Drumm, Don
Drummond, (I G). Concrete
Dryfoos, Nancy. Marble
Dubin, Ralph
Duca, Alfred Milton. Polymers, Metals
Duhme, H Richard, Jr. Bronze, Stone, Terra-cotta
Dunwiddie, Charlotte
Du Pen, Everett George. Bronze, Wood, Terra-cotta, Marble
Dworzan, George R. Wood
Earl, Jack Eugene. Ceramics
East, N S, Jr. Metals
Edmonds, Nicholas Biddle (Nick). Wood
Egri, Ted. Metals, Wood, Mixed Media
Eide, Palmer. Acrylics, Wood, Stone, Mixed Media
Elder, Muldoon
Eldredge, Mary Agnes. Copper, Stone, Wood
Eliscu, Frank
Eloul, Kosso. Stainless Steel, Concrete
Elsky, Herb. Cast Polyester Resin
Elsner, Larry Edward. Wood
Emery, Lin (Lin Emery Braselman). Kinetics, Metals
Escobedo, Augusto Ortega. Bronze, Marble
Escobedo, Helen
Etrog, Sorel
Eversley, Frederick John. Multicolored Cast Transparent Plastic

Sculptor (cont)

Facci, Domenico (Aurelio)
Falk, Gathie. Clay
Falkenstein, Claire
Falzone, Michael Joseph. Acrylics, Mixed Media
Farr, Fred White. Bronze
Fasano, Clara. Terra-cotta, Bronze
FeBland, Harriet. Acrylics, Plexiglas
Feigenbaum, Harriet (Mrs Neil Chamberlain). Hay
Felguerez, Manuel. Acrylics, Plastics, Metals
Fenci, Renzo. Bronze
Fenton, Beatrice. Bronze
Ferber, Herbert
Fernie, John Chipman. Wood, Paper, Cardboard
Ferrara, Frank Vincent. Marble, Bronze, Terra-cotta
Fiero, Emilie Louise. Bronze, Marble
Filipovic, Augustin. Bronze
Filipowski, Richard E. Bronze, Brass, Silver, Steel, Aluminum
Filkosky, Josefa. Aluminum, Plexiglas
Fine, Jud. Mixed Media
Fingesten, Peter. Concrete, Watercolors
Finke, Leonda Froelich. Bronze, Wood
Finkelstein, Max. Metals
Fischer, John J
Fish, Robert (Robert James Field). Rubber
Fite, Harvey, Stone, Wood
Florio, Sal Erseny. Bronze, Marble
Fogel, Seymour
Fonelli, J Vincent
Fontanini, Clare. Stone, Wood, Metals
Forakis, Peter
Forrestall, Thomas De Vany. Tempera, Steel, Iron, Bronze
Fowler, Mary Blackford
Fox, Terry Alan. Mixed Media
Frank, Mary
Frankel, Dextra
Frazier, Le Roy Dyyon
Frazier, Paul D. Metals, Plastics
Fredericks, Marshall Maynard. Granite, Bronze, Marble, Stone, Aluminum, Wood, Polyesters
Fredman, Faiya R. Poly-foam
Freeland, William Lee. Wood, Steel, Plastics
French, Jared
Fried, Howard Lee
Friedeberg, Pedro. Wood
Friedman, Kenneth Scott
Frishmuth, Harriet Whitney
Frudakis, Evangelos William
Fuge, Paul H. Electronic Environments, Video Communication
Fuhrman, Esther. Bronze, Acrylics
Fuller, Sue. Plastics
Gabriel, Robert A
Gach, George. Wax, Wood, Plastic, Bronze
Gage, Frances M
Gaines, Natalie Evelyn. Metal, Plastics
Gallo, Frank
Gasparro, Frank
Gates, Harry Irving
Gaylord, Frank Chalfant. Granite
Geber, Hana. Silver, Bronze
Gebhardt, Harold
Gebhardt, Peter Martin. Metals
Gebhardt, Roland. Marble, Fiber Glass, Concrete
Geissbuhler, Arnold
Geist, Sidney. Wood, Stone
Gellman, Beah (Mrs William C McNulty)
Getz, Dorothy
Giamberstone, Paul. Welded & Cast Bronze
Giambruni, Tio
Gibran, Kahlil George. Steel
Gilhooly, David James, III. Clay
Gill, James (Francis)
Gill, Sue May
Ginnever, Charles. Steel
Giusti, George. Metals

Glickman, Maurice. Bronze, Wood, Stone
Glinsky, Vincent
Glover, Euphemia W. Bronze, Stone
Godwin, Robert Lawrence. Metals
Goeritz, Mathias. Concrete, Steel
Golubic, Theodore Roy. Stone, Plastics, Metals
Gonzales, Carlotta (Mrs Richard Lahey). Stone
Gonzalez, Xavier
Goo, Benjamin. Metals, Stone, Wood
Goodman, Estelle
Goodridge, Lawrence Wayne. Acrylics, Electronics
Gorski, Daniel Alexander. Mixed Media
Goto, Joseph
Gould, Stephen. Bronze
Goulet, Lorrie (Lorrie H De Creeft). Stone, Wood, Ceramics
Granlund, Paul Theodore
Grasso, Doris (Ten-Eyck). Terra-cotta
Grausman, Philip. Metals, Stone
Graves, Nancy Stevenson
Gray, Cleve
Graziano, Florence V Mercolino. Clays
Greco, Anthony Joseph
Green, David Oliver. Stone, Wood, Metals
Greenamyer, George Mossman. Steel, Aluminum
Greenbaum, Dorothea Schwarcz. Lead, Stone, Bronze
Greene-Mercier, Marie Zoe. Bronze, Steel
Greenwood, Paul Anthony. Bronze, Plastic
Gregory, Angela. Stone, Bronze, Aluminum
Gressel, Michael L
Grieger, (Walter) Scott
Grigor, Margaret Christian. Plasteline, Plaster
Grimley, Oliver Fetterolf. Papier-Mâché, Bronze, Wood, Stone
Grippe, Peter J
Gross, Alice (Alice Gross Fish). Terra-cotta, Wood, Bronze
Gross, Chaim
Gross, Irene (Irene Gross Berzon)
Grossman, Nancy
Grosvenor, Robert
Groth, Bruno. Welded Steel, Stainless Steel, Bronze, Wood
Grove, Edward Ryneal
Grove, Jean Donner (Mrs Edward R). Bronze, Stone, Wood, Plastics
Gruber, Aaronel De Roy. Lighted-kinetic, Acrylics, Metal
Gruppe, Karl Heinrich. Marble, Bronze
Guite, Suzanne. Bronze, Stone, Wood
Gussow, Roy. Stainless Steel, Bronze
Habergritz, George Joseph
Hadzi, Dimitri. Bronze
Halberstadt, Ernst
Hale, Nathan Cabot
Haley, John Charles. Bronze
Halkin, Theodore
Hall, Michael David. Aluminum
Hambleton, Bud. Steel, Wood
Hammon, Bill J
Hanbury, Una. Bronze, Stone
Hancock, Walker (Kirtland)
Hanes, Ursula Ann
Hansen, James Lee. Bronze
Hanson, Duane. Polyester Resin, Fiber Glass
Hardin, Adlai S. Wood, Bronze
Hardy, Thomas (Austin). Bronze
Hare, David
Harkavy, Minna
Harman, Jack Kenneth. Bronze
Harmon, Lily. Constructions
Harootian, Khoren Der
Harris, Julian Hoke
Harris, Margo Liebes
Harris, Paul
Harrison, Newton A
Hartwig, Cleo. Stone
Harvey, Donald Gilbert. Mixed Media
Hatchett, Duayne. Metal
Hatgil, Paul. Plastics

Hausman, Fred S. Acrylics
Hay, Dick. Clay
Hayes, David Vincent. Metal, Ceramics
Hayward, Peter. Bronze
Hebald, Milton Elting
Hebert, Julien
Helman, Phoebe. Steel, Formica
Hendler, Raymond. Acrylics, Polystyrene
Henkle, James Lee. Wood, Metals
Henry, John Raymond. Metals
Henselmann, Caspar
Herard, Marvin T
Heric, John F. Stone, Steel, Plastics, Bronze
Herron, Jason
Herschler, David. Stainless Steel, Gold
Hesketh
Hess, Emil John. Metal
Hicks, Harold Jon (Jack). Steel, Aluminum, Wood
Higgins, (George) Edward
Hill, Jim. Plexiglas, Metals
Hill, Megan Lloyd. Leather, Ceramics, Beads, Feathers
Hilts, Alvin. Wood, Stone
Hinman, Charles B. Acrylics
Hirsch, Willard Newman
Hoare, Tyler James. Wood, Metals
Hobbs, (Carl) Fredric. Steel, Fiber Glass, Acrylics
Hobson, Katherine Thayer
Hoffman, Edward Fenno, III. Bronze
Holbrook, Elizabeth Bradford. Clay, Wax, Stone, Bronze
Holmes, Ruth Atkinson
Holt, Charlotte Sinclair
Holvey, Samuel Boyer. Metal Direct Construction, Lumia
Hood, Ethel Painter
Horn, Milton. Bronze, Wood, Stone
Horne, (Arthur Edward) Cleeve
Horwitt, Will
Hostetler, David. Wood
House, James Charles, Jr. Wood
Houser, Vic Carl
Hovell, Joseph
Howard, Cecil Ray. Collage, Assemblage
Howard, Robert A. Welded Steel, Fiber Glass
Howard, Robert Boardman
Hsiao, Chin. Metal Constructions, Acrylics
Hubbard, Robert
Hudson, Robert H
Hueter, James Warren. Wood
Humes, Ralph H. Bronze
Hunt, Kari
Hunt, Richard Howard. Metals
Hunter, Robert Howard. Mixed Media
Huntington, Jim
Hurst, Ralph N. Alabaster, Wood
Hurtig, Martin Russell
Hyslop, Alfred John
Icaza (Francisco De Icaza). Acrylics, Woods, Bronzes
Indiana, Robert. Steel
Inukai, Kyohei. Acrylics, Metals
Iselin, Lewis. Bronze
Isen, Harold Bernard. Bronze, Polyester Resins, Fiber Glass, Clay
Jackson, Harry Andrew. Bronze
Jackson, Hazel Brill
Jacobs, David (Theodore). Aluminum, Rubber, Sound
Jacobs, Harold. Mixed Media, Multimedia
Jacobson, Yolande (Mrs J Craig Sheppard), Bronze, Wood
Janowsky, Bela
Jenkins, Paul Ripley. Wood
Jennewein, C Paul
Jennings, Francis
Jensen, Hank. Steel, Wood, Fiber Glass
Jensen, Leo (Vernon). Bronze, Polychrome, Wood
Jiménez, Luis Alfonso, Jr. Fiber Glass, Epoxy Coating
Johanson, Patricia (Maureen)
Johnson, Daniel LaRue

Johnston, Richard M. Metals
Jolley, Jerry (Geraldine Hazel Jolley)
Jones, Benjamin Franklin
Jones, (Charles) Dexter (Weatherbee), III
Jones, Edward Powis. Bronze
Jones, Elizabeth. Wax, Plaster, Silver,
  Gold, Bronze
Jones, Howard William
Jones, Jacobine. Stone, Bronze
Jones, W Louis. Acrylics, Wood
Judd, Donald Clarence. Metals, Wood,
  Concrete, Plexiglas
Judson, Sylvia Shaw. Bronze, Stone
Kahane, Anne. Wood
Kaish, Luise. Metals, Stone
Kalinowski, Eugene M
Kallem, Herbert
Kallweit, Helmut G
Kaltenbach, Stephen James
Kammerer, Herbert Lewis. Bronze, Stone,
  Terra-cotta, Steel
Kane, Margaret Brassler
Kangas, Gene. Metal, Mixed Media
Kapsalis, Thomas Harry
Karaberi, Marianthe
Karesh, Ann Bamberger. Acrylics
Karoly, Fredric
Kasak, Nikolas
Kassoy, Hortense. Wood, Marble, Bronze
Kasuba, Aleksandra
Katzen, Lila (Pell). Steel, Other Metals,
  Plastics
Kauffman, (Camille) Andrene
Kauffman, Robert Craig. Acrylics, Plastic
Kaufman, Mico. Bronze, Stainless Steel,
  Plastics
Kaz, Nathaniel
Kearl, Stanley Brandon. Cast Bronze
Kearney, John (W). Bronze, Silver, Gold,
  Steel
Kearns, James Joseph. Bronze, Fiber
  Glass
Keene, Maxine M. Bronze
Keene, Paul
Kelly, Ellsworth
Kelly, Lee. Metals
Kelsey, Muriel Chamberlin. Stone
Kepalas (Elena Kepalaite). Bronze
Kern, Arthur (Edward)
Key-Oberg, Ellen Burke. Wood, Stone,
  Terra-cotta
Kimmelman, Harold. Stainless Steel,
  Bronze
King, William Dickey
Kingsbury, Robert David
Kington, Louis Brent. Iron, Steel, Silver,
  Gold
Kipp, Lyman
Kiselewski, Joseph
Kissel, William Thorn, Jr. Bronze, Marble
Klavans, Minnie
Klein, Doris
Klein, Sandor C
Kline, Alma
Knapp, Sadie Magnet. Enamels
Knobler, Nathan. Stone, Wood, Bronze
Knorr, Lester
Knowlton, Grace Farrar. Clay
Koblick, Freda. Plastics
Koepnick, Robert Charles
Kohn, Gabriel
Komodore, Bill
Koni, Nicolaus. Wood, Marble, Bronze,
  Jade, Gold
Konzal, Joseph. Metals, Wood, Construc-
  tions
Kopmanis, Augusts A
Koras, George. Bronze
Koscielny-Parker, Margaret. Plexiglas
Kowal, Dennis J. Stone, Wood, Metal,
  Plastic
Kramer, Reuben. Bronze
Kratina, K George
Krebs, Rockne
Krentzin, Earl. Silver
Kreznar, Richard J
Kriensky (Morris) (E)

Krueger, Jack
Kruger, Louise. Wood, Bronze
Kuntz, Roger Edward. Bronze
Kupferman, Murray
Kurhajec, Joseph A
Kussoy, Bernice (Helen)
Kyriakos, Aleko. Bronze
Labino, Dominick. Glass
Lacroix, Richard. Acrylics
Lafon, Dee J. Mixed Media
Lagorio, Irene R
Lagunes, Maria (Maria Lagunes Hernandez)
La Malfa, James Thomas. Iron
Lamis, Leroy. Plastics
Lamont, Frances (Kent)
La More, Chet Harmon. Steel, Bronze
Landau, Rom. Bronze
Landis, Lily. Bronze, Stone, Epoxy
Landsman, Stanley
Landwehr, William Charles. Mixed Media
Langlais, Bernard. Wood
La Noue, Terence David. Wood, Tobacco
  Cloth
Lantz, Michael F. Bronze, Limestone,
  Marble
Larson, Sidney
Laslo, Patricia Louise. Bronze, Aluminum
Lassaw, Ibram
Lathrop, Gertrude K
Lauck, Anthony Joseph, CSC. Wood, Stone,
  Watercolors
Lazzari, Pietro. Concrete, Bronze, Mixed
  Media
Leaf, June
Ledyard, Walter William. Marble,
  Alabaster, Wood
Leeber, Sharon Corgan. Steel, Aluminum,
  Marble
Leeper, Doris Marie. Metal, Wood, Fiber
  Glass
Lehman, Irving
Leiferman, Silvia W
Lekakis, Michael Nicholas
Lekberg, Barbara Hult. Bronze, Steel
Lennie, Beatrice E C
Leon, Dennis
Lepper, Robert Lewis. Mixed Media
Levee, John H. Acrylics, Plexiglas
Leventhal, Ruth Lee. Bronze
Levine, Les. Gold
Levine, Marilyn Anne. Ceramics
Levinson, Mon
Levitan, Israel (Jack)
Lewis, Golda. Compages
Lewis, Stanley
Lewitt, Sol
Liberi, Dante
Liberman, Alexander
Lichtenstein, Roy
Liles, Raeford Bailey
Lionni, Leo. Bronze
Lipchitz, Jacques
Lipman-Wulf, Peter
Lipofsky, Marvin B. Glass
Lippold, Richard. Wire, Metals
Lipton, Seymour
Little, John. Bronze
Littleton, Harvey K. Glass
Littman, Frederic F. Bronze
Lloyd, Tom
Lochrie, Elizabeth
Lo Medico, Thomas Gaetano
London, Jeff. Mixed Media
Long, C Chee. Wood
Lopez, Domingo
Lopez, Rhoda Le Blanc. Clay
Lorcini, Gino. Aluminum, Stainless Steel
Lorenzani, Arthur Emanuele. Bronze,
  Marble
Lothrop, Kristin Curtis. Bronze, Wood,
  Stone
Love, Jim
Lovet-Lorski, Boris
Lowe, J Michael. Welded Metal
Lubbers, Leland Eugene. Metals
Ludwig, Eva. Wood, Ceramics
Lucchesi, Bruno

Lux, Gwen (Gwen Lux Creighton). Polyester
  Resin, Concrete, Metals
Lye, Len
Lyford, Cabot. Stone, Metal
Lynds, Clyde William
McCloy, William Ashby. Collage, Steel
McClure, Thomas F. Metals
McCracken, John Harvey. Fiber Glass,
  Wood
McCracken, Philip
McDonnell, Joseph Anthony. Bronze, Steel,
  Marble
Mc Elcheran, William Hodd
Mc Geoch, Lillian Jean. Bronze
McGowin, William Ed. Plexiglas, Urethane
  Foam
Machlin, Sheldon M
Mack, Rodger Allen. Cast Metals, Stone,
  Wood, Plastics
McKesson, Malcolm Forbes. Wood, Wood
  Constructions
MacLean-Smith, Elizabeth. Wood, Stone,
  Clay, Bronze, Plastics
McVey, Leza. Clay
McVey, William M. Stone
McWhorter, Elsie Jean
Makarenko, Zachary Philipp. Acrylics,
  Granite, Marble, Wood
Maki, Robert Richard
Malkasian, Gregor. Stone
Mallary, Robert
Mallory, Ronald
Manca, Albino
Mandel, Howard
Mangum, William (Goodson). Bronze
Manhold, John Henry. Marble, Bronze
Mankowski, Bruno
Manship, John Paul. Mosaics
Manton, Jock (Archimedes Aristides
  Giacomantonio). Bronze, Marble
Marans, Moissaye. Wood, Stone
Margo, Boris
Marisol, Escobar
Mark, Phyllis
Marozzi, Eli Raphael. Marble, Synthetic
  Stone
Martin, Knox
Martin, William Henry (Bill)
Martinelli, Ezio
Martino, Eva E. Woods
Mason, John. Ceramics
Mattiello, Roberto. Mixed Media
Mayhall, Dorothy A. Wood
Mayorga, Gabriel Humberto. Epoxy Plas-
  tics, Polyester Plastics
Mazzone, Domenico
Meadmore, Clement L. Steel
Medrich, Libby E. Bronze
Meizner, Paula. Fieldstone, Aluminum
Melcarth, Edward
Melchert, James Frederick. Clay
Mellor, George Edward
Messeguer, Villoro Benito
Metcalf, James
Meyer, Fred (Robert). Bronze, Terra-cotta
Meyer, Seymour W. Bronze
Meyer, Ursula. Metal
Michael, Glen
Midener, Walter. Metal, Wood, Clay, Bronze
Miles, Jeanne Patterson
Miller, Daniel Dawson
Miller, Donald Richard. Bronze, Stone,
  Wood, Terra-cotta
Miller, H McRae
Miller, Leon Gordon
Miller, Nancy. Plexiglas, Paper
Miller, Richard McDermott. Wax, Bronze
Millonzi, Victor. Neon
Mintich, Mary Ringelberg. Metals, Plastics,
  Clay
Miss, Mary
Mitchell, Henry (Weber)
Mochi, Ugo. Graphics
Mol, Leo. Bronze
Molinari, Guido
Montana, Pietro
Moore, E Bruce

Sculptor (cont)

Moquin, Richard Attilio. Clay, Plastic, Fiberboard
Morgan, Arthur C. Bronze, Marble
Morgan, Frances Mallory. Bronze, Marble, Wood
Morgan, Helen Bosart. Bronze, Plastic, Lead, Stone
Morin, Thomas Edward. Metals
Morris, George Lik. Marble
Morris, Hilda. Bronze, Cement, Sumi
Morris, Robert
Mose, Carl C. Bronze, Stone, Ceramic
Moskowitz, Shirley (Mrs Jacob W Gruber). Acrylics, Woods
Moss, Joe (Francis). Plastics, Metal, Wood
Mount, (Pauline) Ward
Mueller, Henrietta Waters. Acrylics, Steel, Aluminum
Mueller, M Gerardine, OP
Mundt, Ernest Karl
Murray, Richard Deibel. Acrylics, Stone
Murray, Robert (Gray). Steel, Aluminum
Myer, Peter Livingston
Myers, Forrest Warden
Myers, Legh. Marble
Nakian, Reuben
Nardin, Mario. Bronze
Nash, Katherine E. Metals
Natzler, Otto. Ceramics
Naylor, John Geoffrey. Aluminum
Neill, T Joseph. Wood, Plastics
Nelson, Carey Boone. Bronze, Marble
Neubert, George Walter
Nevelson, Louise
Nevelson, Mike. Metals
Newman, (John) Christopher. Aluminum
Newmark, Marilyn (Marilyn Newmark Meiselman). Bronze
Nickerson, Ruth (Ruth Nickerson Greacen). Stone
Nickford, Juan. Metals, Mixed Media
Nicodemus, Chester Roland. Ceramics, Bronze
Nierman, Leonardo M. Acrylics, Onyx, Bronze
Niizuma, Minoru. Marble
Nivola, Constantino
Noguchi, Isamu
Noordhoek, Harry Cecil
Norman, Emile. Acrylics, Wood, Bronze, Gold, Silver, Concrete
Norton, Ann. Stone, Wood, Bronze, Charcoal
Notaro, Anthony. Bronze, Marble, Wood
O'Doherty, Brian
Odorfer, Adolf. Ceramics, Wood
Oesterle, Leonhard Friedrich. Stone, Bronze
Offner, Elliot. Wood, Bronze
O'Hanlon, Richard E. Stone, Bronze, Copper, Brass, Aluminum
Ohashi, Yutaka. Collage
Oldenburg, Claes Thure
Olsen, Frederick L. Ceramics
Omwake, Leon, Jr. Acrylics
Oppenheim, Dennis A
Ordoñez, Efren. Concrete, Iron
Ortiz, Ralph. Mixed Media
Ortman, George Earl. Constructions
Ortmayer, Constance. Wood, Ceramic
Ossorio, Alfonso A
Ottiano, John William. Bronze, Gold, Silver
Padovano, Anthony John. Metal, Concrete
Paeff, Bashka (Bashka Paeff Waxman). Bronze, Marble
Papashvily, George. Stone
Paradise, Phil (Herschel)
Paris, Harold Persico. Plastics, Bronze, Graphics
Parks, Charles Cropper
Parks, Christopher Cropper
Parks, Eric Vernon. Bronze, Steel
Passuntino, Peter Zaccaria. Sculptor
Pattison, Abbott
Peabody, Amelia. Stone, Bronze, Ceramics
Pearson, Louis O. Stainless Steel

Pederson, Molly Fay. Acrylics, Brass, Copper
Peeler, Richard. Potter, Sculptor
Peiperl, Adam. Plastics, Light, Water
Pepper, Beverly. Steel, Acrylics
Perless, Robert. Bronze, Stainless Steel
Perry, Charles Owen. Metals, Plastics
Pershing, Louise. Stainless Steel, Brass, Aluminum, Cor-ten Steel
Pfeifer, Bodo
Picard, Lil
Pinardi, Enrico Vittorio. Wood
Pineda, Marianna (Marianna Pineda Tovish). Bronze, Wood, Stone, Ivory, Wax
Pinto, James. Acrylics, Bronze
Plamondon, Marius Gerald
Platt, Eleanor
Politinsky, F Augusta (Flora). Wax, Papier Maché
Portanova, Joseph Domenico. Bronze
Porter, (Edwin) David
Portmann, Frieda Bertha Anne
Posey, Leslie Thomas. Stone
Poucher, Elizabeth Morris. Graphics
Pratt, Dudley
Prestini, James Libero. Steel, Aluminum, Wood
Price, Kenneth
Proctor, Gifford MacGregor. Bronze
Pruitt, A Kelly. Oils, Bronze
Puccinelli, Raimondo
Purves, Austin. Tempera, Aluminum Casting
Quisgard, Liz Whitney
Rabinovich, Raquel. Glass
Rabkin, Leo. Sculptural Constructions
Rachelski, Florian W. Wood, Stone, Bronze, Marble
Ramirez, Eduardo Villamizar. Metal Constructions, Concrete Constructions
Randall, (Lillian) Paula. Wood, Stone, Plastics
Randall, Theodore A
Randell, Richard K
Rankine, V V. Plexiglas
Ratkai, George
Ray, Robert (Donald)
Rebeck, Steven Augustus
Recchia, Richard (Henry). Bronze, Marble
Reed, Hal. Acrylics, Bronze
Reeve, John Sebastian. Mixed Media
Regat, Mary E. Stone
Reginato, Peter. Steel
Reiback, Earl M
Reibel, Bertram. Wood, Bronze, Stone
Reimann, William P(age). Plexiglas, Stainless Steel, Pencil
Remsing, (Joseph) Gary
Renk, Merry (Merry Curtis)
Rennels, F M. Steel, Aluminum
Renouf, Edward Pechmann. Acrylics, Steel
Reopel, Joyce
Reynolds, Nancy Du Pont. Bronze, Lucite
Reynolds, Richard (Henry). Stone, Wood, Metal, Acrylics, Polymers
Rhoden, John W
Rich, Frances L. Bronze
Richard, Betti. Bronze
Richardson, Gretchen (Gretchen Rose Freelander). Stone, Marble, Alabaster
Richenburg, Robert Bartlett
Rickey, George W. Stainless Steel
Ridlon, James A
Risley, John Hollister
Riu, Victor. Granite
Roberts, Gilroy
Robles, Julian
Roche, Jim. Ceramics, Wire, Plastic, Ink
Rockburne, Dorothea
Rocklin, Raymond, Bronze, Steel, Wood
Rogers, John H. Bronze, Wood
Rohm, Robert
Roller, Marion Bender. Terra-cotta, Bronze
Romano, Salvatore Michael. Acrylics, Plaster, Plastics, Wood, Metals, Water

Romano, Umberto Roberto. Acrylics, Bronze, Marble
Romoser, Ruth Amelia
Rosati, James
Rose, Arthur. Steel
Rose, Thomas Albert. Plastics, Polyester, Fiber Glass
Roseberg, Carl Andersson
Rosenblum, Sadie Skoletsky
Rosenthal, Bernard J. Metal
Rosin, Harry. Bronze
Ross, Charles
Rosse, Maryvonne. Clay, Plaster, Wood, Bronze
Roster, Fred Howard
Roszak, Theodore
Rotan, Walter
Rothschild, Lincoln. Wood
Roussel, Claude Patrice. Wood, Stone, Steel, Plastics
Rovelstad, Trygve A
Rowe, Reginald M
Rubins, David Kresz
Rudy, Charles. Stone, Bronze, Wood, Terra-cotta
Rumsey, David MacIver. Television, Film, Electronics, Light, Sound
Russin, Robert I. Marble, Bronze
Rust, Edwin C
Rutsch, Alexander
Safer, John. Acrylics, Brass
Saito, Seiji. Stone, Bronze, Wood
Sakoaka, Yasue. Bronze, Marble, Steel
Salerno, Charles. Stone
Salter, John Randall. Acrylics, Wood
Samaras, Lucas
Samstag, Gordon
Sarnoff, Lolo. Fibers, Acrylics
Sato, Tadashi
Savoy, Chyrl Lenore. Woods, Metals
Scanga, Italo
Scaravaglione, Concetta Maria. Wood, Stone, Bronze, Copper, Terra-cotta
Scarpitta, Salvatore
Schaeffler, Lizbeth. Terra-cotta
Schlemowitz, Abram
Schmeckebier, Laurence E
Schmidt, Arnold Alfred. Acrylics
Schmidt, Julius. Bronze, Iron
Schmidt, Randall Bernard. Ceramics, Vinyls
Schmutzhart, Berthold Josef. Wood, Steel, Bronze
Schnackenberg, Roy
Schneider, Noel. Wood, Stone, Steel
Schnier, Jacques. Bronze, Plexiglas
Schnittmann, Sascha S. Marble, Bronze
Schonberger, Fred. Fiber Glass, Steel
Schreck, Michael Henry. Bronze
Schreiber, Martin. Acrylics, Steel
Schuller, Grete. Stone, Wood
Schultz, Roger d. Acrylics, Copper, Bronze
Schwalbach, Mary Jo. Mixed Media
Schwartz, Aubrey E
Schweitzer, Gertrude
Scriver, Robert Macfie (Bob). Clay, Bronze
Scuris, Stephanie
Searles, Stephen. Bronze, Stone
Secunda, (Holland) Arthur
Segal, George
Seidenberg, (Jacob) Jean. Bronze, Lead, Mixed Media, Wood
Seley, Jason
Sellers, William Freeman. Metals, Wood, Plastics
Serra, Richard
Seyfried, John Louis
Seyler, David W. Stone, Ceramics, Bronze
Shacknove, Reta. Mixed Media, Collage
Shapiro, Joel (Elias). Mixed Media
Shapshak, Rene
Shaw, Donald Edward. Mixed Media
Shaw, Richard Blake. Ceramics, Wood, Mixed Media
Shead, S Ray. Acrylics, Epoxy
Sheppard, Joseph Sherly
Sherbell, Rhoda. Bronze

Sherry, William Grant. Wax
Sherwood, A
Sherwood, Bette (Wilson)
Shimoda, Osamu. Iron
Shonnard, Eugenie F
Shore, Richard Paul
Shostak, Edwin Bennett. Wood
Sider, Deno. Clay
Silvercruys, Suzanne (Mrs Edward Ford Stevenson)
Simon, Bernard
Simon, Sidney
Simpson, Maxwell Stewart
Sims, Agnes
Sinaiko, (Avrom) Arlie. Wood, Bronze
Sine, David William
Sing Hoo (Sing Hoo Yuen). Bronze, Marble, Wood, Clay, Wax
Singer, William Earl
Sinnard, Elaine (Janice)
Sister Thomasita (Mary Thomasita Fessler, OSF)
Skop, Michael. Bronze, Polyester, Wood, Stone
Slick, James Nelson
Slivka, David. Bronze, Wood, Marble
Slobodkin, Louis
Small, Amy Gans. Wood, Stone, Metal
Smith, George W. Steel, Bronze
Smith, Gord
Smith, Leon Polk
Smith, Tony
Smithson, Robert I
Smyth, David Richard
Snelson, Kenneth D. Steel
Soffer, Sasson. Glass
Soleri, Paolo
Solowey, Ben
Sommerburg, Miriam. Wood, Stone, Stained Glass
Spampinato, Clemente. Bronze, Marble
Spaventa, George
Sponenburgh, Mark Ritter
Sprague, Nancy Kunzman
Squier, Jack Leslie. Resin, Fiber Glass, Bronze
Squires, Norma-Jean. Wood, Aluminum, Mirrors, Motors
Stankiewicz, Richard Peter. Metals
Staprans, Raimonds. Plastics
Stark, George King. Brass
Steczynski, John Myron
Steele, Ivy (Newman). Bronze, Wood, Resins
Steig, William. Wood
Stein, Ronald Jay. Plastic
Stein, Walter. Aluminum, Plastic
Steinbomer, Dorothy H
Steiner, Michael. Steel, Aluminum, Brass
Stelzer, Michael Norman
Stephens, Nancy Anne. Magnets, Ceramics, Plastics, Fluids
Stephens, Thomas Michael. Plastics, Steel, Aluminum
Stephenson, John H. Mixed Media, Ceramics, Metals
Stern, Jan Peter. Highly Polished Stainless Steel, Metals
Sterne, Dahli
Stevens, Lawrence Tenney. Marble, Bronze, Wood
Stevenson, Robert Bruce. Plexiglas
Stewart, Albert T
Stewart, John P
Stoloff, Irma
Stone, Sylvia. Plexiglas
Storm, Larue. Graphics
Strawn, Melvin Nicholas
Streeter, Tal. Steel
Streett, Tylden Westcott
Strider, Marjorie Virginia. Plastics
Struppeck, Jules
Sufi, Ahmad Antung. Bronze, Concrete, Polyester, Resin
Sugarman, George. Acrylics, Metal
Summer, (Emily) Eugenia. Acrylics, Polyesters, Wood, Metal
Sunkel, Robert Cleveland. Wood

Suttman, Paul. Bronze, Marble
Svenson, John Edward, Wood, Bronze
Swarz, Sahl, Bronze, Steel
Tait, Cornelia Damian
Tajiri, Shinkichi
Takemoto, Henry Tadaaki. Ceramics
Talbot, William (H M). Concrete, Stained Glass
Tambellini, Aldo. Mixed Media
Tania (Schreiber)
Tarr, William. Steel
Tascona, Antonio Tony
Tatschl, John. Wood, Glass, Bronze
Tatti, Benedict Michael
Tauch, Waldine Amanda
Taylor, Frederick Bourchier
Taylor, Marie
Taysom, Wayne Pendleton
Teichman, Sabina. Clay
Teller, Jane (Simon). Wood, Graphics
Terken, John. Bronze
Terrell, Allen Townsend
Tewi, Thea. Stone
Thek, Paul
Thomas, Lionel Arthur John
Thomas, Reynolds
Thomas, Robert Chester. Stone, Wood, Bronze
Thomas, Steffen Wolfgang. Bronze
Thompson, Joanne. Conté
Thompson, Malcolm Barton
Tobias, Abraham Joel. Plastics, Metals, Stones
Tobias, Julius. Concrete
Todd, Michael Cullen. Steel, Aluminum
Tolgesy, Victor. Steel
Tolpo, Carl (Axel Edward). Plaster
Tolpo, Lily. Plaster
Torres, John, Jr. Stone
Tovish, Harold. Bronze
Townley, Hugh. Wood, Concrete
Triester, Kenneth
Trifon, Harriette
Trova, Ernest Tind
Trudeau, Yves. Bronze, Plexiglas, Steel
Truitt, Anne (Dean). Woods, Acrylics
Tsai, Wen-Ying. Stainless Steel
Tsutakawa, George. Bronze
Tubis, Seymour. Intaglio, Bronze, Wood, Bone
Turano, Don. Bronze, Wood
Turnbull, Grace Hill. Marble, Wood
Turner, Raymond. Wood, Bronze
Turoff, Muriel Pargh. Metals, Enamels
Udinotti, Agnese. Steel, Oils
Udvardy, John Warren. Wood, Canvas, Metals, Plastic
Uhl, Emmy
Umlauf, Charles. Bronze, Marble
Unterseher, Chris Christian. Ceramics
Urban, Mychajlo Raphael. Plywood, Acrylics, Welded Steel
Urban, Reva. Aluminum
Urquhart, Tony. Plywood
Urry, Steven. Aluminum
Valentine, DeWain. Polyester Resin
Van Buren, Richard
Vance, George Wayne. Clay
Van De Bogart, Willard George. Hardware
Van Hook, Nell. Clays, Stone, Bronze
Van Loen, Alfred. Stone
Van Roijen, Hildegarde Graham. Metal, Graphics
Van Wolf, Henry
Varga, Ferenc. Bronze, Marble, Wood
Vargas, Rudolph
Vasa (Vasa Velizar Mihich). Plastics
Vass, Gene. Woods
Vilder, Roger. Kinetics
Viner, Frank Lincoln. Vinyl, Cheesecloth, Dyes
Vodicka, Ruth Kessler. Bronze, Brass, Wood
Voigt, Roben. Steel
Vollmer, Ruth. Plastics
von Meyer, Michael
Von Neumann, Robert A. Clay, Wood, Metals

Von Schlegell, David. Stainless Steel, Aluminum
Von Schneidau, Christian
Voulkos, Peter
Vrana, Albert S. Bronze, Concrete
Waddell, John Henry. Bronze
Wadsworth, Frances Laughlin
Wagner, G Noble. Stainless Steel
Walker, Herbert Brooks. Sheet Metals, Bronze
Walter, Valerie Harrisse. Marble, Teak, Mahogany, Bronze
Walton, Marion (Marion Walton Putnam). Marble, Bronze, Wood
Warneke, Heinz. Granite
Warsinske, Norman George, Jr. Metal, Bronze, Steel
Wasey, Jane. Stone, Wood
Washington, James W, Jr. Granite, Marble
Weaver, John Barney
Weber, Idelle Lois. Plexiglas
Weems, Katharine Lane. Bronze
Weill, Erna. Stone, Metal, Concrete
Wein, Albert W. Bronze, Marble
Weinbaum, Jean. Stained Glass
Weinberg, Elbert. Wood, Bronze, Marble
Weiner, Egon. Bronze
Weinman, Robert Alexander. Bronze, Stone, Wood, Metals
Weiss, Harvey. Bronze, Welded Brass
Welch, Livingston. Lead, Brass
Wells, Charles Arthur, Jr
Werner, Nat
Weschler, Anita. Stone, Aluminum, Plastic, Wood, Terra-cotta, Bronze
Westermann, Horace Clifford. Woods, Metals
Wheeler, Orson Shorey
Whinston, Charlotte
White, Bruce Hilding. Aluminum, Steel
White, Norman Triplett. Electronics, Plastics
White, Robert (Winthrop). Bronze, Terra-cotta, Stone, Wood, Tempera, Water-colors
Whitley, Philip Waff. Steel, Bronze
Widstrom, Edward Frederick. Bronze, Metals
Wille, O Louis. Wood, Stone, Bronze
Willenbecher, John
Willer, Jim
Williams, Gerald. Clays
Williams, Shirley C. Wood
Williams, Warner
Willson, Robert. Glass, Enamel, Ceramics
Wilmarth, Christopher Mallory. Glass, Steel, Wood
Wilson, Albert Leon
Wilson, Edward N. Metals, Concrete
Wilson, May
Wimberley, Frank Walden. Collage
Winer, Arthur Howard. Steel
Wines, James N
Wingate, Arline (Hollander)
Winkel, Nina. Copper, Terra-cotta
Winsor, V Jacqueline
Winter, Clark
Winter, Lumen Martin
Witt, Nancy Camden
Wojcik, Gary Thomas. Welded Metal
Wolfe Ann (Ann Wolfe Graubard). Bronze
Wolfson, Sidney
Woodham, Derrick James. Mixed Media
Woodham, Jean. Metals
Woods, Gurdon Grant. Concrete
Woods, Theodore Nathaniel, III. Plastics, Wood
Woody, (Thomas) Howard. Bronze, Assemblage
Worth, Peter John
Worthen, William Marshall. Steel, Bronze
Wright, G Alan. Bronze, Stone
Wright, Russel
Wyse, Alexander John. Wood, Glass, Tin
Young, Joseph Louis. Multi-Media
Zajac, Jack
Zammitt, Norman

Sculptor (cont)

Zavel (Zavel Silber)
Zemer, Yigal
Ziolkowski, Korczak
Zona, Rinaldo A
Zucker, Murray Harvey
Zuniga, Francisco. Bronze, Marble
Zwick, Rosemary G. Ceramics

SERIGRAPHER
See also Printmaker

Azuma, Norio
Bradford, Howard
Greenleaf, Esther (Hargrave)
Jensen, Marit
Kent, Corita, IHM
Ranson, Nancy Sussman
Shokler, Harry

SILVERSMITH
See also Craftsman & Designer

Krentzin, Earl. Silver
Wardle, Alfred H. Sterling Silver, Gold

Stage Designer see Designer

Tapestry Artist see Weaver

WEAVER
See also Craftsman

Beauchemin, Micheline. Wool, Acrylics,
  Metallic Threads
Cornfeld, Melissa Marein
Elliott, Lillian. Textiles
Fischer, Mildred (Gertrude). Fibers
Gregor, Helen Frances
Hoffmann, Lilly Elisabeth. Textiles
Lindgren, Charlotte. Fibers
Matson, Elina
Meredith, Dorothy Laverne. Fibers
Palau, Marta
Tawney, Lenore. Cloth, Collages
Tiffany, Marguerite Bristol

WRITER

Aach, Herb
Airola, Paavo
Albright, Thomas
Allen, Clarence Canning
Amaya, Mario Anthony
Ames, Lee Judah
Arnason, H Harvard
Arnheim, Rudolf
Aronson, Joseph
Artz, Frederick B
Ayre, Robert Hugh
Bach, Otto Karl
Bacon, Peggy
Baer, Jo
Baird, Joseph Armstrong, Jr
Baker, Charles Edwin
Ballinger, Harry Russell
Ballinger, Louise Bowen
Barker, Walter William
Barr-Sharrar, Beryl
Bartlett, Jennifer Losch
Barzun, Jacques
Bates, Maxwell Bennett
Baur, John I H
Benson, Elaine K G
Benson, Gertrude Acherman
Benton, Thomas Hart
Beny, (Wilfred) Roloff
Berenstain, Stanley
Berger, Klaus
Bier, Justus

Bookbinder, Jack
Borgzinner, Jon
Boros, Billi (Mrs Philip Bisaccio)
Botkin, Henry
Boyd, E
Brandon, Warren Eugene
Brandt, Rexford Elson
Brennan, Francis Edwin
Brewington, Marion Vernon
Brooks, Frank Leonard
Brown, Harry Joe, Jr
Brown, William Ferdinand, II
Brumbaugh, Thomas Brendle
Bruner, Louise Katherine
Burch, Claire R
Burt, David Sill
Bush-Brown, Albert
Butler, Joseph Thomas
Calas, Nicolas
Cameron, Duncan F
Campbell, (James) Lawrence
Campbell, Vivian (Vivian Campbell Stoll)
Caniff, Milton Arthur
Caswell, Helen Rayburn
Chamberlain, Betty
Chamberlain, Samuel
Chapin, Louis (Le Bourgeois)
Chase, Alice Elizabeth
Cheney, Sheldon
Christensen, Erwin Ottomar
Coates, Robert M
Cohoe, Grey
Cole, Sylvan, Jr
Coletti, Joseph Arthur
Constable, Rosalind
Constable, William George
Cooke, Donald Ewin
Cooney, Barbara (Mrs Charles Talbot
  Porter)
Cooney, John Ducey
Coplan, Kate M
Coze-Dabija, Paul
Crane, Roy (Campbell)
Cresson, Margaret French
Criquette (Ruth DuBarry Montague)
Crist, Richard
Cutler, Grayce E
Dal Fabbro, Mario
Damaz, Paul F
Dame, Lawrence
D'Amico, Victor Edmond
Danikian, Caron Le Brun
Danson, Edward B
Daugherty, James Henry
D'Aulaire, Ingri (Mortenson) Parin
Davidson, Abraham A
Davidson, Marshall Bowman
Dawley, Joseph William
Dean, Abner
De Angeli, Marguerite
De Borhegyi, Stephan
DeForest, Julie Morrow
De Jong, Gerrit, Jr
de Kolb, Eric
de Kooning, Elaine Marie Catherine
Delaney, Joseph
De Leeuw, Cateau Wilhelmina
Dentzel, Carl Schaefer
De Ruth, Jan
De Tolnay, Charles
Dickson, Harold Edward
Diller, Mary Black
Donohoe, Victoria
Dulcan, Caril E
Dunn, Alan (Cantwell)
Dutton, Bertha P
Duvoisin, Roger
Edgerly, Beatrice (Beatrice Edgerly
  Macpherson)
Eliasoph, Paula
Emmerich, Andre
Ets, Marie Hall
Evett, Kenneth Warnock
Fabri, Ralph
Farnham, Alexander
Farnsworth, Jerry
Farrell, Patric

Faul, Roberta Heller
Faulkner, Ray N
Fax, Elton Clay
Feininger, T Lux
Flavin, Daniel Nicholas, Jr
Flexner, James Thomas
Forsyth, William, II
Fosburgh, James Whitney
Foushee, Ola Maie (Mrs John M, Sr)
Franck, Frederick S
Freeman, Margaret B
Friedman, Bernard Harper
Frinta, Mojmir Svatopluk
Gablik, Suzi
Garver, Thomas H
Gary, Dorothy Hales
Gasser, Henry Martin
Geisel, Theodor Seuss (Dr Seuss)
Getty, J Paul
Giraudier, Antonio
Glickman, Maurice
Glimcher, Arnold B
Glueck, Grace (Helen)
Goldberg, Norman Lewis
Goldsmith, Barbara
Goodrich, Lloyd
Gowans, Alan
Grafly, Dorothy (Mrs Charles H Drummond)
Gramatky, Hardie
Graves, Maitland
Gray, Francine Du Plessix
Greenburg, Clement
Griffin, Rachael S
Grove, Richard
Groves, Naomi Jackson
Grube, Ernst J
Guggenheimer, Richard Henry
Gussow, Alan
Hackenbroch, Yvonne Alix
Hader, Elmer (Stanley)
Hale, Nathan Cabot
Halvorsen, Ruth Elise
Haskell, Douglas
Hastie, Reid
Hay, George Austin
Hayes, Bartlett Harding, Jr
Helck, (Clarence) Peter
Held, Julius S
Henrickson, Paul Robert
Herman, Vic
Herring, Jan(et Mantel)
Hess, Thomas B
Hirsch, Richard Teller
Hoff, (Syd)
Hogue, Alexandre
Holty, Carl Robert
Hooton, Bruce Duff
Hoover, F Herbert
Horn, Milton
Hornung, Clarence Pearson
Horton, Jan E
Howland, Richard Hubbard
Hunt, Kari
Hurd, Peter
Iselos, Dimitri Theodore
Jackson, Suzanne (Fitzallen)
Janis, Sidney
Jellico, John Anthony
Johnson, Crockett
Johnson, Pauline B
Jones, Elizabeth Orton
Jorn, Asger
Kaufman, Edgar, Jr
Kaufman, Mico
Kayser, Stephen S
Kenny, Bettie Ilene (Bik)
Key, Donald D
Klebe, Gene (Charles Eugene)
Kleinholz, Frank
Klitgaard, Georgina
Koch, Robert
Kootz, Samuel M
Kouwenhoven, John A
Kubler, George Alexander
Kurdian, Haroutiun Harry
Labino, Dominick
Labrie, Rose

Landau, Rom
Lariar, Lawrence
Lathrop, Dorothy
Laury, Jean Ray (Jean Ray Bitters)
Lecoque
Leighton, Clare
Lenski, Lois
Lent, Blair
Lerman, Leo
Lewison, Florence (Mrs Maurice Glickman)
Libby, William C
Lindsay, Kenneth C
Lipman, Juan
Lippard, Lucy Rowland
Logan, Frederick Manning
Loran, Erle
Lunde, Karl Roy
Luntz, Irving
Lynes, Russell
McCloskey, Eunice LonCoske
McFee, June King
McLanathan, Richard B K
Mainardi, Patricia M
Manning, Reg (West)
Mattil, Edward L
Mauldin, Bill
Mayer, Ralph
Meiss, Millard
Mendelowitz, Daniel Marcus
Michelson, Annette
Miller, Donald
Mills, George Thompson
Millsaps, Daniel
Moore, Ethel
Morgan, Charles H
Morley, Grace L McCann
Morris, Jack Austin, Jr
Muensterberger, Werner
Mugnaini, Joseph Anthony
Neal, (Minor) Avon
Newhall, Beaumont
Newman, Elias
Norman, Dorothy (S)
O'Doherty, Brian
Olsen, Herb
Olten, Carol (Carol Mirabile)
Packer, Clair Lange
Papashvily, George
Paris, Jeanne C
Parish, Betty Waldo
Parkhurst, Charles

Parsons, Kitty (Kitty Parsons Recchia)
Perret, George Albert
Petersham, Maud Feller
Phillips, Dorothy W
Phillips, Gifford
Pincus-Witten, Robert A
Pitz, Henry Clarence
Plath, Iona
Plaut, James S
Pollack, Peter
Pollack, Reginald Murray
Preuss, Roger
Pride, Joy
Putnam, Wallace (Bradstreet)
Rainey, Froelich Gladstone
Randolph, Gladys Conrad
Raveson, Sherman Harold
Reaves, Angela Westwater
Rembski, Stanislav
Rey, H A
Rice, Harold Randolph
Richman, Robert M
Robertson, Bryan
Rodman, Selden
Rosenberg, Harold
Rosenberg, Jakob
Rothschild, Lincoln
Sawyer, Helen (Helen Sawyer Farnsworth)
Scheibe, Fred Karl
Scholz, Janos
Schroeder, Eric
Schutz, Anton
Schwartz, Therese
Seiberling, Dorothy Buckler
  Lethbridge
Selvig, Forrest Hall
Shapley, Fern Rusk
Shaw, Charles Green
Shepler, Dwight (Clark)
Sipiora, Leonard Paul
Slate, Joseph Frank
Slive, Seymour
Sloane, Eric
Smith, Ralph Alexander
Snyder, James Wilbert (Wilb)
Soby, James Thrall
Spaeth, Eloise O'Mara
Spencer, Eleanor Patterson
Stampfle, Felice
Steinitz, Kate Trauman
Stern, Harold Phillip

Stevens, Elisabeth Goss
Stewart, John Lincoln
Stilwell, Wilber Moore
Stites, Raymond Somers
Sutherland, Sandy
Swarzenski, Hanns Peter
Sweney, Fred
Swinton, George
Sylvester, Lucille
Sylvestre, Guy
Taubes, Frederic
Taylor, Robert
Terry, Hilda (Hilda Terry D'Alessio)
Thiessen, (Charles) Leonard
Thompson, F Raymond
Thorndike, Charles Jesse (Chuck)
Torbert, Marguerite Birch
Town, Harold Barling
Tracy, (Lois) Bartlett
Trosky, Helene Roth
Tucker, Peri
Tudor, Tasha
Tunis, Edwin
Varga, Margit
Vermeule, Cornelius Clarkson, III
Von Wiegand, Charmion
Walsh, John Stanley
Wang, Yinpao
Ward, Lynd (Kendall)
Warner, Harry Backer, Jr
Waugh, Coulton
Wechsler, Herman J
Weisgard, Leonard Joseph
Weisman, Winston Robert
Werner, Alfred
Whipple, Barbara (Mrs Grant Heilman)
Whitaker, Frederic
Whitehill, Walter Muir
Wiese, Lucie
Willard, Charlotte
Williams, Hermann Warner, Jr
Wingert, Paul Stover
Winternitz, Emanuel
Wofford, Philip
Wolff, Robert Jay
Wolle, Muriel Sibell
Wright, Catharine Morris
Wyrick, Pete (Charles Lloyd
  Wyrick, Jr)
Ziegfeld, Edwin
Zigrosser, Carl

OPEN
EXHIBITIONS

OPEN EXHIBITIONS
NATIONAL, REGIONAL, AND STATE-WIDE

ALABAMA

DIXIE ANNUAL, Montgomery. Annual, Mar. Drawings, prints, watercolors, gouaches, only (matted). Open to artists of 13 states—Ala, Ark, Fla, Ga, Ky, La, Miss, Mo, N C, S C, Tenn, Tex & Va. Jury, prizes & mus purchases. Fee $4, three works per artist; maximum 5 ft by 5 ft. Entries & entry cards due Feb. For further information write Registrar, Montgomery Museum of Fine Arts, 440 S McDonough St, Montgomery, AL 36104

ARIZONA

DOUGLAS ART ASSOCIATION TWO FLAGS ART FESTIVAL. Annual, Oct. Open to all artists of U S & Mex. Cash awards. Prizes & purchase awards. Entry fee $3, limit two, 20% comn. For further information write Douglas Art Association, Douglas, AZ 85607.

HEARD MUSEUM GUILD, Phoenix. Annual, Nov-Dec. All original arts & crafts. Open to Indians of N Am, Indian students & those of Indian descent. Cash awards & ribbons. Fee 20% comn. Entry forms & work due Oct 9-Nov 6. For further information write Florence Knight, Chmn, Heard Museum Guild Indian Arts & Crafts Exhibition, 22 E Monte Vista Rd, Phoenix, AZ 85004.

PHOENIX ART MUSEUM CRAFTS EXHIBITION. Biennial, May. Crafts. Open to craftsmen of Ariz, Colo, N Mex & Utah. Jury, awards. Fee. Entries due as announced. For further information write Registrar, Phoenix Art Museum, 1625 N Central Ave, Phoenix, AZ 85004.

PHOENIX ART MUSEUM PAINTING & SCULPTURE EXHIBITION. Biennial, May-June. Painting & Sculpture. Open to artists of Ariz, Colo, N Mex & Utah. Jury, awards. Fee. Entries due as announced. For further information write Registrar, Phoenix Art Museum, 1625 N Central Ave, Phoenix, AZ 85004.

PHOENIX ART MUSEUM PHOTOGRAPHY EXHIBITION. Biennial, Oct. Open to Ariz photographers. Jury, awards. Fee. Entries due as announced. For furthur information write Registrar, Phoenix Art Museum, 1625 N Central Ave, Phoenix, AZ 85004.

PHOENIX ART MUSEUM WATERCOLOR & GRAPHICS EXHIBITION. Biennial, Jan-Feb. Open to Ariz artists. Jury, awards. Fee. Entries due as announced. For further information write Registrar, Phoenix Art Museum, 1625 N Central Ave, Phoenix, AZ 85004.

TUCSON FESTIVAL EXHIBITION. Biennial, Apr-May. All craft media. Open to all residents of Ariz. Juror, $2000 awards. Fee $4 per work. Entries due Mar 1-3. For further information write Jason D Wong, Exec Dir, Tucson Art Center, 325 W Franklin, Tucson, AZ 85705.

ARKANSAS

ARKANSAS ARTS CENTER DELTA ART EXHIBITION, Little Rock. Annual, Oct-Nov. All paintings & sculpture (not over 500 pounds). Open to artists born in or residing in Ark, La, Miss, Mo, Okla, Tenn & Tex. Cash awards & purchase awards. Fee $5, 10% comn. Entry cards & work due in Sept. For further information write Townsend Wolfe, Dir, The Arkansas Arts Center, Mac-Arthur Park, Little Rock, AR 72203.

ARKANSAS ARTS CENTER PRINTS, DRAWINGS & CRAFTS EXHIBITION, Little Rock. Annual, May-June. Prints in all media; drawings in all media; photographs in color and/or monochrome; crafts in metal, clay, textile, glass, wood, plastics & combined media. Open to artists born in or residing in Ark, La, Miss, Mo, Okla, Tenn & Tex. Cash awards & purchase awards. Fee $5, 10% comn. Entry cards & work due in Apr. For further information write Townsend Wolfe, Dir, The Arkansas Arts Center, Mac-Arthur Park, Little Rock, AR 72203.

FORT SMITH ART CENTER. Annual, Mar. Painting, watercolor, drawing. Open to artists of Ark, Kans, La, Mo, Okla, Miss, Tenn & Tex. Jury, prizes & purchase awards. Fee $5. Entry cards & work due Feb. For further information write Registrar, Fort Smith Art Center, 423 N Sixth St, Fort Smith, AR 72901.

CALIFORNIA

ALL-CALIFORNIA PRINT EXHIBITION, Los Angeles. Annual, Jan. All prints. Open to living Calif artists. Jury, over $1500 awards. Fee, limit on entries. Fees, forms & work due Nov 18. For further information write Betty Anderson, Los Angeles Print-making Society, 1028 Mission St, South Pasadena, CA 91030.

CALIFORNIA NATIONAL WATERCOLOR SOCIETY, Los Angeles. Annual, Sept. All water-based media. Open to all U S artists. Jury, purchase awards & cash awards. Work due Sept 13. For further information write Julon Moser, Secy, 10790 Wilshire Blvd, Los Angeles, CA 90024.

CALIFORNIA SMALL IMAGES EXHIBITION, Los Angeles. Biennial, Jan. Painting, prints, drawing, any media, sculpture (maximum size 18 inches). Open to residents of Calif. Jury, purchase awards. Fee $2 plus $2 handling per work, payable to Cart & Crate. Entries due around Nov 24-Dec 9. For further information write Josine Ianco, Gallery Dir, Art Dept, California State University at Los Angeles, 5151 State College Dr, Los Angeles, CA 90032.

LAGUNA BEACH ALL CALIFORNIA SHOW. Annual, July-Aug. Painting, graphics, sculpture. Open to members & residents of Calif. Cash awards & purchase awards. Fee $3, comn 33⅓%. Entry cards & work due June 22. For further information write Laguna Beach Museum of Art, 307 Cliff Dr, Laguna Beach, CA 92651.

MANY MEDIA MINI EXHIBITION, Redlands. Annual, Oct. All media, original work, total size not to exceed 15 inches in any direction (no photog). Open to all Calif artists. Fee $3 per entry, limit three. For further information write Redlands Art Association, 12 E Vine St, Redlands, CA 92373.

California (cont)

RICHMOND ART CENTER. Biennial, Dec-May (dates change). Painting, alternating with sculpture. Open to all artists. Jury, awards. Fee. Work to be hand delivered. For further information write Richmond Art Center, Civic Center Plaza, Richmond, CA 94804.

RICHMOND ART CENTER DESIGNER-CRAFTSMAN EXHIBITION. Annual, Sept-Nov (dates change). All craft media. Open to all artists. Jury, awards. Fee. Work to be hand delivered. For further information write Richmond Art Center, Civic Center Plaza, Richmond, CA 94804.

SAN BERNARDINO ART ASSOCIATION INLAND EXHIBITION. Annual, Oct. Oil, acrylic, watercolor, mixed, collage, graphics (no sculpture or photog). Open to all Calif artists. Cash awards & purchase awards. Fee $3 per entry, limit two, 30% comn. Entry cards & work due Sept 30. For further information write San Bernardino Art Association, P O Box 2272, San Bernardino, CA 92406.

SANTA CRUZ ART LEAGUE. Annual, Mar. Oil, watercolor, pastels. Open to all residents of Calif. Jury, awards announced on entry blanks. Fee $1.50 each entry; two of each category may be submitted but only one of each hung if passed by jury. For further information write Santa Cruz Art League, 526 Broadway, Santa Cruz, CA 95060.

SOUTHERN CALIFORNIA CHAPTER INDUSTRIAL GRAPHICS INTERNATIONAL, Los Angeles. Annual, Sept. All media. Open to any illusr, designer, photogr or painter. Prizes & ribbons. Fee $5 plus $15 for hanging. Work due July 4. For further information write O L Hopper, Industrial Graphics International, 6515 Wilshire Blvd, Suite 7, Los Angeles, CA 90048.

COLORADO

WESTERN COLORADO CENTER FOR THE ARTS, Grand Junction. Biennial (74-76-78-80), July. All painting & graphics. Open to artists of Ariz, Colo, Kans, Nebr, N Mex, Okla, Utah & Wyo. Cash awards. Fee $5, limit two, 25% comn. For further information write 8 West Biennial, Western Colorado Center for the Arts, 1803 N Seventh St, Grand Junction, CO 81501.

CONNECTICUT

CONNECTICUT ACADEMY OF FINE ARTS, Hartford. Annual, Aug. All media except watercolor. Open to all artists. Prizes. Fee $7 non-mem, 20% comn. Entry cards & work due July 28. For further information write Secy, Connecticut Academy of Fine Arts, Box 204, Hartford, CT 06101.

CONNECTICUT SOCIETY OF WOMEN PAINTERS, West Hartford. Annual, May. All original work. Open to women who reside in Conn. Cash awards. Fee $5 mem, $8 non-mem, per entry, limit two. Entry cards & work due Apr 27 & 28, St Joseph College, West Hartford. For further information write Vincenza Uccello, Chmn, 207 Branford St, Hartford, CT 06112.

NEW HAVEN PAINT AND CLAY CLUB. Annual, Mar-Apr. Oil, watercolor, acrylic, graphics & sculpture. Open to artists from the N Eng states & N Y. Prizes & purchase awards. Fee $6 for first entry, $4 for second. For further information write Mrs M C Greeley, 51 Trumbull St, New Haven, CT 06510.

SILVERMINE GUILD OF ARTISTS NATIONAL PRINT EXHIBITION, New Canaan. Biennial, Mar (next show, 74). All print media except monotypes. Open to all artists. Jury, purchase prizes. Fee; three works per artist allowed. For further information write Exhib Secy, Silvermine Guild of Artists, Inc, 1037 Silvermine Rd, New Canaan, CT 06840.

SILVERMINE GUILD OF ARTISTS NEW ENGLAND EXHIBITION OF PAINTING AND SCULPTURE, New Canaan. Annual, June. Oil, Watercolor, casein, polymer, pastel, mixed & sculpture. Open to artists of the six New Eng States & N Y, N J & Pa. Jury; more than $6000 in cash awards. Fee. For further information write Exhib Secy, Silvermine Guild of Artists, Inc, 1037 Silvermine Rd, New Canaan, CT 06840.

SLATER MEMORIAL MUSEUM, Norwich. Annual, Apr. All media. Open to all resident Conn artists. Jury, prizes. Fee $3 per piece, limit two; sculpture limited to 200 pounds. Entry cards & work due Mar 25. For further information write The Slater Memorial Museum, 108 Crescent St, Norwich, CT 06360.

WASHINGTON, D C

LIBRARY OF CONGRESS, PRINTS AND PHOTOGRAPHS DIVISION, NATIONAL EXHIBITION OF PRINTS, Washington, D C. Biennial, date varies. All fine print media, original prints, black & white or color, exclusive of monotypes, drawings, photographs or prints colored after printing. Open to printmakers of U S. Jury, purchases for the J & E R Pennell Collection. No fee. For further information write Prints & Photographs Div, Library of Congress, Washington, DC 20540.

MINIATURE PAINTERS, SCULPTORS & GRAVERS SOCIETY, Washington, D C. Annual, Oct. All media, size limited to 8 by 10, heads not more than $1\frac{1}{2}$ inches. Open to all prof artists. Prizes. Fee, out-of-town entries $6, local entries $5; 30% comn. Entry cards due Sept 15; work due Sept 23. For further information write Mary Elizabeth King, 5506 Greentree Rd, Bethesda, MD 20034.

FLORIDA

ART GUILD OF BOCA RATON. Annual, Feb. Original painting & sculpture. Open to all artists. Jury. Entries due Feb to be delivered by hand only. For further information write Art Guild of Boca Raton, 801 W Palmetto Park Rd, Boca Raton, FL 33432.

CAPE CORAL NATIONAL. Annual, Jan. All paintings (maximum size 50 by 50 inches). Open to all U S artists. Jury, cash awards. Fee $3 per entry or 2 for $5 plus $5 per crate, limit four. Forms & work due Jan 4. For further information write Cape Coral Art League, Box 425, Cape Coral, FL 33904.

LATIN QUARTER ART GALLERY, Tampa. Annual, Mar. All media. Open to all artists. Jury, prizes. Fee $5 one entry, $8 two entries. Entry cards & work due Feb, all work must be hand delivered. For further information write Oscar Aguayo, P O Box 5287, Tampa, FL 33605.

SOCIETY OF THE FOUR ARTS EXHIBITION OF CONTEMPORARY AMERICAN PAINTINGS, Palm Beach. Annual, Dec. Oils, watercolor, drawings, mixed, & flat collages completed since Jan, 72. Open to artists residing in the U S. Cash awards. Fee $3, limit 2 entries (fee refunded if entry accepted); comn 10%. Specific dates on which entry cards & work are due are announced in prospectus available upon request in Sept. For further information write The Society of the Four Arts, Four Arts Plaza, Palm Beach, FL 33480.

HAWAII

ARTISTS OF HAWAII, PART I & PART II, Honolulu. Annual, Part I in Dec, Part II in Mar. Part I includes work of whatever material, having a basically frontal viewpoint; Part II includes work of whatever material, intended to be seen in the round. Open to all artists residing in Hawaii. Juror. Fee $2 per entry, limited to three. Entries due for Part I, mid-Nov; Part II, mid-Feb. For further information write Selden Washington, Asst Dir, Honolulu Academy of Arts, 900 S Beretania St, Honolulu, HI 96814.

HAWAII NATIONAL PRINT EXHIBITION, Honolulu. Biennial, Apr-May. All media except monoprints. Open to all artists living in the U S. Jury. Fee $3 per artist, three entries per artist. Entries due no later than Feb 2. For further information write Joseph Feher, Honolulu Academy of Arts, 900 S Beretania St, Honolulu, HI 96814.

IDAHO

BOISE GALLERY OF ART. Annual, Mar or Apr. All media (two-dimensional, three-dimensional). Open to current residents of Idaho only. Jury, purchase awards, special mention. Fee $3 per object. Entries due mid-Feb or mid-Mar. For further information write Dir, Boise Gallery of Art, P O Box 1505, Boise, ID 83701.

ILLINOIS

ART INSTITUTE OF CHICAGO. Biennial, Mar-May. All media, not over 7 by 10 by 5 feet or weigh over 1000 pounds. Open to artists, 18 or over, legal residents of 100-mile radius of Chicago. Jury, awards. Fee none. Entries due Feb. For further information write Painting & Sculpture Dept, The Art Institute of Chicago, Michigan & Adams, Chicago, IL 60603.

NORTH SHORE ART LEAGUE NEW HORIZONS IN ART, Chicago. Annual, June. Painting, sculpture, graphics, photog. Open to Ill artists. Cash awards, purchase awards & ribbons. Fee 15% comn. Entry cards & work due mid-May. For further information write North Shore Art League, 620 Lincoln Ave, Winnetka, IL 60093.

ROCKFORD ART ASSOCIATION. Annual, Mar. Oil, watercolor, sculpture, graphic arts. Open to artists of Northern Ill & Southern Wis, exclusive of Chicago & Milwaukee. Jury, awards. Fee $5 per piece, limited to two, $3 for mem. Entries due Feb 10 & 11. For further information write Rockford Art Association, 737 N Main St, Rockford, IL 61103.

INDIANA

BALL STATE UNIVERSITY DRAWING & SMALL SCULPTURE SHOW, Muncie. Annual, May 6-June 30. Drawings & small sculpture not to exceed 150 pounds & no dimensions more than 36 inches. Open to all artists. Jury, awards. Fee $3, one entry per artist. Entry cards & work due Apr 1. For further information write William E Story, Dir, Art Gallery, Ball State University, Muncie, IN 47306.

EVANSVILLE MUSEUM OF ARTS & SCIENCE MID-STATES ART EXHIBITION. Annual, Nov. Painting, sculpture, watercolor, graphic arts, collage & mobiles (no photographs). Open to artists within a 200 mile radius of Evansville. Jury, awards. Fee $3 per work, limit of two works in any combination of categories. Entries due in Oct. For further information write Art Comt, Evansville Museum of Arts & Science, 411 S E Riverside Dr, Evansville, IN 47713.

EVANSVILLE MUSEUM OF ARTS & SCIENCE MID-STATES CRAFT EXHIBITION. Annual, Feb. Ceramics, textiles, silver & metal work, wood, enamel, glass & others. Open to artists within a 200 mile radius of Evansville. Jury, awards. Fee $3 for three objects or less. Entries due Jan. For further information write Craft Comt, Evansville Museum of Arts & Science, 411 S E Riverside Dr, Evansville, IN 47713.

HOOSIER SALON, Indianapolis. Annual, Jan-Feb. All media & sculpture. Open to Indiana artists, native or by residence in the state for one yr minimum. Jury, awards $4000-$5000. Fee $7.50. Entry due early Jan. For further information write Hoosier Salon Patrons Association, 201 Thomas Bldg, 15 E Washington St, Indianapolis, IN 46204.

INDIANAPOLIS MUSEUM OF ART INDIANA ARTISTS SHOW. Annual, Apr-May. Painting & sculpture. Open to artists who reside or have resided in Ind. Jury, awards. Two entries per artist. Entries due mid-Mar. For further information write Miss Suzanne Stafford, Indianapolis Museum of Art, 1200 W 38th St, Indianapolis, IN 46208.

INDIANAPOLIS MUSEUM OF ART OBJECTS & CRAFTS EXHIBITION. Biennial, Apr-May (73). Hand-crafted medium. Open to Ind artists. Jury, awards. Fee $3 per artist, limit three. Entries due mid-Mar. For further information write Miss Suzanne Stafford, Indianapolis Museum of Art, 1200 W 38th St, Indianapolis, IN 46208.

INDIANAPOLIS MUSEUM OF ART WORKS ON PAPER EXHIBITION. Biennial, Apr-May (74). Open to any artist who resides in or has resided in Ind. Jury, awards. Fee $3, limit three per artist. Entries due mid-Mar. For further information write Miss Suzanne Stafford, Indianapolis Museum of Art, 1200 W 38th St, Indianapolis, IN 46208.

MICHIANA REGIONAL ART EXHIBITION, South Bend. Biennial, May. Painting, sculpture, graphics & crafts. Open to artists in Mich & Ind, or former residents. Jury, awards. Fee $5, limited to two entries. Entries due one mo in advance (Apr). For further information write South Bend Art Center, South Bend, IN 46601.

WABASH VALLEY EXHIBITION, Terre Haute. Annual, Mar. All media. Open to artists within a 160 mile radius of Terre Haute. Jury, awards. Fee $3 for first entry, $2 for second and third, limit to three. Entries due Feb. For further information write Curator, The Sheldon Swope Art Gallery, 25 S Seventh St, Terre Haute, IN 47807.

IOWA

SIOUX CITY ART CENTER. Annual, Fall. All painting media. Open to residents of Iowa, Nebr, Minn & S Dak. One-man jury, up to $1200 in purchase & cash awards. Fee $3. Slides due Sept 24 to Oct 14. For further information write Dir, Sioux City Art Center, 513 Nebraska St, Sioux City, IA 51101.

KANSAS

KANSAS WATERCOLOR SOCIETY EXHIBITION, Wichita. Annual, Dec. Transparent aqueous on paper. Open to all artists living in Kan. Cash awards, prizes & purchase awards. Fee $5; comn 20%. Entry cards due before Oct 1 & work due Oct 1. For further information write Charles H Sanderson, Pres, Kansas Watercolor Society, 902 Waddington, Wichita, KS 67212.

WICHITA ART ASSOCIATION NATIONAL DECORATIVE ARTS & CERAMICS EXHIBITION. Biennial. Ceramics, textiles, small sculpture, glass, enameling, jewelry, metalry. Fee $10 for first entry, $7.50 for each additional entry. For further information write Wichita Art Association, 9112 E Central, Wichita, KS 67206.

WICHITA ART ASSOCIATION NATIONAL GRAPHIC ARTS & DRAWING EXHIBITION. Biennial, Apr & May. Print media & original drawings done within previous two yrs. Open to all living American artists. Fee $4, limit two entries. For further information write Wichita Art Association, 9112 E Central, Wichita, KS 67206.

LOUISIANA

LOUISIANA WATERCOLOR SOCIETY INTERNATIONAL, Baton Rouge. Annual, Nov-Dec. Water based, recent original paintings on paper. Open to all artists. Cash awards & purchase prizes. Fee $3 per entry, no limit to number of entries. Work due Oct 9-Nov 6. For further information write Carol Bailey, Corresp Secy, 238 Atherton Dr, Metairie, LA 70005.

NEW ORLEANS MUSEUM OF ART. Biennial, Spring. Focus on contemporary painting or sculpture by prof artists from thirteen-state region of Southeastern U S. Single juror, purchase awards. No fee. For further information write Artists' Biennial, New Orleans Museum of Art, Lelong Ave, City Park, New Orleans, LA 70119.

MAINE

OGUNQUIT ART CENTER NATIONAL PAINTING EXHIBITION. Annual, June-Sept. Oil, watercolor, mixed (originals only). Open to all U S artists. Cash awards. Fee $10, 25% comn. Entry cards due June 1 & work due June 10. For further information write Mrs F Nims, The Ogunquit Art Center, Hoyt's Lane, Ogunquit, ME 03907.

MARYLAND

ACADEMY OF THE ARTS MARYLAND ART EXHIBITION, Easton. Annual, Apr 15 to May 1. All painting, collages, graphics, sculpture. Open to artists born or residing in Md, students at Md art schs & members of Acad. Jury, cash prizes & purchase awards. No fee. Entry cards due Mar 29 & work due Mar 31. For further information write The Academy of the Arts, P O Box 605, Easton, MD 21601.

BALTIMORE MUSEUM OF ART ANNUAL EXHIBITION. Annual, usually in Dec. All media (slides or photographs of work not acceptable). Open to artists born or currently residing in Md. Jury, prizes & awards. No fee. Entries due as announced, usually a mo before exhib. For further information write Mrs Alice C Steinbach, Dir Pub Info, Baltimore Museum of Art, Art Museum Dr, Baltimore, MD 21218.

MASSACHUSETTS

ARTS ATLANTIC NATIONAL, Gloucester. Annual, Sept-Oct. Oil, watercolor, sculpture & graphics. Open internationally to all artists. Cash awards & medals. Fee $10 first entry, $5 each addn entry, 25% comn. Entry cards and work due by mid-Sept. For further information write to Arts Atlantic, Box 281, Rockport, MA 01966.

BERKSHIRE ART ASSOCIATION, Pittsfield. Annual, Oct. All painting, pastels, graphics, collages, sculpture. Open to artists of New Eng & N Y only. Cash awards, prizes & purchase awards. Fee $6. Entry cards & work due on published date in Sept. For further information write Mrs Samuel Boxer, Pres, 19 Paisley Terr, Pittsfield, MA 01201.

BOSTON PRINTMAKERS, Lincoln. Annual, Mar 18-May 6. All print media except monotypes. Open to all printmakers. Jury, awards. Fee $5, limit two. Entry cards & fees due Feb 3, work due Feb 10. For further information write Mrs S M Rantz, Secy, 299 High Rock St, Needham, MA 02192.

CULTURAL AFFAIRS COMMISSION NATIONAL PRINT EXHIBITION, Springfield. Annual, May. All print, no monotypes. Open to all U S artists. Jury, purchase prizes and one-man show award. Fee $4, limit two. Entry cards and work due Apr 19. For further information write Prof Josephine L Cecco, Springfield College, 263 Alden St, Springfield, MA 01109.

GREATER FALL RIVER ART ASSOCIATION NATIONAL. Annual, May. Painting, graphics, sculpture, pottery, glass, textiles. Open to all artists in the U S & Can. Jury, prizes & purchase awards. Fee $5 per entry. Entry cards & slides due Mar 1. For further information write Mrs Ralph L Gordon, 80 Belmont St, Fall River, MA 02720.

MARION ART CENTER BISTATE SHOW. Annual, Aug-Sept. Painting, print, sculpture, photog. Open to artists of Mass & R I. Jury, prizes. Fee $5 for two entries. Entry cards & fee due Aug 15 & work due Aug 23. For further information write Marion Art Center, Front St, Marion, MA 02738.

SPRINGFIELD ART LEAGUE FALL REGIONAL EXHIBITION. Annual, Nov-Dec. Oil, watercolor, casein, pastel, gouache, prints, drawings & sculpture. Open to New Eng States only. Jury, awards. Fee $6. Entry cards & work due Nov. For further information write Rena Anderson, 57 Sherwood Ave, West Springfield, MA 01103.

SPRINGFIELD ART LEAGUE SPRING EXHIBITION. Annual, Apr-May. Oil, watercolor, mixed, graphics, sculpture. Open to all artists residing in U S. Jury, prizes. Fee $6. Entry card & work due Mar 30. For further information write Rena Anderson, 57 Sherwood Ave, West Springfield, MA 01103.

MICHIGAN

HARTLAND ART COUNCIL. Annual, Apr. Open to all Mich artists. Jury, prizes & purchase awards. Fee. Work due Apr 15, hand delivered. For further information write Dorothy Gheen, Dir, Hartland Art Council, Box 126, Hartland, MI 48029.

MICHIGAN ARTIST-CRAFTSMEN EXHIBITION, Detroit. Biennial, Nov (next 73). Ceramics, metal, wood, textiles & plastics. Open to all Mich craftsmen. Jury, awards. Fee $3 per artist, maximum of five works per artist. Entries & cards due Oct. For further information write Dept of Contemporary Art, Detroit Institute of Arts, 5200 Woodward Ave, Detroit, MI 48202.

MICHIGAN ARTISTS EXHIBITION, Detroit. Biennial, Nov (next 74). Painting (any media), sculpture, prints, drawings & photos. Open to all Mich artists. Jury, awards. Fee $3 per artist, maximum two entries per artist. Entries & cards due Oct. For further information write Dept of Contemporary Art, Detroit Institute of Arts, 5200 Woodward Ave, Detroit, MI 48202.

MICHIGAN PAINTERS-PRINTMAKERS EXHIBITION, Grand Rapids. Biennial (with craftsmen show in off yrs), Sept-Oct. Paintings & prints. Open to Mich residents. Jury, prizes to $3000. Fee $2 per work, limit of three works. Entries due Aug 14-24 (except Aug 20). For further information write Miss Idamarie Holmer, Grand Rapids Art Museum, 230 E Fulton, Grand Rapids, MI 49502.

MINNESOTA

MINNESOTA MUSEUM OF ART, Saint Paul. Biennial, Apr-Aug. Drawings, one color—line, wash, tone or combination. Open to living artists work in U S, original work executed since Dec 1, 70. $5000 in awards & purchases. Fee $5 per artist. Entry cards due Jan 26 & entries due Feb 2. For further information write Mary Kelly Theuer, Minnesota Museum of Art, 305 Saint Peter St, Saint Paul, MN 55102.

MISSOURI

MID-AMERICA EXHIBITION, St Louis. Biennial. Oil, tempera, painting, sculpture & others. Open to residents of Mo & the states bordering Mo. Jury, prizes. Fee $4. For further information write The St Louis Art Museum, Curator's Office, Forest Park, St Louis, MO 63110.

WATERCOLOR U S A, Springfield. Annual, Apr-June. Watercolor only. Open to artists from all fifty states. Jury, $10,000 in purchase & cash awards. Fee $5. Entries due Apr 10. For further information write Kenneth M Shuck, Dir, Springfield Art Museum, 1111 E Brookside Dr, Springfield, MO 65804.

NEBRASKA

JOSLYN ART MUSEUM MIDWEST BIENNIAL, Omaha. Biennial, held in even-numbered yrs, late winter or spring. Painting, sculpture, graphics. Open to artists in Ark, Colo, Ill, Iowa, Kans, La, Minn, Mo, Mont, Nebr, N Mex, N Dak, Okla, S Dak, Tex & Wyo. Jury, awards. Fee $5. Entries due Feb, or as announced. For further information write Midwest Biennial, Joslyn Art Museum, 2200 Dodge St, Omaha, NE 68102.

NORTH PLATTE VALLEY ARTISTS' GUILD, Scottsbluff. Annual, Apr. All media. Open to residents of Mont, Nebr, N Dak, S Dak & Wyo. Prizes, purchase awards & ribbons. Fee $3 per entry for adults & $1.50 for youths. Entry cards due Apr 7 & work due Apr 14. For further information write Ethel Vincent, North Platte Valley Artists' Guild, P O Box 1041, Scottsbluff, NE 69361.

NEVADA

LAS VEGAS ART LEAGUE NATIONAL ART ROUND-UP. Annual, (next Apr 7-May 2, 74). All painting, graphics, textiles, sculpture, ceramics, jewelry. Open to all artists. $2000 in cash awards, purchase awards & ribbons. Fee $8 for one or two entries, 20% comn. Entry cards & color slides (2 x 2 in) due Feb 1 & work due Mar 18. For further information write Las Vegas Art League, 3333-6 W Washington, Las Vegas, NV 89107.

NEW JERSEY

ART CENTRE OF THE ORANGES, East Orange. Annual, Mar 25-Apr 13. Oil, watercolor, graphics, sculpture. Open to artists of Conn, N J, N Y & Pa. Jury, prizes. Fee $4 per entry. Entry cards due Mar 1 & work due Mar 10-11. For further information write Ruth Joraleman, Art Centre of the Oranges, 16 Washington St, East Orange, NJ 07017.

ART FROM NEW JERSEY, Trenton. Annual, Mar-May. Painting, graphics, sculpture. Open to all artists living or working in N J. Jury, purchase prizes. No fee. For further information write Al Hilborn, Publ Ed, New Jersey State Museum, W State St, Trenton, NJ 08625.

HUNTERDON ART CENTER NATIONAL PRINT EXHIBITION, Clinton. Annual, Apr-May. All print media except monotype. Open to all printmakers. Jury, awards. Fee $7 for two prints (members $5 for two). Entry cards & work due Mar. For further information write Dir, Hunterdon Art Center, Clinton, NJ 08809.

HUNTERDON ART CENTER NEW JERSEY STATE-WIDE EXHIBITION, Clinton. Annual, June-July. Oil, watercolor, sculpture. Open to all N J artists and those born in the state. Jury, awards. Fee $3 each for two works. Entry cards & work due May. For further information write Dir, Hunterdon Art Center, Clinton, NJ 08809.

MINIATURE ART SOCIETY OF NEW JERSEY, Paramus. Annual, Apr. All media. Open to all artists. Jury, prizes & purchase awards. Fee $6 for three entries & $10 for six. Entry cards due Mar 30 & work due Apr 6. For further information write Miniature Art Society of New Jersey, 451 Lookout Ave, Hackensack, NJ 07601.

NEW JERSEY CHAPTER AMERICAN ARTISTS PROFESSIONAL LEAGUE, West Orange. Annual, Nov. Oil, watercolor, mixed, graphics. Open to all realistic artists. Cash awards. Fee members $3 for one entry, $5 for two, non-members $5 for one, $7 for two. Entry cards due Sept & work due Oct 21. For further information write Mrs Patricia Sprouls, 188 Kaywin Dr, Paramus, NJ 07652.

NEW JERSEY WATERCOLOR SOCIETY, alternate yrs Morris Museum, Morristown & Monmouth Museum, Lincroft. Annual, Nov-Dec. Watercolor, casein, tempera. Open to all present or former residents of N J. Jury, awards. Fee subject to yearly decision of board. For further information write Mrs Nat Lewis, 51 Overlook Rd, Caldwell, NJ 07006.

PAINTERS & SCULPTORS' SOCIETY OF NEW JERSEY, Jersey City. Annual, Mar. Oil, watercolor, casein, pastels, graphics, sculpture. Open to all artists of U S & Can. Jury, cash awards & medals. Fee $5. Entry due Feb at Jersey City Museum. For further information write Painters & Sculptors' Society of New Jersey, c/o Elena Scola, Secy, 281 Springfield Ave, Hasbrook Heights, NJ 07604.

WESTFIELD ART ASSOCIATION, Cranford. Annual, Mar-Apr. All painting, original work only. Open to all N J residents. Jury, prizes & cash awards. Fee $5 per entry. Work due Mar 18. For further information write Mrs Elven Sheahan, 721 Clark St, Westfield, NJ 07090.

NEW MEXICO

MUSEUM OF NEW MEXICO, Santa Fe. Biennial (New Mexico Biennial & Southwestern Biennial held alternate yrs), Apr-May. All painting & sculpture media. Open to artists of South-Southwest. Jury, awards. Works selected for traveling exhib. For further information write Carlos Nagel, Dir, Museum of New Mexico, P O Box 2087, Santa Fe, NM 87501.

NEW MEXICO ART LEAGUE SMALL PAINTING SHOW, Albuquerque. Annual, Feb. All media. Open to all artists. Jury, prizes. Fee $3 per entry non-members, $2 members, limit two. Entry cards due Jan 10, work due Jan 15. For further information write New Mexico Art League, Old Town Gallery, 400 Romero St N W, Albuquerque, NM 87104.

NEW MEXICO ARTS AND CRAFTS FAIR, Albuquerque. Annual, last weekend in June. All media except home arts or crafts. Open to all artists & craftsmen residing in N Mex. Jury. Fee $30 one exhibitor & booth, $15 additional exhibitor. Entry cards & 3 samples of work due Mar 3 & 4. For further information write Mrs Karen Pharris, P O Box 8801, Albuquerque, NM 87108.

NEW YORK

ALLIED ARTISTS OF AMERICA, New York. Annual, Oct-Nov. Oil, watercolor, casein, polymer, pastel, sculpture. Open to American artists. Jury, awards. Fee $5. Entry cards & work due Oct. For further information write Allied Artists of America, 1083 Fifth Ave, New York, NY 10028.

AMERICAN WATERCOLOR SOCIETY, New York. Annual, Apr. Watercolor & gouache. Open to all artists. Jury, awards. Fee $5, limit two (not to exceed 34 by 42 inches framed). Color slides submitted by artists 100 miles or more from New York are due Feb 11; entry cards & work by artists within 100 miles due Mar 23. For further information write American Watercolor Society, 1083 Fifth Ave, New York, NY 10028.

ART DIRECTORS CLUB, New York. Annual Exhibition of Advertising & Editorial Art & Design, Spring. Open to advertising or editorial materials, promotion, posters, packaging & others. Jury, medals & certificates. Fee $2 per proof; $7.50 each TV film. Entries due Dec. For further information write The Art Directors Club, 488 Madison Ave, New York, NY 10022.

AUDUBON ARTISTS, New York. Annual, Jan-Feb. Oil, watercolor, graphics, sculpture. Open to all artists. Jury, awards. Fee $8, one entry per artist. Entry due Jan. For further information write Secy, Audubon Artists, 1083 Fifth Ave, New York, NY 10028.

CATHARINE LORILLARD WOLFE ART CLUB, New York. Annual, Nov. Oil, watercolor, graphics, sculpture. Open to all prof women artists working in realistic manner. Jury, prizes. Fee. Entry cards due Oct 23 & work due Oct 30. For further information and a prospectus next year, write Mrs Mae Berlind Bach, Co-chmn, 470 Park Ave, New York, NY 10022.

CHAUTAUGUA EXHIBITION OF AMERICAN ART. Annual, July. Oil, polymer, watercolor, tempera, casein, mixed. Open to all artists residents of U S & territories. Jury, cash prizes. Fee $6. Entry cards & slides due Apr 10 & work due June 1. For further information write Dr Helen Cleveland, 1192 Parkside Dr, Alliance, OH 44601.

COOPERSTOWN ART ASSOCIATION NATIONAL EXHIBITION. Annual, July-Aug. Painting, graphics, sculpture & crafts (no photog). Open to any adult in the U S. $2700 in prizes. Fee $3 first arts entry, $2 each addn, $3 for three craft entries, 20% comn. Entry cards & work due June 22 by mail, June 28-July 1 if hand delivered. For further information write Mrs Theodore Bellows, Secy, Cooperstown Art Association, Cooperstown, NY 13326.

EVERSON MUSEUM OF ART NATIONAL CERAMIC EXHIBITION, Syracuse. Biennial, Nov-Dec. Ceramics. Open to potters & enamelists in the U S & Can. Jury, purchase prizes. Fee. For further information write Everson Museum of Art, 401 Harrison St, Syracuse, NY 13202.

New York (cont)

HUDSON VALLEY ART ASSOCIATION, White Plains. Annual, May. All media including sculpture. Open to all artists in traditional works. Jury, awards. Fee for non-mem, $8, limit one. Entry due Apr. For further information write Rayma Spaulding, Pres, 15 Minivale Rd, Stamford, CT 06907.

LONG BEACH ART ASSOCIATION. Annual, May. All media. Open to all adults. July, prizes. Fee. Entry cards & work due Apr 21. For further information write Mrs Carol Merzer, 111 McKinley Ave, Island Park, NY 11558.

NATIONAL ACADEMY OF DESIGN, New York. Annual, Feb-Mar. Oil, sculpture, watercolors, graphics. Open to all artists. Jury, awards. No fee. Entry due Feb. For further information write National Academy of Design, 1083 Fifth Ave, New York, NY 10028.

NATIONAL SCULPTURE SOCIETY, New York. Annual, Mar. Sculpture only. Open to all American sculptors on a juried basis. Jury, prizes & awards. No fee. Write for prospectus approx Jan 1. For further information write National Sculpture Society, 250 E 51st St, New York, NY 10022.

NATIONAL SOCIETY OF PAINTERS IN CASEIN & ACRYLIC, New York. Annual, Feb. Casein & acrylic. Open to all artists. Jury, cash awards & medals. Fee $6. Entries due Feb. For further information write Lily Shuff, 465 West End Ave, New York, NY 10024.

NEW ROCHELLE ART ASSOCIATION. Annual, Apr. Oil, watercolor, graphics, collage, acrylic, sculpture. Open to all artists. Jury, ribbons & cash awards. Fee; only uncrated work accepted. For further information write Irene Gross Berzon, 87 Disbrow Lane, New Rochelle, NY 10804.

PRINT CLUB OF ALBANY NATIONAL PRINT EXHIBITION. Biennial, Nov. All print media except monotypes. Open to all printmakers residing in the U S. Jury, awards. Fee $4 each, limit of four. Entries due Sept. For further information write Alice Pauline Schafer, 33 Hawthorne Ave, Albany, NY 12203.

PRINT CLUB OF ALBANY SMALL PRINT EXHIBITION. Biennial, Dec. All print media except monotypes. Open to all printmakers residing in the U S. Jury, awards. Fee $4 each, limit of four. Entries due Nov. For further information write Alice Pauline Schafer, 33 Hawthorne Ave, Albany, NY 12203.

SOCIETY OF AMERICAN GRAPHIC ARTISTS, New York. Annual. All prints except monotype. Open to all printmakers. Jury, awards. Fee $5, limit one (30 inches maximum). For further information write Society of American Graphic Artists, 1083 Fifth Ave, New York, NY 10028.

SUFFOLK COUNTY ARTISTS LEAGUE, Babylon. Annual, Mar. Oils, watercolor, acrylic, sculpture. Open to all artists. Jury, cash awards. Fee $4 per entry, limit two. For further information write Mario Grimaldi, Dir, Suffolk County Artists League, 39 E Main St, Babylon, NY 11702.

NORTH CAROLINA

DAVIDSON NATIONAL PRINT & DRAWING COMPETITION. Annual, Mar-Apr. All prints & drawings. Open to all U S artists. Jury, prizes & purchase awards. Fee $4, limit two. Entry cards & work due Feb. For further information write Herb Jackson, Box 2495, Davidson College, Davidson, NC 28036.

NORTH CAROLINA ARTISTS EXHIBITION, Raleigh. Annual, Dec-Jan. Painting, graphics, sculpture. Open to natives & residents of N C for 12 months preceeding show. Cash awards, prizes & purchase awards. Fee $5 per artist, limit three works. Entry cards & work due Oct 23. For further information write Cur of Art, North Carolina Museum of Art, 107 E Morgan St, Raleigh, NC 27601.

NORTH DAKOTA

NORTH DAKOTA PRINT & DRAWING EXHIBITION, Grand Forks. Annual, Apr. All print & drawing. Open to all U S artists. Jury, prizes. Fee $5. Work due Mar 31. For further information write North Dakota Annual, Art Dept, University of North Dakota, Grand Forks, ND 58201.

OHIO

ALL-OHIO GRAPHICS, PHOTOGRAPHY & FILM MAKING EXHIBITION, Dayton. Annual, Nov-Dec. Prints, drawings, photographs, films. Jury, awards. Entry due Nov. For further information write Mark A. Clark, Registrar, Dayton Art Institute, 405 Riverview Ave, Dayton, OH 45401.

ALL-OHIO PAINTING & SCULPTURE EXHIBITION, Dayton. Biennial, Feb-Mar (next 73). Painting & sculpture. Open to artists residing in Ohio. Jury, awards. No fee; limit, two in either media or total of three. Entry due Jan. For further information write Mark A Clark, Registrar, Dayton Art Institute, 405 Riverview Ave, Dayton, OH 45401.

BUTLER INSTITUTE OF AMERICAN ART MIDYEAR SHOW, Youngstown. Annual, July-Sept. Oil, watercolor, acrylic, casein. Open to artists of the U S. Jury, awards. Fee $8. Entry cards & work due June. For further information write Secy, Butler Institute of American Art, 524 Wick Ave, Youngstown, OH 44502.

MAINSTREAMS, MARIETTA COLLEGE COMPETITION. Annual, Apr-May. Open to all painters & sculptors. Jury, prizes & purchase awards. Fee $10, limit five. Entry cards due Feb 17 & work due Mar 24. For further information write William Gerhold, Dir, Mainstreams, Marietta College, Marietta, OH 45750.

MASSILLON MUSEUM REGIONAL PAINTING EXHIBITION. Annual, Mar. Oil, watercolor, collage, polymer, acrylic & mixed media. Open to residents of Ohio & former residents. Jury, prizes & purchase awards. Fee $2. Work due Feb 11. For further information write Miss Mary Merwin, The Massillon Museum, 212 Lincoln Way E, Massillon, OH 44646.

OHIO ARTISTS & CRAFTSMEN SHOW, Massillon. Biennial, July-Aug (next 74). Print, drawing, photog, all crafts & sculpture. Open to all present & former residents of Ohio. Prizes & purchase awards. Fee $2, 10% comn. Work due June 11. For further information write Miss Mary Merwin, The Massillon Museum, 212 Lincoln Way E, Massillon, OH 44646.

OHIO CERAMIC & SCULPTURE SHOW, Youngstown. Annual, Jan-Feb. Ceramic, enamel, sculpture. Open to present & former Ohio residents. Jury, purchase awards. Fee $3 per class plus $3 per shipping container. Entries due Nov 2-Dec 12. For more information write Secy, Butler Institute of American Art, 534 Wick Ave, Youngstown, OH 44502.

OKLAHOMA

GREEN COUNTRY ART ASSOCIATION DOGWOOD ART FESTIVAL, Poteau. Annual, Easter-Mothers Day. Paintings & sculpture only. Open to artists of Ark, Kans, Mo, Okla & Tex. Jury. Fee. Entry cards due Apr 2, work due Apr 14. For further information write Eloise J Schellstede, Pres, Green Country Art Association, 1307 S Main, Tulsa, OK 74119.

GREEN COUNTRY ART ASSOCIATION PLUS 65 ART SHOW, Tulsa. Annual, Mar. Paintings & sculpture only. Open to artists of Ark, Kans, Mo, Okla & Tex. No fee to artists 65 yrs & older or mem, others $10; 10% comn. Entries due Mar 5-17. For further information write Eloise J Schellstede, Pres, Green Country Art Association, 1307 S Main, Tulsa, OK 74119.

LAWTON-FORT SILL ART COUNCIL INTERNATIONAL. Annual, Sept. All media. Open to all adult artists. Jury, awards, prizes, purchase awards & ribbons. Fee $2 per entry, limit three. Entry cards due Sept 10 & work due Sept 13. For further information write Jerry Ponder, 5111 Elm Ave, Lawton, OK 73501.

LAWTON JUNIOR SERVICE LEAGUE EXHIBITION OF PAINTING & SCULPTURE. Annual, Mar. All painting & sculpture. Open to all artists. Jury, cash prizes & purchase awards. Fee $2 per entry, limit three. Entry cards & work due Feb 5. For further information write Mrs Ben Ansley, 5005 Meadowbrook Dr, Lawton, OK 73501.

NATIONAL COMPETITION FOR AMERICAN INDIAN ARTISTS, Tulsa. Annual, May. Painting, sculpture and graphics. Open to artists of American Indian descent living in the U S. Jury, prizes. No fee. Entries due first Sat in Apr. For further information write Dr Donald G Humphrey, Dir, Philbrook Art Center, 2727 S Rockford Rd, Tulsa, OK 74114.

OKLAHOMA ART CENTER EIGHT STATE EXHIBITION OF PAINTING & SCULPTURE, Oklahoma City. Annual, Sept-Oct. Painting & sculpture. Open to residents of Ark, Colo, Kans, La, Mo, N Mex, Okla & Tex. Jury, purchase awards. Fee $4. Entries due by Aug. For further information write Registrar, Oklahoma Art Center, 3113 Pershing Blvd, Oklahoma City, OK 73107.

OKLAHOMA ART CENTER NATIONAL PRINT & DRAWING EXHIBITION, Oklahoma City. Annual, May. Prints & drawings. Open to any resident of the U S. Jury, purchase awards. Fee $5. For further information write Registrar, Oklahoma Art Center, 3113 Pershing Blvd, Oklahoma City, OK 73107.

OKLAHOMA MUSEUM OF ART ARTISTS SALON, Oklahoma City. Annual, May. Oil, watercolor, graphics, sculpture. Open to artists of Okla & surrounding states. Jury, cash prizes. Fee $1.50 per entry. Entry cards due Apr 10 & work due Apr 17. For further information write Anna Belle Birckett, Dir, 5500 Lincoln, Oklahoma City, OK 73105.

PHILBROOK ART CENTER OKLAHOMA ANNUAL, Tulsa. Annual, Apr. Painting, sculpture and graphics. Open to residents of Okla or former residents who have lived in the state at least one year. Jury, prizes. Fee $1 per entry. Entries due first Sat in Mar. For further information write Dr Donald G Humphrey, Dir, Philbrook Art Center, 2727 S Rockford Rd, Tulsa, OK 74114.

PENNSYLVANIA

AMERICAN COLOR PRINT SOCIETY, Philadelphia. Annual, Mar. All print media in color. Open to all printmakers working in color. Jury, awards. Fee $2.75. Entry due Feb. For further information write American Color Print Society, 2022 Walnut St, Philadelphia, PA 19103.

WASHINGTON & JEFFERSON COLLEGE NATIONAL PAINTING SHOW, Washington. Annual, Mar-Apr. All painting. Open to any U S artist, 18 yrs old. Prizes & purchase awards. Fee $3 for one or two slide entries. Entry cards due Feb 7 & work due Mar 6. For further information write Paul B Edwards, Art Dept, Washington & Jefferson College, Washington, PA 15301.

RHODE ISLAND

ART ASSOCIATION OF NEWPORT. Annual, July. Oil, watercolor, prints, drawings, photographs (alternate with small sculpture). Open to all American artists. Jury, awards. Fee $4 ($2 for photographs). Entry due early June. For further information write Mrs Paul C Rogers, Exec Secy, Art Association of Newport, 76 Bellevue Ave, Newport, RI 02840.

PROVIDENCE ART CLUB OPEN DRAWING SHOW—MONOCHROMATIC. Annual, Nov. All media; work must have been done in last two yrs, & not previously shown in Providence. Open to all New Eng artists. Awards. Fee $2 for each drawing, limit of two. Entries due Nov 9. For further information write Mrs Tore Dalenius, Providence Art Club, 11 Thomas St, Providence, RI 02903.

PROVIDENCE WATERCOLOR CLUB. Annual, Oct-Nov. Watercolor. Open to New Eng artists. Cash awards, prizes & ribbons. Fee $5, 15% comn. Work due Oct 14. For further information write Barbara Besson, 6 Thomas St, Providence, RI 02906.

TENNESSEE

BROOKS MEMORIAL ART GALLERY MID-SOUTH EXHIBITION, Memphis. Annual, Mar. Paintings, drawings, sculpture, prints. Open to artists residing within 250 air miles of Memphis. Jury, awards. Entries received Jan 2-20. For further information write Mid-South Exhibition, Brooks Memorial Art Gallery, Overton Park, Memphis, TN 38112.

DULIN NATIONAL PRINT & DRAWING COMPETITION, Knoxville. Annual, Jan-Feb. Prints & drawings. Open to all artists living & working in the U S. Prizes. Fee $5. Entry cards due Nov 14 & work due Nov 20. For further information write Dulin Gallery of Art, 3100 Kingston Pike, Knoxville, TN 37919.

MISSISSIPPI RIVER CRAFT SHOW, Memphis. Annual, Oct-Nov. Open to craftsmen residing within the ten mid-continent states bordering the Mississippi River. Entries received Aug 1 through Sept 1. For further information write Mississippi River Craft Show, Brooks Memorial Art Gallery, Overton Park, Memphis, TN 38112.

TENNESSEE ALL-STATE ARTISTS EXHIBITION, Nashville. Annual, Nov. Oil, mixed, pastel, watercolor, graphics & sculpture. Open to all artists residing in Tenn. Purchase awards. Fee $3 per entry; 10% comn. Entry cards & work due Sept 25-Oct 13. For further information write Watkins Institute, Sixth & Church, Nashville, TN 37219.

TENNESSEE ART LEAGUE & PARTHENON OF NASHVILLE CENTRAL STATES ART EXHIBITION. Annual, May. Painting, graphics, sculpture. Open to artists of Ala, Ark, Ga, Ky, Miss, N C, S C, Tenn, Va & other areas within 300 miles of Nashville. Jury, purchase awards & prizes. Fee $3 per entry, limit three. Work due Mar 25-Apr 2. For further information write Central States Art Exhibition, The Parthenon, Nashville, TN 37203.

TEXAS

DEL MAR COLLEGE DRAWING & SMALL SCULPTURE SHOW, Corpus Christi. Annual, May. Any drawing or sculpture. Open to all U S artists. Jury, prizes & purchase awards. Fee $5 for one entry, limit two. Entry cards due Mar 1, work due Apr 1. For further information write Joseph A Cain, Chmn, Dept of Art, Del Mar College, Corpus Christi, TX 78404.

EL PASO MUSEUM OF ART NATIONAL SUN CARNIVAL. Annual, Dec. All painting. Open to any U S citizen residing in the U S and its territories. Jury, purchase awards. For further information write Secy to Cur of Collections, El Paso Museum of Art, 1211 Montana, El Paso, TX 79902.

RIO GRANDE VALLEY ARTS & CRAFTS EXPOSITION, Brownsville. Annual, Nov. All media. Open to all artists & craftsmen. Fee $3, 10% comn. Entry cards due Oct 16 & work due Nov 3. For further information write Mrs F S Owens, Gen Chmn, Brownsville Art League, P O Box 3404, Brownsville, TX 78520.

TEXAS FINE ARTS ASSOCIATION, University of Texas at Arlington. Annual, Feb (73). All media. Open to all artists residing in Tex. Jury, prizes. Fee mem $3, non-mem $5. Slides due Jan 12, work due Feb 12. For further information write Box 826 UTA Sta, University of Texas at Arlington, Arlington, TX 76010.

UTAH

SALT LAKE ART CENTER, Salt Lake City. Biennial (alternate yrs with Utah State & Intermountain Regional; no biennial 73 owing to construction of new facility; 74 biennial, spec regional event), Mar. Painting & sculpture. Open to Utah artists (regional open to artists of Colo, Idaho, Mont, Nev & Utah). Jury, awards. No fee. Entries due mid-Feb. For further information write to Roger Bailey, Dir, Salt Lake Art Center, 54 Finch Lane, Salt Lake City, UT 84102.

Utah (cont)

UTAH STATEWIDE COMPETITION AND EXHIBIT, Salt Lake City. Annual, June through Labor Day. Painting, drawing, watercolor. Open to residents of Utah. Jury, $1000 purchase award, other awards as merited. Fee $2. Entries due approx May 15 (varies each yr). For further information write Utah State Division of Fine Arts, 609 E South Temple St, Salt Lake City, UT 94108.

VIRGINIA

AMERICAN DRAWING EXHIBITION, Norfolk. Biennial, Jan-Feb odd years (none in 73). Drawing. Open to all adult artists residing in the U.S. Jury, awards. Entries due Nov. For further information write American Drawing Biennial, Chrysler Museum at Norfolk, Olney Road and Mowbray Arch, Norfolk, VA 23510.

IRENE LEACHE MEMORIAL EXHIBITION, Norfolk. Biennial, Mar-Apr (even yrs). All painting & drawing media (pastels not acceptable). Open to artists residing in Del, Md, N C, Va, Washington, D C & W Va & natives of those states. Jury, cash awards. Limit of three. Entry & cards due Jan. For further information write Irene Leache Memorial Exhibition, Chrysler Museum of Norfolk, Olney Rd & Mowbray Arch, Norfolk, VA 23510.

JAMES RIVER JURIED ART EXHIBITION, Newport News. Annual, Oct-Nov. All painting, drawing, sculpture, graphics. Open to adults who are residents of Md, N C, Va & Washington, D C. Jury, cash awards & purchase awards. Fee $7. Entry cards & work due Sept. For further information write James River Juried Art Exhibition, Mariners Museum, Newport News, VA 23606.

NATIONAL SEAWALL ART SHOW, Portsmouth. Annual, May. All original oil, acrylic, watercolor, graphics, photog, sculpture & crafts. Open to all artists. Over $4500 in cash awards, prizes, purchase awards & ribbons. Fee $10. Entry cards due May 11 & work due May 26. For further information write Mrs Ellen G Wise, Recreation Dept, 1 High St, Portsmouth, VA 23704.

VIRGINIA ARTISTS, Richmond. Biennial, May-June odd years. Original paintings, drawings, watercolor, collages, sculpture & all types of graphics. Jury, awards. Limit three works. Entries due Jan 1. For further information write Virginia Museum of Fine Arts, Boulevard & Grove Aves, Richmond, VA 23221.

VIRGINIA CRAFTSMEN, Richmond. Biennial, Mar-Apr. Personally designed crafts in metal, textile, wood, ceramics & leather. Open to natives & residents of Va & those former residents who lived in Va for five years. Jury, awards. Limit of three works. Entries due by Feb. For further information write Virginia Museum of Fine Arts, Boulevard & Grove Aves, Richmond, VA 23221.

VIRGINIA DESIGNERS, Richmond. Biennial, Jan-Feb. Magazine & newspaper advertisements, brochures, folders, catalogues, programs, posters & others. Open to natives & residents of Va & those former residents who lived in Va for five years. Jury, awards. Fee $3, limit of ten panels. Entries due by Nov. For further information write Virginia Museum of Fine Arts, Boulevard & Grove Aves, Richmond, VA 23221.

VIRGINIA PHOTOGRAPHERS, Richmond. Biennial, Oct-Nov. Monochrome & color photographic prints & color transparencies. Open to natives & residents of Va & those former residents who lived in Va for five years. Jury, awards. Fee $3 for non-mem (mem free); limit eight prints & eight transparencies. Entries by Aug. For further information write Virginia Museum of Fine Arts, Boulevard & Grove Aves, Richmond, VA 23221.

WASHINGTON

NORTHWEST WATERCOLOR EXHIBITION, Seattle. Annual, Feb 23-Mar 25. All aqueous. Open to all artists of Alaska, Idaho, Mont, Ore & Wash. Jury, cash awards & purchase awards. Fee $3, 10% comn. Entry cards & work due Jan 25-Feb 8. For further information write Flora Correa, Chmn, 8253 S E 29th St, Mercer Island, WA 98040.

SEATTLE PRINT INTERNATIONAL. Biennial, June-July. All fine print media, not including monotypes. Open to all nat & int artists of fine print media. Jury, awards. Fee $3. Entry & cards due in Spring (date to be determined). For further information write Secy, Seattle Art Museum, Volunteer Park, Seattle, WA 98102.

WESTERN WASHINGTON STATE COLLEGE SMALL SCULPTURE & DRAWING EXHIBITION, Bellingham. Annual, May-June. All media. Open to all U S residents. Purchase awards. Fee $4. Entry cards & work due in Apr. For further information write Art Dept, Western Washington State College, Bellingham, WA 98225.

WEST VIRGINIA

HUNTINGTON GALLERIES PHOTOGRAPHY & CINEMATOGRAPHY 280. Biennial, Nov (73). Open to photographers above high school age, living within 280 miles of Huntington. Jury, awards. Fee. Entry due Oct. For further information write Photography & Cinematography 280, Huntington Galleries, Huntington, WV 25701.

HUNTINGTON GALLERIES REGIONAL EXHIBITION 280. Biennial, Oct (74). Paintings, graphics, sculpture, crafts. Open to artists above high school age, living within 280 miles of Huntington. Jury, awards. Fee. Entry due Sept. For further information write Exhibition 280, Huntington Galleries, Huntington, WV 25701.

WISCONSIN

STEVENS POINT FINE ARTS EXHIBITION. Annual, Oct. Painting, drawing, graphics. Open to all artists residing in Wis. Jury, $500 top award, other cash & purchase awards. Fee $5. Entry cards & work due Oct 6-8. For further information write Mrs James Delzell, 1124 Ridge Rd, Stevens Point, WI 54481.

WISCONSIN DESIGNER-CRAFTSMEN, Milwaukee. Biennial (74). All media. Open to all craftsmen of Wis over 18 yrs of age. Jury, award. Fee $5 per artist, limit of three. Entry due Jan. For further information write Wisconsin Exhibitions, Milwaukee Art Center, 750 N Lincoln Memorial Dr, Milwaukee, WI 53202.

WISCONSIN PAINTERS & SCULPTORS, Milwaukee. Biennial, Mar-Apr (73). Oil, watercolor, pastel, sculpture (no prints or drawings). Open to all artists of Wis 21 yrs of age & over. Jury, awards. Fee $5 per artist. For further information write Wisconsin Exhibitions, Milwaukee Art Center, 750 N Lincoln Memorial Dr, Milwaukee, WI 53202.

WYOMING

WESTERN STATES ART EXHIBITION, Cody. Annual, June-July. Oil, watercolor, graphics, pastels, sculpture, ceramics & other (all work must be suitable for hanging). Open to all artists. Cash awards & ribbons. Fee $3.50 prof, $2.50 amateur for each work, limit three. For further information write Cody County Art League, P O Box 1524, Cody, WY 82414.

CANADA

ONTARIO

WESTERN ONTARIO EXHIBITION, London. Annual, May. All painting media, sculpture, prints, drawings, wall hangings (batik or woven). Open to all residents of Southwestern Ont. Jury, prizes & awards. No fee ($2 charge for handling of work shipped in). Entries due early Apr. For further information write Secy, Annual Western Ontario Exhibition, London Public Library and Art Museum, 305 Queen's Ave, London, Ont N6B 1X2, Can.

SOUTHWEST 33, Windsor. Annual, Feb. All media. Open to artists of the Southwestern Ont Region. Jury, prizes. Fee $3. Entries due Jan 22. For further information write Art Gallery of Windsor, Willistead Park, Windsor 15, Ont, Can.